Scott Publishing Co.
911 VANDEMARK ROAD, SIDNEY, OHIO 45365 513-498-0802
SCOTT®

Dear Catalogue User:

Welcome to the *1993 Scott Catalogue*. There are numerous firsts and user friendly improvements in store for you in this edition.

Attention topicalists. A new 13-page section starting on page 34A provides country-by-country listings of topical stamps showing **birds** and **trains** for Volume Three countries. Volumes 1 and 2 had a similar section and Volume 4 will contain listings for its countries. The new topical listings are presented by Scott in cooperation with the American Topical Association.

The Mission continues. More listings of both older stamps and newer issues. In Germany, listings for the post-World War II occupation stamps of the Soviet-controlled areas of Berlin-Brandenberg, Mecklenberg-Vorpommern, Saxony, East Saxony, West Saxony and Thuringia have been added. New issues for the recently independent countries of Latvia and Lithuania are provided. Listings also have been added for Jordan and Laos for items previously mentioned in "For the Record." Other previously unlisted items have been added in Madagascar and Mauritania. Minor-variety listings have been added for many se-tenant issues in Mexico, Italy and Japan.

Focus on clarity. In our crusade to make catalogue listings completely clear and easier to use, we have grouped some sets of minor varieties separately from their major variety counterparts. And to make life even better, we have moved all watermark illustrations to the beginning of each country. Now you will not have to hunt for these illustrations over decades of issues as was sometimes the case in the past.

What about catalogue values? Catalogue values this year show a true market response, as both increases and decreases are noted with no clear pattern of movement. As an example of the diversity, East Germany values continue to rise as a result of collectors rushing to fill their albums now that Germany is re-united. At the same time, Nicaragua values for most issues of the 1980's have been changed. Some are down greatly as a result of the country's collapsing currency.

Germany value changes are both up and down. Iran records numerous decreases, some of which are substantial. Although most of the increases for Iran are among earlier items, some issues of the Islamic Republic show upward movement. There are value increases in Iceland prior to 1925, but some values show decreases for modern issues.

More information added. Among the many footnotes added to the Mexico listings are those designed to make it easier to distinguish between watermarked and unwatermarked 3-peso and 20-peso definitives of the 1960's and 1970's. Notes have been provided for the East German listings to improve the explanation of which items are valued as canceled-to-order. Footnotes also have been added to expand perforation data for Indonesia's 1950 overprints. And, footnotes have been added throughout most of this volume to direct users to surcharged and overprinted items.

Despite our reluctance to implement catalogue number changes, some have been necessary. Among the most prominent are Germany's 1986-91 Famous Women, Israel's 1988-90 Archaeology, Japan's 1980-82 coil stamps, Monaco's 1985-88 Rainier and Albert and 1989-91 Rainier definitive sets, and Morocco's 1974-85 postage dues. The addition of stamps previously in the "For the Record" section cause three sets in Jordan and one in Laos to change numbers. Mexico's 1-centavo value of the 1934 National University set has been renumbered as Scott RA13B to reflect statements in the official publication of the Mexican Posts and Telegraphs Department indicating that this stamp was intended to be used as a postal tax stamp in place of the obligatory Pro Infancia stamps.

The number and breadth of changes in this volume are so great that only those affecting the most stamps or the most popular collecting areas can be noted in this brief letter. You are advised to review the listings of areas of particular interest to you for changes. This is but one more year of thousands of individual changes to a volume as we incorporate suggestions and information from our outside experts, users of our catalogues and our own staff to continue our steady improvement of what we offer.

Please let us know your thoughts and further suggestions for improvement.

Sincerely,

Richard L. Sine
Editorial Director

PS: If you appreciate the efforts of your favorite dealer, write and let him know. And, if you're lucky enough to have a local dealer with a shop, thank him profusely.

SCOTT®

1993 Standard Postage Stamp Catalogue

ONE HUNDRED AND FORTY-NINTH EDITION IN FOUR VOLUMES

VOLUME 3

EUROPEAN COUNTRIES and COLONIES,
INDEPENDENT NATIONS of
AFRICA, ASIA, LATIN AMERICA

G-O

VICE PRESIDENT/PUBLISHER	**Stuart J. Morrissey**
EDITORIAL DIRECTOR	**Richard L. Sine**
EDITOR	**William W. Cummings**
ASSISTANT EDITOR	**William H. Hatton**
VALUING EDITOR	**Martin J. Frankevicz**
NEW ISSUES EDITOR	**David C. Akin**
COMPUTER CONTROL COORDINATOR	**Denise Oder**
VALUING ANALYSTS	**Jose R. Capote** **Roger L. Listwan**
EDITORIAL ASSISTANTS	**Judith E. Bertrand** **Beth Brown**
ART/PRODUCTION DIRECTOR	**Edward Heys**
PRODUCTION COORDINATOR	**Nancy S. Martin**
DIRECTOR OF MARKETING & SALES	**Jeff Lawrence**
PRODUCT SALES SUPERVISOR	**Bill Fay**
ADVERTISING MANAGER	**David Lodge**

Scott Publishing Co.

911 Vandemark Road, Sidney, Ohio 45365

A division of AMOS PRESS INC., publishers of *Linn's Stamp News, Coin World, Cars & Parts* magazine and *The Sidney Daily News.*

Table of Contents

See Volumes II and IV for nations of Africa, Asia, Europe, Latin America and their affiliated territories, A-F and P-Z.

See Volume I for United States and Affiliated Territories, United Nations, and British Commonwealth of Nations.

Copyright Notice

Trademark Notice

ISBN 0-89487-180-3

Library of Congress Card No. 2-3301

Catalogue Information

Catalogue Value

The Scott Catalogue value is a retail price, what you could expect to pay for the stamp in a grade of Fine-Very Fine. The value listed is a reference which reflects recent actual dealer selling prices.

Dealer retail price lists, public auction results, published prices in advertising, and individual solicitation of retail prices from dealers, collectors, and specialty organizations have been used in establishing the values found in this catalogue.

Use this catalogue as a guide in your own buying and selling. The actual price you pay for a stamp may be higher or lower than the catalogue value because of one or more of the following: the amount of personal service a dealer offers, increased interest in the country or topic represented by the stamp or set, whether an item is a "loss leader," part of a special sale, or otherwise is being sold for a short period of time at a lower price, or if at a public auction you are able to obtain an item inexpensively because of little interest in the item at that time.

For unused stamps, more recent issues are valued as never-hinged, with the beginning point determined on a country-by-country basis. Notes to show the beginning points are prominently noted in the text.

Grade

A stamp's grade and condition are crucial to its value. Values quoted in this catalogue are for stamps graded at Fine-Very Fine and with no faults. Exceptions are noted in the text. The accompanying illustrations show an example of a Fine-Very Fine grade between the grades immediately below and above it: Fine and Very Fine.

FINE stamps have the design noticeably off-center on two sides. Imperforate stamps may have small margins and earlier issues may show the design touching one edge of the stamp. Used stamps may have heavier than usual cancellations.

FINE-VERY FINE stamps may be somewhat off-center on one side, or only slightly off-center on two sides. Imperforate stamps will have two margins at least normal size and the design will not touch the edge. *Early issues of a country may be printed in such a way that the design naturally is very close to the edges.* Used stamps will not have a cancellation that detracts from the design. This is the grade used to establish Scott Catalogue values.

VERY FINE stamps may be slightly off-center on one side, with the design well clear of the edge. Imperforate stamps will have three margins at least normal size. Used stamps will have light or otherwise neat cancellations.

Condition

The above definitions describe *grade,* which is centering and (for used stamps) cancellation. *Condition* refers to the soundness of the stamp, i.e., faults, repairs, and other factors influencing price.

Copies of a stamp which are of a lesser grade and/or condition trade at lower prices. Those of exceptional quality often command higher prices.

Factors that can increase the value of a stamp include exceptionally wide margins, particularly fresh color, and the presence of selvage.

Factors other than faults that decrease the value of a stamp include loss of gum or regumming, hinge remnant, foreign object adhering to gum, natural inclusion, or a straight edge.

Faults include a missing piece, tear, clipped perforation, pin or other hole, surface scuff, thin spot, crease, toning, oxidation or other form of color changeling, short or pulled perforation, stains or such man-made changes as reperforation or the chemical removal or lightening of a cancellation.

Scott Publishing Co. recognizes that there is no formal, enforced grading scheme for postage stamps, and that the final price you pay for a stamp or obtain for a stamp you are selling will be determined by individual agreement at the time of the transaction.

Catalogue Listing Policy

It is the intent of Scott Publishing to list all postage stamps of the world in the *Scott Standard Postage Stamp Catalogue.* The only strict criteria for listing is that stamps be decreed legal for postage by the issuing country. Whether the primary intent of issuing a given stamp or set was for sale to postal patrons or to stamp collectors is not part of our listing criteria. Scott's role is to provide comprehensive stamp information. It is up to each stamp collector to choose which items to include in a collection.

It is Scott's objective to seek reasons why a stamp should be listed, rather than why it should not. Nevertheless, there are certain types of items which will not be listed:

1. Unissued items, even if they "accidentally" are distributed to the philatelic or even postal market. If such items later are officially issued by the country, they will be listed. Unissued items consist of those which have been printed and then held from sale for reasons such as change in government, error found on stamp, or even something objectionable about a stamp subject or design.
2. Stamps "issued" by non-existent entities or fantasy countries, such as Nagaland, Occusi-Ambeno, South Moluccas and others.
3. Semi-official or unofficial items not required for postage. Examples are items issued by private agencies for their own express services. When such items are required or valid as prepayment of postage, they will be listed.
4. Local stamps issued for local use only. Stamps issued by government specifically for "domestic" use, such as Haiti Scott 219-228 or the U.S. non-denominated stamps, are not considered to be locals.
5. Items not valid for postal use. For example, a few countries have issued souvenir sheets not valid for postage.
6. Intentional varieties, such as imperforate stamps issued in very small quantities with the same design as perforate stamps.
7. Items distributed by the issuing government only to a limited group, such as a stamp club or a single stamp dealer, and then brought to market at inflated prices. These items normally will be included in a footnote.

The fact that a stamp has been used successfully as postage, even on international mail, is not sufficient to prove that it was legitimately issued. Numerous examples of "stamps" from non-existent countries are known to have been used to post letters that have passed through the international mail.

Those items that will still not appear in the catalogue represent a very small percentage, perhaps as little as two percent, of the more than 400,000 stamps currently listed in the Scott catalogue system, or the 8,000 or so new issues that are listed each year.

There are certain items that are subject to interpretation. When a stamp falls outside our specifications, it will be listed and a cautionary footnote added.

A series of factors are considered in our approach to how a stamp is listed. Following is a list of various factors, presented here primarily to share with catalogue users the complexity of the listing process.

Additional printings — "additional printings" of a previously issued stamp may range from something that is totally different to cases where it is virtually impossible to differentiate it from the original. We will assign at least a minor number (a small-letter suffix) if there is a distinct change in stamp color, the design is noticeably redrawn, or the perforation measurement is different. A major number (numeral or numeral and capital-letter combination) will be assigned if we believe the "additional printing" is sufficiently different from the original that it constitutes a whole new issue.

Commemoratives — where practical, or where advance information is available, like commemoratives will be placed in a set, for example, the U.S. Credo issue of 1960-61 and the Constitution Bicentennial series of 1989-90. Japan and Korea issue such material on a regular basis, with an announced or, at least, predictable number of stamps known in advance.

Definitive sets — blocks of numbers are reserved for definitive sets, based on previous experience with that country. If more stamps are issued than expected, but it looks as if only a few more stamps will be issued for that series, they will be inserted into the original set with a capital-letter suffix, such as U.S. Scott 1059A. If it appears that many more stamps are yet to be issued in the set, a new block of numbers will be reserved, and the original grouping closed off, as in the case of the U.S. Transportation coil series and the Great Americans series.

New country — the important consideration is correct placement of the listings within the catalogue, either as a separate country listing or as a "state" following the "mother country" listing, for example, Aland Islands following Finland. Membership in the Univeral Postal Union is not a consideration for listing status or order of placement in the Catalogue.

"No release date" items — very complete information is readily available from certain countries for new issues before the stamps are issued; in some cases no information is available; while others fall somewhere in between. Often countries will provide denominations of upcoming stamps or souvenir sheets not released at the time of issue. Sometimes philatelic agencies, private firms employed by postal administrations, will add these later-issued items to sets months or years after the formal release date. If the items are officially issued by the country, the later material will be inserted into the proper set.

In order to understand how new issues come to market, it is important to know how philatelic agents operate. A philatelic agent is employed by a postal administration to perform duties ranging from complete development of all new issues including concept, design, printing and philatelic distribution to simply publicizing and selling new issues. Many countries do not have agents, or use them only for special projects.

Overprints — color of an overprint is always noted if it is other than black. Where more than one color ink is used on overprints of a set, the color used for a particular stamp is noted in the description line of that stamp.

Se-tenants — including pairs and blocks, will be listed in the format most commonly collected. If the stamps are collected as a unit, the major number will be assigned to the multiple and the minor numbers to the individual increments. When the items are usually collected as singles, then each individual stamp is given a major number and the entire se-tenant item is given a minor number of the last item in sequence. The manner in which an item is listed generally depends on the stamp's usage in the country of issue. Where stamps are used widely for postal purposes, even if se-tenant issues will be collected as a unit, each stamp will be given a major number, such as the stamps of the United States, Canada, Germany, and Great Britain.

Understanding the Listings

On the following page is an enlarged "typical" listing from this catalogue. Following are detailed explanations of each of the highlighted parts of the listing.

1 **Scott number** — Stamp collectors use Scott numbers to identify specific stamps when buying, selling, or trading stamps, and for ease in organizing their collections. Each stamp issued by a country has a unique number. Therefore, Germany Scott 99 can only refer to a single stamp. Although the Scott Catalogue usually lists stamps in chronological order by date of issue, when a country issues a set of stamps over a period of time the stamps within that set are kept together without regard of date of issue. This follows the normal collecting approach of keeping stamps in their natural sets.

When a country is known to be issuing a set of stamps over a period of time, a group of consecutive catalogue numbers is reserved for the stamps in that set, as issued. If that group of numbers proves to be too few, capital-letter suffixes are added to numbers to create enough catalogue numbers to cover all items in the set. Scott uses a suffix letter, e.g., "A," "b," etc., only once. If there is a Scott 16A in a set, there will not be a Scott 16a also. Suffix letters are not cumulative. A minor variety of Scott 16A would be Scott 16b, not Scott 16Ab. Any exceptions, such as Great Britain Scott 358cp, are clearly shown.

There are times when the block of numbers is too large for the set, leaving some numbers unused. Such gaps in the sequence also occur when the editors move an item elsewhere in the catalogue or removed from the listings entirely. Scott does not attempt to account for every possible number, but rather it does attempt to assure that each stamp is assigned its own number.

Scott numbers designating regular postage normally are only numerals. Scott numbers for other types of stamps, i.e., air post, semi-postal, and so on, will have a prefix of either a capital letter or a combination of numerals and capital letters.

2 **Illustration number** — used to identify each illustration. For most sets, the lowest face-value stamp is shown. It then serves as an example of the basic design approach for the set. Where more than one stamp in a set uses the same illustration number but has no different design, that number needs to be used with the design paragraph or description line (noted below) to be certain of the exact design on each stamp within the set. Where there are both vertical and horizontal designs in a set, a single illustration may be used, with the exceptions noted in the design paragraph or description line. When an illustration is followed by a lower-case letter in parentheses, such as "A2(b)," the trailing letter indicates which overprint illustration applies from those shown.

Illustrations normally are 75 percent of the original size of the stamp. An effort has been made to note all illustrations not at that percentage. Overprints are shown at 100 percent of the original, unless otherwise noted. In some cases, the illustration will be placed above the set, between listings, or omitted completely. Overprint and surcharge illustrations are not placed in this catalogue for purposes of expertizing stamps.

3 **Paper color** — The color of the paper is noted in italic type when the paper used is not white.

4 **Listing styles** — there are two principal types of catalogue listings: major and minor.

Majors normally are in a larger type style than minor listings. They also may be distinguished by having as their catalogue number a numeral with or without a capital-letter suffix and with or without a prefix.

Minors are in a smaller type style and have a small-letter suffix (or, only have the small letter itself shown if the listing is immediately beneath its major listing). These listings show a variety of the "normal," or major item. Examples include color variation or a different watermark used for that stamp only.

Examples of major numbers are 16, 28A, B97, C13A, 10N5, and 10N6A. Examples of minor numbers are 16a and C13b.

5 **Basic information on stamp or set** — introducing each stamp issue, this section normally includes the date of issue, method of printing, perforation, watermark, and sometimes some additional information. *New information on method of printing, watermark or perforation measurement will appear when that information changes in the sequential order of the listings.* Stamps created by overprinting or surcharging previous stamps are assumed to have the same perforation, watermark and printing method as the original. Dates of issue are as precise as Scott is able to confirm.

6 **Denomination** — normally the face value of the stamp, i.e., the cost of the stamp at the post office at the time of issue. When the denomination is shown in parentheses, it does not appear on the stamp.

7 **Color or other description** — this line provides information to solidify identification of the stamp. Historically, when stamps normally were printed in a single color, only the color appeared here. With modern printing techniques, which include multicolor presses which mix inks on the paper, earlier methods of color identification are no longer applicable. In many cases, a description of the stamp design appears in this space.

8 **Year of issue** — in stamp sets issued over more than one year, the number in parentheses is the year that stamp appeared. Stamps without a date appeared during the first year of the span. Dates are not always given for minor varieties.

9 **Value unused** and **Value used** — the catalogue values are based on stamps which are in a grade of Fine-Very Fine. Unused values refer to items which have not seen postal or other duty for which they were intended. For pre-1900 issue, unused stamps must have at least most of their original gum; for later issues full original gum is expected. It is probably that they will show evidence of hinging if issued before the never-hinged break-point. Stamps issued without gum are noted. Modern issues with PVA gum may appear ungummed. Unused values are for never-hinged stamps beginning at the point immediately following a prominent notice in the actual listing. The same information also appears at the beginning of the country's information. See the section "Catalogue Values" for an explanation of the meaning of these values. Information about catalogue values shown in italics may be found in the section "Understanding Valuing Notations."

10 **Changes in basic set information** — bold type is used to show any change in the basic data on within a set of stamps, i.e., perforation from one stamp to the next or a different paper or printing method or watermark.

11 **Total value of set** — the total value of sets of five or more stamps, issued after 1900, are shown. The line also notes the range of Scott numbers and total number of stamps included in the total. *Set value* is the term used to indicate the value of a set when it is less than the total of the individual stamps.

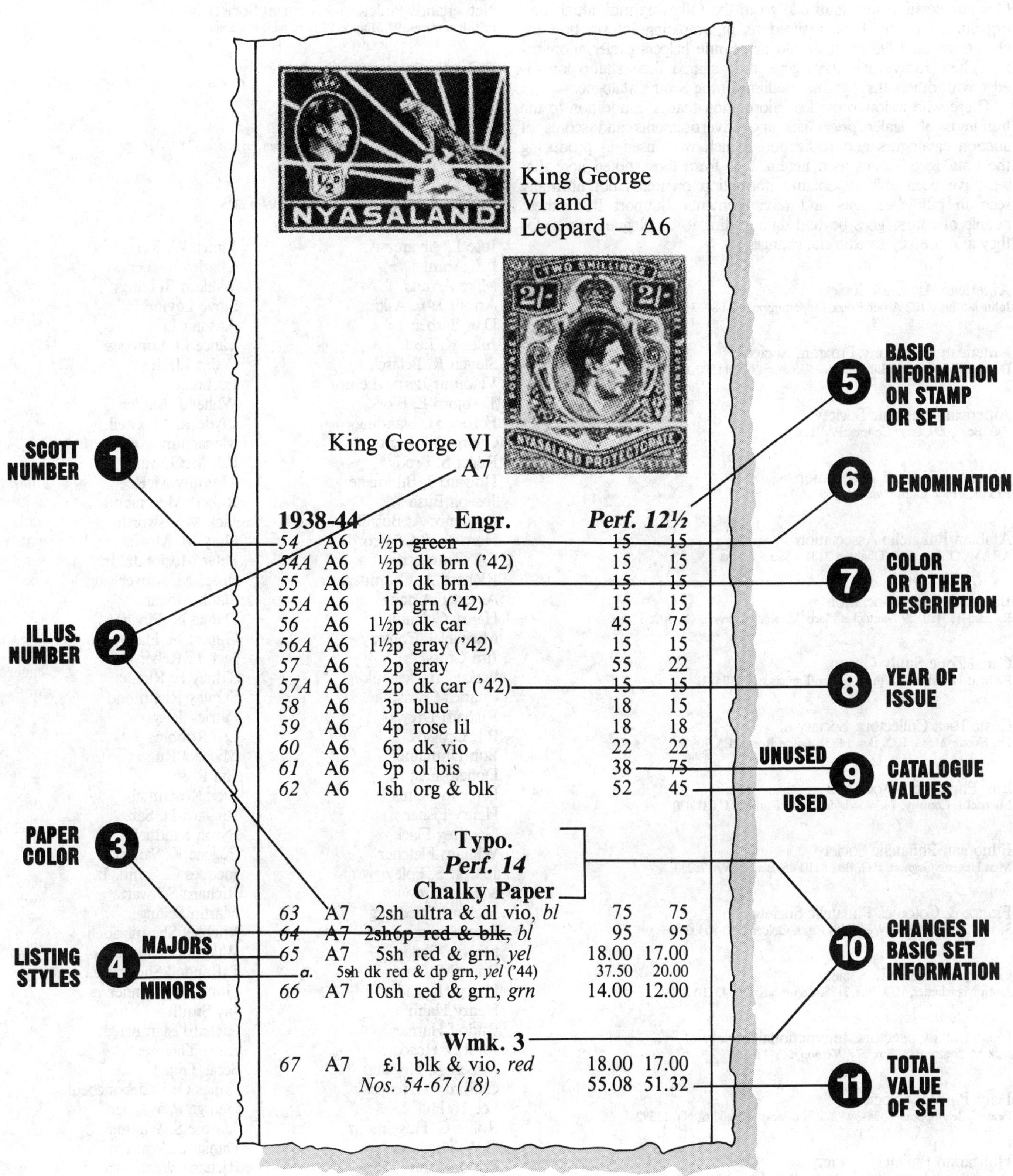
King George VI and Leopard – A6
King George VI – A7
1938-44 Engr. Perf. 12½
54 A6 ½p green 15 15
54A A6 ½p dk brn ('42) 15 15
55 A6 1p dk brn 15 15
55A A6 1p grn ('42) 15 15
56 A6 1½p dk car 45 75
56A A6 1½p gray ('42) 15 15
57 A6 2p gray 55 22
57A A6 2p dk car ('42) 15 15
58 A6 3p blue 18 15
59 A6 4p rose lil 18 18
60 A6 6p dk vio 22 22
61 A6 9p ol bis 38 75
62 A6 1sh org & blk 52 45
Typo.
Perf. 14
Chalky Paper
63 A7 2sh ultra & dl vio, bl 75 75
64 A7 2sh6p red & blk, bl 95 95
65 A7 5sh red & grn, yel 18.00 17.00
a. 5sh dk red & dp grn, yel ('44) 37.50 20.00
66 A7 10sh red & grn, grn 14.00 12.00
Wmk. 3
67 A7 £1 blk & vio, red 18.00 17.00
Nos. 54-67 (18) 55.08 51.32
SCOTT NUMBER 1
ILLUS. NUMBER 2
PAPER COLOR 3
LISTING STYLES 4 MAJORS MINORS
5 BASIC INFORMATION ON STAMP OR SET
6 DENOMINATION
7 COLOR OR OTHER DESCRIPTION
8 YEAR OF ISSUE
UNUSED 9 CATALOGUE VALUES USED
10 CHANGES IN BASIC SET INFORMATION
11 TOTAL VALUE OF SET

Acknowledgments

Our appreciation and gratitude go to the following individuals and organizations who have assisted us in preparing information included in the 1993 Scott Catalogues. Some helpers prefer anonymity. These individuals have generously shared their stamp knowledge with others through the medium of the Scott Catalogue.

Those who follow provided information that is in addition to the hundreds of dealer price lists and advertisements and scores of auction catalogues and realizations which were used in producing the Catalogue Values used herein. It is from those noted here that we have been able to obtain information on items not normally seen in published lists and advertisements. Support from these people of course goes beyond data leading to Catalogue Values, for they also are key to editorial changes.

American Air Mail Society
John J. Smith, 102 Arbor Road, Cinnaminson, NJ 08077

American Ceremony Program Society
David Rosenthal, 48 Hillary Lane, Westbury, NY 11590-1647

American Philatelic Society
P.O. Box 8000, State College, PA 16803

American Topical Association
P.O. Box 630, Johnstown, PA 15907

Arabian Philatelic Association
ARAMCO Box 1929, Dhahran 31311, Saudi Arabia

Bureau Issues Association
Richard T. Hall, 29 Nantucket Place, Manhatten Beach, CA 90266

Canal Zone Study Group
Richard H. Salz, 60 27th Ave., San Francisco, CA 94121

Costa Rica Collectors, Society of
Dr. Hector Mena, P.O. Box 14831, Baton Rouge, LA 70808

Eire Philatelic Association
Michael J. Conway, 74 Woodside Circle, Fairfield, CT 06430

Ethiopian Philatelic Society
Miss Hugette Gagnon, P.O. Box 8110-45, Blaine, WA 98230

France & Colonies Philatelic Society
Stanley J. Luft, 16291 West 56th Place, Golden, CO 80403

Germany Philatelic Society
Jason Manchester, P.O. Box 3128, Columbus, OH 43210

Guatemala Collectors, International Society of
Jack M. Jonza, P.O. Box 271, Vernon, NY 13476

Haiti Philatelic Society
Peter C. Jeannopoulos, 34-38 92 Street, Jackson Heights, NY 11372

Hungarian Philately, Society for
Dr. Stephan I. Frater, 195 George St., Providence, RI 02906

Iran Philatelic Circle
A. John Ultee, 816 Gwynne Ave., Waynesboro, VA 22980

Mexico-Elmhurst Philatelic Society
William E. Shelton, P.O. Box 39838, San Antonio, TX 78218

Netherlands Philately, American Society of
F.H. Rummens, 94 Munroe Pl., Regina, SK Canada S4S 4P7

Philatelic Foundation
21 E. 40th St., New York, NY 10016

Rhodesian Study Circle
William R. Wallace, P.O. Box 16381, San Francisco, CA 94116

Spanish Philatelic Society
Bob Penn, P.O. Box 3804, Gettysburg, PA 17325

Jose L. Alvarez A.
B.J. Ammel
Mike Armus
Arthur L-F. Askins
Dan Barber
Jules K. Beck
Steven R. Belasck
Vladimir Berrio-Lemm
Torbjorn E. Bjork
Forrest H. Blanding
George W. Brett
Roger S. Brody
Howard J. Burkhalter
Joseph Bush
Lawrence A. Bustillo
Herman J. Cestero, Jr.
E.J. Chamberlin
Richard A. Champagne
Albert F. Chang
Henry Chlanda
Michael J. Conway
Jim Cross
Bruce Cruickshank
Charles Cwiakala
Richard Drews
P.J. Drossos
Bob Dumaine
Donald East
Peter R. Feltus
Henry Fisher
Geoffrey Flack
William Fletcher
Joseph E. Foley
Marvin Frey
Richard Friedberg
Peter Georgiadis
Melvin Getlan
Brian M. Green
Harry Hagendorf
Henry Hahn
Rudolf Hamar
John B. Head
Robert R. Hegland
Clifford O. Herrick
Lee H. Hill
Rollin C. Huggins, Jr.
G.W. Hughes
Eric Jackson
Michael Jaffe
Vincent E. Jay
Peter C. Jeannopoulos
Dennis W. Johnson
Jack Jonza
William E. Kahn
Stan Katz
James W. Kerr
Charles Kezbers
William S. Langs
Steve Levine
Anshan Li
Lance D. Limoges
Pedro Llach
Ed Long
Walter J. Mader
Clyde R. Maxwell
Menachim Mayo
P.J. McGowan
Timothy McRee
Robert Meyersburg
Jack Molesworth
Gary M. Morris
Peter Mosiondz, Jr.
Bruce M. Moyer
Stanley Pillar
Daniel N. Pinchot
Gilbert N. Plass
Jack L. Reber
Sidney L. Rich
Stanley Richmond
Patrick Riggs
Lee Robbins
Michael Rogers
Jon Rose
Jack Rosenthal
Richard H. Salz
Byron Sandfield
Eugene K. Sanger
Jacques C. Schiff, Jr.
Richard Schwartz
Martin Sellinger
Michael Shamilzadeh
William E. Shelton
J. Randall Shoemaker
Hubert C. Skinner
Jay Smith
Richard Stambaugh
Ernst Theimer
Scott Trepel
James O. Vadeboncoeur
George P. Wagner
Jerome S. Wagshal
Daniel C. Warren
Richard Washburn
William R. Weiss, Jr.
Hans A. Westphal
John Wilson
Clarke Yarbrough
Nathan Zankel
Joe Zito

Special Notices

Classification of stamps

The *Scott Standard Postage Stamp Catalogue* lists stamps by country of issue. The next level is a listing by section on the basis of the function of the stamps. The principal sections cover regular postage stamps; air post stamps; postage due stamps, registration stamps, special delivery and express stamps, semi-postal stamps, and, so on. Except for regular postage, Catalogue numbers for all sections include a prefix letter (or number-letter combination) denoting the class to which the stamp belongs.

Following is a listing of the most commonly used of the prefixes.

Category	**Prefix**
Air Post	C
Military	M
Newspaper	P
Occupation — Regular Issues	N
Official	O
Parcel Post	Q
Postage Due	J
Postal Tax	RA
Semi-Postal	B
Special Delivery	E
War Tax	MR

Other prefixes used by more than one country are:

Acknowledgment of Receipt	H
Air Post Official	CO
Air Post Parcel Post	CQ
Air Post Postal Tax	RAC
Air Post Registration	CF
Air Post Semi-Postal	CB
Air Post Semi-Postal Official	CBO
Air Post Special Delivery	CE
Authorized Delivery	EY
Franchise	S
Insured Letter	G
Marine Insurance	GY
Military Air Post	MC
Military Parcel Post	MQ
Occupation — Air Post	NC
Occupation — Official	NO
Occupation — Postage Due	NJ
Occupation — Postal Tax	NRA
Occupation — Semi-Postal	NB
Occupation — Special Delivery	NE
Parcel Post Authorized Delivery	QY
Postal-fiscal	AR
Postal Tax Due	RAJ
Postal Tax Semi-Postal	RAB
Registration	F
Semi-Postal Special Delivery	EB
Special Delivery Official	EO
Special Handling	QE

New issue listings

Updates to this catalogue appear each month in the *Scott Stamp Monthly.* Included in this update are additions to the listings of countries found in *Scott Standard Postage Stamp Catalogue* and the *Specialized Catalogue of United States Stamps,* new issues of countries not listed in the catalogues, and corrections and updates to current editions of this catalogue.

From time to time there will be changes in the listings from the *Scott Stamp Monthly* to the next edition of the catalogue, as additional information becomes available.

The catalogue update section of the *Scott Stamp Monthly* is the most timely presentation of this material available. Annual subscription to the *Scott Stamp Monthly* is available from Scott Publishing Co., P.O. Box 828, Sidney, OH 45365.

Number changes

A list of catalogue number changes from the previous edition of the catalogue appears at the back of each volume.

Grade

A stamp's grade and condition are crucial to its value. Values quoted in this catalogue are for stamps graded at Fine-Very Fine and with no faults. Exceptions are noted in the text. The illustrations show an example of a Fine-Very Fine grade between the grades immediately below and above it: Fine and Very Fine.

FINE stamps have the design noticeably off-center on two sides. Imperforate stamps may have small margins and earlier issues may show the design touching one edge of the stamp. Used stamps may have heavier than usual cancellations.

FINE-VERY FINE stamps may be somewhat off-center on one side, or only slightly off-center on two sides. Imperforate stamps will have two margins at least normal size and the design will not touch the edge. *Early issues of a country may be printed in such a way that the design naturally is very close to the edges.* Used stamps will not have a cancellation that detracts from the design.

VERY FINE stamps maybe slightly off-center on one side, with the design well clear of the edge. Imperforate stamps will have three margins at least normal size. Used stamps will have light or otherwise neat cancellations.

Condition

The above definitions describe *grade,* which is centering and (for used stamps) cancellation. *Condition* refers to the soundness of the stamp, i.e., faults, repairs, and other factors influencing price.

Copies of a stamp which are of a lesser grade and/or condition trade at lower prices. Those of exceptional quality often command higher prices.

Factors that can increase the value of a stamp include exceptionally wide margins, particularly fresh color, and the presence of selvage.

Factors other than faults that decrease the value of a stamp include no gum or regumming, hinge remnant, foreign object adhering to gum, natural inclusion, or a straight edge.

Faults include a missing piece, tear, clipped perforation, pin or other hole, surface scuff, thin spot, crease, toning, oxidation or other form of color changeling, short or pulled perforation, stains or such man-made changes as reperforation or the chemical removal or lightening of a cancellation.

Scott Publishing Co. recognizes that there is no formal, enforced grading scheme for postage stamps, and that the final price you pay for a stamp or obtain for a stamp you are selling will be determined by individual agreement at the time of the transaction.

Catalogue Value

The Scott Catalogue value is a retail price, what you could expect to pay for the stamp in a grade of Fine-Very Fine. The value listed is a reference which reflects recent actual dealer selling prices.

Dealer retail price lists, public auction results, published prices in advertising, and individual solicitation of retail prices from dealers, collectors, and specialty organizations have been used in establishing the values found in this catalogue.

Use this catalogue as a guide in your own buying and selling. The actual price you pay for a stamp may be higher or lower than the catalogue value because of one or more of the following: the amount of personal service a dealer offers, increased interest in the country or topic represented by the stamp or set, whether an item is a "loss leader," part of a special sale, or otherwise is being sold for a short period of time at a lower price, or if at a public auction you are able to obtain an item inexpensively because of little interest in the item at that time.

For unused stamps, more recent issues are valued as never-hinged, with the beginning point determined on a country-by-country basis. Notes in the text prominently show the beginning points of these designations.

As a point of philatelic-economic fact, the lower the value shown for an item in this catalogue, the greater the percentage of that value which is attributed to dealer mark-up and profit margin. Thus, a packet of 1,000 different items — each of which has a catalogue value of 15 cents — normally sells for considerably less than 150 dollars!

Persons wishing to establish the specific value of a stamp or other philatelic item may wish to consult with recognized stamp experts (collectors or dealers) and review current information or recent developments which would affect stamp prices.

Scott Publishing Co. assumes no obligation to revise the values during the distribution period of this catalogue or to advise users of other facts, such as stamp availability, political and economic conditions, or collecting preferences, any of which may have an immediate positive or negative impact on values.

Understanding valuing notations

The *absence of a value* does not necessarily suggest that a stamp is scarce or rare. In the U.S. listings, a dash in the value column means that the stamp is known in a stated form or variety, but information is lacking or insufficient for purposes of establishing a usable catalogue value.

Stamp values in *italics* generally refer to items which are difficult to value accurately. For expensive items, i.e., value at $1,000 or more, a value in italics represents an item which trades very seldom, such as a unique item. For inexpensive items, a value in italics represents a warning. One example is a "blocked" issue where the issuing postal administration controlled one stamp in a set in an attempt to make the whole set more valuable. Another example is a single item with a very low face value which sells in the marketplace, at the time of issue, at an extreme multiple of face value. Some countries have released back issues of stamps in a canceled-to-order form, sometimes covering at much as 10 years.

The Scott Catalogue values for used stamps reflect canceled-to-order material when such are found to predominate in the marketplace for the issue involved. Frequently notes appear in the stamp listings to specify items which are valued as canceled-to-order or if there is a premium for postally used examples.

Another example of a warning to collectors is a stamp that used has a value considerably higher than the unused version. Here, the collector is cautioned to be certain the used version has a readable, contemporary cancellation. The type of cancellation on a stamp can be an important factor in determining its sale price. Catalogue values do not apply to fiscal or telegraph cancels, unless otherwise noted.

The *minimum catalogue value* of a stamp is 15 cents, to cover a dealer's costs and then preparing it for resale. As noted, the sum of these values does not properly represent the "value" of sets with a number of minimum-value stamps, or packets of stamps.

Values in the "unused" column are for stamps that have been hinged, unless there is a specific note in a listing after which unused stamps are valued as never-hinged. A similar note will appear at the beginning of the country's listings, noting exactly where the dividing point between hinged and never-hinged is for each section of the listings. Where a value for a used stamp is considerably higher than for the unused stamp, the value applies to a stamp showing a distinct contemporary postmark of origin.

Many countries sell canceled-to-order stamps at a marked reduction of face value. Countries which sell or have sold canceled-to-order stamps at *full* face value include Australia, Netherlands, France, and Switzerland. It may be almost impossible to identify such stamps, if the gum has been removed, because official government canceling devices are used. Postally used copies on cover, of these items, are usually worth more than the canceled-to-order stamps with original gum.

Abbreviations

Scott Publishing Co. uses a consistent set of abbreviations throughout this catalogue to conserve space while still providing necessary information. The first block shown here refers to color names only:

COLOR ABBREVIATIONS

amb	amber	lem	lemon
anil	aniline	lil	lilac
ap	apple	lt	light
aqua	aquamarine	mag	magenta
az	azure	man	manila
bis	bister	mar	maroon
bl	blue	mv	mauve
bld	blood	multi	multicolored
blk	black	mlky	milky
bril	brilliant	myr	myrtle
brn	brown	ol	olive
brnsh	brownish	olvn	olivine
brnz	bronze	org	orange
brt	bright	pck	peacock
brnt	burnt	pnksh	pinkish
car	carmine	Prus	Prussian
cer	cerise	pur	purple
chlky	chalky	redsh	reddish
cham	chamois	res	reseda
chnt	chestnut	ros	rosine
choc	chocolate	ryl	royal
chr	chrome	sal	salmon
cit	citron	saph	sapphire
cl	claret	scar	scarlet
cob	cobalt	sep	sepia
cop	copper	sien	sienna
crim	crimson	sil	silver
cr	cream	sl	slate
dk	dark	stl	steel
dl	dull	turq	turquoise
dp	deep	ultra	ultramarine
db	drab	ven	Venetian
emer	emerald	ver	vermilion
gldn	golden	vio	violet
grysh	grayish	yel	yellow
grn	green	yelsh	yellowish
grnsh	greenish		
hel	heliotrope		
hn	henna		
ind	indigo		
int	intense		
lav	lavender		

When no color is given for an overprint or surcharge, black is the color used. Abbreviations for colors used for overprints and surcharges are: "(B)" or "(Blk)," black; "(Bl)," blue; "(R)," red; "(G)," green; etc.

Additional abbreviations in this catalogue are shown below:

Adm............. Administration
AFL............. American Federation of Labor
Anniv........... Anniversary
APU............. Arab Postal Union
APS............. American Philatelic Society
ASEAN........ Association of South East Asian Nations
ASPCA........ American Society for the Prevention of Cruelty to Animals
Assoc........... Association

b.................. Born
BEP............. Bureau of Engraving and Printing
Bicent.......... Bicentennial
Bklt............. Booklet
Brit.............. British
btwn............ Between
Bur.............. Bureau

c. or ca......... Circa
CAR............ Central African Republic
Cat.............. Catalogue
Cent............ Centennial, century, centenary
CEPT........... Conference Europeenne des Administrations des Postes et des Telecommunications
CIO............. Congress of Industrial Organizations
Conf............ Conference
Cong........... Congress
Cpl.............. Corporal
CTO............ Canceled to order

d.................. Died
Dbl.............. Double
DDR............ German Democratic Republic (East Germany)

ECU............ European currency unit
EEC............ European Economic Community
EKU............ Earliest known use
Engr............ Engraved
Exhib.......... Exhibition
Expo........... Exposition

FAO............ Food and Agricultural Organization of the United Nations
Fed............. Federation
FIP.............. Federation International de Philatelie

GB.............. Great Britain
Gen............. General
GPO............ General post office

Horiz........... Horizontal

ICAO........... International Civil Aviation Organization
ICY............. International Cooperation Year
IEY............. International Education Year
ILO............. International Labor Organization
Imperf.......... Imperforate
Impt............ Imprint
Intl.............. International
Invtd........... Inverted
IQSY........... International Quiet Sun Year
ITU............. International Telecommunications Union
ITY............. International Tourism Year
IWY............ International Women's Year
IYC............. International Year of the Child
IYD............. International Year of the Disabled
IYP............. International Year of Peace
IYSH........... International Year of Shelter for the Homeless
IYY............. International Youth Year

L.................. Left
Lieut............ Lieutenant
Litho............ Lithographed
LL............... Lower left
LR............... Lower right

mm............. Millimeter
Ms............... Manuscript

NASA.......... National Aeronautics and Space Administration
Natl............. National
NATO.......... North Atlantic Treaty Organization
No............... Number
NY.............. New York
NYC............ New York City

OAU............ Organization of African Unity
OPEC........... Organization of Petroleum Exporting Countries
Ovpt............ Overprint
Ovptd.......... Overprinted

P................. Plate number
Perf............. Perforated, perforation
Phil.............. Philatelic
Photo........... Photogravure
PO............... Post office
Pr................ Pair
P.R.............. Puerto Rico
PRC............. People's Republic of China (Mainland China)
Prec............. Precancel, precanceled
Pres............. President
PTT............. Post, Telephone and Telegraph
PUAS........... Postal Union of the Americas and Spain
PUASP........ Postal Union of the Americas, Spain and Portugal

Rio.............. Rio de Janeiro
ROC............ Republic of China (Taiwan)

SEATO........ South East Asia Treaty Organization
Sgt.............. Sergeant
Soc.............. Society
Souv............ Souvenir
SSR............. Soviet Socialist Republic
St................ Saint, street
Surch........... Surcharge

Typo............ Typographed

UAE............ United Arab Emirates
UAMPT....... Union of African and Malagasy Posts and Telecommunications
UL.............. Upper left
UN.............. United Nations
UNCTAD..... United Nations Conference on Trade and Development
UNESCO...... United Nations Educational, Scientific and Cultural Organization
UNICEF....... United Nations Children's Fund

UNPA .... United Nations Postal Administration
Unwmkd....... Unwatermarked
UPAE........... Union Postal de las Americas y Espana
UPU .... Universal Postal Union
UR............... Upper Right
US .... United States
USPO .... United States Post Office Department
USPS .... United States Postal Service
USSR........... Union of Soviet Socialist Republics

Vert............. Vertical
VP................ Vice president

WCY .... World Communications Year
WFUNA....... World Federation of United Nations Associations
WHO........... World Health Organization
Wmk............ Watermark
Wmkd.......... Watermarked
WMO .... World Meteorological Organization
WRY............ World Refugee Year
WWF........... World Wildlife Fund
WWI............ World War I
WWII .... World War II

YAR .... Yemen Arab Republic
Yemen PDR. Yemen People's Democratic Republic

Examination

Scott Publishing Co. will not pass upon the genuiness, grade or condition of stamps, because of the time and responsibility involved. Rather, there are several expertizing groups which undertake this work for both collectors and dealers. Neither can Scott Publishing Co. appraise or identify philatelic material. The Company cannot take responsibility for unsolicited stamps or covers.

How to order from your dealer

It is not necessary to write the full description of a stamp as listed in this catalogue. All that you need is the name of the country, the Scott Catalogue number and whether the item is unused or used. For example, "Japan Scott 422 unused" is sufficient to identify the stamp of Japan listed as "422 A206 5y brown."

Basic Stamp Information

A stamp collector's knowledge of the combined elements that make a given issue of a stamp unique determines his or her ability to identify stamps. These elements include paper, watermark, method of separation, printing, design and gum. On the following pages each of these important areas is described.

PAPER

Paper is a material composed of a compacted web of cellulose fibers formed into sheets. Paper may be manufactured in sheets, or may have been part of a roll before being cut to size. The fibers most often used for the paper on which stamps are printed are bark, wood, straw and certain grasses with linen or cotton rags added for greater strength. Grinding and bleaching these fibers reduces them to a slushy pulp. Sizing and sometimes coloring matter are added to the pulp. Thin coatings of pulp are poured onto sieve-like frames, which allow the water to run off while retaining the matted pulp. Mechanical processes convert the pulp, when it is almost dry, by passing it through smooth or engraved rollers — dandy rolls — or placed between cloth in a press then flattens and dries the product under pressure.

Stamp paper falls broadly into two types: wove and laid. The nature of the surface of the frame onto which the pulp is first fed causes the differences in appearance between the two. If the surface is smooth and even the paper will be of uniform texture throughout, showing no light and dark areas when held to a light. This is known as *wove paper.* Early paper-making machines poured the pulp onto continuously circulating web of felt, but modern machines feed the pulp onto a cloth-like screen made of closely interwoven fine wires. This paper, when held to a light, will show little dots or points very close together. The proper name for this is "wire wove," but the type is still considered wove. Any U.S. or British stamp printed after 1880 will serve as an example of wire wove paper.

Closed spaced parallel wires, with cross wires at wider intervals, make up the frames used for *laid paper.* A greater thickness of the pulp will settle between the wires. The paper, when held to a light, will show alternate light and dark lines. The spacing and the thickess of the lines may vary, but on any one sheet of paper they are all alike. See Russia Scott 31-38 for an example of laid paper.

Batonne, from the French word meaning "a staff," is used if the lines are spaced quite far apart, like the ruling on a writing tablet. Batonne paper may be either wove or laid. If laid, fine laid lines can be seen between the batons. The laid lines, which are a form of watermark, may be geometrical figures such as squares, diamonds, rectangles, or wavy lines.

Quadrille is the term used when the lines form little squares. *Oblong quadrille* is the term used when rectangles rather than squares are formed. See Mexico-Guadalajara Scott 35-37.

Paper also is classified as thick or thin, hard or soft, and by color if dye is added during manufacture. Such colors may be yellowish, greenish, bluish and reddish. Following are brief explanations of other types of paper used for stamps:

Pelure — A very thin, hard and often brittle paper, it is sometimes bluish or grayish. See Serbia Scott 169-170.

Native — A term applied to handmade papers used to produce some of the early stamps of the Indian states. Japanese paper, originally made of mulberry fibers and rice flour, is part of this group. See Japan Scott 1-18.

Manila — Often used to make stamped envelopes and wrappers, it is a coarse textured stock, usually smooth on one side and rough on the other. A variety of colors are known.

Silk — Introduced by the British in 1847 as a safeguard against counterfeiting, bits of colored silk thread are scattered throughout it. Silk-thread paper has uninterrupted threads of colored silk arranged so that one or more threads run through the stamp or postal stationery. See Great Britain Scott 5-6.

Granite — Filled with minute fibers of various colors and lengths, this should not be confused with either type of silk paper. See Austria Scott 172-175.

Chalky — A chalk-like substance coats the surface to discourage the cleaning and reuse of canceled stamps. Because the design is imprinted on the water-soluble coating of the stamp, any attempt to remove a cancellation will destroy the stamp. *Do not soak these stamps in any fluid.* To remove a stamp printed on chalky paper from an envelope, wet the paper from underneath the stamp until the gum dissolves enough to release the stamp from the paper. See St. Kitts-Nevis Scott 89-90.

India — Another name for this paper, originally introduced from China about 1750, is "China Paper." It is a thin, opaque paper often used for plate and die proofs by many countries.

Double — In philately, this has two distinct meanings. The first, used experimentally as a means to discourage reuse, is two-ply paper, usually a combination of a thick and a thin sheet, joined during manufacture. The design is printed on the thin paper. Any attempt to remove a cancellation would destroy the design. The second occurs on the rotary press, when the end of one paper roll is glued to the next roll to save time feeding the paper through the press. Stamp designs are printed over the joined paper and, if overlooked by inspectors, may get into post office stocks.

Goldbeater's Skin — Used for the 1866 issue of Prussia, it was made of a tough translucent paper. The design was printed in reverse on the back of the stamp, and the gum applied over the printing. It is impossible to remove stamps printed on this type of paper from the paper to which they are affixed without destroying the design.

Ribbed — An uneven, corrugated surface made by passing the paper through ridged roller. This type exists on some copies of U.S. Scott 156-165.

Various other substances have been used for stamp manufacture, including wood, aluminum, copper, silver and gold foil; plastic; and silk and cotton fabrics. Stamp collectors and dealers consider most of these as novelties designed for sale to collectors.

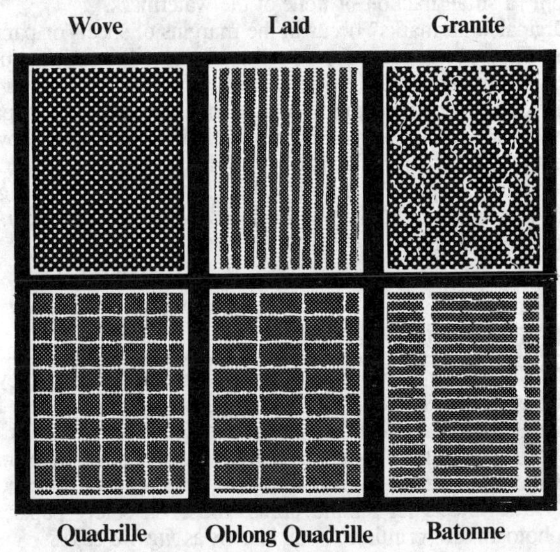

WATERMARKS

Watermarks are an integral part of the paper, for they are formed in the process of paper manufacture. They consist of small designs formed of wire or cut from metal and soldered to the surface of the dandy roll or mold. The designs may be in the form of crowns, stars, anchors, letters, etc. These pieces of metal — known in the paper-making industry as "bits" — impress a design into the paper. The design may be seen by holding the stamp to the light. Some are more easily seen with a watermark detector. This important tool is a small black tray into which the stamp is placed face down and dampened with a watermark detection fluid that brings up the watermark in the form of dark lines against a lighter background.

Multiple watermarks of Crown Agents and Burma

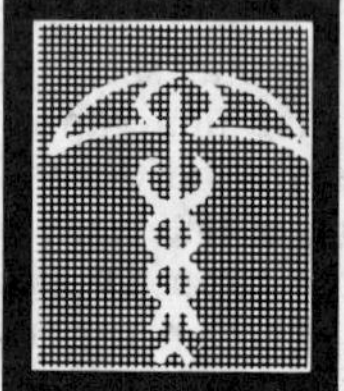

Watermarks of Uruguay, Vatican and Jamaica

WARNING: Some inks used in the photogravure process dissolve in watermark fluids. (See section below on Soluble Printing Inks.) Also, see "chalky paper." There also are electric watermark detectors, which come with plastic filter disks of various colors. The disks neutralize the color of the stamp, permitting the watermark to be seen more easily.

Watermarks may be found reversed, inverted, sideways or diagonal, as seen from the back of the stamp. The relationship of watermark to stamp design depends on the position of the printing plates or how paper is fed through the press. On machine-made paper, watermarks normally are read from right to left. The design is repeated closely throughout the sheet in a "multiple-watermark design." In a "sheet watermark," the design appears only once on the sheet, but extends over many stamps. Individual stamps may carry only a small fraction or none of the watermark.

"Marginal watermarks" occur in the margins of sheets or panes of stamps. They occur outside the border of paper (ostensibly outside the area where stamps are to be printed) a large row of letters may spell the name of the country or the manufacturer of the paper. Careless press feeding may cause parts of these letters to show on stamps of the outer row of a pane.

For easier reference, Scott Publishing Co. identifies and assigns a number to watermarks. See the numerical index of watermarks at the back of this volume.

Soluble Printing Inks

WARNING: Most stamp colors are permanent. That is, they are not seriously affected by light or water. Some colors may fade from excessive exposure to light. There are stamps printed with inks which dissolve easily in water or fluids used to detect watermarks. Use of these inks is intentional to prevent the removal of cancellations. Water affects all aniline prints, those on safety paper, and some photogravure printings — all known as *fugitive colors.*

Separation

"Separation" is the general term used to describe methods of separating stamps. The earliest issues, such as the 1840 Penny Black of Great Britain (Scott 1), did not have any means provided for separating. It was expected they would be cut apart with scissors. These are imperforate stamps. Many stamps first issued imperforate were later issued perforated. Care therefore must be observed in buying imperforate stamps to be certain they were issued imperforate and are not perforated copies that have been altered by having the perforations trimmed away. Imperforate stamps sometimes are valued as singles, as within this catalogue. But, imperforate varieties of normally perforated stamps should be collected in pairs or larger pieces as indisputable evidence of their imperforate character.

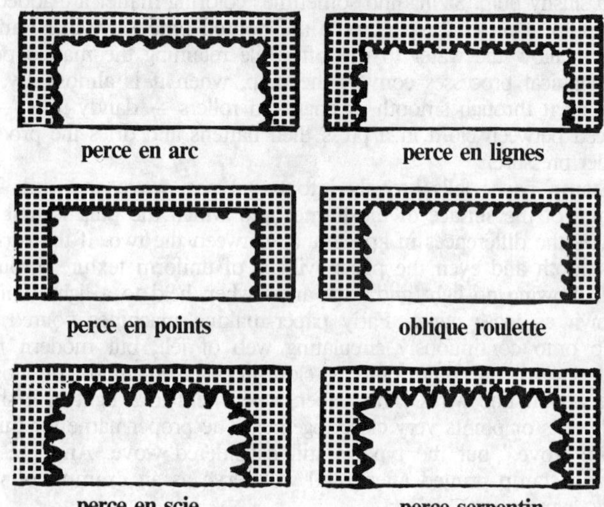

ROULETTING

Separation is brought about by two general methods during stamp production, rouletting and perforating. In rouletting, the paper is cut partly or wholly through, with no paper removed. In perforating, a part of the paper is removed. Rouletting derives its name from the French roulette, a spur-like wheel. As the wheel is rolled over the paper, each point makes a small cut. The number of cuts made in two centimeters determines the gauge of the roulette, just as the number of perforations in two centimeters determines the gauge of the perforation (see below).

The shape and arrangement of the teeth on the wheels varies. Various roulette types generally carry French names:

Perce en lignes — rouletted in lines. The paper receives short, straight cuts in lines. See Mexico Scott 500.

Perce en points — pin-perforated. This differs from a small perforation because no paper is removed, although round, equidistant holes are pricked through the paper. See Mexico Scott 242-256.

Perce en arc and *perce en scie* — pierced in an arc or sawtoothed designs, forming half circles or small triangles. See Hanover (German States) Scott 25-29.

Perce en serpentin — serpentine roulettes. The cuts form a serpentine or wavy line. See Brunswick (German States) Scott 13-18.

PERFORATION

The other chief style of separation of stamps, and the one which is in universal use today, is perforating. By this process, paper between the stamps is cut away in a line of holes, usually round, leaving little bridges of paper between the stamps to hold them together. These little bridges, which project from the stamp when it is torn from the pane are called the teeth of the perforation. As the size of the perforation is sometimes the only way to differentiate between two otherwise identical stamps, it is necessary to be able to measure and describe them. This is done with a perforation gauge, usually a ruler-like device that has dots to show how many perforations may be counted in the space of two centimeters. Two centimeters is the space universally adopted in which to measure perforations.

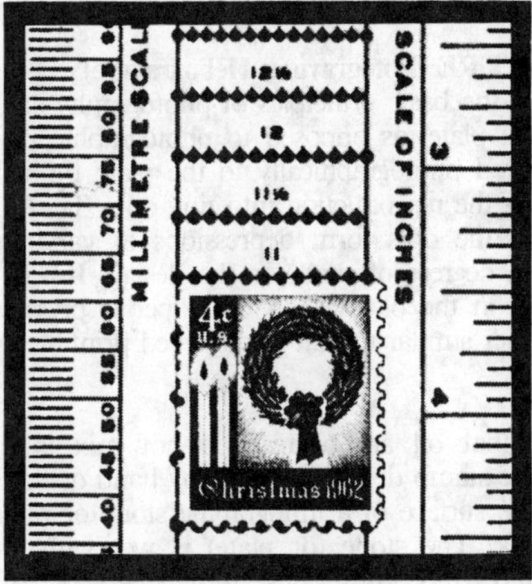

Perforation gauge

To measure the stamp, run it along the gauge until the dots on it fit exactly into the perforations of the stamp. The number to the side of the line of dots which fit the stamp's perforation is the measurement, i.e., an "11" means that 11 perforations fit between two centimeters. The description of the stamp is "perf. 11." If the gauge of the perforations on the top and bottom of a stamp differs from that on the sides, the result is a *compound perforation.* In measuring compound perforations, the gauge at top and bottom is always given first, then the sides. Thus, a stamp that measures 10½ at top and bottom and 11 at the sides is "perf. 10½ x 11." See U.S. Scott 1526.

There are stamps known with perforations different on three or all four sides. Descriptions of such items are in clockwise order, beginning with the top of the stamp.

A perforation with small holes and teeth close together is a "fine perforation." One with large holes and teeth far apart is a "coarse perforation." Holes jagged rather than clean cut, are "rough perforations." *Blind perforations* are the slight impressions left by the perforating pins if they fail to puncture the paper. Multiples of stamps showing blind perforations may command a slight premium over normally perforated stamps.

Printing Processes

ENGRAVING (Intaglio)

Master die — The initial operation in the engraving process is making of the master die. The die is a small flat block of soft steel on which the stamp design is recess engraved in reverse.

Master die

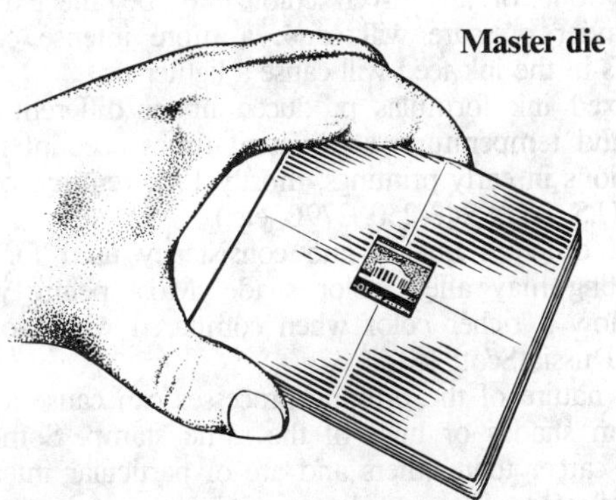

Photographic reduction of the original art is made to the appropriate size, and it serves as a tracing guide for the initial outline of the design. After completion of the engraving, the die is hardened to withstand the stress and pressures of later transfer operations.

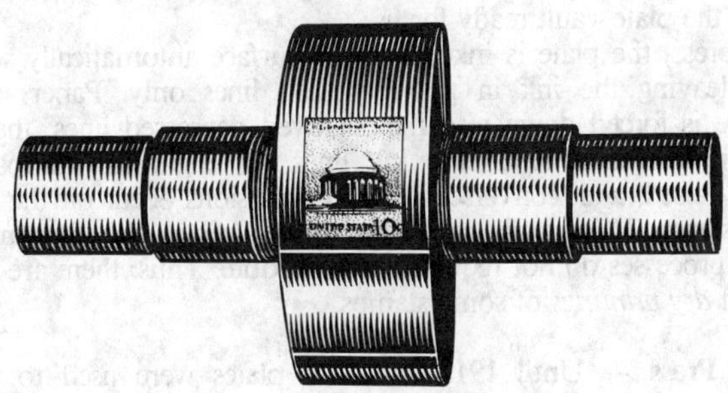

Transfer roll

Transfer roll — Next is production of the transfer roll which, as the name implies, is the medium used to transfer the subject from the die to the plate. A blank roll of soft steel, mounted on a mandrel, is placed under the bearers of the transfer press to allow it to roll freely on its axis. The hardened die is placed on the bed of the press and the face of the transfer roll is applied on the die, under pressure. The bed is then rocked back and forth under increasing pressure until the soft steel of the roll is forced into every engraved line of the die. The resulting impression on the roll is known as a "relief" or a "relief transfer." After the required number of reliefs are "rocked in," the soft steel transfer roll is also hardened.

A "relief" is the normal reproduction of the design on the die in reverse. A "defective relief" may occur during the "rocking in" process because of a minute piece of foreign material lodging on the die, or some other cause. Imperfections in the steel of the transfer roll may result in a breaking away of parts of the design. A damaged relief continued in use will transfer a repeating defect to the plate. Deliberate alterations of reliefs sometimes occur. "Broken reliefs" and "altered reliefs" designate these changed conditions.

Plate — The final step in the procedure is the making of the printing plate. A flat piece of soft steel replaces the die on the bed of the transfer press. One of the reliefs on the transfer roll is applied on this soft steel. "Position dots" determine the position on the plate. The dots have been lightly marked in advance. After the correct position of the relief is determined, pressure is applied. By following the same method used in making the transfer roll, a transfer is entered. This transfer reproduces the design of the relief in reverse and in detail. There are as many transfers entered on the plate as there are subjects printed on the sheet of stamps.

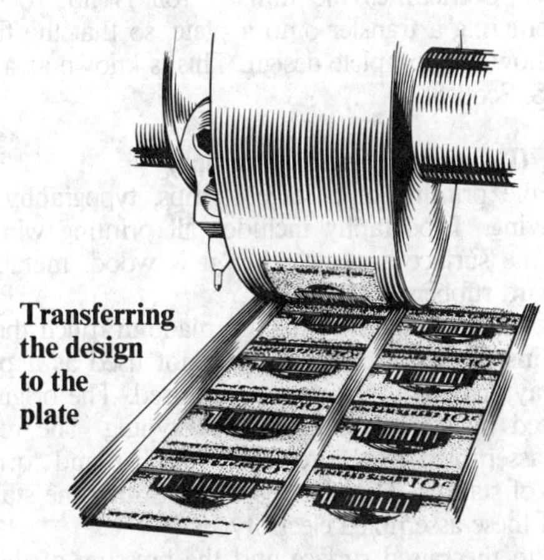

Transferring the design to the plate

Following the entering of the required transfers, the position dots, layout dots and lines, scratches, etc., generally are burnished out. Added at this time are any required *guide lines, plate numbers* or other *marginal markings*. A proof impression is then taken and, if approved, the plate machined for fitting to the press, hardened and sent to the plate vault ready for use.

On press, the plate is inked and the surface automatically wiped clean, leaving the ink in the depressed lines only. Paper under pressure is forced down into the engraved depressed lines, thereby receiving the ink. Thus, the ink lines on engraved stamps are slightly raised; and, conversely, slight depressions occur on the back of the stamp. Historically, paper had been dampened before inking. Newer processes do not require this procedure. Thus, there are both *wet* and *dry printings* of some stamps.

Rotary Press — Until 1915, only flat plates were used to print engraved stamps. Rotary press printing was introduced in 1915. After approval, *rotary press plates* require additional machining. They are curved to fit the press cylinder. "Gripper slots" are cut into the back of each plate to receive the "grippers," which hold the plate securely on the press. The plate is then hardened. Stamps printed from rotary press plates are usually longer or wider than the same stamps printed from flat press plates. The stretching of the plate during the curving process causes this enlargement.

Re-entry — In order to execute a re-entry, the transfer roll is reapplied to the plate, usually at some time after its first use on the press. Worn-out designs can be resharpened by carefully re-entering the transfer roll. If the transfer roll is not precisely in line with the impression of the plate, the registration will not be true and a double transfer will result. After a plate has been curved for the rotary press, it is impossible to make a re-entry.

Double Transfer — This is a description of the condition of a transfer on a plate that shows evidence of a duplication of all, or a portion of the design. It is usually the result of the changing of the registration between the transfer roll and the plate during the rocking-in of the original entry.

It is sometimes necessary to remove the original transfer from a plate and repeat the process a second time. If the finished re-transfer shows indications of the original impression attributable to incomplete erasure, the result is a double transfer.

Re-engraved — Either the die that has been used to make a plate or the plate itself may have it's "temper" drawn (softened) and be re-cut. The resulting impressions from such a re-engraved die or plate may differ slightly from the original issue, and are known as "re-engraved."

Short Transfer — Sometimes the transfer roll is not rocked its entire length in entering a transfer onto a plate, so that the finished transfer fails to show the complete design. This is known as a "short transfer." See U.S. Scott 8.

TYPOGRAPHY (Letterpress, Surface Printing)

As it relates to the printing of postage stamps, typography is the reverse of engraving. Typography includes all printing where the design is above the surface area, whether it is wood, metal, or in some instances hard rubber.

The master die and the engraved die are made in much the same manner. In this instance, however, the area not used as a printing surface is cut away, leaving the surface area raised. The original die is then reproduced by stereotyping or electrotyping. The resulting electrotypes are assembled in the required number and format of the desired sheet of stamps. The plate used in printing the stamps is an electroplate of these assembled electrotypes.

Ink is applied to the raised surface and the pressure of the press transfers the ink impression to the paper. In contrast with engraving, the fine lines of typography are impressed on the surface of the stamp. When viewed from the back (as on a typewritten page), the corresponding linework will be raised slightly above the surface.

PHOTOGRAVURE (Rotogravure, Heliogravure)

In this process, the basic principles of photography are applied to a sensitized metal plate, as opposed to photographic paper. The design is transferred photographically to the plate through a halftone screen, breaking the reproduction into tiny dots. The plate is treated chemically and the dots form depressions of varying depths, depending on the degrees of shade in the design. Ink is lifted out of the depressions in the plate when the paper is pressed against the plate in a manner similar to that of engraved printing.

LITHOGRAPHY

The principle that oil and water will not mix is the basis for lithography. The stamp design is drawn by hand or transferred from engraving to the surface of a lithographic stone or metal plate in a greasy (oily) ink. The stone (or plate) is wet with an acid fluid, causing it to repel the printing ink in all areas not covered by the greasy ink.

Transfer paper is used to transfer the design from the original stone of plate. A series of duplicate transfers are grouped and, in turn, transferred to the final printing plate.

Photolithography — The application of photographic processes to lithography. This process allows greater flexibility of design, related to use of halftone screens combined with linework.

Offset — A development of the lithographic process. A rubber-covered blanket cylinder takes up the impression from the inked lithographic plate. From the "blanket" the impression is *offset* or transferred to the paper. Greater flexibility and speed are the principal reasons offset printing has largely displaced lithography. The term "lithography" covers both processes, and results are almost identical.

Sometimes two or even three printing methods are combined in producing stamps.

EMBOSSED (Relief) Printing

Embossing is a method in which the design first is sunk into the metal of the die. Printing is done against a yielding platen, such as leather or linoleum. The platen is forced into the depression of the die, thus forming the design on the paper in relief.

Embossing may be done without color (see Sardinia Scott 4-6); with color printed around the embossed area (see Great Britain Scott 5 and most U.S. envelopes); and with color in exact registration with the embossed subject (see Canada Scott 656-657).

INK COLORS

Inks or colored papers used in stamp printing usually are of mineral origin. The tone of any given color may be affected by many aspects: heavier pressure will cause a more intense color, slight interruptions in the ink feed will cause a lighter tint.

Hand-mixed ink formulas produced under different conditions (humidity and temperature) at different times account for notable color variations in early printings, mostly 19th century, of the same stamp (see U.S. Scott 248-250, 279B, etc.).

Papers of different quality and consistency used for the same stamp printing may affect color shade. Most pelure papers, for example, show a richer color when compared with wove or laid papers. See Russia Scott 181a.

The very nature of the printing processes can cause a variety of differences in shades or hues of the same stamp. Some of these shades are scarcer than others and are of particular interest to the advanced collector.

Tagged Stamps

Tagging also is known as *luminescence, fluorescence,* and *phosphorescence.* Some tagged stamps have bars (Great Britain and Canada), frames (South Africa), or an overall coating of luminescent material applied after the stamps have been printed (United States). Another tagging method is to incorporate the luminescent material into some or all colors of the printing ink. See Australia Scott 366 and Netherlands Scott 478. A third is to mix the luminescent material with the pulp during the paper manufacturing process or apply it as a surface coating afterwards: "fluorescent" papers. See Switzerland Scott 510-514 and Germany Scott 848.

The treated stamps show up in specific colors when exposed to ultraviolet light. The wave length of light radiated by the luminescent material determines the colors and activates the triggering mechanism of the electronic machinery for sorting, facing or canceling letters.

Various fluorescent substances have been used as paper whiteners, but the resulting "hi-brite papers" show up differently under ultraviolet light and do not trigger the machines. The Scott Catalogue does not recognize these papers.

Many countries now use tagging in its various forms to expedite mail handling, following introduction by Great Britain, on an experimental basis, in 1959. Among these countries, and dates of their introduction, are Germany, 1961; Canada and Denmark, 1962; United States, Australia, Netherlands and Switzerland, 1963; Belgium and Japan, 1966; Sweden and Norway, 1967; Italy, 1968; and Russia, 1969.

Certain stamps were issued with and without the luminescent feature. In those instances, Scott lists the "tagged" variety in the United States, Canada, Great Britain and Switzerland listings and notes the situation in some of the other countries.

Gum

The gum on the back of a stamp may be smooth, rough, dark, white, colored or tinted. It may be either obvious or virtually invisible as on Canada Scott 453 or Rwanda Scott 287-294. Most stamp gumming adhesives use gum arabic or dextrine as a base. Certain polymers such as polyvinyl alcohol (PVA) have been used extensively since World War II. The PVA gum which the security printers Harrison & Sons of Great Britain introduced in 1968 is dull, slightly yellowish and almost invisible.

The *Scott Standard Postage Stamp Catalogue* does not list items by types of gum. The *Scott Specialized Catalogue of United States Stamps* does differentiate among some types of gum for certain issues.

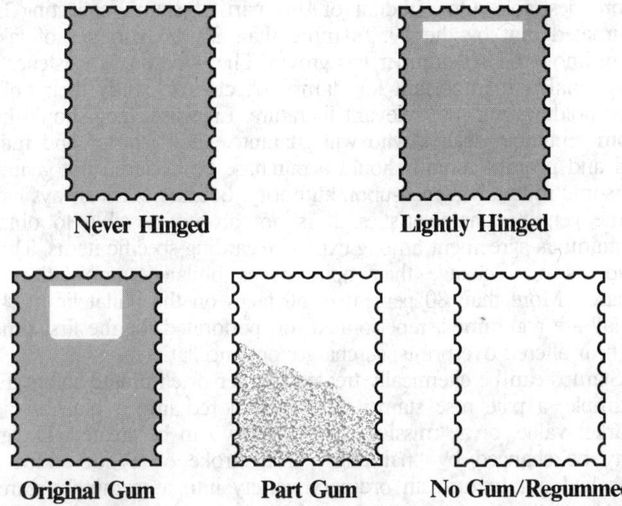

For purposes of determining the grade of an unused stamp, Scott Publishing Co. presents the following (with accompanying illustrations) definitions: **Never Hinged (NH)** — Full original gum with no hinge mark or other blemish or disturbance. The presence of an expertizer's mark does not disqualify a stamp from this designation; **Lightly Hinged (LH)** — Full original gum with a light disturbance of the gum from the removal of a peelable hinge; **Original Gum (OG)** — Hinging and other disturbances should affect 20 percent or less of the original gum. A stamp issued without gum also fits this category; **Part Gum (PG)** — Between 20 and 80 percent of the original gum remains. The stamp may have hinge remnants; **No Gum (NG) or Regummed (RE)** — A stamp with no gum or less than 20 percent of the original gum. A regummed stamp, considered the same as a stamp with none of its original gum, fits this category.

Stamps having full *original gum* sell for more than those from which the gum has been removed. Reprints of stamps may have gum differing from the original issues.

Many stamps have been issued without gum and the catalogue will note this fact. See China Scott 1438-1440. Sometimes, gum may have been removed to preserve the stamp. Germany Scott B68 is valued in the catalogue with gum removed.

Reprints and Reissues

These are impressions of stamps (usually obsolete) made from the original plates or stones. If valid for postage and from obsolete issues, they are *reissues.* If they are from current issues, they are *second, third,* etc., *printings.* If designated for a particular purpose, they are *special printings.*

Scott normally lists those reissues and reprints that are valid for postage.

When reprints are not valid for postage, but made from original dies and plates by authorized persons, they are *official reprints. Private reprints* are made from original plates and dies by private hands. *Official reproductions* or imitations are made from new dies and plates by government authorization.

For the United States' 1876 Centennial, the U.S. government made official imitations of its first postage stamps. Produced were copies of the first two stamps (listed as Scott 3-4), reprints of the demonetized pre-1861 issues and reissues of the 1861 stamps, the 1869 stamps and the then-current 1875 denominations. An example of the private reprint is that of the New Haven, Connecticut, postmaster's provisional.

Most reprints differ slightly from the original stamp in some characteristic, such as gum, paper, perforation, color or watermark. Sometimes the details are followed so meticulously that only a student of that specific stamp is able to distinguish the reprint from the original.

Remainders and Canceled to Order

Some countries sell their stock of old stamps when a new issue replaces them. To avoid postal use, the *remainders* usually are canceled with a punch hole, a heavy line or bar, or a more-or-less regular cancellation. The most famous merchant of remainders was Nicholas F. Seebeck. In the 1880's and 1890's, he arranged printing contracts between the Hamilton Bank Note Co., of which he was a director, and several Central and South American countries. The contracts provided that the plates and all remainders of the yearly issues became the property of Hamilton. Seebeck saw to it that ample stock remained. The "Seebecks," both remainders and reprints, were standard packet fillers for decades.

Some countries also issue stamps *canceled to order (CTO),* either in sheets with original gum or stuck onto pieces of paper or envelopes and canceled. Such CTO items generally are worth less than postally used stamps. Most can be detected by the presence of gum. However, as the CTO practice goes back at least to 1885, the gum inevitably has been washed off some stamps so they could pass for postally used. The normally applied postmarks usually differ slightly and specialists are able to tell the difference. When applied individually to envelopes by philatelically minded persons, CTO material is known as *favor canceled* and generally sells at large discounts.

Cinderellas and Facsimiles

Cinderella is a catchall term used by stamp collectors to describe phantoms, fantasies, bogus items, municipal issues, exhibition seals, local revenues, transportation stamps, labels, poster stamps, and so on. Some cinderella collectors include in their collections local postage issues, telegraph stamps, essays and proofs, forgeries and counterfeits.

A *fantasy* is an adhesive created for a nonexistent stamp issuing authority. Fantasy items range from imaginary countries (Kingdom of Sedang, Principality of Trinidad, or Occusi-Ambeno), to nonexistent locals (Winans City Post), or nonexistent transportation lines (McRobish & Co.'s Acapulco-San Francisco Line).

On the other hand, if the entity exists and might have issued stamps or did issue other stamps, the items are *bogus* stamps. These would include the Mormon postage stamps of Utah, S. Allan Taylor's Guatemala and Paraguay inventions, the propaganda issues for the South Moluccas and the adhesives of the Page & Keyes local post of Boston.

Phantoms is another term for both fantasy and bogus issues.

Facsimiles are copies or imitations made to represent original stamps, but which do not pretend to be originals. A catalogue illustration is such a facsimile. Illustrations from the Moens catalogue of the last century were occasionally colored and passed off as stamps. Since the beginning of stamp collecting, facsimiles have been made for collectors as space fillers or for reference. They often carry the word "facsimile," "falsch" (German), "sanko" or "mozo" (Japanese), or "faux" (French) overprinted on the face or stamped on the back.

Counterfeits or Forgeries

Unauthorized imitations of stamps, intended to deprive the post office of revenue, are *postal counterfeits* or *postal forgeries.* These items often command higher prices in the philatelic marketplace than the genuine stamps they imitate. Sales are illegal. Governments can, and do, prosecute those who trade in them.

The first postal forgery was of Spain's 4-cuarto carmine of 1854 (the real one is Scott 25). The forgers lithographed it, though the original was typographed. Apparently they were not satisfied and soon made an engraved forgery, which is common, unlike the scarce lithographed counterfeit. Postal forgeries quickly followed in Spain, Austria, Naples, Sardinia and the Roman States.

An infamous counterfeit to defraud is the 1-shilling Great Britain "Stock Exchange" forgery of 1872, used on telegraphs at the exchange that year. It escaped detection until a stamp dealer noticed it in 1898. Many postal counterfeits are known of U.S. stamps.

Wartime propaganda stamps of World War I and World War II may be classed as postal counterfeits. They were distributed by enemy governments or resistance groups.

Philatelic forgeries or *counterfeits* are unauthorized imitations of stamps designed to deceive and defraud stamp collectors. Such spurious items first appeared on the market around 1860 and most old-time collections contain one or more. Many are crude and easily spotted, but some can deceive the experts.

An important supplier of these early philatelic forgeries was the Hamburg printer Gebruder Spiro. Many others with reputations in this craft were S. Allan Taylor, George Hussey, James Chute, George Forune, Benjamin & Sarpy, Julius Goldner, E. Oneglia and L.H. Mercier. Among the noted 20th century forgers were Francois Fournier, Jean Sperati, and the prolific Raoul DeThuin.

Fraudulently produced copies are known of most classic rarities, many medium-priced stamps and, in this century, cheap stamps destined for beginners' packets. Few new philatelic forgeries have appeared in recent decades. Successful imitation of engraved work is virtually impossible.

It has proven far easier to produce a fake by altering a genuine stamp than to duplicate a stamp completely.

Repairs, Restoration and Fakes

Scott Publishing Co. bases its catalogue values on stamps which are free of defects and otherwise meet the standards set forth earlier in this introduction. Stamp collectors desire to have the finest copy of an item possible. Even within given grading categories there are variances. This leads to practice that is not universally defined, nor accepted, that of stamp *restoration.*

There are differences of opinion about what is "permissible" when it comes to restoration. Applying a soft eraser carefully to a stamp to remove dirt marks is one form of restoration, as is the washing of the stamp in mild soap and water. More severe forms of restoration are the pressing out of creases, or the removal of stains caused by tape. To what degree each of the above is "acceptable" is dependent on the individual situation. Further along the spectrum is the freshening of a stamp's color by removing oxide build-up or removing toning or the effects of wax paper left next to stamps shipped to the tropics.

At some point along this spectrum the concept of *repair* replaces that of "restoration." Repairs include filling in thin spots, mending tears by reweaving, adding a missing perforation tooth. Regumming stamps may have been acceptable as a restoration technique decades ago, but today it is considered a form of fakery.

Restored stamps may not sell at a discount, and it is possible that the value of individual restored items may be enhanced over that of their pre-restoration state. Specific situations will dictate the resultant value of such an item. Repaired stamps sell at substantial discounts.

When the purchaser of an item has any reason to suspect an item has been repaired, and the detection of such a repair is beyond his own ability, he should seek expert advice. There are services that specialize in such advice.

Fakes are genuine stamps altered in some way to make them more desirable. One student of this part of stamp collecting has estimated that by the 1950's more than 30,000 varieties of fakes were known. That number has grown. The widespread existence of fakes makes it important for stamp collectors to study their philatelic holdings and use relevant literature. Likewise, they should buy from reputable dealers who will guarantee their stamps and make full and prompt refund should a purchase be declared not genuine by some mutually agreed-upon authority. Because fakes always have some genuine characteristics, it is not always possible to obtain unanimous agreement among experts regarding specific items. These students may change their opinions as philatelic knowledge increases. More than 80 percent of all fakes on the philatelic market today are regummed, reperforated (or, perforated for the first time), or bear altered overprints, surcharges or cancellations.

Stamps can be chemically treated to alter or eliminate colors. For example, a pale rose stamp can be recolored into a blue of high market value, or a "missing color" variety can be created. Designs may be changed by "painting," or a stroke or a dot added or bleached out to turn an ordinary variety into a seemingly scarcer stamp. Part of a stamp can be bleached and reprinted in a different version, achieving an inverted center or frame. Margins can be added or repairs done so deceptively that the stamps move from the "repaired" into the "fake" category.

The fakers have not left the backs of the stamps untouched. They may create false watermarks, add fake grills or press out genuine grills. A thin India paper proof may be glued onto a thicker backing to "create" an issued stamp, or a proof printed on cardboard may be shaved down. Silk threads are impressed into paper and stamps have been split so that a rare paper variety is "added" to an otherwise inexpensive stamp. The most common treatment to the back of a stamp, however, is regumming.

Some in the business of faking stamps openly advertise "fool-proof" application of "original gum" to stamps that lack it. This is faking, not counterfeiting. It is believed that few early stamps have survived without being hinged. The large number of never-hinged examples of such earlier material offered for sale thus suggests the widespread extent of regumming activity. Regumming also may be used to hide repairs or thin spots. Dipping the stamp into watermark fluid often will reveal these flaws.

Fakers also tamper with separations. Ingenious ways to add margins are known. Perforated wide-margin stamps may be falsely represented as imperforate when trimmed. Reperforating is commonly done to create scarce coil or perforation varieties and to eliminate the straight-edge stamps found in sheet margin positions of many earlier issues. Custom has made straight edges less desirable. Fakers have obliged by perforating straight-edged stamps so that many are now uncommon, if not rare.

Another fertile field of the faker is that of the overprint, surcharge and cancellation. The forging of rare surcharges or overprints began in the 1880's or 1890's. These forgeries are sometimes difficult to detect, but the experts have identified almost all. Only occasionally are overprints or cancellations removed to create unoverprinted stamps or seemingly unused items. "SPECIMEN" overprints may be removed — scraping and repainting is one way — to create unoverprinted varieties. Fakers use inexpensive revenues or pen-canceled stamps to generate "unused" stamps for further faking by adding other markings. The quartz lamp and a high-powered magnifying glass help in detecting cancellation removal.

The bigger problem, however, is the addition of overprints, surcharges or cancellations — many with such precision that they are very difficult to ascertain. Plating of the stamps or the overprint can be an important method of detection.

Fake postmarks may range from many spurious fancy cancellations, to the host of markings applied to transatlantic covers, to adding "normal" postmarks to World War II-vintage definitives of some countries whose stamps are valued at far more used than unused. With the advance of cover collecting and the widespread interest in postal history, a fertile new field for fakers has come about. Some have tried to create entire covers. Others specialize in adding stamps, tied by fake cancellations, to genuine stampless covers, or replacing less expensive or damaged stamps with more valuable ones. Detailed study of postal rates in effect at the time of the cover in question, including the analysis of each handstamp in the period, ink analysis and similar techniques, usually will unmask the fraud.

Terminology

Booklets — Many countries have issued stamps in small booklets for the convenience of users. This idea is becoming increasingly more popular today in many countries. Booklets have been issued in all sizes and forms, often with advertising on the covers, on the panes of stamps or on the interleaving.

The panes may be printed from special plates or made from regular sheets. All panes from booklets issued by the United States and many from those of other countries contain stamps that are straight edged on the bottom and both sides, but perforated between. Any stamp-like unit in the pane, either printed or blank, which is not a postage stamp, is considered a *label* in the catalogue listings.

Scott lists and values panes only. Complete booklets are listed only in a very few cases. See Grenada Scott 1055. Panes are listed only when they are not fashioned from existing sheet stamps and, therefore, are identifiable from their sheet-stamp counterparts.

Panes usually do not have a "used" value because there is little market activity in used panes, even though many exist used.

Cancellations — the marks or obliterations put on a stamp by the postal authorities to show that the stamp has done service and is no long valid for postage. If made with a pen, the marking is a "pen cancellation." When the location of the post office appears in the cancellation, it is a "town cancellation." When calling attention to a cause or celebration, it is a "slogan cancellation." Many other types and styles of cancellations exist, such as duplex, numerals, targets, etc.

Coil Stamps — stamps issued in rolls for use in dispensers, affixing and vending machines. Those of the United States, Canada, Sweden and some other countries are perforated horizontally or vertically only, with the outer edges imperforate. Coil stamps of some countries, such as Great Britain, are perforated on all four sides.

Covers — envelopes, with or without adhesive postage stamps, which have passed through the mail and bear postal or other markings of philatelic interest. Before the introduction of envelopes in about 1840, people folded letters and wrote the address on the outside. Many people covered their letters with an extra sheet of paper on the outside for the address, producing the term "cover." Used airletter sheets, stamped envelopes, and other items of postal stationery also are considered covers.

Errors — stamps having some unintentional deviation from the normal. Errors include, but are not limited to, mistakes in color, paper, or watermark; inverted centers or frames on multicolor printing, surcharges or overprints, and double impressions. Factually wrong or misspelled information, if it appears on all examples of a stamp, even if corrected later, is not classified as a philatelic error.

Overprinted and Surcharged Stamps — Overprinting is a wording or design placed on stamps to alter the place of use (i.e., "Canal Zone" on U.S. stamps), to adapt them for a special purpose ("Porto" on Denmark's 1913-20 regular issues for use as postage due stamps, Scott J1-J7), or for a special occasion (Guatemala Scott 374-378).

A *surcharge* is an overprint which changes or restates the face value of the item.

Surcharges and overprints may be handstamped, typeset or, occasionally, lithographed or engraved. A few hand-written overprints and surcharges are known.

Precancels — stamps canceled before they are placed in the mail. Precanceling is done to expedite the handling of large mailings.

In the United States, precancellations generally identified the point of origin. That is, the city and state names or initials appeared, usually centered between parallel lines. More recently, bureau precancels retained the parallel lines, but the city and state designation was dropped. Recent coils have a "service inscription" to show the mail service paid for by the stamp. Since these stamps do not receive any further cancellation when used as intended, they fall under the general precancel umbrella.

Such items may not have parallel lines as part of the precancellation.

In France, the abbreviation *Affranchts* in a semicircle together with the word *Postes* is the general form. Belgian precancellations are usually a box in which the name of the city appears. Netherlands' precancellations have the name of the city enclosed between concentric circles, sometimes called a "lifesaver."

Precancellations of other countries usually follow these patterns, but may be any arrangement of bars, boxes and city names.

Precancels are listed in the catalogue only if the precancel changes the denomination (Belgium Scott 477-478); the precanceled stamp is different from the non-precancel version (untagged U.S. stamps); or, if the stamp only exists precanceled (France Scott 1096-1099, U.S. Scott 2265).

Proofs and Essays — Proofs are impressions taken from an approved die, plate or stone in which the design and color are the same as the stamp issued to the public. Trial color proofs are impressions taken from approved dies, plates or stones in varying colors. An essay is the impression of a design that differs in some way from the stamp as issued.

Provisionals — stamps issued on short notice and intended for temporary use pending the arrival of regular issues. They usually are issued to meet such contingencies as changes in government or currency, shortage of necessary postage values, or military occupation.

In the 1840's, postmasters in certain American cities issued stamps that were valid only at specific post offices. In 1861, postmasters of the Confederate States also issued stamps with limited validity. Both of these examples are known as "postmaster's provisionals."

Se-tenant — joined, referring to an unsevered pair, strip or block of stamps differing in design, denomination or overprint. See U.S. Scott 2158a.

Unless the se-tenant item has a continuous design (see U.S. Scott 1451a, 1694a) the stamps do not have to be in the same order as shown in the catalogue (see U.S. Scott 2158a).

Specimens — One of the regulations of the Universal Postal Union requires member nations to send samples of all stamps they put into service to the International Bureau in Switzerland. Member nations of the UPU receive these specimens as samples of what stamps are valid for postage. Many are overprinted, handstamped or initial-perforated "Specimen," "Canceled" or "Muestra." Some are marked with bars across the denominations (China-Taiwan), punched holes (Czechoslovakia) or back inscriptions (Mongolia).

Stamps distributed to government officials or for publicity purposes, and stamps submitted by private security printers for official approval, also may receive such defacements.

These markings prevent postal use, and all such items generally are known as "specimens."

Tete Beche — A pair of stamps in which one is upside down in relation to the other. Some of these are the result of intentional sheet arrangements, e.g. Morocco Scott B10-B11. Others occurred when one or more electrotypes accidentally were placed upside down on the plate. See Colombia Scott 57a. Separation of the stamps, of course, destroys the tete beche variety.

Currency Conversion

Country	Dollar	Pound	S Franc	Guilder	Yen	Lira	HK Dollar	D-Mark	Fr Franc	Cdn Dollar	Aust Dollar
Australia	1.318	2.401	.9029	.7262	.01029	.00109	.1701	.8176	.2435	1.0955	
Canada	1.203	2.192	.8242	.6629	.00939	.00099	.1553	.7463	.2223		.9128
France	5.412	9.861	3.708	2.9822	.04225	.00446	.6985	3.357		4.499	4.107
Germany	1.612	2.937	1.104	.8882	.01258	.00133	.2080		.2979	1.339	1.223
Hong Kong	7.748	14.117	5.308	4.27	.0605	.00638		4.806	1.432	6.441	5.879
Italy	1213.8	2211.5	831.56	668.806	9.4758		156.653	752.947	224.27	1008.936	920.97
Japan	128.09	233.38	87.757	70.5808		.1055	16.53	79.46	23.67	106.48	97.193
Netherlands	1.815	3.30	1.2434		.0142	.0015	.2342	1.126	.3353	1.509	1.377
Switzerland	1.46	2.659		.8043	.0114	.0012	.1883	.9055	.2697	1.213	1.108
U.K.	1.822		.376	.3024	.00428	.00045	.0708	.3405	.1014	.456	.4165
U.S.		1.822	.6851	.5501	.00781	.00082	.1290	.6204	.1848	.8313	.7588

Country	Currency	U.S. $ Equiv.
Gabon	Communicty of French Africa (CFA) franc	.0037
Germany	deutsche mark	.6203
Greece	drachma	.0052
Greenland	krone	.1613
Guatemala	quetzal	.1938
Guinea	CFA franc	.0037
Guinea-Bissau	peso	.0002
Haiti	gourde	.20
Honduras	lempira	.1838
Hungary	forint	.0127
Iceland	krona	.0173
Indonesia	rupiah	.00049
Iran	rial	.00069
Iraq	dinar	32.0
Israel	new shekel	.4042
Italy	lira	.00082
Ivory Coast	CFA franc	.0037
Japan	yen	.0078
Jordan	dollar	14.68
Korea	won	.00128
Laos	kip	.00141
Latvia	ruble	.0118
Lebanon	pound	.0006
Liberia	U.S. dollar	1.00
Libya	dinar	3.623
Liechtenstein	Swiss france	.6851
Lithuania	ruble	.0118
Luxembourg	franc	.0298
Macao	pataca	.1249
Madagascar	franc	.00053
Mali	CFA franc	.0037
Mauritania	ouguiya	.01178
Mexico	peso	.00032
Monaco	French franc	.1848
Mongolia	tugrik	.025
Morocco	dirham	.1172
Mozambique	metical	.00042
Netherlands	guilder	.5510
Netherlands Antilles	guilder	.5586
New Caledonia	Community of French Pacific (CFP) franc	.0102
Nicaragua	gold cordoba	.20
Niger	CFA franc	.0037
Norway	krone	.1592

Source: *Wall Street Journal* June 1, 1992. Figures reflect values as of May 29, 1992.

Common Design Types

Pictured in this section are issues where one illustration has been used for a number of countries in the Catalogue. Not included in this section are overprinted stamps or those issues which are illustrated in each country.

EUROPA

Europa Issue, 1956

The design symbolizing the cooperation among the six countries comprising the Coal and Steel Community is illustrated in each country.

Belgium 496-497
France 805-806
Germany 748-749
Italy 715-716
Luxembourg 318-320
Netherlands 368-369

Europa Issue, 1958

"E" and Dove
CD1

European Postal Union at the service of European integration.

1958, Sept. 13

Belgium 527-528
France 889-890
Germany 790-791
Italy 750-751
Luxembourg 341-343
Netherlands 375-376
Saar 317-318

Europa Issue, 1959

6-Link Endless Chain
CD2

1959, Sept. 19

Belgium 536-537
France 929-930
Germany 805-806
Italy 791-792
Luxembourg 354-355
Netherlands 379-380

Europa Issue, 1960

19-Spoke Wheel
CD3

First anniverary of the establishment of C.E.P.T. (Conference Europeenne des Administrations des Postes et des Telecommunications.)

The spokes symbolize the 19 founding members of the Conference.

1960, Sept.

Belgium 553-554
Denmark 379
Finland 376-377
France 970-971
Germany 818-820
Great Britain 377-378
Greece 688
Iceland 327-328
Ireland 175-176
Italy 809-810
Luxembourg 374-375
Netherlands 385-386
Norway 387
Portugal 866-867
Spain 941-942
Sweden 562-563
Switzerland 400-401
Turkey 1493-1494

Europa Issue, 1961

19 Doves Flying as One
CD4

The 19 doves represent the 19 members of the Conference of European Postal and Telecommunications Administrations C.E.P.T.

1961-62

Belgium 572-573
Cyprus 201-203
France 1005-1006
Germany 844-845
Great Britain 383-384
Greece 718-719
Iceland 340-341
Italy 845-846
Luxembourg 382-383
Netherlands 387-388
Spain 1010-1011
Switzerland 410-411
Turkey 1518-1520

Europa Issue 1962

Young Tree with 19 Leaves
CD5

The 19 leaves represent the 19 original members of C.E.P.T.

1962-63

Belgium 582-583
Cyprus 219-221
France 1045-1046
Germany 852-853
Greece 739-740
Iceland 348-349
Ireland 184-185
Italy 860-861
Luxembourg 386-387
Netherlands 394-395
Norway 414-415
Switzerland 416-417
Turkey 1553-1555

Europa Issue, 1963

Stylized Links, Symbolizing Unity
CD6

1963, Sept.

Belgium 598-599
Cyprus 229-231
Finland 419
France 1074-1075
Germany 867-868
Greece 768-769
Iceland 357-358
Ireland 188-189
Italy 880-881
Luxembourg 403-404
Netherlands 416-417
Norway 441-442
Switzerland 429
Turkey 1602-1603

Europa Issue, 1964

Symbolic Daisy
CD7

5th anniversary of the establishment of C.E.P.T. The 22 petals of the flower symbolize the 22 members of the Conference.

1964, Sept.

Austria 738
Belgium 614-615
Cyprus 244-246
France 1109-1110
Germany 897-898
Greece 801-802
Iceland 367-368
Ireland 196-197
Italy 894-895
Luxembourg 411-412
Monaco 590-591
Netherlands 428-429
Norway 458
Portugal 931-933
Spain 1262-1263
Switzerland 438-439
Turkey 1628-1629

Europa Issue, 1965

Leaves and "Fruit"
CD8

1965

Belgium 636-637
Cyprus 262-264
Finland 437
France 1131-1132
Germany 934-935
Greece 833-834
Iceland 375-376
Ireland 204-205
Italy 915-916
Luxembourg 432-433
Monaco 616-617
Netherlands 438-439
Norway 475-476
Portugal 958-960
Switzerland 469
Turkey 1665-1666

Europa Issue, 1966

Symbolic Sailboat
CD9

1966, Sept.

Andorra, French 172
Belgium 675-676
Cyprus 275-277
France 1163-1164
Germany 963-964
Greece 862-863
Iceland 384-385
Ireland 216-217
Italy 942-943
Liechtenstein 415
Luxembourg 440-441
Monaco 639-640
Netherlands 441-442
Norway 496-497
Portugal 980-982
Switzerland 477-478
Turkey 1718-1719

Europa Issue, 1967

Cogwheels
CD10

1967

Andorra, French 174-175
Belgium 688-689
Cyprus 297-299
France 1178-1179
Greece 891-892
Germany 969-970
Iceland 389-390
Ireland 232-233
Italy 951-952
Liechtenstein 420
Luxembourg 449-450
Monaco 669-670
Netherlands 444-447
Norway 504-505
Portugal 994-996
Spain 1465-1466
Switzerland 482
Turkey B120-B121

Europa Issue, 1968

Golden Key with C.E.P.T. Emblem
CD11

1968

Andorra, French 182-183
Belgium 705-706
Cyprus 314-316
France 1209-1210
Germany 983-984
Greece 916-917
Iceland 395-396

Ireland	242-243
Italy	979-980
Liechtenstein	442
Luxembourg	466-467
Monaco	689-691
Netherlands	452-453
Portugal	1019-1021
San Marino	687
Spain	1526
Turkey	1775-1776

Europa Issue, 1969

"EUROPA" and "CEPT"
CD12

Tenth anniversary of C.E.P.T.

1969

Andorra, French	188-189
Austria	837
Belgium	718-719
Cyprus	326-328
Denmark	458
Finland	483
France	1245-1246
Germany	996-997
Great Britain	585
Greece	947-948
Iceland	406-407
Ireland	270-271
Italy	1000-1001
Liechtenstein	453
Luxembourg	474-475
Monaco	722-724
Netherlands	475-476
Norway	533-534
Portugal	1038-1040
San Marino	701-702
Spain	1567
Sweden	814-816
Switzerland	500-501
Turkey	1799-1800
Vatican	470-472
Yugoslavia	1003-1004

Europa Issue, 1970

Interwoven Threads
CD13

1970

Andorra, French	196-197
Belgium	741-742
Cyprus	340-342
France	1271-1272
Germany	1018-1019
Greece	985, 987
Iceland	420-421
Ireland	279-281
Italy	1013-1014
Liechtenstein	470
Luxembourg	489-490
Monaco	768-770
Netherlands	483-484
Portugal	1060-1062
San Marino	729-730
Spain	1607
Switzerland	515-516
Turkey	1848-1849
Yugoslavia	1024-1025

Europa Issue, 1971

"Fraternity, Cooperation, Common Effort"—CD14

1971

Andorra, French	205-206
Belgium	803-804
Cyprus	365-367
Finland	504
France	1304
Germany	1064-1065
Greece	1029-1030
Iceland	429-430
Ireland	305-306
Italy	1038-1039
Liechtenstein	485
Luxembourg	500-501
Malta	425-427
Monaco	797-799
Netherlands	488-489
Portugal	1094-1096
San Marino	749-750
Spain	1675-1676
Switzerland	531-532
Turkey	1876-1877
Yugoslavia	1052-1053

Europa Issue, 1972

Sparkles, Symbolic of Communications
CD15

1972

Andorra, French	210-211
Andorra, Spanish	62
Belgium	825-826
Cyprus	380-382
Finland	512-513
France	1341
Germany	1089-1090
Greece	1049-1050
Iceland	439-440
Ireland	316-317
Italy	1065-1066
Liechtenstein	504
Luxembourg	512-513
Malta	450-453
Monaco	831-832
Netherlands	494-495
Portugal	1141-1143
San Marino	771-772
Spain	1718
Switzerland	544-545
Turkey	1907-1908
Yugoslavia	1100-1101

Europa Issue, 1973

Post Horn and Arrows
CD16

1973

Andorra, French	319-320
Andorra, Spanish	76
Belgium	839-840
Cyprus	396-398
Finland	526
France	1367
Germany	1114-1115
Greece	1090-1092
Iceland	447-448
Ireland	329-330
Italy	1108-1109
Liechtenstein	528-529
Luxembourg	523-524
Malta	469-471
Monaco	866-867
Netherlands	504-505
Norway	604-605
Portugal	1170-1172
San Marino	802-803
Spain	1753
Switzerland	580-581
Turkey	1935-1936
Yugoslavia	1138-1139

PORTUGAL & COLONIES

Vasco da Gama Issue

Fleet Departing—CD20

Fleet Arriving at Calicut
CD21

Embarking at Rastello—CD22

Muse of History
CD23

Flagship San Gabriel, da Gama and Camoens
CD24

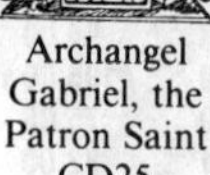

Archangel Gabriel, the Patron Saint
CD25

Flagship San Gabriel
CD26

Vasco da Gama
CD27

Fourth centenary of Vasco da Gama's discovery of the route to India.

1898

Azores	93-100
Macao	67-74
Madeira	37-44
Portugal	147-154
Port. Africa	1-8
Port. india	189-196
Timor	45-52

Pombal Issue
POSTAL TAX

Marquis de Pombal
CD28

Planning Reconstruction of Lisbon, 1755
CD29

Pombal Monument, Lisbon
CD30

Sebastiao Jose' de Carvalho e Mello, Marquis de Pombal (1699-1782), statesman, rebuilt Lisbon after earthquake of 1755. Tax was for the erection of Pombal monument. Obligatory on all mail on certain days throughout the year.

1925

Angola	RA1-RA3
Azores	RA9-RA11
Cape Verde	RA1-RA3
Macao	RA1-RA3
Madeira	RA1-RA3
Mozambique	RA1-RA3
Portugal	RA11-RA13
Port. Guinea	RA1-RA3
Port. India	RA1-RA3
St. Thomas & Prince Islands	RA1-RA3
Timor	RA1-RA3

Pombal Issue
POSTAL TAX DUES

Marquis de Pombal
CD31

Planning Reconstruction of Lisbon, 1755
CD32

Pombal Monument, Lisbon
CD33

1925

Angola	RAJ1-RAJ3

Azores	RAJ2-RAJ4
Cape Verde	RAJ1-RAJ3
Macao	RAJ1-RAJ3
Madeira	RAJ1-RAJ3
Mozambique	RAJ1-RAJ3
Portugal	RAJ2-RAJ4
Port. Guinea	RAJ1-RAJ3
Port. India	RAJ1-RAJ3
St. Thomas & Prince Islands	RAJ1-RAJ3
Timor	RAJ1-RAJ3

Vasco da Gama
CD34

Mousinho de Albuquerque
CD35

Dam
CD36

Prince Henry the Navigator
CD37

Affonso de Albuquerque
CD38

1938-39

Angola	274-291
Cape Verde	234-251
Macao	289-305
Mozambique	270-287
Port. Guinea	233-250
Port. India	439-453
St. Thomas & Prince Islands	302-319, 323-340
Timor	223-239

Plane over Globe
CD39

1938-39

Angola	C1-C9
Cape Verde	C1-C9
Macao	C7-C15
Mozambique	C1-C9
Port. Guinea	C1-C9
Port. India	C1-C8
St. Thomas & Prince Islands	C1-C18
Timor	C1-C9

Lady of Fatima Issue

Our Lady of the Rosary, Fatima, Portugal
CD40

1948-49

Angola	315-318
Cape Verde	266
Macao	336
Mozambique	325-328
Port. Guinea	271
Port. India	480
St. Thomas & Prince Islands	351
Timor	254

A souvenir sheet of 9 stamps was issued in 1951 to mark the extension of the 1950 Holy Year. The sheet contains: Angola No. 316, Cape Verde No. 266, Macao No. 336, Mozambique No. 325, Portuguese Guinea No. 271, Portugese India Nos. 480, 485, St. Thomas & Prince Islands No. 351, Timor No. 254.

The sheet also contains a portrait of Pope Pius XII and is inscribed "Encerramento do Ano Santo, Fatima 1951." It was sold for 11 escudos.

Holy Year Issue

Church Bells and Dove
CD41

Angel Holding Candelabra
CD42

Holy Year, 1950.

1950-51

Angola	331-332
Cape Verde	268-269
Macao	339-340
Mozambique	330-331
Port. Guinea	273-274
Port. India	490-491, 496-503
St. Thomas & Prince Islands	353-354
Timor	258-259

A souvenir sheet of 8 stamps was issued in 1951 to mark the extension of the Holy Year. The sheet contains: Angola No. 331, Cape Verde No. 269, Macao No. 340, Mozambique No. 331, Portuguese Guinea No. 275, Portuguese India No. 490, St. Thomas & Prince Islands No. 354, Timor No. 258, some with colors changed. The sheet contains doves and is inscribed "Encerramento do Ano Santo, Fatima 1951." It was sold for 17 escudos.

Holy Year Conclusion Issue

Our Lady of Fatima
CD43

Conclusion of Holy Year. Sheets contain alternate vertical rows of stamps and labels bearing quotation from Pope Pius XII, different for each colony.

1951

Angola	357
Cape Verde	270
Macao	352
Mozambique	356
Port. Guinea	275
Port. India	506
St. Thomas & Prince Islands	355
Timor	270

Medical Congress Issue

Medical Examination
CD44

First National Congress of Tropical Medicine, Lisbon, 1952.

Each stamp has a different design.

1952

Angola	358
Cape Verde	287
Macao	364
Mozambique	359
Port. Guinea	276
Port. India	516
St. Thomas & Prince Islands	356
Timor	271

POSTAGE DUE STAMPS

CD45

1952

Angola	J37-J42
Cape Verde	J31-J36
Macao	J53-J58
Mozambique	J51-J56
Port. Guinea	J40-J45
Port. India	J47-J52
St. Thomas & Prince Islands	J52-J57
Timor	J31-J36

Sao Paulo Issue

Father Manuel de Nobrega and View of Sao Paulo
CD46

400th anniversary of the founding of Sao Paulo, Brazil.

1954

Angola	385
Cape Verde	297
Macao	382
Mozambique	395
Port. Guinea	291
Port. India	530
St. Thomas & Prince Islands	369
Timor	279

Tropical Medicine Congress Issue

Securidaca Longipedunculata
CD47

Sixth International Congress for Tropical Medicine and Malaria, Lisbon, Sept. 1958.

Each stamp shows a different plant.

1958

Angola	409
Cape Verde	303
Macao	392
Mozambique	404
Port. Guinea	295
Port. India	569
St. Thomas & Prince Islands	371
Timor	289

Sports Issue

Flying
CD48

Each stamp shows a different sport.

1962

Angola	433-438
Cape Verde	320-325
Macao	394-399
Mozambique	424-429
Port. Guinea	299-304
St. Thomas & Prince Islands	374-379
Timor	313-318

Anti-Malaria Issue

Anopheles Funestus and Malaria Eradication Symbol
CD49

World Health Organization drive to eradicate malaria.

1962

Angola	439
Cape Verde	326
Macao	400
Mozambique	430
Port. Guinea	305
St. Thomas & Prince Islands	380
Timor	319

Airline Anniversary Issue

Map of Africa, Super Constellation and Jet Liner
CD50

Tenth anniversary of Transportes Aereos Portugueses (TAP).

1963

Angola	490
Cape Verde	327
Mozambique	434
Port. Guinea	318
St. Thomas & Prince Islands	381

National Overseas Bank Issue

Antonio Teixeira de Sousa
CD51

Centenary of the National Overseas Bank of Portugal.

1964, May 16

Angola	509
Cape Verde	328
Port. Guinea	319
St. Thomas & Prince Islands	382
Timor	320

ITU Issue

ITU Emblem and St. Gabriel
CD52

Centenary of the International Communications Union.

1965, May 17

Angola	511
Cape Verde	329
Macao	402
Mozambique	464
Port. Guinea	320
St. Thomas & Prince Islands	383
Timor	321

National Revolution Issue

St. Paul's Hospital, and Commercial and Industrial School
CD53

40th anniversary of the National Revolution.
Different buildings on each stamp.

1966, May 28

Angola	525
Cape Verde	338
Macao	403
Mozambique	465
Port. Guinea	329
St. Thomas & Prince Islands	392
Timor	322

Navy Club Issue

Mendes Barata and Cruiser Dom Carlos I
CD54

Centenary of Portugal's Navy Club.
Each stamp has a different design.

1967, Jan. 31

Angola	527-528
Cape Verde	339-340
Macao	412-413
Mozambique	478-479
Port. Guinea	330-331
St. Thomas & Prince Islands	393-394
Timor	323-324

Admiral Coutinho Issue

Admiral Gago Coutinho and his First Ship
CD55

Centenary of the birth of Admiral Carlos Viegas Gago Coutinho (1869-1959), explorer and aviation pioneer.
Each stamp has a different design.

1969, Feb. 17

Angola	547
Cape Verde	355
Macao	417
Mozambique	484
Port. Guinea	335
St. Thomas & Prince Islands	397
Timor	335

Administration Reform Issue

Luiz Augusto Rebello da Silva
CD56

Centenary of the administration reforms of the overseas territories.

1969, Sept. 25

Angola	549
Cape Verde	357
Macao	419
Mozambique	491
Port. Guinea	337
St. Thomas & Prince Islands	399
Timor	338

Marshal Carmona Issue

Marshal A.O. Carmona
CD57

Birth centenary of Marshal Antonio Oscar Carmona de Fragoso (1869-1951), President of Portugal.
Each stamp has a different design.

1970, Nov. 15

Angola	563
Cape Verde	359
Macao	422
Mozambique	493
Port. Guinea	340
St. Thomas & Prince Islands	403
Timor	341

Olympic Games Issue

Racing Yachts and Olympic Emblem
CD59

20th Olympic Games, Munich, Aug. 26-Sept. 11.
Each stamp shows a different sport.

1972, June 20

Angola	569
Cape Verde	361
Macao	426
Mozambique	504
Port. Guinea	342
St. Thomas & Prince Islands	408
Timor	343

Lisbon-Rio de Janeiro Flight Issue

"Santa Cruz" over Fernando de Noronha
CD60

50th anniversary of the Lisbon to Rio de Janeiro flight by Arturo de Sacadura and Coutinho, March 30-June 5, 1922.
Each stamp shows a different stage of the flight.

1972, Sept. 20

Angola	570
Cape Verde	362
Macao	427
Mozambique	505
Port. Guinea	343
St. Thomas & Prince Islands	409
Timor	344

WMO Centenary Issue

WMO Emblem
CD61

Centenary of international meterological cooperation.

1973, Dec. 15

Angola	571
Cape Verde	363
Macao	429
Mozambique	509
Port. Guinea	344
St. Thomas & Prince Islands	410
Timor	345

FRENCH COMMUNITY

Colonial Exposition Issue

People of French Empire
CD70

Women's Heads
CD71

France Showing Way to Civilization
CD72

"Colonial Commerce"
CD73

International Colonial Exposition, Paris 1931.

1931

Cameroun	213-216
Chad	60-63
Dahomey	97-100
Fr. Guiana	152-155
Fr. Guinea	116-119
Fr. India	100-103
Fr. Polynesia	76-79
Fr. Sudan	102-105
Gabon	120-123
Guadeloupe	138-141
Indo-China	140-142
Ivory Coast	92-95
Madagascar	169-172
Martinique	129-132
Mauritania	65-68
Middle Congo	61-64
New Caledonia	176-179
Niger	73-76
Reunion	122-125
St. Pierre & Miquelon	132-135
Senegal	138-141
Somali Coast	135-138
Togo	254-257
Ubangi-Shari	82-85
Upper Volta	66-69
Wallis & Futuna Isls.	85-88

Paris International Exposition Issue

Colonial Arts Exposition Issue

"Colonial Resources"
CD74 CD77

Overseas Commerce
CD75

Exposition Building and Women
CD76

"France and the Empire"
CD78

Cultural Treasures of the Colonies
CD79

Souvenir sheets contain one imperf. stamp.

1937

Cameroun	217-222A
Dahomey	101-107
Fr. Equatorial Africa	27-32, 73
Fr. Guiana	162-168
Fr. Guinea	120-126
Fr. India	104-110
Fr. Polynesia	117-123
Fr. Sudan	106-112
Guadeloupe	148-154
Indo-China	193-199
Inini	41
Ivory Coast	152-158
Kwangchowan	132
Madagascar	191-197
Martinique	179-185
Mauritania	69-75
New Caledonia	208-214
Niger	72-83
Reunion	167-173
St. Pierre & Miquelon	165-171
Senegal	172-178
Somali Coast	139-145
Togo	258-264
Wallis & Futuna Isls.	89

Curie Issue

Pierre and Marie Curie
CD80

40th anniversary of the discovery of radium. The surtax was for the benefit of the International Union for the Control of Cancer.

1938

Cameroun	B1
Dahomey	B2
France	B76
Fr. Equatorial Africa	B1
Fr. Guiana	B3
Fr. Guinea	B2
Fr. India	B6
Fr. Polynesia	B5
Fr. Sudan	B1
Guadeloupe	B3
Indo-China	B14
Ivory Coast	B2
Madagascar	B2
Martinique	B2
Mauritania	B3
New Caledonia	B4
Niger	B1
Reunion	B4
St. Pierre & Miquelon	B3
Senegal	B3
Somali Coast	B2
Togo	B1

Caillie Issue

Rene Caille and Map of Northwestern Africa
CD81

Death centenary of Rene Caillie (1799-1838), French explorer.

All three denominations exist with colony name omitted.

1939

Dahomey	108-110
Fr. Guinea	161-163
Fr. Sudan	113-115
Ivory Coast	160-162
Mauritania	109-111
Niger	84-86
Senegal	188-190
Togo	265-267

New York World's Fair Issue

Natives and New York Skyline
CD82

1939

Cameroun	223-224
Dahomey	111-112
Fr. Equatorial Africa	78-79
Fr. Guiana	169-170
Fr. Guinea	164-165
Fr. India	111-112
Fr. Polynesia	124-125
Fr. Sudan	116-117
Guadeloupe	155-156
Indo-China	203-204
Inini	42-43
Ivory Coast	163-164
Kwangchowan	121-122
Madagascar	209-210
Martinique	186-187
Mauritania	112-113
New Caledonia	215-216
Niger	87-88
Reunion	174-175
St. Pierre & Miquelon	205-206
Senegal	191-192
Somali Coast	179-180
Togo	268-269
Wallis & Futuna Isls.	90-91

French Revolution Issue

Storming of the Bastille
CD83

150th anniversary of the French Revolution. The surtax was for the defense of the colonies.

1939

Cameroun	B2-B6
Dahomey	B3-B7
Fr. Equatorial Africa	B4-B8, CB1
Fr. Guiana	B4-B8, CB1
Fr. Guinea	B3-B7
Fr. India	B7-B11
Fr. Polynesia	B6-B10, CB1
Fr. Sudan	B2-B6
Guadeloupe	B4-B8
Indo-China	B15-B19, CB1
Inini	B1-B5
Ivory Coast	B3-B7
Kwangchowan	B1-B5
Madagascar	B3-B7, CB1
Martinique	B3-B7
Mauritania	B4-B8
New Caledonia	B5-B9, CB1
Niger	B2-B6
Reunion	B5-B9, CB1
St. Pierre & Miquelon	B4-B8
Senegal	B4-B8, CB1
Somali Coast	B3-B7
Togo	B2-B6
Wallis & Futuna Isls.	B1-B5

Plane over Coastal Area
CD85

All five denominations exist with colony name omitted.

1940

Dahomey	C1-C5
Fr. Guinea	C1-C5
Fr. Sudan	C1-C5
Ivory Coast	C1-C5
Mauritania	C1-C5
Niger	C1-C5
Senegal	C12-C16
Togo	C1-C5

Colonial Infantryman—CD86

1941

Cameroun	B13B
Dahomey	B13
Fr. Equatorial Africa	B8B
Fr. Guiana	B10
Fr. Guinea	B13
Fr. India	B13
Fr. Polynesia	B12
Fr. Sudan	B12
Guadeloupe	B10
Indo-China	B19B
Inini	B7
Ivory Coast	B13
Kwangchowan	B7
Madagascar	B9
Martinique	B9
Mauritania	B14
New Caledonia	B11
Niger	B12
Reunion	B11
St. Pierre & Miquelon	B8B
Senegal	B14
Somali Coast	B9
Togo	B10B
Wallis & Futuna Isls.	B7

Cross of Lorraine and Four-motor Plane—CD87

1941-5

Cameroun	C1-C7
Fr. Equatorial Africa	C17-C23
Fr. Guiana	C9-C10
Fr. India	C1-C6
Fr. Polynesia	C3-C9
Fr. West Africa	C1-C3
Guadeloupe	C1-C2
Madagascar	C37-C43
Martinique	C1-C2
New Caledonia	C7-C13
Reunion	C18-C24
St. Pierre & Miquelon	C1-C7
Somali Coast	C1-C7

Transport Plane—CD88

Caravan and Plane—CD89

1942

Dahomey	C6-C13
Fr. Guinea	C6-C13
Fr. Sudan	C6-C13
Ivory Coast	C6-C13
Mauritania	C6-C13
Niger	C6-C13
Senegal	C17-C25
Togo	C6-C13

Red Cross Issue

Marianne—CD90

The surtax was for the French Red Cross and national relief.

1944

Cameroun	B28
Fr. Equatorial Africa	B38
Fr. Guiana	B12
Fr. India	B14
Fr. Polynesia	B13
Fr. West Africa	B1
Guadeloupe	B12
Madagascar	B15
Martinique	B11
New Caledonia	B13
Reunion	B15
St. Pierre & Miquelon	B13
Somali Coast	B13
Wallis & Futuna Isls.	B9

Eboue Issue

Felix Eboue—CD91

Felix Eboue, first French colonial administrator to proclaim resistance to Germany after French surrender in World War II.

1945

Cameroun	296-297
Fr. Equatorial Africa	156-157
Fr. Guiana	171-172
Fr. India	210-211
Fr. Polynesia	150-151
Fr. West Africa	15-16
Guadeloupe	187-188
Madagascar	259-260
Martinique	196-197
New Caledonia	274-275
Reunion	238-239
St. Pierre & Miquelon	322-323
Somali Coast	238-239

Victory Issue

Victory—CD92

European victory of the Allied Nations in World War II.

1946, May 8

Cameroun	C8
Fr. Equatorial Africa	C24
Fr. Guiana	C11
Fr. India	C7
Fr. Polynesia	C10
Fr. West Africa	C4
Guadeloupe	C3
Indo-China	C19
Madagascar	C44
Martinique	C3
New Caledonia	C14
Reunion	C25
St. Pierre & Miquelon	C8
Somali Coast	C8
Wallis & Futuna Isls.	C1

Chad to Rhine Issue

Leclerc's Departure from Chad
CD93

Battle at Cufra Oasis
CD94

Tanks in Action, Mareth
CD95

Normandy Invasion
CD96

Entering Paris
CD97

Liberation of Strasbourg
CD98

"Chad to the Rhine" march, 1942-44, by Gen. Jacques Leclerc's column, later French 2nd Armored Division.

1946, June 6

Cameroun	C9-C14
Fr. Equatorial Africa	C25-C30
Fr. Guiana	C12-C17
Fr. India	C8-C13
Fr. Polynesia	C11-C16
Fr. West Africa	C5-C10
Guadeloupe	C4-C9
Indo-China	C20-C25
Madagascar	C45-C50
Martinique	C4-C9
New Caledonia	C15-C20
Reunion	C26-C31
St. Pierre & Miquelon	C9-C14
Somali Coast	C9-C14
Wallis & Futuna Isls.	C2-C7

UPU Issue

French Colonials, Globe and Plane
CD99

75th anniversary of the Universal Postal Union.

1949, July 4

Cameroun	C29
Fr. Equatorial Africa	C34
Fr. India	C17
Fr. Polynesia	C20
Fr. West Africa	C15
Indo-China	C26
Madagascar	C55
New Caledonia	C24
St. Pierre & Miquelon	C18
Somali Coast	C18
Togo	C18
Wallis & Futuna Isls.	C10

Tropical Medicine Issue

Doctor Treating Infant
CD100

The surtax was for charitable work.

1950

Cameroun	B29
Fr. Equatorial Africa	B39
Fr. India	B15
Fr. Polynesia	B14
Fr. West Africa	B3
Madagascar	B17
New Caledonia	B14
St. Pierre & Miquelon	B14
Somali Coast	B14
Togo	B11

Military Medal Issue

Medal, Early Marine and Colonial Soldier
CD101

Centenary of the creation of the French Military Medal.

1952

Cameroun	332
Comoro Isls.	39
Fr. Equatorial Africa	186
Fr. India	233
Fr. Polynesia	179
Fr. West Africa	57
Madagascar	286
New Caledonia	295
St. Pierre & Miquelon	345
Somali Coast	267
Togo	327
Wallis & Futuna Isls.	149

Liberation Issue

Allied Landing, Victory Sign and Cross of Lorraine
CD102

10th anniversary of the liberation of France.

1954, June 6

Cameroun	C32
Comoro Isls.	C4
Fr. Equatorial Africa	C38
Fr. India	C18
Fr. Polynesia	C23
Fr. West Africa	C17
Madagascar	C57
New Caledonia	C25
St. Pierre & Miquelon	C19
Somali Coast	C19
Togo	C19
Wallis & Futuna Isls.	C11

FIDES Issue

Plowmen
CD103

Efforts of FIDES, the Economic and Social Development Fund for Overseas Possessions (Fonds d' Investissement pour le Developpement Economique et Social).

Each stamp has a different design.

1956

Cameroun	326-329
Comoro Isls.	43
Fr. Polynesia	181
Madagascar	292-295
New Caledonia	303
Somali Coast	268
Togo	331

Flower Issue

Euadania
CD104

Each stamp shows a different flower.

1958-9

Cameroun	333
Comoro Isls.	45
Fr. Equatorial Africa	200-201
Fr. Polynesia	192
Fr. So. & Antarctic Terr.	11
Fr. West Africa	79-83
Madagascar	301-302
New Caledonia	304-305
St. Pierre & Miquelon	357
Somali Coast	270
Togo	348-349
Wallis & Futuna Isls.	152

Human Rights Issue

Sun, Dove and U.N. Emblem
CD105

10th anniversary of the signing of the Universal Declaration of Human Rights.

1958

Comoro Isls.	44
Fr. Equatorial Africa	202
Fr. Polynesia	191
Fr. West Africa	85
Madagascar	300
New Caledonia	306
St. Pierre & Miquelon	356
Somali Coast	274
Wallis & Futuna Isls.	153

C.C.T.A. Issue

Map of Africa & Cogwheels—CD106

10th anniversary of the Commission for Technical Cooperation in Africa south of the Sahara.

1960

Cameroun	335
Cent. African Rep.	3
Chad	66
Congo, P.R.	90
Dahomey	138
Gabon	150
Ivory Coast	180
Madagascar	317
Mali	9
Mauritania	117
Niger	104
Upper Volta	89

Air Afrique Issue, 1961

Modern and Ancient Africa, Map and Planes—CD107

Founding of Air Afrique (African Airlines).

1961-62

Cameroun	C37
Cent. African Rep.	C5
Chad	C7
Congo, P.R.	C5
Dahomey	C17
Gabon	C5
Ivory Coast	C18
Mauritania	C17
Niger	C22
Senegal	C31
Upper Volta	C4

Anti-Malaria Issue

Malaria Eradication Emblem—CD108

World Heatlh Organization drive to eradicate malaria.

1962, Apr. 7

Cameroun B36
Cent. African Rep. B1
Chad B1
Comoro Isls. B1
Congo, P.R. B3
Dahomey B15
Gabon B4
Ivory Coast B15
Madagascar B19
Mali B1
Mauritania B16
Niger B14
Senegal B16
Somali Coast B15
Upper Volta B1

Abidjan Games Issue

Relay Race
CD109

Abidjan Games, Ivory Coast, Dec. 24-31, 1961.
Each stamp shows a different sport.

1962

Chad 83-84
Cent. African Rep. 19-20
Congo, P.R. 103-104
Gabon 163-164
Niger 109-111
Upper Volta 103-105

African and Malagasy Union Issue

Flag of African and Malagasy Union
CD110

First anniversary of the Union.

1962, Sept. 8

Cameroun 373
Cent. African Rep. 21
Chad 85
Congo, P.R. 105
Dahomey 155
Gabon 165
Ivory Coast 198
Madagascar 332
Mauritania 170
Niger 112
Senegal 211
Upper Volta 106

Telstar Issue

Telstar and Globe Showing Andover and Pleumeur-Bodou
CD111

First television connection of the United States and Europe through the Telstar satellite, July 11-12, 1962.

1962-63

Andorra, French 154
Comoro Isls. C7
Fr. Polynesia C29
Fr. So. & Antarctic Terr. C5
New Caledonia C33
Somali Coast C31
St. Pierre & Miquelon C26
Wallis & Futuna Isls. C17

Freedom From Hunger Issue

World Map and Wheat Emblem
CD112

United Nations Food and Agriculture Organization's "Freedom from Hunger" campaign.

1963, Mar. 21

Cameroun B37-B38
Cent. African Rep. B2
Chad B2
Congo, P.R. B4
Dahomey B16
Gabon B5
Ivory Coast B16
Madagascar B21
Mauritania B17
Niger B15
Senegal B17
Upper Volta B2

Red Cross Centenary Issue

Centenary Emblem—CD113

Centenary of the International Red Cross.

1963, Sept. 2

Comoro Isls. 55
Fr. Polynesia 205
New Caledonia 328
St. Pierre & Miquelon 367
Somali Coast 297
Wallis & Futuna Isls. 165

African Postal Union Issue

UAMPT Emblem, Radio Masts, Plane and Mail—CD114

Establishment of the African and Malagasy Posts and Telecommunications Union, UAMPT.

1963, Sept. 8

Cameroun C47
Cent. African Rep. C10
Chad C9
Congo, P.R. C13
Dahomey C19
Gabon C13
Ivory Coast C25
Madagascar C75
Mauritania C22
Niger C27
Rwanda 36
Senegal C32
Upper Volta C9

Air Afrique Issue, 1963

Symbols of Flight—CD115

First anniversary of Air Afrique and inauguration of DC-8 service.

1963, Nov. 19

Cameroun C48
Chad C10
Congo, P.R. C14
Gabon C18
Ivory Coast C26
Mauritania C26
Niger C35
Senegal C33

Europafrica Issue

Europe and Africa Linked Together
CD116

Signing of an economic agreement between the European Economic Community and the African and Malagasy Union, Yaounde, Cameroun, July 20, 1963.

1963-64

Cameroun 402
Chad C11
Cent. African Rep. C12
Congo, P.R. C16
Gabon C19
Ivory Coast 217
Niger C43
Upper Volta C11

Human Rights Issue

Scales of Justice and Globe
CD117

15th anniversary of the Universal Declaration of Human Rights.

1963, Dec. 10

Comoro Isls. 58
Fr. Polynesia 206
New Caledonia 329
St. Pierre & Miquelon 368
Somali Coast 300
Wallis & Futuna Isls. 166

PHILATEC Issue

Stamp Album, Champs Elysees Palace and Horses of Marly
CD118

"PHILATEC," International Philatelic and Postal Techniques Exhibition, Paris, June 5-21, 1964.

1963-64

Comoro Isls. 60
France 1078
Fr. Polynesia 207
New Caledonia 341
St. Pierre & Miquelon 369
Somali Coast 301
Wallis & Futuna Isls. 167

Cooperation Issue

Maps of France and Africa and Clasped Hands
CD119

Cooperation between France and the French-speaking countries of Africa and Madagascar.

1964

Cameroun 409-410
Cent. African Rep. 39
Chad 103
Congo, P.R. 121
Dahomey 193
France 1111
Gabon 175
Ivory Coast 221
Madagascar 360
Mauritania 181
Niger 143
Senegal 236
Togo 495

ITU Issue

Telegraph, Syncom Satellite and ITU Emblem
CD120

Centenary of the International Telecommunication Union.

1965, May 17

Comoro Isls. C14
Fr. Polynesia C33
Fr. So. & Antarctic Terr. C8
New Caledonia C40
New Hebrides 124-125
St. Pierre & Miquelon C29
Somali Coast C36
Wallis & Futuna Isls. C20

French Satellite A-1 Issue

Diamant Rocket and Launching Installation
CD121

Launching of France's first satellite, Nov. 26, 1965.

1965-66

Comoro Isls. C15-C16
France 1137-1138
Fr. Polynesia C40-C41
Fr. So. & Antarctic Terr. C9-C10
New Caledonia C44-C45
St. Pierre & Miquelon C30-C31
Somali Coast C39-C40
Wallis & Futuna Isls. C22-C23

French Satellite D-1 Issue

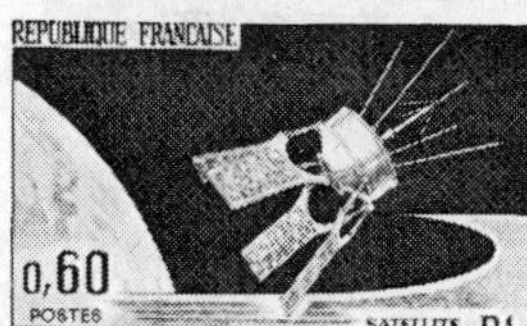

D-1 Satellite in Orbit
CD122

Launching of the D-1 satellite at Hammaguir, Algeria, Feb. 17, 1966.

1966

Comoro Isls.	C17
France	1148
Fr. Polynesia	C42
Fr. So. & Antarctic Terr.	C11
New Caledonia	C46
St. Pierre & Miquelon	C32
Somali Coast	C49
Wallis & Futuna Isls.	C24

Air Afrique Issue, 1966

Planes and Air Afrique Emblem
CD123

Introduction of DC-8F planes by Air Afrique.

1966

Cameroun	C79
Cent. African Rep.	C35
Chad	C26
Congo, P.R.	C42
Dahomey	C42
Gabon	C47
Ivory Coast	C32
Mauritania	C57
Niger	C63
Senegal	C47
Togo	C54
Upper Volta	C31

African Postal Union, 1967

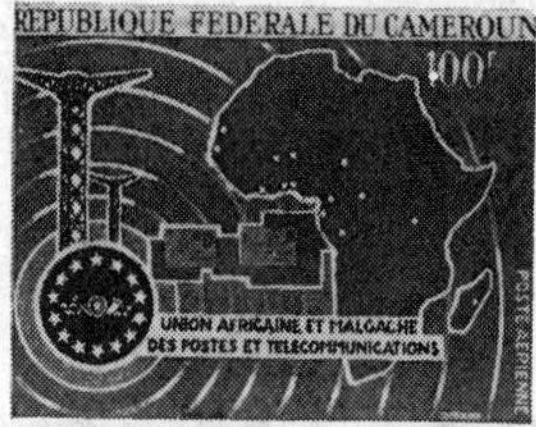

Telecommunications Symbols and Map of Africa
CD124

Fifth anniversary of the establishment of the African and Malagasy Union of Posts and Telecommunications, UAMPT.

1967

Cameroun	C90
Cent. African Rep.	C46
Chad	C37
Congo, P.R.	C57
Dahomey	C61
Gabon	C58
Ivory Coast	C34
Madagascar	C85
Mauritania	C65
Niger	C75
Rwanda	C1-C3
Senegal	C60
Togo	C81
Upper Volta	C50

Monetary Union Issue

Gold Token of the Ashantis, 17-18th Centuries
CD125

Fifth anniversary of the West African Monetary Union.

1967, Nov. 4

Dahomey	244
Ivory Coast	259
Mauritania	238
Niger	204
Senegal	294
Togo	623
Upper Volta	181

WHO Anniversary Issue

Sun, Flowers and WHO Emblem
CD126

20th anniversary of the World Health Organization.

1968, May 4

Afars & Issas	317
Comoro Isls.	73
Fr. Polynesia	241-242
Fr. So. & Antarctic Terr.	31
New Caledonia	367
St. Pierre & Miquelon	377
Wallis & Futuna Isls.	169

Human Rights Year Issue

Human Rights Flame
CD127

International Human Rights Year.

1968, Aug. 10

Afars & Issas	322-323
Comoro Isls.	76
Fr. Polynesia	243-244
Fr. So. & Antarctic Terr.	32
New Caledonia	369
St. Pierre & Miquelon	382
Wallis & Futuna Isls.	170

2nd PHILEXAFRIQUE Issue

Gabon No. 131 and Industrial Plant
CD128

Opening of PHILEXAFRIQUE, Abidjan, Feb. 14. Each stamp shows a local scene and stamp.

1969, Feb. 14

Cameroun	C118
Cent. African Rep.	C65
Chad	C48
Congo, P.R.	C77
Dahomey	C94
Gabon	C82
Ivory Coast	C38-C40
Madagascar	C92
Mali	C65
Mauritania	C80
Niger	C104
Senegal	C68
Togo	C104
Upper Volta	C62

Concorde Issue

Concorde in Flight
CD129

First flight of the prototpye Concorde super-sonic plane at Toulouse, Mar. 1, 1969.

1969

Afars & Issas	C56
Comoro Isls.	C29
France	C42
Fr. Polynesia	C50
Fr. So. & Antarctic Terr.	C18
New Caledonia	C63
St. Pierre & Miquelon	C40
Wallis & Futuna Isls.	C30

Development Bank Issue

Bank Emblem—CD130

Fifth anniversary of the African Development Bank.

1969

Cameroun	499
Chad	217
Congo, P.R.	181-182
Ivory Coast	281
Mali	127-128
Mauritania	267
Niger	220
Senegal	317-318
Upper Volta	201

ILO Issue

ILO Headquarters, Geneva, and Emblem
CD131

50th anniversary of the International Labor Organization.

1969-70

Afars & Issas	337
Comoro Isls.	83
Fr. Polynesia	251-252
Fr. So. & Antarctic Terr.	35
New Caledonia	379
St. Pierre & Miquelon	396
Wallis & Futuna Isls.	172

ASECNA Issue

Map of Africa, Plane and Airport
CD132

10th anniversary of the Agency for the Security of Aerial Navigation in Africa and Madagascar (ASECNA, Agence pour la Securite de la Navigation Aerienne en Afrique et a Madagascar).

1969-70

Cameroun	500
Cent. African Rep.	119
Chad	222
Congo, P.R.	197
Dahomey	269
Gabon	260
Ivory Coast	287
Mali	130
Niger	221
Senegal	321
Upper Volta	204

U.P.U. Headquarters Issue

U.P.U. Headquarters and Emblem
CD133

New Universal Postal Union headquarters, Bern, Switzerland.

1970

Afars & Issas	342
Algeria	443
Cameroun	503-504
Cent. African Rep.	125
Chad	225
Comoro Isls.	84
Congo, P.R.	216
Fr. Polynesia	261-262
Fr. So. & Antarctic Terr.	36
Gabon	258
Ivory Coast	295
Madagascar	444
Mali	134-135
Mauritania	283
New Caledonia	382
Niger	231-232
St. Pierre & Miquelon	397-398
Senegal	328-329
Tunisia	535
Wallis & Futuna Isls.	173

De Gaulle Issue

General de Gaulle 1940
CD134

First anniversary of the death of Charles de Gaulle, (1890-1970), President of France.

1971-72

Afars & Issas	356-357
Comoro Isls.	104-105
France	1322-1325
Fr. Polynesia	270-271
Fr. So. & Antarctic Terr.	52-53
New Caledonia	393-394
Reunion	377, 380
St. Pierre & Miquelon	417-418
Wallis & Futuna Isls.	177-178

African Postal Union Issue, 1971

Carved Stool, UAMPT Building, Brazzaville, Congo
CD135

10th anniversary of the establishment of the African and Malagasy Posts and Telecommunications Union, UAMPT.

Each stamp has a different native design.

1971, Nov. 13

Cameroun	C177
Cent. African Rep.	C89
Chad	C94
Congo, P.R.	C136
Dahomey	C146
Gabon	C120
Ivory Coast	C47
Mauritania	C113
Niger	C164
Rwanda	C8
Senegal	C105
Togo	C166
Upper Volta	C97

West African Monetary Union Issue

African Couple, City, Village and Commemorative Coin
CD136

10th anniversary of the West African Monetary Union.

1972, Nov. 2

Dahomey	300
Ivory Coat	331
Mauritania	299
Niger	258
Senegal	374
Togo	825
Upper Volta	280

African Postal Union Issue, 1973

Telecommunications Symbols and Map of Africa
CD137

11th anniversary of the African and Malagasy Posts and Telecommunications Union (UAMPT).

1973, Sept. 12

Cameroun	574
Cent. African Rep.	194
Chad	272
Congo, P.R.	289
Dahomey	311
Gabon	320
Ivory Coast	361
Madagascar	500
Mauritania	304
Niger	287
Rwanda	540
Senegal	393
Togo	849
Upper Volta	285

Philexafrique II—Essen Issue

Buffalo and Dahomey
No. C33
CD138

Wild Ducks and Baden
No. 1
CD139

Designs: Indigenous fauna, local and German stamps.

Types CD138-CD139 printed horizontally and vertically se-tenant in sheets of 10 (2x5). Label between horizontal pairs alternately commemoratives Philexafrique II, Libreville, Gabon, June 1978, and 2nd International Stamp Fair, Essen, Germany, Nov. 1-5.

1978-1979

Benin	C285-C286
Central Africa	C200-C201
Chad	C238-C239
Congo Republic	C245-C246
Djibouti	C121-C122
Gabon	C215-C216
Ivory Coast	C64-C65
Mali	C356-C357
Mauritania	C185-C186
Niger	C291-C292
Rwanda	C12-C13
Senegal	C146-C147
Togo	C363-C364
Upper Volta	C253-C254

Numerical Index of Vol. 3 Watermark Illustrations

Watermark	Country
3	New Hebrides
47	Iceland
48	Germany
87	Italy
91	Hungary
	Montenegro
92-95	Bavaria 95v-95h
102	Brunswick
106	Hungary
108	Latvia
109	Lithuania
110	Luxembourg
112-114	Iceland
116	Germany
	Wurttemberg
	Liberia
117	Nicaragua
125-127	Germany
128	Hamburg
129	Greece
130	Hanover
131	Haiti
132-133	Hungary
135-137	Hungary
140	Italian Colonies
	Italy
141	Manchukuo
141-142	Japan
143	Liberia
144-147	Lithuania
145	Latvia
148	Lubeck
149	Luxembourg
150-155	Mexico
156	Mexico
157	Modena
158	Netherlands
159-160	Norway
161	Iran
162	Prussia
170	Mongolia
181	Latvia
183	Liechtenstein
184-185	Tuscany
186	Two Sicilies
192	Wurttemberg
	Germany
195	Libya
197	Latvia
198	Lithuania
202	Netherlands
	Netherlands Antilles
	Netherlands Indies

Watermark	Country
209	Honduras
	Lithuania
	Nicaragua
210	Hungary
212	Latvia
213, 216	Luxembourg
223	Germany
228	Indonesia
	Netherlands Indies
232	Macao
237	Germany
238	Lithuania
239	Manchukuo
241	Germany
242	Manchukuo
246-247	Luxembourg
248	Mexico
252	Greece
257	Japan
	Korea
260	Mexico
265	Latvia
266	Hungary
272	Mexico
277	Italy
279	Mexico
283	Hungary
284-286	Germany
292	Germany
	(Russian Zone)
295	Germany
296	Liechtenstein
297	German Dem. Rep.
300	Mexico
301-302	Israel
303	Italy
304	Germany
305	Jordan
306	Iran
310	Libya
312	Korea
313	German Dem. Rep.
314	New Hebrides
316	Iran
317	Korea
328	Jordan
349	Iran
350	Mexico
353	Iran

Selected Topical Listings

This new section has two goals: demonstrate the tremendous breadth of subject areas that can form the basis of a topical stamp collection; and, through the actual topical listings provided here, show the depth that you are able to go (although, of course, you are free to limit your collection in any way you wish).

Topical stamp collections are based on the design of the stamp. As in the case for any type of stamp collection, you may extend your collection as far as you would like, including perforation differences, paper differences, postal markings, and so on. For the Birds topic, as an example, you may choose to limit your collection to sea fowl, or to birds native to only a particular part of the world, or you may wish to extend the collection not only to include all stamps showing birds but also have sections to include the food each bird eats.

What follows

Scott plans to present in each edition of the *Scott Standard Postage Stamp Catalogue* listings of one or two topics. We do not plan to update the listings; that is, we will not include in the 1994 edition an update of the material shown this year. The best way to obtain a continuing update of such information is through the "By Topic" section of *Scott Stamp Monthly,* a regular feature of the magazine that is found in the "Catalogue Update" area.

The listings we present are based on individual handbooks published by the American Topical Association (ATA), and with the organization's permission and cooperation. Because it is our intent to present topical listings as current as the stamp listings in our catalogue, we have supplemented that which is found in the ATA listings with more current information from our own "By Topic" material.

Topical listings found in each volume of the 1993 edition will include items issued by countries found in that volume. Thus, the listings that follow will cover only Volume 3 (non-British Commonwealth beginning with the letters "G" through "O") countries. Further, we have limited our listings to Scott number and brief stamp description, knowing you will only have to turn a few pages to obtain more complete information on any of the stamps noted.

Following the topical listings is information on the ATA, including a list of its available handbooks and checklists. The ATA is a membership organization, offering a variety of services.

Birds

Gabon

279, great egret; 280, gray parrot; 281, woodland kingfisher; 282, red-headed rockfowl; 283, Guinea turaco; 449, African river-martin; 450, red-throated bee-eater; 451, African pitta; 452, Pel's fishing owl; 532, eastern white pelican; 577, South African crowned crane; 578, snowy-breasted hummingbird; 579, keel-billed toucan; 657, white-tufted bittern; 658, Gabon gray parakeet; 659, pygmy hornbill; 660, Pope's martin; C3, African darter; C4, lyre-tailed honeyguide; C14, Johanna's sunbird; C15, blue-headed bee-eater; C16, crowned eagle; C17, narina trogon; C149, bald eagle; C215, gray parrot; C216, white stork.

Germany

774, European robin; 917, owl (unidentified); 1222, greater golden plover; 1355, Eurasian coot; 1380, 1465, 1564, birds (stylized); 1577, eagle (stylized); 1598, marine birds (unidentified); 1649, *philomachus pugnax*; 1650, *sterna albifrons*; 1651, *branta bernicia*; 1652, *haliaeetus albicilla*; B388, hoopoe; B389, Eurasian golden oriole; B390, Eurasian bullfinch; B391, Eurasian kingfisher; B404, Eurasian woodcock; B405, ring-necked pheasant; B406, black grouse; B407, Eurasian capercaillie; B496, osprey; B497, common buzzard; B498, red kite; B499, Montagu's harrier; B721, dove (unidentified).

Germany-Berlin

9N416, bald eagle; 9N495, white stork; 9NB29, Eurasian woodcock; 9NB30, ring-necked pheasant; 9NB31, black grouse; 9NB32, Eurasian capercaillie; 9NB97, northern goshawk; 9NB98, peregrine falcon; 9NB99, Eurasian sparrowhawk; 9NB100, golden eagle; 9NB275b, dalmatian pelican;

Germany-DDR

318, greater flamingo (probable); 434, gray huron; 435, Eurasian bittern; 444, great cormorant; 445, black stork; 446, Eurasian eagle-owl; 447, black grouse; 448, hoopoe; 449, peregrine falcon; 800, red kite; 801, lammergeier; 802, common buzzard; 803, Eurasian kestrel; 804, northern goshawk; 805, golden eagle; 915, common barn-owl; 916, common crane; 917, peregrine falcon; 918, Eurasian bullfinch; 919, Eurasian kingfisher; 920, Eurasian roller; 997, seabird (unidentified); 998, ring-necked pheasant; 999, gray partridge; 1000, mallard; 1001, graylag goose; 1002, Eurasian wood-pigeon; 1244, whale-headed stork; 1430, eastern white pelican (probable); 1448, archaeopteryx; 1453, firecrest; 1454, white-winged crossbill; 1455, Bohemian waxwing;

1456, bluethroat; 1457, Eurasian goldfinch; 1458, Eurasian golden oriole; 1459, gray wagtail; 1460, wall creeper; 1630, blue-and-yellow macaw; 1860, ring-necked pheasant; 1861, mallard; 1976, Eurasian chaffinch; 1977, Eurasian nuthatch; 1978, European robin; 1979, common rosefinch; 1980, blue tit; 1981, Eurasian linnet; 2071, eastern white pelican (probable); 2090, lesser kestrel; 2117, white eared-pheasant; 2265, osprey; 2266, white-tailed eagle; 2267, little owl; 2268, Eurasian eagle-owl; 2481, harpy eagle; 2482, red-breasted goose; 2559, doves (stylized); 2756, exotic birds (unidentified); 2778, 2779, 2780, bird (stylized).

Greece

639, golden eagle; 640, little owl; 709, rock partridge, hoopoe; 754, golden eagle; 755, little owl; 994, rock partridge; 1313, purple heron; 1314, Audouin's gull; 1315, Eleonora's falcon; 1316, Eurasian kingfisher; 1317, eastern white pelican; 1318, white-tailed eagle; 1569, pelicans (unidentified); 1575, 1576, 1577, dove (stylized); 1657, whistling bird (toy); 1681, dove (stylized).

Greenland

16, 25, common eider; 61, common loon, common raven; 65, white-tailed eagle; 114, gyrfalcon; 175a, 175c, northern fulmar; 177, rock ptarmigan; 178, snowy owl; 179, gyrfalcon; 180, common raven; 181, white-tailed eagle; 182, common loon; 183, long-tailed duck; 184, snow bunting; 185, black guillemot; 186, thick-billed murre; 204, snow goose; 209, Arctic skua; B9, king eider; B10, greater shearwater; B14, common eider; B15, birds (stylized).

Guatemala

15, 16, 17, 19, 21, 22, 23, 24, 25, 205, 274, 275, 280, 294, 295, 316, 317, 319, 338a, 354, 367, 368, 369, 370, 371, 372, 373, 380, 381, 382, 382A, 395, 419a, 432, 433, 434, 435, 436, 437, 438, 439, 440, 441, 442, 443, 444, resplendent quetzal; 456, 457, 458, 459, 460, 461, 462, toucan (unidentified); B2, B3, C141, C142, C196, C418, C419, C420, resplendent quetzal; C448, C449, atitlan grebe; C554, C565, C566, C610, C611, resplendent quetzal; C675, ocellated turkey; C677, king vulture; C678, great horned owl; C680, resplendent quetzal, keel-billed toucan; C691, quetzal (stylized); C693, bird (stylized); C714, quetzal (stylized); C747, C828, birds (stylized); C838, quetzal.

Guinea

223, 224, 225, 226, 227, 228, helmeted guineafowl; 263, western crowned crane; 264, gray parrot; 265, abyssinian ground-hornbill; 266, Eurasian spoonbill; 267, bateleur; 268, western crowned crane; 269, gray parrot; 270, abyssinian ground-hornbill; 271, Eurasian spoonbill; 272, bateleur; 273, western crowned crane; 274, gray parrot; 582, violet-crested turaco; 583, Eurasian golden oriole; 584, blue-headed coucal; 585, northern shrike; 586, vulturine guineafowl; 587, southern ground-hornbill; 845A, eagle (stylized); 939, black-billed cuckoo; 940, Carolina parakeet; 941, American anhinga; 942, red-shouldered hawk; 943, eastern screech owl; 944, brown thrasher; 945, mourning dove; 1010, macaw (unidentified); 1073, crowned crane (unidentified);

1075, border includes saddlebilled stork, African jacana; 1088, red-headed bluebill; 1090, red bishop; 1091, beautiful sunbird; 1094, Seychelles parakeet, border includes blue-naped mousebird, scarlet-chested sunbird, variable sunbird, orange-cheeked waxbill, paradise whydah, greater blue-eared glossy starling; 1136, dove (stylized); 1151, eagle (unidentified); B30, B31, B32, B33, B34, B35, helmeted guineafowl; C41, abyssinian ground-hornbill; C42, Eurasian spoonbill; C43, bateleur; C116, violet-crested turaco; C117, Eurasian golden oriole; C118, vulturine guineafowl.

Guinea-Bissau

384A, Eurasian eagle-owl; 384B, secretary bird; 384F, border includes violet turaco; 755, ferruginous pygmy owl; 756, hoopoe; 759, vulturine guineafowl; 888, dove (stylized); 891, rooster, hen (unidentified); 892, turkey (unidentified); 893, duck, ducklings (unidentified); 894, turkey (unidentified); 894, rooster, ducks (unidentified); 912, *kaupifalco monogrammicus*; 913, *balearica pavonina*; 914, *bucorvus abyssinicus*; 915, *ephippiorhynchus senegalensis*; 916, *kaupifalco monogrammicus, balearica pavonina, bucorvus abyssinicus, ephippiorhynchus senegalensis*; 920, 920, doves (stylized); C50, brown pelican; C51, American white pelican; C52, great blue heron; C53, American flamingo.

Haiti

412, American flamingo; 413, mallard; 425, emperor penguin (probable); 611, blue-hooded euphonia; 612, Hispaniolan trogan; 613, palmchat; 614, stripe-headed tanager; 615, blue-hooded euphonia; C103, American flamingo; C104, mallard; C120, emperor penguin (probable); C326, Hispaniolan trogan; C327, black-cowled oriole; C328, stripe-headed tanager; C329, Hispaniolan woodpecker; C344A, Hispaniolan woodpecker; C344B, black-cowled oriole; C344C, striped-headed tanager; C344D, Hispaniolan woodpecker.

Honduras

332, 333, 334, 335, Andean condor; C82, great horned owl; C758, turquoise-browed motmot; C759, keel-billed toucan; C760, yellow-naped amazon; C782, birds (stylized); C798, dove (stylized); C824, toucan (unidentified).

Hungary
1106, heron or egret (unidentified); 1152, mallard; 1214, penguin (unidentified); 1233, great cormorant; 1234, little egret; 1235, purple heron; 1236, great egret; 1237, Eurasian spoonbill; 1238, gray heron; 1239, squacco heron; 1240, glossy ibis; 1342, common raven; 1344, white stork; 1395, Eurasian goldfinch; 1399, Eurasian goldfinch; 1426, nightingale; 1427, great tit; 1428, Eurasian chaffinch; 1429, Eurasian jay; 1430, Eurasian golden oriole; 1431, Eurasian blackbird; 1432, yellowhammer; 1433, northern lapwing; 1626, ring-necked pheasant; 1628, gray partridge; 1633, great bustard; 1665, penguin (unidentified); 1746, barn swallow; 1747, long-tailed tit; 1748, red crossbill; 1749, middle spotted woodpecker; 1750, hoopoe;

1751, northern lapwing; 1889, white stork; 1890, Eurasian golden oriole; 1891, imperial eagle; 1892, red-footed falcon; 1893, Eurasian scops-owl; 1894, great bustard; 1895, Eurasian bee-eater; 1896, graylag goose; 2069, falcon (unidentified); 2071, great bustard; 2078, green peafowl; 2224, Eurasian goldfinch; 2457, Eurasian spoonbill; 2458, white stork; 2459, purple heron; 2460, great bustard; 2461, common crane; 2462, white wagtail; 2463, garganey teal; 2471, common peafowl; 2472, green peafowl; 2473, Congo peafowl; 2474, great argus; 2475, Himalayan monal; 2476, gray peacock-pheasant; 2659, graylag goose; 2660, black-crowned night-heron; 2661, northern shoveler; 2662, white-winged black tern; 2663, great crested grebe;

2664, black-winged stilt; 2665, great egret; 2797, imperial eagle; 2798, lesser spotted eagle; 2799, white-tailed eagle; 2800, red-footed falcon; 2801, Saker falcon; 2802, rough-legged hawk; 2803, common buzzard; 2887, little owl; 2888, common barn owl; 2889, tawny owl; 2890, northern long-eared owl; 2891, snowy owl; 2892, ural owl; 2893, Eurasian eagle-owl; 2928, northern flicker; 2929, Bohemian waxwing; 2930, pileated woodpecker; 2931, northern oriole; 3075, gull (unidentified); 3077, emperor penguin; 3102, Japanese crane; 3136, green-winged teal; 3137, common goldeneye; 3138, Eurasian wigeon; 3138a, green-winged teal, Eurasian wigeon; 3139, red-crested pochard; 3140, gadwall; 3141, mallard; 3178, 3179, birds (stylized);

3206, bird of prey (unidentified); 3224, common kingfisher; 3225, bullfinch; 3226, Syrian woodpecker; 3227, hoopoe; 3228, common bee-eater; 3229, Eurasian common roller; 3239, bird (stylized); 3270, dove (stylized); 3274, eagle as ornament on clock; 3290, 3290, toucan (unidentified); B168, white-tailed eagle; B203, carrier pigeon (stylized); B240, mallard; B302, bird on silver disk (stylized); B338, bird (stylized); B345, bird on tapestry; C53, owl (unidentified); C96, pied avocet; C97, white stork; C98, Eurasian golden oriole; C99, snowy plover; C100, black-winged stilt; C101, lesser gray shrike; C102, red-footed falcon; C104, Eurasian bee-eater; C105, glossy ibis; C106, great egret; C228, Eurasian eagle-owl; C229, osprey;

C230, Eurasian marsh-harrier; C231, booted eagle; C232, African fish-eagle; C233, lammergeier; C234, golden eagle; C235, Eurasian kestrel; C337, winter wren; C338, common rock-thrush; C339, European robin; C340, firecrest; C341, Eurasian linnet; C342, blue tit; C343, bluethroat; C344, gray wagtail; C446, northern flicker; C447, northern cardinal; CB8, common raven.

Iceland
155, 160, gyrfalcon (unidentified); 298, 299, whooper swan; 320, 321, common eider; 323, gyrfalcon; 378, white-tailed eagle; 388, common loon; 500, harlequin duck; 535, Atlantic puffin; 543, winter wren; 544, greater golden plover; 545, common raven; 575, gulls (unidentified); 618, white wagtail; 619, northern pintail; 620, merlin; 621, razorbill; 627, gyrfalcon; 642, short-eared owl; 643, redwing; 644, common oystercatcher; 645, mallard; 665, black-tailed godwit; 666, oldsquaw; 671, red-breasted phalarope; 672, snow bunting; 686, widgeon; 687, pink-footed goose; 688, 692, vulture (stylized); 712, seagull (unidentified); 721, *podiceps auritus*; 725, *sula bassana*; 740, falcon, swans (unidentified); B19, B20, rock ptarmigan; B21, common ringed plover; B22, rock ptarmigan; B23, B24, Arctic tern; C3, gyrfalcon; O56, O61, gyrfalcon (unidentified).

Ifni
61, 64, 67, gull (unidentified); 81, common rock-pigeon; 88, red-legged partridge (probable); 90, white stork; 91, Eurasian goldfinch; 92, Eurasian skylark; 93, white stork; 94, Eurasian goldfinch; 95, Eurasian skylark; 96, white stork; 97, Eurasian goldfinch; 98, Eurasian skylark; B10, B11, B12, common shag; B29, common rock-pigeon; B30, common stock-dove (probable), common rock-pigeon (probable); B33, B34, B35, barn swallow.

Indonesia
599, greater bird-of-paradise; 1104, Pesquet's parrot; 1105, chattering lory; 1106, rainbow lory; 1106A, rainbow lory, Pesquet's parrot, chattering lory; 1163, salmon-crested cockatoo; 1164, greater sulphur-crested cockatoo; 1165, palm cockatoo; 1166a, greater sulphur-crested cockatoo; 1166b, palm cockatoo; 1180, Rothschild's myna; 1181, king bird of paradise; 1181A, Rothchild's myna; 1182, six-plumed parotia; 1183, twelve-wired bird of paradise; 1184, red bird of paradise; 1184A, six-plumed parotia, red bird-of-paradise; 1210, Wilson's bird of paradise; 1211, 1212, 1213, black-billed sicklebill; 1242, Lauterbach's bowerbird; 1243, golden regent bowerbird; 1244, arfak astrapia; 1245, superb bird-of-paradise;

1245a, Lauterbach's bowerbird, superb bird-of-paradise; 1251, 1252, 1273, 1273, 1285, 1286, 1308, 1309, bird (stylized); 1364, 1365, doves (stylized); 1430A, 1439, dove (stylized); B160, pied fantail; B161, zebra dove; B162, black drongo; B163, black-naped oriole; B164, java sparrow.

Iran
1188, 1189, 1428, barn swallow; 1505, Eurasian goldfinch; 1506, green pheasant; 1582, common shelduck; 1583, ruddy shelduck; 1584, greater flamingo; 1587, barn swallow; 1588, hoopoe; 1638, pin-tailed sandgrouse; 1639, chukar; 1640, yellow-bellied waxbill, red-cheeked cordon-bleu; 1782, great bustard; 1784, caucasian blackcock; 2088, 2115, bird (stylized); 2120, birds (stylized); 2143, 2167, bird (stylized); 2172, birds (stylized); 2209, 2217, 2246, bird (stylized); 2283, dove (stylized); 2325, 2394, bird (stylized); 2417, 2417a, glided steel bird; 2428, 2470, birds (unidentified); 2480, 2480, bird (unidentified); C34, C35, C36, C37, C38, C39, C40, C41, C42, C43, C44, C45, C46, C47, C48, C49, C50, C51, C52, C53, C54, C55, C56, C57, C58, C59, C60, C61, C62, C63, C64, C65, C66, C67, eagle (unidentified).

Iraq
463, white-cheeked bulbul; 464, hoopoe; 465, Eurasian jay; 466, peregrine falcon; 467, white stork; 468, black francolin; 469, marbled teal; 787, Eurasian kingfisher; 788, European turtle-dove; 789, pin-tailed sandgrouse; 790, blue rock-thrush; 791, purple heron, gray heron; 1043, 1045, white stork; 1130, 1131, 1132, 1133, 1259, 1260, 1261, 1262, dove (stylized); 1307, 1309, bird (stylized); 1441, 1442, 1443, dove (stylized); O311, white stork; O327, Eurasian kingfisher; O328, European turtle-dove; O329, pin-tailed sandgrouse; O330, blue rock-thrush; O331, purple heron, gray heron.

Israel
577, collared pratincole; 578, spur-winged lapwing; 579, black-winged stilt; 896, lappet-faced vulture; 897, Bonnelli's eagle; 898, sooty falcon; 899, griffon vulture; 956, Eurasian eagle-owl; 957, Bruce's scops-owl; 958, common barn owl; 959, Hume's tawny owl; 960, Scott 956-959 with tab designs in border; 1025a, garganey; 1025b, mallard; 1025c, teal; 1025d, shelduck; 1025E, ducks (unidentified), bird (stylized); 1025f, shelduck; 1025g, mallard; 1025h, garganey; 1025i, teal; 1027, birds (stylized); 1041, bird (stylized); 1052, griffon vulture; 1053, pelican; 1054, winter wren; 1062, bird as ornament; C28, Sinai rosefinch; C29, white-breasted kingfisher; C30, mourning wheatear; C31, Eurasian bee-eater;

C32, graceful prinia; C33, Palestine sunbird; C34, houbara bustard; C35, Eurasian scops-owl; C36, purple heron; C37, white-tailed eagle.

Italian East Africa
C5, C9, bateleur.

Italy
1320, Audouin's gull; 1588, Eurasian bee-eater; 1590, hoopoe; 1600, peafowl (unidentified); 1637, black-winged stilt; 1652d, black swan; 1756, dove (stylized); 1852, *falco pellegrino*; 1LNC2, 1LNC3, 1LNC5, 1LNC6, C107, C109, C111, C113, C130, barn swallow.

Italy-Trieste
C2, C3, C5, C18, C21, barn swallow.

Ivory Coast
231, yellow-bellied green pigeon; 232, spur-winged goose; 233, stone partridge; 234, hammerhead; 235, white-breasted guineafowl; 236, namaqua dove; 237, lizard buzzard; 238, yellow-billed stork; 239, forest francolin; 680, African fish-eagle; 681, gray parrot; 682, violet turaco; 734, 735, bird (stylized); 824, 875, dove (stylized); C64, forest francolin; C65, ring-necked pheasant; C93, red-breasted merganser; C94, American white pelican; C95, wood stork; C96, white-winged scoter.

Japan
46, goose (unidentified); 47, wagtail (unidentified); 50, goshawk (unidentified); 152, 153, Mandarin duck; 299, kite (unidentified); 365, 387, 479, geese (unidentified); 584, Japanese cormorant (probable); 588, Japanese crane; 598, little cuckoo; 611, Mandarin duck; 637, emperor penguin; 654, egrets (unidentified); 677, Japanese cormorant (probable); 680, Japanese crane; 695, Japanese crested ibis; 738, Mandarin duck; 751, copper pheasant; 753, Japanese crane; 788, Lidth's jay; 789, rock ptarmigan; 790, eastern turtle-dove; 791, white stork; 792, Japanese bush-warbler; 792A, meadow bunting; 846, black-tailed gull; 873, 888A, Japanese crane; 985, black-tailed gull; 1060, great tit; 1061, Adelie penguin; 1067, little cuckoo;

1068, mute swan; 1075, copper pheasant; 1077, golden eagle; 1148, Eurasian scops-owl; 1159, 1160, Japanese crane; 1182, Mandarin duck; 1183, northern goshawk; 1199, short-tailed albatross; 1200, Japanese crane; 1201, Bonin Island honeyeater; 1202, Ryukyu robin; 1232, green peafowl; 1257, Japanese crane; 1264, large-billed crow; 1314, Mandarin duck; 1324, Japanese crane; 1347, copper pheasant; 1383, ural owl (probable); 1418, Japanese crane, white-naped crane; 1461, Japanese crested ibis; 1480, eastern turtle-dove; 1487a, greater flamingo (probable); 1487b, king penguin; 1491, blue and white flycatcher; 1534, Okinawa rail; 1535, Blakiston's fish-owl; 1536, Okinawa woodpecker; 1537, Canada goose; 1538, Japanese marsh-warbler;

1539, crested serpent-eagle; 1540, black wood pigeon; 1541, spotted greenshank; 1542, peregrine falcon; 1543, white-backed woodpecker; 1554, Adelie penguin; 1557a, Japanese crane; 1589, golden-breasted starling (hypothetical); 1597, phasianidae (unidentified); 1598, Mandarin duck (wood carving); 1674, bull-headed shrike; 1714, cuckoo (unidentified); 1740, black-billed magpie; 1774, cuckoo (unidentified); 1784, cranes (unidentified); 1811, eagle (unidentified); 1834, bird planter; 1837, Origami crane; 1838, Origami crane; 1845, seagulls (unidentified); 1910, crows (stylized); 1924, swans (unidentified); 1926, ptarmigan; 1930, Japanese cranes; 2058, bird (stylized); 2059b, bluebird; 2072a, zuicho, happy bird (stylized);

2089, dove (stylized); 2103, Latham's snipe; 2104, brown booby; 2105, *larus crassirostris*; 2106, *podiceps ruficollis*; B10, varied tit; B44, bird (unidentified); C9, C10, C11, C12, C13, green pheasant.

Jordan
552, Eurasian goldfinch; 553, rock partridge; 554, ostrich; 555, sand partridge;

558, houbara bustard; 588, white-crowned black wheatear; 589, masked shrike; 590, Palestine sunbird; 702, gyrfalcon (hypothetical); 1285, hoopoe; 1286, northern orange-tufted sunbird; 1287, black-headed bunting; 1288, spur-winged lapwing; 1289, Eurasian greenfinch; 1290, black-winged stilt; 1323, crested lark; 1324, Eurasian stone curlew; 1325, Eurasian redstart; 1326, Eurasian blackbird; 1327, rock dove; 1328, white-breasted kingfisher; 1328A, crested lark, stone curlew, redstart, blackbird, rock dove, smyrna kingfisher; 1411, dove (stylized); C26, four-colored bush-shrike; C27, ornate hawk-eagle; C28, gray-headed kingfisher; C50, mallard.

Korea

101, Japanese crane; 110, black-billed magpie; 122, 129, 175, Japanese crane; 180, black-billed magpie; 311, barn swallow; 340, Tristram's woodpecker; 493, Mandarin duck; 494, Japanese crane; 495, Korean ring-necked pheasant; 643, 805, Japanese crane; 1015, great bustard; 1016, white-naped crane; 1017, Indian pitta; 1018, Tristram's woodpecker; 1019, black wood-pigeon; 1020, common oystercatcher; 1021, black-faced spoonbill; 1022, black stork; 1023, whooper swan; 1024, cinereous vulture; 1088, black-billed magpie; 1090, Japanese crane; 1151, Mandarin duck; 1203, ducks (unidentified); 1204, black-billed magpie; 1212a, Japanese crane; 1250, gulls (unidentified); 1317, black-billed magpie; 1345, whooper swan (probable); 1358, cranes (unidentified);

1385, black-billed magpie; 1477, Japanese waxwing; 1478, black-naped oriole; 1479, black-capped kingfisher; 1480, hoopoe; 1481, eastern broad-billed roller; 1481a, Japanese waxwing, black-naped oriole, black-capped kingfisher, hoopoe, eastern broad-billed roller; 1481B, kingfisher; 1481C, hoopoe; 1481D, roller; 1481E, waxwing; 1481F, oriole; 1504, penguin (unidentified); 1506A, gentoo penguin; 1508a, 1508b, 1508c, 1508d, white-naped crane; 1513, birds (stylized); 1529, birds (unidentified); 1534, 1539, birds (stylized); 1570, 1570a, cranes (stylized); 1585A, bird (stylized); 1615, cranes (stylized); 1637, 1640, 1670, 1670, bird (stylized).

Laos

122, slaty-headed parakeet; 123, white-crested laughing thrush; 124, osprey; 125, Indian roller; 373, barn swallow; 374, hoopoe; 375, Eurasian kingfisher; 376, black-naped monarch; 377, gray wagtail; 378, common tailorbird; 712, greater flamingo; 715, great argus; 716, silver pheasant; 717, ring-necked pheasant; 718, Lady Amherst's pheasant; 719, Reeve's pheasant; 720, golden pheasant; 721, copper pheasant; 744, gray partridge; 800, orange-breasted green pigeon; 812, raptor (unidentified); 864, phororhacus; 866, pteranodon; 877, stork-billed kingfisher; 878, Japanese quail; 879, blossom-headed parakeet; 881, black-crested bulbul; 882, mountain imperial pigeon; 899, 940, dove (stylized); 973, *prosthemadera novaeseelandie*;

974, *alauda arvensis*; 975, variable oystercatcher; 976, *Phalacrocorax carbo*; 977, *demigretta sacra*; 978, *apteryx australis mantelli*; 979, New Zealand king shag.

Lebanon

202, gray heron; 434, Eurasian bullfinch; 435, Eurasian goldfinch; 436, hoopoe; 437, red-legged partridge (probable); 439, 459, Eurasian bee-eater; C107, C108, C109, C110, gray heron; C150, C151, swallow (unidentified).

Liberia

104, great blue turaco; 106, great egret; 114, great blue turaco; 170, palm nut vulture; 193, 207, great Indian hornbill; 253, 264, palm-nut vulture; 271, black-casqued hornbill (probable); 275, 292, little egret; 293, black-casqued hornbill (probable); 341, common bulbul; 342, roller (unidentified); 343, hornbill (unidentified); 344, kingfisher (unidentified); 345, African jacana; 346, broad-tailed whydah; 358, emu; 578, black woodpecker; 580, common murre; 582, Japanese crane; 603, bald eagle; 711, cattle egret; 777, forest francolin; 778, narina trogon; 779, rufous-crowned roller; 780, brown-cheeked hornbill; 781, common bulbul; 782, African fish eagle; 783, Guinea turaco; 842, common bulbul;

1005, white-faced whistling duck, Egyptian goose, African jacana, spur-winged lapwing, fulvous whistling duck; 1017, Bohemian waxwing; 1018, bay-breasted warbler; 1019, white-winged crossbill; 1020, red phalarope; 1021, eastern bluebird; 1022, northern cardinal; 1109, rooster (unidentified); 1127, bald eagle; 1131, 1132, bird (stylized); B10, palm nut vulture; C4, eagle (unidentified); C6, seabird (unidentified); C7, C8, little egret; C11, seabird (unidentied); C12, C17, eagle (unidentified); C18, C19, seabird (unidentified); C20, C21, little egret; C22, C24, seabird (unidentified); C25, C27, eagle (unidentified); C28, C29, seabird (unidentified); C30, C31, little egret; C32, C34, seabird (unidentified);

C35, eagle (unidentified); C45, seabird (unidentified); C46, little egret; C47, seabird (unidentified); C48, little egret; C49, seabird (unidentified); C50, eagle (unidentified); C213, yellow-billed stork; O49, great blue turaco; O51, great egret; O105, palm nut vulture; O125, great Indian hornbill; O139, great Indian hornbill.

Libya

269, long-legged buzzard; 270, Eurasian bee-eater; 271, black-bellied sandgrouse; 272, houbara bustard; 273, spotted sandgrouse; 274, barbary partridge; 607, little bittern; 608, northern shrike; 609, fulvous babbler (probable); 610, Eurasian bee-easter; 611, hoopoe; 616, eagle (unidentified); 1023a, greater flamingo; 1023b, lanner falcon (probable); 1023c, Eurasian hobby (probable); 1023d, swift (unidentified); 1023e, European turtle-dove; 1023f, great whitethroat; 1023g, black-bellied sandgrouse; 1023h, Egyptian vulture; 1023i, Eurasian golden oriole; 1023j, Eurasian bee-eater; 1023k, Eurasian kingfisher; 1023l, Eurasian roller; 1023m, hoopoe; 1023n, cream-colored courser; 1023o, partridge (unidentified); 1023p, common barn-owl; 1048, 1049, 1145, 1146, 1147, 1225, 1226, 1284, 1285, 1300c, 1320, 1321, 1354, 1355, dove (stylized); 1385, 1386, 1387, 1388, eagle (unidentified); B48, ostrich; B52, golden eagle (probable).

Liechtenstein

221, Eurasian capercaillie; 225, golden eagle; 244, black grouse; 508, owl (unidentified); 537, Eurasian crulew; 541, northern three-toed woodpecker; 586, northern lapwing; 588, ring-necked pheasant; 829, barn swallow; 830, European robin; 907, little ringed plover; 945, pheasant; 946, blackcock; 947, mallard drake; 959, dove in flight (stylized); C9, C10, C11, golden eagle; C12, osprey; C13, golden eagle; C17, barn swallow; C18, common black-headed gull; C19, herring gull (probable); C20, northern goshawk (probable); C21, common buzzard (probable); C22, C23, lammergeier (probable).

Lithuania

403, ciconia nigra; 404, grus grus.

Luxembourg

376, great spotted woodpecker; 487, goldcrest; 732, little owl; 765, Eurasian dipper.

Macao

494, Eurasian kingfisher, gray-headed kingfisher; 495, Eurasian jay; 496, Japanese white-eye; 497, hoopoe; 498, red-billed leiothrix; 499, mallard; 549, 550a, common peafowl; 605, 606, 607, 608, 609, 610, bird (stylized); 636, two birds fighting; 657, 657, 657a, falcon (unidentified).

Madagascar

288, 289, long-tailed ground roller; 340, Madagascar blue pigeon; 341, blue coua; 342, red fody; 343, Madagascar pygmy kingfisher; 532, Okinawa woodpecker; 631, hook-billed vanga; 632, cuckoo roller; 633, Madagascar fish-eagle; 773, red-tailed vanga; 774, sicklebill; 775, giant coua; 776, created coua; 777, rufous vanga; 778, cattle egret; 779, Madagascar crested ibis; 780, vasa parrot; 783, black coucal; 840, purple heron; 842, long-tailed ground roller; 853, dove (stylized); 862, blue coua, hoopoe; 864, nelicourvi weaver, red forest fody; 866, crested coua; 868, Madagascar bee-eater, border contains purple heron, Madagascar fish-eagle, green-backed gallinule, red-capped coua, pitta-like ground roller, blue vanga, helmetbird, red fody, sakalava weaver, Madagascar starling;

1000, doves (stylized); 1001, eagle (stylized); C72, helmetbird; C73, pitta-like ground roller; C74, Madagascar crested ibis; C146, Lidth's jay; C191, C192, dove (stylized).

Mali

273, purple indigobird; 274, yellow-breasted barbet; 275, vitelline masked weaver; 276, northern carmine bee-eater; 277, Senegal parrot; 298, red-cheeked cordon-bleu; 299, vinaceous fire finch; 300, red-billed fire finch; 301, African turtle dove; 302, white-billed buffalo weaver; 468, bald eagle; C2, violet-backed starling; C3, bateleur; C4, common gonolek; C5, violet-backed starling; C6, bateleur; C7, C8, common gonolek; C11, cranes (unidentified); C19, C20, South African crowned crane; C25, knysna turaco (hypothetical); C26, abyssinian ground hornbill; C27, Egyptian vulture; C28, goliath heron; C175, western crowned crane; C277, C278, C279, bald eagle; C336, ostrich; C356, Abyssinian ground hornbill;

C357, ruff; C512, Eurasian kingfisher; C513, Stanley bustard; C514, ostrich; C515, Ruppell's vulture.

Martinque

C12, albatross (unidentified).

Mauritania

329, 388, ostrich; 506, eastern white pelican; 507, greater flamingo; 616, Eurasian spoonbill; 617, bridled tern; 634, great cormorant; 635, royal tern; 642, birds (stylized); 677, dove (stylized); C14, greater flamingo; C15, African spoonbill; C16, slender-billed gull; C29, Lichtenstein's sandgrouse; C30, reed cormorant; C31, dark chanting goshawk; C60, South African cornwed crane; C61, great egret; C129, ostrich; C170, yellow-billed stock, sacred ibis; C171, marabou stork; C172, long-crested eagle, martial eagle; C185, South African crowned crane; C186, water rail; C238, scarlet and western tanagers; C239, Bonaparte's gull; C240, blue jay; C241, black skimmer; C242, American anhinga; J26, Ruppell's vulture; J27, common crane;

J28, pink-backed pelican; J29, gargeny teal; J30, Eurasian golden oriole; J31, variable sunbird; J32, northern shoveler; J33, great snipe; J34, Vulturine guineafowl; J35, black stork; J36, gray heron; J37, white stork; J38, red-legged partridge; J39, paradise whydah; J40, little stinit; J41, Arbian bustard.

Mexico

1195, wild turkey; 1234, northern mockingbird; 1236, mountain trogon; 1346, muscovy duck; 1347, black-bellied whistling duck; 1367, 1410, 1411, dove (stylized); 1456, bird (stylized); 1500A, eagle (stylized); 1523, 1524, dove (stylized); 1565, messenger pigeons (stylized); 1593, 1594, 1595, 1596, 1597, 1598, 1600, eagle (stylized); 1650, bird (stylized); 1658, elegant tern; 1667, double-headed eagle (stylized); 1677, eagle (stylized); 1679, parrot (unidentified); 1688, 1689, 1706, dove (stylized); C1, C2, C3, C4, golden eagle (unidentified); C632, American flamingo.

Monaco

511, yellow wagtail; 512, European robin; 513, Eurasian goldfinch; 514, blackcap; 515, great spotted woodpecker; 516, nightingale; 518, Europeam starling; 520, white stork; 754, Japanese crane; 764, white-tailed eagle; 805, razorbill; 853, emperor penguin; 1241, nightingale; 1323, Eurasian nutcracker; 1324, black grouse; 1325, rock partridge; 1326, wall creeper; 1327, rock ptarmigan; 1328, golden eagle; 1339, Eurasian blackbird (probable), passerine birds (unidentified); 1584, 1585, bird (stylized); 1675, magician's bird; 1692, 1693,

doves (stylized); 1701, bird (stylized); 1714, 1715, dove (stylized); 1741, magpie (stylized); 1744, *ciconia abdimii*; 1745, *selasphorus platycercus*; 1746, *anas querquedula*;

1747, *eurystomus orientalis*; 1748, *merops apiaster*, 1776, 1777, 1777, dove (stylized); C40, pelican (unidentified); C41, common tern (probable); C42, gulls (unidentified); C43, albatrosses (unidentified); C44, great cormorant.

Mongolia

137, golden eagle; 144, dalmatian pelican (probable); 183, ring-necked pheasant; 214, rose-colored starling; 215, hoopoe; 216, Eurasian golden oriole; 217, black-billed capercaillie; 218, eastern broad-billed roller; 219, Tibetan sandgrouse; 220, Mandarin duck; 258, 377, golden eagle; 583, common buzzard; 584, twany owl; 585, northern goshawk; 586, white-tailed eagle; 587, peregrine falcon, swallows (unidentified); 588, Eurasian kestrel; 589, black kite; 728, common shelduck; 729, Arctic loon; 730, bar-headed goose; 731, great crested grebe; 732, mallard; 733, mute swan; 734, greater scaup; 798, lesser black-billed gull; 818, northern lapwing; 821, dalmatian pelican; 851, golden eagle; 914, osprey; 915, griffon vulture; 916, lammergeier;

917, Eurasian marsh harrier; 918, cinereous vulture; 919, golden eagle; 920, twany eagle; 1020, gray jay, Tibetan sandgrouse; 1021, common loon, Arctic loon; 1025, northern gannet, lesser black-baked gull; 1137, Adelie penguin; 1139, wandering albatross; 1141, emperor penguin; 1144, Adelie penguin; 1145, emperor penguin; 1311, imperial eagle (hypothetical); 1435, black stork; 1436, white-tailed eagle; 1437, Siberian white crane; 1438, Heude's parrotbill; 1439, hooded crane; 1440, white-naped crane; 1441, raptor (unidentified); 1489, Brandt's and Pelagic cormorants; 1538A, 1538B, Dalmatian pelican; 1538C, 1538D, Eastern white pelican; 1547, water pipit; 1548, redhead; 1549, red grouse; 1550, tundra swan; 1555, gray-faced woodpecker;

1556, Eurasian wryneck; 1557, great spotted woodpecker; 1558, white-backed woodpecker; 1559, lesser spotted woodpecker; 1560, black woodpecker; 1561, northern three-toed woodpecker; 1562, Okinawa woodpecker; 1609, 1610, mute swan; 1611, tundra (Bewick's) swan; 1612, whooper, mute and tundra swans; 1700, 1701, 1702, 1703, white-tailed eagle; 1837, 1850, bird (stylized); 1851, 1852, 1853, 1854, cranes (grus vipio pallas); 1896, 1897, 1898, 1899, 1900, 1901, 1902, 1903, parrots (unidentified); 1913, 1917, 1921, 1934, 1935, 1936, 1937, 1938, 1939, 1940, 1941, 1942, 1943, birds (unidentified); 1944, pheasant (unidentified); 1963, white cranes (unidentified); 1965, *lururus tetrix*; 1966, *tadorna tadorna*;

1967, *phasianus colchicus*; 1968, *clangula byemalis*; 1969, *mergus serator*, 1970, *bucephala clangula*; 1971, *anas crecca*; 2003, kingfisher, African griffon; C114, demoiselle crane; C115, barred warbler; C116, ruddy shelduck; C117, azure-winged magpie; C118, Eurasian goldfinch; C119, great tit; C120, Eurasian golden oriole; C146, white-tailed eagle; C150, snowy owl; C151, Atlantic puffin.

Morocco

233, ruddy shelduck; 234, houbara bustard; 308, Eleonora's falcon; 324, double-spurred francolin; 344, hermit ibis; 383, dark chanting goshawk; 384, purple swamphen; 447, Moussier's redstart; 458, peregrine falcon; 652, desert sparrow; 653, barbary partridge; 665, great bustard; 666, greater flamingo; 680, desert beater; 681, horned lark; 693, tourterelle; 694, huppe fasciee; 728, merops apiaster; 729, ciconia ciconia.

Mozambique

585, violet-crested turaco; 586, lilac-breasted roller; 587, red-headed weaver; 588, violet-backed starling; 589, Peter's twinspot; 590, Eurasian bee-eater; 708, narina trogon; 709, South African crowned crane; 710, red-necked francolin; 711, ostrich; 712, spur-winged goose; 713, African fish eagle; 736, marabou stork; 737, saddle-billed stork; 738, kori bustard; 1017, violet-eared waxbill; 1018, woodland kingfisher; 1019, white-fronted bee-eater; 1020, lesser seed-cracker; 1021, African broad-billed roller; 1022, Neergaard's sunbird; 1070, 1071, 1072, birds (stylized); 1107, bird (stylized); 1138d, chicken (unidentified); RA49, RA50, RA51, RA52, RA53, RA54, RA55, RA56, RA57, RA58, RA59, RA60, RA61, RA62, pelican (unidentified).

Netherlands

247, mute swan; 512a, northern goshawk; 642, Sandwich tern, common eider; 643, barnacle goose; B311, pelican; B354, common oystercatcher; B355, Eurasian curlew; B356, pied avocet; B357, northern lapwing; B386, white stork; B581, great tit; B584, palm cockatoo; B600, northern lapwing; B601, ruff; B602, common redshank; B603, black-tailed godwit; C11, C12, carrion crown.

Netherlands Antilles

242, 298, American flamingo; 302, budgerigar; 333, 342, 344, American flamingo; 459, white-tipped dove; 460, tropical mockingbird; 461, bananaquit; 521, black-faced grassquit; 522, rufous-collared sparrow; 523, blue-tailed emerald; 527, 528, 529, 530, American flamingo; 586, white-tailed tropicbird; 608, crested quail; 638, 638, flamigos (unidentified); 652, songbird (unidentified); 653, flamingo (unidentified); B35, American kestrel; B36, yellow oriole; B37, common ground dove; B38, brown-throated conure; B266, barn owl; B286, parrots (stylized); B288a, owl (stylized).

Netherlands Indies

N34, N35, N36, N37, kite (unidentified).

Netherlands New Guinea

22, 23, greater bird-of-paradise; 24, blue crowned pigeon; 25, raggiana bird-of-paradise (hypothetical); 26, blue crowned pigeon; 27, raggiana bird-of-paradise (hypothetical); 28, blue crowned pigeon; 29, raggiana bird-of-paradise (hypothetical); B4, greater bird of paradise; B5, B6, raggiana bird-of-paradise (hypothetical).

New Caledonia

88, 89, 90, 91, 92, 93, 94, 95, 96, 122, 123, 124, 252, 253, 254, 255, 256, 257, 258, 259, 260, 261, 262, 263, 264, 265, 266, 267, 268, 269, 270, 271, 272, 273, 276, 277, 278, 311, kagu; 345, red-throated parrot-finch; 346, New Caledonia pigeon; 361, New Caledonian grass-warbler; 362, New Caledonian whistler; 363, white-throated pigeon; 364, kagu; 365, New Caledonian horned parakeet; 366, crow honeyeater; 380, New Caldedonian friarbird; 381, sacred kingfisher; 413, brown booby; 414, masked booby; 415, red-footed booby; 420, 430, great frigatebird (probable); 431, black-naped tern; 432, sooty tern; 479, Grey's fruit dove; 480, rainbow lory; 493, common barn owl; 494, osprey; 505, 506, 507, 508, 509, 510, 511, 512, 513, 514, 515, 516, 517, 518, 527, kagu;

533, purple swamphen; 534, island thrush; 545, Australian magpie; 564, green-backed white-eye; 565, peregrine falcon; 584, 585, 586, 587, 588, 591, 591, 592, 592, 593, 593, 594, 595, 598, kagu; 612, marine life latiaxis; 617, La Poule rookery; B1, B2, B3, kagu; C48, uvea horned parakeet; C49, scarlet honeyeater; C49A, cloven-feathered dove; C70, emerald dove; C71, whistling kite; C138, great frigatebird; C186, kagu; C219B, kagu, kiwi.

New Hebrides

1, 2, 6, 7, kagu; 120, cardinal honeyeater; 121, buff-bellied flycatcher; 122, New Hebrides thicket-warbler; 123, white-collared kingfisher; 148, New Hebrides thicket-warbler; 175, Baker's pigeon; 177, red-headed parrot-finch; 180, chestnut-bellied kingfisher; 183, palm lorikeet; 200, chestnut-bellied kingfisher; 201, palm lorikeet; 202, Pacific pigeon; 237, Baker's pigeon; 239, red-headed parrot-finch; 242, chestnut-bellied kingfisher; 245, palm lorikeet; 296, white-bellied honeyeater; 297, scarlet robin; 298, yellow-fronted white-eye; 299, fan-tailed cuckoo.

Nicaragua

963, ruby-throated hummingbird; 1039, black swan; 1101, resplendent quetzal; 1125, lineated woodpecker; 1126, keel-billed toucan; 1127, Finsch's conure; 1128, scarlet macaw; 1813, *apteryx owenii*; 1814, *notornis mantelli*; 1815, *cyanoramphus novazelandiae*; 1816, *gallirallus australis*; 1817, *rhynochetos jubatus*; 1818, *nestor notabilis*; 1819, *strigops habroptilus*; 1861a, yellow-headed amazon; 1861b, toucan (unidentified); 1861c, scarlet macaw; 1861d, quetzel; 1861h, oropendola; 1861i, violet sabrewing; 1861o, white-necked jacobin; 2686, ring-necked pheasant; 2688, helmeted guineafowl; 2690, ocellated turkey; 2724, crimson topaz; 2725, orange-billed nightingale-thrush; 2726, troupial; 2727, painted bunting;

2728, passerine (unidentified); 2729, great horned owl; 2730, great kiskadee; C766, Montezuma oropendola; C768, white-throated magpie-jay; C769, scissor-tailed flycatcher; C770, spot-breasted oriole; C771, rufous-naped wren; C772, great kiskadee; C773, red-legged honeycreeper; C774, great-tailed grackle; C775, belted kingfisher; C776, turquoise-browed motmot; C963, rubythroated hummingbird; C986, slaty-tailed trogon; C987, violet sabrewing; C988, blue-crowned motmot; C1172, *anhinga anhinga*; C1173, *elanoides forficatus*; C1174, *eumomota superciliosa*; C1175, *setophaga picata*; C1176, great antshrike; C1177, *onychorhynchus mexicanus*; C1178, white-flanked antwren; C1179, amazona ochrocephala.

Niger

91, 92, South African crowned crane; 93, 94, saddle-billed stork; 99, 100, ostrich; 184, red-billed hornbill; 185, pied kingfisher; 186, common gonolek; 187, 187A, little weaver; 188, chestnut-bellied sandgrouse; 207, African gray hornbill; 208, woodland kingfisher; 209, Senegal coucal; 210, rose-ringed parakeet; 211, abyssinian roller; 212, cattle egret; 233, African gray hornbill; 234, woodland kingfisher; 235, Senegal coucal; 236, rose-ringed parakeet; 237, red bishop; 244, broad-tailed whydah; 254, cattle egret; 316, abyssinian roller; 391, marabou stork; 425, cattle egret; 443, broad-tailed whydah; 448, 537, ostrich; 540, kori bustard; 695, Sudan golden sparrow; 696, red-billed quelea; C15, northern carmine bee-eater; C86, violet-backed starling;

C87, splendid glossy-starling; C200, common raven; C255, violet-backed starling; C291, South African crowned crane; C292, golden eagle; C352, black-necked stilt; C353, American flamingo; C354, Atlantic puffin; C355, Arctic tern.

Norway

353, 354, whooper swan; 554, white-tailed eagle; 759, common oystercatcher; 760, mallard; 761, Eurasian dipper; 762, great tit; 775, lesser white-fronted goose; 776, peregrine falcon; 777, Atlantic puffin; 778, black guillemot; 800, bluethroat; 801, European robin; 821, barnacle goose; 822, dovekie; 872, Eurasian bullfinch; 885, Eurasian capercaillie; 885C, mute swan; 892, nightingale; 902, doves (stylized); 944, brown leghorn rooster; 959, owl (unidentified); 991, 992, seagulls (unidentified). □

Trains

Gabon

212, diesel railcar; 351, diesel engine; 423, Trans-Gabon Railway diesel engine, passenger cars, railway bridge & map of new & proposed routes; 527, Trans-Gabon Railway, diesel engine, passenger cars & map of railway with proposed extensions; 570, diesel engine & passenger cars of Transgabonais train; 608, 609, diesel engine, passenger cars & map of present route with proposed extension; C46, diesel engine; C76, tracks at Owendo Harbor; C137, diesel engine on transport stamp in orbit around globe; C162, 0-4-0 Marc Seguin engine, 1829; C163, 4-2-2 *The Duke*, 1847; C164, 4-4-0 Rogers engine, USA, 1895; C165, 4-14-4 Class AA engine No. 20-1, Russia, 1935; C206, diesel engine & cars;

C249, 2-8-2 Class D-51 engine, Japan & French National Railway TGV 001; C250, 2-8-8-0 Baltimore & Ohio Railroad engine, USA & 0-6-0 Prussian State railway Type T3 engine; C251, C251a, BB diesel engine, France & Stephenson's *Rocket* & portrait of George Stephenson; C252, Scott C251a overprinted; C274, diesel engine & passenger cars;

German East Africa

N6, N14, N22, Belgian Congo Scott 53 overprinted; N25, Scott N22 surcharged; NB6, Belgian Congo Scott B6 overprinted.

German States-Bavaria

O1, O2, O3, O4, O5, regular issues ovptd. "E" for railway officials' use.

Germany

111, 112, 113, streetcar to left of post office building; 146, 147, 172, 173, 221, 224, 226, 228, mine car; 459, 2-2-2 engine *Der Adler*, 1835, & passenger cars; 460, 4-6-2 Class 03 engine, 1930, & passenger cars; 461, No. VT.04 articulated diesel railcar set *Flying Hamburger*, Berlin-Hamburg line, 1932; 462, 4-6-4 Class 05 engine No. 05.001, 1935; 501, railway terminal, Leipzig; 698, passenger train, semaphore signal & hand signal; 734, track & semaphore signal; 783, Rudolf Diesel & stationary diesel engine; 822, 2-2-2 engine *Der Adler*, 864, map of *Bird Flight Line* railway between Germany & Denmark; 919, railway crossing sign; 923, 2-2-2 engine *Der Adler* & Bo-Bo Class E10.12 electric engine; 968, Werner Von Siemens, designer of first electric engine;

1171, front of ET420/421 electric train set with same design as Scott 9N360; 1191, Maglev monorail with same design as Scott 9N375B; 1210, electric passenger train on the Wuppertal suspension railway; 1249, Siebengebirge Mountains with electric Class 103 engine & passenger cars; 1294, first electric engine & passenger cars, 1879; 1365, Preiser HO gauge model railroad figures forming "100" for "Centenary of Social Insurance"; 1450, *Inauguration of the First German Railway*, painting by Prof. Heim; 1515, loading railway post office cars; 1583, 0-4-0 engine, freight, passenger car & Friedrich List, railway builder; 1619, souvenir sheet border showing two railway bridges; 1646, symbolic design with initals "ICE" (Inter-City Express);

B5, Scott 221 surcharged & overprinted; B113, seatrain *Schwerin* entering Warnemunde with bow raised for unloading; B114, traveling crane & tracks on dock; B226, tracks in lower right; B267, railway artillery car; B359, mine car; B450, 2-2-2 toy tin steam engine, 1835; B517, Class 218 diesel engine No. 218-004; B518, Class 103 electric engine No. 103-101 in "TEE" colors; B519, Class 403 electric railset No. ET403; B520, model of *Transrapid* Maglev train; O22, Scott 224 overprinted "DIENSTIMARKE"; O23, Scott 226 overprinted "DIENSTIMARKE"; 5N12, 5N26, Hollental railway bridge, Black Forest; 5N40, same design as Scott 5N12, without "pf"; 9N90, Werner Von Siemens, designer of first electric engine;

9N112, blacksmith forging billet into rails; 9N145, tracks behind Hansa model town; 9N272, *Borsig Blacksmiths*, drawing by Paul Meyerheim with engine wheel being made, 1878; 9N305, 2-6-0T of Suburban Railway "Wamnsee" engine No. 74-1015 & passenger cars, 1925; 9N306, two four-wheel electric streetcars of street railway, 1890; 9N307, Pferde Street railway horse-drawn four-wheel streetcar No. 247; 9N308, Class ET165.8 electric passenger train of light railway, 1932; 9N309, electric streetcar No. 6200 & trailer, street railway, 1950; 9N310, Berlin subway with railcars & railsets at station, 1971; 9N360, front of ET420/421 electric train set with same design as Germany Scott 1171; 9N375B, Maglev monorail with same design as Scott 1191;

9N573, "Patentee" type steam engine & passenger carriages at station on Berlin-Potsdam Railway, 1838; 9NB65, toy tin railway coach, 1835; 9NB115, 4-4-0 "Drache" (Dragon), 1849; 9NB116, 0-6-0T Class 89.70 No. 89-7452; 9NB117, 2-10-0 Class 050 No. 50-001; 9NB118, 4-6-2 Class 010 No. 10-001; 9NB283, traveling post office car, 1900; 13NB3, 4-6-2 engine in repair shop.

Germany-DDR

164, building steam engine; 172, ore cars under power shovel; 197, same design as Scott 164, redrawn; 286, 287, tracks at Leipzig Fair; 291, electric streetcar, Dresden; 294, traveling cranes; 324, Co-Co Blankenburg-Hanz-Konigshutte Railway Class E251 electric engine; 334, same design as Scott 197; 347, hopper cars at coal mine; 348, electric engine & ore cars; 406, Leipzig railway station; 409, railway postal car; 513, 19th century railway postal car; 529, double deck articulated train, *Young Socialists Express* & signal bridge; 530, train ferry *Sassnitz*, Sassnitz Harbor station & passenger cars; 531, B-B Class V180 hydraulic diesel engine, 1960, double deck passenger cars & 2-2-2 engine *Der Adler*, 615, Rostock railway station;

629, B-B Class V180 hydraulic diesel engine; 661, diesel railcar; 679, loading mail car, passenger car; 724, freight car & traveling crane on dock; 990, Bo-Bo type DE-1 diesel slave unit, built for the Sao Paulo Railway of Brazil; 1038, 0-10-0, diesel engines, freight, passenger cars, signals & bridge, model trains at Leipzig Fair; 1083, Co-Co Class 103 electric engine & railway crossing signal; 1213, railway policeman & class SVT18.16 diesel trainset; 1401, Red Cross car; 1462, Bo-Bo type 211 electric engine No. 200-3 & passenger car; 1463, Waggonbau Dessau refrigerator car, Type MK4-21m; 1464, Ammendorf passenger car, Type 47DK; 1465, Waggonbau Niesky bulk powder freight car; 1466, double deck passenger car; 1467, Type YB/70 passenger car;

1554, railway lines on map; 1574, rail crane lifting Model EDK-2000 diesel engine; 1586, 0-4-0 & diesel engine on UPU centenary issue; 1682, railway crossing sign; 1757, railway bridge over Templin Lake; 1758, Berlin-Adlergestell railway bridge; 1759, railway bridge over the Elbe River at Rosslau; 1760, railway viaduct over the Goltech Valley; 1840, streetcar at "Konsument" department store, Leipzig; 1843, 2-4-0T engine *Muldenthal*, 1861; 1844, Dresden four-wheel streetcar No. 761, 1896; 1889, loading Prussian railway postal car; 1890, loading railway postal car; 1915, traveling crane loading container on flatbed truck; 1916, diesel engines & containers on flat cars; 1917, traveling crane loading containers on ship;

2000, Sheet of two stamps & label with label showing Sachsenring Automobile plant, Zwickau & German Railways auto transporter car; 2001, electric passenger train, Type MXA; 2002, center flow hopper car, Type Us-y; 2003, diesel engine Type BR-110 No. 110836 & passenger car; 2004, automobile transporter car, Type LAAES; 2016, *Rostock*, train ferry; 2017, *Rugen*, train ferry; 2147, Strip of two, 0-4-4T Radebeul-Radeburg Railway Class 99 engine & passenger car, with label showing Moritzburg Castle & railway map of 750mm gauge Radebeul-Radeburg Railway; 2148, Strip of two, 2-8-2T Engine No. 992373 & passenger car, with label between showing steam passenger train & railway map of 900mm gauge Bad Doberan-Ostseebad Railway;

2149a, 0-4-0 toy engine, 1850; 2205, Strip of two, 0-6-4T engine No. 9917618 & baggage car, with label between showing railway map of 750mm gauge Freital-Kurort Kipsdorf Line; 2206, Strip of two, 2-6-0T engine No. 9946328 & passenger car, with label between showing map of 750mm gauge Putbus-Gohren Railway; 2292, attached label with electric engine & freight cars; 2341, Strip of two, 0-4-0 engine & passenger cars, with label between showing the 1000mm gauge Wernigerode-Nordhausen Railway; 2342, Strip of two, steam engine & baggage car, with label between showing map of 750mm gauge Zittau-Kurort Oybin/Kurort Jonsdorf Railway;

2405, Strip of two, 2-10-2T engine No. 99.1775 & passenger coach, with label between showing 750mm gauge Cranzahl-Kurtort Oberwiesenthal Railway & sketch of cable car to Fuchtel Mountain; 2406, Strip of two, 2-6-2T engine No. 99-6001 & passenger coach, with label between showing sketch of Alexisbad & map of 1000 gauge Selke Valley Railway; 2496, signal box Model GS11 & track diagram; 2497, 0-4-2 engine *Saxonia*, 1838, electric engine Model BR250 & Johann Andreas Schubert; 2498, helicopter hoisting material in electrification of Berlin railway network & passenger car; 2499, aerial view of Leipzig Railway Station; 2536, electric engine; 2538, horsedrawn tram, Dresden, 1886; 2539, streetcar, Leipzig, 1896; 2540, streetcar, Berlin, 1919;

2541, streetcar, Halle, 1928; 2574, diesel freight train going onto train ferry *Mukran*; 2575, cross section of two deck train ferry *Mukran*; 2708, railway lift bridge, Magdeburg; 2711, North-South railway bridge over Strelasund River, Rugendamm; 2737, Georg Friedrich List, industrialist, economist; 2738, Dresden railway station, Leipzig, 1839; 2739, steam train, Leipzig railway station, Dresden, 1839; 2844, railway post office cars, 1842 & 1900; B22, loading side-dump cars.

Greece

321, 326, 364, steam engine & passenger car on bridge over Corinth Canal; 1204, steam engine wheel in emblem of European Conference of Ministers of Transportation; 1235, Scott 1204 on envelope; 1251, 2-4-0 engine, mail & passenger cars; 1296, 2-6-0 & diesel engine Piraeus-Athens Frontier Railway; 1377, traveling cranes on dock at Piraeus port; 1502, passenger cars, "Pelion" train; 1503, freight cars on Papadia bridge; 1504, passenger cars, Piraeus-Pelopinnese line; 1505, Calavryta Cog Railway steam passenger train; 1529, streetcar in Salonika, 1912; 1622, Modernistic passenger train & commuter cars; C74, streetcar tracks in Piraeus; C78, streetcar alongside building, Volos; RA55, RA57, Scott 364 overprinted; RA66, RA70, Scott 321 surcharged.

Greece-Cavalla

N169, N175, Bulgaria Scott 94 surcharged.

Guatemala

26, 27, 28, 29, 30, railway tax stamps inscribed "FERROCARRIL AL NORTE" & surcharged; 31, 32, 33, 34, 35, 36, 37, 38, 39, 40, 41, steam engine in upper left corner; 42, Scott 32 surcharged "PROVISIONAL/1886/1/ UN CENTAVO"; 43, 44, 45, 46, 47, 48, 49, 50, same design as Scott 31-41; 51, Scott 38 surcharged & overprinted "1894"; 52, 52a, 53, 53a, 54, 55, 55a, Scott 39-41 surcharged & overprinted "1894"; 56, Scott 44 surcharged & overprinted "1894"; 57, 58, 59, Scott 46 surcharged & overprinted "1895"; 60, 61, 62, 63, 64, 65, 66, 67, 68, 69, 70, 71, 72, 73, steam engine; 74, Scott 64 surcharged & overprinted "1898"; 75, Scott 46 surcharged & overprinted "1898"; 76, Scott 37 surcharged & overprinted "1898"; 77, Scott 46 surcharged & overprinted "1898";

78, Scott 40 surcharged & overprinted "1898"; 79, Scott 35 surcharged & overprinted "1898"; 80, Scott 50 surcharged & overprinted "1898"; 81, Scott 38 surcharged & overprinted "1898"; 82, Scott 48 surcharged & overprinted "1898"; 83, Scott 35 surcharged & overprinted "1898"; 84, Scott 39 surcharged & overprinted "1898"; 85, Scott 41 surcharged & overprinted "1898"; 86, revenue stamp overprinted steam engine & "CORREOS NACIONALES"; 87, Scott 86 surcharged; 97, Scott 46 surcharged & overprinted "1899"; 98, Scott 48 surcharged & overprinted "1900"; 99, 100, 101, 102, 103, 104, 105, 106, 107, same design as Scott 43-50; 108, 109, Scott 49 surcharged &

overprinted "1901"; 110, Scott 50 surcharged "UN/1/Centavo/1901" in black; 111, 112, revenue stamps surcharged & overprinted steam engine; 124, Scott 99 surcharged "1903/25/CENTAVOS"; 125, Scott 100 surcharged "1903/25/CENTAVOS"; 126, Scott 102 surcharged "1903/25/CENTAVOS"; 127, Scott 103 surcharged "1903/25/CENTAVOS"; 128, Scott 38 surcharged "1903/25/CENTAVOS"; 129, Scott 40 surcharged "1903/25/CENTAVOS"; 130, Scott 41 surcharged "1903/25/CENTAVOS"; 162, steam engine; 166, Scott 162 surcharged "1920/2 Centavos"; 174, steam engine & freight cars on La Penitenciaria bridge, Guatemala City; 187, Scott 174 surcharged "1922/DOCE/Y MEDIO/CENTAVOS"; 190, Scott 174 surcharged "1922/25/CENTAVOS"; 191, Scott 174 with same surcharge as Scott 190; 195, Scott 162 with similar surcharge to Scott 190;

201, Scott 174 with similar surcharge to Scott 190; 216, same design as Scott 174; 229, Scott 216 imprinted "Waterlow & Sons, Limited, Londres, 1926"; 245, 246, Scott 227 overprinted "FERROCARRIL ORIENTAL - 1929" & surcharged; 247, 248, 249, 250, 251, Scott 229 overprinted "FERROCARRIL/de los ALTOS/INAUGURADO en 1929" / new value & "DE QUETZAL"; 252, hydroelectric dam at Quetzaltenango for generating electric power for railway;

253, tracks at Los Pirineos; 254, Quetzaltenango railway station; 267, steam engine; C1, C2, C3, C4, Scott 229 overprinted "SERVICIO/POSTAL AEREO/ANO DE 1928" & new values; C5, Scott 216 with same surcharge as Scott C1-C4; C12, Scott 229 overprinted "SERVICIO/ AEREO INTERIOR/10 CENTAVOS/DE QUETZAL/1930";

C23, C24, Scott 229 overprinted "SERVICIO AEREO/INTERIOR-1932/" & new values; C29, steam engine on pier, Port Barrios; C52, C53, railway station, Plaza Barrios; C62, C63, tracks on dock, Port Barrios; C64, C65, tracks on dock, Port San Jose; C89, railway station, Plaza Barrios, overprinted with airplane; C119, railway station, Plaza Barrios, overprinted with Quetzal; C460, C461, C462, C463, steam engine on bridge; C765, steam passenger train crossing trestle over Puente de Las Vacas; C766, diesel engine, 4-4-0 engine & compound type engine, switch tower in yards & portrait of General J.R. Barrios, minister of railways; C767, diesel engine & freight cars crossing Lake Amatitian Dam.

Guinea

661, diesel engine & freight cars; 662, ore cars; 674, passenger monorail on UPU Centenary Issue; 703, diesel engine, freight cars & switch person; 791, child's drawing of steam engine & passenger car; 826, diesel engine & passenger car; 886, 4-8-4+4-8-4 East African Railways Beyer-Garratt engine, 1939; 969, London, Midland & Scottish Railway Class 8F steam engine, U.K.; 970, Bo-Bo German Federal Railway 5500 CH, series III electric engine, Germany; 971, 4-6-2 African Railways *Pacific A-Mazout* No. 270 engine; 972, Suburban *S Bahn* series 420 electric train, Germany; 973, German Federal Railway diesel train "ICE," souvenir sheet border with steam engine *Dragon*, 1848 & German High-Speed train *Vindobona*; 991, Scott 969 surcharged with new value;

992, Scott 970 surcharged with new value; 993, Scott 971 surcharged with new value; 994, Scott 972 surcharged with new value; 1001, Dietrich 640 CV passenger diesel train; 1002, T.13 790lL engine; 1003, Vapeur 01220 engine; 1004, ABH3 type 5020 diesel engine & passenger cars; 1005, 2-2-2 engine *Der Adler*, ICE train, Germany, souvenir sheet border with ABH3 diesel passenger train in Africa; 1135, French National Railway TGV train *Atlantique*.

Guinea-Bissau

412B, British *Stourbridge Lion* steam engine, Japanese *Hikari* train & toy steam engine pulled by child; 619, White Mountain Central Railway steam No. 4, USA, 1926; 620, 2-6-0 Tallalyn Railway, Wales, 1886; 621, Wuppertal Overhead Railway, Germany, 1901; 622, Gurjao Funicular Railway No. 6; 623, Rack engine No. 1 Achenseebahn, Austria; 624, Vitznau-Rigi Railway steam engine; 625, Riggenbach Rack Railway steam engine, 1873; 626, Scott 621, souvenir sheet border with French TGV & several advance design passenger trains; 688g, 150th Anniversary of German Railways-Frankfurt on Main Railway Station, 1914; 795, Rapid Transit train, M2004, Barcelona, Spain; 796, Co-Co TEM 2 diesel engine, Russia;

797, Co-Co Rede Ferroviaria Federal SA diesel engine, Brazil; 798, Rapid Transit train; 799, electric type 593 engine, Czechoslovakia; 800, Bo-Bo Tu7E diesel engine; 801, electric LRV & Scott 797-801; 802, LRV Spanish National Railways Class 593, front cab portion perforated as stamp, design continued in souvenir sheet border.

Haiti

127, 128, streetcar tracks, Iron Market, Port-au-Prince; 134, 135, streetcar tracks at Entrance to Catholic College, Port-au-Prince; 179, Scott 127 handstamped "GL O.Z./ 7 FEV. 1914" & new value; 180, Scott 128 handstamped "GL O.Z./ 7 FEV. 1914" & new value; 185, Scott 134 handstamped "GL O.Z./ 7 FEV. 1914" & new value; 186, Scott 135 handstamped "GL O.Z./ 7 FEV. 1914" & new value; 256, Scott 127 surcharged "2 CTS/ GOURDE"; 257, Scott 134 surcharged "2 CTS/ GOURDE"; 258, Scott 135 surcharged "2 CTS/ GOURDE"; 263, Scott 128 surcharged "2 CTS/ GOURDE"; 270, Scott 135 surcharged "2 CTS/ GOURDE"; 283, Scott 185 "O.Z." surcharged; 284, Scott 186 "O.Z." surcharged; 292, 294, Scott 179 "O.Z." surcharged; 295, Scott 180 "O.Z." surcharged;

310, 311, steam train; 742, 743, 744, 745, 746, 747, Pres. Duvalier & traveling crane on dock; 748, Scott 742 overprinted "1957-1982/25 ANS DE REVOLUTION"; 749, Scott 744 overprinted "1957-1982/25 ANS DE REVOLUTION"; 750, Scott 745 overprinted "1957-1982/25 ANS DE REVOLUTION"; 751, Scott 746 overprinted "1957-1982/25 ANS DE REVOLUTION."

Honduras

103-110, steam engine & passenger cars; 174, 175, 178, 179, Ulua Railway bridge across Ulua River at Pimienta; 237, Scott 175 overprinted "HABILITADO/1926"; 240, Scott 179 overprinted "VALE 6 CTS./1927" & horizontal bar; 285, Scott 174 overprinted "HABILITADO/JULIO. - 1930"; 292, Scott 237 overprinted "HABILITADO/JULIO. - 1930"; C4, Scott 178 overprinted "AERO/CORREO"; C5, Scott 178 overprinted "AERO/CORREO"; C6, C7, Scott 179 overprinted "AERO/CORREO"; C10, Scott 174 surcharged "AERO/CORREO/25"; C12, Scott 178 surcharged "AERO/CORREO/25"; C13, Scott 179 surcharged "AERO/CORREO/25"; C80, Mayo railway bridge; C391, 2-8-2 engine No. 59, Tela Railway, owned by United Fruit Co.;

CO31, CO32, Scott 062 surcharged "AEREO OFICIAL/VALE L.O. 70" 1933; O23, Scott 105 overprinted "OFICIAL"; O24, Scott 107 overprinted "OFICIAL"; O25, Scott 108 overprinted "OFICIAL"; O26, Scott 109 overprinted "OFICIAL"; O27, Scott 110 overprinted "OFICIAL"; O58, Scott 174 overprinted "OFICIAL"; O59, Scott 175 overprinted "OFICIAL"; O62, Scott 178 overprinted "OFICIAL"; O63, Scott 179 overprinted "OFICIAL".

Hungary

472, 573, 574, Count Stephen Szechenyi, railway builder; 577, 4-8-0 Class 424; 702, winged wheel & rail; 785, 4-2-0 Central Hungarian Railway *Heves* No. 69, 1846; 786, 4-8-0 Class 424; 787, 2-DO-2 Class V44 electric engine, 1943; 788, B-B *Arpad* diesel railcar, 1935; 871, electric mine engine & mine cars; 878, 4-6-4 Class 303 & passenger train on bridge; 880, steam engine & train at factory; 881, 4-8-0 Class 424 under traveling crane; 942, diesel railcar & crossing guard with hand held signal, Budapest Pioneer Railway; 945, same design as Scott 871; 952, same design as Scott 878; 954, same design as Scott 880; 955, same design as Scott 881; 962, Ganz railway car factory; 964, Central railway station; 1005, Szekesfehervar railway station;

1008, freight cars at grain elevator; 1012, 4-8-0 Class 424, passenger car & railway crossing guard; 1013, railway construction, Dyplory type track laying car; 1030, subway construction work car; 1031, station & system map; 1052, freight cars at brick factory, Maly; 1056, freight car at foundry, Diosgyor; 1110, steam engine & freight cars at steel mill; 1121, 4-8-0 Class 424, passenger car, railway guard & semaphore signal; 1128, streetcar conductor & part of streetcar; 1141, 1B-2+2-2+2-B1 diesels with diner between; 1145, 4-6-4 Class 303 & passenger cars; 1224, 4-2-0 1/4-inch scale model of engine *Deru*, 1847; 1225, *Hargita* diesel railcar; 1226, semaphore signal (vertical); 1389, steam engine;

1400, George Stephenson, engine builder; 1401, winged railway wheel; 1436, railway target signals; 1508, streetcar; 1510, Budapest West station (Nyugati Palyaudvar); 1511, railway tank car; 1512, Budapest South station (Deli Palyaudvar); 1513, railway mail car; 1519, *Hargita* diesel railcar & passenger car, Keszthely railway station, Lake Balaton; 1522, passenger cars, switch tower under catenary; 1525, loading mail car; 1619, streetcars on Arpad bridge; 1620, streetcars on Margaret bridge & passenger cars below bridge; 1622, streetcars on Elizabeth bridge; 1623, tracks on Liberty bridge; 1624, streetcars on Petofi bridge; 1625, railcar on South Railway bridge; 1679, Elizabeth bridge & tracks along river front;

1737, Count Stephen Szechenyi, railway builder; 1752, 4-2-0 1/4-inch scale model of engine *Deru* & Budapest Railway station, 1846; 1753, B-B Class V43 electric engine & Budapest South station, 1966; 1790, Liberty bridge & Mt. Gellort; 1827, diesel engine & passenger cars; 1833, traveling cranes, Galati shipyards; 1834, traveling cranes, Izmail Harbor; 1862, souvenir sheet border with outline of diesel railcar; 1879, Statue of Kalman Kando, designer of electric engines & electric railways, B-B Class V43 electric engine, passenger car & railway route map; 1897, Co-Co Class M62 diesel engine & refrigerator cars; 1912, 4-8-0 Class 424 No. 424.176; 1921, diesel passenger train; 2017, Budapest Metro train at station;

2018a, 1945 view Liberty, Elizabeth & Margaret bridges; 2018b, 1970 view Liberty, Elizabeth & Margaret bridges; 2076, resistance fighters blowing up railway viaduct; 2086, 2-2-2 engine *Bets* No. 70 & passenger car of first Hungarian railway, map of Central Hungarian Railway system; 2123, 4-6-4 Class 303, 1950, Hungary; 2124, 2-6-0 Prussian State Railway Class P6, Germany; 2125, 0-6-0 Mediterranean System Class 380, Italy; 2126, 4-8-4 Class P36, Russia; 2127, Heisler geared, Japan; 2128, 0-4-4T, Great Britain; 2129, 0-6-0T Austrian State Railway Number 3206, Austria; 2130, 0-6-0 Paris-Strasbourg Railway *Le Continent* No. 80 and passenger cars, France; 2177, Co-Co Class M62 diesel engine, passenger cars & International Railway Union emblem;

2180, diesel passenger train & Margaret bridge; 2181, Elizabeth bridge, Buda, 1872; 2182, Elizabeth bridge, Budapest, 1972; 2184, streetcar, Parliment building, Budapest, 1972; 2271, diesel engine & passenger cars in front of Comecon building, Moscow; 2286, diesel engine & mail cars on UPU Centenary issue; 2296a, steam engine & open passenger car, 1874; 2296b, steam engine & flat car with horses, 1874; 2296c, electric engine & passenger car 1929-73; 2296d, electric engine & passenger car on bridge, 1974; 2350, Postwar poster, *Let us rebuild the Railways*, by Sandor Bortnyk, with steam engine above wrecked trains; 2353, train; 2365, Count Stephen Szechenyi, railway builder; 2368, electric engine, 1902;

2402, Count Stephen Szechenyi on bank note; 2422, Pioneer Railway guard; 2443, 0-6-0 No. 4 & Enese station, 1875; 2444, steam engine No. 17 & passenger cars at Rabatamasi station, 1885; 2445, Railbus *Gysev* & Fertoszentmiklos station, 1925; 2446, 2-4-2 & Kapuvar station; 2447, railcar & trailer, 1926 & first Gyor station, 1855; 2448, railcar & passenger car, 1934 & Fertoboz station; 2449, railcar & passenger cars, 1971 & Sopron station; 2466, Hackney carriage at Budapest East railway station, 1890; 2535, Pioneer Railway type MK45 diesel engine & passenger car; 2540, diesel engine, mail & passenger cars; 2573, 0-4-0 *Rocket*, 1829; 2574, Siemens & Halske first electric engine, 1879, same engine pulling passenger cars at Berlin exhibition.;

2575, 2-2-2 Chicago & Northwestern Railroad *Pioneer*, & passenger car, 1836; 2576, 4-4-0 Class MAV I.e pulling the *Orient Express*, Hungary, 1883; 2577, 4-6-0 pulling the *Trans-Siberian Express*, 1898 & freight car; 2578, Japanese National Railway electric engine & passenger cars of *Hikari*, 1964, Japan; 2579, monorail train *Transrapid 05*, 1979, Germany; 2580, railway map of Europe, souvenir sheet border with electric engine V63002, 1973 & passenger cars; 2608a, 0-2-2T Eibel; 2608b, 4-8-0 Class 424; 2608c, 2-10-0 type 520 No. 520.050; 2608d, diesel type M41 No. M1001; 2697, 0-4-0 *Locomotion* & George Stephenson; 2710, Ship *Felszabadulas* & Hungary Scott 1833; 2711, ship *Rakoczi* & Hungary Scott 1834; 2758, subway train at station;

2863, streetcar at Budapest riverside hotel, Atrium Hyatt; 2865, streetcar at Budapest riverside hotel, Forum; 2868, streetcar at Budapest riverside hotel, Gellert & Liberty bridge; 2903, railway girder bridge, Baja; 2904, Arpad bridge, Budapest; 2906, Reichsbrucke bridge, Vienna; 2909, streetcars on Elizabeth bridge, Budapest & map; 2914, Liberty bridge, Budapest; 2926, Magnetic monorail, Expo '85, Tsukuda, Japan; 2948, Margaret, Elizabeth, Liberty & Petroi bridges, Budapest; 2986, Buda Castle cable railway cars & station; 3082, Railway Officers Training Institute & emblem of Hungarian railways; 3142, 0-4-0 toy engine, passenger & freight cars; 3151, with East Railway Station, Budapest & black control number;

3308, Count Stephen Szechenyi, railway builder; B213, Scott 1121 surcharged with "Red Cross + 40 Filler" in red; B220, Margaret, Arpad & North Railway; B223, Liberty & Petofi bridges; B277, Elizabeth bridge, Budapest; B288d, Margaret bridge, Budapest, 1970; C47, Liberty bridge; C56, 0-4-0 *Locomotion*, George Stephenson & 4-6-4 New York Central Class J-3a; C61, Kalman Kando, electric streetcar & 2-D0-2 Class V44 electric engine; C67, 4-8-0 Class 424; C71, Kossuth & Petofi bridges, Budapest; C73, Tank type steam engine & freight cars at Diosgyor steel mill; C77, 4-6-4 Class 303 & passenger cars; C78, steam engine & freight cars at Matyas Rakesi steel mill, Csepel; C93, Arpad bridge; C167, Scott C78 printed on aluminum foil;

C188, steam engine; C199, streetcars, Academy of Science & Parliament & Margaret bridge; C243, Mongolia Scott 189, diesel mail car; C250, Elizabeth bridge & three streetcars; C262, Helsinki railway station; C353, Elizabeth bridge; J271, diesel engine & mail cars; J279, Railroad mail car.

Indo-China

200-202, Trans-Indo-Chinese Railway 4-6-0 Class 230-200, 1906; 251, 252, steam engine; C18, same design as Scott 200-202.

Indonesia

484, 486, diesel engine; 487, diesel engine & passenger cars; 495, steam engine & sugar cane cars; 631, toy diesel engine & passenger car behind child; 634, Indonesia State Railway B-B diesel hydraulic engine & passenger cars; 659, Scott 634 surcharged; 692, traveling crane; 737, 738, Indonesian Railway Centenary, 2-4-2, diesel engine & passenger cars; 933, tank cars at Pertamina State oil refinery; 1008, diesel engine, passenger cars & flags; 1169, two four-wheel freight cars in design; 1191, traveling cranes on dock.

Iran

793, 2-6-0 & passenger cars on Karun River bridge, Ahwaz; 876, railway bridge over Karun River; 877, same design as Scott 876; 878, 879, Iranian State Railway Veresk viaduct; 882, 883, 2-6-0 Iranian State Railway Class 41, baggage & passenger cars on Karj bridge; 911, freight car on dock, Bandar Shapur; 913, steam train on viaduct over gorge, Veresk; 914, railway line on map of Iran; 920, Railway Square, Teheran; 1074, tracks & railway signal; 1075, Type G12 diesel engine, passenger cars & map of railway; 1076, 2-10-2, 1955, & passenger cars; 1103, steam engine & passenger cars; 1104, steam engine, passenger cars & map; 1498, steam engine & passenger cars; 1613, Iran-Turkey railway diesel engine & freight cars on Ghatour railway bridge; 1704, railway track & globe, emblem of 13th International Railway Conference; 1821, 1832, diesel engine & freight cars on Ghatour railway bridge; 1917, Shahs Riza & Mohammed Riza at railway station, steam engine & passenger cars; 1980, Shah Riza & Crown Prince in doorway of passenger car; 2323, mine car in tunnel; 2357, diesel engine & freight cars.

Iraq

439, cranes, track & electric train on dock; 440, 441, traveling crane & freight cars on dock; 442, same design as Scott 439, yellow added; 672, 673, 50th Anniversary of International Railway Union, emblem; 749, diesel & passenger cars on bridge; 750, diesel No. 511; 751, 0-6-0T & passenger cars; 752, 4-6-0, 1914; 1424, diesel engine; 1425, 1426, diesel engine & passenger cars; C7-C8, steam engine, passenger & freight cars on Dhigala Railway Bridge.

Israel

44, four-wheel dump car; 331, 0-6-0T Hejaz Railway, 1899; 411, Dimona-Oran Railway diesel engine & freight cars; 674, 2-6-0 USA, Jerusalem; 675, 0-6-0, Jezreel Valley; 676, 4-6-0 "P" Class, signal & Lydda station; 677, Israel Railway diesel engine; 848, 0-4-0 & town of Afula.

Italy

410, 411, 412, 2-2-2 & electric railcar set Class ETR-200; 514, diesel railcar; 657, electric train on bridge; 709, steam engine & passenger cars leaving Simplon tunnel; 1031, Bo-Bo Italian National Railway Class E444 electric engine & mail cars; 1198, steam engine driving wheels for 21st meeting of International Railway Conference; 1349, Italy Scott 1031 on stamp for 50th Anniversary of State Printing Works; 1498, envelopes forming railway tracks; 1575, steam engine pulling cars bearing flag designs coming out of envelope by Paolo Bucciarelli; 1707, Rome railway station; 1735, diesel passenger train & station; 1787, 1788, steam engine, passenger cars & bridge.

Italy-Trieste Zone A

40, Italy Scott 514 overprinted "A.M.G.-F.T.T."; 206, Italy Scott 657 overprinted "AMG-FTT."

Ivory Coast

21, 22, 23, 24, 25, Gen. Louis Faidherbe, Builder of Dakar-St. Louis Railway; 229, Abidjan railway station; 240, 0-6-0T, freight car & combination mail & passenger car, 1906; 402, railway bridge over N'zi River, Dimbokro; 481, cheering passengers in passenger cars like television sets drawn by steam engine labeled "PETV"; 514, 4-6-2 Class A4 No. 60074 pulling the *Flying Scotsman*; 515, 0-6-6-0T narrow gauge engine; 516, Santa Fe Railroad diesel engine No. 105, USA; 517, 4-8-4, Japan; 518, French National Railway BB-15000 electric engine & passenger cars, France; 519, 4-6-0 engine, souvenir sheet with border showing original pneumatic car & third rail electric engine with cars *Concorde* entering London post office tunnel;

551, diesel train *Le Belier* (The Ram) on Abidjan- Niger line; 552, Abidjan railway station, 1904; 553, rear view of train leaving Abidjan railway station, with passenger cars & smoke from steam engine, 1908; 554, 4-8-2+2-8-4, Senegal, 1938; 673, Grand Bassam post office, hand trolley & tracks, 1903; 722, diesel passenger train *La Gazelle*; 724, 4-6-2, 1938; 726, 4-6-2 type 10, Belgium; 728, 0-8-8-0T Class GT2, Bavaria; 1424, diesel engine; 1425, diesel engine & passenger cars; 1426, diesel engine; B12, railway bridge & tracks; C15, passenger cars & tracks under Houphouet-Boigny bridge, Abidjan.

Japan

347, 4-6-2 Japanese National Railway Class C59 No. C5928; 396, 2-6-0 Class 7100 *Benkei*, 1880; 436, building steam engine; 475, 477, diesel engine & passenger cars; 521B, same design as Scott 436; 632, Japanese National Railway Class EF58 electric engine & passenger cars; 729, railway bridge, Lake Biwa, Quasi-National Park; 761, Japanese National Railway diesel engine & passenger cars of express train *Hatsukari*, leaving Hokuriku tunnel; 827, Japanese National Railway electric engine & passenger cars of *Hikari* express; 961, Inuyama bridge, Hida-Kisogawa, Quasi-National park; 990, railway tunnel near Yaga; 1059, inside railway post office car; 1092, woodblock print of Tokyo horsedrawn streetcar by Yoshimura;

1109, electric engine & passenger cars of *Hikari* express on bridge; 1127, woodblock print *Inauguration of Railway Service* with 0-6-0 & passenger cars at station; 1128, 4-6-4 Class C62 No. C6222; 1188, 2-8-2 Type D51 *Degoichi* & freight cars; 1189, 4-6-2 Type C57 *Lady* & passenger car on bridge; 1190, 2-8-2 Type D52 *Degoni* & freight cars; 1191, 2-6-2 Type C58 *Shigohachi* & freight cars on bridge; 1192, 4-6-0 Type 8620 *Hachiroku* & passenger cars; 1193, 2-6-4T Type C11 *Cnochonchon* on bridge; 1194, 2-8-0 *Kyuroku* No. 9600 & freight cars; 1195, 4-6-2 Type C51 *Shigoichi*; 1196, 2-6-0 Model 7100 No. 1 & passenger cars at Sapporo Station; 1197, 2-4-0T Model 150 & passenger cars at Shinbashi Station;

1317, subway train at station platform for inauguration of Tokyo subway, 1927; 1318, subway train on the Saishin Line inaugurated, March 1977; 1374a, toy steam engine hauling space rocket, in souvenir sheet border; 1456, traveling crane; 1493, diesel engine of *Hikari* & map of railway; 1494, 60y 0-6-0T Class 1290 *Zenko*, 1881; 1513, *Hikari* train, 1982 1514, 1BB1 Class ED16 electric engine, 1931; 1652, Oonaruto bridge; 1732, four-wheel railway post office car; 1733, postal workers loading railway post office car; 1734, 2-4-2T Japanese National Railway No. 137, 1900; 1735, Maglev electric train No. 002, 1987; 1766, Class ED79 electric engine pulling the *Nihon-Kai* passenger express & map of Seikan Tunnel; 1767, 1768, Kagawa side of bridge;

1769, 1770, Okayama side of bridge; 1860, 75th anniversary of Tokyo railway station; 2002, C+2z (rack & adhesion) Type 10000, 1911; 2003, 2-Co-Co-2 Type EF58 No. 58, 1946, & passenger car; 2004, Bo-Bo+Bo-Bo Type EH10, 1954, & freight car; 2005, B-B Type ED40 (rack & adhesion), 1919; 2006, 2-C0-C0-2 Type EF53, 1932; 2007, Type Co-Co ED70, 1957; 2008, 2-Co-Co-1 Type EF55, 1936; 2009, Bo-Bo Type ED61 & freight cars, 1958; 2010, 2-Co-Co-2 Type EF57, 1940; 2011, Bo-Bo-Bo Type EF30, 1960.

Jordan

245, 246, 247, 248, three diesel engines; 574D, strip of five including 22-fil and 23-fil showing wrecked railway bridges; 874, Scott 574D surcharged; 1010, toy steam engine; 1043, 1044, 1045, Development Plan with steam passenger train in Cog Wheel; 1301, tracks, Amman Industrial Park, Sahab; N18, Scott 245 overprinted "PALESTINE" in English & Arabic; N19, Scott 246 overprinted "PALESTINE" in English & Arabic; N20, Scott 247 overprinted "PALESTINE" in English & Arabic; N21, Scott 248 overprinted "PALESTINE" in English & Arabic.

Korea

107, steam engine & passenger cars of the express train *Sam Chun Li*; 293, diesel type DL701 engine, passenger cars & signals; 301, diesel engine, passenger car & Universal Postal Union monument; 403, electric mine engine & mine cars; 409, diesel engine & passenger cars; 430, three four-wheel mine cars; 570, railway wheel on rail; 602, silhouette of diesel passenger train; 684, 2-6-2T engine, diesel engine type G22 & passenger cars; 685, 2-6-2T engine, 1899; 705, open streetcar of Hansung Electric Co.; 726, diesel engine &

passenger cars; 741, four-wheel coal mine cars; 750, Seoul subway tunnel, map of route & electric passenger train; 905, diesel engine & mail car; 911, subway train in new Chongno line, Seoul;

1003, electric engine type 8001 pulling hopper cars on Inchon-Bukpyong line; 1313, mine car; 1641, destroyed locomotive; 1671, steam locomotive pulling train.

Laos

77, diesel engine & mail train; 266H, 2-6-0 engine, passenger cars & airship; 849, 0-4-0 London & Manchester Railway *Sans Pareil*, 1829; 850, 0-2-2 London & Manchester Railway *Rocket*, 1829; 851, 0-6-0 Stockton & Darlington Railway *Royal George*, 1827; 852, 0-4-0 Trevithick's engine, 1804; 853, 0-4-0 London & Manchester Railway *Novelty*, 1829; 854, 0-4-0 Baltimore & Ohio Railroad *Tom Thumb*, 1829; 855, 0-4-0 Stockton & Darlington Railway *Locomotion*, 1825, souvenir sheet border with schematic drawing of steam engine; 1010, steam locomotive.

Latvia

162, 202, B39, railway bridge, Riga; B96b, Keguma railway bridge; B97, Scott B96 overprinted "1934-1939 & 15/V"; CB19, railway bridge, Riga.

Lebanon

C504, C505, C506, streetcar in front of Veteran's War Memorial, San Francisco, California; C708, mail cars on Universal Postal Union issue.

Liberia

52, 53, steam engine; 298, crane on tracks at Monrovia Harbor; 299, same design as Scott 298, without inscription at top; 518, monorail tracks & train at Expo '70; 522, monorail train, Expo '70; 629, 4-4-2 Great Northern Railway, Great Britain; 630, 4-2-2 Netherlands State Railway, Netherlands; 631, 4-6-0 Peninsular, Lyons & Marseilles Railway, France; 632, 4-6-0 Baltimore & Ohio Railroad No. 1800, USA; 633, 2-4-0T Japanese National Railway, Japan; 634, 4-4-2 Baden State Railway, Germany; 667, Painting of British Advance Passenger train (APT-E) with British Rail emblem & "Royal Mail" on side; 746, British Advance Passenger train, Alexander Graham Bell & Universal Postal Union emblem; 760, diesel engine & iron ore cars;

846, 4-6-2 London, Midland & Scottish Railway *Coronation* Class, Great Britain, 1939; 953, Scott 760 reproduced in smaller size; 1008, diesel engine & iron ore cars; 1085, Bo-Bo Type GP10 diesel engine & ore cars at Nimba; 1086, triple-headed Co-Co diesel iron ore train; 1087, 4-6-0 King Class *King Edward II*, No. 6023, 1930; 1088, 0-6-0 57XX Class No. 3697, 1941, pulling freight train; 1089, 0-4-2T No. 1408, 1932, pulling passenger train; 1090, 4-6-0 Castle Class *Ince Castle*, No. 7034, 1950, pulling the *Bristolean* out of Box tunnel; C52, same design as Scott 298; C53, same design as Scott 299; C73, diesel engine; C84, same design as Scott C73, inscribed "Commemorating Presidential/Visit USA - 1954";

C197, 4-4-0 engine of Swiss Jura-Simplon Railway, souvenir sheet Border with 4-2-0 engine & passenger coaches; O26, same design as Scott 52, overprinted "OS"; O27, same design as Scott 53, overprinted "OS."

Libya

1165c, children & toy steam train; 1190i, 0-6-0 steam engine; 1190j, 2-8-0 steam engine; 1190k, 4-6-2 steam engine; 1190l, 4-6-2 steam engine; 1190m, 2-8-2 steam engine; 1190n, 2-8-2 steam engine; 1190o, 0-8-0 steam engine; 1190p, 4-6-2 steam engine.

Liechtenstein

134, work cars, Binnen Canal Juction; 881, Maglev monorail & computer project map of Liechtenstein; B7, railway bridge between Buchs & Schaan destroyed by flood.

Lithuania

256, 262, railway station, Kaunas.

Luxembourg

128, 129, freight cars at steel mill; 130, 249, Adolphe railway bridge; 264, railway tracks under bridge; 315, two four-wheel freight cars & foundry; 321, Luxembourg Central Station as seen from passenger car window, Bo-Bo electric engine & passenger cars; 356, 2-2-2 engine, 1859, first bars of hymn *De Feierwon* written on day of opening of railway, Luxembourg Railway emblem; 442, Co-Co type 1800 diesel engine; 443, Bo-Bo type 3600 electric engine & station; 445, 447, Adolphe bridge; 459, freight cars & cranes, Mertert; 473, railway bridges; 598, Adolphe bridge; 623, Luxembourg Central station; 682, Monument to civilian & military deportees at Hollerich Railway station; 706, Graphic design of National Railway Network with points, diesel power car & viaduct;

784, Drawing of top of electric engine & tank car; B65G, railway bridge over Alzette; B85a, same design as Scott 128; B241, B244, children's painting of Grand Duke Adolphe Bridge; C1, C2, C3, C4, C5, C6, Adolphe Bridge; O133, Scott 128 overprinted "OFFICIAL"; O134, Scott 129 overprinted "OFFICIAL"; O135, Scott 130 overprinted "OFFICIAL"; O138, Scott 128 overprinted "OFFICIAL"; O140, Scott 130 overprinted "OFFICIAL."

Macao

471, diesel engine & passenger cars; 623, toy steam engine;

Madagascar

79, 80, 81, 82, 83, 84, 85, 86, 87, 88, 89, 90, 91, 92, 93, 94, 95, 96, 97, 98, 99, 100, 101, 102, 103, 104, 105, 106, 107, 108, 109, 110, 111, 112, 113, 114, 0-6-0T Tananarive-Tamatave Railway & passenger car leaving tunnel; 125, Scott 98 surcharged; 126, Scott 107 surcharged; 130, Scott 87 surcharged; 131, 132, Scott 97 surcharged; 133, Scott 98 surcharged; 134, Scott 99 surcharged; 135, Scott 87 surcharged; 136, Scott 113 surcharged; 137, Scott 114 surcharged; 138, 0-6-0T Tananarive-Tamatave Railway & passenger car leaving tunnel, surcharged; 139, Scott 107 surcharged; 140, Scott 99 surcharged; 141, 142, 143, 144, 145, 146, same design as Scott 79-114 surcharged; 178, Scott 113 surcharged; 179, Scott 109 surcharged;

212, Scott 143 with additional overprint "FRANCE/LIBRE"; 213, Scott 145 with additional overprint "FRANCE/LIBRE"; 214, Scott 146 with additional overprint "FRANCE/LIBRE"; 294, tracks at Pangalanes Canal; 325, first diesel engine constructed at Tananarive & passenger cars; 377, early railway mail car; 412, electric engine & passenger cars under highway bridge; 464, flat car laying cable along Malagasy Railway; 472, Malagasy Railway 3600 CV diesel engine; 893, Tananarive-Moramanga line diesel rail car ZM 617 *Tsikirity*; 895, 1020-DES OBB electric & diesel engines, Germany; 896, Malagasy Railways diesel railcar ZE 701 & passenger trailer;

898, diesel railcar, souvenir sheet border shows Tananarive-Tamatave line diesel passenger train *Fandrefiala* at a platform; 985, diesel engine & passenger cars; 999, TGV high speed train; B1, Scott 84 overprinted and surcharged; C59, Antsirabe railway viaduct; C61, sugar cane cars; C114, open sided passenger car *Balladeuse* & tender; C115, 0-4-4-0 engine, 1907; C126, Micheline railcar; C127, gasoline engine rail inspection truck; C128, 2-6-0+0-6-2 engine, 1926.

Mali

140, 0-6-0T *Gallet*, 1882; 141, 0-6-0T *Felou*, 1882; 142, 4-6-0T *Bechevel*, 1882; 143, 4-6-2 Dakar-Niger Railway, 1930; 144, 2-8-2 Dakar-Niger railway Class 40, 1930; 195, 0-6-0T *Bamako*, 1906; 196, 0-4-0T Thies-Bamako line, 1920; 197, 2-8-2 Thies-Bamako line No. 141, 1927; 198, two B-B diesels Dakar-Bamako line, 1947; 218, steam engine & Class BB9200 French National Railway electric train; 230, Scott 218 overprinted "9 OCTOBRE 1974" & surcharged; 396, electric engine & freight cars; 398, diesel engine & passenger cars; 440, diesel engine; 538, James Watt, inventor of the steam engine; C159, Helsinki railway station, Finland; C195, 0-2-2 *Rocket* & 2-2-2 French *Buddicom*;

C196, 4-4-0 Union Pacific Railroad No. 119, 1890 & 4-6-4 Santa Fe Railroad *Blue Goose* No. 3460, 1937; C197, electric & passenger car, French National Railway *Mistral*, Japanese National Railway electric engine & passenger cars of *Hikari*, 1970; C226, 2-10-0 P type, 1939 & Peninsular, Lyons & Marseille Railway C3, 1906; C227, 4-4-0, 1870 & 4-6-2, 1920 USA; C228, 4-8-2 A-1 type, 1925 & 0-4-2, 1847; C229, 4-6-4 New York Central Railroad, 1938 & 2-2-2 *La Gironde*, 1938; C235, C236, electric passenger train, France; C376, diesel engine & passenger cars superimposed on a globe; C381, 150th Anniversary of Liverpool-Manchester Railway & 0-4-0 *Rocket* & Scott 196; C382, 150th Anniversary of Liverpool-Manchester Railway & 0-4-0 *Rocket* & Scott 142;

C396, steam engine & passenger cars, Jules Verne's *Around the World in 80 Days*; C405, Japanese National Railway electric engine & passenger cars of *Hikari*, Japan & Scott 195; C406, Amtrak turbo train, USA, & Scott 140; C407, electric train *Rembrandt*, Germany & Scott 144; C408, French National Railway electric engine & passenger cars of *TVG001*, France & Scott 143; C425, Scott C408 overprinted "26 Fevrier 1981 - RECORD du Monde de Vitesse - 380km/h"; C478b, diesel railcar.

Manchukuo

130, map of states railways in Manchukuo; 131, 4-6-2 Darien-Hsinking line engine pulling *Asia Express*; C3, C4, railway bridge over Sungari River.

Marienwerder

36, 37, 38, Germany Scott 111-113 overprinted "COMMISSION INTERALLIEE MARIENWERDER."

Mauritania

1, 2 3, 4, 5, Gen. Louis Faidherbe, builder of Dakar-St. Louis railway & road bridge over Senegal River; 131, diesel engine & ore cars; 199, 201, diesel engine, Choum Tunnel & tracks; 291, Portion diesel engine from Scott 292 & iron ore cars; 292, three Co-Co diesel engines; 469, 0-4-0T *Gioui Mastodont*, 1850; 470, SNIM-SEM Ore Railway diesel engine & iron ore train; 471, 4-6-2 Milwaukee Road, 1900; 472, Bury engine, Great Britain, 1837; 473, Reseau du Nord Railway Crampton steam engine, France, 1835; 474, 4-2-0, Berlin-Potsdam Railway, Germany, 1840; 580, 2-2-2 *Der Adler*, Germany, 1835; 581, 4-6-2 German Federal Railway Series 10; 641, traveling cranes, Nouakchott Port; C21, ore train, Port Etienne; C236, diesel engine & ore cars.

Memel

14, Germany Scott 112 overprinted "MEMELGIET"; 15, Germany Scott 113 overprinted "MEMELGIET."

Mexico

254, 255, 256, 266, 267, 268, 278, 278A, 289, 290, 291, steam engine & mail cars; 512, 626, 647, map of Mexico showing railways; 870, railway laborer laying rail; 871, diesel engine & map of railway route; 919, railway track & tunnel on Chihuahua Pacific Railway; 942, diesel engines type E8 & cross section of rail; 1005, Mexico city subway train; 1050, 0-6-6-0 engine & freight cars of Mexican railway on trestle at Metlac Point in painting by Jose Maria Velasco; 1257, diesel engine & 15th Pan-American Railway Congress symbol; 1368, toy steam train & Christmas tree; 1530, two diesel engines & freight cars on trestle at Metlac Point; 1638, 2-6-0 engine, Co-Co diesel engine, baggage, passenger car & Felipe Pescador;

1683, locomotive approaching railroad crossing; 1694, electric locomotive; 1695h, 1695i, freight and passenger trains; 1695o, 1695p, railroad cars on wharf siding; C100, steam engine on bridge; C201, two diesel engines & cars crossing Isthmus of Tehuantepec; C202, railway bridge at Coatzacoalcos; C203, steam engine on 75th anniversary of the Universal Postal Union; C242, steam engine blowing up & dead engineer Jesus Garcia at Nacozari; C258, track & map of railway; C259, train on bridge; C279, Sonora-Lower California Railway diesel engine type F2, 4-4-0 engine, horse-drawn streetcar, baggage & freight cars; O20, Scott 254 handstamped "OFICIAL"; O21, Scott 255 handstamped "OFICIAL"; O22, Scott 256 handstamped "OFICIAL";

O39, Scott 278 overprinted "OFICIAL"; O98, Scott 512 with same overprint as Scott O39; O121, O132, O142, O153, O162, Scott 626 overprinted "OFICIAL"; O174, O188, O207, O222, Scott 647 overprinted "OFICIAL"; Q1, Q2, Q3, Q4, Q5, Q6, 4-6-4 Class NR-1 engine & passenger cars; Q7, Q8, Q9, Q10, diesel engine type F2 Class DE-10 No. 6213, Mexican National Railway.

Middle Congo

65, 66, 67, 68, 69, 70, 71, 72, 73, steam engine, freight & passenger cars, Brazzaville-Noire Railway on Mindouli Viaduct.

Monaco

54, steam engine & cars on St. Devote viaduct; 86, 87, 88, same design as Scott 54, but larger in size; 95, Scott 87 surcharged; 96, Scott 88 surcharged; 372, Scott J41 overprinted & surcharged; 382, Scott J50 overprinted & surcharged; 390, Scott J56 overprinted & surcharged; 692, 0-6-0, 1868, nicknamed *Les Bourbonnais*; 693, 4-4-0 Type C, 1898; 694, 4-6-0 Type C, 1910; 695, 4-6-2 Type F, 1925; 696, 4-8-2 Type A, 1932; 697, B-B Electric French National Railway, 1968 & passenger cars; 821, 822, 823, toy steam engine in pack of Father Christmas; 825, 2-8-0 type 743 engine, 1924, TGV-001 electric engine & passenger cars, France & emblem of International Railway Union; 1112, first train arriving at Monaco railway station;

1128, toy diesel train; 1180, arrival of first train in Monaco; 1410, streetcar in painting *Place of Visitation* by Hubert Clerissi, 1910; 1437, steam passenger train & station in painting *Train Entering Monte Carlo Station*, 1910; 1489, streetcar & railway station in painting *Avenue de la Gara Vers* by Hubert Clerissi, 1920; 1523, steam engine at Monaco railway station in painting by Hubert Clerissi, 1912; 1547, streetcar in *Avenue du Beau Rivage* painting by Hubert Clerissi 1925; 1606, Old Monte Carlo station in painting by Hubert Clerissi, 1925; 1624, Atlantique electric engine & passenger cars; 1638, St. Devote railway viaduct Monte Carlo Harbor, 1910; 1639, Monte Carlo railway station, 1910;

1752, streetcar on Place de la Cremaillere; 1754, streetcar on Avenue du Beau Rivage; B93, steam train on St. Devote viaduct; J41, 2-2-2 engine & passenger car; J50, 4-8-2 engine; J56, French National Railway mail car & passenger car; J59, 0-6-0 Peninsular, Lyons & Meditterean Railway Series.

Mongolia

134, 4-8-4 Ulan Bator-Moscow Railway Joseph Stalin Class IS.20, baggage & passenger cars on bridge; 240, 241d, diesel engine type TE2 & passenger cars; 420, steam engine & freight cars; 421, diesel passenger train; 552, Scott 420 overprinted for 45th Anniversary; 553, Scott 421, same overprint as Scott 420; 624, 0-8-0 Narrow gauge engine; 625, diesel engine T32-400, passenger & freight cars; 716, diesel engine & passenger cars; 850A, Scott 624 overprinted for 50 years of communication; 850B, Scott 625 overprinted for 50 years of communication; 927, diesel engine & train; 969, diesel engine & ore cars at Erdenet copper & molybdenum plant; 1027c, Elizabeth Bridge, Budapest, in painting by D. Amgalan;

1077c, London-Birmingham Railway post office car, 1838; 1078, 0-2-2 Liverpool-Manchester Railway *Rocket*, 1829, England; 1079, 2-2-2 Nurmberg-Furth Railway *Der Adler*, 1835, Germany; 1080, 4-4-0 engine, 1860, USA; 1081, 0-8-0 Ulan-Nalajh Railway Class KB4 750mm gauge, engine, 1931, Mongolia; 1082, 0-10-0 Moscow-Ulan Bator Railway Class Er Russia; 1083, Moscow-Ulan Bator Railway Class 2TE 10L diesel, Russia; 1084, Japanese National Railway electric engine & passenger cars of *Hikari*, Japan; 1085, aerotrain *Orleans*, France; 1086, jet engine train *VNIIV Speed*, Russia; 1096a, Brazil Scott 1582; 1174a, Mongolia Scott 240 on stamp for Mongolian National Stamp Exhibit; 1174d, Japan Scott 827 on stamp for Japex Stamp Exhibition;

1178, diesel engine & passenger cars on highway overpass; 1251, diesel train; 1330, diesel railcar; 1368, diesel engine & space rocket on freight cars; 1479, diesel train & space rocket; 1575, diesel engine & passenger car; 1651, diesel engine & coal car; 1740b, French National Railway TGV diesel engine & passenger cars; 1963, Japanese National Railway electric engine & passenger cars of *Hikari*; 2004, electric locomotive and train; C18, diesel engine & passenger cars; C37, Russia Scott 3100; C45, Poland Scott 802; C62, TEE diesel engine & passenger cars, Netherlands; C64, souvenir sheet border with TEE diesel engine & passenger cars, Netherlands; C92, diesel engine & car at factory; C108, souvenir sheet border with France Scott C15.

Morocco

147, diesel engine & passenger cars; 540, diesel engine & passenger cars & railway route map; 562, Santa Fe Railroad diesel engine & passenger cars, USA.

Mozambique

295, Lourenzo Marques Central railway station; 306, 314, Central African Railways Zambezi River bridge, Santos; 360, railway tracks; 384, 385, Scott 360; 387-394, map of Mozambique with Railway Lines in black; 465, Beira railway station; 516, Scott 387 overprinted; 530, Scott 394 overprinted; 636, child's drawing of steam engine & passenger cars; 641A, miner & mine car; 656, 0-6-0T Cape Government Railway 1st Class, 3-foot 6-inch gauge; 657, 0-4-0T Gaza line *Gaza*, narrow gauge; 658, 4-4-0, Beira Railway, 2-foot gauge; 659, 4-6-0 No. 9, 3-foot 6-inch gauge line; 660, 0-6-4T No. 41; 661, 4-8-0 engine; 722, railway tracks; 801, envelope forming railway car; 865, 2-6-6-0 Mozambique Railway, 1947; 866, 2-10-2, 1923;

867, 2-8-2 Congo Ocean Railway, 1950; 868, 0-6-2, 1926; 869, 4-8-2+2-8-4, 1924; 870, 4-8-2T, Mozambique Railway; 879, diesel engine & passenger cars; 891, railway mail caboose; 949, tank cars; 971, Mozambique Company Scott 126; 1064, traveling crane, Quelimane; 1066, traveling cranes & freight cars, Beira; 1067, traveling cranes & freight cars, Nacala; 1068, freight cars, Maputo; 1109A, map of Africa with railway lines.

Mozambique Company

120, steam rail crane & freight cars on dock; 123, 4-8-0 Beira Ry. engine, freight & passenger cars; 126, railway tracks on sisal plantation; 130, same design as Scott 123; 140, same design as Scott 126; 141, same design as Scott 126; 144, same design as Scott 120; 145, same design as Scott 120; 149, Scott 120 surcharged "Um e'meio/ Centavo" in violet; 156, 158, steam engine & freight cars, Beira; 164, Central African Railways steam engine & passenger cars on Zambezi bridge, station & freight cars; 191, design similar to Scott 164.

Netherlands

214, full size scale model of 2-2-2 engine *De Arend* (The Eagle); 215, front of electric passenger train set; 332, 336, steam engine & passenger cars; 425, dwarf signal No. 144 outside Amersfoort station switch tower, track & catenary; 426, Type TT electric engine; 523, subway line on map of Mr. Visser Square, Amsterdam; 603, four-wheel UCES Type hopper car; 616, map of railway yards; 668, Japanese prison camp & Burma Railway construction, 1945; 746, flanged wheel on rail; 747, engines superimposed on one another; 748, passenger cars & station roof; B56, railway bridge at Moerdijk; B277, post office annex to the Hague railway station & viaduct; B278, streetcar tracks by Amsterdam Stock Exchange; B436, railway bridge at Culemborg.

Netherlands Antilles

337, traveling crane at dry dock, Willemstad.

Netherlands Indies

263, railway bridge near Soekaboemi; 270, Scott 263 surcharged.

New Caledonia

388, tank type steam engine & mail cars at Dumbea railway station; 525, Electronic E10B railway switching center; C26, steam engine & hopper cars under nickel mine conveyor; C78, Japanese National Railway electric engine & passenger cars of *Hikari* on viaduct & Mount Fuji.

Nicaragua

20, 21, 22, 23, 24, 25, 26, 27, 28, 29, 4-4-0 engine; 121, 122, 123, 124, 125, 126, 127, 128, 129, 130, 131, 132, 133, 1900 steam engine at dock & Mount Momotombo; 134, Scott 131 overprinted; 135, Scott 133 overprinted; 136, Scott 132 overprinted; 144, Scott 126 overprinted; 145, Scott 126 overprinted; 146, Scott 131 overprinted; 147, Scott 132 overprinted; 148, Scott 126 overprinted; 149, Scott 126 overprinted; 150, Scott 131 overprinted; 151, Scott 133 overprinted; 159, 160, 161, same design as Scott 121-133; 162, Scott 122 overprinted; 163, Scott 121 overprinted; 175, 178, Scott 161 overprinted; 279, 280, 281, 282, 283, 284, 285, 286, railway revenue stamps overprinted on back;

287, 288, 289, railway revenue stamps overprinted on face; 289B, 289D, railway revenue stamps overprinted on back; 290, 291, 292, 293, 293C, railway revenue stamps overprinted on face; 294, Scott O234 overprinted; 325, 326, 327, 328, 329, 330, 331, 332, 333, 334, 335, 336, 337, Province of Zelaya Scott 1L109-1L123 overprinted; 570, tracks on wharf, San Jorge; 571, steam engine & work cars on fill at El Nacascolo; 572, Rivas railway station; 573, train at San Juan del Sur; 574, train at Rivas station; 575, View of El Sauce; 576, railway bridge No. 2 at Santa Lucia; 577, Santa Lucia; 578, railway construction at km 64; 579, track & rock cut at Santa Lucia; 670, mail train; 939, Scott 670 illustrated; 1079, 4-6-0 engine No. 6, 1921;

1080, 2-4-2T narrow gauge engine; 1081, 4-6-0 engine No. 10, 1909; 1082, 2-8-0 engine No. 31, 1906; 1083, 4-6-0 engine No. 21, 1907; 1084, presidential coach at station; 1133, 4-6-0 E93 engine at Lake Granada; 1134, 0-6-0T engine, 1946; 1135, 4-6-0 Philadelphia Iron Works engine, 1911; 1136, wreck crane, 1909; 1137, U-10B diesel engine, 1956; 1138, German diesel rail bus, 1954; 1241, passenger coach; 1242, box car; 1243, tank car; 1244, hopper car; 1245, motor railcar; 1246, ore car; 1247, passenger coach; 1375, diesel engine, Atlantic-Pacific Railway; 1412, Prussian State Railway, EV-1/2 Class electric, 1907; 1413, 0-4-0T Oldenburg State Railway, No. 1 *Landswuhrden*, 1867; 1414, double-deck steam railcar, 1910;

1415, 4-4-0 Prussian State Railway, 1902; 1416, 2-12-0 Wurttemburg Railway, Class K, 1917; 1417, 2-4-0T engine, 1890; 1418, 0-4-2 *Saxonia*, 1838, railway bridge & Chinandega railway station; C67, tracks at La Chocolata Cut; C68, steam engine at El Nacascola; C69, tracks at Cuesta Cut; C70, tracks on dock, San Juan del Sur; C71, view of El Estero; C72, railway bridge, Santa Lucia; C73, fill at Santa Lucia River; C74, Malpaicillo railway station; C75, work car; C76, steam engines at San Andres; C212, tracks at San Juan del Sur; C912, Amtrak jet powered Turboliner train, 1973; C938, 4-6-0 Type S-10 engine No. 33, 1924; C939, 2-8-0 engine No. 36, 1907; C940, 4-4-0 engine; C941, map of railway lines, souvenir sheet border with steam engine & passenger cars;

C943, 4-4-0 engine on Jules Vernes *Around the World in Eighty Days* stamp; C992, Japanese diesel rail bus, 1967; C1005, 2-8-2 engine & box car; C1046, steam engine; C1154, train shed of Friederichstrasse Station, East Berlin; O1, O2, O3, O4, O5, O6, O7, O8, O9, O10, same design as Scott 20 overprinted "FRANQUEO OFICIAL"; O150, Scott 161 overprinted; O151,

O152, Scott 123 overprinted; O153, Scott 161 overprinted; O154, Scott 123 overprinted; O223, O229, O230, O231, O232, O233, O234, O235, O236, O237, O238, O239, O240, O241, O242, O243, O244, railway stamp of 1911 overprinted.

Nicaragua-Province of Zelaya

1L1, Scott 121 overprinted; 1L2, Scott 122 overprinted; 1L3, Scott 123 overprinted; 1L4, Scott 124 overprinted; 1L5, Scott 128 overprinted; 1L6, Scott 129 overprinted; 1L7, Scott 130 overprinted; 1L8, Scott 131 overprinted; 1L9, Scott 132 overprinted; 1L10, Scott 133 overprinted; 1L11, Scott 159 overprinted; 1L12, Scott 160 overprinted; 1L13, Scott 161 overprinted; 1L16, Scott 175 overprinted; 1L17, Scott 178 overprinted; 1L18, Scott 176 overprinted; 1L19, Scott 177 overprinted; 1L20, Scott 151 surcharged; 1L107, Scott 293C ovptd.; 1L107D, Scott 290 ovptd.; 1L107F, Scott 291 ovptd.; 1L108, Scott 289D ovptd.; 1L109, 1L110, 1L111, 1L112, 1L113, 1L114, 1L115, 1L116, 1L117, 1L118, 1L119, 1L120, 1L121, 1L122, 1L123, 4-4-0 engine.

Nicaragua-Cabo Gracias A Dois

2L1, Scott 121 overprinted; 2L2, Scott 122 overprinted; 2L3, Scott 123 overprinted; 2L4, Scott 124 overprinted; 2L5, Scott 128 overprinted; 2L6, Scott 129 overprinted; 2L7, Scott 159 overprinted; 2L8, Scott 161 overprinted; 2L9, Scott 175 overprinted; 2L10, Scott 177 overprinted; 2L16, Scott 121 overprinted; 2L17, Scott 122 overprinted; 2L18, Scott 123 overprinted; 2L19, Scott 124 overprinted; 2L20, Scott 128 overprinted; 2L22, Scott 159 overprinted; 2L23, Scott 161 overprinted; 2L24, Scott 175 overprinted; 2L36, Scott 175 overprinted; 2L37, Scott 161 overprinted; 2L38, Scott 129 overprinted; 2L39, Scott 151 overprinted.

Niger

283, portrait of Rudolf Diesel & diesel; 284, Type BB610 ch; 285, Type 060 DB-1, French National Railway; 286, CC72004, French National Railway; 298, 4-6-0 Class 230K, 1938 & 4-4-4-4 Class T-1, Pennsylvania Railroad, USA, 1948; 299, 4-4-0 C21, Paris, Lyons & Mediterrean Railway, France, 1893; 300, 4-4-0, USA, 1866 & 4-6-2 London North Eastern Railway, Class 4A *Mallard*, 1938; 301, 0-4-0, France, 1829 & 0-2-2 *Rocket*, U.K., 1829; 312, 4-4-0 Great Western Railway *City of Truro*, U.K., 1903; 313, 4-6-4 Deutsche Reichsbahn, Class 5 No. 05.003, Germany, 1937; 314, 4-4-0 Western & Atlantic Railway, *The General*, USA, 1863; 315, BB15.000 French National Railway electric, France, 1971; 477, Advance Passenger Train (APT-E), Great Britain;

478, French electric passenger train; 514, 2-4-0T Shimbashi-Yokohama Railway, 1872; 515, 4-4-0 Milwaukee & Waukesha Railroad, *Fred Merril*, USA, 1870; 516, 4-6-4T Deutsche Reichsbahn, Series 61, 1934; 517, 2-4-0 Prussian State Railway, Type P2, 1900; 518, 2-4-0 *L'Aigle*, France, 1850; 519, the *Rocket*, 1830; 674, Scott 519 overprinted; 687, TGV train over map of Europe & Africa; C72, aerial view of Expo '67 monorail line, Montreal; C113, toy steam train; C241, Head of Japanese woman, envelope & three electic engines; C277, Zeppelin over Essen railway station & streetcar, Germany.

Norway

285, 2-4-0 Hoved Jernbane engine No. 3, 1854; 331, 2-4-0 Kongsvinges Railway *Caroline* engine No. 17 & flat car loaded with lumber; 332, diesel engine & three passenger cars; 333, engineer Alfred Andersen in steam engine cab; 531, diesel railcar; 750, steam engine & passenger cars on Kylling Bridge at Verma, Romsdal; 765b, steam engine, baggage car & coach, 1900; 789, rail ferry *Storegut*, 1956 on Lake Tinnsjo; 852, streetcar in fairy tale *The Rovers in Cardaman Town*; 975, steam engine used to transport Moses cannon during World War II. □

American Topical Association

In addition to the specific American Topical Association (ATA) handbooks used in developing the listings above, considerably more material is available for a wide variety of topics. Following are two sets of such information, one showing handbooks and their prices from ATA and the other showing checklists. Handbooks are large and normally more broad in scope. Checklists may deal with much tighter specialties.

Only ATA members may take advantage of the checklist service, and therefore cost information on checklists is not included here. Membership information is available for a SASE from the ATA Central Office, P.O. Box 630-C, Johnstown, PA 15907.

Handbooks may not be current, based on the publication date of each.

ATA Handbooks

Adventures in Topical Stamp Collecting (HB96), $8.
Americana on Foreign Stamps, volume 1 (HB58), $6.
Americana on Foreign Stamps, volume 2 (HB85), $6.
Astronomy and Philately (HB90), $5.
Bicentennial of American Independence (HB97), $6.
Bicentennial of Postmarks 1972-1984 (HB110), $5.
Birds of the World in Philately (HB106), $14.
Birds of the World in Philately, supplement 1 (HB106-1), $6.
Birds of the World in Philately, supplement 2 (HB106-2), $6.
Christmas Stamps of the World (HB120), $17.
Cooking with Stamps (HB56), $6.
Education on Stamps (HB68), $4.
Fairy Tales and Folk Tales on Stamps (HB73), $4.
Fishes, Amphibia, and Reptiles on Stamps of the World (HB91), $8.
Holy Family on Stamps (HB92), $8.
Horses & Horse Relatives (HB116), $16.
Insects and other Invertebrates of the World on Stamps (HB98), $10.
Lions International Philately (HB59), $4.
Mammals of the World on Stamps (HB79), $5.
Map Stamps of the World (HB104), $7.
Medical Stamps (HB63), $5.
Medicine Stamps (HB66), $7.
Music World of Stamps (HB84), $6.
Old Glory Around the World (HB75), $3.
Orchids on Stamps (HB113), $9.
Pharaceutical Philately (HB114), $9.
Plants on Stamps, volume 1 (HB94), $10.
Plants on Stamps, volume 2 (HB112), $12.
Railway Stamps (HB102), $11.
Railway Stamps, supplement 1 (HB102-1), $5.
Science Stamps (HB87), $7.
Space Stamps (HB99), $11.
Sports & Recreation Checklist (HB83), $4.
Statue of Liberty Stamps and Postmarks (HB111), $5.
Theatre Philatelic (HB67), $5.
Watercraft on Stamps (HB117), $17.
Women on Stamps, volume 1 (HB71), $4.
Women on Stamps, volume 2 (HB93), $7.

ATA Checklists

African Postal Union, 2 pages
AIDS, 1 page
Airlines, 6 pages
Airports, 4 pages
Airships (Zeppelins), 6 pages
Anti-Alcohol, 1 page
Anti-Drug, 1 page
Anti-Malaria (WHO), 4 pages
Anti-Smoking, 2 pages
Arab Postal Union, 1 page
Archery, 7 pages
Audubon, 4 pages
Automobiles, 31 pages
Bach, Johann Sebastian, 1 page
Badger, 1 page
Badminton, 1 page
Ballet, 3 pages
Balloons, 13 pages
Balloons — Toy, 2 pages
Balloons — Weather, 2 pages
Bananas, 3 pages
Baseball, 7 pages
Basketball, 8 pages
Bats, 2 pages
Bears, 8 pages
Bears — Pandas, 1 page
Bears — Teddy Bears, 2 pages
Beauty Queens, 1 page
Bees, 8 pages
Beethoven, 2 pages
Bells, 19 pages
Biathlon, 2 pages
Birds of Prey, 14 pages
Birds — Cockatoos, Lories, Parrots & Parakeets, 7 pages
Birds — Ducks, 5 pages
Birds — Geese, 2 pages
Birds — Hummingbirds, 4 pages
Birds — Loons, 1 page
Birds — Penguins, 4 pages
Birds — Swans, 3 pages
Birds — Woodpeckers, 4 pages
Bison, 2 pages
Blacksmiths, 3 pages
Blood Donations, 3 pages
Bobsled, Luge, Sled & Toboggan, 3 pages
Bonsai, 2 pages
Bowling, 1 page
Boxing, 9 pages
Braille, Louis, 1 page
Breast Feeding, 3 pages
Bridges, 15 pages
Bromeliads (Pineapple Plant), 2 pages
Buffalo, 2 pages
Butterflies, 11 pages
Cameras & Photography, 6 pages
Captain Cook, 4 pages
Carnivals, 2 pages
Castles, 16 pages
Cattle, 9 pages
Cats — Domestic, 9 pages
Cats — Feral, 21 pages
Chess, 8 pages
Civets & Genets, 1 page
Children, Caring for, 8 pages
Children's Drawings, 6 pages
Chopin, 1 page
Churchill, Sir Winston, 4 pages
Circus, 5 pages
Clocks (Timepieces), 11 pages
Clowns, 3 pages
Coffee, 5 pages
Coffee & Tea Service, 4 pages
Columbus, 7 pages
Computers, 5 pages
Copernicus, 4 pages
Costumes, 7 pages
Costumes — Folk (Full Length), 2 pages
Cotton, 3 pages
Crabs, 6 pages
Cricket (Sport), 6 pages
Crocodile, 3 pages
Curies, The, 2 pages
Dams & Hydroelectric Plants, 9 pages
Dance (no Ballet), 11 pages
Darwin, 1 page
Dentistry, 3 pages
Dinosaurs & Flying Reptiles, 4 pages
Diving Competition, 3 pages
Dog Sleds, 1 page
Dolls, 5 pages
Dolphins, 4 pages
Dragonflies (Odonata), 3 pages
Einstein, Albert, 1 page
Esperanto, 2 pages
Europa, 14 pages
Fables, 2 pages
Fairy Tales, Children's Stories, Etc.
Fairy Tales — African & Asian, 1 page
Fairy Tales — Andersen, Hans Christian, 1 page
Fairy Tales — Arabian Nights, 1 page
Fairy Tales — Baltic Fairy Tales, 1 page
Fairy Tales — Children's Classics, 2 pages
Fairy Tales — Children's Stories, 1 page
Fairy Tales — Dickens, Charles, 1 page
Fairy Tales — Disney, Walt, 5 pages
Fairy Tales — Don Quixote, 2 pages
Fairy Tales — European Fairy Tales, 1 page
Fairy Tales — Folktales, 2 pages
Fairy Tales — Grimm Brothers, 2 pages
Fairy Tales — Hercules: Life and Labors, 1 page
Fairy Tales — Japanese Fairy Tales, 1 page
Fairy Tales — Legends, 3 pages
Fairy Tales — Nursery Rhymes, 1 page
Fairy Tales — Perrault, Charles, 1 page
Fairy Tales — Pinocchio, 1 page
Fairy Tales — Russian Folklore, 1 page

Fairy Tales — Scandinavian Fairy Tales, 1 page
Fairy Tales — South & Central American, 1 page
Fairy Tales — Twain, Mark, 1 page
Fairy Tales — Verne, Jules, 2 pages
Fans — Hand Held, 4 pages
Fencing, 8 pages
Fictional Detectives, 1 page
Field Hockey, 3 pages
Firearms, Hunting & Shooting, 6 pages
Fire Fighting, 8 pages
Fireworks, 2 pages
Flowers, 22 pages
Flowers — Hibiscus, 9 pages
Flowers — Iris, 4 pages
Flowers — Peonies, 2 pages
Flowers — Poinsettias, 1 page
Flowers — Roses, 11 pages
Fossils & Prehistoric Animals, 11 pages
Foxes, 3 pages
Frogs & Toads, 5 pages
Fruits & Berries, 18 pages
Galileo, 1 page
Gandhi, Mahatma, 2 pages
Gemstones, 2 pages
Giraffes, 2 pages
Girl Guides & Scouts, 4 pages
Glass, 2 pages
Goats, 3 pages
Golf, 2 pages
Gymnastics — Men, 6 pages
Gymnastics — Women, 8 pages
Halley's Comet, 2 pages
Hammarskjold, Dag, 1 page
Helicopters (Vertical Flight), 7 pages
Hermes (Mercury), 6 pages
Hippopotamus, 2 pages
Horse Racing, 4 pages
Hugo, Victor, 1 page
Hunting Scenes, 2 pages
Ice Hockey, 6 pages
International Education Year, 1 page
International Labor Organization 50th Anniversary, 2 pages
International Letter Writing Week, 2 pages
International Quiet Sun Year, 1 page
International Telecommunications Union Centenary, 4 pages
International Year of the Child, 6 pages
International Year of the Disabled, 3 pages
Jaycees, 1 page
Jazz Musicians, 1 page
Jesuits, 7 pages
Jewelry, 2 pages
Joint Issues, 4 pages
Joint Issues — U.S., 2 pages
Judo, 4 pages
Karate, 2 pages
Kennedy, J.F. Memorial, 3 pages
Kites, 1 page
Koalas, 2 pages
Koch, Dr. Robert, 2 pages
Leonardo da Vinci, 3 pages
Liberty Bell, 1 page
Lifesaving, 1 page
Lindbergh, 2 pages
Lizards, 6 pages
Lobsters & Crayfish, 3 pages
Magnifying Glasses, 2 pages
Maritime Disasters, 6 pages
Martial Arts, 5 pages
Masks, 16 pages
Masks — Comedy/Tragedy, 2 pages
Mermaids, 2 pages
Methodist Religion, 2 pages
Mice & Rats, 2 pages
Microscopes, 7 pages
Minerals, 6 pages
Mining, 4 pages
Mosaics, 6 pages
Motorcycles, 10 pages
Mountain Climbing, 3 pages
Mozart, 2 pages
Mushrooms, 19 pages
Musical Instruments — Bagpipes, 2 pages
Musical Instruments — Brasses, 2 pages
Musical Instruments — Drums, 5 pages
Musical Instruments — Guitar, Mandolin & Zither, 2 pages
Musical Instruments — Keyboard, 1 page
Musical Instruments — Lute, 2 pages
Musical Instruments — Violin Family, 4 pages
Musical Instruments — Wood Winds, 2 pages
Musical Instruments — Xylophone, 1 page
Nobel Chemistry Prize, 3 pages
Nobel Literature Prize, 8 pages
Nobel Medicine Prize, 5 pages
Nobel Peace Prize, 8 pages
Nobel Physics Prize, 6 pages
North American Indians, 5 pages
Nubian Monuments, 3 pages
Nurses & Nursing, 14 pages
Octopus & Squid, 2 pages
Opera, 23 pages
Owls, 5 pages
Parachute, 3 pages
Peace, 7 pages
Pegasus & Winged Horses, 2 pages
Phoenix, 2 pages
Phonographs & Records, 1 page
Picasso, 6 pages
Pigs, Hogs & Wild Boar, 5 pages
Pinnipeds (Seals & Walruses), 4 pages
Pipe Organs, 3 pages
Pirates, 3 pages
Playing Cards, 1 page
Polo, 1 page
Pope John Paul II, 3 pages
Popes, 7 pages
Primates (Apes & Monkeys), 6 pages
Puffins, 2 pages
Puppets, 2 pages
Rabbits, 4 pages
Rainbows, 4 pages
Red Cross Societies, 30 pages
Red Cross Societies, supplement 1, 4 pages
Rockwell, Norman, 3 pages
Roller Skating, 1 page
Rotary International, 6 pages
Rowing, 4 pages
Rugby, 2 pages
St. George & Dragon, 4 pages
Salvation Army, 2 pages
Santa Claus, 3 pages
Scales (Measuring & Weighing), 9 pages
Schweitzer, Albert, 2 pages
Scuba, 5 pages
Sea Horses, 1 page
Seaplanes & Flying Boats, 10 pages
Shakespeare, 3 pages
Sheep, 4 pages
Shells, 5 pages
Side-Saddle Riders, 2 pages
Skating (no Ice Hockey), 8 pages
Skiing, (no Biathlon), 16 pages
Smoking & Tobacco, 6 pages
Snakes, 10 pages
Soccer, 28 pages
Spiders, 1 page
Stained Glass, 6 pages
Streetcars, 4 pages
Submarines, 3 pages
Sugar, 7 pages
Surveying, 6 pages
Swimming, 7 pages
Table Tennis, 3 pages
Telephone Centenary, 2 pages
Tennis, 9 pages
Toys, 4 pages
Track and Field Events — Discus, 5 pages
Track and Field Events — Hammer Throw, 2 pages
Track and Field Events — High Jump, 4 pages
Track and Field Events — Hurdles, 6 pages
Track and Field Events — Javelin, 5 pages
Track and Field Events — Long Jump, 3 pages
Track and Field Events — Pole Vault, 3 pages
Track and Field Events — Relay Race, 2 pages
Track and Field Events — Running, 18 pages
Track and Field Events — Shot Put, 3 pages
Track and Field Events — Triple Jump, 1 page
Track and Field Events — Walking, 1 page
Traffic Safety, 9 pages
Turtles, 9 pages
Umbrellas, 7 pages
Unesco Building in Paris, 1 page
Uniforms, 4 pages
Universal Postal Union, 12 pages
Universities, 11 pages
U.S. Stage & Screen Stars, 5 pages
Vegetables, 5 pages
Volleyball, 5 pages
Wagner, Richard, 2 pages
Waterfalls, 9 pages
Water Polo, 1 page
Water Skiing & Surfing, 2 pages
Whales, 6 pages
Whaleboats, 2 pages
Whisks, Fly, 1 page
Windmills, 6 pages
Windsurfing, 2 pages
Wine, 9 pages
Wolves, 3 pages
World Refugees Year, 2 pages
World Wildlife Fund, 3 pages
Wrestling, 6 pages
X-Ray & Radium, 3 pages
Zebras, 3 pages
Zodiac: Eastern & Western, 4 pages

GABON

LOCATION — West coast of Africa, at the equator
GOVT. — Republic
AREA — 102,089 sq. mi.
POP. — 1,367,000 (est. 1984)
CAPITAL — Libreville

Gabon originally was under the control of French West Africa. In 1886, it was united with French Congo. In 1904, Gabon was granted a certain degree of colonial autonomy which prevailed until 1934, when it merged with French Equatorial Africa. Gabon Republic was proclaimed November 28, 1958.

100 Centimes = 1 Franc

Catalogue values for unused stamps in this country are for Never Hinged items, beginning with Scott 148 in the regular postage section, Scott B4 in the semi-postal section, Scott C1 in the airpost section, Scott CB1 in the airpost semi-postal section, Scott J34 in the postage due section, and Scott O1 in the officials section.

Stamps of French Colonies of 1881-86 Handstamp Surcharged in Black:

a b

1886 Unwmk. *Perf. 14x13½*

1 A9 (a) 5c on 20c red, *grn* 225.00 225.00
2 A9 (b) 10c on 20c red, *grn* 225.00 225.00
3 A9 (b) 25c on 20c red, *grn* 20.00 15.00
e. 56 dots around "GAB" *2,250.* 550.00
4 A9 (b) 50c on 15c bl 800.00 800.00
5 A9 (b) 75c on 15c bl 900.00 850.00

Nos. 1-3 exist with double surcharge of numeral; No. 3 with "GAB" double or inverted, or with "25" double.

On Nos. 3 and 5 the surcharge slants down; on No. 4 it slants up. The number of dots varies.

Counterfeits of Nos. 1-15 exist.

Handstamp Surcharged in Black **15**

1888-89

6 A9 15c on 10c blk, *lav* *2,250.* 450.00
7 A9 15c on 1fr brnz grn, *straw* *1,200.* 525.00
8 A9 25c on 5c grn, *grnsh* 550.00 110.00
9 A9 25c on 10c blk, *lav* *3,000.* 725.00
10 A9 25c on 75c car, *rose* *1,600.* 650.00

Official reprints exist.

Postage Due Stamps of French Colonies Handstamp Surcharged in Black

1889 *Imperf.*

11 D1 15c on 5c black 100.00 70.00
12 D1 15c on 30c blk *3,000.* *2,250.*
13 D1 25c on 20c blk 50.00 40.00

Nos. 11 and 13 exist with "GABON," "TIMBRE" or "25" double; "TIMBRE" or "15" omitted, etc.

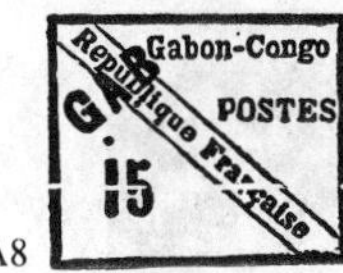

A8

1889 Typeset

14 A8 15c blk, *rose* 1,000. 525.00
15 A8 25c blk, *green* 550.00 375.00

Ten varieties of each. Nos. 14-15 exist with "GAB" inverted or omitted, and with small "f" in "Francaise."

Navigation and Commerce — A9

1904-07 Typo. *Perf. 14x13½*
Name of Colony in Blue or Carmine

16 A9 1c blk, *lil bl* 35 35
a. "GABON" double 175.00
17 A9 2c brn, *buff* 35 35
18 A9 4c claret, *lav* 60 60
19 A9 5c yel grn 90 90
20 A9 10c rose 2.75 2.75
21 A9 15c gray 2.75 2.75
22 A9 20c red, *grn* 4.25 4.25
23 A9 25c blue 2.75 2.75
24 A9 30c yel brn 6.00 6.00
25 A9 35c blk, *yel* ('06) 9.25 9.25
26 A9 40c red, *straw* 6.25 6.25
27 A9 45c blk, *gray grn* ('07) 13.00 13.00
28 A9 50c brn, *az* 4.75 4.75
29 A9 75c dp vio, *org* 8.50 8.50
30 A9 1fr brnz grn, *straw* 15.00 15.00
31 A9 2fr vio, *rose* 37.50 37.50
32 A9 5fr lil, *lav* 67.50 67.50
Nos. 16-32 (17) 182.45 182.45

Perf. 13½x14 stamps are counterfeits.
For surcharges see Nos. 72-84.

Fang Warrior A10

Fang Woman A12

Libreville A11

Inscribed: "Congo Français"

1910 *Perf. 13½x14*

33 A10 1c choc & org 60 60
34 A10 2c blk & choc 90 90
35 A10 4c vio & dp bl 1.00 1.00
36 A10 5c ol gray & grn 1.20 1.20
37 A10 10c red & car 2.25 2.25
38 A10 20c choc & dk vio 2.25 2.25
39 A11 25c dp bl & choc 1.75 1.75
40 A11 30c gray blk & red 14.00 14.00
41 A11 35c dk vio & grn 7.25 7.25
42 A11 40c choc & ultra 10.00 10.00
43 A11 45c car & vio 16.00 16.00
44 A11 50c bl grn & gray 25.00 25.00
45 A11 75c org & choc 45.00 30.00
46 A12 1fr dk brn & bis 47.50 47.50
47 A12 2fr car & brn 130.00 130.00
48 A12 5fr bl & choc 120.00 120.00
Nos. 33-48 (16) 424.70 409.70

For surcharge see No. B1.

A13

A15

A14

Inscribed: "Afrique Equatoriale"

1910-22

49 A13 1c choc & org 15 15
50 A13 2c blk & choc 15 15
a. 2c gray blk & dp ol 15 15
51 A13 4c vio & dp bl 15 15
52 A13 5c ol gray & grn 26 15
53 A13 5c gray blk & ocher ('22) 26 26
54 A13 10c red & car 25 20
55 A13 10c yel grn & bl grn ('22) 26 26
56 A13 15c brn vio & rose ('18) 26 25
57 A13 20c ol brn & dk vio 3.00 2.50
58 A14 25c dp bl & choc 35 25
59 A14 25c Prus bl & blk ('22) 48 48
60 A14 30c gray blk & red 30 25
61 A14 30c rose & red ('22) 30 30
62 A14 35c dk vio & grn 52 32
63 A14 40c choc & ultra 35 25
64 A14 45c car & vio 30 25
65 A14 45c blk & red ('22) 48 48
66 A14 50c bl grn & gray 25 24
67 A14 50c dk bl & bl ('22) 30 30
68 A14 75c org & choc 2.50 2.00
69 A15 1fr dk brn & bis 1.20 1.00
70 A15 2fr car & brn 2.00 1.40
71 A15 5fr bl & choc 3.50 3.00
Nos. 49-71 (23) 17.57 14.59

For overprints and surcharges see Nos. 85-119, B2-B3.

Stamps of 1904-07 Surcharged in Black or Carmine

05 **10**

1912

72 A9 5c on 2c brn, *buff* 35 35
73 A9 5c on 4c cl, *lav* (C) 35 35
74 A9 5c on 15c gray (C) 25 25
75 A9 5c on 20c red, *grn* 25 25
76 A9 5c on 25c bl (C) 25 25
77 A9 5c on 30c pale brn (C) 25 25
78 A9 10c on 40c red, *straw* 25 25
79 A9 10c on 45c blk, *gray grn* (C) 35 35
80 A9 10c on 50c brn, *az*(C) 35 35
81 A9 10c on 75c dp vio, *org* 35 35
82 A9 10c on 1fr brnz grn, *straw* 35 35
83 A9 10c on 2fr vio, *rose* 40 40
a. inverted surch. 175.00 175.00
84 A9 10c on 5fr lil, *lav* 1.40 1.40
Nos. 72-84 (13) 5.15 5.15

Two spacings between the surcharged numerals are found on Nos. 72 to 84.

Stamps of 1910-22 Overprinted in Black, Blue or Carmine **AFRIQUE EQUATORIALE FRANÇAISE**

1924-31

85 A13 1c brn & org 15 15
86 A13 2c blk & choc (Bl) 15 15
87 A13 4c vio & ind 15 15
88 A13 5c gray blk & ocher 15 15
89 A13 10c yel grn & bl grn 15 15
a. Double ovpt. (Bk & Bl) 70.00 70.00
90 A13 10c dk bl & brn ('26) (C) 15 15
91 A13 15c brn vio & rose (Bl) 25 25
92 A13 15c rose & brn vio ('31) (Bl) 50 50
93 A13 20c ol brn & dk vio (C) 25 25
a. Inverted ovpt. 75.00 75.00

Overprinted **AFRIQUE EQUATORIALE FRANÇAISE**

94 A14 25c Prus bl & blk (C) 25 25
95 A14 30c rose & red (Bl) 25 25
96 A14 30c blk & org ('26) 25 25
97 A14 30c dk grn & bl grn ('28) 50 50
98 A14 35c dk vio & grn (Bl) 22 22
99 A14 40c choc & ultra (C) 22 22
100 A14 45c blk & red (Bl) 40 40
101 A14 50c dk bl & bl (C) 22 22
102 A14 50c car & grn ('26) 16 16
103 A14 65c dp bl & red org ('28) 1.65 1.65
104 A14 75c org & brn (Bl) 60 60
105 A14 90c brn red & rose ('30) 1.10 1.10

Overprinted like Nos. 85 to 93

106 A15 1fr dk brn & bis 85 85
107 A15 1.10fr dl grn & rose red ('28) 2.75 2.25
108 A15 1.50fr pale bl & dk bl ('30) 60 60
109 A15 2fr rose & brn 85 85
110 A15 3fr red vio ('30) 3.00 2.75
111 A15 5fr dp bl & choc 2.50 2.50
Nos. 85-111 (27) 18.27 17.52

Types of 1924-31 Issues Surcharged with New Values in Black or Carmine

1925-28

112 A15 65c on 1fr ol grn & brn 50 50
113 A15 85c on 1fr ol grn & brn 50 50
114 A14 90c on 75c brn red & cer ('27) 75 75
115 A15 1.25fr on 1fr dk bl & ultra (C) 50 50
116 A15 1.50fr on 1fr lt bl & dk bl ('27) 65 65
117 A15 3fr on 5fr mag & ol brn 2.25 2.25
118 A15 10fr on 5fr org brn & grn ('27) 6.00 6.00
119 A15 20fr on 5fr red vio & org red ('27) 6.00 6.00
Nos. 112-119 (8) 17.15 17.15

Bars cover the old denominations on Nos. 114-119.

Colonial Exposition Issue
Common Design Types

1931 *Perf. 12½*
Name of Country in Black

120 CD70 40c dp grn 1.00 1.00
121 CD71 50c violet 1.00 1.00
122 CD72 90c red org 1.00 1.00
123 CD73 1.50fr dull blue 1.75 1.75

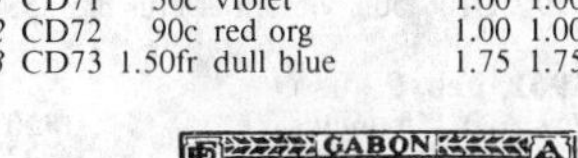

Timber Raft on Ogowe River A16

Count Savorgnan de Brazza — A17

Village of Setta Kemma A18

1932-33 Photo. *Perf. 13x13½*

124 A16 1c brn vio 15 15
125 A16 2c blk, *rose* 15 15
126 A16 4c green 15 15
127 A16 5c grnsh bl 15 15
128 A16 10c red, *yel* 15 15
129 A16 15c red, *grn* 35 25
130 A16 20c dp red 48 35
131 A16 25c brn red 16 15
132 A17 30c yel grn 75 55
133 A17 40c brn vio 60 42
134 A17 45c blk, *dl grn* 80 75
135 A17 50c red brn 52 42

136 A17 65c Prus bl 2.50 1.75
137 A17 75c blk, *red org* 1.20 90
138 A17 90c rose red 1.40 80
139 A17 1fr yel grn, *bl* 10.00 8.00
140 A18 1.25fr dp vio ('33) 1.00 70
141 A18 1.50fr dull blue 1.40 70
142 A18 1.75fr dp grn ('33) 90 60
143 A18 2fr brn red 10.00 8.00
144 A18 3fr yel grn, *bl* 2.25 1.75
145 A18 5fr red brn 2.50 2.00
146 A18 10fr blk, *red org* 11.00 9.00
147 A18 20fr dk vio 20.00 16.00
Nos. 124-147 (24) 68.56 53.84

Catalogue values for all unused stamps in this country are for Never Hinged items.

Republic

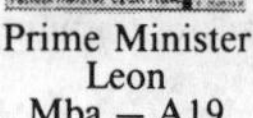

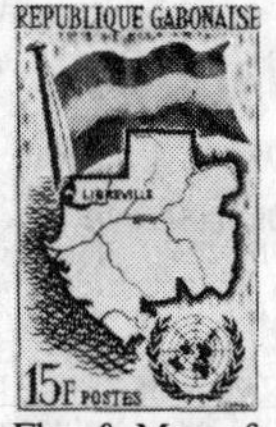

Prime Minister Leon Mba — A19

Flag & Map of Gabon & UN Emblem — A20

Design: 25fr, Leon Mba, profile.

Unwmk.

1959, Nov. 28 Engr. *Perf. 13*
148 A19 15fr chocolate 15 15
149 A19 25fr dk brn & grnsh blk 22 15
Set value 17

Proclamation of the Republic, 1st anniv.

Imperforates
Most Gabon stamps from 1959 onward exist imperforate in issued and trial colors, and also in small presentation sheets in issued colors.

C.C.T.A. Issue
Common Design Type

1960, May 21 Engr. *Perf. 13*
150 CD106 50fr vio brn & Prus bl 55 55

1961, Feb. 9
151 A20 15fr multi 20 15
152 A20 25fr multi 22 20
153 A20 85fr multi 80 60

Gabon's admission to United Nations.

Combretum A21

Designs: 1fr, 5fr, Tulip tree (vert.). 2fr, 3fr, Yellow cassia.

1961, July 4 Unwmk. *Perf. 13*
154 A21 50c rose red & grn 15 15
155 A21 1fr sl grn, red & bis 15 15
156 A21 2fr dk grn & yel 15 15
157 A21 3fr ol grn & yel 15 15
158 A21 5fr multi 16 15
159 A21 10fr grn & rose red 22 16
Set value 66 60

President Leon Mba — A22

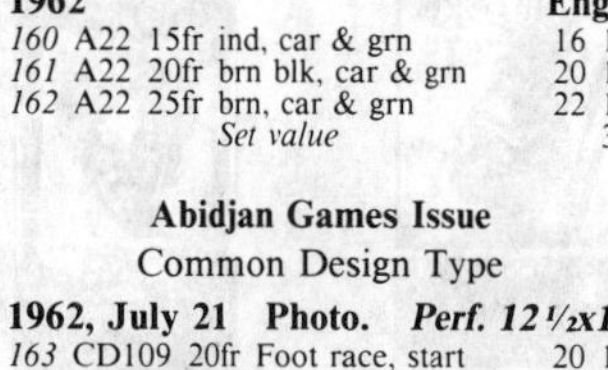

1962 Engr.
160 A22 15fr ind, car & grn 16 15
161 A22 20fr brn blk, car & grn 20 15
162 A22 25fr brn, car & grn 22 15
Set value 31

Abidjan Games Issue
Common Design Type

1962, July 21 Photo. *Perf. 12½x12*
163 CD109 20fr Foot race, start 20 16
164 CD109 50fr Soccer 55 38

See No. C6.

African-Malgache Union Issue
Common Design Type

1962, Sept. 8 *Perf. 12½x12*
165 CD110 30fr emer, bluish grn, red & gold 65 50

Captain Ntchorere and Flags of France and Gabon A23

1962, Nov. 23 *Perf. 12*
166 A23 80fr multi 80 60

Issued to honor Capt. Ntchorere, who died for France, June 7, 1940.

Space Communications Issue

Waves Around Globe A23a

Design: 100fr, Orbit patterns around globe.

1963, Sept. 19 Photo. *Perf. 12½*
167 A23a 25fr ultra, grn & org 25 22
168 A23a 100fr grn, ultra & red brn 1.10 1.10

Issued to publicize space communications.

Human Rights Issue

UNESCO Emblem, Scales and Tree A23b

1963, Dec. 10 Engr. *Perf. 13*
169 A23b 25fr grn, dk gray & red brn 22 20

15th anniv. of the Universal Declaration of Human Rights.

Common Design Types pictured in section at front of book.

World Meteorological Day Issue

Barograph and WMO Emblem A23c

1964, Mar. 23 Unwmk. *Perf. 13*
170 A23c 25fr ol bis, sl grn & ultra 30 25

UN's 4th World Meteorological Day, Mar. 23.

Arms of Gabon — A24

1964, June 15 Photo. *Perf. 13x12½*
171 A24 25fr ocher & multi 22 16

Tarpon A25

Designs: 60fr, Gorilla (vert.). 80fr, Buffalo.

1964, July 15 Engr. *Perf. 13*
172 A25 30fr brn red, bl & blk 35 20
173 A25 60fr brn, grn & brn red 65 35
174 A25 80fr dk bl, grn & red brn 80 60

Cooperation Issue
Common Design Type

1964, Nov. 7
175 CD119 25fr gray, dk brn & lt bl 30 22

Dissotis Rotundifolia — A26

Flowers: 5fr, Gloriosa superba. 15fr, Eulophia horsfallii.

1964, Nov. 16 Photo. *Perf. 12x12½*
Flowers in Natural Colors
176 A26 3fr dp grn 15 15
177 A26 5fr green 15 15
178 A26 15fr dk brn 18 15
Set value 33 24

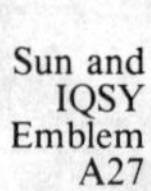

Sun and IQSY Emblem A27

1965, Feb. 25 *Perf. 12½x12*
179 A27 85fr multi 1.10 80

International Quiet Sun Year, 1964-65.

Morse Telegraph A28

1965, May 17 Engr. *Perf. 13*
180 A28 30fr multi 35 25

Cent. of the ITU.

Manganese Crusher, Moanda A29

Design: 60fr, Uranium mining, Mounana.

1965, June 15 Unwmk. *Perf. 13*
181 A29 15fr brt bl, pur & red 15 15
182 A29 60fr brn, brt bl & red 60 40

Issued to publicize Gabon's mineral wealth.

Field Ball — A30

Okoukoue Dance — A31

1965, July 15 Engr. *Perf. 13*
183 A30 25fr brt grn, blk & red 30 20

Issued to commemorate the First African Games, Brazzaville, July 18-25. See No. C35.

1965, Sept. 15 *Perf. 13*

Design: 60fr, Mukudji dance.

184 A31 25fr brn, grn & yel 25 16
185 A31 60fr blk, dk red & brn 60 42

Abraham Lincoln A32

1965, Sept. 28 Photo. *Perf. 12½x13*
186 A32 50fr vio bl, blk, gold & buff 50 35

Centenary of death of Abraham Lincoln.

Old and New Post Offices and Mail Transport A33

1965, Dec. 18 Engr. *Perf. 13*
187 A33 30fr bl, brt grn & choc 30 20

Issued for Stamp Day, 1965.

Balumbu Mask — A34

Designs: 10fr, Fang ancestral figure, Byeri. 25fr, Fang mask. 30fr, Okuyi mask, Myene. 85fr, Bakota leather mask.

1966, Apr. 18 Photo. *Perf. 12x12½*
188 A34 5fr red, brn, blk & buff 15 15
189 A34 10fr brt grnsh bl, dk brn & yel 15 15
190 A34 25fr multi 22 15
191 A34 30fr mar, yel & blk 28 18
192 A34 85fr multi 75 50
Nos. 188-192 (5) 1.55
Set value 94

Intl. Negro Arts Festival, Dakar, Senegal, Apr. 1-24.

WHO Headquarters, Geneva — A35

1966, May 3 Photo. *Perf. 12½x13*
193 A35 50fr org yel, ultra & blk 50 30

Inauguration of the WHO Headquarters, Geneva.

Mother Learning to Write — A36

Soccer Player — A37

1966, June 22 Photo. *Perf. 12x12½*
194 A36 30fr multi 35 20

UNESCO literacy campaign.

1966, July 15 Engr. *Perf. 13*

Design: 90fr, Player facing left.

195 A37 25fr brn, grn & ultra 25 16
196 A37 90fr ultra & dk pur 1.00 60

8th World Cup Soccer Championship, Wembley, England, July 11-30. See No. C45.

Timber Industry — A38

Economic development: 85fr, Offshore oil rigs.

1966, Aug. 17 *Perf. 13*
197 A38 20fr red brn, lil & dk grn 22 15
198 A38 85fr dk brn, brt bl & brt grn 80 42

Woman with Children at Bank Window A39

1966, Sept. 23 Engr. *Perf. 13*
199 A39 25fr brt bl, vio brn & sl grn 22 15

Issued to publicize Savings Banks.

Scouts Around Campfire A40

Design: 50fr, Boy Scout pledging ceremony (vert.).

1966, Oct. 17 Engr. *Perf. 13*
200 A40 30fr sl bl, car & dk brn 30 15
201 A40 50fr Prus bl, brn red & dk brn 55 30

Issued to honor Gabon's Boy Scouts.

Sikorsky S-43 Hydroplane and Map of West Africa A41

1966, Dec. 17 Photo. *Perf. 12½x12*
202 A41 30fr multi 35 16

Issued for Stamp Day and to commemorate the 30th anniversary of the first air-mail service from Libreville to Port Gentil.

Hippopotami — A42

Animals: 2fr, African crocodiles. 3fr, Water chevrotain. 5fr, Chimpanzees. 10fr, Elephants. 20fr, Leopards.

1967, Jan. 5 Photo. *Perf. 13x14*
203 A42 1fr multi 15 15
204 A42 2fr multi 15 15
205 A42 3fr multi 15 15
206 A42 5fr multi 15 15
207 A42 10fr multi 16 15
208 A42 20fr multi 25 15
Set value 65 42

Lions International Emblem A43

Design: 50fr, Lions emblem, map of Gabon and globe.

1967, Jan. 14 *Perf. 12½x13*
209 A43 30fr multi 30 15
210 A43 40fr bl & multi 50 25
a. Strip of 2, #209-210 + label 80 80

50th anniv. of Lions Intl.

Carnival Masks — A44

1967, Feb. 4 Photo. *Perf. 12x12½*
211 A44 30fr brn, yel bis & bl 35 20

Libreville Carnival, Feb. 4-7.

"Transportation" and Tourist Year Emblem — A45

1967, Feb. 15 *Perf. 12½x13*
212 A45 30fr multi 35 20

International Tourist Year, 1967.

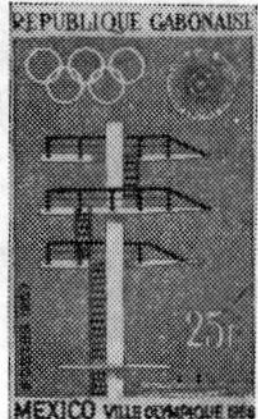

Olympic Diving Tower, Mexico City — A46

Symbolic of Atomic Energy Agency — A47

1968 Olympic Games: 30fr, Sun, snow crystals and Olympic rings. 50fr, Ice skating rink and view of Grenoble.

1967, Mar. 18 Engr. *Perf. 13*
213 A46 25fr dk vio, grnsh bl & ultra 25 15
214 A46 30fr grn, red lil & mar 30 16
215 A46 50fr ultra, grn & brn 55 35

1967, Apr. 15 Engr. *Perf. 13*
216 A47 30fr red brn, dk grn & ultra 35 16

International Atomic Energy Agency.

Pope Paul VI, Papal Arms and Libreville Cathedral A48

1967, June 1 Engr. *Perf. 13*
217 A48 30fr ultra, grn & blk 35 16

Issued to commemorate the "Populorum progressio" encyclical by Pope Paul VI concerning underdeveloped countries.

Flags, Tree, Logger, Map of Gabon and Mask — A49

1967, June 24 Engr. *Perf. 13*
218 A49 30fr multi 35 16

EXPO '67, International Exhibition, Montreal, Apr. 28-Oct. 27, 1967.

Europafrica Issue, 1967

Map of Europe and Africa and Products A50

1967, July 18 Photo. *Perf. 12½x12*
219 A50 50fr multi 50 20

UN Emblem, Women and Child — A51

1967, Aug. 10 Engr. *Perf. 13*
220 A51 75fr brt blue, dk brn & emer 75 40

United Nations Commission for Women.

19th Century Mail Ships — A52

Design: No. 222, Modern mail ships.

1967, Nov. 17 Photo. *Perf. 12½*
221 A52 30fr multi 35 25
222 A52 30fr multi 35 25

Stamp Day. Nos. 221-222 printed se-tenant.

Draconea Fragrans — A53

Trees: 10fr, Pycnanthus angolensis. 20fr, Disthemonanthus benthamianus.

1967, Dec. 5 Engr. *Perf. 13*
Size: 22x36mm
223 A53 5fr bl, emer & brn 15 15
224 A53 10fr grn, dk grn & bl 15 15
225 A53 20fr rose red, grn & ol 22 15
Nos. 223-225,C61-C62 (5) 2.17 1.28

For booklet pane see No. C62a.

WHO Regional Office A54

1968, Apr. 8 Engr. *Perf. 13*
226 A54 20fr multi 22 15

20th anniv. of the WHO.

Dam, Power Station and UNESCO Emblem A55

1968, June 18 Engr. *Perf. 13*
227 A55 15fr lake, org & Prus bl 15 15

Issued to publicize the Hydrological Decade (UNESCO), 1965-1974.

Pres. Albert Bernard Bongo — A56

Design: 30fr, Pres. Bongo and arms of Gabon in background.

1968, June 24 Photo. *Perf. 12x12½*
228 A56 25fr grn, buff & blk 20 15
229 A56 30fr rose lil, lt bl & blk 25 15
Set value 24

Port Gentil Refinery Issue

Tanker, Refinery, and Map of Area Served — A56a

1968, July 30 Photo. *Perf. 12½*
230 A56a 30fr multi 30 16

Issued to commemorate the opening of the Port Gentil (Gabon) Refinery, June 12, 1968.

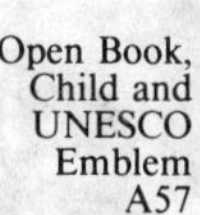

Open Book, Child and UNESCO Emblem A57

1968, Sept. 10 Engr. *Perf. 13*
231 A57 25fr vio bl, dl red & brn 22 15

Issued for International Literacy Day.

Coffee — A58

1968, Oct. 15 Engr. *Perf. 13*
232 A58 20fr shown 20 15
233 A58 40fr Cacao 38 16

"La Junon" A59

1968, Nov. 23 Engr. *Perf. 13*
234 A59 30fr ocher, dk grn & pur 35 20

Issued for Stamp Day.

Lawyer, Globe and Human Rights Flame — A60

1968, Dec. 10
235 A60 20fr blk, bl grn & car 20 15

International Human Rights Year.

Okanda Gap — A61

Designs: 15fr, Barracuda. 25fr, Kinguele Waterfall (vert.). 30fr, Sitatunga trophies (vert.).

1969, Mar. 28 Engr. *Perf. 13*
236 A61 10fr brn, bl & sl grn 15 15
237 A61 15fr brn red, emer & ind 16 15
238 A61 25fr bl, pur & ol 22 15
239 A61 30fr multi 25 15
Set value 40

Year of African Tourism, 1969.

Mvet (Musical Instrument) A62

Musical Instruments: 30fr, Ngombi harp. 50fr, Ebele and Mbe drums. 100fr, Medzang xylophone.

1969, June 6 Engr. *Perf. 13*
240 A62 25fr plum, ol & dp car 22 15
241 A62 30fr red brn, ol & dk brn 25 16
242 A62 50fr plum, ol & dp car 42 25
243 A62 100fr red brn, ol & dk brn 90 45
a. Min. sheet of 4, #240-243 2.50 2.50

Aframomum Polyanthum (Zingiberaceae) A63

Tree of Life A64

African Plants: 2fr, Chlamydocola chlamydantha (Sterculiaceae). 5fr, Costus dinklagei (Zingiberaceae). 10fr, Cola rostrata (Sterculiaceae). 20fr, Dischistocalyx grandifolius (Acanthaceae).

1969, July 15 Photo. *Perf. 12x12½*
244 A63 1fr multi 15 15
245 A63 2fr lt ol & multi 15 15
246 A63 5fr multi 15 15
247 A63 10fr slate & multi 16 15
248 A63 20fr yel & multi 22 16
Set value 56 40

1969, Aug. 17 Photo.
249 A64 25fr multi 22 15

National renovation.

Drilling for Oil on Land A65

Workers and ILO Emblem A66

Design: 50fr, Offshore drilling station.

1969, Sept. 13 *Perf. 12x12½*
250 A65 25fr multi 20 15
251 A65 50fr multi 40 30
a. Strip of 2, #250-251 + label 70 70

20th anniv. of the ELF-SPAFE oil operations in Gabon.

1969, Oct. 29 Engr. *Perf. 13*
252 A66 30fr bl, sl grn & dp car 25 16

50th anniv. of the ILO.

Arms of Port Gentil A67

Canoe Mail Transport A68

Coats of Arms: 20fr, Lambarene. 30fr, Libreville.

1969, Nov. 19 Photo. *Perf. 12*
253 A67 20fr red, gold, sil & blk 16 15
254 A67 25fr bl, blk & gold 20 15
255 A67 30fr bl & multi 22 15
Set value 26

See Nos. 267-269, 291-293, 321-326, 340-348, 409-417, 492-500.

1969, Dec. 18 Engr. *Perf. 13*
256 A68 30fr brt grn, grnsh bl & red brn 30 20

Issued for Stamp Day 1969.

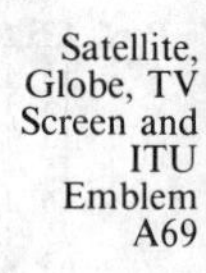

Satellite, Globe, TV Screen and ITU Emblem A69

1970, May 17 Engr. *Perf. 13*
257 A69 25fr dk bl, dk red brn & blk 25 16

International Telecommunications Day.

UPU Headquarters Issue
Common Design Type

1970, May 20 Engr. *Perf. 13*
258 CD133 30fr brt grn, brt rose lil & brn 35 20

Geisha and African Drummer A70

1970, May 27 Photo. *Perf. 12½x12*
259 A70 30fr ultra & multi 25 16

Issued to publicize EXPO '70 International Exhibition, Osaka, Japan, Mar. 15-Sept. 13.

ASECNA Issue
Common Design Type

1970, Aug. 26 Engr. *Perf. 13*
260 CD132 100fr brt grn & bl grn 90 55

UN Emblem, Globe, Dove and Charts A71

1970, Oct. 24 Photo. *Perf. 12½x12*
261 A71 30fr Prus bl & multi 30 20

25th anniversary of the United Nations.

Bushbucks A72

Designs: 15fr, Pels scaly-tailed flying squirrel. 25fr, Gray-cheeked monkey (vert.). 40fr, African golden cat. 60fr, Sevaline genet.

1970, Dec. 14 Photo. *Perf. 12½x13*
262 A72 5fr yel grn & multi 15 15
263 A72 15fr red org & blk 20 15
264 A72 25fr vio & multi 30 16
265 A72 40fr red & multi 40 22
266 A72 60fr bl & multi 60 25
Nos. 262-266 (5) 1.65 93

Arms Type of 1969

Coats of Arms: 20fr, Mouila. 25fr, Bitam. 30fr, Oyem.

1971, Feb. 16 Photo. *Perf. 12*
267 A67 20fr ver, blk, sil & gold 16 15
268 A67 25fr emer, gold & blk 20 15
269 A67 30fr emer, gold, blk & red 22 15
Set value 23

Men of Four Races and Emblem — A73

1971, Mar. 21 Engr. *Perf. 13*
270 A73 40fr multi 35 20

International year against racial discrimination.

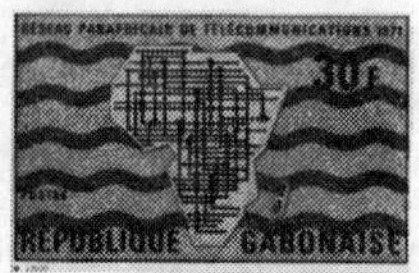

Map of Africa and Telecommunications System — A74

1971, Apr. 30 Photo. *Perf. 13*
271 A74 30fr org & multi 22 16

Pan-African telecommunications system.

Charaxes Smaragdalis — A75

Butterflies: 10fr, Euxanthe crossleyi. 15fr, Epiphora rectifascia. 25fr, Imbrasia bouvieri.

1971, May 26 Photo. *Perf. 13*
272 A75 5fr yel & multi 15 15
273 A75 10fr bl & multi 16 15
274 A75 15fr grn & multi 22 15
275 A75 25fr ol & multi 35 16
Set value 31

Hertzian Center, Nkol Ogoum A76

1971, June 17 Engr. *Perf. 13*
276 A76 40fr grn, blk & dk car 38 22

3rd World Telecommunications Day.

Mother Nursing Child — A77

1971, Aug. 17 Engr. *Perf. 13*
277 A77 30fr lil rose, sep & ocher 25 20

15th anniversary of the Gabonese social security system.

UN Headquarters and Emblem — A78

1971, Sept. 30 Photo. *Perf. 13*
278 A78 30fr red & multi 22 15

10th anniv. of Gabon's admission to the UN.

Large Egret — A79

Birds: 40fr, African gray parrot. 50fr, Woodland Kingfisher. 75fr, Cameroon bare-headed rock-fowl. 100fr, Gold Coast touraco.

1971, Oct. 12 Litho. *Perf. 13*
279 A79 30fr multi 25 16
280 A79 40fr multi 40 22
281 A79 50fr multi 50 25
282 A79 75fr multi 65 30
283 A79 100fr multi 80 38
Nos. 279-283 (5) 2.60 1.31

Asystasia Volgeliana A80

Designs: Flowers of Acanthus Family after paintings by Noel Hallé.

1972, Apr. 4 Photo. *Perf. 13*
284 A80 5fr pale cit & multi 15 15
285 A80 10fr multi 15 15
286 A80 20fr multi 22 16
287 A80 30fr lil rose & multi 35 20
288 A80 40fr dk grn & multi 42 35
289 A80 65fr red & multi 60 42
Nos. 284-289 (6) 1.89 1.43

Louis Pasteur — A81

1972, May 15 Engr. *Perf. 13*
290 A81 80fr dp org, pur & grn 55 20

Sesquicentennial of the birth of Louis Pasteur (1822-1895), scientist and bacteriologist.

Arms Type of 1969

Coats of Arms: 30fr, Franceville. 40fr, Makokou. 60fr, Tchibanga.

1972, June 2 Photo. *Perf. 12*
291 A67 30fr sil & multi 22 15
292 A67 40fr grn & multi 30 15
293 A67 60fr blk, grn & sil 50 16

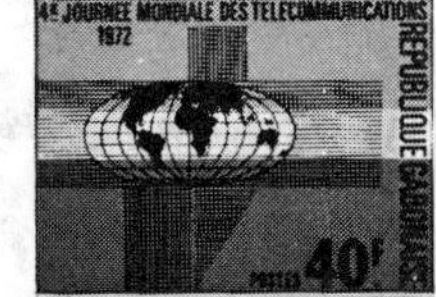

Globe and Telecommunications Symbols — A81a

1972, July 25 *Perf. 13x12½*
294 A81a 40fr blk, yel & org 30 16

4th World Telecommunications Day.

Nat King Cole — A82

Black American Jazz Musicians: 60fr, Sidney Bechet. 100fr, Louis Armstrong.

1972, Sept. 1 Photo. *Perf. 13x13½*
295 A82 40fr bl & multi 35 20
296 A82 60fr org & multi 55 30
297 A82 100fr multi 80 50

Blanding's Rear-fanged Snake — A83

Designs: 2fr, Beauty snake. 3fr, Eggeating snake. 15fr, Striped ground snake. 25fr, Jameson's mamba. 50fr, Gabon viper.

1972, Oct. 2 Litho. *Perf. 13*
298 A83 1fr lem & multi 15 15
299 A83 2fr red brn & multi 15 15
300 A83 3fr brn org & multi 15 15
301 A83 15fr multi 20 15
302 A83 25fr grn & multi 25 15
303 A83 50fr multi 50 22
Set value 1.10 62

Dr. Armauer G. Hansen, Lambarene Leprosarium A84

1973, Jan. 28 Engr. *Perf. 13*
304 A84 30fr Prus grn, sl grn & brn 25 20

Centenary of the discovery of the Hansen bacillus, the cause of leprosy.

Charaxes Candiope — A85

Designs: Various butterflies.

1973, Feb. 23 Litho. *Perf. 13*
305 A85 10fr *shown* 15 15
306 A85 15fr *Eunica pechueli* 15 15
307 A85 20fr *Cyrestis camillus* 20 15
308 A85 30fr *Charaxes castor* 30 16
309 A85 40fr *Charaxes ameliae* 35 20
310 A85 50fr *Pseudacrea boisduvali* 50 22
Nos. 305-310 (6) 1.65
Set value 75

Balloon of Santos-Dumont, 1901 — A86

History of Aviation: 1fr, Montgolfier's balloon, 1783 (vert.). 3fr, Octave Chanute's biplane, 1896. 4fr, Clement Ader's Plane III, 1897. 5fr, Louis Bleriot crossing the Channel, 1909. 10fr, Fabre's hydroplane, 1910.

1973, May 3 Engr. *Perf. 13*
311 A86 1fr grn, sl grn & dk red 15 15
312 A86 2fr sl grn & brt bl 15 15
313 A86 3fr bl, sl & org 15 15
314 A86 4fr lil & dk pur 15 15
315 A86 5fr sl grn & org 15 15
316 A86 10fr rose lil & Prus bl 15 15
Set value 44 30

1977 Coil Stamp
316A A86 10fr aqua 15 15

No. 316A has red control numbers on back of every 10th stamp.

INTERPOL Emblem — A87

1973, June 26 Engr. *Perf. 13*
317 A87 40fr mag & ultra 25 15

50th anniversary of the International Criminal Police Organization (INTERPOL).

Earth Station "2 Decembre" A88

1973, July 2 Engr. *Perf. 13*
318 A88 40fr sl grn, bl & brn 25 15

Party Headquarters, Libreville — A89

1973, Aug. 17 Photo.
319 A89 30fr multi 20 15

African Postal Union Issue
Common Design Type

1973, Sept. 12 Engr. *Perf. 13*
320 CD137 100fr red lil, pur & bl 60 40

Arms Type of 1969

Coats of Arms: 5fr, Gamba. 10fr, Ogowe-Lolo. 15fr, Fougamou. 30fr, Kango. 40fr, Booue. 60fr, Koula-Moutou.

1973-74 Photo. *Perf. 12*
321 A67 5fr bl & multi ('74) 15 15
322 A67 10fr blk, red & gold ('74) 15 15
323 A67 15fr grn & multi ('74) 15 15
324 A67 30fr red & multi 22 15
325 A67 40fr red & multi 25 15
326 A67 60fr emer & multi 40 15
Set value 1.10 40

Issue dates: Nos. 321-323, Feb. 13, 1974; Nos. 324-326, Oct. 4, 1973.

St. Teresa of Lisieux — A90

Human Rights Flame — A91

Design: 40fr, St. Teresa and Jesus carrying cross.

1973, Dec. 4 Photo. *Perf. 13*
327 A90 30fr blk & multi 22 16
328 A90 40fr blk & multi 30 22

St. Teresa of the Infant Jesus (Therese Martin, 1873-97), Carmelite nun.

1973, Dec. 10 Engr.
329 A91 20fr grn, red & ultra 15 15

25th anniversary of the Universal Declaration of Human Rights.

Mangabey A92

Monkeys: 60fr, Cercopithecus cephus. 80fr, Mona monkey.

1974, Mar. 20 Litho. *Perf. 14*
330 A92 40fr gray grn & multi 22 15
331 A92 60fr lt bl & multi 35 20
332 A92 80fr lil rose & multi 42 25

Ogowe River at Lambarene A93

Designs: 50fr, Cape Esterias. 75fr, Poubara rope bridge.

1974, July 30 Photo. *Perf. 13x13½*
333 A93 30fr multi 16 15
334 A93 50fr multi 25 16
335 A93 75fr multi 40 25

Manioc A94

Design: 50fr, Palms and dates.

1974, Nov. 13 Photo. *Perf. 13x12½*
336 A94 40fr org red & multi 22 15
337 A94 50fr bis & multi 25 15

UDEAC Issue

Presidents and Flags of Cameroun, CAR, Congo, Gabon and Meeting Center — A95

1974, Dec. 8 Photo. *Perf. 13*
338 A95 40fr multi 22 15

See No. C156.

Hôtel du Dialogue — A96

1975, Jan. 20 Photo. *Perf. 13*
339 A96 50fr multi 25 16

Opening of Hotel du Dialogue.

Arms Type of 1969

Coats of Arms: 5fr, Ogowe-Ivindo. 10fr, Moabi. No. 342, Moanda. No. 343, Nyanga. 25fr, Mandji. No. 345, Mekambo. No. 346, Omboue. 60fr, Minvoul. 90fr, Mayumba.

1975-77 Photo. *Perf. 12*

340	A67	5fr red & multi	15	15
341	A67	10fr gold & multi	15	15
342	A67	15fr red, sil & blk	15	15
343	A67	15fr bl & multi	15	15
344	A67	25fr grn & multi	15	15
345	A67	50fr blk, gold & red	25	15
346	A67	50fr multi	25	15
347	A67	60fr multi	35	15
348	A67	90fr multi	45	25
		Set value	1.65	85

Issue dates: Nos. 340-342, Jan. 21, 1975. Nos. 343-345, Aug. 17, 1976. Nos. 346-348, July 12, 1977.

Map of Africa with Lion's Head, and Lions Emblem — A97

1975, May 2 Typo. *Perf. 13*
349 A97 50fr grn & multi 25 20

Lions Club 17th congress, District 403, Libreville.

Hertzian Wave Transmitter Network, Map of Gabon A98

1975, July 8 Engr. *Perf. 13*
350 A98 40fr multi 25 16

City and Rural Women, Car, Train and Building — A99

1975, July 22 Engr. *Perf. 13*
351 A99 50fr car, bl & brn 35 20

International Women's Year 1975.

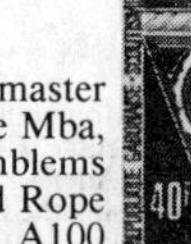

Scoutmaster Ange Mba, Emblems and Rope A100

Design: 50fr, Hand holding rope, Scout, camp, Boy Scout and Nordjamb 75 emblems.

1975, July 29
352 A100 40fr multi 25 16
353 A100 50fr grn, red & dk brn 35 20

Nordjamb 75, 14th Boy Scout Jamboree, Lillehammer, Norway, July 29-Aug. 7.

Lutjanus Goreensis A101

Fish: 40fr, Galeoides decadactylus. 50fr, Sardinella aurita. 120fr, Scarus hoefleri.

1975, Sept. 22 Litho. *Perf. 14*

354	A101	30fr multi	16	15
355	A101	40fr multi	22	16
356	A101	50fr multi	25	20
357	A101	120fr multi	65	45

Agro-Industrial Complex — A102

1975, Dec. 15 Litho. *Perf. 12½*
358 A102 60fr multi 35 22

Inauguration of Agro-Industrial Complex, Franceville.

Tchibanga Bridge — A103

Bridges of Gabon: 10fr, Mouila. 40fr, Kango. 50fr, Lambarene (vert.).

1976, Jan. 30 Engr. *Perf. 13*

359	A103	5fr multi	15	15
360	A103	10fr multi	15	15
361	A103	40fr multi	20	16
362	A103	50fr multi	25	20
		Set value	55	45

Telephones 1876 and 1976, Satellite, A. G. Bell — A104

1976, Mar. 10 Engr. *Perf. 13*
363 A104 60fr dk bl, grn & sl grn 35 22

Centenary of first telephone call by Alexander Graham Bell, Mar. 10, 1876.

Msgr. Jean Remy Bessieux — A105

1976, Apr. 30 Engr. *Perf. 13*
364 A105 50fr grn, bl & sep 25 20

Death centenary of Msgr. Bessieux.

Athletes, Torch, Map of Africa, Games Emblem — A106

1976, June 25 Photo. *Perf. 13x12½*
365 A106 50fr multi 25 20
366 A106 60fr org & multi 35 22

First Central African Games (Zone 5), Libreville, June-July.

Motobecane, France A107

Motorcycles: 5fr, Bultaco, Spain. 10fr, Suzuki, Japan. 20fr, Kawasaki, Japan. 100fr, Harley-Davidson, U.S.

1976, July 20 Litho. *Perf. 12½*

367	A107	3fr multi	15	15
368	A107	5fr org & multi	15	15
369	A107	10fr bl & multi	15	15
370	A107	20fr multi	15	15
371	A107	100fr car & multi	55	40
		Set value	80	60

Rice A108

1976, Oct. 15 Litho. *Perf. 13x13½*
372 A108 50fr shown 25 15
373 A108 60fr Pepper plants 35 22

1977, Apr. 22 Litho. *Perf. 13x13½*

Designs: 50fr, Banana plantation. 60fr, Peanut market.

374 A108 50fr multi 25 20
375 A108 60fr multi 35 22

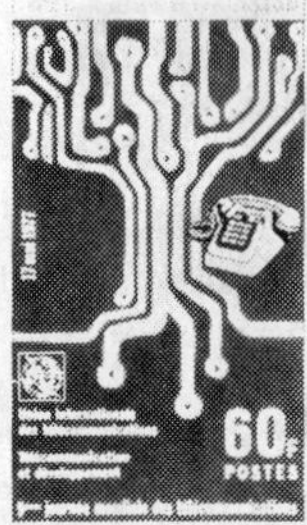

Telecommunications Emblem and Telephone — A109

1977, May 17 *Perf. 13*
376 A109 60fr multi 35 22

World Telecommunications Day.

View of Oyem A110

Designs: 50fr, Cape Lopez. 70fr, Lebamba Cave.

1977, June 9 Litho. *Perf. 12½*

377	A110	50fr multi	25	20
378	A110	60fr multi	35	22
379	A110	70fr multi	38	25

Conference Hall — A111

1977, June 23 Photo. *Perf. 13x12½*
380 A111 100fr multi 55 38

Meeting of the OAU, Libreville.

Arms of Gabon — A112

1977 Engr. *Perf. 13*

Size: 23x36mm

381 A112 50fr blue 25 20

Size: 17x23mm

382 A112 60fr orange 35 15
a. Booklet pane of 5 1.90
383 A112 80fr red 42 35

No. 381 issued in coils, No. 382 in booklets only.

Issue dates: Nos. 381-382, June 23. No. 383, Sept.

Modern Buildings, Libreville — A113

1977, Aug. 17 Litho. *Perf. 12*
387 A113 50fr multi 25 20

National Festival 1977.

Paris to Vienna, 1902 — A114

Renault Automobiles: 10fr, Coupé 1 2 CV, 1921. 30fr, Torpedo Scaphandrier, 1925. 40fr, Reinastella 40 CV, 1929. 100fr, Nerva Grand Sport, 1937. 150fr, Voiturette 1 CV, 1899. 200fr, Alpine Renault V6, 1977.

1977, Aug 30 Engr. *Perf. 13*

388 A114 5fr multi 15 15
389 A114 10fr multi 15 15
390 A114 30fr multi 15 15
391 A114 40fr multi 16 15
392 A114 100fr multi 42 28
Nos. 388-392 (5) 1.03
Set value 60

Miniature Sheet

393 Sheet of 2 + label 2.00 2.00
a. A114 150fr multi 75 75
b. A114 200fr multi 1.00 1.00

Louis Renault, French automobile pioneer, birth centenary. Nos. 383a-393b are perf. on 3 sides, without perforation between stamps and center label showing dark brown portrait of Renault.

See Nos. 395-400.

Globe A115

1978, Feb. 21 Engr. *Perf. 13x12½*

394 A115 80fr multi 42 35

World Leprosy Day.

Automobile Type of 1977

Citroen Cars: 10fr, Cabriolet, 1922. 50fr, Taxi, 1927. 60fr, Berline, 1932. 80fr, Berline, 1934. 150fr, Torpedo, 1919. 200fr, Berline, 1948. 250fr, Pallas, 1975.

1978, May 9 Engr. *Perf. 13*

395 A114 10fr multi 15 15
396 A114 50fr multi 35 22
397 A114 60fr multi 40 25
398 A114 80fr multi 55 35
399 A114 200fr multi 1.40 65
Nos. 395-399 (5) 2.85 1.62

Miniature Sheet

400 Sheet of 2 2.25 2.25
a. A114 150fr multi 75 75
b. A114 250fr multi 1.25 1.25

Andre Citroen (1878-1935), automobile designer and manufacturer.

Ndjole on Ogowe River — A116

Views: 40fr, Lambarene lake district. 50fr, Owendo Harbor.

1978, May 17 Litho. *Perf. 12½*

401 A116 30fr multi 20 15
402 A116 40fr multi 25 16
403 A116 50fr multi 35 20

Sternotomis Mirabilis — A117

Anti- Apartheid Emblem — A118

Various Coleopteras.

1978, June 21 Photo. *Perf. 12½x13*

404 A117 20fr multi 15 15
405 A117 60fr multi 40 25
406 A117 75fr multi 50 30
407 A117 80fr multi 55 35

1978, July 25 Engr. *Perf. 13*

408 A118 80fr multi 55 35

Arms Type of 1969

1978-80 Photo. *Perf. 12*

409 A67 5fr Oyem 15 15
410 A67 5fr Ogowe-Maritime ('79) 15 15
411 A67 10fr Lastoursville ('79) 15 15
412 A67 10fr Haut-Ogooue ('80) 15 15
413 A67 15fr M'Bigou ('79) 15 15
414 A67 20fr Estuaire ('80) 15 15
415 A67 30fr Bitam ('80) 20 15
416 A67 40fr Okondja 25 16
417 A67 60fr Mimongo 40 25
Set value 1.30 80

A119

1978, Oct. 24 Engr. *Perf. 13*

419 A119 80fr multi 55 35

UNESCO campaign to save the Acropolis.

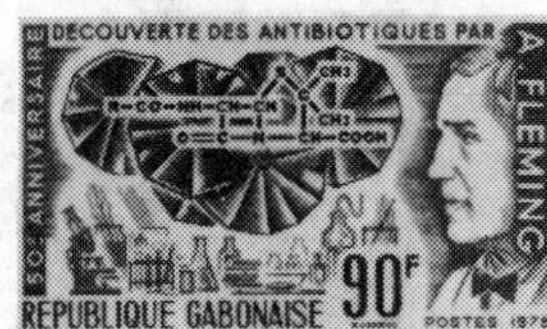

Penicillin Formula, — A120

1978, Nov. 21 Engr. *Perf. 13*

420 A120 90fr multi 60 38

Alexander Fleming's discovery of antibiotics, 50th anniversary.

The Visitation — A121

Designs: 80fr, Massacre of the Innocents. Woodcarvings from St. Michael's Church, Libreville.

1978, Dec. 15 Photo.

421 A121 60fr gold & multi 40 25
422 A121 80fr gold & multi 55 35

Christmas 1978. See Nos. 437-438.

Train and Map A122

1978, Dec. 27 Litho. *Perf. 12½*

423 A122 60fr multi 40 25

Inauguration of Trans-Gabon Railroad, Libreville to Njole.

A123

Pre-Olympic Year (Kremlin Towers, Olympic Emblem, Ancestral Figure and): 80fr, Long jump (vert.). 100fr, Yachts.

1979, May 15 Engr. *Perf. 13*

424 A123 60fr multi 40 25
425 A123 80fr multi 55 35
426 A123 100fr multi 65 40
a. Min. sheet of 3, #424-426 1.60 1.60

Rowland Hill, Messenger and Gabon No. O9 — A124

Allamanda Schottii A125

Designs: 80fr, Bakota mask and tulip tree flowers (vert.). 150fr, Pigeon, UPU emblem, truck and canoe. No. 430b, Gloriosa superba. No. 430c, Phaeomeria magnifica (vert.). No. 430d, Berlinia bracteosa (vert.).

1979, June 8 Photo. *Perf. 13*

427 A124 50fr multi 35 20
428 A124 80fr multi 55 35

Engr.

429 A124 150fr multi 1.00 60

Souvenir Sheet

Photo. *Perf. 14*

430 Sheet of 4 3.00 3.00
a. A125 100fr multi 65
b. A125 100fr multi 65
c. A125 100fr multi 65
d. A125 100fr multi 65

Philexafrique II, Libreville, June 8-17. Nos. 427-429 each printed in sheets of 10 with 5 labels showing exhibition emblem. No. 427 also commemorates Sir Rowland Hill (1795-1879), originator of penny postage. No. 430 has label with exhibition emblem.

IYC Emblem, Globe, Child with Bird — A126

"TELECOM 79" — A127

1979, June 15 Engr. *Perf. 13*

431 A126 100fr multi 65 40

International Year of the Child.

1979, Sept. 18 Litho. *Perf. 13x12½*

432 A127 80fr multi 55 25

3rd World Telecommunications Exhibition, Geneva, Sept. 20-26.

Sugar Cane Harvest — A128

Judo Throw — A129

1979, Oct. 9 Photo. *Perf. 12½x13*

433 A128 25fr shown 16 15
434 A128 30fr Yams 20 15
Set value 18

1979, Oct. 23 Engr. *Perf. 13*

435 A129 40fr multi 25 15

World Judo Championships, Paris, Dec.

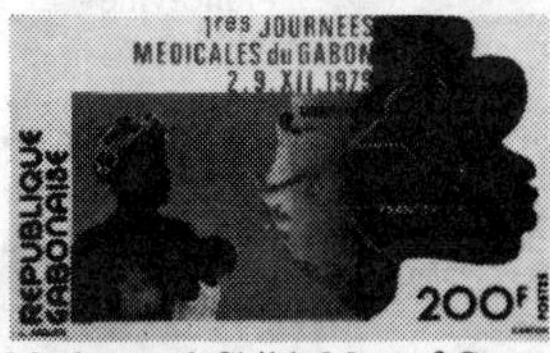

Mother and Child, Map of Congo River Basin — A130

1979, Dec. 2 Litho. *Perf. 12*

436 A130 200fr multi 1.40 65

Medical Week, Dec. 2-9.

Christmas Type of 1978

Wood Carvings, St. Michael's Church, Libreville: 60fr, Flight into Egypt. 80fr, The Circumcision.

1979, Dec. 12 Photo. *Perf. 13*

437 A121 60fr multi 40 20
438 A121 80fr multi 55 25

Set Values

A 15-cent minimum now applies to individual stamps and sets. Where the 15-cent minimum per stamp would increase the "value" of a set beyond retail, there is a "Set Value" notation giving the retail value of the set.

Pres. Omar Bongo, 44th Birthday — A131

OPEC, 20th Anniv. — A132

1979, Dec. 30 Litho. *Perf. 12½*
439 A131 60fr multi 40 20

1980, Feb. 27 Litho. *Perf. 12½*
440 A131 80fr multi 55 25

Pres. Hadj Omar Bongo, re-election and inauguration.

1980, Mar. 27 Litho. *Perf. 13½x13*
441 A132 50fr multi 35 16

Donguila Church — A133

1980 Apr. 3 Litho. *Perf. 12½*
442 A133 60fr shown 40 20
443 A133 80fr Bizengobibere Church 55 25

Easter 1980.

De Brazza (1852-1905), Map of Gabon with Franceville A134

1980, June 30 Litho. *Perf. 12½*
444 A134 165fr multi 1.10 55

Franceville Foundation centenary, founded by Savorgnan De Brazza.

20th Anniversary of Independence — A135

1980, Aug. 17 Photo. *Perf. 13*
445 A135 60fr Leon Mba and Omar Bongo 40 20

Footnotes often refer to other stamps of the same design.

World Tourism Conference, Manila, Sept. 27 — A136

1980, Sept. 10 Engr.
446 A136 80fr multi 55 25

20th Anniversary of OPEC A137

1980, Sept. 15 Litho. *Perf. 12½*
447 A137 90fr shown 60 30
448 A137 120fr Men Holding OPEC emblem, vert. 80 40

Pseudochelidon Eurystomina A138

1980, Oct. 15 Photo. *Perf. 14x14½*
449 A138 50fr *shown* 35 16
450 A138 60fr *Merops nubicus* 40 20
451 A138 80fr *Pitta angolensis* 55 25
452 A138 150fr *Scotopelia peli* 1.00 50

Statue of Bull, Bizangobibere Church — A139

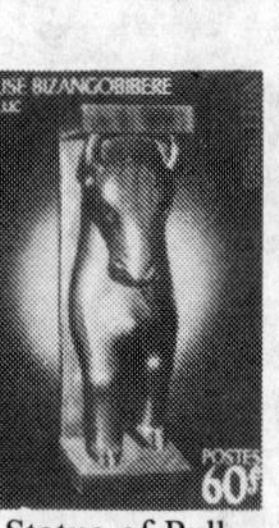
Heinrich von Stephan — A140

1980, Dec. 10 Photo. *Perf. 14x14½*
453 A139 60fr shown 40 20
454 A139 80fr Male statue 55 25

Christmas 1980.

1981, Jan. 7 Engr. *Perf. 13*
455 A140 90fr brn & dk brn 60 30

Von Stephan (1831-97), UPU founder.

13th Anniversary of National Renovation Movement — A141

1981, Mar. 12 Litho. *Perf. 13x12½*
456 A141 60fr multi 40 20

Lion Statue, Bizangobibere A142

Port Gentil Lions Club Banner A143

1981, Apr. 12 Photo. *Perf. 14x14½*
457 A142 75fr multi 50 25
458 A142 100fr multi 65 35

Easter 1981.

1981, May 1 Litho. *Perf. 12½*
459 A143 60fr shown 40 20
460 A143 75fr District 403 50 25
461 A143 80fr Libreville Cocotiers 55 25
462 A143 100fr Libreville Hibiscus 65 35
463 A143 165fr Ekwata 1.10 55
464 A143 200fr Haut-Ogooue 1.40 65
Nos. 459-464 (6) 4.60 2.25

Lions International, 23rd Congress of District 403, Libreville, May 1-3.

13th World Telecommunications Day — A144

1981, May 17 Photo. *Perf. 13*
465 A144 125fr multi 80 42

Unity, Work and Justice A145

R.P. Klaine (Missionary), 70th Death Anniv. A146

1981-86 Photo. *Perf. 13*
466 A145 5fr beige & blk 15 15
467 A145 10fr pale lil & blk 15 15
468 A145 15fr brt yel grn & blk 15 15
469 A145 20fr pink & blk 15 15
470 A145 25fr vio & blk 16 15
471 A145 40fr red org & blk 25 15
472 A145 50fr bluish grn & blk 35 16
473 A145 75fr bis brn & blk 50 25
473A A145 90fr lt bl & blk ('83) 25 15
474 A145 100fr yel & blk 65 35
474A A145 125fr grn & blk ('83) 35 16
474B A145 150fr brt pink & blk ('86) 40 20
Nos. 466-474B (12) 3.51
Set value 1.65

1981, July 2 Litho.

Design: 90fr, Archbishop Walker, 110th birth anniv.

475 A146 70fr multi 45 22
476 A146 90fr multi 60 30

Map of Gabon and Scout Sign — A147

Intl. Year of the Disabled — A148

1981, July 16 *Perf. 12½*
477 A147 75fr multi 50 25

4th Pan-African Scouting Congress, Abidjan, Aug.

No. 477 Overprinted: DAKAR / 28e CONFERENCE / MONDIALE DU / SCOUTISME

1981, July 23
478 A147 75fr multi 50 25

28th World Scouting Conf., Dakar, Aug.

1981, Aug. 6 Engr. *Perf. 13*
479 A148 100fr multi 65 35

Hypolimnas Salmacis — A149

1981, Sept. 10 Litho. *Perf. 14½x14*
480 A149 75fr shown 50 25
481 A149 100fr Euphaedra themis 65 35
482 A149 150fr Amauris niavius 1.00 50
483 A149 250fr Cymothoe lucasi 1.60 80

Paul as Harlequin, by Pablo Picasso (1881-1973) A150

1981, Sept. 25 *Perf. 14½x13½*
484 A150 500fr multi 3.50 1.60

World Food Day — A151

1981, Oct. 16 **Engr.** ***Perf. 13***
485 A151 350fr multi 2.25 1.20

Traditional Hairstyle — A152

Designs: Various hairstyles.

1981, Nov. 12 **Litho.** ***Perf. 14½x15***
486 A152 75fr multi 50 20
487 A152 100fr multi 65 35
488 A152 125fr multi 80 40
489 A152 200fr multi 1.40 65
a. Souv. sheet of 4, #486-489 3.50 1.60

See Nos. 609A, 676.

Christmas 1981 A153

Designs: Children's drawings.

1981, Dec. 10 ***Perf. 14½x14***
490 A153 75fr Girls dancing 50 25
491 A153 100fr Dinner 65 35

Arms Type of 1969
Perf. 12, 13 (#493A-493B)

1982-91 **Photo.**
492 A67 75fr Moyen-Ogooue 50 25
492A A67 90fr Cocobeach ('84) 24 15
493 A67 100fr Woleu-N'tem 65 35
493A A67 100fr Lambarene ('86) 38 18
493B A67 100fr Port Gentil District ('91) 90 45
494 A67 125fr Mouila ('84) 35 16
494A A67 135fr N'Djole ('84) 38 15
495 A67 150fr N'Gounie 1.00 50
500 A67 160fr Leconi ('86) 55 30
Nos. 492-500 (9) 4.95 2.49

Issue dates: Nos. 492, 493, 495, Jan. 13. Nos. 492A, 494, 494A, Aug. 7. No. 493B, Apr. 17.
This is an expanding set. Numbers will change if necessary.

Visit of Pope John Paul II, Feb. 17-19 — A154

1982, Feb. 16 **Litho.** ***Perf. 13***
502 A154 100fr multi 65 35

Alfred de Musset (1810-1857), Writer — A155

1982, Mar. 31 **Engr.** ***Perf. 13***
503 A155 75fr black 50 25

Merchant Navy Ships A156

1982, Apr. 7 **Litho.** ***Perf. 14½x14***
504 A156 75fr Timber carrier 50 25
505 A156 100fr Freighter 65 35
506 A156 200fr Oil tanker 1.40 65

See No. 588.

TB Bacillus Centenary — A157

1982, Apr. 24 **Litho.** ***Perf. 13***
507 A157 100fr multi 65 35

PHILEXFRANCE '82 Stamp Exhibition, Paris, June 11-21 — A158

1982, Apr. 28 ***Perf. 12½***
508 A158 100fr Rope bridge 65 35
509 A158 200fr Sculptured head 1.40 65

Nos. 508-509 se-tenant with label showing show emblem.

14th World Telecommunications Day — A159

1982, May 17 ***Perf. 13***
510 A159 75fr multi 50 25

1982 World Cup — A160

Designs: Various soccer players.

1982, May 19 ***Perf. 14x14½***
511 A160 100fr multi 65 35
512 A160 125fr multi 80 40
513 A160 200fr multi 1.40 65
a. Souvenir sheet of 3, #511-513, perf. 14½ 2.75 1.50

For overprints see Nos. 516-518.

2nd UN Conf. on Peaceful Uses of Outer Space, Vienna, Aug. 9-21 — A161

1982, July 7 **Engr.** ***Perf. 13***
514 A161 250fr Satellites 1.60 80

White Carnations — A162

Designs: Various carnations.

1982, June 9 **Photo.** ***Perf. 14½x14***
515 Strip of 3 2.25 1.10
a. A162 75fr multi 50 25
b. A162 100fr multi 65 35
c. A162 175fr multi 1.10 50

Nos. 511-513a Overprinted in Red with Semi-Finalists or Finalists

1982, Aug. 19 **Litho.** ***Perf. 14x14½***
516 A160 100fr multi 65 35
517 A160 125fr multi 80 40
518 A160 200fr multi 1.40 65
a. Souvenir sheet of 3, #516-518, perf. 14½ 3.00 1.50

Italy's victory in 1982 World Cup.

Phyllonotus Duplex — A163

1982, Sept. 22 ***Perf. 14½x14***
519 A163 75fr shown 50 25
520 A163 100fr Chama crenulata 65 35
521 A163 125fr Cardium hians 80 40

Okouyi Mask — A164 Christmas 1982 — A165

1982, Oct. 13 **Litho.** ***Perf. 14x14½***
522 A164 75fr shown 50 25
523 A164 100fr Ondoumbo reliquary 65 35
524 A164 150fr Tsogho statuette 1.00 50
525 A164 250fr Fang bellows 1.60 80

1983, Dec. 15 **Litho.** ***Perf. 14x14½***
526 A165 100fr St. Francis Xavier Church 65 35

Trans-Gabon Railroad Inauguration — A166

1983, Jan. 18 ***Perf. 12½***
527 A166 75fr multi 50 25

5th African Highway Conference, Libreville, Feb. 6-11 — A167

1983, Feb. 2 ***Perf. 13***
528 A167 100fr multi 65 35

15th Anniv. of Natl. Renewal — A168

Provincial Symbols: a. Bakota mask, Ogowe Ivindo. b. Butterfly, Ogowe Lolo. c. Buffalo, Nyanga. d. Isogho hairdo, Ngounie. e. Tarpon, Ogowe Maritime. f. Manganese, Haut Ogowe. g. Crocodiles, Moyen Ogowe. h. Coffee plant. i. Epitorium trochiformis.

1983, Mar. 12 **Litho.** ***Perf. 13x13½***
529 Strip of 9 + label 6.50 3.50
a. A168 75fr multi 50 25
b. A168 90fr multi 55 30
c. A168 90fr multi 60 30
d. A168 100fr multi 65 35
e. A168 125fr multi 80 40
f. A168 125fr multi 80 40
g. A168 125fr multi 80 40
h. A168 135fr multi 90 45
i. A168 135fr multi 90 45

25th Anniv. of Intl. Maritime Org. — A169

1983, Mar. 17 *Perf. 13*
530 A169 125fr multi 80 40

Pelican A170

1983, Apr. 20 Litho. *Perf. 15x14½*
531 A170 90fr Water musk deer 60 30
532 A170 125fr shown 80 40
533 A170 225fr Elephant 1.50 75
534 A170 400fr Iguana 2.50 1.25
a. Souv. sheet of 4, #531-534 5.75 2.75

25th Anniv. of UN Economic Commission for Africa A171

1983, Apr. 29 Litho. *Perf. 12½*
535 A171 125fr multi 80 40

15th World Telecommunications Day — A172

1983, May 17 Litho. *Perf. 13*
536 A172 90fr multi 60 30
537 A172 90fr multi 60 30
a. Pair, #536-537 1.25 65

Denomination of No. 536 in lower right, No. 537, upper left.

Nkoltang Earth Satellite Station — A173

1983, July 2
538 A173 125fr multi 80 40

10th anniv. of station; World Communications Year.

Ivindo River Rapids — A174

1983, Sept. 7 Engr. *Perf. 13*
539 A174 90fr shown 60 30
540 A174 125fr Ogooue River 80 42
541 A174 185fr Wonga Wongue Preserve 1.20 60
542 A174 350fr Coastal view 2.25 1.20

Hand Drum, Mahongwe A175

Harmful Insects A176

1983, Oct. 12 Litho. *Perf. 14x14½*
543 A175 90fr shown 28 15
544 A175 125fr Okoukoue dancer 40 20
545 A175 135fr Four-stringed fiddle 42 22
546 A175 260fr Ndoumou dancer 80 40

1983, Nov. 9
547 A176 90fr Glossinidae 28 15
548 A176 125fr Belonogaster junceus 40 20
549 A176 300fr Aedes aegypti 1.00 45
550 A176 350fr Mylabris 1.20 60

Christmas 1983 — A177

Wood Carvings, St. Michael's Church, Libreville.

Perf. 14½x13½
1983, Dec. 14 Litho.
551 A177 90fr Adultress 28 15
552 A177 125fr Good Samaritan 40 20

Boeing 737, No. 202 — A178

1984, Jan. 12 *Perf. 13x12½*
553 A178 125fr shown 40 20
554 A178 225fr Lufthansa jet, Germany No. C2 70 38

19th World UPU Congress, Hamburg, June 19-26. Se-tenant with label showing Congress emblem.

3rd Anniv. of Africa 1 Radio Transmitter — A179

1984, Feb. 7 Litho. *Perf. 12½*
555 A179 125fr multi 40 20

Local Flowers — A180

Various flowers.

1984, Apr. 18 Litho. *Perf. 14x15*
556 A180 90fr multi 28 15
557 A180 125fr multi 40 20
558 A180 135fr multi 42 22
559 A180 350fr multi 1.20 60

Fruit Trees A181

1984, Mar. 1 Litho. *Perf. 14½x14*
560 A181 90fr Coconut 28 15
561 A181 100fr Papaya 32 16
562 A181 125fr Mango 40 20
563 A181 250fr Banana 80 40

World Telecommunications Day — A182

1984, May 17 *Perf. 13x13½*
564 A182 125fr multi 40 20

Black Jazz Musicians A183

1984, July 5 *Perf. 12½*
565 A183 90fr Lionel Hampton 28 15
566 A183 125fr Charlie Parker 40 20
567 A183 260fr Erroll Garner 80 40

View of Medouneu — A184

1984, Sept. 1 Litho. *Perf. 13*
568 A184 90fr shown 28 15
569 A184 125fr Canoes, Ogooue River 40 20
570 A184 165fr Railroad 55 25

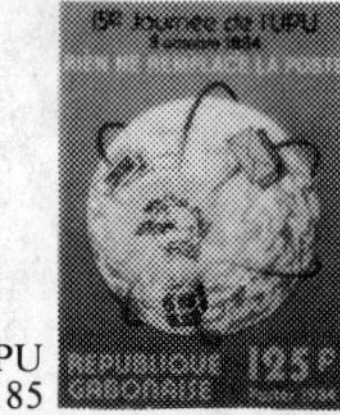

15th World UPU Day — A185

1984, Oct. 9 Litho. *Perf. 13½*
571 A185 125fr UPU emblem, globe, mail 40 20

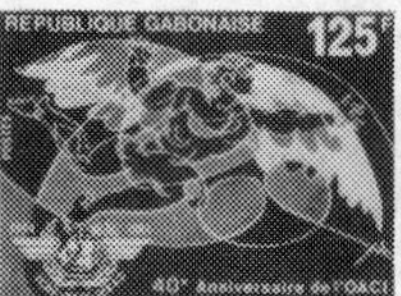

40th Anniv., International Civil Aviation Organization A186

1984, Dec. 1 Litho. *Perf. 13½*
572 A186 125fr Icarus 35 18

Christmas — A187

1984, Dec. 14 Litho. *Perf. 12½*
573 A187 90fr St. Michael's Church Libreville 25 15
574 A187 125fr St. Michael's, diff. 35 18

Issued se-tenant.

World Leprosy Day — A188

1985, Jan. 27 Litho. *Perf. 12½*
575 A188 125fr Hospital, Libreville 35 18

International Youth Year A189

1985, Feb. 6 Litho. *Perf. 13x12½*
576 A189 125fr Silhouttes, wreath 35 18

Birds A190

1984 Litho. *Perf. 15x14*
577 A190 90fr Crowned crane 22 15
578 A190 125fr Hummingbird 35 16
579 A190 150fr Toucan 40 20

Silhouettes, Emblem — A191

1985, Mar. 20 ***Perf. 12½***
580 A191 125fr brt ultra, red & bl 35 16

Cultural and Technical Cooperation Agency, 15th anniv.

Wildlife A192

1985, Apr. 17 ***Perf. 15x14***
581 A192 90fr Aulacode 22 15
582 A192 100fr Porcupine 25 15
583 A192 125fr Giant pangolin 35 16
584 A192 350fr Antelope 90 45
a. Souvenir sheet of 4, #581-584 1.90 90

Georges Damas Aleka, Composer A193

1985, Apr. 30 ***Perf. 13***
585 A193 90fr Portrait, La Concorde score 22 15

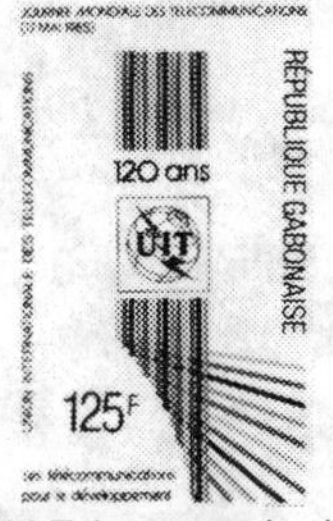

World Telecommunications Day — A194

1985, May 17 ***Perf. 13½***
586 A194 125fr multi 35 16

ITU, 120th anniv.

J.O.C., 30th Anniv. — A195

1985, June 9
587 A195 90fr Emblem 22 15

Merchant Navy Ships Type of 1982

1985, July 1 ***Perf. 15x14***
588 A156 185fr Freighter Mpassa 55 25

Posts and Telecommunications Administration, 20th Anniv. — A196

1985, July 25 ***Perf. 13***
589 A196 90fr Headquarters 25 15

President Bongo — A197

1985, Aug. 17 ***Perf. 14***
590 A197 250fr multi 70 38
591 A197 500fr multi 1.50 80

Imperf

Size: 120x90mm

592 A197 1000fr View of Libreville 3.00 1.50

Natl. Independence, 25th anniv. Nos. 590-591 printed alternately between 3 labels.

No. 592 has non-denominated vignettes of Nos. 590-591.

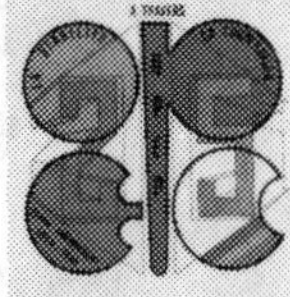

Org. of Petroleum Exporting Countries, 25th Anniv. — A198

1985, Sept. 25 ***Perf. 13½***
593 A198 350fr multi 1.00 50

Intl. Center of the Bantu Civilizations A199

1985, Nov. 16 **Litho.** ***Perf. 15x14***
594 A199 185fr multi 60 32

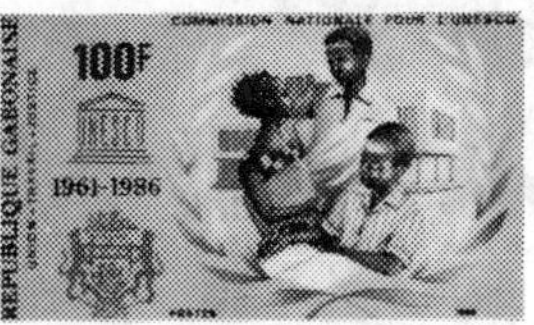

UNESCO, 25th Anniv. — A200

1986, Jan. 5 **Litho.** ***Perf. 12½***
595 A200 100fr multi 52 25

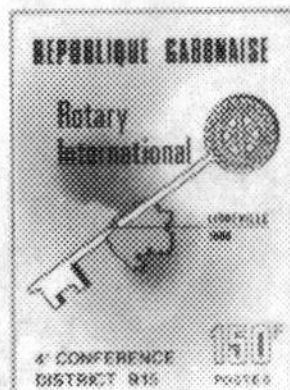

Rotary Intl. District 915, 4th Conf. — A201

1986, May 1 **Litho.** ***Perf. 13½***
596 A201 150fr multi 82 40

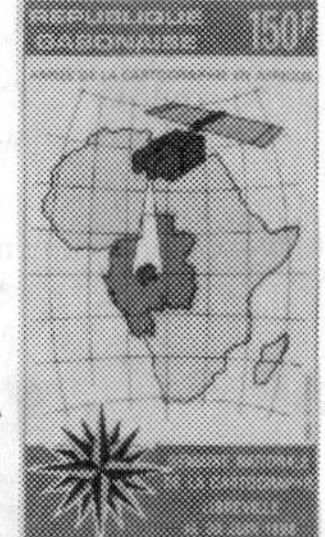

Natl. Week of Cartography, Libreville, June 16-20 — A202

1986, June 16 **Litho.** ***Perf. 12½***
597 A202 150fr multi 82 40

Coffee Flowers, Berries, Beans — A203

1986, Aug. 27 **Litho.** ***Perf. 12½***
598 A203 125fr multi 75 35

Organization of African and Madagascar Coffee Producers, 25th anniv.

Merchantman L'Abanga — A204

1986, June 24 **Litho.** ***Perf. 15x14***
599 A204 250fr multi 1.40 70

Natl. Postage Stamp, Cent. — A205

1986, July 10 ***Perf. 13½x14½***
600 A205 500fr Boats, No. 4 3.00 1.50

Flowering Plants — A206

1986, July 23 ***Perf. 14½x15***
601 A206 100fr Allamanda nerifolia 60 30
602 A206 150fr Musa cultivar 90 45
603 A206 160fr Dissotis decumbens 95 48
604 A206 350fr Campylospermum laeve 2.25 1.10

Butterflies A207

1986, Sept. 18 **Litho.** ***Perf. 15x14***
605 A207 150fr Machaon 82 40
606 A207 290fr Urania 1.60 80

St. Pierre Church, Libreville A208

1986, Dec. 23 **Litho.** ***Perf. 15x14½***
607 A208 500fr multi 2.75 1.40

Christmas.

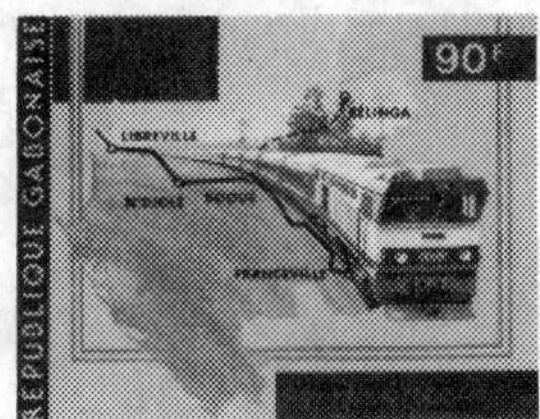

Trans-Gabon Railway from Owendo to Franceville, Inauguration — A209

1986, Dec. 30 ***Perf. 13***
608 A209 90fr multi 50 25

Souvenir Sheet

609 A209 250fr multi 1.40 70

Traditional Hairstyles Type of 1981

1986 **Litho.** ***Perf. 14x15***
609A A152 150fr tan, black & red brown 1.05 52

Fish A210

1987, Jan. 15 ***Perf. 15x14½***
610 A210 90fr Adioryx bastatus 50 25
611 A210 125fr Scarus boefleri 65 32
612 A210 225fr Cephalacanthus volitans 1.25 62
613 A210 350fr Dasyatis marmorata 2.00 95
a. Souv. sheet of 4, Nos. 610-613 5.75 2.90

No. 613a issued Oct. 1987.

The Scott Catalogue value is a retail price, what you could expect to pay for the stamp in a grade of Fine-Very Fine. The value listed is a reference which reflects recent actual dealer selling price.

Raoul Follereau (1903-1977) A211

1987, Jan. 23 *Perf. 12½*
614 A211 125fr multi 70 35

World Leprosy Day.

Pres. Bongo Accepting the 1986 Dag Hammarskjold Peace Prize — A212

1987, Mar. 31 **Litho.** *Perf. 13*
615 A212 125fr multi 70 35

World Telecommunications Day — A213

1987, May 17 **Litho.** *Perf. 13½*
616 A213 90fr multi 50 25

Lions Club of Gabon, 30th Anniv. — A214

Pierre de Coubertin, Father of the Modern Olympics — A215

1987, July 18 **Litho.** *Perf. 12x12½*
617 A214 90fr multi 50 25

1987, Aug. 29
618 A215 200fr multi 1.10 55

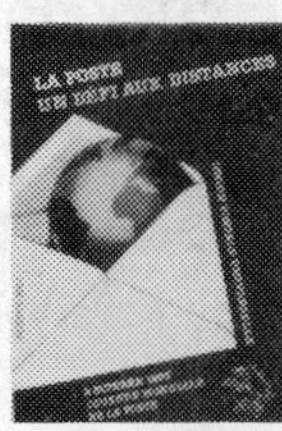

Lions Club Intl., 70th Anniv. — A216

World Post Day — A217

1987, Oct. 1
619 A216 165fr multi 90 45

1987, Oct. 9 **Litho.** *Perf. 13½*
620 A217 125fr multi 85 42

Seashells A218

1987, Oct. *Perf. 15x14*
621 A218 90fr Natica fanel 60 30
622 A218 125fr Natica fulminea cruentata 85 42
a. Souv. sheet of 2, Nos. 621-622 1.50 75

Intl. Year of Shelter for the Homeless — A219

1987, Oct. 5 *Perf. 12½*
623 A219 90fr multi 65 32

Solidarity with the South West African Peoples' Organization (SWAPO) A220

St. Anna of Odimba Mission A221

1987, Sept. 15 **Litho.** *Perf. 14½x15*
624 A220 225fr Pres. Bongo, SWAPO leader 1.60 80

1987, Nov. 2 *Perf. 13½*
625 A221 90fr multi 65 32

Universal Child Immunization — A222

1987, Nov. 16 *Perf. 15x14½*
626 A222 100fr multi 72 35

20th Anniv. of the Presidency of Omar Bongo — A223

1987, Dec. 2 *Perf. 14½x13½*
627 A223 1000fr multi 7.25 3.60

Christmas A224

1987, Dec. 15 *Perf. 15x14½*
628 A224 90fr St. Therese Church, Oyem 65 32

1988 Winter Olympics, Calgary — A225

1987, Dec. 30 *Perf. 13½x14½*
629 A225 125fr multi 90 45

Medicinal Plants — A226

1988, Jan. 26 **Litho.** *Perf. 14x15*
630 A226 90fr Cassia occidentalis 65 32
631 A226 125fr Tabernanthe iboga 90 45
632 A226 225fr Cassia alata 1.60 80
633 A226 350fr Anthocleista schweinfurthii 2.50 1.25
a. Miniature sheet of 4, #630-633 5.75 2.85

World Wildlife Fund — A227

African forest elephant, *Loxodonta africana cyclotis.*

1988, Feb. 29 **Litho.** *Perf. 13½*
634 A227 25fr multi 18 15
635 A227 40fr multi, diff. 30 15
636 A227 50fr multi, diff. 35 18
637 A227 100fr multi, diff. 72 35

Traditional Musical Instruments — A228

1988, Feb. 17 *Perf. 14*
638 A228 90fr Obamba hochet 85 42
639 A228 100fr Fang sanza, vert. 95 48
640 A228 125fr Mitsogho harp, vert. 1.20 60
641 A228 165fr Fang xylophone 1.55 78
a. Souv. sheet of 4, Nos. 638-641 4.55 2.30

World Cup Rugby — A229

1988, Mar. **Litho.** *Perf. 13½x14½*
642 A229 350fr multi 2.50 1.25

Delta Post Office Inauguration — A230

1988, Mar. 9
643 A230 90fr multi 60 30

World Telecommunications Day — A231

1988, May 17 *Perf. 13½*
644 A231 125fr multi 85 42

Storming of the Bastille, July 14, 1789 — A232

1988, May 30 Litho. *Perf. 13*
645 A232 125fr multi 85 42

PHILEXFRANCE '89.

Intl. Fund for Agricultural Development (IFAD), 10th Anniv. — A233

1988, June 20 *Perf. 13½*
646 A233 350fr multi 2.40 1.20

Intl. Red Cross and Red Crescent Organizations, 125th Annivs. — A234

1988, July 15 Litho. *Perf. 12½*
647 A234 125fr multi 80 40

1988 Summer Olympics, Seoul A235

1988, Sept. 17 Litho. *Perf. 15x14*

648	A235	90fr Tennis	62	30
649	A235	100fr Swimming	68	35
650	A235	350fr Running	2.35	1.15
651	A235	500fr Hurdles	3.35	1.65
a.		Souv. sheet of 4, Nos. 648-651	7.00	3.50

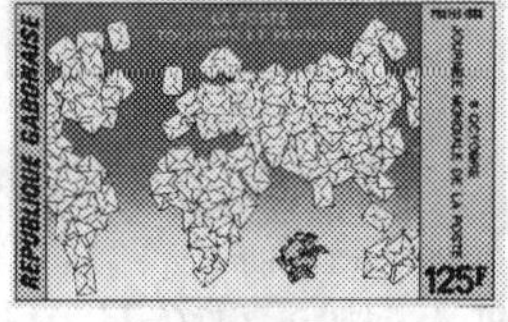

World Post Day A236

1988, Oct. 9 *Perf. 13½*
652 A236 125fr blk, brt yel & brt blue 85 42

Christmas A237

1988, Dec. 20 Litho. *Perf. 15x14*
653 A237 200fr Medouneu Church 1.30 65

Chaine des Rotisseurs in Gabon, 10th Anniv. — A238

1989, Feb. 21 *Perf. 13½*
654 A238 175fr multi 1.15 58

Rabi Kounga Oil Field — A239

1989, Mar. 6 Litho. *Perf. 13½*
655 A239 125fr multi 75 38

Traditional Games — A240

Perf. 13½x14½
1989, Mar. 20 Litho.
656 A240 90fr multicolored 58 30

Birds — A241

1989, Apr. 17 Litho. *Perf. 14x15*

657	A241	100fr White-tufted bittern	60	30
658	A241	175fr Gabon gray parakeet	1.05	52
659	A241	200fr Pygmy hornbill	1.20	60
660	A241	500fr Pope's martin	3.00	1.50
a.		Souv. sheet of 4, Nos. 657-660	5.85	2.95

8th Convention of Lions Intl. District 403, Libreville, Apr. 27-29 — A242

1989, Apr. 27 *Perf. 13*
661 A242 125fr multi 75 38

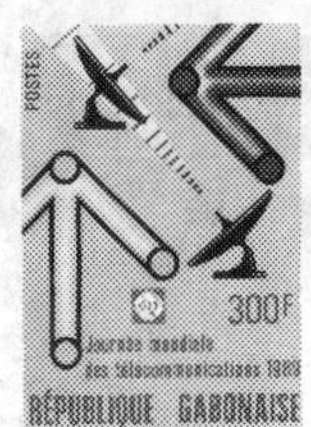

World Telecommunications Day — A243

1989, May 17 *Perf. 13½*
662 A243 300fr multi 1.80 90

PHILEXFRANCE '89 — A244

Symbols of the French revolution, 1789.

Wmk. 385
1989, July 7 Litho. *Perf. 13*
663 A244 175fr multi 1.15 58

French Revolution, Bicent. — A245

1989, July 14
664 A245 500fr multi 3.20 1.60

Fruit — A246

Perf. 14½x15
1989, May 30 Litho. Unwmk.

665	A246	90fr Coconuts	65	32
666	A246	125fr Cabosse	85	42
667	A246	175fr Pineapple	1.25	62
668	A246	250fr Breadfruit	1.75	88
a.		Souv. sheet of 4, #665-668	4.50	2.25

AIMF, 10th Anniv. — A247

1989, July 27 Litho. *Perf. 13*
669 A247 100fr multi 65 32

African Development Bank, 25th Anniv. — A248

1989, Aug. 2 Litho. *Perf. 13*
670 A248 100fr multi 60 30

Apples and Oranges, by Cezanne (1839-1906) — A249

Perf. 13½x14½
1989, June 22 Litho.
671 A249 500fr multicolored 3.20 1.60

1990 World Cup Soccer Championships, Italy — A250

Various athletes.

Perf. 15x14½
1989, Aug. 23 Litho. Unwmk.

672	A250	100fr shown	70	35
673	A250	175fr multi, diff.	1.25	60
674	A250	300fr multi, diff.	2.10	1.05
675	A250	500fr multi, diff.	3.50	1.75
a.		Souv. sheet of 4, #672-675	7.55	3.75

Traditional Hair Style Type of 1981

1989, Sept. 16 *Perf. 14½x15*
676 A152 175fr gray, black & vio 1.25 60

Post Day — A252

1989, Sept. 10 Litho. *Perf. 12*
Granite Paper
677 A252 175fr multicolored 1.40 70

Postal Service, 125th Anniv. (in 1987) — A255

Perf. 13½x14½

1989 Litho. Unwmk.

681 A255 90fr multicolored 65 32

Dated 1988.

St. Louis Church, Port Gentil A256

1989, Dec. 15 Litho. *Perf. 15x14*

682 A256 100fr multicolored 78 40

Christmas.

Libreville Coat of Arms — A257

World Health Day — A258

Wmk. 385

1990, Mar. 12 Litho. *Perf. 13½*

683 A257 100fr multicolored 82 40

1990, Apr. 7 Litho. *Perf. 13*

684 A258 400fr multicolored 3.25 1.60

Souvenir Sheet

Prehistoric Tools A259

1990, Feb. 14 Litho. *Perf. 15x14*

685 Sheet of 4 7.00 3.50
a. A259 100fr Hand axe 72 40
b. A259 175fr Knife blade 1.25 65
c. A259 300fr Arrowhead 2.15 1.10
d. A259 400fr Double bladed hand axe 2.85 1.45

Souvenir Sheet

Fauna — A260

1990, Apr. 13 *Perf. 14*

686 A260 Sheet of 4 8.60 4.25
a. 100fr Cercopitheque 90 45
b. 175fr Potamocherus Porcus 1.55 75
c. 200fr Antelope 1.75 85
d. 500fr Mandrill 4.40 2.20

First Postage Stamps, 150th Anniv. — A261

1991, Jan. 9 Litho. *Perf. 13½x14½*

687 A261 500fr multicolored 4.40 2.20

Independence, 30th Anniv. — A263

1990, Aug. 17 Litho. *Perf. 13*

693 A263 100fr multicolored 90 45

Organization of Petroleum Exporting Countries (OPEC), 30th Anniv. — A264

1990, Sept. 19 Litho. *Perf. 13*

694 A264 200fr multicolored 1.75 90

World Post Day — A265

1990, Oct. 9 *Perf. 13½*

695 A265 175fr bl, yel & blk 1.55 80

Flowers A266

1991, Jan. 9 Litho. *Perf. 15x14*

696 A266 100fr Frangipanier 90 45
697 A266 175fr Boule de feu 1.55 75
698 A266 200fr Flamboyant 1.75 85
699 A266 300fr Rose de porcelaine 2.65 1.30
a. Souvenir sheet of 4, #696-699 7.00 3.50

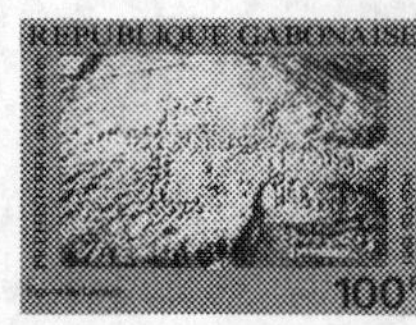

Petroglyphs A267

1991, Feb. 26 Litho. *Perf. 15x14*

700 A267 100fr Lizard figure 90 45
701 A267 175fr Triangular figure 1.55 75
702 A267 300fr Incused lines 2.65 1.30
703 A267 500fr Concentric circles, circles in lines 4.40 2.20
a. Souvenir sheet of 4, #700-703 9.50 4.75

Rubber Trees — A268

1991, Mar. 20 Litho. *Perf. 14x15*

705 A268 100fr multicolored 90 45

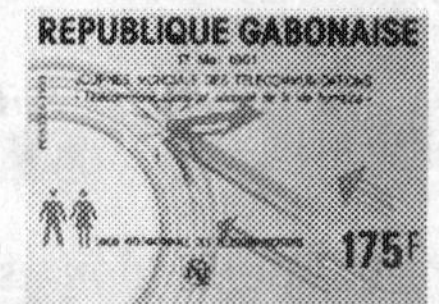

World Telecommunications Day — A269

1991, May 17 Litho. *Perf. 13½*

706 A269 175fr multicolored 1.40 70

Ngounie Women Washing Clothes A271

1991, July 17 Litho. *Perf. 13½*

708 A271 100fr multicolored 90 45

Craftsmen — A272

A273

1991, June 19 *Perf. 14x15*

709 A272 100fr Basket maker 90 45
710 A272 175fr Wood carver 1.55 75
711 A272 200fr Weaver 1.80 90
712 A272 500fr Thatch maker 4.50 2.25

1991, Aug. 18 Litho. *Perf. 14x15*

Gabonese Medals: 100fr, Equatorial Knight's Star. 175fr, Equatorial Officer's Star. 200fr, Equatorial Commander's Star.

713 A273 100fr multicolored 80 40
714 A273 175fr multicolored 1.40 70
715 A273 200fr multicolored 1.60 80

Fishing in Gabon A274

1991, Sept. 18 *Perf. 15x14*

716 A274 100fr Bow-net fishing 80 40
717 A274 175fr Trammel fishing 1.40 70
718 A274 200fr Net fishing 1.60 80
719 A274 300fr Seine fishing 2.40 1.20
a. Souvenir sheet of 4, #716-719 6.20 3.10

World Post Day — A275

Termite Mounds — A276

1991, Oct. 9 *Perf. 13½*

720 A275 175fr multicolored 1.40 70

1991, Nov. 6 *Perf. 14x15*

721 A276 100fr Phallic 80 40
722 A276 175fr Cathedral 1.40 70
723 A276 200fr Mushroom 1.60 80
724 A276 300fr Arboreal 2.40 1.20

SEMI-POSTAL STAMPS

No. 37 Surcharged in Red

1916 Unwmk. *Perf. 13½x14*

B1 A10 10c + 5c red & car 7.25 7.25
a. Double surcharge 70.00 75.00

Same Surcharge on No. 54 in Red

B2 A13 10c + 5c red & car 10.50 10.00
a. Double surcharge 70.00 65.00

No. 54 Surcharged in Red

1917

B3 A13 10c + 5c car & red 40 40

Catalogue values for unused stamps in this section, from this point to the end of the section, are for Never Hinged items.

Republic

Anti-Malaria Issue

Common Design Type

1962, Apr. 7 Engr. *Perf. 12½x12*

B4 CD108 25fr + 5fr yel grn 70 70

WHO drive to eradicate malaria.

Freedom from Hunger Issue

Common Design Type

1963, Mar. 21 Unwmk. *Perf. 13*

B5 CD112 25fr + 5fr dk red, grn & brn 60 60

AIR POST STAMPS

Catalogue values for unused stamps in this section are for Never Hinged items.

Dr. Albert Schweitzer — AP1

Unwmk.

1960, July 23 Engr. *Perf. 13*
C1 AP1 200fr grn, dl red brn & ultra 2.25 1.25

Issued to honor Dr. Albert Schweitzer, medical missionary.
For surcharge see No. C11.

Workmen Felling Tree — AP2

1960, Oct. 8
C2 AP2 100fr red brn, grn & blk 1.40 70

5th World Forestry Cong., Seattle, WA, Aug. 29-Sept. 10.

Olympic Games Issue
French Equatorial Africa No. C37 Surcharged in Red Like Chad No. C1

1960, Dec. 15
C3 AP8 250fr on 500fr grnsh blk, blk & sl 4.00 4.00

Issued to commemorate the 17th Olympic Games, Rome, Aug. 25-Sept. 11.

Lyre-tailed Honey Guide — AP3

1961, May 30 *Perf. 13*
C4 AP3 50fr sl grn, red brn & ultra 60 40

See Nos. C14-C17.

Air Afrique Issue
Common Design Type

1962, Feb. 17 Engr. *Perf. 13*
C5 CD107 500fr sl grn, blk & bis 5.00 3.00

Abidjan Games Issue

Long Jump — AP3a

1962, July 21 Photo. *Perf. 12x12½*
C6 AP3a 100fr dk & lt bl, brn & blk 1.40 70

Issued to publicize the Abidjan Games.

Breguet 14, 1928 — AP4

Development of air transport: 20fr, Dragon biplane transport. 60fr, Caravelle jet. 85fr, Rocket-propelled aircraft.

1962, Sept. 4 Engr. *Perf. 13*
C7 AP4 10fr dl red brn & sl 22 15
C8 AP4 20fr dk bl, sl & ocher 25 18
C9 AP4 60fr dk sl grn, blk & brn 65 50
C10 AP4 85fr dk bl, blk & org 1.10 1.00
a. Souv. sheet of 4, #C7-C10 2.50 2.50

Gabon's 1st phil. exhib., Libreville, Sept. 2-9.

No. C1 Surcharged in Red: "100F/JUBILE GABONAIS/1913-1963"

1963, Apr. 18
C11 AP1 100fr on 200fr 1.10 90

50th anniv. of Dr. Albert Schweitzer's arrival in Gabon.

Post Office, Libreville — AP5

1963, Apr. 28 Photo. *Perf. 13x12*
C12 AP5 100fr multi 90 65

African Postal Union Issue
Common Design Type

1963, Sept. 8 Unwmk. *Perf. 12½*
C13 CD114 85fr brt car, ocher & red 80 60

Bird Type of 1961

Birds: 100fr, Johanna's sunbird. 200fr, Blue-headed bee-eater (vert.). 250fr, Crowned hawk-eagle (vert.). 500fr, Narina trogon (vert.).

1963-64 Engr. *Perf. 13*
C14 AP3 100fr dk grn, vio bl & car 1.20 55
C15 AP3 200fr ol, vio bl & red 2.25 1.20
C16 AP3 250fr grn, blk & dk brn ('64) 3.00 1.50
C17 AP3 500fr multi 5.75 2.75

1963 Air Afrique Issue
Common Design Type

1963, Nov. 19 Photo. *Perf. 13x12*
C18 CD115 50fr lt vio, gray, blk & grn 50 40

Europafrica Issue
Common Design Type

1963, Nov. 30 *Perf. 12x13*
C19 CD116 50fr vio, yel & dk brn 80 50

Chiefs of State Issue

Map and Presidents of Chad, Congo, Gabon and CAR — AP5a

1964, June 23 *Perf. 12½*
C20 AP5a 100fr multi 1.10 70

See note after Central African Republic No. C19.

Europafrica Issue, 1964

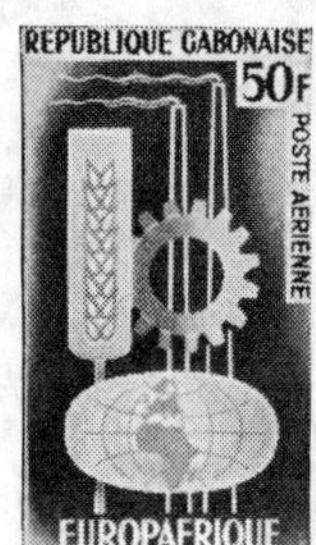

Globe and Emblems of Industry and Agriculture — AP6

1964, July 20 *Perf. 12x13*
C21 AP6 50fr red, ol & bl 55 40

See note after Cameroun No. 402.

Start of Race — AP7

Athletes (Greek): 50fr, Massage at gymnasium (vert.). 100fr, Anointing with oil before game (vert.). 200fr, Four athletes.

1964, July 30 Engr. *Perf. 13*
C22 AP7 25fr sl grn, dk brn & org 22 18
C23 AP7 50fr dk brn, sl grn & org brn 50 35
C24 AP7 100fr vio bl, ol grn & dk brn 1.00 65
C25 AP7 200fr dk brn, mag & org red 2.00 1.40
a. Min. sheet of 4, #C22-C25 3.75 3.75

18th Olympic Games, Tokyo, Oct. 10-25.

Communications Symbols — AP7a

1964, Nov. 2 Litho. *Perf. 12½x13*
C26 AP7a 25fr lt grn, dk brn & lt red brn 22 20

See note after Chad No. C19.

John F. Kennedy (1917-63) — AP8

1964, Nov. 23 Photo. *Perf. 12½*
C27 AP8 100fr grn, org & blk 85 70
a. Souv. sheet of 4 3.50 3.50

Telephone Operator, Nurse and Police Woman — AP9

1964, Dec. 5 Engr. *Perf. 13*
C28 AP9 50fr car, bl & choc 55 35

Social evolution of Gabonese women.

World Map and ICY Emblem — AP10

1965, Mar. 25 Unwmk. *Perf. 13*
C29 AP10 50fr org, Prus bl & grnsh bl 55 38

International Cooperation Year.

Merchant Ship, 17th Century — AP11

Designs: 25fr, Galleon, 16th century (vert.). 85fr, Frigate, 18th century (vert.). 100fr, Brig, 19th century.

1965, Apr. 22 Photo. *Perf. 13*
C30 AP11 25fr lil & multi 35 22
C31 AP11 50fr yel & multi 65 38
C32 AP11 85fr multi 1.00 65
C33 AP11 100fr multi 1.40 80

Red Cross Nurse Carrying Sick Child — AP12

1965, June 25 Engr. *Perf. 13*
C34 AP12 100fr brn, sl grn & red 1.00 65

Issued for the Gabonese Red Cross.

Women's Basketball — AP13

1965, July 15 **Unwmk.**
C35 AP13 100fr sep, red org & brt lil 1.00 65

African Games, Brazzaville, July 18-25.

Maps of Europe and Africa — AP14

1965, July 26 **Photo.** ***Perf. 13x12***
C36 AP14 50fr multi 1.00 30

See note after Cameroun No. 421.

Pres. Leon Mba AP15

1965, Aug. 17 ***Perf. 12½***
C37 AP15 25fr multi 25 20

Fifth anniversary of independence.

Sir Winston Churchill and Microphones — AP16

1965, Sept. 28 **Photo.** ***Perf. 12½***
C38 AP16 100fr gold, blk & bl 1.10 70

Sir Winston Spencer Churchill (1874-1965), statesman and World War II leader.

Dr. Albert Schweitzer — AP17

Embossed on Gold Foil
Die-cut Perf. 14½, Approx.

1965, Dec. 4
C39 AP17 1000fr gold 16.00 16.00

Dr. Albert Schweitzer (1875-1965), medical missionary, theologian and musician.

Pope John XXIII and St. Peter's — AP18

1965, Dec. 10 **Photo.** ***Perf. 13x12½***
C40 AP18 85fr multi 80 60

Issued in memory of Pope John XXIII.

Anti-Malaria Treatment — AP19

1966, Apr. 8 **Photo.** ***Perf. 12½***
C41 AP19 50fr shown 40 25
 a. Min. sheet of 4 1.75 1.75
C42 AP19 100fr First aid 80 45
 a. Min. sheet of 4 3.50 3.50

Issued for the Red Cross.

Diamant Rocket, A-1 Satellite and Map of Africa — AP20

Design: 90fr, FR-1 satellite, Diamant rocket and earth.

1966, May 18 **Engr.** ***Perf. 13***
C43 AP20 30fr dk pur, brt bl & red brn 35 22
C44 AP20 90fr brt lil, red & pur 90 50

French achievements in space.

Soccer and World Map — AP21

1966, July 15 **Engr.** ***Perf. 13***
C45 AP21 100fr sl & brn red 1.20 65

8th World Soccer Cup Championship, Wembley, England, July 11-30.

Symbols of Industry and Transportation AP22

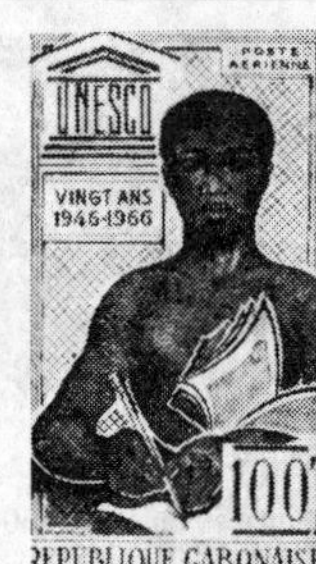

Student and UNESCO Emblem AP23

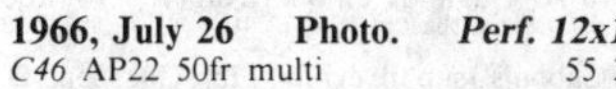

1966, July 26 **Photo.** ***Perf. 12x13***
C46 AP22 50fr multi 55 25

3rd anniv. of the economic agreement between the European Economic Community and the African and Malgache Union.

Air Afrique Issue, 1966
Common Design Type

1966, Aug. 31 **Photo.** ***Perf. 13***
C47 CD123 30fr org, blk & gray 25 15

1966, Nov. 4 **Engr.** ***Perf. 13***
C48 AP23 100fr dl bl, ocher & blk 1.00 55

20th anniv. of UNESCO.

Libreville Airport — AP24

1966, Nov. 21 **Engr.** ***Perf. 13***
C49 AP24 200fr dp bl & red brn 1.75 80

Inauguration of Libreville Airport.

Farman 190 — AP25

Planes: 300fr, De Havilland Heron. 500fr, Potez 56.

1967, Apr. 1 **Engr.** ***Perf. 13***
C50 AP25 200fr ultra, lil & bl grn 1.75 55
C51 AP25 300fr brn, lil & brt bl 2.50 75
C52 AP25 500fr brn car, dk grn & ind 4.00 2.50

For surcharge see No. C128.

Planes, Runways and ICAO Emblem — AP26

1967, May 19 **Engr.** ***Perf. 13***
C53 AP26 100fr plum, brt bl & yel grn 1.00 55

International Civil Aviation Organization.

Blood Donor and Bottles AP27

Jamboree Emblem and Symbols of Orientation AP28

Design: 100fr, Human heart and transfusion apparatus.

1967, June 26 **Photo.** ***Perf. 12½***
C54 AP27 50fr ocher, red & sl 50 25
 a. Souvenir sheet of 4 2.00 2.00
C55 AP27 100fr yel grn, red & gray 1.10 60
 a. Souvenir sheet of 4 4.50 4.50

Issued for the Red Cross. Nos. C54a, C55a each contains 2 vertical tete beche pairs.

1967, Aug. 1 **Engr.** ***Perf. 13***

Design: 100fr, Jamboree emblem, maps and Scouts of Africa and America.

C56 AP28 50fr multi 50 30
C57 AP28 100fr brt grn, dp car & bl 1.00 55

12th Boy Scout World Jamboree, Farragut State Park, Idaho, Aug. 1-9.

African Postal Union Issue, 1967
Common Design Type

1967, Sept. 9 **Engr.** ***Perf. 13***
C58 CD124 100fr dl bl, ol & red brn 90 50

Mission Church — AP29

1967, Oct. 18 **Engr.** ***Perf. 13***
C59 AP29 100fr brt bl, dk grn & blk 90 35

125th anniv. of the arrival of American Protestant missionaries in Baraka-Libreville.

UN Emblem, Sword, Book and People AP30

Konrad Adenauer AP31

1967, Nov. 7 **Photo.** ***Perf. 13***
C60 AP30 60fr dk red, vio bl & bis 65 20

UN Commission on Human Rights.

Tree Type of Regular Issue

Designs: 50fr, Baillonella toxisperma. 100fr, Aucoumea klaineana.

1967, Dec. 5 Engr. *Perf. 13*
Size: 26½x47½mm

C61 A53 50fr grn, brt bl & brn 55 25
C62 A53 100fr multi 1.10 58
a. Bklt. pane (1 each #223-225 & C61-C62 with gutter btwn.) 2.25 2.25

1968, Feb. 20 Photo. *Perf. 12½*

C63 AP31 100fr blk, dl org & red 85 45
a. Souvenir sheet of 4 3.50 3.50

Issued in memory of Konrad Adenauer (1876-1967), chancellor of West Germany (1949-63). No. C63a includes 1967 CEPT (Europa) emblem.

Madonna of the Rosary by Murillo AP32

Paintings: 90fr, Christ in Bonds, by Luis de Morales. 100fr, St. John on Patmos, by Juan Mates (horiz.).

1968, July 9 Photo. *Perf. 12½x12*

C64 AP32 60fr multi 50 25
C65 AP32 90fr multi 70 40
C66 AP32 100fr multi 85 50

See Nos. C77, C102-C104, C132-C133, C146-C148.

Europafrica Issue

Stylized Knot — AP32a

1968, July 23 Photo. *Perf. 13*

C67 AP32a 50fr yel brn, emer & lt ultra 55 25

See note after Congo Republic No. C69.

Support for Red Cross — AP33

Design: 50fr, Distribution of Red Cross gifts.

1968, Aug. 13

C68 AP33 50fr multi 45 22
C69 AP33 100fr multi 1.00 50
a. Bklt. pane of 2 (Nos. C68, C69 with gutter between) 1.50 1.50

Issued for the Red Cross.

High Jump — AP34

Designs: 30fr, Bicycling (vert.). 100fr, Judo (vert.). 200fr, Boxing.

1968, Sept. 3 Engr.

C70 AP34 25fr dk brn, mag & gray 16 15
C71 AP34 30fr brick red, Prus bl & dk brn 22 15
C72 AP34 100fr brt bl, dk brn & dl yel 80 40
C73 AP34 200fr emer, gray & dk brn 1.50 75
a. Bklt. pane (1 each #C70-C71 & C72-C73 with gutter btwn.) 3.50 3.50

Issued to publicize the 19th Summer Olympic Games, Mexico City, Oct. 12-27.

Pres. Mba, Flag and Arms of Gabon AP35

Embossed on Gold Foil

1968, Nov. 28 *Perf. 14½*

C74 AP35 1000fr gold, grn, yel & dk bl 7.00 7.00

1st anniv. of the death of Pres. Léon Mba (1902-67).

Pres. Bongo, Maps of Gabon and Owendo Harbor — AP36

Design: 30fr, Owendo Harbor.

1968, Dec. 16 Photo. *Perf. 12½*

C75 AP36 25fr multi 25 15
C76 AP36 30fr multi 35 16
a. Strip of 2, #C75-C76 + label 65 60

Laying of the foundation stone for Owendo Harbor, June 24, 1968.

PHILEXAFRIQUE Issue
Painting Type of 1968

Design: 100fr, The Convent of St. Mary of the Angels, by Francois Marius Granet.

1969, Jan. 8 Photo. *Perf. 12½x12*

C77 AP32 100fr multi 1.10 1.10

Issued to publicize PHILEXAFRIQUE Philatelic Exhibition in Abidjan, Feb. 14-23. Printed with alternating brown label.

Mahatma Gandhi — AP37

Portraits: 30fr, John F. Kennedy. 50fr, Robert F. Kennedy. 100fr, Martin Luther King, Jr.

1969, Jan. 15 *Perf. 12½*

C78 AP37 25fr pink & blk 20 15
C79 AP37 30fr lt yel grn & blk 22 15
C80 AP37 50fr lt bl & blk 38 18
C81 AP37 100fr brt rose lil & blk 75 32
a. Souv. sheet of 4, #C78-C81 2.00 2.00
Set value 69

Issued to honor exponents of non-violence.

2nd PHILEXAFRIQUE Issue
Common Design Type

1969, Feb. 14 Engr. *Perf. 13*

C82 CD128 50fr grn, ind & red brn 60 35

Battle of Rivoli, by Henri Philippoteaux — AP39

Paintings: 100fr, The Oath of the Army, by Jacques Louis David. 250fr, Napoleon with the Children on the Terrace in St. Cloud, by Louis Ducis.

1969, Apr. 23 Photo. *Perf. 12½x12*

C83 AP39 50fr brn & multi 80 50
C84 AP39 100fr grn & multi 1.50 1.00
C85 AP39 250fr lil & multi 4.00 2.50

Birth bicentenary of Napoleon I.

Red Cross Plane, Nurse and Biafran Children — AP40

Design: 20fr, Dispensary, ambulance and supplies. 25fr, Physician and nurse in children's ward. 30fr, Dispensary and playing children.

1969, June 20 Photo. *Perf. 14x13½*

C86 AP40 15fr lt ultra, dk brn & red 15 15
C87 AP40 20fr emer, blk, brn & red 22 15
C88 AP40 25fr grnsh bl, dk brn & red 25 16
C89 AP40 30fr org yel, dk brn & red 30 16

Red Cross help for Biafra.

A souvenir sheet contains four stamps similar to Nos. C86-C89, but lithographed and rouletted 13x13½. Gray margin with red inscription and Red Cross. Size: 118x75mm. Sold in cardboard folder. Value $1.20.

Astronauts and Lunar Landing Module, Apollo 11 — AP41

Embossed on Gold Foil

1969, July 25 *Die-cut Perf. 10½x10*

C90 AP41 1000fr gold 9.00 9.00

See note after Algeria No. 427.

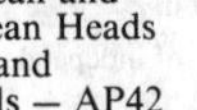

African and European Heads and Symbols — AP42

Icarus and Sun — AP43

Europafrica Issue, 1970

1970, June 5 Photo. *Perf. 12x13*

C91 AP42 50fr multi 50 22

1970, June 10 Engr. *Perf. 13*

Designs: 100fr, Leonardo da Vinci's flying man, 1519. 200fr, Jules Verne's space shell approaching moon, 1865.

C92 AP43 25fr ultra, red & org 20 15
C93 AP43 100fr ocher, plum & sl grn 70 45
C94 AP43 200fr gray, ultra & dk car 2.00 90
a. Min. sheet of 3, #C92-C94 3.25 3.25

UAMPT Emblem AP44

Embossed on Gold Foil

1970, June 18 *Die-cut Perf. 12½*

C95 AP44 200fr gold, yel grn & bl 1.90 1.10

Meeting of the Afro-Malagasy Union of Posts and Telecommuncations (UAMPT), Libreville, June 17-23.

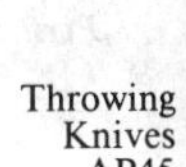

Throwing Knives AP45

Gabonese Weapons: 30fr, Assegai and crossbow (vert.). 50fr, War knives (vert.). 90fr, Dagger and sheath.

1970, July 10 Engr. *Perf. 13*

C96 AP45 25fr multi 18 15
C97 AP45 30fr multi 22 15
C98 AP45 50fr multi 32 20
C99 AP45 90fr multi 70 35
a. Min. sheet of 4, #C96-C99 1.50 1.50
Set value 72

Japanese Masks, Mt. Fuji and Torii at Miyajima AP46

Embossed on Gold Foil

1970, July 31 *Die-cut Perf. 10*

C100 AP46 1000fr multi 10.00 10.00

Issued to publicize EXPO '70 International Exhibition, Osaka, Japan, Mar. 15-Sept. 13.

Pres. Albert Bernard Bongo — AP47

Lithographed; Gold Embossed

1970, Aug. 17 *Perf. 12½*

C101 AP47 200fr multi 2.00 1.10

10th anniversary of independence.

Painting Type of 1968

Paintings: 50fr, Portrait of a Young Man, School of Raphael. 100fr, Portrait of Jeanne d'Aragon, by Raphael. 200fr, Madonna with Blue Diadem, by Raphael.

1970, Oct. 16 Photo. *Perf. 12½x12*

C102 AP32 50fr multi 40 20
C102A AP32 100fr bl & multi 80 40
C102B AP32 200fr brn & multi 1.65 90

Raphael (1483-1520).

Miniature Sheets

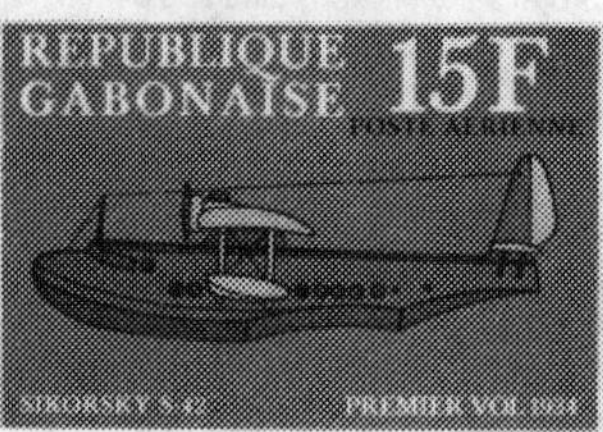
Sikorsky S-32 — AP47a

Hugo Junkers — AP47b

1970, Dec. 5 Litho. *Perf. 12*

C103 Sheet of 8
- *a.* AP47a 15fr shown
- *b.* AP47a 25fr Fokker "Southern Cross"
- *c.* AP47a 40fr Dornier DO-18
- *d.* AP47a 60fr Dornier DO-X
- *e.* AP47a 80fr Breguet "Bizerte"
- *f.* AP47a 125fr Douglas "Cloudster"
- *g.* AP47a 150fr De Havilland DH-2
- *h.* AP47a 200fr Vickers "Vini"

C104 Sheet of 4
- *a.* AP47b 200fr shown
- *b.* AP47b 300fr Claude Dornier
- *c.* AP47b 400fr Anthony Fokker
- *d.* AP47b 500fr Igor Sikorsky

Imperf

C105 Sheet of 8
- *a.* AP47a 10fr Dornier "Spatz"
- *b.* AP47a 20fr Douglas DC-3
- *c.* AP47a 30fr Dornier DO-7 "Wal"
- *d.* AP47a 50fr Sikorsky S-38
- *e.* AP47a 75fr De Havilland "Moth"
- *f.* AP47a 100fr Vickers "Spitfire"
- *g.* AP47a 125fr Breguet XIX
- *h.* AP47a 150fr Fokker "Universal"

Size: 80x90mm

C106 AP47b 1000fr Claude Dornier

Claude Dornier (1884-1969), aviation pioneer. No. C104 exists imperf.

Presidents Bongo and Pompidou — AP48

1971, Feb. 11 Photo. *Perf. 13*

C107 AP48 50fr multi 50 20

Visit of Georges Pompidou, Pres. of France.

Apollo 14 Liftoff AP48a

1971, Feb. 19 *Perf. 14*

Yellow Inscriptions

C108 AP48a 15fr shown
C108A AP48a 25fr Achieving orbit
C108B AP48a 40fr Lunar module descent
C108C AP48a 55fr Lunar landing
C108D AP48a 75fr Lunar liftoff
C108E AP48a 120fr Earth re-entry

Souvenir Sheet

C108F Sheet of 2
- *g.* AP48a 100fr Modules attached
- *h.* AP48a 100fr like #C108E

Nos. C108-C108F exist imperf. with white inscriptions.

Flowers and Plane — AP49

Flowers and Planes: 25fr, Carnations. 40fr, Roses. 55fr, Daffodils. 75fr, Orchids. 120fr, Tulips.

1971, May 7 Litho. *Perf. 13½x14*

C109 AP49 15fr yel & multi 15 15
C109A AP49 25fr multi 20 15
C109B AP49 40fr pink & multi 30 15
C109C AP49 55fr bl & multi 40 20
C110 AP49 75fr multi 60 32
C111 AP49 120fr grn & multi 1.00 50
- *a.* Souvenir sheet of 2, #C110-C111 1.65 1.65

Nos. C109-C111 (6) 2.65 1.47

"Flowers by air."

Napoleon's Death Mask AP50

Designs: 200fr, Longwood, St. Helena, by Jacques Marchand (horiz.). 500fr, Sarcophagus in Les Invalides, Paris.

1971, May 12 Photo. *Perf. 13*

C112 AP50 100fr gold & multi 90 42
C113 AP50 200fr gold & multi 1.65 75
C114 AP50 500fr gold & multi 3.50 1.50

Napoleon Bonaparte (1769-1821).

Souvenir Sheet

Charles de Gaulle — AP51

Designs: 40fr, President de Gaulle. 80fr, General de Gaulle. 100fr, Quotation.

1971, June 18 Photo. *Perf. 12½*

C115 AP51 Sheet of 5 2.50 2.50
- *a.* 40fr dark red & multi 25 25
- *b.* 80fr dark green & multi 25 25
- *c.* 100fr green, brown & yel 65 65

In memory of Gen. Charles de Gaulle (1890-1970), Pres. of France.
For surcharge see No. C126.

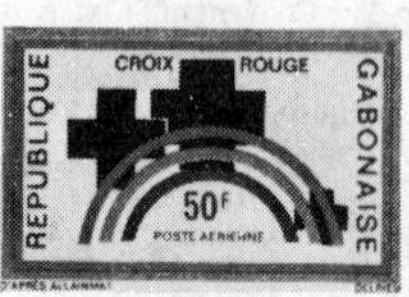
Red Crosses AP52

1971, June 29

C116 AP52 50fr multi 50 25

For the Red Cross of Gabon.
For surcharge see No. C143.

Uranium — AP53

1971, July 20 Photo. *Perf. 13x12½*

C117 AP53 85fr shown 70 40
C118 AP53 90fr Manganese 80 50

Landing Module over Moon — AP54

Embossed on Gold Foil

1971, July 30 ***Die-cut Perf. 10***

C119 AP54 1500fr multi 14.00 14.00

Apollo 11 and 15 US moon missions.

African Postal Union Issue, 1971

Common Design Type

Design: 100fr, Bakota copper mask and UAMPT building, Brazzaville, Congo.

1971, Nov. 13 Photo. *Perf. 13x13½*

C120 CD135 100fr bl & multi 90 45

Ski Jump and Miyajima Torii AP55

Design: 130fr, Speed skating and Japanese temple.

1972, Jan. 31 Engr. *Perf. 13*

C121 AP55 40fr hn brn, sl grn & vio bl 40 16
C122 AP55 130fr hn brn, sl grn & vic bl 1.20 42
- *a.* Strip of 2, #C121-C122 + label 2.00 1.60

11th Winter Olympic Games, Sapporo, Japan, Feb. 3-13.

The Basin and Grand Canal, by Vanvitelli — AP56

Paintings: 70fr, Rialto Bridge, by Canaletto (erroneously inscribed Caffi; vert.) 140fr, Santa Maria della Salute, by Vanvitelli (vert.).

1972, Feb. 7 Photo. *Perf. 13*

C123 AP56 60fr gold & multi 40 15
C124 AP56 70fr gold & multi 60 15
C125 AP56 140fr gold & multi 1.20 35

UNESCO campaign to save Venice.

No. C115 Surcharged in Brown and Gold

Souvenir Sheet

1972, Feb. 11 *Perf. 12½*

C126 AP51 Sheet of 5 4.50 4.50
- *a.* 60fr on 40fr multi 50 50
- *b.* 120fr on 80fr multi 1.00 1.00
- *c.* 180fr on 100fr multi 1.50 1.50

Publicity for the erection of a memorial for Charles de Gaulle. Nos. C126a-C126b have surcharge and Cross of Lorraine in gold, 2 bars obliterating old denomination in brown; No. C126c has surcharge, cross and bars in brown. Two Lorraine Crosses and inscription (MEMORIAL DU GENERAL DE GAULLE) in brown added in margin.

Hotel Inter-Continental, Libreville — AP57

1972, Feb. 26 **Engr.** ***Perf. 13***
C127 AP57 40fr bl, sl grn & org brn 35 15

No. C51 Surcharged

VISITE OFFICIELLE GRAND MAITRE
ORDRE SOUVERAIN DE MALTE
3 MARS 1972

1972, Mar. 3
C128 AP25 50fr on 300fr multi 50 35

Official visit of the Grand Master of the Knights of Malta, March 3.

Discobolus, by Alcamenes — AP58

Designs: 100fr, Doryphoros, by Polycletus. 140fr, Borghese gladiator, by Agasias.

1972, May 10 **Engr.** ***Perf. 13***
C129 AP58 30fr rose cl & gray 20 15
C130 AP58 100fr rose cl & gray 65 18
C131 AP58 140fr rose cl & gray 90 25
a. Min. of sheet of 3, #C129-C131 2.00 2.00

20th Olympic Games, Munich, Aug. 26-Sept. 10.
For surcharges see Nos. C134-C136.

Painting Type of 1968

Paintings: 30fr, Adoration of the Magi, by Peter Brueghel, the Elder (horiz.). 40fr, Madonna and Child, by Marco Basaiti.

1972, Oct. 30 **Photo.** ***Perf. 13***
C132 AP32 30fr gold & multi 25 16
C133 AP32 40fr gold & multi 35 16

Christmas 1972.

Nos. C129-C131 Surcharged with New Value, Two Bars and Names of Athletes.

1972, Dec. 5 **Engr.** ***Perf. 13***
C134 AP58 40fr on 30fr *(Morelon)* 35 20
C135 AP58 120fr on 100fr *(Keino)* 1.00 50
C136 AP58 170fr on 140fr *(Spitz)* 1.50 80

Gold medal winners in 20th Olympic Games: Daniel Morelon, France, Bicycling (C134); Kipchoge Keino, Kenya, steeplechase (C135); Mark Spitz, USA, swimming (C136).

Globe with Space Orbits, Simulated Stamps — AP59

1973, Feb. 20 **Photo.** ***Perf. 13***
C137 AP59 100fr multi 80 42
a. Souv. sheet of 4, perf. 12x12½ 3.75 3.75

PHILEXGABON 1973, Phil. Exhib., Libreville, Feb. 19-26. No. C137a exists imperf.

DC10-30 "Libreville" over Libreville Airport — AP60

1973, Mar. 19 **Typo.** ***Perf. 13***
C138 AP60 40fr blue & multi 35 18

Kinguele Hydroelectric Station — AP61

Design: 40c, Kinguele Dam.

1973, June 19 **Engr.** ***Perf. 13***
C139 AP61 30fr sl grn & dk ol 20 16
C140 AP61 40fr sl grn, dk ol & bl 25 20
a. Strip of 2, #C139-C140 + label 50 50

Hydroelectric installations at Kinguele.

M'Bigou Stone Sculpture, Woman's Head — AP62

Design: 200fr, Sculpture, man's head.

1973, July 5
C141 AP62 100fr blk, bl & grn 80 55
C142 AP62 200fr grn, sep & sl grn 1.60 1.00

No. C116 Surcharged with New Value, 2 Bars, and Overprinted in Ultramarine: "SECHERESSE SOLIDARITE AFRICAINE"

1973, Aug. 16 **Photo.** ***Perf. 12½***
C143 AP52 100fr on 50fr multi 80 50

African solidarity in drought emergency.

Astronauts and Lunar Rover on Moon — AP63

1973, Sept. 6 **Engr.** ***Perf. 13***
C144 AP63 500fr multi 2.75 1.75

Apollo 17 US moon mission, Dec. 7-19, 1973.

Presidents Houphouet Boigny (Ivory Coast) and De Gaulle — AP64

1974, Apr. 30 **Engr.** ***Perf. 13***
C145 AP64 40fr rose lil & ind 22 15

30th anniv. of the Conf. of Brazzaville.

Painting Type of 1968

Impressionist Paintings: 40fr, Pleasure Boats, by Claude Monet (horiz.). 50fr, Ballet Dancer, by Edgar Degas. 130fr, Young Girl with Flowers, by Auguste Renoir.

1974, June 11 **Photo.** ***Perf. 13***
C146 AP32 40fr gold & multi 22 15
C147 AP32 50fr gold & multi 25 16
C148 AP32 130fr gold & multi 70 40

Astronaut on Moon, Eagle and Emblems — AP65

1974, July 20 **Engr.** ***Perf. 13***
C149 AP65 200fr multi 1.10 70

First men on the moon, 5th anniversary.

UPU Emblem, Letters, Pigeon AP66

UPU cent.: 300fr, UPU emblem, letters, pigeons (diff.).

1974, Oct. 9 **Engr.** ***Perf. 13***
C150 AP66 150fr lt bl & Prus bl 75 45
C151 AP66 300fr org & cl 1.50 80

Space Docking, US and USSR Crafts AP67

1974, Oct. 23 **Engr.** ***Perf. 13***
C152 AP67 1000fr grn, red & sl 5.50 3.50

Russo-American space cooperation.
For overprint see No. C169.

Soccer and Games Emblem — AP68

Designs: Soccer actions.

1974, Oct. 25
C153 AP68 40fr grn, red & brn 20 15
C154 AP68 65fr red, brn & grn 30 18
C155 AP68 100fr grn, red & brn 50 30
a. Souv. sheet of 3, #C153-C155 + 3 labels 1.10 1.10

World Cup Soccer Championship, Munich, June 13-July 7.

UDEAC Issue

Presidents and Flags of Cameroun, CAR, Gabon and Congo — AP68a

1974, Dec. 8 **Photo.** ***Perf. 13***
C156 AP68a 100fr gold & multi 60 38

Annunciation, Tapestry, 15th Century — AP69

Christmas: 40fr, Visitation from 15th century tapestry, Notre Dame de Beaune (vert.).

1974, Dec. 11
C157 AP69 40fr gold & multi 25 16
C158 AP69 50fr gold & multi 35 20

Dr. Schweitzer and Lambarene Hospital — AP70

1975, Jan. 14 **Engr.** ***Perf. 13***
C159 AP70 500fr multi 2.50 1.75

Dr. Albert Schweitzer (1875-1965), medical missionary, birth centenary.

Crucifixion, by Bellini — AP71

Paintings: 150fr, Resurrection, Burgundian School, c. 1500.

1975, Apr. 8 **Photo.** ***Perf. 13½***
Size: 26x45mm
C160 AP71 140fr gold & multi 90 50
Size: 36x48mm
Perf. 13
C161 AP71 150fr gold & multi 1.00 50

Easter 1975.

Marc Seguin Locomotive, 1829 — AP72

Locomotives: 25fr, The Iron Duke, 1847. 40fr, Thomas Rogers, 1895. 50fr, The Soviet 272, 1934.

1975, Apr. 8 Engr. *Perf. 13*

C162 AP72 20fr multi 15 15
C163 AP72 25fr multi 15 15
C164 AP72 40fr multi 22 15
C165 AP72 50fr lil & multi 25 16
Set value 47

Swimming Pool, Montreal Olympic Games' Emblem — AP73

Designs: 150fr, Boxing ring and emblem. 300fr, Stadium, aerial view, and emblem.

1975, Sept. 30 Litho. *Perf. 13x12½*

C166 AP73 100fr multi 40 25
C167 AP73 150fr multi 60 40
C168 AP73 300fr multi 1.20 85
a. Min. sheet of 3, #C166-C168 2.25 2.25

Pre-Olympic Year 1975.

No. C152 Surcharged in Violet Blue: "JONCTION / 17 Juillet 1975"

1975, Oct. 20 Engr. *Perf. 13*

C169 AP67 1000fr multi 5.50 3.75

Apollo-Soyuz link-up in space, July 17, 1975.

Annunciation, by Maurice Denis — AP74

Painting: 50fr, Virgin and Child with Two Saints, by Fra Filippo Lippi.

1975, Dec. 9 Photo. *Perf. 13*

C170 AP74 40fr gold & multi 25 16
C171 AP74 50fr gold & multi 35 20

Christmas 1975.

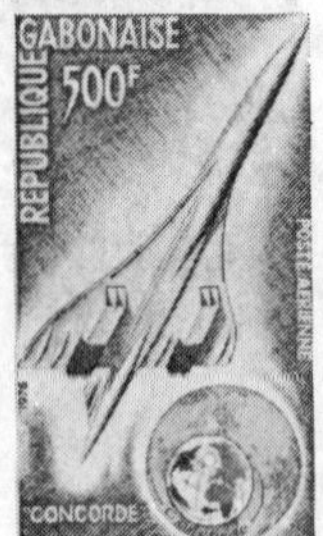

Concorde and Globe — AP75

1975, Dec. 29 Engr. *Perf. 13*

C172 AP75 500fr bl, vio bl & red 2.50 1.90

For overprint see No. C198.

No. C172 Surcharged

= 1000F
21 Janv. 1976
1er Vol
Commercial de
CONCORDE

1976, Jan. 21

C173 AP75 1000fr on 500fr 5.50 3.75

Nos. C172-C173 for the 1st commercial flight of supersonic jet Concorde from Paris to Rio, Jan. 21.

Slalom and Olympic Games Emblem — AP76

Design: 250fr, Speed skating and Winter Olympic Games emblem.

1976, Apr. 22 Engr. *Perf. 13*

C174 AP76 100fr blk, bl & red 40 30
C175 AP76 250fr blk, bl & red 1.00 70
a. Souvenir sheet 1.50 1.50

12th Winter Olympic Games, Innsbruck, Austria, Feb. 4-15. No. C175a contains 100fr and 250fr stamps in continuous design with additional inscription and skier between, but without perforations between the design elements.

Size of perforated area: 125x27mm.; size of sheet: 169x90mm.

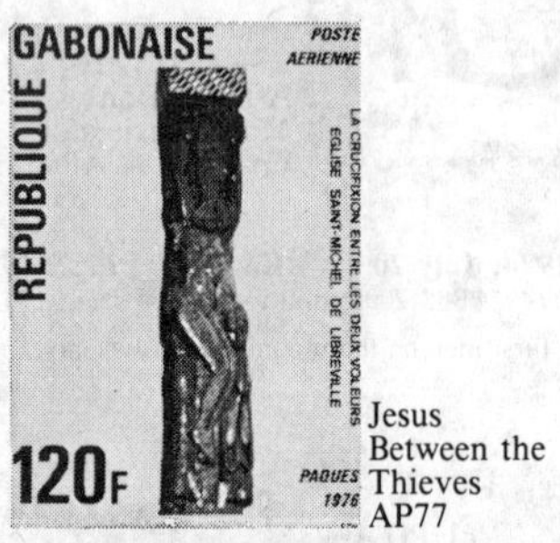

Jesus Between the Thieves AP77

Design: 130fr, St. Thomas putting finger into wounds of Jesus. Both designs after wood carvings in Church of St. Michael, Libreville.

1976, Apr. 28 Litho. *Perf. 12½x13*

C176 AP77 120fr multi 65 42
C177 AP77 130fr multi 70 50

Easter 1976. See #C188-C189, C220-C221.

Boston Tea Party — AP78

Designs: 150fr, Battle of New York. 200fr, Demolition of statue of George III.

1976, May 3 Engr. *Perf. 13*

C178 AP78 100fr multi 55 40
C179 AP78 150fr multi 80 55
C180 AP78 200fr multi 1.10 65
a. Triptych (Nos. C178-C180) +2 labels 2.75 2.25

American Bicentennial. Sheets of 5 triptychs with 10 Prussian blue labels showing Washington and Jefferson.

Nos. C178-C180 Overprinted: "4 JUILLET 1976"

1976, July 4 Engr. *Perf. 13*

C181 AP78 100fr multi 55 40
C182 AP78 150fr multi 80 55
C183 AP78 200fr multi 1.10 65
a. Triptych (Nos. C181-C183) +2 labels 2.75 2.25

Independence Day.

Running — AP79

Designs (Olympic Rings and): 200fr, Soccer. 260fr, High jump.

1976, July 27 Litho. *Perf. 12½*

C184 AP79 100fr multi 40 30
C185 AP79 200fr multi 80 50
C186 AP79 260fr multi 1.00 70
a. Souv. sheet of 3, #C184-C186, perf. 13 2.25 2.25

21st Olympic Games, Montreal, Canada, July 17-Aug. 1.

Presidents Giscard d'Estaing and Bongo — AP80

1976, Aug. 5 Photo. *Perf. 13*

C187 AP80 60fr bl & multi 35 22

Visit of Pres. Valèrie Giscard d'Estaing of France.

Sculpture Type of 1976

Christmas: 50fr, Presentation at the Temple. 60fr, Nativity. Designs after wood Carvings in Church of St. Michael, Libreville.

1976, Dec. 6 Litho. *Perf. 12½x13*

C188 AP77 50fr multi 25 16
C189 AP77 60fr multi 35 22

Oklo Fossil Reactor Station — AP81

1976, Dec. 15 Litho. *Perf. 13*

C190 AP81 60fr red & multi 35 22

The Last Supper, by Juste de Gand — AP82

Painting: 100fr, The Deposition, by Nicolas Poussin.

1977, Mar. 25 Litho. *Perf. 12½*

C191 AP82 50fr gold & multi 25 20
C192 AP82 100fr gold & multi 55 40

Easter 1977.

Air Gabon Plane and Insigne — AP83

1977, June 3 Litho. *Perf. 12½*

C193 AP83 60fr multi 35 22

Air Gabon's first intercontinental route.

Beethoven, Piano and Score — AP84

1977, June 15 Engr. *Perf. 13*

C194 AP84 260fr slate 1.40 90

Ludwig van Beethoven (1770-1827).

Lindbergh and Spirit of St. Louis — AP85

1977, Sept. 13 Engr. *Perf. 13*

C195 AP85 500fr multi 2.50 1.60

Charles A. Lindbergh's solo transatlantic flight from NY to Paris, 50th anniv.

Soccer — AP86

1977, Oct. 18 Photo. *Perf. 13x12½*

C196 AP86 250fr multi 1.40 90

Elimination games, World Soccer Cup, Buenos Aires, 1978.

Viking on Mars AP87

1977, Nov. 17 Engr. *Perf. 13*

C197 AP87 1000fr multi 5.50 2.75

Viking, U.S. space probe.

No. C172 Overprinted: "PARIS NEW-YORK / PREMIER VOL / 22.11.77"

1977, Nov. 22 Engr. *Perf. 13*

C198 AP75 500fr multi 2.75 2.00

Concorde, first commercial flight, Paris to New York.

Lion Hunt, by Rubens — AP88

Rubens Paintings: 80fr, Hippopotamus Hunt. 200fr, Head of Black Man (vert.).

1977, Nov. 24 Litho. *Perf. 13*

C199	AP88	60fr gold & multi	35	22
C200	AP88	80fr gold & multi	42	35
C201	AP88	200fr gold & multi	1.10	80
a.		Souv. sheet of 3, #C199-C201	1.90	1.90

Peter Paul Rubens (1577-1640).

Adoration of the Kings, by Rubens — AP89

Design: 80fr, Flight into Egypt, by Rubens.

1977, Dec. 15 Litho. *Perf. 12½*

C202	AP89	60fr gold & multi	35	22
C203	AP89	800fr gold & multi	42	35

Christmas 1977; 400th birth anniversary of Peter Paul Rubens (1577-1640).

Paul Gauguin, Self-Portrait AP90

Design: 150fr, Flowers in vase and Maori statuette.

1978, Feb. 8 Litho. *Perf. 12½x12*

C204	AP90	150fr multi	80	40
C205	AP90	300fr multi	1.60	80

Paul Gauguin (1848-1903), French painter, 75th death anniversary.

Pres. Bongo, Map of Gabon, Plane and Train AP91

Lithographed; Gold Embossed

1978, Mar. 12 *Perf. 12½*

C206	AP91	500fr multi	2.50	1.40

10th anniversary of national renewal.

Soccer and Argentina '78 Emblem — AP92

Designs (Argentina '78 Emblem and): 120fr, Three soccer players. 200fr, Jules Rimet Cup (vert.).

1978, July 18 Engr. *Perf. 13*

C207	AP92	100fr red, grn & brn	40	20
C208	AP92	120fr grn, red & brn	50	30
C209	AP92	200fr brn & red	80	40
a.		Min. sheet of 3, #C207-C209	1.75	1.75

11th World Cup Soccer Championship, Argentina, June 1-25.

Nos. C207-C209a Overprinted in Ultramarine or Black:
a. ARGENTINE / HOLLANDE / 3-1
b. BRESIL / ITALIE / 2-1
c. CHAMPION / DU MONDE 1978 / ARGENTINE

1978, July 21 Engr. *Perf. 13*

C210	AP92(a)	100fr multi	55	25
C211	AP92(b)	120fr multi	65	35
C212	AP92(c)	200fr multi	1.10	55
a.		Min. sheet of 3 (Bk)	2.50	2.50

Argentina's World Cup victory.

Albrecht Dürer (age 13), Self-portrait AP93

Design: 250fr, Lucas de Leyde, by Dürer.

1978, Sept. 15 Engr. *Perf. 13*

C213	AP93	100fr red brn & sl	55	25
C214	AP93	250fr blk & red brn	1.40	65

Dürer (1474-1528), German painter.

Philexafrique II-Essen Issue
Common Design Types

Designs: No. C215, Gorilla and Gabon No. 280. No. C216, Stork and Saxony No. 1.

1978, Nov. 1 Litho. *Perf. 13x12½*

C215	CD138	100fr multi	55	25
C216	CD139	100fr multi	55	25

Nos. C215-C216 printed se-tenant.

Wright Brothers and Flyer AP94

1978, Dec. 19 Engr. *Perf. 13*

C217	AP94	380fr multi	2.00	1.00

75th anniversary of 1st powered flight.

Pope John Paul II AP95

Design: 200fr, Popes Paul VI and John Paul I, St. Peter's Basilica and Square (horiz.).

1979, Jan. 24 Litho. *Perf. 12½*

C218	AP95	100fr multi	55	25
C219	AP95	200fr multi	1.10	55

Sculpture Type of 1976

Easter: 100fr, Disciples recognizing Jesus in the breaking of the bread. 150fr, Jesus appearing to Mary Magdalene. Designs after wood carvings in Church of St. Michael, Libreville.

1979, Apr. 10 Litho. *Perf. 12½x13*

C220	AP77	100fr multi	65	35
C221	AP77	150fr multi	1.00	50

Capt. Cook and Ships AP96

1979, July 10 Engr. *Perf. 13*

C222	AP96	500fr multi	3.50	1.60

Capt. James Cook (1728-1779), explorer, death bicentenary.

Flags and Map of England and France, Bleriot, Bleriot XI — AP97

Aviation Retrospect: 1000fr, Astronauts walking on moon (gold embossed inset).

Perf. 12½x12, 12

1979, Aug. 8 Litho.

C223	AP97	250fr multi	1.60	80
C224	AP97	1000fr multi	6.50	3.50

1st flight over English Channel, 70th anniv.; Apollo 11 moon landing, 10th anniv.

Rotary Emblem, Map of Africa, Head — AP98

Eugene Jamot, Tsetse Fly — AP99

1979, Sept. 25 Photo. *Perf. 13*

C225	AP98	80fr multi	55	25

Rotary International, 75th anniversary.

1979, Nov. 23 Engr. *Perf. 13*

C226	AP99	300fr multi	2.00	1.00

Eugene Jamot (1879-1937), discoverer of sleeping sickness cure.

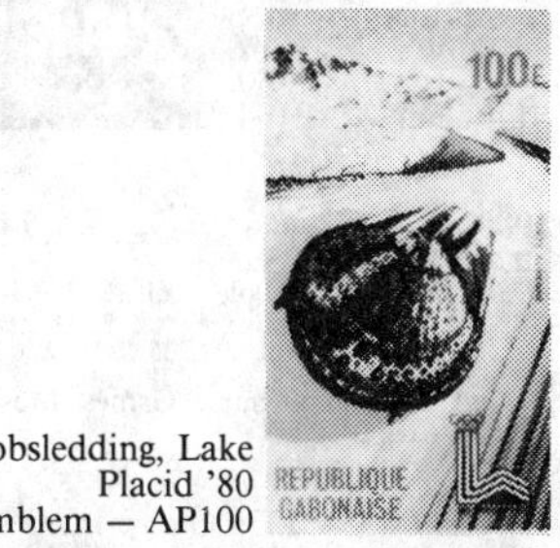
Bobsledding, Lake Placid '80 Emblem — AP100

1980, Feb. 25 Litho. *Perf. 12½*

C227	AP100	100fr shown	60	35
C228	AP100	200fr Ski jump	1.40	65
a.		Souv. sheet of 2, #C227-C228	2.00	1.00

13th Winter Olympic Games, Lake Placid, NY, Feb. 12-24.

Jean Ingres AP101

1980, May 14 Engr. *Perf. 13*

C229	AP101	100fr shown	65	35
C230	AP101	200fr Jacques Offenbach	1.40	65
C231	AP101	360fr Gustave Flaubert	2.25	1.20

12th World Telecommunications Day — AP102

1980, May 17 Litho. *Perf. 12½*

C232	AP102	80fr multi	55	25

Costes, Bellonte and Plane — AP103

Design: 1000fr, Mermoz, sea plane.

1980, July 16 **Engr.** ***Perf. 13***

C233 AP103 165fr multi 1.10 55
C234 AP103 1000fr multi 6.50 3.50

1st North Atlantic crossing, 50th anniv.; 1st South Atlantic air mail service, 50th anniv.

Running, Moscow '80 Emblem — AP104

1980, July 25 **Litho.**

C235 AP104 50fr shown 35 16
C236 AP104 100fr Pole vault 65 35
C237 AP104 250fr Boxing 1.50 80
a. Souv. sheet of 3, #C235-C237 2.50 1.40

22nd Summer Olympic Games, Moscow, July 19-Aug. 3.

Nos. C235-C237a Overprinted in Red, Brown, Ultramarine or Black

50fr: YIFTER (Eth.) / NYAMBUI (Tanz.) / MAANINKA (Finl.) / 5000 Metres

100fr: KOZIAKIEWICZ (Pol.) / (record du monde) / VOLKOV (Urss) et / SLUSARSKI (Pol.)

250fr: WELTERS / ALDAMA (Cuba) / MUGABI (Oug.) / KRUBER (Rda) / et SZCZERDA (Pol.)

1980, Sept. 25 **Litho.** ***Perf. 13***

C238 AP104 50fr (R, vert. & horiz.) 35 16
C239 AP104 100fr (Br) 65 35
C240 AP104 250fr (U) 1.50 80
a. Souv. sheet of 3 (Blk) 2.50 1.40

Pres. Charles de Gaulle AP105

1980, Nov. 9 **Photo.** ***Perf. 13***

C241 AP105 100fr shown 60 35
C242 AP105 200fr Pres. & Mrs. de Gaulle 1.40 65
a. Souv. sheet of 2, #C241-C242 2.00 1.00

Pres. Charles de Gaulle (1890-1970), 10th anniversary of death.

Soccer Players — AP106

1981, Feb. 19 **Litho.** ***Perf. 13***

C243 AP106 60fr shown 40 20
C244 AP106 190fr Soccer player, diff. 1.40 65

ESPANA '82 World Cup Soccer Championship.

200th Anniversary of Discovery of Uranus by William Herschel (1738-1822) AP107

Spacecraft and Astronauts: 250fr, Yuri Gagarin. 500fr, Alan B. Shepard.

1981, Mar. 26 **Litho.** ***Perf. 13***

C245 AP107 150fr multi 1.00 50
C246 AP107 250fr multi 1.60 80
C247 AP107 500fr multi 3.50 1.60
a. Souv. sheet of 3, #C245-C247, perf. 12½ 6.25 3.25

Map of Africa and Emblems AP108

1981, June 1 **Litho.** ***Perf. 12½***

C248 AP108 100fr multi 65 35

Electric Power Distribution Union, 7th Congress, Libreville, June 1-5.

D-51 Steam Locomotive, Japan, and SNCF Turbotrain TGV-001, France — AP109

200th Birth Anniv. of George Stephenson: 100fr, B&O Mallet 7100, US, Prussian T3 steam locomotive. 350fr, Stephenson and his Rocket, BB Alsthom electric locomotive, Central Africa.

1981, June 4 **Engr.** ***Perf. 13***

C249 AP109 75fr multi 50 25
C250 AP109 100fr multi 65 35
C251 AP109 350fr multi 2.25 1.10
a. Souvenir sheet of 3 3.50 1.90

No. C251a contains Nos. C249-C251 in changed colors.

No. C251a Overprinted in 1 line across 3 stamps: 26 fevrier 1981-Record du monde de vitesse 380 km a l'heure
Souvenir Sheet

1981, June 13 **Engr.** ***Perf. 13***

C252 AP109 Sheet of 3 3.50 1.90

New world railroad speed record, set Feb. 26.

Intl. Letter Writing Week, Oct. 9-16 — AP110

1981, Oct. 9 **Photo.** ***Perf. 13***

C253 AP110 200fr multi 1.40 65

Still Life with a Mandolin, by George Braque (1882-1963) — AP111

Design: 350fr, Boy Blowing Bubbles, by Edouard Manet (1832-1883) (vert.).

Perf. 13x12½, 12½x13

1982, Oct. 5 **Litho.**

C254 AP111 300fr multi 2.00 1.00
C255 AP111 350fr multi 2.25 1.20

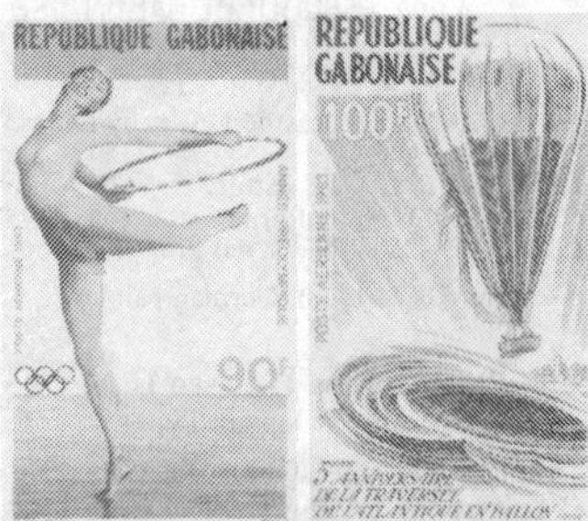

Pre-olympic Year AP112

Manned Flight Bicentenary AP113

1983, Feb. 16 **Litho.** ***Perf. 13***

C256 AP112 90fr Gymnast 45 22
C257 AP112 350fr Wind surfing 1.75 90

1983, June 1 **Engr.** ***Perf. 13***

Balloons.

C258 AP113 100fr Transatlantic flight, 5th anniv. 65 35
C259 AP113 125fr Montgolfiere, 1783 80 40
C260 AP113 350fr Rozier's balloon, 1783 2.25 1.20

Lady with Unicorn, by Raphael (1483-1520) AP114

1983, June 19 ***Perf. 12½x13***

C261 AP114 1000fr multi 6.50 3.50

1984 Winter Olympics — AP115

1984, Feb. 8 **Litho.** ***Perf. 12½***

C262 AP115 125fr Hockey 40 20
C263 AP115 350fr Figure skaters 1.10 55

See No. C268.

Paris-Libreville-Paris Air Race, Mar. 15-28 — AP116

1984, Mar. 15 **Litho.** ***Perf. 13x12½***

C264 AP116 500fr Planes, emblem 1.60 80

The Racetrack, by Edgar Degas — AP117

1984, Mar. 21 ***Perf. 13***

C265 AP117 500fr multi 1.60 80

1984 Summer Olympics AP118

Dr. Albert Schweitzer (1875-1965) AP119

1984, May 31 Litho. *Perf. 12½*

C266 AP118 90fr Basketball 28 15
C267 AP118 125fr Running 40 20

Souvenir Sheet
Nos. C262-C263, C266-C267 with Added Inscriptions

1984, Oct. 3 Litho. *Perf. 13*

C268 Sheet of 4 2.00 1.00
- ***a.*** AP118 90fr MEDAILLE D'OR: U.S.A. 25 15
- ***b.*** AP118 125fr MEDAILLE D'OR: KORIR 35 20
- ***c.*** AP115 125fr Hockey sur glace: U.R.S.S. 35 20
- ***d.*** AP115 350fr Danse couple: J. Torvill-C. Dean 1.00 50

1985, Sept. 5 Litho. *Perf. 12½*

C269 AP119 350fr multi 1.00 50

Flags of Gabon, UN AP120

1985, Sept. 20

C270 AP120 225fr multi 65 35

Admission of Gabon to UN, 25th anniv.

Central Post Office, Libreville, UPU and Gabon Postal Emblems — AP121

1985, Oct. 9

C271 AP121 300fr multi 1.00 50

World Post Day.

UN, 40th Anniv. — AP122

1985, Oct. 24 Litho. *Perf. 12½*

C272 AP122 350fr multi 1.20 55

PHILEXAFRICA '85, Lome, Togo — AP123

1985, Oct. 30 *Perf. 13*

C273 AP123 100fr Scout campsite 35 16
C274 AP123 150fr Telecommunications, transportation 55 25

Nos. C273-C274 printed se-tenant with center labels picturing a map of Africa or UAPT emblem.

Gabon's Gift to the UN — AP124

Design: Mother and Child, carved wood statue, and UN emblem.

1986, Mar. 15 Litho. *Perf. 13½*

C275 AP124 350fr multi 1.75 85

Lastour Arriving in Gabon — AP125

1986, Mar. 25 Litho. *Perf. 12½*

C276 AP125 100fr multi 55 28

Lastoursville, cent.

World Telecommunications Day — AP126

1986, May 17 *Perf. 13½*

C277 AP126 300fr multi 1.65 82

1986 World Cup Soccer Championships, Mexico — AP127

1986, May 31 *Perf. 12½*

C278 AP127 100fr Goal 55 28
C279 AP127 150fr Dribbling, religious carving 82 40
C280 AP127 250fr Players, map, soccer cup 1.40 70
C281 AP127 350fr Stadium, flags 1.90 95
- ***a.*** Souv. sheet of 4, #C278-C281 4.70 2.35

For overprints see Nos. C283-C286.

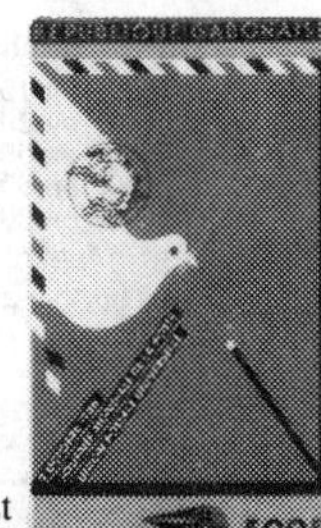

World Post Day — AP128

1986, Oct. 9 Litho. *Perf. 12½*

C282 AP128 500fr multi 2.75 1.40

Nos. C278-C281 Ovptd. "ARGENTINA 3 -R.F.A 2" in One or Two Lines in Red

1986, Oct. 23 Litho. *Perf. 12½*

C283 AP127 100fr multi 55 28
C284 AP127 150fr multi 82 40
C285 AP127 250fr multi 1.40 70
C286 AP127 350fr multi 1.90 95

The Renewal, 19th Anniv. AP129

1987, Mar. 12 Litho. *Perf. 13*

C287 AP129 500fr multi 2.75 1.40

Konrad Adenauer (1876-1967), West German Chancellor AP130

1987, Apr. 15 *Perf. 12x12½*

C288 AP130 300fr mar, chlky bl & blk 1.65 85

Schweitzer and Medical Settlement — AP131

1988, Apr. 17 Litho. *Perf. 12½x12*

C289 AP131 500fr multi 3.50 1.75

Dr. Albert Schweitzer (1875-1965), missionary physician and founder of the hospital and medical settlement, Lambarene, Gabon.

Port Gentil Refinery, 20th Anniv. — AP132

1988, Sept. 1 Litho. *Perf. 13½*

C290 AP132 350fr multi 2.35 1.20

De Gaulle's Call for French Resistance, 50th Anniv. — AP133

1990, June 18 Litho. *Perf. 13*

C291 AP133 500fr multicolored 3.50 1.75

Port of Marseilles by J. B. Jongkind (1819-1891) — AP134

1991, Feb. 9 Litho. *Perf. 13*

C292 AP134 500fr multicolored 4.40 2.20

AIR POST SEMI-POSTAL STAMPS

Catalogue values for unused stamps in this section are for Never Hinged items.

Ramses II Paying Homage to Four Gods, Wadi-es-Sabua — SPAP1

Unwmk.

1964, Mar. 9 Engr. *Perf. 13*

CB1 SPAP1 10fr + 5fr dk bl & bis brn 38 38
CB2 SPAP1 25fr + 5fr dk car rose & vio bl 50 50
CB3 SPAP1 50fr + 5fr sl grn & cl 65 65

UNESCO world campaign to save historic monuments in Nubia.

POSTAGE DUE STAMPS

GABON

Postage Due Stamps of France Overprinted

A. E. F.

1928 Unwmk. *Perf. 14x13½*

J1 D2 5c light blue 15 15
J2 D2 10c gray brn 15 15
J3 D2 20c ol grn 32 32
J4 D2 25c brt rose 55 55
J5 D2 30c lt red 60 60
J6 D2 45c bl grn 65 65
J7 D2 50c brn vio 70 70
J8 D2 60c yel brn 90 90
J9 D2 1fr red brn 90 90
J10 D2 2fr org red 1.10 1.10
J11 D2 3fr brt vio 1.40 1.40
Nos. J1-J11 (11) 7.42 7.42

Chief Makoko, de Brazza's Aide — D3

Count Savorgnan de Brazza — D4

1930 Typo. *Perf. 13½x14*

J12 D3 5c dk bl & ol 55 55
J13 D3 10c dk red & brn 65 65
J14 D3 20c grn & brn 80 80
J15 D3 25c lt bl & brn 80 80
J16 D3 30c bis brn & Prus bl 1.00 1.00
J17 D3 45c Prus bl & ol 1.20 1.20
J18 D3 50c red vio & brn 1.65 1.65
J19 D3 60c gray lil & bl blk 2.75 2.75

J20	D4	1fr bis brn & bl blk	3.75	3.75
J21	D4	2fr vio & brn	5.50	5.50
J22	D4	3fr dp red & brn	6.50	6.50
		Nos. J12-J22 (11)	25.15	25.15

Fang Woman — D5

1932 Photo. *Perf. 13x13½*

J23	D5	5c dk bl, *bl*	45	45
J24	D5	10c red brn	70	70
J25	D5	20c chocolate	1.25	1.25
J26	D5	25c yel grn, *bl*	90	90
J27	D5	30c car rose	1.25	1.25
J28	D5	45c red org, *yel*	4.25	4.25
J29	D5	50c dk vio	1.25	1.25
J30	D5	60c dl bl	1.50	1.50
J31	D5	1fr blk, *red org*	4.25	4.25
J32	D5	2fr dk grn	6.00	6.00
J33	D5	3fr rose lake	5.25	5.25
		Nos. J23-J33 (11)	27.05	27.05

Catalogue values for unused stamps in this section, from this point to the end of the section, are for Never Hinged items.

Republic

Pineapple — D6

Unwmk.

1962, Dec. 10 Engr. *Perf. 11*

J34	D6	50c shown	15	15
J35	D6	50c Mangoes	15	15
J36	D6	1fr Avocados	15	15
J37	D6	1fr Tangerines	15	15
J38	D6	2fr Coconuts	15	15
J39	D6	2fr Grapefruit	15	15
J40	D6	5fr Oranges	30	30
J41	D6	5fr Papaya	30	30
J42	D6	10fr Breadfruit	65	65
J43	D6	10fr Guavas	65	65
J44	D6	25fr Lemons	75	75
J45	D6	25fr Bananas	75	75
		Nos. J34-J45 (12)	4.30	4.30

Stamps of the same denomination are printed together in the sheet, se-tenant at the base.

Charaxes Candiope — D7

Butterflies: 10fr, Charaxes ameliae. 25fr, Cyrestis camillus. 50fr, Charaxes castor. 100fr, Pseudacrea boisduvali.

1978, July 4 Litho. *Perf. 13*

J46	D7	5fr multi	15	15
J47	D7	10fr multi	15	15
J48	D7	25fr multi	15	15
J49	D7	50fr multi	30	18
J50	D7	100fr multi	60	35
		Nos. J46-J50 (5)	1.35	
		Set value		80

OFFICIAL STAMPS

Catalogue values for unused stamps in this section are for Never Hinged items.

Map of Gabon — O1

Flag of Gabon — O2

Designs: 25fr, 30fr, Flag of Gabon. 50fr, 85fr, 100fr, 200fr, Coat of Arms.

1968 Unwmk. Photo. *Perf. 14*

O1	O1	1fr ol & multi	15	15
O2	O1	2fr multi	15	15
O3	O1	5fr lil & multi	15	15
O4	O1	10fr emer & multi	15	15
O5	O1	25fr brn & multi	28	15
O6	O1	30fr org & multi	30	15
O7	O1	50fr multi	50	18
O8	O1	85fr multi	90	32
O9	O1	100fr yel & multi	1.20	42
O10	O1	200fr gray & multi	2.25	1.00
		Nos. O1-O10 (10)	6.03	
		Set value		2.40

1971-84 Typo. *Perf. 13x14*

O11	O2	5fr multi ('81)	15	15
O12	O2	10fr multi	15	15
O13	O2	30fr multi ('78)	25	15
O14	O2	20fr multi ('81)	15	15
O15	O2	25fr multi ('84)	15	15
O16	O2	40fr multi ('72)	45	25
O17	O2	50fr multi ('76)	45	15
O18	O2	60fr multi ('77)	60	25
O19	O2	75fr multi ('81)	30	15
O20	O2	80fr multi ('77)	90	40
O21	O2	100fr multi ('78)	65	25
O22	O2	500fr multi ('78)	3.50	1.25
		Nos. O11-O22 (12)	7.70	
		Set value		3.00

GEORGIA

LOCATION — In the southern part of Russia, bordering on the Black Sea and occupying the entire western part of Trans-Caucasia
GOVT. — A Soviet Socialist Republic
AREA — 25,760 sq. mi. (1920)
POP. — 2,372,403 (1920)
CAPITAL — Tiflis

Georgia was formerly a province of the Russian Empire and later a part of the Transcaucasian Federation of Soviet Republics. Stamps of Georgia were replaced in 1923 by those of Transcaucasian Federated Republics.

100 Kopecks = 1 Ruble

Tiflis

A 6k local stamp, imperforate and embossed without color on white paper, was issued in November, 1857, at Tiflis by authority of the viceroy. The square design shows a coat of arms.

National Republic

St. George
A1 A2

Perf. 11½, Imperf.

1919 Litho. Unwmk.

12	A1	10k blue	18	20
13	A1	40k red org	18	20
a.		Tete beche pair	7.50	7.50
14	A1	50k emerald	18	20
15	A1	60k red	18	22
16	A1	70k claret	18	24
17	A2	1r org brn	18	24

Queen Thamar — A3

1920 *Perf. 11½, Imperf.*

18	A3	2r red brn	18	22
19	A3	3r gray bl	15	25
20	A3	5r orange	20	50

Nos. 12-20 with parts of design inverted, sideways or omitted are fraudulent varieties.

Overprints meaning "Day of the National Guard, 12, 12, 1920" (5 lines) and "Recognition of Independence, 27, 1, 1921" (4 lines) were applied, probably in Italy, to remainders taken by government officials who fled when Russian forces occupied Georgia.

"Constantinople" and new values were unofficially surcharged on stamps of 1919-20 by a consul in Turkey.

Soviet Socialist Republic

Soldier with Flag — A5

Peasant Sowing Grain — A6

Industry and Agriculture — A7

1922 Unwmk. *Perf. 11½*

26	A5	500r rose	1.75	1.90
27	A6	1000r bister brown	1.75	1.90
28	A7	2000r slate	3.00	3.25
29	A7	3000r brown	3.00	3.25
30	A7	5000r green	3.00	3.25
		Nos. 26-30 (5)	12.50	13.55

Nos. 26 to 30 exist imperforate but were not so issued. Value for set, $25.

Nos. 26-30 Handstamped with New Values in Violet

1923

36	A6	10,000r on 1000r	2.50	3.00
a.		Black surcharge	8.00	10.00
b.		20.000r on 1000r	200.00	
37	A7	15,000r on 2000r, blk surch.	4.75	5.50
a.		Violet surcharge	10.00	10.00
38	A5	20,000r on 500r	4.00	5.50
a.		Black surcharge	4.75	3.75
39	A7	40,000r on 5000r	2.50	3.00
a.		Black surcharge	6.50	7.50
40	A7	80,000r on 3000r	4.00	5.50
a.		Black surcharge	6.50	7.50
		Nos. 36-40 (5)	17.75	22.50

There were two types of the handstamped surcharges, with the numerals 5½mm and 6½mm high. The impressions are often too indistinct to measure or even to distinguish the numerals.

Double and inverted surcharges exist, as is usual with handstamps.

Printed Surcharge in Black

43	A6	10,000r on 1000r	5.25	6.00
44	A7	15,000r on 2000r	3.50	3.75
45	A5	20,000r on 500r	1.50	1.90
46	A7	40,000r on 5000r	2.75	3.50
47	A7	80,000r on 3000r	3.25	3.75
		Nos. 43-47 (5)	16.25	18.90

Nos. 43, 45, 46 and 47 exist imperforate but were not so issued. Value $4 each.

Georgia stamps can be mounted in Scott's Soviet Republics Part 1 Album.

Russian Stamps of 1909-18 Handstamp Surcharged

Type I. Surcharge 20x5½mm.
Type II. Surcharge 22x7¼mm.

1923 *Perf. 14½x15*

48	A14	10,000r on 7k lt bl	40.00	40.00
49	A11	15,000r on 15k red brn & bl (I)	4.75	5.50
a.		Type II	4.75	5.50

Type I Surcharge Handstamped on Armenia No. 141

50	A11	15,000r on 5r on 15k red brn & bl	37.50	55.00
a.		Type II		

Russian Stamps and Types of 1909-18 Surcharged in Dark Blue or Black

200000
მან.

1923 *Perf. 11½, 14½x15*

51	A14	75,000r on 1k org	3.00	4.25
a.		Imperf.	100.00	125.00
52	A14	200,000r on 5k cl	3.50	4.75
53	A8	300,000r on 20k bl & car (Bk)	3.50	4.75
a.		Dark blue surcharge	140.00	160.00
54	A14	350,000r on 3k red	5.50	7.25
a.		Imperf.	6.00	7.25

Imperf

55	A14	700,000r on 2k grn	6.50	7.75
a.		Perf. 14½x15	27.50	32.50
		Nos. 51-55 (5)	22.00	28.75

SEMI-POSTAL STAMPS

SP1

SP2

SP3 SP4

Surcharge in Red or Black

1922 Unwmk. *Perf. 11½*

B1	SP1	1000r on 50r vio (R)	30	50
B2	SP2	3000r on 100r brn red	30	50
B3	SP3	5000r on 250r gray grn	30	50
B4	SP4	10,000r on 25r bl (R)	30	50

Nos. B1-B4 exist imperf. but were not so issued. Value about twice that of perf.

GERMAN E. AFRICA

LOCATION — In East Africa, bordering on the Indian Ocean.
GOVT. — Former German Colony
AREA — 384,180 sq. mi.
POP. — 7,680,132 (1913)
CAPITAL — Dar-es Salaam

Following World War I, the greater part of this German Colonial possession was mandated to Great Britain. The British ceded to the Belgians the provinces of Ruanda and Urundi. The Kionga triangle was awarded to the Portuguese and became part of the Mozambique Colony. The remaining area became the British Mandated Territory of Tanganyika.

64 Pesa = 1 Rupee
100 Heller = 1 Rupee (1905)
100 Centimes = 1 Franc (1916)

Numeral of Value — A1   German Imperial Eagle — A2

Stamps of Germany Surcharged in Black

1893 Unwmk. *Perf. 13½x14½*

1	A1	2pes on 3pf brown	40.00	60.00
2	A1	3pes on 5pf green	45.00	60.00
3	A2	5pes on 10pf car	30.00	24.00
4	A2	10pes on 20pf ultra	22.50	17.50
5	A2	25pes on 50pf red brn	40.00	37.50

The surcharge is 14¼, 15¼ or 16¼mm on #2-3; 15¼ or 16¾mm on #4; 16¾ or 17½mm on #5.

A3   A4

Black Surcharge

1896

6	A3	2pes on 3pf dk brn	2.00	*6.75*
a.		2pes on 3pf lt brn	27.50	45.00
b.		2pes on 3pf grysh brn	11.00	5.75
7	A3	3pes on 5pf grn	2.50	5.25
8	A4	5pes on 10pf car	2.50	4.25
9	A4	10pes on 20pf ultra	7.00	5.25
10	A4	25pes on 50pf red brn	25.00	27.50

Kaiser's Yacht "Hohenzollern"
A5   A6

1900 Typo. *Perf. 14*

11	A5	2p brown	3.50	1.65
12	A5	3p green	3.50	1.65
13	A5	5p carmine	3.75	1.90
14	A5	10p ultra	6.50	3.25
15	A5	15p org & blk, *sal*	6.50	4.50
16	A5	20p lake & blk	9.25	12.50
17	A5	25p pur & blk, *sal*	9.25	12.50
18	A5	40p lake & blk, *rose*	11.00	*22.50*

Engr.

Perf. 14½x14

19	A6	1r claret	22.50	*60.00*
20	A6	2r yel grn	11.00	*92.50*
21	A6	3r car & slate	70.00	*165.00*
		Nos. 11-21 (11)	156.75	

Value in Heller

1905 Typo. *Perf. 14*

22	A5	2½h brown	2.50	2.00
23	A5	4h green	7.25	3.75
24	A5	7½h carmine	7.25	1.00
25	A5	15h ultra	13.00	5.50
26	A5	20h org & blk, *yel*	11.00	17.50
27	A5	30h lake & blk	9.00	8.00
28	A5	45h pur & blk	17.00	40.00
29	A5	60h lake & blk, *rose*	24.00	*125.00*
		Nos. 22-29 (8)	91.00	

1905-16 Wmk. Lozenges (125)

31	A5	2½h brn ('06)	85	75
32	A5	4h grn ('06)	85	75
b.		Booklet pane of 4 + 2 labels	50.00	
c.		Booklet pane of 5 + label	*375.00*	
33	A5	7½h car ('06)	85	40
b.		Booklet pane of 4 + 2 labels	50.00	
c.		Booklet pane of 5 + label	*375.00*	
34	A5	15h ultra ('06)	2.00	90
35	A5	20h org & blk, *yel* ('11)	2.50	*12.00*
36	A5	30h lake & blk ('09)	2.75	*7.75*
37	A5	45h pur & blk ('06)	5.00	*50.00*
38	A5	60h lake & blk, *rose*	35.00	*200.00*
		Nos. 31-38 (8)	49.80	

Engr.

Perf. 14½x14

39	A6	1r red ('16)	7.25	*21,500.*
40	A6	2r yel grn	45.00	
41	A6	3r car & sl ('08)	22.50	*215.00*

No. 40 was never placed in use.
Forged cancellations are found on Nos. 35-39, 41.

OCCUPATION STAMPS

Issued under Belgian Occupation

Stamps of Belgian Congo, 1915, Handstamped "RUANDA" in Black or Blue

1916 Unwmk. *Perf. 13½ to 15*

N1	A29	5c grn & blk	13.00
N2	A30	10c car & blk	13.00
N3	A21	15c bl grn & blk	25.00
N4	A31	25c bl & blk	13.00
N5	A23	40c brn red & blk	13.00
N6	A24	50c brn lake & blk	14.00
N7	A25	1fr ol bis & blk	92.50
N8	A27	5fr ocher & blk	*1,500.*
		Nos. N1-N7 (7)	183.50

Stamps of Belgian Congo, 1915, Handstamped "URUNDI" in Black or Blue

N9	A29	5c grn & blk	13.00
N10	A30	10c car & blk	13.00
N11	A21	15c bl grn & blk	25.00
N12	A31	25c bl & blk	13.00
N13	A23	40c brn red & blk	13.00
N14	A24	50c brn lake & blk	14.00
N15	A25	1fr ol bis & blk	92.50
N16	A27	5fr ocher & blk	*1,500.*
		Nos. N9-N15 (7)	183.50

Stamps of Congo overprinted "Karema", "Kigoma" and "Tabora" were not officially authorized.

Nos. N1-N16 exist with forged overprint.

Stamps of Belgian Congo, 1915, Overprinted in Dark Blue

EST AFRICAIN ALLEMAND
OCCUPATION BELGE.

DUITSCH OOST AFRIKA
BELGISCHE BEZETTING.

1916 *Perf. 12½ to 15*

N17	A29	5c grn & blk	30	20
b.		Inverted overprint	72.50	35.00
N18	A30	10c car & blk	40	32
N19	A21	15c bl grn & blk	30	20
N20	A31	25c bl & blk	1.75	1.10
N21	A23	40c brn red & blk	5.00	4.00
N22	A24	50c brn lake & blk	5.50	3.50
N23	A25	1fr ol bis & blk	60	42
N24	A27	5fr ocher & blk	90	70
		Nos. N17-N24 (8)	14.75	10.44

Nos. N17-N18, N20-N22 Surcharged in Black or Red   **•10c**

1922

N25	A24	5c on 50c brn lake & blk	22	22
N26	A29	10c on 5c grn & blk (R)	30	22
N27	A23	25c on 40c brn red & blk (R)	2.00	90
N28	A30	30c on 10c car & blk	20	20
N29	A31	50c on 25c bl & blk (R)	25	20
		Nos. N25-N29 (5)	2.97	1.74

No. N25 has the surcharge at each side.

SEMI-POSTAL STAMPS

Issued under Belgian Occupation

Semi-Postal Stamps of Belgian Congo, 1918, Overprinted   **A. O.**

1918 Unwmk. *Perf. 14, 15*

NB1	A29	5c + 10c grn & bl	20	20
NB2	A30	10c + 15c car & bl	20	20
NB3	A21	15c + 20c bl grn & bl	20	20
NB4	A31	25c + 25c dp bl & pale bl	20	20
NB5	A23	40c + 40c brn red & bl	30	30
NB6	A24	50c + 50c brn lake & bl	30	30
NB7	A25	1fr + 1fr ol bis & bl	1.10	1.10
NB8	A27	5fr + 5fr ocher & bl	6.25	4.00
NB9	A28	10fr + 10fr grn & bl	50.00	50.00
		Nos. NB1-NB9 (9)	58.75	56.50

The letters "A.O." are the initials of "Afrique Orientale" (East Africa).

Stamps issued under British occupation are listed in Volume I.

GERMAN N. GUINEA

LOCATION — A group of islands in the west Pacific Ocean, including a part of New Guinea and adjacent islands of the Bismarck Archipelago.
GOVT. — A former German Protectorate
AREA — 93,000 sq. mi.
POP. — 601,427 (1913)
CAPITAL — Herbertshohe (later Kokopo)

The islands were occupied by Australian troops during World War I and renamed "New Britain." By covenant of the League of Nations they were made a mandated territory of Australia in 1920. The old name of "New Guinea" has since been restored. Postage stamps were issued under all regimes. For other listings see New Britain (1914-15), North West Pacific Islands (1915-22) and New Guinea in Vol. I.

100 Pfennig = 1 Mark

A1   A2

Stamps of Germany Overprinted in Black

1897-99 Unwmk. *Perf. 13½x14½*

1	A1	3pf brown	8.50	11.50
a.		3pf reddish brown ('99)	35.00	65.00
b.		3pf yellow brown ('99)	25.00	50.00
2	A1	5pf green	4.25	6.25
3	A2	10pf carmine	7.25	9.50
4	A2	20pf ultra	11.00	14.00
5	A2	25pf org ('98)	35.00	50.00
a.		Inverted overprint	*2,500.*	
6	A2	50pf red brown	35.00	45.00

Kaiser's Yacht "Hohenzollern"
A3   A4

1901 Typo. *Perf. 14*

7	A3	3pf brown	85	90
8	A3	5pf green	9.25	1.00
9	A3	10pf carmine	30.00	1.75
10	A3	20pf ultra	1.10	*2.00*
11	A3	25pf org & blk, *yel*	1.25	*15.00*
12	A3	30pf org & blk, *sal*	1.25	*22.50*
13	A3	40pf lake & blk	1.25	*24.00*
14	A3	50pf pur & blk, *sal*	1.65	*22.50*
15	A3	80pf lake & blk, *rose*	3.75	*22.50*

Engr.

Perf. 14½x14

16	A4	1m carmine	3.75	*45.00*
17	A4	2m blue	5.50	*60.00*
18	A4	3m blk vio	7.50	*135.00*
19	A4	5m slate & car	150.00	*400.00*
		Nos. 7-19 (13)	217.10	

Fake cancellations exist on Nos. 10-19.

A5   A6

Wmk. Lozenges (125)

1914-19 Typo. *Perf. 14*

20	A3	3pf brown ('19)	65
21	A5	5pf green	1.75
22	A5	10pf carmine	1.75

Engr.

Perf. 14½x14

23	A6	5m slate & car	16.00

Nos. 20 to 23 were never placed in use.
Nos. 21 to 23 have "NEUGUINEA" as one word without a hyphen.

GERMAN S.W. AFRICA

LOCATION — In southwest Africa, bordering on the South Atlantic.
GOVT. — A former German Colony
AREA — 322,450 sq. mi. (1913)
POP. — 94,372 (1913)
CAPITAL — Windhoek

The Colony was occupied by South African troops during World War I and in 1920 was mandated to the Union of South Africa by the League of Nations. See South-West Africa in Vol. I.

100 Pfennig = 1 Mark

A1   A2

Stamps of Germany Overprinted "Deutsch-Südwest-Afrika"

1897 Unwmk. *Perf. 13½x14½*

1	A1	3pf dk brn	6.50	12.00
a.		3pf yellow brown	45.00	
2	A1	5pf green	4.25	4.25
3	A2	10pf carmine	18.00	18.00
4	A2	20pf ultra	4.50	5.00
5	A2	25pf orange	275.00	
6	A2	50pf red brn	275.00	

Nos. 5 and 6 were prepared for issue but were not sent to the Colony.

Overprinted "Deutsch-Südwestafrika"

1899

7	A1	3pf dk brn	4.50	*30.00*
b.		3pf yellow brown	7.50	*9.00*
8	A1	5pf green	3.25	2.50
9	A2	10pf carmine	3.25	3.25
10	A2	20pf ultra	15.00	16.00
11	A2	25pf orange	400.00	500.00
12	A2	50pf red brn	13.00	13.00

Kaiser's Yacht "Hohenzollern"
A3   A4

1900 Typo. *Perf. 14*

13	A3	3pf brown	1.50	1.25
14	A3	5pf green	24.00	75
15	A3	10pf carmine	22.50	75
16	A3	20pf ultra	32.50	1.25
17	A3	25pf org & blk, *yel*	1.75	*5.00*
18	A3	30pf org & blk, *sal*	14.00	2.75
19	A3	40pf lake & blk	1.75	2.75
20	A3	50pf pur & blk, *sal*	1.75	2.25
21	A3	80pf lake & blk, *rose*	1.90	*6.50*

Engr.

Perf. 14½x14

22	A4	1m carmine	18.00	*30.00*
23	A4	2m blue	27.50	*37.50*
24	A4	3m blk vio	30.00	*45.00*
25	A4	5m slate & car	165.00	*135.00*
		Nos. 13-25 (13)	342.15	*270.75*

Wmk. Lozenges (125)

1906-19 Typo. *Perf. 14*

26	A3	3pf brn ('09)	85	80
27	A3	5pf green	85	65
b.		Bklt. pane of 6 (2 #27, 4 #28)	65.00	
c.		Booklet pane of 5 + label	300.00	
28	A3	10pf carmine	85	80
b.		Booklet pane of 5 + label	375.00	
29	A3	20pf ultra ('11)	85	*2.75*
30	A3	30pf org & blk, *buff* ('11)	4.75	*37.50*

Engr.

Perf. 14½x14

31	A4	1m car ('12)	4.75	*15.00*
32	A4	2m bl ('11)	4.75	*17.50*
33	A4	3m blk vio ('19)	9.50	
34	A4	5m slate & car	22.50	*150.00*
		Nos. 26-34 (9)	49.65	

No. 33 was never placed in use.

Forged cancellations are found on Nos. 30-32, 34.

GERMAN STATES

Watermarks

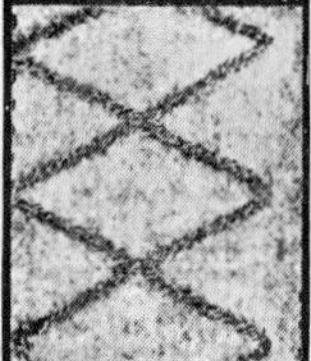

Wmk. 92- 17mm wide

Wmk. 93- 14mm wide

Wmk. 94- Horiz. Wavy Lines Wide Apart

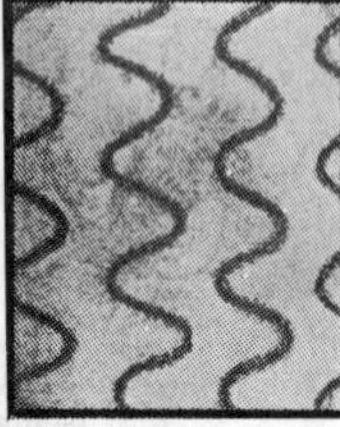

Wmk. 95v- Vert. Wavy Lines Close Together

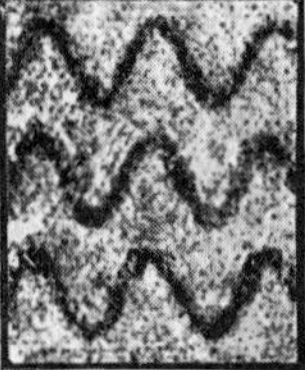

Wmk. 95h- Horiz. Wavy Lines Close Together

Wmk. 102- Post Horn

German South West Africa stamps can be mounted in Scott's Germany Part II Album.

Wmk. 116- Crosses and Circles

Wmk. 128- Wavy Lines

Wmk. 130- Wreath of Oak Leaves

Wmk. 148- Small Flowers

Wmk. 162- Laurel Wreath

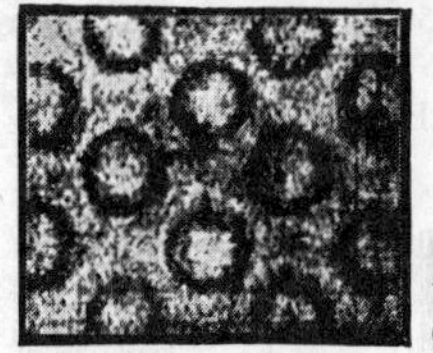

Wmk. 192- Circles

BADEN

LOCATION — In southwestern Germany
GOVT. — Former Grand Duchy
AREA — 5,817 sq. mi.
POP. — 1,432,000 (1864)
CAPITAL — (PRINCIPAL CITY) Karlsruhe

Baden was a member of the German Confederation. In 1870 it became part of the German Empire.

60 Kreuzer = 1 Gulden

Values for 1-9 unused are for copies without gum. Copies with gum sell for about twice as much. No. 10 and following numbers without gum sell for about half the prices.

Nos. 1-9 with margins all around and copies of Nos. 10-14 and 18 with all perforations intact sell considerably higher.

A1

1851-52 Unwmk. Typo. *Imperf.*

1	A1	1kr blk, *dk buff*	175.00	125.00
2	A1	3kr blk, *yellow*	90.00	13.00
3	A1	6kr blk, *yel grn*	400.00	27.50
4	A1	9kr blk, *lil rose*	60.00	14.00

Thin Paper (First Printing, 1851)

1a	A1	1kr blk, *buff*	575.00	625.00
2a	A1	3kr blk, *orange*	250.00	21.00
3a	A1	6kr blk, *bl grn*	1,400.	65.00
4a	A1	9kr blk, *dp rose*	1,700.	110.00
4b	A1	9kr blk, *bl grn* (error)		

1853-58

6	A1	1kr black	135.00	18.00
a.		Tete beche gutter pair		*20,000.*
7	A1	3kr blk, *green*	125.00	5.50
8	A1	3kr blk, *bl* ('58)	200.00	22.50
a.		Printed on both sides		
9	A1	6kr blk, *yellow*	190.00	16.00

Nos. 1-9 with margins all around sell considerably higher.

Reissues (1865) of Nos. 1, 2, 3, 6, 7 and 8 exist on thick paper and No. 9 on thin paper; the color of the last is brighter than that of the original.

Coat of Arms
A2 A3

1860-62 *Perf. 13½*

10	A2	1kr black	60.00	24.00
12	A2	3kr ultra ('61)	60.00	11.00
a.		3kr Prus bl	225.00	11.00
13	A2	6kr red org ('61)	90.00	37.50
a.		6kr yel org ('62)	165.00	60.00
14	A2	9kr rose ('61)	190.00	110.00

Copies of Nos. 10-14 and 18 with all perforations intact sell considerably higher.

1862 *Perf. 10*

15	A2	1kr black	45.00	52.50
a.		1kr silver gray		*6,000.*
16	A2	6kr blue	87.50	47.50
17	A2	9kr brown	75.00	52.50
a.		9kr bister	95.00	100.00

Perf. 13½

18	A3	3kr rose	1,100.	300.00

1862-65 *Perf. 10*

19	A3	1kr blk ('64)	35.00	11.00
a.		1kr silver gray		*1,250.*
20	A3	3kr rose	35.00	90
a.		Imperf.	*35,000.*	*12,000.*
22	A3	6kr ultra ('65)	6.75	15.00
a.		6kr Prus bl ('64)	*275.00*	57.50
23	A3	9kr brn ('64)	12.00	15.00
a.		9kr bister	165.00	19.00
b.		Printed on both sides		*2,750.*
24	A3	18kr green	250.00	500.00
25	A3	30kr orange	21.00	*1,250.*

Forged cancellations are known on Nos. 25 and 28a.

A4

1868

26	A4	1kr green	3.00	2.75
27	A4	3kr rose	1.50	90
28	A4	7kr dull blue	13.00	30.00
a.		7kr sky blue	30.00	85.00

The postage stamps of Baden were superseded by those of the German Empire on Jan. 1, 1872, but Official stamps were used during the year 1905.

Stamps of the Baden sector of the French Occupation Zone of Germany, issued in 1947-49, are listed under Germany, Occupation Issues.

Baden stamps can be mounted in Scott's Germany Part I and II Albums.

RURAL POSTAGE DUE STAMPS

RU1

1862 Unwmk. *Perf. 10*

Thin Paper

LJ1	RU1	1kr blk, *yellow*	5.00	*225.00*
a.		Thick paper	125.00	*450.00*
LJ2	RU1	3kr blk, *yellow*	3.25	*100.00*
a.		Thick paper	75.00	*325.00*
LJ3	RU1	12kr blk, *yellow*	25.00	*15,000.*
a.		Half used as 6kr on cover		*18,000.*
b.		Quarter used as 3kr on cover		*6,500.*

On #LJ3, "LAND-POST" is a straight line.

Paper of #LJ1a, LJ2a is darker yellow.

Forged cancellations abound on #LJ1-LJ3.

OFFICIAL STAMPS

See Germany Nos. OL16-OL21.

BAVARIA

LOCATION — In southern Germany
GOVT. — Former Kingdom
AREA — 30,562 sq. mi. (1920)
POP. — 7,150,146 (1919)
CAPITAL — Munich

Bavaria was a member of the German Confederation and became part of the German Empire in 1870. After World War I, it declared itself a republic. It lost its postal autonomy on Mar. 31, 1920.

60 Kreuzer = 1 Gulden
100 Pfennig = 1 Mark (1874)

Values for unused stamps of 1849-78 issues are for copies with original gum. Copies without gum sell for about half the figures quoted.

A1

Broken Circle — A1a

1849 Unwmk. Typo. *Imperf.*

1	A1	1kr black	500.00	1,200.
a.		1kr deep black	1,750.	2,250.
b.		Tete beche pair	*35,000.*	

With Silk Thread

2	A1a	3kr blue	35.00	1.10
a.		3kr greenish blue	42.50	1.40
b.		3kr deep blue	35.00	1.40
3	A1a	6kr brown	*5,500.*	135.00

No. 1 exists with silk thread but only as an essay.

Complete circle — A2

Coat of Arms — A3

1850-58 With Silk Thread

4	A2	1kr pink	100.00	14.00
5	A2	6kr brown	35.00	1.00
a.		Half used as 3kr on cover		*8,000.*
6	A2	9kr yel grn	60.00	7.25
a.		9kr bl grn ('53)	*3,500.*	*62.50*
7	A2	12kr red ('58)	95.00	90.00
8	A2	18kr yel ('54)	100.00	125.00

1862

No.	Type	Description	Unused	Used
9	A2	1kr yellow	50.00	12.00
10	A1a	3kr rose	62.50	1.25
a.		3kr carmine	30.00	2.75
11	A2	6kr blue	50.00	6.25
a.		6kr ultra	1,750.	
b.		Half used as 3kr on cover		6,000.
12	A2	9kr bister	70.00	9.50
13	A2	12kr yel grn	75.00	52.50
a.		Half used as 6kr on cover		18,000.
14	A2	18kr ver red	525.00	90.00
a.		18kr pale red	125.00	225.00

No. 11a was not put in use.

1867-68 Embossed

No.	Type	Description	Unused	Used
15	A3	1kr yel grn	55.00	5.50
a.		1kr dk bl grn	185.00	20.00
16	A3	3kr rose	45.00	32
a.		Printed on both sides		
17	A3	6kr ultra	30.00	15.00
a.		Half used as 3kr on cover		16,000.
18	A3	6kr bis ('68)	60.00	26.00
a.		Half used as 3kr on cover		20,000.
19	A3	7kr ultra ('68)	340.00	9.00
20	A3	9kr bister	25.00	27.50
21	A3	12kr lilac	325.00	62.50
22	A3	18kr red	100.00	130.00

The paper of the 1867-68 issues often shows ribbed or laid lines.

1870-72 Wmk. 92 *Perf. 11½*

Without Silk Thread

No.	Type	Description	Unused	Used
23	A3	1kr green	1.25	55
24	A3	3kr rose	4.00	25
25	A3	6kr bister	24.00	22.50
26	A3	7kr ultra	1.75	2.00
a.		7kr Prus bl	6.00	5.00
27	A3	9kr pale brn ('72)	2.00	1.50
28	A3	10kr yellow	4.00	10.00
29	A3	12kr lilac, wmk. 93	200.00	600.00
30	A3	18kr red	6.50	7.00

The paper of the 1870-75 issues frequently appears to be laid with the lines either close or wide apart.

See Nos. 33-37.

Reprints exist.

Wmk. 93

No.	Type	Description	Unused	Used
23a	A3	1kr	50.00	5.75
24a	A3	3kr	40.00	1.25
25a	A3	6kr	125.00	40.00
26b	A3	7kr	75.00	22.50
27a	A3	9kr	200.00	350.00
28a	A3	10kr	200.00	225.00
29a	A3	12kr Wmk. 92	575.00	1,500.
30a	A3	18kr	200.00	150.00

A4

1874-75 Wmk. 92 *Imperf.*

No.	Type	Description	Unused	Used
31	A4	1m violet	300.00	65.00

Perf. 11½

No.	Type	Description	Unused	Used
32	A4	1m violet ('75)	130.00	27.50

See Nos. 46-47, 54-57, 73-76.

1875 Wmk. 94

No.	Type	Description	Unused	Used
33	A3	1kr green	25	9.00
34	A3	3kr rose	25	2.00
35	A3	7kr ultra	2.75	190.00
36	A3	10kr yellow	27.50	190.00
37	A3	18kr red	25.00	35.00

False cancellations exist on Nos. 29, 29a, 33-37.

A5

1876-78 Embossed *Perf. 11½*

No.	Type	Description	Unused	Used
38	A5	3pf lt grn	20.00	45
39	A5	5pf dk grn	40.00	5.50
40	A5	5pf lilac ('78)	65.00	9.00
41	A5	10pf rose	32.50	20
42	A5	20pf ultra	35.00	40
43	A5	25pf yel brn	90.00	3.00
44	A5	50pf scarlet	30.00	3.00
45	A5	50pf brn ('78)	225.00	17.00
46	A4	1m violet	1,400.	57.50
47	A4	2m orange	22.50	4.50

The paper of the 1876-78 issue often shows ribbed lines.

See Nos. 48-53, 58-72. For overprints and surcharge see Nos. 237, O1-O5.

1881-1906 Wmk. 95v *Perf. 11½*

No.	Type	Description	Unused	Used
48	A5	3pf green	12.00	20
a.		Imperf.	150.00	225.00
49	A5	5pf lilac	17.50	70
50	A5	10pf carmine	9.00	15
a.		Imperf.	150.00	200.00
51	A5	20pf ultra	12.00	55
52	A5	25pf yel brn	65.00	2.00
53	A5	50pf dp brn	67.50	2.00
54	A4	1m rose lil ('00)	1.75	22
a.		1m red lil, toned paper	25.00	1.25
55	A4	2m org ('01)	2.75	2.75
a.		Toned paper ('90)	18.00	2.75
56	A4	3m ol gray ('00)	19.00	17.50
a.		White paper ('06)	40.00	150.00
57	A4	5m yel grn ('00)	19.00	17.50
a.		White paper ('06)	40.00	125.00

Nos. 56-57 are on toned paper. A 2m lilac was not regularly issued.

1888-1900 Wmk. 95h *Perf. 14½*

No.	Type	Description	Unused	Used
58	A5	2pf gray ('00)	1.25	20
59	A5	3pf green	3.50	40
60	A5	3pf brown ('00)	15	15
61	A5	5pf lilac	6.25	1.40
62	A5	5pf dk grn ('00)	15	15
63	A5	10pf carmine	15	60
64	A5	20pf ultra	15	15
65	A5	25pf yel brn	14.00	1.65
66	A5	25pf org ('00)	16	28
67	A5	30pf ol grn ('00)	16	28
68	A5	40pf yel ('00)	16	70
69	A5	50pf dp brn	22.50	1.65
70	A5	50pf mar ('00)	16	55
71	A5	80pf lilac ('00)	1.50	2.25

Nos. 59, 61, 65, 69 and 70 are on toned paper; Nos. 67-68 on white.

1888-99

Toned Paper

No.	Type	Description	Unused	Used
58a	A5	2pf ('99)	8.00	1.40
60a	A5	3pf ('90)	2.00	15
62a	A5	5pf ('90)	2.00	15
63a	A5	10pf	1.65	15
64a	A5	20pf	2.25	28
66a	A5	25pf ('90)	6.00	75
70a	A5	50pf ('90)	22.50	1.00
71a	A5	80pf ('99)	17.50	4.50

1911 Wmk. 95v

No.	Type	Description	Unused	Used
72	A5	5pf dk grn	50	3.00

1911 Wmk. 95h *Perf. 11½*

No.	Type	Description	Unused	Used
73	A4	1m rose lil	4.00	9.00
74	A4	2m orange	8.00	15.00
75	A4	3m ol gray	8.00	15.00
76	A4	5m pale yel grn	8.00	15.00

A6

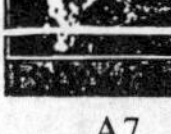
A7

Prince Regent Luitpold
A8

Perf. 14x14½

1911 Wmk. 95h Litho.

No.	Type	Description	Unused	Used
77	A6	3pf brn, *gray brn*	20	15
a.		"911" for "1911"	275.00	275.00
78	A6	5pf dk grn, *grn*	25	15
a.		Tete beche pair	5.00	6.00
b.		Booklet pane of 4 + 2 labels		
c.		Bklt. pane of 5 + label		
d.		Bklt. pane of 6	27.50	
79	A6	10pf scar, *buff*	15	15
a.		Tete beche pair	5.00	7.50
b.		"911" for "1911"	15.00	15.00
d.		Booklet pane of 5 + label		
80	A6	20pf dp bl, *bl*	1.25	15
81	A6	25pf vio brn, *buff*	1.75	75

Perf. 11½

Wmk. 95v

No.	Type	Description	Unused	Used
82	A7	30pf org buff, *buff*	1.00	55
83	A7	40pf ol grn, *buff*	1.50	50
84	A7	50pf cl, *gray brn*	1.75	1.10
84A	A7	60pf dk grn, *buff*	2.00	95
85	A7	80pf vio, *gray brn*	4.00	95
86	A8	1m brn, *gray brn*	1.65	1.25
87	A8	2m dk grn, *grn*	1.65	2.50
88	A8	3m lake, *buff*	10.00	13.00
89	A8	5m dk bl, *buff*	10.00	16.00
90	A8	10m org, *yel*	16.00	35.00
91	A8	20m blk brn, *yel*	14.00	20.00
		Nos. 77-91 (16)	67.15	93.15

90th birthday of Prince Regent Luitpold.

All values exist in 2 types except #84A.

Nos. 77-84, 85-91 exist imperf.

Prince Regent Luitpold
A9

1911, June 10 Unwmk.

No.	Type	Description	Unused	Used
92	A9	5pf grn, yel & blk	30	50
b.		Horiz. pair, imperf. btwn.	110.00	110.00
93	A9	10pf rose, yel & blk	45	1.00
b.		Pair, imperf. between	110.00	110.00

Silver Jubilee of Prince Regent Luitpold.

A10

A11

King Ludwig III
A12 A13

Perf. 14x14½

1914-20 Wmk. 95h Photo.

No.	Type	Description	Unused	Used
94	A10	2pf gray ('18)	15	15
95	A10	3pf brown	15	15
96	A10	5pf yel grn	15	15
a.		5pf dark green	1.60	30
b.		Tete beche pair	6.00	9.00
c.		Booklet pane of 5 + 1 label	50.00	
97	A10	7½pf dp grn ('16)	15	15
a.		Tete beche pair	3.50	5.25
b.		Booklet pane of 6	15.00	
98	A10	10pf vermilion	1.65	15
a.		Tete beche pair	7.50	10.00
b.		Booklet pane of 5 + 1 label	50.00	
99	A10	10pf car rose ('16)	15	15
100	A10	15pf ver ('16)	15	15
a.		Tete beche pair	4.00	5.25
b.		Booklet pane of 5 + 1 label	20.00	
101	A10	15pf car ('20)	1.65	3.00
102	A10	20pf blue	15	15
103	A10	25pf gray	15	15
104	A10	30pf orange	15	15
105	A10	40pf olive grn	15	15
106	A10	50pf red brn	15	15
107	A10	60pf bl grn	22	25
108	A10	80pf violet	25	38

Perf. 11½

Wmk. 95v

No.	Type	Description	Unused	Used
109	A11	1m brown	25	38
110	A11	2m violet	35	90
111	A11	3m scarlet	50	1.50

Wmk. 95h

No.	Type	Description	Unused	Used
112	A12	5m deep blue	1.10	2.25
113	A12	10m yel grn	1.50	15.00
114	A12	20m brown	3.50	17.50
		Nos. 94-114 (21)	12.62	

See Nos. 117-135. For overprints and surcharges see Nos. 115, 136-175, 193-236, B1-B3.

Used Values

of Nos. 94-275 are for postally used stamps. Canceled-to-order stamps, which abound, sell for same prices as unused.

No. 94 Surcharged

1916 Wmk. 95h *Perf. 14x14½*

No.	Type	Description	Unused	Used
115	A13	2½pf on 2pf gray	15	15
a.		Double surcharge		

Ludwig III Types of 1914-20

1916-20 *Imperf.*

No.	Type	Description	Unused	Used
117	A10	2pf gray	15	1.65
118	A10	3pf brown	15	1.65
119	A10	5pf pale yel grn	15	1.65
120	A10	7½pf dp grn	15	1.65
a.		Tete beche pair	5.50	
121	A10	10pf car rose	15	1.65
122	A10	15pf vermilion	15	1.65
a.		Tete beche pair	5.50	
123	A10	20pf blue	15	1.65
124	A10	25pf gray	15	1.65
125	A10	30pf orange	15	1.65
126	A10	40pf olive grn	15	1.65
127	A10	50pf red brn	15	1.65
128	A10	60pf dk grn	15	1.65
129	A10	80pf violet	15	1.65
130	A11	1m brown	25	3.50
131	A11	2m violet	35	5.00
132	A11	3m scarlet	50	5.00
133	A12	5m deep blue	1.00	15.00
134	A12	10m yel grn	1.75	21.00
135	A12	20m brown	2.25	32.50
		Nos. 117-135 (19)	8.05	

Stamps and Type of 1914-20 Overprinted:

Volksstaat Bayern
a

Volksstaat Bayern
b

Wmk. 95h or 95v

1919 *Perf. 14x14½*

Overprint "a"

No.	Type	Description	Unused	Used
136	A10	3pf brown	15	40
137	A10	5pf yel grn	15	16
138	A10	7½pf dp grn	15	40
139	A10	10pf car rose	15	16
140	A10	15pf vermilion	15	16
141	A10	20pf blue	15	40
142	A10	25pf gray	15	40
143	A10	30pf orange	15	40
144	A10	35pf orange	15	1.25
a.		Without overprint	135.00	
145	A10	40pf ol grn	15	32
146	A10	50pf red brn	15	32
147	A10	60pf dk grn	15	40
148	A10	75pf red brn	15	80
a.		Without overprint	35.00	210.00
149	A10	80pf violet	15	65

Perf. 11½

Overprint "a"

No.	Type	Description	Unused	Used
150	A11	1m brown	28	65
151	A11	2m violet	35	1.00
152	A11	3m scarlet	52	2.75

Overprint "b"

No.	Type	Description	Unused	Used
153	A12	5m deep blue	90	4.75
154	A12	10m yel grn	1.25	10.00
155	A12	20m dk brn	2.25	20.00
		Nos. 136-155 (20)	7.65	

Inverted overprints exist on Nos. 137-143, 145-147, 149. Value, each $10.

Double overprints exist on Nos. 137, 139, 143, 145, 150. Values, $20-$50.

Imperf

Overprint "a"

No.	Type	Description	Unused	Used
156	A10	3pf brown	15	60
157	A10	5pf pale yel grn	15	60
158	A10	7½pf dp grn	15	60
159	A10	10pf car rose	15	60
160	A10	15pf vermilion	15	60
161	A10	20pf blue	15	60
162	A10	25pf gray	15	60
163	A10	30pf orange	15	60
164	A10	35pf orange	15	60
a.		Without overprint	14.00	
165	A10	40pf ol grn	15	60
166	A10	50pf red brn	15	60
167	A10	60pf dk grn	15	60
168	A10	75pf red brn	15	60
a.		Without overprint	210.00	
169	A10	80pf violet	20	65
170	A11	1m brown	35	2.00
171	A11	2m violet	42	2.75
172	A11	3m scarlet	55	5.25

Overprint "b"

No.	Type	Description	Unused	Used
173	A12	5m deep blue	1.00	6.25
174	A12	10m yel grn	1.25	20.00
175	A12	20m brown	2.00	20.00
		Nos. 156-175 (20)	7.72	

Stamps of Germany 1906-19 Overprinted

Freistaat Bayern

1919 Wmk. 125 *Perf. 14, 14½*

No.	Type	Description	Unused	Used
176	A22	2½pf gray	15	18
177	A16	3pf brown	15	15
178	A16	5pf green	15	15
179	A22	7½pf orange	15	15
180	A16	10pf carmine	15	15

No.	Type	Description	Unused	Used
181	A22	15pf dk vio	15	15
a.		Double overprint	130.00	*150.00*
182	A16	20pf ultra	15	15
183	A16	25pf org & blk, *yel*	15	48
184	A22	35pf red brn	15	55
185	A16	40pf lake & blk	22	55
186	A16	75pf grn & blk	38	90
187	A16	80pf lake & blk, *rose*	45	1.25
188	A17	1m car rose	95	1.75
189	A21	2m dl bl	1.10	3.50
190	A19	3m gray vio	1.50	4.75
191	A20	5m sl & car	1.90	4.75
a.		Inverted overprint	*2,100.*	
		Nos. 176-191 (16)	7.85	19.56

Bavarian Stamps of 1914-16 Overprinted:

Freistaat Bayern
c

Freistaat Bayern
d

Wmk. 95h or 95v

1919-20 ***Perf. 14x14½***

Overprint "c"

No.	Type	Description	Unused	Used
193	A10	3pf brown	15	52
194	A10	5pf yel grn	15	15
195	A10	7½pf dp grn	15	*3.00*
196	A10	10pf car rose	15	15
197	A10	15pf vermilion	15	15
198	A10	20pf blue	15	20
199	A10	25pf gray	16	60
200	A10	30pf orange	16	60
201	A10	40pf olive grn	25	1.65
202	A10	50pf red brn	16	85
203	A10	60pf dk grn	35	*3.00*
204	A10	75pf olive bister	50	*4.00*
205	A10	80pf violet	35	1.65

Perf. 11½

Overprint "c"

No.	Type	Description	Unused	Used
206	A11	1m brown	35	1.65
207	A11	2m violet	35	2.25
208	A11	3m scarlet	50	4.00

Overprint "d"

No.	Type	Description	Unused	Used
209	A12	5m deep blue	1.10	*6.50*
210	A12	10m yel grn	1.90	*12.00*
211	A12	20m dk brn	2.25	*20.00*
		Nos. 193-211 (19)	9.28	

Imperf

Overprint "c"

No.	Type	Description	Unused	Used
212	A10	3pf brown	15	50
213	A10	5pf pale yel grn	15	50
214	A10	7½pf dp grn	15	*2.50*
215	A10	10pf car rose	15	50
216	A10	15pf vermilion	15	50
217	A10	20pf blue	15	50
a.		Double overprint	47.50	
218	A10	25pf gray	15	50
219	A10	30pf orange	15	50
220	A10	40pf ol grn	32	50
221	A10	50pf red brn	16	50
222	A10	60pf dk grn	32	50
223	A10	75pf ol bis	48	1.00
a.		Without overprint	6.75	
224	A10	80pf violet	20	52
225	A11	1m brown	32	1.65
226	A11	2m violet	32	2.25
227	A11	3m scarlet	60	4.00

Overprint "d"

No.	Type	Description	Unused	Used
228	A12	5m dp bl	90	6.50
229	A12	10m yel grn	2.25	*14.00*
230	A12	20m brown	2.25	*16.00*
		Nos. 212-230 (19)	9.32	

Ludwig Type of 1914, Printed in Various Colors and Surcharged

1,25 M
Freistaat Bayern

1919 ***Perf. 11½***

No.	Type	Description	Unused	Used
231	A11	1.25m on 1m yel grn	15	1.25
232	A11	1.50m on 1m org	15	2.00
233	A11	2.50m on 1m gray	18	4.00

1920 ***Imperf.***

No.	Type	Description	Unused	Used
234	A11	1.25m on 1m yel grn	20	*4.00*
a.		Without surcharge	205.00	
235	A11	1.50m on 1m org	20	*4.75*
a.		Without surcharge	4.50	
236	A11	2.50m on 1m gray	20	*6.50*
a.		Without surcharge	4.50	

20 20

No. 60 Surcharged in Dark Blue

20 20

1920 ***Perf. 14½***

No.	Type	Description	Unused	Used
237	A5	20pf on 3pf brn	15	18
a.		Inverted surcharge	9.75	18.00
b.		Double surcharge	52.50	62.50

Plowman
A14

"Electricity" Harnessing Light to a Water Wheel
A15

Sower
A16

Madonna and Child
A17

von Kaulbach's "Genius" – A18

TWENTY PFENNIG
Type I - Foot of "2" turns downward.
Type II - Foot of "2" turns upward.

Perf. 14x14½

1920 **Wmk. 95h** **Typo.**

No.	Type	Description	Unused	Used
238	A14	5pf yel grn	15	15
239	A14	10pf orange	15	15
240	A14	15pf carmine	15	15
241	A15	20pf vio (I)	15	15
a.		20pf vio (II)	15.00	*250.00*
242	A15	30pf dp bl	15	45
243	A15	40pf brown	15	45
244	A16	50pf vermilion	18	75
245	A16	60pf bl grn	18	75
246	A16	75pf lil rose	18	1.25

Perf. 12x11½

Wmk. 95v

No.	Type	Description	Unused	Used
247	A17	1m car & gray	40	1.25
248	A17	1¼m ultra & ol bis	22	1.25
249	A17	1½m dk grn & gray	22	1.25
250	A17	2½m blk & gray	22	*4.00*

Perf. 11½x12

Wmk. 95h

No.	Type	Description	Unused	Used
251	A18	3m pale blue	35	6.50
252	A18	5m orange	70	6.75
253	A18	10m deep green	1.50	9.25
254	A18	20m black	2.00	13.00
		Nos. 238-254 (17)	7.05	

Imperf., Pair

No.	Type	Description	Unused
238a	A14	5pf yel grn	100.00
239a	A14	10pf orange	225.00
241b	A15	20pf vio (I)	100.00
243a	A15	40pf brown	200.00
244a	A16	50pf vermilion	25.00
245a	A16	60pf blue green	55.00
246a	A16	75pf lil rose	55.00

Wmk. 95v

No.	Type	Description	Unused
247a	A17	1m car & gray	10.00
248a	A17	1¼m ultra & ol bis	10.00
249a	A17	1½m dk grn & gray	10.00
250a	A17	2½m blk & gray	16.00

Wmk. 95h

No.	Type	Description	Unused
251a	A18	3m pale blue	16.00
252a	A18	5m orange	16.00
253a	A18	10m deep green	16.00
254a	A18	20m black	16.00

Perf. 12x11½

1920 **Litho.** **Wmk. 95v**

No.	Type	Description	Unused	Used
255	A17	2½m blk & gray	1.00	*12.00*

On No. 255 the background dots are small, hazy and irregularly spaced. On No. 250 they are large, clear, round, white and regularly spaced in rows. The backs of the typo. stamps usually show a raised impression of parts of the design.

Stamps and Types of Preceding Issue Overprinted

Deutsches Reich

1920

No.	Type	Description	Unused	Used
256	A14	5pf yel grn	15	18
a.		Inverted overprint	16.00	
b.		Imperf., pair	32.50	
257	A14	10pf orange	15	18
a.		Imperf., pair	32.50	
258	A14	15pf carmine	15	18
259	A15	20pf violet	15	18
a.		Inverted overprint	16.00	
b.		Double overprint	16.00	
c.		Imperf., pair	32.50	
260	A15	30pf deep blue	15	18
a.		Inverted overprint	16.00	
b.		Imperf., pair	45.00	
261	A15	40pf brown	15	18
a.		Inverted overprint	22.50	
b.		Imperf., pair	45.00	
262	A16	50pf vermilion	15	18
263	A16	60pf bl grn	15	18
264	A16	75pf lil rose	30	95
265	A16	80pf dark blue	18	45
a.		Without overprint	*120.00*	
b.		Imperf., pair	32.50	

Overprinted in Black or Red

Deutsches Reich

No.	Type	Description	Unused	Used
266	A17	1m car & gray	30	45
a.		Imperf., pair	32.50	
b.		Inverted overprint	22.50	
267	A17	1¼m ultra & ol bis	30	55
a.		Imperf., pair	32.50	
268	A17	1½m dk grn & gray	30	75
a.		Imperf., pair	32.50	
269	A17	2m vio & ol bis	60	1.10
a.		Without overprint	50.00	
b.		Imperf., pair	32.50	
270	A17	2½m (#250) (R)	15	48
c.		Imperf., pair	32.50	
270A	A17	2½m (#255) (R)	55	*60.00*
b.		Imperf., pair	32.50	

Overprinted Deutsches Reich

No.	Type	Description	Unused	Used
271	A18	3m pale blue	2.25	3.00
272	A18	4m dull red	2.50	3.75
a.		Without overprint	60.00	
273	A18	5m orange	2.00	3.00
274	A18	10m dp grn	2.50	4.00
275	A18	20m black	3.75	5.00
		Nos. 256-275 (21)	16.88	

Nos. 256 to 275 were available for postage through all Germany, but were used almost exclusively in Bavaria.

SEMI-POSTAL STAMPS

Regular Issue of 1914-20 Surcharged in Black

5 Pf.
für Kriegs-beschädigte
Freistaat Bayern

1919 **Wmk. 95h** ***Perf. 14x14½***

No.	Type	Description	Unused	Used
B1	A10	10pf + 5pf car rose	40	65
a.		Inverted surcharge	12.00	30.00
b.		Surcharge on back	24.00	
c.		Imperf., pair	325.00	
B2	A10	15pf + 5pf ver	40	65
a.		Inverted surcharge	12.00	30.00
b.		Imperf., pair	160.00	
B3	A10	20pf + 5pf blue	40	85
a.		Inverted surcharge	12.00	30.00
b.		Imperf., pair	200.00	

Surtax was for wounded war veterans.

Bavaria stamps can be mounted in Scott's Germany Part II Album.

POSTAGE DUE STAMPS

D1

D2

With Silk Thread

1862 **Typeset** **Unwmk.** ***Imperf.***

No.	Type	Description	Unused	Used
J1	D1	3kr black	100.00	300.00
a.		"Empfange"	325.00	*650.00*

Without Silk Thread

1870 **Typo.** **Wmk. 93** ***Perf. 11½***

No.	Type	Description	Unused	Used
J2	D1	1kr black	11.00	*575.00*
a.		Wmk 92	25.00	*900.00*
J3	D1	3kr black	11.00	*325.00*
a.		Wmk 92	25.00	440.00

Type of 1876 Regular Issue Overprinted in Red "Vom Empfänger zahlbar"

1876 **Wmk. 94**

No.	Type	Description	Unused	Used
J4	D2	3pf gray	17.50	22.50
J5	D2	5pf gray	12.00	22.50
J6	D2	10pf gray	2.50	65

1883 **Wmk. 95v**

No.	Type	Description	Unused	Used
J7	D2	3pf gray	80.00	100.00
J8	D2	5pf gray	60.00	60.00
J9	D2	10pf gray	60	28
a.		"Empfanper"	100.00	80.00
b.		"zahlbar"	80.00	60.00
c.		Imperf.	100.00	

1895-1903 **Wmk. 95h** ***Perf. 14½***

No.	Type	Description	Unused	Used
J10	D2	2pf gray	55	80
J11	D2	3pf gray ('03)	35	1.00
J12	D2	5pf gray ('03)	70	80
J13	D2	10pf gray ('03)	55	40

Nos. J10-J11 exist with inverted overprint.

1888

Rose-toned Paper

No.	Type	Description	Unused	Used
J10a	D2	2pf gray	75	1.25
J11a	D2	3pf gray	75	75
J12a	D2	5pf gray	1.25	60
J13a	D2	10pf gray	1.25	20
b.		As "a." double overprint		*1,750.*

No. J13b was used at Pirmasens.

Surcharged in Red in Each Corner

1895

J14 D2 2pf on 3pf gray

At least six copies exist, all used in Aichach.

OFFICIAL STAMPS

Nos. 77 to 81, 84, 95, 96, 98, 99 and 102, perforated with a large E were issued for official use in 1912-16.

Regular Issue of 1888-1900 Overprinted

E

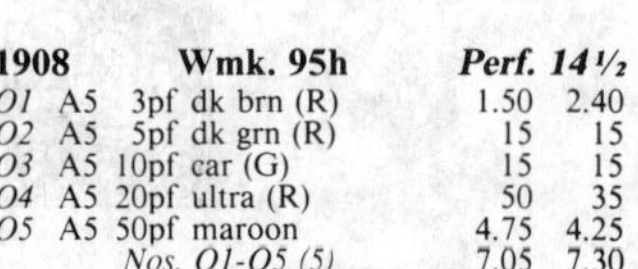

1908 **Wmk. 95h** ***Perf. 14½***

No.	Type	Description	Unused	Used
O1	A5	3pf dk brn (R)	1.50	2.40
O2	A5	5pf dk grn (R)	15	15
O3	A5	10pf car (G)	15	15
O4	A5	20pf ultra (R)	50	35
O5	A5	50pf maroon	4.75	4.25
		Nos. O1-O5 (5)	7.05	7.30

Nos. O1 to O5 were issued for the use of railway officials. "E" stands for "Eisenbahn."

Coat of Arms – O1

1916-17 Typo. *Perf. 11½*

O6 O1 3pf bis brn 15 25
O7 O1 5pf yel grn 15 25
O8 O1 7½pf grn, *grn* 15 25
O9 O1 7½pf grn ('17) 15 20
O10 O1 10pf dp rose 16 25
O11 O1 15pf red, *buff* 15 20
O12 O1 15pf red ('17) 16 40
O13 O1 20pf dp bl, *bl* 1.25 1.25
O14 O1 20pf dp bl ('17) 15 25
O15 O1 25pf gray 15 25
O16 O1 30pf orange 15 25
O17 O1 60pf dk grn 16 30
O18 O1 1m dl vio, *gray* 80 1.75
O19 O1 1m mar ('17) 3.25 *60.00*
Nos. O6-O19 (14) 6.98

Used Values of Nos. O8-O69 are for postally used stamps. Canceled-to-order stamps, which abound, sell for same prices as unused.

Official Stamps and Type of 1916-17 Overprinted **Volksstaat Bayern**

1918

O20 O1 3pf bister brn 15 *3.50*
O21 O1 5pf yel green 15 25
O22 O1 7½pf gray green 15 30
O23 O1 10pf deep rose 15 20
O24 O1 15pf red 15 20
O25 O1 20pf blue 15 20
O26 O1 25pf gray 15 25
O27 O1 30pf orange 15 35
O28 O1 35pf orange 15 35
O29 O1 50pf olive gray 15 35
O30 O1 60pf dark grn 20 1.50
O31 O1 75pf red brown 25 1.50
O32 O1 1m dl vio, *gray* 75 2.50
O33 O1 1m maroon 4.00 *60.00*
Nos. O20-O33 (14) 6.70

O2

O3

O4

1920 Typo. *Perf. 14x14½*

O34 O2 5pf yel grn 15 *3.00*
O35 O2 10pf orange 15 *3.00*
O36 O2 15pf carmine 15 *3.00*
O37 O2 20pf violet 15 *3.00*
O38 O2 30pf dark blue 15 *4.50*
O39 O2 40pf bister 15 *5.00*

Perf. 14½x14
Wmk. 95v

O40 O3 50pf vermilion 15 *10.00*
O41 O3 60pf blue grn 15 *7.50*
O42 O3 70pf dk vio 15 *9.00*
a. Imperf., pair 50.00
O43 O3 75pf dp rose 15 12.50
O44 O3 80pf dl bl 15 20.00
O45 O3 90pf ol grn 15 25.00
O46 O3 1m dk brn 15 22.50
a. Imperf., pair 80.00
O47 O4 1¼m green 15 *27.50*
O48 O4 1½m vermilion 15 *30.00*
a. Imperf. pair 40.00
O49 O4 2½m deep blue 15 *32.50*
a. Imperf. pair 80.00
O50 O4 3m dark red 35 *35.00*
a. Imperf. pair 32.00
O51 O4 5m black 2.00 *45.00*
a. Imperf., pair 80.00
Nos. O34-O51 (18) 4.75

Stamps of Preceding Issue Overprinted **Deutsches Reich**

1920, Apr. 1

O52 O2 5pf yel grn 15 75
a. Imperf., pair 45.00
O53 O2 10pf orange 15 40
O54 O2 15pf carmine 15 40
O55 O2 20pf violet 15 40
O56 O2 30pf dark blue 15 20
O57 O2 40pf bister 15 20
O58 O3 50pf vermilion 15 20
a. Imperf., pair 45.00
O59 O3 60pf bl grn 15 20
O60 O3 70pf dk vio 1.25 1.40
O61 O3 75pf dp rose 32 60
O62 O3 80pf dull blue 15 40
O63 O3 90pf olive grn 80 1.00

Similar Ovpt., Words 8mm apart

O64 O4 1m dk brn 15 20
a. Imperf., pair 45.00
O65 O4 1¼m green 15 20
O66 O4 1½m vermilion 15 20
O67 O4 2½m deep blue 15 40
a. Imperf., pair 60.00
O68 O4 3m dark red 15 50
O69 O4 5m black 4.00 *15.00*
Nos. O52-O69 (18) 8.47

Nos. O52 to O69 could be used in all parts of Germany, but were almost exclusively used in Bavaria.

BERGEDORF

LOCATION — A town in northern Germany.
POP. — 2,989 (1861)

Originally Bergedorf belonged jointly to the Free City of Hamburg and the Free City of Lübeck. In 1867 it was purchased by Hamburg.

16 Schillings = 1 Mark

Values for unused stamps are for copies with gum. Copies without gum sell for about half the figures quoted.

Combined Arms of Lübeck and Hamburg
A1 A2 A3

A4 A5

1861-67 Unwmk. Litho. *Imperf.*

1 A1 ½s blk, *pale bl* 42.50 *375.00*
a. ½s blk, *bl* ('67) 90.00 *2,500.*
2 A3 1s blk, *white* 42.50 *190.00*
a. Tete beche pair 200.00
3 A4 1½s blk, *yellow* 22.50 *550.00*
a. Tete beche pair *175.00*
4 A2 3s blue, *pink* 27.50 *1,000.*
5 A5 4s blk, *brown* 27.50 *1,250.*

Counterfeit cancellations are plentiful.

The ½s on violet and 3s on rose, listed previously, as well as a 1s and 1½s on thick paper and 4s on light rose brown, come from proof sheets and were never placed in use. A 1½ "SCHILLINGE" (instead of SCHILLING) also exists only as a proof.

REPRINTS

½ SCHILLING

There is a dot in the upper part of the right branch of "N" of "EIN". The upper part of the shield is blank or almost blank. The horizontal bar of "H" in "HALBER" is generally defective.

1 SCHILLING

The "1" in the corners is generally with foot. The central horizontal bar of the "E" of "EIN" is separated from the vertical branch by a black line. The "A" of "POSTMARKE" has the horizontal bar incomplete or missing. The horizontal bar of the "H" of "SCHILLING" is separated from the vertical branches by a dark line at each side, sometimes the bar is missing.

1½ SCHILLINGE

There is a small triangle under the right side of the tower, exactly over the "R" of "POSTMARKE."

3 SCHILLINGE

The head of the eagle is not shaded. The horizontal bar of the second "E" of "BERGEDORF" is separated from the vertical branch by a thin line. There is generally a colored dot in the lower half of the "S" of "POSTMARKE."

4 SCHILLINGE

The upper part of the shield is blank or has two or three small dashes. In most of the reprints there is a diagonal dash across the wavy lines of the groundwork at the right of "I" and "E" of "VIER."

Reprints, value $1 each.

These stamps were superseded by those of the North German Confederation in 1868.

BREMEN

LOCATION — In northwestern Germany
AREA — 99 sq. mi.
POP. — 122,402 (1871)

Bremen was a Free City and member of the German Confederation. In 1870 it became part of the German Empire.

22 Grote = 10 Silbergroschen.

Values of Bremen stamps vary according to condition. Quotations are for fine copies. Very fine to superb specimens sell at much higher prices, and inferior or poor copies sell at reduced prices, depending on the condition of the individual specimen.
Values for unused stamps are for copies with gum. Copies without gum sell for about half the figures quoted.

Coat of Arms — A1

THREE GROTE
I II III

Type I. The central part of the scroll below the word Bremen is crossed by one vertical line.
Type II. The center of the scroll is crossed by two vertical lines.
Type III. The center of the scroll is crossed by three vertical lines.

1855 Unwmk. Litho. *Imperf.*
Horizontally Laid Paper

1 A1 3gr blk, *blue* 175.00 250.00

Vertically Laid Paper

1A A1 3gr blk, *blue* 400.00 650.00

Nos. 1 and 1A can be found with parts of a papermaker's watermark, consisting of lilies. Value: unused $500; used $850.

See Nos. 9-10.

A2 A3

FIVE GROTE

Type I. The shading at the left of the ribbon containing "funf Grote" runs downward from the shield.
Type II. The shading at the left of the ribbon containing "funf Grote" runs upward.

1856-60 Wove Paper

2 A2 5gr blk, *rose* 125.00 175.00
a. Printed on both sides
b. "Marken" (not issued) 10.00
3 A2 7gr blk, *yel* ('60) 150.00 *475.00*
4 A3 5sgr green ('59) 125.00 225.00
a. Chalky paper 50.00 *200.00*
b. 5sgr yellow green 100.00 150.00

See Nos. 6, 8, 12-13, 15.

A4 A5

1861-63 *Serpentine Roulette*

5 A4 2gr orange ('63) 150.00 *1,600.*
a. 2gr red orange 150.00 *1,600.*
b. Chalky paper 180.00 *1,400.*
6 A2 5gr blk, *rose* ('62) 90.00 90.00
7 A5 10gr black 350.00 *775.00*
8 A3 5sgr green ('63) 400.00 125.00
a. Chalky paper 425.00 250.00
b. 5sgr yellow green 175.00 115.00

See Nos. 11, 14.

1863
Horizontally (H) or Vertically (V) Laid Paper

9 A1 3gr blk, *blue* (V) 325.00 375.00
a. 3gr black, *blue* (H) 1,000. *1,250.*

1866-67 *Perf. 13*

10 A1 3gr black, *blue* 80.00 150.00

Wove Paper

11 A4 2gr orange 70.00 *200.00*
a. 2gr red orange 125.00 *300.00*
b. Horiz. pair, imperf. btwn. *1,750.*
12 A2 5gr blk, *rose* 100.00 *110.00*
a. Horiz. pair, imperf. btwn.
13 A2 7gr blk, *yel* ('67) 90.00 *4,000.*
14 A5 10gr black ('67) 135.00 *700.00*
15 A3 5sgr green 110.00 *600.00*
a. 5sgr yellow green 110.00 100.00
b. As "a," chalky paper 225.00 175.00

The stamps of Bremen were superseded by those of the North German Confederation on Jan. 1, 1868.

BRUNSWICK

LOCATION — In northern Germany
GOVT. — Former duchy
AREA — 1,417 sq. mi.
POP. — 349,367 (1880)
CAPITAL — Brunswick

Brunswick was a member of the German Confederation and, in 1870 became part of the German Empire.

12 Pfennigs = 1 Gutegroschen
30 Silbergroschen (Groschen) = 24 Gutegroschen = 1 Thaler

Values of Brunswick stamps vary according to condition. Quotations for Nos. 1-22 are for fine copies. Very fine to superb specimens sell at much higher prices, and inferior or poor copies sell at reduced prices, depending on the condition of the individual specimen.
Values for Nos. 1-3 unused are for copies without gum. Copies with gum sell for about three times the prices quoted. Nos. 4-26 without gum sell for about half the figures quoted.

The "Leaping Saxon Horse" — A1

The ½gr has white denomination and "Gr" in right oval.

1852 Unwmk. Typo. *Imperf.*

1 A1 1sgr rose 1,500. 225.00
2 A1 2sgr blue 900.00 150.00
a. Half used as 1sgr on cover
3 A1 3sgr vermilion 900.00 125.00

See Nos. 4-11, 13-22.

1853-63 Wmk. 102

4 A1 ¼ggr blk, *brn* ('56) 200.00 165.00
5 A1 ⅓sgr black ('56) 100.00 250.00
6 A1 ½gr blk, *grn* ('63) 11.00 *150.00*

No.	Type	Description	Unused	Used
7	A1	1sgr blk, *orange*	90.00	32.50
a.		1sgr blk, *org buff*	90.00	32.50
8	A1	1sgr blk, *yel* ('61)	75.00	32.50
9	A1	2sgr blk, *blue*	65.00	40.00
a.		Half used as 1sgr on cover		*6,750.*
10	A1	3sgr blk, *rose*	175.00	40.00
11	A1	3sgr rose ('62)	200.00	165.00

A3

A4

1857

No.	Type	Description	Unused	Used
12	A3	Four 1/4ggr blk, *brn* ('57)	25.00	70.00
a.		Four 1/4ggr blk, *yel brn*	125.00	125.00

The bister on white paper was not issued. Value $12.

1864 ***Serpentine Roulette 16***

No.	Type	Description	Unused	Used
13	A1	1/3sgr black	300.00	*1,900.*
14	A1	1/2gr blk, *green*	200.00	*1,500.*
15	A1	1sgr blk, *yellow*	*1,750.*	*1,000.*
16	A1	1sgr yellow	140.00	125.00
17	A1	2sgr blk, *blue*	250.00	300.00
a.		Half used as 1sgr on cover		*8,000.*
18	A1	3sgr rose	800.00	400.00

Rouletted 12

No.	Type	Description	Unused	Used
20	A1	1sgr blk, *yellow*		*9,000.*
21	A1	1sgr yellow	275.00	200.00
22	A1	3sgr rose	*2,650.*	*1,900.*

Nos. 13, 16, 18, 21 and 22 are on white paper.
Faked roulettes of Nos. 13-22 exist.

Serpentine Roulette
1865 Embossed Unwmk.

No.	Type	Description	Unused	Used
23	A4	1/3gr black	22.50	*250.00*
24	A4	1gr carmine	2.50	*30.00*
25	A4	2gr ultra	6.00	*150.00*
a.		2gr gray blue	6.00	*140.00*
c.		Half used as 1sgr on cover		*7,250.*
26	A4	3gr brown	5.50	*130.00*

Faked cancellations of Nos. 5-26 exist.

Imperf., Pair

No.	Type	Description	Unused
23a	A4	1/3gr	110.00
24a	A4	1gr	32.50
25b	A4	2gr	100.00
26a	A4	3gr	125.00

Stamps of Brunswick were superseded by those of the North German Confederation on Jan. 1, 1868.

HAMBURG

LOCATION — Northern Germany
GOVT. — A former Free City
AREA — 160 sq. mi.
POP. — 453,869 (1880)
CAPITAL — Hamburg

Hamburg was a member of the German Confederation and became part of the German Empire in 1870.

16 Schillings = 1 Mark

> Values of unused stamps are for copies without gum. Copies with gum sell for about twice the figures quoted.

Value Numeral on Arms — A1

1859 Typo. Wmk. 128 ***Imperf.***

No.	Type	Description	Unused	Used
1	A1	1/2s black	45.00	*500.00*
2	A1	1s brown	60.00	*55.00*
3	A1	2s red	55.00	*80.00*
4	A1	3s blue	45.00	*100.00*
5	A1	4s yellow green	50.00	*1,200.*
a.		4s green	75.00	*1,000.*
6	A1	7s orange	50.00	21.00
7	A1	9s yellow	70.00	*1,600.*

See Nos. 13-21.

A2

A3

1864 Litho.

No.	Type	Description	Unused	Used
9	A2	1 1/4s red lilac	50.00	60.00
a.		1 1/4s lilac	65.00	75.00
b.		1 1/4s gray	50.00	42.50
c.		1 1/4s blue	250.00	*500.00*
d.		1 1/4s grnsh gray	50.00	*90.00*
12	A3	2 1/2s green	65.00	*110.00*

See Nos. 22-23.

The 1 1/4s and 2 1/2s have been reprinted on watermarked and unwatermarked paper.

1864-65 Typo. ***Perf. 13 1/2***

No.	Type	Description	Unused	Used
13	A1	1/2s black	3.50	9.00
a.		Imperf. vert., pair	30.00	
14	A1	1s brown	6.00	12.50
a.		Half used as 1/2s on cover		
15	A1	2s red	5.00	17.00
17	A1	3s ultra	15.00	22.50
a.		Imperf., pair	40.00	
b.		Horiz. pair, imperf. vert.		
c.		3s blue	20.00	30.00
18	A1	4s green	5.00	20.00
19	A1	7s orange	85.00	130.00
20	A1	7s vio ('65)	6.00	14.00
a.		Imperf., pair	115.00	
21	A1	9s yellow	10.00	*1,600.*
a.		Vert. pair, imperf. btwn.	325.00	

Litho.

No.	Type	Description	Unused	Used
22	A2	1 1/4s lilac	30.00	9.00
a.		1 1/4s red lilac	30.00	10.00
b.		1 1/4s violet	30.00	9.00
23	A3	2 1/2s yel grn	45.00	25.00
a.		2 1/2s blue green	45.00	25.00

The 1 1/4s has been reprinted on watermarked and unwatermarked paper; the 2 1/2s on unwatermarked paper.

A4

A5

Rouletted 10
1866 Unwmk. Embossed

No.	Type	Description	Unused	Used
24	A4	1 1/4s violet	15.00	22.50
a.		1 1/4s red violet	25.00	30.00
25	A5	1 1/2s rose	4.50	*60.00*

Reprints:

1 1/4s: The rosettes between the words of the inscription have a well-defined open circle in the center of the originals, while in the reprints this circle is filled up.

In the upper part of the top of the "g" of "Schilling", there is a thin vertical line which is missing in the reprints.

The two lower lines of the triangle in the upper left corner are of different thicknesses in the originals while in the reprints they are of equal thickness.

The labels at the right and left containing the inscriptions are 2 3/4mm in width in the originals while they are 2 1/2mm in reprints.

1 1/2s: The originals are printed on thinner paper than the reprints. This is easily seen by turning the stamps over, when on the originals the color and impression will clearly show through, which is not the case in the reprints.

The vertical stroke of the upper part of the "g" in Schilling is very short on the originals, scarcely crossing the top line, while in the reprints it almost touches the center of the "g".

The lower part of the "g" of Schilling in the originals, barely touches the inner line of the frame, in some stamps it does not touch it at all, while in the reprints the whole stroke runs into the inner line of the frame.

A6

> *Hamburg stamps can be mounted in Scott's Germany Part II Album.*

1867 Typo. Wmk. 128 ***Perf. 13 1/2***

No.	Type	Description	Unused	Used
26	A6	2 1/2s dull green	4.00	*65.00*
a.		2 1/2s dark green	12.00	*50.00*
b.		Imperf., pair	65.00	

Forged cancellations exist on almost all stamps of Hamburg, especially on Nos. 4, 7, 21 and 25.

Nos. 1 to 23 and 26 exist without watermark, but they come from the same sheets as the watermarked stamps.

The stamps of Hamburg were superseded by those of the North German Confederation on Jan. 1, 1868.

HANOVER

LOCATION — Northern Germany
GOVT. — A former Kingdom
AREA — 14,893 sq. mi.
POP. — 3,191,000
CAPITAL — Hanover

Hanover was a member of the German Confederation and became in 1866 a province of Prussia.

10 Pfennigs = 1 Groschen
24 Gute Groschen = 1 Thaler
30 Silbergroschen = 1 Thaler (1858)

> Values for unused stamps are for copies with gum. Copies without gum sell for about half the values quoted.

Coat of Arms
A1 A2

Wmk. Square Frame
1850 Rose Gum Typo. ***Imperf.***

No.	Type	Description	Unused	Used
1	A1	1g g blk, *gray bl*	3,000.	40.00

See Nos. 2, 11.

The reprints have white gum and no watermark.

1851-55 Wmk. 130

No.	Type	Description	Unused	Used
2	A1	1g g blk, *gray grn*	20.00	5.75
a.		1g g blk, *yel grn*	165.00	17.50
3	A2	1/30th blk, *salmon*	52.00	32.50
a.		1/30th blk, *crim* ('55)	50.00	32.50
b.		Bisect on cover		
5	A2	1/15th blk, *gray bl*	75.00	37.50
a.		Bisect on cover		
6	A2	1/10th blk, *yellow*	75.00	37.50
a.		1/10th blk, *org*	75.00	37.50

Bisects Nos. 3b, 5a, 12a and 13a were used for 1/2g.
See Nos. 8, 12-13.

The 1/10th has been reprinted on unwatermarked paper, with white gum.

Crown and Numeral — A3

1853 Wmk. 130

No.	Type	Description	Unused	Used
7	A3	3pf rose	225.00	200.00

See Nos. 9, 16-17, 25.

The reprints of No. 7 have white gum.

Fine Network in Second Color
1855 Unwmk.

No.	Type	Description	Unused	Used
8	A2	1/10th blk & org	125.00	80.00
a.		1/10th blk & yel	140.00	110.00

No. 8 with olive yellow network and other values with fine network are essays.

Large Network in Second Color
1856-57

No.	Type	Description	Unused	Used
9	A3	3pf rose & blk	200.00	210.00
a.		3pf rose & gray	225.00	200.00
11	A1	1g g blk & grn	25.00	7.50
12	A2	1/30th blk & rose	65.00	22.50
a.		Bisect on cover		*3,500.*
13	A2	1/15th blk & bl	50.00	47.50
a.		Bisect on cover		*5,000.*
14	A2	1/10th blk & org ('57)	425.00	50.00

The reprints have white gum, and the network does not cover all the outer margin.

Without Network
1859-63

No.	Type	Description	Unused	Used
16	A3	3pf car rose	60.00	75.00
a.		3pf pink	50.00	70.00
17	A3	3pf grn (Drei Zehntel) ('63)	225.00	800.00

Copies of No. 25 with rouletting trimmed off sometimes pretend to be No. 17. Minimum size of No. 17 acknowledged as genuine: 21 1/2x24 1/2mm.

The reprints of No. 16 have pink gum instead of red; the extremities of the banderol point downward instead of outward.

Crown and Post Horn — A7

King George V — A8

1859-61 ***Imperf.***

No.	Type	Description	Unused	Used
18	A7	1/2g blk ('60)	55.00	110.00
a.		Rose gum	200.00	250.00
19	A8	1g rose	3.00	2.00
a.		1g vio rose	20.00	15.00
b.		1g carmine	8.00	12.50
c.		Half used as 1/2g on cover		*3,500.*
20	A8	2g ultra	8.00	22.50
a.		Half used as 1g on cover		*4,000.*
22	A8	3g yellow	125.00	57.50
a.		3g org yel	125.00	52.50
23	A8	3g brn ('61)	10.00	25.00
a.		One third used as 1g on cover		
24	A8	10g grn ('61)	190.00	800.00

Reprints of 1/2g are on thick toned paper with yellowish gum. Originals are on white paper with rose or white gum. Reprints exist tete beche.

Reprints of 3g yellow and 3g brown have white or pinkish gum. Originals have rose or orange gum.

1864 White Gum ***Perce en Arc 16***

No.	Type	Description	Unused	Used
25	A3	3pf grn (Drei Zehntel)	25.00	40.00
26	A7	1/2g black	125.00	200.00
27	A8	1g rose	4.00	2.50
28	A8	2g ultra	60.00	40.00
a.		Half used as 1g on cover		
29	A8	3g brown	60.00	35.00

Reprints of 3g are percè en arc 13 1/2.

Rose Gum

No.	Type	Description	Unused	Used
25a	A3	3pf grn	50.00	65.00
26a	A7	1/2g black	200.00	300.00
27a	A8	1g rose	20.00	20.00
29a	A8	3g brown	*1,250.*	*1,250.*

The stamps of Prussia superseded those of Hanover on Oct. 1, 1866.

LUBECK

LOCATION — Situated on an arm of the Baltic Sea between the former German States of Holstein and Mecklenburg.
GOVT. — Former Free City and State
AREA — 115 sq. mi.
POP. — 136,413
CAPITAL — Lubeck

> *Hanover stamps can be mounted in Scott's Germany Part II Album.*

> *Lubeck stamps can be mounted in Scott's Germany Part II Album.*

Lubeck was a member of the German Confederation and became part of the German Empire in 1870.

16 Schillings = 1 Mark

Values of Lubeck stamps vary according to condition. Quotations are for fine copies. Very fine to superb specimens sell at much higher prices, and inferior or poor copies sell at reduced prices, depending on the condition of the individual specimen.

Values for Nos. 1-7 unused are for copies without gum. Copies with gum sell for about twice the figures quoted. Nos. 8-14 without gum sell for about half the values quoted.

Coat of Arms — A1

1859 Litho. Wmk. 148 *Imperf.*

1	A1	1/2g gray lil	400.00	*1,250.*
2	A1	1s orange	400.00	*1,250.*
3	A1	2s brown	15.00	*200.00*
a.		Value in words reads "ZWEI EIN HALB"	275.00	*6,250.*
4	A1	2 1/2s rose	30.00	*500.00*
5	A1	4s green	15.00	*225.00*

1862 Unwmk.

6	A1	1/2s lilac	20.00	*1,000.*
7	A1	1s yel org	30.00	*1,000.*

The reprints of the 1859-62 issues are unwatermarked and printed in bright colors.

A2

A3

1863 *Rouletted 11 1/2*

Eagle embossed

8	A2	1/2s green	30.00	*65.00*
9	A2	1s orange	90.00	*130.00*
a.		Rouletted 10	175.00	*425.00*
10	A2	2s rose	18.00	*60.00*
11	A2	2 1/2s ultra	40.00	*210.00*
12	A2	4s bister	30.00	*80.00*

The reprints are imperforate and without embossing.

1864 Litho. *Imperf.*

13	A3	1 1/4s brown	18.00	*40.00*

A4

1865 *Rouletted 11 1/2*

Eagle embossed

14	A4	1 1/2s red lilac	18.00	*70.00*

The reprints are imperforate and without embossing.

Counterfeit cancellations are found on Nos. 1 to 14.

The stamps of Lubeck were superseded by those of the North German Confederation on Jan. 1, 1868.

MECKLENBURG-SCHWERIN

LOCATION — In northern Germany, bordering on the Baltic Sea.
GOVT. — A former Grand Duchy
AREA — 5,065 sq. mi. (approx.)
POP. — 674,000 (approx.)
CAPITAL — Schwerin

Mecklenburg-Schwerin was a member of the German Confederation and became part of the German Empire in 1870.

48 Schillings = 1 Thaler

Values of Mecklenburg-Schwerin stamps vary according to condition. Quotations are for fine copies. Very fine to superb specimens sell at much higher prices, and inferior or poor copies sell at reduced prices, depending on the condition of the individual specimen.

Values for unused stamps are for copies without gum.

Coat of Arms
A1 A2

1856 Unwmk. Typo. *Imperf.*

1	A1	Four 1/4s red	100.00	100.00
a.		1/4s red	15.00	12.50
2	A2	3s org yel	75.00	50.00
3	A2	5s blue	200.00	190.00

See Nos. 4, 6-8.

A3

1864-67 *Rouletted 11 1/2*

4	A1	Four 1/4s red	*2,250.*	*2,250.*
a.		1/4s red	110.00	150.00
5	A3	Four 1/4s red	50.00	45.00
a.		1/4s red	8.00	8.00
6	A2	2s gray lil ('67)	150.00	*1,900.*
a.		2s red vio ('66)	200.00	225.00
7	A2	3s org yel, wide margin('67)	35.00	*200.00*
a.		Narrow margin ('65)	150.00	75.00
8	A2	5s bis brn	150.00	*165.00*
a.		Thick paper	200.00	*300.00*

The overall size of #7, including margin, is 24 1/2x24 1/2mm. That of #7a is 23 1/2x23mm.

Counterfeit cancellations exist on those stamps valued higher used than unused.

These stamps were superseded by those of the North German Confederation on Jan. 1, 1868.

MECKLENBURG-STRELITZ

LOCATION — In northern Germany, divided by Mecklenburg-Schwerin
GOVT. — A former Grand Duchy
AREA — 1,131 sq. mi.
POP. — 106,347
CAPITAL — Neustrelitz

Mecklenburg-Strelitz was a member of the German Confederation and became part of the German Empire in 1870.

30 Silbergroschen = 48 Schillings = 1 Thaler

Values of Mecklenburg-Strelitz stamps vary according to condition. Quotations are for fine copies. Very fine to superb specimens sell at much higher prices, and inferior or poor copies sell at reduced prices, depending on the condition of the individual specimen.

Values for unused stamps are for copies without gum.

Coat of Arms
A1 A2

Rouletted 11 1/2

1864 Unwmk. Embossed

1	A1	1/4sg orange	100.00	*2,200.*
a.		1/4sg yellow orange	250.00	*4,000.*
2	A1	1/3sg green	60.00	*1,200.*
a.		1/3sg dark green	100.00	*2,500.*
3	A1	1sch violet	175.00	*3,750.*
4	A2	1sg rose	75.00	180.00
5	A2	2sg ultra	25.00	*850.00*
6	A2	3sg bister	35.00	*1,500.*

Counterfeit cancellations abound.

These stamps were superseded by those of the North German Confederation in 1868.

OLDENBURG

LOCATION — In northwestern Germany, bordering on the North Sea.
GOVT. — A former Grand Duchy
AREA — 2,482 sq. mi.
POP. — 483,042 (1910)
CAPITAL — Oldenburg

Oldenburg was a member of the German Confederation and became part of the German Empire in 1870.

30 Silbergroschen = 1 Thaler
30 Groschen = 1 Thaler

Values of Oldenburg stamps vary according to condition. Quotations for Nos. 1-15 are for fine copies. Very fine to superb specimens sell at much higher prices, and inferior or poor copies sell at reduced prices, depending on the condition of the individual specimen.

Values for Nos. 1-25 unused are for copies without gum.

A1

A2

1852-55 Unwmk. Litho. *Imperf.*

1	A1	1/30th blk, *blue*	200.00	20.00
2	A1	1/15th blk, *rose*	400.00	60.00
3	A1	1/10th blk, *yellow*	450.00	70.00
4	A2	1/3sgr blk, *grn* ('55)	700.00	650.00

There are three types of Nos. 1 and 2.

A3

A4

1859

5	A3	1/3g blk, *green*	1,500.	*3,000.*
6	A3	1g blk, *blue*	425.00	20.00
7	A3	2g blk, *rose*	550.00	450.00
8	A3	3g blk, *yellow*	650.00	550.00
a.		"OLBENBURG"	550.00	825.00

See Nos. 10, 13-15.

1861

9	A4	1/4g orange	150.00	*3,400.*
10	A3	1/3g green	300.00	*750.00*
a.		1/3g bluish green	275.00	*650.00*
b.		1/3g moss green	1,000.	*1,900.*
c.		"OLDEIBURG"	*350.00*	*750.00*
d.		"Dritto"	*350.00*	*750.00*
e.		"Drittd"	*350.00*	*750.00*
f.		Printed on both sides		*3,750.*
12	A4	1/2g redsh brn	200.00	325.00
a.		1/2g dark brown	300.00	400.00

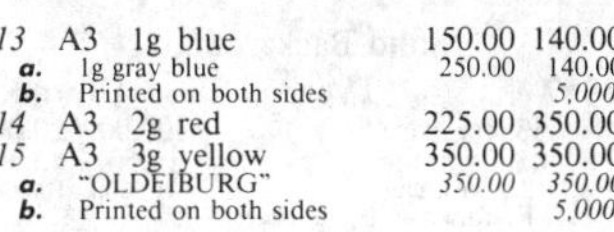

13	A3	1g blue	150.00	140.00
a.		1g gray blue	250.00	140.00
b.		Printed on both sides		*5,000.*
14	A3	2g red	225.00	350.00
15	A3	3g yellow	350.00	350.00
a.		"OLDEIBURG"	*350.00*	*350.00*
b.		Printed on both sides		*5,000.*

Forged cancellations are found on Nos. 9, 10, 12 and their minor varieties.

Coat of Arms — A5

1862 Embossed *Rouletted 11 1/2*

16	A5	1/3g green	140.00	200.00
17	A5	1/2g orange	110.00	100.00
a.		1/2g orange red	140.00	140.00
18	A5	1g rose	65.00	11.00
19	A5	2g ultra	110.00	45.00
20	A5	3g bister	110.00	50.00

1867 *Rouletted 10*

21	A5	1/3g green	10.00	*350.00*
22	A5	1/2g orange	10.00	*275.00*
23	A5	1g rose	4.00	*35.00*
a.		Half used as 1/2g on cover		
24	A5	2g ultra	5.00	*175.00*
25	A5	3g bister	12.50	*275.00*

Forged cancellations are found on Nos. 21-25.

The stamps of Oldenburg were replaced by those of the North German Confederation on Jan. 1, 1868.

PRUSSIA

LOCATION — Formerly the greater part of northern Germany.
GOVT. — A former independent Kingdom
AREA — 134,650 sq. mi.
POP. — 40,165,219 (1910)
CAPITAL — Berlin

Prussia was a member of the German Confederation and became part of the German Empire in 1870.

12 Pfennigs = 1 Silbergroschen
60 Kreuzer = 1 Gulden (1867)

Values for unused stamps are for copies with gum. Copies without gum sell for about half the figures quoted.

King Frederick William IV
A1 A2

1850-56 Engr. Wmk. 162 *Imperf.*

Background of Crossed Lines

1	A1	4pf yel grn ('56)	67.50	47.50
a.		4pf dark green	67.50	55.00
2	A1	6pf (1/2sg) red org	55.00	22.50
3	A2	1sg black, *rose*	60.00	5.00
4	A2	2sg black, *blue*	60.00	7.00
a.		Half used as 1sg on cover		
5	A2	3sg black, *yellow*	70.00	7.75
a.		3sg black, *orange buff*	300.00	25.00

See Nos. 10-13.

Reprints exist on watermarked and unwatermarked paper.

A3

A4

Solid Background

1857 Typo. Unwmk.

No.			Unused	Used
6	A3	1sg rose	300.00	20.00
7	A3	2sg blue	1,050.	42.50
a.		2sg dark blue	1,500.	100.00
b.		Half used as 1sg on cover		
8	A3	3sg orange	105.00	25.00
a.		3sg yellow	215.00	60.00

The reprints of Nos. 6 to 8 inclusive have a period instead of a colon after "SILBERGR."

Background of Crossed Lines

1858-60 Typo.

No.			Unused	Used
9	A4	4pf green	52.50	18.00
		Engr.		
10	A1	6pf (½sg) org ('59)	90.00	80.00
		Typo.		
11	A2	1sg rose	35.00	1.90
12	A2	2sg blue	80.00	11.00
a.		2sg dark blue	125.00	21.00
b.		Half used as 1sg on cover		
13	A2	3sg orange	60.00	9.00
a.		3sg yellow	65.00	11.00

Coat of Arms

A6 A7

1861-65 Embossed *Rouletted 11½*

No.			Unused	Used
14	A6	3pf red lilac ('65)	16.00	17.50
a.		3pf red violet ('65)	40.00	45.00
15	A6	4pf yel grn	6.50	5.75
a.		4pf green	18.00	8.00
16	A6	6pf orange	6.50	7.25
a.		6pf vermilion	60.00	30.00
17	A7	1sg rose	2.50	32
18	A7	2sg ultra	7.00	90
a.		2sg blue	275.00	25.00
20	A7	3sg bister	7.00	1.25
a.		3sg gray brown ('65)	225.00	21.00

A8 A9

Typographed in Reverse on Paper Resembling Goldbeater's Skin

1866 *Rouletted 10*

No.			Unused	Used
21	A8	10sg rose	35.00	60.00
22	A9	30sg blue	50.00	125.00

Perfect copies of Nos. 21 and 22 are extremely rare.

A10

1867 Embossed *Rouletted 16*

No.			Unused	Used
23	A10	1kr green	21.00	14.00
24	A10	2kr orange	37.50	30.00
25	A10	3kr rose	18.00	20.00
26	A10	6kr ultra	18.00	14.00
27	A10	9kr bister brown	18.00	20.00

Imperforate stamps of the above sets are proofs.

The stamps of Prussia were superseded by those of the North German Confederation on Jan. 1, 1868.

OFFICIAL STAMPS.

For stamps formerly listed as Nos. O1-O15, see Germany Nos. OL1-OL15.

SAXONY

LOCATION — In central Germany
GOVT. — A former kingdom
AREA — 5,787 sq. mi.
POP. — 2,500,000 (approx.)
CAPITAL — Dresden

Saxony was a member of the German Confederation and became a part of the German Empire in 1870.

10 Pfennings = 1 Neu-Groschen
30 Neu-Groschen = 1 Thaler

Values of Saxony stamps vary according to condition. Quotations for Nos. 1-14 are for fine copies. Very fine to superb specimens sell at much higher prices, and inferior or poor copies sell at reduced prices, depending on the condition of the individual specimen.

Values for unused stamps are for copies with gum. Copies without gum sell for about half the figures quoted.

A1

1850 Unwmk. Typo. *Imperf.*

No.			Unused	Used
1	A1	3pf red	*5,500.*	*5,000.*
a.		3pf dark red	*10,000.*	*10,000.*

Coat of Arms — A2 Frederick Augustus II — A3

1851

No.			Unused	Used
2	A2	3pf green	70.00	37.50
a.		3pf yellow green	800.00	400.00

Nos. 2 and 2a with margins all around sell considerably higher.

1851-52 Engr.

No.			Unused	Used
3	A3	½ng blk, *gray*	40.00	7.50
a.		½ng pale blue (error)	*16,000.*	
5	A3	1ng blk, *rose*	40.00	6.00
6	A3	2ng blk, *pale bl*	175.00	35.00
7	A3	2ng blk, *dk bl* ('52)	600.00	42.50
8	A3	3ng blk, *yellow*	125.00	10.00

King John I — A4

1855-57

No.			Unused	Used
9	A4	½ng blk, *gray*	8.00	1.75
a.		"11/22" at left or right	375.00	200.00
10	A4	1ng blk, *rose*	8.00	1.75
11	A4	2ng blk, *blue*	10.00	14.00
a.		2ng black, *dark blue*	21.00	6.00
12	A4	3ng blk, *yellow*	13.00	3.50
13	A4	5ng ver ('56)	70.00	22.50
a.		5ng orange brown ('56)	165.00	110.00
b.		5ng deep brown ('57)	*750.00*	200.00
14	A4	10ng blue ('56)	250.00	165.00

The ½ng is found in 3 types, the 1ng in 2.

In 1861 the 5ng and 10ng were printed on hard, brittle, translucent paper.

A5 A6

Typo.; Arms Embossed

1863 *Perf. 13*

No.			Unused	Used
15	A5	3pf blue green	1.50	*9.00*
a.		3pf yellow green	8.00	*16.00*
16	A5	½ng orange	60	1.65
a.		½ng red orange	6.25	3.50
17	A6	1ng rose	75	90
a.		Vert. pair, imperf. between	*150.00*	
b.		Horiz. pair, imperf. between	*275.00*	
18	A6	2ng blue	1.65	3.50
a.		2ng dark blue	7.00	8.50
19	A6	3ng red brown	1.65	4.75
a.		3ng bister brown	5.00	2.75
20	A6	5ng dull violet	9.00	*22.50*
a.		5ng gray violet	9.00	*55.00*
b.		5ng gray blue	7.50	*20.00*
c.		5ng slate	40.00	*100.00*

The stamps of Saxony were superseded on Jan. 1, 1868, by those of the North German Confederation.

SCHLESWIG-HOLSTEIN

LOCATION — In northern Germany.
GOVT. — Former Duchies
AREA — 7,338 sq. mi.
POP. — 1,519,000 (approx.)
CAPITAL — Schleswig

Schleswig-Holstein was an autonomous territory from 1848 to 1851 when it came under Danish rule. In 1864, it was occupied by Prussia and Austria, and in 1866 it became a province of Prussia.

16 Schillings = 1 Mark

Values of Schleswig-Holstein stamps vary according to condition. Quotations for Nos. 1-2, 15-17 are for fine copies. Very fine to superb specimens sell at much higher prices, and inferior or poor copies sell at reduced prices, depending on the condition of the individual specimen.

Values for unused stamps are for copies with gum. Copies without gum sell for about half the figures quoted.

Coat of Arms — A1

Typographed; Arms Embossed

1850 Unwmk. *Imperf.*

With Silk Threads

No.			Unused	Used
1	A1	1s dl bl & grnsh bl	250.00	*3,500.*
a.		1s Prussian blue	425.00	
2	A1	2s rose & pink	350.00	*5,250.*
a.		2s deep pink & rose	450.00	
b.		Double embossing	*500.00*	

Forged cancellations are found on Nos. 1-2, 5-7, 9, 16 and 19.

A2 A3

1865 Typo. *Rouletted 11½*

No.			Unused	Used
3	A2	½s rose	18.00	37.50
4	A2	1¼s green	8.00	9.50
5	A3	1⅓s red lilac	40.00	*100.00*
6	A2	2s ultra	25.00	*165.00*
7	A3	4s bister	50.00	*1,000.*

Schleswig

A4 A5

1864 Typo. *Rouletted 11½*

No.			Unused	Used
8	A4	1¼s green	25.00	9.00
9	A4	4s carmine	60.00	*325.00*

1865 *Rouletted 10, 11½*

No.			Unused	Used
10	A4	½s green	25.00	50.00
11	A4	1¼s red lilac	30.50	10.00
a.		1¼s gray lilac ('67)	225.00	50.00
b.		Half of #11a used as ½s on cover		
12	A5	1⅓s rose	25.00	50.00
13	A4	2s ultra	16.00	32.00
14	A4	4s bister	25.00	55.00

Holstein

A6 A7

Type I- Small lettering in frame. Wavy lines in spandrels close together.
Type II- Small lettering in frame. Wavy lines wider apart.
Type III- Larger lettering in frame and no periods after "H R Z G". Wavy lines as II.

1864 Litho. *Imperf.*

No.			Unused	Used
15	A6	1¼s bl & gray, type I	45.00	32.50
a.		Half used as ½s on cover		*6,250.*
16	A6	1¼s bl & gray, type II	400.00	*2,000.*
a.		Half used as ½s on cover		*22,500.*
17	A6	1¼s bl & gray, type III	32.50	32.50
a.		Half used as ½s on cover		*7,000.*

1864 Typo. *Rouletted 8*

No.			Unused	Used
18	A7	1¼s bl & rose	30.00	12.00
a.		Half used as ½s on cover		*1,200.*

A8

1865 *Rouletted 8*

No.			Unused	Used
19	A8	½s green	50.00	85.00
20	A8	1¼s red lilac	35.00	13.00
21	A8	2s blue	42.50	35.00

A9 A10

1865-66 *Rouletted 7 and 8*

No.			Unused	Used
22	A9	1¼s red lil ('66)	55.00	12.50
a.		Half used as ½s on cover		*3,000.*
23	A10	1⅓s carmine	52.50	25.00
24	A9	2s blue ('66)	110.00	80.00
25	A10	4s bister	50.00	50.00

These stamps were superseded by those of North German Confederation on Jan. 1, 1868.

THURN AND TAXIS

30 Silbergroschen or Groschen = 1 Thaler

A princely house which, prior to the formation of the German Empire, enjoyed the privilege of a postal monopoly. These stamps were superseded on July 1, 1867, by those of Prussia, followed by those of the North German Postal District on Jan. 1, 1868, and later by stamps of the German Empire on Jan. 1, 1872.

Values for unused stamps are for copies with gum. Copies without gum sell for about half the figures quoted.

Values for the imperforate stamps are for fine to very copies with 3 margins. Stamps with 4 clear margins are scarce and command much higher prices.

Northern District

A1 A2

1852-58 Unwmk. Typo. *Imperf.*

1	A1	¼sgr blk, *red brn* ('54)	125.00	55.00
2	A1	⅓sgr blk, *buff* ('58)	52.50	225.00
3	A1	½sgr blk, *green*	200.00	22.50
4	A1	1sgr blk, *dk bl*	325.00	50.00
5	A1	1sgr blk, *lt bl* ('53)	400.00	12.00
6	A1	2sgr blk, *rose*	300.00	14.00
7	A1	3sgr blk, *yellow*	250.00	12.00

Reprints of Nos. 1-12, 15-20, 23-24, were made in 1910. They have "ND" in script on the back. Value, $6 each.

1859-60

8	A1	¼sgr red ('60)	30.00	35.00
9	A1	½gr green	125.00	62.50
10	A1	1sgr blue	125.00	22.50
11	A1	2sgr rose ('60)	65.00	40.00
12	A1	3sgr red brn ('60)	65.00	52.50
13	A2	5sgr lilac	1.00	*250.00*
14	A2	10sgr orange	1.00	*575.00*

Excellent forged cancellations exist on Nos. 13 and 14. For reprints, see note after No. 7.

1862-63

15	A1	¼sgr black ('63)	10.00	*35.00*
16	A1	⅓sgr green ('63)	12.00	*225.00*
17	A1	½sgr org yel	40.00	22.50
18	A1	1sgr rose ('63)	22.50	17.00
19	A1	2sgr blue ('63)	42.50	*45.00*
20	A1	3sgr bis ('63)	12.50	*21.00*

For reprints, see note after No. 7.

1865 *Rouletted*

21	A1	¼sgr black	10.00	*525.00*
22	A1	⅓sgr green	12.50	*275.00*
23	A1	½sgr yellow	14.00	*30.00*
24	A1	1sgr rose	22.50	18.00
25	A1	2sgr blue	1.50	*50.00*
26	A1	3sgr bister	2.00	*17.50*

For reprints, see note after No. 7.

1866 *Rouletted in Colored Lines*

27	A1	¼sgr black	1.25	*950.00*
28	A1	⅓sgr green	1.25	*700.00*
29	A1	½sgr yellow	1.25	*100.00*
30	A1	1sgr rose	1.25	*65.00*
a.		Horizontal pair without rouletting between	85.00	
b.		Half used as ½sgr on cover		*5,250.*
31	A1	2sgr blue	1.25	*750.00*
32	A1	3sgr bister	1.25	*125.00*

Forged cancellations on Nos. 2, 13-14, 15-16, 21-22, 25-32 are plentiful.

Southern District

60 Kreuzer = 1 Gulden

A1 A2

1852-53 Unwmk. *Imperf.*

42	A1	1kr blk, *lt grn*	90.00	12.00
43	A1	3kr blk, *dk bl*	350.00	22.50
44	A1	3kr blk, *bl* ('53)	400.00	9.50
45	A1	6kr blk, *rose*	300.00	13.00
46	A1	9kr blk, *yellow*	300.00	8.75

Reprints of Nos. 42-50, 53-56 were made in 1910. Each has "ND" in script on the back. Value, each $6.

1859

47	A1	1kr green	10.00	6.25
48	A1	3kr blue	250.00	16.00
49	A1	6kr rose	250.00	30.00
50	A1	9kr yellow	250.00	42.50
51	A2	15kr lilac	1.10	*105.00*
52	A2	30kr orange	1.10	*300.00*

Forged cancellations exist on Nos. 51 and 52. For reprints, see note after No. 46.

1862

53	A1	3kr rose	30.00	12.00
54	A1	6kr blue	7.25	13.00
55	A1	9kr bister	7.25	11.00

For reprints, see note after No. 46.

1865 *Rouletted*

56	A1	1kr green	11.00	11.00
57	A1	3kr rose	17.00	7.25
58	A1	6kr blue	1.50	*16.00*
59	A1	9kr bister	1.50	*17.50*

For reprint of No. 56, see note after No. 46.

1867 *Rouletted in Colored Lines*

60	A1	1kr green	1.40	*12.00*
61	A1	3kr rose	1.40	*20.00*
62	A1	6kr blue	1.40	*15.00*
63	A1	9kr bister	1.40	*22.50*

Forged cancellations exist on Nos. 51-52, 58-63.

The Thurn & Taxis Stamps, Northern and Southern Districts, were replaced on July 1, 1867, by those of Prussia.

WURTTEMBERG

LOCATION — In southern Germany
GOVT. — A former Kingdom
AREA — 7,530 sq. mi.
POP. — 2,580,000 (approx.)
CAPITAL — Stuttgart

Württemberg was a member of the German Confederation and became a part of the German Empire in 1870. It gave up its postal autonomy on March 31, 1902, but official stamps were issued until 1923.

16 Kreuzer = 1 Gulden
100 Pfennigs = 1 Mark (1875)

> Values of early Wurttemberg stamps vary according to condition. Quotations for Nos. 1-46 are for fine copies. Very fine to superb specimens sell at much higher prices, and inferior or poor copies sell at reduced prices, depending on the condition of the individual specimen.
>
> Values for Nos. 1-46 unused are for copies without gum. Copies with gum sell for about twice the figures quoted. Nos. 41-54 without gum sell for about half the prices.

A1 A1a

1851-52 Unwmk. Typo. *Imperf.*

1	A1	1kr blk, *buff*	265.00	40.00
a.		1kr blk, *straw*	900.00	275.00
2	A1	3kr blk, *yellow*	150.00	2.75
a.		3kr blk, *org*	1,250.	150.00
4	A1	6kr blk, *yel grn*	600.00	17.50
a.		6kr blk, *bl grn*	1,300.	32.50
5	A1	9kr blk, *rose*	*3,750*	17.50
6	A1a	18kr blk, *dl vio* ('52)	600.00	500.00

On the "reprints" the letters of "Württemberg" are smaller, especially the first "e"; the right branch of the "r's" of Württemberg runs upward in the reprints and downward in the originals.

Coat of Arms — A2

With Orange Silk Threads

1857 Typographed and Embossed

7	A2	1kr yel brn	180.00	60.00
a.		1kr dark brown	425.00	225.00
9	A2	3kr yel org	200.00	5.00
10	A2	6kr green	300.00	27.50
11	A2	9kr car rose	525.00	30.00
12	A2	18kr blue	750.00	575.00

Copies of Nos. 7-12 with margins all around sell considerably higher.

See Nos. 13-46, 53.

The reprints have red or yellow silk threads and are printed 2mm apart, while the originals are ¾mm apart.

1859 Without Silk Threads

13	A2	1kr brown	250.00	50.00
a.		1kr dark brown	600.00	175.00
15	A2	3kr yel org	150.00	3.75
16	A2	6kr green	*3,750.*	57.50
17	A2	9kr car rose	675.00	37.50
18	A2	18kr dark blue	750.00	750.00

The colors of the reprints are brighter; they are also printed 2mm apart instead of 1¼mm.

1860 *Perf. 13½*

19	A2	1kr brown	400.00	60.00
20	A2	3kr yel org	150.00	5.50
21	A2	6kr green	1,200.	40.00
22	A2	9kr carmine	600.00	90.00

1861 Thin Paper

23	A2	1kr brown	275.00	67.50
a.		1kr black brown	390.00	90.00
25	A2	3kr yel org	40.00	17.50
26	A2	6kr green	135.00	32.50
27	A2	9kr rose	350.00	100.00
a.		9kr claret	500.00	180.00
29	A2	18kr dark blue	550.00	550.00

Copies of Nos. 23-29 with all perforations intact sell considerably higher.

1862 *Perf. 10*

30	A2	1kr blk brn	200.00	200.00
31	A2	3kr yel org	200.00	27.50
32	A2	6kr green	195.00	70.00
33	A2	9kr claret	1,150.	550.00

1863

34	A2	1kr yel grn	22.50	6.00
a.		1kr green	150.00	47.50
36	A2	3kr rose	22.50	1.50
a.		3kr dark claret	550.00	225.00
37	A2	6kr blue	80.00	30.00
39	A2	9kr yel brn	225.00	60.00
a.		9kr red brown	125.00	30.00
b.		9kr black brown	300.00	75.00
40	A2	18kr orange	350.00	225.00

1866-68 *Rouletted 10*

41	A2	1kr yel grn	24.00	5.00
a.		1kr dark green	140.00	100.00
42	A2	3kr rose	13.00	1.50
a.		3kr claret	550.00	600.00
43	A2	6kr blue	125.00	30.00
44	A2	7kr sl bl ('68)	465.00	75.00
45	A2	9kr bis brn	425.00	40.00
a.		9kr red brown	365.00	40.00
46	A2	18kr orange	650.00	325.00

A3

1869-73 Typo. & Embossed

47	A3	1kr yel grn	8.00	1.25
48	A3	2kr orange	75.00	40.00
49	A3	3kr rose	8.00	75
50	A3	7kr blue	40.00	14.00
51	A3	9kr lt brn ('73)	50.00	20.00
52	A3	14kr orange	50.00	30.00
a.		14kr lemon yellow	1,000.	325.00

See No. 54.

1873 *Imperf.*

53	A2	70kr red violet	1,050.	1,600.
a.		70kr violet	1,650.	2,000.

Nos. 53 and 53a have single or double lines of fine black dots printed in the gutters between the stamps.

1874 *Perf. 11½x11*

54	A3	1kr yellow green	40.00	32.50

A4 A5

1875-1900 Typo.

55	A4	2pf sl gray ('93)	1.65	48
56	A4	3pf green	6.50	1.00
57	A4	3pf brn ('90)	50	15
a.		Imperf. pair	90.00	
58	A4	5pf violet	8.00	35
59	A4	5pf grn ('90)	1.10	15
a.		5pf bl grn	70.00	12.00
b.		Imperf., pair	90.00	
60	A4	10pf carmine	70	15
a.		10pf rose	40.00	40
b.		Imperf., pair	65.00	
61	A4	20pf ultra	70	15
a.		20pf dull blue	70	15
b.		Imperf., pair	85.00	
62	A4	25pf red brn	35.00	7.25
63	A4	25pf org ('90)	3.00	65
a.		Imperf., pair	80.00	
64	A5	30pf org & blk ('00)	3.50	2.00
65	A5	40pf dp rose & blk ('00)	3.50	3.50
66	A4	50pf gray	250.00	15.00
67	A4	50pf gray grn	25.00	2.00
68	A4	50pf pur brn ('90)	2.00	30
a.		50pf red brn	125.00	20.00
b.		Imperf., pair	100.00	
69	A4	2m yellow	450.00	200.00
70	A4	2m ver, *buff* ('79)	900.00	100.00
71	A5	2m org & blk ('86)	6.00	5.00
a.		2m yel & blk	175.00	15.00
b.		Imperf., pair	90.00	
		Telegraph cancel		1.75
72	A5	5m bl & blk ('81)	60.00	*100.00*
a.		Figure of value inverted		
		Telegraph cancel		45.00

No. 70 has "Unverkauflich" (not for sale) printed on its back to remind postal clerks that it, like No. 69, was for their use and not to be sold to the public.

The regular postage stamps of Württemberg were superseded by those of the German Empire in 1902. Official stamps were in use until 1923.

> Stamps for the Wurttemberg sector of the French Occupation Zone of Germany, issued 1947-1949, are listed under Germany, Occupation Issues.

OFFICIAL STAMPS

For the Communal Authorities

O1

Perf. 11½x11

1875-1900 Typo. Unwmk.

O1	O1	2pf sl gray ('00)	1.00	45
O2	O1	3pf brn ('96)	1.00	16
O3	O1	5pf violet	20.00	1.00
a.		Imperf., pair		*1,750.*
O4	O1	5pf bl grn ('90)	1.50	16
a.		Imperf., pair	32.50	
O5	O1	10pf rose	4.75	16
a.		Imperf., pair	65.00	
O6	O1	25pf org ('00)	12.00	2.75
		Nos. O1-O6 (6)	40.25	4.68

See Nos. O12-O32. For overprints and surcharges see Nos. O7-O11, O40-O52, O59-O93.

> Used Values
> When italicized, used values for Nos. O7-O183 are for favor-canceled copies. Postally used copies command a premium.

Stamps of Previous Issues Overprinted in Black

1806 — 1906

1906, Jan. 30

O7	O1	2pf sl gray	40.00	65.00
O8	O1	3pf dk brn	14.00	7.50
O9	O1	5pf green	3.50	1.40
O10	O1	10pf dp rose	3.50	1.40
O11	O1	25pf orange	52.50	55.00
		Nos. O7-O11 (5)	113.50	130.30

Centenary of Kingdom of Württemberg.

Nos. O7-O11 also exist imperf. but it is doubtful if they were ever issued in that condition.

1906-21 **Wmk. 116**

O12 O1 2pf sl gray 30 15
O13 O1 2½pf gray blk ('16) 30 15
O14 O1 3pf dk brn 30 15
O15 O1 5pf green 30 15
O16 O1 7½pf org ('16) 30 15
O17 O1 10pf dp rose 30 15
O18 O1 10pf org ('21) 15 15
O19 O1 15pf yel brn ('16) 75 18
O20 O1 15pf pur ('17) 40 30
O21 O1 20pf dp ultra ('11) 30 15
O22 O1 20pf dp grn ('21) 15 15
O23 O1 25pf orange 30 15
O24 O1 25pf brn & blk ('17) 40 25
O25 O1 35pf brn ('19) 2.25 7.50
O26 O1 40pf rose red ('21) 15 15
O27 O1 50pf rose lake ('11) 8.00 5.00
O28 O1 50p vio brn ('21) 30 30
O29 O1 60pf ol grn ('21) 40 30
O30 O1 1.25m emer ('21) 25 30
O31 O1 2m gray ('21) 25 30
O32 O1 3m brown ('21) 25 30
Nos. O12-O32 (21) 16.10 16.38

No. O24 contains solid black numerals.
Nos. O12-O32 exist imperf. Value, each pair, $6-$16.

O3

Perf. 14½x14

1916, Oct. 6 **Typo.** **Unwmk.**

O33 O3 2½pf slate 2.75 1.60
O34 O3 7½pf orange 1.90 40
O35 O3 10pf car rose 1.90 40
O36 O3 15pf yel brn 1.90 40
O37 O3 20pf blue 1.90 40
O38 O3 25pf gray blk 5.25 1.25
O39 O3 50pf red brn 9.25 2.00
Nos. O33-O39 (7) 24.85 6.45

25th year of the reign of King Wilhelm II.

Stamps of 1900-06 Surcharged **25 Pf.**

Perf. 11½x11

1916, Sept. 10 **Wmk. 116**

O40 O1 25pf on 25pf org 2.25 2.25
a. Without wmk. 25.00

No. O13 Surcharged in Blue **2**

1919 **Wmk. 116**

O42 O1 2pf on 2½pf gray blk 75 1.25

Volksstaat

Official Stamps of 1906-19 Overprinted

Württemberg

1919

O43 O1 2½pf gray blk 15 20
O44 O1 3pf dk brn 6.25 2.25
O45 O1 5pf green 15 15
O46 O1 7½pf orange 30 20
O47 O1 10pf rose 15 15
O48 O1 15pf purple 15 15
O49 O1 20pf ultra 15 15
O50 O1 25pf brn & blk 15 15
O51 O1 35pf brown 2.75 35
O52 O1 50pf red brn 3.00 40
Nos. O43-O52 (10) 13.20 4.15

Stag — O4

Wmk. 192

1920, Mar. 19 **Litho.** ***Perf. 14½***

O53 O4 10pf maroon 70 75
O54 O4 15pf brown 70 75
O55 O4 20pf indigo 70 75
O56 O4 30pf deep green 70 75
O57 O4 50pf yellow 70 75
O58 O4 75pf bister 70 75
Nos. O53-O58 (6) 4.20 4.50

Deutsches

Official Stamps of 1906-19 Overprinted

Reich

Perf. 11½x11

1920, Apr. 1 **Wmk. 116**

O59 O1 5pf green 3.50 3.00
O60 O1 10pf dp rose 2.25 1.75
O61 O1 15pf dp vio 1.90 1.75
O62 O1 20pf ultra 3.50 3.75
a. Wmk. 192 5.00 5.00
O63 O1 50pf red brn 4.25 5.00
Nos. O59-O63 (5) 15.40 15.25

Nos. O59 to O63 were available for official postage throughout all Germany but were used almost exclusively in Württemberg.

Stamps of 1917-21 Surcharged in Black, Red or Blue **10 Mark**

1923

O64 O1 5m on 10pf org 15 15
O65 O1 10m on 15pf dp vio 15 15
O66 O1 12m on 40pf rose red 18 18
O67 O1 20m on 10pf org 15 18
O68 O1 25m on 20pf grn 15 15
O69 O1 40m on 20pf grn 18 25
O70 O1 50m on 60pf ol grn 15 15

Surcharged **60 Mark**

O71 O1 60m on 1.25m emer 15 15
O72 O1 100m on 40pf rose red 15 15
O73 O1 200m on 2m gray (R) 15 15
O74 O1 300m on 50pf red brn (Bl) 15 15
O75 O1 400m on 3m brn (Bl) 18 35
O76 O1 1000m on 60pf ol grn 18 30
O77 O1 2000m on 1.25m emer 18 15
Nos. O64-O77 (14) 2.25
Set value 2.15

Abbreviations:
Th = (Tausend) Thousand
Mil = (Million) Million
Mlrd = (Milliarde) Billion

Surcharged **20 Tausend**

1923

O78 O1 5th m on 10pf org 18 22
O79 O1 20th m on 40pf rose red 18 15
O80 O1 50th m on 15pf vio 1.40 80
O81 O1 75th m on 2m gray 3.25 28
O82 O1 100th m on 20pf grn 15 28
O83 O1 250th m on 3m brn 15 15

Surcharged **2 Millionen**

O84 O1 1mil m on 60pf ol grn 1.10 80
O85 O1 2mil m on 50pf red brn 22 15
O86 O1 5mil m on 1.25m emer 32 32

Surcharged **10 Milliarden**

O87 O1 4 mlrd m on 50pf red brn 2.75 2.75
O88 O1 10 mlrd m on 3m brn 1.10 1.10
Nos. O78-O88 (11) 10.80 7.00

No. O23 Surcharged with New Values in Rentenpfennig as **3**

1923, Dec.

O89 O1 3pf on 25pf org 1.40 40
O90 O1 5pf on 25pf org 22 15
O91 O1 10pf on 25pf org 22 15
O92 O1 20pf on 25pf org 45 45
O93 O1 50pf on 25pf org 1.50 1.40
Nos. O89-O93 (5) 3.79 2.55

For the State Authorities

O6

Perf. 11½x11

1881-1902 **Typo.** **Unwmk.**

O94 O6 2pf sl gray ('00) 38 22
O95 O6 3pf green 3.25 1.90
O96 O6 3pf dk brn ('90) 38 15
O97 O6 5pf violet 2.25 40
O98 O6 5pf grn ('90) 38 15
O99 O6 10pf rose 1.25 15
O100 O6 20pf ultra 38 15
O101 O6 25pf brown 8.75 2.00
O102 O6 25pf org ('90) 80 15
O103 O6 30pf org & blk ('02) 80 70
O104 O6 40pf dp rose & blk ('02) 80 70
O105 O6 50pf gray grn 16.00 3.50
O106 O6 50pf mar ('90) 80 40
a. 50pf red brown 145.00 625.00
O107 O6 1m yellow 90.00 150.00
O108 O6 1m vio ('90) 11.00 11.00

See Nos. O119-O135. For overprints and surcharges see Nos. O109-O118, O146-O164, O176-O183.

Overprinted in Black **1806 – 1906**

1906

O109 O6 2pf sl gray 32.50 42.50
O110 O6 3pf dk brn 6.00 3.50
O111 O6 5pf green 4.00 85
O112 O6 10pf dp rose 4.00 85
O113 O6 20pf ultra 4.00 2.00
O114 O6 25pf orange 12.00 8.50
O115 O6 30pf org & blk 12.00 8.50
O116 O6 40pf dp rose & blk 35.00 42.50
O117 O6 50pf red brn 35.00 42.50
O118 O6 1m purple 75.00 80.00
Nos. O109-O118 (10) 219.50 231.70

Cent. of the kingdom of Wüttemberg.
Nos. O109 to O118 are also found imperforate, but it is doubtful if they were ever issued in that condition.

1906-19 **Wmk. 116**

O119 O6 2pf sl gray 28 15
O120 O6 2½pf gray blk ('16) 28 15
O121 O6 3pf dk brn 28 15
O122 O6 5pf green 28 15
O123 O6 7½pf org ('16) 28 15
O124 O6 10pf dp rose 28 15
O125 O6 15pf yel brn ('16) 28 15
O126 O6 15pf pur ('17) 40 15
O127 O6 20pf ultra 28 15
O128 O6 25pf orange 28 15
O129 O6 25pf brn & blk ('17) 28 15
O130 O6 30pf org & blk 28 15
O131 O6 35pf brn ('19) 1.10 45
O132 O6 40pf dp rose & blk 28 15
O133 O6 50pf red brn 28 15
O134 O6 1m purple 1.90 2.50
O135 O6 1m sl & blk ('17) 1.90 1.10
Nos. O119-O135 (17) 8.94 6.15

King Wilhelm II — O8

1916 **Unwmk.** **Typo.** ***Perf. 14***

O136 O8 2½pf slate 2.75 70
O137 O8 7½pf orange 1.25 15
O138 O8 10pf carmine 1.25 32
O139 O8 15pf yel brn 1.25 15
O140 O8 20pf blue 1.25 25
O141 O8 25pf gray blk 2.75 32
O142 O8 30pf green 2.75 32
O143 O8 40pf claret 4.00 1.00
O144 O8 50pf red brn 6.25 1.50
O145 O8 1m violet 6.00 1.75
Nos. O136-O145 (10) 29.50 6.46

25th year of the reign of King Wilhelm II.

Stamps of 1890-1906 Surcharged **25 Pf.**

1916-19 **Wmk. 116** ***Perf. 11½x11***

O146 O6 25pf on 25pf org 2.50 2.00
a. Without watermark 35.00 20.00
O147 O6 50pf on 50pf red brn 2.50 1.10
a. Inverted surcharge 30.00

No. O120 Surcharged in Blue

1919 **Wmk. 116**

O149 O6 2pf on 2½pf gray blk 90 70

Volksstaat

Official Stamps of 1890-1919 Overprinted

Württemberg

1919

No.	Type	Denom.	Color	Unused	Used
O150	O6	2½pf	gray blk	28	*15*
O151	O6	3pf	dk brn	5.50	*2.40*
a.			Without watermark	62.50	
O152	O6	5pf	green	18	*15*
O153	O6	7½pf	orange	28	*24*
O154	O6	10pf	rose	18	*15*
O155	O6	15pf	purple	18	*15*
O156	O6	20pf	ultra	20	*15*
O157	O6	25pf	brn & blk	20	*15*
a.			Inverted overprint	70.00	100.00
O158	O6	30pf	org & blk	45	*15*
a.			Inverted overprint	175.00	225.00
O159	O6	35pf	brown	28	*15*
O160	O6	40pf	rose & blk	32	*18*
O161	O6	50pf	claret	32	*24*
O162	O6	1m	sl & blk	70	*48*
			Nos. O150-O162 (13)	9.07	*4.74*

Nos. O151, O151a Surcharged in Carmine **75**

1920 **Wmk. 116**

No.	Type	Denom.	Color	Unused	Used
O164	O6	75pf on 3pf	dk brn	1.00	*65*
a.			Without watermark	27.50	

View of Stuttgart O9

Designs: 10pf, 50pf, 2.50m, 3m, View of Stuttgart. 15pf, 75pf, View of Ulm. 20pf, 1m, View of Tubingen. 30pf, 1.25m, View of Ellwangen.

Wmk. 192

1920, Mar. 25 **Typo.** ***Perf. 14½***

No.	Type	Denom.	Color	Unused	Used
O166	O9	10pf	maroon	45	*40*
O167	O9	15pf	brown	45	*40*
O168	O9	20pf	indigo	45	*40*
O169	O9	30pf	bl grn	45	*40*
O170	O9	50pf	yellow	45	*40*
O171	O9	75pf	bister	45	*50*
O172	O9	1m	org red	45	*50*
O173	O9	1.25m	dp vio	45	*50*
O174	O9	2.50m	dk ultra	80	*75*
O175	O9	3m	yel grn	80	*75*
			Nos. O166-O175 (10)	5.20	*5.00*

Deutsches

Official Stamps of 1906-19 Overprinted

Reich

1920 **Wmk. 116** ***Perf. 11½x11***

No.	Type	Denom.	Color	Unused	Used
O176	O6	5pf	green	20	*38*
O177	O6	10pf	dp rose	15	*15*
O178	O6	15pf	purple	15	*15*
O179	O6	20pf	ultra	15	*15*
a.			Wmk. 192	65.00	*85.00*
O180	O6	30pf	org & blk	15	*20*
O181	O6	40pf	dp rose & blk	15	*20*
O182	O6	50pf	red brn	15	*18*
O183	O6	1m	slate & blk	15	*30*
			Set value	75	

The note after No. O63 will also apply to Nos. O176 to O183.

NORTH GERMAN CONFEDERATION

Northern District
30 Groschen = 1 Thaler
Southern District
60 Kreuzer = 1 Gulden
Hamburg
16 Schillings = 1 Mark

Unused values for Nos. 1-24 are for copies with original gum. Copies without gum sell for about half the figures quoted.

A1

A2

Rouletted 8½ to 10, 11 to 12½ and Compound

1868 **Typo.** **Unwmk.**

No.	Type	Denom.	Color	Unused	Used
1	A1	¼gr	red lilac	15.00	13.00
2	A1	⅓gr	green	7.50	2.00
3	A1	½gr	orange	15.00	90
4	A1	1gr	rose	9.00	30
b.			Half used as ½gr on cover		
5	A1	2gr	ultra	45.00	80
6	A1	5gr	bister	50.00	5.75
7	A2	1kr	green	16.00	6.75
8	A2	2kr	orange	32.50	27.50
9	A2	3kr	rose	32.50	1.50
10	A2	7kr	ultra	125.00	7.50
11	A1	18kr	bister	32.50	42.50

See Nos. 13-23.

Imperf.

No.	Type	Denom.	Color	Unused	Used
1a	A1	¼gr	red lilac	105.00	*275.00*
2a	A1	⅓gr	green	47.50	*210.00*
3a	A1	½gr	orange	67.50	*300.00*
4a	A1	1gr	rose	35.00	*125.00*
5a	A1	2gr	ultra	140.00	*340.00*
6a	A1	5gr	bister	140.00	*300.00*
7a	A2	1kr	green	35.00	*60.00*
8a	A2	2kr	orange	105.00	42.50
9a	A2	3kr	rose	42.50	42.50
10a	A2	7kr	ultra	165.00	*340.00*
11a	A1	18kr	bister	165.00	*340.00*

A3

1868

No.	Type	Denom.	Color	Unused	Used
12	A3	(½s)	vio brn	60.00	25.00

See No. 24.

1869 ***Perf. 13½x14***

No.	Type	Denom.	Color	Unused	Used
13	A1	¼gr	lilac	16.00	9.00
a.		¼gr	red violet	32.50	15.00
14	A1	⅓gr	green	3.00	65
15	A1	½gr	orange	3.00	45
16	A1	1gr	rose	2.50	40
17	A1	2gr	ultra	3.00	40
18	A1	5gr	bister	7.50	2.75
19	A2	1kr	green	12.00	6.00
20	A2	2kr	orange	35.00	*45.00*
21	A2	3kr	rose	6.00	80
22	A2	7kr	ultra	10.00	2.75
23	A2	18kr	bister	75.00	*775.00*

Counterfeit cancels exist on No. 23.

1869

No.	Type	Denom.	Color	Unused	Used
24	A3	(½s)	dull vio brn	2.00	2.50

A4

A5

No.	Type	Denom.	Color	Unused	Used
25	A4	10gr	gray	300.00	400.00
			Pen cancellation		45.00
26	A5	30gr	blue	240.00	*900.00*
			Pen cancellation		*90.00*

Counterfeit cancels exist on No. 26.

OFFICIAL STAMPS

O1

1870 **Unwmk.** **Typo.** ***Perf. 14½x14***

No.	Type	Denom.	Color	Unused	Used
O1	O1	¼gr	blk & buff	24.00	45.00
O2	O1	⅓gr	blk & buff	16.00	13.00
O3	O1	½gr	blk & buff	2.25	2.25
O4	O1	1gr	blk & buff	4.00	35
O5	O1	2gr	blk & buff	6.00	2.50
O6	O1	1kr	blk & gray	21.00	*250.00*
O7	O1	2kr	blk & gray	60.00	*750.00*
O8	O1	3kr	blk & gray	18.00	35.00
O9	O1	7kr	blk & gray	35.00	*265.00*

Counterfeit cancels exist on Nos. O6-O9.

The stamps of the North German Confederation were replaced by those of the German Empire on Jan. 1, 1872.

GERMANY

LOCATION — In northern Europe bordering on the Baltic and North Seas

AREA — 182,104 sq. mi. (until 1945)

POP. — 67,032,242 (1946)

CAPITAL — Berlin

30 Silbergroschen or Groschen = 1 Thaler
60 Kreuzer = 1 Gulden
100 Pfennigs = 1 Mark (1875)
100 Pfennigs = 1 Deutsche Mark (1948)

Catalogue values for unused stamps in this country are for Never Hinged items, beginning with Scott 722 in the regular postage section, Scott B338 in the semi-postal section, Scott C61 in the airpost section, Scott 9N103 in the Berlin regular postage section and Scott 9NB12 in the Berlin semi-postal section.

Watermarks

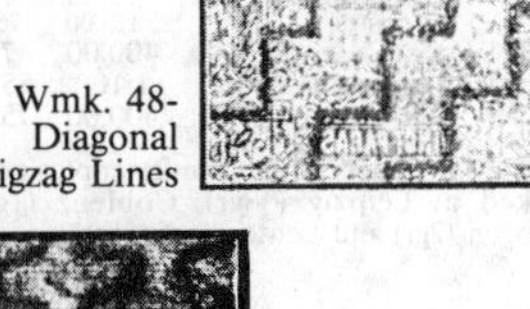

Wmk. 48- Diagonal Zigzag Lines

Wmk. 116- Crosses and Circles

Wmk. 125- Lozenges

Wmk. 126- Network

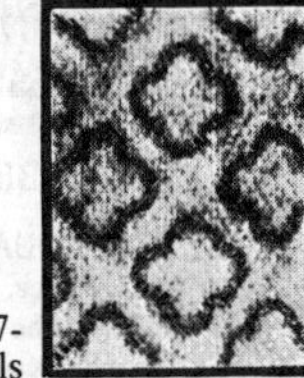

Wmk. 127- Quatrefoils

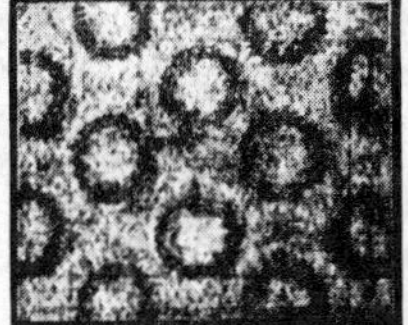

Wmk. 192- Circles

Wmk. 223- Eagle

Wmk. 237- Swastikas

Wmk. 241- Cross

Wmk. 284- "DEUTSCHE POST" Multiple

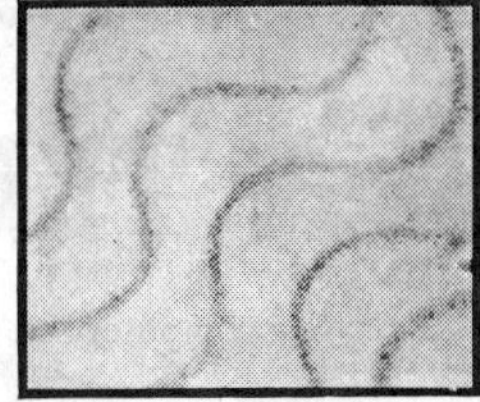

Wmk. 285- Marbleized Pattern

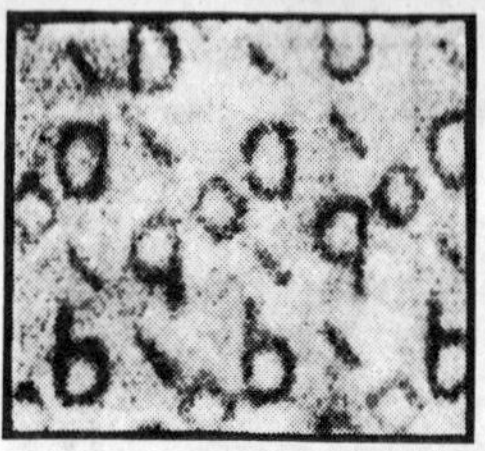

Wmk. 286- D P Multiple

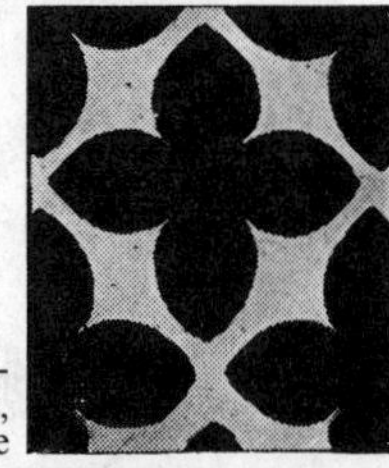
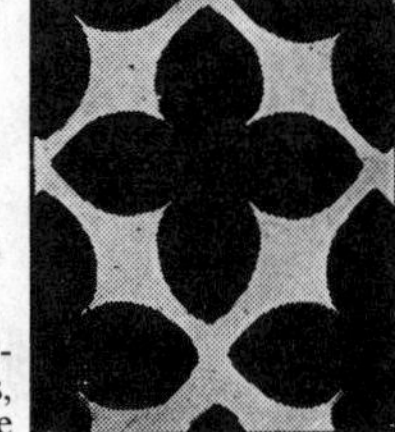

Wmk. 292- Flowers, Multiple

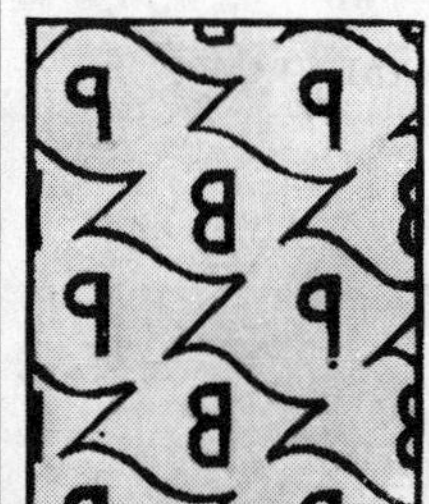

Wmk. 295- B P and Zigzag Lines

Wmk. 304- DBP and Rosettes Multiple

Empire

Values of early German Empire stamps vary according to condition. Quotations for Nos. 1-28 are for fine copies. Very fine to superb specimens sell at much higher prices, and inferior or poor copies sell at reduced prices, depending on the condition of the individual specimen.

Unused values for Nos. 1-13 are for stamps with original gum. Copies without gum sell at lower prices.

Imperial Eagle — A1

Typographed, Center Embossed

1872 Unwmk. *Perf. 13½x14½*

Eagle with small shield

No.	Type	Value	Unused	Used
1	A1	¼gr violet	140.00	55.00
2	A1	⅓gr green	300.00	25.00
a.		Imperf.		
3	A1	½gr red org	850.00	27.50
a.		½gr orange yellow	675.00	30.00
4	A1	1gr rose	200.00	4.00
a.		Imperf.		
5	A1	2gr ultra	650.00	7.50
a.		Imperf.		*8,500.*
6	A1	5gr bister	425.00	57.50
a.		Imperf.		*8,500.*
7	A1	1kr green	350.00	40.00
8	A1	2kr orange	25.00	*100.00*
a.		2kr red orange	325.00	175.00
9	A1	3kr rose	400.00	7.00
10	A1	7kr ultra	1,100.	55.00
11	A1	18kr bister	400.00	275.00

Values for imperforates are for copies postmarked at Leipzig (⅓gr), Coblenz (1gr), Hoengen (2gr) and Leutersdorf (5gr).

A2

A3

1872 Typo. *Perf. 14½x13½*

No.	Type	Value	Unused	Used
12	A2	10gr gray	75.00	*1,000.*
		Pen cancellation		80.00
13	A3	30gr blue	110.00	*2,500.*
		Pen cancellation		*275.00*

A4

A5

Center Embossed

1872 *Perf. 13½x14½*

Eagle with large shield

No.	Type	Value	Unused	Used
14	A4	¼gr violet	42.50	57.50
15	A4	⅓gr yel grn	20.00	9.00
a.		⅓gr blue green	90.00	75.00
16	A4	½gr orange	27.50	3.25
a.		Imperf.		
17	A4	1gr rose	25.00	1.50
a.		Imperf.		*8,500.*
b.		Half used as ½gr on cover		*42,500.*
18	A4	2gr ultra	12.50	3.00
19	A4	2½gr org brn	1,350.	37.50
a.		2½gr lilac brown	*5,250.*	250.00
20	A4	5gr bister	20.00	14.00
a.		Imperf.		*7,750.*
21	A4	1kr yel grn	22.50	20.00
a.		1kr blue green	125.00	150.00
22	A4	2kr orange	350.00	*1,750.*
23	A4	3kr rose	17.50	4.00
24	A4	7kr ultra	22.50	*50.00*
25	A4	9kr red brn	175.00	110.00
a.		9kr lilac brown	1,400.	300.00
26	A4	18kr bister	26.00	*1,500.*

Values for Nos. 17a and 20a are for copies postmarked at Potsdam (1gr), Damgarten or Anklam (5gr).

Nos. 14-26 with embossing inverted are fraudulent.

1874

Brown Surcharge

No.	Type	Value	Unused	Used
27	A5	2½gr on 2½gr brn	23.00	19.00
28	A5	9kr on 9kr brn	55.00	*170.00*

A6

A7

"Pfennige"

1875-77 Typo.

No.	Type	Value	Unused	Used
29	A6	3pf green	45.00	3.50
30	A6	5pf violet	80.00	1.00

Center Embossed

No.	Type	Value	Unused	Used
31	A7	10pf rose	30.00	20
32	A7	20pf ultra	175.00	75
33	A7	25pf red brn	325.00	12.00
34	A7	50pf gray	525.00	9.50
35	A7	50pf sl grn ('77)	2,000.	12.00

See Nos. 37-42. For surcharges see Offices in Turkey Nos. 1-6.

A8

1875-90 Typo. *Perf. 14½x13½*

No.	Type	Value	Unused	Used
36	A8	2m rose lil ('90)	60.00	2.00
a.		2m purple	325.00	9.00
b.		2m dull violet	360.00	27.50

Types of 1875-77, "Pfennig" without final "e"

1880-83 *Perf. 13½x14½*

No.	Type	Value	Unused	Used
37	A6	3pf green	1.65	30
a.		Imperf.		
38	A6	5pf violet	1.25	38

Center Embossed

No.	Type	Value	Unused	Used
39	A7	10pf rose	8.00	15
a.		Imperf.	*350.00*	
40	A7	20pf ultra	5.50	15
41	A7	25pf org brn	12.50	1.65
a.		25pf red brown ('83)	150.00	2.50
42	A7	50pf dp ol grn	6.50	50
a.		50pf gray green	6.50	50

Values for Nos. 37-42 are for stamps on thin paper. Those on thick paper sell for considerably more.

A9

A10

1889-1900 *Perf. 13½x14½*

No.	Type	Value	Unused	Used
45	A9	2pf gray ('00)	30	38
a.		"REIGHSPOST"	75.00	95.00
46	A9	3pf brown	1.90	15
a.		3pf yellow brown	8.00	35
b.		Imperf.	130.00	
c.		3pf reddish brown	50.00	10.00
47	A9	5pf green	90	15
48	A10	10pf carmine	1.50	15
a.		Imperf.	250.00	
49	A10	20pf ultra	7.50	15
a.		20pf Prus blue	350.00	45.00
50	A10	25pf org ('90)	30.00	85
a.		Imperf.	165.00	
51	A10	50pf chocolate	24.00	15
a.		50pf copper brown	250.00	14.00
b.		Imperf.		
		Nos. 45-51 (7)	66.10	1.98

For surcharges and overprints see Offices in China Nos. 1-6, 16, Offices in Morrocco 1-6, Offices in Turkey 8-12.

Germania — A11

1900, Jan. 1 *Perf. 14*

No.	Type	Value	Unused	Used
52	A11	2pf gray	35	15
a.		Imperf.	315.00	
53	A11	3pf brown	35	15
a.		Imperf.	250.00	
54	A11	5pf green	90	15
55	A11	10pf carmine	1.50	15
a.		Imperf.	62.50	
56	A11	20pf ultra	5.50	15
57	A11	25pf org & blk, *yel*	10.50	1.50
58	A11	30pf org & blk, *sal*	16.00	38
59	A11	40pf lake & blk	20.00	75
60	A11	50pf pur & blk, *sal*	20.00	50
61	A11	80pf lake & blk, *rose*	27.50	1.40
		Nos. 52-61 (10)	102.60	5.28

Early printings of Nos. 57-61 had "REICHSPOST" in taller and thicker letters than on the ordinary stamps.

For surcharges see Nos. 65B, Offices in China 17-32, Offices in Morocco 7-15, 32A, Offices in Turkey 13-20, 25-27.

"REICHSPOST" Larger

No.	Type	Value	Unused	Used
57a	A11	25pf	*1,300.*	*2,500.*
58a	A11	30pf	*1,300.*	*2,500.*
59a	A11	40pf	*1,300.*	*2,500.*
60a	A11	50pf	*1,300.*	*2,500.*
61a	A11	80pf	*1,300.*	*2,500.*

General Post Office in Berlin — A12

"Union of North and South Germany" A13

Unveiling Kaiser Wilhelm I Memorial, Berlin — A14

Wilhelm II Speaking at Empire's 25th Anniversary Celebration
A15

Two types of 5m:
I- "5" is thick; "M" has slight serifs.
II- "5" thinner; "M" has distinct serifs.

		Engr.	***Perf. 14½x14***	
62	A12	1m car rose	60.00	1.25
a.		Imperf.	*1,300.*	
63	A13	2m gray blue	60.00	2.75
64	A14	3m blk vio	90.00	30.00
65	A15	5m sl & car, I	700.00	500.00
65A	A15	5m sl & car, II	275.00	250.00

Nos. 62-65 exist perf. 11½.

No. 65 exists with misaligned vignette. White paint was applied to the inner frame. Sometimes red was also used to retouch the vignette. Values, about ⅓ those of No. 65.

For surcharges see Offices in China Nos. 33-36A, Offices in Morrocco 16-19A, Offices in Turkey 21-24B, 28-30.

Half of No. 54 Handstamp Surcharged in Violet **3PF**

1901			***Perf. 14***	
65B	A11	3pf on half of 5pf	*6,500.*	*8,000.*

This provisional was produced at New Orleans when the German cruiser Vineta anchored there. The purser, with the ship commander's approval, surcharged and bisected 300 5pf stamps so the ship's post office could meet the need for a 3pf (printed matter rate). The crew wanted to send home newspapers reporting celebrations of the Kaiser's birthday.

A16

1902				**Typo.**
65C	A16	2pf gray	1.75	24
66	A16	3pf brown	1.00	15
a.		"DFUTSCHES"	8.00	*35.00*
67	A16	5pf green	2.75	15
68	A16	10pf carmine	6.75	15
69	A16	20pf ultra	26.00	18
70	A16	25pf org & blk, *yel*	42.50	1.40
71	A16	30pf org & blk, *sal*	47.50	55
72	A16	40pf lake & blk	65.00	85
73	A16	50pf pur & blk, *buff*	60.00	1.25
74	A16	80pf lake & blk, *rose*	100.00	2.25
		Nos. 65C-74 (10)	353.25	7.17

Nos. 65C-74 exist imperf. Value, set $2,000.

See Nos. 80-91, 118-119, 121-132, 169, 174, 210. For surcharges see Nos. 133-136, B1, Offices in China 37-42, 47-52, Offices in Morrocco 20-28, 33-41, 45-53, Offices in Turkey 31-38, 43-50, 55-59.

A17

A18

A19

A20

		Engr.	***Perf. 14½***	
75	A17	1m car rose	165.00	1.00
a.		Imperf.	925.00	
76	A18	2m gray blue	85.00	70.00
77	A19	3m blk vio	75.00	12.50
a.		Imperf.	925.00	
78	A20	5m slate & car	125.00	15.00
a.		Imperf.	925.00	

See Nos. 92, 94-95, 102, 111-113. For surcharges see Nos. 115-116, Offices in China 43, 45-46, 53, 55-56, Offices in Morrocco 29, 31-32, 42, 44, 54, 56-57, Offices in Turkey 39, 41-42, 51, 53-54.

A21

79	A21	2m gray blue	75.00	2.00
a.		Imperf.	925.00	

See Nos. 93, 114. For surcharges see Nos. 117, Offices in China 44, 54, Offices in Morrocco 30, 43, 55, Offices in Turkey 40, 52.

1905-19		**Typo. Wmk. 125**	***Perf. 14***	
80	A16	2pf gray	1.50	1.50
81	A16	3pf brown	25	15
82	A16	5pf green	15	15
b.		Bklt. pane of 5 + label	400.00	
c.		Bklt. pane of 4 + 2 labels	350.00	
d.		Bklt. pane of 2 + 4 labels	350.00	
e.		Bklt. pane, #82 + 5 #83	130.00	
f.		Bklt. pane, 2 #82 + 4 #83	30.00	
g.		Bklt. pane, 4 #82 + 2 #83	30.00	
83	A16	10pf carmine	75	15
b.		Bklt. pane of 5 + label	775.00	
c.		Bklt. pane of 4 + 2 labels	425.00	
84	A16	20pf bl vio ('18)	25	15
a.		20pf light blue	10.50	3.25
b.		20pf ultramarine	8.00	8.75
c.		Imperf.	350.00	775.00
d.		Half used as 10pf on cover		100.00
85	A16	25pf org & blk, *yel*	40	15
86	A16	30pf org & blk, *buff*	20	15
a.		30pf org & blk, *cr*	16.00	27.50
87	A16	40pf lake & blk	85	15
88	A16	50pf pur & blk, *buff*	30	15
89	A16	60pf mag ('11)	1.50	18
a.		60pf red violet	12.00	8.00
90	A16	75pf grn & blk ('19)	15	15
91	A16	80pf lake & blk, *rose*	1.00	50
		Engr.		
92	A17	1m car rose	2.50	38
a.		1m carmine red	45.00	1.50
93	A21	2m brt bl	5.00	3.75
a.		2m gray blue	45.00	2.50
94	A19	3m vio gray	1.50	2.00
a.		3m blk vio ('11)	47.50	22.50
95	A20	5m sl & car	1.50	1.75
a.		Center inverted	*75,000.*	*100,000.*
		Nos. 80-95 (16)	17.80	11.41

Pre-war printings of Nos. 80-95 have brighter colors and white instead of yellow gum. They sell for considerably more than the wartime printings which are valued here.

Labels in No. 82c contain an "X." The version with advertising is worth 3 times as much. No. 82f has three 10pf stamps in the top row. The version with 3 on the bottom row is worth 4 times as much.

Surcharged and overprinted stamps of designs A16-A22 are listed under Allenstein, Belgium, Danzig, France, Latvia, Lithuania, Marienwerder, Memel, Poland, Romania, Saar and Upper Silesia.

A22

1916-19				**Typo.**
96	A22	2pf lt gray ('18)	15	*2.00*
97	A22	2½pf lt gray	15	15
98	A22	7½pf red org	15	15
b.		Bklt. pane, 4 #98 + 2 #100	165.00	
c.		Bklt. pane, 2 #98 + 4 #99	165.00	
d.		Bklt. pane, 2 #98 + 4 #100	165.00	
e.		Bklt. pane, 2 #82 + 4 #98	32.50	
f.		7½pf yel org	5.00	50
99	A22	15pf yel brn	2.50	35
100	A22	15pf dk vio ('17)	15	15
b.		Bklt. pane, 4 #82 + 2 #100	165.00	
c.		Bklt. pane, 2 #83 + 4 #100	19.00	
101	A22	35pf red brn ('19)	15	35
		Nos. 96-101 (6)	3.25	*3.15*

See No. 120. For surcharge see No. B2.

Nos. 98e and 100c have the 2 stamps first in the bottom row.

Type of 1902

1920		**Engr. Wmk. 192**	***Perf. 14½***	
102	A19	3m blk vio	1,500.	*1,900.*

Republic
National Assembly Issue

Live Stump of Tree Symbolizing that Germany will Survive her Difficulties
A23

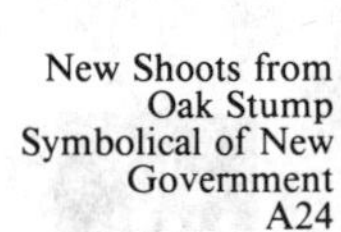

New Shoots from Oak Stump Symbolical of New Government
A24

Rebuilding Germany — A25

Perf. 13x13½

1919-20		**Unwmk.**		**Typo.**
105	A23	10pf carmine rose	15	30
106	A24	15pf choc & blue	15	30
107	A25	25pf green & red	15	30
108	A25	30pf red vio & red ('20)	15	30
		Set value		48

Nos. 107-108 exist with date reading "1019" instead of "1919."

Types of 1902

Perf. 15x14½

1920		**Wmk. 125**		**Offset**
111	A17	1m red	1.10	35
112	A17	1.25m green	1.00	25
113	A17	1.50m yellow brown	15	22
114	A21	2.50m lilac rose	15	20
a.		2.50m magenta	1.10	35
b.		2.50m brown lilac	50	40

Nos. 111, 112 and 113 differ from the illustration in many minor respects. The numerals of Nos. 75 and 92 are outlined, with shaded background. Those of No. 111 are plain, with solid background and flags have been added to the top of the building, at right and left.

Types of 1902, Engraved, Surcharged

*** 1,25m. ***

1920			***Perf. 14½***	
115	A17	1.25m on 1m grn	35	*5.00*
116	A17	1.50m on 1m org brn	35	*5.00*
117	A21	2.50m on 2m lil rose	7.50	*150.00*

Germania Types of 1902-16

1920 Typo. *Perf. 14, 14½*

118 A16 5pf brown 15 15
119 A16 10pf orange 15 15
a. Tete beche pair 65 *2.25*
c. Booklet pane of 6 75
d. Bklt. pane, 4 #119 + 2 #123 1.75
120 A22 15pf vio brn 15 15
a. Imperf. 50.00
b. Booklet pane of 6 6.25
c. Bklt. pane, 4 #84 + 2 #120 10.00
121 A16 20pf green 15 15
a. Imperf. 125.00
123 A16 30pf dl bl 15 15
a. Tete beche pair 65 *2.25*
c. Booklet pane of 6 75
d. Bklt. pane, 2 #123 + 4 #124 1.75
124 A16 40pf car rose 15 15
a. Tete beche pair 65 *2.25*
b. Imperf. 175.00 325.00
c. Booklet pane of 6 75
d. Bklt. pane, 2 #124 + 4 #126 2.25
125 A16 50pf red lilac 65 50
126 A16 60pf ol grn 15 15
a. Tete beche pair 80 *4.00*
b. Booklet pane of 6 1.50
c. Imperf. 175.00
127 A16 75pf red vio 15 20
128 A16 80pf bl vio 15 18
a. Imperf. 175.00
129 A16 1m vio & grn 15 18
a. Imperf. 85.00
130 A16 1¼m ver & mag 15 20
131 A16 2m car & bl 65 20
132 A16 4m blk & rose 15 20
Set value 2.00 2.25

Stamps of 1920 Surcharged:

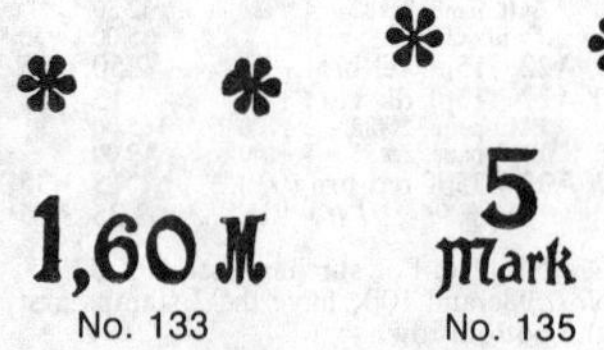

No. 133 No. 135

3 M 3
Nos. 134, 136

1921, Aug.

133 A16 1.60m on 5pf brown 15 28
134 A16 3m on 1¼m ver & mag 15 28
135 A16 5m on 75pf red vio (G) 15 28
136 A16 10m on 75pf red vio 30 45
Set value 56

In 1920 the current stamps of Bavaria were overprinted "Deutsches Reich". These stamps were available for postage throughout Germany, but because they were used almost exclusively in Bavaria, they are listed among the issues of that state.

A26

Iron Workers — A27

Miners A28

Farmers A29

Post Horn A30

Numeral of Value A31

Plowing — A32

Wmk. Lozenges (125)

1921 Typo. *Perf. 14*

137 A26 5pf claret 15 15
138 A26 10pf ol grn 15 15
a. Tete beche pair 70 *5.00*
b. Bklt. pane, 5 #138 + 1 #141 5.50
139 A26 15pf grnsh bl 15 15
140 A26 25pf dk brn 15 15
141 A26 30pf bl grn 15 15
a. Tete beche pair 70 *5.00*
b. Bklt. pane, 2 #124 + 4 #141 3.00
142 A26 40pf red org 15 15
143 A26 50pf violet 40 50
144 A27 60pf red vio 15 15
145 A27 80pf car rose 15 *2.50*
146 A28 100pf yel grn 38 *1.10*
147 A28 120pf ultra 15 18
148 A29 150pf orange 25 *75*
149 A29 160pf sl grn 15 *3.75*
150 A30 2m dp vio & rose 25 *1.25*
151 A30 3m red & yel 25 *5.00*
152 A30 4m dp grn & yel grn 15 *85*

Engr.

153 A31 5m brn org 30 *38*
154 A31 10m car rose 50 *75*
155 A32 20m ind & grn 1.10 *1.00*
a. Green background inverted 175.00 *500.00*
Set value 4.00

See Nos. 136-209, 211, 222-223, 225, 227. For surcharges and overprints see Nos. 241-245, 247-248, 261-262, 273-276, B6-B7, O24.

1922 Litho. *Perf. 14½x14*

156 A31 100m brn vio, *buff* 24 25
157 A31 200m rose, *buff* 15 25
158 A31 300m grn, *buff* 15 15
159 A31 400m bis brn, *buff* 40 *85*
160 A31 500m org, *buff* 15 25
Nos. 156-160 (5) 1.09 *1.75*

Postally Used vs. CTO

Values quoted for canceled copies of the 1921-1923 issues are for postally used stamps. These bring higher prices than the plentiful canceled-to-order specimens made by applying genuine handstamps to remainders. C.T.O. examples sell for about the same price as unused stamps. Certification of postal usage by competent authorities is necessary.

Perf. 14, 14½

1921-22 Typo. Wmk. 126

161 A26 5pf claret 50 *140.00*
162 A26 10pf ol grn 2.00 *115.00*
163 A26 15pf grnsh bl 40 *130.00*
164 A26 25pf dk brn 15 *2.00*
165 A26 30pf bl grn 65 *250.00*
166 A26 40pf red org 15 *2.50*
167 A26 50pf vio ('21) 15 15
168 A27 60pf red vio 15 *16.00*
169 A16 75pf red vio 30 *1.65*
170 A26 75pf dp ultra 15 *1.65*
171 A27 80pf car rose 30 *47.50*
172 A28 100pf yel grn 15 15
a. Imperf. 45.00
173 A28 120pf ultra 65 *65.00*
174 A16 1¼m ver & mag 25 *50*
175 A29 150pf orange 15 15
a. Imperf. 3.50
176 A29 160pf slate grn 75 *125.00*
177 A30 2m vio & rose 15 15
178 A30 3m red & yel ('21) 25 15
a. Imperf. 10.00
179 A30 4m dp grn & yel grn 15 22
180 A30 5m org & yel 15 15
a. Imperf. 150.00
181 A30 10m car & pale rose 15 15
a. Pale rose (background) omitted 21.00
182 A30 20m vio & org 18 20
183 A30 30m brn & yel 15 15
184 A30 50m dk grn & vio 15 15
Set value 7.15

1922-23

SIX MARKS:
Type I- Numerals upright.
Type II- Numerals leaning toward the right and slightly thinner.

EIGHT MARKS:
Type I- Numerals 2½mm wide with thick strokes.
Type II- Numerals 2mm wide with thinner strokes.

185 A30 2m dp vio 15 15
a. Imperf. 110.00
186 A30 3m red 15 15
187 A30 4m dk grn 15 15
a. Imperf. 2.50
188 A30 5m orange 15 15
a. Imperf. 110.00
189 A30 6m dk bl (II) 15 15
a. 6m dark blue (I) 15 25
b. Imperf. 110.00
190 A30 8m ol grn (I) 15 15
a. 8m olive green (II) 35 *17.50*
191 A30 20m dk vio ('23) 15 15
192 A30 30m dp brn ('23) 20 *3.75*
193 A30 40m lt grn 15 15

Engr.

194 A31 5m brn org 25 25
a. Imperf. 150.00
195 A31 10m car rose 65 75
196 A32 20m ind & grn 15 1.25
a. Imperf. 150.00
b. Green background inverted 14.00 *140.00*
Set value 1.65

1922-23 Litho. *Perf. 14½x14*

198 A31 50m indigo 15 25
199 A31 100m brn vio, *buff* ('23) 28 38
200 A31 200m rose, *buff* ('23) 15 15
201 A31 300m grn, *buff* ('23) 15 15
202 A31 400m bis brn, *buff* ('23) 15 15
203 A31 500m org, *buff* ('23) 15 15
204 A31 1000m gray ('23) 15 15
205 A31 2000m bl ('23) 15 18
206 A31 3000m brn ('23) 15 18
207 A31 4000m vio ('23) 15 20
a. Imperf. 27.50
208 A31 5000m gray grn ('23) 50 50
a. Imperf. 40.00

209 A31 100,000m ver ('23) 15 25
a. Imperf. 72.50
Set value 1.65

1920-22 Wmk. 127 Typo.

210 A16 1¼m ver & mag 325.00 350.00
211 A30 50m grn & vio ('22) 1.10 *350.00*

Wmk. 127 was intended for use only in printing revenue stamps.

Arms of Munich — A33

Wmk. Network (126)

1922, Apr. 22 Typo. *Perf. 13x13½*

212 A33 1¼m claret 15 25
213 A33 2m dk vio 15 25
214 A33 3m vermilion 22 32
215 A33 4m dp bl 18 32

Wmk. Lozenges (125)

216 A33 10m brn, *buff* 32 75
217 A33 20m dp rose, *pink* 2.50 6.00
Nos. 212-217 (6) 3.52 7.89

Munich Industrial Fair.

Type of 1921 and

Miners — A34

A35

1922-23 Wmk. 126 *Perf. 14*

221 A34 5m orange 15 *8.25*
222 A29 10m dl bl ('22) 15 15
223 A29 12m ver ('22) 15 15
224 A34 20m red lil 15 15
225 A29 25m ol brn 15 15
226 A34 30m ol grn 15 *32*
227 A29 40m green 15 15
228 A34 50m grnsh bl 35 *80.00*
229 A35 100m violet 15 15
230 A35 200m car rose 15 22
231 A35 300m green 15 22
232 A35 400m dk brn 15 *3.25*
233 A35 500m red org 15 *3.25*
234 A35 1000m slate 15 25
Set value 1.15

The 50m was issued only in vertical coils.
Nos. 222-223 exist imperf.
For surcharges and overprints see Nos. 246, 249-260, 263-271, 277, 310, B5, O22-O23, O25-O28.

Wartburg Castle A36

Cathedral of Cologne A37

1923 **Engr.**

No.	Type	Description	Unused	Used
237	A36	5000m dp bl	25	1.25
a.		Imperf.	325.00	
238	A37	10,000m ol grn	20	1.65

Abbreviations:
Th = (Tausend) Thousand
Mil = (Million) Million
Mlrd = (Milliarde) Billion

A38

1923 **Typo.**

No.	Type	Description	Unused	Used
238A	A38	5th m grnsh bl	15	10.00
b.		Imperf.	100.00	
239	A38	50th m bister	15	25
a.		Imperf.	18.00	
240	A38	75th m dk vio	15	6.50
		Set value	24	

For surcharges see Nos. 272, 278.

Stamps and Types of 1922-23 Surcharged in Black, Blue or Green with Bars over Original Value

8 Tausend

1923 Wmk. Lozenges (125) ***Perf. 14***

No.	Type	Description	Unused	Used
241	A26	8th m on 30pf	15	35
a.		"8" inverted	22.50	275.00

Wmk. Network (126)

No.	Type	Description	Unused	Used
242	A26	5th m on 40pf	15	75
242A	A26	8th m on 30pf	22.50	3,750.
243	A29	15th m on 40m	15	35
244	A29	20th m on 12m	15	35
a.		Inverted surcharge		
245	A29	20th m on 25m	15	2.00
246	A35	20th m on 200m	15	35
a.		Inverted surcharge	85.00	165.00
247	A29	25th m on 25m	15	12.50
248	A29	30th m on 10m dp bl	15	35
a.		Inverted surcharge	150.00	
249	A35	30th m on 200m pale bl (Bl)	15	35
a.		Without surcharge	165.00	
250	A35	75th m on 300m yel grn	15	12.50
a.		Imperf.	15.00	42.50
251	A35	75th m on 400m yel grn	15	35
252	A35	75th m on 1000m yel grn	15	35
a.		Without surcharge	165.00	
253	A35	100th m on 100m	15	75
a.		Double surcharge	22.50	
b.		Inverted surcharge	15.00	
254	A35	100th m on 400m bluish grn (G)	15	35
a.		Imperf.	62.50	
b.		Without surcharge	165.00	
255	A35	125th m on 1000m sal	15	35
256	A35	250th m on 200m	15	3.50
a.		Inverted surcharge	27.50	
b.		Double surcharge	50.00	
257	A35	250th m on 300m dp grn	15	12.50
a.		Inverted surcharge	21.00	
258	A35	250th m on 400m	15	12.50
a.		Inverted surcharge	27.50	
259	A35	250th m on 500m pink	15	35
a.		Imperf.	62.50	
260	A35	250th m on 500m red org	15	10.50
a.		Double surcharge	21.00	
b.		Inverted surcharge	37.50	
261	A26	800th m on 5pf lt grn (G)	15	3.50
a.		Imperf.	8.50	
262	A26	800th m on 10pf lt grn (G)	15	4.25
263	A35	800th m on 200m	15	42.50
a.		Double surcharge	85.00	
b.		Inverted surcharge	50.00	
264	A35	800th m on 300m lt grn (G)	15	4.25
a.		Black surcharge	21.00	
265	A35	800th m on 400m dk brn	15	12.50
a.		Inverted surcharge	67.50	
b.		Double surcharge	70.00	
266	A35	800th m on 400m lt grn (G)	15	3.00
267	A35	800th m on 500m lt grn (G)	15	1,050.
a.		800th m on 500m red org (Bk)	21.00	
268	A35	800th m on 1000m lt grn (G)	15	35
269	A35	2mil m on 200m rose red	15	25
b.		2mil m on 200m car rose (#230)	500.00	
270	A35	2mil m on 300m dp grn	15	85
a.		Inverted surcharge	67.50	
b.		Double surcharge	85.00	
271	A35	2mil m on 500m dl rose	15	4.25
272	A38	2mil m on 5th m dl rose	15	35
b.		Imperf.	42.50	

Nos. 264a, 267a were not put in use.

Serrate Roulette 13 1/2

No.	Type	Description	Unused	Used
273	A26	400th m on 15pf bis (Br)	15	2.00
a.		Imperf.	77.50	
274	A26	400th m on 25pf bis (Br)	15	2.00
a.		Imperf.	425.00	225.00
275	A26	400th m on 30pf bis (Br)	15	2.00
a.		Imperf.	50.00	
276	A26	400th m on 40pf bis (Br)	15	2.00
a.		Imperf.	50.00	
277	A35	2mil m on 200m rose red	15	125.00
278	A38	2mil m on 5th m dl rose	15	6.25

Nos. 273-276 and 278 exist without surcharge. Value, $225-275 each.

A39

A39a

The stamps of types A39 and A39a usually have the value darker than the rest of the design.

1923 **Wmk. 126** ***Perf. 14***

No.	Type	Description	Unused	Used
280	A39	500th m brn	15	2.00
281	A39	1mil m grnsh bl	15	35
a.		Imperf.	60.00	
282	A39	2mil m dl vio	15	22.50
284	A39	4mil m yel grn	15	75
a.		Value double	100.00	
b.		Imperf.	50.00	
285	A39	5mil m rose	15	35
286	A39	10mil m red	15	35
a.		Value double	85.00	300.00
287	A39	20mil m ultra	15	50
288	A39	30mil m red brn	15	10.50
289	A39	50mil m dl grn	15	35
a.		Imperf.	62.50	195.00
b.		Value inverted	35.00	
290	A39	100mil m gray	15	35
291	A39	200mil m bis brn	15	35
a.		Imperf.	6.25	
293	A39	500mil m ol grn	15	35
294	A39a	1mlrd m choc	15	35
295	A39a	2mlrd m pale brn & grn	15	50
296	A39a	5mlrd m yel & brn	15	50
297	A39a	10mlrd m ap grn & grn	15	50
a.		Imperf.	30.00	
298	A39a	20mlrd m bluish grn & brn	15	1.00
299	A39a	50mlrd m bl & dp bl	60	22.50
		Set value	2.00	

The variety "value omitted" exists on Nos. 280-281, 284-287, 290-291, 293-294, 296, 298-299 and 307. Values $90-$175.

See Nos. 301-309. For surcharges and overprints see Nos. 311-321, O40-O46.

Serrate Roulette 13 1/2

No.	Type	Description	Unused	Used
301	A39	10mil m red	15	42.50
302	A39	20mil m ultra	15	300.00
303	A39	50mil m dl grn	15	5.25
304	A39	200mil m bis brn	15	10.50
305	A39a	1mlrd m choc	15	5.00
306	A39a	2mlrd m pale brn & grn	15	2.25
307	A39a	5mlrd m yel & brn	15	1.65
308	A39a	20mlrd m bluish grn & brn	40	10.50
309	A39a	50mlrd m bl & dp bl	1.25	450.00
		Nos. 301-309 (9)	2.70	

Stamps and Types of 1923 Surcharged with New Values

1923 ***Perf. 14***

No.	Type	Description	Unused	Used
310	A35	1mlrd m on 100m vio	15	27.50
a.		Inverted surcharge	62.50	
b.		1mlrd m on 100m dp redsh pur	77.50	3,200.
311	A39	5mlrd m on 2mil m dl vio	35	100.00
a.		Inverted surcharge	30.00	
b.		Double surcharge	62.50	
312	A39	5mlrd m on 4mil m yel grn	15	27.50
a.		Inverted surcharge	42.50	165.00
b.		Double surcharge	50.00	
313	A39	5mlrd m on 10mil m red	15	1.65
a.		Inverted surcharge	27.50	165.00
b.		Double surcharge	30.00	
314	A39	10mlrd m on 20mil m ultra	30	1.65
a.		Double surcharge	72.50	
b.		Inverted surcharge	42.50	
315	A39	10mlrd m on 50mil m dl grn	15	1.65
a.		Inverted surcharge	30.00	
b.		Double surcharge	72.50	
316	A39	10mlrd m on 100mil m gray	15	5.00
a.		Inverted surcharge	37.50	
b.		Double surcharge	70.00	
		Set value	1.33	

No. 310b was issued in Bavaria only and is known as the Hitler provisional. Excellent forgeries exist.

Serrate Roulette 13 1/2

No.	Type	Description	Unused	Used
319	A39	5mlrd m on 10mil m red	1.00	195.00
a.		Inverted surcharge	35.00	
b.		Double surcharge	30.00	
320	A39	10mlrd m on 20mil m ultra	1.25	90.00
321	A39	10mlrd m on 50mil m dl grn	1.00	42.50
a.		Inverted surcharge	35.00	

A40

German Eagle — A41

1923 ***Perf. 14***

No.	Type	Description	Unused	Used
323	A40	3pf brown	30	15
324	A40	5pf dk grn	30	15
325	A40	10pf carmine	30	15
326	A40	20pf dp ultra	75	15
327	A40	50pf orange	1.90	45
328	A40	100pf brn vio	6.25	55
		Nos. 323-328 (6)	9.80	
		Set value		1.30

For overprints see Nos. O47-O52.

Imperf.

No.	Type	Description	Unused	Used
323a	A40	3pf	165.00	250.00
324a	A40	5pf	45.00	250.00
325a	A40	10pf	130.00	130.00
326a	A40	20pf	165.00	235.00
327a	A40	50pf	180.00	300.00
328a	A40	100pf	200.00	

Value Omitted

No.	Type	Description	Unused	Used
323b	A40	3pf	105.00	250.00
324b	A40	5pf	140.00	
325b	A40	10pf	105.00	
326b	A40	20pf	100.00	
327b	A40	50pf	100.00	
328b	A40	100pf	140.00	

1924 **Wmk. 126**

No.	Type	Description	Unused	Used
330	A41	3pf lt brn	24	15
331	A41	5pf lt grn	32	15
332	A41	10pf vermilion	45	15
333	A41	20pf dl bl	1.25	15
334	A41	30pf rose lil	1.90	20
335	A41	40pf ol grn	13.00	45
336	A41	50pf orange	13.00	65
		Nos. 330-336 (7)	30.16	
		Set value		1.50

The values above 5pf have "Pf" in the upper right corner.

For overprints see Nos. O53-O61.

Imperf.

No.	Type	Description	Unused	Used
330a	A41	3pf	160.00	195.00
331a	A41	5pf	210.00	300.00
332a	A41	10pf	195.00	
333a	A41	20pf	195.00	
334a	A41	30pf	195.00	
335a	A41	40pf	200.00	

Rheinstein Castle — A43

View of Cologne — A44

Marienburg Castle — A45

1924 **Engr.** **Wmk. 126**

337 A43 1m green 12.00 1.75
338 A44 2m blue 19.00 1.75
339 A45 3m claret 19.00 4.00

See No. 387.

Dr. Heinrich von Stephan
A46 A47

1924-28 **Typo.**

340 A46 10pf dk green 50 15
341 A46 20pf dark blue 70 35
342 A47 60pf red brown 4.25 15
 a. Chalky paper ('28) 17.50 2.50
343 A47 80pf slate 6.50 85

Universal Postal Union, 50th anniversary.

No. 340 exists imperf. Value $300.

Traffic Wheel — A48

German Eagle Watching Rhine Valley — A49

1925, May 30 ***Perf. 13½x13***

345 A48 5pf dp grn 3.00 3.50
346 A48 10pf vermilion 3.50 5.50

German Traffic Exhibition, Munich, May 30-Oct. 11, 1925.

1925 ***Perf. 14***

347 A49 5pf green 30 15
348 A49 10pf vermilion 50 15
349 A49 20pf deep blue 3.00 70

Issued to commemorate 1000 years' union of the Rhineland with Germany.

Speyer Cathedral A50

1925, Sept. 11 **Engr.**

350 A50 5m dull green 30.00 9.75

Johann Wolfgang von Goethe — A51

Designs: 3pf, 25pf, Goethe. 5pf, Friedrich von Schiller. 8pf, 20pf, Ludwig van Beethoven. 10pf, Frederick the Great. 15pf, Immanuel Kant. 30pf, Gotthold Ephraim Lessing. 40pf, Gottfried Wilhelm Leibnitz. 50pf, Johann Sebastian Bach. 80pf, Albrecht Durer.

1926-27 **Typo.** ***Perf. 14***

351 A51 3pf olive brn 40 15
352 A51 3pf bis ('27) 85 15
353 A51 5pf dk grn 85 15
 b. 5pf light green ('27) 1.00 15
354 A51 8pf bl grn ('27) 1.00 15
355 A51 10pf carmine 85 15
356 A51 15pf vermilion 2.00 15
 a. Booklet pane of 8 + 2 labels 275.00
357 A51 20pf myrtle grn 10.00 60
358 A51 25pf blue 2.50 28
359 A51 30pf olive grn 5.75 16
360 A51 40pf dp vio 10.00 28
361 A51 50pf brown 11.00 4.75
362 A51 80pf chocolate 25.00 3.75
 Nos. 351-362 (12) 70.20 10.72

Nos. 351-354, 356 and 357 exist imperf. Value each $175.

Nos. 354, 356 and 358 Overprinted

I.A.A.

10.-15.10.1927

1927, Oct. 10

363 A51 8pf bl grn 17.00 35.00
364 A51 15pf vermilion 17.00 35.00
365 A51 25pf blue 17.00 35.00

"I.A.A." stands for "Internationales Arbeitsamt," (Intl. Labor Bureau), an agency of the League of Nations. Issued in connection with a meeting of the I.A.A. in Berlin, Oct. 10-15, 1927, they were on sale to the public.

Pres. Friedrich Ebert A60

Pres. Paul von Hindenburg A61

1928-32 **Typo.** ***Perf. 14***

366 A60 3pf bister 15 15
367 A61 4pf lt bl ('31) 25 15
 a. Tete beche pair 6.25 6.25
 b. Bklt. pane of 9 + label 22.50
368 A61 5pf lt grn 32 15
 a. Tete beche pair 6.75 6.75
 b. Imperf. 250.00
 c. Bklt. pane of 6 + 4 labels 19.00
 d. Bklt. pane, 4 #368 + 6 #369 22.50
369 A60 6pf lt ol grn ('32) 32 15
 a. Bklt. pane, 2 #369 + 8 #373 22.50
370 A60 8pf dk grn 15 15
 a. Tete beche pair 7.75 7.75
371 A60 10pf vermilion 1.25 75
372 A60 10pf red vio ('30) 65 15
373 A61 12pf org ('32) 60 15
 a. Tete beche pair 7.75 7.75
374 A61 15pf car rose 50 15
 a. Tete beche pair 10.50 10.50
 b. Bklt. pane 6 + 4 labels 22.50
375 A60 20pf Prus grn 2.75 1.40
 a. Imperf. 500.00
376 A60 20pf gray ('30) 4.50 15
377 A61 25pf blue 6.75 30
378 A60 30pf ol grn 4.00 20
379 A61 40pf violet 10.50 28
380 A60 45pf orange 6.00 1.10
381 A61 50pf brown 6.00 65
382 A60 60pf org brn 6.75 1.10
383 A61 80pf chocolate 16.00 2.00
384 A61 80pf yel bis ('30) 5.00 48
 Nos. 366-384 (19) 72.44 9.61

Stamps of 1928 Overprinted

30. JUNI
1930

1930, June 30

385 A60 8pf dark green 60 15
386 A61 15pf carmine rose 60 20

Issued in commemoration of the final evacuation of the Rhineland by the Allied forces.

View of Cologne — A63

1930 **Engr.** **Wmk. 126**
Inscribed: "Reichsmark"

387 A63 2m dark blue 30.00 8.25

Pres. von Hindenburg A64

Frederick the Great A65

1932, Oct. 1 **Typo.** **Wmk. 126**

391 A64 4pf blue 52 15
392 A64 5pf brt grn 52 15
393 A64 12pf dp org 3.75 15
394 A64 15pf dk red 2.75 6.50
395 A64 25pf ultra 1.00 35
396 A64 40pf violet 8.75 1.00
397 A64 50pf dk brn 6.25 8.50
 Nos. 391-397 (7) 23.54 16.80

85th birthday of von Hindenburg.

See Nos. 401-431, 436-441. For surcharges and overprints see France, Luxembourg and Poland.

1933, Apr. 12 **Photo.**

398 A65 6pf dk grn 42 55
 a. Tete beche pair 12.50 14.00
399 A65 12pf carmine 42 55
 a. Tete beche pair 12.50 14.00
 b. Bklt. pane of 5 + label 42.50
400 A65 25pf ultra 22.50 13.00

Celebration of Potsdam Day.

Hindenburg Type of 1932

1933 **Typo.**

401 A64 3pf ol bis 12.00 50
402 A64 4pf dl bl 3.25 50
403 A64 6pf dk grn 1.40 15
404 A64 8pf dp org 6.50 50
 a. Bklt. pane, 3 #404 + 5 #406 130.00
 b. Open "D" 27.50 3.00
405 A64 10pf chocolate 3.25 50
406 A64 12pf dp car 1.40 15
 a. Bklt. pane, 4 #392 + 4 #406 60.00
407 A64 15pf maroon 4.50 *13.00*
408 A64 20pf brt bl 5.25 65
409 A64 30pf ol grn 6.50 40
410 A64 40pf red vio 24.00 1.25
411 A64 50pf dk grn & blk 15.00 1.65
412 A64 60pf cl & blk 24.00 52
413 A64 80pf dk bl & blk 9.00 90
414 A64 100pf org & blk 18.00 6.50
 Nos. 401-414 (14) 134.05 *27.17*

Hindenburg Type of 1932

1933-36 **Wmk. 237** ***Perf. 14***

415 A64 1pf black 15 15
 a. Bklt. pane, 4 #415, 3 #417, label 5.00
 b. Bklt. pane, 3 #415, 3 #416 + 2 #418 6.00
 c. Bklt. pane, 2 #415, 5 #420, label 6.00
 d. Bklt. pane, 4 #415 + 4 #422 3.50
416 A64 3pf ol bis ('34) 15 15
 a. Bklt. pane, 4 #416 + 4 #418 1.75
 b. Bklt. pane, 4 #416 + 4 #419 2.00
 c. Bklt. pane, 6 #416, 1 #422, label 2.50
417 A64 4pf dl bl ('34) 15 15
 a. Bklt. pane, 3 #417, 4 #422, label 6.00
418 A64 5pf brt grn ('34) 15 15
 a. Bklt. pane, 2 #418, 5 #419, label 5.00
 b. Bklt. pane, 2 #418, 3 #419 + 3 #420 3.50
 c. Bklt. pane, 4 #418 + 4 #420 4.00
419 A64 6pf dk grn ('34) 15 15
 b. Bklt. pane of 7 + label 1.75
 c. Bklt. pane, 1 #419, 6 #422, label 17.00
420 A64 8pf dp org ('34) 15 15
 a. Bklt. pane, 3 #420, 4 #422, label 5.00
 b. Open "D" 6.00 2.50
421 A64 10pf choc ('34) 15 15
422 A64 12pf dp car ('34) 15 15
 a. Bklt. pane of 7 + label 6.00
423 A64 15pf mar ('34) 20 15
424 A64 20pf brt bl ('34) 24 15
425 A64 25pf ultra ('34) 30 15
426 A64 30pf ol grn ('34) 45 15
427 A64 40pf red vio ('34) 45 15
428 A64 50pf dk grn & blk ('34) 70 15
429 A64 60pf cl & blk ('34) 55 15
430 A64 80pf dk bl & blk ('36) 1.75 50
431 A64 100pf org & blk ('34) 3.25 32
 Nos. 415-431 (17) 9.09
 Set value 1.75

Franz Adolf E. Lüderitz A66

Swastika, Sun and Nuremberg Castle A70

Designs: 6pf, Dr. Gustav Nachtigal. 12pf, Karl Peters. 25pf, Hermann von Wissmann.

1934, June 30 ***Perf. 13x13½***

432 A66 3pf brn & choc 1.75 2.75
433 A66 6pf dk grn & choc 75 65
434 A66 12pf dk car & choc 90 38
435 A66 25pf brt bl & choc 5.50 9.00

Issued in remembrance of the lost colonies of Germany.

Hindenburg Memorial Issue
Type of 1932
With Black Border

1934, Sept. 4 ***Perf. 14***

436 A64 3pf ol bis 55 20
437 A64 5pf brt grn 55 32
438 A64 6pf dk grn 90 15
439 A64 8pf vermilion 1.40 20
440 A64 12pf dp car 1.90 20
441 A64 25pf ultra 5.75 4.00
 Nos. 436-441 (6) 11.05 5.07

1934, Sept. 1 **Photo.**

442 A70 6pf dark green 1.50 15
443 A70 12pf dark carmine 3.50 15
 Set value 24

Nazi Congress at Nuremberg.
Imperfs exist. Value, each $400.

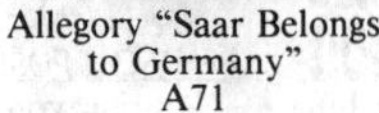

Allegory "Saar Belongs to Germany" A71 — German Eagle A72

1934, Aug. 26 Typo. Wmk. 237

444 A71 6pf dk grn 1.50 15
445 A72 12pf dk car 3.50 15
Set value 24

Issued to mark the Saar Plebiscite.

Friedrich von Schiller A73 — Germania Welcoming Home the Saar A74

1934, Nov. 5

446 A73 6pf green 1.40 15
447 A73 12pf carmine 3.50 15

175th anniv. of the birth of von Schiller.

1935, Jan. 16 Photo.

448 A74 3pf brown 50 35
449 A74 6pf dark green 65 15
450 A74 12pf lake 2.50 15
451 A74 25pf dark blue 8.25 4.00

Return of the Saar to Germany.

German Soldier A75 — Wreath and Swastika A76

1935, Mar. 15

452 A75 6pf dark green 90 85
453 A75 12pf copper red 90 85

Issued to commemorate War Heroes' Day.

1935, Apr. 26 Unwmk.

454 A76 6pf dk grn 85 50
455 A76 12pf crimson 85 50

Issued in connection with the Young Workers' Professional Competitions.

Heinrich Schütz — A77 — "The Eagle" — A80

Wmk. Swastikas (237)

1935, June 21 Engr. *Perf. 14*

456 A77 6pf shown 60 15
457 A77 12pf Bach 70 15
458 A77 25pf Handel 1.25 50
Set value 66

Schutz-Bach-Handel celebration.

1935, July 10 *Perf. 14*

Designs: 12pf, Modern express train. 25pf, "The Hamburg Flyer." 40pf, Streamlined locomotive.

459 A80 6pf dk grn 80 22
460 A80 12pf cop red 80 22
461 A80 25pf ultra 6.50 85
462 A80 40pf red vio 8.00 85

Centenary of railroad in Germany. Exist imperf. Value, $225 each.

Bugler of Hitler Youth Movement A84 — Eagle and Swastika over Nuremberg A85

1935, July 25 Photo.

463 A84 6pf dp grn 1.10 1.50
464 A84 15pf brn lake 1.10 1.50

Hitler Youth Meeting.

1935, Aug. 30 Engr.

465 A85 6pf gray grn 65 15
466 A85 12pf dk car 1.00 15
Set value 18

1935 Nazi Congress at Nuremberg.

Nazi Flag Bearer and Feldherrnhalle at Munich A86 — Airplane A87

1935, Nov. 5 Photo. *Perf. 13½*

467 A86 3pf brown 25 15
468 A86 12pf dk car 40 15

12th anniv. of the 1st Hitler "Putsch" at Munich, Nov. 9, 1923.

1936, Jan. 6

469 A87 40pf sapphire 5.00 90

10th anniv. of the Lufthansa air service.

Gottlieb Daimler A88 — Carl Benz A89

1936, Feb. 15 *Perf. 14*

470 A88 6pf dark green 38 18
471 A89 12pf copper red 55 18

The 50th anniv. of the automobile; Intl. Automobile and Motorcycle Show, Berlin.

Otto von Guericke A90 — Symbolical of Municipalities A91

1936, May 4

472 A90 6pf dk grn 22 15

250th anniv. of the death of the German inventor, Otto von Guericke, May 11, 1686.

1936, June 3

473 A91 3pf dk brn 15 15
474 A91 5pf dp grn 15 15
475 A91 12pf lake 25 15
476 A91 25pf dk ultra 65 65
Set value 90

6th Intl. Cong. of Municipalities, June 7-13.

Allegory of Recreation Congress A92 — Salute to Swastika A93

1936, June 30

477 A92 6pf dk grn 35 28
478 A92 15pf dp claret 50 38

World Congress for Vacation and Recreation held at Hamburg.

1936, Sept. 3 *Perf. 14*

479 A93 6pf deep green 28 15
480 A93 12pf copper red 40 15

The 1936 Nazi Congress.

Shield Bearer A94 — German and Austrian Carrying Nazi Flag A95

1937, Mar. 3 Engr. Unwmk.

481 A94 3pf brown 15 15
482 A94 6pf green 18 15
483 A94 12pf carmine 35 22
Set value 36

The Reich's Air Protection League.

Wmk. Swastikas. (237)

1938, Apr. 8 Photo. *Perf. 14x13½*

Size: 23x28mm

484 A95 6pf dark green 15 15

Unwmk. *Perf. 12½*

Size: 21½x26mm

485 A95 6pf deep green 15 20

Union of Austria and Germany.

Cathedral Island A96 — Hermann Goering Stadium A97

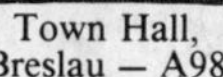
Town Hall, Breslau — A98

Centennial Hall, Breslau — A99

1938, June 21 **Engr.** ***Perf. 14***
486 A96 3pf dk brn 15 15
487 A97 6pf dp grn 24 15
488 A98 12pf cop red 40 15
489 A99 15pf vio brn 65 50
Set value 74

16th German Gymnastic and Sports Festival held at Breslau, July 23-31, 1938.

Nazi Emblem — A100

1939, Apr. 4 **Photo.** **Wmk. 237**
490 A100 6pf dk grn 1.75 2.50
491 A100 12pf dp car 1.75 2.50

Young Workers' Professional Competitions.

St. Mary's Church — A101

The Krantor, Danzig — A102

1939, Sept. 18
492 A101 6pf dk grn 15 22
493 A102 12pf org red 18 32
Set value 26

Unification of Danzig with the Reich.

Johannes Gutenberg and Library at Leipzig — A103

Designs: 6pf, "High House," Leipzig. 12pf, Old Town Hall, Leipzig. 25pf, View of Leipzig Fair.

Inscribed "Leipziger Messe"

Perf. 10½

1940, Mar. 3 **Photo.** **Unwmk.**
494 A103 3pf dk brn 15 22
495 A103 6pf dk gray grn 15 22
496 A103 12pf henna brn 18 15
497 A103 25pf ultra 35 60

Leipzig Fair.

House of Nations, Leipzig — A107

Designs: 6pf, Concert Hall, Leipzig. 12pf, Leipzig Fair Office. 25pf, Railroad Terminal, Leipzig.

Inscribed: "Reichsmesse Leipzig, 1941"

1941, Mar. 1 ***Perf. 14x13½***
498 A107 3pf brown 15 28
499 A107 6pf green 15 28
500 A107 12pf dk red 18 30
501 A107 25pf brt bl 35 60

Leipzig Fair.

Fashion Allegory A111

Vienna Fair Hall A112

"Burgtheater" A113

Monument to Prince Eugene A114

1941, Mar. 8 ***Perf. 13½x14***
502 A111 3pf dk red brn 15 15
503 A112 6pf brt bl grn 15 15
504 A113 12pf scarlet 30 30
505 A114 25pf brt bl 52 52

Vienna Fair.

Adolf Hitler
A115 A116

1941-43 **Typo.** ***Perf. 14***

Size: 18½x22½mm
506 A115 1pf gray blk 15 15
a. Bklt. pane, 4 #506 + 4 #509 2.00
507 A115 3pf lt brn 15 15
a. Bklt. pane, 6 #507 + 2 #510 2.00
508 A115 4pf slate 15 15
a. Bklt. pane, 4 #508, 2 #511 + 2 labels 2.25
509 A115 5pf dp yel grn 15 15
510 A115 6pf purple 15 15
a. Bklt. pane of 7 + label 10.00
511 A115 8pf red 15 15
511A A115 10pf dk brn ('43) 15 15
511B A115 12pf car ('43) 15 15

Engr.
512 A115 10pf dk brn 30 15
513 A115 12pf brt car 30 15
a. Bklt. pane of 6 + 2 labels 6.00
514 A115 15pf brn lake 15 15
515 A115 16pf pck grn 15 55
516 A115 20pf blue 15 15
517 A115 24pf org brn 15 35

Size: 21½x26mm
518 A115 25pf brt ultra 15 15
519 A115 30pf ol grn 15 15
520 A115 40pf brt red vio 15 15
521 A115 50pf myr grn 15 15
522 A115 60pf dk red brn 15 15
523 A115 80pf indigo 15 20

For surcharge see No. MQ3.

1942-44 **Engr.** ***Perf. 14***
524 A116 1m dk slate grn ('44) 15 35
a. Perf. 12½ 1.40 15
525 A116 2m violet ('44) 38 75
a. Perf. 12½ 75 90

Perf. 12½
526 A116 3m copper red 75 1.25
a. Perf. 14 ('44) 1.25 1.75
527 A116 5m dark blue 1.90 4.50
a. Perf. 14 ('44) 2.50 3.50
Set value 4.90

Nos. 507, 510, 511, 511A, 511B, 520, 524-526 exist imperf.

For overprints see Russia Nos. N9-N48.

Storm Trooper Emblem — A117

Adolf Hitler — A118

1942, Aug. 8 **Photo.** ***Perf. 14***
528 A117 6pf purple 15 20

War Effort Day of the Storm Troopers.

1944 **Engr.**
529 A118 42pf brt grn 15 35

Exists imperf. Value $140.

A119

1946 **Typo.** **Wmk. 284** ***Perf. 14***

Size: 18x22mm
530 A119 1pf black 15 15
531 A119 2pf black 15 15
532 A119 3pf yel brn 15 15
533 A119 4pf slate 15 15
534 A119 5pf yel grn 15 15
535 A119 6pf purple 15 15
536 A119 8pf dp ver 15 15
537 A119 10pf chocolate 15 15
538 A119 12pf brt red 15 15
539 A119 12pf sl gray 15 15
a. Bklt. pane, 5 #539 + 3 #542 9.00 *45.00*
540 A119 15pf vio brn 15 15
541 A119 15pf lt yel grn 15 15
542 A119 16pf slate grn 15 15
543 A119 20pf lt blue 15 15
544 A119 24pf org brn 15 15
545 A119 25pf brt ultra 15 20
546 A119 25pf org yel 15 15
547 A119 30pf olive 15 15
548 A119 40pf red vio 15 15
549 A119 42pf emerald 60 1.50
550 A119 45pf brt red 15 15
551 A119 50pf dk ol grn 15 15
552 A119 60pf brn red 15 15
553 A119 75pf dp ultra 15 15
554 A119 80pf dark blue 15 15
555 A119 84pf emerald 15 15

Size: 24½x29½mm
556 A119 1m olive grn 15 15
Set value 1.90 3.35

Imperf. copies of Nos. 543, 544 and 548 are usually from the souvenir sheet No. B295. Most other denominations exist imperf.

For overprints see Nos. 585A-599, 9N64, 10N17-10N21.

Planting Olive A120

Sower A121

Laborer A122

Reaping Wheat A123

Germany Reaching for Peace A124

Heinrich von Stephan A125

1947-48 ***Perf. 14***
557 A120 2pf brn blk 15 15
558 A120 6pf purple 15 15
559 A121 8pf red 15 15
560 A121 10pf yel grn ('48) 15 15
561 A122 12pf gray 15 15
562 A120 15pf choc ('48) 15 20
563 A123 16pf dk bl grn 15 15
564 A121 20pf blue 15 15
565 A123 24pf brn org 15 15
566 A120 25pf org yel 15 15
567 A122 30pf red ('48) 15 24
568 A121 40pf red vio 15 15
569 A123 50pf ultra ('48) 15 40
571 A122 60pf red brn ('48) 15 15
a. 60pf brown red 15 15
572 A122 80pf dk bl 15 15
573 A123 84pf emerald 15 20

Engr.
574 A124 1m olive 15 15
575 A124 2m dk brn vio 15 15
576 A124 3m copper red 15 24
577 A124 5m dk bl ('48) 30 *1.00*
Set value 1.50 *3.00*

For overprints see Nos. 600-633, 9N1-9N34, 9N65-9N67, 10N1-10N16.

1947, May 15 **Litho.**
578 A125 24pf org brn 15 15
579 A125 75pf dark blue 15 18
Set value 15 26

50th anniv. of the death of Heinrich von Stephan, 1st postmaster general of the German Empire.

Leipzig Fair Issues

Type of Semi-Postal Stamp of 1947

Designs: 12pf, Maximilian I granting charter, 1497. 75pf, Estimating and collecting taxes, 1365.

Perf. 13½x13

1947, Sept. 2 **Litho.** **Wmk. 284**
580 SP252 12pf carmine 15 15
581 SP252 75pf dk vio bl 15 15
Set value 15

Type of Semi-Postal Stamp of 1947, Dated 1948

Designs: 50pf, Merchants at customs barrier, 1388. 84pf, Arranging stocks of merchandise, 1433.

1948, Mar. 2 **Engr.**
582 SP252 50pf deep blue 15 15
583 SP252 84pf green 15 15
Set value 15

Exist imperf. Value, each, $400.

Hanover Fair Issue

Weighing Goods for Export — A126

1948, May 22 **Typo.** ***Perf. 14***
584 A126 24pf dp car 15 15
585 A126 50pf ultra 15 22
c. Se-tenant with No. 584 5.50 7.50
Set value 15 30

For Use in the United States and British Zones

Stamps of Germany 1946-47 Overprinted in Black

a 

b 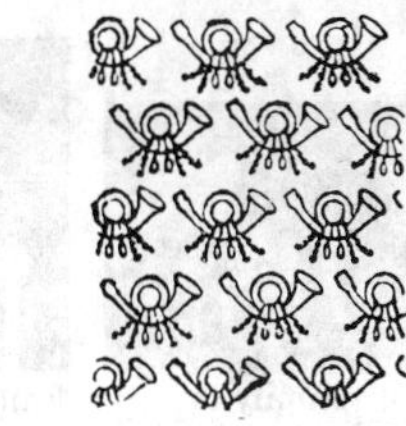

Overprint Type "a" on 1946 Numeral Issue

1948 Wmk. 284 *Perf. 14*

No.	Type	Denomination	Unused	Used
585A	A119	2pf black	2.75	*16.00*
585B	A119	8pf dp ver	5.50	*37.50*
586	A119	10pf chocolate	30	*3.00*
586A	A119	12pf brt red	4.75	*27.50*
586B	A119	12pf sl gray	80.00	*365.00*
586C	A119	15pf vio brn	4.75	*27.50*
587	A119	15pf lt yel grn	4.50	*10.00*
587A	A119	16pf sl grn	24.00	*125.00*
587B	A119	24pf org brn	42.50	*137.50*
587C	A119	25pf brt ultra	7.75	*32.50*
588	A119	25pf org yel	60	*5.00*
589	A119	30pf olive	75	*5.00*
589A	A119	40pf red vio	32.50	*130.00*
590	A119	45pf brt red	1.00	*5.00*
591	A119	50pf dk ol grn	1.00	*5.00*
592	A119	75pf dp ultra	3.00	*12.50*
593	A119	84pf emerald	3.00	*12.50*
		Nos. 585A-593 (17)	218.65	

Same, Overprinted Type "b"

No.	Type	Denomination	Unused	Used
593A	A119	2pf black	7.50	*40.00*
593B	A119	8pf dp ver	16.00	*75.00*
593C	A119	10pf chocolate	14.00	*75.00*
593D	A119	12pf brt red	4.75	*35.00*
593E	A119	12pf sl gray	125.00	*700.00*
593F	A119	15pf vio brn	5.25	*27.50*
594	A119	15pf lt yel grn	30	*4.50*
594A	A119	16pf sl grn	16.00	*95.00*
594B	A119	24pf org brn	21.00	*130.00*
594C	A119	25pf brt ultra	6.25	*35.00*
594D	A119	25pf org yel	19.00	*105.00*
595	A119	30pf olive	65	*4.00*
595A	A119	40pf red vio	26.00	*150.00*
596	A119	45pf brt red	1.00	*7.50*
597	A119	50pf dk ol grn	1.00	*7.50*
598	A119	75pf dp ultra	1.25	*8.50*
599	A119	84pf emerald	1.25	*8.00*
		Nos. 593A-599 (17)	266.20	

Nine other denominations of type A119 (1, 3, 4, 5, 6, 20, 42, 60 and 80pf) were also overprinted with types "a" and "b." These overprints were not authorized, but the stamps were sold at post offices and tolerated for postal use. Forgeries exist.

The overprints on Nos. 585A-599 have been extensively counterfeited.

Overprint Type "a" on Stamps and Types of 1947 Pictorial Issue

No.	Type	Denomination	Unused	Used
600	A120	2pf brn blk	15	15
601	A120	6pf purple	15	15
602	A121	8pf dp ver	15	15
603	A121	10pf yel grn	15	15
604	A122	12pf sl gray	15	15
605	A120	15pf chocolate	4.75	6.75
606	A123	16pf dk bl grn	90	1.25
607	A121	20pf blue	25	50
608	A123	24pf brn org	15	15
609	A120	25pf org yel	25	32
610	A122	30pf red	1.25	2.00
611	A121	40pf red vio	60	70
612	A123	50pf ultra	60	70
614	A122	60pf red brn	60	70
a.		60pf brown red	32.50	*125.00*
615	A122	80pf dk bl	1.00	1.50
616	A123	84pf emerald	2.75	4.00
		Nos. 600-616 (16)	13.85	19.32

Same, Overprinted Type "b"

No.	Type	Denomination	Unused	Used
617	A120	2pf brn blk	50	75
618	A120	6pf purple	50	70
619	A121	8pf red	50	75
620	A121	10pf yel grn	15	15
621	A122	12pf gray	50	75
622	A120	15pf chocolate	15	18
623	A123	16pf dk bl grn	15	15
624	A121	20pf blue	15	15
625	A123	24pf brn org	40	65
626	A120	25pf org yel	5.00	*7.50*
627	A122	30pf red	15	15
628	A121	40pf red vio	20	15
629	A123	50pf ultra	25	18
631	A122	60pf red brn	25	18
a.		60pf brown red	1.40	3.00
632	A122	80pf dark blue	25	15
633	A123	84pf emerald	50	75
		Nos. 617-633 (16)	9.60	

Most of Nos. 585A-633 exist with inverted and double overprints.

Frankfurt Town Hall A127

Our Lady's Church, Munich A128

Cologne Cathedral A129

Brandenburg Gate, Berlin A130

Holsten Gate, Lübeck — A131

Two types of mark values:
I- Four horiz. lines in stairs.
II- Seven horizontal lines.

Perf. 11½x11, 11

1948-51 Litho. Wmk. 286

No.	Type	Denomination	Unused	Used
634	A127	2pf black	15	15
a.		Perf. 14	1.65	4.00
635	A128	4pf org brn	15	15
a.		Perf. 14	75	15
636	A129	5pf blue	15	15
a.		Perf. 14	1.10	15
637	A128	6pf org brn	15	25
638	A128	6pf orange	15	15
a.		Perf. 14	9.75	6.00
639	A127	8pf org yel	15	25
640	A128	8pf dk sl bl	15	15
641	A129	10pf green	14	15
a.		Perf. 14	1.10	15
642	A128	15pf orange	90	2.00
643	A127	15pf violet	55	15
a.		Perf. 14	6.75	15
644	A127	16pf bluish grn	20	50
645	A127	20pf blue	42	1.10
646	A130	20pf carmine	30	15
a.		Perf. 14	2.50	15
647	A130	24pf carmine	15	15
648	A129	25pf vermilion	42	15
a.		Perf. 14	13.00	*25.00*
649	A130	30pf blue	50	15
a.		Perf. 14	14.00	15
650	A128	30pf scarlet	1.25	*3.25*
651	A129	40pf rose lil	70	15
a.		Perf. 14	9.75	15
652	A130	50pf ultra	50	*1.10*
653	A128	50pf bluish grn	70	15
a.		Perf. 14	110.00	15
654	A129	60pf vio brn	25.00	15
a.		Perf. 14	1.50	15
655	A130	80pf red vio	1.25	15
a.		Perf. 14	62.50	15
656	A128	84pf rose vio	1.10	2.50
657	A129	90pf rose lil	1.25	15
a.		Perf. 14	85.00	15

Perf. 11, 11x11½

No.	Type	Denomination	Unused	Used
658	A131	1m yel grn (I)	14.00	55
a.		Perf. 14 (II) ('51)	65.00	15
b.		Perf. 11 (II)	20.00	15
659	A131	2m vio (I)	14.00	55
a.		Type II	30.00	32
660	A131	3m car rose (I)	15.00	2.50
a.		Type II	100.00	85
661	A131	5m bl (I)	20.00	16.00
a.		Type II	125.00	4.75

Imperforates of many values exist.

Specialists collect Nos. 634-661 with watermark in four positions: upright, D's facing left; upright, D's facing right; sideways, D's facing up; sideways, D's facing down.

Two types of perforation: line and comb. Nos. 634-657 are found both perf. 11 and 11½x11.

Herman Hildebrant Wedigh — A132

Wmk. 116

1949, Apr. 22 Engr. *Perf. 14*

No.	Type	Denomination	Unused	Used
662	A132	10pf green	1.25	85
663	A132	20pf car rose	1.25	85
664	A132	30pf blue	1.50	2.25
a.		Sheet of 3, #662-664	50.00	*150.00*

Hanover Export Fair, 1949.
No. 664a sold for 1 mark.

Federal Republic

AREA—95,520 sq. mi.
POP.—62,040,000 (est. 1974)
CAPITAL—Bonn

"Reconstruction" A133

Bavaria Stamp A134

1949, Sept. 7 Litho. Wmk. 286

No.	Type	Denomination	Unused	Used
665	A133	10pf bl grn	21.00	18.00
666	A133	20pf rose car	27.50	21.00

Opening of the first Federal Assembly.
Exist imperf. Value, each $425.

Design: 30pf, Bavaria 6kr.

Wmk. 285

1949, Sept. 30 Litho. *Perf. 14*

No.	Type	Denomination	Unused	Used
667	A134	20pf red & dl bl	22.50	22.50
668	A134	30pf dl bl & choc	27.50	45.00

Centenary of German postage stamps. See No. B309.

Heinrich von Stephan, General Post Office and Guild House, Bern A135

1949, Oct. 9 Wmk. 286

No.	Type	Denomination	Unused	Used
669	A135	30pf ultra	26.00	30.00

75th anniv. of the UPU.

Numeral and Post Horn — A136

1951-52 Typo. Wmk. 295

No.	Type	Denomination	Unused	Used
670	A136	2pf yel grn	20	65
671	A136	4pf yel brn	20	15
a.		Booklet pane, 3 #671 + 3 #673 + 4 #677	125.00	
672	A136	5pf dp rose vio	2.25	15
673	A136	6pf orange	5.50	2.50
674	A136	8pf gray	6.50	6.75
675	A136	10pf dk grn	60	15
a.		Booklet pane, 4 #675 + 5 #677 + label	125.00	
676	A136	15pf purple	10.50	90
677	A136	20pf carmine	60	15
678	A136	25pf dk rose lake	27.50	2.50

Engr.

Size: 20x24½mm

No.	Type	Denomination	Unused	Used
679	A136	30pf blue	16.00	20
680	A136	40pf rose lil ('52)	45.00	20
681	A136	50pf bl gray ('52)	55.00	20
682	A136	60pf brn ('52)	45.00	20
683	A136	70pf dp yel ('52)	180.00	5.00
684	A136	80pf car ('52)	140.00	90
685	A136	90pf yel grn ('52)	200.00	1.10
		Nos. 670-685 (16)	734.85	21.70

Imperfs. exist of #671, 673, 675, 681 & 684.

W. K. Roentgen — A137

Mona Lisa — A138

1951, Dec. 10

No.	Type	Denomination	Unused	Used
686	A137	30pf blue	45.00	10.00

50th anniv. of the awarding of the Nobel prize in physics to Wilhelm K. Roentgen.

Wmk. 285

1952, Apr. 15 Litho. *Perf. 13½*

No.	Type	Denomination	Unused	Used
687	A138	5pf multi	60	50

500th anniv. of the birth of Leonardo da Vinci.

N. A. Otto — A139

Martin Luther — A140

Wmk. 295

1952, July 25 Engr. *Perf. 14*

No.	Type	Denomination	Unused	Used
688	A139	30pf deep blue	16.00	9.00

75th anniv. of the four-cycle gas engine.

1952, July 25

No.	Type	Denomination	Unused	Used
689	A140	10pf green	6.75	3.50

Issued to publicize the Lutheran World Federation Assembly, Hanover, 1952.

Freighter Off Heligoland A141

Carl Schurz A142

1952, Sept. 6

No.	Type	Denomination	Unused	Used
690	A141	20pf red	7.00	4.50

Return of Heligoland, Mar. 1, 1952.

Wmk. 285

1952, Sept. 17 Litho. *Perf. 13½*

No.	Type	Denomination	Unused	Used
691	A142	20pf bl, blk & brn org	10.00	4.25

Issued to commemorate the centenary of Carl Schurz's arrival in America.

Thurn and Taxis Postilion — A143

Philipp Reis — A144

1952, Oct. 25

No.	Type	Denomination	Unused	Used
692	A143	10pf multi	2.50	1.25

1st Thurn and Taxis stamp, cent.

1952, Oct. 27 Photo. *Perf. 14*

No.	Type	Denomination	Unused	Used
693	A144	30pf blue	18.00	11.00

75 years of telephone service in Germany.

"Prevent Traffic Accidents" — A145

1953, Mar. 30 Litho. Wmk. 285
694 A145 20pf blk, red & bl grn 7.25 2.00

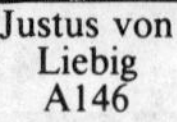
Justus von Liebig A146

Red Cross and Compass A147

1953, May 12 Engr. Wmk. 295
695 A146 30pf dk bl 17.50 12.00

150th anniv. of the birth of Justus von Liebig, chemist.

Perf. 14x13½
1953, May 8 Litho. Wmk. 285
696 A147 10pf dp ol grn & red 8.50 4.00

125th anniv. of the birth of Henri Dunant, founder of the Red Cross.

War Prisoner and Barbed Wire A148

Train and Hand Signal A149

Typographed and Embossed
1953, May 9 Unwmk. *Perf. 14*
697 A148 10pf gray & blk 2.00 15

Issued in memory of the prisoners of war.

Wmk. 295
1953, June 20 Engr. *Perf. 14*

Designs: 10pf, Pigeon and planes. 20pf, Automobiles and traffic signal. 30pf, Ship, barges and buoy.

698 A149 4pf brown 3.25 3.25
699 A149 10pf dp grn 7.75 6.00
700 A149 20pf red 10.00 7.00
701 A149 30pf dp ultra 24.00 13.00

Exhibition of Transport and Communications, Munich, 1953.

Pres. Theodor Heuss — A150

1954-60 Typo. *Perf. 14*
Size: 18½x22mm
702 A150 2pf citron 15 15
a. Booklet pane, 5 #702, 4 #704 + label ('55) 27.50
b. Booklet pane, 3 #702, 6 #704 + label ('56) 2.75
c. Booklet pane, 3 #702, 1 #707, 5 #708 + label ('56) 10.00
703 A150 4pf org brn 15 15
704 A150 5pf rose lil 15 15
a. Booklet pane, 2 #704, 7 #708 + label ('55) 27.50
705 A150 6pf lt brn 15 *30*
706 A150 7pf bluish grn 15 15
707 A150 8pf gray 15 *30*
708 A150 10pf green 15 15
a. Booklet pane, 4 #708, 5 #710 + label ('55) 27.50
709 A150 15pf ultra 16 15
710 A150 20pf dk car rose 15 15
711 A150 25pf red brn 32 30

Engr.
Size: 19½x24mm
712 A150 30pf blue 7.25 1.65
713 A150 40pf red vio 3.25 15
714 A150 50pf gray 130.00 30
715 A150 60pf red brn 27.50 30
716 A150 70pf olive 7.25 65
717 A150 80pf dp rose 1.25 1.65
718 A150 90pf dp grn 7.75 1.00

Size: 24½x29½mm
719 A150 1m ol grn 70 15
720 A150 2m lt vio bl 1.10 65
721 A150 3m dp plum 2.00 75
Nos. 702-721 (20) 189.73 9.20

Coils and sheets of 100 were issued of the 5, 7, 10, 15, 20, 25, 40 and 70pf. Every fifth coil stamp has a control number on the back.

Printings of Nos. 704, 706, 708-711 and 708b were made on fluorescent paper beginning in 1960.

Nos. 702, 709, 714 exist imperf. Value about $375 each.

See Nos. 737b, 755-761.

Catalogue values for unused stamps in this section, from this point to the end of the section, are for Never Hinged items.

Paul Ehrlich and Emil von Behring — A151

15th Century Printer — A152

Wmk. 285
1954, Mar. 13 Litho. *Perf. 13½*
722 A151 10pf dk grn 9.00 2.25

Centenary of the births of Paul Ehrlich and Emil von Behring, medical researchers.

Exists imperf. Value $1,000.

1954, May 5 Typo. Wmk. 295
723 A152 4pf chocolate 90 20

500th anniversary of the publication of Gutenberg's 42-line Bible. Design from woodcut by Jost Amman.

Bishop's Miter and Sword — A153

Carl F. Gauss — A154

Engraved; Center Embossed
1954, June 5 Unwmk. *Perf. 13½x14*
724 A153 20pf gray & red 6.00 4.00

1200th anniversary of the martyrdom of Saint Boniface.

Wmk. 295
1955, Feb. 23 Engr. *Perf. 14*
725 A154 10pf dp grn 3.50 28

Cent. of the death of Carl Friedrich Gauss, mathematician.

Oskar von Miller — A155

Wmk. 304
1955, May 7 Litho. *Perf. 13½*
726 A155 10pf green 3.75 1.00

Cent. of the birth of Oskar von Miller, electrical engineer.

Friedrich von Schiller, poet, 150th Death Anniv. — A156

Engraved and Embossed
1955, May 9 Unwmk. *Perf. 13½x14*
727 A156 40pf blue 11.00 2.75

1906 Automobile A157

Wmk. 304
1955, June 1 Typo. *Perf. 13½*
728 A157 20pf red & blk 8.25 3.50

50th anniversary of German postal motorbus service.

Arms of Baden-Württemberg A158

Globe and Atomic Symbol A159

Perf. 13x13½
1955, June 15 Litho. Wmk. 295
729 A158 7pf lem, blk & brn red 2.75 2.50
730 A158 10pf lem, blk & grn 4.00 2.50
a. Value omitted *325.00 475.00*

Issued to publicize the Baden-Wurttemberg Exhibition, Stuttgart, 1955.

1955, June 24 Photo. *Perf. 13½x14*
731 A159 20pf rose brn 7.00 60

Issued to encourage scientific research.

Orb and Symbols of Battle — A160

Photogravure and Embossed
Perf. 14x13½
1955, Aug. 10 Unwmk.
732 A160 20pf red lilac 7.50 3.00

Issued in honor of Augsburg and the millenium of the Battle on the Lechfeld.

Germany stamps can be mounted in Scott Germany Part I and annually supplemented Part III Albums.

Family in Flight — A161

Railroad Signal, Tracks — A162

1955, Aug. 2 Engr. Wmk. 304
733 A161 20pf brn lake 2.75 25

Issued to commemorate 10 years of German expatriation. See No. 930.

Perf. 13½x14
1955, Oct. 5 Litho. Wmk. 304
734 A162 20pf red & blk 7.25 1.10

European Timetable conf. at Wiesbaden, Oct. 5-15, 1955.

Stifter Monument and Stylized Trees — A163

1955, Oct. 22 Engr.
735 A163 10pf dk grn 3.00 1.25

150th anniversary of the birth of Adalbert Stifter, poet.

United Nations Emblem — A164

Lithographed and Embossed
Perf. 14x13½
1955, Oct. 24 Unwmk.
736 A164 10pf lt grn & red 4.00 3.75

United Nations Day, Oct. 24, 1955.

Numeral A165

Numeral and Signature A166

1955-58 Wmk. 304 Typo. *Perf. 14*
737 A165 1pf gray 20 15
Wmk. 295
737A A165 1pf gray ('58) 8.75 12.00
b. Bklt. pane of 10 (#707, 2 each #737A, #704, #708, 3 #710) 27.50

No. 737A was issued only in the booklet pane, No. 737b. No. 737 was issued on fluorescent paper in 1963.

1956, Jan. 7 Engr. Wmk. 304
738 A166 20pf dk red 5.25 1.65

125th anniv. of the birth of Heinrich von Stephan, co-founder of the UPU.

Clavichord
A167

1956, Jan. 27 **Litho.**
739 A167 10pf dull lilac 40 18

200th anniv. of the birth of Wolfgang Amadeus Mozart, composer.

Heinrich
Heine — A168

Perf. 13x13½
1956, Feb. 17 **Wmk. 295**
740 A168 10pf ol grn & blk 2.00 2.00

Centenary of death of Heinrich Heine, poet.

Old Buildings,
Lüneburg
A169

Wmk. 304
1956, May 2 **Engr.** ***Perf. 14***
741 A169 20pf dull red 6.50 5.75

Millenary of Lüneburg.

Olympic Rings
A170

Robert
Schumann
A171

1956, June 9 ***Perf. 13½x14***
742 A170 10pf sl grn 48 32

Issued to publicize the Olympic year, 1956.

1956, July 28 **Litho.** **Unwmk.**
743 A171 10pf cit, blk & red 40 15

Issued to commemorate the centenary of the death of Robert Schumann, composer.

Synod Emblem
A172

Thomas Mann
A173

Perf. 13½x13
1956, Aug. 8 **Wmk. 304**
744 A172 10pf green 2.25 2.00
745 A172 20pf brn car 2.75 2.25

Issued to honor the meeting of German Protestants (Evangelical Synod), Frankfurt-on-Main, Aug. 8-12.

1956, Aug. 11 **Engr.** ***Perf. 13½x14***
746 A173 20pf pale rose vio 2.00 1.75

Issued to commemorate the first anniversary of the death of Thomas Mann, novelist.

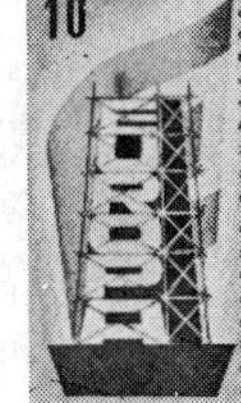

Maria Laach
Abbey
A174

"Rebuilding
Europe"
A175

1956, Aug. 24 **Photo.** ***Perf. 13x13½***
747 A174 20pf brn lake & gray 1.50 1.40

800th anniv. of the dedication of the Maria Laach Abbey.

Europa Issue, 1956

1956, Sept. 15 **Engr.** ***Perf. 14***
748 A175 10pf green 75 15
749 A175 40pf blue 6.75 90

Issued to symbolize the cooperation among the six countries comprising the Coal and Steel Community.

Plan of Cologne
Cathedral and
Hand — A176

1956, Aug. 29 **Litho.** ***Perf. 13x13½***
750 A176 10pf gray grn & red brn 1.50 1.50

Issued to commemorate the 77th meeting of German Catholics, Cologne, Aug. 29.

Map of the
World and
Policeman's
Hand — A177

1956, Sept. 1 ***Perf. 13½x13***
751 A177 20pf red org, grn & blk 2.00 1.50

Issued on the occasion of the International Police Show, Essen, Sept. 1-23.

Pigeon Holding
Letter — A178

Cemetery
Crosses — A179

1956, Oct. 27 **Engr.** ***Perf. 14***
752 A178 10pf green 90 35

Issued to publicize the Day of the Stamp.

1956, Nov. 17 ***Perf. 14x13½***
753 A179 10pf slate 90 35

People of Germany who died during WWII and to promote the Society for the Care of Military Cemeteries.

Saar Coat of
Arms — A180

1957, Jan. 2 **Litho.** ***Perf. 13x13½***
754 A180 10pf bluish grn & brn 40 25

Issued to commemorate the return of the Saar to Germany. See Saar No. 262.

Heuss Type of 1954
1956-57 **Wmk. 304** **Engr.** ***Perf. 14***
Size: 18½x22mm

755	A150 30pf sl grn	60	38
756	A150 40pf lt ultra	2.25	15
757	A150 50pf olive	1.50	15
758	A150 60pf lt brn	2.75	20
759	A150 70pf violet	11.00	15
760	A150 80pf red org	5.75	1.10
761	A150 90pf bluish grn	16.00	30
	Nos. 755-761 (7)	39.85	2.43

Nos. 755-756 were printed on both ordinary and fluorescent paper; Nos. 757-761 only on ordinary paper. Issue dates: 40pf, 1956. Others, 1957.

The 40pf and 70pf were also issued in coils. Every fifth coil stamp has control number on back.

Heinrich Hertz
A181

Paul Gerhardt
A182

1957, Feb. 22 **Litho.** ***Perf. 14***
762 A181 10pf lt grn & blk 1.00 32

Issued to commemorate the centenary of the birth of Heinrich Hertz, physicist.

1957, May 18 **Engr.**
763 A182 20pf car lake 40 28

350th anniv. of the birth of Paul Gerhardt, Lutheran clergyman and hymn writer.

Tulip and Post
Horn — A183

1957, June 8
764 A183 20pf red orange 42 30

Flora & Philately Exhib., Cologne, June 8-10.

Arms of
Aschaffenburg,
1332 — A184

Perf. 13x13½
1957, June 15 **Wmk. 304**
765 A184 20pf dp salmon & blk 42 30

1000th anniv. of the founding of the Abbey and town of Aschaffenburg.

Scholars (Sapiens
Manuscript)
A185

1957, June 24 ***Perf. 13½x13***
766 A185 10pf blk, bl grn & red org 35 15

Issued to commemorate the 500th anniversary of the founding of Freiburg University.

Modern
Passenger
Freighter
A186

1957, June 25 ***Perf. 13½x14***
767 A186 15pf brt bl, blk & red 75 80

Merchant Marine Day, June 25.

Liebig Laboratory
A187

1957, July 3 **Engr.** ***Perf. 14x13½***
768 A187 10pf dk grn 30 20

350th anniv. of the Justus Liebig School at Ludwig University, Giessen.

Albert
Ballin — A188

Television
Screen — A189

Perf. 13½x14
1957, Aug. 15 **Litho.** **Wmk. 304**
769 A188 20pf dk car rose & blk 1.00 28

Issued to commemorate the centenary of the birth of Albert Ballin, founder of the Hamburg-America Steamship Line.

1957, Aug. 23 **Engr.** ***Perf. 14x13½***
770 A189 10pf bl vio & grn 25 18

Issued to publicize the television industry.

Europa Issue, 1957

"United
Europe" — A190

Lithographed; Tree Embossed
1957-58 **Unwmk.** ***Perf. 14x13½***

771	A190 10pf yel grn & lt bl	24	15
a.	Imperf.	*150.00*	*350.00*
772	A190 40pf dk bl & lt bl	4.00	25

Wmk. 304

772A	A190 10pf yel grn & lt bl ('58)	7.50	6.00

A united Europe for peace and prosperity.
Issue dates: Nos. 771-772, Sept. 16, 1957. No. 772A, August, 1958.

Water Lily — A191

European Robin — A192

Wmk. 304

1957, Oct. 4 Litho. *Perf. 14*

773 A191 10pf yel grn & org yel 28 18
774 A192 20pf multi 35 25

Protection of wild animals and plants.

Carrier Pigeons — A193

Baron vom Stein — A194

1957, Oct. 5

775 A193 20pf dp car & blk 60 28

Intl. Letter Writing Week, Oct. 6-12.

1957, Oct. 26 Engr. *Perf. 13½x14*

776 A194 20pf red 1.25 40

200th anniv. of the birth of Baron Heinrich Friedrich vom und zum Stein, Prussian statesman.

Leo Baeck — A195

Landschaft Building, Stuttgart — A196

1957, Nov. 2

777 A195 20pf dk red 1.25 40

1st anniv. of the death of Rabbi Leo Baeck of Berlin.

Perf. 13x13½

1957, Nov. 16 Litho. Wmk. 304

778 A196 10pf dk grn & yel grn 50 35

Issued to commemorate the 500th anniversary of the Wurttemberg Landtag (Assembly).

Coach — A197

"Max and Moritz" — A198

1957, Nov. 26 Engr. *Perf. 14*

779 A197 10pf olive grn 50 32

Issued to commemorate the centenary of the death of Joseph V. Eichendorff, poet.

1958, Jan. 9 Litho. *Perf. 13½x13*

Design: 20pf, Wilhelm Busch.

780 A198 10pf lt ol grn & blk 20 20
781 A198 20pf red & blk 40 28

50th anniv. of the death of Wilhelm Busch, humorist.

"Prevent Forest Fires" — A199

1958, Mar. 5 *Perf. 14*

782 A199 20pf brt red & blk 48 25

Rudolf Diesel A200

1958, Mar. 18 Engr. *Perf. 14*

783 A200 10pf dk bl grn 18 18

Issued to commemorate the centenary of the birth of Rudolf Diesel, inventor.

Giraffe and Lion — A201

View of Old Munich — A202

Perf. 13x13½

1958, May 7 Litho. Wmk. 304

784 A201 10pf brt yel grn & blk 30 28

Zoo at Frankfort on the Main, cent.
Exists imperf. Value $225.

1958, May 22 Engr. *Perf. 14x13½*

785 A202 20pf dk red 30 28

800th anniversary of Munich.

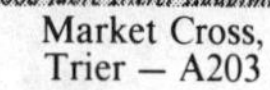

Market Cross, Trier — A203

Heraldic Eagle 5m Coin — A204

1958, June 3

786 A203 20pf dk red & blk 30 28

Millennium of the market of Trier (Treves).

1958, June 20 Litho. *Perf. 13x13½*

787 A204 20pf red & blk 35 28

10th anniv. of the German currency reform.
Exists imperf. Value $400.

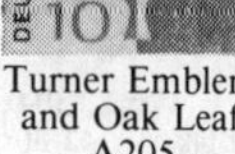

Turner Emblem and Oak Leaf A205

Schulze-Delitzsch A206

Perf. 13½x14

1958, July 21 Wmk. 304

788 A205 10pf gray, blk & dl grn 16 18

150 years of German Turners and on the occasion of the 1958 Turner festival.

1958, Aug. 29 Engr. *Perf. 13½x14*

789 A206 10pf yel grn 16 18

150th anniv. of the birth of Hermann Schulze-Delitzsch, founder of German trade organizations.

Europa Issue, 1958
Common Design Type

1958, Sept. 13 Litho.

Size: 24½x30mm

790 CD1 10pf yel grn & bl 32 15
791 CD1 40pf lt bl & red 2.00 35
Set value 41

Nicolaus Cusanus (Nikolaus Krebs) — A207

Pres. Theodor Heuss A208

1958, Dec. 3 Litho. *Perf. 14x13½*

792 A207 20pf dk car rose & blk 28 15

500th anniv. of the Cusanus Hospice at Kues, founded by Cardinal Nicolaus (1401-64).
Exists imperf. Value $250.

Common Design Types pictured in section at front of book.

1959 Wmk. 304 *Perf. 14*

793 A208 7pf bl grn 22 15
794 A208 10pf green 35 15
795 A208 20pf dk car rose 52 15

Engr.

796 A208 40pf blue 11.00 95
797 A208 70pf dp pur 3.75 32
Nos. 793-797 (5) 15.84
Set value 1.45

Nos. 793-795 were issued in sheets of 100 and in coils. Every fifth coil stamp has a control number on the back.

An experimental booklet containing one pane of 10 of No. 794 was sold at Darmstadt in 1960. Value $650.

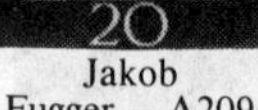

Jakob Fugger — A209

Adam Riese — A210

1959, Mar. 6 *Perf. 13x13½*

798 A209 20pf dk red & blk 24 20

500th anniversary of the birth of Jakob Fugger the Rich, businessman and banker.

1959, Mar. 28 *Perf. 13½x13*

799 A210 10pf ol grn & blk 22 20

Adam Riese (c. 1492-1559), arithmetic teacher, 400th death anniversary.

Alexander von Humboldt A211

Buildings, Buxtehude A212

1959, May 6 Engr. *Perf. 13½x14*

800 A211 40pf blue 80 80

Alexander von Humboldt (1769-1859), naturalist and geographer, death centenary.

1959, June 20 Litho. *Perf. 14*

801 A212 20pf lt bl, ver & blk 18 18

Millennium of town of Buxtehude.

Holy Coat of Trier — A213

Synod Emblem — A214

Lithographed; Coat Embossed

1959, July 18 Wmk. 304 *Perf. 14*

802 A213 20pf dl cl, buff & blk 18 18

Issued to commemorate the showing of the seamless robe of Christ at the Cathedral of Trier, July 19-Sept. 20.

1959, Aug. 12 Litho.

803 A214 10pf grn, brt vio & blk 20 15

Issued to honor the meeting of German Protestants (Evangelical Synod), Munich, Aug. 12-16.

Souvenir Sheet

A215

Portraits: 10pf, George Friedrich Handel. 15pf, Louis Spohr. 20pf, Ludwig van Beethoven. 25pf, Joseph Haydn. 40pf, Felix Mendelssohn-Bartholdy.

Perf. 14x13½

1959, Sept. 8 Engr. Wmk. 304

804 A215 Sheet of 5 27.00 *57.50*
a. 10pf deep green 3.75 5.00
b. 15pf blue 3.75 5.00
c. 20pf dark carmine 3.75 5.00
d. 25pf brown 3.75 5.00
e. 40pf dark blue 3.75 5.00

Opening of Beethoven Hall in Bonn and to honor various anniversaries of German composers.

Europa Issue, 1959
Common Design Type

1959, Sept. 19 Litho. *Perf. 13½x14*

Size: 24x29½mm

805 CD2 10pf ol grn 15 15
806 CD2 40pf dark blue 90 32
Set value 38

Uprooted Oak Emblem — A216

1960, Apr. 7 *Perf. 13½x13*

807 A216 10pf grn, blk & lil 25 15
808 A216 40pf bl, blk & org 1.25 1.40

Issued to publicize World Refugee Year, July 1, 1959-June 30, 1960.

Philipp Melanchthon A217

Symbols of Christ's Sufferings A218

1960, Apr. 19 *Perf. 13½x14*

809 A217 20pf dk car rose & blk 1.00 70

400th anniversary of the death of Philipp Melanchthon, co-worker of Martin Luther in the German Reformation.

1960, May 17 *Perf. 14x13½*

810 A218 10pf Prus grn, gray & ocher 15 15

1960 Passion Play, Oberammergau, Bavaria.

Dove, Chalice and Crucifix — A219

1960, July 30 **Engr.** *Perf. 14x13½*

811 A219 10pf dl grn 32 32
812 A219 20pf maroon 50 50

37th Eucharistic World Congress, Munich.

Wrestlers and Olympic Rings — A220

Hildesheim Cathedral, Miters, Cross and Crosier — A221

Sport scenes from Greek urns: 10pf, Sprinters. 20pf, Discus and Javelin throwers. 40pf, Chariot race.

1960, Aug. 8 **Wmk. 304**

813 A220 7pf red brn 15 15
814 A220 10pf ol grn 18 15
815 A220 20pf vermilion 35 15
816 A220 40pf dk bl 60 95

Issued to commemorate the 17th Olympic Games, Rome, Aug. 25-Sept. 11.

1960, Sept. 6 **Engr.** *Perf. 13½x14*

817 A221 20pf claret 48 38

Issued to commemorate the 1000th anniversary of the birth of St. Bernward (960-1022) and St. Godehard (960-1038), bishops.

Europa Issue, 1960

Common Design Type

1960, Sept. 19 **Wmk. 304**

Size: 30x25mm

818 CD3 10pf ol grn & yel grn 15 15
819 CD3 20pf brt red & lt red 40 15
820 CD3 40pf bl & lt bl 60 75

George C. Marshall A222

Steam Locomotive A223

1960, Oct. 15 **Litho.** *Perf. 13x13½*

821 A222 40pf dp bl & blk 1.40 1.40

Issued to honor George C. Marshall, US general and statesman.

1960, Dec. 7 *Perf. 13½x14*

822 A223 10pf ol bis & blk 15 15

125th anniversary of German railroads.

St. George — A224

Wmk. 304

1961, Apr. 23 **Engr.** *Perf. 14*

823 A224 10pf green 15 15

Honoring Boy Scouts of the world on St. George's Day (patron saint of Boy Scouts).

Albrecht Dürer — A225

Portraits: 5pf, Albertus Magnus. 7pf, St. Elizabeth of Thuringia. 8pf, Johann Gutenberg. 15pf, Martin Luther. 20pf, Johann Sebastian Bach. 25pf, Balthasar Neumann. 30pf, Immanuel Kant. 40pf, Gotthold Ephraim Lessing. 50pf, Johann Wolfgang von Goethe. 60pf, Friedrich von Schiller. 70pf, Ludwig van Beethoven. 80pf, Heinrich von Kleist. 90pf, Prof. Franz Oppenheimer. 1m, Annette von Droste-Hülshoff. 2m, Gerhart Hauptmann.

1961-64 **Typo.** *Perf. 14*

Fluorescent or Ordinary Paper

824 A225 5pf olive 15 15
b. Tete beche pair ('63) 50 60
825 A225 7pf dk bis 15 15
826 A225 8pf lilac 15 15
827 A225 10pf ol grn 15 15
b. Tete beche pair 50 1.00
828 A225 15pf blue 15 15
b. Tete beche pair ('63) 75 1.00
829 A225 20pf dk red 15 15
b. Tete beche pair ('63) 75 1.25
830 A225 25pf org brn 15 15

Engr.

831 A225 30pf gray 15 15
832 A225 40pf blue 15 15
833 A225 50pf red brn 24 15
834 A225 60pf dk car rose ('62) 35 18
835 A225 70pf grnsh blk 22 15
a. 70pf deep green 55 15
836 A225 80pf brown 55 30
837 A225 90pf yel ol ('64) 55 22
838 A225 1m vio bl 95 15
839 A225 2m yel grn ('62) 3.00 25
Nos. 824-839 (16) 7.21
Set value 1.95

Nos. 824-825, 827-830, 832, 834-835, 835a were issued in coils as well as in sheets. Every fifth coil stamp has a black control number on the back.

Nos, 824-839, including booklet panes and tete beche pairs, were printed on fluorescent paper. Nos. 824-829 and 832 were also printed on ordinary paper.

Gottlieb Daimler's Car of 1886 and Signature A226

Design: 20pf, Carl Benz's 3-wheel car of 1886 and signature.

1961, July 3 **Litho.**

840 A226 10pf grn & blk 16 16
841 A226 20pf brick red & blk 22 22

75 years of motorized traffic.

Messenger, Nuremberg, 18th Century A227

Cathedral, Speyer A228

Photogravure and Engraved

1961, Aug. 31 **Wmk. 304** *Perf. 14*

842 A227 7pf brn red & blk 15 15

Issued to publicize the exhibition "The Letter in Five Centuries," Nuremberg.

1961, Sept. 2 **Engr.**

843 A228 20pf vermilion 20 20

900th anniversary of Speyer Cathedral.

Europa Issue, 1961

Common Design Type

1961, Sept. 18 **Litho.**

Size: 28½x18½mm

844 CD4 10pf olive green 15 15
845 CD4 40pf violet blue 30 40
Set value 38 48

No. 844 was printed on both ordinary and fluorescent paper.

Reis Telephone A229

Wmk. 304

1961, Oct. 26 **Engr.** *Perf. 14*

846 A229 10pf green 15 15

Cent. of the demonstration of the 1st telephone by Philipp Reis.

Wilhelm Emanuel von Ketteler — A230

1961, Dec. 22 **Litho.**

847 A230 10pf ol grn & blk 15 15

Sesquicentennial of the birth of von Ketteler, Bishop of Mainz and pioneer in social development.

Fluorescent Paper was introduced for all stamps, starting with No. 848. Of the stamps before No. 848, those issued on both ordinary and fluorescent paper include Nos. 704, 706, 708-711, 737, 755-756, 824-829, 832, 844. Those issued only on fluorescent paper (up to No. 848) include Nos. 708b, 830-831, 833-839 and 842.

Drusus Stone and Old View of Mainz — A231

Notes and Tuning Fork — A232

1962, May 10 **Engr.** **Wmk. 304**

848 A231 20pf deep claret 15 15

The 2000th anniversary of Mainz.

1962, July 12 **Litho.** *Perf. 14*

849 A232 20pf red & blk 15 15

Issued to show appreciation of choral singing. The music is from the choral movement for three voices "In dulci jubilo" from "Musae Sioniae" by Michael Praetorius.

"Faith, Thanksgiving, Service" — A233

1962, Aug. 22 **Engr.** **Unwmk.**

850 A233 20pf magenta 15 15

Issued to commemorate the 79th meeting of German Catholics, Hanover, Aug. 22-29.

Open Bible, Chrismon and Chalice — A234

1962, Sept. 11 **Litho.** **Wmk. 304**

851 A234 20pf ver & blk 15 15

Issued to commemorate the 150th anniversary of the Württemberg Bible Society.

Europa Issue, 1962

Common Design Type

1962, Sept. 17 **Engr.**

Size: 28x23mm

852 CD5 10pf green 15 15
853 CD5 40pf blue 40 40
Set value 46 46

"Bread for the World" — A235

Lithographed and Embossed

1962, Nov. 23 *Perf. 14*

854 A235 20pf brn red & blk 15 15

Issued in connection with the Advent Collection of the Protestant Church in Germany.

Mother and Child Receiving Gift Parcel — A236

1963, Feb. 9 **Engr.**

855 A236 20pf dk car 15 15

Issued to express gratitude to the American organizations, CRALOG (Council of Relief Agencies Licensed to Operate in Germany) and CARE (Cooperative for American Remittances to Everywhere), for help during 1946-1962.

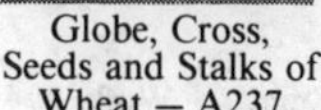

Globe, Cross, Seeds and Stalks of Wheat — A237

Checkered Lily — A238

Lithographed and Engraved

1963, Feb. 27 **Wmk. 304** ***Perf. 14***

856 A237 20pf gray, blk & red 15 15

Issued to publicize the German Catholic "Misereor" (I have compassion) campaign against hunger and illness.

1963, Apr. 28 **Litho.** **Unwmk.**

Flowers: 15pf, Lady's slipper. 20pf, Columbine. 40pf, Beach thistle.

857 A238 10pf multi 15 15
858 A238 15pf multi 15 15
859 A238 20pf multi 15 15
860 A238 40pf multi 28 30
Set value 54 52

Flora and Philately Exhibition, Hamburg.

Heidelberg Catechism A239

1963, May 2 **Litho. & Engr.**

861 A239 20pf dp org, brn org & blk 18 15

400th anniv. of the Heidelberg Catechism, containing the doctrine of the reformed church.

Cross of Golgotha, Darkened Sun and Moon — A240

1963, May 4 **Litho.** **Wmk. 304**

862 A240 10pf grn, dp car, blk & vio 15 15

Consecration of the Regina Martyrum Church, Berlin-Plötzensee, in memory of the victims of Nazism.

Arms of 18 Participating Countries, Paris Conference, 1863 — A241

Map Showing New Railroad Link, German and Danish Flags — A242

1963, May 7 **Engr.**

863 A241 40pf vio bl 25 22

Cent. of the 1st Intl. Postal Conf., Paris, 1863.

1963, May 14 **Litho.** **Unwmk.**

864 A242 20pf multi 15 15

Issued to commemorate the inauguration of the "Bird Flight Line" railroad link between Germany and Denmark.

Cross — A243

Synod Emblem and Crown of Barbed Wire — A244

Lithographed and Embossed

1963, May 24 **Unwmk.** ***Perf. 14***

865 A243 20pf mag, red & yel 15 15

Cent. of the founding of the Intl. Red Cross in connection with the German Red Cross cent. celebrations, Munster, May 24-26.

Perf. 13½x13

1963, July 24 **Litho.** **Wmk. 304**

866 A244 20pf dp org & blk 22 22

Meeting of German Protestants (Evangelical Synod), Dortmund, July 24-28.

Europa Issue, 1963

Common Design Type

1963, Sept. 14 **Engr.** ***Perf. 14***

Size: 28x23½mm

867 CD6 15pf green 15 20
868 CD6 20pf red 15 15
Set value 22 26

Old Town Hall, Hanover — A245

State Capitals: No. 870, Hamburg harbor, 775th anniversary. No. 871, North Ferry pier, Kiel. No. 872, National Theater, Munich. No. 873, Fountain and building, Wiesbaden. No. 874, Reichstag Building, Berlin. No. 875, Gutenberg Museum, Mainz. No. 876, Jan Wellem (Johann Wilhelm II, 1658-1716) statue, Dusseldorf. No. 877, City Hall, Bonn. No. 878, City Hall, Bremen. No. 879, View of Stuttgart. No. 879A, Ludwig's Church, Saarbrucken.

1964-65 **Litho.** **Unwmk.** ***Perf. 14***

869 A245 20pf gray, blk & red 24 15
870 A245 20pf multi 24 15
871 A245 20pf multi 24 15
872 A245 20pf multi 24 15
873 A245 20pf multi 24 15
874 A245 20pf bl, blk, & grn 15 15
875 A245 20pf multi 15 15
876 A245 20pf multi 15 15
877 A245 20pf multi ('65) 15 15
878 A245 20pf multi ('65) 15 15
879 A245 20pf multi ('65) 15 15
879A A245 20pf multi ('65) 15 15
Set value 1.88 1.20

View of Ottobeuren Abbey — A246

Lithographed and Engraved

1964, May 29 ***Perf. 14***

880 A246 20pf pink, red & blk 15 15

Issued to commemorate the 1200th anniversary of the Ottobeuren Benedictine Abbey.

Pres. Heinrich Lübke — A247

Sophie Scholl — A248

1964, July 1 **Litho.** ***Perf. 14***

881 A247 20pf carmine 15 15
882 A247 40pf ultra 16 16
Set value 22 22

Lübke's re-election. See Nos. 974-975.

1964, July 20 **Litho. & Engr.**

Designs: No. 884, Ludwig Beck. No. 885, Dietrich Bonhoeffer. No. 886, Alfred Delp. No. 887, Karl Friedrich Goerdeler. No. 888, Wilhelm Leuschner. No. 889, Count James von Moltke. No. 890, Count Claus Schenk von Stauffenberg.

883 A248 20pf bl gray & blk 1.10 2.00
884 A248 20pf bl gray & blk 1.10 2.00
885 A248 20pf bl gray & blk 1.10 2.00
886 A248 20pf bl gray & blk 1.10 2.00
887 A248 20pf bl gray & blk 1.10 2.00
888 A248 20pf bl gray & blk 1.10 2.00
889 A248 20pf bl gray & blk 1.10 2.00
890 A248 20pf bl gray & blk 1.10 2.00
Nos. 883-890 (8) 8.80 16.00

Issued to honor the German resistance to the Nazis, 1943-45. Printed in sheet of eight, containing one each of Nos. 883-890, se-tenant. Size: 148x105mm. The stamps were valid; the sheet was not, though widely used.

John Calvin — A249

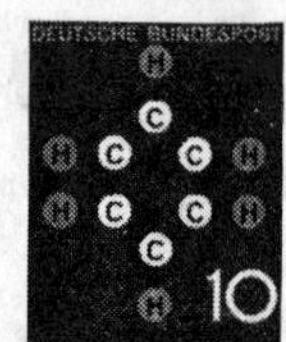

Benzene Ring, Kekule's Formula — A250

1964, Aug. 3 **Litho.** ***Perf. 14***

891 A249 20pf red & blk 15 18

Issued to honor the meeting of the International Union of the Reformed Churches in Germany, Frankfort on the Main, Aug. 3-13.

1964, Aug. 14 **Unwmk.** ***Perf. 14***

Designs: 15pf, Cerenkov radiation, reactor in operation. 20pf, German gas engine.

892 A250 10pf dk brn, brt grn & blk 15 15
893 A250 15pf brt grn, ultra & blk 15 15
894 A250 20pf red, grn & blk 15 15
Set value 23 23

Issued to publicize progress in science and technology: 10pf, centenary of benzene formula by August Friedrich Kekule; 15pf, 25 years of nuclear fission, Hahn and Strassmann; 20pf, centenary of German internal combustion engine, Nikolaus August Otto and Eugen Langen.

Ferdinand Lasalle — A251

Radiating Sun — A252

1964, Aug. 31 **Litho.**

895 A251 20pf sl bl & blk 15 15

Cent. of the death of Ferdinand Lasalle, a founder of the German Labor Movement.

1964, Sept. 2 **Engr.** **Wmk. 304**

896 A252 20pf gray & red 15 15

80th meeting of German Catholics, Stuttgart, Sept. 2-6. The inscription from Romans 12:2: ". . . be ye transformed through the renewing of your mind."

Europa Issue, 1964

Common Design Type

1964, Sept. 14 **Litho.** **Unwmk.**

Size: 23x29mm

897 CD7 15pf yel grn & lil 16 15
898 CD7 20pf rose & lil 16 15
Set value 20

Judo — A253

Prussian Eagle — A254

1964, Oct. 10

899 A253 20pf multi 15 15

18th Olympic Games, Tokyo, Oct. 10-25.

Lithographed and Embossed

1964, Oct. 30 **Unwmk.** ***Perf. 14***

900 A254 20pf brn org & blk 15 15

250 years of the Court of Accounts in Germany, founded as the Royal Prussian Upper Chamber of Accounts.

John F. Kennedy (1917-63) A255

Castle Gate, Ellwangen A256

1964, Nov. 21 **Engr.** **Wmk. 304**

901 A255 40pf dark blue 15 18

1964-66 **Typo.** **Unwmk.**

Designs: (German buildings through 12 centuries): 10pf, Wall pavilion, Zwinger, Dresden. 15pf, Tegel Castle, Berlin. 20pf, Portico, Lorsch. 40pf, Trifels Fortress, Palatinate. 60pf, Treptow Gate, Neubrandenburg. 70pf, Osthofen Gate, Soest. 80pf, Elling Gate, Weissenburg.

903 A256 10pf brn ('65) 15 15
904 A256 15pf dk grn ('65) 15 15
b. Tete beche pair ('65) 1.00 1.00
905 A256 20pf brn red ('65) 15 15
b. Tete beche pair ('66) 1.00 1.00

Engr.

908 A256 40pf vio bl ('65) 32 15
909 A256 50pf ol bis 52 15
910 A256 60pf rose red 70 30

911 A256 70pf dk grn ('65) 80 18
912 A256 80pf chocolate 90 28
Nos. 903-912 (8) 3.69
Set value 1.10

Nos. 903-905, 908, 910-912 were issued in sheets of 100 and in coils. Every fifth coil stamp has a black control number on the back.

Illustrations from the Works of Matthias Claudius
A257

Otto von Bismarck by Franz von Lenbach
A258

1965, Jan. 21 Engr. *Perf. 14*
917 A257 20pf blk & red 15 16

150th anniv. of the death of Matthias Claudius, poet and editor of the "Wandsbecker Bothe." Exists imperf. Value $350.

1965, Apr. 1 Litho. *Perf. 14*
918 A258 20pf blk & dl red 15 16

Prince Otto von Bismarck (1815-1898), Prussian statesman and 1st chancellor of the German Empire.
Exists imperf. Value $250.

Jet Plane and Space Capsule
A259

Bouquet of Flowers
A260

Designs: 5pf, Traffic lights and signs. 10pf, Communications satellite and ground station. 15pf, Old and new post buses. 20pf, Semaphore telegraph and telecommunication tower. 40pf, Old and new railroad engines. 70pf, Sailing ship and ocean liner.

1965
919 A259 5pf gray & multi 15 15
920 A259 10pf multi 15 15
921 A259 15pf multi 15 15
922 A259 20pf mar & multi 15 15
923 A259 40pf dk bl & multi 15 15
924 A259 60pf dl vio, yel & lt bl 20 30
925 A259 70pf multi 25 22
Set value 85 85

Intl. Transport and Communications Exhib., Munich, June 25-Oct. 30. No. 924 also for the 10th anniv. of the reopening of air service by Lufthansa. Issue dates: 60pf, Apr. 1. Others, June 25.
No. 919 exists imperf.

1965, May 1 Litho.
926 A260 15pf multi 15 15

Issued to commemorate the 75th anniversary of May Day celebration in Germany.

ITU Emblem
A261

Adolph Kolping
A262

1965, May 17 Unwmk. *Perf. 14*
927 A261 40pf dp bl & blk 15 15

Cent. of the ITU.

1965, May 26 Typo.
928 A262 20pf blk, gray & red 15 15

Kolping (1813-65), founder of the Catholic Unions of Journeymen, the Kolpingwork.

Rescue Ship
A263

Synod Emblem and Labyrinth
A264

1965, May 29 Litho. & Engr.
929 A263 20pf red & blk 15 15

Issued to commemorate the centenary of the German Sea Rescue Service.

Type of 1955 dated "1945-1965"
Perf. 14x13½
1965, July 28 Engr. Wmk. 304
930 A161 20pf gray 15 15

20 years of German expatriation.

Lithographed and Engraved
Perf. 13½x14
1965, July 28 Unwmk.
931 A264 20pf dp bl, grnsh bl & blk 15 15

Issued to honor the 12th meeting of German Protestants (Evangelical Synod), Cologne, July 28-Aug. 1.

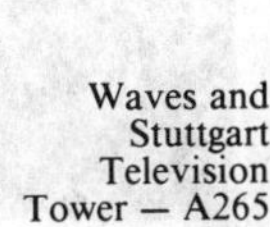

Waves and Stuttgart Television Tower — A265

1965, July 28 Litho. *Perf. 13½x13*
932 A265 20pf dp bl, blk & brt pink 15 15

Issued to publicize the German Radio Exhibition, Stuttgart, Aug. 27-Sept. 5.

Stamps of Thurn and Taxis, 1852-59
A266

1965, Aug. 28 *Perf. 14*
933 A266 20pf multi 15 15

125th anniv. of the introduction of postage stamps in Great Britain.

Europa Issue, 1965
Common Design Type
Perf. 14x13½
1965, Sept. 27 Engr. Wmk. 304
Size: 28x23mm
934 CD8 15pf green 15 16
935 CD8 20pf dl red 15 15
Set value 24 22

Nordertor, Flensburg
A267

Brandenburg Gate
A268

Designs: 5pf, Berlin Gate, Stettin. 10pf, Wall Pavilion, Zwinger, Dresden. 20pf, Portico, Lorsch. 40pf, Trifels Fortress, Palatinate. 50pf, Castle Gate, Ellwangen. 60pf, Treptow Gate, Neubrandenburg. 70pf, Osthofen Gate, Soest. 80pf, Elling Gate, Weissenburg. 90pf, Zschocke Ladies' Home, Königsberg. 1m, Melanchthon House, Wittenberg. 1.10m, Trinity Hospital, Hildesheim. 1.30m, Tegel Castle, Berlin. 2m, Löwenberg, Town Hall, interior view.

1966-69 Unwmk. Engr. *Perf. 14*
936 A267 5pf olive 15 15
937 A267 10pf dk brn ('67) 15 15
939 A267 20pf dk grn ('67) 16 15
940 A267 30pf yel grn 15 15
941 A267 30pf red ('67) 22 15
942 A267 40pf ol bis ('67) 30 15
943 A267 50pf bl ('67) 38 15
944 A267 60pf dp org ('67) 1.75 75
945 A267 70pf sl grn ('67) 55 15
946 A267 80pf red brn ('67) 1.75 60
947 A267 90pf black 60 16
948 A267 1m dl bl 70 15
949 A267 1.10m red brn 90 20
950 A267 1.30m grn ('69) 1.50 38
951 A267 2m purple 1.40 22
Nos. 936-951 (15) 10.66
Set value 2.95

1966-68 Typo. *Perf. 14*
952 A268 10pf chocolate 15 15
a. Bklt. pane, 4 #952, 2 #953, 4 #954 ('67) 3.50
b. Tete beche pair 40 30
c. Bklt. pane, 2 #952, 4 #953 2.00
953 A268 20pf dp grn 15 15
a. Tete beche pair ('68) 48 80
b. Bklt. pane, 2 #953, 2 #954 1.50
954 A268 30pf red 15 15
a. Tete beche pair ('68) 95 90
955 A268 50pf dk bl 65 30
956 A268 100pf dk bl ('67) 5.50 45
Nos. 952-956 (5) 6.60
Set value 90

Nos. 952-956 were issued in sheets of 100 and in coils. Every fifth coil stamp has a black control number on the back.

Nathan Söderblom
A269

Cardinal von Galen
A270

1966, Jan. 15 Litho. *Perf. 13x13½*
959 A269 20pf dl lil & blk 15 15

Soderblom (1866-1931), Swedish Protestant theologian, who worked for the union of Christian churches and received 1930 Nobel Peace Prize.

1966, Mar. 22 Litho. *Perf. 14*
960 A270 20pf dp lil rose, sal pink & blk 15 15

20th anniv. of the death of Clemens August Cardinal Count von Galen (1878-1946), anti-Nazi Bishop of Munster.

"The Miraculous Draught"
A271

G. W. Leibniz
A272

1966, July 13 Litho. *Perf. 14*
961 A271 30pf dp org & blk 15 15

Issued to commemorate the 81st meeting of German Catholics, Bamberg, July 13-17.

1966, Aug. 24 Unwmk. *Perf. 14*
962 A272 30pf rose car, pink & blk 15 15

Gottfried Wilhelm Leibniz (1646-1716), philosopher and mathematician.

Europa Issue, 1966
Common Design Type
1966, Sept. 24 *Perf. 14*
Size: 23x28½mm
963 CD9 20pf multi 15 18
964 CD9 30pf multi 15 15
Set value 24 24

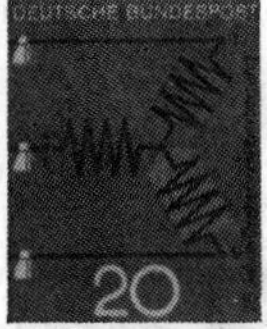
Diagram of Three-Phase Transmission
A273

UNICEF Emblem
A274

1966, Sept. 28 Litho.
965 A273 20pf shown 15 15
966 A273 30pf Dynamo 15 15
Set value 20 24

Issued to publicize progress in science and technology: 20pf, 75th anniversary of three-phase power transmission; 30pf, centenary of discovery by Werner von Siemens of the dynamoelectric principle.

1966, Oct. 24 Litho. *Perf. 14*
967 A274 30pf red, blk & gray 15 15

Awarding of the 1965 Nobel Peace Prize to UNICEF.

Werner von Siemens (1816-92), Electrical Engineer and Inventor — A275

1966, Dec. 13 Engr. *Perf. 14*
968 A275 30pf maroon 15 15

Europa Issue, 1967
Common Design Type
1967, May 2 Photo. *Perf. 14*
Size: 23x28mm
969 CD10 20pf multi 15 16
970 CD10 30pf multi 15 15
Set value 24 21

Franz von Taxis — A276

"Peace Is Among Us" — A277

Lithographed and Engraved

1967, June 3 *Perf. 14*
971 A276 30pf dp org & blk 15 15

Issued to commemorate the 450th anniversary of the death of Franz von Taxis, founder of the Taxis (Thurn and Taxis) postal system.

1967, June 21
972 A277 30pf brt pink & blk 15 15

13th meeting of German Protestants (Evangelical Synod), Hanover, June 21-25.

Friedrich von Bodelschwingh A278

Perf. 13 ½x13

1967, July 1 Litho. Unwmk.
973 A278 30pf redsh brn & blk 15 15

Centenary of Bethel Institution (for the incurable). Friedrich von Bodelschwingh (1877-1946), manager of Bethel (1910-1946) and son of the founder.

Lübke Type of 1964

1967, Oct. 14 Litho. *Perf. 14*
974 A247 30pf carmine 15 15
975 A247 50pf ultra 28 20
Set value 28

Re-election of President Heinrich Lübke.

The Wartburg, Eisenach A279

1967, Oct. 31 Engr. *Perf. 14*
976 A279 30pf red 15 15

450th anniversary of the Reformation.

Cross and Map of South America — A280

Koenig Printing Press — A281

1967, Nov. 17 Photo. *Perf. 14*
977 A280 30pf multi 15 15

"Adveniat," aid movement of German Catholics for the Latin American church.

1968, Jan. 12 Litho. *Perf. 14*

Designs: 20pf, Zinc sulfide and lead sulfide crystals. 30pf, Schematic diagram of a microscope.

978 A281 10pf multi 15 15
979 A281 20pf multi 15 15
980 A281 30pf multi 18 20
Set value 32 34

Progress in science and technology: 10pf, 150th anniv. of the Koenig printing press; 20pf, 1000th anniv. of mining in the Harz Mountains; 30pf, cent. of scientific microscope construction.

Foreign postal stationery (stamped envelopes, postal cards and air letter sheets) lies beyond the scope of this Catalogue, which is limited to adhesive postage stamps.

Symbols of Various Crafts A282

1968, Mar. 8 Litho. *Perf. 14*
981 A282 30pf multi 15 15

Traditions and progress of the crafts. Exists imperf. Value $250.

Souvenir Sheet

Adenauer, Churchill, de Gasperi and Schuman — A283

Portraits: 10pf, Winston S. Churchill. 20pf, Alcide de Gasperi. 30pf, Robert Schuman. 50pf, Konrad Adenauer.

1968, Apr. 19 Litho. *Perf. 14*
Black Inscriptions

982 A283 Sheet of 4 1.90 2.50
a. 10pf dark red brown 40 50
b. 20pf green 40 50
c. 30pf dark red 40 50
d. 50pf bright blue 40 50

1st anniv. of the death of Konrad Adenauer (1876-1967), chancellor of West Germany (1949-63), and honoring leaders in building a united Europe.

Europa Issue, 1968
Common Design Type

1968, Apr. 29 Photo.
Size: 29x24½mm

983 CD11 20pf grn, yel & brn 15 16
984 CD11 30pf car, yel & brn 18 15
Set value 22

Karl Marx (1818-83) A284

Pierre de Coubertin A285

Lithographed and Engraved

1968, Apr. 29 *Perf. 14*
985 A284 30pf red, blk & gray 15 15

1968, June 6 Unwmk. *Perf. 14*
986 A285 30pf lil & dk pur 18 15
Nos. 986,B434-B437 (5) 1.83 1.80

Issued to publicize the 19th Olympic Games, Mexico City, Oct. 12-27.

Opening Bars, "Die Meistersinger von Nurnberg," by Wagner — A286

Lithographed and Photogravure

1968, June 21
987 A286 30pf gray, blk & fawn 15 15

Cent. of the 1st performance of Richard Wagner's "Die Meistersinger von Nurnberg."

Konrad Adenauer (1876-1967) — A287

1968, July 19 Litho. *Perf. 14*
988 A287 30pf dp org & blk 15 15

Cross and Dove in Center of Universe A288

1968, July 19 Litho. & Engr.
989 A288 20pf brt grn, bl blk & yel 15 15

Issued to publicize the 82nd meeting of German Catholics, Essen, Sept. 4-8.

North German Confederation Nos. 4 and 10 — A289

1968, Sept. 5 Engr. *Perf. 14*
990 A289 30pf cop red, gray vio & blk 15 15

Cent. of the stamps of the North German Confederation.

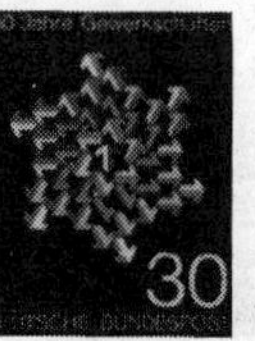

Arrows Symbolizing Determination A290

Human Rights Flame A291

1968, Sept. 26 Photo. *Perf. 14*
991 A290 30pf multi 15 15

Centenary of the German trade unions.

1968, Dec. 10 Photo. *Perf. 14*
992 A291 30pf multi 15 15

International Human Rights Year.

Junkers 52 — A292

Design: 30pf, Boeing 707.

1969, Feb. 6 Litho. *Perf. 14*
993 A292 20pf grn & multi 35 18
994 A292 30pf red & multi 50 18

50th anniv. of German airmail service.

Five-pointed Star — A293

1969, Apr. 28 Litho. *Perf. 13½x13*
995 A293 30pf red & multi 22 15

50th anniv. of the ILO.

Europa Issue, 1969
Common Design Type

1969, Apr. 28 Photo. *Perf. 14*
Size: 29x23mm

996 CD12 20pf grn, bl & yel 28 16
997 CD12 30pf red brn, yel & blk 32 15
Set value 22

Heraldic Eagles of Federal and Weimar Republics A294

1969, May 23 Photo. *Perf. 14*
998 A294 30pf red, blk & gold 38 18

20th anniversary of the German Basic Law, and the 50th anniversary of the proclamation of the Weimar Constitution.

Crosses — A295

1969, June 4 Litho. & Engr.
999 A295 30pf dk vio bl & cr 25 15

Issued to commemorate the 50th anniversary of the German War Graves Commission.

Seashore — A296

1969, June 4 *Perf. 14*
1000 A296 10pf shown 15 15
1001 A296 20pf Foothills 32 30
1002 A296 30pf Mountains 20 15
1003 A296 50pf Riverbed 40 40

Issued to publicize Nature Protection.

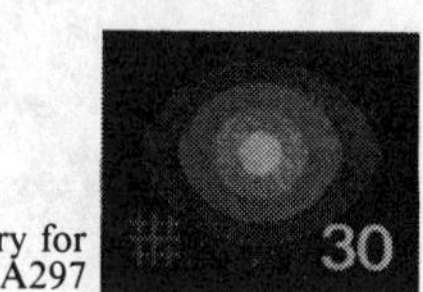

"Hungry for Justice" — A297

1969, July 7 Litho. *Perf. 14*
1004 A297 30pf multi 25 15

14th meeting of German Protestants (Evangelical Synod), Stuttgart, July 16-20.

Electromagnetic Field — A298

Maltese Cross — A299

1969, Aug. 11 Litho. *Perf. 14*
1005 A298 30pf red & multi 25 15

Issued to publicize the German Radio Exhibition, Stuttgart, Aug. 29-Sept. 7.

1969, Aug. 11 *Perf. 13x13½*
1006 A299 30pf red & blk 25 15

Maltese Relief Service, founded 1955, world-wide activities in social services, first aid and disaster assistance.

Souvenir Sheet

Marie Juchacz, Marie-Elisabeth Lüders and Helene Weber — A300

1969, Aug. 11 Engr. *Perf. 14*
1007 A300 Sheet of 3 70 60
a. 10pf olive 15 15
b. 20pf dark green 22 15
c. 30pf lake 32 15

50th anniv. of universal women's suffrage. Marie Juchacz (1879-1956), Marie-Elisabeth Lüders (1878-1966) and Helene Weber (1881-1962) were members of the German Reichstag.

Bavaria No. 16 — A301

Brine Pipe Line — A302

1969, Sept. 4 Litho. & Embossed
1008 A301 30pf gray & rose 25 15

23rd meeting of the Federation of German Philatelists, Sept. 6, the 70th Philatelists' Day, Sept. 7, and the phil. exhib. "120 Years of Bavarian Stamps" in Garmish-Partenkirchen, Sept. 4-7.

1969, Sept. 4 Litho. *Perf. 13½x13*
1009 A302 20pf multi 25 15

350th anniversary of the Brine Pipe Line from Traunstein to Bad Reichenhall.

Rothenburg ob der Tauber — A303

Lithographed and Engraved

1969, Sept. 4 *Perf. 14*
1010 A303 30pf dk red & blk 25 15

See #1047-1049, 1067-1069A, 1106-1110.

Pope John XXIII (1881-1963) A304

Mahatma Gandhi (1869-1948) A305

1969, Oct. 2 Engr. *Perf. 13½x14*
1011 A304 30pf dk red 25 15

1969, Oct. 2 Litho.
1012 A305 20pf yel grn & blk 25 15

Ernst Moritz Arndt A306

Ludwig van Beethoven A307

1969, Nov. 13 Litho. & Engr.
1013 A306 30pf gray & mar 25 15

Arndt (1769-1860), historian, poet and member of German National Assembly.

1970, Mar. 20 *Perf. 13½x14*

Portraits: 20pf, Georg Wilhelm Hegel (1770-1831), philosopher. 30pf, Friedrich Hölderlin (1770-1843), poet.

1014 A307 10pf pale vio & blk 15 15
1015 A307 20pf ol & blk 16 15
1016 A307 30pf rose & blk 25 15
Set value 32

Bicentenary of births of Beethoven, Hegel and Hölderlin.

Saar No. 171 — A308

1970, Apr. 29 Photo. *Perf. 14x13½*
1017 A308 30pf blk, red & gray grn 25 15

Issued to publicize the SABRIA National Stamp Exhibition, Saarbrucken, Apr. 29-May 4. No. 1017 was issued Apr. 29 at the SABRIA post office in Saarbrucken, on May 4 throughout Germany.

Europa Issue, 1970

Common Design Type

1970, May 4 Engr. *Perf. 14x13½*
Size: 28x23mm
1018 CD13 20pf green 28 15
1019 CD13 30pf red 38 15
Set value 22

Münchhausen on His Severed Horse — A309

1970, May 11 Litho. *Perf. 13½x13*
1020 A309 20pf multi 22 15

Count Hieronymus C. F. von Münchhausen (1720-97), soldier and storyteller.

Seagoing Vessel and Underpass A310

Nurse Assisting Elderly Woman A311

1970, June 18 Litho. *Perf. 14*
1021 A310 20pf multi 22 15

Issued to commemorate the 75th anniversary of the North Sea-Baltic Sea Canal.

1970 Photo.

Designs: 5pf, Welder (industrial protection). 10pf, Mountain climbers (rescuer bringing down casualty). 30pf, Fireman. 50pf, Stretcher bearer, casualty and ambulance. 70pf, Rescuer and drowning boy.

1022 A311 5pf dl bl & multi 15 15
1023 A311 10pf brn & multi 15 15
1024 A311 20pf grn & multi 16 15
1025 A311 30pf red & multi 28 15
1026 A311 50pf bl & multi 45 35
1027 A311 70pf grn & multi 52 48
Nos. 1022-1027 (6) 1.71
Set value 1.20

Honoring various voluntary services.
Issue dates: 20pf, 30pf, June 18. Others, Sept. 21.

Pres. Gustav Heinemann A312

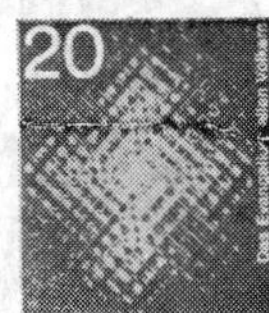

Cross Seen through Glass A313

1970-73 Engr. *Perf. 14*

1028	A312	5pf dk gray	15	15
1029	A312	10pf brown	15	15
1030	A312	20pf green	16	15
1030A	A312	25pf dp yel grn	22	15
1031	A312	30pf red brn	40	15
1032	A312	40pf brn org	45	15
1033	A312	50pf dk bl	1.50	15
1034	A312	60pf blue	1.00	15
1035	A312	70pf dk brn	80	28
1036	A312	80pf sl grn	80	20
1037	A312	90pf magenta	1.50	1.25
1038	A312	1m olive	80	35
1038A	A312	110pf ol gray	1.00	35
1039	A312	120pf ocher	1.00	42
1040	A312	130pf ocher	1.10	35
1040A	A312	140pf dk bl grn	1.25	48
1041	A312	150pf purple	1.25	32
1042	A312	160pf orange	1.40	60
1042A	A312	170pf orange	1.50	32
1043	A312	190pf dp claret	2.25	55
1044	A312	2m dp vio	1.50	40
		Nos. 1028-1044 (21)	20.18	7.07

Issue dates: 5pf, 1m, July 23. 10pf, 20pf, Oct. 23. 30pf, 90pf, 2m, Jan. 7, 1971. 40pf, 50pf, 70pf, 80pf, Apr. 8, 1971. 60pf, June 25, 1971. 25pf, Aug. 27, 1971. 120pf, 160pf, Mar. 8, 1972. 130pf, June 20, 1972. 150pf, July 5, 1972. 170pf, Sept. 11, 1972. 110pf, 140pf, 190pf, Jan. 16, 1973.

1970, Aug. 25 Litho.
1045 A313 20pf emer & yel 18 15

Issued to publicize the world mission of Catholic missionaries who bring the Gospel to all peoples.

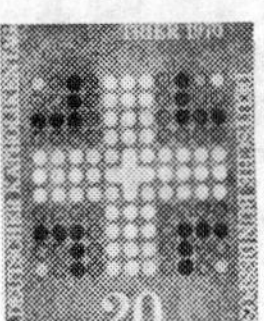

Cross A314

Comenius A315

1970, Sept. 4 *Perf. 13x13½*
1046 A314 20pf multi 18 15

Issued to publicize the 83rd meeting of German Catholics, Trier, Sept. 9-13.

Town Type of 1969

Designs: No. 1047, View of Cochem and Moselle River. No. 1048, Cathedral and view of Freiburg im Breisgau. No. 1049, View of Oberammergau.

1970 Litho. Engr. *Perf. 14*
1047 A303 20pf ap grn & blk 16 15
1048 A303 20pf grn & dk brn 22 15
1049 A303 30pf dp org & blk 25 15
Set value 38

Issue dates: No. 1047, Sept. 21; No. 1048, Nov. 4; No. 1049, May 11.

1970, Nov. 12 *Perf. 13½x14*
1050 A315 30pf dk red & blk 28 15

Issued to commemorate the 300th anniversary of the death of John Amos Comenius (1592-1670), theologian and educator.

Friedrich Engels — A316

Imperial Eagle, 1872 — A317

1970, Nov. 27 Litho. *Perf. 14*
1051 A316 50pf red & vio bl 42 42

Engels (1820-95), socialist, collaborator with Marx.

1971, Jan. 18 Litho. *Perf. 13½x14*
1052 A317 30pf multi 25 15

Centenary of the German Empire.

Friedrich Ebert (Germany No. 378) — A318

Molecule Diagram Textile Pattern — A319

1971, Jan. 18 *Perf. 13*
1053 A318 30pf red brn, ol & blk 25 15

Ebert (1871-1925), 1st Pres. of the German Republic.

1971, Feb. 18 Litho. *Perf. 13½x13*
1054 A319 20pf brt grn, red & blk 18 15

Synthetic textile fiber research, 125th anniversary.

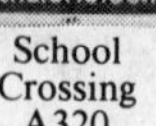

School Crossing A320

Signal to Pass A321

Traffic Signs: 20pf, Proceed with caution. 30pf, Stop. 50pf, Pedestrian crossing.

1971, Feb. 18 ***Perf. 14***

1055 A320 10pf blk, ultra & red 15 15
1056 A320 20pf blk, red & grn 20 15
1057 A320 30pf blk, gray & red 30 15
1058 A320 50pf blk, ultra & red 60 38
Set value 66

New traffic rules, effective Mar. 1, 1971.

1971, Apr. 16 **Photo.** ***Perf. 14***

Traffic Signs: 10pf, Warning signal. 20pf, Drive at right. 30pf, "Observe pedestrian crossings."

1059 A321 5pf bl, blk & car 15 15
1060 A321 10pf multi 15 15
1061 A321 20pf brt grn, blk & car 15 15
1062 A321 30pf car & multi 30 18
Set value 59 42

New traffic rules, effective Mar. 1, 1971.

Luther Facing Charles V, Woodcut by Rabus A322

Thomas à Kempis A323

1971, Mar. 18 ***Perf. 14***

1063 A322 30pf red & blk 28 15

450th anniversary of the Diet of Worms.

Europa Issue, 1971

Common Design Type

1971, May 3 **Photo.** ***Perf. 14***

Size: 28½x23mm

1064 CD14 20pf grn, gold & blk 20 15
1065 CD14 30pf dp car, gold & blk 40 15
Set value 15

1971, May 3 **Engr.**

1066 A323 30pf red & blk 25 15

500th anniversary of the death of Thomas a Kempis (1379-1471), Augustinian monk, author of "The Imitation of Christ."

Town Type of 1969

Designs: 20pf, View of Goslar. No. 1068, View of Nuremberg. No. 1069, Heligoland. 40pf, Heidelberg.

1971-72 **Litho. & Engr.** ***Perf. 14***

1067 A303 20pf brt grn & blk 20 15
1068 A303 30pf ver & blk 35 15
1069 A303 30pf lt grn & blk ('72) 32 15
1069A A303 40pf org & blk ('72) 40 16

Issue dates: 20pf, Sept. 15; No. 1068, May 21; Nos. 1069, 1069A, Oct. 20.

Dürer's Signature — A324

1971, May 21 **Engr.**

1070 A324 30pf cop red & blk 28 15

500th anniversary of the birth of Albrecht Dürer (1471-1528), painter and engraver.

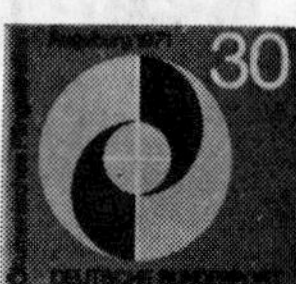

Congress Emblem A325

Illustration from New Astronomy, by Kepler A326

1971, May 28 **Litho.** ***Perf. 13½x13***

1071 A325 30pf red, org & blk 28 15

Ecumenical Meeting at Pentecost of the German Evangelical and Catholic Churches, Augsburg, June 2-5.

1971, June 25 **Photo.** ***Perf. 14***

1072 A326 30pf brt car, gold & blk 28 15

400th anniversary of the birth of Johannes Kepler (1571-1630), astronomer.

Dante Alighieri A327

"Matches Cause Fires" A328

1971, Sept. 3 **Engr.** ***Perf. 14***

1073 A327 10pf black 15 15

650th anniversary of the death of Dante Alighieri (1265-1321), poet.

1971-74 **Typo.** ***Perf. 14***

Designs: 10pf, Broken ladder. 20pf, Hand and circular saw. 25pf, "Alcohol and automobile." 30pf, Safety helmets prevent injury. 40pf, Defective plug. 50pf, Nail sticking from board. 60pf, 70pf, Traffic safety (ball rolling before car). 1m, Hoisted cargo. 1.50m, Fenced-in open manhole.

1074 A328 5pf orange 20 15
a. Bklt. pane, 2 each #1074, 1077-1079 ('74) 6.00
1075 A328 10pf dk brn 15 15
a. Bklt. pane, 4 #1075, 2 #1078 3.25
b. Bklt. pane, 2 each #1075-1076, 1078-1079 ('75) 6.00
c. Bklt. pane, 2 each #1079, 1075, 1078, 1076 19.00
1076 A328 20pf purple 20 15
1077 A328 25pf green 40 15
1078 A328 30pf dk red 22 15
1079 A328 40pf rose cl 28 15
1080 A328 50pf Prus bl 3.00 18
1081 A328 60pf vio blue 2.00 35
1082 A328 70pf grn & vio bl 90 22
1083 A328 100pf olive 1.50 28
1085 A328 150pf red brn 6.00 70
Nos. 1074-1085 (11) 14.85
Set value 2.15

Accident prevention.

Issued in sheets of 100 and in coils. Every fifth coil stamp has a control number on the back.

Issue dates: 25pf, 60pf, Sept. 10. 5pf, Oct. 29. 10pf, 30pf, Mar. 8, 1972. 40pf, June 20, 1972. 20pf, 100pf, July 5, 1972. 150pf, Sept. 11, 1972. 50pf, Jan. 16, 1973. 70pf, June 5, 1973.

Deaconesses A329

Senefelder's Lithography Press A330

1972, Jan. 20 **Litho.** ***Perf. 13x13½***

1087 A329 25pf grn, blk & gray 25 15

Centenary of the death of Wilhelm Löhe (1808-1872), founder of the Deaconesses Training Institute at Neuendettelsau.

1972, Apr. 14 **Litho.** ***Perf. 13½x13***

1088 A330 25pf multi 25 15

175th anniversary of the invention of the lithographic printing process by Alois Senefelder in 1796.

Europa Issue 1972

Common Design Type

1972, May 2 **Photo.** ***Perf. 13½x14***

Size: 23x29mm

1089 CD15 25pf yel grn, dk bl & yel 30 15
1090 CD15 30pf pale rose, dk & lt bl 40 15

Lucas Cranach, by Dürer A331

Archer in Wheelchair A332

Lithographed and Engraved

1972, May 18 ***Perf. 14***

1091 A331 25pf grn, buff & blk 25 15

500th anniversary of the birth of Lucas Cranach (1472-1553), painter and engraver.

1972, July 18 **Litho.** ***Perf. 14***

1092 A332 40pf yel, blk & red brn 38 20

21st Stoke-Mandeville Games for the Paralyzed, Heidelberg, Aug. 1-10.

Kurt Schumacher A333

Post Horn and Decree A334

1972, Aug. 18 **Litho. & Engr.**

1093 A333 40pf red & blk 38 15

Schumacher (1895-1952), 1st chairman of the German Social Democratic Party.

1972, Aug. 18 **Photo.**

1094 A334 40pf gold, car & blk 38 15

Centenary of the German Postal Museum, Berlin. Design shows page from Heinrich von Stephan's decree establishing the museum.

Open Book — A335

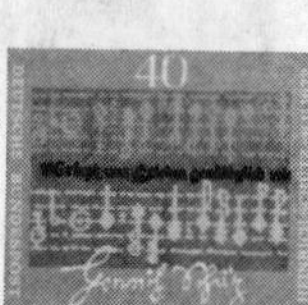

Music by Heinrich Schütz — A336

1972, Sept. 11 **Photo.** ***Perf. 13x13½***

1095 A335 40pf red & multi 38 15

International Book Year 1972.

Lithographed and Engraved

1972, Sept. 29 ***Perf. 14***

1096 A336 40pf multi 38 15

300th anniversary of the death of Heinrich Schütz (1585-1672), composer.

Carnival Dancers A337

1972, Nov. 10 **Litho.** ***Perf. 14***

1097 A337 40pf red & multi 40 15

Cologne Carnival sesquicentennial.

Heinrich Heine (1797-1856), Poet — A338

1972, Dec. 13 **Litho.** ***Perf. 14***

1098 A338 40pf rose, blk & red 38 15

"Bread for the World" A339

1972, Dec. 13 **Photo.** ***Perf. 14***

1099 A339 30pf grn & red 38 38

14th "Bread for the World-Developing Peace" campaign of the Protestant Church in Germany.

Würzburg Cathedral, 13th Century Seal — A340

1972, Dec. 13 **Litho.**

1100 A340 40pf dp car, lil rose & blk 38 15

Synod 72, meeting of Catholic bishoprics, Würzburg.

Colors of France and Germany Interlaced — A340a

1973, Jan. 22 Litho. *Perf. 14*
Size: 51x28mm

1101 A340a 40pf multi 38 18

10th anniversary of the Franco-German Cooperation Treaty.

Meteorological Map — A341

1973, Feb. 19 Litho. *Perf. 14*

1102 A341 30pf multi 30 15

Cent. of intl. meteorological cooperation.

Radio Tower and "Interpol" A342

1973, Feb. 19 *Perf. 13½x13*

1103 A342 40pf blk & red 38 15

50th anniversary of International Criminal Police Organization (INTERPOL).

Copernicus and Solar System A343

1973, Feb. 19 *Perf. 14*

1104 A343 40pf blk & red 38 15

500th anniversary of the birth of Nicolaus Copernicus (1473-1543), astronomer.

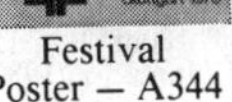

Festival Poster — A344 Maximilian Kolbe — A345

1973, Mar. 15 Photo. *Perf. 14*

1105 A344 40pf multi 38 15

German Turner Festival, Stuttgart, June 12-17.

Town Type of 1969

Designs: 30pf, Saarbrücken. No. 1107, Ship in Hamburg Harbor. No. 1108, Rüdesheim. No. 1109, Aachen. No. 1110, Ships, Bremen Harbor.

1973 Lithographed and Engraved

1106 A303 30pf yel grn & blk 30 15
1107 A303 40pf red & blk 38 15
1108 A303 40pf org & blk 38 15
1109 A303 40pf brn red & blk 40 15
1110 A303 40pf red & blk 40 15
Nos. 1106-1110 (5) 1.86
Set value 60

Issue dates: Nos. 1107-1108, Mar. 15; Nos. 1106, 1109-1110, Oct. 19.

Europa Issue 1973
Common Design Type

1973, Apr. 30 Photo. *Perf. 13½x14*
Size: 38½x21mm

1114 CD16 30pf grn, lt grn & yel 38 15
1115 CD16 40pf dp mag, lil & yel 55 15
Set value 24

1973, May 25 Litho. *Perf. 14*

1116 A345 40pf red, blk & brn 38 15

Maximilian Kolbe (1894-1941), Polish priest who died in Auschwitz and was beatified in 1971.

"R" for Roswitha A346 "Not by Bread Alone" A347

1973, May 25

1117 A346 40pf red, blk & yel 40 15

Millenary of the death of Roswitha of Gandersheim, Germany's first poetess.

1973, May 25 Photo.

1118 A347 30pf multi 35 15

15th meeting of German Protestants (Evangelical Synod), Dusseldorf, June 27-July 1.

Environment Emblem and "Waste" — A348

Designs (Environment Emblem and): 30pf, "Water." 40pf, "Noise." 70pf, "Air."

1973, June 5 Litho.

1119 A348 25pf multi 24 15
1120 A348 30pf multi 30 15
1121 A348 40pf org & multi 42 20
1122 A348 70pf ultra & multi 75 65

International environment protection and Environment Day, June 5.

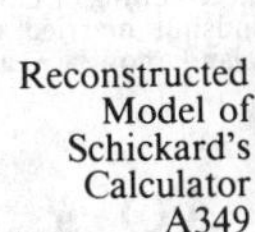

Reconstructed Model of Schickard's Calculator A349

1973, June 12

1123 A349 40pf org & multi 45 45

350th anniv. of the calculator built by Prof. Wilhelm Shickard, University of Tubingen.

Otto Wels (1873-1939), Leader of German Social Democratic Party — A350

1973, Sept. 14 Litho. *Perf. 14*

1124 A350 40pf mag & lil 38 15

Lubeck Cathedral — A351

1973, Sept. 14 Litho. & Engr.

1125 A351 40pf blk & multi 38 15

800th anniversary of Lubeck Cathedral.

Emblems from UN and German Flags A352

1973, Sept. 21 Litho.

1126 A352 40pf multi 52 15

Germany's admission to the UN.

Radio and Speaker, 1923 A353 Luise Otto-Peters A354

1973, Oct. 19 Photo. *Perf. 14*

1127 A353 30pf brt grn & multi 28 15

50 years of German broadcasting.

1974, Jan. 15 Litho. & Engr.

1128 A354 40pf shown 60 35
1129 A354 40pf Helene Lange 60 35
1130 A354 40pf Gertrud Bäumer 60 35
1131 A354 40pf Rosa Luxemburg 60 35

Honoring German women writers and leaders in political and women's movements.

Drop of Blood and Police Car Light A355

1974, Feb. 15 Photo. *Perf. 14*

1132 A355 40pf car & ultra 38 15

Blood donor service in conjunction with accident emergency service.

Handicapped People — A356

1974, Feb. 15 Litho. *Perf. 14*

1133 A356 40pf red & blk 38 15

Rehabilitation of the handicapped.

Thomas Aquinas Teaching — A357

1974, Feb. 15

1134 A357 40pf blk & red 38 15

St. Thomas Aquinas (1225-1274), scholastic philosopher.

Deer in Red, by Franz Marc — A358

Paintings: No. 1136, Girls under Trees, by August Macke, 40pf, Portrait in Blue, by Alexej von Jawlensky (vert.), 50pf, Pechstein (man) Asleep, by Erich Heckel (vert.), 70pf, "Big Still-life," by Max Beckmann. 120pf, Old Farmer, by Ernst Ludwig Kirchner (vert.).

1974 Photo.

1135 A358 30pf multi 28 15
1136 A358 30pf multi 25 15
1137 A358 40pf multi 40 15
1138 A358 50pf multi 52 20
1139 A358 70pf multi 65 45
1140 A358 120pf multi 1.40 95
Nos. 1135-1140 (6) 3.50 2.05

German expressionist painters.

Issue dates: Nos. 1135 and 1137, Feb. 15. Nos. 1136 and 1138, Aug. 16. Nos. 1139-1140, Oct. 29.

Young Man, by Lehmbruck — A359 Immanuel Kant — A360

Europa: 40pf, Kneeling Woman, by Wilhelm Lehmbruck.

1974, Apr. 17 Litho. *Perf. 14*

1141 A359 30pf multi 35 15
1142 A359 40pf multi 45 15
Set value 22

Litho. and Engr. (#1143), Engr. (#1144)

1974 *Perf. 14*

1143 A360 40pf Klopstock 35 16
1144 A360 90pf shown 60 35

Friedrich Gottlieb Klopstock (1724-1803), poet, and Immanuel Kant (1724-1804), philosopher.

Issue dates: 40pf, May 15; 90pf, Apr. 17.

Souvenir Sheet

Federal Eagle and Flag — A361

1974, May 15 Litho. & Embossed

1145 A361 40pf gray & multi 95 95

Federal Republic of Germany, 25th anniv.

Soccer and Games Emblem A362

Design: 40pf, Three soccer players.

1974, May 15 **Litho.**
1146 A362 30pf grn & multi 55 15
1147 A362 40pf org & multi 75 18

World Cup Soccer Championship, Munich, June 13-July 7.

Crowned Cross Emblem of Diaconate A363

Landscape A364

1974, May 15
1148 A363 40pf multi 38 15

125th anniversary of the Diaconal Association of the German Protestant Church.

1974, May 15
1149 A364 30pf multi 30 15

To promote hiking and youth hostels.

Broken Bars of Prison Window A365

1974, July 16 **Litho.** ***Perf. 14x13½***
1150 A365 70pf vio bl & blk 65 30

"Amnesty International," an organization for the protection of the rights of political, non-violent, prisoners.

Hans Holbein, Self-portrait A366

Lithographed and Engraved
1974, July 16 ***Perf. 13½x14***
1151 A366 50pf multi 52 18

450th anniversary of the death of Hans Holbein the Elder (c. 1470-1524), painter.

Man and Woman Looking at Moon, by Friedrich — A367

1974, Aug. 16 **Photo.** ***Perf. 14***
1152 A367 50pf multi 48 22

Caspar David Friedrich (1774-1840), German Romantic painter.

Swiss and German 19th Century Mail Boxes — A368

Mothers and Foundation Emblem — A369

1974, Oct. 29 **Litho.** ***Perf. 14***
1153 A368 50pf red & multi 60 22

Centenary of Universal Postal Union.

1975, Jan. 15 **Litho.** ***Perf. 13***
1154 A369 50pf multi 48 15

Convalescent Mothers' Foundation, 25th anniversary.

Annette Kolb (1875-1967), Writer — A370

German women writers: 40pf, Ricarda Huch (1864-1947), writer. 50pf, Else Lasker-Schüler (1869-1945), poetess. 70pf, Gertrud von Le Fort (1876-1971), writer.

Lithographed and Engraved
1975, Jan. 15 ***Perf. 14***
1155 A370 30pf brn & multi 32 16
1156 A370 40pf multi 40 25
1157 A370 50pf cl & multi 60 28
1158 A370 70pf bl & multi 85 65

Albert Schweitzer A371

Design: 40pf, Hans Böckler.

1975 **Engr.**
1159 A371 40pf grn & blk 35 15
1160 A371 70pf bl & blk 70 30

Birth centenaries of Hans Böckler (1875-1951), German Workers' Union leader, and of Dr. Albert Schweitzer (1875-1965), medical missionary. Issue dates: 40pf, Feb. 14; 70pf, Jan. 15.

Head, by Michelangelo A372

Plan of St. Peter's, Rome A373

1975, Feb. 14 **Photo.** ***Perf. 14***
1161 A372 70pf vio bl & blk 1.25 1.25

500th birth anniversary of Michelangelo Buonarroti (1475-1564), Italian sculptor, painter and architect.

1975, Feb. 14
1162 A373 50pf red & multi 45 18

Holy Year 1975, the "Year of Reconciliation."

Ice Hockey A374

1975, Feb. 14 **Litho.** ***Perf. 14***
1163 A374 50pf bl & multi 48 18

Ice Hockey World Championship, Munich and Düsseldorf, Apr. 3-19.

Concentric Group, by Oskar Schlemmer — A375

Europa: 50pf, Bauhaus Staircase, painting by Oskar Schlemmer (1888-1943) and CEPT emblem.

1975, Apr. 15 **Litho. & Engr.**
1164 A375 40pf gray & multi 50 16
1165 A375 50pf gray & multi 65 16

Eduard Mörike, Weather Vane, Quill and Signature A376

1975, May 15
1166 A376 40pf multi 40 15

Eduard Mörike (1804-75), pastor and poet.

Joust, from Jousting Book of William IV A377

1975, May 15 **Photo.** ***Perf. 14***
1167 A377 50pf multi 48 15

500th anniversary of the Wedding of Landshut, (last Duke of Landshut married the daughter of King of Poland, now a yearly local festival).

Cathedral of Mainz A378

1975, May 15 **Litho. & Engr.**
1168 A378 40pf multi 38 15

Millennium of the Cathedral of Mainz.

View of Neuss, Woodcut A379

Space Laboratory A380

1975, May 15
1169 A379 50pf multi 48 15

500th anniversary of the unsuccessful siege of Neuss by Duke Charles the Bold of Burgundy.

1975-82 **Engr.** ***Perf. 14***
1170 A380 5pf Symphonie satellite 15 15
1171 A380 10pf Electric train 15 15
1172 A380 20pf Old Weser lighthouse 15 15
1173 A380 30pf Rescue helicopter 25 15
1174 A380 40pf Space 25 15
1175 A380 50pf Radar station 35 15
1176 A380 60pf X-ray machine 40 15
1177 A380 70pf Shipbuilding 45 15
1178 A380 80pf Tractor 52 20
1179 A380 100pf Bituminous coal excavator 75 28
1180 A380 110pf Color TV camera 80 30
1181 A380 120pf Chemical plant 80 35
1182 A380 130pf Brewery 95 38
1183 A380 140pf Heating plant, Licterfelde 1.10 38
1184 A380 150pf Power Shovel 1.50 60
1185 A380 160pf Blast furnace, Rhein-hausen 1.65 45
1186 A380 180pf Payloader 1.40 70
1187 A380 190pf Shovel dredger 1.40 52
1188 A380 200pf Oil drilling 1.65 45
1189 A380 230pf Frankfurt Airport 1.90 70
1190 A380 250pf Airport 1.90 70
1191 A380 300pf Electro. RR 2.25 90
1192 A380 500pf Effelsberg radio telescope 3.75 70
Nos. 1170-1192 (23) 24.47 8.81

Issue dates: 40pf, 50pf, 100pf, May 15. 10pf, 30pf, 70pf, Aug. 14. 80pf, 120pf, 160pf, Oct. 15. 5pf, 140pf, 200pf, Nov. 14. 20pf, 500pf, Feb. 17, 1976. 60pf, Nov. 16, 1978. 230pf, May 17, 1979. 150pf, 180pf, July 12, 1979. 110pf, 130pf, 300pf, June 16, 1982. 190pf, 250pf, July 15, 1982.

Market and Town Hall, Alsfeld A381

Designs: No. 1197, Plönlein Corner, Siebers Tower and Kobolzeller Gate, Rothenburg. No. 1198, Town Hall (Steipe), Trier. No. 1199, View of Xanten.

1975, July 15 **Litho. & Engr.**
1196 A381 50pf multi 60 52
1197 A381 50pf multi 60 52
1198 A381 50pf multi 60 52
1199 A381 50pf multi 60 52

European Architectural Heritage Year.

Three Stages of Drug Addiction A382

1975, Aug. 14 **Photo.** ***Perf. 14***
1200 A382 40pf multi 45 15

Fight against drug abuse.

Matthias Erzberger A383

1975, Aug. 14 **Engr.**
1201 A383 50pf red & blk 48 15

Matthias Erzberger (1875-1921), statesman, signer of Compiegne Armistice (1918) at end of World War I.

Sign of Royal Prussian Post, 1776 — A384

1975, Aug. 14 **Litho.**
1202 A384 10pf bl & multi 25 15

Stamp Day, 1975, and 76th German Philatelists' Day, Sept. 21.

Souvenir Sheet

Gustav Stresemann, Ludwig Quidde, Carl von Ossietzky — A385

1975, Nov. 14 **Engr.** ***Perf. 14***
1203 A385 Sheet of 3 1.50 1.50
a.-c. 50pf. single stamp 40 40

German winners of Nobel Peace Prize. No. 1203 has litho. marginal inscription.

Olympic Rings, Symbolic Mountains A386

Konrad Adenauer A387

1976, Jan. 5 **Litho. & Engr.**
1204 A386 50pf red & multi 48 15

12th Winter Olympic Games, Innsbruck, Austria, Feb. 4-15.

1976, Jan. 5 **Engr.**
1205 A387 50pf dk slate grn 48 15

Konrad Adenauer (1876-1967), Chancellor (1949-63), birth centenary.

Books by Hans Sachs — A388

1976, Jan. 5 **Litho.**
1206 A388 40pf multi 40 15

Hans Sachs (1494-1576), poet (meistersinger), 400th death anniversary.

Junkers F 13, 1926 — A389

German Eagle — A390

1976, Jan. 5
1207 A389 50pf multi 55 15

Lufthansa, 50th anniversary.

1976, Feb. 17 **Photo.** ***Perf. 14***
1208 A390 50pf red, blk & gold 55 15

Federal Constitutional Court, 25th anniv.

"EG" A391

1976, Apr. 6 **Photo.** ***Perf. 14***
1209 A391 40pf red & multi 40 15

European Coal and Steel Community, 25th anniversary.

Wuppertal Suspension Train — A392

1976, Apr. 6 **Litho.**
1210 A392 50pf multi 48 15

Wuppertal suspension railroad, 75th anniv.

Girl Selling Trinkets and Prints — A393

Europa: 50pf, Boy selling copperplate prints, and CEPT emblem. Ludwigsburg china figurines, c. 1765.

1976, May 13 **Photo.**
1211 A393 40pf olive & multi 50 15
1212 A393 50pf scar & multi 65 15

Dr. Carl Sonnenschein A394

1976, May 13 **Litho.**
1213 A394 50pf car & multi 48 15

Sonnenschein (1876-1929), Roman Catholic clergyman and social reformer.

Weber Conducting "Freischutz" in Covent Garden — A395

1976, May 13
1214 A395 50pf red brn & blk 48 15

Carl Maria von Weber (1786-1826), composer, 150th death anniversary.

Hymn, by Paul Gerhardt A396

1976, May 13 **Engr. & Litho.**
1215 A396 40pf multi 38 15

Paul Gerhardt (1607-1676), Lutheran hymn writer, 300th death anniversary.

Carl Schurz, American Flag, Capitol A397

1976, May 13 **Litho.**
1216 A397 70pf multi 60 22

American Bicentennial.

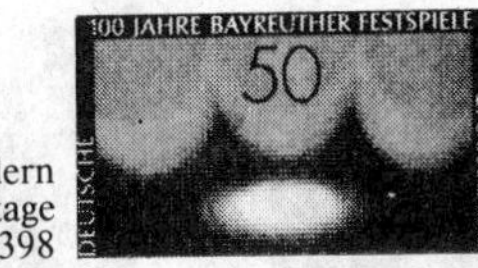

Modern Stage A398

1976, July 14 **Litho.** ***Perf. 14***
1217 A398 50pf multi 48 15

Bayreuth Festival, centenary.

Bronze Ritual Chariot c. 1000 B.C. A399

Archaeological Treasures: 40pf, Celtic gold vessel, 5th-4th centuries B.C. 50pf, Celtic silver torque, 2nd-1st centuries B.C. 120pf, Roman cup with masks, 1st century A.D.

1976, July 14
1218 A399 30pf multi 25 20
1219 A399 40pf multi 38 28
1220 A399 50pf multi 45 35
1221 A399 120pf multi 1.40 1.10

Golden Plover — A400

"Simplicissimus Teutsch" — A401

1976, Aug. 17
1222 A400 50pf multi 60 15

Protection of birds.

1976, Aug. 17
1223 A401 40pf multi 42 15

Johann Jacob Christoph von Grimmelshausen, 300th birth anniversary; author of the "Adventures of Simplicissimus Teutsch."

Imperial Post Emblem, Höchst am Main, 18th Cent. — A402

Caroline Neuber as Medea — A403

1976, Oct. 14 **Litho.** ***Perf. 14***
1224 A402 10pf brn & multi 18 15

Stamp Day.

1976, Nov. 16 **Photo.**

German Actresses: 40pf, Sophie Schröder (1781-1868) as Sappho. 50pf, Louise Dumont (1862-1932) as Hedda Gabler. 70pf, Hermine Körner (1878-1960) as Lady Macbeth.

1225 A403 30pf multi 25 15
1226 A403 40pf multi 35 20
1227 A403 50pf multi 40 20
1228 A403 70pf multi 60 45

Palais de l'Europe, Strasbourg — A404

1977, Jan. 13 **Engr.** ***Perf. 14***
1229 A404 140pf grn & blk 1.25 45

Inauguration of the new Council of Europe Headquarters, Jan. 28.

Values quoted in this catalogue are for stamps graded at Fine-Very Fine and with no faults. An illustrated guide to grade is provided in introductory material, beginning on Page 1A.

Scenes from Till Eulenspiegel
A405

Marksburg Castle
A406

1977, Jan. 13 **Litho.**
1230 A405 50pf multi 60 15

Till Eulenspiegel (d. 1350), roguish fool and hero, his adventures reported in book of same name.

1977-79 **Typo.** ***Perf. 14***

1231 A406 10pf Glucksburg 15 15
  a. Bklt. pane, 4 #1231, 2 each #1234, 1236 3.00
  b. Bklt. pane, 4 #1231, 2 #1234, 2 #1310 2.50
  c. Bklt. pane, 4 #1231, 2 #1310, 2 #1312 3.00
  d. Bklt. pane, 2 each #1231, 1234, 1310-1311 3.00
1232 A406 20pf Pfaueninsel 15 15
1233 A406 25pf Gemen 15 15
1234 A406 30pf Ludwigstein 24 15
1235 A406 40pf Eltz 38 15
1236 A406 50pf Neuschwanstein 75 15
1237 A406 60pf Marksburg 75 18
1238 A406 70pf Mespelbrunn 75 18
1239 A406 90pf Vischerenburg 95 28
1240 A406 190pf Pfaueninsel 1.65 45
1240A A406 200pf Burresheim 1.90 45
1241 A406 210pf Schwanenburg 2.00 60
1242 A406 230pf Lichtenberg 2.00 60
  Nos. 1231-1242 (13) 11.82
  Set value 3.15

See Nos. 1308-1315.

Issued in sheets of 100 and in coils. Every fifth coil stamp has control number on the back.

Issue dates: 60pf, 200pf, Jan. 13. 40pf, 190pf, Feb. 16. 10pf, 30pf, Apr. 14. 50pf, 70pf, May 17. 230pf, Nov. 16, 1978. 25pf, 90pf, Jan. 11, 1979. 20pf, 210pf, Feb. 14, 1979.

Souvenir Sheet

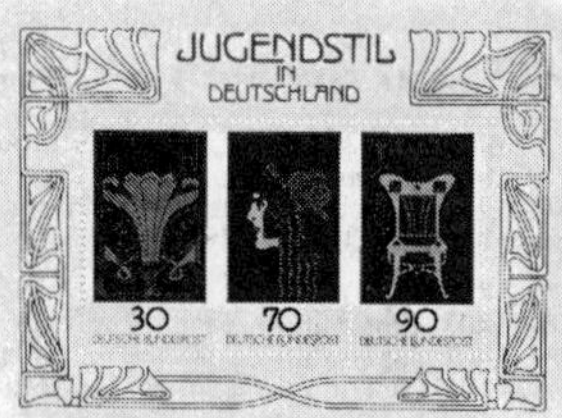

German Art Nouveau — A407

Designs: 30pf, Floral ornament. 70pf, Athena, poster by Franz von Stuck. 90pf, Chair, c. 1902.

1977, Feb. 16 **Litho.** ***Perf. 14***
1243 A407 Sheet of 3 1.75 1.25
  a. 30pf multi 25 20
  b. 70pf multi 48 32
  c. 90pf multi 75 50

1st German Art Nouveau Exhib., 75th anniv.

Jean Monnet
A408

1977, Feb. 16
1244 A408 50pf blk & yel 48 18

Jean Monnet (1888-1979), French proponent of unification of Europe, became first Honorary Citizen of Europe in Apr. 1976.

Flower Show Emblem
A409

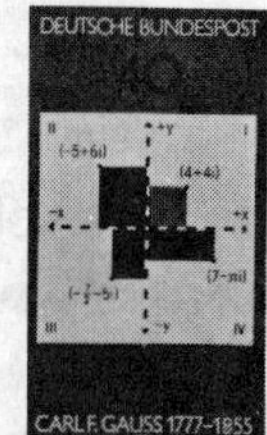

Gauss Plane of Complex Numbers
A410

1977, Apr. 14
1245 A409 50pf green & multi 45 18

25th Federal Horticultural Show, Stuttgart, Apr. 29-Oct. 23.

1977, Apr. 14
1246 A410 40pf silver & multi 42 15

Carl Friedrich Gauss (1777-1855), mathematician, 200th birth anniversary.

Barbarossa Head, Cappenberg Reliquary — A411

1977, Apr. 14
1247 A411 40pf multi 45 15

Staufer Year 1977. "Time of the Hohenstaufen" Exhibition, Stuttgart, Mar. 25-June 5, in connection with the 25th anniversary of Baden-Wurttemberg.

Rhön Highway
A412

Europa: 50pf, Rhine, Siebengebirge and train.

1977, May 7 **Litho. & Engr.**
1248 A412 40pf brt grn & blk 50 15
1249 A412 50pf brt red & blk 65 15
  Set value 24

Rubens, Self-portrait
A413

Ulm Cathedral
A414

1977, May 17 **Engr.**
1250 A413 30pf brn blk 28 15

Peter Paul Rubens (1577-1640), Flemish painter, 400th birth anniversary.

1977, May 17 **Litho. & Engr.**
1251 A414 40pf bl & sepia 42 15

600th anniversary of Ulm Cathedral.

Madonna, Oldest Rector's Seal
A415

Landgrave Philipp, Great Seal of University
A416

1977, May 17 **Photo.**
1252 A415 50pf ind & org red 45 18
1253 A416 50pf ind & org red 45 18

Mainz University, 500th anniversary (No. 1252); Marburg University, 450th anniversary (No. 1253).

Morning, by Runge — A417

1977, July 13 **Litho.** ***Perf. 14***
1254 A417 60pf bl & multi 55 22

Philipp Otto Runge (1777-1810), painter.

Bishop Ketteler's Coat of Arms — A418

1977, July 13
1255 A418 50pf multi 52 15

Wilhelm Emmanuel von Ketteler (1811-1877), Bishop of Mainz, Reichstag member and social reformer, death centenary.

Fritz von Bodelschwingh — A419

1977, July 13 **Litho. & Engr.**
1256 A419 50pf multi 48 15

Pastor Fritz von Bodelschwingh (1877-1946), manager of Bethel Institute (for the incurable sick), birth centenary.

Jesus as Teacher, Great Seal of University — A420

Golden Hat, Schifferstadt, Bronze Age — A421

1977, Aug. 16 **Photo.**
1257 A420 50pf multi 48 15

Tübingen University, 500th anniversary.

1977, Aug. 16 **Litho.**

Archaeological heritage: 120pf, Gilt helmet, from Prince's Tomb, Krefeld-Gellep. 200pf, Bronze Centaur's head, Schwarzenacker.

1258 A421 30pf multi 32 22
1259 A421 120pf multi 1.25 1.25
1260 A421 200pf multi 1.75 1.40

Telephone Operator and Switchboard, 1881 — A422

1977, Oct. 13 **Litho.** ***Perf. 14***
1261 A422 50pf multi 48 15

German telephone centenary.

Arms of Hamburg, Post Emblem, c. 1861 — A423

Wilhelm Hauff — A424

1977, Oct. 13
1262 A423 10pf multi 15 15

Stamp Day.

1977, Nov. 10 **Photo.** ***Perf. 14***
1263 A424 40pf multi 38 15

Wilhelm Hauff (1802-1827), writer and fabulist, 150th death anniversary.

Traveling Surgeon — A425

Book Cover, by Alexander Schröder — A426

1977, Nov. 10 **Litho.**
1264 A425 50pf multi 48 15

Dr. Johann Andreas Eisenbarth (1663-1727), traveling surgeon and adventurer.

1978, Jan. 12 **Litho.** ***Perf. 14***
1265 A426 50pf multi 48 15

Rudolf Alexander Schröder (1878-1962), writer, designer, Lutheran minister.

"Refugees" A427

1978, Jan. 12 **Photo.**
1266 A427 50pf multi 48 15

Friedland Aid Society for displaced Germans, 20th anniversary.

Souvenir Sheet

Gerhart Hauptmann, Hermann Hesse, Thomas Mann — A428

1978, Feb. 16 **Litho.** ***Perf. 14***
1267 A428 Sheet of 3 1.40 1.40
 a. 30pf multi 25 25
 b. 50pf multi 40 40
 c. 70pf multi 60 60

German winners of Nobel Literature Prize.

Martin Buber (1878-1965), Writer and Philosopher A429

1978, Feb. 16
1268 A429 50pf multi 48 15

Museum Tower and Observatory A430

1978, Apr. 13 **Litho.** ***Perf. 14***
1269 A430 50pf multi 48 15

German Museum for Natural Sciences and Technology, Munich, 75th anniversary.

Old City Halls A431

Europa: 40pf, Bamberg. 50pf, Regensburg. 70pf, Esslingen on Neckar.

Lithographed and Engraved

1978, May 22 ***Perf. 14***
1270 A431 40pf multi 65 15
1271 A431 50pf multi 80 20
1272 A431 70pf multi 85 32

Pied Piper of Hamelin A432

1978, May 22 **Litho.**
1273 A432 50pf multi 50 15

The Pied Piper led 130 children of Hamelin away never to be seen again.

Janusz Korczak A433

Fossil Bat A434

1978, July 13 **Litho.** ***Perf. 14***
1274 A433 90pf multi 80 35

Dr. Janusz Korczak (1878-1942), physician, educator, proponent of children's rights.

1978, July 13

Design: 200pf, Eohippus (primitive horse; horiz.).

1275 A434 80pf multi 2.50 2.00
1276 A434 200pf multi 2.50 2.00

Archaeological heritage from Messel opencast mine, c. 50 million years old.

Parliament, Bonn — A435

1978, Aug. 17 **Litho.** ***Perf. 14***
1277 A435 70pf multi 60 24

65th Interparliamentary Conf., Bonn, Sept. 3-14.

Rose Window, Freiburg Cathedral — A436

1978, Aug. 17
1278 A436 40pf multi 38 15

85th Congress of German Catholics, Freiburg, Sept. 13-17.

Brentano as Butterfly, by Luise Duttenhofer A437

1978, Aug. 17
1279 A437 30pf multi 32 15

Clemens Brentano (1778-1842), poet.

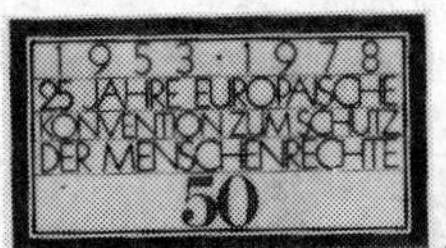
A438

1978, Aug. 17
1280 A438 50pf multi 45 15

European Human Rights Convention, 25th anniversary.

Bavarian Posthouse Sign, c. 1825 — A439

Saxony No. 1 with "World Philatelic Movement" Cancel — A440

1978, Oct. 12 **Litho.** ***Perf. 14***
1281 A439 40pf multi 40 15
1282 A440 50pf multi 50 15
 a. Pair, #1281-1282 90 40

Stamp Day and German Philatelists' Meeting, Frankfurt am Main, Oct. 12-15.

Easter at Walchensee, by Lovis Corinth — A441

Impressionist Paintings: 70pf, Horseman on Shore, by Max Liebermann (vert.). 120pf, Lady with Cat, by Max Slevogt (vert.).

1978, Nov. 16 **Photo.** ***Perf. 14***
1283 A441 50pf multi 48 15
1284 A441 70pf multi 65 40
1285 A441 120pf multi 1.10 70

Child and Building A442

1979, Jan. 11 **Photo.**
1286 A442 60pf blk & rose 65 15

International Year of the Child and 20th anniv. of Declaration of Children's Rights.

Agnes Miegel — A443

Film — A444

1979, Feb. 14 **Photo.** ***Perf. 14***
1287 A443 60pf multi 55 15

Agnes Miegel (1879-1964), poet.

1979, Feb. 14 **Litho.**
1288 A444 50pf blk & grn 45 15

25th German Short-Film Festival, Oberhausen, Apr. 23-28.

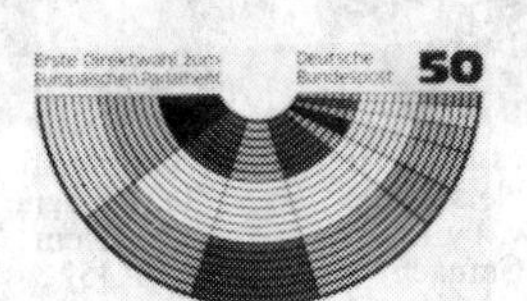
Parliament Benches in Flag Colors of Members — A445

1979, Feb. 14
1289 A445 50pf multi 48 15

European Parliament, first direct elections, June 7-10, 1979.

Emblems of Road Rescue Services — A446

1979, Feb. 14
1290 A446 50pf multi 45 18

Telegraph Office, 1863 — A447

Europa: 60pf, Post Office window, 1854.

1979, May 17 **Litho.** ***Perf. 14***
1291 A447 50pf multi 60 15
1292 A447 60pf multi 85 15

Anne Frank (1929-45), Author, Nazi Victim — A448

1979, May 17 **Photo.**
1293 A448 60pf red & blk 52 18

First Electric Train, 1879 Berlin Exhibition A449

1979, May 17 **Litho.**
1294 A449 60pf multi 52 18

Intl. Transportation Exhib., Hamburg.

Hand Setting Radio Dial A450

1979, July 12 **Litho.** ***Perf. 14***
1295 A450 60pf multi 52 15

World Administrative Radio Conference, Geneva, Sept. 24-Dec. 1.

Moses Receiving Tablets of the Law, by Lucas Cranach A451

Cross and Charlemagne's Emblem A452

1979, July 12 **Litho. & Engr.**
1296 A451 50pf blk & bl grn 45 18

450th anniv. of Martin Luther's Catechism.

1979, July 12 **Litho. & Embossed**
1297 A452 50pf multi 70 35

1979 pilgrimage to Aachen.

The lack of a price for a listed item does not necessarily indicate rarity.

Hildegard von Bingen with Manuscript A453

1979, Aug. 9 **Litho.**
1298 A453 110pf multi 1.00 32

Hildegard von Bingen, Benedictine nun, mystic and writer, 800th death anniversary.

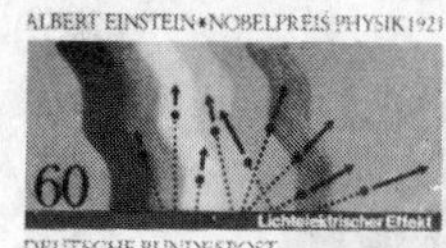

Diagram of Einstein's Photoelectric Effect — A454

Designs: No. 1300, Otto Hahn's diagram of the splitting of the uranium nucleus. No. 1301, Max von Laue's atom arrangement in crystals.

1979, Aug. 9 **Photo.**
1299 A454 60pf multi 55 30
1300 A454 60pf multi 55 30
1301 A454 60pf multi 55 30

Birth centenaries of German Nobel Prize winners: Albert Einstein, physics, 1921; Otto Hahn, chemistry, 1944; Max von Laue, physics, 1914.

Pilot on Board — A455

Lithographed and Engraved

1979, Oct. 11 ***Perf. 14***
1302 A455 60pf multi 52 15

Three centuries of pilots' regulations.

Birds in Garden, by Paul Klee — A456

1979, Nov. 14 **Photo.**
1303 A456 90pf multi 75 30

Paul Klee (1879-1940), Swiss artist.

Mephistopheles and Faust — A457

1979, Nov. 14 **Litho.**
1304 A457 60pf multi 52 20

Doctor Johannes Faust.

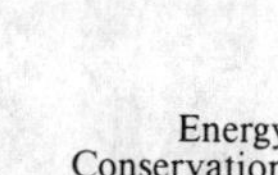

Energy Conservation A458

1979, Nov. 14 ***Perf. 13x13½***
1305 A458 40pf multi 38 15

Castle Type A406 of 1977-79

1979-82 **Typo.** ***Perf. 14***

1308	35pf Lichtenstein	32	15
1309	40pf Wolfsburg	34	15
1310	50pf Inzlingen	40	15
1311	60pf Rheydt	55	15
1312	80pf Wilhelmsthal	65	24
1313	120pf Charlottenburg	1.00	35
1314	280pf Ahrensburg	2.50	85
1315	300pf Herrenhausen Hannover	2.50	90
	Nos. 1308-1315 (8)	8.26	2.94

Issue dates: 60pf, Nov. 14. 40pf, 50pf, Feb. 14, 1980. 35pf, 80pf, 300pf, June 16, 1982. 120pf, 280pf, July 15, 1982.

Iphigenia, by Anselm Feuerbach A459

1980, Jan. 10 **Litho.**
1321 A459 50pf multi 48 18

Anselm Feuerbach (1829-1880), historical and portrait painter.

Flags of NATO and Members A460

1980, Jan. 10
1322 A460 100pf multi 1.00 52

Germany's membership in NATO, 25th anniversary.

Osnabruck, 1,200th Anniversary — A461

1980, Jan. 10 **Litho. & Engr.**
1323 A461 60pf multi 52 20

Götz von Berlichingen, Painting on Glass — A462

1980, Jan. 10 **Litho.**
1324 A462 60pf multi 52 20

Götz von Berlichingen (1480-1562), knight.

Duden Dictionary, Old and New Editions — A463

1980, Jan. 14
1325 A463 60pf multi 52 20

Konrad Duden's German Language Dictionary, centenary of publication.

German Association for Public and Private Social Welfare Centenary — A464

1980, Apr. 10
1326 A464 60pf multi 52 20

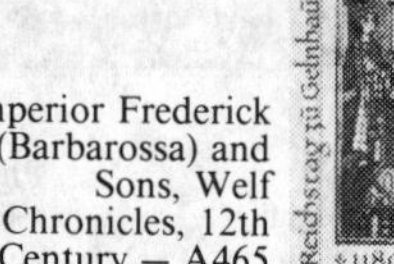

Emperior Frederick I (Barbarossa) and Sons, Welf Chronicles, 12th Century — A465

1980, Apr. 10
1327 A465 60pf multi 52 20

Imperial Diet of Geinhausen, 800th anniv.

Albertus Magnus (1193-1280), Saint and Doctor of the Church — A466

Design: 60pf, Gottfried Wilhelm Leibniz (1646-1716), philosopher.

1980, May 8 **Litho.** ***Perf. 14***
1328 A466 50pf multi 60 16
1329 A466 60pf multi 80 22

Confession of Augsburg, Engraving, 1630 — A467

1980, May 8
1330 A467 50pf multi 45 20

Reading of Confession of Augsburg to Charles V (first official creed of Lutheran Church), 400th anniversary.

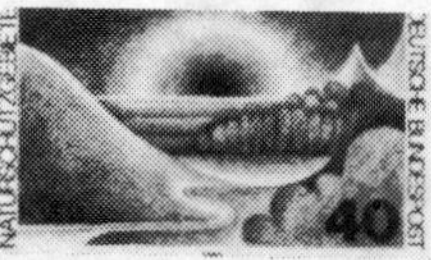

Nature Preserves A468

1980, May 8 **Photo.**
1331 A468 40pf multi 38 15

Oscillogram Pulses and Ear — A469

Lithographed and Embossed

1980, July 10 *Perf. 14*
1332 A469 90pf multi 80 32

16th International Congress for the Training and Education of the Hard of Hearing, Hamburg, Aug. 4-8.

Book of Daily Bible Readings, Title Page, 1731 — A470

1980, July 10 **Litho.**
1333 A470 50pf multi 45 18

Moravian Brethren's Book of Daily Bible Readings, 250th edition.

St. Benedict of Nursia, 1500th Birth Anniv. — A471

1980, July 10 *Perf. 13x13½*
1334 A471 50pf multi 45 20

Helping Hand — A472

1980, Aug. 14 **Litho. & Engr.**
1335 A472 60pf multi 52 20

Dr. Friedrich Joseph Haass (1780-1853), physician and philanthropist.

Marie von Ebner-Eschenbach (1830-1916), Writer — A473

1980, Aug. 14 **Photo.**
1336 A473 60pf multi 52 20

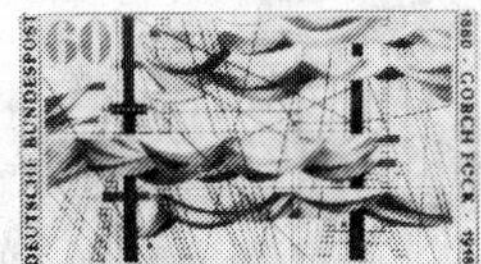
Ship's Rigging A474

1980, Aug. 14 **Litho.**
1337 A474 60pf multi 60 20

Gorch Fock (pen name of Johan Kinau) (1880-1916), poet and dramatist.

Hoeing, Pressing Grapes, Wine Cellar, 14th Century Woodcuts — A475

1980, Oct. 9 **Litho.** *Perf. 14*
1338 A475 50pf multi 45 20

Wine production in Central Europe, 2000th anniversary.

Setting Final Stone in South Tower, Cologne Cathedral — A476

1980, Oct. 9
1339 A476 60pf multi 52 20

Completion of Cologne Cathedral, cent.

Landscape with Fir Trees, by Altdorfer — A477

Lithographed and Engraved

1980, Nov. 13 *Perf. 14*
1340 A477 40pf multi 42 20

Albrecht Altdorfer (1480-1538), painter and engraver.

Elly Heuss-Knapp A478

1981, Jan. 15 **Photo.**
1341 A478 60pf multi 52 20

Elly Heuss-Knapp (1881-1951), founded Elly-Heuss-Knapp Foundation (Rest and Recuperation for Mothers).

International Year of the Disabled — A479

1981, Jan. 15 **Litho.**
1342 A479 60pf multi 52 20

European Urban Renaissance — A480

1981, Jan. 15 **Litho. & Engr.**
1343 A480 60pf multi 52 20

Georg Philipp Telemann, Title Page of "Singet dem Herrn" Cantata — A481

1981, Feb. 12 **Photo.**
1344 A481 60pf multi 52 20

Georg Telemann (1681-1767), composer.

Foreign Guest Worker Integration — A482

1981, Feb. 12 **Litho.**
1345 A482 50pf multi 48 20

Preservation of the Environment — A483

1981, Feb. 12
1346 A483 60pf multi 52 20

European Patent Office Centenary — A484

1981, Feb. 12
1347 A484 60pf multi 52 20

Chest Scintigram A485

1981, Feb. 12 *Perf. 13x13½*
1348 A485 40pf multi 42 20

Early examination for the prevention of cancer.

Europa Issue 1981

South German Couple Dancing in Regional Costumes — A486

1981, May 7 **Litho.** *Perf. 14*
1349 A486 50pf shown 60 20
1350 A486 60pf Northern couple 80 20

19th German Protestant Convention, Hamburg, June 17-21 — A487

1981, May 7 **Photo.**
1351 A487 50pf multi 45 20

Altar Figures, by Tilman Riemenschneider A488

1981, May 7 **Litho.**
1352 A488 60pf multi 52 20

Tilman Riemenschneider (1460-1531), sculptor, 450th death anniversary.

Georg von Neumayer Polar Research Station — A489

1981, July 16 **Litho.** *Perf. 14*
1353 A489 110pf multi 1.10 50

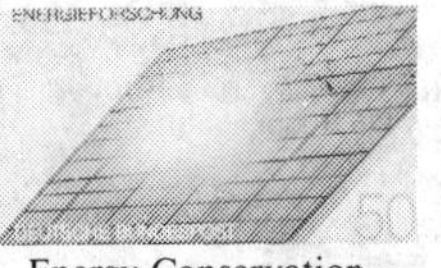
Energy Conservation Research — A490

1981, July 16
1354 A490 50pf Solar generator 45 18

Wildlife Protection A491

1981, July 16
1355 A491 60pf Baby coot 52 20

Cooperation in Third World Development — A492

1981, July 16
1356 A492 90pf multi 80 45

Wilhelm Raabe (1831-1910), Poet — A493

1981, Aug. 13 **Litho. & Engr.**
1357 A493 50pf dk grn & grn 45 18

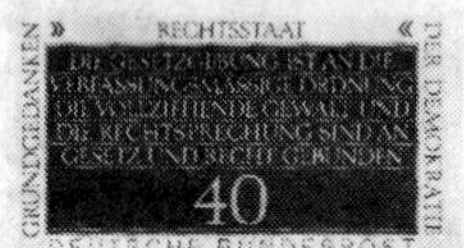

Statement of Constitutional Freedom (Fundamental Concept of Democracy) — A494

1981, Aug. 13 **Litho.** ***Perf. 14***
1358 A494 40pf shown 35 15
1359 A494 50pf Separation of powers 40 15
1360 A494 60pf Sovereignty of the people 52 16
Set value 36

People by Mailcoach, lithograph, 1855 — A495

1981, Oct. 8 **Litho.**
1361 A495 60pf multi 65 25

Stamp Day, Oct. 25.

Antarctic Treaty, 20th Anniv. — A496

1981, Nov. 12 **Litho.** ***Perf. 14***
1362 A496 100pf multi 1.00 45

St. Elizabeth of Thuringia, 750th Anniv. of Death — A497

1981, Nov. 12
1363 A497 50pf multi 50 20

Karl von Clausewitz, by W. Wach — A498

1981, Nov. 12 **Photo.**
1364 A498 60pf multi 65 18

Prussian general and writer, (1780-1831).

Social Insurance Centenary — A499

1981, Nov. 12
1365 A499 60fr multi 65 18

Pear-shaped Pot with Lid, 1715 — A500

1982, Jan. 13 **Litho.**
1366 A500 60pf multi 65 18

Johann Friedrich Bottger (1682-1719), originator of Dresden china, 300th birth anniv.

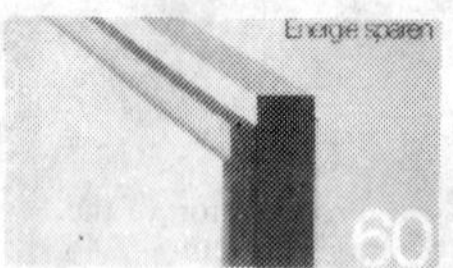

Energy Conservation — A501

1982, Jan. 13
1367 A501 60pf multi 65 18

Illustration from The Town Band of Bremen (folktale) — A502

1982, Jan. 13
1368 A502 40pf red & blk 45 18

Johann Wolfgang von Goethe (1749-1832), by Georg Melchior Kraus, 1776 — A503

1982, Feb. 18 **Photo.**
1369 A503 60pf multi 75 18

Robert Koch (1843-1910), Discoverer of Tubercle Bacillus, (1882) A504

1982, Feb. 18
1370 A504 50pf multi 60 18

Die Fromme Helene, by Wilhelm Busch (1832-1908) — A505

1982, Apr. 15 **Litho.** ***Perf. 13½x14***
1371 A505 50pf multi 55 25

Europa 1982 A506

1982, May 5 **Litho.** ***Perf. 14***
1372 A506 50pf Hambach Meeting sesquicentennial 65 15
1373 A506 60pf Treaties of Rome, 1957-1982 80 20

Kiel Regatta Week Centenary A507

1982, May 5
1374 A507 60pf multi 60 18

Young Men's Christian Assoc. (YMCA) Centenary — A508

1982, May 5
1375 A508 50pf multi 50 18

"Don't Drink and Drive" A509

1982, July 15 **Photo.**
1376 A509 80pf red & blk 90 27

25th Anniv. of German Lepers' Org. — A510

1982, July 15 **Photo.**
1377 A510 80pf multi 90 27

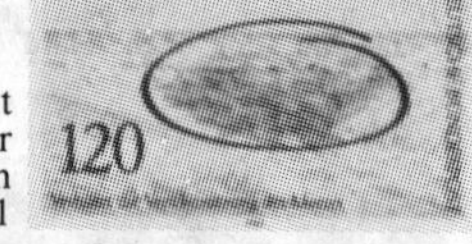

Prevent Water Pollution A511

1982, July 15
1378 A511 120pf multi 1.40 40

Urea Model and Synthesis Formula A512

1982, Aug. 12 **Photo.**
1379 A512 50pf multi 60 18

Friedrich Wohler (1800-1882), chemist, discoverer of organic chemistry.

St. Francis Preaching to the Birds, by Giotto — A513

James Franck, Max Born — A514

1982, Aug. 12 **Litho.**
1380 A513 60pf multi 70 18

800th birth anniv. of St. Francis of Assisi and 87th German Catholics Congress, Dusseldorf, Sept. 1-5.

1982, Aug. 12 **Litho. & Engr.**
1381 A514 80pf multi 75 28

James Franck (1882-1964) and Max Born (1882-1970), Nobel Prize physicists, developed quantum theory.

Stamp Day, Oct. 24 A515

1982, Oct. 14 **Photo.** ***Perf. 14***
1382 A515 80pf Poster 1.10 28

400th Anniv. of the Gregorian Calendar — A516

Design: Calendar illumination, by Johannes Rasch, 1586.

1982, Oct. 14 **Litho.**
1383 A516 60pf multi 65 25

Pres. Theodor Heuss, 1949-1959 A517

Presidents: b. Heinrich Lubke, 1959-69. c. Gustav Heinemann, 1969-74. d. Walter Scheel, 1974-79. e. Karl Carstens, 1979-84.

1982, Nov. 10
1384 Sheet of 5 4.25 4.25
a.-e. A517 80pf. single stamp 75 60

Edith Stein (d. 1942), Philospher and Carmelite Nun — A518

1983, Jan. 13 Litho. *Perf. 14*
1385 A518 80pf gray & blk 1.10 24

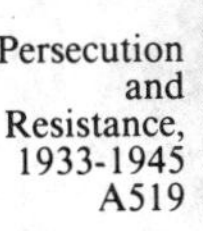

Persecution and Resistance, 1933-1945 A519

1983, Jan. 13
1386 A519 80pf multi 90 24

Light Space Modulator, 1930 — A520

Walter Gropius (1883-1969), Founder of Bauhaus Architecture: 60pf, Sanctuary, zinc lithograph, 1942. 80pf, Bauhaus Archives, Berlin, 1979.

1983, Feb. 8
1387 A520 50pf multi 55 16
1388 A520 60pf multi 70 20
1389 A520 80pf multi 85 24

Federahannes, Swabian-Alemannic Carnival — A521

1983, Feb. 8
1390 A521 60pf multi 70 20

4th Intl. Horticultural Show, Munich, Apr. 28-Oct. 9 — A522

1983, Apr. 12 Litho. *Perf. 14*
1391 A522 60pf multi 70 24

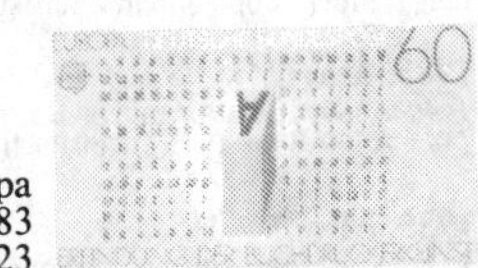
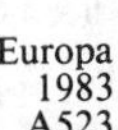
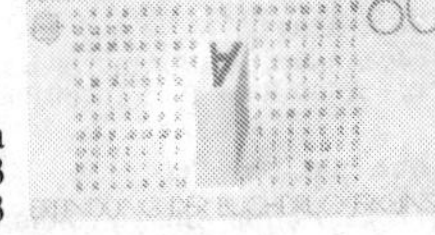

Europa 1983 A523

Discoveries: 60pf, Printing press by Johannes Guttenburg. 80pf, Electromagnetic waves by Heinrich Hertz.

1983, May 5 Litho. *Perf. 14*
1392 A523 60pf Movable type 90 28
1393 A523 80pf Resonant circuit, electric flux lines 1.00 28

Johannes Brahms (1833-1897), Composer A524

1983, May 5 Photo.
1394 A524 80pf multi 1.00 24

Franz Kafka (1883-1924), Writer — A525

1983, May 5
1395 A525 80pf Signature, Tyn Church, Prague 90 24

Beer Pureness Law, 450th Anniv. A526

1983, May 5 Litho.
1396 A526 80pf Brewers, engraving, 1677 90 24

300th Anniv. of Immigration to US. — A527

1983, May 5 Litho. & Engr.
1397 A527 80pf Concord 95 24

See US No. 2040.

Children and Road Safety A528

1983, July 14 Litho. *Perf. 14*
1398 A528 80pf multi 90 20

50th Intl. Auto Show, Frankfurt, Sept. 15-25 A529

1983, July 14
1399 A529 60pf multi 75 20

Otto Warburg A530

Christoph Martin Wieland (1733-1813), Poet A531

1983, Aug. 11 Photo. *Perf. 14*
1400 A530 50pf multi 55 18

Otto Warburg (1883-1970), pioneer of modern biochemistry, 1931 Nobel prize winner in medicine.

1983, Aug. 11 Litho.
1401 A531 80pf multi 90 20

10th Anniv. of UN Membership — A532

1983, Aug. 11 Photo.
1402 A532 80pf multi 1.00 20

Rauhe Haus Orphanage Sesquicentennial — A533

1983, Aug. 11 Litho.
1403 A533 80pf multi 90 20

Survey and Measuring Maps A534

1983, Aug. 11
1404 A534 120pf multi 1.25 30

Intl. Union of Geodesy and Geophysics Gen. Assembly, Hamburg, Aug. 15-26.

Stamp Day — A535

1983, Oct. 13 Litho. *Perf. 13½*
1405 A535 80pf Postrider 1.25 24

Martin Luther (1483-1546) A536

1983, Oct. 13 *Perf. 14*
1406 A536 80pf Engraving by G. Konig 85 24

Customs Union Sesquicentennial — A537

1983, Nov. 10
1407 A537 60pf multi 90 20

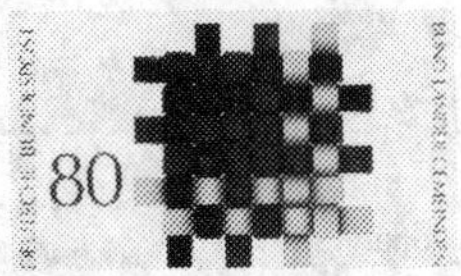

Territorial Authorities (Federation, Land, Communities) — A538

1983, Nov. 10 Litho.
1408 A538 80pf multi 75 24

Trier, 2000th Anniv. A539

1984, Jan. 12 Litho. & Engr.
1409 A539 80pf Black Gate, 175 A.D. 90 24

Philipp Reis (1834-1874) Physicist and Inventor — A540

1984, Jan. 12 Litho.
1410 A540 80pf multi 90 24

Gregor Mendel (1822-1884), Basic Laws of Heredity — A541

1984, Jan. 12 Litho.
1411 A541 50pf multi 70 16

500th Anniv. of Michelstadt Town Hall — A542

1984, Feb. 16 Litho.
1412 A542 60pf multi 70 20

350th Anniv. of Oberammergau Passion Play — A543

1984, Feb. 16 Photo.
1413 A543 60pf multi 70 20

Second Election of Parliament, June 17 — A544

1984, Apr. 12 **Litho.** ***Perf. 13½***
1414 A544 80pf multi 90 22

Europa (1959-1984) A545

1984, May 8 **Photo.** ***Perf. 14***
1415 A545 60pf multi 85 18
1416 A545 80pf multi 1.00 24

Nursery Rhyme Illustration, by Ludwig Richter (1803-84) A546

1984, May 8 **Engr.**
1417 A546 60pf multi 90 22

St. Norbert von Xanten (1080-1134) — A547

1984, May 8
1418 A547 80pf Statue, 1693 90 22

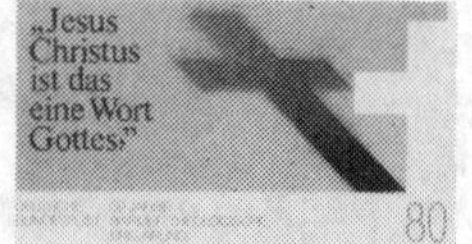

Barmer Theological Declaration, 50th Anniv. — A548

1984, May 8 **Litho.**
1419 A548 80pf Cross, text 90 22

Souvenir Sheet

1984 UPU Congress A549

1984, June 19 **Litho.** ***Perf. 14***
1420 Sheet of 3 3.00 3.00
- ***a.*** A549 60pf Letter sorting, 19th cent. 70 70
- ***b.*** A549 80pf Scanner 80 80
- ***c.*** A549 120pf H. von Stephan, founder 1.40 1.40

City of Neuss Bimillenium A550

1984, June 19 **Litho. & Engr.**
1421 A550 80pf Tomb of Oclatius 90 22

Friedrich Wilhelm Bessel (1784-1846), Astronomer A551

1984, June 19
1422 A551 80pf Bessel function diagram 90 22

88th German Catholic Convention, Munich, July 4-8 — A552

1984, June 19 **Photo.**
1423 A552 60pf Pope Pius XII 65 18

Town Hall, Duderstadt A553

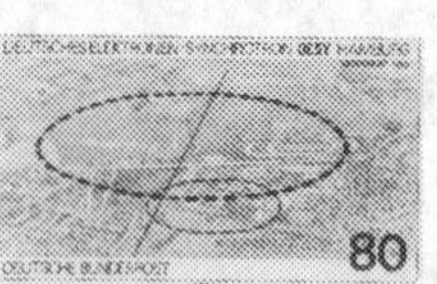

Medieval Document, Computer A554

1984, Aug. 21 **Litho.** ***Perf. 14***
1424 A553 60pf multi 65 18

1984, Aug. 21
1425 A554 70pf multi 70 22

10th Intl. Archives Congress, Bonn.

German Electron Synchrotron (DESY) Research Center, Hamburg — A555

1984, Aug. 21 **Photo.**
1426 A555 80pf multi 90 22

Schleswig-Holstein Canal Bicentenary — A556

1984, Aug. 21 **Litho.**
1427 A556 80pf Knoop lock 90 22

Stamp Day A557

1984, Oct. 18 **Litho.** ***Perf. 14***
1428 A557 80pf Imperial Taxis Posthouse, Augsburg 1.25 22

Anti-smoking Campaign — A558

1984, Nov. 8 **Litho.**
1429 A558 60pf Match, text 90 22

Equal Rights for Men and Women — A559

1984, Nov. 8
1430 A559 80pf Male & female symbols 90 22

Peace and Understanding — A560

1984, Nov. 8
1431 A560 80pf Text 90 22

Augsburg, 2000th Anniversary — A561

1985, Jan. 10 **Litho.**
1432 A561 80pf Roman Emperor Augustus, Augsburg Buildings 90 22

Philipp Jakob Spener, Religious Leader (1635-1705) — A562

1985, Jan. 10 **Litho.**
1433 A562 80pf multi 90 22

Deutches Wortebuch A563

1985, Jan. 10 **Litho.**
1434 A563 80pf Bros. Grimm, text 90 22

Romano Guardini, Theologist (1885-1968) A564

1985, Jan. 10 **Litho.**
1435 A564 80pf multi 90 22

Market and Coinage Rights in Verden, 1000th Anniv. A565

1985, Feb. 21 **Litho.**
1436 A565 60pf multi 70 18

German-Danish Border Areas and Flags — A566

1985, Feb. 21
1437 A566 80pf multi 90 22

Bonn-Copenhagen declarations on mutual minorities, 30th anniv.

Johann Peter Hebel (1760-1826), Poet — A567

1985, Apr. 16 **Litho.**
1438 A567 80pf multi 90 22

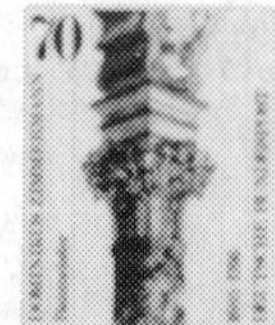

Egon Erwin Kisch (1885-1948), Journalist A568

1985, Apr. 16 **Litho.**
1439 A568 60pf Kisch using telephone 70 20

Europa 1985 A569

Dominikus Zimmermann (1685-1766), Architect A570

European Music Year: 60pf, Georg Friedrich Handel. 80pf, Johann Sebastian Bach.

1985, May 7 **Photo.**
1440 A569 60pf Portrait of Handel 90 15
1441 A569 80pf Portrait of Bach 1.00 18

1985, May 7 **Photo.**
1442 A570 70pf Stucco column 70 20

St. George's Cathedral, 750th Anniv. — A571

1985, May 7 **Litho.** ***Perf. 14***
1443 A571 60pf Cathedral, Limburg 75 20

Father Josef Kentenich (1885-1968) — A572

1985, May 7 **Litho.**
1444 A572 80pf Portrait 90 22

Forest Conservation A573

1985, July 16 **Litho.** ***Perf. 14***
1445 A573 80pf Clock, forest 90 22

Intl. Youth Year A574

1985, July 16 ***Perf. 14***
1446 A574 60pf Scouts, scouting and IYY emblems 65 18

30th World Scouting Conference, Munich, July 15-19.

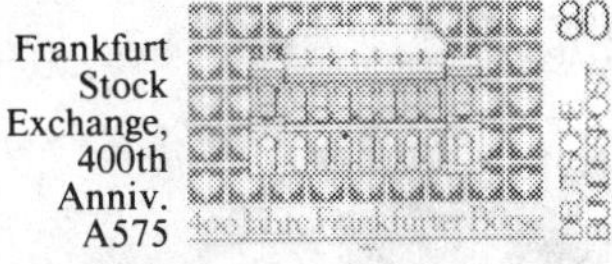

Frankfurt Stock Exchange, 400th Anniv. A575

Design: Bourse, est. 1879, and Frankfurt Eagle, the exchange emblem.

1985, Aug. 13 ***Perf. 14x14½***
1447 A575 80pf multi 90 22

The Sunday Walk, by Carl Spitzweg (1808-85) A576

1985, Aug. 13
1448 A576 60pf multi 70 22

Fritz Reuter (1810-1874), Dialect Author — A577

1985, Oct. 15 **Litho.** ***Perf. 14***
1449 A577 80pf Portrait, manuscript 90 22

Departure of the 1st Train from Nuremberg to Furth, 1835 — A578

1985, Nov. 12 **Litho.** ***Perf. 14x14½***
1450 A578 80pf Adler locomotive 90 22

Founder Johannes Scharrer (1785-1844), German Railways 150th anniv.

Reintegration of German World War II Refugees, 40th Anniv. — A579

1985, Nov. 12 ***Perf. 14***
1451 A579 80pf multi 90 22

Natl. Armed Forces, 30th Anniv. A580

1985, Nov. 12 ***Perf. 14x14½***
1452 A580 80pf Iron Cross, natl. colors 90 22

Benz Tricycle, Saloon Car, 1912, and Modern Automobile — A581

1986, Jan. 16 **Litho.** ***Perf. 14***
1453 A581 80pf multi 90 22

Automobile cent.

Bad Hersfeld, 1250th Anniv. A582

1986, Feb. 13 **Litho.** ***Perf. 14***
1454 A582 60pf multi 70 20

Bach Contata, Detail, by Oskar Kokoschka (1886-1980) — A583

1986, Feb. 13
1455 A583 80pf Self portrait 90 22

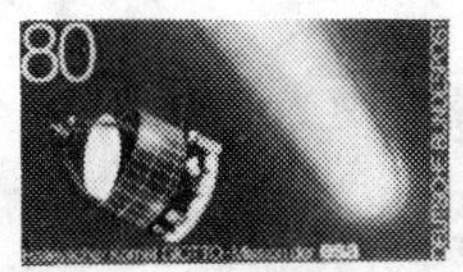

Halley's Comet A584

1986, Feb. 13
1456 A584 80pf multi 90 22

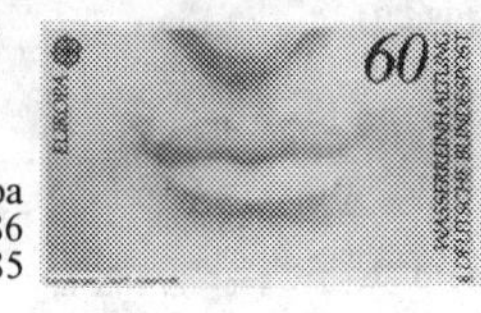

Europa 1986 A585

Details from Michelangelo's David: 60pf, Mouth (pure water). 80pf, Nose, (pure air).

1986, May 5 **Photo.** ***Perf. 14***
1457 A585 60pf multi 80 16
1458 A585 80pf multi 90 22

St. Johannis Monastery, Walsrode — A586

1986, May 5 **Litho. & Engr.**
1459 A586 60pf multi 75 18

Monastery millennium and town of Walsrode, 603rd anniv.

King Ludwig II of Bavaria (1845-1886), Neuschwanstein Castle — A587

1986, May 5 **Litho.**
1460 A587 60pf multi 75 18

Karl Barth (1886-1968), Protestant Theologian A588

1986, May 5 **Engr.**
1461 A588 80pf blk, dk red & red lil 90 22

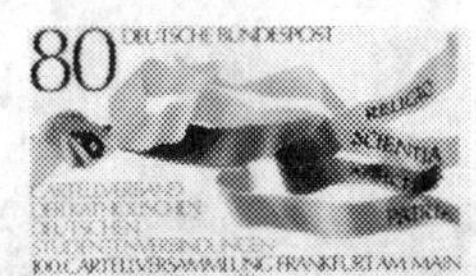

Religion, Science, Friendship and Fatherland — A589

1986, May 5 **Litho.**
1462 A589 80pf multi 90 22

Union of German Catholic Students, 100th assembly, Frankfurt, June 12-15.

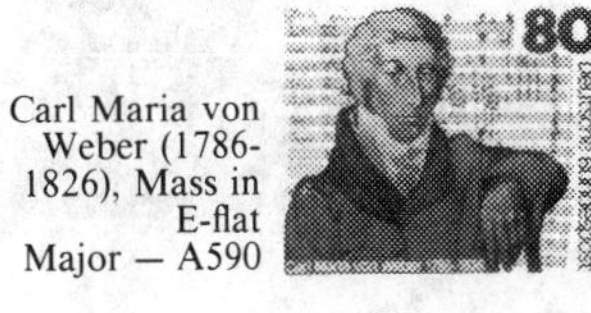

Carl Maria von Weber (1786-1826), Mass in E-flat Major — A590

1986, June 20 **Litho.** ***Perf. 14***
1463 A590 80pf multi 90 22

Franz Liszt and Signature A591

1986, June 20
1464 A591 80pf dk bl & dk org 90 22

Intl. Peace Year A592

1986, June 20
1465 A592 80pf multi 90 22

Souvenir Sheet

Reichstag, Berlin A593

Historic buildings: b, Koening Museum, Bonn. c, Parliament, Bonn.

1986, June 20
1466 Sheet of 3 2.75 2.75
a.-c. A593 80pf, any single 90 30

European Satellite Technology — A594

Design: TV-SAT/TDF-1 over Europe.

1986, June 20
1467 A594 80pf multi 90 28

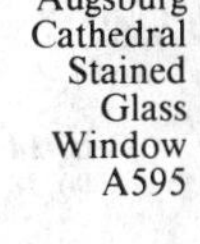

Augsburg Cathedral Stained Glass Window A595

1986, Aug. 14 ***Perf. 14***
1468 A595 80pf multi 90 28

Monuments protection.

King Frederick the Great (1712-1786) A596

German Skat Congress, Cent. A597

1986, Aug. 14
1469 A596 80pf multi 90 28

1986, Aug. 14
1470 A597 80pf Tournament card 90 28

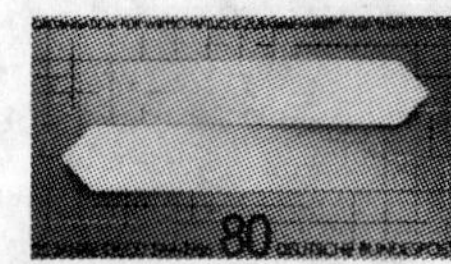

Organization for Economic Cooperation and Development, 25th Anniv. — A598

1986, Aug. 14

1471 A598 80pf multi 90 28

Heidelberg University, 600th Anniv. — A599

1986, Oct. 16 **Litho.**

1472 A599 80pf multi 90 28

Stagecoach, Stamps from 1975-1984 — A600

1986, Oct. 16

1473 A600 80pf multi 90 28

Stamp Day, 50th Anniv.

Mary Wigman (1886-1973), Dancer — A601

1986, Nov. 13 **Litho.** ***Perf. 14***

1474 A601 70pf multi 90 28

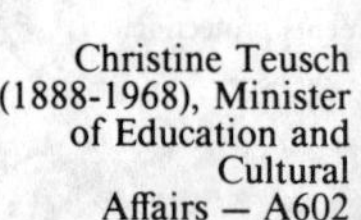

Christine Teusch (1888-1968), Minister of Education and Cultural Affairs — A602

1986-91 **Engr.** ***Perf. 14***

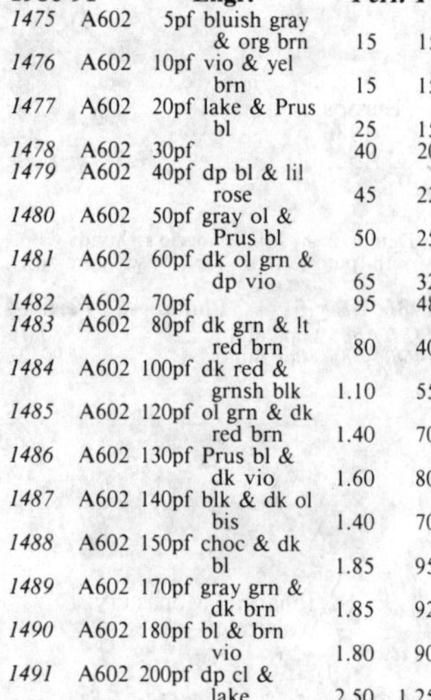

1475	A602	5pf bluish gray & org brn	15	15
1476	A602	10pf vio & yel brn	15	15
1477	A602	20pf lake & Prus bl	25	15
1478	A602	30pf	40	20
1479	A602	40pf dp bl & lil rose	45	22
1480	A602	50pf gray ol & Prus bl	50	25
1481	A602	60pf dk ol grn & dp vio	65	32
1482	A602	70pf	95	48
1483	A602	80pf dk grn & lt red brn	80	40
1484	A602	100pf dk red & grnsh blk	1.10	55
1485	A602	120pf ol grn & dk red brn	1.40	70
1486	A602	130pf Prus bl & dk vio	1.60	80
1487	A602	140pf blk & dk ol bis	1.40	70
1488	A602	150pf choc & dk bl	1.85	95
1489	A602	170pf gray grn & dk brn	1.85	92
1490	A602	180pf bl & brn vio	1.80	90
1491	A602	200pf dp cl & lake	2.50	1.25
1492	A602	240pf Prus bl & yel brn	2.60	1.30
1493	A602	250pf dp lil rose & dp bl	2.50	1.25
1493A	A602	300pf dk vio & sage grn	3.00	1.50
1494	A602	350pf gray grn & lake	3.75	1.90
1494A	A602	500pf slate grn & brt ver	5.75	2.85
		Nos. 1475-1494A (22)	35.40	17.89

Famous Women: 5pf, Emma Ihrer (1857-1911), politician, labor leader. 10pf, Paula Modersohn-Becker (1876-1907), painter. 20pf, Cilly Aussem (1909-1963), tennis champion. 30pf, Kathe Kollwitz (1867-1945), painter, graphic artist. 40pf, Maria Sibylla Merian (1647-1717), naturalist, painter. 60pf, Dorothea Erxleben (1715-62), physician. 70pf, Elisabet Boehm (1859-1943), social organizer. 80pf, Clara Schumann (1819-96), pianist, composer. 100pf, Therese Giehse (1898-1975), actress. 120pf, Elisabeth Selbert (1896-1986), politician. 130pf, Lise Meitner (1878-1968), physicist. 140pf, Cecile Vogt (1875-1962), neurologist. 150pf, Sophie Scholl (1921-1943), member of anti-Nazi resistance. 170pf, Hannah Arendt (1906-75), American political scientist. 180pf, Lotte Lehmann (1888-1976), soprano. 200pf, Bertha von Suttner (1843-1914), 1905 Nobel Peace Prize winner. 240pf, Mathilde Franziska Anneke, (1817-84), American author. 250pf, Queen Louise of Prussia (1776-1810). 300pf, Fanny Hensel (1805-1847), composer-conductor. 350pf, Hedwig Dransfeld (1871-1925), women's rights activist. 500pf, Alice Salomon (1872-1948), feminist and social activist.

Issue dates: 50pf, 80pf, Nov. 18. 40pf, 60pf, Sept. 17, 1987. 120pf, Nov. 7, 1987. 10pf, Apr. 14, 1988. 20pf, 130pf, May 5, 1988. 100pf, 170pf, 240pf, 350pf, Nov. 10, 1988. 500pf, Jan. 12, 1989. 5pf, Feb. 9, 1989. 180pf, 250pf, July 13, 1989. 140pf, 300pf, Aug. 10, 1989. 30pf, 70pf, Jan. 8, 1991. 150pf, 200pf, Feb. 14, 1991.

See No. 1734, Berlin Nos. 9N516-9N532.

Advent Collection for Church Projects in Latin America, 25th Anniv. A603

1986, Nov. 13 **Litho.** ***Perf. 14***

1495 A603 80pf multi 90 25

Berlin, 750th Anniv. — A604

1987, Jan. 15 **Litho.**

1496 A604 80pf multi 90 25

Archbishop's Residence at Wurzburg, 1719-44 — A605

1987, Jan. 15 **Photo.**

1497 A605 80pf multi 90 25

Balthasar Neumann (1687-1753), Baroque architect.

Ludwig Erhard (1897-1977), Economist, Chancellor 1963-66 — A606

1987, Jan. 15

1498 A606 80pf multi 90 25

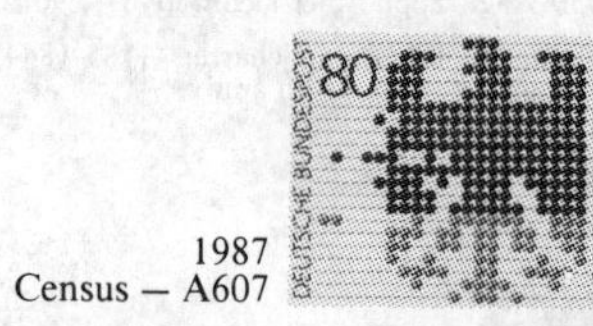

1987 Census — A607

1987, Jan. 15 **Litho.**

1499 A607 80pf Federal Eagle 90 25

Clemenswerth Hunting Castle, 250th Anniv. — A608

1987, Feb. 12 **Litho.**

1500 A608 60pf multi 75 20

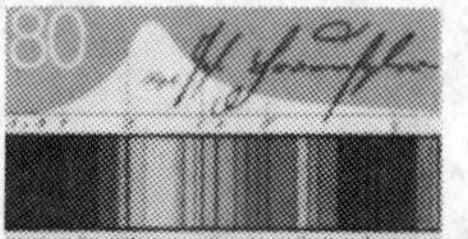

Joseph von Fraunhofer (1787-1826), Optician, Physicist — A609

1987, Feb. 12 **Litho. & Engr.**

1501 A607 80pf Light spectrum diagram 90 25

Karl May (1842-1912), Novelist — A610

1987, Feb. 12 **Photo.**

1502 A610 80pf Apache Chief Winnetou 90 25

Papal Arms, Madonna and Child, Buildings in Kevelaer — A611

1987, Apr. 9 **Litho.**

1503 A611 80pf multi 88 25

State visit of Pope John Paul II, Apr. 30-May 4; 17th Marian and 10th Mariological World Congress, Kevelaer, Sept. 11-20.

German Choral Soc., 125th Anniv. A612

1987, Apr. 9

1504 A612 80pf multi 88 25

Europa 1987 A613

Modern architecture: 60pf, German Pavilion, designed by Ludwig Mies van der Rohe, 1928 World's Fair, Barcelona. 80pf, Kohlbrand Bridge, 1974, Hamburg, designed by Thyssen Engineering.

1987, May 5 **Litho.**

1505 A613 60pf multi 68 20

1506 A613 80pf multi 90 25

Organ Pipes, Signature A614

1987, May 5

1507 A614 80pf multi 90 25

Dietrich Buxtehude (c. 1637-1707), composer.

Wilhelm Kaisen (1887-1979), Bremen City Senate President — A615

1987, May 5

1508 A615 80pf multi 90 25

Johann Albrecht Bengel (1687-1752), Lutheran Theologian A616

1987, May 5 **Photo.** ***Perf. 14***

1509 A616 80pf multi 90 25

Kurt Schwitters (1887-1948), Artist A617

1987, May 5 **Litho.**

1510 A617 80pf multi 90 25

Rotary Intl. Convention, Munich, June 7-10 — A618

1987, May 5 **Photo.**
1511 A618 70pf multi 80 25

Dulmen's Wild Horses, Merfelder Bruch Nature Reserve — A619

1987, May 5
1512 A619 60pf multi 68 25

European Environmental Conservation Year.

Bishopric of Bremen, 1200th Anniv. — A620

Design: Charlemagne, Bremen Cathedral, city arms, Bishop Willehad.

1987, July 16 **Litho.** ***Perf. 14***
1513 A620 80pf multi 90 25

7th European Rifleman's Festival, Lippstadt, Sept. 12-13 — A621

1987, Aug. 20 **Litho.** ***Perf. 14***
1514 A621 80pf multi 90 25

Stamp Day — A622

1987, Oct. 15 **Litho.**
1515 A622 80pf Postmen, 1897 90 25

Historic Sites and Objects — A623

Designs: 5pf, Brunswick Lion. 10pf, Frankfurt Airport. 20pf, No. 1524, Queen Nefertiti of Egypt, bust, Egyptian Museum, Berlin. 30pf, Corner tower, Celle Castle, 14th cent. 33pf, 120pf, Schleswig Cathedral. 38pf, 280pf, Statue of Roland, Bremen. 40pf, Chile House, Hamburg. 45pf, Rastatt Castle. 50pf, Filigree tracery on spires, Freiburg Cathedral. 60pf, Bavaria Munich, bronze statue above the Theresienwiese, Hall of Fame. No. 1524A, Heligoland. 80pf, Entrance to Zollern II coal mine, Dortmund. 90pf, 140pf, Bronze flagon from Reinheim. 100pf, Altotting Chapel, Bavaria. 170pf, Russian church, Wiesbaden. 300pf, Hambach Castle. 350pf, Externsteine Bridge near Horn-Bad Meinberg. 400pf, Opera House, Dresden.

1987-91	**Typo.**	***Perf. 14***	
1515A	5pf Prus bl & gray	15	15
1516	10pf chalky bl & slate bl	15	15
1517	20pf dl bl & tan	22	15
1518	30pf aqua & org brn	35	18
1519	33pf tan & lt grn	40	20
1520	38pf ol bis & brt grnsh bl	45	22
1521	40pf ultra, dk red brn & org red	45	22
1521A	45pf lt grnsh bl & dl org	55	28
1522	50pf ultra & yel brn	58	30
1523	60pf cob & pale gray	68	35
1524	70pf dull bl & tan	85	42
1524A	70pf vio bl & henna brn	85	42
1525	80pf cob & pale gray	90	45
a.	Bklt. pane of 4 10pf, 2 50pf, 2 80pf ('89)	3.45	
1526	90pf dp bis & yel	98	50
1527	100pf brt bluish grn & ol bis	1.10	55
a.	Bklt. pane of 2 each 10, 60, 80, 100pf	5.60	
1528	120pf brn org & lt grnsh bl	1.45	72
1529	140pf dk ol bis & yel	1.60	80
1532	170pf ol bis & brt yel	1.90	95
1537	280pf sky bl & ol bis	3.00	1.50
1538	300pf dk red brn & tan	3.75	1.80
1539	350pf brt ultra & ol bis	3.75	1.90
1540	400pf brn red & dl org	4.80	2.40
	Nos. 1515A-1540 (22)	28.91	14.61

Issue dates: 30pf, 50pf, 60pf, 80pf, Nov. 6. 10pf, 300pf, Jan. 14, 1988. 70pf, 120pf, July 14, 1988. 40pf, 90pf, 280pf, Aug. 11, 1988. 20pf, 33pf, 38pf, 140pf, Jan. 12, 1989. 100pf, 350pf, Feb. 9, 1989. 5pf, Feb. 15, 1990. 45p, No. 1524A, June 21, 1990. 170pf, June 4, 1991. 400pf, Oct. 10, 1991.

See #1655-1663, Berlin #9N543-9N557.

This is an expanding set. Numbers will change if necessary.

Christoph Willibald Gluck (1714-1787), Composer, and Score from the Opera Armide — A624

1987, Nov. 6 ***Perf. 14***
1541 A624 60pf carmine lake & dark gray 68 25

Gerhart Hauptmann (1862-1946), Playwright — A625

1987, Nov. 6 **Litho.**
1542 A625 80pf blk & brick red 90 25

German Agro Action Organization, 125th Anniv. — A626

1987, Nov. 6 **Photo.**
1543 A626 80pf Rice field 90 25

Mainz Carnival, 150th Anniv. — A627

1988, Jan. 14 **Litho.** ***Perf. 14***
1544 A627 60pf Jester 75 20

Jacob Kaiser (1888-1961), Labor Leader — A628

1988, Jan. 14 **Litho. & Engr.**
1545 A628 80pf black 1.00 25

Franco-German Cooperation Treaty, 25th Anniv. — A629

1988, Jan. 14
1546 A629 80pf Adenauer, De Gaulle 1.00 25

See France No. 2086.

Beatification of Edith Stein and Rupert Mayer by Pope John Paul II in 1987 — A630

1988, Jan. 14 **Photo.**
1547 A630 80pf brn, blk & ver 1.00 25

Woodcut (detail) by Ludwig Richter — A631

1988, Feb. 18 **Litho.**
1548 A631 60pf multi 75 20

Woodcut inspired by poem Solitude of the Green Woods, by Baron Joseph von Eichendorff (1788-1857).

Arthur Schopenhauer (1788-1860), Philosopher — A632

1988, Feb. 18 **Photo.**
1549 A632 80pf dk red & brn blk 1.00 25

Friedrich Wilhelm Raiffeisen (1818-1888), Economist — A633

1988, Feb. 18 **Litho.**
1550 A633 80pf blk & brt yel grn 1.00 25

The German Raiffeisen Assoc., an agricultural cooperative credit soc., was founded by Raiffeisen.

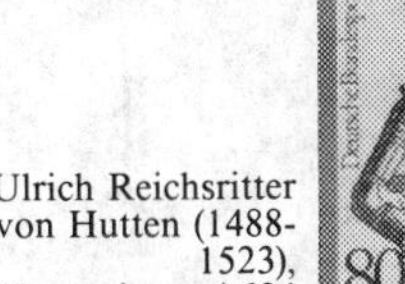

Ulrich Reichsritter von Hutten (1488-1523), Humanist — A634

Design: Detail from an engraving published with Hutten's *Conquestiones.*

1988, Apr. 14 **Litho. & Engr.**
1551 A634 80pf multi 98 25

Europa 1988 A635

Transport and communication: 60pf, Airbus A320. 80pf, Integrated Services Digital Network (ISDN) system.

1988, May 5 **Litho.**
1552 A635 60pf multi 72 20
1553 A635 80pf multi 98 25

City of Dusseldorf, 700th Anniv. — A636

1988, May 5
1554 A636 60pf multi 72 20

Cologne University, 600th Anniv. A637

1988, May 5
1555 A637 80pf multi 98 25

Jean Monnet (1888-1979), French Statesman A638

1988, May 5
1556 A638 80pf multi 98 25

Theodor Storm (1817-1888), Poet, Novelist — A639

1988, May 5
1557 A639 80pf multi 98 25

German Volunteer Service, 25th Anniv. — A640

1988, May 5
1558 A640 80pf multi 98 25

Town of Meersburg, Millennium — A641

1988, July 14 **Litho.** ***Perf. 14***
1559 A641 60pf multi 72 20

Leopold Gmelin (1788-1853), Chemist — A642

1988, July 14 **Litho. & Engr.**
1560 A642 80pf multi 95 25

Vernier Scale as a Symbol of Precision and Quality — A643

1988, July 14 **Litho.**
1561 A643 140pf multi 1.70 75

Made in Germany.

August Bebel (1840-1913), Founder of the Social Democratic Party — A644

1988, Aug. 11 **Photo.**
1562 A644 80pf multi 88 25

Intl. Red Cross, 125th Anniv. — A645

Stamp Day — A646

1988, Oct. 13 **Litho. & Engr.**
1563 A645 80pf scar & blk 88 25

1988, Oct. 13 **Litho.**
1564 A646 20pf Carrier pigeon 22 15

1st Nazi Pogrom, Nov. 9, 1938 A647

Design: Star, "Remembering is the secret of redemption," and burning synagogue in Baden-Baden.

1988, Oct. 13 **Photo.**
1565 A647 80pf dl pale pur & blk 88 25

Postage Stamps for Bethel, Cent. A648

1988, Nov. 10 **Litho.**
1566 A648 60pf multi 65 20

The Postage Stamps for Bethel program was founded by Pastor Friedrich V. Bodelschwingh to employ disabled residents of Bethel.

Samaritan Association of Workers (ASB) Rescue Service, Cent. — A649

1988, Nov. 10
1567 A649 80pf multi 88 25

Bonn Bimillennium — A650

1989, Jan. 12 **Litho.**
1568 A650 80pf multi 92 30

Bonn as capital of the federal republic, 40th anniv.

Bluxao I, 1955, by Willi Baumeister (1889-1955) — A651

1989, Jan. 12
1569 A651 60pf multi 70 25

Misereor and Brot fur die Welt, 30th Annivs. A652

1989, Jan. 12 **Photo.**
1570 A652 80pf Barren and verdant soil 92 30

Church organizations helping Third World nations to become self-sufficient in food production.

Cats in the Attic, Woodcut by Gerhard Marcks (1889-1981) — A653

1989, Feb. 9 **Litho.** ***Perf. 14***
1571 A653 60pf multi 65 25

European Parliament 3rd Elections, June 18 — A654

Flags of member nations.

1989, Apr. 20 **Litho.**
1572 A654 100pf multi 1.10 45

Europa 1989 A655

1989, May 5
1573 A655 60pf Kites 65 32
1574 A655 100pf Puppets 1.10 45

Hamburg Harbor, 800th Anniv. A656

1989, May 5
1575 A656 60pf multi 65 25

Cosmas Damian Asam (1686-1739), Painter, Architect A657

1989, May 5 **Litho. & Engr.**
1576 A657 60pf Fresco 65 25

Federal Republic of Germany, 40th Anniv. — A658

1989, May 5 **Photo.**
1577 A658 100pf Natl. crest, flag, presidents' signatures 1.10 45

Council of Europe, 40th Anniv. — A659

1989, May 5 ***Perf. 14***
1578 A659 100pf Parliamentary Assembly, stars 1.10 45

Franz Xaver Gabelsberger (1789-1849), Inventor of a German Shorthand — A660

1989, May 5 **Litho.**
1579 A660 100pf multi 1.10 45

Sts. Kilian, Colman and Totnan (d. 689), Martyred Missionaries, and Clover — A661

1989, June 15 **Litho.**
1580 A661 100pf multi 1.10 45

See Ireland No. 748.

Friedrich Silcher (1789-1860), Composer, and *Lorelai* Score — A662

1989, June 15
1581 A662 80pf multi 88 30

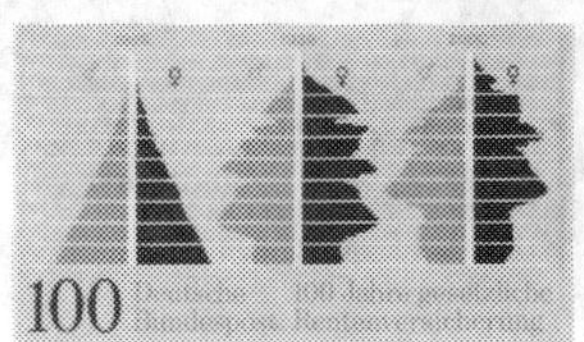

Social Security Pension Insurance, Cent. — A663

1989, June 15
1582 A663 100pf dull ultra, bl & ver 1.10 45

Friedrich List (1789-1846), Economist — A664

1989, July 13 Engr. *Perf. 14*
1583 A664 170pf black & dark red 1.70 75

Summer Evening, 1905, by Heinrich Vogler — A665

1989, July 13 Litho.
1584 A665 60pf multi 60 25

Worpswede Artists' Village, cent.

Reverend Paul Schneider (d. 1939), Martyr of Buchenwald Concentration Camp — A666

1989, July 13 Photo.
1585 A666 100pf slate grn, blk & gray 1.00 45

Frankfurt Cathedral, 750th Anniv. — A667

1989, Aug. 10 Litho.
1586 A667 60pf multi 60 25

Child Welfare A668

1989, Aug. 10 *Perf. 14*
1587 A668 100pf multi 1.00 45

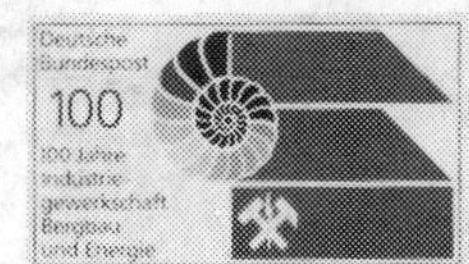

Trade Union of the Mining and Power Industries, Cent. — A669

1989, Aug. 10 *Perf. 14*
1588 A669 100pf multi 1.00 45

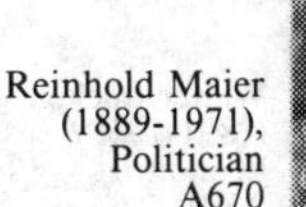

Reinhold Maier (1889-1971), Politician A670

1989, Oct. 12 Litho.
1589 A670 100pf multi 1.10 45

Restoration of St. James Church Organ, Constructed by Arp Schnitger, 1689 — A671

1989, Nov. 16
1590 A671 60pf multi 62 30

Speyer, 2000th Anniv. A672

1990, Jan. 12 Litho. *Perf. 14x14½*
1591 A672 60pf multicolored 65 32

The Young Post Rider, an Engraving by Albrecht Durer — A673

Litho. & Engr.
1990, Jan. 12 *Perf. 14*
1592 A673 100pf buff, vio brn & gray 1.10 45

Postal communications in Europe, 500th anniv. See Austria No. 1486, Belgium No. 1332 and DDR No. 2791.

Riesling Vineyards, 500th Anniv. — A674

1990, Jan. 12 Litho.
1593 A674 100pf multicolored 1.10 45

Addition of Lubeck to the UNESCO World Heritage List, 1987 — A675

1990, Jan. 12 Litho. & Engr.
1594 A675 100pf multicolored 1.10 45

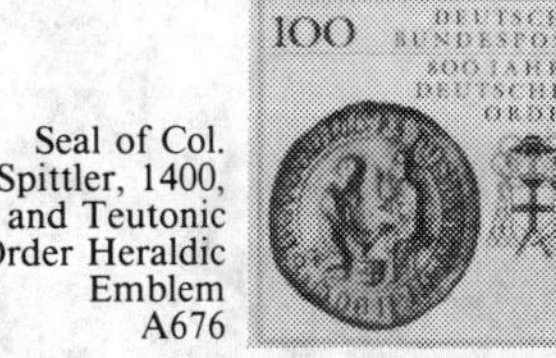

Seal of Col. Spittler, 1400, and Teutonic Order Heraldic Emblem A676

1990, Feb. 15 Litho.
1595 A676 100pf multicolored 1.20 45

Teutonic Order, 800th anniv.

Seal of Frederick II and Galleria Reception Hall at the Frankfurt Fair A677

1990, Feb. 15
1596 A677 100pf multicolored 1.20 45

Granting of fair privileges to Frankfurt by Frederick II, 750th anniv.

Youth Science and Technology Competition, 25th Anniv. — A678

1990, Feb. 15
1597 A678 100pf multicolored 1.20 45

Nature and Environmental Protection — A679

1990, Feb. 15
1598 A679 100pf North Sea 1.20 45

Labor Day, Cent. A680

1990, Apr. 19 Photo. *Perf. 14*
1599 A680 100pf dark red & blk 1.20 45

German Assoc. of Housewives, 75th Anniv. — A681

1990, Apr. 19 Litho.
1600 A681 100pf multicolored 1.20 45

Europa A682

Post offices in Frankfurt am Main: 60pf, Thurn and Taxis Palace. 100pf, Modern Giro office.

1990, May 3 Litho.
1601 A682 60pf multicolored 72 36
1602 A682 100pf multicolored 1.20 45

German Students' Fraternity, 175th Anniv. — A683

1990, May 3 Litho. & Engr.
1603 A683 100pf multicolored 1.20 45

Intl. Telecommunication Union, 125th Anniv. — A684

1990, May 3 Litho.
1604 A684 100pf multicolored 1.20 45

German Life Boat Institution, 125th Anniv. — A685

1990, May 3
1605 A685 60pf multicolored 72 36

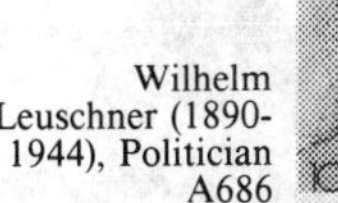

Wilhelm Leuschner (1890-1944), Politician A686

1990, May 3 Litho. & Engr.
1606 A686 100pf lt gray vio 1.20 45

Rummelsberg Diaconal Institution, Cent. — A687

1990, May 3 **Litho.**
1607 A687 100pf multicolored 1.20 45

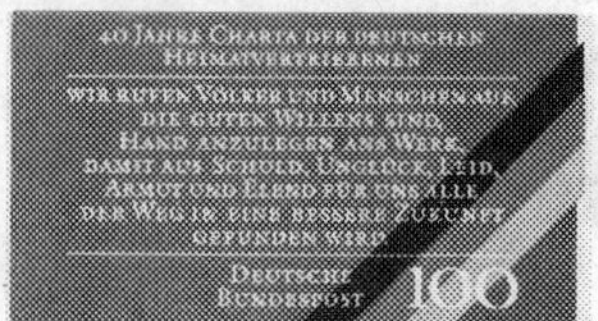

Charter of German Expellees, 40th Anniv. — A688

1990, June 21 **Photo.**
1608 A688 100pf multicolored 1.20 45

Intl. Chamber of Commerce, 30th Universal Congress — A689

1990, June 21 **Litho.**
1609 A689 80pf multicolored 1.00 40

Matthias Claudius (1740-1815), Writer — A691

1990, Aug. 9 **Litho.**
1611 A691 100pf multi 1.20 45

German Reunification — A692

1990, Oct. 3 **Litho.** ***Perf. 14***
1612 A692 50pf blk, red & yel 60 30
1613 A692 100pf blk, red & yel 1.20 60

First Postage Stamps, 150th Anniv. — A693

1990, Oct. 11 **Litho.**
1614 A693 100pf multicolored 1.20 60

Heinrich Schliemann (1822-1890), Archaeologist — A694

1990, Oct. 11
1615 A694 60pf multicolored 70 35

See Greece No. 1705.

Kathe Dorsch (1912-1957), Actress — A695

Opening of Berlin Wall, 1st Anniv. — A696

1990, Nov. 6 **Photo.**
1616 A695 100pf red & violet 1.20 60

1990, Nov. 6 **Photo.** ***Perf. 14***
1617 A696 50pf shown 62 30
1618 A696 100pf Brandenburg Gate 1.25 62

Souvenir Sheet

1619 Sheet of 2 1.87 92
a. A696 50pf like No. 1617 62 30
b. A696 100pf like No. 1618 1.25 62

Rainbow continuous on stamps from #1619.

Pharmacy Profession, 750th Anniv. — A697

1991, Jan. 8 **Litho.**
1620 A697 100pf multicolored 1.35 68

Hanover, 750th Anniv. — A698

1991, Jan. 8
1621 A698 60pf multicolored 80 40

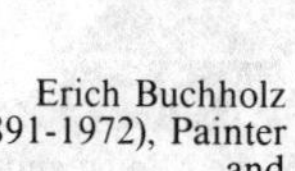

Brandenburg Gate, Bicentennial — A699

1991, Jan. 8 **Litho. & Engr.**
1622 A699 100pf gray, dk bl & red 1.35 68

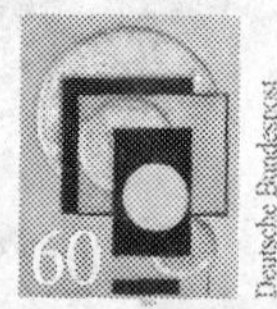
Erich Buchholz (1891-1972), Painter and Architect — A700

1991, Jan. 8 **Photo.**
1623 A700 60pf multicolored 80 40

Walter Eucken (1891-1950), Economist A701

1991, Jan. 8 **Litho.**
1624 A701 100pf multicolored 1.35 68

25th Intl. Tourism Exchange, Berlin — A702

1991, Jan. 8
1625 A702 100pf multicolored 1.35 68

Souvenir Sheet

World Bobsled Championships, Altenberg — A703

1991, Jan. 8 ***Perf. 12½x13***
1626 A703 100pf multicolored 1.35 68

Friedrich Spee von Langenfeld (1591-1635), Poet — A704

1991, Feb. 14 **Litho.** ***Perf. 14***
1627 A704 100pf multicolored 1.15 60

Ludwig Windthorst (1812-1891), Politician A705

1991, Feb. 14
1628 A705 100pf multicolored 1.15 60

Jan von Werth (1591-1652), General — A706

1991, Mar. 12
1629 A706 60pf multicolored 70 35

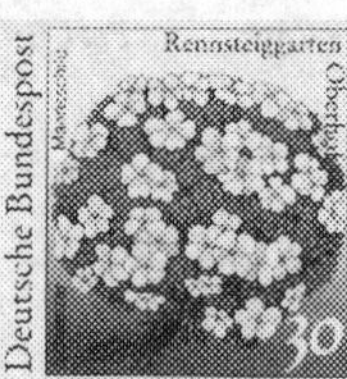
Flowers A707

1991, Mar. 12 ***Perf. 13***
1630 A707 30pf Schweizer mannschild 35 18
1631 A707 50pf Wulfens primel (primula) 60 30
1632 A707 80pf Sommerenzian (gentian) 90 45
1633 A707 100pf Preiselbeere (cranberry) 1.15 60
1634 A707 350pf Alpenedelweiss 4.00 2.00
Nos. 1630-1634 (5) 7.00 3.53

Battle of Legnica, 750th Anniv. A708

1991, Apr. 9 **Litho. & Engr.** ***Perf. 14***
1635 A708 100pf multicolored 1.15 60

See Poland No. 3019.

Choral Singing Academy of Berlin, Bicent. A709

1991, Apr. 9
1636 A709 100pf multicolored 1.15 60

Lette Foundation, 125th Anniv. — A710

1991, Apr. 9 **Photo.**
1637 A710 100pf multicolored 1.15 60

Historic Aircraft A711

1991, Apr. 9

1638 A711	30pf	Junkers F13, 1930	35	18
1639 A711	50pf	Grade Eindecker, 1909	60	30
1640 A711	100pf	Fokker FIII, 1922	1.15	60
1641 A711	165pf	Graf Zeppelin LZ 127, 1928	1.90	95

Europa A712

Satellites: 60pf, ERS-1. 100pf, Copernicus.

1991, May 2 Litho. *Perf. 14*

1642 A712	60pf	multicolored	70	35
1643 A712	100pf	multicolored	1.15	60

Town Charters, 700th Anniv. A713

Design: Arms of Bernkastel, Mayen, Montabaur, Saarburg, Welschbillig, and Wittlich.

1991, May 2

1644 A713	60pf	multicolored	70	35

Max Reger (1873-1916), Composer — A714

1991, May 2

1645 A714	100pf	multicolored	1.15	60

Inter-City Express Railway A715

1991, May 2

1646 A715	60pf	multicolored	70	35

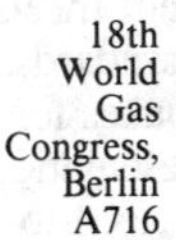

18th World Gas Congress, Berlin A716

Designs: 60pf, Wilhelm August Lampadius (1772-1842), chemist. 100pf, Gas street lamp.

1991, June 4 Litho. *Perf. 13x12½*

1647 A716	60pf	light bl & blk	65	32
1648 A716	100pf	light bl & blk	1.00	50
a.		Pair, #1647-1648 + label	1.65	82

Sea Birds — A717

Designs: 60pf, Kampflaufer, Philomachus pugnax. 80pf, Zwergseeschwalbe, Sterna albifrons. 100pf, Ringelgans, Branta bernicla. 140pf, Seeadler, Haliaeetus albicilla.

1991, June 4 Litho. *Perf. 14*

1649 A717	60pf	multicolored	65	32
1650 A717	80pf	multicolored	90	45
1651 A717	100of	multicolored	1.10	55
1652 A717	140pf	multicolored	1.55	78

Paul Wallot (1841-1912), Architect — A718

Litho. & Engr.

1991, June 4 *Perf. 14*

1653 A718	100pf	multicolored	1.10	55

Historic Sites Type of 1987

1991 Litho. *Die Cut, Imperf.*

Self-Adhesive

1655 A623	10pf	like No. 1516	15	15
1659 A623	60pf	like No. 1523	65	32
1661 A623	80pf	like No. 1525	90	45
1663 A623	100pf	like No. 1527	1.10	55
a.		Bklt. pane, 2 each Nos. 1655, 1659, 1661, 1663	5.75	2.75

Issue date: Nos. 1655, 1659, 1661, 1663, June 4, 1991.

Nos. 1655, 1659, 1661, 1663 issued on peelable paper backing serving as booklet cover.

This is an expanding set. Numbers will change if necessary.

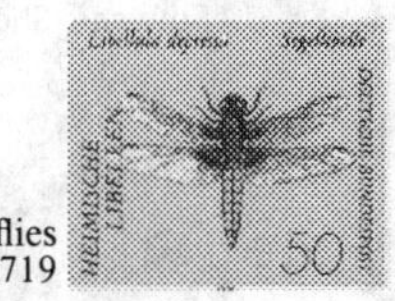

Dragonflies A719

Designs: 50pf, No. 1671, Libellula depressa. No. 1672, 70pf, Sympetrum sanguineum. No. 1673, 80pf, Cordulegaster boltonii. No. 1674, 100pf, Aeshna viridis.

1991, July 9 Photo. *Perf. 14*

1670 A719	50pf	multicolored	55	28
1671 A719	60pf	multicolored	65	32
1672 A719	60pf	multicolored	65	32
1673 A719	60pf	multicolored	65	32
1674 A719	60pf	multicolored	65	32
a.		Block of 4, #1671-1674	2.70	1.35
1675 A719	70pf	multicolored	78	40
1676 A719	80pf	multicolored	90	45
1677 A719	100pf	multicolored	1.10	55
		Nos. 1670-1677 (8)	5.93	2.96

Traffic Safety A720

1991, July 9 Litho.

1678 A720	100pf	multicolored	1.10	55

Geneva Convention on Refugees, 40th Anniv. — A721

1991, July 9

1679 A721	100pf	blk, gray & pink	1.10	55

Intl. Radio Exhibition, Berlin — A722

1991, July 9

1680 A722	100pf	multicolored	1.10	55

Reinold von Thadden-Trieglaff (1891-1976), Founder of German Protestant Convention — A723

1991, Aug. 8 Litho. *Perf. 14*

1681 A723	100pf	multicolored	1.20	60

August Heinrich Hoffman von Fallersleben (1798-1874), Poet and Philologist — A724

1991, Aug. 8
1682 A724 100pf multicolored 1.20 60

German national anthem, 150th anniv.

3-Phase Energy Transmission, Cent. — A725

1991, Aug. 8
1683 A725 170pf multicolored 2.00 1.00

Rhine-Ruhr Harbor, Duisburg, 275th Anniv. — A726

1991, Sept. 12 Litho. *Perf. 14*
1684 A726 100pf multicolored 1.20 60

Souvenir Sheet

Theodor Korner (1791-1813), Poet — A727

1991, Sept. 12 *Perf. 13x12½*
1685 Sheet of 2 1.90 95
a. A727 60pf Sword and pen 70 35
b. A727 100pf Portrait 1.20 60

Hans Albers (1891-1960), Actor — A728

1991, Sept. 12 Photo. *Perf. 14*
1686 A728 100pf multicolored 1.20 60

Postman, Spreewald Region — A729

1991, Oct. 10 Litho. *Perf. 14*
1687 A729 100pf multicolored 1.20 60

Stamp Day.

Bird Monument by Max Ernst — A730

1991, Oct. 10
1688 A730 100pf multicolored 1.20 60

Sorbian Legends A731

1991, Nov. 5 *Perf. 13*
1689 A731 60pf Fiddler, water sprite 75 35
1690 A731 100pf Midday woman, woman from Nochten 1.20 60

Souvenir Sheet

Wolfgang Amadeus Mozart, Death Bicent. — A732

1991, Nov. 5 Litho. *Perf. 14*
1691 A732 100pf multicolored 1.20 60

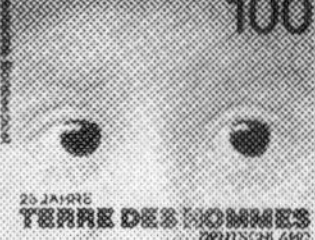

Terre Des Hommes Child Welfare Organization, 25th Anniv. — A737

1992, Jan. 9 Litho. *Perf. 14*
1697 A737 100pf multicolored 1.20 60

Martin Niemoller (1892-1984), Theologian A738

1992, Jan. 9
1698 A738 100pf multicolored 1.20 60

Coats of Arms of States of the Federal Republic of Germany A739

1992 *Perf. 13½*
1699 A739 100pf Baden-Wurttemberg 1.20 60

Issue date: Jan. 9. This is an expanding set. Numbers will change if necessary.

Famous Women Type of 1986

Design: 400pf, Charlotte von Stein (1742-1827), confidant of Goethe.

1992 Engr. *Perf. 14*
1734 A602 400pf lake & blk 4.80 2.40

Issue date: 400pf, Jan. 9, 1992. This is an expanding set. Numbers will change if necessary.

SEMI-POSTAL STAMPS

Issues of the Republic

Regular Issue of 1906-17 Surcharged

1919, May 1 Wmk. 125 *Perf. 14*
B1 A16 10pf + 5pf carmine 15 *4.00*
B2 A22 15pf + 5pf dk vio 20 *3.50*

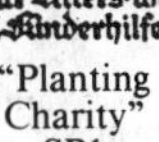

"Planting Charity" SP1

Feeding the Hungry SP2

1922, Dec. 11 Litho. Wmk. 126

B3 SP1 6m + 4m ultra & brn 15 *15.00*
B4 SP1 12m + 8m red org & bl gray 15 *15.00*

Nos. 221, 225 and 196 Surcharged

500 m
Rhein-Ruhr-Hilfe

1923, Feb. 19

B5 A34 5m + 100m 15 *5.00*
B6 A29 25m + 500m 15 *16.00*
a. Inverted surcharge 125.00
B7 A32 20m + 1000m 1.65 *90.00*
a. Inverted surcharge 400.00 *1,250.*
b. Green background inverted 125.00 275.00

Note following No. 160 applies to #B1-B7.

1924, Feb. 25 Typo. *Perf. 14½x15*

Designs: 10pf+30pf, Giving drink to the thirsty. 20pf+60pf, Clothing the naked. 50pf+1.50m, Healing the sick.

B8 SP2 5pf + 15pf dk grn 75 1.90
B9 SP2 10pf + 30pf ver 75 1.50
B10 SP2 20pf + 60pf dk bl 4.00 5.25
B11 SP2 50pf + 1.50m red brn 19.00 40.00

The surtax was used for charity.
See No. B58.

Prussia — SP6

1925, Dec. 15 *Perf. 14*

Inscribed: "1925"

B12 SP6 5pf + 5pf shown 24 45
B13 SP6 10pf + 10pf Bavaria 70 65
B14 SP6 20pf + 20pf Saxony 5.00 11.00
a. Bklt. pane of 2 + 2 labels 225.00

1926, Dec. 1

Inscribed: "1926"

B15 SP6 5pf + 5pf Wurttemberg 75 70
B16 SP6 10pf + 10pf Baden 1.25 1.25
a. Bklt. pane of 6 + 2 labels 150.00
B17 SP6 25pf + 25pf Thuringia 7.75 11.00
B18 SP6 50pf + 50pf Hesse 35.00 42.50

See Nos. B23-B32.

Pres. Paul von Hindenburg — SP13

1927, Sept. 26 Photo.

B19 SP13 8pf dk grn 35 55
a. Bklt. pane, 4 #B19, 3 #B20 + label 70.00
B20 SP13 15pf scarlet 55 90
B21 SP13 25pf dp bl 6.75 11.00
B22 SP13 50pf bis brn 9.25 15.00

80th birthday of Pres. Hindenburg. The stamps were sold at double face value. The surtax was given to a fund for War Invalids.

Arms Type of 1925

Design: 8pf+7pf, Mecklenberg-Schwerin.

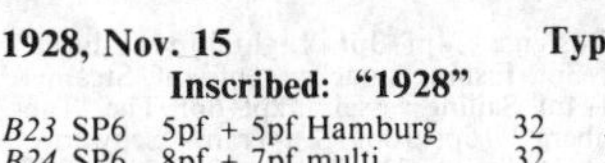

1928, Nov. 15 Typo.

Inscribed: "1928"

B23 SP6 5pf + 5pf Hamburg 32 55
B24 SP6 8pf + 7pf multi 32 55
a. Bklt. pane, 4 #B24, 3 #B25 + label 125.00
B25 SP6 15pf + 15pf Oldenburg 65 90
B26 SP6 25pf + 25pf Brunswick 7.00 14.00
B27 SP6 50pf + 50pf Anhalt 32.50 50.00
Nos. B23-B27 (5) 40.79 66.00

1929, Nov. 4

Coats of Arms: 8pf+4pf, Lippe-Detmold. 25pf+10pf, Mecklenburg-Strelitz. 50pf+40pf, Schaumburg-Lippe.

Inscribed: "1929"

B28 SP6 5pf + 2pf Bremen 40 65
a. Bklt. pane of 6 + 2 labels 30.00
B29 SP6 8pf + 4pf multi 40 65
a. Bklt. pane, 4 #B29, 3 #B30 + label 75.00
B30 SP6 15pf + 5pf Lubeck 55 1.00
B31 SP6 25pf + 10pf multi 8.25 17.00
B32 SP6 50pf + 40pf choc, ocher & red 37.50 42.50
a. "PE" for "PF" 200.00 275.00
Nos. B28-B32 (5) 47.10 61.80

Cathedral of Aachen SP24

Brandenburg Gate, Berlin SP25

Castle of Marienwerder SP26

Statue of St. Kilian and Marienburg Fortress at Würzburg SP27

Souvenir Sheet

Wmk. 223

1930, Sept. 12 Engr. *Perf. 14*

B33 Sheet of 4 300.00 *700.00*
a. SP24 8pf + 4pf dk grn 30.00 50.00
b. SP25 15pf + 5pf car 30.00 50.00
c. SP26 25pf + 10p dk bl 30.00 50.00
d. SP27 50pf + 40pf dk brn 30.00 50.00

Intl. Phil. Exhib., Berlin, Sept. 12-21, 1930.

No. B33 is watermarked Eagle on each stamp and "IPOSTA"-"1930" in the margins. Size: 105x150. Each holder of an admission ticket was entitled to purchase one sheet. The ticket cost 1m and the sheet 1.70m (face value 98pf, charity 59pf, special paper 13pf).

Types of International Philatelic Exhibition Issue

1930, Nov. 1 Wmk. 126

B34 SP24 8 + 4pf dp grn 28 28
a. Bklt. pane of 7 + label 40.00
b. Bklt. pane, 3 #B34, 4 #B35 + label 50.00
B35 SP25 15 + 5pf car 42 38
B36 SP26 25 + 10pf dk bl 8.75 10.50
B37 SP27 50 + 40pf dp brn 22.50 32.50

The surtax was for charity.

The Zwinger at Dresden SP28

Breslau City Hall SP29

Heidelberg Castle — SP30

Holsten Gate, Lübeck — SP31

1931, Nov. 1

B38 SP28 8 + 4pf dk grn 20 32
a. Bklt. pane of 7 + label 40.00
b. Bklt. pane, 3 #B38, 4 #B39 + label 50.00
B39 SP29 15 + 5pf car 30 50
B40 SP30 25 + 10pf dk bl 6.00 12.00
B41 SP31 50 + 40pf dp brn 25.00 37.50

The surtax was for charity.

Nos. B38-B39 Surcharged

1932, Feb. 2

B42 SP28 6 + 4pf on 8 + 4pf 5.00 7.50
B43 SP29 12 + 3pf on 15 + 5pf 5.50 6.50

Wartburg Castle — SP32

Stolzenfels Castle — SP33

Nuremberg Castle — SP34

Lichtenstein Castle — SP35

Marburg Castle — SP36

1932, Nov. 1 Engr.

B44 SP32 4 + 2pf lt bl 20 28
a. Bklt. pane, 5 #B44 + 5 #B45 30.00
B45 SP33 6 + 4pf ol grn 20 55
B46 SP34 12 + 3pf lt red 40 42
b. Bklt. pane of 8 + 2 labels 30.00
B47 SP35 25 + 10pf dp bl 6.50 11.00
B48 SP36 40 + 40pf brn vio 25.00 35.00
Nos. B44-B48 (5) 32.30 47.25

The surtax was for charity.

"Tannhäuser" SP37

Designs: 4pf+2pf, "Der Fliegende Hollander." 5pf+2pf, "Das Rheingold." 6pf+4pf, "Die Meistersinger." 8pf+4pf, "Die Walkure." 12pf+3pf, "Siegfried." 20pf+10pf, "Tristan und Isolde." 25pf+15pf, "Lohengrin." 40pf+35pf "Parsifal."

Wmk. Swastikas (237)

1933, Nov. 1 *Perf. 13½x13*

B49 SP37 3 + 2pf bis brn 1.25 3.75
B50 SP37 4 + 2pf dk bl 95 1.25
b. Bklt. pane, 5 #B50 + 5 #B52 37.50
B51 SP37 5 + 2pf brt grn 2.50 4.25
B52 SP37 6 + 4pf gray grn 95 1.25
B53 SP37 8 + 4pf dp org 1.25 1.75
b. Bklt. pane, 5 #B53, 4 #B53, 4 #B54 + label 82.50
B54 SP37 12 + 3pf brn red 1.50 1.75
B55 SP37 20 + 10pf bl 125.00 130.00
B56 SP37 25 + 15pf ultra 24.00 27.50
B57 SP37 40 + 35pf mag 95.00 110.00
Nos. B49-B57 (9) 252.40 281.50

Perf. 13½x14

B50a SP37 4 + 2pf dk bl 75 1.50
B52a SP37 6 + 4pf gray grn 75 1.50
B53a SP37 8 + 4pf dp org 1.00 2.75
B54a SP37 12 + 3pf brn red 1.25 2.75
B55a SP37 20 + 10pf bl 95.00 95.00
Nos. B50a-B55a (5) 98.75 103.50

Types of Semi-Postal Stamps of 1924 Issue Overprinted "1923-1933"

Souvenir Sheet

1933, Nov. 29 Typo. *Perf. 14½*

B58 Sheet of 4 800.00 *4,000.*
a. SP2 5 + 15pf dk grn 80.00 150.00
b. SP2 10 + 30pf ver 80.00 150.00
c. SP2 20 + 60pf dk bl 80.00 150.00
d. SP2 50pf + 1.50m dk brn 80.00 150.00

The Swastika watermark covers the four stamps and above them appears a further watermark "10 Jahre Deutsche Nothilfe" and "1923-1933" below. Sheet size: 208x148mm.

Businessman SP46

Judge SP54

Designs: 4pf+2pf, Blacksmith. 5pf+2pf, Mason. 6pf+4f, Miner. 8pf+4pf, Architect. 12pf+3pf, Farmer. 20pf+10pf, Agricultural Chemist. 25pf+15pf, Sculptor.

1934, Nov. 5 Engr. *Perf. 13x13½*

B59 SP46 3 + 2pf brn 75 80
B60 SP46 4 + 2pf blk 55 60
a. Bklt. pane, 5 #B60 + 5 #B62 20.00
B61 SP46 5 + 2pf grn 4.25 4.75
B62 SP46 6 + 4pf dl grn 38 35
B63 SP46 8 + 4pf org brn 55 65
a. Bklt. pane, 5 #B63, 4 #B64 + label 30.00
B64 SP46 12 + 3pf hn brn 38 35
B65 SP46 20 + 10pf Prus bl 10.50 14.00
B66 SP46 25 + 15pf ultra 10.50 14.00
B67 SP54 40 + 35pf plum 32.50 45.00
Nos. B59-B67 (9) 60.36 80.50

Souvenir Sheet

SP55

1935, June 23 Wmk. 241 *Perf. 14*

B68 SP55 Sheet of 4 425.00 475.00
a. 3pf red brown 24.00 35.00
b. 6pf dark green 24.00 35.00
c. 12pf dark carmine 24.00 35.00
d. 25pf dark blue 24.00 35.00

Watermarked cross on each stamp and "OSTROPA 1935" in the margins of the sheet. Size: 148x104mm. 1.70m was the price of a ticket of admission to the Intl. Exhib., Königsberg, June 23-July 3, 1935.

Because the gum on No. B68 contains sulphuric acid and tends to damage the sheet, some collectors prefer to remove it. **Catalogue unused values are for sheet and singles without gum.**

East Prussia SP59

Skating SP69

Designs (Costumes of Various Sections of Germany): 4pf+3pf, Silesia. 5pf+3pf, Rhineland. 6pf+4pf, Lower Saxony. 8pf+4pf, Brandenburg. 12pf+6pf, Black Forest. 15pf+10pf, Hesse. 25pf+15pf, Upper Bavaria. 30pf+20pf, Friesland. 40pf+35pf, Franconia.

Wmk. Swastikas (237)

1935, Oct. 4 *Perf. 14x13½*

B69 SP59 3 + 2pf dk brn 15 15
a. Bklt. pane, 4 #B69, 5 #B74 + label 12.00
B70 SP59 4 + 3pf gray 25 55
B71 SP59 5 + 3pf emer 15 38
a. Bklt. pane, 5 #B71 + 5 #B72 3.50
B72 SP59 6 + 4pf dk grn 15 15
B73 SP59 8 + 4pf yel brn 95 75
B74 SP59 12 + 6pf dk car 18 15
B75 SP59 15 + 10pf red brn 2.25 2.50
B76 SP59 25 + 15pf ultra 2.25 3.00
B77 SP59 30 + 20pf ol brn 10.00 10.50
B78 SP59 40 + 35p plum 7.25 6.25
Nos. B69-B78 (10) 23.58 24.38

1935, Nov. 25 *Perf. 13½*

Designs: 12pf+6pf, Ski jump. 25pf+15pf, Bobsledding.

B79	SP69	6 + 4pf green	40	35
B80	SP69	12 + 6pf car	90	50
B81	SP69	25 + 15pf ultra	4.75	7.00

Winter Olympic Games held in Bavaria, Feb. 6-16, 1936.

1936, May 8

Designs: 3pf+2pf, Horizontal bar. 4pf+3pf, Diving. 6pf+4pf, Soccer. 8pf+4pf, Throwing javelin. 12pf+6pf, Torch runner. 15pf+10pf, Fencing. 25pf+15pf, Sculling. 40pf+35pf, Equestrian.

B82	SP69	3 + 2pf brn	15	15
a.		Bklt. pane, 5 #B82 + 5 #B86	8.00	
B83	SP69	4 + 3pf ind	15	50
a.		Bklt. pane, 5 #B83 + 5 #B84	8.00	
B84	SP69	6 + 4pf grn	15	15
B85	SP69	8 + 4pf red org	3.25	90
B86	SP69	12 + 6pf car	28	15
B87	SP69	15 + 10pf brn vio	4.75	2.75
B88	SP69	25 + 15pf ultra	2.75	2.75
B89	SP69	40 + 35pf vio	5.00	5.00
		Nos. B82-B89 (8)	16.48	12.35

Summer Olympic Games, Berlin, Aug. 1-16, 1936.

See Nos. B91-B92.

Souvenir Sheet

Horse Race — SP80

1936, June 22 **Wmk. 237** *Perf. 14*

B90	SP80	42pf brown	4.50	8.75

A surtax of 1.08m was to provide a 100,000m sweepstakes prize. Wmk. 237 appears on the stamp, with "Munchen Riem 1936" watermarked on sheet margin.

For overprint see No. B105.

Type of 1935
Souvenir Sheets

1936, Aug. 1 *Perf. 14x13½*

B91	SP69	Sheet of 4	22.50	35.00
B92	SP69	Sheet of 4	22.50	35.00

11th Olympic Games, Berlin. No. B91 contains Nos. B82-B84, B89. No. B92 contains Nos. B85-B88.

Wmk. 237 appears on each stamp with "XI Olympische Spiele-Berlin 1936" watermarked on sheet margin. Sold for 1m each.

Frontier Highway, Munich — SP81

Designs: 4pf+3pf, Ministry of Aviation. 5pf+3pf, Nuremberg Memorial. 6pf+4pf, Bridge over the Saale, Saxony. 8pf+4pf, Germany Hall, Berlin. 12pf+6pf, German Alpine highway. 15pf+10pf, Fuhrer House, Munich. 25pf+15pf, Bridge over the Mangfall. 40pf+35pf, Museum of German Art, Munich.

Inscribed: "Winterhilfswerk"

Perf. 13½x14

1936, Sept. 21 **Unwmk.**

B93	SP81	3pf + 2pf blk brn	15	15
a.		Bklt. pane, 4 #B93 + 5 #B98 + label	6.00	
B94	SP81	4pf + 3pf blk	15	35
B95	SP81	5pf + 3pf brt grn	15	15
a.		Bklt. pane, 5 #B95 + 5 #B96)	2.25	
B96	SP81	6pf + 4pf dk grn	15	15
B97	SP81	8pf + 4pf brn	45	70
B98	SP81	12pf + 6pf brn car	15	15
B99	SP81	15pf + 10pf vio brn	2.50	2.50
B100	SP81	25pf + 15pf ind	1.40	1.90
B101	SP81	40pf + 35pf rose vio	2.75	3.00
		Nos. B93-B101 (9)	7.85	9.05

Souvenir Sheets

Adolf Hitler — SP90

Wmk. 237

1937, Apr. 5 **Photo.** *Perf. 14*

B102	SP90	Sheet of 4	8.00	7.50
a.		6pf dark green	80	40

48th birthday of Adolf Hitler. Sold for 1m.

See Nos. B103-B104. For overprint see No. B106.

1937, Apr. 16 *Imperf.*

B103	SP90	Sheet of 4	25.00	20.00
a.		6pf dark green	3.50	2.25

German Natl. Phil. Exhib., Berlin, June 16-18, 1937 and the Phil. Exhib. of the Stamp Collectors Group of the Strength Through Joy Organization at Hamburg, Apr. 17-20, 1937.

Sold at the Exhib. post offices for 1.50m.

No. B102 with Marginal Inscriptions

Perf. 14 and Rouletted

1937, June 10 **Wmk. 237**

B104	SP90	Sheet of 4	35.00	50.00
a.		6pf dk grn + 25pf label	5.50	5.50

No. B104 inscribed in the margin beside each stamp "25 Rpf. einschliesslich Kulturspende" in three lines.

The sheets were rouletted to allow for separation of each stamp with its component label. Sold at the post office as individual stamps with labels attached or in complete sheets.

Souvenir Sheet No. B90 Overprinted in Red

1937, Aug. 1 *Perf. 14*

B105	SP80	42pf brown	37.50	75.00

4th running of the "Brown Ribbon" horse race at the Munich-Riem Race Course, Aug. 1, 1937.

Souvenir Sheet No. B104 Overprinted in Black on Each Stamp

Reichsparteitag Nürnberg 1937

Perf. 14 and Rouletted

1937, Sept. 3 **Wmk. 237**

B106	SP90	Sheet of 4	35.00	30.00
a.		6pf dk grn + 25pf label	4.50	2.25

1937 Nazi Congress at Nuremburg.

Lifeboat — SP91

Designs: 4pf+3pf, Lightship "Elbe I." 5pf+3pf, Fishing smacks. 6pf+4pf, Steamer. 8pf+4pf, Sailing vessel. 12pf+6pf, The "Tannenberg." 15pf+10pf, Sea-Train "Schwerin." 25pf+15pf, S. S. Hamburg. 40pf+35pf, S. S. Bremen.

Perf. 13½

1937, Nov. 4 **Engr.** **Unwmk.**

Inscribed: "Winterhilfswerk"

B107	SP91	3pf + 2pf dk brn	15	22
a.		Bklt. pane, 4 #B107 + 5 #B112 + label	6.75	
B108	SP91	4pf + 3pf blk	35	55
B109	SP91	5pf + 3pf yel grn	15	22
a.		Bklt. pane, 5 #B109 + 5 #B110)	2.75	
B110	SP91	6pf + 4pf bl grn	15	22
B111	SP91	8pf + 4pf org	70	90
B112	SP91	12pf + 6pf car lake	16	15
B113	SP91	15pf + 10pf vio brn	2.00	2.50
B114	SP91	25pf + 15pf ultra	3.75	2.50
B115	SP91	40pf + 35pf red vio	5.00	5.00
		Nos. B107-B115 (9)	12.41	12.26

No. B115 actually pictures the S.S. Europa.

Youth Carrying Torch and Laurel — SP100

Adolf Hitler — SP101

Wmk. 237

1938, Jan. 28 **Photo.** *Perf. 14*

B116	SP100	6 + 4pf dk grn	70	55
B117	SP100	12 + 8pf brt car	95	95

5th anniv. of the assumption of power by the Nazis.

1938, Apr. 13 **Engr.** **Unwmk.**

B118	SP101	12 + 38pf cop red	1.75	1.50

Hitler's 49th birthday.

Horsewoman SP102

1938, July 20

B119	SP102	42 + 108pf dp brn	22.50	32.50

5th "Brown Ribbon" at Munich.

Adolf Hitler SP103

Theater at Saarbrücken SP104

1938, Sept. 1

B120	SP103	6 + 19pf dp grn	2.50	2.25

1938 Nazi Congress at Nuremberg. The surtax was for Hitler's National Culture Fund.

1938, Oct. 9 **Photo.** **Wmk. 237**

B121	SP104	6 + 4pf bl grn	75	75
B122	SP104	12 + 8pf dk car	1.75	1.65

Inauguration of the theater of the District of Saarpfalz at Saarbrücken. The surtax was for Hitler's National Culture Fund.

Castle of Forchtenstein SP105

Designs (scenes in Austria and various flowers): 4pf+3pf, Flexenstrasse in Vorarlberg. 5pf+3pf, Zell am See, Salzburg. 6pf+4pf, Grossglockner. 8pf+4pf, Ruins of Aggstein. 12pf+6pf, Prince Eugene Monument, Vienna. 15pf+10pf, Erzberg. 25pf+15pf, Hall, Tyrol. 40pf+35pf, Braunau.

Unwmk.

1938, Nov. 18 **Engr.** *Perf. 14*

Inscribed: "Winterhilfswerk"

B123	SP105	3 + 2pf ol brn	15	15
a.		Bklt. pane, 4 #B123, 5 #B128 + label	12.00	
B124	SP105	4 + 3pf ind	1.25	80
B125	SP105	5 + 3pf emer	15	20
a.		Bklt. pane, 5 #B125 + 5 #B126	3.00	
B126	SP105	6 + 4pf dk grn	15	15
B127	SP105	8 + 4pf red org	1.25	80
B128	SP105	12 + 6pf dk car	18	15
B129	SP105	15 + 10pf dp cl	3.00	2.75
B130	SP105	25 + 15pf dk bl	3.00	2.75
B131	SP105	40 + 35pf plum	5.75	4.75
		Nos. B123-B131 (9)	14.88	12.50

The surtax was for "Winter Help."

Sudeten Couple SP114

Early Types of Automobiles SP115

1938, Dec. 2 **Photo.** **Wmk. 237**

B132	SP114	6 + 4pf bl grn	70	1.00
B133	SP114	12 + 8pf dk car	2.25	2.00

Issued in commemoration of the annexation of the Sudeten Territory. The surtax was for Hitler's National Culture Fund.

1939

Designs: 12pf+8pf, Racing cars. 25pf+10pf, Modern automobile.

B134	SP115	6 + 4pf dk grn	3.50	1.40
B135	SP115	12 + 8pf brt car	3.50	1.65
B136	SP115	25 + 10pf dp bl	5.25	3.50

Berlin Automobile and Motorcycle Exhibition. The surtax was for Hitler's National Culture Fund. For overprints see #B141-B143.

Adolf Hitler SP118

Exhibition Building SP119

Unwmk.

1939, Apr. 13 **Engr.** *Perf. 14*

B137	SP118	12 + 38pf car	1.40	2.25

Hitler's 50th birthday. The surtax was for Hitler's National Culture Fund.

1939, Apr. 22 **Photo.** *Perf. 12½*

B138	SP119	6 + 4pf dk grn	1.10	1.50
B139	SP119	15 + 5pf dp plum	1.10	1.50

Horticultural Exhib. held at Stuttgart. Surtax for Hitler's National Culture Fund.

Adolf Hitler — SP120

Perf. 14x13½

1939, Apr. 28 **Wmk. 237**

B140	SP120	6 + 19pf blk brn	1.75	2.25

Day of National Labor. The surtax was for Hitler's National Culture Fund.
See No. B147.

Nos. B134-B136 Overprinted in Black "Nürburgring-Rennen"

1939, May 18 ***Perf. 14***

B141	SP115	6 + 4pf dk grn	25.00	24.00
B142	SP115	12 + 8pf brt car	25.00	24.00
B143	SP115	25 + 10pf dp bl	25.00	24.00

Nurburgring Auto Races held May 21 and July 23, 1939.

Racehorse "Investment" and Jockey — SP121

1939, June 18 **Engr.** **Unwmk.**

B144	SP121	25 + 50pf ultra	12.00	12.00

70th anniv. of the German Derby. The surtax was divided between Hitler's National Culture Fund and the race promoters.

Man Holding Rearing Horse — SP122

"Venetian Woman" by Albrecht Dürer — SP123

1939, July 12

B145	SP122	42 + 108pf dp brn	14.00	20.00

6th "Brown Ribbon" at Munich.

1939, July 12 **Photo.** **Wmk. 237**

B146	SP123	6 + 19pf dk grn	4.00	5.75

Day of German Art. The surtax was used for Hitler's National Culture Fund.

Hitler Type of 1939
Inscribed "Reichsparteitag 1939"

1939, Aug. 25 ***Perf. 14x13½***

B147	SP120	6 + 19pf blk brn	2.75	4.75

1939 Nazi Congress at Nuremberg.

Meeting in German Hall, Berlin SP124

Designs: 4pf+3pf, Meeting of postal and telegraph employees. 5pf+3pf, Professional competitions. 6pf+4pf, 6pf+9pf, Professional camp. 8pf+4pf, 8pf+12pf, Gold flag competitions. 10pf+5pf, Awarding prizes. 12&f+6pf, 12pf+18pf, Automobile race. 15pf+10pf, Sports. 16pf+10pf, 16pf+20pf, Postal police. 20pf+10pf, 20pf+30pf, Glider workshops. 24pf+10pf, 24pf+36pf, Mail coach. 25pf+15pf, Convalescent home, Konigstein.

Perf. 13½x14

1939-41 **Unwmk.** **Photo.**

Inscribed: "Kameradschaftsblock der Deutschen Reichpost"

B148	SP124	3 + 2pf bis brn	2.00	3.50
B149	SP124	4 + 3pf sl bl	1.75	3.00
B150	SP124	5 + 3pf brt bl grn	60	1.10
B151	SP124	6 + 4pf myr grn	60	1.10
B151A	SP124	6 + 9pf dk grn ('41)	42	95
B152	SP124	8 + 4pf dp org	55	95
B152A	SP124	8 + 12pf hn brn ('41)	35	75
B153	SP124	10 + 5pf dk brn	55	95
B154	SP124	12 + 6pf rose brn	85	1.40
B154A	SP124	12 + 18pf dk car rose ('41)	35	75
B155	SP124	15 + 10pf dp red lil	85	1.40
B156	SP124	16 + 10pf sl grn	1.10	1.90
B156A	SP124	16 + 24pf blk ('41)	1.10	2.50
B157	SP124	20 + 10pf ultra	1.10	1.90
B157A	SP124	20 + 30pf ultra ('41)	1.10	2.00
B158	SP124	24 + 10pf ol grn	1.75	2.50
B158A	SP124	24 + 36pf pur ('41)	3.25	4.50
B159	SP124	25 + 15pf dk bl	1.75	3.00
		Nos. B148-B159 (18)	20.02	34.15

The surtax was used for Hitler's National Culture Fund and the Postal Employees' Fund.
See Nos. B273, B275-B277.

Elbogen Castle — SP136

Buildings: 4pf+3pf, Drachenfels on the Rhine. 5pf+3pf, Kaiserpfalz at Goslar. 6pf+4pf, Clocktower at Graz. 8pf+4pf, Town Hall, Frankfurt. 12pf+6pf, Guild House, Klagenfurt. 15pf+10pf, Ruins of Schreckenstein Castle. 25pf+15pf, Fortress of Salzburg. 40pf+35pf, Castle of Hohentwiel.

1939 **Unwmk.** **Engr.** ***Perf. 14***

Inscribed: "Winterhilfswerk"

B160	SP136	3 + 2pf dk brn	15	22
a.		Bklt. pane, 4 #B160, 5 #B165 + label	9.75	
B161	SP136	4 + 3pf gray blk	1.10	1.25
B162	SP136	5 + 3pf emer	20	22
a.		Bklt. pane, 5 #B162 + 5 #B163	3.25	
B163	SP136	6 + 4pf sl grn	20	22
B164	SP136	8 + 4pf red org	85	75
B165	SP136	12 + 6pf dk car	20	22
B166	SP136	15 + 10pf brn vio	2.75	3.00
B167	SP136	25 + 15pf ultra	1.65	3.00
B168	SP136	40 + 35pf rose vio	2.75	3.25
		Nos. B160-B168 (9)	9.85	12.13

Hall of Honor at Chancellery, Berlin — SP145

Child Greeting Hitler — SP146

1940, Mar. 28

B169	SP145	24 + 76pf dk grn	5.50	9.50

2nd National Stamp Exposition, Berlin.

Perf. 14x13½

1940, Apr. 10 **Photo.** **Wmk. 237**

B170	SP146	12 + 38pf cop red	2.00	2.75

51st birthday of Adolf Hitler.

Armed Warrior SP147

Horseman SP148

1940, Apr. 30 **Unwmk.** ***Perf. 14***

B171	SP147	6 + 4pf sl grn & lt grn	22	40

Issued to commemorate May Day.

Perf. 14x13½

1940, June 22 **Wmk. 237**

B172	SP148	25 + 100pf dp ultra	3.00	5.50

Issued in commemoration of the Blue Ribbon race held at Hamburg, June 30 1940.
The surtax was for Hitler's National Culture Fund.

Chariot — SP149

Unwmk.

1940, July 20 **Engr.** ***Perf. 14***

B173	SP149	42 + 108pf brn	15.00	20.00

7th "Brown Ribbon" at Munich.
The surtax was for Hitler's National Culture Fund and the promoters of the race.

View of Malmedy SP150

Design: 12pf+8pf, View of Eupen.

Perf. 14x13½

1940, July 25 **Photo.** **Wmk. 237**

B174	SP150	6 + 4pf dk grn	55	1.00
B175	SP150	12 + 8pf org red	55	1.00

Issued on the occasion of the reunion of Eupen-Malmedy with the Reich.

Rocky Cliffs of Heligoland SP152

Artushof in Danzig SP153

1940, Aug. 9 **Unwmk.**

B176	SP152	6 + 94pf brt bl grn & red org	3.00	5.00

Heligoland's 50th year as part of Germany.

1940, Nov. 5 **Engr.** ***Perf. 14***

Buildings: 4pf+3pf, Town Hall, Thorn. 5pf+3pf, Castle at Kaub. 6pf+4pf, City Theater, Poznan. 8pf+4pf, Castle at Heidelberg. 12pf+6pf, Porta Nigra Trier. 15pf+10pf, New German Theater, Prague. 25pf+15pf, Town Hall, Bremen. 40pf+35pf, Town Hall, Munster.

Inscribed: "Winterhilfswerk"

B177	SP153	3 + 2pf dk brn	15	15
a.		Bklt. pane, 4 #B177 + 5 #B182 + label	6.50	
B178	SP153	4 + 3pf bluish blk	75	55
B179	SP153	5 + 3pf yel grn	20	28
a.		Bklt. pane, 5 #B179 + 5 #B180	3.00	
B180	SP153	6 + 4pf dk grn	20	15
B181	SP153	8 + 4pf dp org	70	75
B182	SP153	12 + 6pf car	20	15
B183	SP153	15 + 10pf dk vio brn	70	1.40
B184	SP153	25 + 15pf dp ultra	1.00	2.25
B185	SP153	40 + 35pf red lil	2.00	3.50
		Nos. B177-B185 (9)	5.90	9.18

von Behring SP162

Postilion SP163

1940, Nov. 26 **Photo.**

B186	SP162	6 + 4pf dp grn	60	1.25
B187	SP162	25 + 10pf brt ultra	80	1.50

Dr. Emil von Behring (1854-1917), bacteriologist.

1941, Jan. 12 ***Perf. 14x13½***

B188	SP163	6 + 24pf dp grn	48	80

Postage Stamp Day. The surtax was for Hitler's National Culture Fund.

Benito Mussolini and Adolf Hitler SP164

Perf. 13½x14

1941, Jan. 30 **Wmk. 237**

B189	SP164	12 + 38pf rose brn	95	1.50

Issued as propaganda for the Rome-Berlin Axis. The surtax was for Hitler's National Culture Fund.

Adolf Hitler — SP165

Race Horse — SP166

1941, Apr. 17 ***Perf. 14x13½***

B190	SP165	12 + 38pf dk red	1.00	1.75

52nd birthday of Adolf Hitler. The surtax was for Hitler's National Culture Fund.

Perf. 13½x14

1941, June 20 **Engr.** **Unwmk.**

B191	SP166	25 + 100pf saph	2.75	5.50

Issued in commemoration of the Blue Ribbon race held at Hamburg, June 29, 1941.

Amazons SP167

1941, July 20 ***Perf. 14***

B192	SP167	42 + 108pf brown	1.65	3.00

8th "Brown Ribbon" at Munich.

Brandenburg Gate, Berlin — SP168

1941, Sept. 9

B193	SP168	25 + 50pf dp ultra	1.65	3.00

Issued in honor of the Berlin races.

Marburg SP169

Veldes SP170

Pettau SP171

Triglav SP172

1941, Sept. 29 **Photo.**

B194	SP169	3 + 7pf brn	40	80
B195	SP170	6 + 9pf pur	50	90
B196	SP171	12 + 13pf rose brn	65	1.10
B197	SP172	25 + 15pf dk bl	1.10	2.00

Annexation of Styria and Carinthia.

View from Belvedere Palace, Vienna SP173

Belvedere Gardens, Vienna SP174

1941, Sept. 16 **Engr.**

B198	SP173	12 + 8pf dp red	75	1.00
B199	SP174	15 + 10pf vio	75	1.25

Issued to commemorate the Vienna Fair.

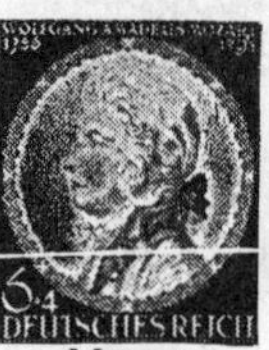

Mozart SP175

Philatelist SP176

1941, Nov. 28

B200	SP175	6 + 4pf dk rose vio	15	22

Wolfgang Amadeus Mozart (1756-91).

1942, Jan. 11 **Photo.**

B201	SP176	6 + 24pf dp pur	40	1.00

To commemorate Stamp Day.

Soldier's Head — SP177

Adolf Hitler — SP178

1942, Mar. 10 ***Perf. 14x13½***

B202	SP177	12 + 38pf slate blk	28	50

To commemorate Hero Memorial Day.

1942, Apr. 13

B203	SP178	12 + 38pf lake	1.25	2.50

To commemorate Hitler's 53rd birthday.

Racing Three-year-old SP179

1942, June 16 **Engr.** ***Perf. 14***

B204	SP179	25 + 100pf dk bl	4.75	8.50

73rd Hamburg Derby.

Race Horses — SP180

1942, July 14

B205	SP108	42 + 108pf brn	1.40	3.00

9th "Brown Ribbon" at Munich.

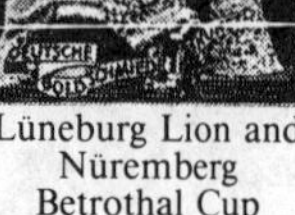

Lüneburg Lion and Nüremberg Betrothal Cup SP181

Henlein Monument, Nüremberg SP182

1942, Aug. 8 **Photo.** ***Perf. 14x13½***

B206	SP181	6 + 4pf cop red	20	38
B207	SP181	12 + 88pf green	30	65

10th anniv. of the German Goldsmiths' Society and the 1st Goldsmiths' Day in Germany.

1942, Aug. 29 ***Perf. 14***

B208	SP182	6 + 24pf rose vio	25	45

To commemorate the 400th anniversary of the death of Peter Henlein, inventor of the pocket watch.

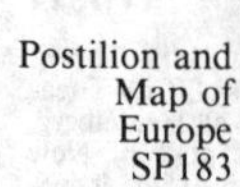

Postilion and Map of Europe SP183

Postilion and Globe — SP184

Postilion SP185

Perf. 13½x14, 14x13½

1942, Oct. 12 **Photo.**

B209	SP183	3 + 7pf dl bl	15	28

Engr.

B210	SP184	6 + 14pf ultra & dp brn	18	40
B211	SP185	12 + 38pf rose red & dp brn	38	75

European Postal Congress, Vienna.

Nos. B209 to B211 Overprinted in Black ***19.Okt.1942***

1942, Oct. 19

B212	SP183	3 + 7pf dl bl	42	85
B213	SP184	6 + 14pf ultra & dp brn	42	90
B214	SP185	12 + 38pf rose red & dp brn	55	1.10

To commemorate the signing of the European postal-telegraph agreement at Vienna.

Mail Coach SP186

1943, Jan. 10 **Engr.**

B215	SP186	6 + 24pf gray, brn & yel	15	15

To commemorate Stamp Day. The surtax went to Hitler's National Culture Fund.

Brandenburg Gate SP187

Nazi Emblem SP188

1943, Jan. 26 **Photo.**

B216	SP187	54 + 96pf cop red	25	38

To commemorate the 10th anniversary of the assumption of power by the Nazis.

1943, Jan. 26

B217	SP188	3 + 2pf olive bis	15	25

Used to secure special philatelic cancellations.

Submarine SP189

Designs: 4pf+3pf, Schutz-Staffel Troops. 5pf+4pf, Motorized marksmen. 6pf+9pf, Signal Corps. 8pf+7pf, Engineer Corps. 12pf+8pf, Grenade assault. 15pf+10pf, Heavy artillery. 20pf+14pf, Anti-aircraft units in action. 25pf+15pf, Dive bombers. 30pf+30pf, Paratroops. 40pf+40pf, Tank. 50pf+50pf, Speed boat.

1943, Mar. 21 **Engr.**

B218	SP189	3 + 2pf dk brn	20	38
B219	SP189	4 + 3pf brown	20	38
B220	SP189	5 + 4pf dk grn	20	38
B221	SP189	6 + 9pf dp vio	20	38
B222	SP189	8 + 7pf brn org	20	38
B223	SP189	12 + 8pf car lake	20	38
B224	SP189	15 + 10pf vio brn	22	35
B225	SP189	20 + 14pf slate bl	30	45
B226	SP189	25 + 15pf indigo	30	70
B227	SP189	30 + 30pf green	45	75
B228	SP189	40 + 40pf red lil	45	90
B229	SP189	50 50pf grnsh blk	85	1.65
		Nos. B218-B229 (12)	3.77	7.08

Army Day and Hero Memorial Day.

Nos. B220 and B224 exist imperf. Value, each $67.50.

Nazi Flag and Children SP201

1943, Mar. 26 **Photo.**

B230	SP201	6 + 4pf dk grn	15	40

To commemorate the Day of Youth Obligation when all German boys and girls had to take an oath of allegiance to Hitler.

Adolf Hitler SP202

1943, Apr. 13

B231	SP202	3 + 7pf brn blk	35	65
B232	SP202	6 + 14pf dk grn	35	65
B233	SP202	8 + 22pf dk chlky bl	35	65
B234	SP202	12 + 38pf cop red	35	65
B235	SP202	24 + 76pf vio brn	60	1.10
B236	SP202	40 + 160pf dk ol grn	65	1.40
		Nos. B231-B236 (6)	2.65	5.10

To commemorate Hitler's 54th birthday. No. B231 exists imperf. Value $100.

Reich Labor Service Corpsmen SP203 SP204

Designs: 6pf+14pf, Corpsman chopping. 12pf+18pf, Corpsman with implements.

1943, June 26 **Engr.**

B237	SP203	3 + 7pf bis brn	15	18
B238	SP204	5 + 10pf pale ol grn	15	18
B239	SP204	6 + 14pf dp bl	15	18
B240	SP204	12 + 18pf dk red	18	38
		Set value		42

Anniversary of Reich Labor Service. Nos. B237-B238, B240 exist imperf.

Rosegger's Birthplace, Upper Styria
SP207

Peter Rosegger
SP208

Perf. 13½x14, 14x13½

1943, July 27 **Photo.**

B241	SP207	6 + 4pf green	15	18
B242	SP208	12 + 8pf cop red	15	18
		Set value	15	

To commemorate the centenary of the birth of Peter Rosegger, Austrian writer.

Hunter — SP209

1943, July 27 **Engr.**

B243	SP209	42 + 108pf brown	15	40

10th "Brown Ribbon" at Munich.
No. B243 exists imperf. Value $300.

Race Horse
SP210

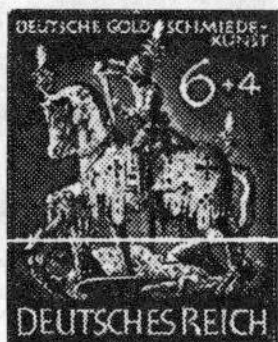

Mother and Children
SP211

1943, Aug. 14

B244	SP210	6 + 4pf vio blk	15	18
B245	SP210	12 + 88pf dk car	15	18
		Set value	24	

Grand Prize of the Freudenau, the Vienna race track, Aug. 15, 1943.

1943, Sept. 1

B246	SP211	12 + 38pf dk red	15	30

10th anniversary of Winter Relief.

St. George in Gold
SP212

Ancient Lübeck
SP213

1943, Oct. 1

B247	SP212	6 + 4pf dk ol grn	15	20
B248	SP212	12 + 88pf vio brn	15	25
		Set value	20	

German Goldsmiths' Society.

1943, Oct. 24 **Photo.**

B249	SP213	12 + 8pf cop red	15	35

800th anniv. of the Hanseatic town of Lubeck.
No. B249 exists imperf. Value, $75.

"And Despite All, You Were Victorious"
SP214

Dr. Robert Koch
SP215

1943, Nov. 5

B250	SP214	24 + 26pf henna	15	35

20th anniv. of the Nazis' Munich beer-hall putsch and to honor those who died for the Nazi movement. #B250 exists imperf.

1944, Jan. 25 **Engr.** **Unwmk.**

B251	SP215	12 + 38pf sepia	15	35

Centenary of the birth of the bacteriologist, Robert Koch (1843-1910).

Hitler and Nazi Emblems
SP216

1944, Jan. 29 **Photo.**

B252	SP216	54 + 96pf yel brn	15	35

Assumption of power by the Nazis, 11th anniv.

Airport Scene — SP217

Seaplane — SP218

Plane Seen from Above — SP219

Perf. 14x13½, 13½x14

1944, Feb. 11 **Photo.** **Unwmk.**

B252A	SP217	6 + 4pf dk grn	15	20
B252B	SP218	12 + 8pf maroon	15	25
B252C	SP219	42 + 108pf dp sl bl	15	35
		Set value	33	

25th anniv. of German air mail. The surtax was for the National Culture Fund.

Infant's Crib — SP220

Assault Boat — SP221

Designs: 6pf+4pf, Public nurse. 12pf+8pf, "Mother and Child" clinic. 15pf+10pf, Expectant mothers.

1944, Mar. 2

B253	SP220	3 + 2pf dk brn	15	15
B254	SP220	6 + 4pf dk grn	15	15
B255	SP220	12 + 8pf dp car	15	15
B256	SP220	15 + 10pf vio brn	15	25
		Set value	26	60

10th anniv. of "Mother and Child" aid.

1944, Mar. 11

Designs: 4pf+3pf, Chain-wheel vehicle. 5pf+3pf, Paratroops. 6pf+4pf, Submarine officer. 8pf+4pf, Schutz-Staffel grenade throwers. 10pf+5pf, Searchlight. 12pf+6pf, Infantry. 15pf+10pf, Self-propelled gun. 16pf+10pf, Speed boat. 20pf+10pf, Sea raider. 24pf+10pf, Railway artillery. 25pf+15pf, Rockets. 30pf+20pf, Mountain trooper.

Inscribed: "Grossdeutsches Reich"

B257	SP221	3 + 2pf yel brn	15	30
B258	SP221	4 + 3pf ryl bl	15	30
B259	SP221	5 + 3pf dp yel grn	15	30
B260	SP221	6 + 4pf dp vio	15	30
B261	SP221	8 + 4pf org ver	15	30
B262	SP221	10 + 5pf choc	15	30
B263	SP221	12 + 6pf car	15	30
B264	SP221	15 + 10pf dp cl	15	30
B265	SP221	16 + 10pf dk bl grn	18	38
B266	SP221	20 + 10pf brt bl	20	45
B267	SP221	24 + 10pf dl org brn	25	52
B268	SP221	25 + 15pf vio bl	35	75
B269	SP221	30 + 20pf ol grn	32	70
		Nos. B257-B269 (13)	2.50	5.20

To commemorate Hero Memorial Day.

Flora Statue in Fulda's Schloss Garden
SP234

Adolf Hitler
SP235

1944, Mar. 11

B270	SP234	12 + 38pf dp brn	15	20

1,200th anniversary of town of Fulda.

1944, Apr. 14 **Engr.** **Unwmk.**

B271	SP235	54 + 96pf rose car	18	50

To commemorate Hitler's 55th birthday.

Type of 1939-41 and

Woman Mail Carrier — SP236

Field Post in the East — SP237

Designs: 8pf+12pf, Mail coach. 16pf+24pf, Automobile race. 20pf+30pf, Postal police. 24pf+36pf, Glider workshops.

1944, May 3 **Photo.**

Designs measure 29½x24½mm

B272	SP236	6 + 9pf vio bl	15	15
B273	SP124	8 + 12pf gray blk	15	15
B274	SP237	12 + 18pf dp plum	15	15
B275	SP124	16 + 24pf dk grn	15	15
B276	SP124	20 + 30pf blue	15	20
B277	SP124	24 + 36pf dk pur	15	20
		Set value	48	

Surtax for the Postal Employees' Fund.

Soldier and Tirolese Rifleman
SP238

Albert I, Duke of Prussia
SP239

1944, July

B278	SP238	6 + 4pf dp grn	15	15
B279	SP238	12 + 8pf brn lake	15	15
		Set value	15	

To commemorate the 7th National Shooting Matches at Innsbruck.

1944, July

B280	SP239	6 + 4pf dk bl grn	15	30

To commemorate the 400th anniversary of Albert University, Königsberg.

Labor Corps Girl
SP240

Labor Corpsman
SP241

1944, June **Engr.**

B281	SP240	6 + 4pf green	15	15
B282	SP241	12 + 8pf carmine	15	15
		Set value	15	

Issued to honor an exhibit of the Reich Labor Service.

Race Horse and Foal — SP242

1944, July 23 ***Perf. 14x13½***

B283	SP242	42 + 108pf brown	15	35

11th "Brown Ribbon" at Munich.

Race Horse's Head in Oak Wreath
SP243

Nautilus Cup in Green Vault, Dresden
SP244

1944, Aug. **Photo.** ***Perf. 14***

B284	SP243	6 + 4pf Prus grn	15	20
B285	SP243	12 + 88pf car lake	15	22
		Set value	15	

Vienna Grand Prize Race.

1944, Sept. 11

B286	SP244	6 + 4pf dk grn	15	20
B287	SP244	12 + 88pf car brn	15	22
		Set value	15	

Issued in honor of the German Goldsmiths' Society.
No. B287 exists imperf. Value $175.

Post Horn and Letter — SP245

1944, Oct. 2
B288 SP245 6 + 24pf dk grn 15 35

To commemorate Stamp Day.

Eagle and Serpent SP246

Count Anton Günther SP247

1944, Nov. 9
B289 SP246 12 + 8pf rose red 15 30

21st anniv. of the Munich putsch.

1945, Jan. 6 Typo. *Perf. 13½x14*
B290 SP247 6 + 14pf brn vio 15 32

600th anniv. of municipal law in Oldenburg.

People's Army — SP248

1945, Feb. Photo. *Perf. 14x13½*
B291 SP248 12 + 8pf rose car 18 48

To commemorate the proclamation of the People's Army (Volkssturm) in East Prussia to fight the Russians.

Elite Storm Trooper (S. S.) — SP249

Storm Trooper (S. A.) — SP250

1945, Apr. 21 *Perf. 13½x14*
B292 SP249 12 + 38pf brt car 6.75 *12.50*
B293 SP250 12 + 38pf brt car 6.75 *12.50*

To commemorate the 12th anniversary of the assumption of power by the Nazis. Nos. B292 and B293 were on sale in Berlin briefly before the collapse of that city.
Exist imperf. Value same as perf.

Souvenir Sheets

SP251

Wmk. 284

1946, Dec. 8 Typo. *Perf. 14*
B294 SP251 Sheet of 3 21.00 *160.00*

Imperf

B295 SP251 Sheet of 3 32.50 *190.00*
a. A119 20pf light blue 6.50 17.50
b. A119 24pf orange brown 6.50 17.50
c. A119 40pf red violet 6.50 17.50

No. B294 contains Nos. 543, 544 and 548.
Nos. B294-B295 sold for 5m each. Surtax for refugees and the aged.

Leipzig Proclaimed Market Place, 1160 — SP252

Design: 60pf+40pf, Foreign merchants displaying their wares, 1268.

Wmk. 48

1947, Mar. 5 Engr. *Perf. 13*
B296 SP252 24 +26pf chnt brn 15 35
B297 SP252 60 + 40pf dp vio bl 15 45
Set value 22

1947 Leipzig Fairs.
No. B296 exists imperf. Value $150.
See Nos. 580-583, 10NB1-10NB2, 10NB4-10NB5, 10NB12-10NB13 and German Democratic Republic Nos. B15-B16.

Madonna SP254

Cathedral Towers SP255

Designs: 12pf+8pf, Three Kings. 24pf+16pf, Cologne Cathedral.

Wmk. 286

1948, Aug. 15 Typo. *Perf. 11*
B298 SP254 6 + 4pf org brn 15 42
a. "1948-1248" 4.00 7.25
B299 SP254 12 + 8pf grnsh bl 50 1.10
a. "1948-1948" 5.75 9.25
B300 SP254 24 + 16pf car 1.00 2.25
B301 SP255 50 + 50pf blue 2.00 5.00

700th anniv. of the laying of the cornerstone of Cologne Cathedral. The surtax was to aid in its reconstruction.
Specialists collect Nos. B298-B301 with watermark in four positions: upright, D's facing left; upright, D's facing right; sideways, D's facing up; sideways, D's facing down. Two types of perforation: line and comb.

Brandenburg Gate, Berlin SP256

Bicycle Racers SP257

Perf. 10½x11½, 11

1948, Dec. Litho.
B302 SP256 10 + 5pf green 1.50 4.00
B303 SP256 20 + 10pf rose car 2.00 4.00

The surtax was for aid to Berlin.

Wmk. 116

1949, May 15 Engr. *Perf. 14*
B304 SP257 10 + 5pf green 1.50 2.75
B305 SP257 20 + 10pf brn org 3.75 *12.00*

1949 Bicycle Tour of Germany.

Goethe at Rome SP258

Goethe SP259

Design: 30pf+15pf, Goethe portrait facing left.

1949, Aug. 15
B306 SP258 10 + 5pf green 1.00 3.00
B307 SP259 20 + 10pf red 1.00 3.25
B308 SP259 30 + 15pf blue 4.50 *12.00*

Issued to commemorate the bicentenary of the birth of Johann Wolfgang von Goethe.
The surtax was for the reconstruction of Goethe House, Frankfurt-on-Main.

Federal Republic

Bavaria Stamp of 1849 SP260

St. Elisabeth SP261

1949, Sept. 30 Litho. Wmk. 285
B309 SP260 10 + 2pf grn & blk 5.00 6.50

Centenary of German postage stamps.

1949, Dec. 14 Engr. Wmk. 286

Designs: 10pf+5pf, Paracelsus. 20pf+10pf, F. W. A. Froebel. 30pf+15pf, J. H. Wichern.

B310 SP261 8 + 2pf brn vio 10.00 20.00
B311 SP261 10 + 5pf yel grn 7.00 10.00
B312 SP261 20 + 10pf red 7.75 10.00
B313 SP261 30 + 15pf vio bl 37.50 90.00

The surtax was for welfare organizations.

Seal of Johann Sebastian Bach SP262

Frescoes from Marienkirche SP263

1950, July 28 *Perf. 14*
B314 SP262 10 + 2pf dk grn 30.00 35.00
B315 SP262 20 + 3pf dk car 35.00 42.50

Bicentenary of the death of Bach.

1951, Aug. 30 Photo. Wmk. 286
Center in Gray
B316 SP263 10 + 5pf green 35.00 55.00
B317 SP263 20 + 5pf brn lake 40.00 70.00

700th anniv. of the construction of Marienkirche, Lübeck.
The surtax aided in its reconstruction.

Stamps Under Magnifying Glass — SP264

St. Vincent de Paul — SP265

Wmk. 295

1951, Sept. 14 Typo. *Perf. 14*
B318 SP264 10 + 2pf yel grn, blk & yel 22.50 40.00
B319 SP264 20 + 3pf dp mag, blk & yel 22.50 40.00

Issued to publicize the National Philatelic Exposition, Wuppertal, 1951.

1951, Oct. 23 Engr.

Portraits: 10pf+3pf, Friedrich von Bodelschwingh. 20pf+5pf, Elsa Brandstrom. 30pf+10pf, Johann Heinrich Pestalozzi.

B320 SP265 4 + 2pf brn 3.25 4.50
B321 SP265 10 + 3pf grn 6.50 5.50
B322 SP265 20 + 5pf rose red 6.50 5.50
B323 SP265 30 + 10pf dp bl 55.00 85.00

The surtax was for charitable purposes.

Nuremberg Madonna SP266

Boy Hikers and Youth Hostel SP267

1952, Aug. 9
B324 SP266 10 + 5pf green 10.00 14.00

Centenary of the founding of the Germanic National Museum, Nuremberg. The surtax was for the museum.

1952, Sept. 17 *Perf. 13½x14*

Design: 20pf+3pf, Girls and Hostel.

B325 SP267 10 + 2pf grn 12.00 16.00
B326 SP267 20 + 3pf dp car 12.00 16.00

The surtax was to aid the youth program of the Federal Republic.

Elizabeth Fry SP268

Owl and Cogwheel SP269

Portraits: 10pf+5pf, Dr. Carl Sonnenschein. 20pf+10pf, Theodor Fliedner. 30pf+10pf, Henri Dunant.

1952, Oct. 1
B327 SP268 4 + 2pf org brn 3.50 5.00
B328 SP268 10 + 5pf grn 3.50 4.00
B329 SP268 20 + 10pf brn car 8.50 9.25
B330 SP268 30 + 10pf dp bl 35.00 60.00

The surtax was for welfare organizations.

1953, May 7 Wmk. 295 *Perf. 14*
B331 SP269 10 + 5pf dp grn 14.00 22.50

50th anniv. of the founding of the German Museum in Munich.

Thurn and Taxis Palace Gate
SP270

August Hermann Francke
SP271

Design: 20pf+3pf, Telecommunications Bldg., Frankfurt-on-Main.

Wmk. 285

1953, July 29 Litho. *Perf. 13½*

B332 SP270 10 + 2pf yel grn, bl & fawn 10.00 18.00
B333 SP270 20 + 3pf fawn, blk & gray 13.00 22.50

The surtax was for the International Stamp Exhibition, Frankfurt-on-Main, 1953.

Wmk. 295

1953, Nov. 2 Engr. *Perf. 14*

Designs: 10pf+5pf, Sebastian Kneipp. 20pf+10pf, Dr. Johann Christian Senckenberg. 30pf+10pf, Fridtjof Nansen.

B334 SP271 4 + 2pf choc 1.90 3.25
B335 SP271 10 + 5pf bl grn 3.25 4.25
B336 SP271 20 + 10pf red 5.25 5.50
B337 SP271 30 + 10pf bl 20.00 37.50

The surtax was for welfare organizations.

Catalogue values for unused stamps in this section, from this point to the end of the section, are for Never Hinged items.

Käthe Kollwitz
SP272

Carrier Pigeon and Magnifying Glass
SP273

Portraits: 10pf+5pf, Lorenz Werthmann. 20pf+10pf, Johann Friedrich Oberlin. 40pf+10pf, Bertha Pappenheim.

1954, Dec. 28 *Perf. 13½x14*

B338 SP272 7pf + 3pf brn 2.25 2.00
B339 SP272 10pf + 5pf grn 1.65 1.10
B340 SP272 20pf + 10pf red 8.00 2.00
B341 SP272 40pf + 10pf bl 27.50 27.50

The surtax was for welfare organizations.

1955, Sept. 14 Wmk. 304 *Perf. 14*

Design: 20pf+3pf, Post horn and stamp tongs.

B342 SP273 10pf + 2pf grn 4.25 5.75
B343 SP273 20pf + 3pf red 8.25 9.25

WESTROPA, 1955, philatelic exhibition at Dusseldorf. The surtax aided the Society of German Philatelists.

Amalie Sieveking – SP274

Portraits: 10pf+5pf, Adolph Kolping. 20pf+10pf, Dr. Samuel Hahnemann. 40pf+10pf, Florence Nightingale.

1955, Nov. 15 Photo. & Litho.

B344 SP274 7 + 3pf ol bis 1.65 1.50
B345 SP274 10 + 5pf dk grn 1.25 65
B346 SP274 20 + 10pf red org 1.65 90
B347 SP274 40 + 10pf grnsh bl 22.50 27.50

The surtax was for independent welfare organizations.

Boy and Geometrical Designs – SP275

Design: 10pf+5pf, Girl playing flute.

Unwmk.

1956, July 21 Litho. *Perf. 14*

B348 SP275 7pf + 3pf multi 2.50 2.00
B349 SP275 10pf + 5pf multi 6.00 7.25

The surtax was for the Youth Hostel Organization.

The Midwife – SP276

Designs: 10pf+5pf, Ignaz Philipp Semmelweis. 20pf+10pf, The mother. 40pf+10pf, The children's nurse.

1956, Oct. 1 Photo.

Design and Inscription in Black

B350 SP276 7pf + 3pf org brn 1.00 1.10
B351 SP276 10pf + 5pf grn 60 42
B352 SP276 20pf + 10pf brt red 70 42
B353 SP276 40pf + 10pf brt bl 12.50 12.00

Issued to honor Ignaz Philipp Semmelweis, the discoverer of the cause of puerperal fever. The surtax was for independent welfare organizations.

Children Leaving SP277

Design: 20pf+10pf, Child arriving.

1957, Feb. 1 Litho. *Perf. 13½x13*

B354 SP277 10pf + 5pf gray grn & red org 1.40 1.25
B355 SP277 20pf + 10pf red org & lt bl 1.90 1.75

The surtax was for vacations for the children of Berlin.

Young Miner
SP278

"The Fox who Stole the Goose"
SP279

Designs: 10pf+5pf, Miner with drill. 20pf+10pf, Miner and conveyor. 40pf+10pf, Miner and coal elevator.

1957, Oct. 1 Wmk. 304 *Perf. 14*

B356 SP278 7pf + 3pf bis brn & blk 1.10 1.10
B357 SP278 10pf + 5pf blk & yel grn 60 42
B358 SP278 20pf + 10pf blk & red 85 42
B359 SP278 40pf + 10pf blk & bl 13.00 13.00

The surtax was for independent welfare organizations.

1958, Apr. 1 Litho.

Design: 20pf+10pf, "A Hunter from the Palatinate."

B360 SP279 10pf + 5pf brn red, grn & blk 1.25 1.10
B361 SP279 20pf + 10pf multi 2.25 2.00

The surtax was to finance young peoples' study trips to Berlin.

Friedrich Wilhelm Raiffeisen
SP280

Dairy Maid
SP281

Designs: 20pf+10pf, Girl picking grapes. 40pf+10pf, Farmer with pitchfork.

1958, Oct. 1 Wmk. 304 *Perf. 14*

B362 SP280 7pf + 3pf gldn brn & dk brn 32 40
B363 SP281 10pf + 5pf grn, red & yel 28 20
B364 SP281 20pf + 10pf red, yel & bl 42 28
B365 SP281 40pf + 10pf bl & ocher 5.50 5.50

The surtax was for independent welfare organizations.

Stamp of Hamburg, 1859 – SP282

Design: 20pf+10pf, Stamp of Lübeck, 1859.

1959, May 22 Engr. Wmk. 304

B366 SP282 10pf + 5pf grn & brn 85 1.10
a. 10pf + 5pf yel grn & brn 15 18
B367 SP282 20pf + 10pf mar & red brn 1.10 1.40
a. 20pf + 10pf red org & red brn 15 35

Issued to publicize the "Interposta" Philatelic Exhibition, Hamburg, May 22-31, 1959. "Interposta" commemorated the centenary of the first stamps of Hamburg and Lübeck.

The surtax on Nos. B366a and B367a was for vacations for the children of Berlin. Issued Aug. 22, 1959.

Girl Giving Bread to Beggar – SP283

Jacob and Wilhelm Grimm – SP284

Designs (from "Star Dollars" fairy tale): 10pf + 5pf, Girl giving coat to boy, 20pf + 10pf, Star-Money from Heaven.

1959, Oct. 1 Litho. *Perf. 14*

B368 SP283 7pf + 3pf brn & yel 15 24
B369 SP283 10pf + 5pf grn & yel 20 18
B370 SP283 20pf + 10pf brick red & yel 32 18
B371 SP284 40pf + 10pf bl, blk, ocher & emer 2.50 3.00

The surtax was for independent welfare organizations.

Little Red Riding Hood and the Wolf – SP285

Various Scenes from Little Red Riding Hood.

1960, Oct. 1 Wmk. 304 *Perf. 14*

B372 SP285 7pf + 3pf brn ol, red & blk 20 28
B373 SP285 10pf + 5pf grn, red & blk 24 15
B374 SP285 20pf + 10pf brick red, emer & blk 30 18
B375 SP285 40pf + 20pf brt bl, red & blk 2.50 2.75

The surtax was for independent welfare organizations.

1961, Oct. 2

Various Scenes from Hansel and Gretel.

B376 SP285 7pf + 3pf multi 15 16
B377 SP285 10pf + 5pf multi 15 15
B378 SP285 20pf + 10pf multi 20 15
B379 SP285 40pf + 20pf multi 1.10 1.40

The surtax was for independent welfare organizations.

See Nos. B384-B387, B392-B395, B400-B403.

Fluorescent Paper was introduced for semipostal stamps, starting with No. B380.

Apollo
SP286

Hoopoe
SP287

Butterflies: 10pf+5pf, Camberwell beauty. 20pf+10pf, Tortoise-shell. 40pf+20pf, Tiger swallowtail.

Wmk. 304

1962, May 25 Litho. *Perf. 14*

Butterflies in Natural Colors, Black Inscriptions

B380 SP286 7pf + 3pf bis brn 24 22
B381 SP286 10pf + 5pf brt grn 25 25
B382 SP286 20pf + 10pf dp crim 70 60
B383 SP286 40pf + 20pf brt bl 1.10 1.10

Issued for the benefit of young people.

Nos. B381-B383 exist without watermark. Value, each $900 unused, $750 used.

Fairy Tale Type of 1960

Various Scenes from Snow White (Schneewittchen).

1962, Oct. 10 *Perf. 14*

B384 SP285 7pf + 3pf multi 15 15
B385 SP285 10pf + 5pf multi 15 15
B386 SP285 20pf + 10pf multi 18 15
B387 SP285 40pf + 20pf multi 70 90

The surtax was for independent welfare organizations.

1963, June 12 Unwmk. *Perf. 14*

Birds: 15pf+5pf, European golden oriole. 20pf+10pf, Bullfinch. 40pf+20pf, European kingfisher.

B388 SP287 10pf + 5pf multi 32 24
B389 SP287 15pf + 5pf multi 32 30
B390 SP287 20pf + 10pf multi 40 30
B391 SP287 40pf + 20pf multi 1.40 1.10

Issued for the benefit of young people.

Fairy Tale Type of 1960

Various Scenes from the Grimm Brothers' "The Wolf and the Seven Kids."

1963, Sept. 23 Litho.

B392 SP285 10pf + 5pf multi 15 15
B393 SP285 15pf + 5pf multi 15 15
B394 SP285 20pf + 10pf multi 16 15
B395 SP285 40pf + 20pf multi 55 65
Set value 93

The surtax was for independent welfare organizations.

Herring SP288 — Woodcock SP289

Fish: 15pf+5pf, Rosefish. 20pf+10pf, Carp. 40pf+20pf, Cod.

1964, Apr. 10 Unwmk. *Perf. 14*

B396 SP288 10pf + 5pf multi 22 22
B397 SP288 15pf + 5pf multi 22 20
B398 SP288 20pf + 10pf multi 35 20
B399 SP288 40pf + 20pf multi 1.00 1.00

Issued for the benefit of young people.

Fairy Tale Type of 1960

Various Scenes from Sleeping Beauty (Dornroschen).

1964, Oct. 6 Litho. *Perf. 14*

B400 SP285 10pf + 5pf multi 15 15
B401 SP285 15pf + 5pf multi 15 15
B402 SP285 20pf + 10pf multi 15 15
B403 SP285 40pf + 20pf multi 55 70

The surtax was for independent welfare organizations.

1965, Apr. 1 Unwmk. *Perf. 14*

Birds: 15pf+5pf, Ring-necked pheasant. 20pf+10pf, Black grouse. 40pf+20pf, Capercaillie.

B404 SP289 10pf + 5pf multi 15 15
B405 SP289 15pf + 5pf multi 15 15
B406 SP289 20pf + 10pf multi 18 15
B407 SP289 40pf + 20pf multi 38 55

Issued for the benefit of young people.

Cinderella Feeding Pigeons — SP290 — Roe Deer — SP291

Various Scenes from Cinderella.

1965, Oct. 6 Litho. *Perf. 14*

B408 SP290 10pf + 5pf multi 15 15
B409 SP290 15pf + 5pf multi 15 15
B410 SP290 20pf + 10pf multi 15 15
B411 SP290 40pf + 20pf multi 48 55
Set value 78

The surtax was for independent welfare organizations.
See Nos. B418-B421, B426-B429.

1966, Apr. 22 Litho. *Perf. 14*

Designs: 20pf+10pf, Chamois. 30pf+15pf, Fallow deer. 50pf+25pf, Red deer.

B412 SP291 10pf + 5pf multi 16 15
B413 SP291 20pf + 10pf multi 20 15
B414 SP291 30pf + 15pf multi 28 20
B415 SP291 50pf + 25pf multi 65 65

Issued for the benefit of young people.
See Nos. B422-B425.

Prussian Letter Carrier — SP292

Design: 30pf+15pf, Bavarian mail coach.

1966 Litho. *Perf. 14*

B416 SP292 30pf + 15pf multi 42 60
B417 SP292 50pf + 25pf multi 32 52

Issued to publicize the meeting of the Federation Internationale de Philatelie (FIP), Munich, Sept. 26-29, and the stamp exhibition, Municipal Museum, Sept. 24-Oct. 1. The surcharge was for the Foundation for the Promotion of Philately and Postal History. Issue dates: No. B416, Sept. 24; No. B417, July 13.

Fairy Tale Type of 1965

Various Scenes from The Princess and the Frog.

1966, Oct. 5 Litho. *Perf. 14*

B418 SP290 10pf + 5pf multi 15 15
B419 SP290 20pf + 10pf multi 15 15
B420 SP290 30pf + 15pf multi 20 15
B421 SP290 50pf + 25pf multi 50 75

The surtax was for independent welfare organizations.

Animal Type of 1966

Designs: 10pf+5pf, Rabbit. 20pf+10pf, Ermine. 30pf+15pf, Hamster. 50pf+25pf, Red fox.

1967, Apr. 4 Litho. *Perf. 14*

B422 SP291 10pf + 5pf multi 20 18
B423 SP291 20pf + 10pf multi 20 22
B424 SP291 30pf + 15pf multi 32 30
B425 SP291 50pf + 25pf multi 1.00 1.10

Issued for the benefit of young people.

Fairy Tale Type of 1965

Various Scenes from Frau Holle.

1967, Oct. 3 Litho. *Perf. 14*

B426 SP290 10pf + 5pf multi 15 16
B427 SP290 20pf + 10pf multi 15 15
B428 SP290 30pf + 15pf multi 25 15
B429 SP290 50pf + 25pf multi 65 90

The surtax was for independent welfare organizations.

Wildcat — SP293

Animals: 20pf+10pf, Otter. 30pf+15pf, Badger. 50pf+25pf, Beaver.

1968, Feb. 2 Photo. Unwmk.

B430 SP293 10pf + 5pf multi 28 35
B431 SP293 20pf + 15pf multi 35 45
B432 SP293 30pf + 15pf multi 65 75
B433 SP293 50pf + 25pf multi 1.75 2.00

The surtax was for the benefit of young people.

Olympic Games Type of Regular Issue

Designs (Olympic Rings and): 10pf+5pf, Karl-Friedrich Freiherr von Langen, equestrian. 20pf+10pf, Rudolf Harbig, runner. 30pf+15pf, Helene Mayer, fencer. 50pf+25pf, Carl Diem, sports organizer.

Lithographed and Engraved

1968, June 6 Unwmk. *Perf. 14*

B434 A285 10pf + 5pf ol & dk brn 15 15
B435 A285 20pf + 10pf dp emer & dk grn 30 30
B436 A285 30pf + 15pf dp rose & dk red 45 45
B437 A285 50pf + 25pf brt bl & dk bl 75 75

The surtax was for the Foundation for the Promotion of the 1972 Olympic Games in Munich.

Doll, c. 1878 — SP294 — Pony — SP295

Designs: Various 19th Century Dolls. Nos. B438-B440 are from Germanic National Museum, Nuremberg; No. B441 is from Altona Museum, Hamburg.

1968, Oct. 3 Litho. *Perf. 14*

B438 SP294 10pf + 5pf multi 15 18
B439 SP294 20pf + 10pf multi 16 15
B440 SP294 30pf + 15pf multi 20 18
B441 SP294 50pf + 25pf multi 60 95

The surtax was for independent welfare organizations.

1969, Feb. 6 Litho. *Perf. 14*

Horses: 20pf+10pf, Work horse. 30pf+15pf, Hotblood. 50pf+25pf, Thoroughbred.

B442 SP295 10pf + 5pf multi 22 28
B443 SP295 20pf + 10pf multi 30 35
B444 SP295 30pf + 15pf multi 65 80
B445 SP295 50pf + 25pf multi 1.50 1.75

Surtax for the benefit of young people.

Track and Olympic Rings SP296 — Toy Locomotive of Tin SP297

Designs (Olympic Rings and): 20pf+10pf, Hockey. 30pf+15pf, Archery. 50pf+25pf, Sailing.

1969, June 4 Photo. *Perf. 14*

B446 SP296 10pf + 5pf dk brn & lem 15 18
B447 SP296 20pf + 10pf bl grn & emer 32 38
B448 SP296 30pf + 15pf mag & dp lil rose 45 55
B449 SP296 50pf + 25pf dp bl & brt bl 1.10 1.25

Issued to publicize the 1972 Olympic Games in Munich. The surtax was for the German Olympic Committee.

1969, Oct. 2 Litho. *Perf. 13½x14*

Tin Toys: 20pf+10pf, Gardener. 30pf+15pf, Bird seller. 50pf+25pf, Knight on horseback.

B450 SP297 10pf + 5pf multi 15 15
B451 SP297 20pf + 10pf multi 18 18
B452 SP297 30pf + 15pf multi 32 32
B453 SP297 50pf + 25pf multi 80 80

The surtax was for independent welfare organizations.

Tin Toy Type of 1969 Inscribed: "Weihnachtsmarke 1969"

Christmas: 10pf+5pf, Jesus in Manger.

1969, Nov. 13 *Perf. 13½x14*

B454 SP297 10pf + 5pf multi 25 25

Heinrich von Rugge — SP298

Minnesingers: 20pf+10pf, Wolfram von Eschenbach. 30pf+15pf, Walther von Metz. 50pf+25pf, Walther von der Vogelweide.

1970, Feb. 5 Photo. *Perf. 13½x14*

B455 SP298 10pf + 5pf multi 25 25
B456 SP298 20pf + 10pf multi 35 35
B457 SP298 30pf + 15pf multi 52 52
B458 SP298 50pf + 25pf multi 1.25 1.25

Surtax was for benefit of young people.

Residenz (Palace), Munich SP299

Munich Buildings: 20pf+10pf, Propylaea. 30pf+15pf, Glyptothek. 50pf+25pf, Bavaria Statue and Colonnade.

1970, June 5 Engr. *Perf. 14*

B459 SP299 10pf + 5pf ol bis 20 20
B460 SP299 20pf + 10pf dk bl grn 40 40
B461 SP299 30pf + 15pf car 50 50
B462 SP299 50pf + 25pf dk bl 1.00 1.00

The surtax was for the Foundation for the Promotion of the 1972 Olympic Games in Munich.

Jester SP300 — King Caspar SP301

Puppets: 20pf+10pf, "Hanswurst." 30pf+15pf, Clown. 50pf+25pf, Harlequin.

1970, Oct. 6 Litho. *Perf. 13½x14*

B463 SP300 10pf + 5pf multi 15 15
B464 SP300 20pf + 10pf multi 16 16
B465 SP300 30pf + 15pf multi 30 30
B466 SP300 50pf + 25pf multi 75 75

The surtax was for independent welfare organizations.

1970, Nov. 12

Christmas: 10pf+5pf, Rococo Angel, from Ursuline Sisters' Convent, Innsbruck.

B467 SP300 10pf + 5pf multi 20 20

1971, Feb. 5 Litho. *Perf. 14*

Children's Drawings: 20pf+10pf, Flea. 30pf+15pf, Puss-in-Boots. 50pf+25pf, Snake.

B468 SP301 10pf + 5pf multi 16 16
B469 SP301 20pf + 10pf multi 35 35
B470 SP301 30pf + 15pf multi 55 55
B471 SP301 50pf + 25pf multi 1.10 1.10

Surtax for the benefit of young people.

Ski Jump
SP302

Women Churning Butter
SP303

Designs: 20pf+10pf, Figure skating. 30pf+15pf, Downhill skiing. 50pf+25pf, Ice hockey.

"1971" at Lower Right

1971, June 4 Litho. *Perf. 14*

B472 SP302 10pf + 5pf brn org & blk	28	28
B473 SP302 20pf + 10pf grn & blk	55	55
B474 SP302 30pf + 15pf rose red & blk	70	70
B475 SP302 50pf + 25pf bl & blk	1.40	1.40
a. Souvenir sheet of 4	3.50	3.50
b. 10pf + 5pf brn org & blk	75	75
c. 20pf + 10pf grn & blk	75	75
d. 30pf + 15pf rose red & blk	75	75
e. 50pf + 25pf bl & blk	75	75

Olympic Games 1972.

No. B475a contains Nos. B475b-B475e which lack the minute date ("1971") at lower right.

1971, Oct. 5 Litho. *Perf. 14*

Wooden Toys: 25pf+10pf, Horseback rider. 30pf+15pf, Nutcracker. 60pf+30pf, Dovecot.

B476 SP303 20pf + 10pf multi	15	15
B477 SP303 25pf + 10pf multi	18	18
B478 SP303 30pf + 15pf multi	24	24
B479 SP303 60pf + 30pf multi	85	85

The surtax was for independent welfare organizations.

1971, Nov. 11

Christmas: 20pf+10pf, Christmas angel with lights.

B480 SP303 20pf + 10pf multi 28 28

Ducks Crossing Road
SP304

Olympic Rings and Wrestling
SP305

Designs: 25pf+10pf, Hunter chasing deer and rabbits. 30pf+15pf, Girl protecting birds from cat. 60pf+30pf, Boy annoying swans.

1972, Feb. 4 Litho. *Perf. 14*

B481 SP304 20pf + 10pf multi	60	60
B482 SP304 25pf + 10pf multi	70	70
B483 SP304 30pf + 15pf multi	90	90
B484 SP304 60pf + 30pf multi	1.75	1.75

Animal protection. Surtax for the benefit of young people.

1972, June 5 Photo. *Perf. 14*

Designs (Olympic Rings and): 25pf+10pf, Sailing. 30pf+15pf, Gymnastics. 60pf+30pf, Swimming.

B485 SP305 20pf + 10pf multi	42	42
B486 SP305 25pf + 10pf multi	52	52
B487 SP305 30pf + 15pf multi	65	65
B488 SP305 60pf + 30pf multi	1.75	1.75

20th Olympic Games, Munich, Aug. 26 Sept. 10. See No. B490.

Souvenir Sheet

Olympic Games Site, Munich — SP306

1972, July 5 Litho. *Perf. 14*

B489 SP306 Sheet of 4	7.50	7.50
a. 25pf + 10pf Gymnastics stadium	1.65	1.65
b. 30pf + 15pf Soccer stadium	1.65	1.65
c. 40pf + 20pf Tent and lake	1.65	1.65
d. 70pf + 35pf Television tower (vert.)	1.65	1.65

20th Olympic Games, Munich. Surcharge was for the Foundation for the Promotion of the Munich Olympic Games.

Olympic Games Type of 1972
Souvenir Sheet

1972, Aug. 18 Litho. *Perf. 14*

B490 Sheet of 4	7.25	7.25
a. SP305 25pf + 5pf Long jump, women's	1.65	1.65
b. SP305 30pf + 10pf Basketball	1.65	1.65
c. SP305 40pf + 10pf Discus, women's	1.65	1.65
d. SP305 70pf + 10pf Canoeing	1.65	1.65
e. Booklet pane of 4	20.00	

20th Olympic Games, Munich. No. B490e contains one each of Nos. B490a-B490d.

Knight
SP307

Adoration of the Kings
SP308

1972, Oct. 5

B491 SP307 25pf + 10pf shown	30	30
B492 SP307 30pf + 15pf Rook	35	35
B493 SP307 40pf + 20pf Queen	45	45
B494 SP307 70pf + 35pf King	1.50	1.50

19th century chess pieces made by Faience Works, Gien, France; now in Hamburg Museum. The surtax was for independent welfare organizations.

1972, Nov. 10 Litho.

B495 SP308 30pf + 15pf multi 52 52

Christmas 1972.

Osprey
SP309

Hesse-Kassel
SP310

Birds of Prey: 30pf+15pf, Buzzard. 40pf+20pf, Red kite. 70pf+35pf, Montagu's harrier.

1973, Feb. 6 Photo. *Perf. 14*

B496 SP309 25pf + 10pf multi	1.25	1.25
B497 SP309 30pf + 15pf multi	1.50	1.50
B498 SP309 40pf + 20pf multi	2.00	2.00
B499 SP309 70pf + 35pf multi	5.00	5.00

Surtax was for benefit of young people.

1973, Apr. 5 Litho. *Perf. 14*

Posthouse Signs: No. B501, Prussia. No. B502a, Württemberg. No. B502b, Bavaria.

B500 SP310 40pf + 20pf multi	1.00	1.00
B501 SP310 70pf + 35pf multi	1.50	1.50

Souvenir Sheet

B502 Sheet of 2	6.50	6.50
a. SP310 40pf + 20pf multi	3.00	3.00
b. SP310 70pf + 35pf multi	3.00	3.00

IBRA München 1973 International Philatelic Exhibition, Munich, May 11-20. No. B502 sold for 2.20 mark.

French Horn, 19th Century
SP311

Christmas Star
SP312

Musical Instruments: 30pf+15pf, Pedal piano, 18th century. 40pf+20pf, Violin, 18th century. 70pf+35pf, Pedal harp, 18th century.

1973, Oct. 5 Litho. *Perf. 14*

B503 SP311 25pf + 10pf multi	35	30
B504 SP311 30pf + 15pf multi	38	35
B505 SP311 40pf + 20pf multi	60	52
B506 SP311 70pf + 35pf multi	1.65	1.50

Surtax was for independent welfare organizations.

1973, Nov. 9 Litho. & Engr.

B507 SP312 30pf + 15pf multi 65 65

Christmas 1973.

Young Builder
SP313

Campion
SP314

Designs: 30pf+15pf, Girl in national costume. 40pf+20pf, Boy studying. 70pf+35pf, Girl with microscope.

1974, Apr. 17 Photo. *Perf. 14*

B508 SP313 25pf + 10pf multi	1.10	1.10
B509 SP313 30pf + 15pf multi	1.25	1.25
B510 SP313 40pf + 20pf multi	2.00	2.00
B511 SP313 70pf + 35pf multi	2.75	2.75

Surtax was for benefit of young people.

1974, Oct. 15 Litho. *Perf. 14*

Flowers: 40pf+20pf, Foxglove. 50pf+25pf, Mallow. 70pf+35pf, Bellflower.

B512 SP314 30pf + 15pf multi	32	32
B513 SP314 40pf + 20pf multi	42	42
B514 SP314 50pf + 25pf multi	55	55
B515 SP314 70pf + 35pf multi	1.50	1.50

Surtax was for independent welfare organizations.

1974, Oct. 29

Christmas: 40pf+20pf, Advent decoration.

B516 SP314 40pf + 20pf multi 65 65

Diesel Locomotive Class 218 — SP315

Locomotives: 40pf+20pf, Electric engine Class 103. 50pf+25pf, Electric rail motor train Class 403. 70pf+35pf, Magnetic suspension train "Transrapid" (model).

1975, Apr. 15 Litho. *Perf. 14*

B517 SP315 30pf + 15pf multi	60	60
B518 SP315 40pf + 20pf multi	80	80
B519 SP315 50pf + 25pf multi	1.25	1.25
B520 SP315 70pf + 35pf multi	1.65	1.65

Surtax was for benefit of young people.

Edelweiss — SP316

Alpine Flowers: 40pf+20pf, Trollflower. 50pf+25pf, Alpine rose. 70pf+35pf, Pasqueflower.

1975, Oct. 15 Litho. *Perf. 14*

B521 SP316 30pf + 15pf multi	35	25
B522 SP316 40pf + 20pf multi	50	40
B523 SP316 50pf + 25pf multi	70	52
B524 SP316 70pf + 35pf multi	1.50	1.10

Surtax was for independent welfare organizations.

1975, Nov. 14

Christmas: 40pf+20pf, Snow rose.

B525 SP316 40pf + 20pf multi 70 70

Basketball — SP317

Designs: 40pf+20pf, Rowing. 50pf+25pf, Gymnastics, women's. 70pf+35pf, Volleyball.

1976, Apr. 6 Litho. *Perf. 14*

B526 SP317 30pf + 15pf multi	65	65
B527 SP317 40pf + 20pf multi	90	90
B528 SP317 50pf + 25pf multi	1.10	1.10
B529 SP317 70pf + 35pf multi	1.50	1.50

Youth training for Olympic Games. Surtax was for benefit of young people.

Swimmer and Olympic Rings
SP318

Designs (Olympic Rings and): 30pf+15pf, Hockey. 50pf+25pf, High jump. 70pf+35pf, Rowing, coxed four.

1976, Apr. 6

B530 SP318 40pf + 20pf multi	55	55
B531 SP318 50pf + 25pf multi	70	70

Souvenir Sheet

B532 Sheet of two	1.75	1.75
a. SP318 30pf + 15pf multi	85	85
b. SP318 70pf + 35pf multi	85	85

21st Olympic Games, Montreal, Canada, July 17-Aug. 1. The surtax was for the German Sports Aid Foundation.

Phlox
SP319

Flowers: 40pf+20pf, Marigolds. 50pf+25pf, Dahlias. 70pf+35pf, Pansies.

1976, Oct. 14 Litho. *Perf. 14*

B533 SP319 30pf + 15pf multi 40 40
B534 SP319 40pf + 20pf multi 52 52
B535 SP319 50pf + 25pf multi 65 65
B536 SP319 70pf + 35pf multi 1.10 1.10

Surtax was for independent welfare organizations.

Souvenir Sheet

Nativity, Window, Frauenkirche, Esslingen — SP320

1976, Nov. 16 Litho. & Engr.

B537 SP320 50pf + 25pf multi 75 75

Christmas 1976.

Wapen von Hamburg, c. 1730 SP321

Historic Ships: 40pf+20pf, Preussen, 5-master, 1902. 50pf+**25pf, Bremen, 1929.** 70pf+35pf, Freighter Sturmfels, 1972.

1977, Apr. 14 Litho. *Perf. 14*

B538 SP321 30pf + 15pf multi 60 60
B539 SP321 40pf + 20pf multi 95 95
B540 SP321 50pf + 25pf multi 1.10 1.10
B541 SP321 70pf + 35pf multi 1.50 1.50

Surtax was for benefit of young people.

Caraway — SP322

Meadow Flowers: 40pf+20pf, Dandelion. 50pf+25pf, Red clover. 70pf+35pf, Meadow sage.

1977, Oct. 13 Litho. *Perf. 14*

B542 SP322 30pf + 15pf multi 45 45
B543 SP322 40pf + 20pf multi 55 55
B544 SP322 50pf + 25pf multi 70 70
B545 SP322 70pf + 35pf multi 1.00 1.00

Surtax was for independent welfare organizations.

See Nos. B553-B556.

15-Cent Minimum Value
The minimum value for a single stamp is 15 cents. This value reflects the costs of the handling of inexpensive stamps.

Souvenir Sheet

King Caspar Offering Gold, Window, St. Gereon's, Cologne — SP323

1977, Nov. 10

B546 SP323 50pf + 25pf multi 75 75

Christmas 1977.

Giant Slalom SP324

Design: No. B548, Steeplechase.

1978 Litho. *Perf. 14*

B547 SP324 50pf + 25pf multi 1.75 1.75
B548 SP324 70pf + 35pf multi 4.50 4.50

Issue dates: No. B547, Jan. 12, No. B548, Apr. 13.

Surtax was for the German Sports Foundation.

Balloon Ascent, Oktoberfest, Munich, 1820 — SP325

Designs: 40pf+20pf, Airship LZ 1, 1900. 50pf+25pf, Bleriot monoplane, 1909. 70pf+35pf, Grade monoplane, 1909.

1978, Apr. 13 Litho. *Perf. 14*

B549 SP325 30pf + 15pf multi 55 55
B550 SP325 40pf + 20pf multi 70 70
B551 SP325 50pf + 25pf multi 95 95
B552 SP325 70pf + 35pf multi 1.25 1.25

Surtax was for benefit of young people.

Flower Type of 1977

Woodland Flowers: 30pf+15pf, Arum. 40pf+20pf, Weaselsnout. 50pf+25pf, Turk's-cap lily. 70pf+35pf, Liverwort.

1978, Oct. 12 Litho. *Perf. 14*

B553 SP322 30pf + 15pf multi 38 38
B554 SP322 40pf + 20pf multi 50 50
B555 SP322 50pf + 25pf multi 60 60
B556 SP322 70pf + 35pf multi 1.10 1.10

Surtax was for independent welfare organizations.

Souvenir Sheet

Christ Child, Window, Frauenkirche, Munich — SP326

1978, Nov. 16 Litho. *Perf. 14*

B557 SP326 50pf + 25pf multi 75 75

Christmas 1978.

Dornier Wal, 1922 SP327

Airplanes: 50pf+25pf, Heinkel HE70, 1932. 60pf+30pf, Junkers W33 Bremen, 1928. 90pf+45pf, Focke-Wulf FW61, 1936.

1979, Apr. 5 Litho. *Perf. 14*

B558 SP327 40pf + 20pf multi 60 60
B559 SP327 50pf + 25pf multi 85 85
B560 SP327 60pf + 30pf multi 1.00 1.00
B561 SP327 90pf + 45pf multi 1.50 1.50

Surtax was for benefit of young people. See Nos. B570-B573.

Handball SP328

Design: 90pf+45pf, Canoeing.

1979, Apr. 5

B562 SP328 60pf + 30pf multi 1.00 1.00
B563 SP328 90pf + 45pf multi 1.40 1.40

Surtax was for German Sports Foundation.

Post House Sign, Altheim, Saar, 1754 — SP329

1979, Oct. 11 Litho. *Perf. 14*

B564 SP329 60pf + 30pf multi 1.00 1.00

Stamp Day. Surtax was for Foundation of Promotion of Philately and Postal History. Issued in sheet of 10.

Red Beech SP330

Woodland Plants: 50pf+25pf, English oak. 60pf+30pf, Hawthorn. 90pf+45pf, Mountain pine.

1979, Oct. 11 Litho. *Perf. 14*

B565 SP330 40pf + 20pf multi 48 48
B566 SP330 50pf + 25pf multi 60 60
B567 SP330 60pf + 30pf multi 65 65
B568 SP330 90pf + 45pf multi 1.10 1.10

Surtax was for independent welfare organizations.

Nativity, Medieval Manuscript SP331

1979, Nov. 14 Litho. *Perf. 13½*

B569 SP331 60pf + 30pf multi 80 80

Christmas 1979.

Aviation Type of 1979

Designs: 40pf+20pf, FS 24 Phoenix, 1957. 50pf+25pf, Lockheed Super Constellation, 1950. 60pf+30pf, Airbus A300, 1972. 90pf+45pf, Boeing 747, 1969.

1980, Apr. 10 Litho. *Perf. 14*

B570 SP327 40 + 20pf multi 55 55
B571 SP327 50 + 25pf multi 75 75
B572 SP327 60 + 30pf multi 95 95
B573 SP327 90 + 45pf multi 1.50 1.50

Surtax was for benefit of young people.

Soccer SP332

Designs: 60pf+30pf, Equestrian. 90pf+45pf, Cross-country skiing.

1980, May 8 Photo. *Perf. 14*

B574 SP332 50 + 25pf multi 70 70
B575 SP332 60 + 30pf multi 90 90
B576 SP332 90 + 45pf multi 1.40 1.40

Surtax was for German Sports Foundation.

Ceratocephalus SP333

Wildflowers: 50pf+25pf, Climbing meadow pea. 60pf+30pf, Corn cockle. 90pf+45pf, Grape hyacinth.

1980, Oct. 9 Litho. *Perf. 14*

B577 SP333 40 + 20pf multi 55 55
B578 SP333 50 + 25pf multi 70 70
B579 SP333 60 + 30pf multi 80 80
B580 SP333 90 + 45pf multi 1.25 1.25

Surtax was for independent welfare organizations.

Post House Sign, 1754, Altheim, Saar — SP334

1980, Nov. 13 Litho. *Perf. 14*

B581 SP334 60 + 30pf multi 70 70

49th FIP Congress (Federation Internationale de Philatelie), Essen, Nov. 12-13.

Nativity, Altomunster Manuscript, 12th Century SP335

1980, Nov. 13 *Perf. 14x13½*

B582 SP335 60 + 30pf multi 75 75

Christmas 1980.

Borda Circle, 1800 — SP336

Historic Optical Instruments: 50pf+25pf, Reflecting telescope, 1770. 60pf+30pf, Binocular microscope, 1860. 90pf+45pf, Octant, 1775.

1981, Apr. 10 **Litho.** *Perf. 13½*

B583 SP336 40 + 20pf multi 60 60
B584 SP336 50 + 25pf multi 75 75
B585 SP336 60 + 30pf multi 1.00 1.00
B586 SP336 90 + 45pf multi 1.50 1.50

Surtax was for benefit of young people.

Rowing SP337

1981, Apr. 10 *Perf. 14*

B587 SP337 60 + 30pf shown 90 90
B588 SP337 90 + 45pf Gliding 1.25 1.25

Surtax was for the German Sports Foundation.

Water Nut — SP338

Endangered Species: 50pf+25pf, Floating heart. 60pf+30pf, Water gillyflower. 90pf+45pf, Water lobelia.

1981, Oct. 8 **Litho.**

B589 SP338 40 + 20pf multi 60 60
B590 SP338 50 + 25pf multi 75 75
B591 SP338 60 + 30pf multi 90 90
B592 SP338 90 + 45pf multi 1.25 1.25

Surtax was for independent welfare organizations.

Nativity, 19th Cent. Painting SP339

1981, Nov. 12 **Litho.**

B593 SP339 60 + 30pf multi 90 90

Christmas 1981.

Antique Cars SP340

Designs: 40+20pf, Benz, 1886. 50+25pf, Mercedes, 1913. 60+30pf, Hanomag, 1925. 90+45pf, Opel Olympia, 1937.

1982, Apr. 15 **Litho.**

B594 SP340 40 + 20pf multi 65 65
B595 SP340 50 + 25pf multi 75 75
B596 SP340 60 + 30pf multi 95 95
B597 SP340 90 + 45pf multi 1.40 1.40

Surtax was for benefit of young people.

Jogging SP341

1982, Apr. 15 **Litho.**

B598 SP341 60 + 30pf shown 85 85
B599 SP341 90 + 45pf Archery 1.40 1.40

Surtax was for the German Sports Foundation.

Tea-rose Hybrid — SP342

Designs: 60pf+30pf, Floribunda. 80pf+40pf, Bourbon rose. 120pf+60pf, Polyantha hybrid.

1982, Oct. 14 **Litho.** *Perf. 14*

B600 SP342 50 + 20pf multi 70 70
B601 SP342 60 + 30pf multi 90 90
B602 SP342 80 + 40pf multi 1.10 1.10
B603 SP342 120 + 60pf multi 1.75 1.75

Surtax was for independent welfare organizations.

Christmas 1982 — SP343

Designs: Nativity, Oak altar, St. Peter's Church, Hamburg, 1380.

1982, Nov. 10

B604 SP343 80 + 40pf multi 1.25 1.25

Historic Motorcycles — SP344

Designs: 50pf+20pf, Daimler-Mayback, 1885. 60+30pf, NSU, 1901. 80+40pf, Megola-Sport, 1922. 120pf+60pf, BMW, 1936.

1983, Apr. 12 **Litho.** *Perf. 14*

B605 SP344 50 + 20pf multi 75 75
B606 SP344 60 + 30pf multi 90 90
B607 SP344 80 + 40pf multi 1.10 1.10
B608 SP344 120 + 60pf multi 1.75 1.75

Surtax was for benefit of young people.

1983 Sports Championships — SP345

Designs: 80pf+40pf, Gymnastics Festival. 120pf+60pf, Modern Pentathlon World Championships.

1983, Apr. 12

B609 SP345 80 + 40pf multi 1.25 1.25
B610 SP345 120 + 60pf multi 1.75 1.75

Surtax was for German Sports Foundation.

Swiss Androsace — SP346

Designs: 60pf+30pf, Krain groundsel. 80pf+40pf, Fleischer's willow herb. 120pf+60pf, Alpine sow-thistle.

1983, Oct. 13 **Litho.** *Perf. 14*

B611 SP346 50 + 20pf multi 70 55
B612 SP346 60 + 30pf multi 90 70
B613 SP346 80 + 40pf multi 1.25 1.00
B614 SP346 120 + 60pf multi 1.75 1.40

Surtax was for welfare organizations.

Christmas 1983 SP347

Insects SP348

1983, Nov. 10 **Litho.**

B615 SP347 80 + 40pf Carolers 1.40 1.25

Surtax was for free welfare work.

1984, Apr. 12 **Litho.**

Designs: 50pf+20pf, Trichodes apoarius. 60pf+30pf, Vanessa atalanta. 80pf+40pf, Apis mellifera. 120pf+60pf, Chrysotoxum festivum.

B616 SP348 50 + 20pf multi 75 55
B617 SP348 60 + 30pf multi 1.00 70
B618 SP348 80 + 40pf multi 1.40 1.00
B619 SP348 120 + 60pf multi 1.90 1.40

Surtax was for German Youth Stamp Foundation.

Women's Discus SP349

Olympic Sports: 80pf+40pf, Rhythmic gymnastics. 120pf+60pf, Wind surfing.

1984, Apr. 12

B620 SP349 60 + 30pf multi 1.00 80
B621 SP349 80 + 40pf multi 1.40 1.10
B622 SP349 120 + 60pf multi 2.00 1.65

Surtax was for German Sports Foundation.

Orchids SP350

Designs: 50pf+20pf, Aceras anthropophorum. 60pf+30pf, Orchis ustulata. 80pf+40pf, Limodorum abortivum. 120+60pf, Dactylorhiza sambucina.

1984, Oct. 18 **Litho.** *Perf. 14*

B623 SP350 50 + 20pf multi 70 60
B624 SP350 60 + 30pf multi 90 80
B625 SP350 80 + 40pf multi 1.25 1.10
B626 SP350 120 + 60pf multi 1.75 1.65

Surtax was for welfare organizations.

Christmas 1984 SP351

1984, Nov. 8 **Litho.**

B627 SP351 80pf + 40pf St. Martin 1.25 1.25

Surtax was for welfare organizations.

Bowling SP352

1985, Feb. 21 **Photo.**

B628 SP352 80pf + 40pf multi 1.40 1.10
B629 SP352 120pf + 60pf Kayaking 1.90 1.65

Surtax was for German Sports Foundation.

Antique Bicycles SP353

Designs: 50pf+20pf, Draisienne, 1817. 60pf+30pf, NSU Germania, 1886. 80pf+40pf, Cross-frame, 1887. 120pf+60pf, Adler tricycle, 1888.

1985, Apr. 16 **Litho.**

B630 SP353 50pf + 20pf multi 75 60
B631 SP353 60pf + 30pf multi 1.00 80
B632 SP353 80pf + 40pf multi 1.40 1.10
B633 SP353 120pf + 60pf multi 1.90 1.65

Surtax was for benefit of young people. Each stamp also shows the International Youth Year emblem.

MOPHILA '85, Hamburg, Sept. 11-15 SP354

1985, Aug. 13 **Litho.** *Perf. 14x14½*

B634 SP354 60 + 20pf Coachman, horses 1.65 1.65
B635 SP354 80 + 20pf Stagecoach 2.00 2.00
a. Pair, #B634-B635 3.75 3.75

Surtax for the benefit of the Philatelic & Postal History Foundation. Printed se-tenant in a continuous design.

SP355

Designs: Various ornamental borders, medieval prayer book, Prussian State Library, Berlin.

1985, Oct. 15 Litho. *Perf. 14*

B636	SP355	50pf + 20pf multi	70	60
B637	SP355	60pf + 30pf multi	90	80
B638	SP355	80pf + 40pf multi	1.25	1.10
B639	SP355	120pf + 60pf multi	1.75	1.65

Surtax for welfare organizations.

Christmas 1985 — SP356

Woodcut: The Birth of Christ, by Hans Baldung Grien (1485-1545), Freiburg Cathedral High Altar.

1985, Nov. 12 Litho. *Perf. 14*

B640	SP356	80pf + 40pf multi	1.25	1.25

Surtax for welfare organizations.

European World Sports Championships — SP357

1986, Feb. 13 Litho. *Perf. 14*

B641	SP357	80 + 40pf Running	1.25	1.25
B642	SP357	120 + 55pf Bobsledding	1.75	1.75

Surtax for the Natl. Sports Promotion Foundation.

Vocational Training SP358

1986, Apr. 10

B643	SP358	50 + 25pf Optician	90	70
B644	SP358	60 + 30pf Mason	1.10	80
B645	SP358	70 + 35pf Beautician	1.40	1.00
B646	SP358	80 + 40pf Baker	1.65	1.10

Surtax for German Youth Stamp Foundation.

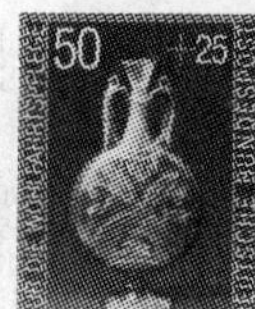
Glassware in German Museums — SP359

1986, Oct. 16 Litho.

B647	SP359	50 + 25pf Ornamental flask, c. 300	85	75
B648	SP359	60 + 30pf Goblet, c. 1650	1.00	90
B649	SP359	70 + 35pf Imperial eagle tankard, c. 1662	1.10	1.05
B650	SP359	80 + 40pf Engraved goblet, c. 1720	1.40	1.20

Surtax for public welfare organizations.

Christmas SP360

Adoration of the Infant Jesus, Ortenberg Altarpiece, c. 1430, Hesse Museum, Darmstadt.

1986, Nov. 13 Litho. *Perf. 14*

B651	SP360	80 + 40pf multi	1.40	1.20

Surtax for public welfare organizations.

World Championships — SP361

1987, Feb. 12 Litho.

B652	SP361	80 + 40pf Sailing	1.35	1.35
B653	SP361	120 + 55pf Cross-country skiing	1.95	1.95

Surtax for the benefit of the national Sports Promotion Foundation.

Youth in Industry SP362

1987, Apr. 9 Litho.

B654	SP362	50 + 25pf Plumber	82	82
B655	SP362	60 + 30pf Dental technician	1.00	1.00
B656	SP362	70 + 35pf Butcher	1.15	1.15
B657	SP362	80 + 40pf Bookbinder	1.30	1.30

Surtax for youth organizations.

Gold and Silver Artifacts SP363

1987, Oct. 15

B658	SP363	50 + 25pf Roman bracelet, 4th cent.	85	85
B659	SP363	60 + 30pf Gothic buckle, 6th cent.	1.00	1.00
B660	SP363	70 + 35pf Merovingian disk fibula, 7th cent.	1.20	1.20
B661	SP363	80 + 40pf Purse-shaped reliquary, 8th cent.	1.35	1.35

Surtax for welfare organizations sonsoring free museum exhibitions.

Christmas SP364

Illustration from Book of Psalms, 13th cent., Bavarian Natl. Museum: Birth of Christ.

1987, Nov. 6

B662	SP364	80 + 40pf multi	1.40	1.40

Surtax for public welfare organizations.

Sports SP365

1988, Feb. 18 Litho.

B663	SP365	60 + 30pf Soccer	1.15	1.15
B664	SP365	80 + 40pf Tennis	1.50	1.50
B665	SP365	120 + 55pf Diving	2.20	2.20

Surtax for Stiftung Deutsche Sporthilfe, a foundation for the promotion of sports in Germany.

Rock Stars SP366

Designs: No. B666, Buddy Holly (1936-1959). No. B667, Elvis Presley (1935-1977). No. B668, Jim Morrison (1943-1971). No. B669, John Lennon (1940-1980).

1988, Apr. 14 Litho. *Perf. 14*

B666	SP366	50 + 25pf multi	1.05	1.05
B667	SP366	60 + 30pf multi	1.10	1.10
B668	SP366	70 + 35pf multi	1.30	1.30
B669	SP366	80 + 40pf multi	1.50	1.50

Surtax for German Youth Stamp Foundation.

Gold and Rock Crystal Reliquary, c. 1200, Schnutgen Museum, Cologne SP367

Gold and silver artifacts: No. B671, Bust of Charlemagne, 14th cent., Aachen cathedral. No. B672, Crown of Otto III, 10th cent., Essen cathedral. No. B673, Flower bouquet, c. 1620, Schmuck Museum, Pforzheim.

1988, Oct. 13 Litho.

B670	SP367	50 + 25pf multi	82	82
B671	SP367	60 + 30pf multi	95	95
B672	SP367	70 + 35pf multi	1.15	1.15
B673	SP367	80 + 40pf multi	1.30	1.30

Surtax for welfare organizations.

Christmas SP368

Illumination from *The Gospel Book of Henry the Lion,* Helmarshausen, 1188, Prussian Cultural Museum, Bavaria: Adoration of the Magi.

1988, Nov. 10 Litho.

B674	SP368	80 + 40pf multi	1.30	1.30

Surtax for public welfare organizations.

World Championship Sporting Events Hosted by Germany — SP369

1989, Feb. 9 Litho.

B675	SP369	100pf + 50pf Table tennis	1.65	1.65
B676	SP369	140pf + 60pf Gymnastics	2.15	2.15

Surtax for the Natl. Sports Promotion Foundation.

IPHLA Philatelic Literature Exhibition, Frankfurt, Apr. 19-23 — SP370

1989, Apr. 20 Litho.

B677	SP370	100 + 50pf multi	1.65	1.65

Surtax benefited the Foundation for the Promotion of Philately and Postal History.

Circus SP371

1989, Apr. 20

B678 SP371 60 +30pf Elephants 1.00 1.00
B679 SP371 70 + 30pf Bareback rider 1.10 1.10
B680 SP371 80 + 35pf Clown 1.30 1.30
B681 SP371 100 +50pf Caravans, big top 1.65 1.65

Surtax for natl. youth welfare organizations.

Mounted Courier of Thurn and Taxis, 18th Cent. — SP372

History of mail carrying: No. B683, Hamburg postal service messenger, 1808. No. B684, Bavarian mail coach, c. 1900.

1989, Oct. 12 **Litho.**

B682 SP372 60 + 30pf multi 98 98
B683 SP372 80 + 35pf multi 1.25 1.25
B684 SP372 100 + 50pf multi 1.65 1.65

Surtax for the benefit of Free Welfare Work.

Christmas SP373

Wood carvings by Veit Stoss in St. Lawrence's Church, Nuremburg, 1517-18.

1989, Nov. 16 **Litho.**

B685 SP373 60 + 30pf Angel 92 92
B686 SP373 100 +50pf Adoration of the Kings 1.55 1.55

Surtax for benefit of the Federal Working Assoc. of Free Welfare Work.

Popular Sports SP374

1990, Feb. 15 **Litho.**

B687 SP374 100 + 50pf Handball 1.80 1.80
B688 SP374 140 + 60pf Physical fitness 2.40 2.40

Surtax for the Natl. Sports Promotion Foundation.

Max and Moritz, by Wilhelm Busch, 125th Anniv. — SP375

1990, Apr. 19 **Litho.**

B689 SP375 60 + 30pf Widow Bolte 1.05 1.05
B690 SP375 70 + 30pf Max 1.20 1.20
B691 SP375 80 + 35pf Max and Moritz 1.35 1.35
B692 SP375 100 + 50pf Max and Moritz, diff. 1.75 1.75

Surcharge for the German Youth Stamp Foundation.

Dusseldorf '90 — SP376

Illustration reduced.

1990, June 21 **Litho.**

B693 Sheet of 6 10.80 10.80
a. SP376 100pf + 50pf multi 1.80 1.80

Surtax for the Foundation for Promotion of Philately and Postal History. 10th Intl. Philatelic Exhibition of Youth and 11th Natl. Philatelic Exhibition of Youth.

Post and Telecommunications — SP377

Designs: 60pf + 30pf, Postal vehicle, 1900. 80pf + 35pf, Telephone exchange, 1890. 100pf + 50pf, Post office, 1900.

1990, Sept. 27 **Litho.** ***Perf. 13½x14***

B694 SP377 60pf + 30pf multi 1.05 1.05
B695 SP377 80pf + 35pf multi 1.35 1.35
B696 SP377 100pf + 50pf multi 1.75 1.75

Surtax for welfare organizations.

Christmas SP378

1990, Nov. 6 **Litho.** ***Perf. 14***

B697 SP378 50pf + 20pf shown 85 85
B698 SP378 60pf + 30pf Smoking manikin 1.05 1.05
B699 SP378 70pf + 30pf Nutcracker 1.20 1.20
B700 SP378 100pf + 50pf Angel, diff. 1.75 1.75

Surtax for welfare organizations.

Sports — SP379

1991, Feb. 14 **Litho.** ***Perf. 14***

B701 SP379 70 +30pf Weight lifting 1.25 1.25
B702 SP379 100 +50pf Cycling 1.85 1.85
B703 SP379 140 +60pf Basketball 2.50 2.50
B704 SP379 170 +80pf Wrestling 3.10 3.10

Surtax for the Foundation for the Promotion of Sports.

Endangered Butterflies SP380

No. B705, Alpen gelbling, alpine sulphur. No. B706, Grosser eisvogel, Viceroy. No. B707, Grosser schillerfalter, purple emperor. No. B708, Blauschillernder beuerfalter, bluish copper. No. B709, Schwalben-schwanz, swallowtail. No. B710, Alpen apollo, alpine apollo. No. B711, Hochmoor gelbling, moor sulphur. No. B712, Grosser feuerfalter, large copper.

1991, Apr. 9 **Litho.** ***Perf. 13½***

B705 SP380 30 +15pf multi 50 50
B706 SP380 50 +25pf multi 90 90
B707 SP380 60 +30pf multi 1.05 1.05
B708 SP380 70 +30pf multi 1.15 1.15
B709 SP380 80 +35pf multi 1.35 1.35
B710 SP380 90 +45pf multi 1.55 1.55
B711 SP380 100 +50pf multi 1.70 1.70
B712 SP380 140 +60pf multi 2.30 2.30
Nos. B705-B712 (8) 10.50 10.50

Surtax for German Youth Stamp Foundation.

Souvenir Sheet

Otto Lilienthal's First Glider Flight, Cent. — SP381

1991, July 9 **Litho.** ***Perf. 14***

B713 SP381 100pf +50pf multi 1.70 1.70

Surtax benefited Foundation of Philately and Postal History.

Christmas SP383

Paintings by Martin Schongauer (c. 1450-1491): 60pf+30pf, Angel of the Annunciation. 70pf+30pf, The Annunciation. 80pf+35pf, Angel. 100pf+50pf, Nativity.

1991, Nov. 5 **Litho.** ***Perf. 14***

B720 SP383 60pf +30pf multi 1.10 1.10
B721 SP383 70pf +30pf multi 1.20 1.20
B722 SP383 80pf +35pf multi 1.40 1.40
B723 SP383 100pf +50pf multi 1.80 1.80

Surtax for Federal Working Association of Free Welfare Work.

AIR POST STAMPS

Issues of the Republic

Post Horn with Wings — AP1

Biplane AP2

Perf. 15x14½

1919, Nov. 10 **Typo.** **Unwmk.**

C1 AP1 10pf orange 15 *1.75*
C2 AP2 40pf dark green 15 *1.75*
a. Imperf. 675.00
Set value 20

No. C2a is ungummed.

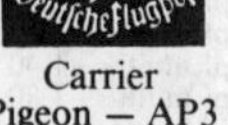

Carrier Pigeon — AP3

German Eagle — AP4

1922-23 Wmk. 126 *Perf. 14, 14½*

Size: 19x23mm

C3	AP3	25(pf) chocolate	30	*10.00*
C4	AP3	40(pf) orange	30	*14.00*
C5	AP3	50(pf) violet	18	*5.00*
C6	AP3	60(pf) carmine	40	*8.25*
C7	AP3	80(pf) bl grn	40	*10.00*

Perf. 13x13½

Size: 22x28mm

C8	AP3	1m dk grn & pale grn	15	*1.65*
C9	AP3	2m lake & gray	15	*1.65*
C10	AP3	3m dk bl & gray	15	*1.65*
C11	AP3	5m red org & yel	15	*1.65*
C12	AP3	10m vio & rose ('23)	15	*5.25*
C13	AP3	25m brn & yel ('23)	15	*4.00*
C14	AP3	100m ol grn & rose ('23)	15	*4.00*
		Nos. C3-C14 (12)	2.63	

1923

C15	AP3	5m vermilion	15	*24.00*
C16	AP3	10m violet	15	*7.25*
C17	AP3	25m dk brn	15	*6.00*
C18	AP3	100m ol grn	15	*5.00*
C19	AP3	200m deep blue	15	*25.00*
a.		Imperf.	72.50	
		Set value	56	

Issue dates: #C15-C18, June 1. #C19, July 25.

Note following #160 applies to #C1-C19.

1924, Jan. 11 *Perf. 14*

Size: 19x23mm

C20	AP3	5(pf) yel grn	1.25	85
C21	AP3	10(pf) carmine	1.25	1.50
C22	AP3	20(pf) vio bl	3.50	4.00
C23	AP3	50(pf) orange	12.50	11.00
C24	AP3	100(pf) dl vio	32.50	32.50
C25	AP3	200(pf) grnsh bl	55.00	52.50
C26	AP3	300(pf) gray	87.50	82.50
a.		Imperf.	*1,900.*	
		Nos. C20-C26 (7)	193.50	184.85

1926-27

C27	AP4	5pf green	65	45
C28	AP4	10pf rose red	65	45
b.		Tete beche pair	120.00	140.00
d.		Bklt. pane 10 (6 No. C28 + 4 No. C29)	110.00	
C29	AP4	15pf lil rose ('27)	1.40	95
a.		Double impression	*1,250.*	
C30	AP4	20pf dl bl	1.40	95
a.		Tete beche pair	120.00	140.00
b.		Bklt. pane 4 (4 No. C30 + 6 labels)	110.00	
c.		Bklt. pane 5 (5 No. C30 + 5 labels)	300.00	
C31	AP4	50pf brn org	20.00	3.50
C32	AP4	1m blk & sal	15.00	4.75
C33	AP4	2m blk & blue	15.00	17.50
C34	AP4	3m blk & ol grn	50.00	55.00
		Nos. C27-C34 (8)	104.10	83.55

"Graf Zeppelin" Crossing Ocean — AP5

1928-31 Photo.

C35	AP5	1m car ('31)	22.50	27.50
C36	AP5	2m ultra	37.50	37.50
C37	AP5	4m blk brn	22.50	27.50

Issue dates: 2m, 4m, Sept. 20, 1928. 1m, May 8, 1931.

For overprints see Nos. C40-C45.

AP6

1930, Apr. 19 Wmk. 126

C38	AP6	2m ultra	165.00	250.00
C39	AP6	4m blk brn	225.00	250.00

First flight of Graf Zeppelin to South America. Nos. C38-C39 exist with watermark vertical or horizontal.

Counterfeits exist of Nos. C38-C45.

Nos. C35-C37 Overprinted in Brown **POLAR-FAHRT 1931**

1931, July 15

C40	AP5	1m carmine	87.50	65.00
C41	AP5	2m ultra	140.00	165.00
C42	AP5	4m blk brn	300.00	500.00

Polar flight of Graf Zeppelin.

Nos. C35-C37 Overprinted **Chicagofahrt Weltausstellung 1933**

1933, Sept. 25

C43	AP5	1m carmine	375.00	*240.00*
C44	AP5	2m ultra	35.00	*125.00*
C45	AP5	4m blk brn	35.00	*125.00*

Graf Zeppelin flight to Century of Progress International Exhibition, Chicago.

Swastika Sun, Globe and Eagle — AP7

Otto Lilienthal — AP8

Design: 3m, Count Ferdinand von Zeppelin.

Perf. 14, 13½x13

1934, Jan. 21 Typo. Wmk. 237

C46	AP7	5(pf) brt grn	32	24
C47	AP7	10(pf) brt car	32	35
C48	AP7	15(pf) ultra	32	35
C49	AP7	20(pf) dl bl	65	65
C50	AP7	25(pf) brown	65	65
C51	AP7	40(pf) red vio	65	45
C52	AP7	50(pf) dk grn	2.00	45
C53	AP7	80(pf) org yel	1.50	1.90
C54	AP7	100(pf) black	2.00	1.40
C55	AP8	2m grn & blk	11.00	12.00
C56	AP8	3m bl & blk	37.50	25.00
		Nos. C46-C56 (11)	56.91	43.44

"Hindenburg" — AP10

Perf. 14, 14½x14

1936, Mar. 16 Engr.

C57	AP10	50pf dark blue	4.50	40
C58	AP10	75pf dull green	5.25	40

Count Zeppelin — AP11

Airship Gondola — AP12

1938, July 5 Unwmk. *Perf. 13½*

C59	AP11	25pf dull blue	2.50	55
C60	AP12	50pf green	3.00	35

Count Ferdinand von Zeppelin (1838-1917), airship inventor and builder.

Catalogue values for unused stamps in this section, from this point to the end of the section, are for Never Hinged items.

Federal Republic

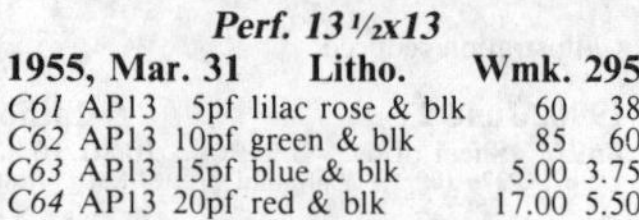

Lufthansa Emblem — AP13

Perf. 13½x13

1955, Mar. 31 Litho. Wmk. 295

C61	AP13	5pf lilac rose & blk	60	38
C62	AP13	10pf green & blk	85	60
C63	AP13	15pf blue & blk	5.00	3.75
C64	AP13	20pf red & blk	17.00	5.50

Re-opening of German air service, Apr. 1.

MILITARY AIR POST STAMP

Junkers 52 Transport MAP1

1942 Unwmk. Typo. *Perf. 13½*

MC1	MAP1	ultra	15	25
a.		Rouletted	15	50

MILITARY PARCEL POST STAMPS

Nazi Emblem — MPP1

1942 Unwmk. Typo. *Perf. 13½*

Size: 28x23mm

MQ1	MPP1	red brown	15	30
a.		Rouletted	15	50

1944 Size: 22½x18mm *Perf. 14*

MQ2	MPP1	bright green	75	*50.00*

See note "Postally Used vs. CTO" after No. 160.

No. 520 Overprinted in Black **FELDPOST 2kg**

1944 Engr.

MQ3	A115	on 40pf brt red vio	90	*65.00*

See note after No. O13.

OFFICIAL STAMPS

Issues of the Republic

In 1920 the Official Stamps of Bavaria and Wurttemberg then current were overprinted "Deutsches Reich" and made available for official use in all parts of Germany. They were, however, used almost exclusively in the two states where they originated and we have listed them among the issues of those states.

O1

O2

O3

O4

O5

O6

O7

O8

O9

O10

O11

O12

1920-21 Typo. Wmk. 125 *Perf. 14*

O1	O1	5pf dp grn	65	*3.25*
O2	O2	10pf car rose	15	15
O3	O2	10pf org ('21)	40	*180.00*
O4	O3	15pf vio brn	15	15
a.		Imperf. ('21)		65.00
O5	O4	20pf dp ultra	15	15
O6	O5	30pf org, *buff*	15	15
O7	O6	40pf carmine	15	15
O8	O7	50pf vio, *buff*	15	15
O9	O8	60pf red brn ('21)	15	25
O10	O9	1m red, *buff*	15	15
O11	O10	1.25m dk bl, *yel*	15	20
O12	O11	2m dk bl	3.25	85
O13	O12	5m brn, *yel*	15	15
		Set value	5.10	

The value of No. O4a is for a copy postmarked at Bautzen.

See No. O15. For surcharges see Nos. O29-O33, O35-O36, O38.

Postally Used vs. CTO

Values quoted for canceled copies of Nos. O1-O46) are for postally used stamps. See note after No. 160.

O13

O14

O15

Wmk. 126, 125 (#O16-O17)

1922-23

O14 O13 75pf dark blue 15 *2.00*
O15 O11 2m dark blue 15 15
a. Imperf. 125.00
O16 O14 3m brown, *rose* 15 15
O17 O15 10m dk grn, *rose* 15 15
O18 O15 10m dk grn, *rose* 15 *6.50*
O19 O15 20m dk bl, *rose* 15 15
O20 O15 50m vio, *rose* 15 15
O21 O15 100m rose red, *rose* 15 15
Set value 68

Issue date: #O18-O21, 1923. Nos. O20-O21 exist imperf.
For surcharges see Nos. O34, O37, O39.

Regular Issue of 1923 Overprinted

a

Dienstmarke

1923

O22 A34 20m red lil 15 *5.00*
O23 A34 30m ol grn 15 *18.00*
O24 A29 40m green 15 *2.25*
O25 A35 200m car rose 15 *32*
O26 A35 300m green 15 *32*
O27 A35 400m dk brn 15 *32*
O28 A35 500m red org 15 *32*
Set value 50

Official Stamps of 1920-23 Surcharged with New Values
Abbreviations:
Th=(Tausend) Thousand
Mil=(Million) Million
Mlrd=(Milliarde) Billion

1923 **Wmk. 125**

O29 O12 5th m on 5m 15 *1.65*
a. Inverted surcharge 52.50
O30 O5 20th m on 30pf 15 *1.25*
a. Inverted surcharge 62.50
b. Imperf. 62.50
O31 O3 100th m on 15pf 15 *1.65*
a. Imperf. 62.50
b. Inverted surcharge 52.50
O32 O2 250th m on 10pf car rose 15 *1.25*
a. Double surcharge 52.50
O33 O5 800th m on 30pf 55 *150.00*

Official Stamps and Types of 1920-23 Surcharged with New Values

Wmk. 126

O34 O15 75th m on 50m 15 *1.65*
a. Inverted surcharge 52.50
O35 O3 400th m on 15pf brn 15 *20.00*
O36 O5 800th m on 30pf org, *buff* 15 *1.65*
O37 O13 1 mil m on 75pf 15 *20.00*
O38 O2 2 mil m on 10pf car rose 15 *1.65*
a. Imperf. 70.00
O39 O15 5 mil m on 100m 15 *3.25*
Set value 1.45

The 10, 15 and 30 pfennig are not known with this watermark and without surcharge.

Nos. 290-291, 295-299 Overprinted Type "a"

1923

O40 A39 100 mil m 15 *100.00*
O41 A39 200 mil m 15 *85.00*
O42 A39a 2 mlrd m 15 *72.50*
O43 A39a 5 mlrd m 15 *57.50*
O44 A39a 10 mlrd m 3.00 *85.00*
O45 A39a 20 mlrd m 2.00 *100.00*
O46 A39a 50 mlrd m 2.00 *150.00*
Nos. O40-O46 (7) 7.60

Same Overprint on Nos, 323-328, Values in Rentenpfennig

1923

O47 A40 3pf brown 22 15
O48 A40 5pf dk grn 22 15
a. Inverted overprint 125.00 110.00
O49 A40 10pf carmine 38 15
a. Inverted overprint 100.00 110.00
b. Imperf. 52.50
O50 A40 20pf dp ultra 75 15
O51 A40 50pf orange 75 48
O52 A40 100pf brn vio 3.50 4.50
Nos. O47-O52 (6) 5.82 5.58

Same Overprint On Issues of 1924

1924

O53 A41 3pf lt brn 28 15
a. Inverted overprint 60.00 160.00
O54 A41 5pf lt grn 28 15
a. Imperf. 62.50
b. Inverted overprint 110.00
O55 A41 10pf vermilion 28 15
O56 A41 20pf blue 28 15
O57 A41 30pf rose lil 55 15
O58 A41 40pf ol grn 55 15
O59 A41 50pf orange 2.50 1.10
O60 A47 60pf red brn 1.10 1.75
O61 A47 80pf slate 6.50 *21.00*
Nos. O53-O61 (9) 12.32 *24.75*

O16

Swastika — O17

1927-33 ***Perf. 14***

O62 O16 3pf bister 32 15
O63 O16 4pf lt bl ('31) 15 15
O64 O16 4pf blue ('33) 1.25 2.00
O65 O16 5pf green 15 15
O66 O16 6pf pale ol grn ('32) 15 15
O67 O16 8pf dk grn 15 15
O68 O16 10pf carmine 5.00 3.00
O69 O16 10pf ver ('29) 8.50 9.25
O70 O16 10pf red vio ('30) 25 15
a. Imperf. 100.00
O71 O16 10pf choc ('33) 1.10 1.65
O72 O16 12pf org ('32) 20 15
O73 O16 15pf vermilion 1.00 20
O74 O16 15pf car ('29) 32 15
O75 O16 20pf Prus grn 2.00 65
O76 O16 20pf gray ('30) 50 32
O77 O16 30pf olive grn 55 15
O78 O16 40pf violet 55 20
O79 O16 60pf red brn ('28) 85 40
Nos. O62-O79 (18) 22.99 19.02

1934, Jan. 18 **Wmk. 237**

O80 O17 3pf bister 15 15
O81 O17 4pf dl bl 15 15
O82 O17 5pf brt grn 15 15
O83 O17 6pf dk grn 15 15
a. Imperf. 90.00
O84 O17 8pf vermilion 30 15
O85 O17 10pf chocolate 25 15
O86 O17 12pf brt car 40 15
a. Unwmkd. 1.50 2.00
O87 O17 15pf claret 75 1.40
O88 O17 20pf light blue 15 24
O89 O17 30pf olive grn 25 24
O90 O17 40pf red vio 25 24
O91 O17 50pf org yel 35 28
Nos. O80-O91 (12) 3.30
Set value 3.00

O83 exists imperf.

1942 **Unwmk.** ***Perf. 14***

O92 O17 3pf bis brn 15 15
O93 O17 4pf dull blue 15 15
O94 O17 5pf deep olive 15 15
O95 O17 6pf deep vio 15 15
O96 O17 8pf vermilion 15 22
O97 O17 10pf chocolate 15 18
O98 O17 12pf rose car 22 32
a. Wmk. 237 1.10 1.90
O99 O17 15pf brn car 1.65 1.90
O100 O17 20pf light blue 15 38
O101 O17 30pf olive grn 15 38
O102 O17 40pf red vio 15 38
O103 O17 50pf dk grn 1.10 1.90
Nos. O92-O103 (12) 4.32 6.26

LOCAL OFFICIAL STAMPS

For Use in Prussia

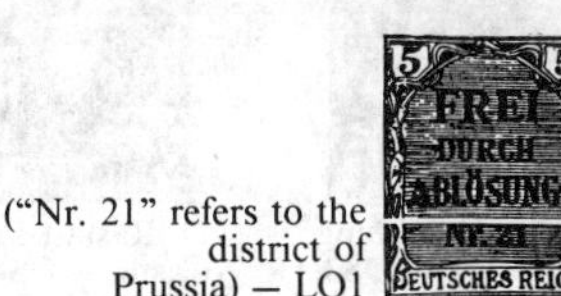

("Nr. 21" refers to the district of Prussia) — LO1

1903 **Unwmk.** **Typo.** ***Perf. 14, 14½***

OL1 LO1 2pf slate 90 1.65
OL2 LO1 3pf bis brn 90 1.65
OL3 LO1 5pf green 22 15
OL4 LO1 10pf carmine 22 15
OL5 LO1 20pf ultra 22 15
OL6 LO1 25pf org & blk, *yel* 22 15
OL7 LO1 40pf lake & blk 22 48
OL8 LO1 50pf pur & blk, *sal* 32 48
Nos. OL1-OL8 (8) 3.22 4.86

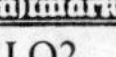
LO2

LO3

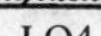
LO4

LO5

LO6

LO7

LO8

1920 **Typo.** **Wmk. 125** ***Perf. 14***

OL9 LO2 5pf green 20 1.50
OL10 LO3 10pf carmine 75 75
OL11 LO4 15pf vio brn 16 35
OL12 LO5 20pf dp ultra 16 35
OL13 LO6 30pf org, *buff* 15 28
OL14 LO7 50pf brn lil, *buff* 28 35
OL15 LO8 1m red, *buff* 5.25 2.25
Nos. OL9-OL15 (7) 6.95 5.83

For Use in Baden

LO9

1905 **Unwmk.** **Typo.** ***Perf. 14, 14½***

OL16 LO9 2pf gray blue 37.50 32.50
OL17 LO9 3pf brown 3.50 3.00
OL18 LO9 5pf green 1.75 2.25
OL19 LO9 10pf rose 38 32
OL20 LO9 20pf blue 1.00 1.00
OL21 LO9 25pf org & blk, *yel* 22.50 22.50
Nos. OL16-OL21 (6) 66.63 61.57

NEWSPAPER STAMPS

Newsboy and Globe — N1

Wmk. Swastikas (237)

1939, Nov. 1 **Photo.** ***Perf. 14***

P1 N1 5pf green 30 50
P2 N1 10pf red brn 30 50

FRANCHISE STAMPS

For use by the National Socialist German Workers' Party

Party Emblem — F1

1938 **Typo.** **Wmk. 237** ***Perf. 14***

S1 F1 1pf black 55 75
S2 F1 3pf bister 55 52
S3 F1 4pf dull blue 90 52
S4 F1 5pf brt grn 55 52
S5 F1 6pf dk grn 55 52
S6 F1 8pf vermilion 2.75 60
S7 F1 12pf brt car 3.50 52
S8 F1 16pf gray 90 *4.00*
S9 F1 24pf citron 1.65 2.50
S10 F1 30pf olive grn 90 2.00
S11 F1 40pf red vio 90 3.25
Nos. S1-S11 (11) 13.70 15.70

1942 **Unwmk.**

S12 F1 1pf gray blk 38 50
S13 F1 3pf bis brn 15 15
S14 F1 4pf dk gray bl 15 15
S15 F1 5pf gray grn 15 30
S16 F1 6pf violet 15 15
S17 F1 8pf dp org 15 15
a. Imperf. 100.00
S18 F1 12pf carmine 18 15
S19 F1 16pf bl grn 2.00 1.50
S20 F1 24pf yel brn 25 55
S21 F1 30pf dp ol grn 25 65
S22 F1 40pf lt rose vio 25 55
Nos. S12-S22 (11) 4.06 4.80

OCCUPATION STAMPS

100 Centimes = 1 Franc
100 Pfennig = 1 Mark

Issued under Belgian Occupation

Belgian Stamps of 1915-20 Overprinted

ALLEMAGNE
DUITSCHLAND

Perf. 11½, 14, 14½

1919-21 **Unwmk.**

1N1 A46 1c orange 40 40
1N2 A46 2c chocolate 40 40
1N3 A46 3c gray blk ('21) 60 1.50
1N4 A46 5c green 80 1.00
1N5 A46 10c carmine 2.25 2.00
1N6 A46 15c purple 1.00 1.00
1N7 A46 20c red vio 1.25 1.25
1N8 A46 25c blue 1.25 1.50
1N9 A54 25c dp bl ('21) 5.00 5.00

Overprinted

ALLEMAGNE
DUITSCHLAND

1N10 A47 35c brn org & blk 1.40 1.25
1N11 A48 40c grn & blk 1.50 2.00
1N12 A49 50c car rose & blk 8.00 10.00
1N13 A56 65c cl & blk ('21) 4.25 8.50
1N14 A50 1fr violet 24.00 24.00
1N15 A51 2fr slate 42.50 45.00
1N16 A52 5fr dp bl 9.50 12.00
1N17 A53 10fr brown 55.00 62.50
Nos. 1N1-1N17 (17) 159.10 179.30

Belgian Stamps of 1915 Surcharged

EUPEN
&
MALMÉDY
5 PF.
Nos. 1N18-1N22

EUPEN
&
MALMÉDY
1 MK 25
Nos. 1N23-1N24

Black Surcharge

1920

1N18 A46 5pf on 5c grn 42 75
1N19 A46 10pf on 10c car 50 75
1N20 A46 15pf on 15c pur 75 90
1N21 A46 20pf on 20c red vio 1.00 1.25
1N22 A46 30pf on 25c bl 1.25 1.50

Red Surcharge

1N23 A49 75pf on 50c car rose & blk 17.50 21.00
1N24 A50 1m25pf on 1fr vio 20.00 22.50
Nos. 1N18-1N24 (7) 41.42 48.65

EUPEN ISSUE

Belgian Stamps of 1915-20 Overprinted:

Eupen — Nos. 1N25-1N36

Eupen — Nos. 1N37-1N41

1920-21 *Perf. 11½, 14, 14½*

1N25	A46	1c orange	42	42
1N26	A46	2c chocolate	42	42
1N27	A46	3c gray blk ('21)	60	1.65
1N28	A46	5c green	70	95
1N29	A46	10c carmine	1.10	1.25
1N30	A46	15c purple	1.25	1.40
1N31	A46	20c red vio	1.25	1.65
1N32	A46	25c blue	1.65	1.90
1N33	A54	25c dp bl ('21)	6.75	9.25
1N34	A47	35c brn org & blk	2.00	2.00
1N35	A48	40c grn & blk	2.25	2.00
1N36	A49	50c car rose & blk	6.75	7.75
1N37	A56	65c cl & blk ('21)	4.50	9.25
1N38	A50	1fr violet	20.00	19.00
1N39	A51	2fr slate	37.50	32.50
1N40	A52	5fr dp bl	14.00	15.00
1N41	A53	10fr brown	55.00	57.50
		Nos. 1N25-1N41 (17)	156.14	163.89

MALMEDY ISSUE

Belgian Stamps of 1915-20 Overprinted:

Malmédy — Nos. 1N42-1N50

Malmédy — Nos. 1N51-1N53

Malmédy — Nos. 1N54-1N58

1920-21

1N42	A46	1c orange	40	40
1N43	A46	2c chocolate	40	40
1N44	A46	3c gray blk ('21)	60	1.50
1N45	A46	5c green	65	1.00
1N46	A46	10c carmine	1.00	1.25
1N47	A46	15c purple	1.10	1.25
1N48	A46	20c red vio	1.25	1.50
1N49	A46	25c blue	1.50	1.75
1N50	A54	25c dp bl ('21)	6.50	9.25
1N51	A47	35c brn org & blk	2.00	2.00
1N52	A48	40c grn & blk	2.25	2.00
1N53	A49	50c car rose & blk	6.50	7.25
1N54	A56	65c cl & blk ('21)	4.25	9.25
1N55	A50	1fr violet	19.00	18.00
1N56	A51	2fr slate	35.00	30.00
1N57	A52	5fr dp bl	13.00	14.00
1N58	A53	10fr brown	52.50	55.50
		Nos. 1N42-1N58 (17)	147.90	156.30

OCCUPATION POSTAGE DUE STAMPS

Belgian Postage Due Stamps of 1919-20, Overprinted Eupen

1920 **Unwmk.** *Perf. 14½*

1NJ1	D3	5c green	1.10	1.50
1NJ2	D3	10c carmine	2.25	2.25
1NJ3	D3	20c gray grn	3.75	3.75
1NJ4	D3	30c brt bl	4.50	4.50
1NJ5	D3	50c gray	11.00	16.00
		Nos. 1NJ1-1NJ5 (5)	22.60	28.00

Belgian Postage Due Stamps of 1919-20, Overprinted Malmédy

1NJ6	D3	5c green	1.25	1.25
1NJ7	D3	10c carmine	2.25	1.75
a.		Inverted overprint	35.00	
1NJ8	D3	20c gray grn	9.25	10.50
1NJ9	D3	30c brt bl	5.75	6.00
1NJ10	D3	50c gray	9.75	10.50
		Nos. 1NJ6-1NJ10 (5)	28.25	30.00

A. M. G. ISSUE

Issued jointly by the Allied Military Government of the United States and Great Britain, for civilian use in areas under Allied occupation.

OS1

Type I. Thick paper, white gum.
Type II. Medium paper, yellow gum.
Type III. Medium paper, white gum.

Perf. 11, 11½ and Compound

1945-46 **Litho.** **Unwmk.**

Type III, Brunswick Printing

Size: 19-19½x22-22½mm

3N1	OS1	1pf sl gray	15	20
3N2	OS1	3pf dull lilac	15	15
3N3	OS1	4pf lt gray	15	15
3N4	OS1	5pf emerald	15	15
3N5	OS1	6pf yellow	15	15
3N6	OS1	8pf orange	60	1.75
3N7	OS1	10pf yel brn	15	15
3N8	OS1	12pf rose vio	15	15
3N9	OS1	15pf rose car	15	15
3N10	OS1	16pf dp Prus grn	15	32
3N11	OS1	20pf blue	15	15
3N12	OS1	24pf chocolate	15	42
3N13	OS1	25pf brt ultra	15	1.40

Size: 21½x25mm

3N14	OS1	30pf olive	18	50
3N15	OS1	40pf dp mag	15	15
3N16	OS1	42pf green	15	15
3N17	OS1	50pf sl grn	15	25
3N18	OS1	60pf vio brn	15	35
3N19	OS1	80pf bl blk	15.00	25.00

Size: 25x29½mm

3N20	OS1	1m dk ol grn ('46)	1.75	4.50
		Nos. 3N1-3N20 (20)	19.93	36.19

Most of Nos. 3N1-3N20 exist imperforate and part-perforate.

Type I, Washington Printing

Size: 19-19½x22-22½mm

Perf. 11

3N2a	OS1	3pf lilac	15	15
3N3a	OS1	4pf lt gray	15	15
3N4a	OS1	5pf emerald	15	15
3N5a	OS1	6pf yellow	15	15
3N6a	OS1	8pf dp org	15	15
3N7a	OS1	10pf brown	15	15
3N8a	OS1	12pf rose vio	15	15
3N9a	OS1	15pf cerise	15	15
3N13a	OS1	25pf brt ultra	15	15
		Set value	45	70

Type II, London Printing

Size: 19-19½x22-22½mm

Photo.

Perf. 14, 14½ and Compound

3N2b	OS1	3pf lilac	15	15
3N3b	OS1	4pf lt gray	15	15
3N4b	OS1	5pf dp emer	30	30
3N5b	OS1	6pf org yel	15	15
3N6b	OS1	8pf dk org	30	38
3N8b	OS1	12pf rose vio	15	15
		Set value	80	1.00

ISSUED UNDER FRENCH OCCUPATION

Coats of Arms

Rhine Province — OS3

Palatinate District — OS4

Saarland OS5

Württemberg OS6

Allied Military Government stamps can be mounted in Scott's Germany Part I Album.

Baden OS7

Johann Wolfgang von Goethe OS8

Friedrich von Schiller OS9

Heinrich Heine OS10

Perf. 14x13½

1945-46 **Unwmk.** **Typo.**

4N1	OS3	1pf blk, grn & lem	15	15
4N2	OS4	3pf dk red, blk & dl yel	15	15
4N3	OS6	5pf brn, blk & org yel	15	15
4N4	OS7	8pf brn, yel & red	15	15
4N5	OS3	10pf brn, grn & lem	5.00	*12.50*
4N6	OS4	12pf red, blk & org yel	15	15
4N7	OS5	15pf blk, ultra & red ('46)	15	15
4N8	OS6	20pf red, org yel & blk	15	15
4N9	OS5	24pf blk, dp ultra & red ('46)	15	15
4N10	OS7	30pf blk, org yel & red	15	15

Engr. *Perf. 13*

4N11	OS8	1m lil brn	1.25	*3.00*
4N12	OS9	2m dp bl ('46)	1.00	*4.50*
4N13	OS10	5m dl red brn ('46)	1.25	*5.00*
		Nos. 4N1-4N13 (13)	9.85	

Exist imperf. Value for set of 13, $300.

BADEN

Johann Peter Hebel — OS1

Girl of Constance — OS2

Hans Baldung Grien — OS3

Rastatt Castle — OS4

Black Forest Scene OS5

Cathedral of Freiburg — OS6

1947 **Unwmk.** **Photo.** *Perf. 14*

5N1	OS1	2pf gray	15	15
5N2	OS2	3pf brown	15	15
5N3	OS3	10pf slate bl	15	15
5N4	OS1	12pf dk grn	15	15
5N5	OS2	15pf purple	15	15
5N6	OS4	16pf olive grn	15	40
5N7	OS3	20pf blue	15	15
5N8	OS4	24pf crimson	15	15
5N9	OS2	45pf cerise	15	15
5N10	OS1	60pf dp org	15	15
5N11	OS3	75pf brt bl	15	25
5N12	OS5	84pf bl grn	20	55
5N13	OS6	1m dk brn	20	15
		Set value	1.00	2.30

Festival Headdress OS7

Grand Duchess Stephanie OS8

1948

5N14	OS1	2pf dp org	15	24
5N15	OS2	6pf vio brn	15	15
5N16	OS7	8dpf bl grn	28	85
5N17	OS3	10pf dk brn	16	15
5N18	OS1	12pf crimson	16	15
5N19	OS2	15pf blue	20	32
5N20	OS4	16dpf violet	52	1.50
5N21	OS3	20dpf brown	2.00	85
5N22	OS4	24pf dk grn	28	15
5N23	OS7	30pf cerise	65	70
5N24	OS8	50pf brt bl	65	15
5N25	OS1	60dpf gray	2.00	24
5N26	OS5	84pf rose brn	4.00	3.00
5N27	OS6	1dm brt bl	4.00	3.00
		Nos. 5N14-5N27 (14)	15.20	11.45

Without "PF"

1948-49

5N28	OS1	2(pf) dp org	38	50
5N29	OS4	4(pf) violet	18	30
5N30	OS2	5(pf) blue	48	60
5N31	OS2	6(pf) vio brn	12.50	8.50
5N32	OS7	8(pf) rose brn	55	50
5N33	OS3	10(pf) dk grn	55	15
5N37	OS3	20(pf) cerise	90	25
5N38	OS4	40(pf) brown	35.00	*47.50*
5N39	OS1	80(pf) red	5.75	4.75
5N40	OS5	90(pf) rose brn	35.00	*65.00*
		Nos. 5N28-5N40 (10)	91.29	128.05

Constance Cathedral and Insel Hotel OS9

Type I. Frameline thick and straight. Inscriptions thick. Shading dark. Upper part of "B" narrow.

Type II. Frameline thin and zigzag. Inscriptions fine. Shading light. Upper part of "B" wide.

1949, June 22

5N41	OS9	30pf dk bl (I)	15.00	*60.00*
a.		Type II	*375.00*	*1,750.*

Issued to publicize the International Engineering Congress, Constance, 1949.

Conradin Kreutzer — OS10

1949, Aug. 27

5N42	OS10	10pf dark green	1.40	*2.50*

Conradin Kreutzer (1780-1849), composer.

Stagecoach OS11

Design: 20pf, Post bus, trailer and plane.

1949, Sept. 17

5N43	OS11	10pf green	2.75	*6.75*
5N44	OS11	20pf red brown	2.75	*6.50*

Centenary of German postage stamps.

Globe, Olive Branch and Post Horn — OS12

1949, Oct. 4

5N45	OS12	20pf dark red	2.50	*10.00*
5N46	OS12	30pf deep blue	2.50	*5.00*

75th anniv. of the UPU.

OCCUPATION SEMI-POSTAL STAMPS

Arms of Baden OSP1

Cornhouse, Freiburg OSP2

Perf. 13½x14

1949, Feb. 25 Photo. Unwmk.

Cross in Red

5NB1	OSP1	10 + 20pf grn	15.00	*52.50*
5NB2	OSP1	20 + 40pf lilac	15.00	*52.50*
5NB3	OSP1	30 + 60pf blue	15.00	*52.50*
5NB4	OSP1	40 + 80pf gray	15.00	*52.50*
a.		Sheet of 4, imperf.	90.00	*1,400.*

The surtax was for the Red Cross.

No. 5NB4a measures 90x101mm. and contains one each of Nos. 5NB1 to 5NB4, with red inscription in upper margin and no gum.

1949, Feb. 24 *Perf. 14*

Designs: 10pf+20pf, Cathedral tower. 20pf+30pf, Trumpeting angel. 30pf+50pf, Fish pool.

5NB5	OSP2	4 + 16pf dk vio	5.00	*25.00*
5NB6	OSP2	10 + 20pf dk grn	7.25	*27.50*
5NB7	OSP2	20 + 30pf car	8.75	*27.50*
5NB8	OSP2	30 + 50pf blue	14.00	*32.50*
a.		Sheet of 4, #5NB5-5NB8	47.50	*175.00*
b.		As "a," imperf.	47.50	*175.00*

The surtax was for the reconstruction of historical monuments in Freiburg.

Carl Schurz at Rastatt OSP3

Goethe OSP4

1949, Aug. 23

5NB9	OSP3	10 + 5pf green	6.00	*22.50*
5NB10	OSP3	20 + 10pf cer	6.00	*22.50*
5NB11	OSP3	30 + 15pf blue	6.00	*22.50*

Centenary of the surrender of Rastatt.

1949, Aug. 12

Various Portraits.

5NB12	OSP4	10 + 5pf green	5.50	*16.00*
5NB13	OSP4	20 + 10pf cer	5.50	*16.00*
5NB14	OSP4	30 + 15pf blue	6.75	*32.50*

Johann Wolfgang von Goethe (1749-1832).

RHINE PALATINATE

Beethoven OS1

Wilhelm E. F. von Ketteler OS2

Girl Carrying Grapes OS3

Porta Nigra, Trier OS4

Karl Marx OS5

"Devil's Table", Near Pirmasens OS6

Street Corner, St. Martin OS7

Cathedral of Worms OS8

Cathedral of Mainz OS9

Statue of Johann Gutenberg OS10

Gutenfels and Pfalzgrafenstein Castles on Rhine — OS11

Statue of Charlemagne — OS12

1947-48 Unwmk. Photo. *Perf. 14*

6N1	OS1	2pf gray	15	15
6N2	OS2	3pf dk brn	15	15
6N3	OS3	10pf slate blue	15	15
6N4	OS4	12pf green	15	15
6N5	OS5	15pf purple	15	15
6N6	OS6	16pf lt ol grn	15	15
6N7	OS7	20pf brt bl	15	15
6N8	OS8	24pf crimson	15	15
6N9	OS10	30pf cerise ('48)	15	30
6N10	OS9	45pf cerise	15	15
6N11	OS9	50pf blue ('48)	15	35
6N12	OS1	60pf deep org	15	15
6N13	OS10	75pf blue	15	15
6N14	OS11	84pf green	20	45
6N15	OS12	1m brown	20	18
		Set value	1.00	2.10

Exist imperf. Value for set, $600.

1948

6N16	OS1	2pf dp org	15	20
6N17	OS2	6pf vio brn	15	20
6N18	OS4	8dpf bl grn	24	1.00
6N19	OS3	10pf dk brn	24	15
6N20	OS4	12pf crim rose	22	15
6N21	OS5	15pf blue	55	50
6N22	OS6	16dpf dk vio	28	85
6N23	OS7	20dpf brown	55	60
6N24	OS8	24pf green	25	15
6N25	OS9	30pf cerise	52	20
6N26	OS10	50pf brt bl	80	20
6N27	OS1	60dpf gray	5.50	22
6N28	OS11	84dpf rose brn	2.75	3.00
6N29	OS12	1dm brt bl	3.00	2.25
		Nos. 6N16-6N29 (14)	15.20	9.67

Exist imperf. Value for set, $600.

Types of 1947 Without "PF"

1948-49

6N30	OS1	2(pf) dp org	18	30
6N31	OS6	4(pf) vio ('49)	28	18
6N32	OS5	5(pf) bl ('49)	48	40
6N33	OS2	6(pf) vio brn	16.00	12.00
6N33A	OS4	8(pf) rose brn ('49)	45.00	*125.00*
6N34	OS3	10(pf) dk grn	50	18
a.		Imperf.	175.00	
6N35	OS7	20(pf) cerise	55	18
6N36	OS8	40(pf) brn ('49)	1.40	2.25
6N37	OS4	80(pf) red ('49)	1.75	3.75
6N38	OS11	90(pf) rose brn ('49)	2.75	*11.00*
		Nos. 6N30-6N38 (10)	68.89	*155.24*

Type of Baden, 1949

Designs as in Baden.

1949, Sept. 17

6N39	OS11	10pf green	3.75	*18.00*
6N40	OS11	20pf red brown	3.75	*18.00*

UPU Type of Baden, 1949

1949, Oct. 4

6N41	OS12	20pf dark red	2.75	*9.25*
6N42	OS12	30pf deep blue	2.75	5.75

OCCUPATION SEMI-POSTAL STAMPS

St. Martin — OSP1

Design: 30pf+50pf, St. Christopher.

1948 Unwmk. Photo. *Perf. 14*

6NB1	OSP1	20pf + 30pf dp cl	65	*3.50*
6NB2	OSP1	30pf + 50pf dp bl	65	*3.50*

The surtax was to aid victims of an explosion at Ludwigshafen.

Type of Baden, 1949, Showing Arms of Rhine Palatinate

1949, Feb. 25 *Perf. 13½x14*

Cross in Red

6NB3	OSP1	10pf + 20pf grn	15.00	*70.00*
6NB4	OSP1	20pf + 40pf lil	15.00	*70.00*
6NB5	OSP1	30pf + 60pf bl	15.00	*70.00*
6NB6	OSP1	40pf + 80pf gray	15.00	*70.00*
a.		Sheet of 4, #6NB3-6NB6, imperf.	80.00	*1,400.*

The surtax was for the Red Cross.

No. 6NB6a measures 90x100mm and has no gum.

Goethe Type of Baden, 1949

Various Portraits.

1949, Aug. 12

6NB7	OSP4	10pf + 5pf green	3.00	*12.50*
6NB8	OSP4	20pf + 10pf cerise	3.00	*12.50*
6NB9	OSP4	30pf + 15pf blue	6.00	*27.50*

WURTTEMBERG

Friedrich von Schiller OS1

Castle of Bebenhausen, near Tübingen OS2

Friedrich Hölderlin OS3

Town Gate of Wangen (Allgäu) OS4

Lichtenstein Castle — OS5

Zwiefalten Church — OS6

1947-48 Unwmk. Photo. *Perf. 14*

8N1	OS1	2pf gray ('48)	15	15
8N2	OS3	3pf brn ('48)	15	15
8N3	OS4	10pf sl bl ('48)	15	15
8N4	OS1	12pf dk grn	15	15
8N5	OS3	15pf pur ('48)	15	15
8N6	OS2	16pf ol grn ('48)	15	18
8N7	OS4	20pf bl ('48)	15	15
8N8	OS2	24pf crimson	15	15
8N9	OS3	45pf cerise	15	15
8N10	OS1	60pf dp org ('48)	15	35
8N11	OS4	75pf brt bl	15	35
8N12	OS5	84pf bl grn	20	55
8N13	OS6	1m dk brn	30	35
		Set value	1.10	2.40

The 12pf and 60pf exist imperf. Value, each $35.

Waldsee OS7

Ludwig Uhland OS8

1948

8N14	OS1	2pf dp org	15	48
8N15	OS3	6pf vio brn	15	15
8N16	OS7	8dpf bl grn	48	*1.10*
8N17	OS4	10pf dk brn	15	28
8N18	OS1	12pf crimson	15	15
8N19	OS3	15pf blue	35	22
8N20	OS2	16dpf dk vio	42	*1.10*
8N21	OS4	20dpf brown	1.00	70
8N22	OS2	24pf dk grn	38	15
8N23	OS7	30pf cerise	60	22
8N24	OS8	50pf dull blue	1.25	22
8N25	OS1	60dpf gray	6.25	22
8N26	OS5	84dpf rose brn	2.50	2.00
8N27	OS6	1dm brt bl	2.50	2.00
		Nos. 8N14-8N27 (14)	16.33	8.99

The 2pf, 10pf, 24pf and 30pf exist imperf. Value, each $35.

Without "PF"

1948-49

8N28	OS1	2(pf) dp org	65	25
8N29	OS2	4(pf) violet	65	25
8N30	OS3	5(pf) blue	1.10	60
8N31	OS3	6(pf) vio brn	3.75	3.00
8N32	OS7	8(pf) rose brn	3.75	90
8N33	OS4	10(pf) dk grn	3.75	15
8N34	OS4	20(pf) cerise	3.75	15
8N35	OS2	40(pf) brown	11.00	*27.50*
8N36	OS1	80(pf) red	30.00	27.50
8N37	OS5	90(pf) rose brn	37.50	*75.00*
		Nos. 8N28-8N37 (10)	95.90	*135.30*

The 4pf and 6pf exist imperf. Value, respectively $100 and $37.50.

Type of Baden, 1949

Designs as in Baden.

1949, Sept. 17

8N38	OS11	10pf green	3.75	*6.25*
8N39	OS11	20pf red brown	3.75	*8.50*

UPU Type of Baden, 1949

1949, Oct. 4

8N40	OS12	20pf dark red	2.75	*9.00*
8N41	OS12	30pf deep blue	2.75	3.50

OCCUPATION SEMI-POSTAL STAMPS

Type of Baden, 1949

Design: Arms of Württemberg.

Perf. 13½x14

1949, Feb. 25 Photo. Unwmk.

Cross in Red

8NB1	OSP1	10 + 20pf grn	22.50	*85.00*
8NB2	OSP1	20 + 40pf lilac	22.50	*85.00*
8NB3	OSP1	30 + 60pf blue	22.50	*85.00*
8NB4	OSP1	40 + 80pf gray	22.50	*85.00*
a.		Sheet of 4, imperf.	125.00	*1,250.*

The surtax was for the Red Cross.

No. 8NB4a measures 90x100mm and contains one each of Nos. 8NB1 to 8NB4, with red inscription in upper margin and no gum.

View of Isny OSP1

Design: 20pf+6pf, Skier and village.

Wmk. 116

1949, Feb. 11 Typo. *Perf. 14*

8NB5	OSP1	10 + 4pf dl grn	2.50	*6.50*
8NB6	OSP1	20 + 6pf red brn	2.50	*6.50*

Issued to commemorate the 1948-49 German Ski Championship at Isny im Allgau.

Gustav Werner — OSP2

1949, Sept. 4

8NB7	OSP2	10 + 5pf bl grn	3.00	*7.25*
8NB8	OSP2	20 + 10pf claret	3.00	*7.25*

Issued to commemorate the centenary of the founding of Gustav Werner's "Christianity in Action" and "House of Brotherhood."

Goethe Type of Baden, 1949

Various Portraits.

1949, Aug. 12

8NB9	OSP4	10 + 5pf green	4.00	*11.50*
8NB10	OSP4	20 + 10pf cerise	5.00	*18.00*
8NB11	OSP4	30 + 15pf blue	6.50	*27.50*

BERLIN

Issued for Use in the American, British and French Occupation Sectors of Berlin

Germany Nos. 557-569, 571-573 Overprinted Diagonally in Black

a

Wmk. 284

1948, Sept. 1 Typo. *Perf. 14*

9N1	A120	2pf brn blk	90	*1.50*
9N2	A120	6pf purple	60	50
9N3	A121	8pf red	60	50
9N4	A121	10pf yel grn	38	26
9N5	A122	12pf gray	38	26
9N6	A120	15pf chocolate	3.50	*26.00*
9N7	A123	16pf dk bl grn	65	55
9N8	A121	20pf blue	1.40	*2.50*
9N9	A123	24pf brn org	52	25
9N10	A120	25pf org yel	9.50	*30.00*
9N11	A122	30pf red	1.50	*3.25*
9N12	A121	40pf red vio	1.10	1.10
9N13	A123	50pf ultra	3.50	*9.00*
9N14	A122	60pf red brn	1.10	15
9N15	A122	80pf dark blue	3.25	*14.00*
9N16	A123	84pf emerald	7.75	*57.50*

Germany Nos. 574-577 Overprinted Diagonally in Black

b

Engr.

9N17	A124	1m olive	19.00	*82.50*
9N18	A124	2m dk brn vio	27.50	*300.00*
9N19	A124	3m cop red	35.00	*425.00*
9N20	A124	5m dark blue	35.00	*450.00*
		Nos. 9N1-9N20 (20)	153.13	

Forged overprints and cancellations are found on Nos. 9N1-9N20.

Stamps of Germany 1947-48 with "a" Overprint in Red

1948-49 Wmk. 284 Typo. *Perf. 14*

9N21	A120	2pf brn blk ('49)	1.00	1.40
9N22	A120	6pf pur ('49)	5.25	1.40
9N23	A121	8pf red ('49)	19.00	2.75
9N24	A121	10pf yel grn	1.00	42
9N25	A120	15pf chocolate	2.50	1.40
9N26	A121	20pf blue	1.00	55
9N27	A120	25pf org yel ('49)	47.50	30.00
9N28	A122	30pf red ('49)	30.00	4.50
9N29	A121	40pf red vio ('49)	30.00	7.50
9N30	A123	50pf ultra ('49)	30.00	4.50
9N31	A122	60pf red brn	3.75	42
9N32	A122	80pf dk bl ('49)	52.50	5.75

With "b" Overprint in Red

Engr.

9N33	A124	1m olive	225.00	300.00
9N34	A124	2m dk brn vio	125.00	110.00
		Nos. 9N21-9N34 (14)	573.50	470.59

Forgeries exist of the overprints on Nos. 9N21-9N34. No. 9N33 exists imperf.

Statue of Heinrich von Stephan

OS1 OS2

1949, Apr. 9 Litho. *Perf. 14*

9N35	OS1	12pf gray	4.50	3.25
9N36	OS1	16pf bl grn	11.00	4.75
9N37	OS1	24pf org brn	8.75	28
9N38	OS1	50pf brn ol	65.00	10.00
9N39	OS1	60pf brn red	67.50	10.00
9N40	OS2	1m olive	37.50	47.50
9N41	OS2	2m brn vio	45.00	24.00
		Nos. 9N35-9N41 (7)	239.25	99.78

75th anniv. of the UPU.

Brandenburg Gate, Berlin — OS3

Tempelhof Airport — OS4

Designs: 4pf, 8pf, 40pf, Schoeneberg, Rudolf Wilde Square. 5pf, 25pf, 5m, Tegel Castle. 6pf, 50pf, Reichstag Building. 10pf, 30pf, Cloisters, Kleist Park. 15pf, Tempelhof Airport. 20pf, 80pf, 90pf, Polytechnic College, Charlottenburg. 60pf, National Gallery. 2m, Gendarmen Square. 3m, Brandenburg Gate.

1949 Typo. Wmk. 284

Size: 22x18mm

9N42	OS3	1pf black	15	15
a.		Bklt. pane 5 + label	10.00	
b.		Tete beche	48	60
9N43	OS3	4pf yel brn	20	15
a.		Bklt. pane 5 + label	10.00	
b.		Tete beche	1.50	1.75
9N44	OS3	5pf bl grn	20	15
9N45	OS3	6pf red vio	35	70
9N46	OS3	8pf red org	52	70
9N47	OS3	10pf yel grn	42	15
a.		Bklt. pane 5 + label	42.50	
9N48	OS4	15pf chocolate	2.75	35
9N49	OS3	20pf red	1.90	15
a.		Bklt. pane 5 + label	42.50	
9N50	OS3	25pf orange	8.00	35
9N51	OS3	30pf vio bl	3.00	35
a.		Imperf.	*850.00*	
9N52	OS3	40pf lake	5.50	25
9N53	OS3	50pf olive	5.50	25
9N54	OS3	60pf red brn	19.00	15
9N55	OS3	80pf dark blue	4.50	60
9N56	OS3	90pf emerald	4.50	60

Engr.

Size: 29¼-29¾x24-24½mm

9N57	OS4	1m olive	8.00	35
9N58	OS4	2m brn vio	22.50	55
9N59	OS4	3m hn brn	80.00	2.25
9N60	OS4	5m dp bl	47.50	7.00
		Nos. 9N42-9N60 (19)	214.49	15.20

See Nos. 9N101-9N102, 9N108-9N110.

Goethe and "Iphigenie" — OS5

Statue of Atlas, New York — OS6

Designs (Goethe and scenes from his works): 20pf, "Reineke Fuchs." 30pf, "Faust."

1949, July 29 Litho. *Perf. 14*

9N61	OS5	10pf green	55.00	40.00
9N62	OS5	20pf carmine	55.00	50.00
9N63	OS5	30pf ultra	10.00	25.00

Bicentenary of the birth of Johann Wolfgang von Goethe.

Germany Nos. 550, 565, 572 and 576 Surcharged "BERLIN" and New Value in Dark Green

1949, Aug. 1 Typo.

9N64	A119	5pf on 45pf	1.50	15
9N65	A123	10pf on 24pf	4.00	20
9N66	A122	20pf on 80pf	20.00	15.00

Engr.

9N67	A124	1m on 3m	62.50	16.00

1950, Oct. 1 Engr. Wmk. 116

9N68	OS6	20pf dk car	42.50	35.00

European Recovery Plan.

Albert Lortzing — OS7

Freedom Bell, Berlin — OS8

1951, Apr. 22

9N69	OS7	20pf red brown	30.00	47.50

Centenary of the death of Albert Lortzing, composer.

1951 *Perf. 14*

9N70	OS8	5pf chocolate	1.25	*1.50*
9N71	OS8	10pf dp grn	4.25	*7.25*
9N72	OS8	20pf rose red	1.50	*3.25*
9N73	OS8	30pf blue	16.00	*27.50*
9N74	OS8	40pf rose vio	6.75	*16.00*
		Nos. 9N70-9N74 (5)	29.75	55.50

Re-engraved

1951-52

9N75	OS8	5pf ol bis ('52)	1.25	85
9N76	OS8	10pf yel grn	3.00	3.50
9N77	OS8	20pf brt red	12.00	12.50
9N78	OS8	30pf bl ('52)	24.00	26.00
9N79	OS8	40pf dp car ('52)	10.00	12.00
		Nos. 9N75-9N79 (5)	50.25	54.85

Bell clapper moved from left to right. Imprint "L. Schnell" in lower margin.

No. 9N76 exists imperf. Value $900.

See Nos. 9N94-9N98.

Ludwig van Beethoven OS9

Olympic Symbols OS10

1952, Mar. 26 Engr. Unwmk.

9N80	OS9	30pf blue	22.50	20.00

125th anniversary of the death of Ludwig van Beethoven.

1952, June 20 Litho. Wmk. 116

9N81	OS10	4pf yel brn	45	50
9N82	OS10	10pf green	4.50	5.00
9N83	OS10	20pf rose red	8.00	9.25

Issued to publicize the pre-Olympic Festival Day, June 20, 1952.

Carl Friedrich Zelter — OS11

Arms Breaking Chains — OS12

Portraits: 5pf, Otto Lilienthal. 6pf, Walter Rathenau. 8pf, Theodor Fontane. 10pf, Adolph von Menzel. 15pf, Rudolf Virchow. 20pf, Werner von Siemens. 25pf, Karl Friedrich Schinkel. 30pf, Max Planck. 40pf, Wilhelm von Humboldt.

1952-53 Engr. Wmk. 284

9N84	OS11	4pf brown	15	15
9N85	OS11	5pf dp bl ('53)	25	32
9N86	OS11	6pf choc ('53)	2.00	5.25
9N87	OS11	8pf hn brn ('53)	1.10	1.65
9N88	OS11	10pf dp grn	1.25	45
9N89	OS11	15pf pur ('53)	5.00	9.25
9N90	OS11	20pf brn red	1.25	52
9N91	OS11	25pf dp ol ('53)	19.00	3.75
9N92	OS11	30pf brn vio ('53)	6.00	4.50
9N93	OS11	40pf blk ('53)	10.00	2.00
		Nos. 9N84-9N93 (10)	46.00	27.84

Bell Type of 1951-1952

Second Re-engraving

1953 Wmk. 284 *Perf. 14*

9N94	OS8	5pf brown	60	60
9N95	OS8	10pf dp grn	1.40	1.40
9N96	OS8	20pf brt red	3.50	3.00
9N97	OS8	30pf blue	6.25	10.00
9N98	OS8	40pf rose vio	24.00	25.00
		Nos. 9N94-9N98 (5)	35.75	40.00

Bell clapper hangs straight down. Marginal imprint omitted.

For overprint and surcharge see Nos. 9N106, 9NB17.

1953, Aug. 17 **Typo.**

Design: 30pf, Brandenburg Gate.

9N99	OS12	20pf black	1.90	1.00
9N100	OS12	30pf dp car	10.00	15.00

Issued to commemorate the strike of East German workers, June 17, 1953.

Similar to Type of 1949

Designs: 4pf, Exposition halls. 20pf, Olympic Stadium, Berlin.

1953-54 **Wmk. 284** ***Perf. 14***

9N101	OS3	4pf yel brn ('54)	1.40	1.25
9N102	OS3	20pf red	30.00	25

Catalogue values for unused stamps in this section, from this point to the end of the section, are for Never Hinged items.

Allied Council Building — OS13

1954, Jan. 25 **Litho.**

9N103	OS13	20pf red	7.00	4.00

Issued to publicize the Four Power Conference, Berlin, 1954.

Prof. Ernst Reuter (1889-1953), Mayor of Berlin (1948-53) OS14

1954, Jan. 18 **Engr.** **Wmk. 284**

9N104	OS14	20pf chocolate	7.00	1.25

See No. 9N174.

Ottmar Mergenthaler and Linotype — OS15

1954, May 11

9N105	OS15	10pf dk bl grn	1.75	1.75

Issued to commemorate the centenary of the birth of Ottmar Mergenthaler.

No. 9N96 Overprinted in Black

Wahl des Bundespräsidenten in Berlin 17. Juli 1954

1954, July 17 ***Perf. 13½x14***

9N106	OS8	20pf brt red	3.00	3.00

Issued to publicize the West German presidential election held in Berlin July 17, 1954.

Berlin stamps can be mounted in Scott's Germany Part III Album.

Germany in Bondage OS16

Richard Strauss OS17

1954, July 20 **Typo.**

9N107	OS16	20pf car & gray	4.00	4.25

10th anniv. of the attempted assassination of Adolf Hitler.

Similar to Type of 1949

Designs: 7pf, Exposition halls. 40pf, Memorial library. 70pf, Hunting lodge, Grunewald.

1954 **Wmk. 284** ***Perf. 14***

9N108	OS3	7pf aqua	6.00	24
9N109	OS3	40pf rose lil	10.00	3.25
9N110	OS3	70pf ol grn	90.00	17.50

1954, Sept. 18 **Engr.**

9N111	OS17	40pf vio bl	9.50	2.50

5th anniv. of the death of Richard Strauss, composer.

Early Forge — OS18

1954, Sept. 25

9N112	OS18	20pf redsh brn	7.50	2.00

Issued to commemorate the centenary of the death of August Borsig, industrial leader.

M. S. Berlin and Arms of Berlin OS19

Wilhelm Furtwängler OS20

1955, Mar. 12 **Wmk. 284**

9N113	OS19	10pf Prus grn	95	28
9N114	OS19	25pf vio bl	5.00	2.50

Issued to publicize the resumption of shipping under West German ownership.

Perf. 13½x14

1955, Sept. 17 **Unwmk.**

9N115	OS20	40pf ultra	15.00	12.00

Issued to honor the conductor Wilhelm Furtwangler and to publicize the Berlin Music Festival, September 1955.

Arms of Berlin OS21 OS22

1955, Oct. 17 **Litho.** **Wmk. 304**

9N116	OS21	10pf red, org yel & blk	45	18
9N117	OS21	20pf red, org yel & blk	4.00	3.75

Meeting of the German Bundestag in Berlin, Oct. 17-22, 1955.

1956, Mar. 16

9N118	OS22	10pf red, ocher & blk	1.10	25
9N119	OS22	25pf red, ocher & blk	3.50	2.50

Meeting of the German Bundesrat in Berlin Mar. 16, 1956.

Radio Station, Berlin (OS23 has no top inscription. OS24 has top inscription.) OS23 OS24

Free University OS25

Monument of the Great Elector Frederick William OS26

Designs: 1pf, 3pf, Brandenburg Gate. 5pf, General Post Office. 8pf, City Hall, Neukölln. 10pf, Kaiser Wilhelm Memorial Church. 15pf, Airlift memorial. 25pf, Lilienthal Monument. 30pf, Pfaueninsel Castle. 40pf, Charlottenburg Castle. 50pf, Reuter power plant. 60pf, Chamber of Commerce and Industry and Stock Exchange. 70pf, Schiller Theater. 3m, Congress Hall.

Typo.; Litho. (3pf, #9N122)

1956-63 **Wmk. 304** ***Perf. 14***

9N120	OS25	1pf gray ('57)	15	15
9N120A	OS25	3pf brt pur ('63)	15	15
9N121	OS25	5pf rose lil ('57)	15	15
9N122	OS23	7pf bl grn	5.00	1.50
9N123	OS24	7pf bl grn	15	15
9N124	OS24	8pf gray	18	35
9N125	OS24	8pf red org ('59)	15	15
9N126	OS24	10pf emerald	15	15
9N127	OS24	15pf chlky bl	15	16
9N128	OS25	20pf rose car	15	15
9N129	OS24	25pf dl red brn	18	35

Engr.

9N130	OS24	30pf gray grn ('57)	20	40
9N131	OS25	40pf lt ultra ('57)	4.75	4.00
9N132	OS24	50pf olive	42	60
9N133	OS25	60pf lt brn ('57)	55	75
9N134	OS25	70pf violet	17.50	7.50
9N135	OS26	1m olive	1.00	1.10

Size: 29x24½mm

9N136	OS25	3m rose cl ('58)	3.50	4.75
		Nos. 9N120-9N136 (18)	34.48	22.51

No. 9N120 exists on both ordinary and fluorescent paper; No. 9N120A on fluorescent paper only; others on ordinary paper.

Engineers' Society Emblem OS27

Paul Lincke OS28

1956, May 12 **Engr.** ***Perf. 14***

9N140	OS27	10pf dk grn	1.40	1.00
9N141	OS27	20pf dk red	3.25	3.50

Cent. of Soc. of German Civil Engineers.

1956, Sept. 3

9N142	OS28	20pf dk red	2.00	2.25

Issued to commemorate the 10th anniversary of the death of Paul Lincke, composer.

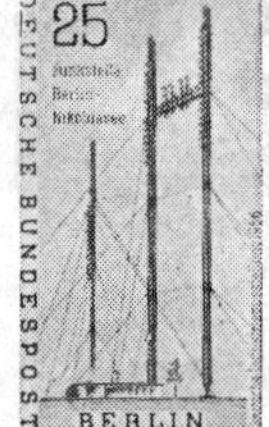

Radio Station, Berlin-Nikolassee OS29

Spandau, 1850 OS30

1956, Sept. 15

9N143	OS29	25pf brown	5.50	5.75

Issued to publicize the German Industrial Fair, Berlin, Sept. 15-30.

1957, Mar. 7

9N144	OS30	20pf gray ol & brn red	55	45

725th anniversary of Spandau.

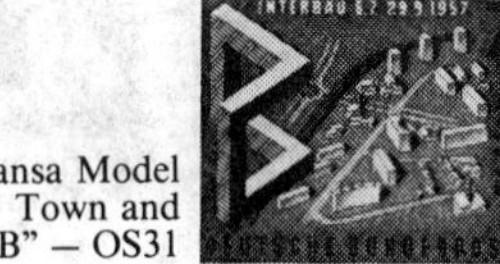

Hansa Model Town and "B" — OS31

Designs: 20pf, View of exposition grounds and "B." 40pf, Auditorium and "B."

1957 **Engr.**

9N145	OS31	7pf vio brn	15	15
9N146	OS31	20pf carmine	45	45
9N147	OS31	40pf vio bl	75	85

Issued to publicize the International Building Show, Berlin, July 6-Sept. 29, 1957.

Friedrich Karl von Savigny, Law Teacher OS32

Uta Statue, Naumburg Cathedral OS33

Portraits: 7pf, Theodor Mommsen, historian. 8pf, Heinrich Zille, painter. 10pf, Ernst Reuter, mayor of Berlin. 15pf, Fritz Haber, chemist. 20pf, Friedrich Schleiermacher, theologian. 25pf, Max Reinhardt, theatrical director. 40pf, Alexander von Humboldt, naturalist and geographer. 50pf, Christian Daniel Rauch, sculptor.

1957-59 **Wmk. 304** ***Perf. 14***

Portraits in Brown

9N148	OS32	7pf bl grn ('58)	15	15
9N149	OS32	8pf gray ('58)	15	15
9N150	OS32	10pf grn ('58)	15	15
9N151	OS32	15pf dk bl	45	35
9N152	OS32	20pf car ('58)	15	15
9N153	OS32	25pf magenta	58	52
9N154	OS32	30pf ol grn	90	90
9N155	OS32	40pf blue ('59)	26	28
9N156	OS32	50pf olive	3.00	2.50
		Nos. 9N148-9N156 (9)	5.79	5.15

Issued to honor famous men of Berlin.

See No. 9NB19.

1957, Aug. 6
9N157 OS33 25pf brn red 45 45

Issued to publicize the annual meeting of the East German Culture Society in Berlin.

"Unity and Justice and Liberty" OS34

Postilion 1897-1925 OS35

1957, Oct. 15 **Litho.**
9N158 OS34 10pf multi 32 40
9N159 OS34 20pf multi 1.50 1.90

Issued to commemorate the first meeting of the third German Bundesrat, Berlin, Oct. 15.

1957, Oct. 23 **Wmk. 304** ***Perf. 14***
9N160 OS35 20pf multi 50 45

Issued for Stamp Day and BEPHILA stamp exhibition, Berlin, Oct. 23-27.

World Veterans' Federation Emblem OS36

Christ and the Cosmos OS37

1957, Oct. 28
9N161 OS36 20pf bl grn, ol grn & yel 55 45

Issued to publicize the 7th General Assembly of the World Veterans' Federation, Berlin, Oct. 24 - Nov. 1.

1958, Aug. 13
9N162 OS37 10pf lt bl grn & blk 20 22
9N163 OS37 20pf rose lil & blk 50 50

Issued in honor of the 78th German Catholics Meeting, Berlin, Aug. 13-17.

Prof. Otto Suhr (1894-1957), Mayor of Berlin (1955-57) OS38

1958, Aug. 30 **Engr.** ***Perf. 14***
9N164 OS38 20pf rose red 60 70

Pres. Heuss Type of Germany, 1959

1959 **Litho., Engraved (40pf, 70pf)**
9N165 A208 7pf bl grn 15 15
9N166 A208 10pf green 28 15
9N167 A208 20pf dk car rose 65 15
9N168 A208 40pf blue 2.00 2.50
9N169 A208 70pf dl pur 6.75 8.50
Nos. 9N165-9N169 (5) 9.83 11.45

Nos. 9N168-9N169 were issued in sheets of 100 and in coils. Every fifth coil stamp has a control number on the back.

An enhanced introduction to the Scott Catalogue begins on Page 1A. A thorough understanding of the material presented there will greatly aid your use of the catalogue itself.

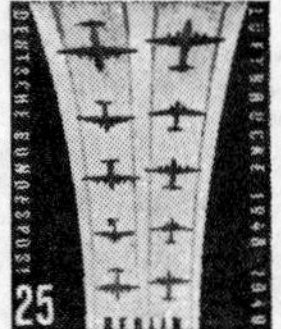
Aerial Bridge to Berlin — OS39

Globe and Brandenburg Gate — OS40

1959, May 12 **Engr.**
9N170 OS39 25pf mar & blk 22 20

10th anniversary of Berlin Airlift.

1959, June 18 **Litho.** ***Perf. 14***
9N171 OS40 20pf lt bl & red 18 20

Issued to publicize the 14th International Municipal Congress, Berlin, June 18-23.

Friedrich von Schiller (1759-1805), Poet — OS41

1959, Nov. 10 **Engr.** **Wmk. 304**
9N172 OS41 20pf dl red & brn 15 15

Dr. Robert Koch (1843-1910), Bacteriologist OS42

Hans Böckler (1875-1951), Labor Leader OS43

1960, May 27 ***Perf. 14***
9N173 OS42 20pf rose lake 15 15

Mayor Type of 1954

Portrait: Dr. Walther Carl Rudolf Schreiber, Mayor of Berlin, 1953-54.

1960, June 30 **Wmk. 304** ***Perf. 14***
9N174 OS14 20pf brn car 42 42

1961, Feb. 16 **Litho.** ***Perf. 14***
9N175 OS43 20pf dk brick red & blk 15 15

Issued to honor Hans Böckler (1875-1951), labor leader, on the 10th anniversary of his death, Feb. 26, 1961.

Fluorescent Paper
was introduced for all stamps, starting with No. 9N176, and including Nos. 9N120 and 9N120A.

Albrecht Dürer — OS44

Louise Schroeder — OS45

Portraits: 5pf, Albertus Magnus. 7pf, St. Elizabeth of Thuringia. 8pf, Johann Gutenberg. 15pf, Martin Luther. 20pf, Johann Sebastian Bach. 25pf, Balthasar Neumann. 30pf, Immanuel Kant. 40pf, Gotthold Ephraim Lessing. 50pf, Johann Wolfgang von Goethe. 60pf, Friedrich von Schiller. 70pf, Ludwig van Beethoven. 80pf, Heinrich von Kleist. 1m, Annette von Droste-Hülshoff. 2m, Gerhart Hauptmann.

1961-62 **Typo.** **Wmk. 304**
9N176 OS44 5pf olive 15 15
9N177 OS44 7pf dk bis 15 15
9N178 OS44 8pf lilac 15 15
9N179 OS44 10pf ol grn 15 15
b. Tete beche pair 70 65
9N180 OS44 15pf blue 15 15
9N181 OS44 20pf dk red 15 15
9N182 OS44 25pf org brn 15 15

Engr.
9N183 OS44 30pf gray 18 32
9N184 OS44 40pf blue 38 52
9N185 OS44 50pf red brn 38 52
9N186 OS44 60pf dk car rose ('62) 38 52
9N187 OS44 70pf green 48 45
9N188 OS44 80pf brown 3.00 3.00
9N189 OS44 1m vio bl 1.25 1.25
9N190 OS44 2m yel grn ('62) 1.65 1.50
Nos. 9N176-9N190 (15) 8.75 9.13

Nos. 9N176-9N182, 9N184 and 9N187 were issued in sheets and in coils. Every fifth coil stamp has a black control number on the back.

1961, June 3 **Engr.** ***Perf. 14***
9N192 OS45 20pf dk brn 15 15

Issued to honor Louise Schroeder, acting mayor of Berlin (1947-1948).

Synod Emblem and St. Mary's Church — OS46

Berlin Bear with Record, TV Set and Radio Tower — OS47

Design: 20pf, Emblem and Kaiser Wilhelm Memorial Church.

1961, July 19 **Litho.** **Wmk. 304**
9N193 OS46 10pf grn & vio 15 15
9N194 OS46 20pf rose cl & vio 16 18
Set value 24 26

10th meeting of German Protestants (Evangelical Synod), Berlin, July 19-23.

1961, Aug. 3 **Engr.**
9N195 OS47 20pf brn red & dk brn 15 15

German Radio, Television and Phonograph Exhibition, Berlin, Aug. 25-Sept. 3.

Berlin, 1650 — OS48

Views of Old Berlin: 10pf, Spree and Waisenbrücke (Orphans' Bridge). 15pf, Mauer Street, 1780. 20pf, Berlin Palace, 1703. 25pf, Potsdam Square, 1825. 40pf, Bellevue Palace, 1800. 50pf, Fischer Bridge, 1830. 60pf, Halle Gate, 1880. 70pf, Parochial Church, 1780. 80pf, University, 1825. 90pf, Opera House, 1780. 1m, Grunewald Lake, 1790.

1962-63 **Wmk. 304** ***Perf. 14***
9N196 OS48 7pf dk gray & gldn brn 15 15
9N197 OS48 10pf grn & dk gray 15 15
9N198 OS48 15pf bluish gray & dk bl ('63) 15 15
9N199 OS48 20pf org brn & sep 15 15
9N200 OS48 25pf ol & gray ('63) 15 15
9N201 OS48 40pf bluish gray & ultra 18 15
9N202 OS48 50pf gray & dk brn ('63) 18 18
9N203 OS48 60pf gray & car rose ('63) 20 24
9N204 OS48 70pf dk gray & lil 22 28
9N205 OS48 80pf dk gray & dk red ('63) 24 30
9N206 OS48 90pf sep & brn org ('63) 24 35
9N207 OS48 1m ol gray & dp grn 45 60
Set value 2.05 2.40

Gelber Hund, 1912, and Boeing 707 — OS49

Berlin Bear and Radio Tower — OS50

1962, Sept. 12 **Litho.**
9N208 OS49 60pf brt bl & blk 28 35

50th anniv. of German airmail service.

1963, July 24 **Unwmk.** ***Perf. 14***
9N209 OS50 20pf bl, vio bl & gray 15 16

German Radio, Television and Phonograph Exhibition, Berlin, Aug. 30-Sept. 8.

Schöneberg City Hall, John F. Kennedy Place, Berlin — OS51

1964, May 30 **Engr.** **Wmk. 304**
9N210 OS51 20pf dk brn, *cr* 15 16

700th anniv. of the Schöneberg district of Berlin. The Senate and House of Representatives of West Berlin meet at Schöneberg City Hall.

Lübke Type of Germany, 1964

1964, July 1 **Litho.** **Unwmk.**
9N211 A247 20pf carmine 15 15
9N212 A247 40pf ultra 18 18
Set value 26 26

See Nos. 9N263-9N264.

Capitals Type of Germany

Design: Reichstag Building, Berlin.

1964, Sept. 14 **Litho.** ***Perf. 14***
9N213 A245 20pf bl, blk & grn 15 16

Kennedy Type of Germany

1964, Nov. 21 **Engr.** **Wmk. 304**
9N214 A255 40pf dk bl 16 15

Castle Gate, Ellwangen — OS52

Designs (German buildings through 12 centuries): 10pf, Wall pavilion, Zwinger, Dresden. 15pf, Tegel Castle, Berlin. 20pf, Portico, Lorsch. 40pf, Trifels Fortress, Palatinate. 60pf, Treptow Gate, Neubrandenburg. 70pf, Osthofen Gate, Soest. 80pf, Elling Gate, Weissenburg.

1964-65 **Typo.** **Unwmk.**
9N215 OS52 10pf brn ('65) 15 15
b. Tete beche pair 50 50
9N216 OS52 15pf dk grn ('65) 15 15
9N217 OS52 20pf brn red ('65) 15 15

Engr.
9N218 OS52 40pf vio bl ('65) 35 40
9N219 OS52 50pf ol bis 75 85
9N220 OS52 60pf rose red 55 60
9N221 OS52 70pf dk grn ('65) 1.25 1.40
9N222 OS52 80pf chocolate 70 75
Nos. 9N215-9N222 (8) 4.05 4.45

Nos. 9N215-9N218, 9N221 were issued in sheets of 100 and in coils. Every fifth coil stamp has a black control number on the back.

Kaiser Wilhelm Memorial Church OS53

Nordertor, Flensburg OS54

The New Berlin: 15pf, German Opera House (horiz.). 20pf, Philharmonic Hall (horiz.). 30pf, Jewish Community Center (horiz.). 40pf, Regina Martyrum Memorial (horiz.). 50pf, Ernst Reuter Square (horiz.). 60pf, Europa Center. 70pf, School of Engineering (horiz.). 80pf, City Highway. 90pf, Planetarium and observatory (horiz.). 1m, Schaeferberg radio tower, Wannsee. 1.10m, University clinic, Steglitz (horiz.).

Engraved and Lithographed

1965-66 Unwmk. *Perf. 14*

9N223 OS53 10pf multi 15 15
9N224 OS53 15pf multi 15 15
9N225 OS53 20pf multi 15 15
9N226 OS53 30pf multi ('66) 16 15
9N227 OS53 40pf multi ('66) 28 20
9N228 OS53 50pf multi 30 22
9N229 OS53 60pf multi ('66) 30 25
9N230 OS53 70pf multi ('66) 38 30
9N231 OS53 80pf multi 42 30
9N232 OS53 90pf multi ('66) 50 35
9N233 OS53 1m multi ('66) 55 45
9N234 OS53 1.10m multi ('66) 60 60
Nos. 9N223-9N234 (12) 3.94 3.27

1966-69 Engr. *Perf. 14*

Designs: 5pf, Berlin Gate, Stettin. 8pf, Castle, Kaub on the Rhine. 10pf, Wall Pavilion, Zwinger, Dresden. 20pf, Portico, Lorsch. 40pf, Trifels Fortress, Palatinate. 50pf, Castle Gate, Ellwangen. 60pf, Treptow Gate, Neubrandenburg. 70pf, Osthofen Gate, Soest. 80pf, Elling Gate, Weissenburg. 90pf, Zschocke Ladies' Home, Königsberg. 1m, Melanchthon House, Wittenberg. 1.10m, Trinity Hospital, Hildeshelm. 1.30m, Tegel Castle, Berlin. 2m, Löwenberg Town Hall, interior view.

9N235 OS54 5pf olive 15 15
9N236 OS54 8pf car rose 15 15
9N237 OS54 10pf dk brn ('67) 15 15
9N238 OS54 20pf dk grn ('67) 15 15
9N239 OS54 30pf yel grn 15 15
9N240 OS54 30pf red ('67) 16 15
9N241 OS54 40pf ol bis ('67) 48 52
9N242 OS54 50pf bl ('67) 40 42
9N243 OS54 60pf dp org ('67) 1.25 1.25
9N244 OS54 70pf sl grn ('67) 55 60
9N245 OS54 80pf red brn ('67) 95 1.00
9N246 OS54 90pf black 55 60
9N247 OS54 1m dl bl 52 24
9N248 OS54 1.10m red brn 90 75
9N249 OS54 1.30m grn ('69) 1.25 1.25
9N250 OS54 2m purple 1.25 1.10
Nos. 9N235-9N250 (16) 9.01 8.63

Brandenburg Gate Type of Germany

1966-70 Typo. *Perf. 14*

9N251 A268 10pf chocolate 15 15
a. Bklt. pane of 10 (4 #9N251, 2 #9N252, 4 #9N253) 3.00
b. Tete beche pair 45 45
c. Bklt. pane of 6 (4 #9N251, 2 #9N253) ('70) 2.00
9N252 A268 20pf dp grn 15 15
a. Bklt pane of 4 (2 #9N252, 2 #9N253) ('70) 2.00
9N253 A268 30pf red 15 15
a. Tete beche pair 1.25 1.25
9N254 A268 50pf dk bl 60 50
9N255 A268 100pf dk bl ('67) 4.00 2.25
Nos. 9N251-9N255 (5) 5.05 3.20

Nos. 9N251-9N255 were issued in sheets of 100 and in coils. Every fifth coil stamp has a black control number on the back.

Young Man, by Conrat Meit, 1520 — OS55

Designs: 20pf, The Great Elector Friedrich Wilhelm (1640-88), head from monument by Andreas Schlüter. 30pf, The Evangelist Mark, by Tilman Riemenschneider. 50pf, Head of "Victory" from Brandenburg Gate, by Gottfried Schadow, 1793. 1m, Madonna, by Joseph Anton Feuchtmayer. 1.10m, Jesus and John, wood sculpture, anonymous, c. 1320.

1967 Engr. *Perf. 14*

9N256 OS55 10pf sep & lem 15 15
9N257 OS55 20pf sl grn & bluish gray 15 15
9N258 OS55 30pf brn & ol 15 15
9N259 OS55 50pf blk & gray 22 20
9N260 OS55 1m bl & chlky bl 40 38

Size: 22x40mm

9N261 OS55 1.10m brn & buff 48 50
Nos. 9N256-9N261 (6) 1.55 1.53

Issued to publicize Berlin art treasures.

Berlin Radio Tower and Television Screens — OS56

Lithographed and Engraved

1967, July 19 Unwmk. *Perf. 14*

9N262 OS56 30pf multi 15 15

25th German Radio, Television and Phonograph Exhibition, Berlin, Aug. 25-Sept. 3.

Lübke Type of Germany, 1964

1967, Oct. 14 Litho.

9N263 A247 30pf carmine 16 20
9N264 A247 50pf ultra 30 45

Old Court Building (Berlin Museum) OS57

Turners' Emblem OS58

1968, Mar. 16 Engr. *Perf. 14*

9N265 OS57 30pf black 18 20

500th anniv. of the Berlin Court of Appeal.

1968, Apr. 29 Litho. *Perf. 14*

9N266 OS58 20pf gray, blk & red 15 16

Issued to publicize the German Turner Festival, Berlin, May 28-June 3.

Newspaper Vendor by Christian Wilhelm Allers — OS59

19th Century Berliners: 5pf, Hack, by Heinrich Zille (horiz.). No. 9N269, Horse omnibus, coachman and passengers, 1890, by C. W. Allers. No. 9N270, Cobbler's apprentice, by Franz Kruger. No. 9N271, Cobbler, by Adolph von Menzel. No. 9N272, Blacksmiths, by Paul Meyerheim. No. 9N273, Three Ladies, by Franz Kruger. 50pf, Strollers at Brandenburg Gate, by Christian W. Allers.

1969 Engr. *Perf. 14*

9N267 OS59 5pf black 15 15
9N268 OS59 10pf dp brn 15 15
9N269 OS59 10pf brown 15 15
9N270 OS59 20pf dk ol grn 15 15
9N271 OS59 20pf green 15 15
9N272 OS59 30pf dk red brn 22 18
9N273 OS59 30pf red brn 16 15
9N274 OS59 50pf ultra 95 75
Set value 1.75 1.45

Souvenir Sheet

Berlin Zoo Animals — OS60

Designs: 10pf, Orangutan family. 20pf, White pelicans. 30pf, Gaur and calf. 50pf, Zebra and foal.

Engraved and Lithographed

1969, June 4 *Perf. 14*

9N275 OS60 Sheet of 4 1.75 1.75
a. 10pf bister & black 40 40
b. 20pf light green & black 40 40
c. 30pf lilac rose & black 40 40
d. 50pf blue & black 40 40

Issued to commemorate the 125th anniversary of the Berlin Zoo. The sheet was sold with a 20pf surtax for the benefit of the Zoo.

Australian Postman OS61

Joseph Joachim OS62

Designs: 20pf, African telephone operator. 30pf, Middle East telecommunications engineer. 50pf, Loading mail on plane.

1969, July 21 Litho. *Perf. 14*

9N276 OS61 10pf ol & ap grn 15 15
9N277 OS61 20pf dk brn, bis & brn 18 15
9N278 OS61 30pf vio blk & bis 25 20
9N279 OS61 50pf dk bl & bl 50 42

20th Congress of the Post Office Trade Union Federation, Berlin, July 7-11.

1969, Sept. 12 Photo. *Perf. 14*

Design: 50pf, Alexander von Humboldt, painting by Joseph Stieler.

9N280 OS62 30pf multi 30 28
9N281 OS62 50pf multi 45 42

Cent. of the Berlin Music School and honoring its 1st director, Joseph Joachim (1831-1907), violinist, conductor and composer; Alexander von Humboldt (1769-1859), naturalist and explorer.

1970, Jan. 7

Design: 20pf, Theodor Fontane, painting by Hanns Fechner.

9N282 OS62 20pf multi 20 16

150th anniv. of the birth of Theodor Fontane (1819-1898), poet and writer.
See No. 9N303.

Film Frame — OS63

Symbols of Dance, Theater & Art — OS64

1970, June 18 Photo. *Perf. 14*

9N283 OS63 30pf multi 30 25

20th International Film Festival.

President Heinemann Type of Germany Inscribed "Berlin"

1970-73 Engr. *Perf. 14*

9N284 A312 5pf dk gray 15 15
9N285 A312 8pf ol bis 65 80
9N286 A312 10pf brown 15 15
9N286A A312 15pf olive 15 15
9N287 A312 20pf green 15 15
9N288 A312 25pf dp yel grn 70 90
9N289 A312 30pf red brn 1.00 40
9N290 A312 40pf brn org 32 20
9N291 A312 50pf dk bl 35 24
9N292 A312 60pf blue 50 48
9N293 A312 70pf dk brn 45 55
9N294 A312 80pf sl grn 52 55
9N295 A312 90pf magenta 1.65 1.25
9N296 A312 1m olive 65 40
9N296A A312 110pf ol gray 70 65
9N297 A312 120pf ocher 65 75
9N298 A312 130pf ocher 90 80
9N298A A312 140pf dk bl grn 90 80
9N299 A312 150pf purple 1.00 80
9N300 A312 160pf orange 90 80
9N300A A312 170pf orange 1.10 80
9N300B A312 190pf dp cl 1.25 1.00
9N301 A312 2m dp vio 1.25 80
Nos. 9N284-9N301 (23) 16.04 13.57

Issue dates: 5pf, 1m, July 23. 10pf, 20pf, Oct. 23. 30pf, 90pf, 2m, Jan. 7, 1971. 8pf, 40pf, 50pf, 70pf, 80pf, Apr. 8, 1971. 60pf, June 25, 1971. 25pf, Aug. 27, 1971. 120pf, 160pf, Mar. 8, 1972. 15pf, 130pf, June 20, 1972. 150pf, July 5, 1972. 170pf, Sept. 11, 1972. 110pf, 140pf, 190pf, Jan. 16, 1973.

1970, Sept. 4 Litho. *Perf. 13½x14*

9N302 OS64 30pf gray & multi 28 28

20th Berlin Festival Weeks.

Portrait Type of 1969

Design: 30pf, Leopold von Ranke, by Julius Schrage.

1970, Oct. 23 Photo. *Perf. 13½x14*

9N303 OS62 30pf multi 32 32

175th anniversary of the birth of Leopold von Ranke (1795-1886), historian.

Imperial Eagle Type of Germany

1971, Jan. 18 Litho. *Perf. 13½x14*

9N304 A317 30pf org, red, gray & blk 25 25

Metropolitan Train, 1932 — OS65

Designs: 5pf, Suburban train, 1925. 10pf, Street cars, 1890. 20pf, Horsedrawn trolley. 50pf, Street car, 1950. 1m, Subway train, 1971.

1971 Litho. *Perf. 14*

9N305 OS65 5pf multi 15 15
9N306 OS65 10pf multi 15 15
9N307 OS65 20pf multi 20 20
9N308 OS65 30pf multi 35 35
9N309 OS65 50pf multi 1.00 1.00
9N310 OS65 1m multi 1.00 1.00
Nos. 9N305-9N310 (6) 2.85 2.85

Issue dates: 30pf, 1m, Jan. 18. Others, May 3.

Bagpipe Player, by Dürer — OS66

1971, May 21 Engr. *Perf. 14*

9N311 OS66 10pf blk & brn 16 16

500th anniversary of the birth of Albrecht Dürer (1471-1528), painter and engraver.

Score from 2nd Brandenburg Concerto and Bach — OS67

1971, July 14 Litho. *Perf. 14*

9N312 OS67 30pf buff, brn & sl 28 28

250th anniv. of 1st performance of Johann Sebastian Bach's 2nd Brandenburg Concerto.

Telecommunications Tower, Berlin — OS68

1971, July 14 Photo.

9N313 OS68 30pf dk bl, blk & car 28 28

Intl. Broadcasting Exhibition, Berlin.

Hermann von Helmholtz (1821-94), Scientist — OS69

1971, Aug. 27

9N314 OS69 25pf multi 30 30

See Nos. 9N332-9N333, 9N341.

Souvenir Sheet

Racing Cars — OS70

1971, Aug. 27 Litho. *Perf. 14*

9N315 OS70	Sheet of 4	1.25	1.25
a.	10pf Opel racer	30	30
b.	25pf Auto Union racer	30	30
c.	30pf Mercedes-Benz SSKL. 1931	30	30
d.	60pf Mercedes and Auto Union cars racing on North embankment	30	30

50th anniversary of Avus Race Track.

Accident Prevention Type of Germany

Designs: 5pf, "Matches cause fires." 10pf, Broken ladder. 20pf, Hand and circular saw. 25pf, "Alcohol and automobile." 30pf, Safety helmets prevent injury. 40pf, Defective plug. 50pf, Nail sticking from board. 60pf, 70pf, Traffic safety (ball rolling before car). 100pf, Hoisted cargo. 150pf, Fenced-in open manhole.

1971-73 Typo. *Perf. 14*

9N316	A328	5pf orange	22	20
9N317	A328	10pf dk brn	22	15
a.		Bklt. pane of 8 (2 each #9N317-9N318, 9N320-9N321) ('74)	6.50	
9N318	A328	20pf purple	18	15
9N319	A328	25pf green	55	28
9N320	A328	30pf dk red	38	15
9N321	A328	40pf rose cl	30	24
9N322	A328	50pf Prus bl	2.00	45
9N323	A328	60pf vio blue	1.50	75
9N323A	A328	70pf grn & vio bl	90	50
9N324	A328	100pf olive	1.50	70
9N325	A328	150pf red brn	4.25	1.50
		Nos. 9N316-9N325 (11)	12.00	5.07

Issued in sheets of 100 and coils. Every fifth coil stamp has a control number on the back.

Issue dates: 25pf, 60pf, Sept. 10. 5pf, Oct. 29. 10pf, 30pf, Mar. 8, 1972. 40pf, June 20, 1972. 20pf, 100pf, July 5, 1972. 150pf, Sept. 11, 1972. 50pf, Jan. 16, 1973. 70pf, June 5, 1973.

Microscope and Metal Slide OS71

Friedrich Gilly, by Gottfried Schadow OS72

1971, Oct. 26 Photo. *Perf. 14*

9N326 OS71 30pf multi 25 25

Materials Testing Laboratory centenary.

1972, Feb. 4 Engr. *Perf. 14*

9N327 OS72 30pf blk & bl 28 28

Friedrich Gilly (1772-1800), sculptor.

Grunewaldsee, by Alexander von Riesen — OS73

Paintings of Berlin Lakes: 25pf, Wannsee, by Max Liebermann. 30pf, Schlachtensee, by Walter Leistikow.

1972, Apr. 14 Photo. *Perf. 14*

9N328 OS73	10pf bl & multi	15	15
9N329 OS73	25pf grn & multi	25	25
9N330 OS73	30pf blk & multi	35	35

E. T. A. Hoffmann — OS74

1972, May 18

9N331 OS74 60pf vio & blk 55 45

E. T. A. Hoffmann (1776-1822), writer and composer. (Portrait by Wilhelm Hensel.)

Portrait Type of 1971

Designs: No. 9N332, Max Liebermann (1847-1935), self-portrait. No. 9N333, Karl August, Duke of Hardenberg (1750-1822), Prussian statesman, by J. H. W. Tischbein.

1972 Photo. *Perf. 14*

9N332 OS69 40pf multi 40 40

9N333 OS69 40pf multi 40 40

Issue dates: No. 9N332, July 18; No. 9N333, Nov. 10.

Stamp-Printing Press — OS75

1972, Oct. 20 Engr. & Litho.

9N334 OS75 20pf dk red, blk & lt bl 18 18

Stamp Day 1972, and for the 5th National Youth Philatelic Exhib., Berlin, Oct. 26-29.

Streetcar, 1907 OS76

Designs: No. 9N336, Double-decker bus, 1919. No. 9N337, Double-decker bus, 1925. No. 9N338, Electrobus, 1933. No. 9N339, Double-decker bus, 1970. No. 9N340, Elongated bus, 1973.

1973, Apr. 30 Litho. *Perf. 14*

9N335 OS76	20pf gray & multi	32	28
9N336 OS76	30pf gray & multi	45	40
9N337 OS76	40pf gray & multi	60	52

1973, Sept. 14

9N338 OS76	20pf gray & multi	32	28
9N339 OS76	30pf gray & multi	45	40
9N340 OS76	40pf gray & multi	60	52
	Nos. 9N335-9N340 (6)	2.74	2.40

Public transportation in Berlin.

Portrait Type of 1971

Design: 40pf, Ludwig Tieck (1773-1853), poet and writer, by Carl Christian Vogel von Vogelstein.

1973, May 25 Photo. *Perf. 14*

9N341 OS69 40pf multi 40 40

Johann Joachim Quantz (1697-1773), Flutist and Composer — OS77

1973, June 12 Engr. *Perf. 14*

9N342 OS77 40pf black 40 40

Souvenir Sheet

50 Years of Broadcasting — OS78

1973, Aug. 23 Litho. *Perf. 14*

9N343 OS78	Sheet of 4	3.50	3.50
a.	20pf Speaker, set, 1926	75	75
b.	30pf Hans Bredow	75	75
c.	40pf Girl, TV, tape recorder	75	75
d.	70pf TV camera	75	75

50 years of German broadcasting. Sold for 1.80m.

Georg W. von Knobelsdorff OS79

Gustav R. Kirchhoff OS80

1974, Feb. 15 Engr. *Perf. 14*

9N344 OS79 20pf chocolate 18 18

275th anniversary of the birth of Georg Wenzelslaus von Knobelsdorff (1699-1753), architect.

1974, Feb. 15 Litho. & Engr.

9N345 OS80 30pf gray & dk grn 28 28

Sesquicentennial of the birth of Gustav Robert Kirchhoff (1824-1887), physicist.

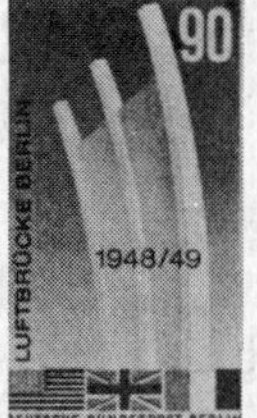

Airlift Memorial, Allied Flags — OS81

Adolf Slaby and Waves — OS82

1974, Apr. 17 Photo. *Perf. 14*

9N346 OS81 90pf multi 75 65

25th anniversary of the end of the Allied airlift into Berlin.

1974, Apr. 17 Litho. *Perf. 14*

9N347 OS82 40pf blk & red 38 38

125th anniversary of the birth of Adolf Slaby (1849-1913), radio pioneer.

School Seal Showing Athena and Hermes — OS83

1974, July 13 Photo. *Perf. 14*

9N348 OS83 50pf multi 50 50

400th anniversary of the Gray Brothers' School, a secondary Franciscan school.

Berlin-Tegel Airport — OS84

Lithographed and Engraved

1974, Oct. 15 *Perf. 14*

9N349 OS84 50pf multi 50 50

Opening of Berlin-Tegel Airport and Terminal, Nov. 1, 1974.

Venus, by F. E. Meyer, c. 1775
OS85

Gottfried Schadow
OS86

Berlin Porcelain: 40pf, "Astronomy," by W. C. Meyer, c. 1772. 50pf, "Justice," by J. G. Müller, c. 1785.

1974, Oct. 29 Litho. *Perf. 14*

9N350 OS85 30pf car & multi 28 28
9N351 OS85 40pf car & multi 35 35
9N352 OS85 50pf car & multi 48 48

1975, Jan. 15 Engr. *Perf. 14*

9N353 OS86 50pf maroon 50 50

Johann Gottfried Schadow (1764-1850), sculptor.

S.S. Princess Charlotte
OS87

Ships: 40pf, S.S. Siegfried. 50pf, S.S. Sperber. 60pf, M.S. Vaterland. 70pf, M.S. Moby Dick.

1975, Feb. 14 Litho. *Perf. 14*

9N354 OS87 30pf gray & multi 32 32
9N355 OS87 40pf ol & multi 38 38
9N356 OS87 50pf ultra & multi 40 40
9N357 OS87 60pf red brn & multi 48 48
9N358 OS87 70pf dk bl & multi 65 65
Nos. 9N354-9N358 (5) 2.23 2.23

Berlin passenger ships

Industry Type of 1975

1975-82 Engr. *Perf. 14*

Type A380

9N359	5pf	Symphonie satellite	15	15
9N360	10pf	Electric train	15	15
9N361	20pf	Old Weger lighthouse	15	15
9N362	30pf	Rescue helicopter	22	15
9N363	40pf	Space	28	15
9N364	50pf	Radar station	35	15
9N365	60pf	X-ray machine	55	15
9N366	70pf	Shipbuilding	55	24
9N367	80pf	Tractor	65	35
9N368	100pf	Coal excavator	80	42
9N368A	110pf	TV camera	90	38
9N369	120pf	Chemical plant	1.00	55
9N369A	130pf	Brewery	1.10	45
9N370	140pf	Heating plant	1.25	60
9N371	150pf	Power shovel	1.50	55
9N372	160pf	Blast furnace	1.40	90
9N373	180pf	Payloader	1.50	70
9N373A	190pf	Shovel dredger	1.50	65
9N374	200pf	Oil drill platform	1.50	75
9N375	230pf	Frankfort airport	2.25	70
9N375A	250pf	Airport	2.25	90
9N375B	300pf	Electric railroad	2.50	1.00
9N376	500pf	Radio telescope	4.25	2.50
Nos. 9N359-9N376 (23)			26.75	12.69

Issue dates: 40pf, 50pf, 100pf, May 15. 10pf, 30pf, 70pf, Aug. 14. 80pf, 120pf, 160pf, Oct. 15. 5pf, 140pf, 200pf, Nov. 14. 20pf, 500pf, Feb. 17, 1976. 60pf, Nov. 16, 1978. 230pf, May 17, 1979. 150pf, 180pf, July 12, 1979. 110pf, 130pf, 300pf, June 16, 1982. 190pf, 250pf, July 15, 1982.

Ferdinand Sauerbruch
OS88

Gymnasts' Emblem
OS89

Lithographed and Engraved

1975, May 15 *Perf. 13½x14*

9N379 OS88 50pf dl red & dk brn 48 48

Ferdinand Sauerbruch (1875-1951) surgeon, birth centenary.

1975, May 15 Photo. *Perf. 14*

9N380 OS89 40pf grn, gold & blk 38 38

6th Gymnaestrada, Berlin, July 1-5.

Lovis Corinth (1858-1925), Self-portrait, 1900 — OS90

1975, July 15 Photo. *Perf. 14*

9N381 OS90 50pl multi 48 48

Architecture Type of 1975

Design: Houses, Naunynstrasse, Berlin-Kreuzberg.

1975, July 15 Litho. & Engr.

9N382 A381 50pf multi 48 48

European Architectural Heritage Year.

Paul Löbe and Reichstag
OS92

1975, Nov. 14 Engr. *Perf. 14*

9N383 OS92 50pf cop red 48 48

Paul Löbe (1875-1967), president of German Parliament 1920-1932, birth centenary.

Grain — OS93

1976, Jan. 5 Photo. *Perf. 14*

9N384 OS93 70pf grn & yel 60 60

Green Week International Agricultural Exhibition, Berlin, 50th anniversary.

Hockey
OS94

1976, May 13 Engr. *Perf. 14*

9N385 OS94 30pf green 28 28

Women's World Hockey Championships.

Treble Clef — OS95

Berlin Fire Brigade Emblem — OS96

1976, May 13 Photo.

9N386 OS95 40pf multi 38 38

German Choir Festival.

1976, May 13 Litho.

9N387 OS96 50pf red & multi 48 48

Berlin Fire Brigade, 125th anniversary.

Sailboat on Havel River — OS97

Berlin Views: 40pf, Spandau Castle. 50pf, Tiergarten.

1976, Nov. 16 Engr. *Perf. 14*

9N388 OS97 30pf bl & blk 30 30
9N389 OS97 40pf brn & blk 38 38
9N390 OS97 50pf grn & blk 55 55

See Nos. 9N422-9N424.

Castle Type of Germany

1977-79 Typo. *Perf. 14*

Castles: 10pf, Glücksburg. 20pf, 190pf, Pfaueninsel. 25pf, Gemen. 30pf, Ludwigstein. 40pf, Eltz. 50pf, Neuschwanstein. 60pf, Marksburg. 70pf, Mespelbrunn. 90pf, Vischering. 200pf, Bürresheim. 210pf, Schwanenburg. 230pf, Lichtenberg.

9N391	A406	10pf gray bl	15	15
a.		Booklet pane of 8 (4 #9N391, 2 each #9N394, 9N396)	2.50	
b.		Bklt. pane of 8 (4#9N391, 2 #9N394, 2 #9N440)	2.25	
c.		Bklt. pane (4 #9N391, 2 #9N440, 2 #9N442)	2.25	
d.		Bklt. pane (2 each #9N391, 9N394, 9N440-9N441)	2.50	
9N392	A406	20pf orange	15	15
9N393	A406	25pf crimson	18	15
9N394	A406	30pf olive	22	15
9N395	A406	40pf bl grn	40	15
9N396	A406	50pf rose car	48	15
9N397	A406	60pf brown	55	20
9N398	A406	70pf blue	55	30
9N399	A406	90pf dk bl	90	40
9N400	A406	190pf red brn	1.50	85
9N401	A406	200pf green	1.75	70
9N402	A406	210pf red brn	2.00	90
9N403	A406	230pf dk grn	2.25	1.00
Nos. 9N391-9N403 (13)			11.08	5.25

Issued in sheets of 100 and coils. Every fifth coil stamp has a control number on the back.

Issue dates: 60pf, 200pf, Jan. 13. 40pf, 190pf, Feb. 16. 10pf, 20pf, 30pf, Apr. 14. 50pf, 70pf, May 17. 230pf, Nov. 16, 1978. 25pf, 90pf, Jan. 11, 1979. 210pf, Feb. 14, 1979.

See Nos. 9N438-9N445.

15-Cent Minimum Value

The minimum catalogue value is 15 cents. Separating se-tenant pieces into individual stamps does not increase the "value" of the stamps... since demand for the separated stamps may be small.

Eugenie d'Alton, by Rausch — OS98

Eduard Gaertner (1801-77), Painter — OS99

1977, Jan. 13 Photo. *Perf. 14*

9N404 OS98 50pf vio blk 48 48

Christian Daniel Rausch (1777-1857), sculptor, birth bicentenary.

1977, Feb. 16 Litho. & Engr.

9N405 OS99 40pf lt grn, grn & blk 38 38

Fountain, by Georg Kolbe
OS100

"Bear each other's burdens"
OS101

1977, Apr. 14 Photo. *Perf. 14*

9N406 OS100 30pf dk ol 28 28

Georg Kolbe (1877-1947), sculptor.

1977, May 17 Litho. *Perf. 14*

9N407 OS101 40pf grn blk & yel 38 38

17th meeting of German Protestants (Evangelical Synod), Berlin.

Patent Office, Berlin-Kreuzberg — OS102

1977, July 13 Litho. & Engr.

9N408 OS102 60pf gray & red 50 50

Centenary of German patent laws.

Telephones, 1905 and 1977
OS103

Painting by George Grosz (1893-1959)
OS104

1977, July 13 Litho.

9N409 OS103 50pf multi 50 50

International Broadcasting Exhibition, Berlin, Aug. 26-Sept. 4, and centenary of telephone in Germany.

1977, July 13

9N410 OS104 70pf multi 65 65

15th European Art Exhibition, Berlin, Aug. 14-Oct. 16.

Rhinecanthus Aculeatus — OS105

Designs: 30pf, Paddlefish. 40pf, Tortoise. 50pf, Rhinoceros iguana. Designs include statue of iguanodon from Aquarium entrance.

1977, Aug. 16 Photo. Perf. 14

9N411 OS105 20pf multi 16 15
9N412 OS105 30pf multi 28 24
9N413 OS105 40pf multi 35 30
9N414 OS105 50pf multi 45 40

25th anniversary of the reopening of Berlin Aquarium.

Walter Kollo (1878-1940), Composer — OS106

1978, Jan. 12 Engr. Perf. 14

9N415 OS106 50pf brn, red & dk brn 50 50

Chamber of Commerce Emblem OS107

1978, Apr. 13 Engr. Perf. 14

9N416 OS107 90pf dk bl & red 80 80

American Chamber of Commerce in Germany, 75th anniversary.

Albrecht von Graefe OS108

Friedrich Ludwig Jahn OS109

1978, May 22 Engr. Perf. 14

9N417 OS108 30pf red brn & blk 28 28

Dr. Albrecht von Graefe (1828-1870) ophthalmologist.

1978, July 13 Engr. Perf. 14

9N418 OS109 50pf dk car 50 50

Friedrich Ludwig Jahn (1778-1852), founder of organized gymnastics.

Swimmers — OS110

1978, Aug. 17 Litho. Perf. 14

9N419 OS110 40pf multi 38 38

3rd World Swimming Championships, Berlin, Aug. 18-28.

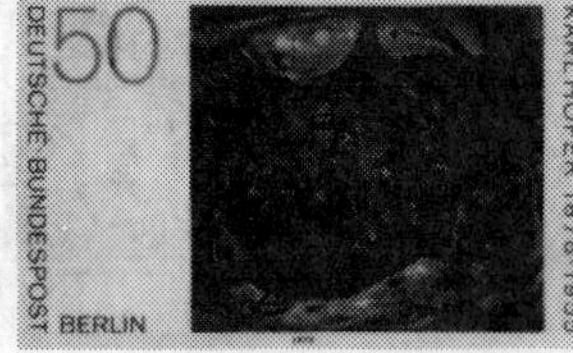

The Boat, by Karl Hofer — OS111

1978, Oct. 12 Photo. Perf. 14

9N420 OS111 50pf multi 50 50

Karl Hofer (1878-1955), painter.

National Library OS112

1978, Nov. 16 Engr. Perf. 14

9N421 OS112 90pf red & ol 80 80

Opening of new National Library building.

Views Type of 1976

Berlin Views: 40pf, Belvedere, Charlottenburg Castle. 50pf, Shell House on Landwehr Canal. 60pf, Village Church, Alt-Lichtenrade.

1978, Nov. 16

9N422 OS97 40pf grn & blk 40 40
9N423 OS97 50pf lil & blk 45 45
9N424 OS97 60pf brn & blk 60 60

International Conference Center — OS113

Photogravure and Engraved

1979, Feb. 14 Perf. 14

9N425 OS113 60pf multi 55 55

Opening of International Conference Center in Berlin.

German Eagles — OS114

1979, May 17 Litho. Perf. 14

9N426 OS114 60pf multi 55 55

Cent. of German Natl. Printing Bureau.

TV Screen and Emblem — OS115

1979, July 12 Photo. Perf. 14

9N427 OS115 60pf multi 55 55

Intl. Broadcasting Exhibition, Berlin.

Target and Arrows OS116

1979, July 12

9N428 OS116 50pf multi 50 50

World Archery Championships, Berlin.

Moses Mendelssohn OS117

1979, Aug. 9 Engr. Perf. 14

9N429 OS117 90pf black 80 80

Mendelssohn (1729-86), philosopher.

Gas Lamp — OS118

Historic Street Lanterns: 40pf, Carbon arc lamp. 50pf, Hanging gas lamps. 60pf, 5-armed candelabra.

1979, Aug. 9 Litho.

9N430 OS118 10pf multi 15 15
9N431 OS118 40pf multi 38 38
9N432 OS118 50pf multi 50 50
9N433 OS118 60pf multi 60 60

300 years of street lighting in Berlin.

Orchid OS119

1979, Aug. 9

9N434 OS119 50pf multi 50 50

Botanical Gardens, Berlin, 300th anniv.

Berlin Poster Columns, 125th Anniversary OS120

Lithographed and Engraved

1979, Nov. 14 Perf. 14

9N435 OS120 50pf multi 50 50

Castle Type of 1977

1979-82 Typo. Perf. 14

9N438	A406	35pf	Lichtenstein	35	15
9N439	A406	40pf	Wolfsburg	38	15
9N440	A406	50pf	Inzlingen	50	18
9N441	A406	60pf	Rheydt	60	15
9N442	A406	80pf	Wilhelmsthal	75	30
9N443	A406	120pf	Charlottenburg	1.10	45
9N444	A406	280pf	Ahrensburg	2.50	1.10
9N445	A406	300pf	Herrenhausen	2.75	1.10
			Nos. 9N438-9N445 (8)	8.93	3.58

Issue dates: 60pf, Nov. 14. 40pf, 50pf, Feb. 14, 1980. 35pf, 80pf, 300pf, June 16, 1982. 120pf, 280pf, July 15, 1982.

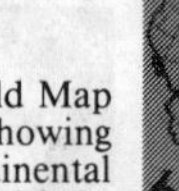
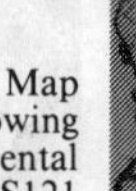

World Map Showing Continental Drift — OS121

1980, Feb. 14 Litho. Perf. 14

9N451 OS121 60pf multi 70 65

Alfred Wegener (1880-1930), geophysicist and meteorologist; founded theory of continental drift.

Cardinal Count Preysing (1880-1950) — OS122

1980, May 8 Engr. Perf. 14

9N452 OS122 50pf blk & car rose 50 50

German Catholics Day.

Angel, Enamel Medallion, 12th Century OS123

Prussian Museum, Berlin, 150th Anniversary: 60pf, Monks Reading, oak sculpture, by Ernest Barlach (1870-1938).

1980, July 10 Litho. Perf. 14

9N453 OS123 40pf multi 40 40
9N454 OS123 60pf multi 60 60

Von Steuben Leading Troops OS124

Robert Stolz Conducting OS125

1980, Aug. 14 Litho. Perf. 14

9N455 OS124 40pf multi 45 45

Friedrich Wilhelm von Steuben (1730-94).

1980, Aug. 14

9N456 OS125 60pf dk bl & bis 55 55

Robert Stolz (1880-1975), composer.

Lilenthal Memorial — OS126

Designs: 50pf, Grosse Neugierde Memorial, 1835. 60pf, Lookout tower, Grunewald Memorial to Kaiser Wilhelm I.

1980, Nov. 13 Engr. Perf. 14

9N457 OS126 40pf dk grn & blk 40 40
9N458 OS126 50pf brn & blk 45 45
9N459 OS126 60pf dk bl & blk 60 60

Von Gontard and Kleist Park Colonnades, Berlin — OS127

1981, Jan. 15 Litho. *Perf. 14*
9N460 OS127 50pf multi 50 50

Karl Philipp von Gontard (1731-91), architect.

Achim von Arnim OS128

Adelbert von Chamisso OS129

1981, Jan. 15 Engr.
9N461 OS128 60pf dk grn 55 55

Achim von Arnim (1781-1831), poet.

1981, Jan. 15 Litho.
9N462 OS129 60pf brn & gldn brn 55 55

Adelbert von Chamisso (1781-1838), poet.

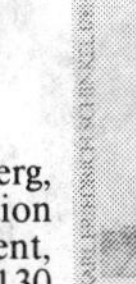

Berlin-Kreuzberg, Liberation Monument, 1813 — OS130

1981, Feb. 12 Engr. *Perf. 14*
9N463 OS130 40pf brown 40 40

Karl Friedrich Schinkel (1781-1841), architect, 400th anniversary of birth.

Arts and Science Medal, Awarded 1842-1933 OS131

Amor and Psyche, by Reinhold Begas (1831-1911) OS132

1981, July 16 Litho. *Perf. 14*
9N464 OS131 40pf multi 40 40

"Prussia—an attempt at a balance" exhibition.

1981, July 16 Photo.
9N465 OS132 50pf multi 50 50

Intl. Telecommunications Exhibition — OS133

1981, July 16 Litho.
9N466 OS133 60pf multi 55 55

Peter Beuth (1781-1853), Constitutional Law Expert — OS134

Nijinsky, by Georg Kolbe, 1914 — OS135

Lithographed and Engraved

1981, Nov. 12 *Perf. 14*
9N467 OS134 60pf gold & blk 55 55

1981, Nov. 12 Photo.

20th Century Sculptures: 60pf, Mother Earth II, by Ernst Barlach, 1920. 90pf, Flora Kneeling, by Richard Scheibe, 1930.

9N468 OS135 40pf multi 32 32
9N469 OS135 60pf multi 50 50
9N470 OS135 90pf multi 85 85

750th Anniv. of Spandau OS136

Lithographed and Engraved

1982, Feb. 18 *Perf. 14*
9N471 OS136 60pf multi 55 55

Berlin Philharmonic Centenary A137

Salzburg Emigration to Prussia, 250th Anniv. A138

Lithographed and Embossed

1982, Apr. 15 *Perf. 14*
9N472 A137 60pf multi 55 55

1982, May 5 Litho. Engr.
9N473 A138 50pf multi 50 50

Italian Stone Carriers, by Max Pechstein — A139

Design: 80pf, Two Girls Bathing, by Otto Mueller.

1982, July 15 Litho. *Perf. 14*
9N474 A139 50pf multi 55 50
9N475 A139 80pf multi 85 75

Villa Borsig — A140

1982, Nov. 10 Engr. *Perf. 14*
9N476 A140 50pf shown 50 50
9N477 A140 60pf Sts. Peter and Paul Church 60 60
9N478 A140 80pf Villa von der Heydt 80 80

State Theater, Charlottenburg, 1790 — A141

1982, Nov. 10 Litho. & Engr.
9N479 A141 80pf multi 85 80

Carl Gotthard Langhans (1732-1808), architect.

Street Pump, 1900 — A142

Various street pumps and fire hydrants, 1900.

1983, Jan. 13 Litho. *Perf. 14*
9N480 A142 50pf multi 55 35
9N481 A142 60pf multi 70 45
9N482 A142 80pf multi 80 55
9N483 A142 120pf multi 1.25 85

Berlin-Koblenz Telegraph Service Sesquicentennial A142a

1983, Feb. 8 Engr. *Perf. 14*
9N484 A142a 80pf dk brn 90 55

Portrait of Barbara Campanini, 1745, by Antoine Pesne (1683-1757) — A143

1983, May 5 Photo. *Perf. 14*
9N485 A143 50pf multi 55 35

Joachim Ringelnatz (1883-1934), Painter and Writer — A144

1983, July 14 Litho. *Perf. 14*
9N486 A144 50pf Silhouette 55 35

Intl. Radio Exhibition, Sept. 2-11 — A145

1983, July 14
9N487 A145 80pf Nipkow's phototelegraphy diagram 90 55

Ancient Artwork, Berlin Museum A146

Designs: 30pf, Bust of Queen Cleopatra VII, 69-30 B.C. 50pf, Statue of Egyptian Couple, Giza, 2400 B.C. 60pf, Stone God with Beaded Turban, Mexico, 300 B.C. 80pf, Enamel Plate, 16th century.

1984, Jan. 12 Litho. *Perf. 14*
9N488 A146 30pf multi 32 22
9N489 A146 50pf multi 50 35
9N490 A146 60pf multi 70 45
9N491 A146 80pf multi 80 55

Electricity Centenary A147

Conference Emblem A148

Design: Allegorical figure holding light bulb (symbol of electric power).

1984, May 8 Litho. *Perf. 14*
9N492 A147 50pf blk & org 55 18

1984, May 8
9N493 A148 60pf multi 65 22

European Ministers of Culture, 4th Conf.

Erich Klausener (1885-1934), Chairman of Catholic Action — A149

1984, May 8 Engr. *Perf. 14x13½*
9N494 A149 80pf dk grn 90 30

Alfred Brehm (1829-1884), Zoologist — A150

Lithographed and Engraved

1984, Apr. 18 *Perf. 14*
9N495 A150 80pf Brehm, white stork 90 30

Ernst Ludwig Heim (1747-1834), Botanist — A151

1984, Aug. 21 Engr. *Perf. 14*
9N496 A151 50pf brn & blk 55 18

Sunflowers, by Karl Schmidt-Rottluff (1884-1976) — A152

1984, Nov. 8 Litho. *Perf. 14*

9N497 A152 60pf multi 65 22

Bettina von Arnim, Writer (1785-1859) — A153

1985, Feb. 21 Litho. & Engr.

9N498 A153 50pf multi 55 18

Wilhelm von Humboldt, Statesman (1767-1835) A154

1985, Feb. 21 Engr.

9N499 A154 80pf bl, blk & red 90 30

1985 Berlin Horticultural Show — A155

1985, Apr. 16 Litho. *Perf. 14*

9N500 A155 80pf Symbolic flower 90 28

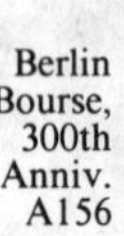

Berlin Bourse, 300th Anniv. A156

1985, May 7 Litho. & Engr.

9N501 A156 50pf multi 55 18

Otto Klemperer (1885-1973), Conductor — A157

1985, May 7 Engr.

9N502 A157 60pf dp bl vio 65 20

Telefunken Camera, 1936 — A158

1985, July 16 Litho. *Perf. 14*

9N503 A158 80pf multi 90 28

German Television, 50th anniv., Intl. Telecommunications Exhibition, Berlin.

9th World Gynecological Congress — A159

Design: Emblem of the Intl. Federation for Gynecology and birth aid.

1985, July 16 Photo. *Perf. 13½x14*

9N504 A159 60pf pale yel, ap grn & dp grn 65 20

Edict of Potsdam, 300th Anniv. A160

Lithographed and Engraved

1985, Oct. 15 *Perf. 14*

9N505 A160 50pf dk bluish lil 55 20

Kurt Tucholsky (1890-1935), Novelist, Journalist — A161

1985, Nov. 12 Litho. *Perf. 14*

9N506 A161 80pf multi 90 30

Wilhelm Furtwangler (1886-1954), Composer — A162

Score from Sonata in D Sharp.

Lithographed and Engraved

1986, Jan. 16 *Perf. 14*

9N507 A162 80pf multi 90 30

Ludwig Mies van der Rohe (1886-1969), Architect — A163

1986, Feb. 13

9N508 A163 50pf multi 55 20

New Natl. Gallery, Berlin

16th European Communities Day — A164

1986, Apr. 10 Litho. *Perf. 14*

9N509 A164 60pf Flags 55 25

Leopold von Ranke (1795-1886), Historian A165

Gottfried Benn (1886-1956), Writer and Physician A166

1986, May 5 Litho.

9N510 A165 80pf brn blk & tan 90 35

Engr.

9N511 A166 80pf brt bl 90 35

Portals and Gateways A167

1986, June 20 Litho. & Engr.

9N512 A167 50pf Charlotte Gate 55 22

9N513 A167 60pf Gryphon Gate, Glienicke Castle 65 28

9N514 A167 80pf Elephant Gate, Berlin Zoo 90 38

King Frederick the Great — A168

Painting: The Flute Concert (detail), by Adolph von Menzel.

1986, Aug. 14 Litho. *Perf. 14*

9N515 A168 80pf multi 90 38

Famous Women Type of 1986

Designs: 5pf, Emma Ihrer (1857-1911), politician, labor leader. 10pf, Paula Modersohn-Becker (1876-1907), painter. 20pf, Cilly Aussem (1909-63), tennis champion. 40pf, Maria Sibylla Merian. 50pf, Christine Teusch. 60pf, Dorothea Erxleben (1715-62), physician. 80pf, Clara Schumann. 100pf, Therese Giehse (1898-1975), actress. 130pf, Lise Meitner (1878-1968), physicist. 140pf, Cecile Vogt (1875-1962), neurologist. 170pf, Hannah Arendt (1906-75), American political scientist. 180pf, Lotte Lehmann (1888-1976), soprano. 240pf, Mathilde Franziska Anneke, (1817-84), American author. 250pf, Queen Louise of Prussia (1776-1810). 300pf, Fanny Hensel (1805-1847), composer-conductor. 350pf, Hedwig Dransfeld (1871-1925), women's rights activist. 500pf, Alice Salomon (1872-1948), feminist and social activist.

1986-89 Engr. *Perf. 14*

Type A602

9N516	5pf bluish gray & org brn	15	15
9N517	10pf vio & yel brn	15	15
9N518	20pf lake & Prus bl	20	15
9N519	40pf dp bl & dk lil rose	38	22
9N520	50pf gray ol & Prus bl	48	25
9N521	60pf dp vio & grnsh blk	55	32
9N522	80pf dk grn & lt red brn	75	40
9N523	100pf dk red & grnsh blk	95	55
9N524	130pf Prus bl & dk vio	1.25	80
9N525	140pf blk & dk ol bis	1.40	70
9N526	170pf gray grn & dk brn	1.65	92
9N527	180pf bl & brn vio	1.75	90
9N528	240pf Prus bl & yel brn	2.25	1.30
9N529	250pf dp lil rose & dp bl	2.50	1.25
9N530	300pf dk vio & sage grn	2.75	1.50
9N531	350pf gray grn & lake	3.25	1.90
9N532	500pf slate grn & brt ver	4.75	2.85
	Nos. 9N516-9N532 (17)	25.16	14.31

Issue dates: 50pf, 80pf, Nov. 1. 40pf, Sept. 17, 1987. 10pf, Apr. 4, 1988. 20pf, 130pf, May 5, 1988. 60pf, 100pf, 170pf, 240pf, 350pf, Nov. 10, 1988. 500pf, Jan. 12, 1989. 5pf, Feb. 9, 1989. 180pf, 250pf, July 13, 1989. 140pf, 300pf, Aug. 10, 1989.

Berlin 750th Anniv. Type of 1987

Designs: a, Berlin, 1650, engraving by Caspar Merian. b, Charlottenburg Castle, c. 1830. c, AEG Company turbine construction building, by architect Walter Behrens, 1909. d, Philharmonic Concert Hall and Chamber Music Rooms on the Kemperplatz, 1987.

1987, Jan. 15 Litho. *Perf. 14*

9N536 A604 80pf like #1496 85 85

Souvenir Sheet

Perf. 14x14½

9N537	Sheet of 4	2.50	2.50
a.	A604 40pf multi	42	42
b.	A604 50pf multi	52	52
c.	A604 60pf multi	65	65
d.	A604 80pf multi	85	85

No. 9N537 contains four 43x25mm stamps.

Louise Schroeder (1887-1957), Politican — A169

1987, Feb. 12 Engr. *Perf. 14*

9N538 A169 50pf sep & dk red 55 28

Settlement of Bohemians at Rixdorf, 250th Anniv. — A170

Design: Bohemian refugees, bas-relief detail from monument to King Friedrich Wilhelm I of Prussia, 1912.

1987, May 5 Litho. & Engr.

9N539 A170 50pf sep & pale gray grn 58 30

1987 Intl. Architecture Exhibition — A171

1987, May 5 Litho. *Perf. 14x14½*

9N540 A171 80pf lt ultra, sil & blk 90 45

14th Int'l. Botanical Congress — A172

1987, July 16 Litho. *Perf. 14*

9N541 A172 60pf multicolored 68 35

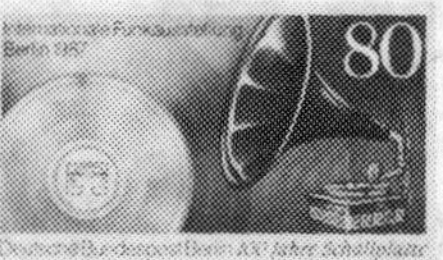

Int'l. Radio Exhibition A173

1987, Aug. 20
9N542 A173 80pf Gramophone, compact disc 90 45

Historic Sites and Objects Type

Designs: 5pf, Brunswick Lion. 10pf, Frankfurt Airport. 20pf, No. 9N550, Queen Nefertiti, bust, Egyptian Museum, Berlin. 30pf, Corner tower, Celle Castle, 14th cent. 40pf, Chile House, Hamburg. 50pf, Filigree tracery on spires, Freiburg Cathedral. 60pf, Bavaria Munich, bronze statue above the Theresienwiese, Hall of Fame. No. 9N551, Heligoland. 80pf, Entrance to Zollern II, coal mine, Dortmund. 100pf, Altotting Chapel, Bavaria. 120pf, Schleswig Cathedral. 140pf, Bronze flagon from Reinheim. 300pf, Hambach Castle. 350pf, Externsteine Bridge near Horn-Bad Meinberg.

1987-90 Typo. *Perf. 14*
Type A623

9N543	5pf Prus bl & gray	15	15
9N544	10pf lt chalky bl & slate bl	15	15
9N545	20pf dull bl & tan	22	15
9N546	30pf agua & org brn	35	18
9N547	40pf ultra, dk red brn & org red	45	22
9N548	50pf ultra & yel brn	58	30
9N549	60pf cob & pale gray	68	35
9N550	70pf dull bl & fawn	85	42
9N551	70pf vio bl & henna brn	85	42
9N552	80pf cob & pale gray	90	45
a.	Bklt. pane of 8 (4 10pf, 2 50pf, 2 80pf) ('89)	3.45	
9N553	100pf brt bluish grn & olive bis	1.10	55
a.	Bklt. pane of 8 (2 each 10pf, 60pf, 80pf, 100pf)	5.60	
9N554	120pf brn org & lt grnsh bl	1.45	72
9N555	140pf tan & lt grn	1.60	80
9N556	300pf dk red brn & tan	3.75	1.80
9N557	350pf brt ultra & ol bis	3.75	1.90
	Nos. 9N543-9N557 (15)	16.83	8.56

Issue dates: 30pf, 50pf, 60pf, 80pf, Nov. 6. 10pf, 300pf, Jan. 14, 1988. No. 9N550, 120pf, July 14, 1988. 20pf, 140pf, Jan. 12, 1989. 100pf, 350pf, Feb. 9, 1989. 5pf, Feb. 15, 1990. No. 9N551, June 21, 1990.

European Culture — A175

1988, Jan. 14 Litho. *Perf. 14*
9N568 A175 80pf Berlin Bear 1.00 50

Urania Science Museum, Cent. A176

1988, Feb. 18
9N569 A176 50pf multicolored 65 32

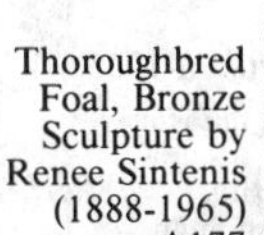

Thoroughbred Foal, Bronze Sculpture by Renee Sintenis (1888-1965) A177

1988, Feb. 18
9N570 A177 60pf multicolored 75 38

The Great Elector with Family in Berlin Castle Gardens — A178

1988, May 5 Litho. & Engr.
9N571 A178 50pf multicolored 60 30

The Great Elector of Brandenburg (d. 1688), founder of the Hohenzollern Dynasty.

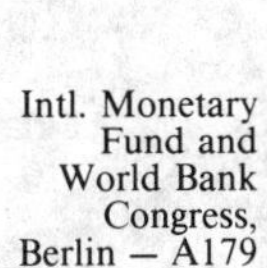

Intl. Monetary Fund and World Bank Congress, Berlin — A179

1988, Aug. 11 Litho.
9N572 A179 70pf multicolored 78 40

Berlin-Potsdam Railway, 150th Anniv. — A180

1988, Oct. 13 Litho.
9N573 A180 10pf multicolored 15 15

The Collector, 1913, by Ernst Barlach (1870-1938) A181

1988, Oct. 13
9N574 A181 40pf multicolored 45 22

Airlift, 40th Anniv. — A182

1989, May 5 Photo. *Perf. 14*
9N575 A182 60pf multicolored 68 35

13th Intl. Congress of the Supreme Audit Office, Berlin A183

1989, May 5 Litho.
9N576 A183 80pf multicolored 90 45

Ernst Reuter (1889-1953), Mayor of Berlin — A184

Litho. & Engr.
1989, July 13 *Perf. 14x14½*
9N577 A184 100pf multicolored 1.10 55

Intl. Radio Exhibition, Berlin — A185

1989, July 13 Litho.
9N578 A185 100pf multicolored 1.10 55

Plans of the Zoological Gardens, Berlin, and Designer Peter Joseph Lenne (1789-1866) — A186

Litho. & Engr.
1989, Aug. 10 *Perf. 14*
9N579 A186 60pf multicolored 60 30

Carl von Ossietzky (1889-1938), Awarded Nobel Peace Prize of 1935 — A187

1989, Aug. 10 Photo.
9N580 A187 100pf multicolored 1.00 50

450th Anniv. of the Reformation A188

Design: Nikolai Church, Spandau District.

1989, Oct. 12 Litho.
9N581 A188 60pf multicolored 60 30

French Gymnasium, 300th Anniv. — A189

Design: School from 1701 to 1873 and frontispiece of *Leges Gymnasie Gallici,* published in 1689.

1989, Oct. 12 Litho. & Engr.
9N582 A189 40pf multicolored 40 20

Journalists, 1925, by Hannah Hoch (1889-1978) A190

1989, Oct. 12 Litho. *Perf. 13½*
9N583 A190 100pf multicolored 1.00 50

European Postal Service 500th Anniv. Type

Litho. & Engr.
1990, Jan. 12 *Perf. 14*
9N584 A673 100pf *The Young Post Rider* 1.10 55

Public Transportation, 250th Anniv. — A191

1990, Jan. 12 Litho.
9N585 A191 60pf multicolored 65 32

Ernst Rudorff (1840-1916), Conservationist — A192

1990, Jan. 12
9N586 A192 60pf multicolored 65 32

People's Free Theater Organization, Cent. — A193

1990, Feb. 15 *Perf. 13½*
9N587 A193 100pf multicolored 1.10 55

Parliament House, 40th Anniv. A194

1990, Feb. 15 *Perf. 14x14½*
9N588 A194 100pf multicolored 1.10 55

Bicent. of the Invention of the Barrel Organ — A195

1990, May 3 Litho. *Perf. 14*
9N589 A195 100pf multicolored 1.20 60

90th German Catholics Day — A196

1990, May 3
9N590 A196 60pf multicolored 70 35

German Pharmaceutical Society, Cent. — A197

1990, Aug. 9 Litho. *Perf. 14*
9N591 A197 100pf multicolored 1.20 60

Adolph Diesterweg (1790-1866), Educator — A198

1990, Sept. 27
9N592 A198 60pf multicolored 70 35

Stamps for Berlin were discontinued Oct. 3, 1990, when Germany and the German Democratic Republic merged. The stamps remained valid until Dec. 31, 1991.

OCCUPATION SEMI-POSTAL STAMPS

Offering Plate and Berlin Bear — OSP1

Wmk. 284

1949, Dec. 1 Litho. *Perf. 14*
9NB1 OSP1 10 + 5pf grn 42.50 *150.00*
9NB2 OSP1 20 + 5pf car 42.50 *150.00*
9NB3 OSP1 30 + 5pf blue 42.50 *150.00*
a. Souv. sheet of 3, #9NB1-9NB3 525.00 *2,200.*

The surtax was for Berlin victims of currency devaluation.

Harp and Laurel Branch OSP2

"Singing Angels" OSP3

1950, Oct. 29 Engr. Wmk. 116
9NB4 OSP2 10 + 5pf grn 22.50 32.50
9NB5 OSP3 30 + 5pf dk sl bl 37.50 *62.50*

The surtax was to aid in reestablishing the Berlin Philharmonic Orchestra.

Young Stamp Collectors OSP4

Reconstructed Kaiser Wilhelm Memorial Church OSP5

1951, Oct. 7 *Perf. 14*
9NB6 OSP4 10 + 3pf grn 10.00 *18.00*
9NB7 OSP4 20 + 2pf brn red 12.00 *22.50*

Stamp Day, Berlin, Oct. 7, 1951.

1953, Aug. 9 Wmk. 284

Design: 20pf+10pf, 30pf+15pf, Ruins of Kaiser Wilhelm Memorial Church.

9NB8 OSP5 4 + 1pf choc 15 32
9NB9 OSP5 10 + 5pf grn 75 *2.75*
9NB10 OSP5 20 + 10pf car 75 *2.50*
9NB11 OSP5 30 + 15pf dp bl 8.25 *35.00*

The surtax was to aid in reconstructing the church.

Catalogue values for unused stamps in this section, from this point to the end of the section, are for Never Hinged items.

Prussian Postilion — OSP6

Prussian Field Postilion — OSP7

1954, Aug. 4 Litho. Wmk. 284
9NB12 OSP6 20 + 10pf multi 14.00 *18.00*

National Stamp Exhibition, Berlin, Aug. 4-8.

Perf. 13½x14

1955, Oct. 27 Wmk. 304
9NB13 OSP7 25 + 10pf multi 5.50 7.50

The surtax was for the benefit of philately.

St. Otto, Bishop of Bamberg — OSP8

Statues: 10pf+5pf, St. Hedwig, Duchess of Silesia. 20pf+10pf, St. Peter.

1955, Nov. 26 Engr. *Perf. 14*
9NB14 OSP8 7 + 3pf brown 60 1.10
9NB15 OSP8 10 + 5pf gray grn 1.10 1.25
9NB16 OSP8 20 + 10pf rose lil 1.25 1.65

25th anniv. of the Bishopric of Berlin.
The surtax was for the reconstruction of destroyed churches throughout the bishopric.

Bell Type of 1951 Surcharged

+10
Berlinhilfe
für die
Hochwassergeschädigten
DEUTSCHE BUNDESPOST·BERLIN

Perf. 13½x14

1956, Aug. 9 Wmk. 284
9NB17 OS8 20pf + 10pf citron 1.75 2.50

The surtax was for help for flood victims.

Postrider of Brandenburg, 1700 — OSP9

Ludwig Heck — OSP10

Wmk. 304

1956, Oct. 26 Litho. *Perf. 14*
9NB18 OSP9 25pf + 10pf multi 1.50 2.00

The surtax was for the benefit of philately.

1957, Sept. 7 Engr. *Perf. 13½x14*
9NB19 OSP10 20pf + 10pf red & dk brn 25 35

Issued in honor of Dr. Ludwig Heck, zoologist and long-time director of the Berlin Zoo. The surtax was for the Zoo.

Elly Heuss-Knapp and Relaxing Mothers OSP11

Boy at Window OSP12

1957, Nov. 30 *Perf. 14*
9NB20 OSP11 20pf + 10pf dk red 1.00 1.25

The surtax was for welfare work among mothers.

1960, Sept. 15 Litho. Wmk. 304

Designs: 10pf+5pf, Girl going to school. 20pf+10pf, Girl with flower and mountains. 40pf+20pf, Girls at seashore.

9NB21 OSP12 7pf + 3pf dk brn & brn 15 15
9NB22 OSP12 10pf + 5pf ol grn & sl grn 15 15
9NB23 OSP12 20pf + 10pf dk car & brn blk 20 16
9NB24 OSP12 40pf + 20pf bl & ind 70 90

The surtax was for vacations for the children of Berlin.

Fluorescent Paper was introduced for semipostal stamps, starting with Nos. 9NB25-9NB28.

Fairy Tale Type of 1960

Various Scenes from Sleeping Beauty

1964, Oct. 6 Unwmk. *Perf. 14*
9NB25 SP285 10pf + 5pf multi 15 16
9NB26 SP285 15pf + 5pf multi 15 15
9NB27 SP285 20pf + 10pf multi 15 15
9NB28 SP285 40pf + 20pf multi 60 90
Set value 90

The surtax was for independent welfare organizations.

Beginning with 9NB25-9NB28 semipostals are types of Germany inscribed "Berlin" unless otherwise noted.

Bird Type of 1965

Birds: 10pf+5pf, Woodcock. 15pf+5pf, Ring-necked pheasant. 20pf+10pf, Black grouse. 40pf+20pf, Capercaillie.

1965, Apr. 1 Litho. *Perf. 14*
9NB29 SP289 10pf + 5pf multi 15 15
9NB30 SP289 15pf + 5pf multi 15 20
9NB31 SP289 20pf + 10pf multi 20 25
9NB32 SP289 40pf + 20pf multi 45 70

Issued for the benefit of young people.

Fairy Tale Type of 1965

Various Scenes from Cinderella

1965, Oct. 6 Litho. *Perf. 14*
9NB33 SP290 10pf + 5pf multi 15 15
9NB34 SP290 15pf + 5pf multi 15 15
9NB35 SP290 20pf + 10pf multi 15 15
9NB36 SP290 40pf + 20pf multi 45 90
Set value 78

The surtax was for independent welfare organizations.

Animal Type of 1966

Designs: 10pf+5pf, Roe deer. 20pf+10pf, Chamois. 30pf+15pf, Fallow deer. 50pf+25pf, Red deer.

1966, Apr. 22 Litho. *Perf. 14*
9NB37 SP291 10pf + 5pf multi 15 15
9NB38 SP291 20pf + 10pf multi 15 15
9NB39 SP291 30pf + 15pf multi 18 18
9NB40 SP291 50pf + 25pf multi 40 75

Issued for the benefit of young people.

Fairy Tale Type of 1965

Various Scenes from The Princess and the Frog.

1966, Oct. 5 Litho. *Perf. 14*
9NB41 SP290 10pf + 5pf multi 15 15
9NB42 SP290 20pf + 10pf multi 15 15
9NB43 SP290 30pf + 15pf multi 20 15
9NB44 SP290 50pf + 25pf multi 40 70
Set value 76

The surtax was for independent welfare organizations.

Animal Type of 1966

Designs: 10pf+5pf, Rabbit. 20pf+10pf, Ermine. 30pf+15pf, Hamster. 50pf+25pf, Red fox.

1967, Apr. 4 Unwmk.
9NB45 SP291 10pf + 5pf multi 15 15
9NB46 SP291 20pf + 10pf multi 18 20
9NB47 SP291 30pf + 15pf multi 22 24
9NB48 SP291 50pf + 25pf multi 65 85

Issued for the benefit of young people.

Fairy Tale Type of 1965

Various Scenes from Frau Holle.

1967, Oct. 3 Litho. *Perf. 14*
9NB49 SP290 10pf + 5pf multi 15 18
9NB50 SP290 20pf + 10pf multi 15 15
9NB51 SP290 30pf + 15pf multi 18 16
9NB52 SP290 50pf + 25pf multi 45 95

The surtax was for independent welfare organizations.

Animal Type of 1968

Animals: 10pf+5pf, Wildcat. 20pf+10pf, Otter. 30pf+15pf, Badger. 50pf+25pf, Beaver.

1968, Feb. 2 Photo. *Perf. 14*
9NB53 SP293 10pf + 5pf multi 30 32
9NB54 SP293 20pf + 10pf multi 35 35
9NB55 SP293 30pf + 15pf multi 60 60
9NB56 SP293 50pf + 25pf multi 1.50 1.75

Surtax for benefit of young people.

Doll Type of 1968

Designs: Various 19th century dolls in sitting position.

1968, Oct. 3 Litho. *Perf. 14*
9NB57 SP294 10pf + 5pf multi 15 20
9NB58 SP294 20pf + 10pf multi 15 15
9NB59 SP294 30pf + 15pf multi 18 18
9NB60 SP294 50pf + 25pf multi 55 1.00

The surtax was for independent welfare organizations.

Horse Type of 1969

Horses: 10pf+5pf, Pony. 20pf+10pf, Work horse. 30pf+15pf, Hotblood. 50pf+25pf, Thoroughbred.

1969, Feb. 6 Litho. *Perf. 14*
9NB61 SP295 10pf + 5pf multi 16 16
9NB62 SP295 20pf + 10pf multi 22 22
9NB63 SP295 30pf + 15pf multi 38 38
9NB64 SP295 50pf + 25pf multi 1.25 1.25

Surtax for benefit of young people.

Tin Toy Type of 1969

Tin Toys: 10pf+5pf, Coach. 20pf+10pf, Woman feeding chickens. 30pf+15pf, Woman grocer. 50pf+25pf, Postilion on horseback.

1969, Oct. 2 Litho. *Perf. 13½x14*
9NB65 SP297 10pf + 5pf multi 15 15
9NB66 SP297 20pf + 10pf multi 16 16
9NB67 SP297 30pf + 15pf multi 25 25
9NB68 SP297 50pf + 25pf multi 65 65

The surtax was for independent welfare organizations.

1969, Nov. 13 Litho. *Perf. 13½x14*

Christmas: 10pf+5pf, The Three Kings.

9NB69 SP297 10pf + 5pf multi 35 35

Minnesinger Type of 1970

Minnesingers (and their Ladies): 10pf+5pf, Heinrich von Stretlingen. 20pf+10pf, Meinloh von Sevelingen. 30pf+15pf, Burkhart von Hohenfels. 50pf+25pf, Albrecht von Johansdorf.

1970, Feb. 5 Photo. *Perf. 13½x14*
9NB70 SP298 10pf + 5pf multi 15 15
9NB71 SP298 20pf + 10pf multi 30 30
9NB72 SP298 30pf + 15pf multi 48 48
9NB73 SP298 50pf + 25pf multi 95 95

Surtax for benefit of young people.

Puppet Type of 1970

Puppets: 10pf+5pf, "Kasperl." 20pf+10pf, Polichinelle. 30pf+5pf, Punch. 50pf+25pf, Pulcinella.

1970, Oct. 6 Litho. *Perf. 13½x14*
9NB74 SP300 10pf + 5pf multi 15 15
9NB75 SP300 20pf + 10pf multi 16 16
9NB76 SP300 30pf + 15pf multi 22 22
9NB77 SP300 50pf + 25pf multi 80 80

The surtax was for independent welfare organizations.

1970, Nov. 12

Christmas: 10pf+5pf, Rococo angel, from Ursuline Sisters' Convent, Innsbruck.

9NB78 SP300 10pf + 5pf multi 35 35

Drawings Type of 1971

Children's Drawings: 10pf+5pf, Fly. 20pf+10pf, Fish. 30pf+15pf, Porcupine. 50pf+25pf, Cock. All stamps horizontal.

1971, Feb. 5 Litho. *Perf. 14*
9NB79 SP301 10pf + 5pf multi 15 15
9NB80 SP301 20pf + 10pf multi 30 30
9NB81 SP301 30pf + 15pf multi 40 40
9NB82 SP301 50pf + 25pf multi 80 80

Surtax for the benefit of young people.

Wooden Toy Type of 1971

Wooden Toys: 10pf+5pf, Movable dolls in box. 25pf+10pf, Knight on horseback. 30pf+15pf, Jumping jack. 60pf+30pf, Nurse rocking babies.

1971, Oct. 5
9NB83 SP303 10pf + 5pf multi 15 15
9NB84 SP303 25pf + 10pf multi 18 18
9NB85 SP303 30pf + 15pf multi 28 28
9NB86 SP303 60pf + 30pf multi 70 70

1971, Nov. 11

Christmas: 10pf+5pf, Christmas angel with candles.

9NB87 SP303 10pf + 5pf multi 35 35

Animal Protection Type of 1972

Designs: 10pf+5pf, Boy trying to rob bird's nest. 25pf+10pf, Girl with kittens to be drowned. 30pf+15pf, Watch dog and man with whip. 60pf+30pf, Hedgehog and deer passing before car at night.

1972, Feb. 4
9NB88 SP304 10pf + 5pf multi 15 15
9NB89 SP304 25pf + 10pf multi 25 25
9NB90 SP304 30pf + 15pf multi 42 42
9NB91 SP304 60pf + 30pf multi 1.00 1.00

Surtax for the benefit of young people.

Chess Type of 1972

1972, Oct. 5 Litho. *Perf. 14*
9NB92 SP307 20pf + 10 Knight 22 22
9NB93 SP307 30pf + 15 Rook 32 32
9NB94 SP307 40pf + 20 Queen 40 40
9NB95 SP307 70pf + 35 King 95 95

The surtax was for independent welfare organizations.

Christmas Type of 1972

Design: 20pf+10pf, Holy Family.

1972, Nov. 10 Litho. *Perf. 14*
9NB96 SP308 20pf + 10pf multi 35 35

Bird Type of 1973

Birds of Prey: 20pf+10pf, Goshawk. 30pf+15pf, Peregrine falcon. 40pf+20pf, Sparrow hawk. 70pf+35pf, Golden eagle.

1973, Feb. 6 Photo. *Perf. 14*
9NB97 SP309 20pf + 10pf multi 40 40
9NB98 SP309 30pf + 15pf multi 65 65
9NB99 SP309 40pf + 20pf multi 1.00 1.00
9NB100 SP309 70pf + 35pf multi 1.50 1.50

Surtax was for benefit of young people.

Instrument Type of 1973

Musical Instruments: 20pf+10pf, Hurdy-gurdy, 17th century. 30pf+15pf, Drum, 16th century. 40pf+20pf, Archlute, 18th century. 70pf+35pf, Organ, 16th century.

1973, Oct. 5 Litho. *Perf. 14*
9NB101 SP311 20pf + 10pf multi 24 24
9NB102 SP311 30pf + 15pf multi 38 38
9NB103 SP311 40pf + 20pf multi 48 48
9NB104 SP311 70pf + 35pf multi 95 95

Surtax was for independent welfare organizations.

Star Type of 1973

Christmas: 20pf+10pf, Christmas star.

1973, Nov. 9 Litho. & Engr.
9NB105 SP312 20pf + 10pf multi 35 35

Youth Type of 1974

Designs: 20pf+10pf, Boy photographing. 30pf+15pf, Boy athlete. 40pf+20pf, Girl violinist. 70pf+35pf, Nurse's aid.

1974, Apr. 17 Photo. *Perf. 14*
9NB106 SP313 20pf + 10pf multi 40 40
9NB107 SP313 30pf + 15pf multi 55 55
9NB108 SP313 40pf + 20pf multi 1.00 1.00
9NB109 SP313 70pf + 35pf multi 1.40 1.40

Surtax was for benefit of young people.

Flower Type of 1974

Designs: 30pf+15pf, Spring bouquet. 40pf+20pf, Autumn bouquet. 50pf+25pf, Roses. 70pf+35pf, Winter flowers. All horizontal.

1974, Oct. 15 Litho. *Perf. 14*
9NB110 SP314 30pf + 15pf multi 32 32
9NB111 SP314 40pf + 20pf multi 40 40
9NB112 SP314 50pf + 25pf multi 55 55
9NB113 SP314 70pf + 35pf multi 75 75

Surtax was for independent welfare organizations.

1974, Oct. 29

Christmas: 30pf+15pf, Christmas bouquet (horiz.).

9NB114 SP314 30pf + 15pf multi 45 45

Locomotive Type of 1975

Steam Locomotives: 30pf+15pf, Dragon. 40pf+20pf, Class 89 (70-75). 50pf+25pf, Class O50. 70pf+35pf, Class O10.

1975, Apr. 15 Litho. *Perf. 14*
9NB115 SP315 30pf + 15pf multi 60 55
9NB116 SP315 40pf + 20pf multi 75 70
9NB117 SP315 50pf + 25pf multi 1.10 95
9NB118 SP315 70pf + 35pf multi 1.90 1.65

Surtax was for benefit of young people.

Flower Type of 1975

Alpine Flowers: 30pf+15pf, Yellow gentian. 40pf+20pf, Arnica. 50pf+25pf, Cyclamen. 70pf+35pf, Blue gentian.

1975, Oct. 15 Litho. *Perf. 14*
9NB119 SP316 30pf + 15pf multi 35 35
9NB120 SP316 40pf + 20pf multi 45 45
9NB121 SP316 50pf + 25pf multi 55 55
9NB122 SP316 70pf + 35pf multi 75 75

Surtax was for independent welfare organizations.

1975, Nov. 14

Christmas: 30pf+15pf, Snow heather.

9NB123 SP316 30pf + 15pf multi 38 38

Sports Type of 1976

Designs: 30pf+15pf, Shot put, women's. 40pf+20pf, Hockey. 50pf+25pf, Handball. 70pf+35pf, Swimming.

1976, Apr. 6 Litho. *Perf. 14*
9NB124 SP317 30pf + 15pf multi 40 40
9NB125 SP317 40pf + 20pf multi 52 52
9NB126 SP317 50pf + 25pf multi 65 65
9NB127 SP317 70pf + 35pf multi 1.00 1.00

Youth training for Olympic Games. The surtax was for the benefit of young people.

Iris — OSP13

Flowers: 40pf+20pf, Wallflower. 50pf+25pf, Dahlia. 70pf+35pf, Larkspur.

1976, Oct. 14 Litho. *Perf. 14*
9NB128 OSP13 30pf + 15pf 32 32
9NB129 OSP13 40pf + 20pf 45 45
9NB130 OSP13 50pf + 25pf 55 55
9NB131 OSP13 70pf + 35pf 90 90

Surtax was for independent welfare organizations.

Souvenir Sheet
Christmas Type of 1976

Christmas: 30pf+15pf, Annunciation to the Shepherds, stained-glass window, Frauenkirche, Esslingen.

1976, Nov. 16 Litho. & Engr.
9NB132 SP320 30pf + 15pf multi 48 48

Ship Type of 1977

Historic Ships: 30pf+15pf, Bremer Kogge, c. 1380. 40pf+20pf, Helena Sloman, 1850. 50pf+25pf, Passenger ship, Cap Polonio, 1914. 70pf+35pf, Freighter Widar, 1971.

1977, Apr. 14 Litho. *Perf. 14*
9NB133 SP321 30pf + 15pf 40 40
9NB134 SP321 40pf + 20pf 52 52
9NB135 SP321 50pf + 25pf 65 65
9NB136 SP321 70pf + 35pf 1.00 1.00

Surtax was for benefit of young people.

Flower Type of 1977

Meadow Flowers: 30pf+15pf, Daisy. 40pf+20pf, Cowslip. 50pf+25pf, Sainfoin. 70pf+35pf, Forget-me-not.

1977, Oct. 13 Litho. *Perf. 14*
9NB137 SP322 30pf + 15pf 35 35
9NB138 SP322 40pf + 20pf 45 45
9NB139 SP322 50pf + 25pf 55 55
9NB140 SP322 70pf + 35pf 85 85

Surtax was for independent welfare organizations.

See Nos. 9NB148-9NB151.

Souvenir Sheet
Christmas Type of 1977

Christmas: 30pf+15pf, Virgin and Child, stained-glass window, Sacristy of St. Gereon Basilica, Cologne.

1977, Nov. 10
9NB141 SP323 30pf + 15pf multi 45 45

Aviation Type of 1978

Designs: 30pf+15pf, Montgolfier balloon, 1783. 40pf+20pf, Lilienthal's glider, 1891. 50pf+25pf, Wright brothers' plane, 1909. 70pf+35pf, Etrich/Rumpler Taube, 1910.

1978, Apr. 13 Litho. *Perf. 14*
9NB142 SP325 30pf + 15pf 40 40
9NB143 SP325 40pf + 20pf 48 48
9NB144 SP325 50pf + 25pf 60 60
9NB145 SP325 70pf + 35pf 90 90

Surtax was for benefit of young people.

Sports Type of 1978

Designs: 50pf+25pf, Bicycling. 70pf+35pf, Fencing.

1978, Apr. 13 Litho. *Perf. 14*
9NB146 SP324 50pf + 25pf 70 70
9NB147 SP324 70pf + 35pf 1.10 1.10

Surtax was for German Sports Foundation.

Flower Type of 1977

Woodland Flowers: 30pf+15pf, Solomon's-seal. 40pf+20pf, Wood primrose. 50pf+25pf, Cephalanthera rubra (orchid). 70pf+35pf, Bugle.

1978, Oct. 12 Litho. *Perf. 14*
9NB148 SP322 30pf + 15pf 35 35
9NB149 SP322 40pf + 20pf 42 42
9NB150 SP322 50pf + 25pf 55 55
9NB151 SP322 70pf + 35pf 75 75

Surtax was for independent welfare organizations.

Souvenir Sheet
Christmas Type of 1978

Christmas: 30pf+15pf, Adoration of the Kings, stained glass window, Frauenkirche, Munich.

1978, Nov. 16 Litho. *Perf. 14*
9NB152 SP326 30pf + 15pf multi 45 45

Aviation Type of 1979

Airplanes: 40pf+20pf, Vampyr, 1921. 50pf+25pf, Junkers JU52/3M, 1932. 60pf+30pf, Messerschmitt BF/ME 108, 1934. 90pf+45pf, Douglas DC3, 1935.

1979, Apr. 5 Litho. *Perf. 14*
9NB153 SP327 40pf + 20pf 40 40
9NB154 SP327 50pf + 25pf 55 55
9NB155 SP327 60pf + 30pf 65 65
9NB156 SP327 90pf + 45pf 1.25 1.25

Surtax was for benefit of young people.

Sports Type of 1979

Designs: 60pf+30pf, Runners. 90pf+45pf, Archers.

1979, Apr. 5
9NB157 SP328 60pf + 30pf 70 70
9NB158 SP328 90pf + 45pf 1.00 1.00

Surtax was for German Sports Foundation.

Plant Type of 1979

Woodland Plants: 40pf+20pf, Larch. 50pf+25pf, Hazelnut. 60pf+30pf, Horse chestnut. 90pf+45pf, Blackthorn.

1979, Oct. 11 Litho. *Perf. 14*
9NB159 SP330 40pf + 20pf 45 45
9NB160 SP330 50pf + 25pf 55 55
9NB161 SP330 60pf + 30pf 65 65
9NB162 SP330 90pf + 45pf 1.00 1.00

Surtax was for independent welfare organizations.

Christmas Type of 1979

Christmas: Nativity, medieval manuscript, Cistercian Abby, Altenberg.

1979, Nov. 14 Litho. *Perf. 13½*
9NB163 SP331 40pf + 20pf multi 50 50

Aviation Type of 1979

Designs: 40pf+20pf, Vickers Viscount, 1950. 50pf+25pf, Fokker 27 Friendship, 1955. 60pf+30pf, Sud Aviation Caravelle, 1955. 90pf+45pf, Sikorsky-55, 1949.

1980, Apr. 10 Litho. *Perf. 14*
9NB164 SP327 40 + 20pf multi 42 42
9NB165 SP327 50 + 25pf multi 55 55
9NB166 SP327 60 + 30pf multi 60 60
9NB167 SP327 90 + 45pf multi 1.00 1.00

Surtax was for benefit of young people.

Sports Type of 1980

Designs: 50pf+25pf, Javelin. 60pf+30pf, Weight lifting. 90pf+45pf, Water polo.

1980, May 8 Photo. *Perf. 14*
9NB168 SP332 50 + 25pf multi 48 48
9NB169 SP332 60 + 30pf multi 65 65
9NB170 SP332 90 + 45pf multi 1.00 1.00

Surtax was for German Sports Foundation.

Wildflower Type of 1980

Wildflowers: 40pf+20pf, Orlaya. 50pf+25pf, Yellow gagea. 60pf+30pf, Summer pheasant's eye. 90pf+45pf, Small-flowered Venus' looking-glass.

1980, Oct. 9 Litho. *Perf. 14*
9NB171 SP333 40 + 20pf multi 45 45
9NB172 SP333 50 + 25pf multi 55 55
9NB173 SP333 60 + 30pf multi 65 65
9NB174 SP333 90 + 45pf multi 1.10 1.10

Surtax was for independent welfare organizations.

Christmas Type of 1980

Christmas: 40pf+20pf, Annunciation to the Shepherds, from Altomunster manuscript, 12th century.

1980, Nov. 13 Litho. *Perf. 14x13½*
9NB175 SP335 40 + 20pf multi 55 55

Optical Instrument Type of 1981

Designs: 40pf+20pf, Theodolite, 1810. 50pf+25pf, Equatorial telescope, 1820. 60pf +30pf, Microscope, 1790. 90pf+45pf, Sextant, 1830.

1981, Apr. 10 Litho. *Perf. 13½*
9NB176 SP336 40 + 20pf multi 55 55
9NB177 SP336 50 + 25pf multi 70 70
9NB178 SP336 60 + 30pf multi 85 85
9NB179 SP336 90 + 45pf multi 1.40 1.40

Surtax for benefit of young people.

Sports Type of 1981

Designs: 60pf+30pf, Women's gymnastics. 90pf+45pf, Cross-county running.

1981, Apr. 10 *Perf. 14*
9NB180 SP337 60 + 30pf multi 80 80
9NB181 SP337 90 + 45pf multi 1.10 1.10

Surtax for the German Sports Foundation.

Plant Type of 1981

Designs: 40pf+20pf, Common bistort. 50pf+25pf, Pedicularis sceptrum-carolinum. 60pf+30pf, Gladiolus palustris. 90pf+45pf, Iris sibirica.

1981, Oct. 8 Litho.
9NB182 SP338 40 + 20pf multi 55 55
9NB183 SP338 50 + 25pf multi 65 65
9NB184 SP338 60 + 30pf multi 80 80
9NB185 SP338 90 + 45pf multi 1.25 1.25

Surtax was for independent welfare organizations.

Christmas Type of 1981

Christmas: Adoration of the Kings, 19th cent. painting.

1981, Nov. 12 Litho.
9NB186 SP339 40 + 20pf multi 55 55

Antique Car Type of 1982

Designs: 40pf+20pf, Daimler, 1889. 50pf+25pf, Wanderer, 1911. 60pf+30pf, Adler limousine, 1913. 90pf+45pf, DKW-F, 1931.

1982, Apr. 15 Litho.
9NB187 SP340 40 + 20pf multi 55 55
9NB188 SP340 50 + 25pf multi 70 70
9NB189 SP340 60 + 30pf multi 80 80
9NB190 SP340 90 + 45pf multi 1.25 1.25

Surtax was for benefit of young people.

Sports Type of 1982

Designs: 60pf+30pf, Sprinting. 90pf+45pf, Volleyball.

1982, Apr. 15 Litho.
9NB191 SP341 60 + 30pf multi 90 90
9NB192 SP341 90 + 45pf multi 1.40 1.40

Surtax was for the German Sports Foundation.

Flower Type of 1982

Designs: 50pf+20pf, Floribunda grandiflora. 60pf+30pf, Tea-rose hybrid (diff.). 80pf+40pf, Floribunda (diff.). 120pf+60pf, Miniature rose.

1982, Oct. 14 Litho. *Perf. 14*
9NB193 SP342 50 + 20pf multi 65 65
9NB194 SP342 60 + 30pf multi 85 85
9NB195 SP342 80 + 40pf multi 1.10 1.10
9NB196 SP342 120 + 60pf multi 1.65 1.65

Surtax was for independent welfare organizations.

Christmas Type of 1982

Christmas: Adoration of the Kings, Oak altar, St. Peter's Church, Hamburg, 1380.

1982, Nov. 10
9NB197 SP343 50 + 20pf multi 80 80

Motorcycle Type of 1983

Designs: 50pf+20pf, Hildebrand & Wolfmuller, 1894. 60pf+30pf, Wanderer, 1908. 80pf+40pf, DKW-Lomos, 1922. 120pf+60pf, Mars, 1925.

1983, Apr. 12 Litho. *Perf. 14*
9NB198 SP344 50 + 20pf multi 75 50
9NB199 SP344 60 + 30pf multi 1.00 65
9NB200 SP344 80 + 40pf multi 1.25 85
9NB201 SP344 120 + 60pf multi 1.90 1.25

Surtax was for benefit of young people.

Sports Type of 1983

Designs: 80pf+40pf, European Latin American Dance Championship. 120pf+60pf, World Hockey Championship.

1983, Apr. 12
9NB202 SP345 80 + 40pf multi 1.25 1.00
9NB203 SP345 120 + 60pf multi 1.90 1.40

Surtax was for German Sports Foundation.

Flower Type of Germany

Designs: 50pf+20pf, Mountain wildflower. 60pf+30pf, Alpine auricula. 80pf+40pf, Little primrose. 120pf+60pf, Einsele's aquilegia.

1983, Oct. 13 Litho. *Perf. 14*
9NB204 SP346 50 + 20pf multi 65 55
9NB205 SP346 60 + 30pf multi 80 75
9NB206 SP346 80 + 40pf multi 1.00 1.00
9NB207 SP346 120 + 60pf multi 1.65 1.40

Surtax was for welfare organizations.

Christmas Type of Germany

1983, Nov. 10 Litho.
9NB208 SP347 50 + 20pf Nativity 85 80

Surtax was for free welfare work.

Insect Type of 1984

Designs: 50pf+20pf, Trichius fasciatus. 60pf+30pf, Agrumenia carniolioa. 80pf+40pf, Bombus terrestris. 120pf+60pf, Eristalis tenax.

1984, Apr. 12 Litho.
9NB209 SP348 50 + 20pf multi 70 55
9NB210 SP348 60 + 30pf multi 90 70
9NB211 SP348 80 + 40pf multi 1.25 1.00
9NB212 SP348 120 + 60pf multi 1.75 1.50

Surtax was for German Youth Stamp Foundation.

Olympic Type of 1984

Women's Events: 60pf+30pf, Hurdles. 80pf+40pf, Cycling. 120pf+60pf, Kayak.

1984, Apr. 12
9NB213 SP349 60 + 30pf multi 90 75
9NB214 SP349 80 + 40pf multi 1.25 1.00
9NB215 SP349 120 + 60pf multi 1.75 1.50

Surtax was for German Sports Foundation.

Orchid Type of 1984

Designs: 50+20pf, Listera cordata. 60pf+30pf, Ophrys insectifera. 80pf+40pf, Epipactis palustris. 120pf+60pf, Ophrys coriophora.

1984, Oct. 18 Litho. *Perf. 14*
9NB216 SP350 50 + 20pf multi 70 55
9NB217 SP350 60 + 30pf multi 90 70
9NB218 SP350 80 + 40pf multi 1.25 1.00
9NB219 SP350 120 + 60pf multi 1.75 1.50

Surtax was for welfare organizations.

Christmas Type of 1984

1984, Nov. 8 Litho.
9NB220 SP351 50pf + 20pf St. Nicholas 65 55

Surtax was for welfare organizations.

Sport Type of 1985

1985, Feb. 21 Photo.
9NB221 SP352 80 + 40pf Basketball 1.25 90
9NB222 SP352 120 + 60pf Table Tennis 1.75 1.30

Surtax was for German Sport Foundation.

Bicycle Type of 1985

Designs: 50pf+20pf, Bussing bicycle, 1868. 60pf+30pf, Child's tricycle, 1885. 80pf+40pf, Jaray bicycle, 1925. 120pf+60pf, Opel racer, 1925.

1985, Apr. 16 Litho.
9NB223 SP353 50 + 20pf multi 70 48
9NB224 SP353 60 + 30pf multi 90 60
9NB225 SP353 80 + 40pf multi 1.25 80
9NB226 SP353 120 + 60pf multi 1.90 1.20

Surtax was for benefit of young people. Each stamp also shows the International Youth Year emblem.

Prayer Book Type of 1985

1985, Oct. 15 Litho. *Perf. 14*
9NB227 SP355 50 + 20pf multi 75 55
9NB228 SP355 60 + 30pf multi 90 70
9NB229 SP355 80 + 40pf multi 1.25 95
9NB230 SP355 120 + 60pf multi 1.90 1.40

Surtax for welfare organizations.

Christmas Type of 1985

Woodcut: Worship of the Kings, Epiphany Altar, Frieburg Cathedral, by Hans Baldung Grien (1485-1545).

1985, Nov. 12 Litho. *Perf. 14*
9NB231 SP356 50 + 20pf multi 72 55

Surtax for welfare organizations.

European Sports Championships Type of 1986

1986, Feb. 13 Litho. *Perf. 14*
9NB232 SP357 80 + 40pf Swimming 1.25 1.10
9NB233 SP357 120 + 55pf Show jumping 1.75 1.50

Surtax for the Natl. Sports Promotion Foundation.

Vocational Training Type of 1986

1986, Apr. 10
9NB234 SP358 50 + 25pf Glazier 80 65
9NB235 SP358 60 + 30pf Mechanic 95 80
9NB236 SP358 70 + 35pf Tailor 1.10 90
9NB237 SP358 80 + 40pf Carpenter 1.40 1.10

Surtax for German Youth Stamp Foundation.

Glassware Type of 1986

1986, Oct. 16 Litho. *Perf. 13x13½*
9NB238 SP359 50 + 25pf Cantharus, 1st cent. 75 75
9NB239 SP359 60 + 30pf Tumbler, c. 200 90 95
9NB240 SP359 70 + 35pf Jug, 3rd cent. 1.05 1.05
9NB241 SP359 80 + 40pf Diatreta, 4th cent. 1.20 1.20

Surtax for public welfare organizations.

Christmas Type of 1986

Christmas: Adoration of the Magi, Ortenberg Altarpiece, c. 1420.

1986, Nov. 13 Litho. *Perf. 14*
9NB242 SP360 50 + 25pf multi 75 75

Surtax for public welfare organizations.

Sports Championships Type of 1987

1987, Feb. 12 Litho.
9NB243 SP361 80 + 40pf Gymnastics 1.35 1.35
9NB244 SP361 120 + 55pf Judo 1.95 1.95

Surtax for the benefit of the national Sports Promotion Foundation.

Industry Type of 1987

1987, Apr. 9 Litho.
9NB245 SP362 50 + 25pf Cooper 82 82
9NB246 SP362 60 + 30pf Stonemason 1.00 1.00
9NB247 SP362 70 + 35pf Furrier 1.15 1.15
9NB248 SP362 80 + 40pf Painter 1.30 1.30

Surtax for youth organizations.

Gold and Silver Artifacts Type of 1987

1987, Oct. 15
9NB249 SP363 50 + 25pf Bonnet ornament, 5th cent. 85 85
9NB250 SP363 60 + 30pf Athena plate, 1st cent. B.C. 1.00 1.00
9NB251 SP363 70 + 35pf Armilla armlet, c. 1180 1.20 1.20
9NB252 SP363 80 + 40pf Snake bracelet, 300 B.C. 1.35 1.35

Surtax for welfare organizations sponsoring free museum exhibitions.

Christmas Type of 1987

Illustration from Book of Psalms, 13th cent., Bavarian Natl. Museum: Adoration of the Magi.

1987, Nov. 6
9NB253 SP364 50 + 25pf multi 85 85

Surtax for public welfare organizations.

Sports Type of 1988

1988, Feb. 18 Litho.
9NB254 SP365 60 + 30pf Trapshooting 1.15 1.15
9NB255 SP365 80 + 40pf Figure skating 1.50 1.50
9NB256 SP365 120 + 55pf Hammer throw 2.20 2.20

Music Type of 1988

Designs: No. 9NB257, Piano terzet. No. 9NB258, Wind quintet. No. 9NB259, Guitar, mandolin, recorder. No. 9NB260, Children's choir.

1988, Apr. 14 Litho. *Perf. 14*
9NB257 SP366 50 +25pf multi 1.05 1.05
9NB258 SP366 60 +30pf multi 1.10 1.10
9NB259 SP366 70 +35pf multi 1.30 1.30
9NB260 SP366 80 +40pf multi 1.50 1.50

Surtax for German Youth Stamp Foundation.

Artifacts Type of 1988

Designs: No. 9NB261, Brooch, c. 1700, Schmuck Museum, Pforzheim. No. 9NB262, Lion, 1540, Kunstgewerbe Museum, Berlin. No. 9NB263, Lidded goblet, 1536, Kunstgewerbe Museum. No. 9NB264, Cope clasp, c. 1400, Aachen cathedral.

1988, Oct. 13 Litho.
9NB261 SP367 50 +25pf multi 82 82
9NB262 SP367 60 +30pf multi 95 95
9NB263 SP367 70 +35pf multi 1.15 1.15
9NB264 SP367 80 +40pf multi 1.30 1.30

Surtax for welfare organizations.

Christmas Type of 1988

Illumination from *The Gospel Book of Henry the Lion*, Helmarshausen, 1188, Prussian Cultural Museum, Bavaria: Angels announce the birth of Christ to the shepherds.

1988, Nov. 10 Litho.
9NB265 SP368 50 +25pf multi 82 82

Surtax for public welfare organizations.

Sports Type of 1989

1989, Feb. 9 Litho.
9NB266 SP369 100pf +50pf Volleyball 1.65 1.65
9NB267 SP369 140pf +60pf Hockey 2.15 2.15

Surtax for the Natl. Sports Promotion Foundation.

Circus Type of 1989

1989, Apr. 20 Litho.
9NB268 SP371 60 +30pf Tamer and tigers 1.00 1.00
9NB269 SP371 70 +30pf Trapeze artists 1.10 1.10
9NB270 SP371 80 +35pf Seals 1.30 1.30
9NB271 SP371 100 +50pf Jugglers 1.65 1.65

Surtax for natl. youth welfare organizations.

Mail Carrying Type of 1989

Designs: No. 9NB272, Messenger, 15th cent. No. 9NB273, Brandenburg mail wagon, c. 1700. No. 9NB274, Prussian postal workers, 19th cent.

1989, Oct. 12 Litho.
9NB272 SP372 60 +30pf multi 98 98
9NB273 SP372 80 +35pf multi 1.25 1.25
9NB274 SP372 100 +50pf multi 1.65 1.65

Surtax for the benfit of Free Welfare Work.

Christmas Type of 1989

1989, Nov. 16 Litho.
9NB275 SP373 40 +20pf Angel 62 62
9NB276 SP373 60 +30pf Nativity 92 92

Surtax for the benefit of the Federal Working Assoc. of Free Welfare Work.

Sports Type of 1990

Designs: No. 9NB277, Water polo. No. 9NB278, Wheelchair basketball.

1990, Feb. 15 Litho.
9NB277 SP374 100 +50pf multi 1.80 1.80
9NB278 SP374 140 +60pf multi 2.40 2.40

Surtax for the Natl. Sports Promotion Foundation.

Max and Moritz Type of 1990

1990, Apr. 19 Litho.
9NB279 SP375 60 +30pf Max, Moritz 1.05 1.05
9NB280 SP375 70 +30pf Max, Moritz, diff. 1.20 1.20
9NB281 SP375 80 +35pf Moritz 1.35 1.35
9NB282 SP375 100 +50pf Bug, Uncle 1.75 1.75

Surcharge for the German Youth Stamp Foundation.

Post and Telecommunications Type of 1990

Designs: 60pf + 30pf, Railway mail car, 1900. 80pf + 35pf, Telephone installation, 1900. 100pf + 50pf, Mail truck, 1900.

1990, Sept. 27 Litho. *Perf. 13½x14*
9NB283 SP377 60 +30pf multi 1.05 1.05
9NB284 SP377 80 +35pf multi 1.35 1.35
9NB285 SP377 100 +50pf multi 1.75 1.75

Surtax for welfare organizations.

ISSUED UNDER RUSSIAN OCCUPATION

Germany under Russian Occupation stamps can be mounted in Scott's Germany Part I and Soviet Republics Part I Albums.

When the mark was revalued in June, 1948, a provisional overprint, consisting of various city and town names and post office or zone numerals, was applied by hand in black, violet or blue at innumerable post offices to their stocks.

For Use in All Provinces in the Russian Zone

Germany Nos. 557 to 573 Overprinted in Black

Sowjetische Besatzungs Zone

1948, July 3 Wmk. 284 *Perf. 14*
10N1 A120 2pf brn blk 15 15
10N2 A120 6pf purple 15 15
10N3 A121 8pf red 15 15
10N4 A121 10pf yel grn 15 15
10N5 A122 12pf gray 15 15
10N6 A120 15pf chocolate 15 15
10N7 A123 16pf dk bl grn 15 15
10N8 A121 20pf blue 15 15
10N9 A123 24pf brn org 15 15
10N10 A120 25pf org yel 15 15
10N11 A122 30pf red 15 18
10N12 A121 40pf red vio 15 18
10N13 A123 50pf ultra 22 28
10N14 A122 60pf red brn 30 30
a. 60pf brown red 19.00 *40.00*
10N15 A122 80pf dk bl 35 40
10N16 A122 84pf emerald 35 40
Set value 2.30 2.30

Same Overprint on Numeral Stamps of Germany, 1946

1948, Sept.
10N17 A119 5pf yel grn 15 15
10N18 A119 30pf olive 22 42
10N19 A119 45pf brt red 15 24
10N20 A119 75pf dp ultra 15 24
10N21 A119 84pf emerald 25 24
Nos. 10N17-10N21 (5) 92 1.29

Nos 10N1-10N21 all exist with inverted overprint, and majority with double overprint.

Bear from Berlin Arms — OS1

Design differs for each stamp.
All inscribed: "Stadt Berlin"
Overprint in Black

1948, Sept. Unwmk. Litho. *Perf. 14*
10N22 OS1 5(pf) green 15 15
a. Serrate roulette 15 15
10N23 OS1 6pf violet 15 15
10N24 OS1 8(pf) red 15 15
10N25 OS1 10pf brown 15 15
10N26 OS1 12pf rose 15 35
10N27 OS1 20(pf) blue 15 20
10N28 OS1 30(pf) olive 15 30
Set value 85 1.25

The overprint made #10N22-10N28 valid for postage throughout the Russian Zone.

Käthe Kollwitz — OS2

Designs: 60pf, 40pf, Gerhard Hauptmann. 8pf, 50pf, Karl Marx. 10pf, 84pf, August Bebel. 12pf, 30pf, Friedrich Engels. 15pf, 60pf, G. W. F. Hegel. 16pf, 25pf, Rudolf Virchow. 20pf, Käthe Kollwitz. 24pf, 80pf, Ernst Thälmann.

Perf. 13x12½

1948 Typo. Wmk. 292
10N29 OS2 2pf gray 15 15
10N30 OS2 6pf violet 15 15
10N31 OS2 8pf red brn 18 15
10N32 OS2 10pf bl grn 15 15
10N33 OS2 12pf blue 1.90 15
10N34 OS2 15pf brown 25 40
10N35 OS2 16pf turquoise 18 15
10N36 OS2 20pf maroon 18 30
10N37 OS2 24pf carmine 2.25 15
10N38 OS2 25pf ol grn 35 65
10N39 OS2 30pf red 38 50
10N40 OS2 40pf red vio 25 30
10N41 OS2 50pf dk ultra 30 20
10N42 OS2 60pf dl grn 95 20
10N43 OS2 80pf dk bl 55 20
10N44 OS2 84pf brn lake 80 85
Nos. 10N29-10N44 (16) 8.97 4.65

See German Democratic Republic Nos. 122-136.

Karl Liebknecht and Rosa Luxemburg OS3

Perf. 13½x13

1949, Jan. 15 Litho. Wmk. 292
10N45 OS3 24pf rose 15 40

30th anniv. of the death of Karl Liebknecht and Rosa Luxemburg, German socialists.

Dove and Laurel — OS4

1949
10N46 OS4 24pf carmine rose 38 95

Overprinted in Black: "3. Deutscher Volkskongress 29.-30. Mai 1949"

1949, May 29
10N47 OS4 24pf car rose 30 70

Nos. 10N46 and 10N47 were issued for the 3rd German People's Congress.
For succeeding issues see German Democratic Republic.

RUSSIAN OCCUPATION SEMI-POSTAL STAMPS

Leipzig Fair Issue

Type of German Semi-Postal Stamps of 1947

Designs: 16pf+9pf, First New Year's Fair, 1459. 50pf+25pf, Arrival of clothmakers from abroad, 1469.

Wmk. 292

1948, Aug. 29 Litho. *Perf. 13½*
10NB1 SP252 16 + 9pf dk vio brn 15 15
10NB2 SP252 50 + 25pf dl vio bl 15 18
Set value 18

The 1948 Leipzig Autumn Fair.

Emblem of Philatelic Institute OSP1

Goethe OSP2

1948, Oct. 23 *Perf. 13x13½*
10NB3 OSP1 12 + 3pf red 15 20

Stamp Day, Oct. 26, 1948.

Leipzig Fair Issue

Type of German Semi-Postal Stamps of 1947

Designs: 30pf+15pf, First fair in newly built Town Hall, 1556. 50pf+25pf, Italians at the Fair, 1536.

1949, Mar. 6 Litho. *Perf. 13½*
10NB4 SP252 30 + 15pf red 1.10 1.75
10NB5 SP252 50 + 25pf blue 1.50 2.25

1949 Leipzig Spring Fair.

1949, July 20 Wmk. 292 *Perf. 13*

Designs: Different Goethe portraits.

10NB6 OSP2 6 + 4pf dl vio 1.00 1.10
10NB7 OSP2 12 + 8pf dl brn 1.00 1.10
10NB8 OSP2 24 + 16pf red brn 90 90
10NB9 OSP2 50 + 25pf dk bl 90 90
10NB10 OSP2 84 + 36pf ol gray 1.50 1.65
Nos. 10NB6-10NB10 (5) 5.30 5.65

Issued to commemorate the bicentenary of the birth of Johann Wolfgang von Goethe.

Souvenir Sheet

Profile of Goethe OSP3

1949, Aug. 22 Engr. *Perf. 14*
10NB11 OSP3 50pf + 4.50m blue 125.00 200.00

The sheet measures 106x105mm. The surtax was for the reconstruction of Weimar.

Leipzig Fair Issue

Type of German Semi-Postal Stamps of 1947

Designs: 12pf+8pf, Russian merchants at the Fair, 1650. 24pf+16pf, Young Goethe at the Fair, 1765.

1949, Aug. 30 Litho. *Perf. 13½*
10NB12 SP252 12 + 8pf gray 1.50 2.50
10NB13 SP252 24 + 16pf lake brown 2.25 2.75

1949 Leipzig Autumn Fair.

BERLIN-BRANDENBURG

Berlin Bear — OS1

1945 Litho. *Perf. 14*
11N1 OS1 5pf shown 15 15
11N2 OS1 6pf Bear holding spade 15 15
11N3 OS1 8pf Bear on shield 15 15
11N4 OS1 10pf Bear holding brick 15 15
11N5 OS1 12pf Bear carrying board 15 15
11N6 OS1 20pf Bear on small shield 15 20
11N7 OS1 30pf Oak sapling, ruins 15 25
Set value 50 1.00

Issue dates: 5pf, 8pf, June 9. 12pf, July 5. Others, July 18.

1945, Dec. 6 *Serrate Roulette 13½*
11N1a OS1 5pf 4.00
11N2a OS1 6pf 4.00
11N3a OS1 8pf 3.00
11N4a OS1 10pf 5.00
11N5a OS1 12pf 4.00

11N6a	OS1	20pf	4.00
11N7a	OS1	30pf	4.00
		Nos. 11N1a-11N7a (7)	28.00

MECKLENBURG-VORPOMMERN

OS1

Plowman — OS2

Design: 12pf, Wheat.

1945-46 Typo. *Perf. 10½*

12N1	OS1	6pf black, *green*	25
12N2	OS1	6pf purple	25
12N3	OS1	6pf purple, *green*	25
12N4	OS2	8pf red, *rose*	25
a.		8pf red lilac, *rose*	35
12N5	OS2	8pf black, *rose*	25
12N6	OS2	8pf red lilac, *green*	25
12N7	OS2	8pf black, *green*	25
12N8	OS2	8pf brown	25
12N9	OS2	12pf black, *rose*	25
12N10	OS2	12pf brown lilac	25
12N11	OS2	12pf red	1.25
12N12	OS2	12pf red, *rose*	25
		Nos. 12N1-12N12 (12)	4.00

Issue dates: Nos. 12N1, 12N9, Aug. 28. No. 12N4, Oct. 6. No. 12N5, Oct. 19. No. 12N7, Nov. 2. No. 12N6, Nov. 3. No. 12N10, Nov. 9. No. 12N2, Nov. 16. No. 12N11, Dec. 20. No. 12N8, Jan. 7, 1946. No. 12N3, Jan. 11, 1946. No. 12N12, Jan. 30, 1946.

Buildings — OS3

Designs: 4pf, Deer. 5pf, Fishing boats. 6pf, Harvesting grain. 8pf, Windmill. 10pf, Two-horse plow. 12pf, Bricklayer on scaffolding. 15pf, Tractor plowing field. 20pf, Ship, warehouse. 30pf, Factory. 40pf, Woman spinning.

1946 Typo. *Imperf.*

12N13	OS3	3pf brown	1.25
12N14	OS3	4pf blue	5.00
12N15	OS3	4pf red brown	1.25
12N16	OS3	5pf green	1.25
12N17	OS3	8pf orange	40
12N18	OS3	10pf brown	40

Perf. 10½

12N19	OS3	6pf purple	20
12N20	OS3	6pf blue	3.50
12N21	OS3	12pf red	20
12N22	OS3	15pf brown	30
12N23	OS3	20pf blue	25
12N24	OS3	30pf blue green	25
12N25	OS3	40pf red violet	20

Issue dates: 3pf, No. 12N14, 5pf, 6pf, 8pf, Jan. 17. 10pf, 12pf, 40pf, Jan. 22. 15pf, Jan. 24. 30pf, Jan. 26. 20pf, Jan. 29. No. 12N15, Feb. 25.

Nos. 12N13-12N21 exist on both white and toned paper.

MECKLENBURG-VORPOMMERN SEMI-POSTAL STAMPS

Rudolf Breischeid (1874-1944), Politician OSP1

Designs: 8pf+22pf, Dr. Erich Klausener (1885-1934), theologian. 12pf+28pf, Ernst Thalmann (1886-1944), politician.

1945, Oct. 21 Typo. *Perf. 10½x11*

12NB1	OSP1	6 +14pf green	3.00
12NB2	OSP1	8 +22pf purple	3.00
12NB3	OSP1	12 +28pf red	3.00

Horsedrawn plow — OSP2

Child Welfare — OSP3

Designs: 8pf+22pf, Sower. 12pf+28pf, Reaper.

1945

12NB4	OSP2	6 +14pf bl grn	1.75
12NB5	OSP2	6 +14pf grn	1.75
12NB6	OSP2	8 +22pf brn	1.75
12NB7	OSP2	8 +22pf yel brn	1.75
12NB8	OSP2	12 +28pf red	1.75
12NB9	OSP2	12 +28pf org	1.75
		Nos. 12NB4-12NB9 (6)	10.50

Issue dates: Nos. 12NB4, 12NB6, 12NB8, Dec. 8, others Dec. 31.

1945, Dec. 31 *Perf. 11*

12NB10	OSP3	6 +14pf Child in hand	50
12NB11	OSP3	8 +22pf Girl in winter	50
12NB12	OSP3	12 +28pf Boy	50

SAXONY

Coat of Arms — OS1

Land Reform — OS2

Perf. 13x12½

1945-46 Typo. Wmk. 48

13N1	OS1	1pf slate	15
a.		Imperf.	30
13N2	OS1	3pf yellow brown	15
a.		Imperf.	30
13N3	OS1	5pf green	15
a.		Imperf.	30
13N4	OS1	6pf purple	15
a.		Imperf.	30
13N5	OS1	8pf orange	15
a.		Imperf.	30
13N6	OS1	10pf brown	15
a.		Imperf.	2.00
13N7	OS1	12pf red	15
a.		Imperf.	30
13N8	OS1	15pf red brown	15
13N9	OS1	20pf blue	15
13N10	OS1	24pf orange brown	15
13N11	OS1	30pf olive green	15
13N12	OS1	40pf lake	15
		Set value	1.00

Issue dates: Nos. 13N1-13N12, Dec. 1945. Nos. 13N1a-13N5a, 13N7a, Oct. 10, 1945. No. 13N6a, Jan. 1946.

1945-46 Unwmk. *Imperf.*

13N13	OS2	6pf green	15
13N14	OS2	12pf red	15

On Thin Transparent Paper

Wmk. *Perf. 13x13½*

13N15	OS2	6pf green	15
13N16	OS2	12pf red	15
		Set value, Nos. 13N13-13N16	30

Issue dates: Nos. 13N13-13N14, Dec. 17, 1945. Others Feb. 21, 1946.

SAXONY SEMI-POSTAL STAMPS

Reconstruction OSP1

Designs: 6+4pf, Housing construction. 12+8pf, Bridge repair. 42+28pf, Locomotives.

1946 Typo. *Perf. 13*

13NB1	OSP1	6pf +4pf green	15
a.		Imperf.	15
13NB2	OSP1	12pf +8pf red	15
a.		Imperf.	15
13NB3	OSP1	42pf +28pf violet	15
a.		Imperf.	15
		Set value	18

Issue dates: Perf., Jan. 19. Imperf., Feb. 21.

WEST SAXONY

OS1

Leipzig Fair — OS2

1945 Typo. Wmk. 48 *Perf. 13x12½*

14N1	OS1	3pf brown	15	15
14N2	OS1	4pf slate	15	15
14N3	OS1	5pf green	15	15
a.		Imperf.	15	
14N4	OS1	6pf violet	15	15
a.		Imperf.	15	
14N5	OS1	8pf orange	15	15
a.		Imperf.	15	
14N6	OS1	10pf gray	15	15
14N7	OS1	12pf red	15	15
a.		Imperf.	15	
14N8	OS1	15pf red brown	15	15
14N9	OS1	20pf blue	25	25
14N10	OS1	30pf olive green	25	35
14N11	OS1	40pf red lilac	25	35
14N12	OS1	60pf maroon	35	45
		Set value	1.40	2.00

Issue dates: 3pf, 4pf, 20pf, 30pf, Nov. 9. 5pf, 6pf, 8pf, 12pf, Nov. 12. 10pf, 15pf, 40pf, 60pf, Nov. 15. Imperfs., Sept. 28.

1945, Oct. 18

14N13	OS2	6pf green	15
14N14	OS2	12pf red	15

Leipzig Arms — OS3

Designs: 5pf, 6pf, St. Nicholas Church. 8pf, 12pf, Leipzig Town Hall.

1946, Feb. 12

14N15	OS3	3pf brown	15
a.		Unwatermarked	15
14N16	OS3	4pf slate	15
a.		Unwatermarked	15
14N17	OS3	5pf green	15
a.		Unwatermarked	15
14N18	OS3	6pf violet	15
a.		Unwatermarked	15
14N19	OS3	8pf orange	15
a.		Unwatermarked	15
14N20	OS3	12pf red	15
a.		Unwatermarked	15
		Set value	35
		Set value, unwatermarked	30

WEST SAXONY SEMI-POSTAL STAMPS

OSP1

Market, Old Town Hall — OSP2

Perf. 13x12½

1946, Jan. 7 Typo. Wmk. 48

14NB1	OSP1	3 +2pf yel brn	15
14NB2	OSP1	4 +3pf slate	15
14NB3	OSP1	5 +3pf green	15
14NB4	OSP1	6 +4pf violet	15
14NB5	OSP1	8 +4pf orange	15
14NB6	OSP1	10 +5pf gray	15
14NB7	OSP1	12 +6pf red	15
14NB8	OSP1	15 +10pf red brn	15
14NB9	OSP1	20 +10pf blue	15
14NB10	OSP1	30 +20pf olive grn	15
14NB11	OSP1	40 +30pf red lilac	15
14NB12	OSP1	60 +40pf lake	15
		Set value	1.25

Issue dates: Nos. 14NB1, 14NB4, 14NB7, 14NB11, Jan. 7; others, Jan. 28.

1946, May 8 *Perf. 13*

14NB13	OSP2	6 +14pf violet	15
a.		Imperf.	25
b.		Unwatermarked	20
14NB14	OSP2	12 +18pf bl gray	15
a.		Imperf.	25
b.		Unwatermarked	20
14NB15	OSP2	24 +26pf org brn	15
a.		Imperf.	25
b.		Unwatermarked	25
14NB16	OSP2	84 +66pf green	15
a.		Imperf.	25
c.		Sheet of 4, #15NB13a-15NB16a	*100.00*
		Set value	30

Issue date: Imperf., May 20.

EAST SAXONY

Type OS1 Inscribed "NOYTA"

1945, June 23 Photo. *Imperf.*

15N1	OS1	12pf red	

OS1

Litho. (3pf, #15N9), Photo.

1945-46

15N2	OS1	3pf sepia	15
15N3	OS1	4pf blue gray	15
a.		4pf gray	15
15N4	OS1	5pf brown	20
15N5	OS1	6pf green	1.00
15N6	OS1	6pf violet	15
15N7	OS1	8pf dark violet	30
15N8	OS1	10pf dark brown	18
15N9	OS1	10pf gray	18
15N10	OS1	12pf red	15
15N11	OS1	15pf lemon	25
15N12	OS1	20pf gray blue	15
a.		20pf blue	15
15N13	OS1	25pf blue	20
15N14	OS1	30pf yellow	15
15N15	OS1	40pf lilac	30

Typo.

Perf. 13x12½

15N16	OS1	3pf brown	15
15N17	OS1	5pf green	15
15N18	OS1	6pf violet	15
15N19	OS1	8pf orange	15
15N20	OS1	12pf vermilion	15

Issue dates: 12pf, June 28. #15N5, June 30. 8pf, #15N8, July 3. 25pf, July 5. 5pf, July 6. 40pf, July 7. 15pf, July 10. #15N12, July 26. #15N9, 15N12a, 15N17-15N20, Nov. 3. #15N3, 30pf, Nov. 5. 3pf, Dec. 5. #15N15, Dec. 21. #15N6, Jan. 22, 1946.

EAST SAXONY SEMI-POSTAL STAMPS

Zwinger, Dresden — OSP1

Design: 12pf+88pf, Rathaus, Dresden.

1946, Feb. 6 Photo. *Perf. 11*

15NB1	OSP1	6pf +44pf green	15
15NB2	OSP1	12pf +88pf red	15

THURINGIA

Fir Trees — OS1

Designs: 6pf, 8pf, Posthorn. 12pf, Schiller. 20pf, 30pf, Goethe.

1945-46 Typo. *Perf. 11*

16N1 OS1 3pf brown 15
16N2 OS1 4pf black 15
16N3 OS1 5pf green 15
a. Souvenir sheet of 3, #16N1-16N3 *150.00*
16N4 OS1 6pf dark green 15
16N5 OS1 8pf orange 15
16N6 OS1 12pf red 15
16N7 OS1 20pf blue 15
a. Imperf. 15
b. Souv. sheet of 4, #16N2, 16N4, 16N6-16N7, rouletted by imperf. between *500.00*
16N8 OS1 30pf gray 30
a. Imperf. 75
Nos. 16N1-16N8 (8) 1.35

Issue dates: 6pf, Oct. 1. 12pf, Oct. 19. 5pf, Oct. 20. 8pf, Nov. 3. 20pf, Nov. 24. Nos. 16N3a, 16N7b, Dec. 18. 30pf, Dec. 22. 3pf, 4pf, Jan. 4, 1946.

Souvenir Sheet

Rebuilding of German Natl. Theater, Weimar — OS2

Designs: a, 6pf, Schiller. b, 10pf, Goethe. c, 12pf, Liszt. d, 16pf, Wieland. e, 40pf, Natl. Theater.

1946, Mar. 27 Wmk. 48 *Imperf.*

16N9 OS2 Sheet of 5, #a.-e. 10.00
f. Sheet, unwatermarked 25.00

Sold for 7.50 marks.

THURINGIA SEMI-POSTAL STAMPS

Bridge Reconstruction OSP1

Designs: 10pf+60pf, Saalburg Bridge. 12pf+68pf, Camsdorf Bridge, Jena. 16pf+74pf, Goschwitz Bridge. 24pf+76pf, Ilm Bridge, Mellingen.

1946, Mar. 30 Typo. *Imperf.*

16NB1 OSP1 10 +60pf red brown 15
16NB2 OSP1 12 +68pf red 15
16NB3 OSP1 16 +74pf dark green 15
16NB4 OSP1 24 +76pf brown 15
a. Souv. sheet of 4, #16NB1-16NB4 *125.00*
Set value 30

GERMAN DEMOCRATIC REPUBLIC

LOCATION — Eastern Germany
GOVT. — Republic
AREA — 41,659 sq. mi.
POP. — 16,701,500 (1983)
CAPITAL — Berlin (Soviet sector)

100 Pfennigs = 1 Deutsche Mark (East)
100 Pfennigs = 1 Mark of the Deutsche Notenbank (MDN) (1965)
100 Pfennigs = 1 Mark of the National Bank (M) (1969)
100 Pfennigs = 1 Deutsche Mark (West) (1990)

Catalogue values for all unused stamps in this country are for Never Hinged items.

Watermarks

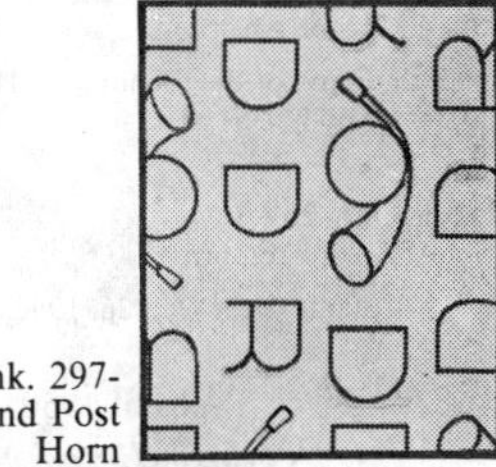
Wmk. 297- DDR and Post Horn

Wmk. 313- Quatrefoil and DDR

Pigeon, Letter and Globe A5

Wmk. Flowers Multiple (292)

1949, Oct. 9 Litho. *Perf. 13½*

48 A5 50pf lt bl & dk bl 6.75 3.25

75th anniv. of the UPU.

Letter Carriers A6

Skier A7

1949, Oct. 27 *Perf. 13*

49 A6 12pf blue 5.00 3.00
50 A6 30pf red 9.00 5.00

"Day of the International Postal Workers' Trade Union," October 27-29, 1949.

1950, Mar. 2 *Perf. 13*

51 A7 12pf shown 4.75 3.00
52 A7 24pf Skater 6.25 4.25

1st German Winter Sport Championship Matches, Schierke, 1950.

Globe and Sun — A8

1950, May 1 Typo.

53 A8 30pf deep carmine 11.00 8.00

60th anniv. of Labor Day.

Pres. Wilhelm Pieck A9 A10

1950-51 Wmk. 292 *Perf. 13x12½*

54 A9 12pf dark blue 7.75 90
55 A9 24pf red brown 14.00 60

Perf. 13x13½

56 A10 1m olive green 14.00 2.25

Litho.

57 A10 2m red brown 7.00 2.25

Engr.

57A A10 5m deep blue ('51) 1.50 20
Nos. 54-57A (5) 44.25 6.20

See Nos. 113-117, 120-121.

Leonhard Euler — A11

Miner — A12

Portraits: 5pf, Alexander von Humboldt. 6pf, Theodor Mommsen. 8pf, Wilhelm von Humboldt. 10pf, H. L. F. von Helmholtz. 12pf, Max Planck. 16pf, Jacob Grimm. 20pf, W. H. Nernst. 24pf, Gottfried von Leibnitz. 50pf, Adolf von Harnack.

Wmk. 292

1950, July 10 Litho. *Perf. 12½*

58 A11 1pf gray 3.00 1.40
59 A11 5pf dp grn 4.50 3.75
60 A11 6pf purple 7.50 4.50
61 A11 8pf org brn 13.00 8.75
62 A11 10pf dk gray grn 10.00 8.75
63 A11 12pf dk bl 3.00 1.40
64 A11 16pf Prus bl 15.00 11.00
65 A11 20pf vio brn 13.00 8.75
66 A11 24pf red 13.00 2.75
67 A11 50pf dp ultra 18.00 10.50
Nos. 58-67 (10) 100.00 61.55

250th anniv. of the founding of the Academy of Science, Berlin.
See Nos. 352-354.

Canceled to Order

The government stamp agency started about 1950 to sell canceled sets of new issues.

Used values are for CTO's from No. 68 to No. 2831.

1950, Sept. 1 *Perf. 13*

Design: 24pf, Smelting copper.

68 A12 12pf blue 3.25 60
69 A12 24pf dark red 4.75 90

750th anniv. of the opening of the Mannsfeld copper mines.

Symbols of a Democratic Vote — A13

Hand Between Dove and Tank — A14

1950, Sept. 28

70 A13 24pf brn red 9.00 60

Publicizing the election of Oct. 15, 1950.

1950, Dec. 15 Litho. *Perf. 13*

Designs show hand shielding dove from: 8pf, Exploding shell, 12pf, Atomic explosion, 24pf, Cemetery.

71 A14 6pf vio bl 2.75 1.10
72 A14 8pf brown 2.50 55
73 A14 12pf blue 4.25 95
74 A14 24pf red 4.00 45

Issued to publicize the "Fight for Peace."

Tobogganing A15

Design: 24pf, Ski jump.

1951, Feb. 3 Litho. *Perf. 13*

76 A15 12pf blue 6.00 1.50
77 A15 24pf rose 8.00 2.25

Issued to publicize the second Winter Sports Championship Matches at Oberhof.

A16

1951, Mar. 4 Wmk. 292 *Perf. 13*

78 A16 24pf rose car 13.00 3.50
79 A16 50pf vio bl 13.00 3.50

Issued to publicize the 1951 Leipzig Fair.

Pres. Wilhelm Pieck and Pres. Boleslaw Bierut Shaking Hands Across Oder-Neisse Frontier — A17

1951, Apr. 22 *Perf. 13*

80 A17 24pf scarlet 17.50 4.50
81 A17 50pf blue 17.50 4.50

Issued to commemorate the visit of Pres. Boleslaw Bierut of Poland to the Russian Zone of Germany.

Mao Tse-tung — A18

Redistribution of Chinese Land — A19

1951, June 27 ***Perf. 13***

82	A18	12pf dark green	*65.00*	7.25
83	A19	24pf deep carmine	*100.00*	13.00
84	A18	50pf violet blue	*60.00*	5.00

Issued to publicize East Germany's friendship toward Communist China.

Boy Raising Flag A20

5-Year Plan Symbolism A21

Design: 24pf, 50pf, Girls dancing.

1951, Aug. 3

Grayish Paper, Except 30pf

85	A20	12pf choc & org brn	9.00	1.75
86	A20	24pf dk car & yel grn	9.50	1.25
87	A20	30pf dk bl grn & org brn, *cit*	12.00	2.25
88	A20	50pf vio bl & dk car	10.00	1.90

3rd World Youth Festival, Berlin, 1951.

1951, Sept. 2 **Typo.** **Wmk. 292**

89	A21	24pf multi	3.50	50

East Germany's Five-Year Plan.

Karl Liebknecht A22

Father and Children with Stamp Collection A23

1951, Oct. 7 **Litho.** ***Perf. 13½x13***

90	A22	24pf red & bl gray	3.50	50

80th anniversary of the birth of Karl Liebknecht, socialist.

1951, Oct. 28 ***Perf. 13***

91	A23	12pf deep blue	3.00	60

Stamp Day, Oct. 28, 1951.

Stalin and Wilhelm Pieck A24

Design: 12pf, Pavel Bykov and Erich Wirth.

1951

92	A24	12pf deep blue	3.75	90
93	A24	24pf red	4.75	1.10

Month of East German-Soviet friendship.
Issue dates: 12pf, Dec. 15, 24pf, Dec. 1.

Skier A25

Beethoven A26

Design: 24pf, Ski jump.

1952, Jan. 12 **Wmk. 292**

94	A25	12pf bl grn	3.75	70
95	A25	24pf deep blue	3.75	90

Winter Sports Championship Matches, Oberhof, 1952.

1952, Mar. 26 ***Perf. 13½***

Design: 12pf, Beethoven full face.

96	A26	12pf bl gray & vio bl	1.25	15
97	A26	24pf gray & red brn	1.50	15

125th anniversary of the death of Ludwig van Beethoven.

See Nos. 100-102.

Cyclists — A27

Klement Gottwald — A28

1952, May 5 **Photo.** ***Perf. 13x13½***

98	A27	12pf blue	1.50	15

Issued to publicize the 5th International Bicycle Peace Race, Warsaw-Berlin-Prague.

1952, May 1

99	A28	24pf violet blue	1.90	35

Friendship between German Democratic Republic and Czechoslovakia.

Similar to A26

Portraits: 6pf, G. F. Handel. 8pf, Albert Lortzing. 50pf, C. M. von Weber.

1952, July 5 **Litho.** **Wmk. 297**

100	A26	6pf brn buff & choc	1.10	28
101	A26	8pf pink & dp rose pink	2.00	32
102	A26	50pf bl gray & dp bl	3.00	40

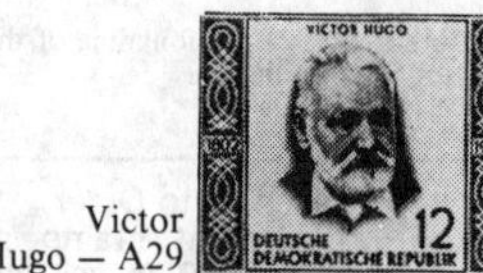

Victor Hugo — A29

Portraits: 20pf, Leonardo da Vinci. 24pf, Nicolai Gogol. 35pf, Avicenna.

Wmk. 292

1952, Aug. 11 **Photo.** ***Perf. 13***

103	A29	12pf brown	2.00	50
104	A29	20pf green	2.00	50
105	A29	24pf rose	2.00	50
106	A29	35pf blue	2.75	75

Machine, Globe and Dove — A30

Friedrich Ludwig Jahn — A31

1952, Sept. 7 **Wmk. 297** ***Perf. 13***

108	A30	24pf red	1.50	15
109	A30	35pf deep blue	1.50	48

Issued to publicize the 1952 Leipzig Fair.

1952, Oct. 15 **Litho.**

110	A31	12pf blue	1.40	15

Jahn (1778-1852), introduced gymnastics to Germany, and was a politician.

Halle University A32

Stamp, Flags, Wreath, Dove and Hammer A33

1952, Oct. 18 **Photo.**

111	A32	24pf green	1.40	15

450th anniv. of the founding of Halle University, Wittenberg.

1952, Oct. 26

112	A33	24pf red brn	1.50	24

Stamp Day, Oct. 26, 1952.

Pieck Types of 1950

Perf. 13x12½

1952-53 **Wmk. 297** **Typo.**

113	A9	5pf bl grn	6.25	38
114	A9	12pf dark blue	19.00	18
115	A9	24pf red brn	17.00	18

Perf. 13x13½

116	A10	1m ol grn	22.50	2.75

Litho. ***Perf. 13***

117	A10	2m red brn ('53)	22.50	90
		Nos. 113-117 (5)	87.25	4.39

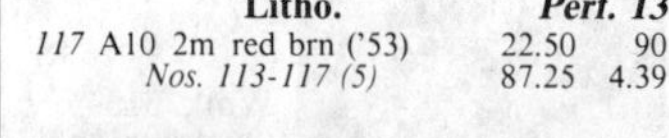

Globe, Dove and St. Stephen's Cathedral — A34

Pres. Wilhelm Pieck — A35

1952, Dec. 8 **Photo.** ***Perf. 13***

118	A34	24pf brt car	90	22
119	A34	35pf deep blue	1.10	28

Issued to publicize the Congress of Nations for Peace, Vienna, Dec. 12-19, 1952.

1953 **Wmk. 297** ***Perf. 13x13½***

120	A35	1m olive	12.00	15
a.		1m dark olive ('55)	20.00	15
121	A35	2m red brown	12.00	15
		Set value		15

See Nos. 339-340, 532.

Portrait Types of Russian Occupation, 1948

Designs as before.

1953 **Typo.** ***Perf. 13x12½***

122	OS2	2pf gray	90	38
123	OS2	6pf purple	1.50	30
124	OS2	8pf red brn	90	30
125	OS2	10pf bl grn	2.00	30
126	OS2	15pf brown	6.50	2.50
127	OS2	16pf turquoise	2.75	48
128	OS2	20pf maroon	1.50	30
129	OS2	25pf ol grn	45.00	15.00
130	OS2	30pf red	4.00	1.00
131	OS2	40pf red vio	1.25	48
132	OS2	50pf dk ultra	13.00	4.25
133	OS2	60pf dl grn	2.75	45
134	OS2	80pf dark blue	1.50	35
a.		Varnish coating	3.00	1.40
135	OS2	80pf crimson	8.00	2.00
136	OS2	84pf brn lake	35.00	12.00
		Nos. 122-136 (15)	126.55	40.09

"Industry" and Red Flag — A36

Marx and Engels — A37

Karl Marx Speaking A38

Karl Marx Medallion A39

Designs: 12pf, Spasski tower and communist flag. 16pf, Marching workers. 24pf, Portrait of Karl Marx. 35pf, Marx addressing audience. 48pf, Karl Marx and Friedrich Engels. 60pf. Red banner above heads and shoulders of workers.

1953 **Photo.** ***Perf. 13***

137	A36	6pf grnsh gray & red	40	15
138	A37	10pf grnsh gray & dk brn	2.50	15
139	A36	12pf grn, dp plum & dk grn	40	15
140	A37	16pf vio bl & dk car	1.90	38
141	A38	20pf brn & buff	65	20
142	A38	24pf brn & red	1.90	15
143	A36	35pf dp pur & cr	1.90	65
144	A36	48pf dk ol grn & red brn	80	20
a.		Souvenir sheet of 6	110.00	25.00
145	A37	60pf vio brn & red	2.50	65
146	A39	84pf bl & brn	1.90	48
a.		Souvenir sheet of 4	110.00	25.00
		Nos. 137-146 (10)	14.85	3.16

No. 144a contains one each of the denominations in types A36 and A38. Perf. and imperf.

No. 146a contains one each of the denominations in types A37 and A39. Perf. and imperf.

Maxim Gorky — A40

Bicycle Racers — A41

1953, Mar. 28

147	A40	35pf brown	25	15

1953, May 2 **Wmk. 297** ***Perf. 13***

Designs: 35pf, 60pf, Different views of bicycle race.

148	A41	24pf bluish grn	1.25	25
149	A41	35pf dp ultra	85	25
150	A41	60pf chocolate	1.25	30

6th International Bicycle Peace Race.

Heinrich von Kleist A42

Coal Miner A43

Designs: 20pf, Evangelical Marienkirche. 24pf, Sailboat on Oder River. 35pf, City Hall, Frankfurt-on-Oder.

1953, July 6 **Litho.**
151 A42 16pf chocolate 95 22
152 A42 20pf bl grn 55 15
153 A42 24pf rose red 95 22
154 A42 35pf vio bl 95 22

700th anniversary of the founding of Frankfurt-on-Oder.

1953 **Litho.** ***Perf. 13x12½***

Designs: 5pf, Woman mariner. 6pf, German and Soviet workers. 8pf, Mother teaching Marxist principles. 10pf, Machinists. 12pf, Worker, peasant and intellectual. 15pf, Teletype operator. 16pf, Steel worker. 20pf, Bad Elster. 24pf, Stalin Boulevard. 25pf, Locomotive building. 30pf, Dancing couple. 35pf, Sports Hall, Berlin. 40pf, Laboratory worker. 48pf, Zwinger Castle, Dresden. 60pf, Launching ship. 80pf, Agricultural workers. 84pf, Dove and East German family.

155 A43 1pf blk brn 80 15
156 A43 5pf emerald 1.10 15
157 A43 6pf violet 1.10 15
158 A43 8pf org brn 1.40 15
159 A43 10pf bl grn 1.10 15
160 A43 12pf blue 1.10 15
161 A43 15pf purple 2.25 15
162 A43 16pf dk vio 2.50 15
163 A43 20pf olive 2.50 15
163A A43 24pf carmine 6.00 15
164 A43 25pf dk grn 3.50 15
165 A43 30pf dp car 3.50 15
166 A43 35pf vio bl 7.00 15
167 A43 40pf rose red 6.25 15
168 A43 48pf rose red 6.00 15
169 A43 60pf deep blue 6.00 15
170 A43 80pf aqua 8.50 15
171 A43 84pf chocolate 8.50 15
Nos. 155-171 (18) 69.10
Set value 90

See Nos. 187-204, 216-223A, 227-230A, 330-338, 476-482.

Used values of Nos. 155-171 are for cto reprints with printed cancellations. The reprints differ slightly from originals in design and shade.

Power Shovel — A44

Design: 35pf, Road-building machine.

1953, Aug. 29 **Photo.** ***Perf. 13***
172 A44 24pf red brn 1.10 16
173 A44 35pf dp grn 1.65 35

The 1953 Leipzig Fair.

G. W. von Knobelsdorff and Berlin State Opera House — A45

Design: 35pf, Balthasar Neumann and Wurzburg bishop's palace.

1953, Sept. 16 ***Perf. 13x12½***
174 A45 24pf cerise 85 15
175 A45 35pf dk sl bl 1.65 32

200th anniv. of the deaths of G. W. von Knobelsdorff and Balthasar Neumann, architects.

Lucas Cranach — A46

Nurse Applying Bandage — A47

1953, Oct. 16 ***Perf. 13x13½***
176 A46 24pf brown 1.90 28

400th anniversary of the death of Lucas Cranach (1472-1553), painter.

Perf. 13½x13
1953, Oct. 23 **Wmk. 297**
177 A47 24pf brown & red 1.50 15

Issued to honor the Red Cross.

Mail Delivery A48

Lion and Lioness A49

1953, Oct. 25 **Photo.**
178 A48 24pf blue gray 90 15

Issued to publicize Stamp Day, Oct. 24, 1953.

1953, Nov. 2 ***Perf. 13x13½***
179 A49 24pf olive brn 90 15

75th anniversary of Leipzig Zoo.

Thomas Muntzer and Attackers A50

Designs: 16pf, H. F. K. vom Stein. 20pf, Ferdinand von Schill leading cavalry. 24pf, G. L. Blucher and battle scene. 35pf, Students fighting for National Unity. 48pf, Revolution of 1848.

1953, Nov. **Photo.** ***Perf. 13x12½***
180 A50 12pf brown 85 15
181 A50 16pf dp brn 85 15
182 A50 20pf dk car rose 65 15
183 A50 24pf deep blue 70 15
184 A50 35pf dk grn 1.25 28
185 A50 48pf dk brn 1.50 25
Nos. 180-185 (6) 5.80
Set value 88

Issued to honor German patriots.

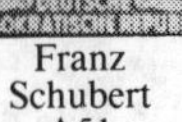
Franz Schubert A51

Gotthold E. Lessing A52

1953, Nov. 13 ***Perf. 13½x13***
186 A51 48pf brt org brn 1.90 25

125th anniversary of the death of Franz Schubert.

Types of 1953 Redrawn

Designs as before.

1953-54 **Typo.** ***Perf. 13x12½***
187 A43 1pf blk brn 50 15
188 A43 5pf emerald 2.25 15
a. Bklt. pane. 3 #188 + 3 #227
b. Bklt. pane. 3 #188 + 3 #228
189 A43 6pf purple 3.25 15
190 A43 8pf org brn 3.25 15
191 A43 10pf bl grn 5.25 15
192 A43 12pf grnsh bl 3.00 15
193 A43 15pf brt vio ('54) 5.25 15
194 A43 16pf dk pur 1.90 15
195 A43 20pf olive ('54) 6.50 15
196 A43 24pf carmine 5.25 15
197 A43 25pf dk bl grn 1.75 15
198 A43 30pf dp car 2.25 15
199 A43 35pf dp vio bl 2.25 15
200 A43 40pf rose red ('54) 6.00 15
201 A43 48pf rose vio 8.00 15
202 A43 60pf blue 8.00 15
203 A43 80pf aqua 3.00 15
204 A43 84pf chocolate 12.50 15
Nos. 187-204 (18) 80.15
Set value 90

Nos. 155-171 were printed from screened halftones, and shading consists of dots. Shading in lines without screen on Nos. 187-204. Designers' and engravers' names added below design on all values except 6, 12, 16 and 35pf. There are many other minor differences.

See note on used values after No. 171.

1954, Jan. 20 **Photo.** ***Perf. 13***
205 A52 20pf dk grn 1.75 15

225th anniversary of the birth of G. E. Lessing, dramatist.

Dove Over Conference Table — A53

Joseph V. Stalin — A54

1954, Jan. 25 ***Perf. 12½x13***
206 A53 12pf blue 1.25 15

Four Power Conference, Berlin, 1954.

1954, Mar. 5 **Typo.** ***Perf. 13x12½***
207 A54 20pf gray, dk brn & red org 1.90 15

1st anniv. of the death of Joseph V. Stalin.

Cyclists A55

Design: 24pf, Cyclists passing farm.

1954, Apr. 30 **Photo.**
208 A55 12pf brown 80 18
209 A55 24pf dl grn 1.10 22

7th International Bicycle Peace Race.

Dancers — A56

Fritz Reuter — A57

Design: 24pf, Boy, two girls and flag.

1954, June 3 ***Perf. 13***
210 A56 12pf emerald 95 15
211 A56 24pf rose brn 95 15

Issued to publicize the 2nd German youth meeting for peace, unity and freedom.

1954, July 12
212 A57 24pf sepia 1.10 16

80th anniversary of the death of Fritz Reuter, writer.

Ernst Thälmann A58

Hall of Commerce, Leipzig Fair A59

1954, Aug. 18 ***Perf. 13½x13***
213 A58 24pf red org & ind 90 15

10th anniv. of the death of Ernst Thälmann (1886-1944), Communist leader.

1954, Sept. 4 ***Perf. 13x13½***
214 A59 24pf dk red 40 15
215 A59 35pf gray bl 50 15
Set value 20

Issued to publicize the 1954 Leipzig Fair.

Redrawn Types of 1953-54 Surcharged with New Value and "X" in Black

1954 **Typo.** ***Perf. 13x12½***
216 A43 5pf on 6pf purple 15 15
217 A43 5pf on 8pf org brn 15 15
218 A43 10pf on 12pf grnsh bl 32 15
219 A43 15pf on 16pf dk pur 15 15
220 A43 20pf on 24pf car 32 15
221 A43 40pf on 48pf rose vio 55 15
222 A43 50pf on 60pf blue 75 15
223 A43 70pf on 84pf choc 2.25 15
Nos. 216-223 (8) 4.64
Set value 40

See note on used values after No. 171.

No. 163A Surcharged with New Value and "X" in Black

1955 **Litho.**
223A A43 20pf on 24pf car 32 15

Counterfeit surcharges exist on other values of the lithographed set (Nos. 155-171).

Pres. Wilhelm Pieck and Flags A60

1954, Oct. 6 **Photo.**
224 A60 20pf brown 30 15
225 A60 35pf greenish blue 60 15
Set value 20

5th anniv. of the founding of the German Democratic Republic.

Cologne Cathedral, Leipzig Monument and Unissued Stamp Design — A61

1954, Oct. 23 ***Perf. 13x13½***
226 A61 20pf brt car rose 35 15
a. Souvenir sheet, imperf. 30.00 14.00

Stamp Day. No. 226a has frame and inscription in blue. Size: 60x80mm.

Redrawn Types of 1953-54

Designs: 10pf, Worker, peasant and intellectual. 15pf, Steelworker. 20pf, Stalin Boulevard. 40pf, Zwinger Castle, Dresden. 50pf, Launching ship. 70pf, Dove and East German family.

1955 **Typo.** ***Perf. 13x12½***
227 A43 10pf blue 1.25 15
a. Bklt. pane. 4 #227 + 2 #228
227B A43 15pf violet 1.50 15
228 A43 20pf carmine 1.10 15
229 A43 40pf rose vio 1.75 15

230 A43 50pf deep blue 1.75 15
230A A43 70pf chocolate 4.50 15
Nos. 227-230A (6) 11.85
Set value 20

See note on used values after No. 171.

Soviet Pavilion, Leipzig Spring Fair — A62

Women of Three Nations — A63

Design: 35pf, Chinese pavilion.

Perf. 13x13½

1955, Feb. 21 Photo. Wmk. 297

231 A62 20pf rose vio 20 15
232 A62 35pf vio bl 50 16
Set value 25

Issued to publicize the Leipzig Spring Fair.

1955, Mar. 1 ***Perf. 13x13½***

233 A63 10pf green 75 15
234 A63 20pf red 1.00 15
Set value 15

International Women's Day, 45th year.

Workers' Demonstration — A64

1955, Mar. 15 ***Perf. 13x12½***

235 A64 10pf blk & red 90 15

Intl. Trade Union Conference, Apr., 1955.

Monument to the Victims of Fascism — A65

1955, Apr. 9 ***Perf. 13½x13***

236 A65 10pf vio bl 70 15
237 A65 20pf cerise 85 15
a. Souv. sheet of 2, #236-237, imperf. 12.00 6.00
Set value 20

No. 237a sold for 50pf.

Russian War Memorial, Berlin — A66

1955, Apr. 15 ***Perf. 12½x13***

238 A66 20pf lilac rose 90 15

Nos. 236-238 issued for 10th anniv. of liberation, No. 237a for reconstruction of natl. memorial sites.

German Democratic Republic (East Germany) stamps can be mounted in Scott's Germany Part IV Album.

Cyclists — A67

Friedrich von Schiller — A68

1955 Wmk. 297 ***Perf. 13½x13***

239 A67 10pf bl grn 20 15
240 A67 20pf car rose 50 15
Set value 25

Issued to publicize the 8th International Bicycle Peace Race, Prague-Berlin-Warsaw.

Starting with the 1955 issues, commemorative stamps which are valued in italics were sold on a restricted basis.

1955, Apr. 20

Various Portraits of Schiller.

241 A68 5pf dk gray grn *2.50* *50*
242 A68 10pf brt bl 20 15
243 A68 20pf chocolate 20 15
a. Souv. sheet, #241-243, imperf. *19.00* *6.75*
Set value 65

150th anniv. of the death of Friedrich von Schiller, poet.

No. 243a sold for 50pf.

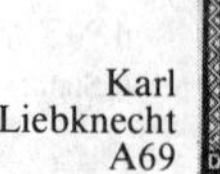

Karl Liebknecht A69

Portraits: 10pf, August Bebel. 15pf, Franz Mehring. 20pf, Ernst Thalmann. 25pf, Clara Zetkin. 40pf, Wilhelm Liebknecht. 60pf, Rosa Luxemburg.

1955, June 20 Photo. ***Perf. 13x12½***

244 A69 5pf bl grn 15 15
245 A69 10pf deep blue 15 15
246 A69 15pf violet *5.00* *1.00*
247 A69 20pf red 15 15
248 A69 25pf slate 15 15
249 A69 40pf rose car 1.00 15
250 A69 60pf dk brn 24 15
Nos. 244-250 (7) 6.84
Set value 1.50

Issued to honor German communists.

Optical Goods — A70

Design: 20pf, Pottery and china.

1955, Aug. 29 Photo. ***Perf. 13x13½***

253 A70 10pf dark blue 40 15
254 A70 20pf slate grn 40 15
Set value 15

Issued to publicize the 1955 Leipzig Fair.

Farmer Receiving Deed — A71

Harvesters — A72

Design: 10pf, Construction of new farm community.

1955, Sept. 3 ***Perf. 13½x13, 13x13½***

255 A71 5pf dl grn *4.50* *1.90*
256 A71 10pf ultra 70 15
257 A72 20pf lake 70 15

10th anniv. of the Land-Reform Program.

Man Holding Badge of Peoples' Solidarity — A73

Engels at "First International," 1864 — A74

Perf. 13½x13

1955, Oct. 10 Wmk. 297

258 A73 10pf dark blue 30 15

10th anniv. of the "Peoples' Solidarity."

1955, Nov. 7 ***Perf. 13½x13***

Designs: 10pf, Marx and Engels writing the Communist Manifesto. 15pf, Engels as newspaper editor. 20pf, Friedrich Engels. 30pf, Friedrich Engels. 70pf, Engels on the barricades in 1848.

259 A74 5pf Prus bl & ol 18 15
260 A74 10pf dk bl & yel 18 15
261 A74 15pf dk grn & ol 18 15
262 A74 20pf brn vio & org 1.25 25
263 A74 30pf org brn & lt bl *5.50* *1.50*
264 A74 70pf gray grn & rose car 1.25 25
a. Souv. sheet of 6, #259-264 *57.50* *27.50*
Nos. 259-264 (6) 8.54 2.45

Friedrich Engels, 135th birth anniv.

Cathedral at Magdeburg A75

Georgius Agricola A76

German Buildings: 10pf, German State Opera. 15pf, Old City Hall, Leipzig. 20pf, City Hall, Berlin. 30pf, Cathedral at Erfurt. 40pf, Zwinger at Dresden.

1955, Nov. 14

265 A75 5pf blk brn 55 15
266 A75 10pf gray grn 55 15
267 A75 15pf purple 55 15
268 A75 20pf carmine 55 15
269 A75 30pf dk red brn *7.00* *1.90*
270 A75 40pf indigo 80 30
Nos. 265-270 (6) *10.00* *2.80*

For surcharges see Nos. B29-B30.

1955, Nov. 21 Wmk. 297

271 A76 10pf brown 35 15

400th anniv. of the death of Georgius Agricola, mineralogist and scholar.

Portrait of a Young Man, by Dürer — A77

Mozart — A78

Famous Paintings: 10pf, Chocolate Girl, Liotard. 15pf, Portrait of a Boy, Pinturicchio. 20pf, Self-portrait with Saskia, Rembrandt. 40pf, Girl with Letter, Vermeer. 70pf, Sistine Madonna, Raphael.

1955, Dec. 15 ***Perf. 13½x13***

272 A77 5pf dk red brn 1.25 15
273 A77 10pf chestnut 1.25 15
274 A77 15pf pale pur *24.00* *3.25*
275 A77 20pf brown 1.65 15
276 A77 40pf ol grn 1.65 16
277 A77 70pf deep blue 4.25 25
Nos. 272-277 (6) *34.05* *4.11*

Issued to publicize the return of famous art works to the Dresden Art Gallery.

See Nos. 355-360, 439-443.

1956, Jan. 27 Photo.

Designs: 20pf, Portrait facing left.

278 A78 10pf gray grn *5.50* *1.25*
279 A78 20pf cop brn 1.50 15

200th anniv. of the birth of Wolfgang Amadeus Mozart, composer.

Flag and Schoenefeld Airport, Berlin — A79

Lufthansa Plane A80

Designs: 15pf, Plane facing right. 20pf, Plane facing down and left.

1956, Feb. 1 ***Perf. 13x12½***

280 A79 5pf multi *7.00* *1.40*
281 A80 10pf gray grn 24 15
282 A80 15pf dl bl 24 15
283 A80 20pf brn red 24 15

Issued to commemorate the opening of passenger service of the German Lufthansa.

Heinrich Heine — A81

Railroad Cranes — A82

Design: 20pf, Heine (different portrait.)

1956, Feb. 17 ***Perf. 13½x13***

284 A81 10pf Prus grn *5.25* *85*
285 A81 20pf dk red 2.50 40

Cent. of the death of Heinrich Heine, poet.

1956, Feb. 26 ***Perf. 13x13½***

286 A82 20pf brn red 55 15
287 A82 35pf vio bl 55 15
Set value 20

Issued to publicize the Leipzig Spring Fair.

Ernst Thälmann — A83

1956, Apr. 16 Litho. ***Perf. 13x13½***

288 A83 20pf blk ol & red 30 15
a. Souv. sheet of 1 *5.25* *5.25*

70th anniv. of the birth of Ernst Thälmann.

No. 288a was sold at double face value. The proceeds were used for national memorials at former concentration camps.

Wheel, Hand and Olive Branch — A84

City Hall and Old Market — A85

Design: 20pf, Wheel and coats of arms of Warsaw, Berlin, Prague.

Perf. 13½x13

1956, Apr. 30	Wmk. 297		
289 A84 10pf lt grn		45	15
290 A84 20pf brt car		45	15
Set value			20

9th International Bicycle Peace Race, Warsaw-Berlin-Prague, May 1-15, 1956.

1956, June 1

Designs: 20pf, Hofkirche and Elbe Bridge. 40pf, Technical College.

291 A85 10pf green	18	15
292 A85 20pf car rose	18	15
293 A85 40pf brt pur	*2.25*	*75*
Set value		*80*

750th anniversary of Dresden.

Worker Holding Cogwheel Emblem — A86

Robert Schumann (Music by Schubert) — A87

1956, June 30	*Perf. 13½x13*	
294 A86 20pf rose red	35	15

10th anniversary of nationalized industry.

1956, July 20	*Perf. 13x13½*	
295 A87 10pf brt grn	*80*	*40*
296 A87 20pf rose red	20	15
Set value		*45*

Centenary of the death of Robert Schumann, composer. See Nos. 303-304.

Soccer Players — A88

Thomas Mann — A89

Designs: 10pf, Javelin Thrower. 15pf, Women Hurdlers. 20pf, Gymnast.

1956, July 25	*Perf. 13½x13*	
297 A88 5pf green	15	15
298 A88 10pf dk vio bl	15	15
299 A88 15pf red vio	*1.50*	*48*
300 A88 20pf rose red	15	15
Set value	*1.75*	*60*

Second Sports Festival, Leipzig, Aug. 2-5.

1956, Aug. 13	Wmk. 297	
301 A89 20pf bluish blk	70	15

Issued to commemorate the first anniversary of the death of Thomas Mann, novelist.

Jakub Bart Cisinski A90

Robert Schumann (Music by Schumann) A91

1956, Aug. 20	Photo.	
302 A90 50pf claret	50	15

Birth centenary of Jakub Bart Cisinski, poet.

1956, Oct. 8	*Perf. 13x13½*	
303 A91 10pf brt grn	*1.25*	*15*
304 A91 20pf rose red	25	15
Set value	*1.50*	*16*

See Nos. 295, 296.

Lace — A92

Olympic Rings, Laurel and Torch — A93

Design: 20pf, Sailboat.

1956, Sept. 1 Typo.	*Perf. 13½x13*	
305 A92 10pf grn & blk	15	15
306 A92 20pf rose red & blk	15	15
Set value	15	15

Leipzig Fair, Sept. 2-9.

1956, Sept. 28 **Litho.**

Design: 35pf, Classic javelin thrower.

307 A93 20pf brn red	15	15
308 A93 35pf slate bl	18	15
Set value		15

Issued to publicize the 16th Olympic Games at Melbourne, Nov. 22-Dec. 8, 1956.

Post Runner of 1450 — A94

Greifswald University Seal — A95

1956, Oct. 27		
309 A94 20pf red	25	15

Issued to publicize the Day of the Stamp.

1956, Oct. 17	*Perf. 13x13½*	
310 A95 20pf magenta	25	15

500th anniv. of Greifswald University.

Ernst Abbe — A96

Zeiss Works, Jena A97

Portrait: 25pf, Carl Zeiss.

Perf. 12½x13, 13x12½

1956, Nov. 9 Photo.	Wmk. 297	
311 A96 10pf dk grn	15	15
312 A97 20pf brn red	15	15
313 A96 25pf bluish blk	15	15
Set value	35	15

110th anniversary of the Carl Zeiss Optical Works in Jena.

Chinese Girl with Flowers — A98

Designs: 10pf, Negro woman and child. 25pf, European man and dove.

1956, Dec. 10 Litho.	*Perf. 13*	
314 A98 5pf ol, *pale lem*	*95*	*30*
315 A98 10pf brn, *pink*	15	15
316 A98 25pf vio bl, *pale vio bl*	15	15
Set value	*1.10*	*38*

Issued for Human Rights Day.

Elephants A99

1956, Dec. 17 Photo. *Perf. 13x12½*
Design in Gray

317 A99 5pf shown	15	15
318 A99 10pf Flamingoes	15	15
319 A99 15pf White rhinoceros	*3.50*	*75*
320 A99 20pf Mouflon	15	15
321 A99 25pf Bison	15	15
322 A99 30pf Polar bear	15	15
Set value	*4.00*	*90*

Issued to publicize the Berlin Zoo.

Freighter A100

Design: 25pf, Electric Locomotive.

1957, Mar. 1 Litho.	Wmk. 313	
323 A100 20pf rose red	18	15
324 A100 25pf brt bl	18	15
Set value	15	15

Leipzig Spring Fair.

Silver Thistle A101

Designs: 10pf, Emerald lizard. 20pf, Lady's-slipper.

1957, Apr. 12 Photo.	Wmk. 313	
325 A101 5pf chocolate	15	15
326 A101 10pf dk sl grn	*1.75*	*60*
327 A101 20pf red brn	15	15
Set value	*1.90*	*65*

Nature Conservation Week, Apr. 14-20.

Children at Play — A102

Design: 20pf, Friedrich Froebel and Children.

1957, Apr. 18 Litho.	*Perf. 13*	
328 A102 10pf dk sl grn & ol	*70*	*32*
329 A102 20pf blk & brn red	30	18

175th anniv. of the birth of Friedrich Froebel, educator.

Redrawn Types of 1953

Designs: 5pf, Woman mariner. 10pf, Worker, peasant and intellectual. 15pf, Steel worker. 20pf, Stalin Boulevard. 25pf, Locomotive building. 30pf, Dancing couple. 40pf, Zwinger Castle, Dresden. 50pf, Launching ship. 70pf, Dove and East German family.

Imprint: "E. Gruner K. Wolf"
No imprint on 10pf, 15pf

Perf. 13x12½

1957-58 Typo.	Wmk. 313	
330 A43 5pf emerald	15	15
a. Bklt. pane, 3 #330 + 3 #331		
b. Bklt. pane, 3 #330 + 3 #333		
c. Booklet pane of 6	85	
331 A43 10pf blue	70	15
a. Bklt. pane, 4 #331 + 2 #333		
b. Perf. 14 ('58)	15	15
332 A43 15pf violet	15	15
a. Perf. 14 ('58)	15	15
333 A43 20pf carmine	15	15
a. Bklt. pane (5 #333 + 1 #477)		
334 A43 25pf bluish grn	15	15
335 A43 30pf dl red	38	15
336 A43 40pf rose vio	55	15
337 A43 50pf brt bl	75	15
338 A43 70pf chocolate	80	15

See Nos. 476-482.

Pieck Type of 1953

Photo.	*Perf. 13x13½*	
339 A35 1m dk ol grn ('58)	1.25	15
340 A35 2m red brn ('58)	1.90	15
Nos. 330-340 (11)	6.93	
Set value		50

Bicycle Race Route — A103

Perf. 13x13½

1957, Apr. 30 Litho.	Wmk. 313	
346 A103 5pf orange	25	15

Issued to publicize the 10th International Bicycle Peace Race, Prague-Berlin-Warsaw.

Steam Shovel A104

Miner — A105

Design: 20pf, Coal conveyor.

Perf. 13x12½, 13½x13 (25pf)

1957, May 3		
347 A104 10pf green	15	15
348 A104 20pf redsh brn	15	15
349 A105 25pf bl vio	*85*	*28*
Set value		*40*

Issued in honor of the coal mining industry.

Henri Dunant and Globe A106

Design: 25pf, Henri Dunant facing right and globe.

1957, May 7 Photo. *Perf. 13x12½*

350 A106 10pf grn, red & blk 16 15
351 A106 25pf brt bl, red & blk 20 15
Set value 15

Tenth Red Cross world conference.

Portrait Type of 1950, Redrawn

Portraits: 5pf, Joachim Jungius. 10pf, Leonhard Euler. 20pf, Heinrich Hertz.

1957, June 7 Litho.

352 A11 5pf brown *55* *30*
353 A11 10pf green 15 15
354 A11 20pf henna brn 15 15
Set value *70* *40*

Issued to honor famous German scientists.

Painting Type of 1955.

Famous Paintings: 5pf, Holy Family, Mantegna. 10pf, The Dancer Campani, Carriera. 15pf, Portrait of Morette, Holbein. 20pf, The Tribute Money, Titian. 25pf, Saskia with Red Flower, Rembrandt. 40pf, Young Standard Bearer, Piazetta.

Perf. 13½x13

1957, June 26 Photo. Wmk. 313

355 A77 5pf dk brn 15 15
356 A77 10pf lt yel grn 15 15
357 A77 15pf brn ol 15 15
358 A77 20pf rose brn 15 15
359 A77 25pf deep claret 15 15
360 A77 40pf dk bl gray *2.25* *85*
Nos. 355-360 (6) *3.00*
Set value *1.00*

Clara Zetkin A107

Bertolt Brecht A108

1957, July 5 *Perf. 13x13½*

361 A107 10pf dk grn & red 40 15

Centenary of the birth of Clara Zetkin, politician and founder of the socialist women's movement.

1957, Aug. 14 *Perf. 13½x13*

362 A108 10pf dk grn 25 15
363 A108 25pf deep blue 25 15
Set value 15

Brecht (1898-1956), playwright and poet.

Congress Emblem A109

Fair Emblem A110

1957, Aug. 23 Litho.

364 A109 20pf brt red & blk 35 15

Issued to publicize the fourth International Trade Union Congress, Leipzig, Oct. 4-15.

1957, Aug. 30 Wmk. 313

365 A110 20pf crim & ver 18 15
366 A110 25pf brt bl & lt bl 18 15
Set value 15

Issued to publicize the 1957 Leipzig Fair.

Savings Book — A111

Postrider, 1563 — A112

1957, Oct. 10 *Perf. 13½x13*

367 A111 10pf grn & blk, *gray* *55* *15*
368 A111 20pf rose car & blk, *gray* 35 15
Set value *25*

Issued to publicize "Savings Weeks."

1957, Oct. 25 Wmk. 313

369 A112 5pf blk, *pale sep* 25 15

Issued for the Day of the Stamp.

Sputnik I A113

Storming of the Winter Palace A114

Designs: 20pf, Stratospheric balloon above clouds. 25pf, Ship with plumb line exploring deep sea.

1957-58 *Perf. 12½x13*

370 A113 10pf bl blk 20 15
371 A113 20pf car rose ('58) 35 15
372 A113 25pf brt bl ('58) *1.25* *35*
Set value *45*

IGY. The 10pf also for the launching of the 1st artificial satellite.

1957, Nov. 7 Photo.

373 A114 10pf yel grn & red 15 15
374 A114 25pf brt bl & red 15 15
Set value 15

40th anniv. of the Russian Revolution.

Guenther Ramin — A115

Dove and Globe — A116

Portrait: 20pf, Hermann Abendroth.

Perf. 13½x13

1957, Nov. 22 Litho. Wmk. 313

375 A115 10pf yel grn & blk *60* *26*
376 A115 20pf red org & blk 32 15

Ramin (1898-1956) and Abendroth (1883-1956), musicians, on the 1st anniv. of their death.

1958, Feb. 27 *Perf. 13x13½*

377 A116 20pf rose red 18 15
378 A116 25pf blue 18 15
Set value 15

Issued to publicize the 1958 Leipzig Fair.

Radio Tower, Morse Code and Post Horn A117

Design: 20pf, Radio tower and small post horn.

1958, Mar. 6 *Perf. 13x12½*

379 A117 5pf gray & blk *42* *20*
380 A117 20pf crim rose & dk red 15 15
Set value *50* *25*

Conf. of Postal Ministers of Communist countries, Moscow, Dec. 3-17, 1957.

Sketch by Zille A118

Symbolizing Quantum Theory A119

Design: 20pf, Self-portrait of Zille.

1958, Mar. 20 *Perf. 13½x13*

381 A118 10pf grn & gray *1.50* *20*
382 A118 20pf dp car & gray 40 15
Set value *25*

Centenary of the birth of Heinrich Zille, artist.

1958, Apr. 23 Litho.

Design: 20pf, Max Planck.

383 A119 10pf gray grn *1.00* *25*
384 A119 20pf magenta 40 15
Set value *30*

Issued to commemorate the centenary of the birth of Max Planck, physicist.

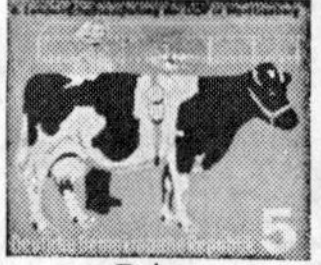
Prize Cow — A120

Charles Darwin — A121

Designs: 10pf, Mowing machine. 20pf, Beet harvester.

Perf. 13x13½

1958, June 4 Wmk. 313

Size: 28x23mm

385 A120 5pf gray & blk *1.25* *25*

Size: 39x22mm

Perf. 13x12½

386 A120 10pf brt grn 15 15
387 A120 20pf rose red 18 15
Set value *30*

6th Agricultural Show, Markkleeberg.

1958, June 19 *Perf. 13x13½*

Portrait: 20pf, Carl von Linné.

388 A121 10pf grn & blk *75* *32*
389 A121 20pf dk red & blk 30 15
Set value *40*

Cent. of Darwin's theory of evolution and the bicent. of Linne's botanical system.

Seven Towers of Rostock and Ships — A122

Congress Emblem — A123

Designs: 10pf, Ship at pier. 25pf, Ships in harbor.

1958 *Perf. 13½x13*

390 A122 10pf emerald 15 15
391 A122 20pf red org 15 15
392 A122 25pf lt bl *75* *16*
Set value *90* *20*

Establishment of Rostock as a seaport.
Issue dates: 20pf, July 5; 10pf and 25pf, Nov. 24.
For overprint see No. 500.

1958, June 25 *Perf. 13x13½*

393 A123 10pf rose red 15 15

5th congress of the Socialist Party of the German Democratic Republic (SED).

Mare and Foal A124

Designs: 10pf, Trotter. 20pf, Horse race.

1958, July 22 Photo. *Perf. 13x12½*

394 A124 5pf blk brn *1.25* *22*
395 A124 10pf dk ol grn 15 15
396 A124 20pf dk red brn 15 15
Set value *26*

Issued to publicize the Grand Prize of the DDR, 1958.

Jan Amos Komensky (Comenius) A125

Design: 20pf, Teacher and pupils, 17th cent.

1958, Aug. 7 Litho. *Perf. 13x13½*

397 A125 10pf brt bl grn & blk *1.10* *32*
398 A125 20pf org brn & blk 16 15
Set value *40*

University Seal A126

Design: 20pf, Schiller University, Jena.

1958, Aug. 19 *Perf. 13x12½*

399 A126 5pf gray & blk *1.10* *55*
400 A126 20pf dk red & gray 16 15

400th anniversary of Friedrich Schiller University in Jena.

Soldier on Obstacle Course A127

Arms Breaking A-Bomb A128

Design: 20pf, Spartacist emblem. 25pf, Marching athletes, map and flag.

Perf. 13½x13

1958, Sept. 19 Litho. Wmk. 313

401 A127 10pf emer & brn 95 28
402 A127 20pf brn red & yel 15 15
403 A127 25pf lt bl & red 15 15
Set value 35

Issued to publicize the first Spartacist Sports Meet of Friendly Armies, Leipzig, Sept. 20-28.

1958, Sept. 19 ***Perf. 13x13½***

404 A128 20pf rose red 20 15
405 A128 25pf blue 20 15
Set value 15

Issued to publicize the people's fight against atomic death.

Woman and Leipzig Railroad Station A129

Design: 25pf, Woman in Persian lamb coat and old City Hall, Leipzig.

1958, Aug. 29 ***Perf. 13x12½***

406 A129 10pf grn, brn & blk 15 15
407 A129 25pf bl & blk 15 15
Set value 15

Issued to publicize the 1958 Leipzig Fair.

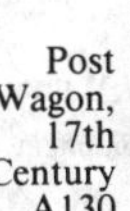

Post Wagon, 17th Century A130

Design: 20pf, Mail train and plane.

1958, Oct. 23 Wmk. 313

408 A130 10pf green 52 45
409 A130 20pf lake 15 15
Set value 57 50

Issued for the Day of the Stamp.

Brandenburg Gate, Berlin — A131

Head from Greek Tomb — A132

1958, Nov. 29 ***Perf. 13x13½***

410 A131 20pf rose red 15 15
411 A131 25pf dark blue 1.25 55
Set value 60

Issued to commemorate 10 years of democratic city administration of Berlin.

1958, Dec. 2 ***Perf. 13½x13***

Design: 20pf, Giant's head from Pergamum frieze.

412 A132 10pf bl grn & blk 90 40
413 A132 20pf dp rose & blk 15 15
Set value 45

Issued to commemorate the return of art treasures from Russia. See Nos. 484-486.

Negro and Caucasian Men A133

Design: 25pf, Chinese and Caucasian girls.

1958, Dec. 10 ***Perf. 13x12½***

414 A133 10pf brt bl grn & blk 15 15
415 A133 25pf bl & blk 90 35
Set value 40

10th anniv. of the signing of the Universal Declaration of Human Rights.

Worker and Soldier A134

Otto Nuschke A135

1958, Nov. 7 ***Perf. 12½x13***

416 A134 20pf blk, ver & dl pur 8.00 3.25

40th anniv. of the Revolution of Nov. 7. (Stamp inscribed Nov. 9.) Withdrawn from sale on day of issue.

Perf. 13½x13

1958, Dec. 27 Wmk. 313

417 A135 20pf red 15 15

First anniversary of the death of Otto Nuschke, vice president of the republic.

Communist Newspaper, "The Red Flag" — A136

1958, Dec. 30 ***Perf. 13x12½***

418 A136 20pf red 15 15

Issued to commemorate the 40th anniversary of the German Communist Party.

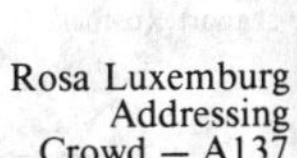

Rosa Luxemburg Addressing Crowd — A137

Design: 20pf, Karl Liebknecht addressing crowd.

Perf. 13x13½

1959, Jan. 15 Wmk. 313

419 A137 10pf bl grn 1.25 52
420 A137 20pf hn brn & blk 32 15
Set value 60

40th anniversary of the death of Rosa Luxemburg and Karl Liebknecht.

Gewandhaus, Leipzig — A138

President Wilhelm Pieck — A139

Design: 25pf, Opening theme of Mendelssohn's A Major symphony.

1959, Feb. 28 Engr. ***Perf. 14***

421 A138 10pf grn, *grnsh* 15 15
422 A138 25pf bl, *bluish* 90 26
Set value 30

Issued to commemorate the 150th anniversary of the birth of Felix Mendelssohn-Bartholdy, composer.

1959, Jan. 3 Photo. ***Perf. 13½x13***

423 A139 20pf henna brn 25 15

Issued to commemorate the 83rd birthday of President Wilhelm Pieck. See No. 511.

"Black Pump" Plant A140

Design: 25pf, Photographic equipment.

1959, Feb. 28 Litho. ***Perf. 13x12½***

424 A140 20pf car rose 25 15
425 A140 25pf lt ultra 25 15
Set value 15

1959 Leipzig Spring Fair.

Boy and Girl — A141

Statue of Handel, Halle — A142

1959, Apr. 2 ***Perf. 13½x13***

426 A141 10pf blk, *lt grn* 1.00 32
427 A141 20pf blk, *salmon* 15 15
Set value 35

Issued to commemorate five years of the Youth Consecration ceremony.

1959, Apr. 27 Wmk. 313

Design: 20pf, Handel by Thomas Hudson, 1749.

428 A142 10pf bluish grn & blk 1.00 32
429 A142 20pf rose & blk 15 15
Set value 35

Bicentenary of the death of George Frederick Handel, composer.

Alexander von Humboldt and Central American View — A143

Post Horn — A144

Design: 20pf, Portrait and Siberian view.

1959, May 6

430 A143 10pf bluish grn 1.00 32
431 A143 20pf rose 15 15
Set value 35

Centenary of the death of Alexander von Humboldt, naturalist and geographer.

1959, May 30 ***Perf. 13½x13***

432 A144 20pf scar, yel & blk 15 15
433 A144 25pf lt bl, yel & blk 45 30
Set value 50 35

Conference of socialist postal ministers.

Gray Heron A145

Designs: 10pf, Bittern. 20pf, Lily of the valley and butterfly. 25pf, Beaver. 40pf, Pussy willows and bee.

1959, June 26 ***Perf. 13x12½***

434 A145 5pf lt bl, blk & lil 15 15
435 A145 10pf grnsh bl, dk brn & org 15 15
436 A145 20pf org red, grn & vio 15 15
437 A145 25pf lil, yel & blk 15 15
438 A145 40pf gray bl, yel & blk 3.00 75
Nos. 434-438 (5) 3.60
Set value 85

Issued to publicize wildlife protection.

Painting Type of 1955.

Famous Paintings: 5pf, Portrait, Angelica Kauffmann. 10pf, The Lady Lace Maker, Gabriel Metsu. 20pf, Mademoiselle Lavergne, Liotard. 25pf, Old Woman with Brazier, Rubens. 40pf, Young Man in Black Coat, Hals.

1959, June 29 Photo. ***Perf. 13½x13***

439 A77 5pf olive 15 15
440 A77 10pf green 15 15
441 A77 20pf dp org 15 15
442 A77 25pf chestnut 15 15
443 A77 40pf dp magenta 3.00 60
Nos. 439-443 (5) 3.60
Set value 72

Great Cormorant A146

Youths of Three Races A147

Birds: 10pf, Black Stork. 15pf, Eagle owl. 20pf, Black grouse. 25pf, Hoopoe. 40pf, Peregrine falcon.

Perf. 13x13½

1959, July 2 Litho. Wmk. 313

Designs in Black

444 A146 5pf yellow 15 15
445 A146 10pf lt grn 15 15
446 A146 15pf pale vio 1.75 60
447 A146 20pf dp pink 15 15
448 A146 25pf blue 15 15
449 A146 40pf vermilion 15 15
Set value 2.00 70

Protection of native birds.

Perf. 12½x13, 13x12½

1959, July 25

Design: 25pf, Swedish girl kissing African girl (horiz.).

450 A147 20pf crimson 15 15
451 A147 25pf brt bl 25 15
Set value 15

Issued to publicize the 7th World Youth Festival, Vienna, July 26-Aug. 14.

Glass Tea Service A148

Design: 25pf, Distilling apparatus (vert.).

1959, Sept. 1 ***Perf. 13x12½, 12½x13***

452 A148 10pf bluish brn 15 15
453 A148 25pf brt bl 40 22
Set value 45 25

75 years of Jena glassware.

Lunik 2 Hitting Moon — A149

1959, Sept. 21 ***Perf. 13½x13***
454 A149 20pf rose red 28 15

Landing of the Soviet rocket Lunik 2 on the moon, Sept. 13, 1959.

New Buildings, Leipzig, Globe and Fair Emblem
A150

1959, Aug. 17 ***Perf. 13x12½***
455 A150 20pf gray & rose 18 15

1959 Leipzig Fall Fair.

Flag and Harvester
A151

Johannes R. Becher
A152

Designs (Flag and): 10pf, Fritz Heckert rest home. 15pf, Zwinger, Dresden. 20pf, Steelworker. 25pf, Chemist. 40pf, Central Stadium, Leipzig. 50pf, Woman tractor driver. 60pf, Airplane. 70pf, Merchant ship. 1m, First atomic reactor of the DDR.

1959, Oct. 6 ***Perf. 13½x13***
Flag in Black, Red & Orange Yellow Inscription and Design in Black & Red

456 A151 5pf yellow 15 15
457 A151 10pf gray 15 15
458 A151 15pf citron 15 15
459 A151 20pf gray 15 15
460 A151 25pf lt gray ol 15 15
461 A151 40pf citron 15 15
462 A151 50pf salmon 15 15
463 A151 60pf pale bluish grn 15 15
464 A151 70pf pale grnsh yel 15 15
465 A151 1m bis brn 18 15
Set value *90* *40*

Issued to commemorate the 10th anniversary of the German Democratic Republic.

1959, Oct. 28 **Litho.** ***Perf. 13x13½***
466 A152 20pf red & slate 70 15

1st anniversary of the death of Johannes R. Becher, writer.
Printed with alternating yellow labels. The label carries in blue a verse from the national anthem and Becher's signature.

Schiller's Home, Weimar
A153

Post Rider and Mile Stone, 18th Century
A154

Design: 20pf, Friedrich von Schiller.

1959, Nov. 10 **Engr.** ***Perf. 14***
467 A153 10pf dl grn, *grnsh* 90 40
468 A153 20pf lake, *pink* 15 15
Set value *45*

Issued to commemorate the 200th anniversary of the birth of Friedrich von Schiller.

1959, Nov. 17 **Litho.** ***Perf. 13½x13***

Design: 20pf, Motorized mailman.

469 A154 10pf green 80 25
470 A154 20pf dk car rose 15 15
Set value *28*

Issued for the Day of the Stamp.

Red Squirrels
A155

1959, Nov. 27 ***Perf. 13x12½***
471 A155 5pf shown 15 15
472 A155 10pf Hares 15 15
473 A155 20pf Roe deer 15 15
474 A155 25pf Red deer 15 15
475 A155 40pf Lynx *2.75* 85
Nos. 471-475 (5) *3.35*
Set value *95*

Redrawn Types of 1953
Without Imprint

1959-60 **Wmk. 313** **Typo.** ***Perf. 14***
476 A43 5pf emerald 15 15
477 A43 10pf lt bl grn *(Machin-ists)* 32 15
a. Perf. 13x12½ 15 15
b. Bklt. pane of 6 #477a 1.00
478 A43 20pf carmine 15 15
a. Se-tenant with DEBRIA label 75 15
479 A43 30pf dl red 15 15
480 A43 40pf rose vio 15 15
481 A43 50pf brt bl 15 15
482 A43 70pf choc ('60) 15 15
Set value 85 35

No. 478a was issued Sept. 3, 1959, to commemorate the 2nd German Stamp Exhibition, Berlin. Sheet contains 60 stamps, 40 labels.
Two other stamps without imprint are Nos. 331-332.

Type of 1958 and

Pergamum Altar of Zeus — A156

Designs: 5pf, Head of an Attic goddess, 580 B.C. 10pf, Head of a princess from Tell el Amarna, 1360 B.C. 20pf, Bronze figure from Toprak-Kale (Armenia), 7th century B.C.

1959, Dec. 29 **Litho.** ***Perf. 13½x13***
484 A132 5pf yel & blk 15 15
485 A132 10pf bluish grn & blk 15 15
486 A132 20pf rose & blk 15 15
487 A156 25pf lt bl & blk *1.10* 25
Set value *34*

Boxing — A157

Designs: 10pf, Sprinters. 20pf, Ski jump. 25pf, Sailboat.

Perf. 13x13½

1960, Jan. 27 **Wmk. 313**
488 A157 5pf brn & ocher *3.75* *1.10*
489 A157 10pf grn & ocher 15 15
490 A157 20pf car & ocher 15 15
491 A157 25pf ultra & ocher 15 15
Set value *1.25*

Issued to publicize the 1960 Winter and Summer Olympic Games.

Technical Fair, North Entrance
A158

Design: 25pf, "Ring" Fair building.

1960, Feb. 17 ***Perf. 13x12½***
492 A158 20pf red & gray 15 15
493 A158 25pf lt bl & gray 15 15
Set value 25 15

1960 Leipzig Spring Fair.

Purple Foxglove
A159

Lenin
A160

Medicinal Plants: 10pf, Camomile. 15pf, Peppermint. 20pf, Poppy. 40pf, Dog rose.

1960, Apr. 7 ***Perf. 12½x13***
494 A159 5pf grn, gray & car rose 15 15
495 A159 10pf cit, gray & grn 15 15
496 A159 15pf fawn, gray & grn 15 15
497 A159 20pf grnsh bl, gray & vio 15 15
498 A159 40pf brn, gray, grn & red *2.75* *60*
Set value *3.00* *68*

1960, Apr. 22 **Engr.** ***Perf. 14***
499 A160 20pf lake 18 15

90th anniversary of the birth of Lenin.

No. 390 Overprinted:
"Inbetriebnahme des Hochseehafens 1.Mai 1960"

1960, Apr. 28 **Litho.** ***Perf. 13½x13***
500 A122 10pf emerald 15 15

Inauguration of the seaport Rostock.

Russian Soldier and Liberated Prisoner — A161

1960, May 5 **Litho.** ***Perf. 13x13½***
501 A161 20pf rose red 15 15

Issued to commemorate the 15th anniversary of Germany's liberation from fascism.

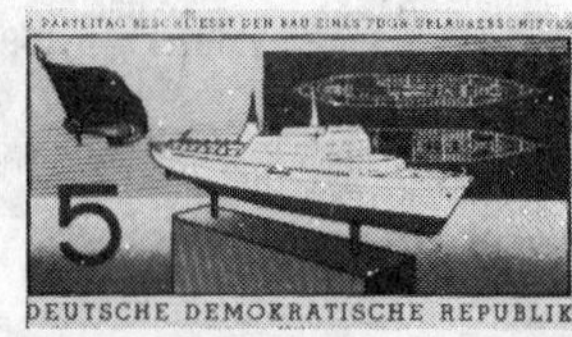

Model of Vacation Ship — A162

Designs: 25pf, Ship before Leningrad.

Perf. 13½x13

1960, June 23 **Wmk. 313**
502 A162 5pf sl, cit & blk 15 15
503 A162 25pf blk, yel & ultra *2.25* *1.25*

Issued to commemorate the launching of the trade union (FDGB) vacation ship. June 25, 1960. See Nos. B58-B59.

Masked Dancer in Porcelain — A163

Lenin Monument, Eisleben — A164

Meissen porcelain: 10pf, Plate with Meissen mark and date. 15pf, Otter. 20pf, Potter. 25pf, Coffee pot.

1960, July 28 ***Perf. 12½x13***
504 A163 5pf bl & org 15 15
505 A163 10pf bl & emer 15 15
506 A163 15pf bl & pur *2.75* *1.10*
507 A163 20pf bl & org red 15 15
508 A163 25pf bl & ap grn 15 15
Set value *3.00* *1.25*

Meissen porcelain works, 250th anniv.

Perf. 13x13½

1960, July 2 **Wmk. 313**

Design: 20pf, Thälmann monument, gift for Pushkin, USSR.

509 A164 10pf dk grn 15 15
510 A164 20pf brt red 15 15
Set value 20 15

Pieck Type of 1959

1960, Sept. 10 **Litho.** ***Perf. 13½x13***
511 A139 20pf black 20 15
a. Souv. sheet of 1, imperf. 60 30

Pres. Wilhelm Pieck (1876-1960).

Modern Postal Trucks
A165

Design: 25pf, Railroad mail car, 19th cent.

1960, Oct. 6 ***Perf. 13x12½***
512 A165 20pf car rose, blk & yel 15 15
513 A165 25pf bl, gray & blk *55* *32*

Issued for the Day of the Stamp, 1960.

New Opera House, Leipzig
A166

Design: 25pf, Car, sailboat, tent, campers.

1960, Aug. 29 **Wmk. 313**
514 A166 20pf rose brn & gray 15 15
515 A166 25pf bl & grysh brn 15 15
Set value 25 15

1960 Leipzig Fall Fair.

Hans Burkmair Medal, 1518 A167

Neidhardt von Gneisenau A168

Design: 25pf, Dancing Peasants by Albrecht Dürer.

1960, Oct. 20 Litho. *Perf. 12½x13*

516 A167 20pf buff, grn & ocher 24 15
517 A167 25pf lt bl & blk *1.25* 35

400th anniv. of the Dresden Art Gallery.

Perf. 13x12½, 12½x13
1960, Oct. 27

Design: 20pf, Neidhardt von Gneisenau (horiz.).

518 A168 20pf dk car & blk 15 15
519 A168 25pf ultra *1.25* 40
Set value 45

200th anniversary of the birth of Count August Neidhardt von Gneisenau, Prussian Field Marshal.

Rudolf Virchow A169

Humboldt University, Berlin A170

Designs: 10pf, Robert Koch. 25pf, Wilheim and Alexander von Humboldt medal. 40pf, Wilheim Griesinger.

1960, Nov. 4 Litho. *Perf. 13x12½*

520 A169 5pf ocher & blk 15 15
521 A169 10pf grn & blk 15 15
522 A170 20pf cop red, gray & blk 15 15
523 A170 25pf brt bl & blk 15 15
524 A169 40pf car rose & blk *1.75* 35
Set value *2.00* 48

Nos. 520, 521, 524 for the 250th anniv. of the Charite (hospital), Berlin; Nos. 522-523 the 150th anniv. of Humboldt University, Berlin.

Nos. 520 and 523, and Nos. 521 and 522 are printed se-tenant.

Scientist and Chemical Formula — A171

Designs: 10pf, Chemistry worker (fertilizer). 20pf, Woman worker (automobile). 25pf, Laboratory assistant (synthetic fabrics).

Perf. 13x13½
1960, Nov. 10 Wmk. 313

525 A171 5pf dk red & gray 15 15
526 A171 10pf org & brt grn 15 15
527 A171 20pf bl & red 15 15
528 A171 25pf yel & ultra *1.50* *52*
Set value *1.70* *60*

Day of the Chemistry Worker.

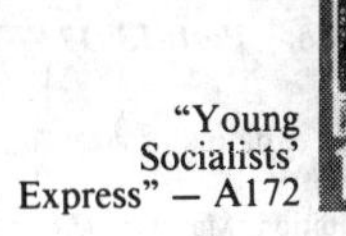

"Young Socialists' Express" — A172

Designs: 20pf, Sassnitz Harbor station and ferry. 25pf, Diesel locomotive and 1835 "Adler."

Perf. 13x13½; 13x12½ (20pf)
1960, Dec. 5
Sizes: 10pf, 25pf, 28x23mm
20pf, 38½x22mm

529 A172 10pf emer & blk 15 15
530 A172 20pf red & blk 15 15
531 A172 25pf bl & blk *2.50* *1.50*

125th anniv. of German railroads. No. 530 exists imperf. Value $1.

Pieck Type of 1953 with Dates Added

1961, Jan. 3 Photo. *Perf. 13x13½*

532 A35 20pf hn brn & blk 20 15

Issued on the 85th anniversary of the birth of Pres. Wilhelm Pieck (1876-1960).

380 Kilovolt Switch A173

Lilienstein A174

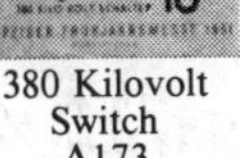

Design: 25pf, Leipzig Press Center.

1961, Mar. 3 Litho. *Perf. 13½x13*

533 A173 10pf brt grn & dk gray 20 15
534 A173 25pf vio bl & dk gray 25 15
Set value 15

Leipzig Spring Fair of 1961.

1961 Typo. *Perf. 14*

Designs: 5pf, Rudelsburg on Saale. 10pf, Wartburg. No. 538, City Hall, Wernigerode. 25pf, Brocken, Harz Mts. (horiz.).

535 A174 5pf gray 15 15
536 A174 10pf bl grn 15 15
537 A174 20pf red brn 15 15
538 A174 20pf dl red 15 15
539 A174 25pf dark blue 15 15
Set value 35 15

Issue dates: No. 538, 25pf, Mar. 14. 5pf, 10pf, No. 537, June 22.

Trawler — A176

Designs: 20pf, Fishermen. 25pf, S.S. Robert Koch. 40pf, Cannery worker.

1961, Apr. 4 Engr. Wmk. 313

545 A176 10pf gray grn 15 15
546 A176 20pf claret 15 15
547 A176 25pf slate 15 15
548 A176 40pf dl vio *1.65* *65*
Set value *1.75* *75*

Deep-sea fishing industry.

Vostok 1 Leaving Earth A177

Designs: 20pf, Astronaut in capsule. 25pf, Parachute landing of capsule.

1961, Apr. Litho. *Perf. 13x12½*

549 A177 10pf lt bl grn & red 22 15
550 A177 20pf red 30 15
551 A177 25pf lt bl *2.25* *1.50*

Issued to commemorate the first man in space, Yuri A. Gagarin, Apr. 12, 1961.
Issue dates: 10pf, Apr. 18; others, Apr. 20.

Zebra A178

Dresden Zoo cent.: 20pf, Black-and-white colobus monkeys.

1961, May 9

552 A178 10pf grn & blk *1.90* *90*
553 A178 20pf lil rose & blk 40 15

Engels, Marx, Lenin and Crowd — A179

1961, Apr. 20 Litho. *Perf. 13½x13*

554 A179 20pf red 20 15

15th anniversary of Socialist Unity Party of Germany (SED).

Stag Leap — A180

Designs: 20pf, Arabesque. 25pf, Exercise on parallel bars (horiz.).

1961, June 3 *Perf. 13½x13, 13x13½*

555 A180 10pf bl grn 15 15
556 A180 20pf rose pink 15 15
557 A180 25pf brt bl *3.00* *1.25*

3rd Europa Cup for Women's Gymnastics.

Salt Miners and Castle Giebichenstein — A181

Design: 20pf, Chemist and "Five Towers" of Halle.

1961, June 22 *Perf. 13x12½*

558 A181 10pf blk, grn & yel *1.00* *35*
559 A181 20pf blk, dk red & yel 15 15

1000th anniv. of the founding of Halle.

Kayak Slalom A182

Designs: 10pf, Canoe. 20pf, Two seater canoe.

1961, July 6 Litho. Wmk. 313

560 A182 5pf gray & Prus bl *1.50* *90*
561 A182 10pf gray & sl grn 15 15
562 A182 20pf gray & dk car rose 15 15

Issued to commemorate the Canoe Slalom and Rapids World Championships.

Target Line Casting A183

Design: 20pf, River fishing.

1961, July 21

563 A183 10pf grn & bl *1.25* *75*
564 A183 20pf dk red brn & bl 15 15

World Fishing Championships, Dresden.

Tulip — A184

"Alte Waage," Historical Building, Leipzig — A185

1961, Sept. 13 Photo. *Perf. 14*

565 A184 10pf shown 15 15
566 A184 20pf Dahlia 20 15
567 A184 40pf Rose *5.25* *3.00*

Intl. Horticulture Exhibition, Erfurt.

Perf. 13½x13
1961, Aug. 23 Litho. Wmk. 313

Design: 25pf, Old Exchange Building.

568 A185 10pf cit & bl grn 15 15
569 A185 25pf lt bl & ultra 35 15
Set value 40 15

Issued to publicize the 1961 Leipzig Fall Fair. See Nos. 595-597.

Liszt's Hand, French Sculpture A186

Television Camera and Screen A187

Designs: 5pf, Liszt and Hector Berlioz. 20pf, Franz Liszt, medallion by Ernst Rietschel, 1852. 25pf, Liszt and Frederic Chopin.

1961, Oct.-Nov. Engr. *Perf. 14*

570 A186 5pf gray 15 15
571 A186 10pf bl grn *1.25* *48*
572 A186 20pf dl red 15 15
573 A186 25pf chlky bl *2.00* *80*

Issued to commemorate the 150th anniversary of the birth of Franz Liszt, composer.

1961, Oct. 25 *Perf. 13x13½*

Design: 20pf, Microphone and radio dial.

574 A187 10pf brt grn & blk *1.25* 35
575 A187 20pf brick red & blk 15 15
Set value *40*

Issued for Stamp Day, 1961.

Maj. Gherman Titov and Young Pioneers A188

Designs: 10pf, Titov in Leipzig (vert.). 15pf, Titov in spaceship. 20pf, Titov and Walter Ulbricht. 25pf, Spaceship Vostok 2. 40pf, Titov and Ulbricht in Berlin.

1961, Dec. 11 Litho. *Perf. 13½*

576 A188 5pf car & vio 15 15
577 A188 10pf ol grn & car 15 15
578 A188 15pf bl & lil *4.75* *2.50*
579 A188 20pf bl & car rose 18 15
580 A188 25pf car & bl 15 15
581 A188 40pf car & dk bl 55 15
Nos. 576-581 (6) 5.93
Set value *2.70*

Issued to commemorate the visit of Russian Maj. Gherman Titov to the German Democratic Republic.

Chairman Walter Ulbricht A189

Red Ants A190

1961-67 Wmk. 313 Typo. *Perf. 14*
Size: 17x21mm

582 A189 5pf slate 15 15
a. Bklt. pane of 8
583 A189 10pf brt grn 15 15
a. Bklt. pane of 8
584 A189 15pf red lilac 15 15
585 A189 20pf dk red 15 15
586 A189 25pf dl bl ('63) 15 15
587 A189 30pf car rose ('63) 15 15
588 A189 40pf brt vio ('63) 20 15
589 A189 50pf ultra ('63) 28 15
589A A189 60pf dp yel grn ('64) 32 15
590 A189 70pf red brn ('63) 48 15
590A A189 80pf brt bl ('67) 60 15

Engr.
Size: 24x28½mm

590B A189 1dm dl grn ('63) 50 15
590C A189 2dm brown ('63) 1.00 15
Nos. 582-590C (13) 4.28
Set value 45

See Nos. 751-752, 1112A-1114A, 1483. Currency abbreviation is "DM" on Nos. 590B-590C, "MDN" on Nos. 751-752, and "M" on Nos. 1113-1114A.

1962, Feb. 16 Photo.

591 A190 5pf shown *2.50* *95*
592 A190 10pf Weasels 16 15
593 A190 20pf Shrews 16 15
594 A190 40pf Bat 42 16

See Nos. 663-667.

Type of 1961

Buildings: 10pf, "Coffee Tree House." 20pf, Gohlis Castle. 25pf, Romanus House.

1962, Feb. 22 Litho. *Perf. 13x13½*

595 A185 10pf ol grn & brn 18 15
596 A185 20pf org red & blk 28 15
597 A185 25pf brt bl & brn 45 15
Set value 20

Leipzig Spring Fair of 1962.

Air Defense A191

Designs: 10pf, Motorized infantry. 20pf, Soldier and worker as protectors. 25pf, Sailor and destroyer escort. 40pf, Tank and tankman.

1962, Mar. 1 *Perf. 13x12½*

598 A191 5pf lt bl 15 15
599 A191 10pf brt grn 15 15
600 A191 20pf red 15 15
601 A191 25pf ultra 15 15
602 A191 40pf brown *1.65* *55*
Set value *1.90* *65*

National People's Army, 6th anniv.

Cyclists and Hradcany, Prague A192

Design: 25pf, Cyclist, East Berlin City Hall and dove.

1962, Apr. 26 Litho. Wmk. 313

603 A192 10pf multi 15 15
604 A192 25pf multi *1.65* *45*
Set value 50

Issued to commemorate the 15th International Bicycle Peace Race, Berlin-Warsaw-Prague. See No. B89.

Johann Gottlieb Fichte — A193

Design: 10pf, Fichte's birthplace in Rammenau.

1962, May 17 *Perf. 13x13½*

605 A193 10pf brt grn & blk 65 26
606 A193 20pf ver & blk 15 15
Set value 32

Issued to commemorate bicentenary of the birth of Johann Gottlieb Fichte, philosopher.

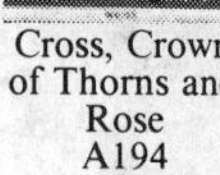

Cross, Crown of Thorns and Rose A194

George Dimitrov at Reichstag Trial, Leipzig A195

1962, June 7 *Perf. 12½x13*

607 A194 20pf red & blk 15 15
608 A194 25pf brt bl & blk *65* *30*
Set value *36*

20th anniversary of the destruction of Lidice in Czechoslovakia by the Nazis.

1962, June 18 Photo. *Perf. 14*

Design: 20pf, Dimitrov as Premier of Bulgaria.

609 A195 5pf bl grn & blk *55* *20*
610 A195 20pf car rose & blk 15 15
Set value *60* *24*

George Dimitrov, (1882-1949), communist leader and premier of the Bulgarian Peoples' Republic.

Nos. 609-610 also printed se-tenant, divided by a label inscribed with a Dimitrov quotation.

Corn Planter A196

Designs: 20pf, Milking machine. 40pf, Combine harvester.

1962, June 26 Litho. *Perf. 13x12½*

611 A196 10pf multi 15 15
612 A196 20pf multi 15 15
613 A196 40pf yel, grn & dk red *1.40* *70*
Set value *80*

10th Agricultural Exhibition, Markkleeberg.

Map of Baltic Sea and Emblem — A197

Brandenburg Gate, Berlin — A198

Designs: 20pf, Hotel, Rostock (vert.). 25pf, Cargo ship "Frieden" in Rostock harbor.

Perf. 13x13½, 13½x13 (20pf)

1962, July 2 Wmk. 313

614 A197 10pf bluish grn & ultra 15 15
615 A197 20pf dk red & yel 15 15
616 A197 25pf bl & bis *1.75* *65*
Set value *75*

Issued to commemorate the Fifth Baltic Sea Week, Rostock, July 7-15.

1962, July 17 *Perf. 13½x13*

Designs: No. 618 Heads of youths of three races. No. 619, Peace dove. No. 620, National Theater, Helsinki.

617 A198 5pf multi *1.40* *65*
618 A198 5pf multi *1.40* *65*
619 A198 20pf multi *1.40* *65*
620 A198 20pf multi *1.40* *65*

Issued to publicize the 8th Youth Festival for Peace and Friendship, Helsinki, July 28-Aug. 6, 1962.

Printed in sheets of 60 incorporating all four designs arranged in blocks to form the festival flower emblem. See Nos. B90-B91.

Free Style Swimming A199

Municipal Store, Leipzig A200

Designs: 10pf, Back stroke. 25pf, Butterfly stroke. 40pf, Breast stroke. 70pf, Water polo.

1962, Aug. 7 Litho. *Perf. 13x13½*
Design in Greenish Blue

621 A199 5pf orange 15 15
622 A199 10pf grnsh bl 15 15
623 A199 25pf ultra 15 15
624 A199 40pf brt vio *1.40* *1.40*
625 A199 70pf red brn 15 15
Set value, #621-625, B92 *1.65* *1.65*

Issued to publicize the 10th European Swimming Championships, Leipzig, Aug. 18-25.

Nos. 621-625 and B92 were also printed in the same sheet, arranged in se-tenant blocks of six.

Engr. & Photo.
1962, Aug. 28 Wmk. 313 *Perf. 14*

Buildings: 20pf, Mädler Passage. 25pf, Leipzig Air Terminal and plane.

626 A200 10pf blk & emer 15 15
627 A200 20pf blk & red 28 15
628 A200 25pf blk & bl 48 18
Set value 25

Leipzig Fall Fair of 1962.

"Transportation and Communication" — A201

1962, Oct. 3 Litho. *Perf. 13½x13*

629 A201 5pf lt bl & blk 25 15

10th anniv. of the Friedrich List Transportation College.

Souvenir Sheet

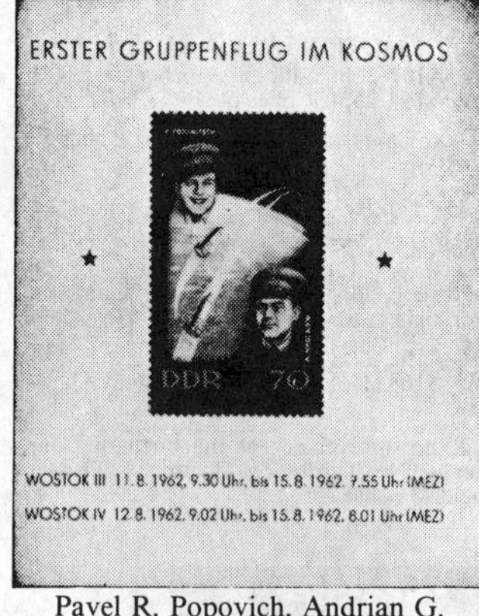

Pavel R. Popovich, Andrian G. Nikolayev and Space Capsules — A202

1962, Sept. 13 Wmk. 313 *Imperf.*

630 A202 70pf dk bl, lt grn & yel *1.90* *70*

1st Russian group space flight of Vostoks III and IV, Aug. 11-13, 1962.

DDR Television Signal — A203

Young Collectors and World Map — A204

1962, Oct. 25 *Perf. 13½x13*

631 A203 20pf grn & gray 18 15
632 A204 40pf brt pink & blk *1.40* *45*
Set value *48*

No. 631 commemorates the 10th anniversary of television in the German Democratic Republic; No. 632 is for Stamp Day.

Gerhart Hauptmann A205

1962, Nov. 15 *Perf. 13x13½*

633 A205 20pf red & blk 30 15

Issued to commemorate the centenary of the birth of Gerhart Hauptmann, playwright.

Souvenir Sheet

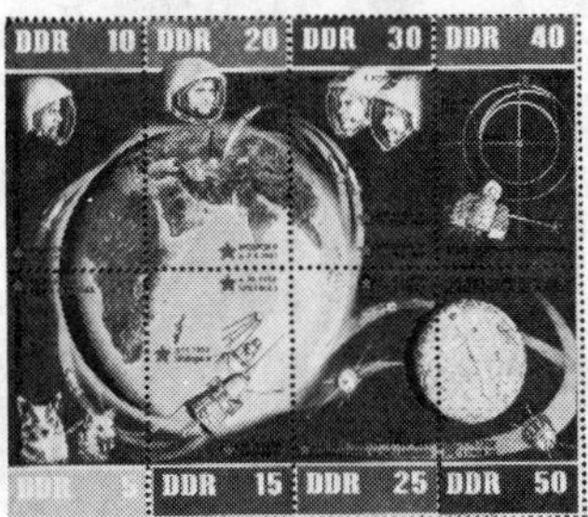

Russian Space Flights and Astronauts — A206

1962, Dec. 28 Litho. *Perf. 12½x13*

634	A206 Sheet of 8	*25.00*	*15.00*
a.	5pf yellow	*1.75*	*1.10*
b.	10pf emerald	*1.75*	*1.10*
c.	15pf magenta	*1.75*	*1.10*
d.	20pf red	*1.75*	*1.10*
e.	25pf greenish blue	*1.75*	*1.10*
f.	30pf red brown	*1.75*	*1.10*
g.	40pf crimson	*1.75*	*1.10*
h.	50pf ultramarine	*1.75*	*1.10*

Issued to show the development of Russian space flights from Sputnik 1 to Vostoks 3 and 4, and to honor the Russian astronauts Gagarin, Titov, Nikolayev and Popovich.

Pierre de Coubertin A207

Congress Emblem, Flag with Marx, Engels and Lenin A208

Design: 25pf, Stadium and Olympic rings.

1963, Jan. 2 *Perf. 13½x13*

635	A207 20pf car & gray	28	15
636	A207 25pf bl & bis	*1.65*	*30*
	Set value		*32*

Issued to commemorate the centenary of the birth of Baron Pierre de Coubertin, organizer of the modern Olympic Games.

1963, Jan. 15 *Perf. 13x13½*

637	A208 10pf yel, org, red & blk	25	15

6th congress of Socialist Unity Party of Germany (SED).

World Map and Exterminator — A209

Designs: 25pf, Map, cross and staff of Aesculapius. 50pf, Map, cross, mosquito.

1963, Feb. 6 *Perf. 13x12½*

638	A209 20pf dp org, dk red & blk	15	15
639	A209 25pf multi	15	15
640	A209 50pf multi	*85*	*48*
	Set value	*1.00*	*55*

WHO drive to eradicate malaria.

Silver Fox A210

Design: 25pf, Karakul.

1963, Feb. 14 Photo. *Perf. 14*

641	A210 20pf rose & blk	15	15
642	A210 25pf bl & blk	*65*	*28*
	Set value		*30*

Issued to publicize the International Fur Auctions. Leipzig, Feb. 14-15, Apr. 21-24.

Barthels House, Leipzig — A211

Designs: 20pf, New Leipzig City Hall. 25pf, Belltower Building.

Engr. & Photo.

1963, Feb. 26 Wmk. 313 *Perf. 14*

643	A211 10pf blk & citron	15	15
644	A211 20pf blk & red org	20	15
645	A211 25pf blk & blue	55	28
	Set value		40

1963 Leipzig Spring Fair.

Souvenir Sheet

On March 12, 1963, a souvenir sheet publicizing "Chemistry for Peace and Socialism" was issued. It contains two imperforate stamps, 50pf and 70pf, printed on ungummed synthetic tissue. Size: 105x74mm. Value $1.50.

Richard Wagner and "The Flying Dutchman" A213

Designs (Portrait and Scene from Play): 5pf, Johann Gottfried Seume (1763-1810). 10pf, Friedrich Hebbel (1813-1863). 20pf, Georg Büchner (1813-1837).

1963, Apr. 9 Litho. *Perf. 13x12½*

647	A213 5pf brt cit & blk	15	15
648	A213 10pf brt grn & blk	15	15
649	A213 20pf org & blk	15	15
650	A213 25pf dl bl & blk	*1.10*	*45*
	Set value		*55*

Issued to commemorate anniversaries of German dramatists and the 150th anniversary of the birth of Richard Wagner, composer.

First Aid Station A214

Design: 20pf, Ambulance and hospital.

1963, May 14 Wmk. 313

651	A214 10pf multi	*1.00*	*45*
652	A214 20pf red, blk & gray	15	15
	Set value		*50*

Centenary of International Red Cross.

Eugene Pottier, Writer — A215

Design: 25pf, Pierre-Chretien Degeyter, composer.

1963, June 18 *Perf. 13x13½*

653	A215 20pf ver & blk	15	15
654	A215 25pf vio bl & blk	*60*	*30*
	Set value		*32*

75th anniv. of the communist song "The International."

Valentina Tereshkova and Vostok 6 — A216

Motorcyclist in "Motocross" at Apolda — A217

Design: No. 656, Valeri Bykovski and Vostok 5.

1963, July 18 Photo. *Perf. 13½*

655	A216 20pf bl, blk & gray bl	85	15
656	A216 20pf bl, blk & gray bl	85	15
	Set value		15

Space flights of Valeri Bykovski, June 14-19, and Valentina Tereshkova, 1st woman cosmonaut, June 16-19, 1963.

Nos. 655-656 printed se-tenant.

Engr. & Photo.

1963, July 30 *Perf. 14*

Designs: 20pf, Motorcyclist at Sachsenring (horiz.). 25pf, Two motorcyclists at Sachsenring (horiz.).

Size: 23x28mm

657	A217 10pf lt grn & dk grn	*2.50*	*1.00*

Size: 48½x21mm

658	A217 20pf rose & dk red	15	15
659	A217 25pf lt bl & dk bl	20	15
	Set value		*1.10*

Motorcycle World Championships.

Monument at Treblinka — A218

Globe, Car and Train — A219

Perf. 13x13½

1963, Aug. 20 Litho. Wmk. 313

660	A218 20pf brick red & dk bl	25	15

Issued to commemorate the erection of a memorial at Treblinka (Poland) concentration camp.

1963, Aug. 27 *Perf. 13½x13*

Design: No. 662, Globe, plane and bus.

661	A219 10pf multi	1.00	15
662	A219 10pf multi	1.00	15
	Set value		15

Issued to publicize the 1963 Leipzig Fall Fair. Nos. 661-662 printed se-tenant.

Fauna Type of 1962

Designs: 10pf, Stag beetle. 20pf, Fire salamander. 30pf, Pond turtle. 50pf, Green toad. 70pf, Hedgehogs.

1963, Sept. 10 Photo. *Perf. 14*

663	A190 10pf emer, brn & blk	15	15
664	A190 20pf crim, blk & yel	15	15
665	A190 30pf multi	16	15
666	A190 50pf multi	*2.75*	*90*
667	A190 70pf cl brn, brn & bis	35	15
	Nos. 663-667 (5)	*3.56*	
	Set value		*1.10*

Neidhardt von Gneisenau and Gebhard Leberecht von Blücher — A220

Designs: 10pf, Cossacks and home guard, Berlin. 20pf, Ernst Moritz Arndt and Baron Heinrich vom Stein. 25pf, Lützow's volunteers before battle. 40pf, Gerhard von Scharnhorst and Prince Mikhail I. Kutuzov.

1963, Oct. 10 Litho. *Perf. 13½x13*

Center in Tan and Black

668	A220 5pf brt yel	15	15
669	A220 10pf emerald	15	15
670	A220 20pf dp org	20	15
671	A220 25pf dp ultra	20	15
672	A220 40pf dk red	*1.40*	*35*
	Nos. 668-672 (5)	*2.10*	
	Set value		*52*

150th anniversary of War of Liberation.

Valentina Tereshkova and Space Craft — A221

Burning Synagogue and Star of David in Chains — A222

Designs: No. 674, Tereshkova and map of DDR (vert.). No. 675, Yuri A. Gagarin and map of DDR (vert.). 25pf, Tereshkova in space capsule.

1963 *Perf. 13½x13, 13x13½*

Size: 28x28mm (10pf, 25pf); 28x37mm (20pf)

673	A221 10pf ultra & grn	15	15
674	A221 20pf red, blk & ocher	15	15
675	A221 20pf red, grn & ocher	15	15
676	A221 25pf org & bl	*1.65*	*65*
	Set value		*70*

Issued to commemorate the visit of astronauts Valentina Tereshkova and Yuri A. Gagarin to the German Democratic Republic.

Perf. 13½x13

1963, Nov. 8 Wmk. 313

677	A222 10pf multi	25	15

Issued to mark the 25th anniversary of the "Crystal Night," the start of the systematic persecution of the Jews in Germany. Inscribed: "Never again Crystal Night."

Letter Sorting Machine A223

Design: 20pf, Mechanized mail loading.

1963, Nov. 25 *Perf. 13x12½*

678	A223 10pf multi	*75*	*32*
679	A223 20pf multi	15	15
	Set value		*35*

Issued for Stamp Day.

Ski Jump and Olympic Rings A224

1963, Dec. 16 Litho. *Perf. 13½x13*

No.	Type	Description	Unused	Used
680	A224	5pf shown	15	15
681	A224	10pf Start	15	15
682	A224	25pf Landing	*1.65*	*52*
		Set value		*58*

9th Winter Olympic Games, Innsbruck, Jan. 29-Feb. 9, 1964. See No. B111.

Admiral — A225

Butterflies: 15pf, Alpine Apollo. 20pf, Swallowtail. 25pf, Postilion. 40pf, Great fox.

Wmk. 313

1964, Jan. 15 Photo. *Perf. 14*

Butterflies in Natural Colors

No.	Type	Description	Unused	Used
683	A225	10pf cit & blk	15	15
684	A225	15pf pale vio & blk	15	15
685	A225	20pf lt brick red & blk	20	15
686	A225	25pf lt bl & dk brn	25	15
687	A225	40pf lt ultra & blk	*2.50*	*65*
		Nos. 683-687 (5)	*3.25*	
		Set value		*80*

William Shakespeare A226

Designs: 20pf, Quadriga, Brandenburg Gate, Berlin. 25pf, Keystone, History Museum (Zeughaus), Berlin.

1964, Feb. 6 Litho. *Perf. 13x12½*

No.	Type	Description	Unused	Used
688	A226	20pf rose & dk bl	15	15
689	A226	25pf lt bl & mag	15	15
690	A226	40pf lt vio & dk bl grn	*85*	*55*
		Set value		*63*

200th anniv. of the birth of the sculptor Johann Gottfried Schadow (20pf); 300th anniv. of the birth of the sculptor Andreas Schlüter (25pf); 400th anniv. of the birth of William Shakespeare, dramatist (40pf).

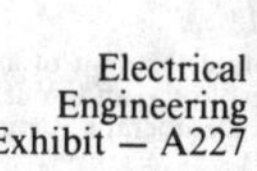

Electrical Engineering Exhibit — A227

Design: 20pf, Bräunigkes Court, exhibition hall, 1700.

Perf. 13x13½

1964, Feb. 26 Wmk. 313

No.	Type	Description	Unused	Used
691	A227	10pf brt grn & blk	5.00	15
692	A227	20pf red & blk	6.00	15
		Set value		15

Issued to publicize the Leipzig Spring Fair, Mar. 1-10, 1964. Nos. 691-692 printed in same sheet with alternating yellow and black label.

Khrushchev and Inventors A228

Youth Training for Leadership A229

Design: 40pf, Khrushchev, Tereshkova and Bykovski.

1964, May 15 *Perf. 13x13½*

No.	Type	Description	Unused	Used
693	A228	25pf blue	15	15
694	A228	40pf lil & grnsh blk	*2.25*	*48*
		Set value		*52*

Issued in honor of Premier Nikita S. Khrushchev of the Soviet Union.

1964, May 13 Litho.

Designs: 20pf, Young athletes. 25pf, Accordion player and girl with flowers.

Center in Black

No.	Type	Description	Unused	Used
695	A229	10pf ultra, mag & emer	15	15
696	A229	20pf emer, ultra & mag	15	15
697	A229	25pf mag, emer & ultra	*60*	*28*
		Set value	*75*	*33*

German Youth Meeting, Berlin.

Television Antenna and Puppets — A230

Children's Day: Various characters from children's television programs.

1964, June 1 *Perf. 13x13½*

No.	Type	Description	Unused	Used
698	A230	5pf multi	15	15
699	A230	10pf multi	15	15
700	A230	15pf multi	15	15
701	A230	20pf multi	15	15
702	A230	40pf multi	*1.00*	*65*
		Set value	*1.30*	*75*

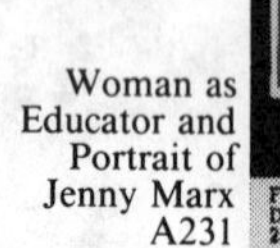

Woman as Educator and Portrait of Jenny Marx A231

Designs: 25pf, Women in industry and transistor diagram. 70pf, Women in agriculture.

Perf. 13½x13

1964, June 26 Litho. Wmk. 313

No.	Type	Description	Unused	Used
703	A231	20pf crim, gray & yel	15	15
704	A231	25pf lt bl, gray & red	*1.25*	*42*
705	A231	70pf emer, gray & yel	18	15
		Set value		*50*

Congress of Women of the German Democratic Republic, June 25-27.

Bicycling — A232

Diving — A233

Litho. & Engr.

1964, July 15 *Perf. 14*

No.	Type	Description	Unused	Used
706	A232	5pf shown	15	15
707	A232	10pf Volleyball	15	15
708	A232	20pf Judo	15	15
709	A232	25pf Woman diver	15	15
710	A232	70pf Equestrian	*1.65*	*70*
		Set value, #706-710, B118	*2.20*	*90*

Litho.

Perf. 13x13½

No.	Type	Description	Unused	Used
711	A233	10pf shown	1.65	1.10
712	A233	10pf Volleyball	1.65	1.10
713	A233	10pf Bicycling	1.65	1.10
714	A233	10pf Judo	1.65	1.10
a.		Block of 6, #711-714, B119-B120	14.00	9.25

18th Olympic Games, Tokyo, Oct. 10-25, 1964. See Nos. B118-B120. No. 714a printed in 2 horiz. rows: (1st: #711, #B119, #712. 2nd: #713, #B120, #714). The Olympic rings extend over the 6 stamps.

Monument, Leningrad — A234

1964, Aug. 8 Litho. *Perf. 13x13½*

No.	Type	Description	Unused	Used
715	A234	25pf brt bl, blk & yel	35	15

Issued to honor the victims of the siege of Leningrad, Sept. 1941-Jan. 1943.

Bertha von Suttner A235

Medieval Glazier and Goblet A236

Designs: 20pf, Frederic Joliot Curie. 50pf, Carl von Ossietzky.

1964, Sept. 1 *Perf. 14*

No.	Type	Description	Unused	Used
716	A235	20pf red & blk	15	15
717	A235	25pf ultra & blk	15	15
718	A235	50pf lil & blk	*80*	*42*
		Set value		*50*

Issued to promote World Peace.

1964, Sept. 3 *Perf. 14*

Design: 15pf, Jena glass for chemical industry.

No.	Type	Description	Unused	Used
719	A236	10pf lt ultra & multi	95	15
720	A236	15pf red & multi	95	15
		Set value		20

Issued for the Leipzig Fall Fair, 1964. Nos. 719-720 printed as triptychs with label inscribed "800 years Leipzig Fair" between.

Handstamp of First Socialist International, 1864 — A237

1964, Sept. 16 Photo. Wmk. 313

No.	Type	Description	Unused	Used
721	A237	20pf org red & blk	15	15
722	A237	25pf dl bl & blk	*60*	*35*
		Set value		*38*

Centenary of First Socialist International.

Stamp of 1955 (Dürer's Portrait of Young Man) — A238

1964, Sept. 23 Litho. *Perf. 13x13½*

No.	Type	Description	Unused	Used
723	A238	50pf gray & dk red brn	*85*	*45*

Natl. Stamp Exhibition, Berlin, Oct. 3-18. See Nos. B124-B125.

Navigation A239

Man from Mönchgut, Rügen A240

Designs: No. 725, Flag and new Berlin buildings. No. 726, Bituminous coal transport and surveyors level. No. 727, Chemist. No. 728, Soldier. No. 729, Farm woman and cows. No. 730, Steel worker. No. 731, Woman scientist and lecture hall. No. 732, Heavy industry. No. 733, Optical industry. No. 734, Consumer goods (woman examining cloth). No. 735, Foreign trade, Leipzig fair emblem. No. 736, Buildings industry. No. 737, Sculptor. No. 738, Woman skier.

Perf. 13½x13

1964, Oct. 6 Litho. Wmk. 313

No.	Type	Description	Unused	Used
724	A239	10pf bl & multi	15	15
725	A239	10pf bl & multi	15	15
726	A239	10pf gray & multi	15	15
727	A239	10pf red & multi	15	15
728	A239	10pf red & multi	15	15
729	A239	10pf yel grn & multi	15	15
730	A239	10pf red & multi	15	15
731	A239	10pf red & multi	15	15
732	A239	10pf gray & multi	15	15
733	A239	10pf gray & multi	15	15
734	A239	10pf bl & multi	15	15
735	A239	10pf bl & multi	15	15
736	A239	10pf yel grn & multi	15	15
737	A239	10pf yel grn & multi	15	15
738	A239	10pf bl & multi	15	15
		Set value	1.60	90

German Democratic Republic, 15th anniv. A souvenir sheet contains 15 imperf. stamps similar to #724-738. Size: 210x287mm. Value, $17.50.

For surcharge see No. B134.

1964, Nov. 25 Photo. *Perf. 14*

Regional Costumes: No. 740, Woman from Mönchgut, Rügen. No. 741, Man from Spreewald. No. 742, Woman from Spreewald. No. 743, Man from Thuringia. No. 744, Woman from Thuringia.

No.	Type	Description	Unused	Used
739	A240	5pf multi	*6.75*	*4.25*
740	A240	5pf multi	*6.75*	*4.25*
741	A240	10pf multi	16	15
742	A240	10pf multi	16	15
743	A240	20pf multi	25	15
744	A240	20pf multi	25	15
		Nos. 739-744 (6)	*14.32*	*9.10*

The male and female costume stamps of the same denomination are printed se-tenant in checkerboard arrangement.

See Nos. 859-864.

Souvenir Sheets

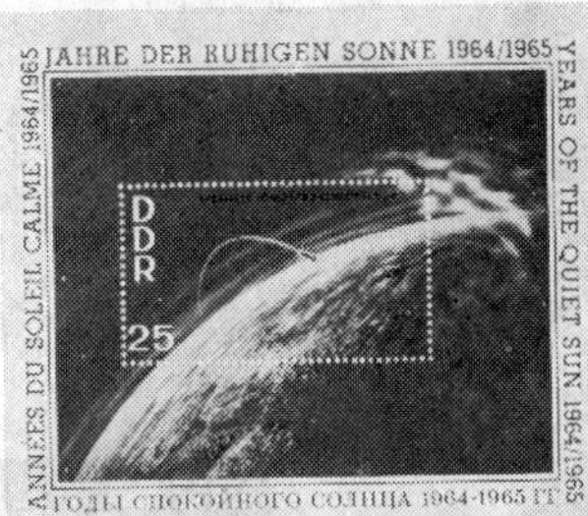

Exploration of Ionosphere — A241

Designs: 40pf, Exploration of sun activities. 70pf, Exploration of radiation belt.

1964, Dec. 29 Litho. *Perf. 13½x13*

745	A241	25pf vio bl & yel	*5.25*	*1.75*
746	A241	40pf vio bl, yel & red	*1.25*	*35*
747	A241	70pf dp grn, vio bl & yel	*1.50*	*42*

Intl. Quiet Sun Year, 1964-65.

Albert Schweitzer as Physician — A242

August Bebel — A243

Designs (Schweitzer): 20pf, As fighter against war and atom bomb. 25pf, At the organ with score of Organ Prelude by Bach.

Wmk. 313

1965, Jan. 14 Photo. *Perf. 14*

748	A242	10pf emer, blk & bis	15	15
749	A242	20pf crim, blk & bis	15	15
750	A242	25pf bl, blk & bis	*2.25*	*1.10*
		Set value		*1.20*

Issued to commemorate the 90th birthday of Dr. Albert Schweitzer, medical missionary.

Ulbricht Type of 1961-63
Currency in "Mark of the Deutsche Notenbank" (MDN)

1965, Feb. 10 Engr.

Size: 24x28½mm

751	A189	1mdn dl grn	70	15
752	A189	2mdn brown	70	15
		Set value		15

See note below Nos. 590B-590C.

1965 Photo. *Perf. 14*

Portraits: 10pf, Wilhelm Conrad Roentgen. No. 753A, Adolph von Menzel. 25pf, Wilhelm Külz. 40pf, Erich Weinert. 50pf, Dante Alighieri.

753	A243	10pf dk brn, yel & emer	15	15
753A	A243	10pf dk brn, yel & org	15	15
754	A243	20pf ol brn, red & buff	18	15
754A	A243	25pf ol brn, yel & bl	18	15
754B	A243	40pf ol brn, buff & car rose	28	15
755	A243	50pf dk brn, yel & org	35	15
		Nos. 753-755 (6)	1.29	
		Set value		30

Roentgen (1845-1923), physicist, discoverer of X-rays. Sesquicentennial of the birth of Adolph von Menzel, painter and graphic artist. Bebel, labor leader (1840-1913). 90th anniv. of the birth of Wilhelm Külz, politician. 75th anniv. of the birth of Erich Weinert, poet. Alighieri (1265-1321), Italian poet.

Issue dates: No. 753, Mar. 24; No. 753A, Dec. 8; 20pf, Feb. 22; 25pf, July 5; 40pf, July 28; 50pf, Apr. 15.

Gold Medal, Leipzig Fair — A244

Designs: 15pf, Obverse of medal, arms of German Democratic Republic. 25pf, Chemical plant.

1965, Feb. 25 Wmk. 313

756	A244	10pf lil rose & gold	15	15
757	A244	15pf lil rose & gold	20	15
758	A244	25pf brt bl, yel & gold	38	15
		Set value		15

1965 Leipzig Spring Fair and 800th anniv. of the Fair.

Giraffe — A245

Designs: 25pf, Common iguana (horiz.). 30pf, White-tailed gnu.

1965, Mar. 24

759	A245	10pf grn & gray	15	15
760	A245	25pf dk vio bl & gray	32	15
761	A245	30pf brn & gray	*1.50*	*42*
		Set value		*50*

10th anniversary of Berlin Zoo.

Col. Pavel Belyayev and Lt. Col. Alexei Leonov A246

Boxing Glove and Laurel Wreath A247

Design: 25pf, Lt. Col. Leonov floating in space.

Perf. 13½x13

1965, Apr. 15 Litho. Wmk. 313

762	A246	10pf red	24	15
763	A246	25pf dk ultra	*1.75*	*40*
		Set value		*45*

Space flight of Voskhod 2 and the first man walking in space, Lt. Col. Alexel Leonov.

1965, Apr. 27 Photo. *Perf. 14*

764	A247	20pf blk, red & gold	*80*	*32*

16th European Boxing Championship, Berlin, May, 1965. See No. B126.

Walter Ulbricht and Erich Weinert Distributing "Free Germany" Leaflets on the Eastern Front — A248

Designs: 50pf, Liberation of concentration camps. 60pf, Russian soldiers raising flag on Reichstag, Berlin. 70pf, Political demonstration.

1965, May 5 Photo. *Perf. 14*

Flags in Red, Black & Yellow

765	A248	40pf bl grn & red	15	15
766	A248	50pf dl bl & red	15	15
767	A248	60pf brn & red	*1.75*	*1.25*
768	A248	70pf vio bl & red	15	15
		Nos. 765-768,B127-B131 (9)	*2.95*	*2.45*

20th anniv. of liberation from fascism.

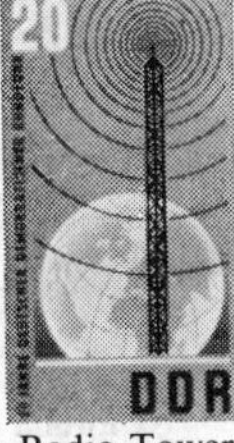

Radio Tower and Globe A249

ITU Emblem and Frequency Diagram A250

Design: 40pf, Workers and broadcasting equipment.

1965, May 12 Litho. *Perf. 12½x13*

769	A249	20pf dk car rose & blk	15	15
770	A249	40pf vio bl & blk	*60*	*35*
		Set value	*65*	*40*

20th anniv. of the German Democratic broadcasting system.

1965, May 17

Design: 25pf, ITU emblem and telephone diagram.

771	A250	20pf ol, yel & blk	15	15
772	A250	25pf vio, pale vio & blk	*1.00*	*28*
		Set value		*32*

Cent. of the ITU.

Emblem of Free German Trade Union — A251

Hemispheres with Crowd of Workers — A252

1965, June 10 Photo. *Perf. 14*

773	A251	20pf red & gold	15	15
774	A252	25pf gold, bl & blk	*60*	*32*
		Set value	*65*	*35*

20th anniv. of the Free German Trade Union (FDGB) and of the World Organization of Trade Unions.

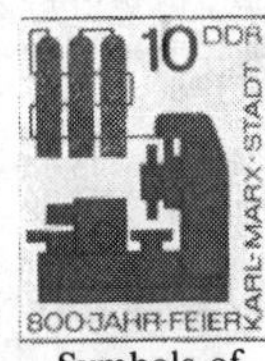

Symbols of Industry A253

Marx and Lenin A254

Designs: 20pf, Red Tower. 25pf, City Hall.

1965, June 16

775	A253	10pf gold & emer	15	15
776	A253	20pf gold & crim	15	15
777	A253	25pf gold & brt bl	*60*	*35*
		Set value	*75*	*45*

800th anniv. of Chemnitz (Karl Marx City).

1965, June 21 Litho. *Perf. 13½x13*

778	A254	20pf red, blk & buff	15	15

6th Conference of Postal Ministers of Communist Countries, Peking, June 21-July 15.

"Alte Waage" and New Building, Leipzig — A255

Designs: 25pf, Old City Hall. 40pf, Opera House and General Post Office. 70pf, Hotel "Stadt Leipzig."

Unwmk.

1965, Aug. 25 Photo. *Perf. 14*

781	A255	10pf gold, cl brn & ultra	15	15
a.		Souv. sheet of 2, #781, 784	*2.50*	*90*
782	A255	25pf gold, brn, & ocher	15	15
a.		Souv. sheet of 2, #782-783	*1.00*	*38*
783	A255	40pf gold, brn, ocher & yel grn	15	15
784	A255	70pf gold & ultra	*1.40*	*75*
		Set value	*1.60*	*90*

800th anniv. of the City of Leipzig. No. 781a sold for 90pf; No. 782a for 80pf. The souvenir sheets were issued Sept. 4, 1965.

Cameras A256

Equestrian A257

Leipzig Fall Fair: 15pf, Electric guitar and organ. 25pf, Microscope.

1965, Sept. 9 *Perf. 14*

785	A256	10pf grn, blk & gold	15	15
786	A256	15pf multi	15	15
787	A256	25pf multi	50	15
		Set value	70	20

Perf. 13½x13

1965, Sept. 15 Litho. Unwmk.

789	A257	10pf shown	15	15
790	A257	10pf Swimmer	15	15
791	A257	10pf Runner	*1.90*	*65*
		Set value, #789-791, B135-B136		*80*

Issued to commemorate the International Modern Pentathlon Championships, Leipzig.

Alexei Leonov and Brandenburg Gate — A258

Memorial Monument, Putten — A259

Designs: No. 793, Pavel Belyayev and Berlin City Hall. 25pf, Leonov floating in space and space ship.

Wmk. 313

1965, Nov. 1 Litho. *Perf. 14*

Size: 23½x28½mm

792 A258 20pf bl, sil & red *1.00 42*
793 A258 20pf bl, sil & red *1.00 42*

Size: 51x28½mm

794 A258 25pf bl, sil & red *1.00 42*

Visit of the Russian astronauts to the German Democratic Republic. Nos. 792-794 printed se-tenant.

1965, Nov. 19 *Perf. 13x13½*

795 A259 25pf brt bl, pale yel & blk 30 15

Issued in memory of the victims of a Nazi attack on Putten, Netherlands, Sept. 30, 1944.

Furnace A260

Designs (after old woodcuts): 15pf, Ore miners. 20pf, Proustite crystals. 25pf, Sulphur crystals.

Perf. 13x12½

1965, Nov. 11 Litho. Unwmk.

796 A260 10pf blk & multi 15 15
797 A260 15pf blk & multi *65 32*
798 A260 20pf blk & multi 15 15
799 A260 25pf blk & multi 15 15
Set value 90 40

Issued to commemorate the bicentenary of the Mining Academy in Freiberg.

Red Kite A261

Otto Grotewohl A262

Birds: 10pf, Lammergeier. 20pf, Buzzard. 25pf, Kestrel. 40pf, Northern goshawk. 70pf, Golden eagle.

1965, Dec. 8 Photo. *Perf. 14*

Gold Frame

800 A261 5pf org & blk 15 15
801 A261 10pf emer, brn & blk 15 15
802 A261 20pf car, red brn & blk 15 15
803 A261 25pf bl, red brn & blk 15 15
804 A261 40pf lil, blk & dk red 15 15
805 A261 70pf brn, blk & yel *3.50 1.00*
Nos. 800-805 (6) 4.25
Set value 1.25

1965, Dec. 14 Photo. Wmk. 313

806 A262 20pf black 20 15

Issued in memory of Otto Grotewohl (1894-1964), prime minister (1949-1964).

Souvenir Sheet

Spartacus Letter, Karl Liebknecht and Rosa Luxemburg — A263

1966, Jan. 3 Unwmk.

807 A263 Sheet of 2 1.10 42
a. 20pf red & black 48 18
b. 50pf red & black 48 18

50th anniv. of the natl. conf. of the Spartacus organization.

Tobogganing, Women's Singles — A264

Tobogganing: 20pf, Men's doubles. 25pf, Men's singles.

Perf. 13½x13

1966, Jan. 25 Litho. Unwmk.

808 A264 10pf cit & dp grn 15 15
809 A264 20pf car rose & dk vio bl 16 15
810 A264 25pf bl & dk bl *70 38*
Set value 45

10th Intl. Tobogganing Championships, Friedrichroda, Feb. 8-13.

Electronic Computer A265

Design: 15pf, Drill and milling machine.

1966, Feb. 24 *Perf. 13x12½*

811 A265 10pf multi 15 15
812 A265 15pf multi 16 15
Set value 24 15

Leipzig Spring Fair, 1966.

Jan Arnost Smoler and Linden Leaf — A266

Soldier and National Gallery, Berlin — A267

Design: 25pf, House of the Sorbs, Bautzen, Saxony.

1966, Mar. 1 *Perf. 13x13½*

813 A266 20pf brt bl, blk & brt red 15 15
814 A266 25pf brt red, blk & brt bl *42 22*
Set value 25

Smoler (1816-84), philologist of the Sorbian language. The Sorbs are a small group of slavic people in Saxony.

Wmk. 313

1966, Mar. 1 Photo. *Perf. 14*

Designs (Soldier and): 10pf, Brandenburg Gate. 20pf, Factory. 25pf, Combine.

815 A267 5pf ol gray, blk & yel 15 15
816 A267 10pf ol gray, blk & yel 15 15
817 A267 20pf ol gray, blk & yel 15 15
818 A267 25pf ol gray, blk & yel *90 32*
Set value 1.25 42

National People's Army, 10th anniversary.

Luna 9 on Moon A268

Medal for Scholarship A269

1966, Mar. 7 Unwmk.

819 A268 20pf multi 95 15

Issued to commemorate the first soft landing on the moon by Luna 9, Feb. 3, 1966.

1966, Mar. 7 Litho. *Perf. 13½x13*

820 A269 20pf multi 15 15

20th anniv. of the State Youth Organization.

Traffic Signs — A270

Traffic safety: 15pf, Automobile and child with scooter. 25pf, Bicyclist and signaling hand. 50pf, Motorcyclist, ambulance and glass of beer.

1966, Mar. 28 Litho. *Perf. 13*

821 A270 10pf dk & lt bl, red & blk 15 15
822 A270 15pf brt grn, cit & blk 15 15
823 A270 25pf ol bis, brt bl & blk 15 15
824 A270 50pf car, yel, gray & blk *70 42*
Set value 88 55

Marx, Lenin and Crowd — A271

Designs: 5pf, Party emblem and crowd (vert.). 15pf, Marx, Engels and title page of Communist Manifesto (vert.). 20pf, Otto Grotewohl and Wilhelm Pieck shaking hands, and Party emblem (vert.). 25pf, Chairman Walter Ulbricht receiving flowers.

1966, Mar. 31 Photo. *Perf. 14*

825 A271 5pf multi 15 15
826 A271 10pf multi 15 15
827 A271 15pf grn & blk 15 15
828 A271 20pf dk car & blk 15 15
829 A271 25pf multi *1.25 70*
Nos. 825-829 (5) 1.85
Set value 90

20th anniversary of Socialist Unity Party of Germany (SED).

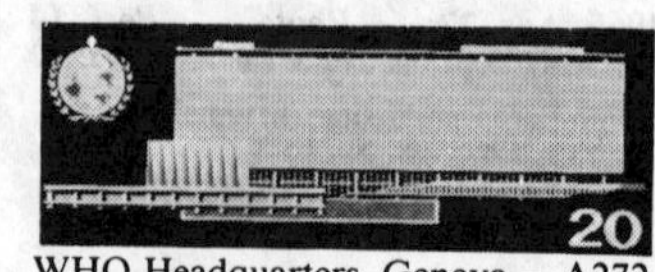

WHO Headquarters, Geneva — A272

Perf. 13x12½

1966, Apr. 26 Litho. Unwmk.

830 A272 20pf multi 20 15

Inauguration of WHO Headquarters, Geneva.

Rügen Island, Königsstuhl — A273

National Parks: 10pf, Spree River woodland. 20pf, Saxon Switzerland. 25pf, Dunes at Westdarss. 30pf, Thale in Harz, Devil's Wall. 50pf, Feldberg Lakes, Mecklenburg.

Perf. 13x12½

1966, May 17 Litho. Unwmk.

831 A273 10pf multi 15 15
832 A273 15pf multi 15 15
833 A273 20pf multi 15 15
834 A273 25pf multi 15 15
835 A273 30pf multi 15 15
836 A273 50pf multi *1.50 65*
Set value 1.75 80

Plauen Lace — A274

Various Lace Designs.

1966, May 26 *Perf. 13x13½*

837 A274 10pf grn & lt grn 15 15
838 A274 20pf dk bl & lt bl 15 15
839 A274 25pf brn red & ver 15 15
840 A274 50pf dk vio & bluish lilac *1.40 90*
Set value 1.60 98

Rhododendron A275

Parachutist Landing on Target A276

Flowers: 20pf, Lilies of the Valley. 40pf, Dahlias. 50pf, Cyclamen.

Photo. & Engr.

1966 Unwmk. *Perf. 14x13½*

841 A275 20pf multi 15 15
842 A275 25pf multi 15 15
843 A275 40pf multi 15 15
844 A275 50pf multi *2.75 1.10*
Set value 1.25

Intl. Flower Show, Erfurt. Issue dates: 20pf, Aug. 16; others, June 28.

1966, July 12 Litho. *Perf. 12½x13*

Designs: 15pf, Group parachute jump. 20pf, Free fall.

845 A276 10pf bl, blk & ol 15 15
846 A276 15pf multi *55 28*
847 A276 20pf sky bl, blk & ol 15 15
Set value 70 35

Issued to publicize the 8th International Parachute Championships, Leipzig.

Hans Kahle, Song of German Fighters and Medal of Spanish Republic — A277

Design: 15pf, Hans Beimler and street fighting in Madrid.

1966, July 15 **Photo.** ***Perf. 14***

848 A277 5pf multi 15 15
849 A277 15pf multi 15 15
Set value, #848-849, B137-B140 *1.60* *80*

Issued to honor the German fighters in the Spanish Civil War.

Television Set
A278

Design: 15pf, Electric typewriter.

Perf. 13x12½

1966, Aug. 29 **Litho.** **Unwmk.**

850 A278 10pf brt grn, blk & gray 15 15
851 A278 15pf red, blk & gray 15 15
Set value 25 15

1966 Leipzig Fall Fair.

Women's Doubles Kayak Race — A279

1966, Aug. 16

852 A279 15pf brt bl & multi *1.10* *25*

7th Canoe World Championships, Berlin. See No. B141.

Oradour sur Glane Memorial and French Flag
A280

Emblem of the Committee for Health Education
A281

Perf. 13x13½

1966, Sept. 9 **Wmk. 313**

853 A280 25pf ultra, blk & red 25 15

Issued in memory of the victims of the Nazi attack on Oradour, France, June 10, 1944.

1966, Sept. 13 ***Perf. 14***

Designs: 5pf, Symbolic blood donor and recipient (horiz.).

854 A281 5pf brt brn & red 15 15
855 A281 40pf brt bl & red *70* *50*
Set value *55*

Issued to publicize blood donations and health education. See No. B142.

Weight Lifter — A282

Perf. 13½x13

1966, Sept. 22 **Litho.** **Unwmk.**

856 A282 15pf lt brn & blk *1.50* *42*

Intl. and European Weight Lifting Championships, Berlin. See No. B143.

Congress Hall
A283

Emblem
A284

1966, Oct. 10 ***Perf. 13***

857 A283 10pf multi *50* *15*
858 A284 20pf dk bl & yel 15 15
Set value *15*

6th Congress of the International Organization of Journalists, Berlin.

Costume Type of 1964

Regional Costumes: 5pf, Woman from Altenburg. No. 860, Man from Altenburg. No. 861, Woman from Mecklenburg. 15pf, Man from Mecklenburg. 20pf, Woman from Magdeburg area. 30pf, Man from Magdeburg area.

1966, Oct. 25 **Photo.** ***Perf. 14***

859 A240 5pf multi 15 15
860 A240 10pf multi 15 15
861 A240 10pf lt grn & multi 15 15
862 A240 15pf lt grn & multi 15 15
863 A240 20pf yel & multi *3.25* *1.25*
864 A240 30pf yel & multi *3.25* *1.25*
Nos. 859-864 (6) *7.10*
Set value *2.65*

The male and female costume designs of the same region are printed se-tenant in checkerboard arrangement.

Megalamphodus Megalopterus — A285

Various Tropical Fish in Natural Colors.

1966, Nov. 8 **Litho.** ***Perf. 13x12½***

865 A285 5pf lt bl & gray 15 15
866 A285 10pf bl & ind 15 15
867 A285 15pf cit & blk *2.00* *80*
868 A285 20pf grn & blk 15 15
869 A285 25pf ultra & blk 15 15
870 A285 40pf emer & blk 22 15
Nos. 865-870 (6) *2.82*
Set value *1.00*

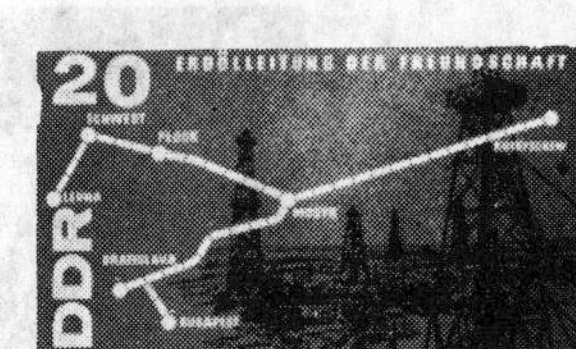

Map of Oil Pipeline and Oil Field — A286

Design: 25pf, Map of oil pipelines and "Walter Ulbricht" Leuna chemical factory.

1966, Nov. 8 ***Perf. 13½x13***

871 A286 20pf red & blk 15 15
872 A286 25pf bl & blk *42* *22*
Set value *25*

Chemical industry.

Detail from Ishtar Gate, Babylon, 580 B.C. — A287

Designs from Babylon c. 580 B.C.: 20pf, Mythological animal from Ishtar Gate. 25pf, Lion facing right and ornaments (vert.). 50pf, Lion facing left and ornaments (vert.).

Perf. 13½x14, 14x13½

1966, Nov. 23 **Photo.**

873 A287 10pf multi 15 15
874 A287 20pf multi 15 15
875 A287 25pf multi 15 15
876 A287 50pf multi *1.00* *55*
Set value *1.20* *66*

Near East Museum, Berlin.

Wartburg, Thuringia
A288

Gentian
A289

Design: 25pf, Wartburg, Palace.

1966, Nov. 23 **Litho.** ***Perf. 13x13½***

877 A288 20pf olive 15 15
878 A288 25pf vio brn *40* *22*
Set value *48* *26*

900th anniv. (in 1967) of the Wartburg (castle) near Eisenach, Thuringia. See No. B145.

1966, Dec. 8 **Litho.** ***Perf. 12½x13***

Protected Flowers: 20pf, Cephalanthera rubra (orchid). 25pf, Mountain arnica.

Black Background

879 A289 10pf yel, grn & bl 15 15
880 A289 20pf yel, grn & red 15 15
881 A289 25pf red, yel & grn *90* *45*
Set value *56*

Son Leaving Home
A290

City Hall, Stralsund
A291

Various Scenes from Fairy Tale "The Table, the Ass and the Stick."

1966, Dec. 8 ***Perf. 13½x13***

882 A290 5pf multi 45 18
883 A290 10pf multi 45 18
884 A290 20pf multi 45 20
885 A290 25pf multi 45 20
886 A290 30pf multi 45 18
887 A290 50pf multi 45 18
Nos. 882-887 (6) 2.70 1.12

Nos. 882-887 printed together in sheets of six. See Nos. 968-973, 1063-1068, 1339-1344.

Perf. 14x13½, 13½x14

1967, Jan. 24 **Photo.**

Buildings: 5pf, Wörlitz Castle (horiz.). 15pf, Chorin Convent. 20pf, Ribbeck House, Berlin (horiz.). 25pf, Moritzburg, Zeitz. 40pf, Old City Hall, Potsdam.

888 A291 5pf multi 15 15
889 A291 10pf multi 15 15
890 A291 15pf multi 15 15
891 A291 20pf multi 15 15
892 A291 25pf multi 15 15
893 A291 40pf multi *1.10* *52*
Set value *1.50* *65*

See Nos. 1018, 1020, 1071-1076.

Rifle Shooting, Prone — A292

Designs: 20pf, Shooting on skis. 25pf, Relay race with rifles on skis.

1967, Feb. 15 **Litho.** ***Perf. 13x12½***

894 A292 10pf Prus bl gray & brt pink 15 15
895 A292 20pf sl grn, brt bl & grn 15 15
896 A292 25pf ol grn, ol & grnsh bl *75* *32*
Set value *40*

World Biathlon Championships (skiing and shooting), Altenberg, Feb. 15-19.

Circular Knitting Machine — A293

Mother and Child — A294

Design: 15pf, Zeiss telescope and galaxy.

1967, Mar. 2 ***Perf. 13½x13***

897 A293 10pf dl mag & brt grn 15 15
898 A293 15pf ultra & gray 15 15
Set value 23 15

Leipzig Spring Fair of 1967.

1967, Mar. 7 ***Perf. 13x13½***

Design: 25pf, Working women.

899 A294 20pf rose brn, red & gray 15 15
900 A294 25pf dk bl, brt bl & brn *75* *35*
Set value *40*

20th anniv. of the Democratic Women's Federation of Germany.

Marx, Engels, Lenin and Electronic Control Center — A295

Designs (Portraits and): 5pf, Farmer driving combine. No. 903, Students and teacher. 15pf, Family. No. 905, Soldier, sailor and aviator. No. 906, Ulbricht among workers. 25pf, Soldier, sailor, aviator and factories. 40pf, Farmers with modern equipment. Nos. 901, 903-905 are vertical.

1967 **Photo.** ***Perf. 14***

901 A295 5pf multi 15 15
902 A295 10pf multi 15 15
903 A295 10pf multi 15 15
904 A295 15pf multi *35* *25*
905 A295 20pf multi 15 15
906 A295 20pf multi 15 15

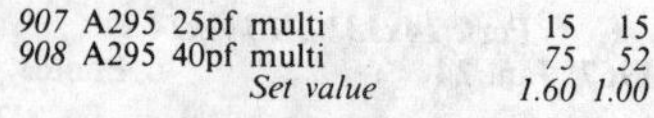

907 A295 25pf multi 15 15
908 A295 40pf multi *75* *52*
Set value *1.60* *1.00*

7th congress of Socialist Unity Party of Germany (SED), Apr. 17.
Nos. 902, 906-908 issued Mar. 22; Nos. 901, 903-905, Apr. 6.

Tahitian Women, by Paul Gauguin — A296

Paintings from Dresden Gallery: 20pf, Young Woman, by Ferdinand Hodler. 25pf, Peter in the Zoo, by H. Hakenbeck. 30pf, Venetian Episode (woman feeding pigeons), by R. Bergander. 50pf, Grandmother and Granddaughter, by J. Scholtz. 70pf, Cairn in the Snow, by Caspar David Friedrich. 20pf, 25pf, 30pf, 50pf are vertical.

1967, Mar. 29

909 A296 20pf multi 15 15
910 A296 25pf multi 15 15
911 A296 30pf multi 15 15
912 A296 40pf multi 15 15
913 A296 50pf multi *2.00* *1.40*
914 A296 70pf multi 15 15
Nos. 909-914 (6) *2.75*
Set value *1.75*

Barn Owl — A297

Protected Birds: 10pf, Eurasian crane. 20pf, Peregrine falcon. 25pf, Bullfinches. 30pf, European kingfisher. 40pf, European roller.

1967, Apr. 27 Photo. *Perf. 14*
Birds in Natural Colors

915 A297 5pf gray blue 15 15
916 A297 10pf gray blue 15 15
917 A297 20pf gray blue 15 15
918 A297 25pf gray blue 15 15
919 A297 30pf gray blue *1.90* *95*
920 A297 40pf gray blue 15 15
Nos. 915-920 (6) *2.65*
Set value *1.25*

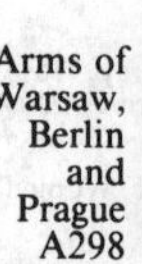
Arms of Warsaw, Berlin and Prague A298

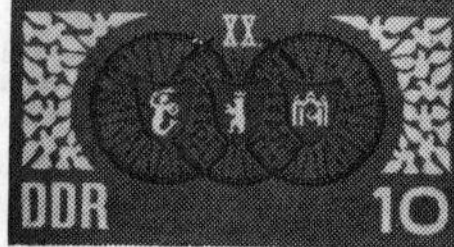

Design: 25pf, Bicyclists and doves.

Perf. 13x12½
1967, May 10 Litho. Wmk. 313

921 A298 10pf org, blk & lil 15 15
922 A298 25pf lt bl & dk car *32* *24*
Set value *40* *27*

20th Intl. Bicycle Peace Race, Berlin-Warsaw-Prague.

Cat A299

Children's Drawings: 10pf, Snow White and the Seven Dwarfs. 15pf, Fire truck. 20pf, Cock. 25pf, Flowers in vase. 30pf, Children playing ball.

1967, June 1 Unwmk.

923 A299 5pf multi 15 15
924 A299 10pf blk & multi 15 15
925 A299 15pf dk bl & multi 15 15
926 A299 20pf org & multi 15 15
927 A299 25pf multi 15 15
928 A299 30pf multi *65* *45*
Set value *1.00* *63*

Issued for International Children's Day.

Girl with Straw Hat, by Salomon Bray — A300

Exhibition Emblem and Map of DDR — A301

Paintings: 5pf, Three Horsemen, by Rubens (horiz.). 10pf, Girl Gathering Grapes, by Gerard Dou. 20pf, Spring Idyl, by Hans Thoma (horiz.). 25pf, Wilhelmine Schroder-Devrient, by Karl Begas. 50pf, The Four Evangelists, by Jacob Jordaens.

1967, June 7 Photo. *Perf. 14*

929 A300 5pf lt & dk bl 15 15
930 A300 10pf lt red brn & red brn 15 15
931 A300 20pf lt & dp yel grn 15 15
932 A300 25pf pale rose & rose lil 15 15
933 A300 40pf pale grn & ol grn 15 15
934 A300 50pf tan & sep *1.65* *95*
Set value *1.95* *1.12*

Issued to publicize paintings missing from museums since World War II.

Perf. 12½x13
1967, June 14 Litho. Unwmk.

935 A301 20pf dk grn, ocher & red 20 15

15th Agricultural Exhib., Markkleeberg.

Marie Curie — A302

German Playing Cards — A303

Portraits: 5pf, Georg Herwegh, poet. 20pf, Käthe Kollwitz. 25pf, Johann J. Winckelmann, archaeologist. 40pf, Theodor Storm, writer.

1967 Engr. *Perf. 14*

936 A302 5pf brown 15 15
937 A302 10pf dk bl 15 15
938 A302 20pf dl red 15 15
939 A302 25pf gray 15 15
940 A302 40pf sl grn *60* *38*
Set value *90* *52*

150th anniv. of the birth of Herwegh, Winckelmann and Storm, and the birth centenaries of Curie and Kollwitz.

1967, July 18 Photo.

Designs: Various German playing cards.

941 A303 5pf red & multi 15 15
942 A303 10pf grn & multi 15 15
943 A303 20pf multi 22 15
944 A303 25pf multi *3.00* *1.10*
Set value *1.25*

Mare and Foal A304

Horses: 10pf, Stallion. 20pf, Horse race finish. 50pf, Colts (vert.).

Perf. 13½x13, 13x13½
1967, Aug. 15 Litho. Unwmk.

945 A304 5pf multi 15 15
946 A304 10pf org, blk & dk brn 15 15
947 A304 20pf bl & multi 15 15
948 A304 50pf multi *2.25* *80*
Set value *95*

Thoroughbred Horseshow of Socialist Countries, Hoppegarten, Berlin.

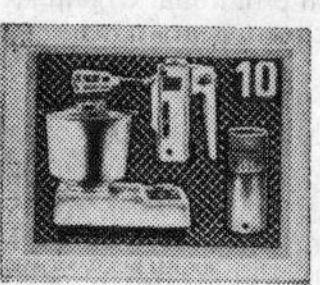

Small Electrical Appliances A305

Leipzig Fall Fair: 15pf, Woman's fur coat and furrier's trademark.

Perf. 14x13½
1967, Aug. 8 Photo. Unwmk.

949 A305 10pf brt bl, blk & yel 15 15
950 A305 15pf yel, brn & blk 18 15
Set value 15

Max Reichpietsch and Warship — A306

Designs: 15pf, Albin Köbis and warship. 20pf, Sailors marching with red flag, and warship.

1967, Sept. 5 Litho. *Perf. 13½x13*
Bluish Paper

951 A306 10pf dk bl, gray & red 15 15
952 A306 15pf dk bl, gray & red *32* *22*
953 A306 20pf dk bl, gray & red 15 15
Set value *45* *30*

50th anniv. of the sailors' uprising at Kiel.

Monument at Kragujevac A307

1967, Sept. 20 *Perf. 13x13½*

954 A307 25pf dk red, yel & blk 20 15

Issued in memory of the victims of the Nazis at Kragujevac, Yugoslavia, Oct. 21, 1941.

Worker and Symbols of Electrification — A308

Designs (Communist Emblem and): 5pf, Worker, and Communist newspaper masthead. 15pf, Russian War Memorial, Berlin-Treptow. 20pf, Russian and German soldiers, and coat of arms. 40pf, Lenin and cruiser Aurora.

1967, Oct. 6 Photo. *Perf. 14x14½*

955 A308 5pf multi 15 15
956 A308 10pf multi 15 15
957 A308 15pf multi 15 15
958 A308 20pf multi 15 15
959 A308 40pf multi *1.90* *1.10*
a. Souvenir sheet of 2 90 80
Nos. 955-959 (5) *2.50*
Set value *1.25*

50th anniv. of the Russian October Revolution. No. 959a contains 2 imperf. stamps similar to Nos. 958-959 with simulated perforations. It commemorates the Red October Jubilee Stamp Exhibition, Karl-Marx-Stadt, Oct. 6-15. Sold for 85pf.

Martin Luther, by Lucas Cranach A309

Young Inventors and Fair Emblem A310

Designs: 25pf, Luther's House, Wittenberg (horiz.). 40pf, Castle Church, Wittenberg.

Engraved and Photogravure
1967, Oct. 17 *Perf. 14*

960 A309 20pf blk & rose lil 15 15
961 A309 25pf blk & bl 15 15
962 A309 40pf blk & lem *75* *52*
Set value *90* *60*

450th anniversary of the Reformation.

1967, Nov. 15 Unwmk. *Perf. 14*

Designs: No. 964, Boy's and girl's heads and emblem of the Free German Youth Organization. 25pf, Young workers receiving awards, and medal.

Size: 23x28½mm

963 A310 20pf multi 80 45
964 A310 20pf multi 80 45

Size: 51x28½mm

965 A310 25pf multi 80 45
a. Strip of 3, #963-965 2.50 1.40

Issued to publicize the 10th Masters of Tomorrow Fair, Leipzig, Nov. 15-26.

Goethe House, Weimar A311

Design: 25pf, Schiller House, Weimar.

1967, Nov. 27 Litho. *Perf. 13x12½*

966 A311 20pf gray, blk & brn 15 15
967 A311 25pf cit, dk grn & brn *55* *24*
Set value *28*

Honoring German classical humanism.

Fairy Tale Type of 1966

Various Scenes from King Drosselbart.

1967, Nov. 27 *Perf. 13½x13*

968 A290 5pf multi 45 18
969 A290 10pf multi 45 18
970 A290 15pf multi 45 22
971 A290 20pf multi 45 22

972	A290	25pf multi	45	18
973	A290	30pf multi	45	18
		Nos. 968-973 (6)	2.70	1.16

Nos. 968-973 printed together in sheets of 6.

Farmers, Stables and Silos — A312

Perf. 13x12½

1967, Dec. 6 Litho. Unwmk.

974	A312	10pf multi	15	15

Issued to publicize the 15th anniversary of the first agricultural co-operatives.

Nutcracker and Figurines A313

Speed Skating A314

Design: 20pf, Candle holders: angel and miner.

1967, Dec. 6 Photo. *Perf. 13½x14*

975	A313	10pf grn & multi	50	15
976	A313	20pf red & multi	25	15
		Set value		22

Issued to publicize local handicrafts of the Erzgebirge in Saxony (Ore Mountains).

Perf. 13½x13

1968, Jan. 17 Litho. Unwmk.

Sport and Olympic Rings: 15pf, Slalom. 20pf, Ice hockey. 25pf, Figure skating, pair. 30pf, Long-distance skiing.

977	A314	5pf bl, dk bl & red	15	15
978	A314	15pf multi	15	15
979	A314	20pf grnsh bl, dk bl & red	15	15
980	A314	25pf multi	15	15
981	A314	30pf grnsh bl, vio bl & red	1.40	70
		Set value, #977-981, B146	1.90	90

10th Winter Olympic Games, Grenoble, France, Feb. 6-18.

Antenna, Cloud Formation and Map of Europe — A315

Designs: 10pf, Actinometer, Sun and Potsdam Meteorological Observatory. 25pf, Weather influence on farming (fields by day and night, produce).

1968, Jan. 24 *Perf. 13½x13*

Size: 23x28mm

982	A315	10pf brt mag, org & blk	90	20

Size: 50x28mm

983	A315	20pf multi	90	20

Size: 23x28mm

984	A315	25pf ol, blk & yel	90	20
a.		Strip of 3, Nos. 982-984	3.00	85

75th anniversary of the Meteorological Observatory in Potsdam.

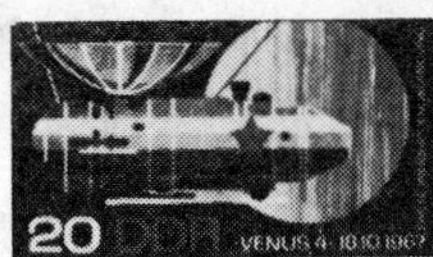

Venus 4 Interplanetary Station — A316

Design: 25pf, Earth satellites Kosmos 186 and 188 orbiting earth.

1968, Jan. 24 Photo. *Perf. 14*

985	A316	20pf multi	15	15
986	A316	25pf multi	38	24
		Set value	45	30

Russian space explorations.

Fighters of The Underground A317

Designs: 20pf, "The Liberation." 25pf, "The Partisans."

1968, Feb. 21 Photo. *Perf. 14x13½*

987	A317	10pf blk & multi	15	15
988	A317	20pf blk & multi	15	15
989	A317	25pf blk & multi	52	48
		Set value	70	60

The designs are from the stained glass window triptych by Walter Womacka in the Sachsenhausen Memorial Museum.

Diesel Locomotive — A318

Design: 15pf, Refrigerator fishing ship.

1968, Feb. 29 *Perf. 14*

990	A318	10pf multi	25	15
991	A318	15pf multi	42	24
		Set value		30

The 1968 Leipzig Spring Fair.

Woman from Hoyerswerda A319

Maxim Gorky and View of Gorky A320

Sorbian Regional Costumes: 20pf, Woman from Schleife. 40pf, Woman from Crostwitz. 50pf, Woman from Spreewald.

1968, Mar. 14

992	A319	10pf cit & multi	15	15
993	A319	20pf fawn & multi	15	15
994	A319	40pf bl grn & multi	15	15
995	A319	50pf grn & multi	90	65
		Set value	1.15	80

1968, Mar. 14 Engr.

Design: 25pf, Stormy petrel and toppling towers.

996	A320	20pf brn p rose car	15	15
997	A320	25pf brn & rose car	35	24
		Set value	43	30

Maxim Gorky (1868-1936), Russian writer.

Ring-necked Pheasants A321

Designs: 15pf, Gray partridges. 20pf, Mallards. 25pf, Graylag geese. 30pf, Wood pigeons. 40pf, Hares.

1968, Mar. 26 Litho. *Perf. 13½x13*

998	A321	10pf gray & multi	15	15
999	A321	15pf gray & multi	15	15
1000	A321	20pf gray & multi	20	15
1001	A321	25pf gray & multi	24	15
1002	A321	30pf gray & multi	30	15
1003	A321	40pf gray & multi	2.50	65
		Nos. 998-1003 (6)	3.54	
		Set value		85

Karl Marx A322

Fritz Heckert A323

Designs: 10pf, Title page of the "Communist Manifesto." 25pf, Title page of "Das Kapital."

1968, Apr. 25 Photo. *Perf. 14*

1004	A322	10pf yel grn & blk	50	18
1005	A322	20pf mag, yel & blk	50	18
1006	A322	25pf lem, blk & red brn	50	18
a.		Souvenir sheet of 3	80	80

Karl Marx (1818-83). Nos. 1004-1006 are printed se-tenant. No. 1006a contains 3 imperf. stamps similar to Nos. 1004-1006 with simulated perforations.

1968, Apr. 25

Design: 20pf, Young workers, new apartment buildings and Congress emblem.

1007	A323	10pf multi	15	15
1008	A323	20pf multi	24	15
		Set value		15

Issued to publicize the 7th Congress of the Free German Trade Unions.

"Right to Work" — A324

Designs: 10pf, "Right to Live," tree and globe. 25pf, "Right for Peace," dove and sun.

1968, May 8 Litho. *Perf. 13½x13*

1009	A324	5pf mar & pink	18	15
1010	A324	10pf brn ol & ol bis	15	15
1011	A324	15pf Prus bl & lt bl	55	24
		Set value		40

International Human Rights Year.

Angler A325

Designs: No. 1013, Rowing (woman). No. 1014, High jump (woman).

Unwmk.

1968, June 6 Photo. *Perf. 14*

1012	A325	20pf ol grn, sl bl & dk red	15	15
1013	A325	20pf Prus bl, dk bl & ol	15	15
1014	A325	20pf cop red, dp cl & bl	65	28
		Set value		36

Issued to publicize: World angling championships, Gustrow (No. 1012); European women's rowing championships, Berlin (No. 1013); second European youth athletic competition, Leipzig (No. 1014).

Brandenburg Gate, Torch A326

Youth Festival Emblem A327

Design: 25pf, Stadium and torch.

1968, June 20 Litho. *Perf. 13½x13*

1015	A326	10pf multi	15	15
1016	A326	25pf multi	75	32
		Set value		35

Issued to publicize the 2nd Children's and Youths' Spartakiad, Berlin.

1968, June 20

1017	A327	25pf multi	45	25

Issued to publicize the 9th Youth Festival for Peace and Friendship, Sofia.
See No. B148.

Type of 1967 and

Moritzburg Castle, Dresden — A328

Buildings: 10pf, City Hall, Wernigerode. 25pf, City Hall, Greifswald. 30pf, Sanssouci Palace, Potsdam.

1968, June 25 Photo. *Perf. 13½x14*

1018	A291	10pf multi	15	15
1019	A328	20pf multi	15	15
1020	A291	25pf multi	15	15
1021	A328	30pf multi	60	42
		Set value	85	52

Walter Ulbricht and Arms of Republic A329

Photo. & Engr.

1968, June 27 *Perf. 14*

1022	A329	20pf org, dp car & blk	20	15

75th birthday of Walter Ulbricht, chairman of the Council of State, Communist party secretary and deputy prime minister.

Old Rostock and Arms A330

Design: 25pf, Historic and modern buildings, 1968, and arms of Rostock.

1968, July 9 **Photo.**
1023 A330 20pf multi 15 15
1024 A330 25pf multi *45 32*

750th anniv. of Rostock and to publicize the 11th Baltic Sea Week.

Karl Landsteiner, M.D. (1868-1943) A331

"Trener" Stunt Plane A332

Portraits: 15pf, Emanuel Lasker (1868-1941), chess champion and writer. 20pf, Hanns Eisler (1898-1962), composer. 25pf, Ignaz Semmelweis, M.D. (1818-1865). 40pf, Max von Pettenkofer (1818-1901), hygienist.

1968, July 17 **Engr.** ***Perf. 14***
1025 A331 10pf gray grn 15 15
1026 A331 15pf black 15 15
1027 A331 20pf brown 15 15
1028 A331 25pf gray bl 15 15
1029 A331 40pf rose lake *75 52*
Set value *1.05 70*

1968, Aug. 13 **Litho.** ***Perf. 12½x13***

Design: 25pf, Two "Trener" stunt planes in parallel flight.

1030 A332 10pf multi 15 15
1031 A332 25pf bl & multi *35 25*
Set value *40 28*

Peasant Woman, by Wilhelm Leibl — A333

Paintings from Dresden Gallery: 10pf, "On the Beach," by Walter Womacka (horiz.). 15pf, Mountain Farmers Mowing, by Albin Egger-Lienz (horiz.). 40pf, The Artist's daughter, by Venturelli. 50pf, High School Girl, by Michaelis. 70pf, Girl with Guitar, by Castelli.

Perf. 14x13½, 13½x14

1968, Aug. 20 **Photo.**
1032 A333 10pf multi 15 15
1033 A333 15pf multi 15 15
1034 A333 20pf multi 15 15
1035 A333 40pf multi 15 15
1036 A333 50pf multi 18 15
1037 A333 70pf multi *1.50 1.10*
Set value *1.95 1.50*

Model Trains — A334

1968, Aug. 29 ***Perf. 14x13½***
1038 A334 10pf lt ultra, red & blk 15 15

The 1968 Leipzig Fall Fair.

Spremberg Dam A335

Designs: 10pf, Pöhl Dam (vert.). 15pf, Ohra Dam (vert.). 20pf, Rappbode Dam.

Perf. 13x12½, 12½x13

1968, Sept. 11 **Litho.**
1039 A335 5pf multi 15 15
1040 A335 10pf multi 15 15
1041 A335 15pf multi *40 22*
1042 A335 20pf multi 15 15
Set value *58 30*

Issued to publicize dams built since 1945.

Runner A336

Designs: 25pf, Woman gymnast (vert.). 40pf, Water polo (vert.). 70pf, Sculling.

1968, Sept. 18 **Photo.** ***Perf. 14***
1043 A336 5pf multi 15 15
1044 A336 25pf multi 15 15
1045 A336 40pf multi 16 15
1046 A336 70pf bl & multi *1.65 70*
Set value *80*

19th Olympic Games, Mexico City, Oct. 12-27. See Nos. B149-B150.

Monument, Fort Breendonk, Belgium — A337

Tiger Beetle — A338

1968, Oct. 10 **Litho.** ***Perf. 13x13½***
1047 A337 25pf multi 20 15

Issued in memory of the victims of the Nazis at the Fort Breendonk Concentration Camp.

1968, Oct. 16 ***Perf. 13½x13***

Insects: 15pf, Ground beetle (Cychrus caraboides). 20pf, Ladybug. 25pf, Ground beetle (Carabus arcensis hrbst.). 30pf, Hister beetle. 40pf, Checkered beetle.

1048 A338 10pf yel & multi 15 15
1049 A338 15pf bluish lil & blk 15 15
1050 A338 20pf multi 15 15
1051 A338 25pf lt lil & blk *1.50 90*
1052 A338 30pf lt grn, blk & red 15 15
1053 A338 40pf pink & blk 18 15
Set value *1.95 1.15*

Lenin and Letter to Spartacists — A339

Designs: 20pf, Workers, soldiers and sailors with masthead and slogans. 25pf, Karl Liebknecht and Rosa Luxemburg.

1968, Oct. 29 **Litho.** ***Perf. 13x12½***
1054 A339 10pf lem, red & blk 15 15
1055 A339 20pf lem, red & blk 15 15
1056 A339 25pf lem, red & blk *38 28*
Set value *52 36*

50th anniv. of the November Revolution in Germany.

Cattleya — A340

Orchids: 10pf, Paphiopedilum albertianum. 15pf, Cattleya fabia. 20pf, Cattleya aclandiae. 40pf, Sobralia macrantha. 50pf, Dendrobium alpha.

1968, Nov. 12 **Photo.** ***Perf. 13***

Flowers in Natural Colors

1057 A340 5pf bluish lilac 15 15
1058 A340 10pf green 15 15
1059 A340 15pf bister 15 15
1060 A340 20pf green 15 15
1061 A340 40pf light brown 22 15
1062 A340 50pf gray *1.90 75*
Set value *1.00*

Fairy Tale Type of 1966

Various Scenes from Puss in Boots.

1968, Nov. 27 **Litho.** ***Perf. 13½x13***
1063 A290 5pf multi 50 15
1064 A290 10pf multi 50 15
1065 A290 15pf multi 50 26
1066 A290 20pf multi 50 26
1067 A290 25pf multi 50 15
1068 A290 30pf multi 50 15
Nos. 1063-1068 (6) 3.00 1.12

#1063-1068 printed together in sheets of 6.

Young Pioneers — A341

Design: 15pf, Five Young Pioneers.

1968, Dec. 3 ***Perf. 13x13½***
1069 A341 10pf bl & multi 15 15
1070 A341 15pf multi *24 16*
Set value *30 20*

20th anniv. of the founding of the Ernst Thalmann Young Pioneers' organization.

Buildings Type of 1967

Buildings: 5pf, City Hall, Tangermunde. 10pf, German State Opera, Berlin (horiz.). 20pf, Wall Pavilion, Dresden. 25pf, Burgher's House, Luckau. 30pf, Rococo Palace, Dornburg (horiz.). 40pf, "Stockfish" House, Erfurt.

1969, Jan. 1 **Photo.** ***Perf. 14***
1071 A291 5pf multi 15 15
1072 A291 10pf multi 15 15
1073 A291 20pf multi 15 15
1074 A291 25pf multi *85 52*
1075 A291 30pf multi 15 15
1076 A291 40pf multi 15 15
Set value *1.25 75*

Martin Andersen Nexö, Danish Writer — A342

Portraits: 20pf, Otto Nagel (1894-1967), painter. 25pf, Alexander von Humboldt (1769-1859), naturalist, traveler, statesman. 40pf, Theodor Fontane (1819-1898), writer.

1969, Feb. 5 **Engr.** ***Perf. 14***
1077 A342 10pf grnsh blk 15 15
1078 A342 20pf dp brn 15 15
1079 A342 25pf vio bl *48 32*
1080 A342 40pf brown 15 15
Set value *75 45*

Issued to honor famous men.

Be Attentive and Considerate! A343

Designs: 10pf, Watch ahead! (car, truck and traffic signal). 20pf, Watch railroad crossings! (train and car at crossing). 25pf, If in doubt don't pass! (cars and truck).

1969, Feb. 18 **Litho.** ***Perf. 13x13½***
1081 A343 5pf lt bl & multi 15 15
1082 A343 10pf yel & multi 15 15
1083 A343 20pf pink & multi 15 15
1084 A343 25pf multi *40 25*
Set value *60 40*

Traffic safety campaign.

Combine A344

Leipzig Spring Fair: 15pf, Planeta-Variant offset printing press.

1969, Feb. 26 **Photo.** ***Perf. 14***
1085 A344 10pf multi 15 15
1086 A344 15pf crim, blk & bl 16 15
Set value 22 15

Jorinde and Joringel A345

Various Scenes from Fairy Tale "Jorinde and Joringel."

1969, Mar. 18 **Litho.** ***Perf. 13½x13***
1087 A345 5pf blk & multi 25 16
1088 A345 10pf blk & multi 25 16
1089 A345 15pf blk & multi 25 22
1090 A345 20pf blk & multi 25 22
1091 A345 25pf blk & multi 25 16
1092 A345 30pf blk & multi 25 16
Nos. 1087-1092 (6) 1.50 1.08

#1087-1092 printed together in sheets of 6. See Nos. 1176-1181.

Spring Snowflake A346

Red Cross, Crescent, Lion and Sun Emblems A347

Protected Plants: 10pf, Adonis. 15pf, Globeflowers. 20pf, Garden Turk's-cap. 25pf, Button snakeroot. 30pf, Dactylorchis latifolia.

1969, Apr. 4 Photo. *Perf. 14*

No.	Type	Description	Unused	Used
1093	A346	5pf grn & multi	15	15
1094	A346	10pf grn & multi	15	15
1095	A346	15pf grn & multi	15	15
1096	A346	20pf grn & multi	20	15
1097	A346	25pf grn & multi	*1.90*	*75*
1098	A346	30pf grn & multi	28	15
		Nos. 1093-1098 (6)	*2.83*	
		Set value		*1.00*

1969, Apr. 23 Litho. *Perf. 12½x13*

Design: 15pf, Large Red Cross, Red Crescent and Lion and Sun Emblems.

No.	Type	Description	Unused	Used
1099	A347	10pf gray, red & yel	15	15
1100	A347	15pf multi	*32*	*16*
		Set value	*40*	*20*

Issued to commemorate the 50th anniversary of the League of Red Cross Societies.

Conifer Nursery A348

Erythrite from Schneeberg A349

Designs: 10pf, Forests as natural resources (timber and resin). 20pf, Forests as regulators of climate. 25pf, Forests as recreation areas (tents along lake).

1969, Apr. 23

No.	Type	Description	Unused	Used
1101	A348	5pf multi	15	15
1102	A348	10pf multi	15	15
1103	A348	20pf multi	15	15
1104	A348	25pf multi	*40*	*30*
		Set value	*60*	*40*

Prevention of forest fires.

1969, May 21 Photo. *Perf. 13½x14*

Minerals: 10pf, Fluorite from Halsbrücke. 15pf, Galena from Neudorf. 20pf, Smoky quartz from Lichtenberg. 25pf, Calcite from Niederrabenstein. 50pf, Silver from Freiberg.

No.	Type	Description	Unused	Used
1105	A349	5pf tan & multi	15	15
1106	A349	10pf multi	15	15
1107	A349	15pf gray & multi	15	15
1108	A349	20pf lem & multi	15	15
1109	A349	25pf multi	*85*	*52*
1110	A349	50pf lt bl & multi	18	15
		Set value	*1.25*	*65*

Women and Symbols of Agriculture, Science and Industry — A350

Design: 25pf, Woman's head and symbols.

1969, May 28 Engr. *Perf. 14*

No.	Type	Description	Unused	Used
1111	A350	20pf dk red & bl	15	15
1112	A350	25pf bl & dk red	*40*	*22*
		Set value		*28*

2nd Women's Congress of the German Democratic Republic.

Ulbricht Type of 1961-67

1969-71 Wmk. 313 Typo. *Perf. 14*

Size: 17x21mm

No.	Type	Description	Unused	Used
1112A	A189	35pf Prus bl ('71)	40	15

Engr. Unwmk.

Size: 24x28½mm

No.	Type	Description	Unused	Used
1113	A189	1m dull green	30	22
1114	A189	2m brown	60	45

See note below Nos. 590B-590C.

Coil Stamp

1970, Jan. 20 Typo. Wmk. 313

Size: 17x21mm

No.	Type	Description	Unused	Used
1114A	A189	1m olive	40	15

Emblem of DDR Philatelic Society A351

Worker Protecting Children A352

1969, June 4 Photo. Unwmk.

No.	Type	Description	Unused	Used
1115	A351	10pf red, gold & ultra	15	15

National Philatelic Exhibition "20 Years DDR," Magdeburg, Oct. 31-Nov. 9.

1969, June 4 Litho. *Perf. 13*

Designs: 25pf, Workers of various races. 20pf+5pf, Berlin buildings: Brandenburg Gate, Council of State, Soviet Cenotaph, Town Hall Tower, Television Tower, Teachers' Building and Hall.

Size: 23x28mm

No.	Type	Description	Unused	Used
1116	A352	10pf lem & multi	70	48

Size: 50x28mm

No.	Type	Description	Unused	Used
1117	A352	20pf + 5pf multi	70	48

Size: 23x28mm

No.	Type	Description	Unused	Used
1118	A352	25pf lem & multi	70	48
a.		Strip of 3, Nos. 1116-1118	2.25	1.50

Intl. Peace Meeting, Berlin. Nos. 1116-1118 printed se-tenant. The surtax on No. 1117 was for the Peace Council of the German Democratic Republic.

Opening Ceremony before Battle of Leipzig Monument — A353

Designs: 15pf, Parading athletes and stadium. 25pf, Running, hurdling, javelin and flag waving. 30pf, Presentation of colors before old Leipzig Town Hall.

Photo. & Engr.

1969, June 18 *Perf. 14*

No.	Type	Description	Unused	Used
1119	A353	5pf multi & blk	15	15
1120	A353	15pf multi & blk	15	15
1121	A353	25pf multi & blk	*80*	*60*
1122	A353	30pf multi & blk	15	15
		Set value, #1119-1122, B152-B153	*1.10*	*81*

Issued to publicize the 5th German Gymnastic and Sports Festival, Leipzig.

Pierre de Coubertin, by Wieland Forster A354

Knight A355

Design: 25pf, Coubertin column, Memorial Grove, Olympia.

1969, June 6 *Perf. 14x13½*

No.	Type	Description	Unused	Used
1123	A354	10pf blk & lt bl	15	15
1124	A354	25pf blk & sal pink	*80*	*26*
		Set value		*30*

75th anniversary of the revival of the Olympic Games.

1969, July 29 Photo. *Perf. 14*

Designs: No. 1126, Bicycle wheel. No. 1127, Volleyball.

No.	Type	Description	Unused	Used
1125	A355	20pf red, gold & dk brn	16	15
1126	A355	20pf grn, gold & red	16	15
1127	A355	20pf multi	16	15
		Set value		35

16th Students' Chess World Championships, Dresden (No. 1125); Indoor Bicycle World Championships, Erfurt (No. 1126); 2nd Volleyball World Cup (No. 1127).

Merchandise — A356

1969, Aug. 27 Litho. *Perf. 12½x13*

No.	Type	Description	Unused	Used
1128	A356	10pf multi	15	15

Leipzig Fall Fair, Aug. 31-Sept. 7, 1969.

Arms of Republic and View of Rostock A357

Design: 1m, DDR Arms, Town Hall, Marienkirche and Television Tower, Berlin (vert.).

1969, Sept. 23 Photo. *Perf. 14*

No.	Type	Description	Unused	Used
1129	A357	10pf Rostock	15	15
1130	A357	10pf Neubrandenburg	15	15
1131	A357	10pf Potsdam	15	15
1132	A357	10pf Eisenhüttenstadt	15	15
1133	A357	10pf Hoyerswerda	15	15
1134	A357	10pf Magdeburg	15	15
1135	A357	10pf Halle-Neustadt	15	15
1136	A357	10pf Suhl	15	15
1137	A357	10pf Dresden	15	15
1138	A357	10pf Leipzig	15	15
1139	A357	10pf Karl-Marx-Stadt	15	15
1140	A357	10pf Berlin	15	15
		Set value	96	70

Souvenir Sheet

No.	Type	Description	Unused	Used
1141	A357	1m multi	1.25	75

#1129-1141, 1142-1145 for 20th anniv. of the German Democratic Republic.

No. 1141 contains one 29x52mm stamp.

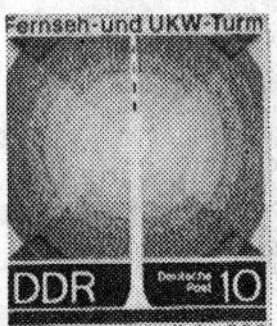

Television Tower, Berlin — A358

People and Flags A359

Designs: 20pf, Sphere of Television Tower and TV test picture. No. 1144, Television Tower and TV test picture.

1969, Oct. 6 *Perf. 14*

No.	Type	Description	Unused	Used
1142	A358	10pf multi	15	15
1143	A358	20pf multi	20	15
		Set value	35	15

Souvenir Sheets

No.	Type	Description	Unused	Used
1144	A358	1m dk bl & multi	1.40	1.00

Perf. 13x12½

No.	Type	Description	Unused	Used
1145	A359	1m red & multi	1.10	80

No. 1144 contains one 21½x60mm stamp.

Cathedral, Otto von Guericke Monument and Hotel International, Magdeburg — A360

1969, Oct. 28 Litho. *Perf. 13x12½*

No.	Type	Description	Unused	Used
1146	A360	20pf multi	15	15

Natl. Postage Stamp Exhibition in honor of the 20th anniv. of the German Democratic Republic, Magdeburg, Oct. 31-Nov. 9. See No. B154.

UFI Emblem — A361

1969, Oct. 28 *Perf. 13x13½*

No.	Type	Description	Unused	Used
1147	A361	10pf multi	15	15
1148	A361	15pf multi	*55*	*15*
		Set value		*18*

36th UFI Congress (Union des Foires Internationales), Leipzig, Oct. 28-30.

Memorial Monument, Copenhagen-Ryvangen A362

Rostock University Seal and Building A363

1969, Oct. 28 *Perf. 13*

No.	Type	Description	Unused	Used
1149	A362	25pf multi	25	15

Issued in memory of the victims of the Nazis in Denmark.

1969, Nov. 12 ***Perf. 12½x13***

Design: 15pf, Steam turbine, curve and Rostock University emblem.

1150 A363 10pf brt bl & multi 15 15
1151 A363 15pf vio & multi *32 16*
Set value *40 20*

550th anniversary of Rostock University.

ILO Emblem A364

Mold for Christmas Cookies A365

1969, Nov. 12 ***Perf. 13½x14***

1152 A364 20pf dp grn & sil 15 15
1153 A364 25pf lil rose & sil *40 26*
Set value *45 30*

50th anniv. of the ILO.

1969, Nov. 25 Litho. ***Perf. 13½x13***

Design: 50pf, Negro couple, shaped spice cookie.

1154 A365 10pf dl org, bl & red brn 1.10 60
1155 A365 50pf lt bl & multi 1.65 90

Issued to publicize folk art of Lusatia. Nos. 1154-1155 printed se-tenant. See No. B155.

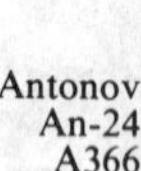

Antonov An-24 A366

Planes: 25pf, Ilyushin Il-18. 30pf, Tupolev Tu-134. 50pf, Mi-8 helicopter.

1969, Dec. 2 ***Perf. 13x12½***

1156 A366 20pf bl, red & blk 15 15
1157 A366 25pf vio, red & blk *90 80*
1158 A366 30pf ultra, red & blk 15 15
1159 A366 50pf ol, red & blk 15 15
Set value *1.20 1.00*

Siberian Teacher, by D. K. Sveshnikov A367

Russian Paintings from Dresden Gallery of Modern Masters: 10pf, Steelworker, by V. A. Serov. 20pf, Still Life, by E. A. Aslamasjan. 25pf, Hot Day (boats on river), by J. D. Romas. 40pf, Spring is Coming (young woman and snow-covered street), by L. V. Kabatchek. 50pf, Man on River Bank, by V. J. Makovskij.

1969, Dec. 10 Photo. ***Perf. 13***

1160 A367 5pf gray & multi 15 15
1161 A367 10pf gray & multi 15 15
1162 A367 20pf gray & multi 15 15
1163 A367 25pf gray & multi *1.10 75*
1164 A367 40pf gray & multi 15 15
1165 A367 50pf gray & multi 16 15
Set value *1.50 1.00*

Ernst Barlach (1870-1938), Sculptor and Writer — A368

Portraits: 10pf, Johann Gutenberg (1400-68). 15pf, Kurt Tucholsky (1890-1935), writer. 20pf, Ludwig van Beethoven. 25pf, Friedrich Hölderlin (1770-1843), poet. 40pf, Georg Wilhelm Friedrich Hegel (1770-1831), philosopher.

1970, Jan. 20 Engr. ***Perf. 14***

1166 A368 5pf blue vio 15 15
1167 A368 10pf gray brn 15 15
1168 A368 15pf vio blue 15 15
1169 A368 20pf rose lilac 15 15
1170 A368 25pf blue green *65 55*
1171 A368 40pf rose claret 15 15
Set value *1.10 75*

Rabbit — A369

1970, Feb. 5 Photo. ***Perf. 13½x14***

1172 A369 10pf shown 15 15
1173 A369 20pf Red fox 15 15
1174 A369 25pf Mink *90 75*
1175 A369 40pf Hamster 15 15
Set value *1.12 85*

Issued to publicize the 525th International Fur Auctions, Leipzig.

Fairy Tale Type of 1969

Various Scenes from Fairy Tale "Little Brother and Sister."

1970, Feb. 17 Litho. ***Perf. 13½x13***

1176 A345 5pf lil & multi 42 16
1177 A345 10pf lil & multi 42 16
1178 A345 15pf lil & multi 42 30
1179 A345 20pf lil & multi 42 30
1180 A345 25pf lil & multi 42 16
1181 A345 30pf lil & multi 42 16
Nos. 1176-1181 (6) 2.52 1.24

#1176-1181 printed together in sheets of 6.

Telephone Coordinating Station — A370

Design: 15pf, High voltage testing transformer (vert.).

Perf. 13x12½, 12½x13

1970, Feb. 24

1182 A370 10pf multi 15 15
1183 A370 15pf multi 16 15
Set value 25 15

Leipzig Spring Fair, Mar. 1-10, 1970.

Horseman's Tombstone (700 A.D.) A371

Treasures from the Halle Museum: 20pf, Helmet (500 A.D.). 25pf, Bronze basin (1000 B.C.). 40pf, Clay drum (2500 B.C.).

1970, Mar. 3 Photo. ***Perf. 13***

1184 A371 10pf dp grn, gray & dk brn 15 15
1185 A371 20pf multi 15 15
1186 A371 25pf yel & multi *75 50*
1187 A371 40pf multi 15 15
Set value *1.00 65*

Lenin and Clara Zetkin — A372

Designs: 10pf, Lenin, "ISKRA" (newspaper's name), composing frame and printing press. 25pf, Lenin and title page of German edition of "State and Revolution." 40pf, Lenin statue, Eisleben. 70pf, Lenin monument and Lenin Square, Berlin. 1m, Lenin portrait (vert.).

Photogravure and Engraved

1970, Apr. 16 ***Perf. 14***

1188 A372 10pf multi 15 15
1189 A372 20pf multi 15 15
1190 A372 25pf multi *1.00 65*
1191 A372 40pf multi 15 15
1192 A372 70pf multi 20 15
Nos. 1188-1192 (5) *1.65*
Set value *90*

Souvenir Sheet

1193 A372 1m dk car & multi 1.25 1.00

Lenin (1870-1924), Russian communist leader. No. 1193 contains one vertical stamp.

Sea Kale — A373

Red Army Soldier Raising Flag over Berlin Reichstag — A374

Protected Plants: 20pf, European pasqueflower. 25pf, Fringed gentian. 30pf, Galeate orchis. 40pf, Marsh tea. 70pf, Round-leaved wintergreen.

1970, Apr. 28 **Photo.**

1194 A373 10pf multi 15 15
1195 A373 20pf vio & multi 15 15
1196 A373 25pf multi *2.25 1.10*
1197 A373 30pf multi 15 15
1198 A373 40pf multi 15 15
1199 A373 70pf multi 16 15
Nos. 1194-1199 (6) *3.01*
Set value *1.30*

1970, May 5 Litho. ***Perf. 13x13½***

Designs: 20pf, Spasski Tower, Kremlin; State Council Building, Berlin; coats of arms of USSR and German Democratic Republic, and newspaper clipping about friendship treaty with USSR. 25pf, Mutual Economic Aid Building, Moscow, and flags of member countries. 70pf, Memorial monument, Buchenwald (horiz.).

1200 A374 10pf multi 15 15
1201 A374 20pf multi 15 15
1202 A374 25pf multi *52 38*
Set value *60 45*

Souvenir Sheet

1203 A374 70pf multi 1.00 65

25th anniv. of liberation from Fascism.

Shortwave Antenna, RBI Emblem and Globe — A375

Grain and Globe — A376

Designs: 15pf, Berlin Radio Station, emblems of Radio Berlin International (RBI), Radio DDR and Radio Germany.

1970, May 13 Litho. ***Perf. 13½x13***

Size: 23x28mm

1204 A375 10pf ap grn, vio bl & bl 55 42

Size: 50x28mm

1205 A375 15pf vio bl, dp rose & ap grn 1.10 80

25th anniv. of the German Democratic Republic broadcasting system.

1970, May 19

Design: 25pf, House of Culture, Dresden, and grain.

1206 A376 20pf vio bl, yel & bl 1.25 85
1207 A376 25pf vio bl, yel & bl 1.25 85
a. Strip of 2 (#1206-1207) + label 3.75 2.50

Issued to publicize the 5th World Cereal and Bread Congress, Dresden, May 24-29. Nos. 1206-1207 printed se-tenant with label in between carrying name of congress in German, English, French and Russian.

Fritz Heckert Medal A377

Design: 25pf, Globes and "FSM."

1970, June 9 ***Perf. 13x12½***

1208 A377 20pf red, yel & brn 15 15
1209 A377 25pf red, bl & yel *40 26*
Set value *45 30*

25th anniv. of the Free German Trade Union and of the World Organization of Trade Unions.

Traffic Policeman A378

Designs: 10pf, Young Pioneers congratulating police woman. 15pf, Volga police car. 20pf, Railroad policeman with radio-telephone. 25pf, River police in Volga wing-type boat.

1970, June 23 Litho. ***Perf. 13x12½***

1210 A378 5pf ocher & multi 15 15
1211 A378 10pf grn & multi 15 15
1212 A378 15pf ultra & multi 15 15
1213 A378 20pf multi 15 15
1214 A378 25pf multi *65 48*
Set value *80 60*

25th anniversary of the People's Police.

Gods Amon, Shu and Tefnut — A379

Designs from Lion Temple in Musawwarat: 15pf, Head of King Arnekhamani. 20pf, Cow from cattle frieze. 25pf, Head of Prince Arka. 30pf, Head of God Arensnuphis (vert.). 40pf, Elephants and prisoners of war. 50pf, Lion God Apedemak.

Perf. 13½x14, 14x13½

1970, June 23 **Photo.**

1215 A379 10pf multi 15 15
1216 A379 15pf multi 15 15
1217 A379 20pf multi 15 15
1218 A379 25pf multi *1.50 90*
1219 A379 30pf multi 15 15

1220 A379 40pf multi 15 15
1221 A379 50pf multi 15 15
Set value *1.95 1.10*

Issued to publicize the archaeological work in the Sudan by the Humboldt University, Berlin.

Arms and Flags of DDR and Poland — A380

1970, July 1 Litho. *Perf. 13x12½*
1222 A380 20pf multi 15 15

20th anniversary of the Görlitz Agreement concerning the Oder-Neisse border.

Culture Association Emblem A381

Athlete on Pommel Horse A382

Design: 25pf, Johannes R. Becher medal.

1970, July 1 Photo. *Perf. 14*
1223 A381 10pf ultra, sil & brn 3.00 2.00
1224 A381 25pf ultra, gold & brn 3.00 2.00
a. Strip of 2, #1223-1224 + label 9.00 4.50

25th anniv. of the German Kulturbund.

1970, July 1 *Perf. 14x13½*
1225 A382 10pf blk, yel & brn red 15 15

Issued to publicize the 3rd Children's and Youths' Spartakiad. See No. B156.

Meeting of the American, British and Russian Delegations — A383

Designs: 10pf, Cecilienhof Castle. 20pf, "Potsdam Agreement" in German, English, French and Russian.

1970, July 28 Litho. *Perf. 13*
Size: 23x28mm
1226 A383 10pf blk, cit & red 38 18
1227 A383 20pf blk, cit & red 38 18
Size: 77x28mm
1228 A383 25pf red & blk 38 18
a. Strip of 3, #1226-1228 1.20 60

25th anniv. of the Potsdam Agreement among the Allies concerning Germany at the end of WW II.

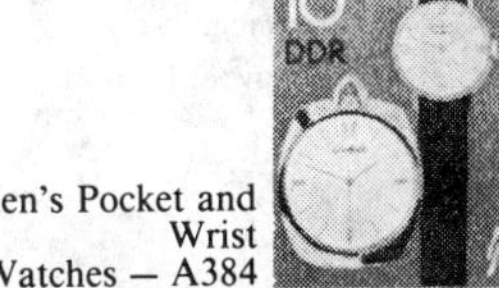

Men's Pocket and Wrist Watches — A384

1970, Aug. 25 Photo. *Perf. 13½x14*
1229 A384 10pf ultra, blk & gold 20 15

Leipzig Fall Fair, 1970.

Theodor Neubauer and Magnus Poser A385

"Homeland" from Soviet Cenotaph, Berlin-Treptow A386

1970, Sept. 2 *Perf. 13x12½, 12½x13*
1230 A385 20pf dk bl, car & pale grn 16 15
1231 A386 25pf dp car, pale bl 28 16
Set value 25

Issued in memory of fighters against "fascism and imperialistic wars."

Competition Map and Compass — A387

Design: 25pf, Competition map and runner at 3 different stations.

1970, Sept. 15 Litho. *Perf. 13x12½*
1232 A387 10pf yel & multi 15 15
1233 A387 25pf yel & multi *35 22*
Set value *40 25*

World Orienting Championships.

Mother and Child, by Käthe Kollwitz — A388

Works of Art: 10pf, Forest Worker Scharf's Birthday, by Otto Nagel. 20pf, Portrait of a Girl, by Otto Nagel. 25pf, No More War, (Woman with raised arm) by Käthe Kollwitz. 40pf, Head from Gustrow Memorial, by Ernst Barlach. 50pf, The Flutist, by Ernst Barlach.

Photo.; Litho. (25pf, 30pf)
1970, Sept. 22 *Perf. 14x13½*
1234 A388 10pf multi 15 15
1235 A388 20pf multi 15 15
1236 A388 25pf pink & dk brn *1.65 1.00*
1237 A388 30pf sal & blk 15 15
1238 A388 40pf yel & blk 15 15
1239 A388 50pf yel & blk 15 15
Set value *1.90 1.20*

Issued in memory of the artists Otto Nagel, Käthe Kollwitz and Ernst Barlach.

"The Little Trumpeter" A389

1970, Oct. 1 Photo.
1240 A389 10pf dp ultra, brn & org 25 15

2nd Natl. Youth Stamp Exhib., Karl-Marx-Stadt, Oct. 4-11. The design shows the memorial in Halle for Fritz Weineck, trumpeter for the Red War Veterans' Organization. See No. B160.

Emblem with Flags of East Block Nations — A390

1970, Oct. 1 Litho. *Perf. 13x12½*
1241 A390 10pf car & multi 15 15
1242 A390 20pf multi 22 15
Set value 30 15

Issued to publicize the Brothers in Arms maneuvers of the East Bloc countries in the territory of the German Democratic Republic.

Musk Ox — A391

Berlin Zoo: 15pf, Shoebill. 20pf, Addax. 25pf, Malayan sun bear.

1970, Oct. 6 Photo. *Perf. 14*
1243 A391 10pf bl & multi 15 15
1244 A391 15pf grn & multi 15 15
1245 A391 20pf org & multi 18 15
1246 A391 25pf multi *2.75 65*
Set value *75*

UN Headquarters and Emblem A392

1970, Oct. 20 Photo. *Perf. 13*
1247 A392 20pf ultra & multi 50 15

25th anniversary of the United Nations.

Friedrich Engels A393

Epiphyllum A394

Designs: 20pf, Friedrich Engels and Karl Marx. 25pf, Engels and title page of his polemic against Dühring.

Photogravure and Engraved
1970, Nov. 24 *Perf. 14*
1248 A393 10pf ver, gray & blk 15 15
1249 A393 20pf ver, dk grn & blk 15 15
1250 A393 25pf ver, dk car rose & blk *50 32*
Set value *60 42*

150th anniversary of the birth of Friedrich Engels (1820-1895), socialist, collaborator with Karl Marx.

1970, Dec. 2 Photo. *Perf. 14*

Flowering Cactus Plants: 10pf, Astrophytum myriostigma. 15pf, Echinocereus salm-dyckianus. 20pf, Selenicereus grandiflorus. 25pf, Hamatocactus setispinus. 30pf, Mamillaria boolii.

1251 A394 5pf multi 15 15
1252 A394 10pf dk bl & multi 15 15
1253 A394 15pf multi 15 15
1254 A394 20pf multi 15 15
1255 A394 25pf dk bl & multi *1.65 75*
1256 A394 30pf pur & multi 15 15
Set value *2.00 90*

Souvenir Sheet

Ludwig van Beethoven — A395

1970, Dec. 10 Engr. *Perf. 14*
1257 A395 1m gray 1.10 90

Bicentenary of the birth of Ludwig van Beethoven (1770-1827), composer.

Dancer's Mask, South Seas A396

Works from Ethnological Museum, Leipzig: 20pf, Bronze head, Africa. 25pf, Tea pot, Asia. 40pf, Clay figure (jaguar), Mexico.

1971, Jan. 12 Photo. *Perf. 13*
1258 A396 10pf multi 15 15
1259 A396 20pf multi 15 15
1260 A396 25pf multi *75 65*
1261 A396 40pf multi 15 15
Set value *1.00 80*

The Catalogue editors cannot undertake to appraise, identify or judge the genuineness or condition of stamps.

Venus 5, Soft-landing on Moon — A397

Designs: No. 1263, Model of space station. No. 1264, Luna 16 and Luna 10 satellites. No. 1265, Group flight of Sojuz 6, 7 and 8. No. 1266, Proton 1, radiation measuring satellite. No. 1267, Communications satellite Molniya 1. No. 1268, Yuri A. Gagarin, first flight of Vostok 1. No. 1269, Alexei Leonov walking in space, Voskhod 2.

1971, Feb. 11 Litho. *Perf. 13x12½*

1262 A397 20pf dk bl & multi 40 20
1263 A397 20pf dk bl & multi 40 20
1264 A397 20pf dk bl & multi 40 35
1265 A397 20pf dk bl & multi 40 35
1266 A397 20pf dk bl & multi 40 35
1267 A397 20pf dk bl & multi 40 35
1268 A397 20pf dk bl & multi 40 20
1269 A397 20pf dk bl & multi 40 20
Nos. 1262-1269 (8) 3.20 2.20

Soviet space research. Nos. 1262-1269 printed together in sheets of eight.

Johannes R. Becher A398

Karl Liebknecht A399

Portraits: 10pf, Heinrich Mann. 15pf, John Heartfield. 20pf, Willi Bredel. 25pf, Franz Mehring. 40pf, Rudolf Virchow. 50pf, Johannes Kepler.

1971 Engr. *Perf. 14*

1270 A398 5pf brown 15 15
1271 A398 10pf vio bl 15 15
1272 A398 15pf black 15 15
1273 A398 20pf rose lake 15 15
1274 A398 25pf green *80 48*
1274A A398 40pf pale pur 25 15
1275 A398 50pf dp blk 15 15
Set value 1.30 60

Honoring prominent Germans. See Nos. 1349-1353.

1971, Feb. 23 Photo.

Design: 25pf, Rosa Luxemburg.

1276 A399 20pf gold, mag & blk 28 25
1277 A399 25pf gold, mag & blk 28 25

Karl Liebknecht (1871-1919) and Rosa Luxemburg (1871-1919), leaders of Spartacist Movement. Printed se-tenant.

Soldier and Army Emblem — A400

1971, Mar. 1 *Perf. 13½x14*

1278 A400 20pf gray & multi 25 15

15th anniv. of the National People's Army.

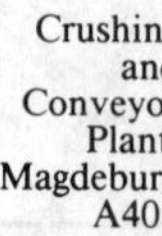

Crushing and Conveyor Plant, Magdeburg A401

Leipzig Spring Fair: 15pf, Dredger for low temperature work.

1971, Mar. 9 Litho. *Perf. 13x12½*

1279 A401 10pf grn & multi 15 15
1280 A401 15pf multi 18 15
Set value 15

Proclamation of the Commune, Town Hall, Paris A402

Designs: 20pf, Barricade at Place Blanche, defended by women. 25pf, Illustration by Theophile A. Steinlen for the International. 30pf, Title page for "The Civil War in France," by Karl Marx.

1971, Mar. 9 *Perf. 13*

1281 A402 10pf red, bis & blk 15 15
1282 A402 20pf red, bis & blk 15 15
1283 A402 25pf red, buff & blk *75 55*
1284 A402 30pf red, gray & blk 15 15
Set value 90 65

Centenary of the Paris Commune.

Lunokhod 1 on Moon — A403

1971, Mar. 30 Photo. *Perf. 14*

1285 A403 20pf multi 25 15

Luna 17 unmanned, automated moon mission, Nov. 10-17, and the 24th Communist Party Congress of the Soviet Union.

Discobolus — A404

1971, Apr. 6 Litho. *Perf. 13½x13*

1286 A404 20pf dl bl, lt bl & buff 20 15

20th anniversary of the Olympic Committee of German Democratic Republic.

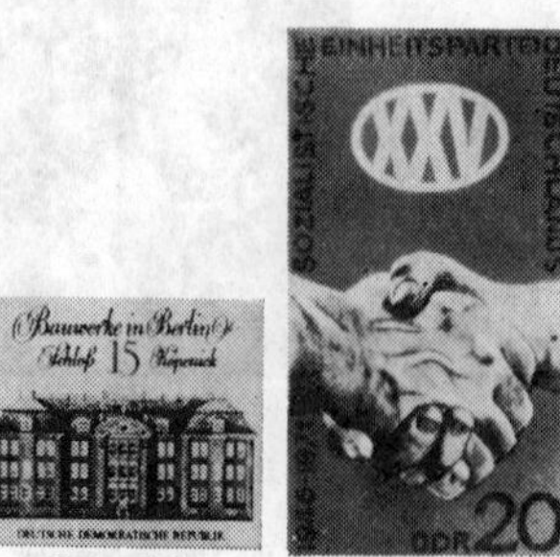

Köpenick Castle — A405 Clasped Hands — A406

Berlin Buildings: 10pf, St. Mary's Church (vert.). 20pf, Old Library. 25pf, Ermeler House (vert.). 50pf, New Guard Memorial. 70pf, National Gallery of Art.

Perf. 13½x14, 14x13½

1971, Apr. 6 Photo.

1287 A405 10pf multi 15 15
1288 A405 15pf multi 15 15
1289 A405 20pf multi 15 15
1290 A405 25pf multi *2.50 1.10*
1291 A405 50pf multi 15 15
1292 A405 70pf multi 20 15
Set value 2.90 1.25

Lithographed and Embossed

1971, Apr. 20 *Perf. 13x13½*

1293 A406 20pf red, blk & gold 25 15

25th anniversary of Socialist Unity Party of Germany (SED).

Dance Costume, Schleife — A407

Self-Portrait, by Dürer — A408

Sorbian Dance Costumes from: 20pf, Hoyerswerda. 25pf, Cottbus. 40pf, Kamenz.

1971, May 4 Litho. *Perf. 13*

Size: 33x42mm

1294 A407 10pf multi 15 15
1295 A407 20pf grn & multi 15 15
1296 A407 25pf bl & multi *1.00 80*
1297 A407 40pf multi 15 15
Set value 1.20 90

1971, Nov. 23 *Perf. 13½x13*

Size: 23x28mm

1297A A407 10pf multi 20 15
c. Booklet pane of 4 90
d. Booklet pane, 2 #1297A, 2 #1297B 1.75
1297B A407 20pf multi 50 32

Nos. 1297A-1297B were issued only in booklets.

1971, May 18 *Perf. 12½x13*

Art Works by Dürer: 40pf, Three Peasants. 70pf, Portrait of Philipp Melanchthon.

1298 A408 10pf multi 15 15
1299 A408 40pf brn & multi 15 15
1300 A408 70pf gray & multi *1.50 95*
Set value 1.60 1.00

500th anniversary of the birth of Albrecht Dürer (1471-1528), painter and engraver.

Building Industry A409

Congress Emblem A410

Designs: 10pf, Science and technology. No. 1303, Farming. 25pf, Civilian defense.

1971, June 9 Photo. *Perf. 14*

1301 A409 5pf cr, red & blk 15 15
1302 A409 10pf cr, red & blk 15 15
1303 A409 20pf cr, red, bl & blk 15 15
1304 A410 20pf gold, dp car & red 22 15
1305 A409 25pf cr, red & blk *52 38*
Set value 85 52

8th Congress of Socialist Unity Party of Germany (SED).

Golden Fleece, 1730 A411

Treasures from the Green Vault, Dresden: 5pf, Cherry stone with 180 heads carved on it, 1590. 15pf, Tankard, Nuremberg, 1530. 20pf, Moor with drums on horseback, 1720. 25pf, Decorated writing box, 1562. 30pf, St. George pendant, 1570.

1971, June 22 *Perf. 13*

1306 A411 5pf dp car & multi 15 15
1307 A411 10pf grn & multi 15 15
1308 A411 15pf vio & multi 15 15
1309 A411 20pf multi 15 15
1310 A411 25pf multi *1.00 70*
1311 A411 30pf multi 15 15
Set value 1.25 85

Prisoners, by Fritz Cremer — A412

Design: 25pf, Brutality in Buchenwald Concentration Camp, by Fritz Cremer.

1971, June 22 Litho. *Perf. 13*

1312 A412 20pf bis & blk 50 42
1313 A412 25pf lt bl & blk 50 42

International Federation of Resistance Fighters (FIR), 20th anniversary. Nos. 1312-1313 printed se-tenant with embossed label with commemorative inscription in between.

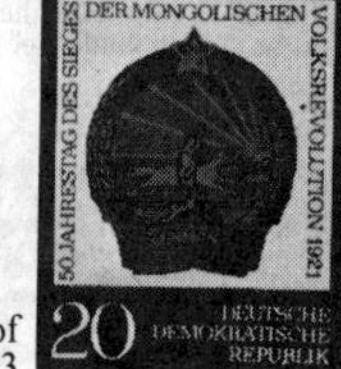

Coat of Arms of Mongolia — A413

1971, July 6 Litho. *Perf. 13*

1314 A413 20pf dk red, yel & blk 20 15

50th anniversary of the Mongolian People's Revolution.

Child's Head, UNICEF Emblem A414

1971, July 13 Photo.

1315 A414 20pf multi 20 15

25th anniv. of UNICEF.

Militiaman, Soldier and Brandenburg Gate — A415

Design: 35pf, Brandenburg Gate and new buildings in East Berlin.

1971, Aug. 12

1316	A415	20pf red & multi	35	15
1317	A415	35pf yel & multi	60	20
		Set value		30

10 years of Berlin Wall.

Passenger Ship Iwan Franko — A416

Ships: 15pf, Freighter, type 17. 20pf, Freighter Rostock, type XD. 25pf, Fish processing ship "Junge Welt." 40pf, Container cargo ship. 50pf, Explorer ship Akademik Kurtschatow.

1971, Aug. 24 **Engr.**

1318	A416	10pf pale pur	15	15
1319	A416	15pf pale brn & ind	15	15
1320	A416	20pf gray grn	15	15
1321	A416	25pf slate	*1.65*	*1.10*
1322	A416	40pf maroon	15	15
1323	A416	50pf grysh bl	15	15
		Set value	*1.90*	*1.40*

Shipbuilding industry.

Butadiene Plant — A417

Leipzig Fall Fair: 25pf, Refinery.

1971, Sept. 2 **Photo.** ***Perf. 13***

1324	A417	10pf ol, vio & mag	15	15
1325	A417	25pf bl, vio & ol	28	15
		Set value		20

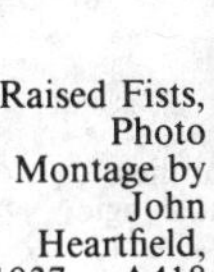

Raised Fists, Photo Montage by John Heartfield, 1937 — A418

1971, Sept. 23

1326	A418	35pf grnsh bl, blk & sil	30	15

Intl. Year Against Racial Discrimination.

Karl Marx Monument A419

1971, Oct. 5 **Photo.** ***Perf. 14x13½***

1327	A419	35pf vio brn, pink & buff	35	15

Unveiling of Karl Marx memorial at Karl-Marx-Stadt (Chemnitz).

Wiltz Memorial, Flag of Luxembourg A420

1971, Oct. 5

1328	A420	25pf multi	20	15

Memorial for victims of the Nazis, Wiltz, Luxembourg.

Postal Milestones, Saxony, and Zürner's Surveyor Carriage — A421

Photo. & Engr.

1971, Oct. 5 ***Perf. 14***

1329	A421	25pf bl, olive & lil	*50*	*30*

Philatelists' Day 1971. See No. B162.

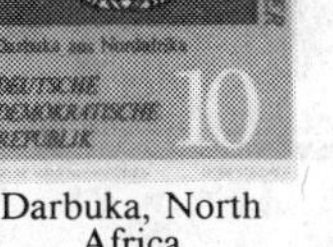

Darbuka, North Africa A422

Geodetic Apparatus A423

Musical Instruments: 15pf, Two morin chuur, Mongolia. 20pf, Violin, Germany. 25pf, Mandolin, Italy. 40pf, Bagpipes, Bohemia. 50pf, Kasso, Sudan.

1971, Oct. 26 **Photo.** ***Perf. 14x13½***

1330	A422	10pf multi	15	15
1331	A422	15pf multi	15	15
1332	A422	20pf ocher & multi	15	15
1333	A422	25pf bl & multi	15	15
1334	A422	40pf gray & multi	15	15
1335	A422	50pf multi	*1.50*	*1.10*
		Set value	*1.75*	*1.30*

Instruments from the Music Museum in Markneukirchen.

1971, Nov. 9 **Photo.** ***Perf. 13½x14***

Designs: 20pf, Ergaval microscope. 25pf, Planetarium.

Size: 23½x28½mm

1336	A423	10pf bl, blk & red	65	40
1337	A423	20pf bl, blk & red	65	40

Size: 50½x28½mm

1338	A423	25pf bl, vio bl & yel	65	40
a.		Strip of 3, Nos. 1336-1338	2.00	1.25

125th anniversary of the Carl Zeiss optical works in Jena.

Fairy Tale Type of 1966

Designs: Various Scenes from Fairy Tale "The Bremen Town Musicians."

1971, Nov. 23 **Litho.** ***Perf. 13½x13***

1339	A290	5pf multi	42	16
1340	A290	10pf ocher & multi	42	16
1341	A290	15pf gray & multi	42	30
1342	A290	20pf ver & multi	42	30
1343	A290	25pf vio & multi	42	16
1344	A290	30pf yel & multi	42	16
		Nos. 1339-1344 (6)	2.52	1.24

#1339-1344 printed together in sheets of 6.

Olympic Rings and Sledding — A424

Olympic Rings and: 20pf, Long-distance skiing. 25pf, Biathlon. 70pf, Ski jump.

1971, Dec. 7 **Photo.** ***Perf. 13½x14***

1345	A424	5pf grn, car & blk	15	15
1346	A424	20pf car rose, vio & blk	15	15
1347	A424	25pf vio, car & blk	*1.75*	*1.25*
1348	A424	70pf vio bl, vio & blk	20	16
		Set value, #1345-1348, B163-B164	*2.10*	*1.55*

11th Winter Olympic Games, Sapporo, Japan, Feb. 3-13, 1972.

Portrait Type of 1971.

Portraits: 10pf, Johannes Tralow (1882-1968), playwright. 20pf, Leonhard Frank (1882-1961), writer. 25pf, K. A. Kocor (1822-1904), composer. 35pf, Heinrich Schliemann (1822-1890), archaeologist. 50pf, F. Caroline Neuber (1697-1760), actress.

1972, Jan. 25 **Engr.** ***Perf. 14***

1349	A398	10pf green	15	15
1350	A398	20pf rose claret	15	15
1351	A398	25pf dk bl	15	15
1352	A398	35pf brown	15	15
1353	A398	50pf rose vio	*1.40*	*1.25*
		Set value	*1.60*	*1.40*

Honoring famous personalities.

Gypsum, Eisleben A425

Minerals found in East Germany: 10pf, Zinnwaldite, Zinnwald. 20pf, Malachite, Ullersreuth. 25pf, Amethyst, Wiesenbad. 35pf, Halite, Merkers. 50pf, Proustite, Schneeberg.

1972, Feb. 22 **Photo.** ***Perf. 13***

1354	A425	5pf grnsh bl & brn blk	15	15
1355	A425	10pf cit, brn & blk	15	15
1356	A425	20pf multi	15	15
1357	A425	25pf multi	15	15
1358	A425	35pf lt grn, ind & blk	15	15
1359	A425	50pf gray & multi	*1.75*	*1.10*
		Set value	*2.00*	*1.25*

Russian Pavilion and Fair Emblem A426

Design: 25pf, Flags of East Germany and Russia, and Fair emblem.

1972, Mar. 3 **Photo.** ***Perf. 14***

1360	A426	10pf vio bl & multi	15	15
1361	A426	25pf cl & multi	20	15
		Set value	28	16

50 years of Russian participation in the Leipzig Fair.

Miniature Sheets

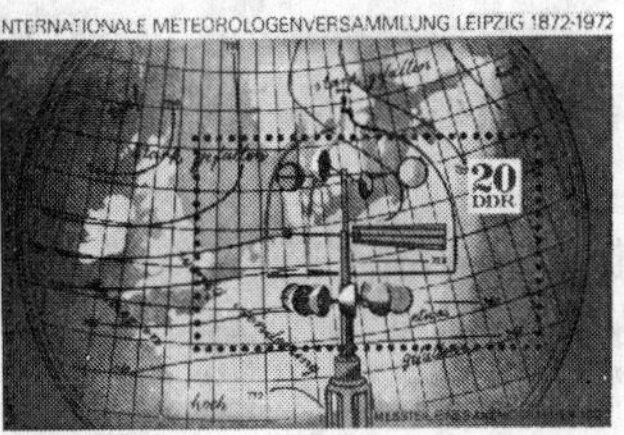

Anemometer, 1896, and Meteorological Chart, 1876 — A427

Designs: 35pf, Dipole and cloud photograph taken by satellite. 70pf, Meteor weather satellite and weather map.

1972, Mar. 23 **Litho.** ***Perf. 13x12½***

1362	A427	20pf multi	60	45
1363	A427	35pf multi	60	45
1364	A427	70pf grn & multi	60	45

Intl. Meteorologists' Cent. Meeting, Leipzig.

World Health Organization Emblem A428

1972, Apr. 4 **Photo.** ***Perf. 13***

1365	A428	35pf lt bl, vio bl & sil	32	15

World Health Day.

Kamov Helicopter A429

Aircraft: 10pf, Agricultural spray plane. 35pf, Ilyushin jet. 1m, Jet and tail with Interflug emblem.

1972, Apr. 25 ***Perf. 14***

1366	A429	5pf bl & multi	15	15
1367	A429	10pf multi	15	15
1368	A429	35pf bl grn & multi	15	15
1369	A429	1m multi	*1.90*	*1.25*
		Set value	*2.00*	*1.30*

Wrestling and Olympic Rings — A430

Sport and Olympic Rings: 20pf, Pole vault. 35pf, Volleyball. 70pf, Women's gymnastics.

1972, May 16 Photo. *Perf. 13½x14*

1370 A430 5pf bl, gold & blk 15 15
1371 A430 20pf mag, gold & blk 15 15
1372 A430 35pf ol bis, gold & blk 15 15
1373 A430 70pf yel grn, gold & blk *1.65 1.50*
Set value, #1370-1373, B166-B167 *1.90 1.80*

20th Olympic Games, Munich, Aug. 26-Sept. 11.

Flags of USSR and German Democratic Republic — A431

Design: 20pf, Flags, Leonid Brezhnev and Erich Honecker.

1972, May 24 Engr. & Photo.

1374 A431 10pf red, yel & blk 16 15
1375 A431 20pf red, yel & blk 24 15
Set value 24

Society for German-Soviet Friendship, 25th anniversary.

Workers — A432

Design: 35pf, Students.

1972, May 24 Litho. *Perf. 13*

1376 A432 10pf dl yel, org & mag 35 20
1377 A432 35pf dl yel & ultra 35 20
a. Strip of 2, #1376-1377 + label 80 50

8th Congress of Free German Trade Unions, Berlin.

Karneol Rose A433

1972, June 13 Photo. *Perf. 13*

Size: 36x36mm

1378 A433 5pf shown 15 15
1379 A433 10pf Berger's Erfurt Rose 15 15
1380 A433 15pf Charme *1.65 1.00*
1381 A433 20pf Izetka Spree-Athens 15 15
1382 A433 25pf Kopenick summer 15 15
1383 A433 35pf Prof. Knoll 15 15
Set value *1.90 1.25*

International Rose Exhibition.

Redrawn

1972, Aug. 22 *Perf. 13½x13*

Size: 23x28mm

1383A A433 10pf multi 15 15
d. Booklet pane of 4 55
1383B A433 25pf multi 30 18
e. Booklet pane of 4 (2 #1383B, 2 #1383C) 3.00
1383C A433 35pf multi 30 18

International Rose Exhibition. Nos. 1383A-1383C were issued only in booklets.

Young Mother and Child, by Cranach A434

Paintings by Lucas Cranach: 5pf, Young man. 35pf, Margarete Luther (Martin's mother). 70pf, Reclining nymph (horiz.).

1972, July 4 *Perf. 14x13½, 13½x14*

1384 A434 5pf gold & multi 15 15
1385 A434 20pf gold & multi 15 15
1386 A434 35pf gold & multi 15 15
1387 A434 70pf gold & multi *1.75 1.40*

500th anniversary of the birth of Lucas Cranach (1472-1553), painter.

Compass and Motorcyclist — A435

Designs: 10pf, Parachute and light plane. 20pf, Target and military obstacle race. 25pf, Amateur radio transmitter, Morse key and tape. 35pf, Propeller and sailing ship.

1972, Aug. 8 Photo. *Perf. 14*

1388 A435 5pf multi 15 15
1389 A435 10pf multi 15 15
1390 A435 20pf multi 15 15
1391 A435 25pf multi *1.00 75*
1392 A435 35pf multi 15 15
Set value *1.20 85*

Society for Sport and Technology.

Young Worker Reading, by Jutta Damme — A436

1972, Aug. 22 Photo. *Perf. 13½x14*

1393 A436 50pf multi 50 20

International Book Year 1972.

Polylux Writing Projector A437

George Dimitrov A438

Design: 25pf, Pentacon-audiovision projector (horiz.).

Perf. 12½x13, 13x12½

1972, Aug. 29 Litho.

1394 A437 10pf crim & blk 15 15
1395 A437 25pf brt grn & blk 28 15
Set value 18

Leipzig Fall Fair, 1972.

1972, Sept. 19 *Perf. 13x13½*

1396 A438 20pf rose red & blk 25 15

George Dimitrov (1882-1949), Bulgarian Communist party leader.

Bird Catchers, Egypt, c. 2400 B.C. — A439

Red Cross Trainees and Red Cross — A440

Design: 20pf, Tapestry with animal design, Anatolia, c. 1400 A.D.

1972, Sept. 19 Photo. *Perf. 14*

1397 A439 10pf multi 15 15
1398 A439 20pf multi 15 15
Set value 25 15

Interartes Philatelic Exhibition, Berlin, Oct. 4-Nov. 11. See Nos. B168-B169.

1972, Oct. 3 Litho. *Perf. 13*

Designs: 15pf, Red Cross rescue launch in the Baltic. 35pf, Red Cross with world map, ship, plane and vehicles.

Size: 23x28mm

1399 A440 10pf grnsh bl, dk bl & red 40 30
1400 A440 15pf grnsh bl, dk bl & red 40 30

Size: 50x28mm

1401 A440 35pf grnsh bl, dk bl & red 40 30
a. Strip of 3, Nos. 1399-1401 1.25 1.10

Red Cross at work in the DDR.

Arab Celestial Globe, 1279 A441

Anti-Fascists Monument A442

Designs: 10pf, Globe, by Joachim R. Praetorius, 1568. 15pf, Globe clock, by Reinhold and Roll, 1586. 20pf, Globe clock, by J. Bürgi, c. 1590. 25pf, Armillary sphere, by J. Moeller, 1687. 35pf, Heraldic celestial globe, 1690.

1972, Oct. 17 Photo. *Perf. 14x13½*

1402 A441 5pf gray & multi 15 15
1403 A441 10pf gray & multi 15 15
1404 A441 15pf gray & multi *2.25 95*
1405 A441 20pf gray & multi 15 15
1406 A441 25pf gray & multi 15 15
1407 A441 35pf gray & multi 22 15
Nos. 1402-1407 (6) *3.07*
Set value *1.10*

Celestial and terrestrial globes from the National Mathematical and Physics Collection, Dresden.

1972, Oct. 24 Litho. *Perf. 12½x13*

1408 A442 25pf multi 30 15

Monument for Polish soldiers and German anti-Fascists, unveiled in Berlin, May 14, 1972.

Young Workers Receiving Technical Education — A443

Design: 25pf, Workers with modern welding machine.

1972, Nov. 2 Photo. *Perf. 13½x14*

1409 A443 10pf bl & multi 25 22
1410 A443 25pf bl & multi 25 22
a. Strip of 2, #1409-1410 + label 55 50

15th Central Fair of Masters of Tomorrow.

Mauz and Hoppel — A444

Designs: Children's television characters.

1972, Nov. 28 Litho. *Perf. 13½x13*

1411 A444 5pf shown 42 20
1412 A444 10pf Fox and magpie 42 20
1413 A444 15pf Mr. Owl 42 32
1414 A444 20pf Mrs. Hedgehog and Borstel 42 32
1415 A444 25pf Schnuffel and Peips 42 20
1416 A444 35pf Paul from the Library 42 20
Nos. 1411-1416 (6) 2.52 1.44

#1411-1416 printed together in sheets of 6.

Grandmother, Children, Magic Mirror — A445

Scenes from Hans Christian Andersen's "Snow Queen": 10pf, Kay and Snow Queen. 15pf, Gerda in magic garden. 20pf, Gerda and crows at palace. 25pf, Gerda and reindeer in Lapland. 35pf, Gerda and Kay at Snow Queen's palace.

1972, Nov. 28 *Perf. 13x13½*

1417 A445 5pf multi 42 20
1418 A445 10pf multi 42 32
1419 A445 15pf multi 42 20
1420 A445 20pf multi 42 20
1421 A445 25pf multi 42 32
1422 A445 35pf multi 42 20
Nos. 1417-1422 (6) 2.52 1.44

#1417-1422 printed together in sheets of 6.

Souvenir Sheet

Heinrich Heine — A446

1972, Dec. 5 *Perf. 12½x13*

1423	A446	1m brn ol, blk & red	1.50	1.10

150th anniversary of the birth of Heinrich Heine (1797-1856), poet.

Coat of Arms of USSR A447

Michelangelo da Caravaggio A448

1972, Dec. 5 **Photo.** *Perf. 13½x14*

1424	A447	20pf red & multi	25	15

50th anniversary of the Soviet Union.

1973 **Litho.** *Perf. 13½x13*

1425	A448	5pf brown	*1.00*	*80*
1426	A448	10pf dl grn	15	15
1427	A448	20pf rose lil	15	15
1428	A448	25pf blue	15	15
1429	A448	35pf brn red	15	15
1429A	A448	40pf rose claret	30	15
		Set value	*1.60*	*90*

Michelangelo da Caravaggio (1565(?)-1609), Italian painter (5pf). Friedrich Wolf (1888-1953), writer (10pf). Max Reger (1873-1916), composer (20pf). Max Reinhardt (1873-1943), Austrian theatrical director (25pf). Johannes Dieckmann (1893-1969), member and president of People's Chamber (35pf). Hermann Matern (1893-1971), vice-president of DDR (40pf).

Lenin Square, Berlin — A449

Coat of Arms of DDR — A449a

Designs: 5pf, Pelican, Berlin Zoo. 10pf, Neptune Fountain, City Hall Street. 15pf, Fisherman's Island, Berlin. 25pf, World clock, Alexander Square, Berlin. 30pf, Workers' Memorial, Halle. 35pf, Marx monument, Karl-Marx-Stadt. 40pf, Brandenburg Gate, Berlin. 50pf, New Guardhouse, Berlin. 60pf, Zwinger, Dresden. 70pf, Old Town Hall, Office Building, Leipzig. 80pf, Old and new buildings, Rostock-Warnemunde. 1m, Soviet War Memorial, Treptow.

1973-74 **Engr.** *Perf. 14x13½*
Size: 29x23½mm

1430	A449	5pf bl grn	15	15
1431	A449	10pf emerald	15	15
1432	A449	15pf rose lil	15	15
1433	A449	20pf rose mag	20	15
1434	A449	25pf grnsh bl	28	15
1435	A449	30pf orange	28	15
1436	A449	35pf grnsh bl	32	15
1437	A449	40pf dl vio	35	15
1438	A449	50pf bl, *bluish*	45	15
1439	A449	60pf lil ('74)	60	15
1440	A449	70pf redsh brn	70	15
1441	A449	80pf vio bl ('74)	65	15
1442	A449	1m olive	90	15
1443	A449a	2m lake	1.90	15
1443A	A449a	3m rose lil ('74)	2.50	60
		Nos. 1430-1443A (15)	9.58	
		Set value		1.25

See Nos. 1610-1617, 2071-2085.

Lebachia Speciosa (Oldest Conifer) A450

Fossils from Natural History Museum, Berlin: 15pf, Sphenopteris hollandica (carbon fern). 20pf, Pterodactylus kochi (flying reptile). 25pf, Botryopteris (permian fern). 35pf, Archaeopteryx lithographica (primitive reptile-like bird). 70pf, Odontopieura ovata (trilobite).

1973, Feb. 6 **Photo.** *Perf. 13*

1444	A450	10pf multi	15	15
1445	A450	15pf ultra, gray & blk	15	15
1446	A450	20pf yel & multi	15	15
1447	A450	25pf emer, blk & brn	15	15
1448	A450	35pf ocher & multi	15	15
1449	A450	70pf ind, blk & yel	*2.00*	*1.75*
		Set value	*2.25*	*2.00*

Bobsled Track, Oberhof — A451

1973, Feb. 13 **Litho.** *Perf. 12½x13*

1450	A451	35pf dk bl, bl & org	30	20

15th Bobsledding Championships, Oberhof.

Combines — A452

Leipzig Spring Fair: 25pf, Computerized threshing and silage producing machine.

1973, Mar. 6 **Litho.** *Perf. 13x12½*

1451	A452	10pf ol & multi	15	15
1452	A452	25pf bl & multi	18	18
		Set value		23

Firecrests A453

Songbirds: 10pf, White-winged crossbill. 15pf, Waxwing. 20pf, White-spotted and red-spotted bluethroats. 25pf, Goldfinch. 35pf, Golden oriole. 40pf, Gray wagtail. 50pf, Wall creeper.

1973, Mar. 20 **Photo.** *Perf. 14x13½*

1453	A453	5pf multi	15	15
1454	A453	10pf multi	15	15
1455	A453	15pf multi	15	15
1456	A453	20pf multi	15	15
1457	A453	25pf multi	15	15
1458	A453	35pf multi	15	15
1459	A453	40pf multi	15	15
1460	A453	50pf ocher & multi	*3.00*	*2.25*
		Set value	*3.50*	*2.75*

Copernicus and Title Page — A454

1973, Feb. 13 **Litho.** *Perf. 13½x13*

1461	A454	70pf multi	65	32

500th anniversary of the birth of Nicolaus Copernicus (1473-1543), astronomer.

Electric Locomotive — A455

Railroad Cars Manufactured in DDR: 10pf, Refrigerator car. 20pf, Long-distance coach. 25pf, Multiple tank car with pneumatic filling device. 35pf, Two-story coach. 85pf, International coaches.

1973, May 22 **Litho.** *Perf. 13x12½*

1462	A455	5pf gray & multi	15	15
1463	A455	10pf brt bl & multi	15	15
1464	A455	20pf dk bl & multi	15	15
1465	A455	25pf gray & multi	15	15
1466	A455	35pf multi	15	15
1467	A455	85pf grn & multi	*2.25*	*1.75*
		Nos. 1462-1467 (6)	*3.00*	
		Set value		*2.00*

King Lear, Staged by Wolfgang Langhoff A456

Great Theatrical Productions: 25pf, Midsummer Marriage, staged by Walter Felsenstein. 35pf, Mother Courage, staged by Bertolt Brecht.

1973, May 29 **Photo.** *Perf. 13*

1468	A456	10pf mar, rose & yel	15	15
1469	A456	25pf vio bl, lt bl & rose	15	15
1470	A456	35pf dk gray, bis & bl	*85*	*70*
		Set value	*1.00*	*80*

Goethe and his Home in Weimar — A457

Fireworks, TV Tower, World Clock — A458

Designs (Portraits and Houses): 15pf, Christoph Martin Wieland. 20pf, Friedrich von Schiller. 25pf, Johann Gottfried Herder. 35pf, Lucas Cranach, the Elder. 50pf, Franz Liszt.

1973, June 26 **Litho.** *Perf. 12½x13*

1471	A457	10pf bl & multi	15	15
1472	A457	15pf multi	15	15
1473	A457	20pf multi	15	15
1474	A457	25pf multi	15	15
1475	A457	35pf grn & multi	15	15
1476	A457	50pf multi	*1.65*	*90*
		Set value	*2.00*	*1.25*

Famous men and their homes in Weimar.

1973

Designs (Festival Emblem and): 15pf, Vietnamese and European men, book and girder. 20pf, Construction workers and valve. 30pf, Negro and European students, dam and retort. 35pf, Emblems of World Federation of Democratic Youth and International Students Union. 50pf, Brandenburg Gate.

1477	A458	5pf vio bl & multi	15	15
a.		Bklt. pane of 4	70	
1478	A458	15pf ol & multi	15	15
1479	A458	20pf multi	15	15
a.		Bklt. pane of 4	75	
1480	A458	30pf bl & multi	*1.25*	*90*
1481	A458	35pf grn & multi	15	15
		Set value	*1.50*	*1.00*

Souvenir Sheet

1482	A458	50pf aqua & multi	80	60

10th Festival of Youths and Students, Berlin, July 1973.

Issue dates: Nos. 1477-1481, July 3; No. 1482, July 26.

Ulbricht Type of 1961-67

1973, Aug. 8 **Engr.** *Perf. 14*
Size: 24x28½mm

1483	A189	20pf black	25	15

In memory of Walter Ulbricht (1893-1973), chairman of Council of State.

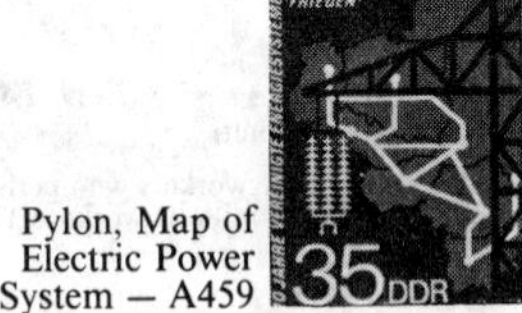

Pylon, Map of Electric Power System — A459

1973, Aug. 14 **Photo.** *Perf. 14*

1484	A459	35pf mag, org & lt bl	40	20

10th anniversary of the united East European electric power system "Peace."

Sports Equipment A460

Design: 25pf, Sailboat, guitar, electric drill.

1973, Aug. 28 **Photo.** *Perf. 14*

1485	A460	10pf multi	15	15
1486	A460	25pf multi	28	15
		Set value		20

Leipzig Fall Fair and EXPOVITA exhibition for leisure time equipment.

Militiaman and Emblem — A461

Designs: 20pf, Militia guarding border at Brandenburg Gate. 50pf, Representatives of Red Veterans' League, International Brigade in Spain and Workers' Militia in DDR (vert.).

1973, Sept. 11 **Litho.** *Perf. 13x12½*

1487	A461	10pf multi	15	15
1488	A461	20pf tan, red & blk	26	15
		Set value	35	20

Souvenir Sheet
Perf. 12½x13

1489 A461 50pf multi 75 48

20th anniversary of Workers' Militia of the German Democratic Republic.

Globe and Red Flag Emblem — A462

1973, Sept. 11 Photo. *Perf. 13½x14*
1490 A462 20pf gold & red 25 15

15th anniversary of the review "Problems of Peace and Socialism," published in Prague in 28 languages.

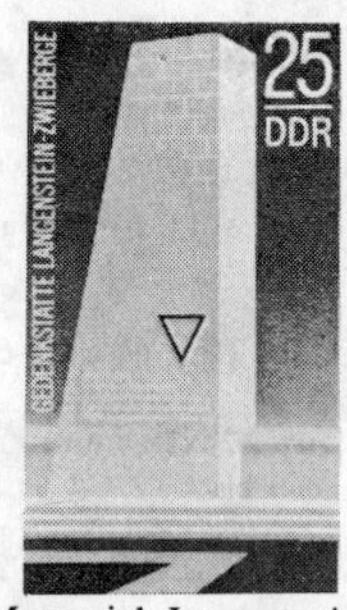

Memorial, Langenstein-Zwieberge — A463

1973, Sept. 18 *Perf. 14x13½*
1491 A463 25pf multi 35 15

In memory of the workers who perished in the subterranean munitions works at Langenstein-Zwieberge.

UN Headquarters, NY, UN and DDR Emblems — A464

1973, Sept. 21 *Perf. 13*
1492 A464 35pf multi 50 15

Admission of the DDR to the UN.

Union Emblem A465 Rocket Launching A466

1973, Oct. 11 Photo. *Perf. 14x13½*
1493 A465 35pf sil & multi 35 15

8th Congress of the World Federation of Trade Unions, Varna, Bulgaria.

1973, Oct. 23 *Perf. 14*

Designs: 20pf, Emblem with map of Russia and hammer and sickle (horiz.). 25pf, Oil refinery, Ryazan.

1494 A466 10pf vio bl & multi 15 15
1495 A466 20pf vio bl, red & sil 15 15
1496 A466 25pf multi *90 60*
Set value *1.00 68*

Soviet Science and Technology Days in German Democratic Republic.

Child with Doll, by Christian L. Vogel — A467

Paintings: 15pf, Madonna with the Rose, by Parmigianino. 20pf, Woman with Plaited Blond Hair, by Rubens. 25pf, Lady in White, by Titian. 35pf, Archimedes, by Domenico Fetti. 70pf, Bouquet with Blue Iris, by Jan D. de Heem.

1973, Nov. 13 Photo. *Perf. 14*
1497 A467 10pf gold & multi 15 15
1498 A467 15pf gold & multi 15 15
1499 A467 20pf gold & multi 15 15
1500 A467 25pf gold & multi 15 15
1501 A467 35pf gold & multi 16 15
1502 A467 70pf gold & multi *2.50 1.75*
Set value *2.90 2.10*

Human Rights Flame A468

1973, Nov. 20 *Perf. 13*
1503 A468 35pf dp rose, dk car & sil 40 15

25th anniv. of the Universal Declaration of Human Rights.

Boy Holding Pike — A469 Edwin Hoernle — A470

Designs: Various scenes from Russian Folktale "At the Bidding of the Pike."

1973, Dec. 4 Litho. *Perf. 13x13½*
1504 A469 5pf multi 42 30
1505 A469 10pf multi 42 48
1506 A469 15pf multi 42 30
1507 A469 20pf multi 42 30
1508 A469 25pf multi 42 48
1509 A469 35pf multi 42 30
Nos. 1505-1509 (5) 2.10 1.86

#1504-1509 printed together in sheets of 6.

1974 Litho. *Perf. 13½x13*

Portraits: No. 1511, Etkar Andre. No. 1512, Paul Merker. No. 1513, Hermann Duncker. No. 1514, Fritz Heckert. No. 1515, Otto Grotewohl. No. 1516, Wilhelm Florin. No. 1517, Georg Handke. No. 1518, Rudolf Breitscheid. No. 1519, Kurt Bürger. No. 1519A Carl Moltmann.

1510 A470 10pf gray grn 15 15
1511 A470 10pf rose vio 15 15
1512 A470 10pf dark blue 15 15
1513 A470 10pf brown 15 15
1514 A470 10pf dl grn 15 15
1515 A470 10pf red brn 15 15
1516 A470 10pf vio bl 15 15
1517 A470 10pf olive brn 15 15
1518 A470 10pf slate grn 15 15
1519 A470 10pf dull vio 15 15
1519A A470 10pf brown 15 15
Set value 1.30 90

Leaders of German labor movement.
Issue dates: Nos. 1510-1517, Jan. 8; others July 9.

Flags of Comecon Members A471

1974, Jan. 22 Photo. *Perf. 13*
1520 A471 20pf red & multi 20 15

25th anniversary of the Council of Mutual Economic Assistanče (Comecon).

Pablo Neruda and Chilean Flag A472

1974, Jan. 22 *Perf. 14*
1521 A472 20pf multi 20 15

Pablo Neruda (Neftali Ricardo Reyes, 1904-1973), Chilean poet.

Echinopsis Multiplex A473 Fieldball A474

Various Flowering Cacti: 10pf, Lobivia haageana. 15pf, Parodia sanguiniflora. 20pf, Gymnocal. monvillei. 25pf, Neoporteria rapifera. 35pf, Notocactus concinnus.

1974, Feb. 12 Photo. *Perf. 14*
1522 A473 5pf multi 15 15
1523 A473 10pf tan & multi 15 15
1524 A473 15pf grn & multi *2.00 1.40*
1525 A473 20pf multi 15 15
1526 A473 25pf vio & multi 18 15
1527 A473 35pf multi 25 15
Nos. 1522-1527 (6) *2.88*
Set value *1.70*

1974, Feb. 26 Litho. *Perf. 13*

Design: Various fieldball scenes.

1528 A474 5pf grn & multi *35 28*
1529 A474 10pf grn & multi *35 28*
1530 A474 35pf grn & multi *35 28*
a. Strip of 3. Nos. 1528-1530 *1.25 1.00*

8th World Fieldball Championships for Men.

Power Testing Station A475 Rhodophyllus Sinuatus A476

Leipzig Spring Fair: 25pf, Robotron EC 2040 data processer (horiz.).

1974, Mar. 5 Photo. *Perf. 14*
1531 A475 10pf multi 15 15
1532 A475 25pf multi 28 15
Set value 20

1974, Mar. 19 Litho. *Perf. 13x13½*

European Poisonous Mushrooms: 10pf, Boletus satanas. 15pf, Amanita pantherina. 20pf, Amanita muscaria. 25pf, Gyromitra esculenta. 30pf, Inocybe patouillardii. 35pf, Amanita phalloides. 40pf, Clitocybe dealbata.

1533 A476 5pf buff & multi 15 15
1534 A476 10pf buff & multi 15 15
1535 A476 15pf buff & multi 15 15
1536 A476 20pf buff & multi 15 15
1537 A476 25pf buff & multi 18 15
1538 A476 30pf buff & multi 22 15
1539 A476 35pf buff & multi 22 15
1540 A476 40pf buff & multi *1.75 1.25*
Nos. 1533-1540 (8) *2.97*
Set value *1.75*

Gustav Robert Kirchhoff — A477

Portraits: 10pf, Immanuel Kant. 20pf, Ehm Welk. 25pf, Johann Gottfried Herder. 35pf, Lion Feuchtwanger.

1974, Mar. 26 Litho. *Perf. 13½x13*
1541 A477 5pf blk & gray 15 15
1542 A477 10pf vio bl & dl bl 15 15
1543 A477 20pf mar & rose 15 15
1544 A477 25pf sl grn & grn 16 15
1545 A477 35pf brn & lt brn *80 52*
Set value *1.20 75*

"Peace" A477a

1974, Apr. 16 *Perf. 13*
1548 A477a 35pf sil & multi 35 15

25th anniv. of the 1st World Peace Congress.

Truck Driver and Arms of DDR A477b

1974, Apr. 30 Photo. *Perf. 13*

1549	A477b	10pf shown	15	15
1550	A477b	20pf Students	15	15
1551	A477b	25pf Woman worker	15	15
1552	A477b	35pf Family	*95*	*80*
		Set value		*90*

25th anniv. of the DDR.

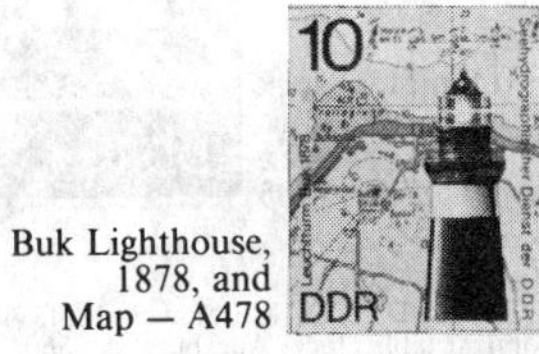

Buk Lighthouse, 1878, and Map — A478

Lighthouses, Maps and Nautical Charts: 15pf, Warnemünde, 1898. 20pf, Darsser Ort, 1848. 35pf, Arkona, 1827 and 1902. 40pf, Greifswalder Oie, 1855.

1974, May 7 Litho. *Perf. 14*

1553	A478	10pf multi	15	15
1554	A478	15pf multi	15	15
1555	A478	20pf multi	15	15
1556	A478	35pf multi	15	15
1557	A478	40pf multi	*1.10*	*90*
		Set value	*1.50*	*1.10*

Hydrographic Service of German Democratic Republic. See Nos. 1645-1649.

The Ages of Man, by C. D. Friedrich — A479

C. D. Friedrich, Self-portrait — A480

Paintings by Friedrich: 10pf, Two Men Observing Moon. 25pf, The Heath near Dresden. 35pf, View of Elbe Valley.

1974, May 21 Photo. *Perf. 13½*

1558	A479	10pf gold & multi	15	15
1559	A479	20pf gold & multi	15	15
1560	A479	25pf gold & multi	*1.10*	*1.00*
1561	A479	35pf gold & multi	20	15
		Set value		*1.10*

Souvenir Sheet

Engr.

Perf. 14x13½

1562	A480	70pf sepia	*1.25*	*1.25*

200th anniversary of the birth of Caspar David Friedrich (1774-1840), German Romantic painter.

Plauen Lace — A481

Designs: Various Plauen lace patterns.

1974, June 11 Litho. *Perf. 13*

1563	A481	10pf vio, lil & blk	15	15
1564	A481	20pf brn ol & blk	15	15
1565	A481	25pf bl, lt bl & blk	*1.10*	*80*
1566	A481	35pf lil rose, rose & blk	24	15
		Set value		*1.00*

Trotter — A482

Designs: 10pf, Thoroughbred hurdling (vert.). 25pf, Haflinger breed horses. 35pf, British thoroughbred race horse.

Perf. 14x13½, 13½x14

1974, Aug. 13 Photo.

1570	A482	10pf ol & multi	15	15
1571	A482	20pf multi	15	15
1572	A482	25pf lt bl & multi	*80*	*70*
1573	A482	35pf ocher & multi	20	15
		Set value		*95*

International Horse Breeders' of Socialist Countries Congress, Berlin.

Crane Lifting Diesel Locomotive — A483

Leipzig Fall Fair: 25pf, Sugar beet harvester, type KS6.

1974, Aug. 27 Litho. *Perf. 13x12½*

1574	A483	10pf multi	15	15
1575	A483	25pf org & multi	28	15
		Set value		20

Miniature China and Mirror Exhibits — A484

Designs: Scenes from 18th century Thuringia, Dolls' Village, Arnstadt Castle Museum.

1974, Sept. 10 Photo. *Perf. 14x13½*

1576	A484	5pf shown	15	15
1577	A484	10pf Harlequin barker at Fair	15	15
1578	A484	15pf Wine tasters	15	15
1579	A484	20pf Cooper and apprentice	15	15
1580	A484	25pf Bagpiper	*1.50*	*1.40*
1581	A484	35pf Butcher and beggar, women	22	18
		Nos. 1576-1581 (6)	*2.32*	
		Set value		*1.75*

Bound Guerrillas, Ardeatine Caves, Rome — A485

Design: No. 1583, Resistance Fighters, monument near Chateaubriant, France.

1974, Sept. 24 *Perf. 13½x14*

1582	A485	35pf grn, blk & red	40	32
1583	A485	35pf bl, blk & red	40	32

International war memorials.

Souvenir Sheet

Family and Flag — A486

1974, Oct. 3 Photo. *Perf. 13*

1584	A486	1m multi	1.50	90

25th anniv. of the DDR.

Freighter and Paddle Steamer A487

"In Praise of Dialectics" A488

Cent. of the UPU: 20pf, Old steam locomotive and modern Diesel. 25pf, Bi-plane and jet. 35pf, Mail coach and truck.

1974, Oct. 9 *Perf. 14*

1585	A487	10pf grn & multi	15	15
1586	A487	20pf multi	15	15
1587	A487	25pf bl & multi	18	15
1588	A487	35pf multi	*1.00*	*65*
		Set value		*80*

1974, Oct. 24 Litho. *Perf. 13x13½*

Designs: 10pf+5pf, "Praise to the Revolutionaries." 25pf, "Praise to the Party." Designs are from bas-reliefs by Rossdeutscher, Jastram and Wetzel, illustrating poems by Bertholt Brecht.

1589	A488	10pf + 5pf multi	*28*	*22*
1590	A488	20pf multi	*28*	*22*
1591	A488	25pf multi	*28*	*22*
a.		Strip of 3, #1589-1591	*1.00*	*80*

DDR '74 Natl. Stamp Exhib., Karl-Marx-Stadt.

Souvenir Sheet

Drawings by Young Pioneers — A489

1974, Nov. 26 Litho. *Perf. 14*

1592	A489	Sheet of 4	*1.40*	*1.10*
a.		20pf Sun shines on everybody	*35*	*28*
b.		20pf My Friend Sascha	*35*	*28*
c.		20pf Carsten, the Best Swimmer	*35*	*28*
d.		20pf Me at the Blackboard	*35*	*28*

Young Pioneers' drawings (7-10 years old).

Man Cutting Tree, and Bird — A490

Meditating Girl, by Wilhelm Lachnit — A491

Designs: Various scenes from Russian folktale "Twittering To and Fro."

1974, Dec. 3 *Perf. 13x13½*

1593	A490	10pf multi	*50*	*30*
1594	A490	15pf multi	*50*	*45*
1595	A490	20pf multi	*50*	*30*
1596	A490	30pf multi	*50*	*30*
1597	A490	35pf multi	*50*	*45*
1598	A490	40pf multi	*50*	*30*
		Nos. 1593-1598 (6)	*3.00*	*2.10*

#1593-1598 printed together in sheets of 6.

Perf. 13½x14, 14x13½

1974, Dec. 10

Paintings: 10pf, Still Life, by Ronald Paris (horiz.). 20pf, Fisherman's House, Vitte, by Harald Hakenbeck. 35pf, Girl in Red, by Rudolf Bergander (horiz.). 70pf, The Artist's Parents, by Willi Sitte.

1599	A491	10pf multi	15	15
1600	A491	15pf multi	15	15
1601	A491	20pf multi	15	15
1602	A491	35pf multi	25	15
1603	A491	70pf multi	*1.90*	*1.25*
		Nos. 1599-1603 (5)	*2.60*	
		Set value		*1.42*

Paintings in Berlin Museums.

Banded Jasper — A492

Minerals from the collection of the Mining Academy in Freiberg: 15pf, Smoky quartz. 20pf, Topaz. 25pf, Amethyst. 35pf, Aquamarine. 70pf, Agate.

1974, Dec. 17 Photo. *Perf. 14*

1604	A492	10pf lt yel & multi	15	15
1605	A492	15pf lt yel & multi	15	15
1606	A492	20pf lt yel & multi	15	15
1607	A492	25pf lt yel & multi	20	15
1608	A492	35pf lt yel & multi	25	15
1609	A492	70pf lt yel & multi	*2.00*	*1.40*
		Nos. 1604-1609 (6)	*2.90*	
		Set value		*1.80*

Type of 1973 Coil Stamps

1974-75 Photo. *Perf. 14*

Designs: 5pf, Pelican. 10pf, Neptune Fountain. 20pf, Lenin Square. 25pf, World clock. 50pf, New Guard House. 1m, Soviet War Memorial.

Size: 21x17½mm

1610	A449	5pf bl grn ('74)	15	15
1611	A449	10pf emerald	15	15
1612	A449	20pf rose mag	24	16
1613	A449	25pf grn ('75)	22	15
1615	A449	50pf blue ('74)	50	32
1617	A449	1m olive ('74)	1.10	55
		Nos. 1610-1617 (6)	2.36	1.48

Black control number on back of every fifth stamp.

The 20pf was issued in sheets of 100 in 1975.

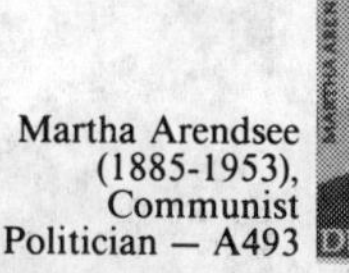

Martha Arendsee (1885-1953), Communist Politician — A493

1975, Jan. 14 Litho. *Perf. 13½x13*

1618 A493 10pf dull red 15 15

Souvenir Sheet

Peasants' War, Contemporary Woodcuts — A494

1975, Feb. 11 *Perf. 12½x13*

1619 A494 Sheet of 6 + label *3.00 1.75*
- ***a.*** 5pf Forced labor *48 24*
- ***b.*** 10pf Peasant paying tithe *48 24*
- ***c.*** 20pf Thomas Munzer *48 24*
- ***d.*** 25pf Armed peasants *48 38*
- ***e.*** 35pf Peasant, "Liberty" flag *48 38*
- ***f.*** 50pf Peasant on trial *48 24*

Peasants' War, 450th anniversary.

Black Women — A495

Designs: 20pf, Caucasian women. 25pf, Indian woman and child.

1975, Feb. 25 Litho. *Perf. 13*

1620 A495 10pf red & multi *26 20*
1621 A495 20pf red & multi *26 20*
1622 A495 25pf red & multi *26 20*
- ***a.*** Strip of 3. Nos. 1620-1622 *1.00 70*

International Women's Year 1975. Nos. 1620-1622 printed se-tenant.

Microfilm Pentakta Camera A496

Leipzig Spring Fair: 25pf, Sket cement plant.

1975, Mar. 4 Photo. *Perf. 14*

1623 A496 10pf ultra & multi 15 15
1624 A496 25pf org & multi 22 15
Set value 30 15

Hans Otto (1900-33) Actor — A497

Portraits: 10pf, Thomas Mann (1875-1955), writer. 20pf, Albert Schweitzer (1875-1965), medical missionary. 25pf, Michelangelo (1475-1564), painter and sculptor. 35pf, Andre Marie Ampere (1775-1836), scientist.

1975, Mar. 18 Litho. *Perf. 13½x13*

1625 A497 5pf dk bl 15 15
1626 A497 10pf dk car rose 15 15
1627 A497 20pf dk grn 15 15
1628 A497 25pf sepia 15 15
1629 A497 35pf vio bl *1.25 70*
Set value 1.60 90

Famous men, birth anniversaries.

Blue and Yellow Macaws, Magdeburg Zoo — A498

German Zoological Gardens: 10pf, Orangutan family, Dresden. 15pf, Siberian chamois, Halle. 20pf, Rhinoceros, Berlin. 25pf, Dwarf hippopotamus, Erfurt. 30pf, Baltic seal and pup, Rostock. 35pf, Siberian tiger, Leipzig. 50pf, Boehm's zebra, Cottbus. 20pf, 25pf, 30pf, 35pf are horiz.

Perf. 13½x13, 13x13½

1975, Mar. 25

1630 A498 5pf multi 15 15
1631 A498 10pf multi 15 15
1632 A498 15pf multi 15 15
1633 A498 20pf multi 15 15
1634 A498 25pf multi 16 15
1635 A498 30pf multi 18 15
1636 A498 35pf multi 26 15
1637 A498 50pf multi *2.00 1.00*
Nos. 1630-1637 (8) 3.20
Set value 1.50

Soldiers, Industry and Agriculture — A499

1975, May 6 Photo. *Perf. 13½x14*

1638 A499 20pf multi 20 15

20th anniversary of the signing of the Warsaw Treaty (Bulgaria, Czechoslovakia, German Democratic Rep., Hungary, Poland, Romania, USSR).

Soviet War Memorial, Berlin-Treptow A500

Ribbons, Youth Organization Emblems of DDR and USSR A501

Designs (Arms of German Democratic Rep. and): 20pf, Buchenwald Memorial (detail). 25pf, Woman reconstruction worker. 35pf, Skyscraper and statue at Orenburg (economic integration). 50pf, Soldier raising Red Flag on Reichstag Building, Berlin.

1975, May 6 *Perf. 14x13½*

1639 A500 10pf red & multi 15 15
1640 A500 20pf red & multi 15 15
1641 A500 25pf red & multi 18 15
1642 A500 35pf red & multi *75 65*
Set value 1.10 90

Souvenir Sheet

Imperf

1643 A500 50pf red & multi 65 55

30th anniversary of liberation from fascism.

1975, May 13 *Perf. 14*

1644 A501 10pf multi 15 15

Third Friendship Festival of Russian and German Youths, Halle, 1975.

Lighthouse Type of 1974

Lighthouses, Maps and Nautical Charts: 5pf, Timmendorf, 1872. 10pf, Gellen, 1905. 20pf, Sassnitz, 1904. 25pf, Dornbush, 1888. 35pf, Peenemünde, 1954.

1975, May 13 Litho. *Perf. 14*

1645 A478 5pf multi 15 15
1646 A478 10pf multi 15 15
1647 A478 20pf multi 15 15
1648 A478 25pf multi 20 15
1649 A478 35pf multi *1.10 75*
Set value 1.50 95

Hydrographic Service of the DDR.

Wilhelm Liebknecht, August Bebel — A502

Designs: 20pf, Tivoli House and front page of Protocol of Gotha. 25pf, Karl Marx and Friedrich Engels.

1975, May 21 Photo.

1650 A502 10pf buff, brn & red *20 16*
1651 A502 20pf sal, brn & red *20 16*
1652 A502 25pf buff, brn & red *20 16*

Centenary of the Congress of Gotha, the beginning of German Socialist Workers' Party. Nos. 1650-1652 printed se-tenant.

Construction Workers, Union Emblem — A503

1975, June 10 Photo. *Perf. 14*

1653 A503 20pf red & multi 25 15

Free German Association of Trade Unions (FDGB), 30th anniversary.

"Socialist Scientific Cooperation" Mosaic by Walter Womacka — A504

1975, June 10 Litho. *Perf. 13*

1654 A504 20pf multi 25 15

Eisenhüttenstadt, first socialist city of DDR, 25th anniversary.

Automatic Clock by Paulus Schuster, 1585 — A505

Clocks, Dresden Museums: 10pf, Astronomical table clock, Augsburg, c. 1560. 15pf, Automatic clock, Hans Schlottheim, c. 1600. 20pf, Table clock, Johann Heinrich Köhler, c. 1720. 25pf, Table clock, Köhler, c. 1700. 35pf, Astronomical clock, Johannes Klein, 1738.

1975, June 24 Photo. *Perf. 14*

1655 A505 5pf multi 15 15
1656 A505 10pf ultra & multi 15 15
1657 A505 15pf red & multi *1.65 1.25*
1658 A505 20pf ol & multi 15 15
1659 A505 25pf multi 15 15
1660 A505 35pf ocher & multi 22 15
Nos. 1655-1660 (6) 2.47
Set value 1.48

Dictionary, Compiled by Jacob and Wilhelm Grimm — A506

Designs: 20pf, Karl-Schwarzschild Observatory, Tautenburg near Jena. 25pf, Electron microscope and chemical plant (scientific and practical cooperation). 35pf, Intercosmos 10 satellite.

1975, July 2 Litho. *Perf. 13½x13*

1661 A506 10pf plum, ol & blk 15 15
1662 A506 20pf vio bl & blk 15 15
1663 A506 25pf grn, yel & blk 16 15
1664 A506 35pf bl & multi *95 85*
Set value 1.25 1.00

German Academy of Sciences, 275th anniversary.

Torch Bearer — A507

Designs: 20pf, Hurdling. 25pf, Diving. 35pf, Gymnast on bar.

1975, July 15 *Perf. 13½x13*

1665 A507 10pf sal rose & blk 15 15
1666 A507 20pf yel & blk 15 15
1667 A507 25pf ultra & blk 16 15
1668 A507 35pf yel grn & blk *95 75*
Set value 1.25 90

5th Children and Youths Spartakiad.

Map of Europe A508

1975, July 30 **Photo.** ***Perf. 13***

1669 A508 20pf multi 22 15

European Security and Cooperation Conference, Helsinki, July 30-Aug. 1.

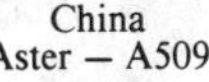
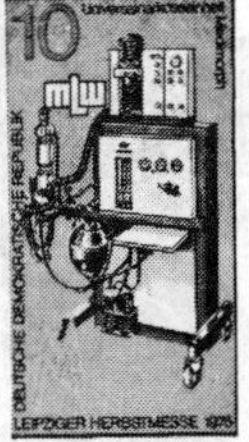

China Aster — A509

Medimorph Anesthesia Unit — A510

1975, Aug. 19 **Photo.** ***Perf. 13½x14***

1670 A509 5pf shown 15 15
1671 A509 10pf Geranium 15 15
1672 A509 20pf Transvaal daisies 15 15
1673 A509 25pf Carnation 15 15
1674 A509 35pf Chrysanthemum 20 15
1675 A509 70pf Pansies *2.50 1.25*
Nos. 1670-1675 (6) *3.30*
Set value *1.60*

1975, Aug. 28 ***Perf. 14***

Leipzig Fall Fair: 25pf, Motorcycle, type MZ TS 250 (horiz.).

1676 A510 10pf multi 15 15
1677 A510 25pf yel & multi 28 15
Set value 20

Children and Child Crossing Guard A511

Designs: 15pf, Traffic policewoman. 20pf, Policeman helping, motorist. 25pf, Motor vehicle inspection. 35pf, Volunteer instructor.

1975, Sept. 9 **Litho.** ***Perf. 13x12½***

1678 A511 10pf multi 15 15
1679 A511 15pf grn & multi *1.10* *85*
1680 A511 20pf brn & multi 15 15
1681 A511 25pf vio & multi 15 15
1682 A511 35pf multi 18 15
Set value *1.55 1.10*

Traffic police serving and instructing the public.

Soyuz Take-off — A512

Designs: 20pf, Soyuz and Apollo in space. 70pf, Spacecraft after link-up (horiz.; 79x28mm.).

Perf. 14x13½, 13½x14

1975, Sept. 15 **Photo.**

1683 A512 10pf multi 15 15
1684 A512 20pf multi 15 15
1685 A512 70pf multi *1.40* *90*
Set value *1.00*

Apollo Soyuz space test project (Russo-American space cooperation), launching July 15; link-up, July 17.

Weimar, 1630, after Merian — A513

Designs: 20pf, Buchenwald Liberation Monument (vert.). 35pf, Composite view of old and new buildings in Weimar.

1975, Sept. 23 **Litho.** ***Perf. 13½x13***

1686 A513 10pf grn, gray & blk 15 15
1687 A513 20pf red & multi 15 15
1688 A513 35pf ultra & multi *60* *45*
Set value *75* *55*

Millennium of Weimar.

Monument, Vienna — A514

1975, Oct. 14 **Photo.** ***Perf. 14x13½***

1689 A514 35pf red & multi 30 15

Memorial for the victims of the struggle for a free Austria, 1934-1945.

Louis Braille and Dots — A515

Designs: 35pf, Hands reading Braille. 50pf, Eyeball and protective glasses.

1975, Oct. 14

1690 A515 20pf gray & multi 15 15
1691 A515 35pf multi 20 15
1692 A515 50pf multi *1.25* *85*
Set value *1.00*

World Braille Year 1975. Sesquicentennial of the invention of Braille system of writing for the blind, by Louis Braille (1809-1852).

Post Office Bärenfels — A516

1975, Oct. 21 **Photo.** ***Perf. 14***

1693 A516 20pf multi 15 15

Philatelists' Day 1975. See No. B177.

Emperor Ordering Clothes — A517

Designs: Scenes from "The Emperor's New Clothes," by Hans Christian Andersen and Andersen portrait.

1975, Nov. 18 **Litho.** ***Perf. 14x13***

1694 A517 20pf ocher & multi *75* *38*
1695 A517 35pf ocher & multi *75* *75*
1696 A517 50pf ocher & multi *75* *38*
a. Sheet of 3, Nos. 1694-1696 *2.25* *1.65*

Nos. 1694-1696 issued in sheet of 3.

Tobogganing and Olympic Rings — A518

Designs (Olympic Rings and): 20pf, Speed-skating Rink, Berlin. 35pf, Figure-skating Hall, Karl-Marx Stadt. 70pf, Mass skiing at Schmiedefeld. 1m, Innsbruck and surrounding mountains.

1975, Dec. 2 **Photo.** ***Perf. 14***

1697 A518 5pf multi 15 15
1698 A518 20pf ol & multi 15 15
1699 A518 35pf multi 22 15
1700 A518 70pf multi *1.25 1.00*
Nos. 1697-1700,B178-B179 (6) *2.14 1.75*

Souvenir Sheet

1701 A518 1m ultra & multi *1.40 1.10*

12th Winter Olympic Games, Innsbruck, Austria, Feb. 4-15, 1976. No. 1701 contains one stamp (size: 32x27mm).

Wilhelm Pieck A519

Ernst Thälmann (1886-1944) A520

1975, Dec. 30 **Litho.** ***Perf. 13½x13***

1702 A519 10pf lt ultra & blk 15 15

Pres. Pieck (1876-1960), birth cent.

1976, Jan. 13 ***Perf. 13½x13***

Labor Leaders: No. 1704, Georg Schumann (1886-1945). No. 1705, Wilhelm Koenen (1886-1963). No. 1706, John Schehr (1896-1934).

1703 A520 10pf rose & blk 15 15
1704 A520 10pf emer & blk 15 15
1705 A520 10pf ocher & blk 15 15
1706 A520 10pf vio & blk 15 15
Set value 32 25

See Nos. 1852-1854.

Silbermann Organ, Rötha — A521

Silbermann Organs: 20pf, Freiberg. 35pf, Fraureuth. 50pf, Dresden.

1976, Jan. 27 **Photo.** ***Perf. 14***

1707 A521 10pf grn & multi 15 15
1708 A521 20pf red & multi 15 15
1709 A521 35pf multi 18 15
1710 A521 50pf brn & multi *1.25* *95*

Organs built by Gottfried Silbermann (1683-1753).

Souvenir Sheet

Richard Sorge — A522

1976, Feb. 3 **Litho.** ***Imperf.***

1711 A522 1m multi *1.50 1.00*

Dr. Richard Sorge (1895-1944), Soviet intelligence agent. No. 1711 contains one stamp with simulated perforations.

Military Flag, Sailor, Soldier, Aviator — A523

Design: 20pf, Military flag, ships, tanks, missile and planes.

1976, Feb. 24 **Litho.** ***Perf. 13½x14***

1712 A523 10pf multi 15 15
1713 A523 20pf multi 25 15
Set value 15

National People's Army, 20th anniversary.

Telephone A524

Apartment House, Leipzig A525

1976, Mar. 2 ***Perf. 13***

1714 A524 20pf lt bl 25 15

Centenary of first telephone call by Alexander Graham Bell, March 10, 1876.

1976, Mar. 9 **Photo.** ***Perf. 14***

Design: 25pf, Ocean super trawler (horiz.).

1715 A525 10pf grn & multi 15 15
1716 A525 25pf vio bl, blk & grn 32 15
Set value 15

Leipzig Spring Fair.

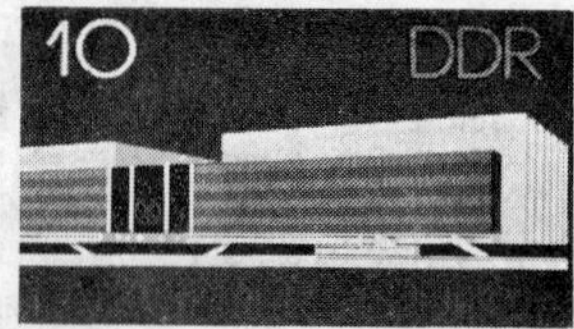

Palace of the Republic — A526

1976, Apr. 22 Photo. *Perf. 14*
1717 A526 10pf vio bl & multi 40 15

Inauguration of Palace of the Republic, Berlin. See No. 1721.

Post Office Radar Station — A527

Marx, Engels, Lenin and Party Flag — A528

1976, Apr. 27 Photo. *Perf. 13½x14*
1718 A527 20pf multi 25 15

Intersputnik 1976.

Perf. 14x13½, 13½x14
1976, May 11

Designs: 20pf, New factories and apartment houses, party flag (horiz.). 1m, Palace of the Republic.

1719 A528 10pf dp mag, gold & red 18 15
1720 A528 20pf multi 35 15
Set value 15

Souvenir Sheet
Perf. 14
1721 A526 1m multi *1.50 1.10*

9th Congress of Unity Party (SED).

Peace Bicycle Race and Olympic Rings — A529

Designs: 20pf, Town and sport halls, Suhl. 25pf, Regatta course, Brandenburg. 70pf, 1500-meter race. 1m, Central Stadium, Leipzig.

1976, May 18 Photo. *Perf. 13½x14*
1722 A529 5pf grn & multi 15 15
1723 A529 20pf bl & multi 15 15
1724 A529 25pf multi 16 15
1725 A529 70pf ultra & multi *2.00 1.40*
Nos. 1722-1725,B180-B181 (6) 2.86
Set value 1.85

Souvenir Sheet
Perf. 14
1726 A529 1m multi *1.65 1.25*

21st Olympic Games, Montreal, Canada, July 17-Aug. 1. No. 1726 contains one stamp (32x27mm).

Ribbons and Emblem A530

Design: 20pf, Young man and woman, industrial installations.

1976, May 25 *Perf. 14*
1727 A530 10pf bl & multi 15 15
1728 A530 20pf multi 25 15
Set value 15

10th Parliamentary Meeting of the Free German Youth Organization.

Himantoglossum Hircinum A531

Dancer at Rest, by Walter Arnold A532

Designs: European orchids.

1976, June 15 Litho. *Perf. 12½x13*
1729 A531 10pf *shown* 15 15
1730 A531 20pf *Dactylorhiza incarnata* 15 15
1731 A531 25pf *Anacamptis pyramidalis* 15 15
1732 A531 35pf *Dactylorhiza sambucina* 20 15
1733 A531 40pf *Orchis coriophora* 22 16
1734 A531 50pf *Cypripedium calceolus* *2.00 1.50*
Nos. 1729-1734 (6) 2.87 2.26

1976, June 22 Photo. *Perf. 14*

Small Sculptures: 10pf, Shetland Pony, by Heinrich Drake (horiz.). 25pf, "At the Beach," by Ludwig Engelhardt. 35pf, Hermann Duncker, by Walter Howard. 50pf, "The Conversation," by Gustav Weidanz.

1735 A532 10pf blk & bl grn 15 15
1736 A532 20pf ocher & blk 15 15
1737 A532 25pf ocher & blk 15 15
1738 A532 35pf yel grn & blk 15 15
1739 A532 50pf brick red & blk *2.00 1.00*
Nos. 1735-1739 (5) 2.60
Set value 1.20

Marx, Engels, Lenin, Red Flags, Berlin Buildings A533

1976, June 29 Photo. *Perf. 14*
1740 A533 20pf bl, red & dk red 25 15

European Communist Workers' Congress, Berlin.

Coronation Coach, 1790 A534

Historic Coaches: 20pf, Open carriage, Russia, 1800. 25pf, Court landau, Saxony, 1840. 35pf, State carriage, Saxony, 1860. 40pf, Mail coach, 1850. 50pf, Town carriage, Saxony, 1889.

1976, July 27
1741 A534 10pf multi 15 15
1742 A534 20pf multi 15 15
1743 A534 25pf multi 15 15
1744 A534 35pf multi 18 15
1745 A534 40pf multi 20 15
1746 A534 50pf multi *2.50 1.90*
Nos. 1741-1746 (6) 3.33 2.65

View of Gera A535

Design: 10pf+5pf, View of Gera, c. 1652.

1976, Aug. 5 Litho. *Perf. 13*
1747 A535 10pf + 5pf multi 22 20
1748 A535 20pf multi 22 20
a. Pair, #1747-1748 + label 50 45

4th German Youth Philatelic Exhib., Gera.

Boxer — A536

Dogs: 10pf, Airedale terrier. 20pf, German shepherd. 25pf, Collie. 35pf, Giant schnauzer. 70pf, Great Dane.

1976, Aug. 17 *Perf. 14*
1749 A536 5pf multi 15 15
1750 A536 10pf multi 15 15
1751 A536 20pf multi 15 15
1752 A536 25pf multi 15 15
1753 A536 35pf multi 18 15
1754 A536 70pf multi *2.50 1.25*
Nos. 1749-1754 (6) 3.28
Set value 1.65

Oil Distillery A537

Design: 25pf, German Library, Leipzig.

1976, Sept. 1 *Perf. 13x12½*
1755 A537 10pf multi 15 15
1756 A537 25pf multi 24 15
Set value 22

Leipzig Fall Fair.

Templin Lake Bridge — A538

Designs: 15pf, Overpass, Berlin-Adlergestell. 20pf, Elbe River Bridge, Rosslau. 25pf, Göltzschtal Viaduct. 35pf, Elbe River Bridge, Magdeburg. 50pf, Grosser Dreesch Overpass, Schwerin.

1976, Sept. 21 Photo. *Perf. 14*
1757 A538 10pf multi 15 15
1758 A538 15pf multi 15 15
1759 A538 20pf multi 15 15
1760 A538 25pf multi 16 15
1761 A538 35pf multi 20 15
1762 A538 50pf multi *2.50 1.75*
Nos. 1757-1762 (6) 3.31
Set value 2.10

Memorial Monument (detail), Budapest — A539

1976, Oct. 5 Photo. *Perf. 14*
1763 A539 35pf tan & multi 40 15

Memorial to World War II victims.

Brass Jug, c. 1500 — A540

Guppy — A541

Artistic Handicraft Works: 20pf, Faience vase with lid, c. 1710. 25pf, Porcelain centerpiece (woman carrying bowl), c. 1768. 35pf, Porter, gilded silver, c. 1700. 70pf, Art Nouveau glass vase, c. 1900.

1976, Oct. 19
1764 A540 10pf dk car multi 15 15
1765 A540 20pf ultra & multi 15 15
1766 A540 25pf grn & multi 15 15
1767 A540 35pf vio bl & multi 20 15
1768 A540 70pf red brn & multi *2.25 1.75*
Nos. 1764-1768 (5) 2.90
Set value 2.00

1976, Nov. 9 Litho. *Perf. 13½x13*

Designs: Various guppies.

1769 A541 10pf multicolored 15 15
1770 A541 15pf multicolored 15 15
1771 A541 20pf multicolored 15 15
1772 A541 25pf multicolored 15 15
1773 A541 35pf multicolored 15 15
1774 A541 70pf multicolored *1.90 1.50*
Nos. 1769-1774 (6) 2.65
Set value 1.75

Vessels, c. 3000 B.C. — A542

Designs: 20pf, Cult cart, c. 1300 B.C. 25pf, Roman gold coin, 270-273 A.D. 35pf, Gold pendant, 950 A.D. 70pf, Glass cup, 3rd century A.D.

1976, Nov. 23 Photo. *Perf. 13*
1775 A542 10pf multicolored 15 15
1776 A542 20pf multicolored 15 15
1777 A542 25pf multicolored 15 15
1778 A542 35pf multicolored 16 15
1779 A542 70pf multicolored *1.90 1.40*
Nos. 1775-1779 (5) 2.51
Set value 1.60

Archaeological finds in DDR.

"Air," by Rosalba Carriera – A543

Rumpelstiltskin and King – A544

Paintings, Dresden Museum: 15pf, Virgin and Child, by Murillo. 20pf, Woman Viola da Gamba Player, by Bernardo Strozzi. 25pf, Ariadne Forsaken, by Angelica Kauffmann. 35pf, Old Man with Black Cap, by Bartolomeo Nazzari. 70pf, Officer Reading a Letter, by Gerard Terborch.

1976, Dec. 14 Photo. *Perf. 13½x14*

1780 A543 10pf multicolored 15 15
1781 A543 15pf multicolored 15 15
1782 A543 20pf multicolored 15 15
1783 A543 25pf multicolored 15 15
1784 A543 35pf multicolored 22 15
1785 A543 70pf multicolored *2.75 1.75*
Nos. 1780-1785 (6) *3.57*
Set value *2.00*

1976, Dec. 14 Litho. *Perf. 13*

Designs: Scenes from fairy tale "Rumpelstiltskin."

1786 A544 5pf multicolored 42 20
1787 A544 10pf multicolored 42 28
1788 A544 15pf multicolored 42 20
1789 A544 20pf multicolored 42 20
1790 A544 25pf multicolored 42 28
1791 A544 30pf multicolored 42 20
Nos. 1786-1791 (6) 2.52 1.36

#1786-1791 printed se-tenant in sheet of 6.

Arnold Zweig and Quotation A545

Designs: 20pf, Otto von Guericke and Magdeburg hemispheres. 35pf, Albrecht D. Thaer, wheat, plow and sheep. 40pf, Gustav Hertz and diagram of separation of isotopes.

1977, Feb. 8 Litho. *Perf. 13x12½*

1792 A545 10pf rose & blk 15 15
1793 A545 20pf gray & blk 15 15
1794 A545 35pf lt grn & blk 18 15
1795 A545 40pf bl & blk *95 75*
Set value *95*

Honoring Arnold Zweig (1887-1968), novelist; Otto von Guericke (1602-1686), physicist; Albrecht D. Thaer (1752-1828), agronomist and physician; Gustav Hertz (1887-1975), physicist.

Spring near Plaue – A546

Natural Monuments: 20pf, Small Organ, Johnsdorf. 25pf, Ivenacker Oaks, Reuterstadt. 35pf, Stone Rose, Saalburg. 50pf, Rauenscher Stein (boulder), Furstenwalde.

1977, Feb. 24 Litho. *Perf. 12½x13*

1796 A546 10pf multicolored 15 15
1797 A546 20pf multicolored 15 15
1798 A546 25pf multicolored 15 15
1799 A546 35pf multicolored 18 15
1800 A546 50pf multicolored *1.75 1.00*
Nos. 1796-1800 (5) *2.38*
Set value *1.25*

Fair Building, Book Fair A547

Leipzig Spring Fair: 25pf, Wide aluminum roll casting machine, Nachterstedt factory.

1977, Mar. 8 Photo. *Perf. 14*

1801 A547 10pf multicolored 15 15
1802 A547 25pf multicolored 28 15
Set value 20

Costume Senftenberg A548

Start after Wheel Change A549

Sorbian Costumes from: 20pf, Bautzen. 25pf, Klitten. 35pf, Nochten. 70pf, Muskau.

1977, Mar. 22

1803 A548 10pf multicolored 15 15
1804 A548 20pf multicolored 15 15
1805 A548 25pf multicolored 15 15
1806 A548 35pf multicolored 18 15
1807 A548 70pf multicolored *2.00 1.40*
Nos. 1803-1807 (5) *2.63 2.00*

1977, Apr. 19 Photo. *Perf. 14*

Designs: 20pf, Sprint. 35pf, At finish line.

1808 A549 10pf multicolored *30 24*
1809 A549 20pf multicolored *30 24*
1810 A549 35pf multicolored *30 24*

30th International Peace Bicycling Race. Nos. 1808-1810 printed se-tenant.

Carl Friedrich Gauss A550

1977, Apr. 19 Litho. *Perf. 13x12½*

1811 A550 20pf lt ultra & blk 25 15

Carl Friedrich Gauss (1777-1855), mathematician, 200th birth anniversary.

Flags and Handshake A551

1977, May 3 Photo. *Perf. 13*

1812 A551 20pf vio bl & multi 25 15

9th German Trade Union Congress, Berlin.

VKM Channel Converter, Filter and ITU Emblem – A552

1977, May 17 Litho. *Perf. 14*

1813 A552 20pf multi 25 15

International Telecommunications Day.

Pistol Shooting A553

Designs: 20pf, Deep-sea diver. 35pf, Radio controlled model boat.

1977, May 17 Photo.

1814 A553 10pf lt grn & multi 15 15
1815 A553 20pf lt bl & multi 15 15
1816 A553 35pf sal & multi *75 52*
Set value *90 60*

Organization for Physical and Technical Training.

Accordion, c. 1900 – A554

Designs: 20pf, Treble viola da gamba, 1747. 25pf, Oboe, 1785, Clarinet, 1830 and flute, 1817. 35pf, Concert zither, 1891. 70pf, Trumpet, 1860.

1977, June 14

1817 A554 10pf multicolored 15 15
1818 A554 20pf multicolored 15 15
1819 A554 25pf multicolored 15 15
1820 A554 35pf multicolored 16 15
1821 A554 70pf multicolored *2.25 1.90*
Nos. 1817-1821 (5) *2.86*
Set value *2.15*

Vogtland musical instruments from Markneukirchen Museum.

Mercury and Argus, by Rubens – A555

Rubens Paintings in Dresden Gallery: 10pf, Bath of Bathsheba (vert.). 20pf, The Drunk Hercules (vert.). 25pf, Diana Returning from the Hunt. 35pf, Old Woman with Brazier (vert.). 50pf, Leda and the Swan.

1977, June 28 Photo. *Perf. 14*

1822 A555 10pf multicolored 15 15
1823 A555 15pf multicolored 15 15
1824 A555 20pf multicolored 15 15
1825 A555 25pf multicolored 15 15
1826 A555 35pf multicolored 18 15
1827 A555 50pf multicolored *2.25 1.25*
Nos. 1822-1827 (6) *3.03*
Set value *1.45*

Peter Paul Rubens (1577-1640), Flemish painter, 400th birth anniversary.

Souvenir Sheet

Wreath, Flags of USSR and DDR – A556

1977, June 28

1828 A556 50pf multicolored *1.00* *70*

Society for German-Soviet Friendship, 30th anniversary.

Tractor with Plow – A557

Designs: 20pf, Fertilizer-spreader. 25pf, Potato digger and loader. 35pf, High-pressure harvester. 50pf, Rotating milking machine.

1977, July 12 Litho. *Perf. 13x12½*

1829 A557 10pf multicolored 15 15
1830 A557 20pf multicolored 15 15
1831 A557 25pf multicolored 15 15
1832 A557 35pf multicolored 18 15
1833 A557 50pf multicolored *2.00 1.40*
Nos. 1829-1833 (5) *2.63*
Set value *1.55*

Motorized modern agriculture.

High Jump A558

Designs: 20pf, Hurdles, girls. 35pf, Dancing. 40pf, Torch bearer and flags.

1977, July 19

1834 A558 5pf red & multi 15 15
1835 A558 20pf lt grn & multi 15 15
1836 A558 35pf grn & multi 18 15
1837 A558 40pf bl & multi *1.90 1.00*
Nos. 1834-1837,B183-B184 (6) *4.33*
Set value *1.30*

6th Gymnastics and Sports Festival and 6th Children's and Youth Spartacist Games.

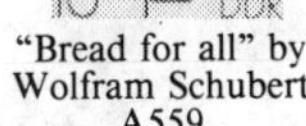

"Bread for all" by Wolfram Schubert A559

Konsument Department Store, Leipzig A560

Design: 25pf, "When Communists Dream," by Walter Womacka (detail) and Sozphilex emblem.

1977, Aug. 16 Photo. *Perf. 14*

1838 A559 10pf multicolored 18 15
 a. Souvenir sheet of 4 1.00 60
1839 A559 25pf multicolored 42 28
 a. Souvenir sheet of 4 2.50 1.50

SOZPHILEX '77 Philatelic Exhibition, Berlin, Aug. 19-28. See No. B185.

1977, Aug. 30

Design: 25pf, Glasses and wooden plate.

1840	A560	10pf bl & multi	15	15
1841	A560	25pf multicolored	25	15
		Set value	35	15

Leipzig Fall Fair.

Souvenir Sheet

Dzerzhinski and Quotation from Mayakovsky — A561

1977, Sept. 6 Litho. *Perf. 12½x13*

1842	A561	Sheet of 2	*1.00*	*70*
a.		20pf multi	*32*	*22*
b.		35pf multi	*55*	*42*

Feliks E. Dzerzhinski (1877-1926), organizer and head of Russian Secret Police (Cheka), birth centenary.

Muldenthal Locomotive, 1861 — A562

Designs: 10pf, Trolley car, Dresden, 1896. 20pf, First successful German plane, 1909. 25pf, 3-wheel car "Phäno-mobile," 1924. 35pf, Passenger steamship on the Elbe, 1837.

1977, Sept. 13 Photo. *Perf. 14*

1843	A562	5pf grn & multi	15	15
1844	A562	10pf grn & multi	15	15
1845	A562	20pf grn & multi	18	15
1846	A562	25pf grn & multi	22	15
1847	A562	35pf grn & multi	*2.00*	*70*
		Nos. 1843-1847 (5)	*2.70*	
		Set value		*85*

Transportation Museum, Dresden.

Cruiser "Aurora" A563

Designs: 25pf, Storming of the Winter Palace. 1m, Lenin (vert.).

1977, Sept. 20

1848	A563	10pf multicolored	*20*	*15*
1849	A563	25pf multicolored	*50*	*25*

Souvenir Sheet

Perf. 12½x13

1850	A563	1m car & blk	*1.50*	*1.10*

60th anniversary of the Russian Revolution.

Set Values

A 15-cent minimum now applies to individual stamps and sets. Where the 15-cent minimum per stamp would increase the "value" of a set beyond retail, there is a "Set Value" notation giving the retail value of the set.

Mother Russia and Obelisk — A564

1977, Sept. 20 Litho. *Perf. 14*

1851	A564	35pf multicolored	35	15

Soviet soldiers' memorial, Berlin-Schönholz.

Labor Leaders Type of 1976

Portraits: No. 1852, Ernst Meyer (1887-1930). No. 1853, August Fröhlich (1877-1966). No. 1854, Gerhart Eisler (1897-1968).

1977, Oct. 18 Litho. *Perf. 14*

1852	A520	10pf ol & brn	15	15
1853	A520	10pf rose & brn	15	15
1854	A520	10pf lt bl & blk brn	15	15
		Set value	30	20

Souvenir Sheet

Heinrich von Kleist, by Peter Friedl, 1801 — A565

1977, Oct. 18

1855	A565	1m multicolored	*1.90*	*1.40*

Heinrich von Kleist (1777-1811), poet and playwright, birth bicentenary.

Rocket A566

Design: 20pf, as 10pf, design reversed.

1977, Nov. 8 Photo. *Perf. 14*

1856	A566	10pf red, blk & sil	*20*	*16*
1857	A566	20pf ultra, blk & gold	*20*	*16*
a.		Pair, #1856-1857 + label	*52*	*42*

20th Central Young Craftsmen's Exhibition (Masters of Tomorrow).

Mouflons A567

Children Visiting Firehouse A568

Hunting in East Germany: 15pf, Red deer. 20pf, Retriever with pheasant, hunter. 25pf, Red fox, wild duck. 35pf, Tractor driver saving fawn. 70pf, Wild boars.

1977, Nov. 15

1858	A567	10pf multicolored	15	15
1859	A567	15pf multicolored	*2.50*	*1.40*
1860	A567	20pf multicolored	15	15
1861	A567	25pf multicolored	15	15
1862	A567	35pf multicolored	16	15
1863	A567	70pf multicolored	32	18
		Nos. 1858-1863 (6)	*3.43*	
		Set value		*1.75*

1977, Nov. 22 Litho. *Perf. 14*

Firemen's Activities: 10pf, Firemen racing with ladders (horiz.). 25pf, Fire engines fighting forest and brush fires (horiz.). 35pf, Artificial respiration. 50pf, Fireboat alongside freighter (horiz.).

1864	A568	10pf multicolored	15	15
1865	A568	20pf multicolored	15	15
1866	A568	25pf multicolored	15	15
1867	A568	35pf multicolored	16	15
1868	A568	50pf multicolored	*1.90*	*1.50*
		Nos. 1864-1868 (5)	*2.51*	*2.10*

Knight and King — A569

Designs: Various scenes from fairytale: "Six Men Around the World."

1977, Nov. 22 *Perf. 13x13½*

1869	A569	5pf blk & multi	50	28
1870	A569	10pf blk & multi	50	42
1871	A569	20pf blk & multi	50	28
1872	A569	25pf blk & multi	50	28
1873	A569	35pf blk & multi	50	42
1874	A569	60pf blk & multi	50	28
		Nos. 1869-1874 (6)	3.00	1.96

#1869-1874 printed together in sheets of 6.

Hips and Dog Rose A570

Medicinal Plants: 15pf, Birch. 20pf, Chamomile. 25pf, Coltsfoot. 35pf, Linden. 50pf, Elder.

1978, Jan. 10 Photo. *Perf. 14*

1875	A570	10pf multicolored	15	15
1876	A570	15pf multicolored	15	15
1877	A570	20pf multicolored	15	15
1878	A570	25pf multicolored	18	15
1879	A570	35pf multicolored	22	15
1880	A570	50pf multicolored	*2.50*	*1.50*
		Nos. 1875-1880 (6)	*3.35*	
		Set value		*1.85*

Amilcar Cabral A571

Town Hall, Suhl-Heinrichs A572

1978, Jan. 17 Litho. *Perf. 14*

1881	A571	20pf multicolored	25	15

Amilcar Cabral (1924-1973), freedom movement leader from Guinea-Bissau.

1978, Jan. 24 Photo. *Perf. 14*

Half-timbered Buildings, 17th-18th Centuries: 20pf, Farmhouse, Niederoderwitz. 25pf, Farmhouse, Strassen. 35pf, Townhouse, Quedlinburg. 40pf, Townhouse, Eisenach.

1882	A572	10pf multicolored	15	15
1883	A572	20pf multicolored	15	15
1884	A572	25pf multicolored	15	15
1885	A572	35pf multicolored	18	15
1886	A572	40pf multicolored	*2.00*	*1.40*
		Nos. 1882-1886 (5)	*2.63*	
		Set value		*1.80*

Mail Truck, 1921 A573

Past and Present Mail Transport: 20pf, Mail truck, 1978. 25pf, Railroad mail car, 1896. 35pf, Railroad mail car, 1978.

1978, Feb. 9 Litho. *Perf. 13x12½*

1887	A573	10pf brn & multi	20	18
1888	A573	20pf brn & multi	32	28
1889	A573	25pf brn & multi	45	38
1890	A573	35pf brn & multi	60	52
a.		Block of 4, #1887-1890	1.60	1.60

Earring, 11th Century A574

Royal House, Leipzig A575

Archaeological Artifacts: 20pf, Earring, 10th century. 25pf, Bronze sheath, 10th century. 35pf, Bronze horse, 12th century. 70pf, Arabian coin, 8th century.

1978, Feb. 21 Photo. *Perf. 14*

1891	A574	10pf multicolored	15	15
1892	A574	20pf multicolored	15	15
1893	A574	25pf multicolored	15	15
1894	A574	35pf multicolored	18	15
1895	A574	70pf multicolored	*2.00*	*1.50*
		Nos. 1891-1895 (5)	*2.63*	
		Set value		*1.80*

Treasures found on Slavic sites.

1978, Mar. 7

Leipzig Spring Fair: 25pf, Universal measuring instrument by Carl Zeiss.

1896	A575	10pf multicolored	15	15
1897	A575	25pf multicolored	28	15
		Set value		20

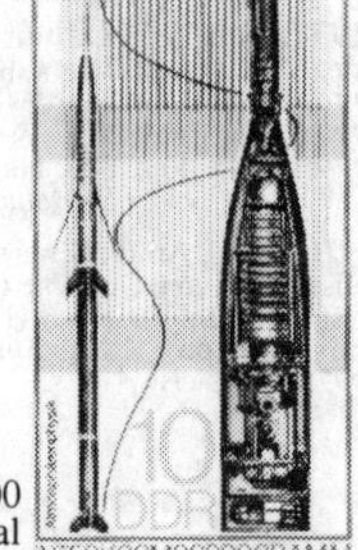

M-100 Meteorological Rocket — A576

Designs: 20pf, Intercosmos I satellite. 35pf, Meteor satellite with spectometric complex. 1m, MFK-6 multi-spectral camera over city.

1978, Mar. 21 Photo. *Perf. 14x13½*

1898	A576	10pf multicolored	15	15
1899	A576	20pf multicolored	15	15
1900	A576	35pf multicolored	*80*	*75*
		Set value	*95*	*85*

Souvenir Sheet

1901	A576	1m multicolored	*1.90*	*1.75*

Achievements in atmospheric and space research.

Samuel Heinicke, Leipzig, c. 1800 A577

Design: 25pf, Deaf child learning sign language.

1978, Apr. 4 Litho. *Perf. 13x12½*
1902 A577 20pf multicolored 15 15
1903 A577 25pf multicolored 52 44
Set value 50

National Institute for the Education of the Deaf, established by Samuel Heinicke, 200th anniversary.

Radio Tower, Dequede, TV Truck A578

Saxon Miner, 19th Century A579

Design: 20pf, TV equipment and tower (vert.).

Perf. 13½x14, 14x13½

1978, Apr. 25
1904 A578 10pf multicolored 15 15
1905 A578 20pf multicolored 32 26
Set value 38 30

World Telecommunications Day.

1978, May 9 *Perf. 12½x13*

Dress Uniforms, 19th Century: 20pf, Foundry worker, Freiberg. 25pf, Mining Academy student. 35pf, Chief Inspector of Mines.

1906 A579 10pf sil & multi 15 15
1907 A579 20pf sil & multi 15 15
1908 A579 25pf sil & multi 15 15
1909 A579 35pf sil & multi 1.00 80
Set value 1.00

Lion Cub — A580

Young Animals: 20pf, Leopard. 35pf, Tiger. 50pf, Snow leopard.

1978, May 23 Photo. *Perf. 14*
1910 A580 10pf multicolored 15 15
1911 A580 20pf multicolored 15 15
1912 A580 35pf multicolored 16 15
1913 A580 50pf multicolored 1.25 95
Set value 1.10

Centenary of Leipzig Zoo.

Loading Container A581

Ceramic Bull A582

Designs: 20pf, Loading container on flatbed truck. 35pf, Container trains in terminal. 70pf, Loading container on ship.

1978, June 13 Litho. *Perf. 12½x13*
1914 A581 10pf multicolored 15 15
1915 A581 20pf multicolored 15 15
1916 A581 35pf multicolored 15 15
1917 A581 70pf multicolored 1.65 1.10
Set value 1.30

Perf. 14x13½, 13½x14

1978, June 20 Photo.

Designs: 10pf, Woman's head, ceramic. 20pf, Gold armband (horiz.). 25pf, Animal head, gold ring. 35pf, Seated family from signet ring. 40pf, Necklace (horiz.).

1918 A582 5pf multicolored 15 15
1919 A582 10pf multicolored 15 15
1920 A582 20pf multicolored 15 15
1921 A582 25pf multicolored 15 15
1922 A582 35pf multicolored 16 15
1923 A582 40pf multicolored 2.00 1.10
Nos. 1918-1923 (6) 2.76
Set value 1.50

African art from 1st and 2nd centuries in Berlin and Leipzig Egyptian museums.

Old and New Buildings, Cottbus A583

Design: 10pf + 5pf, View of Cottbus, 1730.

1978, July 18 Litho. *Perf. 13x12½*
1924 A583 10pf + 5pf multi 30 28
1925 A583 20pf multicolored 30 28
a. Strip of 2, #1924-1925 + label 75 70

5th Youth Philatelic Exhibition, Cottbus.

Justus von Liebig, Wheat and Retort A584

Famous Germans: 10pf, Joseph Dietzgen (1828-1888) and title page. 15pf, Alfred Döblin (1878-1957) and title page. 20pf, Hans Loch (1898-1960) and signature, president of Liberal Democratic Party. 25pf, Dr. Theodor Brugsch (1878-1963), and blood circulation. 35pf, Friedrich Ludwig Jahn (1778-1852) and gymnast. 70pf, Dr. Albrecht von Graefe (1828-1870) and ophthalmological instruments.

1978, July 18
1926 A584 5pf yel & blk 15 15
1927 A584 10pf gray & blk 15 15
1928 A584 15pf yel grn & blk 15 15
1929 A584 20pf ultra & blk 15 15
1930 A584 25pf sal & blk 15 15
1931 A584 35pf lt grn & blk 16 15
1932 A584 70pf ol & blk 1.90 1.25
Nos. 1926-1932 (7) 2.81
Set value 1.65

Festival Emblem and New Buildings, Havana — A585

Design: 35pf, Balloons and new buildings, Berlin.

1978, July 25 Litho. *Perf. 13x12½*
1933 A585 20pf multicolored 45 40
1934 A585 35pf multicolored 45 40
a. Strip of 2, #1933-1934 + label 1.00 90

11th World Youth Festival, Havana, July 28-Aug. 5.

Foot Soldier, by Hans Schäufelein A586

Fair Building "Three Kings," Leipzig A587

Etchings: 20pf, Woman Reading Letter, by Jean Antoine Watteau. 25pf, Seated Boy, by Gabriel Metsu. 30pf, Seated Young Man, by Cornelis Saftleven. 35pf, St. Anthony, by Matthias Grunewald. 50pf, Seated Man, by Abraham van Diepenbeeck.

1978, July 25 *Perf. 13½x14*
1935 A586 10pf lem & blk 60 32
1936 A586 20pf lem & blk 60 52
1937 A586 25pf lem & blk 60 32
1938 A586 30pf lem & blk 60 32
1939 A586 35pf lem & blk 60 52
1940 A586 50pf lem & blk 60 32
Nos. 1935-1940 (6) 3.60 2.32

Etchings from Berlin Museums. Nos. 1935-1940 printed together in sheets of 6.

1978, Aug. 29 Photo. *Perf. 14*

Leipzig Fall Fair: 10pf, IFA Multicar 25 truck (horiz.).

1941 A587 10pf multicolored 15 15
1942 A587 25pf multicolored 24 15

Mauthausen Memorial — A588

1978, Sept. 5 *Perf. 13½x14*
1943 A588 35pf multicolored 40 15

International war memorials.

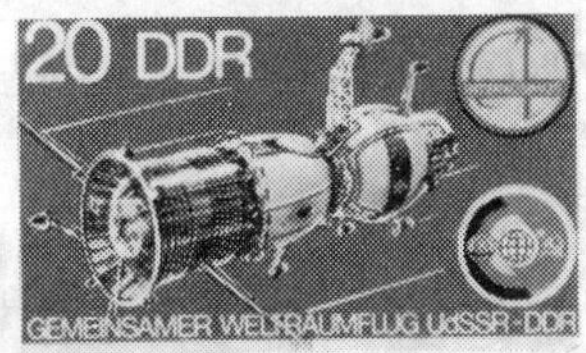

Soyuz, Intercosmos and German-Soviet Space Flight Emblems — A589

Soyuz, Camera and Space Complex A590

Designs: 10pf, Soyuz and Albert Einstein. 20pf, Sigmund Jähn, 1st German cosmonaut (vert.). 35pf, Salyut-Soyuz space station, Otto Lilienthal and his glider. 1m, Cosmonauts Bykovsky and Jähn and space ships.

1978, Sept. Photo. *Perf. 14*
1944 A589 20pf multicolored 22 15

Litho.

Perf. 13½x13
1945 A590 5pf multicolored 15 15
1946 A590 10pf multicolored 15 15
1947 A590 20pf multicolored 15 15
1948 A590 35pf multicolored 95 80
Set value 1.35 95

Souvenir Sheet

Perf. 13½x14
1949 A590 1m multicolored 1.90 1.65

1st German cosmonaut on Russian space mission. #1949 contains 1 54x33mm stamp.

Issue dates: #1944, Sept. 4; others, Sept. 21.

Marching Soldiers, Tractor, Factory A591

Design: 35pf, Russian and German Soldiers, Communist war veteran, 1933.

1978, Sept. 19 Photo. *Perf. 14*
1950 A591 20pf multicolored 45 35
1951 A591 35pf multicolored 45 35
a. Strip of 2, #1950-1951 + label 95 75

Workers' military units, 25th anniv.

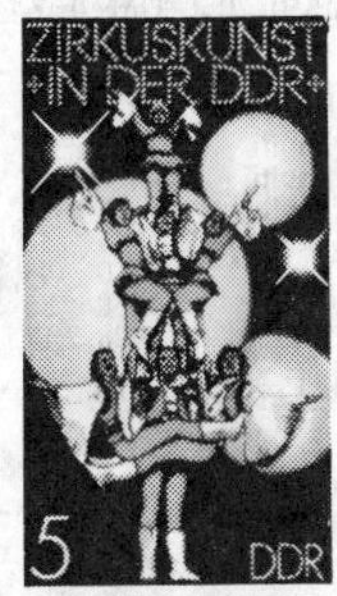

Seven-person Pyramid — A592

Designs: 10pf, Elephant on tricycle. 20pf, Dressage. 35pf, Polar bear kissing woman trainer.

1978, Sept. 26 Photo. *Perf. 14*
1952 A592 5pf blk & multi 32 15
1953 A592 10pf blk & multi 60 24
1954 A592 20pf blk & multi 1.10 45
1955 A592 35pf blk & multi 1.90 75
a. Block of 4, #1952-1955 *4.50* *1.75*

Circus in German Democratic Republic.

Construction of Gas Pipe Line, Drushba Section — A593

1978, Oct. 3 Litho. *Perf. 13x12½*
1956 A593 20pf multicolored 25 15

German youth helping to build gas pipe line from Orenburg to Russian border.

African Behind Barbed Wire A594

Papilio Hahneli A595

1978, Oct. 3 Litho. *Perf. 12½x13*
1957 A594 20pf multicolored 25 15

Anti-Apartheid Year.

1978, Oct. 24 Photo. *Perf. 14*

Designs: 20pf, Agama lehmanni (lizards). 25pf, Agate from Wiederau. 35pf, Paleobatrachus diluvianus. 40pf, Clock, 1720. 50pf, Table telescope, 1750.

1958	A595	10pf multicolored	15	15
1959	A595	20pf multicolored	15	15
1960	A595	25pf multicolored	15	15
1961	A595	35pf multicolored	15	15
1962	A595	40pf multicolored	20	15
1963	A595	50pf multicolored	*2.50*	*1.75*
		Nos. 1958-1963 (6)	*3.30*	
		Set value		*2.00*

Dresden Museum of Natural History, 250th anniversary.

Wheel Lock Gun, 1630 — A596

Hunting Guns: 10pf, Double-barreled gun, 1978. 20pf, Spring-cock gun, 1780. 25pf, Superimposed double-barreled gun, 1978. 35pf, Percussion gun, 1850. 70pf, Three-barreled gun, 1978.

1978, Nov. 21 Photo. *Perf. 14*

1964	A596	5pf sil & multi	15	15
1965	A596	10pf sil & multi	20	15
1966	A596	20pf sil & multi	38	25
1967	A596	25pf sil & multi	45	32
1968	A596	35pf sil & multi	60	45
1969	A596	70pf sil & multi	1.50	85
		Nos. 1964-1969 (6)	3.28	2.17

5pf, 20pf, 35pf printed se-tenant in sheets of 9, as are 10pf, 25pf, 70pf.

Rapunzel's Rescuer and Witch — A597

Designs: Scenes from fairy tale "Rapunzel."

1978, Nov. 21 Litho. *Perf. 13*

1970	A597	10pf multicolored	60	32
1971	A597	15pf multicolored	60	52
1972	A597	20pf multicolored	60	32
1973	A597	25pf multicolored	60	32
1974	A597	35pf multicolored	60	52
1975	A597	50pf multicolored	60	32
		Nos. 1970-1975 (6)	3.60	2.32

Printed se-tenant in sheets of 6.

Chaffinches A598

Chabo Cock A599

Song Birds: 10pf, Nuthatch. 20pf, Robin. 25pf, Bullfinches. 35pf, Blue tit. 50pf, Red linnets.

1979, Jan. 9 Photo. *Perf. 13½x14*

1976	A598	5pf multicolored	15	15
1977	A598	10pf multicolored	15	15
1978	A598	20pf multicolored	15	15
1979	A598	25pf multicolored	15	15
1980	A598	35pf multicolored	20	15
1981	A598	50pf multicolored	*1.90*	*1.65*
		Nos. 1976-1981 (6)	*2.70*	
		Set value		*2.00*

1979, Jan. 23 *Perf. 14x13½*

German Cocks: 15pf, Kraienkopp. 20pf, Porcelain-colored bantam. 25pf, Saxonian. 35pf, Phoenix. 50pf, Striped Italian.

1982	A599	10pf multicolored	15	15
1983	A599	15pf multicolored	15	15
1984	A599	20pf multicolored	15	15
1985	A599	25pf multicolored	15	15
1986	A599	35pf multicolored	18	15
1987	A599	50pf multicolored	*2.25*	*1.90*
		Nos. 1982-1987 (6)	*3.03*	
		Set value		*2.25*

Telephone Operators, 1900 and 1979 — A600

Design: 35pf, Telegraph operators, 1880 and 1979.

1979, Feb. 6 Photo. *Perf. 13½x14*

1988	A600	20pf multicolored	15	15
1989	A600	35pf multicolored	*60*	*52*
		Set value		*56*

Development of German postal telephone and telegraph service.

Souvenir Sheet

Albert Einstein (1879-1955), Theoretical Physicist A601

1979, Feb. 20 Litho. *Perf. 14*

1990	A601	1m multicolored	*2.50*	*1.75*

Max Klinger House, Leipzig — A602

Leipzig Spring Fair: 25pf, Horizontal drilling and milling machine (horiz.).

1979, Mar. 6 Litho. *Perf. 14*

1991	A602	10pf multicolored	15	15
1992	A602	25pf multicolored	28	18
		Set value		25

Container Ship, Tug, World Map and IMCO Emblem — A603

1979, Mar. 20 Photo.

1993	A603	20pf multicolored	24	15

World Navigation Day.

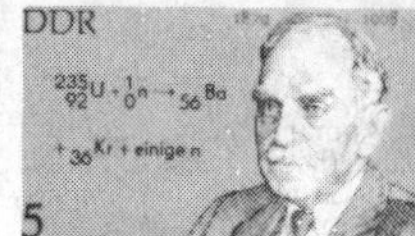

Otto Hahn and Equation of Nuclear Fission A604

Famous Germans: 10pf, Max von Laue (1879-1969) and diagram of sulphide zinc. 20pf, Arthur Scheunert (1879-1957), symbol of nutrition and health. 25pf, Friedrich August Kekulé (1829-1896), and benzene ring. 35pf, George Forster (1754-1794) and Capt. Cook's ship Resolution. 70pf, Gotthold Ephraim Lessing (1729-1781) and title page for Nathan the Wise.

1979, Mar. 20 Litho. *Perf. 13x12½*

1994	A604	5pf pale sal & blk	15	15
1995	A604	10pf bl gray & blk	15	15
1996	A604	20pf lem & blk	15	15
1997	A604	25pf lt grn & blk	15	15
1998	A604	35pf lt bl & blk	16	15
1999	A604	70pf pink & blk	*2.00*	*1.50*
		Nos. 1994-1999 (6)	*2.76*	
		Set value		*1.80*

See Nos. 2088-2093.

Miniature Sheet

Horch 8, 1911 — A605

Design: 35pf, Trabant 601S de luxe, 1978.

1979, Apr. 3 Litho. *Perf. 14*

2000		Sheet of 2 + label	*1.50*	*1.25*
a.		A605 20pf multi	*55*	*45*
b.		A605 35pf multi	*90*	*75*

Sachsenring automobile plant, Zwickau.

Self-Propelled Car — A606

DDR Railroad Cars: 10pf, Self-unloading freight car Us-y. 20pf, Diesel locomotive BR 110. 35pf, Laaes automobile carrier.

1979, Apr. 17 Litho. *Perf. 13*

2001	A606	5pf multicolored	15	15
2002	A606	10pf multicolored	15	15
2003	A606	20pf multicolored	15	15
2004	A606	35pf multicolored	*1.25*	*1.10*
		Set value	*1.45*	*1.20*

Durga, 18th Century — A607

Indian Miniatures in Berlin Museums: 35pf, Mahavira, 15th-16th centuries. 50pf, Todi Ragini, 17th century. 70pf, Asavari Ragini, 17th century.

1979, May 8 Photo. *Perf. 14x13½*

2005	A607	20pf multicolored	15	15
2006	A607	35pf multicolored	25	15
2007	A607	50pf multicolored	35	20
2008	A607	70pf multicolored	*2.50*	*1.90*

Youth Gathering A608

Design: 10pf + 5pf, Torchlight parade of German youth, Oct. 7, 1949.

1979, May 22 Photo. *Perf. 14*

2009	A608	10pf + 5pf multi	*30*	*28*
2010	A608	20pf multicolored	*30*	*28*
a.		Strip of 2, #2009-2010 + label	*70*	*65*

National Youth Festival, Berlin.

Housing Project, Berlin A609

Design: 20pf, Berlin-Marzahn building site and surveyors.

1979, May 22 Litho. *Perf. 13x12½*

2011	A609	10pf multicolored	15	15
2012	A609	20pf multicolored	*38*	*32*
		Set value	*44*	*35*

Berlin Project of Free German Youth.

Children Playing and Reading A610

Exhibition Emblem A611

Design: 20pf, Doctor with black and white children.

1979, May 22 Photo. *Perf. 14*

2013	A610	10pf multi	15	15
2014	A610	20pf multi	*60*	*45*
		Set value	*65*	*50*

International Year of the Child.

1979, June 5

2015	A611	10pf multi	20	15

Agra '79 Agricultural Exhib., Markkleeberg.

Ferry Boats A612

1979, June 26 Photo. *Perf. 14*

2016	A612	20pf Rostock	60	52
2017	A612	35pf Rugen	*60*	*52*
a.		Strip of 2, #2016-2017 + label	*1.40*	*1.20*

Railroad ferry from Sassnitz, DDR, to Trelleborg, Sweden, 70th anniversary.

Hospital Classroom — A613

Design: 35pf, Handicapped workers.

1979, June 26 Litho. ***Perf. 13x12½***

2018 A163 10pf multi		15	15
2019 A163 35pf multi		*60*	*52*
	Set value	*66*	*55*

Rehabilitation in DDR.

Bicyclists A614

Design: 20pf, Roller skating.

1979, July 3

2020 A614 10pf multi		15	15
2021 A614 20pf multi		*50*	*42*
	Set value	*56*	*46*

7th Children's and Youth Spartakiad, Berlin.

Dahlia "Rubens" A615

Dahlias: 20pf, Rosalie. 25pf, Corinna. 35pf, Enzett-Dolli. 50pf, Enzett-Carola. 70pf, Don Lorenzo.

1979, July 17 Photo. ***Perf. 13***

2022 A615 10pf multi	15	15
2023 A615 20pf multi	15	15
2024 A615 25pf multi	18	15
2025 A615 35pf multi	20	15
2026 A615 50pf multi	32	16
2027 A615 70pf multi	*2.75*	*1.90*
Nos. 2022-2027 (6)	*3.75*	*2.66*

Dahlias shown at International Garden Exhibition, Erfurt.

Russian Alphabet Around Congress Emblem A616

1979, Aug. 7 Photo. ***Perf. 13***

2028 A616 20pf multi	20	15

4th International Congress of Teachers of Russian Language and Literature, Berlin.

Dandelion Fountain, Dresden — A617

Composite of Dresden Buildings — A618

1979, Aug. 7 ***Perf. 14***

2029 A617 20pf multi	15	15

Souvenir Sheet

Litho. ***Perf. 13x12½***

2030 A618 1m multi	*2.00*	*1.50*

DDR '79, Natl. Stamp Exhib., Dresden. See No. B187.

Italian Lira da Gamba, 1592 — A619

Musical Instruments, Leipzig Museum: 25pf, French "serpent," 17th-18th centuries. 40pf, French barrel lyre, 18th century. 85pf, German tenor trumpet, 19th century.

1979, Aug. 21 ***Perf. 14***

2031 A619 20pf multi	15	15
2032 A619 25pf multi	20	15
2033 A619 40pf multi	30	15
2034 A619 85pf multi	*2.75*	*2.00*

Galloping — A620

1979, Aug. 21

2035 A620 10pf shown	15	15
2036 A620 25pf Dressage	*90*	*75*

30th International Horse-breeding Congress of Socialist Countries, Berlin.

Memorial Monument, Nordhausen — A621

Teddy Bear — A622

1979, Aug. 28 Photo. ***Perf. 14***

2037 A621 35pf dl vio & blk	40	35

Memorial to World War II victims.

1979, Aug. 28

Leipzig Autumn Fair: 25pf, Grosser Blumenberg (building), Leipzig (horiz.).

2038 A622 10pf multi		15	15
2039 A622 25pf multi		*60*	*48*
	Set value	*66*	*52*

Philipp Dengel (1888-1948) — A623

Working-Class Movement Leaders: No. 2041, Heinrich Rau (1899-1961). No. 2042, Otto Buchwitz (1879-1964). No. 2043, Bernard Koenen (1889-1964).

1979, Sept. 11 **Litho.**

2040 A623 10pf multi		22	15
2041 A623 10pf multi		22	15
2042 A623 10pf multi		22	15
2043 A623 10pf multi		22	15
	Set value		50

See Nos. 2166-2169, 2249-2253, 2314-2318, 2390-2392, 2452-2454.

DDR Arms and Flag, Worker A624

DDR Arms, Flag and: 10pf, Young man and woman. 15pf, Soldiers. 20pf, Workers.

1979, Oct. 2 Photo. ***Perf. 13***

2044 A624 5pf multi		15	15
2045 A624 10pf multi		15	15
2046 A624 15pf multi		*50*	*35*
2047 A624 20pf multi		15	15
	Set value	*70*	*50*

Souvenir Sheet

2048 A624 1m multi	*1.75*	*1.50*

DDR, 30th anniv. No. 2048 contains one stamp (33x55mm).

Altozier Porcelain Coffee Pot — A625

Meissen Porcelain and Hallmark, 18th-20th Centuries: 5pf, Woman applying make-up, 1967. 15pf, "Grosser Ausschnitt" coffee pot, 1974. 20pf, Covered vase. 25pf, Parrot. 35pf, Harlequin drinking. 50pf, Woman selling flowers. 70pf, Sake bottle.

1979, Nov. 6 Photo. ***Perf. 14***

2049 A625 5pf multi	*15*	*15*
2050 A625 10pf multi	*20*	*15*
2051 A625 15pf multi	*32*	*24*
2052 A625 20pf multi	*42*	*30*
2053 A625 25pf multi	*50*	*35*
2054 A625 35pf multi	*70*	*52*
2055 A625 50pf multi	*1.00*	*75*
2056 A625 70pf multi	*1.50*	*1.10*
Nos. 2049-2056 (8)	*4.79*	*3.56*

Nos. 2049-2052 and 2053-2056 printed se-tenant in blocks of 4, sheets of 16.

Rag Doll, 1800 — A626

Historic Dolls: 15pf, Ceramic, 1960. 20pf, Wooden, 1780. 35pf, Straw, 1900. 50pf, Jointed, 1800. 70pf, Tumbler, 1820.

1979, Nov. 20 **Litho.**

2057 A626 10pf multi	*65*	*38*
2058 A626 15pf multi	*65*	*55*
2059 A626 20pf multi	*65*	*38*
2060 A626 35pf multi	*65*	*38*
2061 A626 50pf multi	*65*	*55*
2062 A626 70pf multi	*65*	*38*
Nos. 2057-2062 (6)	*3.90*	*2.62*

#2057-2062 printed se-tenant in sheets of 6.

Bobsledding, by Gunter Rechn, Olympic Rings — A627

Olympic Rings and: 20pf, Figure Skating, by Johanna Stake (vert.). 35pf, Speed Skating, by Axel Wunsch (vert.). 1m, Cross-country Skiing, by Lothar Zitzmann.

1980, Jan. 18 Photo. ***Perf. 14***

2063 A627 10pf multi		15	15
2064 A627 20pf multi		15	15
2065 A627 35pf multi		*1.25*	*1.10*
	Set value		*1.20*

Souvenir Sheet

2066 A627 1m multi	*1.75*	*1.40*

13th Winter Olympic Games, Lake Placid, NY, Feb. 12-24. No. 2066 contains one 29x23½mm stamp. See Nos. 2098-2099, 2119-2121, B189, B190, B192.

"Quiet Music," Grossedlitz — A628

Baroque Gardens: 20pf, Orange grove, Belvedere, Weimar. 50pf, Flower garden, Dornburg Castle. 70pf, Park, Rheinsberg Castle.

1980, Jan. 29

2067 A628 10pf multi	15	15
2068 A628 20pf multi	15	15
2069 A628 50pf multi	28	15
2070 A628 70pf multi	*1.90*	*1.50*

Type of 1973

1980-81 Engr. ***Perf. 14***

Size: 22x17mm

2071 A449 5pf bl grn	15	15
2072 A449 10pf emerald	15	15
2073 A449 15pf rose lilac	15	15
2074 A449 20pf rose mag	15	15
2075 A449 25pf grnsh bl	20	15
2076 A449 30pf org ('81)	28	15
2077 A449 35pf blue	28	15
2078 A449 40pf dl vio	32	15
2079 A449 50pf blue	42	22
2080 A449 60pf lilac ('81)	65	25
2081 A449 70pf redsh brn ('81)	80	35
2082 A449 80pf vio bl ('81)	85	38
2083 A449 1m olive	1.00	45
2084 A449 2m red	1.90	80
2085 A449a 3m rose lil ('81)	3.50	1.25
Nos. 2071-2085 (15)	10.80	4.90

Cable-Laying Vehicle, Dish Antenna — A629

Design: 20pf, Radio tower, television screen.

1980, Feb. 5 **Photo.**

2086 A629 10pf multi 15 15
2087 A629 20pf multi 16 15
Set value 24 15

Famous Germans Type of 1979

Designs: 5pf, Johann Wolfgang Dobereiner (1780-1849), chemist. 10pf, Frederic Joliot-Curie (1900-1958), French physicist. 20pf, Johann Friedrich Naumann (1780-1857), ornithologist. 25pf, Alfred Wegener (1880-1930), geophysicist and meteorologist. 35pf, Carl von Clausewitz (1780-1831), Prussian major general. 70pf, Helene Weigel (1900-1971), actress.

1980, Feb. 26 **Litho.** ***Perf. 13x12½***

2088 A604 5pf pale yel & blk 15 15
2089 A604 10pf multi 15 15
2090 A604 20pf lt yel grn & blk 15 15
2091 A604 25pf multi 15 15
2092 A604 35pf lt bl & blk 15 15
2093 A604 70pf lt red brn & blk *1.40 1.25*
Set value *1.85 1.50*

Type ZT-303 Tractor A630

1980 Leipzig Spring Fair: 10pf, Karl Marx University, Leipzig (vert.).

1980, Mar. 4 **Photo.** ***Perf. 14***

2094 A630 10pf multi 15 15
2095 A630 25pf multi 28 18

Werner Eggerath (1900-1977), Labor Leader — A631

1980, Mar. 18 **Litho.**

2096 A631 10pf brick red & blk 15 15

Souvenir Sheet

Cosmonauts, Salyut 6 and Soyuz — A632

1980, Apr. 11 **Litho.** ***Perf. 14***

2097 A632 1m multi *1.90 1.50*

Intercosmos cooperative space program.

Olympic Type of 1980

Designs: 10pf, On the Bars, by Erich Wurzer. 50pf, Scull's Crew, by Wilfried Falkenthal.

1980, Apr. 22 **Photo.** ***Perf. 14***

2098 A627 10pf multi 15 15
2099 A627 50pf multi *90 75*

22nd Summer Olympic Games, Moscow, July 19-Aug. 3. See No. B190.

Flags of Member Countries A633

Bauhaus Cooperative Society Building, 1928, Gropius A634

1980, May 13 **Photo.**

2100 A633 20pf multi 24 15

Signing of Warsaw Pact (Bulgaria, Czechoslovakia, German Democratic Rep., Hungary, Poland, Romania, USSR), 25th anniversary.

1980, May 27

Bauhaus Architecture: 10pf, Socialists' Memorial, 1926, by Mies van der Rohe (horiz.). 15pf, Monument, 1922, by William Gropius. 20pf, Steel building, 1926, by Muche and Paulick (horiz.). 50pf, Trade-Union School, 1928, by Meyer. 70pf, Bauhaus Building, 1926, by Gropius (horiz.).

2101 A634 5pf multi 15 15
2102 A634 10pf multi 15 15
2103 A634 15pf multi 15 15
2104 A634 20pf multi 15 15
2105 A634 50pf multi 28 15
2106 A634 70pf multi *1.90 1.40*
Nos. 2101-2106 (6) *2.78*
Set value *1.70*

Rostock View A635

1980, June 10 **Photo.** ***Perf. 14***

2107 A635 10pf shown 15 15
2108 A635 20pf Dancers 20 15
Set value 30 15

18th Workers' Festival, Rostock, June 27-29.

Dish Antenna, Interflug Airlines A636

1980, June 10 **Litho.** ***Perf. 13x12½***

2109 A636 20pf shown *45 26*
2110 A636 25pf Jet *60 32*
2111 A636 35pf Agricultural plane *80 48*
2112 A636 70pf Aerial photography *1.65 95*

Interflug Airlines. Nos. 2109-2112 se-tenant. See No. B191

Okapi — A637

1980, June 24 ***Perf. 14***

2113 A637 5pf shown 15 15
2114 A637 10pf Wild cats 15 15
2115 A637 15pf Prairie wolf 15 15
2116 A637 20pf Arabian oryx 15 15
2117 A637 25pf White-eared pheasant 20 15
2118 A637 35pf Musk oxen *1.75 1.25*
Nos. 2113-2118 (6) *2.55*
Set value *1.50*

Olympic Type of 1980

Designs: 10pf, Judo, by Erhard Schmidt. 50pf, Final Spurt, by Siegfried Schreiber. 1m, Spinnaker Yachts, by Karl Raetsch.

1980, July 8 **Photo.** ***Perf. 14***

2119 A627 10pf multi 15 15
2120 A627 50pf multi *1.10 95*

Souvenir Sheet

2121 A627 1m multi *1.65 1.40*

22nd Summer Olympic Games, Moscow, July 19-Aug. 3. No. 2121 contains one stamp (29x24mm). See No. B192.

Old and New Buildings, Suhl A638

Design: 10pf + 5pf, View of Suhl, 1700.

1980, July 22 **Litho.** ***Perf. 13x12½***

2122 A638 10pf + 5pf multi *24 20*
2123 A638 20pf multi *24 20*
a. Strip of 2, #2122-2123 + label *55 48*

6th National Youth Philatelic Exhibition, Suhl. Surtax for East German Association of Philatelists.

Huntley Microscope, London, 1740 — A639

Optical Museum, Karl Zeiss Foundation, Jena: 25pf, Magny microscope, Paris, 1751. 35pf, Amici microscope, Modena, 1845. 70pf, Zeiss microscope, Jena, 1873.

1980, Aug. 12 **Photo.** ***Perf. 14***

2124 A639 20pf multi 42 32
2125 A639 25pf multi 50 40
2126 A639 35pf multi 65 52
2127 A639 70pf multi 1.50 1.10
a. Block of 4, #2124-2127 2.60 2.60

Maidenek Memorial — A640

1980, Aug. 26

2128 A640 35pf multi 35 15

Leipzig 1980 Autumn Fair, Information Center — A641

1980, Aug. 26

2129 A641 10pf shown 15 15
2130 A641 25pf Carpet loom 32 18
Set value 25

67th Interparliamentary Conference, Berlin — A642

1980, Sept. 9 **Photo.** ***Perf. 14***

2131 A642 20pf Republic Palace, Berlin 22 15

Laughing Boy with Flute — A643

Designs: Paintings by Frans Hals (1580-1666).

1980, Sept. 23

2132 A643 10pf *shown* 15 15
2133 A643 20pf *Man in Gray Coat* 15 15
2134 A643 25pf *The Mulatto* 16 15
2135 A643 35pf *Man in Black Coat* *1.10 90*

Souvenir Sheet

2136 A643 1m *Self-portrait*, horiz. *1.90 1.40*

Leccinum Testaceo Scabrum — A644

Edible Mushrooms: 10pf, Boletus erythropus. 15pf, Agaricus campester. 20pf, Xerocomus badius. 35pf, Boletus edulis. 70pf, Cantharellus cibarius.

1980, Oct. 28 **Litho.** ***Perf. 13x13½***

2137 A644 5pf multi 15 15
2138 A644 10pf multi 15 15
2139 A644 15pf multi 15 15
2140 A644 20pf multi 15 15
2141 A644 35pf multi 22 15
2142 A644 70pf multi *2.25 1.90*
Nos. 2137-2142 (6) *3.07*
Set value *2.25*

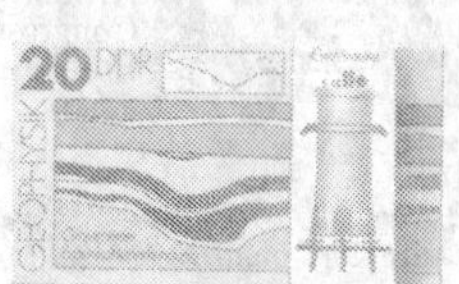

Exploration of Lignite Deposits (Gravimetry) — A645

Geophysical Exploration: 25pf, Bore-hole measuring (water). 35pf, Seismic geology (mineral oil, natural gas). 50pf, Seismology. Nos. 2143-2146 se-tenant.

1980, Nov. 11 **Litho.** ***Perf. 13***

2143 A645 20pf multi 38 30
2144 A645 25pf multi 48 38
2145 A645 35pf multi 70 55
2146 A645 50pf multi 95 75

Radebeul-Radeburg Railroad Locomotive — A646

1980, Nov. 25 ***Perf. 13x12½***

2147 Strip of 2 + label *90 75*
a. A646 20pf shown
b. A646 25pf Passenger car

2148 Strip of 2 + label *90 75*
a. A646 20pf Bad Doberan-Ostseebad Kuhlungsborn Locomotive
b. A646 35pf Passenger car

Labels show maps of routes and Moritzburg Castle (No. 2147), Bad Doberan Street (No. 2148).

See Nos. 2205-2206.

Toy Locomotive, 1850 — A647

1980, Dec. 9 ***Perf. 14***
2149 Sheet of 6 *3.00 2.25*
a. A647 10pf shown *50 32*
b. A647 20pf Airplane, 1914 *50 45*
c. A647 25pf Steam roller, 1920 *50 32*
d. A647 35pf Ship, 1825 *50 32*
e. A647 40pf Car, 1900 *50 45*
f. A647 50pf Balloon, 1920 *50 32*

Souvenir Sheet

Mozart — A648

1981, Jan. 13 **Litho.**
2150 A648 1m multi *2.00 1.25*

225th birth anniversary of Wolfgang Amadeus Mozart.

St. John's Apple — A649

Heinrich von Stephan — A650

1981, Jan. 13 **Photo.**
2151 A649 5pf shown 15 15
2152 A649 10pf Snow drop, horiz. 15 15
2153 A649 20pf Bladder bush 15 15
2154 A649 25pf Paulownia tomentose 15 15
2155 A649 35pf German honeysuckle, horiz. 22 15
2156 A649 50pf Genuine spice bush *2.25 1.50*
Nos. 2151-2156 (6) *3.07*
Set value *1.90*

1981, Jan. 20 **Litho.** ***Perf. 13x13½***
2157 A650 10pf lt lem & blk 15 15

Von Stephan (1831-97), founder of UPU.

Dedication of National Commemorative Plaza, Sachsenhausen — A651

1981, Jan. 27 **Photo.** ***Perf. 14***
2158 A651 10pf shown 15 15
2159 A651 20pf Changing of guard 20 15
Set value 30 15

National People's Forces, 25th anniversary.

Socialist Union Party, 10th Congress — A652

1981, Feb. 10
2160 A652 10pf multi 15 15

Postal and Newspaper Apprentice Training — A653

1981, Feb. 10 **Litho.**
2161 A653 5pf shown 15 15
2162 A653 10pf Telephone and telex service 15 15
2163 A653 15pf Radio communications 15 15
2164 A653 20pf School of Engineering, Leipzig 15 15
2165 A653 25pf Communications Academy, Dresden *90 80*
Set value *1.20 1.00*

Working-class Leader Type of 1979

Designs: No. 2166, Erich Baron (1881-1933). No. 2167, Conrad Blenkle (1901-1943). No. 2168, Arthur Ewert (1890-1959). No. 2169, Walter Stoecker (1891-1939).

1981, Feb. 24 **Litho.** ***Perf. 14***
2166 A623 10pf gray grn & blk 15 15
2167 A623 10pf bl vio & blk 15 15
2168 A623 10pf lem & blk 15 15
2169 A623 10pf lt red brn & blk 15 15
Set value 48 18

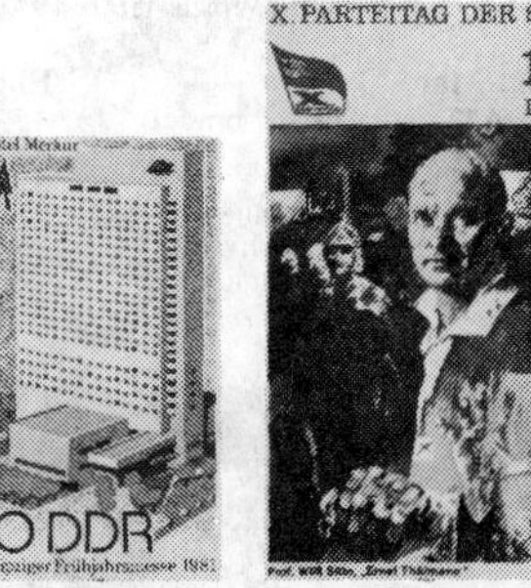

Merkur Hotel, Leipzig A654

Ernst Thälmann, by Willi Sitte A655

1981 Leipzig Spring Fair: 25pf, Takraf mining conveyor system (horiz.).

1981, Mar. 10 **Photo.** ***Perf. 14***
2170 A654 10pf multi 15 15
2171 A654 25pf multi 30 15
Set value 20

1981, Mar. 24

10th Communist Party Congress (Paintings): 20pf, Worker, by Bernhard Heising. 25pf, Festivities, by Rudolf Bergander. 35pf, Brotherhood in Arms, by Paul Michaelis. 1m, When Communists Dream, by Walter Womacka.

2172 A655 10pf multi 15 15
2173 A655 20pf multi 15 15
2174 A655 25pf multi *1.10 85*
2175 A655 35pf multi 18 15
Set value *1.10*

Souvenir Sheet

2176 A655 1m multi *1.50 1.50*

Souvenir Sheet

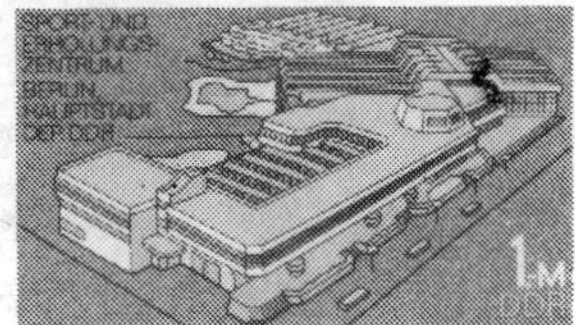

Opening of Sport and Recreation Center, Berlin — A656

1981, Mar. 24 **Litho.**
2177 A656 1m multi *1.75 1.40*

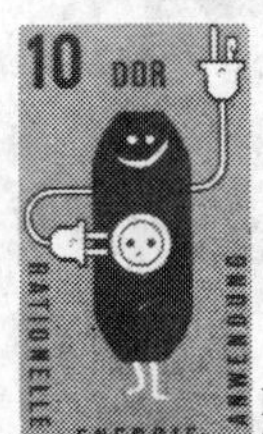

Energy Conservation — A657

1981, Apr. 21 **Litho.** ***Perf. 12½x13***
2178 A657 10pf org & blk 15 15

Heinrich Barkhausen (1881-1956), Physicist — A658

Famous Men: 20pf, Johannes R. Becher (1891-1958), poet. 25pf, Richard Dedekind (1831-1916), mathematician. 35pf, Georg Philipp Telemann (1681-1767), composer. 50pf, Adelbert V. Chamisso (1781-1838), botanist. 70pf, Wilhelm Raabe (1831-1910), writer.

1981, May 5 ***Perf. 13x12½***
2179 A658 10pf dl bl & blk 15 15
2180 A658 20pf brick red & blk 15 15
2181 A658 25pf dl brn & blk *1.65 1.50*
2182 A658 35pf lt vio & blk 16 15
2183 A658 50pf yel grn & blk 24 15
2184 A658 70pf ol bis & blk 35 20
Nos. 2179-2184 (6) *2.70 2.30*

Free German Youth Members A659

1981, May 19
2185 A659 10pf shown *25 22*
2186 A659 20pf Youths, diff. *25 22*

Free German Youth, 11th Parliament, Berlin. Nos. 2185-2186 se-tenant with label showing parliament emblem.

View and Map of Worlitz Park — A660

1981, June 9 **Litho.** ***Perf. 12½x13***
2187 A660 5pf shown 15 15
2188 A660 10pf Tiefurt 15 15
2189 A660 15pf Marxwalde 15 15
2190 A660 20pf Branitz 15 15
2191 A660 25pf Treptow *1.25 95*
2192 A660 35pf Wiesenburg 15 15
Set value *1.75 1.25*

Artistic Gymnastics — A661

8th Children's and Youth Spartacist Games: No. 2193, children and youths.

1981, June 23 **Photo.** ***Perf. 14***
2193 A661 10pf + 5pf multi *42 32*
2194 A661 20pf multi 15 15

Javelin Throwers A662

1981, June 23 **Litho.** ***Perf. 13x12½***
2195 A662 5pf shown 18 16
2196 A662 15pf Men at museum 18 16

Intl. Year of the Disabled. Nos. 2195-2196 se-tenant with label showing IYD emblem.

Schinkel's Berlin Playhouse A663

Karl Friedrich Schinkel, (1781-1841), Architect: 25pf, Old Museum, Berlin.

1981, June 23 **Litho. & Engr.**
2197 A663 10pf tan & blk 15 15
2198 A663 25pf tan & blk *50 45*
Set value *56 50*

Sugar Loaf House, Gross Zicker — A664

Frame Houses: 10pf, Zaulsdorf, 19th cent. (vert.). 25pf, Farmhouse, stable, Weckersdorf (vert.). 35pf, Restaurant (former farmhouse), Pillgram. 50pf, Eschenbach (vert.). 70pf, Farmhouse, Lüdersdorf.

1981, July 7 **Photo.**
2199 A664 10pf multi 15 15
2200 A664 20pf multi 15 15
2201 A664 25pf multi 15 15
2202 A664 35pf multi 24 15
2203 A664 50pf multi 20 15
2204 A664 70pf multi *2.00 1.90*
Nos. 2199-2204 (6) *2.89*
Set value *2.30*

Railroad Type of 1980

1981, July 21 **Litho.** ***Perf. 13x12½***
2205 Strip of 2 + label *50 38*
a. A646 5pf Locomotive, Freital-Kurort-Kipsdorf line
b. A646 15pf Luggage car
2206 Strip of 2 + label *50 38*
a. A646 5pf Locomotive, Putbus-Gohren line
b. A646 20pf Passenger car

Labels show maps of train routes.

Ebers Papyrus (Egyptian Medical Text, 1600 B.C.), Leipzig — A665

Chemical Plant — A666

Literary Treasures in DDR Libraries: 35pf, Maya manuscript, 12th cent., Dresden. 50pf, Petrarch sonnet illustration, 16th century French manuscript, Berlin.

1981, Aug. 18 Photo. *Perf. 14*

2207 A665 20pf multi 15 15
2208 A665 35pf multi 20 15
2209 A665 50pf multi *1.10 1.00*

1981, Aug. 18

Leipzig 1981 Autumn Fair: 25pf, Concert Hall, Leipzig (horiz.).

2210 A666 10pf multi 15 15
2211 A666 25pf multi 30 15
Set value 20

Anti-Fascist Resistance Monument, Sassnitz — A667

Forceps, 18th Cent., Speculum, 17th Cent. — A668

1981, Sept. 8 Photo. *Perf. 14*

2212 A667 35pf multi 45 18

1981, Sept. 22

Historic Medical Instruments, Karl Sudhoff Institute, Leipzig: 10pf, Henbana, censer, 16th cent. 20pf, Pelican, dental elevator and extractors, 17th cent. 25pf, Seton forceps, 17th cent. 35pf, Lithotomy knife, 18th cent., hernia scissors, 17th cent. 85pf, Elevators, 17th cent. 10pf, 20pf, 25pf, 35pf horiz.

2213 A668 10pf multi 15 15
2214 A668 20pf multi 15 15
2215 A668 25pf multi 15 15
2216 A668 35pf multi 15 15
2217 A668 50pf multi *2.25 1.90*
2218 A668 85pf multi 38 18
Nos. 2213-2218 (6) *3.23 2.68*

Philatelists' Day — A669

1981, Oct. 6 Photo. *Perf. 14*

2219 A669 10pf + 5pf Letter by Engels, 1840 *45 38*
2220 A669 20pf Postcard by Marx, 1878 15 15

River Boat A670

1981, Oct. 20

2221 A670 10pf Tugboat 15 15
2222 A670 20pf Tugboat, diff. 15 15
2223 A670 25pf Diesel paddle liner 16 15
2224 A670 35pf Ice breaker 18 15
2225 A670 50pf Motor freighter 26 15
2226 A670 85pf Bucket dredger *2.75 1.75*
Nos. 2221-2226 (6) *3.65 2.50*

Windmill, Dabel — A671

Toys — A672

1981, Nov. 10 Photo. *Perf. 14*

2227 A671 10pf shown 15 15
2228 A671 20pf Pahrenz 15 15
2229 A671 25pf Dresden-Gohlis 15 15
2230 A671 70pf Ballstadt *1.25 1.25*
Set value *1.50 1.40*

1981, Nov. 24 Litho. *Perf. 13½*

2231 Sheet of 6 *3.50 2.75*
a. A672 10pf Jointed snake, 1850 *55 38*
b. A672 20pf Teddy bear, 1910 *55 38*
c. A672 25pf Fish, 1935 *55 55*
d. A672 35pf Hobby horse, 1850 *55 55*
e. A672 40pf Cuckoo, 1800 *55 38*
f. A672 70pf Frog, 1930 *55 38*

Meissen Porcelain Teapot, 1715 — A673

1982, Jan. 26 Photo. *Perf. 14*

2232 A673 10pf shown 16 16
2233 A673 20pf Vase, 1715 35 32
2234 A673 25pf Oberon figurine, 1969 45 40
2235 A673 35pf Day and Night vase, 1979 55 50

Souvenir Sheet

2236 Sheet of 2 *1.50 1.40*
a. A673 50pf Portrait *70 65*
b. A673 50pf Emblem *70 65*

Johann Friedrich Bottger (1682-1719), inventor of Dresden china. Nos. 2232-2235 se-tenant. No. 2236 contains 2 stamps (24x29mm.); multicolored margin shows Albrechtsburg Castle, Meissen.

Post Offices — A674

1982, Feb. 9

2237 A674 20pf Liebenstein 15 15
2238 A674 25pf Berlin 15 15
2239 A674 35pf Erfurt 15 15
2240 A674 50pf Dresden *1.40 1.10*

Intl. Fur Auction, Leipzig A675

1982, Feb. 23 Photo. *Perf. 14*

2241 A675 10pf Marmot, vert. 15 15
2242 A675 20pf Polecat 15 15
2243 A675 25pf Mink 16 15
2244 A675 35pf Stone marten *1.25 1.00*

Souvenir Sheet

Goethe-Schiller Awards, 1980-1984 — A676

1982, Mar. 9 Litho.

2245 Sheet of 2 *2.50 1.40*
a. A676 50pf Goethe *1.00 65*
b. A676 50pf Schiller *1.00 65*

1982 Leipzig Spring Fair A677

1982, Mar. 9 *Perf. 13x12½*

2246 A677 10pf Entrance 15 15
2247 A677 25pf Exhibit 35 22
Set value 30

Souvenir Sheet

TB Bacillus Centenary A678

1982, Mar. 23 *Perf. 14*

2248 A678 1m multi *2.50 1.50*

Working-class Leader Type of 1979

Designs: No. 2249, Max Fechner (1892-1973). No. 2250, Ottomar Greschke (1882-1957). No. 2251, Helmut Lehmann (1882-1959). No. 2252, Herbert Warnke (1902-1975). No. 2253, Otto Winzer (1902-1975).

1982, Mar. 23 Engr.

2249 A623 10pf dk red brn 15 15
2250 A623 10pf green 15 15
2251 A623 10pf violet 15 15
2252 A623 10pf dull blue 15 15
2253 A623 10pf gray olive 15 15
Set value 50 20

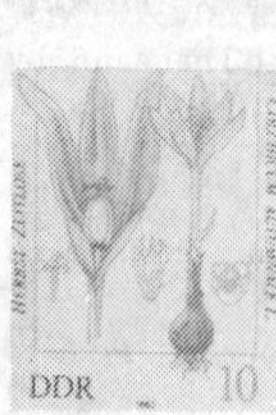

Poisonous Plants — A679

Free Federation of German Trade Unions, 10th Congress — A680

1982, Apr. 6 Litho. *Perf. 14*

2254 A679 10pf Meadow saffron 15 15
2255 A679 15pf Water arum 15 15
2256 A679 20pf Marsh tea 15 15
2257 A679 25pf White bryony 15 15
2258 A679 35pf Common monkshood 18 15
2259 A679 50pf Henbane *1.90 1.50*
Nos. 2254-2259 (6) *2.68*
Set value *1.85*

1982, Apr. 20 Photo.

Paintings: 10pf, Mother and Child, by Walter Womacka. 20pf, Discussion at the Innovator Collective, by Willi Neubert (horiz.). 25pf, Young Couple, by Karl-Heinz Jacob.

2260 A680 10pf multi 15 15
2261 A680 20pf multi 15 15
2262 A680 25pf multi *75 52*
Set value *60*

Intl. Book Art Exhibition, Leipzig — A681

1982, Apr. 20

2263 A681 15pf "I" *45 42*
2264 A681 35pf Emblem *45 42*

Se-tenant with label showing quotation.

Sea Eagle — A682

Designs: Protected species. 10pf, 25pf, 35pf vert.

Perf. 13½x14, 14x13½

1982, May 18 Photo.

2265 A682 10pf Fish hawk 15 15
2266 A682 20pf shown 15 15
2267 A682 25pf Tawny eagle 16 15
2268 A682 35pf Eagle owl *1.10 85*
Set value *1.00*

19th Workers' Festival, Neubrandenburg — A683

1982, June 8 Photo. *Perf. 14*

2269 A683 10pf View of Neubrandenburg 15 15
2270 A683 20pf Traditional costumes 25 16

Souvenir Sheet

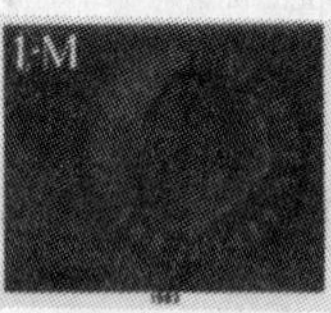

Dimitrov Memorial Medal — A684

1982, June 8

2271 A684 1m multi *1.50 1.40*

George Dimitrov (1882-1947), first prime minister of Bulgaria.

Cargo Ship Frieden — A685

1982, June 22

2272 A685 5pf shown 15 15
2273 A685 10pf Fichtelberg 15 15
2274 A685 15pf Brocken 15 15
2275 A685 20pf Weimar 18 15

2276 A685 25pf Vorwarts 22 15
2277 A685 35pf Berlin *1.40 1.00*
Nos. 2272-2277 (6) *2.25*
Set value *1.30*

Technology — A686

1982, June 22 Litho. ***Perf. 13x12½***
2278 A686 20pf multi 25 15

Bird Wedding A687

Sorbian Folklore: 20pf, Zampern masqueraders. 25pf, Easter egg game. 35pf, Painting Easter eggs. 40pf, St. John's Day parade. 50pf, Christmas celebration.

1982, July 6 Litho. ***Perf. 13x12½***
2279 Block of 6 *4.00 2.75*
a. A687 10pf multi *25 18*
b. A687 20pf multi *38 28*
c. A687 25pf multi *50 35*
d. A687 35pf multi *70 55*
e. A687 40pf multi *75 60*
f. A687 50pf multi *90 75*

View of Schwerin A688

7th Youth Stamp Exhibition, Schwerin: 10pf + 5pf, View, 1640. Nos. 2280-2281 se-tenant with label showing arms of Schwerin.

1982, July 6
2280 A688 10pf + 5pf multi *40 35*
2281 A688 20pf multi *40 35*

7th Pioneer Meeting, Dresden A689

1982, July 20 Photo. ***Perf. 14x13½***
2282 A689 10pf + 5pf Pioneers, banner *50 45*
2283 A689 20pf Bugle, pennant 15 15

Seascape, by Ludolf Backhuysen (1631-1708) — A690

17th Cent. Paintings in Natl. Museum, Schwerin: 10pf, Music Making at Home, by Frans van Mieris (1635-1681) (vert.). 20pf, The Gate Guard, by Carel Fabritius (1622-1654) (vert.). 25pf, Farmers Company, by Adriaen Brouwer (1606-1638). 35pf, Breakfast Table with Ham, by Willem Clacsz Heda (1593-1680). 70pf, River Landscape, by Jan van Goyen (1596-1656).

1982, Aug. 10 ***Perf. 14***
2284 A690 5pf multi 15 15
2285 A690 10pf multi 15 15
2286 A690 20pf multi 15 15
2287 A690 25pf multi 15 15
2288 A690 35pf multi 18 15
2289 A690 70pf multi *2.00 1.50*
Nos. 2284-2289 (6) *2.78*
Set value *1.85*

1982 Leipzig Autumn Fair A691

1982, Aug. 24 Litho. ***Perf. 13x12½***
2290 A691 10pf Exhibition Hall 15 15
2291 A691 25pf Decorative box, ring 22 15
Set value 25

Karl-Marx-Stadt Buildings and Monument — A692

1982, Aug. 24 Photo. ***Perf. 14***
2292 A692 10pf multi 20 15

Org. for the Cooperation of Socialist Countries and Posts and Telecommunications Dept., 13th Conference, Karl-Marx-Stadt, Sept. 6-11. Se-tenant with label showing modes of communication.

Emblem A693

Auschwitz-Birkenau Intl. Memorial A694

1982, Sept. 7 Litho. ***Perf. 14***
2293 A693 10pf multi 15 15

Intl. Federation of Resistance Fighters, 9th Congress, Berlin.

1982, Sept. 7 **Photo.**
2294 A694 35pf multi 35 15

Autumn Flowers — A695

1982, Sept. 21
2295 A695 5pf Autumn anemones 15 15
2296 A695 10pf Student flowers 15 15
2297 A695 15pf Hybrid gazanias 15 15
2298 A695 20pf Sunflowers 15 15
2299 A695 25pf Chrysanthemums 16 15
2300 A695 35pf Cosmos bipinnatus *1.25 1.10*
Set value *1.70 1.40*

Ambulance — A696

1982, Oct. 5 Litho. ***Perf. 13x12½***
2301 A696 5pf shown 15 15
2302 A696 10pf Street cleaner 15 15
2303 A696 20pf Bus 15 15
2304 A696 25pf Platform truck 16 15
2305 A696 35pf Platform truck, diff. 20 15
2306 A696 85pf Milk truck *1.75 1.65*
Nos. 2301-2306 (6) *2.56*
Set value *2.05*

25th Masters of Tomorrow Central Fair — A697

1982, Oct. 19 ***Perf. 14***
2307 A697 20pf multi 15 15

Martin Luther (1483-1546) A698

Toy Carpenter, 1830 A699

Designs: 10pf, Seal of Eisleben (town of birth and death). 20pf, Portrait, Eisenach, 1521. 35pf, Wittenberg seal, 1500. 85pf, Portrait, after Cranach, 1528.

1982, Nov. 23 Photo. ***Perf. 14x13½***
2308 A698 10pf multi 15 15
2309 A698 20pf multi 15 15
a. Miniature sheet of 10 2.75 2.50
2310 A698 35pf multi 20 15
2311 A698 85pf multi *1.40 1.25*
Set value *1.45*

1982, Nov. 23 Litho. ***Perf. 14***
2312 Sheet of 6 *3.50 2.50*
a. A699 10pf shown *55 32*
b. A699 20pf Cobbler *55 50*
c. A699 25pf Baker *55 32*
d. A699 35pf Cooper *55 32*
e. A699 40pf Tanner *55 50*
f. A699 70pf Carter *55 32*

Souvenir Sheet

Johannes Brahms (1833-1897), Composer — A700

1983, Jan. 11 Litho. ***Perf. 14***
2313 A700 1.15m multi *1.90 1.65*

Working-class Leader Type of 1979

Designs: No. 2314, Franz Dahlem (1892-1981). No. 2315, Karl Maron (1903-1975). No. 2316, Josef Miller (1883-1964). No. 2317, Fred Oelssner (1903-1977). No. 2318, Siegfried Radel (1893-1943).

1983, Jan. 25 **Photo.**
2314 A623 10pf dk brn 15 15
2315 A623 10pf dk grn 15 15
2316 A623 10pf dk ol grn 15 15
2317 A623 10pf dp plum 15 15
2318 A623 10pf dk bl 15 15
Set value 40 20

World Communications Year — A701

1983, Feb. 8 Photo. ***Perf. 14***
2319 A701 5pf Telephone receiver, buttons 15 15
2320 A701 10pf Rugen radio 15 15
2321 A701 20pf Surface and air mail 15 15
2322 A701 35pf Optical conductors *70 65*
Set value *92 80*

Otto Nuschke (1883-1957), Statesman A702

1983, Feb. 8
2323 A702 20pf red brn, bl & blk 20 15

Town Hall, Gera, 1576 — A703

1983 Leipzig Spring Fair — A704

1983, Feb. 22 Photo. ***Perf. 14***
2324 A703 10pf Stolberg, 1482, horiz. 15 15
2325 A703 20pf shown 15 15
2326 A703 25pf Possneck, 1486 16 15
2327 A703 35pf Berlin, 1869, horiz. *95 90*
Set value *1.10*

1983, Mar. 8
2328 A704 10pf Fair building 16 15
2329 A704 25pf Robotron microcomputer 32 15
Set value 25

Paul Robeson (1898-1976), Singer — A705

1983, Mar. 22 Litho. ***Perf. 13x12½***
2330 A705 20pf multi 20 15

Souvenir Sheet

Schulze-Boysen/Harnack Resistance Org. — A706

Design: Arvid Harnack (1901-1942), Harro Schulze-Boysen (1909-1942), John Sieg (1903-1942).

1983, Mar. 22
2331 A706 85pf multi 1.40 1.10

Karl Marx (1818-1883), and Newspaper Mastheads — A707

Portraits and: 20pf, Lyons silk weavers' revolt, 1831, French-German Yearbook. 35pf, Engels, Communist Manifesto. 50pf, Das Kapital titlepage. 70pf, Program of German Workers' Movement text. 85pf, Engels, Lenin, globe. 1.15m Portrait (24x29mm).

1983, Apr. 11 Photo. *Perf. 13x12½*
2332 A707 10pf multi 15 15
2333 A707 20pf multi 15 15
2334 A707 35pf multi 15 15
2335 A707 50pf multi 20 15
2336 A707 70pf multi 25 15
2337 A707 85pf multi *2.00 1.90*
Nos. 2332-2337 (6) *2.90 2.65*

Souvenir Sheet

Litho. *Perf. 14*
2338 A707 1.15m multi *1.75 1.50*

Works of Art from Berlin State Museums — A708

1983, Apr. 19 Photo. *Perf. 14*
2339 A708 10pf Athena 15 15
2340 A708 20pf Amazon, bronze, 430 BC 24 15
Set value 15

Narrow-Gauge Railroads — A709

1983, May 17 Litho. *Perf. 13x12½*
2341 Pair, Wernigerode-Nordhausen line 90 85
a. A709 15pf Locomotive 42 40
b. A709 20pf Passenger car 42 40
2342 Pair, Zittau-Oybin/Johnsdorf line 98 85
a. A709 20pf Locomotive 42 40
b. A709 50pf Freight car 42 40

Nos. 2341 and 2342 se-tenant with labels showing maps. See Nos. 2405-2406.

Sand Glasses and Sundials A710

Cacti A711

1983, June 7 Photo. *Perf. 14*
2343 A710 5pf Sand glass, 1674 15 15
2344 A710 10pf Sand glass, 1700 15 15
2345 A710 20pf Sundial, 1611 15 15
a. Sheet of 8 *2.75 2.25*
2346 A710 30pf Sundial, 1750 22 15
2347 A710 50pf Sundial, 1760 30 18
2348 A710 85pf Sundial, 1800 *3.00 1.90*
Nos. 2343-2348 (6) *3.97 2.68*

1983, June 21
2349 A711 5pf Coryphantha elephantidens 15 15
2350 A711 10pf Thelocactus schwarzii 15 15
2351 A711 20pf Leuchtenbergia principis 15 15
2352 A711 25pf Submatucana madisoniorum 15 15
2353 A711 35pf Oroya peruviana 20 16
2354 A711 50pf Copiapoa cinerea *2.00 1.65*
Nos. 2349-2354 (6) *2.80*
Set value *2.00*

Naumberg Cathedral Statues, 15th Cent. A712

1983, July 5 Photo. *Perf. 13*
2355 A712 20pf Thimo and Wilhelm *45 40*
2356 A712 25pf Gepa and Gerburg *55 50*
2357 A712 35pf Hermann and Reglindis *80 72*
2358 A712 85pf Eckehard and Uta *1.90 1.75*

Nos. 2355-2358 se-tenant.

Technical Training, by Harald Metzkes (b. 1929) A713

SOZPHILEX '83 Junior Stamp Exhibition, Berlin: 10pf+5pf, Glasewaldt and Zinna Defending the Barricade-18th March, 1848, by Theodor Hosemann (vert.). Surtax was for exhibition.

1983, July 5 Litho. *Perf. 13x12½*
2359 A713 10pf + 5pf multi *55 45*
2360 A713 20pf multi 15 15

Volleyball A714

1983, July 19 Photo. *Perf. 14*
2361 A714 10pf + 5pf Passing beach balls *38 28*
2362 A714 20pf shown 15 15

7th Gymnastic and Sports Meeting; 9th Children's and Youth Spartikiade, Leipzig.

Simon Bolivar (1783-1830) — A715

1983, July 19
2363 A715 35pf Bolivar, Alexander von Humboldt 50 30

City Arms — A716

1983 Leipzig Autumn Fair — A717

1983, Aug. 9
2364 A716 50pf Berlin *90 50*
2365 A716 50pf Cottbus *90 50*
2366 A716 50pf Dresden *90 50*
2367 A716 50pf Erfurt *90 50*
2368 A716 50pf Frankfurt *90 50*
Nos. 2364-2368 (5) *4.50 2.50*

See Nos. 2398-2402, 2464-2468.

1983, Aug. 30
2369 A717 10pf Central Palace 15 15
2370 A717 25pf Microelectronic pattern 28 25

Leonhard Euler (1707-1783), Mathematician — A718

1983, Sept. 6
2371 A718 20pf multi 35 15

Souvenir Sheet

30th Anniv. of Working-Class Brigade Groups — A719

1983, Sept. 6 Litho. *Perf. 12½x13*
2372 A719 1m multi *1.25 1.00*

Governmental Palaces, Potsdam Gardens — A720

1983, Sept. 20 *Perf. 13x12½*
2373 A720 10pf Sanssouci Palace 15 15
2374 A720 20pf Chinese tea-house 15 15
2375 A720 40pf Charlottenhof Palace 25 22
2376 A720 50pf Royal Stables, Film Museum *1.60 1.50*

Monument, Mamajew-Kurgan Hill — A721

1983, Oct. 4 *Perf. 14*
2377 A721 35pf Mother Home 50 30

Souvenir Sheet

Martin Luther — A722

1983, Oct. 18 Litho. *Perf. 14*
2378 A722 1m multi *1.90 1.65*

Margin shows title page from Luther Bible, 1541.

Thuringian Glass — A723

1983, Nov. 8 Photo. *Perf. 13½x14*
2379 A723 10pf Cock 15 15
2380 A723 20pf Cup 15 15
2381 A723 25pf Vase 15 15
2382 A723 70pf Ornamental Glass *1.25 1.10*

Souvenir Sheet

New Year 1984 — A724

1983, Nov. 22 Litho. *Perf. 14*
2383 Sheet of 4 *1.40 1.25*
a. A724 10pf multi *15 15*
b. A724 20pf multi *28 25*
c. A724 25pf multi *40 35*
d. A724 35pf multi *60 55*

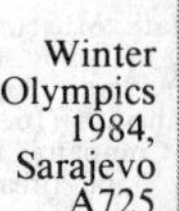

Winter Olympics 1984, Sarajevo A725

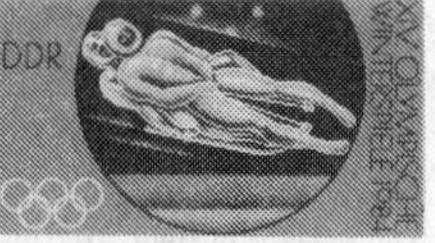

1983, Nov. 22 Photo. *Perf. 14*
2384 A725 10pf + 5pf 2-man luge 15 15
2385 A725 20pf + 10pf Ski jump 15 15
2386 A725 25pf Skiing 15 15

2387 A725 35pf Biathlon *1.25 1.10*

Souvenir Sheet

2388 A725 85pf Olympic Center *1.40* 1.25

Jena Glass Centenary — A726

1984, Jan. 10 Litho. *Perf. 12½x13*

2389 A726 20pf Otto Schott 30 28

Working-class Leader Type of 1979

Designs: No. 2390, Friedrich Ebert (1894-1979). No. 2391, Fritz Grosse (1904-1957). No. 2392, Albert Norden (1904-1982).

1984, Jan. 24 Engr. *Perf. 14*

2390 A623 10pf black 16 15
2391 A623 10pf dk grn 16 15
2392 A623 10pf dk bl 16 15

Souvenir Sheet

Felix Mendelssohn (1809-1847), Composer — A727

1984, Jan. 24 Litho.

2393 A727 85pf multi 1.25 1.00

Margin shows Song Without Words score.

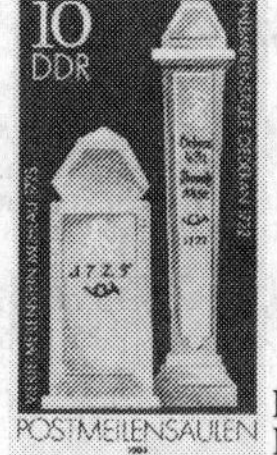

Postal Milestones — A728

Designs: 10pf, Muhlau, 1725; Oederan, 1722. 20pf, Johanngeorgenstadt, 1723; Schonbrunn, 1724. 35pf, Freiberg, 1723. 85pf, Pegau, 1723.

1984, Feb. 7 Photo. *Perf. 14*

2394 A728 10pf multi 15 15
2395 A728 20pf multi 18 16
2396 A728 35pf multi 30 28
2397 A728 85pf multi 70 65

City Arms Type of 1983

1984, Feb. 21

2398 A716 50pf Gera 48 42
2399 A716 50pf Halle 48 42
2400 A716 50pf Karl-Marx-Stadt 48 42
2401 A716 50pf Leipzig 48 42
2402 A716 50pf Magdeburg 48 42
Nos. 2398-2402 (5) 2.40 2.10

1984 Leipzig Spring Fair A729

1984, Mar. 6 *Perf. 14*

2403 A729 10pf Old Town Hall 15 15
2404 A729 25pf Factory 20 16
Set value 30 23

Railroad Type of 1983

1984, Mar. 20 Litho. *Perf. 13x12½*

2405 Pair, Cranzahl Oberwiesenthal line 95 85
a. A709 30pf Locomotive 28 25
b. A709 80pf Passenger car 65 55
2406 Pair, Selke Valley line 85 75
a. A709 40pf Locomotive 32 28
b. A709 60pf Passenger car 50 45

Labels show maps of routes.

Stone Door, Rostock A730

Council Building A731

Intl. Society of Monument Preservation 7th General Meeting: 10pf, Town Hall, Rostock. 15pf, Albrecht Castle, Meissen. 85pf, Stable Courtyard, Dresden. 10pf, 15pf, 85pf horiz.

1984, Apr. 24 Photo. *Perf. 14*

2407 A730 10pf multi 15 15
2408 A730 15pf multi 16 15
2409 A730 40pf multi 42 35
2410 A730 85pf multi 80 70

1984, May 8

2411 A731 70pf multi 60 55

Standing Commission of Posts and Telecommunications of Council of Mutual Economic Aid, 25th meeting.

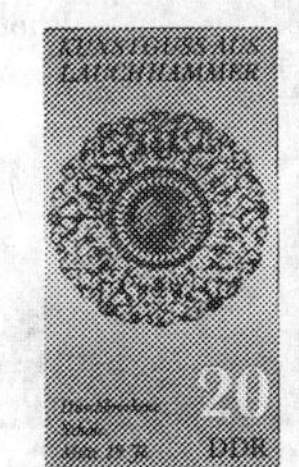

Cast-iron Bowl, 19th Cent. A732

Marionette A733

Cast-Iron, Lauchhammer: 85pf, Ascending Man, by Fritz Cremer, 1967.

1984, May 22

2412 A732 20pf multi 15 15
2413 A732 85pf multi 75 70

1984, June 5

2414 A733 50pf shown 35 40
2415 A733 80pf Puppet 65 65

Natl. Youth Festival A734

1984, June 5 Litho. *Perf. 13x12½*

2416 A734 10pf + 5pf Demonstration 15 15
2417 A734 20pf Construction workers 15 15
Set value 24

Nos. 2416-2417 se-tenant with label showing emblem and text.

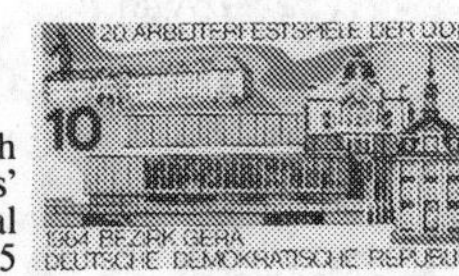

20th Workers' Festival A735

1984, June 19

2418 A735 10pf View of Gera 15 15
2419 A735 20pf Traditional costumes 22 15
Set value 22

Nos. 2418-2419 se-tenant with label showing arms, text.

Natl. Stamp Exhib., Halle — A736

Historic Seals, 1442 — A737

1984, July 3 *Perf. 13½x14*

2420 A736 10pf + 5pf Salt carrier 15 15
2421 A736 20pf Wedding couple 15 15
Set value 24

1984, Aug. 7 Litho. *Perf. 14*

2422 A737 5pf Baker, Berlin *30* 15
2423 A737 10pf Wool weaver, Berlin *60* 15
2424 A737 20pf Wool weaver, Cologne *1.10* 15
2425 A737 35pf Shoemaker, Cologne *2.00* 25
Set value *4.00* 50

Nos. 2422-2425 printed se-tenant.

Building Renovation and Construction A738

Ironwork Collective Combine East — A739

Litho., Photo. (#2427, 2429, 25pf)

1984 *Perf. 14x13½*

2426 A738 10pf shown 15 15
2427 A739 10pf shown 15 15
2428 A738 20pf Surface mining 18 16
2429 A739 20pf Armed forces 18 16
2430 A739 25pf Petro-chemical Collective Combine, Schwedt 20 18
Set value 72 64

Souvenir Sheets

2431 A738 1m Privy Council Building 95 80
2432 A739 1m Family 95 80

35th anniv. of DDR. Issue dates: A738, Aug. 21; A739, Sept. 11.

1984 Leipzig Autumn Fair — A740

1984, Aug. 28 Photo. *Perf. 14*

2433 A740 10pf Frege House, Katharine St. 15 15
2434 A740 25pf Crystal bowl, Olbernhau 32 16
Set value 24

Members of the Resistance, Sculpture by Arno Wittig — A741

1984, Sept. 18 Photo. *Perf. 14*

2435 A741 35pf multi 30 22

View of Magdeburg — A742

1984, Oct. 4 Litho. *Perf. 13x12½*

2436 A742 10pf + 5pf shown 18 15
2437 A742 20pf Old & modern buildings 22 15
Set value 24

8th Youth Stamp Exhibition, Magdeburg. Se-tenant with label showing arms.

35th Anniv. of Republic — A743

1984, Oct. 4 Photo. *Perf. 14*

2438 A743 10pf Construction 15 15
2439 A743 20pf Military 15 15
2440 A743 25pf Heavy industry 20 18
2441 A743 35pf Agriculture 25 22

Souvenir Sheet

2442 A743 1m Arms, dove, vert. 75 70

Figurines, Green Vault of Dresden — A744

1984, Oct. 23

2443 A744 10pf Spring 15 15
2444 A744 20pf Summer 15 15
a. Miniature sheet of 8, litho., perf. 12½x13 1.75 1.50
2445 A744 35pf Autumn 25 22
2446 A744 70pf Winter 50 45

Falkenstein Castle — A745

1984, Nov. 6 Litho. *Perf. 14*

2447 A745 10pf shown 15 15
2448 A745 20pf Kriebstein 15 15
2449 A745 35pf Ranis 25 22
2450 A745 80pf Neuenburg 65 60

See Nos. 2504-2507.

Dead Tsar's Daughter and the Seven Warriors
A746

Various scenes from the fairytale.

1984, Nov. 27 Litho. *Perf. 13*

2451	Sheet of 6	1.25	1.10
a.	A746 5pf multi	15	15
b.	A746 10pf multi	15	15
c.	A746 15pf multi	15	15
d.	A746 20pf multi	18	16
e.	A746 35pf multi	30	28
f.	A746 50pf multi	45	40

Working-class Leader Type of 1979

Designs: No. 2452, Anton Ackermann (1905-1973). No. 2453, Alfred Kurella (1895-1975). No. 2454, Otto Schon (1905-1968).

1985, Jan. 8 Engr. *Perf. 14*

2452	A623 10pf blk brn	15	15
2453	A623 10pf red brn	15	15
2454	A623 10pf gray vio	15	15
	Set value	24	22

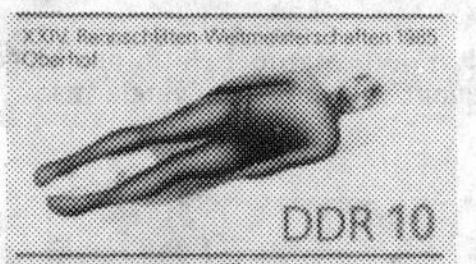

24th World Luge Championship — A747

1985, Jan. 22 Photo.

2455	A747 10pf Single seat luge	15	15

Antique Mailboxes — A748

1985, Feb. 5 Litho. *Perf. 14*

2456	A748 10pf 1850	15	15
2457	A748 20pf 1860	18	16
2458	A748 35pf 1900	30	28
2459	A748 50pf 1920	42	38
a.	Block of 4, Nos. 2456-2459	1.00	90

Souvenir Sheet

Dresden Opera House Reopening — A749

Litho. & Engr.

1985, Feb. 12 *Perf. 13*

2460	A749 85pf multicolored	75	70

1985 Leipzig Spring Fair — A750

Bach, Handel and Schutz Tribute — A751

1985, Mar. 5 Photo. *Perf. 14*

2461	A750 10pf Statue of Bach, Leipzig	15	15
2462	A750 25pf Porcelain pot, Meissen	20	16
	Set value	30	23

Souvenir Sheet

1985, Mar. 19 Litho.

2463	Sheet of 3	1.10	1.00
a.	A751 10pf Bach	15	15
b.	A751 20pf Handel	15	15
c.	A751 85pf Heinrich Schutz (1585-1672)	80	75

City Arms Type of 1983

1985, Apr. 9 Photo. *Perf. 14*

2464	A716 50pf Neubrandenburg	48	42
2465	A716 50pf Potsdam	48	42
2466	A716 50pf Rostock	48	42
2467	A716 50pf Schwerin	48	42
2468	A716 50pf Suhl	48	42
	Nos. 2464-2468 (5)	2.40	2.10

Seelow Heights Memorial — A752

1985, Apr. 16 Photo. *Perf. 14*

2469	A752 35pf multi	32	28

Egon Erwin Kisch, Journalist (1885-1948) — A753

1985, Apr. 23 Photo. *Perf. 14*

2470	A753 35pf multi	32	28

No. 2470 was printed se-tenant with label showing the house where Kisch was born.

Liberation from Fascism, 40th Anniv. — A754

Designs: 10pf, German and Soviet astronauts. 20pf, Coal miner Adolf Hennecke, symbols of industry and energy. 25pf, farm workers, symbols of socialist agriculture. 50pf, Technicians manufacturing microchips, science and technology.

1985, May 7 Photo. *Perf. 14x13½*

2471	A754 10pf multi	15	15
2472	A754 20pf multi	18	16
2473	A754 25pf multi	20	18
2474	A754 50pf multi	42	38

Souvenir Sheet

Perf. 12½x13

2475	A754 1m Berlin-Treptow Soviet Heroes Monument	85	75

Warsaw Treaty, 30th Anniv. — A755

1985, May 14 Litho. *Perf. 13x12½*

2476	A755 20pf Flags of pact nations	30	15

Historical and Modern Buildings
A756

12th Youth Parliament, Berlin: 20pf, Ernst Thalmann, flags.

1985, May 21 Litho.

2477	A756 10pf + 5pf multi	15	15
2478	A756 20pf multi	18	15
	Set value	30	23

Nos. 2477-2478 printed se-tenant with central label picturing youth parliament logo.

Intl. Olympic Committee 90th Meeting — A757

1985, May 28 Litho. *Perf. 14*

2479	A757 35pf Flag	30	28

No. 2479 was printed se-tenant with label.

Free German Trade Unions, 40th Anniv. — A758

1985, June 11 Photo.

2480	A758 20pf Red flags	25	22

Wildlife Preservation
A759

1985, June 25 Photo.

2481	A759 5pf Harpy eagle, vert.	15	15
2482	A759 10pf Red-necked goose	15	15
2483	A759 20pf Spectacled bear	18	16
2484	A759 50pf Banteng (Javanese) buffalo	42	38
2485	A759 85pf Sunda Straits crocodile	70	65
	Nos. 2481-2485 (5)	1.60	1.49

19th Century Steam Engines
A760

1985, July 9 Photo.

2486	A760 10pf Bock engine, vert.	15	15
2487	A760 85pf Beam engine	65	60

12th World Youth and Student Festival, Moscow
A761

1985, July 23 Litho. *Perf. 13x12½*

2488	A761 20pf + 5pf Students reading	20	15
2489	A761 50pf Student demonstration	50	35

Nos. 2488-2489 printed se-tenant with center label picturing festival emblem.

2nd World Orienteering and Deep-sea Diving Championship — A762

1985, Aug. 13 Photo. *Perf. 14*

2490	A762 10pf Diver at turning buoy	15	15
2491	A762 70pf Long-distance divers	60	45
	Set value	70	52

Bose House Fair Building, St. Thomas Churchyard — A763

1985, Apr. 27 Photo.

2492	A763 10pf shown	15	15
2493	A763 25pf Bach trumpet	25	18
	Set value	35	25

Leipzig Autumn Fair.

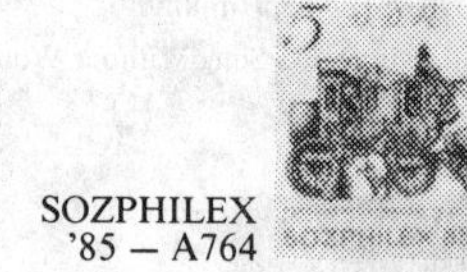

SOZPHILEX '85 — A764

Design: 19th century coach and team, 1878, bas-relief by Hermann Steinemann, in the court of the former Berlin Post Office.

1985, Sept. 10 Litho. *Perf. 13x12½*

2494	A764 5pf multi	15	15
2495	A764 20pf + 5pf multi	20	18
a.	Miniature sheet of 8, 4 each	1.00	90
	Set value	25	22

No. 2495a has a continuous design.

Socialist Railway Org. — A765

Designs: 20pf, GS II signal box, track diagram. 25pf, 1838 Saxonia, first German locomotive, designer Johann Andreas Schubert (1808-1870), Model 250 electric locomotive. 50pf, Helicopter lifting cable drum, section electrification. 85pf, Leipzig Central Station.

1985, Sept. 24 Litho. *Perf. 12½x13*

2496	A765 20pf multi	25	18
2497	A765 25pf multi	32	22
2498	A765 50pf multi	65	45
2499	A765 85pf multi	1.00	70

German Railways 150th anniv.

Bridges in East Berlin A766

Photo.; Litho. (#2501a)

1985, Oct. 8 *Perf. 14*

2500 A766 10pf Gertrauden 15 15
2501 A766 20pf Jungfern 20 18
a. Min. sheet of 8, perf. 13x12½ 1.25 1.40
2502 A766 35pf Weidendammer 35 32
2503 A766 70pf Marx-Engels 70 60

Castles Type of 1984

1985, Oct. 15 **Litho.**

2504 A745 10pf Hohnstein 15 15
2505 A745 20pf Rochsburg 16 15
2506 A745 35pf Schwarzenberg 32 28
2507 A745 80pf Stein 70 65

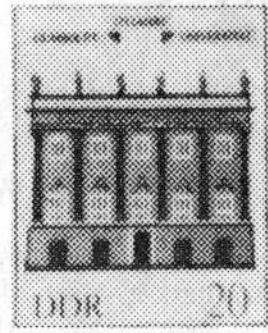

Humboldt University, 175th Anniv. — A767

Anniversaries: 85pf, Charity Hospital, Berlin, 275th anniv.

1985, Oct. 22 *Perf. 14*

2508 A767 20pf Administration bldg. 16 15
2509 A767 85pf Buildings, 1897, 1982 75 70

Castle Cacilienhof, UN Emblem A768

1985, Oct. 22 **Photo.** *Perf. 13*

2510 A768 85pf multi 75 70

UN, 40th Anniv.

Circus Art — A769

1985, Nov. 12 *Perf. 14*

2511 A769 10pf Elephant training 15 15
2512 A769 20pf Trapeze artist 45 25
2513 A769 35pf Acrobats on unicycles 80 42
2514 A769 50pf Tiger training 1.10 65

Nos. 2511-2514 se-tenant.

Souvenir Sheet

Brothers Grimm, Fabulists & Philologists A770

Fairy tales compiled by Wilhelm (1786-1859) and Jacob (1785-1863) Grimm.

1985, Nov. 26 **Litho.** *Perf. 13½x13*

2515 Sheet of 6 1.75 1.65
a. A770 5pf multi 15 15
b. A770 10pf Valiant Tailor 15 15
c. A770 20pf Lucky John 18 16
d. A770 25pf Puss-in-Boots 22 20
e. A770 35pf Seven Ravens 32 28
f. A770 85pf Sweet Porridge 75 70

Monuments to Water Power — A772

Postal Uniforms, c. 1850 — A773

Designs: 10pf, Cast iron hand pump, c. 1900. 35pf, Berlin-Altglienicke water tower, c. 1900. 50pf, Berlin-Friedrichshagen waterworks, 1893. 70pf, Rapphoden Hydro-electric Dam, 1959.

Engr., Photo. & Engr. (35pf)

1986, Jan. 21 *Perf. 14*

2516 A772 10pf dk grn & lake 15 15
2517 A772 35pf buff, blk & dk grn 30 28
2518 A772 50pf dk red brn & lt ol grn 42 38
2519 A772 70pf dk bl & brn 58 52

1986, Feb. 4 **Photo.** *Perf. 14½x14*

2520 A773 10pf Saxon postillion 15 15
a. Litho., perf. 12½x13 15 15
2521 A773 20pf Prussian postman 18 16
a. Litho., perf. 12½x13 18 16
2522 A773 85pf Prussian P.O. clerk 75 70
a. Litho., perf. 12½x13 75 70
2523 A773 1m Mecklenburg clerk 85 75
a. Litho., perf. 12½x13 85 75
b. Block of 4, #2520a-2523a 1.90 1.75

Natl. People's Army, 30th Anniv. A774

1986, Feb. 18 *Perf. 14*

2524 A774 20pf multi 25 16

No. 2524 printed se-tenant with gold and red inscribed label.

Free German Youth Org., 40th Anniv. — A775

1986, Feb. 18

2525 A775 20pf multi 25 16

Leipzig Spring Fair A776

1986, Mar. 11 **Litho.** *Perf. 13x12½*

2526 A776 35pf Fair grounds entrance, 1946 32 28
2527 A776 50pf Trawler Atlantik 488 48 42

Manned Space Flight, 25th Anniv. — A777

Designs: 40pf, Yuri Gagarin, Soviet cosomonaut, Vostok rocket, 1961. 50pf, Cosmonauts W. Bykowski, USSR, and S. Jahn, DDR, Vega probe, 1986, Intercosmos emblem. 70pf, Venera probe, Venus, spectrometer. 85pf, MKF-6 multi-spectral reconnaissance camera.

1986, Mar. 25 *Perf. 14*

2528 A777 40pf multi 38 35
2529 A777 50pf multi 48 42
2530 A777 70pf multi 65 60
2531 A777 85pf multi 78 70

Nos. 2528-2531 printed se-tenant.

Socialist Unity 11th Party Day — A778

Designs: 10pf, Marx, Engels and Lenin. 20pf, Ernst Thalmann. 50pf, Wilhelm Pieck and Otto Grotewohl, Uniting Party Day, 1946. 85pf, Family, motto. 1m, Construction worker, key to economic progress.

1986, Apr. 8 *Perf. 13½x13*

2532 A778 10pf multi 15 15
2533 A778 20pf multi 20 18
2534 A778 50pf multi 48 42
2535 A778 85pf multi 80 75

Souvenir Sheet

Perf. 13x14

2536 A778 1m multi 95 85

Ernst Thalmann Park Opening, Berlin — A779

1986, Apr. 15 **Photo.** *Perf. 14*

2537 A779 20pf Memorial statue 20 18

Trams and Streetcars A780

Designs: 10pf, Dresden horse-drawn tram, 1886. 20pf, Leipzig streetcar, 1896. 40pf, Berlin streetcar, 1919. 70pf, Halle streetcar, 1928.

1986, May 20 **Photo.** *Perf. 14*

2538 A780 10pf multi 15 15
2539 A780 20pf multi 22 16
2540 A780 40pf multi 42 32
2541 A780 70pf multi 75 60

Dresden Zoo, 125th Anniv. — A781

Berlin, 750th Anniv. — A782

1986, May 27 **Litho.** *Perf. 14*

2542 A781 10pf Orangutan 15 15
2543 A781 20pf Colobus monkey 18 16
2544 A781 50pf Mandrill 55 50
2545 A781 70pf Lemur 75 68

Litho. & Engr., Engr. (70pf, 1m)

1986, June 3 *Perf. 12½x13, 13x12½*

20pf, 50pf are horiz.

2546 A782 10pf City seal, 1253 15 15
2547 A782 20pf Map, 1648 18 16
2548 A782 50pf City arms, 1253 45 40
2549 A782 70pf Nicholas Church, 1832 65 60

Souvenir Sheet

2550 A782 1m Royal Palace, 1986 95 85

21st Workers' Games, Magdeburg — A783

Designs: 20pf, Couple in folk dress, house construction. 50pf, Magdeburg Port, River Elbe.

1986, June 17 **Litho.** *Perf. 13x12½*

2551 A783 20pf multi 18 16
2552 A783 50pf multi 45 40

#2551-2552 printed se-tenant with center label picturing Workers' Party emblem.

9th Youth Stamp Exhibition, Berlin — A784

1986, July 22 **Litho.** *Perf. 13x12½*

2553 A784 10pf + 5pf Berlin, c. 1652 15 15
2554 A784 20pf Art, architecture, 1986 20 18

Nos. 2553-2554 printed se-tenant with center label picturing Berlin city seal, 1338.

Castles A785

1986, July 29 *Perf. 13x12½*

2555 A785 10pf Schwerin 15 15
a. Miniature sheet of 4 50 35
2556 A785 20pf Gustrow 20 18
a. Miniature sheet of 4 80 70
2557 A785 85pf Rheinsberg 85 70
2558 A785 1m Ludwigslust 1.00 90

Intl. Peace Year A786

1986, Aug. 5 **Photo.** ***Perf. 13***
2559 A786 35pf multi 35 32

Berlin Wall, 25th Anniv. — A787

1986, Aug. 5 **Litho.** ***Perf. 14***
2560 A787 20pf Soldiers, Brandenburg Gate 20 18

Souvenir Sheet

Leipzig Autumn Fair — A788

1986, Aug. 19
2561 A788 Sheet of 2 1.00 90
a. 25pf Fair building 50 18
b. 85pf Cloth merchants, 15th cent. 50 70

City Coins A789

1986, Sept. 2 **Photo.** ***Perf. 13***
2562 A789 10pf Rostock, 1637 15 15
2563 A789 35pf Nordhausen, 1660 35 32
2564 A789 50pf Erfurt, 1633 48 42
2565 A789 85pf Magdeburg, 1638 82 75
2566 A789 1m Stralsund, 1622 95 85
Nos. 2562-2566 (5) 2.75 2.49

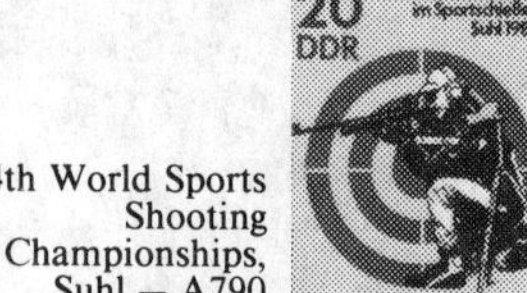

44th World Sports Shooting Championships, Suhl — A790

1986, Sept. 2 ***Perf. 14***
2567 A790 20pf Rifle shooting 20 18
2568 A790 70pf Woman firing handgun 68 60
2569 A790 85pf Skeet-shooting 80 70

11th World Trade Unions Congress, Berlin — A791

Border Guards, 40th Anniv. — A792

1986, Sept. 9
2570 A791 70pf multi 68 60

No. 2570 printed se-tenant with label continuing the design.

1986, Sept. 9
2571 A792 20pf multi 20 18

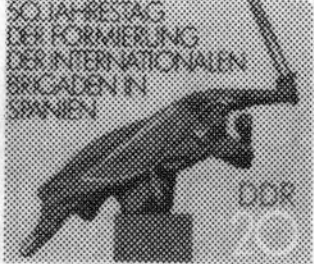

Intl. Brigades in Spain, 50th Anniv. — A793

1986, Sept. 11
2572 A793 20pf Memorial, Friedrichshain 20 18

Natl. Memorial for Concentration Camp Victims, Sachsenhausem, 25th Anniv. — A794

1986, Sept. 23
2573 A794 35pf multi 35 32

Mukran-Klaipeda Train-Ferry, Inauguration — A795

1986, Sept. 23
2574 A795 50pf Pier, Mukran 48 42
2575 A795 50pf Ferry 48 42

Printed se-tenant.

Souvenir Sheet

Carl Maria von Weber (1786-1826), Composer — A796

1986, Nov. 4 **Litho.** ***Perf. 14***
2576 A796 85pf multi 85 75

Indira Gandhi (1917-1984), Prime Minister of India — A797

1986, Nov. 18 **Photo.**
2577 A797 10pf multi 15 15

Miniature Sheet

Chandeliers from the Ore Mountains A798

Wrought iron candle-carrying chandeliers presented to Johann Georgenstadt miners annually by the mine blacksmith.

1986, Nov. 18 **Photo.** ***Perf. 14***
2578 Sheet of 6 2.25 1.90
a. A798 10pf 1778 35 15
b. A798 20pf 1796 35 18
c. A798 25pf 1810 35 22
d. A798 35pf 1821 35 32
e. A798 40pf 1830 35 35
f. A798 85pf 1925 35 75

Statues of Roland, Medieval Hero — A799

1987, Jan. 20 **Photo.** ***Perf. 14½x14***
2579 A799 10pf Stendal, 1525 15 15
2580 A799 20pf Halle, 1719 22 20
2581 A799 35pf Brandenburg, 1474 40 35
2582 A799 50pf Quedlinburg, 1460 55 50

See Nos. 2782-2785.

Historic Post Offices A800

1987, Feb. 3 **Photo.** ***Perf. 14x14½***
2583 A800 10pf Freiberg, 1889 15 15
2584 A800 20pf Perleberg, 1897 20 18
2585 A800 70pf Weimar, 1889 65 60
2586 A800 1.20m Kirschau, 1926 1.10 1.00
a. Block of 4, #2583-2586 2.25 2.00

Nos. 2583-2586 printed in sheets of fifty and se-tenant in sheets of 40.

Berlin, 750th Anniv. A801

Architecture: 20pf, Reconstructed Palais Ephraim, Nikolai Quarter, demolished 1936, reopened 1987, vert. 35pf, Old Marzahn Village, modern housing. 70pf, Marx-Engels Forum, Central Berlin. 85pf, Reconstructed Friedrichstadt Palace Theater, reopened 1984.

Perf. 12½x13, 13x12½
1987, Feb. 17 **Engr.**
2587 A801 20pf vio brn & bluish grn 25 20
2588 A801 35pf sage grn & dk rose brn 45 32
2589 A801 70pf org & dk bl 80 65
2590 A801 85pf dk ol grn & yel grn 1.10 85

See Nos. 2628-2631.

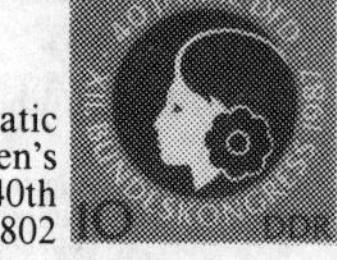

Democratic Women's Federation, 40th Anniv. — A802

1987, Mar. 3 **Litho.** ***Perf. 13½***
2591 A802 10pf sil, dk bl & brt red 18 16

Leipzig Spring Fair A803

1987, Mar. 10 ***Perf. 13x12½***
2592 A803 35pf New Fair Hall No. 20 38 35
2593 A803 50pf Traders at market, c. 1804 55 50

Leaders of the German Workers' Movement — A804

Portraits: No. 2594, Fritz Gabler (1897-1974). No. 2595, Robert Siewert (1887-1973). No.2596, Walter Vesper (1897-1978). No. 2597, Clara Zetkin (1857-1933).

1987, Mar. 24 **Engr.** ***Perf. 14***
2594 A804 10pf dark gray 15 15
2595 A804 10pf dark green 15 15
2596 A804 10pf black 15 15
2597 A804 10pf vio black 15 15
Set value 48 40

See Nos. 2721-2724.

K.A. Lingner (1861-1916), Museum — A805

1987, Apr. 7 **Photo.** ***Perf. 14***
2598 A805 85pf multi 90 80

German Hygiene Museum, Dresden, 75th anniv.

Free German Trade Unions 11th Congress A806

1987, Apr. 7 **Litho.** ***Perf. 13x12½***
2599 A806 20pf Construction 22 20
2600 A806 50pf Computer, ship 58 52

Printed se-tenant with center label picturing unions emblem and text.

German Red Cross 10th Congress A807

1987, Apr. 7 Photo. *Perf. 14*
2601 A807 35pf multi 40 35

Agricultural Cooperative, 35th Anniv. — A808

1987, Apr. 21 Litho. *Perf. 13x12½*
2602 A808 20pf multi 24 22

Famous Men A809

Designs: 10pf, Ludwig Uhland (1787-1862), poet, philologist. 20pf, Arnold Zweig (1887-1968), novelist. 35pf, Gerhart Hauptmann (1862-1946), 1912 Nobel laureate for literature, and scene from The Weavers. 50pf, Gustav Hertz (1887-1975), physicist, and atomic energy transmission diagram.

1987, May 5
2603 A809 10pf multi 15 15
2604 A809 20pf multi 24 22
2605 A809 35pf multi 40 35
2606 A809 50pf multi 58 52

Freshwater Fish A810

1987, May 19 Litho. *Perf. 13x12½*
2607 A810 5pf Abramis brama 15 15
2608 A810 10pf Salmo trutta fario 15 15
2609 A810 20pf Silurus glanis 24 22
2610 A810 35pf Thymallus thymallus 40 35
2611 A810 50pf Barbus barbus 58 52
2612 A810 70pf Esox lucius 80 70
Nos. 2607-2612 (6) 2.32 2.09

Nos. 2608-2609 exist in sheets of 4.

Fire Engines A811

1987, June 16
2613 A811 10pf Hand-operated, 1756 15 15
2614 A811 25pf Steam, 1903 28 25
2615 A811 40pf LF 15, 1919 45 40
2616 A811 70pf LF 16-TS 8, 1971 78 70
a. Block of 4, Nos. 2613-2616 1.65 1.50

Souvenir Sheet

Esperanto Movement, Cent. — A812

1987, July 7 Litho. *Perf. 14*
2617 A812 85pf L.L. Zamenhof, globe 95 85

World Wildlife Fund A813

1987, July 7 Photo.
2618 A813 10pf Two otters 15 15
2619 A813 25pf Otter swimming 28 25
2620 A813 35pf Otter 38 35
2621 A813 60pf Close-up of head 68 60

8th Sports Festival and 11th Youth Sports Championships, Leipzig — A814

1987, July 21
2622 A814 5pf Tug-of-war 15 15
2623 A814 10pf Handball 15 15
2624 A814 20pf + 5pf Girls' long jump 28 25
2625 A814 35pf Table tennis 38 35
2626 A814 40pf Bowling 45 40
2627 A814 70pf Running 78 70
Nos. 2622-2627 (6) 2.19 2.00

Berlin Anniversary Type of 1987
Perf. 12½x13, 13x12½
1987, Feb. 17 Engr.
2628 A801 10pf like No. 2587 15 15
a. Miniature sheet of 4 48 42
2629 A801 10pf like No. 2588 15 15
a. Miniature sheet of 4 48 42
2630 A801 20pf like No. 2589 24 22
a. Miniature sheet of 4 1.00 90
2631 A801 20pf like No. 2590 24 22
a. Miniature sheet of 4 1.00 90

Assoc. of Sports and Science, 35th Anniv. A815

1987, Aug. 4 Litho. *Perf. 13x12½*
2632 A815 10pf multi 15 15

Stamp Day A816

Designs: 10pf+5pf, Court Post Office, Berlin, 1760. 20pf, Wartenberg Palace, former Prussian General Post Office, 1770.

1987, Aug. 11 Photo. *Perf. 14*
2633 A816 10pf +5pf multi 18 16
2634 A816 20pf multi 24 22

Nos. 2633-2634 printed se-tenant with center label picturing two-wheel post wagon.

Souvenir Sheet

Leipzig Autumn Fair — A817

1987, Aug. 25 Litho. *Perf. 13½*
2635 A817 Sheet of 2 1.10 1.00
a. 40pf multi 48 42
b. 50pf multi 60 55

Intl. War Victims' Memorial, Budapest A818

1987, Sept. 8 Photo. *Perf. 14*
2636 A818 35pf Statue of Jozsef Somogyi 40 35

Souvenir Sheet

Thalmann Memorial — A819

Litho. & Engr.
1987, Sept. 8 *Perf. 14*
2637 A819 1.35m buff, ver & blk 1.50 1.40

City of Berlin, 750th anniv.

10th Natl. Art Exhibition, Berlin — A820

Designs: 10pf, Weidendamm Bridge, Berlin, 1986, by Arno Mohr. 50pf, They Only Wanted to Learn How to Read and Write, Nicaragua, 1985-86, by Willi Sitte. 70pf, Large Figure of a Man in Mourning, 1983, scupture by Wieland Forster. 1m, Ceramic bowl, 1986, by Gerd Lucke. Nos. 2638-2640, vert.

1987, Sept. 28 Litho.
2638 A820 10pf multi 15 15
2639 A820 50pf multi 55 50
2640 A820 70pf multi 80 70
2641 A820 1m multi 1.15 1.00

Lenin, Flag, Smolny Institute, Cruiser Aurora A821

1987, Oct. 27 Photo. *Perf. 14*
2642 A821 10pf shown 15 15
2643 A821 20pf Spasski Tower 22 20

October Revolution, Russia, 70th anniv.

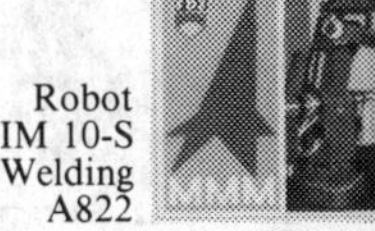

Robot ZIM 10-S Welding A822

1987, Nov. 3 Litho. *Perf. 13x12½*
2644 A822 10pf Personal computer 15 15
2645 A822 20pf shown 22 20

30th MMM Science Fair and 10th Central Industrial Fair for Students and Youth Scientists, Leipzig.

Miniature Sheet

Christmas Candle Carousels from the Ore Mountains — A823

Designs: 10pf, Annaberg, c. 1810. 20pf, Freiberg, c. 1830. 25pf, Neustadtel, c. 1870. 35pf, Schneeberg, c. 1870. 40pf, Lossnitz, c. 1880. 85pf, Seiffen, c. 1910.

1987, Nov. 3 Litho. *Perf. 12½x13*
2646 Sheet of 6 2.75 2.50
a. A823 10pf multi 15 15
b. A823 20pf multi 25 22
c. A823 25pf multi 32 28
d. A823 35pf multi 45 40
e. A823 40pf multi 50 45
f. A823 85pf multi 1.05 95

1988 Winter Olympics, Calgary — A824

1988, Jan. 19 Photo. *Perf. 14½x14*
2647 A824 5pf Ski jumping 15 15
2648 A824 10pf Speed skating 15 15
2649 A824 20pf +10pf 4-Man bobsled 42 38
2650 A824 35pf Biathlon 48 42

Souvenir Sheet
Perf. 13x12½
2651 A824 1.20m Single and double luge 1.65 1.50

No. 2649 surtaxed for the Olympic Promotion Society.

Postal Buildings, East Berlin A825

1988, Feb. 2 ***Perf. 14***

2652 A825 15pf Berlin-Buch post office 22 20
2653 A825 20pf Natl. Postal Museum 28 25
2654 A825 50pf General post office, Berlin-Marzahn 70 65

Souvenir Sheet

Bertolt Brecht (1898-1956), Playwright — A826

1988, Feb. 2 Litho. ***Perf. 13x12½***

2655 A826 70pf multi 1.00 90

Flowering Plants — A827

Leipzig Spring Fair — A828

1988, Feb. 16 Photo. ***Perf. 14***

2656 A827 10pf Tillandsia macrochlamys 15 15
2657 A827 25pf Tillandsia bulbosa 30 28
2658 A827 40pf Tillandsia kalmbacheri 50 45
2659 A827 70pf Guzmania blassii 85 75

1988, Mar. 8 Litho. ***Perf. 12½x13***

Designs: 20pf, Entrance No. 8. 70pf, Faust and Mephistopheles, bronze statue by Matthieu Molitor.

2660 A828 20pf multi 24 22
2661 A828 70pf multi 85 75

Madler Passage (arcade), 75th anniv.

Souvenir Sheet

Joseph von Eichendorff (1788-1857), Poet — A829

1988, Mar. 8 ***Perf. 14***

2662 A829 70pf multi 85 75

Seals — A830

1988, Mar. 22 Photo. ***Perf. 14***

2663 A830 10pf Muhlhausen saddler, 1565 15 15
2664 A830 25pf Dresden butcher, 1564 30 28
2665 A830 35pf Nauen smith, 16th cent. 42 38
2666 A830 50pf Frankfurt-Oder clothier, 16th cent. 60 55
a. Block of 4, Nos. 2663-2666 1.45 1.25

Georg Forster Antarctic Research Station A831

1988, Mar. 22 Litho. ***Perf. 13x12½***

2667 A831 35pf multi 42 38

District Capitals A832

1988, Apr. 5 Photo. ***Perf. 14***

2668 A832 5pf Wismar 15 15
2669 A832 10pf Anklam 15 15
2670 A832 25pf Ribnitz-Damgarten 30 28
2671 A832 60pf Stralsund 72 65
2672 A832 90pf Bergen 1.10 1.00
2673 A832 1.20m Greifswald 1.45 1.25
Nos. 2668-2673 (6) 3.87 3.48

Souvenir Sheet

Ulrich von Hutten (1488-1523), Promulgator of the Lutheran Movement — A833

1988, Apr. 5 Litho. ***Perf. 12½x13***

2674 A833 70pf multi 85 75

USSR-DDR Manned Space Flight, 10th Anniv. — A834

Designs: 5pf, Cosmonauts S. Jahn and Valery Bykowski, Soyuz-29 landing, Sept. 3, 1978. 10pf, MKS-M multi-channel spectrometer. 20pf, MIR space station.

1988, June 21 Litho. ***Perf. 14***

2675 A834 5pf multi 15 15
2676 A834 10pf multi 15 15
2677 A834 20pf multi 24 22
Set value 42 38

See Nos. 2698-2700.

10th Youth Stamp Exhibitions in Erfurt and Karl-Marx-Stadt — A835

Designs: 10pf+5pf, Erfurt, c. 1520. 20+5pf, Chemnitz, c. 1620. 25pf, Historic and modern buildings of Erfurt. 50pf, Historic and modern buildings of Karl-Marx-Stadt.

1988, June 21 **Photo.**

2678 A835 10pf +5pf multi 18 16
2679 A835 20pf +5pf multi 28 25
2680 A835 25pf multi 28 25
2681 A835 50pf multi 58 52

Nos. 2678, 2680 and Nos. 2679, 2681 printed se-tenant with center labels picturing Erfurt and Karl-Marx-Stadt municipal coats of arms, repectively. Nos. 2678-2679 surtaxed to benefit the Philatelists' League of the DDR Cultural Union.

22nd Workers' Games, Frankfurt-on-Oder — A836

1988, July 7 Litho. ***Perf. 13x12½***

2682 A836 20pf multi 24 22
2683 A836 50pf multi, diff. 58 52

Nos. 2682-2683 printed se-tenant in a continuous design with center label picturing Games emblem and folk dancers.

Workers' Militia, 35th Anniv. — A837

1988, July 5 Photo. ***Perf. 14***

2684 A837 5pf Oath 15 15
2685 A837 10pf Ernst Thalmann tribute 15 15
2686 A837 15pf Roll call 18 16
2687 A837 20pf Weapons exchange 24 22
Set value 60 54

8th Young Pioneers' Congress, Karl-Marx-Stadt — A838

1988, July 19 Litho. ***Perf. 13x12½***

2688 A838 10pf shown 15 15
2689 A838 10pf +5pf Youths playing musical instruments 18 16

Nos. 2688-2689 printed se-tenant with center label picturing Ernst Thalmann badge, the emblem of the Young Pioneers. Surtax financed the congress.

1988 Summer Olympics, Seoul A839

1988, Aug. 9 Photo. ***Perf. 14***

2690 A839 5pf Swimming 15 15
2691 A839 10pf Handball 15 15
2692 A839 20pf +10pf Hurdles 32 28
2693 A839 25pf Rowing 28 25
2694 A839 35pf Boxing 38 35
2695 A839 50pf +20pf Cycling 78 70
Nos. 2690-2695 (6) 2.06 1.88

Souvenir Sheet
Litho.
Perf. 13x12½

2696 A839 85pf Relay race 95 85

Souvenir Sheet

Leipzig Autumn Fair — A840

1988, Aug. 30 Litho. ***Perf. 14***

2697 A840 Sheet of 3 1.50 1.40
a. 5pf Fair, c. 1810 15 15
b. 15pf Battle of Leipzig Memorial 18 16
c. 1m Fair, c. 1820 1.20 1.10

DDR-USSR Manned Space Flight Type of 1988

1988, Aug. 30 Litho. ***Perf. 14***

2698 A834 10pf like No. 2675 15 15
a. Sheet of 4 50 45
2699 A834 20pf like No. 2676 22 20
a. Sheet of 4 90 80
2700 A834 35pf like No. 2677 38 35
a. Sheet of 4 1.55 1.40

Issued in sheets of four.

Fascism Resistance Memorial, Como, Italy — A841

1988, Sept. 13 **Photo.**

2701 A841 35pf multi 38 35

Memorial at Buchenwald, 30th Anniv. — A842

1988, Sept. 13 ***Perf. 14***

2702 A842 10pf multi 15 15

Mariner's Soc., Stralsund, 500th Anniv. — A843

Paintings: 5pf, *Adolph Friedrich* at Stralsund, by C. Leplow. 10pf, *Die Gartenlaube* (built in 1872) at Stralsund, by J.F. Kruger. 70pf, Brigantine *Auguste Mathilde* (built in 1830) at Stralsund, by I.C. Grunwaldt. 1.20m, Brig *Hoffnung* at Cologne, by G.A. Luther.

1988, Sept. 20 Litho. ***Perf. 13½x13***

2703 A843 5pf multi 15 15
2704 A843 10pf multi 15 15
2705 A843 70pf multi 78 70
2706 A843 1.20m multi 1.30 1.10

Ship Lifts and Bridges A844

1988, Oct. 18 Photo. *Perf. 14x14½*

2707 A844 5pf Magdeburg 15 15
2708 A844 10pf Magdeburg-Rothensee 15 15
2709 A844 35pf Niederfinow 42 38
2710 A844 70pf Altfriesack 82 75
2711 A844 90pf Rugendamm 1.05 95
Nos. 2707-2711 (5) 2.59 2.38

1st Nazi Pogrom (Kristallnacht), Nov. 9, 1938 — A845

1988, Nov. 8 *Perf. 14*

2712 A845 35pf Menorah 42 38

Paintings by Max Lingner (1888-1959) A846

1988, Nov. 8

2713 A846 5pf *In the Boat, 1931* 15 15
2714 A846 10pf *Yvonne, 1939* 15 15
2715 A846 20pf *Free, Strong and Happy, 1944* 22 20
2716 A846 85pf *New Harvest, 1951* 1.00 90

Souvenir Sheet

Friedrich Wolf (1888-1953), Playwright — A847

1988, Nov. 22 Litho.

2717 A847 1.10m multi 1.25 1.10

WHO, 40th Anniv. A848

Bone Lace from Erzgebirge A849

1988, Nov. 22 Photo.

2718 A848 85pf multi 1.00 90

Miniature Sheet

Various lace designs.

1988, Nov. 22 Litho. *Perf. 12½x13*

2719 Sheet of 6 3.00 2.75
a. A849 20pf multi 22 20
b. A849 25pf multi 28 25
c. A849 35pf multi 40 35
d. A849 40pf multi 45 40
e. A849 50pf multi 58 52
f. A849 85pf multi 1.00 90

Council for Mutual Economic Aid, 40th Anniv. A850

1989, Jan. 10 Photo. *Perf. 13*

2720 A850 20pf multi 22 20

Labor Leaders Type of 1987

Portraits: No. 2721, Edith Baumann (1909-1973). No. 2722, Otto Meier (1889-1962). No. 2723, Fritz Selbmann (1899-1975). No. 2724, Alfred Oelssner (1879-1962).

1989, Jan. 24 Engr. *Perf. 14*

2721 A804 10pf dark vio brn 15 15
2722 A804 10pf dark grn 15 15
2723 A804 10pf dark blue 15 15
2724 A804 10pf brn blk 15 15
Set value 48 40

Telephones A851

Designs: 10pf, Philipp Reis, 1861. 20pf, Siemens & Halske wall model, 1882. 50pf, Wall model OB 03, 1903. 85pf, Table model OB 05, 1905.

1989, Feb. 7 Litho.

2725 A851 10pf shown 15 15
2726 A851 20pf multi 22 20
2727 A851 50pf multi 55 50
2728 A851 85pf multi 95 85
a. Block of 4, Nos. 2725-2728 1.85 1.75

Famous Men A852

1989, Feb. 28 Photo.

2729 A852 10pf Ludwig Renn (1889-1979) 15 15
2730 A852 10pf Carl von Ossietzky (1889-1938) 15 15
2731 A852 10pf Adam Scharrer (1889-1948) 15 15
2732 A852 10pf Rudolf Mauersberger (1889-1971) 15 15
2733 A852 10pf Johann Beckmann (1739-1811) 15 15
Set value 60 55

Leipzig Spring Fair — A853

1989, Mar. 7 Litho.

2734 A853 70pf shown 78 70
2735 A853 85pf Buildings, 1690 95 85

Handelshof, 80th anniv. (70pf).

Souvenir Sheet

Thomas Munzer (c. 1468-1525), Religious Reformer — A854

1989, Mar. 21 *Perf. 13x12½*

2736 A854 1.10m multi 1.25 1.10

1st Long-distance German Railway, Leipzig-Dresden, Sesquicentennial A855

Designs: 15pf, Georg Friedrich List (1789-1846), industrialist, economist. 20pf, Dresden Station in Leipzig, 1839. 50pf, Leipzig Station in Dresden, 1839.

1989, Apr. 4 *Perf. 14*

2737 A855 15pf multi 18 16
2738 A855 20pf multi 22 20
2739 A855 50pf multi 55 50

Meissen Onion-pattern Porcelain, 250th Anniv., and Sword Emblem — A856

1989, Apr. 18 Litho. *Perf. 12½x13*

2740 A856 10pf Tea caddy 15 15
2741 A856 20pf Vase 22 20
2742 A856 35pf Breadboard 38 35
2743 A856 70pf Teapot 78 70

Size: 33x56mm

Perf. 14

2744 Block of 4 1.50 1.40
a. A856 10pf like No. 2740 15 15
b. A856 20pf like No. 2741 22 20
c. A856 35pf like No. 2742 38 35
d. A856 70pf like No. 2743 78 70

Intl. Book Fair (IBA), Leipzig — A857

1989, May 2 Photo. *Perf. 14½x14*

2745 A857 20pf "I" 22 20
2746 A857 50pf "B" 55 50
2747 A857 1.35m "A" 1.50 1.40

Student Government — A858

1989, May 9 Litho. *Perf. 13½x12½*

2748 A858 20pf 8th World Youth Festival, Pyongyang 22 20
2749 A858 20pf +5pf Whitsun meeting of Free German Youth 28 25

Nos. 2748-2749 printed se-tenant with center label picturing FDJ emblem.

Princess Luise — A859

Carl Zeiss Foundation, Jena, Cent. — A860

Sculptures by Johann Gottfried Schadow (1764-1850), Prussian Court Sculptor.

1989, May 16 Photo. *Perf. 14½x14*

2750 A859 50pf shown 55 50
2751 A859 85pf Princess Friederike 90 80

1989, May 16

Modern medical technology: 50pf, Interference microscope Jenaval. 85pf, Bicoordinate measuring instrument ZKM 01-250C.

2752 A860 50pf multi 55 50
2753 A860 85pf multi 90 80

Nos. 2752-2753 printed se-tenant with center label picturing founder Ernst Abbe (1840-1905).

Jena University Inaugural Address, Bicent. — A861

1989, May 23 Photo. *Perf. 14*

2754 A861 25pf Frontispiece 26 24
2755 A861 85pf Excerpt 88 80

Nos. 2754-2755 printed se-tenant with center label picturing a bust of Friedrich Schiller, author of the address.

Souvenir Sheet

Zoologists — A862

1989, June 13 **Litho.**

2756 A862 Sheet of 2 1.40 1.25

a. 50pf Alfred Brehm (1829-1884) 52 45

b. 85pf Christian Brehm (1787-1864) 88 80

French Revolution, Bicent. — A863

Designs: 5pf, Storming of the Bastille, July 14, 1789. 20pf, Revolutionaries, flag bearer. 90pf, Storming Tuileries Palace, Aug. 10, 1792.

1989, July 4 **Photo.** ***Perf. 13***

2757 A863 5pf multi 15 15

2758 A863 20pf multi 20 18

2759 A863 90pf multi 90 80

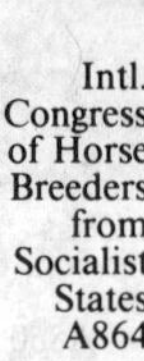

Intl. Congress of Horse Breeders from Socialist States A864

1989, July 18 **Litho.** ***Perf. 13½***

2760 A864 10pf Haflinger 15 15

2761 A864 20pf English thoroughbred 20 18

2762 A864 70pf Cold blood 70 65

2763 A864 110pf Noble warm blood 1.10 1.00

Natl. Stamp Exhibition, Magdeburg — A865

1989, Aug. 8 **Litho.** ***Perf. 13x12½***

2764 A865 20pf Owlglass Fountain 22 20

2765 A865 70pf +5pf Demons Fountain 82 75

No. 2765 surtaxed for the philatelic unit of the Kulturbund.

For unused stamps, more recent issues are valued as never hinged, with the beginning point determined on a country-by-country basis. Notes to show the beginning points are prominently placed in the text.

Souvenir Sheet

Leipzig Autumn Fair — A866

1989, Aug. 22 ***Perf. 14***

2766 A866 Sheet of 2 1.50 1.40

a. 50pf Fairground 55 55

b. 85pf Fairground, diff. 92 85

Thomas Munzer (1489-1525), Religious Reformer A867

Various details of the painting *Early Bourgeois Revolution in Germany in 1525,* by W. Tubke.

1989, Aug. 22

2767 A867 5pf Globe 15 15

2768 A867 10pf Fountain 15 15

2769 A867 20pf Battle scene 22 20

a. Souv. sheet of 4 90 80

2770 A867 50pf Ark 55 50

2771 A867 85pf Rainbow, battle 92 85

Nos. 2767-2771 (5) 1.99 1.85

Muttergruppe, 1965, Bronze Statue in the Natl. Memorial, Ravensbruck A868

1989, Sept. 5 **Photo.** ***Perf. 14***

2772 A868 35pf multi 38 35

Natl. Memorial, Ravensbruck, 30th anniv.

Flowering Cacti (*Epiphyllum*) A869

1989, Sept. 19 **Litho.** ***Perf. 13***

2773 A869 10m Adriana 15 15

2774 A869 35m Feuerzauber 38 35

2775 A869 50m Franzisko 55 50

DDR, 40th Anniv. — A870

1989, Oct. 3 ***Perf. 14***

2776 A870 5pf Education 15 15

2777 A870 10pf Agriculture 15 15

2778 A870 20pf Construction 22 20

2779 A870 25pf Machinist, computer user 28 25

Set value 66 60

Souvenir Sheet

2780 A870 135pf Two workers 1.50 1.40

Jawaharlal Nehru, 1st Prime Minister of Independent India — A871

1989, Nov. 7 **Photo.** ***Perf. 14***

2781 A871 35pf multicolored 38 35

Statues of Roland Type of 1987

1989, Nov. 7 ***Perf. 14½x14***

2782 A799 5pf Zerbst, 1445 15 15

2783 A799 10pf Halberstadt, 1433 15 15

2784 A799 20pf Buch-Altmark, 1611 22 20

2785 A799 50pf Perleberg, 1546 55 50

a. Block of 4, #2782-2785 95 85

Set value 94 84

Miniature Sheet

Chandeliers from Erzgebirge — A872

Designs: a, Schneeburg, circa 1860. b, Schwarzenberg, circa 1850. c, Annaberg, circa 1880. d, Seiffen, circa 1900. e, Seiffen, circa 1930. f, Annaberg, circa 1925.

Litho. & Engr.

1989, Nov. 28 ***Perf. 14***

2786 Sheet of 6 2.35 2.25

a. A872 10pf multicolored 15 15

b. A872 20pf multicolored 22 20

c. A872 25pf multicolored 28 25

d. A872 35pf multicolored 38 35

e. A872 50pf multicolored 55 50

f. A872 70pf multicolored 78 70

Bees Collecting Nectar — A873

1990, Jan. 9 **Litho.**

2787 A873 5pf Apple blossom 15 15

2788 A873 10pf Blooming heather 15 15

2789 A873 20pf Rape blossom 24 22

2790 A873 50pf Red clover 60 55

Set value 92

The Young Post Rider, an Engraving by Albrecht Durer — A874

1990, Jan. 12 **Litho.** ***Perf. 13***

2791 A874 35pf multi 42 38

Postal communications in Europe, 500th anniv.

See Austria No. 1486, Belgium No. 1332, Germany No. 1592 and Berlin No. 9N584.

Labor Leaders — A875

Coats of Arms — A876

Portraits: No. 2792, Bruno Leuschner (1910-1965). No. 2793, Erich Weinert (1890-1953).

1990, Jan. 16 ***Perf. 14***

2792 A875 10pf gray brown 15 15

2793 A875 10pf deep blue 15 15

Set value 24 22

1990, Feb. 6 **Photo.** ***Perf. 14***

Early postal agency insignia: 10pf, Schwarzburg-Rudolstadt and Thurn & Taxis. 20pf, Royal Saxon letter collection. 50pf, Imperial Postal Agency. 1.10pf, Auxiliary post office.

2794 A876 10pf multicolored 15 15

2795 A876 20pf multicolored 24 22

2796 A876 50pf multicolored 60 55

2797 A876 110pf multicolored 1.30 1.10

Size: 32x42mm

Perf. 13½

Litho.

2798 Block of 4 2.25 2.00

a. A876 10pf like No. 2794 15 15

b. A876 20pf like No. 2795 24 22

c. A876 50pf like No. 2796 60 55

d. A876 110pf like No. 2797 1.30 1.10

Posts & Telecommunications Workers' Day.

August Bebel (1840-1913), Co-founder of the Social Democratic Party — A877

1990, Feb. 20 **Photo.**

2799 A877 20pf multicolored 24 22

Flying Machine Designed by Leonardo da Vinci A878

1990, Feb. 20 **Litho.** ***Perf. 13½x13***

2800 A878 20pf shown 24 22

2801 A878 35pf +5pf Melchior Bauer 48 42

2802 A878 50pf Albrecht Berblinger 58 52

2803 A878 90pf Otto Lilienthal 1.05 95

LILIENTHAL '91 airmail exhibition. No. 2792 surtaxed for philatelic promotion.

Leipzig Spring Fair Seals A879

Dying Warriors A880

1990, Mar. 6 *Perf. 12½x13*

2804 A879 70pf Seal, 1268 82 75
2805 A879 85pf Seal, 1497 1.00 90

City of Leipzig and the Leipzig Spring Fair, 825th annivs.

1990, Mar. 6 Photo. *Perf. 13½x14*

Sculptures by Andreas Schluter.

2806 A880 40pf shown 48 42
2807 A880 70pf multi, diff. 82 75

Museum of German History in the Zeughaus of Berlin.

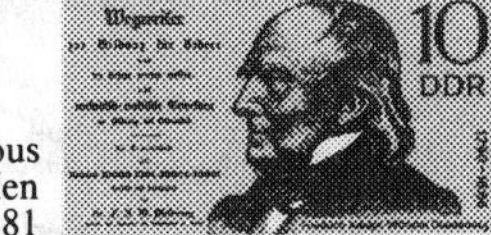

Famous Men A881

Portraits: No. 2808, Friedrich Diesterweg (1790-1866), educator. No. 2809, Kurt Tucholsky (1890-1935), novelist, journalist.

1990, Mar. 20 Photo. *Perf. 14*

2808 A881 10pf multicolored 15 15
2809 A881 10pf multicolored 15 15
Set value 24 20

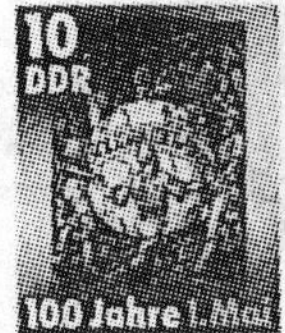

Labor Day, Cent. – A882

1990, Apr. 3

2810 A882 10pf shown 15 15
2811 A882 20pf Flower, "1890/1990" 24 22

Dicraeosaurus – A883

Perf. 13x12½, 12½x13

1990, Apr. 17 **Litho.**

2812 A883 10pf shown 15 15
2813 A883 25pf Kentrurosaurus 30 28
a. Miniature sheet of 4 1.30 1.10
2814 A883 35pf Dysalotosaurus 42 38
2815 A883 50pf Brachiosaurus 60 55
2816 A883 85pf Brachiosaurus skull 1.10 1.00

Natural History Museum of Berlin, cent. Nos. 2815-2816 vert.

Penny Black, 150th Anniv. – A884

1990, May 8 *Perf. 14*

2817 A884 20pf shown 24 22
2818 A884 35pf +15pf Saxony No. 1 60 55
2819 A884 110pf No. 48 1.35 1.25

Intl. Telecommunications Union, 125th Anniv. – A885

Designs: 10pf, David Edward Hughes (1831-1900), type-printing telegraph, 1855. 20pf, Distribution linkage, Berlin-Kopenick post office. 25pf, TV and microwave tower. 50pf, Molniya news satellite, globe. 70pf, Philipp Reis (1834-1874), physicist, designed sound transmission equipment.

1990, May 15

2820 A885 10pf multicolored 15 15
2821 A885 20pf multicolored 24 22
2822 A885 25pf multicolored 30 28
2823 A885 50pf multicolored 60 55

Souvenir Sheet

2824 A885 70pf multicolored 90 80

Pope John Paul II, 70th Birthday – A886

1990, May 15

2825 A886 35pf multicolored 45 40

11th Youth Stamp Exhibition, Halle – A887

1990, June 5 *Perf. 13x12½*

2826 A887 10pf +5pf 18th cent. Halle 18 16
2827 A887 20pf 20th cent. Halle 24 22
a. Pair, #2826-2827 + label 42 40

Treasures in the German State Library, Berlin A888

Designs: 20pf, Rules of an order, 1264. 25pf, Rudimentum novitiorum, 1475. 50pf, Chosrou wa Schirin, 18th cent. 110pf, Bookcover of Amalienbibliothek, 18th cent.

1990, June 19

2828 A888 20pf multicolored 24 22
2829 A888 25pf multicolored 30 28
2830 A888 50pf multicolored 60 55
2831 A888 110pf multicolored 1.35 1.25

100 pfennig = 1 Deutsche Mark

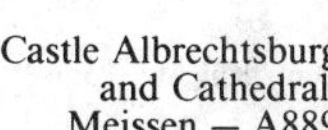

Castle Albrechtsburg and Cathedral, Meissen – A889

Designs: 30pf, Goethe-Schiller Monument, Weimar. 50pf, Brandenburg Gate, Berlin. 60pf, Kyffhauser Monument. 70pf, Semper Opera, Dresden. 80pf, Castle Sanssouci, Potsdam. 100pf, Wartburg, Eisenach. 200pf, Magdeburg Cathedral. 500pf, Schwerin Castle.

1990, July 2 Photo. *Perf. 14*

2832 A889 10pf ultramarine 15 15
2833 A889 30pf olive green 36 18
2834 A889 50pf bluish green 60 30
2835 A889 60pf violet brown 72 36
2836 A889 70pf dark brown 85 42
2837 A889 80pf red brown 95 48
2838 A889 100pf dark carmine 1.20 60
2839 A889 200pf dark violet 2.40 1.20
2840 A889 500pf green 6.00 3.00
Nos. 2832-2840 (9) 13.23 6.69

Nos. 2832-2840 have face values based on the Federal Republic's Deutsche mark and were valid for postage in both countries.

Postal System, 500th Anniv. A890

Designs: 30pf, 15th century postman. 50pf, 16th century postrider. 70pf, Post carriages c. 1595, 1750. 100pf, Railway mail carriages 1842, 1900.

1990, Aug. 28 Litho. *Perf. 13x13½*

2841 A890 30pf multicolored 40 20
2842 A890 50pf multicolored 70 35
2843 A890 70pf multicolored 95 48
2844 A890 100pf multicolored 1.40 70

Louis Lewandowski (1821-1894), Composer – A891

Design: 50pf+15pf, New Synagogue, Berlin.

1990, Sept. 18 *Perf. 14*

2845 A891 30pf multicolored 40 20
2846 A891 50pf +15pf multi 90 45

Heinrich Schliemann (1822-1890), Archaeologist A892

Design: 50pf, Schliemann, double pot c. 2600-1900 B.C., horiz.

1990, Oct. 2 **Photo.**

2847 A892 30pf multicolored 40 20
2848 A892 50pf multicolored 70 35

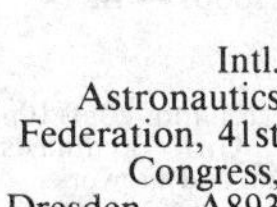

Intl. Astronautics Federation, 41st Congress, Dresden – A893

1990, Oct. 2

2849 A893 30pf Dresden skyline 40 20
2850 A893 50pf Globe 70 35
2851 A893 70pf Moon 95 48
2852 A893 100pf Mars 1.40 70

Stamps of the German Democratic Republic were replaced starting Oct. 3, 1990 by those of the Federal Republic of Germany. #2832-2852 remained valid until Dec. 31, 1991.

SEMI-POSTAL STAMPS

Some se-tenants include a semi-postal stamp. To avoid splitting the se-tenant piece the semi-postal is listed with the regular issue.

Bavaria No. 1 and Magnifier – SP4

Wmk. 292

1949, Oct. 30 Litho. *Perf. 14*

B14 SP4 12pf + 3pf gray blk 6.00 3.00

Stamp Day, 1949. See No. B21a.

Leipzig Fair Issue.
German Type of 1947
Inscribed: "Deutsche Demokratische Republik"

Leipzig Spring Fair: 24pf+12pf, First porcelain at Fair, 1710. 30pf+14pf, First Fair at Municipal Store, 1894.

1950, Mar. 5 *Perf. 13*

B15 SP252 24 + 12pf red vio 7.00 6.25
B16 SP252 30 + 14pf rose car 7.50 6.50

Shepherd Boy with Double Flute – SP5

"Bach Year": 24pf+6pf, Girl with hand organ. 30pf+8pf, Johann Sebastian Bach. 50pf+16pf, Chorus.

1950, June 14 *Perf. 14*

B17 SP5 12pf + 4pf bl grn 3.00 2.50
B18 SP5 24pf + 6pf ol 3.00 2.50
B19 SP5 30pf + 8pf dk red 7.50 6.25
B20 SP5 50pf + 16pf bl 10.00 8.25

Saxony No. 1, Globe and Dove – SP6

1950, July 1 Photo. Wmk. 292

B21 SP6 84 + 41pf brn red 25.00 9.00
a. Souv. sheet of 2, #B14, B21, imperf. *100.00 100.00*

German Stamp Exhib. (DEBRIA) held at Leipzig for the cent. of Saxony's 1st postage stamp.

Canceled to Order
Used values are for CTO's from No. B22 to No. B203.

Clearing Land – SP7

Reconstruction program: 24pf+6pf, Bricklaying. 30pf+10pf, Carpentry. 50pf+10pf, Inspecting plans.

1952, May 1 **Litho.**

B22 SP7 12pf + 3pf brt vio 70 70
B23 SP7 24pf + 6pf henna brn 75 90
B24 SP7 30pf + 10pf dp grn 75 90
B25 SP7 50pf + 10pf vio bl 1.10 1.50

Dam — SP8

1954, Aug. 16 **Unwmk.**
B26 SP8 24pf + 6pf green 28 15

The surtax was for flood victims.

No. B26 Surcharged with New Value and "X" in Black

1955, Feb. 25
B27 SP8 20 +5pf on 24+6pf 28 18

The surtax was for flood victims.

Buchenwald Memorial — SP9

Perf. 13½x13

1956, Sept. 8 **Wmk. 297**
B28 SP9 20pf + 80pf rose red *85 60*

The surtax was for the erection of national memorials at the concentration camps of Buchenwald, Ravensbruck and Sachsenhausen. See No. B43.

Type of 1955 Surcharged "HELFT AGYPTEN +10" (#B29) or "HELFT DEM SOZIALISTISCHEN UNGARN +10" (#B30)

Perf. 13½x13

1956, Dec. 20 **Wmk. 313**
B29 A75 20pf + 10pf carmine 15 15
B30 A75 20pf + 10pf carmine 15 15
Set value 20 15

Monument to Ravensbrück SP10

Memorial Park and Lake — SP11

Perf. 13x13½, 13½x13

1957, Apr. 25 **Litho.**
B31 SP10 5pf + 5pf grn *15 15*
B32 SP11 20pf + 10pf rose red *15 15*
Set value *25 18*

Issued for the International Day of Liberation. See Nos. B54, B70.

Ernst Thälmann SP12

Bugler, Flag and Camp SP13

Portraits: 25pf+15pf, Rudolf Breitscheid. 40pf+20pf, Rev. Paul Schneider.

1957, Dec. 3 **Photo.** ***Perf. 13***

Portraits in Gray

B33 SP12 20pf + 10pf dp plum 15 15
B34 SP12 25pf + 15pf dk bl 15 15
B35 SP12 40pf + 20pf vio 15 15
a. Souv. sheet of 3, #B33-B35, imperf. ('58) 35.00 25.00
Set value 25

1958, July 11 **Wmk. 313** ***Perf. 13***

Portraits: 5pf+5pf, Albert Kuntz. 10pf+5pf, Rudi Arndt. 15pf+10pf, Kurt Adams. 20pf+10pf, Rudolf Renner. 25pf+15pf, Walter Stoecker.

Portraits in Gray

B36 SP12 5pf + 5pf brn blk 15 15
B37 SP12 10pf + 5pf dk sl grn 15 15
B38 SP12 15pf + 10pf dp vio 15 25
B39 SP12 20pf + 10pf dk red brn 15 15
B40 SP12 25pf + 15pf bl blk *55 60*
Set value *90 1.00*

Issued to honor the murdered victims of the Nazis at Buchenwald. The surtax was for the erection of national memorials.

See Nos. B49-B53, B55-B57, B60-B64, B71-B75, B79-B81.

1958, Aug. 7 **Litho.** ***Perf. 12½***

Design: 20pf+10pf, Pioneers and flag.

B41 SP13 10pf + 5pf grn 22 15
B42 SP13 20pf + 10pf red 22 15
Set value 18

Pioneer organization, 10th anniversary.

Type of 1956 Overprinted in Black "14. September 1958"

Perf. 13½x13

1958, Sept. 15 **Unwmk.**
B43 SP9 20pf + 20pf rose red *40 15*

Dedication of the memorial at Buchenwald concentration camp, Sept. 14, 1958.

Exercises with Hoops — SP14

Designs: 10pf+5pf, High jump. 20pf+10pf Vaulting. 25pf+10pf, Girl gymnasts. 40pf+20pf, Leipzig stadium and fireworks.

Perf. 13x13½

1959, Aug. 10 **Litho.** **Wmk. 313**
B44 SP14 5pf + 5pf org 15 15
B45 SP14 10pf + 5pf grn 15 15
B46 SP14 20pf + 10pf brt car 15 15
B47 SP14 25pf + 10pf brt bl 15 15
B48 SP14 40pf + 20pf red vio *1.40 90*
Set value *1.60 1.10*

3rd German Sports Festival, Leipzig.

Portrait Type of 1957-58

Portraits: 5pf+5pf, Tilde Klose. 10pf+5pf, Kathe Niederkirchner. 15pf+10pf, Charlotte Eisenblatter. 20pf+10pf, Olga Benario-Prestes. 25pf+15pf, Maria Grollmuss.

1959, Sept. 3 **Photo.** ***Perf. 13***

Portraits in Gray

B49 SP12 5pf + 5pf sep 15 15
B50 SP12 10pf + 5pf dp grn 15 15
B51 SP12 15pf + 10pf dp vio 15 15
B52 SP12 20pf + 10pf mag 15 15
B53 SP12 25pf + 15pf dk bl *25 30*
Set value *70 40*

Issued to honor women murdered by the Nazis at Buchenwald.

Ravensbrück Type of 1957 Dated: "12. September 1959"

Perf. 13½x13

1959, Sept. 11 **Litho.** **Wmk. 313**
B54 SP11 20pf + 10pf dp car & blk 35 15

Portrait Type of 1957-58

Portraits: 5pf+5pf, Lothar Erdmann. 10pf+5pf, Ernst Schneller. 20pf+10pf, Lambert Horn.

1960, Feb. 25 **Photo.** ***Perf. 13½x13***

Portraits in Gray

B55 SP12 5pf + 5pf ol bis 15 15
B56 SP12 10pf + 5pf dk grn 15 15
B57 SP12 20pf + 10pf dl mag 15 15
Set value 25 15

Issued to honor murdered victims of the Nazis at Sachsenhausen.

Type of Regular Issue, 1960

Designs: 10pf+5pf, Vacation ship under construction, Wismar. 20pf+10pf, Ship before Stubbenkammer and sailboat.

Wmk. 313

1960, June 23 **Litho.** ***Perf. 13***
B58 A162 10pf + 5pf blk, yel & red 15 15
B59 A162 20pf + 10pf blk, red & bl 15 15
Set value 15 15

Portrait Type of 1957-58

Portraits: 10pf+5pf, Max Lademann. 15pf+5pf, Lorenz Breunig. 20pf+10pf, Mathias Thesen. 25pf+10pf, Gustl Sandtner. 40pf+20pf, Hans Rothbarth.

1960 **Wmk. 313** ***Perf. 13½x13***

Portraits in Gray

B60 SP12 10pf + 5pf grn 15 15
B61 SP12 15pf + 5pf dp vio *32 42*
B62 SP12 20pf + 10pf mar 15 15
B63 SP12 25pf + 10pf dk bl 15 15
B64 SP12 40pf + 20pf lt red brn *1.50 85*
Set value *2.00 1.50*

Issued to honor the murdered victims of the Nazis at Sachsenhausen.

Bicyclist — SP15

Design: 25pf+10pf, Bicyclists and spectators.

1960, Aug. 3 ***Perf. 13x13½, 13x12½***

Size: 28x23mm

B65 SP15 20pf + 10pf multi 15 15

Size: 38½x21mm

B66 SP15 25pf + 10pf bl, gray & brn *85 60*
Set value *65*

Issued to publicize the Bicycling World Championships, Aug. 3-14.

Rook and Congress Emblem — SP16

Designs: 20pf+10pf, Knight. 25pf+10pf, Bishop.

Perf. 14x13½

1960, Sept. 19 **Engr.** **Wmk. 313**
B67 SP16 10pf + 5pf blue green 15 15
B68 SP16 20pf + 10pf rose claret 15 15
B69 SP16 25pf + 10pf blue *80 52*
Set value *95 60*

14th Chess Championships, Leipzig.

Type of 1957

Design: Monument and memorial wall of Sachsenhausen National Memorial.

1960, Sept. 8 **Litho.** ***Perf. 13x13½***
B70 SP10 20pf + 10pf dp car 20 15

No. B70 was re-issued Apr. 20, 1961, with gray label adjoining each stamp in sheet, to commemorate the dedication of Sachsenhausen National Memorial.

Type of 1957

Portraits: 5pf+5pf, Werner Kube. 10pf+5pf, Hanno Gunther. 15pf+5pf, Elvira Eisenschneider. 20pf+10pf, Hertha Lindner. 25pf+10pf, Herbert Tschäpe.

1961, Feb. 6 ***Perf. 13½x13***

Portraits in Black

B71 SP12 5pf + 5pf brt brn 15 15
B72 SP12 10pf + 5pf bl grn 15 15
B73 SP12 15pf + 5pf brt lil *1.25 1.10*
B74 SP12 20pf + 10pf dp rose 15 15
B75 SP12 25pf + 10pf brt bl 15 15
Set value *1.40 1.25*

Surtax for the erection of natl. memorials.

Pioneers Playing Volleyball SP17

Designs: 20pf+10pf, Folk dancing. 25pf+10pf, Building model airplanes.

1961, May 25 ***Perf. 13x12½***
B76 SP17 10pf + 5pf multi 15 15
B77 SP17 20pf + 10pf multi 15 15
B78 SP17 25pf + 10pf multi *1.25 85*
Set value *90*

Young Pioneers' meeting, Erfurt.

Type of 1957 and

Sophie and Hans Scholl SP18

Portraits: 5pf+5pf, Carlo Schönhaar. 10pf+5pf, Herbert Baum. 20pf+10pf, Liselotte Herrmann. 40pf+20pf, Hilde and Hans Coppi.

Perf. 13½x13, 13x13½

1961, Sept. 7 **Litho.** **Wmk. 313**

Portraits in Black

B79 SP12 5pf + 5pf green 15 15
B80 SP12 10pf + 5pf bl grn 15 15
B81 SP12 20pf + 10pf rose car 15 15
B82 SP18 25pf + 10pf blue 15 15
B83 SP18 40pf + 20pf rose brn *1.25 1.25*
Nos. B79-B83 (5) *1.85*
Set value *1.50*

The surtax was for the support of national memorials at Buchenwald, Ravensbrück and Sachsenhausen.

Danielle Casanova of France — SP19

Portraits: 10pf+5pf, Julius Fucik, Czechoslovakia. 20pf+10pf, Johanna Jannetje Schaft, Netherlands. 25pf+10pf, Pawel Finder, Poland. 40pf+20pf, Soya Anatolyevna Kosmodemyanskaya, Russia.

1962, Mar. 22 **Engr.** ***Perf. 13½***
B84 SP19 5pf + 5pf gray 15 15
B85 SP19 10pf + 5pf grn 15 15
B86 SP19 20pf + 10pf mar 15 15

B87 SP19 25pf + 10pf dp bl 22 15
B88 SP19 40pf + 20pf sepia *1.65 75*
Set value *2.00 1.00*

Issued in memory of foreign victims of the Nazis.

Type of Regular Issue, 1962

Design: 20pf+10pf, Three cyclists and Warsaw Palace of Culture and Science.

Perf. 13x12½

1962, Apr. 26 Litho. Wmk. 313

B89 A192 20pf + 10pf ver, bl, blk & yel 15 15

Folk Dance — SP20

Design: 15pf+5pf, Youths of three nations parading.

1962, July 17 Wmk. 313 *Perf. 14*

B90 SP20 10pf + 5pf multi 50 20
B91 SP20 15pf + 5pf multi 50 20

Issued to publicize the 8th Youth Festival for Peace and Friendship, Helsinki, July 28-Aug. 6, 1962.

Nos. B90-B91 are printed se-tenant forming the festival emblem.

Type of Regular Issue, 1962

Design: 20pf+10pf, Springboard diving.

1962, Aug. 7 Wmk. 313 *Perf. 13*

B92 A199 20pf + 10pf lil rose & grnsh bl 15 15

René Blieck of Belgium — SP21

Seven Cervi Brothers of Italy SP22

Portraits: 10pf+5pf, Dr. Alfred Klahr, Austria. 15pf+5pf, Jose Diaz, Spain. 20pf+10pf, Julius Alpari, Hungary.

1962, Oct. 4 Engr. *Perf. 14*

B93 SP21 5pf + 5pf dk bl gray 15 15
B94 SP21 10pf + 5pf green 15 15
B95 SP21 15pf + 5pf brt vio 15 15
B96 SP21 20pf + 10pf dl red brn 15 15
B97 SP22 70pf + 30pf sepia *1.40 1.10*
Set value *1.75 1.25*

Issued to commemorate foreign victims of the Nazis.

Walter Bohne, Runner SP23

Gymnasts SP24

Portraits: 10pf+5pf, Werner Seelenbinder, wrestler. 15pf+5pf, Albert Richter, bicyclist. 20pf+10pf, Heinz Steyer, soccer player. 25pf+10pf, Kurt Schlosser, mountaineer.

Engr. & Photo.

1963, May 27 Wmk. 313 *Perf. 14*

B98 SP23 5pf + 5pf yel & blk 15 15
B99 SP23 10pf + 5pf pale yel grn & blk 15 15
B100 SP23 15pf + 5pf rose lil & blk 15 15
B101 SP23 20pf + 10pf pink & blk 16 15
B102 SP23 25pf + 10pf pale bl & blk *1.65 1.50*
Nos. B98-B102 (5) *2.26*
Set value *1.70*

Issued to commemorate sportsmen victims of the Nazis. Each stamp printed with alternating label showing sporting events connected with each person honored. The surtax went for the maintenance of national memorials. See Nos. B106-B110.

1963, June 13 Litho. *Perf. 12½x13*

Designs: 20pf+10pf, Women gymnasts. 25pf+10pf, Relay race.

B103 SP24 10pf + 5pf blk, yel grn & lem 15 15
B104 SP24 20pf + 10pf blk, red & vio 15 15
B105 SP24 25pf + 10pf blk, bl, & gray *2.00 1.65*

Issued to commemorate the 4th German Gymnastic and Sports Festival, Leipzig. The surtax went to the festival committee.

Type of 1963

Portraits: 5pf+5pf, Hermann Tops, gymnastics instructor. 10pf+5pf, Käte Tucholla, field hockey players. 15pf+5pf, Rudolph Seiffert, long-distance swimmers. 20pf+10pf, Ernst Grube, sportsmen demonstrating for peace. 40pf+20pf, Kurt Biedermann, kayak in rapids.

Engraved and Photogravure

1963, Sept. 24 Wmk. 313 *Perf. 14*

B106 SP23 5pf + 5pf yel & blk 15 15
B107 SP23 10pf + 5pf grn & blk 15 15
B108 SP23 15pf + 5pf lil & blk 15 15
B109 SP23 20pf + 10pf pale pink & blk 15 15
B110 SP23 40pf + 20pf lt bl & blk *1.65 1.65*
Nos. B106-B110 (5) *2.25 2.25*

See note after No. B102.

Type of Regular Issue, 1963

Design: 20pf+10pf, Ski jumper in mid-air.

Perf. 13½x13

1963, Dec. 16 Litho. Wmk. 313

B111 A224 20pf + 10pf multi 15 15

Surtax for the Natl. Olympic Committee.

Anton Saefkow SP25

Designs: 10pf+5pf, Franz Jacob. 15pf+5pf, Bernhard Bästlein. 20pf+5pf, Harro Schulze-Boysen. 25pf+10pf, Adam Kuckhoff. 40pf+10pf, Mildred and Arvid Harnack. Nos. B112-B114 show group posting anti-Hitler and pacifist posters. Nos. B115-B117 show production of anti-fascist pamphlets.

1964, Mar. 24 Wmk. 313 *Perf. 13*

Size: 41x32mm

B112 SP25 5pf + 5pf dk red brn & chlky bl 15 15
B113 SP25 10pf + 5pf dk red brn & gray ol 15 15
B114 SP25 15pf + 5pf dk red brn & lt vio 15 15
B115 SP25 20pf + 5pf car rose & gray ol 18 15
B116 SP25 25pf + 10pf brt bl & gray ol 24 15

Size: 48½x28mm

B117 SP25 40pf + 10pf dl red brn & gray ol *1.25 85*
Nos. B112-B117 (6) *2.12*
Set value *1.20*

The surtax was for the support of national memorials for victims of the Nazis.

Olympic Types of Regular Issues

Designs: 40pf+20pf, Two runners. #B119, Equestrian. #B120, Three runners.

Lithographed and Engraved

1964, July 15 Wmk. 313 *Perf. 14*

B118 A232 40pf + 20pf multi 28 15

Litho.

Perf. 13

B119 A233 10pf + 5pf multi 1.65 1.10
B120 A233 10pf + 5pf multi 1.65 1.10

See note after No. 714.

Pioneers Studying — SP26

Designs: 20pf+10pf, Pioneers planting tree. 25pf+10pf, Pioneers playing.

1964, July 29

B121 SP26 10pf + 5pf multi 15 15
B122 SP26 20pf + 10pf multi 15 15
B123 SP26 25pf + 10pf multi *80 65*
Set value *96 72*

Issued to commemorate the Fifth Young Pioneers Meeting, Karl-Marx-Stadt.

Stamp Exhibition Type of 1964

Designs: 10pf+5pf, Stamp of 1958 (No. 390). 20pf+10pf, Stamp of 1950 (No. 73).

Perf. 13x13½

1964, Sept. 23 Litho. Wmk. 313

B124 A238 10pf + 5pf org & emer 15 15
B125 A238 20pf + 10pf brt pink & bl 15 15
Set value 20 15

Boxing Type of Regular Issue

Design: 10pf+5pf, Two boxing gloves and laurel.

Perf. 13½x14

1965, Apr. 27 Photo. Wmk. 313

B126 A247 10pf + 5pf blk, gold, red & blue 15 15

The surtax went to the German Turner and Sport Organization.

Type of Regular Issue, 1965

Designs: 5pf+5pf, George Dimitrov at Leipzig trial and communist newspaper. 10pf+5pf, Anti-fascists clandestinely distributing leaflets. 15pf+5pf, Fighting in Spanish Civil War. 20pf+10pf, Ernst Thalman behind bars and demonstration for his release. 25pf+10pf, Founding of National Committee for Free Germany and signatures.

Wmk. 313

1965, May 5 Photo. *Perf. 14*

Flags in Red, Black and Yellow

B127 A248 5pf + 5pf blk, org & red 15 15
B128 A248 10pf + 5pf grn & red 15 15
B129 A248 15pf + 5pf lil, red & yel 15 15
B130 A248 20pf + 10pf blk & red 15 15
B131 A248 25pf + 10pf ol grn, yel & blk 15 15
Set value 38 25

The surtax went for the maintenance of national memorials.

Doves, Globe and Finnish Flag — SP27

1965, July 5 Litho. *Perf. 13x13½*

B132 SP27 10pf + 5pf vio bl & emer 15 15
B133 SP27 20pf + 5pf red & vio bl *42 22*
Set value *50 25*

World Peace Congress, Helsinki, July 10-17. The surtax went to the peace council of the DDR.

Hilfe für
VIETNAM

No. 725 Surcharged

+10

Perf. 13½x13

1965, Aug. 23 Wmk. 313

B134 A239 10pf + 10pf multi 25 15

Surtax was for North Viet Nam.

Sports Type of Regular Issue

Sport: No. B135, Fencer. No. B136, Pistol shooter.

Perf. 13½x13

1965, Sept. 15 Litho. Unwmk.

B135 A257 10pf + 5pf vio bl & grnsh bl 18 15
B136 A257 10pf + 5pf dk car rose, gray & blk 18 15
Set value 15

International Modern Pentathlon Championships, Leipzig.

Type of Regular Issue

Designs: 10pf+5pf, Willi Bredel and instruction of International Brigade. 20pf+10pf, Heinrich Rau and parade after battle of Brunete. 25pf+10pf, Hans Marchwitza, international fighters and globe. 40pf+10pf, Artur Becker and battle on the Ebro.

1966, July 15 Photo. *Perf. 14*

B137 A277 10pf + 5pf multi 15 15
B138 A277 20pf + 10pf multi 15 15
B139 A277 25pf + 10pf multi 15 15
B140 A277 40pf + 10pf multi *1.25 65*
Set value *1.50 70*

The surtax was for the maintenance of national memorials.

Canoe Type of Regular Issue

Design: 10pf+5pf, Men's single canoe race.

Perf. 13x12½

1966, Aug. 16 Litho. Unwmk.

B141 A279 10pf + 5pf multi 15 15

Red Cross Type of Regular Issue

Design: ICY Red Crescent, Red Cross, and Red Lion and Sun emblems (horiz.).

1966, Sept. 13 Wmk. 313 *Perf. 14*

B142 A281 20pf + 10pf vio & red 15 15

International health cooperation. Surtax for German Red Cross.

Sports Type of Regular Issue

Design: 20pf+5pf, Weight lifter.

Perf. 13½x13

1966, Sept. 22 Litho. Unwmk.

B143 A282 20pf + 5pf ultra & blk 15 15

Armed Woman Planting Flower — SP28

1966, Oct. 25 *Perf. 13½x13*

B144 SP28 20pf + 5pf blk & pink 22 15

Surtax was for North Viet Nam.

Wartburg Type of Regular Issue

Design: Wartburg, view from the East.

1966, Nov. 23 ***Perf. 13x13½***
B145 A288 10pf + 5pf slate 15 15

See note after No. 878.

Olympic Type of Regular Issue

Design: 10pf+5pf, Tobogganing.

1968, Jan. 17 Litho. ***Perf. 13½x13***
B146 A314 10pf + 5pf grnsh bl, vio bl & red 15 15

The surtax was for the Olympic Committee of the German Democratic Republic.

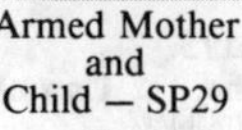

Armed Mother and Child — SP29

Armed Vietnamese Couple — SP30

1968, May 8 ***Perf. 13½x13***
B147 SP29 10pf + 5pf yel & multi 20 15

Surtax was for North Viet Nam.

Festival Type of Regular Issue

1968, June 20 Litho. ***Perf. 13½x13***
B148 A327 20pf + 5pf multi 15 15

Olympic Games Type of Regular Issue, 1968

Designs: 10pf+5pf, Pole vault (vert.). 20pf+10pf, Soccer (vert.).

1968, Sept. 18 Photo. ***Perf. 14***
B149 A336 10pf + 5pf multi 15 15
B150 A336 20pf + 10pf multi 15 15
Set value 15 15

The surtax was for the Olympic Committee.

1969, June 4
B151 SP30 10pf + 5pf multi 20 15

Surtax was for North Viet Nam.

Sports Type of Regular Issue, 1969

Designs: 10pf+5pf, Gymnastics. 20pf+5pf, Art Exhibition with sports motifs.

Photo. & Engr.

1969, June 18 ***Perf. 14***
B152 A353 10pf + 5pf multi 15 15
B153 A353 20pf + 5pf multi 15 15
Set value 15 15

The surtax was for the German Gymnastic and Sports League.

Otto von Guericke's Vacuum Test with Magdeburg Hemispheres — SP31

1969, Oct. 28 Litho. ***Perf. 13x12½***
B154 SP31 40pf + 10pf multi *50 40*

See note after No. 1146.

Folk Art Type of Regular Issue

Design: 20pf+5pf, Decorative plate.

1969, Nov. 25 Litho. ***Perf. 13½x13***
B155 A365 20pf + 5pf yel blk & ultra 80 40

Sports Type of Regular Issue

Design: 20pf+5pf, Children hurdling.

1970, July 1 Photo. ***Perf. 14x13½***
B156 A382 20pf + 5pf multi 22 15

Pioneer Waving Kerchief, and Pioneer Activities — SP32

Design: 25pf+5pf, Girl Pioneer holding kerchief, and Pioneer activities.

1970, July 28 Litho. ***Perf. 13x12½***
B157 SP32 10pf + 5pf multi 45 15
B158 SP32 25pf + 5pf multi 45 15
Set value 20

6th Youth Pioneer Meeting, Cottbus. Printed se-tenant in continuous design.

Ho Chi Minh — SP33

German Democratic Republic No. 460 — SP34

1970, Sept. 2 ***Perf. 13x13½***
B159 SP33 20pf + 5pf rose, blk & red 25 15

Surtax was for North Viet Nam.

1970, Oct. 1 Photo. ***Perf. 14x13½***
B160 SP34 15pf + 5pf multi 20 15

2nd National Youth Philatelic Exhibition, Karl-Marx-Stadt, Oct. 4-11.

Mother and Child SP35

Vietnamese Farm Woman SP36

Photo. & Engr.

1971, Sept. 2 ***Perf. 14***
B161 SP35 10pf + 5pf multi 18 15

Surtax was for North Viet Nam.

Type of Regular Issue

Design: 10pf+5pf, Loading and unloading mail at airport.

Photo. & Engr.

1971, Oct. 5 ***Perf. 14***
B162 A421 10pf + 5pf multi 15 15

Olympic Games Type of Regular Issue

Olympic Rings and: 10pf+5pf, Figure skating, pairs. 15pf+5pf, Speed skating.

1971, Dec. 7 Photo. ***Perf. 13½x14***
B163 A424 10pf + 5pf bl, car & blk 15 15
B164 A424 15pf + 5pf grn, blk & bl 15 15
Set value 15 15

1972, Feb. 22 Litho. ***Perf. 13½x13***
B165 SP36 10pf + 5pf multi 20 15

Surtax was for North Viet Nam.

Olympic Games Type of Regular Issue

Sport and Olympic Rings: 10pf+5pf, Diving. 25pf+10pf, Rowing.

1972, May 16 Photo. ***Perf. 13½x14***
B166 A430 10pf + 5pf grnsh bl, gold & blk 15 15
B167 A430 25pf + 10pf multi 15 15
Set value 15 15

Interartes Type of Regular Issue

Designs: 15pf+5pf, Spear carrier, Persia, 500 B.C. 35pf+5pf, Grape Sellers, by Max Lingner, 1949 (horiz.).

1972, Sept. 19 Photo. ***Perf. 14***
B168 A439 15pf + 5pf multi *1.25 85*
B169 A439 35pf + 5pf multi 15 15

Flags and World Time Clock SP37

Young Couple, by Günter Glombitza SP38

Design: 25pf+5pf, Youth group with guitar and dove.

1973, Feb. 13 Litho. ***Perf. 12½x13***
B170 SP37 10pf + 5pf multi 16 15
B171 SP37 25pf + 5pf multi 35 22
Set value 30

10th World Youth Festival, Berlin.

1973, Oct. 4 Photo. ***Perf. 13½x14***
B172 SP38 20pf + 5pf multi 25 15

Philatelists' Day and for the 3rd National Youth Philatelic Exhibition, Halle.

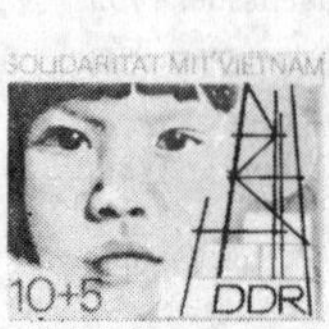

Child, Symbols of Reconstruction SP39

Luis Corvalan, Red Flag SP40

1973, Oct. 11 ***Perf. 14x13½***
B173 SP39 10pf + 5pf multi 20 15

Surtax was for North Viet Nam.

1973, Nov. 5 ***Perf. 13½x14***

Design: 25pf+5pf, Salvador Allende and Chilean flag.

B174 SP40 10pf + 5pf multi *24 18*
B175 SP40 25pf + 5pf multi *45 35*

Solidarity with the people of Chile.

Raised Fist and Star — SP41

Restored Post Gate, Wurzen, 1734 — SP42

1975, Sept. 23 Litho. ***Perf. 13x13½***
B176 SP41 10pf + 5pf multi 20 15

Surtax was for the Solidarity Committee of the German Democratic Republic.

1975, Oct. 21 Photo. ***Perf. 14***
B177 SP42 10pf + 5pf multi *32 30*

Philatelists' Day 1975.

Olympic Games Type of 1975

Designs: 10pf+5pf, Luge run, Oberhof. 25pf+5pf, Ski jump, Rennsteig at Oberhof.

1975, Dec. 2 Photo. ***Perf. 14***
B178 A518 10pf + 5pf multi 15 15
B179 A518 25pf + 5pf multi 22 15
Set value 20

Olympic Games Type of 1976

Designs: 10pf+5pf, Swimming pool, High School for Physical Education, Leipzig. 35pf+10pf, Rifle range, Suhl.

1976, May 18 Photo. ***Perf. 13½x14***
B180 A529 10pf + 5pf multi 15 15
B181 A529 35pf + 10pf multi 25 15
Set value 33 20

TV Tower, Berlin, and Perforations SP43

Hand Holding Torch SP44

1976, Oct. 19 Litho. ***Perf. 13***
B182 SP43 10pf + 5pf org & bl 16 15

Surtax was for Sozphilex 77, Philatelic Exhibition of Socialist Countries, in connection with 60th anniversary of October Revolution.

Sports Type of 1977

Designs: 10pf+5pf, Young milers. 25pf+5pf, Girls artistic gymnastic performance.

1977, July 19 Litho. ***Perf. 13x12½***
B183 A558 10pf + 5pf multi 15 15
B184 A558 25pf + 5pf multi 15 15
Set value 27 15

Sozphilex Type of 1977

Souvenir Sheet

Design: 50pf+20pf, World Youth Song, by Lothar Zitzmann (horiz.).

1977, Aug. 16 Photo. ***Perf. 13***
B185 A559 50pf + 20pf multi *1.25 95*

1977, Oct. 18 Litho. ***Perf. 14***
B186 SP44 10pf + 5pf multi 16 15

Surtax was for East German Solidarity Committee.

Fountain Type of 1979

Design: 10pf+5pf, Goose Boy Fountain.

1979, Aug. 7 Photo. ***Perf. 14***
B187 A617 10pf + 5pf multi *35 35*

Vietnamese Soldier, Mother and Child — SP45

1979, Nov. 6 Litho. *Perf. 14*

B188 SP45 10pf + 5pf red org & blk 20 15

Surtax was for Vietnam.

Olympic Type of 1980

Design: Ski Jump, sculpture by Gunther Schutz.

1980, Jan. 15 Photo.

B189 A627 25pf + 10pf multi 15 15

1980, Apr. 22 Photo. *Perf. 14*

Design: 20pf+5pf, Runners at the Finish, by Lothar Zitzmann.

B190 A627 20 + 5pf multi 15 15

Interflug Type of 1980

Souvenir Sheet

1980, June 10 Litho. *Perf. 13x12½*

B191 A636 1m + 10pf Jet, globe *1.90 1.50*

AEROSOZPHILEX 1980 International Airpost Exhibition, Berlin, Aug. 1-10.

Olympic Type of 1980

Design: Swimmer, by Willi Sitte (vert.).

1980, July 8 Photo. *Perf. 14*

B192 A627 20pf + 10pf multi 15 15

22nd Summer Olympic Games, Moscow, July 19-Aug. 3.

International Solidarity

SP46 SP47

1980, Oct. 14 Photo. *Perf. 14*

B193 SP46 10pf + 5pf multi 16 15

1981, Oct. 6 Photo. *Perf. 14*

B194 SP47 10pf + 5pf multi 18 15

Palestinian Family, Tree of Life — SP48

1982, Sept. 21 Litho. *Perf. 14*

B195 SP48 10pf + 5pf multi 18 15

Palestinian solidarity.

Literacy, Home Defense — SP49

1983, Nov. 8 Litho. *Perf. 14x13½*

B196 SP49 10pf + 5pf multi 18 15

Nicaraguan solidarity.

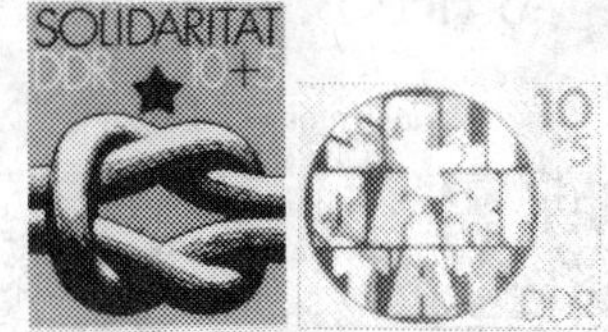

Solidarity

SP50 SP51

1984, Oct. 23 Photo. *Perf. 14*

B197 SP50 10pf + 5pf Knot 25 15

1985, May 28 Photo.

B198 SP51 10pf + 5pf Globe, peace dove 25 15

Surtax for the Solidarity Committee.

Technical Assistance to Developing Nations — SP52

1986, Nov. 4 Photo.

B199 SP52 10pf + 5pf multi 25 15

Surtax for the Solidarity Committee.

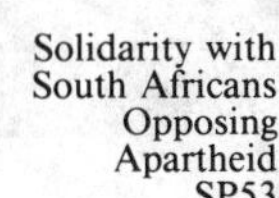

Solidarity with South Africans Opposing Apartheid SP53

1987, June 16 Litho. *Perf. 14*

B200 SP53 10pf +5pf multi 25 15

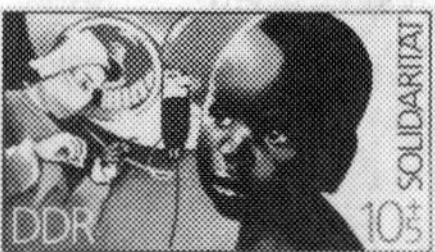

Solidarity SP54

1988, Oct. 4 Photo. *Perf. 14*

B201 SP54 10pf +5pf multi 18 15

Surtax for the Solidarity Committee. No. B201 printed se-tenant with label containing a Wilhelm Pieck quote.

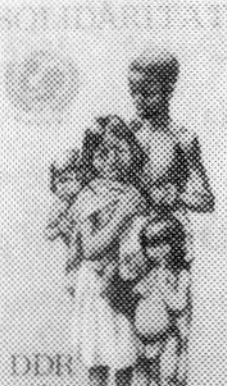

UNICEF Emblem and Children of Africa — SP55

1989, Sept. 5 Photo. *Perf. 14½x14*

B202 SP55 10pf +5pf multi 16 15

Surtax for the Solidarity Committee.

Leipzig Church, Municipal Arms SP56

1990, Feb. 28 Photo. *Perf. 13*

B203 SP56 35pf +15pf multicolored 60 55

We are the People.

Intl. Literacy Year — SP57

1990, July 24 Photo. *Perf. 14*

B204 SP57 30pf+5pf on 10pf+5pf 45 45

Not issued without surcharge.

AIR POST STAMPS

Canceled to Order
Used values are for CTO's.

Stylized Plane

AP1 AP2

Perf. 13x12½, 13x13½ (AP2)

1957, Dec. 13 Litho. Wmk. 313

C1	AP1	5pf gray & blk	15	15
C2	AP1	20pf brt car & blk	15	15
C3	AP1	35pf vio & blk	15	15
C4	AP1	50pf mar & blk	15	15
C5	AP2	1m olive & yel	65	15
C6	AP2	3m choc & yel	1.75	15
C7	AP2	5m dk bl & yel	3.75	15
		Nos. C1-C7 (7)	6.75	
		Set value		50

Plane and Envelope — AP3

1982-87 Photo. *Perf. 14*

C8	AP3	5pf lt bl & blk	15	15
C9	AP3	15pf brt rose lil & blk	18	15
C10	AP3	20pf ocher & blk	15	15
C11	AP3	25pf ol bis & blk	28	15
C12	AP3	30pf brt grn & blk	25	15
C13	AP3	40pf ol grn & blk	30	18
C14	AP3	1m blue & blk	70	42
C15	AP3	3m brn & blk	2.75	90
C16	AP3	5m dk red & blk	4.50	35
		Nos. C8-C16 (9)	9.26	2.60

Issue dates: 30pf, 40pf, 1m, Oct. 26. 5pf, 20pf, Oct. 4, 1983. 3m, Apr. 10, 1984. 5m, Sept. 10, 1985. 15pf, 25pf, Oct. 6, 1987.

OFFICIAL STAMPS

While valid, these Official stamps were not sold to the public unused. After their period of use, some sets were sold abroad by the government stamp sales agency.

Arms of Republic — O1

Perf. 13x12½

1954 Wmk. 297 Litho.

O1	O1	5pf emerald	5.75	15
O2	O1	6pf violet	2.50	15
O3	O1	8pf org brn	5.75	15
O4	O1	10pf lt bl grn	5.75	15
O5	O1	12pf blue	5.75	15
O6	O1	15pf dk vio	5.75	15
O7	O1	16pf dk vio	2.50	15
O8	O1	20pf olive	2.50	15
O9	O1	24pf brn red	2.50	15
O10	O1	25pf sage grn	4.00	15
O11	O1	30pf brn red	1.75	15
O12	O1	40pf red	4.00	15
O13	O1	48pf rose lil	2.00	50
O14	O1	50pf rose lil	2.00	15
O15	O1	60pf brt bl	2.00	15
O16	O1	70pf brown	2.00	15
O17	O1	84pf brown	2.00	90
		Nos. O1-O17 (17)	58.50	
		Set value		1.90

Type of 1954 Redrawn

Arc of compass projects at right except on No. O22.

1954-56 Typo.

O18	O1	5pf emer ('54)	60	15
O19	O1	10pf bl grn	60	15
O20	O1	12pf dk bl ('54)	50	15
O21	O1	15pf dk vio	60	15
O22	O1	20pf ol, arc at left ('55)	*4.00*	15
a.		Arc of compass projects at right ('56)	175.00	15
O23	O1	25pf dk grn	30	15
O24	O1	30pf brn red	80	15
O25	O1	40pf red	50	15
O26	O1	50pf rose lil	40	15
O27	O1	70pf brown	50	15
		Nos. O18-O27 (10)	8.80	
		Set value		45

Shaded background of emblem consists of vertical lines; on Nos. O1-O17 it consists of dots.

Granite paper was used for a 1956 printing of the 5pf, 10pf, 15pf, 20pf and 40pf. Value for set unused $300, used 30 cents.

See Nos. O37-O43.

O2 O3

1956 Wmk. 297 *Perf. 13x12½*

O28	O2	5pf black	15	15
O29	O2	10pf black	15	15
O30	O2	20pf black	15	15
O31	O2	40pf black	25	15
O32	O2	70pf black	35	15
		Set value	82	25

1956 Litho. Wmk. 297

O33	O3	10pf lilac & black	20	18
O34	O3	20pf lilac & black	*25.00*	15
O35	O3	40pf lilac & black	20	18
O36	O3	70pf lilac & black	60	55

Nos. O33-O36 exist also with black or violet overprint of 4-digit control number.

See Nos. O44-O45.

No. O34 was reprinted with watermark sideways ("DDR" vertical). Value $2.

Redrawn Type of 1954-56

Perf. 13x12½, 14

1957-60 Typo. Wmk. 313

Granite Paper

O37	O1	5pf emerald	15	15
O38	O1	10pf bl grn	15	15
O39	O1	15pf dk vio	15	15
O40	O1	20pf olive	15	15
O41	O1	30pf dk red ('58)	15	15
O42	O1	40pf red	15	15
O42A	O1	50pf rose lil ('60)	40	15
O43	O1	70pf brn ('58)	40	15
		Set value	1.20	50

Nos. O37-O43 were all issued in perf. 13x12½. Nos. O37-O40 were also issued perf. 14. Values are the same.

Type of 1956

1957 Litho. *Perf. 13x12½*

O44	O3	10pf lilac & black	25	35
O45	O3	20pf lilac & black	25	55

Nos. O44-O45 have black or violet overprint of four-digit control number.

Stamps similar to type O3 were issued later, with denomination expressed in dashes: one for 10pf, two for 20pf.

GERMAN OFFICES ABROAD

OFFICES IN CHINA

100 Pfennings = 1 Mark
100 Cents = 1 Dollar (1905)

Stamps of Germany, 1889-90, Overprinted in Black at 56 degree Angle

1898		Unwmk.	Perf. 13½x14½	
1	A9	3pf dark brown	4.25	3.50
a.		3pf yellow brown	7.50	7.50
b.		3pf reddish brown	21.00	30.00
2	A9	5pf green	2.25	2.25
3	A10	10pf carmine	6.00	6.00
4	A10	20pf ultramarine	15.0	16.00
5	A10	25pf orange	25.00	27.50
6	A10	50pf red brown	13.00	13.00

Overprinted at 45 degree Angle

1c	A9	3pf yellow brown	130.00	*25,000.*
1d	A9	3pf reddish brown	165.00	
2a	A9	5pf green	12.00	12.00
3a	A10	10pf carmine	15.00	10.00
4a	A10	20pf ultramarine	13.00	10.00
5a	A10	25pf orange	52.50	55.00
6a	A10	50pf red brown	22.50	18.00

Foochow Issue

Nos. 3 and 3a Handstamp Surcharged **5 pf**

16	A10	5pf on 10pf, #3	415.00	525.00
a.		On No. 3a	465.00	650.00

For similar 5pf surcharges on 10pf carmine, see Tsingtau Issue, Kiauchau.

Tientsin Issue

German Stamps of 1900 Issue Handstamped

1900				
17	A11	3pf brown	525.00	600.00
18	A11	5pf green	265.00	400.00
19	A11	10pf carmine	675.00	650.00
20	A11	20pf ultra	650.00	475.00
21	A11	30pf org & blk, *sal*	*7,750.*	*7,750.*
22	A11	50pf pur & blk, *sal*	*30,000.*	*17,500.*
23	A11	80pf lake & blk, *rose*	*4,750.*	*4,250.*

This handstamp is known inverted and double on most values.
Excellent faked handstamps are plentiful.

Regular Issue

A3

A4

A5

A6

A7

Overprinted Horizontally in Black

1901			Perf. 14, 14½	
24	A3	3pf brown	1.75	1.75
a.		3pf light red brown	90.00	110.00
25	A3	5pf green	1.75	1.00
26	A3	10pf carmine	2.75	80
27	A3	20pf ultra	3.25	1.50
28	A3	25pf org & blk, *yel*	11.50	16.00
29	A3	30pf org & blk, *sal*	11.50	13.00
30	A3	40pf lake & blk	11.50	8.75
31	A3	50pf pur & blk, *sal*	11.50	8.75
32	A3	80pf lake & blk, *rose*	14.00	13.00

Overprinted in Black or Red

33	A4	1m car rose	35.00	32.50
34	A5	2m gray blue	30.00	30.00
35	A6	3m blk vio (R)	50.00	65.00
36	A7	5m sl & car, type I	300.00	450.00
36A	A7	5m sl & car, type II	200.00	300.00
		Nos. 24-36A (14)	684.50	942.05

Retouched copies of No. 36 sell for ⅔ as much. See note after Germany No. 65A.

Surcharged on German Stamps of 1902 in Black or Red

a

* 1 Dollar *
China
b

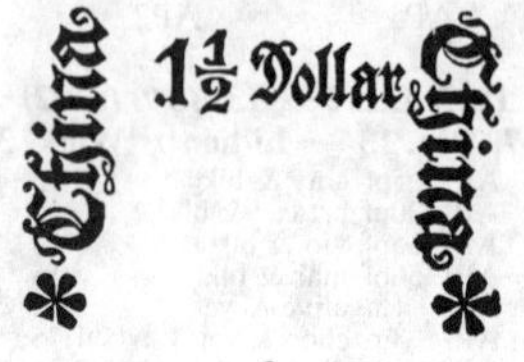

c

1905				
37	A16(a)	1c on 3pf brn	2.50	2.50
38	A16(a)	2c on 5pf grn	2.50	1.10
39	A16(a)	4c on 10pf car	6.00	1.10
40	A16(a)	10c on 20pf ultra	2.50	1.50
41	A16(a)	20c on 40pf lake & blk	20.00	5.75
42	A16(a)	40c on 80pf lake & blk, *rose*	30.00	12.00
43	A17(b)	½d on 1m car rose	12.00	13.00
44	A21(b)	1d on 2m gray bl	15.00	14.00
45	A19(c)	1½d on 3m blk vio (R)	10.50	*40.00*
46	A20(b)	2½d on 5m sl & car	82.50	*225.00*
		Nos. 37-46 (10)	183.50	*315.95*

Surcharged on German Stamps of 1905 in Black or Red

1906-13			Wmk. 125	
47	A16(a)	1c on 3pf brn	45	70
48	A16(a)	2c on 5pf grn	45	70
49	A16(a)	4c on 10pf car	45	70
50	A16(a)	10c on 20pf ultra	1.00	*5.25*
51	A16(a)	20c on 40pf lake & blk	1.40	*2.75*
52	A16(a)	40c on 80pf lake & blk, *rose*	1.40	*30.00*
53	A17(b)	½d on 1m car rose	2.75	*27.50*
54	A21(b)	1d on 2m gray bl	4.50	*27.50*
55	A19(c)	1½d on 3m blk vio (R)	5.25	*75.00*
56	A20(b)	2½d on 5m sl & car	22.50	*37.50*
		Nos. 47-56 (10)	40.15	

Forged cancellations exist.

German Offices Abroad stamps can be mounted in Scott's Germany Part I Album.

OFFICES IN MOROCCO

100 Centimos = 1 Peseta

A1

A2

Stamps of Germany Surcharged in Black

1899		Unwmk.	Perf. 13½x14½	
1	A1	3c on 3pf dk brn	3.25	2.00
2	A1	5c on 5pf grn	3.25	2.50
3	A2	10c on 10pf car	7.50	7.00
4	A2	25c on 20pf ultra	12.50	12.50
5	A2	30c on 25pf org	25.00	27.50
6	A2	60c on 50pf red brn	20.00	24.00

Before Nos. 1-6 were issued, the same six basic stamps of Germany's 1889-1900 issue were overprinted "Marocco" diagonally without the currency-changing surcharge line, but were not issued. Value, $1,500.

A3

A4

A5

A6

A7

Black or Red Surcharge

1900			Perf. 14, 14½	
7	A3	3c on 3pf brn	1.25	1.25
8	A3	5c on 5pf grn	1.25	1.00
9	A3	10c on 10pf car	2.00	1.00
10	A3	25c on 20pf ultra	2.75	2.25
11	A3	30c on 25pf org & blk, *yel*	10.00	11.50
12	A3	35c on 30pf org & blk, *sal*	7.25	5.25
13	A3	50c on 40pf lake & blk	7.25	5.25
14	A3	60c on 50pf pur & blk, *sal*	16.00	30.00
15	A3	1p on 80pf lake & blk, *rose*	11.50	11.50
16	A4	1p25c on 1m car rose	30.00	35.00
17	A5	2p50c on 2m gray bl	32.50	40.00
18	A6	3p75c on 3m blk vio (R)	42.50	60.00
19	A7	6p25c on 5m sl & car, type I	230.00	475.00
19A	A7	6p25c on 5m sl & car, type II	215.00	215.00
		Nos. 7-19A (14)	609.25	894.00

A 1903 printing of Nos. 8, 16-18 and 19A differs in the "M" and "t" of the surcharge. Values are for 1900 printing: Nos. 8, 16-18. 1903 printing: No. 19A.

Retouched copies of No. 19 sell for ⅔ as much. See note after Germany No. 65A.

German Stamps of 1902 Surcharged in Black or Red

Marocco
3 Centimos
a

Marocco 1 Pes. 25 Cts.
b

Marocco 3 Pes. 75 Cts.
c

1905				
20	A16(a)	3c on 3pf brn	3.25	3.00
21	A16(a)	5c on 5pf grn	5.25	1.10
22	A16(a)	10c on 10pf car	10.50	75
23	A16(a)	25c on 20pf ultra	21.00	3.00
24	A16(a)	30c on 25pf org & blk, *yel*	7.00	4.75
25	A16(a)	35c on 30pf org & blk, *buff*	10.50	5.75
26	A16(a)	50c on 40pf lake & blk	9.75	9.25
27	A16(a)	60c on 50pf pur & blk, *buff*	35.00	25.00
28	A16(a)	1p on 80pf lake & blk, *rose*	35.00	22.50
29	A17(b)	1p25c on 1m car rose	45.00	27.50
30	A21(b)	2p50c on 2m gray bl	100.00	150.00
31	A19(c)	3p75c on 3m blk vio (R)	52.50	50.00
32	A20(b)	6p25c on 5m sl & car	140.00	165.00
		Nos. 20-32 (13)	474.75	467.60

Surcharged on Germany No. 54

32A	A11(a)	5c on 5pf grn	6.50	*25.00*

German Stamps of 1905 Surcharged

1906-11			Wmk. 125	
33	A16(a)	3c on 3pf brn	9.50	2.25
34	A16(a)	5c on 5pf grn	9.50	1.10
35	A16(a)	10c on 10pf car	9.50	1.10
36	A16(a)	25c on 20pf ultra	16.00	2.25
37	A16(a)	30c on 25pf org & blk, *yel*	18.00	11.00
38	A16(a)	35c on 30pf org & blk, *buff*	18.00	11.00
39	A16(a)	50c on 40pf lake & blk	35.00	*185.00*
40	A16(a)	60c on 50pf pur & blk, *buff*	24.00	16.00
41	A16(a)	1p on 80pf lake & blk, *rose*	125.00	225.00
42	A17(b)	1p25c on 1m car rose	60.00	*185.00*
43	A21(b)	2p50c on 2m gray bl	60.00	*185.00*
44	A20(b)	6p25c on 5m sl & car	125.00	*375.00*
		Nos. 33-44 (12)	509.50	*1,199.*

Excellent forgeries exist of No. 41.

Surcharge Spelled "Marokko" in Black or Red

1911				
45	A16(a)	3c on 3pf brn	50	70
46	A16(a)	5c on 5pf grn	50	90
47	A16(a)	10c on 10pf car	50	1.00
48	A16(a)	25c on 20pf ultra	65	1.00
49	A16(a)	30c on 25pf org & blk, *yel*	1.25	*15.00*
50	A16(a)	35c on 30pf org & blk, *buff*	1.25	*8.00*
51	A16(a)	50c on 40pf lake & blk	1.25	*5.00*
52	A16(a)	60c on 50pf pur & blk, *buff*	1.50	*32.50*
53	A16(a)	1p on 80pf lake & blk, *rose*	1.75	*26.00*
54	A17(b)	1p25c on 1m car rose	2.00	*60.00*
55	A21(b)	2p50c on 2m gray bl	3.50	*52.50*
56	A19(c)	3p75c on 3m blk vio (R)	6.00	*125.00*
57	A20(b)	6p25c on 5m sl & car	15.00	*200.00*
		Nos. 45-57 (13)	35.65	

Forged cancellations exist.

OFFICES IN THE TURKISH EMPIRE

Unused values for Nos. 1-6 are for stamps with original gum. Copies without gum sell for about one-third of the figures quoted.

40 Paras = 1 Piaster

A1

A2

German Stamps of 1880-83 Surcharged in Black or Blue

1884 Unwmk. *Perf. 13 ½x14 ½*

No.	Type	Description	Unused	Used
1	A1	10pa on 5pf vio	20.00	18.00
2	A2	20pa on 10pf rose	50.00	18.00
3	A2	1pi on 20pf ultra (Bk)	45.00	2.50
4	A2	1pi on 20pf ultra (Bl)	600.00	45.00
5	A2	1 ¼pi on 25pf brn	125.00	125.00
6	A2	2 ½pi on 50pf gray grn	125.00	70.00
a.		2 ½pi on 50pf dp ol grn	240.00	200.00

There are two types of the surcharge on the 1 ¼pi and 2 ½pi stamps, the difference being in the spacing between the figures and the word "PIASTER".

There are re-issues of these stamps which vary only slightly from the originals in overprint measurements.

A3

A4

A5

German Stamps of 1889-1900 Surcharged in Black

1889

No.	Type	Description	Unused	Used
8	A3	10pa on 5pf grn	2.00	60
9	A4	20pa on 10pf car	3.50	1.80
10	A4	1pi on 20pf ultra	4.50	65
11	A5	1 ¼pi on 25pf org	21.00	14.00
12	A5	2 ½pi on 50pf choc	35.00	18.00
a.		2 ½pi on 50pf copper brn	150.00	100.00

A6

A7

A8

A9

A10

A11

1900 *Perf. 14, 14 ½*

Black or Red Surcharge

No.	Type	Description	Unused	Used
13	A6	10pa on 5pf grn	2.00	2.00
14	A6	20pa on 10pf car	2.50	2.50
15	A6	1pi on 20pf ultra	4.75	1.50
16	A7	1 ¼pi on 25pf org & blk, *yel*	6.25	3.50
17	A7	1 ½pi on 30pf org & blk, *sal*	6.25	3.50
18	A6	2pi on 40pf lake & blk	6.25	3.50
19	A7	2 ½pi on 50pf pur & blk, *sal*	14.00	14.00
20	A6	4pi on 80pf lake & blk, *rose*	14.00	14.00
21	A8	5pi on 1m car rose	35.00	35.00
22	A9	10pi on 2m gray bl	35.00	40.00
23	A10	15pi on 3m blk vio (R)	60.00	80.00
24	A11	25pi on 5m sl & car, type I	250.00	440.00
a.		Double surcharge	*12,500.*	*15,000.*
24B	A11	25pi on 5m sl & car, type II	190.00	325.00
c.		Double surcharge	*11,000.*	*9,000.*
		Nos. 13-24B (13)	626.00	964.50

Retouched copies of No. 24 sell for ⅔ as much. See note after Germany No. 65A.

German Stamps of 1900 Surcharged in Black — **1 PIASTER 1**

1903-05

No.	Type	Description	Unused	Used
25	A11	10pa on 5pf green	14.00	10.00
26	A11	20pa on 10pf car	32.50	18.00
27	A11	1pi on 20pf ultra	8.50	3.50

5 PIASTER 5

No.	Type	Description	Unused	Used
28	A12	5pi on 1m car rose	65.00	52.50
29	A13	10pi on 2m bl ('05)	135.00	225.00
30	A15	25pi on 5m sl & car	275.00	*700.00*
a.		Double surcharge	*4,250.*	
		Nos. 25-30 (6)	530.00	*1,009.*

The 1903-05 surcharges may be easily distinguished from those of 1900 by the added bar at the top of the letter "A".

German Stamps of 1902 Surcharged in Black or Red

a **10 10 Para**

b **5 Piaster 5**

1905 Unwmk.

No.	Type	Description	Unused	Used
31	A16(a)	10pa on 5pf grn	4.50	2.50
32	A16(a)	20pa on 10pf car	10.00	3.25
33	A16(a)	1pi on 20pf ultra	11.00	2.50
34	A16(a)	1 ¼pi on 25pf org & blk, *yel*	11.00	7.00
35	A16(a)	1 ½pi on 30pf org & blk, *buff*	20.00	18.00
36	A16(a)	2pi on 40pf lake & blk	32.50	18.00
37	A16(a)	2 ½pi on 50pf pur & blk, *buff*	12.00	*27.50*
38	A16(a)	4pi on 80pf lake & blk, *rose*	35.00	16.00
39	A17(b)	5pi on 1m car rose	30.00	27.50
40	A21(b)	10pi on 2m gray bl	42.50	47.50
41	A19(b)	15pi on 3m blk vio (R)	55.00	47.50
42	A20(b)	25pi on 5m sl & car	250.00	325.00
		Nos. 31-42 (12)	513.50	542.25

German Stamps of 1905 Surcharged in Black or Red

1906-12 Wmk. 125

No.	Type	Description	Unused	Used
43	A16(a)	10pa on 5pf grn	2.00	45
44	A16(a)	20pa on 10pf car	2.75	45
45	A16(a)	1pi on 20pf ultra	3.50	50
46	A16(a)	1 ¼pi on 25pf org & blk, *yel*	16.00	12.50
47	A16(a)	1 ½pi on 30pf org & blk, *buff*	10.00	5.00
48	A16(a)	2pi on 40pf lake & blk	4.50	1.25
49	A16(a)	2 ½pi on 50pf pur & blk, *buff*	11.50	8.00
50	A16(a)	4pi on 80pf lake & blk, *rose*	10.00	*24.00*
51	A17(b)	5pi on 1m car rose	20.00	30.00
52	A21(b)	10pi on 2m gray bl	20.00	*40.00*
53	A19(b)	15pi on 3m blk vio (R)	22.50	*450.00*
54	A20(b)	25pi on 5m sl & car	27.50	*55.00*
		Nos. 43-54 (12)	150.25	

German Stamps of 1905 Surcharged Diagonally in Black — **10 Centimes**

1908

No.	Type	Description	Unused	Used
55	A16	5c on 5pf grn	1.25	1.50
56	A16	10c on 10pf car	3.00	2.00
57	A16	25c on 20pf ultra	7.25	*27.50*
58	A16	50c on 40pf lake & blk	32.50	*80.00*
59	A16	100c on 80pf lake & blk, *rose*	65.00	90.00
		Nos. 55-59 (5)	109.00	*201.00*

Forged cancellations exist on Nos. 37, 53-54, 57-59.

GRAND COMORO

LOCATION — One of the Comoro Islands in the Mozambique Channel between Madagascar and Mozambique.
GOVT. — Former French Colony
AREA — 385 sq. mi. (approx.)
POP. — 50,000 (approx.)
CAPITAL — Moroni

See Comoro Islands

100 Centimes = 1 Franc

Navigation and Commerce — A1

Perf. 14x13 ½

1897-1907 Typo. Unwmk.

Name of Colony in Blue or Carmine

No.	Type	Description	Unused	Used
1	A1	1c blk, *lil bl*	55	55
2	A1	2c brn, *buff*	60	60
3	A1	4c claret, *lav*	80	80
4	A1	5c grn, *grnsh*	1.50	1.50
5	A1	10c blk, *lavender*	3.50	3.00
6	A1	10c red ('00)	4.50	4.50
7	A1	15c blue, quadrille paper	6.00	4.50
8	A1	15c gray, *lt gray* ('00)	4.50	4.50
9	A1	20c red, *grn*	6.00	5.75
10	A1	25c blk, *rose*	7.00	5.75
11	A1	25c blue ('00)	7.50	4.50
12	A1	30c brn, *bister*	8.00	5.75
13	A1	35c blk, *yel* ('06)	7.50	6.25
14	A1	40c red, *straw*	9.00	5.75
15	A1	45c blk, *gray grn* ('07)	39.00	32.50
16	A1	50c car, *rose*	16.00	8.00
17	A1	50c brn, *bluish* ('00)	18.00	16.00
18	A1	75c dp vio, *org*	25.00	16.00
19	A1	1fr brnz grn, *straw*	15.00	12.00
		Nos. 1-19 (19)	179.95	138.20

Perf. 13 ½x14 stamps are counterfeits.

Issues of 1897-1907 Surcharged in Black or Carmine

05 10

1912

No.	Type	Description	Unused	Used
20	A1	5c on 2c brn, *buff*	45	45
a.		Inverted surcharge	80.00	
21	A1	5c on 4c cl, *lav* (C)	60	60
22	A1	5c on 15c blue (C)	45	45
23	A1	5c on 20c red, *grn*	50	50
24	A1	5c on 25c blk, *rose* (C)	50	50
25	A1	5c on 30c brn, *bis* (C)	60	60
26	A1	10c on 40c red, *straw*	60	60
27	A1	10c on 45c blk, *gray grn* (C)	60	60
28	A1	10c on 50c car, *rose*	65	65
29	A1	10c on 75c dp vio, *org*	65	65
		Nos. 20-29 (10)	5.60	5.60

Two spacings between the surcharged numerals are found on Nos. 20 to 29.

Nos. 20 to 29 were available for use in Madagascar and the entire Comoro archipelago.

Stamps of Grand Comoro were superseded by those of Madagascar, and in 1950 by those of Comoro Islands.

GREECE

(Hellas)

LOCATION — Southern part of the Balkan Peninsula in southeastern Europe, bordering on the Ionian, Aegean and Mediterranean Seas
GOVT. — Republic
AREA — 50,949 sq. mi.
POP. — 9,740,417 (1981)
CAPITAL — Athens

In 1923 the reigning king was forced to abdicate and the following year Greece was declared a republic. In 1935, the king was recalled by a "plebiscite" of the people. Greece became a republic in June 1973. The country today includes the Aegean Islands of Chios, Mytilene (Lesbos), Samos, Icaria (Nicaria) and Lemnos, the Ionian Islands (Corfu, etc.) Crete, Macedonia, Western Thrace and part of Eastern Thrace, the Mount Athos District, Epirus and the Dodecanese Islands.

100 Lepta = 1 Drachma

Catalogue values for unused stamps in this country are for Never Hinged items, beginning with Scott 601 in the regular postage section, Scott B1 in the semi-postal section, Scott C67 in the airpost section, Scott CB1 in the airpost semi-postal section, Scott RA69 in the postal tax section, and Scott N239 in the occupation and annexation section.

Watermarks

Wmk. 129-Crown and ET

Wmk. 252-Crowns

Values of early Greek stamps vary according to condition. Quotations for Nos. 1-58 are for fine copies. Very fine to superb specimens sell at much higher prices, and inferior or poor copies sell at reduced prices, depending on the condition of the individual specimen.

Values for Nos. 1-7 unused are for specimens without gum. Stamps with original gum are worth considerably more.

Hermes (Mercury) — A1

Paris Print, Fine Impression

The enlarged illustrations show the head in various states of the plates. The differences are best seen in the shading lines on the cheek and neck.

1861 Unwmk. Typo. *Imperf.*

Without Figures on Back

1 A1 1 l choc, *cream* 150.00 275.00
- *a.* 1 l red brown, *cream* 165.00 300.00

2 A1 2 l ol bis, *straw* 21.00 35.00
- *a.* 2 l brown buff, *buff* 20.00 32.50

3 A1 5 l emer, *grnsh* 150.00 100.00

4 A1 20 l bl, *bluish* 375.00 52.50
- *a.* 20 l dp bl, *bluish* 500.00 160.00
- *b.* On pelure paper 250.00

5 A1 40 l vio, *bl* 165.00 100.00

6 A1 80 l rose, *pink* 110.00 70.00
- *a.* 80 l carmine, *pink* 110.00 70.00

Large Figures, 8mm high, on Back

7 A1 10 l red org, *bl* 275.00 275.00
- *a.* "O1" on back
- *b.* Without "10" on back 475.00
- *c.* "O" of "10" inverted on back 675.00
- *d.* "1" of "10" inverted on back 775.00

No. 7b was not regularly issued.

Trial impressions of Paris prints exist in many shades, some being close to those of the issued stamps. The gum used was thin and smooth instead of thick, brownish and crackly as on the issued stamps.

See Nos. 8-58. For surcharges see Nos. 130, 132-133, 137-139, 141-143, 147-149, 153-154, 157-158.

Athens Print, Clear Impression

1861-62

Without Figures on Back

Fine Printing, #9

Coarse Printing, #9a

8 A1 1 l choc, *cr* ('62) 375.00 225.00
- *a.* 1 l dk choc, *cr* 675.00 428.00

9 A1 2 l bis brn, *cr* 35.00 47.50
- *a.* 2 l dk brn, *straw*

10 A1 20 l dk bl, *bluish* (coarse print) 10,000.

No. 10 often shows a quadrille appearance in the background.

With Figures on Back

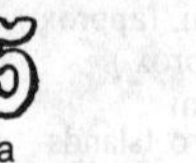

Fine Printing, #11-14

Coarse Printing, #11a-14a

11 A1 (a) 5 l grn, *grnsh* 175.00 65.00
- *a.* 5 l grn, *grnsh* 215.00 65.00
- *b.* Double "5" on back 475.00

12 A1 10 l org, *grnsh* 400.00 67.50
- *a.* 10 l org, *grnsh* 725.00 87.50

13 A1 20 l dk bl, *bluish* 2,500. 55.00
- *a.* 20 l dl bl, *bluish* 2,750. 80.00

14 A1 40 l red vio, *bl* 1,500. 190.00
- *a.* 40 l red vio, *bl* 1,600. 200.00

15 A1 80 l dl rose, *pink* ('62) 550.00 100.00
- *a.* 80 l car, *pink* ('62) 550.00 100.00

The fine stamps can be distinguished by the delicate lines of the numerals on the back as compared with the coarser ones of later printings.

Nos. 15 and 15a have vermilion figures on the back, while those of all later printings are carmine.

Athens Print, Coarse Impression

1862-67

With Figures on Back, Except 1 l and 2 l

16 A1 1 l choc, *cr* 35.00 24.00
- *a.* 1 l red brn, *cr* (poor print) 140.00 70.00
- *b.* 1 l brn, *cr* (poor print) 45.00 22.50

17 A1 2 l brnsh bis, *cr* 7.25 6.50
- *a.* 2 l bis, *cr* 7.25 6.50

18 A1 (b) 5 l grn, *grnsh* 125.00 8.00
- *a.* 5 l yelsh grn, *grnsh* 125.00 8.00

19 A1 10 l yel org, *bluish* 150.00 8.75
- *a.* 10 l org, *bl* (1864) 325.00 10.00
- *b.* "10" on face instead of back (No. 19a) 5,500.
- *c.* 10 l red org, *bl* (Dec. 1865) 300.00 10.00
- *d.* "01" on back 500.00

20 A1 20 l bl, *bluish* 125.00 5.50
- *a.* 20 l lt bl, *bluish* (fine print) 125.00 14.00
- *b.* 20 l dk bl, *bluish* 375.00 14.00
- *c.* 20 l bl, *grnsh* 1,000. 10.00
- *d.* "80" on back 1,300.
- *e.* Double "20" on back 175.00
- *f.* Without "20" on back 1,400.

21 A1 40 l red vio, *bl* 225.00 12.00
- *a.* 40 l brn vio, *bl* 225.00 12.00
- *b.* 40 l lil brn, *lil gray* 1,000. 14.00
- *c.* Double "40" on back 225.00

22 A1 80 l car, *pale rose* 50.00 10.00
- *a.* 80 l rose, *pale rose* 55.00 10.00
- *b.* "8" on back inverted 1,000. 175.00
- *c.* "80" on back inverted 225.00
- *d.* "8" only on back 185.00

Faint vertical lines are visible in the background of Nos. 16, 16a and 16b.

Many stamps of this and succeeding issues which are normally imperforate are known rouletted, pin-perforated, percé en scie, etc., all of which are unofficial.

1868-69

Athens Print, From Cleaned Plates

23 A1 1 l redsh brn, *cr* 25.00 22.50
- *a.* 1 l dk redsh brn, *cr* 22.50 27.50

24 A1 2 l gray bis, *cr* 12.00 11.00

25 A1 (b) 5 l grn, *grnsh* 1,100. 40.00

26 A1 10 l pale org, *bluish* 900.00 9.00
- *a.* "10" on back inverted 500.00

27 A1 20 l pale bl, *bluish* 1,000. 7.00
- *a.* Double "20" on back 200.00

28 A1 40 l rose vio, *bl* 225.00 17.00
- *a.* "20" on back, corrected to "40" 1,400. 600.00

29 A1 80 l rose car, *pale rose* 125.00 72.50

The "0" on the back of No. 29 is printed more heavily than the "8".

1870

Special Athens Printing Made Under Supervision of German Workmen

Good Impression

30 A1 1 l redsh brn, *cr* 60.00 70.00
- *a.* 1 l dp redsh brn, *cr* 80.00 95.00

31 A1 20 l lt bl, *bluish* 1,500. 13.00
- *a.* 20 l blue, *bluish* 1,600. 14.00
- *b.* "02" on back 225.00
- *c.* "20" on back inverted 190.00

Nos. 30 and 30a have short lines of shading on cheek. The spandrels of No. 31 are very pale with the lines often broken or missing.

1870-71

Medium to Thin Paper Without Mesh

32 A1 1 l brn, *cr* 57.50 40.00
- *a.* 1 l pur brn, *cr* 47.50 35.00

33 A1 2 l sal bis, *cr* 8.00 8.00

34 A1 (b) 5 l grn, *grnsh* 2,000. 30.00

35 A1 10 l lt red org, *grnsh* 1,100. 27.50

36 A1 20 l bl, *bluish* 1,000. 7.25
- *a.* "02" on back 190.00
- *b.* Double "20" on back 200.00

37 A1 40 l sal, *grnsh* 475.00 40.00
- *a.* 40 l lilac, *grnsh*

The stamps of this issue have rather coarse figures on back.

No. 37a is printed in the exact shade of the numerals on the back of No. 37.

1872-75

Thin Transparent Paper Showing Mesh

38 A1 1 l red brn, *yelsh* 32.50 30.00
- *a.* 1 l grysh brn, *straw* 37.50 32.50

39 A1 (b) 5 l grn, *grnsh* 425.00 13.00
- *a.* 5 l dk grn, *grnsh* 400.00 20.00
- *b.* Double "5" on back 100.00

40 A1 10 l red org, *grnsh* 650.00 5.00
- *a.* 10 l red org, *pale lil* 2,750. 32.50
- *b.* "10" on back inverted (No. 40) 450.00 60.00
- *c.* Double "10" on back 160.00
- *d.* "0" on back 67.50

41 A1 20 l dk bl, *bluish* 750.00 5.50
- *a.* 20 l blue, *bluish* 700.00 5.50
- *b.* 20 l dark blue, *blue* 800.00 18.00

42 A1 40 l brn, *bl* 18.00 20.00
- *a.* 40 l olive brn, *bl* 18.50 20.00
- *b.* 40 l red vio, *bl* 600.00 18.00
- *c.* 40 l gray vio, *bl* 400.00 16.00
- *d.* Figures on back bis 60.00 16.00

The mesh is not apparent on Nos. 38, 38a.

1875-80

On Cream Paper Unless Otherwise Stated

43 A1 1 l gray brn 17.50 15.00
- *a.* 1 l dk gray brn 17.50 15.00
- *b.* 1 l blk brn 22.50 20.00
- *c.* 1 l red brn 22.50 20.00
- *d.* 1 l dk red brn 22.50 20.00
- *e.* 1 l pur brn 30.00 20.00

44 A1 2 l bister 19.00 17.00

45 A1 (b) 5 l dk yel grn 100.00 12.00
- *a.* 5 l pale yel grn 100.00 12.00

46 A1 10 l orange 125.00 6.00
- *a.* 10 l org, *yel* 150.00 8.00
- *c.* "00" on back 135.00 65.00
- *d.* "1" on back 150.00 67.50
- *e.* "0" on back 175.00 67.50
- *f.* "01" on back 67.50
- *g.* Double "10" on back 140.00

47 A1 20 l ultra 80.00 4.00
- *a.* 20 l blue 175.00 8.00
- *b.* 20 l dull blue 275.00 10.00
- *c.* "02" on back 135.00
- *d.* "20" on back inverted
- *e.* As "c," inverted
- *f.* Double "20" on back

48 A1 40 l salmon 18.00 30.00

The back figures are found in many varieties, including "1" and "0" inverted in "10."

1876

Without Figures on Back

Paris Print, Clear Impression

49 A1 30 l ol brn, *yelsh* 140.00 25.00
- *a.* 30 l brn, *yelsh* 200.00 47.50

50 A1 60 l grn, *grnsh* 24.00 32.50

Athens Print, Coarse Impression, Yellowish Paper

51 A1 30 l dk brn 32.50 3.00
- *a.* 30 l blk brn 35.00 3.50

52 A1 60 l green 260.00 30.00

1880-82 Cream Paper

53 A1 5 l green 6.50 2.25

54 A1 10 l orange 11.00 2.50
- *a.* 10 l yellow 11.00 2.50
- *b.* 10 l red orange 2,250. 35.00

55 A1 20 l ultra 225.00 65.00

56 A1 20 l rose (aniline ink) ('82) 3.00 1.00
- *a.* 20 l pale rose (aniline ink) ('82) 3.00 1.00
- *b.* 20 l dp car 125.00 8.00

57 A1 30 l ultra ('82) 110.00 10.00
- *a.* 30 l slate blue 110.00 10.00

58 A1 40 l lilac 40.00 5.00
- *a.* 40 l violet 40.00 5.00

Stamps of type A1 were not regularly issued with perf. 11½ but were freely used on mail.

Hermes — A2

Lepta denominations have white numeral tablets.

Belgian Print, Clear Impression

1886-88 *Imperf.*

64 A2 1 l brown ('88) 1.25 75
65 A2 2 l bister ('88) 3.00 45.00
66 A2 5 l yel grn ('88) 4.50 1.00
67 A2 10 l yellow ('88) 9.50 1.00
68 A2 20 l car rose ('88) 25.00 1.00
69 A2 25 l blue 95.00 1.00
70 A2 40 l vio ('88) 47.50 17.50
71 A2 50 l gray grn 4.00 1.00
72 A2 1d gray 50.00 1.00

See Nos. 81-116. For surcharges see Nos. 129, 134, 140, 144, 150, 151-152, 155-156.

1891 *Perf. 11½*

81 A2 1 l brown 2.75 1.40
82 A2 2 l bister 10.50 5.00
83 A2 5 l yel grn 13.00 4.50
84 A2 10 l yellow 18.00 4.50
85 A2 20 l car rose 30.00 4.50
86 A2 25 l blue 125.00 22.50
87 A2 40 l violet 95.00 30.00
88 A2 50 l gray grn 12.00 4.50
89 A2 1d gray 125.00 3.00

The Belgian Printings perf. 13½ and most of the values perf. 11½ (Nos. 82-86) were perforated on request of philatelists at the main post office in Athens. While not regularly issued they were freely used for postage.

Athens Print, Poor Impression

Wmk. Greek Words in Some Sheets

1889-95 *Imperf.*

90 A2 1 l blk brn 80 20
- *a.* 1 l brown 80 20

No.	Type	Description	Unused	Used
91	A2	2 l pale bis	1.00	65
a.		2 l buff	1.00	65
92	A2	5 l green	2.50	30
a.		Double impression		
b.		5 l deep green	3.75	30
93	A2	10 l yellow	18.00	25
a.		10 l orange	35.00	25
b.		10 l dull yellow	12.00	25
94	A2	20 l carmine	3.25	15
a.		20 l rose	3.25	15
95	A2	25 l brt bl	40.00	75
a.		25 l indigo	75.00	2.50
b.		25 l ultra	75.00	2.50
c.		25 l dull blue	40.00	2.00
96	A2	25 l red vio ('93)	2.40	25
a.		25 l lilac	2.40	25
97	A2	40 l red vio ('91)	47.50	25.00
98	A2	40 l blue ('93)	6.25	2.00
99	A2	1d gray ('95)	190.00	5.00

Perf. 13½

No.	Type	Description	Unused	Used
100	A2	1 l brown	7.50	7.50
101	A2	2 l buff	1.25	1.25
103	A2	10 l orange	35.00	5.00
104	A2	20 l carmine	10.00	3.75
a.		20 l rose	10.00	3.75
105	A2	40 l red vio	75.00	30.00

Other denominations of type A2 were not officially issued with perf. 13½.

Perf. 11½

No.	Type	Description	Unused	Used
107	A2	1 l brown	1.25	70
a.		1 l black brown	2.75	1.00
108	A2	2 l pale bister	2.00	1.00
a.		2 l buff	2.00	1.00
109	A2	5 l pale grn	3.75	50
a.		5 l dp grn	5.75	50
110	A2	10 l yellow	10.00	1.00
a.		10 l dull yellow	19.00	1.00
b.		10 l orange	40.00	1.50
111	A2	20 l carmine	4.50	50
a.		20 l rose	4.50	50
112	A2	25 l dull blue	47.50	3.50
a.		25 l indigo	80.00	5.50
b.		25 l ultra	125.00	7.50
c.		25 l bright blue	47.50	3.75
113	A2	25 l red vio	3.75	50
a.		25 l lilac	3.75	50
114	A2	40 l red vio	60.00	30.00
115	A2	40 l blue	10.00	3.50
116	A2	1d gray	225.00	10.00

Partly-perforated varieties sell for about twice as much as normal copies.

The watermark on Nos. 90-116 consists of three Greek words meaning Paper for Public Service. It is in double-lined capitals, measures 270x35mm, and extends across three panes.

Boxers A3

Discobolus by Myron A4

Vase Depicting Pallas Athene (Minerva) — A5

Chariot Driving A6

Stadium and Acropolis A7

Statue of Hermes by Praxiteles A8

Statue of Victory by Paeonius A9

Acropolis and Parthenon A10

Perf. 14x13½, 13½x14

1896 **Unwmk.**

No.	Type	Description	Unused	Used
117	A3	1 l ocher	60	30
118	A3	2 l rose	60	30
a.		Without engraver's name	10.00	6.00
119	A4	5 l lilac	90	45
120	A4	10 l slate gray	1.25	50
121	A5	20 l red brn	10.00	20
122	A6	25 l red	12.00	45
123	A5	40 l violet	8.00	2.75
124	A6	60 l black	15.00	5.50
125	A7	1d blue	40.00	6.25
126	A8	2d bister	60.00	25.00
a.		Horiz. pair, imperf. btwn.		
127	A9	5d green	200.00	135.00
128	A10	10d brown	210.00	175.00
		Nos. 117-128 (12)	558.35	351.70

1st intl. Olympic Games of the modern era, held at Athens. Counterfeits of Nos. 123-124 and 126-128 exist.

For surcharges see Nos. 159-164.

Preceding Issues Surcharged

ΛΕΠΤΑ
20

1900 ***Imperf.***

No.	Type	Description	Unused	Used
129	A2	20 l on 25 l dl bl (No. 95c)	75	50
a.		20 l on 25 l ind (No. 95a)	47.50	7.50
b.		20 l on 25 l ultra (No. 95b)	67.50	20.00
c.		Double surcharge	50.00	30.00
d.		Triple surcharge	60.00	
e.		Inverted surcharge	50.00	30.00
f.		"20" above word	50.00	30.00
g.		Pair, one without surcharge	100.00	
h.		"20" without word		
130	A1	30 l on 40 l vio, *cr* (No. 58a)	4.50	4.00
a.		30 l on 40 l lil (No. 58)	5.25	4.50
b.		Broad "0" in "30"	6.00	5.25
c.		First letter of word is "A"	50.00	45.00
d.		Double surcharge	*250.00*	
132	A1	40 l on 2 l bis, *cr* (No. 44)	5.25	4.00
a.		Broad "0" in "40"	6.00	6.00
b.		First letter of word is "A"	50.00	45.00
133	A1	50 l on 40 l sal, *cr* (No. 48)	6.00	3.75
a.		Broad "0" in "50"	5.25	5.25
b.		First letter of word is "A"	50.00	45.00
c.		"50" without word		
d.		"50" above word		
134	A2	1d on 40 l red vio (No. 97)	10.00	9.25
137	A1	3d on 10 l org, *cr* (No. 54)	50.00	25.00
a.		3d on 10 l yel (No. 54a)	50.00	25.00
138	A1	5d on 40 l red vio, *bl* (No. 21)	90.00	65.00
a.		5d on 40 l red vio, *bl* (#28)	90.00	65.00
b.		"20" on back corrected to "40"		
139	A1	5d on 40 l red vio, *bl* (No. 42b)	300.00	

Perf. 11½

No.	Type	Description	Unused	Used
140	A2	20 l on 25 l dl bl (No. 112)	2.25	1.25
a.		20 l on 25 l ind (No. 112a)	67.50	17.50
b.		20 l on 25 l ultra (No. 112b)	55.00	20.00
c.		Double surcharge	50.00	25.00
d.		Triple surcharge	60.00	40.00
e.		Inverted surcharge	50.00	25.00
f.		"20" above word	75.00	
141	A1	30 l on 40 l vio, *cr* (No. 58a)	6.50	6.00
a.		30 l on 40 l lilac (No. 58)	6.50	6.00
b.		Broad "0" in "30"	9.25	9.25
c.		First letter of word "A"	50.00	45.00
d.		Double surcharge		
142	A1	40 l on 2 l bis, *cr* (No. 44)	6.50	6.00
a.		Broad "0" in "40"	9.25	9.25
b.		First letter of word "A"	50.00	45.00
143	A1	50 l on 40 l sal, *cr* (No. 48)	8.00	6.50
a.		Broad "0" in "50"	9.25	9.25
b.		First letter of word "A"	50.00	45.00
c.		"50" without word		
144	A2	1d on 40 l red vio (No. 114)	13.00	10.50
147	A1	3d on 10 l org, *cr* (No. 54)	57.50	20.00
a.		3d on 10 l yel, *cr* (No. 54a)	57.50	20.00
148	A1	5d on 40 l red vio, *bl* (No. 21)	80.00	62.50
a.		5d on 40 l red vio, *bl* (No. 28)	80.00	62.50
149	A1	5d on 40 l red vio, *bl* (No. 42)	315.00	

Perf. 13½

No.	Type	Description	Unused	Used
150	A2	2d on 40 l red vio (No. 105)	6.50	6.50

The 1d on 40 l perf. 13½ and the 2d on 40 l, both imperf. and perf. 13½, were not officially issued.

Surcharge Including "A M"

"A M" = "Axia Metalliki" or "Value in Metal (gold)."

1900 ***Imperf.***

No.	Type	Description	Unused	Used
151	A2	25 l on 40 l vio (#70)	6.00	5.00
152	A2	50 l on 25 l bl (#69)	27.50	22.50
153	A1	1d on 40 l brn, *bl* (#42b)	125.00	115.00
154	A1	2d on 5 l grn, *cr* (#53)	15.00	11.50

Perf. 11½

No.	Type	Description	Unused	Used
155	A2	25 l on 40 l vio (#87)	10.00	10.00
156	A2	50 l on 25 l bl (#86)	47.50	40.00
157	A1	1d on 40 l brn, *bl* (#42b)	140.00	125.00
158	A1	2d on 5 l grn, *cr* (#53)	18.00	17.50

Partly-perforated varieties of Nos. 129-158 sell for about two to three times as much as normal copies.

Surcharge Including "A M" on Olympic Issue in Red

1900-01 ***Perf. 14x13½***

No.	Type	Description	Unused	Used
159	A7	5 l on 1d blue	11.00	8.00
a.		Wrong font "M" with serifs	40.00	37.50
b.		Double surcharge	250.00	225.00
160	A5	25 l on 40 l vio	65.00	40.00
161	A8	50 l on 2d bis	45.00	32.50
a.		Broad "0" in "50"	50.00	40.00
162	A9	1d on 5d grn ('01)	250.00	150.00
a.		Greek "D" instead of "A" as 3rd letter	500.00	450.00
163	A10	2d on 10d brn ('01)	45.00	45.00
a.		Greek "D" instead of "A" as 3rd letter	250.00	250.00
		Nos. 159-163 (5)	416.00	275.50

Black Surcharge on No. 160

No.	Type	Description	Unused	Used
164	A5	50 l on 25 l on 40 l vio (R + Bk)	475.00	450.00
a.		Broad "0" in "50"	450.00	525.00

Nos. 151-164 and 179-183, gold currency stamps, were generally used for parcel post and foreign money orders. They were also available for use on letters, but cost about 20 per cent more than the regular stamps of the same denomination.

Counterfeit surcharges exist of #159-164.

Giovanni da Bologna's Hermes

A11 A12

A13

FIVE LEPTA.

Type I- Letters of "ELLAS" not outlined at top and left. Only a few faint horizontal lines between the outer vertical lines at sides.

Type II- Letters of "ELLAS" fully outlined. Heavy horizontal lines between the vertical frame lines.

Perf. 11½, 12½, 13½

1901 **Engr.** **Wmk. 129**

No.	Type	Description	Unused	Used
165	A11	1 l yel brn	30	15
166	A11	2 l gray	40	15
167	A11	3 l orange	55	15
168	A12	5 l grn, type I	55	15
a.		5 l yel grn, type I	55	15
b.		5 l yel grn, type II	55	15
169	A12	10 l rose	1.65	15
170	A11	20 l red lilac	1.75	15
171	A12	25 l ultra	2.25	15
172	A11	30 l dl vio	10.00	1.75
173	A11	40 l dk brn	18.00	1.75
174	A11	50 l brn lake	16.00	1.75

Perf. 12½, 14 and Compound

No.	Type	Description	Unused	Used
175	A13	1d black	45.00	2.75
a.		Horiz. pair, imperf. btwn.	300.00	
c.		Horiz. pair, imperf. vert.	300.00	
d.		Vert. pair, imperf. horiz.	300.00	

Litho.

Perf. 12½

No.	Type	Description	Unused	Used
176	A13	2d bronze	6.00	6.00
177	A13	3d silver	6.00	6.00
a.		Horiz. pair, imperf. btwn.	450.00	
178	A13	5d gold	7.50	7.50
		Nos. 165-178 (14)	115.95	28.55

For overprints and surcharges see Nos. RA3-RA13, N16, N109.

Imperf., Pair

No.	Type	Denomination	Value
165a	A11	1 l	25.00
166a	A11	2 l	30.00
167a	A11	3 l	30.00
168c	A12	5 l	25.00
169a	A12	10 l	25.00
170a	A11	20 l	30.00
171a	A12	25 l	30.00
172a	A11	30 l	125.00
173a	A11	40 l	130.00
174a	A11	50 l	80.00
175b	A13	1d	300.00

Hermes — A14

1902, Jan. 1 **Engr.** ***Perf. 13½***

No.	Type	Description	Unused	Used
179	A14	5 l dp org	2.50	48
a.		Imperf., pair	45.00	
180	A14	25 l emerald	30.00	1.40
181	A14	50 l ultra	30.00	3.00
a.		Imperf., pair	300.00	
182	A14	1d rose red	30.00	4.75
183	A14	2d org brn	40.00	32.50
		Nos. 179-183 (5)	132.50	42.13

See note after No. 164. In 1913 remainders of Nos. 179-183 were used as postage dues.

Apollo Throwing Discus — A15

Jumper, with Jumping Weights — A16

Victory A17

Atlas and Hercules A18

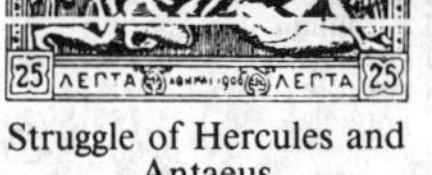

Struggle of Hercules and Antaeus A19

Wrestlers A20

Daemon of the Games A21

Foot Race A22

Nike, Priest and Athletes in Pre-Games Offering to Zeus — A23

Wmk. Crown and ET (129)

1906, Mar. Engr. *Perf. 13½, 14*

184	A15	1 l brown	1.90	48
a.		Imperf., pair	*150.00*	
185	A15	2 l gray	65	24
a.		Imperf., pair	*150.00*	
186	A16	3 l orange	65	24
a.		Imperf., pair	*180.00*	
187	A16	5 l green	1.10	20
a.		Imperf., pair	*60.00*	
188	A17	10 l rose red	2.50	20
a.		Imperf., pair	*150.00*	
189	A18	20 l magenta	5.00	20
a.		Imperf., pair	*350.00*	
190	A19	25 l ultra	6.25	40
a.		Imperf., pair	*350.00*	
191	A20	30 l dl pur	6.25	4.50
a.		Double impression	*900.00*	
192	A21	40 l dk brn	5.00	4.50
193	A18	50 l brn lake	8.25	3.25
194	A22	1d gray blk	52.50	5.25
a.		Imperf., pair	*800.00*	
195	A22	2d rose	60.00	14.00
196	A22	3d olive yel	75.00	70.00
197	A23	5d dull blue	75.00	70.00
		Nos. 184-197 (14)	300.05	173.46

Greek Special Olympic Games of 1906 at Athens, celebrating the 10th anniv. of the modern Olympic Games.

Surcharged stamps of this issue are revenues.

A24

Iris Holding Caduceus — A25

Hermes Donning Sandals — A26

Hermes Carrying Infant Arcas — A27

Hermes, from Old Cretan Coin — A28

Designs A24 to A28 are from Cretan and Arcadian coins of the 4th Century, B.C.

Serrate Roulette 13½

1911-21 Engr. Unwmk.

198	A24	1 l green	30	15
199	A25	2 l car rose	30	15
200	A24	3 l vermilion	20	15
201	A26	5 l green	1.15	15
202	A24	10 l car rose	8.00	15
203	A25	20 l gray lilac	1.75	20
204	A25	25 l ultra	14.00	20
a.		Rouletted in black	90.00	
205	A26	30 l car rose	2.25	70
206	A25	40 l deep blue	6.75	5.00
207	A26	50 l dl vio	14.00	1.50
208	A27	1d ultra	16.00	30
209	A27	2d vermilion	22.50	60
210	A27	3d car rose	25.00	1.00
a.		Size 20¼x25½mm ('21)	75.00	17.50
211	A27	5d ultra	40.00	3.50
a.		Size 20¼x25½mm ('21)	125.00	17.00
212	A27	10d dp bl ('21)	35.00	17.00
a.		Size 20x26½mm ('11)	250.00	175.00
213	A28	25d deep blue	50.00	45.00
		Nos. 198-213 (16)	237.20	75.75

The 1921 reissues of the 3d, 5d and 10d measure 20¼x25½mm instead of 20x26½mm.

See Nos. 214-231. For overprints see Nos. 233-248B, N1, N10-N15, N17-N52A, N110-N148.

Imperf., Pair

198a	A24	1 l	40.00
200a	A24	3 l	*100.00*
201a	A26	5 l	25.00
202a	A24	10 l	35.00
203a	A25	20 l	80.00
204b	A25	25 l	110.00
206a	A25	40 l	125.00
207a	A26	50 l	150.00
208a	A27	1d	175.00
209a	A27	2d	175.00
210b	A27	3d	175.00
211b	A27	5d	175.00
212b	A27	10d As "a"	*900.00*
213a	A28	25d	*450.00*

Serrate Roulette 10½x13½, 13½

1913-23 Litho.

214	A24	1 l green	15	15
a.		Without period after "Ellas"	40.00	40.00
215	A25	2 l rose	15	15
216	A24	3 l vermilion	15	15
217	A26	5 l green	15	15
218	A24	10 l carmine	15	15
219	A25	15 l dl bl ('18)	15	15
220	A25	20 l slate	15	15
221	A25	25 l ultra	2.50	15
a.		25 l blue	15	
c.		Double impression	50.00	
222	A26	30 l rose ('14)	55	15
223	A25	40 l indigo ('14)	1.00	30
224	A26	50 l vio brn ('14)	2.50	15
225	A26	80 l vio brn ('23)	2.50	60
226	A27	1d ultra ('19)	2.75	15
227	A27	2d ver ('19)	6.50	20
228	A27	3d car rose ('20)	7.25	20
229	A27	5d ultra ('22)	11.00	30
230	A27	10d dp bl ('22)	5.50	60
231	A28	25d indigo ('22)	5.50	2.50
		Nos. 214-231 (18)	48.60	6.35

Nos. 221, 223 and 226 were re-issued in 1926, printed in Vienna from new plates. There are slight differences in minor details.

The 10 lepta brown, on thick paper, type A28, is not a postage stamp. It was issued in 1922 to replace coins of this denomination during a shortage of copper.

Imperf., Pair

214b	A24	1 l	22.50
215a	A25	2 l	30.00
216a	A24	3 l	60.00
217a	A26	5 l	30.00
218a	A24	10 l	30.00
220a	A25	20 l	40.00
221b	A25	25 l	60.00
222a	A26	30 l	65.00
224a	A26	50 l	90.00
225b	A26	80 l	50.00
227a	A27	2d	75.00
228b	A27	3d	90.00
229a	A27	5d	140.00

Raising Greek Flag at Suda Bay, Crete A29

1913, Dec. 1 Engr. *Perf. 14½*

232	A29	25 l bl & blk	4.50	3.50
a.		Imperf., pair	*600.00*	

Union of Crete with Greece. Used only in Crete.

Stamps of 1911-14 Overprinted in Red or Black

Serrate Roulette 13½

1916, Nov. 1 Litho.

233	A24	1 l grn (R)	15	15
234	A25	2 l rose	20	20
235	A24	3 l vermilion	20	20
236	A26	5 l grn (R)	35	15
237	A24	10 l carmine	35	15
238	A25	20 l slate (R)	70	20
239	A25	25 l blue (R)	70	15
a.		25 l ultra	60.00	3.00
240	A26	30 l rose	70	20
a.		Pair, one without overprint		
241	A25	40 l indigo (R)	9.00	2.25
242	A26	50 l vio brn (R)	37.50	2.25

Engr.

243	A24	3 l vermilion	70	70
244	A26	30 l car rose	1.00	1.00
245	A27	1d ultra (R)	32.50	60
a.		Rouletted in blk	150.00	
246	A27	2d vermilion	25.00	3.50
247	A27	3d car rose	12.50	3.50
248	A27	5d ultra (R)	47.50	6.75
248B	A27	10d dp bl (R)	15.00	15.00
		Nos. 233-248B (17)	184.05	36.95

Most of Nos. 233-248B exist with overprint double, inverted, etc. Values 2 to 3 times those of normal examples, minimum $3. Excellent counterfeits of the overprint varieties exist.

Issued by the Venizelist Provisional Government

Iris — A32

1917, Feb. 5 Litho. *Perf. 14*

249	A32	1 l dp grn	30	18
250	A32	5 l yel grn	30	25
251	A32	10 l rose	60	25
252	A32	25 l lt bl	95	40
253	A32	50 l gray vio	7.25	1.50
254	A32	1d ultra	1.50	50
255	A32	2d lt red	3.50	1.25
256	A32	3d claret	15.00	5.00
257	A32	5d gray bl	3.00	2.00
258	A32	10d dk bl	57.50	12.00
259	A32	25d slate	80.00	80.00
		Nos. 249-259 (11)	169.90	103.33

The 4d, type A32, was used only as a revenue stamp.

Imperf., Pair

249a	A32	1 l	6.00
250a	A32	5 l	6.00
251a	A32	10 l	6.00
252a	A32	25 l	12.50
253a	A32	50 l	22.50
254a	A32	1d	25.00
255a	A32	2d	25.00
256a	A32	3d	60.00
257a	A32	5d	65.00
258a	A32	10d	125.00
259a	A32	25d	125.00

Stamps of 1917 Surcharged

ΕΠΑΝΑΣΤΑΣΙΣ
1922
ΛΕΠΤΑ 10

1923

260	A32	5 l on 10 l rose	15	15
a.		Inverted surcharge	7.00	
261	A32	50 l on 50 l gray vio	15	15
262	A32	1d on 1d ultra	15	15
a.		1d on 1d gray	25	25
263	A32	2d on 2d lt red	25	25
264	A32	3d on 3d claret	1.40	1.40
265	A32	5d on 5d dk bl	1.25	1.25
266	A32	25d on 25d slate	25.00	25.00

Same Surcharge on Occupation of Turkey Stamps, 1913

Perf. 13½

267	O2	5 l on 3 l org	15	15
a.		Inverted surcharge	10.00	
268	O1	10 l on 20 l vio	40	40
a.		Inverted surcharge	20.00	
269	O2	10 l on 25 l pale bl	25	25
270	O1	10 l on 30 l gray grn	25	25
271	O2	10 l on 40 l ind	30	30
272	O1	50 l on 50 l dk bl	25	25
a.		Inverted surcharge	20.00	
273	O1	2d on 2d gray brn	55.00	55.00
274	O2	3d on 3d dl bl	2.75	2.75
a.		Imperf., pair	325.00	
275	O1	5d on 5d gray	3.00	3.00
276	O2	10d on 1d vio brn	6.00	6.00
276A	O2	10d on 10d car	900.00	

Dangerous counterfeits of No. 276A exist.

Same Surcharge on Stamps of Crete

Perf. 14

On Crete #50, 52, 59

276B	A6	5 l on 1 l red brn	35.00	30.00
277	A8	10 l on 10 l red	20	20
277B	A8	10 l on 25 l bl	150.00	

On Crete #66-69, 71

278	A8	10 l on 25 l blue	20	20
279	A6	50 l on 50 l lilac	25	25
279A	A6	50 l on 50 l ultra	3.75	3.75
280	A9	50 l on 1d gray vio	1.75	1.75
280A	A11	50 l on 5d grn & blk	35.00	

On Crete #77-82

281	A15	10 l on 20 l bl grn	120.00	120.00
282	A16	10 l on 25 l ultra	40	40
a.		Double surcharge	20.00	
283	A17	50 l on 50 l yel brn	30	30
284	A18	50 l on 1d rose car & brn	2.50	2.50
a.		Imperf., pair		
285	A19	3d on 3d org & blk	7.50	7.50
286	A20	5d on 5d ol grn & blk	7.50	7.50

On Crete #83-84

287	A21	10 l on 25 l bl & blk	1.10	1.10
a.		Imperf., pair		
287B	A22	50 l on 1d grn & blk	3.00	3.00

On Crete #96

288	A23	10 l on 10 l brn red	20	20
a.		Inverted surcharge	12.00	

On Crete #91

288B	A17	50 l on 50 l yel brn	*1,000.*	

Dangerous counterfeits of the overprint on No. 288B are plentiful. Copies with the surcharge on top of the overprint sell for more.

On Crete #109

289	A19	3d on 3d org & blk	14.00	14.00

On Crete #111, 113-120

290	A6	5 l on 1 l vio brn	15	15
a.		Inverted surcharge	12.00	12.00
291	A13	5 l on 5 l grn	20	20
a.		Inverted surcharge	12.00	
292	A23	10 l on 10 l brn red	20	20
a.		Inverted surcharge	12.00	
293	A15	10 l on 20 l bl grn	25	25
a.		Inverted surcharge	12.00	
294	A16	10 l on 25 l ultra	30	30
a.		Inverted surcharge	12.00	12.00
295	A17	50 l on 50 l yel brn	35	35
296	A18	50 l on 1d rose car & brn	3.00	3.00
a.		Inverted surcharge		
b.		Double surcharge	70.00	
c.		Double surch., one invtd.		
d.		Imperf., pair		
297	A19	3d on 3d org & blk	12.00	12.00
298	A20	5d on 5d ol grn & blk	130.00	130.00

Dangerous counterfeits of No. 298 exist.

Crete #J2-J9

299	D1	5 l on 5 l red	15	15
a.		Inverted surcharge	5.00	5.00
300	D1	5 l on 10 l red	15	15
301	D1	10 l on 20 l red	10.00	10.00
a.		Inverted surcharge		
302	D1	10 l on 40 l red	20	20
303	D1	50 l on 50 l red	20	20
304	D1	50 l on 1d red	50	50
a.		Double surcharge		
305	D1	50 l on 1d on 1d red	6.75	6.75
306	D1	2d on 2d red	75	75

On Crete #J11-J13

307	D1	5 l on 5 l red	3.50	3.50
308	D1	5 l on 10 l red	90	90
a.		"Ellas" inverted	5.00	
309	D1	10 l on 20 l red	32.50	32.50

On Crete #J20-J22, J24-J26

310	D1	5 l on 5 l red	50	50
311	D1	5 l on 10 l red	50	50
a.		Inverted surcharge	10.00	
312	D1	10 l on 20 l red	50	50
313	D1	50 l on 50 l red	1.10	1.10
314	D1	50 l on 1d red	1.40	1.40
315	D1	2d on 2d red	6.00	6.00

These surcharged Postage Due stamps were intended for the payment of ordinary postage.

Nos. 260 to 315 were surcharged in commemoration of the revolution of 1922.

Nos. 59, 91, 109, 111, 113-120, J11-J13, J20-J22, J24-J26 are on stamps previously overprinted by Crete.

Issues of the Republic

Lord Byron — A33

Byron at Missolonghi — A34

1924, Apr. 16 Engr. *Perf. 12*

316 A33	80 l dark blue	50	25
317 A34	2d dk vio & blk	1.00	70

Death of Lord Byron (1788-1824) at Missolonghi.

Tomb of Markos Botsaris — A35

Serrate Roulette 13½

1926, Apr. 24 Litho.

318 A35	25 l lilac	45	45

Centenary of the defense of Missolonghi against the Turks.

Corinth Canal A36

Dodecanese Costume A37

Macedonian Costume A38

Monastery of Simon Peter on Mt. Athos A39

White Tower of Salonika A40

Temple of Hephaestus A41

The Acropolis — A42

Cruiser "Georgios Averoff" — A43

Academy of Sciences, Athens — A44

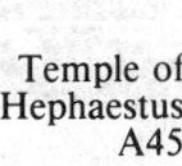

Temple of Hephaestus A45

Acropolis A46

Perf. 12½x13, 13, 13x12½, 13½, 13½x13

1927, Apr. 1 Engr.

321 A36	5 l dk grn	15	15
a.	Vert. pair, imperf. horiz.	50.00	
322 A37	10 l org red	15	15
a.	Horiz. pair, imperf. between	67.50	
c.	Double impression	20.00	
323 A38	20 l violet	15	15
324 A39	25 l slate bl	15	15
a.	Imperf., pair	67.50	67.50
b.	Vert. pair, imperf. between	67.50	
325 A40	40 l slate bl	60	15
326 A36	50 l violet	1.90	15
327 A36	80 l dk bl & blk	95	15
a.	Imperf., pair	115.00	
328 A41	1d dk bl & bis brn (I)	1.90	15
a.	Imperf., pair	175.00	
b.	Center inverted		*5,000.*
c.	Double impression of center		*1,200.*
d.	Double impression of frame	125.00	
329 A42	2d dk grn & blk	2.75	18
a.	Imperf., pair	150.00	
330 A43	3d dp vio & blk	3.75	18
a.	Double impression of center		200.00
b.	Center inverted		*3,500.*
331 A44	5d yel & blk	6.25	55
a.	Imperf., pair	375.00	
b.	Center inverted		*1,350.*
c.	5d yellow & green	100.00	35.00
332 A45	10d brn car & blk	19.00	1.10
333 A44	15d brt yel grn & blk	19.00	6.75
334 A46	25d grn & blk	40.00	6.75
a.	Double impression		100.00
	Nos. 321-334 (14)	96.70	16.71

See Nos. 364-371 and notes preceding No. 364. For overprints see Nos. RA55, RA57, RA60, RA66, RA70-RA71.

This series as prepared, included a 1 lepton dark brown, type A37, but that value was never issued. Most copies were burned. Value $250.

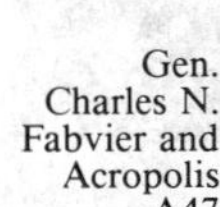

Gen. Charles N. Fabvier and Acropolis A47

1927, Aug. 1 *Perf. 12*

335 A47	1d red	95	20
336 A47	3d dark blue	2.25	60
337 A47	6d green	6.75	6.75

Cent. of the liberation of Athens from the Turks in 1826.

For surcharges see Nos. 376-377.

Bay of Navarino and Pylos — A48

Battle of Navarino A49

"Edward" omitted A50

"Edward" added A51

Admiral de Rigny — A52

Admiral van der Heyden — A53

Designs: Nos. 340-341, Sir Edward Codrington.

Perf. 13½x12½, 12½x13½, 13x12½, 12½x13

1927-28 Litho.

338 A48	1.50d gray grn	1.25	15
a.	Imperf., pair	225.00	
b.	Horiz. pair, imperf. btwn.	225.00	
c.	Horiz. pair, imperf. vert.	225.00	
339 A49	4d dk gray bl ('28)	4.50	35
340 A50	5d dk brn & gray	4.50	2.00
a.	5d blk brn & blk ('28)	10.50	6.00
341 A51	5d dk brn & blk ('28)	18.00	6.50
342 A52	5d vio bl & blk ('28)	13.00	3.00
343 A53	5d lake & blk ('28)	7.25	3.00
	Nos. 338-343 (6)	48.50	15.00

Centenary of the naval battle of Navarino.

For surcharges see Nos. 372-375.

Independence Centenary Issue

Admiral Lascarina Bouboulina A54

Athanasios Diakos A55

Map of Greece in 1830 and 1930 A56

Sortie from Missolonghi A58

Patriots Declaring Independence — A57

Portraits: 10 l, Constantine Rhigas Ferreos. 20 l, Gregorios V. 40 l, Prince Alexandros Ypsilantis. No. 345, Bouboulina. No. 355, Diakos. No. 346, Theodoros Kolokotronis. No. 356, Konstantinos Kanaris. No.347, Georgios Karaiskakis. No. 357, Markos Botsaris. 2d, Andreas Miaoulis. 3d, Lazaros Koundouriotis. 5d, Count John Capo d'Istria (Capodistria), statesman and doctor. 10d, Petros Mavromichalis. 15d, Dionysios Solomos. 20d, Adamantios Korais.

Various Frames

1930, Apr. 1 Engr. *Perf. 13½, 14*

Imprint of Perkins, Bacon & Co.

344 A55	10 l brown	15	15
345 A54	50 l red	15	15
346 A54	1d car rose	24	15
347 A55	1.50d lt bl	20	15
348 A55	2d orange	30	16
349 A55	5d purple	1.25	1.25
350 A54	10d gray blk	7.00	3.75
351 A54	15d yel grn	7.00	5.50
352 A55	20d bl blk	9.00	7.25

Imprint of Bradbury, Wilkinson & Co.

Perf. 12

353 A55	20 l black	15	15
354 A55	40 l bl grn	15	15
355 A55	50 l brt bl	20	15
356 A55	1d brn org	30	15
357 A55	1.50d dk red	24	15
358 A55	3d dk brn	85	18
359 A56	4d dk bl	1.90	65
360 A57	25d black	9.00	7.00
361 A58	50d red brn	27.50	*35.00*
	Nos. 344-361 (18)	65.58	*62.09*

Centenary of Greek independence. Some exist imperf.

Arcadi Monastery and Abbot Gabriel (Mt. Ida in Background) A60

1930, Nov. 8 *Perf. 12*

363 A60	8d dp vio	8.00	50

Issue of 1927 Re-engraved

50 l, Design is clearer, especially "50" and the 10 letters.

Type I 1927

Type II 1931

1d. Type I- Greek letters "L," "A," "D" have sharp pointed tops; numerals "1" are 1½mm wide at the foot, and have a straight slanting serif at top.

1d. Type II- Greek letters "L," "A," "D" have flat tops; numerals "1" are 2mm wide at foot and the serif at top is slightly curved. Perf. 14.

There are many minor differences in the lines of the two designs.

1d. Type III- The "1" in lower left corner has no serif at left of foot. Lines of temple have been deepened, so details stand out more clearly.

2d. On 1927 stamp the Parthenon is indistinct and blurred. On 1933 stamp it is strongly outlined and clear. Between the two pillars at lower right are four blocks of marble. These blocks are clear and distinct on the 1933 stamp but run together on the 1927 issue.

3d. Design is clearer, especially vertical lines of shading in smoke stacks and reflections in the water. Two or more sides perf. 11½.

10d. Background and shading of entire stamp have been lightened. Detail of frame is clearer and more distinct.

15d. Many more lines of shading in sky and foreground. Engraving is sharp and clear, particularly in frame. Two or more sides perf. 11½.

25d. Background has been lightened and foreground reduced until base of larger upright column is removed and fallen column appears nearly submerged.

Sizes in millimeters:

50 l, 1927, 18x24¾. 1933, 18½x24½.

1d, 1927, 24¾x17¾. 1931, 24¾x17¼. 1933, 24½x18¼.

2d, 1927, 24½x17¾. 1933, 24½x18½.

Perf. 11½, 11½x12½, 12½x10, 13, 13x12½, 14

1931-35

364 A36	50 l dk vio ('33)	3.00	50
365 A41	1d dk bl & org brn, type II	6.00	35
366 A41	1d dk bl & org brn, type III ('33)	4.25	22
367 A42	2d dk grn & blk ('33)	2.00	22
368 A43	3d red vio & blk ('34)	2.50	22
a.	Imperf., pair		
369 A45	10d brn car & blk ('35)	30.00	95
370 A44	15d pale yel grn & blk ('34)	57.50	9.00
a.	Imperf., pair		
371 A46	25d dk grn & blk ('35)	9.25	6.00
	Nos. 364-371 (8)	114.50	17.46

Stamps of 1927-28 and 1927 Surcharged in Red

ΔP.1.50

1932	Perf. 12½x13½, 12½x13		
372 A52	1.50d on 5d dk bl & blk	1.75	20
373 A53	1.50d on 5d lake & blk	1.65	20
a.	Double surcharge	60.00	
374 A50	2d on 5d blk brn & blk	2.00	20
375 A51	2d on 5d blk brn & blk	6.25	20
	Perf. 12		
376 A47	2d on 3d dk bl	2.50	20
a.	Double surcharge	60.00	
377 A47	4d on 6d grn	3.75	1.00
	Nos. 372-377 (6)	17.90	2.00

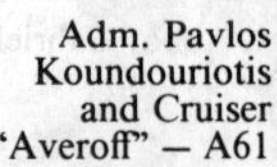

Adm. Pavlos Koundouriotis and Cruiser "Averoff" — A61

Pallas Athene A62

Youth of Marathon A63

1933	Perf. 13½x13, 13x13½		
378 A61	50d blk & ind	27.50	3.00
379 A62	75d blk & vio brn	82.50	*120.00*
a.	Imperf., pair	450.00	
380 A63	100d brn & dl grn	275.00	26.00

For surcharges see Nos. 386-387.

Approach to Athens Stadium A64

Perf. 11½, 11½x10, 13½x11½

1934, Dec. 10			
381 A64	8d blue	37.50	50

Perforations on No. 381 range from 10½ to 13, including compounds.

Church of Pantanassa, Mistra — A65

1935, Nov. 1	Perf. 13x12½		
382 A65	4d brown	10.00	40
a.	Horizontal pair, imperf. between	350.00	
b.	Imperf., pair	600.00	

Issues of the Monarchy

Postage Due Stamp and Type of 1913 Surcharged in Red or Blue

Serrate Roulette 13½

1935, Nov. 24		Litho.	
383 D3	50 l on 40 l ind (R)	20	15
a.	Double surcharge		25.00
384 D3	3d on 3d ver (Bl)	50	35

Surcharged on No. 182

Perf. 13

385 D3	3d on 3d rose red (Bl)	2.50	75

Nos. 380, 379 Surcharged in Red or Blue

386 A63	5d on 100d brn & dl grn (R)	1.50	1.00
387 A62	15d on 75d blk & vio brn (Bl)	5.25	4.25

King Constantine A66

Center Engr., Frame Litho.

Perf. 12x13½

1936, Nov. 18		Wmk. 252	
389 A66	3d blk & brn	50	30
a.	Pair with printer's name in Greek	40.00	
b.	Pair with printer's name in English	40.00	
390 A66	8d blk & bl	1.00	1.25
a.	Pair with printer's name in Greek	40.00	
b.	Pair with printer's name in English	40.00	

Re-burial of the remains of King Constantine and Queen Sophia.

Two printings exist, the first containing varieties "a" and "b" with gray border; second with black border.

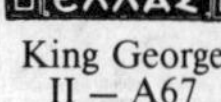
King George II — A67

Pallas Athene — A68

1937, Jan. 24	Engr.	Perf. 12½x12	
391 A67	1d green	15	15
392 A67	3d red brn	18	15
393 A67	8d dp bl	55	35
394 A67	100d car lake	7.25	7.25

For surcharges see Nos. 484-487, 498-500, RA86-RA87, N241-N242.

1937, Apr. 17	Unwmk.	Perf. 11½	
395 A68	3d yel brn	45	35

Centenary of the University of Athens.

Contest with Bull — A69

Lady of Tiryns — A70

Zeus of Dodona A71

Coin of Amphictyonic League A72

Diagoras of Rhodes, Victor at Olympics — A73

Venus of Melos — A74

Battle of Salamis — A75

Chariot of Panathenaic Festival — A76

Alexander the Great at Battle of Issos — A77

St. Paul Preaching to Athenians A78

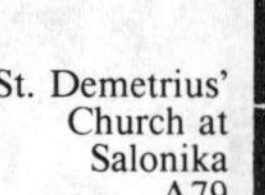

St. Demetrius' Church at Salonika A79

Leo III Victory over Arabs — A80

Allegorical Figure of Glory — A81

Perf. 13½x12, 12x13½

1937, Nov. 1	Litho.	Wmk. 252	
396 A69	5 l brn red & bl	15	15
a.	Double impression of frame	60.00	
397 A70	10 l bl & brn red	15	15
a.	Double impression of frame	20.00	
398 A71	20 l blk & grn	15	15
399 A72	40 l grn & blk	15	15
a.	Green impression doubled	20.00	
400 A73	50 l brn & blk	15	15
401 A74	80 l ind & yel brn	15	15
	Engr.		
402 A75	2d ultra	15	15
403 A76	5d red	15	15
a.	Printer's name omitted	8.00	8.00
404 A77	6d ol brn	55	40
405 A78	7d dk brn	1.10	45
406 A79	10d red brn	15	15
407 A80	15d green	15	20
408 A81	25d dk bl	15	20
	Set value	2.50	1.90

See Nos. 413, 459-466. For overprints and surcharges see Nos. 455-458, 476-477, RA75-RA78, RA83-RA85, N202-N217, N246-N247.

Cerigo, Paxos, Lefkas

Greek stamps with Italian overprints for the islands of Cerigo (Kithyra), Paxos and Lefkas (Santa Maura) are fraudulent.

Royal Wedding Issue

Princess Frederika-Louise and Crown Prince Paul — A82

1938	Wmk. 252	Perf. 13½x12	
409 A82	1d green	15	15
410 A82	3d org brn	38	32
411 A82	8d dark blue	1.00	1.00

Arms of Greece, Romania, Yugoslavia and Turkey A83

Statue of King Constantine A84

Perf. 12x12½

1938, Feb. 8	Litho.	Unwmk.	
412 A83	6d blue	4.00	1.40

Balkan Entente.

Tiryns Lady Type of 1937 Corrected Inscription

1938	Wmk. 252	Perf. 12x13½	
413 A70	10 l blue & brn red	65	65

The first four letters of the third word of the inscription read "TIPY" instead of "TYPI".

Perf. 12x13½

1938, Oct. 8	Engr.	Unwmk.	
414 A84	1.50d green	55	55
415 A84	30d org brn	3.00	3.00

For overprint see No. N218.

Coats of Arms of Ionian Islands — A85

Fort at Corfu — A86

King George I of Greece and Queen Victoria of England A87

Perf. 12½x12, 13½x12

1939, May 21 Engr. Unwmk.

416 A85 1d dk bl 85 20
417 A86 4d green 1.65 85
418 A87 20d yel org 12.50 13.00
419 A87 20d dl bl 12.50 13.00
420 A87 20d car lake 12.50 13.00
Nos. 416-420 (5) 40.00 40.05

75th anniv. of the union of the Ionian Islands with Greece.

Runner with Shield — A88

10th Pan-Balkan Games: 3d, Javelin thrower. 6d, Discus thrower. 8d, Jumper.

Perf. 12x13½

1939, Oct. 1 Litho. Unwmk.

421 A88 50 l slate grn & grn 20 20
422 A88 3d hn brn & dl rose 80 80
423 A88 6d cop brn & dl org 2.00 2.25
424 A88 8d ultra & gray 2.00 2.25

Arms of Greece, Romania, Turkey and Yugoslavia — A92

Perf. 13x12½

1940, May 27 Wmk. 252

425 A92 6d blue 3.00 1.00
426 A92 8d blue gray 3.00 1.00

Balkan Entente.

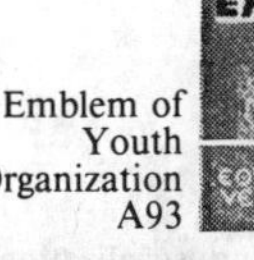

Emblem of Youth Organization A93

Boy Member — A94

Designs: 3d, 100d, Emblem of Greek Youth Organization. 10d, Girl member. 15d, Javelin Thrower. 20d, Column of members. 25d, Flag bearers and buglers. 30d, Three youths. 50d, Line formation. 75d, Coat of arms.

Perf. 12½, 13½x12½

1940, Aug. 3 Litho. Wmk. 252

427 A93 3d sil, dp ultra & red 2.25 2.25
428 A94 5d dk bl & blk 6.25 6.00
429 A94 10d red org & blk 7.75 6.50
430 A94 15d dk grn & blk 45.00 45.00
431 A94 20d lake & blk 20.00 17.00
432 A94 25d dk bl & blk 24.00 20.00
433 A94 30d rose vio & blk 26.00 26.00
434 A94 50d lake & blk 26.00 26.00
435 A94 75d dk bl, brn & gold 26.00 27.50
436 A93 100d sil, dp ultra & red 37.50 35.00
Nos. 427-436,C38-C47 (20) 399.75 380.00

4th anniv. of the founding of the Greek Youth Organization. The stamps were good for postal duty Aug. 3-5, 1940, only. They remained on sale until Feb. 3, 1941.

For overprints see Nos. N219-N238.

Windmills on Mykonos A103

Bourtzi Fort — A104

Aspropotamos River — A105

Candia Harbor, Crete — A106

Houses at Hydra — A107

Meteora Monasteries A108

Edessa — A109

Pantokratoros Monastery and Port — A110

Bridge at Konitsa A111

Ekatontapiliani Church, Paros — A112

Ponticonissi, Corfu (Mouse Island) — A113

Perf. 12½, 13½x12½

1942-44 Litho. Wmk. 252

437 A103 2d red brn 15 15
438 A104 5d lt bl grn 15 15
a. "NAYO . . ." 10.00 10.00
439 A105 10d lt bl 15 15
440 A106 15d red vio 15 15
441 A107 25d org red 15 15
442 A108 50d saph 15 15
443 A109 75d dp rose 15 15
444 A110 100d black 15 15
445 A110 200d ultra 15 15
a. Imprint omitted 3.00 3.00
446 A111 500d dk olive 15 15
447 A112 1000d org brn 15 15
448 A113 2000d dp bl 15 15
449 A111 5000d rose red 15 15
450 A112 15,000d rose lil 15 15
451 A113 25,000d green 15 15
452 A105 500,000d blue 20 20
453 A103 2,000,000d turq grn 20 20
454 A104 5,000,000d rose brn 20 20
Set value 1.85 1.85

Double impressions exist of 10d, 25d, 50d, 100d, 200d, 1,000d and 2,000d. Value, each $30.

Issue dates: Nos. 439-442, Sept. 1. 200d, Dec. 1. Nos. 446-448, Mar. 15, 1944. Nos. 449-451, July 1, 1944. Nos. 452-454, Sept. 15, 1944.

For surcharges and overprint see Nos. 472C, 473B-475, 478-481, 501-505, B1-B5, B11-B15, RA72-RA74, N239-N240, N243-N245, N248.

Imperf., Pair

439a A105 10d 70.00
440a A106 15d 70.00
441a A107 25d 70.00
442a A108 50d 50.00
446a A111 500d 70.00
447a A112 1000d 70.00
448a A113 2000d 70.00
449a A111 5000d 70.00
450a A112 15.000d 70.00
451a A113 25.000d 70.00
452a A105 500.000d 90.00
454a A104 5.000.000d 90.00

Nos. 400, 402-404 Surcharged in Blue Black

ΔΡΑΧΜΑΙ ΝΕΑΙ

1944-45 ***Perf. 13½x12***

455 A73 50 l brn & blk 15 15
a. Double surcharge 12.00 12.00
456 A75 2d ultra 15 15
457 A76 5d red 15 15
a. Inverted surcharge 20.00
b. Double surcharge 20.00
c. Printer's name omitted (403a) 10.00 10.00
d. Pair, one without surcharge 15.00
458 A77 6d olive brn ('45) 25 25
Set value 45 45

Glory Type of 1937

Perf. 12½x13½

1945 Litho. Wmk. 252

459 A81 1d dl rose vio 15 15
460 A81 3d rose brn 15 15
a. Imperf., pair 50.00
461 A81 5d ultra 15 15
a. Imperf., pair 50.00
462 A81 10d dl brn 15 15
463 A81 20d dl vio 15 15
464 A81 50d olive blk 15 15
465 A81 100d pale blue 2.50 3.25
a. Imperf., pair 175.00
466 A81 200d slate 2.00 1.25
Nos. 459-466 (8) 5.40 5.40

Doric Column and Greek Flag A114

Franklin D. Roosevelt A115

1945, Oct. 28 Unwmk.

467 A114 20d org brn 15 15
468 A114 40d blue 18 18
a. Double impression 20.00

Vote of Oct. 28, 1940, refusing Italy's ultimatum. "OXI" means "No."

Exist imperf.

1945, Dec. 21 Unwmk.

469 A115 30d blk & red brn 15 15
a. Center double 65.00 65.00
c. Inverted frame 65.00
d. Imperf., pair 70.00
470 A115 60d blk & sl gray 15 15
a. Center double 60.00 60.00
b. 60d black & blue gray 10.00 10.00
c. Imperf., pair 100.00
d. Inverted frame 60.00
471 A115 200d blk & vio brn 15 15
a. Center double 70.00 70.00
b. Imperf., pair 125.00
Set value 33 33

Death of Pres. Franklin D. Roosevelt.

Nos. C61, C63, 447-451, 453, 398, 401, 454 and 452 Surcharged in Black or Carmine

ΔΡΧ. 10

Perf. 12½, 12x13½, 13½x12½

1946 Wmk. 252

472 AP35 10d on 10d rose red 15 15
a. Inverted surcharge 30.00 30.00
b. Double surcharge 20.00
472C A113 10d on 2000d dp bl (C) 15 15
473 AP35 20d on 50d vio bl (C) 15 15
a. Inverted surcharge 30.00
473B A112 20d on 1000d org brn 20 15
474 A113 50d on 25,000d grn (C) 20 15
475 A103 100d on 2,000,000d turq grn (C) 25 15
476 A71 130d on 20 l blk & grn (C) 40 15
b. Double surcharge 25.00
476A A71 250d on 20 l blk & grn (C) 1.00 15
c. Double surcharge 25.00
477 A74 300d on 80 l ind & yel brn 45 35
a. Purple brown surcharge 10.00 7.00
b. Double surcharge 30.00
478 A104 500d on 5,000,000d rose brn 1.75 25
a. Inverted surcharge 35.00
b. Double surcharge 30.00
479 A105 1000d on 500,000d bl (C) 5.25 22
a. Double surcharge 40.00
480 A111 2000d on 5000d rose red 14.00 2.50
481 A112 5000d on 15,000d rose lil 35.00 22.50
a. Blue surcharge 45.00 45.00
Nos. 472-481 (13) 58.95 27.02

The surcharge exists in various shades on most denominations. A 150d on 20 l is fraudulent.

Eleutherios K. Venizelos A116

Panaghiotis Tsaldaris A117

Perf. 12x13½

1946, Mar. 25 Litho. Wmk. 252

482 A116 130d brn ol & buff 15 15
a. Double impression of brn olive 15.00
483 A116 300d red brn & pale brn 25 25
a. Double impression of red brown 15.00

Venizelos (1864-1936), statesman.

Nos. 391 to 394 Surcharged in Blue Black

1-9-1946

1946, Sept. 28 ***Perf. 12½x12***

484 A67 50d on 1d grn 15 15
485 A67 250d on 3d red brn 20 15
a. Date omitted 25.00
b. Inverted surcharge 40.00 40.00
486 A67 600d on 8d dp bl 75 75
a. Additional surcharge on back, inverted 30.00
b. Carmine surcharge 100.00
487 A67 3000d on 100d car lake 3.75 85

Plebiscite of Sept. 1, 1946, which resulted in the return of King George II to Greece.

Perf. 12½x13½

1946, Nov. 15 Litho. Unwmk.

488 A117 250d red brn & buff 55 15
489 A117 600d dp bl & pale bl 1.25 1.10
a. Double impression 55.00

Naval Convoy — A118

Torpedoing of Cruiser Helle — A119

Women Carrying Ammunition in Pindus Mountains A120

Troops in Albania — A121

Campaign of Greek Troops in Italy — A122

Allegory of Flight — A123

Greek Torpedo Boat Towing Captive Submarine A124

Design: 5000d, Memorial Tomb, El Alamein.

1946-47 Unwmk. Engr. *Perf. 13*

490 A118	50d dk bl grn	15	15
491 A119	100d dp ultra	15	15
492 A120	250d yel grn ('46)	15	15
493 A121	500d yel brn	48	15
494 A122	600d dk brn	1.10	22
495 A123	1000d dl lil	1.25	22
496 A124	2000d dp ultra	3.75	3.00
497 A119	5000d dk car	7.75	48
a.	Imperf., pair	400.00	
	Nos. 490-497 (8)	14.78	4.52

1947 stamps issued May 1.

King George II Memorial Issue

Nos. 391 to 393 Surcharged in Black

Perf. 12½x12

1947, Apr. 15 Wmk. 252

498 A67	50d on 1d grn	15	15
a.	Double surcharge	20.00	
499 A67	250d on 3d red brn	28	15
a.	Double surcharge	25.00	
b.	Pair, one without surcharge	12.50	
500 A67	600d on 8d dp bl	80	50
a.	Double surcharge	20.00	
	Set value		62

Nos. 446, 438, 442, 439 and 443 Surcharged in Carmine or Black

1947 *Perf. 12½*

501 A111	20d on 500d dk ol	15	15
a.	Double surcharge	25.00	
502 A104	30d on 5d lt bl grn	15	15
503 A108	50d on 50d saph	15	15
504 A105	100d on 10d lt bl	20	15
505 A109	450d on 75d dp rose (Bk)	80	1.00
	Set value	1.25	1.10

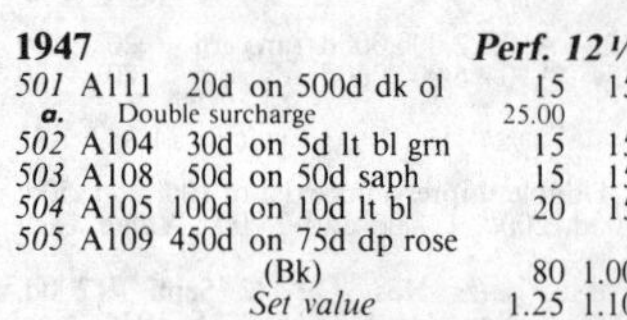

Castellorizo Castle — A126

Dodecanese Vase A127

Dodecanese Costume A128

Monastery where St. John Preached, Patmos A129

Emanuel Xanthos A130

Sailing Vessel of 1824 A131

Revolutionary Stamp of 1912 — A132

Statue of Hippocrates A133

Colossus of Rhodes A134

Perf. 12½x13½, 13½x12½

1947-48 Litho. Wmk. 252

506 A126	20d ultra	15	15
507 A127	30d blk brn & buff	15	15
508 A128	50d chlky bl	15	15
509 A129	100d blk grn & pale grn	15	15
510 A130	250d gray grn & pale grn	18	15
511 A132	450d dp bl ('48)	75	15
512 A131	450d dp bl & pale bl ('48)	75	15
a.	Imperf., pair	150.00	
513 A132	500d red	30	15
514 A133	600d vio brn & pale pink	55	15
515 A134	1000d brn & cream	85	15
a.	Imperf., pair	150.00	
	Nos. 506-515 (10)	3.98	
	Set value		68

Return of the Dodecanese to Greece. See Nos. 520-522, 525-534.

Battle of Crete — A135

1948, Sept. 15 Engr. *Perf. 13x13½*

516 A135	1000d dark green	1.00	25

Battle of Crete, 7th anniversary.

Abduction of Children A136

Concentration Camp — A137

Protective Mother — A138

Perf. 13½x12½, 12½x13½

1949, Feb. 1 Litho. Wmk. 252

517 A136	450d dk & lt vio	75	50
518 A137	1000d dk & lt brn	1.75	25
519 A138	1800d dk red & cr	2.00	25

Types of 1947

1950, Apr. 5 *Perf. 12½x13½*

520 A127	2000d org brn & sal	8.75	15
a.	Imperf., pair	85.00	
521 A133	5000d rose vio	21.00	45
522 A134	10,000d ultra	8.75	30

Map of Crete and Flags A139

Perf. 13½x13

1950, Apr. 28 Engr. Wmk. 252

523 A139	1000d deep blue	1.50	25
a.	Imperf., pair	*425.00*	

Battle of Crete, 9th anniversary.

Youth of Marathon — A140

Engraved and Lithographed

1950, May 21 *Perf. 13x13½*

524 A140	1000d cr & dp grn	50	20
a.	Without dates	90.00	
b.	"1949" only	80.00	
c.	Dates inverted	80.00	
d.	Dates doubled	80.00	

75th anniv. (in 1949) of the UPU. Exists imperf., used only.

Types of 1947-48

Perf. 12½x13½, 13½x12½

1950 Litho. Wmk. 252

525 A130	200d orange	30	15
526 A128	300d orange	30	15
527 A129	400d blue	1.65	15
528 A133	700d lil rose	1.65	15
529 A133	700d bl grn	1.65	15
a.	Imperf., pair	110.00	
530 A131	800d pur & pale grn	75	15
531 A132	1300d carmine	5.00	15
532 A126	1500d brn org	7.50	15
533 A127	1600d ultra & bl gray	1.65	15
534 A134	2600d emer & pale grn	3.50	42
	Nos. 525-534 (10)	23.95	
	Set value		1.35

Altar and Sword — A141

St. Paul — A142

St. Paul by El Greco A143

Preaching to Athenians A144

Perf. 13½x12, 12x13½

1951, June 15 Engr. Unwmk.

535 A141	700d red vio	1.40	35
536 A142	1600d lt bl	3.00	3.00
537 A143	2600d dk ol bis	5.25	4.50
538 A144	10,000d red brn	40.00	30.00

1900th anniv. of St. Paul's visit to Athens.

Industrialization A145

Designs: 800d, Fishing. 1300d, Rebuilding. 1600d, Farming. 2600d, Home Industries. 5000d, Electrification and map of Greece.

Perf. 12½x13½

1951, Sept. 20 Wmk. 252

539 A145	700d red org	2.25	15
540 A145	800d aqua	3.75	50
541 A145	1300d grnsh bl	6.75	32
542 A145	1600d ol grn	11.50	32
543 A145	2600d vio gray	35.00	50
544 A145	5000d dp plum	32.50	70
	Nos. 539-544 (6)	91.75	2.49

Issued to publicize Greek recovery under the Marshall Plan.

King Paul I — A146

Allegorical Figure and Medal — A147

1952, Dec. 14 Engr. *Perf. 12½x12*

No.	Type	Value	Color	Unused	Used
545	A146	200d	dp grn	40	15
546	A146	1000d	red	95	15
547	A147	1400d	blue	4.75	1.00
548	A146	10,000d	dk red lil	20.00	8.75

50th birthday of King Paul I.

Oranges A148

Tobacco — A149

National Products: 1000d, Olive oil, Pallas Athene. 1300d, Wine. 2000d, Figs. 2600d, Grapes and bread. 5000d, Bacchus holding grapes.

1953, July 1 *Perf. 13½x13, 13x13½*

No.	Type	Value	Color	Unused	Used
549	A148	500d	dp car & org	40	16
550	A149	700d	dk brn & org yel	70	16
551	A148	1000d	bl & lt ol grn	85	16
a.			Imperf., pair	100.00	
552	A149	1300d	dp plum & org brn	4.00	16
553	A149	2000d	dk brn & lt grn	6.25	20
554	A149	2600d	vio & ol bis	8.25	1.00
555	A149	5000d	dk brn & yel grn	9.25	35
			Nos. 549-555 (7)	29.70	2.19

Pericles A150

Homer A151

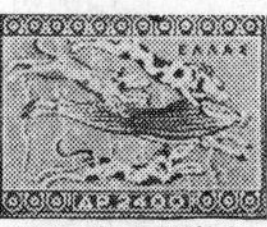

Hunting Wild Boar — A152

Shepherd Carrying Calf — A152a

Designs: 200d, Mycenaean oxhead vase. 500d, Zeus of Istiaea. 600d, Head of a youth. 1000d, Alexander the Great. 1200d, Charioteer of Delphi. 2000d, Vase of Dipylon. 4000d, Voyage of Dionysus. 20,000d, Pitcher bearers.

Perf. 13½x13, 12½x12, 13x13½

1954, Jan. 15 Litho.

No.	Type	Value	Color	Unused	Used
556	A150	100d	red brn	18	15
557	A150	200d	black	30	15
558	A151	300d	bl vio	80	15
559	A151	500d	green	80	15
560	A151	600d	rose pink	1.00	15
561	A151	1000d	dl bl & blk	1.00	15
562	A150	1200d	ol grn	1.00	15
563	A150	2000d	red brn	2.50	15
564	A152	2400d	grnsh bl	4.00	20
a.			Double impression	125.00	
565	A152a	2500d	dk bl grn	4.00	15
566	A151	4000d	dk car	4.00	24
567	A150	20,000d	rose lil	42.50	1.50
			Nos. 556-567 (12)	62.08	
			Set value		2.70

See Nos. 574-581, 632-638, and 689.

British Parliamentary Debate and Ink Blot — A153

1954, Sept. *Perf. 12½*

Center in Black

No.	Type	Value	Color	Unused	Used
568	A153	1.20d	cream	1.75	15
569	A153	2d	orange	4.50	4.00
570	A153	2d	lt bl	4.50	3.50
571	A153	2.40d	lilac	4.50	60
572	A153	2.50d	pink	4.50	60
573	A153	4d	citron	5.75	1.25
			Nos. 568-573 (6)	25.50	10.10

Document in English on Nos. 569, 572, 573; in French on Nos. 570, 571 and in Greek on No. 568.

Issued to promote the proposed union between Cyprus and Greece.

Types of 1954

Perf. 13½x13, 12½x12, 13x13½

1955 Litho. Wmk. 252

Designs: 20 l, Mycenaean oxhead vase. 30 l, Pericles. 50 l, Zeus of Istiaea. 1d, Head of a youth. 2d, Alexander the Great. 3d, Hunting wild boar. 3.50d, Homer. 4d, Voyage of Dionysus.

No.	Type	Value	Color	Unused	Used
574	A150	20 l	dk grn	55	15
575	A150	30 l	yel brn	75	15
576	A151	50 l	car lake	1.50	15
577	A151	1d	bl grn	1.90	15
578	A151	2d	brn & blk	4.75	15
579	A152	3d	red org	5.75	15
580	A151	3.50d	rose crim	9.25	24
581	A151	4d	vio bl	13.00	24
			Nos. 574-581 (8)	37.45	
			Set value		1.15

Samos Coin Picturing Pythagoras A154

Pythagorean Theorem A155

Samos Mapped in Antique Style — A156

1955, Aug. 20 *Perf. 12x13½*

No.	Type	Value	Color	Unused	Used
582	A154	2d	green	2.25	30
583	A155	3.50d	int blk	6.25	2.75
584	A154	5d	plum	13.00	1.10
585	A156	6d	blue	6.25	*15.00*

2500th anniv. of the founding of the 1st School of Philosophy by Pythagoras on Samos.

Globe and Rotary Emblem — A157

Perf. 12x13½

1956, May 15 Litho. Wmk. 252

No.	Type	Value	Color	Unused	Used
586	A157	2d	ultra	2.25	35

50th anniv. of Rotary Intl. (in 1955).

King Alexander A158

Crown Prince Constantine — A159

Portraits: 30 l, George I. 50 l, Queen Olga. 70 l, King Otto. 1d, Queen Amalia. 1.50d, King Constantine. 2d, 7.50d, King Paul. 3d, George II. 3.50d, Queen Sophia. 4d, Queen Frederica. 5d, King Paul and Queen Frederica. 10d, King, Queen and Crown Prince.

Perf. 13½x12, 12x13½

1956, May 21 Engr.

No.	Type	Value	Color	Unused	Used
587	A158	10 l	bl vio	16	15
588	A159	20 l	dl pur	16	15
589	A159	30 l	sepia	16	15
590	A159	50 l	red brn	16	15
591	A159	70 l	lt ultra	40	15
592	A159	1d	grnsh bl	40	15
593	A159	1.50d	gray bl	48	15
594	A159	2d	black	48	15
595	A159	3d	brown	80	15
596	A159	3.50d	cop brn	1.90	15
597	A159	4d	gray grn	1.90	15
598	A158	5d	rose car	1.90	15
599	A159	7.50d	ultra	4.00	1.25
600	A158	10d	dk bl	5.75	70
			Nos. 587-600 (14)	18.65	
			Set value		2.85

See Nos. 604-617.

Catalogue values for unused stamps in this section, from this point to the end of the section, are for Never Hinged items.

Dionysios Solomos and Nicolaos Mantzaros A160

Dionysios Solomos A161

Design: 5d, View on Zante and bust of Solomos.

Perf. 13½x12, 12x13½

1957, Mar. 26 Litho. Wmk. 252

No.	Type	Value	Color	Unused	Used
601	A160	2d	red brn & ocher	4.00	18
602	A161	3.50d	bl & gray	7.75	3.25
603	A160	5d	dk grn & ol bis	8.00	4.75

Centenary of the death of Dionysios Solomos, composer of the Greek national anthem.

Types of 1956

Designs as before.

Perf. 13½x12

1957 Wmk. 252 Engr.

No.	Type	Value	Color	Unused	Used
604	A158	10 l	rose lake	40	15
605	A159	20 l	orange	40	15
606	A159	30 l	gray blk	40	15
607	A159	50 l	grnsh blk	40	15
608	A159	70 l	rose lil	1.00	60
609	A159	1d	rose red	85	15
610	A159	1.50d	lt ol grn	1.40	15
611	A159	2d	carmine	1.40	15
612	A159	3d	dk bl	2.00	15
613	A159	3.50d	blk vio	5.25	20
a.			Imperf., pair		
614	A159	4d	red brn	5.25	18
615	A158	5d	gray bl	5.25	15

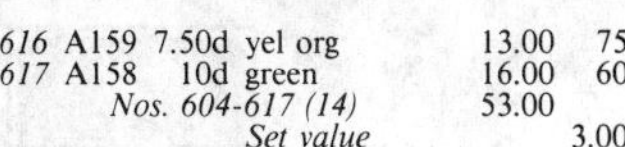

No.	Type	Value	Color	Unused	Used
616	A159	7.50d	yel org	13.00	75
617	A158	10d	green	16.00	60
			Nos. 604-617 (14)	53.00	
			Set value		3.00

Oil Tanker A162

Ships: 1d, Ocean liner. 1.50d, Sailing ship, 1820. 2d, Byzantine vessel. 3.50d, Ship from 6th century B. C. 5d, "Argo."

1958, Jan. 30 Litho. *Perf. 13½x12*

No.	Type	Value	Color	Unused	Used
618	A162	50 l	multi	15	15
619	A162	1d	ultra, blk & bis	22	18
620	A162	1.50d	blk & car	25	20
a.			Double impression of blk	100.00	
621	A162	2d	vio bl, blk & red brn	35	30
622	A162	3.50d	lt bl, blk & red	1.10	1.00
a.			Double impression of blk	150.00	120.00
623	A162	5d	bl grn, blk & car	7.25	6.00
			Nos. 618-623 (6)	9.32	7.83

Issued to honor the Greek merchant marine.

Narcissus — A163

Designs: 30 l, Daphne (laurel) and Apollo. 50 l, Adonis (hibiscus) and Aphrodite. 70 l, Pitys (pine) and Pan. 1d, Crocus. 2d, Iris. 3.50d, Tulips. 5d, Cyclamen.

1958, Sept. 15 Wmk. 252 *Perf. 13*

Size: 22½x38mm

No.	Type	Value	Color	Unused	Used
624	A163	20 l	multi	15	15
625	A163	30 l	multi	15	15
626	A163	50 l	multi	15	15
627	A163	70 l	multi	20	15

Perf. 12½x12

Size: 21½x26mm

No.	Type	Value	Color	Unused	Used
628	A163	1d	multi	35	24

Perf. 12x13½

Size: 22x32mm

No.	Type	Value	Color	Unused	Used
629	A163	2d	multi	25	16
630	A163	3.50d	multi	1.25	90
a.			Imperf., pair	250.00	
631	A163	5d	multi	1.75	1.25
			Nos. 624-631 (8)	4.25	3.15

International Congress for the Protection of Nature, held in Athens.

Types of 1954

Designs: 10 l, Pericles. 20 l, Mycenaean oxhead vase. 50 l, Zeus of Istiaea. 70 l, Charioteer of Delphi. 1d, Head of a youth. 1.50d, Pitcher bearers. 2.50d, Alexander the Great.

Two types of 2.50d:

I- 9 dots in upper half of right border.

II- 10 dots.

Perf. 13½x13, 12½x12

1959 Litho. Wmk. 252

No.	Type	Value	Color	Unused	Used
632	A150	10 l	emerald	18	18
633	A150	20 l	magenta	42	15
634	A151	50 l	lt bl grn	1.50	15
635	A150	70 l	red org	42	15
636	A151	1d	redsh brn	4.00	15
637	A150	1.50d	brt bl	7.00	15
638	A151	2.50d	mag & blk (II)	12.00	15
a.			Type I	55.00	52
			Nos. 632-638 (7)	25.52	1.08

Zeus-Eagle Coin A164

Helios-Rose Coin — A165

Ancient Greek Coins: 20 l, Athena & Owl. 50 l, Nymph Arethusa & Chariot. 70 l, Hercules & Zeus. 1.50d, Griffin & Square. 2.50d, Apollo & Lyre. 4.50d, Apollo & Labyrinth. 6d, Aphrodite & Apollo. 8.50d, Ram's Head & Incuse Squares.

1959, Mar. 24 Wmk. 252 *Perf. 14*

Coins in Various Shades of Gray

No.	Type	Value	Color	Unused	Used
639	A164	10 l	red brn & blk	50	15
640	A164	20 l	dp bl & blk	50	15
641	A164	50 l	plum & blk	1.25	15
642	A164	70 l	ultra & blk	1.25	15
643	A165	1d	dk car rose & blk	2.50	15
644	A164	1.50d	ocher & blk	2.50	15
645	A164	2.50d	dp mag & blk	3.00	15
646	A165	4.50d	Prus grn & blk	4.50	22
647	A165	6d	ol grn & blk	5.00	22
648	A165	8.50d	dp car & blk	4.50	1.00
			Nos. 639-648 (10)	25.50	
			Set value		1.95

See Nos. 750-758.

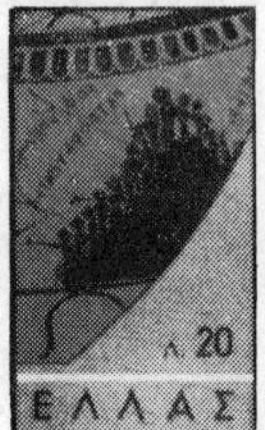

Audience, Vase 580 B. C. — A166

Theater, Delphi A167

Designs: 50 l, Clay tragedy mask, 3rd cent. B.C. 1d, Flute, drum and lyre. 2.50d, Clay statue of an actor, 3rd cent. B.C. 4.50d, Andromeda, vase, 4th cent. B.C. 6d, Actors, bowl 410 B.C.

Perf. 13x13½, 13½x13

1959, June 20 Litho. Wmk. 252

No.	Type	Value	Color	Unused	Used
649	A166	20 l	blk, fawn & gray	15	15
650	A166	50 l	dk red brn & ol bis	20	15
651	A166	1d	grn, brn & ocher	20	15
652	A166	2.50d	brn & bl	35	28
653	A167	3.50d	red brn, grn & sep	8.75	6.50
654	A167	4.50d	blk & fawn	1.25	90
655	A166	6d	blk, fawn & gray	1.25	90
			Nos. 649-655 (7)	12.15	9.03

Ancient Greek theater.

"Victory" and Soldiers — A168

Perf. 13x13½

1959, Aug. 29 Wmk. 252

No.	Type	Value	Color	Unused	Used
656	A168	2.50d	red brn, ultra & blk	2.50	25

10th anniversary of civil war.

Aesculapius — A169

The Good Samaritan A170

Designs: 20 l, Plane tree of Hippocrates. 70 l, St. Basil. 2.50d, Achilles and Patroclus. 3d, Globe and Red Cross over people receiving help. 4.50d, Henri Dunant.

Perf. 13½x12, 12x13½

1959, Sept. 21 Litho.

No.	Type	Value	Color	Unused	Used
657	A170	20 l	multi	15	15
658	A169	50 l	multi	15	15
659	A169	70 l	multi	15	15
660	A169	2.50d	multi	15	15
661	A169	3d	multi	8.00	6.50
662	A169	4.50d	multi	42	35
663	A170	6d	multi	52	45
			Nos. 657-663 (7)	9.54	7.90

Cent. of the Red Cross idea. Sizes: Nos. 658-660, 662 24½x32mm, No. 661 32x47mm.

Imre Nagy A171

Costis Palamas A172

Perf. 13x13½

1959, Dec. 8 Wmk. 252

No.	Type	Value	Color	Unused	Used
664	A171	4.50d	org brn & dk brn	1.00	1.00
665	A171	6d	brt bl, bl & blk	1.00	1.00

3rd anniv. of the crushing of the 1956 Hungarian Revolution, and to honor Premier Imre Nagy, its leader.

1960, Jan. 25 *Perf. 12x13½*

No.	Type	Value	Color	Unused	Used
666	A172	2.50d	multi	2.75	20

Issued to commemorate the centenary of the birth of Costis Palamas (1859-1943), poet.

Ship Battling Storm A173

Design: 4.50d, Ship in calm sea and rainbow.

Perf. 13½x13

1960, Apr. 7 Wmk. 252

No.	Type	Value	Color	Unused	Used
667	A173	2.50d	multi	35	15
668	A173	4.50d	multi	1.00	85

Issued to publicize World Refugee Year, July 1, 1959-June 30, 1960.

Boy Scout on Horseback, St. George and Dragon — A174

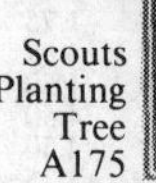

Scouts Planting Tree A175

Designs: 30 l, Scout taking oath and boy of ancient Athens. 40 l, Scouts helping in disaster. 70 l, Scouts reading map and tent. 1d, Boy Scout, Sea Scout and Air Scout. 2.50d, Crown Prince Constantine. 6d, Scout flag of Greece and Military Merit medal.

Perf. 13x13½, 13½x13

1960, Apr. 23 Litho.

No.	Type	Value	Color	Unused	Used
669	A174	20 l	multi	15	15
670	A174	30 l	multi	15	15
671	A174	40 l	multi	15	15
672	A175	50 l	multi	18	15
673	A175	70 l	multi	18	15
674	A175	1d	multi	18	15
675	A174	2.50d	multi	40	15
676	A175	6d	multi	2.00	1.10
			Nos. 669-676 (8)	3.39	
			Set value		1.65

Issued to commemorate the 50th anniversary of the Greek Boy Scout Organization.

Greek Holding Sacred Disk Proclaiming Armistice During Games — A176

Lighting Olympic Flame A177

Designs: 70 l, Youth taking oath. 80 l, Boy cutting olive branches for Olympic prizes. 1d, Judges entering stadium. 1.50d, Long jump. 2.50d, Discus thrower. 4.50d, Sprinters. 5d, Javelin thrower. 6d, Crowning the victors. 12.50d, Victor in chariot entering home town.

Perf. 13x13½, 13½x13

1960, Aug. 12 Wmk. 252

No.	Type	Value	Color	Unused	Used
677	A176	20 l	multi	15	15
678	A177	50 l	multi	22	15
679	A176	70 l	multi	22	15
680	A177	80 l	multi	22	15
a.			Imperf., pair	225.00	
681	A177	1d	multi	22	15
682	A177	1.50d	multi	22	15
683	A176	2.50d	multi	50	15
684	A177	4.50d	multi	1.00	52
a.			Dbl. impression of black	160.00	160.00
685	A176	5d	multi	55	42
686	A177	6d	multi	65	52
687	A177	12.50d	multi	7.75	5.00
			Nos. 677-687 (11)	11.70	7.51

Issued to commemorate the 17th Olympic Games, Rome, Aug. 25-Sept. 11.

Europa Issue, 1960

Common Design Type

Perf. 13½x12

1960, Sept. 19 Litho. Wmk. 252

Size: 33x23mm

No.	Type	Value	Color	Unused	Used
688	CD3	4.50d	ultra	3.50	1.65
a.			Double impression	100.00	

Common Design Types pictured in section at front of book.

Shepherd Type of 1954

1960, Sept. 1 Wmk. 252 *Perf. 13*

No.	Type	Value	Color	Unused	Used
689	A152a	3d	ultra	2.50	20

Crown Prince Constantine and Yacht — A178

1961, Jan. 18 *Perf. 13½x13*

No.	Type	Value	Color	Unused	Used
690	A178	2.50d	multi	1.50	20

Victory of Crown Prince Constantine and his crew at the 17th Olympic Games, Rome (Gold medal, Yachting, Dragon class).

Castoria A179

Delphi — A180

Landscapes and Ancient Monuments: 20 l, Meteora. 50 l, Hydra harbor. 70 l, Acropolis, Athens. 80 l, Mykonos. 1d, St. Catherine's Church, Salonika. 1.50d, Olympia. 2.50d, Knossos. 3.50d, Rhodes. 4d, Epidauros amphitheater. 4.50d, Temple of Poseidon, Sounion. 5d, Temple of Zeus, Athens. 7.50d, Aslan's mosque, Ioannina. 8d, Mount Athos. 8.50d, Santorini. 12.50d, Marble lions, Delos.

Perf. 13½x12½, 12½x13½

1961, Feb. 15 Engr. Wmk. 252

No.	Type	Value	Color	Unused	Used
691	A179	10 l	dk gray bl	20	15
692	A179	20 l	dk pur	20	15
693	A179	50 l	blue	20	15
694	A179	70 l	dk pur	48	15
695	A179	80 l	brt ultra	28	15
696	A179	1d	red brn	52	15
697	A179	1.50d	brt grn	80	15
698	A179	2.50d	carmine	5.25	15
699	A179	3.50d	purple	1.10	15
700	A179	4d	sl grn	1.10	15
701	A179	4.50d	dk bl	1.10	15
702	A179	5d	claret	2.25	15
703	A180	6d	slate grn	2.75	15
704	A179	7.50d	black	2.75	24
705	A180	8d	dk vio bl	2.75	45
706	A180	8.50d	org ver	2.75	45
707	A179	12.50d	dk brn	3.25	60
			Nos. 691-707 (17)	27.73	
			Set value		2.50

Issued for tourist publicity.

Lily Vase — A181

Partridge and Fig Pecker A182

Minoan Art: 1d, Fruit dish. 1.50d, Rhyton bearer. 2.50d, Ladies of Knossos Palace. 4.50d, Sarcophagus of Hagia Trias. 6d, Dancer. 10d, Two vessels with spouts.

Perf. 13x13½, 13½x13

1961, June 30 **Litho.**

708 A181 20 l multi 42 35
709 A182 50 l multi 55 35
710 A182 1d multi 85 22
711 A181 1.50d multi 1.25 28
712 A182 2.50d multi 1.50 15
713 A181 4.50d multi 3.50 2.75
714 A182 6d multi 3.75 2.25
715 A182 10d multi 12.00 4.00
Nos. 708-715 (8) 23.82 10.35

Democritus Nuclear Research Center A183

Democritus A184

1961, July 31 ***Perf. 13½x13***

716 A183 2.50d dp lil rose & rose lil 60 15
717 A184 4.50d vio bl & pale vio bl 1.10 95

Inauguration of the Democritus Nuclear Research Center at Aghia Paraskevi.

Europa Issue, 1961
Common Design Type

1961, Sept. 18 ***Perf. 13½x12***
Size: 32½x22mm

718 CD4 2.50d ver & pink 15 15
a. Pink omitted (inscriptions white) 10.00 10.00
719 CD4 4.50d ultra & lt ultra 20 20

Nicephoros Phocas A185

Hermes Head of 1861 A186

1961, Sept. 22 **Wmk. 252**

720 A185 2.50d multi 85 32

1000th anniv. of the liberation of Crete from the Saracens by the Byzantine general (later emperor) Phocas.

1961, Dec. 20 **Litho.** ***Perf. 13x13½***

Each denomination shows a different stamp of 1861 issue.

721 A186 20 l brn, red brn & cream 15 15
722 A186 50 l brn, bis & straw 15 15
723 A186 1.50d emer & gray 15 15
724 A186 2.50d red org & ol bis 18 15
725 A186 4.50d dk bl, bl & gray 22 15
726 A186 6d rose lil, pale rose & bl 25 16
727 A186 10d car, rose & cr 1.75 1.10
Nos. 721-727 (7) 2.85
Set value 1.75

Centenary of Greek postage stamps.

Tauropos Dam and Lake — A187

Ptolemais Power Station A188

Designs: 50 l, Ladhon river hydroelectric plant. 1.50d, Louros river dam. 2.50d, Aliverion power plant. 4.50d, Salonika hydroelectric sub-station. 6d, Agra river hydroelectric station, interior.

Perf. 13x13½, 13½x13

1962, Apr. 14 **Wmk. 252**

728 A187 20 l multi 15 15
729 A187 50 l multi 15 15
730 A188 1d multi 40 15
731 A188 1.50d multi 40 15
732 A188 2.50d multi 48 15
733 A188 4.50d multi 1.90 1.25
734 A188 6d multi 2.50 1.75
Nos. 728-734 (7) 5.98 3.75

National electrification project.

Youth with Shield and Helmet from Ancient Vase — A189

Designs: 2.50d, Zappion hall (horiz.). 4.50d, Kneeling soldier from Temple of Aphaea, Aegina. 6d, Standing soldier from stele of Ariston.

Perf. 13½x12, 12x13½

1962, May 3 **Litho.** **Wmk. 252**
Sizes: 22x33mm, 33x22mm

735 A189 2.50d grn, bl, red & brn 38 15
736 A189 3d brn, buff & red brn 48 20
737 A189 4.50d bl & gray 60 35

Size: 21x37mm

738 A189 6d brn red & blk 60 35

Ministerial congress of NATO countries, Athens, May 3-5.

Europa Issue, 1962
Common Design Type

1962, Sept. 17 ***Perf. 13½x12***
Size: 33x23mm

739 CD5 2.50d ver & blk 55 25
740 CD5 4.50d ultra & blk 1.10 52

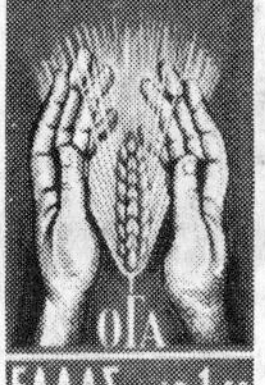

Hands and Grain A190

Demeter A191

1962, Oct. 30 ***Perf. 13x13½***

741 A190 1.50d dp car, blk & brn 38 15
742 A190 2.50d brt grn, blk & brn 95 25

Agricultural Insurance Program.

Perf. 12x13½

1963, Apr. 25 **Wmk. 252**

Design: 4.50d, Wheat and globe.

743 A191 2.50d brn car, gray & blk 35 15
744 A191 4.50d multi 1.00 65

FAO "Freedom from Hunger" campaign.

George I, Constantine XII, Alexander I, George II and Paul I — A192

Perf. 13½x12½

1963, June 29 **Engr.**

745 A192 50 l rose car 22 15
746 A192 1.50d green 55 15
747 A192 2.50d redsh brn 70 15
748 A192 4.50d dk bl 3.25 90
749 A192 6d violet 2.75 45
Nos. 745-749 (5) 7.47
Set value 1.55

Centenary of the Greek dynasty.

Coin Types of 1959

Ancient Greek Coins: 50 l, Nymph Arethusa & Chariot. 80 l, Hercules & Zeus. 1d, Helios & Rose. 1.50d, Griffin & Square. 3d, Zeus & Eagle. 3.50d, Athena & Owl. 4.50d, Apollo & Labyrinth. 6d, Aphrodite & Apollo. 8.50d, Ram's head & Incuse Squares.

Perf. 13½x13, 13x13½

1963, July 5 **Litho.** **Wmk. 252**
Coins in Various Shades of Gray

750 A164 50 l vio bl 15 15
751 A164 80 l dp mag 24 15
752 A165 1d emerald 48 15
753 A164 1.50d lil rose 48 15
754 A164 3d olive 60 15
755 A164 3.50d vermilion 75 15
756 A165 4.50d redsh brn 1.10 15
757 A165 6d bl grn 1.10 15
758 A165 8.50d brt bl 1.50 50
Nos. 750-758 (9) 6.40
Set value 1.15

"Acropolis at Dawn" by Lord Baden-Powell — A193

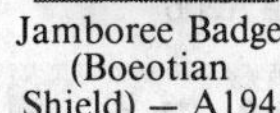

Jamboree Badge (Boeotian Shield) — A194

Athenian Treasury, Delphi — A195

Designs: 2.50d, Crown Prince Constantine, Chief Scout. 3d, Athanassios Lefkadites (founder of Greek Scouts) and Lord Baden-Powell. 4.50d, Scout bugling with conch shell.

1963, Aug. 1

759 A193 1d bl, sal & ol 15 15
760 A194 1.50d dk bl, org brn & brn 15 15
761 A194 2.50d multi 15 15
762 A193 3d multi 32 15
763 A194 4.50d multi 1.50 80
Nos. 759-763 (5) 2.27
Set value 1.15

11th Boy Scout Jamboree, Marathon, July 29-Aug. 16, 1963.

1963, Sept. 16 ***Perf. 12x13½***

Designs: 2d, Centenary emblem. 2.50d, Queen Olga, founder of Greek Red Cross. 4.50d, Henri Dunant.

764 A195 1d multi 15 15
765 A195 2d multi 15 15
766 A195 2.50d multi 20 15
767 A195 4.50d multi 1.25 70
Set value 96

International Red Cross Centenary.

Europa Issue, 1963
Common Design Type

1963, Sept. 16 ***Perf. 13½x12***
Size: 33x23mm

768 CD6 2.50d green 1.50 50
769 CD6 4.50d brt mag 3.00 1.50

Vatopethion Monastery A196

King Paul I (1901-1964) A197

Designs: 80 l, St. Denys' Monastery. 1d, "Protaton" (Founder's) Church (horiz.). 2d, Stavronikita Monastery. 2.50d, Jeweled cover of Nicephoros Phocas Gospel. 3.50d, Fresco of St. Athanassios, founder of community. 4.50d, Presentation of Christ, 11th century manuscript. 6d, Great Lavra Church (horiz.).

Perf. 13x13½, 13½x13

1963, Dec. 5 **Litho.** **Wmk. 252**

770 A196 30 l multi 15 15
771 A196 80 l multi 22 15
772 A196 1d multi 50 15
773 A196 2d multi 65 15
774 A196 2.50d multi 65 15
775 A196 3.50d multi 1.00 40
776 A196 4.50d multi 1.10 40
777 A196 6d multi 1.50 52
Nos. 770-777 (8) 5.77 2.07

Millennium of the founding of the monastic community on Mt. Athos.

1964, May 6 ***Perf. 12x13½***

778 A197 30 l brown 15 15
779 A197 50 l purple 18 15
780 A197 1d green 18 15
781 A197 1.50d orange 30 15
782 A197 2d blue 35 15
783 A197 2.50d chocolate 60 15
784 A197 3.50d red brn 1.10 18
785 A197 4d ultra 1.10 18
786 A197 4.50d bluish blk 1.40 25
787 A197 6d rose pink 2.25 38
Nos. 778-787 (10) 7.61
Set value 1.50

Archangel Michael — A198

Designs: 1d, Bulgaroctonus coin of Emperor Basil II. 1.50d, Two armed saints from ivory triptych by Harbaville, Louvre. 2.50d, Lady, fresco by Panselinos, Protaton Church, Mt. Athos. 4.50d, Angel, mosaic, Daphni Church, Athens.

1964, June 10 ***Perf. 12x13½***

788 A198 1d multi 15 15
789 A198 1.50d multi 15 15
790 A198 2d multi 18 15
791 A198 2.50d multi 28 15
792 A198 4.50d multi 1.50 1.00
Nos. 788-792 (5) 2.26
Set value 1.20

Issued to commemorate Byzantine Art and in connection with the Byzantine Art Exhibition, Athens, April-June, 1964.

Exist imperf.

Birth of Aphrodite, Emblem of Kythera A199

Designs (emblems of islands): 20 l, Trident, Paxos. 1d, Head of Ulysses, Ithaca. 2d, St. George slaying dragon, Lefkas. 2.50d, Zakyntnos, Zante. 4.50d, Cephalus, dog and spear, Cephalonia. 6d, Trireme, Corfu.

Perf. 13½x12

1964, July 20 Litho. Wmk. 252

793 A199 20 l multi 15 15
794 A199 30 l multi 15 15
795 A199 1d multi 15 15
796 A199 2d multi 16 15
797 A199 2.50d sl grn & dl grn 20 15
798 A199 4.50d multi 75 55
799 A199 6d multi 90 38
Nos. 793-799 (7) 2.46
Set value 1.30

Centenary of the union of the Ionian Islands with Greece.

Child and Sun — A200

1964, Sept. 10 Wmk. 252

800 A200 2.50d multi 85 25

50th anniv. of the Natl. Institute of Social Welfare for the Protection of Children and Mothers (P.I.K.P.A.).

Europa Issue, 1964

Common Design Type

1964, Sept. 14 Litho. *Perf. 13x13½*

Size: 23x39mm

801 CD7 2.50d lt grn & dk red 75 18
802 CD7 4.50d gray & brn 1.10 80

King Constantine II and Queen Anne-Marie A201

Peleus and Atalante Fighting, 6th Cent. B.C. Vase A202

1964, Sept. 18 Engr. *Perf. 13½x14*

803 A201 1.50d green 15 15
804 A201 2.50d rose car 15 15
805 A201 4.50d brt ultra 65 40
Set value 55

Wedding of King Constantine II and Princess Anne-Marie of Denmark, Sept. 18, 1964.

Perf. 12x13½, 13½x12

1964, Oct. 24 Litho. Wmk. 252

Designs: 1d, Runners on amphora (horiz.). 2d, Athlete on vase (horiz.). 2.50d, Discus thrower and judge, pitcher. 4.50d, Charioteer, sculpture (horiz.). 6d, Boxers, vase (horiz.). 10d, Apollo, frieze from Zeus Temple at Olympia.

806 A202 10 l multi 15 15
807 A202 1d multi 15 15
808 A202 2d multi 15 15
809 A202 2.50d multi 15 15
810 A202 4.50d multi 32 18
811 A202 6d multi 32 15
812 A202 10d multi 90 55
Nos. 806-812 (7) 2.14
Set value 1.15

18th Olympic Games, Tokyo, Oct. 10-25.

Detail from "Christ Stripped of His Garments" by El Greco A203

Aesculapius Theatre, Epidauros A204

Paintings by El Greco: 1d, Concert of the Angels. 1.50d, El Greco's painted signature (horiz.). 2.50d, Self-portrait. 4.50d, Storm-lashed Toledo.

Perf. 12x13½, 13½x12

1965, Mar. 6 Litho. Wmk. 252

813 A203 50 l sep & multi 15 15
814 A203 1d gray & multi 15 15
a. Double impression of black
815 A203 1.50d multi 15 15
816 A203 2.50d sl & multi 15 15
817 A203 4.50d multi 40 32
Set value 82 68

350th anniv. of the death of Domenico Theotocopoulos, El Greco (1541-1614).

1965, Apr. 30 Litho. *Perf. 12x13½*

Design: 4.50d, Herod Atticus Theatre, and Acropolis, Athens.

818 A204 1.50d multi 32 15
819 A204 4.50d multi 40 25

Epidauros and Athens theatrical festivals.

ITU Emblem, Old and New Telecommunication Equipment — A205

1965, Apr. 30 *Perf. 13½x12*

820 A205 2.50d multi 30 15

Cent. of the ITU.

Swearing-in Ceremony A206

Flag of Philiki Hetaeria, the Friends' Society A207

Perf. 13½x12

1965, May 31 Litho. Wmk. 252

821 A206 1.50d multi 20 15
822 A207 4.50d gray & multi 25 22

Issued to commemorate the 150th anniversary of the Friends' Society, a secret organization for the liberation of Greece from Turkey.

Emblem of A.H.E.P.A. A208

1965, June 30

823 A208 6d lt bl, blk & ol 55 25

Congress of the American Hellenic Educational Progressive Association, Athens.

Eleutherios Venizelos, Therissos, 1905 — A209

Designs: 2d, Venizelos signing Treaty of Sevres, 1920. 2.50d, Venizelos portrait.

1965, June 30 Engr. *Perf. 12½x13*

824 A209 1.50d green 16 15
825 A209 2d dk bl 40 25
826 A209 2.50d brown 48 20

Issued to commemorate the centenary of the birth of Eleutherios Venizelos (1864-1963), statesman and prime minister.

Symbols of Planets A210

Astronaut in Space A211

Design: 6d, Two space ships over globe.

Perf. 12½x13½

1965, Sept. 11 Litho. Wmk. 252

827 A210 50 l multi 15 15
828 A211 2.50d multi 15 15
829 A211 6d multi 25 22
Set value 46 46

Issued to commemorate the 16th Astronautical Congress, Athens, Sept. 12-18.

Victory Medal — A212

Stadium, Phaleron A213

Design: 1d, Games' emblem and "JBA."

Perf. 13½x13, 13x13½

1965, Sept. 11

830 A213 1d multi 15 15
831 A212 2d multi 15 15
832 A213 6d multi 25 22
Set value 46 40

24th Balkan Games, Sept. 1-10.

Europa Issue, 1965

Common Design Type

1965, Oct. 21 *Perf. 13½x12*

Size: 33x23mm

833 CD8 2.50d bl gray, blk & dk bl 28 15
834 CD8 4.50d ol, blk & grn 55 40

Hipparchus and Astrolabe A214

1965, Oct. 21 Litho. Wmk. 252

835 A214 2.50d bl grn, blk & dk red 22 15

Issued to commemorate the opening of the Evghenides Planetarium, Athens.

St. Andrew's Church, Patras A215

St. Andrew A216

1965, Nov. 30 *Perf. 12x13½*

836 A215 1d multi 15 15
837 A216 5d multi 18 15
Set value 27 15

Return of the head of St. Andrew from St. Peter's, Rome to St. Andrew's, Patras. The design of the 5d is from an 11th cent. mosaic at St. Luke's Monastery, Boeotia.

Ants and Anthill — A217

Savings Bank and Book — A218

1965, Nov. 30 Litho. Wmk. 252

838 A217 10 l grn, blk & bis 15 15
839 A218 2.50d multi 38 15
Set value 25

50th anniv. of the Post Office Savings Bank.

Theodore Brysakes A219

Jean Gabriel Eynard A220

Banknote of 1867 — A221

Painters: 1d, Nikeforus Lytras. 2.50d, Constantin Volonakes. 4d, Nicolas Gyses. 5d, George Jacobides.

Perf. 13x13½

1966, Feb. 28 Litho. Wmk. 252

840 A219 80 l multi 15 15
841 A219 1d multi 15 15
842 A219 2.50d multi 15 15

843 A219 4d multi 15 15
844 A219 5d multi 18 15
Set value 63 50

Issued to honor Greek painters.

Perf. 12x13½

1966, Mar. 30 Engr. Wmk. 252

Designs: 2.50d, Georgios Stavros. 4d, Bank's first headquarters, etching by Yannis Kefallinos.

845 A220 1.50d gray grn 15 15
846 A220 2.50d brown 15 15
847 A221 4d ultra 15 15
848 A221 6d black 28 18
Set value 56 36

National Bank of Greece, 125th anniv.

Symbolic Water Cycle A222

UNESCO Emblem A223

WHO Headquarters, Geneva A224

Perf. 12x13½, 13½x12

1966, Apr. 18 Litho.

849 A222 1d multi 15 15
850 A223 3d multi 15 15
851 A224 5d multi 28 22
Set value 48 40

Hydrological Decade (UNESCO), 1965-74, (1d); 20th anniv. of UNESCO (3d); inauguration of the WHO Headquarters, Geneva (5d).

Geannares Michael (Hatzes) A225

Explosion at Arkadi Monastery A226

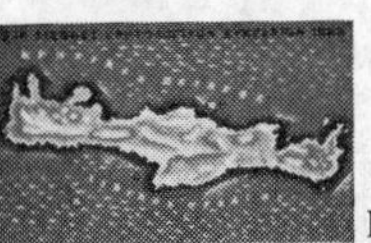

Map of Crete — A227

1966, Apr. 18

852 A225 2d multi 15 15
853 A226 2.50d multi 15 15
854 A227 4.50d multi 28 22
Set value 48 40

Cent. of the Cretan revolt against the Turks. Geannares Michael (Hatzes), the leader of the revolt, was a member of Cretan government and a writer.

Copper Mask, 4th Century, B.C. — A228

Dionysus on a Thespian Ship-Chariot — A229

Designs: 2.50d, Old Theater of Dionysus, Athens, 6th Century B.C. 4.50d, Dancing Dionysus, from vase by Kleophrades, c. 500 B.C.

Perf. 12x13½, 13½x12

1966, May 26 Litho. Wmk. 252

855 A228 1d multi 15 15
856 A229 1.50d multi 15 15
857 A229 2.50d multi 15 15
858 A228 4.50d multi 25 22
Set value 52 50

2500th anniversary of Greek theater.

Boeing 707-320 over New York Buildings and Greek Column A230

1966, May 26 *Perf. 13x12½*

859 A230 6d bl & dk bl 38 18

Issued to commemorate the inauguration of transatlantic flights of Olympic Airways.

Tobacco Worker — A231

Design: 5d, Woman sorting tobacco leaves.

Perf. 12½x13½

1966, Sept. 19 Litho. Wmk. 252

860 A231 1d multi 22 15
861 A231 5d multi 42 15
Set value 23

Issued to publicize the Greek tobacco industry, in connection with the 4th International Scientific Tobacco Congress, Athens, Sept. 19-26.

Europa Issue, 1966

Common Design Type

1966, Sept. 19 Litho. Wmk. 252

Size: 23x33mm

862 CD9 1.50d olive 25 15
863 CD9 4.50d lt red brn 52 38

Carved Cases for Knitting Needles — A232

Bridegroom, Embroidery from Epirus A233

Designs (Popular Art): 50 l, Lyre, Crete. 1d, Massa (stringed instrument). 1.50d, Basrelief (cross and angels). 2d, Icon (Sts. Constantine and Helena). 2.50d, Virgin (wood carving, Church of St. Nicholas, Galaxeidon). 3d, Embroidery (sailing ship from Skyros). 4d, Embroidery (wedding parade). 4.50d, Carved wooden distaff (Sts. George and Barbara). 5d, Silver and agate necklace and earrings. 20d, Handwoven cloth, Cyprus.

Perf. 12x13½, 13½x12

1966, Nov. 21 Litho. Wmk. 252

864 A232 10 l multi 15 15
865 A233 30 l multi 15 15
866 A232 50 l multi 15 15
867 A232 1d multi 15 15
868 A232 1.50d multi 15 15
869 A232 2d multi 1.10 15
870 A232 2.50d multi 18 15
871 A233 3d multi 20 15
872 A233 4d multi 22 15
873 A232 4.50d multi 30 18
874 A232 5d multi 30 15
875 A233 20d multi 4.00 50
Nos. 864-875 (12) 7.05
Set value 1.40

King Constantine II, Queen Anne-Marie and Princess Alexia — A234

Designs: 2d, Princess Alexia. 3.50d, Queen Anne-Marie and Princess Alexia.

Perf. 13½x14

1966, Dec. 19 Engr. Wmk. 252

876 A234 2d green 15 15
877 A234 2.50d brown 15 15
878 A234 3.50d ultra 30 20
Set value 35

Issued to honor Princess Alexia, successor to the throne of Greece.

"Night" by John Cossos (1830-73) — A235

Sculptures: 50 l, Penelope by Leonides Drosses (1836-1882). 80 l, Shepherd by George Fytales. 2d, Woman's torso by Constantine Demetriades (1881-1943). 2.50d, "Colocotrones" (equestrian statue) by Lazarus Sochos (1862-1911). 3d, Sleeping Young Lady by John Halepas (1851-1938) (horiz.). 10d, Woodcutter by George Filippotes (1839-1919; horiz.).

Perf. 12x13½, 13½x12

1967, Feb. 28 Litho. Wmk. 252

879 A235 20 l Prus bl, gray & blk 15 15
880 A235 50 l brn, gray & blk 15 15
881 A235 80 l brn red, gray & blk 18 15
882 A235 2d vio bl, gray & blk 15 15
883 A235 2.50d ultra, blk & grn 18 15
884 A235 3d bl, lt bl, gray & blk 18 15
885 A235 10d bl & multi 20 18
Set value 96 62

Issued to honor modern Greek sculptors.

World Map and Olympic Rings A236

Discus Thrower by C. Demetriades A237

Designs: 1.50d, Runners on ancient clay vessel. 2.50d, Hurdler and map of Europe and Near East. 6d, Rising sun over Altis ruins at Olympia.

Perf. 13½x12, 12x13½

1967, Apr. 6 Litho. Wmk. 252

886 A236 1d multi 15 15
887 A236 1.50d multi 15 15
888 A236 2.50d multi 15 15
889 A237 5d multi 25 22
890 A236 6d multi 28 20
Set value 82 64

Olympic Games Day, Apr. 6 (1d); Classic Marathon Race, Apr. 6 (1.5d); athletic qualifying rounds for the Cup of Europe, June 24-25 (2.50d); 9th contest for the European Athletic Championships, 1969 (5d); founding of the International Academy at Olympia and the 7th meeting of the Academy, July 29-Aug. 14, 1967 (6d).

Europa Issue, 1967

Common Design Type

Perf. 12x13½

1967, May 2 Litho. Wmk. 252

Size: 23x33½mm

891 CD10 2.50d buff, lt & dk brn 38 15
892 CD10 4.50d grn, lt & dk grn 55 50

Chapel, Skopelos Island — A238

Plaka District, Athens — A239

Intl. Tourist Year: 4.50d, Doric Temple of Epicurean Apollo, by Itkinus, c. 430 B.C.

Perf. 13½x12, 12x13½

1967, June 26 Litho. Wmk. 252

893 A238 2.50d multi 15 15
894 A238 4.50d multi 28 22
a. Double impression of black
895 A239 6d multi 30 25

Destroyer and Sailor — A240

Training Ship, Merchant Marine Academy — A241

Maritime Week: 2.50d, Merchant Marine Academy, Aspropyrgos, Attica, and rowing crew. 3d, Cruiser Georgios Averoff and Naval School, Poros. 6d, Merchant ship and bearded figurehead.

1967, June 26

896 A240 20 l multi 15 15
897 A241 1d multi 15 15
898 A240 2.50d multi 15 15
899 A240 3d multi 30 20
900 A240 6d multi 30 20
Nos. 896-900 (5) 1.05
Set value 50

Soldier and Rising Phoenix A242

Blast Furnaces A243

Perf. 12x13½

1967, Aug. 30 Litho. Wmk. 252

901 A242 2.50d bl & multi 15 15
902 A242 3d org & multi 15 15
903 A242 4.50d multi 38 38
Set value 56

Revolution of Apr. 21, 1967.

1967, Nov. 29 ***Perf. 13x14***

904 A243 4.50d brt bl & dk vio bl 50 35

1st meeting of the UN Industrial Development Organization, Athens, Nov. 29-Dec. 20.

Sailboats A244

Children's Drawings: 1.50d, Steamship and island. 3.50d, Farmhouse. 6d, Church on hill.

1967, Dec. 20 ***Perf. 13½x12½***

905 A244 20 l multi 30 15
906 A244 1.50d grn, dk bl & blk 20 15
907 A244 3.50d multi 32 30
908 A244 6d multi 65 32

Javelin — A245

Apollo, Olympic Academy Seal A246

Discus Thrower by Demetriades A247

Designs: 1d, Jumping. 2.50d, Attic vase showing lighting of Olympic torch. 4d, Olympic rings and map of Europe (horiz.). 6d, Long-distance runners (vert.).

Wmk. 252

1968, Feb. 28 Litho. ***Perf. 12½***

909 A245 50 l ultra & bis 15 15
910 A245 1d grn, yel, blk & gray 15 15
911 A246 1.50d blk, bl & buff 15 15
912 A246 2.50d ol grn, blk & org brn 15 15
913 A246 4d gray & multi 42 18
914 A247 4.50d bl, grn, yel & blk 65 42
915 A245 6d brn, red & bl 32 18
Nos. 909-915 (7) 1.99
Set value 1.00

50 l, 1d, 6d, 27th Balkan Games, Athens, Aug. 29-Sept. 1; 1.50d, Meeting of the Intl. Olympic Academy; 2.50d, Lighting of the Olympic torch for 19th Olympic Games, Mexico City; 4d, Olympic Day, Apr. 6; 4.50d, 9th European Athletic Championships, 1969.

Europa Issue, 1968

Common Design Type

Perf. 13½x12

1968, Mar. 29 Litho. Wmk. 252

Size: 33x23mm

916 CD11 2.50d cop red, bis & blk 52 35
917 CD11 4.50d vio, bis & blk 1.25 75

Emblems of Greek and International Automobile Clubs — A248

1968, Mar. 29 ***Perf. 13x14***

918 A248 5d ultra & org brn 52 35

General Assembly of the International Automobile Federation, Athens, Apr. 8-14.

Athena Defeating Alkyoneus, from Pergamos Altar, 180 B.C. — A249

Athena, 2nd Century, B.C. — A250

Winged Victory of Samothrace, c. 190 B.C. — A251

Designs: 50 l, Alexander the Great on horseback, from sarcophagus, c. 310 B.C. 1.50d, Emperors Constantine and Justinian bringing offerings to Virgin Mary, Byzantine mosaic. 2.50d, Emperor Constantine Paleologos, lithograph by D. Tsokos, 1859. 3d, Greece in Missolonghi, by Delacroix. 4.50d, Greek Soldier (evzone), by G. B. Scott.

Perf. 13½x13, 13x13½, 13½x14 (A249)

1968, Apr. 27

919 A249 10 l gray & multi 15 15
920 A250 20 l grn & multi 15 15
921 A250 50 l pur & multi 15 15
922 A249 1.50d gray & multi 15 15
923 A250 2.50d multi 15 15
924 A251 3d multi 15 15
925 A251 4.50d multi 50 28
926 A251 6d multi 65 50
Set value 1.70 1.10

Issued to publicize an exhibition "The Hellenic Fight for Civilization."

Monument to the Unknown Priest and Teacher, Rhodes A252

Map & Flag of Greece — A253

Cross and Globe — A254

Perf. 14x13½, 13½x14

1968, July 11 Litho. Wmk. 252

927 A252 2d multi 30 15
928 A253 5d multi 40 40

20th anniv. of the union of the Dodecanese Islands with Greece.

1968, July 11 ***Perf. 13½x14***

929 A254 6d multi 55 35

19th Biennial Congress of the Greek Orthodox Archdiocese of North and South America.

Antique Lamp (GAPA Emblem) A255

1968, July 11 ***Perf. 14x13½***

930 A255 6d multi 50 35

Issued to publicize the Regional Congress of the Greek-American Progressive Association, G.A.P.A.

Fragment of Bas-relief, Temple of Aesculapius, Athens — A256

Perf. 13½x14

1968, Sept. 8 Litho. Wmk. 252

931 A256 4.50d multi 2.00 90

Issued to publicize the 5th European Cardiology Congress, Athens, Sept. 8-14.

View of Olympia, Site of Ancient Games A257

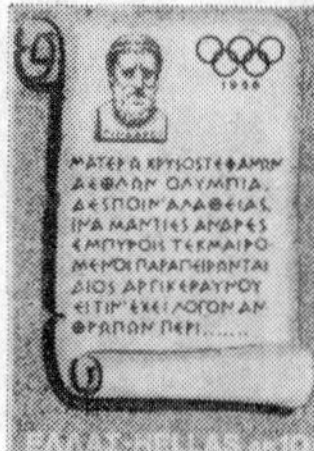

Pindar and Olympic Ode A258

Hygeia and WHO Emblem A259

Design: 2.50d, Panathenaic Stadium, site of 1896 Olympic Games.

Perf. 14x13½, 13x13½

1968, Sept. 25 Litho. Wmk. 252

932 A257 2.50d multi 15 15
933 A257 5d grn & multi 15 15
934 A258 10d bl, yel & brn 1.75 1.00

Issued to publicize the 19th Olympic Games, Mexico City, Oct. 12-27.

On 10d, hyphen is omitted at end of 5th line of ode on 5 of 50 stamps in each sheet.

1968, Nov. 8 ***Perf. 13½x14***

935 A259 5d gray & multi 55 32

20th anniv. of WHO.

Mediterranean, Breguet 19 and Flight Route, 1928 — A260

Farman, 1912, Plane and F-104G Jet A261

St. Zeno, The Letter Bearer A262

Design: 2.50d, Greek air force pilot ramming enemy plane over Langada.

1968, Nov. 8 ***Perf. 14x13½, 13½x14***

936 A260 2.50d ultra, blk & yel 15 15
937 A260 3.50d multi 15 15
938 A261 8d multi 1.25 90

Exploits of Royal Hellenic Air Force.

Perf. 13½x14

1969, Feb. 10 Litho. Wmk. 252

939 A262 2.50d multi 45 20

Establishment of the feast day of St. Zeno as the day of Greek p.o. personnel.

Hephaestus and Cyclops, Bas-relief A263

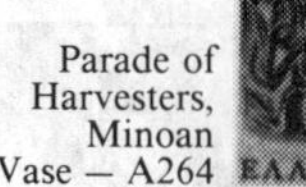

Parade of Harvesters, Minoan Vase — A264

1969, Feb. 10 ***Perf. 13½x12½***

940 A263 1.50d multi 35 15
941 A264 10d multi 1.00 65

50th anniv. of the ILO.

Yachts in Vouliagmeni Harbor — A265

Athens Festival, Chorus of Elders — A266

View of Astypalaia — A267

Perf. 13½x12½, 12½x13½

1969, Mar. 3

No.	Type	Denom.	Description	Unused	Used
942	A265	1d	multi	15	15
943	A266	5d	multi	85	70
944	A267	6d	multi	45	15

Issued for tourist publicity.

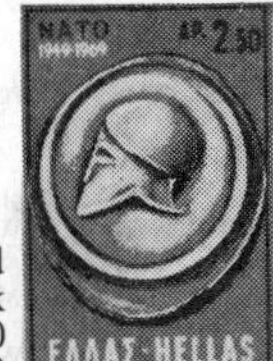
Attic Shield and Helmet on Greek Coin, 461-450 B.C. — A268

Hoplites and Flutist, from Proto-Corinthian Pitcher, 640-630 B.C. — A269

Perf. 12½x13½, 13½x12½

1969, Apr. 4 Litho. Wmk. 252

No.	Type	Denom.	Description	Unused	Used
945	A268	2.50d	rose red, blk & sl	35	15
946	A269	4.50d	multi	85	65

20th anniv. of NATO.

Europa Issue, 1969

Common Design Type

1969, May 5 ***Perf. 13½x12½***

Size: 33x23mm

No.	Type	Denom.	Description	Unused	Used
947	CD12	2.50d	multi	65	15
948	CD12	4.50d	multi	1.10	90

Victory Medal — A270

Pole Vault and Pentathlon (from Panathenaic Amphora) — A271

Designs: 5d, Relay race and runners from amphora, 525 B.C. (horiz.). 8d, Modern and ancient (Panathenaic amphora, c. 480 B.C.) discus throwers.

Perf. 12½x13½, 13½x12½

1969, May 5

No.	Type	Denom.	Description	Unused	Used
949	A270	20 l	red & multi	15	15
950	A271	3d	gray & multi	16	15
951	A271	5d	multi	16	15
952	A271	8d	multi	1.40	75
			Set value		1.00

Issued to publicize the 9th European Athletic Championships, Athens, Sept. 16-21.

Greece and the Sea Issue

Oil Tanker A272

Merchant Vessels and Warships, 1821 A273

Designs: 80 l, Brig and steamship, painting by Ioannis Poulakas (vert.). 4.50d, Warships on maneuvers. 6d, Battle of Salamis, 480 B.C., painting by Constantine Volonakis.

Perf. 12½x13½, 13½x12½, 13½x13

1969, June 28 Litho. Wmk. 252

No.	Type	Denom.	Description	Unused	Used
953	A272	80 l	multi	15	15
954	A272	2d	blk, bl & gray	15	15
955	A273	2.50d	dk bl & multi	15	15
956	A272	4.50d	brn, gray & bl	75	35
957	A273	6d	multi	90	45
			Nos. 953-957 (5)	2.10	
			Set value		1.00

Raising Greek Flag — A274

1969, Aug. 31 ***Perf. 13x13½***

No.	Type	Denom.	Description	Unused	Used
958	A274	2.50d	bl & multi	55	20

20th anniv. of the Grammos-Vitsi victory.

Athena Promachos and Map of Greece A275

"National Resistance" A276

Greek Participation in World War II — A277

Perf. 13x13½, 13½x14

1969, Oct. 12 Litho. Wmk. 252

No.	Type	Denom.	Description	Unused	Used
959	A275	4d	multi	15	15
960	A276	5d	multi	60	50
961	A277	6d	multi	45	20

25th anniv. of the liberation of Greece in WW II.

No. 960 exists imperf.

Demetrius Tsames Karatasios, by G. Demetriades A278

Pavlos Melas, by P. Mathiopoulos A279

Designs: 2.50d, Emmanuel Pappas, statue by Nicholas Perantinos. 4.50d, Capetan Kotas.

Perf. 12x13½

1969, Nov. 12 Litho. Wmk. 252

No.	Type	Denom.	Description	Unused	Used
962	A278	1.50d	multi	15	15
963	A278	2.50d	bl & multi	15	15
964	A279	3.50d	gray & multi	22	15
965	A279	4.50d	multi	95	55
			Set value		85

Issued to honor Greek heroes in Macedonia's struggle for liberation.

Angel of the Annunciation, Daphni Church, 11th Century — A280

Dolphins, Delos, 110 B.C. A281

Christ's Descent into Hell, Nea Moni Church, 11th Cent. A282

Greek Mosaics: 1.50d, The Holy Ghost (dove), Hosios Loukas Monastery, 11th century. 2d, The Hunter, Pella, 4th century B.C. 5d, Bird, St. George's Church, Salonica, 5th century.

Perf. 12x13½, 13½x12 (1d), 13x13½ (6d)

1970, Jan. 16 Litho. Wmk. 252

No.	Type	Denom.	Description	Unused	Used
966	A280	20 l	multi	15	15
967	A281	1d	multi	15	15
968	A280	1.50d	bl & multi	15	15
969	A280	2d	gray & multi	15	15
970	A280	5d	bis & multi	32	15
971	A282	6d	multi	2.25	1.00
			Nos. 966-971 (6)	3.17	
			Set value		1.25

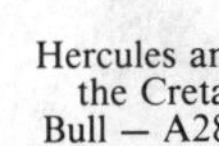

Hercules and the Cretan Bull — A283

Hercules and the Erymanthian Boar — A284

Labors of Hercules: 30 l, Capture of Cerberus. 1d, Capture of the golden apples of the Hesperides. 1.50d, Lernean Hydra. 2d, Slaying of Geryon. 3d, Centaur Nessus. 4.50d, Fight with the river god Achelos. 5d, Nemean lion. 6d, Stymphalian birds. 20d, Giant Antaeus. Designs of 20 l and 1d are from Temple of Zeus, Olympia; others from various vessels; all from 7th-5th cent. B.C.

Perf. 13½x12, 12x13½

1970, Mar. 16 Litho. Wmk. 252

No.	Type	Denom.	Description	Unused	Used
972	A283	20 l	gray, blk & yel	15	15
973	A283	30 l	ocher & multi	15	15
974	A284	1d	bl gray, blk & bl	15	15
975	A283	1.50d	dk brn, bis & sl grn	15	15
976	A283	2d	ocher & multi	1.65	15
977	A284	2.50d	ocher, dk brn & dl red	32	15
978	A284	3d	multi	1.25	15
979	A283	4.50d	dk bl & multi	70	15
980	A283	5d	multi	90	15
981	A283	6d	multi	90	15
982	A283	20d	blk & multi	4.00	70
			Nos. 972-982 (11)	10.32	
			Set value		1.50

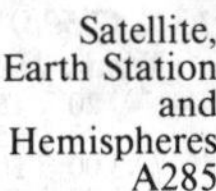
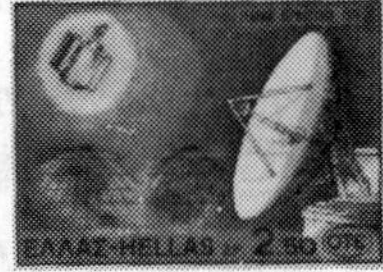
Satellite, Earth Station and Hemispheres A285

1970, Apr. 21 ***Perf. 13½x12***

No.	Type	Denom.	Description	Unused	Used
983	A285	2.50d	bl, gray & yel	70	20
984	A285	4.50d	brn, ol & bl	1.10	85

Issued to publicize the opening of the Earth Satellite Telecommunications Station "Thermopylae," Apr. 21, 1970.

Europa Issue, 1970

Common Design Type and

Owl (Post Horns and CEPT) — A287

Perf. 13½x12, 12x13½

1970, Apr. 21

No.	Type	Denom.	Description	Unused	Used
985	CD13	2.50d	rose red & org	55	20
986	A287	3d	brt bl, gray & vio bl	95	38
987	CD13	4.50d	ultra & org	2.00	1.25

St. Demetrius with Cyril and Methodius as Children A288

Emperor Michael III with Sts. Cyril and Methodius A290

St. Cyril A289 St. Methodius A291

Perf. 13½x14 (50 l); 12x13½ (2d, 10d); 13x13½ (5d)

1970, Apr. 17 Litho. Wmk. 252

No.	Type	Denom.	Description	Unused	Used
988	A288	50 l	multi	20	15
989	A289	2d	multi	65	25
990	A290	5d	multi	65	25
991	A291	10d	multi	1.25	75

Issued to commemorate Sts. Cyril and Methodius who translated the Bible into Slavonic. No. 989 and 991 printed se-tenant.

Greek Fir
A292

Jankaea
Heldreichii
A293

Designs: 6d, Rock partridge (horiz.). 8d, Wild goat.

Perf. 13x14, 14x13, 12x13½ (2.50d)

1970, June 16 Litho. Wmk. 252

No.	Type	Value	Color	Unused	Used
992	A292	80 l	multi	20	15
993	A293	2.50d	multi	32	15
994	A292	6d	multi	3.00	50
995	A292	8d	multi	5.00	2.50

European Nature Conservation Year, 1970.

Map Showing Link Between AHEPA Members and Greece
A294

1970, Aug. 1 ***Perf. 13½x13***

No.	Type	Value	Color	Unused	Used
996	A294	6d	bl & multi	1.10	25

Issued to publicize the 48th annual AHEPA (American Hellenic Educational Progressive Association) Congress, Athens, Aug. 1970.

UPU Headquarters, Bern — A295

Education Year Emblem — A296

Mahatma Gandhi — A297

United Nations Emblem
A298

Ludwig van Beethoven
A299

Perf. 13½x12, 13x14, 12x13½

1970, Oct. 7 Litho. Wmk. 252

No.	Type	Value	Color	Unused	Used
997	A295	50 l	bis & multi	15	15
998	A296	2.50d	bl & multi	15	15
999	A297	3.50d	multi	95	30
1000	A298	4d	bl & multi	95	25
1001	A299	4.50d	blk & multi	1.65	1.00
	Nos. 997-1001 (5)			3.85	1.85

Inauguration of the UPU Headquarters, Bern (50 l); Intl. Education Year (2.50d); cent. of the birth of Mohandas K. Gandhi (1869-1948), leader in India's struggle for independence (3.50d); 25th anniv. of the UN (4d); Ludwig van Beethoven (1770-1827), composer (4.50d).

The Shepherds (Mosaic) — A300

Christmas (from Mosaic in the Monastery of Hosios Loukas, Boetia, 11th century): 4.50d, The Three Kings and Angel. 6d, Nativity (horiz.).

1970, Dec. 5 ***Perf. 13x14, 14x13***

No.	Type	Value	Color	Unused	Used
1002	A300	2d	bis & multi	28	18
1003	A300	4.50d	bis & multi	80	42
1004	A300	6d	bis & multi	80	42

"Leonidas"
A301

Priest Sworn in as Fighter, from Commemorative Medal — A302

Eugenius Voulgaris (1716-1806)
A303

Battle of Corinth
A304

Kaltetsi Monastery, Seal of Peloponnesian Senate — A305

Death of Bishop Isaias, Battle of Alamana — A306

Designs: No. 1009, *Pericles.* No. 1010, Sacrifice of Kapsalis. 1.50d, *Terpsichore.* No. 1012, Patriarch Grigorius IV. No. 1013, Suliot women in battle (horiz.). No. 1015, *Karteria.* No. 1016, Adamantios Korias, M.D. No. 1017, Memorial column, provincial administrative seal of Epidaurus. 3d, Naval battle, Samos (horiz.). 5d, Battle of Athens. 6d, Naval battle, Yeronda. 6.50d, Battle of Maniaki. 9d, Battle of Karpenisi, death of Marcos Botsaris. 10d, Bishop Germanos blessing flag. 15d, *Secret School.* 20d, John Capodistrias' signature and seal.

1971 Litho. Wmk. 252

No.	Type	Value	Color	Unused	Used
1005	A301	20 l	multi	15	15
1006	A302	50 l	multi	15	15
1007	A303	50 l	multi	15	15
1008	A304	50 l	multi	15	15
1009	A301	1d	multi	20	15
1010	A304	1d	multi	15	15
1011	A301	1.50d	multi	20	15
1012	A302	2d	multi	20	15
1013	A304	2d	multi	20	15
1014	A305	2d	multi	20	15
1015	A301	2.50d	multi	20	15
1016	A303	2.50d	multi	70	35
1017	A305	2.50d	multi	20	15
1018	A304	3d	multi	42	22
1019	A306	4d	multi	32	15
1020	A304	5d	multi	65	22
1021	A301	6d	multi	65	32
1022	A301	6.50d	multi	85	38
1023	A301	9d	multi	90	42
1024	A306	10d	multi	90	42
1025	A306	15d	multi	1.25	60
1026	A305	20d	multi	1.50	60
	Nos. 1005-1026 (22)			10.29	
	Set value				4.60

Sesquicentennial of Greece's uprising against the Turks. Emphasize role of Navy (Nos. 1005, 1009, 1011, 1015, 1018, 1021), issued Mar. 15; Church (Nos. 1006, 1012, 1019, 1024), Feb. 8; Instructors (Nos. 1007, 1016, 1025), June 21; Land Forces (Nos. 1008, 1010, 1013, 1020, 1022-1023), Sept. 21; Provincial Administrations (Nos. 1014, 1017, 1026), Oct. 19.

Sizes: 37x24mm: (Nos. 1005, 1009, 1011, 1015); 40x27½mm (No. 1021); 48x33mm (Nos. 1022, 1023).

Perfs.: 14x13 (Nos. 1005, 1009, 1011, 1013, 1015, 1018); 13½x14 (Nos. 1006, 1012); 12x13½ (Nos. 1007, 1016, 1019, 1022-1025); 13x14 (Nos. 1008, 1010, 1020); 13½x13 (Nos. 1014, 1017, 1021, 1026).

Spyridon Louis, Winner of 1896 Marathon Race, Arriving at Stadium
A307

Pierre de Coubertin and Memorial Column — A308

Perf. 13½x13, 13x13½

1971, Apr. 10 Litho. Wmk. 252

No.	Type	Value	Color	Unused	Used
1027	A307	3d	multi	38	28
1028	A308	8d	multi	55	52

Olympic Games revival, 75th anniv.

Europa Issue, 1971

Common Design Type

1971, May 18 ***Perf. 13½x12***

Size: 33x22½mm

No.	Type	Value	Color	Unused	Used
1029	CD14	2.50d	grn, yel & blk	1.00	32
1030	CD14	5d	org, yel & blk	1.25	85

Hosios Lukas Monastery
A309

Monasteries and Churches: 1d, Daphni Church. 2d, St. John the Divine, Patmos. 2.50d, Koumbelidiki Church, Kastoria. 4.50d, Chalkeon Church, Thessalonica. 6.50d, Paregoritissa Church, Arta. 8.50d, St. Paul's Monastery, Mt. Athos.

1972, Jan. 17 ***Perf. 14x13***

No.	Type	Value	Color	Unused	Used
1031	A309	50 l	multi	15	15
1032	A309	1d	multi	15	15
1033	A309	2d	multi	15	15
1034	A309	2.50d	multi	15	15
1035	A309	4.50d	multi	40	20
1036	A309	6.50d	multi	40	15
1037	A309	8.50d	multi	1.10	70
	Nos. 1031-1037 (7)			2.50	
	Set value				1.35

Cretan Costume — A310

Designs: Greek regional costumes.

1972, Mar. 1 ***Perf. 12½x13½***

No.	Type	Value	Description	Unused	Used
1038	A310	50 l	shown	15	15
1039	A310	1d	Woman, Pindus	16	15
1040	A310	2d	Man, Missolonghi	18	15
1041	A310	2.50d	Woman, Sarakatsan, Attica	25	15
a.			"1972" omitted	3.00	3.00
1042	A310	3d	Woman, Island of Nisyros	25	15
1043	A310	4.50d	Woman, Megara	50	15
1044	A310	6.50d	Woman, Trikeri	70	15
1045	A310	10d	Woman, Pylaia, Macedonia	1.40	55
	Nos. 1038-1045 (8)			3.59	
	Set value				1.05

See Nos. 1073-1089, 1121-1135.

Memorial Medal, Science and Industry
A311

Flag and Map of Greece — A312

Honeycomb, Transportation and Industry — A313

Perf. 13½x13, 13x13½

1972, Apr. 21 Wmk. 252

No.	Type	Value	Color	Unused	Used
1046	A311	2.50d	bl & multi	15	15
1047	A312	4.50d	ocher & multi	25	25
1048	A313	5d	multi	38	38

5th anniversary of the revolution.

Europa Issue 1972

Common Design Type

1972, May 2 ***Perf. 12x13½***

Size: 23x33mm

No.	Type	Value	Color	Unused	Used
1049	CD15	3d	multi	50	15
1050	CD15	4.50d	bl & multi	1.25	1.00

Acropolis and Car — A314

Route of Automobile Rally — A315

1972, May 26 ***Perf. 13½x12***

1051	A314	4.50d	multi	65	50
1052	A315	5d	bl & multi	65	50

20th Acropolis Automobile Rally, May 26-29.

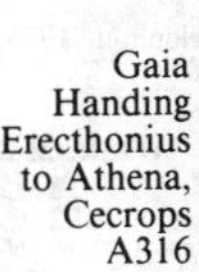

Gaia Handing Erecthonius to Athena, Cecrops A316

Designs: 2d, Uranus, from altar of Zeus at Pergamum. 2.50d, Gods defeating the Giants, Treasury of Siphnos. 5d, Zeus of Dodona.

1972, June 26 **Litho.** ***Perf. 14x13½***

1053	A316	1.50d	yel grn & blk	15	15
1054	A316	2d	dk bl & blk	15	15
1055	A316	2.50d	org brn & blk	15	15
1056	A316	5d	dk brn & blk	40	30
			Set value		54

Greek mythology. No. 1056 issued only se-tenant with Nos. 1053-1055 in sheets of 40 (4x10). Nos. 1053-1055 issued also in sheets of 50 each.

Olympic Rings, Wrestlers A317

Designs: 50 l, Young athlete, crowning himself, c. 480 B.C. (vert.). 3.50d, Spartan woman running, Archaic period (vert.). 4.50d, Episkyros ball game, 6th century B.C. 10d, Running youths, from Panathenaic amphora.

Perf. 13½x14, 14x13½

1972, July 28 **Litho.** **Wmk. 252**

1057	A317	50 l	mar, blk & gray	15	15
1058	A317	1.50d	brn, gray & blk	15	15
1059	A317	3.50d	ocher & multi	15	15
1060	A317	4.50d	grn, buff & blk	40	25
1061	A317	10d	blk & fawn	60	38
			Set value	1.25	80

20th Olympic Games, Munich, Aug. 26-Sept. 11.

Young Stamp Collector — A318

Three Kings and Angels — A319

1972, Nov. 15 ***Perf. 13x14***

1062	A318	2.50d	multi	18	15

Stamp Day.

1972, Nov. 15

1063	A319	2.50d	shown	15	15
1064	A319	4.50d	Nativity	15	15

Christmas 1972. Printed se-tenant in sheets of 50.

Technical University, 1885, by Luigi Lanza — A320

1973, Mar. 30 ***Perf. 13½x13***

1065	A320	2.50d	multi	18	15

Centenary of the Metsovion National Technical University.

"Spring," Fresco — A321

Breast-form Jug — A322

"Wooing and Twittering Swallows" Fresco A323

Designs: 30 l, "Blue Apes" fresco. 1.50d, Jug decorated with birds. 5d, "Wild Goats" fresco. 6.50d, Wrestlers, fresco.

Perf. 13x13½, 13½x13

1973, Mar. 30

1066	A321	10 l	multi	15	15
1067	A322	20 l	multi	15	15
1068	A323	30 l	multi	15	15
1069	A322	1.50d	grn & multi	15	15
1070	A323	2.50d	multi	15	15
1071	A323	5d	multi	25	25
1072	A323	6.50d	multi	1.50	1.50
			Set value	2.15	2.15

Archaeological treasures from Santorini Island (Thera).

Costume Type of 1972

Designs: Women's costumes except 10 l, 20 l, 50 l, 5d, 15d.

1973, Apr. 18 ***Perf. 12½x13½***

1073	A310	10 l	Peloponnesus	15	15
1074	A310	20 l	Central Greece	15	15
1075	A310	30 l	Locris	15	15
1076	A310	50 l	Skyros	15	15
1077	A310	1d	Spetsai	15	15
1078	A310	1.50d	Almyros	15	15
1079	A310	2.50d	Macedonia	15	15
1080	A310	3.50d	Salamis	18	15
1081	A310	4.50d	Epirus	24	15
1082	A310	5d	Lefkas	28	15
1083	A310	6.50d	Skyros	24	15
1084	A310	8.50d	Corinth	35	15
1085	A310	10d	Corfu	35	15
1086	A310	15d	Epirus	45	15
1087	A310	20d	Thessaly	90	18
1088	A310	30d	Macedonia	1.10	50
1089	A310	50d	Thrace	1.75	65
			Nos. 1073-1089 (17)	6.89	
			Set value		2.80

Europa Issue 1973

Common Design Type

1973, May 2 ***Perf. 13½x12½***

Size: 35x22mm

1090	CD16	2.50d	dp bl & lt bl	25	15
1091	CD16	3d	dp car & dp org	50	30
1092	CD16	4.50d	ol grn & yel	75	45

Zeus Battling Typhoeus, from Amphora A324

Designs: 1d, Mount Olympus, after photograph. 2.50d, Zeus battling Giants, from Pergamum Altar. 4.50d, Punishment of Atlas and Prometheus, from vase.

Perf. 14x13½

1973, June 25 **Wmk. 252**

1093	A324	1d	gray & blk	15	15
1094	A324	2d	multi	15	15
1095	A324	2.50d	gray, blk & buff	20	15
1096	A324	4.50d	ocher & multi	30	22
a.			Strip of 4, #1093-1096	1.25	1.00
			Set value	64	48

Greek mythology.

Dr. George Papanicolaou A325

Icon, The Annunciation A326

Perf. 13x13½

1973, Aug. 10 **Litho.** **Wmk. 252**

1097	A325	2.50d	multi	30	30
1098	A325	6.50d	multi	35	30

Dr. George Papanicolaou (1883-1962), cytologist and cancer researcher.

1973, Aug. 10

1099	A326	2.50d	multi	22	15

Miraculous icon of Our Lady of the Annunciation found on Tinos, 1823.

Triptolemus Holding Wheat on Chariot — A327

Perf. 13x14

1973, Oct. 22 **Litho.** **Wmk. 252**

1100	A327	4.50d	buff, dk brn & red	25	22

5th Symposium of the European Conf. of Transport Ministers, Athens, Oct. 22-25.

Georgios Averoff — A328

National Benefactors: 2d, Apostolos Arsakis. 2.50d, Constantine Zappas. 4d, Andrea Sygros. 6.50d, John Varvakis.

1973, Nov. 15 **Engr.**

1101	A328	1.50d	dk red brn	15	15
1102	A328	2d	car rose	15	15
1103	A328	2.50d	sl grn	15	15
1104	A328	4d	purple	15	15
1105	A328	6.50d	black	15	15
			Set value	57	48

Child Examining Stamp — A329

1973, Nov. 15 **Litho.** ***Perf. 14x13***

1106	A329	2.50d	multi	18	15

Stamp Day.

Lord Byron in Souliot Costume — A330

Byron Taking Oath at Grave of Botsaris — A331

Perf. 13x14

1974, Apr. 4 **Wmk. 252** **Litho.**

1107	A330	2.50d	multi	15	15
1108	A331	4.50d	multi	15	15
			Set value	22	16

George Gordon, Lord Byron (1788-1824), English poet involved in Greek struggle for independence.

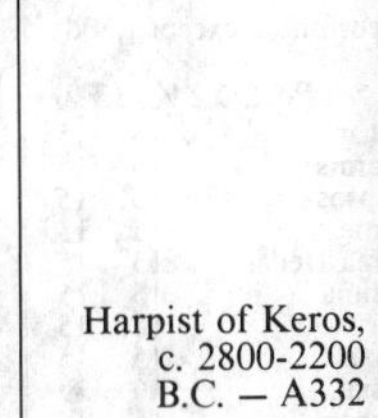

Harpist of Keros, c. 2800-2200 B.C. — A332

Europa: 4.50d, Statue of Young Women, c. 510 B.C. 6.50d, Charioteer of Delphi, c. 480-450 B.C.

1974, May 10 ***Perf. 13x14***

1109	A332	3d	dp bl & multi	16	15
1110	A332	4.50d	dl red & multi	20	15
1111	A332	6.50d	yel & multi	38	25

Zeus and Hera Enthroned, and Iris A333

Design from Mycenean Vase and UPU Emblem A334

Greek mythology (from Vases, 5th Cent. B.C.): 2d, Birth of Athena (horiz.). 2.50d, Artemis, Apollo, Leto (horiz.). 10d, Hermes, the messenger.

1974, June 24 ***Perf. 13x14, 14x13***

1112	A333	1.50d	ocher, blk & brn	15	15
1113	A333	2d	blk, ocher & brn	15	15
1114	A333	2.50d	blk, ocher & brn	15	15
1115	A333	10d	blk, ocher & brn	20	15
			Set value	54	36

1974, Sept. 14 ***Perf. 12½x13½***

UPU cent.: 4.50d, Hermes on the Move (horiz.). 6.50d, Woman reading letter.

1116	A334	2d	vio & blk	15	15
1117	A334	4.50d	vio & blk	15	15
1118	A334	6.50d	vio & blk	15	15

Crete No. 80 A335

1974, Nov. 15 Litho. ***Perf. 13½x13***

1119	A335	2.50d	multi	18	15

Stamp Day.

Flight into Egypt — A336

1974, Nov. 15 ***Perf. 13½x14***

1120	A336		Strip of 3	38	30
a.		2d	ocher & multi	15	15
b.		4.50d	ocher & multi	15	15
c.		8.50d	ocher & multi	15	15

Christmas 1974. Design is from 11th cent. Codex of Dionysos Monastery on Mount Athos.

Costume Type of 1972

Designs: Women's costumes, except 1.50d.

1974, Dec. 5 ***Perf. 12½x13½***

1121	A310	20 l	Megara	15	15
1122	A310	30 l	Salamis	15	15
1123	A310	50 l	Edipsos	15	15
1124	A310	1d	Kyme	15	15
1125	A310	1.50d	Sterea Hellas	15	15
1126	A310	2d	Desfina	15	15
1127	A310	3d	Epirus	15	15
1128	A310	3.50d	Naousa	15	15
1129	A310	4d	Hasia	16	15
1130	A310	4.50d	Thasos	16	15
1131	A310	5d	Skopelos	18	15
1132	A310	6.50d	Epirus	18	15
1133	A310	10d	Pelion	20	15
1134	A310	25d	Kerkyra	48	18
1135	A310	30d	Boeotia	65	30
			Set value	2.75	1.60

Secret Vostitsa Assembly, 1821 — A337

Grigorios Dikeos-Papaflessas A338

Aghioi Apostoli Church, Kalamata A339

Perf. 13½x12½, 12½x13½

1975, Mar. 24

1136	A337	4d	multi	15	15
1137	A338	7d	multi	15	15
1138	A339	11d	multi	20	15
			Set value		32

Grigorios Dikeos-Papaflessas (1788-1825), priest and leader in Greece's uprising against the Turks, sesquicentennial of death.

Vase with Flowers — A340 Erotokritos and Aretussa — A341

Design: 11d, Girl with Hat. All designs are after paintings by Theophilos Hatzimichael (d. 1934).

Perf. 12½x13½

1975, May 10 Litho. Wmk. 252

1139	A340	4d	multi	20	15
1140	A341	7d	multi	32	25
1141	A340	11d	multi	50	38

House, Kastoria A342

Greek Houses, 18th Cent.: 40 l, Arnea, Halkidiki. 4d, Veria. 6d, Siatista. 11d, Ambelakia, Thessaly.

1975, June 26 ***Perf. 13½x12½***

1142	A342	10 l	brt bl & blk	15	15
1143	A342	40 l	red org & blk	15	15
1144	A342	4d	bis & blk	28	15
1145	A342	6d	ultra & multi	20	18
1146	A342	11d	org & blk	55	35
			Nos. 1142-1146 (5)	1.33	
			Set value		80

IWY Emblem, Neolithic Goddess — A343 "Looking to the Future" — A344

Design: 8.50d, Confrontation between Antigone and Creon.

Perf. 12½x13½

1975, Sept. 29 Litho. Wmk. 252

1147	A343	1.50d	lil & dk brn	15	15
1148	A343	8.50d	bis, blk & brn	18	15
1149	A344	11d	bl & blk	20	18
			Set value	46	38

International Women's Year 1975.

Papanastasiou and University Buildings — A345

First University Building A346

University City Plan A347

1975, Sept. 29 ***Perf. 14x13½***

1150	A345	1.50d	tan & sepia	15	15
1151	A346	4d	multi	15	15
1152	A347	11d	multi	18	15
			Set value	42	28

Thessaloniki University, 50th anniversary. Alexandros Papanastasiou (1876-1936), founded University while Prime Minister.

Evangelos Zappas and Zappeion Building — A348

National Benefactors: 4d, Georgios Rizaris and Rizarios Ecclesiastical School. 6d, Michael Tositsas and Metsovion Technical University. 11d, Nicolaos Zosimas and Zosimea Academy.

Perf. 14x13

1975, Nov. 15 Litho. Wmk. 252

1153	A348	1d	blk & grn	15	15
1154	A348	4d	blk & brn	15	15
1155	A348	6d	blk & org	15	15
1156	A348	11d	blk & brick red	20	20
			Set value	52	46

Greece No. 380 — A349

1975, Nov. 15 ***Perf. 13x14***

1157	A349	11d	dull grn & brn	25	20

Stamp Day 1975.

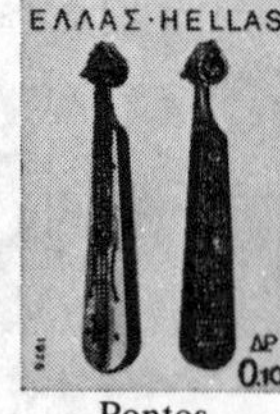

Pontos Lyre — A350 Musicians, Byzantine Mural — A351

Designs: 1d, Cretan lyre. 1.50d, Tambourine. 4d, Guitarist, from amphora (horiz.). 6d, Bagpipes. 7d, Lute. 10d, Barrel organ. 11d, Pipes and zournadas. 20d, Musicians and singers praising God, Byzantine mural (horiz.). 25d, Drums. 30d, Kanonaki (horiz.).

Perf. 12½x13½, 13½x12½

1975, Dec. 15 Litho. Wmk. 252

1158	A350	10 l	multi	15	15
1159	A351	20 l	multi	15	15
1160	A350	1d	ultra & multi	15	15
1161	A350	1.50d	multi	15	15
1162	A351	4d	multi	15	15
1163	A350	6d	multi	16	15
1164	A350	7d	multi	20	15
1165	A350	10d	multi	30	15
1166	A350	11d	red & multi	30	15
1167	A351	20d	multi	28	15
1168	A350	25d	multi	30	15
1169	A350	30d	multi	45	20
			Nos. 1158-1169 (12)	2.74	
			Set value		1.20

Popular musical instruments.

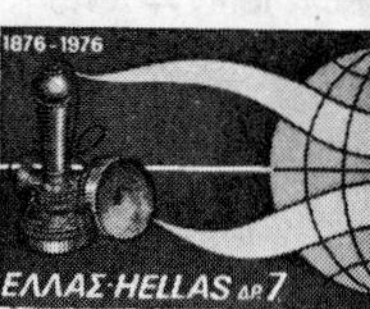

Early Telephone, Globe, Waves A352

Design: 11d, Globe, waves, telephone 1976.

Perf. 13½x12½

1976, Mar. 23 Litho. Wmk. 252

1170	A352	7d	blk & multi	18	15
1171	A352	11d	blk & multi	22	15
a.			Pair, Nos. 1170-1171	60	60

Centenary of first telephone call by Alexander Graham Bell, Mar. 10, 1876. Nos. 1170-1171 printed se-tenant in sheets of 50.

Sortie of Missolonghi — A353

1976, Mar. 23 ***Perf. 13½x13***

1172	A353	4d	multi	15	15

Sortie of the garrison of Missolonghi, sesquicentennial.

Florina Jugn — A354 Avramidis Plate — A355

Europa: 11d, Egina pitcher with Greek flags.

Perf. 13x14, 12½x12 (A355)

1976, May 10 Litho. Wmk. 252

1173	A354	7d	buff & multi	15	15
1174	A355	8.50d	blk & multi	18	15
1175	A354	11d	gray & multi	35	24
			Set value		46

Lion Attacking Bull — A356 Head of Silenus — A357

Designs: 4.50d, Flying aquatic birds. 7d, Wounded bull. 11d, Cow feeding calf (horiz.). Designs from Creto-Mycenaean engraved seals, c. 1400 B.C.

Perf. 13x12½, 13½x14, 14x13½

1976, May 10

1176	A356	2d	bis & multi	15	15
1177	A356	4.50d	multi	20	15
1178	A356	7d	multi	16	15
1179	A357	8.50d	pur & multi	16	15
1180	A357	11d	brn & multi	20	15
			Nos. 1176-1180 (5)	87	
			Set value		48

Long Jump A358

Montreal and Athens Stadiums — A359

Designs (Classical and Modern Events): 2d, Basketball. 3.50d, Wrestling. 4d, Swimming. 25d, Lighting Olympic flame and Montreal Olympic Games torch.

Perf. 14x13½, 12½x13½ (A359)

1976, June 25 Litho. Wmk. 252

1181 A358	50 l	org & multi	15	15
1182 A358	2d	org & multi	15	15
1183 A358	3.50d	org & multi	15	15
1184 A358	4d	bl & multi	15	15
1185 A359	11d	multi	24	15
1186 A358	25d	org & multi	50	25
		Set value	1.10	68

21st Olympic Games, Montreal, Canada, July 17-Aug. 1.

Lesbos, View and Map A360

Designs (Views and Maps): 30d, Lemnos (vert.). 75d, Chios. 100d, Samos.

Perf. 13½x14, 14x13½

1976, July 26 Litho. Wmk. 252

1187 A360	30d	bl & multi	1.00	25
1188 A360	50d	bl & multi	1.50	38
1189 A360	75d	bl & multi	2.50	50
1190 A360	100d	bl & multi	3.00	65

Greek Aegean Islands.

Three Kings Speaking to the Jews — A361

Christmas: 7d, Nativity. Designs from manuscripts in Esfigmenou Monastery, Mount Athos.

1976, Dec. 8 ***Perf. 13½x14***

1191 A361	4d	yel & multi	15	15
1192 A361	7d	yel & multi	16	15
		Set value		24

Greek Grammar of 1478 — A362

1976, Dec. 8 ***Perf. 14x13***

1193 A362	4d	multi	15	15

500th anniversary of printing of first Greek book by Constantin Lascaris, Milan.

Heinrich Schliemann A363

Brooch with Figure of Goddess A364

Designs: 4d, Gold bracelet (horiz.). 7d, Gold diadem (horiz.). 11d, Gold mask (Agamemnon). Treasures from Mycenaean tombs.

1976, Dec. 8 ***Perf. 13x14, 14x13***

1194 A363	2d	multi	15	15
1195 A364	4d	multi	15	15
1196 A364	5d	grn & multi	15	15
1197 A364	7d	multi	15	15
1198 A364	11d	multi	22	16
		Set value	66	50

Cent. of the discovery of the Mycenaean royal shaft graves by Heinrich Schliemann.

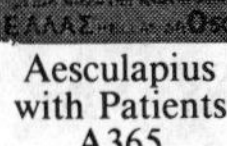
Aesculapius with Patients A365

Patient in Clinic A366

Designs: 1.50d, Aesculapius curing young man. 2d, Young Hercules with old nurse. 20d, Old man with votive offering of large leg.

Perf. 12½x13½ (A365); 13x12 (A366)

1977, Mar. 15 Litho. Wmk. 252

1199 A365	50 l	multi	15	15
1200 A366	1d	multi	15	15
1201 A366	1.50d	multi	15	15
1202 A366	2d	multi	15	15
1203 A365	20d	multi	22	18
		Set value	52	42

International Rheumatism Year.

Winged Wheel, Modern Transportation — A367

1977, May 16 Litho. ***Perf. 14x13½***

1204 A367	7d	multi	20	15

European Conference of Ministers of Transport (E.C.M.T.), Athens, June 1-3.

Mani Castle, Vathia A368

Europa: 7d, Santorini (vert.). 15d, Windmills on Lasithi plateau.

Perf. 14x13½, 13½x14

1977, May 16 Litho. Wmk. 252

1205 A368	5d	multi	15	15
1206 A368	7d	multi	15	15
1207 A368	15d	multi	30	22
		Set value		40

Alexandria Lighthouse, from Roman Coin — A369

Designs: 1d, Alexander places Homer's works into Achilles' tomb, fresco by Raphael. 1.50d, Alexander descends to the bottom of the sea, Flemish miniature. 3d, Alexander searching for water of life, Hindu plate. 7d, Alexander on horseback, Coptic carpet. 11d, Alexander hearing oracle that his days are numbered, Byzantine manuscript. 30d, Death of Alexander, Persian miniature. All designs include gold coin of Lysimachus with Alexander's head.

1977, July 23 ***Perf. 14x13***

1208 A369	50 l	sil & multi	15	15
1209 A369	1d	sil & multi	15	15
1210 A369	1.50d	sil & multi	15	15
1211 A369	3d	sil & multi	15	15
1212 A369	7d	sil & multi	18	15
1213 A369	11d	sil & multi	18	15
1214 A369	30d	sil & multi	55	32
		Set value	1.20	88

Cultural influence of Alexander the Great (356-323 B.C.), King of Macedonia.

"Greece Rising Again" A370

People in Front of University A371

Greek Flags, Laurel, University A372

Perf. 13½x12½, 12x12½, 12½x12

1977, July 23 Unwmk.

1215 A370	4d	multi	15	15
1216 A371	7d	multi	15	15
1217 A372	20d	multi	25	20
		Set value		40

Restoration of Democracy in Greece.

Archbishop Makarios, Map of Cyprus — A373

Design: 4d, Archbishop Makarios (vert.).

Perf. 13x13½, 13½x13

1977, Sept. 10 Litho. Unwmk.

1218 A373	4d	sepia & blk	15	15
1219 A373	7d	buff, brn & blk	15	15
		Set value		22

Archbishop Makarios (1913-1977), President of Cyprus.

Old Athens Post Office A374

Neo-Hellenic architecture: 1d, Institution for the Blind, Salonika. 1.50d, Townhall, Syros. 2d, National Bank of Greece, Piraeus. 5d, Byzantine Museum, Athens. 50d, Municipal Theater, Patras.

1977, Sept. 22 ***Perf. 13½x13***

1220 A374	50 l	multi	15	15
1221 A374	1d	multi	15	15
1222 A374	1.50d	multi	15	15
1223 A374	2d	multi	15	15
1224 A374	5d	multi	15	15
1225 A374	50d	multi	60	30
		Set value	1.00	70

Battle of Navarino, Lithograph — A375

Adm. Van Heyden, Sir Edward Codrington, Count de Rigny — A376

1977, Oct. 20 ***Perf. 13½x13***

1226 A375	4d	brn, buff & blk	15	15
1227 A376	7d	multi	15	15
		Set value	24	21

150th anniversary of Battle of Navarino.

Parthenon and Refinery — A377

Caryatid and Factories — A379

Fish and Birds Suffering from Pollution A378

Design: 7d, Birds and trees in polluted air.

Perf. 13½x14, 14x13½

1977, Oct. 20

1228 A377	3d	org & blk	15	15
1229 A378	4d	multi	20	15
1230 A378	7d	multi	30	20
1231 A379	30d	blk, gray & slate	42	28

Protection of the environment.

Map of Greece and Ships — A380

Globe and Swallows A381

Letter with Flags, Swallow A382

Designs: 5d, Globe with Greek flag. 13d, World map showing dispersion of Greeks abroad.

1977, Dec. 15 *Perf. 13½x12½*

1232	A380	4d multi		15	15
1233	A380	5d multi		15	15
1234	A381	7d multi		18	15
1235	A382	11d multi		18	15
1236	A380	13d multi		22	15
	Nos. 1232-1236 (5)			88	
	Set value				50

Greeks living abroad.

Kalamata Harbor, by Constantine Parthenis — A383

Greek Paintings: 2.50d, Boats, Arsanas, by Spyros Papaloucas (vert.). 4d, Santorini, by Constantine Maleas. 7d, The Engagement, by Nicolaus Gyzis. 11d, Woman with Straw Hat, by Nicolaus Lytras (vert.). 15d, "Spring" (nude), by Georgio Iacovidis.

Perf. 13½x13, 13x13½

1977, Dec. 15

1237	A383	1.50d	yel & multi	15	15
1238	A383	2.50d	yel & multi	15	15
1239	A383	4d	yel & multi	15	15
1240	A383	7d	yel & multi	15	15
1241	A383	11d	yel & multi	16	15
1242	A383	15d	yel & multi	30	15
	Set value			88	56

Ebenus Cretica — A384

Greek Flora: 2.50d, Dwarf lily. 3d, Campanula oreadum. 4d, Tiger lily. 7d, Viola delphinantha. 25d, Paeonia rhodia.

1978, Mar. 30 **Litho.** *Perf. 13x13½*

1243	A384	1.50d	multi	15	15
1244	A384	2.50d	multi	15	15
1245	A384	3d	multi	15	15
1246	A384	4d	multi	15	15
1247	A384	7d	multi	24	15
1248	A384	25d	multi	24	16
	Set value			86	64

Postrider, Cancellation A385

Designs: 5d, S.S. Maximilianos and Hermes Head. 7d, 19th century mail train and No. 122. 30d, Mailmen on motorcycles and No. 1062.

1978, May 15 *Perf. 13½x12½*

1249	A385	4d	buff & multi	15	15
1250	A385	5d	buff & multi	18	15
1251	A385	7d	buff & multi	30	15
1252	A385	30d	buff & multi	30	15
a.	Souvenir sheet of 4			1.10	1.10
	Set value				48

150th anniv. of Greek postal service.

No. 1252a issued Sept. 25, contains Nos. 1249-1252 in slightly changed colors. Sold for 60d.

Lighting Olympic Flame, Olympia — A386

Start of 100-meter Race — A387

1978, May 15 *Perf. 13x14*

1253	A386	7d	multi	20	15
1254	A387	13d	multi	28	20

80th session of International Olympic Committee, Athens, May 10-21.

Europa Issue 1978

St. Sophia, Salonica A388

Lysicrates Monument, Athens — A389

1978, May 15 *Perf. 13x14, 14x13*

1255	A388	4d	multi	15	15
1256	A389	7d	multi	18	15
	Set value				20

Aristotle, Roman Bust — A390

School of Athens, by Raphael — A391

Map of Chalcidice, Base of Statue from Attalus Arcade — A392

Aristotle the Wise, Byzantine Fresco, St. George's Church, Ioannina — A393

Perf. 13x13½, 13½x14 (20d)

1978, July 10 **Litho.**

1257	A390	2d	multi	15	15
1258	A391	4d	multi	15	15
1259	A392	7d	multi	15	15
1260	A393	20d	multi	38	25
	Set value			68	48

Aristotle (384-322 B.C.), systematic philosopher.

Rotary Emblem A394

Surgeons Operating — A395

Ugo Foscolo, View of Zante — A396

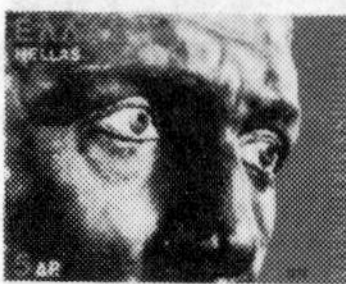

Hellenistic Bronze Head — A397

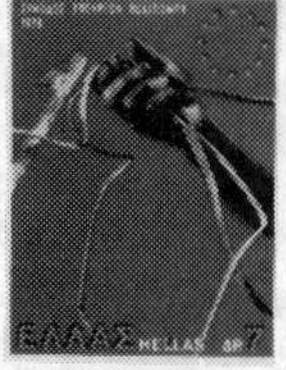

Charioteer's Hand, Delphi — A398

Wright Brothers' Plane, Daedalus and Icarus — A399

1978, Sept. 21 **Litho.** *Perf. 12½*

1261	A394	1d	multi	15	15
1262	A395	1.50d	multi	15	15
1263	A396	2.50d	multi	15	15
1264	A397	5d	multi	15	15
1265	A398	7d	multi	15	15
1266	A399	13d	multi	16	15
	Set value			68	46

Rotary in Greece, 50th anniv. (1d); 11th Greek Surgery Cong., Salonica (1.50d); Ugo Foscolo (1778-1827), Italian writer (2.50d); European Convention on Human Rights, 25th anniv. (5d); 2nd Conf. of Ministers of Culture of the Council of Europe member countries, Athens, Oct. 23-27 (7d); 75th anniv. of 1st powered flight (13d).

Poor Woman and her 5 Children A400

Scenes from Fairy Tale "The 12 Months": 3d, The poor woman and the 12 months. 4d, The poor woman and the gold coins. 20d, Punishment of the greedy woman.

1978, Nov. 6 **Litho.** *Perf. 13½x13*

1267	A400	2d	multi	15	15
1268	A400	3d	multi	15	15
1269	A400	4d	multi	15	15
1270	A400	20d	multi	28	15
	Set value			56	38

"Transplants" A401

The Miracle of St. Anarghiri A402

1978, Nov. 6 *Perf. 12½x13½*

1271	A401	4d	multi	15	15
1272	A402	10d	multi	20	15
	Set value			30	20

Advancements in organ transplants.

Cruiser A403

New and Old Greek Naval Ships: 1d, Torpedo boats. 2.50d, Submarine Papanicolis. 4d, Battleship Psara. 5d, Sailing ship "Madonna of Hydra." 7d, Byzantine corvette. 50d, Archaic trireme.

1978, Dec. 15 **Litho.** *Perf. 13½x12*

1273	A403	50 l	multi	15	15
1274	A403	1d	multi	15	15
1275	A403	2.50d	multi	15	15
1276	A403	4d	multi	15	15
1277	A403	5d	multi	15	15
1278	A403	7d	multi	15	15
1279	A403	50d	multi	65	40
	Set value			1.20	88

Cadet Officer, Military School, Nauplia A404

Cadet Officers' School Emblem — A405

Design: 10d, Cadet Officers Military School, Athens, Cadet's uniform, 1978.

Perf. 13½x12, 12x13½

1978, Dec. 15

1280	A404	1.50d	multi	15	15
1281	A405	2d	multi	15	15
1282	A404	10d	multi	16	15
	Set value			32	20

Cadet Officers Military School, 150th anniv.

Virgin and Child — A406

Baptism of Christ — A407

Designs from 16th century icon stands in Stavronikita Monastery.

1978, Dec. 15 *Perf. 13x13 ½*

1283	A406	4d multi	15	15
1284	A407	7d multi	15	15
		Set value	24	20

Christmas 1978.

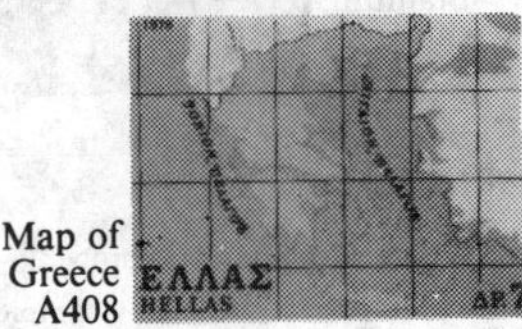
Map of Greece A408

1978, Dec. 28 *Perf. 14x13*

1285	A408	7d multi	16	15
1286	A408	11d multi	16	15
1287	A408	13d multi	16	15
		Set value		32

Kitsos Tzavellas A409

Souli Castle A410

Designs: 10d, Fighting Souliots. 20d, Fight of Zalongo.

Perf. 12 ½x13 ½, 13 ½x12 ½

1979, Mar. 12 **Litho.**

1288	A409	1.50d buff, blk & brn	15	15
1289	A410	3d multi	15	15
1290	A410	10d multi	20	15
1291	A409	20d buff, blk & brn	32	20
		Set value	72	50

Struggle of the Souliots, 18th century fighters for freedom from Turkey.

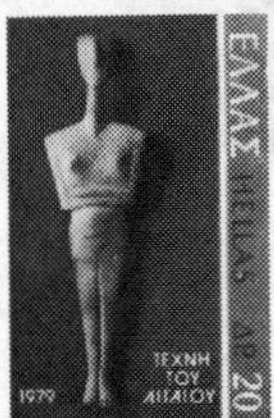
Cycladic Figure from Amorgos A411

Mailmen from Crete A412

1979, Apr. 26 **Litho.** *Perf. 12x13 ½*

1292	A411	20d multi	40	25

Aegean art.

1979, May 11 *Perf. 13 ½x14*

Europa: 7d, Rural mailman on horseback, Crete.

1293	A412	4d multi	15	15
1294	A412	7d multi	22	15
		Set value	30	21

Printed se-tenant in sheets of 50.

Nicolas Scoufas A413

Basketball A415

Locomotives A414

Mene Psarianosi Symeonidis Fossil A416

Temple of Hephaestus and Byzantine Church — A417

Victory of Paeonius Statue, Flags of Balkan Countries — A418

1979, May 12 *Perf. 13x14, 14x13*

1295	A413	1.50d multi	15	15
1296	A414	2d multi	15	15
1297	A415	3d multi	15	15
1298	A416	4d multi	15	15
1299	A417	10d multi	15	15
1300	A418	20d multi	24	15
		Set value	76	48

Nicolas Scoufas (1779-1818), founder of (patriotic) Friendly Society; Piraeus-Athens-to-the-frontier railroad, 75th anniversary; European Basketball Championship; 7th International Congress for the Study of the Neocene Period in the Mediterranean; Balkan Tourist Year 1979; 50 years of track and field competitions in Balkan countries.

Wheat with Members' Flags, Greek Coins — A419

European Parliament, Strasbourg — A420

Perf. 13x14, 14x13

1979, May 28 **Litho.**

1301	A419	7d multi	20	20
1302	A420	30d multi	30	30

Greece's entry into European Economic Community and Parliament.

Statue of a Girl, IYC Emblem — A421

International Year of the Child: 8d, Girl and pigeons. 20d, Mother and Children, painting by Iacovides.

1979, June 27 **Litho.** *Perf. 13x14*

1303	A421	5d multi	20	15
1304	A421	8d multi	24	15
1305	A421	20d multi	24	15

Philip II, Bust — A422

Purple Heron — A423

Designs: 8d, Golden wreath. 10d, Copper vessel. 14d, Golden casket (horiz.). 18d, Silver ewer. 20d, Golden quiver (detail). 30d, Gold and iron cuirass.

Perf. 13 ½x14, 14x13 ½

1979, Sept. 15 **Litho.**

1306	A422	6d multi	15	15
1307	A422	8d multi	15	15
1308	A422	10d multi	20	15
1309	A422	14d multi	22	15
1310	A422	18d multi	30	15
1311	A422	20d multi	32	18
1312	A422	30d multi	42	25
		Nos. 1306-1312 (7)	1.76	
		Set value		96

Archaeological finds from Vergina, Macedonia.

1979, Oct. 15

Protected Birds: 8d, Gull. 10d, Falcon (horiz.). 14d, Kingfisher (horiz.). 20d, Pelican. 25d, White-tailed sea eagle.

1313	A423	6d multi	15	15
1314	A423	8d multi	15	15
1315	A423	10d multi	22	15
1316	A423	14d multi	30	20
1317	A423	20d multi	32	22
1318	A423	25d multi	32	22
		Nos. 1313-1318 (6)	1.46	1.09

Council of Europe wildlife and natural habitat protection campaign.

Agricultural Bank — A424

St. Cosmas — A425

Basil the Great — A426

Balkan Countries, Magnifier A427

Aristotelis Valaoritis A428

Golfer A429

Hippocrates A430

Parliament in Session A431

Perf. 14x13 ½, 13 ½x14

1979, Nov. 24 **Litho.**

1319	A424	3d multi	15	15
1320	A425	4d multi	15	15
1321	A426	6d multi	15	15
1322	A427	8d multi	15	15
1323	A427	10d multi	18	15
1324	A428	12d multi	22	15
1325	A429	14d multi	18	15
1326	A430	18d multi	18	15
1327	A431	25d multi	32	18
		Nos. 1319-1327 (9)	1.68	
		Set value		1.00

Agricultural Bank of Greece, 50th anniversary; Cosmas the Aetolian (1714-1779), Greek missionary and martyr; Basil the Great (330-379), Archbishop of Caesarea; Balkanfila, Balkan Stamp Exhibition, Athens, Nov. 24-Dec. 2; Aristotelis Valaoritis (1824-1879), Greek poet; 27th World Golf Championship, Nov. 8-11; International Hippocratic Foundation of Cos; Greek Parliament, 104th anniversary.

Parnassus — A432

Tempe Valley — A433

Perf. 12 ½x13 ½, 13 ½x12 ½

1979, Dec. 15 **Litho.**

1328	A432	50 l shown	15	15
1329	A433	1d shown	15	15
1330	A432	2d Melos	15	15
1331	A432	4d VikosGorge	15	15
1332	A433	5d Missolonghi Salt Lake	15	15
1333	A432	6d Louros Aqueduct	15	15
1334	A432	7d Samothrace	15	15
1335	A433	8d Sithonia-Halkidiki	18	15
1336	A433	10d Samarias Gorge, vert	20	15
1337	A432	12d Siphnos	22	15
1338	A433	14d Kyme	25	15
1339	A432	18d Ios	32	15
1340	A432	20d Thasos	30	28
1341	A433	30d Paros	48	18
1342	A432	50d Cephalonia	55	35
		Set value	3.15	1.80

Byzantine Castle of Thessalonica A434

Designs: 4d, Aegosthena Castle (vert.). 8d, Cave of Perama Ioannina (vert.). 10d, Cave of Dyros, Mani (vert.). 14d, Arta Bridge. 20d, Kalogiros Bridge, Epirus.

Perf. 12½x14, 14x12½

1980, Mar. 15 **Litho.**

1343 A434	4d multi		15	15
1344 A434	6d multi		15	15
1345 A434	8d multi		20	15
1346 A434	10d multi		20	15
1347 A434	14d multi		20	15
1348 A434	20d multi		22	15
	Nos. 1343-1348 (6)		1.12	
	Set value			72

Gate of Galerius A435

1980, Mar. 15

1349 A435 8d multi 18 15

1st Hellenic Congress of Nephrology, Thessalonica, Mar. 20-22.

Solar System A436

Design: 10d, Temple of Hera, Aristarchus' theory and diagram.

1980, May 5 Litho. ***Perf. 13½x12½***

1350 A436	10d multi	22	18
1351 A436	20d multi	25	20

Aristarchus of Samos, first astronomer to discover heliocentric theory of universe, 2300th birth anniv.; Intl. Scientific Congress on Aristarchus, Samos, June 17-19.

Maria Callas (1923-1977), Opera Singer — A437

Europa: 8d, Georges Seferis (1900-1971), writer and diplomat.

1980, May 5

1352 A437	8d multi	18	15
1353 A437	14d multi	30	22

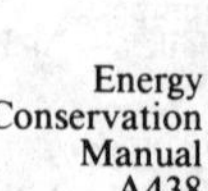

Energy Conservation Manual A438

Perf. 13½x12½, 12½x13½

1980, May 5

1354 A438	8d shown	20	18
1355 A438	20d Candle in bulb, vert.	28	24

Firemen — A439

St. Demetrius, Angel, Fresco — A440

Soldiers Marching through Crete — A441

Ancient Vase, Olives — A442

Federation Emblem, Newspaper A443

Constantinos Ikonomos A444

1980, July 14 **Litho.** ***Perf. 12½***

1356 A439	4d multi		15	15
1357 A440	6d multi		15	15
1358 A441	8d multi		18	15
1359 A442	10d multi		18	15
1360 A443	14d multi		20	18
1361 A444	20d multi		24	20
	Nos. 1356-1361 (6)		1.10	
	Set value			72

Fire Brigade, 50th anniv.; St. Demetrius, 1700th birth anniv.; Therissos Revolution, 75th anniv.; 2nd Intl. Olive Oil Year; Intl. Federation of Journalists, 15th Cong., Athens, May 12-16; Constantinos Ikonomos (1780-1857), writer and revolutionary.

Elis Gold Coin, Olympia Stadium, Olympic Rings A445

Olympic Rings and: 14d, Stadium and coin of Delphi 18d, Epidaurus theater, coin of Olympia 20d, Rhodes Stadium, Cos coin. 50d, Panathenean Stadium; 1st Olympic Games medal.

1980, Aug. 11 **Litho.** ***Perf. 13½x13***

1362 A445	8d multi	18	15
1363 A445	14d multi	30	15
1364 A445	18d multi	32	18
1365 A445	20d multi	35	20
1366 A445	50d multi	60	40
	Nos. 1362-1366 (5)	1.75	1.08

22nd Summer Olympic Games, Moscow, July 19-Aug. 3.

Asbestos A446

Perf. 13½x12½

1980, Sept. 22 **Litho.**

1367 A446	6d shown	16	15
1368 A446	8d Gypsum, vert.	20	15
1369 A446	10d Copper ore	24	15
1370 A446	14d Barite, vert.	30	15
1371 A446	18d Chromite	30	15
1372 A446	20d Mixed sulphides, vert.	28	15
1373 A446	30d Bauxite, vert.	28	15
	Nos. 1367-1373 (7)	1.76	1.05

Tow Truck — A447

Air Force Jet — A448

Airplane and Hangar — A449

Ships in Port A450

Students' Association Headquarters A451

1980, Oct. 31 **Litho.** ***Perf. 12½***

1374 A447	6d multi	20	15
1375 A448	8d multi	25	18
1376 A449	12d multi	25	15
1377 A450	20d multi	25	15
1378 A451	25d multi	25	16
	Nos. 1374-1378 (5)	1.20	79

Road Assistance Service of Automobile and Touring Club of Greece, 20th anniv.; Air Force, 50th anniv.; Flyers' Club of Thessaloniki, 50th anniv.; Piraeus Port Organization, 50th anniv.; Association for Macedonian Studies, 40th anniv.

Madonna and Child, by Theodore Poulakis — A452

Christmas 1980: He is Happy Thanks to You, by Theodore Poulakis. Nos. 1379-1381 se-tenant in continuous design in sheet of 12.

1980, Dec. 10 ***Perf. 13½***

1379 A452	6d multi	18	15
1380 A452	14d multi	24	18
1381 A452	20d multi	30	22

Vegetables for Export — A453

1981, Mar. 16 **Litho.** ***Perf. 12½***

1382 A453	9d shown	28	15
1383 A453	17d Fruits	35	22
1384 A453	20d Cotton	35	22
1385 A453	25d Marble	35	20

Europa Issue 1981

Kira Maria Folk Dance, Alexandria — A454

1981, May 4 **Litho.** ***Perf. 14x13***

1386 A454	12d shown	28	20
1387 A454	17d Cretan Sousta (dance)	35	25

Runner, Olympic Stadium, Kalogreza A455

1981, May 4

1388 A455	12d shown	30	24
1389 A455	17d Runners, Europe	30	24

13th European Athletic Championship, Athens, 1982.

Torso Showing Kidneys A456

Sky Diver and Airplanes A457

Views of Thessaly and Epirus — A458

Oil Rig and Map of Thassos Island — A460

Vase with Painted Eyes A459

Globes and Ancient Coin A461

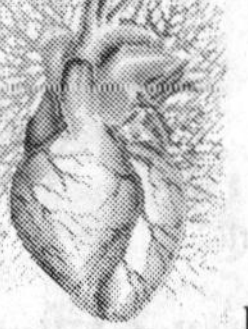

Heart and Vessels — A462

Perf. 13½x14, 14x13½

1981, May 22 **Litho.**

1390 A456 2d multi 15 15
1391 A457 3d multi 15 15
1392 A458 6d multi 20 15
1393 A459 9d multi 30 20
1394 A460 12d multi 32 20
1395 A461 21d multi 32 18
1396 A462 40d multi 40 22
Nos. 1390-1396 (7) 1.84 1.25

8th Intl. Nephrology Conf., Athens, June 7-12; Greek National Air Club, 50th anniv.; Intl. Historical Symposium, Volos, Sept. 27-30; Greek Ophthalmological Society, 50th anniv.; inauguration of oil production at Thassos Island; World Assoc. for Intl. Relations, Athens, 2nd anniv.; 15th Intl. Cardiovascular Surgery Conference, Athens, Sept. 6-10.

Cockles
A463

1981, June 30 **Litho.** *Perf. 14x13½*

1397 A463 4d shown 15 15
1398 A463 5d Parrot fish 15 15
1399 A463 12d Painted comber 30 20
1400 A463 15d Common dentex 35 25
1401 A463 17d Parnassius apollo 42 30
1402 A463 50d Colias hyale 1.50 1.00
Nos. 1397-1402 (6) 2.87 2.05

Bell Tower, Epirus
A464

Altar Gate, St. Paraskevi's Church
A465

Bell Towers and Wood Altar Gates (Iconostases): 9d, Pelion (horiz.). 12d, Church of Sts. Constantine and Helen, Epirus. 17d, St. Nicolas Church, Velvendos (horiz.). 30d, St. Jacob icon, Church Museum, Alexandroupolis. 40d, St. nicholas Church, Makrinitsa.

1981, Sept. 30 **Litho.**

1403 A464 4d multi 16 15
1404 A465 6d multi 18 15
1405 A465 9d multi 28 15
1406 A464 12d multi 38 18
1407 A465 17d multi 38 18
1408 A465 30d multi 38 18
1409 A465 40d multi 38 18
Nos. 1403-1409 (7) 2.14 1.17

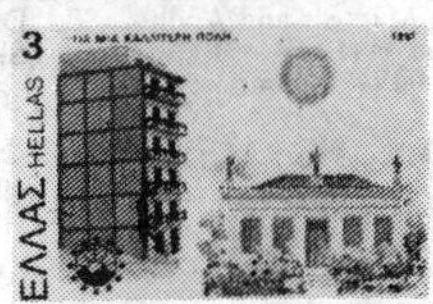

European Urban Renaissance Year — A466

St. Simeon, Archbishop of Thessalonica
A467

Promotion of Breastfeeding
A468

Gina Bachauer, Pianist, 5th Death Anniv.
A469

Constantine Broumidis, Artist, Death Centenary
A470

Sesquicentennial of Greek Banknotes — A471

Perf. 14x13½, 13½x14

1981, Nov. 20 **Litho.**

1410 A466 3d multi 18 15
1411 A467 9d multi 24 15
1412 A468 12d multi 30 15
1413 A469 17d multi 45 22
1414 A470 21d multi 50 22
1415 A471 50d multi 52 25
Nos. 1410-1415 (6) 2.19 1.14

Old Parliament Building, Athens
A472

Angelos Sikelianos (1884-1951), Poet
A473

Harilaos Tricoupis, Politician, Birth Sesquicentennial
A474

Aegean Islands Exhib., Rhodes, Athens
A475

Petralona Cave and Skull
A477

Olympic Airlines, 25th Anniv.
A476

Perf. 13½x12½, 12½x13½

1982, Mar. 15 **Litho.**

1416 A472 2d multi 15 15
1417 A473 9d multi 30 15
1418 A474 15d multi 42 20
1419 A475 21d multi 55 20
1420 A476 30d multi 55 22
1421 A477 50d multi 60 18
Nos. 1416-1421 (6) 2.57 1.10

Historical and Ethnological Society centennial (2d); 3rd European Anthropology Congress, Halkidiki, Sept. (50d).

Europa 1982 — A478

13th European Athletic Championships, Athens — A479

1982, May 10 **Litho.** *Perf. 13½x14*

1422 A478 21d Battle of Marathon, 490 BC 55 25
1423 A478 30d 1826 Revolution 75 38

Perf. 14x13½, 13½x14

1982, May 10

1424 A479 21d Pole vaulting, horiz. 32 20
1425 A479 25d Running 40 28
1426 A479 40d Sports, horiz. 75 55

Byzantine Book Illustrations
A480

Perf. 13½x12½, 12½x13½

1982, June 26 **Litho.**

1427 A480 4d Gospel book heading 15 15
1428 A480 6d Illuminated "E," vert. 15 15
1429 A480 12d Illuminated "T," vert. 30 18
1430 A480 15d Gospel reading canon table, vert. 38 24
1431 A480 80d Zoology book heading 1.50 90
Nos. 1427-1431 (5) 2.48 1.62

George Caraiskakis (1782-1827), Liberation Hero — A481

Amnesty Intl. — A482

Designs: 12d, Camp in Piraeus, by von Krazeisen. 50d, Meditating.

1982, Sept. 20 **Litho.** *Perf. 13x13½*

1432 A481 12d multi 28 16
1433 A481 50d multi 1.00 60

1982, Sept. 20 *Perf. 13x14*

1434 A482 15d Vigil 32 20
1435 A482 75d Prisoners 1.50 75

Natl. Resistance Movement, 1941-44 — A483

Designs: 1d, Demonstration of Mar. 24, 1942. 2d, Sacrifice of Inhabitants of Kalavrita, by S. Vasiliou. 5d, Resistance Fighters in Thrace, by A. Tassos. 9d, The Start of Resistance in Crete, by P. Gravalos. 12d, Partisan Men and Women, by P. Gravalos. 21d, Blowing Up a Bridge, by A. Tassos. 30d, Fighters at a Barricade, by G. Sikeliotis. 50d, The Fight in Northern Greece, by B. Katraki, 5d, 9d, 12d, 21d vert.

1982, Nov. 8 **Litho.** *Perf. 12½*

1436 A483 1d multi 15 15
1437 A483 2d multi 15 15
1438 A483 5d multi 15 15
1439 A483 9d multi 18 15
1440 A483 12d multi 24 15
1441 A483 21d multi 40 18
a. Souv. sheet. 5d, 9d, 12d, 21d 3.25 3.75
1442 A483 30d multi 60 22
1443 A483 50d multi 90 32
a. Souv. sheet. 1d, 2d, 30d, 50d 2.25 2.25
Nos. 1436-1443 (8) 2.77
Set value 1.10

Christmas 1982 — A484

Designs: Various Byzantine Nativity bas-reliefs, Byzantine Museum. Se-tenant.

1982, Dec. 6 **Litho.** *Perf. 13½x12½*

1444 A484 9d multi 20 15
1445 A484 21d multi 35 25

25th Anniv. of Intl. Maritime Org.
A485

Ship Figureheads. 15d, 18d, 25d, 40d vert.

Perf. 14x13½, 13½x14

1983, Mar. 14

1446 A485 11d Ares, Tsamados 30 15
1447 A485 15d Ares, Miaoulis 42 18
1448 A485 18d Female figure 45 20
1449 A485 25d Spetses, Boubou-lina 55 24
1450 A485 40d Epameinondas, K. Babas 55 24
1451 A485 50d Carteria 1.10 48
Nos. 1446-1451 (6) 3.37 1.49

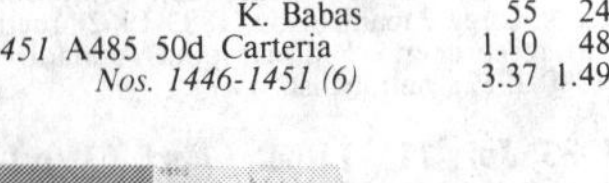

Postal Code Inauguration
A486

1983, Mar. 14 **Litho.** *Perf. 12½*

1452 A486 15d Cover, map 35 22
1453 A486 25d Hermes, post horn, vert. 42 28

Rowing
A487

1983, Apr. 28 *Perf. 14x13, 13x14*

1454 A487 15d shown 32 20
1455 A487 18d Water skiing, vert. 40 22
1456 A487 27d Wind surfing, vert. 65 35
1457 A487 50d Skiiers on chair-lift, vert. 1.10 45
1458 A487 80d Skiing 1.50 75
Nos. 1454-1458 (5) 3.97 1.97

Europa Issue 1983

Acropolis — A488

Archimedes and His Hydrostatic Principle — A489

Perf. 12½x13½, 13x13½

1983, Apr. 28 **Litho.**

1459 A488 25d multi			85	32
1460 A489 80d multi			2.25	75

Marinos Antypas (1873-1907), Farmers' Movement Leader — A490

Designs: 9d, Nicholas Plastiras (1883-1953), prime minister. 15d, George Papandreou (1888-1968), statesman. 20d, Constantine Cavafy (1863-1933), poet. 27d, Nikos Kazantzakis (1883-1957), writer. 32d, Manolis Calomiris (1883-1962), composer. 40d, George Papanicolaou (1883-1962), medical researcher. 50d, Despina Achladioti (1890-1982), nationalist.

1983, July 11 Litho. ***Perf. 13½x14***

1461 A490 6d multi	15	15
1462 A490 9d multi	18	15
1463 A490 15d multi	25	15
1464 A490 20d multi	38	16
1465 A490 27d multi	48	20
1466 A490 32d multi	75	24
1467 A490 40d multi	80	25
1468 A490 50d multi	95	30
Nos. 1461-1468 (8)	3.94	1.60

First Intl. Conference on the Works of Democritus (Philosopher, 460-370 BC), Xanthe, Oct. — A491

1983, Sept. 26 Litho. ***Perf. 13½x13***

1469 A491 50d Portrait bust	1.00	50

Polytechnic School Uprising, 1st Anniv. — A492

1983, Nov. 17 **Litho.** ***Perf. 13***

1470 A492 15d Poster	38	25
1471 A492 30d Flight from school	52	32

The Deification of Homer — A493

Homer Inspired Artworks: 3d, The Abduction of Helen by Paris, horiz. 4d, The Wooden Horse, horiz. 5d, Achilles Throwing Dice with Ajax, horiz. 6d, Achilles, vert. 10d, Hector Receiving His Arms from His Parents. 14d, Single-handed Battle Between Ajax and Hector, horiz. 15d, Priam Requesting the Body of Hector, horiz. 20d, The Blinding of Polyphemus, vert. 27d, Ulysses Escaping from Polyphemus' Cave, horiz. 30d, Ulysses Meeting with Nausica. 32d, Ulysses on the Island of the Sirens, horiz. 50d, Ulysses Slaying the Suitors, horiz. 75d, The Heroes of the Iliad, horiz. 100d, Homer.

1983, Dec. 19 **Litho.** ***Perf. 13***

1472 A493 2d multi	15	15
1473 A493 3d multi	15	15
1474 A493 4d multi	15	15
1475 A493 5d multi	15	15
1476 A493 6d multi	15	15
1477 A493 10d multi	16	15
1478 A493 14d multi	20	15
1479 A493 15d multi	24	15
1480 A493 20d multi	32	15
1481 A493 27d multi	40	15
1482 A493 30d multi	48	15
1483 A493 32d multi	52	15
1484 A493 50d multi	75	30
1485 A493 75d multi	1.25	45
1486 A493 100d multi	1.50	85
Nos. 1472-1486 (15)	6.57	
Set value		2.60

Horse's Head from Chariot of Seline — A494

Horsemen and Heroes A495

1984, Mar. 15 Litho. ***Perf. 14½x14***

1487 A494 14d shown	22	15
1488 A494 15d Dionysus	24	15
1489 A494 20d Hestia, Dione, Aphrodite	48	15
1490 A494 27d Ilissus	60	25
1491 A494 32d Lapith, centaur	80	30
Nos. 1487-1491 (5)	2.34	1.00

Souvenir Sheet

Perf. 13x13½

1492 Sheet of 4	3.35	1.50
a. A495 15d multi	40	20
b. A495 21d multi	55	32
c. A495 27d multi	70	40
d. A495 32d multi	80	48

Marble from the Parthenon. No. 1492 sold for 107d.

Europa (1959-84) A496

1984, Apr. 30 Litho. ***Perf. 14x13½***

1493 A496 15d multi	1.00	28
1494 A496 27d multi	1.50	50

Nos. 1493-1494 exist se-tenant.

1984 Summer Olympics — A497

Designs: 14d, Ancient Olympic stadium crypt. 15d, Athletes training. 20d, Broad jump, discus thrower. 32d, Athletes, diff. 80d, Stadium, Demetrius Bikelos, poet, organizer of 1896 Athens games. Nos. 1495-1499 exist se-tenant.

1984, Apr. 30 ***Perf. 13½x14***

1495 A497 14d multi	32	20
1496 A497 15d multi	35	25
1497 A497 20d multi	60	35
1498 A497 32d multi	90	50
1499 A497 80d multi	2.25	1.10
Nos. 1495-1499 (5)	4.42	2.40

Also issued in booklets.

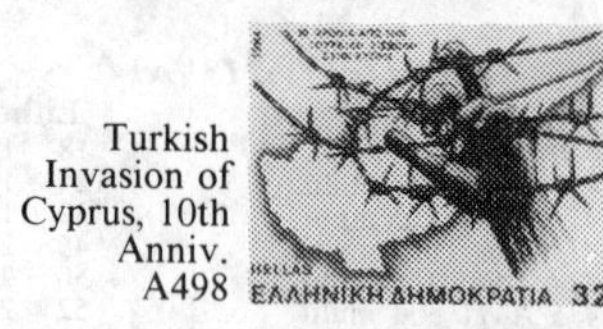

Turkish Invasion of Cyprus, 10th Anniv. A498

1984, July 10 **Litho.** ***Perf. 13***

1500 A498 20d Tank, map, vert.	40	15
1501 A498 32d Map, barbed wire	70	25

Exist se-tenant. Also issued in booklets.

Greek Railway Centenary A499

Perf. 13x13½, 13½x13

1984, July 20 **Litho.**

1502 A499 15d Pelion	24	15
1503 A499 20d Papadia Bridge, vert.	32	15
1504 A499 30d Piraeus-Peloponnese	70	22
1505 A499 50d Cogwheel Calavryta, vert.	1.25	35

Sesquicentenary of Athens as Capitol City — A500

Designs: 15d, 4d silver coin, 5th cent. BC, city plan (vert.). 100d, Views of ancient and modern Athens.

Perf. 13½x13, 13x13½

1984, Oct. 12 **Litho.**

1506 A500 15d multi	65	15
1507 A500 100d multi	1.65	50

10th Anniv. of Democratic Govt. — A501

1984, Oct. 12 Litho. ***Perf. 13x13½***

1508 A501 95d "10" on flag	2.00	50

Christmas 1984 — A502

Scenes from 18th cent. icon by Athanasios Tountas.

1984, Dec. 6 **Litho.** ***Perf. 13½x13***

1509 A502 14d Annunciation	25	15
1510 A502 20d Nativity	35	18
1511 A502 25d Presentation in the Temple	55	22
1512 A502 32d Baptism of Christ	1.00	30

Nos. 1509-1512 exist se-tenant. Also issued in booklets.

Runner A503

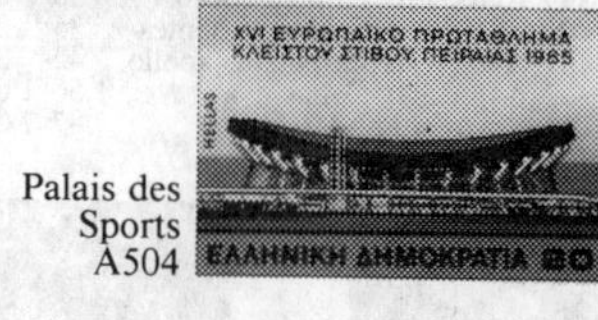

Palais des Sports A504

Perf. 13, 13x13½ (#1515)

1985, Mar. 1 **Litho.**

1513 A503 12d shown	22	15
1514 A503 15d Shot put	28	15
1515 A504 20d shown	32	18
1516 A503 25d Hurdles	55	20
1517 A503 80d Women's high jump	1.65	75
Nos. 1513-1517 (5)	3.02	1.43

European Indoor Athletics Championships, Palais des Sports, New Phaleron.

Europa 1985 — A505

CEPT emblem and: 27d, Musical contest between Marsyas and Apollo. 80d, Dimitris Mitropoulos (1896-1960) and Nikos Skalkottas (1904-1949), composers.

1985, Apr. 29 ***Perf. 14x14½***

1518 A505 27d multi	40	30
1519 A505 80d multi	1.40	1.25

Exist se-tenant. Also issued in booklets.

Melos Catacombs, A.D. 2nd Cent., Trypete A506

1985, Apr. 29 ***Perf. 14½x14***

1520 A506 15d Niche	22	15
1521 A506 20d Altar, Central Gallery	55	20
1522 A506 100d Catacombs	1.75	65

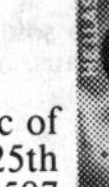
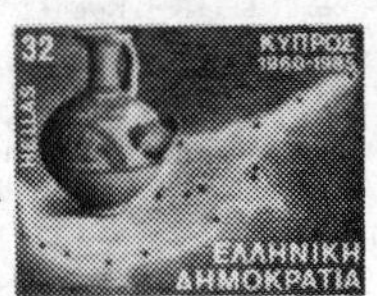

Republic of Cyprus, 25th Anniv. — A507

1985, June 24 *Perf. 13x13½*

1523 A507 32d Map of Cyprus, urn 70 30

Coin of King Cassander (315 B.C.), Personification of Salonika, Galerius Era Bas-relief
A508

Sts. Demetrius and Methodius, Mosaics — A509

Designs: 15d, Emperor sacrificing at Altar, Arch of Galerius, Roman era. 20d, Eastern walls of Salonika, Byzantine era. 32d, Houses in the Upper City. 50d, Liberation of Salonika by the Greek Army, 1912. 80d, German occupation, 1941-44, the Old Mosque. 95d, View of city, Trade Fair grounds, Aristotelian University tower.

Perf. 14½x14 (A508), 14x14½ (A509)

1985, June 24

1524 A508 1d multi 18 15
1525 A509 5d multi 45 15
1526 A508 15d multi 50 15
1527 A508 20d multi 55 18
1528 A508 32d multi 60 20
1529 A508 50d multi 80 22
1530 A508 80d multi 1.10 38
1531 A509 95d multi 1.50 45
Nos. 1524-1531 (8) 5.68 1.88

Salonika City, 2300th anniv. Aristotelian University, Trade Fair, 60th annivs.

Athenian Cultural Heritage — A510

Ancient art and architecture: 15d, Democracy Crowning the City, bas-relief from a column, Ancient Agora of Athens, vert. 20d, Mosaic pavement of tritons, nereids, dolphins, etc., Roman baths at Hieratus, Isthmia, A.D. 2nd cent. 32d, Angel, fresco, Grotto of Pentheli, A.D. 13th cent., vert. 80d, Capodistrian University, Athens.

1985, Oct. 7 *Perf. 13½x13, 13x13½*

1532 A510 15d multi 22 15
1533 A510 20d multi 28 15
1534 A510 32d multi 45 25
1535 A510 80d multi 1.10 65

Intl. Youth Year
A511

UN 40th Anniv.
A512

Design: No. 1540, Girl crowned with flowers, Stadium of Peace and Friendship, Athens.

1985, Oct. 7 *Perf. 14x14½*

1536 A511 15d Children, olive wreath 28 15
1537 A511 25d Children, doves 50 15
1538 A512 27d UN General Assembly, dove 55 18
1539 A512 100d UN building, emblem 2.00 60

Souvenir Sheet

1985, Nov. 22 *Perf. 14x13 on 3 sides*

1540 A511 100d multi 1.65 50

No. 1540 contains one 43x47mm stamp.

Pontic Hellenism Cultural Reformation
A513

Perf. 14x12½, 12½x14

1985, Dec. 9 **Litho.**

1541 A513 12d Folk dance 18 15
1542 A513 15d Our Lady Soumela Monastery 24 15
1543 A513 27d Folk costumes, vert. 50 16
1544 A513 32d Trapezus High School 60 20
1545 A513 80d Sinope Castle 1.50 50
Nos. 1541-1545 (5) 3.02 1.16

Greek Gods — A514

1986, Feb. 17 **Litho.** *Perf. 13 Horiz.*

1546 A514 5d Hestia 15 15
1547 A514 18d Hermes 22 15
1548 A514 27d Aphrodite 35 20
1549 A514 32d Ares 38 22
1550 A514 35d Athena 42 22
1551 A514 40d Hephaestus 45 25
1552 A514 50d Artemis 60 25
1553 A514 110d Apollo 1.25 60
1554 A514 150d Demeter 1.90 1.00
1555 A514 200d Poseidon 2.50 1.25
1556 A514 300d Hera 3.75 2.00
1557 A514 500d Zeus 6.25 3.25
Nos. 1546-1557 (12) 18.22 9.54

Each denomination sold in bklts. containing 20 panes of 5 stamps. Also issued perf. 13.

Youth of Antikythera
A515

Soccer Players
A517

Diadoumenos, by Polycleitus
A516

Wrestlers, Hellenic Era Statue — A518

Cyclists — A520

Volleyball Players — A519

Commemorative Design for 1st Modern Olympic Games — A521

1986, Mar. 3 *Perf. 12*

1558 A515 18d multi 35 18
1559 A516 27d multi 50 22
1560 A517 32d multi 55 25
1561 A518 35d multi 65 25
1562 A519 40d multi 75 30
1563 A520 50d multi 95 38
1564 A521 110d multi 2.25 90
Nos. 1558-1564 (7) 6.00 2.48

First World Junior Athletic Championships. Pan-European Junior Soccer Championships. Pan-European Free-style and Greco-Roman Wrestling Championships. Men's World Volleyball Championships. Sixth International Round-Europe Cycling Meet. Modern Olympic Games, 90th anniv.

European Traffic Safety Year — A522

1986, Mar. 3 *Perf. 12½x14*

1565 A522 18d Seat belts 30 15
1566 A522 27d Motorcycle 45 18
1567 A522 110d Speed limits 1.75 70

Prevention of Forest Fires
A523

1986, Apr. 23 **Litho.** *Perf. 14x13½*

1568 A523 35d shown 75 30
1569 A523 110d Prespa Lakes wetlands 1.75 70
a. Bklt. pane. 2 each 35d, 110d *22.50*

Europa. Nos. 1568-1569 printed se-tenant.

New Postal Services
A524

May Day Strike, Chicago, Cent.
A525

Perf. 13½x14, 14x13½

1986, Apr. 23

1570 A524 18d Intelpost 50 20
1571 A524 110d Express mail, horiz. 1.75 70

1986, Apr. 23 *Perf. 12½*

1572 A525 40d Strikers, monument 65 30

Eleutherios K. Venizelos (1864-1936), Premier
A526

Designs: 18d, Venizelos, Ministers taking oath of office, 1917. 110d, Old Hania Harbor, Crete.

1986, June 30 **Litho.** *Perf. 14x12½*

1573 A526 18d multi 30 15
1574 A526 110d multi 1.90 70

6th Intl. Cretological Conference, Crete.

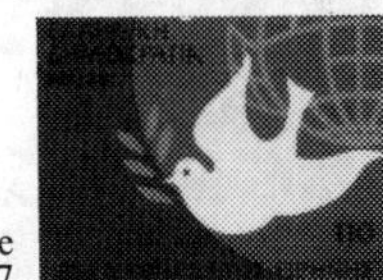

Intl. Peace Year — A527

1986, Oct. 6 **Litho.** *Perf. 12½*

1575 A527 18d Dove, sun, vert. 28 15
1576 A527 35d Flags, dove, vert. 55 22
1577 A527 110d World cage, dove 1.75 70

Christmas
A528

Aesop's Fables
A529

Religious art in the Benaki Museum: 22d, Madonna and Child Enthroned, triptych center panel, 15th cent. 46d, Adoration of the Magi, 15th cent. 130d, Christ Enthroned with St. John the Evangelist, triptych panel.

1986, Dec. 1 **Litho.** *Perf. 13½x14*

1578 A528 22d multi 30 15
1579 A528 46d multi 65 25
1580 A528 130d multi 1.80 70

Size of No. 1579: 27x35mm.

Perf. 12½ Horiz.

1987, Mar. 5 **Litho.**

1581 A529 2d Fox and the Grapes 15 15
1582 A529 5d North Wind and the Sun 15 15
1583 A529 10d Stag and the Lion 15 15
1584 A529 22d Zeus and the Snake 32 15
1585 A529 32d Crow and the Fox 48 20

1586 A529 40d Woodcutter and Hermes 60 24
1587 A529 46d Ass in a Lion's Skin 68 28
1588 A529 130d Tortoise and the Hare 2.00 80
Nos. 1581-1588 (8) 4.53
Set value 1.85

Each denomination sold in booklets containing 20 panes of 5 stamps. Also issued perf. 12½x13.

Europa 1987 — A530

Modern art: 40d, Composition, by Achilleas Apergis. 130d, Delphic Light, by Gerassimos Sklavos.

1987, May 4 Litho. *Perf. 12½*
1589 A530 40d multi 68 35
1590 A530 130d multi 2.15 1.10
a. Bklt. pane, 2 each #1589-1590 6.50

Printed se-tenant.

25th European Basketball Championships, Stadium of Peace and Friendship — A531

A532

1987, May 4 *Perf. 13½x14, 12½*
1591 A531 22d Jump shot, stadium, vert. 38 15
1592 A532 25d Emblem, spectators 42 18
1593 A531 130d Two players, vert. 2.15 85

Higher Education Sesquicentenary — A533

Perf. 14x13½, 13½x14
1987, May 4 Litho.
1594 A533 3d Students, tapestry 15 15
1595 A533 23d Owl, medallion 40 16
1596 A533 40d Institute, symbols of science 70 28
1597 A533 60d Institute, students 1.00 40

Capodistrias University of Athens (Nos. 1594-1595); The Natl. Metsovio Polytechnic Institute (Nos. 1596-1597). #1596-1597 vert.

Souvenir Sheet

25th European Men's Basketball Championships A534

1987, June 3 Litho. *Perf. 13x14*
1598 Sheet of 3 2.75 2.75
a. A534 40d Jump ball 52 52
b. A534 60d Layup 75 75
c. A534 100d Dunk shot 1.25 1.25

Architecture A535

Designs: 2d, Ionic and Corinthian capitals, Archaic Era. 26d, Doric capital, the Parthenon (detail). 40d, Ionic capital and the Erechteum. 60d, Corinthian capital and the Tholos in Epidaurus.

1987, July 1 Litho. *Perf. 13½x12½*
1599 A535 2d multi 15 15
1600 A535 26d multi 38 15
1601 A535 40d multi 55 25
1602 A535 60d multi 85 38

Engraving by Yiannis Kephalinos — A536

Panteios School A537

Perf. 12½x14, 14x12½
1987, Oct. 1 Litho.
1603 A536 26d multi 38 15
1604 A537 60d multi 85 38

School of Fine Arts, 150th anniv. (26d), and Panteios School of Political Science, 60th anniv. (60d).

Greek Natl. Team, Winner, 25th European Men's Basketball Championship A538

1987, Oct. 1 *Perf. 13x14*
1605 A538 40d multi 60 25

Traditional and Modern Greek Theater — A539

Designs: 2d, Eleni Papadaki in Hecuba, by Euripides, and outdoor theater, Philippi. 4d, Christopher Nezer in The Wasps, by Aristophane, and outdoor theater, Dodona. 7d, Emilios Veakis in Oedipus Rex and theater, Delphi. 26d, Marika Cotopouli in The Shepherdess's Love, by Dimitris Koromilas. 40d, Katina Paxinou in Abraham's Sacrifice, by Vitzentzos Cornaros. 50d, Kyveli in Countess Valeraina's Secret, by Gregory Xenopoulos. 60d, Director Carolos Koun, stage setting. 100d, Dimitris Rontiris teaching ancient dance, Greek National Theater.

1987, Dec. 2 Litho. *Perf. 14x13½*
1606 A539 2d multi 15 15
1607 A539 4d multi 15 15
1608 A539 7d multi 15 15
1609 A539 26d multi 40 16
1610 A539 40d multi 60 25
1611 A539 50d multi 75 35
1612 A539 60d multi 90 45
1613 A539 100d multi 1.50 75
Nos. 1606-1613 (8) 4.60
Set value 2.10

Christmas — A540

1987, Dec. 2 *Perf. 13x12½*
1614 A540 26d Angel facing right 40 16
1615 A540 26d Angel facing left 40 16
a. Bklt. pane of 10, 5 each Nos. 1614-1615 4.00

Nos. 1614-1615 printed se-tenant.

Marine Life — A541

1988, Mar. 2 *Perf. 12½ Vert.*
1616 A541 30d Codonellina 50 20
1617 A541 40d Diaperoecia major 65 28
1618 A541 50d Artemia 82 38
1619 A541 60d Posidonia oceanica 1.00 45
1620 A541 100d Padina pavonica 1.65 80
Nos. 1616-1620 (5) 4.62 2.11

Each denomination sold in bklts. containing 20 panes of 5 stamps. Also issued perf. 14x12½ in sheets of 50.

Europa 1988 — A542

Communication and transport: 60d, Telecommunications satellite, telephone and facsimile machine. 150d, Passenger trains.

1988, May 6 Litho. *Perf. 12½*
1621 A542 60d multi 1.00 45
1622 A542 150d multi 2.50 1.10
a. Bklt. pane of 4, 2 each Nos. 1621-1622, perf. 14 vert. 7.00

Se-tenant. Single stamps also issued in strips of 5, perf. 14 vert.

1988 Olympics A543

Designs: 4d, Ancient Olympia and Temple of Zeus. 20d, Javelin thrower and and ancient Olympians in open-air gymnasium. 30d, Centenary emblem of the modern Games (cent. in 1996). 60d, Wrestlers, runners and other ancient athletes in training. 170d, Modern torch-bearer.

1988, May 6 *Perf. 14x12*
1623 A543 4d multi 15 15
1624 A543 20d multi 32 15
1625 A543 30d multi 50 20
1626 A543 60d multi 1.00 45
1627 A543 170d multi 2.80 1.40
a. Strip of 5, Nos. 1623-1627 4.75
b. Bklt. pane of 5, perf. 12½ vert. 4.75
Nos. 1623-1627 (5) 4.77 2.35

Each denomination also sold in bklts. containing 20 panes of 5 stamps, perf. 12½ vert. See Korea No. B53.

Waterfalls A544

20th Pan-European Postal Trade Unions Congress A545

Designs: 10d, Catarractis village falls at the foot of the Tzoumerca Mountain Range. 60d, Edessa Waterfalls. 100d, Edessaios River cascades.

1988, July 4 Litho. *Perf. 12½x14*
1628 A544 10d multi 16 15
1629 A544 60d multi 95 40
1630 A544 100d multi 1.60 75

Each denomination also sold in bklts. containing 20 panes of 5 stamps, perf. 14 vert.

1988, July 4 *Perf. 13x12½*
1631 A545 60d multi 95 40

No. 1631 also sold in bklts. containing 20 panes of 5 stamps, perf. 14 vert.

Premier Eleutherios Venizelos (1864-1936), Natl. Flag and Map — A546

Designs: 70d, Lady liberty, flag and map.

1988, Oct. 7 Litho. *Perf. 12½x13*
1632 A546 30d shown 45 18
1633 A546 70d multi 1.05 50

Union of Crete with Greece and liberation of Epirus and Macedonia from Turkish rule, 75th annivs.

Each denomination also sold in bklts. containing 20 panes of 5 stamps, perf. 14 horiz.

Departmental Seats — A547

Designs: 2d, Mytilene-Lesbos Harbor, painting by Theophilos. 3d, Alexandroupolis lighthouse. 4d, St. Nicholas bell tower, Kozane. 5d, Labor Center, Hermoupolis. 7d, Sparta Town Hall. 8d, Pegasus of Leukas. 10d, Castle of the Knights, Rhodes. 20d, The Acropolis, Athens. 25d, Kavalla aqueduct. 30d, Statue of Athanasios Diakos and castle, Lamia. 50d, Preveza cathedral bell tower and Venetian clock. 60d, Corfu promenade. 70d, Harbor view of Hagios Nicolaos. 100d, Poligiros public fountains. 200d, Church of the Apostle Paul, Corinth.

1988, Oct. 7 *Perf. 13 Vert. or Horiz.*
1634 A547 2d multi 15 15
1635 A547 3d multi 15 15
1636 A547 4d multi 15 15
1637 A547 5d multi 15 15
1638 A547 7d multi 15 15
1639 A547 8d multi 15 15
1640 A547 10d multi 15 15
1641 A547 20d multi 30 15
a. Bklt. pane of 16 (4 each 3d, 5d, 10d, 20d) 2.35
1642 A547 25d multi 38 16
1643 A547 30d multi 45 20
1644 A547 50d multi 75 30
1645 A547 60d multi 90 38
1646 A547 70d multi 1.05 50

1647 A547 100d multi 1.50 65
1648 A547 200d multi 3.00 1.50
Nos. 1634-1648 (15) 9.38
Set value 4.00

3d-5d, 10d-20d, 30d-50d vert. Nos. 1634-1648 issued in panes of 20, perf. 13 vert. or horiz. and in sheets, perf. 13.

Council of Europe, Rhodes, Dec. 2-3
A548

Christmas
A549

Designs: 60d, Map and Castle of the Knights, Rhodes. 100d, Head of Helios, Rhodian 2nd-3rd cent. B.C. coin, and flags.

1988, Dec. 2 Litho. *Perf. 12½*
1649 A548 60d multi 90 38
1650 A548 100d multi 1.50 65

Nos. 1649-1650 also issued in bklt. panes of 5, perf. 14 horiz.

1988, Dec. 2 *Perf. 12½ on 3 Sides*

Paintings: 30d, *Adoration of the Magi*, by El Greco. 70d, *The Annunciation*, by Costas Parthenis, horiz.

1651 A549 30d multi 45 20
a. Bklt. pane of 10 4.50

Perf. 14

1652 A549 70d multi 1.05 50

No. 1651 issued in booklets. No. 1652 also issued in bklts. containing 20 panes of 5 stamps, perf. 14 vert.

Modern Olympics, Cent. (in 1996) — A550

Athens '96 emblem and: 30d, High jumper and ancient Olympia. 60d, Wrestlers and view of Delphi. 70d, Swimmers and The Acropolis, Athens. 170d, Sports complex.

Perf. 13½ Vert.
1989, Mar. 17 Litho.
1653 A550 30d multi 42 18
1654 A550 60d multi 85 36
1655 A550 70d multi 1.00 45
1656 A550 170d multi 2.45 1.25
a. Strip of 4, Nos. 1653-1656, perf. 14x13½ 4.75
b. Bklt. pane of 4, #1653-1656 4.75

Europa 1989 — A551

Children's toys.

1989, May 22 Litho. *Perf. 12½x14*
1657 A551 60d Whistling bird 85 36
1658 A551 170d Butterfly 2.45 1.25
a. Bklt. pane, 2 each #1657-1658 6.60

Printed se-tenant in sheets of 16. Nos. 1657-1658 also issued separately in booklets containing 20 panes of 5 stamps, perf. 14 vert.

Anniversaries — A552

1989, May 22 *Perf. 14x13½*
1659 A552 30d Flags 38 16
1660 A552 50d Flag, La Liberte 65 25
1661 A552 60d Flag, ballot box 75 30
1662 A552 70d Coin, emblem 90 38
1663 A552 200d Flag, "40" 2.50 1.25
Nos. 1659-1663 (5) 5.18 2.34

Six-nation Initiative for Peace and Disarmament, 5th anniv. (30d); French revolution, bicent. (50d); European Parliament Elections in Greece, 10th anniv. (60d); Interparliamentary Union, cent. (70d); and Council of Europe, 40th anniv. (200d).

Nos. 1659-1663 also issued in bklts. containing 20 panes of 5 stamps, perf. 13½ horiz.

A553

BALKANFILA XII, Sept. 30-Oct. 8, Salonica — A554

1989, Sept. 25 Litho. *Perf. 14x12½*
1664 A553 60d shown 72 28
1665 A553 70d Eye, magnifying glass 82 35

Souvenir Sheet
Perf. 14x13

1666 A554 200d shown 2.40 2.40

Wildflowers
A555

1989, Dec. 8 Litho. *Perf. 14x12½*
1667 A555 8d Wild rose 15 15
1668 A555 10d Common myrtle 15 15
1669 A555 20d Field poppy 24 15
1670 A555 30d Anemone 35 15
1671 A555 60d Dandelion, chicory 72 28
1672 A555 70d Mallow 82 35
1673 A555 200d Thistle 2.35 1.10
Nos. 1667-1673 (7) 4.78
Set value 2.00

Ursus arctos
A556

Rare and endangered species.

1990, Mar. 16 Litho. *Perf. 14x12½*
1674 A556 40d shown 50 22
1675 A556 70d *Caretta caretta* 90 38
1676 A556 90d *Monachus monachus* 1.15 45
1677 A556 100d *Lynx lynx* 1.25 50

Europa
1990 — A557

Post offices: 70d, Old Central P.O. interior. 210d, Contemporary p.o. exterior.

Perf. 13½x12½
1990, May 11 Litho.
1678 A557 70d multicolored 85 35
1679 A557 210d multicolored 2.55 1.00
a. Bklt. pane, 2 each #1678-1679 6.80
b. Pair, #1678-1679 3.40 1.50

Natl. Reconcilation
A558

Political Reformers
A559

1990, May 11 *Perf. 12½x13½*
1680 A558 40d Flag, handshake 50 20
1681 A558 70d Dove, ribbon 85 35
1682 A558 100d Map, gift of flowers 1.20 48

1990, May 11
1683 A559 40d Gregoris Lambrakis (1912-63) 50 20
1684 A559 40d Pavlos Bakoyiannis (1935-89) 50 20

Trikala Fort and Clock Tower — A560

Department Seats: 2d, Karditsa, the commercial-animal fair. 8d, Veria, street with traditional architecture. 10d, Missolonghi, Central Monument of Fallen Heroes in the Exodus. 15d, Chios, view. 20d, Tripoli, street with neoclassical architecture. 25d, Volos, view with town hall, woodcut by A. Tassou. 40d, Kalamata, neoclassical town hall. 50d, Pirgos, central marketplace. 70d, Yannena, view of lake and island. 80d, Rethymnon, sculpture at the port. 90d, Argostoli, view before earthquake. 100d, Nauplio, Bourtzi with Palamidi in the background. 200d, Patras, central lighthouse. 250d, Florina, street with neoclassical architecture. Nos. 1685, 1687, 1695, 1698 vert.

Perf. 13½ Horiz. or Vert.
1990, June 20 Litho.
1685 A560 2d multicolored 15 15
1686 A560 5d multicolored 15 15
1687 A560 8d multicolored 15 15
1688 A560 10d multicolored 15 15
1689 A560 15d multicolored 18 15
1690 A560 20d multicolored 24 15
1691 A560 25d multicolored 30 15
1692 A560 40d multicolored 48 20
1693 A560 50d multicolored 60 24
1694 A560 70d multicolored 85 32
1695 A560 80d multicolored 95 38
1696 A560 90d multicolored 1.10 45
1697 A560 100d multicolored 1.20 48
1698 A560 200d multicolored 2.40 95
1699 A560 250d multicolored 3.00 1.20
Nos. 1685-1699 (15) 11.90 5.27

Each denomination sold in booklets containing 20 panes of 5 stamps. Also issued perf. 13x12, 12x13.

1996 Summer Olympics — A561

1990, July 13 *Perf. 12½x13½*
1700 A561 20d Sailing 24 15
1701 A561 50d Wrestling 60 24
1702 A561 80d Sprinting 95 38
1703 A561 100d Basketball 1.20 48
1704 A561 250d Soccer 3.00 1.20
a. Strip of 5, #1700-1704 6.00
Nos. 1700-1704 (5) 5.99 2.45

Athens, proposed site for centennial Summer Olympic Games. Exists perf. 13½ vert.

Heinrich Schliemann (1822-1890), Archaeologist — A562

1990, Oct. 11 Litho. *Perf. 14x13½*
1705 A562 80d multicolored 95 38

See Germany No. 1615.

Greco-Italian War, 50th Anniv. — A563

1990, Oct. 11 *Perf. 12½*
1706 A563 50d Woman knitting 60 20
1707 A563 80d Virgin Mary, soldier 95 38
1708 A563 100d Women volunteers 1.25 42

Souvenir Sheet

Stamp Day — A564

1990, Dec. 14 Litho. *Perf. 14x13*
1709 A564 300d multicolored 4.00 4.00

The Muses — A565

Designs: 50d, Calliope, Euterpe, Erato. 80d, Terpsichore, Polyhymnia, Melpomene. 250d, Thalia, Clio, Urania.

1991, Mar. 11 Litho. *Perf. 12½*
1710 A565 50d multicolored 60 20
1711 A565 80d multicolored 95 38
1712 A565 250d multicolored 3.00 1.20

Battle of Crete by Ioannis Anousakis — A566

Design: 300d, Map, flags of participating allied armies.

Perf. 12½x13½

1991, May 20			**Litho.**	
1713	A566	60d multicolored	75	25

Size: 32x24mm

Perf. 12½

1714	A566	300d multicolored	3.60	1.20

Battle of Crete, 50th anniv.

Europa A567

Designs: 80d, Icarus pushing modern satellite. 300d, Chariot of the Sun.

1991, May 20			*Perf. 12½*	
1715	A567	80d multicolored	95	38
1716	A567	300d multicolored	3.60	1.20
a.		Pair, #1715-1716	4.60	1.60
b.		Bklt. pane, 2 ea. #1715-1716	9.20	3.20

No. 1716a printed in continuous design.

1991 Mediterranean Games, Athens — A568

1991, June 25		**Litho.**	*Perf. 13½x14*	
1717	A568	10d Swimming	15	15
1718	A568	60d Basketball	75	25
1719	A568	90d Gymnastics	1.10	38
1720	A568	130d Weight lifting	1.60	52
1721	A568	300d Hammer throw	3.60	1.20
		Nos. 1717-1721 (5)	7.20	2.50

Athenian Democracy, 2500th Anniv. — A569

1991, Sept. 20		**Litho.**	*Perf. 13½x14*	
1722	A569	100d multicolored	1.05	35

Souvenir Sheet

Greek Presidency of CEPT — A570

Europe with Zeus metmorphosed into a bull, from Attic vase, c. 500 B.C.

1991, Sept. 20			*Perf. 14x13*	
1723	A570	300d multicolored	3.10	1.05

Greek Membership in EEC, 10th Anniv. — A571

Designs: 50d, Pres. Konstantin Karamanlis signing Treaty of Greek entrance into EEC. 80d, Map showing EEC members, Pres. Karamanlis.

1991, Dec. 9		**Litho.**	*Perf. 13x14*	
1724	A571	50d multicolored	55	18
1725	A571	80d multicolored	90	30

80 16th Winter Olympics, Albertville — A572

1991, Dec. 9			*Perf. 12½x13½*	
1726	A572	80d Speed skaters	90	30
1727	A572	300d Slalom skier	3.30	1.10
a.		Pair, #1726-1727	4.20	1.40

Year Sets

Year set values are determined from price lists offering complete sets for each year. Not all dealers offer these sets. Values may be lower or higher than the total value of the individual stamps. Contents of the sets being offered may differ (complete booklets by some, singles from the booklets by others).

1959	#632-665	46.50
1960	#666-689	20.00
1961	#690-727	45.00
1962	#728-742	10.90
1963	#743-777	24.00
1964	#778-812	14.25
1965	#813-839	6.40
1966	#840-878	10.00
1967	#879-908	7.50
1968	#909-938	12.00
1969	#939-965	10.25
1970	#966-1004	33.75
1971	#1005-1030	10.50
1972	#1031-1064	13.00
1973	#1065-1106	12.75
1974	#1107-1135	4.50
1975	#1136-1169	6.50
1976	#1170-1198	8.25
1977	#1199-1242	5.25
1978	#1243-1287	7.50
1979	#1288-1342	11.50
1980	#1343-1381	8.00
1981	#1382-1415	10.75
1982	#1416-1445	17.25
1983	#1446-1486	19.75
1984	#1487-1512	20.00
1985	#1513-1545	20.00
1986	#1546-1580	32.50
1987	#1581-1615	21.00
1988	#1616-1652	35.00
1989	#1653-1673	25.00
1990	#1674-1709	35.00

SEMI-POSTAL STAMPS

Catalogue values for unused stamps in this section are for Never Hinged items.

Nos. 440-444 Surcharged in Blue

ΒΟΜΒΑΡΔΙΣΜΟΣ
ΠΕΙΡΑΙΩΣ
11-1-1944
ΔΡ. 100.000

1944		**Wmk. 252**	*Perf. 12½*	
B1	A106	100,000d on 15d	90	60
B2	A107	100,000d on 25d	90	60
B3	A108	100,000d on 50d	90	60
B4	A109	100,000d on 75d	90	60
B5	A110	100,000d on 100d	90	60
		Nos. B1-B5,CB1-CB5 (10)	7.75	6.00

The proceeds aided victims of the Piraeus bombing, Jan. 11, 1944. The exceptionally high face value discouraged the use of these stamps.

Nos. 437 to 441 Surcharged in Blue

ΠΑΙΔΙΚΑΙ ΕΞΟΧΑΙ
ΔΡΧ.
50,000+450,000

1944, July 20				
B11	A103	50,000d + 450,000d on 2d	70	50
B12	A104	50,000d + 450,000d on 5d	70	50
B13	A105	50,000d + 450,000d on 10d	70	50
B14	A106	50,000d + 450,000d on 15d	70	50
a.		Pair, one without surcharge	50.00	
B15	A107	50,000d + 450,000d on 25d	70	50
		Nos. B11-B15,CB6-CB10 (10)	7.75	5.00

The surtax aided children's camps.

AIR POST STAMPS

Italy-Greece-Turkey-Rhodes Service

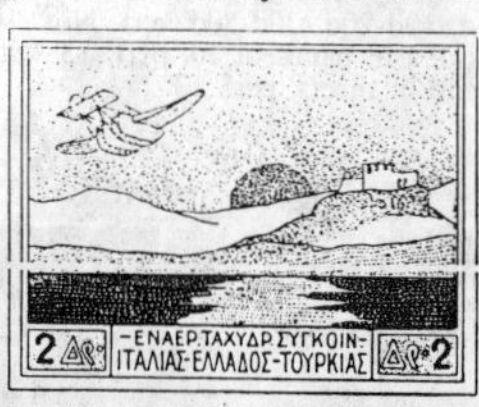

Flying Boat off Phaleron Bay — AP1

Flying Boat over Acropolis — AP2

Flying Boat over Map of Southern Europe — AP3

Flying Boat Seen through Colonnade — AP4

Perf. 11½

1926, Oct. 20		**Unwmk.**	**Litho.**	
C1	AP1	2d multi	40	25
a.		Horiz. pair, imperf. vert.	450.00	
C2	AP2	3d multi	4.50	3.50
C3	AP3	5d multi	40	50
C4	AP4	10d multi	4.50	3.75

Graf Zeppelin Issue

Zeppelin over Acropolis AP5

1933, May 2			*Perf. 13½x12½*	
C5	AP5	30d rose red	7.00	7.00
C6	AP5	100d deep blue	35.00	35.00
C7	AP5	120d dark brown	35.00	35.00

Propeller and Pilot's Head AP6

Temple of Apollo, Corinth AP7

Plane over Hermoupolis, Syros — AP8

Allegory of Flight
AP9 AP12

Map of Italy-Greece-Turkey-Rhodes Airmail Route — AP10

Head of Hermes and Airplane — AP11

1933, Oct. 10 **Engr.** ***Perf. 12***

C8	AP6	50 l grn & org	16	15
C9	AP7	1d bl & brn org	25	22
C10	AP8	3d dk vio & org brn	38	42
C11	AP9	5d brn org & dk bl	3.75	3.25
C12	AP10	10d dp red & blk	1.25	1.10
C13	AP11	20d blk & grn	3.75	2.50
C14	AP12	50d dp brn & dp bl	37.50	42.50
		Nos. C8-C14 (7)	47.04	50.14

By error the 1d stamp is inscribed in the plural "Draxmai" instead of the singular "Draxmh." This stamp exists bisected, used as a 50 lepta denomination.

All values of this set exist imperforate but were not regularly issued.

For General Air Post Service

Airplane over Map of Greece — AP13

Airplane over Map of Icarian Sea — AP14

Airplane over Acropolis AP15

Perf. 13x13½, 13x12½, 13½x13, 12½x13

1933, Nov. 2

C15	AP13	50 l green	16	25
C16	AP13	1d red brn	28	48
C17	AP14	2d lt vio	52	75
C18	AP15	5d ultra	2.75	2.75
a.		Imperf., pair	500.00	500.00
b.		Horiz. pair, imperf. vert.	500.00	
C19	AP14	10d car rose	3.75	4.50
C20	AP13	25d dark blue	27.50	18.00
C21	AP15	50d dark brn	27.50	*37.50*
a.		Imperf., pair	600.00	600.00
		Nos. C15-C21 (7)	62.46	64.23

Helios Driving the Sun Chariot AP16

Iris — AP17

Daedalus Preparing Icarus for Flying AP18

Pallas Athene Holding Pegasus AP19

Hermes AP20

Zeus Carrying off Ganymede AP21

Triptolemos, King of Eleusis AP22

Bellerophon and Pegasus — AP23

Phrixos and Helle on the Ram Flying over the Hellespont AP24

Perf. 13x12½, 12½x13

1935, Nov. 10 **Engr.**

Grayish Paper

Size: 34x23½mm, 23½x34mm

C22	AP16	1d dp red	35	35
C23	AP17	2d dl bl	80	50
C24	AP18	5d dk vio	6.25	1.10
C25	AP19	7d bl vio	8.75	2.50
C26	AP20	10d bis brn	2.00	2.00
C27	AP21	25d rose	3.25	*3.25*
C28	AP22	30d dk grn	40	40
C29	AP23	50d violet	2.75	*3.25*
C30	AP24	100d brown	60	*90*
		Nos. C22-C30 (9)	25.15	*14.25*

Re-engraved

1937-39

White Paper

Size: 34¼x24mm, 24x34¼mm

C31	AP16	1d red	20	20
C32	AP17	2d gray bl	20	20
C33	AP18	5d violet	20	20
C34	AP19	7d dp ultra	20	20
C35	AP20	10d brn org ('39)	1.75	1.40
		Nos. C31-C35 (5)	2.55	2.20

No. C35, Mar. 1, 1939, others Aug. 3, 1937.

Postage Due Stamp, 1913, Overprinted in Red

Serrate Roulette 13½

1938, Aug. 8 **Litho.** **Unwmk.**

C36	D3	50 l vio brn	15	15
a.		"O" for "P" in word at foot	27.50	27.50

Same Overprint on No. J79 in Red

1939, June 26 ***Perf. 13½x12½***

C37	D3	50 l dark brown	15	15

Meteora Monasteries, near Trikkala — AP25

Designs: 4d, Simon Peter Monastery. 6d, View of Santorin. 8d, Church of Pantanassa. 16d, Santorin view. 32d, Ponticonissi, Corfu. 45d, Acropolis, Athens. 55d, Erechtheum. 65d, Temple of Nike Apteros. 100d, Temple of the Olympian Zeus, Athens.

Wmk. Crowns (252)

1940, Aug. 3 **Litho.** ***Perf. 12½***

C38	AP25	2d red org & blk	2.00	1.75
C39	AP25	4d dk grn & blk	10.00	10.50
C40	AP25	6d lake & blk	10.00	10.50
C41	AP25	8d dk bl & blk	16.00	16.00
C42	AP25	16d rose vio & blk	16.00	16.00
C43	AP25	32d red org & blk	20.00	21.00
C44	AP25	45d dk grn & blk	22.50	21.00
C45	AP25	55d lake & blk	27.50	24.00
C46	AP25	65d dk bl & blk	27.50	24.00
C47	AP25	100d rose vio & blk	27.50	24.00
		Nos. C38-C47 (10)	179.00	168.75

4th anniv. of the founding of the Greek Youth Organization. The stamps were good for postal duty on Aug. 3-5, 1940, only. They remained on sale until Feb. 3, 1941.

For overprints see Nos. N229-N238.

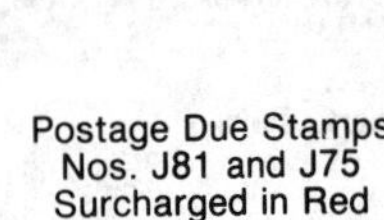

Postage Due Stamps Nos. J81 and J75 Surcharged in Red

1941-42 **Unwmk.** ***Perf. 13x12½***

C48	D3	1d on 2d lt red	15	15
a.		Inverted surcharge	20.00	

Serrate Roulette 13½

C49	D3	1d on 2d ver ('42)	15	15
a.		Inverted surcharge	20.00	
b.		Double surcharge	20.00	
		Set value	24	24

Nos. J83, J84, J86, J87 Overprinted in Red

1941-42 ***Perf. 13, 12½x13***

C50	D3	5d gray bl ('42)	20	20
a.		Inverted overprint	20.00	
b.		Double overprint	20.00	
c.		Pair, one without ovpt.	20.00	
d.		Surcharge on back	20.00	
e.		On No. J78 ('42)	120.00	*150.00*
C51	D3	10d gray grn	30	30
a.		Inverted overprint	15.00	
b.		Vert. pair, imperf. btwn.	250.00	
C52	D3	25d lt red	75	75
a.		Inverted overprint	30.00	
C53	D3	50d orange	1.40	1.40

Boreas, North Wind — AP35

Winds: 5d, Notus, South. 10d, Apeliotes, East. 20d, Lips, Southwest. 25d, Zephyrus, West. 50d, Kaikias, Northeast.

Wmk. 252

1942, Aug. 15 **Litho.** ***Perf. 12½***

C55	AP35	2d emerald	15	15
C56	AP35	5d red org	15	15
a.		Imperf., pair	175.00	
b.		Double impression	50.00	25.00
C57	AP35	10d red brn	15	15
C58	AP35	20d brt bl	15	15
C59	AP35	25d dk red org	15	15
C60	AP35	50d gray blk	2.50	2.50
a.		Double impression	140.00	
		Nos. C55-C60 (6)	3.25	3.25

1943, Sept. 15

Winds: 10d, Apeliotes, East. 25d, Zephyrus, West. 50d, Kaikias, Northeast. 100d, Boreas, North. 200d, Eurus, Southeast. 400d, Skiron, Northwest.

C61	AP35	10d rose red	15	15
C62	AP35	25d Prus grn	15	15
C63	AP35	50d vio bl	15	15
C64	AP35	100d slate blk	15	15
C65	AP35	200d claret	15	15
C66	AP35	400d steel blue	20	20
		Set value	75	75

Double impressions exist of 10d and 400d. Value, each $30.

For surcharges see Nos. 472, 473, CB1-CB10.

Imperf., Pair

C61a	AP35	10d	85.00
C62a	AP35	25d	75.00
C63a	AP35	50d	75.00
C64a	AP35	100d	80.00
C65a	AP35	200d	120.00
C66a	AP35	400d	90.00

Catalogue values for unused stamps in this section, from this point to the end of the section, are for Never Hinged items.

Priest Blessing Troops on Summit of Mt. Grammos AP36

Torchbearer AP37

Designs: 1700d, Victory above Mt. Vitsi. 2700d, Battle Scene. 7000d, Victory leading infantry.

1952, Aug. 29 **Engr.** ***Perf. 12x13½***

C67	AP36	1000d deep blue	85	22
C68	AP36	1700d dp bl grn	3.00	90
C69	AP36	2700d brown	8.25	3.00
C70	AP36	7000d olive grn	25.00	8.25

Greek army's struggle against communism.

1954, May 15 ***Perf. 13***

Designs: 2400dr, Coin of Amphictyonic League. 4000dr, Pallas Athene.

C71	AP37	1200d dp org	7.00	20
C72	AP37	2400d dk grn	27.50	6.25
C73	AP37	4000d dp ultra	65.00	2.50

5th anniv. of the signing of the North Atlantic Treaty.

Piraeus AP38

Harbors: 15d, Salonika. 20d, Patras. 25d, Hermoupolis (Syra). 30d, Volos. 50d, Cavalla. 100d, Herakleion (Candia).

Perf. 13½x13

1958, July 1 Wmk. 252 Litho.

C74 AP38 10d multi 6.00 18
C75 AP38 15d multi 1.00 32
C76 AP38 20d multi 5.75 25
C77 AP38 25d multi 1.00 50
C78 AP38 30d multi 1.00 32
C79 AP38 50d multi 2.50 32
C80 AP38 100d multi 17.00 2.50
Nos. C74-C80 (7) 34.25 4.39

AIR POST SEMI-POSTAL STAMPS

Catalogue values for unused stamps in this section are for Never Hinged items.

Nos. C61 to C65 Surcharged in Blue like Nos. B1-B5

1944, June Wmk. 252 *Perf. 12½*

CB1 AP35 100,000d on 10d 65 60
CB2 AP35 100,000d on 25d 65 60
CB3 AP35 100,000d on 50d 65 60
a. Inverted overprint 50.00
CB4 AP35 100,000d on 100d 65 60
CB5 AP35 100,000d on 200d 65 60
Nos. CB1-CB5 (5) 3.25 3.00

The exceptionally high face value discouraged the use of these stamps.

The proceeds aided victims of the Piraeus bombing, January 11, 1944.

Nos. C61 to C65 Surcharged in Blue like Nos. B11-B15

1944, July

CB6 AP35 50,000d + 450,000d on 10d 85 50
CB7 AP35 50,000d + 450,000d on 25d 85 50
CB8 AP35 50,000d + 450,000d on 50d 85 50
CB9 AP35 50,000d + 450,000d on 100d 85 50
CB10 AP35 50,000d + 450,000d on 200d 85 50
Nos. CB6-CB10 (5) 4.25 2.50

The surtax aided children's camps. Surcharge exists inverted or double. Value, each $55.

POSTAGE DUE STAMPS

D1

D2

Perf. 9, 9½, and 10, 10½ and Compound

1875 Litho. Unwmk.

J1 D1 1 l grn & blk 2.25 2.00
J2 D1 2 l grn & blk 2.25 2.00
J3 D1 5 l grn & blk 2.25 2.00
J4 D1 10 l grn & blk 8.50 6.00
J5 D1 20 l grn & blk 45.00 27.50
J6 D1 40 l grn & blk 10.00 5.75
J7 D1 60 l grn & blk 20.00 17.50
J8 D1 70 l grn & blk 11.00 8.50
J9 D1 80 l grn & blk 11.00 8.50
J10 D1 90 l grn & blk 11.00 8.50
J11 D1 1d grn & blk 15.00 8.00
J12 D1 2d grn & blk 27.50 14.00

Imperforate and part perforated, double and inverted center varieties of Nos. J1-J12 are believed to be printers' waste.

Perf. 12, 13 and 10½x13

J13 D1 1 l grn & blk 2.25 80
J14 D1 2 l grn & blk 2.25 2.00
J15 D1 5 l grn & blk 14.00 8.50
J16 D1 10 l grn & blk 6.00 5.75
J17 D1 20 l grn & blk 40.00 22.50
J18 D1 40 l grn & blk 8.50 2.75
J19 D1 60 l grn & blk 17.50 14.00
J20 D1 70 l grn & blk 8.50 7.00
J21 D1 80 l grn & blk 8.50 6.00
J22 D1 90 l grn & blk 18.00 14.00
J23 D1 1d grn & blk 14.00 14.00
J24 D1 2d grn & blk 27.50 14.00

Redrawn
"Lepton" or "Lepta" in Larger Greek Letters

1876 *Perf. 9, 9½, and 10, 10½*

J25 D2 1 l grn & blk 3.00 2.75
J26 D2 2 l dk grn & blk 3.00 2.75
J27 D2 5 l dk grn & blk 375.00 250.00
J28 D2 10 l grn & blk 2.50 1.75
J29 D2 20 l grn & blk 5.25 3.25
J30 D2 40 l grn & blk 25.00 10.50
J31 D2 60 l grn & blk 11.00 7.25
J32 D2 70 l grn & blk 27.50 20.00
J33 D2 80 l grn & blk 22.50 12.50
J34 D2 90 l grn & blk 35.50 25.00
J35 D2 100 l grn & blk 27.50 12.50
J36 D2 200 l grn & blk 22.50 12.50

Perf. 11½ to 13

J37 D2 1 l yel grn & blk 1.75 70
J38 D2 2 l yel grn & blk 1.75 70
J39 D2 5 l yel grn & blk 3.50 90
J40 D2 10 l yel grn & blk 2.00 90
a. Perf. 10-10½x11½-13 3.00
J41 D2 20 l yel grn & blk 2.00 90
J42 D2 40 l yel grn & blk 30.00 16.00
J43 D2 60 l yel grn & blk 9.00 6.25
J47 D2 100 l yel grn & blk 11.00 7.25
J48 D2 200 l yel grn & blk 15.00 7.25

Footnote below No. J12 applies also to Nos. J25-J48.

D3

1902 Engr. Wmk. 129 *Perf. 13½*

J49 D3 1 l chocolate 20 20
J50 D3 2 l gray 20 20
J51 D3 3 l orange 20 20
J52 D3 5 l yel grn 20 20
J53 D3 10 l scarlet 25 20
J54 D3 20 l lilac 30 20
J55 D3 25 l ultra 4.00 1.75
J56 D3 30 l dp vio 30 30
J57 D3 40 l dk brn 35 25
J58 D3 50 l red brn 35 20
J59 D3 1d black 90 60

Litho.

J60 D3 2d bronze 2.25 60
J61 D3 3d silver 2.00 2.00
J62 D3 5d gold 6.00 5.00
Nos. J49-J62 (14) 17.50 11.90

See Nos. J63-J88, J90-J93. For overprints and surcharges see Nos. 383-385, J89, RA56, RA58-RA59, NJ1-NJ31.

Imperf., Pairs

J50a D3 2 l 22.50
J51a D3 3 l 22.50
J52a D3 5 l 22.50
J55a D3 25 l 22.50
J56a D3 30 l 35.00
J58a D3 50 l 35.00
J59a D3 1d 40.00

Serrate Roulette 13½

1913-26 Unwmk.

J63 D3 1 l green 15 15
J64 D3 2 l carmine 15 15
J65 D3 3 l vermilion 15 15
J66 D3 5 l green 15 15
a. Imperf., pair 40.00
b. Double impression 40.00
c. "o" for "p" in lowest word 3.00 3.00
J67 D3 10 l carmine 15 15
J68 D3 20 l slate 20 15
J69 D3 25 l ultra 15 15
J70 D3 30 l carmine 15 15
J71 D3 40 l indigo 20 15
J72 D3 50 l vio brn 30 25
a. "o" for "p" in lowest word 25.00 20.00
J73 D3 80 l lil brn ('24) 40 20
J74 D3 1d blue 2.00 60
a. 1d ultramarine 9.00 3.50
J75 D3 2d vermilion 1.75 35
J76 D3 3d carmine 5.25 3.25
J77 D3 5d ultra 17.50 3.50
J78 D3 5d gray bl ('26) 3.50 90
Nos. J63-J78 (16) 32.15 10.40

In 1922-23 and 1941-42 some postage due stamps were used for ordinary postage.

In 1916 Nos. J52, and J63 to J75 were surcharged for the Mount Athos District (see note after No. N166) but were never issued there. By error some of them were put in use as ordinary postage due stamps in Dec., 1924. In 1932 the balance of them was burned.

Type of 1902 Issue

Perf. 13, 13½x12½, 13½x13

1930 Litho.

J79 D3 50 l dk brn 30 30
J80 D3 1d lt bl 30 30
J81 D3 2d lt red 30 30
J82 D3 3d rose red 35.00 22.50
J83 D3 5d gray bl 30 30
J84 D3 10d gray grn 30 30
J85 D3 15d red brn 30 30
J86 D3 25d lt red 65 65
Nos. J79-J86 (8) 37.45 24.95

Type of 1902 Issue

1935 Engr. *Perf. 12½x13*

J87 D3 50d orange 30 30
J88 D3 100d slate green 30 30

No. J70 Surcharged with New Value in Black

1942

J89 D3 50 (l) on 30 l carmine 90 90

Type of 1902

1943 Wmk. 252 Litho. *Perf. 12½*

J90 D3 10d red orange 15 15
J91 D3 25d ultramarine 15 15
J92 D3 100d black brown 15 15
J93 D3 200d violet 15 15
Set value 40 40

POSTAL TAX STAMPS

"The Tragedy of War" — PT1

Red Cross, Nurses, Wounded and Bearers — PT1a

Serrate Roulette 13½

1914 Litho. Unwmk.

RA1 PT1 2 l carmine 15 15
a. 2 l red 15 15
b. Imperf., pair 50.00
RA2 PT1 5 l blue 25 20
a. Imperf., pair
Set value 33 28

1915 *Serrate Roulette 13*

RA2B PT1a (5 l) dk bl & red 10.00 1.50

The tax was for the Red Cross.

Women's Patriotic League Badge — PT1b

1915, Nov. *Perf. 11½*

RA2C PT1b (5 l) dk bl & car 50 50
d. Horiz. pair, imperf. btwn. 50.00

The tax was for the Greek Women's Patriotic League.

Regular Issue of 1901 Surcharged in Black or Brown:

Κ. Π.
λεπτοῦ
1
a

Κ. Π.
λεπτοῦ
1
b

In type "b" the letters, especially those in the first line, are thinner than in type "a", making them appear taller.

Perf. 11½, 12½, 13½ and Compound

1917 Engr. Wmk. 129

RA3 A11(a) 1 l on 1 l brn 2.00 1.75
a. Double surcharge 5.00
RA4 A11(a) 1 l on 1 l brn (Br) 20.00 20.00
RA5 A11(a) 1 l on 3 l org 30 30
RA6 A11(b) 1 l on 3 l org 30 30
a. Triple surcharge 5.00
b. Dbl. surch., one invtd. 5.00
c. "K.M." for "K.II." 5.00 5.00
RA7 A11(a) 5 l on 1 l brn 2.00 2.00
a. Double surcharge 5.00
b. Dbl. surch., one invtd. 5.00
c. Inverted surcharge 5.00
RA8 A11(a) 5 l on 20 l red lil 65 65
a. Double surcharge 5.00
b. Dbl. surch., one invtd. 5.00
RA9 A11(b) 5 l on 40 l dk brn 65 65
a. Imperf.
RA10 A11(b) 5 l on 50 l brn lake 65 65
a. Double surcharge 5.00
b. Dbl. surch., one invtd. 5.00
RA11 A13(b) 5 l on 1d blk 1.25 1.25
a. Imperf.
b. Inverted surcharge 10.00
RA12 A11(a) 10 l on 30 l dl vio 90 90
a. Imperf.
b. Double surcharge 6.00
RA13 A11(a) 30 l on 30 l dl vio 90 90
a. Double surcharge 6.00
Nos. RA3-RA13 (11) 29.60 29.35

Same Surcharge On Occupation Stamps of 1912

Serrate Roulette 13½

1917 Litho. Unwmk.

RA14 O2 (b) 5 l on 25 l pale bl 45 45
a. Triple surch., one invtd. 6.00
b. Double surcharge 6.00
RA15 O2 (b) 5 l on 40 l indigo 45 45
a. Double surch., one invtd. 6.00
b. Double surcharge 6.00
RA16 O1 (b) 5 l on 50 l dk bl 45 45
a. Double surcharge 10.00
b. Inverted surcharge 10.00

There are many wrong font, omitted and misplaced letters and punctuation marks and similar varieties in the surcharges on Nos. RA3 to RA16.

Revenue Stamps Surcharged in Brown

"Victory" — R1

Κ. Π.
λεπτοῦ
1

1917

RA17 R1 1 l on 10 l blue 60 60
RA18 R1 1 l on 80 l blue 60 60
RA19 R1 5 l on 10 l blue 12.00 8.00
RA20 R1 5 l on 60 l blue 2.50 1.75
a. Perf. vert. through middle 4.25 2.50
RA21 R1 5 l on 80 l blue 1.75 1.75
a. Perf. vert. through middle 7.50 4.00
b. Inverted surcharge
RA22 R1 10 l on 70 l blue 12.50 4.00
a. Perf. vert. through middle 4.25 2.00
RA23 R1 10 l on 90 l blue 4.75 2.00
a. Perf. vert. through middle 12.50 11.00
RA24 R1 20 l on 20 l blue 650.00 475.00
RA25 R1 20 l on 30 l blue 3.50 2.75
RA26 R1 20 l on 40 l blue 9.50 6.75
RA27 R1 20 l on 50 l blue 4.50 3.00
RA28 R1 20 l on 60 l blue 250.00 150.00
RA29 R1 20 l on 80 l blue 32.50 24.00
RA30 R1 20 l on 90 l blue 3.00 1.50
a. Inverted surcharge 45.00
Nos. RA17-RA30 (14) 987.70 681.70

No. RA19 is known only with vertical perforation through the middle.

Counterfeits exist of Nos. RA17-RA43, used.

Surcharged in Brown or Black

Κ. Π.
5 λεπτ. 5

RA31 R1 1 l on 50 l vio (Bk) 95 30
RA32 R1 5 l on 10 l bl (Br) 95 30
a. Inverted surcharge 30.00
b. Left "5" invert. 30.00
RA33 R1 5 l on 10 l vio (Br) 95 30
RA34 R1 10 l on 50 l vio (Br) 1.90 90
RA35 R1 10 l on 50 l vio (Bk) 22.50 7.00

RA36 R1 20 l on 2d bl (Bk) 5.00 3.00
a. Surcharged "20 lept. 30" 30.00 25.00
b. Horiz. pair, imperf. btwn.
Nos. RA31-RA36 (6) 32.25 11.80

The "t," fourth Greek letter of the denomination in the surcharge ("Lept."), is normally omitted on Nos. RA31, RA34-RA36.

Corfu Issue

Surcharged in Black — Κ.Π. / 1 ΛΕΠΤΟΝ 1

1917

RA37	R1	1 l on 10 l blue	95	70
RA38	R1	5 l on 50 l blue	32.50	22.50
RA39	R1	10 l on 50 l blue	280.00	200.00
RA40	R1	20 l on 50 l blue	450.00	380.00

Surcharged in Black — Κ.Π. / 20 ΛΕΠΤΑ 20

RA41	R1	10 l on 50 l blue	5.50	2.25
RA42	R1	20 l on 50 l blue	13.00	5.25
RA43	R1	30 l on 50 l blue	7.75	6.00

Surcharged in Black — Κ. Π. / 5 Λεπτὰ 5

RA44 R1 5 l on 10 l vio & red 5.25 2.00
a. "K" with serifs 7.50 3.50

Counterfeits exist of Nos. RA17-RA44.
Similar stamps with denominations higher than 30 lepta were for revenue use.

Wounded Soldier — PT2

1918 ***Serrate Roulette 13½, 11½***

RA45 PT2 5 l bl, yel & red 5.25 2.50

Overprinted — Π.Ι.Π.

RA46 PT2 5 l bl, yel & red 6.00 2.50

The letters are the initials of Greek words equivalent to "Patriotic Relief Institution." The proceeds were given to the Patriotic League, for the aid of disabled soldiers.
Counterfeits exist of Nos. RA45-RA46.

PT3

Surcharge in Red

1922 **Litho.** ***Perf. 11½***

Dark Blue & Red

RA46A	PT3	5 l on 10 l	*250.00*	2.50
RA46B	PT3	5 l on 20 l	37.50	19.00
RA46C	PT3	5 l on 50 l	190.00	60.00
RA46D	PT3	5 l on 1d	3.25	*30.00*

Counterfeit surcharges exist. Copies of Nos. RA46A-RA46C without surcharge, each 50 cents.

Red Cross Help to Soldier and Family PT3a

St. Demetrius PT4

1924 ***Perf. 11½, 13½ x 12½***

RA47 PT3a 10 l bl, buff & red 30 15
a. Imperf., pair 24.00
b. Horiz. pair, imperf. btwn. 24.00
c. Double impression of cross 24.00

Proceeds were given to the Red Cross.

1934 ***Perf. 11½***

RA48 PT4 20 l brown 15 15
a. Horizontal pair, imperf. between 10.00
b. Vertical pair, imperf. between 15.00
c. Imperf., pair 20.00

No. RA48 was obligatory as a tax on all interior mail, including air post, mailed from Salonika.
For surcharge see No. RA69.

"Health"
PT5 PT6

1934, Dec. 28 ***Perf. 13, 13x13½***

RA49 PT5 10 l bl grn, org & buff 15 15
a. Vert. pair, imperf. horiz.
RA50 PT5 20 l ultra, org & buff 45 20
RA51 PT5 50 l grn, org & buff 1.25 40

For surcharge see No. RA67.

1935

RA52 PT6 10 l yel grn, org & buff 15 15
RA53 PT6 20 l ultra, org & buff 15 15
RA54 PT6 50 l grn, org & buff 50 35

The use of Nos. RA49 to RA54 was obligatory on all mail during four weeks each year including Christmas, the New Year and Easter, and on parcel post packages at all times. For the benefit of the tubercular clerks and officials of the Post, Telephone and Telegraph Service.
See No. RA64. For surcharge see No. RA68.

No. 364 Overprinted in Red

ΠΡΟΝΟΙΑ

1937, Jan. 20 **Engr.** ***Perf. 13x12½***

RA55 A36 50 l violet 1.25 15
a. Inverted overprint 75 15

No. RA55a first appeared as an error, then was issued deliberately in quantity to avoid speculation.

Same Overprint in Blue on No. J67

Litho.

Serrate Roulette 13½

RA56 D3 10 l carmine 15 15
a. Inverted overprint 50.00

No. RA56 with blue overprint double exists only with additional black overprint of Ionian Islands No. NRA1a.

Same Overprint in Green on No. 364

1937 **Engr.** ***Perf. 13x12½***

RA57 A36 50 l violet 75 15

Same Overprint, with Surcharge of New Value, on Nos. J66, J68 and 323 in Blue or Black

Serrate Roulette 13½

1938 **Litho.** **Unwmk.**

RA58 D3 50 l on 5 l grn 40 25
a. "o" for "p" in lowest word 25.00 25.00
b. Vert. pair, imperf. horiz. 50.00
RA59 D3 50 l on 20 l slate 90 50

Engr. ***Perf. 13x12½***

RA60 A38 50 l on 20 l vio (Bk) 75 15

Surcharge on No. RA60 is 14½x16½mm.

Queens Olga and Sophia — PT7

1939, Feb. 1 **Litho.** ***Perf. 13½x12***

RA61 PT7 10 l brt rose, *pale rose* 15 15
RA62 PT7 50 l gray grn, *pale grn* 15 15
RA63 PT7 1d dl bl, *lt bl* 20 20
Set value 40 40

For overprints and surcharges see Nos. RA65, RA79-RA81A, NRA1-NRA3.

"Health" Type of 1935

1939 ***Perf. 12½***

RA64 PT6 50 l brn & buff 40 30

No. RA62 Overprinted in Red

ΠΡΟΣΤΑΣΙΑ ΦΥΜΑΤΙΚΩΝ ΤΤΤ

1940 ***Perf. 13½x12***

RA65 PT7 50 l gray grn, *pale grn* 25 25
a. Inverted overprint 25.00
b. Pair, one without surcharge 20.00

Proceeds of Nos. RA64 and RA65 were used for the benefit of tubercular clerks and officials of the Post, Telephone and Telegraph Service. No. RA65 was used in Albania during the Greek occupation, 1940-41 without additional overprint.

No. 321 Surcharged in Carmine — Κ.Π. / λεπτῶν / 50

1941 **Unwmk.** **Engr.** ***Perf. 13½x13***

RA66 A36 50 l on 5 l dk grn 15 15
a. Inverted surcharge 15.00

No. RA49 and Type of 1935 Surcharged with New Value in Black

Perf. 12½x13, 13x13½

Litho.

RA67 PT5 50 l on 10 l 2.00 2.00
RA68 PT6 50 l on 10 l dp bl grn, dl org & buff 15 15
a. Inverted surcharge 20.00
b. Double surcharge 20.00

Catalogue values for unused stamps in this section, from this point to the end of the section, are for Never Hinged items.

No. RA48 Surcharged in Green — ΔΡ. 1

1942 ***Perf. 11½***

RA69 PT4 1d on 20 l brn 15 15
a. Pair, one without surcharge 10.00
b. Imperf., pair 15.00
c. Double surcharge 15.00

Nos. 321, 324 Surcharged In Red or Carmine

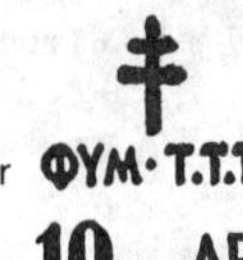
ΦΥΜ·Τ.Τ.Τ. / 10 ΔΡ

1942-43 **Engr.** ***Perf. 13½x13***

RA70 A36 10d on 5 l dk grn ('43) 15 15
a. Double surcharge 15.00
RA71 A39 10d on 25 l sl bl (C) 15 15
a. Inverted surcharge 15.00
Set value 20 20

No. 444 Overprinted in Red

1944 **Wmk. 252** **Litho.** ***Perf. 12½***

RA72 A110 100d black 15 15
a. Double overprint 9.00
b. Inverted overprint 9.00

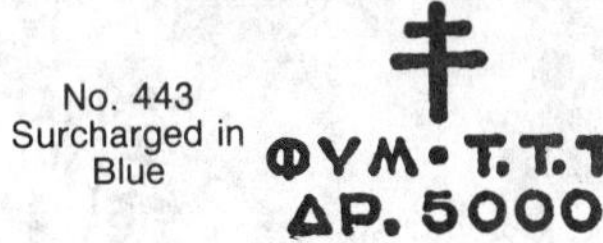

No. 443 Surcharged in Blue

RA73 A109 5000d on 75d dp rose 15 15
a. Double surcharge 20.00

No. 437 Surcharged in Blue — ΥΠΕΡ ΤΩΝ ΦΥΜΑΤΙΚΩΝ Τ.Τ.Τ. ΔΡΧ. 25.000

RA74 A103 25000d on 2d red brn 15 15
a. Double surcharge 15.00
b. Additional surcharge on back 17.50

No. 399 Surcharged in Blue or Carmine — ΥΠΕΡ ΤΩΝ ΦΥΜΑΤΙΚΩΝ Τ.Τ.Τ. ΔΡΑΧΜΗ 1

1945 ***Perf. 13½x12***

RA75 A72 1d on 40 l grn & blk 15 15
a. Double surcharge 10.00
RA76 A72 2d on 40 l grn & blk (C) 15 15
a. Vert. pair, one without surch. 8.00
b. Surcharged on back 10.00
c. Inverted surcharge 10.00
Set value 20 20

Tax on Nos. RA67, RA68-RA70 to RA76 aided the postal clerks' tuberculosis fund.

Nos. 396 and 399 Surcharged in Carmine — ΠΡΟΝΟΙΑ ΠΡΟΣΩΠΙΚΟΥ Τ.Τ.Τ. ΔΡΑΧΜΑΙ 20

1946

RA77 A72 20d on 40 l grn & blk 20 20
a. Pair, one without surcharge 15.00
RA78 A69 20d on 5 l brn red & bl 30 20

Same Surcharge in Carmine on Nos. RA62 and RA63

1946-47 **Unwmk.** ***Perf. 13½x12***

RA79 PT7 50d on 50 l gray grn, *pale grn* ('47) 15 15
a. Inverted surcharge 25.00
RA80 PT7 50d on 1d dl bl, *lt bl* 15 15
a. Violet black surcharge 4.00 1.00
Set value 25 25

The tax on Nos. RA77 to RA80 was for the Postal Clerks' Welfare Fund.

Nos. RA65 and RA62 Surcharged in Carmine

ΔΡ. ▬ 50

1947

RA81 50d on 50 l (RA65) 35 15
RA81A 50d on 50 l (RA62) 32.50 32.50

The tax was for the postal clerks' tuberculosis fund.

St. Demetrius — PT8

1948 **Litho.** ***Perf. 12x13½***

RA82 PT8 50d yel brn 20 15

Obligatory on all domestic mail. The tax was for restoration of historical monuments and churches destroyed during World War II.

Nos. 397 and 413 Surcharged in Blue

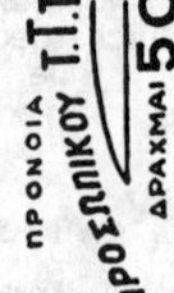

1950 **Wmk. 252**

RA83 A70 50d on 10 l (#397) 20 15
a. Stamp with double frame 8.00
b. Surcharge reading down 18.00 18.00
RA84 A70 50d on 10 l (#413) 25 15
a. Surcharge reading down 16.00 16.00
Set value 20

Tax for the Postal Clerks' Welfare Fund.

No. 396 Surcharged in Carmine

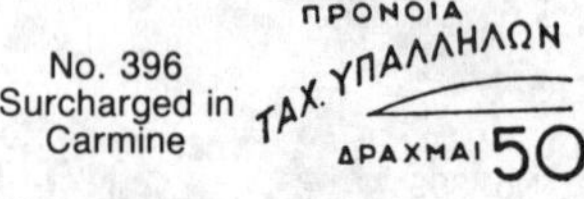

1951 ***Perf. 13½x12***

RA85 A69 50d on 5 l brn red & bl 25 15

The tax was for the Postal Employees' Welfare Fund.

No. 392 Surcharged in Black

✝ 50

1951 **Wmk. 252** ***Perf. 12½x12***

RA86 A67 50d on 3d red brn 15 15
a. Pair, one without surcharge 15.00
b. "50" omitted 18.00

Tax for the postal clerks' tuberculosis fund.

No. 393 Surcharged in Carmine

ΠΡΟΣΘΕΤΟΝ
ΔΡ. 100

1952

RA87 A67 100d on 8d deep blue 15 15

The tax was for the State Welfare Fund.

> *Greek Occupation and Annexation stamps can be mounted in Scott's Greece Album.*

Ruins of Church of Phaneromeni, Zante — PT9

Zeus on Macedonian Coin of Philip II — PT10

Design: 500d, Map and scene of destruction, Argostoli.

1953 **Wmk. 252** **Litho.** ***Perf. 12½***

RA88 PT9 300d ind & pale grn 30 15
RA89 PT9 500d dk brn & buff 60 40

The tax was for the reconstruction of Cephalonia, Ithaca, and Zante, Ionian Islands destroyed by earthquake.

1956 ***Perf. 13½***

Design: 1d, Aristotle.

RA90 PT10 50 l dk car rose 35 15
a. Imperf., pair 100.00
RA91 PT10 1d brt blue 90 60

Tax for archaeological research in Macedonia. The coin on No. RA90 portrays Zeus despite inscription of Philip's name.

POSTAL TAX SEMI-POSTAL STAMPS

Child — PTSP1

Mother and Child — PTSP2

Virgin and Christ Child — PTSP3

Perf. 12x13½

1943 **Wmk. 252** **Litho.**

RAB1 PTSP1 25d + 25d bl grn 15 15
RAB2 PTSP2 100d + 50d rose vio 15 15
RAB3 PTSP3 200d + 100d red brn 15 15
Set value 30 30

Surtax aided needy children. These stamps were compulsory on domestic mail in Oct. 1943.

OCCUPATION AND ANNEXATION STAMPS

During the Balkan wars, 1912-13, Greece occupied certain of the Aegean Islands and part of Western Turkey. She subsequently acquired these territories and they were known as the New Greece.

Most of the special issues for the Aegean Islands were made by order of the military commanders.

For Use in the Aegean Islands Occupied by Greece

CHIOS

Greece No. 221 Overprinted in Red

Serrate Roulette 13½

1913 **Litho.** **Unwmk.**

N1 A25 25 l ultra 65.00 55.00
a. Inverted overprint 100.00 100.00
b. Greek "L" instead of "D" 90.00 90.00

ICARIA (NICARIA)

Penelope — I1

1912 **Unwmk.** **Litho.** ***Perf. 11½***

N2 I1 2 l orange 80 80
N3 I1 5 l bl grn 80 80
N4 I1 10 l rose 80 80
N5 I1 25 l ultra 80 1.25
N6 I1 50 l gray lil 1.75 2.00
N7 I1 1d dk brn 2.50 *8.25*
N8 I1 2d claret 3.00 *11.00*
N9 I1 5d slate 6.00 *19.00*
Nos. N2-N9 (8) 16.45 *43.90*

Counterfeits of Nos. N1-N15 are plentiful.

Stamps of Greece, 1911-23, Overprinted Reading Up

ΕΛΛΗΝΙΚΗ ΔΙΟΙΚΗΣΙΣ

1913 **Engr.**

On Issue of 1911-21

N10 A25 2 l car rose 19.00 19.00
N11 A24 3 l vermilion 19.00 19.00

Litho.

On Issue of 1912-23

N12 A24 1 l green 19.00 19.00
N13 A24 3 l vermilion 19.00 19.00
N14 A26 5 l green 19.00 19.00
N15 A24 10 l carmine 19.00 19.00
Nos. N10-N15 (6) 114.00 114.00

LEMNOS

Regular Issues of Greece Overprinted in Black

ΛΗΜΝΟΣ

On Issue of 1901

1912 **Wmk. 129** **Engr.** ***Perf. 13½***

N16 A11 20 l red lilac 75 75

On Issue of 1911-21

Unwmk.

Serrate Roulette 13½

N17 A24 1 l green 15 15
N18 A25 2 l car rose 15 15
N19 A24 3 l vermilion 15 15
N20 A26 5 l green 30 30
N21 A24 10 l car rose 65 65
N22 A25 20 l gray lil 35 35
N23 A25 25 l ultra 85 85
N24 A26 30 l car rose 85 85
N25 A25 40 l dp bl 1.50 1.50
N26 A26 50 l dl vio 1.50 1.50
N27 A27 1d ultra 2.00 2.00
N28 A27 2d vermilion 7.00 7.00
N29 A27 3d car rose 10.00 10.00
N30 A27 5d ultra 12.50 12.50
N31 A27 10d dp bl 110.00 110.00
N32 A28 25d dp bl 85.00 85.00

On Issue of 1912-23

Litho.

N33 A24 1 l green 15 15
a. Without period after "Ellas" 85.00 85.00
N34 A26 5 l green 15 15
N35 A24 10 l carmine 25 25
N36 A25 25 l ultra 1.00 1.00
Nos. N16-N36 (21) 235.25 235.25

Red Overprint

On Issue of 1911-21

Engr.

N37 A25 2 l car rose 50 50
N38 A24 3 l vermilion 50 50
N39 A25 20 l gray lil 1.00 1.00
N40 A26 30 l car rose 1.50 1.50
N41 A25 40 l dp bl 1.50 1.50
N42 A26 50 l dl vio 1.50 1.50
N43 A27 1d ultra 1.50 1.50
N44 A27 2d vermilion 9.00 9.00
N45 A27 3d car rose 10.00 10.00
N46 A27 5d ultra 20.00 20.00
N47 A27 10d dp bl 110.00 110.00
N48 A28 25d dp bl 85.00 85.00

On Issue of 1912-23

Litho.

N49 A24 1 l green 50 50
a. Without period after "Ellas" 85.00 85.00
N50 A26 5 l green 30 30
N51 A24 10 l carmine 1.40 1.40
N52 A25 25 l ultra 80 80
Nos. N37-N52 (16) 245.00 245.00

The overprint is found inverted or double on many of Nos. N16-N52. There are several varieties in the overprint: Greek "D" for "L", large Greek "S" or "O", and small "O".

No. N49 with Added "Greek Administration" Overprint, as on Nos. N109-N148, in Black

1913

N52A A24 1 l green 15.00 12.50

Counterfeits of Nos. N16-N52A are plentiful.

MYTILENE (LESBOS)

Turkey Nos. 162, 158 Overprinted in Blue

'Ελληνική Κατοχὴ Μυτιλήνης

Perf. 12, 13½ and Compound

1912 **Typo.** **Unwmk.**

N53 A21 20pa rose 22.50 22.50
N54 A21 10pi dull red 125.00 125.00

On Turkey Nos. P68, 151-155, 137, 157-158 in Black

N55 A21 2pa ol grn 75 75
N56 A21 5pa ocher 1.50 1.50
N57 A21 10pa bl grn 1.50 1.50
N58 A21 20pa rose 75 75
N59 A21 1pi ultra 2.25 2.25
N60 A21 2pi bl blk 15.00 15.00
N61 A19 2½pi dk brn 8.50 8.50
N62 A21 5pi dk vio 19.00 19.00
N63 A21 10pi dl red 110.00 110.00
Nos. N55-N63 (9) 159.25 159.25

On Turkey Nos. 161-163, 145 in Black

N64 A21 10pa bl grn 4.00 4.00
a. Double overprint 15.00
N65 A21 20pa rose 3.00 3.00
N66 A21 1pi ultra 3.00 3.00
N67 A19 2pi bl blk 52.50 52.50

Nos. N55, N58, N65, N59 Surcharged in Blue or Black

N68 A21 25 l on 2pa 4.50 4.50
a. New value inverted 22.50
N69 A21 50 l on 20pa 5.75 5.75
b. New value inverted 22.50
N70 A21 1d on 20pa (N65) (Bk) 15.00 15.00
a. New value inverted 45.00
N71 A21 2d on 1pi (Bk) 20.00 20.00
a. New value inverted

Same Overprint on Turkey No. J49

N72 A19 1pi blk, *dp rose* 50.00 50.00

The overprint is found on all values reading up or down with inverted "i" in the first word and inverted "e" in the third word.

No. N72 was only used for postage.

Counterfeits of Nos. N53-N72 are plentiful.

SAMOS

Issues of the Provisional Government

Map of Samos OS1

1912 Unwmk. Typo. *Imperf.*

N73	OS1	5 l gray grn	20.00	5.50
N74	OS1	10 l red	25.00	6.25
N75	OS1	25 l blue	37.50	9.00
a.		25 l green (error)	*500.00*	*600.00*

Nos. N73-N75 exist in tete beche pairs. Value per set, $500 unused, $250 used.

Counterfeits exist of Nos. N73 to N75.

Hermes — OS2

1912 Litho. *Perf. 11½*

Without Overprint

N76	OS2	1 l gray	3.75	85
N77	OS2	5 l lt grn	3.75	85
N78	OS2	10 l rose	47.50	85
b.		Half used as 5 l on cover		15.00
N79	OS2	25 l lt bl	4.25	1.50
N80	OS2	50 l vio brn	12.50	5.50

With Overprint

N81	OS2	1 l gray	50	50
N82	OS2	5 l bl grn	50	50
N83	OS2	10 l rose	1.00	1.00
b.		Half used as 5 l on cover		20.00
N84	OS2	25 l blue	2.00	1.00
N85	OS2	50 l vio brn	10.50	6.00
N86	OS2	1d orange	10.00	6.00
		Nos. N76-N86 (11)	96.25	24.55

For overprints and surcharge see Nos. N92-N103.

Imperf., Pairs

Without Overprint

N76a	OS2	1 l	40.00	
N77a	OS2	5 l	40.00	
N78a	OS2	10 l	40.00	
N79a	OS2	25 l	40.00	
N80a	OS2	50 l	40.00	

With Overprint

N81a	OS2	1 l	80.00	
N82a	OS2	5 l	80.00	
N83a	OS2	10 l	80.00	
N85a	OS2	50 l	60.00	60.00

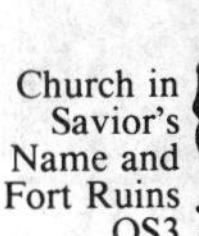

Church in Savior's Name and Fort Ruins OS3

Manuscript Initials in Red or Black

1913

N87	OS3	1d brn (R)	14.00	11.50
N88	OS3	2d dp bl (R)	14.00	11.50
N89	OS3	5d gray grn (R)	27.50	22.50
N90	OS3	10d yel grn (R)	100.00	90.00
a.		Black initials	300.00	
N91	OS3	25d red (Bk)	67.50	67.50
a.		Red initials	210.00	
		Nos. N87-N91 (5)	223.00	203.00

Victory of the Greek fleet in 1824 and the union with Greece of Samos in 1912. The manuscript initials are those of Pres. Themistokles Sofulis.

Values the same for copies without initials.

Exist imperf. Counterfeits of Nos. N87-N91 are plentiful.

For overprints see Nos. N104-N108.

Nos. N76 to N80 Overprinted ΕΛΛΑΣ

1914

N92	OS2	1 l gray	4.00	3.00
N93	OS2	5 l lt grn	4.00	3.00
N94	OS2	10 l rose	4.25	3.00
a.		Double overprint	60.00	
N95	OS2	25 l lt bl	12.00	10.50
N96	OS2	50 l vio brn	12.00	5.00
a.		Double overprint	60.00	
		Nos. N92-N96 (5)	36.25	24.50

Charity Issues of Greek Administration

Nos. N81 to N86 Overprinted in Red or Black

1915

N97	OS2	1 l gray (R)	18.00	18.00
a.		Black overprint	100.00	
b.		Without overprint	60.00	
N98	OS2	5 l bl grn (Bk)	80	80
a.		Red overprint	85.00	
b.		Double overprint	80.00	
N99	OS2	10 l rose (Bk)	90	90
a.		Red overprint	90.00	
b.		Inverted overprint	80.00	
N100	OS2	25 l bl (Bk)	80	80
a.		Red overprint	90.00	
N101	OS2	50 l vio brn (Bk)	1.00	1.00
a.		Red overprint	85.00	
N102	OS2	1d org (R)	2.00	2.00
a.		Inverted overprint	90.00	
b.		Black overprint	100.00	
c.		Double black overprint	90.00	

No. N102 With Additional Surcharge in Black ΛΕΠΤΟΝ

N103	OS2	1 l on 1d org	7.00	7.00
a.		Black surcharge double	90.00	
b.		Black surcharge inverted	100.00	
		Nos. N97-N103 (7)	30.50	30.50

Issue of 1913 Overprinted in Red or Black

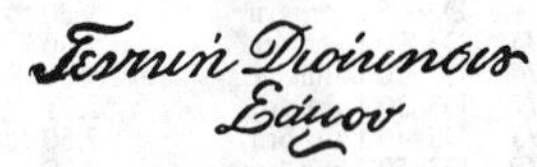

1915

N104	OS3	1d brn (R)	18.00	10.00
N105	OS3	2d dp bl (R)	24.00	14.00
a.		Double overprint		
N106	OS3	5d gray grn (R)	40.00	25.00
N107	OS3	10d yel grn (Bk)	55.00	50.00
a.		Inverted overprint		
N108	OS3	25d red (Bk)	550.00	400.00
		Nos. N104-N108 (5)	687.00	499.00

Nos. N97 to N108 inclusive have an embossed control mark, consisting of a cross encircled by a Greek inscription.

Most copies of Nos. N104-N108 lack the initials.

Counterfeits of Nos. N104-N108 are plentiful.

FOR USE IN PARTS OF TURKEY OCCUPIED BY GREECE (NEW GREECE)

Regular Issues of Greece Overprinted

ΕΛΛΗΝΙΚΗ ΔΙΟΙΚΗΣΙΣ

Black Overprint Meaning "Greek Administration"

On Issue of 1901

1912 Wmk. 129 Engr. *Perf. 13½*

N109	A11	20 l red lilac	1.50	50

On Issue of 1911-21

Unwmk.

Serrate Roulette 13½

N110	A24	1 l green	40	20
N111	A25	2 l car rose	30	20
N112	A24	3 l vermilion	30	20
N113	A26	5 l green	35	20
N114	A24	10 l car rose	55	30
N115	A25	20 l gray lil	90	30
N116	A25	25 l ultra	1.50	50
N117	A26	30 l car rose	1.50	1.40
N118	A25	40 l dp bl	3.25	1.40
N119	A26	50 l dl vio	3.00	1.40
N120	A27	1d ultra	6.50	1.40
N121	A27	2d vermilion	35.00	20.00
N122	A27	3d car rose	35.00	20.00
N123	A27	5d ultra	11.00	7.00
N124	A27	10d dp bl	275.00	200.00
N125	A28	25d dp bl, ovpt. horiz.	175.00	140.00

On Issue of 1913-23

Litho.

N126	A24	1 l green	30	18
b.		Without period after "Ellas"	60.00	60.00
N127	A26	5 l green	28	18
N128	A24	10 l carmine	70	24
N129	A25	25 l blue	3.25	1.10
		Nos. N109-N129 (21)	555.58	396.70

Red Overprint

On Issue of 1911-21

Engr.

N130	A24	1 l green	60	35
N131	A25	2 l car rose	7.00	6.00
N132	A24	3 l vermilion	9.00	6.00
N133	A26	5 l green	90	70
N134	A25	20 l gray lil	7.00	1.50
N135	A25	25 l ultra	60.00	40.00
N136	A26	30 l car rose	24.00	20.00
N137	A25	40 l dp bl	3.00	2.25
N138	A26	50 l dl vio	4.00	2.75
N139	A27	1d ultra	14.00	5.00
N140	A27	2d vermilion	50.00	40.00
N141	A27	3d car rose	25.00	20.00
N142	A27	5d ultra	315.00	250.00
N143	A27	10d dp bl	25.00	20.00
N144	A28	25d dp bl, ovpt. horiz.	47.50	47.50
a.		Vertical overprint	200.00	200.00

On Issue of 1913-23

Litho.

N145	A24	1 l green	700	6.00
a.		Without period after "Ellas"	85.00	
N146	A26	5 l green	85	85
N147	A24	10 l carmine	55.00	45.00
N148	A25	25 l blue	2.25	1.75
		Nos. N130-N148 (19)	657.10	515.65

The normal overprint is vertical, reading upward on N109-N124, N126-N143, N145-N148. It is often double or reading downward. There are numerous broken, missing and wrong font letters with a Greek "L" instead of "D" as the first letter of the second word.

Counterfeits exist of Nos. N109-N148.

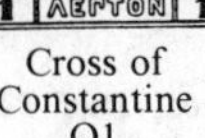
Cross of Constantine O1

Eagle of Zeus O2

1912 Litho.

N150	O1	1 l brown	25	20
N151	O2	2 l red	25	20
a.		2 l rose	30	22
N153	O2	3 l orange	30	25
N154	O1	5 l green	60	15
N155	O1	10 l rose red	1.10	15
N156	O1	20 l violet	6.50	1.50
N157	O2	25 l pale bl	1.75	50
N158	O1	30 l gray grn	42.50	1.40
N159	O2	40 l indigo	3.50	1.50
N160	O1	50 l dk bl	2.50	1.00
N161	O2	1d vio brn	4.00	1.75
N162	O1	2d gray brn	40.00	4.00
N163	O2	3d dl bl	125.00	20.00
N164	O1	5d gray	125.00	25.00
N165	O2	10d carmine	135.00	170.00
N166	O1	25d gray blk	135.00	170.00
		Nos. N150-N166 (16)	623.25	397.60

Occupation of Macedonia, Epirus and some of the Aegean Islands.

Sold only in New Greece.

Dangerous forgeries of #N165-N166 exist.

In 1916 some stamps of this issue were overprinted in Greek: "I (era) Koinotis Ag (iou) Orous" for the Mount Athos Monastery District. They were never placed in use and most of them were destroyed.

For surcharges see Nos. RA14-RA16.

Imperf., Pairs

Without Overprint

N150a	O1	1 l	175.00	
N151b	O2	2 l	175.00	
N153a	O2	3 l	125.00	
N154a	O1	5 l	70.00	
N155a	O1	10 l	70.00	
N156a	O1	20 l	275.00	
N157a	O2	25 l	275.00	
N158a	O1	30 l	375.00	
N159a	O2	40 l	275.00	
N163a	O2	3d	900.00	

CAVALLA

ΕΛΛΗΝΙΚΗ ΔΙΟΙΚΗΣΙΣ

Bulgaria Nos. 89-97 Surcharged in Red

25 ΛΕΠΤΑ 25

1913 Unwmk. Engr. *Perf. 12*

N167	A20	5 l on 1s myr grn	*13.50*	*13.50*
N169	A25	10 l on 15s brn bis	*50.00*	*50.00*
N170	A26	10 l on 25s ultra & blk	*15.00*	*15.00*
N171	A21	15 l on 2s car & blk	*25.00*	*25.00*
N172	A22	20 l on 3s lake & blk	*18.00*	*18.00*
N173	A23	25 l on 5s grn & blk	*10.50*	*8.50*
N174	A24	50 l on 10s red & blk	*13.50*	*8.50*
N175	A25	1d on 15s brn bis	*30.00*	*25.00*
N176	A27	1d on 30s bl & blk	*60.00*	*30.00*
N177	A28	1d on 50s ocher & blk	*100.00*	*50.00*

Blue Surcharge

N178	A24	50 l on 10s red & blk	*13.50*	*9.00*
		Nos. N167-N178 (11)	*349.00*	*252.50*

The counterfeits and reprints of Nos. N167-N178 are difficult to distinguish from originals. Many overprint varieties exist.

Some specialists question the status of Nos. N167-N178.

DEDEAGATCH

(Alexandroupolis)

ΕΛΛΗΝΙΚΗ
ΔΙΟΙΚΗΣΙΣ
ΔΕΔΕΑΓΑΤΣ
ΔΕΚΑ ΛΕΠΤΑ

D1-(10 lepta)

1913 Unwmk. Typeset *Perf. 11½*

Control Mark in Red

N179	D1	5 l black	35.00	27.50
N180	D1	10 l black	3.00	3.00
N181	D1	25 l black	4.00	4.00
a.		Sheet of 8	100.00	100.00

Nos. N179-N181 issued without gum in sheets of 8, consisting of one 5 l, three 10 l normal, one 10 l inverted, three 25 l and one blank. The sheet yields se-tenant pairs of 5 l & 10 l, 10 l & 25 l; tete beche pairs of 5 l & 10 l, 10 l & 25 l and 10 l & 10 l.

Also issued imperf., value $175 unused, $125 canceled.

The 5 l reads "PENTE LEPTA" in Greek letters; the 10 l is illustrated; the 25 l carries the numeral "25."

ΕΛΛΗΝΙΚΗ
ΔΙΟΙΚΗΣΙΣ
ΔΕΔΕΑΓΑΤΣ
10
ΛΕΠΤΑ

Bulgaria Nos. 89-90, 92-93, 95 Surcharged

Red Surcharge

1913 *Perf. 12*

N182	A20	5 l on 1s myr grn	72.50	42.50
N183	A26	1d on 25s ultra & blk	72.50	42.50

Blue Surcharge

N184 A24 10 l on 10s red & blk 27.50 17.00
N185 A23 25 l on 5s grn & blk 32.50 17.00
N187 A21 50 l on 2s car & blk 72.50 42.50
Nos. N182-N185,N187 (5) 277.50 161.50

The surcharges on Nos. N182 to N187 are printed from a setting of eight, which was used for all, with the necessary changes of value. No. 6 in the setting has a Greek "L" instead of "D" for the third letter of the third word of the surcharge.

The 25 l surcharge also exists on 8 copies of the 25s, Bulgaria No. 95.

ΠΡΟΣΩΡΙΝΟΝ
ΕΛΛΗΝΙΚΗ
ΔΙΟΙΚΗΣΙΣ
ΔΕΔΕΑΓΑΤΣ
1 ΛΕΠΤΟΝ 1
D2

ΠΡΟΣΩΡΙΝΟΝ
ΕΛΛΗΝΙΚΗ
ΔΙΟΙΚΗΣΙΣ
ΔΕΔΕΑΓΑΤΣ
5 ΛΕΠΤΑ 5
D3

1913, Sept. 15 Typeset *Perf. 11½*
Control Mark in Blue

N188 D2 1 l blue 65.00
N189 D2 2 l blue 65.00
N190 D2 3 l blue 65.00
N191 D2 5 l blue 65.00
N192 D2 10 l blue 65.00
N193 D2 25 l blue 65.00
N194 D2 40 l blue 65.00
N195 D2 50 l blue 65.00

Nos. N188 to N195 were issued without gum in sheets of eight containing all values.

1913, Sept. 25 Typeset
Control Mark in Blue

N196 D3 1 l blue, *gray bl* 65.00
N197 D3 5 l blue, *gray bl* 65.00
N198 D3 10 l blue, *gray bl* 65.00
N199 D3 25 l blue, *gray bl* 65.00
N200 D3 30 l blue, *gray bl* 65.00
N201 D3 50 l blue, *gray bl* 65.00

Nos. N196 to N201 were issued without gum in sheets of six containing all values.

Counterfeits of Nos. N182-N201 are plentiful.

FOR USE IN NORTH EPIRUS (ALBANIA)

Greek Stamps of 1937-38 Overprinted in Black

ΕΛΛΗΝΙΚΗ
ΔΙΟΙΚΗΣΙΣ

Perf. 13½x12, 12x13½
1940 Litho. Wmk. 252

N202 A69 5 l brn red & bl 15 15
a. Inverted overprint 20.00
N203 A70 10 l bl & brn red (No. 413) 15 15
a. Double impression of frame 10.00
N204 A71 20 l blk & grn 15 15
a. Inverted overprint 25.00
N205 A72 40 l grn & blk 15 15
a. Inverted overprint 30.00
N206 A73 50 l brn & blk 18 18
N207 A74 80 l ind & yel brn 18 18
N208 A67 1d green 22 22
a. Inverted overprint 35.00
N209 A75 2d ultra 15 15
N210 A67 3d red brn 15 15
N211 A76 5d red 18 18
N212 A77 6d ol brn 22 22
N213 A78 7d dk brn 38 38
N214 A67 8d dp bl 55 55
N215 A79 10d red brn 55 55
N216 A80 15d green 95 95
N217 A81 25d dk bl 1.10 1.10
a. Inverted overprint 45.00

Engr.
Unwmk.

N218 A84 30d org brn 2.75 2.75
Nos. N202-N218 (17) 8.16 8.16

Same Overprinted in Carmine on National Youth Issue

1941 Litho. *Perf. 12½, 13½x12½*

N219 A93 3d sil, dp ultra & red 1.00 1.00
N220 A94 5d dk bl & blk 1.60 1.60
N221 A94 10d red org & blk 2.00 2.00
N222 A94 15d dk grn & blk 26.00 26.00
N223 A94 20d lake & blk 3.25 3.25
N224 A94 25d dk bl & blk 6.50 6.50
N225 A94 30d rose vio & blk 6.50 6.50
N226 A94 50d lake & blk 6.50 6.50
N227 A94 75d dk bl, brn & gold 6.50 6.50
N228 A93 100d sil, dp ultra & red 6.50 6.50
a. Inverted overprint *175.00*
Nos. N219-N228 (10) 66.35 66.35

Same Overprint in Carmine on National Youth Air Post Stamps

N229 AP25 2d red org & blk 65 65
a. Inverted overprint 75.00
N230 AP25 4d dk grn & blk 3.25 3.25
a. Inverted overprint *75.00*
N231 AP25 6d lake & blk 3.25 3.25
a. Inverted overprint *75.00*
N232 AP25 8d dk bl & blk 3.25 3.25
N233 AP25 16d rose vio & blk 5.00 5.00
N234 AP25 32d red org & blk 5.00 5.00
N235 AP25 45d dk grn & blk 6.50 6.50
N236 AP25 55d lake & blk 6.50 6.50
N237 AP25 65d dk bl & blk 6.50 6.50
N238 AP25 100d rose vio & blk 6.50 6.50
Nos. N229-N238 (10) 46.40 46.40

Some specialists have questioned the status of Nos. N230a and N231a.

For other stamps issued by Greece for use in occupied parts of Epirus and Thrace, see the catalogue listings of those countries.

Catalogue values for unused stamps in this section, from this point to the end of the section, are for Never Hinged items.

FOR USE IN THE DODECANESE ISLANDS

Greece, No. 472C, with Additional Overprint in Carmine or Silver

Σ. Δ. Δ.

1947 Wmk. 252 Litho. *Perf. 12½*

N239 A113 10d on 2,000d dp bl (C) 30 30
N240 A113 10d on 2,000d dp bl (S) 30 30

These stamps sold for 5 lire (100 drachmas) and paid postage for that amount.

King George II Memorial Issue

Greece, Nos. 484 and 485, With Additional Overprint in Black

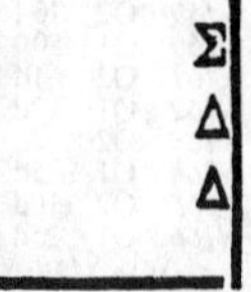

1947 Engr. *Perf. 12½x12*

N241 A67 50d on 1d grn 75 75
N242 A67 250d on 3d red brn 75 75

The letters are initials of the Greek words for "Military Administration of the Dodecanese."

Greece, Nos. 501 and 502 Overprinted in Carmine

Σ. Δ. Δ.

1947 Wmk. 252 Litho. *Perf. 12½*

N243 A111 20d on 500d dk ol 40 40
N244 A104 30d on 5d lt bl grn 60 60

Greece, Nos. 437, 406, 407 and 445, Surcharged in Black or Carmine

1947 *Perf. 12½, 13½x12*

N245 A103 50d on 2d 70 70

Engr.

N246 A79 250d on 10d 1.40 1.40
N247 A80 400d on 15d (C) 1.75 1.75
a. Inverted surcharge 125.00

Litho.

N248 A110 1000d on 200 (C) 85 85
a. Imprint omitted 70.00

POSTAGE DUE STAMPS

FOR USE IN PARTS OF TURKEY OCCUPIED BY GREECE (NEW GREECE)

Postage Due Stamps of Greece, 1902, Overprinted

ΕΛΛΗΝΙΚΗ
ΔΙΟΙΚΗΣΙΣ

1912 Wmk. 129 Engr. *Perf. 13½*
Black Overprint

NJ1 D3 1 l chocolate 20 20
NJ2 D3 2 l gray 20 20
NJ3 D3 3 l orange 20 20
NJ4 D3 5 l yel grn 30 30
NJ5 D3 10 l scarlet 30 30
NJ6 D3 20 l lilac 60 60
NJ7 D3 30 l dp vio 2.75 1.75
NJ8 D3 40 l dk brn 2.50 2.50
NJ9 D3 50 l red brn 3.00 3.00
NJ10 D3 1d black 17.50 14.00
NJ11 D3 2d bronze 17.50 11.00
NJ12 D3 3d silver 42.50 27.50
NJ13 D3 5d gold 100.00 85.00
Nos. NJ1-NJ13 (13) 187.55 146.55

Red Overprint

NJ14 D3 1 l chocolate 60 60
NJ15 D3 2 l gray 60 60
NJ16 D3 3 l orange 22.50 22.50
NJ17 D3 5 l yel grn 60 50
NJ18 D3 10 l scar, down 3.00 3.00
NJ19 D3 20 l lilac 60 60
NJ20 D3 30 l dp vio 2.25 2.25
NJ21 D3 40 l dk brn 60 50
NJ22 D3 50 l red brn 60 50
NJ23 D3 1d black 4.00 4.00
NJ24 D3 2d bronze 7.00 6.00
NJ25 D3 3d silver 17.50 17.50
NJ26 D3 5d gold 35.00 35.00
Nos. NJ14-NJ26 (13) 94.85 93.55

The normal position of the overprint is reading upward but it is often reversed. Some of the varieties of lettering which occur on the postage stamps are also found on the postage due stamps. Double overprints exist on some denominations.

FOR USE IN NORTH EPIRUS (ALBANIA)

Postage Due Stamps of Greece, 1930, Surcharged or Overprinted in Black:

ΕΛΛΗΝΙΚΗ
ΔΙΟΙΚΗΣΙΣ
50
ΛΕΠΤΑ
a

ΕΛΛΗΝΙΚΗ
ΔΙΟΙΚΗΣΙΣ
b

Perf. 13, 13x12½
1940 Litho. Unwmk.

NJ27 D3(a) 50 l on 25d lt red 20 30
NJ28 D3(b) 2d light red 25 25
a. Inverted overprint 30.00
NJ29 D3(b) 5d blue gray 25 25
NJ30 D3(b) 10d green 45 45
NJ31 D3(b) 15d red bowrn 60 60
Nos. NJ27-NJ31 (5) 1.75 1.85

POSTAL TAX STAMPS

FOR USE IN NORTH EPIRUS (ALBANIA)

Postal Tax Stamps of Greece, Nos. RA61-RA63, Overprinted Type "b" in Black

1940 Unwmk. Litho. *Perf. 13½x12*

NRA1 PT7 10 l 15 15
NRA2 PT7 50 l 15 15
a. Inverted overprint 35.00
NRA3 PT7 1d 20 20

GREENLAND

LOCATION — North Atlantic Ocean
GOVT. — Danish
AREA — 840,000 sq. mi.
POP. — 52,347 (1984)

In 1953 the colony of Greenland became an integral part of Denmark.

100 Ore = 1 Krone

Catalogue values for unused stamps in this country are for Never Hinged items, beginning with Scott 48 in the regular postage section, Scott B4 in the semi-postal section.

Christian X — A1

Polar Bear — A2

Perf. 13x12½
1938-46 Unwmk. Engr.

1 A1 1o olive blk 22 32
2 A1 5o rose lake 1.40 65
3 A1 7o yel green 1.75 2.75
4 A1 10o purple 95 65
5 A1 15o red 95 65
6 A1 20o red ('46) 95 75
7 A2 30o blue 6.00 7.50
8 A2 40o blue ('46) 17.50 7.50
9 A2 1k light brn 6.50 9.50
Nos. 1-9 (9) 36.22 30.27

Issue dates: Nov. 1, 1938, Aug. 1, 1946.

For surcharges see Nos. 39-40.

Harp Seal — A3

Christian X — A4

Dog Team — A5

Designs: 1k, Polar bear. 2k, Eskimo in kayak. 5k, Eider duck.

1945, Feb. 1 *Perf. 12*

10 A3 1o ol blk & vio 15.00 17.50
11 A3 5o rose lake & ol bister 15.00 17.50
12 A3 7o grn & blk 15.00 17.50
13 A4 10o pur & olive 15.00 17.50
14 A4 15o red & brt ultra 15.00 17.50
15 A5 30o dk bl & red brn 15.00 17.50
16 A5 1k brn & gray blk 15.00 17.50
17 A5 2k sep & dp grn 15.00 17.50
18 A5 5k dk pur & dl brn 15.00 17.50
Nos. 10-18 (9) 135.00 157.50

Nos. 10-18 Overprinted in Carmine or Blue

DANMARK BEFRIET 5 MAJ 1945

1945

19	A3	1o (C)	21.00	22.50
20	A3	5o (Bl)	21.00	22.50
21	A3	7o (C)	21.00	22.50
22	A4	10o (Bl)	37.50	55.00
a.		Overprint in carmine	150.00	225.00
23	A4	15o (C)	35.00	55.00
a.		Overprint in blue	75.00	100.00
24	A5	30o (Bl)	35.00	55.00
a.		Overprint in carmine	75.00	100.00
25	A5	1k (C)	35.00	55.00
a.		Overprint in blue	75.00	100.00
26	A5	2k (C)	35.00	55.00
a.		Overprint in blue	75.00	100.00
27	A5	5k (Bl)	35.00	55.00
a.		Overprint in carmine	75.00	100.00
		Nos. 19-27 (9)	275.50	397.50
		Nos. 22a-27a (6)	525.00	725.00

Liberation of Denmark from the Germans. Overprint illustrated as on Nos. 19-21. Larger type and different settings used for Types A4 and A5. Overprint often smudged.

Nos. 19-27 exist with overprint inverted. Value, each $375.

Frederik IX — A6

Polar Ship "Gustav Holm" — A7

1950-60 Unwmk. Engr. *Perf. 13*

28	A6	1o dk olive grn	15	15
29	A6	5o deep car	18	15
30	A6	10o green	28	28
31	A6	15o purple ('60)	55	45
a.		15o dull purple	2.00	1.00
32	A6	25o vermilion	1.10	90
33	A6	30o dk bl ('53)	16.00	1.65
34	A6	30o ver ('59)	48	32
35	A7	50o deep blue	15.00	14.00
36	A7	1k brown	6.50	1.65
37	A7	2k dull red	3.75	1.65
38	A7	5k gray ('58)	1.90	1.40
		Nos. 28-38 (11)	45.89	22.60

Issue dates: Nos. 28-30, 31a, 32, 35-37, Aug. 15. No. 33, Dec. 1. No. 38, Aug. 14. No. 34, Oct. 29. No. 31, Oct.

For surcharges see Nos. B1-B2.

Nos. 8 and 9 Surcharged

60 øre

1956, Mar. 8

39	A2	60o on 40o blue	6.75	1.40
40	A2	60o on 1k lt brn	22.50	6.50

Drum Dancer — A8

Designs: 50o, The Boy and the Fox. 60o, The Mother of the Sea. 80o, The Girl and the Eagle. 90o, The Great Northern Diver and the Raven.

1957-69 Engr. *Perf. 13*

41	A8	35o gray olive	1.25	1.00
42	A8	50o brown red	1.25	1.40
43	A8	60o blue	2.75	1.40
44	A8	80o light brn	1.25	1.40
45	A8	90o dark blue	2.75	3.25
		Nos. 41-45 (5)	9.25	8.45

Issue dates: 35o, Mar. 16, 1961. 50o, Sept. 22, 1966. 60o, May 2, 1957. 80o, Sept. 18, 1969. 90o, Nov. 23, 1967.

Hans Egede — A9

Knud Rasmussen — A10

1958, Nov. 5

46	A9	30o henna brown	6.00	1.65

200th anniv. of death of Hans Egede, missionary to Eskimos in Greenland.

1960, Nov. 24 *Perf. 13*

47	A10	30o dull red	1.65	1.00

50th anniv. of establishment by Rasmussen of the mission and trading station at Thule (Dundas).

Catalogue values for unused stamps in this section, from this point to the end of the section, are for Never Hinged items.

Northern Lights and Crossed Anchors — A11

Frederick IX — A12

Polar Bear — A13

1963-68 Engr.

48	A11	1o gray	15	15
49	A11	5o rose claret	15	15
50	A11	10o green	42	42
51	A11	12o yel grn	45	45
52	A11	15o rose vio	60	60
53	A12	20o ultra	4.00	4.00
54	A12	25o lt brn ('64)	40	40
55	A12	30o grn ('68)	28	28
56	A12	35o dl red ('64)	20	20
57	A12	40o gray ('64)	40	40
58	A12	50o grnsh bl ('64)	8.00	7.75
59	A12	50o dk red ('65)	40	28
60	A12	60o rose cl ('68)	42	28
61	A12	80o orange	85	75
62	A13	1k brown	60	28
63	A13	2k dull red	2.50	75
64	A13	5k dark blue	2.50	1.10
65	A13	10k dl sl grn	2.50	1.10
		Nos. 48-65 (18)	24.82	19.34

Issue dates: Nos. 48-52, Mar. 7. Nos. 53, 61, July 25. Nos. 62-65, Sept. 17. Nos. 54, 56-58, Mar. 11. No. 59, Sept. 9. No. 60, Feb. 29. No. 55, Nov. 21.

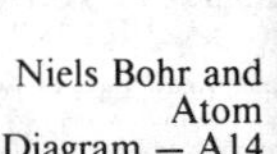

Niels Bohr and Atom Diagram — A14

1963, Nov. 21 Unwmk.

66	A14	35o red brown	45	45
67	A14	60o dark blue	4.00	4.00

50th anniv. of atom theory of Prof. Bohr (1885-1962).

Samuel Kleinschmidt (1814-1886), Philologist — A15

1964, Nov. 26

68	A15	35o brown red	50	50

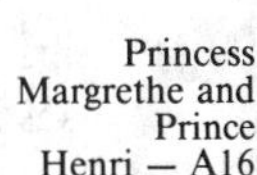

Princess Margrethe and Prince Henri — A16

1967, June 10

69	A16	50o red	3.75	3.75

Wedding of Crown Princess Margrethe and Prince Henri de Monpezat.

Frederik IX and Map of Greenland — A17

1969, Mar. 11 Engr. *Perf. 13*

70	A17	60o dull red	1.50	1.50

70th birthday of King Frederik IX.

Musk Ox A18

Liberation Celebration at Jakobshaven A19

Designs: 1k, Right whale diving off Disko Island. 2k, Narwhal. 5k, Polar bear. 10k, Walruses.

1969-76 Engr. *Perf. 13*

71	A18	1k dark blue	42	35
72	A18	2k gray green	55	42
73	A18	5k blue	1.40	85
74	A18	10k sepia	2.75	1.40
75	A18	25k greenish gray	7.00	2.75
		Nos. 71-75 (5)	12.12	5.77

Issue dates: 1k, Mar. 5, 1970. 2k, Feb. 20, 1975. 5k, Feb. 19, 1976. 10k, Feb. 15, 1973. 25k, Nov. 27, 1969.

1970, May 4

76	A19	60o red brown	2.25	2.25

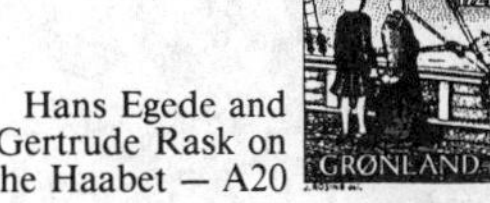

Hans Egede and Gertrude Rask on the Haabet — A20

1971, May 6 Engr. *Perf. 13*

77	A20	60o brown red	1.65	1.65

250th anniversary of arrival of Hans Egede in Greenland and the beginning of its colonization.

Mail-carrying Kayaks — A21

Designs: 70o, Umiak (women's rowboat). 80o, Catalina seaplane dropping mail by parachute. 90o, Dog sled. 1k, Coaster

Kununguak and pilot boat. 1.30k, Schooner Sokongen. 1.50k, Longboat off Greenland coast. 2k, Helicopter over mountains.

1971-77 Engr. *Perf. 13*

78	A21	50o green	25	22
79	A21	70o dl red ('72)	25	25
80	A21	80o black ('76)	45	45
81	A21	90o blue ('72)	35	25
82	A21	1k red ('76)	48	48
83	A21	1.30k dl bl ('75)	60	48
84	A21	1.50k gray grn ('74)	45	45
85	A21	2k blue ('77)	65	65
		Nos. 78-85 (8)	3.48	3.23

Issue dates: No. 78, Nov. 4. No. 81, Feb. 29. No. 79, Sept. 21. No. 84, Feb. 21. No. 83, Apr. 17. Nos. 80, Oct. 11. No. 85, Feb. 24.

Queen Margrethe — A22

1973-79 Engr. *Perf. 13*

86	A22	5o car rose ('78)	15	15
87	A22	10o slate grn	15	15
88	A22	60o sepia	35	24
89	A22	80o sepia ('79)	24	24
90	A22	90o red brn ('74)	60	35
91	A22	1k dk red ('77)	24	24
a.		Bklt. pane of 10 (4 10k, 6 1k)	2.00	
92	A22	1.20k dk bl ('74)	60	60
93	A22	1.20k mar ('78)	30	30
94	A22	1.30k dk bl ('77)	40	40
95	A22	1.30k red ('79)	35	35
96	A22	1.60k blue ('79)	60	60
97	A22	1.80k dl grn ('78)	75	75
		Nos. 86-97 (12)	4.73	4.37

Nos. 86, 89, 93, 95-97 inscribed "Kalaallit Nunaat."

Issue dates: Nos. 87-88, Apr. 16. Nos. 90, 92, Oct. 24. Nos. 91, 94, May 26. Nos. 86, 93, 97, Apr. 17. Nos. 89, 95-96, Mar. 29.

Trawler and Kayaks — A23

Falcon and Radar — A24

Design: 2k, Old Trade Buildings, Copenhagen (vert.).

1974, May 16 Engr. *Perf. 13*

98	A23	1k lt red brn	60	45
99	A23	2k sepia	70	60

Royal Greenland Trade Dept. Bicentennial.

1975, Sept. 4 Engr. *Perf. 13*

100	A24	90o red	42	42

50th anniversary of Greenland's telecommunications system.

Sirius Sled Patrol A25

1975, Oct. 16 Engr. *Perf. 13*

101	A25	1.20k sepia	42	42

Sirius sled patrol in northeast Greenland, 25th anniversary.

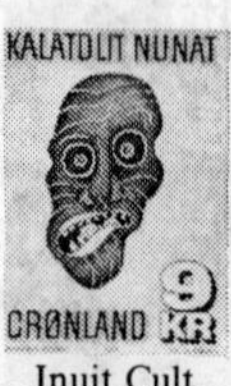

Inuit Cult Mask — A26

Jorgen Bronlund, Jakobshavn, Disko Bay — A27

Designs: 6k, Tupilac, a magical creature, carved whalebone. 7k, Soapstone sculpture. 8k, Eskimo with Family, driftwood sculpture, by Johannes Kreutzmann (1862-1940).

1977-80

102	A26	6k dp rose lil	1.75	1.75
103	A26	7k gray olive	1.75	1.75
104	A26	8k dark blue	2.00	2.00
105	A26	9k black	3.25	2.75

Issue dates: 6k, Oct. 5, 1978. 7k, Sept. 6, 1979. 8k, Feb. 29, 1980. 9k, Sept. 6, 1977.

The 6k, 7k, 8k are inscribed "Kalaallit Nunaat."

1977, Oct. 20

106	A27	1k red brown	28	25

Jorgen Bronlund, arctic explorer, birth centenary.

Meteorite — A28

1978, Jan. 20 Engr. *Perf. 13*

107	A28	1.20k dull red	40	40

Scientific Research Commission, centenary.

Sun Rising over Mountains — A29

1978, June 5 Engr. *Perf. 13*

108	A29	1.50k dark blue	50	40

25th anniversary of Constitution.

Hans Egede, Settlers, Troops and Drummer A30

1978, Aug. 29 Engr. *Perf. 13*

109	A30	2.50k red brown	75	75

Founding of Godthaab, 250th anniversary.

Navigator — A31

1979, May 1 Engr.

110	A31	1.10k sepia	42	42

Establishment of home rule, May 1, 1979.

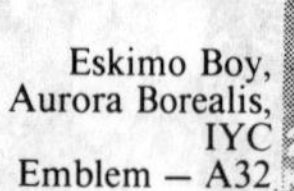

Eskimo Boy, Aurora Borealis, IYC Emblem — A32

1979, Oct. 18 Engr. *Perf. 13*

111	A32	2k olive green	60	60

International Year of the Child.

The Legend of the Reindeer and the Larva, by Jens Kreutzmann, 1860 — A33

Designs: 2.70k, Harpooning a Walrus, Jakob Danielsen. No. 114, Life in Thule, c. 1900, by Aninaaq. No. 115, Landscape, Ammassalik Fjord, Eastern Greenland, Peter Rosing (1892-1965). 3k, Footrace, woodcut by Aron from Kagec (1822-1869). 3.70k, Polar Bear Killing Seal Hunter, K. Andreassen (1890-1934). 9k, Hares Hunting, Gerhard Kleist (1855-1931).

1980-87 Engr. *Perf. 13*

112	A33	1.60k red	45	45
113	A33	2.70k dp vio	75	75
114	A33	2.80k lake	60	60
115	A33	2.80k lake	40	40
116	A33	3k black	95	95
117	A33	3.70k bl blk	95	95
118	A33	9k dk grn	2.00	2.00
		Nos. 112-118 (7)	6.10	6.10

Issue dates: 1.60k, Mar. 26, 1981. 2.70k, June 24, 1982. No. 114, Sept. 4, 1986. No. 115, Apr. 9, 1987. 3k, Sept. 4, 1980. 3.70k, Feb. 9, 1984. 9k, Sept. 5, 1985.

This is an expanding set. Numbers will change if necessary.

Queen Margrethe, Map of Greenland — A34

1980-89 Engr. *Perf. 13*

120	A34	50o pur ('81)	15	15
121	A34	80o sepia	28	28
122	A34	1.30k red	52	52
123	A34	1.50k royal bl ('82)	45	45
124	A34	1.60k ultra	1.00	1.00
125	A34	1.80k dl red ('82)	38	38
126	A34	2.30k dk grn ('81)	55	55
127	A34	2.50k red ('83)	52	52
128	A34	2.80k cop red ('85)	60	60
129	A34	3k fawn ('88)	70	70
130	A34	3.20k rose ('89)	90	90
a.		Bklt. pane of 10 (4 50o, 6 3.20k)	6.00	
131	A34	3.80k sl bl ('85)	70	70
132	A34	4.10k brt bl ('88)	95	95
133	A34	4.40k ultra ('89)	1.25	1.25
		Nos. 120-133 (14)	8.95	8.95

Issue dates: Nos. 121-122, 124, Apr. 16. Nos. 120, 126, Jan. 29. Nos. 123, 125, May 13. No. 127, Mar. 30. Nos. 128, 131, Feb. 7. Nos. 129, 132, Feb. 4. Nos. 130, 133, Jan. 30.

Rasmus Berthelsen (Teacher, Hymnist), in Training College Library, 1830 — A35

1980, May 29 Engr. *Perf. 13*

134	A35	2k brown, *cream*	65	65

Greenland Public Library Service, 150th anniversary.

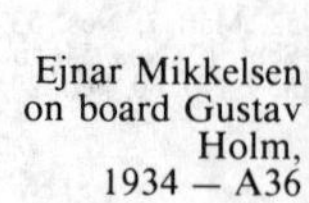

Ejnar Mikkelsen on board Gustav Holm, 1934 — A36

1980, Oct. 16 Engr. *Perf. 13*

135	A36	4k slate green	1.25	1.25

Ejnar Mikkelsen, inspector of East Greenland, birth centenary.

Pandalus Borealis — A37

Designs: No. 137, Anarhicas minor. No. 138, Reinhardtius Hippoglossoides. No. 139, Mallotus villosus. 25k, Codfish. 50k, Salmo salar.

1981-86 Engr. *Perf. 13*

136	A37	10k multi	2.25	2.25
137	A37	10k dk bl & blk	3.75	3.25
138	A37	10k multi	2.25	2.25
139	A37	10k grnsh blk & blk	2.25	2.25
140	A37	25k multi	5.00	5.00
141	A37	50k multi	10.00	10.00
		Nos. 136-141 (6)	25.50	25.00

Issue dates: 25k, May 21. No. 136, Apr. 1, 1982. 50k, Jan. 27, 1983. No. 137, Oct. 11, 1984. No. 138, Oct. 10, 1985. No. 139, Oct. 16, 1986.

This is an expanding set. Numbers will change if necessary.

Saqqaq Eskimo in Kayak, Reindeer — A38

Design: 5k, Tunit-Dorset hunters hauling seal.

1981, Oct. 15 Engr. *Perf. 12½*

146	A38	3.50k dark blue	1.05	1.05
147	A38	5k brown	1.50	1.50

Thule District Eskimos Catching Whale, 1000AD — A39

Greenland history: No. 149, Bishop Joen Smyrill's house and staff, 12th cent. No. 150, Wooden dolls, 13th cent. No. 151, Eskimo mummy, sacrificial stones, 14th cent. No. 152, Hans Pothorst, explorer, 15th cent. No. 153, Glass pearls, 16th cent. No. 154, Apostle spoons, 17th cent. No. 155, Key, trading station, 18th cent. No. 156, Trade Ship Hvalfisken, masthead, 19th cent. No. 157, Communications satellite, Earth, 20th cent.

1982, Sept. 30

148	A39	2k brown red	45	45
149	A39	2.70k dark blue	60	60

1983, Sept. 15

150	A39	2.50k red	55	55
151	A39	3.50k brown	80	80
152	A39	4.50k blue	1.00	1.00

1984, Mar. 29

153	A39	2.70k red brown	70	70
154	A39	3.70k dark blue	90	90
155	A39	5.50k brown	1.40	1.40

1985, Mar. 21

156	A39	2.80k violet	55	55
157	A39	6k blue black	1.10	1.10
		Nos. 148-157,B10 (11)	8.95	8.95

250th Anniv. of Settlement of New Herrnhut A40

1983, Nov. 2 Engr.

158	A40	2.50k brown	90	90

Henrik Lund, Natl. Anthem Score, Lichtenau Fjord — A41

1984, Sept. 6 Engr.

159	A41	5k dark green	1.10	1.10

Henrik Lund (1875-1948), natl. anthem composer, artist, only Greenlander to win Ingenio et Arti medal.

Greenland stamps can be mounted in Scott's Scandinavia and Finland Album.

Prince Henrik, 50th Birthday — A42

1984, June 6 Engr. *Perf. 13*
160 A42 2.70k dull red 1.10 1.10

Town of Christianshab, 250th Anniv. — A43

1984, July 25 Engr. *Perf. 13*
161 A43 3.70k Danish grenadier, 1734 80 80

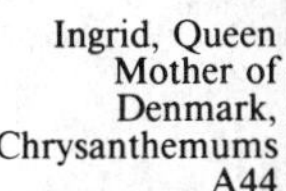

Ingrid, Queen Mother of Denmark, Chrysanthemums A44

1985, May 21 Litho. & Engr.
162 A44 2.80k multi 95 95

Arrival in Denmark of Princess Ingrid, 50th anniv. See Denmark No. 775.

Intl. Youth Year — A45

1985, June 27 Litho.
163 A45 3.80k Emblem, birds nesting, fiord 1.25 1.25

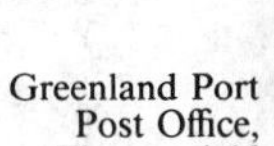

Greenland Port Post Office, Flags — A46

1986, Mar. 6 Engr. *Perf. 13*
164 A46 2.80k dark red 75 75

Transfer of postal control under Greenland Home Rule, Jan. 1, 1986.

Artifacts — A47

1986-88 Engr. *Perf. 13*
165 A47 2.80k Sewing needles, case 55 55
165A A47 3k Buckets, bowl, scoop 88 88
166 A47 3.80k Ulos 1.10 1.10
167 A47 3.80k Masks 75 75
168 A47 5k Harpoon points 1.45 1.45
169 A47 6.50k Lard lamps 2.00 2.00
172 A47 10k Carved faces 2.90 2.90
Nos. 165-172 (7) 9.63 9.63

Issue dates: No. 166, 6.50k, May 22. 2.80k, 3.80k, June 11, 1987. 3k, 5k, 10k, Oct. 27, 1988.

This is an expanding set. Numbers will change if necessary.

Souvenir Sheet

HAFNIA '87 — A48

1987, Jan. 23 Litho. *Perf. 13*
175 A48 Sheet of 3 5.50 5.50
a. 2.80k Gull in flight 1.50 1.50
b. 3.80k Mountain 1.75 1.75
c. 6.50k Gulls in water 2.00 2.00

No. 175 sold for 19.50k.

See No. 199.

Year of the Fishing, Sealing and Whaling Industries — A49

1987, Apr. 9 Litho. *Perf. 13*
176 A49 3.80k multi 75 75

Lagopus Mutus — A50 Birds of Prey — A51

1987-90 Litho. *Perf. 13*
177 A51 3k Falco rusticolus 95 95
178 A51 3.20k Clangula hyemalis 90 90
179 A51 4k Anser caerulescens 1.15 1.15
180 A51 4.10k Corvus corax 1.30 1.30
181 A51 4.40k Plectrophenax nivalis 1.25 1.25
182 A50 5k shown 1.25 1.25
183 A51 5.50k Haliaeetus albicilla 1.75 1.75
184 A51 5.50k Cepphus grylle 1.55 1.55
185 A51 6.50k Uria lomvia 1.85 1.85
186 A51 7k Gavia immer 2.25 2.25
187 A51 7.50k Stercorarius longicaudus 2.15 2.15
188 A50 10k Nyctea scandiaca 2.50 2.50
Nos. 177-188 (12) 18.85 18.85

Issue dates: 5k, 10k, Sept. 3. 3k, 4.10k, No. 183, 7k, Apr. 14, 1988. 3.20k, 4.40k, No. 184, 6.50k, Mar. 16, 1989. 4k, 7.50k, Jan. 15, 1990.

Plants — A52

1989-92 Litho. *Perf. 13*
189 A52 4k *Campanula gieseckiana* 1.25 1.25
190 A52 4k *Pedicularis hirsuta* 1.25 1.25
191 A52 5k *Eriophorum scheuchzeri* 1.40 1.40
192 A52 5.50k *Ledum groenlandicum* 1.75 1.75
193 A52 6.50k *Cassiope tetragona* 2.00 2.00
194 A52 7.25k *Saxifraga oppositifolia* 2.25 2.25
196 A52 10k *Papaver radicatum*, vert. 2.75 2.75
Nos. 189-196 (7) 12.65 12.65

Issue dates: 5k, 10k, Oct. 12, 1989. No. 189, 5.50k, 6.50k, June 7, 1990; No. 190, 7.25k, Mar. 26, 1992. Nos. 189-190 vert.

This is an expanding set. Numbers will change if necessary.

HAFNIA Type of 1987
Souvenir Sheet

Design: Uummannaq Mountain in winter, horiz.

1987, Oct. 16 Litho. *Perf. 13x12½*
199 A48 2.80k slate blue & lake 1.25 1.25

No. 199 sold for 4k.

Greenland Home Rule, 10th Anniv.
A53 A54

1989, May 1 Litho. *Perf. 13*
200 A53 3.20k Flag, landscape 90 90
201 A54 4.40k Coat of arms 1.25 1.25

Queen Margrethe — A55

1990, Apr. 5 Engr. *Perf. 13*
214 A55 25o green 15 15
217 A55 1k brown 32 32
a. Bklt. pane of 10, 4 #214, 6 #217 2.25
224 A55 4k car rose 1.25 1.25
228 A55 6.50k blue 2.00 2.00

No. 217a issued May 3.

This is an expanding set. Numbers will change if necessary.

Frederik Lynge (1889-1957), Politician — A56

Design: 25k, Augo Lynge (1899-1959), politician

1990, Oct. 18 Engr. *Perf. 13x12½*
231 A56 10k rose brn & dk bl 3.25 3.25
232 A56 25k vio & dk bl 8.00 8.00

See Nos. 242-243.

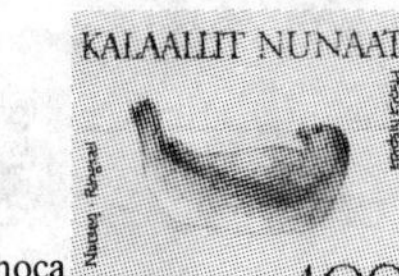

Phoca Hispida — A57

Walrus and Seals.

Litho. & Engr.
1991, Mar. 14 *Perf. 13*
233 A57 4k shown 1.25 1.25
234 A57 4k Pagophilus groenlandicus 1.25 1.25
235 A57 7.25k Cystophora cristata 2.25 2.25
236 A57 7.25k Odobenus rosmarus 2.25 2.25
237 A57 8.50k Erignatus barbatus 2.65 2.65
238 A57 8.50k Phoca vitulina 2.65 2.65
a. Min. sheet of 8, #233-238 12.30 12.30
Nos. 233-238 (6) 12.30 12.30

Village of Ilulissat, 250th Anniv. — A58

1991, May 15 Litho. *Perf. 13*
239 A58 4k multicolored 1.25 1.25

Tourism — A59

1991, May 15 *Perf. 12½x13*
240 A59 4k Iceberg 1.25 1.25
241 A59 8.50k Skiers, sled dogs 2.65 2.65

Famous Men Type of 1990

Designs: 10k, Jonathan Petersen (1881-1961), musician. 50k, Hans Lynge (1906-1988), artist and writer.

1991, Sept. 5 Engr. *Perf. 13x12½*
242 A56 10k black & dk blue 3.10 3.10
243 A56 50k red brn & blue 15.50 15.50

SEMI-POSTAL STAMPS

No. 35 Surcharged in Red

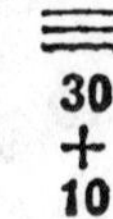

1958, May 22 Engr. *Perf. 13*
B1 A7 30o + 10o on 50o dp bl 3.25 1.75

The surtax was for the campaign against tuberculosis in Greenland.

No. 32 Surcharged: "Gronlandsfonden 30+10" and Bars

1959, Feb. 23 Unwmk.
B2 A6 30o + 10o on 25o ver 3.50 3.50

The surtax was for the benefit of the Greenland Fund.

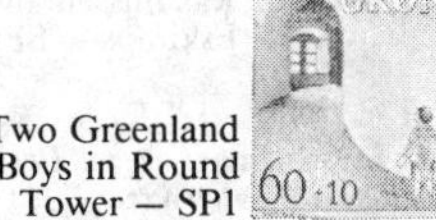

Two Greenland Boys in Round Tower — SP1

1968, Sept. 12 Engr. *Perf. 13*
B3 SP1 60o + 10o dark red 1.50 2.00

Surtax for child welfare work in Greenland.

Catalogue values for unused stamps in this section, from this point to the end of the section, are for Never Hinged items.

A particular stamp may be scarce, but if few collectors want it, its market value may remain relatively low.

Hans Egede Explaining Bible to Natives — SP2

1971, July 3 **Engr.** ***Perf. 13***
B4 SP2 60o + 10o red brown 2.50 2.50

See footnote after No. 77.

Frederik IX, "Dannebrog" off Umanak — SP3

1972, Apr. 20
B5 SP3 60o + 10o dull red 1.65 1.65

In memory of King Frederik IX (1899-1972). The surtax was for humanitarian and charitable purposes.

Heimaey Town and Volcano — SP4

1973, Oct. 18 **Engr.** ***Perf. 13***
B6 SP4 70o + 20o gray & red 1.65 1.65

The surtax was for the victims of the eruption of Heimaey Volcano.

Arm Pulling, by Hans Egede — SP5

1976, Apr. 8 **Engr.** ***Perf. 12½***
B7 SP5 100o + 20o multi 60 60

Surtax for the Greenland Athletic Union.

Rasmussen and Eskimos — SP6

1979, July **Engr.** ***Perf. 13***
B8 SP6 1.30k + 20o brown red 80 80

Knud Rasmussen (1879-1933), arctic explorer and ethnologist.

Stone Tent Ring, Polar Wolf, King Eider Ducks — SP7

1981, Sept. 3 **Engr.** ***Perf. 13***
B9 SP7 1.60k + 20o lt red brn 75 75

Surtax was for Peary Land Expeditions.

History Type of 1982

Design: Eric the Red sailing for Greenland.

1982, Aug. 2 **Engr.** ***Perf. 12½***
B10 A39 2k + 40o dk red brn 90 90

Surtax was for Cultural House, Julianehab.

Blind Man — SP8

1983, May 19 **Engr.**
B11 SP8 2.50k + 40o multi 1.00 1.00

Surtax was for the handicapped.

Greenland Sports Union — SP9

1986, Apr. 17 **Litho.**
B12 SP9 2.80k + 50o Water game 85 85

Surtax for the Sports Union.

Greenland PO, 50th Anniv. — SP10

1988, Sept. 16 **Litho.** ***Perf. 12½x13***
B13 SP10 3k +50o multi 1.00 1.00

Surtax for the purchase of postal artifacts.

Sled Dog, Common Eider — SP11

Litho. & Engr.

1990, Sept. 6 ***Perf. 13***
B14 SP11 400o + 50o multi 1.45 1.45

Surtax for the Greenland Environmental Foundation.

Blue Cross of Greenland, 75th Anniv. — SP12

1991, Sept. 5 **Litho.** ***Perf. 13***
B15 SP12 4k +50o multi 1.40 1.40

Surtax benefits Blue Cross of Greenland.

PARCEL POST STAMPS

Arms of Greenland — PP1

Perf. 11, 11½

1905-37 **Unwmk.** **Typo.**
Q1 PP1 1o ol grn ('16) 32.50 30.00
  a. Perf. 12½ ('05) 400.00 450.00
Q2 PP1 2o yel ('16) 110.00 65.00
Q3 PP1 5o brn ('16) 65.00 57.50
  a. Perf. 12½ ('05) 450.00 525.00
Q4 PP1 10o bl ('37) 25.00 40.00
  a. Perf. 12½ ('05) 425.00 375.00
  b. Perf. 11½ ('16) 32.50 35.00
Q5 PP1 15o vio ('16) 100.00 92.50
Q6 PP1 20o red ('16) 12.00 10.00
  a. Perf. 11 ('37) 26.00 35.00
Q7 PP1 70o vio ('37) 25.00 *55.00*
  a. Perf. 11½ ('30) 110.00 110.00
Q8 PP1 1k yel ('37) 25.00 *110.00*
  a. Perf. 11½ ('30) 40.00 40.00
Q9 PP1 3k brn ('30) 80.00 100.00

1937 **Litho.** ***Perf. 11***
Q10 PP1 70o pale vio 27.50 *65.00*
Q11 PP1 1k yellow 25.00 55.00

On lithographed stamps, PAKKE-PORTO is slightly larger, hyphen has rounded ends and lines in shield are fine, straight and evenly spaced.

On typographed stamps, hyphen has squared ends and shield lines are coarse, uneven and inclined to be slightly wavy.

Used values are for postally used stamps. Numeral cancels indicate use as postal savings stamps.

Sheets of 25. Certain printings of Nos. Q1-Q2, Q3a, Q4a, and Q5-Q6 were issued without sheet margins. Stamps from the outer rows are straight edged.

GUADELOUPE

LOCATION — In the West Indies lying between Montserrat and Dominica
GOVT. — Former French colony
AREA — 688 sq. mi.
POP. — 271,262 (1946)
CAPITAL — Basse-Terre

Guadeloupe consists of two large islands, Guadeloupe proper and Grande-Terre, together with five smaller dependencies. Guadeloupe became an integral part of the Republic, acquiring the same status as the departments in metropolitan France, under a law effective Jan. 1, 1947.

100 Centimes = 1 Franc

Catalogue values for unused stamps in this country are for Never Hinged items, beginning with Scott 168 in the regular postage section, Scott B12 in the semi-postal section, Scott C1 in the airpost section, and Scott J38 in the postage due section.

See France Nos. 850, 909, 1280, 1913 for French stamps inscribed "Guadeloupe."

Stamps of French Colonies Surcharged

G P.E.
20

1884 **Unwmk.** ***Imperf.***
1 A8 20c on 30c brn, *bis* 27.50 20.00
  a. Large "2" 150.00 110.00
2 A8 25c on 35c blk, *org* 27.50 20.00
  a. Large "2" 150.00 110.00
  b. Large "5" 65.00 60.00

The 5c on 4c (French Colonies No. 40) was not regularly issued. Value $150.

c

d

1889 ***Perf. 14x13½***

Surcharged Type c

3 A9 3c on 20c red, *grn* 1.65 1.65
4 A9 15c on 20c red, *grn* 14.00 14.00
5 A9 25c on 20c red, *grn* 12.50 12.00

Surcharged Type d

6 A9 5c on 1c blk, *lil bl* 6.25 6.25
  a. Inverted surcharge *450.00*
  b. Double surcharge *90.00* *90.00*
7 A9 10c on 40c red, *straw* 14.00 13.00
  a. Double surcharge 160.00 150.00
8 A9 15c on 20c red, *grn* 14.00 11.50
  a. Double surcharge 160.00 150.00
9 A9 25c on 30c brn, *bis* 22.50 17.50
  a. Double surcharge 160.00 150.00

The word "centimes" in surcharges "b" and "c" varies from 10 to 12½mm.

Issue dates: No. 6, June 25, others, Mar. 22.

5 C.
GPE

1891
10 A9 5c on 10c blk, *lav* 6.75 6.25
11 A9 5c on 1fr brnz grn, *straw* 6.75 6.25

Stamps of French Colonies Overprinted in Black **GUADELOUPE**

1891 ***Imperf.***
12 A7 30c brn, *yelsh* 175.00 175.00
13 A7 80c car, *pnksh* 525.00 525.00

Perf. 14x13½

14 A9 1c blk, *lil bl* 70 70
  a. Double overprint 12.50 11.00
  b. Inverted overprint 60.00 60.00
15 A9 2c brn, *buff* 1.00 65
  a. Double overprint 14.00 11.00
16 A9 4c claret, *lav* 2.25 1.75
17 A9 5c grn, *grnsh* 3.00 3.00
  a. Double overrinpt 15.00 11.00
  b. Inverted overprint 62.50 62.50
18 A9 10c blk, *lavender* 5.50 5.00
19 A9 15c blue 15.00 2.00
  a. Double overprint 42.50 42.50
20 A9 20c red, *grn* 15.00 11.00
  a. Double overprint 90.00 80.00
21 A9 25c blk, *rose* 15.00 2.00
  a. Double overprint 90.00 85.00
  b. Inverted overprint 80.00 80.00
22 A9 30c brn, *bis* 16.00 14.00
  a. Double overprint 90.00 90.00
23 A9 35c dp vio, *org* 35.00 27.50
24 A9 40c red, *straw* 20.00 19.00
  a. Double overprint 350.00 225.00
25 A9 75c car, *rose* 60.00 57.50
26 A9 1fr brnz grn, *straw* 37.50 35.00

The following errors may be found in all values of Nos. 12-26: "GNADELOUPE," "GUADELOUEP," "GUADELONPE" and "GUADBLOUPE."

Navigation and Commerce — A7

Perf. 14x13½

1892-1901 **Typo.** **Unwmk.**

Colony Name in Blue or Carmine

27 A7 1c blk, *lil bl* 62 40
28 A7 2c brn, *buff* 60 40
29 A7 4c claret, *lav* 60 45
30 A7 5c grn, *grnsh* 1.40 40
31 A7 5c yel grn ('01) 1.50 62
32 A7 10c blk, *lavender* 4.00 1.20
33 A7 10c red ('00) 2.50 1.00
  a. Imperf. 45.00
34 A7 15c blue, quadrille paper 4.00 40

35 A7 15c gray, *lt gray* ('00) 4.00 62
36 A7 20c red, *grn* 3.25 1.60
37 A7 25c blk, *rose* 3.25 60
38 A7 25c blue ('00) 45.00 45.00
39 A7 30c brn, *bister* 7.50 5.00
40 A7 40c red, *straw* 7.50 4.50
41 A7 50c car, *rose* 14.00 7.00
42 A7 50c brn, *az* ('00) 18.00 11.00
43 A7 75c dp vio, *org* 12.00 8.25
44 A7 1fr brnz grn, *straw* 16.00 14.00
Nos. 27-44 (18) 145.72 102.44

Perf. 13½x14 stamps are counterfeits.
For surcharges see Nos. 45-53, 83-85.

Nos. 39-41, 43-44 Surcharged in Black:

G & D 5 — f
G et D 10 — g
G & D 1 fr. — h

1903
45 A7 (f) 5c on 30c 1.50 1.50
a. "C" instead of "G" 12.00 12.00
b. Inverted surcharge 15.00 15.00
c. Double surcharge 62.50 62.50
d. Double surch., inverted 65.00
46 A7 (g) 10c on 40c 2.50 2.50
a. "C" instead of "G" 12.00 12.00
b. "1" inverted 20.00 20.00
c. Inverted surcharge 17.50 17.50
47 A7 (f) 15c on 50c 3.50 3.50
a. "C" instead of "G" 15.00 15.00
b. Inverted surcharge 40.00 40.00
c. "15" inverted 150.00 150.00
48 A7 (g) 40c on 1fr 4.00 4.00
a. "C" instead of "G" 16.00 16.00
b. "4" inverted 45.00 45.00
c. Inverted surcharge 45.00 45.00
d. Double surcharge 100.00 100.00
49 A7 (h) 1fr on 75c 16.00 16.00
a. "C" instead of "G" 60.00 60.00
b. "1" inverted 75.00 75.00
c. Value above "G & D" 150.00 150.00
d. Inverted surcharge 45.00 45.00
Nos. 45-49 (5) 27.50 27.50

Letters and figures from several fonts were used for these surcharges, resulting in numerous minor varieties.

Nos. 48-49 With Additional Overprint "1903" in a Frame

1904, Mar.

Red Overprint
50 A7 (g) 40c on 1fr 22.50 22.50
51 A7 (h) 1fr on 75c 27.50 27.50

Blue Overprint
52 A7 (g) 40c on 1fr 16.00 16.00
53 A7 (h) 1fr on 75c 27.50 27.50

The date "1903" may be found in 19 different positions and type faces within the frame. These stamps may also be found with the minor varieties of Nos. 48-49.
The 40c exists with black overprint.

Harbor at Basse-Terre A8

View of La Soufriere A9

Pointe-a-Pitre, Grand-Terre — A10

1905-27 Typo. *Perf. 14x13½*
54 A8 1c blk, *bluish* 15 15
55 A8 2c vio brn, *straw* 15 15
56 A8 4c bis brn, *az* 15 15
57 A8 5c green 45 28
58 A8 5c dp bl ('22) 15 15
59 A8 10c rose 45 15
60 A8 10c grn ('22) 15 15
61 A8 10c red, *bluish* ('25) 15 15
62 A8 15c violet 20 15
63 A9 20c red, *grn* 15 15
64 A9 20c bl grn ('25) 15 15
65 A9 25c blue 15 15
66 A9 25c ol grn ('22) 15 15
67 A9 30c black 1.25 90
68 A9 30c rose ('22) 15 15
69 A9 30c brn ol, *lav* ('25) 15 15
70 A9 35c blk, *yel* ('06) 22 15
71 A9 40c red, *straw* 35 35
72 A9 45c ol gray, *lil* ('07) 25 22
73 A9 45c rose ('25) 30 30
74 A9 50c gray grn, *straw* 1.60 90
75 A9 50c dp bl ('22) 38 38
76 A9 50c vio ('25) 15 15
77 A9 65c blue ('27) 30 30
78 A9 75c car, *bl* 42 32
79 A10 1fr blk, *green* 65 65
80 A10 1fr lt bl ('25) 55 55
81 A10 2fr car, *org* 70 65
82 A10 5fr dp bl, *org* 2.50 2.50
Nos. 54-82 (29) 12.52 10.70

Nos. 57 and 59 exist imperf.
For surcharges see Nos. 86-95, 167, B1-B2.

Nos. 29, 39 and 40 Surcharged in Carmine or Black

05 10

1912, Nov.
83 A7 5c on 4c cl, *lav* (C) 35 35
84 A7 5c on 30c brn, *bis* (C) 60 60
85 A7 10c on 40c red, *straw* 80 80

Two spacings between the surcharged numerals are found on Nos. 83 to 85.

Stamps and Types of 1905-27 Surcharged with New Value and Bars

1924-27
86 A10 25c on 5fr dp bl, *org* 30 30
87 A10 65c on 1fr gray grn 60 60
88 A10 85c on 1fr gray grn 60 60
89 A9 90c on 75c dl red 60 60
90 A10 1.05fr on 2fr ver (Bl) 30 30
91 A10 1.25fr on 1fr lt bl (R) 15 15
92 A10 1.50fr on 1fr dk bl 60 60
93 A10 3fr on 5fr org brn 52 52
94 A10 10fr on 5fr vio rose, *org* 4.00 4.00
95 A10 20fr on 5fr rose lil, *pnksh* 4.75 4.75
Nos. 86-95 (10) 12.42 12.42

Years issued: Nos. 87-88, 1925. Nos. 90-91, 1926. Nos. 89, 92-95, 1927.

Sugar Mill — A11

Saints Roadstead A12

Harbor Scene A13

Perf. 14x13½
1928-40 Unwmk. Typo.
96 A11 1c yel & vio 15 15
97 A11 2c blk & lt red 15 15
98 A11 3c yel & red vio ('40) 15 15
99 A11 4c yel grn & org brn 15 15
100 A11 5c ver & grn 15 15
101 A11 10c bis brn & dp bl 15 15
102 A11 15c brn red & blk 15 15
103 A11 20c lil & ol brn 15 15
104 A12 25c grnsh bl & olvn 15 15
105 A12 30c gray grn & yel grn 15 15
106 A12 35c bl grn ('38) 15 15
107 A12 40c yel & vio 15 15
108 A12 45c vio brn & slate 35 35
109 A12 45c bl grn & dl grn ('40) 30 30
110 A12 50c dl grn & org 30 15
111 A12 55c ultra & car ('38) 35 28
112 A12 60c ultra & car ('40) 15 15
113 A12 65c gray blk & ver 15 15
114 A12 70c gray blk & ver ('40) 15 15
115 A12 75c dl red & bl grn 35 30
116 A12 80c car & brn ('38) 22 22
117 A12 90c dl red & dl rose 80 80
118 A12 90c rose red & bl ('39) 40 40
119 A13 1fr lt rose & lt bl 2.00 1.00
120 A13 1fr rose red & org ('38) 45 45
121 A13 1fr bl gray & blk brn ('40) 20 20
122 A13 1.05fr lt bl & rose 60 60
123 A13 1.10fr lt red & grn 1.20 1.00
124 A13 1.25fr bl gray & blk brn ('33) 15 15
125 A13 1.25fr brt rose & red org ('39) 35 35
126 A13 1.40fr lt bl & lil rose ('40) 22 22
127 A13 1.50fr dl bl & bl 15 15
128 A13 1.60fr lil rose & yel brn ('40) 22 22
129 A13 1.75fr lil rose & yel brn ('33) 1.75 1.00
130 A13 1.75fr vio bl ('38) 2.25 1.60
131 A13 2fr bl grn & dk brn 15 15
132 A13 2.25fr vio bl ('39) 30 30
133 A13 2.50fr pale org & grn ('40) 40 40
134 A13 3fr org brn & sl 20 15
135 A13 5fr dl bl & org 35 28
136 A13 10fr vio & ol brn 42 38
137 A13 20fr grn & mag 50 50
Nos. 96-137 (42) 17.03 14.15

Nos. 96-97 exist imperf.
For surcharges see Nos. 161-166.

Colonial Exposition Issue
Common Design Types

1931, Apr. 13 Engr. *Perf. 12½*
Name of Country in Black
138 CD70 40c dp grn 1.25 1.25
139 CD71 50c violet 1.40 1.40
140 CD72 90c red org 2.50 2.50
141 CD73 1.50fr dull blue 2.00 2.00

Cardinal Richelieu Establishing French Antilles Co., 1635 — A14

Victor Hugues and his Corsairs — A15

1935 *Perf. 13*
142 A14 40c gray brn 4.00 4.00
143 A14 50c dl red 4.00 4.00
144 A14 1.50fr dull blue 4.00 4.00
145 A15 1.75fr lil rose 4.00 4.00
146 A15 5fr dk brn 4.00 4.00
147 A15 10fr bl grn 4.00 4.00
Nos. 142-147 (6) 24.00 24.00

Tercentenary of the establishment of the French colonies in the West Indies.

Paris International Exposition Issue
Common Design Types

1937 *Perf. 13*
148 CD74 20c dp vio 52 52
149 CD75 30c dk grn 52 52
150 CD76 40c car rose 75 75
151 CD77 50c dk brn & blk 75 75
152 CD78 90c red 75 75
153 CD79 1.50fr ultra 75 75
Nos. 148-153 (6) 4.04 4.04

Common Design Types pictured in section at front of book.

Colonial Arts Exhibition Issue
Souvenir Sheet
Common Design Type

1937 *Imperf.*
154 CD75 3fr dark blue 2.50 2.50

New York World's Fair Issue
Common Design Type

1939 Engr. *Perf. 12½x12*
155 CD82 1.25fr car lake 45 45
156 CD82 2.25fr ultra 45 45

For surcharges see Nos. 159-160.

La Soufriere View and Marshal Petain A16

1941 Engr. *Perf. 12½x12*
157 A16 1fr lilac 35
158 A16 2.50fr blue 35

Nos. 157-158 were issued by the Vichy government and were not placed on sale in Guadeloupe. This is also true of a 10c stamp, type A11 without "RF," released in 1944.

Nos. 155, 156, 113, 117 and 118 Surcharged with New Values in Black

1943 *Perf. 14x13½, 12½x12*
159 CD82 40c on 1.25fr car lake 35 35
160 CD82 40c on 2.25fr ultra 62 62
161 A12 50c on 65c gray blk & ver 42 42
162 A12 1fr on 90c dl red & dl rose 65 65
163 A12 1fr on 90c rose red & bl 42 42
Nos. 159-163 (5) 2.46 2.46

Nos. 104, 106, 113 and 90 Surcharged with New Values in Black

1944 *Perf. 14x13½*
164 A12 40c on 35c 35 35
165 A12 50c on 25c 15 15
166 A12 1fr on 65c 42 42
a. Double surcharge 60.00
167 A10 4fr on 1.05fr on 2fr 80 80

The surcharge on No. 166 is spelled out.

Catalogue values for unused stamps in this section, from this point to the end of the section, are for Never Hinged items.

Dolphins A17

1945 Unwmk. Photo. *Perf. 11½*
168 A17 10c chlky bl & red org 15 15
169 A17 30c lt yel grn & red 15 15
170 A17 40c lt bl & car 30 22
171 A17 50c red org & yel grn 15 15
172 A17 60c ol bis & lt bl 15 15
173 A17 70c lt gray & yel grn 30 25
174 A17 80c lt bl grn & yel 30 25
175 A17 1fr brn vio & grn 15 15
176 A17 1.20fr brt red vio & yel grn 15 15
177 A17 1.50fr dl brn & car 28 15
178 A17 2fr cer & bl 28 20
179 A17 2.40fr sal & yel grn 62 55
180 A17 3fr gray brn & bl vio 20 20
181 A17 4fr ultra & buff 15 15
182 A17 4.50fr brn org & grn 20 15
183 A17 5fr dk vio & grn 28 22
184 A17 10fr gray grn & red vio 28 22
185 A17 15fr sl gray & org 55 40
186 A17 20fr pale gray & dl org 80 65
Set value 4.75 3.85

Eboue Issue
Common Design Type

1945 Engr. *Perf. 13*
187 CD91 2fr black 22 22
188 CD91 25fr Prus green 60 60

Basse-Terre Harbor and Woman A18

Cutting Sugar Cane — A19

Pineapple Bearer — A20

Guadeloupe Woman A21

Gathering Coffee A22

Guadeloupe Woman — A23

1947 Unwmk. Engr. *Perf. 13*

189 A18	10c red brown	15	15
190 A18	30c sepia	15	15
191 A18	50c bl grn	15	15
192 A19	60c blk brn	15	15
193 A19	1fr dp car	25	22
194 A19	1.50fr dk gray bl	60	40
195 A20	2fr bl grn	65	55
196 A20	2.50fr dp car	60	40
197 A20	3fr deep blue	65	55
198 A21	4fr violet	60	45
199 A21	5fr bl grn	60	45
200 A21	6fr red	60	40
201 A22	10fr dp bl	60	40
202 A22	15fr dk vio brn	70	55
203 A22	20fr rose red	80	70
204 A23	25fr bl grn	1.40	90
205 A23	40fr red	1.50	1.10
	Nos. 189-205 (17)	10.15	7.67

SEMI-POSTAL STAMPS

Nos. 59 and 62 Surcharged in Red ✚5c

1915-17 Unwmk. *Perf. 14 x 13½*

B1 A8	10c + 5c rose	2.25	1.20
B2 A8	15c + 5c vio	1.50	1.25
a.	Double surcharge	60.00	60.00

Curie Issue
Common Design Type

1938, Oct. 24 *Perf. 13*

B3 CD80	1.75fr + 50c brt ultra	5.25	5.25

French Revolution Issue
Common Design Type
Name and Value Typo. in Black

1939, July 5 Photo. *Perf. 13*

B4 CD83	45c + 25c green	3.25	3.25
B5 CD83	70c + 30c brown	3.75	3.75
B6 CD83	90c + 35c red org	3.75	3.75
B7 CD83	1.25fr + 1fr rose pink	3.75	3.75
B8 CD83	2.25fr + 2fr blue	3.75	3.75
	Nos. B4-B8 (5)	18.25	18.25

Common Design Type and

Colonial Artillery SP1

Colonial Infantry — SP2

1941 Photo. *Perf. 13½*

B9 SP1	1fr + 1fr red	55	
B10 CD86	1.50fr + 3fr maroon	55	
B11 SP2	2.50fr + 1fr blue	55	

Nos. B9-B11 were issued by the Vichy government, and were not placed on sale in Guadeloupe.

Nos. 157-158 were surcharged "OEUVRES COLONIALES" and surtax (including change of denomination of the 2.50fr to 50c). These were issued in 1944 by the Vichy government, and not placed on sale in Guadeloupe.

Catalogue values for unused stamps in this section, from this point to the end of the section, are for Never Hinged items.

Red Cross Issue
Common Design Type

1944 *Perf. 14½x14*

B12 CD90	5fr + 20fr ultra	55	55

The surtax was for the French Red Cross and national relief.

AIR POST STAMPS

Catalogue values for unused stamps in this section are for Never Hinged items.

Common Design Type

1945 Unwmk. Photo. *Perf. 14½x14*

C1 CD87	50fr green	45	45
C2 CD87	100fr deep plum	60	60

Victory Issue
Common Design Type

1946, May 8 Engr. *Perf. 12½*

C3 CD92	8fr redsh brn	60	60

Chad to Rhine Issue
Common Design Types

1946, June 6

C4 CD93	5fr dk slate grn	70	70
C5 CD94	10fr deep blue	70	70
C6 CD95	15fr brt vio	70	70
C7 CD96	20fr brown car	70	70
C8 CD97	25fr black	70	70
C9 CD98	50fr red brown	70	70
	Nos. C4-C9 (6)	4.20	4.20

Gathering Bananas — AP1

Seaplane at Roadstead — AP2

Pointe-a-Pitre Harbor and Guadeloupe Woman — AP3

1947 Unwmk. *Perf. 13*

C10 AP1	50fr dk brn vio	3.50	2.00
C11 AP2	100fr deep blue	4.00	2.50
C12 AP3	200fr red	5.00	3.00

AIR POST SEMI-POSTAL STAMPS

Stamps of the design shown above and stamp of Cameroun type V10 inscribed "Guadeloupe" were issued in 1942 by the Vichy Government, but were not placed on sale in Guadeloupe.

POSTAGE DUE STAMPS

D1 D2 D3

1876 Unwmk. Typeset *Imperf.*

J1 D1	25c black	500.00	400.00
J2 D2	40c black, *blue*		*16,000.*
J3 D3	40c black	600.00	500.00

Twenty varieties of each.

Nos. J1 and J3 have been reprinted on thinner and whiter paper than the originals.

D4

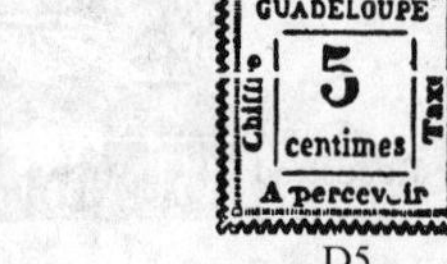

D5

1879

J4 D4	15c black, *blue*	19.00	14.00
a.	Period after "c" omitted	82.50	82.50
J5 D4	30c black	42.50	27.50
a.	Period after "c" omitted	120.00	110.00

Twenty varieties of each.

1884

J6 D5	5c black	9.00	9.00
J7 D5	10c blk, *blue*	22.50	15.00
J8 D5	15c blk, *violet*	42.50	25.00
J9 D5	20c blk, *rose*	65.00	45.00
a.	Italic "2" in "20"	450.00	375.00
J10 D5	30c blk, *yellow*	60.00	57.50
J11 D5	35c blk, *gray*	19.00	16.00
J12 D5	50c blk, *green*	9.00	7.50

There are ten varieties of the 35c, and fifteen of each of the other values, also numerous wrong font and missing letters.

Postage Due Stamps of French Colonies Surcharged in Black

1903

J13 D1	30c on 60c brn, *cr*	140.00	140.00
a.	"3" with flat top	325.00	325.00
b.	Inverted surcharge	400.00	400.00
c.	As "a," inverted	650.00	650.00
J14 D1	30c on 1fr rose, *cr*	160.00	160.00
a.	Inverted surcharge	425.00	425.00
b.	"3" with flat top	425.00	425.00
c.	As "b," inverted	700.00	700.00

Gustavia Bay — D6

Avenue of Royal Palms — D7

1905-06 Typo. *Perf. 14x13½*

J15 D6	5c blue	15	15
J16 D6	10c brown	15	15
J17 D6	15c green	25	25
J18 D6	20c blk, *yel* ('06)	28	28
J19 D6	30c rose	38	38
J20 D6	50c black	1.40	1.40
J21 D6	60c brn org	60	60
J22 D6	1fr violet	1.50	1.50
	Nos. J15-J22 (8)	4.71	4.71

Type of 1905-06 Issue Surcharged **2 francs à percevoir**

1926-27

J23 D6	2fr on 1fr gray	70	70
J24 D6	3fr on 1fr ultra ('27)	1.00	1.00

1928, June 18

J25 D7	2c olive brn & lil	15	15
J26 D7	4c bl & org brn	15	15
J27 D7	5c gray grn & dk brn	15	15
J28 D7	10c dl vio & yel	15	15
J29 D7	15c rose & olive grn	15	15
J30 D7	20c brn org & ol grn	15	15
J31 D7	25c brn red & bl grn	20	20
J32 D7	30c slate & olivine	20	20
J33 D7	50c ol brn & lt red	28	28
J34 D7	60c dp bl & blk	45	45
J35 D7	1fr green & orange	1.40	1.40
J36 D7	2fr bis brn & lt red	1.00	1.00
J37 D7	3fr vio & bl blk	45	45
	Set value	4.35	4.35

Stamps of type D7 without "RF" monogram were issued in 1944 by the Vichy Government, but were not placed on sale in Guadeloupe.

Catalogue values for unused stamps in this section, from this point to the end of the section, are for Never Hinged items.

D8

Perf. 14x13

1947, June 2 Unwmk. Engr.

J38 D8	10c black	15	15
J39 D8	30c dl bl grn	15	15
J40 D8	50c brt ultra	15	15
J41 D8	1fr dk grn	15	15
J42 D8	2fr dark blue	35	35
J43 D8	3fr blk brn	42	42
J44 D8	4fr lil rose	55	55
J45 D8	5fr purple	62	62
J46 D8	10fr red	80	80
J47 D8	20fr dk vio	1.00	1.00
	Nos. J38-J47 (10)	4.34	4.34

GUATEMALA

LOCATION — Central America, bordering on Atlantic and Pacific Oceans
GOVT. — Republic
AREA — 42,042 sq. mi.
POP. — 6,577,000 (est. 1984)
CAPITAL — Guatemala City

100 Centavos = 8 Reales = 1 Peso
100 Centavos de Quetzal = 1 Quetzal (1927)

Catalogue values for unused stamps in this country are for Never Hinged items, beginning with Scott 316 in the regular postage section, Scott B5 in the semi-postal section, Scott C137 in the air post section, Scott CB5 in the air post semi-postal section and Scott E2 in the special delivery section.

Coat of Arms
A1 A2

Two types of 10c:
Type I- Both zeros in "10" are wide.
Type II- Left zero narrow.

Perf. 14x13½

1871, Mar. 1 Typo. Unwmk.
1 A1 1c ocher 75 *10.00*
a. Imperf., pair 5.00
b. Printed on both sides, imperf. 75.00
2 A1 5c lt bister brn 4.00 *7.50*
a. Imperf., pair 35.00
b. Tete beche pair 150.00
c. Tete beche pair, imperf. 2,600.
3 A1 10c blue (I) 5.00 *8.00*
a. Imperf., pair (I) 45.00
b. Type II 8.00 10.00
c. Imperf. pair (II) 60.00
4 A1 20c rose 4.00 *7.50*
a. Imperf., pair 45.00
b. 20c blue (error) 130.00 125.00
c. As "b," imperf. *800.00*

Forgeries exist. Forged cancellations abound. See No. C458.

1873 Litho. *Perf. 12*
5 A2 4r dull red vio 300.00 75.00
6 A2 1p dull yellow 150.00 100.00

Forgeries exist.

Liberty
A3 A4

A5 A6

1875, Apr. 15 Engr.
7 A3 ¼r black 1.00 *3.50*
8 A4 ½r blue green 1.00 *3.00*
9 A5 1r blue 1.00 *3.00*
a. Half used as ½r on cover *1,700.*
10 A6 2r dull red 1.00 *3.00*

Nos. 7-10 normally lack gum.
Forgeries and forged cancellations exist.

Indian Woman A7 Quetzal A8

Typographed on Tinted Paper

1878, Jan. 10 *Perf. 13*
11 A7 ½r yel grn 75 *3.00*
12 A7 2r car rose 1.25 *4.00*
13 A7 4r violet 1.25 *4.50*
14 A7 1p yellow 2.00 *9.00*
c. Half used as 4r on cover *2,200.*

Some sheets of Nos. 11-14 have papermaker's watermark, "LACROIX FRERES," in double-lined capitals appearing on six stamps.
Part perforate pairs of Nos. 11, 12 and 14 exist. Value for each, about $100.
Forgeries of Nos. 11-14 are plentiful. Forged cancellations exist.
For surcharges see Nos. 18, 20.

Imperf., Pairs
11a A7 ½r yel grn 50.00
12a A7 2r car rose 50.00
13a A7 4r violet 50.00
14a A7 1p yellow 50.00

1879 Engr. *Perf. 12*
15 A8 ¼r brn & grn 2.50 2.75
16 A8 1r blk & grn 2.50 3.75
a. Half used as ½r on cover *1,800.*

For similar types see A11, A72, A103, A121, A146. For surcharges see Nos. 17, 19.

Nos. 11, 12, 15, 16 Surcharged in Black

1 centavo.

1881 *Perf. 12 and 13*
17 A8 1c on ¼r brn & grn 5.00 6.00
a. "ecntavo." 30.00 20.00
b. Pair, one without surch. 200.00
18 A7 5c on ½r yel grn 5.00 7.50
a. "ecntavos." 35.00 35.00
b. "5" omitted 100.00
c. Double surcharge 75.00 85.00
19 A8 10c on 1r blk & grn 7.50 7.50
a. "s" of "centavos" missing 75.00 75.00
b. "ecntavos" 40.00 45.00
20 A7 20c on 2r car rose 35.00 40.00
a. Horiz. pair, imperf. btwn. 425.00

The 5c had three settings.
Surcharge varieties found on Nos. 17-20 include: Period omitted; comma instead of period; "ecntavo." or "ecntavos."; "s" omitted; spaced "centavos."; wider "0" in "20."
Counterfeits of Nos. 17-20 are plentiful.

Quetzal — A11

1881, Nov. 7 Engr. *Perf. 12*
21 A11 1c blk & grn 75 50
22 A11 2c brn & grn 50 50
a. Center inverted 175.00 150.00
23 A11 5c red & grn 2.25 75
a. Center inverted *3,000.* 1,300.
24 A11 10c gray vio & grn 75 50
25 A11 20c yel & grn 75 1.00
a. Center inverted 275.00 200.00
Nos. 21-25 (5) 5.00 3.25

Gen. Justo Rufino Barrios — A12

Black Surcharge

Correos Nacionales
25 c. 25 c.
Guatemala.
25 c. 25 c.
25 centavos.

1886, Mar. 6
26 A12 25c on 1p ver 50 50
a. "centovos" 1.00
b. "centanos" 1.00
c. "255" instead of "25" 150.00
d. Inverted "S" in "Nacionales" 20.00
f. "cen avos" 20.00
h. "Corre cionales" 20.00
i. Inverted surcharge 75.00
27 A12 50c on 1p ver 50 50
a. "centovos" 1.00
b. "centanos" 1.00
c. "Carreos" 1.00
d. Inverted surcharge 50.00
e. Double surcharge 75.00
f. Inverted "S" in "Nacionales" 10.00
g. "centavo" 20.00
h. "cen avos" 20.00
28 A12 75c on 1p ver 50 50
a. "centovos" 1.00
b. "centanos" 1.00
c. "Carreos" 1.00
d. "50" for "75" at upper right 1.50
e. Inverted "S" in "Nacionales" 10.00
f. Double surcharge 75.00
g. "ales" inverted 100.00
29 A12 100c on 1p ver 75 60
a. "110" at upper left and "a" at lower left, instead of "100" 4.00
b. Inverted surcharge 75.00
c. "Guatemala" bolder; 23mm instead of 18½mm wide 1.50
d. Double surch., one diagonal 100.00
30 A12 150c on 1p ver 50 50
a. Inverted "G" 5.00
b. "Guetemala" and italic "5" in upper 4 numerals 5.00
d. Inverted surcharge 90.00
e. Pair, one without surcharge 100.00
f. Double surcharge 100.00
Nos. 26-30 (5) 2.75 2.60

There are many other minor varieties, such as wrong font letters, etc. The surcharge on Nos. 29 and 30 has different letters and ornaments. On No. 29, "Guatemala," normally is 18½mm wide.
Used values of Nos. 26-30 are for canceled to order stamps. Postally used sell for much more.

National Emblem — A13

1886, July 1 Litho. *Perf. 12*
31 A13 1c dull blue 5.00 2.00
32 A13 2c brown 5.00 3.00
33 A13 5c purple 37.50 75
34 A13 10c red 10.00 75
35 A13 20c emerald 15.00 1.25
36 A13 25c orange 15.00 1.50
37 A13 50c ol grn 10.00 2.00
38 A13 75c car rose 10.00 3.00
39 A13 100c red brn 10.00 3.00
40 A13 150c dark blue 15.00 3.75
41 A13 200c org yel 17.50 4.75
Nos. 31-41 (11) 150.00 25.75

Used values of Nos. 38-41 are for canceled to order stamps. Postally used sell for more.
See Nos. 43-50, 99-107. For surcharges see Nos. 42, 51-59, 75-85, 97-98, 108-110, 124-130.

No. 32 Surcharged in Black

PROVISIONAL.
1886
1
UN CENTAVO

Two settings:
I- "1886" (no period).
II- "1886." (period).

1886, Nov. 12
42 A13 1c on 2c brn, I 2.00 2.50
a. Date inverted, I 75.00
b. Date double, I 75.00
c. Date omitted, I 60.00
d. Date double, one invtd., I 100.00
e. Date triple, one inverted, I 100.00

f. Setting II 1.50 1.00
g. Inverted surcharge, II 4.00
h. Double surcharge, II 100.00

Forgeries exist.

Type I Type II

Two types of 5c:
I- Thin "5"
II- Larger, thick "5"

1886-95 Engr. *Perf. 12*
43 A13 1c blue 75 15
44 A13 2c yel brn 2.25 15
a. Half used as 1c on cover 100.00
45 A13 5c pur (I) 50.00 1.00
46 A13 5c vio (II) ('88) 1.50 15
47 A13 6c lilac ('95) 60 20
48 A13 10c red ('90) 1.50 15
49 A13 20c green ('93) 3.00 75
50 A13 25c red org ('93) 7.50 1.25
Nos. 43-44,46-50 (7) 17.10 2.80

The impression of the engraved stamps is sharper than that of the lithographed. On the engraved stamps the top four lines at left are heavier than those below them. (This is also true of the 1c litho., which is distinguished from the engraved only by a slight color difference and the impression.) The "2" and "5" (I) are more open than the litho. numerals. The "10" of the engraved is wider. The 20c and 25c of the engraved have a vertical line at right end of the "centavos" ribbon.

No. 38 Surcharged in Blue Black

1894

2
CENTAVOS

"1894" 14½mm wide

1894, Apr. 25
51 A13 10c on 75c car rose 4.50 4.50
a. Double surcharge 75.00
b. Inverted surcharge 100.00

Same on Nos. 38-41 in Blue or Red
"1894" 14mm wide

1894, June 13
52 A13 2c on 100c 7.50 4.25
53 A13 6c on 150c (R) 7.50 3.50
54 A13 10c on 75c 550.00 500.00
55 A13 10c on 200c 7.50 4.25
c. Inverted surcharge 75.00

Nos. 54-55 exist with thick or thin "1" in new value.

Same on Nos. 39-41 in Black or Red
"1894" 12mm wide

1894, July 14
52a A13 2c on 100c red brn (Bk) 4.00 3.50
b. Vert. pair, one without surch. 150.00
53a A13 6c on 150c dk bl (R) 4.50 3.50
55a A13 10c on 200c org yel (Bk) 5.00 3.50
d. Inverted surcharge 100.00
e. Vert. pair, one without surch. 150.00

Nos. 44 and 46 Surcharged in Black, Blue Black, or Red:

1894
1
CENTAVO
b

1895
1
CENTAVO
c

1
CENTAVO
1895
d

1
CENTAVO
1895
e

1894-96
56 A13 (b) 1c on 2c (Bk) 75 30
a. "Centav" 5.00 5.00
b. Double surcharge 75.00
c. As "a," dbl. surcharge 150.00
d. Blue black surcharge 20.00 20.00
e. Dbl. surch., one inverted 150.00
57 A13 (c) 1c on 5c (R) ('95) 50 20
a. Inverted surcharge 3.00 3.00
b. "1894" instead of "1895" 3.50 3.00
c. Double surcharge 50.00
58 A13 (d) 1c on 5c (R) ('95) 75 20
a. Inverted surcharge 50.00 50.00
b. Double surcharge 50.00
59 A13 (e) 1c on 5c (R) ('96) 1.25 40
a. Inverted surcharge 50.00 50.00
b. Double surcharge 50.00

Nos. 56-58 may be found with thick or thin "1" in the new value.

National Arms and President J. M. Reyna Barrios
A21

1897, Jan. 1 Engr. Unwmk.
60 A21 1c blk, *lil gray* 50 50
61 A21 2c blk, *grnsh gray* 50 50
62 A21 6c blk, *brn org* 50 50
63 A21 10c blk, *dl bl* 50 50
64 A21 12c blk, *rose red* 50 50
65 A21 18c blk, *grysh white* 8.00 7.50
66 A21 20c blk, *scarlet* 1.00 1.00
67 A21 25c blk, *bis brn* 1.50 1.00
68 A21 50c blk, *redsh brn* 1.00 1.00
69 A21 75c blk, *gray* 50.00 50.00
70 A21 100c blk, *bl grn* 1.00 1.00
71 A21 150c blk, *dl rose* 100.00 125.00
72 A21 200c blk, *magenta* 1.00 1.00
73 A21 500c blk, *yel grn* 1.00 1.00
Nos. 60-73 (14) 167.00 191.00

Issued for Central American Exposition.

Stamps often sold as Nos. 65, 69 and 71 are copies with telegraph overprint removed.

Used values for Nos. 60-73 are for canceled-to-order copies. Postally used examples are worth more.

The paper of Nos. 64 and 66 was originally colored on one side only, but has "bled through" on some copies.

No. 64 Surcharged in Violet

UN
CENTAVO
1898

1897, Nov.
74 A21 1c on 12c *rose red* 1.00 1.00
a. Inverted surcharge 30.00 30.00
b. Pair, one without surcharge 75.00
c. Dbl. surch., one invtd. 100.00

Stamps of 1886-93 Surcharged in Red

1898
1
centavo
f

1898
10
centavos
g

1898
75 (f) 1c on 5c vio 1.00 1.00
a. Inverted surcharge 75.00
76 (f) 1c on 50c ol grn 1.50 1.25
a. Inverted surcharge 100.00 100.00
77 (f) 6c on 5c vio 4.50 1.50
a. Inverted surcharge 75.00
b. Double surcharge 100.00
78 (f) 6c on 150c dk bl 4.50 3.25
79 (g) 10c on 20c emer 5.00 4.00
a. Double surch., one inverted 125.00 125.00
b. Inverted surcharge 75.00
Nos. 75-79 (5) 16.50 11.00

Black Surcharge

80 (f) 1c on 25c red org 2.00 2.00
81 (f) 1c on 75c car rose 1.50 1.50
a. Double surcharge 100.00
82 (f) 6c on 10c red 10.00 9.00
a. Inverted surcharge 75.00
83 (f) 6c on 20c emer 5.00 4.00
84 (f) 6c on 100c red brn 5.00 4.00
85 (f) 6c on 200c org yel 5.00 4.00
a. Inverted surcharge 50.00 50.00
Nos. 80-85 (6) 28.50 24.50

National Emblem
A24 A25

Revenue Stamp Overprinted or Surcharged in Carmine

Perf. 12, 12x14, 14x12

1898, Oct. 8 Litho.
86 A24 1c dark blue 75 50
a. Inverted overprint 12.50 12.50
87 A24 2c on 1c dk bl 1.00 50
a. Inverted surcharge 12.50 12.50

Counterfeits exist.
See type A26.

Revenue Stamps Surcharged in Carmine

1898 Engr. *Perf. 12½ to 16*
88 A25 1c on 10c bl gray 75 75
a. "ENTAVO" 5.00 5.00
89 A25 2c on 5c pur 1.25 1.00
90 A25 2c on 10c bl gray 6.50 7.00
a. Double surch., car & blk 100.00 75.00
91 A25 2c on 50c dp bl 8.00 9.00
a. Double surch., car & blk 100.00 100.00

Black Surcharge

92 A25 2c on 1c lil rose 3.50 2.00
93 A25 2c on 25c red 7.50 8.00
94 A25 6c on 1p pur 4.00 4.50
95 A25 6c on 5p gray vio 7.50 7.50
96 A25 6c on 10p emer 7.50 7.50
Nos. 92-96 (5) 30.00 29.50

Nos. 88 and 90 are found in shades ranging from Prussian blue to slate blue.

Varieties other than those listed are bogus. Counterfeits exist of No. 92.

Soaking in water causes marked fading.
See type A27.

No. 46 Surcharged in Red

Un I Centavo
1899

1899, Sept. *Perf. 12*
97 A13 1c on 5c violet 40 25
a. Inverted surcharge 7.50 7.50
b. Double surcharge 15.00 15.00
c. Double surcharge, one inverted 15.00 15.00

No. 48 Surcharged in Black

1900
1
CENTAVO

1900, Jan.
98 A13 1c on 10c red 50 50
a. Inverted surcharge 10.00 10.00
b. Double surcharge 75.00 75.00

Quetzal Type of 1886

1900-02 Engr.
99 A13 1c dk grn 60 25
100 A13 2c carmine 60 25
101 A13 5c blue (II) 2.25 1.25
102 A13 6c lt grn 75 25
103 A13 10c bister brn 7.50 1.00
104 A13 20c purple 7.50 7.50
105 A13 20c bis brn ('02) 7.50 7.50
106 A13 25c yellow 7.50 7.50
107 A13 25c bl grn ('02) 7.50 7.50
Nos. 99-107 (9) 41.70 33.00

No. 49 Surcharged in Black

1901
1
CENTAVO

1901, May
108 A13 1c on 20c green 50 50
a. Inverted surcharge 20.00 20.00
b. Double surch., one diagonal 50.00
109 A13 2c on 20c green 1.50 1.50

No. 50 Surcharged in Black

UN
1
CENTAVO
1901

1901, Apr.
110 A13 1c on 25c red org 60 60
a. Inverted surcharge 25.00 25.00
b. Double surcharge 50.00 50.00

A26

A27

Revenue Stamps Surcharged in Carmine or Black

1902, July *Perf. 12, 14x12, 12x14*
111 A26 1c on 1c dk bl 1.00 1.00
a. Double surcharge 20.00
b. Inverted surcharge 20.00
112 A26 2c on 1c dk bl 1.00 1.00
a. Double surcharge 75.00
b. Inverted surcharge 25.00

Perf. 14, 15

113 A27 6c on 25c red (Bk) 2.00 2.50
a. Double surch., one invtd. 75.00 75.00

National Emblem — A28

Statue of Justo Rufino Barrios — A29

"La Reforma" Palace — A30

Temple of Minerva — A31

Lake Amatitlán A32

Cathedral in Guatemala A33

Columbus Theater — A34

Artillery Barracks — A35

Monument to Columbus — A36

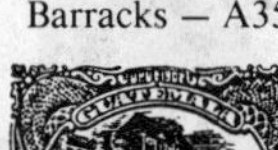

School for Indians — A37

1902 Engr. *Perf. 12 to 16*
114 A28 1c grn & claret 15 15
a. Horiz. pair, imperf. vert. 100.00
115 A29 2c lake & blk 15 15
a. Horiz. or vert. pair, imperf. between 150.00
116 A30 5c bl & blk 20 15
a. 5c ultra & blk 60 15
b. Imperf., pair 100.00 100.00
c. Horiz. pair, imperf. vert. 100.00
117 A31 6c bis & grn 20 15
a. Horiz. pair, imperf. btwn. 150.00
118 A32 10c org & bl 22 15
a. Horiz. pair, imperf. vert. 100.00
119 A33 20c rose lil & blk 40 15
a. Horiz. pair, imperf. vert. 100.00
120 A34 50c red brn & bl 32 15
a. Vert. pair, imperf. btwn. 350.00
121 A35 75c gray lil & blk 32 15
a. Horiz. pair, imperf. btwn. 150.00
b. Horiz. pair, imperf. vert. 100.00
122 A36 1p brn & blk 55 20
a. Horiz. pair, imperf. btwn. 150.00
123 A37 2p ver & blk 65 40
Nos. 114-123 (10) 3.16
Set value 1.55

See Nos. 210, 212-214, 219, 223, 239-241, 243. For overprints and surcharges see Nos. 133, 135-139, 144-157, 168, 170-171, 178, 192-194, 298-299, 301, C19, C27, C123.

Issues of 1886-1900 Surcharged in Black or Carmine

1903
25
CENTAVOS

1903, Apr. 18 *Perf. 12*
124 A13 25c on 1c dk grn 1.25 50
a. Inverted surcharge 40.00 40.00
125 A13 25c on 2c car 1.50 50
126 A13 25c on 6c lt grn 2.50 1.75
a. Inverted surcharge 40.00 40.00
127 A13 25c on 10c bis brn 7.50 7.00
128 A13 25c on 75c rose 10.00 10.00
129 A13 25c on 150c dk bl (C) 9.00 9.00
130 A13 25c on 200c yel 10.00 10.00
Nos. 124-130 (7) 41.75 38.75

Forgeries and bogus varieties exist.

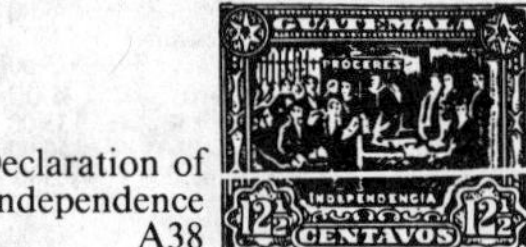
Declaration of Independence A38

1907, Jan. 1 *Perf. 13½ to 15*
132 A38 12½c ultra & blk 25 15
a. Horiz. pair, imperf. btwn. 150.00

For surcharge see No. 134.

Nos. 118, 119 and 132 Surcharged in Black or Red

1908
UN 1 UN
CENTAVO

1908, May
133 A32 1c on 10c org & bl 30 25
a. Double surcharge 25.00
b. Inverted surcharge 15.00 15.00
c. Pair, one without surcharge 50.00
134 A38 2c on 12½c ultra & blk (R) 25 25
a. Horiz. or vert. pair, imperf. between 100.00
b. Inverted surcharge 15.00 10.00
c. Double surcharge 30.00
135 A33 6c on 20c rose lil & blk 40 25
a. Inverted surcharge 20.00 20.00

Similar Surcharge, Dated 1909, in Red or Black on Nos. 121 and 120

1909, Apr.
136 A35 2c on 75c (R) 50 50
137 A34 6c on 50c (R) 50.00 50.00
a. Double surcharge 100.00 100.00
138 A34 6c on 50c (Bk) 30 30

Counterfeits exist of Nos. 137, 137a.

No. 123 Surcharged in Black

12½
CENTAVOS
1909.

139 A37 12½c on 2p ver & blk 30 30
a. Inverted surcharge 25.00 25.00
b. Period omitted after "1909" 12.50 12.50

Counterfeits exist.

Gen. Miguel Garcia Granados, Birth Cent. (in 1909) — A39

1910, Feb. 11 ***Perf. 14***
140 A39 6c bis & indigo 50 40
a. Imperf., pair 50.00

Some sheets used for this issue contained a two-line watermark, "SPECIAL POSTAGE PAPER / LONDON." For surcharge see No. 143.

General Post Office — A40

Pres. Manuel Estrada Cabrera — A41

1911, June ***Perf. 12***
141 A40 25c bl & blk 50 15
a. Center inverted *1,750.* 650.00
142 A41 5p red & blk 65 65
a. Center inverted 25.00 27.50

Nos. 116, 118 and 140 Surcharged in Black or Red:

1911
Un Centavo
h

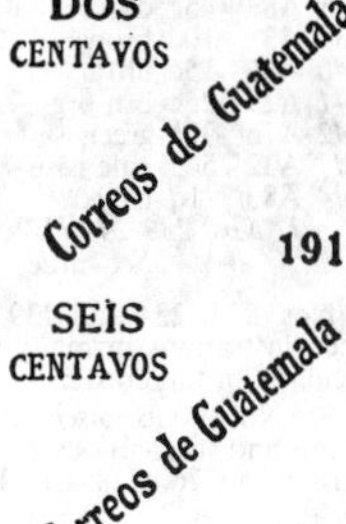

DOS
CENTAVOS
Correos de Guatemala
1911
i

SEIS
CENTAVOS
Correos de Guatemala
1911
j

1911 ***Perf. 14***
143 A39 (h) 1c on 6c 20.00 7.50
a. Double surcharge 75.00
144 A30 (i) 2c on 5c (R) 1.50 75
145 A32 (j) 6c on 10c 1.25 1.25
a. Double surcharge 50.00

See watermark note after No. 140. Forgeries exist.

Nos. 119-121 Surcharged in Black:

1912
k

1 UN CENTAVO 1
1912 1912
l

2 CENTAVOS 2
5 5
m
CINCO CENTAVOS 1912

1912, Sept.
147 A33 1c on 20c 30 30
a. Inverted surcharge 7.50 7.50
b. Double surcharge 15.00 15.00
148 A34 2c on 50c 30 30
a. Inverted surcharge 10.00 10.00
b. Double surcharge 12.50
c. Double inverted surcharge 25.00
149 A35 5c on 75c 75 75
a. "191" for "1912" 7.50 7.50
b. Double surcharge 15.00 15.00
c. Inverted surcharge 10.00

Forgeries exist.

Nos. 120, 122 and 123 Surcharged in Blue, Green or Black:

1913
UN CENTAVO
n

1913
Seis centavos
o

1913
12½ CENTAVOS
p

1913, July
151 A34 (n) 1c on 50c (Bl) 25 25
a. Inverted surcharge 10.00
b. Double surcharge 17.50
c. Horiz. pair, imperf. btwn. 100.00
152 A36 (o) 6c on 1p (G) 30 30
153 A37 (p) 12½c on 2p (Bk) 30 30
a. Inverted surcharge 15.00 15.00
b. Double surcharge 40.00
c. Horiz. pair, imperf. btwn. 100.00

Forgeries exist.

Nos. 114 and 115 Surcharged in Black:

DOS CENTAVOS
q

SEIS CENTAVOS
r

12½ CENTAVOS
s

VEINTICINCO CENTAVOS
t

1916-17
154 A28 (q) 2c on 1c ('17) 20 20
155 A28 (r) 6c on 1c 20 20
156 A28 (s) 12½c on 1c 20 20
157 A29 (t) 25c on 2c 20 20

Numerous errors of value and color, inverted and double surcharges and similar varieties are in the market. They were not regularly issued, but were surreptitiously made and sold.

Counterfeit surcharges abound.

"Liberty" and President Estrada Cabrera A51

Estrada Cabrera and Quetzal A52

1917, Mar. 15 ***Perf. 14, 15***
158 A51 25c dp bl & brn 25 15

Re-election of President Estrada Cabrera.

1918 ***Perf. 12***
161 A52 1.50p dark blue 20 15

Radio Station — A54

"Joaquina" Maternity Hospital — A55

"Estrada Cabrera" Vocational School — A56

National Emblem — A57

1919, May 3 ***Perf. 14, 15***
162 A54 30c red & blk 2.00 75
163 A55 60c ol grn & blk 75 50
164 A56 90c red brn & blk 75 75
165 A57 3p dp grn & blk 1.50 50

See Nos. 215, 227. For surcharges see Nos. 166-167, 179-185, 188, 195-198, 245-246, C8-C11, C21-C22.

No. 162 Surcharged

1920
2 centavos

Blue Overprint and Black Surcharge

1920, Jan. **Unwmk.**
166 A54 2c on 30c red & blk 25 25
a. Inverted surcharge 12.50 12.50
b. "1920" double 10.00 10.00
c. "1920" omitted 15.00 15.00
d. "2 centavos" omitted 20.00

Nos. 123 and 163 Surcharged:

2 centavos
u

1920
25
Centavos
v

1920
167 A55 2c on 60c (Bk & R) 25 25
a. Inverted surcharge 10.00 10.00
b. "1920" inverted 7.50 7.50
c. "1920" omitted 10.00 10.00
d. "1920" only 10.00
e. Double surcharge 25.00
168 A37 25c on 2p (Bk) 30 25
a. "35" for "25" 7.50 7.50
b. Large "5" in "25" 7.50 7.50
c. Inverted surcharge 15.00 15.00
d. Double surcharge 25.00

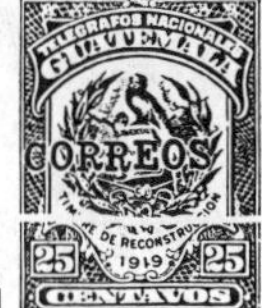

A61

1920
169 A61 25c green 25 15
a. Double overprint 50.00
b. Double overprint, inverted 75.00

See types A65-A66.

No. 119 Surcharged

1921
Doce y medio
centavos

1921, Apr.
170 A33 12½c on 20c 25 15
a. Double surcharge 15.00
b. Inverted surcharge 15.00

No. 121 Surcharged

1921
Cincuenta
centavos

1921, Apr.
171 A35 50c on 75c lil & blk 40 30
a. Double surcharge 15.00
b. Inverted surcharge 25.00 25.00

Mayan Stele at Quirigua — A62

Monument to President Granados — A63

"La Penitenciaria" Bridge — A64

1921, Sept. 1 ***Perf. 13½, 14, 15***
172 A62 1.50p bl & org 75 25
173 A63 5p brn & grn 2.50 1.25
174 A64 15p blk & ver 9.00 5.00

See Nos. 216, 228, 229. For surcharges see Nos. 186-187, 189-191, 199-201, 207, 231, 247-251, C1-C5, C12, C23-C24.

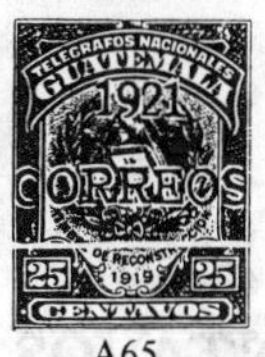

A65 A66

Telegraph Stamps Overprinted or Surcharged in Black or Red

1921 ***Perf. 14***
175 A65 25c green 25 20
176 A66 12½c on 25c grn (R) 20 20
177 A66 12½c on 25c grn 15.00 15.00

Nos. 119, 163 and 164 Surcharged in Black or Red:

1922
DOCE Y
MEDIO
CENTAVOS
w

1922
25
CENTAVOS

x

1922, Mar.

178 A33(w) 12½c on 20c — 20 20
a. Inverted surcharge — 10.00
179 A55(w) 12½c on 60c (R) — 50 50
a. Inverted surcharge — 15.00
180 A56(w) 12½c on 90c — 50 50
a. Inverted surcharge — 25.00
181 A55(x) 25c on 60c — 1.00 1.00
a. Inverted surcharge — 20.00
182 A55(x) 25c on 60c (R) — 125.00 125.00
183 A56(x) 25c on 90c — 1.00 1.00
a. Inverted surcharge — 25.00
184 A56(x) 25c on 90c (R) — 4.00 4.00
Nos. 178-181,183-184 (6) — 7.20 7.20

Counterfeits exist.

Nos. 165, 173-174 Surcharged in Red or Dark Blue

1922
DOCE
Y MEDIO
CENTAVOS

1922, May

185 A57 12½c on 3p grn & blk (R) — 20 15
186 A63 12½c on 5p brn & grn — 50 45
187 A64 12½c on 15p blk & ver — 50 45

Nos. 165, 173-174 Surcharged in Red or Black

1922
25
CENTAVOS

25 25 25 25
I II III IV

1922

188 A57 25c on 3p (I) (R) — 20 20
a. Type II — 60 60
b. Type III — 60 60
c. Type IV — 30 30
d. Inverted surcharge — 40.00
e. Horiz. or vert. pair, imperf. between (I) — 125.00
189 A63 25c on 5p (I) — 1.00 2.00
a. Type II — 2.00 3.00
b. Type III — 2.00 3.00
c. Type IV — 1.00 2.00
190 A64 25c on 15p (I) — 1.00 1.50
a. Type II — 2.00 3.00
b. Type III — 2.00 3.00
c. Type IV — 1.00 1.50
191 A64 25c on 15p (I) (R) — 22.50 30.00
a. Type II — 40.00 45.00
b. Type III — 45.00 45.00
c. Type IV — 30.00 35.00

Stamps of 1902-21 Surcharged in Dark Blue or Red

1922
25
CENTAVOS

25 25 25
V VI VII
25 25
VIII IX

1922, Aug. **On Nos. 121-123**

192 A35 25c on 75c (V) — 35 35
a. Type VI — 35 35
b. Type VII — 1.75 1.75
c. Type VIII — 5.50 4.00
d. Type IX — 6.50 6.00
193 A36 25c on 1p (V) — 30 30
a. Type VI — 30 30
b. Type VII — 1.25 1.25
c. Type VIII — 2.50 2.50
d. Type IX — 4.00 3.50
e. Inverted surcharge — 40.00
194 A37 25c on 2p (V) — 45 45
a. Type VI — 45 45
b. Type VII — 1.25 1.25
c. Type VIII — 4.00 4.00
d. Type IX — 6.50 6.50

On Nos. 162-165

195 A54 25c on 30c (V) — 45 45
a. Type VI — 45 45
b. Type VII — 1.25 1.25
c. Type VIII — 5.50 5.50
d. Type IX — 6.50 6.50
196 A55 25c on 60c (V) — 1.00 1.50
a. Type VI — 1.00 1.50
b. Type VII — 5.50 7.50
c. Type VIII — 8.00 9.00
d. Type IX — 10.00 11.00
197 A56 25c on 90c (V) — 1.00 1.50
a. Type VI — 1.50 2.00
b. Type VII — 5.50 6.50
c. Type VIII — 8.00 9.00
d. Type IX — 10.00 11.00
198 A57 25c on 3p (R) (V) — 35 35
a. Type VI — 35 35
b. Type VII — 1.25 1.00
c. Type VIII — 6.00 4.50
d. Type IX — 6.50 6.00
e. Invtd. surch. — 50.00

On Nos. 172-174

199 A62 25c on 1.50p (V) — 30 25
a. Type VI — 30 25
b. Type VII — 1.25 1.00
c. Type VIII — 3.00 3.00
d. Type IX — 4.50 4.00
e. Invtd. surch. — 40.00
200 A63 25c on 5p (V) — 75 90
a. Type VI — 80 1.00
b. Type VII — 3.00 3.50
c. Type VIII — 5.50 6.00
d. Type IX — 8.00 8.50
201 A64 25c on 15p (V) — 85 90
a. Type VI — 1.50 1.50
b. Type VII — 5.00 5.50
c. Type VIII — 6.50 6.50
d. Type IX — 12.00 12.00

Centenary Palace — A69

National Palace at Antigua — A70

1922 *Perf. 14, 14½*

Printed by Waterlow & Sons

202 A69 12½c green — 15 15
a. Horiz. or vert. pair, imperf. btwn. — 100.00
203 A70 25c brown — 15 15
Set value — 20

See Nos. 211, 221, 234.

Columbus Theater A71

Quetzal A72

Granados Monument — A73

Litho. by Castillo Bros.

1924, Feb. *Perf. 12*

204 A71 50c rose — 50 20
a. Imperf., pair — 7.50
b. Horiz. or vert. pair, imperf. btwn. — 25.00
205 A72 1p dk grn — 75 20
a. Imperf. vertically — 15.00
b. Vertical pair, imperf. between — 20.00
c. Imperf., pair — 7.50
206 A73 5p orange — 1.25 50
a. Imperf., pair — 7.50
b. Horizontal pair, imperf. between — 20.00

For surcharges see Nos. 208-209.

Nos. 172 and 206 Surcharged

1924
—
UN PESO
25 Cents.

1924, July

207 A62 1p on 1.50p bl & org — 30 20
208 A73 1.25p on 5p org — 50 50
a. "UN PESO 25 Cents." omitted — 40.00
b. Horiz. pair, imperf. btwn. — 25.00

#208 with two bars over "25 Cents."

1924

209 A73 1p on 5p orange — 50 50

Types of 1902-22 Issues

Engr. by Perkins Bacon & Co.

1924, Aug. **Re-engraved** *Perf. 14*

210 A31 6c bister — 15 15
211 A70 25c brown — 20 15
212 A34 50c red — 25 15
213 A36 1p org brn — 25 15
214 A37 2p orange — 35 25
215 A57 3p dp grn — 2.00 50
216 A64 15p black — 2.25 75
Nos. 210-216 (7) — 5.45 2.10

The designs of the stamps of 1924 differ from those of the 1902-22 issues in many details which are too minute to illustrate. The re-engraved issue may be readily distinguished by the imprint "Perkins Bacon & Co. Ld. Londres."

Pres. Justo Rufino Barrios A74

Lorenzo Montufar A75

1924, Aug.

217 A74 1.25p ultra — 20 15
218 A75 2.50p dk vio — 1.00 25

See Nos. 224, 226. For surcharges see Nos. 232, C6, C20.

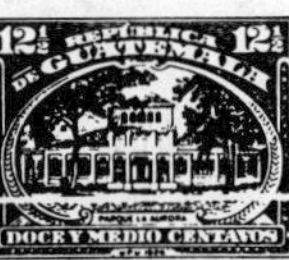
Aurora Park — A76

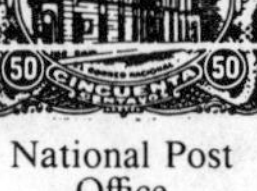
National Post Office A77

National Observatory A78

Types of 1921-24 Re-engraved and New Designs Dated 1926

Engraved by Waterlow & Sons, Ltd.

1926, July-Aug. *Perf. 12½*

219 A31 6c ocher — 15 15
220 A76 12½c green — 15 15
221 A70 25c brown — 15 15
222 A77 50c red — 15 15
223 A36 1p org brn — 20 15
224 A74 1.50p dk bl — 20 15
225 A78 2p orange — 1.25 1.00
226 A75 2.50p dk vio — 1.50 1.25
227 A57 3p dk grn — 45 20
228 A63 5p brn vio — 1.00 40
229 A64 15p black — 1.25 60
Nos. 219-229 (11) — 6.45 4.35

These stamps may be distinguished from those of the same designs in preceding issues by the imprint "Waterlow & Sons, Limited, Londres," the date, "1926," and the perforation.

See Nos. 233, 242. For surcharge see No. 230.

Nos. 225-226, 228 Surcharged in Various Colors

1928
½ CENTAVO
DE QUETZAL

1928

230 A78 ½c on 2p (Bl) — 60 45
a. Inverted surcharge — 12.50
231 A63 ½c on 5p (Bk) — 30 20
a. Inverted surcharge — 10.00 10.00
b. Double surcharge — 50.00
c. Blue surcharge — 45.00 45.00
d. Blue and black surcharge — 50.00 50.00
232 A75 1c on 2.50p (R) — 30 20
b. Double surcharge — 50.00

Barrios A79

Montufar A80

Granados A81

General Orellana A82

Coat of Arms of Guatemala City — A83

Engraved by T. De la Rue & Co.

1929, Jan. *Perf. 14*

233 A78 ½c yel grn — 75 15
234 A70 1c dk brn — 25 15
235 A79 2c dp bl — 25 15
236 A80 3c dk vio — 20 15
237 A81 4c orange — 25 15
238 A82 5c dk car — 50 15
239 A31 10c brown — 40 15
240 A36 15c ultra — 50 15
241 A29 25c brn org — 1.00 25
242 A76 30c green — 90 40
243 A32 50c pale rose — 2.00 75
244 A83 1q black — 3.00 50
Nos. 233-244 (12) — 10.00
Set value — 2.70

Nos. 233, 234 and 239 to 243 differ from the illustrations in many minor details, particularly in the borders.

See No. 300 for bisect of No. 235. For overprints and surcharges see Nos. 297, C13, C17-C18, C25-C26, C28, E1, RA17-RA18.

No. 227 Surcharged in Black or Red

1929, Dec. 28 *Perf. 12½, 13*

245 A57 3c on 3p dk grn (Bk) — 1.25 1.75
a. Inverted surcharge — 15.00 15.00
246 A57 5c on 3p dk grn (R) — 1.25 1.75
a. Inverted surcharge — 15.00 15.00

Inauguration of the Eastern Railroad connecting Guatemala and El Salvador.

No. 229 Surcharged in Red

FERROCARRIL
DE LOS ALTOS
Inaugurado en 1929
2 CENTAVOS
DE QUETZAL

1930, Mar. 30 **Unwmk.**

No.	Type	Description	Unused	Used
247	A64	1c on 15p black	50	50
248	A64	2c on 15p black	50	75
249	A64	3c on 15p black	60	75
250	A64	5c on 15p black	60	75
251	A64	15c on 15p black	60	75
		Nos. 247-251 (5)	2.80	3.50

Opening of Los Altos electric railway.

Hydroelectric Dam — A85

Los Altos Railway — A86

Railroad Station — A87

1930, Mar. 30 **Typo.** ***Perf. 12***

No.	Type	Description	Unused	Used
252	A85	2c brn vio & blk	1.00	1.40
a.		Horiz. pair, imperf. btwn.	125.00	
253	A86	3c dp red & blk	1.75	2.00
a.		Vert. pair, imperf. btwn.	125.00	
254	A87	5c buff & dk bl	1.75	2.00

Opening of Los Altos electric railway. Exist imperf.

Mayan Stele at Quirigua — A91

1932, Apr. 8 **Engr.**

No.	Type	Description	Unused	Used
258	A91	3c carmine rose	1.00	15

See Nos. 302-303.

Flag of the Race, Columbus and Tecum Uman A92

1933, Aug. 3 **Litho.** ***Perf. 12½***

No.	Type	Description	Unused	Used
259	A92	½c dk grn	50	75
260	A92	1c dl brn	1.00	1.25
261	A92	2c dp bl	1.00	1.25
262	A92	3c dl vio	1.00	75
263	A92	5c rose	1.00	1.00
		Nos. 259-263 (5)	4.50	5.00

Commemorating the Day of the Race and the 441st anniversary of the sailing of Columbus from Palos, Spain, August 3rd, 1492, on his first voyage to the New World.

The 3c and 5c exist imperf.

Birthplace of Barrios A93

View of San Lorenzo A94

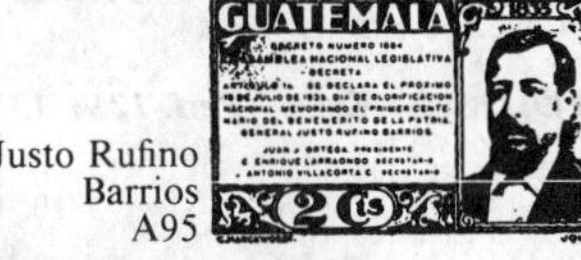
Justo Rufino Barrios A95

National Emblem and Locomotive A96

General Post Office — A97

Telegraph Building and Barrios A98

Military Academy A99

National Police Headquarters — A100

Jorge Ubico and J. R. Barrios A101

1935, July 19 **Photo.**

No.	Type	Description	Unused	Used
264	A93	½c yel grn & mag	50	60
265	A94	1c org red & pck bl	50	60
266	A95	2c org & blk	50	70
267	A96	3c car rose & pck bl	1.00	1.00
268	A97	4c pck bl & org red	5.00	6.00
269	A98	5c bl grn & brn	4.00	5.00
270	A99	10c slate grn & rose lake	6.00	7.00
271	A100	15c ol grn & org brn	5.00	6.00
272	A101	25c scar & bl	5.00	6.00
		Nos. 264-272 (9)	27.50	32.90

General Barrios. See Nos. C29-C31.

Lake Atitlan A102

Quetzal A103

Legislative Building — A104

1935, Oct. 10

No.	Type	Description	Unused	Used
273	A102	1c brn & crim	25	15
274	A103	3c rose car & pck grn	50	15
275	A103	3c red org & pck grn	50	15
276	A104	4c brt bl & dp rose	35	15
		Set value		40

See No. 277. For surcharges see Nos. B1-B3.

No. 273 perforated diagonally through the center

1935, July ***Perf. 12½x12***

No.	Type	Description	Unused	Used
277	A102	(½c) brn & crimson	20	15
a.		Unsevered pair	50	60

Bureau of Printing — A105

Map of Guatemala A106

1936, Sept. 24 ***Perf. 12½***

No.	Type	Description	Unused	Used
278	A105	½c grn & pur	15	15
279	A106	5c bl & dk brn	1.00	15
		Set value		25

For surcharge see No. B4.

Quetzal A107

Union Park, Quezaltenango A108

Gen. Jorge Ubico on Horseback A109

Designs: 1c, Tower of the Reformer. 3c, National Post Office. 4c, Government Building, Retalhuleu. 5c, Legislative Palace entrance. 10c, Custom House. 15c, Aurora Airport Custom House. 25c, National Fair. 50c, Residence of Presidential Guard. 1.50q, General Ubico, portrait standing, no cap.

1937, May 20

No.	Type	Description	Unused	Used
280	A107	½c pck bl & car rose	25	30
281	A107	1c ol gray & red brn	50	30
282	A108	2c vio & car rose	50	35
283	A108	3c brn vio & brt bl	50	20
284	A108	4c yel & dl ol grn	2.00	2.25
285	A107	5c crim & brt vio	1.90	1.75
286	A107	10c mag & brn blk	3.00	3.50
287	A108	15c ultra & cop red	2.50	3.50
288	A108	25c red org & vio	3.00	3.75
289	A108	50c dk grn & org red	4.50	5.50
290	A109	1q mag & blk	22.50	25.00
291	A109	1.50q red brn & blk	22.50	25.00
		Nos. 280-291 (12)	63.65	71.40

Second term of President Ubico.

Mayan Calendar A119

Natl. Flower (White Nun Orchid) A120

Quetzal — A121

Map of Guatemala A122

1939, Sept. 7 ***Perf. 13x12, 12½***

No.	Type	Description	Unused	Used
292	A119	½c grn & red brn	25	15
293	A120	2c bl & gray blk	1.50	20
294	A121	3c red org & turq grn	1.00	15
295	A121	3c ol bis & turq grn	1.00	15
296	A122	5c blue & red	1.75	1.75
		Nos. 292-296 (5)	5.50	2.40

For overprints see Nos. 324, C157.

No. 235 Surcharged with New Value in Red

1939, Sept. ***Perf. 14***

No.	Type	Description	Unused	Used
297	A79	1c on 2c deep blue	20	15

Stamps of 1929 Surcharged in Blue:

1 1
y
UN CENTAVO
5 5
z

1940, June

No.	Type	Description	Unused	Used
298	A29 (y)	1c on 25c brn org	25	15
299	A32 (z)	5c on 50c pale rose (bar 10x¾mm)	25	15
a.		Bar 12½x2mm	30	15
b.		Bar 12½x1mm	50.00	5.00
		Set value		25

No. 235 perforated diagonally through the center

1941, Aug. 16 ***Perf. 14x11½***

No.	Type	Description	Unused	Used
300	A79	(1c) deep blue	15	15
a.		Unsevered pair	40	40

No. 241 Surcharged in Black

½ ½
MEDIO CENTAVO

1941, Dec. 24 ***Perf. 14***

No.	Type	Description	Unused	Used
301	A29	½c on 25c brn org	15	15

Type of 1932 Inscribed "1942"

1942 **Engr.** ***Perf. 12***

No.	Type	Description	Unused	Used
302	A91	3c green	1.00	15
303	A91	3c deep blue	1.00	15
		Set value		20

Issued to publicize the coffee of Guatemala.

Vase of Guastatoya
A123

Home for the Aged
A124

1942, July 13 **Unwmk.**

304 A123	½c red brn	35	15
305 A124	1c car rose	35	15
	Set value		20

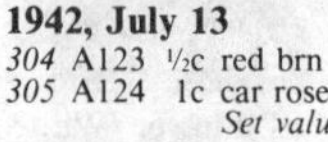
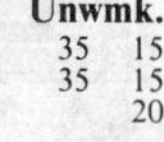

National Printing Works
A125

Rafael Maria Landivar
A126

1943, Jan. 25 **Engr.** ***Perf. 11, 12***

307 A125	2c scarlet	25	15
a.	Vert. pair, imperf. horiz.	35.00	

1943, Aug. ***Perf. 11***

308 A126	5c brt ultra	20	15

Issued to commemorate the 150th anniversary of the death of Rafael Landivar, poet.

National Palace
A127

1944, June 30 ***Perf. 11***

309 A127	3c dk bl grn	15	15

Inauguration of the Natl. Palace, Nov. 10, 1943.

See Nos. C137A-C139. For overprints see Nos. 311-311A, C133.

Ruins of Zakuleu — A128

1945, Jan. 6

310 A128	½c blk brn	15	15

Type of 1944 Overprinted in Blue

25 de junio de 1944

PALACIO NACIONAL

1945, Jan. 15

311 A127	3c deep blue	25	15

Overprint Bar 1mm Thick

311A A127	3c deep blue	75	40
	Set value		45

> ***Buying Sets***
> *Frequently it is less expensive to purchase complete sets rather than the individual stamps that make up the set. "Set Values" are provided for many such sets.*

Allegory of the Revolution
A129

Torch
A130

1945, Feb. 20

312 A129	3c grysh bl	15	15

Issued to commemorate the Revolution of Oct. 20, 1944. See Nos. C128-C131.

1945, Oct. 20

313 A130	3c deep blue	15	15

1st anniv. of the Revolution of Oct. 20, 1944. See No. C135-C136.

José Milla y Vidaurre
A131

Payo Enriquez de Rivera
A132

1945 ***Perf. 11, 12½***

314 A131	1c dp grn	15	15
315 A132	2c dull lilac	15	15
	Set value		15

See Nos. 343-346, 379, C134-C134A, C137, C269, C311-C315.

> **Catalogue values for unused stamps in this section, from this point to the end of the section, are for Never Hinged items.**

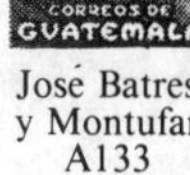

José Batres y Montufar
A133

UPU Monument Bern, Switzerland
A134

1946 **Unwmk.**

316 A133	½c sepia	15	15
317 A133	3c deep blue	15	15
	Set value		15

See Nos. 319, C142.

1946, Aug. 5 **Photo.** ***Perf. 14x13***

318 A134	1c vio & gray brn	25	15

Issued to commemorate the centenary of the first postage stamp. See Nos. C140-C141.

Batres Type of 1946

1947, Nov. 11 **Engr.** ***Perf. 11, 12½***

319 A133	3c dl grn	15	15

Symbolical of Labor
A135

Bartolomé de las Casas and Indian
A136

1948, May 14 **Unwmk.** ***Perf. 11***

320 A135	1c dp grn	15	15
a.	Perf. 12½	5.00	
321 A135	2c sepia	15	15
a.	Perf. 12½	5.00	
322 A135	3c dp ultra	15	15
a.	Perf. 12½	5.00	
323 A135	5c rose car	15	15
a.	Perf. 12½	5.00	
	Set value		20

Labor Day, May 1, 1948. Other perfs. and compound perfs. exist.

No. 296 Overprinted "1948" in Carmine at Lower Right

1948, May 14 ***Perf. 12½***

324 A122	5c bl & red	20	15

1949, Oct. 8 **Engr.** ***Perf. 12½, 13½***

325 A136	½c red	15	15
326 A136	1c blk brn	20	15
327 A136	2c dk bl grn	20	15
a.	2c green, perf. 11, 11½ ('60)	20	15
328 A136	3c rose pink	20	15
a.	3c car perf. 11, 12½, 13½ ('64)	30	15
329 A136	4c ultra	25	15
	Nos. 325-329 (5)	1.00	
	Set value		50

See Nos. 384-386.

Gathering Coffee — A137

Designs: 1c, Poptun Agricultural Colony. 2c, Banana trees. 3c, Sugar cane field. 6c, International Bridge.

1950, Feb. **Photo.** ***Perf. 14***

330 A137	½c vio bl, pink & ol gray	20	15
331 A137	1c red brn, yel & grnsh gray	20	15
332 A137	2c ol grn, pink & bl gray	20	15
333 A137	3c pur, bl & org brn	20	15
334 A137	6c dp org, aqua & vio	35	15
	Nos. 330-334 (5)	1.15	
	Set value		55

See Nos. 347-349.

Badge of Public and Social Assistance Ministry — A138

Nurse — A139

Map Showing Hospitals — A140

1950-51 **Litho.** ***Perf. 12, 12½x12***

335 A138	1c car rose & bl	20	15
336 A139	3c dl grn & rose red	30	15

Perf. 12

337 A140	5c dk bl & choc ('51)	40	20
a.	Souv. sheet, #335-337	2.50	2.50

Issued to publicize the National Hospitals Fund.

No. 337a exists perf. and imperf., same values.

A perforated souvenir sheet is known which is similar to No. 337a, but with the 5c stamp like the basic stamp of No. C232 (with "BRITISH HONDURAS" inscription).

See Nos. C177-C180a. For overprint see No. C232.

Motorcycle Messenger
A141

1951, May 22 ***Perf. 14x12½***

337B A141	4c bl grn & gray blk	50	20

Issued for regular postage, although inscribed "Expreso." See No. E2.

Souvenir Sheet

A142

Typographed and Engraved

1951, Oct. 22 ***Imperf.***

338 A142	Sheet of two	75	1.00
a.	1c rose carmine	25	25
b.	10c deep ultramarine	25	25

75th anniv. (in 1949) of the UPU.

For overprint see No. 419.

A143

Modern Model Schools
A144

1951, Oct. 22 **Photo.** ***Perf. 13½x14***

339 A143	½c pur & sepia	15	15
340 A144	1c brn car & dl grn	15	15
341 A143	2c grnsh bl & red brn	15	15
342 A144	4c blk brn & rose vio	15	15
	Set value		40

Enriquez de Rivera Type of 1945 Re-engraved

1952, June 4 ***Perf. 12½***

343 A132	½c violet	15	15
344 A132	1c rose car	15	15
345 A132	2c green	15	15
346 A132	4c orange	20	15
	Set value	50	20

A panel containing the dates "1660-1951" has been added below the portrait.

Produce Type of 1950

Designs: ½c, Sugar cane field. 1c, Banana trees. 2c, Poptun Agricultural Colony.

1953, Feb. 11 **Photo.** ***Perf. 13½***

347 A137	½c dk brn & dp bl	15	15
348 A137	1c red org & ol grn	15	15
349 A137	2c dk car & gray blk	15	15
	Set value		15

Issued to publicize farming.

Rafael Alvarez Ovalle and Jose Joaquin Palma
A145

1953, May 13
350 A145 ½c pur & blk 25 15
351 A145 1c dk grn & org brn 30 15
352 A145 2c org brn & ol grn 30 15
353 A145 3c dk bl & ol brn 30 15
Set value 45

Authors of Guatemala's national anthem.
For overprints see Nos. 374-378.

Quetzal — A146

1954, Sept. 27 Engr. *Perf. 12½, 11*
354 A146 1c dp vio blue 15 15

See Nos. 367-373, 380-382A, 434-444. For overprint see No. 395.

Mario Camposeco A147 — Globe and Red Cross A148

Designs: 10c, Carlos Aguirre Matheu. 15c, Goalkeeper.

1955-56 Unwmk. *Perf. 12½*
355 A147 4c violet 1.00 25
356 A147 4c car ('56) 1.00 25
357 A147 4c bl grn ('56) 1.00 25
358 A147 10c bluish grn 3.00 75
359 A147 15c dk bl 3.00 2.00
Nos. 355-359 (5) 9.00 3.50

50 years of Soccer in Guatemala.

1956, May 23 *Perf. 13x12½*

Designs: 3c, Red Cross, Telephone and "5110." 4c, Nurse, patient and Red Cross flag.

360 A148 1c brn & car 25 20
361 A148 3c dk grn & red 25 20
362 A148 4c dk sl grn & red 25 20

Red Cross. See Nos. B5-B7, CB5-CB7. For surcharges see Nos. CB8-CB10.

Dagger-Cross of the Liberation — A149

Designs: 1c, Map showing 2,000 km. (1,243 miles) of new roads. 3c, Oil production.

1956 Engr. *Perf. 12½*
363 A149 ½c violet 15 15
364 A149 1c dk bl grn 15 15

Perf. 11
365 A149 3c sepia 15 15
Set value 35 20

Liberation of 1954-55. Issue dates: ½c, 1c, July 27; 3c, Oct. 31. See Nos. C210-C218.

Quetzal Type of 1954

1957-58 *Perf. 11, 12½*
367 A146 2c violet 15 15
368 A146 3c car rose 15 15
369 A146 3c ultra 15 15
a. 3c dk bl, perf. 11½ ('72) 5.00 5.00
370 A146 4c orange 25 15
371 A146 5c brown 30 15
372 A146 5c org ver ('58) 30 15
373 A146 6c yel grn 30 20
Nos. 367-373 (7) 1.60
Set value 70

No. 368 is only perf. 12½. The 2c, 4c and No. 369 are found in perf. 11 and 12½. Other values are only perf. 11.

No. 350 Overprinted in Blue, Black, Carmine, Red Orange or Green:

1858 1958

CENTENARIO

1958, Nov.-Dec. Photo. *Perf. 13½*
374 A145 ½c pur & blk (Bl) 15 60
375 A145 ½c pur & blk (Bk) 15 60
376 A145 ½c pur & blk (C) 15 60
377 A145 ½c pur & blk (RO) 15 60
378 A145 ½c pur & blk (G) 15 60
Nos. 374-378 (5) 75 3.00

Cent. of the birth of Rafael Alvarez Ovalle, composer of Guatemala's national anthem.

Re-engraved Rivera Type of 1945

1959, Sept. 12 Engr. *Perf. 11, 12½*
379 A132 4c gray blue 15 15

See note after No. 346.

Quetzal Type of 1954

1960-63 Unwmk. *Perf. 11*
380 A146 2c brn ('61) 15 15
381 A146 4c lt vio 15 15
382 A146 5c bl grn 25 15

Perf. 12½
382A A146 5c slate gray ('63) 50 40
Set value 70

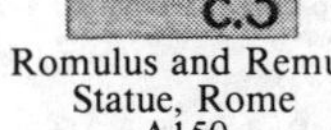

Romulus and Remus Statue, Rome A150 — 1871 Stamp A151

1961 Photo. *Perf. 14*
383 A150 3c blue 15 15

Inauguration of the Plaza Italia.

Las Casas Type of 1949

Perf. 11, 11½, 12½, 13½
1962-64 Engr.
384 A136 ½c blue 15 15
385 A136 1c brt vio ('64) 15 15
386 A136 4c brn ('64) 15 15
Set value 15

1963-66 Unwmk. *Perf. 11*
387 A151 10c carmine 20 15
388 A151 10c slate ('64) 25 15

Perf. 11½
389 A151 10c ol brn ('66) 20 15
390 A151 20c dp pur ('64) 30 25
391 A151 20c dk bl ('65) 30 25
Nos. 387-391 (5) 1.25
Set value 70

For souvenir sheet, see No. C310.

Pedro Bethancourt Comforting Sick Man — A152

1964, Jan. 6 Engr. *Perf. 11*
394 A152 2½c olive bister 15 15

Beatification (1962-63) of Pedro Bethancourt (1626-67). See Nos. C319-C322. For overprints see Nos. C381-C382.

Quetzal Type of 1957-58 Overprinted in Blue

HOMENAJE
A LA
"I. S. G. C."
1948—1963

1964, Dec. 29 Engr. *Perf. 12½*
395 A146 4c orange 25 15

15th anniv. (in 1963) of the Intl. Soc. of Guatemala Collectors.

Map of Guatemala and British Honduras — A153 — Quetzal, Mayan Ball Game Goal — A154

1967, Apr. 28 Litho. *Perf. 14x13½*
396 A153 4c ol, vio bl & dp rose 25 25
397 A153 5c ocher, vio bl & dp org 20 15
398 A153 6c dp org, vio bl & gray 20 15

Issued to state Guatemala's claim to British Honduras.
For overprints see Nos. C411-C413.

Lithographed and Engraved
1968, Oct. 15 *Perf. 11½*
399 A154 1c blk, lt grn & red 15 15
400 A154 5c yel, lt grn & red 20 15
401 A154 8c org, lt grn & red 20 15
402 A154 15c bl, lt grn & red 30 15
403 A154 30c lt vio, lt grn & red 75 1.00
Nos. 399-403 (5) 1.60
Set value 1.30

Issued to commemorate the 19th Olympic Games, Mexico City, Oct. 12-27.
See Nos. 412-415. For overprints see Nos. 408-411, C431-C435.

Child and Poinsettia — A155

1968-70 Typo. *Perf. 13½*
404 A155 2½c grn, dp bis & car 15 15
405 A155 2½c grn, org & car ('70) 40 50
406 A155 5c grn, gray & car 20 15
407 A155 21c grn, lil & car 50 50

Issued to help abandoned children.

Type of 1968 Overprinted in Black or Red

Cincuentenario
O. I. T.

1970, Mar. 19 Litho. *Perf. 13½*
408 A154 8c org, lt grn & red 25 50
409 A154 8c org, lt grn & red (R) 25 50

Perf. 12½
410 A154 15c bl, lt grn & red 40 75
411 A154 15c bl, lt grn & red (R) 40 75

50th anniv. of ILO. Gold overprint believed to be a trial color.

Type of 1968

1971 Typo. & Engr. *Perf. 11½*
412 A154 1c gray, yel grn & red 20 15

Typo.
413 A154 5c brt pink, yel grn & red 35 20
414 A154 5c brn, grn & red 35 20
415 A154 5c dk bl, grn & red 35 20

Mayas and CARE Package — A156

1971-72 Typo. *Perf. 13½*
416 A156 1c blk & multi 15 15

Perf. 11½
417 A156 1c vio & multi ('72) 15 15
418 A156 1c brn & multi ('72) 15 15
Set value 30 35

10th anniversary of CARE in Guatemala, a US-Canadian Cooperative for American Relief Everywhere. Exist imperf. See No. C459.

No. 338 (trimmed) Overprinted in Orange with Olympic Rings and: "JUEGOS OLIMPICOS / MUNICH 1972"
Souvenir Sheet

Typo. & Engr.
1972, Oct. 23 *Imperf.*
419 A142 Sheet of two 50 75
a. 1c rose carmine ("Munich") 15 25
b. 10c deep ultra ("1972") 30 50

20th Olympic Games, Munich, Aug. 26-Sept. 11. Commemorative inscriptions on No. 338 at left, top and right have been trimmed off. Size: 61x45mm (approximately). Many varieties exist. Gold overprints probably are proofs.

Pres. Carlos Arana Osorio A157

Designs: 3c, 5c, President Osorio seated (vert.). 8c, Pres. Osorio standing (vert.).

1973-74 Typo. *Perf. 12½*
420 A157 2c bl & blk 15 15
421 A157 3c org & brn 20 15
422 A157 5c rose car & blk 25 15
423 A157 8c blk & brt grn 30 15
a. Lithographed ('74) 20 15
Set value 45

8th population and 3rd dwellings census, Mar. 26-Apr. 7, 1973.

Francisco Ximenez — A158

Typographed, Lithographed (#426)
1973-77 *Perf. 11½, 13½ (#426)*
424 A158 2c blk & emer 15 15
425 A158 3c dk brn & org 15 15
426 A158 3c blk & yel 25 15
427 A158 6c blk & brt bl 25 20
Set value 40

Brother Francisco Ximenez, discoverer and translator of National Book of Guatemala. No. 427 issued for Intl. Book Year 1972.
Issue dates: 6c, Aug. 2, 1973; 2c, Jan. 14, 1975; No. 425, Mar. 5, 1975; No. 426, Sept. 26, 1977.

Sculpture of Christ, by Pedro de Mendoza, 1643 — A159

Design: 8c, Sculpture by Lanuza Brothers, 18th century.

1977, Apr. 4 Litho. *Perf. 11*

428 A159 6c pur & multi	15	15
429 A159 8c pur & multi	25	15
Nos. 428-429,C614-C619 (8)	2.35	2.15

Holy Week 1977.

INTERFER 77 Emblem — A160

1977, Oct. 31 Litho. *Perf. 11½*

430 A160 7c black & multi	15	15

INTERFER 77, 4th International Fair, Guatemala, Oct. 31-Nov. 13.

Rotary Intl., 75th Anniv. A161

1980, July 31 Litho. *Perf. 11½*

431 A161 4c shown	15	15
432 A161 6c Diamond and Quetzal	15	15
433 A161 10c Paul P. Harris	25	15
Set value		15

Quetzal Type of 1954

1984-86 Engr. *Perf. 12½*

434 A146 1c dp grn	15	15
435 A146 2c deep blue	15	15
436 A146 3c olive green	15	15
437 A146 3c sepia	15	15
438 A146 3c blue	15	15
439 A146 3c red	15	15
440 A146 3c orange	15	15
441 A146 3c vermilion	15	15
442 A146 4c lt red brn	15	15
443 A146 5c magenta	15	15
444 A146 6c deep blue	15	15
Set value	1.10	55

Issue dates: Nos. 436-439, Feb. 20. No. 441, 6c, Apr. 25, 1986. 1c, 4c, 5c, Feb. 16, 1987. 2c, Mar. 25, 1987.

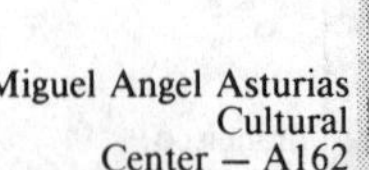

Miguel Angel Asturias Cultural Center — A162

1987-91 Litho. *Perf. 12½, 11½ (9c)*

446 A162 2c bister brown	15	15
447 A162 3c ultra	15	15
449 A162 5c orange	15	15
451 A162 7c ver	15	15
452 A162 8c brt pink	15	15
453 A162 9c black	15	15
454 A162 10c pale grn	15	15
Set value	75	35

Miguel Angel Asturias (1899-1974), 1967 Nobel laureate in literature.

Issue dates: 3c, Nov. 24; 7c, Nov. 17; 8c, Nov. 27; 10c, Dec. 8; 2c, Mar. 2, 1988; 5c, Mar. 23, 1990; 9c, Oct. 1, 1991.

This is an expanding set. Numbers will change if necessary.

Central American and Caribbean University Games A163

Toucan as a participant in various events.

1990 Litho. *Perf. 12½*

455 A163 15c shown	30	15
456 A163 20c Torch bearer, vert.	40	15
457 A163 25c Volleyball	50	15
458 A163 30c Soccer	60	20
459 A163 45c Karate	90	30
460 A163 1q Baseball	2.00	66
461 A163 2q Basketball	4.00	1.30
462 A163 3q Hurdles	6.00	2.00
Nos. 455-462 (8)	14.70	4.91

Issue dates: 20c, Aug. 22; 30c, 3q, July 10; others, Apr. 25.

SEMI-POSTAL STAMPS

Regular Issues of 1935-36 Surcharged in Blue or Red similar to illustration

EXPOSICION
1937
FILATELICA
+1

1937, Mar. 15 Unwmk. *Perf. 12½*

B1 A102 1c + 1c brn & crim	75	1.00
B2 A103 3c + 1c rose car & pck grn	75	1.00
B3 A103 3c + 1c red org & pck grn	75	1.00
B4 A106 5c + 1c bl & dk brn (R)	75	1.00

1st Phil. Exhib. held in Guatemala, Mar. 15-20.

Catalogue values for unused stamps in this section, from this point to the end of the section, are for Never Hinged items.

Type of Regular Issue, 1956

Designs: 5c+15c, Nurse, Patient and Red Cross Flag. 15c+50c, Red Cross, telephone and "5110." 25c+50c, Globe and Red Cross.

1956, June 19 Engr. *Perf. 13x12½*

B5 A148 5c + 15c ultra & red	90	1.25
a. Imperf. pair	75.00	
B6 A148 15c + 50c dk vio & red	2.00	2.50
B7 A148 25c + 50c bluish blk & car	2.00	2.50

The surtax was for the Red Cross.

Jesus and Esquipulas Cathedral — SP1

1957, Oct. 29 *Perf. 13*

B8 SP1 1½c + ½c blk & brn	50	20

The tax was for the Esquipulas highway. See Nos. CB12-CB14.

Type of Air Post Semi-Postal Stamps and

Arms — SP2

Design: 3c+3c, Wounded man, Battle of Solferino.

1960, Apr. 9 Photo. *Perf. 13½x14*
Cross in Rose Red

B9 SP2 1c + 1c red brn & bl	20	30
B10 SPAP2 3c + 3c lil, bl & pink	20	30
B11 SP2 4c + 4c blk & bl	20	30

Cent. (in 1959) of the Red Cross idea. The surtax went to the Red Cross. Exist imperf. See Nos. CB15-CB21.

AIR POST STAMPS

AP1

AP2

Surcharged in Red on No. 229

1929, May 20 Unwmk. *Perf. 12½*

C1 AP1 3c on 15p blk	50	60
C2 AP1 5c on 15p blk	30	15
C3 AP1 15c on 15p blk	75	20
a. Double surcharge (G & R)	100.00	
C4 AP1 20c on 15p blk	1.00	1.00
a. Inverted surcharge	100.00	
b. Double surcharge	100.00	

Surcharged in Red on No. 216

1929, May 20 *Perf. 14*

C5 AP1 5c on 15p black	1.50	1.00

Surcharged in Black on No. 218

1929, Oct. 9

C6 AP2 3c on 2.50p dk vio	1.00	1.00

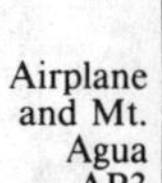
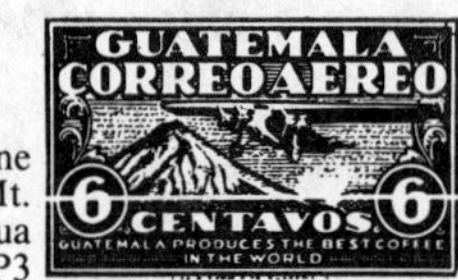

Airplane and Mt. Agua AP3

1930, June 4 Litho. *Perf. 12½*

C7 AP3 6c rose red	60	40
a. Double impression	25.00	25.00
b. Imperf., pair	350.00	

For overprint see No. C14.

Nos. 227, 229 Surcharged in Black or Red

SERVICIO
AEREO INTERIOR
10 Centavos
DE QUETZAL
1930

1930, Dec. 9 *Perf. 12½*

C8 A57 1c on 3p grn (Bk)	30	30
a. Double surcharge	100.00	
C9 A57 2c on 3p grn (Bk)	75	1.00
C10 A57 3c on 3p grn (R)	75	1.00
C11 A57 4c on 3p grn (R)	75	1.00
C12 A64 10c on 15p blk (R)	1.00	1.00
a. Double surcharge	125.00	
Nos. C8-C12 (5)	3.55	4.30

No. 237 Overprinted

AEREO
EXTERIOR
1931

1931, May 19 *Perf. 14*

C13 A81 4c orange	25	15
a. Double overprint	40.00	50.00

No. C7 Overprinted

EXTERIOR - 1931

Perf. 12½

C14 AP3 6c rose red	1.00	1.00
a. On No. C7a	30.00	30.00
b. Inverted overprint	6.00	7.50

AP4

AP5

Red Overprint

1931, Oct. 21 *Perf. 14*

C15 AP4 15c ultra	1.50	20
a. Double overprint	100.00	100.00
C16 AP5 30c green	2.50	85
a. Double overprint	75.00	75.00

Nos. 235-236 Overprinted in Red or Green

Primer Vuelo
Postal
BARRIOS-
MIAMI
1931

1931, Dec. 5

C17 A79 2c dp bl (R)	2.50	3.00
C18 A80 3c dk vio (G)	2.50	3.00

No. 240 Overprinted in Red

Primer Vuelo Postal
BARRIOS-MIAMI
1931

C19 A36 15c ultra	2.50	3.00

Nos. C17-C19 were issued in connection with the 1st postal flight from Barrios to Miami.

No. 224 Surcharged in Red

SERVICIO
AEREO
INTERIOR
1932
Q0.02

1932-33 *Perf. 12½*

C20 A74 2c on 1.50p dk bl	65	50

Nos. 227, 229 Surcharged in Violet, Red or Blue

SERVICIO AEREO
INTERIOR — 1932
Q0.03

C21 A57 3c on 3p grn (V)	75	15
a. Inverted surcharge	40.00	40.00
b. Vert. pair, imperf. horiz.	750.00	
C22 A57 3c on 3p grn (R)	75	20
C23 A64 10c on 15p blk (R)	7.50	6.00
b. First "I" of "Interior" missing	10.00	10.00
C24 A64 15c on 15p blk (Bl)	9.00	8.00
a. First "I" of "Interior" missing	15.00	15.00
Nos. C20-C24 (5)	18.65	14.85

Issue dates: No. C22, Jan. 1, 1933; others, Feb. 11, 1932.

AP6

Green Overprint

1933, Jan. 1 *Perf. 14*

C25	AP6	4c orange	25	15
a.		Double overprint	40.00	40.00

AEREO
EXTERIOR
1934

Nos. 235, 238 and 240 Overprinted in Red or Black

1934, Aug. 7

C26	A82	5c dk car (Bk)	1.50	15
C27	A36	15c ultra (R)	1.50	15

AEREO
INTERIOR
1934

Overprinted in Red

C28	A79	2c deep blue	50	15

View of Port Barrios — AP7

Designs: 15c, Tomb of Barrios. 30c, Equestrian Statue of Barrios.

1935, July 19 **Photo.** *Perf. 12½*

C29	AP7	10c yel brn & pck grn	2.00	2.00
C30	AP7	15c gray & brn	2.00	2.00
C31	AP7	30c car rose & bl vio	2.00	1.50

Birth cent. of Gen. Justo Rufino Barrios.

Lake Amatitlán AP10

Designs: Nos. C36, C37, C45, C46. Different views of Lake Amatitlan. 3c, Port Barrios. No. C34, C35, Ruins of Port San Felipe. 10c, Port Livingston. No. C39, C40, Port San Jose. No. C41, C42, View of Atitlan. No. C43, C44, Aurora Airport.

Overprinted with Quetzal in Green

1935-37 **Size: 37x17mm**

C32	AP10	2c org brn	15	15
C33	AP10	3c blue	20	15
C34	AP10	4c black	25	15
C35	AP10	4c ultra ('37)	20	15
C36	AP10	6c yel grn	22	15
C37	AP10	6c blk vio ('37)	4.00	15
C38	AP10	10c claret	50	25
C39	AP10	15c red org	65	40
C40	AP10	15c yel grn ('37)	65	65
C41	AP10	30c olive grn	6.00	6.50
C42	AP10	30c ol bis ('37)	75	50
C43	AP10	50c rose vio	17.50	15.00
C44	AP10	50c Prus bl ('36)	4.00	3.00
C45	AP10	1q scarlet	17.50	20.00
C46	AP10	1q car ('36)	4.50	3.00
		Nos. C32-C46 (15)	57.07	50.20

Issue dates follow No. C69.

For overprints and surcharges see Nos. C70-C79, CB1-CB2.

Central Park, Antigua AP11

Designs: 1c, Guatemala City. 2c, Central Park, Guatemala City. 3c, Monastery. Nos. C50-C51, Mouth of Dulce River. Nos. C52-C53, Plaza Barrios. Nos. C54-C55, Los Proceres Monument. No. C56, Central Park, Antigua. No. C57, Dulce River. Nos. C58-C59, Quezaltenango. Nos. C60-C61, Ruins at Antigua. Nos. C62-C63, Dock at Port Barrios. Nos. C64-C65, Port San Jose. Nos. C66-C67, Aurora Airport. 2.50q, Island off Atlantic Coast. 5q, Atlantic Coast view.

Overprinted with Quetzal in Green

Size: 34x15mm

C47	AP11	1c yel brn	15	15
C48	AP11	2c vermilion	15	15
C49	AP11	3c magenta	50	25
C50	AP11	4c org yel ('36)	1.75	1.50
C51	AP11	4c car lake ('37)	1.00	75
C52	AP11	5c dl bl	20	15
C53	AP11	5c org ('37)	15	15
C54	AP11	10c red brn	50	35
C55	AP11	10c ol grn ('37)	50	30
C56	AP11	15c rose red	25	15
C57	AP11	15c ver ('37)	22	15
C58	AP11	20c ultra	2.50	3.00
C59	AP11	20c dp cl ('37)	50	25
C60	AP11	25c gray blk	3.00	3.50
C61	AP11	25c bl grn ('37)	45	25
a.		Quetzal omitted		2,000.
C62	AP11	30c yel grn	1.50	1.50
C63	AP11	30c rose red ('37)	75	15
C64	AP11	50c car rose	7.00	8.00
C65	AP11	50c pur ('36)	6.50	7.50
C66	AP11	1q dk bl	22.50	25.00
C67	AP11	1q dk grn ('36)	7.50	7.50

Size: 46x20mm

C68	AP11	2.50q rose red & ol grn ('36)	5.00	3.00
C69	AP11	5q org & ind ('36)	7.00	4.00
a.		Quetzal omitted	1,500.	1,250.
		Nos. C47-C69 (23)	69.57	67.70

Issue dates of Nos. C32-C69: Nov. 1, 1935; Oct. 1, 1936; Jan. 1, 1937.

For overprints and surcharges see Nos. C80-C91, CB3-CB4.

Types of Air Post Stamps, 1935 Overprinted with Airplane in Blue

Designs: 2c, Quezaltenango. 3c, Lake Atitian. 4c, Progressive Colony, Lake Amatitlan. 6c, Carmen Hill. 10c, Relief map. 15c, National University. 30c, Espana Plaza. 50c, Police Station, Aurora Airport. 75c, Amphitheater, Aurora Airport. 1q, Aurora Airport.

1937, May 18

Center in Brown Black

C70	AP10	2c carmine	15	15
C71	AP10	3c blue	1.00	1.25
C72	AP10	4c citron	15	15
C73	AP10	6c yel grn	35	25
C74	AP10	10c red vio	2.00	2.25
C75	AP10	15c orange	1.50	1.00
C76	AP10	30c ol grn	3.75	3.00
C77	AP10	50c pck bl	5.00	4.25
C78	AP10	75c dk vio	10.00	11.00
C79	AP10	1q dp rose	11.00	12.00
		Nos. C70-C79 (10)	34.90	35.30

Overprinted with Airplane in Black

Designs: 1c, 7th Ave., Guatemala City. 2c, Los Proceres Monument. 3c, National Printing Office. 5c, National Museum. 10c, Central Park. 15c, Escuintla. 20c, Motorcycle Police. 25c, Slaughterhouse, Escuintla. 30c, Exhibition Hall. 50c, Barrios Plaza. 1q, Polytechnic School. 1.50q, Aurora Airport.

Size: 33x15mm

C80	AP11	1c yel brn & brt bl	15	15
C81	AP11	2c crim & dp vio	15	15
C82	AP11	3c red vio & red brn	50	50
C83	AP11	5c pck grn & cop red	4.00	3.00
C84	AP11	10c car & grn	1.25	1.00
C85	AP11	15c rose & dl ol grn	50	25
C86	AP11	20c ultra & blk	3.00	1.75
C87	AP11	25c dk gray & scar	2.50	2.50
C88	AP11	30c grn & dp vio	1.25	1.25
C89	AP11	50c mag & ultra	10.00	12.00

Size: 42x19mm

C90	AP11	1q ol grn & red vio	10.00	12.00
C91	AP11	1.50q scar & ol brn	10.00	12.00
		Nos. C80-C91 (12)	43.30	46.55

Second term of President Ubico.

Souvenir Sheet

AP12

1938, Jan. 10 *Perf. 12½*

C92	AP12	Sheet of four	1.50	1.50
a.		15c George Washington	30	30
b.		4c Franklin D. Roosevelt	30	30
c.		4c Map of the Americas	30	30
d.		15c Pan American Union Building, Washington, DC	30	30

150th anniv. of US Constitution.

President Arosemena, Panama AP13

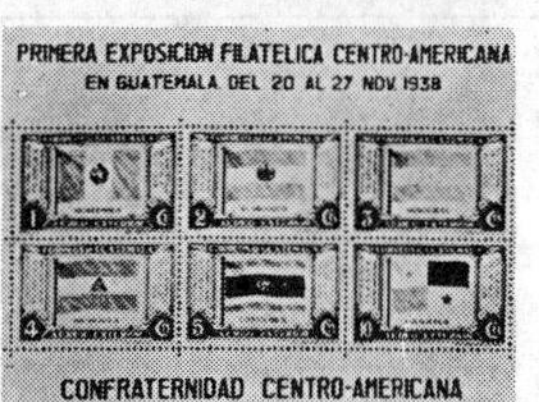

Flags of Central American Countries — AP19

Designs: 2c, Pres. Cortés Castro, Costa Rica. 3c, Pres. Somoza, Nicaragua. 4c, Pres. Carias Andino, Honduras. 5c, Pres. Martinez, El Salvador. 10c, Pres. Ubico, Guatemala.

1938, Nov. 20 **Unwmk.**

C93	AP13	1c org & ol brn	15	15
C94	AP13	2c scar, pale pink & sl grn	15	15
C95	AP13	3c grn, buff & ol brn	25	30
C96	AP13	4c dk cl, pale lil & brn	30	35
C97	AP13	5c bis, pale grn & ol brn	50	60
C98	AP13	10c ultra, pale bl & brn	1.00	1.25
		Nos. C93-C98 (6)	2.35	2.80

Souvenir Sheet

C99	AP19	Sheet of six	1.00	1.00
a.		1c Guatemala	15	15
b.		2c El Salvador	15	15
c.		3c Honduras	15	15
d.		4c Nicaragua	15	15
e.		5c Costa Rica	15	15
f.		10c Panama	15	15

1st Central American Phil. Exhib., Guatemala City, Nov. 20-27.

For overprints see Nos. CO1-CO7.

La Merced Church, Antigua AP20

Designs: 2c, Ruins of Christ School, Antigua. 3c, Aurora Airport. 4c, Drill ground, Guatemala City. 5c, Cavalry barracks. 6c, Palace of Justice. 10c, Customhouse, San Jose. 15c, Communications Building, Retalhuleu. 30c, Municipal Theater, Quezaltenango. 50c, Customhouse, Retalhuleu. 1q, Departmental Building.

Inscribed "Aéreo Interior" Overprinted with Quetzal in Green

1939, Feb. 14

C100	AP20	1c ol bis & chnt	20	15
C101	AP20	2c rose red & sl grn	20	15
C102	AP20	3c dl bl & bis	25	15
C103	AP20	4c rose pink & yel grn	25	15
C104	AP20	5c brn lake & brt ultra	30	15
C105	AP20	6c org & gray brn	35	15
C106	AP20	10c bis brn & gray blk	50	20
C107	AP20	15c dl vio & blk	75	15
C108	AP20	30c dp bl & dk car	1.10	25
C109	AP20	50c org & brt vio	1.50	40
a.		Quetzal omitted		1,750.
C110	AP20	1q yel grn & brt ultra	2.50	1.25
		Nos. C100-C110 (11)	7.90	3.15

See Nos. C111-C122. For overprint and surcharge see No. C124, C132.

1939, Feb. 14

Designs: 1c, Mayan Altar, Aurora Park. 2c, Sanitation Building. 3c, Lake Amatitlan. 4c, Lake Atitlan. 5c, Tamazulapa River bridge. 10c, Los proceres Monument. 15c, Palace of Captains General. 20c, Church on Carmen Hill. 25c, Barrios Park. 30c, Mayan Altar. 50c, Charles III fountain. 1q, View of Antigua.

Inscribed "Aéreo International" or "Aérea Exterior"

Overprinted with Quetzal in Green

C111	AP20	1c ol grn & gldn brn	20	15
C112	AP20	2c lt grn & blk	30	20
C113	AP20	3c ultra & cob bl	20	15
C114	AP20	4c org brn & yel grn	20	15
C115	AP20	5c sage grn & red org	35	15
C116	AP20	10c lake & sl blk	1.75	15
C117	AP20	15c ultra & brt rose	1.75	15
C118	AP20	20c yel grn & ap grn	60	20
C119	AP20	25c dl vio & lt ol grn	60	15
C120	AP20	30c dl rose & blk	80	15
C121	AP20	50c scar & brt yel	1.50	20
C122	AP20	1q org & yel grn	2.50	35
		Nos. C111-C122 (12)	10.75	
		Set value		1.70

No. 240 Overprinted in Carmine

UNION PANAMERICANA
1890 - 1940
CORREO AEREO

1940, Apr. 14 *Perf. 14*

C123	A36	15c ultra	55	15

Pan American Union, 50th anniversary.

No. C112 Overprinted in Carmine

DICIEMBRE 2
1941
SEGUNDO DIA PAN-
AMERICANO DE LA SALUD

1941, Dec. 2 *Perf. 12½*

C124	AP20	2c lt grn & blk	40	20

Second Pan American Health Day.

San Carlos University, Antigua AP21

1943, June 25 **Engr.** *Perf. 11*

C125	AP21	15c dk red brn	40	15
a.		Imperf., pair	100.00	

Don Pedro de Alvarado AP22

Type I- Diagonal shading lines at inner edges of commemorative tablet.
Type II- Overall shading added to tablet.

1943, Mar. 10 Unwmk. *Perf. 11½*

C126	AP22	15c dp ultra (II)	40	15
a.		Type I	15.00	10.00

400th anniv. of the founding of Antigua.

National Police Building AP23

1943, Aug. 3 *Perf. 11*

C127	AP23	10c dp rose vio	35	15

Allegory of 1944 Revolution — AP24

1945, Apr. 27 Engr.

C128	AP24	5c dp rose	25	15
C129	AP24	6c dk bl grn	25	20
a.		Imperf., pair	110.00	
C130	AP24	10c violet	25	15
C131	AP24	15c aqua	25	20

Revolution of October 20, 1944.

No. C113 Surcharged in Red

1945
FERIA DEL LIBRO
2½ CENTAVOS

1945, July 25 *Perf. 12½*

C132	AP20	2½c on 3c	1.00	1.25

The 1945 Book Fair.

National Palace AP25

Carmine Overprint

1945, Aug. Engr. *Perf. 11*

C133	AP25	5c rose car	20	15
a.		Triple ovpt., one inverted	50.00	25.00
b.		Double ovpt., one inverted	65.00	

See Nos. C137A-C139.

Jose Milla y Vidaurre AP26

Torch AP27

AP28

1945

C134	AP26	7½c sepia	75	1.00
C134A	AP26	7½c dark blue	40	25

Issue dates: No. C134, Sept. 28. No. C134A, Dec. 6.
For overprint see No. C230.

1945, Oct. 19

C135	AP27	5c brt red vio	30	15

Souvenir Sheet
Imperf

C136	AP28	Sheet of two	1.20	1.20
a.		5c brt red vio	50	50

1st anniv. of the Revolution of Oct. 20, 1944.
See Nos. C147-C150.

Catalogue values for unused stamps in this section, from this point to the end of the section, are for Never Hinged items.

Payo Enriquez de Rivera — AP29

1946, Jan. 22 Unwmk. *Perf. 11*

C137	AP29	5c rose pink	25	15

See Nos. C269, C311-C315.

Palace Type of 1945

1946-47 Without Overprint

C137A	AP25	5c rose car ('47)	50	15
C138	AP25	10c dp lil	25	15
a.		Imperf., pair	100.00	
C139	AP25	15c blue	50	15
a.		Imperf., pair	100.00	
		Set value		35

Sir Rowland Hill — AP30

Globes, Quetzal — AP31

1946, Aug. 5 Photo. *Perf. 14x13*

C140	AP30	5c slate & brn (blk ovpt.)	35	15
a.		Without "AEREO" ovpt.	*400.00*	*400.00*
C141	AP31	15c car lake, ultra & emer	50	20

Centenary of the first postage stamp.

José Batres y Montufar AP32

Signing the Declaration of Independence AP33

1946, Sept. 16 Engr. *Perf. 11*

C142	AP32	10c Prus grn	25	15
a.		Perf. 12½	10.00	15

1946, Dec. 19 *Perf. 11*

C143	AP33	5c rose car	15	15
C144	AP33	6c ol brn	20	15
C145	AP33	10c violet	25	15
C146	AP33	20c blue	30	20
		Set value		55

125th anniv. of the signing of the Declaration of Independence.

Torch Type of 1945
Dated 1944-1946

1947, Feb. 3 Engr.

C147	AP27	1c green	15	15
C148	AP27	2c carmine	15	15
C149	AP27	3c violet	15	15
C150	AP27	5c dp bl	15	15
		Set value		40

Inscribed "II Aniversario de la Revolucion." "Aereo" in color on a white background.
2nd anniv. of the Revolution of Oct. 20, 1944.

Franklin D. Roosevelt — AP34

1947, June 6

C151	AP34	5c rose car	20	15
C152	AP34	6c blue	20	15
C153	AP34	10c dp ultra	35	25
C154	AP34	30c gray blk	1.50	1.00
C155	AP34	50c lt vio	2.50	2.50
a.		Imperf., pair	125.00	
C156	AP34	1q gray grn	4.00	4.00
a.		Imperf., pair	125.00	
		Nos. C151-C156 (6)	8.75	8.05

No. 296 Overprinted in Carmine

1948
AEREO

1948, May 14 *Perf. 12½*

C157	A122	5c blue & red	15	15

Soccer Game AP35

1948, Aug. 31 Engr.

Center in Black

C158	AP35	3c brt car	65	30
C159	AP35	5c bl grn	75	40
C160	AP35	10c dk vio	90	90
C161	AP35	30c dp bl	3.00	3.50
C162	AP35	50c bister	4.00	4.50
		Nos. C158-C162 (5)	9.30	9.60

4th Central American and Caribbean Soccer Championship, Mar., 1948.

Seal, University of Guatemala — AP36

1949, Nov. 29 *Perf. 12½*

Center in Blue

C163	AP36	3c carmine	50	40
C164	AP36	10c green	75	75
C165	AP36	50c yellow	2.75	3.25

1st Latin American Congress of Universities.

Lake Atitlan AP37

Tecum Uman Monument AP38

Designs: 8c, San Cristobal Church. 13c, Weaver. 35c, Momostenango Cliffs.

1950, Feb. 17 Photo. *Perf. 14*

Multicolored Centers

C166	AP37	3c car rose	35	15
C167	AP38	5c red brn	35	15
C168	AP37	8c dk sl grn	40	15
C169	AP38	13c brown	60	25
C170	AP37	35c purple	2.25	2.75
		Nos. C166-C170 (5)	3.95	3.45

See No. C181.

Soccer AP39

Pole Vault AP40

Designs: 3c, Foot race. 8c, Tennis. 35c, Diving. 65c, Stadium.

1950, Feb. 25 Engr. *Perf. 12½*

Center in Black

C171	AP39	1c purple	50	20
C172	AP39	3c carmine	60	20
C173	AP40	4c org brn	75	25
C174	AP39	8c red vio	90	30
C175	AP40	35c lt bl	2.00	2.75

Center in Green

C176	AP40	65c dk sl grn	4.25	4.50
		Nos. C171-C176 (6)	9.00	8.20

6th Central American and Caribbean Games.

Nurse and Patient AP41

Designs: 10c, School of Nurses. 50c, Zacapa Hospital. 1q, Roosevelt Hospital.

1950, Sept. 6 Litho. *Perf. 12*

Quetzal in Blue Green

C177	AP41	5c rose vio & car	25	15
a.		Double impression (frame)	25.00	
C178	AP41	10c ol brn & emer	60	35
C179	AP41	50c ver & red vio	2.00	2.50
C180	AP41	1q org yel & sage grn	2.50	2.75
a.		Souv. sheet, #C177-C180	6.50	7.50

National Hospital Fund.
Nos. C177-C180 exist with colors reversed, perf. and imperf. These are proofs.

No. C168 perf. 12½ or 12 diagonally through center

1951, Apr. *Perf. 14*

C181	AP37	(4c) multi	10.00	7.50
a.		Unservered pair	25.00	15.00

Counterfeits of diagonal perforation exist.

Ceremonial Stone Ax
AP42

National Flag and Emblem
AP43

1953, Feb. 11 Photo. *Perf. 14x13½*

C182	AP42	3c dk bl & ol gray	20	15
C183	AP42	5c dk gray & hn brn	25	15
C184	AP42	10c dk pur & slate	35	25
		Set value		45

1953, Mar. 14 *Perf. 13½*

Multicolored Center

C185	AP43	1c maroon	20	15
C186	AP43	2c sl grn	25	15
C187	AP43	4c dk brn	30	15

Issued to mark the passing of the presidency from J. J. Arevalo to Col. Jacobo Arbenz Guzman.

Regional Dance — AP44

Horse Racing
AP45

Designs: 4c, White nun - national flower. 5c, Allegory of the fair. 20c, Zakuleu ruins. 30c, Symbols of Agriculture. 50c, Champion bull. 65c, Bicycle racing. 1q, Quetzal.

1953, Dec. 18 Engr. *Perf. 12½*

C188	AP44	1c dp ultra & car	15	15
C189	AP44	4c org & grn	50	25
C190	AP44	5c emer & choc	30	20
C191	AP45	15c choc & dk pur	1.25	1.00
C192	AP45	20c car & ultra	75	1.00
C193	AP44	30c dp ultra & choc	1.25	1.50
C194	AP45	50c pur & blk	1.50	1.50
C195	AP45	65c lt bl & dk grn	2.50	2.75
C196	AP44	1q dk bl grn & dk red	4.00	4.75
		Nos. C188-C196 (9)	12.20	13.10

National Fair, Oct. 20, 1953.

Indian — AP46

1954, Apr. 21 Unwmk. *Perf. 12½*

C197	AP46	1c carmine	25	15
C198	AP46	2c dp bl	25	15
C199	AP46	4c yel grn	25	15
C200	AP46	5c aqua	50	20
C201	AP46	6c orange	50	20
C202	AP46	10c violet	75	25
C203	AP46	20c blk brn	2.75	3.00
		Nos. C197-C203 (7)	5.25	4.10

Guatemala and ODECA Flags
AP47

Rotary Emblem, Map of Guatemala
AP48

1954, Oct. 13 Photo. *Perf. 14x13½*

C204	AP47	1c multi	15	15
C205	AP47	2c multi	15	15
C206	AP47	4c multi	20	15
		Set value		30

3rd anniv. of the formation of the Organization of Central American States.

1956, Sept. 8 Engr.

C207	AP48	4c bl & dl yel	25	20
C208	AP48	6c lt bl grn & dl yel	25	15
C209	AP48	35c pur & dl yel	1.50	2.00

50th anniv. of Rotary Intl. (in 1955).

Mayan Warrior Holding Dagger Cross of the Liberation — AP49

Designs: 4c, Family looking into the sun. 5c, The dagger of the Liberation destroying communist symbols. 6c, Hands holding cogwheel and map of Guatemala. 20c, Monument to the victims of communism and flag. 30c, Champerico harbor. 65c, Radio tower, Mercury and map of Guatemala. 1q, Flags of the American nations. 5q, Pres. Carlos Castillo Armas.

1956, Oct. 10 Photo. *Perf. 14x13½*

C210	AP49	2c dp grn, red, bl & brn	15	15
C211	AP49	4c dp car & gray blk	15	15
C212	AP49	5c bl & red brn	20	20
C213	AP49	6c dk brn & dp ultra	15	15
C214	AP49	20c vio, brn & bl	1.20	1.50
C215	AP49	30c dp bl & ol	1.50	1.75
C216	AP49	65c chnt brn & grn	2.25	2.75
C217	AP49	1q dk brn & multi	3.25	3.50
C218	AP49	5q multi	13.00	14.00
		Nos. C210-C218 (9)	21.85	24.15

Liberation of 1954-55.

For overprints see Nos. C233, C243, C265-C266, C417.

Red Cross, Map and Quetzal
AP50

Designs: 2c, José Ruiz Augulo and woman with child (vert.) 3c, Pedro de Bethancourt with sick man. 4c, Rafael Ayau.

Perf. 13½x14, 14x13½

1958, May 13 Unwmk.

C219	AP50	1c multi	22	15
C220	AP50	2c multi	22	15
C221	AP50	3c multi	22	15
C222	AP50	4c multi	22	15

Issued in honor of the Red Cross.

For overprints and surcharges see Nos. C235-C242, C251-C254, C283-C298, C390-C394.

Col. Carlos Castillo Armas
AP51

Galleon of 1532 and Freighter "Quezaltenango"
AP52

1959, Feb. 27 *Perf. 14x13½*

Center in Dark Blue and Yellow

C223	AP51	1c black	15	15
C224	AP51	2c rose red	15	15
C225	AP51	4c brown	15	15
C226	AP51	6c dk bl grn	15	15
C227	AP51	10c dk pur	25	25
C228	AP51	20c bl grn	75	75
C229	AP51	35c gray	1.20	1.25
		Nos. C223-C229 (7)	2.80	2.85

Pres. Carlos Castillo Armas (1914-1957).

No. C134A Overprinted in Carmine: "HOMENAJE A LAS NACIONES UNIDAS"

1959, Mar. 4 Engr. *Perf. 11*

C230	AP26	7½c dk bl	80	1.00

Issued to honor the United Nations.

1959, May 15 Litho. *Perf. 11*

C231	AP52	6c ultra & rose red	20	15

Issued to honor the formation of the Guatemala-Honduras merchant fleet.

For overprint see No. C467.

Type of 1950 Overprinted in Dark Blue

BELICE ES NUESTRO
A E R E O

1959, Oct. 9 *Perf. 12*

C232	A140	5c dk bl & lt brn	50	20
a.		Inverted overprint	200.00	35.00

Issued to state Guatemala's claim to British Honduras. Overprint reads: "Belize is ours." Map includes "BRITISH HONDURAS" and its borderline, and excludes bit extending above "A" of "GUATEMALA" on No. 337.

No. C232 is known without overprint in multiples.

No. C213 Overprinted in Red: "1859 Centenario Primera Exportacion de Cafe 1959"

1959, Oct. 26 Photo. *Perf. 14x13½*

C233	AP49	6c dk brn & dp ultra	50	30

Centenary of coffee export.

Pres. and Mrs. Villeda of Honduras
AP53

1959, Nov. 3 Litho. *Perf. 11*

C234	AP53	6c pale brn	15	15

Visit of President Ramon Villeda Morales of Honduras, Oct. 12, 1958.

For overprint see No. C415.

Nos. C219-C222 Overprinted: "AÑO MUNDIAL DE REFUGIADOS" in Green, Violet, Blue or Brown

Perf. 13½x14, 14x13½

1960, Apr. 23 Photo. Unwmk.

C235	AP50	1c multi (G)	60	85
C236	AP50	2c multi (V)	60	85
C237	AP50	3c multi (Bl)	60	85
C238	AP50	4c multi (Br)	60	85

Nos. C219-C222 Overprinted as Above and Surcharged with New Value

C239	AP50	6c on 1c multi	2.25	2.00
C240	AP50	7c on 2c multi	2.25	2.00
C241	AP50	10c on 3c multi	3.75	4.00
C242	AP50	20c on 4c multi	4.00	4.00
		Nos. C235-C242 (8)	14.65	15.40

Nos. C235-C242 issued to publicize World Refugee Year, July 1, 1959-June 30, 1960.

No. C213 Overprinted in Red: "Fundacion de la ciudad Melchor de Mencos, 30-IV-1960"

1960, Apr. 30 *Perf. 14x13½*

C243	AP49	6c dk brn & dp ultra	1.00	1.25

Founding of the city of Melchor de Mencos.

UNESCO and Eiffel Tower, Paris — AP54

1960, Nov. 4 Photo. *Perf. 12½*

C244	AP54	5c dp mag & vio	15	15
C245	AP54	6c ultra & vio brn	15	15
C246	AP54	8c emer & mag	30	15
C247	AP54	20c red brn & dl bl	1.25	1.25

Issued to honor UNESCO.

For overprints see Nos. C258, C267-C268.

Abraham Lincoln — AP55

1960, Oct. 29 Engr. *Perf. 11*

C248	AP55	5c vio bl	20	20
C249	AP55	30c violet	1.00	1.25
C250	AP55	50c gray	5.00	6.00

Issued to commemorate the sesquicentenary of the birth of Abraham Lincoln.

An 8c was also printed, but was not issued and all copies were destroyed.

Nos. C219-C222 Overprinted "Mayo de 1960" in Green, Blue or Brown

Perf. 13½x14, 14x13½

1961, Apr. 20 Photo. Unwmk.

C251	AP50	1c multi (G)	35	25
C252	AP50	2c multi (Bl)	35	25
C253	AP50	3c multi (Bl)	35	25
C254	AP50	4c multi (Br)	35	25

Issued to honor the Red Cross.

Proclamation of Independence — AP56

1962 Engr. *Perf. 11*

C255	AP56	4c sepia	20	15
C256	AP56	5c vio bl	25	15
C257	AP56	15c brt vio	75	50

140th anniv. of Independence (in 1961).

Issue dates: 4c, 5c, May 23; 15c, Aug. 10.

No. C245 Overprinted in Red: "1962 / EL MUNDO UNIDO / CONTRA LA MALARIA"

1962, Oct. 4 Photo. *Perf. 12½*

C258	AP54	6 ultra & vio brn	80	1.25

WHO drive to eradicate malaria.

Dr. José Luna — AP57

Guatemalan physicians: 4c, Rodolfo Robles. 5c, Narciso Esparragoza y Gallardo. 6c, Juan J. Ortega. 10c, Dario Gonzalez. 20c, Jose Felipe Flores.

1962, Dec. 12 Photo. *Perf. 14x13½*

C259	AP57	1c ol bis & dl pur	40	15
C260	AP57	4c org yel & gray ol	40	15
C261	AP57	5c pale bl & red brn	40	15
C262	AP57	6c sal & blk	40	15
C263	AP57	10c pale grn & red brn	60	20
C264	AP57	20c pale pink & bl	70	60
		Nos. C259-C264 (6)	2.90	
		Set value		1.20

No. C213 Overprinted in Red: "PRESIDENTE/ YDIGORAS/ FUENTES/ RECORRE POR TIERRA/ CENTRO AMERICA/ 14 A 20 DIC. 1962"

1962, Dec. Photo. *Perf. 14x13½*

C265	AP49	6c dk brn & dp ultra	1.00	75

Issued to commemorate Pres. Ydigoras' tour of Central America, Dec. 14-20, 1962.

No. C213 Overprinted in Vermilion: "Reunion Presidents: Kennedy, EE. UU. - Ydigoras F., Guat. - Rivera. Salv. -Villeda M., Hond. - Somoza, Nic. - Orlich, C. R. - Chiari, Panama - San Jose, Costa Rica, 18 A 21 de Marzo de 1963"

Perf. 14x13½

1963, Mar. 18 Unwmk.

C266	AP49	6c dk brn & dp ultra	3.50	2.50

Meeting of Pres. John F. Kennedy with the Presidents of the Central American Republics, San Jose, Costa Rica, Mar. 18-21.

Nos. C245-C246 Overprinted "CONMEMORA / CION FIRMA / NUEVA CARTA / ODECA. - 1962" in Magenta or Black

1963, Mar. 14 *Perf. 12½*

C267	AP54	6c ultra & vio brn (M)	25	15
C268	AP54	8c emer & mag	35	15

Issued to commemorate the signing of the new charter of the Organization of Central American States (ODECA).

Enriquez de Rivera Type of 1946

Perf. 11, 11½, 12½

1963, Mar. 26 Engr.

C269	AP29	5c olive bister	15	15

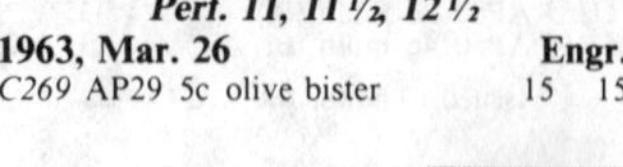

Woman Carrying Fruit Basket — AP58

1963, Mar. 14 Litho. *Perf. 11, 12½*

C270	AP58	1c multi	15	15

Spring Fair, 1960.

Reaper AP59

Ceiba Tree AP60

1983, July 25 Photo. *Perf. 14*

C271	AP59	5c Prus grn	20	20
C272	AP59	10c dk bl	35	20

FAO "Freedom from Hunger" campaign.

1963 Unwmk. *Perf. 12*

C273	AP60	4c brn & grn	25	15

Patzun Palace AP61

Buildings: 3c, Coban. 4c, Retalhuleu. 5c, San Marcos. 6c, Captains General of Antigua.

1964, Jan. 15 *Perf. 13½x14*

C274	AP61	1c rose red & brn	15	15
C275	AP61	3c rose cl & Prus grn	15	15
C276	AP61	4c vio bl & rose lake	15	15
C277	AP61	5c brn & blue	22	20
C278	AP61	6c grn & slate	22	20
		Nos. C274-C278 (5)	89	
		Set value		70

City Hall, Guatemala City — AP62

Design: 4c, Social Security Institute.

1964, Jan. 15 Photo. *Perf. 12x11½*

C279	AP62	3c brt bl & brn	15	15
C280	AP62	4c brn & brt bl	15	15
		Set value		20

See Nos. C281-C282A. For overprints see Nos. C360-C361, C421.

1964-65 Engr. *Perf. 11½*

Designs: 3c, Social Security Institute. 4c, University administration building. No. C282, City Hall, Guatemala City. No. C282A, Engineering School.

Different Frames

C281	AP62	3c dl grn	16	15
C281A	AP62	4c gray ('65)	16	15
C282	AP62	7c blue	22	15
C282A	AP62	7c ol bis ('65)	20	20

Nos. C219-C222 Overprinted in Green, Blue or Black with Olympic Rings and: "OLIMPIADAS / TOKIO - 1964"

1964 Photo. *Perf. 13½x14, 14x13½*

C283	AP50	1c multi (G)	75	1.00
C284	AP50	2c multi (Bl)	75	1.00
C285	AP50	3c multi (G)	75	1.00
C286	AP50	4c multi (Bk)	75	1.00

Issued to publicize the 18th Olympic Games, Tokyo, Oct. 10-25, 1964.

Nos. C219-C222 Surcharged in Green, Blue or Black with New Value and: "HABILITADA - 1964"

1964

C287	AP50	7c on 1c multi (G)	20	20
C288	AP50	9c on 2c multi (Bl)	25	35
C289	AP50	13c on 3c multi (Bl)	35	45
C290	AP50	21c on 4c multi (Bk)	65	75

Nos. C219-C222 Overprinted "FERIA MUNDIAL / DE NEW YORK" in Green, Blue or Black

1964, June 25

C291	AP50	1c multi (G)	50	75
C292	AP50	2c multi (Bl)	50	75
C293	AP50	3c multi (G)	50	75
C294	AP50	4c multi (Bk)	50	75

New York World's Fair.

Nos. C219-C222 Overprinted in Green, Blue or Black: "VIII VUELTA / CICLISTICA"

1964

C295	AP50	1c multi (G)	50	75
C296	AP50	2c multi (Bl)	50	75
C297	AP50	3c multi (G)	50	75
C298	AP50	4c multi (Bk)	1.00	1.25

Eighth Bicycle Race.

Pres. John F. Kennedy AP63

Centenary Emblem AP64

1964 Engr. *Perf. 11½*

C299	AP63	1c violet	60	60
C300	AP63	2c yel grn	60	60
C301	AP63	3c brown	60	60
C302	AP63	7c dp bl	60	60
C303	AP63	50c dk gray	6.00	6.50
		Nos. C299-C303 (5)	8.40	8.90

John F. Kennedy (1917-63). Minute letters "TEOK" are in lower right corner of 1c, 2c, 3c and 50c.

Issue dates: 7c, July 10; others, Aug. 21.

Perf. 11x12

1964, Sept. 9 Unwmk. Photo.

C304	AP64	7c ultra, sil & red	40	25
C305	AP64	9c org, sil & red	40	40
C306	AP64	13c pur, sil & red	55	55
C307	AP64	21c brt grn, sil & red	75	1.00
C308	AP64	35c brn, sil & red	1.20	1.40
C309	AP64	1q lem, sil & red	2.50	3.00
		Nos. C304-C309 (6)	5.80	6.60

Centenary (in 1963) of the Intl. Red Cross.

For overprints see Nos. C323-C327, C395-C400.

Type of Regular Issue 1963

Souvenir Sheet

1964 Engr. *Imperf.*

C310	Sheet of 2	3.50	3.75
a.	A151 10c violet blue	1.40	1.50
b.	A151 20c carmine	1.40	1.50

15th UPU Congress, Vienna, May-June, 1964.

Enriquez de Rivera Type of 1946

1964, Dec. 18 Engr. *Perf. 11½*

C311	AP29	5c gray	15	15
C312	AP29	5c orange	15	15
C313	AP29	5c lt grn	15	15
C314	AP29	5c lt ultra	15	15
C315	AP29	5c dl vio	15	15
		Nos. C311-C315 (5)	75	
		Set value		50

Bishop Francisco Marroquin AP65

Guatemalan Boy Scout Emblem AP66

1965, Jan. 21 Photo. Unwmk.

C316	AP65	4c lil & brn	15	15
C317	AP65	7c gray & sep	20	15
C318	AP65	9c vio bl & blk	25	15
		Set value		35

Issued to honor Bishop Francisco Marroquin.

Bethancourt Type of Regular Issue, 1964

1965, Apr. 20 Engr. *Perf. 11½*

C319	A152	2½c vio bl	15	15
C320	A152	3c orange	15	15
C321	A152	4c purple	15	15
C322	A152	5c yel grn	15	15
		Set value	50	40

For overprints see Nos. C381-C382.

Nos. C304-C308 Overprinted in Red: "AYUDENOS / MAYO 1965"

1965, June 18 Photo. *Perf. 11x12*

C323	AP64	7c ultra, sil & red	35	35
C324	AP64	9c org, sil & red	40	40
C325	AP64	13c pur, sil & red	50	50
C326	AP64	21c brt grn, sil & red	65	65
C327	AP64	35c brn, sil & red	1.00	1.10
		Nos. C323-C327 (5)	2.90	3.00

1966, Mar. 3 Photo. *Perf. 14x13½*

Designs: 9c, Campfire and Scouts. 10c, Scout emblem and Scout carrying torch and flag. 15c, Scout emblem, flags and Scout giving Scout sign. 20c, Lord Baden-Powell.

C328	AP66	5c multi	50	50
C329	AP66	9c multi	50	50
C330	AP66	10c multi	70	70
C331	AP66	15c multi	80	80
C332	AP66	20c multi	1.00	1.00
		Nos. C328-C332 (5)	3.50	3.50

5th Interamerican Regional Training Conf., Guatemala City, Mar. 1-3.

For overprints see Nos. C376-C380.

Central American Independence Issue

Flags of Central American States — AP67

1966, Mar. 9 *Perf. 12½x13½*

C333	AP67	6c multi	20	15

Queen Nefertari Temple, Abu Simbel AP68

1966, Oct. 3 Photo. *Perf. 12*

C334	AP68	21c vio & ocher	55	30

UNESCO world campaign to save historic monuments in Nubia.

Coat of Arms — AP69

1966-70 Engr. *Perf. 13½*

C335 AP69 5c orange 25 15
C336 AP69 5c green 25 15
a. 5c yel grn, perf. 11½ ('69) 25 15

Perf. 11½

C337 AP69 5c bl ('67) 25 15
a. 5c dk bl, perf. 12½ ('69) 25 15

Perf. 12½

C338 AP69 5c gray ('67) 25 15
C339 AP69 5c pur ('67) 25 15
a. 5c bright violet ('69) 25 15

Perf. 11½

C339B AP69 5c dp mag ('70) 25 15
C339C AP69 5c grn, *yel* ('70) 30 15
Nos. C335-C339C (7) 1.80
Set value 80

Issue dates: No. C335, Oct. 3; No. C336, Dec. 15, 1966; No. C337, Feb. 9, 1967; Nos. C338-C339, Apr. 28, 1967; No. C336a, Dec. 3, 1969; No. C339a, Dec. 11, 1969; No. C339B, July 8, 1970; No. C339C, Oct. 16, 1970.

Msgr. Mariano Rossell y Arellano — AP70

1966, Nov. 3 Engr. *Perf. 13½*

C340 AP70 1c dp vio 15 15
C341 AP70 2c green 20 15
C342 AP70 3c brown 20 15
C343 AP70 7c blue 35 15
C344 AP70 50c gray 1.40 1.40
Nos. C340-C344 (5) 2.30 2.00

Issued to honor Msgr. Mariano Rossell y Arellano, apostolic delegate.

Mario Mendez Montenegro AP71

Morning Glory and Map of Guatemala AP72

1966-67 *Perf. 13½*

C345 AP71 2c rose red ('67) 15 15
C346 AP71 3c org ('67) 15 15
C347 AP71 4c rose cl ('67) 20 15
C348 AP71 5c gray 35 20
C349 AP71 5c lt ultra ('67) 35 20
C350 AP71 5c grn ('67) 35 20
C351 AP71 5c bluish blk ('67) 35 20
Nos. C345-C351 (7) 1.90 1.25

Mario Mendez Montenegro (1910-65), founder of the Revolutionary Party.

1967, Jan. 12 Photo. *Perf. 12*

Flowers: 8c, Bird of paradise (horiz.). 10c, White nun orchid, national flower (horiz.). 20c, Nymphs of Amatitlan.

Flowers in Natural Colors

C352 AP72 4c orange 35 25
C353 AP72 8c green 35 15
C354 AP72 10c dk bl 50 50
C355 AP72 20c dk red 1.00 1.00

Pan-American Institute Emblem — AP73

1967, Apr. 13 Photo. *Perf. 13½*

C356 AP73 4c lt brn, lil & blk 20 15
C357 AP73 5c ol, bl & blk 35 15
C358 AP73 7c org yel, bl & blk 50 15

8th Gen. Assembly of the Pan-American Geographical and Historical Institute in 1965.

No. C281 Overprinted

GUATEMALA
CAMPEON
III Norceca Foot-Ball

1967, Apr. 28 Engr. *Perf. 11½*

C360 AP62 3c dull green 50 40

Issued to commemorate Guatemala's victory in the 3rd Norceca Soccer Games (Caribbean, Central and North American).

No. C281A Overprinted in Red: "REUNION JEFES DE ESTADO / AMERICANO, PUNTA DEL ESTE, / MONTEVIDEO, URUGUAY 1967"

1967, June 28 Engr. *Perf. 11½*

C361 AP62 4c gray 65 65

Meeting of American Presidents, Punta del Este, Apr. 10-12.

Handshake AP74

1967, June 28 Photo. *Perf. 12*

C362 AP74 7c pink, brn & grn 30 15
C363 AP74 21c lt bl, grn & brn 50 50

Issued to publicize "Peace and Progress through Cooperation."
For overprint see No. C416.

Church of Santo Domingo AP75

Designs: 1c, Yurrita Church (vert.). 3c, Church of St. Francis. 4c, Antonio Josede Irisarri (vert.). 5c, Church of the Convent (vert.). 7c, Mercy Church, Antigua. 10c, Metropolitan Cathedral.

1967, Aug. *Perf. 11½x12, 12x11½*

C364 AP75 1c grn, lt bl & dk brn 16 15
C365 AP75 2c plum, sal pink & brn 22 15
C366 AP75 3c brt rose, gray & blk 22 15
C367 AP75 4c mar, sl grn & org 22 15
C368 AP75 5c lil, pale grn & dk brn 22 15
C369 AP75 7c ultra, lil rose & blk 35 20
C370 AP75 10c pur, yel & blk 50 22
Nos. C364-C370 (7) 1.89
Set value 95

Abraham Lincoln — AP76

1967 Engr. *Perf. 13½, 11½ (9c)*

C371 AP76 7c gray & dp org 35 20
C372 AP76 9c dk grn & grysh 40 22
C373 AP76 11c brn org & sl 40 30
C374 AP76 15c ultra & vio brn 65 35
C375 AP76 30c mag & grn 1.50 1.50
Nos. C371-C375 (5) 3.30 2.57

Issued to commemorate the centenary of the death of Abraham Lincoln (1809-1865).
Issue dates: 7c, 9c, Oct. 9. Others, Dec. 12.
For surcharge see No. C554.

Nos. C328-C332 Overprinted: "VIII Camporee Scout / Centroamericano / Diciembre 1-8/1967"

1967, Dec. 1 Photo. *Perf. 14x13½*

C376 AP66 5c multi 35 35
C377 AP66 9c multi 50 50
C378 AP66 10c multi 65 65
C379 AP66 15c multi 65 65
C380 AP66 20c multi 80 80
Nos. C376-C380 (5) 2.95 2.95

Issued to commemorate the 8th Central American Boy Scout Camporee, Dec. 1-8.

Nos. C320-C321 Overprinted in Four Lines: "Premio Nobel de Literatura - 10 diciembre 1967 - Miguel Angel Asturias"

1967, Dec. 11 Engr. *Perf. 11½*

C381 A152 3c orange 50 50
C382 A152 4c purple 50 50

Issued to commemorate the awarding of the Nobel Prize for Literature to Miguel Angel Asturias, Guatemalan writer.

Institute Emblem — AP77

1967, Dec. 12 Engr. *Perf. 11½*

C383 AP77 9c blk & grn 65 65
C384 AP77 25c car & brn 1.40 1.40
C385 AP77 1q ultra & bl 3.50 3.50

25th anniv. of the Inter-American Agriculture Institute.

UNESCO Emblem and Children AP78

1967, Dec. 12

C386 AP78 4c bl grn 20 20
C387 AP78 5c blue 20 20
C388 AP78 7c gray 30 30
C389 AP78 21c brt rose lil 80 80

20th anniv. (in 1966) of UNESCO.

Nos. C219-C221 and C304-C308 Overprinted in Black or Yellow Green: "III REUNION DE / PRESIDENTES / Nov. 15-18, 1967"

Perf. 13½x14, 14x13½, 11x12

1968, Jan. 23 Photo.

C390 AP50 1c multi 65 50
C391 AP50 1c multi (G) 65 75
C392 AP50 2c multi 65 75
C393 AP50 2c multi (G) 65 75
C394 AP50 3c multi 65 75
C395 AP50 3c multi (G) 65 75
C396 AP64 7c multi 65 75
C397 AP64 9c multi 1.00 1.00
C398 AP64 13c multi 1.40 1.00
C399 AP64 21c multi 2.00 1.00
C400 AP64 35c multi 1.60 1.75
Nos. C390-C400 (11) 10.55 9.75

3rd meeting of Central American Presidents, Nov. 15-18, 1967.

Our Lady of the Coro — AP79

Miguel Angel Asturias, Flags of Guatemala and Sweden — AP80

1968-74 Engr. *Perf. 13½, 11½*

C403 AP79 4c ultra 40 15
C404 AP79 7c slate 35 15
C405 AP79 9c green 50 15
C406 AP79 9c lil ('73) 20 15
C407 AP79 10c brick red 65 20
C408 AP79 10c gray 50 20
C408A AP79 10c vio bl ('74) 35 15
C409 AP79 1q vio brn 3.50 3.00
C410 AP79 1q org yel 3.50 3.00
Nos. C403-C410 (9) 9.95 7.15

Perf. 13½ applies to 4c and Nos. C407, C409-C410; perf. 11½ to 4c, 7c, 9c and Nos. C408, C408A.

Nos. 396-398 Overprinted: "AEREO / XI VUELTA / CICLISTICA / 1967"

1968, Mar. 25 Litho. *Perf. 14x13½*

C411 A153 4c multi 50 50
C412 A153 5c multi 50 50
C413 A153 6c multi 40 40

The 11th Bicycle Race.

1968, June 18 Engr. *Perf. 11½*

C414 AP80 20c ultra 1.00 35

Awarding of the Nobel Prize for Literature to Miguel Angel Asturias.

No. C234 Overprinted in Carmine: "1968. - AÑO INTERNACIONAL / DERECHOS HUMANOS. - ONU"

1968, July 18 Litho. *Perf. 11*

C415 AP53 6c pale brn 50 25

International Human Rights Year.

No. C362 Overprinted: "AYUDA A CONSERVAR / LOS BOSQUES. - 1968"

1968, July 18 Photo. *Perf. 12*

C416 AP74 7c pink, brn & grn 35 15

Issued to publicize forest conservation.

No. C213 Overprinted in Brown: "Expedicion / Cientifica / Nahakin / Guatemala-Peru / Ruta de los / Mayas"

1968, Aug. 23 Photo. *Perf. 14x13½*

C417 AP49 6c dk brn & dp ultra 25 15

Issued to commemorate the Nahakin scientific expedition along the route of the Mayas undertaken jointly with Peru.

Views, Quetzal and White Nun Orchid — AP81

1968, Aug. 23 Engr. *Perf. 13½*

C418 AP81 10c dp cl & grn 50 20
C419 AP81 20c dp org & blk 75 50
C420 AP81 50c ultra & car 1.25 1.25

Issued for tourist publicity.

No. C281A Overprinted in Carmine: "CONFEDERACION / DE UNIVERSIDADES / CENTROAMERICANAS / 1948 1968"

1968, Nov. 4 ***Perf. 11½***

C421 AP62 4c gray 25 25

20th anniv. of the Federation of Central American Universities.

Presidents Gustavo Diaz Ordaz and Julio Cesar Mendez Montenegro AP82

1968, Dec. 3 **Litho.** ***Perf. 14x13½***

C422 AP82 5c multi 15 15
C423 AP82 10c multi 35 20
C424 AP82 25c multi 80 75

Mutual visits of the Presidents of Mexico and Guatemala.

ITU Emblem, Old and New Communication Equipment — AP83

Engraved and Photogravure

1968-74 ***Perf. 11½, 12½ (21c)***

C425 AP83 7c vio bl 25 15
C426 AP83 15c gray & emer 35 25
C426A AP83 15c vio brn & org ('74) 50 25
C427 AP83 21c magenta 50 35
C428 AP83 35c rose red & emer 90 50
C429 AP83 75c grn & red 2.00 2.00
C430 AP83 3q brn & red 6.50 6.50
Nos. C425-C430 (7) 11.00 10.00

Cent. (in 1965) of the ITU.

Nos. C425, C427 are engr. only; on others denominations are photo.. No. C426A is on thin, toned paper.

Dates of issue: No: C426A, Feb. 18, 1974; others Dec. 13, 1968.

For surcharges see Nos. C454, C516.

Nos. 399-403 Overprinted in Red, Black or Gold **AEREO**

Lithographed and Engraved

1969 ***Perf. 11½, 13½ (1c)***

C431 A154 1c blk, lt grn & red (R) 50 50
C432 A154 5c yel, lt grn & red 65 65
C433 A154 8c org, lt grn & red 80 80
C434 A154 15c bl, lt grn & red 1.00 1.00
C435 A154 30c lt vio, lt grn & red (G) 1.40 1.40
Nos. C431-C435 (5) 4.35 4.35

Dante Alighieri — AP84

1969, July 17 **Engr.** ***Perf. 12½***

C436 AP84 7c rose vio & ultra 15 15
C437 AP84 10c dk bl 25 15
C438 AP84 20c green 40 15
C439 AP84 21c gray & brn 70 70
C440 AP84 35c pur & brt grn 1.50 1.50
Nos. C436-C440 (5) 3.00 2.65

Dante Alighieri (1265-1321), Italian poet.

Map of Latin America — AP85

Design: 9c, Seal of University.

1969, Oct. 29 **Typo.** ***Perf. 13***

Size: 44x27mm

C441 AP85 2c brt pink & blk 15 15

Size: 35x27mm

C442 AP85 9c gray & blk 30 20

Souvenir Sheet

Imperf

C443 AP85 Sheet of 2 50 50
a. 2c light blue & black 20 20
b. 9c orange & black 20 20

20th anniv. of the Union of Latin American Universities.

Moon Landing Issue

Moon Landing — AP86

1969-70 **Engr.** ***Perf. 11½***

C444 AP86 50c mar & blk 2.00 2.00
C445 AP86 1q ultra & blk 3.50 3.75

Souvenir Sheet

Imperf

C446 AP86 1q yel grn & ultra 3.75 4.00

See note after US No. C76. No. C446 contains one stamp with simulated perforations.

Issue dates: Nos. C445-C446, Dec. 19, 1969; No. C444, Jan. 6, 1970.

Giant Grebe Family on Lake Atitlan AP87

Designs: 4c, Lake Atitlan. 20c, Grebe chick, eggs atop floating nest (vert.).

1970, Mar. 31 **Litho.** ***Perf. 13½***

C447 AP87 4c red & multi 25 15
C448 AP87 9c red & multi 50 30
a. Souv. sheet of 2, #C447-C448 1.25 1.25
C449 AP87 20c red & multi 75 75

Protection of zambullidor ducks.

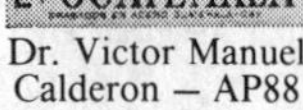

Dr. Victor Manuel Calderon — AP88

Hand Holding Bible — AP89

1970 **Litho. & Engr.** ***Perf. 13, 12½***

C450 AP88 1c lt bl & blk 15 15
C451 AP88 2c pale grn & blk 15 15

Perf. 13

C452 AP88 9c yel & blk 30 25
Set value 50 42

Issued in memory of Dr. Victor Manuel Calderon (1889-1969), who described microfilaria, a blood parasite.

1970 **Litho. & Typo.** ***Perf. 13x13½***

C453 AP89 5c red & multi 25 25

Fourth centenary of the Bible in Spanish.

No. C430 Surcharged

VALE Ø0.50

1971, Mar. 11 **Engr.** ***Perf. 11½***

C454 AP83 50c on 3q brn & red 1.75 1.75

Arms of Guatemala, Newspapers — AP90

Official Decree of First Issue — AP91

1971 **Litho.** ***Perf. 11½, 12½***

C455 AP90 2c dk bl & red 15 15
C456 AP90 5c brn & red 16 15
C457 AP90 25c brt bl & red 50 25
Set value 37

Souvenir Sheet

Lithographed and Engraved

Imperf

C458 AP91 Sheet of 5 1.50 1.50

Cent. of Guatemala's postage stamps.

Nos. C456-C457 have white value tablet.

No. C458 contains a litho. 4c black and engr. reproductions of Nos. 1-4 in colors similar to 1871 issue. Simulated perforations.

In 1974 No. C458 was overprinted "Conmemorativa / al Campeonato Mundial de Foot Ball / Munich 1974" and Munich Games emblem in black. Overprint in gold or other colors was not authorized.

See Nos. C569-C570.

Mayas with CARE Package — AP92

1971 **Typo.** ***Perf. 11½***

C459 AP92 5c multi 30 30
a. Souv. sheet of 2 1.50 1.50

25th aniversary of CARE, a U.S.-Canadian Cooperative for American Relief Everywhere.

No. C459a contains imperf. stamps similar to Nos. 416 and C459.

J. Rufino Barrios, M. Garcia Granados, Map of Guatemala, Quetzal — AP93

1971, June 30 ***Perf. 11½***

Value in Red

C460 AP93 2c blk & multi 25 15
a. Value in pink ('72) 15 15
C461 AP93 10c grn & multi 40 20
a. Value in pink, perf. 12½ ('72) 25 20
C462 AP93 50c brn & multi 1.50 1.50
C463 AP93 1q vio & multi 3.00 3.00

Centenary of the liberal revolution of 1871.

Chavarry Arrué and León Bilak — AP94

Perf. 11½, 11x12½, 12½

1971-72 **Engr.**

C464 AP94 1c grn & blk ('72) 15 15
C465 AP94 2c lt brn & blk ('72) 15 15
C466 AP94 5c org & blk 25 15
Set value 30

Honoring J. Arnoldo Chavarry Arrué, stamp engraver; León Bilak, philatelist.

No. C231 Overprinted

FERIA INTERNACIONAL "INTERFER—71" 30 Oct. al 21 Nov.

1971, Oct. 25 **Litho.** ***Perf. 11***

C467 AP52 6c ultra & rose red 25 25

INTERFER 71, Intl. Fair, Guatemala, Oct. 30-Nov. 21.

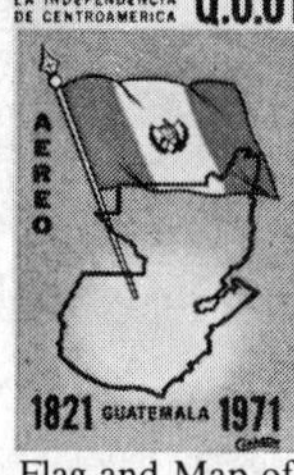

Flag and Map of Guatemala AP95

UNICEF Emblem and Mayan Figure AP96

Perf. 13½ (1c), 12½ (3c, 9c), 11 (5c)

1971-75 **Typo.**

C468 AP95 1c blk, bl & lil 15 15
a. Lithographed ('75) 15 15
C469 AP95 3c brn, brt pink & bl 15 15
C470 AP95 5c brn, org & bl 15 15
a. Lithographed, perf. 12½ ('74) 15 15
C471 AP95 9c blk, emer & bl 20 15
Set value 47 20

Sesquicentennial of Central American independence.

Date of issue: #C469-C471, July 10, 1972.

1971-75 Engr. *Perf. 11½*
C472 AP96 1c yel grn 15 15
C472A AP96 2c purple 15 15
C473 AP96 50c vio brn 1.75 1.75
C474 AP96 1q ultra 3.00 3.00

25th anniv. UNICEF.

Issue dates: 2c, Feb. 24, 1975, others, Nov. 1971.

Early Boeing Planes — AP97

Design: 10c, Bleriot's plane.

1972 Typo. *Perf. 11½*
C475 AP97 5c lt brn & brt bl 25 15
C476 AP97 10c dark blue 50 15

Military aviation in Guatemala, 50th anniv.

Arches, Antigua — AP98

1972-73 Typo. *Perf. 11½*

Dark Blue and Light Blue
C480 AP98 1c shown 16 15
C481 AP98 1c Cathedral 16 15
C482 AP98 1c Fountain, Central Park 16 15
C483 AP98 1c Capuchin Monastery 16 15
C484 AP98 1c Fountain and Santa Clara 16 15
C485 AP98 1c Portal of San Francisco 16 15
Nos. C480-C485 (6) 96
Set value 60

Black, Lilac Rose, and Silver
C486 AP98 2½c shown 35 15
C487 AP98 2½c Catherdral 35 15
C488 AP98 2½c Fountain and Santa Clara 35 15
C489 AP98 2½c Portal of San Francisco 35 15
C490 AP98 2½c Fountain 35 15
C491 AP98 2½c Capuchin Monastery 35 15
Nos. C486-C491 (6) 2.10 90

Blue, Orange and Black
C492 AP98 5c shown 65 15
C493 AP98 5c Cathedral 65 15
C494 AP98 5c Santa Clara 65 15
C495 AP98 5c Portal of San Francisco 65 15
C496 AP98 5c Fountain 65 15
C497 AP98 5c Capuchin Monastery 65 15
Nos. C492-C497 (6) 3.90 90

Nos. C492-C497 exist perf. 12½, same value.

Perf. 12½

Red, Blue and Black
C498 AP98 1q Fountain 3.50 2.50
C499 AP98 1q Capuchin Monastery 3.50 2.50
C500 AP98 1q shown 3.50 2.50
C501 AP98 1q Cathedral 3.50 2.50
C502 AP98 1q Fountain and Santa Clara 3.50 2.50
C503 AP98 1q Portal of San Francisco 3.50 2.50
Nos. C498-C503 (6) 21.00 15.00
Nos. C480-C503 (25) 27.96 18.30

Earthquake ruins of Antigua. 1c printed se-tenant in sheets of 90 (10x9); 2½c, 5c se-tenant in sheets of 30 (5x6); 1q se-tenant in sheets of 6 (3x2).

On Nos. C498-C503 the inks were applied by a thermographic process giving a shiny raised effect.

Issue dates: Nos. C480-C485, Dec. 14, 1972; Nos. C486-C491, Jan. 22, 1973; Nos. C492-C497, Mar. 12, 1973; Nos. C498-C503, Aug. 22, 1973.

Nos. C480-C485 were overprinted "II Feria Internacional" / INTERFER/73 / 31 Octubre - Noviembre 18 / 1973 / GUATEMALA in lilac rose and issued Nov. 3, 1973. Value $3.

The Interfer overprint exists in black on Nos. C480-C485, but these stamps were not decreed or issued.

See Nos. C528-C545, C770-C775F. For overprints see Nos. C517-C523.

Simon Bolivar and Map of Americas AP99

1973-74 *Perf. 11½*
C504 AP99 3c brt lil rose & blk 15 15
C505 AP99 3c org & dk bl ('74) 15 15
C506 AP99 5c yel & multi 18 15
C507 AP99 5c brt grn & blk 18 15
Set value 25

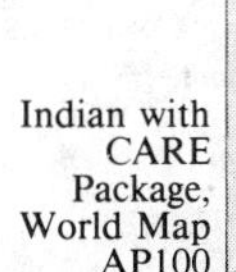

Indian with CARE Package, World Map AP100

CARE Package — AP101

1973, June 14 Typo. *Perf. 12½*
C508 AP100 2c blk & multi 20 20
C509 AP101 10c blk & multi 40 40
a. Souvenir sheet of 2 80 90

25th anniversary of CARE (in 1971), a US-sponsored relief organization and 10th anniversary of its work in Guatemala.

No. C509a contains 2 stamps similar to Nos. C508-C509 with simulated perforations.

Guatemala No. 1, Laurel AP102

1973-74 Engr. *Perf. 12½, 11½ (1q)*
C510 AP102 1c yel brn ('74) 20 15
C511 AP102 1q rose cl 2.50 2.50

Centenary (in 1971) of Guatemala postage stamps. See Nos. C574-C576A.

Oak Wreath and Star AP103

1973, Aug. 22 Typo. *Perf. 12½*
C512 AP103 5c brn, yel & bl 15 15

Centenary of Escuela Politecnica, Guatemala's military academy.

See Nos. C552-C553.

Eleanor Roosevelt AP104

1973, Sept. 11 Engr. *Perf. 12½*
C513 AP104 7c blue 20 15

Eleanor Roosevelt (1884-1962), lecturer, writer, UN delegate.

Boys' School, Chiquimula AP105

1973-74 Typo. *Perf. 12½*
C514 AP105 3c blk & bl 15 15
C515 AP105 5c blk & dp lil rose 15 15
Set value 25 25

Centenary of the Instituto Varones in Chiquimula.

Issue dates: 5c, Dec. 5, 1973, 3c, June 13, 1974.

No. C430 Surcharged in Red: "Desvalorizadas a Q0.50" and Ornamental Obliteration of Old Denomination

1974 Engr. & Photo. *Perf. 11½*
C516 AP83 50c on 3q brn & red 1.25 1.25

Nos. C480-C485 and C509a Overprinted with UPU Emblem, "UPU / HOMENAJE CENTENARIO / 1874 1974"

1974, June 13 Typo. *Perf. 11½*
C517 AP98 1c dk bl & lt bl 22 30
C518 AP98 1c dk bl & lt bl 22 30
C519 AP98 1c dk bl & lt bl 22 30
C520 AP98 1c dk bl & lt bl 22 30
C521 AP98 1c dk bl & lt bl 22 30
C522 AP98 1c dk bl & lt bl 22 30
Nos. C517-C522 (6) 1.32 1.80

Souvenir Sheet
C523 Sheet of 2 6.50 7.50

Centenary of Universal Postal Union.

No. C523 consists of an overprint on No. C509a, including "UNIVERSAL POSTAL UNION" instead of "UPU."

The overprint on No. C523 in red was not authorized by the Post Office.

Antigua Type of 1972-73

1974, Oct. 8 Typo. *Perf. 11½*

Black and Light Brown
C528 AP98 2c Capuchin Monastery 15 15
C529 AP98 2c Arches 15 15
C530 AP98 2c Cathedral 15 15
C531 AP98 2c Fountain and Santa Clara 15 15
C532 AP98 2c Portal of San Francisco 15 15
C533 AP98 2c Fountain 15 15
Nos. C528-C533 (6) 90
Set value 60

1974, Sept. 24

Black and Yellow
C540 AP98 20c Capuchin Monastery 50 50
C541 AP98 20c Arches 50 50
C542 AP98 20c Cathedral 50 50
C543 AP98 20c Fountain and Santa Clara 50 50
C544 AP98 20c Portal of San Francisco 50 50
C545 AP98 20c Fountain 50 50
Nos. C540-C545 (6) 3.00 3.00

Earthquake ruins of Antigua. Each group of six printed se-tenant in sheets of 30 (5x6).

Nos. C528-C533 were printed in 1975 in black and bister se-tenant in sheets of 24 (4x6) on whiter paper.

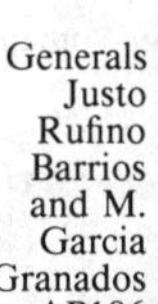

Generals Justo Rufino Barrios and M. Garcia Granados AP106

Polytechnic School — AP107

Perf. 12½, 11½ (25c)

1974-75 Typo.
C552 AP106 6c red, gray & bl 15 15
C553 AP107 25c multi 35 25
Set value 30

Centenary (in 1973) of Escuela Politecnica, Guatemala's military academy.

Issue dates: 6c, Sept. 17, 1974; 25c, Jan. 14, 1975.

No. C373 Surcharged in Black and Green

1974, Dec. 3 Engr. *Perf. 13½*
C554 AP76 10c on 11c multi 25 15

Nature protection. The quetzal, Guatemala's national bird.

Costume San Martin Sacatepequez AP108

Costumes of Women: 2c, Solola. 9c, Coban. 20c, Chichicastenango.

1974-75 Typo. *Perf. 12½*

C556 AP108	2c car & multi	15	15
C557 AP108	2½c bl, car & brn	15	15
C559 AP108	9c bl & multi	30	15
a.	Perf. 12½x13½	30	15
C561 AP108	20c red & multi	50	25
	Set value		45

Issue dates: 2½c, Dec. 16, 1974; 20c, Jan. 14, 1975; 2c, 9c, May 19, 1975.

Quetzals and Maya Quekchi Woman Wearing Huipil — AP109

1975, June 25 Litho. *Perf. 13½*

C565 AP109	8c bl & multi	35	15
C566 AP109	20c red & multi	65	15
	Set value		25

International Women's Year 1975.

Rotary Emblem AP110

1975-76 Typo. *Perf. 13½*

C567 AP110	10c bl & multi	20	15

Perf. 11½

C568 AP110	15c bl & multi	40	15
	Set value		22

Guatemala City Rotary Club, 50th anniversary. Issue dates: 10c, Oct. 1, 1975; 15c, Dec. 21, 1976.

Gaceta Type of 1971 Redrawn

1975-76 Typo. *Perf. 12½*

C569 AP90	5c brn & red	15	15
C570 AP90	50c brt rose & brn	1.25	1.25

The white background around numeral and on right of arms has been filled in.

Issue dates: 5c, Dec. 12, 1975; 50c, Dec. 1, 1976.

IWY Emblem and White Nun Orchid — AP111

1975-76 *Perf. 12½x13½*

C571 AP111	1c multi	15	15
C572 AP111	8c yel & multi	25	15
C573 AP111	26c rose & multi	65	20
	Set value		40

International Women's Year 1975.

Issue dates: 1c, Dec. 19; 8c, Dec. 12; 26c, May 10, 1976.

Stamp Centenary Type of 1973

1975-77 Engr. *Perf. 11½*

C574 AP102	6c orange	15	15
C575 AP102	6c green ('76)	15	15
C576 AP102	6c gray ('77)	15	15
C576A AP102	6c vio bl ('77)	15	15
	Set value		40

Centenary (in 1971) of Guatemala's postage stamps.

Issue dates: No. C574, Dec. 31. No. C575, May 10. Others, Aug. 10.

Destroyed Joyabaj Village — AP112

Designs (Guatemala Flag and): 3c, Emergency food distribution. 5c, Jaguar Temple, Tikal. 10c, Destroyed bridge. 15c, Outdoors emergency hospital. 20c, Sugar cane harvest. 25c, Destroyed house. 30c, New building, Tecpan. 50c, Destroyed Cerro del Carmen church. 75c, Cleaning up debris. 1q, Military help. 2q, Lake Atitlan.

1976, June 4 Litho. *Perf. 12½*

C577 AP112	1c red & multi	15	15
C578 AP112	3c multi	15	15
C579 AP112	5c pink & multi	15	15
C580 AP112	10c red & multi	25	15
C581 AP112	15c multi	35	15
C582 AP112	20c pink & multi	45	30
C583 AP112	25c red & multi	60	35
C584 AP112	30c multi	75	20
C585 AP112	50c red & multi	1.25	75
C586 AP112	75c multi	2.00	1.00
C587 AP112	1q multi	2.50	1.25
C588 AP112	2q multi	5.00	3.00
	Nos. C577-C588 (12)	13.60	7.60

Earthquake of Feb. 4, 1976, and gratitude for foreign help. Inscriptions in colored panels vary. 3 imperf. souvenir sheets exist (50c, 1q, 2q). Size: 112x83mm.

Allegory of Independence — AP113

Designs: 2c, Boston Tea Party. 3c, Thomas Jefferson (vert.). 4c, 20c, 35c, Allegory of Independence (each different; 4c, 35c, vert.). 5c, Warren's Death at Bunker Hill. 10c, Washington at Valley Forge. 15c, Washington at Monmouth. 25c, The Generals at Yorktown. 30c, Washington Crossing the Delaware. 40c, Declaration of Independence. 45c, Patrick Henry (vert.). 50c, Congress Voting Independence. 1q, Washington (vert.). 2q, Lincoln (vert.). 3q, Franklin (vert.). 5q, John F. Kennedy (vert.). The historical designs and portraits are after paintings.

1976, July 4 Litho. *Perf. 12½*

Size: 46x27mm, 27x46mm

C592 AP113	1c multicolored	15	15
C593 AP113	2c multicolored	15	15
C594 AP113	3c multicolored	15	15
C595 AP113	4c multicolored	15	15
C596 AP113	5c multicolored	15	15
C597 AP113	10c multicolored	20	15
C598 AP113	15c multicolored	30	15
C599 AP113	20c multicolored	40	15
C600 AP113	25c multicolored	50	16
C601 AP113	30c multicolored	65	20
C602 AP113	35c multicolored	70	50
C603 AP113	40c multicolored	90	60
C604 AP113	45c multicolored	1.00	75
C605 AP113	50c multicolored	1.20	50
C606 AP113	1q multicolored	2.25	2.25
a.	Souvenir sheet	2.25	2.50
C607 AP113	2q multicolored	4.00	4.00
a.	Souvenir sheet	5.00	5.25
C608 AP113	3q multicolored	6.00	6.00
a.	Souvenir sheet	6.50	6.75

Size: 35x55mm

C609 AP113	5q multicolored	10.00	3.75
a.	Souvenir sheet	12.00	12.50
	Nos. C592-C609 (18)	28.85	19.91

American Bicentennial. Souvenir sheets contain one imperf. stamp each.

1974 Quetzal Coin AP114

Lithographed and Engraved

1976, Dec. 1 *Perf. 11½*

C610 AP114	8c org, blk & bl	16	15

Perf. 13½

C611 AP114	20c brt rose, bl & blk	40	15
	Set value		25

50th anniversary of introduction of Quetzal currency.

Engineers at Work AP115

1976, Dec. 21 Engr. *Perf. 11½*

C612 AP115	9c ultra	16	15
C613 AP115	10c green	16	15
	Set value		15

School of Engineering, Guatemala City, centenary.

Holy Week Type of 1977

Designs: Sculptures of Christ from various Guatemalan churches. 4c, 7c, 9c, 20c, vert.

1977, Apr. 4 Litho. *Perf. 11*

C614 A159	3c pur & multi	15	15
C615 A159	4c pur & multi	15	15
C616 A159	7c pur & multi	20	15
C617 A159	9c pur & multi	30	25
C618 A159	20c pur & multi	50	50
C619 A159	26c pur & multi	65	65
	Nos. C614-C619 (6)	1.95	1.85

Souvenir Sheet

Roulette 7½

C620 A159	30c pur & multi	65	1.00

Holy Week 1977.

City Hall and Bank of Guatemala — AP116

Designs: 6c, Deed to original site (vert.). 8c, Church and farm house, site of first legislative session. 9c, Coat of arms of Pedro Cortes, first archbishop. 22c, Arms of Guatemala City (vert.).

Perf. 13½ (6c); 11½ (others)

1977, Aug. 10 Litho.

C621 AP116	6c multicolored	15	15
C622 AP116	7c multicolored	16	15
C623 AP116	8c multicolored	16	15
C624 AP116	9c multicolored	22	15
a.	Souvenir sheet	25	50
C625 AP116	22c multicolored	40	25
a.	Souvenir sheet	50	75
	Nos. C621-C625 (5)	1.09	
	Set value		64

Bicentenary of the founding of Nueva Guatemala de la Asuncion (Guatemala City). Nos. C624a-C625a contain one stamp each with simulated perforations.

Arms of Quetzaltenango AP117

City Hall and Torch AP118

1977, Sept. 11 Litho. *Perf. 11½*

C626 AP117	7c blk & sil	20	15
C627 AP118	30c bl & yel	80	20

150th anniversary of the founding of Quetzaltenango.

Mayan Bas-relief AP119

1977, Nov. 7

C628 AP119	10c brt car & blk	20	15

14th Intl. Cong. of Latin Notaries.

Children Bringing Gifts to Christ Child — AP120

Christmas: 1c, Mother and children (horiz.). 4c, Guatemalan children's Nativity scene.

1977, Dec. 16 Litho. *Perf. 11½*

C629 AP120	1c multicolored	15	15
C630 AP120	2c multicolored	15	15
C631 AP120	4c multicolored	15	15
	Set value	30	20

Almolonga Costume, Cancer League Emblem AP121

Virgin of Sorrows, Antigua AP122

Regional Costumes after Paintings by Carlos Merida and Cancer League Emblem: 2c, Nebaj woman. 5c, San Juan Cotzal couple. 6c, Todos Santos couple. 20c, Regidores men. 30c, San Cristobal woman.

Perf. 14 (1c, 5c, No. C636); Perf. 12 (2c, 6c, No. C636a, 30c)

1978, Apr. 3 Litho.

C632 AP121	1c gold & multi	15	15
C633 AP121	2c gold & multi	15	15
C634 AP121	5c gold & multi	15	15
C635 AP121	6c gold & multi	16	15
C636 AP121	20c gold & multi	65	50
a.	Souv. sheet of 1	65	75
C637 AP121	30c gold & multi	65	50
	Nos. C632-C637 (6)	1.91	
	Set value		1.40

Part of proceeds from sale of stamps went to National League to Fight Cancer.

1978 Litho. *Perf. 11½*

Statues from Various Churches: 4c, Virgin of Mercy, Antigua. 5c, Virgin of Anguish, Yurrita. 6c, Virgin of the Rosary, Santo Domingo. 8c, Virgin of Sorrows, Santo Domingo. 9c, Virgin of the Rosary, Quetzaltenango. 10c, Virgin of the Immaculate Conception, Church of St. Francis. 20c, Virgin of the Immaculate Conception, Cathedral Church.

C638 AP122	2c multicolored	15	15
C639 AP122	4c multicolored	15	15
C640 AP122	5c multicolored	15	15
C641 AP122	6c multicolored	15	15
C642 AP122	8c multicolored	16	15
C643 AP122	9c multicolored	20	15

C644 AP122 10c multicolored 22 15
C645 AP122 20c multicolored 50 20
Nos. C638-C645 (8) 1.68
Set value 85

Holy Week 1978. A 30c imperf. souvenir sheet shows the Pieta from Calvary Church, Antigua. Size: 71x101mm.

Issue dates: 6c, 10c, 20c, Sept. 28. Others, May 22.

Soccer Player, Argentina '78 Emblem AP123

Gymnastics AP124

1978, July 3 Litho. *Perf. 12*
C646 AP123 10c multicolored 20 15

11th World Cup Soccer Championship, Argentina, June 1-25.

1978, Sept. 4 *Perf. 12*
C647 AP124 6c shown 15 15
C648 AP124 6c Volleyball 15 15
C649 AP124 6c Target shooting 15 15
C650 AP124 6c Weight lifting 15 15
C651 AP124 8c Track & field 16 15
Set value 56 30

13th Central American and Caribbean Games, Medellin, Colombia. Nos. C647-C650 printed se-tenant in panes of 50.

Cattleya Pachecoi AP125

Designs: Orchids.

1978, Dec. 7 Litho. *Perf. 12*
C652 AP125 1c shown 15 15
C653 AP125 1c Sobralia 15 15
C654 AP125 1c Cypripedium 15 15
C655 AP125 1c Oncidium 15 15
C656 AP125 3c Cattleya bowrigiana 15 15
C657 AP125 3c Encyclia 15 15
C658 AP125 3c Epidendrum 15 15
C659 AP125 3c Barkeria 15 15
C660 AP125 8c Spiranthes 25 25
C661 AP125 20c Lycaste 65 65
Set value 1.50 1.50

Stamps of same denomination printed se-tenant. Sheets of 60.

Seal of University AP126

Students of Different Departments AP127

Designs: 12c, Student in 17th cent. clothes. 14c, Students, 1978, and molecular model.

1978, Dec. 7
C662 AP126 6c multicolored 15 15
C663 AP127 7c multicolored 15 15
C664 AP126 12c multicolored 20 15
C665 AP126 14c multicolored 25 15
Set value 40

San Carlos University of Guatemala, tercentenary.

Brown and White Children AP128

A Helping Hand AP129

Designs: 7c, Child at play. 14c, Hands sheltering Indian girl.

1978, Dec. 7
C666 AP128 6c multicolored 15 15
C667 AP128 7c multicolored 15 15
C668 AP129 12c multicolored 20 15
C669 AP129 14c multicolored 25 15
Set value 40

Year of the Children of Guatemala.

Tree Planting and FAO Emblem — AP130

Forest protection: 8c, Burnt forest. 9c, Watershed, river and trees. 10c, Sawmill. 26c, Forests, river and cultivated terraces.

1979, Apr. 16 Litho. *Perf. 13½*
C670 AP130 6c multicolored 15 15
C671 AP130 8c multicolored 15 15
C672 AP130 9c multicolored 15 15
C673 AP130 10c multicolored 15 15
C674 AP130 26c multicolored 35 20
a. Souv. sheet of 5, #C670-C674 90 1.25
Set value 80 40

Peten Wild Turkey AP131

Clay Jar, 50-100 A.D. AP132

Wildlife conservation: 3c, White-tailed deer (horiz.). 5c, King buzzard. 7c, Horned owl. 9c, Young wildcat. 30c, Quetzal.

1979, June 14 Litho. *Perf. 13½*
C675 AP131 1c multicolored 15 15
C676 AP131 3c multicolored 15 15
C677 AP131 5c multicolored 15 15
C678 AP131 7c multicolored 20 15
C679 AP131 9c multicolored 25 15
Set value 75 35

Souvenir Sheet

C680 AP131 30c multicolored 50 75

1979, Sept. 19 Litho. *Perf. 13*

Archaeological Treasures from Tikal: 3c, Mayan woman, ceramic head, 900 A.D. 4c, Earring, 50-100 A.D. 5c, vase, 700 A.D. 6c, Boy, 200-50 B.C. 7c, Bone carving, 700 A.D. 8c, Striped vase, 700 A.D. 10c, Covered vase on tripod, 450 B.C.

C681 AP132 2c multi 15 15
C682 AP132 3c multi 15 15
C683 AP132 4c multi 15 15
C684 AP132 5c multi 15 15
C685 AP132 6c multi 15 15
C686 AP132 7c multi 15 15
C687 AP132 8c multi 15 15
C688 AP132 10c multi 15 15
Set value 70 40

Presidential Guard Patches — AP133

Presidential Guard, 30th anniv.: 10c, Guard Headquarters.

1979, Dec. 6 Litho. *Perf. 11½*
C689 AP133 8c multi 15 15
C690 AP133 10c multi 15 15
Set value 24 15

National Coat of Arms — AP134

Arms of Guatemalan Municipalities.

1979, Dec. 27 Litho. *Perf. 13½*
C691 AP134 8c shown 25 15
C692 AP134 8c Alta Verapaz 25 15
C693 AP134 8c Baja Verapaz 25 15
C694 AP134 8c Chimal Tenango 25 15
C695 AP134 8c Chiquimula 25 15
C696 AP134 8c Escuintla 25 15
C697 AP134 8c Flores 25 15
C698 AP134 8c Guatemala 25 15
C699 AP134 8c Huehuetenango 25 15
C700 AP134 8c Izabal 25 15
C701 AP134 8c Jalapa 25 15
C702 AP134 8c Jutiapa 25 15
C703 AP134 8c Mazatenango 25 15
C704 AP134 8c Progreso 25 15
C705 AP134 8c Quezaltenango 25 15
C706 AP134 8c Quiche 25 15
C707 AP134 8c Retalhuleu 25 15
C708 AP134 8c Sacatepequez 25 15
C709 AP134 8c San Marcos 25 15
C710 AP134 8c Santa Rosa 25 15
C711 AP134 8c Solola 25 15
C712 AP134 8c Totonicapan 25 15
C713 AP134 8c Zacapa 25 15
Nos. C691-C713 (23) 5.75 3.45

Miniature Sheet

Imperf

C714 AP134 50c 1st & current natl. arms 1.50 50

No. C714 is horizontal.

The Creation of the World — AP135

Designs: Scenes from The Creation, Popul Vuh (Sacred Book of the Ancient Quiches of Guatemala): No. C716, Origin of the Twin Semi-gods. No. C717, Populating the earth. No. C718, Balam Quitze. No. C719, Quiche monarch Cotuha. No. C720, Birth of the Stick Men. No. C721, Princess Xquic's punishment. No. C722, Caha Paluma. No. C723, Cotuha and Iztayul invincible. No. C724, Odyssey of Hun Ahpu and Xbalanque. No. C725, Balam Acab. No. C726, Chief of all Nations. No. C727, Destruction of the Stick Men. No. C728, The Test in Xibalba. No. C729, Chomiha. No. C730, Warrior with captive. No. C731, Creation of the Corn Men. No. C732, Multiplication of the Prodigies. No. C733, Mahucutah. No. C734, Undefeatable king. No. C735, Thanksgiving. No. C736, Deification of Hun Ahpu and Xbalanque. No. C737, Tzununiha. No. C738, Greatness of the Quiches (battle scene).

1981 Litho. *Perf. 12*
C715 AP135 1c multi 15 15
C716 AP135 1c multi 15 15
C717 AP135 2c multi 15 15
C718 AP135 2c multi 15 15
C719 AP135 3c multi 15 15
C720 AP135 4c multi 15 15
C721 AP135 4c multi 15 15
C722 AP135 4c multi 15 15
C723 AP135 4c multi 15 15
C724 AP135 6c multi 15 15
C725 AP135 6c multi 15 15
C726 AP135 6c multi 15 15
C727 AP135 8c multi 20 15
C728 AP135 8c multi 20 15
C729 AP135 8c multi 20 15
C730 AP135 8c multi 20 15
C731 AP135 10c multi 25 15
C732 AP135 10c multi 25 15
C733 AP135 10c multi 25 15
C734 AP135 10c multi 25 15
C735 AP135 22c multi 50 15
C736 AP135 26c multi 60 15
C737 AP135 30c multi 75 25
C738 AP135 50c multi 1.25 30
Set value 6.00 2.00

Issue dates: Nos. C715, C717, 3c, C727, C731, 22c, Jan. 29. Nos. C716, C718, C721-C722, C724-C725, C728-C729, C732-C733, 26c, 30c, Mar. 16. Other, 1981.

Thomas Edison (Phonograph Centenary) AP136

Talking Movies, 50th Anniv. — AP137

Telephone Centenary (1976) — AP138

Lindbergh's Atlantic Flight, 50th Anniv. (1977) — AP139

Designs: 12c, Jose Cecilio del Valle, patriot. 25c, Jesus Castillo (1877-1949), composer.

Perf. 11½, 12½ (25c)

1981, June 1 Litho.
C739 AP136 3c multi 15 15
C740 AP137 5c multi 15 15
C741 AP138 6c multi 18 15
C742 AP139 7c multi 20 15
C743 AP139 12c multi 30 15
C744 AP139 25c multi 60 15
Nos. C739-C744 (6) 1.58
Set value 40

First Police Chief Roderico Toledo and Present Chief German Chupina AP140

1981, Sept. 12 Litho. *Perf. 11½*

C745	AP140	2c shown	15	15
C746	AP140	4c Headquarters	15	15
		Set value	20	20

Mayan Rock of the Sun Calendar AP141

1981, Oct. 9

C747	AP141	1c multi	15	15

Gen. Jose Gervasio Artigas of Uruguay — AP142

Liberators of the Americas: 2c, Bernardo O'Higgins (Chile). 4c, Jose de San Martin (Argentina). 10c, Miguel Garcia Granados. 2c, 4c, 10c, 31x47mm.

1982, Apr. 2 Litho. *Perf. 11½*

C748	AP142	2c multi	15	15
C749	AP142	3c multi	15	15

Perf. 12½

C750	AP142	4c multi	15	15
C751	AP142	10c tan & blk	15	15
		Set value	32	20

Occidents Bank Centenary (1981) AP143

Designs: 1c, Justo Rufino Barrios (first pres.), Main Office, Quezaltenango. 2c, Main Office, 3c, Emblem (vert.). 4c, Commemorative medals (vert.).

1982, July 28 Litho. *Perf. 11½*

C752	AP143	1c multi	15	15
C753	AP143	2c multi	15	15
C754	AP143	3c multi	15	15
C755	AP143	4c multi	15	15
		Set value	24	20

50th Anniv. of Natl. Mortgage Bank (1980) AP144

Various emblems. 5c vert.

1982, Oct. 18 Litho. *Perf. 11½*

C756	AP144	1c multi	15	15
C757	AP144	2c multi	15	15
C758	AP144	5c multi	15	15
C759	AP144	10c multi	15	15
		Set value	24	20

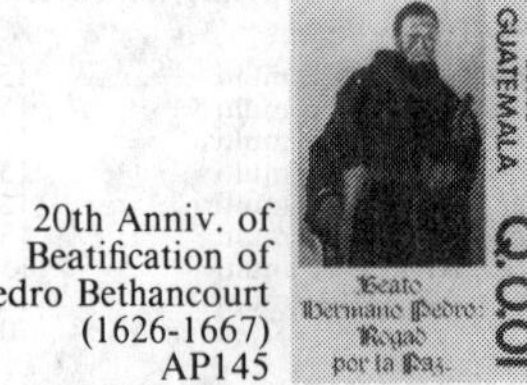

20th Anniv. of Beatification of Pedro Bethancourt (1626-1667) AP145

1983, May 16 Litho. *Perf. 11½*

C760	AP145	1c Portrait	15	15
C761	AP145	20c Aparition, horiz.	25	15
		Set value	30	15

World Telecommunications and Health Day, May 17, 1981 — AP146

1983, July 25 Litho. *Perf. 11½*

C762	AP146	10c multi	15	15

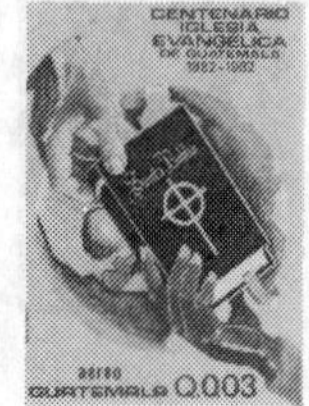

Evangelical Church Centenary (1982) — AP147

1983, Aug. 9

C763	AP147	3c Hands holding bible	15	15
C764	AP147	5c Church	15	15
		Set value	15	15

Natl. Railroad Centenary AP148

Designs: 10c, First locomotive crossing Puenta de Las Vacas. 25c, General Justo Rufino Barrios, Railroad Yard. 30c, Spanish Diesel, Amatitlan crossing.

1983, Sept. 28 Litho. *Perf. 11½*

C765	AP148	10c multi	15	15
C766	AP148	25c multi	25	15
C767	AP148	30c multi	40	15
		Set value		18

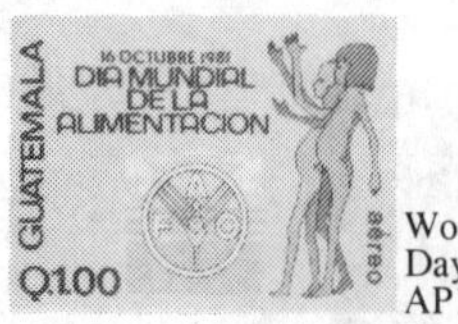

World Food Day AP149

1983, Oct. 16 Photo. *Perf. 11½*

C768	AP149	8c Globe, wheat, vert.	15	15
C769	AP149	1q shown	1.40	1.00

Architecture Type of 1972

1984, Feb. 20 Typo. *Perf. 12½*

Black and Green

C770	AP98	1c like #C480	15	15
C771	AP98	1c like #C481	15	15
C772	AP98	1c like #C482	15	15
C773	AP98	1c like #C483	15	15
C774	AP98	1c like #C484	15	15
C775	AP98	1c like #C485	15	15
g.		Strip of 6. #C770-C775	30	30

Black, Brown and Orange Brown

C775A	AP98	5c like #C484	15	15
C775B	AP98	5c like #C485	15	15
C775C	AP98	5c like #C482	15	15
C775D	AP98	5c like #C483	15	15
C775E	AP98	5c like #C480	15	15
C775F	AP98	5c like #C481	15	15
g.		Strip of 6. #C775A-C775F	60	60
		Set value	90	90

Visit of Pope John Paul II, Mar. 8-9, 1983 AP150

1984, Mar. 26 Litho. *Perf. 11½*

C776	AP150	4c Pope, arms	15	15
C777	AP150	8c Receiving Mayan indian	15	15
		Set value	23	15

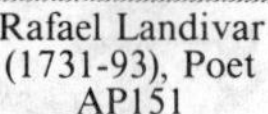

Rafael Landivar (1731-93), Poet AP151

Cardinal Mario Casariego y Acevedo AP152

1984, Aug. 6 Litho. *Perf. 11½*

C778	AP151	2c Portrait, vert.	15	15
C779	AP151	4c Tomb	15	15
		Set value	15	15

1984, Aug. 6

C780	AP152	10c 16th archbishop of Guat. (1909-83)	15	15

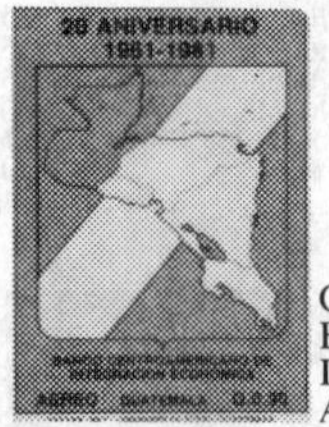

Central American Bank for Economic Integration, 20th Anniv. — AP153

1984, Sept. 10 Litho. *Perf. 11½*

C781	AP153	30c Bank emblem, map	40	15

Coffee Production, 1870 AP154

Modern Coffee Production AP155

Designs: 1c, Planting coffee. 2c, Harvesting. 3c, Drying beans. 4c, Loading beans on steamer. 5c, Reyna plant grafting method. 10c, Picking beans, coffee cup. 12c, Drying unripened beans, Gardiola Freeze-drying machine. 25c, Cargo transports.

1984, Dec. 19 *Perf. 11½*

C782	AP154	1c sep & pale brn	15	15
C783	AP154	2c sep & pale org brn	15	15
C784	AP154	3c sep & beige	15	15
C785	AP154	4c sep & pale yel brn	15	15
C786	AP155	5c multi	15	15
C787	AP155	10c multi	15	15
C788	AP155	12c multi	16	15
C789	AP155	25c multi	35	15
		Set value	1.00	50

Natl. coffee production and export. An 86x112mm 25c stamp of Type AP154 and a 105x85mm 30c stamp of Type AP155 exist.

Natl. Scouting Assoc. — AP156

Scouting emblems and: 5c, Beaver scout, Pyramid of Tikal. 6c, Wolf scout, Palace of the Captains-General and Ahua Volcano. 8c, Scout, San Pedro Volcano and Marimba player. 10c, Rover scout and conquest mask dance. 20c, Lord Baden-Powell and Col. Carlos Cipriani, natl. founder.

1985, July 1

C792	AP156	5c multi	15	15
C793	AP156	6c multi	15	15
C794	AP156	8c multi	15	15
C795	AP156	10c multi	15	15
C796	AP156	20c multi	25	15
		Set value	68	40

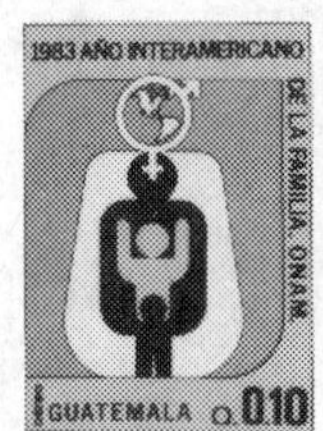

Inter-American Family Unity Year — AP157

Central American Aeronautics Admin., 25th Anniv. — AP158

1985, Oct. 16

C797	AP157	10c multi	15	15

1985, Nov. 11

C798	AP158	10c multi	15	15

Natl. Telegraph, Cent. — AP159

Portraits: Samuel Morse, telegraph inventor, and Justo Rufino Barrios, communications pioneer.

1985, Nov. 20 *Perf. 12*

C799	AP159	4c brn & blk	15	15

Intl. Olympic Committee, 90th Anniv. AP160

Designs: 8c, Mayan bust of ancient sportsman. 10c, Baron Pierre de Coubertin (1863-1937), father of modern Games, 1st committee president.

1986, Jan. 28 Litho. *Perf. 11½*

C800 AP160 8c multi 16 15
C801 AP160 10c multi 20 15
Set value 15

Volunteer Fire Department AP161

1986, Feb. 6 Litho. *Perf. 11½*

C802 AP161 6c multi 15 15

Temple of Minerva — AP162

Quetzeltenango Coat of Arms, City Hall — AP163

Perf. 12½, 11½

1986, July 16 Litho.

C803 AP162 8c multi 16 15
C804 AP163 10c multi 20 15
Set value 15

Quetzeltenango Independence Fair, cent.

Volunteer Fire Department AP164

1986, Oct. 10 Litho. *Perf. 11½*

C805 AP164 8c Rescue 16 15
C806 AP164 10c Ruins 20 15
Set value 15

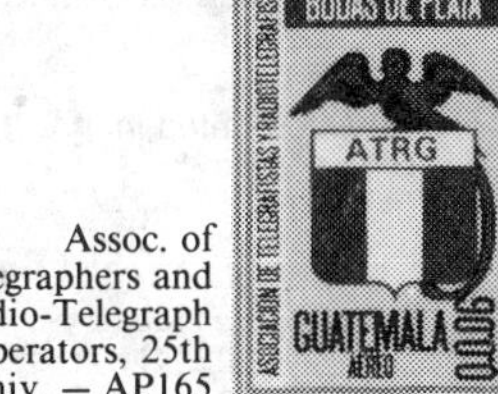

Assoc. of Telegraphers and Radio-Telegraph Operators, 25th Anniv. — AP165

1986, Oct. 10 *Perf. 12*

C807 AP165 6c multi 15 15

San Carlos University School of Architecture, 25th Anniv. AP166

1987, Feb. 16 Litho. *Perf. 11½*

C808 AP166 10c multi 20 15

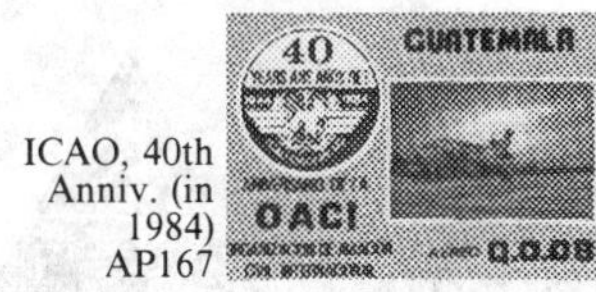

ICAO, 40th Anniv. (in 1984) AP167

1987, Apr. 2 Litho. *Perf. 11½*

C809 AP167 8c Aviateca Airlines jet 16 15
C810 AP167 10c Jet, vert. 20 15
Set value 15

Chixoy Hydroelectric Power Plant — AP168

1987, May 18 Litho. *Perf. 11½*

C811 AP168 2c multi 15 15

Nat'l. Electrification Institute inauguration (in 1985).

San Jose de los Infantes College, 200th Anniv. (in 1981) AP169

Designs: 8c, Portrait of Archbishop Cayetano Francos y Monroy, founder, vert. 10c, College crest.

1987, June 10

C812 AP169 8c multi 16 15
C813 AP169 10c multi 20 15
Set value 15

Promotion of Literacy in Latin America and Caribbean AP170

1987, Aug. 20 Litho. *Perf. 11½*

C814 AP170 12c apple grn, blk & brt org 25 15

19th Natl. Folklore Carnival of Coban, Alta Verapaz, July 25 — AP171

1987, Oct. 12

C815 AP171 1q Three girls from Tamahu 2.10 70

1987, Dec. 8

C816 AP171 50c Girl weaving 1.00 50

See No. C831.

9th Pan American Games, Caracas AP172

1987, Nov. 5 *Perf. 12½*

C817 AP172 10c blk & sky blue 20 15

Writers and Historians AP173

Esquipulas II AP174

Designs: 1c, Flavio Herrera, poet, novelist. 2c, Rosendo Santa Cruz, novelist. 3c, Werner Ovalle Lopez, poet. 4c, Enrique A. Hidalgo, poet, humorist. 5c, Enrique Gomez Carrillo (1873-1927), novelist. 6c, Cesar Branas (1899-1976), journalist. 7c, Clemente Marroquin Rojas, historian. 8c, Rafael Arevalo Martinez (1884-1975), poet. 9c, Jose Milla y Vidaurre (1822-1882), historian. 10c, Miguel Angel Asturias, Nobel laureate for literature.

1987-90 *Perf. 11½*

C818 AP173 1c blk & lil 15 15
C819 AP173 2c blk & dl org 15 15
C820 AP173 3c blk & brt bl 15 15
C821 AP173 4c blk & ver 15 15
C822 AP173 5c blk & org brn 15 15
C823 AP173 6c blk & org 15 15
C824 AP173 7c blk & grn 15 15
C825 AP173 8c blk & brt red 16 15
C826 AP173 9c blk & brt rose lil 18 15
C827 AP173 10c blk & yel 20 15
Set value 1.10 52

Issue dates: 6c, 8c, 9c, Nov. 5. 4c, 5c, Jan. 13, 1988. 7c, Mar. 23, 1990. 1c, 2c, 3c, 10c, Apr. 9, 1990.

1988, Jan. 15 *Perf. 12½*

C828 AP174 10c dark olive grn 20 15
C829 AP174 40c plum 85 30
C830 AP174 60c deep blue vio 1.25 40

2nd Meeting of the Central American Peace Plan. Nos. C828-C829 horiz.

Folklore Festival Type of 1987

1988, Dec. 6 Litho. *Imperf.*

Souvenir Sheet

C831 AP171 2q Music ensemble, horiz. 4.00 1.35

St. John Bosco (1815-1888), Educator — AP175

1989, Feb. 1 Litho. *Perf. 11½*

C832 AP175 40c gold & blk 80 28

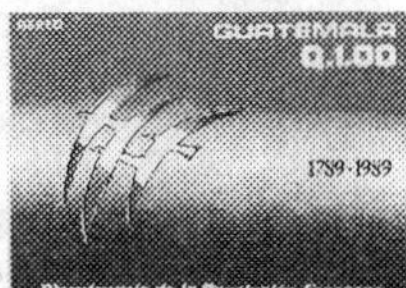

French Revolution, Bicent. AP176

1989, Oct. 18 Litho. *Perf. 11½*

C833 AP176 1q dark red, blk & deep blue 2.00 68

America Issue — AP177

UPAE emblem and: 10c, Detail of the *Madrid Codex*. 20c, Temple of the Gran Jaguar of Tikal, Tikal Natl. Park.

1990, Jan. 25 Litho. *Perf. 11½*

C834 AP177 10c shown 25 15
C835 AP177 20c brown & multi 52 18
C836 AP177 20c black & muiti 52 18

Institute of Nutrition of Central America and Panama, 40th Anniv. AP178

1990, May 18

C837 AP178 20c multicolored 40 15

Red Cross, Red Crescent Societies, 125th Anniv. AP179

1990, June 8

C838 AP179 50c multicolored 1.00 34

Defense Ministry General Staff, Cent. AP180

1991, May 8 Litho. *Perf. 11½*

C839 AP180 20c multicolored 40 15

America
AP181

UPAE: 10c, Pacaya Volcano Erupting at Night. 60c, Lake Atitlan.

1991, July 30 Litho. *Perf. 11½*

C840	AP181	10c multicolored	20	15
C841	AP181	60c multicolored	1.20	30

AIR POST SEMI-POSTAL STAMPS

Air Post Stamps of 1937 Surcharged in Red or Blue

1937

EXPOSICION FILATELICA

+1

1937, Mar. 15 Unwmk. *Perf. 12½*

CB1	AP10	4c + 1c ultra (R)	75	85
CB2	AP10	6c + 1c blk vio (R)	75	85
CB3	AP11	10c + 1c ol grn (Bl)	75	85
CB4	AP11	15c + 1c ver (Bl)	75	85

1st Phil. Exhib. held in Guatemala, Mar. 15-20.

Catalogue values for unused stamps in this section, from this point to the end of the section, are for Never Hinged items.

Type of Regular Issue, 1956

Designs: 35c+1q, Red Cross, Ambulance and Volcano. 50c+1q, Red Cross, Hospital and Nurse. 1q+1q, Nurse and Red Cross.

Perf. 13x12½

1956, June 19 Engr. Unwmk.

CB5	A148	35c + 1q red & ol grn	5.00	5.50
CB6	A148	50c + 1q ultra & red	5.00	5.50
CB7	A148	1q + 1q dk grn & dk red	5.00	5.50

The surtax was for the Red Cross.

Nos. B5-B7 Overprinted AEREO - 1957

1957, May 11

CB8	A148	5c + 15c	6.50	7.00
a.		Imperf., pair	225.00	
CB9	A148	15c + 50c	6.50	7.00
a.		Overprint inverted	110.00	
CB10	A148	25c + 50c	6.50	7.00

The surtax was for the Red Cross.

Type of Semi-Postal Stamps, 1957 and

Esquipulas Cathedral
SPAP1

Designs: 15c+1q, Cathedral and crucifix. 20c+1q, Christ with crown of thorns and part of globe. 25c+1q, Archbishop Mariano Rossell y Arellano.

Perf. 13½x14½, 13

1957, Oct. 29 Engr. Unwmk.

CB11	SPAP1	10c + 1q choc & emer	6.25	6.75
CB12	SP1	15c + 1q dl grn & sep	6.25	6.75
CB13	SP1	20c + 1q bl gray & brn	6.25	6.75
CB14	SP1	25c + 1q lt vio & car	6.25	6.75

The tax was for the Esquipulas highway.

Wounded Man, Battle of Solferino
SPAP2

Designs: 6c+6c, 20c+20c, Flood disaster. 10c+10c, 25c+25c, Earth, moon and stars. 15c+15c, 30c+30c, Red Cross headquarters.

1960, Apr. 9 Photo. *Perf. 13½x14*

CB15	SPAP2	5c + 5c multi	2.25	2.50
CB16	SPAP2	6c + 6c multi	2.25	2.50
CB17	SPAP2	10c + 10c multi	2.25	2.50
CB18	SPAP2	15c + 15c multi	2.25	2.50
CB19	SPAP2	20c + 20c multi	2.25	2.50
CB20	SPAP2	25c + 25c multi	2.25	2.50
CB21	SPAP2	30c + 30c multi	2.25	2.50
		Nos. CB15-CB21 (7)	15.75	17.50

Cent. (in 1959) of the Red Cross idea. The surtax went to the Red Cross. Exist imperf.

AIR POST OFFICIAL STAMPS

Nos. C93-C98 Overprinted in Black

1939, Apr. 29 Unwmk. *Perf. 12½*

CO1	AP13	1c org & ol brn	1.00	1.10
CO2	AP13	2c multi	1.00	1.10
CO3	AP13	3c multi	1.00	1.10
CO4	AP13	4c multi	1.00	1.10
CO5	AP13	5c multi	1.00	1.10
CO6	AP13	10c multi	1.00	1.10
		Nos. CO1-CO6 (6)	6.00	6.60

No. C99 with Same Overprint on each Stamp

1939

CO7	AP19	Sheet of six	2.50	2.50
a.		1c yel org, bl & blk	30	25
b.		2c lake, org, bl & blk	30	25
c.		3c ol, bl & org	30	25
d.		4c dk cl, bl, org & blk	30	25
e.		5c grnsh bl, bl, red, org & blk	30	25
f.		10c ol bis, red & org	30	25

SPECIAL DELIVERY STAMPS

No. 237 Overprinted in Red EXPRESO

1940, June Unwmk. *Perf. 14*

E1	A81	4c orange	1.25	30

No. E1 paid for express service by motorcycle messenger between Guatemala City and Coban.

Catalogue values for unused stamps in this section, from this point to the end of the section, are for Never Hinged items.

Motorcycle Messenger
SD1

Black Surcharge

1948, Sept. 3 Photo. *Perf. 14x12½*

E2	SD1	10c on 4c bl grn & gray blk	1.50	85

No. E2 without surcharge was issued for regular postage, not special delivery. See No. 337B.

OFFICIAL STAMPS

O1

National Emblem — O2

1902, Dec. 18 Typeset *Perf. 12*

O1	O1	1c green	3.75	1.75
O2	O1	2c carmine	3.75	1.75
O3	O1	5c ultra	4.50	1.50
O4	O1	10c brn vio	5.00	1.50
O5	O1	25c orange	5.25	1.50
a.		Horiz. pair, imperf. between	100.00	
		Nos. O1-O5 (5)	22.25	8.00

Nos. O1-O5 printed on thin paper with sheet watermark "AMERICAN LINEN BOND." Nos. O1-O3 also printed on thick paper with sheet watermark "ROYAL BANK BOND." Values are for copies that do not show the watermark. Counterfeits of Nos. O1-O5 exist.

During the years 1912 to 1926 the Post Office Department perforated the word "OFICIAL" on limited quantities of the following stamps: Nos. 114-123, 132, 141-149, 151-153, 158, 202, 210-229 and RA2. The perforating was done in blocks of four stamps at a time and was of two types.

A rubber handstamp "OFICIAL" was also used during the same period and was applied in violet, red, blue or black to stamps No. 117-118, 121-123, 163-165, 172 and 202-218.

Both perforating and handstamping were done in the post office at Guatemala City and use of the stamps was limited to that city.

1929, Jan. Engr. *Perf. 14*

O6	O2	1c pale grnsh bl	25	25
O7	O2	2c dark brown	25	25
O8	O2	3c green	25	25
O9	O2	4c dp vio	35	35
O10	O2	5c brn car	35	35
O11	O2	10c brn org	60	60
O12	O2	25c dark blue	1.25	1.00
		Nos. O6-O12 (7)	3.30	3.05

POSTAL TAX STAMPS

National Emblem — PT1

Perf. 13½, 14, 15

1919, May 3 Engr. Unwmk.

RA1	PT1	12½c carmine	16	15

Tax for rebuilding post offices.

G. P. O. and Telegraph Building — PT2

1927, Nov. 10 Typo. *Perf. 14*

RA2	PT2	1c olive green	15	15

Tax to provide a fund for building a post office in Guatemala City.

No. RA2 Overprinted in Green

1871
30 DE JUNIO
1936

1936, June 30

RA3	PT2	1c olive green	50	40

Liberal revolution, 65th anniversary.

No. RA2 Overprinted in Blue

1821
15 de SEPTIEMBRE
1936

1936, Sept. 15

RA4	PT2	1c olive green	40	30

115th anniv. of the Independence of Guatemala.

No. RA2 Overprinted in Red Brown

FERIA NACIONAL
1936

1936, Nov. 15

RA5	PT2	1c olive green	50	40

National Fair.

No. RA2 Overprinted in Red

EXPOSICION
FILATELICA
1937

1937, Mar. 15

RA6	PT2	1c olive green	40	40

No. RA2 Overprinted in Blue

1787-1789
CL ANIVERSARIO DE LA
CONSTITUCION EE. UU.
1937-1939

1938, Jan. 10 *Perf. 14x14½*

RA7	PT2	1c olive grn	22	16
a.		"1937-1939" omitted	110.00	

150th anniv. of the US Constitution.

No. RA2 Overprinted in Blue or Red 1938

1938 *Perf. 14*

RA8	PT2	1c olive grn (Bl)	30	20
RA9	PT2	1c olive grn (R)	30	15

No. RA2 Overprinted in Violet

Primera Expo-
sicion Filatélica
Centroamericana
1938

1938, Nov. 20

RA10	PT2	1c olive green	30	15

Issued in commemoration of the First Central American Philatelic Exposition.

No. RA2 Overprinted in Green or Black 1939

1939

RA11 PT2	1c olive grn (G)	35	15
RA12 PT2	1c olive grn (Bk)	35	15

No. RA2 Overprinted in Violet or Brown — **1940**

1940

RA13 PT2	1c olive grn (V)	35	15
RA14 PT2	1c olive grn (Br)	35	15

No. RA2 Overprinted in Red — **Conmemorativo Unión Panamericana 1890-1940**

1940, Apr. 14

RA15 PT2	1c olive green	25	15

Pan American Union, 50th anniversary.

No. RA2 Overprinted in Red — **1941**

1941

RA16 PT2	1c olive green	50	15

No. 235 Surcharged in Red — **CONSTRUCCION CONSTRUCCION UN CENTAVO**

RA17 A79	1c on 2c deep blue	25	15

No. 235 Surcharged in Carmine — **CONSTRUCCION 1942 UN CENTAVO**

1942, Jan.

RA18 A79	1c on 2c deep blue	50	15

Arch of Communications Building
PT3 PT4

With Imprint Below Design

1942, June 3 Engr. *Perf. 11, 12x11*

RA19 PT3	1c black brown	5.00	1.00

No imprint; Thin Paper

Perf. 11, 12x11, 11x12, 11x12x11x11

1942, July 18

RA20 PT3	1c black brown	35	15

1943 ***Perf. 11, 12x11, 12***

RA21 PT4	1c orange	25	15

PT5

Perf. 11, 12½ and Compound

1945, Feb. Unwmk.

RA22 PT5	1c orange	20	15

1949 ***Perf. 12½***

RA23 PT5	1c deep ultra	30	15

GUINEA

LOCATION — Coast of West Africa, between Guinea-Bissau and Sierra Leone
GOVT. — Republic
AREA — 94,926 sq. mi.
POP. — 5,412,000 (est. 1983)
CAPITAL — Conakry

This former French Overseas Territory of French West Africa proclaimed itself an independent republic on October 2, 1958.

100 Centimes = 1 Franc
100 Caury = 1 Syli (1973)
100 Centimes = 1 CFA Franc (1986)

Catalogue values for all unused stamps in this country are for Never Hinged items.

French West Africa No. 79 Overprinted — **REPUBLIQUE DE GUINEE**

1959 Unwmk. Photo. *Perf. 12x12½*

168 CD104	10fr multi	1.00	1.10

French West Africa No. 78 Surcharged in Red — **45 F REPUBLIQUE DE GUINEE**

Engr.
Perf. 13

169 A33	45fr on 20fr multi	1.00	1.10

Common Design Types pictured in section at front of book.

Map, Dove and Pres. Sékou Toure A12

1959 Unwmk. Engr. *Perf. 13*

170 A12	5fr rose car	15	15
171 A12	10fr ultramarine	20	15
172 A12	20fr orange	38	25
173 A12	65fr slate green	1.00	65
174 A12	100fr violet	1.90	1.40
	Nos. 170-174 (5)	3.63	2.60

Proclamation of independence, Oct. 2, 1958.

Bananas — A13

Flag Raising, Labe — A15

Fishing Boats and Tamara Lighthouse A14

Fruits: 15fr, Grapefruit. 20fr, Lemons. 25fr, Avocados. 50fr, Pineapple.

1959 Litho. *Perf. 11½*
Fruits in Natural Colors

175 A13	10fr red	15	15
176 A13	15fr green & pink	15	15
177 A13	20fr red brn & bl	20	15
178 A13	25fr blue & yel	25	20
179 A13	50fr dark vio bl	42	22
	Nos. 175-179 (5)	1.17	
	Set value		68

For overprints see Nos. 209-213.

1959 Engr. *Perf. 13½*

Designs: 5fr, Coco palms and sailboat (vert.). 10fr, Launching fishing pirogue. 15fr, Elephant's head. 20fr, Pres. Sekou Toure and torch (vert.). 25fr, Elephant.

180 A14	1fr rose	15	15
181 A14	2fr green	15	15
182 A14	3fr brown	15	15
183 A14	5fr blue	15	15
184 A14	10fr claret	15	15
185 A14	15fr light brn	25	15
186 A14	20fr claret	38	15
187 A14	25fr red brown	40	15
	Set value	1.25	60

1959 Litho. *Perf. 12*

188 A15	50fr multicolored	42	20
189 A15	100fr multicolored	90	50

For overprints see Nos. 201-202.

UN Headquarters, New York, and People of Guinea — A16

1959 ***Perf. 12***

190 A16	1fr vio blue & org	15	15
191 A16	2fr red lil & emer	15	15
192 A16	3fr brn & crimson	15	15
193 A16	5fr brn & grnsh bl	15	15
	Set value, #190-193, C22-C23	1.40	1.00

Guinea's admission to the UN, first anniv.
For overprints see Nos. 205-208, C27-C28.

Uprooted Oak Emblem — A17

1960 Photo. *Perf. 11½*
Granite Paper

194 A17	25fr multicolored	20	18
195 A17	50fr multicolored	28	20

World Refugee Year, July 1, 1959-June 30, 1960.

For surcharges see Nos. B17-B18.

UPU Monument, Bern — A18

1960 Granite Paper Unwmk.

196 A18	10fr gray brn & blk	15	15
197 A18	15fr lil & purple	15	15
198 A18	20fr ultra & dk blue	16	15
199 A18	25fr yel grn & sl grn	25	15
200 A18	50fr red org & brown	45	20
	Nos. 196-200 (5)	1.16	80

Nos. 199-200 are vertical.
Admission to the UPU, first anniv.

Nos. 188-189 Overprinted in Black, Orange or Carmine: "Jeux Olympiques Rome 1960" and Olympic Rings

1960 Litho. *Perf. 12*

201 A15	50fr multi (Bk)	2.50	2.50
202 A15	100fr multi (O or C)	4.00	4.00
	Nos. 201-202,C24-C26 (5)	28.50	26.00

17th Olympic Games, Rome, Aug. 25-Sept. 11.

Map and Flag of Guinea — A19

1960 Photo. *Perf. 11½*

203 A19	25fr multicolored	20	16
204 A19	30fr multicolored	25	20

Second anniversary of independence.

Nos. 190-193 Overprinted — **XVÈME ANNIVERSAIRE DES NATIONS UNIES**

1961 Litho. *Perf. 12*

205 A16	1fr vio blue & org	15	15
206 A16	2fr red lil & emer	15	15
207 A16	3fr brn & crimson	15	15
208 A16	5fr brn & grnsh bl	15	15

Nos. 175-179 Overprinted in Black or Orange — **XVEME ANNIVERSAIRE**

DES NATIONS UNIES

Perf. 11½
Fruits in Natural Colors

209 A13	10fr red	15	15
210 A13	15fr grn & pink	16	15
211 A13	20fr red brn & bl	22	20
212 A13	25fr bl & yel (O)	25	22
213 A13	50fr dk vio blue	50	45
	Nos. 205-213,C27-C28 (11)	2.98	2.70

15th anniversary of United Nations.

Defassa Waterbuck A20

1961, Sept. 1 Photo. *Perf. 11½*
Multicolored Design; Granite Paper

214 A20	5fr bright grn	15	15
215 A20	10fr emerald	15	15
216 A20	25fr lilac	18	15

217 A20 40fr orange 30 16
218 A20 50fr red orange 40 25
219 A20 75fr ultramarine 65 25
Nos. 214-219 (6) 1.83
Set value 85

For surcharges see Nos. B19-B24.

Exhibition Hall A21

1961, Oct. 2 ***Perf. 11½***
Flag in Red, Yellow & Green
Granite Paper

220 A21 5fr ultra & red 15 15
221 A21 10fr brown & red 15 15
222 A21 25fr gray grn & red 15 15
Set value 27 27

First Three-Year Plan.

Gray-breasted Helmet Guinea Fowl — A22

1961 **Unwmk.** ***Perf. 13x14***

223 A22 5fr rose lil, sep & bl 15 15
224 A22 10fr dp org, sep & bl 15 15
225 A22 25fr cerise, sep & bl 15 15
226 A22 40fr ocher, sep & bl 25 15
227 A22 50fr lem, sepia & bl 35 16
228 A22 75fr ap grn, sep & bl 70 30
Nos. 223-228 (6) 1.75
Set value 72

For surcharges see Nos. B30-B35.

Patrice Lumumba and Map of Africa — A23

1962, Feb. 13 **Photo.** ***Perf. 11½***

229 A23 10fr multicolored 38 25
230 A23 25fr multicolored 50 25
231 A23 50fr multicolored 30 25

Death anniv. (on Feb. 12, 1961) of Patrice Lumumba, Premier of the Congo Republic.

King Mohammed V of Morocco and Map of Africa — A24

1962, Mar. 15 **Litho.** ***Perf. 13***

232 A24 25fr multicolored 42 16
233 A24 75fr multicolored 90 30

First anniv. of the conference of African heads of state at Casablanca.
For surcharges see Nos. B36-B37.

The Scott Catalogue value is a retail price, what you could expect to pay for the stamp in a grade of Fine-Very Fine. The value listed is a reference which reflects recent actual dealer selling price.

African Postal Union Issue

Map of Africa and Post Horn — A24a

1962, Apr. 23 **Photo.** ***Perf. 13½x13***

234 A24a 25fr org, blk & grn 50 15
235 A24a 100fr deep brn & org 1.25 25

Establishment of African Postal Union.

Bolon Player A26

Musical Instruments: 30c, 25fr, 50fr, Bote, vert. 1fr, 10fr, Flute, vert. 1.50fr, 3fr, Koni. 2fr, 20fr, Kora. 40fr, 75fr, Bolon.

Perf. 13½x13, 13x13½
1962, June 15

236 A26 30c bl, dk grn & red 15 15
237 A26 50c sal, brn & brt grn 15 15
238 A26 1fr yel grn, grn & lil 15 15
239 A26 1.50fr yel, red & bl 15 15
240 A26 2fr rose lil, red lil & grn 15 15
241 A26 3fr brn grn, grn & lil 15 15
242 A26 10fr org, brn & bl 15 15
243 A26 20fr ol, dk ol & car 15 15
244 A26 25fr ol, dk ol & lil 20 15
245 A26 40fr bl, grn & red lil 30 20
246 A26 50fr rose, dp rose & Prus bl 40 25
247 A26 75fr dl yel, brn & Prus bl 50 35
Nos. 236-247,C32-C34 (15) 7.35
Set value 4.25

Hippopotamus — A27

Designs: 25fr, 75fr, Lion. 30fr, 100fr, Leopard.

1962, Aug. 25 **Litho.** ***Perf. 13x13½***

248 A27 10fr org, grn & brn 15 15
249 A27 25fr emer, blk & brn 25 15
250 A27 30fr yel grn, dk brn & yel 30 15
251 A27 50fr vio bl, dk brn & grn 42 25
252 A27 75fr lil, lt lil & red brn 55 35
253 A27 100fr grnsh bl, dk brn & yel 65 50
Nos. 248-253 (6) 2.32 1.55

See Nos. 340-345

Child at Blackboard A28

Alfa Yaya A29

Designs: 10fr, 20fr, Adult class.

1962, Sept. 19 **Photo.** ***Perf. 13½x13***

254 A28 5fr yel, dk brn & org 15 15
255 A28 10fr org & dk brn 15 15
256 A28 15fr yel grn, dk brn & red 15 15
257 A28 20fr bl & dk brn 15 15
Set value 38 24

Campaign against illiteracy.

> Imperforates
> From late 1962 onward, most Guinea stamps exist imperforate.

1962, Oct. 2 ***Perf. 13½***

Portraits: 30fr, King Behanzin. 50fr, King Ba Bemba. 75fr, Almamy Samory. 100fr, Tierno Aliou.

Gold Frame

258 A29 25fr brt bl & sep 22 15
259 A29 30fr yel & sep 35 16
260 A29 50fr brt pink & sep 42 22
261 A29 75fr yel grn & sep 1.00 40
262 A29 100fr org, red & sep 1.20 60
Nos. 258-262 (5) 3.19 1.53

Heroes and martyrs of Africa.

Gray Parrot A30

Birds: 30c, 3fr, 50fr, Crowned crane (vert). 1fr, 20fr, Abyssinian ground hornbill. 1.50fr, 25fr, White spoonbill. 2fr, 40fr, Bateleur eagle.

1962, Dec. ***Perf. 13½x13, 13x13½***

263 A30 30c multicolored 15 15
264 A30 50c multicolored 15 15
265 A30 1fr multicolored 15 15
266 A30 1.50fr multicolored 15 15
267 A30 2fr multicolored 15 15
268 A30 3fr multicolored 15 15
269 A30 10fr multicolored 15 15
270 A30 20fr multicolored 16 15
271 A30 25fr multicolored 20 15
272 A30 40fr multicolored 30 20
273 A30 50fr multicolored 40 25
274 A30 75fr multicolored 50 35
Nos. 263-274,C41-C43 (15) 8.51
Set value 4.40

Wheat Emblem and Globe A31

1963, Mar. 21 **Photo.** ***Perf. 13x14***

275 A31 5fr red & yellow 15 15
276 A31 10fr emerald & yel 15 15
277 A31 15fr brown & yel 15 15
278 A31 25fr dark ol & yel 20 15
Set value 40 26

FAO "Freedom from Hunger" campaign.

Basketball — A32

Designs: 50c, 4fr, 30fr, Boxing. 1fr, 5fr, Running. 1.50fr, 10fr, Bicycling. 2fr, 20fr, Single sculls.

1963, Mar. 16 **Unwmk.** ***Perf. 14***

279 A32 30c ver, dp cl & grn 15 15
280 A32 50c lil & bl 15 15
281 A32 1fr dl org, sep & grn 15 15
282 A32 1.50fr org, ultra & mag 15 15
283 A32 2fr aqua, dk bl & mag 15 15
284 A32 3fr ol, dp cl & grn 15 15
285 A32 4fr car rose, pur & bl 15 15
286 A32 5fr brt grn, ol & mag 15 15
287 A32 10fr lil rose, ultra & mag 15 15
288 A32 20fr red org, dk bl & crim 15 15
289 A32 25fr emer, dp cl & dk grn 25 15
290 A32 30fr gray, pur & bl 30 20
Nos. 279-290,C44-C46 (15) 7.20
Set value 3.75

For overprints and surcharges see Nos. 312-314, C58-C60.

A33

Various Butterflies.

1963, May 10 **Photo.** ***Perf. 12***

291 A33 10c dp rose, blk & gray 15 15
292 A33 30c rose, blk & yel 15 15
293 A33 40c yel grn, brn & yel 15 15
294 A33 50c pale vio, blk & grn 15 15
295 A33 1fr yel, blk & emer 15 15
296 A33 1.50fr bluish grn, blk & sep 15 15
297 A33 2fr multi 15 15
298 A33 3fr multi 15 15
299 A33 10fr rose lil, blk & grn 15 15
300 A33 20fr gray, blk & grn 20 15
301 A33 25fr yel grn, blk & gray 30 15
302 A33 40fr multi 40 16
303 A33 50fr ultra, blk & yel 50 20
304 A33 75fr yel, blk & grn 60 35
Nos. 291-304,C47-C49 (17) 9.50
Set value 3.75

Handshake, Map and Dove — A34

1963, May 22 ***Perf. 13½x14***

305 A34 5fr bluish grn & dk brn 15 15
306 A34 10fr org yel & dk brn 15 15
307 A34 15fr ol & dk brn 15 15
308 A34 25fr bis brn & dk brn 18 15
Set value 40 28

Conference of African heads of state for African Unity, Addis Ababa.

Globe Encircled by Satellite — A35

1963, July 25 Engr. *Perf. 10½*
309 A35 5fr green & car 15 15
310 A35 10fr vio bl & car 15 15
311 A35 15fr yellow & car 15 15
Set value 25 22

Centenary of the International Red Cross. See Nos. C50-C51.

Nos. 279-281 Surcharged in Carmine, Yellow or Orange: "COMMISSION PRÉPARATOIRE AUX JEUX OLYMPIQUES À CONAKRY," New Value and Olympic Rings

1963, Nov. 20 Photo. *Perf. 14*
312 A32 40fr on 30c (C or Y) 1.10 1.00
313 A32 50fr on 50c (C or O) 1.50 1.40
314 A32 75fr on 1fr (C or O) 2.50 2.00
Nos. 312-314,C58-C60 (6) 15.25 12.80

Meeting of the Olympic Games Preparatory Commission at Conakry. The overprint is in a circular line on No. 312, in three lines on each side on Nos. 313-314.

Jewelfish A36

Fish: 40c, 30fr, Golden pheasant. 50c, 40fr, Blue gularis. 1fr, 75fr, Banded Jewelfish. 1.50fr, African lyretail. 2fr, Six-barred epiplatys. 5fr, Jewelfish.

1964, Feb. 15 Litho. *Perf. 14x13½*
315 A36 30c car rose & multi 15 15
316 A36 40c pur & multi 15 15
317 A36 50c car rose & multi 15 15
318 A36 1fr blue & multi 15 15
319 A36 1.50fr blue & multi 15 15
320 A36 2fr pur & multi 15 15
321 A36 5fr blue & multi 15 15
322 A36 30fr grn & multi 20 15
323 A36 40fr pur & multi 50 22
324 A36 75fr multi 65 35
Set value, #315-324, C54-C55 4.35 2.40

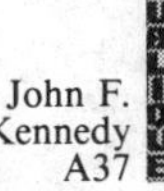

John F. Kennedy A37

1964, Mar. 5 Engr. *Perf. 10½*
Flag in Red and Blue
325 A37 5fr blk & pur 15 15
326 A37 25fr grn & pur 16 15
327 A37 50fr brn & pur 40 25
Set value 42

Issued in memory of John F. Kennedy. Issued in sheets of 20 with marginal quotations in English and French. Two sheets for each denomination. See No. C56.

Workers Welding Pipe — A38

Designs: 5fr, Pipe line over mountains (vert.). 10fr, Waterworks. 30fr, Transporting pipe. 50fr, Laying pipe.

1964, May 1 Photo. *Perf. 11½*
328 A38 5fr deep mag 15 15
329 A38 10fr bright pur 15 15
330 A38 20fr org red 15 15
331 A38 30fr ultra 15 15
332 A38 50fr yel grn 25 15
Set value 54 35

Completion of the water-supply pipeline to Conakry, Mar. 1964.

Ice Hockey — A39

1964, May 15 *Perf. 13x12½*
333 A39 10fr shown 15 15
334 A39 25fr Ski jump 30 15
335 A39 50fr Slalom 60 35
Set value 55

9th Winter Olympic Games, Innsbruck, Jan. 29-Feb. 9, 1964. See No. C57.

Eleanor Roosevelt Reading to Children — A40

1964, June 1 Engr. *Perf. 10½*
336 A40 5fr green 15 15
337 A40 10fr red org 15 15
338 A40 15fr bright bl 15 15
339 A40 25fr car rose 18 15
Nos. 336-339,C61 (5) 1.03
Set value 52

Eleanor Roosevelt, 15th anniv. of the Universal Declaration of Human Rights (in 1963).

Animal Type of 1962

Designs: 5fr, 30fr, Striped hyenas. 40fr, 300fr, Black buffaloes. 75fr, 100fr, Elephants.

1964, Oct. 8 Litho. *Perf. 13x13½*
340 A27 5fr yellow & blk 15 15
341 A27 30fr light bl & blk 18 15
342 A27 40fr lil rose & blk 25 15
343 A27 75fr yel grn & blk 55 22
344 A27 100fr bister & blk 65 38
345 A27 300fr orange & blk 1.90 1.10
Nos. 340-345 (6) 3.68 2.15

Guinea Exhibit, World's Fair — A41

1964, Oct. 26 Engr. *Perf. 10½*
346 A41 30fr vio & emerald 20 15
347 A41 40fr red lil & emer 30 15
348 A41 50fr sepia & emer 40 18
349 A41 75fr rose red & dk bl 60 25

New York World's Fair, 1964-65. See Nos. 372-375, C62-C63, C69-C70.

Queen Nefertari Crowned by Isis and Hathor — A42

Weight Lifter and Caucasian, Japanese and Negro Children — A43

Designs: 25fr, Ramses II in battle. 50fr, Submerged sphinxes, sailboat, Wadies-Sebua. 100fr, Ramses II holding crook and flail, Abu Simbel. 200fr, Feet and legs of Ramses statues, Abu Simbel.

1964, Nov. 19 Photo. *Perf. 12*
350 A42 10fr dk bl, red brn & cit 15 15
351 A42 25fr blk, dl red & brn 15 15
352 A42 50fr dk brn, bl & vio 22 15
353 A42 100fr dk brn, yel & pur 38 30
354 A42 200fr pur, dl grn & buff 90 55
Nos. 350-354,C64 (6) 3.70 2.40

UNESCO campaign to preserve Nubian monuments.
For overprint see No. 415.

1965, Jan. 18 Photo. *Perf. 13x12½*

Designs: 10fr, Runner carrying torch. 25fr, Pole vaulting and flags. 40fr, Runners. 50fr, Judo. 75fr, Japanese woman, flags and stadium.

355 A43 5fr gold, cl & blk 15 15
356 A43 10fr gold, blk, ver & bl 15 15
357 A43 25fr gold, blk, yel grn & red 15 15
358 A43 40fr gold, blk, brn & yel 20 15
359 A43 50fr gold, blk & grn 35 22
360 A43 75fr gold & multi 60 35
Nos. 355-360,C65 (7) 2.60
Set value 1.25

18th Olympic Games, Tokyo, Oct. 10-25, 1964.
For overprints see Nos. 410-414.

Doudou Mask, Boke — A44

Designs: 40c, 1fr, 15fr, Various Niamou masks, N'Zerekore region. 60c, "Yoki," woodcarved statuette of a girl, Boke. 80c, Masked woman dancer from Guekedou. 2fr, Masked dancer from Macenta. 20fr, Beater from Tamtam. 60fr, Bird dancer from Macenta. 80fr, Bassari dancer from Koundara. 100fr, Sword dancer from Karana.

1965, Feb. 15 Unwmk. *Perf. 14*
361 A44 20c multicolored 15 15
362 A44 40c multicolored 15 15
363 A44 60c multicolored 15 15
364 A44 80c multicolored 15 15
365 A44 1fr multicolored 15 15
366 A44 2fr multicolored 15 15
367 A44 15fr multicolored 15 15
368 A44 20fr multicolored 20 15
369 A44 60fr multicolored 50 35
370 A44 80fr multicolored 50 38
371 A44 100fr multicolored 70 40
Set value, #361-371, C68 4.50 2.40

World's Fair Type of 1964 Inscribed "1965"

1965, Mar. 24 Engr. *Perf. 10½*
372 A41 30fr grn & orange 15 15
373 A41 40fr car & brt grn 22 15
374 A41 50fr brt grn & vio 35 25
375 A41 75fr brown & vio 50 40

See Nos. C69-C70.

Blacksmith A45

Handicrafts: 20fr, Potter. 60fr, Cloth dyers. 80fr, Basketmaker.

1965, May 1 Photo. *Perf. 14*
376 A45 15fr multicolored 15 15
377 A45 20fr multicolored 15 15
378 A45 60fr multicolored 38 25
379 A45 80fr multicolored 45 35
Nos. 376-379,C71-C72 (6) 3.73 2.05

ITU Emblem, Old and New Communication Equipment — A46

1965, May 17 Unwmk.
380 A46 25fr yel, gray, gold & blk 15 15
381 A46 50fr yel, grn, gold & blk 30 22

ITU centenary. See Nos. C73-C74.

Maj. Virgil I. Grissom A47

Moon from 258mi. A48

Sputnik Over Earth — A49

American Achievements in Space: 10fr, Lt. Com. John W. Young. 25fr, Moon from 115mi. 30fr, Moon from 58mi. 100fr, Grissom and Young in Gemini 2 spaceship.

1965, July 19 Photo. *Perf. 13*
Size: 21x29mm
382 A47 5fr dk red & multi 15 15
383 A47 10fr dk red & multi 15 15
384 A48 15fr gold, bl & dk bl 15 15
Size: 39x28mm
385 A48 25fr gold, bl & dk bl 15 15
Size: 21x29mm
386 A48 30fr gold, bl & dk bl 16 15
Size: 39x28mm
387 A47 100fr multi & dk red 52 40
a. Sheet of 15, #382-387 4.00

Russian Achievements in Space: 5fr, Col. Pavel Belyayev. 10fr, Lt. Col. Alexei Leonov. 15fr, Vostoks 3 & 4 in space. 30fr, Vostoks 5 & 6 over Earth. 100fr, Leonov floating in space.

Size: 21x29mm
388 A47 5fr bl & multi 15 15
389 A47 10fr bl & multi 15 15
390 A49 15fr bl & multi 15 15
Size: 39x28mm
391 A49 25fr bl & multi 15 15
Size: 21x29mm
392 A49 30fr bl & multi 16 15
Size: 39x28mm
393 A47 100fr blk, dk red & gold 52 40
a. Sheet of 15, #388-393 4.00
Set value, #382-393 2.00 1.50

American and Russian achievements in space. Nos. 387a and 393a contain five triptychs each: four rows with 5fr, 100fr and 10fr, and a center row with 15fr, 25fr and 30fr stamps each.

ICY Emblem, UN Headquarters and Skyline, New York — A50

1965, Sept. 8 *Perf. 10½*

394 A50 25fr yel grn & ver 15 15
395 A50 45fr vio & orange 25 18
396 A50 75fr red brn & org 40 25

Intl. Cooperation Year, 1965. See No. C75.

Polytechnic Institute, Conakry — A51

New Projects, Conakry: 30fr, Hotel Camayenne. 40fr, Gbessia Airport. 75fr, Stadium "28 September."

1965, Oct. 2 **Photo.** *Perf. 13½*

397 A51 25fr multicolored 16 15
398 A51 30fr multicolored 22 15
399 A51 40fr multicolored 42 25
400 A51 75fr multicolored 52 35
Nos. 397-400,C76-C77 (6) 7.07 3.70

Seventh anniversary of independence.

Photographing Far Side of Moon — A52

Designs: 10fr, Trajectories of Ranger VII on flight to moon. 25fr, Relay satellite. 45fr, Vostoks I & II and globe.

1965, Nov. 15 **Litho.** *Perf. 14x13½*

401 A52 5fr blk, pur & ocher 15 15
402 A52 10fr red brn, lt grn & yel 15 15
403 A52 25fr blk, bl & bis 20 15
404 A52 45fr blk, lt ultra & bis 38 20
Nos. 401-404,C78-C79 (6) 3.13
Set value 1.30

For overprints and surcharges see Nos. 529-530, C112-C112B.

Sword Dance, Karana — A53

Designs: 30c, Dancing girls, Lower Guinea. 50c, Behore musicians of Tiekere playing "Eyoro" (horiz.). 5fr, Doundouba dance of Kouroussa. 40fr, Bird man's dance of Macenta.

1966, Jan. 5 **Photo.** *Perf. 13½*

Size: 26x36mm

405 A53 10c multicolored 15 15
406 A53 30c multicolored 15 15

Size: 36x28½mm

407 A53 50c multicolored 15 15

Size: 26x36mm

408 A53 5fr multicolored 15 15
409 A53 40fr multicolored 35 18
Set value, #405-409, C80 1.25 70

Festival of African Art and Culture. See Nos. 436-441.

Engraved Overprint in Red or Orange on Nos. 355-356 and Nos. 358-360

1966, Mar. 14 *Perf. 13x12½*

410 A43 5fr multi (R) 15 15
411 A43 10fr multi (R) 15 15
412 A43 40fr multi (O) 35 25
413 A43 50fr multi (R) 45 35
414 A43 75fr multi (R) 80 58
Nos. 410-414,C81 (6) 2.70 1.86

4th Pan Arab Games, Cairo, Sept. 2-11, 1965. The same overprint was also applied to imperf. sheets of No. 357.

Engraved Red Orange Overprint on No. 352: "CENTENAIRE DU TIMBRE CAIRE 1966"

1966, Mar. 14 *Perf. 12*

415 A42 50fr dk brn, bl & vio 35 35

First Egyptian postage stamps, cent. See No. C82.

Vonkou Rock, Telimélé — A54

Views: 25fr, Artificial lake, Coyah. 40fr, Kale waterfalls. 50fr, Forecariah bridge. 75fr, Liana bridge.

1966, Apr. 4 **Photo.** *Perf. 13½*

416 A54 20fr multicolored 15 15
417 A54 25fr multicolored 15 15
418 A54 40fr multicolored 20 15
419 A54 50fr multicolored 30 15
420 A54 75fr multicolored 42 25
Nos. 416-420,C83 (6) 1.92
Set value 98

See Nos. 475-478, C90-C91. For overprints see Nos. 482-488, C93-C95.

UNESCO Emblem — A55

1966, May 2 **Photo.** **Unwmk.**

421 A55 25fr multicolored 20 15

20th anniv. of UNESCO. See Nos. C84-C85.

Woman of Guinea and Morning Glory — A56

Symbolic Water Cycle and UNESCO Emblem — A57

Designs: Women and Flowers of Guinea.

1966, May 30 **Photo.** *Perf. 13½*

Size: 23x34mm

422 A56 10c multicolored 15 15
423 A56 20c multicolored 15 15
424 A56 30c multicolored 15 15
425 A56 40c multicolored 15 15
426 A56 3fr multicolored 15 15
427 A56 4fr multicolored 15 15
428 A56 10fr multicolored 15 15
429 A56 25fr multicolored 25 15

Size: 28x43mm

430 A56 30fr multicolored 30 15
431 A56 50fr multicolored 40 22
432 A56 80fr multicolored 58 30
Nos. 422-432,C86-C87 (13) 6.68
Set value 2.75

1966, Sept. 26 **Engr.** *Perf. 10½*

433 A57 5fr bl & dp org 15 15
434 A57 25fr grn & dp org 15 15
435 A57 100fr brt rose lil & dp org 58 35
Set value 75 48

Hydrological Decade (UNESCO), 1965-74.

Dance Type of 1966

Designs: Various folk dances. 25fr, 75fr, horizontal.

1966, Oct. 24 **Photo.** *Perf. 13½*

Sizes: 26x36mm (vert.); 36x28½mm (horiz.)

436 A53 60c multicolored 15 15
437 A53 1fr multicolored 15 15
438 A53 1.50fr multicolored 15 15
439 A53 25fr multicolored 15 15
440 A53 50fr multicolored 35 18
441 A53 75fr multicolored 45 35
Set value 1.10 75

Guinean National Dancers.

Child's Drawing and UNICEF Emblem — A58

Children's Drawings: 2fr, Elephant. 3fr, Girl. 20fr, Village (horiz.). 25fr, Boy playing soccer. 40fr, Still life. 50fr, Bird in a tree.

1966, Dec. 12 **Photo.** *Perf. 13½*

442 A58 2fr multicolored 15 15
443 A58 3fr multicolored 15 15
444 A58 10fr multicolored 15 15
445 A58 20fr multicolored 15 15
446 A58 25fr multicolored 16 15
447 A58 40fr multicolored 25 15
448 A58 50fr multicolored 35 20
Set value 1.10 62

20th anniv. of UNICEF. Printed in sheets of 10 stamps and 2 labels with ornamental borders and inscriptions.

Laboratory Technician — A59

Designs (WHO Emblem and): 50fr, Physician examining infant. 75fr, Pre-natal care and instruction. 80fr, WHO Headquarters, Geneva.

1967, Jan. 20 **Photo.** *Perf. 13½*

449 A59 30fr multicolored 15 15
450 A59 50fr multicolored 25 15
451 A59 75fr multicolored 38 22
452 A59 80fr multicolored 45 35

Inauguration (in 1966) of WHO Headquarters, Geneva.

Niamou Mask, N'Zerekore — A60

Designs: 10c, 1fr, 30fr, Small Banda mask, Kanfarade, Boke region. 1.50fr, 50fr, Like 30c. 50c, 5fr, 75fr, Bearded Niamou mask. 60c, 25fr, 100fr, Horned Yinadjinkele mask, Kankan region.

1967, Mar. 25 **Photo.** *Perf. 14x13*

453 A60 10c org & multi 15 15
454 A60 30c cit & brn blk 15 15
455 A60 50c dp lil rose, blk & red 15 15
456 A60 60c dp org, blk & bis 15 15
457 A60 1fr yel grn & multi 15 15
458 A60 1.50fr sal pink & brn blk 15 15
459 A60 5fr ap grn, blk & red 15 15
460 A60 25fr red lil, blk & bis 16 15
461 A60 30fr bis & multi 25 15
462 A60 50fr grnsh bl & brn blk 40 15
463 A60 75fr yel, blk & red 60 25
464 A60 100fr lt ultra, blk & bis 90 40
Set value 2.70 1.25

Ball Python A61

Designs: 20c, Pastoria Research Institute. 50c, 75fr, Extraction of snake venom. 1fr, 50fr, Rock python. 2fr, Men holding rock python. 5fr, 30fr, Gaboon viper. 20fr, West African mamba.

1967, May 15 **Litho.** *Perf. 13½*

Size: 43½x20mm

465 A61 20c multicolored 15 15
466 A61 30c multicolored 15 15
467 A61 50c multicolored 15 15
468 A61 1fr multicolored 15 15
469 A61 2fr multicolored 15 15
470 A61 5fr multicolored 15 15

Size: 56x26mm

471 A61 20fr multicolored 15 15
472 A61 30fr multicolored 35 15
473 A61 50fr multicolored 42 15
474 A61 75fr multicolored 65 20
Nos. 465-474,C88-C89 (12) 6.12
Set value 2.50

Research Institute for Applied Biology of Guinea (Pastoria). For Souvenir sheet see No. C88a.

Scenic Type of 1966

Views: 5fr, Loos Island. 30fr, Tinkisso Waterfalls. 70fr, "The Elephant's Trunk" Hotel, Mt. Kakoulima. 80fr, Evening at the shore, Ratoma.

1967, June 20 **Photo.** *Perf. 13½*

475 A54 5fr multicolored 15 15
476 A54 30fr multicolored 16 15
477 A54 70fr multicolored 42 15
478 A54 80fr multicolored 58 15
Nos. 475-478,C90-C91 (6) 3.31
Set value 1.40

People's Palace, Conakry — A62

Elephant A63

1967, Sept. 28 Photo. Perf. 13½

479 A62 5fr silver & multi 15 15
480 A63 30fr silver & multi 22 16
481 A62 55fr gold & multi 40 20
Set value 66 40

20th anniv. of the Democratic Party of Guinea and the opening of the People's Palace, Conakry. See No. C92.

Nos. 418-420 and 475-478 Overprinted with Lions Emblem and: "AMITIE DES PEUPLES GRACE AU TOURISME 1917-1967"

1967, Nov. 6

482 A54 5fr multicolored 16 15
483 A54 30fr multicolored 38 15
484 A54 40fr multicolored 35 15
485 A54 50fr multicolored 45 20
486 A54 70fr multicolored 55 25
487 A54 75fr multicolored 80 38
488 A54 80fr multicolored 1.00 38
Nos. 482-488,C93-C95 (10) 6.79 3.16

50th anniversary of Lions International.

WHO Office for Africa — A64

1967, Dec. 4 Photo. Perf. 13½

489 A64 30fr lt ol grn, bis & dk grn 25 15
490 A64 75fr red org, bis & dk bl 55 25

Inauguration of the WHO Regional Office for Africa in Brazzaville, Congo.

Human Rights Flame — A65

1968, Jan. 15 Photo. Perf. 13½

491 A65 30fr ocher, grn & dk car 22 15
492 A65 40fr vio, grn & car 30 15
Set value 22

International Human Rights Year, 1968.

Coyah, Dubréka Region — A66

Homes and People: 30c, 30fr, Kankan Region. 40c, Kankan, East Guinea. 50c, 15fr, Woodlands Region. 60c, Fulahmori, Gaoual Region. 5fr, Cognagui, Kundara Region. 40fr, Fouta Djallon, West Guinea. 100fr, Labe, West Guinea.

1968, Apr. 1 Photo. Perf. 13½x14
Size: 36x27mm

493 A66 20c gold & multi 15 15
494 A66 30c gold & multi 15 15
495 A66 40c gold & multi 15 15
496 A66 50c gold & multi 15 15

Perf. 14x13½
Size: 57x36mm

497 A66 60c gold & multi 15 15
498 A66 5fr gold & multi 15 15
499 A66 15fr gold & multi 15 15
500 A66 20fr gold & multi 16 15
501 A66 30fr gold & multi 25 15
502 A66 40fr gold & multi 38 15
503 A66 100fr gold & multi 90 22
Set value, #493-503, C100 4.00 1.60

The Storyteller — A67

African Legends: 15fr, The Little Genie of Mt. Nimba. No. 506, The Legend of the Moons and the Stars. No. 507, Lan, the Child Buffalo (vert.). 40fr, Nianablas and the Crocodiles. 50fr, Leuk the Hare Playing the Drum (vert.). 75fr, Leuk the Hare Selling his Sister (vert.). 80fr, The Hunter and the Antelope-woman. The designs are from paintings by students of the Academy of Fine Arts in Bellevue.

1968 Photo. Perf. 13½

504 A67 15fr multicolored 15 15
505 A67 25fr multicolored 15 15
506 A67 30fr multicolored 15 15
507 A67 30fr multicolored 20 15
508 A67 40fr multicolored 30 15
509 A67 50fr multicolored 40 15
a. Souv. sheet of 4 3.75 3.75
510 A67 75fr multicolored 42 25
511 A67 80fr multicolored 65 25
Nos. 504-511,C101-C104 (12) 7.57
Set value 2.50

Issued in sheets of 10 plus 2 labels. No. 509a contains 4 imperf. stamps similar to Nos. 508-509, C101 and C104. "Poste Aerienne" omitted on the 70fr and 300fr of the souvenir sheet.

Issue dates: May 16, Nos. 505-506, 510-511. Sept. 16, Nos. 504, 507-509.

Anubius Baboon — A68

African Animals: 10fr, Leopards. 15fr, Hippopotami. 20fr, Nile crocodile. 30fr, Ethiopian wart hog. 50fr, Defassa waterbuck. 75fr, Cape buffaloes.

1968, Nov. 25 Photo. Perf. 13½
Size: 44x31mm

512 A68 5fr gold & multi 15 15
513 A68 10fr gold & multi 15 15
514 A68 15fr gold & multi 15 15
a. Souv. sheet of 3, #512-514 30 30
515 A68 20fr gold & multi 22 15
516 A68 30fr gold & multi 30 15
517 A68 50fr gold & multi 40 15
a. Souv. sheet of 3, #515-517 90 90
518 A68 75fr gold & multi 60 25
a. Souv. sheet of 3 3.25 3.25
Nos. 512-518,C105-C106 (9) 4.37
Set value 1.50

No. 518a contains one No. 518 and one each similar to Nos. C105-C106 without "POSTE AERIENNE" inscription. The three souvenir sheets contain 3 stamps and one green and gold label inscribed "FAUNE AFRICAINE."

Senator Robert F. Kennedy — A69

Portraits: 75fr, Rev. Martin Luther King, Jr. 100fr, Pres. John F. Kennedy.

1968, Dec. 16

519 A69 30fr yel & multi 16 15
520 A69 75fr multicolored 50 15
521 A69 100fr multicolored 65 25
Nos. 519-521,C107-C109 (6) 3.96
Set value 1.15

Robert F. Kennedy, John F. Kennedy and Martin Luther King, Jr., martyrs for freedom.

The stamps are printed in sheets of 15 (3x5) containing 10 stamps and five yellow-green and gold center labels. Sheets come either with English or French inscriptions on label.

Sculpture and Runner A70

Sculpture and Soccer — A71

Designs (Sculpture and): 10fr, Boxing. 15fr, Javelin. 30fr, Steeplechase. 50fr, Hammer throw. 75fr, Bicycling.

1969, Feb. 18 Photo. Perf. 13½

522 A70 5fr multicolored 15 15
523 A70 10fr multicolored 15 15
524 A70 15fr multicolored 22 15
525 A71 25fr multicolored 25 15
526 A70 30fr multicolored 25 15
527 A70 50fr multicolored 42 15
528 A70 75fr multicolored 55 18
Nos. 522-528,C110-C111A (10) 6.29
Set value 1.85

19th Olympic Games, Mexico City, Oct. 12-27.

No. 404 Surcharged and Overprinted in Red

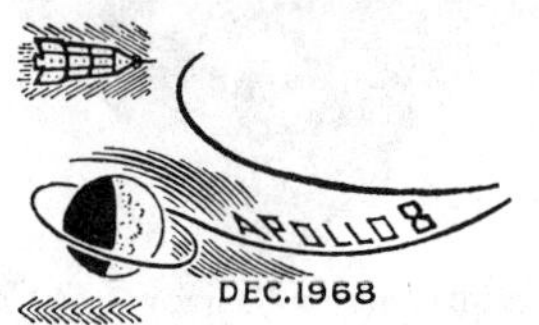

1969, Mar. 17 Litho. Perf. 14x13½

529 A52 30fr on 45fr multi 35 35
530 A52 45fr multicolored 35 35
Nos. 529-530,C112-C112B (5) 3.55 2.50

US Apollo 8 mission, the first men in orbit around the moon, Dec. 21-27, 1968.

Nos. 529-530 also exist with surcharge and overprint in black. These sell for about 10% more.

Tarzan — A72

Designs: 30fr, Tarzan sitting in front of Pastoria Research Institute gate. 75fr, Tarzan and his family. 100fr, Tarzan sitting in a tree.

1969, June 6 Photo. Perf. 13½

531 A72 25fr orange & multi 16 15
532 A72 30fr bl grn & multi 22 15
533 A72 75fr yel grn & multi 50 18
534 A72 100fr yellow & multi 80 30
Set value 66

Tarzan was a Guinean chimpanzee with superior intelligence and ability.

Campfire — A73

Designs: 25fr, Boy Scout and tents. 30fr, Marching Boy Scouts. 40fr, Basketball. 45fr, Senior Scouts, thatched huts and mountain. 50fr, Guinean Boy Scout badge.

1969, July 1

535 A73 5fr gold & multi 15 15
536 A73 25fr gold & multi 16 15
537 A73 30fr gold & multi 20 15
538 A73 40fr gold & multi 30 15
539 A73 45fr gold & multi 35 15
540 A73 50fr gold & multi 40 18
a. Min. sheet of 6, #535-540 2.00 2.00
Nos. 535-540 (6) 1.56
Set value 58

Issued to honor the Boy Scouts of Guinea.

Launching Apollo 11 — A74

Designs: 30fr, Earth showing Africa as seen from moon. 50fr, Separation of lunar landing module and spaceship. 60fr, Astronauts and module on moon. 75fr, Module on moon and earth. 100fr, Module leaving moon. 200fr, Splashdown. "a" stamps are inscribed in French. "b" stamps are inscribed in English.

1969, Aug. 20 Photo. Perf. 13½
Size: 34x55mm

541 25fr Pair, #541a, 541b 35 15
542 30fr Pair, #542a, 542b 45 15
543 50fr Pair, #543a, 543b 65 18
544 60fr Pair, #544a, 544b 1.15 30
545 75fr Pair, #545a, 545b 1.30 36

Size: 34x71mm

546 100fr Pair, #546a, 546b 2.10 50

Size: 34x55mm

547 200fr Pair, #547a, 547b 4.25 1.20
Nos. 541-547 (7) 10.25 2.84

Man's 1st landing on the moon, July 20, 1969.

Harvest and ILO Emblem A75

ILO, 50th Anniv.: 25fr, Power lines and blast furnaces. 30fr, Women in broadcasting studio. 200fr, Potters.

1969, Oct. 28 Photo. *Perf. 13½*

548	A75	25fr gold & multi	16	15
549	A75	30fr gold & multi	20	15
550	A75	75fr gold & multi	50	15
551	A75	200fr gold & multi	1.50	50
		Set value		75

Mother and Sick Child — A76

Designs: 25fr, Sick child. 40fr, Girl receiving vaccination. 50fr, Boy receiving vaccination. 60fr, Mother receiving vaccination. 200fr, Edward Jenner, M.D.

1970, Jan. 15 Photo. *Perf. 13½*

552	A76	25fr multicolored	15	15
553	A76	30fr multicolored	20	15
554	A76	40fr multicolored	25	15
555	A76	50fr multicolored	40	18
556	A76	60fr multicolored	45	18
557	A76	200fr multicolored	1.50	75
		Nos. 552-557 (6)	2.95	1.56

Campaign against smallpox and measles.

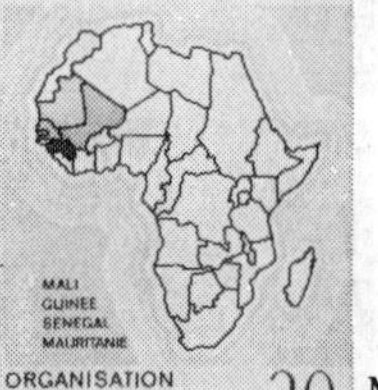

Map of Africa — A77

1970, Feb. 3 Litho. *Perf. 14½x14*

558	A77	30fr lt bl & multi	20	15
559	A77	200fr lt vio & multi	1.40	75

Meeting of statesmen of countries bordering on Senegal River: Mali, Guinea, Senegal and Mauritania.

Open Book and Radar A78

1970, July 6 Litho. *Perf. 14*

560	A78	5fr lt bl & blk	15	15
561	A78	10fr rose & blk	15	15
562	A78	50fr yellow & blk	38	15
563	A78	200fr lilac & blk	1.40	75
		Set value		90

International Telecommunications Day.

Lenin — A79

Designs: 20fr, Meeting with Lenin, by V. Serov. 30fr, Lenin Addressing Workers, by V. Serov. 40fr, Lenin with Red Guard Soldier and Sailor, by P. V. Vasiliev. 100fr, Lenin Speaking from Balcony, by P. V. Vasiliev. 200fr, Like 5fr.

1970, Nov. 16 Photo. *Perf. 13*

564	A79	5fr gold & multi	15	15
565	A79	20fr gold & multi	16	15
566	A79	30fr gold & multi	22	15
567	A79	40fr gold & multi	38	15
568	A79	100fr gold & multi	80	25
569	A79	200fr gold & multi	1.60	65
		Nos. 564-569 (6)	3.31	
		Set value		1.20

Lenin (1870-1924), Russian communist leader.

Phenecogrammus Interruptus — A80

Designs: Various fish from Guinea.

1971, Apr. 1 Photo. *Perf. 13*

570	A80	5fr gold & multi	15	15
571	A80	10fr gold & multi	15	15
572	A80	15fr gold & multi	15	15
573	A80	20fr gold & multi	15	15
574	A80	25fr gold & multi	20	15
575	A80	30fr gold & multi	25	15
576	A80	40fr gold & multi	25	15
577	A80	45fr gold & multi	30	18
578	A80	50fr gold & multi	35	18
579	A80	75fr gold & multi	60	25
580	A80	100fr gold & multi	70	35
581	A80	200fr gold & multi	1.40	80
		Nos. 570-581 (12)	4.65	
		Set value		2.25

Violet-crested Touraco — A81

Birds: 20fr, European golden oriole. 30fr, Blue-headed coucal. 40fr, Northern shrike. 75fr, Vulturine guinea fowl. 100fr, Southern ground hornbill.

1971, June 18 Photo. *Perf. 13*

Size: 34x34mm

582	A81	5fr gold & multi	15	15
583	A81	20fr gold & multi	15	15
584	A81	30fr gold & multi	16	15
585	A81	40fr gold & multi	30	15
586	A81	75fr gold & multi	70	22
587	A81	100fr gold & multi	90	35
		Nos. 582-587,C113-C113B (9)	5.31	2.17

UNICEF Emblem, Map of Africa — A82

1971, Dec. 24 *Perf. 12x12½*

Map in Olive

588	A82	25fr orange & blk	15	15
589	A82	30fr pink & black	16	15
590	A82	50fr gray grn & blk	35	15
591	A82	60fr gray bl & blk	42	15
592	A82	100fr lil rose & blk	70	25
		Nos. 588-592 (5)	1.78	
		Set value		62

UNICEF, 25th anniv.

For overprints see Nos. 625-629.

Imaginary Prehistoric Space Creature — A83

Designs: Various imaginary prehistoric space creatures.

1972, Apr. 1 *Perf. 13½x13*

593	A83	5fr multicolored	15	15
594	A83	20fr multicolored	15	15
595	A83	30fr multicolored	15	15
596	A83	40fr multicolored	25	15
597	A83	100fr multicolored	60	30
598	A83	200fr multicolored	1.10	58
		Nos. 593-598 (6)	2.40	
		Set value		1.15

Black Boy, Men of 4 Races, Emblem — A84

Designs: 20fr, Oriental boy. 30fr, Indian youth. 50fr, Caucasian girl. 100fr, Men of 4 races and Racial Equality emblem.

1972, May 14 *Perf. 13x13½*

599	A84	15fr gold & multi	15	15
600	A84	20fr gold & multi	15	15
601	A84	30fr gold & multi	15	15
602	A84	50fr gold & multi	25	15
603	A84	100fr gold & multi	50	25
		Nos. 599-603,C119 (6)	1.80	
		Set value		92

Intl. Year Against Racial Discrimination, 1971.

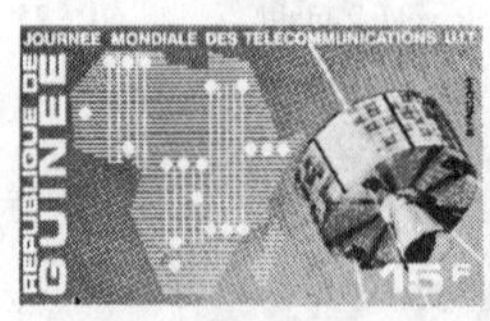

Map of Africa, Syncom Satellite A85

Designs (Map of Africa and Satellites): 30fr, Relay. 75fr, Early Bird. 80fr, Telstar.

1972, May 17 Litho. *Perf. 13*

604	A85	15fr multicolored	15	15
605	A85	30fr red org & multi	15	15
606	A85	75fr grn & multi	38	20
607	A85	80fr multicolored	45	30
		Nos. 604-607,C120-C121 (6)	2.63	1.55

4th World Telecommunications Day.

Carrier Pigeon, UPAF Emblem A86

1972, July 10

608	A86	15fr brt bl & multi	15	15
609	A86	30fr multicolored	15	15
610	A86	75fr lil & multi	38	20
611	A86	80fr multicolored	45	30
		Nos. 608-611,C122-C123 (6)	2.93	1.70

Book Year Emblem, Reading Child — A87

Designs (Book Year Emblem and): 15fr, Book as sailing ship. 40fr, Young woman with flower and book. 50fr, Book as key. 75fr, Man reading and globe. 200fr, Book and laurel.

1972, Aug. 2 Photo. *Perf. 14x13½*

612	A87	5fr red & multi	15	15
613	A87	15fr multicolored	15	15
614	A87	40fr yel & multi	20	15
615	A87	50fr blue & multi	30	15
616	A87	75fr dk red & multi	50	30
617	A87	200fr org & multi	90	60
		Nos. 612-617 (6)	2.20	
		Set value		1.20

International Book Year 1972.

Javelin, Olympic Emblems, Arms of Guinea — A88

1972, Aug. 26 Photo. *Perf. 13*

618	A88	5fr shown	15	15
619	A88	10fr Pole vault	15	15
620	A88	25fr Hurdles	15	15
621	A88	30fr Hammer throw	15	15
622	A88	40fr Boxing	25	15
623	A88	50fr Vaulting	25	15
624	A88	75fr Running	40	25
		Nos. 618-624,C124-C125 (9)	3.25	
		Set value		1.60

20th Olympic Games, Munich, Aug. 26-Sept. 11.

Nos. 588-592 Overprinted 

1972, Sept. 28 Photo. *Perf. 12x12½*

Map in Olive

625	A82	25fr org & blk	15	15
626	A82	30fr pink & blk	15	15
627	A82	50fr gray grn & blk	25	15
628	A82	60fr gray bl & blk	38	15
629	A82	100fr lil rose & blk	45	25
		Nos. 625-629 (5)	1.38	
		Set value		62

UN Conference on Human Environment, Stockholm, June 5-16.

Dimitrov at Leipzig Trial — A89

1972, Sept. 28 *Perf. 13*

Gold, Dark Green & Black

630 A89 5fr shown 15 15
631 A89 25fr In Moabit Prison, 1933 15 15
632 A89 40fr Writing his memoirs 20 15
633 A89 100fr Portrait 55 25
Set value 50

George Dimitrov (1882-1949), Bulgarian Communist party leader and Premier.

Emperor Haile Selassie — A90

Syntomeida Epilais — A91

Design: 200fr, Emperor facing right.

1972, Oct. 2

634 A90 40fr blk & multi 22 18
635 A90 200fr multicolored 1.10 65

1973, Mar. 5 **Photo.** *Perf. 14x13½*

Designs: Various insects.

636 A91 5fr shown 15 15
637 A91 15fr Ladybugs 15 15
638 A91 30fr Green locust 15 15
639 A91 40fr Honey bee 20 15
640 A91 50fr Photinus pyralis 25 15
641 A91 200fr Ancyluris formosissima 1.10 70
Nos. 636-641 (6) 2.00
Set value 1.10

Kwame Nkrumah A92

Designs: Various portraits of Kwame Nkrumah.

1973, May 25 **Photo.** *Perf. 13½*

642 A92 1.50s lt grn, gold & brn 15 15
643 A92 2.50s lt grn, gold & brn 15 15
644 A92 5s lt grn, gold & brn 25 20
645 A92 10s gold & dark vio 50 35
Set value 68

OAU, 10th anniversary.

Institute for Applied Biology, Kindia A93

Designs (WHO Emblem and): 2.50s, Technicians inoculating egg. 3s, Filling vaccine into ampules. 4s, Sterilization of vaccine. 5s, Assembling of vaccine and vaccination gun. 10s, Inoculation of steer. 20s, Vaccination of woman.

1973, Nov. 16 **Photo.** *Perf. 13½*

Size: 40x36mm

646 A93 1s gold & multi 15 15
647 A93 2.50s gold & multi 15 15
648 A93 3s gold & multi 20 15
649 A93 4s gold & multi 22 15

Size: 47½x31mm

650 A93 5s gold & multi 35 18
651 A93 10s gold & multi 50 25
652 A93 20s gold & multi 1.20 55
Nos. 646-652 (7) 2.77 1.58

WHO, 25th anniversary.

Copernicus, Heliocentric System, Primeval Landscape — A94

Nicolaus Copernicus A95

Designs (Copernicus and): 2s, Sun rising over volcanic desert, and spacecraft. 4s, Earth, moon and spacecraft. 5s, Moon scape and spacecraft. 10s, Jupiter and spacecraft. 20s, Saturn and heliocentric system.

1973, Dec. 17 **Photo.** *Perf. 13½*

653 A94 50c gold & multi 15 15
654 A94 2s gold & multi 15 15
655 A94 4s gold & multi 18 15
656 A94 5s gold & multi 30 15
657 A94 10s gold & multi 60 25
658 A94 20s gold & multi 1.20 62
Nos. 653-658 (6) 2.58
Set value 1.20

Souvenir Sheet

659 Sheet of 4 6.50 6.50
a. A95 20s Single stamp 1.40 1.00

Nicolaus Copernicus (1473-1543), Polish astronomer. No. 659 contains center label showing rocket and heliocentric system in gold margin.

Loading Bauxite on Freighter — A96

1974, Mar. 1 **Litho.** *Perf. 13½*

660 A96 4s shown 20 15
661 A96 6s Freight train 30 20
662 A96 10s Mining 50 30

Bauxite mining, Boke.

Clappertonia Ficifolia — A97

1974, May 20 **Photo.** *Perf. 13*

Size: 25x36mm

663 A97 50c shown 15 15
664 A97 1s Rothmannia longiflora 15 15
665 A97 2s Oncoba spinosa 15 15
666 A97 3s Venidium fastuosum 15 15

Size: 31x42mm

667 A97 4s Bombax costatum 18 15
668 A97 5s Clerodendrum splendens 25 15
669 A97 7.50s Combretuni grandiflorum 38 20
670 A97 10s Mussaendra erythrophylla 55 30

Size: 38x38mm (Diamond)

671 A97 12s Argemone mexicana 65 40
Nos. 663-671,C127-C129 (12) 6.86
Set value 3.50

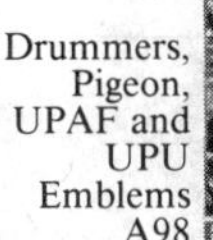

Drummers, Pigeon, UPAF and UPU Emblems A98

Designs (Carrier Pigeon, African Postal Union and UPU Emblems): 6s, Runner with letter stick. 7.50s, Monorail and mail truck. No. 675, Jet and ocean liner. No. 676, Balloon and dugout canoe. 20s, Satellites over earth.

1974, Oct. 16 **Photo.** *Perf. 13½x14*

672 A98 5s mag & multi 25 15
673 A98 6s grn & multi 35 20
674 A98 7.50s ver & multi 45 25
675 A98 10s Prus bl & multi 55 45

Souvenir Sheets

Perf. 13½

676 A98 10s ocher & multi 3.50
677 Sheet of 4, multi 4.00
a. A98 20s Single stamp 90 70

Centenary of Universal Postal Union. No. 676 contains one 70x60mm stamp.

Rope Bridge — A99

Designs (Pioneers): 2s, Field observation. 4s, Communication. 5s, Cooking in camp. 7.50s, Salute. 10s, Basketball.

1974, Nov. 22 **Photo.** *Perf. 14x13½*

678 A99 50c multicolored 15 15
679 A99 2s multicolored 15 15
680 A99 4s multicolored 18 15
681 A99 5s multicolored 25 15
682 A99 7.50s multicolored 38 20
683 A99 10s multicolored 50 30
a. Souv. sheet of 2, #682-683 1.60 1.60
Nos. 678-683 (6) 1.61
Set value 75

National Pioneer Movement.

Souvenir Sheet

Fruit — A100

1974, Nov. 22 **Photo.** *Perf. 13x14*

684 A100 Sheet of 5 3.50
a. 4s Limes 25
b. 4s Oranges 25
c. 5s Bananas 35
d. 5s Mangos 35
e. 12s Pineapple 80

Chimpanzee — A101

1975, May 14 **Photo.** *Perf. 13½*

685 A101 1s shown 15 15
686 A101 2s Impala 15 15
687 A101 3s Wart hog 15 15
688 A101 4s Kobus defassa 18 15
a. Souv. sheet of 4, #685-688 65 65
689 A101 5s Leopard 20 15
690 A101 6s Greater kudu 25 20
691 A101 6.50s Zebra 30 22
692 A101 7.50s Cape buffalo 35 25
a. Souv. sheet of 4, #689-692 1.40 1.40
693 A101 8s Hippopotamus 38 25
694 A101 10s Lion 42 30
695 A101 12s Black rhinoceros 50 35
696 A101 15s Elephant 65 50
a. Souv. sheet of 4, #693-696 2.25 2.25
Nos. 685-696 (12) 3.68 2.82

Sheets exist perf. and imperf.

Stamps in Nos. 692a, 696a are inscribed "Poste Aerienne."

Lions, Pipe Line and ADB Emblem A102

Designs (African Development Bank Emblem, Pipe Line and): 7s, Elephants. 10s, Male lions. 20s, Elephant and calf.

1975, June 16 **Photo.** *Perf. 13½*

697 A102 5s gold & multi 25 15
698 A102 7s gold & multi 30 16
699 A102 10s gold & multi 45 25
700 A102 20s gold & multi 1.00 60

African Development Bank, 10th anniv.

Demand, as well as supply, determines a stamp's market value. One is as important as the other.

Women Musicians, IWY Emblem — A103

Designs (IWY Emblem and): 7s, Women banjo and guitar players. 9s, Woman railroad shunter and train. 15s, Woman physician examining infant. 20s, Male and female symbols.

1976, Apr. 12 Photo. *Perf. 13½*

No.	Type	Description	Unused	Used
701	A103	5s multicolored	25	15
702	A103	7s multicolored	38	20
703	A103	9s blue & multi	45	30
704	A103	15s multicolored	70	50
a.		Souvenir sheet	80	80
705	A103	20s vio bl & multi	1.00	70
a.		Souvenir sheet of 4	4.25	4.25
		Nos. 701-705 (5)	2.78	1.85

International Women's Year 1975. No. 704a contains one stamp similar to No. 704 with gold frame. No. 705a contains 4 stamps similar to No. 705 with gold frame.

Woman Gymnast A104

Designs (Montreal Olympic Games Emblem and): 4s, Long jump. 5s, Hammer throw. 6s, Discus. 6.50s, Hurdles. 7s, Javelin. 8s, Running. 8.50s, Bicycling. 10s, High jump. 15s, Shot put. 20s, Pole vault. No. 717, Soccer. No. 718, Swimming.

1976, May 17 Photo. *Perf. 13½*

Size: 38x38mm

No.	Type	Description	Unused	Used
706	A104	3s multicolored	15	15
707	A104	4s grn & multi	20	15
708	A104	5s yel & multi	25	15
709	A104	6s multicolored	30	20
710	A104	6.50s plum & multi	35	20
711	A104	7s blue & multi	38	22
712	A104	8s ultra & multi	90	25
713	A104	8.50s org & multi	42	25
714	A104	10s multicolored	50	30
715	A104	15s multicolored	70	50
716	A104	20s multicolored	1.00	80
717	A104	25s grn & multi	1.40	80
		Nos. 706-717 (12)	6.55	3.97

Souvenir Sheet

No.	Type	Description	Unused	Used
718	A104	25s multicolored	2.25	2.25

21st Olympic Games, Montreal, Canada, July 17-Aug. 1. No. 718 contains one 32x32mm stamp. See No. C130.

A. G. Bell, Telephone, 1900 — A105

Designs: 7s, Wall telephone, 1910. 12s, Syncom telecommunications satellite. No. 722, Telstar satellite. No. 723, Telephone switchboard operator, 1914.

1976, Nov. 15 Photo. *Perf. 13*

No.	Type	Description	Unused	Used
719	A105	5s multicolored	25	15
720	A105	7s multicolored	38	20
721	A105	12s multicolored	65	40
722	A105	15s multicolored	80	55
a.		Souvenir sheet of 4, #719-722	2.25	2.25

Souvenir Sheet

No.	Type	Description	Unused	Used
723	A105	15s multicolored	1.00	1.00

Centenary of first telephone call by Alexander Graham Bell, Mar. 10, 1876.

Collybia Fusipes — A106

Mushrooms: 7s, Lycoperdon perlatum. 9s, Boletus edulis. 9.50s, Lactarius deliciosus. 11.50s, Agaricus campestris.

1977, Feb. 6 Photo. *Perf. 13*

Size: 48x26mm

No.	Type	Description	Unused	Used
724	A106	5s multicolored	25	15
725	A106	7s multicolored	38	18
726	A106	9s multicolored	45	22
a.		Souvenir sheet of 2, #724, 726	1.00	1.00
727	A106	9.50s multicolored	55	30

Size: 48x31mm

No.	Type	Description	Unused	Used
728	A106	11.50s multicolored	65	40
		Nos. 724-728,C131-C133 (8)	4.33	2.38

Hexaplex Hoplites — A107

Sea Shells: 2s, Perrona lineata. 4s, Marginella pseudofaba. 5s, Tympanotonos radula. 7s, Marginella strigata. 8s, Harpa doris. 10s, Demoulia pinguis. 20s, Bursa scrobiculator. 25s, Marginella adansoni.

1977, Apr. 25 Photo. *Perf. 13*

Size: 50x25mm

No.	Type	Description	Unused	Used
729	A107	1s gold & multi	15	15
730	A107	2s gold & multi	15	15
731	A107	4s gold & multi	25	16
732	A107	5s gold & multi	35	20
733	A107	7s gold & multi	45	28
734	A107	8s gold & multi	55	32

Size: 50x30mm

No.	Type	Description	Unused	Used
735	A107	10s gold & multi	65	40
736	A107	20s gold & multi	1.40	80
737	A107	25s gold & multi	1.60	1.00
		Nos. 729-737 (9)	5.55	3.46

Farmers and Ox Plow A108

Designs: 5s, Pres. Touré addressing rally. 20s, Soldier driving farm tractor. 25s, Pres. Touré addressing UN General Assembly. 30s, 40s, Pres. Sekou Touré (vert.).

Perf. 13½x13, 13x13½

1977, May 14

No.	Type	Description	Unused	Used
738	A108	5s gold & multi	35	20
739	A108	10s gold & multi	65	40
740	A108	20s gold & multi	1.40	80
741	A108	25s gold & multi	1.60	1.00
a.		Souvenir sheet of 4, #738-741	4.25	3.50
742	A108	30s gold & dk brn	2.00	1.20
743	A108	40s gold & sl grn	2.50	1.60
a.		Souvenir sheet of 2, #742-743	5.00	4.00
		Nos. 738-743 (6)	8.50	5.20

Democratic Party of Guinea, 30th anniv.

Nile Monitor — A109

Reptiles and Snakes: 4s, Frogs. 5s, Lizard (uromastix). 6s, Sand skink. 6.50s, Agama. 7s, Black-lipped spitting cobra. 8.50s, Ball python. 20s, Toads.

1977, Oct. 10 Photo. *Perf. 13½*

Size: 46x20mm

No.	Type	Description	Unused	Used
744	A109	3s multi	20	15
745	A109	4s multi	25	16
746	A109	5s multi	35	20

Size: 46x30mm

No.	Type	Description	Unused	Used
747	A109	6s multi	40	22
748	A109	6.50s multi	42	25
749	A109	7s multi	45	28
750	A109	8.50s multi	55	35
751	A109	20s multi	1.40	80
		Nos. 744-751,C134-C136 (11)	7.27	4.41

Eland — A110

Endangered Animals: 2s, Chimpanzee. 2.50s, Pygmy elephant. 3s, Lion. 4s, Palm squirrel. 5s, Hippopotamus. Each animal shown male, female and young.

1977, Dec. 12 Photo. *Perf. 14x13½*

No.	Type	Description	Unused	Used
752	A110	1s Strip of 3	22	15
a.-c.		Single stamp	15	
753	A110	2s Strip of 3	42	22
a.-c.		Single stamp	15	
754	A110	2.50s Strip of 3	50	30
a.-c.		Single stamp	16	
755	A110	3s Strip of 3	60	38
a.-c.		Single stamp	20	
756	A110	4s Strip of 3	80	50
a.-c.		Single stamp	25	
757	A110	5s Strip of 3	1.05	60
a.-c.		Single stamp	35	
		Nos. 752-757,C137-C142 (12)	15.24	8.85

Lenin Speaking, 1917 A111

Designs: 2.50s, First Lenin debate, Moscow. 7.50s, Lenin and people. 8s, Lenin in first parade on Red Square.

1978, Feb. 27 Photo. *Perf. 14*

No.	Type	Description	Unused	Used
758	A111	2.50s gold & multi	16	15
759	A111	5s gold & multi	35	20
760	A111	7.50s gold & multi	50	30
761	A111	8s gold & multi	55	35
		Nos. 758-761,C143-C144 (6)	4.21	2.60

Russian October Revolution, 60th anniv.

Pres. Giscard d'Estaing at Microphones — A112

Pres. Valery Giscard d'Estaing of France and Pres. Sekou Toure of Guinea: 5s, 10s, In conference. 6.50s, Signing agreement. 7s, Attending official meeting. 8.50s, With their wives. 20s, Drinking a toast.

1979, Sept. 14 Photo. *Perf. 13*

No.	Type	Description	Unused	Used
762	A112	3s lt brn & brn	20	15
763	A112	5s green & brn	35	20
764	A112	6.50s red lil & brn	42	25
765	A112	7s ultra & brn	45	28
766	A112	8.50s dk red & brn	55	35
767	A112	10s vio & brown	65	40
768	A112	20s yel grn & brn	1.40	80
		Nos. 762-768,C145 (8)	5.62	3.43

Visit of Pres. Valery Giscard d'Estaing to Guinea.

Twenty Thousand Leagues Under the Sea — A113

Jules Verne Stories: 3s, Children of Capt. Grant. 5s, Mysterious Island. 7s, A Captain at Fifteen. 10s, The Borsac Mission.

1979, Nov. 8 Litho. *Perf. 12x12½*

No.	Type	Description	Unused	Used
769	A113	1s multicolored	15	15
770	A113	3s multicolored	20	15
771	A113	5s multicolored	35	20
772	A113	7s multicolored	45	28
773	A113	10s multicolored	65	40
		Nos. 769-773,C146-C147 (7)	4.80	2.98

Jules Verne (1828-1905), French science fiction writer.

"Aerial Steam Carriage," 1842 — A114

Aviation Retrospect: 5s, Wright's Flyer 1 1903. 6.50s, Caudron, 1934. 7s, Spirit of St. Louis, 1927. 8.50s, Bristol Beaufighter, 1940. 10s, Bleriot XI, 1909. No. 780, Concorde. No. 781, Boeing 727, 1963.

1979, Nov. 22 Photo. *Perf. 14*

No.	Type	Description	Unused	Used
774	A114	3s multi	22	15
775	A114	5s multi	40	20
776	A114	6.50s multi	50	30
777	A114	7s multi	55	32
778	A114	8.50s multi	65	38
779	A114	10s multi	80	40
780	A114	20s multi	1.60	80
781	A114	20s multi	1.60	80
		Nos. 774-781 (8)	6.32	3.35

Hafia Soccer Team — A115

Designs: 2s, Players and Sekou Touré cup (vert.). 5s, Pres. Touré presenting cup. 7s, Pres. Touré and player holding cup (vert.). 8s, Sekou Touré cup (vert.). 10s, Team captains and referees (vert.). 20s, The winning goal.

Perf. 12½x12, 12x12½

1979, Dec. 18 Litho.

No.	Type	Description	Unused	Used
782	A115	1s multicolored	15	15
783	A115	2s multicolored	16	15
784	A115	5s multicolored	40	20
785	A115	7s multicolored	55	28
786	A115	8s multicolored	65	35
787	A115	10s multicolored	80	40
788	A115	20s multicolored	1.60	65
		Nos. 782-788 (7)	4.31	2.18

Hafia Soccer Team, African triple champions, 1977.

Train, IYC Emblem A116

IYC Emblem and: 2s, Children dancing around tree (vert.). 4s, "1979" and leaves (vert.). 7s, Village. 10s, Boy climbing tree. 25s, Boys of different races, flowers, sun.

Perf. 13x13½, 13½x13

1980, Jan. 14

789	A116	2s multicolored	20	15
790	A116	4s multicolored	40	16
791	A116	5s multicolored	50	20
792	A116	7s multicolored	65	28
793	A116	10s multicolored	1.00	40
794	A116	25s multicolored	2.50	1.00
		Nos. 789-794 (6)	5.25	2.19

International Year of the Child (1979).

Butterflyfish — A117

1980, Apr. 1 ***Perf. 12½x12, 12x12½***

795	A117	1s shown	15	15
796	A117	2s Porgy	15	15
797	A117	3s Zeus conchifer, vert.	20	15
798	A117	4s Grouper	25	16
799	A117	5s Sea horse, vert.	35	20
800	A117	6s Hatchet fish	40	22
801	A117	7s Pisodonophis semicinctus	45	28
802	A117	8s Flying gurnard, vert.	55	35
803	A117	9s Squirrelfish	60	38
804	A117	10s Psettus sebae, vert.	65	40
805	A117	12s Abudefuf hoeffleri	80	50
806	A117	15s Triggerfish	1.00	60
		Nos. 795-806 (12)	5.55	3.54

Apollo 11 Take-Off — A118

1980, July 20 **Photo.** ***Perf. 14***

807	A118	1s shown	15	15
808	A118	2s Earth from moon	16	15
809	A118	4s Armstrong leaving module	35	16
810	A118	5s Armstrong on moon	42	20
811	A118	7s Collecting samples	60	28
812	A118	8s Re-entry	65	35
813	A118	12s Recovery	1.00	50
814	A118	20s Crew	1.60	80
		Nos. 807-814 (8)	4.93	2.59

Apollo 11 moon landing, 10th anniv. (1979).

Intl. Palestinian Solidarity Day — A119

1981, Nov. 21 **Photo.** ***Perf. 13½***

815	A119	8s multicolored	65	35
816	A119	11s multicolored	1.00	42

Soccer — A120

1982 **Litho.** ***Perf. 12½x12***

817	A120	1s shown	15	15
818	A120	2s Basketball	15	15
819	A120	3s Diving	20	15
820	A120	4s Gymnast	25	16
821	A120	5s Boxing	35	20
822	A120	6s Pole vault	40	25
823	A120	7s Running	45	30
824	A120	8s Long jump	55	35
		Nos. 817-824,C148-C152 (13)	7.45	4.81

22nd Summer Olympic Games, Moscow, July 19-Aug. 3, 1980.

5th Anniv. of West African Economic Community — A121

1982, May 14 ***Perf. 13½***

825	A121	6s multicolored	50	25
826	A121	7s multicolored	65	35
827	A121	9s multicolored	80	50

Kemal Ataturk Birth Centenary A122

1982, July 19 **Photo.** ***Perf. 13½***

828	A122	7s multi	45	28
829	A122	10s multi, diff.	65	40
830	A122	25s multi, horiz.	1.60	1.00

See No. C153.

1982 World Cup — A123

Designs: Various soccer players.

1982, Aug. 23

831	A123	6s multicolored	40	25
832	A123	8s multicolored	55	35
833	A123	9s multicolored	60	38
834	A123	10s multicolored	65	40
		Nos. 831-834,C154-C156 (7)	5.85	3.58

Soccer Type of 1982 Nos. 831-834 Overprinted in Green: "CHAMPION ITALIE-11 JUILLET 1982"

1982, Aug. 23 **Photo.** ***Perf. 13½***

835	A123	6s multicolored	40	25
836	A123	8s multicolored	55	35
837	A123	9s multicolored	60	38
838	A123	10s multicolored	65	40
		Nos. 835-838,C157-C159 (7)	5.85	3.58

Italy's victory in 1982 World Cup.

23rd Olympic Games, Los Angeles, July 28-Aug. 12, 1984 — A124

1983, July 1 **Litho.** ***Perf. 13½***

839	A124	5s Wrestling	35	20
840	A124	7s Weightlifting	45	28
841	A124	10s Gymnastics	65	40
842	A124	15s Discus	1.00	60
843	A124	20s Kayak	1.40	80
844	A124	25s Equestrian	1.60	1.00
		Nos. 839-844 (6)	5.45	3.28

Litho. & Embossed

Size: 39x58mm

844A	A124	100s Running		

Souvenir Sheets

Litho.

845	A124	30s Running	2.00	1.40

Litho. & Embossed

845A	A124	100s Show jumping		

Nos. 844A, 845A are airmail. No. 845A contains one 58x39mm stamp.

First Manned Balloon Flight, 200th Anniv. — A125

Designs: 5s, Marquis D'Arlandes, Pilatre de Rozier. 7s, Marie Antoinette Balloon, Rozier. 10s, Dirigible, Dupuy De Lome (horiz.). 15s, Dirigible, Major A. Perseval (horiz.).

1983, Aug. 1 **Litho.** ***Perf. 13½***

846	A125	5s multicolored	35	20
847	A125	7s multicolored	45	28
848	A125	10s multicolored	65	50
849	A125	15s multicolored	1.00	60
		Nos. 846-849,C160-C161 (6)	5.45	3.38

Intl. Year of the Handicapped — A126

1983, Aug. 24 **Litho.**

850	A126	10s multicolored	80	40
851	A126	20s multicolored	1.60	80

Dr. Robert Koch (1843-1910), TB Bacillus A127

Various phases of research.

1983, Aug. 24 **Litho.**

852	A127	6s multicolored	40	25
853	A127	10s multicolored	65	40
854	A127	11s multicolored	70	42
855	A127	12s multicolored	80	45
856	A127	15s multicolored	1.10	60
857	A127	20s multicolored	1.40	80
858	A127	25s multicolored	1.60	1.00
		Nos. 852-858 (7)	6.65	3.92

Mosque, Conakry A128

1983, Oct. 2 **Litho.** ***Perf. 13½***

859	A128	1s multicolored	15	15
860	A128	2s multicolored	15	15
861	A128	5s multicolored	30	15
862	A128	10s multicolored	60	30
		Set value		56

Souvenir Sheet

863	A128	25s multicolored	1.50	70

Natl. independence, 25th anniv. No. 863 airmail.

Mano River Union, 10th Anniv. A129

Designs: 2s, Development program graduates. 7s, Emblem. 8s, Pres. Toure of Guinea, Stevens of Sierra Leone, Doe of Liberia. 10s, 20s, Signing treaty.

1983, Oct. 3

864	A129	2s multicolored	15	15
865	A129	7s multicolored	40	20
866	A129	8s multicolored	50	22
867	A129	10s multicolored	60	30

Souvenir Sheet

868	A129	20s multicolored	1.10	55

No. 868 airmail.

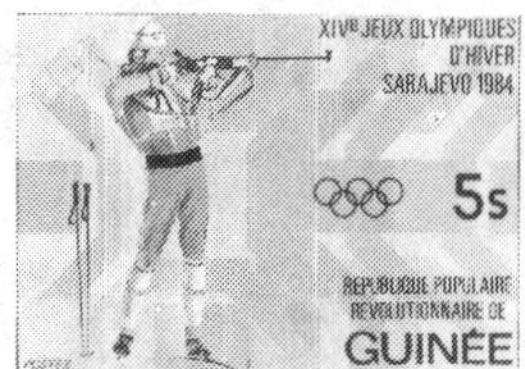

14th Winter Olympics, Sarajevo, Feb. 8-19, 1984 — A130

1983, Dec. 5 **Litho.** ***Perf. 13½***

869	A130	5s Biathlon	35	20
870	A130	7s Bobsledding	45	30
871	A130	10s Downhill skiing	65	40
872	A130	15s Speed skating	1.00	60

873 A130 20s Ski jumping 1.40 80
874 A130 25s Figure skating 1.60 1.00
Nos. 869-874 (6) 5.45 3.30

Litho. & Embossed

Size: 58x39mm

874A A130 100s Downhill skiing

Souvenir Sheets

Litho.

875 A130 30s Hockey 2.00 1.40

Litho. & Embossed

875A A130 100s 4-man bobsled

Nos. 873-875A airmail. No. 875A contains one 58x39mm stamp.

Self-portrait and Virgin with Blue Diadem, by Raphael A131

Designs: 7s, Self-portrait and Holy Family, by Rubens. 10s, Self-portrait and Portrait of Saskia, by Rembrandt. 15s, Portrait of Goethe and scene from Young Werther. 20s, Scouting Year. 25s, Paul Harris, Rotary emblem. 30s, J.F. Kennedy, Apollo XI. 100s, Paul Harris, 3 other men in Rotary meeting.

1984, Jan 2 Litho. *Perf. 13*

876 A131 5s multicolored 35 20
877 A131 7s multicolored 45 30
878 A131 10s multicolored 65 40
879 A131 15s multicolored 1.00 60
880 A131 20s multicolored 1.40 80
881 A131 25s multicolored 1.60 1.20
Nos. 876-881 (6) 5.45 3.50

Souvenir Sheets

882 A131 30s multicolored 2.00 1.40

Litho. & Embossed

Perf. 13½

882A A131 100s gold & multi

Nos. 880-882A airmail. No. 882A contains one 51x42mm stamp.

For overprints see Nos. C164-C165.

Transportation — A132

1984, May 7 Litho. *Perf. 13½*

883 A132 5s Congo River steamer 25 16
884 A132 7s Graf Zeppelin LZ 127 38 20
885 A132 10s Daimler automobile, 1886 55 32
886 A132 15s E. African RR Beyer-Garrat 70 45
887 A132 20s Latecoere 28, 1929 1.10 60
888 A132 25s Sial Marchetti S.M. 73, 1934 1.40 80
Nos. 883-888 (6) 4.38 2.53

Souvenir Sheet

889 A132 30s Series B locomotive 1.60 90

Nos. 887-889 airmail.

Anniversaries and Events — A133

Famous men: 5s, Abraham Lincoln, log cabin, the White House. 7s, Jean-Henri Dunant, Red Cross at Battle of Solferino. 10s, Gottlieb Daimler, 1892 Motor Carriage. 15s, Louis Bleriot, monoplane. 20s, Paul Harris, Rotary Intl. 25s, Auguste Piccard, bathyscaphe Trieste. 30s, Anatoly Karpov, world chess champion, chessboard and knight. 100s, Paul Harris, Rotary Intl. emblem.

1984, Aug. 20 Litho. *Perf. 13½*

890 A133 5s multicolored 30 15
891 A133 7s multicolored 40 20
892 A133 10s multicolored 60 30
893 A133 15s multicolored 90 45
894 A133 20s multicolored 1.10 55
895 A133 25s multicolored 1.50 70
Nos. 890-895 (6) 4.80 2.35

Litho. & Embossed

Size: 60x30mm

895A A133 100s gold & multi
b. Miniature sheet of 1, 91x70mm
c. Miniature sheet of 1, 121x70mm

Souvenir Sheet

896 A133 30s multicolored 1.90 90

Nos. 894-896 are airmail.
For overprints see Nos. C163, C166.

The Holy Family, by Durer — A134

Painting details: 5s, The Mystic Marriage of St. Catherine and St. Sebastian, by Correggio. 10s, The Veiled Woman, by Raphael. 15s, Portrait of a Young Man, by Durer. 20s, Portrait of Soutine, by Modigliani. 25s, Esterhazy Madonna, by Raphael. 30s, Impannata Madonna, by Raphael.

1984, Aug. 23

897 A134 5s multicolored 25 15
898 A134 7s multicolored 38 22
899 A134 10s multicolored 55 32
900 A134 15s multicolored 70 45
901 A134 20s multicolored 1.10 62
902 A134 25s multicolored 1.40 80
Nos. 897-902 (6) 4.38 2.56

Souvenir Sheet

903 A134 30s multicolored 1.60 90

Nos. 901-903 airmail.

1984 Winter Olympics, Sarajevo A135

Gold medalists: 5s, East German two-man bobsled. 7s, Thomas Wassberg, Sweden, 50-kilometer cross-country. 10s, Gaetan Boucher, Canada, 1000 and 1500-meter speed skating. 15s, Katarina Witt, DDR, singles figure skating. 20s, Bill Johnson, US, men's downhill. 25s, Soviet Union, ice hockey. 30s, Jens Weissflog, DDR, 70-meter ski jump. No. 909A, Phil Mahre, US, slalom skiing. No. 910A, Jayne Torvill & Christopher Dean, Great Britain, ice dancing.

1985, Sept. 23 Litho. *Perf. 13½*

904 A135 5s multicolored 30 15
905 A135 7s multicolored 40 20
906 A135 10s multicolored 60 30
907 A135 15s multicolored 90 45
908 A135 20s multicolored 1.10 55
909 A135 25s multicolored 1.50 70
Nos. 904-909 (6) 4.80 2.35

Litho. & Embossed

Size: 51x36mm

909A A135 100s gold & multi

Souvenir Sheets

Litho.

910 A135 30s multicolored 1.90 90

Litho. & Embossed

910A A135 100s gold & multi

Nos. 908A-910A are airmail. No. 910A contains one 51x36mm stamp.

1984 Los Angeles Summer Olympics — A136

Medalists and various satellites: 5s, T. Ruiz and C. Costie, US, synchronized swimming. 7s, West Germany, team dressage. 10s, US, yachting, flying Dutchman class. 15s, Mark Todd, New Zealand, individual 3-day equestrian event. 20s, Daley Thompson, G.B., decathlon. 25s, US, team jumping. 30s, Carl Lewis, US, long jump, 100 and 200-meter run, 4x100 relay.

1985, Mar. 18 Litho. *Perf. 13½*

911 A136 5s multicolored 20 15
912 A136 7s multicolored 28 16
913 A136 10s multicolored 40 22
914 A136 15s multicolored 60 38
915 A136 20s multicolored 70 45
916 A136 25s multicolored 1.00 60
Nos. 911-917 (7) 4.58 2.76

Souvenir Sheet

917 A136 30s multicolored 1.40 80

Nos. 915-917 airmail.

Fungi — A137

1985, Mar. 21 Litho. *Perf. 13½*

918 A137 5s Rhodophyllus callidermus 25 15
919 A137 7s Agaricus niger 38 18
920 A137 10s Thermitomyces globulus 55 25
921 A137 15s Amanita robusta 80 40
922 A137 20s Lepiota subradicans 1.10 55
923 A137 25s Cantharellus rhodophyllus 1.40 65
Nos. 918-923 (6) 4.48 2.18

Souvenir Sheet

924 A137 30s Phlebopus sylvaticus 1.60 80

Nos. 922-924 airmail.
For surcharges see Nos. 962-968.

Scientist Herman J. Oberth, and Two-Stage Rocket — A138

Space achievements: 10s, Lunik 1, USSR, 1959. 15s, Lunik 2 on the Moon, 1959. 20s, Lunik 3 photographing the Moon, 1959. 30s, US astronauts Armstrong, Aldrin, Collins and Apollo 11, 1969. 35s, Sally Ride, 1st American woman in space, 1983. 50s, Recovering a Palapa B satellite, 1984. No. 930A, Guion S. Bluford, 1st black American astronaut. No. 931A, Viking probe on Mars.

1985, May 26 Litho. *Perf. 13½*

925 A138 7s multicolored 28 16
926 A138 10s multicolored 40 22
927 A138 15s multicolored 60 38
928 A138 20s multicolored 70 45
929 A138 30s multicolored 1.40 80
930 A138 35s multicolored 1.50 85
Nos. 925-930 (6) 4.88 2.86

Litho. & Embossed

Size: 51x36mm

930A A138 200s gold & multi

Souvenir Sheet

Litho.

931 A138 50s multicolored 2.00 1.10

Litho. & Embossed

931A A138 200s gold & multi

Nos. 929-931A are airmail. No. 931A contains one 51x36mm stamp.

Maimonides (1135-1204), Jewish Scholar, Cordoba Jewish Quarter — A139

Anniversaries and events: 10s, Christopher Columbus departing from Palos for New World, 1492. 15s, Frederic Auguste Bartholdi (1834-1904), sculptor, architect, and Statue of Liberty, cent. 20s, Queen Mother, 85th birthday. 30s, Ulf Merbold, German physicist, US space shuttle Columbia. 35s, Wedding of Prince Charles and Lady Diana, 1981. 50s, Charles, Diana, Princes Henry and William. 100s, Queen Mother Elizabeth's 85th birthday.

1985, Sept. 23

932 A139 7s multicolored 38 18
933 A139 10s multicolored 55 25
934 A139 15s multicolored 80 40
935 A139 20s multicolored 1.10 55
936 A139 30s multicolored 1.60 80
937 A139 35s multicolored 1.90 90
Nos. 932-937 (6) 6.33 3.08

Litho. & Embossed

Size: 42x51mm

937A A139 100s gold & multi

Souvenir Sheet

Litho.

938 A139 50s multicolored 2.50 1.40

Nos. 936-938 airmail. No. 938 contains one 51x36mm stamp.

Audubon Birth Bicent. — A140

Illustrations of bird species from Birds of America.

1985, Sept. 23 Litho. *Perf. 13½*

939 A140 7s Coccizus erythrophtalmus 40 20
940 A140 10s Conuropsis carolinensis 60 30
941 A140 15s Anhinga anhinga 90 45
942 A140 20s Buteo lineatus 1.10 60
943 A140 30s Otus asio 1.90 90
944 A140 35s Toxostoma rufum 2.00 1.10
Nos. 939-944 (6) 6.90 3.55

Souvenir Sheet

945 A140 50s Zenaidura macroura 3.00 2.25

Nos. 941, 944 vert. Nos. 943-945 are airmail. No. 945 contains one 51x36mm stamp.

1986 World Cup Soccer Championships, Mexico — A141

Famous soccer players: 7s, Bebeto, Brazil. 10s, Rinal Dassaev, USSR. 15s, Phil Neal, Great Britain. 20s, Jean Tigana, France. 30s, Fernando Chalana, Portugal. 35s, Michel Platini, France. 50s, Karl Heinz Rummenigge, West Germany.

1985, Oct. 26

946 A141 7s multicolored 38 18
947 A141 10s multicolored 55 25
948 A141 15s multicolored 80 40
949 A141 20s multicolored 1.10 55
950 A141 30s multicolored 1.60 80
951 A141 35s multicolored 1.90 90
Nos. 946-951 (6) 6.33 3.08

Souvenir Sheet

952 A141 50s multicolored 2.50 1.40

Nos. 950-952 airmail.

Cats and Dogs A142

1985, Oct. 26

953 A142 7s Blue-point Siamese 38 18
954 A142 10s Cocker spaniel 55 25
955 A142 15s Poodles 80 40
956 A142 20s Blue Persian 1.10 55
957 A142 25s European red-and-white tabby 1.40 65
958 A142 30s German shepherd 1.60 80
959 A142 35s Abyssinians 1.90 90
960 A142 40s Boxer 2.25 1.10
Nos. 953-960 (8) 9.98 4.83

Souvenir Sheet

961 A142 50s Pyrenean mountain dog, chartreux cat 2.50 1.40

Nos. 958-961 airmail. No. 961 contains one 51x30mm stamp.

Nos. 918-924 Surcharged with 4 Bars

1985, Nov. 15

962 A137 1s on 5s multi 15 15
963 A137 2s on 7s multi 15 15
964 A137 8s on 10s multi 42 22
965 A137 30s on 15s multi 1.60 80
966 A137 35s on 20s multi 1.90 90
967 A137 40s on 25s multi 2.25 1.10
Nos. 962-967 (6) 6.47 3.32

Souvenir Sheet

968 A137 50s on 30s multi 2.50 1.40

Nos. 966-968 airmail.

Locomotives — A143

Designs: 7s, 8F Class steam, Great Britain. 15s, Bobo 5500 Series III electric, German Fed. Railways. 25s, Pacific A Mazout No. 270, African Railways. 35s, Serie 420 electric train set, Suburban S-Bahn, Germany. 50s, ICE high-speed train, German Fed. Railways.

1985, Dec. 18 Litho. *Perf. 13½*

969 A143 7s multicolored 38 20
970 A143 15s multicolored 80 40
971 A143 25s multicolored 1.40 65
972 A143 35s multicolored 1.90 90

Souvenir Sheet

973 A143 50s multicolored 2.50 1.40

Nos. 972-973 airmail.
For surcharges see Nos. 991-995.

Columbus Discovering America, 1492 — A144

1985, Dec. 18

974 A144 10s Pinta 55 25
975 A144 20s Santa Maria 1.10 55
976 A144 30s Nina 1.60 80
977 A144 40s Santa Maria, sighting land 2.25 1.10

Souvenir Sheet

978 A144 50s Columbus and Nina 2.50 1.40

Nos. 976-979 airmail.

Intl. Youth Year — A145

1986, Jan. 21

979 A145 10s Chopin 80 40
980 A145 20s Botticelli 1.60 80
981 A145 25s Picasso 2.00 1.00
982 A145 35s Rossini 2.75 1.40

Souvenir Sheet

983 A145 50s Michelangelo 4.00 2.00

Nos. 981-983 airmail.
For surcharges see Nos. 996-1000.

Halley's Comet — A146

Sightings: 5fr, Bayeux Tapestry (detail), c. 1092, France. 30fr, Arab, astrolabe, 1400. 40fr, Montezuma II, Aztec deity. 50fr, Edmond Halley, trajectory diagram. 300fr, Halley, Sir Isaac Newton. 500fr, Giotto, Soviet and NASA space probes, comet. 600fr, Hally commemorative medal, Giotto probe.

1986, July 1 Litho. *Perf. 13½*

5fr-500fr Surcharged with New Currency in Silver or Black

984 A146 5fr multi 15 15
985 A146 30fr multi 16 15
986 A146 40fr multi 22 15
987 A146 50fr multi 28 15
988 A146 300fr multi 1.65 82
989 A146 500fr multi 2.75 1.40
Nos. 984-989 (6) 5.21 2.82

Souvenir Sheet

990 A146 600fr multi 3.25 1.65

Nos. 988-990 are airmail. Nos. 984-989 not issued without surcharge.

Nos. 969-973 Surcharged in Black or Black on Silver

1986, Aug. 25 Litho. *Perf. 13½*

991 A143 2fr on 7s multi (B on S) 15 15
992 A143 25fr on 15s multi 15 15
993 A143 50fr on 25s multi 28 15
994 A143 90fr on 35s multi 50 25
Set value 50

Souvenir Sheet

995 A143 500fr on 50s multi 2.75 1.40

Nos. 979-983 Surcharged

1986, Aug. 25

996 A145 5fr on 10s multi 15 15
997 A145 35fr on 20s multi 20 15
998 A145 50fr on 25s multi 28 15
999 A145 90fr on 35s multi 50 25
Set value 52

Souvenir Sheet

1000 A145 500fr on 50s multi 2.75 1.40

Locomotives — A147

Designs: 20fr, Dietrich 640 CV. 100fr, T.13 7906. 300fr, Vapeur 01220. 400fr, ABH Type 3 5020. 600fr, Renault ABH 3 (300 CV).

1986, Nov. 1

1001 A147 20fr multi 15 15
1002 A147 100fr multi 55 28
1003 A147 300fr multi 1.65 82
1004 A147 400fr multi 2.25 1.10

Souvenir Sheet

1005 A147 600fr multi 3.25 1.65

Nos. 1004-1005 are airmail.

Discovery of America, 500th Anniv. (in 1992) — A148

Designs: 40fr, Columbus at Ft. Navidad construction, Santa Maria, 1492. 70fr, Landing at Hispaniola, 2nd voyage, 1494. 200fr, Aboard ship, 3rd voyage, 1498. 500fr, Trading with Indians. 600fr, At court of Ferdinand and Isabella, 1493.

1986, Nov. 1

1006 A148 40fr multi 22 15
1007 A148 70fr multi 40 20
1008 A148 200fr multi 1.10 55
1009 A148 500fr multi 2.75 1.40

Souvenir Sheet

1010 A148 600fr multi 3.25 1.65

Nos. 1009-1010 are airmail.

Anniversaries & Events — A149

Designs: 30fr, Prince Charles and Diana, 5th wedding anniv. 40fr, Alain Prost, San Marino, 1985 Formula 1 Grand Prix world champion. 100fr, Wedding of Prince Andrew and Sarah Ferguson. 300fr, Elvis Presley (1935-1977). 500fr, Michael Jackson (b. 1958). 600fr, M. Dassault (1892-1986), aerospace engineer.

1986, Nov. 12

1011 A149 30fr multi 16 15
1012 A149 40fr multi 22 15
1013 A149 100fr multi 55 28
1014 A149 300fr multi 1.65 82
1015 A149 500fr multi 2.75 1.40
Nos. 1011-1015 (5) 5.33 2.80

Souvenir Sheet

1016 A149 600fr multi 3.30 1.65

Nos. 1015-1016 are airmail.

1986 World Cup Soccer Championships — A150

Various players and final scores.

1986, Nov. 12

1017 A150 100fr Pfaff 55 28
1018 A150 300fr Platini 1.65 82
1019 A150 400fr Matthaus 2.20 1.10
1020 A150 500fr D. Maradona 2.75 1.40

Souvenir Sheet

1021 A150 600fr Maradona, trophy 3.30 1.65

Nos. 1020-1021 are airmail. No. 1021 contains one 51x42mm stamp.

1988 Summer Olympics, Seoul — A151

Pierre de Coubertin (1863-1937), Seoul Stadium, Telecommunications Satellite — A151A

1987, Jan. 17 Litho. *Perf. 13½*

1022 A151 20fr Judo 15 15
1023 A151 30fr High jump 15 15
1024 A151 40fr Team handball 16 15
1025 A151 100fr Women's gymnastics 40 20
1026 A151 300fr Javelin 1.20 60
1027 A151 500fr Equestrian 2.00 1.00
Nos. 1022-1027 (6) 4.06 2.25

Souvenir Sheet

1028 A151A 600fr multi 2.25 1.20

Dated 1986. Nos. 1026-1028 are airmail.

1988 Winter Olympics, Calgary — A152

1987, Mar. 23 Litho. *Perf. 13½*

1029 A152 50fr on 40fr Biathlon 28 15
1030 A152 100fr Cross-country skiing 55 28
1031 A152 400fr Ski jumping 2.25 2.25

1032	A152	500fr	Two-man bob-sled	2.75	1.40

Souvenir Sheet

1033	A152	600fr	Woman skater, satellite	3.50	1.75

No. 1029 not issued without overprint. Nos. 1031-1033 are airmail.

1988 Winter Olympics, Calgary A153

Telecommunications satellite, athletes and emblem.

1987, May 1

1034	A153	25fr	Women's slalom	15	15
1035	A153	50fr	Hockey	28	15
1036	A153	100fr	Men's figure skating	55	28
1037	A153	150fr	Men's downhill skiing	85	42
1038	A153	300fr	Speed skating	1.75	90
1039	A153	500fr	Four-man bob-sled	2.75	1.40
			Nos. 1034-1039 (6)	6.33	3.30

Souvenir Sheet

1040	A153	600fr	Ski jumping	3.50	1.75

Nos. 1038-1040 are airmail.

Famous Men — A154

Intl. Cardiology Congresses in Chicago, Washington and New York — A155

Designs: 50fr, Lafayette, military leader during American and French revolutions. 100fr, Ettore Bugatti (1881-1947), Italian automobile manufacturer. 200fr, Garri Kasparov, Russian chess champion. 300fr, George Washington. 400fr, Boris Becker, 1987 Wimbledon tennis champion. 500fr, Sir Winston Churchill.

1987, Nov. 1 Litho. *Perf. 13½*

1041	A154	50fr	multi	35	18
1042	A154	100fr	multi	70	35
1043	A154	200fr	multi	1.40	70
1044	A154	300fr	multi	2.05	1.00
1045	A154	400fr	multi	2.75	1.40
1046	A154	500fr	multi	3.50	1.75
			Nos. 1041-1046 (6)	10.75	5.38

Souvenir Sheet

1047	A155	1500fr	multi	10.25	5.00

Nos. 1045-1047 are airmail. Stamp in No. 1047 divided into three sections by simulated perforations.

Cave Bear — A156

Prehistoric Animals — A157

1987, Nov. 1

1048	A156	50fr	Dimetrodon	35	18
1049	A156	100fr	Iguanodon	70	35
1050	A156	200fr	Tylosaurus	1.40	70
1051	A156	300fr	shown	2.05	1.00
1052	A156	400fr	Saber-tooth tiger	2.75	1.40
1053	A156	500fr	Stegosaurus	3.50	1.75
			Nos. 1048-1053 (6)	10.75	5.38

Souvenir Sheet

1054	A157	600fr	Triceratops	4.25	2.10

Nos. 1052-1054 are airmail.

1988 Summer Olympics, Seoul — A158

Male and female tennis players in action.

1987, Nov. 28

1055	A158	50fr	multi	35	18
1056	A158	100fr	multi, diff.	72	35
1057	A158	150fr	multi, diff.	1.10	55
1058	A158	200fr	multi, diff.	1.45	72
1059	A158	300fr	multi, diff.	2.15	1.10
1060	A158	500fr	multi, diff.	3.60	1.80
			Nos. 1055-1060 (6)	9.37	4.70

Souvenir Sheet

1061	A158	600fr	multi	4.50	2.25

Reintroduction of tennis as an Olympic event. Nos. 1059-1061 are airmail.

1992 Summer Olympics, Barcelona A159

Athletes participating in events, Barcelona highlights: 50fr, Discus, courtyard of St. Croix and St. Paul Hospital. 100fr, High jump, Pablo Casals playing cello. 150fr, Long jump, Labyrinth of Horta. 170fr, Javelin, lizard from Guell Park. 400fr, Gymnastics, Mercy Church. 500fr, Tennis, Picasso Museum. 600fr, Running, tapestry by Miro.

1987, Dec. 28 Litho. *Perf. 13½*

1062	A159	50fr	multi	35	18
1063	A159	100fr	multi	70	35
1064	A159	150fr	multi	1.05	55
1065	A159	170fr	multi	1.20	60
1066	A159	400fr	multi	2.75	1.40
1067	A159	500fr	multi	3.50	1.75
			Nos. 1062-1067 (6)	9.55	4.83

Souvenir Sheet

1068	A159	600fr	multi	4.25	2.15

Nos. 1066-1068 are airmail.

Wildlife A160

1987, Dec. 28

1069	A160	50fr	African wild dog pups	35	18
1070	A160	70fr	Adult	42	20
1071	A160	100fr	Adults circling gazelle	70	35
1072	A160	170fr	Chasing gazelle	1.20	60
1073	A160	400fr	Crown cranes	2.75	1.40
1074	A160	500fr	Derby elands	3.50	1.75
			Nos. 1069-1074 (6)	8.92	4.48

Souvenir Sheet

1075	A160	600fr	Vervet monkeys	4.25	2.15

Nos. 1069-1072 picture World Wildlife Fund emblem; Nos. 1073, 1075, picture Scouting trefoil and No. 1074 pictures Rotary Intl. emblem. Nos. 1073-1075 are airmail.

Reconciliation Summit Conference, July 11-12, 1986 — A161

Heads of state and natl. flags: Dr. Samuel Kanyon Doe of Liberia, Colonel Lansana Conte of Guinea and Maj.-Gen. Joseph Saidu Momoh of Sierra Leone.

1987 Litho. *Perf. 13½*

1076	A161	40fr	multi	35	18
1077	A161	50fr	multi	42	20
1078	A161	75fr	multi	65	32
1079	A161	100fr	multi	85	42
1080	A161	150fr	multi	1.25	62
			Nos. 1076-1080 (5)	3.52	1.74

Space Exploration — A162

1988, Apr. 16

1081	A162	50fr	Galaxie-Grasp	35	16
1082	A162	150fr	Energia-Mir	1.05	52
1083	A162	200fr	NASA Space Station	1.40	70
1084	A162	300fr	Ariane 5-E.S.A.	2.10	1.05
1085	A162	400fr	Mars-Rover	2.80	1.40
1086	A162	450fr	Venus-Vega	3.25	1.65
			Nos. 1081-1086 (6)	10.95	5.48

Souvenir Sheet

1087	A162	500fr	Mars-Phobos	3.50	1.75

Nos. 1085-1087 are airmail.

Boy Scouts Watching Birds and Butterflies A163

1988, July 5 Litho. *Perf. 13½*

1088	A163	50fr	Spermophaga ruficapilla	32	16
1089	A163	100fr	Medon nymphalidae	65	32
1090	A163	150fr	Euplecte orix	98	50
1091	A163	300fr	Nectarinia pulchella	1.95	1.00
1092	A163	400fr	Sophia nymphalidae	2.60	1.30
1093	A163	450fr	Rumia nymphalidae	2.90	1.45
			Nos. 1088-1093 (6)	9.40	4.73

Souvenir Sheet

1094	A163	750fr	Opis nymphalidae, Psittacula krameri	4.85	2.45

Nos. 1092-1094 are airmail. No. 1094 contains one 35x50mm stamp.

Famous People — A164

Designs: 200fr, Queen Elizabeth II, Prince Philip and crown jewels. 250fr, Fritz von Opel (1899-1971), German automotive industrialist, and 1928 RAK 2 Opel. 300fr, Wolfgang Amadeus Mozart (1756-1791), composer, and Masonic emblem. 400fr, Steffi Graf, tennis champion. 450fr, Buzz Aldrin and Masonic emblem. 500fr, Paul Harris (1868-1947), Rotary Intl. founder, and organization emblem. 750fr, Thomas Jefferson (1743-1826), horiz.

1988, July 5

1095	A164	200fr	multi	1.30	65
1096	A164	250fr	multi	1.60	80
1097	A164	300fr	multi	1.95	1.00
1098	A164	400fr	multi	2.60	1.30
1099	A164	450fr	multi	2.90	1.45
1100	A164	500fr	multi	3.25	1.65
			Nos. 1095-1100 (6)	13.60	6.85

Souvenir Sheet

1101	A164	750fr	multi	4.85	2.45

40th wedding anniv. of Queen Elizabeth II and Prince Philip (200fr).

Nos. 1099-1101 are airmail. No. 1101 contains one 42x36mm stamp.

1988 Winter Olympics Gold Medalists — A165

Designs: 50fr, Vreni Schneider, Switzerland, women's giant slalom and slalom. 100fr, Frank-Peter Roetsch, East Germany, 10 and 20-kilometer biathlon. 150fr, Matti Nykaenen, Finland, 70 and 90-meter ski jumping. 250fr, Marina Kiehl, West Germany, women's downhill. 400fr, Frank Piccard, France, super giant slalom. 450fr, Katarina Witt, East Germany, women's figure skating. 750fr, Pirmin Zurbriggen, Switzerland, men's downhill. Nos. 1102-1107 vert.

1988, Oct. 2 Litho. *Perf. 13½*

1102 A165 50fr multi 32 16
1103 A165 100fr multi 65 32
1104 A165 150fr multi 98 50
1105 A165 250fr multi 1.60 80
1106 A165 400fr multi 2.60 1.30
1107 A165 450fr multi 2.90 1.45
Nos. 1102-1107 (6) 9.05 4.53

Souvenir Sheet

1108 A165 750fr multi 4.85 2.45

Nos. 1103, 1107-1108 are airmail.

African Postal Union, 25th Anniv. A165a

1988 Litho. *Perf. 13½*

1108A A165a 50fr multicolored 35 18
1108B A165a 75fr multicolored 55 28
1108C A165a 100fr multicolored 70 35
1108D A165a 150fr multicolored 1.10 55

World Health Day — A165b

1988 Litho. *Perf. 13½*

1108E A165b 50fr Medical research 40 20
1108F A165b 150fr Immunization 1.15 58
1108G A165b 500fr Dentistry 3.85 1.95

1992 Summer Olympics, Barcelona — A166

1989, May 3 Litho. *Perf. 13½*

1109 A166 50fr Diving 32 16
1110 A166 100fr Running, vert. 65 32
1111 A166 150fr Shooting 98 50
1112 A166 250fr Tennis, vert. 1.60 80
1113 A166 400fr Soccer 2.60 1.30
1114 A166 500fr Equestrian, vert. 3.25 1.60
Nos. 1109-1114 (6) 9.40 4.68

Souvenir Sheet

1115 A166 750fr Yachting, vert. 4.85 2.45

Nos. 1113-1115 are airmail.

French Revolution, Bicent. — A167

Personalities of and scenes from the revolution: 250fr, Jean-Sylvain Bailly (1736-1793) leading proceedings in Tennis Court, June 20, 1789. 300fr, Count Mirabeau (1749-1791) at royal session, June 23, 1789. 400fr, Lafayette (1757-1834), federation anniversary celebration, July 18, 1790. 450fr, Jerome Petion de Villeneuve (1756-1794), king's arrest at Varennes-en-Argonne, June 21, 1791. 750fr, Camille Desmoulins (1760-1794), destruction of the Bastille, July 1789.

1989, July 7 Litho. *Perf. 13½*

1116 A167 250fr multi 1.50 75
1117 A167 300fr multi 1.75 88
1118 A167 400fr multi 2.35 1.20
1119 A167 450fr multi 2.65 1.35

Souvenir Sheet

1120 A167 750fr multi 4.50 2.25

Nos. 1119-1120 airmail.

Planting A168

1989 Litho. *Perf. 13½*

1121 A168 25fr shown 18 15
1122 A168 50fr Irrigation 35 18
1123 A168 75fr Milking 52 25
1124 A168 100fr Fishing 70 35
1125 A168 150fr Farmers in corn field 1.05 52
1126 A168 300fr Public well 2.10 1.05
Nos. 1121-1126 (6) 4.90 2.50

Natl. Campaign for Self-sufficiency in Food Production and 10th anniv. of the Intl. Fund for Agricultural Development (in 1988). Dated 1988.

African Development Bank, 25th Anniv. — A169

1989, Nov. 4 Litho. *Perf. 13½*

1127 A169 300fr multicolored 2.15 1.10

Mano River Union, 15th Anniv. A170

Design: 300fr, Map of Guinea, Sierra Leone and Liberia, leaders' portraits.

1989, Nov. 4

1128 A170 150fr multicolored 1.10 55
1129 A170 300fr multicolored 2.15 1.10

World Cup Soccer, Italy — A171

Various soccer plays and: 200fr, Spire of San Domenico, Naples. 250fr, Piazza San Carlo, Turin. 300fr, Church of San Cataldo. 450fr, Church of San Francesco, Utine. 750fr, Statue of Dante, Florence and World Cup Soccer Trophy.

1990, Aug. 3 Litho. *Perf. 13½*

1130 A171 200fr multicolored 1.50 75
1131 A171 250fr multicolored 1.90 95
1132 A171 300fr multicolored 2.25 1.15
1133 A171 450fr multicolored 3.40 1.70

Souvenir Sheet

1134 A171 750fr multicolored 5.75 2.85

No. 1133-1134 airmail.

Concorde, TGV Atlantic — A172

1990, Aug. 3

1135 A172 400fr multicolored 3.00 1.50

No. 1135 exists in a souvenir sheet of 1.

Pope John Paul II, Pres. Gorbachev — A173

1990, Aug. 3

1136 A173 300fr multicolored 2.30 1.15

Summit Meeting, Dec. 2, 1989. No. 1136 exists in a souvenir sheet of 1.

1992 Winter Olympics, Albertville A174

1990, Aug. 3

1137 A174 150fr Downhill skiing 1.15 58
1138 A174 250fr Cross country skiing 1.90 1.00
1139 A174 400fr Two-man bobsled 3.00 1.50
1140 A174 500fr Speedskating 3.75 1.90

Souvenir Sheet

1141 A174 750fr Slalom skiing 5.65 2.85

Nos. 1140-1141 airmail. Nos. 1137-1140 exist in souvenir sheets of 1.

Pres. Bush, Pres. Gorbachev — A175

1990 Litho. *Perf. 13½*

1142 A175 200fr multicolored 1.50 75

Summit Meeting Dec. 3, 1989. No. 1142 exists in a souvenir sheet of 1.

De Gaulle's Call for French Resistance, 50th Anniv. — A176

1990

1143 A176 250fr multicolored 1.90 95

No. 1143 exists in a souvenir sheet of 1.

A177

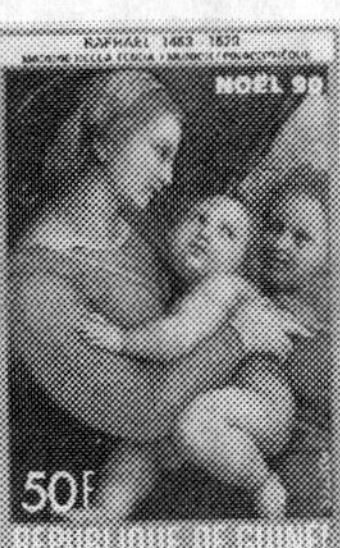

World Cup Soccer Championships, Italy 1990 — A178

Designs: No. 1152, Player, Chateau Saint-Ange.

1991, Apr. 1 Litho. *Perf. 13½*

1144 A177 200fr Rudi Voller 1.50 75
1145 A177 250fr Uwe Bein 1.90 95
1146 A177 300fr Pierre Littbarski 2.30 1.15
1147 A177 400fr Jurgen Klinsmann 3.00 1.50
1148 A177 450fr Lothar Matthaus 3.40 1.70
1149 A177 500fr Andreas Brehme 3.75 1.90
Nos. 1144-1149 (6) 15.85 7.95

Litho. & Embossed

1150 A178 1500fr gold & multi

Souvenir Sheets

Litho.

1151 A177 750fr Brehme, diff. 5.65 2.85

Litho. & Embossed

1152 A178 1500fr gold & multi

Nos. 1148-1152 are airmail. Nos. 1144-1150 exist in souvenir sheets of 1.

Christmas A179

Paintings by Raphael: 50fr, Della Tenda Madonna. 100fr, Cowper Madonna. 150fr, Tempi Madonna. 250fr, Niccolini Madonna. 300fr, Orleans Madonna. 500fr, Solly Madonna. 750fr, Madonna of the Fish.

1991, Apr. 1 Litho.

1153 A179 50fr multi 38 20
1154 A179 100fr multi 75 40
1155 A179 150fr multi 1.15 58

1156 A179 250fr multi 1.90 95
1157 A179 300fr multi 2.30 1.15
1158 A179 500fr multi 3.75 1.90

Souvenir Sheet

1159 A179 750fr multi 5.65 2.85

Nos. 1157-1159 are airmail. Nos. 1153-1158 exist in souvenir sheets of 1.

A180

World War II Battles — A181

Designs: No. 1160, Sinking of the Bismarck, May 27, 1941, Adm. Raeder and Adm. Tovey. No. 1161, Battle of Midway, June 3, 1942, Adm. Yamamoto and Adm. Nimitz. 200fr, Guadalcanal, Oct. 7, 1942, Adm. Kondo and Adm. Halsey. 250fr, Battle of El Alamein, Oct. 23, 1942, Field Marshal Erwin Rommel, Field Marshal Montgomery. 300fr, Battle of the Bulge, Dec. 16, 1944, Gen. Guderian and Gen. Patton. 450fr, Sinking of the Yamato, Apr., 7, 1945, Adm. Kogo and Gen. MacArthur. No. 1166, Review of Free French Forces, July 14, 1940, Gen. Charles De Gaulle. 750fr, Boeing B-17G, Gen. Dwight Eisenhower. No. 1168, De Gaulle's Call for French Resistance, June 18, 1940.

1991, Apr. 8 Litho. *Perf. 13½*

1160 A180 100fr multicolored 75 40
1161 A180 150fr multicolored 1.15 58
1162 A180 200fr multicolored 1.50 75
1163 A180 250fr multicolored 1.90 95
1164 A180 300fr multicolored 2.30 1.15
1165 A180 450fr multicolored 4.90 2.45
a. Sheet of 6, #1160-1165 12.50 6.25
Nos. 1160-1165 (6) 12.50 6.28

Litho. & Embossed

1166 A181 1500fr gold & multi

Souvenir Sheets

Litho.

1167 A180 750fr multicolored 5.65 2.85

Litho. & Embossed

1168 A181 1500fr gold & multi

Nos. 1164-1168 are airmail. No. 1160-1166 exist in souvenir sheets of 1.

Doctors Without Borders A182

1991 Litho. *Perf. 13½*

1169 A182 300fr multicolored 2.40 1.20

Telecom '91 A183

1991

1170 A183 150fr multi, vert. 2.00 1.00
1171 A183 300fr shown 4.00 2.00

6th World Forum and Exposition on Telecommunications, Geneva, Switzerland.

American Entertainers and Films — A184

Designs: 100fr, Nat King Cole Trio. 150fr, Yul Brynner, The Magnificent Seven. 250fr, Judy Garland, The Wizard of Oz. 300fr, Steve McQueen, Papillon. 500fr, Gary Cooper, Sergeant York. 600fr, Bing Crosby, High Society. 750fr, John Wayne, How the West Was Won.

1991, Oct. 2 Litho. *Perf. 13½*

1172 A184 100fr multicolored 75 40
1173 A184 150fr multicolored 1.15 58
1174 A184 250fr multicolored 1.90 95
1175 A184 300fr multicolored 2.30 1.15
1176 A184 500fr multicolored 3.75 1.90
1177 A184 600fr multicolored 8.00 4.00
Nos. 1172-1177 (6) 17.85 8.98

Souvenir Sheet

1178 A184 750fr multicolored 5.65 2.85

Nos. 1176-1178 are airmail. No. 1172-1177 exist in souvenir sheets of 1.

SEMI-POSTAL STAMPS

Eye Examination SP1

Microscopic Examination SP2

Designs: 30fr+20fr, Medical laboratory. 40fr+20fr, Insect control. 100fr+100fr, Surgical operation.

Engraved and Lithographed

1960 Unwmk. *Perf. 11½*

B12 SP1 20fr + 10fr ultra & car 45 45
B13 SP1 30fr + 20fr brn org & violet 45 45
B14 SP1 40fr + 20fr rose lil & blue 55 55
B15 SP2 50fr + 50fr grn & brn 90 90
B16 SP2 100fr + 100fr lil & grn 1.10 1.10
Nos. B12-B16 (5) 3.45 3.45

Issued for national health propaganda.
For overprints see Nos. B25-B29.

Nos. 194-195 Surcharged "1961" and New Value in Red or Orange

1961, June 6 Photo.

B17 A17 25fr + 10fr (R or O) 2.75 2.75
B18 A17 50fr + 20fr (R or O) 2.75 2.75

Nos. B17-B18 exist with orange surcharges transposed: "1961 + 10FRS." on 50fr and "1961 + 20FRS." on 25fr.

Nos. 214-219 Surcharged in Green, Lilac, Orange or Blue: "POUR LA PROTECTION DE NOS ANIMAUX +5 FRS"

Photo., Surcharge Engr.

1961, Dec. 8

Multicolored Design; Granite Paper

B19 A20 5fr + 5fr brt grn (G) 15 15
B20 A20 10fr + 5fr emer (G) 15 15
B21 A20 25fr + 5fr lilac (L) 32 18
B22 A20 40fr + 5fr org (O) 40 22
B23 A20 50fr + 5fr red org (O) 55 35
B24 A20 75fr + 5fr ultra (B) 80 45
Nos. B19-B24 (6) 2.37 1.50

The surtax was for animal protection.

Nos. B12-B16 Overprinted in Red or Orange

Engr. & Litho.

1962, Feb. *Perf. 11½*

B25 SP1 20fr + 10fr (R or O) 25 25
B26 SP1 30fr + 20fr (R or O) 35 35
B27 SP1 40fr + 20fr (R or O) 38 38
B28 SP2 50fr + 50fr (R or O) 80 80
B29 SP2 100fr + 100fr (R or O) 1.60 1.60
Nos. B25-B29 (5) 3.38 3.38

WHO drive to eradicate malaria.
No. B25 also exists with black overprint.

Nos. 223-228 Surcharged in Red: "POUR LA PROTECTION DE NOS OISEAUX + 5 FRS"

Photo., Surcharge Engr.

1962, May 14 *Perf. 13x14*

B30 A22 5fr + 5fr multi 15 15
B31 A22 10fr + 5fr multi 15 15
B32 A22 25fr + 5fr multi 22 16
B33 A22 40fr + 5fr multi 35 22
B34 A22 50fr + 5fr multi 62 38
B35 A22 75fr + 5fr multi 1.40 70
Nos. B30-B35 (6) 2.89 1.76

The surtax was for bird protection.

Nos. 232-233 Surcharged in Orange or Red and Overprinted: "Aide aux Refugies Algeriens"

1962, Nov. 1 Litho. *Perf. 13*

B36 A24 25fr + 15fr multi 40 40
B37 A24 75fr + 25fr multi 80 80

Issued to help Algerian refugees.

Astronomers and Space Phenomena — SP3

1989, Mar. 7 Litho. *Perf. 13½*

B38 SP3 100fr +25fr Helical nebula 82 40
B39 SP3 150fr +25fr Orion nebula 1.15 58
B40 SP3 200fr +25fr Eagle nebula 1.50 75
B41 SP3 250fr +25fr Trifide nebula 1.80 90
B42 SP3 300fr +25fr Eta-carinae nebula 2.10 1.05
B43 SP3 500fr +25fr NGC-2264 nebula 3.40 1.70
Nos. B38-B43 (6) 10.77 5.38

Souvenir Sheet

B44 SP3 750fr +50fr Horse's Head nebula 5.25 2.60

Nos. B42-B44 are airmail.

AIR POST STAMPS

Lockheed Constellation — AP1

Design: 500fr, Plane on ground.

Lithographed and Engraved

1959, July 13 Unwmk. *Perf. 11½*

Size: 52½x24mm

C14 AP1 100fr dp car, ultra & emer 1.00 65
C15 AP1 200fr emer, brn & lil 1.40 1.00

Size: 56½x26mm

C16 AP1 500fr multicolored 3.50 2.00

For overprints see Nos. C24-C26, C52-C53.

Doves with Letter and Olive Twig — AP2

1959, Oct. 16 Engr. *Perf. 13½*

C17 AP2 40fr blue 20 20
C18 AP2 50fr emerald 38 30
C19 AP2 100fr dk car rose 70 50
C20 AP2 200fr rose red 1.20 1.00
C21 AP2 500fr red orange 3.50 2.50
Nos. C17-C21 (5) 5.98 4.50

For overprints see Nos. C35-C38.

Admission to UN Type of 1959

Engr. & Litho.

1959, Dec. 12 *Perf. 12*

Size: 44x26mm

C22 A16 50fr multicolored 55 40
C23 A16 100fr multicolored 65 50

For overprints see Nos. C27-C28.

Nos. C14-C16 Overprinted in Carmine, Orange or Blue: "Jeux Olympiques Rome 1960" and Olympic Rings

1960 Litho. & Engr. *Perf. 11½*

Size: 52½x24mm

C24 AP1 100fr multi (C or O) 2.50 2.00
C25 AP1 200fr multi (Bl) 5.50 3.50

Size: 56½x26mm

C26 AP1 500fr multi (C or O) 14.00 14.00

17th Olympic Games, Rome, Aug. 25-Sept. 11.

Nos. C22-C23 Overprinted XVÈME ANNIVERSAIRE DES NATIONS UNIES

Engr. & Litho.

1961, Oct. 24 *Perf. 12*

C27 A16 50fr multicolored 45 38
C28 A16 100fr multicolored 65 55

United Nations, 15th anniversary.

Mosquito and Malaria Eradication Emblem AP3

1962, Apr. 7 Engr. *Perf. 10½*

C29 AP3 25fr orange & blk 25 15
C30 AP3 50fr car rose & blk 38 25
C31 AP3 100fr green & blk 70 45

WHO drive to eradicate malaria.
A souvenir sheet exists containing a 100fr green & sepia stamp, imperf. Sepia coat of arms in margin. Size: 102x76mm.

Musician Type of Regular Issue

Musical Instruments: 100fr, 200fr, Kora. 500fr, Balafon.

1962, June 15 Photo. *Perf. 13x13½*

C32 A26 100fr brt pink, dk car & Prus bl 50 40
C33 A26 200fr lt & dk ultra & car rose 1.00 60
C34 A26 500fr dl org, pur & Prus bl 3.25 2.00

Nos. C17-C20 Overprinted in Carmine, Orange or Black: "La Conquete De L'Espace"

Perf. 13½

1962, Nov. 15 Unwmk. Engr.

C35 AP2 40fr bl (C or O) 40 22
C36 AP2 50fr emer (C or O) 40 22
C37 AP2 100fr dk car rose (B) 65 45
C38 AP2 200fr rose red (B) 1.20 90

The conquest of space. Two types of overprint: Straight lines on 40fr and 50fr in carmine, 100fr (black). Curved lines on 40fr and 50fr in orange, 200fr (black).

Bird Type of Regular Issue

Birds: 100fr, Hornbill. 200fr, White spoonbill. 500fr, Bateleur eagle.

1962, Dec. Photo. *Perf. 13x13½*

C41 A30 100fr multicolored 90 40
C42 A30 200fr multicolored 1.50 70
C43 A30 500fr multicolored 3.50 2.00

Sports Type of Regular Issue, 1963

Designs: 100fr, Running. 200fr, Bicycling. 500fr, Single sculls.

1963, Mar. 16 *Perf. 14*

C44 A32 100fr dp rose, sep & grn 65 30
C45 A32 200fr ol bis, ultra & mag 1.50 70
C46 A32 500fr ocher, dk bl & red 3.00 2.00

Butterfly Type of Regular Issue, 1963

Various Butterflies.

1963, May 10 Unwmk. *Perf. 12*

C47 A33 100fr cit, dk brn & gray 65 30
C48 A33 200fr sal pink, blk & green 2.00 70
C49 A33 500fr multicolored 3.50 1.60

Red Cross Type of Regular Issue

1963, July 25 Engr. *Perf. 10½*

C50 A35 25fr black & car 25 15

Souvenir Sheet

Imperf

C51 A35 100fr green & car 1.50 1.50

Nos. C14-C15 Overprinted:

PREMIER SERVICE DIRECT
CONAKRY-NEW YORK
PAN AMERICAN
30, JUILLET 1963

Lithographed and Engraved

1963, Oct. 28 *Perf. 11½*

C52 AP1 100fr dp car, ultra & emer 1.10 70
C53 AP1 200fr emer, brn & lil 2.50 1.20

1st Pan American air service from Conakry to New York, July 30, 1963.

Fish Type of Regular Issue, 1964

Designs: 100fr, African lyretail. 300fr, Six-barred epiplatys.

1964, Feb. 15 Litho. *Perf. 14x13½*

C54 A36 100fr grn & multi 70 40
C55 A36 300fr brn & multi 2.00 1.00

Kennedy Type of Regular Issue, 1964

1964, Mar. 5 Engr. *Perf. 10½*

C56 A37 100fr multicolored 80 80

See note after No. 327.

Olympic Type of Regular Issue

Design: 100fr, Women's ice skating.

1964, May 15 Photo. *Perf. 13x12½*

C57 A39 100fr gold, brn org & ind 65 42

Nos. C44-C46 Overprinted in Carmine or Orange: "Jeux Olympiques Tokyo 1964" and Olympic Rings

1964, May 15 Unwmk. *Perf. 14*

C58 A32 100fr (C or O) 1.65 1.40
C59 A32 200fr (C or O) 2.50 2.00
C60 A32 500fr (C or O) 6.00 5.00

18th Olympic Games, Tokyo, Oct. 10-25.

Mrs. Roosevelt Type of Regular Issue, 1964

1964, June 1 Engr. *Perf. 10½*

C61 A40 50fr violet 40 25

Souvenir Sheets

Unisphere, "Rocket Thrower" and Guinea Pavilion — AP4

1964, Oct. 26 Engr. *Imperf.*

C62 AP4 100fr dk bl & org 80 80
C63 AP4 200fr rose red & emer 1.90 1.90

New York World's Fair, 1964-65. See Nos. C69-C70.

Nubian Monuments Type of Regular Issue, 1964

Design: 300fr, Queen Nefertari, Abu Simbel.

1964, Nov. 19 Photo. *Perf. 12*

C64 A42 300fr gold, dl red brn & sal 1.90 1.10

For overprint see No. C82.

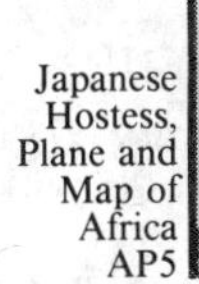

Japanese Hostess, Plane and Map of Africa AP5

1965, Jan. 18 *Perf. 12½x13*

C65 AP5 100fr gold, blk & red lil 1.00 35

18th Olympic Games, Tokyo, Oct. 10-25, 1964. Two multicolored souvenir sheets (200fr vert. and 300fr horiz.) exist, showing different views of Mt. Fuji. Sizes: 86x119mm, 119x86mm.
For overprint see No. C81.

Mask Type of Regular Issue

Design: 300fr, Niamou mask from N'Zerekore.

1965, Feb. 15 Photo. *Perf. 14*

C68 A44 300fr multicolored 2.25 90

World's Fair Type of 1964
Souvenir Sheets

1965, Mar. 24 Engr. *Imperf.*

C69 AP4 100fr green & brn 1.00 1.00
C70 AP4 200fr grn & car rose 2.00 2.00

Handicraft Type of Regular Issue

Handicrafts: 100fr, Cabinetmaker. 300fr, Ivory carver.

1965, May 1 Photo. *Perf. 14*

C71 A45 100fr multicolored 60 35
C72 A45 300fr multicolored 2.00 80

ITU Type of Regular Issue, 1965

1965, May 17 Unwmk.

C73 A46 100fr multicolored 65 30
C74 A46 200fr multicolored 1.60 50

Exist imperf.

ICY Type of Regular Issue, 1965

1965, Sept. 8 Engr. *Perf. 10½*

C75 A50 100fr bl & yel org 80 35

West Facade, Polytechnic Institute — AP6

Design: 200fr, North facade.

1965, Oct. 2 Photo. *Perf. 13½*

C76 AP6 200fr gold & multi 1.50 80
C77 AP6 500fr gold & multi 4.25 2.00

Seventh anniversary of independence.
For overprints see Nos. C84-C85.

Moon Type of 1965

Designs: 100fr, Ranger VII approaching moon (vert.). 200fr, Launching of Ranger VII, Cape Kennedy (vert.).

1965, Nov. 15 Litho. *Perf. 13½x14*

C78 A52 100fr rose red, yel & dk brown 65 30
C79 A52 200fr multicolored 1.60 60

For overprints and surcharge see Nos. C112-C112B.

Dancer Type of Regular Issue, 1966

Design: 100fr, Kouyate Kandia, national singer (horiz.).

1966, Jan. 5 Photo. *Perf. 13½*

Size: 36x28½mm

C80 A53 100fr multicolored 70 35

Engraved Overprint on No. C65

1966, Mar. 14 Photo. *Perf. 12½x13*

C81 AP5 100fr gold, blk & red lil 80 38

Fourth Pan Arab Games, Cairo, Sept. 2-11, 1965. The same overprint was applied to two souvenir sheets noted after No. C65 (red ovpt. on 200fr, black ovpt. on 300fr).

Engraved Dark Blue Overprint on No. C64: "CENTENAIRE DU TIMBRE / CAIRE 1966"

1966, Mar. 14 *Perf. 12*

C82 A42 300fr gold, dl red brn & sal 2.00 1.20

Centenary of first Egyptian postage stamp.

Scenic Type of Regular Issue

View: Boulbinet Lighthouse.

1966, Apr. 4 *Perf. 13½*

C83 A54 100fr multicolored 70 35

See Nos. C90-C91. For overprints see Nos. C93-C95.

Nos. C76-C77 Overprinted in Blue or Yellow

1966, May 2 Photo. *Perf. 13½*

C84 AP6 200fr multi (Bl) 1.40 90
C85 AP6 500fr multi (Y) 3.25 2.00

UNESCO, 20th anniv.

Woman-Flower Type of Regular Issue

Designs: Women and flowers of Guinea.

1966, May 30 Photo. *Perf. 13½*

Size: 28x34mm

C86 A56 200fr multicolored 1.60 60
C87 A56 300fr multicolored 2.50 1.10

Snake Type of Regular Issue

Designs: 200fr, Pastoria Research Institute. 300fr, Men holding rock python.

1967, May 15 Litho. *Perf. 13½*

Size: 56x20mm

C88 A61 200fr multicolored 1.40 70
a. Souv. sheet of 3, #471, 474, C88 4.00 3.50
C89 A61 300fr multicolored 2.25 1.10

Scenic Type of Regular Issue

Views: 100fr, House of explorer Olivier de Sanderval. 200fr, Conakry.

1967, June 20 Photo. *Perf. 13½*

C90 A54 100fr multicolored 60 40
C91 A54 200fr multicolored 1.40 70

For overprints see Nos. C94-C95.

Elephant Type of Regular Issue, 1967

1967, Sept. 28 Photo. *Perf. 13½*

C92 A63 200fr gold & multi 1.40 65

Nos. C83 and C90-C91 Overprinted with Lions Emblem and: "AMITIE DES PEUPLES GRACE AU TOURISME 1917-1967"

1967, Nov. 6

C93 A54 100fr multi (#C83) 80 40
C94 A54 100fr multi (#C90) 80 40
C95 A54 200fr multi (#C91) 1.50 70

50th anniversary of Lions International.

Detail from Mural by José Vela Zanetti — AP7

Family, Mural by Per Krohg — AP8

The designs of the 30fr, 50fr and 200fr show mankind's struggle for a lasting peace after the mural in the lobby of the UN Conference Building, N.Y. The designs of the 100fr and of Nos. C98a-C98b show mankind's hope for the future after a mural in the UN Security Council Chamber.

1967, Nov. 11

C96 AP7 30fr multicolored 22 15
C97 AP7 50fr multicolored 30 15
C98 AP8 100fr multicolored 65 30
a. Souv. sheet of 3, English inscription 1.50 1.50
b. Souv. sheet of 3, French inscription 1.50 1.50
C99 AP7 200fr multi 1.40 45

Nos. C98a and C98b each contain a 100fr stamp similar to No. C98 and two 50fr stamps showing festival scenes. The 50fr stamps have not been issued individually.

People and Dwellings Type of Regular Issue

Design: 300fr, People and village of Les Bassari, Kundara Region.

1968, Apr. 1 Photo. *Perf. 14x13½*

Size: 57x36mm

C100 A66 300fr gold & multi 2.00 80

Legends Type of Regular Issue

Designs: 70fr, The Girl and the Hippopotamus. 100fr, Old Faya's Inheritance (vert.). 200fr, Soumangourou Kante Killed by Djegue (woman on horseback). 300fr, Little Goune, Son of the Lion (vert.).

1968 Photo. *Perf. 13½*

C101 A67 70fr multicolored 50 15
C102 A67 100fr multicolored 80 20
C103 A67 200fr multicolored 1.60 38
a. Souv. sheet of 4 4.00 4.00
C104 A67 300fr multicolored 2.25 80

Issued in sheets of 10 plus 2 labels. No. C103a contains 4 imperf. stamps similar to Nos. 510-511 and C102-C103.;
For souvenir sheet see No. 509a.
Issue dates: May 16, Nos. C102-C103. Sept. 16, Nos. C101, C104.

African Animal Type of Regular Issue

1968, Nov. 25 Photo. *Perf. 13½*

Size: 49x35mm

C105 A68 100fr Lions 90 30
C106 A68 200fr Elephant 1.50 60

For souvenir sheet see No. 518a.

Robert F. Kennedy Type of Regular Issue, 1968

Portraits: 50fr, Senator Robert F. Kennedy. 100fr, Rev. Martin Luther King, Jr. 200fr, Pres. John F. Kennedy.

1968, Dec. 16
C107 A69 50fr yel & multi 35 15
C108 A69 100fr multicolored 70 20
C109 A69 200fr multicolored 1.60 45

The stamps are printed in sheets of 15 (3x5) containing 10 stamps and five green and gold center labels. Sheets come either with English or French inscriptions on label.

Olympic Type of Regular Issue

Designs (Sculpture and): 100fr, Gymnast on vaulting horse. 200fr, Gymnast on rings. 300fr, High jump.

1969, Feb. 1 Photo. *Perf. 13½*
C110 A71 100fr multicolored 65 25
C111 A71 200fr multicolored 1.40 40
C111A A71 300fr multicolored 2.25 60

Nos. C78-C79 Surcharged and Overprinted in Red

1969, Mar. 17 Litho. *Perf. 13½x14*
C112 A52 25fr on 200fr multi 35 15
C112A A52 100fr multicolored 90 65
C112B A52 200fr multicolored 1.60 1.00

See note after No. 530.

Nos. C112-C112B also exist with surcharge and overprint in orange (25fr, 200fr) or black (100fr). These sell for a small premium.

Bird Type of Regular Issue

Birds: 50fr, Violet-crested touraco. 100fr, European golden oriole. 200fr, Vulturine guinea fowl.

1971, June 18 Photo. *Perf. 13*
Size: 41x41mm
C113 A81 50fr gold & multi 55 20
C113A A81 100fr gold & multi 80 30
C113B A81 200fr gold & multi 1.60 50

John and Robert Kennedy, Martin Luther King, Jr. — AP9

Embossed on Metallic Foil
1972 *Die Cut Perf. 10½*
C114 AP9 300fr silver

Embossed & Typo.
C114A AP9 1500fr gold, cream & green

Jules Verne, Moon Rocket — AP10

Embossed on Metallic Foil
1972 *Die Cut Perf. 10½*
C115 AP10 300fr silver
C115A AP10 1200fr gold

Richard Nixon — AP11

Nixon and Mao — AP12

Nixon's Trip to People's Republic of China: a. Nixon. b. Chinese table tennis player. c. American table tennis player, Capitol dome. d. Mao Tse-tung.

Embossed on Metallic Foil
1972 *Die Cut Perf. 10½*
C116 AP11 90fr Block of 4, #C116a-C126d, silver
C117 AP11 290fr Block of 4, #C117a-C117d, gold

Embossed & Typo.
C118 AP12 1200fr gold & red

Perforations within blocks of 4 are perf. 11.

Racial Equality Year Type of Regular Issue

Design: 100fr, Men of 4 races and racial equality emblem (like No. 603).

1972, May 14 Photo. *Perf. 13x13½*
C119 A84 100fr gold & multi 60 35

Satellite Type of Regular Issue

Designs: 100fr, Map of Africa and Relay. 200fr, Map of Africa and Early Bird.

1972, May 17 Litho. *Perf. 13*
C120 A85 100fr yel & multi 50 25
C121 A85 200fr multicolored 1.00 50

African Postal Union Type of Regular Issue

Designs: 100fr, 200fr, Air mail envelope and UPAF emblem.

1972, July 10
C122 A86 100fr multicolored 60 30
C123 A86 200fr multicolored 1.20 60

Olympic Type of Regular Issue

1972, Aug. 26 Photo. *Perf. 13*
C124 A88 100fr Gymnast on rings 65 30
C125 A88 200fr Bicycling 1.10 60

Souvenir Sheet
C126 A88 300fr Soccer 1.90 1.90

Flower Type of 1974

1974, May 20 Photo. *Perf. 13*
Size: 38x38mm (Diamond)
C127 A97 20s Thunbergia alata 90 45
C128 A97 25s Diascia barberae 1.10 60
C129 A97 50s Kigelia africana 2.25 1.20

Olympic Games Type of 1976
Souvenir Sheet

1976, May 17 Photo. *Perf. 13½*
C130 Sheet of 4 6.50 6.50
a. A104 25s Soccer 1.40 80

No. C130 contains 32x32mm stamps.

Mushroom Type of 1977

Mushrooms: 10s, Morchella esculenta. 12s, Lepiota procera. 15s, Cantharellus cibarius.

1977, Feb. 6 Photo. *Perf. 13*
Size: 48x31mm
C131 A106 10s multicolored 60 30
C132 A106 12s multicolored 65 38
C133 A106 15s multicolored 80 45

Reptile Type of 1977

Reptiles: 10s, Flap-necked chameleon. 15s, Nile crocodiles. 25s, Painted tortoise.

1977, Oct. 10 Photo. *Perf. 13½*
Size: 46x30mm
C134 A109 10s multicolored 65 40
C135 A109 15s multicolored 1.00 60
C136 A109 25s multicolored 1.60 1.00

Animal Type of 1977

Endangered Animals: 5s, Eland. 8s, Pygmy elephant. 9s, Hippopotamus. 10s, Chimpanzee. 12s, Palm squirrel. 13s, Lion. Male, female and young of each animal shown.

1977, Dec. 12 Photo. *Perf. 14x13½*
C137 A110 5s Strip of 3 1.05 60
a.-c. Single stamp 35
C138 A110 8s Strip of 3 1.65 90
a.-c. Single stamp 55
C139 A110 9s Strip of 3 1.80 1.10
a.-c. Single stamp 60
C140 A110 10s Strip of 3 2.00 1.20
a.-c. Single stamp 65
C141 A110 12s Strip of 3 2.40 1.40
a.-c. Single stamp 80
C142 A110 13s Strip of 3 2.75 1.50
a.-c. Single stamp 90
Nos. C137-C142 (6) 11.65 6.70

Russian Revolution Type, 1978

Designs: 10s, Russian ballet. 30s, Pushkin Monument.

1978, Feb. 27 Photo. *Perf. 14*
C143 A111 10s gold & multi 65 40
C144 A111 30s gold & multi 2.00 1.20

Giscard d'Estaing Type of 1979

Design: Pres. Valery Giscard d'Estaing of France (vert.).

1979, Sept. 14 Photo. *Perf. 13*
C145 A112 25s multicolored 1.60 1.00

Jules Verne Type of 1979

Designs: 20s, Five Weeks in a Balloon. 25s, Robur the Conqueror.

1979, Nov. 8 Litho. *Perf. 12x12½*
C146 A113 20s multicolored 1.40 80
C147 A113 25s multicolored 1.60 1.00

Olympic Type of 1982

1982 Litho. *Perf. 12½x12, 12x12½*
C148 A120 9s Fencing 60 38
C149 A120 10s Soccer, vert. 65 40
C150 A120 11s Basketball, vert. 70 42
C151 A120 20s Diving, vert. 1.40 80
C152 A120 25s Boxing, vert. 1.60 1.10

Ataturk Type of 1982

1982, July 19 Photo. *Perf. 13½*
C153 A122 25s like #830 1.60 1.00

World Cup Type of 1982

Designs: Various soccer players.

1982, Aug. 23
C154 A123 10s multicolored 65 40
C155 A123 20s multicolored 1.40 80
C156 A123 25s multicolored 1.60 1.00

Nos. C154-C156 Overprinted in Green "CHAMPION ITALIE - 11 JUILLET 1982"

1982, Aug. 23 Photo. *Perf. 13½*
C157 A123 10s multicolored 65 40
C158 A123 20s multicolored 1.40 80
C159 A123 25s multicolored 1.60 1.00

Balloon Type

Designs: 20s, Graf Zeppelin, Airship (horiz.). 25s, Double Eagle II, L. Newman, B. Abruzzo, M. Anderson. 30s, Le Geant Hot Air Balloon, Nadar; Dirigible, Dumont.

1983, Aug. 1 Litho. *Perf. 13½*
C160 A125 20s multicolored 1.40 80
C161 A125 25s multicolored 1.60 1.00

Souvenir Sheet
C162 A125 30s multicolored 2.00 1.20

Nos. 894, 880-881 and 896 Overprinted

1985, Nov. 5 Litho. *Perf. 13½*
C163 A133 20s "80c Anniversaire / 1905-1985" 1.10 60
C164 A131 20s "Rassemblement / Jambville-1985" 1.10 60
C165 A131 25s "80e Anniversaire / 1905-1985" 1.50 70

Souvenir Sheet
C166 A133 30s "Kasparov / champion / du Monde" 1.90 90

US Space Shuttle Challenger Explosion, Jan. 28, 1986 — AP13

Designs: 100fr, Lift-off, crew names. 170fr, Shuttle design, Christa McAuliffe holding shuttle model. 600fr, Lift-off, vert.

1986, July 1
100fr, 170fr Surcharged in Silver and Black
C167 AP13 100fr multicolored 55 28
C168 AP13 170fr multicolored 95 48

Souvenir Sheet
C169 AP13 600fr multicolored 3.30 1.65

Nos. C167-C168 not issued without surcharge.

Souvenir sheets of one exist containing Nos. C167 and C168.

Robin Yount, Milwaukee Brewers Baseball Player — AP14

1990, Aug. 3 Litho. *Perf. 13½*
C170 AP14 450fr multicolored 3.45 1.75

No. C170 exists in a souvenir sheet of 1.

Souvenir Sheet

Armstrong, Aldrin, Collins and Apollo 11 Emblem — AP15

1990, Aug. 3 Litho. *Perf. 13½*
C171 AP15 750fr multicolored 5.75 2.85

Galileo Spacecraft — AP16

1990, Aug. 3
C172 AP16 500fr multicolored 3.75 1.90

No. C172 exists as a souvenir sheet of 1.

POSTAGE DUE STAMPS

D5 D6

1959	Unwmk.	Litho.	Perf. 11½	
J36 D5	1fr emerald		15	15
J37 D5	2fr lilac rose		15	15
J38 D5	3fr brown		15	15
J39 D5	5fr blue		16	16
J40 D5	10fr orange		60	60
J41 D5	20fr rose lilac		1.10	1.10
	Nos. J36-J41 (6)		2.31	2.31

1960	Engr.		Perf. 13½	
J42 D6	1fr dark carmine		15	15
J43 D6	2fr brn orange		15	15
J44 D6	3fr dark car rose		25	20
J45 D6	5fr bright green		45	40
J46 D6	10fr dark brown		90	65
J47 D6	20fr dull blue		1.90	1.50
	Nos. J42-J47 (6)		3.80	3.05

GUINEA-BISSAU

LOCATION — West coast of Africa between Senegal and Guinea
GOVT. — Republic
AREA — 13,948 sq. mi.
POP. — 844,000 (est. 1984)
CAPITAL — Bissau

Guinea-Bissau, the former Portuguese Guinea, attained independence on September 10, 1974. The state includes the Bissagos Islands.

100 Centavos = 1 Escudo
100 Centavos = 1 Peso

Catalogue values for all unused stamps in this country are for Never Hinged items.

Amilcar Cabral, Map of Africa and Flag — A27

Design: Flag of the PAIGC (African Party of Independence of Guinea-Bissau and Cape Verde) shows location of Guinea-Bissau on map of Africa.

Perf. 11x10½

1974, Sept. 10	Litho.	Unwmk.	
345 A27	1p brn & multi	50	40
346 A27	2.50p brn & multi	70	60
347 A27	5p brn & multi	*16.00*	*8.00*
348 A27	10p brn & multi	1.90	1.50

First anniv. of Proclamation of Independence, Sept. 24, 1973.

WMO Emblem — A28

Portuguese Guinea No. 344 Overprinted in Black

1975 Litho. *Perf. 13*
349 A28 2c brown & multi 50 50

No. 349 exists with overprint in brown.

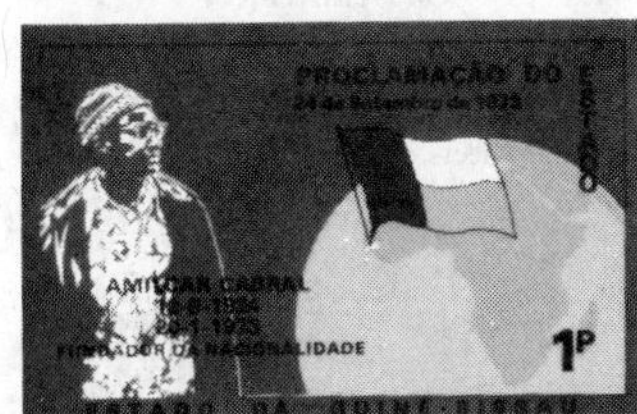

Amilcar Cabral, Map of Africa, Flag — A29

1975	Litho.	Perf. 11	
350 A29	1p brown & multi		
351 A29	2.50p brown & multi		
352 A29	5p brown & multi		
353 A29	10p brown & multi		
	Nos. 350-353 (4)	9.00	6.75

Flag and Arms of Guinea-Bissau and Amilcar Cabral — A30

Designs: (Flag, Arms and): 2e, No. 358, Family. 3e, 5e, Pres. Luiz Cabral. No. 359, like 1e.

1975, Sept.		Perf. 14	
354 A30	1e yel & multi	15	15
355 A30	2e multicolored	15	15
356 A30	3e red & multi	15	15
357 A30	5e yel & multi	20	15
358 A30	10e red & multi	38	25
359 A30	10e brt grn & multi	35	25
	Nos. 354-359 (6)	1.38	
	Set value		80

Amilcar Cabral's 51st birth anniv. (1e, No. 359); African Party of Independence of Guinea-Bissau and Cape Verde, 19th anniv. (2e, No. 358); Proclamation of Independence, 2nd anniv. (3e, 5e).
For surcharges see Nos. 367-367E.

Henry Knox, Cannons of Ticonderoga — A30a

Designs: 10e, Israel Putnam, Battle of Bunker Hill. 15e, Washington crossing the Delaware. 20e, Tadeusz Kosciuszko, Battle of Saratoga. 30e, Von Steuben, winter at Valley Forge. 40e, Lafayette, Washington rallying troops at Monmouth. 50e, Signing the Declaration of Independence.

1976, May 5 Litho. *Perf. 13½*
360 A30a 5e multicolored
360A A30a 10e multicolored
360B A30a 15e multicolored
360C A30a 20e multicolored
360D A30a 30e multicolored
360E A30a 40e multicolored

Souvenir Sheet

360F A30a 50e multicolored

American Revolution, bicentennial. Nos. 360D-360F are airmail. Nos. 360-360E exist in miniature sheets of 1, perf. and imperf. No. 360F contains one 75x45mm stamp and exists imperf.
See Nos. 371-371A.

Masked Dancer A30b

1976, May 10 *Perf. 11*
Denomination in Black on Silver Block

361 A30b 2p shown
361A A30b 3p Dancer, drummer
361B A30b 5p Dancers on stilts
361C A30b 10p Dancer with spear, bow
361D A30b 15p Masked dancer, diff.
361E A30b 20p Dancer with striped cloak

Souvenir Sheet

361F A30b 50p Like No. 361E

Nos. 361C-361F are airmail. Silver block obliterates original denomination. Not issued without surcharge.

Nos. 361-361F Ovptd. in Black

1976, June 8 *Perf. 11*
362 A30b 2p on No. 361
362A A30b 3p on No. 361A
362B A30b 5p on No. 361B
362C A30b 10p on No. 361C
362D A30b 15p on No. 361D
362E A30b 20p on No. 361E

Souvenir Sheet

362F A30b 50p on No. 361F

Nos. 362C-362F are airmail. UPU cent. (in 1974). Nos. 362-362F exist perf. imperf. and Nos. 362-362E in imperf. miniature sheets of 1, all with black or red overprints.

Cabral, Guinean Mother and Children — A31

1976, Aug.	Litho.	Perf. 13½	
363 A31	3p multicolored	15	15
364 A31	5p multicolored	18	15
365 A31	6p multicolored	22	15
366 A31	10p multicolored	38	20
	Set value		47

3rd anniv. of assassination of Amilcar Cabral (1924-1973), revolutionary leader.

Nos. 354-359 Surcharged in Black on Silver **1P00 PESOS**

1976, Sept. 12 Litho. *Perf. 14*
367 A30 1p on 1e No. 354
367A A30 2p on 2e No. 355
367B A30 3p on 3e No. 356
367C A30 5p on 5e No. 357
367D A30 10p on 10e No. 358
367E A30 10p on 10e No. 359

1876 Bell Telephone and Laying First Trans-Atlantic Cable — A31a

Telephones of: 3p, France, 1890, and first telephone booth, 1893. 5p, Germany, 1903, and automatic telephone, 1898. 10p, England, 1910, and relay station, 1963. 15p, France, 1924, and communications satellite. 20p, Modern telephone, 1970, and Molniya satellite. 50p, Picture phone.

1976, Oct. 18 *Perf. 13½*
368 A31a 2p multicolored
368A A31a 3p multicolored
368B A31a 5p multicolored
368C A31a 10p multicolored
368D A31a 15p multicolored
368E A31a 20p multicolored

Souvenir Sheet

368F A31a 50p multicolored

Nos. 368C-368F are airmail. No. 368F contains one 68x42mm stamp. No. 368F exists imperf. Nos. 368-368E exist in souvenir sheets of one, perf. and imperf.

1976 Winter Olympics, Innsbruck — A31b

1976, Nov. 3 *Perf. 14x13½*
369 A31b 1p Women's figure skating
369A A31b 3p Ice hockey
369B A31b 5p Two-man bobsled
369C A31b 10p Pairs figure skating
369D A31b 20p Cross country skiing

369E A31b 30p Speed skating

Souvenir Sheet

369F A31b 50p Downhill skiing

Nos. 369C-369F are airmail. No. 369F exists imperf. Nos. 369-369E exist in souvenir sheets of one, perf. and imperf.

1976 Summer Olympics, Montreal A31c

1976, Nov. 24 *Perf. 13½*

370 A31c 1p Soccer
370A A31c 3p Pole vault
370B A31c 5p Women's hurdles
370C A31c 10p Discus
370D A31c 20p Sprinting
370E A31c 30p Wrestling

Souvenir Sheet

370F A31c 50p Cycling, horiz.

Nos. 370E-370F are airmail. No. 370F contains one 47x38mm stamp. No. 370F exists imperf. Nos. 370-370E exist in souvenir sheets of one, perf. and imperf.

American Revolution Type of 1976

Designs: 3.50p, Crispus Attucks, Boston Massacre. 5p, Martin Luther King, US Capitol.

1977, Jan. 27 *Perf. 13½*

Denomination in Black on Gold Block

371 A30a 3.50p multicolored
371A A30a 5p multicolored

Gold block obliterates original denomination. Not issued without surcharge. Exist in souvenir sheets of one, perf. and imperf.

Cabral Addressing UN General Assembly A32

Design: 50c, Cabral and guerrilla fighters.

1977, July **Litho.** *Perf. 13½*

372 A32 50c multicolored	15	15
373 A32 3.50p multicolored	30	15
Set value		15

For surcharges see Nos. C12-C13.

Henri Dunant, Nobel Peace Prize, 1901 — A32a

Nobel Prize Winners: 5p, Einstein, Physics, 1921. 6p, Irene and Frederic Joliot-Curie, Chemistry, 1935. 30p, Fleming, Medicine, 1945. 35p, Hemingway, Literature, 1954. 40p, J. Tinbergen, Economics, 1969. 50p, Nobel Prize Medal.

1977, July 27

374 A32a 3.50p multicolored
374A A32a 5p multicolored
374B A32a 6p multicolored
374C A32a 30p multicolored
374D A32a 35p multicolored
374E A32a 40p multicolored

Souvenir Sheet

374F A32a 50p multicolored

Nos. 374D-374F are airmail. No. 374F contains one 57x39mm stamp. No. 374F exists imperf. Nos. 374-374E exist in souvenir sheets of one, perf. and imperf.

Postal Runner, Telstar Satellite — A32b

UPU Centenary (in 1974): 5p, Biplane, satellites encircle globe. 6p, Mail truck, satellite control room. 30p, Stagecoach, astronaut canceling letters on Moon. 35p, Steam locomotive, communications satellite. 40p, Space shuttle, Apollo-Soyuz link-up. 50p, Semaphore signalling system, satellite dish.

1977, Sept. 30

375 A32b 3.50p multicolored
375A A32b 5p multicolored
375B A32b 6p multicolored
375C A32b 30p multicolored
375D A32b 35p multicolored
375E A32b 40p multicolored

Souvenir Sheet

375F A32b 50p multicolored

Nos. 375D-375F are airmail. No. 375F exists imperf. Nos. 375-375E exist in souvenir sheets of one, perf. and imperf.

Torch and Party Emblem — A33

1977, Sept. **Litho.** *Perf. 14*

376 A33 3p yel & multi	15	15
377 A33 15p sal & multi	60	40
378 A33 50p lt grn & multi	1.50	1.00

African Party of Independence of Guinea-Bissau and Cape Verde, 20th anniversary.

Queen Elizabeth II, Silver Jubilee — A33a

Designs: 5p, Coronation ceremony. 10p, Yeoman of the Guard, Crown Jewels. 20p, Trumpeter. 25p, Royal Horse Guard. 30p, Royal Family. 50p, Queen Elizabeth II.

1977, Oct. 15

379 A33a 3.50p multicolored
379A A33a 5p multicolored
379B A33a 10p multicolored
379C A33a 20p multicolored
379D A33a 25p multicolored
379E A33a 30p multicolored

Souvenir Sheet

379F A33a 50p multicolored

Nos. 379D-379F are airmail. No. 379F contains one 42x39mm stamp. No. 379F exists imperf. Nos. 379-379E exist in souvenir sheets of one, perf. and imperf.

Massacre of the Innocents by Rubens A33b

Paintings by Peter Paul Rubens: 5p, Rape of the Daughters of Leukippos. 6p, Lamentation of Christ, horiz. 30p, Francisco IV Gonzaga, Prince of Mantua. 35p, The Four Continents. 40p, Marquise Brigida Spinola Doria. 50p, The Wounding of Christ.

1977, Nov. 15

380 A33b 3.50p multicolored
380A A33b 5p multicolored
380B A33b 6p multicolored
380C A33b 30p multicolored
380D A33b 35p multicolored
380E A33b 40p multicolored

Souvenir Sheet

380F A33b 50p multicolored

Nos. 380D-380F are airmail. Nos. 380-380F exist imperf. Nos. 380-380E exist in souvenir sheets of one, perf. and imperf.

Congress Emblem — A34

1977, Nov. 15 **Litho.** *Perf. 14*

381 A34 3.50p multicolored	15	15

3rd PAIGC Congress, Bissau, Nov. 15-20.

Santos-Dumont's Airship, 1901 — A34a

Airships: 5p, R-34 crossing the Atlantic, 1919. 10p, Norge over North Pole, 1926. 20p, Graf Zeppelin over Abu Simbel, 1931. 25p, Hindenburg over New York, 1937. 30p, Graf Zeppelin, Concorde, space shuttle. 50p, Ferdinand von Zeppelin, horiz.

1978, Feb. 27

382 A34a 3.50p multicolored
382A A34a 5p multicolored
382B A34a 10p multicolored
382C A34a 20p multicolored
382D A34a 25p multicolored
382E A34a 30p multicolored

Souvenir Sheet

382F A34a 50p multicolored

Nos. 382D-382F are airmail. No. 382F exists imperf. Nos. 382-382E exist in souvenir sheets of one, perf. and imperf.

World Cup Soccer Championships, Argentina — A34b

Soccer players and posters from previous World Cup Championships: 3.50p, 1930. 5p, 1938. 10p, 1950. 20p, 1962. 25p, 1970. 30p, 1974. 50p, Argentina '78 emblem.

1978, Mar. 15

383 A34b 3.50p multicolored
383A A34b 5p multicolored
383B A34b 10p multicolored
383C A34b 20p multicolored
383D A34b 25p multicolored
383E A34b 30p multicolored

Souvenir Sheet

383F A34b 50p multicolored

Nos. 383D-383F are airmail. Nos. 383-383F exist imperf. Nos. 383-383E exist in miniature sheets of one, perf. and imperf.

For surcharges see Nos. 393-393F.

Endangered Species A34c

1978, Apr. 17

384 A34c 3.50p Black antelope
384A A34c 5p Fennec
384B A34c 6p Secretary bird
384C A34c 30p Hippopotami
384D A34c 35p Cheetahs
384E A34c 40p Gorillas

Souvenir Sheet

384F A34c 50p Cercopithecus erythotis

Nos. 384D-384F are airmail. No. 384F contains one 39x42mm stamp. No. 384F exists imperf. Nos. 384-384E exist in souvenir sheets of one, perf. and imperf.

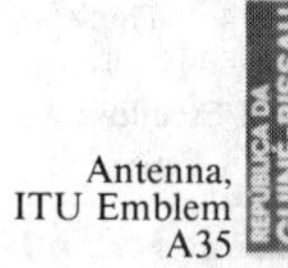

Antenna, ITU Emblem A35

1978, May 17 **Litho.** *Perf. 13½*

385 A35 3.50p silver & multi	15	15
386 A35 10p gold & multi	42	25

10th World Telecommunications Day.

Boy — A36

Designs: 3p, Infant and grandfather. 5p, Boys. 30p, Girls.

1978 *Perf. 14*

387 A36 50c yel grn & dk bl	15	15
388 A36 3p cl & car rose	15	15
389 A36 5p ocher & brown	20	15
390 A36 30p car & ocher	1.10	65
Set value		90

Children's Day.

Queen Elizabeth II, Silver Jubilee A36a

Elizabeth, Imperial State Crown — A36b

Designs: 5p, Queen, Prince Philip in Coronation Coach. 10p, Queen, Prince Philip. 20p, Mounted drummer. 25p, Imperial State Crown, St. Edward's Crown. 30p, Queen holding orb and scepter. 50p, Queen on Throne flanked by Archbishops. No. 391H, Coronation Coach.

1978, June 15

391 A36a 3.50p multicolored
391A A36a 5p multicolored
391B A36a 10p multicolored
391C A36a 20p multicolored
391D A36a 25p multicolored
391E A36a 30p multicolored

Litho. & Embossed

391F A36b 100p gold & multi

Souvenir Sheets

391G A36a 50p multicolored

Litho. & Embossed

391H A36b 100p gold & multi

Nos. 391D-391H are airmail. Nos. 391-391E exist in souvenir sheets of one, perf. and imperf. Nos. 391F-391H exist imperf.

History of Aviation — A36c

1978, June 15 **Litho.** ***Perf. 13½***

392 A36c 3.50p Wright Brothers
392A A36c 10p Santos-Dumont
392B A36c 15p Bleriot
392C A36c 20p Lindbergh, Spirit of St. Louis
392D A36c 25p Lunar module
392E A36c 30p Space shuttle

Souvenir Sheet

392F A36c 50p Concorde

Nos. 392D-392F are airmail. Nos. 392-392E exist in souvenir sheets of one, perf. and imperf. No. 392F exists imperf.

Nos. 383-383F Ovptd. in Gold

1º ARGENTINA
2º HOLANDA
3º BRASIL

1978, Oct. 2

393 A34b 3.50p on No. 383
393A A34b 5p on No. 383A
393B A34b 10p on No. 383B
393C A34b 20p on No. 383C
393D A34b 25p on No. 383D
393E A34b 30p on No. 383E

Souvenir Sheet

393F A34b 50p on No. 383F

Nos. 393D-393F are airmail. Nos. 393-393F exist imperf. Nos. 393-393E exist in miniature sheets of 1 perf. and imperf. No. 393F exists overprinted in silver.

Virgin and Child by Albrecht Durer — A36d

Different Paintings of the Virgin and Child (Virgin only on 30p) by Durer.

1978, Nov. 14

394 A36d 3.50p multicolored
394A A36d 5p multicolored
394B A36d 6p multicolored
394C A36d 30p multicolored
394D A36d 35p multicolored
394E A36d 40p multicolored

Souvenir Sheet

394F A36d 50p multicolored

Nos. 394D-394F are airmail. No. 394F contains one 51x56mm stamp. Nos. 394-394E exist in souvenir sheets of one, perf. and imperf. No. 394F exists imperf.

Sir Rowland Hill (1795-1879), Wurttemberg No. 53 — A36e

Hill and: 5p, Belgium #1. 6p, Monaco #10. 30p, Spain 2r stamp of 1851 in blue. 35p, Switzerland #5. 40p, Naples #8. 50p, Portuguese Guinea #13 in brown.

1978, Dec. 15

395 A36e 3.50p multicolored
395A A36e 5p multicolored
395B A36e 6p multicolored
395C A36e 30p multicolored
395D A36e 35p multicolored
395E A36e 40p multicolored

Souvenir Sheet

395F A36e 50p multicolored

Nos. 395D-395F are airmail. No. 395F contains one 51x42mm stamp. Nos. 395-395E exist in souvenir sheets of one, perf. and imperf. No. 395F exists imperf.

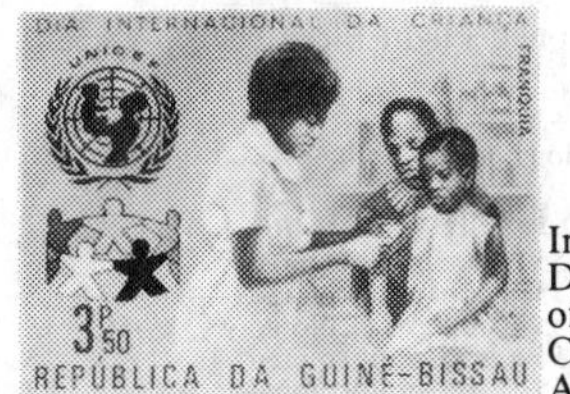

Intl. Day of the Child A36f

1979, Jan. 15 ***Perf. 14***

396 A36f 3.50p shown
396A A36f 10p Children drinking
396B A36f 15p Child with book
396C A36f 20p Space plane
396D A36f 25p Skylab
396E A36f 30p Children playing chess

Souvenir Sheet

396F A36f 50p Children watching spaceship

Nos. 396C-396F are airmail. Nos. 396-396E exist in souvenir sheets of one, perf. and imperf. No. 396F exists imperf.

Massacre of Pindjiguiti, 20th Anniv. — A36g

1979 **Litho.** ***Perf. 13***

397 A36g 4.50p multicolored

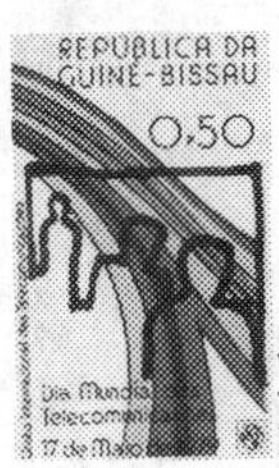

World Telecommunications Day — A36h

1979 **Litho.** ***Perf. 14***

397A	A36h	50c	shown	16
397B	A36h	4p	People, rainbow, diff.	1.35

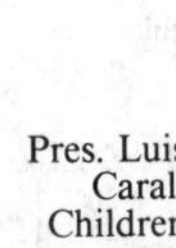

Family A37

1979, May **Litho.** ***Perf. 12x11½***

398	A37	50c	multicolored	15	15
399	A37	2p	multicolored	15	15
400	A37	4p	multicolored	20	15
			Set value	35	28

General population census, Apr. 16-30.

Ernst Udet and Fokker D.VII — A38

1980 **Litho.** ***Perf. 13½***

401	A38	3.50p	shown	15	15
401A	A38	5p	Charles Nungesser, Nieuport 17	20	15
401B	A38	6p	von Richthofen, Fokker DR.1	25	20
401C	A38	30p	Francesco Baracca, Spad XIII	1.00	55
			Nos. 401-401C,C14-C14A (6)	4.35	2.35

Lake Placid Emblem, Speed Skating A39

1980

402	A39	3.50p	shown	15	15
402A	A39	5p	Downhill skiing	20	15
402B	A39	6p	Luge	25	20
402C	A39	30p	Cross-country skiing	1.00	55
			Nos. 402-402C,C15-C16 (6)	4.35	2.35

13th Winter Olympic Games, Lake Placid, NY, Feb. 12-24.

Shot-put A40

1980, Aug. **Litho.** ***Perf. 13½***

403	A40	3.50p	shown	15	15
403A	A40	5p	Athlete on rings	20	15
403B	A40	6p	Running	25	20
403C	A40	30p	Fencing	1.00	55
			Nos. 403-403C,C18-C19 (6)	4.35	2.35

22nd Summer Olympic Games, Moscow, July 19-Aug. 3.

Pres. Luis Caral, Children and Workers A41

Literacy Campaign: 5p, Pres. Caral holding books.

1980, Aug. **Litho.** ***Perf. 13½***

404	A41	3.50p	multicolored	15	15
405	A41	5p	multicolored	25	15
			Set value		20

See Nos. C21-C22.

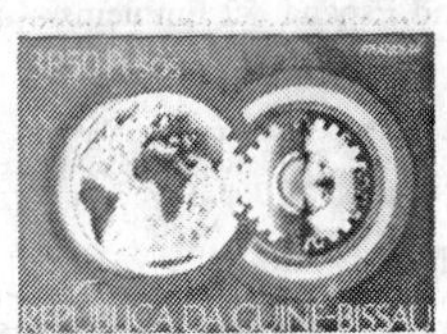

Cooperation Among Developing Countries — A42

1980, Aug.

406	A42	3.50p	multicolored	15	15
407	A42	6p	multicolored	18	15
408	A42	10p	multicolored	38	20
			Set value		35

Baskets — A43

1980, Aug. Litho. *Perf. 13½*

409 A43 3p Bird, family wood statues, vert. 15 15
410 A43 6p shown 20 15
411 A43 20p Head, doll carvings 70 40
Set value 55

Infant and Toy Train, Locomotive, IYC Emblem A44

1980

412 A44 6p Classroom, horiz. 25 20
412A A44 10p Boy reading Jules Verne story 38 30
412B A44 25p shown 90 50
412C A44 35p Archer, boy with bow 1.40 70

Souvenir Sheet

412D A44 50p Students in lab 2.00 1.00

International Year of the Child (1979).

Columbia Space Shuttle and Crew — A45

Space Exploration: 3.50p, Galileo, satellites. 5p, Wernher von Braun. 6p, Jules Verne, rocket.

1981, May Litho. *Perf. 13½*

413 A45 3.50p multicolored 20 15
413A A45 5p multicolored 25 15
413B A45 6p multicolored 30 18
413C A45 30p multicolored 1.50 80
Nos. 413-413C,C23-C24 (6) 5.00 2.58

Soccer Players, World Cup, Argentina '78 and Espana '82 Emblems — A46

Soccer scenes and famous players: 3.50p, Platini, France. 5p, Bettega, Italy. 6p, Rensenbrink, Netherlands. 30p, Rivelino, Brazil.

1981, May

414 A46 3.50p multicolored 20 15
414A A46 5p multicolored 25 15
414B A46 6p multicolored 30 18
414C A46 30p multicolored 1.50 60
Nos. 414-414C,C26-C27 (6) 5.00 2.38

Prince Charles and Lady Diana, St. Paul's Cathedral A47

Royal Wedding (Couple and): 3.50p, Diana leading horse. 5p, Charles crowned Prince of Wales. 6p, Diana with kindergarten children.

1981 Litho. *Perf. 13½*

415 A47 3.50p multicolored 20 15
415A A47 5p multicolored 25 15
415B A47 6p multicolored 30 18
415C A47 30p multicolored 1.50 80
Nos. 415-415C,C29-C30 (6) 6.15 3.53

Woman Before a Mirror, by Picasso (1881-1973) A48

Picasso Birth Centenary: Various paintings.

1981, Dec. Litho. *Perf. 13½*

416 A48 3.50p multi 20 15
417 A48 5p multi 25 15
418 A48 6p multi 30 18
419 A48 30p multi 1.50 80
Nos. 416-419,C32-C33 (6) 6.15 3.53

Henrique Vermelho and his Ship, Drakkar A49

Navigators and their ships: 5p, Vasco de Gama, St. Gabriel. 6p, Ferdinand Magellan, Victoria. 30p, Jacques Cartier, Emerillon.

1981 Litho. *Perf. 13½*

420 A49 3.50p multicolored 20 15
421 A49 5p multicolored 25 15
422 A49 6p multicolored 30 18
423 A49 30p multicolored 1.50 80
Nos. 420-423,C35-C36 (6) 6.15 3.53

Christmas — A50

Designs: Virgin and Child paintings.

1981

424 A50 3.50p Mantegna 20 15
425 A50 5p Bellini 25 15
426 A50 6p Mantegna, diff. 30 18
427 A50 25p Correggio 1.50 80
Nos. 424-427,C38-C39 (6) 6.15 3.53

Scouting Year — A51

1982, June 9 Litho. *Perf. 13½*

428 A51 3.50p Archery 15 15
429 A51 5p First aid training 20 15
430 A51 6p Bugler 25 15
431 A51 30p Cub scouts 1.40 60
Nos. 428-431,C41-C42 (6) 5.40 2.75

1982 World Cup — A52

Various soccer players and cup.

1982, June 13 Litho. *Perf. 13½*

432 A52 3.50p Keegan 15 15
433 A52 5p Rossi 20 15
434 A52 6p Zico 25 15
435 A52 30p Arconada 1.40 60
Nos. 432-435,C44-C45 (6) 5.40 2.75

21st Birthday of Princess Diana — A53

Portraits and scenes of Diana.

1982

436 A53 3.50p multicolored 15 15
437 A53 5p multicolored 20 15
438 A53 6p multicolored 25 15
439 A53 30p multicolored 1.40 60
Nos. 436-439,C47-C48 (6) 5.40 2.75

For overprints see Nos. 450-456.

Manned Flight Bicentenary — A55

Various hot air balloons.

1983, Jan. 15 Litho. *Perf. 11*

442 A55 50c multicolored 15 15
443 A55 2.50p multicolored 15 15
444 A55 3.50p multicolored 18 15
445 A55 5p multicolored 22 15
446 A55 10p multicolored 45 22
447 A55 20p multicolored 1.00 40
448 A55 30p multicolored 1.50 60
Nos. 442-448 (7) 3.65
Set value 1.50

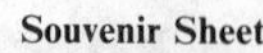

Souvenir Sheet

Perf. 12½

449 A55 50p multicolored 2.50 1.25

No. 449 contains one 47x47mm stamp.

Nos. 436-439, C47-C48 Overprinted: "21 DE JULHO . GUILHERMO ARTUR FILIPE LUIS PRINCIPE DE GALES"

1982 Litho. *Perf. 13½*

450 A53 3.50p multicolored 15 15
451 A53 5p multicolored 22 15
452 A53 6p multicolored 25 15
453 A53 30p multicolored 1.40 65
454 A53 35p multicolored 1.60 80
455 A53 40p multicolored 1.90 1.00
Nos. 450-455 (6) 5.52 2.90

Souvenir Sheet

456 A53 50p multicolored 2.75 1.20

Nos. 454-456 airmail.

African Apes and Monkeys — A56

1983, Mar. 15 Litho. *Perf. 13½*

457 A56 1p Comopithecus hamadryas 15 15
458 A56 1.50p Gorilla gorilla 15 15
459 A56 3.50p Theropithecus gelada 18 15
460 A56 5p Mandrillus sphinx 25 15
461 A56 8p Pan trogladytes 42 20
462 A56 20p Colobus abyssinicus 1.10 50
463 A56 30p Cercopithecus diana 1.60 70
Nos. 457-463 (7) 3.85
Set value 1.70

Souvenir Sheet

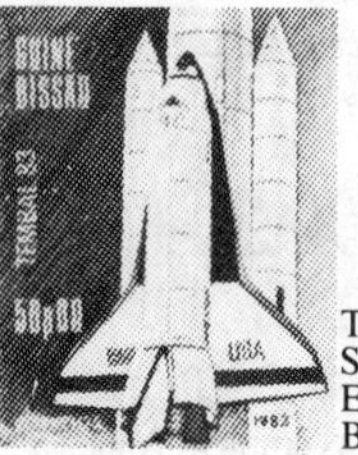

TEMBAL '83, Stamp Exhibition, Basel — A57

1983, May 21

464 A57 50p Space shuttle 2.00 1.25

A58

Designs: Various telecommunications satellites and space shuttles.

1983, May 25 Litho. *Perf. 13½*

465 A58 1p multicolored 15 15
466 A58 1.50p multicolored 15 15
467 A58 3.50p multicolored 18 15
468 A58 5p multicolored 25 15
469 A58 8p multicolored 42 20
470 A58 20p multicolored 1.00 42
471 A58 30p multicolored 1.50 65
Nos. 465-471 (7) 3.65
Set value 1.55

Souvenir Sheet

472 A58 50p multicolored 2.50 1.25

History of Chess — A59

Early Chess Game — A60

Various chess pieces.

1983, June 13 Litho. *Perf. 12*

No.	Type	Value	Description	Unused	Used
473	A59	1p	multicolored	15	15
474	A59	1.50p	multicolored	15	15
475	A59	3.50p	multicolored	15	15
476	A59	5p	multicolored	25	15
477	A59	10p	multicolored	55	25
478	A59	20p	multicolored	1.10	50
479	A59	40p	multicolored	2.25	1.00
			Nos. 473-479 (7)	4.60	
			Set value		2.00

Souvenir Sheet

No.	Type	Value	Description	Unused	Used
480	A60	50p	brown & blk	2.50	1.25

Raphael, 500th Birth Anniv. A61

Various paintings.

1983, June 30 Litho. *Perf. 12½*

No.	Type	Value	Description	Unused	Used
481	A61	1p	gold & multi	15	15
482	A61	1.50p	gold & multi	15	15
483	A61	3.50p	gold & multi	18	15
484	A61	5p	gold & multi	25	15
485	A61	8p	gold & multi	42	22
486	A61	15p	gold & multi	90	40
487	A61	30p	gold & multi	1.60	65
			Nos. 481-487 (7)	3.65	
			Set value		1.50

Souvenir Sheet

No.	Type	Value	Description	Unused	Used
488	A61	50p	gold & multi	2.50	1.20

1984 Summer Olympics, Los Angeles — A62

1983, July 20 Litho. *Perf. 12½*

No.	Type	Value	Description	Unused	Used
489	A62	1p	Swimming	15	15
490	A62	1.50p	Jumping	15	15
491	A62	3.50p	Fencing	15	15
492	A62	5p	Weightlifting	22	15
493	A62	10p	Running	50	22
494	A62	20p	Equestrian	1.00	50
495	A62	40p	Bicycling	2.00	1.00
			Nos. 489-495 (7)	4.17	
			Set value		2.00

Souvenir Sheet

No.	Type	Value	Description	Unused	Used
496	A62	50p	Stadium	2.50	1.25

Souvenir Sheet

BRASILIANA '83, Philatelic Exhibition A63

1983, July 29 Litho. *Perf. 13*

No.	Type	Value	Description	Unused	Used
497	A63	50p	multicolored	2.50	1.25

Local Fish A64

Perf. 12x11½, 11½x12

1983, Dec. 8 Litho.

No.	Type	Value	Description	Unused	Used
498	A64	1p	Monodactylus sebae, vert.	15	15
499	A64	1.50p	Botia macracanthus	15	15
500	A64	3.50p	Ctenopoma acutirostre	18	15
501	A64	5p	Roloffia bertholdi	25	15
502	A64	8p	Aphyosemion bualanum	42	20
503	A64	10p	Aphyosemion bivittatum	62	30
504	A64	30p	Aphyosemion australe	1.90	90
			Nos. 498-504 (7)	3.67	
			Set value		1.75

1984 Winter Olympics, Sarajevo — A65

1983, Oct. 10 Litho. *Perf. 13*

No.	Type	Value	Description	Unused	Used
505	A65	1p	Speed skating	15	15
506	A65	1.50p	Ski jumping	15	15
507	A65	3p	Biathlon	15	15
508	A65	5p	Bobsledding	18	15
509	A65	10p	Hockey	32	18
510	A65	15p	Figure skating	60	30
511	A65	20p	Luge	75	38
			Nos. 505-511 (7)	2.30	
			Set value		1.10

Souvenir Sheet

No.	Type	Value	Description	Unused	Used
512	A65	50p	Downhill skiing	2.50	1.25

No. 512 contains one 31x40mm stamp.

First Anniv. of Women's Federation — A66

1983, Nov. 7 *Perf. 12½*

No.	Type	Value	Description	Unused	Used
513	A66	4.50p	Emblem	15	15
514	A66	7.50p	Woman, flag	20	15
515	A66	9p	Sewing	25	15
516	A66	12p	Farm workers	32	15
			Set value		42

Local Flowers — A67

1983, Nov. 12 Litho. *Perf. 13*

No.	Type	Value	Description	Unused	Used
517	A67	1p	Canna coccinea	15	15
518	A67	1.50p	Bouganville litoralis	15	15
519	A67	3.50p	Euphorbia milii	18	15
520	A67	5p	Delonix regia	25	15
521	A67	8p	Bauhinia variegata	40	20
522	A67	10p	Spathodea campanulata	55	20
523	A67	30p	Hibiscus rosa sinensis	1.50	70
			Nos. 517-523 (7)	3.18	
			Set value		1.40

JAAC Congress, Sept. 8-12 A68

1983, Sept. 1 Litho. *Perf. 13*

No.	Type	Value	Description	Unused	Used
524	A68	4p	shown	15	15
524A	A68	5p	Emblem	15	15
			Set value		22

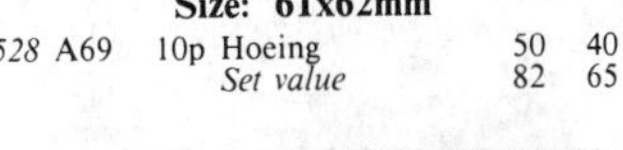

World Food Day A69

1983, Oct. 16 Litho. *Perf. 12½x12*

No.	Type	Value	Description	Unused	Used
525	A69	1.50p	multicolored	15	15
526	A69	2p	multicolored	15	15
527	A69	4p	multicolored	18	15

Imperf

Size: 61x62mm

No.	Type	Value	Description	Unused	Used
528	A69	10p	Hoeing	50	40
			Set value	82	65

1984 Winter Olympics, Sarajevo — A70

1984, Feb. 8 *Perf. 12*

No.	Type	Value	Description	Unused	Used
529	A70	50c	Ski jumping	15	15
530	A70	2.50p	Speed skating	15	15
531	A70	3.50p	Hockey	15	15
532	A70	5p	Biathlon	25	15
533	A70	6p	Downhill skiing	35	20
534	A70	20p	Figure skating	1.00	50
535	A70	30p	Bobsledding	1.60	70
			Nos. 529-535 (7)	3.65	
			Set value		1.70

Souvenir Sheet

Perf. 11½

No.	Type	Value	Description	Unused	Used
536	A70	50p	Skiing	2.50	1.25

No. 536 contains one 32x43mm stamp.

World Communications Year — A71

1983, Aug. 30 Litho. *Perf. 12½*

No.	Type	Value	Description	Unused	Used
537	A71	50c	Rowland Hill	15	15
538	A71	2.50p	Samuel Morse	15	15
539	A71	3.50p	H.R. Hertz	18	15
540	A71	5p	Lord Kelvin	25	15
541	A71	10p	Alex. Graham Bell	50	20
542	A71	20p	G. Marconi	1.00	50
543	A71	30p	V. Zworykin	1.40	65
			Nos. 537-543 (7)	3.63	
			Set value		1.70

Souvenir Sheet

No.	Type	Value	Description	Unused	Used
544	A71	50p	Satellites	2.50	1.25

No. 544 contains one stamp 31x39mm.

Vintage Cars A72

1984, Mar. 20 *Perf. 12*

No.	Type	Value	Description	Unused	Used
545	A72	5p	Duesenberg, 1928	15	15
546	A72	8p	MG Midget, 1932	25	15
547	A72	15p	Mercedes, 1928	42	20
548	A72	20p	Bentley, 1928	60	35
549	A72	24p	Alfa Romeo, 1929	70	35
550	A72	30p	Datsun, 1932	80	40
551	A72	35p	Lincoln, 1932	1.00	50
			Nos. 545-551 (7)	3.92	2.10

Souvenir Sheet

No.	Type	Value	Description	Unused	Used
552	A72	100p	Gottlieb Daimler	2.50	1.50

No. 552 contains one stamp 50x42mm.

Madonna and Child, by Morales — A73

Paintings by Spanish Artists (Espana '84): 6p, Dona Tadea Arias de Enriquez, by Goya. 10p, Santa Cassilda, by Zurbaran. 12p, Saints Andrew and Francis, by El Greco. 15p, Infanta Isabel Clara Eugenia, by Coello. 35p, Queen Maria of Austria, by Velazquez. 40p, Holy Trinity, by El Greco. 100p, Clothed Maja, by Goya.

1984, Apr. 20

No.	Type	Value	Description	Unused	Used
553	A73	3p	multicolored	15	15
554	A73	6p	multicolored	20	15
555	A73	10p	multicolored	30	15
556	A73	12p	multicolored	35	20
557	A73	15p	multicolored	42	25
558	A73	35p	multicolored	1.10	60
559	A73	40p	multicolored	1.25	65
			Nos. 553-559 (7)	3.77	2.15

Souvenir Sheet

No.	Type	Value	Description	Unused	Used
560	A73	100p	multicolored	3.00	1.50

No. 560 contains one stamp 29x50mm.

Carnivorous Animals — A74

1984, June 28

561 A74 3p Panthera tigris 15 15
562 A74 6p Panthera leo 20 15
563 A74 10p Neofelis nebulosa 35 15
564 A74 12p Acinonyx jubatus 35 20
565 A74 15p Lynx lynx 42 25
566 A74 35p Panthera pardus 1.10 60
567 A74 40p Uncia uncia 1.25 60
Nos. 561-567 (7) 3.82 2.10

Intl. Civil Aviation Org., 40th Anniv. — A75

1984, Apr. 4 Litho. *Perf. 12½*

568 A75 8p Caravelle 15
569 A75 22p DC-6B 40
570 A75 80p IL-76 1.50

1984 Summer Olympics, Los Angeles A76

1984, May 24 *Perf. 12*

571 A76 6p Soccer 15
572 A76 8p Dressage 18
573 A76 15p Yachting 35
574 A76 20p Field hockey 45
575 A76 22p Women's team handball 52
576 A76 30p Canoeing 70
577 A76 40p Boxing 90
Nos. 571-577 (7) 3.25

Souvenir Sheet

Perf. 11½

578 A76 100p Windsurfing 2.25

World Heritage — A77

Amilcar Cabral, 60th Birth Anniv. — A78

Wood sculptures: 3p, Pearl throne, Cameroun and Central Africa. 6p, Antelope, South Sudan. 10p, Kneeling woman, East Africa. 12p, Mask, West African coast. 15p, Leopard, Guinea coast. 35p, Standing woman, Zaire. 40p, Funerary statues, Southeast Africa and Madagascar.

1984, Aug. 15 *Perf. 12½*

579 A77 3p multicolored 15
580 A77 6p multicolored 15
581 A77 10p multicolored 22
582 A77 12p multicolored 28
583 A77 15p multicolored 35
584 A77 35p multicolored 80
585 A77 40p multicolored 90
Nos. 579-585 (7) 2.85

1984, Sept. 12 *Perf. 13*

586 A78 5p Public speaking 15
587 A78 12p In combat fatigues 20
588 A78 20p Memorial building, Bafata 35
589 A78 50p Mausoleum, Bissau 90

Independence, 11th Anniv. — A79

1984, Sept. 24

590 A79 3p Mechanic 15
591 A79 6p Student 15
592 A79 10p Mason 22
593 A79 12p Health care, vert. 28
594 A79 15p Seamstress, vert. 35
595 A79 35p Telecommunications 80
596 A79 40p PAIGC building 90
Nos. 590-596 (7) 2.85

Whales A80

1984, Sept. 30 *Perf. 12*

597 A80 5p Eschrichtius gibbosus 15
598 A80 8p Balaenoptera musculus 18
599 A80 15p Tursiops truncatus 35
600 A80 20p Physeter macrocephalus 45
601 A80 24p Orcinus orca 55
602 A80 30p Balaena mysticetus 70
603 A80 35p Balaenoptera borealis 80
Nos. 597-603 (7) 3.18

Butterflies A81

1984, Oct. 6 *Perf. 12½x13*

604 A81 3p Hypolimnas dexithea 15
605 A81 6p Papilio arcturus 15
606 A81 10p Morpho menelaus terrestris 22
607 A81 12p Apaturina erminea papuana 28
608 A81 15p Prepona praeneste 35
609 A81 35p Ornithoptera paradisea 80
610 A81 40p Morpho hecuba obidona 90
Nos. 604-610 (7) 2.85

1984 Olympic Winners — A82

National flag, medal and: 6p, Carl Lewis, 4x100 relay, US. 8p, Koji Gushiken, gymnastics, Japan. 15p, Reiner Klimke, equestrian, Federal Republic of Germany. 20p, Tracie Ruiz, synchronized swimming, US. 22p, Mary Lou Retton, gymnastics, US. 30p, Michael Gross, swimming, Federal Republic of Germany. 40p, Edwin Moses, hurdler, US. 100p, Daley Thompson, decathlon, Great Britain.

1984, Nov. 27 *Perf. 13*

611 A82 6p multicolored 15
612 A82 8p multicolored 18
613 A82 15p multicolored 35
614 A82 20p multicolored 45
615 A82 22p multicolored 52
616 A82 30p multicolored 70
617 A82 40p multicolored 90
Nos. 611-617 (7) 3.25

Souvenir Sheet

618 A82 100p multicolored 2.25

No. 618 contains one stamp 32x40mm, perf. 12½.

Locomotives — A83

1984, Dec. 15

619 A83 5p White Mountain Central No. 4 15
620 A83 8p Kessler 2-6-OT, 1886 18
621 A83 15p Langen tram, 1901 35
622 A83 20p Gurjao No. 6 45
623 A83 24p Achenseebahn 55
624 A83 30p Vitznau-Rigi steam locomotive 70
625 A83 35p Riggenbach rackrail, 1873 80
Nos. 619-625 (7) 3.18

Souvenir Sheet

Perf. 12½

625A A83 100p like #621 2.25

No. 625A contains one stamp 40x32mm.

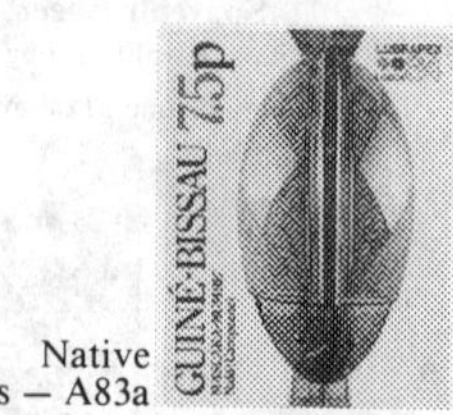

Native Crafts — A83a

Designs: a, Numbe mask. b, Sono statue. c, Erande statue. d, Kokumba arms. e, Oma mask. f, Koni mask.

1984 Litho. *Perf. 13½*

626 A83a 7.50p Strip of 6, #a.-f.

Motorcycle Cent. — A84

1985, Feb. 20 *Perf. 13x12½*

627 A84 5p Harley-Davidson 15
628 A84 8p Kawasaki 18
629 A84 15p Honda 35
630 A84 20p Yamaha 45
631 A84 25p Suzuki 55
632 A84 30p BMW 70
633 A84 35p Moto Guzzi 80
Nos. 627-633 (7) 3.18

Souvenir Sheet

634 A84 100p Daimler Motorized Bicycle, 1885, vert. 2.25

No. 634 contains one stamp 32x40mm, perf. 12½.

Miniature Sheet

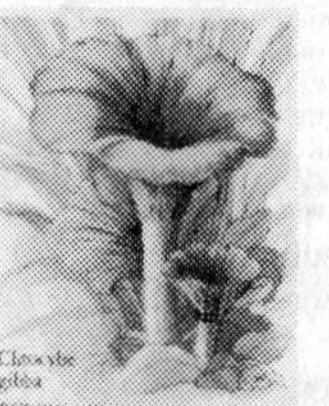

Mushrooms A85

1985, May 15 *Perf. 13*

635 Sheet of 6 3.10
a. A85 7p Clitocybe gibba 16
b. A85 9p Morchella elata 22
c. A85 12p Lepista nuda 28
d. A85 20p Lactarius deliciosus 45
e. A85 30p Russula virescens 70
f. A85 35p Chroogomphus rutilus 80

Henri Dunant (1828-1910), Red Cross Founder, Plane — A87

1985, June 12 *Perf. 12½*

643 A87 20p shown 45
644 A87 25p Ambulance 52
645 A87 40p Helicopter 90
646 A87 80p Speed boat 2.00

Cats — A88

1985, July 5 *Perf. 13*

647 A88 7p multicolored 16
648 A88 10p multicolored 22
649 A88 12p multicolored 28
650 A88 15p multicolored 35
651 A88 20p multicolored 45
652 A88 40p multicolored 90
653 A88 45p multicolored 1.20
Nos. 647-653 (7) 3.56

Souvenir Sheet

654 A88 100p multicolored 2.25

ARGENTINA '85. No. 654 contains one 40x32mm stamp.

Composers and Musical Instruments A89

Designs: 4p, Vincenzo Bellini (1801-1835), harp, 1820, and descant viol, 16th cent. 5p, Schumann (1810-1856) and Viennese pyramid piano, 1829. 7p, Chopin (1810-1849) and piano-forte, 1817. 12p, Luigi Cherubini (1760-1842) and 18th cent. Baryton violin and Quinton viol. 20p, G. B. Pergolesi (1710-1736) and double-manual harpsichord, 1734. 30p, Handel (1685-1759), valve trumpet, 1825, and timpani drum, 18th cent. 50p, Heinrich Schutz (1585-1672), bass viol and two-stop oboe, 17th cent. 100s, Bach (1685-1750) and St. Thomas Church organ, Leipzig.

1985, Aug. 5 *Perf. 12*

655 A89 4p multicolored 15
656 A89 5p multicolored 15
657 A89 7p multicolored 16
658 A89 12p multicolored 28
659 A89 20p multicolored 45
660 A89 30p multicolored 70
661 A89 50p multicolored 1.10
Nos. 655-661 (7) 2.99

Souvenir Sheet

Perf. 11½

662 A89 100p multicolored 2.25

No. 662 contains one 30x50mm stamp 30x50mm.

Santa Maria, 15th Cent., Spain — A90

Ships: 15p, Carack, 16th cent., Netherlands. 20p, Mayflower, 17th cent., Great Britain. 30p, St. Louis, 17th cent., France. 35p, Royal Sovereign, 1635, Great Britain. 45p, Soleil Royal, 17th cent., France. 80p, English brig, 18th-19th cent.

1985, Sept. 12 *Perf. 13*

663 A90 8p multicolored 20
664 A90 15p multicolored 35
665 A90 20p multicolored 45
666 A90 30p multicolored 70
667 A90 35p multicolored 80
668 A90 45p multicolored 1.10
669 A90 80p multicolored 2.00
Nos. 663-669 (7) 5.60

UN, 40th Anniv. A91

1985, Oct. 17

670 A91 10p Emblem, doves, vert. 22
671 A91 20p Emblem, 40 45

Venus and Mars, by Sandro Botticelli (1445-1510) A92

Botticelli paintings (details): 7p, Virgin with Child and St. John. 12p, St. Augustine in the Work Hall. 15p, Awakening of Spring. 20p, Virgin and Child. 40p, Virgin with Child and St. John, diff. 45p, Birth of Venus. 100p, Virgin and Child with Two Angels.

1985, Oct. 25 *Perf. 12½x13*

672 A92 7p multicolored 16
673 A92 10p multicolored 22
674 A92 12p multicolored 28
675 A92 15p multicolored 35
676 A92 20p multicolored 45
677 A92 40p multicolored 90
678 A92 45p multicolored 1.10

Size: 73x106mm

Imperf

679 A92 100p multicolored 2.25
Nos. 672-679 (8) 5.71

ITALIA '85.

Intl. Youth Year A93

1985, Nov. 29 **Litho.** *Perf. 12½*

680 A93 7p Dance 15
681 A93 13p Wind surfing 22
682 A93 15p Rollerskating 25
683 A93 25p Hang gliding 40
684 A93 40p Surfing 65
685 A93 50p Skateboarding 80
686 A93 80p Parachuting 1.40
Nos. 680-686 (7) 3.87

Souvenir Sheet

Perf. 13

687 A93 100p Self-defense 1.60

No. 687 contains one 40x32mm stamp.

Miniature Sheet

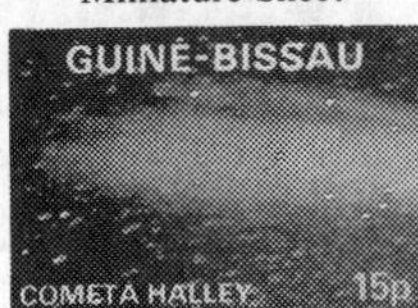
Halley's Comet — A94

1986 World Cup Soccer Championships, Mexico — A95

24th Summer Olympics, Seoul, 1988 — A96

Italian Automobile Industry, Cent. — A97

German Railways, 150th Anniv. A98

Discovery of America, 500th Anniv. (in 1992) A99

First American Manned Space Flight, 25th Anniv. — A100

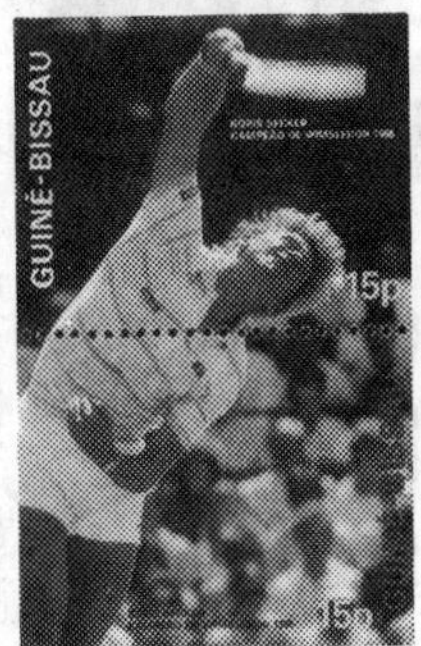
1986 Wimbledon Tennis Championships — A101

1986 Masters Tennis Championships — A102

Giotto Space Probe A103

Designs: a, Comet tail. b, Comet. c, Trophy. d, Trophy base. e, Five-ring Olympic emblem. f, Alfa Tourer, Italy, c. 1905. g, Railway station, Frankfurt-on Main, c. 1914. h, Barcelona, site of Discovery of America exhibition and 1992 Olympics. i, Space station solar panels and tanks. j, Space station. k, Removing cargo from space shuttle. l, Docking facility, station panels. m, Boris Becker swinging tennis racket. n, Becker, diff. o, Ivan Lendl holding racket. p, Lendl, diff.

1986, Dec. 30 **Litho.** *Perf. 13½*

688 Sheet of 16 *30.00*
a.-p. A94-A102 15p any single

Souvenir Sheet

689 A103 100p multicolored 6.50

Nos. 688a-688b, 688c-688d, 688i-688l, 688m-688n, 688o-688p are se-tenant in continuous designs. Inscription on Nos. 688i-688l incorrect; should read "TRIPULADO MERCURY / 5-5-1961."

Discovery of America, 500th Anniv. (in 1992) — A104

Designs: No. 690, Christopher Columbus aboard caravelle. No. 691, Guadalquivir Port, Seville, c. 1490. No. 692, Pedro Alvars Cabral landing at Bahia, Brazil. No. 693, Bridge over the Guadalquivir River, Seville. No. 694, Port, Lisbon, 15th cent.

1987, Feb. 27

690 A104 50p multicolored 1.50
691 A104 50p multicolored 1.50
692 A104 50p multicolored 1.50
693 A104 50p multicolored 1.50

Souvenir Sheet

694 A104 150p multicolored 10.00

No. 694 exists with pink or yellow anniv. emblem pictured in vignette.

Portuguese Guinea Nos. 306-309, 313, 316-317, Ovptd., Guinea-Bissau No. 349 Surcharged

1987, July **Litho.** *Perf. 13½*

696 A21 100p on 20c #306 *3.00*
697 A21 200p on 35c #307 *6.00*
698 A21 300p on 70c #308 *9.00*
699 A21 400p on 80c #309 *12.00*
700 A21 500p on 3.50e #313 *15.00*
701 A21 1000p on 15e #316 *30.00*
702 A21 2000p on 20e #317 *60.00*

Perf. 13

703 CD61 2500p on 2e #349 *75.00*
Nos. 696-703 (8) *210.00*

Placement of "Bissau," new denomination and obliterating bar varies.

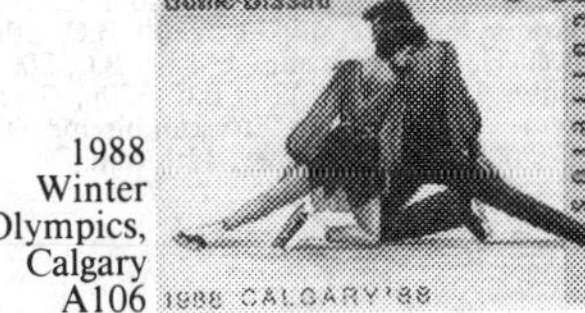
1988 Winter Olympics, Calgary A106

1988, Jan. 15 Litho. *Perf. 13*

704 A106 5p Pairs figure skating 15
705 A106 10p Luge 15
706 A106 50p Skiing 15
707 A106 200p Slalom skiing 36
708 A106 300p Skibobbing 55
709 A106 500p Ski jumping, vert. 90
710 A106 800p Speed skating, vert. 1.45
Nos. 704-710 (7) 3.71

Souvenir Sheet

710A A106 900p Two-man luge 1.60

No. 710A contains one 40x32mm stamp.

Soccer — A107

Various soccer plays.

1988, Apr. 14 Litho. *Perf. 13*

711 A107 5p multi 15
712 A107 10p multi, diff. 15
713 A107 50p multi, diff. 15
714 A107 200p multi, diff. 60
715 A107 300p multi, diff. 88
716 A107 500p multi, diff. 1.50
717 A107 800p multi, diff. 2.35
Nos. 711-717 (7) 5.78

Souvenir Sheet

718 A107 900p multi, diff. 2.65

ESSEN '88 stamp exhibition. No. 718 contains one 32x40mm stamp.

1988 Summer Olympics, Seoul — A108

Perf. 12½x12, 12x12½
1988, Feb. 26 Litho.

719 A108 5p Yachting, vert. 15
720 A108 10p Equestrian 15
721 A108 50p High jump 18
722 A108 200p Shooting 72
723 A108 300p Long jump, vert. 1.10
724 A108 500p Tennis, vert. 1.80
725 A108 800p Women's archery, vert. 2.90
Nos. 719-725 (7) 7.00

Souvenir Sheet
Perf. 12½

726 A108 900p Soccer 3.25

No. 726 contains one 40x32mm stamp.

Ancient Ships — A109

Designs: 5p, Egyptian, c. 3300 B.C. 10p, Pharaoh Sahure's ship, c. 2700 B.C. 50p, Queen Hatsepsowe's ship, c. 1500 B.C. 200p, Ramses III's ship, c. 1200 B.C. 300p, Greek trireme, 480 B.C. 500p, Etruscan bireme, 600 B.C. 800p, Venetian galley, 12th cent.

1988 Litho. *Perf. 13x12½*

727 A109 5p multi 15
728 A109 10p multi 15
729 A109 50p multi 18
730 A109 200p multi 72
731 A109 300p multi 1.10
732 A109 500p multi 1.80
733 A109 800p multi 2.90
Nos. 727-733 (7) 7.00

FINLANDIA '88 — A110

Chess champions, board and chessmen.

1988 Litho. *Perf. 12x12½*

734 A110 5p Philidor 15
735 A110 10p Staunton 15
736 A110 50p Anderssen 18
737 A110 200p Morphy 72
738 A110 300p Steinitz 1.10
739 A110 500p Lasker 1.80
740 A110 800p Capablanca 2.90
Nos. 734-740 (7) 7.00

Souvenir Sheet
Perf. 13

741 A110 900p Ruy Lopez 3.25

No. 741 contains one 40x32mm stamp.

Dogs A111

1988 *Perf. 13x12½*

742 A111 5p Basset hound 15
743 A111 10p Great blue of Gascony 15
744 A111 50p Sabujo of Italy 18
745 A111 200p Yorkshire terrier 72
746 A111 300p Small musterlander 1.10
747 A111 500p Pointer 1.80
748 A111 800p German setter 2.90
Nos. 742-748 (7) 7.00

Souvenir Sheet
Perf. 12½

749 A111 900 German shepherd 3.25

No. 749 contains one 40x32mm stamp.

Intl. Red Cross and Red Crescent Organizations, 125th Annivs. — A112

1988 *Perf. 13*

750 A112 10p Jean-Henri Dunant 15
751 A112 50p Dr. T. Maunoir 18
752 A112 200p Dr. Louis Appia 72
753 A112 800p Gustave Moynier 2.90

Maps and Fauna — A113

1988 *Perf. 12½x13, 13x12½*

754 A113 5p *Panthera leo* 15
755 A113 10p *Glaucidium brasilianum* 15
756 A113 50p *Upupa epops* 18
757 A113 200p *Equus burchelli antiquorum* 72
758 A113 300p *Loxodonta africana* 1.10
759 A113 500p *Acryllium vulturinum* 1.80
760 A113 800p *Diceros bicornis* 2.90
Nos. 754-760 (7) 7.00

Nos. 754-755, 758-760 vert. The genus *"Upupa"* is misspelled on the 50p and *"Loxodonta"* is misspelled on the 300p.

Samora Machel (1933-1986), Pres. of Mozambique A114

1988 *Perf. 13*

761 A114 10p shown 15
762 A114 50p Raising fist 18
763 A114 200p With sentry 75
764 A114 300p Wearing earphones at UN 1.15

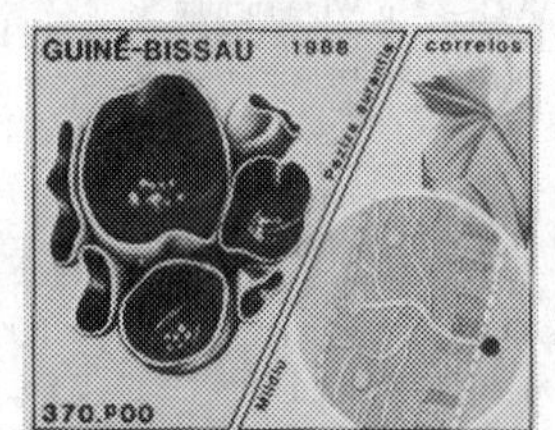

Mushrooms — A115

1988 Litho. *Perf. 13x12½*

765 A115 370p *Peziza aurantia* 1.20
766 A115 470p *Morchella* 1.55
767 A115 600p *Amanita caesarea* 2.00
768 A115 780p *Amanita muscaria* 2.60
769 A115 800p *Amanita phalloides* 2.65
770 A115 900p *Agaricus bisporus* 3.00
771 A115 945p *Cantharellus cibarius* 3.15
Nos. 765-771 (7) 16.15

1992 Winter Olympics, Albertville — A116

1989, Oct. 12 Litho. *Perf. 12½x12*

772 A116 50p Speed skating 15
773 A116 100p Women's figure skating 22
774 A116 200p Ski jumping 45
775 A116 350p Skiing 78
776 A116 500p Skiing, diff. 1.15
777 A116 800p Bobsled 1.80
778 A116 1000p Ice hockey 2.25
Nos. 772-778 (7) 6.80

Souvenir Sheet
Perf. 12½

779 A116 1500p Ice hockey, diff. 3.40

No. 779 contains one 32x40mm stamp.

World Cup Soccer Championships, Italy — A117

Various soccer players.

1989 Litho. *Perf. 12½*

780 A117 50p multicolored 15 15
781 A117 100p multicolored 22 22
782 A117 200p multicolored 45 45
783 A117 350p multicolored 80 80
784 A117 500p multicolored 88 88
785 A117 800p multicolored 1.85 1.85
786 A117 1000p multicolored 2.30 2.30
Nos. 780-786 (7) 6.65 6.65

Souvenir Sheet
Perf. 13

786A A117 1500p multicolored 4.90 4.90

No. 786A contains one 40x32mm stamp.

Lilies — A118

1989 *Perf. 12½*

787 A118 50p Lilium Limelight 15 15
788 A118 100p Lilium candidum 22 22
789 A118 200p Lilium pardalinum 45 45
790 A118 350p Lilium auratum 80 80
791 A118 500p Lilium canadense 88 88
792 A118 800p Lilium Enchantment 1.85 1.85
793 A118 1000p Lilium Black Dragon 2.30 2.30
Nos. 787-793 (7) 6.65 6.65

Souvenir Sheet

794 A118 1500p Lilium pyrenaicum 4.90 4.90

No. 794 contains one 32x40mm stamp.

Trains A119

Various railroad engines.

1989, May 24 Litho. *Perf. 13*

795 A119 50p multicolored 17 17
796 A119 100p multicolored 34 34
797 A119 200p multicolored 68 68
798 A119 350p multicolored 1.25 1.25
799 A119 500p multicolored 1.75 1.75
800 A119 800p multicolored 2.75 2.75

Perf. 12½
Size: 68x27mm

801 A119 1000p multicolored 3.40 3.40
Nos. 795-801 (7) 10.34 10.34

Souvenir Sheet
Perf. 12½

802 A119 1500p multicolored 5.00 5.00

No. 802 contains one 32x40mm stamp.

La Marseillaise by Francois Rude
A120

Paintings: 100p, Armed mob. 200p, Storming the Bastille. 350p, Lafayette, Liberty, vert. 500p, Dancing around the Liberty tree. 800p, Rouget de Lisle singing La Marseillaise by Pils. 1000p, Storming the Bastille, diff. 1500p, Arms of the Republic of France.

Perf. 12½, 12x12½ (350p)

1989, July 5
803 A120 50p shown 17 17
804 A120 100p multicolored 34 34
805 A120 200p multicolored 68 68
806 A120 350p multicolored, 27x44mm 1.25 1.25
807 A120 500p multicolored 1.75 1.75
808 A120 800p multicolored 2.75 2.75
809 A120 1000p multicolored 3.40 3.40
Nos. 803-809 (7) 10.34 10.34

Souvenir Sheet
Perf. 13

810 A120 1500p multicolored 5.00 5.00

Pioneers Organization — A122

1989 *Perf. 13*
819 A122 10p Children presenting flag, vert. 15 15
820 A122 50p Children saluting, vert. 21 21
821 A122 200p shown 85 85
822 A122 300p Children playing ball 1.25 1.25

Town of Cacheu, 400th Anniv.
A123

1989, Nov. 30
823 A123 10p Monument, vert. 15 15
824 A123 50p shown 21 21
825 A123 200p Old building 85 85
826 A123 300p Church 1.25 1.25

Dated 1988.

Prehistoric Creatures — A124

Perf. 13, 12½x12 (100p)

1989, Sept. 15
827 A124 50p Trachodon 15 15
828 A124 100p Edaphosaurus, 68x27mm 24 24
829 A124 200p Mesosaurus 48 48
830 A124 350p Elephas primigenius 80 80
831 A124 500p Tyrannosaurus 1.15 1.15
832 A124 800p Stegosaurus 1.85 1.85
833 A124 1000p Cervus megaceros 2.25 2.25
Nos. 827-833 (7) 6.92 6.92

Nos. 828, 831-833 horiz.

Musical Instruments — A125

1989, Apr. 10 **Litho.** *Perf. 13*
834 A125 50p Bombalon 15
835 A125 100p Flauta 30
836 A125 200p Tambor 60
837 A125 350p Dondon 1.05
838 A125 500p Balafon 1.50
839 A125 800p Kora 2.40
840 A125 1000p Nhanhero 3.00
Nos. 834-840 (7) 9.00

Indian Artifacts — A126

1989, July 13 *Perf. 12x12½*
841 A126 50p Teotihuacan 15 15
842 A126 100p Mochica 24 24
843 A126 200p Jaina 48 48
844 A126 350p Nayarit 80 80
845 A126 500p Inca 1.15 1.15
846 A126 800p Hopewell 1.85 1.85
847 A126 1000p Taina 2.25 2.25
Nos. 841-847 (7) 6.92 6.92

Souvenir Sheet
Perf. 12½

848 A126 1500p Indian statuette 3.50 3.50

Brasiliana '89 Philatelic Exhibition. Nos. 841-847 printed se-tenant with multicolored label showing scenes of colonization. No. 848 contains one 32x40mm stamp.

1992 Summer Olympics, Barcelona
A127

1989, June 3 *Perf. 12½x13*
849 A127 50p Hurdles 15 15
850 A127 100p Boxing 16 16
851 A127 200p High jump 32 32
852 A127 350p Sprinters in the blocks 52 52
853 A127 500p Woman sprinter 75 75
854 A127 800p Gymnastics 1.25 1.25
855 A127 1000p Pole vault 1.50 1.50
856 A127 1500p Soccer 2.25 2.25
Nos. 849-855 (7) 4.65 4.65

Wild Animals — A128

1989, Nov. 24 *Perf. 12½*
857 A128 50p Syncerus caffer 15 15
858 A128 100p Equus quagga 16 16
859 A128 200p Diceros bicornis 32 32
860 A128 350p Okapia johnstoni 52 52
861 A128 500p Macaca mulatta 75 75
862 A128 800p Hippopotamus amphibius 1.25 1.25
863 A128 1000p Acinonyx jubatus 1.50 1.50
864 A128 1500p Panthera leo 2.25 2.25
Nos. 857-864 (8) 6.90 6.90

Christmas
A129

Paintings of the Madonna and Child (50p) and the Adoration of the Magi.

1989, Dec. 10 *Perf. 13*
865 A129 50p Fra Filippo Lippi 15 15
866 A129 100p Pieter Brueghel 15 15
867 A129 200p Mostaert 20 20
868 A129 350p Durer 35 35
869 A129 500p Rubens 50 50
870 A129 800p Van der Weyden 80 80
871 A129 1000p Francia, horiz. 1.00 1.00
Nos. 865-871 (7) 3.15 3.15

Womens' Hairstyles
A130

Various hairstyles.

1989, Mar. 8 *Perf. 12½x13*
872 A130 50p multicolored 15 15
873 A130 100p multicolored 16 16
874 A130 200p multicolored 32 32
875 A130 350p multicolored 52 52
876 A130 800p multicolored 1.25 1.25
877 A130 1000p multicolored 1.50 1.50
Nos. 872-877 (6) 3.90 3.90

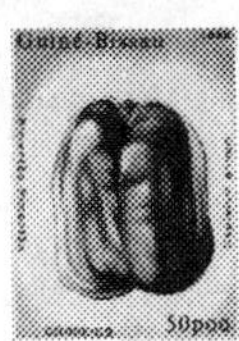

Vegetables — A131

1989, May 20 *Perf. 12½*
878 A131 50p Capisium annum 15 15
879 A131 100p Solanium 15 15
880 A131 200p Curcumis peco 20 20
881 A131 350p Solanium licopersicum 35 35
882 A131 500p Solanium itiopium 50 50
883 A131 800p Hibiscus esculentus 80 80
884 A131 1000p Oseille de guine 1.00 1.00
Nos. 878-884 (7) 3.15 3.15

Visit of Pope John Paul II — A132

1990, Jan. 27 **Litho.** *Perf. 13½*
885 A132 500p shown 1.50 1.50
886 A132 1000p multi, diff. 3.00 3.00

Souvenir Sheet

887 A132 1500p multi, diff., vert. 4.50 4.50

Souvenir Sheet

Belgica '90 — A133

1990, June 1 *Perf. 14½*
888 A133 3000p multicolored 4.05 4.05

World Meteorology Day — A134

1990, Oct. 1 **Litho.** *Perf. 13*
889 A134 1000p Radar weather map 1.30
890 A134 3000p Heliograph 3.90

LUBRAPEX '90 — A135

1990, Sept. 21 *Perf. 14*
891 A135 500p Rooster, hen 65
892 A135 800p Turkey 1.05
893 A135 1000p Duck, ducklings 1.30

Souvenir Sheet
Perf. 13½

894 A135 1500p Rooster, turkey, ducks 2.00

UN Development Program, 40th Anniv. — A136

1990 **Litho.** *Perf. 14*
895 A136 1000p multicolored 1.35

Fight against AIDS.

Textile Manufacturing
A137

No. 896: a, Gossypium hirsutum. b, Processing cotton. c, Spinning thread. d, Picking cotton. e, Moth, silkworms. f, Dyeing thread. g, Weaving. h, Animal design. i, Multi-colored stripes design. j, Stripes, dots design.

1990

896 Sheet of 10 1.50
a.-j. A137 150p any single 15
897 A137 400p like #896a 35
898 A137 500p like #896g 45
899 A137 600p like #896h 55

Carnival Masks A138

1990 Litho. *Perf. 14*

900 A138 200p Mickey Mouse 18
901 A138 300p Hippopotamus 28
902 A138 600p Bull 55
903 A138 1200p Bull, diff. 1.10

Fish A139

Designs: 300p, Pentanemus quinquarius. 400p, Psettias sabae. 500p, Chaetodipterus goreensis. 600p, Trachinotus goreensis.

1991, Mar. 10 Litho. *Perf. 14*

904 A139 300p multicolored 25 25
905 A139 400p multicolored 35 35
906 A139 500p multicolored 42 42
907 A139 600p multicolored 50 50

Fire Trucks A140

1991, Aug. 19 Litho. *Perf. 14*

908 A140 200p shown 15 15
909 A140 500p Ladder truck 38 38
910 A140 800p Rescue vehicle 62 62
911 A140 1500p Ambulance 1.15 1.15

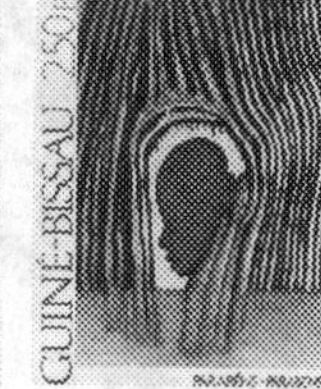

Birds — A141 Messages — A142

Designs: 100p, Kaupifalco monogrammicus. 250p, Balearica pavonina. 350p, Bucorvus abyssinicus. 500p, Ephippiorhynchus senegalensis. 1500p, Kaupifalco monogrammicus, diff.

1991, Sept. 10

912 A141 100p multicolored 15 15
913 A141 250p multicolored 20 20
914 A141 350p multicolored 30 30
915 A141 500p multicolored 38 38

Souvenir Sheet

Perf. 14½

916 A141 1500p multicolored 1.15 1.15

No. 916 contains one 40x50mm stamp.

1991, Oct. 28 Litho. *Perf. 14*

917 A142 250p Congratulations 20 20
918 A142 400p With love 32 32
919 A142 800p Happiness 65 65
920 A142 1000p Seasons Greetings 80 80

AIR POST STAMPS

Liftoff of Soyuz Spacecraft AP1

Apollo-Soyuz mission: 10p, Launch of Apollo spacecraft. 15p, Leonov, Stafford and meeting in space. 20p, Eclipse of the sun. 30p, Infra-red photo of Earth. 40p, Return to Earth. 50p, Apollo and Soyuz docked, horiz.

1976, Oct. 4 *Perf. 13½*

C10 AP1 5p multicolored
C10A AP1 10p multicolored
C10B AP1 15p multicolored
C10C AP1 20p multicolored
C10D AP1 30p multicolored
C10E AP1 40p multicolored

Souvenir Sheet

C10F AP1 50p multicolored

No. C10F contains one 60x42mm stamp. Nos. C10-C10E exist in souvenir sheets of one, perf. and imperf.

Viking Spacecraft Orbiting Mars — AP2

Design: 35p, Viking gathering Martian soil samples.

1977, Jan. 27

C11 AP2 25p multicolored
C11A AP2 35p multicolored

Nos. 372-373 Surcharged with New Value and "CORREIO AEREO" in Black on Silver Panels

1978 Litho. *Perf. 13½*

C12 A32 15p on 3.50p multi 80 42
C13 A32 30p on 50c multi 1.00 60

History of Aviation Type of 1980

1980 Litho. *Perf. 13½*

C14 A38 35p Willy de Houthulst, Hanriot HD.1 1.25 60
C14A A38 40p Charles Guynemer, Spad S. VII 1.50 70

Souvenir Sheet

C14B A38 50p Comdr. de Rose, Nieuport 2.00 1.00

No. C14B contains one stamp 37x55mm.

Winter Olympics Type of 1980

1980

C15 A39 35p Slalom 1.25 60
C16 A39 40p Figure skating 1.50 70

Souvenir Sheet

C17 A39 50p Ice hockey, horiz. 2.00 1.00

Summer Olympics Type of 1980

1980, Aug. Litho. *Perf. 13½*

C18 A40 35p Somersault 1.25 60
C19 A40 40p Running 1.50 70

Souvenir Sheet

C20 A40 50p Emblem 2.00 1.00

Literacy Type of 1980

1980, Aug. Litho. *Perf. 13½*

C21 A41 15p like #391 60 30
C22 A41 25p like #392 1.00 50

Space Type of 1981

Designs: 35p, Viking 1 and 2. 40p, Apollo-Soyuz craft and crew. 50p, Apollo 11 crew, craft and emblem.

1981, May Litho. *Perf. 13½*

C23 A45 35p multicolored 1.25 60
C24 A45 40p multicolored 1.50 70

Souvenir Sheet

C25 A45 50p multicolored 2.25 1.25

No. C25 contains one stamp 60x42mm.

Soccer Type of 1981

Designs: 35p, Rummenigge, Germany. 40p, Kempes, Argentina. 50p, Juanito, Spain.

1981, May

C26 A46 35p multicolored 1.25 60
C27 A46 40p multicolored 1.50 70

Souvenir Sheet

C28 A46 50p multicolored 2.25 1.25

No. C28 contains one stamp 56x40mm.

Royal Wedding Type of 1981

1981 Litho. *Perf. 13½*

C29 A47 35p Palace 1.90 1.00
C30 A47 40p Prince of Wales arms 2.00 1.25

Souvenir Sheet

C31 A47 50p Couple 2.25 1.25

Picasso Type of 1981

1981, Dec. Litho. *Perf. 13½*

C32 A48 35p multicolored 1.90 1.00
C33 A48 40p multicolored 2.00 1.25

Souvenir Sheet

C34 A48 50p multicolored 2.25 1.25

No. C34 contains one stamp 41x50mm.

Navigator Type of 1981

Designs: 35p, Francis Drake, Golden Hinde. 40p, James Cook, Endeavor. 50p, Columbus, Santa Maria.

1981 Litho. *Perf. 13½*

C35 A49 35p multicolored 1.90 1.00
C36 A49 40p multicolored 2.00 1.25

Souvenir Sheet

C37 A49 50p multicolored 2.25 1.25

Christmas Type of 1981

1981

C38 A50 30p Memling 1.90 1.00
C39 A50 35p Bellini, diff. 2.00 1.25

Souvenir Sheet

C40 A50 50p Fra Angelico 2.25 1.25

No. C40 contains one stamp 35x59mm.

Scout Type of 1982

1982, June 9 Litho. *Perf. 13½*

C41 A51 35p Canoeing 1.50 70
C42 A51 40p Flying model planes 1.90 1.00

Souvenir Sheet

C43 A51 50p Playing chess 2.25 1.25

No. C43 contains one stamp 48x38mm.

Soccer Type of 1982

1982, June 13 Litho. *Perf. 13½*

C44 A52 35p Kempes 1.50 70
C45 A52 40p Kaltz 1.90 1.00

Souvenir Sheet

C46 A52 50p Stadium 2.25 1.25

Diana Type of 1982

1982

C47 A53 35p multicolored 1.50 70
C48 A53 40p multicolored 1.90 1.00

Souvenir Sheet

C49 A53 50p multi, vert. 2.25 1.25

Audubon Birth Bicent. — AP3

1985, Apr. 16 Litho. *Perf. 12*

C50 AP3 5p Brown pelican 15
C51 AP3 10p American white pelican 22
C52 AP3 20p Great blue heron 45
C53 AP3 40p American flamingo 90

HAITI

LOCATION — Western part of Hispaniola
GOVT. — Republic
AREA — 10,700 sq. mi.
POP. — 5,198,000 (est. 1984)
CAPITAL — Port-au-Prince

100 Centimes = 1 Piaster (1906)
100 Centimes = 1 Gourde

Catalogue values for unused stamps in this country are for Never Hinged items, beginning with Scott 370 in the regular postage section, Scott B2 in the semi-postal section, Scott C33 in the air post section, Scott CB10 in the air post semi-postal section, Scott CO6 in the air post official section, Scott CQ1 in the air post parcel post seciton, Scott E1 in the special delivery section, Scott J21 in the postage due section, Scott Q1 in the parcel post section, Scott RA1 in the postal tax section, and Scott RAC1 in the air post postal tax section.

Watermark

Wmk. 131- RH

Liberty Head — A1

1881 Unwmk. Typo. *Imperf.*

1 A1 1c ver, *yelsh* 5.25 3.50
2 A1 2c dk vio, *pale lil* 7.00 3.75
3 A1 3c bis, *pale bis* 12.00 4.50
4 A1 5c grn, *grnsh* 21.00 7.75
5 A1 7c bl, *grysh* 14.00 2.75
6 A1 20c red brn, *yelsh* 52.50 17.50

Nos. 1-6 were printed from plate I, Nos. 7-13 from plates II and III.

1882 *Perf. 13½*

7 A1 1c ver, *yelsh* 3.50 1.25
c. Horiz. pair, imperf. btwn. 125.00
d. Vert. pair imperf. btwn. 115.00 100.00

8 A1 2c dk vio, *pale lil* 5.25 1.75
a. 2c dk vio 7.00 4.25
b. 2c red vio, *pale lil* 5.25 2.00
c. Horiz. or vert. pair, imperf. vert. 100.00
e. Horiz. pair, imperf. between 120.00 120.00
9 A1 3c bis, *pale bis* 7.00 2.75
10 A1 5c grn, *grnsh* 4.25 85
a. 5c yel grn, *grnsh* 4.25 85
b. 5c dp grn, *grnsh* 4.25 85
c. Horiz. pair, imperf. vert. 110.00
d. Horiz. or vert. pair, imperf. btwn. 120.00
11 A1 7c bl, *grysh* 6.25 1.40
a. Horiz. pair, imperf. between
12 A1 7c ultra, *grysh* 10.00 2.00
a. Vert. pair, imperf. between
b. Horiz. pair, imperf. vert.
13 A1 20c pale brn, *yelsh* 5.00 1.10
a. 20c red brn, *yelsh* 10.50 2.00
b. Horiz. pair, imperf. vert 90.00
c. Vert. pair, imperf. horiz. 110.00
d. Horiz. or vert. pair, imperf. between 120.00 110.00

Stamps perf. 14, 16 are forgeries which were made to defraud the government and used freely in the mails.

A3

A4

1886-87 ***Perf. 13½***
18 A3 1c ver, *yelsh* 3.50 1.10
a. Horiz. pair, imperf. vert. 120.00
b. Horiz. pair, imperf. between 120.00 120.00
19 A3 2c dk vio, *lil* 27.50 4.25
20 A4 5c grn ('87) 10.50 1.40

Differences between Nos. 18-20 (which were printed from new dies) and the preceding issues are too small to illustrate clearly. These stamps can be identified by the numerals of value, which are larger than the earlier ones and differ slightly in shape. Nos. 18 and 19 show crossed lines of dots on face.

General Louis Etienne Félicité Salomon — A5

1887 **Engr.** ***Perf. 14***
21 A5 1c lake 28 28
22 A5 2c violet 70 52
23 A5 3c blue 52 35
24 A5 5c green 3.50 35

Some experts believe the imperfs. of Nos. 21-24 are plate proofs. Value per pair, $20.

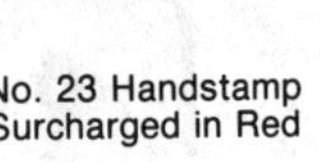
No. 23 Handstamp Surcharged in Red

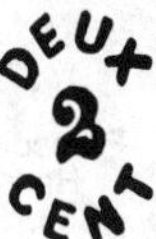

1890
25 A5 2c on 3c blue 42 35

This surcharge being handstamped is to be found double, inverted, etc. This applies to succeeding surcharged issues.

Coat of Arms — A7

Coat of Arms (Leaves Drooping) — A9

1891 ***Perf. 13***
26 A7 1c violet 35 25
27 A7 2c blue 52 28
28 A7 3c gray lilac 70 35
a. 3c slate 70 42
29 A7 5c orange 2.50 28
30 A7 7c red 5.50 2.00
Nos. 26-30 (5) 9.57 3.16

Nos. 26-30 exist imperf. Value of unused pairs, each $20.

The 2c, 3c and 7c exist imperf. vertically.

No. 28 Surcharged Like No. 25 in Red

1892
31 A7 2c on 3c gray lilac 90 70
a. 2c on 3c slate 90 70

1892-95 **Engr., Litho. (20c)** ***Perf. 14***
32 A9 1c lilac 18 15
a. Imperf., pair
33 A9 2c deep blue 18 15
34 A9 3c gray 52 35
35 A9 5c orange 1.75 25
36 A9 7c red 25 18
a. Imperf., pair 4.50
37 A9 20c brown 1.25 75
Nos. 32-37 (6) 4.13 1.83

Nos. 32, 33, 35 exist in pairs, imperf. vert., No. 35, pair, imperf. horiz.

1896 **Engr.** ***Perf. 13½***
38 A9 1c light blue 15 15
39 A9 2c red brown 20 15
40 A9 3c lilac brown 15 15
41 A9 5c slate green 15 15
42 A9 7c dark gray 15 15
43 A9 20c orange 18 18
Nos. 38-43 (6) 98
Set value 75

Nos. 32-37 are 23¾mm high, Nos. 38-43 23¼mm to 23½mm. The "C" is closed on Nos. 32-37, open on Nos. 38-43. Other differences exist. The stamps of the two issues may be readily distinguished by their colors and perfs.

Nos. 38-43 exist imperf. and in horiz. pairs, imperf. vert. The 1c, 3c, 5, 7c exist in vert. pairs, imperf. horiz. or imperf. between. The 5c, 7c exist in horiz. pairs, imperf. between. Value of unused pairs, $5 and up.

Nos. 37 and 43 Surcharged Like No. 25 in Red

1898
44 A9 2c on 20c brown 90 42
45 A9 2c on 20c orange 52 35

No. 45 exists in various part perf. varieties.

Coat of Arms — A11

1898 **Wmk. 131** ***Perf. 11***
46 A11 1c ultra 1.00 70
47 A11 2c brn car 35 15
48 A11 3c dl vio 85 52
49 A11 5c dk grn 35 20
50 A11 7c gray 2.00 1.40
51 A11 20c orange 2.00 1.40
Nos. 46-51 (6) 6.55 4.37

All values exist imperforate. They are plate proofs.

Pres. T. Augustin Simon Sam — A12

Coat of Arms — A13

1898-99 **Unwmk.** ***Perf. 12***
52 A12 1c ultra 15 15
53 A13 1c yel grn ('99) 15 15
54 A12 2c dp org 15 15
55 A13 2c car lake ('99) 15 15
56 A12 3c green 15 15
57 A13 4c red 18 15
58 A12 5c red brn 15 15
59 A13 5c pale bl ('99) 15 15
60 A12 7c gray 15 15
61 A13 8c carmine 18 15
62 A13 10c org red 18 15
63 A13 15c ol grn 52 35
64 A12 20c black 50 35
65 A12 50c rose brn 55 35
66 A12 1g red vio 1.50 1.40
Nos. 52-66 (15) 4.81
Set value 3.50

For overprints see Nos. 67-81, 110-124, 169, 247-248.

Stamps of 1898-99 Handstamped in Black

1902
67 A12 1c ultra 45 45
68 A13 1c yel grn 35 18
69 A12 2c dp org 70 70
70 A13 2c car lake 35 15
71 A12 3c green 35 35
72 A13 4c red 45 45
73 A12 5c red brn 1.00 1.00
74 A13 5c pale bl 35 35
75 A12 7c gray 70 70
76 A13 8c carmine 70 70
77 A13 10c org red 70 70
78 A13 15c ol grn 3.50 2.50
79 A12 20c black 3.50 2.75
80 A12 50c rose brn 8.75 4.25
81 A12 1g red vio 10.50 8.75
Nos. 67-81 (15) 32.35 23.98

Many forgeries exist of this overprint.

Centenary of Independence Issues

Coat of Arms — A14

Pierre D. Toussaint L'Ouverture — A15

Emperor Jean Jacques Dessalines — A16

Pres. Alexandre Sabes Pétion — A17

1904 **Engr.** ***Perf. 13½, 14***
82 A14 1c green 15 15

Center Engr., Frame Litho.
83 A15 2c rose & blk 15 15
84 A15 5c dl bl & blk 15 15
85 A16 7c plum & blk 15 15
86 A16 10c yel & blk 15 15
87 A17 20c slate & blk 15 15
88 A17 50c olive & blk 15 15
Nos. 82-88 (7) 1.05
Set value 84

Nos. 82 to 88 exist imperforate.

Nos. 83-88 exist with centers inverted. Some are known with head omitted.

Forgeries exist.

Same Handstamped in Blue

1904
89 A14 1c green 25 25
90 A15 2c rose & blk 28 28
91 A15 5c dl bl & blk 28 28
92 A16 7c plum & blk 35 35
93 A16 10c yel & blk 35 35
94 A17 20c slate & blk 35 35
95 A17 50c olive & blk 35 35
Nos. 89-95 (7) 2.21 2.21

Two dies were used for the handstamped overprint on Nos. 89-95. Letters and figures are larger on one than on the other. All values exist imperforate.

Pres. Pierre Nord-Alexis — A18

1904 **Engr.** ***Perf. 13½, 14***
96 A18 1c green 15 15
97 A18 2c carmine 15 15
98 A18 5c dk bl 15 15
99 A18 10c org brn 15 15
100 A18 20c orange 15 15
101 A18 50c claret 15 15
a. Tete beche pair 35.00
Set value 45 45

Nos. 96 to 101 exist imperforate.

For overprints and surcharges see Nos. 102-109, 150-161, 170-176, 217-218, 235-238, 240-242, 302-303.

Reprints or very accurate imitations of this issue exist, including No. 101a.

They are printed in very bright colors on very white paper and are found both perforated and imperforate.

Same Handstamped in Blue

1904
102 A18 1c green 42 35
103 A18 2c carmine 42 35
104 A18 5c dk bl 42 35
105 A18 10c org brn 42 35
106 A18 20c orange 42 35
107 A18 50c claret 42 35
Nos. 102-107 (6) 2.52 2.10

The note after No. 95 applies also to Nos. 102-107. All values exist imperf.

Regular Issue of 1904 Handstamp Surcharged in Black:

1906, Feb. 20
108 A18 1c on 20c orange 18 15
a. 1c on 50c claret 800.00
109 A18 2c on 50c claret 18 15
Set value 20

No. 108a is known only with inverted surcharge.

Forgeries exist.

Nos. 52-66 Handstamped in Red

1906
110 A12 1c ultra 90 70
111 A13 1c yel grn 52 52
112 A12 2c dp org 1.75 1.75
113 A13 2c car lake 1.00 1.00
114 A12 3c green 1.00 1.00
115 A13 4c red 4.25 3.50
116 A12 5c red brn 5.25 4.25
117 A13 5c pale bl 70 42
118 A12 7c gray 3.50 3.50
119 A13 8c carmine 70 70
120 A13 10c org red 1.40 90
121 A13 15c ol grn 1.75 1.00
122 A12 20c black 4.25 3.50
123 A12 50c rose brn 4.25 2.75
124 A12 1g red vio 7.00 5.50
Nos. 110-124 (15) 38.22 30.99

Forgeries of this overprint are plentiful.

Coat of Arms
A19

President Nord-Alexis
A20

Market at Port-au-Prince
A21

Sans Souci Palace
A22

Independence Palace at Gonaives
A23

Entrance to Catholic College at Port-au-Prince
A24

Monastery and Church at Port-au-Prince
A25

Seat of Government at Port-au-Prince
A26

Presidential Palace at Port-au-Prince
A27

For Foreign Postage
(centimes de piastre)

1906-13 *Perf. 12*

125	A19	1c de p grn	18	15
126	A20	2c de p ver	35	18
127	A21	3c de p brn	52	18
128	A21	3c de p org yel ('11)	5.00	2.75
129	A22	4c de p car lake	52	28
130	A22	4c de p lt ol grn ('13)	7.00	4.25
131	A20	5c de p dk bl	1.75	18
132	A23	7c de p gray	1.40	70
133	A23	7c de p org red ('13)	21.00	14.00
134	A24	8c de p car rose	1.40	60
135	A24	8c de p ol grn ('13)	12.00	8.50
136	A25	10c de p org red	90	18
137	A25	10c de p red brn ('13)	12.00	8.50
138	A26	15c de p sl grn	1.75	70
139	A26	15c dp p yel ('13)	5.25	2.75
140	A20	20c de p bl grn	1.75	70
141	A19	50c de p red	2.75	2.00
142	A19	50c de p org yel ('13)	6.00	4.25
143	A27	1p claret	5.50	3.50
144	A27	1p red ('13)	6.00	5.00
		Nos. 125-144 (20)	93.02	59.35

All 1906 values exist imperf. These are plate proofs.

For overprints and surcharges see Nos. 177-195, 213-216, 239, 245, 249-260, 263, 265-277, 279-284, 286-301, 304.

Nord-Alexis
A28

Coat of Arms
A29

For Domestic Postage
(centimes de gourde)

1906-10

145	A28	1c de g blue	18	15
146	A29	2c de g org yel	35	15
147	A29	2c de g lemon ('10)	52	15
148	A28	3c de g slate	28	15
149	A29	7c de g green	90	35
		Nos. 145-149 (5)	2.23	
		Set value		78

For overprints see Nos. 196-197.

Regular Issue of 1904 Handstamp Surcharged in Red:

1907

150	A18	1c on 5c dk bl	28	20
151	A18	1c on 20c org	20	15
152	A18	2c on 10c org brn	25	18
153	A18	2c on 50c claret	35	20

Black Surcharge

154	A18	1c on 5c dk bl	35	18
155	A18	1c on 10c org brn	25	15
156	A18	2c on 20c org	20	18

Brown Surcharge

157	A18	1c on 5c dk bl	35	35
158	A18	1c on 10c org brn	55	35
159	A18	2c on 20c org	1.75	1.40
160	A18	2c on 50c claret	17.50	16.00

Violet Surcharge

161	A18	1c on 20c org	70.00	

The handstamps are found sideways, diagonal, inverted and double.

Forgeries exist.

President Antoine T. Simon
A30 A31

For Foreign Postage

1910

162	A30	2c de p rose red & blk	52	35
163	A30	5c de p bl & blk	8.75	52
164	A30	20c de p yel grn & blk	7.00	5.50

For Domestic Postage

165	A31	1c de g lake & blk	15	15

For overprint and surcharges see Nos. 198, 262, 278, 285.

A32

A33

Pres. Cincinnatus Leconte — A34

1912

166	A32	1c de g car lake	20	18
167	A33	2c de g dp org	25	18

For Foreign Postage

168	A34	5c de p dp bl	52	18

For overprints see Nos. 199-201.

Stamps of Preceding Issues Handstamped Vertically

Gl. O.Z.
7 FÉV. 1914

1914

On Stamp of 1898-99

169	A13	8c carmine	8.75	7.00

On Regular Issue of 1904

170	A18	1c green	25.00	21.00
171	A18	2c carmine	25.00	21.00
172	A18	5c dk bl	45	25
173	A18	10c org brn	45	25
174	A18	20c orange	70	35
175	A18	50c claret	2.00	90

Perforation varieties of Nos. 172-175 exist.

On Stamp of 1904
With "Poste Paye" Handstamp

176	A18	50c claret	*10,000.*	*10,000.*

Horizontally on Stamps of 1906-13

177	A19	1c de p grn	35	25
178	A20	2c de p ver	52	25
179	A21	3c de p brn	70	52
180	A21	3c de p org yel	35	25
181	A22	4c de p car lake	70	60
182	A22	4c de p lt ol grn	1.25	65
183	A23	7c de p gray	2.00	2.00
184	A23	7c de p org red	2.75	2.75
185	A24	8c de p car rose	3.50	3.50
186	A24	8c de p ol grn	3.50	3.50
187	A25	10c de p org red	90	52
188	A25	10c de p red brn	1.40	90
189	A26	15c de p sl grn	2.75	2.75
190	A26	15c de p yel	1.25	70
191	A20	20c de p bl grn	2.50	90
192	A19	50c de p red	4.25	4.25
193	A19	50c de p org yel	4.25	4.25
194	A27	1p claret	4.25	4.25
195	A27	1p red	4.25	4.25
196	A29	2c de g lemon	35	18
197	A28	3c de g slate	35	21
		Nos. 177-197 (21)	42.12	37.43

On Stamp of 1910

198	A30	20c de p yel grn & blk	2.75	2.75

Vertically on Stamps of 1912

199	A32	1c de g car lake	25	18
200	A33	2c de g dp org	45	35
201	A34	5c de p dp bl	70	20

Two handstamps were used for the overprints on Nos. 169 to 201. They may be distinguished by the short and long foot of the "L" of "GL" and the position of the first "1" in "1914" with regard to the period above it. Both handstamps are found on all these stamps.

Handstamp Surcharged

Gl. O.Z.
1 CENT DE PIASTRE
7 FÉV. 1914

On Nos. 141 and 143

213	A19	1c de p on 50c de p red	28	20
214	A27	1c de p on 1p claret	45	42

On Nos. 142 and 144

215	A19	1c de p on 50c de p org yel	45	35
216	A27	1c de p on 1p red	52	42

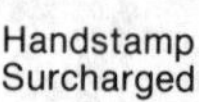
Handstamp Surcharged

On Nos. 100 and 101

217	A18	7c on 20c orange	42	20
218	A18	7c on 50c claret	35	20

The initials on the preceding handstamps are those of Gen. Oreste Zamor; the date is that of his triumphal entry into Port-au-Prince.

Pres. Oreste Zamor — A35

Coat of Arms — A36

Pres. Tancrede Auguste — A37

Coat of Arms — A38

Zamor — A39

For Foreign Postage

1914

219	A35	1c de p dk grn & blk	1.40	
221	A36	3c de p dl grn & blk	15	
223	A35	5c de p bl & blk	25	
224	A37	7c de p org & blk	60	
226	A35	10c de p blk brn & blk	18	
227	A35	15c de p ol gray & blk	25	
228	A36	20c de p yel brn & blk	25	

For Domestic Postage

230	A39	2c de g yel & blk	45	
231	A38	5c de g yel grn & blk	70	
232	A39	7c de g rose & blk	42	
		Nos. 219-232 (10)	4.65	

Owing to the theft of a large quantity of Nos. 219-232 while in transit from the printers, the stamps were never placed on sale at post offices. A few copies have been canceled through carelessness or favor.

Preceding Issues Handstamp Surcharged in Carmine or Blue

On Nos. 98-101

1915-16

235	A18	1c on 5c dk bl (C)	1.40	1.40
236	A18	1c on 10c org brn	15	15
237	A18	1c on 20c org	42	35
238	A18	1c on 50c claret	15	15

On No. 132

239	A23	1c on 7c de p gray (C)	15	15

On Nos. 106-107

240	A18	1c on 20c org	52	70
241	A18	1c on 50c claret	1.75	52
242	A18	1c on 50c cl (C)	27.50	21.00

Nos. 240-242 are known with two types of the "Post Paye" overprint. No. 237 with red surcharge and any stamps with violet surcharge are unofficial.

No. 143 Handstamp Surcharged in Red

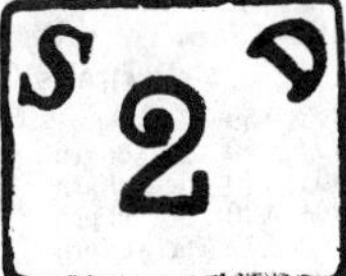

1917-19
245 A27 2c on 1p claret 18 15

Stamps of 1906-14 Handstamp Surcharged in Various Colors

1c, 5c

On Nos. 123-124
247 A12 1c on 50c (R) 17.50 12.50
248 A12 1c on 1g (R) 21.00 16.00

On Nos. 127, 129, 134, 136, 138, 140-141
249 A22 1c on 4c de p (Br) 15 15
250 A25 1c on 10c de p (Bl) 15 15
251 A25 1c on 10c de p (Bk) 70 70
252 A20 1c on 20c de p (R) 18 15
253 A20 1c on 20c de p (Bk) 25 15
254 A19 1c on 50c de p (R) 18 15
255 A19 1c on 50c de p (Bk) 25 15
256 A21 2c on 3c de p (R) 28 18
257 A24 2c on 8c de p (R) 18 15
258 A24 2c on 8c de p (Bk) 25 15
259 A26 2c on 15c de p (R) 18 15
260 A20 2c on 20c de p (R) 25 15
Nos. 249-260 (12) 3.00 2.38

On Nos. 164, 128
262 A30 1c on 20c de p (Bk) 3.50 3.50
263 A21 2c on 3c de p (R) 42 28

On Nos. 130, 133, 135, 137, 139, 142, 144
265 A22 1c on 4c de p (R) 28 28
266 A23 1c on 7c de p (Br) 42 28
267 A26 1c on 15c de p (R) 42 28
268 A19 1c on 50c de p (Bk) 90 90
269 A27 1c on 1p (Bk) 90 90
270 A24 2c on 8c de p (R) 35 35
271 A25 2c on 10c de p (Br) 35 15
272 A26 2c on 15c de p (R) 45 45
273 A25 5c on 10c de p (Bl) 70 70
274 A25 5c on 10c de p (VBk) 45 45
275 A26 5c on 15c de p (R) 3.50 3.50
Nos. 265-275 (11) 8.72 8.24

"O. Z." Stamps of 1914 Handstamp Surcharged in Red or Brown

1 1CT GOURDE

276 A26 1c on 15c de p sl grn 18 18
277 A20 1c on 20c de p bl grn 18 18
278 A30 1c on 20c de p yel grn & blk 35 35
279 A27 1c on 1p claret (Br) 22 15
280 A27 1c on 1p claret 1.25 1.25
281 A27 5c on 1p red (Br) 35 35
Nos. 276-281 (6) 2.53 2.46

"O. Z." Stamps of 1914 Handstamp Surcharged in Various Colors as in 1917-19 and

1919-20
282 A22 2c on 4c de p car lake (V) 35 35
283 A24 2c on 8c de p car rose (G) 28 15
284 A24 2c on 8c de p ol grn (R) 18 15
285 A30 2c on 20c de p yel grn & blk (R) 28 15
286 A19 2c on 50c de p red (G) 15 15
288 A19 2c on 50c de p red (R) 45 35
289 A19 2c on 50c de p org yel (R) 25 18
290 A27 2c on 1pi claret (R) 2.00 1.75
291 A27 2c on 1pi red (R) 1.50 1.50
292 A21 3c on 3c de p brn (R) 35 35
293 A23 3c on 7c de p org red (R) 35 18
294 A21 5c on 3c de p brn (R) 42 18
295 A21 5c on 3c de p org yel (R) 1.40 1.40
296 A22 5c on 4c de p car lake (R) 45 45
297 A22 5c on 4c de p ol grn (R) 25 25
298 A23 5c on 7c de p gray (V) 28 28
299 A23 5c on 7c de p org red (V) 35 35
300 A25 5c on 10c de p org red (V) 25 25
301 A26 5c on 15c de p yel (M) 35 35
Nos. 282-301 (19) 9.89 8.77

Nos. 217 and 218 Handstamp Surcharged with New Value
302 A18 5c on 7c on 20c org (M) 35 35
303 A18 5c on 7c on 50c cl (M) 2.75 2.75

No. 187 Handstamp Surcharged

5 CTS = PIASTRE

304 A25 5c de p on 10c de p (M) 45 45

Postage Due Stamps of 1906-14 Handstamp Surcharged

POSTE -5 CTS- GOURDE

On Stamp of 1906
305 D2 5c on 50c ol gray (Bk) 10.50 8.50

On Stamp of 1914
306 D2 5c on 10c vio (Bk) 35 35
307 D2 5c on 50c ol gray (Bk) 45 45
308 D2 5c on 50c ol gray (M) 1.75 1.75

Nos. 299 with red surcharge and 306 and 307 with violet are trial colors or essays.

Allegory of Agriculture A40

Allegory of Commerce A41

1920, Apr. **Engr.** ***Perf. 12***
310 A40 3c dp org 18 15
311 A40 5c green 18 15
312 A41 10c vermilion 42 28
313 A41 15c violet 35 25
314 A41 25c dp bl 42 15
Nos. 310-314 (5) 1.55 98

Stamps of this issue overprinted "T. M." are revenue stamps. The letters are the initials of "Timbre-Mobile".

President Louis J. Borno — A42

Christophe's Citadel — A43

Old Map of West Indies — A44

Borno — A45

National Capitol — A46

1924, Sept. 3
315 A42 5c dp grn 15 15
316 A43 10c carmine 28 15
317 A44 20c vio bl 65 15
318 A45 50c org & blk 65 18
319 A46 1g olive grn 1.25 25
Nos. 315-319 (5) 2.98
Set value 73

For surcharge see No. 359.

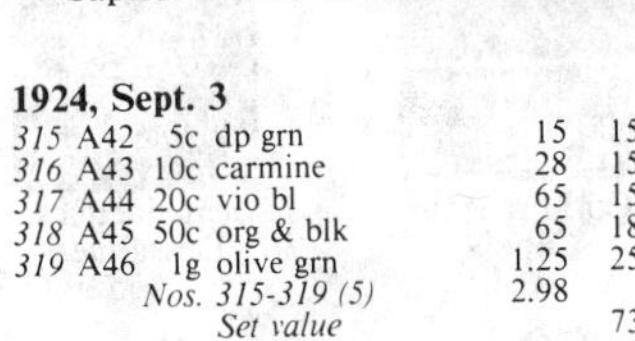

Coffee Beans and Flowers — A47

1928, Feb. 6
320 A47 35c deep green 2.75 35

For surcharge see No. 337.

Pres. Louis Borno — A48

1929, Nov. 4
321 A48 10c car rose 25 15

Signing of the "Frontier" treaty between Haiti and the Dominican Republic.

Presidents Salomon and Vincent — A49

Pres. Stenio Vincent — A50

1931, Oct. 16
322 A49 5c dp grn 90 35
323 A50 10c car rose 90 35

50th anniv. of Haiti's joining the UPU.

President Vincent A52

Aqueduct at Port-au-Prince A53

Fort National — A54

Palace of Sans Souci — A55

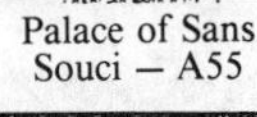

Christophe's Chapel at Milot — A56

King's Gallery Citadel — A57

Vallieres Battery — A58

1933-40
325 A52 3c orange 15 15
326 A52 3c dp ol grn ('39) 15 15
327 A53 5c green 15 15
328 A53 5c ol grn ('40) 42 15
329 A54 10c rose car 35 15
a. 10c vermilion 52 15
330 A54 10c red brn ('40) 35 15
331 A55 25c blue 65 18
332 A56 50c brown 1.75 35
333 A57 1g dk grn 1.75 35
334 A58 2.50g ol bis 2.75 52
Nos. 325-334 (10) 8.47
Set value 1.85

For surcharges see Nos. 357-358, 360.

Alexandre Dumas, His Father and Son — A59

1935, Dec. 29 **Litho.** ***Perf. 11½***
335 A59 10c rose pink & choc 65 25
336 A59 25c bl & choc 1.25 28

Issued in honor of the visit of a delegation from France to Haiti. See No. C10.

The only foreign revenue stamps listed in this Catalogue are those authorized for prepayment of postage.

No. 320 Surcharged in Red

= 25c =

1939, Jan. 24 *Perf. 12*

337 A47 25c on 35c dp grn	70	28

Statue of Liberty, Map of Haiti and Flags of American Republics A60

1941, June 30 **Engr.** *Perf. 12*

338 A60 10c rose car	75	28
339 A60 25c dark blue	65	35

3rd Inter-American Caribbean Conf., held at Port-au-Prince. See Nos. C12-C13.

Patroness of Haiti, Map and Coat of Arms — A61

1942, Dec. 8

Size: 26x36¼mm

340 A61 3c dl vio	30	24
341 A61 5c brt grn	45	24
342 A61 10c rose car	45	24
343 A61 15c orange	60	45
344 A61 20c brown	60	48
345 A61 25c dp bl	1.25	48
346 A61 50c red org	1.75	75
347 A61 2.50g ol blk	6.00	1.50

Size: 32x45mm

348 A61 5g purple	12.00	3.00
Nos. 340-348,C14-C18 (14)	27.80	8.93

Issued in honor of Our Lady of Perpetual Help, patroness of Haiti.

For surcharges see Nos. 355-356.

Adm. Hammerton Killick and Destruction of "La Crete-à-Pierrot" — A62

1943, Sept. 6

349 A62 3c orange	28	15
350 A62 5c turq grn	35	18
351 A62 10c car rose	35	15
352 A62 25c dp bl	42	18
353 A62 50c olive	90	28
354 A62 5g brn blk	4.50	2.50
Nos. 349-354,C22-C23 (8)	8.82	4.94

Nos. 343 and 345 Surcharged with New Value and Bars in Red

1944, July 19

355 A61 10c on 15c org	28	20
356 A61 10c on 25c dp bl	28	20

Nos. 319, 326 and 334 Surcharged with New Values and Bars in Red

1944-45

357 A52 2c on 3c dp ol grn	15	15
358 A52 5c on 3c dp ol grn	20	18
359 A46 10c on 1g ol grn	35	15
a. Surcharged "01.0"		
360 A58 20c on 2.50g ol bis	35	28

Nurse and Wounded Soldier on Battlefield — A63

1945, Feb. 20

Cross in Rose

361 A63 3c gray blk	15	15
362 A63 5c dk bl grn	15	15
363 A63 10c red org	18	15
364 A63 20c blk brn	15	15
365 A63 25c dp bl	25	15
366 A63 35c orange	25	18
367 A63 50c car rose	42	20
368 A63 1g ol grn	65	28
369 A63 2.50g pale vio	2.00	35
Nos. 361-369,C25-C32 (17)	12.33	5.06

Issued to honor the Intl. Red Cross.

20c, 1g, 2.50g, Aug. 14. Others, Feb. 20.

For overprints and surcharges see Nos. 456-457, C153-C160.

Catalogue values for unused stamps in this section, from this point to the end of the section, are for Never Hinged items.

Col. François Capois A64

Jean Jacques Dessalines A65

Unwmk.

1946, July 18 **Engr.** *Perf. 12*

370 A64 3c red org	15	15
371 A64 5c Prus grn	15	15
372 A64 10c red	15	15
373 A64 20c ol blk	15	15
374 A64 25c dp bl	15	15
375 A64 35c orange	18	15
376 A64 50c red brn	25	15
377 A64 1g ol brn	35	15
378 A64 2.50g gray	1.00	35
Nos. 370-378,C35-C42 (17)	5.88	
Set value		3.15

For surcharges see Nos. 383, 392, C43-C45, C49-C51, C61-C62.

1947-54

379 A65 3c org yel	15	15
380 A65 5c green	15	15
380A A65 5c dp vio ('54)	42	15
381 A65 10c car rose	15	15
382 A65 25c dp bl	18	15
Set value, #379-382, C46	98	34

No. 375 Surcharged with New Value and Rectangular Block in Black

1948

383 A64 10c on 35c orange	18	15

Arms of Port-au-Prince A66

Engraved and Lithographed

1950, Feb. 12 *Perf. 12½*

384 A66 10c multi	20	15

200th anniv. (in 1949) of the founding of Port-au-Prince. See Nos. C47-C48.

Nos. RA10-RA12 and RA16 Surcharged or Overprinted in Black

U P U

1874 1949

1950, Oct. 4 **Unwmk.** *Perf. 12*

385 PT2 3c on 5c ol gray	15	15
386 PT2 5c green	25	15
387 PT2 10c on 5c car rose	25	20
388 PT2 20c on 5c blue	35	35
Nos. 385-388,C49-C51 (7)	2.27	2.05

75th anniv. (in 1949) of the UPU.

Exist with inverted or double surcharge and 10c on 5c green.

Cacao — A67

Pres. Paul E. Magloire and Day Nursery, Saline — A68

1951, Sept. 3 **Photo.** *Perf. 12½*

389 A67 5c dk brn	25	15

See Nos. C52-C54.

1953, May 4 **Engr.** *Perf. 12*

Design: 10c, Applying asphalt.

390 A68 5c green	15	15
391 A68 10c rose car	15	15
Nos. 390-391,C57-C60 (6)	2.28	
Set value		1.40

7 AVRIL

1803 - 1953

50

No. 375 Surcharged in Black

1953, Apr. 7

392 A64 50c on 35c org	35	20

Issued to commemorate the 150th anniversary of the death of Gen. Pierre Dominique Toussaint L'Ouverture (1743-1803), liberator.

J. J. Dessalines and Paul E. Magloire — A69

Alexandre Sabes Pétion — A70

Battle of Vertieres — A71

Design: No. 395, Larmartiniere. No. 396, Boisrond-Tonnerre. No. 397, Toussaint L'Ouverture. No. 399, Capois. No. 401, Marie Jeanne and Lamartiniere leading attack.

1954, Jan. 1 **Photo.** *Perf. 11½*

Portraits in Black

393 A69 3c bl gray	15	15
394 A70 5c yel grn	18	15
395 A70 5c yel grn	15	15
396 A70 5c yel grn	18	15
397 A70 5c yel grn	15	15
398 A69 10c crimson	15	15
399 A70 15c rose lil	20	15

Perf. 12½

400 A71 25c dk gray	20	15
401 A71 25c dp org	20	15
Nos. 393-401 (9)	1.56	
Set value		78

150th anniv. of Haitian independence. See Nos. C63-C74, C95-C96.

Mme. Yolette Magloire — A72

1954, Jan. 1 *Perf. 11½*

402 A72 10c orange	15	15
403 A72 10c blue	15	15
Set value		18

See Nos. C75-C80.

Henri Christophe, Paul Magloire and Citadel A73

Tomb and Arms of Henri Christophe — A74

Perf. 13½x13

1954, Dec. 6 **Litho.** **Unwmk.**

404 A73 10c carmine	15	15

Perf. 13

405 A74 10c red, blk & car	15	15
Set value		18

Restoration of Christophe's Citadel. See Nos. C81-C90.

J. J. Dessalines A75

Pres. Magloire and Dessalines Memorial, Gonaives A76

1955-57 **Photo.** *Perf. 11½*

406 A75 3c ocher & blk	15	15
407 A75 5c pale vio & blk ('56)	15	15
408 A75 10c rose & blk	15	15
a. 10c salmon pink & blk ('57)	15	15
409 A75 25c chalky bl & blk ('56)	20	15
a. 25c blue & blk ('57)	20	15
Set value, #406-409, C93-C94	63	35

1955, Aug. 1

410 A76 10c dp bl & blk	25	20
411 A76 10c crim & blk	25	20

21st anniv. of the new Haitian army. Nos. 410-411 were printed in a single sheet of 20 (5x4). The two upper rows are of No. 410, the two lower No. 411, providing five se-tenant pairs.

See Nos. C97-C98.

Flamingo A77

Mallard A78

1956, Apr. 14 Photo. *Perf. 11½*

Granite Paper

412 A77 10c bl & ultra 18 15
413 A78 25c dk grn & bluish grn 42 18

See Nos. C99-C104.

Immanuel Kant — A79

1956, July 19 *Perf. 12*

Granite Paper

414 A79 10c brt ultra 15 15

10th anniv. of the 1st Inter-American Philosophical Congress. See Nos. C105-C107a.

Zim Waterfall A80

J. J. Dessalines and Dessalines Memorial, Gonaives A81

1957, Dec. 16 Unwmk. *Perf. 11½*

Granite Paper

415 A80 10c org & bl 15 15

See Nos. C108-C111. For surcharge and overprint see Nos. CB49, CQ2.

1958, July 1 Photo.

416 A81 5c yel grn & blk 15 15

Bicentenary of birth of J. J. Dessalines. See Nos. 470-471, C112, C170. For overprints see Nos. 480-482, C183-C184, CQ1, Q1-Q3.

"Atomium" — A82

View of Brussels Exposition A83

Perf. 13x13½, 13½x13

1958, July 22 Litho. Unwmk.

417 A82 50c brown 18 15
418 A83 75c brt grn 18 15
419 A82 1g purple 52 18
420 A83 1.50g red org 42 20
Nos. 417-420,C113-C114 (6) 2.85 1.75

Issued for the Universal and International Exposition at Brussels.
For surcharges see Nos. B2-B3, CB9.

Sylvio Cator — A84

U. S. Satellite — A85

1958, Aug. 16 Photo. *Perf. 11½*

Granite Paper

421 A84 5c green 15 15
422 A84 10c brown 15 15
423 A84 20c lilac 15 15
Nos. 421-423,C115-C118 (7) 2.53
Set value 1.15

30th anniversary of the world championship record broad jump of Sylvio Cator.

1958, Oct. 8 *Perf. 14x13½*

Designs: 20c, Emperor penguins. 50c, Modern observatory. 1g, Ocean exploration.

424 A85 10c brt bl & brn red 15 15
425 A85 20c blk & dp org 28 20
426 A85 50c grn & rose brn 42 20
427 A85 1g blk & bl 60 18
Nos. 424-427,C119-C121 (7) 3.98 1.61

Issued for the International Geophysical Year 1957-58. See No. C121a.

President François Duvalier — A86

Engraved and Lithographed

1958, Oct. 22 Unwmk. *Perf. 11½*

Commemorative Inscription in Ultramarine

428 A86 10c blk & dp pink 15 15
429 A86 50c blk & lt grn 28 15
430 A86 1g blk & brick red 42 25
431 A86 5g blk & sal 1.75 1.25
Nos. 428-431,C122-C125 (8) 7.15 4.70

1st anniv. of the inauguration of Pres. Dr. François Duvalier. See note on souvenir sheets after No. C125.

Regular Issue
Without Commemorative Inscription

1958 Nov. 20

432 A86 5c blk & lt vio bl 15 15
433 A86 10c blk & dp pink 15 15
434 A86 20c blk & yel 15 15
435 A86 50c blk & lt grn 18 15
436 A86 1g blk & brick red 28 15
437 A86 1.50g blk & rose pink 42 28
438 A86 2.50g blk & gray vio 65 42
439 A86 5g blk & sal 1.25 90
Nos. 432-439 (8) 3.23 2.35

For surcharges see Nos. B13, B22-B24.

Map of Haiti — A87

1958, Dec. 5 Photo. *Perf. 11½*

Granite Paper

440 A87 10c rose pink 15 15
441 A87 25c green 15 15
Nos. 440-441,C133-C135 (5) 1.00
Set value 59

Tribute to the UN. See No. C135a. For overprints and surcharges see Nos. 442-443, B4-B5, CB11-CB12.

Nos. 440-441 Overprinted "10th ANNIVERSARY OF THE / UNIVERSAL DECLARATION / OF HUMAN RIGHTS" in English (a), French (b), Spanish (c) or Portuguese (d)

1959, Jan. 28

442 A87 10c Block of 4 35 35
a.-d. Single 15 15
443 A87 25c Block of 4 90 70
a.-d. Single 20 15
Nos. 442-443,C136-C138 (5) 10.65 10.45

10th anniv. of the signing of the Universal Declaration of Human Rights.

Pope Pius XII and Children — A88

Designs: 50c, Pope praying. 2g, Pope on throne.

1959, Feb. 28 Photo. *Perf. 14x13½*

444 A88 10c vio bl & ol 15 15
445 A88 50c grn & dp brn 20 15
446 A88 2g dp cl & dk brn 65 35
Nos. 444-446,C139-C141 (6) 2.15
Set value 1.00

Issued in memory of Pope Pius XII.
For surcharges see Nos. B6-B8.

Abraham Lincoln A89

1959, May 12 Photo. *Perf. 12*

447 A89 50c lt bl & dp cl 25 15

Sesquicentennial of the birth of Abraham Lincoln. Imperf. pairs exist. See Nos. C142-C144a. For surcharges see #B9, CB16-CB18.

Chicago's Skyline and Dessables House A90

Jean Baptiste Dessables and Map of American Midwest, c. 1791 — A91

Design: 50c, Discus thrower and flag of Haiti.

1959, Aug. 27 Unwmk. *Perf. 14*

448 A90 25c blk brn & lt bl 18 15
449 A90 50c multi 42 28
450 A91 75c brn & bl 52 42
Nos. 448-450,C145-C147 (6) 2.89 1.66

Issued to commemorate the 3rd Pan American Games, Chicago, Aug. 27-Sept. 7.
For surcharges see #B10-B12, CB19-CB21.

No. 449 Overprinted

1960, Feb. 29

451 A90 50c multi 1.25 1.00

Issued to commemorate the 8th Olympic Winter Games, Squaw Valley, Calif., Feb. 18-29, 1960. See Nos. C148-C150.

Uprooted Oak Emblem and Hands — A92

1960, Apr. 7 Litho. *Perf. 12½x13*

452 A92 10c sal & grn 15 15
453 A92 50c vio & mag 18 15
Set value 21

Issued to publicize World Refugee Year, July 1, 1959-June 30, 1960. See Nos. 489-490, C151-C152a, C191-C192. For surcharges see Nos. B14-B17, B28-B29, CB24-CB27, CB45-CB46.

No. 406 Surcharged with New Values

1960, Apr. 27 Photo. *Perf. 11½*

454 A75 5c on 3c ocher & blk 15 15
455 A75 10c on 3c ocher & blk 15 15
Set value 21 15

No. 369 Surcharged or Overprinted in Red: "28eme ANNIVERSAIRE"

1960, May 8 Engr. *Perf. 12*

Cross in Rose

456 A63 1g on 2.50g pale vio 65 32
457 A63 2.50g pale vio 90 70

28th anniversary of the Haitian Red Cross. See Nos. C153-C160.

Claudinette Fouchard, Miss Haiti, Sugar Queen — A93

Sugar Queen and: 20c, Sugar harvest. 50c, Beach. 1g, Sugar plantation.

Perf. 11½

1960, May 30 Photo. Unwmk.

Granite Paper

458 A93 10c ol bis & vio 15 15
459 A93 20c red brn & blk 18 15
460 A93 50c brt bl & brn 35 15
461 A93 1g grn & brn 70 20
Nos. 458-461,C161-C162 (6) 2.63
Set value 85

Haitian sugar industry.

Olympic Victors, Athens, 1896, Melbourne Stadium and Olympic Torch — A94

Designs: 20c, Discus thrower and Rome stadium. 50c, Pierre de Coubertin and victors, Melbourne, 1956. 1g, Athens stadium, 1896.

1960, Aug. 18 Photo. *Perf. 12*

462 A94 10c blk & org 15 15
463 A94 20c dk bl & crim 15 15
464 A94 50c grn & ocher 18 15
465 A94 1g dk brn & grnsh bl 28 15
Nos. 462-465,C163-C165 (7) 2.01
Set value 1.00

17th Olympic Games, Rome, Aug. 25-Sept. 11. See No. C165a. For surcharges see Nos. B18-B19, CB28-CB29.

Occide Jeanty and Score from "1804" A95

Designs: 20c, Occide Jeanty and National Capitol.

1960, Oct. 19 *Perf. 14x14½*

466 A95 10c org & red lil 15 15
467 A95 20c bl & red lil 18 15
468 A95 50c grn & sepia 42 18
Nos. 466-468,C166-C167 (5) 1.55
Set value 64

Issued to commemorate the centenary of the birth of Occide Jeanty, composer. Printed in sheets of 12 (3x4) with commemorative inscription and opening bars of "1804," Jeanty's military march, in top margin.

UN Headquarters, NYC — A96

1960, Nov. 25 Engr. *Perf. 10½*

469 A96 1g grn & blk 25 18

15th anniv. of the UN. See Nos. C168-C169a. For surcharges see Nos. B20-B21, CB30-CB31, CB35-CB36.

Dessalines Type of 1958

Perf. 11½

1960, Nov. 5 Unwmk. Photo.

Granite Paper

470 A81 10c red org & blk 15 15
471 A81 25c ultra & blk 18 15
Set value 15

See No. C170.

Alexandre Dumas Pere and Musketeer — A97

Designs: 5c, Map of Haiti and birthplace of General Alexandre Dumas (horiz.) 50c, Alexandre Dumas, father and son and French and Haitian flags (horiz.)

1961, Feb. 10 *Perf. 11½*

Granite Paper

472 A97 5c lt bl & choc 15 15
473 A97 10c rose, blk & sep 15 15
474 A97 50c dk bl & crim 20 15
Nos. 472-474,C177-C179 (6) 1.28
Set value 80

Gen. Dumas (Alexandre Davy de la Pailleterie), born in Jeremie, Haiti, and his son and grandson, French authors.

Privateer in Battle — A98

Tourist publicity: 5c, Map of Tortuga. 10c, Three Pirates. 15c, Pirates. 50c, Pirate with cutlass in rigging.

1961, Apr. 4 Litho. *Perf. 12*

475 A98 5c bl & yel 15 15
476 A98 10c lake & yel 15 15
477 A98 15c ol grn & org 15 15
478 A98 20c choc & org 15 15
479 A98 50c vio bl & org 20 18
Set value, #475-479, C180-C182 1.10 75

For surcharges and overprints see Nos. 484-485, C186-C187.

Nos. 416, 470-471 and 378 Overprinted: "Dr. F. Duvalier / President / 22 Mai 1961"

1961, May 22 Photo. *Perf. 11½*

480 A81 5c yel grn & blk 15 15
481 A81 10c red org & blk 15 15
482 A81 25c ultra & blk 18 15

Engr.

Perf. 12

483 A64 2.50g gray 70 52
Set value, #480-483, C183-C185 1.55 1.20

Re-election of Pres. Francois Duvalier.

No. 475 Surcharged: "EXPLORATION SPATIALE JOHN GLENN," Capsule and New Value

1962, May 10 Litho.

484 A98 50c on 5c bl & yel 28 20
485 A98 1.50g on 5c bl & yel 1.00 70

Issued to honor the United States' achievement in space exploration and to commemorate the first orbital flight of a US astronaut, Lt. Col. John H. Glenn, Jr., Feb. 20, 1962. See Nos. C186-C187.

Malaria Eradication Emblem — A99

Design: 10c, Triangle pointing down.

Unwmk.

1962, May 30 Litho. *Perf. 12*

486 A99 5c crim & dp bl 15 15
487 A99 10c red brn & emer 15 15
488 A99 50c bl & crim 18 15
Set value, #486-488, C188-C190 88 60

WHO drive to eradicate malaria.
Sheets of 12 with marginal inscription.
For surcharges see Nos. B25-B27, CB42-CB44.

WRY Type of 1960 Dated "1962"

1962, June 22 *Perf. 12½x13*

489 A92 10c lt bl & org 15 15
490 A92 50c rose lil & ol grn 15 15
Set value 19 19

Issued to publicize the plight of refugees. For souvenir sheet see note after #C191-C192.

Haitian Scout Emblem — A100

Designs: 5c, 50c, Scout giving Scout sign. 10c, Lord and Lady Baden-Powell (horiz.).

Perf. 14x14½, 14½x14

1962, Aug. 6 Photo.

491 A100 3c blk, ocher & pur 15 15
492 A100 5c cit, red brn & blk 15 15
493 A100 10c ocher, blk & grn 15 15
494 A100 25c mar, ol & bl 15 15
495 A100 50c vio, grn & red 25 15
Set value, #491-495, C193-C195 1.20 75

22nd anniv. of the Haitian Boy Scouts.
For surcharges and overprints see Nos. B31-B34, C196-C199.

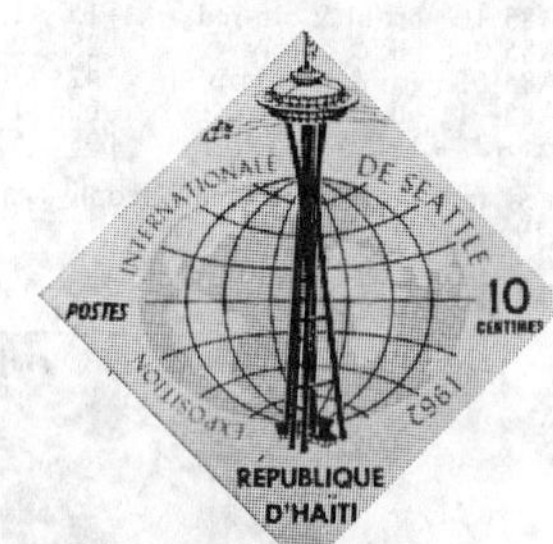

Space Needle, Space Capsule and Globe — A101

1962, Nov. 19 Litho. *Perf. 12½*

496 A101 10c red brn & lt bl 15 15
497 A101 20c vio bl & pink 15 15
498 A101 50c emer & yel 20 15
499 A101 1g car & lt grn 35 15
Nos. 496-499,C200-C202 (7) 1.82 1.10

"Century 21" International Exposition, Seattle, Wash., Apr. 21-Oct. 21.
For overprints see #503-504, C206-C207.

Plan of Duvalier Ville and Stamp of 1904 — A102

1962, Dec. 10 Photo. *Perf. 14x14½*

500 A102 5c vio, yel & blk 15 15
501 A102 10c car rose, yel & blk 15 15
502 A102 25c bl gray, yel & blk 15 15
Nos. 500-502,C203-C205 (6) 1.52
Set value 1.05

Issued to publicize Duvalier Ville.
For surcharge see No. B30.

Nos. 498-499 with Vertical Overprint in Black Similar to

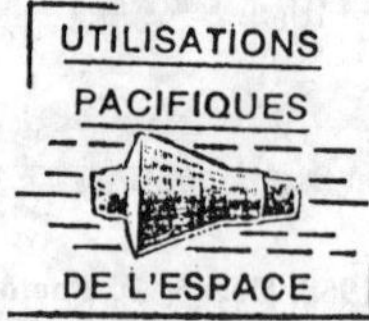

1963, Jan. 23 Litho. *Perf. 12½*

503 A101 50c emer & yel 28 28
a. Claret overprint, horiz. 35 28
504 A101 1g car & lt grn 52 35
a. Claret overprint, horiz. 60 42

Issued to publicize "Peaceful Uses of Outer Space." The black vertical overprint has no outside frame lines and no broken shading lines around capsule. Nos. 503a and 504a were issued Feb. 20.
See Nos. C206-C207a.

Symbolic Harvest A103

1963, July 12 Photo. *Perf. 13x14*

505 A103 10c org & blk 15 15
506 A103 20c bluish grn & blk 15 15
Set value 17 15

FAO "Freedom from Hunger" campaign. See Nos. C208-C209.

J. J. Dessalines A104

Weight Lifter A105

1963, Oct. 17 *Perf. 14x14½*

507 A104 5c tan & ver 15 15
508 A104 10c yel & blue 15 15
Set value 15 15

See Nos. C214-C215. For overprints see Nos. 509, C216-C217.

No. 508 Overprinted: "FETE DES MERES / 1964"

1964, July 22

509 A104 10c yel & blue 15 15

Issued for Mother's Day, 1964. See Nos. C216-C218.

1964, Nov. 12 Photo. *Perf. 11½*

Granite Paper

Design: 50c, Hurdler.

510 A105 10c lt bl & dk brn 15 15
511 A105 25c sal & dk brn 15 15
512 A105 50c pale rose lil & dk brn 15 15
Set value, #510-512, C223-C226 1.12 78

Issued to commemorate the 18th Olympic Games, Tokyo, Oct. 10-25. Printed in sheets of 50 (10x5), with map of Japan in background extending over 27 stamps.
For surcharges see #B35-B37, CB51-CB54.

Madonna of Haiti and International Airport, Port-au-Prince A106

Unisphere, NY World's Fair A107

1964, Dec. 15 *Perf. 14½x14*

513 A106 10c org yel & blk 15 15
514 A106 25c bl grn & blk 18 15
515 A106 50c brt yel grn & blk 25 15
516 A106 1g ver & blk 35 25
Nos. 513-516,C227-C229 (7) 2.45

Same Overprinted "1965"

1965, Feb. 11

517 A106 10c org, yel & blk 15 15
518 A106 25c bl grn & blk 18 15
519 A106 50c brt yel grn & blk 25 15
520 A106 1g ver & blk 35 25
Nos. 517-520,C230-C232 (7) 2.35
Set value 1.42

1965, Mar. 22 Photo. *Perf. 13½*

Design: 20c, "Rocket Thrower" by Donald De Lue.

521 A107 10c grn, yel ol & dk red 15 15
522 A107 20c plum & org 15 15
523 A107 50c dk brn, dk red, yel & grn 25 15
Nos. 521-523,C233-C235 (6) 2.83 2.38

New York World's Fair, 1964-65.

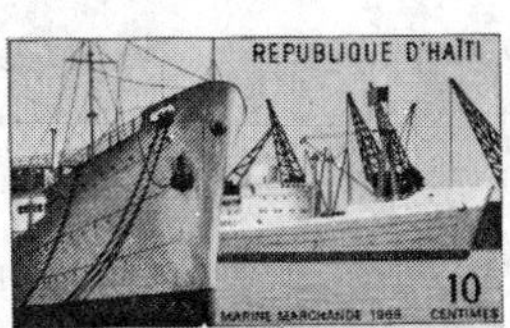

Merchantmen — A108

1965, May 13 Unwmk. *Perf. 11½*

524 A108 10c blk, lt grn & red 15 15
525 A108 50c blk, lt bl & red 15 15
Set value 19 15

Issued to honor the merchant marine. See Nos. C236-C237.

ITU Emblem, Old and New Communication Equipment — A109

1965, Aug. 16 Litho. *Perf. 13½*

526 A109 10c gray & multi 15 15
527 A109 25c multi 15 15
528 A109 50c multi 18 15
Nos. 526-528,C242-C245 (7) 1.98
Set value 1.40

Cent. of the ITU.
For overprints see #537-539, C255-C256.

Statue of Our Lady of the Assumption A110

Passionflower A111

Designs: 5c, Cathedral of Port-au-Prince (horiz.). 10c, High altar.

Perf. 14x13, 13x14

1965, Nov. 19 Photo.

Size: 39x29mm, 29x39mm

529 A110 5c multi 15 15
530 A110 10c multi 15 15
531 A110 25c multi 15 15
Nos. 529-531,C246-C248 (6) 2.93
Set value 2.15

200th anniv. of the Metropolitan Cathedral of Port-au-Prince.

1965, Dec. 20 Photo. *Perf. 11½*

Granite Paper

Flowers: 5c, 15c, American elder. 10c, Okra.

532 A111 3c dk vio, lt vio bl & grn 15 15
533 A111 5c grn, lt bl & yel 15 15
534 A111 10c multi 15 15
a. "0.10" omitted
535 A111 15c grn, pink & yel 15 15
536 A111 50c dk vio, yel & grn 20 15
Nos. 532-536,C249-C254 (11) 3.49
Set value 2.60

For surcharges see Nos. 566, B38-B40, CB55-CB56.

Nos. 526-528 Overprinted in Red: "20e. Anniversaire / UNESCO"

1965, Aug. 27 Litho. *Perf. 13½*

537 A109 10c gray & multi 15 15
538 A109 25c yel brn & multi 35 35
539 A109 50c pale grn & multi 70 70
Nos. 537-539,C255-C256 (5) 4.20 2.25

20th anniversary of UNESCO.

Amulet — A112

Ceremonial Stool A113

Perf. 14x½x14, 14x14½

1966, Mar. 14 Photo. Unwmk.

540 A112 5c grnsh bl, blk & yel 15 15
541 A113 10c multi 15 15
542 A112 50c scar, yel & blk 15 15
Nos. 540-542,C257-C259 (6) 2.07
Set value 1.25

For overprints and surcharges see Nos. 543, 567-570, C260-C261, C280-C281.

No. 541 Overprinted in Red: "Hommage / a Haile Selassieler / 24-25 Avril 1966"

1966, Apr. 24

543 A113 10c multi 18 18

Visit of Emperor Haile Selassie of Ethiopia, Apr. 24-25. See Nos. C260-C262.

Walter M. Shirra, Thomas P. Stafford, Frank A. Borman, James A. Lovell and Gemini VI A114

1966, May 3 *Perf. 13½*

544 A114 5c vio bl, brn & lt bl 15 15
545 A114 10c pur, brn & lt bl 15 15
546 A114 25c grn, brn & lt bl 15 15
547 A114 50c dk red, brn & lt bl 20 15
Set value, #544-547, C263-C265 1.50 1.10

Rendezvous in space of US spacecraft Gemini VI and VII, Dec. 15, 1965.
For overprint see No. 584.

Soccer Ball within Wreath and Pres. Duvalier — A115

Design: 10c, 50c, Soccer player within wreath and Duvalier.

Lithographed and Photogravure

1966, June 16 *Perf. 13x13½*

Portrait in Black; Gold Inscription; Green Commemorative Inscription in Two Lines

548 A115 5c pale sal & grn 15 15
549 A115 10c lt ultra & grn 15 15
550 A115 15c lt grn & grn 15 15
551 A115 50c pale lil rose & grn 20 15

Green Commemorative Inscription in 3 Lines; Gold Inscription Omitted

552 A115 5c pale sal & grn 15 15
553 A115 10c lt ultra & grn 15 15
554 A115 15c lt grn & grn 15 15
555 A115 50c pale lil rose & grn 18 15
Set value, #548-555, C266-C269 2.10 1.50

Issued to commemorate the Caribbean Soccer Festival, June 10-22. Nos. 548-551 also commemorate the National Soccer Championships, May 8-22.
For surcharges and overprint see Nos. 578-579, C288, CB57.

"ABC," Boy and Girl — A116

Designs: 10c, Scout symbols. 25c, Television set, book and communications satellite (horiz.).

Perf. 14x13½, 13½x14

1966, Oct. 18 Litho. & Engr.

556 A116 5c grn, sal pink & brn 15 15
557 A116 10c red brn, lt brn & blk 15 15
558 A116 25c grn, bl & dk vio 15 15
Set value, #556-558, C270-C272 1.00 95

Issued to publicize education through literacy, Scouting and by audio-visual means.

Dr. Albert Schweitzer, Maps of Alsace and Gabon A117

Designs: 10c, Dr. Schweitzer and pipe organ. 20c, Dr. Schweitzer and Albert Schweitzer Hospital, Deschapelles, Haiti.

Perf. 12½x13

1967, Apr. 20 Photo. Unwmk.

559 A117 5c pale lil & multi 15 15
560 A117 10c buff & multi 15 15
561 A117 20c gray & multi 15 15
Nos. 559-561,C273-C276 (7) 2.13
Set value 1.80

Issued in memory of Dr. Albert Schweitzer (1875-1965), medical missionary to Gabon, theologian and musician.

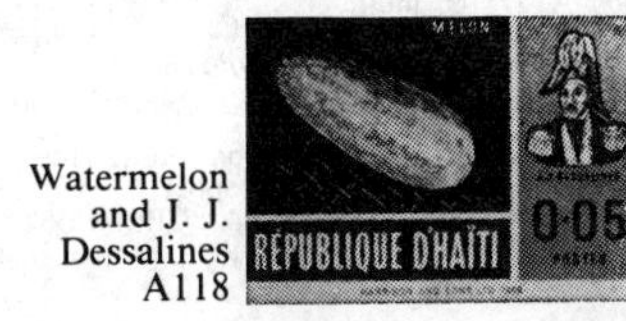

Watermelon and J. J. Dessalines A118

1967, July 4 Photo. *Perf. 12½*

562 A118 5c shown 15 15
563 A118 10c Cabbage 15 15
564 A118 20c Tangerine 15 15
565 A118 50c Chayote 15 15
Set value, #562-565, C277-C279 1.15 90

No. 532 Surcharged

1967, Aug. 21 Photo. *Perf. 11½*

566 A111 50c on 3c multi 18 15
Nos. 566,B38-B40,CB55-CB56 (6) 1.16 1.10

12th Boy Scout World Jamboree, Farragut State Park, Idaho, Aug. 1-9.

Nos. 540-542 Overprinted and Surcharged

Perf. 14½x14, 14x14½

1967, Aug. 30 Photo.

567 A112 5c grnsh bl, blk & yel 15 15
568 A113 10c multi 15 15
569 A112 50c scar, yel & blk 15 15
570 A112 1g on 5c multi 28 25
Nos. 567-570,C280-C281 (6) 1.95
Set value 1.40

Issued to commemorate EXPO '67 International Exhibition, Montreal, Apr. 28-Oct. 27.

Pres. Duvalier and Brush Turkey A119

1967, Sept. 22 Photo. *Perf. 14x13*

571 A119 5c car rose & gold 15 15
572 A119 10c ultra & gold 15 15
573 A119 25c dk red brn & gold 15 15
574 A119 50c dp red lil & gold 15 15
Set value, #571-574, C282-C284 1.90 1.50

10th anniversary of Duvalier revolution.

Writing Hands A120

Designs: 10c, Scout emblem and Scouts (vert.). 25c, Audio-visual teaching of algebra.

1967, Dec. 11 Litho. *Perf. 11½*

575 A120 5c multi 15 15
576 A120 10c multi 15 15
577 A120 25c dk grn, lt bl & yel 15 15
Set value, #575-577, C285-C287 1.00 85

Issued to publicize the importance of education.
For surcharges see Nos. CB58-CB60.

Nos. 552 and 554 Surcharged

15-Cent Minimum Value
The minimum value for a single stamp is 15 cents. This value reflects the costs of the handlling of inexpensive stamps.

Lithographed and Photogravure

1968, Jan. 18 *Perf. 13x13½*

578 A115 50c on 15c lt grn & grn 15 15
579 A115 1g on 5c pale sal & grn 25 20

Issued to publicize the 19th Olympic Games, Mexico City, Oct. 12-27. See No. C288, CB57.

The 1968 date is missing on 2 stamps in every sheet of 50.

Caiman Woods, by Raoul Dupoux
A121

1968, Apr. 22 **Photo.** *Perf. 12*

Size: 36x26mm

580 A121 5c multi 15 15
581 A121 10c rose red & multi 15 15
582 A121 25c multi 15 15
583 A121 50c dl lil & multi 15 15
Nos. 580-583,C289-C295 (11) 3.98 3.40

Caiman Woods ceremony during the Slaves' Rebellion, Aug. 14, 1791.

Xème JEUX OLYMPIQUES
D'HIVER–GRENOBLE 1968

No. 547 Overprinted

1968, Apr. 19 **Photo.** *Perf. 13½*

584 A114 50c dk red, brn & lt bl 70 70

Issued to commemorate the 10th Winter Olympic Games, Grenoble, France, Feb. 6-18, 1968. See Nos. C296-C298.

Monument to the Unknown Maroon
A122

Palm Tree and Provincial Coats of Arms
A123

Madonna, Papal Arms and Arms of Haiti — A124

1968, May 22 *Perf. 11½*

Granite Paper

585 A122 5c bl & blk 15 15
586 A122 10c rose brn & blk 15 15
587 A122 20c vio & blk 15 15
588 A122 25c lt ultra & blk 15 15
589 A122 50c brt bl grn & blk 25 15
Set value, #585-589, C299-C301 1.65 1.10

Issued to commemorate the unveiling of the monument to the Unknown Maroon, Port-au-Prince.

For surcharges see Nos. C324-C325.

Perf. 13x14, 12½x13½

1968, Aug. 16 **Photo.**

Design: 25c, Cathedral, arms of Pope Paul VI and arms of Haiti.

590 A123 5c grn & multi 15 15
591 A124 10c brn & multi 15 15
592 A124 25c multi 15 15
Nos. 590-592,C302-C305 (7) 2.00
Set value 1.25

Issued to commemorate the consecration of the Bishopric of Haiti, Oct. 28, 1966.

Air Terminal, Port-au-Prince — A125

1968, Sept. 22 **Photo.** *Perf. 11½*

Portrait in Black

593 A125 5c brn & lt ultra 15 15
594 A125 10c brn & lt bl 15 15
595 A125 25c brn & pale lil 15 15
Set value, #593-595, C306-C308 1.45 1.25

Issued to commemorate the inauguration of the Francois Duvalier Airport in Port-au-Prince.

Slave Breaking Chains, Map of Haiti, Torch, Conch — A126

1968, Oct. 28 **Litho.** *Perf. 14½x14*

596 A126 5c brn, lt bl & brt pink 15 15
597 A126 10c brn, lt ol & brt pink 15 15
598 A126 25c brn, bis & brt pink 15 15
Set value, #596-598, C310-C313 1.55 1.30

Slaves' Rebellion, of 1791.

Children Learning to Read
A127

Designs: 10c, Children watching television. 50c, Hands setting volleyball and sports medal.

1968, Nov. 14 *Perf. 11½*

599 A127 5c multi 15 15
600 A127 10c multi 15 15
601 A127 50c multi 15 15
Set value, #599-601, C314-C316 1.20 90

Issued to publicize education through literacy, audio-visual means and sport.

For surcharges see #B41-B42, CB61-CB62.

Winston Churchill — A128

Churchill: 5c, as painter. 10c, as Knight of the Garter. 15c, and soldiers at Normandy. 20c, and early seaplane. 25c, and Queen Elizabeth II. 50c, and Big Ben, London.

1968, Dec. 23 **Photo.** *Perf. 13*

602 A128 3c gold & multi 15 15
603 A128 5c gold & multi 15 15
604 A128 10c gold & multi 15 15
605 A128 15c gold & multi 15 15
606 A128 20c gold & multi 15 15
607 A128 25c gold & multi 15 15
608 A128 50c gold & multi 18 15
Set value, #602-608, C319-C322 1.50 1.25

Issued in memory of Sir Winston Spencer Churchill (1874-1965), statesman and World War II leader. Exist imperforate.

For surcharge see No. 828.

1968 Winter Olympics, Grenoble
A128a

Designs: 5c, 1.50g, Peggy Fleming, US, figure skating. 10c, Harold Groenningen, Norway, cross-country skiing. 20c, Belousova & Protopopov, USSR, pairs figure skating. 25c, Toini Gustafsson, Sweden, cross country skiing. 50c, Eugenio Monti, Italy, 4-man bobsled. 2g, Erhard Keller, Germany, speed skating. 4g, Jean-Claude Killy, France, downhill skiing.

1968 **Litho.** *Perf. 14x13½*

609 A128a 5c brt bl & multi
609A A128a 10c bl grn & multi
609B A128a 20c brt rose & multi
609C A128a 25c sky bl & multi
609D A128a 50c ol bis & multi
609E A128a 1.50g vio & multi

Size: 36x65mm

Perf. 12x12½

609F A128a 2g emer grn & multi

Souvenir Sheet

609G A128a 4g brn & multi

No. 609G contains one 36x65mm stamp. Nos. 609F-609G are airmail. No. 609G exists imperf. with green, brown and blue margin.

No. 589 Surcharged with New Value and Rectangle

1969, Feb. 21 **Photo.** *Perf. 11½*

610 A122 70c on 50c 32 20

See Nos. C324-C325.

Blue-headed Euphonia
A129

Power Lines and Light Bulb
A131

Olympic Marathon Winners, 1896-1968 — A130

Birds of Haiti: 10c, Hispaniolan trogon. 20c, Palm chat. 25c, Stripe-headed tanager. 50c, Like 5c.

1969, Feb. 26 *Perf. 13½*

611 A129 5c lt grn & multi 15 15
612 A129 10c yel & multi 15 15
613 A129 20c cream & multi 15 15
614 A129 25c lt lil & multi 15 15
615 A129 50c lt gray & multi 25 15
Nos. 611-615,C326-C329 (9) 2.25
Set value 1.50

For overprints see Nos. C344A-C344D.

1969, Oct. 6 *Perf. 12½x12*

Designs: Games location, date, winner, country and time over various stamp designs.

Souvenir sheets do not show location, date, country or time.

Size: 66x35mm (Nos. 616, 616C, 616F, 616O)

616 A130 5c like Greece #124
616A A130 10c like France #124
616B A130 15c US #327
616C A130 20c like Great Britain #142
616D A130 20c Sweden #68
616E A130 25c Belgium #B49
616F A130 25c like France #198
616G A130 25c Netherlands #B30
616H A130 30c US #718
616I A130 50c Germany #B86
616J A130 60c Great Britain #274
616K A130 75c like Finland #B110
616L A130 75c like Australia #277
616M A130 90c Italy #799
616N A130 1g like Japan #822
616O A130 1.25g like Mexico #C328

Souvenir Sheets

616P A130 1.50g US #718, diff.

Imperf

616Q A130 1.50g Germany #B86, diff.

Nos. 616H-616O are airmail. Nos. 616P-616Q contain one 66x35mm stamp. A 2g souvenir sheet exists, perf. & imperf.

1969, May 22 **Litho.** *Perf. 13x13½*

617 A131 20c lilac & blue 15 15

Issued to publicize the Duvalier Hydroelectric Station. See Nos. C338-C340.

Learning to Write — A132

Designs: 10c, children playing (vert.). 50c, Peace poster on educational television (vert.).

1969, Aug. 12 **Litho.** *Perf. 13½*

618 A132 5c multi 15 15
619 A132 10c multi 15 15
620 A132 50c multi 15 15
Set value, #618-620, C342-C344 1.25 82

Issued to publicize national education.

ILO Emblem
A133

1969, Sept. 22 *Perf. 14*

621 A133 5c bl grn & blk 15 15
622 A133 10c brn & blk 15 15
623 A133 20c vio bl & blk 15 15
Set value, #621-623, C345-C347 1.25 75

50th anniv. of the ILO.

Apollo Space Missions — A133a

Designs: 10c, Apollo 7 rendezvous of command module, third stage. 15c, Apollo 7, preparation for re-entry. 20c, Apollo 8, separation of third stage. 25c, Apollo 8, midcourse correction. 70c, Apollo 8, approaching moon. 1g, Apollo 8, orbiting moon, Christmas 1968, vert. 1.25, Apollo 8, leaving moon. 1.50g, Apollo 8, crew, vert. 1.75g, 2g, Apollo 11, first lunar landing.

1969, May 16 ***Perf. 12x12½***

624 A133a 10c brt rose & multi
624A A133a 15c vio & multi
624B A133a 20c ver & multi
624C A133a 25c emer grn & multi
624D A133a 70c brt bl & multi
624E A133a 1g bl grn & multi
624F A133a 1.25g dk bl & multi
624G A133a 1.50g dp rose lil & multi
624H A133a 2g sky bl & multi

Souvenir Sheet

624I A133a 1.75g grn & multi

Nos. 624D-624I are airmail. No. 624I exists imperf. in different colors.

Papilio Zonaria — A134

Butterflies: 20c, Zerene cesonia cynops. 25c, Papilio machaonides.

1969, Nov. 14 **Photo.** ***Perf. 13½***

625 A134 10c pink & multi 15 15
626 A134 20c gray & multi 15 15
627 A134 25c lt bl & multi 15 15
Nos. 625-627,C348-C350 (6) 1.57
Set value 1.10

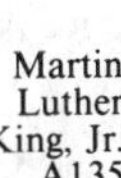

Martin Luther King, Jr. A135

Perf. 12½x13½

1970, Jan. 12 **Litho.**

628 A135 10c bis, red & blk 15 15
629 A135 20c grnsh bl, red & blk 15 15
630 A135 25c brt rose, red & blk 15 15
Set value, #628-630, C351-C353 1.25 88

Martin Luther King, Jr. (1929-1968), American civil rights leader.

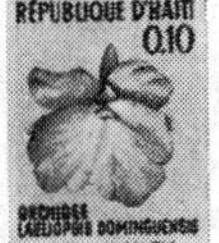

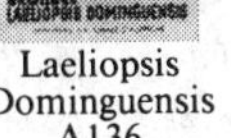

Laeliopsis Dominguensis A136 — UPU Monument and Map of Haiti A137

Haitian Orchids: 20c, Oncidium Haitiense. 25c, Oncidium calochilum.

1970, Apr. 3 **Litho.** ***Perf. 13x12½***

631 A136 10c yel, lil & blk 15 15
632 A136 20c lt bl grn, yel & brn 20 15
633 A136 25c bl & multi 28 15
Nos. 631-633,C354-C356 (6) 1.85
Set value 1.20

1970, June 23 **Photo.** ***Perf. 11½***

Designs: 25c, Propeller and UPU emblem (vert.). 50c, Globe and doves.

634 A137 10c blk, brt grn & ol bis 15 15
635 A137 25c blk, brt rose & ol bis 18 15
636 A137 50c blk & bl 35 25
Nos. 634-636,C357-C359 (6) 2.08 1.55

16th Cong. of the UPU, Tokyo, Oct. 1-Nov. 16, 1970.
For overprints see Nos. 640, C360-C362.

Map of Haiti, Dam and Generator A138

Design: 25c, Map of Haiti, dam and pylon.

1970 **Litho.** ***Perf. 14x13½***

637 A138 20c lt grn & multi 15 15
638 A138 25c lt bl & multi 18 15
Set value 17

Issued to publicize the François Duvalier Central Hydroelectric Plant.
For surcharges see #B43-B44, RA40-RA41.

Apollo 12 — A138a

1970, Sept. ***Perf. 13½x14***

639 A138a 5c Lift-off
639A A138a 10c 2nd stage ignition
639B A138a 15c Docking preparations
639C A138a 20c Heading for moon
639D A138a 25c like 639B
639E A138a 25c Lunar exploration
639F A138a 30c Landing on Moon
639G A138a 30c Lift-off from Moon
639H A138a 40c 3rd stage separation
639I A138a 40c Lunar module, crew
639J A138a 50c Lunar orbital activities
639K A138a 50c Leaving Moon orbit
639L A138a 75c In Earth orbit
639M A138a 1g Re-entry
639N A138a 1.25g Landing at sea
639O A138a 1.50g Docking with lunar module

Nos. 639E, 639G, 639I, 639K-639O are airmail. Nos. 639-639O exist imperf. with brighter colors.
For overprints see Nos. 656-656O.

No. 636 Overprinted in Red with UN Emblem and: "XXVe ANNIVERSAIRE / O.N.U."

1970, Dec. 14 **Photo.** ***Perf. 11½***

640 A137 50c blk & bl 20 15

UN, 25th anniv. See Nos. C360-C362.

Fort Nativity, Drawing by Columbus A139 — Ascension, by Castera Bazile A140

1970, Dec. 22

641 A139 3c dk brn & buff 15 15
642 A139 5c dk grn & pale grn 18 15
Set value 23 19

Christmas 1970.

1971, Apr. 29 **Litho.** ***Perf. 12x12½***

Paintings: 5c, Man with Turban, by Rembrandt. 20c, Iris in a Vase, by Van Gogh. 50c, Baptism of Christ, by Castera Bazile. No. 647, Young Mother Sewing, by Mary Cassatt. No. 648, The Card Players, by Cezanne.

Size: 20x40mm

643 A140 5c multi 15 15
644 A140 10c multi 15 15

Perf. 13x12½

Size: 25x37mm

645 A140 20c multi 15 15

Perf. 12x12½

Size: 20x40mm

646 A140 50c multi 28 15
Nos. 643-646,C366-C368 (7) 1.78
Set value 1.10

Souvenir Sheets

Imperf

647 A140 3g multi 1.00 1.00
648 A140 3g multi 1.00 1.00

No. 647 contains one stamp, size: 20x40mm. No. 648 contains one stamp, size: 25x37mm.

Soccer Ball — A141

Design: No. 651, 1g, 5g, Jules Rimet cup.

1971, June 14 **Photo.** ***Perf. 11½***

649 A141 5c sal & blk 15 15
650 A141 50c tan & blk 20 15
651 A141 50c rose pink, blk & gold 20 15
652 A141 1g lil, blk & gold 38 28
653 A141 1.50g gray & blk 52 42
654 A141 5g gray, blk & gold 1.75 1.50
Nos. 649-654 (6) 3.20 2.65

Souvenir Sheet

Imperf

655 Sheet of 2 8.50 7.00
a. A141 70c lt vio & blk
b. A141 1g lt grn, bl & gold

9th World Soccer Championships for the Jules Rimet Cup, Mexico City, May 30-June 21, 1970. The surface tint of the sheets of 50 (10x5) of Nos. 649-654 includes a map of Brazil covering 26 stamps. Positions 27, 37 and 38 inscribed "Brasilia," "Santos," "Rio de Janeiro" respectively. On soccer ball design the 4 corner stamps are inscribed "Pele."

Nos. 655a and 655b have portions of map of Brazil in background; No. 655a inscribed "Pele" and "Santos," No. 655b "Brasilia."

Nos. 639-639O Ovptd. in Gold

APOLLO XIII RETOUR SUR LA TERRE

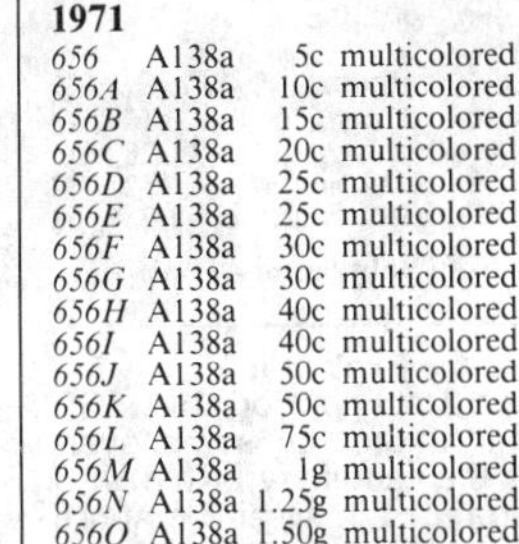

1971

656 A138a 5c multicolored
656A A138a 10c multicolored
656B A138a 15c multicolored
656C A138a 20c multicolored
656D A138a 25c multicolored
656E A138a 25c multicolored
656F A138a 30c multicolored
656G A138a 30c multicolored
656H A138a 40c multicolored
656I A138a 40c multicolored
656J A138a 50c multicolored
656K A138a 50c multicolored
656L A138a 75c multicolored
656M A138a 1g multicolored
656N A138a 1.25g multicolored
656O A138a 1.50g multicolored

Nos. 656E, 656G, 656I, 656K-656O are airmail.
Exist overprinted in silver.

J. J. Dessalines A142 — "Sun" and EXPO '70 Emblem A143

1972, Apr. 28 **Photo.** ***Perf. 11½***

657 A142 5c grn & blk 15 15
658 A142 10c brt bl & blk 15 15
659 A142 25c org & blk 15 15
Set value, #657-659, C378-C379 1.25 75

See Nos. 697-700, C448-C458, 727, C490-C493, C513-C514. For surcharges see Nos. 692, 705-709, 724-726, C438, C512.

1972, Oct. 27 **Photo.** ***Perf. 11½***

660 A143 10c ocher, brn & grn 15 15
661 A143 25c ocher, brn & mar 15 15
Nos. 660-662,C378-C379 (4) 1.38
Set value 1.25

EXPO '70 International Exposition, Osaka, Japan, Mar. 15-Sept. 13, 1970.

Gold Medalists, 1972 Summer Olympics, Munich — A143a

Designs: 5c, L. Linsenhoff, dressage, W. Ruska, judo. 10c, S. Kato, gymnastics, S.Gould, women's swimming. 20c, M. Peters, women's pentathlon, K. Keino, steeplechase. 25c, L. Viren, 5,000, 10,000m races, R. Milburn, 110m hurdles. No. 662D, D. Morelon, cycling, J. Akii-Bua, 400m hurdles. No. 662E, R. Williams, long jump. 75c, G. Mancinelli, equestrian. 1.50g, W. Nordwig, pole vault. 2.50g, K. Wolferman, javelin. 5g, M. Spitz, swimming.

1972, Dec. 29 ***Perf. 13½***

662 A143a 5c multicolored
662A A143a 10c multicolored
662B A143a 20c multicolored
662C A143a 25c multicolored
662D A143a 50c multicolored
662E A143a 50c multicolored
662F A143a 75c multicolored
662G A143a 1.50g multicolored
662H A143a 2.50g multicolored
662I A143a 5g multicolored

Nos. 662E-662I are airmail.

Basket Vendors A144

Designs: 80c, 2.50g, Postal bus.

1973, Jan. Photo. *Perf. 11 1/2*

665 A144	50c blk & multi	18	15
666 A144	80c blk & multi	28	16
667 A144	1.50g blk & multi	52	32
668 A144	2.50g blk & multi	1.25	52

20th anniv. of Caribbean Travel Assoc.

Space Exploration

A set of 12 stamps for US-USSR space exploration, the same overprinted for the centenary of the UPU and 3 overprinted in silver for Apollo 17 exist but we have no evidence that they were printed with the approval of the Haitian postal authorities.

Micromelo Undata A145

Designs: Marine life; 50c horizontal.

1973, Sept. 4 Litho. *Perf. 14*

669 A145	5c *shown*	15	15
670 A145	10c *Nemaster rubiginosa*	15	15
671 A145	25c *Cyerce cristallina*	15	15
672 A145	50c *Desmophyllum risei*	15	15
	Set value, #669-672, C395-C398	1.65	1.25

For surcharge see No. C439/

Gramma Loreto — A146

1973 *Perf. 13 1/2*

673 A146	10c *shown*	15	15
674 A146	50c *Acanthurus coeruleus*	18	15
	Nos. 673-674,C399-C402 (6)	2.55	1.95

For surcharges see Nos. 693, C440.

Soccer Stadium A147

Design: 20c, Haiti No. 654.

1973, Nov. 29 *Perf. 14x13*

675 A147	10c bis, blk & emer	15	15
676 A147	20c rose lil, blk & tan	15	15
	Nos. 675-676,C407-C410 (6)	3.92	2.98

Caribbean countries preliminary games of the World Soccer Championships, Munich, 1974.

Jean Jacques Dessalines A148

Nicolaus Copernicus A149

1974, Apr. 22 Photo. *Perf. 14*

677 A148	10c lt bl & emer	15	15
678 A148	20c rose & blk	15	15
679 A148	25c yel & vio	15	15
	Set value, #677-679, C411-C414	1.30	1.00

For surcharges see Nos. 694, C443.

1974, May 24 Litho. *Perf. 14x13 1/2*

Design: 10c, Symbol of heliocentric system.

680 A149	10c multi	15	15
681 A149	25c brt grn & multi	15	15
	Set value, #680-681, C415-C419	1.35	1.00

500th anniversary of the birth of Nicolaus Copernicus (1473-1543), Polish astronomer.
For overprint and surcharges see Nos. 695, C444, C460-C463.

Pres. Jean-Claude Duvalier — A151

1974 Photo. *Perf. 14x13 1/2*

689 A151	10c grn & gold	15	15
690 A151	20c car rose & gold	15	15
691 A151	50c bl & gold	15	15
	Nos. 689-691,C421-C426 (9)	3.42	2.65

For surcharge and overprints see Nos. C445, C487-C489.

Audubon Birds

In 1975 or later various sets of bird paintings by Audubon were produced by government employees without official authorization. They were not sold by the Haiti post office and were not valid for postage. The first set consisted of 23 values and was sold in 1975. A second set containing some of the original stamps and some new stamps appeared unannounced several years later. More sets may have been printed as there may be as many as 63 different stamps in the original 15 designs.

Nos. 659, 673 and 679-680 Surcharged with New Value and Bar

Perf. 11 1/2, 13 1/2, 14, 14x13 1/2

1976 Photo.; Litho.

692 A142	80c on 25c	35	20
693 A146	80c on 10c	35	20
694 A148	80c on 25c	35	20
695 A149	80c on 10c	35	20

Haiti No. C11 and Bicentennial Emblem — A152

1976, Apr. 22 Photo. *Perf. 11 1/2*

Granite Paper

696 A152	10c multi	15	15
	Nos. 696,C434-C437 (5)	2.94	2.28

American Bicentennial.

Dessalines Type of 1972

1977 Photo. *Perf. 11 1/2*

697 A142	10c rose & blk	15	15
698 A142	20c lem & blk	15	15
699 A142	50c vio & blk	15	15
700 A142	50c tan & blk	15	15
	Set value	40	30

Dessalines Type of 1972 Surcharged in Black or Red

1978 Photo. *Perf. 11 1/2*

705 A142	1g on 20c (#698)	28	20
706 A142	1g on 1.75g (#C454)	28	20
707 A142	1.25g on 75c (#C448)	35	26
708 A142	1.25g on 1.50g (#C453)	35	26
709 A142	1.25g on 1.50g (#C453; R)	35	26
	Nos. 705-709 (5)	1.61	1.18

Rectangular bar obliterates old denomination on Nos. 705-709 and "Par Avion" on Nos. 706-709.

J. C. Duvalier Earth Telecommunications Station — A153

Designs: 20c, Video telephone. 50c, Alexander Graham Bell (vert.).

1978, June 19 Litho. *Perf. 13 1/2*

710 A153	10c multi	15	15
711 A153	20c multi	15	15
712 A153	50c multi	15	15
	Set value, #710-712, C466-C468	1.42	1.05

Centenary of first telephone call by Alexander Graham Bell, March 10, 1876.

Athletes' Inaugural Parade — A154

1978, Sept. 4 Litho. *Perf. 13 1/2x13*

713 A154	5c shown	15	15
714 A154	25c Bicyclists	15	15
715 A154	50c High jump	15	15
	Nos. 713-715,C469-C471 (6)	2.90	
	Set value		1.72

21st Olympic Games, Montreal, July 17-Aug. 1, 1976.

Mother Nursing Child — A155

Mother Feeding Child — A156

1979, Jan. 15 Photo. *Perf. 14x14 1/2*

716 A155	25c multi	15	15

Inter-American Children's Institute, 50th anniversary. See Nos. C472-C473.

1979, May 11 Photo. *Perf. 11 1/2*

717 A156	25c multi	15	15
718 A156	50c multi	15	15
	Nos. 717-718,C474-C476 (5)	1.48	1.18
	Set value		

30th anniversary of CARE (Cooperative for American Relief Everywhere).

Human Rights Emblem — A157

1979, July 20 Litho. *Perf. 14*

719 A157	25c multi	15	15

30th anniversary of declaration of human rights. See Nos. C477-C479.

Anti-Apartheid Year Emblem, Antenor Firmin, "On the Equality of Human Races" A158

1979, Nov. 22 Photo. *Perf. 12x11 1/2*

720 A158	50c tan & black	15	15

Anti-Apartheid Year (1978). See Nos. C480-C482.

Children Playing, IYC Emblem A159

1979, Dec. 19 Photo. *Perf. 12*

721 A159	10c multi	15	15
722 A159	25c multi	15	15
723 A159	50c multi	15	15
	Nos. 721-723,C483-C486 (7)	3.18	2.43

International Year of the Child.

Nos. C379, C449, C454 Surcharged

TIMBRE POSTE G. 1.00

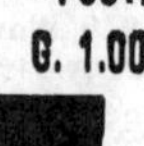

1980 Photo. *Perf. 11 1/2*

Granite Paper

724 A142	1g on 2.50g lil & blk	28	20
725 A142	1.25g on 80c emer & blk	35	32
726 A142	1.25g on 1.75g rose & blk	35	32

Dessalines Type of 1972

1980, Aug. 27 Photo. *Perf. 11 1/2*

Granite Paper

727 A142	25c org yel & blk	15	15
	Nos. 727,C490-C493 (5)	2.73	2.03

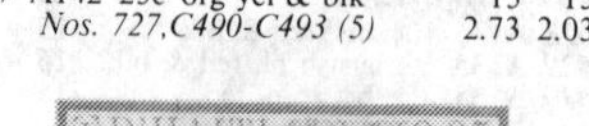

Henry Christophe Citadel — A160

1980, Dec. 2 Litho. *Perf. 12 1/2x12*

728 A160	5c shown	15	15
729 A160	25c Sans-Souci Palace	15	15
730 A160	50c Vallieres market	15	15
	Nos. 728-730,C494-C498 (8)	2.75	2.10

World Tourism Conf., Manila, Sept. 27.
For surcharges see Nos. 738, C511.

Soccer Players, World Cup, Flag of Uruguay (1930 Champion) — A161

1980, Dec. 30 Litho. *Perf. 14*

731	A161	10c shown	15	15
732	A161	20c Italy, 1934	15	15
733	A161	25c Italy, 1938	15	15
		Nos. 731-733,C499-C506 (11)	4.30	
		Set value		3.00

World Cup Soccer Championship, 50th anniversary.

For surcharges see Nos. 741, 829.

Going to Church, by Gregoire Etienne A162

Paintings: 5c, Woman with Birds and Flowers, by Hector Hyppolite (vert.). 20c, Street Market, by Petion Savain. 25c, Market Vendors, by Michele Manuel.

1981, May 12 Photo. *Perf. 11½*

734	A162	5c multi	15	15
735	A162	10c multi	15	15
736	A162	20c multi	15	15
737	A162	25c multi	15	15
		Set value, #734-737, C507-C510	2.65	1.95

For surcharges see Nos. 739-740.

Nos. 728, 734-735, 732 Surcharged

Perf. 12½x12, 14, 11½

1981, Dec. 30 Litho., Photo.

738	A160	1.25g on 5c multi	35	28
739	A162	1.25g on 5c multi	35	28
740	A162	1.25g on 10c multi	35	28
741	A161	1.25g on 20c multi	35	28
		Nos. 738-741,C511-C512 (6)	2.30	1.85

10th Anniv. of Pres. Duvalier Reforms — A163

1982, June 21 Photo. *Perf. 11½x12*

Granite Paper

742	A163	25c yel grn & blk	15	15
743	A163	50c ol & blk	15	15
744	A163	1g rose & blk	28	20
745	A163	1.25g bl & blk	35	28
746	A163	2g org red & blk	55	42
747	A163	5g org & blk	1.40	1.00
		Nos. 742-747 (6)	2.88	2.20

Nos. 742, 744-746 Overprinted in Blue: "1957-1982 / 25 ANS DE REVOLUTION"

1982, Nov. 29 Photo. *Perf. 11½x12*

Granite Paper

748	A163	25c yel grn & blk	15	15
749	A163	1g rose & blk	28	20
750	A163	1.25g bl & blk	35	28
751	A163	2g org red & blk	55	42

25th anniv. of revolution.

Scouting Year A164

Perf. 13½x14, 14x13½

1983, Feb. 26 Litho.

752	A164	5c Building campfire	15	15
753	A164	10c Baden-Powell, vert.	15	15
754	A164	25c Boat building	15	15
755	A164	50c like 10c	15	15
756	A164	75c like 25c	20	18
757	A164	1g like 5c	28	20
758	A164	1.25g like 25c	35	28
759	A164	2g like 10c	55	42
		Set value	1.65	1.30

Nos. 756-759 airmail.

For surcharge see No. 824.

Patroness of Haiti — A165

1983, Mar. 9 Litho. *Perf. 14*

760	A165	10c multi	15	15
761	A165	20c multi	15	15
762	A165	25c multi	15	15
763	A165	50c multi	15	15
764	A165	75c multi	20	18
765	A165	1g multi	28	20
766	A165	1.25g multi	35	28
767	A165	1.50g multi	42	35
768	A165	1.75g multi	50	38
769	A165	2g multi	55	42
770	A165	5g multi	1.40	1.00
a.		Souvenir sheets	1.40	1.00
		Nos. 760-770 (11)	4.30	3.41

Centenary of the Miracle of Our Lady of Perpetual Help. Nos. 764-770 airmail. Sizes of Nos. 770a: 116x90mm; 90x116mm.

UPU Admission, 100th Anniv. A165a

1983, June 10 Litho. *Perf. 15x14*

770B	A165a	5c shown	15	15
770C	A165a	10c L.F. Salomon, J.C. Duvalier	15	15
770D	A165a	25c No. 1, UPU emblem	15	15
770E	A165a	50c like 5c	15	15
770F	A165a	75c like 10c	20	18
770G	A165a	1g like 5c	28	20
770H	A165a	1.25g like 25c	35	28
770I	A165a	2g like 25c	55	42
		Set value	1.65	1.30

Nos. 770F-770I airmail.

For surcharge see No. 825.

1982 World Cup — A166

Games and scores. Nos. 776-780 airmail, horiz.

1983, Nov. 22 Litho. *Perf. 14*

771	A166	5c Argentina, Belgium	15	15
772	A166	10c Northern Ireland, Yugoslavia	15	15
773	A166	20c England, France	15	15
774	A166	25c Spain, Northern Ireland	15	15
775	A166	50c Italy (champion)	15	15
776	A166	1g Brazil, Scotland	28	20
777	A166	1.25g Northern Ireland, France	35	28
778	A166	1.50g Poland, Cameroun	42	32
779	A166	2g Italy, Germany	55	42
780	A166	2.50g Argentina, Brazil	70	70
		Set value	2.65	2.20

For surcharge see No. 826.

Haiti Postage Stamp Centenary — A167

1984, Feb. 29 Litho. *Perf. 14½*

781	A167	5c #1	15	15
782	A167	10c #2	15	15
783	A167	25c #3	15	15
784	A167	50c #5	15	15
785	A167	75c Liberty, Salomon	20	16
786	A167	1g Liberty, Salomon	28	20
787	A167	1.25g Liberty, Duvalier	35	28
788	A167	2g Liberty, Duvalier	55	42
		Set value	1.65	1.30

Nos. 785-788 airmail.

For surcharge see No. 826A.

World Communications Year — A168

1984, May 30 Photo. *Perf. 11½*

Granite Paper

789	A168	25c Broadcasting equipment, horiz.	15	15
790	A168	50c like 25c	15	15
791	A168	1g Drum	28	20
792	A168	1.25g like 1g	35	28
793	A168	2g Globe	55	42
794	A168	2.50g like 2g	70	55
		Nos. 789-794 (6)	2.18	1.75

1984 Summer Olympics — A169

1984, July 27

Granite Paper

795	A169	5c Javelin, running, pole vault, horiz.	15	15
796	A169	10c like 5c	15	15
797	A169	25c Hurdles, horiz.	15	15
798	A169	50c like 25c	15	15
799	A169	1g Long jump	28	20
800	A169	1.25g like 1g	35	28
801	A169	2g like 1g	55	42
		Set value	1.45	1.15

Souvenir Sheet

802	A169	2.50g like 1g	70	52

No. 802 exists imperf.

Arrival of Europeans in America, 500th Anniv. A170

The Unknown Indian, detail or full perspective of statue. Nos. 807-809 are vert. and airmail.

1984, Dec. 5 Litho. *Perf. 14*

803	A170	5c multi	15	15
804	A170	10c multi	15	15
805	A170	25c multi	15	15
806	A170	50c multi	15	15
807	A170	1g multi	25	20
808	A170	1.25g multi	30	22
809	A170	2g multi	48	38
		Set value	1.30	1.00

Simon Bolivar and Alexander Petion — A171

Designs: 25c, 1.25g, 7.50g, Portraits reversed. 50c, 4.50g, Bolivar, flags of Grand Colombian Confederation member nations.

1985, Aug. 30 *Perf. 13½x14*

810	A171	5c multi	15	15
811	A171	25c multi	15	15
812	A171	50c multi	15	15
813	A171	1g multi	25	20
814	A171	1.25g multi	30	22
815	A171	2g multi	48	38
816	A171	7.50g multi	1.75	1.40
		Nos. 810-816 (7)	3.23	2.65

Souvenir Sheet

Imperf

817	A171	4.50g multi	1.10	80

Nos. 813-817 airmail.

Arrival of Europeans in America, 500th Anniv. — A172

Designs: 10c, 25c, 50c, Henri, cacique of Bahoruco, hero of the Spanish period, 1492-1625. 1g, 1.25g, 2g, Henri in tropical forest.

1986, Apr. 11 Litho. *Perf. 14*

818	A172	10c multi	15	15
819	A172	25c multi	15	15
820	A172	50c multi	15	15
821	A172	1g multi	28	20
822	A172	1.25g multi	35	26
823	A172	2g multi	55	42
		Set value	1.45	1.10

Nos. 821-823 are airmail. A 3g souvenir sheet exists picturing Henri in tropical forest.

Nos. 770B, 771, 781, 756, C322, C500 Surcharged

1986, Apr. 18

825	A165a	25c on 5c No. 770B	15	15
826	A166	25c on 5c No. 771	15	15
826A	A167	25c on 5c No. 781	15	15
827	A164	25c on 75c No. 756	15	15
828	A128	25c on 1.50g No. C322	15	15
829	A161	25c on 75c No. C500	15	15
		Set value	36	30

A little time given to the study of the arrangement of the Scott Catalogue can make it easier to use effectively.

Intl. Youth Year — A173

UNESCO, 40th Anniv. (in 1986) — A174

1986, May 20 Litho. *Perf. 14x15*

830 A173 10c Afforestation 15 15
831 A173 25c IYY emblem 15 15
832 A173 50c Girl Guides 15 15
833 A173 1g like 10c 28 20
834 A173 1.25g like 25c 35 26
835 A173 2g like 50c 55 42
Nos. 830-835 (6) 1.63
Set value 1.08

Souvenir Sheet

836 A173 3g multi *3.50 3.50*

Nos. 833-836 are airmail.

1987, May 29 Photo. *Perf. 11½*

Granite Paper

837 A174 10c multi 15 15
838 A174 25c multi 15 15
839 A174 50c multi 20 15
840 A174 1g multi 40 30
841 A174 1.25g multi 50 38
842 A174 2.50g multi 1.00 75
Nos. 837-842 (6) 2.40 1.88

Souvenir Sheet

Granite Paper

843 A174 2g multi *1.05 1.05*

Nos. 840-842 are airmail.

Charlemagne Peralte, Resistance Leader — A175

1988 Litho. *Perf. 14*

844 A175 25c multi 15 15
845 A175 50c multi 22 16
846 A175 1g multi 45 35
847 A175 2g multi 90 68
a. Souvenir sheet 90 90
848 A175 3g multi 1.35 1.00
Nos. 844-848 (5) 3.07 2.34

Nos. 846-848, 847a are airmail.

SEMI-POSTAL STAMPS

Pierre de Coubertin SP1

Unwmk.

1939, Oct. 3 Engr. *Perf. 12*

B1 SP1 10c + 10c multi 20.00 20.00

Pierre de Coubertin, organizer of the modern Olympic Games. The surtax was used to build a Sports Stadium at Port-au-Prince.

See Nos. CB1-CB2.

Catalogue values for unused stamps in this section, from this point to the end of the section, are for Never Hinged items.

Nos. 419-420 Surcharged in Deep Carmine

+ 50 CENTIMES

Perf. 13x13½, 13½x13

1958, Aug. 30 Litho. Unwmk.

B2 A82 1g + 50c pur 1.75 1.75
B3 A83 1.50g + 50c red org 1.75 1.75

The surtax was for the Red Cross. Overprint arranged horizontally on No. B3. See No. CB9.

Similar Surcharge in Red on One Line on Nos. 440-441

1959, Apr. 7 Photo. *Perf. 11½*

Granite Paper

B4 A87 10c + 25c rose pink 18 15
B5 A87 25c + 25c grn 25 20

Nos. 444-446 Surcharged Like Nos. B2-B3 in Red

Perf. 14x13½

B6 A88 10c + 50c vio bl & ol 52 35
B7 A88 50c + 50c grn & dp brn 52 42
B8 A88 2g + 50c dp cl & dk brn 70 70
Nos. B4-B8 (5) 2.17 1.82

The surtax from Nos. B4-B8 was for the Red Cross. See Nos. CB10-CB15.

No. 447 Surcharged Diagonally

Nations Unies
ANNEE DES REFUGIES
1959-1960
+ 20
Centimes

Unwmk.

1959, July 23 Photo. *Perf. 12*

B9 A89 50c + 20c lt bl & dp cl 52 52

Issued for the World Refugee Year, July 1, 1959-June 30, 1960. See Nos. CB16-CB18.

Nos. 448-450 Surcharged in Dark Carmine

POUR LE SPORT
+ 0.75
CENTIMES

1959, Oct. 30 *Perf. 14*

B10 A90 25c + 75c blk brn & lt bl 50 50
B11 A90 50c + 75c multi 65 52
B12 A91 75c + 75c brn & bl 65 52
Nos. B10-B12,CB19-CB21 (6) 3.75 3.23

The surtax was for Haitian athletes.
On No. B12, surcharge lines are spaced to total depth of 16mm.

No. 436 Surcharged in Red: "Hommage a l'UNICEF +G. 0,50"

Engraved and Lithographed

1960, Feb. 2 *Perf. 11½*

B13 A86 1g + 50c blk & brick red 65 65

UNICEF. See Nos. CB22-CB23.

Nos. 452-453 Surcharged with Additional Value and Overprinted "ALPHABETISATION" in Red or Black

Perf. 12½x13

1960, July 12 Litho. Unwmk.

B14 A92 10c + 20c sal & grn (R) 18 15
B15 A92 10c + 30c sal & grn 20 18
B16 A92 50c + 20c vio & mag (R) 28 20
B17 A92 50c + 30c vio & mag 42 35
Nos. B14-B17,CB24-CB27 (8) 3.08 2.46

Olympic Games Issue

Nos. 464-465 Surcharged with Additional Value

1960, Sept. 9 Photo. *Perf. 12*

B18 A94 50c + 25c grn & ocher 25 18
B19 A94 1g + 25c dk brn & grnsh bl 28 20

See Nos. CB28-CB29.

No. 469 Surcharged "UNICEF +25 centimes"

1961, Jan. 14 Engr. *Perf. 10½*

B20 A96 1g + 25c grn & blk 28 20

UNICEF0. See Nos. CB30-CB31.

No. 469 Surcharged: "OMS SNEM +20 CENTIMES"

1961, Dec. 11

B21 A96 1g + 20c grn & blk 55 52

Issued to publicize Haiti's participation in the UN malaria eradication drive. See Nos. CB35-CB36.

Nos. 434, 436 and 438 Surcharged in Black or Red:

(Surcharge arranged to fit shape of stamp.)

1961-62 Engr. & Litho. *Perf. 11½*

B22 A86 20c + 25c blk & yel 18 15
B23 A86 1g + 50c blk & brick red (R) ('62) 42 35
B24 A86 2.50g + 50c blk & gray vio (R) ('62) 65 52
Nos. B22-B24,CB37-CB41 (8) 3.70 3.27

The surtax was for the benefit of the urban rehabilitation program in Duvalier Ville.

Nos. 486-488 Surcharged: "+25 centimes"

1962, Sept. 13 Litho. *Perf. 12*

B25 A99 5c + 25c crim & dp bl 15 15
B26 A99 10c + 25c red brn & emer 18 18
B27 A99 50c + 25c bl & crim 20 18
Nos. B25-B27,CB42-CB44 (6) 1.16 1.01

Nos. 489-490 Surcharged in Red: "+0.20"

1962 Unwmk. *Perf. 12½x13*

B28 A92 10c + 20c bl & org 15 15
B29 A92 50c + 20c rose lil & ol grn 20 15
Set value 24

See Nos. CB45-CB46.

No. 502 Surcharged: "ALPHABETISATION" and "+0,10"

1963, Mar. 15 Photo. *Perf. 14x14½*

B30 A102 25c + 10c bl gray, yel & blk 15 15

See Nos. CB47-CB48.

Nos. 491-494 Surcharged and Overprinted in Black or Red With Olympic Emblem and: "JEUX OLYMPIQUES / D'HIVER / INNSBRUCK 1964"

Perf. 14x14½, 14½x14

1964, July 27 Unwmk.

B31 A100 50c + 10c on 3c (R) 28 18
B32 A100 50c + 10c on 5c 28 18
B33 A100 50c + 10c on 10c (R) 28 18
B34 A100 50c + 10c on 25c 28 18
Nos. B31-B34,CB49 (5) 1.64 1.14

9th Winter Olympic Games, Innsbruck, Austria, Jan. 20-Feb. 9, 1964. The 10c surtax went for charitable purposes.

Nos. 510-512 Surcharged: "+ 5c." in Black

1965, Mar. 15 Photo. *Perf. 11½*

Granite Paper

B35 A105 10c + 5c lt bl & dk brn 15 15
B36 A105 25c + 5c sal & dk brn 18 15
B37 A105 50c + 5c pale rose lil & dk brn 25 18
Nos. B35-B37,CB51-CB54 (7) 1.65 1.55

Nos. B35-B37 and CB51-CB54 also exist with this surcharge (with period after "c") in red or green. They also exist with a similar black surcharge which lacks the period and is in a thinner, lighter type face.

Nos. 533 and 535-536 Surcharged and Overprinted with Haitian Scout Emblem and "12e Jamboree / Mondial 1967" Like Regular Issue

1967, Aug. 21 Photo. *Perf. 11½*

B38 A111 10c + 10c on 5c multi 15 15
B39 A111 15c + 10c multi 15 15
B40 A111 50c + 10c multi 18 18
Set value 35 35

12th Boy Scout World Jamboree, Farragut State Park, Idaho, Aug. 1-9. The surcharge on No. B38 includes 2 bars through old denomination. See Nos. CB55-CB56.

Nos. 600-601 Surcharged in Red with New Value, Red Cross and: "50ème. Anniversaire / de la Ligue des / Societes de la / Croix Rouge"

1969, June 25 Litho. *Perf. 11½*

B41 A127 10c + 10c multi 15 15
B42 A127 50c + 20c multi 18 18

50th anniv. of the League of Red Cross Societies. See Nos. CB61-CB62.

Nos. 637-638 Surcharged with New Value and: "INAUGURATION / 22-7-71"

1971, Aug. 3 Litho. *Perf. 14x13½*

B43 A138 20c + 50c multi 25 20
B44 A138 25c + 1.50g multi 65 42

Inauguration of the François Duvalier Central Hydroelectric Plant, July 22, 1971.

AIR POST STAMPS

Plane over Port-au-Prince — AP1

1929-30 Unwmk. Engr. *Perf. 12*

C1 AP1 25c dp grn ('30) 28 25
C2 AP1 50c dp vio 42 18
C3 AP1 75c red brn ('30) 1.25 1.00
C4 AP1 1g dp ultra 1.40 1.25

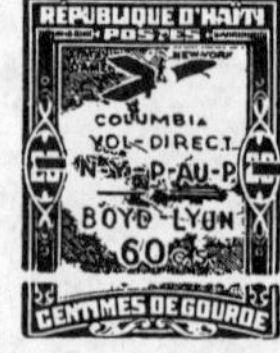

AP1a

Red Surcharge

1933, July 6

C4A AP1a 60c on 20c blue 35.00 35.00

Issued to commemorate the non-stop flight of Capt. J. Errol Boyd and Robert G. Lyon from New York to Port-au-Prince.

Plane over Christophe's Citadel — AP2

1933-40

C5	AP2	50c org brn	3.50	65
C6	AP2	50c ol grn ('35)	3.25	65
C7	AP2	50c car rose ('37)	2.00	1.25
C8	AP2	50c blk ('38)	1.50	65
C8A	AP2	60c choc ('40)	65	15
C9	AP2	1g ultra	1.25	35
		Nos. C5-C9 (6)	12.15	3.70

For surcharge see No. C24.

Alexandre Dumas, His Father and Son — AP3

1936, Mar. 1 Litho. *Perf. 11½*

C10 AP3 60c brt vio & choc 3.25 1.90

Visit of delegation from France to Haiti.

Arms of Haiti and Portrait of George Washington — AP4

1938, Aug. 29 Engr. *Perf. 12*

C11 AP4 60c deep blue 42 20

150th anniv. of the US Constitution.

Caribbean Conference Type of Regular Issue

1941, June 30

C12	A60	60c olive	2.50	65
C13	A60	1.25g purple	2.25	42

Madonna Type of Regular Issue

1942, Dec. 8 *Perf. 12*

C14	A61	10c dk ol	28	15
C15	A61	25c brt ultra	42	28
C16	A61	50c turq grn	70	28
C17	A61	60c rose car	1.00	42
C18	A61	1.25g black	2.00	42
		Nos. C14-C18 (5)	4.40	1.55

Souvenir Sheets
Perf. 12, Imperf.

C19	A61	Sheet of 2, #C14, C16	3.50	3.50
C20	A61	Sheet of 2, #C15, C17	3.50	3.50
C21	A61	Sheet of 1, #C18	3.50	3.50

Our Lady of Perpetual Help, patroness of Haiti.

Killick Type of Regular Issue

1943, Sept. 6

C22	A62	60c purple	52	25
C23	A62	1.25g black	1.50	1.25

No. C8A Surcharged with New Value and Bars in Red

1944, Nov. 25

C24	AP2	10c on 60c choc	35	25
a.		Bars at right vertical	1.75	
b.		Double surcharge	52.50	

Red Cross Type of Regular Issue

1945 Cross in Rose

C25	A63	20c yel org	15	15
C26	A63	25c brt ultra	15	15
C27	A63	50c ol blk	18	15
C28	A63	60c dl vio	25	15
C29	A63	1g yellow	1.00	15
C30	A63	1.25g carmine	70	20
C31	A63	1.35g green	70	35
C32	A63	5g black	5.00	2.00
		Nos. C25-C32 (8)	8.13	3.30

Issue dates: 1g, Aug. 14; others, Feb. 20.
For surcharges see Nos. C153-C160.

Catalogue values for unused stamps in this section, from this point to the end of the section, are for Never Hinged items.

Franklin D. Roosevelt — AP11

1946, Feb. 5 Unwmk. *Perf. 12*

C33	AP11	20c black	15	15
C34	AP11	60c black	18	15
		Set value		17

Capois Type of Regular Issue

1946, July 18 Engr.

C35	A64	20c car rose	15	15
C36	A64	25c dk grn	15	15
C37	A64	50c orange	15	15
C38	A64	60c purple	18	15
C39	A64	1g gray blk	28	15
C40	A64	1.25g red vio	42	25
C41	A64	1.35g black	52	35
C42	A64	5g rose car	1.50	1.00
		Nos. C35-C42 (8)	3.35	2.35

For surcharges see Nos. C43-C45, C49-C51, C61-C62.

Nos. C37 and C41 Surcharged with New Value and Bar or Block in Red or Black

1947-48

C43	A64	5c on 1.35g blk (R) ('48)	42	18
C44	A64	30c on 50c org	32	20
C45	A64	30c on 1.35g blk (R)	32	25

Dessalines Type of 1947-54 Regular Issue

1947, Oct. 17 Engr.

C46 A65 20c chocolate 18 15

Christopher Columbus and Fleet — AP14

Pres. Dumarsais Estiméand Exposition Buildings — AP15

1950, Feb. 12 *Perf. 12½*

C47	AP14	30c ultra & gray	70	35
C48	AP15	1g black	70	28

200th anniversary (in 1949) of the founding of Port-au-Prince.

Nos. C36, C39 and C41 Surcharged or Overprinted in Carmine

1874 1949

30

1950, Oct. 4 *Perf. 12*

C49	A64	30c on 25c dk grn	20	20
a.		30c on 1g gray black	70.00	
C50	A64	1g gray blk	42	35
a.		"P" of overprint omitted	42.50	42.50
C51	A64	1.50g on 1.35g blk	65	65

75th anniv. (in 1949) of the UPU.

Bananas AP16

Coffee AP17

Sisal — AP18

1951, Sept. 3 Photo. *Perf. 12½*

C52	AP16	30c dp org	35	15
C53	AP17	80c dk grn & sal pink	90	42
C54	AP18	5g gray	3.25	2.75

For surcharge see No. C218.

Isabella I AP19

Cap Haitien Roadstead AP20

1951, Oct. 12 *Perf. 13*

C55	AP19	15c brown	18	15
C56	AP19	30c dl bl	32	32

Issued to commemorate the 500th anniversary of the birth of Queen Isabella I of Spain.

1953, May 4 Engr. *Perf. 12*

Designs: 30c, Workers' housing, St. Martin. 1.50g, Restored cathedral. 2.50g, School lunchroom.

C57	AP20	20c dp bl	15	15
C58	AP20	30c red brn	28	15
C59	AP20	1.50g gray blk	55	35
C60	AP20	2.50g violet	1.00	70

Nos. C38 and C41 Surcharged in Black

18 MAI

1803 - 1953

50

1953, May 18

C61	A64	50c on 60c pur	28	15
a.		Double surcharge	20.00	20.00
C62	A64	50c on 1.35g blk	28	20
a.		Double surcharge	20.00	

Issued to commemorate the 150th anniversary of the adoption of the national flag.

Henri Christophe — AP21

J. J. Dessalines and Paul E. Magloire — AP22

1954, Jan. 1 Photo. *Perf. 11½*

C63	AP21	50c shown	25	18
C64	AP21	50c Toussaint L'Ouverture	25	18
C65	AP21	50c Dessalines	25	18
C66	AP21	50c Petion	25	18
C67	AP21	50c Boisrond-Tonerre	25	18
C68	AP21	1g Petion	50	18
C69	AP21	1.50g Lamartiniere	1.00	65
C70	AP22	7.50g shown	3.25	3.25
		Nos. C63-C70 (8)	6.00	4.98

150th anniv. of Haitian independence. See Nos. C95-C96.

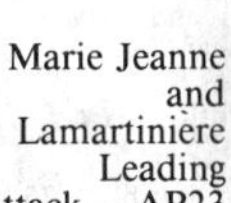

Marie Jeanne and Lamartiniere Leading Attack — AP23

Design: Nos. C73, C74, Battle of Vertieres.

1954, Jan. 1 *Perf. 12½*

C71	AP23	50c black	18	15
C72	AP23	50c carmine	18	15
C73	AP23	50c ultra	18	15
C74	AP23	50c sal pink	18	15
		Set value		40

150th anniv. of Haitian independence.

Mme. Magloire Type of Regular Issue

1954, Jan. 1 *Perf. 11½*

C75	A72	20c red org	15	15
C76	A72	50c brown	18	18
C77	A72	1g gray grn	35	28
C78	A72	1.50g crimson	42	35
C79	A72	2.50g bl grn	70	65
C80	A72	5g gray	1.90	1.50
		Nos. C75-C80 (6)	3.70	3.11

Christophe Types of Regular Issue

1954, Dec. 6 Litho. *Perf. 13½x13*

Portraits in Black

C81	A73	50c orange	25	18
C82	A73	1g blue	42	35
C83	A73	1.50g green	65	52
C84	A73	2.50g gray	1.25	70
C85	A73	5g rose car	2.00	1.40

Perf. 13

Flag in Black and Carmine

C86	A74	50c orange	28	18
C87	A74	1g dp bl	42	35
C88	A74	1.50g bl grn	65	52
C89	A74	2.50g gray	1.25	70
C90	A74	5g red org	2.00	1.50
		Nos. C81-C90 (10)	9.17	6.40

Fort Nativity, Drawing by Christopher Columbus — AP27

1954, Dec. 14 Engr. *Perf. 12*

C91	AP27	50c dk rose car	42	20
C92	AP27	50c dk gray	42	20

Dessalines Type of 1955-57 Issue

Perf. 11½

1955, July 14 Unwmk. Photo.

C93 A75 20c org & blk 15 15
C94 A75 20c yel grn & blk 15 15
Set value 20 16

For overprint see No. C183a.

Portrait Type of 1954
Dates omitted

Design: J. J. Dessalines.

1955, July 19

Portrait in Black

C95 AP21 50c gray 20 15
C96 AP21 50c blue 20 15
Set value 20

Dessalines Memorial Type of Regular Issue

1955, Aug. 1

C97 A76 1.50g gray & blk 42 18
C98 A76 1.50g grn & blk 52 20

Types of 1956 Regular Issue and

Car and Coastal View — AP30

Designs: No. C100, 75c, Plane, steamship and Haiti map. 1g, Car and coastal view. 2.50g, Flamingo. 5g, Mallard.

1956, Apr. 14 Unwmk. *Perf. 11½*

Granite Paper

C99 AP30 50c hn brn & lt bl 25 15
C100 AP30 50c blk & gray 20 15
C101 AP30 75c dp grn & bl grn 35 28
C102 AP30 1g ol grn & lt bl 35 20
C103 A77 2.50g dp org & org 2.00 70
C104 A78 5g red & buff 3.50 1.75
Nos. C99-C104 (6) 6.65 3.23

For overprint see No. C185.

Kant Type of Regular Issue

1956, July 19 Photo. *Perf. 12*

Granite Paper

C105 A79 50c chestnut 18 15
C106 A79 75c dp yel grn 25 18
C107 A79 1.50g dp mag 90 35
a. Miniature sheet of 3 2.50 1.90

No. C107a exists both perf. and imperf. Each sheet contains Nos. C105, C106 and a 1.25g gray black of same design.

Waterfall Type of Regular Issue

1957, Dec. 16 *Perf. 11½*

Granite Paper

C108 A80 50c grn & grnsh bl 15 15
C109 A80 1.50g ol grn & grnsh bl 35 28
C110 A80 2.50g dk bl & brt bl 65 52
C111 A80 5g bluish blk & saph 1.50 1.25

For surcharge and overprint see Nos. CB49, CQ2.

Dessalines Type of Regular Issue

1958, July 2

C112 A81 50c org & blk 18 15

For overprints see Nos. C184, CQ1.

Brussels Fair Types of Regular Issue, 1958

Perf. 13x13½, 13½x13

1958, July 22 Litho. Unwmk.

C113 A82 2.50g pale car rose 65 42
C114 A83 5g brt bl 90 65
a. Souv. sheet of 2, #C113-C114, imperf. 2.50 2.50

For surcharge see No. CB9.

Sylvio Cator — AP33

1958, Aug. 16 Photo. *Perf. 11½*

Granite Paper

C115 AP33 50c green 15 15
C116 AP33 50c blk brn 15 15
C117 AP33 1g org brn 28 18
C118 AP33 5g gray 1.50 70
Set value 1.00

30th anniversary of the world championship record broad jump of Sylvio Cator.

IGY Type of Regular Issue, 1958

Designs: 50c, US Satellite. 1.50g, Emperor penguins. 2g, Modern observatory.

1958, Oct. 8 *Perf. 14x13½*

C119 A85 50c dp ultra & brn red 28 18
C120 A85 1.50g brn & crim 1.00 35
C121 A85 2g dk bl & crim 1.25 35
a. Souv. sheet of 4, #427, C119-C121, imperf. 3.00 2.50

President Francois Duvalier AP34

Engraved and Lithographed

1958, Oct. 22 Unwmk. *Perf. 11½*

Commemorative Inscription in Ultramarine

C122 AP34 50c blk & rose 65 15
C123 AP34 2.50g blk & ocher 90 35
C124 AP34 5g blk & rose lil 1.25 1.00
C125 AP34 7.50g blk & lt bl grn 1.75 1.40

See note after No. 431.

Souvenir sheets of 3 exist, perf. and imperf., containing one each of Nos. C124-C125 and No. 431. Sheets measure 132x77mm. with marginal inscription in ultramarine. Value, $6.25 each.

For surcharges see Nos. CB37-CB39.

Same Without Commemorative Inscription

1958, Nov. 20

C126 AP34 50c blk & rose 18 15
C127 AP34 1g blk & vio 35 20
C128 AP34 1.50g blk & pale brn 52 28
C129 AP34 2g blk & rose pink 65 28
C130 AP34 2.50g blk & ocher 65 35
C131 AP34 5g blk & rose lil 1.25 90
C132 AP34 7.50g blk & lt bl grn 1.90 1.25
Nos. C126-C132 (7) 5.50 3.41

For surcharges see Nos. CB22-CB23, CB40-CB41.

Type of Regular Issue and

Flags of Haiti and UN — AP35

Perf. 11½

1958, Dec. 5 Unwmk. Photo.

Granite Paper

C133 AP35 50c pink, car & ultra 15 15
C134 A87 75c brt bl 20 15
C135 A87 1g brown 35 18
a. Souv. sheet of 2, #C133, C135, imperf. 2.25 2.25

Issued in tribute to the United Nations.

For surcharges see Nos. CB10-CB12.

Nos. C133-C135 Overprinted: "10th ANNIVERSARY OF THE UNIVERSAL DECLARATION OF HUMAN RIGHTS," in English (a), French (b), Spanish (c) or Portuguese (d)

1959, Jan. 28

C136 AP35 50c Block of 4 1.90 1.90
a.-d. Single 35 35
C137 A87 75c Block of 4 2.50 2.50
a.-d. Single 45 45
C138 A87 1g Block of 4 5.00 5.00
a.-d. Single 1.00 1.00

Pope Pius XII — AP36

Designs: 1.50g, Pope praying. 2.50g, Pope on throne.

1959, Feb. 28 Photo. *Perf. 14x13½*

C139 AP36 50c grn & lil 15 15
C140 AP36 1.50g ol & red brn 35 15
C141 AP36 2.50g pur & dk bl 65 28
Set value 48

Issued in memory of Pope Pius XII.

For surcharges see Nos. CB13-CB15.

Lincoln Type of Regular Issue, 1959

Designs: Various Portraits of Lincoln.

1959, May 12 *Perf. 12*

C142 A89 1g lt grn & chnt 20 15
C143 A89 2g pale lem & sl grn 35 18
C144 A89 2.50g buff & vio bl 42 28
a. Min. sheet of 4, #447, C142-C144, imperf. 2.00 2.00

Imperf. pairs exist.

For surcharges see Nos. CB16-CB18.

Pan American Games Types of Regular Issue

Designs: 50c, Jean Baptiste Dessables and map of American Midwest, c. 1791. 1g, Chicago's skyline and Dessables house. 1.50g, Discus thrower and flag of Haiti.

Unwmk.

1959, Aug. 27 Photo. *Perf. 14*

C145 A91 50c hn brn & aqua 42 18
C146 A90 1g lil & aqua 65 28
C147 A90 1.50g multi 70 35

For surcharges see Nos. CB19-CB21.

Nos. C145-C147 Overprinted

1960, Feb. 29

C148 A91 50c hn brn & aqua 70 70
C149 A90 1g lil & aqua 1.25 1.25
C150 A90 1.50g multi 1.40 1.40

Issued to commemorate the 8th Olympic Winter Games, Squaw Valley, Calif., Feb. 18-29, 1960.

WRY Type of Regular Issue, 1960

1960, Apr. 7 Litho. *Perf. 12½x13*

C151 A92 50c bl & blk 15 15
C152 A92 1g lt grn & mar 28 18
a. Souv. sheet of 4, #452-453, C151-C152, imperf. 3.00 3.00

See Nos. C191-C192. For surcharges see Nos. CB24-CB27, CB45-CB46.

Nos. C31, C28 and 369 Surcharged or Overprinted in Red: "28eme ANNIVERSAIRE"

1960, May 8 Engr. *Perf. 12*

Cross in Rose

C153 A63 20c on 1.35g grn 18 15
C154 A63 50c on 60c dl vio 20 18
C155 A63 50c on 1.35g grn 20 18
C156 A63 50c on 2.50g pale vio 20 18
C157 A63 60c dl vio 25 18
C158 A63 1g on 1.35g grn 28 28
C159 A63 1.35g green 52 42
C160 A63 2g on 1.35g grn 90 70
Nos. C153-C160 (8) 2.73 2.27

28th anniv. of the Haitian Red Cross. Additional overprint "Avion" on No. C156.

Sugar Type of Regular Issue

Designs (Miss Fouchard and): 50c, Harvest. 2.50g, Beach.

Perf. 11½

1960, May 30 Unwmk. Photo.

Granite Paper

C161 A93 50c lil rose & brn 35 15
C162 A93 2.50g ultra & brn 90 35

Olympic Type of Regular Issue

Designs: 50c, Pierre de Coubertin, Melbourne stadium and torch. 1.50g, Discus thrower and Rome stadium. 2.50g, Victors' parade, Athens, 1896, and Melbourne, 1956.

1960, Aug. 18 *Perf. 12*

C163 A94 50c mar & bis 18 15
C164 A94 1.50g rose car & yel grn 42 20
C165 A94 2.50g sl grn & mag 65 28
a. Souv. sheet of 2, #465, C165, imperf. 2.00 2.00

For surcharges see Nos. CB28-CB29.

Jeanty Type of Regular Issue

Designs: 50c, Occide Jeanty and score from "1804." 1.50g, Occide Jeanty and National Capitol.

1960, Oct. 19 *Perf. 14x14½*

C166 A95 50c yel & bl 28 15
C167 A95 1.50g lil rose & sl grn 52 20

Printed in sheets of 12 (3x4) with commemorative inscription and opening bars of "1804," Jeanty's military march, in top margin.

UN Type of Regular Issue, 1960

1960, Nov. 25 Engr. *Perf. 10½*

C168 A96 50c red org & blk 15 15
C169 A96 1.50g dk bl & blk 35 25
a. Souv. sheet of 3, #469, C168-C169, imperf. 1.75 1.75
Set value 32

For surcharges see Nos. CB30-CB31, CB35-CB36.

Dessalines Type of Regular Issue

1960, Nov. 5 Photo. *Perf. 11½*

Granite Paper

C170 A81 20c gray & blk 15 15

For overprint see No. C183.

Sud-Caravelle Jet Airliner and Orchid — AP37

Designs: 50c, Boeing 707 jet airliner, facing left, and Kittyhawk. 1g, Sud-Caravelle jet airliner and Orchid. 1.50g, Boeing 707 jet airliner and air post stamp of 1933.

1960, Dec. 17 Photo. Unwmk.

Granite Paper

C171 AP37 20c dp ultra & car 15 15
C172 AP37 50c rose brn & grn 20 15
C173 AP37 50c brt grnsh bl & ol grn 20 15
C174 AP37 50c gray & grn 20 15
C175 AP37 1g gray ol & ver 28 20
C176 AP37 1.50g brt pink & dk bl 52 28
a. Souv. sheet of 3, #C174-C176, imperf. 1.00 70
Nos. C171-C176 (6) 1.55 1.08

Issued for Aviation Week, Dec. 17-23.

Nos. C172-C174 are dated 17 Decembre 1903.

For overprints and surcharges see Nos. CB32-CB34, CO1-CO5.

Dumas Type of Regular Issue.

Designs: 50c, The Three Musketeers and Dumas pere (horiz.) 1g, The Lady of the Camellias and Dumas fils. 1.50g, The Count of Monte Cristo and Dumas pere.

1961, Feb. 10 Photo. *Perf. 11½*

Granite Paper

C177 A97 50c brt bl & blk 18 15
C178 A97 1g blk & red 25 18
C179 A97 1.50g brt grn & bl blk 35 25

Type of Regular Issue, 1961

Tourist publicity: 20c, Privateer in Battle. 50c, Pirate with cutlass in rigging. 1g, Map of Tortuga.

1961, Apr. 4 Litho. *Perf. 12*

C180 A98 20c dk bl & yel 15 15
C181 A98 50c brt pur & org 18 15
C182 A98 1g Prus grn & yel 25 18
Set value 34

For overprint and surcharge see Nos. C186-C187.

Nos. C170, C112 and C101 Overprinted: "Dr. F. Duvalier President 22 Mai 1961"

1961, May 22 Photo. *Perf. 11½*

C183 A81 20c gray & blk 15 15
a. On No. C93
C184 A81 50c org & blk 18 15
C185 AP30 75c dp grn & bl grn 28 25
Set value 45

Re-election of Pres. Francois Duvalier.

No. C182 Overprinted or Surcharged: "EXPLORATION SPATIALE JOHN GLENN" and Capsule

1962, May 10 Litho. *Perf. 12*

C186 A98 1g Prus grn & yel 35 28
C187 A98 2g on 1g Prus grn & yel 90 75

See note after No. 485.

Malaria Type of Regular Issue

Designs: 20c, 1g, Triangle pointing down. 50c, Triangle pointing up.

1962, May 30 Unwmk.

C188 A99 20c lil & red 15 15
C189 A99 50c emer & rose car 18 15
C190 A99 1g org & dk vio 28 15
a. Souv. sheet of 3 1.40 1.40
Set value 35

Printed in sheets of 12 with marginal inscription.

No. C190a contains stamps similar to Nos. 488 and C189-C190 in changed colors and imperf. Issued July 16.

A similar sheet without the "Contribution . . ." inscription was issued May 30.

For surcharges see Nos. CB42-CB44.

WRY Type of 1960 Dated "1962"

1962, June 22 *Perf. 12½x13*

C191 A92 50c lt bl & red brn 15 15
C192 A92 1g bis & blk 20 20

Issued to publicize the plight of refugees. A souvenir sheet exists containing one each of Nos. 489-490 and C191-C192, imperf. Value, $2.

For surcharges see Nos. CB45-CB46.

Boy Scout Type of 1962

Designs: 20c, Scout giving Scout sign. 50c, Haitian Scout emblem. 1.50g, Lord and Lady Baden-Powell (horiz.).

Perf. 14x14½, 14½x14

1962, Aug. 6 Photo. Unwmk.

C193 A100 20c multi 15 15
C194 A100 50c multi 20 15
C195 A100 1.50g multi 35 28
Set value 42

A souvenir sheet contains one each of Nos. C194-C195 imperf. Value, 90 cents.

A similar sheet inscribed in gold, "Epreuves De Luxe," was issued Dec. 10. Value $2.

Nos. 495 and C193-C195 Overprinted: "AÉROPORT INTERNATIONAL 1962"

Perf. 14x14½, 14½x14

1962, Oct. 26

C196 A100 20c multi, #C193 15 15
C197 A100 50c multi, #495 15 15
C198 A100 50c multi, #C194 15 15
C199 A100 1.50g multi, #C195 20 15
Set value 40

Proceeds from the sale of Nos. C196-C199 were for the construction of new airport at Port-au-Prince. The overprint on No. C197 has "Poste Aérienne" added.

Seattle Fair Type of 1962

Design: Denomination at left, "Avion" at right.

1962, Nov. 19 Litho. *Perf. 12½*

C200 A101 50c blk & pale lil 20 15
C201 A101 1g org brn & gray 35 15
C202 A101 1.50g red lil & org 42 20
Set value 40

An imperf. sheet of two exists containing one each of Nos. C201-C202 with simulated gray perforations. Size: 133x82mm. Value, $2.50.

Street in Duvalier Ville and Stamp of 1881 — AP38

1962, Dec. 10 Photo. *Perf. 14x14½*

Stamp in Dark Brown

C203 AP38 50c orange 20 15
C204 AP38 1g blue 35 28
C205 AP38 1.50g green 52 42

Issued to publicize Duvalier Ville.

For surcharges see Nos. CB47-CB48.

Nos. C201-C202 with Vertical Overprint in Black Similar To

1963, Jan. 23 Litho. *Perf. 12½*

C206 A101 1g org brn & gray 52 45
a. Claret ovpt., horiz. 90 60
C207 A101 1.50g red lil & org 70 70
a. Claret ovpt., horiz. 1.10 1.10

Issued to publicize "Peaceful Uses of Outer Space." The black vertical overprint has no outside frame lines and no broken shading lines around capsule. Nos. C206a and C207a were issued Feb. 20.

Hunger Type of Regular Issue

Perf. 13x14

1963, July 12 Unwmk. Photo.

C208 A103 50c lil rose & blk 15 15
C209 A103 1g lt ol grn & blk 28 15
Set value 22

Dag Hammarskjold and UN Emblem — AP39

Lithographed and Photogravure

1963, Sept. 28 *Perf. 13½x14*

Portrait in Slate

C210 AP39 20c buff & brn 15 15
C211 AP39 50c lt bl & car 20 18
a. Souvenir sheet of 2 1.25 1.25
C212 AP39 1g pink & bl 28 18
C213 AP39 1.50g gray & grn 45 35

Dag Hammarskjold, Sec. Gen. of the UN, 1953-61. Printed in sheets of 25 (5x5) with map of Sweden extending over 9 stamps in second and third vertical rows. No. C211a contains 2 imperf. stamps: 50c blue and carmine and 1.50g ocher and brown with map of southern Sweden in background.

For overprints see Nos. C219-C222, C238-C241, CB50.

Dessalines Type of Regular Issue, 1963

1963, Oct. 17 Photo. *Perf. 14x14½*

C214 A104 50c bl & lil rose 15 15
C215 A104 50c org & grn 15 15
Set value 20

Nos. C214-C215 and C53 Overprinted in Black or Red: "FETE DES MERES / 1964"

1964, July 22 *Perf. 14x14½, 12½*

C216 A104 50c bl & lil rose 20 15
C217 A104 50c org & grn 20 15
C218 AP17 1.50g on 80c dk grn & sal pink (R) 35 20

Issued for Mother's Day, 1964.

Nos. C210-C213 Overprinted in Red

Lithographed and Engraved

1964, Oct. 2 *Perf. 13½x14*

Portrait in Slate

C219 AP39 20c buff & brn 20 15
C220 AP39 50c lt bl & car 20 15
C221 AP39 1g pink & bl 35 28
C222 AP39 1.50g gray & grn 42 35
Nos. C219-C222,CB50 (5) 2.07 1.63

Issued to commemorate the centenary (in 1963) of the International Red Cross.

Olympic Type of Regular Issue

Designs: No. C223, Weight lifter. Nos. C224-C226, Hurdler.

1964, Nov. 12 Photo. *Perf. 11½*

Granite Paper

C223 A105 50c pale lil & dk brn 15 15
C224 A105 50c pale grn & dk brn 15 15
C225 A105 75c buff & dk brn 20 18
C226 A105 1.50g gray & dk brn 35 18
a. Souv. sheet of 4 90 90

Printed in sheets of 50 (10x5), with map of Japan in background extending over 27 stamps.

No. C226a contains four imperf. stamps similar to Nos. C223-C226 in changed colors and with map of Tokyo area in background.

For surcharges see Nos. CB51-CB54.

Airport Type of Regular Issue, 1964

1964, Dec. 15 *Perf. 14½x14*

C227 A106 50c org & blk 20 15
C228 A106 1.50g brt lil rose & blk 42 20
C229 A106 2.50g lt vio & blk 90 52

Same Overprinted "1965"

1965, Feb. 11 Photo.

C230 A106 50c org & blk 20 15
C231 A106 1.50g brt lil rose & blk 52 25
C232 A106 2.50g lt vio & blk 70 52

World's Fair Type of Regular Issue, 1965

Designs: 50c, 1.50g, "Rocket Thrower" by Donald De Lue. 5g, Unisphere, N.Y. World's Fair.

1965, Mar. 22 Unwmk. *Perf. 13½*

C233 A107 50c dp bl & org 18 15
C234 A107 1.50g gray & org 35 28
C235 A107 5g multi 1.75 1.50

Merchant Marine Type of Regular Issue, 1965

1965, May 13 Photo. *Perf. 11½*

C236 A108 50c blk, lt grnsh bl & red 15 15
C237 A108 1.50g blk, lt vio & red 42 28

O. N. U.

Nos. C210-C213 Overprinted

1945-1965

Lithographed and Photogravure

1965, June 26 *Perf. 13½x14*

Portrait in Slate

C238 AP39 20c buff & brn 15 15
C239 AP39 50c lt bl & car 15 15
C240 AP39 1g pink & bl 25 20
C241 AP39 1.50g gray & grn 20 28
Set value 64

20th anniversary of the United Nations.

ITU Type of Regular Issue

Perf. 13½

1965, Aug. 16 Unwmk. Litho.

C242 A109 50c multi 15 15
C243 A109 1g multi 28 25
C244 A109 1.50g bl & multi 42 35
C245 A109 2g pink & multi 65 50

A souvenir sheet, released in 1966, contains 50c and 2g stamps resembling Nos. C242 and C245, with simulated perforations.

For overprints see Nos. C255-C256.

Cathedral Type of Regular Issue, 1965

Designs: 50c, Cathedral, Port-au-Prince (horiz.). 1g, High Altar. 7.50g, Statue of Our Lady of the Assumption.

Perf. 14x13, 13x14

1965, Nov. 19 Photo.

Size: 39x29mm, 29x39mm

C246 A110 50c multi 20 15
C247 A110 1g multi 28 18

Size: 38x52mm

C248 A110 7.50g multi 2.00 1.75

Flower Type of Regular Issue

Flowers: No. C249, 5g, Passionflower. Nos. C250, C252, Okra. Nos. C251, C253, American elder.

1965, Dec. 20 Photo. *Perf. 11½*

Granite Paper

C249 A111 50c dk vio, yel & grn 15 15
C250 A111 50c multi 15 15
C251 A111 50c grn, gray & yel 15 15
C252 A111 1.50g multi 42 35
C253 A111 1.50g grn, tan & yel 42 35
C254 A111 5g dk vio, yel grn & grn 1.40 1.25
Nos. C249-C254 (6) 2.69 2.40

For surcharges see Nos. CB55-CB56.

Nos. C242-C243 Overprinted in Red: "20e. Anniversaire / UNESCO"

1965, Aug. 27 Litho. *Perf. 13½*

C255 A109 50c lt vio & multi 1.00 35
C256 A109 1g cit & multi 2.00 70

20th anniversary of UNESCO.

The souvenir sheet noted below No. C245 was also overprinted "20e. Anniversaire / UNESCO" in red.

Culture Types of Regular Issue and

Modern Painting — AP40

Designs: 50c, Ceremonial stool. 1.50g, Amulet.

Perf. 14x14½, 14½x14, 14

1966, Mar. 14 Photo. Unwmk.

C257 A113 50c lil, brn & brnz 20 15
C258 A112 1.50g brt rose lil, yel & blk 52 35
C259 AP40 2.50g multi 90 60

For overprints and surcharge see Nos. C260-C262, C280-C281.

Nos. C257-C259 Overprinted in Black or Red: "Hommage / a Haile SelassieIer / 24-25 Avril 1966"

1966, Apr. 24

C260	A112	50c (R)	20	15
C261	A113	1.50g (vert. ovpt.)	52	42
C262	AP40	2.50g (R)	90	70

See note after No. 543.

Walter M. Schirra, Thomas P. Stafford, Frank A. Borman, James A. Lovell and Gemini VI and VII — AP41

1966, May 3 ***Perf. 13½***

C263	AP41	50c vio bl, brn & lt bl	20	15
C264	AP41	1g grn, brn & lt bl	35	28
C265	AP41	1.50g car, brn & bl	52	42

See note after No. 547.

For overprints see Nos. C296-C298.

Soccer Type of Regular Issue

Designs: 50c, Pres. Duvalier and soccer ball within wreath. 1.50g, President Duvalier and soccer player within wreath.

Lithographed and Photogravure

1966, June 16 ***Perf. 13x13½***

Portrait in Black; Gold Inscription; Green Commemorative Inscription in Two Lines

C266	A115	50c lt ol grn & plum	15	15
C267	A115	1.50g rose & plum	52	42

Green Commemorative Inscription in 3 Lines; Gold Inscription Omitted

C268	A115	50c lt ol grn & plum	15	15
C269	A115	1.50g rose & plum	52	42

Caribbean Soccer Festival, June 10-22. Nos. C266-C267 also for the National Soccer Championships, May 8-22.

For overprint and surcharge see Nos. C288, CB57.

Education Type of Regular Issue

Designs: 50c, "ABC", boy and girl. 1g, Scout symbols. 1.50g, Television set, book and communications satellite (horiz.).

Perf. 14x13½, 13½x14

1966, Oct. 18 **Litho. and Engraved**

C270	A116	50c grn, yel & brn	15	15
C271	A116	1g dk brn, org & blk	28	28
C272	A116	1.50g grn, bl grn & dk bl	42	42

Schweitzer Type of Regular Issue

Designs (Schweitzer and): 50c, 1g, Albert Schweitzer Hospital, Deschapelles, Haiti. 1.50g, Maps of Alsace and Gabon. 2g, Pipe organ.

Perf. 12½x13

1967, Apr. 20 **Photo.** **Unwmk.**

C273	A117	50c multi	18	40
C274	A117	1g multi	35	28
C275	A117	1.50g lt bl & multi	50	42
C276	A117	2g multi	65	55

Fruit-Vegetable Type of Regular Issue, 1967

1967, July 4 **Photo.** ***Perf. 12½***

C277	A118	50c Watermelon	15	15
C278	A118	1g Cabbage	28	20
C279	A118	1.50g Tangerine	42	35

No. C258 Overprinted or Surcharged Like EXPO '67 Regular Issue

1967, Aug. 30 **Photo.** ***Perf. 14½x14***

C280	A112	1.50g multi	52	42
C281	A112	2g on 1.50g multi	70	55

Issued to commemorate EXPO '67 International Exhibition, Montreal, Apr. 28-Oct. 27.

Duvalier Type of Regular Issue, 1967

1967, Sept. 22 **Photo.** ***Perf. 14x13***

C282	A119	1g brt grn & gold	35	28
C283	A119	1.50g vio & gold	52	42
C284	A119	2g org & gold	70	55

Education Type of Regular Issue, 1967

Designs: 50c, Writing hands. 1g, Scout emblem and Scouts (vert.). 1.50g, Audio-visual teaching of algebra.

1967, Dec. 11 **Litho.** ***Perf. 11½***

C285	A120	50c multi	15	15
C286	A120	1g multi	28	25
C287	A120	1.50g multi	42	35

For surcharges see Nos. CB58-CB60.

No. C269 Overprinted

MEXICO 1968

Lithographed and Photogravure

1968, Jan. 18 ***Perf. 13x13½***

C288	A115	1.50g rose & plum	52	42

See note after No. 579.

Caiman Woods Type of Regular Issue

1968, Apr. 22 **Photo.** ***Perf. 12***

Size: 36x26mm

C289	A121	50c multi	15	15
C290	A121	1g multi	28	28

Perf. 12½x13½

Size: 49x36mm

C291	A121	50c multi	15	15
C292	A121	1g multi	28	25
C293	A121	1.50g multi	42	42
C294	A121	2g gray & multi	70	55
C295	A121	5g multi	1.40	1.00
		Nos. C289-C295 (7)	3.38	2.80

Nos. C263-C265 Overprinted

Xème JEUX OLYMPIQUES D'HIVER-GRENOBLE 1968

1968, Apr. 19 ***Perf. 13½***

C296	AP41	50c multi	52	25
C297	AP41	1g multi	1.00	52
C298	AP41	1.50g multi	1.75	90

See note after No. 584.

Monument Type of Regular Issue

1968, May 22 ***Perf. 11½***

Granite Paper

C299	A122	50c ol bis & blk	20	15
C300	A122	1g brt rose & blk	35	25
C301	A122	1.50g org & blk	52	35

For surcharges see Nos. C324-C325.

Types of Regular Bishopric Issue

Designs: 50c, Palm tree and provincial coats of arms. 1g, 2.50g, Madonna, papal arms and arms of Haiti. 1.50g, Cathedral, arms of Pope Paul VI and arms of Haiti.

Perf. 13x14, 12½x13½

1968, Aug. 16 **Photo.**

C302	A123	50c lil & multi	15	15
C303	A124	1g multi	28	25
C304	A124	1.50g multi	42	35
C305	A124	2.50g multi	70	65

Airport Type of Regular Issue

Design: 50c, 1.50g, 2.50g, Front view of air terminal.

1968, Sept. 22 **Photo.** ***Perf. 11½***

Portrait in Black

C306	A125	50c rose lake & pale vio	15	15
C307	A125	1.50g rose lake & bl	42	35
C308	A125	2.50g rose lake & lt grnsh bl	70	65

Pres. Francois Duvalier — AP42

Embossed & Typo. on Gold Foil

1968, Sept. 22 ***Die Cut Perf. 14***

C309	AP42	30g black & red		

Freed Slaves' Type of Regular Issue

1968, Oct. 28 **Litho.** ***Perf. 14½x14***

C310	A126	50c brn, lil & brt pink	15	15
C311	A126	1g brn, yel grn & brt pink	28	25
C312	A126	1.50g brn, lt vio bl & brt pink	42	35
C313	A126	2g brn, lt grn & brt pink	55	45

Education Type of Regular Issue, 1968

Designs: 50c, 1.50g, Children watching television. 1g, Hands throwing ball, and sports medal.

1968, Nov. 14 ***Perf. 11½***

C314	A127	50c multi	15	15
C315	A127	1g multi	28	25
C316	A127	1.50g multi	52	35

For surcharges see Nos. CB61-CB62.

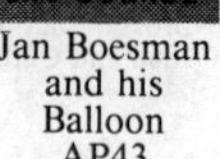

Jan Boesman and his Balloon AP43

Cachet of May 2, 1925 Flight AP44

1968, Nov. 28 **Litho.** ***Perf. 13½***

C317	AP43	70c lt yel grn & sep	35	28
C318	AP43	1.75g grnsh bl & sep	90	70

Dr. Jan Boesman's balloon flight, Mexico City, Nov. 1968.

Miniature Sheet

1968, Nov. 28 **Litho.** ***Perf. 13½x14***

Black Cachets, Magenta Inscriptions and Rose Lilac Background

C318A	Sheet of 12	5.50	7.50
b.	AP44 70c 2 Mai 1925	35	45
c.	AP44 70c 2 Septembre 1925	35	45
d.	AP44 70c 28 Mars 1927	35	45
e.	AP44 70c 12 Juillet 1927	35	45
f.	AP44 70c 13 Septembre 1927	35	45
g.	AP44 70c 6 Fevrier 1928	35	45

Galiffet's 1784 balloon flight and pioneer flights of the 1920's. No. C318A contains 2 each of Nos. C318b-C318g. The background of the sheet shows in white outlines a balloon and the inscription "BALLON GALIFFET 1784." The design of each stamp shows a different airmail cachet, date of a special flight and part of the white background design.

Churchill Type of Regular Issue

Churchill: 50c, and early seaplane. 75c, and soldiers at Normandy. 1g, and Queen Elizabeth II. 1.50g, and Big Ben, London. 3g, and coat of arms (horiz.)

1968, Dec. 23 **Photo.** ***Perf. 13***

C319	A128	50c gold & multi	15	15
C320	A128	75c gold & multi	20	18
C321	A128	1g gold & multi	28	25
C322	A128	1.50g gold & multi	42	35

Souvenir Sheet

Perf. 12½x13, Imperf.

C323	A128	3g sil, blk & red	1.00	1.00

Nos. C319-C322 exist imperf.

No. C323 contains one horizontal stamp, size: 38x25½mm.

Nos. C299-C300 Surcharged with New Value and Rectangle

1969, Feb. 21 **Photo.** ***Perf. 11½***

C324	A122	70c on 50c	20	18
C325	A122	1.75g on 1g	52	42

Bird Type of Regular Issue

Birds of Haiti: 50c, Hispaniolan trogon. 1g, Black-cowled oriole. 1.50g, Stripe-headed tanager. 2g, Striated woodpecker.

1969, Feb. 26 ***Perf. 13½***

C326	A129	50c multi	15	15
C327	A129	1g lt bl & multi	28	25
C328	A129	1.50g multi	42	35
C329	A129	2g gray & multi	55	50

For overprints see Nos. C344A-C344D.

Electric Power Type of 1969

1969, May 22 **Litho.** ***Perf. 13x13½***

C338	A131	20c dk bl & lil	15	15
C339	A131	25c grn & rose red	15	15
C340	A131	25c rose red & grn	15	15
		Set value	28	23

Education Type of 1969

Designs: 50c, Peace poster on educational television (vert.). 1g, Learning to write. 1.50g, Playing children (vert.).

1969, Aug. 12 **Litho.** ***Perf. 13½***

C342	A132	50c multi	15	15
C343	A132	1g multi	35	18
C344	A132	1.50g multi	52	35

Nos. C326-C329 Overprinted

1969, Aug. 29 **Photo.** ***Perf. 13½***

C344A	A129	50c multi		
C344B	A129	1g lt bl & multi		
C344C	A129	1.50g multi		
C344D	A129	2g gray & multi		

ILO Type of Regular Issue

1969, Sept. 22 ***Perf. 14***

C345	A133	25c red & blk	15	15
C346	A133	70c org & blk	25	15
C347	A133	1.75g brt pur & blk	65	42
		Set value		62

Butterfly Type of Regular Issue

Butterflies: 50c, Danaus eresimus kaempfferi. 1.50g, Anaea marthesia nemesis. 2g, Prepona antimache.

1969, Nov. 14 **Photo.** ***Perf. 13½***

C348	A134	50c multi	15	15
C349	A134	1.50g multi	42	35
C350	A134	2g yel & multi	55	50

King Type of Regular Issue

Perf. 12½x13½

1970, Jan. 12 **Litho.**

C351	A135	50c emer, red & blk	18	15
C352	A135	1g brick red, red & blk	35	25
C353	A135	1.50g brt bl, red & blk	52	35

Orchid Type of Regular Issue

Haitian Orchids: 50c, Tetramicra elegans. 1.50g, Epidendrum truncatum. 2g, Oncidium desertorum.

1970, Apr. 3 **Litho.** ***Perf. 13x12½***

C354	A136	50c buff, brn & mag	15	15
C355	A136	1.50g multi	42	35
C356	A136	2g lil & multi	65	50

UPU Type of Regular Issue

Designs: 50c, Globe and doves. 1.50g, Propeller and UPU emblem (vert.). 2g, UPU Monument and map of Haiti.

1970, June 23 **Photo.** ***Perf. 11½***

C357	A137	50c blk & vio	18	15
C358	A137	1.50g multi	52	35
C359	A137	2g multi	70	50
a.		Souvenir sheet of 3, #C357-C359, imperf.	1.50	

Nos. C357-C359a Overprinted in Red with UN Emblem and: "XXVe ANNIVERSAIRE / O.N.U."

1970, Dec. 14 Photo. *Perf. 11½*

C360 A137 50c blk & vio 18 15
C361 A137 1.50g multi 52 35
C362 A137 2g multi 70 50
a. Souvenir sheet of 3 1.90

United Nations, 25th anniversary.

Haitian Nativity AP45

1970, Dec. 22

C363 AP45 1.50g sep & multi 52 35
C364 AP45 1.50g ultra & multi 52 35
C365 AP45 2g multi 90 50

Christmas 1970.

Painting Type of Regular Issue

Paintings: 50c, Nativity, by Rigaud Benoit. 1g, Head of a Negro, by Rubens. 1.50g, Ascension, by Castera Bazile (like No. 648).

1971, Apr. 29 Litho. *Perf. 12x12½*
Size: 20x40mm

C366 A140 50c multi 18 15
C367 A140 1g multi 35 28
C368 A140 1.50g multi 52 42

Balloon and Haiti No. C2 — AP46

Designs: No. C370, as No. C369. No. C373, Haiti No. C2. 1g, 1.50g, Supersonic transport and Haiti No. C2.

1971, Dec. 22 Photo. *Perf. 11½*

C369 AP46 20c bl, red org & blk 15 15
C370 AP46 50c ultra, red org & blk 20 15
C371 AP46 1g org & blk 42 20
C372 AP46 1.50g lil rose & blk 70 32
Set value 66

Souvenir Sheet
Imperf

C373 AP46 50c brt grn & blk 3.50

40th anniv. (in 1969) of air post service in Haiti.
For overprints see #C374-C377, C380-C386.

Nos. C369-C372 Overprinted

INTERPEX 72

1972, Mar. 17 *Perf. 11½*

C374 AP46 20c multi 15
C375 AP46 50c multi 18
C376 AP46 1g org & blk 35
C377 AP46 1.50g lil rose & blk 52

14th INTERPEX, NYC, Mar. 17-19.

Dessalines Type of Regular Issue

1972, Apr. 28 Photo. *Perf. 11½*

C378 A142 50c yel grn & blk 18 15
C379 A142 2.50g lil & blk 90 52

For surcharge see No. C438.

Nos. C369-C372 Overprinted

HAIPEX 5ème. CONGRES

1972, May 4

C380 AP46 20c multi 15 15
C381 AP46 50c multi 18 15
C382 AP46 1g org & blk 35 20
C383 AP46 1.50g lil rose & blk 52 28
Set value 62

HAIPEX, 5th Congress.

Nos. C370-C372 Overprinted

1972, July

C384 AP46 50c multi 18 15
C385 AP46 1g org & blk 35 20
C386 AP46 1.50g lil rose & blk 52 32

Belgica '72, International Philatelic Exhibition, Brussels, June 24-July 9.

Tower of the Sun, EXPO '70 Emblem AP47

1972, Oct. 27

C387 AP47 50c bl, plum & dk bl 15 15
C388 AP47 1g bl, plum & red 35 20
C389 AP47 1.50g bl, plum & blk 42 32
C390 AP47 2.50g bl, plum & grn 90 52

EXPO '70 International Exposition, Osaka, Japan, Mar. 15-Sept. 13, 1970.
For surcharge see No. C447.

Souvenir Sheets

1972 Summer Olympics, Munich — AP47a

Designs: 2.50g, Israeli delegation, opening ceremony in Munich Stadium. 5g, Assassinated Israeli athlete David Berger.

1973 *Perf. 13½*

C390A AP47a 2.50g multi
C390B AP47a 5g multi

No. C390B contains one 22½x34mm stamp.

Headquarters and Map of Americas — AP48

1973, Aug. Litho. *Perf. 14½*

C391 AP48 50c dk bl & multi 15 15
C392 AP48 80c multi 22 18
C393 AP48 1.50g vio & multi 42 32
C394 AP48 2g brn & multi 55 42

70th anniversary (in 1972) of the Panamerican Health Organization.

Marine Life Type of Regular Issue

Designs: Marine life; 50c, 1.50g horizontal.

1973, Sept. 4 *Perf. 14*

C395 A145 50c *Platypodia spectabilis* 15 15
C396 A145 85c *Goniaster tessellatus* 25 18
C397 A145 1.50g *Stephanocyathus diadema* 42 32
C398 A145 2g *Phyllangia americana* 55 42

For surcharge see No. C439.

Fish Type of Regular Issue

Designs: Tropical fish.

1973 *Perf. 13½*

C399 A146 50c *Gramma melacara* 15 15
C400 A146 85c *Holacanthus tricolor* 25 18
C401 A146 1.50g *Liopropoma rubre* 42 32
C402 A146 5g *Clepticus parrai* 1.40 1.00

For surcharge see No. C440.

Haitian Flag — AP49

Designs: Nos. C404, C405, Haitian flag and coat of arms. No. C406, Flag and Pres. Jean-Claude Duvalier.

1973, Nov. 18 *Perf. 14½x14*
Size: 35x22½mm

C403 AP49 80c blk & red 22 18
C404 AP49 80c red & blk 22 18

Perf. 14x13½
Size: 42x27mm

C405 AP49 1.85g blk & red 52 32
C406 AP49 1.85g red & blk 52 32

For overprints and surcharges see Nos. C427-C428, C432-C433, C441-C442.

Soccer Type of Regular Issue

Designs: 50c, 80c, Soccer Stadium. 1.75g, 10g, Haiti No. 654.

1973, Nov. 29 *Perf. 14x13*

C407 A147 50c multi 15 15
C408 A147 80c multi 22 18
C409 A147 1.75g multi 50 35
C410 A147 10g multi 2.75 2.00

Dessalines Type of 1974

1974, Apr. 22 Photo. *Perf. 14*

C411 A148 50c brn & grnsh bl 15 15
C412 A148 80c gray & brn 22 18
C413 A148 1g lt grn & mar 28 20
C414 A148 1.75g lil & ol brn 50 35

For surcharge see No. C443.

Copernicus Type of 1974

Designs: No. C415, 80c, 1.50g, 1.75g, Symbol of heliocentric system. No. C416, 1g, 2.50g, Nicolaus Copernicus.

1974, May 24 Litho. *Perf. 14x13½*

C415 A149 50c org & multi 15 15
C416 A149 50c yel & multi 15 15
C417 A149 80c multi 22 18
C418 A149 1g multi 28 20
C419 A149 1.75g brn & multi 50 35

Souvenir Sheet
Imperf

C420 Sheet of 2 1.25
a. A149 1.50g lt grn & multi 42
b. A149 2.50g dp org & multi 70

For overprint and surcharges see Nos. C444, C460-C463.

Pres. Duvalier Type of 1974

1974 Photo. *Perf. 14x13½*

C421 A151 50c vio brn & gold 15 15
C422 A151 80c rose red & gold 22 18
C423 A151 1g red lil & gold 28 20
C424 A151 1.50g Prus bl & gold 42 32
C425 A151 1.75g brt vio & gold 50 35
C426 A151 5g ol grn & gold 1.40 1.00
Nos. C421-C426 (6) 2.97 2.20

For surcharge and overprints see Nos. C445, C487-C489.

Nos. C405-C406 Surcharged in Violet Blue

G. 0.80 

1975, July 15 Litho. *Perf. 14x13½*

C427 AP49 80c on 1.85g, #C405
C428 AP49 80c on 1.85g, #C406

Nos. C405-C406 Overprinted in Blue

1874 UPU 1974

100 ANS

1975, July 15 Litho. *Perf. 14x13½*

C432 AP49 1.85g blk & red 52 32
C433 AP49 1.85g red & blk 52 32

Centenary of Universal Postal Union. "100 ANS" in 2 lines on No. C433.

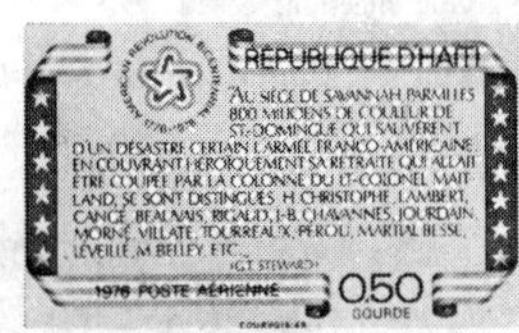

Names of Haitian Participants at Siege of Savannah — AP50

1976, Apr. 22 Photo. *Perf. 11½*
Granite Paper

C434 AP50 50c multi 15 15
C435 AP50 80c multi 22 16
C436 AP50 1.50g multi 42 32
C437 AP50 7.50g multi 2.00 1.50

American Bicentennial.

Stamps of 1972-74 Surcharged with New Value and Bar in Black or Violet Blue

Perf. 11½, 13½, 14x13½, 14
1976 Photogravure; Lithographed

C438 A142 80c on 2.50g, #C379 22 16
C439 A145 80c on 85c, #C396 22 16
C440 A146 80c on 85c, #C400 22 16
C441 AP49 80c on 1.85g, #C405 22 16
C442 AP49 80c on 1.85g, #C406 22 16
C443 A148 80c on 1.75g, #C414 (VB) 22 16
C444 A149 80c on 1.75g, #C419 (VB) 22 16
C445 A151 80c on 1.75g, #C425 22 16
C446 AP50 80c on 1.50g, #C436 22 16
C447 AP47 80c on 1.50g, #C389
Nos. C438-C446 (9) 1.98 1.44

Black surcharge of Nos. C441-C442 differs from the violet blue surcharge of Nos. C427-C428 in type face, arrangement of denomination and bar, and size of bar (10x6mm.).

Dessalines Type of 1972

1976-77 Photo. *Perf. 11½*
Granite Paper

C448 A142 75c yel & blk 20 18
C449 A142 80c emer & blk 22 15
C450 A142 1g bl & blk 28 20
C451 A142 1g red brn & blk 28 20
C452 A142 1.25g yel grn & blk 35 26
C453 A142 1.50g bl gray & blk 42 32
C454 A142 1.75g rose & blk 50 38
C455 A142 2g yel & blk 55 42
C457 A142 5g bl grn & blk 1.40 1.00
C458 A142 10g ocher & blk 2.75 2.00
Nos. C448-C458 (10) 6.95 5.11

Issue dates: 75c, 80c, No. C451, 1.75g, 5g, 10g, 1977.

Nos. C415-C416, C418-C419 Overprinted or Surcharged in Black, Dark Blue or Green

1977, July 6 Litho. *Perf. 14x13½*

C460	A149	1g (Bk)	28	20
C461	A149	1.25g on 50c (DB)	35	26
C462	A149	1.25g on 50c (G)	35	26
C463	A149	1.25g on 1.75g (Bk)	35	26

Charles A. Lindbergh's solo transatlantic flight from NY to Paris, 50th anniv.

Telephone Type of 1978

Designs: 1g, Telstar over globe. 1.25g, Duvalier Earth Telecommunications Station. 2g, Wall telephone, 1890 (vert.).

1978, June 19 Litho. *Perf. 13½*

C466	A153	1g multi	28	20
C467	A153	1.25g multi	35	26
C468	A153	2g multi	55	42

Olympic Games Type of 1978

Designs (Montreal Olympic Games' Emblem and): 1.25g, Equestrian. 2.50g, Basketball. 5g, Yachting.

1978, Sept. 4 Litho. *Perf. 13½x13*

C469	A154	1.25g multi	35	26
C470	A154	2.50g multi	70	52
C471	A154	5g multi	1.40	75

Children's Institute Type, 1979

Designs: 1.25g, Mother nursing child. 2g, Nurse giving injection.

1979, Jan. 15 Photo. *Perf. 14x14½*

C472	A155	1.25g multi	35	26
C473	A155	2g multi	55	42

Haitians Spinning Cotton, CARE Workshop AP51

1979, May 11 Photo. *Perf. 11½*

C474	AP51	1g multi	28	20
C475	AP51	1.25g multi	35	26
C476	AP51	2g multi	55	42

30th anniversary of CARE.

Human Rights Type of 1979

1979, July 20 Litho. *Perf. 14*

C477	A157	1g multi	28	20
C478	A157	1.25g multi	35	26
C479	A157	2g multi	55	42

Anti-Apartheid Year Type of 1979

1979, Nov. 22 Photo. *Perf. 12x11½*

C480	A158	1g yel grn & blk	28	20
C481	A158	1.25g bl & blk	35	26
C482	A158	2g gray ol	55	42

IYC Type of 1979

1979, Dec. 19 Photo. *Perf. 12*

C483	A159	1g multi	28	20
C484	A159	1.25g multi	35	26
C485	A159	2.50g multi	70	52
C486	A159	5g multi	1.40	1.00

Nos. C421, C424-C425 Overprinted:

27 JOUR
5
80 FASTE

1980, May 17 Photo. *Perf. 14x13½*

C487	A151	50c multi	15	15
C488	A151	1.50g multi	42	32
C489	A151	1.75g multi	50	38

Wedding of Pres. Duvalier, May 27.

Dessalines Type of 1972

1980, Aug. 27 Photo. *Perf. 11½*

Granite Paper

C490	A142	1g gray vio & blk	28	20
C491	A142	1.25g sal pink & blk	35	26
C492	A142	2g pale grn & blk	55	42
C493	A142	5g lt bl & blk	1.40	1.00

For surcharge see No. C512.

Tourism Type

1980, Dec. 2 Litho. *Perf. 12½x12*

C494	A160	1g like #728	28	20
C495	A160	1.25g like #729	35	25
C496	A160	1.50g Carnival dancers	42	28
C497	A160	2g Vendors	55	42
C498	A160	2.50g like #C497	70	50

For surcharge see No. C511.

Soccer Type of 1980

1980, Dec. 30 Litho. *Perf. 14*

C499	A161	50c Uruguay, 1950	15	15
C500	A161	75c Germany, 1954	20	18
C501	A161	1g Brazil, 1958	28	20
C502	A161	1.25g Brazil, 1962	35	26
C503	A161	1.50g Gt. Britain, 1966	42	32
C504	A161	1.75g Brazil, 1970	50	38
C505	A161	2g Germany, 1974	55	42
C506	A161	5g Argentina, 1978	1.40	1.00

Painting Type of 1981

1981, May 12 Photo. *Perf. 11½*

C507	A162	50c like #734	15	15
C508	A162	1.25g like #735	35	26
C509	A162	2g like #736	55	42
C510	A162	5g like #737	1.40	1.00

Nos. C496, C493 Surcharged

Perf. 12½x12, 11½

1981, Dec. 30 Litho., Photo.

C511	A160	1.25g on 1.50g multi	35	28
C512	A142	2g on 5g multi	55	45

Dessalines Type of 1972

1982, Jan. 25 Photo. *Perf. 11½*

Granite Paper

C513	A142	1.25g lt brn & blk	35	28
C514	A142	2g lil & blk	55	45

AIR POST SEMI-POSTAL STAMPS

Coubertin Semipostal Type of 1939

Unwmk.

1939, Oct. 3 Engr. *Perf. 12*

CB1	SP1	60c + 40c multi	15.00	15.00
CB2	SP1	1.25g + 60c multi	15.00	15.00

Mosquito and National Sanatorium — SPAP2

1949, July 22 Cross in Carmine

CB3	SPAP2	20c + 20c sep	7.00	5.00
CB4	SPAP2	30c + 30c dp grn	7.00	5.00
CB5	SPAP2	45c + 45c lt red brn	7.00	5.00
CB6	SPAP2	80c + 80c pur	7.00	5.00
CB7	SPAP2	1.25g + 1.25g car rose	7.00	5.00
a.		Souvenir sheet	24.00	18.00
CB8	SPAP2	1.75g + 1.75g bl	7.00	5.00
a.		Souvenir sheet	24.00	18.00
		Nos. CB3-CB8 (6)	42.00	30.00

The surtax was used for fighting tuberculosis and malaria.

No. C113 Surcharged in Deep Carmine

+ 50 CENTIMES

1958, Aug. 30 Litho. *Perf. 13x13½*

CB9	A82	2.50g + 50c	2.00	2.00

The surtax was for the Red Cross.

Catalogue values for unused stamps in this section, from this point to the end of the section, are for Never Hinged items.

Similar Surcharge in Red on One Line on Nos. C133-C135

1959, Apr. 7 Photo. *Perf. 11½*

Granite Paper

CB10	AP35	50c + 25c pink, car & ultra	25	18
CB11	A87	75c + 25c brt bl	28	25
CB12	A87	1g + 25c brn	42	35

Nos. C139-C141 Surcharged Like No. CB9 in Red

CB13	AP36	50c + 50c grn & lil	65	65
CB14	AP36	1.50g + 50c ol & red brn	65	65
CB15	AP36	2.50g + 50c pur & dk bl	70	70
		Nos. CB10-CB15 (6)	2.95	2.78

Surtax for the Red Cross.

Nos. C142-C144 Surcharged Diagonally

Nations Unies
ANNEE DES REFUGIES
1959-1960
+ 20
Centimes

1959, July 23 Unwmk. *Perf. 12*

CB16	A89	1g + 20c	65	52
CB17	A89	2g + 20c	65	65
CB18	A89	2.50g + 20c	70	70

Issued for the World Refugee Year, July 1, 1959-June 30, 1960. A similar surcharge of 50c was applied horizontally to stamps in No. C144a. Value $17.50.

C145-C147 Surcharged in Dark Carmine

POUR LE SPORT
+ 0.75
CENTIMES

1959, Oct. 30 Photo. *Perf. 14*

CB19	A91	50c + 75c hn brn & aqua	65	52
CB20	A90	1g + 75c lil & aqua	65	52
CB21	A90	1.50g + 75c multi	65	65

The surtax was for Haitian athletes.

On No. CB19, surcharge lines are spaced to total depth of 16mm.

Nos. C129-C130 Surcharged in Red: "Hommage a l'UNICEF +G. 0,50"

Engraved and Lithographed

1960, Feb. 2 *Perf. 11½*

CB22	AP34	2g + 50c	70	70
CB23	AP34	2.50g + 50c	1.25	1.25

Issued to honor UNICEF.

Nos. C151-C152 Surcharged and Overprinted: "ALPHABETISATION" in Red or Black.

1960, July 12 Litho. *Perf. 12½x13*

CB24	A92	50c + 20c (R)	28	20
CB25	A92	50c + 30c	42	28
CB26	A92	1g + 20c (R)	65	55
CB27	A92	1g + 30c	65	55

Olympic Games Issue

Nos. C163-C164 Surcharged

1960, Sept. 9 Photo. *Perf. 12*

CB28	A94	50c + 25c	18	15
CB29	A94	1.50g + 25c	35	28

Nos. C168-C169 Surcharged: "UNICEF +25 centimes"

1961, Jan. 14 Engr. *Perf. 10½*

CB30	A96	50c + 25c red org & blk	20	15
CB31	A96	1.50g + 25c dk bl & blk	35	25

Issued for the UNICEF.

Nos. C171, C175-C176 Surcharged with Additional Value, Scout Emblem and: "18e Conference Internationale du Scoutisme Mondial Lisbonne Septembre 1961"

1961, Sept. 30 Photo. *Perf. 11½*

CB32	AP37	20c + 25c	18	15
CB33	AP37	1g + 25c	20	18
CB34	AP37	1.50g + 25c	28	28

Issued to commemorate the 18th Boy Scout World Conference, Lisbon, Sept. 19-24, 1961.

The surtax was for the Red Cross. Additional proceeds from the sale of Nos. CB32-CB34 benefited the Port-au-Prince airport project.

The same surcharge was also applied to No. C176a.

Nos. C168-C169 Surcharged: "OMS SNEM +20 CENTIMES"

1961, Dec. 11 Engr. *Perf. 10½*

CB35	A96	50c + 20c	90	90
CB36	A96	1.50g + 20c	1.25	1.25

Issued to publicize Haiti's participation in the UN malaria eradication drive.

Nos. C123, C126-C127 and C131-C132 Surcharged in Black or Red:

Duvalier-Ville
+ 25
CENTIMES

Engraved and Lithographed

1961-62 *Perf. 11½*

CB37	AP34	50c + 25c	15	15
CB38	AP34	1g + 50c	18	15
CB39	AP34	2.50g + 50c (R) ('62)	42	35
CB40	AP34	5g + 50c	70	70
CB41	AP34	7.50g + 50c (R) ('62)	1.00	90
		Nos. CB37-CB41 (5)	2.45	2.25

The surtax was for the benefit of the urban rehabilitation program in Duvalier Ville.

Nos. C188-C190 Surcharged: "+25 centimes"

1962, Sept. 13 Litho. *Perf. 12*

CB42	A99	20c + 25c lil & red	15	15
CB43	A99	50c + 25c emer & rose car	20	15
CB44	A99	1g + 25c org & dk vio	28	20

Nos. C191-C192 Surcharged in Red: "+0.20"

1962 *Perf. 12½x13*

CB45	A92	50c + 20c lt bl & red brn	20	15
CB46	A92	1g + 20c bis & blk	28	20

Nos. C203 and C205 Surcharged: "ALPHABETISATION" and "0, 10"

1963, Mar. 15 Photo. *Perf. 14x14½*

CB47	AP38	50c + 10c	20	15
CB48	AP38	1.50g + 10c	28	28

No. C110 Surcharged in Red with Olympic Emblem and: "JEUX OLYMPIQUES / D'HIVER / INNSBRUCK 1964"

1964, July 27 Photo. *Perf. 11½*

CB49	A80	2.50g + 50c + 10c	52	42

See note after No. B34. The 50c+10c surtax went for charity.

No. C213 Surcharged in Red

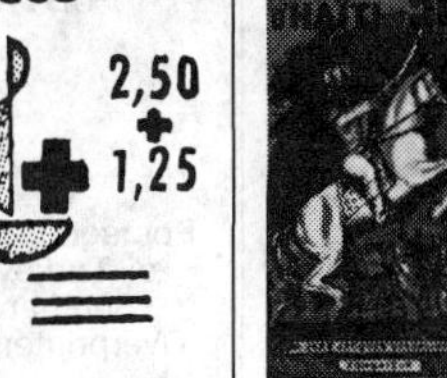

Engraved and Photogravure

1964, Oct. 2 *Perf. 13½x14*

CB50 AP39 2.50g + 1.25g on 1.50g 90 70

Issued to commemorate the centenary (in 1963) of the International Red Cross.

Nos. C223-C226 Surcharged: "+ 5c." in Black

1965, Mar. 15 Photo. *Perf. 11½*

CB51 A105 50c + 5c pale lil & dk brn 15 15
CB52 A105 50c + 5c pale grn & dk brn 15 15
CB53 A105 75c + 5c buff & dk brn 25 25
CB54 A105 1.50g + 5c gray & dk brn 52 52

The souvenir sheet No. C226a was surcharged "+25c."
See note following No. B37.

Nos. C251 and C253 Surcharged and Overprinted with Haitian Scout Emblem and "12e Jamboree / Mondial 1967" Like Regular Issue

1967, Aug. 21 Photo. *Perf. 11½*

CB55 A111 50c + 10c multi 15 15
CB56 A111 1.50g + 50c multi 42 35

See note after No. B40.

No. C269 Surcharged Like Regular Issue

Lithographed and Photogravure

1968, Jan. 18 *Perf. 13x13½*

CB57 A115 2.50g + 1.25g on 1.50g 1.00 90

See note after No. 579.

Nos. C285-C287 Surcharged "CULTURE + 10"

1968, July 4 Litho. *Perf. 11½*

CB58 A120 50c + 10c multi 15 15
CB59 A120 1g + 10c multi 28 28
CB60 A120 1.50g + 10c multi 35 35

Nos. C314 and C316 Surcharged in Red with New Value, Red Cross and: "50eme. Anniversaire / de la Ligue des / Societes de la / Croix Rouge"

1969, June 25 Litho. *Perf. 11½*

CB61 A127 50c + 20c multi 25 25
CB62 A127 1.50g + 25c multi 65 42

Issued to commemorate the 50th anniversary of the League of Red Cross Societies.

AIR POST OFFICIAL STAMPS

Nos. C172-C176 and C176a Overprinted: "OFFICIEL"

Perf. 11½

1961, Mar. Unwmk. Photo.

CO1 AP37 50c rose brn & grn 18
CO2 AP37 50c brt grnsh bl & ol grn 18
CO3 AP37 50c gray & grn 18
CO4 AP37 1g gray ol & ver 28
CO5 AP37 1.50g brt pink & dk bl 42
a. Sheet of 3 1.40
Nos. CO1-CO5 (5) 1.24

Nos. CO1-CO5a only available canceled.

Catalogue values for unused stamps in this section, from this point to the end of the section, are for Never Hinged items.

Jean Jacques Dessalines — OA1

1962, Mar. 7 Photo. *Perf. 14x14½*

Size: 20½x38mm

CO6 OA1 50c dk bl & sepia 18 15
CO7 OA1 1g lt bl & mar 35 26
CO8 OA1 1.50g bister & bl 42 35

Size: 30x40mm

CO9 OA1 5g rose & ol grn 1.25 1.10

Inscription at bottom of #CO9 is in 2 lines.

AIR POST PARCEL POST STAMPS

Catalogue values for unused stamps in this section are for Never Hinged items.

Nos. C112 and C111 Overprinted in Red **COLIS POSTAUX**

Perf. 11½

1960, Nov. 21 Unwmk. Photo.

CQ1 A81 50c org & blk 25 18
CQ2 A80 5g bluish blk & saph 2.00 1.75

Type of Parcel Post Stamps, 1961 Inscribed "Poste Aerienne"

1961, Mar. 24 *Perf. 14*

CQ3 PP1 2.50g yel grn & mar 90 70
CQ4 PP1 5g org & grn 1.75 1.40

SPECIAL DELIVERY STAMP

The catalogue value for the unused stamp in this section is for Never Hinged.

Postal Administration Building — SD1

Unwmk.

1953, May 4 Engr. *Perf. 12*

E1 SD1 25c vermilion 70 60

POSTAGE DUE STAMPS

D1

D2

1898, May Unwmk. Engr. *Perf. 12*

J1 D1 2c black 25 25
J2 D1 5c red brn 35 35
J3 D1 10c brn org 52 20
J4 D1 50c slate 1.50 70

For overprints see Nos. J5-J9, J14-J16.

Stamps of 1898 Handstamped

1902 Black Overprint

J5 D1 2c black 70 52
J6 D1 5c red brn 70 52
J7 D1 10c brn org 85 52
J8 D1 50c slate 6.00 3.50

Red Overprint

J9 D1 2c black 85 85
Nos. J5-J9 (5) 9.10 5.91

1906

J10 D2 2c dl red 60 45
J11 D2 5c ultra 1.75 1.75
J12 D2 10c violet 1.75 1.75
J13 D2 50c ol gray 7.50 4.25

For overprints see Nos. J17-J20.

Preceding Issues Handstamped

Gl O.Z.
7 Fév. 1914

1914 On Stamps of 1898

J14 D1 5c red brn 60 45
J15 D1 10c brn org 55 55
J16 D1 50c slate 3.75 2.50

On Stamps of 1906

J17 D2 2c dl red 45 30
J18 D2 5c ultra 75 45
J19 D2 10c violet 3.00 2.50
J20 D2 50c olive gray 5.50 3.50

The note after No. 201 applies to Nos. J14-J20 also.

Catalogue values for unused stamps in this section, from this point to the end of the section, are for Never Hinged items.

Unpaid Letter — D3

1951, July Litho. *Perf. 11½*

J21 D3 10c carmine 15 15
J22 D3 20c red brown 15 15
J23 D3 40c green 25 25
J24 D3 50c orange yellow 35 35

PARCEL POST STAMPS

Catalogue values for unused stamps in this section are for Never Hinged items.

Nos. 416, 470-471 and 378 Overprinted in Red **COLIS POSTAUX**

Photogravure, Engraved

Perf. 11½, 12

1960, Nov. 21 Unwmk.

Q1 A81 5c yel grn & blk 15 15
Q2 A81 10c red org & blk 15 15
Q3 A81 25c ultra & blk 15 15
Q4 A64 2.50g gray 1.00 1.00
Set value 1.25 1.25

Coat of Arms — PP1

Unwmk.

1961, Mar. 24 Photo. *Perf. 14*

Q5 PP1 50c bister & pur 35 15
Q6 PP1 1g pink & dark bl 52 28

See Nos. CQ3-CQ4.

POSTAL TAX STAMPS

Catalogue values for unused stamps in this section, are for Never Hinged items.

Haitian Woman, War Invalids and Ruined Buildings
PT1

Unwmk.

1944, Aug. 16 Engr. *Perf. 12*

RA1 PT1 5c dull purple 70 28
RA2 PT1 5c dark blue 70 28
RA3 PT1 5c olive green 70 28
RA4 PT1 5c black 70 28

1945, Dec. 17

RA5 PT1 5c dark green 70 28
RA6 PT1 5c sepia 70 28
RA7 PT1 5c red brown 70 28
RA8 PT1 5c rose carmine 70 28

The proceeds from the sale of Nos. RA1 to RA8 were for United Nations Relief.

George Washington, J. J. Dessalines and Simon Bolivar — PT2

1949, Sept. 20

RA9 PT2 5c red brown 20 15
RA10 PT2 5c olive gray 20 15
RA11 PT2 5c blue 20 15
RA12 PT2 5c green 20 15
RA13 PT2 5c violet 20 15
RA14 PT2 5c black 20 15
RA15 PT2 5c orange 20 15
RA16 PT2 5c carmine rose 20 15
Nos. RA9-RA16 (8) 1.60
Set value 96

Bicentenary of Port-au-Prince.
For overprint and surcharges see #385-388.

Helicopter Inspection of Hurricane Damage
PT3

Helicopter
PT4

1955, Jan. 3 Photo. *Perf. 11½*

RA17 PT3 10c bright grn 15 15
RA18 PT3 10c bright bl 15 15
RA19 PT3 10c gray blk 15 15
RA20 PT3 10c orange 15 15

RA21	PT3 20c rose carmine	15	15
RA22	PT3 20c deep green	15	15
	Set value	60	30

1955, May 3

RA23	PT4 10c black, *gray*	15	15
RA24	PT4 20c vio blue, *blue*	15	15
	Set value	24	15

The surface tint of the sheets of 50, (10x5) of #RA23-RA24, RAC1-RAC2 includes a map of Haiti's southern peninsula which extends over the three center rows of stamps.

The tax was for reconstruction.

See Nos. RAC1-RAC2.

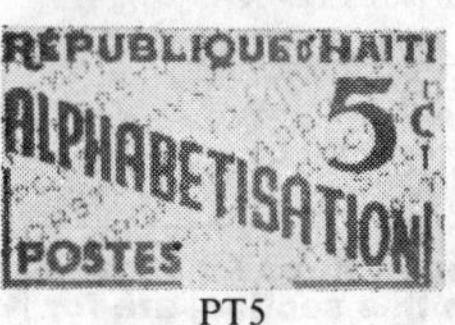

PT5

PT6

1959-60 Unwmk. Photo. *Perf. 11½*

Size: 38x22½mm

RA25	PT5 5c green	15	15
RA26	PT5 5c black ('60)	15	15
RA27	PT5 10c red	15	15
	Set value	24	16

1960-61

Size: 28x17mm

RA28	PT5 5c green	15	15
RA29	PT5 10c red	15	15
RA30	PT5 10c blue ('61)	15	15
	Set value	18	15

1963, Sept. *Perf. 14½x14*

Size: 13½x21mm

RA31	PT6 10c red orange	15	15
RA32	PT6 10c bright blue	15	15
RA33	PT6 10c olive	15	15
	Set value, #RA31-RA33, RAC6-RAC8	33	30

1966-69 Photo. *Perf. 14x14½*

Size: 17x25mm

RA34	PT6 10c bright green	15	15
RA35	PT6 10c violet	15	15
RA36	PT6 10c violet blue	15	15
RA37	PT6 10c brown ('69)	15	15
	Set value, #RA34-RA37, RAC9-RAC15	62	55

Nos. RA25-RA37 represent a tax for a literacy campaign.

See Nos. RA42-RA45, RAC20-RAC22.

Duvalier de Peligre Hydroelectric Works — PT7

1970-72

RA38	PT7 20c vio & olive	15	15
RA39	PT7 20c ultra & blk ('72)	15	15
	Set value	18	15

See Nos. RA46, RAC16-RAC19, RAC23.

Nos. 637-638 Surcharged: "ALPHABETISATION +10"

1971, Dec. 23 Litho. *Perf. 14x13½*

RA40	A138 20c + 10c multi	15	15
a.	Inverted surcharge		2.00
RA41	A138 25c + 10c multi	15	15
	Set value	18	15

Tax was for the literacy campaign.

"CA" Type of 1963

1972-74 Photo. *Perf. 14x14½*

Size: 17x25mm

RA42	PT6 5c violet blue	15	15
RA43	PT6 5c deep carmine	15	15
RA44	PT6 5c ultra ('74)	15	15
RA45	PT6 5c carmine rose ('74)	15	15
	Set value	20	20

Tax was for literacy campaign.

Hydroelectric Type of 1970

1980 Photo. *Perf. 14x14½*

RA46	PT7 25c choc & green	22	15

AIR POST POSTAL TAX STAMPS

Catalogue values for unused stamps in this section, are for Never Hinged items.

Helicopter Type of 1955

1955 Unwmk. Photo. *Perf. 11½*

RAC1	PT4 10c red brn, *pale sal*	15	15
RAC2	PT4 20c rose pink, *pink*	15	15
	Set value		15

See note after No. RA24.

Type of Postal Tax Stamps, 1960-61

1959

Size: 28x17mm

RAC3	PT5 5c yellow	15	15
RAC4	PT5 10c dull salmon	15	15
RAC5	PT5 10c blue	15	15
	Set value	17	15

Type of Postal Tax Stamps, 1963

1963, Sept. *Perf. 14½x14*

Size: 13½x21mm

RAC6	PT6 10c dark gray	15	15
RAC7	PT6 10c violet	15	15
RAC8	PT6 10c brown	15	15
	Set value	15	15

1966-69 *Perf. 14x14½*

Size: 17x25mm

RAC9	PT6 10c orange	15	15
RAC10	PT6 10c sky blue	15	15
RAC11	PT6 10c yel ('69)	15	15
RAC12	PT6 10c car ('69)	15	15
RAC13	PT6 10c gray grn ('69)	15	15
RAC14	PT6 10c lilac ('69)	15	15
RAC15	PT6 10c dp claret ('69)	15	15
	Set value	40	35

Nos. RAC3-RAC15, RAC20-RAC21 represent a tax for a literacy campaign.

Hydroelectric Type of 1970

1970-74

RAC16	PT7 20c tan & sl	15	15
RAC17	PT7 20c brt bl & dl vio	15	15
RAC18	PT7 25c sal & bluish blk ('74)	18	15
RAC19	PT7 25c yel ol & bluish blk ('74)	18	15
	Set value		24

"CA" Type of 1963

1973 Photo. *Perf. 14x14½*

Size: 17x26mm

RAC20	PT6 10c brn & bl	15	15
RAC21	PT6 10c brn & grn	15	15
RAC22	PT6 10c brn & org	15	15
	Set value		15

Hydroelectric Power Type of 1970

1980 Photo. *Perf. 14x14½*

RAC23	PT7 25c blue & vio brn	18	15

HATAY

(Formerly Alexandretta)

LOCATION — Northwest of Syria, bordering on Mediterranean Sea.
GOVT. — Former semi-independent republic
AREA — 10,000 sq. mi. (approx.)
POP. — 273,350 (1939)
CAPITAL — Antioch

Alexandretta, a semi-autonomous district of Syria under French mandate, was renamed Hatay in 1938 and transferred to Turkey in 1939.

100 Santims = 1 Kurush
40 Paras = 1 Kurush (1939)

Stamps of Turkey, 1931-38, Surcharged in Black:

HATAY DEVLETİ 75 Sant.
On A77

HATAY DEVLETİ 25 Sant.
On A78

1939 Unwmk. *Perf. 11½x12*

1	A77	10s on 20pa dp org	32	32
a.		"Sent" instead of "Sant"	20.00	20.00
2	A78	25s on 1ku dk sl grn	32	32
a.		Small "25"	35	35
3	A78	50s on 2ku dk vio	32	32
a.		Small "50"	35	35
4	A77	75s on 2½ku grn	32	32
5	A78	1ku on 4ku slate	32	32
6	A78	1ku on 5ku rose red	32	32
7	A78	1½ku on 3ku brn org	55	55
8	A78	2½ku on 4ku slate	70	70
9	A78	5ku on 8ku brt bl	2.25	2.25
10	A77	12½ku on 20ku ol grn	3.25	3.25
11	A77	20ku on 25ku Prus bl	3.50	3.50
		Nos. 1-11 (11)	12.17	12.17

Map of Hatay — A1

Lions of Antioch A2

Flag of Hatay — A3

Post Office A4

1939 Unwmk. Typo. *Perf. 12*

12	A1	10p org & aqua	24	24
13	A1	30p lt vio & aqua	30	30
14	A1	1½ku ol & aqua	32	32
15	A2	2½ku turq grn	42	42
16	A2	3ku light blue	50	50
17	A2	5ku chocolate	55	55
18	A3	6ku brt bl & car	65	65
19	A3	7½ku dp grn & car	55	55
20	A3	12ku vio & car	90	90
21	A3	12½ku dk bl & car	95	95
22	A4	17½ku brn car	2.25	2.25
23	A4	25ku olive brn	3.00	3.00
24	A4	50ku slate blue	6.25	6.25
		Nos. 12-24 (13)	16.88	16.88

Stamps of 1939 Overprinted in Black

T. C.
ilhak tarihi
30-6-1939

1939

25	A1	10p org & aqua	22	22
a.		Overprint reading up	20.00	
26	A1	30p lt vio & aqua	32	32
27	A1	1½ku ol & aqua	32	32
28	A2	2½ku turq grn	45	45
29	A2	3ku light blue	55	55
30	A2	5ku chocolate	60	60
a.		Overprint inverted	20.00	
31	A3	6ku brt bl & car	60	60
32	A3	7½ku dp grn & car	60	60
33	A3	12ku vio & car	75	75
34	A3	12½ku dk bl & car	90	90
35	A4	17½ku brn car	1.75	1.75
a.		Overprint inverted	20.00	
36	A4	25ku olive brn	3.50	3.50
37	A4	50ku slate bl	7.25	7.25
		Nos. 25-37 (13)	17.81	17.81

The overprint reads "Date of annexation to the Turkish Republic, June 30, 1939."

On Nos. 25-27, the overprint reads down. On Nos. 28-37, it is horizontal.

POSTAGE DUE STAMPS

Postage Due Stamps of Turkey, 1936, Surcharged or Overprinted in Black

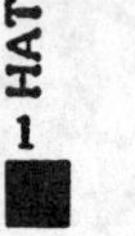

1939 Unwmk. *Perf. 11½*

J1	D6	1ku on 2ku lt bl	45	45
J2	D6	3ku brt vio	70	70
J3	D6	4ku on 5ku Prus bl	95	95
J4	D6	5ku on 12ku brt rose	1.25	1.25
J5	D6	12ku brt rose	14.00	14.00
		Nos. J1-J5 (5)	17.35	17.35

Castle at Antioch D1

1939 Typo. *Perf. 12*

J6	D1	1ku red orange	50	50
J7	D1	3ku dk olive brn	70	70
J8	D1	4ku turq green	85	85
J9	D1	5ku slate blk	1.10	1.10

Nos. J6-J9 Overprinted in Black like Nos. 25-37

1939

J10	D1	1ku red org	80	80
J11	D1	3ku dk ol brn	95	95
J12	D1	4ku turq grn	1.00	1.00
J13	D1	5ku sl blk	1.25	1.25
a.		Overprint inverted	20.00	

HONDURAS

LOCATION — Central America, between Guatemala on the north and Nicaragua on the south
GOVT. — Republic
AREA — 43,277 sq. mi.
POP. — 4,092,174 (est. 1983)
CAPITAL — Tegucigalpa

8 Reales = 1 Peso
100 Centavos = 1 Peso (1878)
100 Centavos = 1 Lempira (1933)

Catalogue values for unused stamps in this country are for Never Hinged items, beginning with Scott 344 in the regular postage section, Scott C309 in the airpost section, Scott CE3 in the airpost special delivery section, Scott CO110 in the airpost official section, and Scott RA6 in the postal tax section.

Watermark

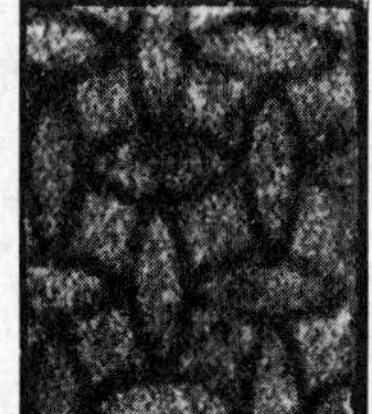

Wmk. 209- Multiple Ovals

Coat of Arms — A1

1865, Dec. Unwmk. Litho. *Imperf.*

1	A1	2r black, *green*	60
2	A1	2r black, *pink*	60

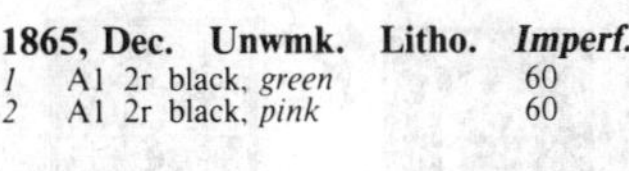

A2

A3

The actual surcharges are very blurry, distorted and generally unreadable. The above illustrations are only intended to show what the surcharges would look like based on the type face used.

Comayagua Issue

1877, Apr.

Red Surcharge

3	A2	½r on 2r blk, *grn*	60.00

Blue Surcharge

5	A2	2r on 2r blk, *grn*	95.00
6	A2	2r on 2r blk, *pink*	95.00

Black Surcharge

7	A2	1r on 2r blk, *grn*	75.00
9	A2	2r on 2r blk, *pink*	95.00

Tegucigalpa Issue

1877, June

Black Surcharge

13	A3	1r on 2r blk, *grn*	14.00	16.00
14	A3	1r on 2r blk, *pink*	14.00	
16	A3	2r on 2r blk, *pink*	12.50	

Blue Surcharge

18	A3	½r on 2r blk, *grn*	12.00	
19	A3	½r on 2r blk, *pink*	12.00	
20	A3	1r on 2r blk, *pink*	14.00	
23	A3	2r on 2r blk, *pink*	14.00	16.00

Red Surcharge

24	A3	½r on 2r blk, *grn*	12.00	14.00
25	A3	½r on 2r blk, *pink*	14.00	

#3-25 have been extensively counterfeited.

Regular Issue

President Francisco Morazan — A4

Thin, hard paper, colorless gum
Various Frames

1878, July Engr. *Perf. 12*

Printed by National Bank Note Co. of N.Y.

30	A4	1c violet	42	42
31	A4	2c brown	42	42
32	A4	½r black	42	42
33	A4	1r green	1.40	1.40
34	A4	2r deep blue	3.00	3.00
35	A4	4r vermilion	2.75	*2.50*
36	A4	1p orange	3.25	*3.25*
		Nos. 30-36 (7)	11.66	*11.41*

Various counterfeit cancellations exist on Nos. 30-36.

Re-Issue
Soft paper, yellowish gum
Various Frames

1889

Printed by American Bank Note Co. of N.Y.

30a	A4	1c deep violet	28
31a	A4	2c red brown	18
32a	A4	½r black	18
33a	A4	1r blue green	22
34a	A4	2r ultramarine	22
35a	A4	4r scarlet ver	28
36a	A4	1p orange yel	35
		Nos. 30a-36a (7)	1.71

Nos. 30a-36a were not for postal use.

Arms of Honduras — A5

1890, Jan. 6

40	A5	1c yellow green	25	28
41	A5	2c red	25	28
42	A5	5c blue	25	28
43	A5	10c orange	32	35
44	A5	20c ocher	32	35
45	A5	25c rose red	32	35
46	A5	30c purple	42	52
47	A5	40c dark blue	42	*70*
48	A5	50c brown	50	*70*
49	A5	75c blue green	50	*1.75*
50	A5	1p carmine	60	*2.00*
		Nos. 40-50 (11)	4.15	*7.56*

The tablets and numerals of Nos. 40 to 50 differ for each denomination.
For overprints see Nos. O1-O11.

Used values of Nos. 40-94 are for stamps with genuine cancellations applied while the stamps were valid. Various counterfeit cancellations exist.

President Luis Bogran
A6 A7

1891, July 31

51	A6	1c dark blue	25	28
52	A6	2c yel brown	25	28
53	A6	5c blue green	25	28
54	A6	10c vermilion	25	28
55	A6	20c brown red	25	28
56	A6	25c magenta	35	50
57	A6	30c slate	35	50
58	A6	40c blue green	35	50
59	A6	50c black brown	42	*70*
60	A6	75c purple	42	*1.10*
61	A6	1p brown	42	*1.40*
62	A7	2p brn & black	70	*4.25*
a.		Head inverted	125.00	
63	A7	5p pur & black	70	*5.00*
a.		Head inverted	42.50	
64	A7	10p green & blk	70	*5.00*
a.		Head inverted	42.50	
		Nos. 51-64 (14)	5.66	*20.35*

Nos. 62 and 64 exist with papermakers watermark.
For overprints see Nos. O12-O22.

Columbus Sighting Honduran Coast
A8

General Trinidad Cabanas
A9

1892, July 31

65	A8	1c slate	35	40
66	A8	2c deep blue	35	40
67	A8	5c yellow grn	35	40
68	A8	10c blue green	35	40
69	A8	20c red	35	40
70	A8	25c orange brn	45	50
71	A8	30c ultramarine	45	52
72	A8	40c orange	45	*80*
73	A8	50c brown	52	*75*
74	A8	75c lake	52	*1.10*
75	A8	1p purple	52	*1.25*
		Nos. 65-75 (11)	4.66	*6.92*

Discovery of America by Christopher Columbus, 400th anniv.

1893, Aug.

76	A9	1c green	22	22
77	A9	2c scarlet	22	22
78	A9	5c dark blue	22	22
79	A9	10c orange brn	22	26
80	A9	20c brown red	22	28
81	A9	25c dark blue	28	28
82	A9	30c red orange	40	*52*
83	A9	40c black	40	*70*
84	A9	50c olive brn	40	*80*
85	A9	75c purple	52	*1.00*
86	A9	1p deep magenta	52	*1.10*
		Nos. 76-86 (11)	3.62	*5.60*

"Justice"
A10

President Celio Arias
A11

1895, Jan. 25

87	A10	1c vermilion	28	28
88	A10	2c deep blue	28	28
89	A10	5c slate	28	42
90	A10	10c brown rose	35	42
91	A10	20c violet	35	45
92	A10	30c deep vio	35	*75*
93	A10	50c olive brn	42	*1.10*
94	A10	1p dark green	50	*1.40*
		Nos. 87-94 (8)	2.81	*5.10*

The tablets and numerals of Nos. 76-94 differ for each denomination.

1896, Jan. 1 Litho. *Perf. 11½*

95	A11	1c dark blue	30	35
96	A11	2c yellow brn	30	35
97	A11	5c purple	1.10	28
a.		5c red violet	55	1.10
98	A11	10c vermilion	42	42
99	A11	20c emerald	75	52
a.		20c deep green		
100	A11	30c ultramarine	65	70
101	A11	50c rose	90	*1.00*
102	A11	1p black brown	1.25	*1.50*
		Nos. 95-102 (8)	5.67	*5.12*

Counterfeits are plentiful. Nos. 95-102 exist imperf. between horiz. or vertically.
Originals of Nos. 95 to 102 are on both thin, semi-transparent paper and opaque paper; reprints are on thicker, opaque paper and usually have a black cancellation "HONDURAS" between horizontal bars.

Railroad Train — A12

1898, Aug. 1

103	A12	1c brown	40	18
104	A12	2c rose	40	18
105	A12	5c dull ultra	75	22
b.		5c red violet (error)	1.00	70
106	A12	6c red violet	60	25
b.		6c dull rose (error)		
107	A12	10c dark blue	75	28
108	A12	20c dull orange	1.00	75
109	A12	50c orange red	1.50	1.25
110	A12	1p blue green	3.00	3.00
		Nos. 103-110 (8)	8.40	6.11

Excellent counterfeits of Nos. 103-110 exist.
For overprints see Nos. O23-O27.

Laid Paper

103a	A12	1c	60	32
104a	A12	2c	65	32
105a	A12	5c	75	32
106a	A12	6c	70	40
107a	A12	10c	75	55

General Santos Guardiola
A13

President José Medina
A14

1903, Jan. 1 Engr. *Perf. 12*

111	A13	1c yellow grn	30	18
112	A13	2c car rose	30	25
113	A13	5c blue	30	25
114	A13	6c dk violet	35	25
115	A13	10c brown	35	28
116	A13	20c dull ultra	40	32
117	A13	50c vermilion	1.00	1.00
118	A13	1p orange	1.00	1.00
		Nos. 111-118 (8)	4.00	3.53

"PERMITASE" handstamped on stamps of 1896-1903 was applied as a control mark by the isolated Pacific Coast post office of Amapala to prevent use of stolen stamps.

1907, Jan. 1 *Perf. 14*

119	A14	1c dark green	25	25
120	A14	2c scarlet	28	25
120A	A14	2c carmine	6.00	3.00
121	A14	5c blue	32	28
122	A14	6c purple	35	28
a.		6c dark violet	70	52
123	A14	10c gray brown	35	35
124	A14	20c ultra	75	75
a.		20c blue violet	100.00	100.00
125	A14	50c deep lake	1.00	1.00
126	A14	1p orange yel	1.25	1.25
		Nos. 119-126 (9)	10.55	7.41

All values of the above set exist imperforate, imperforate horizontally and in horizontal pairs, imperforate between.
For surcharges see Nos. 128-130.

1909 Typo. *Perf. 11½*

127	A14	1c green	1.25	1.00
a.		Imperf., pair	3.50	3.50
b.		Printed on both sides	7.50	

The 1909 issue is roughly typographed in imitation of the 1907 design. It exists pin perf. 8, 13, etc.

No. 124 Handstamp Surcharged in Black, Green or Red:

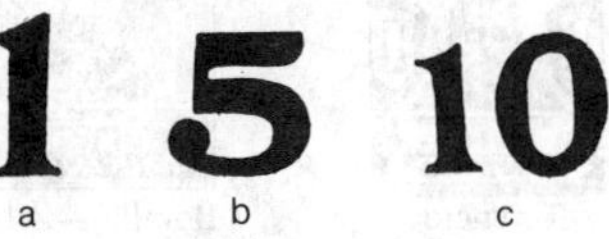

1910, Nov. *Perf. 14*

128	A14	1c on 20c ultra	6.00	5.00
129	A14	5c on 20c ultra (G)	6.00	5.00
130	A14	10c on 20c ultra (R)	6.00	5.00

As is usual with handstamped surcharges inverts and double exist.

Honduran Scene — A15

1911, Jan. Litho. *Perf. 14, 12 (1p)*

131	A15	1c violet	30	15
132	A15	2c green	30	15
a.		Perf. 12	1.75	1.00
133	A15	5c carmine	35	15
a.		Perf. 12	7.00	3.00
134	A15	6c ultramarine	35	28
135	A15	10c blue	50	35
136	A15	20c yellow	50	42
137	A15	50c brown	1.75	1.50
138	A15	1p olive green	2.00	1.75
		Nos. 131-138 (8)	6.05	4.75

For overprints and surcharges see Nos. 139, 141-147, O28-O47.

No. 132a Overprinted in Red

XC
Aniversario de la
Independencia

1911, Sept. 19 *Perf. 12*

139	A15	2c green	14.00	14.00
a.		Inverted overprint	20.00	20.00

90th anniversary of Independence.
Counterfeit overprints on perf. 14 stamps exist.

President Manuel Bonilla — A16

1912, Feb. 1 Typo. *Perf. 11½*

140	A16	1c org red	12.00	12.00

Election of Pres. Manuel Bonilla.

Stamps of 1911 Surcharged in Black, Red or Blue:

2 CENTAVOS (a) 5 cts. (b)

1913 **Litho.** ***Perf. 14***

141	A15(a) 2c on 1c vio	1.00	65
a.	Double surcharge		2.75
b.	Inverted surcharge	4.00	
c.	Double surch., one invtd.	6.00	
d.	Red surcharge	35.00	35.00
142	A15(b) 2c on 1c vio	6.00	5.00
a.	Inverted surcharge	12.50	
143	A15(b) 2c on 10c bl	2.50	2.00
a.	Double surcharge	5.00	5.00
b.	Inverted surcharge		
144	A15(b) 2c on 20c yel	6.00	6.00
145	A15(b) 5c on 1c vio	2.00	65
146	A15(b) 5c on 10c bl (Bl)	2.50	1.25
147	A15(b) 6c on 1c vio	2.50	2.00
	Nos. 141-147 (7)	22.50	17.55

Counterfeit surcharges exist.

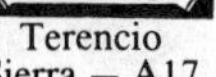
Terencio Sierra — A17

Bonilla — A18

ONE CENTAVO:
Type I - Solid border at sides below numerals.
Type II - Border of light and dark stripes.

1913-14 **Typo.** ***Perf. 11½***

151	A17 1c dark brn, I	20	15
a.	1c brown, type II	35	25
152	A17 2c carmine	25	20
153	A18 5c blue	40	20
154	A18 5c ultra ('14)	40	20
155	A18 6c gray vio	50	25
156	A18 6c pur ('14)	40	25
a.	6c red lilac	60	35
157	A17 10c blue	75	75
158	A17 10c brn ('14)	1.25	50
159	A17 20c brown	1.00	75
160	A18 50c rose	2.00	2.00
161	A18 1p gray green	2.25	2.25
	Nos. 151-161 (11)	9.40	7.50

For overprints and surcharges see Nos. 162-173, O48-O57.

Surcharged in Black or Carmine — 1 cent.

1914

162	A17 1c on 2c carmine	75	75
163	A17 5c on 2c carmine	1.25	90
164	A18 5c on 6c gray vio	2.00	2.00
165	A17 10c on 2c carmine	2.00	2.00
166	A18 10c on 6c gray vio	2.00	2.00
a.	Double surcharge	10.00	
167	A18 10c on 6c gray vio (C)	2.00	2.00
168	A18 10c on 50c rose	6.50	5.00
	Nos. 162-168 (7)	16.50	14.65

No. 158 Surcharged with New Value

1915

173	A17 5c on 10c brown	2.50	1.75

Ulua Bridge — A19 Bonilla Theater — A20

1915-16 **Typo.**

174	A19 1c chocolate	20	15
175	A19 2c carmine	20	15
a.	Tete beche pair	1.00	1.00
176	A20 5c bright blue	25	15
177	A20 6c deep purple	35	18
178	A19 10c dull blue	70	25
179	A19 20c red brown	1.25	1.00
a.	Tete beche pair	4.00	4.00
180	A20 50c red	1.50	1.50
181	A20 1p yellow grn	2.50	2.50
	Nos. 174-181 (8)	6.95	5.88

For overprints and surcharges see Nos. 183, 231-232, 237, 239-240, 285, 292, C1-C13, C25, C28, C31, C36, C57, CO21, CO30-CO32, CO42, O58-O65.

Imperf., Pairs

174a	A19 1c	2.00	2.00
175b	A19 2c	2.00	2.00
176a	A20 5c	3.50	
178a	A19 10c	3.50	
179b	A19 20c	5.25	
180b	A20 50c	7.00	
181a	A20 1p	8.75	8.75

Francisco Bertrand A21

Statue to Francisco Morazan A22

1916, Feb. 1

182	A21 1c orange	2.00	2.00

Election of Pres. Francisco Bertrand.
Unauthorized reprints exist.

Official Stamp No. O60 Overprinted — CORRIENTE

1918

183	A20 5c bright blue	2.00	1.50
a.	Inverted overprint	5.00	5.00

1919 **Typo.**

184	A22 1c brown	15	15
a.	Printed on both sides	2.00	
b.	Imperf., pair	70	
185	A22 2c carmine	25	15
186	A22 5c lilac rose	25	15
187	A22 6c bright vio	35	15
188	A22 10c dull blue	75	25
189	A22 15c light blue	75	20
190	A22 15c dark vio	60	20
191	A22 20c orange brn	75	30
a.	20c gray brown	75	30
b.	Imperf., pair	2.75	
192	A22 50c light brn	1.75	1.25
a.	Imperf. pair	6.00	
193	A22 1p yellow grn	5.00	3.00
a.	Imperf. pair	7.50	
b.	Printed on both sides	7.50	
c.	Tete beche pair	9.00	
	Nos. 184-193 (10)	10.60	5.80

Unauthorized reprints exist.

For overprints and surcharges see Nos. 201-210C, 230, 235-236, 238, 241-243, 287, 289, C58, C61, CO23, CO25, CO33, CO36-CO38, CO39, CO40, O66-O74.

"Dawn of Peace" — A23

1920, Feb. 1

Size: 27x21mm

194	A23 2c rose	2.50	2.50
a.	Tete beche pair	12.50	12.50
b.	Imperf., pair	12.50	12.50

Size: 51x40mm

195	A23 2c gold	10.00	10.00
196	A23 2c silver	10.00	10.00
197	A23 2c bronze	10.00	10.00
198	A23 2c red	10.00	10.00
	Nos. 194-198 (5)	42.50	42.50

Assumption of power by Gen. Rafael Lopez Gutierrez.
Nos. 195-198 exist imperf.
Unauthorized reprints of #195-198 exist.

Type of 1919, Dated "1920"

1921

201	A22 6c dark violet	5.00	*3.00*
a.	Tete beche pair	15.00	
b.	Imperf. pair	15.00	

Unauthorized reprints exist.

No. 185 Surcharged in Antique Letters — VALE SEIS CTS.

1922

202	A22 6c on 2c car	40	40
a.	"ALE" for "VALE"	2.00	2.00
b.	Comma after "CTS"	2.00	2.00
c.	Without period after "CTS"	2.00	2.00
d.	"CT" for "CTS"	2.00	2.00
e.	Double surcharge	4.25	
f.	Inverted surcharge	4.25	

Stamps of 1919 Surcharged in Roman Figures and Antique Letters in Green — $ 0.50 HABILITADO VALE CTA. CTS.

1923

203	A22 10c on 1c brown	1.50	1.50
204	A22 50c on 2c car	2.00	2.00
a.	Inverted surcharge	6.00	6.00
b.	"HABILTADO"	6.00	6.00

Surcharged in Black or Violet Blue — $ 1.00 HABILITADO VALE UN PESO

205	A22 1p on 5c lil rose (Bk)	3.50	3.50
a.	"PSEO"	20.00	20.00
b.	Inverted surcharge	20.00	20.00
206	A22 1p on 5c lil rose (VB)	20.00	20.00
a.	"PSEO"	70.00	

On Nos. 205-206, "Habilitado Vale" is in Antique letters, "Un Peso" in Roman.

No. 185 Surcharged in Roman Letters in Green — VALE SEIS CTS

207	A22 6c on 2c carmine	3.50	2.75

Nos. 184-185 Surcharged in Roman Letters in Green — $ 0.50 HABILITADO VALE CTA CTS

208	A22 10c on 1c brown	1.75	1.25
a.	"DIES"	4.00	
b.	"DEIZ"	4.00	
c.	"DEIZ CAS"	4.00	
d.	"TTS" for "CTS"	4.00	
e.	"HABILTADO"	4.00	
f.	"HABILITAD"	4.00	
g.	"HABILITA"	4.00	
h.	Inverted surcharge	15.00	
209	A22 50c on 2c carmine	3.75	2.75
a.	"CAT" for "CTA"	7.50	
b.	"TCA" for "CTA"	7.50	
c.	"TTS" for "CTS"	7.50	
d.	"CAS" for "CTS"	7.50	
e.	"HABILTADO"	7.50	

Surcharge on No. 209 is found in two spacings between value and HABILITADO: 5mm (illustrated) and 1½mm.

No. 186 Surcharged in Antique Letters in Black — $ 1.00 HABILITADO VALE UN PESO

210	A22 1p on 5c lil rose	25.00	*25.00*
a.	"PFSO"	75.00	

In the surcharges on Nos. 202 to 210 there are various wrong font, inverted and omitted letters.

No. 184 Surcharged in Large Antique Letters in Green — $ 0.10 HABILITADO VALE DIEZ CTS

210C	A22 10c on 1c brown	15.00	15.00
d.	"DIFZ"	55.00	55.00

Dionisio de Herrera — A24

Pres. Miguel Paz Baraona — A25

1924, June **Litho.** ***Perf. 11, 11½***

211	A24 1c olive green	30	15
212	A24 2c deep rose	30	15
213	A24 6c red violet	35	15
214	A24 10c blue	35	15
215	A24 20c yellow brn	70	30
216	A24 50c vermilion	1.50	1.00
217	A24 1p emerald	3.50	2.50
	Nos. 211-217 (7)	7.00	4.40

In 1924 a facsimile of the signatures of Santiago Herrera and Francisco Caceres, covering four stamps, was handstamped in violet to prevent the use of stamps that had been stolen during a revolution.

For overprints and surcharges see Nos. 280-281, 290-291, C14-C24, C26-C27, C29-C30, C32-C35, C56, C60, C73-C76, CO1-CO5, CO22, CO24, CO28-CO29, CO34-CO35, CO38A, CO39A, CO41, CO43, O75-O81.

1925, Feb. 1 **Typo.** ***Perf. 11½***

218	A25 1c dull blue	2.00	2.00
a.	1c dark blue	2.00	2.00
219	A25 1c car rose	5.25	5.25
a.	1c brown carmine	5.25	5.25
220	A25 1c olive brn	14.00	14.00
a.	1c orange brown	14.00	14.00
b.	1c dark brown	14.00	14.00
c.	1c black brown	14.00	14.00
221	A25 1c buff	12.00	12.00
222	A25 1c red	52.50	52.50
223	A25 1c green	35.00	35.00
	Nos. 218-223 (6)	120.75	120.75

Imperf

225	A25 1c dull blue	5.50	5.50
a.	1c dark blue	5.50	5.50
226	A25 1c car rose	8.75	8.75
a.	1c brown carmine	8.75	8.75
227	A25 1c olive brn	8.75	8.75
a.	1c orange brown	8.75	8.75
b.	1c deep brown	8.75	8.75
c.	1c black brown	8.75	8.75
228	A25 1c buff	8.75	8.75
229	A25 1c red	50.00	50.00
229A	A25 1c green	27.50	27.50
	Nos. 225-229A (6)	109.25	109.25

Inauguration of President Baraona.
Counterfeits and unauthorized reprints exist.

No. 187 Overprinted in Black and Red — Acuerdo Mayo 3 de 1926 HABILITADO

1926, June ***Perf. 11½***

230	A22 6c bright violet	1.25	1.00

Many varieties of this two-part overprint exist: one or both inverted or double, and various combinations. Value, each $10.

Nos. 177 and 187 Overprinted in Black or Red — 1926

1926

231	A20 6c deep pur (Bk)	2.00	2.00
a.	Inverted overprint	5.50	5.50
b.	Double overprint	5.50	5.50
232	A20 6c deep pur (R)	2.50	2.50
a.	Double overprint	5.00	5.00
233	A22 6c lilac (Bk)	60	60
a.	6c violet	75	75
b.	Inverted overprint	5.00	5.00
c.	Double overprint	5.00	5.00
d.	Double ovpt., one inverted	5.00	5.00
e.	"192"	7.50	7.50
f.	Double ovpt., both inverted	7.50	7.50

Same Overprint on No. 230

235	A22 6c violet	16.00	16.00
a.	"1926" inverted	16.00	16.00
b.	"Habilitado" triple, one invtd.	16.00	16.00

No. 188 Surcharged in Red or Black

Vale 6 Cts.
1926

No.	Type	Description	Unused	Used
236	A22	6c on 10c blue (R)	50	20
c.		Double surcharge	2.00	2.00
d.		Without bar		
e.		Inverted surcharge	2.50	2.50
f.		"Vale" omitted		
g.		"6cts" omitted		
h.		"cts" omitted		
k.		Black surcharge	50.00	50.00

Nos. 175 and 185 Overprinted in Green

HABILITADO
1926

No.	Type	Description	Unused	Used
237	A19	2c carmine	20	20
a.		Tete beche pair	70	70
b.		Double overprint	2.00	1.40
c.		"HARILITADO"	2.00	1.40
d.		"1926" only	2.75	2.75
e.		Double overprint, one inverted	2.75	2.75
f.		"1926" omitted	3.50	3.50
g.		Triple overprint, two inverted	5.25	5.25
h.		Double on face, one on back	5.25	5.25
238	A22	2c carmine	20	20
a.		"HARILITADO"	90	90
b.		Double overprint	1.40	1.40
c.		Inverted overprint	2.00	2.00

No. 177 Overprinted in Red

1926

Large Numerals, 12x5mm

1927

No.	Type	Description	Unused	Used
239	A20	6c deep purple	25.00	25.00
a.		"1926" over "1927"	35.00	35.00
b.		Invtd. ovpt. on face of stamp, normal ovpt. on back	30.00	

No. 179 Surcharged

vale 6 cts.
1927

1927

No.	Type	Description	Unused	Used
240	A19	6c on 20c brown	75	75
a.		Tete beche pair	2.75	2.75
c.		Interted surcharge	2.00	2.00
d.		Double surcharge	8.50	8.50

Nos. 8 and 10 in the setting have no period after "cts" and No. 50 has the "t" of "cts" inverted.

Same Surcharge on Nos. 189-191

No.	Type	Description	Unused	Used
241	A22	6c on 15c blue	27.50	27.50
a.		"c" of "cts" omitted		
242	A22	6c on 15c vio	70	70
a.		Double surcharge	1.75	1.75
b.		Double surch., one invtd.	2.00	2.00
c.		"L" of "Vale" omitted		
243	A22	6c on 20c yel brn	60	60
a.		6c on 20c deep brown		
b.		"6" omitted	1.75	1.75
c.		"Vale" and "cts" omitted	3.50	3.50

On Nos. 242 and 243 stamps Nos. 12, 16 and 43 in the setting have no period after "cts" and No. 34 often lacks the "s". On No. 243 the "c" of "cts" is missing on stamp No. 38. On No. 241 occur the varieties "ct" or "ts" for "cts." and no period.

Southern Highway — A26

Ruins of Copan — A27

Pine Tree — A28

Presidential Palace — A29

Ponciano Leiva — A30

Pres. M.A. Soto — A31

Lempira A32

Map of Honduras A33

President Juan Lindo — A34

Statue of Columbus — A35

1927-29 Typo. Wmk. 209

No.	Type	Description	Unused	Used
244	A26	1c ultramarine	30	15
a.		1c blue	30	18
245	A27	2c carmine	30	15
246	A28	5c dull violet	30	15
247	A28	5c bl gray ('29)	8.00	4.00
248	A29	6c blue black	75	52
a.		6c gray black	75	52
249	A29	6c dark bl ('29)	40	15
a.		6c light blue	40	15
250	A30	10c blue	70	18
251	A31	15c deep blue	1.00	50
252	A32	20c dark blue	1.25	60
253	A33	30c dark brown	1.50	1.00
254	A34	50c light blue	2.50	1.50
255	A35	1p red	5.00	2.50
		Nos. 244-255 (12)	22.00	11.40

In 1929 a quantity of imperforate sheets of No. 249 were stolen from the Litografia Nacional. Some of them were perforated by sewing machine and a few copies were passed through the post. To prevent the use of stolen stamps of the 1927-29 issues they were declared invalid and the stock on hand was overprinted "1929 a 1930."

For overprints and surcharges see Nos. 259-278, CO19-CO20B.

Pres. Vicente Mejia Colindres and Vice-Pres. Rafael Diaz Chavez A36

President Mejia Colindres — A37

1929, Feb. 25

No.	Type	Description	Unused	Used
256	A36	1c dk carmine	2.75	2.75
257	A37	2c emerald	2.75	2.75

Installation of Pres. Vicente Mejia Colindres. Printed in sheets of ten.

Nos. 256 and 257 were surreptitiously printed in transposed colors. They were not regularly issued.

Stamps of 1927-29 Overprinted in Various Colors

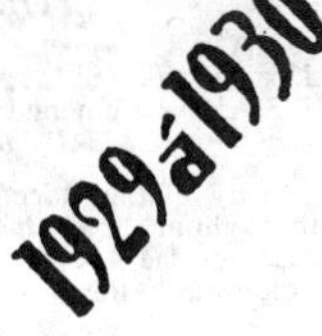

1929, Oct.

No.	Type	Description	Unused	Used
259	A26	1c blue (R)	20	15
a.		1c ultramarine (R)	50	15
b.		Double overprint	2.50	1.75
c.		As "a", double overprint	2.50	1.75
260	A26	1c blue (Bk)	6.50	6.50
a.		1c ultramarine (Bk)		
261	A27	2c car (R Br)	3.50	3.50
a.		Double overprint		
262	A27	2c car (Bl Gr)	1.00	1.00
a.		Double overprint		
263	A27	2c car (Bk)	1.00	50
264	A27	2c car (V)	50	25
a.		Double overprint		
b.		Double ovpt., one inverted		
265	A27	2c org red (V)	1.50	
266	A28	5c dl vio (R)	40	30
a.		Double overprint (R+V)		
267	A28	5c bl gray (R)	1.00	75
a.		Double overprint (R+Bk)		
269	A29	6c gray blk (R)	2.50	2.00
a.		Double overprint	6.00	6.00
272	A29	6c dk blue (R)	40	15
a.		6c light blue (R)	40	15
b.		Double overprint	2.00	2.00
c.		Double overprint (R+V)		
273	A30	10c blue (R)	40	15
a.		Double overprint	2.50	1.75
274	A31	15c dp blue (R)	50	25
a.		Double overprint	3.50	2.50
275	A32	20c dark bl (R)	50	35
276	A33	30c dark brn (R)	75	60
a.		Double overprint	3.50	2.50
277	A34	50c light bl (R)	1.00	1.00
278	A35	1p red (V)	2.50	2.50
		Nos. 259-278 (17)	24.15	
		Nos. 259-264, 266-278		19.95

Nos. 259 to 278 exist in numerous shades. There are also various shades of the red and violet overprints. The overprint may be found reading upwards, downwards, inverted, double, triple, tete beche or combinations.

Status of both 6c stamps with overprint in black is questioned.

A38

1929, Dec. 10

No.	Type	Description	Unused	Used
279	A38	1c on 6c lilac rose	70	70
a.		"1992" for "1929"		
b.		"9192" for "1929"		
c.		Surcharge reading down		
d.		Dbl. surch., one reading down		

Varieties include "1992" reading down and pairs with one surcharge reading down, double or with "1992."

No. 214 Surcharged in Red

Vale 2
cts. 1930

Perf. 11, 11½

1930, Mar. 26 Unwmk.

No.	Type	Description	Unused	Used
280	A24	1c on 10c blue	35	32
a.		"1093" for "1930"	1.40	
b.		"tsc" for "cts"	1.40	
281	A24	2c on 10c blue	35	32
a.		"tsc" for "cts"	2.00	
b.		"Vale 2" omitted		

Official Stamps of 1929 Overprinted in Red or Violet

Habilitado para el servicio públi- co. 1930

1930, Mar. Wmk. 209 *Perf. 11½*

No.	Type	Description	Unused	Used
282	O1	1c blue (R)	50	50
a.		Double overprint	2.00	2.00
284	O1	2c carmine (V)	90	90

Stamps of 1915-26 Overprinted in Blue

Habilitado
julio.—1930

On No. 174

1930, July 19 Unwmk.

No.	Type	Description	Unused	Used
285	A19	1c chocolate	28	25
a.		Double overprint	1.00	1.00
b.		Inverted overprint	1.40	1.40
c.		Dbl. ovpt., one inverted	1.40	1.40

On No. 184

No.	Type	Description	Unused	Used
287	A22	1c brown	14.00	14.00
a.		Double overprint	14.00	14.00
c.		Inverted overprint		

On No. 204

No.	Type	Description	Unused	Used
289	A22	50c on 2c car	100.00	100.00
b.		Inverted surcharge	100.00	100.00

On Nos. 211 and 212

No.	Type	Description	Unused	Used
290	A24	1c olive grn	20	18
a.		Double overprint	1.75	1.75
b.		Inverted overprint	1.75	1.75
d.		On No. O75	12.00	
291	A24	2c car rose	25	25
a.		Double overprint	1.75	1.75
b.		Inverted overprint	1.75	1.75

On No. 237

No.	Type	Description	Unused	Used
292	A19	2c car (G & Bl)	90.00	90.00

From Title Page of Government Gazette, First Issue — A39

1930, Aug. 11 Typo. Wmk. 209

No.	Type	Description	Unused	Used
295	A39	2c orange	90	90
296	A39	2c ultramarine	90	90
297	A39	2c red	90	90

Publication of the 1st newspaper in Honduras, cent. The stamps were on sale and available for postage on Aug. 11th, 1930, only. Not more than 5 copies of each color could be purchased by an applicant.

Nos. 295-297 exist imperf. and part-perforate. Unauthorized reprints exist.

For surcharges see Nos. CO15-CO18A.

Paz Baraona A40

Manuel Bonilla A41

Lake Yojoa — A42

View of Palace at Tegucigalpa A43

City of Amapala A44

Mayan Stele at Copan A45

Christopher Columbus A46

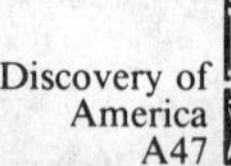

Discovery of America A47

Loarque Bridge A48

Unwmk.

1931, Jan. 2 Engr. *Perf. 12*

298	A40	1c black brown	20	15
299	A41	2c carmine rose	20	15
300	A42	5c dull violet	30	15
301	A43	6c deep green	30	15
302	A44	10c brown	50	25
303	A45	15c dark blue	50	15
304	A46	20c black	1.00	30
305	A47	50c olive green	2.00	1.00
306	A48	1p slate black	3.50	2.00
		Nos. 298-306 (9)	8.50	4.30

Regular Issue of 1931 Overprinted in Black or Various Colors **T.S.de C.**

1931

307	A40	1c black brown	25	15
308	A41	2c carmine rose	40	15
309	A45	15c dark blue	60	20
310	A46	20c black	1.00	25

Overprinted T. S. de C.

311	A42	5c dull violet	35	18
312	A43	6c deep green	35	15
315	A44	10c brown	50	28
316	A47	50c olive green	4.00	3.50
317	A48	1p slate black	5.00	5.00
		Nos. 307-317 (9)	12.45	9.86

The overprint is a control mark. It stands for "Tribunal Superior de Cuentas" (Superior Tribunal of Accounts).

Overprint varieties include: inverted; double; double, one or both inverted; on back; pair, one without overprint; differing colors (6c exists with overprint in orange, yellow and red).

See Nos. C51-C55.

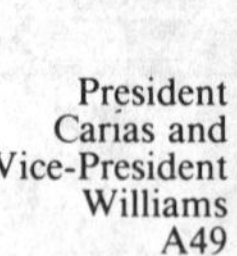

President Carias and Vice-President Williams A49

1933, Apr. 29

318	A49	2c carmine rose	50	35
319	A49	6c deep green	75	40
320	A49	10c deep blue	1.00	50
321	A49	15c red orange	1.25	75

Inauguration of President Tiburico Carias Andino and Vice-President Abraham Williams, Feb. 1, 1933.

Columbus' Fleet and Flag of the Race A50

Wmk. 209

1933, Aug. 3 Typo. *Perf. 11½*

322	A50	2c ultramarine	1.00	65
323	A50	6c yellow	1.00	65
324	A50	10c lemon	1.40	85

Perf. 12

325	A50	15c violet	2.00	1.50
326	A50	50c red	4.00	3.50
327	A50	1 l emerald	7.00	7.00
		Nos. 322-327 (6)	16.40	14.15

"Day of the Race," an annual holiday throughout Spanish-American countries. Also for the 441st anniv. of the sailing of Columbus to the New World, Aug. 3, 1492.

Masonic Temple, Tegucigalpa — A51

Designs: 2c, President Carias. 5c, Flag. 6c, Tomas Estrada Palma.

Unwmk.

1935, Jan. 12 Engr. *Perf. 12*

328	A51	1c green	40	15
329	A51	2c carmine	40	18
330	A51	5c dark blue	40	25
331	A51	6c black brown	40	25
a.		Vert. pair, imperf. btwn.	20.00	20.00

See Nos. C77-C83.

Gen. Carias Bridge — A55

1937, June 4

332	A55	6c car & ol green	75	35
333	A55	21c grn & violet	1.25	65
334	A55	46c orange & brn	1.75	1.25
335	A55	55c ultra & black	2.50	2.00

Prolongation of the Presidential term to Jan. 19, 1943.

Seal of Honduras A56

Central District Palace — A57

Designs: 3c, Map of Honduras. 5c, Bridge of Choluteca. 8c, Flag.

1939, Mar. 1 *Perf. 12½*

336	A56	1c orange yellow	20	15
337	A57	2c red orange	20	15
338	A57	3c carmine	30	15
339	A57	5c orange	30	20
340	A56	8c dark blue	50	20
		Nos. 336-340 (5)	1.50	85

Nos. 336-340 exist imperf.

See #C89-C98. For overprints see #342-343.

Nos. 336 and 337 Overprinted in Green **HABILITADO 1944-45**

1944 *Perf. 12½*

342	A56	1c orange yellow	30	28
a.		Inverted overprint	5.00	5.00
343	A57	2c red orange	1.25	75
a.		Inverted overprint	5.00	5.00

Catalogue values for unused stamps in this section, from this point to the end of the section, are for Never Hinged items.

International Peace Movement — A58

1984, Feb. 15 Litho. *Perf. 12*

344	A58	78c multi	70	70
345	A58	85c multi	80	35
346	A58	95c multi	85	40
347	A58	1.50 l multi	1.40	60
348	A58	2 l multi	1.75	80
349	A58	5 l multi	4.50	2.00
		Nos. 344-349 (6)	10.00	4.85

Central American Aeronautics Corp., 25th Anniv. — A59

Designs: 2c, Edward Warner Award issued by the Intl. Civil Aviation Organization, vert. 5c, Corp. emblem, flags of Guatemala, Honduras, El Salvador, Costa Rica and Panama. 60c, Transmission tower, plane. 75c, Corp. emblem, vert. 1 l, 1.50 l, Emblem, flags, diff.

1987, Feb. 26 Litho. *Perf. 12*

350	A59	2c multi	15	15
351	A59	5c multi	15	15
352	A59	60c multi	52	25
353	A59	75c multi	65	30
354	A59	1 l multi	90	40
		Nos. 350-354 (5)	2.37	
		Set value		1.00

Souvenir Sheet

355	A59	1.50 l multi	1.40	

Housing Institute (INVA), 30th Anniv. A60

1987, Oct. 9 Litho. *Perf. 13½*

356	A60	5c shown	15	15
357	A60	95c Map, emblem, text	85	40
		Set value		45

EXFILHON '88 — A61

1988, Sept. 11 Litho. *Imperf.*

358	A61	3 l dull red brn & brt ultra	3.00	3.00

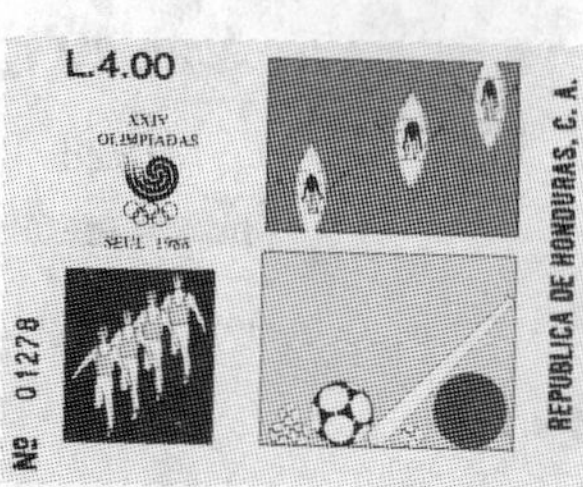

1988 Summer Olympics, Seoul — A62

1988, Sept. 30 Litho. *Imperf.*

359	A62	4 l multi	4.75	4.75

See Nos. C772-C773.

Luis Bogran Technical Institute, Cent. — A63

Design: 85c, Cogwheel, map, flag of Honduras.

1990, Sept. 28 Litho. *Perf. 10½*

360	A63	20c multicolored	15	
361	A63	85c multicolored	55	

Size: 114x82mm

Imperf

362	A63	2 l like #360	1.25	

Nos. 360-361 are airmail.

America Issue A64

UPAE emblem, land and seascapes showing produce and fish.

1990, Oct. 31 Litho. *Perf. 13½*

363	A64	20c multi, vert.	15	
364	A64	1 l multicolored	60	

AIR POST STAMPS

Regular Issue of 1915-16 Overprinted in Black, Blue or Red **AERO CORREO**

1925 Unwmk. *Perf. 11½*

C1	A20	5c lt blue (Bk)	87.50	87.50
C2	A20	5c lt blue (Bl)	300.00	300.00
a.		Inverted overprint	*400.00*	
b.		Vertical overprint	*600.00*	
c.		Double overprint	*800.00*	
C3	A20	5c lt blue (R)	*7,000.*	

Value for No. C3 is for copy without gum.

C4	A19	10c dk blue (R)	175.00	
a.		Inverted overprint	325.00	
b.		Overprint tete beche, pair	*800.00*	
C5	A19	10c dk blue (Bk)	*1,850.*	
C6	A19	20c red brn (Bk)	175.00	175.00
a.		Inverted overprint	250.00	
b.		Tete beche pair	400.00	
c.		Overprint tete beche, pair	*725.00*	
d.		"AFRO"	*1,400.*	
e.		Double overprint	600.00	
C7	A19	20c red brn (Bl)	175.00	175.00
a.		Inverted overprint	*500.00*	
b.		Tete beche pair	*800.00*	
c.		Vertical overprint	600.00	
C8	A20	50c red (Bk)	300.00	300.00
a.		Inverted overprint	*600.00*	
b.		Overprint tete beche, pair	*800.00*	
C9	A20	1p yel grn (Bk)	1,000.	1,000.

Surcharged in Black or Blue

AERO
CORREO
25

C10 A19 25c on 1c choc 125.00 125.00
a. Inverted surcharge 600.00
C11 A20 25c on 5c lt bl (Bl) 225.00 225.00
a. Inverted surcharge 550.00
b. Double inverted surcharge 525.00
C12 A19 25c on 10c dk bl 60,000.
C13 A19 25c on 20c brn (Bl) 200.00 200.00
a. Inverted surcharge 325.00
b. Tete beche pair 500.00

Counterfeits of Nos. C1-C13 are plentiful.

Monoplane and Lisandro Garay
AP1

1929, June 5 Engr. *Perf. 12*

C13C AP1 50c carmine 2.00 1.75

No. 216 Surcharged in Blue

Servicio aéreo
Vale 25 centavos oro.—1929.

1929 *Perf. 11, 11½*

C14 A24 25c on 50c ver 4.25 3.50

In the surcharges on Nos. C14 to C40 there are various wrong font and defective letters and numerals, also periods omitted.

AP2

Surcharged in Green, Black or Red

1929, Oct.

C15 AP2 5c on 20c yel brn (G) 1.40 1.40
a. Double surcharge (R+G) 45.00
C16 AP2 10c on 50c ver (Bk) 2.25 1.90
C17 AP2 15c on 1p emer (R) 3.50 3.50

Nos. 214 and 216 Surcharged Vertically in Red or Black

Servicio Aéreo Internacional
Vale 5 cts. oro
1929
a

Servicio Aéreo Internacional.—Vale
20.cts. oro.—1929
b

1929, Dec. 10

C18 A24(a) 5c on 10c bl (R) 50 50
C19 A24(b) 20c on 50c ver 95 95
a. "1299" for "1929" 190.00
b. "cts. cts." for "cts. oro." 190.00
c. "r" of "Aereo" omitted 2.00
d. Horiz. pair, imperf. btwn. 20.00

Nos. 214, 215 and 180 Surcharged in Various Colors

Servicio Aéreo Internacional
Vale 25 cts. oro
1930

1930, Feb.

C20 A24 5c on 10c bl (R) 52 52
a. "1930" reading down 3.50
b. "1903" for "1930" 3.50
c. Surcharge reading down 10.00

d. Double surcharge 14.00
e. Dbl. surch., one downward 14.00
C21 A24 5c on 10c bl (Y) *450.00 450.00*
C22 A24 5c on 20c yel brn (Bl) 125.00 125.00
C23 A24 10c on 20c yel brn (Bk) 70 70
a. "0" for "10" 3.50
b. Double surcharge 8.75
c. Dbl. surch., one downward 12.00
d. Horiz. pair, imperf. btwn. 70.00
C24 A24 10c on 20c yel brn (V) *650.00 650.00*
a. "0" for "10" *1,600.*
C25 A20 25c on 50c red (Bk) 95 95
a. "Internaoicnal" 3.50
b. "o" for "oro" 3.50
c. Inverted surcharge 17.50
d. As "a," invtd. surch. *175.00*
e. As "b," invtd. surch. *175.00*

Surcharge on No. C25 is horizontal.

Nos. 214, 215 and 180 Surcharged

Servicio aéreo
Vale 15 centavos oro.—Marzo —1930

1930, Apr. 1

C26 A24 5c on 10c blue 50 50
a. Double surcharge 9.50
b. "Servicioa" 3.50
C27 A24 15c on 20c yel brn 52 52
a. Double surcharge 7.00
C28 A20 20c on 50c red, surch. reading down 95 95
a. Surcharge reading up 7.00

Nos. C22 and C23 Surcharged Vertically in Red

Vale 10
cts. oro

1930

C29 A24 10c on 5c on 20c yel brn (Bl+R) 90 90
a. "1930" reading down 9.00 9.00
b. "1903" for "1930" 9.00 9.00
c. Red surch. reading down 14.00
C30 A24 10c on 10c on 20c yel brn (Bk+R) 87.50 87.50
a. "0" for "10" 190.00

No. 181 Surcharged as No. C25 and Resurcharged

Vale 50
cts. oro

C31 A20 50c on 25c on 1p grn 4.25 4.25
a. "Internaoicnal" 7.00
b. "o" for "oro" 7.00
c. 25c surcharge inverted 17.50 17.50
d. 50c surcharge inverted 17.50 17.50
e. As "a" and "c"
f. As "a" and "d"
g. As "b" and "c"
h. As "b" and "d"

No. 215 Surcharged in Dark Blue

Servicio aéreo
Vale 5 centavos oro.
Mayo.

1930, May 22

C32 A24 5c on 20c yel brn 1.00 1.00
a. Double surcharge 5.25 5.25
b. Horiz. pr., imperf. btwn. 60.00 60.00
c. Vertical pair, imperf. between 20.00 20.00

Nos. O78-O80 Surcharged like Nos. C20 to C25 in Various Colors

1930

C33 A24 5c on 10c bl (R) 350.00 350.00
a. "1930" reading down *875.00*
b. "1903" for "1930" *875.00*
C34 A24 5c on 20c yellow brown (Bl) 400.00 400.00
C35 A24 25c on 50c ver (Bk) 175.00 175.00
a. 55c on 50c vermilion 325.00 325.00

No. C35 exists with inverted surcharge.

No. O64 Surcharged like No. C28

C36 A20 20c on 50c red (dbl. surch., reading up) *350.00 350.00*
a. Dbl. surch., reading down *350.00 350.00*

No. O87 Overprinted

HABILITADO
Servicio Aéreo Internacional
1930

1930, Feb. 21 Wmk. 209 *Perf. 11½*

C37 O1 50c yel, grn & blue 1.25 1.25
a. "Internacional" 5.25
b. "Iuternacional" 5.25
c. Double overprint 5.25

Nos. O86-O88 Overprinted in Various Colors

HABILITADO
Servicio Aéreo
MAYO 1930

1930, May 23

C38 O1 20c dark blue (R) 1.00 90
a. Double overprint 8.75
b. Triple overprint 12.00
C39 O1 50c org, grn & bl (Bk) 1.00 90
C40 O1 1p buff (Bl) 1.25 1.25
a. Double overprint 10.50

National Palace
AP3

Unwmk.

1930, Oct. 1 Engr. *Perf. 12*

C41 AP3 5c yel orange 50 30
C42 AP3 10c carmine 75 60
C43 AP3 15c green 1.00 75
C44 AP3 20c dull violet 1.25 60
C45 AP3 1p light brown 4.00 4.00
Nos. C41-C45 (5) 7.50 6.25

Same Overprinted in Various Colors

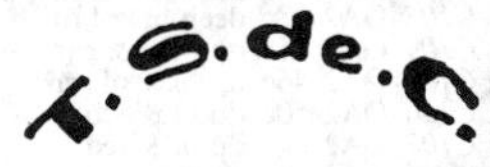

T.S.de.C.

1931 *Perf. 12*

C51 AP3 5c yel orange (R) 2.00 1.50
C52 AP3 10c carmine (Bk) 3.00 2.50
C53 AP3 15c green (Br) 5.00 4.00
C54 AP3 20c dull vio (O) 5.00 4.25
C55 AP3 1p lt brown (G) 10.00 8.75
Nos. C51-C55 (5) 25.00 21.00

See note after No. 317.

Stamps of Various Issues Surcharged

Servicio aéreo
interior.
Vale 15 cts.
Octubre 1931.

Blue Surcharge

1931, Oct. *Perf. 11½*

On No. 215

C56 A24 15c on 20c yel brn 3.50 2.75
a. Horiz. pr., imperf. btwn. 42.50
b. Green surcharge 20.00 20.00

On No. O64

C57 A20 15c on 50c red 4.25 3.50
a. Inverted surcharge 10.50 10.50

On No. O72

C58 A22 15c on 20c brn 4.25 4.25
a. Vert. pair, imperf. between 12.00

On Nos. C57 and C58 the word "OFICIAL" is canceled by two bars.

Black Surcharge

On No. O88

Wmk. 209

C59 O1 15c on 1p buff 4.25 4.25
a. Imperf. horizontally, pair 8.75
b. "Sevricio" 14.00 14.00

The varieties "Vaie" for "Vale", "aereo" with circumflex accent on the first "e" and "Interior" with initial capital "I" are found on Nos. C56, C58 and C59. No. C57 is known with initial capital in "Interior."

A similar surcharge, in slightly larger letters and with many minor varieties, exists on Nos. 215, O63, O64 and O73. The authenticity of this surcharge is questioned.

Various Designs Surcharged in Green, Red or Black

S.—Aéreo
VI. 15 cts.
XI 1931.

1931, Nov. Unwmk.

On No. 215

C60 A24 15c on 20c yel brn (G) 3.50 2.75
a. Inverted surcharge 6.25
b. "XI" omitted 6.25
c. "X" for "XI" 6.25
d. "PI" for "XI" 6.25

On No. O73

C61 A22 15c on 50c lt brn (R) 3.50 2.75
a. "XI" omitted 6.75
b. "PI" for "XI" 6.75
c. Double surcharge 20.00 20.00

On No. C61 the word "OFICIAL" is not barred out.

On Nos. O87 and O88

Wmk. 209

C62 O1 15c on 50c org, grn & blue (Bk) 2.75 2.50
a. "1391" for "1931" 10.50 10.50
b. Double surcharge 8.75 8.75
C63 O1 15c on 1p buff (Bk) 2.50 2.25
a. "1391" for "1931" 12.50
b. Surcharged on both sides 7.00

Nos. O76-O78 Surcharged in Black or Red

Aéreo
interior
VALE
15 Cts.
1932

1932 Unwmk. *Perf. 11, 11½*

C73 A24 15c on 2c dp rose 50 50
a. Double surcharge 5.50
b. Inverted surcharge 4.25
c. "Ae" of "Aero" omitted 70
d. On No. 212 (no "Official")
C74 A24 15c on 6c red vio 50 50
a. Double surcharge 3.50
b. Horiz. pair, imperf. btwn. 17.50
c. "Aer" omitted
d. "A" omitted 70
e. Inverted surcharge 3.50
C75 A24 15c on 10c dp blue (R) 50 50
a. Double surcharge 5.50
b. Inverted surcharge 3.50
c. "r" of "Aereo" omitted 70

Same Surcharge on No. 214 in Red

C76 A24 15c on 10c dp bl *87.50 87.50*

There are various broken and missing letters in the setting.

A similar surcharge with slightly larger letters exists.

Post Office and National Palace
AP4

View of Tegucigalpa — AP5

Designs: 15c, Map of Honduras. 20c, Mayo Bridge. 40c, View of Tegucigalpa. 50c, Owl. 1 l, Coat of Arms.

1935, Jan. 10 *Perf. 12*

C77 AP4 8c blue 15 15
C78 AP5 10c gray 25 15
C79 AP5 15c olive gray 40 15
C80 AP5 20c dull green 50 15
C81 AP5 40c brown 70 20
C82 AP4 50c yellow 4.00 1.25
C83 AP4 1 l green 2.50 2.25
Nos. C77-C83 (7) 8.50 4.30

Flags of US and Honduras — AP11

Engr. & Litho.

1937, Sept. 17 **Unwmk.**

C84 AP11 46c multicolored 1.00 1.00

US Constitution, 150th anniv..

Comayagua Cathedral AP12

Founding of Comayagua AP13

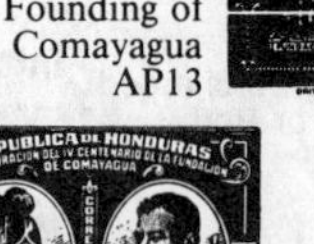

Alonzo Cáceres and Pres. Carias — AP14

Lintel of Royal Palace — AP15

1937, Dec. 7 **Engr.**

C85	AP12	2c copper red	15	15
C86	AP13	8c dark blue	35	15
C87	AP14	15c slate black	50	50
C88	AP15	50c dark brown	3.00	2.00

City of Comayagua founding, 400th anniv.
For surcharges see Nos. C144-C146.

Mayan Stele at Copan — AP16

Mayan Temple, Copan — AP17

Designs: 15c, President Carias. 30c, Jose C. de Valle. 40c, Presidential House. 46c, Lempira. 55c, Church of Our Lady of Suyapa. 66c, J. T. Reyes. 1 l, Hospital at Choluteca. 2 l, Ramon Rosa.

1939, Mar. 1 ***Perf. 12½***

C89	AP16	10c orange brn	25	15
C90	AP16	15c greenish bl	25	15
C91	AP17	21c gray	50	15
C92	AP16	30c dark bl grn	50	15
C93	AP17	40c dull vio	1.00	15
C94	AP16	46c dk gray brn	1.00	50
C95	AP16	55c green	1.25	65
a.		Imperf., pair	22.50	
C96	AP16	66c black	1.75	1.25
C97	AP16	1 l olive grn	3.00	1.00
C98	AP16	2 l henna red	4.50	2.50
		Nos. C89-C98 (10)	14.00	6.65

For surcharges see #C118-C119, C147-C152.

Souvenir Sheets

AP26

Designs: 14c, Francisco Morazan. 16c, George Washington. 30c, J. C. de Valle. 40c, Simon Bolivar.

1940, Apr. 13 **Engr.** ***Perf. 12***

Centers of Stamps Lithographed

C99	AP26	Sheet of four	2.25	2.25
a.		14c blk, yel, ultra & rose	35	28
b.		16c blk, yel, ultra & rose	42	35
c.		30c blk, yel, ultra & rose	65	55
d.		40c blk, yel, ultra & rose	75	70

Imperf

C100	AP26	Sheet of four	2.25	2.25
a.		14c blk, yel ultra & rose	35	28
b.		16c blk, yel ultra & rose	42	35
c.		30c blk, yel ultra & rose	65	55
d.		40c blk, yel ultra & rose	75	70

Pan American Union, 50th anniv.
For overprints see Nos. C153-C154, C187.

Air Post Official Stamps of 1939 Overprinted in Red

Correo Aéreo
Habilitado para
Servicio Publico
Pro-Faro Colon-1940

1940, Oct. 12 ***Perf. 12½***

C101	OA2	2c dp bl & green	20	20
C102	OA2	5c dp blue & org	20	20
C103	OA2	8c deep bl & brn	20	20
C104	OA2	15c dp blue & car	40	40
C105	OA2	46c dp bl & ol grn	70	70
C106	OA2	50c dp bl & vio	80	80
C107	OA2	1 l dp bl & red brn	3.50	3.50
C108	OA2	2 l dp bl & red org	7.00	7.50
		Nos. C101-C108 (8)	13.00	13.50

Erection and dedication of the Columbus Memorial Lighthouse.

Air Post Official Stamps of 1939 Overprinted in Black

Habilitada para el
Servicio Público
1941

1941, Aug. 2

C109	OA2	5c deep bl & org	2.50	24
C110	OA2	8c dp blue & brn	5.00	24
a.		Overprint inverted		*225.00*

Air Post Official Stamps of 1939 Surcharged in Black

Rehabilitada para
el Servicio Público
1941
Vale tres cts.

1941, Oct. 28

C111	OA2	3c on 2c dp bl & grn	40	18
C112	OA2	8c on 2c dp bl & grn	50	50
C113	OA2	8c on 15c dp bl & car	50	20
C114	OA2	8c on 46c dp bl & ol green	60	60
C115	OA2	8c on 50c dp bl & vio	75	52
C116	OA2	8c on 1 l dp bl & red brown	1.25	70
C117	OA2	8c on 2 l dp bl & red orange	2.00	1.50
		Nos. C111-C117 (7)	6.00	4.20

Once in each sheet a large "h" occurs in "ocho" on Nos. C112-C117.

Nos. C90, C94 Surcharged in Red

Correo Aéreo
L 0.08

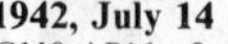

1942, July 14

C118	AP16	8c on 15c	70	25
a.		"Cerreo"	2.00	2.00
b.		Double surcharge	25.00	25.00
c.		As "a," double surch.	*175.00*	
C119	AP16	16c on 46c	70	25
a.		"Cerreo"	2.00	2.00

Plaque AP27

Morazan's Tomb, San Salvador AP28

Designs: 5c, Battle of La Trinidad. 8c, Morazan's birthplace. 16c, Statue of Morazan. 21c, Church where Morazan was baptized. 1 l, Arms of Central American Federation. 2 l, Gen. Francisco Morazan.

1942, Sept. 15 ***Perf. 12***

C120	AP27	2c red orange	15	15
C121	AP27	5c turq green	15	15
C122	AP27	8c sepia	15	15
C123	AP28	14c black	30	30
C124	AP27	16c olive gray	20	20
C125	AP27	21c light blue	85	65
C126	AP27	1 l brt ultra	2.75	2.25
C127	AP28	2 l dl ol brn	7.25	7.25
		Nos. C120-C127 (8)	11.80	11.10

Gen. Francisco Morazan (1799-1842).
For surcharges see Nos. C349-C350.

Coat of Arms AP35

Cattle AP36

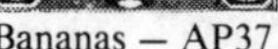

Bananas — AP37

Pine Tree — AP38

Tobacco Plant AP39

Orchid AP40

Coco Palm — AP41

Map of Honduras AP42

Designs: 2c, Flag. 8c, Rosario. 16c, Sugar cane. 30c, Oranges. 40c, Wheat. 1 l, Corn. 2 l, Map of Americas.

1943, Sept. 14 ***Perf. 12½***

C128	AP35	1c light grn	15	15
C129	AP35	2c blue	15	15
C130	AP36	5c green	30	15
C131	AP37	6c dark bl grn	25	15
C132	AP36	8c lilac	30	15
C133	AP38	10c lilac brn	30	15
C134	AP39	15c dp claret	35	15
C135	AP38	16c dark red	35	15
C136	AP40	21c deep blue	75	15
C137	AP39	30c org brown	60	15
C138	AP40	40c red orange	60	15
C139	AP41	55c black	1.00	48
C140	AP41	1 l dark olive	1.50	1.25
C141	AP37	2 l brown red	5.00	3.75
C142	AP42	5 l orange	12.50	12.50
a.		Vert. pair, imperf. btwn.	150.00	
		Nos. C128-C142 (15)	24.10	19.63

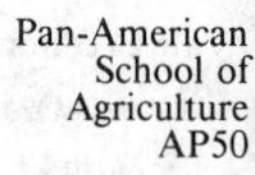

Pan-American School of Agriculture AP50

1944, Oct. 12 ***Perf. 12***

C143 AP50 21c dark bl grn 32 16

Inauguration of the Pan-American School of Agriculture, Tegucigalpa.

Air Post Stamps of 1937-39 Surcharged in Red or Green

Correo Aéreo
HABILITADO
Acd. № 798-1945
L 0.01

1945, Mar. 13 ***Perf. 11, 12½***

C144	AP15	1c on 50c dk brn	15	15
C145	AP12	2c on 2c cop red	20	15
C146	AP14	8c on 15c sl blk	25	15
C147	AP16	10c on 10c org brown (G)	40	40
C148	AP16	15c on 15c grnsh blue (G)	25	25
C149	AP17	30c on 21c gray (G)	5.00	3.00
C150	AP17	40c on 40c dull violet (G)	2.00	2.00
C151	AP16	1 l on 46c dk gray brown (G)	2.00	1.50
C152	AP16	2 l on 66c blk (G)	2.75	2.75
		Nos. C144-C152 (9)	13.00	10.35

Souvenir Sheets

Nos. C99 and C100 Overprinted in Red "VICTORIA DE LAS NACIONES UNIDAS, ALEMANIA SE RINDE INCONDICIONALMENTE 8 DE MAYO DE 1945. ACDO. No. 1231 QUE AUTORIZA LA CONTRAMARCA"

1945, Oct. 1 ***Perf. 12***

C153 AP26 Sheet of 4 1.90 1.90

Imperf

C154 AP26 Sheet of 4 3.75 3.00

Allied Nations' victory and Germany's unconditional surrender, May 8, 1945.

Seal of Honduras AP51

Arms of Gracias and Trujillo AP52

Franklin D. Roosevelt ("F.D.R." under Column) AP53

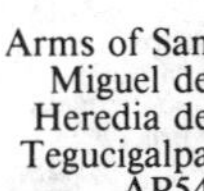

Arms of San Miguel de Heredia de Tegucigalpa AP54

Designs (Coats of Arms): 5c, Comayagua and San Jorge de Olancho. 15c, Province of Honduras and San Juan de Puerto Caballas. 21c, Comayagua and Tencoa. 1 l, Jerez de la Frontera de Choluteca and San Pedro de Zula.

Perf. 12½

1946, Oct. 15 Unwmk. Engr.

C155	AP51	1c red	15	15
a.		Vert. pair, imperf. between	17.50	
b.		Imperf., pair	70.00	
C156	AP52	2c red orange	15	15
a.		Imperf., pair	70.00	
C157	AP52	5c violet	18	15
C158	AP53	8c brown	70	25
a.		Horiz. pair, imperf. btwn.	70.00	
C159	AP52	15c sepia	35	18
C160	AP52	21c deep blue	35	28
a.		Horiz. pair, imperf. btwn.	15.00	
b.		Imperf., pair	70.00	
C161	AP52	1 l green	1.75	1.25
C162	AP54	2 l dark grn	2.50	2.00
		Nos. C155-C162 (8)	6.13	4.41

No. C158 commemorates the death of Franklin D. Roosevelt and the Allied victory over Japan in World War II.

Type AP53 Redrawn ("Franklin D. Roosevelt" under Column) AP59

1947, Oct. ***Perf. 12½***

C163	AP59	8c brown	42	28
a.		Vert. pair, imperf. between	87.50	
b.		Horiz. pair, imperf. between		
c.		Perf. 12x6	*175.00*	

Map, Ancient Monuments and Conference Badge AP60

1947, Oct. 20 ***Perf. 11x12½***

Various Frames

C164	AP60	16c green	40	15
C165	AP60	22c orange yel	35	15
C166	AP60	40c orange	75	28
C167	AP60	1 l deep blue	1.00	75
C168	AP60	2 l lilac	3.50	3.00
C169	AP60	5 l brown	9.00	7.50
		Nos. C164-C169 (6)	15.00	11.83

1st Intl. Archeological Conference of the Caribbean.

For overprints and surcharges see Nos. C181-C186, C351, C353-C354, C379, C544.

Flag and Arms of Honduras AP61

Juan Manuel Galvez AP62

J. M. Galvez, Gen. Tiburcio Carias A. and Julio Lozano AP63

National Stadium AP64

Designs: 5c, 15c, Julio Lozano. 9c, Juan Manuel Galvez. 40c, Custom House. 1 l, Recinto Hall. 2 l, Gen. Tiburcio Carias A. 5 l, Galvez and Lozano.

Various Frames

Inscribed: "Conmemorativa de la Sucesion Presidencial para el Periodo de 1949-1955."

1949, Sept. 17 Engr. ***Perf. 12***

C170	AP61	1c deep blue	15	15
C171	AP62	2c rose car	15	15
C172	AP62	5c deep blue	15	15
C173	AP62	9c sepia	15	15
C174	AP62	15c red brown	25	15
C175	AP63	21c gray black	50	15
C176	AP64	30c olive gray	60	15
C177	AP64	40c slate gray	70	18
C178	AP61	1 l red brown	1.00	35
C179	AP62	2 l violet	2.50	1.50
C180	AP64	5 l rose car	7.00	6.25
		Nos. C170-C180 (11)	13.15	9.33

Presidential succession for the 1949-1955 term.

For overprints and surcharges see Nos. C188-C197, C206-C208, C346, C355, C419-C420, C478, C545.

Nos. C164-C169 Overprinted in Carmine

U. P. U.
75 Aniversario
1874-1949

1951, Feb. 26 ***Perf. 11x12½***

C181	AP60	16c green	50	50
a.		Inverted overprint	45.00	45.00
C182	AP60	22c orange yel	75	75
a.		Inverted overprint	45.00	
C183	AP60	40c orange	75	75
C184	AP60	1 l deep blue	2.00	2.00
C185	AP60	2 l lilac	3.00	2.50
a.		Inverted overprint	60.00	
C186	AP60	5 l brown	22.50	18.00
		Nos. C181-C186 (6)	29.50	24.50

Souvenir Sheets

Same Overprint in Carmine on Nos. C99 and C100

Perf. 12

C187	AP26	Sheet of 4	2.75	2.25
a.		Imperf.	*250.00*	*250.00*

UPU, 75th anniv. (in 1949).

Nos. C170 to C179 Overprinted in Carmine

Conmemorativa
Fundación
Banco Central
Administración
Gálvez—Lozano
Julio 1º. de 1950

1951, Feb. 27 ***Perf. 12***

C188	AP61	1c deep blue	15	15
C189	AP62	2c rose car	15	15
C190	AP62	5c deep blue	15	15
C191	AP62	9c sepia	15	15
C192	AP62	15c red brown	20	15
C193	AP63	21c gray black	25	20
C194	AP64	30c olive gray	60	30
C195	AP64	40c slate gray	75	50
C196	AP61	1 l red brown	1.75	1.25
C197	AP62	2 l violet	6.00	4.50
		Nos. C188-C197 (10)	10.15	7.50

Founding of Central Bank, July 1, 1950.

Discovery of America AP65

Queen Isabella I — AP66

Designs: 2c, 1 l, Columbus at court. 8c, Surrender of Granada. 30c, Queen Isabella offering her jewels.

Perf. 13½x14, 14x13½

1952, Oct. 11 Engr. Unwmk.

C198	AP65	1c red org & blk	15	15
C199	AP65	2c bl & red brn	15	15
C200	AP65	8c dk grn & dk brown	30	15
C201	AP66	16c dk bl & blk	50	40
C202	AP65	30c pur & dk grn	1.00	60
C203	AP65	1 l dp car & blk	2.50	2.50
C204	AP65	2 l brn & vio	5.00	5.00
C205	AP66	5 l rose lil & ol	8.50	8.50
		Nos. C198-C205 (8)	18.10	17.45

500th birth anniv. of Isabella I of Spain.

For overprints and surcharges see Nos. C209-C221, C377-C378, C404-C406, C489.

No. C175 Surcharged in Carmine

HABILITADO 1953
L 0.05

1953, May 13 ***Perf. 12***

C206	AP63	5c on 21c gray blk	15	15
C207	AP63	8c on 21c gray blk	50	15
C208	AP63	16c on 21c gray blk	80	18
		Set value		36

Nos. CO52-CO54 Surcharged "HABILITADO 1953" and New Value in Red

1953, Dec. 8 ***Perf. 13½x14, 14x13½***

C209	AP65	10c on 1c	15	15
a.		Inverted surcharge	45.00	45.00
C210	AP65	12c on 1c	15	15
C211	AP65	15c on 2c	20	15
C212	AP65	20c on 2c	30	20
C213	AP65	24c on 2c	30	20
a.		Inverted surcharge	45.00	45.00
C214	AP65	25c on 2c	30	25
C215	AP65	30c on 8c	35	25
C216	AP65	35c on 8c	45	45
C217	AP65	50c on 8c	60	45
C218	AP65	60c on 8c	80	55

Same Overprint on Nos. CO57-CO59

C219	AP65	1 l dk grn & dk brown	2.00	1.75
C220	AP65	2 l bl & red brn	6.00	5.00
C221	AP66	5 l red org & blk	12.00	12.00
a.		Date inverted	150.00	
		Nos. C209-C221 (13)	23.60	21.55

Flags of UN and Honduras AP67

Designs: 2c, UN emblem. 3c, UN building. 5c, Shield. 15c, Juan Manuel Galvez. 30c, UNICEF. 1 l, UNRRA. 2 l, UNESCO. 5 l, FAO.

Engraved; Center of 1c Litho.

1953, Dec. 18 ***Perf. 12½***

Frames in Black

C222	AP67	1c ultra & vio bl	15	15
C223	AP67	2c blue	15	15
C224	AP67	3c rose lilac	16	15
C225	AP67	5c green	15	15
C226	AP67	15c red brown	32	22
C227	AP67	30c brown	80	50
C228	AP67	1 l dp carmine	6.25	4.50
C229	AP67	2 l orange	7.00	5.00
C230	AP67	5 l blue green	17.50	15.00
		Nos. C222-C230 (9)	32.48	25.82

Issued to honor the United Nations.

For overprints and surcharges see Nos. C231-C249, C331-C335, C472, C490.

Nos. CO60-CO66 Overprinted in Red

1955, Feb. 23 Unwmk. ***Perf. 12½***

Frames in Black

C231	AP67	1c ultra & vio bl	15	15
C232	AP67	2c deep bl grn	15	15
C233	AP67	3c orange	15	15
C234	AP67	5c dp carmine	16	16
C235	AP67	15c dk brown	28	28
C236	AP67	30c purple	85	85
C237	AP67	1 l olive gray	17.00	17.00

Overprint exists inverted on 1c, 3c.

Nos. C231 to C233 Surcharged with New Value in Black

C238	AP67	8c on 1c	15	15
C239	AP67	10c on 2c	15	15
C240	AP67	12c on 3c	20	20
		Nos. C231-C240 (10)	19.24	19.24

50th anniv. of the founding of Rotary International (Nos. C231-C240).

Nos. CO60-CO63, C226-C230 Overprinted

O N U
X ANIVERSARIO
1945 - 1955

1956, July 14 Unwmk. ***Perf. 12½***

Frames in Black

C241	AP67	1c ultra & vio bl	15	15
C242	AP67	2c dp bl grn	15	15
C243	AP67	3c orange	18	18
C244	AP67	5c dp car	22	22
C245	AP67	15c red brn	26	26
C246	AP67	30c brown	40	40
C247	AP67	1 l dp car	3.00	2.50
C248	AP67	2 l orange	4.50	4.50
C249	AP67	5 l bl grn	12.00	12.00
		Nos. C241-C249 (9)	20.86	20.36

10th anniv. of UN (in 1955). The red "OFICIAL" overprint was not obliterated.

The "ONU" overprint exists inverted on 1c, 3c, 5c and 1-lempira.

Basilica of Suyapa — AP68

Pres. Julio Lozano Diaz — AP69

Designs: 3c, Southern Highway. 4c, Genoveva Guardiola de Estrada Palma. 5c, Maria Josefa Lastiri de Morazan. 8c, Landscape and cornucopia (5-Year Plan). 10c, National Stadium. 12c, U. S. School. 15c, Central Bank. 20c, Legislative Palace. 25c, Development Bank (projected). 30c, Toncontin Airport. 40c, Juan Ramon Molina Bridge. 50c, Peace Monument. 60c, Treasury Palace. 1 l, Blood bank. 2 l, Communications Building. 5 l, Presidential Palace.

Engraved; #C255 Litho.

1956, Oct. 3 ***Perf. 13x12½, 12½x13***

C250	AP68	1c blk & vio bl	15	15
C251	AP69	2c blk & dk bl	15	15
C252	AP68	3c blk & brown	15	15
C253	AP69	4c blk & lilac	15	15
C254	AP69	5c blk & dk red	15	15
C255	AP68	8c brn & multi	15	15
C256	AP68	10c blk & emer	15	15
C257	AP68	12c blk & green	15	15
C258	AP68	15c dk red & blk	16	15
C259	AP68	20c blk & ultra	16	15
C260	AP69	24c black & lil	22	16

C261 AP68 25c blk & green 25 22
C262 AP68 30c blk & car rose 28 22
C263 AP68 40c blk & red brn 32 25
C264 AP69 50c blk & bl grn 38 32
C265 AP68 60c blk & orange 48 45
C266 AP68 1 l blk & rose vio 1.25 1.00
C267 AP69 2 l black & mag 2.50 2.25
C268 AP69 5 l blk & brn car 5.75 5.00
Nos. C250-C268 (19) 12.95 11.37

Issued to publicize the Five-Year Plan.

For overprints and surcharges see Nos. C414-C418, C491-C493, C537-C538, C542, C550.

Flag of Honduras — AP70

Designs: 2c, 8c, Monument and mountains. 10c, 15c, 1 l, Lempira. 30c, 2 l, Coat of arms.

1957, Oct. 21 Litho. *Perf. 13*
Frames in Black

C269 AP70 1c buff & ultra 15 15
C270 AP70 2c org, pur & emerald 15 15
C271 AP70 5c pink & ultra 15 15
C272 AP70 8c org, vio & ol 18 15
C273 AP70 10c vio & brown 18 15
C274 AP70 12c lt grn & ultra 25 18
C275 AP70 15c green & brn 32 20
C276 AP70 30c pink & slate 42 25
C277 AP70 1 l blue & brn 1.75 1.50
C278 AP70 2 l lt grn & slate 3.25 3.00
Nos. C269-C278 (10) 6.80 5.88

First anniv. of the October revolution.

Control marks were handstamped in violet on many current stamps in July and August, 1958, following fire and theft of stamps at Tegucigalpa in April. All post offices were ordered to honor only stamps overprinted with the facsimile signature of their departmental revenue administrator. Honduras has 18 departments.

For surcharge see No. C551.

Flags of Honduras and US — AP71

1958, Oct. 2 Engr. *Perf. 12*
Flags in National Colors

C279 AP71 1c light blue 15 15
C280 AP71 2c red 15 15
C281 AP71 5c green 15 15
C282 AP71 10c brown 15 15
C283 AP71 20c orange 28 20
C284 AP71 30c deep rose 28 25
C285 AP71 50c gray 42 42
C286 AP71 1 l orange yel 1.10 1.10
C287 AP71 2 l gray olive 2.25 2.25
C288 AP71 5 l vio blue 4.50 4.50
Nos. C279-C288 (10) 9.43 9.32

Honduras Institute of Inter-American Culture. The proceeds were intended for the Binational Center, Tegucigalpa.

For overprints see Nos. C320-C324.

Abraham Lincoln — AP72

REPUBLICA DE HONDURAS
1809 AEREO 1959
CONMEMORATIVA DEL CL ANIVERSARIO DEL NACIMIENTO DE LINCOLN
DOS CENTAVOS DE LEMPIRA

Lincoln's Birthplace AP73

Designs: 3c, 50c, Gettysburg Address. 5c, 1 l, Freeing the slaves. 10c, 2 l, Assassination. 12c, 5 l, Memorial, Washington.

1959, Feb. 12 Unwmk. *Perf. 13½*
Flags in National Colors

C289 AP72 1c green 15 15
C290 AP73 2c dark blue 15 15
C291 AP73 3c purple 16 16
C292 AP73 5c dk carmine 16 16
C293 AP73 10c black 24 16
C294 AP73 12c dark brown 24 16
C295 AP72 15c red orange 32 16
C296 AP73 25c dull pur 50 26
C297 AP73 50c ultra 65 50
C298 AP73 1 l red brown 1.40 1.25
C299 AP73 2 l gray olive 2.25 2.00
C300 AP73 5 l ocher 4.75 4.75
a. Miniature sheet 5.75 5.75
Nos. C289-C300 (12) 10.97 9.86

Birth sesquicentennial of Abraham Lincoln.

No. C300a contains one each of the 1c, 3c, 10c, 25c, 1 l and 5 l, imperf.

For overprints and surcharges see Nos. C316-C319, C325-C330, C345, C347-C348, C352, C356-C364, C494-C495, C539-C541, C552-C553.

Constitution AP74

Designs: 2c, 12c, Inauguration of Pres. Villeda Morales (horiz). 3c, 25c, Pres. Ramon Villeda Morales. 5c, 50c, Allegory of Second Republic (Torch and olive branches).

Engr.; Seal Litho. on 1c, 10c
1959, Dec. 21 *Perf. 13½*

C301 AP74 1c red brn, car & ultra 15 15
C302 AP74 2c bister brn 15 15
C303 AP74 3c ultra 15 15
C304 AP74 5c orange 18 15
C305 AP74 10c dull green, car & ultra 22 15
C306 AP74 12c rose red 35 15
C307 AP74 25c dull lilac 85 20
C308 AP74 50c dark blue 1.10 1.10
Nos. C301-C308 (8) 3.15
Set value 1.80

Second Republic of Honduras, 2nd anniv.

For surcharge see No. C543.

Catalogue values for unused stamps in this section, from this point to the end of the section, are for Never Hinged items.

King Alfonso XIII and Map AP75

Designs: 2c, 1906 award of King Alfonso XIII of Spain. 5c, Arbitration commission delivering its award, 1907. 10c, Intl. Court of Justice. 20c, Verdict of the Court, 1960. 50c, Pres. Morales, Foreign Minister Puerto and map. 1 l, Pres. Davila and Pres. Morales.

1961, Nov. 18 Engr. *Perf. 14½x14*

C309 AP75 1c dark blue 15 15
C310 AP75 2c magenta 15 15
C311 AP75 5c deep green 15 15
C312 AP75 10c brn orange 20 15
C313 AP75 20c vermilion 32 16
C314 AP75 50c brown 95 48
C315 AP75 1 l vio black 1.25 80
Nos. C309-C315 (7) 3.17
Set value 1.70

Judgment of the Intl. Court of Justice at The Hague, Nov. 18, 1960, returning a disputed territory to Honduras from Nicaragua.

Nos. C295-C297 and CO105 Surcharged **L 0.06**

1964, Apr. 7 *Perf. 13½*
Flags in National Colors

C316 AP72 6c on 15c red org 22 15
C317 AP73 8c on 25c dl pur 22 15
C318 AP73 10c on 50c ultra 32 16
C319 AP73 20c on 25c black 48 32

The red "OFICIAL" overprint on No. C319 was not obliterated.

See Nos. C345-C355, C419-C421.

Nos. C279-C281, C284 and C287 Overprinted: "FAO / Lucha Contra / el Hambre"

1964, Mar. 23 Unwmk. *Perf. 12*
Flags in National Colors

C320 AP71 1c light blue 16 16
C321 AP71 2c red 16 16
C322 AP71 5c green 20 20
C323 AP71 30c deep rose 1.00 1.00
C324 AP71 2 l gray olive 5.50 5.50
Nos. C320-C324 (5) 7.02 7.02

FAO "Freedom from Hunger Campaign" (1963).

Nos. CO98-CO101, CO104 and CO106 Overprinted in Blue or Black: "IN MEMORIAM / JOHN F. KENNEDY / 22 NOVEMBRE 1963"

1964, May 29 *Perf. 13½*
Flags in National Colors

C325 AP72 1c ocher (Bl) 15 15
C326 AP73 2c gray ol (Bl) 16 16
C327 AP73 3c red brn (Bl) 18 18
C328 AP73 5c ultra (Bk) 32 32
C329 AP72 15c dk brn (Bl) 1.25 1.25
C330 AP73 50c dk car (Bl) 6.25 6.25
Nos. C325-C330 (6) 8.31 8.31

Pres. John F. Kennedy (1917-63). The red "OFICIAL" overprint was not obliterated. The same overprint was applied to the stamps in miniature sheet No. C300a and seal of Honduras and Alliance for Progress emblem added in margin.

Nos. C222-C224, C226 and CO67 Overprinted with Olympic Rings and "1964"

Engr.; Center of 1c Litho.
1964, July 23 *Perf. 12½*
Frames in Black

C331 AP67 1c ultra & vio bl 15 15
C332 AP67 2c blue 18 18
C333 AP67 3c rose lilac 25 25
C334 AP67 15c red brown 48 48
C335 AP67 2 l lilac rose 6.25 6.25
Nos. C331-C335 (5) 7.31 7.31

18th Olympic Games, Tokyo, Oct. 10-25. The red "OFICIAL" overprint on No. C335 was not obliterated.

The same overprint was applied in black to the six stamps in No. CO108a, with additional rings and "1964" in margins of souvenir sheet. Value $50.

View of Copan AP76

Designs: 2c, 12c, Stone marker from Copan. 5c, 1 l, Mayan ball player (stone). 8c, 2 l, Olympic Stadium, Tokyo.

Unwmk.
1964, Nov. 27 Photo. *Perf. 14*
Black Design and Inscription

C336 AP76 1c yellow grn 15 15
C337 AP76 2c pale rose lil 15 15
C338 AP76 5c light ultra 15 15
C339 AP76 8c bluish green 24 24
C340 AP76 10c buff 35 28
C341 AP76 12c lemon 52 35
C342 AP76 1 l light ocher 1.40 1.25
C343 AP76 2 l pale ol grn 3.50 3.50
C344 AP76 3 l rose 4.00 4.00
Nos. C336-C344 (9) 10.46 10.07

18th Olympic Games, Tokyo, Oct. 10-25. Perf. and imperf. souvenir sheets of four exist containing one each of Nos. C338-C339, C341 and C344. Size: 129x110mm.

Nos. C292, C174, CO106, CO104, C124-C125, C165, CO105, C167-C168 and C178 Surcharged **L. 0.12**

1964-65

C345 AP73 4c on 5c dk car, bl & red 15 15
C346 AP62 10c on 15c red brn 18 15
C347 AP73 10c on 50c dk car, bl & red 18 15
C348 AP72 12c on 15c dk brn, bl & red 28 15
C349 AP27 12c on 16c ol gray 28 15
C350 AP27 12c on 21c lt blue 28 15
C351 AP60 12c on 22c org yel 28 15
C352 AP73 12c on 25c blk, bl & red 28 15
C353 AP60 30c on 1 l deep bl 50 22
C354 AP60 40c on 2 l lil ('65) 70 50
C355 AP61 40c on 1 l red brown ('65) 70 28
Nos. C345-C355 (11) 3.81
Set value 1.65

The red "OFICIAL" overprint on Nos. C347-C348 and C352 was not obliterated.

Nos. C289, CO99, C291-C292, C295-C296, CO106 and C299-C300 Overprinted in Black or Green: "Toma de Posesion / General / Oswaldo Lopez A. / Junio 6, 1965"

1965, June 6 Engr. *Perf. 13½*
Flags in National Colors

C356 AP72 1c green 15 15
C357 AP73 2c gray ol (G) 15 15
C358 AP73 3c pur (G) 15 15
C359 AP73 5c dk car (G) 15 15
C360 AP72 15c red orange 25 25
C361 AP73 25c dull pur (G) 40 40
C362 AP73 50c dk car (G) 85 85
C363 AP73 2 l gray ol (G) 3.00 3.00
C364 AP73 5 l ocher (G) 7.50 7.50
Nos. C356-C364 (9) 12.60 12.60

Inauguration of Gen. Oswaldo Lopez Arellano as president. The red "OFICIAL" overprint on Nos. C358 and C362 was not obliterated.

Ambulance and Maltese Cross AP77

Designs (Maltese Cross and): 5c, Hospital of Knights of Malta. 12c, Patients treated in village. 1 l, Map of Honduras.

1965, Aug. 30 Litho. *Perf. 12x11*

C365 AP77 1c ultra 18 18
C366 AP77 5c dark green 32 32
C367 AP77 12c dark brown 48 48
C368 AP77 1 l brown 1.90 1.90

Knights of Malta; campaign against leprosy.

Father Manuel de Jesus Subirana — AP78

Designs: 1c, Jicaque Indian. 2c, Preaching to the Indians. 10c, Msgr. Juan de Jesus Zepeda. 12c, Pope Pius IX. 20c, Tomb of Father Subirana, Yore. 1 l, Mission church. 2 l, Jicaque mother and child.

Perf. 13½x14
1965, July 27 Litho. Unwmk.

C369 AP78 1c blk, vio & gold 15 15
C370 AP78 2c blk, sal & gold 15 15
C371 AP78 8c blk, sal pink & gold 15 15
C372 AP78 10c blk, lil rose & gold 15 15
C373 AP78 12c blk, tan & gold 18 15

C374 AP78 20c blk, emer & gold 35 28
C375 AP78 1 l blk, yel grn & gold 1.75 1.50
C376 AP78 2 l blk, brt bl & gold 3.50 3.00
a. Souv. sheet of 4, #C371, C373, C375-C376 17.50 17.50
Nos. C369-C376 (8) 6.38 5.53

Centenary (in 1964) of the death of Father Manuel de Jesus Subirana (1807-64), Spanish missionary to the Central American Indians.

For overprints and surcharges see Nos. C380-C386, C407-C413, C487-C488, C554.

Nos. C198-C199 and C168 Overprinted: "IN MEMORIAM / Sir Winston Churchill / 1874-1965."

1965, Dec. 20 Engr. *Perf. 13½x14*
C377 AP65 1c red org & blk 35 35
C378 AP65 2c bl & red brn 70 70
C379 AP60 2 l lilac 7.00 7.00

Sir Winston Spencer Churchill (1874-1965), statesman and World War II leader.

Nos. C369-C375 Overprinted

CONMEMORATIVA
Visita S. S.
Pablo VI
a la ONU.
4-X-1965

1966, Mar. 10 Litho. *Perf. 13½x14*
C380 AP78 1c multicolored 15 15
C381 AP78 2c multicolored 15 15
C382 AP78 8c multicolored 25 15
C383 AP78 10c multicolored 25 15
C384 AP78 12c multicolored 28 15
C385 AP78 20c multicolored 35 35
C386 AP78 1 l multicolored 3.25 3.25
Nos. C380-C386 (7) 4.68 4.35

Visit of Pope Paul VI to the UN, New York City, Oct. 4, 1965.

Stamp of 1866, No. 1 — AP79

Tomas Estrada Palma — AP80

Post Office, Tegucigalpa AP81

Designs: 2c, Air post stamp of 1925, #C1. 5c, Locomotive. 6c, 19th cent. mail transport with mules. 7c, 19th cent. mail room. 8c, Sir Rowland Hill. 9c, Modern mail truck. 10c, Gen. Oswaldo Lopez Arellano. 12c, Postal emblem. 15c, Heinrich von Stephan. 20c, Mail plane. 30c, Flag of Honduras. 40c, Coat of Arms. 1 l, UPU monument, Bern. 2 l, Jose Maria Medina.

Perf. 14½x14, 14x14½
1966, May 31 Litho. Unwmk.
C387 AP79 1c gold, blk & grnsh gray 15 15
C388 AP79 2c org, blk & lt bl 15 15
C389 AP80 3c brt rose, gold & dp plum 15 15
C390 AP81 4c bl, gold & blk 15 15
C391 AP81 5c pink, gold & blk 52 15
C392 AP81 6c lil, gold & blk 15 15
C393 AP81 7c lt bl grn, gold & black 15 15
C394 AP80 8c lt bl, gold & blk 15 15
C395 AP81 9c lt ultra, gold & black 15 15
C396 AP80 10c cit, gold & blk 15 15
C397 AP79 12c gold, blk, yel & emerald 15 15
C398 AP80 15c brt pink, gold & dp claret 25 25
C399 AP81 20c org, gold & blk 32 32
C400 AP79 30c gold & bl 35 35
C401 AP79 40c multi 52 52
C402 AP79 1 l emer, gold & dk green 1.25 1.00
C403 AP80 2 l gray, gold & black 2.75 2.75
a. Souv. sheet of 6, #C387-C388, C396-C397, C402-C403 3.50 3.50
Nos. C387-C403 (17) 7.46 6.84

Centenary of the first Honduran postage stamp. No. C403a exists perf. and imperf. See No. CE3. For surcharges see Nos. C473-C474, C479, C486, C496.

Nos. CO53, C201 and C204 Overprinted: "CAMPEONATO DE FOOTBALL Copa Mundial 1966 Inglaterra-Alemania Wembley, Julio 30"

Perf. 13½x14, 14x13½
1966, Nov. 25 Engr.
C404 AP65 2c brown & vio 16 16
C405 AP66 16c dk bl & blk 32 32
C406 AP65 2 l brn & vio 8.50 8.50

Final game between England and Germany in the World Soccer Cup Championship, Wembley, July 30, 1966. The overprint on the 2c and 2 l is in 5 lines, it is in 8 lines on the 16c. There is no hyphen between "Inglaterra" and "Alemania" on the 16c.

Nos. C369-C371 and C373-C376 Overprinted in Red: "CONMEMORATIVA / del XX Aniversario / ONU 1966"

1967, Jan. 31 Litho. *Perf. 13½x14*
C407 AP78 1c black, vio & gold 16 16
C408 AP78 2c blk, sal & gold 18 18
C409 AP78 8c blk, sal pink & gold 32 32
C410 AP78 12c black, tan & gold 48 40
C411 AP78 20c blk, emer & gold 65 55
C412 AP78 1 l blk, yel grn & gold 1.50 1.50
C413 AP78 2 l blk, brt bl & gold 3.25 3.25
Nos. C407-C413 (7) 6.54 6.36

UN, 20th anniversary.

Nos. C250, C252, C258, C261 and C267 Overprinted in Red: "Simeon Canas y Villacorta / Libertador de los esclavos / en Centro America / 1767-1967"

1967, Feb. 27 Engr.
C414 AP68 1c blk & vio bl 15 15
C415 AP68 3c blk & brown 25 25
C416 AP68 15c dk red & blk 35 35
C417 AP68 25c blk & grn 70 70
C418 AP69 2 l blk & mag 2.50 2.50
Nos. C414-C418 (5) 3.95 3.95

Birth bicentenary of Father José Simeon Canas y Villacorta, D.D. (1767-1838), emancipator of the Central American slaves. The overprint is in 6 lines on the 2 l, in 4 lines on all others.

Nos. C178-C179 and CE2 Surcharged **L. 0.10**

1967
C419 AP61 10c on 1 l red brown 35 15
C420 AP62 10c on 2 l violet 35 15
C421 APSD1 10c on 20c blk & red 35 15
Set value 30

José Cecilio del Valle, Honduras AP82

Designs: 12c, Ruben Dario, Nicaragua. 14c, Batres Montufar, Guatemala. 20c, Francisco Antonio Gavidia, El Salvador. 30c, Juan Mora Fernandez, Costa Rica. 40c, Federation Emblem with map of Americas. 50c, Map of Central America.

1967, Aug. 4 Litho. *Perf. 13*
C422 AP82 11c gold, ultra & blk 15 15
C423 AP82 12c lt bl, yel & blk 15 15
C424 AP82 14c sil, grn & blk 15 15
C425 AP82 20c pink, grn & blk 25 25
C426 AP82 30c bluish lil, yel & black 40 35
C427 AP82 40c pur, lt bl & gold 70 70
C428 AP82 50c lem, grn & car rose 70 70
Nos. C422-C428 (7) 2.50 2.45

Founding of the Federation of Central American Journalists.

For surcharges see Nos. C475-C476.

Olympic Rings, Flags of Mexico and Honduras AP83

Olympic Rings and Winners of 1964 Olympics: 2c, Like 1c. 5c, Italian flag and boxers. 10c, French flag and women skiers. 12c, German flag and equestrian team. 50c, British flag and women runners. 1 l, US flag and runners (Bob Hayes).

1968, Mar. 4 Litho. *Perf. 14x13½*
C429 AP83 1c gold & multi 15 15
C430 AP83 2c gold & multi 18 18
C431 AP83 5c gold & multi 25 25
C432 AP83 10c gold & multi 32 25
C433 AP83 12c gold & multi 48 25
C434 AP83 50c gold & multi 1.90 1.10
C435 AP83 1 l gold & multi 6.25 6.25
Nos. C429-C435 (7) 9.53 8.43

19th Olympic Games, Mexico City, Oct. 12-27. Perf. and imperf. souvenir sheets of 2 exist containing 20c and 40c stamps in design of 1c. Value $4.50 each.

For surcharge see No. C499.

John F. Kennedy, Rocket at Cape Kennedy AP84

ITU Emblem and: 2c, Radar and telephone. 3c, Radar and television set. 5c, Radar and globe showing Central America. 8c, Communications satellite. 10c, 20c, like 1c.

1968, Nov. 28 *Perf. 14x13½*
C436 AP84 1c vio & multi 15 15
C437 AP84 2c sil & multi 20 20
C438 AP84 3c multicolored 25 25
C439 AP84 5c org & multi 30 30
C440 AP84 8c multicolored 35 35
C441 AP84 10c olive & multi 40 40
C442 AP84 20c multicolored 50 50
Nos. C436-C442 (7) 2.15 2.15

ITU, cent. A 30c in design of 2c, a 1 l in design of 5c and a 1.50 l in design of 1c exist; also two souvenir sheets, one containing 10c, 50c and 75c, the other one 1.50 l.

For overprints see Nos. C446-C453.

Nos. C436, C441-C442 Overprinted: "In Memoriam / Robert F. Kennedy / 1925-1968"

1968, Dec. 23
C446 AP84 1c vio & multi 20 20
C447 AP84 10c ol & multi 30 30
C448 AP84 20c multicolored 50 50

In memory of Robert F. Kennedy. Same overprint was also applied to a 1.50 l and to a souvenir sheet containing one 1.50 l.

Nos. C437-C440 Overprinted in Blue or Red with Olympic Rings and: "Medalias de Oro / Mexico 1968"

1969, Mar. 3
C450 AP84 2c multi (Bl) 20 20
C451 AP84 3c multi (Bl) 30 30
C452 AP84 5c multi (Bl) 40 40
C453 AP84 8c multi (R) 50 50

Gold medal winners in 19th Olympic Games, Mexico City. The same red overprint was also applied to a 30c and a 1 l. The souvenir sheet of 3 noted after No. C442 exists with this overprint in black.

Rocket Blast-off AP85

Designs: 10c, Close-up view of moon. 12c, Spacecraft (horiz.). 20c, Astronaut and module on moon (horiz.). 24c, Lunar landing module.

Perf. 14½x13½, 13½x14
1969, Oct. 29
C454 AP85 5c multicolored 20 20
C455 AP85 10c multicolored 30 30
C456 AP85 12c multicolored 40 40
C457 AP85 20c multicolored 50 50
C458 AP85 24c multicolored 1.00 1.00
Nos. C454-C458 (5) 2.40 2.40

Man's first landing on the moon, July 20, 1969. A 30c showing re-entry of capsule, a 1 l in design of 20c and a 1.50 l in design of 24c exist. Two souvenir sheets exist, one containing Nos. C454-C455 and 1.50 l, and the other No. C456, 30c and 1 l.

For the safe return of Apollo 13, overprints were applied in 1970 to Nos. C454-C458, the three unlisted denominations and the two souvenir sheets.

For overprints and surcharges see Nos. C500-C504, C555.

Nos. C224, C393, C395, C422, C424, CE2 and C178 Surcharged with New Value

1970, Feb. 20 Engr.; Litho.
C472 AP67 4c on 3c blk & rose lil 20 15
C473 AP81 5c on 7c multi 25 15
C474 AP81 10c on 9c multi 30 15
C475 AP82 10c on 11c multi 30 15
C476 AP82 12c on 14c multi 35 20
C477 APSD1 12c on 20c blk & red 35 20
C478 AP61 12c on 1 l red brn 35 20
Nos. C472-C478 (7) 2.10 1.20

No. CE3 Overprinted "HABILITADO"

1970 Litho. *Perf. 14x14½*
C479 AP81 20c bis brn, brn & gold 75 35

Julio Adolfo Sanhueza AP86

Emblems, Map and Flag of Honduras AP87

Designs: 8c, Rigoberto Ordoñez Rodriguez. 12c, Forest Fire Brigade emblem (with map of Honduras) and emblems of fire fighters, FAO and Alliance for Progress (horiz.). 1 l, Flags of Honduras, UN and US, Arms of Honduras and emblems as on 12c.

Perf. 14½x14, 14x14½
1970, Aug. 15 Litho.
C480 AP86 5c gold, emer & ind 15 15
C481 AP86 8c gold, org brn & indigo 16 15
C482 AP87 12c bl & multi 24 15
C483 AP87 20c yel & multi 40 24
C484 AP87 1 l gray & multi 1.40 1.40
a. Souvenir sheet of 5 2.00 2.00
Nos. C480-C484 (5) 2.35 2.09

Campaign against forest fires and in memory of the men who lost their lives fighting forest fires. No. C484a contains 5 imperf. stamps with simulated perforations and without gum similar to Nos. C480-C484. Sold for 1.45 l.

For surcharges see Nos. C497-C498.

Hotel Honduras Maya
AP88

1970, Oct. 24 **Litho.** ***Perf. 14***
C485 AP88 12c sky bl & blk 30 22

Opening of the Hotel Honduras Maya, Tegucigalpa.

Stamps of 1952-1968 Surcharged

1971 **Litho.; Engr.**
C486 AP79 4c on 1c (#C387) 15
C487 AP78 5c on 1c (#C369) 15
C488 AP78 8c on 2c (#C370) 25
C489 AP65 10c on 2c (#C199) 35
C490 AP67 10c on 3c (#C224) 35
a. Inverted surcharge
C491 AP68 10c on 3c (#C252) 35
C492 AP68 10c on 3c (#CO71) 35
C493 AP69 10c on 2c (#C251) 35
C494 AP73 10c on 2c (#CO99) 35
C495 AP73 10c on 3c (#CO100) 35
C496 AP80 10c on 3c (#C389) 35
C497 AP87 15c on 12c (#C482) 50
C498 AP87 30c on 12c (#C482) 1.00
C499 AP83 40c on 50c (#C434) 1.25
C500 AP85 40c on 24c (#C458) 1.25
Nos. C486-C500 (15) 7.35

Red "OFICIAL" overprint was not obliterated on Nos. C492, C494-C495.
No. C491 exists with inverted surcharge.

Nos. C454, C456-C458 Overprinted and Surcharged

Aniversario Gran Logia de Honduras 1922-1972

L 1.00

Perf. 14½x13½, 13½x14½
1972, May 15 **Litho.**
C501 AP85 5c multi 70 40
C502 AP85 12c multi 1.00 75
C503 AP85 1 l on 20c multi 2.00 1.00
C504 AP85 2 l on 24c multi 4.00 2.00

Masonic Grand Lodge of Honduras, 50th anniv. Overprint varies to fit stamp shape.

Soldier's Bay, Guanaja
AP89

Designs: 5c, 7c, 9c, 10c, 2 l, vertical.

1972, May 19 ***Perf. 13***
C505 AP89 4c shown 15 15
C506 AP89 5c Taps 15 15
C507 AP89 6c Yojoa Lake 15 15
C508 AP89 7c Banana Carrier, by Roberto Aguilar 15 15
C509 AP89 8c Military parade 15 15
C510 AP89 9c Orchid, national flower 25 15
C511 AP89 10c like 9c 25 15
C512 AP89 12c Soldier with machine gun 20 15
C513 AP89 15c Sunset over beach 30 15
C514 AP89 20c Litter bearers 30 15
C515 AP89 30c Landscape, by Antonio Velasquez 50 25
C516 AP89 40c Ruins of Copan 75 40
a. Souv. sheet of 4, #C508, C513, C515-C516 1.40 1.40

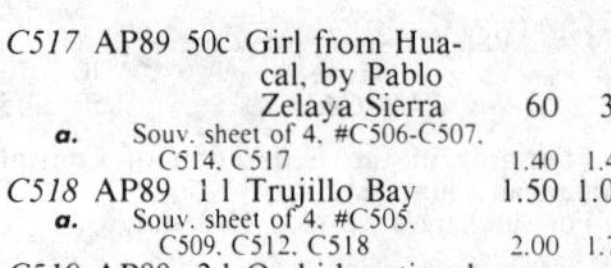

C517 AP89 50c Girl from Huacal, by Pablo Zelaya Sierra 60 35
a. Souv. sheet of 4, #C506-C507, C514, C517 1.40 1.40
C518 AP89 1 l Trujillo Bay 1.50 1.00
a. Souv. sheet of 4, #C505, C509, C512, C518 2.00 1.75
C519 AP89 2 l Orchid, national flower 4.00 3.00
a. Souv. sheet of 3, #C510-C511, C519 4.50 3.25
Nos. C505-C519,CE4 (16) 9.70 6.80

Sesquicentennial of independence (stamps inscribed 1970).
For surcharge see No. CE5.

Sister Maria Rosa and Child — AP90

Designs: 15c, SOS Children's Village emblem (horiz.). 30c, Father José Trinidad Reyes. 40c, Kennedy Center, first SOS village in Central America (horiz.). 1 l, Boy.

Perf. 13½x13, 13x13½
1972, Nov. 10 **Photo.**
C520 AP90 10c grn, gold & brn 18 15
C521 AP90 15c grn, gold & brn 25 15
C522 AP90 30c grn, gold & brn 42 15
C523 AP90 40c grn, gold & brn 50 18
C524 AP90 1 l grn, gold & brn 2.00 1.50
Nos. C520-C524 (5) 3.35 2.13

Children's Villages in Honduras (Intl. SOS movement to save homeless children).
For overprints and surcharges see #C531, C534-C536, C546-C549, C556, C560-C561.

Map of Honduras and Society Emblem
AP91

Design: 12c, Map of Honduras, emblems of National Geographic Institute and Interamerican Geodesic Service.

1973, Mar. 27 **Litho.** ***Perf. 13***
C525 AP91 10c multicolored 55 28
C526 AP91 12c multicolored 65 28

25th annivs. of Natl. Cartographic Service (10c) and of joint cartographic work (12c).
For overprints and surcharges see Nos. C532-C533, C557-C558.

Juan Ramon Molina
AP92

Designs: 8c, Illustration from Molina's book "Habitante de la Osa." 1 l, Illustration from "Tierras Mares y Cielos." 2 l, "UNESCO."

1973, Apr. 17 **Litho.** ***Perf. 13½***
C527 AP92 8c brn org, blk & red brn 18 15
C528 AP92 20c brt bl & multi 70 25
C529 AP92 1 l green & multi 1.40 1.00
C530 AP92 2 l org & multi 2.75 2.75
a. Sheet of 4 5.25 5.25

Molina (1875-1908), poet, and 25th anniv. (in 1971) of UNESCO. No. C530a contains 4 stamps similar to Nos. C527-C530. Exists perf. and imperf.

For surcharge see No. C559.

Nos. C520-C523, C525-C526 Overprinted in Red or Black: "Censos de Poblaciọn y Vivienda, marzo 1974. 1974, Ano Mundial de Poblaciọn"

Perf. 13½x13, 13x13½, 13
1973, Dec. 28 **Photo; Litho.**
C531 AP90 10c multi (R) 15 15
C532 AP91 10c multi (B) 15 15
C533 AP91 12c multi (B) 15 15
C534 AP90 15c multi (R) 15 15
C535 AP90 30c multi (R) 28 25
C536 AP90 40c multi (R) 35 35
Set value 96 90

1974 population and housing census; World Population Year. The overprint is in 7 lines on vertical stamps, in 5 lines on horizontal.

Issues of 1947-59 Surcharged in Red or Black

Perf. 13x12½, 13½, 11x12½, 12
1974, June 28 **Engr.**
C537 AP68 2c on 1c (#C250) (R) 15 15
C538 AP68 2c on 1c (#CO69) 15 15
C539 AP72 2c on 1c (#C289) 15 15
C540 AP72 2c on 1c (#CO98) 15 15
C541 AP72 3c on 1c (#C289) 15 15
C542 AP68 3c on 1c (#C250) (R) 15 15
C543 AP74 1 l on 50c (#C308) 1.40 1.40
C544 AP60 1 l on 2 l (#C168) 1.40 1.40
C545 AP62 1 l on 2 l (#C179) (R) 1.40 1.40
Nos. C537-C545 (9) 5.10 5.10

Red "OFICIAL" overprint was not obliterated on Nos. C538 and C540.

Nos. C520-C523 Overprinted in Bright Green: "1949-1974 SOS Kinderdorfer International Honduras-Austria"

1974, July 25 **Photo.**
C546 AP90 10c grn, gold & brn 15 15
C547 AP90 15c grn, gold & brn 18 18
C548 AP90 30c grn, gold & brn 25 25
C549 AP90 40c grn, gold & brn 35 35

25th anniversary of Children's Villages in Honduras. Overprint in 6 lines on 10c and 30c, in 4 lines on 15c and 40c.

Stamps of 1956-73 Surcharged

1975, Feb. 24 **Litho.; Engr.**
C550 AP68 16c on 1c (#C250) 20 15
C551 AP70 16c on 1c (#C269) 20 15
C552 AP72 16c on 1c (#C289) 20 15
C553 AP72 16c on 1c (#CO98) 20 15
C554 AP78 16c on 1c (#C369) 30 30
C555 AP85 18c on 12c (#C456) 40 22
C556 AP90 18c on 10c (#C520) 25 18
C557 AP91 18c on 10c (#C525) 25 18
C558 AP91 18c on 12c (#C526) 25 18
C559 AP92 18c on 8c (#C527) 25 18
C560 AP90 50c on 30c (#C522) 75 52
C561 AP90 1 l on 30c (#C522) 1.25 90
Nos. C550-C561,CE5 (13) 5.35 3.86

Denominations not obliterated on Nos. C551, C553-C558, C560-C561; "OFICIAL" overprint not obliterated on No. C553.

Flags of Germany and Austria
AP93

Designs (Flags): 2c, Belgium and Denmark. 3c, Spain and France. 4c, Hungary and Russia. 5c, Great Britain and Italy. 10c, Norway and Sweden. 12c, Honduras. 15c, United States and Switzerland. 20c, Greece and Portugal. 30c, Romania and Serbia. 1 l, Egypt and Netherlands. 2 l, Luxembourg and Turkey.

1975, June 18 **Litho.** ***Perf. 13***
Gold & Multicolored; Colors Listed are for Shields
C562 AP93 1c lilac 15 15
C563 AP93 2c gold 15 15
C564 AP93 3c rose gray 15 15
C565 AP93 4c light blue 15 15
C566 AP93 5c yellow 15 15
C567 AP93 10c gray 16 16
C568 AP93 12c lilac rose 22 22
C569 AP93 15c bluish green 32 32
C570 AP93 20c bright blue 32 32
C571 AP93 30c pink 48 48
C572 AP93 1 l salmon 1.50 1.50
C573 AP93 2 l yellow green 3.25 3.25
Nos. C562-C573 (12) 7.00 7.00

Souvenir Sheet

C574 AP93 Sheet of 12 *9.50 9.50*

UPU, cent. (in 1974). No. C574 contains 12 stamps similar to Nos. C562-C573 with shields in different colors.

Humuya Youth Center and Mrs. Arellano
AP94

Designs (Portrait of First Lady, Gloria de Lopez Arellano, IWY Emblem and): 16c, Jalteva Youth Center. 18c, Mrs. Arellano (diff. portrait) and IWY emblem. 30c, El Carmen de San Pedro Sula Youth Center. 55c, Flag of National Social Welfare Organization (vert.). 1 l, La Isla sports and recreational facilities. 2 l, Women's Social Center.

1976, Mar. 5 **Litho.** ***Perf. 13½***
C575 AP94 8c sal & multi 15 15
C576 AP94 16c yel & multi 18 18
C577 AP94 18c pink & multi 18 18
C578 AP94 30c org & multi 35 35
C579 AP94 55c multicolored 52 52
C580 AP94 1 l multicolored 1.10 1.10
C581 AP94 2 l multicolored 2.00 2.00
Nos. C575-C581 (7) 4.48 4.48

International Women's Year (1975).
For surcharges see #C736-C737, C781, C798.

"CARE" and Globe
AP95

Designs: 1c, 16c, 30c, 55c, 1 l, Care package and globe (vert.). Others like 5c.

1976, May 24 **Litho.** ***Perf. 13½***
C582 AP95 1c blk & lt blue 15 15
C583 AP95 5c rose brn & blk 15 15
C584 AP95 16c black & org 18 18
C585 AP95 18c lemon & blk 22 22
C586 AP95 30c blk & blue 35 35
C587 AP95 50c yel grn & blk 52 52
C588 AP95 55c blk & buff 52 52
C589 AP95 70c brt rose & blk 70 70
C590 AP95 1 l blk & lt grn 1.10 1.10
C591 AP95 2 l ocher & blk 2.00 2.00
Nos. C582-C591 (10) 5.89 5.89

20th anniversary of CARE in Honduras.
For surcharges see Nos. C735, C738, C788.

Fawn in Burnt-out Forest — AP96

"Sons of Liberty" — AP97

Forest Protection: 16c, COHDEFOR emblem (Corporacion Hondurena de Desarollo Forestal). 18c, Forest (horiz.). 30c, 2 l, Live and burning trees. 50c, like 10c. 70c, Emblem. 1 l, Young forest (horiz.).

1976, May 28 **Litho.** ***Perf. 13½***
C592 AP96 10c multicolored 15 15
C593 AP96 16c multicolored 25 15
C594 AP96 18c multicolored 25 15
C595 AP96 30c grn & multi 50 20
C596 AP96 50c multicolored 75 30
C597 AP96 70c brn & multi 1.00 40

C598	AP96	1 l yel & multi	1.60	75
C599	AP96	2 l vio & multi	3.00	3.00
		Nos. C592-C599,CE6 (9)	8.10	5.55

For surcharges see Nos. C784, C787.

1976, Aug. 29 Litho. *Perf. 12*

American Bicentennial: 2c, Raising flag of "Liberty and Union." 3c, Bunker Hill flag. 4c, Washington's Cruisers' flag. 5c, 1st Navy Jack. 6c, Flag of Honduras over Presidential Palace, Tegucigalpa. 18c, US flag over Capitol. 55c, Grand Union flag. 2 l, Bennington flag. 3 l, Betsy Ross and her flag.

C601	AP97	1c multicolored	15	15
C602	AP97	2c multicolored	15	15
C603	AP97	3c multicolored	15	15
C604	AP97	4c multicolored	15	15
C605	AP97	5c multicolored	15	15
C606	AP97	6c multicolored	15	15
C607	AP97	18c multicolored	30	35
C608	AP97	55c multicolored	75	70
a.		Souv. sheet of 4, #C603, C606-C608	*1.50*	*1.50*
C609	AP97	2 l multicolored	2.00	1.75
a.		Souv. sheet of 3, #C601, C604, C609	*3.25*	*3.25*
C610	AP97	3 l multicolored	4.50	4.50
a.		Souv. sheet of 3, #C602, C605, C610	*4.75*	*4.75*
		Nos. C601-C610 (10)	8.45	8.20

Queen Sophia of Spain — AP98

Designs: 18c, King Juan Carlos. 30c, Queen Sophia and King Juan Carlos. 2 l, Arms of Honduras and Spain (horiz.).

1977, Sept. 13 Litho. *Perf. 14*

C611	AP98	16c multicolored	15	15
C612	AP98	18c multicolored	15	15
C613	AP98	30c multicolored	30	22
C614	AP98	2 l multicolored	1.90	1.90

Visit of King and Queen of Spain.

Mayan Steles, Exhibition Emblems AP99

Designs: 18c, Giant head. 30c, Statue. 55c, Sun god. 1.50 l, Mayan pelota court.

1978, Apr. 28 Litho. *Perf. 12*

C615	AP99	15c multi	18	18
C616	AP99	18c multi	25	25
C617	AP99	30c multi	35	35
C618	AP99	55c multi	70	70

Imperf

C619	AP99	1.50 l multi	1.75	1.75

Honduras '78 Philatelic Exhibition.
For overprints and surcharge see Nos. C642-C645, C786.

Del Valle's Birthplace AP100

Designs: 14c, La Merced Church, Choluteca, where del Valle was baptized. 15c, Baptismal font (vert.). 20c, Del Valle reading independence acts. 25c, Portrait, documents, map of Central America. 40c, Portrait (vert.). 1 l, Monument, Central Park, Choluteca (vert.). 3 l, Bust (vert.).

1978, Apr. 11 Litho. *Perf. 14*

C620	AP100	8c multicolored	15	15
C621	AP100	14c multicolored	15	15
C622	AP100	15c multicolored	15	15
C623	AP100	20c multicolored	20	20
C624	AP100	25c multicolored	26	26
C625	AP100	40c multicolored	38	38
C626	AP100	1 l multicolored	95	95
C627	AP100	3 l multicolored	3.25	3.25
		Nos. C620-C627 (8)	5.49	5.49

Bicentenary of the birth of José Cecilio del Valle (1780-1834), Central American patriot and statesman.
For surcharges see Nos. C739, C793, C795.

Rural Health Center AP101

Designs: 6c, Child at water pump. 10c, Los Laureles Dam, Tegucigalpa. 20c, Rural aqueduct. 40c, Teaching hospital, Tegucigalpa. 2 l, Parents and child. 3 l, National vaccination campaign. 5 l, Panamerican Health Organization Building, Washington, DC.

1978, May 10 Litho. *Perf. 14*

C628	AP101	5c multi	15	15
C629	AP101	6c multi	15	15
C630	AP101	10c multi	15	15
C631	AP101	20c multi	22	22
C632	AP101	40c multi	45	45
C633	AP101	2 l multi	1.90	1.90
C634	AP101	3 l multi	3.00	3.00
C635	AP101	5 l multi	4.50	4.50
		Nos. C628-C635 (8)	10.52	10.52

75th anniv. of Panamerican Health Organization (in 1977).
For surcharge see No. C783.

Luis Landa and his "Botanica" AP102

Designs (Luis Landa and): 16c, Map of Honduras showing St. Ignacio. 18c, Medals received by Landa. 30c, Landa's birthplace in St. Ignacio. 2 l, Brassavola (orchid), national flower. 3 l, Women's Normal School.

1978, Aug. 29 Photo. *Perf. 13x13½*

C636	AP102	14c multi	20	16
C637	AP102	16c multi	20	16
C638	AP102	18c multi	20	16
C639	AP102	30c multi	40	20
C640	AP102	2 l multi	3.00	1.00
C641	AP102	3 l multi	3.50	3.50
		Nos. C636-C641 (6)	7.50	5.18

Prof. Luis Landa (1875-1975), botanist.
For surcharges see Nos. C740, C794.

Nos. C615-C618 Overprinted in Red with Argentina '78 Soccer Cup Emblem and: "Argentina Campeon / Holanda Sub-Campeon / XI Campeonato Mundial / de Football"

1978, Sept. 6 Litho. *Perf. 12*

C642	AP99	15c multicolored	15	15
C643	AP99	18c multicolored	25	18
C644	AP99	30c multicolored	35	28
C645	AP99	55c multicolored	75	52

Argentina's victory in World Cup Soccer Championship. Same overprint was applied to No. C619.

Central University and Coat of Arms — AP103

Designs show for each denomination a 19th century print and a contemporary photograph of same area (except 1.50 l, 5 l): No. C647, University City. 8c, Manuel Bonilla Theater. No. C650, Court House (vert.). No. C651, North Boulevard highway intersection (vert.). No. C652, National Palace. No. C653, Presidential Palace. 20c, Hospital. 40c, Cathedral. 50c, View of Tegucigalpa. 1.50 l, Aerial view of Tegucigalpa. No. C660, Arms of San Miguel de Tegucigalpa, 18th century (vert.). No. C661, Pres. Marco Aurelio Soto (1846-1908) (painting; vert.).

1978, Sept. 29

C646	AP103	6c blk & brn	15	15
C647	AP103	6c multi	15	15
C648	AP103	8c blk & brn	15	15
C649	AP103	8c multi	15	15
C650	AP103	10c blk & brn	15	15
C651	AP103	10c multi	15	15
C652	AP103	16c blk & brn	25	16
C653	AP103	16c multi	25	16
C654	AP103	20c blk & brn	30	16
C655	AP103	20c multi	30	16
C656	AP103	40c blk & brn	60	45
C657	AP103	40c multi	60	45
C658	AP103	50c blk & brn	75	48
C659	AP103	50c multi	75	48
C660	AP103	5 l blk & brn	6.00	6.00
C661	AP103	5 l multi	6.00	6.00
		Nos. C646-C661 (16)	16.70	15.40

Souvenir Sheet

C662	AP103	1.50 l multi	2.00	2.00

400th anniv. of the founding of Tegucigalpa.
In the listing the first number is for the 19th cent. design, the second for the 20th cent. design. Stamps of same denomination se-tenant.
For overprints and surcharges see Nos. C724-C725, C740A-C746, C766-C769, C779-C780.

Goalkeeper — AP104

Designs: Various soccer scenes.

1978, Nov. 26 Litho. *Perf. 12*

C663	AP104	15c multi, vert.	16	16
C664	AP104	30c multi	32	32
C665	AP104	55c multi, vert.	50	50
C666	AP104	1 l multi	1.00	1.00
C667	AP104	2 l multi	2.00	2.00
		Nos. C663-C667 (5)	3.98	3.98

7th Youth Soccer Championship, Nov. 26.
For surcharge see No. C797.

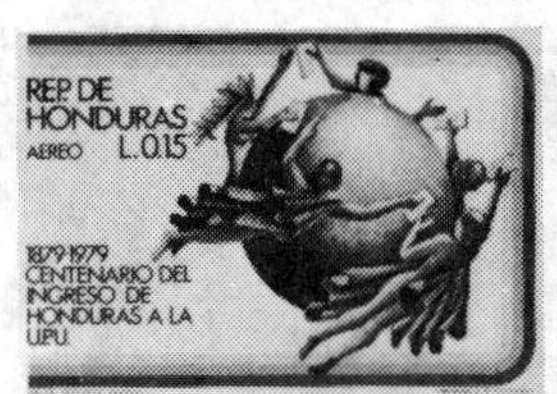

UPU Emblem — AP105

Designs: 2c, Postal emblem of Honduras. 25c, Dr. Ramon Rosa (vert.). 50c, Pres. Marco Aurelio Soto (vert.).

1979, Apr. 1 Litho. *Perf. 12*

C668	AP105	2c multicolored	15	15
C669	AP105	15c multicolored	15	15
C670	AP105	25c multicolored	20	20
C671	AP105	50c multicolored	42	42

Centenary of Honduras joining UPU.

Rotary Emblem and "50" AP106

1979, Apr. 26 Litho. *Perf. 14*

C672	AP106	3c multi	15	15
C673	AP106	5c multi	15	15
C674	AP106	50c multi	42	42
C675	AP106	2 l multi	1.65	1.65

Rotary Intl. of Honduras, 50th anniv.

Map of Caratasca Lagoon AP107

Designs: 10c, Fort San Fernando de Omoa. 24c, Institute anniversary emblem (vert.). 5 l, Map of Santanilla islands.

1979, Sept. 15 Litho. *Perf. 13½*

C676	AP107	5c multi	15	15
C677	AP107	10c multi	15	15
C678	AP107	24c multi	18	18
C679	AP107	5 l multi	3.75	3.75

Panamerican Institute of History and Geography, 50th anniversary.

General Post Office, 1979 — AP108

UPU Membership Centenary: 3 l, Post Office, 19th century.

1980, Feb. 20 Litho. *Perf. 12*

C680	AP108	24c multi	20	20
C681	AP108	3 l multi	2.50	2.50

Workers in the Field, IYC Emblem AP109

1980, Dec. 9 Litho. *Perf. 14½*

C682	AP109	1c shown	15	15
C683	AP109	5c Landscape, vert.	15	15
C684	AP109	15c Sitting boy, vert.	15	15
C685	AP109	20c IYC emblem, vert.	20	20
C686	AP109	30c Beach scene	30	30
		Set value		74

Souvenir Sheet

C687	AP109	1 l UNICEF and IYC emblems, vert.	1.00	1.00

International Year of the Child (1979).

Maltese Cross, Hill
AP110

1980, Dec. 17

C688 AP110 1c shown 15 15
C689 AP110 2c Penny Black 15 15
C690 AP110 5c Honduras type A1 15 15
C691 AP110 10c Honduras type A1 15 15

Size: 47x34mm

C692 AP110 15c Postal emblem 15 15
C693 AP110 20c Flags of Honduras, Gt. Britain 18 18
Set value 54 54

Souvenir Sheet

C694 AP110 1 l Honduras #C402 85 85

Sir Rowland Hill (1795-1879), originator of penny postage. No. C694 contains one stamp 47x34mm.

Intibucana Mother and Child
AP111

Bernardo O'Higgins, by Jose Gil de Castro
AP112

Inter-American Women's Commission, 50th Anniv.: 2c, Visitacion Padilla, Honduras Section founder. 10c, Maria Trinidad del Cid, Section member. 1 l, Emblem (horiz.).

1981, June 15 Litho. *Perf. 14½*

C695 AP111 2c multicolored 15 15
C696 AP111 10c multicolored 15 15
C697 AP111 40c multicolored 32 32
C698 AP111 1 l multicolored 80 80

1981, June 29

Paintings of O'Higgins: 16c, Liberation of Chile, by Cosme San Martin (horiz.). 20c, Portrait of Ambrosio O'Higgins (father). 1 l, Abdication of Office, by Antonio Caro (horiz.).

C699 AP112 16c multicolored 15 15
C700 AP112 20c multicolored 16 16
C701 AP112 30c multicolored 25 25
C702 AP112 1 l multicolored 85 50

For surcharge see No. C785.

CONCACAF 81 Soccer Cup — AP113

1981, Dec. 30 Litho. *Perf. 14*

C703 AP113 20c Emblem 16 16
C704 AP113 50c Player 42 25
C705 AP113 70c Flags 60 40
C706 AP113 1 l Stadium 85 85

Souvenir Sheet

C707 AP113 1.50 l like #C703 1.25 1.25

For overprint see No. C797.

50th Anniv. of Air Force (1981)
AP114

Designs: 3c, Curtis CT-32 Condor. 15c, North American NA-16. 25c, Chance Vought F4U-5. 65c, Douglas C47. 1 l Cessna A37-B. 2 l, Super Mister SMB-11.

1983, Jan. 14 Litho. *Perf. 12*

C708 AP114 3c multi 15 15
C709 AP114 15c multi 15 15
C710 AP114 25c multi 22 20
C711 AP114 65c multi 55 35
C712 AP114 1 l multi 85 50
C713 AP114 2 l multi 1.75 1.75
Nos. C708-C713 (6) 3.67 3.10

Souvenir Sheet

C714 AP114 1.55 l Helicopter 1.50 1.50

UPU Executive Council Membership, 3rd Anniv. — AP115

1983, Jan. 14

C715 AP115 16c UPU monument 15 15
C716 AP115 18c 18th UPU Congress emblem 16 16
C717 AP115 30c Natl. Postal Service emblem 28 28
C718 AP115 55c Rio de Janeiro 45 45
C719 AP115 2 l Dove on globe 1.75 1.75
Nos. C715-C719 (5) 2.79 2.79

Souvenir Sheet

C720 AP115 1 l like 2 l 90 90

Natl. Library and Archives Centenary (1980)
AP116

1983, Feb. 11 Litho. *Perf. 12*

C721 AP116 9c Library 15 15
C722 AP116 1 l Books 80 40

Intl. Year of the Disabled (1979)
AP117

1983, Feb. 11

C723 AP117 25c Emblem 22 22

Nos. C656-C657 Overprinted in Red: "CONMEMORATIVA DE LA VISITA / DE SS. JUAN PABLO II / 8 de marzo de 1983"

1983, Mar. 8

C724 AP103 40c multicolored 1.50 1.00
C725 AP103 40c multicolored 1.50 1.00

Visit of Pope John Paul II.

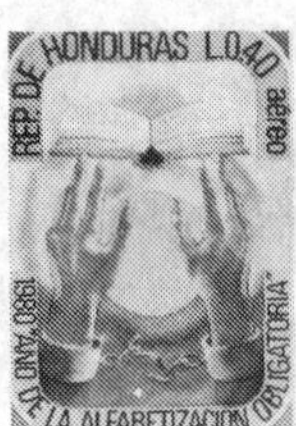

Literacy Campaign (1980) — AP118

World Food Day, Oct. 16, 1981 — AP119

1983, May 18 Litho. *Perf. 12*

C726 AP118 40c Hands, open book 35 35
C727 AP118 1.50 l People holding books 1.40 1.40

1983, May 18

C728 AP119 65c Produce, emblem 60 60

20th Anniv. of Inter-American Development Bank (1980) — AP120

1983, June 17 Litho. *Perf. 12*

C729 AP120 1 l Comayagua River Bridge 85 50
C730 AP120 2 l Luis Bogran Technical Institute of Physics 1.65 1.00

2nd Anniv. of Return to Constitutional Government — AP121

1984, Jan. 27 Litho. *Perf. 12*

C731 AP121 20c Arms, text 18 15
C732 AP121 20c Pres. Suazo Cordova 18 15
a. Pair, #C731-C732 36 30
Set value 20

La Gaceta Newspaper Sesquicentenary (1980) — AP122

1984, May 25 Litho. *Perf. 12*

C733 AP122 10c Masthead, pen & ink 15 15
C734 AP122 20c like 10c 18 15
Set value 27 16

Nos. C582 and C575-C576 Surcharged

1985, June 26 Litho. *Perf. 13½*

C735 AP95 5c on 1c #C582 15 15
C736 AP94 10c on 8c #C575 15 15
C737 AP94 20c on 16c #C576 18 15
C738 AP95 1 l on 1c #C582 90 40
Set value 64

Nos. C621, C636 and C646-C647 Surcharged

Litho., Photo. (No. C740)

1986, Aug. 21 *Perfs. as before*

C739 AP100 50c on 14c #C621 45 25
C740 AP102 60c on 14c #C636 55 30
C740A AP103 85c on 6c #C646 75 40
C740B AP103 85c on 6c #C647 75 40
C741 AP103 95c on 6c #C646 85 45
C742 AP103 95c on 6c #C647 85 45
Nos. C739-C742 (6) 4.20 2.25

Black bar obliterating old values on Nos. C739-C740 also cover "aereo." Nos. C741-C742 se-tenant.

Nos. C656-C657 Ovptd. in Red "EXFILHON '86," "MEXICO '86" and:
No. C743 "ARGENTINA CAMPEON"
No. C744 "ALEMANIA FEDERAL Sub Campeon"
No. C745 "FRANCIA TERCER LUGAR"
No. C746 "BELGICA CUARTO LUGAR"

1986, Sept. 12 Litho. *Perf. 12*

C743 AP103 40c No. C656 40 20
C744 AP103 40c No. C657 40 20
C745 AP103 40c No. C657 40 20
C746 AP103 40c No. C656 40 20
a. Block of 4, #C743-C746 1.60

AP123

San Fernando de Omoa Castle — AP124

Designs: 20c, Phulapanzak Falls, vert. 78c, Bahia Isls. beach. 85c, Bahia Isls. cove. 95c, Yojoa Lake, vert. 1 l, Woman painting pottery, vert.

Perf. 13½x14, 14x13½

1986, Nov. 10 Litho.

C747 AP123 20c multi 18 15
C748 AP123 78c multi 70 35
C749 AP123 85c multi 75 35
C750 AP123 95c multi 85 40
C751 AP123 1 l multi 90 45

Size: 84x59mm

Imperf

C752 AP124 1.50 l multi 1.40 1.40
Nos. C747-C752 (6) 4.78 3.10

For overprint see No. C782.

National Flag, Pres. Jose Azcona Hoyo — AP125

1987, Feb. 2 Litho. *Perf. 13½*

C753 AP125 20c multicolored 18 15
C754 AP125 85c multicolored 75 30

Democratic government, 1st anniv.

Flora — AP126

Birds — AP127

1987, July 8 Litho. *Perf. 13½x14*

C755 AP126 10c Eupatorium cyrillinelsonii 15 15
C756 AP126 20c Salvia ernesti-vargasii 18 15

C757 AP126 95c Robinsonella erasmi-sosae 85 40
Set value 55

1987, Sept. 10 Litho. *Perf. 13½x14*

C758 AP127 50c Eumomota superciliosa 45 25
C759 AP127 60c Ramphastos sulfuratus 60 30
C760 AP127 85c Amazona autumnalis 75 40

Natl. Autonomous University of Honduras, 30th Anniv. — AP128

1987, Dec. 10 Litho. *Perf. 13½*

C761 AP128 1 l blk, brt yel & dark red 90 45

Natl. Red Cross, 50th Anniv. — AP129

1987, Dec. 23 Litho. *Perf. 13½*

C762 AP129 20c red & dk ultra 18 15

17th Regional Meeting of Lions Intl. — AP130

1988, Jan. 27 Litho. *Perf. 13½*

C763 AP130 95c brt blue & org yel 85 40

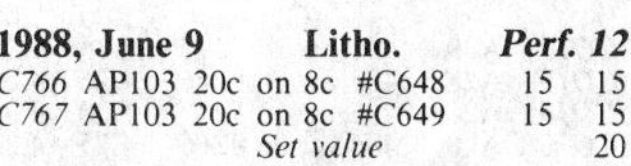

Atlantida Bank, 75th Anniv. AP131

Main offices: 10c, La Ceiba, Atlantida, 1913. 85c, Tegucigalpa, 1988.

1988, Feb. 10

C764 AP131 10c multi 15 15
C765 AP131 85c mutli 75 40
a. Souv. sheet of 2, #358-359, imperf. 90 90
Set value 45

No. C765a sold for 1 l.

L.0.20

Nos. C648-C649 Surcharged

1988, June 9 Litho. *Perf. 12*

C766 AP103 20c on 8c #C648 15 15
C767 AP103 20c on 8c #C649 15 15
Set value 20

L.0.05

Nos. C646-C647 Surcharged

1988, July 8 Litho. *Perf. 12*

C768 AP103 5c on 6c #C646 15 15
C769 AP103 5c on 6c #C647 15 15
Set value 15 15

Postman — AP132

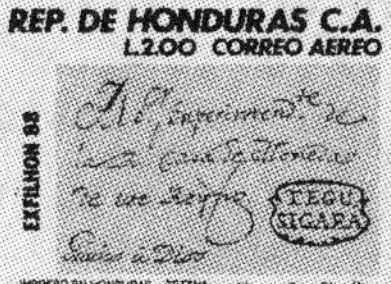

Tegucigalpa Postmark on Stampless Cover, 1789 AP133

1988, Sept. 11 Litho. *Perf. 13½*

C770 AP132 85c dull red brn 1.05 40
C771 AP133 2 l dull red brn & ver 2.50 1.00

EXFILHON '88.

Summer Olympics Type of 1988

1988, Sept. 30 Litho. *Perf. 13½*

C772 A62 85c Running, vert. 1.05 40
C773 A62 1 l Baseball, soccer, basketball 1.20 50

Discovery of America, 500th Anniv. (in 1992) AP134

Pre-Colombian pottery artifacts: 10c, Footed vase, vert. 25c, Bowl. 30c, Footed bowl. 50c, Pitcher, vert. 1 l, Rectangular footed bowl.

1988 Litho. *Perf. 13½*

C774 AP134 10c multicolored 15 15
C775 AP134 25c multicolored 38 15
C776 AP134 30c multicolored 45 15
C777 AP134 50c multicolored 75 25

Size: 115x83mm

Imperf

C778 AP134 1 l multicolored 1.50

Nos. C652-C653 and C576 Surcharged

1988 Litho. *Perf. 12, 13½*

C779 AP103 10c on 16c #C652 15 15
C780 AP103 10c on 16c #C653 15 15
C781 AP94 50c on 16c #C576 60 40

Issue dates: 10c, Apr. 7, 50c, May 25.

No. C752 Overprinted

"BICENTENARIO DE LA REVOLUCION FRANCESA", 1789-1989

1989, July 14 Litho. *Imperf.*

C782 AP124 1.50 l multi 1.80

French revolution, bicent.

Nos. C629 and C593 Surcharged

L.0.15 L. 0.15

Type I- Old denomination covered by an "X."
Type II- Covered by a rectangle.

1989 Litho. *Perf. 14, 13½*

C783 AP101 15c on 6c #C629, I 18
C783A AP101 15c on 6c #C629, II 1.00
C784 AP96 1 l on 16c #C593 1.25

Issue date: 1 l, June 15.

Nos. C699 and C616 Surcharged

1989 Litho. *Perf. 14½, 12*

C785 AP112 20c on 16c #C699 20
C786 AP99 95c on 18c #C616 75

Nos. C594 and C585 Surcharged with New Denomination and "IV Juegos / Olimpicos / Centroamericanos"

1989 *Perf. 13½*

C787 AP96 75c on 18c #C594 (S) 98
C788 AP95 85c on 18c #C585 1.10

World Wildlife Fund — AP135

Various *Mono ateles.*

1990 Litho. *Perf. 13½*

C789 AP135 10c shown 25
C790 AP135 10c Adult, young 25
C791 AP135 20c Adult hanging, diff. 50
C792 AP135 20c Adult, young, diff. 50

No. C621 Surcharged

1990 Litho. *Perf. 14*

C793 AP100 20c on 14c multi 15

Nos. C621 and C636 Surcharged "50 Aniversario / IHCI" / 1939-1989

1990

C794 AP102 20c on 14c No. 636 15
C795 AP100 1 l on 14c No. 621 45

No. C665 Surcharged

ITALIA'90 L.1.00

1990 Litho. *Perf. 12*

C796 AP104 1 l on 55c multi 45

World Cup Soccer Championships, Italy.

No. C707 Ovptd. in Margin "CAMPEONATO MUNDIAL DE FUTBOL Italia '90," and Character Trademark
Souvenir Sheet

1990 *Perf. 14*

C797 AP113 1.50 l multi 70

No. C577 Surcharged in Black

L. 0.20

1990 Litho. *Perf. 13½*

C798 AP94 20c on 18c multi 15

FAO, 45th Anniv. AP136

1990, Oct. 16 Litho. *Perf. 13½*

C799 AP136 95c yel, blk, bl, grn 55

17th Interamerican Congress of Industry and Construction — AP137

1990, Nov. 21 Litho. *Perf. 13½*

C800 AP137 20c Map, vert. 15
C801 AP137 1 l Jose Cecilio Del Valle Palace 60

AP138

Christmas — AP139

1990, Nov. 30 Litho. *Perf. 13½*

C802 AP138 20c shown 15
C803 AP138 95c Madonna and Child, vert. 55

Size: 112x82mm

Imperf

C804 AP139 3 l Poinsettia 1.75

Salesian Order in Honduras, 80th Anniv. AP140

1990, Dec. 28 Litho. *Perf. 13½*

C805 AP140 75c St. John Bosco 45
C806 AP140 1 l Natl. Youth Sanctuary 60

Pres. Rafael Leonardo Callejas — AP141

1991, Jan. 31

C807 AP141 30c Taking oath 18
C808 AP141 2 l Portrait 1.20

Moths and Butterflies AP142

1991, Feb. 28 Litho. *Perf. 13½*

C809 AP142 85c Strymon melinus 50
C810 AP142 90c Diorina sp. 55
C811 AP142 1.50 l Hyalophora cecropia 90

Size: 114x82mm

Imperf

C812 AP142 5 l Papilio polixenes 3.00

Notary Day — AP143

1991, May 22 Litho. *Perf. 13½*

C813 AP143 50c multicolored 35

Rafael Heliodoro Valle, Birth Cent. — AP144

1991, July 26 Litho. *Perf. 13½*

C815 AP144 2 l pale pink & blk 1.25

Churches AP145

Discovery of America, 500th Anniv. emblem and: 30c, Church of St. Manuel of Colohete, Gracias. 95c, Church of Our Lady of Mercy, Gracias. 1 l, Comayagua Cathedral.

1991 Litho. *Perf. 13½*

C816 AP145 30c multicolored 18
C817 AP145 95c multicolored 55
C818 AP145 1 l multicolored 60

Latin American Institute, 25th Anniv. AP146

1991, June 20

C819 AP146 1 l multicolored 60

Flowers AP147

1991, Apr. 30

C820 AP147 30c Rhyncholaelia glauca 18
C821 AP147 50c Oncidium splendidum, vert. 30
C822 AP147 95c Laelia anceps, vert. 55
C823 AP147 1.50 l Cattleya skinneri 90

Espamer '91, Buenos Aires AP148

1991, July 1

C824 AP148 2 l multicolored 1.20

Size: 101x82mm

Imperf

C825 AP148 5 l like #C824 3.00

Discovery of America, 500th anniv. (in 1992).

11th Pan American Games, Havana AP149

1991, Aug. 8

C826 AP149 30c Equestrian 18
C827 AP149 85c Judo 50
C828 AP149 95c Men's swimming 55

Size: 114x83mm

Imperf

C829 AP149 5 l Women's swimming 3.00

Pre-Columbian Culture — AP150

UPAEP emblem, artifacts and: 25c, ears of corn. 40c, ear of corn, map. 1.50 l, map.

1991 Litho. *Perf. 13½*

C830 AP150 25c multicolored 15
C831 AP150 40c multicolored 25
C832 AP150 1.50 l multicolored 90

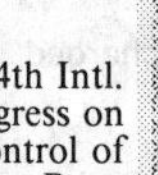

4th Intl. Congress on Control of Insect Pests AP151

Designs: 30c, Tactics to control pests. 75c, Integration of science. 1 l, Cooperation between farmers and scientists. 5 l, Pests and biological controls.

1991

C833 AP151 30c multicolored 18
C834 AP151 75c multicolored 45
C835 AP151 1 l multicolored 60

Size: 115x83mm

Imperf

C836 AP151 5 l multicolored 3.00

AIR POST SEMI-POSTAL STAMPS

No. C13C Surcharged with Plus Sign and Surtax in Black

Unwmk.

1929, June 5 Engr. *Perf. 12*

CB1 AP1 50c + 5c carmine 42 28
CB2 AP1 50c + 10c carmine 52 35
CB3 AP1 50c + 15c carmine 70 52
CB4 AP1 50c + 20c carmine 90 70

AIR POST SPECIAL DELIVERY STAMPS

No. CO52 Surcharged in Red

ENTREGA INMEDIATA 1953 L 0.20

Perf. 13½x14

1953, Dec. 8 Engr. Unwmk.

CE1 AP65 20c on 1c rose lil & olive 2.50 1.00

Transport Plane APSD1

1956, Oct. 3 *Perf. 13x12½*

CE2 APSD1 20c black & red 75 42

Surcharges on No. CE2 (see Nos. C421, C477) eliminate its special delivery character.

Catalogue values for unused stamps in this section, from this point to the end of the section, are for Never Hinged items.

Stamp Centenary Type of Air Post Issue

Design: 20c, Mailman on motorcycle.

1966, May 31 Litho. *Perf. 14x14½*

CE3 AP81 20c bis brn, brn & gold 60 42

Centenary (in 1965) of the first Honduran postage stamp.

The "HABILITADO" overprint on No. CE3 (see No. C479) eliminates its special delivery character.

Independence Type of Air Post Issue

1972, May 19 Litho. *Perf. 13*

CE4 AP89 20c Corsair plane 30 30

Same Surcharged

1975

CE5 AP89 60c on 20c 85 60

Forest Protection Type of Air Post Issue

Design: Stag in forest.

1976, May 28 Litho. *Perf. 13½*

CE6 AP96 60c org & multi 60 45

AIR POST OFFICIAL STAMPS

Official Stamps Nos. O78 to O81 Overprinted in Red, Green or Black

Servicio aéreo Habilitado VI—1930

1930 *Perf. 11, 11½*

CO1 A24 10c deep blue (R) 1.25 1.25
CO2 A24 20c yel brown 1.25 1.25
a. Vertical pair, imperf. between 14.00
CO3 A24 50c ver (Bk) 1.40 1.40
CO4 A24 1p emerald (R) 1.25 1.25

OA1

Green Surcharge

CO5 OA1 5c on 6c red vio 1.00 1.00
a. "1910" for "1930" 2.75 2.75
b. "1920" for "1930" 2.75 2.75

The overprint exists in other colors and on other denominations but the status of these is questioned.

Official Stamps of 1931 Overprinted

Servicio Aéreo Exterior. Habilitado X. 1931.

1931 Unwmk. *Perf. 12*

CO6 O2 1c ultra 35 35
CO7 O2 2c black brn 85 85
CO8 O2 5c olive gray 1.00 1.00
CO9 O2 6c orange red 1.00 1.00
a. Inverted overprint 24.00 24.00
CO10 O2 10c dark green 1.25 1.25
CO11 O2 15c olive brn 2.00 1.75
a. Inverted overprint 20.00 20.00
CO12 O2 20c red brown 2.00 1.75
CO13 O2 50c gray vio 1.40 1.40
CO14 O2 1p dp orange 2.00 1.75
Nos. CO6-CO14 (9) 11.85 11.10

In the setting of the overprint there are numerous errors in the spelling and punctuation, letters omitted and similar varieties.

This set is known with blue overprint. A similar overprint is known in larger type, but its status has not been fully determined.

Postage Stamps of 1918-30 Surcharged Type "a" or Type "b" (#CO22-CO23) in Green, Black, Red and Blue

a **Aéreo Oficial Vale L. 0.70 1933**

b **Aéreo oficial Vale L. 0.90 1933**

1933 Wmk. 209, Unwmk.

CO15 A39 20c on 2c #295 (G) 3.25 3.25
CO16 A39 20c on 2c #296 (G) 3.25 3.25
CO17 A39 20c on 2c #297 (G) 3.25 3.25
CO17A A39 40c on 2c #295 2.00 2.00
CO18 A39 40c on 2c #297 (G) 7.00 7.00
CO18A A39 40c on 2c #297 4.25 4.25
CO19 A28 40c on 5c #246 4.25 4.25
CO19A A28 40c on 5c #247 7.00 7.00
CO20 A28 40c on 5c #266 4.25 4.25

CO20A A28 40c on 5c #267 9.00 9.00
CO20B A28 40c on 5c #267 (R) 14.00 14.00
CO21 A20 70c on 5c #183 3.00 3.00
CO22 A24 70c on 10c #214 (R) 3.25 3.25
CO23 A22 1 l on 20c #191 (Bl) 3.25 3.25
CO24 A24 1 l on 50c #216 (Bl) 14.00 14.00
CO25 A22 1.20 l on 1p #193 (Bl) 1.00 1.00
Nos. CO15-CO25 (16) 86.00 86.00

Official Stamps of 1915-29 Surcharged Type "a" or Type "b" (#CO28-CO29, CO33-CO41, CO43) in Black, Red, Green, Orange, Carmine or Blue

CO26 O1 40c on 5c #O84 (Bk) 95 95
CO27 O1 40c on 5c #O84 (R) 25.00 25.00
CO28 A24 60c on 6c #O77 (Bk) 70 70
CO29 A24 60c on 6c #O77 (G) 25.00 25.00
CO30 A20 70c on 5c #O60 (Bk) 5.25 5.25
CO31 A19 70c on 10c #O62 (R) 9.00 9.00
CO32 A19 70c on 10c #O62 (Bk) 7.75 7.75
CO33 A22 70c on 10c #O70 (R) 4.50 4.00
CO34 A24 70c on 10c #O78 (O) 3.50 3.50
CO35 A24 70c on 10c #O78 (C) 4.50 4.50
CO36 A22 70c on 15c #O71 (R) 87.50 87.50
CO37 A22 90c on 10c #O70 (R) 5.25 5.25
CO38 A22 90c on 15c #O71 (R) 3.75 3.75
CO38A A24 1 l on 2c #O76 1.40 1.40
CO39 A22 1 l on 20c #O72 2.50 2.50
CO39A A24 1 l on 20c #O79 3.75 3.75
CO40 A22 1 l on 50c #O73 1.90 1.90
CO41 A24 1 l on 50c #O80 4.25 4.25

CO42 A20 1.20 l on 1p #O65 9.00 7.00
CO43 A24 1.20 l on 1p #O81 1.50 1.50
Nos. CO26-CO43 (20) 206.95 204.45

Varieties of foregoing surcharges exist.

Merchant Flag and Seal of Honduras OA2

1939, Feb. 27 Unwmk. *Perf. 12½*
CO44 OA2 2c dp bl & grn 15 15
CO45 OA2 5c dp bl & org 15 15
CO46 OA2 8c dp bl & brn 15 15
CO47 OA2 15c dp bl & car 28 20
CO48 OA2 46c dp bl & ol grn 38 28
CO49 OA2 50c dp bl & vio 48 28
CO50 OA2 1 l dp bl & red brown 1.75 1.25
CO51 OA2 2 l dp bl & red orange 3.75 2.25
Nos. CO44-CO51 (8) 7.09 4.71

For overprints and surcharges see Nos. C101-C117.

Types of Air Post Stamps of 1952 Overprinted in Red — OFICIAL

Perf. 13½x14, 14x13½
1952 Engr. Unwmk.
CO52 AP65 1c rose lil & ol 15 15
CO53 AP65 2c brn & vio 15 15
CO54 AP65 8c dp car & blk 15 15
CO55 AP66 16c pur & dk grn 25 25
CO56 AP65 30c dk bl & blk 52 52
CO57 AP65 1 l dk grn & dk brown 1.75 1.75
CO58 AP65 2 l bl & red brn 3.50 3.50
CO59 AP66 5 l red org & blk 8.50 8.50
Nos. CO52-CO59 (8) 14.97 14.97

Queen Isabella I of Spain, 500th birth anniv.
For surcharge see No. CE1.

No. C222 and Types of Air Post Stamps of 1953 Overprinted in Red — OFICIAL

Engraved; Center of 1c Litho.
1953, Dec. 18 *Perf. 12½*
Frames in Black
CO60 AP67 1c ultra & vio bl 15 15
CO61 AP97 2c dp bl grn 15 15
CO62 AP67 3c orange 15 15
CO63 AP67 5c deep car 16 16
CO64 AP67 15c dk brown 22 22
CO65 AP67 30c purple 40 40
CO66 AP67 1 l ol gray 3.75 2.50
CO67 AP67 2 l lilac rose 4.50 3.25
CO68 AP67 5 l ultra 10.50 8.00
Nos. CO60-CO68 (9) 19.98 14.98

Issued to honor the United Nations.

Types of Air Post Stamps Overprinted in Red — OFICIAL

Engraved; 8c Lithographed
1956, Oct. 3 *Perf. 13x12½*
CO69 AP68 1c blk & brn car 15 15
CO70 AP69 2c blk & mag 15 15
CO71 AP68 3c blk & rose vio 15 15
CO72 AP69 4c blk & org 15 15
CO73 AP69 5c blk & bl grn 15 15
CO74 AP68 8c vio & multi 15 15
CO75 AP68 10c blk & red brn 15 15
CO76 AP68 12c blk & car rose 15 15
CO77 AP68 15c car & blk 15 15
CO78 AP68 20c blk & ol brn 15 15
CO79 AP69 24c blk & blue 18 18
CO80 AP68 25c blk & rose vio 18 18
CO81 AP68 30c blk & grn 20 20
CO82 AP68 40c blk & red org 26 26
CO83 AP69 50c blk & brn red 32 32
CO84 AP68 60c blk & rose vio 38 38
CO85 AP68 1 l blk & brn 1.40 1.10
CO86 AP69 2 l blk & dk bl 2.75 2.25
CO87 AP69 5 l blk & vio bl 5.75 5.25
Nos. CO69-CO87 (19) 12.92 11.62

Nos. C269-C278 Overprinted Vertically in Red (Horizontally on Nos. CO89 and CO91) — OFICIAL

1957, Oct. 21 Litho. *Perf. 13*
Frames in Black
CO88 AP70 1c buff & aqua 15 15
CO89 AP70 2c org, pur & emer 15 15
CO90 AP70 5c pink & ultra 15 15
a. Inverted overprint
CO91 AP70 8c org, vio & ol 15 15
CO92 AP70 10c vio & brn 15 15
CO93 AP70 12c lt grn & ultra 15 15
CO94 AP70 15c grn & brn 16 15
CO95 AP70 30c pink & sl 55 22
CO96 AP70 1 l bl & brn 1.40 1.00
CO97 AP70 2 l lt grn & sl 2.75 2.25
Nos. CO88-CO97 (10) 5.76 4.52

Types of Lincoln Air Post Stamps 1959 Overprinted in Red — OFICIAL

1959 Engr. *Perf. 13½*
Flags in National Colors
CO98 AP72 1c ocher 15 15
CO99 AP73 2c gray olive 15 15
a. Inverted overprint
CO100 AP73 3c red brown 15 15
CO101 AP73 5c ultra 15 15
CO102 AP73 10c dull pur 15 15
a. Overprint omitted
CO103 AP73 12c red org 15 15
CO104 AP72 15c dark brn 15 15
CO105 AP73 25c black 20 15
CO106 AP73 50c dark car 32 25
CO107 AP73 1 l purple 75 65
CO108 AP73 2 l dark bl 1.40 1.10
a. Min. sheet of 6, 2c, 5c, 12c, 15c, 50c, 2 l, imperf. 2.50 2.00
CO109 AP73 5 l green 4.50 3.75
Nos. CO98-CO109 (12) 8.22 6.95

Catalogue values for unused stamps in this section, from this point to the end of the section, are for Never Hinged items.

No. CO55 Overprinted: "IN MEMORIAM / Sir Winston / Churchill / 1874-1965"

1965, Dec. 20 *Perf. 14x13½*
CO110 AP66 16c pur & dk grn 70 70

See note after No. C379.

Nos. C336-C344 Overprinted in Red: — OFICIAL

1965 Photo. *Perf. 14*
Black Design and Inscription
CO111 AP76 1c yel grn 15 15
CO112 AP76 2c pale rose lil 15 15
CO113 AP76 5c lt ultra 15 15
CO114 AP76 8c bluish grn 15 15
CO115 AP76 10c buff 25 25
CO116 AP76 12c lemon 32 32
CO117 AP76 1 l lt ocher 3.50 3.25
CO118 AP76 2 l pale ol grn 7.75 7.00
CO119 AP76 3 l rose 9.50 8.50
Nos. CO111-CO119 (9) 21.92 19.92

OFFICIAL STAMPS

Type of Regular Issue of 1890 Overprinted in Red — OFICIAL

1890 Unwmk. *Perf. 12*
O1 A5 1c pale yellow 18
O2 A5 2c pale yellow 18
O3 A5 5c pale yellow 18
O4 A5 10c pale yellow 18
O5 A5 20c pale yellow 18
O6 A5 25c pale yellow 18
O7 A5 30c pale yellow 18
O8 A5 40c pale yellow 18
O9 A5 50c pale yellow 18
O10 A5 75c pale yellow 18
O11 A5 1p pale yellow 18
Nos. O1-O11 (11) 1.98

Type of Regular Issue of 1891 Overprinted in Red

1891
O12 A6 1c yellow 18
O13 A6 2c yellow 18
O14 A6 5c yellow 18
O15 A6 10c yellow 18
O16 A6 20c yellow 18
O17 A6 25c yellow 18
O18 A6 30c yellow 18
O19 A6 40c yellow 18
O20 A6 50c yellow 18
O21 A6 75c yellow 18
O22 A6 1p yellow 18
Nos. O12-O22 (11) 1.98

Nos. O1 to O22 were never placed in use. Cancellations were applied to remainders. They exist with overprint inverted, double, triple and omitted; also, imperf. and part perf.

Regular Issue of 1898 Overprinted — OFICIAL

1898-99 *Perf. 11½*
O23 A12 5c dl ultra 20
O24 A12 10c dark bl 20
O25 A12 20c dull org 28
O26 A12 50c org red 35
O27 A12 1p blue grn 60
Nos. O23-O27 (5) 1.63

Counterfeits of basic stamps and of overprint exist.

Regular Issue of 1911 Overprinted — OFICIAL

1911-15 *Perf. 12, 14*
Carmine Overprint
O28 A15 1c violet 1.50 60
a. Inverted overprint 2.00
b. Double overprint 2.00
O29 A15 6c ultra 2.50 2.00
a. Inverted overprint 2.50
O30 A15 10c blue 1.50 1.25
a. "OFICAIL" 2.50
b. Double overprint 3.50
O31 A15 20c yellow 10.00 7.50
O32 A15 50c brown 7.00 6.00
O33 A15 1p ol grn 12.00 10.00
Nos. O28-O33 (6) 34.50 27.35

Black Overprint
O34 A15 2c green 1.00 70
a. "CFICIAL" 5.00
O35 A15 5c carmine 1.50 1.00
a. Perf. 12 7.50 5.00
O36 A15 6c ultra 4.50 4.50
O37 A15 10c blue 3.50 3.50
O38 A15 20c yellow 1.75 1.75
O39 A15 50c brown 5.50 4.00
Nos. O34-O39 (6) 17.75 15.45

Counterfeits of overprint of Nos. O28-O39 exist.

With Additional Surcharge — 10 cts.

1913-14
O40 A15 1c on 5c car 1.75 1.50
O41 A15 2c on 5c car 2.00 1.50
O42 A15 10c on 1c vio 4.00 3.50
a. "OFICIAL" inverted 7.50
O43 A15 20c on 1c vio 3.00 2.50

On No. O40 the surcharge reads "1 cent." Nos. O40-O43 exist with double surcharge.

No. O43 Surcharged Vertically in Black, Yellow or Maroon — OFICIAL 10 cts.

1914
O44 A15 10c on 20c on 1c 7.00 7.00
a. Maroon surcharge 20.00 20.00
O45 A15 10c on 20c on 1c (Y) 30.00 30.00

No. O35 Surcharged — 10c

1915
O46 A15 10c on 5c car *20.00 20.00*

No. O39 Surcharged — OFICIAL $ 0.20

O47 A15 20c on 50c brn 5.00 5.00

Regular Issues of 1913-14 Overprinted in Red or Black — OFICIAL

1915 *Perf. 11½*
O48 A17 1c brn (R) 40 40
a. "OFICAIL" 3.00
O49 A17 2c car (Bk) 40 40
a. "OFICAIL" 3.50
b. Double overprint 4.00
O50 A18 5c ultra (Bk) 40 40
a. "OFIC" 4.00
O51 A18 5c ultra (R) 1.00 1.00
a. "OFIC"
b. "OFICAIL"
O52 A18 6c pur (Bk) 1.50 1.50
a. 6c red lil (Bk)
O53 A17 10c brn (Bk) 1.25 1.25
O54 A17 20c brn (Bk) 3.00 3.00
O55 A17 20c brn (R) 3.00 3.00
a. Double overprint (R+Bk) 10.00
b. "OFICAIL"
O56 A18 50c rose (Bk) 6.00 6.00
Nos. O48-O56 (9) 16.95 16.95

The 10c blue, formerly listed, had the overprint "OFICIAL" in different type from the other stamps of the series. It is stated that forty copies were overprinted for the Postmaster General but the stamp was never put in use or on sale at the post office.

No. 152 Surcharged — OFICIAL. $ 0,01

O57 A17 1c on 2c car 2.00 2.00
a. "0.10" for "0.01" 4.25 4.25
b. "0.20" for "0.01" 4.25 4.25
c. Double surcharge 8.50 8.50
d. As "a," double surcharge 77.50
e. As "b," double surcharge 77.50

Regular Issue of 1915-16 Overprinted in Black or Red. — OFICIAL

1915-16
O58 A19 1c choc (Bk) 20 20
O59 A19 2c car (Bk) 20 20
a. Tete beche pair 1.25 1.25
b. Double overprint 2.00
c. Double overprint, one inverted 2.00
d. "b" and "c" in tete beche pair
O60 A20 5c brt blue (R) 30 30
a. Inverted overprint 3.00
O61 A20 6c deep pur (R) 40 40
a. Black overprint 3.00
b. Inverted overprint 2.00 2.00
O62 A19 10c dl bl (R) 40 40
O63 A19 20c red brn (Bk) 60 60
a. Tete beche pair 2.50
O64 A20 50c red (Bk) 1.75 1.75
O65 A20 1p yel grn (C) 3.75 3.75
Nos. O58-O65 (8) 7.60 7.60

The 6c, 10c and 1p exist imperf.

Regular Issue of 1919 Overprinted OFICIAL

1921

No.	Type	Description	Unused	Used
O66	A22	1c brown	*2.25*	*2.25*
a.		Inverted overprint	3.00	3.00
O67	A22	2c carmine	*6.50*	*6.50*
a.		Inverted overprint	3.00	3.00
O68	A22	5c lilac rose	*6.50*	*6.50*
a.		Inverted overprint	3.00	
O69	A22	6c brt vio	50	50
a.		Inverted overprint		
O70	A22	10c dull blue	60	60
a.		Double overprint		
O71	A22	15c light blue	70	70
a.		Inverted overprint	2.00	
b.		Double ovpt., one inverted	4.00	
O72	A22	20c brown	1.00	1.00
O73	A22	50c light brown	1.50	1.50
O74	A22	1p yellow green	3.00	3.00
		Nos. O66-O74 (9)	22.55	22.55

Regular Issue of 1924 Overprinted

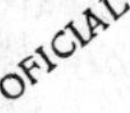

1924 *Perf. 11, 11½*

No.	Type	Description	Unused	Used
O75	A24	1c olive brn	15	15
O76	A24	2c deep rose	20	20
O77	A24	6c red vio	30	30
O78	A24	10c deep bl	50	50
O79	A24	20c yel brn	60	60
O80	A24	50c vermilion	1.25	1.25
O81	A24	1p emerald	2.00	2.00
		Nos. O75-O81 (7)	5.00	5.00

J. C. del Valle — O1

Designs: 2c, J. R. Molina. 5c, Coffee tree. 10c, J. T. Reyes. 20c, Tegucigalpa Cathedral. 50c, San Lorenzo Creek. 1p, Radio station.

1929 Litho. Wmk. 209 *Perf. 11½*

No.	Type	Description	Unused	Used
O82	O1	1c blue	15	15
O83	O1	2c carmine	20	20
a.		2c rose	20	20
O84	O1	5c purple	35	35
O85	O1	10c emerald	50	35
O86	O1	20c dk bl	60	60
O87	O1	50c org, grn & bl	1.00	1.00
O88	O1	1p buff	1.75	1.75
		Nos. O82-O88 (7)	4.55	4.40

Nos. O82-O88 exist imperf.

For overprints and surcharges see Nos. 282, 284, C37-C40, C59, C62-C63, CO26-CO27.

View of Tegucigalpa O2

1931 Unwmk. Engr. *Perf. 12*

No.	Type	Description	Unused	Used
O89	O2	1c ultra	30	20
O90	O2	2c black brn	30	20
O91	O2	5c olive gray	35	25
O92	O2	6c orange red	40	32
O93	O2	10c dark green	50	35
O94	O2	15c olive brn	65	42
O95	O2	20c red brown	75	50
O96	O2	50c gray vio	1.00	65
O97	O2	1p dp orange	1.75	1.75
		Nos. O89-O97 (9)	6.00	4.64

For overprints see Nos. CO6-CO14, O98-O105.

Official Stamps of 1931 Overprinted in Black

HABILITADO
1935-1938

1936-37

No.	Type	Description	Unused	Used
O98	O2	1c ultra	25	25
O99	O2	2c black brn	25	25
a.		Inverted overprint	10.00	
O100	O2	5c olive gray	30	30
O101	O2	6c red orange	40	40
O102	O2	10c dark green	40	40
O103	O2	15c olive brn	50	50
a.		Inverted overprint	5.00	
O104	O2	20c red brown	1.00	1.00
a.		"1938-1935"		
O105	O2	50c gray vio	4.00	3.00
		Nos. O98-O105 (8)	7.10	6.10

Double overprints exist on 1c and 2c. No. O97 with this overprint is fraudulent.

POSTAL TAX STAMPS

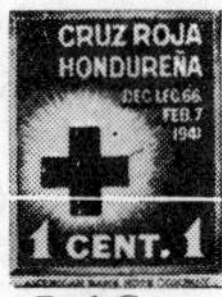

Red Cross PT1

Francisco Morazan PT2

Engr.; Cross Litho.

1941 Unwmk. *Perf. 12*

No.	Type	Description	Unused	Used
RA1	PT1	1c blue & carmine	25	15

Obligatory on all domestic or foreign mail, the tax to be used by the Honduran Red Cross.

1941 Engr.

No.	Type	Description	Unused	Used
RA2	PT2	1c copper brown	32	15

Francisco Morazan, 100th anniv. of death.

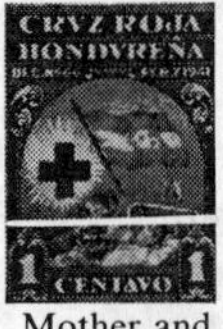

Mother and Child — PT3

Henri Dunant — PT4

1945 Engr.; Cross Litho.

No.	Type	Description	Unused	Used
RA3	PT3	1c ol brn, car & bl	25	15

The tax was for the Honduran Red Cross.

Similar to Type of 1945
Large Red Cross

1950

No.	Type	Description	Unused	Used
RA4	PT3	1c olive brn & red	25	15

The tax was for the Honduran Red Cross.

1959 *Perf. 13x13½*

No.	Type	Description	Unused	Used
RA5	PT4	1c blue & red	20	15

The tax was for the Red Cross.

Henri Dunant — PT5

Design: No. RA7, as PT5, but redrawn; country name panel at bottom, value at right, "El poder . . ." at top.

1964, Dec. 15 Litho. *Perf. 11*

No.	Type	Description	Unused	Used
RA6	PT5	1c brt grn & red	20	15
RA7	PT5	1c brown & red	20	15
		Set value		16

The tax was for the Red Cross.

Nurse and Patient — PT6

1969, June Litho. *Perf. 13½*

No.	Type	Description	Unused	Used
RA8	PT6	1c light blue & red	20	15

The tax was for the Red Cross.

HORTA

LOCATION — An administrative district of the Azores, consisting of the islands of Pico, Fayal, Flores and Corvo

GOVT. — A district of the Republic of Portugal

AREA — 305 sq. mi.

POP. — 49,000 (approx.)

CAPITAL — Horta

1000 Reis = 1 Milreis

King Carlos
A1 A2

Chalk-surfaced Paper

Perf. 11½, 12½, 13½

1892-93 Typo. Unwmk.

No.	Type	Description	Unused	Used
1	A1	5r yellow	1.50	1.00
2	A1	10r redsh vio	1.50	1.25
3	A1	15r chocolate	2.00	1.40
4	A1	20r lavender	2.50	1.75
5	A1	25r dp grn, perf. 11½	2.00	40
a.		Perf. 13½	2.50	1.40
6	A1	50r blue	3.00	1.75
a.		Perf. 13½	5.00	3.00
7	A1	75r carmine	4.75	4.00
8	A1	80r yel grn	8.00	6.00
9	A1	100r brn, *yel* ('93)	6.00	3.50
a.		Perf. 12½	90.00	45.00
10	A1	150r car, *rose* ('93)	30.00	22.50
11	A1	200r dk bl, *bl* ('93)	30.00	20.00
12	A1	300r dk bl, ('93)	35.00	24.00
		Nos. 1-12 (12)	126.25	87.55

Bisects of No. 1 were used in Aug. 1894.

The reprints have shiny white gum and clean-cut perforation 13½. The white paper is thinner than that of the originals.

1897-1905 *Perf. 11½*

Name and Value in Black Except 500r

No.	Type	Description	Unused	Used
13	A2	2½r gray	45	28
14	A2	5r orange	45	28
15	A2	10r lt grn	45	28
16	A2	15r brown	5.25	3.00
17	A2	15r gray grn ('99)	1.00	70
18	A2	20r gray vio	1.00	70
19	A2	25r sea grn	1.90	45
20	A2	25r car rose ('99)	90	48
21	A2	50r blue	1.90	70
22	A2	50r ultra ('05)	7.50	5.25
23	A2	65r slate bl ('98)	60	52
24	A2	75r rose	1.90	95
25	A2	75r brn, *yel* ('05)	9.00	7.00
26	A2	80r violet	1.10	95
27	A2	100r dk bl, *bl*	1.75	95
28	A2	115r org brn, *pink* ('98)	1.40	75
29	A2	130r gray brn, *buff* ('98)	1.40	75
30	A2	150r lt brn, *buff*	1.40	75
31	A2	180r sl, *pnksh* ('98)	1.50	90
32	A2	200r red vio, *pale lil*	4.50	3.00
33	A2	300r dk bl, *rose*	7.50	5.25
34	A2	500r blk & red, *bl*	10.50	6.75
		Nos. 13-34 (22)	63.35	40.64

Stamps of Portugal replaced those of Horta.

HUNGARY

LOCATION — Central Europe

GOVT. — Republic

AREA — 35,911 sq. mi.

POP. — 10,679,000 (est. 1984)

CAPITAL — Budapest

Prior to World War I, Hungary together with Austria comprised the Austro-Hungarian Empire. During 1850-1871 stamps listed under Austria were also used in Hungary. Copies showing clear Hungarian cancels sell for substantially more.

100 Krajczár (Kreuzer) = 1 Forint
100 Filler = 1 Korona (1900)
100 Filler = 1 Pengö (1926)
100 Filler = 1 Forint (1946)

Catalogue values for unused stamps in this country are for Never Hinged items, beginning with Scott 631 in the regular postage section, Scott B175 in the semi-postal section, Scott C45 in the airpost section, Scott CB1 in the airpost semi-postal section, Scott J167 in the postage due section, and Scott Q9 in the parcel post section.

Watermarks

Wmk. 91- "ZEITUNGS-MARKEN" in Double-lined Capitals across the Sheet

Wmk. 106- Multiple Star

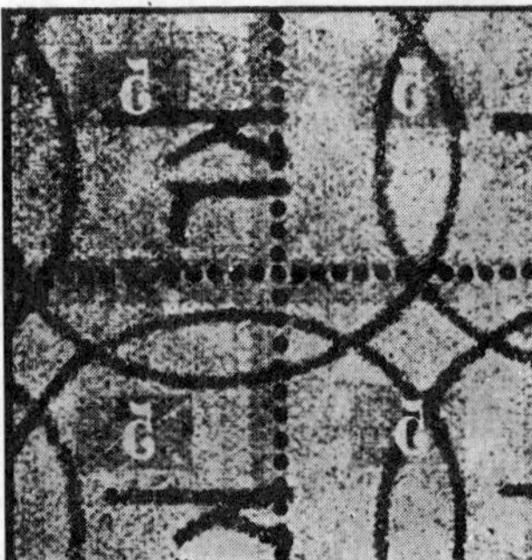

Wmk. 132- kr in Oval

Wmk. 133- Four Double Crosses

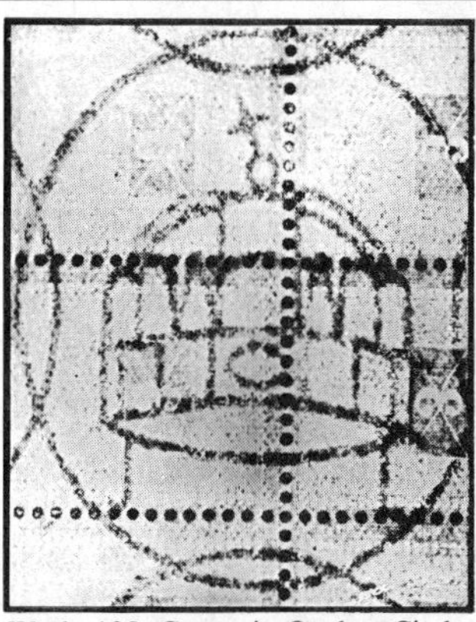

Wmk. 135- Crown in Oval or Circle, Sideways

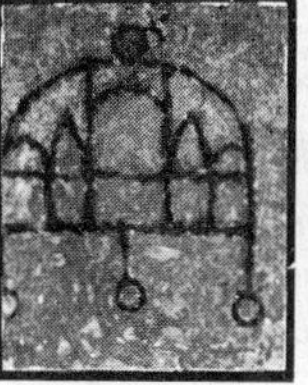

Wmk. 136

Wmk. 136a

Wmk. 137- Double Cross

Wmk. 210- Double Cross on Pyramid

Wmk. 266- Double Barred Cross, Wreath and Crown

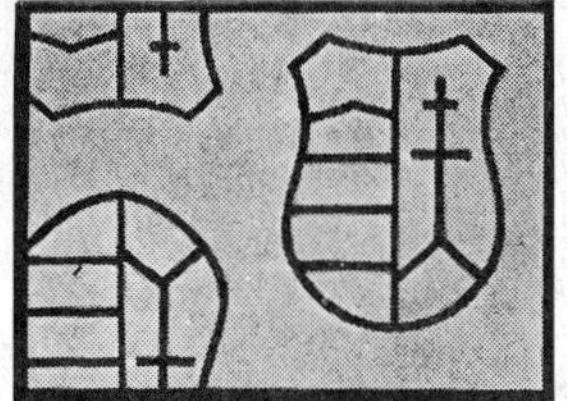

Wmk. 283- Double Barred Cross on Shield, Multiple

Perforations of Nos. 1-12 usually cut into the designs. Well-centered stamps sell at much higher prices.

Issues of the Monarchy

Franz Josef I — A1

1871 Unwmk. Litho. *Perf. 9½*

No.	Design	Description	Unused	Used
1	A1	2k orange	160.00	80.00
a.		2k yellow	600.00	150.00
2	A1	3k lt grn	425.00	300.00
3	A1	5k rose	150.00	20.00
a.		5k brick red	500.00	45.00
4	A1	10k blue	400.00	95.00
a.		10k pale blue	400.00	100.00
5	A1	15k yel brn	475.00	125.00
6	A1	25k violet	450.00	125.00
a.		25k bright violet	550.00	200.00

The first printing of No. 1, in dark yellow, was not issued because of spots on the King's face. A few copies were used at Pest in 1873.

1871-72 Engr.

No.	Design	Description	Unused	Used
7	A1	2k orange	30.00	8.50
a.		2k yellow	175.00	18.00
b.		Bisect on cover		*425.00*
8	A1	3k green	37.50	20.00
a.		3k blue green	50.00	22.50
9	A1	5k rose	30.00	2.00
a.		5k brick red	100.00	11.00
10	A1	10k dp bl	175.00	9.00
11	A1	15k brown	175.00	16.00
a.		15k copper brown	1,400.	850.00
b.		15k black brown	500.00	75.00
12	A1	25k lilac	85.00	35.00

Reprints are perf. 11½ and watermarked "kr" in oval. Value, set $300.

Crown of St. Stephen
A2 A3

Design A3 has an overall burelage of dots.

1874-76 *Perf. 12½ to 13½*

No.	Design	Description	Unused	Used
13	A2	2k rose lilac	22.50	1.50
14	A2	3k yel grn	25.00	1.50
a.		3k blue green	32.50	1.50
15	A2	5k rose	12.50	25
a.		5k dull red	27.50	95
16	A2	10k blue	50.00	1.00
17	A2	20k slate	350.00	7.00

Perf. 11½ and Compound

No.	Design	Description	Unused	Used
13a	A2	2k rose lilac	57.50	3.00
14b	A2	3k yellow green	40.00	5.75
c.		3k blue green	40.00	5.75
d.		Perf. 9½	*750.00*	*425.00*
15b	A2	5k rose	30.00	70
c.		5k dull red	35.00	70
d.		Perf. 9½	*290.00*	*190.00*
16a	A2	10k blue	70.00	2.75
17a	A2	20k slate	775.00	40.00

1881 Wmk. 132 *Perf. 11½, 12x11½*

No.	Design	Description	Unused	Used
18	A2	2k violet	1.75	25
a.		2k rose lilac	1.75	25
b.		2k slate	8.50	42
19	A2	3k blue green	1.65	15
20	A2	5k rose	10.00	15
21	A2	10k blue	5.00	32
22	A2	20k slate	8.50	65

Perf. 12½ to 13½ and Compound

No.	Design	Description	Unused	Used
18c	A2	2k violet	85.00	4.00
19a	A2	3k blue green	62.50	1.40
20a	A2	5k rose	60.00	1.40
21a	A2	10k blue	42.50	1.75
22b	A2	20k slate	425.00	8.50

1888-98 Typo. *Perf. 11½, 12x11½*

Numerals in Black

No.	Design	Description	Unused	Used
22A	A3	1k blk, one plate	90	20
c.		"1" printed separately	9.50	1.05
23	A3	2k red violet	90	32
a.		Perf. 11½	50.00	3.50
24	A3	3k green	1.40	38
a.		Perf. 11½	27.50	1.75
25	A3	5k rose	1.65	15
a.		Perf. 11½	27.50	1.40
26		8k orange	4.50	25
a.		"8" double	*62.50*	
27	A3	10k blue	4.00	65
a.		Perf. 11½	125.00	87.50
28	A3	12k brn & grn	6.50	25
29	A3	15k claret & bl	6.25	15
30	A3	20k gray	7.00	2.25
a.		Perf. 11½	250.00	160.00
31	A3	24k brn vio & red	14.00	35
32	A3	30k ol grn & brn	14.00	15
33	A3	50k red & org	24.00	60

Numerals in Red

No.	Design	Description	Unused	Used
34	A3	1fo gray bl & sil	150.00	1.50
a.		Perf. 11½	165.00	1.75
35	A3	3fo lil brn & gold	17.50	6.00

Most of Nos. 22A to 103 exist imperforate, but were never so issued.

Perf. 12x11½, 11½

1898-99 Wmk. 135

Numerals in Black

No.	Design	Description	Unused	Used
35A	A3	1k black	75	18
36	A3	2k violet	4.00	18
37	A3	3k green	3.75	18
38	A3	5k rose	2.75	15
39	A3	8k orange	11.00	1.75
40	A3	10k blue	4.00	35
41	A3	12k red brn & grn	57.50	2.00
a.		Perf. 11½	125.00	19.00
42	A3	15k rose & blue	3.50	28
43	A3	20k gray	10.00	1.10
a.		Perf. 11½	140.00	14.50
44	A3	24k vio brn & red	5.00	1.20
a.		Perf. 11½	175.00	45.00
45	A3	30k ol grn & brn	4.50	1.25
a.		Perf. 11½	65.00	19.00
46	A3	50k dl red & org	9.50	4.50
a.		Perf. 11½	*225.00*	*55.00*
		Nos. 35A-46 (12)	116.25	13.12

In the watermark with circles, a four-pointed star and "VI" appear four times in the sheet in the large spaces between the intersecting circles. The paper with the circular watermark is often yellowish and thinner than that with the oval watermark and sell for much higher prices.

See note after No. 35.

"Turul" and Crown of St. Stephen — A4

Franz Josef I Wearing Hungarian Crown — A5

1900-04 Wmk. 135

Numerals in Black

No.	Design	Description	Unused	Used
47	A4	1f gray	42	35
a.		1f dull lilac	55	35
48	A4	2f ol yel	42	15
49	A4	3f orange	45	22
50	A4	4f violet	45	15
a.		Booklet pane of 6	60.00	
51	A4	5f emerald	4.25	15
a.		Booklet pane of 6	35.00	
52	A4	6f claret	50	18
a.		6f violet brown	50	18
53	A4	6f bister ('01)	10.00	70
54	A4	6f ol grn ('04)	3.75	40
55	A4	10f carmine	3.50	15
a.		Booklet pane of 6	35.00	
56	A4	12f vio ('04)	2.25	35
57	A4	20f brn ('01)	2.75	28
58	A4	25f blue	1.65	28
a.		Booklet pane of 6	60.00	
59	A4	30f org brn	25.00	22
60	A4	35f red vio ('01)	10.50	18
a.		Booklet pane of 6	70.00	
61	A4	50f lake	9.50	90
62	A4	60f green	50.00	42
a.		Perf. 11½	200.00	15.00
63	A5	1k brn red	32.50	55
a.		Perf. 11½	35.00	2.00
64	A5	2k gray bl ('01)	175.00	7.00
a.		Perf. 11½	225.00	45.00
65	A5	3k sea green	25.00	2.50
66	A5	5k vio brn ('01)	30.00	10.00
a.		Perf. 11½	275.00	125.00
		Nos. 47-66 (20)	387.89	25.13

The watermark on Nos. 47 to 66 is always the circular form of Wmk. 135 described in the note following No. 46.

Pairs imperforate between were favor prints made for an influential Budapest collector.

For overprints and surcharges see Nos. B35-B52, 2N1-2N3, 6N1-6N6, 6NB127N1-7N6, 7NB1, 10N1.

See note after No. 35.

1908-13 Wmk. 136 *Perf. 15*

No.	Design	Description	Unused	Used
67	A4	1f slate	35	15
68	A4	2f olive yel	20	15
69	A4	3f orange	30	15
70	A4	5f emerald	15	15
c.		Booklet pane of 6		
71	A4	6f olive grn	25	15
72	A4	10f carmine	15	15
c.		Booklet pane of 6		
73	A4	12f violet	65	18
74	A4	16f gray grn ('13)	38	35
75	A4	20f dk brn	2.50	15
76	A4	25f blue	2.10	15
77	A4	30f org brn	1.75	15
78	A4	35f red vio	3.50	15
79	A4	50f lake	70	25
80	A4	60f green	2.10	15
81	A5	1k brn red	5.50	15
82	A5	2k gray blue	42.50	55
83	A5	5k vio brn	60.00	7.00
		Nos. 67-83 (17)	123.08	10.13

See note after No. 35.

1904-05 Wmk. 136a *Perf. 12x11½*

No.	Design	Description	Unused	Used
67a	A4	1f slate	95	85
68a	A4	2f olive yellow	3.50	18
69a	A4	3f orange	52	35
70a	A4	5f emerald	1.90	15
71a	A4	6f olive green	1.40	20
72a	A4	10f carmine	4.00	15
73a	A4	12f violet	1.65	1.40
75a	A4	20f dark brown	9.50	55
76a	A4	25f blue	19.00	42
77a	A4	30f orange brown	4.50	22
78a	A4	35f red violet	15.00	28
79a	A4	50f lake	13.00	2.50
c.		50f magenta	65	90
80a	A4	60f green	190.00	90
81a	A5	1k brown red	125.00	1.40
82a	A5	2k gray blue	*350.00*	40.00
c.		Perf. 11½	*425.00*	52.50
83a	A5	5k violet brown	140.00	50.00

1906 *Perf. 15*

No.	Design	Description	Unused	Used
67b	A4	1f slate	1.00	35
68b	A4	2f olive yellow	42	15
69b	A4	3f orange	90	15
70b	A4	5f emerald	42	15
71b	A4	6f olive green	1.00	15
72b	A4	10f carmine	1.00	15
73b	A4	12f violet	1.75	18
75b	A4	20f dark brown	3.50	22
76b	A4	25f blue	2.50	18
77b	A4	30f orange brown	3.25	15
78b	A4	35f red violet	19.00	15
79b	A4	50f lake	1.90	30
80b	A4	60f green	30.00	35
81b	A5	1k brown red	30.00	55
82b	A5	2k gray blue	105.00	6.50
		Nos. 67b-82b (15)	201.64	9.68

1913-16 Wmk. 137 Vert. *Perf. 15*

No.	Type	Description	Unused	Used
84	A4	1f slate	25	18
85	A4	2f olive yel	15	15
86	A4	3f orange	15	15
87	A4	5f emerald	40	15
88	A4	6f olive grn	15	15
89	A4	10f carmine	15	15
90	A4	12f vio, *yel*	18	15
91	A4	16f gray grn	28	28
92	A4	20f dk brn	22	15
93	A4	25f ultra	22	15
94	A4	30f org brn	22	15
95	A4	35f red vio	22	15
96	A4	50f lake, *bl*	28	18
a.		Cliche of 35f in plate of 50f	165.00	165.00
97	A4	60f green	3.50	1.75
98	A4	60f grn, *salmon*	70	15
99	A4	70f red brn, *grn* ('16)	22	15
100	A4	80f dl vio ('16)	22	15
101	A5	1k dull red	1.05	15
102	A5	2k dull blue	3.50	28
103	A5	5k vio brn	10.00	3.50
		Nos. 84-103 (20)	22.06	
		Set value		7.20

See note after No. 35.

For overprints and surcharges see Nos. 2N1-2N3, 6N1-6N6, 6NB127N1-7N6, 7NB1, 10N1.

Wmk. 137 Horiz.

No.	Type	Description	Unused	Used
84a	A4	1f slate	1.05	1.05
85a	A4	2f olive yellow	2.50	1.05
87a	A4	5f emerald	70	52
88a	A4	6f olive green	90	52
89b	A4	10f carmine	1.05	28
90a	A4	12f violet, *yellow*	3.25	35
92a	A4	20f dark brown	7.75	42
94a	A4	30f orange brown	52.50	28
95a	A4	35f red violet	175.00	70
96b	A4	50f lake, *blue*	15.00	11.50
97a	A4	60f green	2.25	2.10
98a	A4	60f green, *salmon*	2.00	28
101a	A5	1k dull red	22.50	42
102a	A5	2k dull blue	175.00	2.10

A5a

1916, July 1 *Perf. 15*

No.	Type	Description	Unused	Used
103A	A5a	10f violet brown		50

Although issued as a postal savings stamp, No. 103A was also valid for postage. Used value is for postal usage.

For overprints and surcharges see Nos. 2N59, 5N23, 6N50, 8N13, 10N42.

Queen Zita — A6

Charles IV — A7

1916, Dec. 30

No.	Type	Description	Unused	Used
104	A6	10f violet	40	25
105	A7	15f red	40	25

Coronation of King Charles IV and Queen Zita on Dec. 30, 1916.

Harvesting (White Numerals) — A8

1916

No.	Type	Description	Unused	Used
106	A8	10f rose	20	15
107	A8	15f violet	20	15
		Set value		15

For overprints and surcharges see Nos. B56-B57, 2N4-2N5, 5N1.

Harvesting Wheat — A9

Parliament Building at Budapest — A10

1916-18 *Perf. 15*

No.	Type	Description	Unused	Used
108	A9	2f brn org	15	15
109	A9	3f red lilac	15	15
110	A9	4f slate gray ('18)	15	15
111	A9	5f green	15	15
112	A9	6f grnsh bl	15	15
113	A9	10f rose red	24	15
114	A9	15f violet	15	15
115	A9	20f gray brn	15	15
116	A9	25f dull blue	15	15
117	A9	35f brown	15	15
118	A9	40f olive grn	15	15

Perf. 14

No.	Type	Description	Unused	Used
119	A10	50f red vio & lil	15	15
120	A10	75f brt bl & pale bl	15	15
121	A10	80f grn & pale grn	15	15
122	A10	1k red brn & cl	15	15
123	A10	2k ol brn & bis	15	15
124	A10	3k dk vio & ind	22	15
125	A10	5k dk brn & lt brn	24	15
126	A10	10k vio brn & vio	42	16
		Set value	2.00	1.10

See Nos. 335-377, 388-396. For overprints and surcharges see Nos. 153, 167, C1-C5, J76-J99, 1N1-1N21, 1N26-1N30, 1N33, 1N36-1N39, 2N6-2N27, 2N33-2N38, 2N41, 2N43-2N48, 4N1-4N4, 5N2-5N17, 6N7-6N24, 6N29-6N39, 7N7-7N30, 7N38, 7N41-7N42, 8N1-8N4, 9N1-9N2, 9N4, 10N2-10N16, 10N25-10N29, 10N31, 10N33-10N41, Szeged 1-15, 20-24, 27, 30, 32-33.

During 1921-24 various stamps then current were punched with three holes forming a triangle. These were sold at post offices and collectors and dealers who wanted them unpunched would have to purchase them through the philatelic agency at a 10% advance over face value.

Charles IV — A11

Queen Zita — A12

1918 *Perf. 15*

No.	Type	Description	Unused	Used
127	A11	10f scarlet	15	15
128	A11	15f dp vio	15	15
129	A11	20f dk brn	15	15
130	A11	25f brt bl	15	15
131	A12	40f olive grn	15	15
132	A12	50f lilac	15	15
		Set value	45	45

For overprints see Nos. 168-173, 1N32, 1N34-1N35, 2N28-2N32, 2N39-2N40, 2N42, 2N49-2N51, 5N18-5N22, 6N25-6N28, 6N40-6N43, 7N31-7N37, 7N39-7N40, 8N5, 9N3, 10N17-10N21, 10N30, 10N32, Szeged 16-19, 25-26, 28-29, 31.

Issues of the Republic

Hungarian Stamps of 1916-18 Overprinted in Black

1918-19 Wmk. 137 *Perf. 15, 14*

On Stamps of 1916-18

No.	Type	Description	Unused	Used
153	A9	2f brn org	15	15
154	A9	3f red lilac	15	15
155	A9	4f slate gray	15	15
156	A9	5f green	15	15
157	A9	6f grnsh bl	15	15
158	A9	10f rose red	15	15
159	A9	20f gray brn	22	22
162	A9	40f olive grn	15	15
163	A10	1k red brn & cl	15	15
164	A10	2k ol brn & bis	15	15
165	A10	3k dk vio & ind	20	20
166	A10	5k dk brn & lt brn	75	60
167	A10	10k vio brn & vio	80	80

On Stamps of 1918

No.	Type	Description	Unused	Used
168	A11	10f scarlet	15	15
169	A11	15f dp vio	15	15
170	A11	20f dk brn	15	15
171	A11	25f brt bl	20	20
172	A12	40f olive grn	20	20
173	A12	50f lilac	22	22
		Set value	3.30	3.10

Nos. 153-162 and 168-173 exist with overprint inverted.

A13

A14

1919-20 *Perf. 15*

No.	Type	Description	Unused	Used
174	A13	2f brn org	15	15
176	A13	4f slate gray	15	15
177	A13	5f yel grn	15	15
178	A13	6f grnsh bl	15	15
179	A13	10f red	15	15
180	A13	15f violet	15	15
181	A13	20f dk brn	15	15
182	A13	20f grn ('20)	15	15
183	A13	25f dull blue	15	15
184	A13	40f olive grn	15	15
185	A13	40f rose red ('20)	15	15
186	A13	45f orange	15	15

Perf. 14

No.	Type	Description	Unused	Used
187	A14	50f brn vio & pale vio	15	15
188	A14	60f brn & bl ('20)	15	15
189	A14	95f dk bl & bl	15	15
190	A14	1k red brn	15	15
191	A14	1k dk bl & dl bl ('20)	15	15
192	A14	1.20k dk grn & grn	15	15
193	A14	1.40k yel grn	15	15
194	A14	2k ol brn & bis	15	15
195	A14	3k dk vio & ind	15	15
196	A14	5k dk brn & brn	15	15
197	A14	10k vio brn & red vio	50	55
		Set value	1.70	1.80

The 3f red lilac, type A13, was never regularly issued without overprint (Nos. 204 and 312). In 1923 a small quantity was sold by the Government at public auction. Value $2.50.

For overprints see Nos. 203-222, 306-330, 1N40, 2N52-2N58, 6N44-6N49, 8N6-8N12, 10N22-10N24, Szeged 34-35.

Issues of the Soviet Republic

Karl Marx — A15

Sándor Petőfi — A16

Ignác Martinovics A17

György Dózsa A18

Friedrich Engels — A19

Wmk. 137 Horiz.

1919, June 14 Litho. *Perf. 12½x12*

No.	Type	Description	Unused	Used
198	A15	20f rose & brn	26	40
199	A16	45f brn org & dk grn	26	40
200	A17	60f bl gray & brn	65	90
201	A18	75f cl & vio brn	70	1.10
202	A19	80f ol db & blk brn	65	90
		Nos. 198-202 (5)	2.52	3.70

The 3f red lilac, type A13, was never regularly issued without overprint (Nos. 204 and 312). In 1923 a small quantity was sold by the Government at public auction. Value $2.50. Values are for favor cancels.

Wmk. Vertical

No.	Type	Description	Unused	Used
198a	A15	20f	2.25	
199a	A16	45f	4.75	
200a	A17	60f	2.25	
201a	A18	75f	2.25	
202a	A19	80f	27.50	
		Nos. 198a-202a (5)	39.00	

Nos. 198a-202a were not used postally.

Stamps of 1919 Overprinted in Red

MAGYAR
TANÁCS-
KÖZTÁRSASÁG.

1919, July 21 Typo. *Perf. 15*

No.	Type	Description	Unused	Used
203	A13	2f brn org	15	15
204	A13	3f red lilac	15	15
205	A13	4f slate gray	15	15
206	A13	5f yel grn	15	15
207	A13	6f grnsh bl	15	15
208	A13	10f red	15	15
209	A13	15f violet	15	15
210	A13	20f dk brn	15	15
211	A13	25f dull blue	15	15
212	A13	40f olive grn	15	15
213	A13	45f orange	15	15

Overprinted in Red

MAGYAR
TANÁCSKÖZTÁRSASÁG

Perf. 14

No.	Type	Description	Unused	Used
214	A14	50f brn vio & pale vio	15	15
215	A14	95f dk bl & bl	15	15
216	A14	1k red brn	15	15
217	A14	1.20k dk grn & grn	15	15
218	A14	1.40k yel grn	15	15
219	A14	2k ol brn & bister	28	28
220	A14	3k dk vio & ind	28	28
221	A14	5k dk brn & brn	35	35
222	A14	10k vio brn & red vio	60	60
		Set value	2.50	2.50

"Magyar Tanacsköztarsasag" on Nos. 198 to 222 means "Hungarian Soviet Republic."

Issues of the Kingdom

Stamps of 1919 Overprinted in Black

A nemzeti
hadsereg
bevonulása.
1919. XI/16.

1919, Nov. 16

No.	Type	Description	Unused	Used
306	A13	5f green	50	50
307	A13	10f rose red	50	50
308	A13	15f violet	50	50
309	A13	20f gray brn	50	50
310	A13	25f dull blue	50	50
		Nos. 306-310 (5)	2.50	2.50

Issued to commemorate the Romanian evacuation. The overprint reads: "Entry of the National Army-November 16, 1919".

Nos. 203 to 213 Overprinted in Black

1920, Jan. 26 *Perf. 15*

No.	Type	Description	Unused	Used
311	A13	2f brn org	35	35
312	A13	3f red lilac	15	15
313	A13	4f slate gray	35	35
314	A13	5f yel grn	15	15
315	A13	6f bl grn	15	15
316	A13	10f red	15	15
317	A13	15f violet	15	15
318	A13	20f dk brn	15	15
319	A13	25f dull blue	15	15
320	A13	40f olive grn	45	45
321	A13	45f orange	45	45

Nos. 214 to 222 Overprinted in Black

Perf. 14

322 A14 50f brn vio & pale vio 45 45
323 A14 95f dk bl & bl 45 45
324 A14 1k red brn 45 45
325 A14 1.20k dk grn & grn 1.10 1.10
326 A14 1.40k yel grn 1.10 1.10
327 A14 2k ol brn & bis 1.65 1.65
328 A14 3k dk vio & ind 1.65 1.65
329 A14 5k dk brn & brn 35 35
330 A14 10k vio brn & red vio 2.50 2.50
Nos. 311-330 (20) 12.35 12.35

Counterfeit overprints exist.

Types of 1916-18 Issue
Denomination Tablets Without Inner Frame on Nos. 350 to 363

1920-24 **Wmk. 137** ***Perf. 15***

335 A9 5f brn org 15 15
336 A9 10f red vio 15 15
337 A9 40f rose red 15 15
338 A9 50f yel grn 15 15
339 A9 50f bl vio ('22) 15 15
340 A9 60f black 15 15
341 A9 1k grn ('22) 15 15
342 A9 1½k brn vio ('22) 15 15
343 A9 2k grnsh bl ('22) 15 15
344 A9 2½k dp grn ('22) 15 15
345 A9 3k brn org ('22) 15 15
346 A9 4k lt red ('22) 15 15
347 A9 4½k dl vio ('22) 32 15
348 A9 5k dp brn ('22) 15 15
349 A9 6k dk bl ('22) 16 15
350 A9 10k brown ('23) 15 15
351 A9 15k slate ('23) 15 15
352 A9 20k red vio ('23) 15 15
353 A9 25k org ('23) 15 15
354 A9 40k gray grn ('23) 15 15
355 A9 50k dk bl ('23) 15 15
356 A9 100k claret ('23) 15 15
357 A9 150k dk grn ('23) 15 15
358 A9 200k grn ('23) 15 15
359 A9 300k rose red ('24) 15 15
360 A9 350k vio ('23) 32 15
361 A9 500k dk gray ('24) 35 15
362 A9 600k ol bis ('24) 35 16
363 A9 800k org yel ('24) 60 20

Perf. 14

364 A10 2.50k bl & gray bl 15 15
365 A10 3.50k gray 15 15
366 A10 10k brn ('22) 15 15
367 A10 15k dk gray ('22) 15 15
368 A10 20k red vio ('22) 15 15
369 A10 25k org ('22) 15 15
370 A10 30k claret ('22) 15 15
371 A10 40k gray grn ('22) 15 15
372 A10 50k dp bl ('22) 15 15
373 A10 100k yel brn ('22) 15 15
374 A10 400k turq bl ('23) 48 28
375 A10 500k brt vio ('23) 40 15
376 A10 1000k lilac ('24) 40 15
377 A10 2000k car ('24) 1.40 20
Set value 7.00 3.00

Nos. 372 to 377 have colored numerals.

Madonna and Child — A23

1921-25 **Typo.** ***Perf. 12***

378 A23 50k dk brn & bl 48 20
379 A23 100k ol bis & yel brn 80 40

Wmk. 133

380 A23 200k dk bl & ultra 32 18
381 A23 500k vio brn & vio 40 22
382 A23 1000k vio & red vio 40 30
383 A23 2000k grnsh bl & vio 42 45
384 A23 2500k ol brn & buff 52 35
385 A23 3000k brn red & vio 65 35
386 A23 5000k dk grn & yel grn 65 35
a. Center inverted 6,000. 4,000.
387 A23 10000k gray vio & pale bl 1.65 1.25
Nos. 378-387 (10) 6.29 4.05

Issue dates: 50k, 100k, Feb. 27, 1921, 2500k, 10,000k, 1925, others, 1923.

Types of 1916-18
Denomination Tablets Without Inner Frame on Nos. 388-394

1924 **Wmk. 133** ***Perf. 15***

388 A9 100k claret 45 28
389 A9 200k yel grn 22 15
390 A9 300k rose red 22 15
391 A9 400k dp bl 22 15
392 A9 500k dk gray 22 18
393 A9 600k ol bis 22 22
a. "800" in upper right corner 140.00 140.00
394 A9 800k org yel 48 35

Perf. 14½x14

395 A10 1000k lilac 75 18
396 A10 2000k carmine 95 28
Nos. 388-396 (9) 3.73 1.94

Nos. 395 and 396 have colored numerals.

Maurus Jókai (1825-1904), Novelist — A24

1925, Feb. 1 **Unwmk.** ***Perf. 12***

400 A24 1000k dp grn & blk brn 1.00 1.65
401 A24 2000k lt brn & blk brn 65 55
402 A24 2500k dk bl & blk brn 1.00 1.90

Crown of St. Stephen A25

Matthias Cathedral A26

Palace at Budapest — A27

Perf. 14, 15

1926-27 **Wmk. 133** **Litho.**

403 A25 1f dk gray 20 15
404 A25 2f lt bl 20 15
405 A25 3f orange 20 15
406 A25 4f violet 20 15
407 A25 6f lt grn 28 15
408 A25 8f lil rose 40 15

Typo.

409 A26 10f dp bl 35 15
410 A26 16f dk vio 35 15
411 A26 20f carmine 35 15
412 A26 25f lt brn 35 18

Perf. 14½x14

413 A27 32f dp vio & brt vio 1.00 20
414 A27 40f dk bl & bl 1.25 18
Nos. 403-414 (12) 5.13
Set value 1.20

See Nos. 428-436. For surcharges see Nos. 450-456, 466-467.

Madonna and Child — A28

1926-27 **Engr.** ***Perf. 14***

415 A28 1p violet 16.00 50
416 A28 2p red 9.00 80
417 A28 5p blue ('27) 16.00 2.75

Palace at Budapest A29

St. Stephen A30

1926-27 **Typo.**

418 A29 30f bl grn ('27) 1.00 15
419 A29 46f ultra ('27) 1.50 28
420 A29 50f brn blk ('27) 1.00 15
421 A29 70f scarlet 1.50 15

For surcharge see No. 480.

1928-29 **Engr.** ***Perf. 15***

422 A30 8f yel grn 42 30
423 A30 8f rose lake ('29) 42 30
424 A30 16f org red 55 30
425 A30 16f vio ('29) 42 28
426 A30 32f ultra 1.10 1.10
427 A30 32f bis ('29) 1.10 1.10
Nos. 422-427 (6) 4.01 3.38

890th death anniversary of St. Stephen, the first king of Hungary.

Types of 1926-27 Issue

Perf. 14, 15

1928-30 **Typo.** **Wmk. 210**

428 A25 1f black 24 15
429 A25 2f blue 20 15
430 A25 3f orange 20 15
431 A25 4f violet 20 15
432 A25 6f bl grn 20 15
433 A25 8f lil rose 24 15
434 A26 10f dp bl ('30) 2.50 15
435 A26 16f violet 50 15
436 A26 20f dl red 38 15
Nos. 428-436 (9) 4.66
Set value 60

On Nos. 428 to 433 the numerals have thicker strokes than on the same values of the 1926-27 issue.

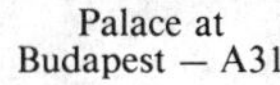

Palace at Budapest — A31

Admiral Nicholas Horthy — A32

Type A31 resembles A27 but the steamer is nearer the right of the design.

1928-31 ***Perf. 14***

437 A31 30f emer ('31) 70 20
438 A31 32f red vio 95 32
439 A31 40f dp bl 80 15
440 A31 46f apple grn 80 20
441 A31 50f ocher ('31) 80 16
Nos. 437-441 (5) 4.05 1.03

1930, Mar. 1 **Litho.** ***Perf. 15***

445 A32 8f myr grn 1.40 28
446 A32 16f purple 1.40 32
447 A32 20f carmine 3.75 1.05
448 A32 32f ol brn 3.75 3.75
449 A32 40f dl bl 7.00 1.65
Nos. 445-449 (5) 17.30 7.05

10th anniv. of the election of Adm. Nicholas Horthy as Regent, Mar. 1, 1920.

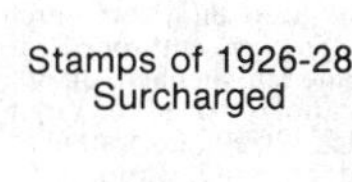

Stamps of 1926-28 Surcharged

1931, Jan. 1 ***Perf. 14, 15***

450 A25 2f on 3f org 80 40
451 A25 6f on 8f mag 80 18
a. Perf. 14 24.00 24.00
452 A26 10f on 16f vio 65 16

Wmk. 133

453 A25 2f on 3f org 3.75 3.00
454 A25 6f on 8f mag 3.00 3.00
a. Perf. 14 75.00 75.00
455 A26 10f on 16f dk vio 2.50 1.50
456 A26 20f on 25f lt brn 2.50 1.25
a. Perf. 14 1.65 1.50
Nos. 450-456 (7) 14.00 9.49

For surcharges see Nos. 466-467.

St. Elizabeth A33

Ministering to Children A34

Wmk. 210

1932, Apr. 21 **Photo.** ***Perf. 15***

458 A33 10f ultra 65 30
459 A33 20f scarlet 65 30

Perf. 14

460 A34 32f dp vio 1.90 2.10
461 A34 40f dp bl 1.50 1.25

700th anniv. of the death of St. Elizabeth of Hungary.

Madonna, Patroness of Hungary — A35

1932, June 1 ***Perf. 12***

462 A35 1p yel grn 14.00 60
463 A35 2p carmine 14.00 85
464 A35 5p dp bl 57.50 3.50
465 A35 10p ol bis 85.00 37.50

Nos. 451 and 454 Surcharged **2**

1932, June 14 **Wmk. 210** ***Perf. 15***

466 A25 2f on 6f on 8f mag 1.50 40

Wmk. 133

467 A25 2f on 6f on 8f mag 35.00 35.00

Imre Madach — A36

Designs: 2f, Janos Arany. 4f, Dr. Ignaz Semmelweis. 6f, Baron Roland Eotvos. 10f, Count Stephen Szechenyi. 16f, Ferenc Deak. 20f, Franz Liszt. 30f, Louis Kossuth. 32f, Stephen Tisza. 40f, Mihaly Munkacsy. 50f, Alexander Csoma. 70f, Farkas Bolyai.

1932 **Wmk. 210** ***Perf. 15***

468 A36 1f slate vio 16 18
469 A36 2f orange 15 15
470 A36 4f ultra 15 15
471 A36 6f yel grn 15 15
472 A36 10f Prus grn 15 15
473 A36 16f dull vio 28 22
474 A36 20f dp rose 15 15
475 A36 30f brown 52 15
476 A36 32f brn vio 80 45
477 A36 40f dull blue 80 15
478 A36 50f deep green 1.25 15
479 A36 70f cerise 1.65 18
Nos. 468-479 (12) 6.21
Set value 1.75

Issued in honor of famous Hungarians. See Nos. 509-510.

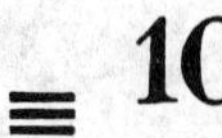

No. 421 Surcharged ≡ **10** ≡

1933, Apr. 15 **Wmk. 133** ***Perf. 14***

480 A29 10f on 70f scar 40 20

Leaping Stag and Double Cross — A47

Wmk. 210

1933, July 10 **Photo.** ***Perf. 15***

481 A47 10f dk grn 90 1.00
482 A47 16f vio brn 2.50 2.25
483 A47 20f car lake 1.65 1.25
484 A47 32f yellow 3.75 4.00
485 A47 40f dp bl 3.75 4.00
Nos. 481-485 (5) 12.55 12.50

Boy Scout Jamboree at Gödöllö, Hungary, July 20 to Aug. 20, 1933.

Souvenir Sheet

Franz Liszt A48

1934, May 6 *Perf. 15*

486	A48	20f lake	50.00	45.00

Second Hungarian Philatelic Exhibition, Budapest, and Jubilee of the First Hungarian Philatelic Society. Sold for 90f, including entrance fee. Size: 64x76mm.

Francis II Rakoczy (1676-1735), Prince of Transylvania — A49

1935, Apr. 8 *Perf. 12*

487	A49	10f yel grn	60	52
488	A49	16f brt vio	3.00	2.50
489	A49	20f dk car	60	52
490	A49	32f brn lake	5.00	4.50
491	A49	40f blue	5.00	4.00
		Nos. 487-491 (5)	14.20	12.04

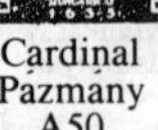

Cardinal Pazmany A50

Signing the Charter A51

1935, Sept. 25

492	A50	6f dl grn	1.10	1.00
493	A51	10f dk grn	40	40
494	A50	16f slate vio	1.40	1.25
495	A50	20f magenta	40	40
496	A51	32f dp claret	3.00	1.65
497	A51	40f dk bl	2.75	1.65
		Nos. 492-497 (6)	9.05	6.35

Tercentenary of the founding of the University of Budapest by Peter Cardinal Pazmany.

Ancient City and Fortress of Buda — A52

Guardian Angel over Buda — A53

Shield of Buda, Cannon and Massed Flags — A54

First Hungarian Soldier to Enter Buda A55

1936, Sept. 2 *Perf. 11½x12½*

498	A52	10f dk grn	55	32
499	A53	16f dp vio	2.10	2.00
500	A54	20f car lake	55	32
501	A55	32f dk brn	2.40	2.50
502	A52	40f dp bl	2.40	2.50
		Nos. 498-502 (5)	8.00	7.64

250th anniv. of the recapture of Budapest from the Turks.

Budapest International Fair — A56

1937, Feb. 22 *Perf. 12*

503	A56	2f dp org	15	18
504	A56	6f yel grn	20	18
505	A56	10f myr grn	24	18
506	A56	20f dp cer	40	28
507	A56	32f dk vio	80	70
508	A56	40f ultra	1.00	70
		Nos. 503-508 (6)	2.79	2.22

Portrait Type of 1932

Designs: 5f, Ferenc Kolcsey. 25f, Mihaly Vorosmarty.

1937, May 5 *Perf. 15*

509	A36	5f brn org	15	15
510	A36	25f ol grn	38	20

Pope Sylvester II, Archbishop Astrik A59

Admiral Horthy A67

Designs: 2f, 16f, Stephen the Church builder. 4f, 20f, St. Stephen enthroned. 5f, 25f, Sts. Gerhardt, Emerich, Stephen. 6f, 30f, St. Stephen offering holy crown to Virgin Mary. 10f, same as 1f. 32f, 50f, Portrait of St. Stephen. 40f, Madonna and Child. 70f, Crown of St. Stephen.

1938, Jan. 1 *Perf. 12*

511	A59	1f dp vio	15	22
512	A59	2f ol brn	15	15
513	A59	4f brt bl	32	15
514	A59	5f magenta	38	28
515	A59	6f dp yel grn	32	18
516	A59	10f red org	38	15
517	A59	16f gray vio	65	52
518	A59	20f car lake	50	15
519	A59	25f dk grn	1.00	52
520	A59	30f olive bister	1.40	18
521	A59	32f dp cl, *buff*	2.00	1.05
522	A59	40f Prus grn	1.40	18
523	A59	50f rose vio, *grnsh*	2.00	32
524	A59	70f ol grn, *bluish*	2.25	42
		Nos. 511-524 (14)	12.90	4.47

900th anniv. of the death of St. Stephen. For overprints see Nos. 535-536.

1938, Jan. 1 *Perf. 12½x12*

525	A67	1p peacock grn	90	15
526	A67	2p brown	1.65	25
527	A67	5p saph blue	5.75	1.75

Souvenir Sheet

St. Stephen — A68

1938, May 22 **Wmk. 210** *Perf. 12*

528	A68	20f car lake	10.00	9.50

3rd Hungarian Phil. Exhib., Budapest. Sheet sold only at exhibition with 1p ticket.

College of Debrecen A69

Three Students — A71

George Marothy — A73

Designs: 10f, 18th century view of College. 20f, 19th century view of College. 40f, Stephen Hatvani.

Perf. 12x12½, 12½x12

1938, Sept. 24 **Wmk. 210**

529	A69	6f dp grn	15	15
530	A69	10f brown	15	15
531	A71	16f brn car	18	18
532	A69	20f crimson	15	15
533	A73	32f slate grn	50	45
534	A73	40f brt bl	55	30
		Nos. 529-534 (6)	1.68	1.38

400th anniversary of the founding of Debrecen College.

Types of 1938 Overprinted in Blue or Carmine:

a

HAZATÉRÉS
1938

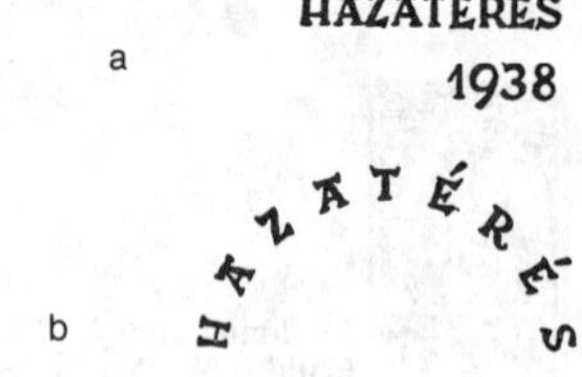

b

HAZATÉRÉS
19 38

1938 *Perf. 12*

535	A59(a)	20f sal pink (Bl)	65	25
536	A59(b)	70f brn, *grnsh* (C)	75	25

Restoration of the territory ceded by Czechoslovakia.

The 70f exists without overprint. Value, unused, $3500; used, $3000. Forgeries exist.

Crown of St. Stephen A75

St. Stephen A76

Madonna, Patroness of Hungary A77

Coronation Church, Budapest A78

Reformed Church, Debrecen A79

Cathedral, Esztergom A80

Deak Square Evangelical Church, Budapest A81

Cathedral of Kassa A82

Wmk. 210

1939, June 1 **Photo.** *Perf. 15*

537	A75	1f brn car	15	15
538	A75	2f Prus grn	15	15
539	A75	4f ocher	15	15
540	A75	5f brn vio	15	15
541	A75	6f yel grn	15	15
542	A75	10f bis brn	15	15
543	A75	16f rose vio	15	15
544	A76	20f rose red	15	15
545	A77	25f bl gray	15	15

Perf. 12

546	A78	30f red vio	30	15
547	A79	32f brown	28	15
548	A80	40f greenish blue	30	15
549	A81	50f olive	30	15
550	A82	70f henna brown	35	15
		Set value	2.00	85

See Nos. 578-596. For overprints see Nos. 559-560.

Girl Scout Sign and Olive Branch — A83

Designs: 6f, Scout lily, Hungary's shield, Crown of St. Stephen. 10f, Girls in Scout hat and national headdress. 20f, Dove and Scout emblems.

1939, July 20 **Photo.** *Perf. 12*

551	A83	2f brn org	42	42
552	A83	6f green	45	42
553	A83	10f brown	75	42
554	A83	20f lil rose	1.00	70

Girl Scout Jamboree at Gödöllö.

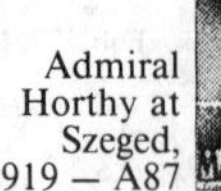

Admiral Horthy at Szeged, 1919 — A87

Admiral Nicholas Horthy — A88

Cathedral of Kassa and Angel Ringing "Bell of Liberty" A89

1940, Mar. 1

555	A87	6f green	24	15
556	A88	10f ol blk & ol bis	24	15
557	A89	20f brt rose brn	55	35

20th anniversary of the election of Admiral Horthy as Regent of Hungary.

Crown of St. Stephen — A90

1940, Sept. 5

558	A90	10f dk grn & yel	15	15

Issued in commemoration of the recovery of northeastern Transylvania from Romania.

Nos. 542, 544 Overprinted in Red or Black

DÉL-VISSZATÉR

1941, Apr. 21 ***Perf. 15***

559	A75	10f bis brn (R)	20	15
560	A76	20f rose red (Bk)	20	15
		Set value		24

Return of the Bacska territory from Yugoslavia.

Admiral Nicholas Horthy A92

Wmk. 210

1941, June 18 **Photo.** ***Perf. 12***

570	A92	1p dk grn & buff	20	18
571	A92	2p dk brn & buff	45	32
572	A92	5p dk rose vio & buff	1.50	1.40

See Nos. 597-599.

Count Stephen Széchenyi A93

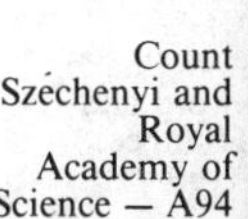

Count Széchenyi and Royal Academy of Science — A94

Representation of the Narrows of Kazán — A95

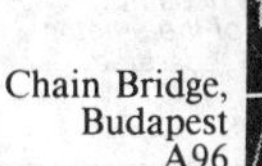

Chain Bridge, Budapest A96

Mercury, Train and Boat — A97

1941, Sept. 21

573	A93	10f dk ol grn	15	15
574	A94	16f ol brn	15	15
575	A95	20f car lake	16	16
576	A96	32f red org	25	25
577	A97	40f ryl bl	20	20
		Nos. 573-577 (5)	91	91

Count Stephen Szechenyi (1791-1860).

Types of 1939

Perf. 12x12½, 12½x12, 15

1941-43 **Wmk. 266**

578	A75	1f rose lake ('42)	15	15
579	A75	3f dk brn	15	15
580	A75	5f vio gray ('42)	15	15
581	A75	6f lt grn ('42)	15	15
582	A75	8f slate grn	15	15
583	A75	10f ol brn ('42)	15	15
584	A75	12f red org	15	15
585	A76	20f rose red ('42)	15	15
586	A76	24f brn vio	15	15
587	A78	30f lilac ('42)	15	15
588	A82	30f rose red ('43)	15	15
589	A80	40f bl grn ('42)	15	15
590	A79	40f gray blk ('43)	15	15
591	A81	50f ol grn ('42)	15	15
592	A80	50f brt bl ('43)	15	15
593	A82	70f cop red ('42)	15	15
594	A81	70f gray grn ('43)	15	15
595	A77	80f brn bister	15	15
596	A78	80f bis brn ('43)	15	15
		Set value	1.40	90

Horthy Type of 1941

Perf. 12x12½

1941, Dec. 18 **Wmk. 266**

597	A92	1p dk grn & buff	45	15
598	A92	2p dk brn & buff	15	15
599	A92	5p dk rose vio & buff	38	28
		Set value		50

Stephen Horthy — A98

1942, Oct. 15 ***Perf. 12***

600	A98	20f black	30	20

Death of Stephen Horthy (1904-42), son of Regent Nicholas Horthy, who died in a plane crash.

Arpád — A99

A109

Portraits: 2f, King Ladislaus I. 3f, Miklós Toldi. 4f, János Hunyadi. 5f, Paul Kinizsi. 6f, Count Miklós Zrinyi. 8f, Francis II Rakoczy. 10f, Count Andrew Hadik. 12f, Arthur Görgei. 18f, 24f, Virgin Mary, Patroness of Hungary.

1943-45 ***Perf. 15***

601	A99	1f grnsh blk	15	15
602	A99	2f red org	15	15
603	A99	3f ultra	15	15
604	A99	4f brown	15	15
605	A99	5f vermilion	15	15
606	A99	6f slate bl	15	15
607	A99	8f dk ol grn	15	15
608	A99	10f brown	15	15
609	A99	12f dp bl grn	15	15
610	A99	18f dk gray	15	15
611	A109	20f chnt brn	15	15
612	A99	24f rose vio	15	15
613	A109	30f brt car	15	15
614	A109	50f blue	15	15
615	A109	80f yel brn	15	15
616	A109	1p green	15	15
616A	A109	2p brn ('45)	18	15
616B	A109	5p dk red vio ('45)	32	32
		Set value	1.40	1.25

For overprints and surcharges see Nos. 631-658, 660-661, 664, 666-669, 671-672, 674-677, 679, 680, 682, 685-689, 691-698, 801-803, 805-806, 810-815, F2, Q2-Q3, Q7.

Message to the Shepherds A110

St. Margaret A113

Designs: 20f, Nativity. 30f, Adoration of the Magi.

1943, Dec. 1 ***Perf. 12x12½***

617	A110	4f dk grn	15	18
618	A110	20f dl bl	15	18
619	A110	30f brn org	15	18

1944, Jan. 19 ***Perf. 15***

620	A113	30f dp car	15	15

Canonization of St. Margaret of Hungary.
For surcharges see Nos. 662, 673A.

Kossuth with Family A114

Lajos Kossuth A117

Honvéd Drummer A115

Design: 30f, Kossuth orating.

Perf. 12½x12, 12x12½

1944, Mar. 20

621	A114	4f yel brn	15	15
622	A115	20f dk ol grn	15	15
623	A115	30f henna brown	15	15
624	A117	50f slate blue	15	15
		Set value	30	27

To commemorate the 50th anniversary of the death of Louis (Lajos) Kossuth (1802-94).
For surcharges see Nos. B175-B178.

St. Elizabeth — A118

Portraits: 24f, St. Margaret. 30f, Elizabeth Szilágyi. 50f, Dorothy Kanuizsai. 70f, Susanna Lorántffy. 80f, Ilona Zrinyi.

1944, Aug. 1 ***Perf. 15***

625	A118	20f olive	15	15
626	A118	24f rose vio	15	15
627	A118	30f copper red	15	15
628	A118	50f dark blue	15	15
629	A118	70f org red	15	15
630	A118	80f brn car	15	15
		Set value	38	44

For overprints and surcharges see Nos. 659, 663, 665, 670, 673, 678, 681, 683-684, 690, 804, 807-809, F1, F3, Q1, Q4-Q6, Q8.

Catalogue values for unused stamps in this section, from this point to the end of the section, are for Never Hinged items.

Issues of the Republic

Types of Hungary, 1943 Surcharged in Carmine

1945, May 1 **Wmk. 266**

Blue Surface-tinted Paper

631	A99	10f on 1f grnsh blk	1.50	1.50
632	A99	20f on 3f ultra	1.50	1.50
633	A99	30f on 4f brn	1.50	1.50
634	A99	40f on 6f sl bl	1.50	1.50
635	A99	50f on 8f dk ol grn	1.50	1.50
636	A99	1p on 10f brn	1.50	1.50
637	A99	150f on 12f dp bl grn	1.50	1.50
638	A99	2p on 18f dk gray	1.50	1.50
639	A109	3p on 20f chnt brn	1.50	1.50
640	A99	5p on 24f rose vio	1.50	1.50
641	A109	6p on 50f blue	1.50	1.50
642	A109	10p on 80f yel brn	1.50	1.50
643	A109	20p on 1p grn	1.50	1.50

Yellow Surface-tinted Paper

644	A99	10f on 1f grnsh blk	1.50	1.50
645	A99	20f on 3f ultra	1.50	1.50
646	A99	30f on 4f brn	1.50	1.50
647	A99	40f on 6f sl bl	1.50	1.50
648	A99	50f on 8f dk ol grn	1.50	1.50
649	A99	1p on 10f brn	1.50	1.50
650	A99	150f on 12f dp bl grn	1.50	1.50
651	A99	2p on 18f dk gray	1.50	1.50
652	A109	3p on 20f chnt brn	1.50	1.50
653	A99	5p on 24f rose vio	1.50	1.50
654	A109	6p on 50f bl	1.50	1.50
655	A109	10p on 80f yel brn	1.50	1.50
656	A109	20p on 1p grn	1.50	1.50
		Nos. 631-656 (26)	39.00	39.00

Hungary's liberation.

Types of Hungary, 1943-45, Surcharged in Carmine or Black

1945
10
fillér

1945

Blue Surface-tinted Paper

657	A99	10f on 4f brn (C)	15	15
658	A99	10f on 10f brn (C)	45	45
659	A118	20f on 20f ol (C)	15	15
660	A99	28f on 5f ver	15	15
661	A109	30f on 30f brt car	15	15
662	A113	30f on 30f dp car	15	15
663	A118	30f on 30f cop red	15	15
664	A99	40f on 10f brn	15	15
665	A118	1p on 70f org red	25	25
666	A109	1p on 80f yel brn (C)	15	15
667	A99	2p on 4f brn	15	15
668	A109	2p on 2p brn (C)	15	15
669	A109	4p on 30f brt car	15	15
670	A118	8p on 20f olive	15	15
671	A99	10p on 2f red org	7.25	7.25
672	A109	10p on 80f yel brn	15	15
673	A118	20p on 30f cop red	15	15

Same Surcharge with Thinner Unshaded Numerals of Value

673A	A113	300p on 30f dp car	15	15

Surcharged as Nos. 657-673 Yellow Surface-tinted Paper

674	A99	10f on 12f dp bl grn (C)	15	15
675	A99	20f on 1f grnsh blk (C)	15	15
676	A99	20f on 18f dk gray (C)	15	15
a.		Double surcharge		
677	A99	40f on 24f rose vio (C)	15	15
678	A118	40f on 24f rose vio (C)	15	15
679	A109	42f on 20f chnt brn (C)	15	15
680	A109	50f on 50f bl (C)	15	15
681	A118	50f on 50f dk bl (C)	15	15
682	A99	60f on 8f dk ol grn (C)	15	15
683	A118	80f on 24f rose vio	20	20
684	A118	80f on 80f brn car (C)	15	15
685	A109	1p on 20f chnt brn	15	15
686	A109	1p on 1p grn (C)	15	15
687	A99	150f on 6f sl bl (C)	90	90
688	A99	1.60p on 12f dp bl grn	15	15
689	A99	3p on 3f ultra (C)	32	32
690	A118	3p on 50f dk bl	15	15
691	A99	5p on 8f dk ol grn	15	15
692	A109	5p on 5p dk red vio (C)	25	25

693	A109	6p on 50f blue	15	15
694	A109	7p on 1p grn	15	15
695	A99	9p on 1f grnsh blk	15	15

Same Surcharge with Thinner, Unshaded Numerals of Value

696	A99	40p on 8f dk ol grn	15	15
697	A99	60p on 18f dk gray	15	15
698	A99	100p on 12f dp bl grn	15	15
		Set value, #657-698	11.50	11.50

Various shades and errors of overprint exist on Nos. 657-698.

These surface-tinted stamps exist without surcharge, but were not so issued.

Construction
A124

Designs: 1.60p, Manufacturing. 2p, Railroading. 3p, Building. 5p, Agriculture. 8p, Communications. 10p, Architecture. 20p, Writing.

Wmk. 266

1945, Sept. 11 Photo. *Perf. 12*

700	A124	40f gray blk	4.50	4.50
701	A124	1.60p ol bis	4.50	4.50
702	A124	2p sl grn	4.50	4.50
703	A124	3p dk pur	4.50	4.50
704	A124	5p dk red	4.50	4.50
705	A124	8p brown	4.50	4.50
706	A124	10p dp claret	4.50	4.50
707	A124	20p slate bl	4.50	4.50
		Nos. 700-707 (8)	36.00	36.00

World Trade Union Conf., Paris, Sept. 25 to Oct. 10, 1945.

"Reconstruction" — A132

1945-46

708	A132	12p brn olive	24	24
709	A132	20p brt grn	15	15
710	A132	24p org brn	24	24
711	A132	30p gray blk	15	15
712	A132	40p olive grn	15	15
713	A132	60p red org	15	15
714	A132	100p org yel	15	15
715	A132	120p brt ultra	15	15
716	A132	140p brt red	38	38
717	A132	200p olive brn	15	15
718	A132	240p brt bl	15	15
719	A132	300p dk car	15	15
720	A132	500p dl grn	15	15
721	A132	1000p red vio	15	15
722	A132	3000p brt red ('46)	15	15
		Set value	1.80	1.80

Nos. 708 to 721 exist tete beche. Value: 4 times the value of a single.

"Liberation"
A133

Postrider
A134

1946, Feb. 12

723	A133	3ez p dk red	15	15
724	A133	15ez p ultra	15	15
		Set value	20	20

1946 Photo.; Values Typo. *Perf. 15*

725	A134	4ez p brn org	15	15
726	A134	10ez p brt red	15	15
727	A134	15ez p ultra	15	15
728	A134	20ez p dk brn	15	15
729	A134	30ez p red vio	15	15
730	A134	50ez p gray blk	15	15
731	A134	80ez p brt ultra	15	15
732	A134	100ez p rose car	15	15
733	A134	160ez p gray grn	15	15
734	A134	200ez p yel grn	15	15
735	A134	500ez p red	15	15
736	A134	640ez p ol bis	15	15
737	A134	800ez p rose vio	15	15
		Set value	1.25	1.25

Abbreviations:
Ez (Ezer) = Thousand
Mil (Milpengo) = Million
Mlrd (Milliard) = Billion
Bil (Billio-pengo) = Trillion

Arms of Hungary — A135

1946 Wmk. 210

738	A135	1mil p vermilion	15	20
739	A135	2mil p ultra	15	20
740	A135	3mil p brown	15	15
741	A135	4mil p slate gray	15	15
742	A135	5mil p rose vio	15	15
743	A135	10mil p green	15	15
744	A135	20mil p car	15	15
745	A135	50mil p olive	15	15

Arms and Post Horn
A136 A137

746	A136	100mil p hn brn	15	15
747	A136	200mil p hn brn	15	15
748	A136	500mil p hn brn	15	15
749	A136	1000mil p hn brn	15	15
750	A136	2000mil p hn brn	15	15
751	A136	3000mil p hn brn	15	15
752	A136	5000mil p hn brn	15	15
753	A136	10,000mil p hn brn	15	15
754	A136	20,000mil p hn brn	15	15
755	A136	30,000mil p hn brn	15	15
756	A136	50,000mil p hn brn	22	28

Denomination in Carmine

757	A137	100mlrd p olive	15	15
758	A137	200mlrd p olive	15	15
759	A137	500mlrd p olive	15	15

Dove and Letter — A138

Denomination in Carmine

760	A138	1bil p grnsh blk	15	20
761	A138	2bil p grnsh blk	15	20
763	A138	5bil p grnsh blk	15	20
764	A138	10bil p grnsh blk	15	20
765	A138	20bil p grnsh blk	15	20
766	A138	50bil p grnsh blk	15	20
767	A138	100bil p grnsh blk	15	20
768	A138	200bil p grnsh blk	15	20
769	A138	500bil p grnsh blk	15	20
770	A138	1000bil p grnsh blk	15	20
771	A138	10,000bil p grnsh blk	20	20
772	A138	50,000bil p grnsh blk	22	22
773	A138	100,000bil p grnsh blk	22	22
774	A138	500,000bil p grnsh blk	22	22

Denomination in Black

775	A137	5ez ap green	15	15
776	A137	10ez ap green	15	15
777	A137	20ez ap green	15	15
778	A137	50ez ap green	15	15
779	A137	80ez ap green	15	15
780	A137	100ez ap green	15	15
781	A137	200ez ap green	15	15
782	A137	500ez ap green	15	15
783	A137	1mil ap vermilion	15	15
784	A137	5mil ap vermilion	15	15
		Set value	5.60	7.00

Denominations are expressed in "ado" or "tax" pengos.

Early Steam Locomotive
A139

Designs: 20,000ap, Recent steam locomotive. 30,000ap, Electric locomotive. 40,000ap, Diesel locomotive.

1946, July 15 Wmk. 266 *Perf. 12*

785	A139	10,000ap vio brn	3.00	3.00
786	A139	20,000ap dk bl	3.00	3.00
787	A139	30,000ap dp yel grn	3.00	3.00
788	A139	40,000ap rose car	3.00	3.00

Centenary of Hungarian railways.

Industry
A143

Agriculture
A144

1946 Wmk. 210 Photo. *Perf. 15*

788A	A143	8f henna brn	15	15
789	A143	10f henna brn	15	15
790	A143	12f henna brn	15	15
791	A143	20f henna brn	15	15
792	A143	30f henna brn	15	15
793	A143	40f henna brn	15	15
794	A143	60f henna brn	16	15
795	A144	1fo dp yel grn	30	15
796	A144	1.40fo dp yel grn	42	15
797	A144	2fo dp yel grn	52	15
798	A144	3fo dp yel grn	4.00	15
799	A144	5fo dp yel grn	1.50	15
800	A144	10fo dp yel grn	3.50	35
		Nos. 788A-800 (13)	11.30	
		Set value		1.10

For surcharges see Nos. Q9-Q11.

Stamps and Types of 1943-45 Overprinted in Carmine or Black to Show Class of Postage for which Valid

"Any." or "Nyomtatv."=Printed Matter.
"Hl" or "Helyi level"=Local Letter.
"Hlp." or "Helyi lev.-lap"=Local Postcard.
"Tl." or "Tavolsagi level"=Domestic Letter.
"Tlp." or "Tavolsági lev.-lap"=Domestic Postcard.

a

Nyomtatv
20 gr.
b

1946 Wmk. 266

801	A99(a)	"Any 1." on 1f grnsh blk (#601;C)	15	15
802	A99(a)	"Any 2," on 1f grnsh blk (#601;C)	15	15
803	A99(b)	"Nyomtatv. 20gr" on 60f on 8f dk ol grn, *yel* (#682;Bk + C)	15	15
804	A118(a)	"Hl. 1" on 50f dk bl (#628;C)	15	15
805	A99(a)	"Hl. 2" on 40f on 10f brn, *bl* (#664;C + Bk)	15	15
806	A99(b)	"Helyi level" on 10f brn, *bl* (Bk)	15	15
807	A118(a)	"Hlp.1" on 8p on 20f ol, *bl* (#670;C + Bk)	15	15
808	A118(a)	"Hlp.2." on 8p on 20f ol. *bl* (#670;C + Bk)	15	15
809	A118(b)	"Helyi lev.-lap" on 20f ol, *bl* (C)	15	15
810	A99(a)	"Tl.1" on 10f brn (#608;Bk)	15	15
811	A99(a)	"Tl.2." on 10f on 4f brn, *bl* (#657;Bk + C)	15	15
812	A99(b)	"Tavolsagi level" on 18f dk gray (#610;C)	15	15
813	A99(a)	"Tlp.1." on 4f brn (#604;Bk)	15	15
814	A99(a)	"Tlp.2." on 4f brn (#604;Bk)	15	15
815	A99(b)	"Tavolsagi lev.-lap" on 4f brn (#604;Bk)	15	15
		Set value	90	1.35

Nos. 806 and 809 were not issued without overprint.

György Dózsa — A145

Designs: 10f, Antal Budai-Nagy. 12f, Tamas Esze. 20f, Ignac Martinovics. 30f, Janos Batsanyi. 40f, Lajos Kossuth. 60f, Mihaly Tancsics. 1fo, Alexander Petöfi. 2fo, Andreas Ady. 4fo, Jozsef Attila.

1947, Mar. 15 Photo. Wmk. 210

816	A145	8f rose brn	22	15
817	A145	10f dp ultra	22	15
818	A145	12f dp brn	22	15
819	A145	20f dk yel grn	25	15
820	A145	30f dk ol bis	18	15
821	A145	40f brn car	18	15
822	A145	60f cerise	35	15
823	A145	1fo dp grnsh bl	42	15
824	A145	2fo dk vio	1.10	35
825	A145	4fo grnsh blk	1.50	70
		Nos. 816-825 (10)	4.64	
		Set value		1.50

Peace and Agriculture
A155

Postal Savings Emblem
A156

1947, Sept. 22 *Perf. 12*

826	A155	60f brt red	30	20

Peace treaty.

1947, Oct. 31

Design: 60f, Postal Savings Bank, Budapest.

827	A156	40f rose brn	15	15
828	A156	60f brt rose car	38	15
		Set value		22

Savings Day, Oct. 31, 1947.

Hungarian Flag — A157

1848 Printing Press — A158

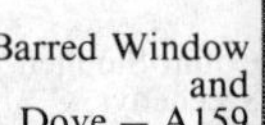

Barred Window and Dove — A159

1848 Shako, Sword and Trumpet
A160

15-Cent Minimum Value
The minimum catalogue value is 15 cents. Separating se-tenant pieces into individual stamps does not increase the "value" of the stamps... since demand for the separated stamps may be small.

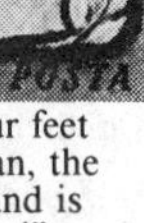

"On your feet Hungarian, the Homeland is Calling!" A161

Arms of Hungary A162

Perf. 12½x12, 12x12½

1948 Wmk. 283 Photo.

829	A157	8f dk rose red	24	16
830	A158	10f ultra	24	16
831	A159	12f cop brn	38	24
832	A160	20f dp grn	80	15
833	A161	30f ol brn	38	15
834	A157	40f dk vio brn	60	15
835	A161	60f car lake	1.00	15
836	A162	1fo brt ultra	1.00	15
837	A162	2fo red brn	1.40	24
838	A162	3fo green	1.65	60
839	A162	4fo scarlet	4.25	80
		Nos. 829-839 (11)	11.94	
		Set value		2.55

Cent. of the beginning of Hungary's war for independence.

No. 834 is inscribed "Kossuth," No. 835 "Petofi".

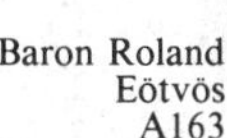

Baron Roland Eötvös A163

1948, July 27

840	A163	60f dp red	50	25

Issued to commemorate the centenary of the birth of Roland Eötvös, physicist.

Hungarian Workers — A164

1948, Oct. 17 Wmk. 283 *Perf. 12*

841	A164	30f dk car rose	40	30
a.		Sheet of 4	20.00	20.00

The 17th Trade Union Congress, Budapest, October 1948. No. 841a was sold for 2 forint.

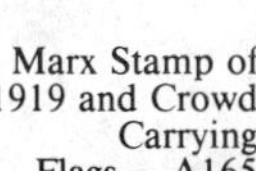

Marx Stamp of 1919 and Crowd Carrying Flags — A165

Petőfi Stamp of 1919 and Flags — A166

1949, Mar. 19

Flags in Carmine

842	A165	40f brown	30	25
843	A166	60f ol gray	30	25

Issued to commemorate the 30th anniversary of the first Hungarian Soviet Republic.

Workers of the Five Continents and Flag — A167

1949, June 29 *Perf. 12x12½*

Flag in Red

844	A167	30f yel brn	2.50	2.50
845	A167	40f brn vio	2.50	2.50
846	A167	60f lil rose	2.50	2.50
847	A167	1fo vio bl	2.50	2.50

2nd Congress of the World Federation of Trade Unions, Milan, 1949.

Sándor Petőfi — A168

Youth of Three Races — A169

Perf. 12½x12

1949, July 31 Engr. Unwmk.

848	A168	40f claret	30	30
849	A168	60f dk red	22	15
850	A168	1fo dp bl	30	16

Cent. of the death of Sándor Petőfi, poet.

See Nos. 867-869.

Perf. 12½x12

1949, Aug. 14 Photo. Wmk. 283

Designs: 30f, Three fists. 40f, Soldier breaking chain. 60f, Soviet youths carrying flags. 1fo, Young workers displaying books.

851	A169	20f dk vio brn	70	70
a.		20f blue green	2.25	2.25
852	A169	30f bl grn	80	80
a.		30f violet brown	2.25	2.25
853	A169	40f ol bis	1.00	1.00
a.		40f ultramarine	2.25	2.25
854	A169	60f rose pink	1.00	1.00
855	A169	1fo ultra	1.50	1.50
a.		1fo olive bister	2.75	2.75
b.		Souv. sheet of 5, #851a-855a	25.00	22.50
		Nos. 851-855 (5)	5.00	5.00

Issued to publicize the World Festival of Youth and Students, Budapest, August 14-28, 1949.

Arms of Hungarian People's Republic A170

1949 Wmk. 283

Arms in Bister, Carmine Blue and Green

856	A170	20f green	85	48
857	A170	60f carmine	35	20
858	A170	1fo blue	85	55

Adoption of the Hungarian People's Republic constitution. Nos. 856-858 also exist unwatermarked; same values as watermarked.

Imperforates

Nearly all Hungarian stamps from No. 859 on were issued imperforate as well as with perforations. In most cases the imperforate quantities were smaller than the perforated ones. The imperforates were sold at five times face value, and all issued before Feb. 22, 1958, were invalid. Late in 1958, Philatelica Hungarica started selling the imperforates at four to six times face value.

Symbols of the UPU — A171

1949, Nov. 1 *Perf. 12x12½*

859	A171	60f rose red	15	15
a.		Booklet pane of 6	2.50	
860	A171	1fo blue	30	30
a.		Booklet pane of 6	4.00	

75th anniv. of the UPU.

Nos. 859 and 860 exist imperf. and stamps from 859a and 860a in horiz. pairs, imperf. between.

See Nos. C63, C81.

Chain Bridge — A172

1949, Nov. 20 Wmk. 283

861	A172	40f bl grn	15	15
862	A172	60f red brn	18	18
863	A172	1fo blue	24	24
		Nos. 861-863,C64-C65 (5)	1.54	1.54

Issued to commemorate the centenary of the opening of the Chain Bridge at Budapest to traffic. For souvenir sheet see No. C66.

Joseph V. Stalin — A173

Perf. 12½x12

1949, Dec. 21 Engr. Unwmk.

864	A173	60f dk red	42	15
865	A173	1fo dp bl	48	32
866	A173	2fo brown	90	65

70th anniv. of the birth of Joseph V. Stalin.

See Nos. 1034-1035.

Petőfi Type of 1949

1950, Feb. 5 *Perf. 12½x12*

867	A168	40f brown	15	15
868	A168	60f dk car	24	18
869	A168	1fo dk grn	65	28

Philatelic Museum, Budapest A174

Perf. 12x12½

1950, Mar. 12 Photo. Wmk. 283

870	A174	60f gray & brn	2.25	2.25

20th anniv. of the establishment of the Hungarian PO Phil. Museum. See No. C68.

Coal Mining A175

Designs: 10f, Heavy industry. 12f, Power production. 20f, Textile industry. 30f, "Cultured workers." 40f, Mechanized agriculture. 60f, Village cooperative. 1fo, Train. 1.70fo, "Holiday." 2fo, Defense. 3fo, Shipping. 4fo, Livestock. 5fo, Engineering. 10fo, Sports.

1950 Wmk. 283

871	A175	8f gray	45	20
872	A175	10f claret	45	15
873	A175	12f org ver	70	38
874	A175	20f bl grn	28	15
875	A175	30f rose vio	35	15
876	A175	40f sepia	45	15
877	A175	60f red	42	15
878	A175	1fo gray brn, yel & lil	1.90	26
879	A175	1.70fo dk grn & yel	5.50	40
880	A175	2fo vio brn & cr	2.75	20
881	A175	3fo sl & cr	4.50	18
882	A175	4fo blk brn & sal	19.00	4.00
883	A175	5fo rose vio & yel	9.75	1.90
884	A175	10fo dk brn & yel	45.00	11.00
		Nos. 871-884 (14)	91.50	19.27

Issued to publicize Hungary's Five Year Plan. See Nos. 945-958.

Citizens Welcoming Liberators A176

1950, Apr. 4 Unwmk. *Perf. 12*

885	A176	40f gray blk	60	48
886	A176	60f rose brn	40	15
887	A176	1fo dp bl	48	20
888	A176	2fo brown	80	60

Fifth anniversary of Hungary's liberation.

Chess Players A177

Design: 1fo, Iron Workers Union building and chess emblem.

1950, Apr. 9 Wmk. 106

889	A177	60f dp mag	70	42
890	A177	1fo dp bl	1.25	85

Issued to publicize the World Chess Championship Matches, Budapest. See No. C69.

Workers Symbolizing International Proletariat — A178

Design: 60f, Blast furnace, tractor, workers holding Maypole.

1950, May 1

891	A178	40f org brn	35	35
892	A178	60f rose car	22	15
893	A178	1fo dp bl	70	42

Issued to publicize Labor Day, May 1, 1950.

Liberty, Cogwheel, Dove and Globes A179

Inscribed: "1950. V. 10.-24."

Design: 60f, Three workers and flag.

1950, May 10 Photo. *Perf. 12x12½*

No.	Type	Description	Unused	Used
894	A179	40f ol grn	16	15
895	A179	60f dk car	28	15
		Set value		23

Issued to publicize the meeting of the World Federation of Trade Unions, Budapest, May 1950.

Doctor Inspecting Baby's Bath A180

Children's Day: 30f, Physical Culture. 40f, Education. 60f, Boys' Camp. 1.70fo, Model plane building.

1950, June 4 Wmk. 106

No.	Type	Description	Unused	Used
896	A180	20f gray & brn	85	55
897	A180	30f brn & rose lake	42	15
898	A180	40f ind & dk grn	42	15
899	A180	60f SZABAD	42	15
a.		UTANPOTLASUNK . .	*1,100.*	*850.00*
900	A180	1.70fo dp grn & gray	1.65	55
		Nos. 896-900 (5)	3.76	1.55

Youths Marching on Globe A181

Working Man and Woman — A182

Designs: 30f, Foundry worker. 60f, Workers on Mt. Gellert. 1.70fo, Worker, peasant and student; flags.

Inscribed: "Budapest 1950. VI. 17-18."

Perf. 12x12½, 12½x12

1950, June 17

No.	Type	Description	Unused	Used
901	A181	20f dk grn	45	40
902	A181	30f dp red org	18	15
903	A182	40f dk brn	18	15
904	A182	60f dp claret	28	15
905	A182	1.75fo dk ol grn	75	32
		Nos. 901-905 (5)	1.84	1.17

Issued to publicize the First Congress of the Working Youth, Budapest, June 17-18, 1950.

Peonies — A183

Designs: 40f, Anemones. 60f, Pheasant's-eye. 1fo, Geraniums. 1.70fo, Bluebells.

Engraved and Lithographed

Perf. 12½x12

1950, Aug. 20 Unwmk.

No.	Type	Description	Unused	Used
906	A183	30f rose brn, rose pink & grn	75	24
907	A183	40f dk grn, lil & yel	75	28
908	A183	60f red brn, yel & grn	1.10	45
909	A183	1fo pur, red & grn	2.75	2.00
910	A183	1.70fo dk vio & grn	3.50	2.50
		Nos. 906-910 (5)	8.85	5.47

Miner — A184

Designs: 60f, High speed lathe. 1fo, Prefabricated building construction.

Perf. 12x12½

1950, Oct. 7 Photo. Wmk. 106

No.	Type	Description	Unused	Used
911	A184	40f brown	18	18
912	A184	60f car rose	20	18
913	A184	1fo brt bl	60	45

Issued to publicize the 2nd National Exhibition of Inventions.

Gen. Josef Bem and Battle at Piski A185

Perf. 12½x12

1950, Dec. 10 Engr. Unwmk.

No.	Type	Description	Unused	Used
914	A185	40f dk brn	80	60
915	A185	60f dp car	70	28
916	A185	1fo dp bl	1.00	65

Gen. Josef Bem, death centenary.
See No. C80.

Signing Petition — A186

Peace Demonstrator Holding Dove — A187

Design: 1fo, Mother and Children with soldier.

Wmk. 106

1950, Nov. 23 Photo. *Perf. 12*

No.	Type	Description	Unused	Used
917	A186	40f ultra & red brn	8.75	6.50
918	A187	60f red org & dk grn	2.00	1.50
919	A186	1fo ol grn & dk brn	8.75	5.50

Women Swimmers A188

Designs: 20f, Vaulting. !fo, Mountain climbing. 1.70fo, Basketball. 2fo, Motorcycling.

1950, Dec. 2 *Perf. 12x12½*

No.	Type	Description	Unused	Used
920	A188	10f bl & gray	16	15
921	A188	20f sal & dk brn	16	15
922	A188	1fo ol & grn	48	45
923	A188	1.70fo ver & brn car	80	55
924	A188	2fo sal & pur	1.65	1.00
		Nos. 920-924,C82-C86 (10)	8.57	6.20

Canceled to Order

The government stamp agency started about 1950 to sell canceled sets of new issues. Values in the second ("used") column are for these canceled-to-order stamps. Postally used copies are worth more.

The practice was to end Apr. 1, 1991.

A189

Worker, Peasant, Soldier and Party Flag — A190

Designs: 60f, Matthias Rakosi and allegory. 1fo, House of Parliament, columns of workers and banner.

Inscribed: "Budapest * 1951 * Februar 24."

Perf. 12½x12, 12x12½

1951, Feb. 24

No.	Type	Description	Unused	Used
925	A189	10f yel grn	15	15
926	A190	30f brown	15	15
927	A190	60f car rose	22	22
928	A189	1fo blue	60	35

Issued to publicize the 2nd Congress of the Hungarian Workers' Party.

Mare and Foal — A191

Designs: 30f, Sow and shoats. 40f, Ram and ewe. 60f, Cow and calf.

1951, Apr. 5 *Perf. 12x12½*

No.	Type	Description	Unused	Used
929	A191	10f ol bis & rose brn	30	15
930	A191	30f rose brn & ol bis	45	32
931	A191	40f dk grn & brn	45	24
932	A191	60f brn org & brn	60	32
		Nos. 929-932,C87-C90 (8)	5.87	3.90

Issued to encourage increased livestock production.

Flags of Russia and Hungary A192

Russian Technician Teaching Hungarians A193

1951, Apr. 4 *Perf. 12½x12, 12x12½*

No.	Type	Description	Unused	Used
933	A192	60f brnsh car	18	15
934	A193	1fo dl vio	28	15
		Set value		21

Issued to publicize the "Month of Friendship" between Hungary and Russia, 1951.

Worker Holding Olive Branch and Mallet — A194

Workers Carrying Flags — A195

Design: 1fo, Workers approaching Place of Heroes.

Perf. 12x12½, 12½x12

1951, May 1 Photo. Wmk. 106

No.	Type	Description	Unused	Used
935	A194	40f brown	15	15
936	A195	60f scarlet	22	15
937	A194	1fo blue	38	16
		Set value		32

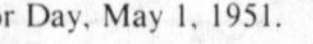

Issued to publicize Labor Day, May 1, 1951.

Leo Frankel A196

Children of Various Races A198

Paris Street Fighting, 1871 — A197

1951, May 20

No.	Type	Description	Unused	Used
938	A196	60f dk brn	22	18
939	A197	1fo bl & red	28	28

80th anniv. of the Commune of Paris.

1951, June 3 *Perf. 12½x12*

Designs: 40f, Boy and girl at play. 50f, Street car and Girl Pioneer. 60f, Chemistry students. 1.70fo, Pioneer bugler.

Inscribed:
"Nemzetkozi Gyermeknap 1951"

No.	Type	Description	Unused	Used
940	A198	30f dk brn	25	15
941	A198	40f green	25	18
942	A198	50f brn red	35	25
943	A198	60f plum	50	35
944	A198	1.70fo blue	95	95
		Nos. 940-944 (5)	2.30	1.88

Issued to publicize the International Day of Children, June 3, 1951.

5-Year-Plan Type of 1950

Designs as before.

1951-52 Wmk. 106 *Perf. 12x12½*

No.	Type	Description	Unused	Used
945	A175	8f gray	40	15
946	A175	10f claret	24	15
947	A175	12f org ver	24	15
948	A175	20f bl grn	24	15
949	A175	30f rose vio	24	15
950	A175	40f sepia	45	15
951	A175	60f red	55	15
952	A175	1fo gray brn, yel & lil	55	15
953	A175	1.70fo dk grn & yel	1.25	18
954	A175	2fo vio brn & cr	1.40	15
955	A175	3fo sl & cr	2.00	25
956	A175	4fo blk brn & sal	2.25	35
957	A175	5fo rose vio & yel ('52)	2.75	60
958	A175	10fo dk brn & yel ('52)	5.75	1.90
		Nos. 945-958 (14)	18.31	
		Set value		4.00

Maxim Gorky — A199

Perf. 12½x12

1951, June 17 Engr. Unwmk.

No.	Type	Description	Unused	Used
959	A199	60f cop red	18	15
960	A199	1fo dp bl	32	22
961	A199	2fo rose vio	1.00	75

15th anniversary of the death of Gorky.

Budapest Buildings

Railroad Workshop A200

Building in Lehel Street A201

Suburban Bus Terminal
A202

Rakosi House of Culture
A203

George Kilian Street School
A204

Central Construction Headquarters
A205

1951 Wmk. 106 Photo. *Perf. 15*
962 A200 20f green 20 15
963 A201 30f red org 20 15
964 A202 40f brown 25 15
965 A203 60f red 32 15
966 A204 1fo blue 65 15
967 A205 3fo dp plum 2.00 15
Nos. 962-967 (6) 3.62
Set value 32

The original size of Nos. 962-967, 22x18mm, was changed to 21x17mm starting in 1958. Values are the same.
See Nos. 1004-1011, 1048-1056C.

Tractor Manufacture
A206

Designs: 30f, Fluoroscope examination. 40f, Checking lathework. 60f, Woman tractor operator.

1951, Aug. 20 *Perf. 12x12½*
968 A206 20f blk brn 16 15
969 A206 30f dp bl 16 15
970 A206 40f crim rose 38 15
971 A206 60f brown 45 16
Nos. 968-971,C91-C93 (7) 3.15 1.56

Issued to publicize the successful conclusion of the first year under Hungary's 5-year plan.

Soldiers of the People's Army — A207

1951, Sept. 29
972 A207 1fo brown 85 30

Issued to publicize Army Day, Sept. 29, 1951. See No. C94.

Stamp of 1871, Portrait Replaced by Postmark
A208

Cornflower
A209

Perf. 12½x12
1951, Sept. 12 Engr. Unwmk.
973 A208 60f ol grn 2.00 1.75

80th anniv. of Hungary's 1st postage stamp. See Nos. B207-B208, C95, CB13-CB14.

1951, Nov. 4 Engr. & Litho.
974 A209 30f shown 60 20
975 A209 40f Lily of the Valley 75 55
976 A209 60f Tulip 65 20
977 A209 1fo Poppy 1.25 40
978 A209 1.70fo Cowslip 2.50 1.40
Nos. 974-978 (5) 5.75 2.75

Storming of the Winter Palace — A210

Designs: 60f, Lenin speaking to soldiers. 1fo, Lenin and Stalin.

Perf. 12x12½
1951, Nov. 7 Photo. Wmk. 106
979 A210 40f gray grn 38 24
980 A210 60f dp bl 45 16
981 A210 1fo rose lake 80 40

Issued to commemorate the 34th anniversary of the Russian Revolution.

Marchers Passing Stalin Monument
A211

1951, Dec. 16 Wmk. 106
982 A211 60f henna brn 20 16
983 A211 1fo deep blue 55 32

Joseph V. Stalin, 72nd birthday.

Grand Theater, Moscow
A212

Views of Moscow: 1fo, Lenin Mausoleum. 1.60fo, Kremlin.

1952, Feb. 20 *Perf. 12*
984 A212 60f ol grn & rose brn 28 16
985 A212 1fo lil rose & ol brn 55 28
986 A212 1.60fo red brn & ol 90 55

Hungarian-Soviet Friendship Month.

Rakosi and Farmers
A213

Matyas Rakosi — A214

Design: 2fo, Rakosi and Workers.

Perf. 12x12½, 12½x12
1952, Mar. 9 Engr. Unwmk.
987 A213 60f dp plum 20 15
988 A214 1fo dk red brn 26 20
989 A213 2fo dp vio bl 85 50

60th anniv. of the birth of Matyas Rakosi, communist leader.

Lajos Kossuth and Speech at Debrecen
A215

Designs: 30f, Sándor Petöfi. 50f, Gen. Josef Bem. 60f, Michael Tancsics. 1fo, Gen. Janos Damjanich. 1.50fo, Gen. Alexander Nagy.

1952, Mar. 15 *Perf. 12*
990 A215 20f green 15 15
991 A215 30f rose vio 15 15
992 A215 50f grnsh blk 24 24
993 A215 60f brn car 38 16
994 A215 1fo blue 45 28
995 A215 1.50fo redsh brn 52 48
Nos. 990-995 (6) 1.89 1.46

Heroes of the 1848 revolution.

No. B204 Surcharged in Black with Bars Obliterating Inscription and Surtax

Perf. 12½x12
1952, Apr. 27 Photo. Wmk. 283
996 SP121 60f magenta 37.50 32.50

Budapest Philatelic Exhibition. Counterfeits exist.

Girl Drummer Leading Parade
A216

Designs: 60f, Workers and soldier. 1fo, Worker, flag-encircled globe and dove.

Perf. 12x12½
1952, May 1 Photo. Wmk. 106
997 A216 40f dk grn & dl red 30 24
998 A216 60f dk red brn & dl red 30 24
999 A216 1fo sep & dl red 45 40

Issued to publicize Labor Day, May 1, 1952.

Runner — A217

Designs: 40f, Swimmer. 60f, Fencer. 1fo, Woman gymnast.

1952, May 26 *Perf. 11*
1000 A217 30f dk red brn 30 15
1001 A217 40f dp grn 35 15
1002 A217 60f dp lil rose 45 25
1003 A217 1fo dp bl 75 50
Nos. 1000-1003,C107-C108 (6) 4.20 2.65

Issued to publicize Hungary's participation in the Olympic Games, Helsinki, 1952

Building Types of 1951

Buildings: 8f, School, Stalinvarost. 10f, Szekesfehervar Station. 12f, Building, Ujpest. 50f, Metal works, Inotai. 70f, Grain elevator, Hajdunanas. 80f, Tiszalok dam. 4fo, Miners' union headquarters. 5fo, Workers' apartments, Ujpest.

1952 Wmk. 106 *Perf. 15*
1004 A202 8f green 24 15
1005 A200 10f purple 30 15
1006 A202 12f carmine 24 15
1007 A202 50f gray bl 38 15
1008 A202 70f yel brn 48 15
1009 A200 80f maroon 85 15
1010 A202 4fo ol grn 1.50 15
1011 A202 5fo gray blk 2.75 20
Nos. 1004-1011 (8) 6.74
Set value 60

The original size of Nos. 1004-1011 was 22x18mm. Starting in 1958, this was changed to 21x17mm. Values are the same.

Approaching Train — A218

Railroad Day: 1fo, Railroad Construction.

1952, Aug. 10 *Perf. 12x12½*
1012 A218 60f red brn 60 18
1013 A218 1fo dp ol grn 65 35

Coal Excavator
A219

Miners' Day: 1fo, Coal breaker.

1952, Sept. 7
1014 A219 60f brown 48 16
1015 A219 1fo dk grn 75 24

Lajos Kossuth
A220

Janos Hunyadi
A221

Design: 60f, Kossuth statue.

1952, Sept. 19 *Perf. 12½x12*
1016 A220 40f ol brn, *pink* 40 28
1017 A220 60f blk brn, *bl* 18 15
1018 A220 1fo pur, *citron* 40 18

150th anniv. of the birth of Lajos Kossuth.

1952, Sept. 28 Engr. Unwmk.

Portraits: 30f, Gyorgy Dozsa. 40f, Miklos Zrinyi. 60f, Ilona Zriuyi. 1fo, Bottyan Vak. 1.50fo, Aurel Stromfeld.

1019 A221 20f purple 15 15
1020 A221 30f dk grn 15 15
1021 A221 40f indigo 15 15
1022 A221 60f dk vio brn 20 15
1023 A221 1fo dk bl grn 48 32
1024 A221 1.50fo dk brn 1.25 90
Nos. 1019-1024 (6) 2.38
Set value 1.38

Army Day, Sept. 28, 1952.

Lenin and Conference at Smolny Palace — A222

Designs: 60f, Stalin and Cavalry Attack. 1fo, Marx, Engels, Lenin and Stalin.

1952, Nov. 7 Wmk. 106
Portraits in Olive Gray
1025 A222 40f deep claret 60 40
1026 A222 60f gray 32 15
1027 A222 1fo rose red 80 28

Russian Revolution, 35th anniversary.

Peasant Woman Holding Wheat — A223

Peace Meeting A224

Perf. 12½x12, 12x12½

1952, Nov. 22

1028	A223 60f brn red, *citron*	38	20
1029	A224 1fo brown, *blue*	60	38

Third Hungarian Peace Congress, 1952.

Subway Construction A225

Design: 1fo, Station and map.

1953, Jan. 19 Photo. ***Perf. 12x12½***

1030	A225 60f dk sl grn	55	25
1031	A225 1fo brn red	75	45

Issued to commemorate the completion of the Budapest subway extension.

Tank and Flag A226

Stalin A227

Design: 60f, Map of Central Europe and Soldier.

1953, Feb. 18

1032	A226 40f dk car rose	48	24
1033	A226 60f chocolate	48	15

Battle of Stalingrad, 10th anniversary.

Perf. 12x11½

1953 Engr. Wmk. 106

1034	A227 60f pur blk	30	15

Souvenir Sheet

1035	A227 2fo pur blk	16.00	16.00

Death of Joseph Stalin (1879-1953).
Issue dates: #1034, Mar. 27. #1035, Mar. 9.

Workers' Rest Home, Galyateto A228

Designs: 40f, Home at Mecsek. 50f, Parad Mineral Baths. 60f, Home at Kekes. 70f, Balatonfured Mineral Baths.

1953, Apr. Photo. ***Perf. 12x12½***

1036	A228 30f fawn	28	15
1037	A228 40f dp bl	28	15
1038	A228 50f dk ol bis	35	15
1039	A228 60f dp yel grn	38	18
1040	A228 70f scarlet	55	22
	Nos. 1036-1040 (5)	1.84	
	Set value		72

Young Workers with Red Flags — A229

Karl Marx — A230

1953, May 1 ***Perf. 12½x12***

1041	A229 60f brn & red, *yel*	25	15

Issued to publicize Labor Day, May 1, 1953.

1953, May 1 Engr. ***Perf. 11½x12***

1042	A230 1fo blk, *pink*	30	15

70th anniv. of the death of Karl Marx. See No. 1898.

Insurgents in the Forest — A231

Designs: 30f, Drummer and fighters. 40f, Battle scene. 60f, Cavalry attack. 1fo, Francis Rakoczy II.

1953, June 14 Photo. ***Perf. 11***

1043	A231 20f dk ol grn & org red, *grnsh*	35	28
1044	A231 30f vio brn & red org	48	40
1045	A231 40f gray bl & red org, *pink*	65	40
1046	A231 60f dk ol brn & org, *yel*	85	75
1047	A231 1fo dk red brn & org red, *yel*	1.10	1.00
	Nos. 1043-1047 (5)	3.43	2.83

250th anniv. of the insurrection of 1703.

Building Types of 1951

Buildings: 8f, Day Nursery, Ozd. 10f, Medical research institute, Szombathely. 12f, Apartments, Komlo. 20f, Department store, Ujpest. 30f, Brick factory, Maly. 40f, Metropolitan hospital. 50f, Sports building, Stalinvaros. 60f, Post office, Csepel. 70f, Blast furnace, Diosgyor. 1.20fo, Agricultural school, Ajkacsinger Valley. 1.70fo, Iron Works School, Csepel. 2fo, Optical works house of culture.

1953 Wmk. 106 ***Perf. 15***

1048	A204	8f ol grn	28	15
1049	A204	10f purple	38	15
1050	A205	12f rose car	38	15
1051	A204	20f dk grn	38	15
1052	A204	30f orange	38	15
1053	A204	40f dk brn	38	15
1054	A205	50f bl vio	60	15
1055	A205	60f rose red	60	15
1056	A204	70f yel brn	90	15
1056A	A205	1.20fo red	1.40	15
1056B	A204	1.70fo blue	1.25	15
1056C	A204	2fo green	1.40	15
		Nos. 1048-1056C (12)	8.33	
		Set value		75

The original size of Nos. 1048-1056C was 22x18mm. Starting in 1958, this was changed to 21x17mm. Values are the same.

Hungary stamps can be mounted in Scott's annual Hungary Supplement.

Cycling — A232

1953, Aug. 20 ***Perf. 11***

1057	A232 20f shown	40	24
1058	A232 30f Swimming	15	15
1059	A232 40f Calisthenics	28	15
1060	A232 50f Discus	35	16
1061	A232 60f Wrestling	40	20
	Nos. 1057-1061 (5)	1.58	90

Opening of the People's Stadium, Budapest. See Nos. C123-C127.

Kazar Costume — A233

Lenin — A234

Provincial Costumes: 30f, Ersekcsanad. 40f, Kalocsa. 60f, Sioagard. 1fo, Sarkoz. 1.70fo, Boldog. 2fo, Orhalom. 2.50fo, Hosszuheteny.

1953, Sept. 12 Engr. ***Perf. 12***

1062	A233	20f bl grn	50	28
1063	A233	30f chocolate	50	20
1064	A233	40f ultra	50	28
1065	A233	60f red	65	42
1066	A233	1fo grnsh bl	1.10	85
1067	A233	1.70fo brt grn	2.25	1.25
1068	A233	2fo car rose	4.00	2.00
1069	A233	2.50fo purple	7.00	4.25
		Nos. 1062-1069 (8)	16.50	9.53

See No. 1189.

1954, Jan. 21 Wmk. 106 ***Perf. 12***

Designs: 60f, Lenin and Stalin at meeting. 1fo, Lenin, facing left.

1073	A234 40f dk bl grn	55	55
1074	A234 60f blk brn	52	22
1075	A234 1fo dk car rose	85	65

30th anniversary, death of Lenin.

Worker Reading A235

Revolutionary and Red Flag — A236

Design: 1fo, Soldier.

Perf. 12x12½, 12½x12

1954, Mar. 21 **Photo.**

1076	A235 40f gray bl & red	1.25	65
1077	A236 60f brn & red	1.75	1.50
1078	A235 1fo gray & red	2.50	2.25

35th anniversary of the "First Hungarian Communist Republic."

Blood Test A237

Maypole A238

Designs: 40f, Mother receiving newborn baby. 60f, Medical examination of baby.

1954, Mar. 8 ***Perf. 12***

1079	A237 30f brt bl	20	15
1080	A237 40f brn bister	25	15
1081	A237 60f purple	35	15
	Nos. 1079-1081,C146-C148 (6)	2.35	1.60

1954, May 1 ***Perf. 12½x12***

Design: 60f, Flag bearer.

1082	A238 40f olive	24	15
1083	A238 60f orange red	28	15
	Set value		24

Issued to publicize Labor Day, May 1, 1954.

Farm Woman with Fruit A239

1954, May 24 ***Perf. 12***

1084	A239 60f red org	25	15

Issued to publicize the 3rd Congress of the Hungarian Workers Party, Budapest, May 24, 1954.

Natl. Museum, Budapest — A240

Peppers — A241

Designs: 60f, Arms of People's Republic. 1fo, Dome of Parliament Building.

1954, Aug. 20 ***Perf. 12½x12***

1085	A240 40f brt bl	22	17
1086	A240 60f redsh brn	18	15
1087	A240 1fo dk brn	38	22

Fifth anniversary of the People's Republic Constitution.

1954, Sept. 11 Engr., Fruit Litho.

Fruit: 50f, Tomatoes. 60f, Grapes. 80f, Apricots. 1fo, Apples. 1.20fo, Plums. 1.50fo, Cherries. 2fo, Peaches.

Fruit in Natural Colors

1088	A241	40f gray bl	28	18
1089	A241	50f plum	28	18
1090	A241	60f gray bl	28	18
1091	A241	80f chocolate	38	18
1092	A241	1fo rose vio	40	24
1093	A241	1.20fo dl bl	80	38

1094 A241	1.50fo	plum	1.40	1.25
1095 A241	2fo	gray bl	1.10	75
		Nos. 1088-1095 (8)	4.92	3.34

National agricultural fair.

Maurus Jokai — A242 Janos Apacai Csere — A243

1954, Oct. 17 **Engr.**

1096 A242	60f	dk brn ol	42	25
1097 A242	1fo	deep claret	85	70

Issued to commemorate the 50th anniversary of the death of Maurus Jokai, writer.

No. 1097 in violet blue is from the souvenir sheet. No. C157.

1954, Dec. 5 **Photo.** ***Perf. 12x12½***

Scientists: 10f, Csoma Sandor Korosi. 12f, Anyos Jedlik. 20f, Ignaz Semmelweis. 30f, Janos Irinyi. 40f, Frigyes Koranyi. 50f, Armin Vambery. 60f, Karoly Than. 1fo, Otto Herman. 1.70fo, Tivadar Puskas. 2fo, Endre Hogyes.

1098 A243	8f	dk vio brn, *yel*	15	15
1099 A243	10f	brn, car, *pink*	20	15
1100 A243	12f	gray, *bl*	15	15
1101 A243	20f	brn, *yel*	15	15
1102 A243	30f	vio bl, *pink*	15	15
1103 A243	40f	dk grn, *yel*	15	15
1104 A243	50f	red brn, *pale grn*	15	15
1105 A243	60f	bl, *pink*	15	15
1106 A243	1fo	olive	38	16
1107 A243	1.70fo	rose brn, *yel*	60	32
1108 A243	2fo	bl grn	80	48
		Nos. 1098-1108 (11)	3.03	
		Set value		1.70

Readers in Industrial Library A244 Industry A245

Designs: 1fo, Agriculture. 2fo, Liberation monument.

1955, Apr. 4 ***Perf. 12½x12, 12x12½***

1109 A244	40f	dk car & ol brn	22	16
1110 A245	60f	dk grn & red	22	16
1111 A245	1fo	choc & grn	38	16
1112 A244	2fo	bl grn & brn	65	48

10th anniversary of Hungary's liberation.

Date, Flags and Farm — A246

1955, May 1 ***Perf. 12x12½***

1113 A246	1fo	rose car	45	15

Labor Day, May 1, 1955.

Government Printing Plant — A247

1955, May 28 **Wmk. 106**

1114 A247	60f	gray grn & hn brn	25	20

Issued to commemorate the centenary of the establishment of the government printing plant.

Young Citizens and Hungarian Flag A248

1955, June 15 ***Perf. 12***

1115 A248	1fo	red brn	35	15

Issued to publicize the second national congress of the Hungarian Youth Organization.

Truck Farmer A249

Designs: 10f, Fisherman. 12f, Bricklayer. 20f, Radio assembler. 30f, Woman potter. 40f, Railwayman and train. 50f, Clerk and scales. 60f, Postman emptying mail box. 70f, Cattle and herdsman. 80f, Textile worker. 1fo, Riveter. 1.20fo, Carpenter. 1.40fo, Streetcar conductor. 1.70fo, Herdsman and pigs. 2fo, Welder. 2.60fo, Woman tractor driver. 3fo, Herdsman in national costume and horse. 4fo, Bus driver. 5fo, Lineman. 10fo, Coal miner.

1955 **Wmk. 106** ***Perf. 12x12½***

1116 A249	8f	chestnut	16	15
1117 A249	10f	Prus grn	16	15
1118 A249	12f	red org	15	15
1119 A249	20f	ol grn	15	15
1120 A249	30f	dk red	42	15
1121 A249	40f	brown	15	15
1122 A249	50f	vio bl	15	15
1123 A249	60f	brn red	35	15
1124 A249	70f	olive	35	15
1125 A249	80f	purple	45	15
1126 A249	1fo	blue	22	15
1127 A249	1.20fo	ol bis	22	15
1128 A249	1.40fo	dp grn	42	15
1129 A249	1.70fo	purple	42	15
1130 A249	2fo	rose brn	42	15
1131 A249	2.60fo	vermilion	50	15
1132 A249	3fo	green	90	15
1133 A249	4fo	pck bl	1.10	16
1134 A249	5fo	org brn	1.50	26
1135 A249	10fo	violet	2.50	52
		Nos. 1116-1135 (20)	10.69	
		Set value		1.75

For surcharges see Nos. B211-B216.

Postrider Blowing Horn — A250

1955, June 25 ***Perf. 12½x12***

1136 A250	1fo	rose vio	35	15

Hungarian Postal Museum, 25th anniv.

Exists tete-beche. Value: 2½ times the value of a single.

Mihaly Csokonai Vitez — A251

Portraits: 1fo, Mihaly Vorosmarty. 2fo, Attila József.

1955, July 28 ***Perf. 12***

1137 A251	60f	ol blk	40	32
1138 A251	1fo	dk bl	70	24
1139 A251	2fo	rose brn	90	65

Issued to honor three Hungarian poets.

Bela Bartok — A252

1955, Oct. 9

1140 A252	60f	lt brn	70	50

10th anniversary of the death of Bela Bartok, composer. See Nos. C168-C169.

Diesel Train A253

Designs: 60f, Bus. 80f, Motorcycle. 1fo, Truck. 1.20fo, Steam locomotive. 1.50fo, Dump truck. 2fo, Freighter.

1955, Dec. 20 ***Perf. 14½***

1141 A253	40f	grn & vio brn	15	15
1142 A253	60f	dp grn & ol	16	15
1143 A253	80f	ol grn & brn	25	15
1144 A253	1fo	ocher & grn	45	28
1145 A253	1.20fo	sal & blk	65	32
1146 A253	1.50fo	grnsh blk & red brn	80	48
1147 A253	2fo	aqua & brn	1.10	90
		Nos. 1141-1147 (7)	3.56	2.43

Puli (Sheepdog) — A254

Puli and Steer A255

Hungarian Pointer — A256

Hungarian Dogs: 60f, Pumi (sheepdog). 1fo, Retriever with fowl. 1.20fo, Kuvasz (sheepdog). 1.50fo, Komondor (sheepdog) and cottage. 2fo, Komondor (head).

Perf. 11x13 (A254), 12

1956, Mar. 17 **Engr. & Litho.**

1148 A254	40f	yel, blk & red	20	15
1149 A254	50f	bl, bis & blk	20	15
1150 A254	60f	yel grn, blk & red	20	15
1151 A254	80f	bluish grn, ocher & blk	24	15
1152 A254	1fo	turq, ocher & blk	32	18
1153 A254	1.20fo	sal, blk & chnt	48	18
1154 A254	1.50fo	ultra, blk & buff	90	52
1155 A254	2fo	cer, blk & chnt	1.25	80
		Nos. 1148-1155 (8)	3.79	2.28

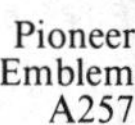

Pioneer Emblem A257

Perf. 12x12½

1956, June 2 **Photo.** **Wmk. 106**

1156 A257	1fo	red	25	15
1157 A257	1fo	gray	25	15
		Set value		24

Pioneer movement, 10th anniversary.

Janos Hunyadi Statue — A258 Miner — A259

1956, Aug. 12 ***Perf. 12***

1158 A258	1fo	brn, *yelsh*	50	35

500th anniv. of the defeat of the Turks at the battle of Pecs under Janos Hunyadi.

Printed in sheets of 50 with alternate vertical rows inverted and center row of perforation omitted, providing 25 tete beche pairs, of which 5 are imperf. between.

1956, Sept. 2

1159 A259	1fo	dk bl	30	15

Issued in honor of Miners' Day 1956.

Kayak Racer A260

Sports: 30f, Horse jumping hurdle. 40f, Fencing. 60f, Women hurdlers. 1fo, Soccer. 1.50fo, Weight lifting. 2fo, Gymnastics. 3fo, Basketball.

1956, Sept. 25 **Wmk. 106** ***Perf. 11***

Figures in Brown Olive

1160 A260	20f	lt bl	15	15
1161 A260	30f	lt ol grn	15	15
1162 A260	40f	dp org	16	15
1163 A260	60f	bluish grn	15	15
1164 A260	1fo	vermilion	24	15
1165 A260	1.50fo	bl vio	32	22
1166 A260	2fo	emerald	45	28
1167 A260	3fo	rose lil	80	60
		Nos. 1160-1167 (8)	2.42	
		Set value		1.55

16th Olympic Games at Melbourne, Nov. 22-Dec. 8, 1956.

Franz Liszt
A261

Portrait: 1fo, Frederic Chopin facing left.

1956, Oct. 7 Photo. *Perf. 12x12½*

1168 A261 1fo vio bl 90 90
1169 A261 1fo magenta 90 90

Nos. 1168 and 1169 alternate in the sheet, forming horizontal se-tenant pairs.
Issued for the 29th Day of the Stamp and sold only at the Philatelic Exhibition together with entrance ticket for 4fo.

Janos Arany A262 Arms of Hungary A263

1957, Sept. 15 Wmk. 106 *Perf. 12*

1170 A262 2fo brt bl 50 15

Issued in honor of the 75th anniversary of the death of Janos Arany, poet.

1957, Oct. 1

1171 A263 60f brt red 20 15
1172 A263 1fo dp yel grn 30 15
Set value 19

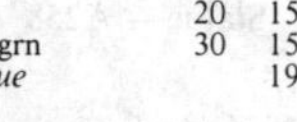

Trade Union Congress Emblem A264

1957, Oct. 4

1173 A264 1fo dk car 25 15

Issued to publicize the fourth International Trade Union Congress, Leipzig, Oct. 4-15.

Dove and Colors of Communist Countries — A265

Design: 1fo, Lenin.

1957, Nov. 7 Litho. *Perf. 12*

1174 A265 60f gray, blk & multi 24 15
1175 A265 1fo ol bis & ind 25 16
Set value 24

Russian Revolution, 40th anniversary.

Komarom Tumbler Pigeons A266

Pigeons: 40f, Two short-beaked Budapest pigeons. 60f, Giant domestic pigeon. 1fo, Three Szeged pigeons. 2fo, Two Hungarian fantails.

Perf. 12x12½

1957-58 Photo. Wmk. 106

1176 A266 30f yel grn, cl & ocher 20 15
1177 A266 40f ocher & blk 20 15
1178 A266 60f bl & gray 20 15
1179 A266 1fo gray & red brn 45 16
1180 A266 2fo brt pink & gray 1.00 60
Nos. 1176-1180,C175 (6) 2.80 1.71

Issued to publicize the International Pigeon Exhibition, Budapest, Dec. 14-16.
Issue dates: No. 1176, Jan. 12, 1958, others, Dec. 14, 1957.

Television Station — A267

1958, Feb. 22 Engr. *Perf. 11*

1181 A267 2fo rose vio 90 65
a. Perf. 12 2.00 2.00

Souvenir Sheet

1182 A267 2fo green 22.50 22.50

Issued to publicize the television industry. No. 1182 sold for 25fo.

Mother and Child A268

Designs: 30f, Old man feeding pigeons. 40f, School boys. 60f, "Working ants and fiddling grasshopper." 1fo, Honeycomb and bee. 2fo, Handing over money.

1958, Mar. 9 Photo. *Perf. 12*

1183 A268 20f yel grn & ol gray 22 15
1184 A268 30f lt ol & mar 22 15
1185 A268 40f yel bis & brn 22 15
1186 A268 60f rose car & grnsh blk 30 18
1187 A268 1fo ol gray & dk brn 52 35
1188 A268 2fo org & ol gray 1.40 70
Nos. 1183-1188 (6) 2.88 1.68

Issued to publicize the value of savings and insurance.

Kazar Costume Type of 1953
Souvenir Sheet

1958, Apr. 17 Engr. *Perf. 12*

1189 A233 10fo magenta 20.00 20.00

Issued for the Universal and International Exposition at Brussels.

Arms of Hungary — A269

1958, May 23 Litho. Wmk. 106
Arms in Original Colors

1190 A269 60f lt red brn & red 15 15
1191 A269 1fo gray grn & grn 16 15
1192 A269 2fo gray & dk brn 48 20
Set value 38

Issued to commemorate the first anniversary of the law amending the constitution.

Youth Holding Book — A270

Post Horn and Town Hall, Prague — A271

1958, June 14 Photo. *Perf. 12½x12*

1193 A270 1fo brn car 45 20

Issued to publicize the 5th Hungarian Youth Festival at Keszthely.
Printed with alternating label, inscribed: V. IFJUSAGI TALALKOZO KESZTHELY 1958.

1958, June 30

1194 A271 60f green 20 15
a. Se-tenant with No. C184 60 42

Conference of Postal Ministers of Communist Countries at Prague, June 30-July 8.

Dolomite Flax — A272

Hungarian Thistles — A273

Flowers: 30f, Kitaibelia vitifolia. 60f, Crocuses. 1fo, Hellebore. 2fo, Lilies. 2.50fo, Pinks. 3fo, Dog roses.

Perf. 11x13, 12½x12 (A273)

1958, Aug. 12 Photo. Wmk. 106

1195 A272 20f red vio & yel 1.00 20
1196 A272 30f bl, yel & grn 15 15
1197 A273 40f brn & bis 22 15
1198 A273 60f bl grn & pink 30 15
1199 A273 1fo rose car & yel grn 52 22
1200 A273 2fo grn & yel 95 20
1201 A272 2.50fo vio bl & pink 1.25 42
1202 A272 3fo grn & pink 2.00 70
a. Souvenir sheet of 4, perf. 12 20.00 20.00
Nos. 1195-1202 (8) 6.39 2.19

No. 1202a and a similar imperf. sheet were issued for the International Philatelic Congress at Brussels, Sept. 15-17, 1958. They contain the triangular 20f, 30f, 2.50fo and 3fo stamps printed in different colors. Sheets measure 111x111mm. and are printed on unwatermarked, linen-finish paper. Background of stamps, marginal inscriptions and ornaments in green. No. 1202a also exists perf. 11; same value.

Paddle, Ball and Olive Branch A274

Designs: 30f, Table tennis player (vert.). 40f, Wrestlers (vert.). 60f, Wrestlers (horiz.). 1fo, Water polo player (vert.). 2.50fo, High dive (vert.). 3fo, Swimmer.

1958, Aug. 30 Wmk. 106 *Perf. 12*

1203 A274 20f rose red, *pnksh* 15 15
1204 A274 30f olive, *grnsh* 15 15
1205 A274 40f mag, *yel* 18 15
1206 A274 60f brn, *bluish* 22 15
1207 A274 1fo ultra, *bluish* 38 22
1208 A274 2.50fo dk red, *yel* 75 42
1209 A274 3fo grnsh bl, *grnsh* 1.10 75
Nos. 1203-1209 (7) 2.93 1.99

The International Wrestling and European Swimming and Table Tennis Championships, held at Budapest.

Red Flag — A275

Design: 2fo, Hand holding newspaper.

1958, Nov. 21 *Perf. 12½x12*

1210 A275 1fo brn & red 15 15
1211 A275 2fo dk gray bl & red 28 15
Set value 20

40th anniversary of the founding of the Hungarian Communist Party and newspaper.

Satellite, Sputnik and American Rocket A276

Designs: 10f, Eötvös Torsion Balance and Globe. 20f, Deep sea exploration. 30f, Icebergs, penguins and polar light. 40f, Soviet Antarctic camp and map of Pole. 60f, "Rocket" approaching moon. 1fo, Sun and observatory.

1959, Mar. 14 *Perf. 12x12½*
Size: 32x21mm

1212 A276 10f car rose & sep 30 15
1213 A276 20f brt bl & gray 18 15
1214 A276 30f dk sl grn & bis 28 15

Perf. 12
Size: 35x26mm

1215 A276 40f sl bl & lt bl 18 15

Perf. 15
Size: 58x21mm

1216 A276 60f Prus bl & lem 40 20

Perf. 12
Size: 35x26mm

1217 A276 1fo scar & yel 65 32
1218 A276 5fo brn & red brn 1.50 80
Nos. 1212-1218 (7) 3.49 1.92

Intl. Geophysical Year. See No. 1262.

"Revolution" — A277

1959, Mar. 21 *Perf. 12½x12*

1219 A277 20f vio brn & red 20 15
1220 A277 60f bl & red 15 15
1221 A277 1fo brn & red 45 15
Set value 28

40th anniv. of the proclamation of the Hungarian Soviet Republic.

Rose — A278

1959, May 1 Photo. *Perf. 11*
1222 A278 60f lil, dp car & grn 30 15
1223 A278 1fo lt brn, dl red & grn 48 18

Issued for Labor Day, May 1, 1959.

Early Locomotive — A279

Designs: 30f, Diesel coach. 40f, Early semaphore (vert.). 60f, Csonka automobile. 1fo, Icarus bus. 2fo, First Lake Balaton steamboat. 2.50fo, Stagecoach.

1959, May 26 Litho. *Perf. 14½x15*
1224 A279 20f multi 28 15
1225 A279 30f multi 22 16
1226 A279 40f multi 22 16
1227 A279 60f multi 22 16
1228 A279 1fo multi 28 20
1229 A279 2fo multi 55 38
1230 A279 2.50fo multi 85 70
Nos. 1224-1230,C201 (8) 3.87 2.86

Transport Museum, Budapest.

Perf. 10½x11½
1959, May 29 Wmk. 106
1231 A279 2.50fo multi 2.00 2.00

Designer's name on No. 1231. Printed in sheets of four with four labels to commemorate the congress of the International Federation for Philately in Hamburg.

Post Horn and World Map A280

1959, June 1 Photo. *Perf. 12*
1232 A280 1fo cerise 40 30

Postal Ministers Conference, Berlin.
Printed in sheets of 25 stamps with 25 alternating gray labels showing East Berlin Opera House.

Great Cormorant A281

Warrior, 10th Century A282

Birds: 20f, Little egret and nest. 30f, Purple heron and nest. 40f, Great egret. 60f, White spoonbill. 1fo, Gray heron. 2fo, Squacco heron and nest. 3fo, Glossy ibis.

1959, June 14
1233 A281 10f grn & ind 15 15
1234 A281 20f gray bl & ol grn 22 15
1235 A281 30f org, grnsh blk & vio 15 15
1236 A281 40f dk grn & gray 22 20
1237 A281 60f dp cl & pale rose 35 20
1238 A281 1fo dp bl grn & blk 42 30
1239 A281 2fo dp org & gray 85 30
1240 A281 3fo bis & brn lake 1.50 95
Nos. 1233-1240 (8) 3.86 2.40

1959, July 11

Designs: 20f, Warrior, 15th century. 30f, Soldier, 18th century. 40f, Soldier, 19th century. 60f, Cavalry man, 19th century. 1fo, Fencer, assault. 1.40fo, Fencer on guard. 3fo, Swordsman saluting.

1241 A282 10f gray & bl 18 15
1242 A282 20f gray & dl yel 20 15
1243 A282 30f gray & gray vio 18 15
1244 A282 40f gray & ver 18 15
1245 A282 60f gray & rose lil 18 18
1246 A282 1fo ind & lt bl grn 35 22
1247 A282 1.40fo org & blk 75 25
1248 A282 3fo blk & ol grn 1.10 70
Nos. 1241-1248 (8) 3.12 1.95

24th World Fencing Championships, Budapest.

Sailboat, Lake Balaton — A283

Designs: 40f, Vintager and lake (horiz.). 60f, Bathers. 1.20fo, Fishermen. 2fo, Summer guests and ship.

1959, July 11 Photo. Wmk. 106
1249 A283 30f bl, *yel* 15 15
1250 A283 40f car rose 15 15
1251 A283 60f dp red brn 15 15
1252 A283 1.20fo violet 35 15
1253 A283 2fo red org, *yel* 70 35
Nos. 1249-1253,C202-C205 (9) 2.57
Set value 1.42

Issued to publicize Lake Balaton and the opening of the Summer University.

Haydn's Monogram A284

Esterhazy Palace A285

Haydn and Schiller Monograms — A286

Design: 1fo, Joseph Haydn and score.

1959, Sept. 20 Wmk. 106 *Perf. 12*
1254 A284 40f dp cl & yel 20 15
1255 A285 60f Prus bl, gray & yel 80 48
1256 A284 1fo dk vio, lt brn & org 65 40

Designs: 40f, Schiller's monogram. 60f, Pegasus rearing from flames. 1fo, Friedrich von Schiller.

1257 A284 40f ol grn & org 20 15
1258 A285 60f vio bl & lil 40 38
1259 A284 1fo dp cl & org brn 80 40
Nos. 1254-1259 (6) 3.05 1.96

Souvenir Sheet

Imperf

1260 A286 Sheet of two 8.75 8.75
a. 3fo magenta 2.25 2.25
b. 3fo green 2.25 2.25

150th anniv. of the death of Joseph Haydn, Austrian composer, Nos. 1254-1256; 200th anniv. of the birth of Friedrich von Schiller, German poet and dramatist, Nos. 1257-1259; No. 1260 honors both Haydn and Schiller.

Shepherd — A287

1959, Sept. 25 Engr. *Perf. 12*
1261 A287 2fo dp claret 1.65 1.65
a. With ticket 2.00 2.00

Day of the Stamp and Natl. Stamp Exhib. Issued in sheets of 8 with alternating ticket. The 4fo sale price marked on the ticket was the admission fee to the Natl. Stamp Exhib.

Type of 1959 Overprinted in Red

1959, Sept. 24 Photo. *Perf. 15*
1262 A276 60f dl bl & lemon 45 25

Landing of Lunik 2 on moon, Sept. 14.

Handing over Letter A288

1959, Oct. 4 Litho. *Perf. 12*
1263 A288 60f multi 25 15

Intl. Letter Writing Week, Oct. 4-10.

Szamuely and Lenin — A289

Designs: 40pf, Aleksander Pushkin. 60pf, Vladimir V. Mayakovsky. 1fo, Hands holding peace flag.

1959, Nov. 14 Photo. Wmk. 106
1264 A289 20f dk red & bis 15 15
1265 A289 40f brn & rose lil, *bluish* 15 15
1266 A289 60f dk bl & bis 20 16
1267 A289 1fo bl, car, buff, red & grn 32 28
Set value 60

Soviet Stamp Exhibition, Budapest.

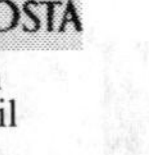

European Swallowtail A290

Worker with Banner A291

Butterflies: 30f, Arctia hebe (horiz.). 40f, Lysandra hylas (horiz.). 60f, Apatura ilia.

Perf. 11½x12, 12x11½
1959, Nov. 20
Butterflies in Natural Colors
1268 A290 20f blk & yel grn 16 15
1269 A290 30f lt bl & blk 24 15
1270 A290 40f dk gray & org brn 25 16
1271 A290 60f dk gray & dl yel 32 20
Nos. 1268-1271,C206-C208 (7) 5.07 2.55

1959, Nov. 30 *Perf. 14½*

Design: 1fo, Congress flag.

1272 A291 60f brn, grn & red 15 15
1273 A291 1fo brn, red, red & grn 18 15
Set value 15

Issued to commemorate the 7th Congress of the Hungarian Socialist Workers' Party.

Teacher Reading Fairy Tales A292

Sumeg Castle A293

Fairy Tales: 30f, Sleeping Beauty. 40f, Matt, the Goose Boy. 60f, The Cricket and the Ant. 1fo, Mashenka and the Three Bears. 2fo, Hansel and Gretel. 2.50fo, Pied Piper. 3fo, Little Red Riding Hood.

1959, Dec. 15 Litho. *Perf. 11½*
Designs in Black
1274 A292 20f gray & multi 15 15
1275 A292 30f brt pink 15 15
1276 A292 40f lt bl grn 18 15
1277 A292 60f lt bl 15 16
1278 A292 1fo yellow 24 24
1279 A292 2fo brt yel grn 45 24
1280 A292 2.50fo orange 60 38
1281 A292 3fo crimson 90 60
Nos. 1274-1281 (8) 2.82 2.07

Wmk. 106
1960, Feb. 1 Photo. *Perf. 14½*

Castles: 20fr, Tata. 30f, Diosgyor. 60f, Saros-Patak. 70f, Nagyvazsony. 1.40fo, Siklos. 1.70fo, Somlo. 3fo, Csesznek (vert.). 5fo, Koszeg (vert.). 10fo, Sarvar (vert.).

Size: 21x17½mm
1282 A293 8f purple 15 15
1283 A293 20f dk yel grn 15 15
1284 A293 30f org brn 15 15
1285 A293 60f rose red 15 15
1286 A293 70f emerald 18 15

Perf. 12x11½, 11½x12
Size: 28x21mm, 21x28mm
1287 A293 1.40fo ultra 18 15
1288 A293 1.70fo dl vio ("Somlo") 22 15
b. 1.70fo dl vio ("Somlyo") 45 15
1289 A293 3fo red brn 38 15
1290 A293 5fo yel grn 75 18
1291 A293 10fo car rose 1.65 38
Nos. 1282-1291 (10) 3.96
Set value 1.00

Tinted Paper
Perf. 14½
Size: 21x17½mm
1282a A293 8f pur, *bluish* 15 15
1283a A293 20f dk yel grn, *grnsh* 20 15
1284a A293 30f org brn, *yel* 28 15

1285a A293 60f rose red, *pnksh* 20 15
1286a A293 70f emer, *bluish* 50 15

Perf. 12x11½

Size: 28x21mm

1287a A293 1.40fo ultra, *bluish* 55 28
1288a A293 1.70fo dl vio, *bluish* 70 28
Nos. 1282a-1288a (7) 2.58
Set value 88

See Nos. 1356-1365, 1644-1646.

Halas Lace — A294

Cross-country Skier — A295

Designs: Various Halas lace patterns.

Wmk. 106

1960, Feb. 15 Litho. *Perf. 11½*

Sizes: 20f, 60f, 1fo, 3fo: 27x37mm
30f, 40f, 1.50fo, 2fo: 37½x43½mm

Inscriptions in Orange

1292 A294 20f brn blk 15 15
1293 A294 30f violet 15 15
1294 A294 40f Prus bl 38 15
1295 A294 60f dk brn 20 15
1296 A294 1fo dk grn 22 15
1297 A294 1.50fo green 38 18
1298 A294 2fo dk bl 85 22
1299 A294 3fo dk car 1.50 55
Nos. 1292-1299 (8) 3.83
Set value 1.32

See Nos. 1570-1577.

Souvenir Sheet

Design as on No. 1299.

1960, Sept. 3

Inscriptions in Orange

1300 Sheet of 4 + 4 labels 6.75 6.75
a. 3fo brown olive 1.25 1.25
b. 3fo bright violet 1.25 1.25
c. 3fo emerald 1.25 1.25
d. 3fo bright blue 1.25 1.25

Fédération Internationale de Philatélie Congress, Warsaw, Sept. 3-11. No. 1300 contains 4 stamps and 4 alternating labels, printed in colors of adjoining stamps.

1960, Feb. 29 Photo. *Perf. 11½x12*

Sports: 40f, Ice hockey player. 60f, Ski jumper. 80f, Woman speed skater. 1fo, Downhill skier. 1.20fo, Woman figure skater.

Inscriptions and Figures in Bister

1301 A295 30f dp bl 15 15
1302 A295 40f brt grn 15 15
1303 A295 60f scarlet 15 15
1304 A295 80f purple 22 15
1305 A295 1fo brt grnsh bl 45 22
1306 A295 1.20fo brn red 55 45
Nos. 1301-1306,B217 (7) 2.92
Set value 1.45

8th Olympic Winter Games, Squaw Valley, Calif., Feb. 18-29, 1960.

Clara Zetkin — A296

Portraits: No. 1308, Kato Haman. No. 1309, Lajos Tükory. No. 1310, Giuseppe Garibaldi. No. 1311, Istvan Türr. No. 1312, Otto Herman. No. 1313, Ludwig van Beethoven. No. 1314, Ferenc Mora. No. 1315, Istvan Toth Bucsoki. No. 1316, Donat Banki. No. 1317, Abraham G. Pattantyus. No. 1318, Ignaz Semmelweis. No. 1319, Frederic Joliot-Curie. No. 1320, Ferenc Erkel. No. 1321, Janos Bolyai. No. 1322, Lenin.

1960 Photo. *Perf. 10½*

1307 A296 60f lt red brn 15 15

Engr.

1308 A296 60f pale pur 15 15
1309 A296 60f rose red 15 15
1310 A296 60f violet 15 15
1311 A296 60f bl grn 15 15
1312 A296 60f blue 15 15
1313 A296 60f gray brn 15 15
1314 A296 60f sal pink 15 15
1315 A296 60f gray 15 15
1316 A296 60f rose lil 15 15
1317 A296 60f green 15 15
1318 A296 60f vio bl 15 15
1319 A296 60f brown 15 15
1320 A296 60f rose brn 15 15
1321 A296 60f grnsh bl 15 15
1322 A296 60f dl red 15 25
Set value 1.75 1.00

Nos. 1307-1308 commemorate International Women's Day, Mar. 8.

Flower and Quill — A297

Soviet Capt. Ostapenko Statue — A298

Wmk. 106

1960, Apr. 2 Photo. *Perf. 12*

1323 A297 2fo brn, yel & grn 1.25 1.25
a. With ticket 1.50 1.50

Issued for the stamp show of the National Federation of Hungarian Philatelists. The olive green 4fo ticket pictures the Federation's headquarters and served as entrance ticket to the show. Printed in sheets of 35 stamps and 35 tickets.

Perf. 12½x11½, 11½x12½

1960, Apr. 4

Designs: 60f, Youth holding flag (horiz.).

1324 A298 40f dp car & brn 15 15
1325 A298 60f red brn, red & grn 16 15
Set value 16

Issued to commemorate the 15th anniversary of Hungary's liberation from the Nazis.

Boxers — A299

Sports: 10f, Rowers. 30f, Archer. 40f, Discus thrower. 50f, Girls playing ball. 60f, Javelin thrower. 1fo, Rider. 1.40fo, Wrestlers. 1.70fo, Swordsmen. 3fo, Hungarian Olympic emblem.

1960, Aug. 21 *Perf. 11½x12*

Designs in Ocher and Black

1326 A299 10f blue 15 15
1327 A299 20f salmon 15 15
1328 A299 30f lt vio 15 15
1329 A299 40f yellow 15 15
1330 A299 50f dp pink 15 15
1331 A299 60f gray 15 15
1332 A299 1fo pale brn vio 24 15
1333 A299 1.40fo lt vio bl 30 15
1334 A299 1.70fo ocher 48 22
1335 A299 3fo multi 1.40 90
Nos. 1326-1335,B218 (11) 4.27
Set value 2.10

17th Olympic Games, Rome, Aug. 25-Sept. 11.

Souvenir Sheet

Romulus and Remus Statue and Olympic Flame — A300

1960, Aug. 21

1336 A300 10fo multi 10.00 12.00

Winter and Summer Olympic Games, 1960.

Woman of Mezokovesd Writing Letter — A301

Perf. 11½x12

1960, Oct. 15 Photo. Wmk. 106

1337 A301 2fo multi 1.40 1.40
a. With ticket 1.75 1.75

Day of the Stamp and Natl. Stamp Exhib. Issued in sheets of 8 with alternating ticket. The 4fo sale price marked on the ticket was the admission fee to the Natl. Stamp Exhib.

The Turnip, Russian Fairy Tale — A302

Kangaroo — A303

Fairy Tales: 30f, Snow White and the Seven Dwarfs. 40f, The Miller, His Son and the Donkey. 60f, Puss in Boots. 80f, The Fox and the Raven. 1fo, The Maple-Wood Pipe. 1.70fo, The Fox and the Stork. 2fo, Momotaro (Japanese).

1960, Dec. 1 *Perf. 11½x12*

1338 A302 20f multi 15 15
1339 A302 30f multi 15 15
1340 A302 40f multi 15 15
1341 A302 60f multi 15 15
1342 A302 80f multi 18 15
1343 A302 1fo multi 40 15
1344 A302 1.70fo multi 75 40
1345 A302 2fo multi 1.19 70
Nos. 1338-1345 (8) 3.12
Set value 1.40

1961, Feb. 24 *Perf. 11½x12*

Animals: 30f, Bison. 40f, Brown bear. 60f, Elephants. 80fr, Tiger with cubs. 1fo, Ibex. 1.40fo, Polar bear. 2fo, Zebra and young. 2.60fo, Bison cow with calf. 3fo, Main entrance to Budapest Zoological Gardens. 30f, 60f, 80f, 1.40fo, 2fo, 2.60fo are horizontal.

1346 A303 20f org & blk 15 15
1347 A303 30f yel grn & blk brn 15 15
1348 A303 40f org brn & brn 15 15
1349 A303 60f lil rose & gray 15 15
1350 A303 80f gray & yel 15 15
1351 A303 1fo bl grn & brn 15 15
1352 A303 1.40fo grnsh bl, gray & blk 30 18
1353 A303 2fo pink & blk 40 24
1354 A303 2.60fo brt vio & brn 60 38
1355 A303 3fo multi 1.10 75
Nos. 1346-1355 (10) 3.30
Set value 1.90

Issued for the Budapest Zoo.

Castle Type of 1960

Castles: 10f, Kisvárda. 12f, Szigliget. 40f, Simon Tornya. 50f, Füzer. 80f, Egervar. 1fo, Vitany. 1.20fo, Sirok. 2fo, Boldogkö. 2.60fo, Hollokö. 4fo, Eger.

1961, Mar. 3 Photo. *Perf. 14½*

Size: 21x17½mm

1356 A293 10f org brn 15 15
1357 A293 12f vio bl 15 15
1358 A293 40f brt grn 15 15
1359 A293 50f brown 15 15
1360 A293 80f dl claret 15 15

Perf. 12x11½

Size: 28x21mm

1361 A293 1fo brt bl 15 15
1362 A293 1.20fo rose vio 28 15
1363 A293 2fo ol bis 45 15
1364 A293 2.60fo dl bl 70 15
1365 A293 4fo brt vio 85 20
Nos. 1356-1365 (10) 3.18
Set value 84

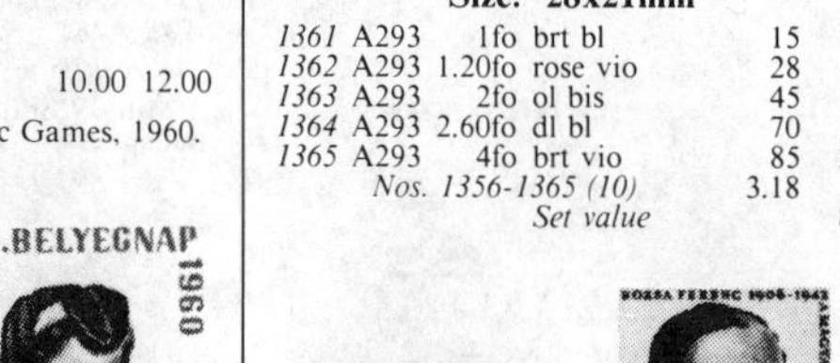

Child Chasing Butterfly A304

Ferenc Rozsa, Journalist A305

Designs: 40f, Man on operating table. 60f, Ambulance and stretcher. 1fo, Traffic light and scooter. 1.70fo, Syringe. 4fo, Emblem of Health Information Service (torch and serpent).

1961, Mar. 17 Litho. *Perf. 10½*

Cross in Red

Size: 18x18mm

1366 A304 30f org brn & blk 15 15
1367 A304 40f bl grn, bl & sepia 15 15

Size: 25x30mm

1368 A304 60f multi 16 15
1369 A304 1fo multi 18 15
1370 A304 1.70fo multi 60 22
1371 A304 4fo gray & yel grn 1.40 55
Nos. 1366-1371 (6) 2.64
Set value 1.10

Health Information Service.

Wmk. 106, Unwmk.

1961 Photo. *Perf. 12*

Portraits: No. 1373, Gyorgy Kilian. No. 1374, Jozsef Rippl-Ronai. No. 1375, Sandor Latinka. No. 1376, Mate Zalka. No. 1377, Jozsef Katona.

1372 A305 1fo red brn 15 15
1373 A305 1fo grnsh bl 15 15
1374 A305 1fo rose brn 15 15
1375 A305 1fo ol bis 15 15
1376 A305 1fo ol grn 15 15
1377 A305 1fo maroon 15 15
Set value 72 35

Issued to commemorate variously: Press Day (No. 1372); the inauguration of the Gyorgy Kilian Sports Movement (No. 1373); the birth centenary of Jozsef Rippl-Ronai, painter (No. 1374); the 75th anniversary of the death of Sandor Latinka, revolutionary leader (No. 1375); Mate Zalka, author and revolutionist (No. 1376); Jozsef Katona, dramatist (No. 1377).

Nos. 1374, 1375, 1377 are unwmkd. Others in this set have wmk. 106.

Yuri A. Gagarin and Vostok 1 — A306

Roses — A307

Design: 1fo, Launching Vostok 1.

Perf. 11½x12

1961, Apr. 25 **Wmk. 106**

1381 A306 1fo dk bl & bis brn 52 52
1382 A306 2fo dp ultra & bis brn 2.50 2.50

Issued to commemorate the first man in space, Yuri A. Gagarin, Apr. 12, 1961.

1961, Apr. 29 ***Perf. 12½x11½***

Design: 2fo, as 1fo, design reversed.

1383 A307 1fo grn & dp car 22 15
1384 A307 2fo grn & dp car 28 15

Issued for May Day, 1961. Nos. 1383-1384 are printed se-tenant in sheet.

"Venus" and Moon A308

Designs: Various Stages of Rocket.

1961, May 24 **Wmk. 106** ***Perf. 14½***

1385 A308 40f grnsh bl, bis & blk 40 22
1386 A308 60f brt bl, bis & blk 52 22
1387 A308 80f ultra & blk 1.00 70
1388 A308 2fo vio & yel 3.00 2.25

Issued to commemorate the Soviet launching of the Venus space probe, Feb. 12, 1961. No. 1388 was also printed in sheets of four, perf. and imperf. Size: 130x76mm.

Warsaw Mermaid, Letter and Sea, Air and Land Transport A309

Mermaid and: 60f, Television screen and antenna. 1fo, Radio.

1961, June 19 **Photo.** ***Perf. 13½***

1389 A309 40f red org & blk 15 15
1390 A309 60f lil & blk 24 15
1391 A309 1fo brt bl & blk 38 15
Set value 27

Conference of Postal Ministers of Communist Countries held at Warsaw.

Flag and Parliament A310

Designs: 1.70fo, Orchid. 2.60fo, Small tortoise-shell butterfly. 3fo, Goldfinch.

1961, June 23 ***Perf. 11***

Background in Silver

1392 A310 1fo grn, red & blk 38 38
1393 A310 1.70fo red & multi 52 52
1394 A310 2.60fo pur & multi 85 85
1395 A310 3fo bl & multi 1.10 1.10

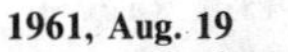

1961, Aug. 19

Background in Gold

1396 A310 1fo grn & blk 38 38
1397 A310 1.70fo red & multi 48 48
1398 A310 2.60fo pur & multi 85 85
1399 A310 3fo bl & multi 1.10 1.10
Nos. 1392-1399 (8) 5.66 5.66

Issued to publicize the International Stamp Exhibition, Budapest, Sept. 23-Oct. 3, 1961.

Each denomination of Nos. 1392-1399 printed in sheets of four.

In gold background issue the top left inscription is changed on 1fo and 3fo.

George Stephenson A311

Winged Wheel, Steering Wheel and Road A312

Design: 2fo, Jenö Landler.

Perf. 12½x11½

1961, July 4 **Photo.** **Wmk. 106**

1400 A311 60f yel olive 15 15
1401 A312 1fo bl & bister 24 15
1402 A311 2fo yel brn 42 24

Conference of Transport Ministers of Communist Countries held at Budapest.

Soccer A313

1961, July 8 **Unwmk.** ***Perf. 14½***

1403 A313 40f shown 15 15
1404 A313 60f Wrestlers 15 15
1405 A313 1fo Gymnast 32 20
Set value 54 37

50th anniv. of the Steel Workers Sport Club (VASAS). See No. B219.

Galloping Horses — A314

Designs: 40f, Hurdle Jump. 60f, Two trotters. 1fo, Three trotters. 1.70fo, Mares and foals. 2fo, Race horse "Baka." 3fo, Race horse "Kincsem."

1961, July 22

1406 A314 30f multi 15 15
1407 A314 40f multi 15 15
1408 A314 60f multi 15 15
1409 A314 1fo multi 35 15
1410 A314 1.70fo multi 60 18
1411 A314 2fo multi 95 40
1412 A314 3fo multi 1.50 70
Nos. 1406-1412 (7) 3.85 1.88

Keyboard, Music and Liszt Silhouette A315

Liszt Monument, Budapest — A316

Designs: 2fo, Academy of Music, Budapest, and bar of music. 10fo, Franz Liszt.

1961, Oct. 2 **Unwmk.** ***Perf. 12***

1413 A315 60f gold & blk 18 15
1414 A316 1fo dk gray 35 20
1415 A315 2fo dk bl & gray grn 50 40

Souvenir Sheet

1416 A316 10fo multi 6.00 6.00

150th anniv. of the birth, and the 75th anniv. of the death of Franz Liszt, composer.

Lenin — A317

Monk's Hood — A318

1961, Oct. 22 ***Perf. 11½***

1417 A317 1fo dp brn 25 15

22nd Congress of the Communist Party of the USSR, Oct. 17-31.

Wmk. 106

1961, Nov. 4 **Photo.** ***Perf. 12***

1418 A318 20f shown 15 15
1419 A318 30f Centaury 15 15
1420 A318 40f Blue iris 15 15
1421 A318 60f Thorn apple 15 15
1422 A318 1fo Purple hollyhock 28 15
1423 A318 1.70fo Hop 45 20
1424 A318 2fo Poppy 95 40
1425 A318 3fo Mullein 1.40 65
Nos. 1418-1425 (8) 3.68
Set value 1.50

Nightingale A319

Mihaly Karolyi A320

Birds: 40f, Great titmouse. 60f, Chaffinch (horiz.). 1fo, Eurasian jay. 1.20fo, Golden oriole (horiz.). 1.50fo, European blackbird (horiz.). 2fo, Yellowhammer. 3fo, Lapwing (horiz.).

1961, Dec. 18 **Unwmk.** ***Perf. 12***

1426 A319 30f multi 15 15
1427 A319 40f multi 20 15
1428 A319 60f multi 15 15
1429 A319 1fo multi 15 15
1430 A319 1.20fo multi 18 15
1431 A319 1.50fo multi 48 15
1432 A319 2fo multi 60 24
1433 A319 3fo multi 1.25 48
Nos. 1426-1433 (8) 3.16
Set value 1.30

1962, Mar. 18

1434 A320 1fo black 20 15

Issued in memory of Mihaly Karolyi, (1875-1955), Prime Minister of Hungarian Republic (1918-19).

1962, Mar. 29

Portrait: No. 1435, Ferenc Berkes.

1435 A320 1fo red brn 16 15

Fifth Congress of the Hungarian Cooperative Movement, and to honor Ferenc Berkes, revolutionary. See Nos. 1457, 1459.

Map of Europe, Train Signals and Emblem — A321

1962, May 2 **Photo.**

1436 A321 1fo bl grn 20 15

Issued to commemorate the 14th International Esperanto Congress of Railway Men.

Xiphophorus Helleri — A322

Tropical Fish: 30f, Macropodus opercularis. 40f, Lebistes reticulatus. 60f, Betta splendens. 80c, Puntius tetrazona. 1fo, Pterophyllum scalare. 1.20fo, Mesogonistius chaetodon. 1.50fo, Aphyosemion australe. 2fo, Hyphessobrycon innesi. 3fo, Symphysodon aequifasciata haraldi.

1962, May 5 ***Perf. 11½x12***

Fish in Natural Colors, Black Inscriptions

1437 A322 20f blue 15 15
1438 A322 30f citron 15 15
1439 A322 40f lt bl 15 15
1440 A322 60f lt yel grn 15 15
1441 A322 80f bl grn 28 15
1442 A322 1fo brt bl grn 16 15
1443 A322 1.20fo bl grn 22 15
1444 A322 1.50fo grnsh bl 28 15
1445 A322 2fo green 60 28
1446 A322 3fo gray grn & yel 90 70
Nos. 1437-1446 (10) 3.04
Set value 1.65

Globe, Soccer Ball and Flags of Colombia and Uruguay — A323

Goalkeeper — A324

Flags of: 40f, USSR and Yugoslavia. 60f, Switzerland and Chile. 1fo, Germany and Italy. 1.70fo, Argentina and Bulgaria. 3fo, Brazil and Mexico.

Unwmk.

1962, May 21 Photo. *Perf. 11*

Flags in National Colors

1447 A323 30f rose & bis 15 15
1448 A323 40f pale grn & bis 15 15
1449 A323 60f pale lil & bis 15 15
1450 A323 1fo bl & bis 38 18
1451 A323 1.70fo ocher & bis 30 24
1452 A323 3fo pink & bl bis 90 45
Nos. 1447-1452,B224,C209A (8) 4.13
Set value 1.70

Souvenir Sheet

Perf. 12

1453 A324 10fo multi 7.00 7.00

World Cup Soccer Championship, Chile, May 30-June 17.

Type of 1961 and

Johann Gutenberg — A325

Portraits: No. 1456, Miklós Misztófalusi Kis, Hungarian printer (1650-1702). No. 1457, Jozsef Pach. No. 1458, Andras Chazar. No. 1459, Dr. Ferenc Hutyra. No. 1460, Gabor Egressy and National Theater.

1962 Unwmk. Photo. *Perf. 12*

1455 A325 1fo bl blk 18 15
1456 A325 1fo red brn 18 15
1457 A320 1fo blue 18 15
1458 A325 1fo violet 18 15
1459 A320 1fo dp bl 18 15
1460 A325 1fo rose red 18 15
Nos. 1455-1460 (6) 1.08
Set value 42

Cent. of Printers' and Papermakers' Union (Nos. 1455-1456). 75th anniv. of founding, by Jozsef Pech, of Hungarian Hydroelectric Service (No. 1457). Andras Chazar, founder of Hungarian deaf-mute education (No. 1458). Dr. Ferenc Hutyra, founder of Hungarian veterinary medicine (No. 1459). 125th anniv. of National Theater (No. 1460).

Malaria Eradication Emblem — A327

1962, June 25 *Perf. 15*

1461 A327 2.50fo lem & blk 50 40
a. 2.50fo grn & blk, sheet of 4, perf. 11 5.00 5.00

WHO drive to eradicate malaria. Imperf. sheets with control numbers exist.

Sword-into-Plowshare Statue, United Nations, NY — A328

1962, July 7 *Perf. 12*

1462 A328 1fo brown 15 15

Issued to commemorate the World Congress for Peace and Disarmament, Moscow, July 9-14.

Floribunda Rose A329

Festival Emblem A330

1962 *Perf. 12½x11½*

Various Roses in Natural Colors

1465 A329 20f org brn 15 15
1466 A329 40f sl grn 15 15
1467 A329 60f violet 15 15
1468 A329 80f rose red 18 15
1469 A329 1fo dk grn 24 15
1470 A329 1.20fo orange 28 18
1471 A329 2fo dk bl grn 75 52
1472 A330 3fo multi 1.10 42
Nos. 1465-1472 (8) 3.00
Set value 1.45

No. 1472 was issued to commemorate the 8th World Youth Festival, Helsinki, July 28-Aug. 6.

Weight Lifter — A331

Oil Derrick and Primitive Oil Well — A332

1962, Sept. 16 *Perf. 12*

1473 A331 1fo copper red 30 15

Issued to commemorate the European Weight Lifting Championships.

Perf. 12x11½

1962, Oct. 8 Photo. Unwmk.

1474 A332 1fo green 20 15

Issued to commemorate the 25th anniversary of the Hungarian oil industry.

Racing Motorcyclist — A333

Designs: 30f, Stunt racing. 40f, Uphill race. 60f, Cyclist in curve. 1fo, Start. 1.20fo, Speed racing. 1.70fo, Motorcyclist with sidecar. 2fo, Motor scooter. 3fo, Racing car.

1962, Dec. 28 *Perf. 11*

1475 A333 20f multi 15 15
1476 A333 30f multi 15 15
1477 A333 40f multi 15 15
1478 A333 60f multi 15 15
1479 A333 1fo multi 18 15
1480 A333 1.20fo multi 22 15
1481 A333 1.70fo multi 42 15
1482 A333 2fo multi 60 24
1483 A333 3fo multi 1.10 55
Nos. 1475-1483 (9) 3.12
Set value 1.32

Ice Skater — A334

Designs: 20f-3fo, Various figure skating and ice dancing positions. (20f, 3fo horiz.). 10fo, Figure skater and flags of participating nations.

Perf. 12x11½, 11½x12

1963, Feb. 5 Photo. Unwmk.

1484 A334 20f multi 18 15
1485 A334 40f multi 18 15
1486 A334 60f multi 18 15
1487 A334 1fo multi 30 15
1488 A334 1.40fo multi 30 22
1489 A334 2fo multi 42 35
1490 A334 3fo multi 1.00 70
Nos. 1484-1490 (7) 2.56
Set value 1.55

Souvenir Sheet

Perf. 11½x12

1491 A334 10fo multi 4.75 4.25

European Figure Skating and Ice Dancing Championships, Budapest, Feb. 5-10.

János Batsányi (1763-1845) — A335

Designs: No. 1493, Helicon Monument. No. 1494, Actors before Szeged Cathedral. No. 1495, Leo Weiner, composer. No. 1496, Ferenc Entz, horticulturist. No. 1497, Ivan Markovits, inventor of Hungarian shorthand, 1863. No. 1498, Dr. Frigyes Koranyi. No. 1499, Ferenc Erkel (1810-93), composer. No. 1500, Geza Gardonyi (1863-1922), writer of Hungarian historical novels for youth. No. 1501, Pierre de Coubertin, Frenchman, reviver of Olympic Games. No. 1502, Jozsef Eötvös, author, philosopher, educator. No. 1503, Budapest Industrial Fair emblem. No. 1504, Stagecoach and Arc de Triomphe, Paris. No. 1505, Hungary map and power lines. No. 1506, Roses.

1963 Unwmk. *Perf. 11*

1492 A335 40f dk car rose 15 15
1493 A335 40f blue 15 15
1494 A335 40f vio bl 15 15
1495 A335 40f olive 15 15
1496 A335 40f emerald 15 15
1497 A335 40f dk bl 15 15
1498 A335 60f dl vio 15 15
1499 A335 60f bis brn 15 15
1500 A335 60f gray grn 15 15
1501 A335 60f red brn 42 18
1502 A335 60f lilac 15 15
1503 A335 1fo purple 22 15
1504 A335 1fo rose red 25 15
1505 A335 1fo gray 25 15
1506 A335 2fo multi 60 15
Nos. 1492-1506 (15) 3.24
Set value 1.00

No. 1493, 10th Youth Festival, Keszthely. No. 1494, Outdoor plays, Szeged. No. 1495, Budapest Music Competition. No. 1496, Cent. of professional horticultural training. No. 1498, 50th anniv. of the death of Prof. Koranyi, pioneer in fight against tuberculosis. No. 1499, Erkel Memorial Festival, Gyula. No. 1501, 10th anniv. of the People's Stadium, Budapest. No. 1502, 150th anniv. of birth of Jozsef Eötvös, organizer of modern public education in Hungary. No. 1504, Paris Postal Conf., 1863. No. 1505, Rural electrification. No. 1506, 5th Natl. Rose Show.

Ship and Chain Bridge, Budapest A336

Bus and Parliament A337

Designs: 20f, Trolley. 30f, Sightseeing bus and National Museum. 40f, Bus and trailer. 50f, Railroad tank car. 60f, Trolley bus. 70f, Railroad mail car. 80f, Motorcycle messenger. No. 1516, Mail plane (vert.). No. 1517, Television transmitter, Miskolc (vert.). 1.40fo, Mobile post office. 1.70fo, Diesel locomotive. 2fo, Mobile radio transmitter and stadium. 2.50fo, Tourist bus. 2.60fo, Passenger train. 3fo, P.O. parcel conveyor. 4fo, Television transmitters, Pecs (vert.). 5fo, Hydraulic lift truck and mail car. 6fo, Woman teletypist. 8fo, Map of Budapest and automatic dial phone. 10fo, Girl pioneer and woman letter carrier.

1963-64 Photo. *Perf. 11*

1507 A336 10f brt bl 15 15
1508 A336 20f dp yel grn 15 15
1509 A336 30f violet 15 15
1510 A336 40f orange 15 15
1511 A336 50f brown 15 15
1512 A336 60f crimson 15 15
1513 A336 70f ol gray 15 15
1514 A336 80f red brn ('64) 28 15

Perf. 12x11½, 11½x12

1515 A337 1fo rose claret 15 15
1516 A337 1.20fo org brn 1.00 70
1517 A337 1.20fo dp vio ('64) 18 15
1518 A337 1.40fo dp yel grn 24 18
1519 A337 1.70fo maroon 35 15
1520 A337 2fo grnsh bl 40 15
1521 A337 2.50fo lilac 42 15
1522 A337 2.60fo olive 42 15
1523 A337 3fo dk bl ('64) 35 15
1524 A337 4fo blue ('64) 42 15
1525 A337 5fo ol brn ('64) 55 15
1526 A337 6fo dk ol bis ('64) 70 15
1527 A337 8fo red lil ('64) 1.00 24
1528 A337 10fo emer ('64) 1.00 50
Nos. 1507-1528 (22) 8.51
Set value 2.75

Size of 20f, 60f: 20½-21x16¾-17mm.

Minute inscription in lower margin includes year date, number of stamp in set and designer's name (Bokros F. or Legrady S.).

See Nos. 1983-1983B, 2196-2204.

Coil Stamps

1965-67 *Perf. 14*

Size: 21½x16½mm

1508a A336 20f dp yel grn 15 15
1512a A336 60f crimson ('67) 38 15
Set value 20

Black control number on back of every fifth stamp.

Motorboat — A338

Girl, Steamer and Castle — A339

Design: 60f, Sailboat.

1963, July 13 *Perf. 11*

1529 A338 20f sl grn, red & blk 22 15
1530 A339 40f multi 22 18
1531 A338 60f bl, blk, brn & org 38 25

Centenary of the summer resort Siofok.

Child with Towel and Toothbrush A340

Karancssag Woman A341

Designs: 40f, Child with medicines. 60f, Girls of 3 races. 1fo, Girl and heart. 1.40fo, Boys of 3 races. 2fo, Medical examination of child. 3fo, Hands shielding plants.

1963, July 27 ***Perf. 12x11½***

1532	A340	30f	multi	15	15
1533	A340	40f	multi	15	15
1534	A340	60f	multi	15	15
1535	A340	1fo	multi	15	15
1536	A340	1.40fo	multi	18	15
1537	A340	2fo	multi	30	28
1538	A340	3fo	multi	75	60
			Nos. 1532-1538 (7)	1.83	
			Set value		1.30

Centenary of the International Red Cross.

1963, Aug. 18 **Engr.** ***Perf. 11½***

Provincial Costumes: 30f, Kapuvár man. 40f, Debrecen woman. 60f, Hortobagy man. 1fo, Csököly woman. 1.70fo, Dunantul man. 2fo, Bujak woman. 2.50fo, Alföld man. 3fo, Mezökövesd bride.

1539	A341	20f	claret	15	15
1540	A341	30f	green	15	15
1541	A341	40f	brown	15	15
1542	A341	60f	brt bl	16	15
1543	A341	1fo	brn red	22	15
1544	A341	1.70fo	purple	35	22
1545	A341	2fo	dk bl grn	48	22
1546	A341	2.50fo	dk car	60	32
1547	A341	3fo	vio bl	1.10	55
			Nos. 1539-1547 (9)	3.36	
			Set value		1.65

Issued in connection with the Popular Art Exhibition in Budapest.

Slalom and 1964 Olympic Emblem — A342

Sports: 60f, Downhill skiing. 70f, Ski jump. 80f, Rifle shooting on skis. 1fo, Figure skating pair. 2fo, Ice hockey. 2.60fo, Speed ice skating. 10fo, Skier and mountains (vert.).

1963-64 **Photo.** ***Perf. 12***

1964 Olympic Emblem in Black and Red

1548	A342	40f	yel grn & bis	15	15
1549	A342	60f	vio & bis	15	15
1550	A342	70f	ultra & bis	15	15
1551	A342	80f	emer & bis	15	15
1552	A342	1fo	brn org & bis	18	15
1553	A342	2fo	brt bl & bis	45	22
1554	A342	2.60fo	rose lake & bis	70	45
			Nos. 1548-1554,B234 (8)	2.83	
			Set value		1.40

Souvenir Sheet

Perf. 11½x12

1555	A342	10fo	grnsh bl, red & brn ('64)	5.00	4.75

9th Winter Olympic Games, Innsbruck, Austria, Jan. 29-Feb. 9, 1964.

Four-Leaf Clover A343

Moon Rocket A344

Good Luck Symbols: 20f, Calendar and mistletoe (horiz.). 30f, Chimneysweep and clover. 60f, Top hat, pig and clover. 1fo, Clown with balloon and clover (horiz.). 2fo, Lanterns, mask and clover.

Perf. 12x11½, 11½x12

1963, Dec. 12 **Photo.** **Unwmk.**

Sizes: 28x22mm (20f, 1fo); 22x28mm (40f); 28x39mm (30f, 60f, 2fo)

1556	A343	20f	multi	15	15
1557	A343	30f	multi	15	15
1558	A343	40f	multi	15	15
1559	A343	60f	multi	15	15
1560	A343	1fo	multi	20	15
1561	A343	2fo	multi	48	22
			Nos. 1556-1561,B235-B236 (8)	2.63	
			Set value		1.25

New Year 1964. The 20f and 40f issued in booklet panes of 10, perf. and imperf.; sold for 2 times and 1½ times face respectively.

1964, Jan. 8 ***Perf. 11½x12, 12x11½***

American and Russian Spacecraft: 40f, Venus space probe. 60f, Vostok I (horiz.). 1fo, Friendship 7. 1.70fo, Vostok III & IV. 2fo, Telstar 1 & 2 (horiz.). 2.60fo, Mars I. 3fo, Radar, rockets and satellites (horiz.).

1562	A344	30f	grn, yel & brnz	15	15
1563	A344	40f	pur, bl & sil	15	15
1564	A344	60f	bl, blk, yel, sil & red	15	15
1565	A344	1fo	dk brn, red & sil	18	15
1566	A344	1.70fo	vio bl, blk, tan & red	28	15
1567	A344	2fo	sl grn, yel & sil	50	18
1568	A344	2.60fo	dp bl, yel & brnz	75	35
1569	A344	3fo	dp vio, lt bl & sil	1.00	60
			Nos. 1562-1569 (8)	3.16	
			Set value		1.45

Achievements in space research.

Lace Type of 1960

Various Halas Lace Designs.

Sizes: 20f, 2.60fo: 38x28mm. 30f, 40f, 60f, 1fo, 1.40fo, 2fo: 38x45mm.

Engr. & Litho.

1964, Feb. 28 ***Perf. 11½***

1570	A294	20f	emer & blk	15	15
1571	A294	30f	dl yel & blk	15	15
1572	A294	40f	dp rose & blk	15	15
1573	A294	60f	ol & blk	16	15
1574	A294	1fo	red org & blk	32	15
1575	A294	1.40fo	bl & blk	45	22
1576	A294	2fo	bluish grn & blk	70	28
1577	A294	2.60fo	lt vio & blk	1.10	60
			Nos. 1570-1577 (8)	3.18	
			Set value		1.45

Special Anniversaries-Events Issue

Imre Madach (1823-64) A345

Shakespeare A346

Karl Marx and Membership Card of International Working Men's Association — A347

Michelangelo — A348

Lajos Kossuth and György Dózsa — A349

Budapest Fair Buildings — A350

Designs: No. 1579, Ervin Szabo. No. 1580, Writer Andras Fay (1786-1864). No. 1581, Aggtelek Cave scene. No. 1582, Excavating bauxite. No. 1584, Equestrian statue, Szekesfehervar. No. 1585, Bowler. No. 1586, Waterfall and forest. No. 1587, Architect Miklos Ybl (1814-91) and Budapest Opera. No. 1590, Armor, saber, sword and foil. No. 1592, Galileo Galilei. No. 1593, Women basketball players. No. 1595, Two runners breaking tape.

Perf. 11½x12, 12x11½, 11

1964 **Photo.** **Unwmk.**

Inscribed: "ÉVFORDULÓK-ESEMÉNYEK"

1578	A345	60f	brt pur	15	15
1579	A345	60f	olive	15	15
1580	A345	60f	ol grn	15	15
1581	A346	60f	bluish grn	20	15
1582	A346	60f	Prus bl	15	15
1583	A347	60f	rose red	15	15
1584	A348	60f	sl bl	16	15
1585	A345	1fo	car rose	20	15
1586	A346	1fo	dl bl grn	20	15
1587	A348	1fo	org brn	15	15
1588	A349	1fo	ultra	15	15
1589	A350	1fo	brt grn	15	15
1590	A345	2fo	yel brn	25	15
1591	A346	2fo	magenta	38	15
1592	A346	2fo	red brn	32	15
1593	A346	2fo	brt bl	32	15
1594	A348	2fo	gray brn	38	15
1595	A348	2fo	brn red	32	15
			Nos. 1578-1595 (18)	3.93	
			Set value		1.00

No. 1579, Municipal libraries, 60th anniv., and librarian Szabo (1877-1918). No. 1582, Bauxite mining in Hungary, 30th year. No. 1583, Cent. of 1st Socialist Intl. No. 1584, King Alba Day in Szekesfehervar. No. 1585, 1st European Bowling Championship, Budapest.

No. 1586, Cong. of Natl. Forestry Federation. No. 1588, City of Cegled, 600th anniv. No. 1589, Opening of 1964 Budapest Intl. Fair. No. 1590, Hungarian Youth Fencing Association, 50th anniv. Nos. 1591-1592, Shakespeare and Galileo, 400th birth anniversaries. No. 1593, 9th European Women's Basketball Championship. No. 1594, Michelangelo's 400th death anniv. No. 1595, 50th anniv. of 1st Hungarian-Swedish athletic meet.

Eleanor Roosevelt — A351

Design (horiz.): a, d, Portrait at right. b, c, Portrait at left.

1964, Apr. 27 ***Perf. 12½***

1596	A351	2fo	gray, blk & buff	30	22

Miniature Sheet

Perf. 11

1597			Sheet of 4	3.75	3.75
a.	A351	2fo	dp cl, brn & blk	75	75
b.	A351	2fo	dk bl, brn & blk	75	75
c.	A351	2fo	grn, brn & blk	75	75
d.	A351	2fo	ol, brn & blk	75	75

Fencing — A352

Sport: 40f, Women's gymnastics. 60f, Soccer. 80f, Equestrian. 1fo, Running. 1.40fo, Weight lifting. 1.70fo, Gymnast on rings. 2fo, Hammer throw and javelin. 2.50fo, Boxing.

1964, June 12 **Photo.** ***Perf. 11***

Multicolored Design and Inscription

1598	A352	30f	lt ver	15	15
1599	A352	40f	blue	15	15
1600	A352	60f	emerald	15	15
1601	A352	80f	tan	15	15
1602	A352	1fo	yellow	15	15
1603	A352	1.40fo	bis brn	15	15
1604	A352	1.70fo	bluish gray	28	15
1605	A352	2fo	gray grn	40	22
1606	A352	2.50fo	vio gray	65	52
			Nos. 1598-1606,B237 (10)	2.98	
			Set value		2.10

Issued to publicize the 18th Olympic Games, Tokyo, Oct. 10-25.

Elberta Peaches — A353

Peaches: 40h, Blossoms (J. H. Hale). 60h, Magyar Kajszi. 1fo, Mandula Kajszi. 1.50fo, Borsi Rozsa. 1.70fo, Blossoms (Alexander). 2fo, Champion. 3fo, Mayflower.

1964, July 24 ***Perf. 11½***

1607	A353	40f	multi	15	15
1608	A353	60f	multi	15	15
1609	A353	1fo	multi	18	15
1610	A353	1.50fo	multi	22	18
1611	A353	1.70fo	multi	28	18
1612	A353	2fo	multi	40	18
1613	A353	2.60fo	multi	48	40
1614	A353	3fo	multi	75	60
			Nos. 1607-1614 (8)	2.61	
			Set value		1.75

Issued to publicize the National Peach Exhibition, Szeged.

Crossing Street in Safety Zone — A354

Designs: 60f, "Watch out for Children" (child and ball). 1fo, "Look before Crossing" (mother and child).

1964, Sept. 27 *Perf. 11*

1615 A354 20f multi 18 15
1616 A354 60f multi 18 15
1617 A354 1fo lil & multi 28 15
Set value 36

Issued to publicize traffic safety.

Souvenir Sheet

Voskhod 1 and Globe — A355

1964, Nov. 6 *Perf. 12x11½*

1618 A355 10fo multi 4.50 4.50

Russian space flight of Vladimir M. Komarov, Boris B. Yegorov and Konstantine Feoktistov.

Arpad Bridge — A356

Danube Bridges, Budapest: 30f, Margaret Bridge. 60f, Chain Bridge. 1fo, Elizabeth Bridge. 1.50fo, Freedom Bridge. 2fo, Petöfi Bridge. 2.50fo, Railroad Bridge.

1964, Nov. 21 Photo. *Perf. 11x11½*

1619 A356 20f multi 18 15
1620 A356 30f multi 18 15
1621 A356 60f multi 18 15
1622 A356 1fo multi 25 15
1623 A356 1.50fo multi 35 15
1624 A356 2fo multi 60 22
1625 A356 2.50fo multi 1.10 55
Nos. 1619-1625 (7) 2.84
Set value 1.25

Opening of the reconstructed Elizabeth Bridge. See No. C250.

Ring-necked Pheasant and Hunting Rifle — A357

Designs: 30f, Wild boar. 40f, Gray partridges. 60f, Varying hare. 80f, Fallow deer. 1fo, Mouflon. 1.70fo, Red deer. 2fo, Great bustard. 2.50fo, Roebuck and roe deer. 3fo, Emblem of National Federation of Hungarian Hunters (antlers).

1964, Dec. 30 Photo. *Perf. 12x11½*

1626 A357 20f multi 15 15
1627 A357 30f multi 15 15
1628 A357 40f multi 15 15
1629 A357 60f multi 15 15
1630 A357 80f multi 15 15
1631 A357 1fo multi 15 15
1632 A357 1.70fo multi 25 15
1633 A357 2fo multi 35 15
1634 A357 2.50fo multi 70 30
1635 A357 3fo multi 1.00 60
Nos. 1626-1635 (10) 3.20
Set value 1.55

Castle Type of 1960

Castles: 3fo, Czesznek (vert.). 4fo, Eger. 5fo, Koszeg (vert.).

1964 *Perf. 11½x12, 12x11½*

Size: 21x28mm, 28x21mm

1644 A293 3fo red brn 38 15
1645 A293 4fo brt vio 50 15
1646 A293 5fo yel grn 65 15
Set value 16

Equestrian, Gold and Bronze Medals — A358

Designs: 30f, Women's gymnastics, silver and bronze medals. 50f, Small-bore rifle, gold and bronze medals. 60f, Water polo, gold medal. 70f, Shot put, bronze medal. 80f, Soccer, gold medal. 1fo, Weight lifting, 1 bronze and 2 silver medals. 1.20fo, Canoeing, silver medal. 1.40fo, Hammer throw, silver medal. 1.50fo, Wrestling, 2 gold medals. 1.70fo, Javelin, 2 silver medals. 3fo, Fencing, 4 gold medals.

1965, Feb. 20 *Perf. 12*

Medals in Gold, Silver or Bronze

1647 A358 20f lt ol grn & dk brn 15 15
1648 A358 30f vio & dk brn 15 15
1649 A358 50f ol & dk brn 15 15
1650 A358 60f lt bl & red brn 15 15
1651 A358 70f lt gray & red brn 15 15
1652 A358 80f yel grn & dk brn 15 15
1653 A358 1fo lil, vio & red brn 15 15
1654 A358 1.20fo lt bl, ultra & red brn 18 18
1655 A358 1.40fo gray & red brn 22 15
1656 A358 1.50fo tan, lt brn & red brn 35 25
1657 A358 1.70fo pink & red brn 70 28
1658 A358 3fo grnsh bl & brn 90 60
Set value 3.00 2.00

Issued to commemorate the victories won by the Hungarian team in the 1964 Olympic Games, Tokyo, Oct. 10-25.

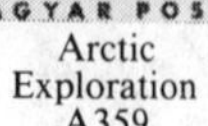

Arctic Exploration A359

Chrysanthemums A360

Designs: 30f, Radar tracking rocket, ionosphere research. 60f, Rocket and earth with reflecting layer diagrams, atmospheric research. 80f, Telescope and map of Milky Way, radio astronomy. 1.50fo, Earth, compass rose and needle, earth magnetism. 1.70fo, Weather balloon and lightning, meteorology. 2fo, Aurora borealis and penguins, arctic research. 2.50fo, Satellite, earth and planets, space research. 3fo, IQSY emblem and world map. 10fo, Sun with flares and corona, snow crystals and rain.

Perf. 11½x12

1965, Mar. 25 Photo. Unwmk.

1659 A359 20f bl, org & blk 15 15
1660 A359 30f gray, blk & emer 15 15
1661 A359 60f lil, blk & yel 15 15
1662 A359 80f lt grn, yel & blk 15 15
1663 A359 1.50fo lem, bl & blk 16 15
1664 A359 1.70fo bl, pink & blk 22 15
1665 A359 2fo ultra, sal & blk 25 15
1666 A359 2.50fo org brn, yel & blk 38 22
1667 A359 3fo lt bl, cit & blk 70 50
Nos. 1659-1667 (9) 2.31
Set value 1.25

Souvenir Sheet

1668 A359 10fo ultra, org & blk 3.00 3.00

Intl. Quiet Sun Year, 1964-65.

1965, Apr. 4

Designs: 30f, Peonies. 50f, Carnations. 60f, Roses. 1.40fo, Lilies. 1.70fo, Anemones. 2fo, Gladioli. 2.50fo, Tulips. 3fo, Mixed flower bouquet.

Flowers in Natural Colors

1669 A360 20f gold & gray 15 15
1670 A360 30f gold & gray 15 15
1671 A360 50f gold & gray 15 15
1672 A360 60f gold & gray 15 15
1673 A360 1.40fo gold & gray 15 15
1674 A360 1.70fo gold & gray 18 15
1675 A360 2fo gold & gray 20 15
1676 A360 2.50fo gold & gray 38 16
1677 A360 3fo gold & gray 80 60
Nos. 1669-1677 (9) 2.31
Set value 1.25

Issued to commemorate the 20th anniversary of liberation from the Nazis.

"Head of a Combatant" by Leonardo da Vinci — A361

Perf. 11½x12

1965, May 4 Photo. Unwmk.

1678 A361 60f bis & org brn 30 15

Issued to publicize the First International Renaissance Conference, Budapest.

Nikolayev, Tereshkova and View of Budapest A362

1965, May 10 *Perf. 11*

1679 A362 1fo dl bl & brn 25 15

Visit of the Russian astronauts Andrian G. Nikolayev and Valentina Tereshkova (Mr. & Mrs. Nikolayev) to Budapest.

ITU Emblem, Old and New Communication Equipment A363

1965, May 17

1680 A363 60f vio bl 15 15

Cent. of the ITU.

Souvenir Sheet

Austrian WIPA Stamp of 1933 — A363a

1965, June 4 Photo. *Perf. 11*

1681 A363a Sheet of 2 + 2 labels 4.00 4.00
a. 2fo gray & dp ultra 1.50 1.50

1965 Vienna Intl. Phil. Exhib. WIPA, June 4-13.

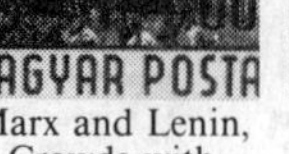

Marx and Lenin, Crowds with Flags — A364

ICY Emblem and Pulley — A365

1965, June 15 *Perf. 11½x12*

1682 A364 60f red, blk & yel 15 15

6th Conference of Ministers of Post of Socialist Countries, Peking, June 21-July 15.

1965, June 25

1683 A365 2fo dk red 20 15
a. Min. sheet of 4, perf. 11 2.75 2.75

Intl. Cooperation Year, 1965. No. 1683a contains rose red, olive, Prussian green and violet stamps.

Musical Clown A366

Dr. Semmelweis A367

Circus Acts: 20f, Equestrians. 40f, Elephant. 50f, Seal balancing ball. 60f, Lions. 1fo, Wildcat jumping through burning hoops. 1.50fo, Black leopards. 2.50fo, Juggler. 3fo, Leopard and dogs. 4fo, Bear on bicycle.

1965, July 26 Photo. *Perf. 11½x12*

1684 A366 20f multi 15 15
1685 A366 30f multi 15 15
1686 A366 40f multi 15 15
1687 A366 50f multi 15 15
1688 A366 60f multi 15 15
1689 A366 1fo multi 15 15
1690 A366 1.50fo multi 22 15
1691 A366 2.50fo multi 38 15
1692 A366 3fo multi 60 32
1693 A366 4fo multi 80 48
Nos. 1684-1693 (10) 2.90
Set value 1.50

1965, Aug. 20 Photo. Unwmk.

1694 A367 60f red brn 15 15

Dr. Ignaz Philipp Semmelweis (1818-1865), discoverer of the cause of puerperal fever and introduced antisepsis into obstetrics.

Runner — A368

Sport: 30f, Swimmer at start. 50f, Woman diver. 60f, Modern dancing. 80f, Tennis. 1.70fo, Fencing. 2fo, Volleyball. 2.50fo, Basketball. 4fo, Water polo. 10fo, People's Stadium, Budapest (horiz.).

1965, Aug. 20 *Perf. 11*

Size: 38x38mm

No.	Type	Value & Color	Unused	Used
1695	A368	20f multi	15	15
1696	A368	30f bl & red brn	15	15
1697	A368	50f bl grn, blk & red brn	15	15
1698	A368	60f vio, blk & red brn	15	15
1699	A368	80f tan, ol & red brn	18	15
1700	A368	1.70fo multi	30	15
1701	A368	2fo multi	35	18
1702	A368	2.50fo gray, blk & red brn	60	35
1703	A368	4fo bl, red brn & blk	1.00	60
		Nos. 1695-1703 (9)	3.03	
		Set value		1.60

Souvenir Sheet

Perf. 12x11½

No.	Type	Value & Color	Unused	Used
1704	A368	10fo bis, red brn & gray	3.25	3.00

Intl. College Championships, "Universiade," Budapest. No. 1704 contains one 38x28mm stamp.

Hemispheres and Warsaw Mermaid — A369

1965, Oct. 8 **Photo.** *Perf. 12x11½*

No.	Type	Value & Color	Unused	Used
1705	A369	60f brt bl	20	15

Sixth Congress of the World Federation of Trade Unions, Warsaw.

Phyllocactus Hybridus — A370

Flowers from Botanical Gardens: 30f, Cattleya Warszewiczii (orchid). 60f, Rebutia calliantha. 70f, Paphiopedilum hybridium. 80f, Opuntia cactus. 1fo, Laelia elegans (orchid). 1.50fo, Christmas cactus. 2fo, Bird-of-paradise flower. 2.50fo, Lithops Weberi. 3fo, Victoria water lily.

1965, Oct. 11 *Perf. 11½x12*

No.	Type	Value & Color	Unused	Used
1706	A370	20f gray & multi	18	15
1707	A370	30f gray & multi	18	15
1708	A370	60f gray & multi	15	15
1709	A370	70f gray & multi	15	15
1710	A370	80f gray & multi	15	15
1711	A370	1fo gray & multi	18	15
1712	A370	1.50fo gray & multi	24	15
1713	A370	2fo gray & multi	30	18
1714	A370	2.50fo gray & multi	48	30
1715	A370	3fo gray & multi	75	42
		Nos. 1706-1715 (10)	2.76	
		Set value		1.35

"The Black Stallion" A371

Tales from the Arabian Nights: 30f, Shahriar and Scheherazade. 50f, Sinbad's Fifth Voyage (ship). 60f, Aladdin, or The Wonderful Lamp. 80f, Harun al-Rashid. 1fo, The Flying Carpet. 1.70fo, The Fisherman and the Genie. 2fo, Ali Baba and the Forty Thieves. 3fo, Sinbad's Second Voyage (flying bird).

1965, Dec. 15 **Litho.** *Perf. 11½*

No.	Type	Value & Color	Unused	Used
1716	A371	20f multi	15	15
1717	A371	30f multi	15	15
1718	A371	50f multi	15	15
1719	A371	60f multi	15	15
1720	A371	80f multi	22	15
1721	A371	1fo multi	22	15
1722	A371	1.70fo multi	38	15
1723	A371	2fo multi	50	25
1724	A371	3fo multi	1.10	60
		Nos. 1716-1724 (9)	3.02	
		Set value		1.45

Congress Emblem A372

Callimorpha Dominula A373

1965, Dec. 9 **Photo.** *Perf. 11½x12*

No.	Type	Value & Color	Unused	Used
1725	A372	2fo dark blue	30	15

Fifth Congress of the International Federation of Resistance Fighters (FIR), Budapest.

1966, Feb. 1 **Photo.** *Perf. 11½x12*

Various Butterflies in Natural Colors; Black Inscription

No.	Type	Value & Color	Unused	Used
1726	A373	20f lt aqua	16	15
1727	A373	60f pale vio	15	15
1728	A373	70f tan	22	15
1729	A373	80f lt ultra	22	15
1730	A373	1fo gray	15	15
1731	A373	1.50fo emerald	45	15
1732	A373	2fo dl rose	35	15
1733	A373	2.50fo bister	50	30
1734	A373	3fo blue	75	60
		Nos. 1726-1734 (9)	2.95	
		Set value		1.68

Lal Bahadur Shastri A374

Designs: 60f, Bela Kun. 2fo, Istvan Szechenyi and Chain Bridge.

Lithographed; Photogravure (#1736)

1966 *Perf. 11½x12, 12x11½*

No.	Type	Value & Color	Unused	Used
1735	A374	60f red & blk	15	15
1736	A374	1fo brt vio	22	15
1737	A374	2fo dl yel, buff & sep	30	15
		Set value		19

Kun (1886-1939), communist labor leader; Shastri (1904-66), Indian Prime Minister; Count Istvan Szechenyi (1791-1860), statesman.

See Nos. 1764-1765, 1769-1770.

Luna 9 — A375

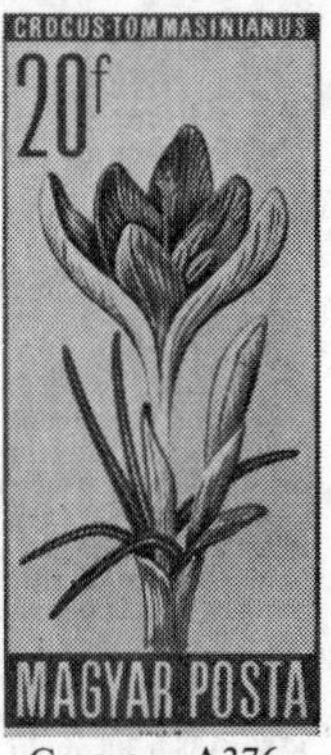

Crocus — A376

Design: 3fo, Luna 9 sending signals from moon to earth (horiz.).

1966, Mar. 12 **Photo.** *Perf. 12*

No.	Type	Value & Color	Unused	Used
1738	A375	2fo vio, blk & yel	45	18
1739	A375	3fo lt ultra, blk & yel	85	60

1st soft landing on the moon by the Russian satellite Luna 9, Feb. 3, 1966.

1966, Mar. 12 *Perf. 11*

Flowers: 30f, Cyclamen. 60f, Ligularia sibirica. 1.40fo, Lilium bulbiferum. 1.50fo, Snake's head. 3fo, Snapdragon and emblem of Hungarian Nature Preservation Society.

Flowers in Natural Colors

No.	Type	Value & Color	Unused	Used
1740	A376	20f brown	15	15
1741	A376	30f aqua	15	15
1742	A376	60f rose claret	24	15
1743	A376	1.40fo gray	35	24
1744	A376	1.50fo ultra	50	30
1745	A376	3fo mag & sepia	1.00	52
		Nos. 1740-1745 (6)	2.39	1.51

1966, Apr. 16

Designs: 20f, Barn swallows. 30f, Long-tailed tits. 60f, Red crossbill and pine cone. 1.40fo, Middle spotted woodpecker. 1.50fo, Hoopoe feeding young. 3fo, Forest preserve, lapwing and emblem of National Forest Preservation Society.

Birds in Natural Colors

No.	Type	Value & Color	Unused	Used
1746	A376	20f brt grn	24	15
1747	A376	30f vermilion	15	15
1748	A376	60f brt grn	24	17
1749	A376	1.40fo vio bl	30	28
1750	A376	1.50fo blue	90	50
1751	A376	3fo brn, mag & grn	1.10	90
		Nos. 1746-1751 (6)	2.93	2.15

Nos. 1740-1751 issued to promote protection of wild flowers and birds.

Locomotive, 1947; Monoplane, 1912; Autobus, 1911; Steamer, 1853, and Budapest Railroad Station, 1846 — A377

Designs: 2fo, Transportation, 1966: electric locomotive V.43; turboprop airliner IL-18; Ikarusz autobus; Diesel passenger ship, and Budapest South Railroad Station.

1966, Apr. 2 **Photo.** *Perf. 12*

No.	Type	Value & Color	Unused	Used
1752	A377	1fo yel, brn & grn	22	15
1753	A377	2fo pale grn, bl & brn	38	22

Issued to commemorate the re-opening of the Transport Museum, Budapest.

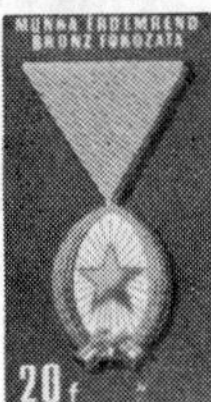

Bronze Order of Labor — A378

Decorations: 30f, Silver Order of Labor. 50f, Banner Order, third class. 60f, Gold Order of Labor. 70f, Banner Order, second class. 1fo, Red Banner Order of Labor. 1.20fo, Banner Order, first class. 2fo, Order of Merit. 2.50fo, Hero of Socialist Labor. Sizes: 20f, 30f, 60f, 1fo, 2fo, 2.50fo: 19½x38mm. 50f: 21x29mm. 70f, 25x31mm. 1.20fo: 28x38mm.

1966, Apr. 2 **Unwmk.** *Perf. 11*

Decorations in Original Colors

No.	Type	Value & Color	Unused	Used
1754	A378	20f dp ultra	15	15
1755	A378	30f lt brn	15	15
1756	A378	50f bl grn	15	15
1757	A378	60f violet	15	15
1758	A378	70f carmine	15	15
1759	A378	1fo vio bl	15	15
1760	A378	1.20fo brt bl	15	15
1761	A378	2fo olive	28	18
1762	A378	2.50fo dl bl	34	24
		Set value	1.30	85

Portrait Type of 1966 and

Dubna Nuclear Research Institute A379

WHO Headquarters, Geneva — A380

Designs: No. 1764, Pioneer girl. No. 1765, Tamas Esze (1666-1708), military hero. No. 1767, Old view of Buda and UNESCO emblem. No. 1768, Horse-drawn fire pump and emblem of Sopron Fire Brigade. No. 1769, Miklos Zrinyi (1508-66), hero of Turkish Wars. No. 1770, Sandor Koranyi (1866-1944), physician and scientist.

1966 **Litho.** *Perf. 11½x12*

No.	Type	Value & Color	Unused	Used
1763	A379	60f bl grn & blk	15	15
1764	A374	60f multi	15	15
1765	A374	60f brt bl & blk	15	15
1766	A380	2fo lt ultra & blk	20	15
1767	A380	2fo lt bl & pur	30	15
1768	A380	2fo org & blk	30	15
1769	A374	2fo ol bis & brn	24	15
1770	A374	2fo multi	24	15
		Set value	1.50	50

No. 1763, 10th anniv. of the United Institute for Nuclear Research, Dubna, USSR; No. 1764, 20th anniv. of Pioneer Movement; No. 1766, Inauguration of the WHO Headquarters, Geneva; No. 1767, 20th anniv. of UNESCO and 72nd session of Executive Council, Budapest, May 30-31; No. 1768, Cent. of Volunteer Fire Brigade.

Hungarian Soccer Player and Soccer Field — A381

Jules Rimet, Cup and Soccer Ball — A382

Designs (Views of Soccer play): 30f, Montevideo 1930 (Uruguay 4, Argentina 2). 60f, Rome 1934 (Italy 2, Czechoslovakia 1). 1fo, Paris 1938 (Italy 4, Hungary 2). 1.40fo, Rio de Janeiro 1950 (Uruguay 2, Brazil 1). 1.70fo, Bern 1954 (Germany 3, Hungary 2). 2fo, Stockholm 1958 (Brazil 5, Sweden 2). 2.50fo, Santiago 1962 (Brazil 3, Czechoslovakia 1).

Souvenir Sheet

1966, May 16 Photo. *Perf. 11½x12*

1771	A381	10fo multi	3.75	3.50

1966, June 6 *Perf. 12x11½*

1772	A382	20f bl & multi	24	15
1773	A382	30f org & multi	24	15
1774	A382	60f multi	20	15
1775	A382	1fo multi	20	15
1776	A382	1.40fo multi	15	15
1777	A382	1.70fo multi	20	15
1778	A382	2fo multi	24	18
1779	A382	2.50fo multi	60	50
		Nos. 1772-1779,B258 (9)	2.67	
		Set value		1.75

World Cup Soccer Championship, Wembley, England, July 11-30.

European Red Fox — A383

Hunting Trophies: 60f, Wild boar. 70f, Wildcat. 80f, Roebuck. 1.50fo, Red deer. 2.50fo, Fallow deer. 3fo, Mouflon.

1966, July 4 Photo. *Perf. 11½x12*

Animals in Natural Colors

1780	A383	20f gray & lt brn	15	15
1781	A383	60f buff & gray	15	15
1782	A383	70f lt bl & gray	20	15
1783	A383	80f pale grn & yel bis	25	15
1784	A383	1.50fo pale lem & brn	32	16
1785	A383	2.50fo gray & brn	60	32
1786	A383	3fo pale pink & gray	95	65
		Nos. 1780-1786 (7)	2.62	
		Set value		1.50

The 80f and 1.50fo were issued with and without alternating labels, which show date and place when trophy was taken; the 2.50fo was issued only with labels, 20f, 60f, 70f and 3fo without labels only.

Discus Thrower and Matthias Cathedral A384

Designs: 30f, High jump and Agriculture Museum. 40f, Javelin (women's) and Parliament. 50f, Hammer throw, Mt. Gellert and Liberty Bridge. 60f, Broad jump and view of Buda. 1fo, Shot put and Chain Bridge. 2fo, Pole vault and Stadium. 3fo, Long distance runners and Millenium Monument.

1966, Aug. 30 Photo. *Perf. 12x11½*

1787	A384	20f grn, brn & org	15	15
1788	A384	30f multi	28	15
1789	A384	40f multi	18	15
1790	A384	50f multi	16	15
1791	A384	60f multi	16	15
1792	A384	1fo multi	28	16
1793	A384	2fo multi	60	25
1794	A384	3fo multi	1.10	70
		Nos. 1787-1794 (8)	2.91	
		Set value		1.55

8th European Athletic Championships, Budapest, Aug. 30-Sept. 4. See No. C261.

Girl in the Forest by Miklos Barabas A385

Paintings: 1fo, Mrs. Istvan Bitto by Miklos Barabas (1810-98). 1.50fo, Hunyadi's Farewell by Gyula Benczur (1844-1920). 1.70fo, Reading Woman by Gyula Benczur (horiz.). 2fo, Woman with Fagots by Mihaly Munkacsi (1844-1900). 2.50fo, Yawning Boy by Mihaly Munkacsi. 3fo, Lady in Violet by Pal Szinyei Merse (1845-1920). 10fo, Picnic in May by Pal Szinyei Merse (horiz.).

1966, Dec. 9 *Perf. 12½*

Gold Frame

1795	A385	60f multi	15	15
1796	A385	1fo multi	15	15
1797	A385	1.50fo multi	25	15
1798	A385	1.70fo multi	55	15
1799	A385	2fo multi	55	15
1800	A385	2.50fo multi	75	20
1801	A385	3fo multi	1.65	1.10
		Nos. 1795-1801 (7)	4.05	2.05

Souvenir Sheet

1802	A385	10fo multi	8.25	8.25

Issued to honor Hungarian painters. Size of stamp in No. 1802: 56x51mm.

Vostoks 3 and 4 — A386

Space Craft: 60f, Gemini 6 and 7. 80f, Vostoks 5 and 6. 1fo, Gemini 9 and target rocket. 1.50fo, Alexei Leonov walking in space. 2fo, Edward White walking in space. 2.50fo, Voskhod. 3fo, Gemini 11 docking Agena target.

1966, Dec. 29 *Perf. 11*

1803	A386	20f lt ultra, red & blk	15	15
1804	A386	60f brt bl, red & blk	15	15
1805	A386	80f grnsh bl, red & blk	15	15
1806	A386	1fo grnsh bl, red & blk	18	15
1807	A386	1.50fo lt grn, red & blk	28	18
1808	A386	2fo aqua, sal & blk	40	20
1809	A386	2.50fo ultra, red & blk	60	35
1810	A386	3fo sky bl, red & blk	1.00	50
		Nos. 1803-1810 (8)	2.91	
		Set value		1.60

American and Russian twin space flights.

Pal Kitaibel and Kitaibelia Vitifolia — A387

Flowers of the Carpathian Basin: 60f, Dentaria glandulosa. 1fo, Edraianthus tenuifolius. 1.50fo, Althaea pallida. 2fo, Centaurea mollis. 2.50fo, Sternbergia colchiciflora. 3fo, Iris Hungarica.

1967, Feb. 7 Photo. *Perf. 11½x12*

Flowers in Natural Colors

1811	A387	20f rose, blk & gold	15	15
1812	A387	60f green	15	15
1813	A387	1fo vio gray	15	15
1814	A387	1.50fo blue	25	16
1815	A387	2fo lt ol	32	20
1816	A387	2.50fo gray grn	60	32
1817	A387	3fo yel grn	1.10	65
		Nos. 1811-1817 (7)	2.72	
		Set value		1.50

Issued to commemorate the 150th anniversary of the death of Pal Kitaibel (1757-1817), botanist, chemist and physician.

Militiaman A388

1967, Feb. 18 Photo. *Perf. 11½x12*

1818	A388	2fo bl gray	40	15

Workers' Militia, 10th anniversary.

Mme. Du Barry and Louis XV, by Gyula Benczur (1844-1920) — A390

Souvenir Sheet

Painting: 10fo, Milton dictating "Paradise Lost" to his daughters, by Soma Orlai Petrics.

1967, May 6 Photo. *Perf. 12½*

1819	A390	10fo multi	5.75	5.00

1967, June 22

Paintings: 60f, Franz Liszt by Mihaly Munkacsi (1844-1900). 1fo, Samuel Lanyi, self-portrait, 1840. 1.50fo, Lady in Fur-lined Jacket by Jozsef Borsos (1821-1883). 1.70fo, The Lovers, by Pal Szinyei Merse (1845-1920; horiz.). 2fo, Portrait of Szidonia Deak, 1861, by Alajos Gyorgyi (1821-1863). 2.50fo, National Guardsman, 1848, by Jozsef Borsos.

Gold Frame

1820	A390	60f multi	15	15
1821	A390	1fo multi	18	15
1822	A390	1.50fo multi	22	15
1823	A390	1.70fo multi	35	15
1824	A390	2fo multi	42	15
1825	A390	2.50fo multi	55	22
1826	A390	3fo multi	90	70
		Nos. 1820-1826 (7)	2.77	
		Set value		1.40

Issued to honor Hungarian painters. No. 1819 commemorates AMPHILEX 67 and the F.I.P. Congress, Amsterdam, May 11-21. No. 1819 contains one 56x50mm stamp.

See #1863-1870, 1900-1907, 1940-1947.

Map of Hungary, Tourist Year Emblem, Plane, Train, Car and Ship A391

1967, May 6 *Perf. 12x11½*

1827	A391	1fo brt bl & blk	20	15

International Tourist Year, 1967.

S.S. Ferencz Deak, Schönbüchel Castle, Austrian Flag — A392

Designs: 60f, Diesel hydrobus, Bratislava Castle and Czechoslovak flag. 1fo, Diesel ship Hunyadi, Buda Castle and Hungarian flag. 1.50fo, Diesel tug Szekszard, Golubac Fortress and Yugoslav flag. 1.70fo, Towboat Miskolc, Vidin Fortress and Bulgarian flag. 2fo, Cargo ship Tihany, Galati shipyard and Romanian flag. 2.50fo, Hydrofoil Siraly I, Izmail Harbor and Russian flag.

1967, June 1 *Perf. 11½x12*

Flags in National Colors

1828	A392	30f lt bl grn	38	22
1829	A392	60f org brn	38	28
1830	A392	1fo grnsh bl	75	32
1831	A392	1.50fo lt grn	75	38
1832	A392	1.70fo blue	1.40	52
1833	A392	2fo rose lil	3.00	1.00
1834	A392	2.50fo lt ol grn	5.25	2.25
		Nos. 1828-1834 (7)	11.91	4.97

25th session of the Danube Commission.

Poodle A393

Collie — A394

Dogs: 1fo, Hungarian pointer. 1.40fo, Fox terriers. 2fo, Pumi, Hungarian sheep dog. 3fo, German shepherd. 4fo, Puli, Hungarian sheep dog.

1967, July 7 Litho. *Perf. 12*

1835	A393	30f multi	24	15
1836	A394	60f multi	24	15
1837	A393	1fo multi	20	15
1838	A394	1.40fo multi	24	24
1839	A393	2fo multi	38	18

1840	A394	3fo multi	60	50
1841	A393	4fo multi	95	70
		Nos. 1835-1841 (7)	2.85	2.07

Sterlets A395

Fish: 60f, Pike perch. 1fo, Carp. 1.70fo, European catfish. 2fo, Pike. 2.50fo, Rapfin.

1967, Aug. 22 Photo. *Perf. 12x11½*

1842	A395	20f multi	20	15
1843	A395	60f bis & multi	15	15
1844	A395	1fo multi	15	15
1845	A395	1.70fo multi	15	15
1846	A395	2fo grn & multi	30	15
1847	A395	2.50fo gray & multi	75	55
		Nos. 1842-1847,B263 (7)	2.60	1.75

Issued to commemorate the 14th Congress of the International Federation of Anglers (C.I.P.S.), Dunaujvaros, Aug. 20-28.

Prince Igor, by Aleksandr Borodin — A396

Opera Scenes: 30f, Freischütz, by Karl Maria von Weber. 40f, The Magic Flute, by Mozart. 60f, Prince Bluebeard's Castle, by Bela Bartok. 80f, Carmen, by Bizet (vert.). 1fo, Don Carlos, by Verdi (vert.). 1.70fo, Tannhäuser, by Wagner (vert.). 3fo. Laszlo Hunyadi, by Ferenc Erkel (vert.).

1967, Sept. 26 Photo. *Perf. 12*

1848	A396	20f multi	20	15
1849	A396	30f multi	20	15
1850	A396	40f multi	20	15
1851	A396	60f multi	20	15
1852	A396	80f multi	20	15
1853	A396	1fo multi	25	20
1854	A396	1.70fo multi	48	32
1855	A396	3fo multi	1.10	80
		Nos. 1848-1855 (8)	2.83	
		Set value		1.65

Teacher, Students and Stone from Pecs University, 14th Century — A397

1967, Oct. 9 Photo. *Perf. 11½x12*

1856	A397	2fo gold & dp grn	40	15

Issued to commemorate the 600th anniversary of higher education in Hungary; University of Pecs was founded in 1367.

Eötvös University, and Symbols of Law and Justice A398

1967, Oct. 12 *Perf. 12x11½*

1857	A398	2fo slate	40	15

Issued to commemorate the 300th anniversary of the School of Political Science and Law at the Lorand Eötvös University, Budapest.

Lenin as Teacher, by Sandor Legrady A399

Paintings by Sandor Legrady: 1fo, Lenin. 3fo, Lenin on board the cruiser Aurora.

1967, Oct. 31 *Perf. 12½*

1858	A399	60f gold & multi	15	15
1859	A399	1fo gold & multi	15	15
1860	A399	3fo gold & multi	55	35
		Set value		52

Issued to commemorate the 50th anniversary of the Russian October Revolution.

Venus 4 Landing on Venus — A400

1967, Nov. 6 *Perf. 12*

1861	A400	5fo gold & multi	1.25	1.10

Issued to commemorate the landing of the Russian automatic space station Venus 4 on the planet Venus.

Souvenir Sheet

19th Century Mail Coach and Post Horn — A401

Photogravure; Gold Impressed

1967, Nov. 21 *Perf. 12½*

1862	A401	10fo multi	3.50	3.50

Hungarian Postal Administration, cent.

Painting Type of 1967

Paintings: 60f, Brother and Sister by Adolf Fenyes (1867-1945). 1fo, Wrestling Boys by Oszkar Glatz (1872-1958). 1.50fo, "October" by Karoly Ferenczy (1862-1917). 1.70fo, Women at the River Bank by Istvan Szönyi (1894-1960) (horiz.). 2fo, Godfather's Breakfast by Istvan Csok (1865-1961). 2.50fo, "Eviction Notice" by Gyula Derkovits (1894-1934). 3fo, Self-portrait by M. T. Czontvary Kosztka (1853-1919). 10fo, The Apple Pickers by Bela Uitz (1887-).

1967, Dec. 21 Photo. *Perf. 12½*

1863	A390	60f multi	15	15
1864	A390	1fo multi	15	15
1865	A390	1.50fo multi	18	15
1866	A390	1.70fo multi	30	15
1867	A390	2fo multi	38	18
1868	A390	2.50fo multi	50	30
1869	A390	3fo multi	95	60
		Nos. 1863-1869 (7)	2.61	1.68

Miniature Sheet

1870	A390	10fo multi	3.00	3.00

Issued to honor Hungarian painters.

Biathlon — A402

Sport (Olympic Rings and): 60f, Figure skating, pair. 1fo, Bobsledding. 1.40fo, Slalom. 1.70fo, Women's figure skating. 2fo, Speed skating. 3fo, Ski jump. 10fo, Ice hockey.

1967, Dec. 30 Photo. *Perf. 12½*

Souvenir Sheet

1871	A402	10fo lil & multi	3.00	3.00

1968, Jan. 29 *Perf. 11*

1872	A402	30f multi	15	15
1873	A402	60f multi	15	15
1874	A402	1fo multi	15	15
1875	A402	1.40fo rose & multi	16	16
1876	A402	1.70fo multi	20	15
1877	A402	2fo multi	32	16
1878	A402	3fo ol & multi	80	38
		Nos. 1872-1878,B264 (8)	2.63	
		Set value		1.45

Issued to publicize the 10th Winter Olympic Games, Grenoble, France, Feb. 6-18. No. 1871 contains one stamp, size: 43x43mm.

Kando Statue, Miskolc, Kando Locomotive and Map of Hungary A403

1968, Mar. 30 Photo. *Perf. 11½x12*

1879	A403	2fo dk bl	35	15

Issued in memory of Kalman Kando (1869-1931), engineer, inventor of Kando locomotive.

Domestic Cat — A404

1968, Mar. 30 *Perf. 11*

1880	A404	20f shown	15	15
1881	A404	60f Cream Persian	18	15
1882	A404	1fo Smoky Persian	22	15
1883	A404	1.20fo Domestic kitten	22	15
1884	A404	1.50fo White Persian	32	15
1885	A404	2fo Brown-striped Persian	32	28
1886	A404	2.50fo Siamese	52	32
1887	A404	5fo Blue Persian	1.25	75
		Nos. 1880-1887 (8)	3.18	
		Set value		1.80

Zoltan Kodaly, by Sandor Legrady A405

1968, Apr. 17 Photo. *Perf. 12½*

1888	A405	5fo gold & multi	1.00	75

Issued in memory of Zoltan Kodaly (1882-1967), composer and musicologist.

White Storks A406

Birds: 50f, Golden orioles. 60f, Imperial eagle. 1fo, Red-footed falcons. 1.20fo, Scops owl. 1.50fo, Great bustard. 2fo, European bee-eaters. 2.50fo, Graylag goose.

1968, Apr. 25

Birds in Natural Colors

1889	A406	20f ver & lt ultra	20	20
1890	A406	50f ver & gray	15	15
1891	A406	60f ver & lt bl	20	15
1892	A406	1fo ver & yel grn	25	15
1893	A406	1.20fo ver & brt grn	25	15
1894	A406	1.50fo ver & lt vio	28	18
1895	A406	2fo ver & pale lil	60	28
1896	A406	2.50fo ver & bl grn	1.25	70
		Nos. 1889-1896 (8)	3.18	1.96

International Bird Preservation Congress.

City Hall, Kecskemet A407

Student and Agricultural College A408

1968, Apr. 25 *Perf. 12x11½*

1897	A407	2fo brn org	30	15

600th anniversary of Kecskemet.

Marx Type of 1953

1968, May 5 Engr. *Perf. 12*

1898	A230	1fo claret	15	15

Issued to commemorate the 150th anniversary of the birth of Karl Marx (1818-1883).

1968, May 24 Photo. *Perf. 12x11½*

1899	A408	2fo dk ol grn	30	15

Issued to commemorate the 150th anniversary of the founding of the Agricultural College at Mosonmagyarovar.

Painting Type of 1967

Paintings: 40f, Girl with Pitcher, by Goya (1746-1828). 60f, Head of an Apostle, by El Greco (c. 1541-1614). 1fo, Boy with Apple Basket and Dogs, by Pedro Nunez (1639-1700) (horiz.). 1.50fo, Mary Magdalene, by El Greco. 2.50fo, The Breakfast, by Velazquez

(1599-1660) (horiz.). 4fo, The Virgin from The Holy Family, by El Greco. 5fo, The Knife Grinder, by Goya. 10fo, Portrait of a Girl, by Palma Vecchio (1480-1528).

1968, May 30 *Perf. 12½*

1900	A390	40f multi	15	15
1901	A390	60f multi	15	15
1902	A390	1fo multi	15	15
1903	A390	1.50fo multi	22	15
1904	A390	2.50fo multi	50	20
1905	A390	4fo multi	70	22
1906	A390	5fo multi	1.00	45
		Nos. 1900-1906 (7)	2.87	
		Set value		1.18

Souvenir Sheet

1907	A390	10fo multi	3.50	3.50

Issued to publicize art treasures in the Budapest Museum of Fine Arts and to publicize an art exhibition.

Lake Balaton at Badacsony A409

Views on Lake Balaton: 40f like 20f. 60f, Tihanyi Peninsula. 1fo, Sailboats at Almadi. 2fo, Szigliget Bay.

1968-69 **Litho.** *Perf. 12*

1908	A409	20f multi	15	15
1908A	A409	40f multi ('69)	15	15
b.		Bklt. pane of 6 (2 each #1908A, 1910, 1 each #1909, 1911)	75	
c.		Bklt. pane of 6 (3 #1908A, 1 each #1909-1911)	75	
d.		Bklt. pane of 6 (3 #1908A, 2 #1909, 1 #1911)	75	
1909	A409	60f multi	15	15
1910	A409	1fo multi	20	15
1911	A409	2fo multi	45	22
		Set value	92	45

Locomotive, Type 424 — A410

1968, July 14 **Photo.** *Perf. 12x11½*

1912	A410	2fo gold, lt bl & sl	50	15

Centenary of the Hungarian State Railroad.

Horses Grazing — A411

Designs: 40f, Horses in storm. 60f, Horse race on the steppe. 80f, Horsedrawn sleigh. 1fo, Four-in-hand and rainbow. 1.40fo, Farm wagon drawn by 7 horses. 2fo, One rider driving five horses. 2.50fo, Campfire on the range. 4fo, Coach with 5 horses.

1968, July 25 *Perf. 11*

1913	A411	30f multi	15	15
1914	A411	40f multi	15	15
1915	A411	60f multi	15	17
1916	A411	80f multi	15	15
1917	A411	1fo multi	22	15
1918	A411	1.40fo multi	35	15
1919	A411	2fo multi	35	16
1920	A411	2.50fo multi	50	28
1921	A411	4fo multi	1.10	60
		Nos. 1913-1921 (9)	3.12	
		Set value		1.70

Horse breeding on the Hungarian steppe (Puszta).

Mihály Tompa (1817-68), Poet — A412

1968, July 30 **Photo.** *Perf. 12x11½*

1922	A412	60f blue black	20	15

Festival Emblem, Bulgarian and Hungarian National Costumes — A413

1968, Aug. 3 **Litho.** *Perf. 12*

1923	A413	60f multi	20	15

Issued to publicize the 9th Youth Festival for Peace and Friendship, Sofia, Bulgaria.

Souvenir Sheet

Runners and Aztec Calendar Stone — A414

1968, Aug. 21 **Photo.** *Perf. 12½*

1924	A414	10fo multi	3.00	3.00

19th Olympic Games, Mexico City, Oct. 12-27.

Scientific Society Emblem A415

Hesperis A416

Perf. 12½x11½

1968, Dec. 10 **Photo.**

1925	A415	2fo brt bl & blk	35	15

Issued to publicize the work of the Society for the Popularization of Scientific Knowledge.

1968, Oct. 29 *Perf. 11½x12*

Garden Flowers: 60f, Pansy. 80f, Zinnias. 1fo, Morning-glory. 1.40fo, Petunia. 1.50fo, Portulaca. 2fo, Michaelmas daisies. 2.50fo, Dahlia.

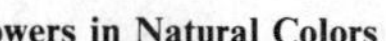

Flowers in Natural Colors

1926	A416	20f gray	16	16
1927	A416	60f lt grn	16	16
1928	A416	80f bluish lil	28	16
1929	A416	1fo buff	28	16
1930	A416	1.40fo lt grnsh bl	20	16
1931	A416	1.50fo lt bl	28	20
1932	A416	2fo pale pink	34	28
1933	A416	2.50fo lt bl	90	60
		Nos. 1926-1933 (8)	2.60	1.88

Pioneers Saluting Communist Party — A417

Children's Paintings: 60f, Four pioneers holding banner saluting Communist Party. 1fo, Pioneer camp.

1968, Nov. 16 **Photo.** *Perf. 12x11½*

1934	A417	40f buff & multi	22	15
1935	A417	60f buff & multi	22	15
1936	A417	1fo buff & multi	32	22

Issued to commemorate the 50th anniversary of the Communist Party of Hungary. The designs are from a competition among elementary school children.

Workers, Monument by Z. Olcsai-Kiss A418

Design: 1fo, "Workers of the World Unite!" poster by N. Por (vert.).

Perf. 11½x12, 12x11½

1968, Nov. 24 **Photo.**

1937	A418	1fo gold, red, & blk	15	15
1938	A418	2fo gold & multi	18	15
		Set value	27	16

Issued to commemorate the 50th anniversary of the Communist Party of Hungary.

Human Rights Flame — A419

1968, Dec. 10 *Perf. 12½x11½*

1939	A419	1fo dk red brn	25	15

International Human Rights Year.

Painting Type of 1967

Italian Paintings: 40f, Esterhazy Madonna, by Raphael. 60f, The Annunciation, by Bernardo Strozzi. 1fo, Portrait of a Young Man, by Raphael. 1.50fo, The Three Graces, by Battista Naldini. 2.50fo, Portrait of a Man, by Sebastiano del Piombo. 4fo, The Doge Marcantonio Trevisani, by Titian. 5fo, Venus, Cupid and Jealousy, by Angelo Bronzino. 10fo, Bathsheba Bathing, by Sebastiano Ricci (horiz.).

1968, Dec. 10 **Photo.** *Perf. 12½*

1940	A390	40f multi	15	15
1941	A390	60f multi	15	15
1942	A390	1fo multi	15	15
1943	A390	1.50fo multi	20	15
1944	A390	2.50fo multi	45	15
1945	A390	4fo multi	75	30
1946	A390	5fo multi	1.25	52
		Nos. 1940-1946 (7)	3.10	
		Set value		1.20

Miniature Sheet

Perf. 11

1947	A390	10fo multi	3.00	3.00

Issued to publicize art treasures in the Budapest Museum of Fine Arts. No. 1947 contains one stamp size of stamp: 62x45mm.

1869 and 1969 Emblems of Athenaeum Press — A420

Endre Ady (1877-1919), Lyric Poet — A421

1969, Jan. 27 *Perf. 12½x11½*

1948	A420	2fo gold, gray, lt bl & blk	30	15

Centenary of Athenaeum Press, Budapest.

1969, Jan. 27 *Perf. 11½x12*

1949	A421	1fo multi	20	15

Olympic Medal and Women's Javelin — A422

Olympic Medal and: 60f, Canadian singles (canoeing). 1fo, Soccer. 1.20fo, Hammer throw. 2fo, Fencing. 3fo, Greco-Roman Wrestling. 4fo, Kayak single. 5fo, Equestrian. 10fo, Head of Mercury by Praxiteles and Olympic torch.

1969, Mar. 7 **Photo.** *Perf. 12*

1950	A422	40f multi	15	15
1951	A422	60f multi	15	15
1952	A422	1fo multi	15	15
1953	A422	1.20fo multi	15	15
1954	A422	2fo multi	20	15
1955	A422	3fo multi	35	15
1956	A422	4fo multi	1.10	20
1957	A422	5fo multi	1.10	70
		Nos. 1950-1957 (8)	3.35	
		Set value		1.50

Souvenir Sheet

Litho. *Perf. 11½*

1958	A422	10fo multi	3.75	3.75

Issued to commemorate the victories won by the Hungarian team in the 1968 Olympic Games, Mexico City, Oct. 12-27, 1968. No. 1958 contains one stamp, size: 45x33mm.

1919 Revolutionary Poster — A423

Revolutionary Posters: 60f, Lenin. 1fo, Man breaking chains. 2fo, Industrial worker looking at family and farm. 3fo, Militia recruiter. 10fo, Shouting revolutionist with red banner (horiz.).

1969, Mar. 21 **Photo.** *Perf. 11½x12*

Gold Frame

1960	A423	40f red & blk	15	15
1961	A423	60f red & blk	15	15
1962	A423	1fo red & blk	15	15

1963 A423 2fo blk, gray & red 28 15
1964 A423 3fo multi 40 20
Set value 92 42

Souvenir Sheet

Perf. 12½

1965 A423 10fo red, gray & blk 1.50 1.50

50th anniv. of the proclamation of the Hungarian Soviet Republic.

The 60f red lilac with 4-line black printing on back was given away by the Hungarian PO.

No. 1965 contains one 51x38½mm stamp.

Jersey Tiger A424

Designs: Various Butterflies and Moths.

1969, Apr. 15 Litho. *Perf. 12*

1966 A424 40f shown 15 15
1967 A424 60f Eyed hawk moth 15 15
1968 A424 80f Painted lady 15 15
1969 A424 1fo Tiger moth 15 15
1970 A424 1.20fo Small fire moth 24 18
1971 A424 2fo Large blue 38 18
1972 A424 3fo Belted oak egger 75 45
1973 A424 4fo Peacock 1.10 70
Nos. 1966-1973 (8) 3.07
Set value 1.85

ILO Emblem A426

1969, May 22 Photo. *Perf. 12x11½*

1974 A426 1fo car lake & lake 20 15

50th anniv. of the ILO.

Black Pigs, by Paul Gauguin A427

French Paintings: 60f, These Women, by Toulouse-Lautrec (horiz.). 1fo, Venus in the Clouds, by Simon Vouet. 2fo, Lady with Fan, by Edouard Manet (horiz.). 3fo, La Petra Camara (dancer), by Theodore Chasseriau. 4fo, The Cowherd, by Constant Troyon (horiz.). 5fo, The Wrestlers, by Gustave Courbet. 10fo, Pomona, by Nicolas Fouche.

1969, May 28 Photo. *Perf. 12½*

1975 A427 40f multi 15 15
1976 A427 60f multi 15 15
1977 A427 1fo multi 15 15
1978 A427 2fo multi 28 15
1979 A427 3fo multi 50 18
1980 A427 4fo multi 70 25
1981 A427 5fo multi 1.25 52
Nos. 1975-1981 (7) 3.18
Set value 1.25

Miniature Sheet

1982 A427 10fo multi 3.50 3.25

Art treasures in the Budapest Museum of Fine Arts. No. 1982 contains one 40x62mm stamp.

Hotel Budapest A428

Budapest Post Office 100 A429

1969, May Photo. *Perf. 11*

1983 A428 1fo brown 15 15

Coil Stamps

1970, Aug. 3 *Perf. 14*

1983B A429 40f gray 24 15
1983a A428 1fo brown 30 15

Yellow control number on back of every 5th stamp.

Arms and Buildings of Vac A430

Towns of the Danube Bend: 1fo, Szentendre. 1.20fo, Visegrad. 3fo, Esztergom.

1969, June 9 Litho. *Perf. 12*

1984 A430 40f multi 15 15
a. Bklt. pane of 6 (4 #1984, 1 each #1985, 1987) 2.75
b. Bklt. pane of 6 (1986, 3 #1984, 2 #1985) 2.75
1985 A430 1fo multi 15 15
1986 A430 1.20fo multi 22 15
1987 A430 3fo multi 38 28
Set value 58

Stamps in booklet panes Nos. 1984a-1984b come in two arrangements.

"PAX" and Men Holding Hands – A431

1969, June 17 Photo. *Perf. 11½x12*

1988 A431 1fo lt bl, dk bl & gold 20 15

20th anniversary of Peace Movement.

The Scholar, by Rembrandt A432

Fossilized Zelkova Leaves A433

1969, Sept. 15 *Perf. 11½x12*

1989 A432 1fo sepia 20 15

Issued to publicize the 22nd International Congress of Art Historians, Budapest.

1969, Sept. 21 Photo.

Designs: 60f, Greenockit calcite sphalerite crystals. 1fo, Fossilized fish, clupea hungarica. 1.20fo, Quartz crystals. 2fo, Ammonite. 3fo, Copper. 4fo, Fossilized turtle, placochelys placodonta. 5fo, Cuprite crystals.

1990 A433 40f red, gray & sep 15 15
1991 A433 60f vio, yel & blk 15 15
1992 A433 1fo bl, tan & brn 15 15
1993 A433 1.20fo emer, gray & lil 15 15
1994 A433 2fo ol, tan & brn 16 15
1995 A433 3fo org, brt & dk grn 32 22
1996 A433 4fo dl blk grn, brn & blk 60 30
1997 A433 5fo multi 1.00 48
Nos. 1990-1997 (8) 2.68
Set value 1.35

Issued to commemorate the centenary of the Hungarian State Institute of Geology.

Steeplechase – A434

Designs: 60f, Fencing. 1fo, Pistol shooting. 2fo, Swimmers at start. 3fo, Relay race. 5fo, Pentathlon.

1969, Sept. 15 Photo. *Perf. 12x11½*

1998 A434 40f bl & multi 15 15
1999 A434 60f multi 15 15
2000 A434 1fo multi 15 15
2001 A434 2fo vio & multi 34 15
2002 A434 3fo lem & multi 58 34
2003 A434 5fo bluish grn, gold & dk red 1.25 70
Nos. 1998-2003 (6) 2.62
Set value 1.42

Hungarian Pentathion Championshipa.

First Hungarian Postal Card A435

1969, Oct. 1

2004 A435 60f ver & ocher 15 15

Issued to commemorate the centenary of the postal card. Hungary and Austria both issued cards in 1869.

Mahatma Gandhi – A436

1969, Oct. 1 *Perf. 11½x12*

2005 A436 5fo grn & multi 1.25 70

Mohandas K. Gandhi (1869-1948), leader in India's fight for independence.

World Trade Union Emblem A437

1969, Oct. 17 Photo. *Perf. 12x11½*

2006 A437 2fo fawn & dk bl 30 15

Issued to publicize the 7th Congress of the World Federation of Trade Unions.

Janos Balogh Nagy, Self-portrait A438

1969, Oct. 17 *Perf. 11½x12*

2007 A438 5fo gold & multi 1.50 80

Issued to commemorate the 50th anniversary of the death of Janos Balogh Nagy (1874-1919), painter.

St. John the Evangelist, by Anthony Van Dyck A439

Dutch Paintings: 60f, Three Fruit Pickers (by Pieter de Molyn?). 1fo, Boy Lighting Pipe, by Hendrick Terbrugghen. 2fo, The Feast, by Jan Steen. 3fo, Woman Reading Letter, by Pieter de Hooch. 4fo, The Fiddler, by Dirk Hals. 5fo, Portrait of Jan Asselyn, by Frans Hals. 10fo, Mucius Scaevola before Porsena, by Rubens and Van Dyck.

1969-70 Photo. *Perf. 12½*

2008 A439 40f multi 15 15
2009 A439 60f multi 15 15
2010 A439 1fo multi 15 15
2011 A439 2fo multi 24 15
2012 A439 3fo multi 45 18
2013 A439 4fo multi 60 40
2014 A439 5fo multi 1.10 70
Nos. 2008-2014 (7) 2.84
Set value 1.60

Miniature Sheet

2015 A439 10fo multi 3.75 3.75

Treasures in the Museum of Fine Arts, Budapest and the Museum in Eger.

Issue Dates: Nos. 2008-2014, Dec. 2, 1969; No. 2015, Jan. 1970.

Kiskunfelegyhaza Circling Pigeon – A440

1969, Dec. 12 Photo. *Perf. 11½x12*

2016 A440 1fo multi 20 15

Issued to publicize the International Pigeon Show, Budapest, Dec. 1969.

Subway A441

1970, Apr. 3 Photo. *Perf. 12*

2017 A441 1fo blk, lt grn & ultra 20 15

Opening of new Budapest subway.

Souvenir Sheet

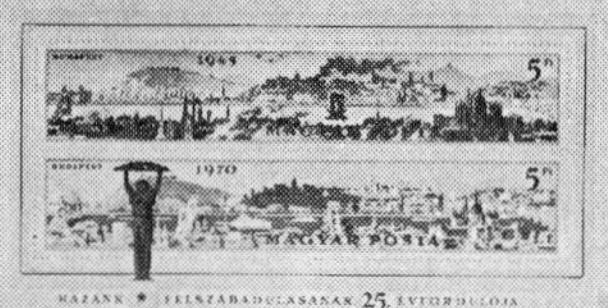

Panoramic View of Budapest 1945 and 1970, and Soviet Cenotaph — A442

Illustration reduced.

1970, Apr. 3 ***Perf. 12x11½***

2018	A442	Sheet of 2	3.00	3.00
a.		5fo "1945"	1.10	1.10
b.		5fo "1970"	1.10	1.10

25th anniv. of the liberation of Budapest.

Cloud Formation, Satellite, Earth and Receiving Station A443

Lenin Statue, Budapest A444

1970, Apr. 8 **Litho.** ***Perf. 12***

2019	A443	1fo dk bl, yel & blk	20	15

Issued to commemorate the centenary of the Hungarian Meteorological Service.

1970, Apr. 22 **Photo.** ***Perf. 11***

Design: 2fo, Lenin portrait.

2020	A444	1fo gold & multi	15	15
2021	A444	2fo gold & multi	18	15
		Set value	27	15

Issued to commemorate the centenary of the birth of Lenin (1870-1924), Russian communist leader.

Franz Lehar and "Giuditta" Music — A445

1970, Apr. 30 **Photo.** ***Perf. 12***

2022	A445	2fo multi	50	20

Issued to commemorate the centenary of the birth of Franz Lehar (1870-1948), composer.

Samson and Delilah, by Michele Rocca A446

Paintings: 60f, Joseph Telling Dream, by Giovanni Battista Langetti. 1fo, Clio, by Pierre Mignard. 1.50fo, Venus and Satyr, by Sebastiano Ricci (horiz.). 2.50fo, Andromeda, by Francesco Furini. 4fo, Venus, Adonis and Cupid, by Luca Giordano. 5fo, Allegorical Feast, by Corrado Giaquinto. 10fo, Diana and Callisto, by Abraham Janssens (horiz.).

1970, June 2 **Photo.** ***Perf. 12½***

2023	A446	40f gold & multi	15	15
2024	A446	60f gold & multi	15	15
2025	A446	1fo gold & multi	24	15
2026	A446	1.50fo gold & multi	28	15
2027	A446	2.50fo gold & multi	40	20
2028	A446	4fo gold & multi	85	40
2029	A446	5fo gold & multi	1.10	60
		Nos. 2023-2029 (7)	3.17	
		Set value		1.58

Miniature Sheet

Perf. 11

2030	A446	10fo gold & multi	3.50	3.50

No. 2030 contains one 63x46mm horizontal stamp.

Beethoven Statue, by Janos Pasztor, at Martonvasar A447

1970, June 27 **Litho.** ***Perf. 12***

2031	A447	1fo plum, gray grn & org yel	75	20

Ludwig van Beethoven (1770-1827), composer. The music in the design is from Sonata 37.

Foundryman A448

King Stephen I A449

1970, July 28 **Litho.** ***Perf. 12***

2032	A448	1fo multi	25	15

200th anniversary of the first Hungarian steel foundry at Diosgyor, now the Lenin Metallurgical Works.

1970, Aug. 19 **Photo.** ***Perf. 11½x12***

2033	A449	3fo multi	1.50	50

Issued to commemorate the millenary of the birth of Saint Stephen, first King of Hungary.

Women's Four on Lake Tata and Tata Castle A450

1970, Aug. 19 **Litho.** ***Perf. 12***

2034	A450	1fo multi	35	15

Issued to commemorate the 17th European Women's Rowing Championships, Lake Tata.

Mother Giving Bread to her Children, FAO Emblem A451

1970, Sept. 21 **Litho.** ***Perf. 12***

2035	A451	1fo lt bl & multi	20	15

7th European Regional Cong. of the UNFAO, Budapest, Sept. 21-25.

Boxing and Olympic Rings A452

Designs (Olympic Rings and): 60f, Canoeing. 1fo, Fencing. 1.50fo, Water polo. 2fo, Woman gymnast. 2.50fo, Hammer throwing. 3fo, Wrestling. 5fo, Swimming, butterfly stroke.

1970, Sept. 26 **Photo.** ***Perf. 11***

2036	A452	40f lt vio & multi	15	15
2037	A452	60f sky bl & multi	15	15
2038	A452	1fo org & multi	15	15
2039	A452	1.50fo multi	20	15
2040	A452	2fo multi	35	15
2041	A452	2.50fo multi	40	18
2042	A452	3fo multi	60	34
2043	A452	5fo multi	1.10	55
		Nos. 2036-2043 (8)	3.10	
		Set value		1.45

Issued to commemorate the 75th anniversary of the Hungarian Olympic Committee. The 5fo also publicizes the 1972 Olympic Games in Munich.

Flame and Family A453

1970, Sept. 28 **Litho.** ***Perf. 12***

2044	A453	1fo ultra, org & emer	20	15

5th Education Congress, Budapest.

Chalice, by Benedek Suky, 1440 — A454

Hungarian Goldsmiths' Art: 60f, Altar burette, 1500. 1fo, Nadasdy goblet, 16th century. 1.50fo, Coconut goblet, 1600. 2fo, Silver tankard, by Mihaly Toldalaghy, 1623. 2.50fo, Communion cup of Gyorgy Rakoczy I, 1670. 3fo, Tankard, 1690. 4fo, Bell-flower cup, 1710.

1970, Oct. **Photo.** ***Perf. 12***

2045	A454	40f gold & multi	15	15
2046	A454	60f gold & multi	15	15
2047	A454	1fo gold & multi	15	15
2048	A454	1.50fo gold & multi	15	15
2049	A454	2fo gold & multi	20	15
2050	A454	2.50fo gold & multi	24	18
2051	A454	3fo gold & multi	60	42
2052	A454	4fo gold & multi	1.00	60
		Nos. 2045-2052 (8)	2.64	
		Set value		1.60

Virgin and Child, by Giampietrino — A455

Paintings from Christian Museum, Esztergom: 60f, "Love" (woman with 3 children), by Gregorio Lazzarini. 1fo, Legend of St. Catherine, by Master of Bat. 1.50fo, Adoration of the Shepherds, by Francesco Fontebasso (horiz.). 2.50fo, Adoration of the Kings, by Master of Aranyosmarot. 4fo, Temptation of St. Anthony the Hermit, by Jan de Cock. 5fo, St. Sebastian, by Marco Palmezzano. 10fo, Lady with the Unicorn, by Painter of Lombardy.

1970, Dec. 7 **Photo.** ***Perf. 12½***

2053	A455	40f sil & multi	15	15
2054	A455	60f sil & multi	15	15
2055	A455	1fo sil & multi	15	15
2056	A455	1.50fo sil & multi	18	15
2057	A455	2.50fo sil & multi	40	20
2058	A455	4fo sil & multi	75	30
2059	A455	5fo sil & multi	1.10	70
		Nos. 2053-2059 (7)	2.88	
		Set value		1.55

Souvenir Sheet

2060	A455	10fo sil & multi	3.50	3.25

No. 2060 contains one 50½x56mm stamp.

Monument to Hungarian Martyrs, by A. Makrisz — A456

1970, Dec. 30 **Photo.** ***Perf. 12x11½***

2061	A456	1fo ultra & sep	15	15

The 25th anniversary of the liberation of the concentration camps at Auschwitz, Mauthausen and Dachau.

Marseillaise, by Francois Rude A457

Béla Bartók (1881-1945), Composer A458

1971, Mar. 18 **Litho.** ***Perf. 12***

2062	A457	3fo bis & grn	40	20

Centenary of the Paris Commune.

1971

Design: No. 2064, Andras L. Achim (1871-1911), peasant leader.

2063	A458	1fo gray & dk car	55	18
2064	A458	1fo gray & grn	20	15
		Set value		25

Dates of issue: No. 2063, Mar. 25; No. 2064, Apr. 17.

Györ Castle, 1594 A459

1971, Mar. 27

2065	A459	2fo lt bl & multi	40	15

700th anniversary of Györ.

Bison Hunt — A460

Designs: 60f, Wild boar hunt. 80f, Deer hunt. 1fo, Falconry. 1.20fo, Felled stag and dogs. 2fo, Bustards. 3fo, Net fishing. 4fo, Angling.

1971, May **Photo.** ***Perf. 12***

2066	A460	40f ver & multi	15	15
2067	A460	60f plum & multi	15	15
2068	A460	80f multi	15	15
2069	A460	1fo lil & multi	16	15
2070	A460	1.20fo multi	25	22
2071	A460	2fo multi	45	20
2072	A460	3fo multi	80	30
2073	A460	4fo grn & multi	1.10	65
		Nos. 2066-2073 (8)	3.21	
		Set value		1.70

World Hunting Exhibition, Budapest, Aug. 27-30. See No. C313.

Souvenir Sheet

Portrait of a Man, by Dürer — A461

1971, May 21 ***Perf. 12½***

2074	A461	10fo gold & multi	3.50	3.25

Albrecht Dürer (1471-1528), German painter and etcher.

Carnation and Pioneers' Emblem — A462

1971, June 2 **Photo.** ***Perf. 12***

2075	A462	1fo dk red & multi	20	15

25th anniversary of the Hungarian Pioneers' Organization.

FIR Emblem, Resistance Fighters A463

1971, July 3

2076	A463	1fo brn & multi	20	15

International Federation of Resistance Fighters (FIR), 20th anniversary.

Walking in Garden, Tokyo School A464

Japanese Prints from Museum of East Asian Art, Budapest: 60f, Geisha in Boat, by Yeishi (1756-1829). 1fo, Woman with Scroll, by Yeishi. 1.50fo, Courtesans, by Kiyonaga (1752-1815). 2fo, Awabi Fisher Women, by Utamaro (1753-1806). 2.50fo, Seated Courtesan, by Harunobu (1725-1770). 3fo, Peasant Woman Carrying Fagots, by Hokusai (1760-1849). 4fo, Women and Girls Walking, by Yeishi.

1971, July 9 ***Perf. 12½***

2077	A464	40f gold & multi	15	15
2078	A464	60f gold & multi	15	15
2079	A464	1fo gold & multi	15	15
2080	A464	1.50fo gold & multi	18	15
2081	A464	2fo gold & multi	24	15
2082	A464	2.50fo gold & multi	30	20
2083	A464	3fo gold & multi	55	24
2084	A464	4fo gold & multi	1.25	60
		Nos. 2077-2084 (8)	2.97	
		Set value		1.50

Locomotive, Map of Rail System and Danube — A465

1971, July 15 **Litho.** ***Perf. 12***

2086	A465	1fo multi	30	15

125th anniversary of first Hungarian railroad between Pest and Vac.

Griffin Holding Ink Balls A466

1971, Sept. 11 **Photo.** ***Perf. 12x11½***

2087	A466	1fo multi	75	60

Centenary of stamp printing in Hungary. Printed se-tenant with 2 labels showing printing presses of 1871 and 1971 and Hungary Nos. P1 and 1171.

OIJ Emblem and Printed Page — A467

1971, Sept. 21 ***Perf. 11½x12***

2088	A467	1fo dk bl, bl & gold	25	15

25th anniversary of the International Organization of Journalists (OIJ).

Josef Jacob Winterl and Barren Strawberry — A468

Plants: 60f, Bromeliaceae. 80f, Titanopsis calcarea. 1fo, Periwinkle. 1.20fo, Gymnocalycium. 2fo, White water lily. 3fo, Iris arenaria. 5fo, Peony.

1971, Oct. 29 **Litho.** ***Perf. 12***

2089	A468	40f lt vio & multi	15	15
2090	A468	60f gray & multi	15	15
2091	A468	80f multi	15	15
2092	A468	1fo multi	15	15
2093	A468	1.20fo lil & multi	18	15
2094	A468	2fo gray & multi	40	15
2095	A468	3fo multi	70	35
2096	A468	5fo multi	1.25	55
		Nos. 2089-2096 (8)	3.13	
		Set value		1.50

Bicentenary of Budapest Botanical Gardens.

Galloping — A469

Equestrian Sports: 60f, Trotting. 80f, Horses fording river. 1fo, Jumping. 1.20fo, Start. 2fo, Polo. 3fo, Steeplechase. 5fo, Dressage.

1971, Nov. 22 **Photo.** ***Perf. 12***

2097	A469	40f bl & multi	15	15
2098	A469	60f ocher & multi	15	15
2099	A469	80f ol & multi	15	15
2100	A469	1fo red & multi	18	15
2101	A469	1.20fo multi	28	15
2102	A469	2fo multi	40	18
2103	A469	3fo vio & multi	60	40
2104	A469	5fo bl & multi	1.00	70
		Nos. 2097-2104 (8)	2.91	
		Set value		1.75

Beheading of Heathen Chief Koppany A470

Designs: 60f, Samuel Aba pursuing King Peter. 1fo, Basarad's victory over King Charles Robert. 1.50fo, Strife between King Salomon and Prince Geza. 2.50fo, Founding of Obuda Church by King Stephen I and Queen Gisela. 4fo, Reconciliation of King Koloman and his brother Almos. 5fo, Oradea Church built by King Ladislas I. 10fo, Funeral of Prince Emeric and blinding of Vazul.

1971, Dec. 10 **Litho.**

2105	A470	40f buff & multi	15	15
2106	A470	60f buff & multi	15	15
2107	A470	1fo buff & multi	18	15
2108	A470	1.50fo buff & multi	18	15
2109	A470	2.50fo buff & multi	30	16
2110	A470	4fo buff & multi	60	32
2111	A470	5fo buff & multi	1.10	60
		Nos. 2105-2111 (7)	2.66	
		Set value		1.45

Miniature Sheet

Perf. 11½

2112	A470	10fo buff & multi	3.25	3.00

History of Hungary, from miniatures from Illuminated Chronicle of King Louis the Great, c. 1370. No. 2112 contains one stamp (size 44½x52mm).

Equality Year Emblem — A471

1971, Dec. 30 **Litho.** ***Perf. 12***

2113	A471	1fo bister & multi	20	15

Intl. Year Against Racial Discrimination.

Ice Hockey and Sapporo '72 Emblem — A472

Sport and Sapporo '72 Emblem: 60f, Men's slalom. 80f, Women's figure skating. 1fo, Ski jump. 1.20fo, Long-distance skiing. 2fo, Men's figure skating. 3fo, Bobsledding. 4fo, Biathlon. 10fo, Buddha.

1971, Dec. 30 ***Perf. 12***

2114	A472	40f blk & multi	15	15
2115	A472	60f blk & multi	15	15
2116	A472	80f blk & multi	15	15
2117	A472	1fo blk & multi	15	15
2118	A472	1.20fo blk & multi	24	15
2119	A472	2fo blk & multi	40	20
2120	A472	3fo blk & multi	60	40
2121	A472	4fo blk & multi	1.25	65
		Nos. 2114-2121 (8)	3.09	
		Set value		1.65

Souvenir Sheet

Perf. 11½

2122	A472	10fo gold & multi	3.50	3.25

11th Winter Olympic Games, Sapporo, Japan, Feb. 3-13, 1972. No. 2122 contains one stamp (size 86x48mm).

Hungarian Locomotive — A473

Locomotives: 60f, Germany. 80f, Italy. 1fo, Soviet Union. 1.20fo, Japan. 2fo, Great Britain. 4fo, Austria. 5fo, France.

1972, Feb. 23 Photo. *Perf. 12x11½*

2123	A473	40f multi	15	15
2124	A473	60f ocher & multi	15	15
2125	A473	80f multi	15	15
2126	A473	1fo ol & multi	15	15
2127	A473	1.20fo ultra & multi	40	30
2128	A473	2fo ver & multi	25	16
2129	A473	4fo multi	55	30
2130	A473	5fo multi	1.00	50
		Nos. 2123-2130 (8)	2.80	
		Set value		1.50

Janus Pannonius, by Andrea Mantegna — A474

1972, Mar. 27 Litho. *Perf. 12*

2131	A474	1fo gold & multi	25	15

500th anniversary of the death of Janus Pannonius (Johannes Czezmiczei, 1434-1472), humanist and poet.

Mariner 9 — A475

Design: No. 2133, Mars 2 and 3 spacecraft.

1972, Mar. 30 Photo. *Perf. 11½x12*

2132	A475	2fo dk bl & multi	45	45
2133	A475	2fo multi	45	45
a.		Strip #2132-2133 + label	1.35	1.35

Exploration of Mars by Mariner 9 (US), and Mars 2 and 3 (USSR). Issued in sheets containing 4 each of Nos. 2132-2133 and 4 labels inscribed in Hungarian, Russian and English.

13th Century Church Portal — A476

1972, Apr. 11

2134	A476	3fo greenish black	40	15

Centenary of the Society for the Protection of Historic Monuments.

Hungarian Greyhound — A477

Hounds: 60f, Afghan hound (head). 80f, Irish wolfhound. 1.20fo, Borzoi. 2fo, Running greyhound. 4fo, Whippet. 6fo, Afghan hound.

1972, Apr. 14 Litho. *Perf. 12*

2135	A477	40f multi	15	15
2136	A477	60f brn & multi	15	15
2137	A477	80f multi	16	15
2138	A477	1.20fo multi	16	15
2139	A477	2fo multi	35	15
2140	A477	4fo multi	80	24
2141	A477	6fo multi	1.25	90
		Nos. 2135-2141 (7)	3.02	
		Set value		1.55

József Imre, Emil Grósz, László Blaskovics (Ophthalmologists) — A478

Design: 2fo, Allvar Gullstrand, V. P. Filatov, Jules Gonin, ophthalmologists.

1972, Apr. 17

2142	A478	1fo red, brn & blk	45	20
2143	A478	2fo bl, brn & blk	1.10	50

First European Ophthalmologists' Congress, Budapest.

Girl Reading and UNESCO Emblem — A479

Roses — A480

1972, May 27 Photo. *Perf. 11½x12*

2144	A479	1fo multi	40	15

International Book Year 1971.

1972, June 1

2145	A480	1fo multi	40	15

15th Rose Exhibition, Budapest.

George Dimitrov A481

1972, June 18 Litho. *Perf. 12*

2146	A481	3fo blk & multi	40	15

90th anniversary, birth of George Dimitrov (1882-1949), communist leader.

Souvenir Sheet

St. Martin and the Beggar, Stained-glass Window A482

1972, June 20 *Perf. 10½*

2147	A482	10fo multi	3.50	3.25

Belgica 72, International Philatelic Exhibition, Brussels, June 24-July 9.

Gyorgy Dozsa (1474-1514), Peasant Leader — A483

1972, June 25 Photo. *Perf. 11½x12*

2148	A483	1fo red & multi	20	15

Olympic Rings, Soccer — A484

Designs (Olympic Rings and): 60f, Water polo. 80f, Javelin, women's. 1fo, Kayak, women's. 1.20fo, Boxing. 2fo, Gymnastics, women's. 5fo, Fencing.

1972, July 15 *Perf. 11*

2149	A484	40f multi	15	15
2150	A484	60f multi	15	15
2151	A484	80f multi	15	15
2152	A484	1fo lil & multi	15	15
2153	A484	1.20fo bl & multi	22	15
2154	A484	2fo multi	50	25
2155	A484	5fo grn & multi	1.00	65
		Nos. 2149-2155,B299 (8)	2.87	
		Set value		1.70

20th Olympic Games, Munich, Aug. 26-Sept. 11. See No. C325.

Prince Geza Selecting Site of Szekesfehervar — A485

Designs: 60f, St. Stephen, first King of Hungary. 80f, Knights (country's defense). 1.20fo, King Stephen dictating to scribe (legal organization). 2fo, Sculptor at work (education). 4fo, Merchants before king (foreign relations). 6fo, View of castle and town of Székesfehérvár, 10th century. 10fo, King Andreas II presenting Golden Bull to noblemen.

1972, Aug. 20 Photo. *Perf. 12*

2156	A485	40f sl & multi	15	15
2157	A485	60f multi	20	15
2158	A485	80f lil & multi	15	15
2159	A485	1.20fo multi	25	15
2160	A485	2fo bis & multi	45	18
2161	A485	4fo bl & multi	75	35
2162	A485	6fo pur & multi	1.10	70
		Nos. 2156-2162 (7)	3.05	
		Set value		1.55

Souvenir Sheet

Perf. 12½

2163	A485	10fo blk & multi	3.50	3.25

Millenium of the town of Székesfehérvár and 750th anniversary of the Golden Bull granting rights to lesser nobility. No. 2163 contains one stamp (94x45mm).

Parliament, Budapest — A486

Design: 6fo, Session room of Parliament.

1972, Aug. 20 Litho.

2164	A486	5fo dk bl & multi	60	20
2165	A486	6fo multi	95	30

Constitution of 1949.

Eger, 17th Century View, and Bottle of Bull's Blood — A487

Design: 2fo, Contemporary view of Tokay and bottle of Tokay Aszu.

1972, Aug. 21 Litho. *Perf. 12*

2166	A487	1fo buff & multi	28	15
2167	A487	2fo grn & multi	65	20
		Set value		27

1st World Wine Exhibition, Budapest, Aug. 1972.

Georgikon Emblems, Grain, Potato Flower A488

1972, Sept. 3

2168	A488	1fo multi	20	15

175th anniversary of the founding of the Georgikon at Keszthely, the first scientific agricultural academy.

Covered Candy Dish — A489

Herend Porcelain: 40f, Vase with bird. 80f, Vase with flowers and butterflies. 1fo, Plate with Mexican landscape. 1.20fo, Covered dish. 2fo, Teapot, cup and saucer. 4fo, Plate with flowers. 5fo, Baroque vase showing Herend factory.

1972, Sept. 15
Sizes: 23x46mm (40f, 80f, 2fo, 5fo); 33x36mm, others

2169	A489	40f gray & multi	15	15
2170	A489	60f ocher & multi	15	15
2171	A489	80f multi	15	15
2172	A489	1fo multi	15	15
2173	A489	1.20fo grn & multi	18	15
2174	A489	2fo multi	35	20
2175	A489	4fo red & multi	70	40
2176	A489	5fo multi	1.10	60
		Nos. 2169-2176 (8)	2.93	
		Set value		1.70

Herend china factory, founded 1839.

UIC Emblem and M-62 Diesel Locomotive — A490

1972, Sept. 19 Photo. ***Perf. 11½x12***
2177 A490 1fo dk red 35 15

50th anniversary of International Railroad Union Congress, Budapest, Sept. 19.

"25" and Graph — A491

1972, Sept. ***Perf. 11½x12***
2178 A491 1fo yel & brn 35 15

Planned national economy, 25th anniv.

View of Obuda, 1872 A492

Designs: No. 2180, Budapest, 1972. No. 2181, Buda, 1872. No. 2182, Budapest, 1972. No. 2183, Pest, 1872. No. 2184, Budapest, 1972.

1972, Sept. 26 ***Perf. 12x11½***

2179	A492	1fo Prus bl & rose car	16	15
2180	A492	1fo rose car & Prus bl	16	15
2181	A492	2fo ocher & ol	28	15
2182	A492	2fo ol & ocher	28	15
2183	A492	3fo grn & lt brn	42	18
2184	A492	3fo lt brn & grn	42	18
		Nos. 2179-2184 (6)	1.72	
		Set value		70

Centenary of unification of Obuda, Buda and Pest into Budapest. Stamps of same denomination printed se-tenant.

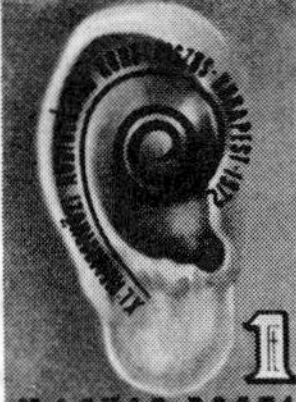

Ear and Congress Emblem — A493

Flora Martos — A494

1972, Oct. 3 ***Perf. 11½x12***
2185 A493 1fo brn, yel & blk 20 15

11th Intl. Audiology Cong., Budapest.

1972 Photo. ***Perf. 11½x12***

Portrait: No. 2187, Miklós Radnóti.

2186	A494	1fo grn & multi	15	15
2187	A494	1fo brn & multi	15	15
		Set value		15

Flora Martos (1897-1938), Hungarian Labor Party leader, and Miklós Radnóti (1909-1944), poet

Issue dates: No. 2186, Nov. 5; No. 2187, Nov. 11.

Muses, by Jozsef Rippl-Ronai A495

Stained-glass Windows, 19th-20th Centuries: 60f, 16th century scribe, by Ferenc Sebesteny. 1fo, Flight into Egypt, by Karoly Lotz and Bertalan Szekely. 1.50fo, Prince Arpad's Messenger, by Jenö Percz. 2.50fo, Nativity, by Lili Sztehlo. 4fo, Prince Arpad and Leaders, by Karoly Kernstock. 5fo, King Matthias and Jester, by Jenö Haranghy.

1972, Nov. 15 ***Perf. 12***

2188	A495	40f multi	15	15
2189	A495	60f multi	15	15
2190	A495	1fo multi	15	15
2191	A495	1.50fo multi	22	15
2192	A495	2.50fo multi	38	16
2193	A495	4fo multi	75	32
2194	A495	5fo multi	1.25	60
		Nos. 2188-2194 (7)	3.05	
		Set value		1.38

Weaver, Cloth and Cogwheel A496

1972, Nov. 27 Litho. ***Perf. 12***
2195 A496 1fo sil & multi 30 15

Opening of Museum of Textile Techniques, Budapest.

Main Square, Szarvas A497

Church and City Hall, Vac A498

Designs: 1fo, Modern buildings, Salgotarjan. 3fo, Tokay and vineyard. 4fo, Esztergom Cathedral. 7fo, Town Hall, Kaposvar. 20fo, Veszprem.

1972 Litho. ***Perf. 11***

2196	A497	40f brown & orange	15	15
2197	A497	1fo dk & lt blue	22	15

1973 ***Perf. 12x11½***

2198	A498	3fo dk & lt grn	60	15
2199	A498	4fo red brn & org	75	15
2200	A498	7fo bl vio & lil	1.40	15
2200A	A498	20fo multi	3.75	55
		Nos. 2196-2200A (6)	6.87	
		Set value		85

See Nos. 2330-2335.

Coil Stamps
Type of 1963-64

Designs as before

1972, Nov. Photo. ***Perf. 14***
Size: 21½x17½mm, 17½x21½mm

2201	A336	2fo bl grn	38	15
2202	A336	3fo dk bl	55	15
2203	A336	4fo blue, vert.	75	25
2204	A336	6fo bister	1.10	40

Black control number on back of every 5th stamp.

Minute inscription centered in lower margin: "Legrady Sandor".

Arms of Soviet Union — A498a

1972, Dec. 30 Photo. ***Perf. 11½x12***
2205 A498a 1fo multi 15 15

50th anniversary of Soviet Union.

Petöfi Speaking at Pilvax Cafe — A499

Designs: 2fo, Portrait. 3fo, Petöfi on horseback, 1848-49.

1972, Dec. 30 Engr. ***Perf. 12***

2206	A499	1fo rose car	18	15
2207	A499	2fo violet	35	15
2208	A499	3fo Prus grn	50	24
		Set value		45

Sesquicentennial of the birth of Sandor Petöfi (1823-49), poet and revolutionary.

Postal Zone Map of Hungary and Letter-carrying Crow — A500

1973, Jan. 1 Litho. ***Perf. 12***
2209 A500 1fo red & blk 20 15

Introduction of postal code system.

Imre Madách (1823-64), Poet and Dramatist A501

1973, Jan. 20 Photo. ***Perf. 11½x12***
2210 A501 1fo multi 20 15

Busho Mask — A502

Designs: Various Busho masks.

1973, Feb. 17 Litho. ***Perf. 12***

2211	A502	40f tan & multi	15	15
2212	A502	60f dl grn & multi	15	15
2213	A502	80f lil & multi	15	15
2214	A502	1.20fo multi	20	15
2215	A502	2fo tan & multi	32	16
2216	A502	4fo multi	80	38
2217	A502	6fo lil & multi	1.25	55
		Nos. 2211-2217 (7)	3.02	
		Set value		1.40

Busho Walk at Mohacs, ancient ceremony to drive out winter.

Nicolaus Copernicus A503

1973, Feb. 19 Engr. ***Perf. 12***
2218 A503 3fo brt ultra 75 60

500th anniversary of the birth of Nicolaus Copernicus (1473-1543), Polish astronomer. Printed with alternating label showing heliocentric system and view of Torun.

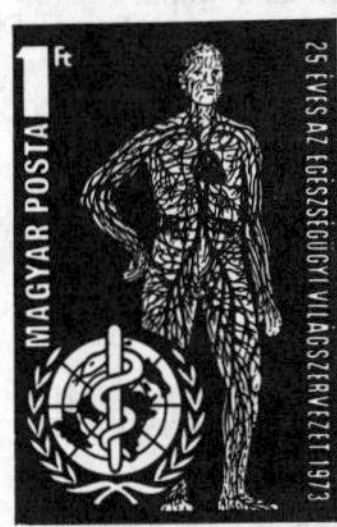

Vascular System and WHO Emblem — A504

1973, Apr. 16 Photo. ***Perf. 12***
2219 A504 1fo sl grn & brn red 25 15

25th anniv. of WHO.

The first price column gives the catalogue value of an unused stamp, the second that of a used stamp.

Tank, Rocket, Radar, Plane, Ship and Soldier A505

1973, May 9 Litho. *Perf. 12*
2220 A505 3fo bl & multi 40 15

Philatelic Exhibition of Military Stamp Collectors of Warsaw Treaty Member States. No. 2220 was printed with alternating label showing flags of Warsaw Treaty members.

Hungary No. 1396 and IBRA '73 Emblem — A506

1973, May 11 Litho. *Perf. 12*
2221 A506 40f shown 15 15
2222 A506 60f No. 1397, POLSKA '73 15 15
2223 A506 80f No. 1398, IBRA '73 15 15
2224 A506 1fo No. 1399, POLSKA 15 15
2225 A506 1.20fo No. B293a, IBRA 16 15
2226 A506 2fo No. B293b, POLSKA 32 16
2227 A506 4fo No. B293c, IBRA 80 38
2228 A506 5fo No. B293d, POLSKA 1.15 50
Nos. 2221-2228 (8) 3.03
Set value 1.40

Publicity for IBRA '73 International Philatelic Exhibition, Munich, May 11-20; and POLSKA '73, Poznan, Aug. 15-Sept. 2. See No. C345.

Typesetting, from "Orbis Pictus," by Comenius A507

Design: 3fo, Printer and wooden screw press, woodcut from Hungarian translation of Gospels.

1973, June 5 Photo. *Perf. 11½x12*
2229 A507 1fo blk & gold 18 15
2230 A507 3fo blk & gold 42 18
Set value 25

500th anniv. of book printing in Hungary.

Storm over Hortobagy Puszta, by Csontvary — A508

Paintings: 60f, Mary's Well, Nazareth. 1fo, Carriage Ride by Moonlight in Athens (vert.). 1.50fo, Pilgrimage to Cedars of Lebanon (vert.). 2.50fo, The Lonely Cedar. 4fo, Waterfall at Jajce. 5fo, Ruins of Greek Theater at Taormina. 10fo, Horseback Riders on Shore.

1973, June 18 *Perf. 12½*
2231 A508 40f gold & multi 15 15
2232 A508 60f gold & multi 15 15
2233 A508 1fo gold & multi 15 15
2234 A508 1.50fo gold & multi 22 15
2235 A508 2.50fo gold & multi 48 16
2236 A508 4fo gold & multi 80 45
2237 A508 5fo gold & multi 95 70
Nos. 2231-2237 (7) 2.90
Set value 1.60

Souvenir Sheet

2238 A508 10fo gold & multi 3.75 3.25

Paintings by Tividar Kosztka Csontvary (1853-1919). No. 2238 contains one stamp (size: 90x43mm).

Hands Holding Map of Europe — A509

Flowers — A510

1973, July 3 Photo. *Perf. 11½x12*
2239 A509 2.50fo blk & gldn brn 3.00 3.00
a. Souv. sheet of 4 + 2 labels 14.50 14.50

Conference for European Security and Cooperation. Helsinki, July 1973. No. 2239 was printed in souvenir sheet of 4 stamps and 2 blue labels showing conference sites.

1973, Aug. 4
2240 A510 40f Provence roses 15 15
2241 A510 60f Cyclamen 15 15
2242 A510 80f Lungwort 15 15
2243 A510 1.20fo English daisies 16 15
2244 A510 2fo Buttercups 32 18
2245 A510 4fo Violets 80 35
2246 A510 6fo Poppies 1.25 65
Nos. 2240-2246 (7) 2.98
Set value 1.55

"Let's be Friends in Traffic" — A511

Designs: 60f, "Not even one drink." 1fo, "Light your bicycle."

1973, Aug. 18 Photo. *Perf. 12x11½*
2247 A511 40f grn & org 15 15
2248 A511 60f pur & org 15 15
2249 A511 1fo indigo & org 16 15
Set value 30 17

To publicize traffic rules.

Adoration of the Kings A512

Paintings: 60f, Angels playing violin and lute. 1fo, Adoration of the Kings. 1.50fo, Annunciation. 2.50fo, Angels playing organ and harp. 4fo, Visitation of Mary. 5fo, Legend of St. Catherine of Alexandria. 10fo, Nativity.

1973, Nov. 3 Photo. *Perf. 12½*
2250 A512 40f gold & multi 15 15
2251 A512 60f gold & multi 15 15
2252 A512 1fo gold & multi 18 15
2253 A512 1.50fo gold & multi 25 15
2254 A512 2.50fo gold & multi 48 22
2255 A512 4fo gold & multi 70 38
2256 A512 5fo gold & multi 1.00 65
Nos. 2250-2256 (7) 2.91
Set value 1.55

Souvenir Sheet

Perf. 11

2257 A512 10fo gold & multi 3.50 3.25

Paintings by Hungarian anonymous early masters from the Christian Museum at Esztergom. No. 2257 contains one 49x74mm stamp.

Mihaly Csokonai Vitez — A513

José Marti and Cuban Flag — A514

1973, Nov. 17 Photo. *Perf. 11½x12*
2258 A513 2fo bis & multi 35 15

Bicentenary of the birth of Mihaly Csokonai Vitez (1773-1805), poet.

1973, Nov. 30
2259 A514 1fo dk brn, red & bl 15 15

José Marti (1853-1895), Cuban national hero and poet.

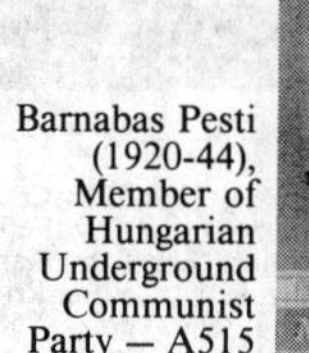

Barnabas Pesti (1920-44), Member of Hungarian Underground Communist Party — A515

1973, Nov. 30
2260 A515 1fo bl, brn & buff 15 15

Women's Double Kayak — A516

Designs: 60f, Water polo. 80f, Men's single kayak. 1.20fo, Butterfly stroke. 2fo, Men's fours kayak. 4fo, Men's single canoe. 6fo, Men's double canoe.

1973, Dec. 29 Litho. *Perf. 12x11*
2261 A516 40f red & multi 15 15
2262 A516 60f bl & multi 15 15
2263 A516 80f multi 15 15
2264 A516 1.20fo grn & multi 22 15
2265 A516 2fo car & multi 40 16
2266 A516 4fo vio & multi 80 38
2267 A516 6fo multi 1.10 60
Nos. 2261-2267 (7) 2.97
Set value 1.40

Hungarian victories in water sports at Tampere and Belgrade.

Souvenir Sheet

Map of Europe — A517

1974, Jan. 15 Photo. *Perf. 12x11½*
2268 Sheet of 2 + label 10.00 10.00
a. A517 5fo multi 2.25 2.25

European Peace Conference (Arab-Israeli War), Geneva, Jan. 1974.

Lenin A518

1974, Jan. 21 Photo. *Perf. 11½x12*
2269 A518 2fo gold, dl bl & brn 25 15

50th anniversary of the death of Lenin (1870-1924).

Jozsef Boczor, Imre Bekes, Tamas Elek A519

1974, Feb. 21 *Perf. 12½*
2270 A519 3fo brn & multi 25 15

30th anniversary of the death in France of Hungarian resistance fighters.

Comecon Building, Moscow and Flags A520

1974, Feb. 26 Photo. *Perf. 12x11½*
2271 A520 1fo multi 25 15

25th anniversary of the Council of Mutual Economic Assistance.

Bank Emblem, Coins and Banknote A521

1974, Mar. 1 *Perf. 11½x12*
2272 A521 1fo lt grn & multi 25 15

25th anniversary of the State Savings Bank.

Spacecraft on Way to Mars — A522

Designs: 60f, Mars 2 over Mars. 80f, Mariner 4. 1fo, Mars and Mt. Palomar Observatory. 1.20fo, Soft landing of Mars 3. 5fo, Mariner 9 with Mars satellites Phobos and Deimos.

1974, Mar. 11 Photo. *Perf. 12½*

2273 A522 40f gold & multi 15 15
2274 A522 60f sil & multi 15 15
2275 A522 80f gold & multi 15 15
2276 A522 1fo sil & multi 22 15
2277 A522 1.20fo gold & multi 28 15
2278 A522 5fo sil & multi 95 50
Nos. 2273-2278,C347 (7) 3.00
Set value 1.55

Exploration of Mars. See No. C348.

Salvador Allende (1908-73), Pres. of Chile — A523

1974, Mar. 27 Photo. *Perf. 11½x12*

2279 A523 1fo blk & multi 15 15

Mona Lisa, by Leonardo da Vinci A524

1974, Apr. 19 *Perf. 12½*

2280 A524 4fo gold & multi 7.75 7.50

Exhibition of the Mona Lisa in Asia.
Printed in sheets of 6 stamps and 6 labels with commemorative inscription.

Souvenir Sheet

Issue of 1874 and Flowers — A525

Designs: a, Mallow. b, Aster. c, Daisy. d, Columbine.

1974, May 11 Litho. *Perf. 11½*

2281 A525 Sheet of 4 3.50 3.50
a.-d. 2.50fo any single 48 48

Centenary of the first issue inscribed "Magyar Posta" (Hungarian Post).

Carrier Pigeon, World Map, UPU Emblem — A526

1974, May 22 Litho. *Perf. 12*

2282 A526 40f shown 15 15
2283 A526 60f Mail coach 15 15
2284 A526 80f Old mail automobile 15 15
2285 A526 1.20fo Balloon post 20 16
2286 A526 2fo Mail train 42 25
2287 A526 4fo Mail bus 90 50
Nos. 2282-2287,C349 (7) 2.13
Set value 1.20

Centenary of the Universal Postal Union.

Dove of Basel, Switzerland No. 3L1, 1845 — A527

1974, June 7 Photo. *Perf. 11½x12*

2288 A527 3fo gold & multi 1.20 1.20

INTERNABA 1974 Philatelic Exhibition, Basel, June 7-16. No. 2288 issued in sheets of 3 stamps and 3 labels showing Internaba 1974 emblem. Size: 104x125mm.

Chess Players, from 13th Century Manuscript A528

Designs: 60f, Chess players, 15th century English woodcut. 80f, Royal chess party, 15th century Italian chess book. 1.20fo, Chess players, 17th century copper engraving by Selenus. 2fo, Farkas Kempelen's chess playing machine, 1769. 4fo, Hungarian Grand Master Geza Maroczy (1870-1951). 6fo, View of Nice and emblem of 1974 Chess Olympiad.

1974, June 6 Litho. *Perf. 12*

2289 A528 40f multi 15 15
2290 A528 60f multi 15 15
2291 A528 80f multi 24 15
2292 A528 1.20fo multi 30 20
2293 A528 2fo multi 30 18
2294 A528 4fo multi 75 35
2295 A528 6fo multi 1.25 70
Nos. 2289-2295 (7) 3.14 1.88

50th anniversary of International Chess Federation and 21st Chess Olympiad, Nice, June 6-30.

Souvenir Sheet

Cogwheel Railroad — A529

Designs: a, Passenger train, 1874. b, Freight train, 1874. c, Electric train, 1929-73. d, Twin motor train, 1973.

1974, June 25 Litho. *Perf. 12*

2296 A529 Sheet of 4 3.75 3.75
a.-d. 2.50fo, any single 50 50

Cent. of Budapest's cogwheel railroad.

Congress Emblem (Globe and Parliament) A530

1974, Aug. 18 Photo. *Perf. 12*

2297 A530 2fo sil, dk & lt bl 35 15

4th World Congress of Economists, Budapest, Aug. 19-24.

Bathing Woman, by Karoly Lotz A531

Paintings of Nudes: 60f, Awakening, by Karoly Brocky. 1fo, Venus and Cupid, by Brocky (horiz.). 1.50fo, After the Bath, by Lotz. 2.50fo, Resting Woman, by Istvan Csok (horiz.). 4fo, After the Bath, by Bertalan Szekely. 5fo, "Devotion," by Erzsebet Korb. 10fo, Lark, by Pál Szinyei Merse.

1974, Aug. *Perf. 12½*

2298 A531 40f gold & multi 15 15
2299 A531 60f gold & multi 15 15
2300 A531 1fo gold & multi 18 15
2301 A531 1.50fo gold & multi 35 15
2302 A531 2.50fo gold & multi 45 20
2303 A531 4fo gold & multi 85 30
2304 A531 5fo gold & multi 1.00 55
Nos. 2298-2304 (7) 3.13
Set value 1.40

Souvenir Sheet

Perf. 11

2305 A531 10fo gold & multi 3.75 3.75

No. 2305 contains one stamp (45x70mm).

Mimi, by Bela Czobel A532

1974, Sept. 4

2306 A532 1fo multi 40 20

91st birthday of Béla Czóbel, Hungarian painter.

Intersputnik Tracking Station A533

High Voltage Line "Peace" and Pipe Line "Friendship" A534

Perf. 11½x12, 12x11½

1974, Sept. 5 Litho.

2307 A533 1fo bl & vio 18 15
2308 A534 3fo multi 60 18
Set value 25

Technical assistance and cooperation between Hungary and USSR, 25th anniversary.

Pablo Neruda A535

Sweden No. 1 and Lion from Royal Palace, Stockholm A536

1974, Sept. 11 Photo. *Perf. 11½x12*

2309 A535 1fo multi 15 15

70th anniversary of the birth of Pablo Neruda (Neftali Ricar do Reyes, 1904-1973), Chilean poet.

1974, Sept. 21 *Perf. 12x11½*

2310 A536 3fo ultra, yel grn & gold 1.25 1.25

Stockholmia 74 International Philatelic Exhibition, Stockholm, Sept. 21-29. No. 2310 issued in sheets of 3 stamps and 3 labels showing Stockholmia emblem. White margin inscribed "UPU" multiple in white. Size: 126x104mm.

Values quoted in this catalogue are for stamps graded at Fine-Very Fine and with no faults. An illustrated guide to grade is provided in introductory material, beginning on Page 1A.

Tank Battle and Soldier with Anti-tank Grenade — A537

1974, Sept. 28 Litho. *Perf. 12*

2311	A537	1fo gold, org & blk	15	15

Army Day. See Nos. C351-C352.

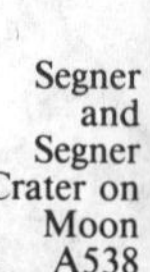

Segner and Segner Crater on Moon A538

1974, Oct. 5

2312	A538	3fo multi	60	25

270th anniversary of the birth of Janos Andras Segner, naturalist. No. 2312 printed se-tenant with label arranged checkerwise in sheet. Label shows Segner wheel.

Rhyparia Purpurata A539

Lepidoptera: 60f, Melanargia galathea. 80f, Parnassius Apollo. 1fo, Celerio euphorbia. 1.20fo, Catocala fraxini. 5fo, Apatura iris. 6fo, Palaeochrysophanus hyppothoe.

1974, Nov. 11 Photo. *Perf. 12½*

2313	A539	40f multi	15	15
2314	A539	60f vio & multi	15	15
2315	A539	80f multi	16	15
2316	A539	1fo brn & multi	16	15
2317	A539	1.20fo bl & multi	30	22
2318	A539	5fo pur & multi	1.00	42
2319	A539	6fo multi	1.25	65
		Nos. 2313-2319 (7)	3.17	
		Set value		1.60

Motherhood A540

Robert Kreutz A541

1974, Dec. 24 Litho. *Perf. 12*

2320	A540	1fo lt bl, blk & yel	25	15

1974, Dec. 24

2321	A541	1fo shown	15	15
2322	A541	1fo István Pataki	15	15
		Set value	20	15

30th death anniversary of anti-fascist martyrs Robert Kreutz (1923-1944) and Istvan Pataki (1914-1944).

Puppy — A542

Young Animals: 60f, Siamese kittens (horiz.). 80f, Rabbit. 1.20fo, Foal (horiz.). 2fo, Lamb. 4fo, Calf (horiz.). 6fo, Piglet.

1974, Dec. 30

2323	A542	40f lt bl & multi	15	15
2324	A542	60f multi	15	15
2325	A542	80f ol & multi	15	15
2326	A542	1.20fo grn & multi	24	15
2327	A542	2fo brn & multi	35	15
2328	A542	4fo org & multi	75	40
2329	A542	6fo vio & multi	1.25	60
		Nos. 2323-2329 (7)	3.04	
		Set value		1.35

See Nos. 2403-2409.

Building Type of 1973

Designs: 4fo, Szentendre. 5fo, View of Szolnok across Tisza River. 6fo, Skyscraper, Dunaujvaros. 10fo, City Hall, Kiskunfelegyhaza. 50fo, Church (Turkish Mosque), Hunyadi Statue and TV tower, Pecs.

1974-80 Litho. *Perf. 12x11½*

2330	A498	4fo red brn & pink	80	15
2331	A498	5fo dk bl & ultra	1.00	15
2332	A498	6fo dk brn & org	1.25	15
2333	A498	8fo dk & brt grn	1.65	15
2334	A498	10fo brown & yel	2.00	15
2335	A498	50fo multi	10.00	1.75
		Nos. 2331-2335 (5)	15.90	2.35

Issue dates: 8fo, Dec. 7. 10fo, 50fo, Dec. 30. 5fo, Mar. 8, 1975. 6fo, June 10, 1975. 4fo, June 20, 1980.

Hospital, Lambarene — A544

Designs: 60f, Dr. Schweitzer, patient and microscope. 80f, Patient arriving by boat. 1.20fo, Hospital supplies arriving by ship. 2fo, Globe, Red Cross, carrier pigeons. 4fo, Nobel Peace Prize medal. 6fo, Portrait and signature of Dr. Schweitzer, organ pipes and "J. S. Bach."

1975, Jan. 14 Photo. *Perf. 12*

2340	A544	40f gold & multi	15	15
2341	A544	60f gold & multi	15	15
2342	A544	80f gold & multi	15	15
2343	A544	1.20fo gold & multi	24	15
2344	A544	2fo gold & multi	35	18
2345	A544	4fo gold & multi	75	40
2346	A544	6fo lil & multi	1.25	60
		Nos. 2340-2346 (7)	3.04	
		Set value		1.45

Dr. Albert Schweitzer (1875-1965), medical missionary and musician, birth centenary.

Farkas Bolyai — A545

1975, Feb. 7 Litho. *Perf. 11½x12*

2347	A545	1fo gray & red brn	20	15

Bicentenary of the birth of Farkas Bolyai (1775-1856), mathematician.

Mihály Károlyi — A546

1975, Mar. 4 Litho. *Perf. 12*

2348	A546	1fo lt bl & brn	20	15

Birth centenary of Count Mihály Károlyi (1875-1955), prime minister, 1918-1919.

Woman, IWY Emblem A547

1975, Mar. 8 *Perf. 12x11½*

2349	A547	1fo aqua & blk	15	15

International Women's Year 1975.

"Let us Build up the Railroads" — A548

Posters: 60f, "Bread starts here." 2fo, "Hungarian Communist Party-a Party of Action." 4fo, "Heavy Industry-secure base of Three-year Plan." 5fo, "Our common interest-a developed socialist society."

1975, Mar. 17 Photo. *Perf. 11*

2350	A548	40f red & multi	15	15
2351	A548	60f red & multi	15	15
2352	A548	2fo red & multi	20	15
2353	A548	4fo red & multi	48	20
2354	A548	5fo red & multi	70	40
		Nos. 2350-2354 (5)	1.68	
		Set value		75

Hungary's liberation from Fascism, 30th anniversary.

Arrow, 1915, Pagoda and Mt. Fuji — A549

Antique Cars: 60f, Swift, 1911, Big Ben and Tower of London. 80f, Model T Ford, 1908, Capitol and Statue of Liberty. 1fo, Mercedes, 1901, Towers of Stuttgart. 1.20fo, Panhard Levassor, 1912, Arc de Triomphe and Eiffel Tower. 5fo, Csonka, 1906, Fishermen's Bastion and Chain Bridge. 6fo, Emblems of Hungarian Automobile Club, Alliance Internationale de Tourisme and Federation Internationale de l'Automobile.

1975, Mar. 27 Litho. *Perf. 12*

2355	A549	40f lt bl & multi	15	15
2356	A549	60f lt grn & multi	15	15
2357	A549	80f pink & multi	15	15
2358	A549	1fo lil & multi	18	15
2359	A549	1.20fo org & multi	25	15
2360	A549	5fo ultra & multi	90	42
2361	A549	6fo lil rose & multi	1.40	70
		Nos. 2355-2361 (7)	3.18	
		Set value		1.62

Hungarian Automobile Club, 75th anniv.

The Creation of Adam, by Michelangelo — A550

1975, Apr. 23 Photo. *Perf. 12½*

2362	A550	10fo gold & multi	4.00	3.75

Michelangelo Buonarroti (1475-1564), Italian painter, sculptor and architect.

Academy of Science — A551

Design: 2fo, Dates "1975 1825." 3fo, Count Istvan Szechenyi.

1975, May 5 Litho. *Perf. 12*

2363	A551	1fo grn & multi	15	15
2364	A551	2fo grn & multi	28	15
2365	A551	3fo grn & multi	50	28

Sesquicentennial of Academy of Science, Budapest, founded by Count Istvan Szechenyi.

Emblem of 1980 Olympics and Proposed Moscow Stadium — A553

1975, May 8 Photo. *Perf. 11½x12*

2366	A553	5fo lt bl & multi	1.50	1.25

Socfilex 75 International Philatelic Exhibition, Moscow, May 8-18. No. 2366 issued in sheets of 3 stamps and 3 labels showing Socfilex 75 emblem (War Memorial, Berlin-Treptow). Size: 104x125mm.

France No. 1100 and Venus of Milo — A554

1975, June 3 Photo. *Perf. 11½x12*

2367	A554	5fo lil & multi	1.50	1.25

ARPHILA 75 International Philatelic Exhibition, Paris, June 6-16. No. 2367 issued in sheets of 3 stamps and 3 labels showing ARPHILA 75 emblem. Size: 104x125mm.

Early Transformer, Kando Locomotive, 1902, Pylon — A555

1975, June 10 Litho. *Perf. 12*

2368	A555	1fo multi	30	15

Hungarian Electrotechnical Association, 75th anniversary.

Epée, Saber, Foil and Globe — A556

1975, July 11

2369	A556	1fo multi	25	15

32nd World Fencing Championships, Budapest, July 11-20.

Souvenir Sheet

Whale Pavilion, Oceanexpo 75 — A557

1975, July 21 Photo. *Perf. 12½*

2370	A557	10fo gold & multi	3.50	3.50

Oceanexpo 75, International Exhibition, Okinawa, July 20, 1975-Jan. 1976.

Dr. Agoston Zimmermann (1875-1963), Veterinarian A558

1975, Sept. 4 Litho. *Perf. 12*

2371	A558	1fo brn & bl	20	15

Symbolic of 14 Cognate Languages A559

1975, Sept. 9

2372	A559	1fo gold & multi	20	15

International Finno-Ugrian Congress.

Voters — A560

Design: No. 2374, Map of Hungary with electoral districts.

1975, Oct. 1

2373	A560	1fo multi	15	15
2374	A560	1fo multi	15	15
		Set value		15

Hungarian Council System, 25th anniv.

Fish and Waves (Ocean Pollution) — A561

Designs: 60f, Skeleton hand reaching for rose in water glass. 80f, Fish gasping for raindrop. 1fo, Carnation wilting in polluted soil. 1.20fo, Bird dying in polluted air. 5fo, Sick human lung and smokestack. 6fo, "Stop Pollution" (raised hand protecting globe from skeleton hand).

1975, Oct. 16 Litho. *Perf. 11½*

2375	A561	40f multi	15	15
2376	A561	60f multi	15	15
2377	A561	80f multi	15	15
2378	A561	1fo multi	20	15
2379	A561	1.20fo multi	28	18
2380	A561	5fo multi	85	32
2381	A561	6fo multi	1.25	55
		Nos. 2375-2381 (7)	3.03	
		Set value		1.35

Environmental Protection.

Mariska Gárdos (1885-1973) A562

Portraits: No. 2383, Imre Mezö (1905-56). No. 2384, Imre Tarr (1900-37).

1975, Nov. 4 Litho. *Perf. 12*

2382	A562	1fo blk & red org	15	15
2383	A562	1fo blk & red org	15	15
2384	A562	1fo blk & red org	15	15
		Set value	30	15

Famous Hungarians, birth anniversaries.

Treble Clef, Organ and Orchestra — A563

1975, Nov. 14

2385	A563	1fo multi	30	15

Franz Liszt Musical Academy, centenary.

Szigetcsep Icon A564

Virgin and Child, 18th Century Icons: 60f, Graboc. 1fo, Esztergom. 1.50fo, Vatoped. 2.50fo, Tottos. 4fo, Gyor. 5fo, Kazan.

1975, Nov. 25 Photo. *Perf. 12½*

2386	A564	40f gold & multi	15	15
2387	A564	60f gold & multi	20	15
2388	A564	1fo gold & multi	16	15
2389	A564	1.50fo gold & multi	25	15
2390	A564	2.50fo gold & multi	40	15
2391	A564	4fo gold & multi	80	35
2392	A564	5fo gold & multi	1.25	90
		Nos. 2386-2392 (7)	3.21	
		Set value		1.70

Members' Flags, Radar, Mother and Child — A565

1975, Dec. 15 Litho. *Perf. 12*

2393	A565	1fo multi	20	15

20th anniversary of the signing of the Warsaw Treaty (Bulgaria, Czechoslovakia, German Democratic Rep., Hungary, Poland, Romania, USSR).

Ice Hockey, Winter Olympics' Emblem — A566

Designs (Emblem and): 60f, Slalom. 80f, Ski race. 1.20fo, Ski jump. 2fo, Speed skating. 4fo, Cross-country skiing. 6fo, Bobsled. 10fo, Figure skating, pair.

1975, Dec. 29 Photo. *Perf. 12x11½*

2394	A566	40f sil & multi	15	15
2395	A566	60f sil & multi	15	15
2396	A566	80f sil & multi	15	15
2397	A566	1.20fo sil & multi	24	15
2398	A566	2fo sil & multi	35	18
2399	A566	4fo sil & multi	85	35
2400	A566	6fo sil & multi	1.25	65
		Nos. 2394-2400 (7)	3.14	
		Set value		1.50

Souvenir Sheet

Perf. 12½

2401	A566	10fo sil & multi	3.50	3.50

12th Winter Olympic Games, Innsbruck, Austria, Feb. 4-15, 1976. No. 2401 contains one stamp (59x36mm).

"P," 5-pengö and 500-pengö Notes — A567

1976, Jan. 16 Litho. *Perf. 12*

2402	A567	1fo multi	25	15

Hungarian Bank Note Co., 50th anniversary.

Animal Type of 1974

Young Animals: 40f, Wild boars (horiz.). 60f, Squirrels. 80f, Lynx (horiz.). 1.20fo, Wolves. 2fo, Foxes (horiz.). 4fo, Bears. 6fo, Lions (horiz.).

1976, Jan. 26

2403	A542	40f multi	15	15
2404	A542	60f bl & multi	15	15
2405	A542	80f multi	15	15
2406	A542	1.20fo multi	24	15
2407	A542	2fo vio & multi	38	18
2408	A542	4fo yel & multi	85	35
2409	A542	6fo multi	1.25	55
		Nos. 2403-2409 (7)	3.17	
		Set value		1.30

A.G. Bell, Telephone, Molniya I and Radar — A568

1976, Mar. 10 Litho. *Perf. 11½x12*

2410	A568	3fo multi	75	75

Centenary of first telephone call by Alexander Graham Bell, Mar. 10, 1876. Issued in sheets of 4.

Battle of Kuruc-Labantz — A569

Paintings: 60f, Meeting of Rakoczi and Tamas Esze, by Endre Veszprem. 1fo, Diet of Onod, by Mor Than. 2fo, Camp of the Kurucs. 3fo, Ilona Zrinyi (Rakoczi's mother; vert.). 4fo, Kuruc officers (vert.). 5fo, Prince Francis II Rakoczy, by Adam Manyoki (vert.). Painters of 40f, 2fo, 3fo, 4fo, are unknown.

1976, Mar. 27 Photo. *Perf. 12½*

2411	A569	40f gold & multi	15	15
2412	A569	60f gold & multi	15	15
2413	A569	1fo gold & multi	28	15
2414	A569	2fo gold & multi	65	18
2415	A569	3fo gold & multi	85	25
2416	A569	4fo gold & multi	1.40	35
2417	A569	5fo gold & multi	1.75	70
		Nos. 2411-2417 (7)	5.23	1.93

Francis II Rakoczy (1676-1735), leader of Hungarian Protestant insurrection, 300th birth anniversary.

Canceled-to-order stamps are often from remainders. Most collectors of canceled stamps prefer postally used specimens.

Standard Meter, Hungarian Meter Act — A570

Designs: 2fo, Istvan Krusper, his vacuum balance, standard kilogram. 3fo, Interferometer and rocket.

1976, Apr. 5 *Perf. 11½x12*

2418	A570	1fo multi	18	15
2419	A570	2fo multi	28	18
2420	A570	3fo multi	42	28

Centenary of introduction of metric system in Hungary.

US No. 1353 and Independence Hall, Philadelphia — A571

Photogravure and Foil Embossed

1976, May 29 *Perf. 11½x12*

2421	A571	5fo bl & multi	1.40	1.25

Interphil 76 International Philatelic Exhibition, Philadelphia, Pa., May 29-June 6. No. 2421 issued in sheets of 3 stamps and 3 labels showing bells. Size: 115x125mm.

"30" and Various Pioneer Activities A572

1976, June 5 **Litho.** *Perf. 12*

2422	A572	1fo multi	25	15

Hungarian Pioneers, 30th anniversary.

Trucks, Safety Devices, Trade Union Emblem — A573

1976, June *Perf. 12½*

2423	A573	1fo multi	15	15

Labor safety.

Intelstat 4, Montreal Olympic Emblem, Canadian Flag — A574

Designs: 60f, Equestrian. 1fo, Butterfly stroke. 2fo, One-man kayak. 3fo, Fencing. 4fo, Javelin. 5fo, Athlete on vaulting horse.

1976, June 29 **Photo.** *Perf. 11½x12*

2424	A574	40f dk bl & multi	15	15
2425	A574	60f sl grn & multi	15	15
2426	A574	1fo bl & multi	18	15
2427	A574	2fo grn & multi	35	15
2428	A574	3fo brn & multi	55	20
2429	A574	4fo bis & multi	75	35
2430	A574	5fo mar & multi	95	55
		Nos. 2424-2430 (7)	3.08	
		Set value		1.40

21st Olympic Games, Montreal, Canada, July 17-Aug. 1. See No. C365.

Denmark No. 2 and Mermaid, Copenhagen — A575

1976, Aug. 19 **Photo.** *Perf. 11½x12*

2431	A575	3fo multi	1.25	1.25

HAFNIA 76 Intl. Phil. Exhib., Copenhagen, Aug. 20-29. No. 2431 issued in sheets of 3 stamps and 3 labels showing HAFNIA emblem.

Souvenir Sheet

Discovery of Body of Lajos II, by Bertalan Székely — A576

1976, Aug. 27 **Photo.** *Perf. 12½*

2432	A576	20fo multi	3.50	3.50

450th anniversary of the Battle of Mohacs against the Turks.

Flora, by Titian A577

1976, Aug. 27

2433	A577	4fo gold & multi	75	25

Titian (1477-1576), Venetian painter.

Hussar, Herend China — A578

1976, Sept. 28 **Litho.** *Perf. 12*

2434	A578	4fo multi	75	25

Herend China manufacture, sesqui.

Daniel Berzsenyi (1776-1836), Poet — A579

1976, Sept. 28

2435	A579	2fo blk, gold & yel	25	15

Pal Gyulai (1826-1909), Poet and Historian A580

1976, Sept. 28

2436	A580	2fo org & blk	25	15

Tuscany No. 1 and Emblem — A581

1976, Oct. 13 **Photo.** *Perf. 11½x12*

2437	A581	5fo org & multi	2.25	2.25

ITALIA 76 International Philatelic Exhibition, Milan, Oct. 14-24. No. 2437 issued in sheets of 3 stamps and 3 labels showing Italia 76 emblem. Size: 106x127mm.

Jozsef Madzsar, M.D. — A582

Labor leaders: No. 2439, Ignac Bogar (1876-1933), secretary of printers' union. No. 2440, Rudolf Golub (1901-44), miner.

1976, Nov. 4 **Litho.** *Perf. 12*

2438	A582	1fo dp brn & red	15	15
2439	A582	1fo dp brn & red	15	15
2440	A582	1fo dp brn & red	15	15
		Set value		15

Science and Culture House, Georgian Dancer, Hungarian and USSR Flags A583

1976, Nov. 4 *Perf. 12½x12*

2441	A583	1fo multi	40	15

House of Soviet Science and Culture, Budapest, 2nd anniversary.

Koranyi Sanitarium and Statue — A584

1976, Nov. 11 *Perf. 12*

2442	A584	2fo multi	35	15

Koranyi TB Sanitarium, founded by Dr. Frigyes Koranyi, 75th anniversary.

Locomotive, 1875, Enese Station — A585

Designs: 60f, Steam engine No. 17, 1885, Rabatamasi Station. 1fo, Railbus, 1925, Fertoszentmiklos Station. 2fo, Express steam engine, Kapuvar Station. 3fo, Engine and trailer, 1926, Gyor Station. 4fo, Eight-wheel express engine, 1934, and Fertoboz Station. 5fo, Raba-Balaton engine, Sopron Station.

1976, Nov. 26 **Litho.** *Perf. 12*

2443	A585	40f multi	15	15
2444	A585	60f multi	15	15
2445	A585	1fo multi	18	15
2446	A585	2fo multi	35	15
2447	A585	3fo multi	48	20
2448	A585	4fo multi	75	55
2449	A585	5fo multi	1.00	60
		Nos. 2443-2449 (7)	3.06	
		Set value		1.65

Gyor-Sopron Railroad, centenary.

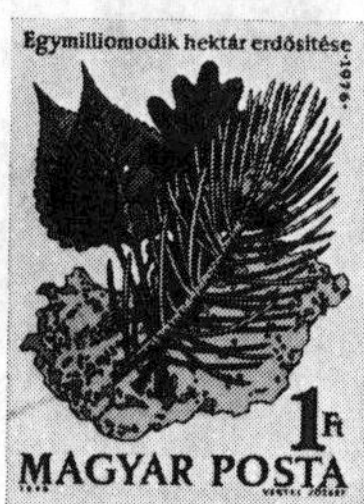

Poplar, Oak, Pine and Map of Hungary A586

1976, Dec. 14

2450	A586	1fo multi	25	15

Millionth hectare of reforestation.

Weight Lifting and Wrestling, Silver Medals — A587

Designs: 60f, Kayak, men's single and women's double. 1fo, Horse vaulting. 4fo, Women's fencing. 6fo, Javelin. 20fo, Water polo.

1976, Dec. 14 Photo. *Perf. 11½x12*

2451	A587	40f multi	15	15
2452	A587	60f multi	15	15
2453	A587	1fo multi	18	15
2454	A587	4fo multi	85	35
2455	A587	6fo multi	1.10	55
		Nos. 2451-2455 (5)	2.43	
		Set value		1.05

Souvenir Sheet

Perf. 12½x11½

2456	A587	20fo multi	3.50	3.50

Hungarian medalists in 21st Olympic Games.

Spoonbills — A588

Birds: 60f, White storks. 1fo, Purple herons. 2fo, Great bustard. 3fo, Common cranes. 4fo, White wagtails. 5fo, Garganey teals.

1977, Jan. 3 Litho. *Perf. 12*

2457	A588	40f multi	18	15
2458	A588	60f multi	18	15
2459	A588	1fo multi	28	15
2460	A588	2fo multi	40	18
2461	A588	3fo multi	50	28
2462	A588	4fo multi	1.10	40
2463	A588	5fo multi	1.40	65
		Nos. 2457-2463 (7)	4.04	1.96

Birds from Hortobagy National Park.

1976 World Champion Imre Abonyi Driving Four-in-hand — A589

Designs: 60f, Omnibus on Boulevard, 1870. 1fo, One-horse cab at Budapest Railroad Station, 1890. 2fo, Mail coach, Buda to Vienna route. 3fo, Covered wagon of Hajduszoboszlo. 4fo, Hungarian coach, by Jeremias Schemel, 1563. 5fo, Post chaise, from a Lübeck wood panel, 1430.

1977, Jan. 31 Litho. *Perf. 12x11½*

2464	A589	40f multi	15	15
2465	A589	60f multi	15	15
2466	A589	1fo multi	18	15
2467	A589	2fo multi	35	18
2468	A589	3fo multi	50	20
2469	A589	4fo multi	70	48
2470	A589	5fo multi	85	60
		Nos. 2464-2470 (7)	2.88	
		Set value		1.65

History of the coach.

Peacock A590

Birds: 60f, Green peacock. 1fo, Congo peacock. 3fo, Argus pheasant. 4fo, Impeyan pheasant. 6fo, Peacock pheasant.

1977, Feb. 22 Litho. *Perf. 12*

2471	A590	40f multi	18	15
2472	A590	60f multi	18	15
2473	A590	1fo multi	20	15
2474	A590	3fo multi	50	22
2475	A590	4fo multi	80	35
2476	A590	6fo multi	1.25	65
		Nos. 2471-2476 (6)	3.11	
		Set value		1.45

Newspaper Front Page, Factories A591

1977, Mar. 3 Litho. *Perf. 12*

2477	A591	1fo gold, blk & ver	15	15

Nepszava newspaper, centenary.

Flowers, by Mihaly Munkacsy A592

Flowers, by Hungarian Painters: 60f, Jakab Bogdany. 1fo, Istvan Csok (horiz.). 2fo, Janos Halapy. 3fo, Jozsef Rippl-Ronai (horiz.). 4fo, Janos Tornyai. 5fo, Jozsef Koszta.

1977, Mar. 18 Photo. *Perf. 12½*

2478	A592	40f gold & multi	15	15
2479	A592	60f gold & multi	15	15
2480	A592	1fo gold & multi	16	15
2481	A592	2fo gold & multi	32	16
2482	A592	3fo gold & multi	48	20
2483	A592	4fo gold & multi	65	38
2484	A592	5fo gold & multi	95	52
		Nos. 2478-2484 (7)	2.86	
		Set value		1.48

Newton and Double Convex Lens — A593

1977, Mar. 31 Litho. *Perf. 12*

2485	A593	3fo tan & multi	1.00	1.00

Isaac Newton (1643-1727), natural philosopher and mathematician, 250th death anniversary. No. 2485 issued in sheets of 4 stamps and 4 blue and black labels showing illustration from Newton's "Principia Mathematica," and Soviet space rocket.

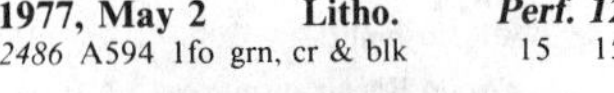

Janos Vajda (1827-97), Poet — A594

1977, May 2 Litho. *Perf. 12*

2486	A594	1fo grn, cr & blk	15	15

Netherlands No. 1 and Tulips — A595

1977, May 23 Photo. *Perf. 11½x12*

2487	A595	3fo multi	1.25	1.25

AMPHILEX '77, International Stamp Exhibition, Amsterdam, May 26-June 5. Issued in sheets of 3 stamps and 3 yellow, brown and ocher labels showing Amphilex poster.

Scene from "Wedding at Nagyrede" A596

1977, June 14 Litho. *Perf. 12*

2488	A596	3fo multi	50	20

State Folk Ensemble, 25th anniversary.

Souvenir Sheet

Bath of Bathsheba, by Rubens — A597

1977, June 14 Photo. *Perf. 11*

2489	A597	20fo multi	4.00	4.00

Peter Paul Rubens (1577-1640), Flemish painter.

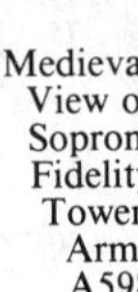

Medieval View of Sopron, Fidelity Tower, Arms A598

1977, June 25 Litho. *Perf. 12x11½*

2490	A598	1fo multi	1.50	1.50

700th anniversary of Sopron. Printed se-tenant with label showing European Architectural Heritage medal awarded Sopron in 1975.

Race Horse Kincsem A599

1977, July 16 Litho. *Perf. 12*

2491	A599	1fo multi	1.00	90

Sesquicentennial of horse racing in Hungary. Printed se-tenant with label showing portrait of Count Istvan Szechenyi and vignette from his 1827 book "Rules of Horse Racing in Hungary."

German Democratic Republic No. 370 — A600

1977, Aug. 18 Photo. *Perf. 12x11½*

2492	A600	3fo multi	1.25	1.10

SOZPHILEX 77 Philatelic Exhibition, Berlin, Aug. 19-28. No. 2492 issued in sheets of 3 stamps and 3 labels showing SOZPHILEX emblem.

Scythian Iron Bell, 6th Century B.C. — A601

Panel, Crown of Emperor Constantin Monomakhos A602

Designs: No. 2494, Bronze candlestick in shape of winged woman, 12th-13th centuries. No. 2495, Centaur carrying child, copper aquamanile, 12th century. No. 2496, Gold figure of Christ, from 11th century Crucifix. Designs show art treasures from Hungarian National Museum, founded 1802.

1977, Sept. 3 Litho. *Perf. 12*

2493 A601 2fo multi 75 75
2494 A601 2fo multi 75 75
2495 A601 2fo multi 75 75
2496 A601 2fo multi 75 75
a. Horiz. strip of 4, #2493-2496 3.00 3.00

Souvenir Sheet

2497 A602 10fo multi 3.50 3.00

50th Stamp Day.

Sputnik — A603

Spacecraft: 60f, Skylab. 1fo, Soyuz-Salyut 5. 3fo, Luna 24. 4fo, Mars 3. 6fo, Viking.

1977, Sept. 20

2498 A603 40f multi 15 15
2499 A603 60f multi 15 15
2500 A603 1fo multi 18 15
2501 A603 3fo multi 48 24
2502 A603 4fo multi 80 38
2503 A603 6fo multi 1.25 55
Nos. 2498-2503 (6) 3.01
Set value 1.35

Space explorations, from Sputnik to Viking. See No. C375.

Janos Szanto Kovacs (1852-1908), Agrarian Movement Pioneer — A604

Ervin Szabo (1877-1918), Revolutionary Workers' Movement Pioneer — A605

1977, Nov. 4 Litho. *Perf. 12*

2504 A604 1fo red & blk 15 15
2505 A605 1fo red & blk 15 15
Set value 16

Monument to Hungarian October Revolutionists, Omsk — A606

1977, Nov. 4

2506 A606 1fo blk & red 15 15

60th anniversary of Russian October Revolution.

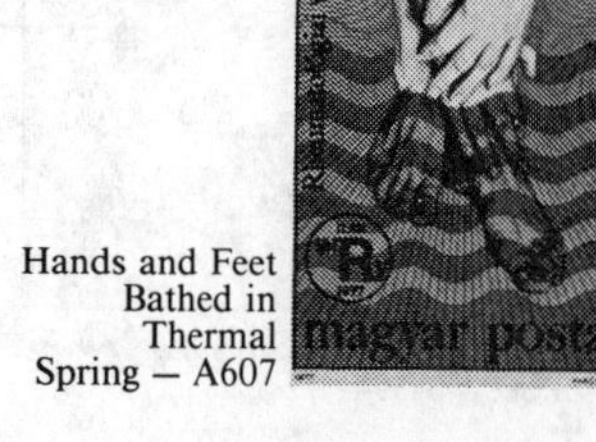

Hands and Feet Bathed in Thermal Spring — A607

1977, Nov. 1

2507 A607 1fo multi 25 15

World Rheumatism Year.

Endre Ady — A608

1977, Nov. 22 Engr. *Perf. 12*

2508 A608 1fo vio bl 35 35

Endre Ady (1877-1919), lyric poet. Issued in sheets of 4.

Lesser Panda — A609

Designs: 60f, Giant panda. 1fo, Asiatic black bear. 4fo, Polar bear. 6fo, Brown bear.

1977, Dec. 16 Litho. *Perf. 11½x12*

2509 A609 40f yel & multi 15 15
2510 A609 60f yel & multi 15 15
2511 A609 1fo yel & multi 35 15
2512 A609 4fo yel & multi 95 35
2513 A609 6fo yel & multi 1.40 70
Nos. 2509-2513 (5) 3.00
Set value 1.25

Souvenir Sheet

Flags and Ships along Intercontinental Waterway — A610

Flags: a, Austria. b, Bulgaria. c, Czechoslovakia. d, France. e, Luxembourg. f, Yugoslavia. g, Hungary. h, Fed. Rep. of Germany. i, Romania. j, Switzerland. k, USSR.

1977, Dec. 28 Litho. *Perf. 12*

2514 A610 Sheet of 11 15.00 15.00
a.-k. 2fo, any single 1.25 1.25

European Intercontinental Waterway: Danube, Main and Rhine.

Lancer, 17th Century A611

Hussars: 60f, Kuruts, 1710. 1fo, Baranya, 1762. 2fo, Palatine officer, 1809. 4fo, Sandor, 1848. 6fo, Trumpeter, 5th Honved Regiment, 1900.

1978, Jan. Litho. *Perf. 11½x12*

2515 A611 40f lil & multi 15 15
2516 A611 60f yel grn & multi 15 15
2517 A611 1fo red & multi 18 15
2518 A611 2fo dl bl & multi 35 18
2519 A611 4fo ol bis & multi 75 40
2520 A611 6fo gray & multi 1.40 60
Nos. 2515-2520 (6) 2.98
Set value 1.40

School of Arts and Crafts A612

1978, Mar. 31 Litho. *Perf. 12*

2521 A612 1fo multi 20 15

School of Arts and Crafts, 200th anniv.

Soccer Players, Flags of West Germany and Poland A613

Designs (Various Soccer Scenes and Flags): No. 2523, Hungary and Argentina. No. 2524, France and Italy. No. 2525, Tunisia and Mexico. No. 2526, Sweden and Brazil. No. 2527, Spain and Austria. No. 2528, Peru and Scotland. No. 2529, Iran and Netherlands. Flags represent first round of contestants. 20fo, Argentina '78 emblem.

1978, May 25 Litho. *Perf. 12*

2522 A613 2fo multi 35 15
2523 A613 2fo multi 35 15
2524 A613 2fo multi 35 15
2525 A613 2fo multi 35 15
2526 A613 2fo multi 35 15
2527 A613 2fo multi 35 15
2528 A613 2fo multi 35 35
2529 A613 2fo multi 1.00 50
Nos. 2522-2529 (8) 3.45 1.75

Souvenir Sheet

Perf. 11½

2530 A613 20fo multi 4.00 4.00

Argentina '78 11th World Cup Soccer Championships, Argentina, June 2-25.

Vase, Star and Glass Blower's Tube A614

1978, May 20 Litho. *Perf. 12*

2531 A614 1fo multi 20 15

Ajka Glass Works, centenary.

Canada No. 1 and Trillium — A615

1978, June 2

2532 A615 3fo multi 1.00 90

CAPEX '78, Canadian International Philatelic Exhibition, Toronto, Ont., June 9-18. Issued in sheets of 3 stamps and 3 labels showing CAPEX '78 emblem.

Souvenir Sheets

Leif Ericson and his Ship — A616

Explorers and their ships: #2533b, Columbus. c, Vasco da Gama. d, Magellan. #2534a, Drake. b, Hudson. c, Cook. d, Peary.

1978, June 10 Litho. *Perf. 12x11½*

2533 Sheet of 4 4.50 4.50
a.-d. A616 2fo, any single 75 75
2534 Sheet of 4 4.50 4.50
a.-d. A616 2fo, any single 75 75

Diesel Train, Pioneer's Kerchief — A617

Congress Emblem as Flower — A618

1978, June 10 *Perf. 12*

2535 A617 1fo multi 20 15

30th anniversary of Pioneer Railroad.

1978, June

Design: No. 2537, Congress emblem, "Cuba" and map of Cuba.

2536 A618 1fo multi 25 15
2537 A618 1fo multi 25 15

11th World Youth Festival, Havana. Nos. 2536-2537 printed se-tenant.

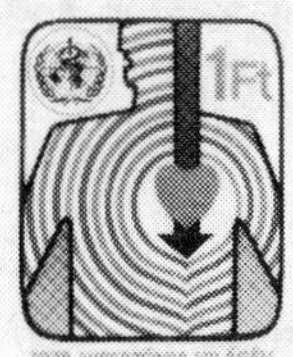

WHO Emblem, Stylized Body and Heart — A619

Clenched Fist, Dove and Olive Branch — A620

1978, Aug. 21 Litho. *Perf. 12*
2538 A619 1fo multi 25 15

Drive against hypertension.

1978, Sept. 1 Litho. *Perf. 12*
2539 A620 1fo gray, red & blk 20 15

Publication of review "Peace and Socialism," 20th anniversary.

Train, Telephone, Space Communication — A621

1978, Sept. 8 Litho. *Perf. 12*
2540 A621 1fo multi 25 15

20th anniversary of Organization for Communication Cooperation of Socialist Countries.

"Toshiba" Automatic Letter Sorting Machine — A622

1978, Sept. 15 Litho. *Perf. 11½x12*
2541 A622 1fo multi 25 20

Introduction of automatic letter sorting. No. 2541 printed with se-tenant label showing bird holding letter.

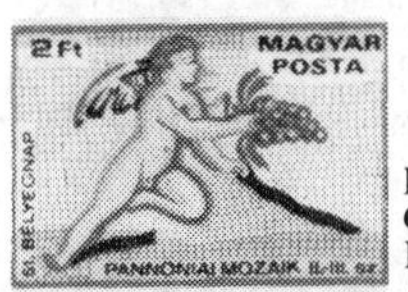

Eros Offering Grapes, Villa Hercules A623

Roman Mosaics Found in Hungary: No. 2543, Tiger (Villa Hercules, Budapest). No. 2544, Bird eating berries (Balacapuszta). No. 2545, Dolphin (Aquincum). 10fo, Hercules aiming at Centaur fleeing with Deianeira (Villa Hercules).

Photogravure and Engraved
1978, Sept. 16 *Perf. 11½*
2542 A623 2fo multi 2.00 2.00
2543 A623 2fo multi 2.00 2.00
2544 A623 2fo multi 2.00 2.00
2545 A623 2fo multi 2.00 2.00

Souvenir Sheet
2546 A623 10fo multi 12.00 12.00

Stamp Day. No. 2546 contains one stamp (52x35mm).

Count Imre Thököly — A624

1978, Oct. 1 Photo. *Perf. 12½*
2547 A624 1fo blk & yel 25 15

300th anniversary of Hungary's independence movement, led by Imre Thököly (1657-1705).

Souvenir Sheet

Hungarian Crown Jewels — A625

1978, Oct. 10
2548 A625 20fo gold & multi 7.00 6.75

Return of Crown Jewels from United States, Jan. 6, 1978.

"The Red Coach" A626

1978, Oct. 21 Litho. *Perf. 12*
2549 A626 3fo red & blk 50 15

Gyula Krudy, 1878-1933, novelist.

St. Ladislas I Reliquary, Györ Cathedral A627

1978, Nov. 15 *Perf. 11½x12½*
2550 A627 1fo multi 20 15

Ladislas I (1040-1095), 900th anniversary of accession to throne of Hungary.

Miklos Jurisics Statue, Köszeg — A628

1978, Nov. 15 *Perf. 12*
2551 A628 1fo multi 20 15

650th anniversary of founding of Köszeg.

Samu Czaban and Gizella Berzeviczy — A629

Photogravure and Engraved
1978, Nov. 24 *Perf. 11½x12*
2552 A629 1fo brn, buff & red 20 15

Samu Czaban (1878-1942) and Gizella Berzeviczy (1878-1954), Communist teachers during Soviet Republic (1918-1919).

Communist Party Emblem A630

1978, Nov. 24 Litho. *Perf. 12*
2553 A630 1fo gray, red & blk 15 15

Hungarian Communist Party, 60th anniv.

Woman Cutting Bread — A631

Ceramics by Margit Kovacs (1902-1976): 2fo, Woman with pitcher. 3fo, Potter.

1978, Nov. 30 Litho. *Perf. 11½x12*
2554 A631 1fo multi 15 15
2555 A631 2fo multi 32 15
2556 A631 3fo multi 80 60

Virgin and Child, by Dürer A632

Dürer Paintings: 60f, Adoration of the Kings (horiz.). 1fo, Self-portrait, 1500. 2fo, St. George. 3fo, Nativity (horiz.). 4fo, St. Eustatius. 5fo, The Four Apostles. 20fo, Dancing Peasant Couple, 1514 (etching).

1979, Jan. 8 Photo. *Perf. 12½*
2557 A632 40f gold & multi 15 15
2558 A632 60f gold & multi 15 15
2559 A632 1fo gold & multi 16 15
2560 A632 2fo gold & multi 32 18
2561 A632 3fo gold & multi 40 22
2562 A632 4fo gold & multi 80 35
2563 A632 5fo gold & multi 1.00 90
Nos. 2557-2563 (7) 2.98 2.10

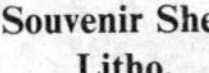
Souvenir Sheet
Litho.
2564 A632 20fo buff & brn 3.75 3.50

Albrecht Dürer (1471-1528), German painter and engraver.

Human Rights Flame — A633

1979, Feb. 8 Litho. *Perf. 11½x12*
2565 A633 1fo dk & lt bl 1.50 1.50

Universal Declaration of Human Rights, 30th anniversary. No. 2565 issued in sheets of 12 stamps (3x4) and 4 labels. Alternating horizontal rows inverted.

Child at Play — A634

IYC Emblem and: No. 2567, Family. No. 2568, 3 children (international friendship).

1979, Feb. 26 *Perf. 12*
2566 A634 1fo multi 2.00 75
2567 A634 1fo multi 2.00 75
2568 A634 1fo multi 6.00 6.50

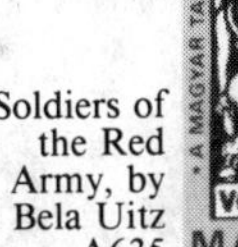

Soldiers of the Red Army, by Bela Uitz A635

1979, Mar. 21 Litho. *Perf. 12*
2569 A635 1fo sil, blk & red 15 15

60th anniv. of Hungarian Soviet Republic.

Calvinist Church, Nyirbator — A636

1979, Mar. 28 *Perf. 11*
2570 A636 1fo brn & yel 15 15

700th anniversary of Nyirbator.
See No. 2601.

Chessmen, Gold Cup, Flag — A637

1979, Apr. 12 Litho. *Perf. 12*
2571 A637 3fo multi 50 50

Hungarian victories in 23rd Chess Olympiad, Buenos Aires, 1978.

Alexander Nevski Cathedral, Sofia, Bulgaria No. 1 — A638

1979, May 18 Litho. *Perf. 11½x12*

2572 A638 3fo multi 75 75

Philaserdica '79 Philatelic Exhibition, Sofia, Bulgaria, May 18-27. No. 2572 issued in sheets of 3 stamps and 3 labels showing Philaserdica emblem and arms of Sofia.

Stephenson's Rocket, 1829, IVA '79 Emblem — A639

Railroad Development: 60f, Siemens' first electric locomotive, 1879. 1fo, "Pioneer," Chicago & Northwestern Railroad, 1836. 2fo, Orient Express, 1883. 3fo, Trans-Siberian train, 1898. 4fo, Express train on Tokaido line, 1964. 5fo, Transrapid-O5 train, exhibited 1979. 20fo, Map of European railroad network.

1979, June 8 Litho. *Perf. 12x11½*

2573	A639	40f multi	15	15
2574	A639	60f multi	15	15
2575	A639	1fo multi	20	15
2576	A639	2fo multi	35	22
2577	A639	3fo multi	50	35
2578	A639	4fo multi	65	52
2579	A639	5fo multi	1.00	65
		Nos. 2573-2579 (7)	3.00	2.19

Souvenir Sheet

Perf. 12½x11½

2580 A639 20fo multi 4.50 4.50

International Transportation Exhibition (IVA '79), Hamburg. No. 2580 contains one stamp (47x32mm).

Natural Gas Pipeline and Compressor A640

Designs: 2fo, Lenin power station and dam, Dniepropetrovsk and pylon. 3fo, Comecon Building, Moscow, and star symbolizing ten member states.

1979, June 26 *Perf. 11½x12*

2581	A640	1fo multi	15	15
2582	A640	2fo multi	28	15
2583	A640	3fo multi	40	20
		Set value		40

30th anniversary of the Council of Mutual Economic Assistance, Comecon.

Zsigmond Moricz (1879-1942), Writer, by Jozsef Ripple-Ronai A641

1979, June 29 *Perf. 12*

2584 A641 1fo multi 20 15

Town Hall, Helsinki, Finnish Flag, Moscow '80 Emblem A642

Designs (Moscow '80 Emblem and): 60f, Colosseum, Rome, Italian flag. 1fo, Asakusa Temple, Tokyo, Japanese flag. 2fo, Mexico City Cathedral, Mexican flag. 3fo, Our Lady's Church, Munich, German flag. 4fo, Skyscrapers, Montreal, Canadian flag. 5fo, Lomonosov University, Misha the bear and Soviet flag.

1979, July 31 *Perf. 12x11½*

2585	A642	40f multi	15	15
2586	A642	60f multi	15	15
2587	A642	1fo multi	18	15
2588	A642	2fo multi	28	20
2589	A642	3fo multi	35	24
2590	A642	4fo multi	48	30
2591	A642	5fo multi	85	55
		Nos. 2585-2591 (7)	2.44	
		Set value		1.50

Pre-Olympic Year.

Boy with Horse and Greyhounds, by Janos Vaszary — A643

Paintings of Horses: 60f, Coach and Five, by Karoly Lotz. 1fo, Boys on Horseback, by Celesztin Pallya. 2fo, Farewell, by Lotz. 3fo, Horse Market, by Pallya. 4fo, Wanderer, by Bela Ivanyi-Grunwald. 5fo, Ready for the Hunt, by Karoly Sterio.

1979, Aug. 11 Photo. *Perf. 12½*

2592	A643	40f multi	15	15
2593	A643	60f multi	15	15
2594	A643	1fo multi	20	15
2595	A643	2fo multi	28	15
2596	A643	3fo multi	50	20
2597	A643	4fo multi	65	35
2598	A643	5fo multi	1.00	50
		Nos. 2592-2598 (7)	2.93	
		Set value		1.42

Sturgeons, Map of Danube, "Calypso" A644

1979, Aug. 11

2599 A644 3fo multi 50 15

Environmental protection of rivers and seas.

Pentathlon A645

1979, Aug. 12 Litho. *Perf. 12*

2600 A645 40f multi 50 20

Pentathlon World Championship, Budapest, Aug. 12-18.

Architecture Type of 1979

Design: Vasvar Public Health Center.

1979, Aug. 15 Litho. *Perf. 11*

2601 A636 40f multi 15 15

700th anniversary of Vasvar.

Denarius of Stephen I, 1000-1038, Reverse A646

Hungarian Coins: 2fo, Copper coin of Bela III, 1172-1196. 3fo, Golden groat of King Louis the Great, 1342-1382. 4fo, Golden forint of Matthias I, 1458-1490. 5fo, Silver gulden of Wladislaw II, 1490-1516.

Engraved and Photogravure

1979, Sept. 3 *Perf. 12x11½*

2602	A646	1fo multi	18	20
2603	A646	2fo multi	28	35
2604	A646	3fo multi	35	35
2605	A646	4fo multi	48	35
2606	A646	5fo multi	1.00	85
		Nos. 2602-2606 (5)	2.29	2.10

9th International Numismatic Congress, Berne, Switzerland.

Souvenir Sheet

Unofficial Stamp, 1848 — A647

1979, Sept. 15 Litho. *Perf. 12*

2607 A647 10fo dk brn, blk & red 3.00 3.00

Stamp Day. Multicolored margin shows Rowland Hill (1795-1879) and Mor Than (1828-1899).

Souvenir Sheet

Elbel Locomotive A648

1979, Oct. 19 Litho. *Perf. 12*

2608		Sheet of 4	3.50	3.50
a.	A648	5fo shown	70	70
b.	A648	5fo Type 424 steam engine	70	70
c.	A648	5fo "War Locomotive"	70	70
d.	A648	5fo Hydraulic diesel locomotive	70	70

Gyor-Sopron-Ebenfurt rail service, cent.

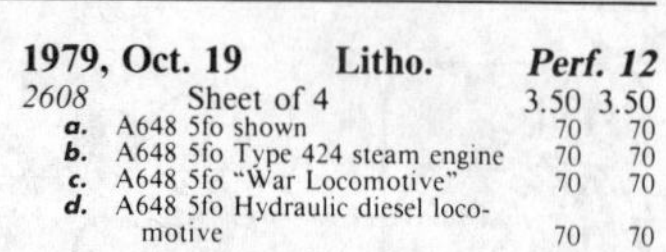

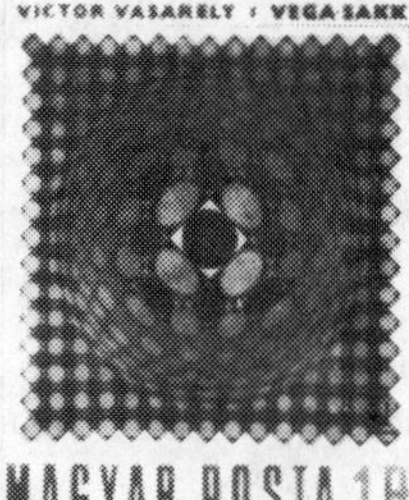

Vega-Chess, by Victor Vasarely A649

1979, Oct. 29

2609 A649 1fo multi 15 15

International Savings Day — A650

1979, Oct. 29 Litho. *Perf. 12*

2610 A650 1fo multi 15 15

Otter — A651

Wildlife Protection: 60f, Wild cat. 1fo, Pine marten. 2fo, Eurasian badger. 4fo, Polecat. 6fo, Beech marten.

1979, Nov. 20

2611	A651	40f multi	15	15
2612	A651	60f multi	15	15
2613	A651	1fo multi	18	15
2614	A651	2fo multi	35	20
2615	A651	4fo multi	65	28
2616	A651	6fo multi	1.00	65
		Nos. 2611-2616 (6)	2.48	
		Set value		1.35

Tom Thumb, IYC Emblem A652

IYC Emblem and Fairy Tale Scenes: 60f, The Ugly Duckling. 1fo, The Fisherman and the Goldfish. 2fo, Cinderella. 3fo, Gulliver's Travels. 4fo, The Little Pigs and the Wolf. 5fo, Janos the Knight. 20fo, The Fairy Ilona.

1979, Dec. 29 Litho. *Perf. 12x11½*

2617	A652	40f multi	15	15
2618	A652	60f multi	15	15
2619	A652	1fo multi	20	15
2620	A652	2fo multi	35	20

2621	A652	3fo multi	50	28
2622	A652	4fo multi	70	40
2623	A652	5fo multi	1.00	70
		Nos. 2617-2623 (7)	3.05	2.03

Souvenir Sheet

2624	A652	20fo multi	4.50	4.25

Trichodes Apairius and Yarrow — A653

Insects Pollinating Flowers: 60f, Bumblebee and blanketflower. 1fo, Red admiral butterfly and daisy. 20fo, Cetonia aurata and rose. 4fo, Graphosoma lineatum and petroselinum hortense. 6fo, Chlorophorus varius and thistle.

1980, Jan. 25 Litho. *Perf. 12*

2625	A653	40f multi	15	15
2626	A653	60f multi	15	15
2627	A653	1fo multi	15	15
2628	A653	2fo multi	30	18
2629	A653	4fo multi	70	32
2630	A653	6fo multi	95	45
		Nos. 2625-2630 (6)	2.40	
		Set value		1.15

Hanging Gardens of Semiramis, 6th Century B.C., Map showing Babylon A654

Seven Wonders of the Ancient World (and Map): 60f, Temple of Artemis, Ephesus, 6th century B.C. 1fo, Zeus, by Phidias, Olympia. 2fo, Tomb of Maussolos, Halikarnassos, 3rd century B.C. 3fo, Colossos of Rhodes. 4fo, Pharos Lighthouse, Alexandria, 3rd century B.C. 5fo, Pyramids, 26th-24th centuries B.C.

1980, Feb. 29 Litho. *Perf. 12x11½*

2631	A654	40f multi	15	15
2632	A654	60f multi	15	15
2633	A654	1fo multi	15	15
2634	A654	2fo multi	30	18
2635	A654	3fo multi	42	30
2636	A654	4fo multi	60	38
2637	A654	5fo multi	75	60
		Nos. 2631-2637 (7)	2.52	1.91

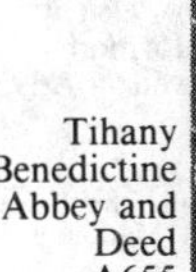

Tihany Benedictine Abbey and Deed A655

1980, Mar. 19 Litho. *Perf. 12*

2638	A655	1fo multi	15	15

Benedictine Abbey, Tihany, 925th anniversary of deed (oldest document in Hungarian).

Gabor Bethlen, Copperplate Print — A656

1980, Mar. 19

2639	A656	1fo multi	15	15

Gabor Bethlen (1580-1629), Prince of Transylvania (1613-1629) and King of Hungary (1620-1629), 400th anniversary of birth.

Easter Casket of Garamszentbenedek, 15th Century (Restoration) — A657

1980, Mar. 19

2640	A657	1fo shown	15	15
2641	A657	2fo Three Marys	30	30
2642	A657	3fo Apostle James	42	42
2643	A657	4fo Thaddeus	60	60
2644	A657	5fo Andrew	85	60
		Nos. 2640-2644 (5)	2.32	2.07

Liberation from Fascism, 35th Anniversary A658

1980, Apr. 3 Litho. *Perf. 12*

2645	A658	1fr multi	20	15

Jozsef Attila, poet and lyricist. — A659

1980, Apr. 11

2646	A659	1fo rose car & olive	20	15

Hungary No. 386a — A660

1980, Apr. 28 *Perf. 11½x12*

2647	A660	1fo multi	2.25	1.50

Hungarian Postal Museum, 50th anniv.

Two Pence Blue, Mounted Guardsman, London 1980 Emblem — A661

1980, Apr. 30 *Perf. 11½x12*

2648	A661	3fo multi	1.10	1.10

London 1980 International Stamp Exhibition, May 6-14. No. 2648 issued in sheets of 3 stamps and 3 labels showing London 1980 emblem and arms of city. Size: 104x125mm.

Norway No. B51, Mother with Child, by Gustav Vigeland — A662

1980, June 9 Litho. *Perf. 11½x12*

2649	A662	3fo multi	1.10	1.10

NORWEX '80 Stamp Exhibition, Oslo, June 13-22. No. 2649 issued in sheets of 3 stamps and 3 labels showing NORWEX emblem. Size: 108x125mm.

Margit Kaffka (1880-1918), Writer — A663

1980, June 9 *Perf. 12*

2650	A663	1fo blk & pur, *cr*	25	15

Zoltan Schönherz (1905-42), Anti-fascist Martyr A664

1980, July 25 Litho.

2652	A664	1fo multi	15	15

Dr. Endre Hogyes and Congress Emblem — A665

Decanter, c. 1850 — A666

1980, July 25

2653	A665	1fo multi	15	15

28th International Congress of Physiological Sciences, Budapest. Dr. Hogyes (1847-1906) first described equilibrium reflex-curve and modified Pasteur's rabies vaccine.

1980, Sept. Litho. *Perf. 12*

2654	A666	1fo shown	25	25
2655	A666	2fo Decorated glass	38	38
2656	A666	3fo Stem glass	65	65

Souvenir Sheet

2657	A666	10fo Pecs glass	2.50	2.25

53rd Stamp Day.

Bertalan Por, Self-portrait — A667

Graylag Goose — A668

1980, Nov. 4 Litho. *Perf. 12*

2658	A667	1fo Artist (1880-1964)	35	18

1980, Nov. 11 *Perf. 11½x12*

2659	A668	40f shown	15	15
2660	A668	60f Black-crowned night heron	15	15
2661	A668	1fo Shoveler	16	15
2662	A668	2fo Chlidonias leucopterus	32	22
2663	A668	4fo Great crested grebe	65	42
2664	A668	6fo Black-necked stilt	1.00	60
		Nos. 2659-2664 (6)	2.43	
		Set value		1.45

Souvenir Sheet

2665	A668	20fo Great white heron	4.75	4.50

European Nature Protection Year. No. 2665 contains one stamp (37x59mm).

Souvenir Sheet

Dove on Map of Europe — A669

1980, Nov. 11 *Perf. 12½x11½*

2666	A669	20fo multi	4.75	4.50

European Security and Cooperation Conference, Madrid.

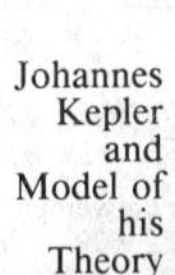

Johannes Kepler and Model of his Theory A670

1980, Nov. 21 Litho. *Perf. 12*

2667	A670	1fo multi	35	20

Johannes Kepler (1571-1630), German astronomer, 350th anniversary of death. No. 2667 printed se-tenant with label showing rocket and satellites orbiting earth.

Karoly Kisfaludy (1788-1830), Poet and Dramatist A671

1980, Nov. 21

2668	A671	1fo brn red & dl brn	15	15

UN Headquarters, New York — A672

UN membership, 25th anniversary.

Photogravure and Engraved

1980, Dec. 12 *Perf. 11½x12*

2669 A672 40f shown 15 15
2670 A672 60f Geneva headquarters 15 15
2671 A672 1fo Vienna headquarters 15 15
2672 A672 2fo UN & Hungary flags 28 18
2673 A672 4fo UN, Hungary arms 55 35
2674 A672 6fo World map 95 60
Nos. 2669-2674 (6) 2.23
Set value 1.30

Ferenc Erdei (1910-71), Economist and Statesman A673

1980, Dec. 23 **Litho.** *Perf. 12*

2675 A673 1fo dk grn & brn 15 15

Bela Szanto — A674

Count Lajos Batthyany — A675

1981, Jan. 31 **Litho.** *Perf. 12*

2676 A674 1fo multi 15 15

Bela Szanto (1881-1951), labor movement leader.

1981, Feb. 14

2677 A675 1fo multi 15 15

Count Lajos Batthyany (1806-1849), prime minister, later executed.

Bela Bartok (1881-1945), Composer A677

Design: b, Cantata Profana illustration.

1981, Mar. 25 **Litho.** *Perf. 12½*

2685 Sheet of 2 3.00 3.00
a.-b. A677 10fo any single 1.40 1.40

Telephone Exchange System Cent. — A678

Belling Stag — A679

1981, Apr. 29 **Litho.** *Perf. 12*

2686 A678 2fo multi 25 15

1981, Apr. 29

2687 A679 2fo multi 25 15

Flag of the House of Arpad, 11th Cent. — A680

1981, Apr. 29

2688 A680 40f shown 15 15
2689 A680 60f Hunyadi family, 15th cent. 15 15
2690 A680 1fo Gabor Bethlen, 1600 15 15
2691 A680 2fo Ferenc Rakoczi II, 1716 28 15
2692 A680 4fo Honved, 1848 75 28
2693 A680 6fo Troop flag, 1919 1.00 40
Nos. 2688-2693 (6) 2.48
Set value 1.00

Red Cross and Ambulance Vehicles A681

Map of Europe and J. Henry Dunant (Red Cross Founder) — A682

1981, May 4

2694 A681 2fo multi 25 15

Souvenir Sheet

Perf. 12½x11½

2695 A682 20fo multi 2.75 2.75

Hungarian Red Cross cent. (2fo); 3rd European Red Cross Conf., Budapest, May 4-7 (20fo).

Souvenir Sheet

1933 WIPA Exhibition Seals — A683

1981, May 15 *Perf. 12x12½*

2696 Sheet of 4 2.75 2.75
a.-d. A683 5fo single 65 65

WIPA 1981 Phil. Exhib., Vienna, May 22-31.

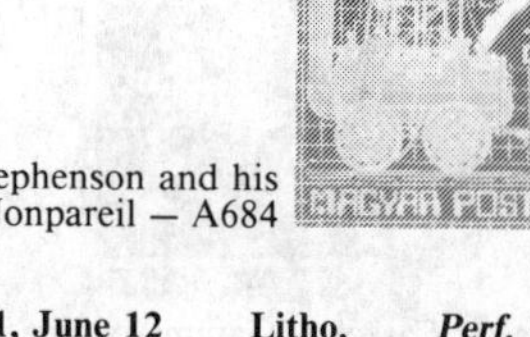

Stephenson and his Nonpareil — A684

1981, June 12 **Litho.** *Perf. 12*

2697 A684 2fo multi 25 15

George Stephenson (1781-1848), British railroad engineer, birth bicentenary.

Bela Vago (1881-1939), Anti-fascist Martyr — A685

1981, Aug. 7 **Litho.** *Perf. 12*

2698 A685 2fo ocher & brn ol 25 15

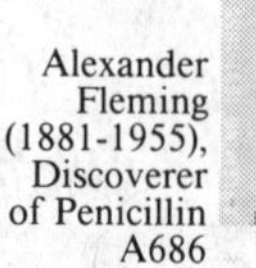

Alexander Fleming (1881-1955), Discoverer of Penicillin A686

1981, Aug. 7

2699 A686 2fo multi 25 15

Bridal Chest A687

Designs: Bridal chests.

1981, Sept. 12 **Litho.** *Perf. 12*

2700 A687 1fo Szentgal, 18th cent. 15 15
2701 A687 2fo Hodmezovasarhely, 19th cent. 30 18

Souvenir Sheet

2702 A687 10fo Bacs County, 17th cent. 2.00 2.00

54th Stamp Day. No. 2702 contains one stamp (44x25mm).

Calvinist College, Papa, 450th Anniv. A688

1981, Oct. 3 **Litho.** *Perf. 12*

2703 A688 2fo multi 25 15

World Food Day — A689

1981, Oct. 16

2704 A689 2fo multi 25 15

Passenger Ship Rakoczi, 1964, No. 1834 A690

Designs: Sidewheelers and Hungarian stamps.

1981, Nov. 25 *Perf. 12x11½*

2705 A690 1fo Franz I, #1828 16 15
2706 A690 1fo Arpad, #1829 16 15
2707 A690 2fo Szechenyi, #1830 32 16
2708 A690 2fo Grof Szechenyi Istvan, #1831 32 16
2709 A690 4fo Sofia, #1832 65 32
2710 A690 6fo Felszabadulas, #1833 95 48
2711 A690 8fo shown 1.25 65
Nos. 2705-2711 (7) 3.81 2.07

Souvenir Sheet

Perf. 13

2712 A690 20fo Hydrofoil Solyom, #1830 3.50 3.50

European Danube Commission, 125th anniv.

Souvenir Sheet

Slovakian Natl. Costumes — A691

Perf. 12½x11½

1981, Nov. 18 **Litho.**

2713 Sheet of 4 2.25 2.25
a. A691 1fo shown 20 20
b. A691 2fo German 40 40
c. A691 3fo Croatian 60 60
d. A691 4fo Romanian 80 80

Christmas 1981 — A692

Pen Pals, by Norman Rockwell — A693

Sculptures: 1fo, Mary Nursing the Infant Jesus, by Margit Kovacs. 2fo, Madonna of Csurgo.

1981, Dec. 4 *Perf. 12½x11½*

2714 A692 1fo multi 15 15
2715 A692 2fo multi 30 15
Set value 15

1981, Dec. 29 *Perf. 11½x12*

Norman Rockwell Illustrations.

2716 A693 1fo shown 15 15
2717 A693 2fo Courting Under the Clock at Midnight 25 15
2718 A693 2fo Maiden Voyage 25 15
2719 A693 4fo Threading the Needle 52 30
Nos. 2716-2719,C435-C437 (7) 3.47 2.60

Souvenir Sheet

La Toilette, by Pablo Picasso (1881-1973) — A694

1981, Dec. 29 Litho. Perf. 11½
2720 A694 20fo multicolored 2.75 2.75

25th Anniv. of Worker's Militia — A695

1982, Jan. 26 Litho. Perf. 12
2721 A695 1fo Shooting practice 18 15
2722 A695 4fo Members, 3 generations 50 35
Set value 43

10th World Trade Union Cong., Havana, Feb. 10-15 — A696

Gyula Alpri (1882-1944), Anti-fascist Martyr — A697

1982, Feb. 12 Litho. Perf. 12x11½
2723 A696 2fo multicolored 25 15

1982, Mar. 24 Perf. 12
2724 A697 2fo multicolored 25 15

TB Bacillus Centenary — A698

1982, Mar. 24 Litho. Perf. 12
2725 A698 2fo multicolored 25 15

1982 World Cup — A699

Designs: Hungary in competition with other World Cup teams.
No. 2733a, Barcelona Stadium. b, Madrid Stadium.

1982, Apr. 16 Perf. 11
2726 A699 1fo Egypt, 1934 15 15
2727 A699 1fo Italy, 1938 15 15
2728 A699 2fo Germany, 1954 25 16
2729 A699 2fo Mexico, 1958 25 16
2730 A699 4fo England, 1962 50 30
2731 A699 6fo Brazil, 1966 80 45
2732 A699 8fo Argentina, 1978 1.00 60
Nos. 2726-2732 (7) 3.10 1.97

Souvenir Sheet

2733 Sheet of 2 3.00 3.00
a.-b. A699 10fo any single 1.40 1.40

No. 2733 contains 44x44mm stamps.

European Table Tennis Championship, Budapest, Apr. 17-25 — A700

1982, Apr. 16 Litho. Perf. 11½x12
2734 A700 2fo multi 25 15

Roses — A701

25 Years of Space Travel — A702

1982, Apr. 30 Perf. 12
2735 A701 1fo Pascali 20 15
2736 A701 1fo Michele Meilland 20 15
2737 A701 2fo Diorama 38 18
2738 A701 2fo Wendy Cussons 38 18
2739 A701 3fo Blue Moon 52 28
2740 A701 3fo Invitation 52 28
2741 A701 4fo Tropicana 75 35
Nos. 2735-2741 (7) 2.95 1.57

Souvenir Sheet

2742 A701 10fo Bouquet 2.50 2.50

No. 2742 contains one stamp (34x59mm, perf. 11).

1982, May 18 Photo. Perf. 11½
2743 A702 1fo Columbia shuttle, 1981 15 15
2744 A702 1fo Armstrong, Apollo 11, 1969 15 15
2745 A702 2fo A. Leonov, Voskhod 2, 1965 28 18
2746 A702 2fo Yuri Gagarin, Vostok 28 18
2747 A702 4fo Laika, Sputnik 2, 1957 55 35
2748 A702 4fo Sputnik I, 1957 55 35
2749 A702 6fo Space researcher K.E. Ciolkovski 85 50
Nos. 2743-2749 (7) 2.81 1.86

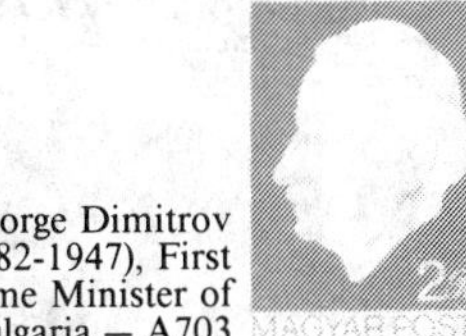

George Dimitrov (1882-1947), First Prime Minister of Bulgaria — A703

1982, May 7 Litho. Perf. 12
2750 A703 2fo multi 25 15

SOZPHILEX '82 Stamp Exhibition, Sofia, Bulgaria, May. No. 2750 se-tenant with label showing Bulgarian 1300th anniv. emblems.

Diosgyor Paper Mill Bicent. — A704

1982, May 27 Litho. Perf. 12x11½
2751 A704 2fo multi 25 15

First Rubik's Cube World Championship, Budapest, June 5 — A705

1982, June 4 Perf. 11½x12
2752 A705 2fo multi 25 15

Souvenir Sheet

George Washington, by F. Kemmelmeyer A706

Washington's 250th Birth Anniv.: a, Michael Kovats de Fabricy (1724-1779), Cavalry Commandant, by Sandor Finta.

1982, July 2 Litho. Perf. 11
2753 Sheet of 2 2.50 2.50
a.-b. A706 5fo any single 75 75

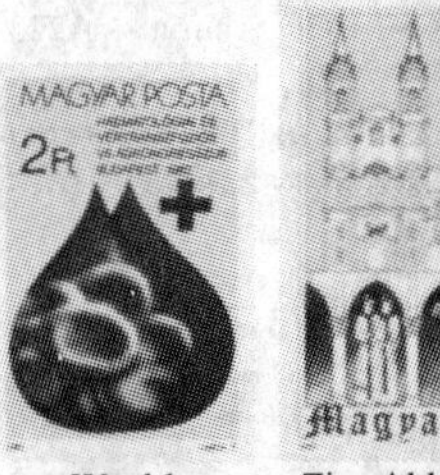

World Hematology Congress, Budapest A707

Zirc Abbey, 800th Anniv. A708

1982, July 30 Perf. 12½x11½
2754 A707 2fo multi 25 15

1982, Aug. 19 Perf. 11½x12
2755 A708 2fo multi 25 15

KNER Printing Office, Gyoma, Centenary — A709

1982, Sept. 23 Litho. Perf. 12x11½
2756 A709 2fo Emblem 25 15

AGROFILA '82 Intl. Agricultural Stamp Exhibition, Godollo — A710

1982, Sept. 24 Perf. 11½x12
2757 A710 5fo Map 1.00 95

Issued in sheets of 3 stamps and 3 labels showing Godollo Agricultural University, emblem. Size: 109x127mm.

Public Transportation Sesquicentennial — A711

1982, Oct. 5 Litho. Perf. 12x11½
2758 A711 2fo multi 25 15

Vuk and a Bird — A712

Scenes from Vuk the Fox Cub, Cartoon by Attila Dargay.

1982, Nov. 11 Perf. 12½
2759 A712 1fo shown 15 15
2760 A712 1fo Dogs 15 15
2761 A712 2fo Rooster 28 18
2762 A712 2fo Owl 28 18
2763 A712 4fo Geese 55 35
2764 A712 6fo Frog 80 60
2765 A712 8fo Master fox 1.10 80
Nos. 2759-2765 (7) 3.31 2.41

Engineering Education Bicentenary A713

Gyorgy Boloni (1882-1959), Writer and Journalist A714

1982, Oct. 13 Perf. 12
2766 A713 2fo Budapest Polytechnical Univ. 25 15

1982, Oct. 29
2767 A714 2fo multi 25 15

Footnotes often refer to other stamps of the same design.

October Revolution, 65th Anniv. A715

Works of Art in Hungarian Chapel, Vatican A716

1982, Nov. 5 Litho. ***Perf. 11½x12***
2768 A715 5fo Lenin 75 42

1982, Nov. 30 ***Perf. 12x11½***

Designs: No. 2769, St. Stephen, first King of Hungary (1001-1038). No. 2770, Pope Sylvester II making donation to St. Stephen. No. 2771, Pope Callixtus III ordering noon victory bell ringing by St. John of Capistrano, 1456. No. 2772, Pope Paul VI showing Cardinal Lekai location of Hungarian Chapel. No. 2773, Pope John Paul II consecrating chapel, 1980. No. 2774, Madonna and Child. Nos. 2769, 2774 sculptures by Imre Varga; others by Amerigo Tot. Nos. 2770-2773 in continuous design (37x18mm); Nos. 2769-2774 se-tenant.

2769 A716 2fo multi 38 38
2770 A716 2fo multi 38 38
2771 A716 2fo multi 38 38
2772 A716 2fo multi 38 38
2773 A716 2fo multi 38 38
2774 A716 2fo multi 38 38
Nos. 2769-2774 (6) 2.28 2.28

Souvenir Sheet

Zoltan Kodaly (1882-1967), Composer A717

1982, Dec. 16 ***Perf. 11½***
2775 A717 20fo multi 2.75 2.75

New Year 1983 — A718

Perf. 12½x11½
1982, Dec. 16 **Litho.**
2776 A718 2fo multi 25 15

Johann Wolfgang Goethe (1749-1832), German Poet, by Heinrich Kolbe — A719

1982, Dec. 29 ***Perf. 11½x12½***
2777 A719 20fo multi 3.00 2.75

10th Anniv. of Postal Code — A720

1983, Jan. 24 ***Perf. 11½x12***
2778 A720 2fo multi 25 15

3rd Budapest Spring Festival, Mar. 18-27 A721

1983, Mar. 18 Litho. ***Perf. 12x11½***
2779 A721 2fo Ship of Peace, by Engre Szasz 25 15

Gyula Juhasz (1883-1937), Poet — A722

1983, Apr. 15 ***Perf. 12***
2780 A722 2fo multi 25 15

City of Szentgotthard, 800th Anniv. — A723

1983, May 4 Litho. ***Perf. 11½***
2781 A723 2fo Monastery, seal, 1489 25 15

Malomto Lake, Tapolca — A724

1983, May 17 ***Perf. 11½x12***
2782 A724 5fo multi 80 80

TEMBAL '83 Intl. Topical Stamp Exhibition, Basel, May 21-29. Issued in sheets of 3 stamps and 3 labels.

Souvenir Sheet

5th Interparliamentary Union Conference on European Cooperation, Budapest, May 30-June 5 — A725

1983, May 30 Litho. ***Perf. 12½***
2783 A725 20fo Budapest Parliament 3.50 3.50

Jeno Hamburger (1883-1936) A726

1983, May 31 ***Perf. 12***
2784 A726 2fo multi 25 15

Lady with Unicorn, by Raphael (1483-1517) A727

Paintings: No. 2786, John of Aragon. No. 2787, Granduca Madonna. No. 2788, Madonna and Child with St. John. 4fo, La Muta. 6fo, La Valeta. 8fo, La Fornarina. 20fo, Esterhazy Madonna.

Perf. 11½x12½
1983, June 29 **Litho.**
2785 A727 1fo multi 15 15
2786 A727 1fo multi 15 15
2787 A727 2fo multi 24 15
2788 A727 2fo multi 24 15
2789 A727 4fo multi 50 28
2790 A727 6fo multi 75 35
2791 A727 8fo multi 85 50
Nos. 2785-2791 (7) 2.88 1.73

Souvenir Sheet

2792 A727 20fo multi 3.00 3.00

No. 2792 contains one stamp (24x37mm).

Simon Bolivar (1783-1830) — A728

1983, July 22 Litho. ***Perf. 12***
2793 A728 2fo multi 25 15

Istvan Vagi (1883-1940), Anti-fascist Martyr — A729

1983, July 22 ***Perf. 11½x12½***
2794 A729 2fo multi 25 15

68th World Esperanto Congress, Budapest, July 30-Aug. 6 — A730

1983, July 29 ***Perf. 12***
2795 A730 2fo multi 25 15

Souvenir Sheet

Martin Luther (1483-1546) — A731

1983, Aug. 12 ***Perf. 12½***
2796 A731 20fo multi 2.75 2.50

Protected Birds of Prey and World Wildlife Fund Emblem — A732

1983, Aug. 18 ***Perf. 11½x12***
2797 A732 1fo Aquila heliaca 16 15
2798 A732 1fo Aquila pomarina 16 15
2799 A732 2fo Haliaetus albicilla 25 16
2800 A732 2fo Falco vespertinus 25 16
2801 A732 4fo Falco cherrug 50 32
2802 A732 6fo Buteo lagopus 75 40
2803 A732 8fo Buteo buteo 90 85
Nos. 2797-2803 (7) 2.97 2.19

Bee Collecting Pollen — A733

1983, Aug. 25 ***Perf. 12***
2804 A733 1fo multi 15 15

29th Intl. Apicultural Congress, Budapest, Aug. 25-31.

Fruit, by Bela Czobel (1883-1976) — A734

1983, Sept. 15 Litho. ***Perf. 12x11½***
2805 A734 2fo multi 25 15

World Communications Year — A735

Designs: No. 2806, Telecommunications Earth Satellite. No. 2807, Intersputnik Earth Station. 2fo, TMM-81 Telephone Service. 3fo, Intelligent Terminal System. 5fo, OCR Optical Reading Instrument. 8fo, Teletext. 20fo, Molina Communications Satellite.

1983, Oct. 7 Litho. ***Perf. 11½x12***
2806 A735 1fo multi 18 15
2807 A735 1fo multi 18 15
2808 A735 2fo multi 28 18
2809 A735 3fo multi 42 25

2810 A735	5fo multi		70	42
2811 A735	8fo multi		1.10	65
	Nos. 2806-2811 (6)		2.86	1.80

Souvenir Sheet

Perf. 12x12½

2812 A735 20fo multi 3.00 3.00

34th Intl. Astronautical Federation Congress — A736

1983, Oct. 10 Photo. *Perf. 12*

2813 A736 2fo multi 25 15

SOZPHILEX 83, Moscow — A737

1983, Oct. 14 Litho. *Perf. 12*

2814 A737 2fo Kremlin 50 50

Issued in sheets of 3 stamps and 3 labels showing emblem. Size: 101x133mm.

Mihaly Babits (1883-1941), Poet and Translator — A738

1983, Nov. 25

2815 A738 2fo multi 25 15

Souvenir Sheet

European Security and Cooperation Conference, Madrid — A739

Perf. 12½x11½

1983, Nov. 10 Litho.

2816 A739 20fo multi 3.75 3.75

1984 Winter Olympics, Sarajevo — A740

Designs: Ice dancers representing the seven phases of a figure cut.

1983, Dec. 22 Litho. *Perf. 12x12½*

2817 A740	1fo	Emblem upper right	15	15
2818 A740	1fo	Emblem upper left	15	15
2819 A740	2fo	Arms extended	28	15
2820 A740	2fo	Arms bent	28	15
2821 A740	4fo	Man looking down	55	30
2822 A740	4fo	Girl looking up	55	30
2823 A740	6fo	multi	85	45
a.		Strip of 7, #2817-2823	3.00	2.00
		Nos. 2817-2823 (7)	2.81	1.65
		Set value		

Souvenir Sheet

Perf. 12½

2824 A740 20fo multi 3.00 3.00

No. 2824 contains one 49x39mm stamp.

Christmas — A741

Resorts and Spas — A742

Designs: 1fo, Madonna with Rose, Kassa, 1500. 2fo, Altar piece, Csikmenasag, 1543.

1983, Dec. 13 Litho. *Perf. 11½x12*

2825 A741 1fo multi	15	15
2826 A741 2fo multi	30	15
Set value		22

1983, Dec. 18

2827 A742	1fo	Zanka, Lake Balaton	16	15
2828 A742	2fo	Hajduszoboszlo	32	15
2829 A742	5fo	Heviz	80	40
		Set value		50

Virgin with Six Saints, by Giovanni Battista Tiepolo — A743

Rest During Flight into Egypt, by Giovanni Domenico Tiepolo — A744

Paintings Stolen and Later Recovered, Museum of Fine Arts, Budapest: b, Esterhazy Madonna, by Raphael. c, Portrait of Giorgione, 16th cent. d, Portrait of a Woman, by Tintoretto. e, Pietro Bempo, by Raphael. f, Portrait of a Man, by Tintoretto.

1984, Feb. 16 *Perf. 12½x12*

2839	Sheet of 7	3.75	3.75
a.-f.	A743 2fo multi	35	
g.	A744 8fo multi	1.50	

Energy Conservation — A745

1984, Mar. 30 Litho. *Perf. 11½x12*

2840 A745 1fo multi 25 15

Sandor Korosi Csoma (1784-1842), Master of Tibetan Philology A746

1984, Mar. 30 *Perf. 11½x12½*

2841 A746 2fo multi 25 18

Stamps with silver inscription and with back inscription "Gift of the Hungarian Post" issued to members of Natl. Fed. of Hungarian Philatelists.

Miniature Sheet

No. 1900 — A747

Designs: b, No. 1346. c, No. 1259.

1984, Apr. 20 Litho. *Perf. 12x11½*

2842	Sheet of 3	2.75	2.75
a.-c.	A747 4fo multi	70	

Espana '84; Ausipex '84; Philatelia '84.

Post-Roman Archaeological Discoveries — A748

Designs: No. 2843, Round gold disc hair ornaments, Rakamaz. No. 2844, Saber belt plates, Szolnok-Strazsahalom and Galgocz. No. 2845, Silver disc hair ornaments, Sarospatak. No. 2846, Swords. 4fo, Silver and gold bowl, Ketpo. 6fo, Bone walking stick handles, Hajdudorog and Szabadbattyan. 8fo, Ivory saddle bow, Izsak; bit, stirrups, Muszka.

1984, May 15 *Perf. 12*

2843 A748 1fo dk brn & tan	15	15
2844 A748 1fo dk brn & tan	15	15
2845 A748 2fo dk brn & tan	28	15
2846 A748 2fo dk brn & tan	28	15
2847 A748 4fo dk brn & tan	55	22
2848 A748 6fo dk brn & tan	80	32
2849 A748 8fo dk brn & tan	1.10	42
Nos. 2843-2849 (7)	3.31	
Set value		1.15

View of Cracow A749

Butterflies A750

Perf. 12½x11½

1984, May 21 Litho.

2850 A749 2fo multi 25 15

Permanent Committee of Posts and Telecommunications, 25th Session, Cracow.

1984, June 7 *Perf. 11½x12*

2851 A750	1fo	Epiphille dilecta	15	15
2852 A750	1fo	Agra sara	15	15
2853 A750	2fo	Morpho cypris	26	15
2854 A750	2fo	Ancylusis formossissima	26	15
2855 A750	4fo	Danaus chrysippus	52	22
2856 A750	6fo	Catagramma cynosura	85	35
2857 A750	8fo	Ornithoptera paradisea	1.10	48
		Nos. 2851-2857 (7)	3.29	
		Set value		1.30

Archer, by Kisfaludy Strobl (1884-1975) — A751

Perf. 12½x11½

1984, July 26 Litho.

2858 A751 2fo multicolored 25 15

Akos Hevesi (1884-1937), Revolutionary — A752

1984, July 26

2859 A752 2fo multicolored 25 15

See Nos. 2884-2885, 2910, 2915, 2962.

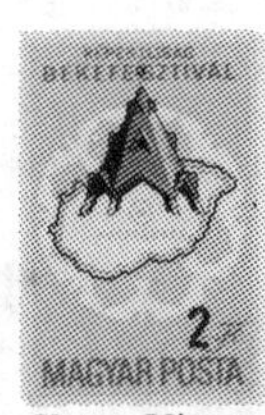

Kepes Ujsag Peace Festival A753

Aerobatic Championship A754

1984, Aug. 3 Litho. *Perf. 12½x11½*

2860 A753 2fo Map, building 25 15

1984, Aug. 14

2861 A754 2fo Plane, map 25 15

Horse Team World Championship, Szilvasvarad, Aug. 17-20 — A755

1984, Aug. 17 *Perf. 12*

2862 A755 2fo Horse-drawn wagon 25 15

Budapest Riverside Hotels — A756

1984, Sept.

2863 A756	1fo	Atrium Hyatt	18	15
2864 A756	2fo	Duna Intercontinental	26	15
2865 A756	4fo	Forum	52	26
2866 A756	4fo	Thermal Hotel, Margaret Isld.	52	26

2867 A756 5fo Hilton 70 35
2868 A756 8fo Gellert 1.00 52
Nos. 2863-2868 (6) 3.18 1.69

Souvenir Sheet

2869 A756 20fo Hilton, diff. 3.00 3.00

14th Conference of Postal Ministers, Budapest — A757

1984, Sept. 10 ***Perf. 12½x11½***
2870 A757 2fo Building, post horn 25 15

57th Stamp Day — A758

1984, Sept. 21 ***Perf. 12***
2871 A758 1fo Four-handled vase, Zsolnay 15 15
2872 A758 2fo Platter, vert. 30 15
Set value 20

Souvenir Sheet

2872A A758 10fo #19 on cover 2.00 2.00

No. 2872A contains one stamp (44x27mm, perf. 11).

Edible Mushrooms A759

Photogravure and Engraved

1984, Oct. ***Perf. 12x11½***
2873 A759 1fo Boletus edulis 20 15
2874 A759 1fo Marasmius oreades 20 15
2875 A759 2fo Morchella esculenta 30 15
2876 A759 2fo Agaricus campester 30 15
2877 A759 3fo Macrolepiota procera 45 24
2878 A759 3fo Cantharellus cibarius 45 24
2879 A759 4fo Armillariella mellea 65 30
Nos. 2873-2879 (7) 2.55 1.38

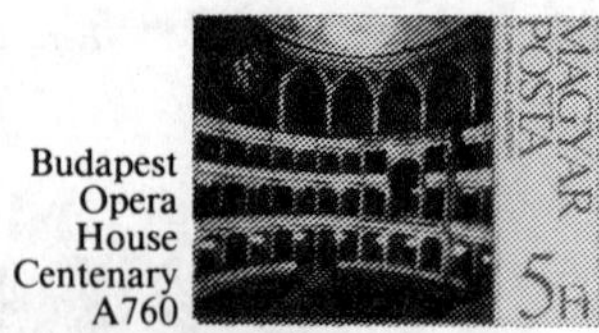

Budapest Opera House Centenary A760

1984, Sept. 27 ***Perf. 12x11½***
2880 A760 1fo Fresco by Mor Than 15 15
2881 A760 2fo Hallway 30 15
2882 A760 5fo Auditorium 75 30
Set value 48

Souvenir Sheet

2883 A760 20fo Building 2.75 2.75

No. 2883 contains one stamp (49x40mm, perf. 12½).

Famous Hungarians Type of 1984

Designs: No. 2884, Bela Balazs, writer (1884-1949); No. 2885, Kato Haman, labor leader (1884-1936).

1984, Dec. 3 Litho. ***Perf. 12½x11½***
2884 A752 2fo multi 25 15
2885 A752 2fo multi 25 15
Set value 20

Madonna and Child, Trensceny A763

Owls A764

1984, Dec. 17 Litho. ***Perf. 11½x12***
2886 A763 1fo multi 15 15

Photogravure and Engraved

1984, Dec. 28 ***Perf. 12½x11½***
2887 A764 1fo Athene Noctua 18 15
2888 A764 1fo Tyto alba 18 15
2889 A764 2fo Strix aluco 28 15
2890 A764 2fo Asio otus 28 15
2891 A764 4fo Nyctea scadiaca 55 28
2892 A764 6fo Strix uralensis 85 40
2893 A764 8fo Bubo bubo 1.00 55
Nos. 2887-2893 (7) 3.32
Set value 1.55

Torah Crown, Buda — A765

19th Cent. Art from Jewish Museum, Budapest.

1984, Dec. Litho. ***Perf. 12***
2894 A765 1fo shown 15 15
2895 A765 1fo Chalice, Moscow 15 15
2896 A765 2fo Torah shield, Vienna 30 15
2897 A765 2fo Chalice, Warsaw 30 15
2898 A765 4fo Container, Augsburg 60 24
2899 A765 6fo Candlestick holder, Warsaw 90 38
2900 A765 8fo Funeral urn, Pest 1.25 48
Nos. 2894-2900 (7) 3.65
Set value 1.40

Souvenir Sheet

Olympics A766

1985, Jan. 2 Photo. ***Perf. 12x12½***
2901 A766 20fo Long jump 3.00 3.00

Novi Sad, Yugoslavia — A767

Danube Bridges: No. 2903, Baja. No. 2904, Arpad Bridge, Budapest. No. 2905, Bratislava, Czechoslovakia. 4fo, Reichsbrucke, Vienna. 6fo, Linz, Austria. 8fo, Regensburg, Federal Rep. of Germany. 20fo, Elizabeth Bridge, Budapest, and map.

1985, Feb. 12 Litho. ***Perf. 12x11½***
2902 A767 1fo multi 15 15
2903 A767 1fo multi 15 15
2904 A767 2fo multi 24 15
2905 A767 2fo multi 24 15
2906 A767 4fo multi 52 24
2907 A767 6fo multi 75 38
2908 A767 8fo multi 1.00 48
Nos. 2902-2908 (7) 3.05
Set value 1.40

Souvenir Sheet

Perf. 12½

2909 A767 20fo multi 3.00 3.00

Famous Hungarians Type of 1984

Design: Laszlo Rudas (1885-1950), communist philosopher.

1985, Feb. 21 ***Perf. 12½x11½***
2910 A752 2fo gold & brn 25 15

Intl. Women's Day, 75th Anniv. A769

Perf. 11½x12½

1985, Mar. 5 **Photo.**
2911 A769 2fo gold & multi 25 15

OLYMPHILEX '85, Lausanne A770

1985, Mar. 14 Litho. ***Perf. 11½x12***
2912 A770 4fo No. B81 50 25
2913 A770 5fo No. B82 65 32

Souvenir Sheet

Liberation of Hungary From German Occupation Forces, 40th Anniv. A771

Design: Liberty Bridge, Budapest and silhouette of the Liberation Monument on Gellert Hill illuminated by fireworks.

1985, Mar. 28 ***Perf. 12½***
2914 A771 20fo multi 3.25 3.25

Famous Hungarians Type of 1984

Design: Gyorgy Lukacs (1885-1971) communist philosopher, educator.

1985, Apr. 12 ***Perf. 12½x11½***
2915 A752 2fo gold & brn 25 15

Totfalusi Bible, 300th Anniv. — A773

1985, Apr. 25 ***Perf. 12***
2916 A773 2fo gold & blk 25 15

1st Bible printed in Hungarian by Nicolas Totfalusi Kis (1650-1702), publisher, in 1685.

Lorand Eotvos Univ., 350th Anniv. A774

26th European Boxing Championships, Budapest A775

Design: Archbishop Peter Pazmany (1570-1637), founder.

1985, May 14
2917 A774 2fo mag & gray 25 15

No. 2917 printed se-tenant with label picturing obverse and reverse of university commemorative medal.

1985, May 25
2918 A775 2fo multi 25 15

Intl. Youth Year — A776

1985, May 29 ***Perf. 11½x12***
2919 A776 1fo Girl's soccer 15 15
2920 A776 2fo Windsurfing 24 15
2921 A776 2fo Aerobic exercise 24 15
2922 A776 4fo Karate 52 24
2923 A776 4fo Go-kart racing 52 24
2924 A776 5fo Hang gliding 70 30
2925 A776 6fo Skateboarding 75 38
Nos. 2919-2925 (7) 3.12
Set value 1.40

Electro-magnetic High-speed Railway — A777

EXPO '85, Tsukuba, Japan: futuristic technology.

1985, May 29 ***Perf. 12x11½***
2926 A777 2fo shown 25 15
2927 A777 4fo Fuyo (robot) Theater 50 20
Set value 28

Audubon Birth Bicentenary A778

Audubon illustrations

1985, June 19 *Perf. 12*
2928 A778 2fo Colaptes cafer 28 15
2929 A778 2fo Bombycilla garrulus 28 15
2930 A778 2fo Dryocopus pileatus 28 15
2931 A778 4fo Icterus galbula 58 28
Set value 58

See Nos. C446-C447.

Mezohegyes Stud Farm, Bicent. — A779

Horses: No. 2932, Nonius-36, 1883, a dark chestnut. No. 2933, Furioso-23, 1889, a light chestnut. No. 2934, Gidrian-1, 1935, a blond breed. No. 2935, Ramses-3, 1960, gray sporting horse. No. 2936, Krozus-1, 1970, chestnut sporting horse.

1985, June 28
2932 A779 1fo multi 15 15
2933 A779 2fo multi 28 15
2934 A779 4fo multi 55 22
2935 A779 4fo multi 55 22
2936 A779 6fo multi 85 35
Nos. 2932-2936 (5) 2.38
Set value 94

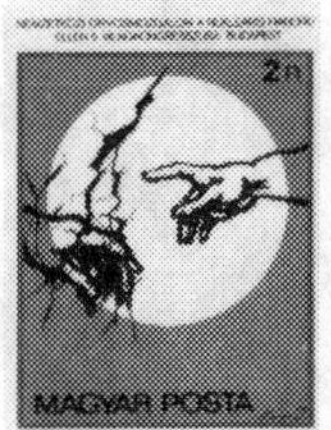

Prevention of Nuclear War — A780

European Music Year — A781

Design: Illustration of a damaged globe and hands, by Imre Varga (b. 1923), 1973 Kossuth prize-winner.

1985, June 28 *Perf. 11½x12*
2937 A780 2fo multi 25 15

Intl. Physician's Movement for the Prevention of Nuclear War, 5th Congress.

1985, July 10 *Perf. 11*

Composers and instruments: 1fo, George Frideric Handel (1685-1759), kettle drum, horn. 2fo, Johann Sebastian Bach (1685-1750), Thomas Church organ. No. 2940, Luigi Cherubini (1760-1842), harp, bass viol, baryton. No. 2941, Frederic Chopin (1810-1849), piano, 1817. 5fo, Gustav Mahler (1860-1911), pardessus de viole, kettle drum, double horn. 6fo, Erkel Ferenc (1810-1893), bass tuba, violin.

2938 A781 1fo multi 15 15
2939 A781 2fo multi 28 15
2940 A781 4fo multi 55 22
2941 A781 4fo multi 55 22
2942 A781 5fo multi 70 28
2943 A781 6fo multi 85 35
Nos. 2938-2943 (6) 3.08 1.37

Souvenir Sheet

12th World Youth Festival, Moscow A782

1985, July 22 *Perf. 12½*
2944 A782 20fo Emblem, Red Square 3.00 3.00

Souvenir Sheet

Helsinki Agreement, 10th Anniv. — A783

1985, Aug. 1 *Perf. 11*
2945 A783 20fo Finlandia Hall, Helsinki 4.00 4.00

World Tourism Day — A784

COMNET '85 — A785

Perf. 12½x11½
1985, Sept. 27 **Litho.**
2946 A784 2fo Key, globe, heart 30 15

1985, Oct. 1 *Perf. 11½*
2947 A785 4fo Computer terminal 60 30

3rd Computer Sciences Conference, Budapest, Oct. 1-4.

Souvenir Sheet

Danube River, Budapest Bridges — A786

1985, Oct. 15 *Perf. 12*
2948 A786 20fo multi 3.50 3.50

European Security and Cooperation Conference and Cultural Forum, Budapest, Oct. 15-Nov. 25. Exists inscribed "Kuturalis Forum Resztvevoi Tiszteletere" in gold on front and "Gift of the Hungarian Post" on back. Not valid for postage.

EUROPHILEX '85, Oct. 14-31 — A787

16-17th century ceramics: 1fo, Faience water jar and dispenser, 1609. 2fo, Tankard, 1670. 10fo, Hexagonal medicine jar, 1774.

1985, Oct. 18 *Perf. 12½x11½*
2949 A787 1fo multi 15 15
2950 A787 2fo multi 35 15
Set value 16

Souvenir Sheet

2951 A787 10fo multi 1.75 1.75

Italy No. 799, View of Rome — A788

1985, Oct. 21 *Perf. 12x11½*
2952 A788 5fo multi 90 90

Italia '85, Rome, Oct. 25-Nov. 3. Issued in sheets of 3 stamps and 3 labels showing emblem.

UN, 40th Anniv. — A789

1985, Oct. 24 *Perf. 11½x12*
2953 A789 4fo Dove, globe, emblem 60 30

Indigenous Lilies — A790

Photogravure and Engraved
1985, Oct. 28 *Perf. 12x11½*
2954 A790 1fo Lilium bulbiferum 15 15
2955 A790 2fo Lilium martagon 28 15
2956 A790 2fo Erythronium dens-canis 28 15
2957 A790 4fo Fritillaria meleagris 55 22
2958 A790 4fo Lilium tigrinum 55 22
2959 A790 5fo Hemerocallis lilio-asphodelus 70 28
2960 A790 6fo Bulbocodium vernum 85 35
Nos. 2954-2960 (7) 3.36
Set value 1.30

Christmas 1985 A791

1985, Nov. 6 **Litho.** *Perf. 13½x13*
2961 A791 2fo Youths caroling 30 15

Famous Hungarians Type of 1984

Design: Istvan Ries (1885-1950), Minister of Justice (1949), labor movement.

1985, Nov. 11 *Perf. 12½x11½*
2962 A752 2fo gold & ol brn 25 15

Motorcycle Centenary — A793

Photogravure & Engraved
1985, Dec. 28 *Perf. 11½x12*
2963 A793 1fo Fantic Sprinter, 1984 18 15
2964 A793 2fo Suzuki Katana GSX, 1983 28 15
2965 A793 2fo Harley-Davidson Duo-Glide, 1960 28 15
2966 A793 4fo Rudge-Whitworth, 1935 55 20
2967 A793 4fo BMW R47, 1927 55 20
2968 A793 5fo NSU, 1910 75 24
2969 A793 6fo Daimler, 1885 85 28
Nos. 2963-2969 (7) 3.44
Set value 1.15

Bela Kun (1886-1939), Communist Party Founder — A794

Perf. 12½x11½
1986, Feb. 20 **Litho.**
2970 A794 4fo multi 50 30

Souvenir Sheet

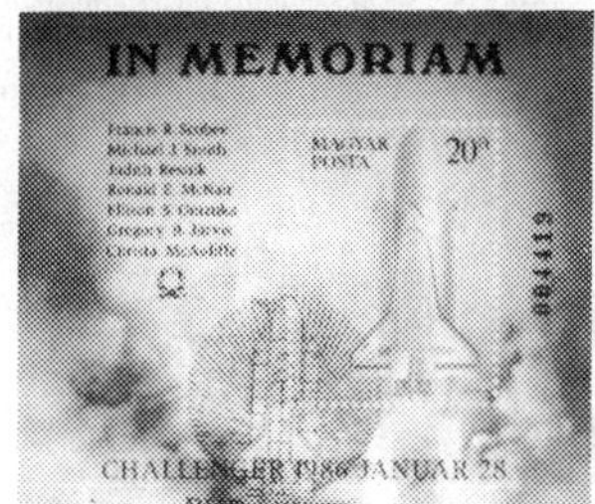

US Shuttle Challenger — A795

1986, Feb. 21 *Perf. 11½*
2971 A795 20fo multi 3.50 3.50

Memorial to the US astronauts who died when the Challenger exploded during takeoff, Jan. 28.

An enhanced introduction to the Scott Catalogue begins on Page 1A. A thorough understanding of the material presented there will greatly aid your use of the catalogue itself.

Halley's Comet — A796

Designs: No. 2972, US Ice satellite, dinosaurs. No. 2973, USSR Vega and Bayeaux tapestry detail, 1066, France. No. 2974, Japanese Suisei and German engraving, 1507. No. 2975, European Space Agency Giotto and The Three Magi, tapestry by Giotto. No. 2976, USSR Astron and Apianis constellation, 1531. No. 2977, US space shuttle and Edmond Halley.

Perf. 11½x13½

1986, Feb. 14 **Litho.**

2972 A796 2fo multi 30 15
2973 A796 2fo multi 30 15
2974 A796 2fo multi 30 15
2975 A796 4fo multi 60 24
2976 A796 4fo multi 60 24
2977 A796 6fo multi 90 38
Nos. 2972-2977 (6) 3.00 1.31

Seeing-eye Dog, Red Cross — A797

Soccer Players in Blue and Red Uniforms — A798

Perf. 12½x11½

1986, Mar. 20 **Litho.**

2978 A797 4fo multi 60 15

Assistance for the blind.

1986, Apr. 2 ***Perf. 11***

Color of Uniforms

2979 A798 2fo shown 35 15
2980 A798 2fo Blue & green 35 15
2981 A798 4fo Red & black 75 24
2982 A798 4fo Yellow & red 75 24
2983 A798 4fo Yellow & green 75 24
2984 A798 6fo Orange & white 1.00 38
Nos. 2979-2984 (6) 3.95 1.40

Souvenir Sheet

Perf. 12½

2985 A798 20fo Victors 4.00 4.00

1986 World Cup Soccer Championships, Mexico. No. 2979 contains one stamp (size: 41x32mm). Also exists with added inscription "In honor of the winner . . ." and red control number.

Buda Castle Cable Railway Station Reopening — A799

1986, Apr. 30 ***Perf. 11½x12***

2986 A799 2fo org, brn & pale yel 50 15

Souvenir Sheet

AMERIPEX '86, Chicago, May 22-June 1 — A800

Designs: a, Yankee doodle rose. b, America rose. c, George Washington, statue by Gyula Bezeredy (1858-1935), Budapest.

1986, Apr. 30 ***Perf. 12½x11½***

2987 Sheet of 3 4.00 4.00
a.-b. A800 5fo any single 1.00 1.00
c. A800 10fo multi 2.00 2.00

Size of No. 2987c: 27x74mm.

Hungary Days in Tokyo — A801

1986, May 6 ***Perf. 11½x12***

2988 A801 4fo Folk dolls 60 30

Andras Fay (1786-1864), Author, Politician — A802

Lithographed and Engraved

1986, May 29 ***Perf. 12***

2989 A802 4fo beige & fawn 60 30

Printed se-tenant with label picturing First Hungarian Savings Bank Union, founded by Fay.

Automobile, Cent. A803

Designs: No. 2990, 1961 Ferrari Tipo 156, 1985 race car. No. 2991, 1932 Alfa Romeo Tipo B, 1984 race car. No. 2992, 1936 Volkswagen, 1986 Porsche 959. No. 2993, 1902 Renault 14CV, 1985 Renault 5 GT Turbo. No. 2994, 1899 Fiat 3½, 1985 Fiat Ritmo. 6fo, 1886 Daimler, 1986 Mercedes-Benz 230SE.

1986, July 24 **Litho.** ***Perf. 12***

2990 A803 2fo multi 30 15
2991 A803 2fo multi 30 15
2992 A803 2fo multi 30 15
2993 A803 4fo multi 60 24
2994 A803 4fo multi 60 24
2995 A803 6fo multi 90 38
Nos. 2990-2995 (6) 3.00
Set value 1.00

Wasa, 1628, Warship — A804

1986, Aug. 15 **Litho.** ***Perf. 11½x12***

2996 A804 2fo multi 50 50

STOCKHOLMIA '86, Aug. 28-Sept. 7. printed se-tenant with label (size: 27x34mm) picturing exhibition emblem. Printed in sheets of 3.

14th Intl. Cancer Congress, Budapest — A805

Design: Moritz Kaposi (1837-1902), Austrian cancer researcher.

1986, Aug. 21 ***Perf. 12½x11½***

2997 A805 4fo multi 60 30

Recapture of Buda Castle, by Gyula Benzcur (1844-1920) — A806

1986, Sept. 2 ***Perf. 12***

2998 A806 4fo multi 60 30

Recapture of Buda from the Turks, 300th anniv.

Tranquility — A807

Hope — A808

Stamp Day: Paintings by Endre Szasz.

1986, Sept. 5

2999 A807 2fo shown 30 15
3000 A807 2fo Confidence 30 15
Set value 20

Souvenir Sheet

Perf. 11½

3001 A808 10fo shown 1.75 1.75

5th Intl. Conference on Oriental Carpets, Vienna and Budapest A809

1986, Sept. 17 **Litho.** ***Perf. 11***

3002 A809 4fo Anatolia crivelli, 15th cent. 60 30

Franz Liszt, Composer A810

1986, Oct. 21 **Engr.** ***Perf. 12***

3003 A810 4fo grysh grn 60 30

Intl. Peace Year — A811

1986, Oct. 24 **Litho.**

3004 A811 4fo multi 60 30

No. 3004 printed se-tenant with label in a continuous design.

Souvenir Sheet

Hofburg Palace, Vienna, and Map — A812

1986, Nov. 4 ***Perf. 11***

3005 A812 20fo multi 2.75 2.75

European Security and Cooperation Conference, Vienna.

Fruits — A813

Photogravure & Engraved

1986, Nov. 25 ***Perf. 12x11½***

3006 A813 2fo Sour cherries 28 15
3007 A813 2fo Apricots 28 15
3008 A813 4fo Peaches 55 28
3009 A813 4fo Raspberries 55 28
3010 A813 4fo Apples 55 28
3011 A813 6fo Grapes 85 40
Nos. 3006-3011 (6) 3.06 1.54

Natl. Heroes — A814

Designs: No. 3012, Jozseph Pogany (1886-1939), journalist, martyr. No. 3013, Ferenc Munnich (1886-1967), prime minister, 1958-61.

1986 Litho. *Perf. 12½x11½*

3012 A814 4fo multi 65 32
3013 A814 4fo multi 65 32

Issue dates: No. 3012, Nov. 6. No. 3013, Nov. 14.

World Communist Youth Fed., 12th Congress A815

1986, Nov. 21 *Perf. 12*

3014 A815 4fo multi 60 30

Castles — A816

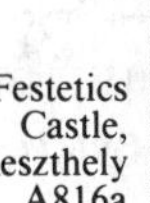

Festetics Castle, Keszthely A816a

Designs: 2fo, Forgach, Szecseny. 3fo, Savoya, Rackeve. 4fo, Batthyany, Kormend. 5fo, Szechenyi, Nagycenk. 6fo, Rudnyanszky, Nagyteteny. 7fo, Esterhazy, Papa. 8fo, Szapary, Buk. 10fo, Festetics, Keszthely. 12fo, Dory Castle, Mihalyi. 20fo, Brunswick, Martonvasar. 30fo, De la Motte, Nosvaj. 40fo, L'Huillier-Coborg, Edeleny. 50fo, Teleki-Degenfeld, Szirak. 70fo, Magochy, Pacin. 100fo, Eszterhazy, Fertod.

Perf. 12x11½, 11½x12½ (7fo)

1986-91 Litho.

3015 A816 2fo yel & ol bis 20 15
3016 A816 3fo pale grn & grn 28 15
3017 A816 4fo pale bl & bl 38 20
3018 A816 5fo pale pink & pink 45 22
3019 A816 6fo pale org & brn org 55 28
3019A A816 7fo brn olive & dk brn 90 45
3020 A816 8fo ver & dk red 70 38
3021 A816 10fo beige & choc 1.10 55
3021A A816 12fo lt vio & dk vio 1.50 75
3022 A816 20fo greenish yel & pale olive green 2.25 1.10
3023 A816 30fo lt blue green & blue green 3.50 1.65
3024 A816 40fo lt ultra & blue 4.25 2.25
3025 A816 50fo pale rose & lake 5.75 2.75
3026 A816 70fo gray & dark gray 7.00 4.00
3027 A816 100fo lt vio & vio 11.00 5.75
Nos. 3015-3027 (15) 39.81 20.63

Issue dates: 2fo-6fo, 8fo, Nov. 28. 10fo, 20fo, 30fo, 100fo, May 28, 1987. 40fo-60fo, July 30, 1987. 7fo, June 27, 1991. 12fo, Sept. 6, 1991.

For overprint see No. 3320.

Litho. & Engr.

1989, Feb. 28 *Perf. 12*

3028 A816a 10fo lt lem & brn blk 1.65 85

This is an expanding set. Numbers will change if necessary.

Wildlife Conservation A817

1986, Dec. 15 *Perf. 12*

3035 A817 2fo Felis silvestris 30 15
3036 A817 2fo Lutra lutra 30 15
3037 A817 2fo Mustela erminea 30 15
3038 A817 4fo Sciurus vulgaris 60 30
3039 A817 4fo Erinaceus concolor 60 30
3040 A817 6fo Emys orbicularis 90 45
Nos. 3035-3040 (6) 3.00 1.50

Portraits of Hungarian Kings in the Historical Portrait Gallery — A818

King and reign: No. 3041, St. Steven, 997-1038. No. 3042, Geza I, 1074-1077. No. 3043, St. Ladislas, 1077-1095. No. 3044, Bela III, 1172-1196. No. 3045, Bela IV, 1235-1270.

1986, Dec. 10 *Perf. 11½x12*

3041 A818 2fo multi 30 15
3042 A818 2fo multi 30 15
3043 A818 4fo multi 60 30
3044 A818 4fo multi 60 30
3045 A818 6fo multi 90 45
Nos. 3041-3045 (5) 2.70 1.35

See Nos. 3120-3122.

Fungi — A819

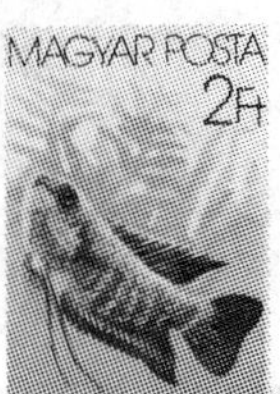

Saltwater Fish — A820

Lithographed and Engraved

1986, Dec. 30 *Perf. 11½*

3046 A819 2fo Amanita phalloides 30 15
3047 A819 2fo Inocybe patouillardi 30 15
3048 A819 2fo Amanita muscaria 30 15
3049 A819 4fo Omphalotus olearius 60 30
3050 A819 4fo Amanita pantherina 60 30
3051 A819 6fo Gyromitra esculenta 90 45
Nos. 3046-3051 (6) 3.00 1.50

1987, Jan. 15 Photo. *Perf. 11½*

3052 A820 2fo Colisa fasciata 30 15
3053 A820 2fo Pseudotropheus zebra 30 15
3054 A820 2fo Iriatherina werneri 30 15
3055 A820 4fo Aphyosemion multicolor 60 30
3056 A820 4fo Papiliochromis ramirezi 60 30
3057 A820 6fo Hyphessobrycon erythrostigma 90 45
Nos. 3052-3057 (6) 3.00 1.50

Seated Woman, 1918, by Bela Uitz (1887-1972), Painter A821

Abstract, 1960, by Lajos Kassak (1887-1967) A822

1987, Mar. 6 Litho. *Perf. 12*

3058 A821 4fo multi 60 30

1987, Mar. 20

3059 A822 4fo blk & red 60 30

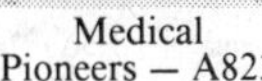

Medical Pioneers — A823

Neolithic and Copper Age Artifacts — A824

Designs: 2fo, Hippocrates (460-377 B.C.), Greek physician. No. 3061, Avicenna or Ibn Sina (A.D. 980-1037), Islamic pharmacist, diagnostician. No. 3062, Ambroise Pare (1510-1590), French surgeon. No. 3063, William Harvey (1578-1657), English physician, anatomist. 6fo, Ignaz Semmelweis (1818-1865), Hungarian obstetrician.

1987, Mar. 31

3060 A823 2fo blk & dk red brn 30 15
3061 A823 4fo blk & dk grn 60 30
3062 A823 4fo blk & steel bl 60 30
3063 A823 4fo blk & ol blk 60 30
3064 A823 6fo blk & grn blk 90 45
Nos. 3060-3064 (5) 3.00 1.50

1987, Apr. 15 Litho. *Perf. 12*

Designs: 2fo, Urn, Hodmezovasarhely. No. 3066, Altar, Szeged. No. 3067, Deity, Szegvar-Tuzkoves. 5fo, Vase, Center.

3065 A824 2fo pale bl grn & sep 30 15
3066 A824 4fo buff & sep 60 30
3067 A824 4fo pale org & sep 60 30
3068 A824 5fo pale yel grn & sep 90 45

Souvenir Sheet

Esztergom Cathedral Treasury Reopening — A825

1987, Apr. 28 *Perf. 11*

3069 A825 20fo Calvary of King Matthias 4.50 4.50

No. 3069 margin pictures the Horn Chalice of King Sigismund, Rhineland, 1408 (UL), Crozier of Archbishop Miklos Olah, Hungary, c. 1490 (UR), Monstrance of Imre Eszterhazy, by Gaspar Meichl, Vienna, 1728 (LL), and the Chalice of Matthias, Hungary, c. 1480.

Hungarian First Aid Assoc., Cent. — A826

1987, May 5 *Perf. 11½x12*

3070 A826 4fo Ambulances, 1887-1987 60 30

Souvenir Sheet

CAPEX '87, Toronto A827

Stamp exhibitions: b, OLYMPHILEX '87, Rome. c, HAFNIA '87, Copenhagen.

1987, May 20 Litho. *Perf. 11*

3071 Sheet of 3 + 3 labels 4.00 3.00
a.-c. A827 5fo any single 1.25 90

Nos. 3071a-3071c printed se-tenant with labels picturing exhibition emblems.

Jozsef Marek (1886-1952), Veterinarian — A828

1987, May 25 *Perf. 12x11½*

3072 A828 4fo multi 60 30

Veterinary education, bicent.

Teleki's African Expedition, Cent. — A829

1987, June 10

3073 A829 4fo multi 60 30

Samuel Teleki (1845-1916), explorer.

Woodcut by Abraham von Werdt, 18th Cent. — A830

Antarctic Research, 75th Anniv. — A831

Helicopter Landing, Mirnij Research Station — A832

Litho. & Engr.

1987, June 25 *Perf. 12*

3074 A830 4fo beige & sepia 60 30

Hungarian Printing, Paper and Press Workers' Union, 125th anniv.

1987, June 30 **Litho.**

Map, explorer and scene: No. 3075, James Cook (1728-1779) and ship. No. 3076, Fabian von Bellingshausen (1778-1852) and seals. No. 3077, Ernest H. Shackleton (1874-1922) and penguins. No. 3078, Roald Amundsen (1872-1928) discovering South Pole, dog team. No. 3079, Robert F. Scott (1868-1912) and ship. No. 3080, Richard E. Byrd (1888-1957) and Floyd Bennett monoplane.

3075 A831	2fo multi		30	15
3076 A831	2fo multi		30	15
3077 A831	2fo multi		30	15
3078 A831	4fo multi		60	30
3079 A831	4fo multi		60	30
3080 A831	6fo multi		90	45
	Nos. 3075-3080 (6)		3.00	1.50

Souvenir Sheet

Perf. 11½

3081 A832 20fo multi 3.00 3.00

Railway Officers Training Institute, Cent. — A833

Stamp Day, 60th Anniv. — A834

1987, Sept. 4 **Litho.** *Perf. 11½x12*

3082 A833 4fo blue & black 1.00 50

Litho. & Engr.

1987, Sept. 18 *Perf. 12*

Masonry of the medieval Buda Castle: 2fo, Flowers, dolphin. 4fo, Arms of King Matthias. 10fo, Capital inscribed "ONDIDIT/GENEROSVM".

3083 A834 2fo multi 50 25
3084 A834 2fo multi 1.00 50

Souvenir Sheet

Perf. 11

3085 A834 10fo multi 2.50 2.50

A835

Orchids — A836

A837

1987, Sept. 30 **Litho.** *Perf. 12*

3086 A835 4fo multi 1.00 50
a. Se-tenant with label 1.00 50

No 3086 printed in sheet of 50 and in sheet of 25 plus 25 labels picturing 13th cent. church at Gyongyospata which houses the altar.

1987, Oct. 29 **Litho.** *Perf. 11*

3087 A836	2fo	Cypripedium calceolus	50	25
3088 A836	2fo	Orchis purpurea	50	25
3089 A836	4fo	Himantoglossum hircinum	1.00	50
3090 A836	4fo	Ophrys scolopax cornuta	1.00	50
3091 A836	5fo	Cephalanthera rubra	1.25	62
3092 A836	6fo	Epipactis atrorubens	1.50	75
		Nos. 3087-3092 (6)	5.75	2.87

Miniature Sheet

3093 A837 20fo shown 5.00 5.00

1988 Winter Olympics, Calgary — A838

1987, Nov. 24

3094 A838	2fo	Speed skating	50	25
3095 A838	2fo	Cross-country skiing	50	25
3096 A838	4fo	Biathlon	1.00	50
3097 A838	4fo	Ice hockey	1.00	50
3098 A838	4fo	4-Man bobsled	1.00	50
3099 A838	6fo	Ski-jumping	1.50	75
		Nos. 3094-3099 (6)	5.50	2.75

Souvenir Sheet

3100 A838 20fo Slalom 5.00 5.00

Souvenir Sheet

US-Soviet Summit, Dec. 7-10 — A839

1987, Dec. 7 *Perf. 12*

3101 A839 20fo Shaking hands 5.00 5.00

Meeting of Gen. Secretary Gorbachev and Pres. Reagan to discuss and sign nuclear arms reduction treaty.

Fairy Tales — A840

Designs: No. 3102, The White Crane, from Japan. No. 3103, The Fox and the Crow, Aesop's Fables. No. 3104, The Tortoise and the Hare, Aesop's Fables. No. 3105, The Ugly Duckling, by Hans Christian Andersen. No. 3106, The Steadfast Tin Soldier, by Andersen.

1987, Dec. 11

3102 A840	2fo multi	50	25
3103 A840	2fo multi	50	25
3104 A840	4fo multi	1.00	50
3105 A840	4fo multi	1.00	50
3106 A840	6fo multi	1.50	75
	Nos. 3102-3106 (5)	4.50	2.25

Count Ferdinand von Zeppelin (1838-1917), Designer of Dirigibles A841

1988, Jan. 29 **Litho.** *Perf. 12*

3107 A841	2fo	LZ-2, 1905	50	25
3108 A841	4fo	LZ-4, 1908	1.00	50
3109 A841	4fo	LZ-10, Schwaben, 1911	1.00	50
3110 A841	8fo	LZ-127, Graf Zeppelin, 1928	2.00	1.00

1988 World Figure Skating Championships, Budapest — A842

Various athletes wearing period costumes.

1988, Feb. 29 **Photo.** *Perf. 11½*

3111 A842	2fo	Male, 20th cent.	50	25
3112 A842	2fo	Male, (cap), 19th cent.	50	25
3113 A842	4fo	Male (hat), 18th cent.	1.00	50
3114 A842	4fo	Woman, c. 1930	1.00	50
3115 A842	5fo	Woman (contemporary)	1.25	62
3116 A842	6fo	Pair	1.50	75
		Nos. 3111-3116 (6)	5.75	2.87

Souvenir Sheet

Perf. 12x11½

3117 A842 20fo Death spiral 5.00 5.00

No. 3117 contains one stamp (size: 37x52mm).

Illes Monus (1888-1944), Party Leader — A843

1988, Mar. 11 **Litho.** *Perf. 11½x12*

3118 A843 4fo multi 1.00 50

See Nos. 3152, 3160.

Miniature Sheet

Postmaster's Coat, Hat and Post Horn, 18th Cent. — A844

1988, Mar. 18 **Litho.** *Perf. 13*

3119 A844 4fo + 4 labels 1.00 1.00

Intl. stamp exhibitions, 1988. No. 3119 contains 4 labels picturing exhibition emblems: JUVALUX '88, Luxembourg, Mar. 29-Apr. 4 (UL), SYDPEX '88, Sydney, Australia, July 30-Aug.7 (UR), FINLANDIA '88, Helsinki, Finland, June 1-12 (LR), and PRAGA '88, Prague, Czechoslovakia, Aug. 26-Sept. 4 (LL).

King Type of 1986

Portraits of Hungarian kings in the Historical Portrait Gallery. King and reign: 2fo, Charles Robert (1308-1342). 4fo, Louis I (1342-1382). 6fo, Sigismund (1387-1437).

1988, Mar. 31 *Perf. 11½x12*

3120 A818	2fo pale grn, sep & red	50	25
3121 A818	4fo pale ultra, sep & red	1.00	50
3122 A818	6fo pale vio, sep & red	1.50	75

1988 Summer Olympics, Seoul A845

Computer Animation A846

1988, Apr. 20 **Litho.** *Perf. 13½x13*

3123 A845	2fo	Rowing	50	25
3124 A845	4fo	Hurdling	1.00	50
3125 A845	4fo	Fencing	1.00	50
3126 A845	6fo	Boxing	1.50	75

Souvenir Sheet

Perf. 12½

3127 A845 20fo Tennis 5.00 5.00

1988, May 12 *Perf. 12*

Design: Graphic from the computer-animated film *Dilemma,* 1972, by graphic artist Janos Kass (b. 1927) and cartoon film director John Halas (b. 1912).

3128 A846 4fo blk, pur & ver 1.00 50

Eurocheck Congress, June 10, Budapest A847

1988, June 10 **Litho.** *Perf. 12*

3129 A847 4fo multi 1.00 50

Eurocheck as legal tender, 20th anniv.

Sovereign of the Seas
A848

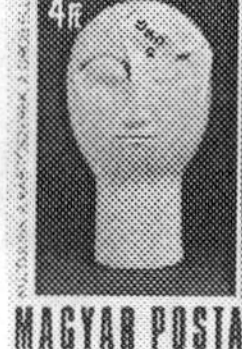

Fight Drug Abuse
A849

1988, June 30

3130	A848	2fo shown	50	25
3131	A848	2fo *Santa Maria*	50	25
3132	A848	2fo *Mayflower*	50	25
3133	A848	4fo *Jylland*	1.00	50
3134	A848	6fo *St. Jupat*	1.50	75
		Nos. 3130-3134 (5)	4.00	2.00

1988, July 7 Litho. *Perf. 12*
3135 A849 4fo multi 1.00 50

Ducks
A850

1988, July 29 Litho. *Perf. 13x13½*

3136	A850	2fo Anas crecca	50	25
3137	A850	2fo Bucephala clangula	50	25
3138	A850	4fo Anas penelope	1.00	50
a.		Pane of 10 No. 3136+10 No. 3138 with gutter between	15.00	
3139	A850	4fo Netta rufina	1.00	50
3140	A850	6fo Anas strepera	1.50	75
		Nos. 3136-3140 (5)	4.50	2.25

Souvenir Sheet

Perf. 12½x11½

3141 A850 20fo Anas platyrhynchos 5.00 5.00

No. 3141 contains one 52x37mm stamp.
For surcharges see Nos. 3199-3200.

Antique Toys — A851

Calvinist College, Debrecen, 450th Anniv. — A852

1988, Aug. 12 *Perf. 12*

3142	A851	2fo Train	50	25
3143	A851	2fo See-saw	50	25
3144	A851	4fo +2fo Pecking chickens	1.50	75
3145	A851	5fo String-manipulated soldier	1.25	62

Surtax for youth philately programs.

1988, Aug. 16 Litho. *Perf. 13½x13*
3146 A852 4fo multi 1.00 50

58th American Society of Travel Agents World Congress, Oct. 23-29, Budapest
A853

1988, Aug. 30 *Perf. 12*
3147 A853 4fo multi 1.00 50

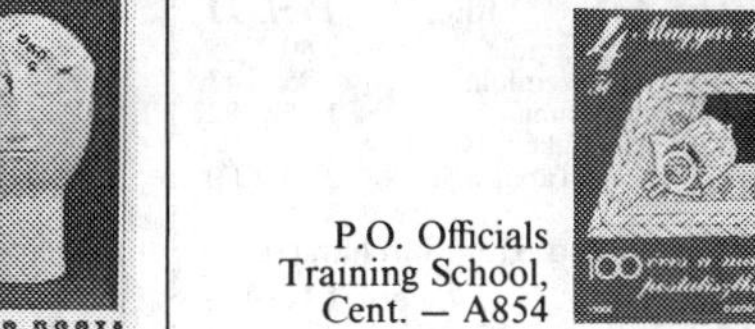

P.O. Officials Training School, Cent. — A854

1988, Sept. 9 Litho. *Perf. 12*
3148 A854 4fo Badge on collar 1.00 50

Gabor Baross (1848-1892), Minister of Commerce and Communication — A855

Portrait and: 2fo, Postal Savings Bank, Budapest, emblem and postal savings stamp. 4fo, Telephone and telegraph apparatus, registration label and cancellations. 10fo, East Railway Station, Budapest.

1988, Sept. 16

3149	A855	2fo multi	50	25
3150	A855	4fo multi	1.00	50

Souvenir Sheet

Perf. 11½

3151 A855 10fo multi 2.50 2.50

No. 3151 contains one 50x29mm stamp.

Famous Hungarians Type of 1988

Design: Gyula Lengyel (1888-1941), political writer.

1988, Oct. 7 *Perf. 11½x12*
3152 A843 4fo multi 1.00 50

Christmas
A857

Nobel Prize Winners
A858

Perf. 12½x11½

1988, Nov. 10 Litho.
3153 A857 2fo multi 50 25

Litho. & Engr.

1988, Nov. 30 *Perf. 12*

Designs: No. 3154, Richard Adolf Zsigmondy (1865-1929), Germany, chemistry (1925). No. 3155, Robert Barany (1876-1936), Austria, medicine (1914). No. 3156, Georg von Hevesy (1885-1966), Hungary, chemistry (1943). No. 3157, Albert Szent-Gyorgyi (1893-1986), Hungary-US, medicine (1937). No. 3158, Georg von Bekesy (1899-1972), US, medicine (1961). 6fo, Denis Gabor (1900-1979), Great Britain, physics (1971).

3154	A858	2fo red brn	50	25
3155	A858	2fo grn	50	25
3156	A858	2fo deep claret	50	25
3157	A858	4fo rose lake	1.00	50
3158	A858	4fo steel blue	1.00	50
3159	A858	6fo sepia	1.50	75
		Nos. 3154-3159 (6)	5.00	2.50

Famous Hungarians Type of 1988

Design: Arpad Szakasits (1888-1965), party leader.

1988, Dec. 6 *Perf. 11½x12*
3160 A843 4fo multi 1.00 50

Souvenir Sheet

Medals Won by Hungarian Athletes at the 1988 Seoul Olympic Games — A860

1988, Dec. 19 Litho. *Perf. 12*
3161 A860 20fo multi 5.00 5.00

Silver and Cast Iron — A861

1988, Dec. 28 Litho. & Engr.

3162	A861	2fo Teapot, Pest, 1846	50	25
3163	A861	2fo Coffee pot, Buda, 18th cent.	50	25
3164	A861	4fo Sugar bowl, Pest, 1822	1.00	50
3165	A861	5fo Cast iron plate, Romania, 1850	1.25	62

Postal Savings Bank Inauguration — A862

1989, Jan. 20 Litho. *Perf. 12x11½*
3166 A862 5fo royal blue, blk & silver 1.25 62

Kalman Wallisch (1889-1934), Labor Leader — A863

1989, Feb. 28 Litho. *Perf. 12*
3167 A863 3fo dk red & brt bl 75 38

See No. 3170.

World Indoor Sports Championships, Budapest, Mar. 3-5 — A864

1989, Mar. 3 *Perf. 13x13½*
3168 A864 3fo multi 75 38

Souvenir Sheet

Interparliamentary Union Cent. and 81st Session, Budapest, Mar. 13-18 — A865

Designs: a, Parliament, Big Ben and Tower Bridge, London. b, Parliament and Chain Bridge, Budapest.

1989, Mar. 13 Litho. *Perf. 11*

3169	A865	Sheet of 2	5.00	5.00
a.-b.		10fo any single	2.50	2.50

Exists with red inscriptions and control number.

Famous Hungarians Type of 1989

Design: Janos Gyetvai (1889-1967), journalist, diplomat.

1989, Apr. 7 Litho. *Perf. 12*
3170 A863 3fo dark red & brt grn 75 38

Stud Farm at Babolna, 200th Anniv. — A867

Horses: a, O Bajan. b, Meneskari Csikos. c, Gazal II.

1989, May 18 Litho. *Perf. 12*

3171		Strip of 3	2.25	1.15
a.-c.	A867	3fo any single	75	38

ART '89, May 23-27, Budapest
A868

1989, May 23 *Perf. 12x11½*
3172 A868 5fo multi 1.25 62

Exhibition for disabled artists.

Flower Arrangements — A869

1989, May 31 *Perf. 12*

3173	A869	2fo multi, vert.	50	25
3174	A869	3fo multi, vert.	75	38
3175	A869	3fo shown	75	38
3176	A869	5fo multi, diff.	1.25	62
3177	A869	10fo multi, vert.	2.50	1.25
		Nos. 3173-3177 (5)	5.75	2.88

French Revolution, Bicent. — A870

1989, June 1 *Perf. 12*

3178	A870	5fo brt blue, blk & red	1.25	62

Souvenir Sheet

Perf. 11½

3179	A870	20fo like 5fo	5.00	5.00

No. 3179 contains one 50x30mm stamp.

Medieval Church of the Csolts Near Veszto — A871

Photography, 150th Anniv. — A872

1989, June 15 **Litho.** *Perf. 12*

3180	A871	3fo multi	60	30

1989, June 15

3181	A872	5fo multi	1.00	50

Old Mills — A873

Designs: 2fo, Water mill, Turistvandi, 18th cent. 3fo, Horse-driven mill, Szarvas, 1836. 5fo, Windmill, Kiskunhalas, 18th cent. 10fo, Water wheel on the Drava River.

1989, June 20

3182	A873	2fo multi	40	20
3183	A873	3fo multi	60	30
3184	A873	5fo multi	1.00	50
3185	A873	10fo multi	2.00	1.00

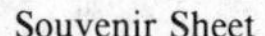
Souvenir Sheet

1st Moon Landing, 20th Anniv. — A874

1989, July 12 **Litho.** *Perf. 12½*

3186	A874	20fo multi	6.00	6.00

Gliders — A875

1989, July 20 *Perf. 12*

3187	A875	3fo Futar	60	30
3188	A875	5fo Cimbora	1.00	60

17th Intl. Old Timers Rally, Budakeszi Airport, and 60th anniv. of glider flying in Hungary.

Reptiles — A876

1989, July 26 *Perf. 11*

3189	A876	2fo *Lacerta agilis*	40	20
3190	A876	3fo *Lacerta viridis*	60	30
3191	A876	5fo *Vipera rakosiensis*	1.00	50
3192	A876	5fo *Natrix natrix*	1.00	50
3193	A876	10fo *Emys orbicularis*	2.00	1.00
		Nos. 3189-3193 (5)	5.00	2.50

31st Modern Pentathlon World Championships, Aug. 30-Sept. 4, Budapest — A877

1989, July 31 *Perf. 13½x13*

3194	A877	5fo multi	1.00	50

10th World Speleology Congress, Aug. 13-20, Sofia — A878

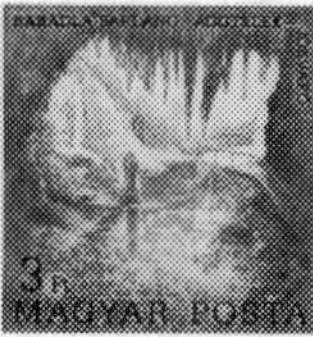

Caves.

1989, Aug. 14 **Litho.** *Perf. 11*

3195	A878	3fo Baradla	50	25
3196	A878	5fo Szemlohegy	85	42
3197	A878	10fo Anna	1.65	82
3198	A878	12fo Lake Cave of Tapolca	2.00	1.00

Nos. 3136 and 3138 Surcharged

1989, Aug. 14 *Perf. 13x13½*

3199	A850	3fo on 2fo #3136	50	25
3200	A850	5fo on 4fo #3138	85	42

Third World Two-in-Hand Carriage-driving Championships, Balatonfenyves, Aug. 24-27 — A879

1989, Aug. 24 *Perf. 12*

3201	A879	5fo multi	88	45

Stamp Day — A880

Nurses: 5fo, Zsuzsanna Kossuth (1820-1854) and emblem. 10fo, Florence Nightingale (1820-1910) and medal awarded in her name by the Red Cross.

1989, Sept. 8 **Litho.** *Perf. 12*

3202	A880	5fo multi	88	45
3203	A880	10fo multi	1.65	82

See No. B341.

Pro-Philatelia 1989 — A881

1989, Oct. 10 **Litho.** *Imperf.*

3204	A881	50fo Nos. 2665, C426, 2742, 3005, B233	8.00	8.00

Dismantling of the Electronic Surveillance System (Iron Curtain) on the Hungary-Austria Border — A882

1989, Oct. 30 *Perf. 11*

3205	A882	5fo multi	90	45

Conquest of Hungary, by Mor Than — A883

1989, Oct. 31

3206	A883	5fo multi	90	45

Arpad, chief who founded the 1st Magyar dynasty of Hungary in 889.

Christmas — A884

1989, Nov. 10 **Litho.** *Perf. 11½x12*

3207	A884	3fo Flight to Egypt	52	25

Jawaharlal Nehru, 1st Prime Minister of Independent India — A885

Litho. & Engr.

1989, Nov. 14 *Perf. 12*

3208	A885	3fo buff & rose brn	52	25

Modern Art — A886

Paintings: 3fo, *Mike,* by Dezso Korniss. 5fo, *Sunrise,* by Lajos Kassak. 10fo, *Grotesque Burial,* by Endre Balint. 12fo, *Memory of Toys,* by Tihamer Gyarmathy.

1989, Dec. 18 **Litho.** *Perf. 12*

3209	A886	3fo multicolored	62	30
3210	A886	5fo multicolored	1.05	55
3211	A886	10fo multicolored	2.10	1.05
3212	A886	12fo multicolored	2.50	1.25

Medical Pioneers — A887

Designs: No. 3213, Galen (129-c.199), Greek physician. No. 3214, Paracelsus (1493-1541), German alchemist. 4fo, Andreas Vesalius (1514-1564), Belgian anatomist. 6fo, Rudolf Virchow (1821-1902), German pathologist. 10fo, Ivan Petrovich Pavlov (1849-1936), Russian physiologist.

1989, Dec. 29 Engr. *Perf. 12*

3213	A887	3fo olive gray	65	32
3214	A887	3fo brown	65	32
3215	A887	4fo black	1.15	58
3216	A887	6fo intense black	1.30	65
3217	A887	10fo brown violet	2.15	1.10
		Nos. 3213-3217 (5)	5.90	2.97

Hungarian Savings Bank, 150th Anniv. — A888

1990, Jan. 11 Litho.

3218	A888	5fo multicolored	88	45

Singer Sewing Machine, 125th Anniv. A889

Telephone, Budapest Exchange A890

1990, Jan. 15 *Perf. 12*

3219	A889	5fo brown & sepia	88	45

1990, Jan. 29

Designs: 5fo, Mailbox and main p.o., Budapest, c. 1900.

3220	A890	3fo shown	38	20
3221	A890	5fo multicolored	62	30

Coil Stamps
Size: 17x22mm
Perf. 14
Photo.

3222	A890	3fo shown	38	20
3223	A890	5fo multi	62	30

Nos. 3220-3221 inscribed "Pj 1989." Nos. 3222-3223 inscribed "1989."
Nos. 3222-3223 do not exist imperf.

Protected Bird Species — A891

1990, Feb. 20 Litho. *Perf. 11½x12*

3224	A891	3fo *Alcedo atthis*	70	35
3225	A891	3fo *Pyrrhula pyrrhula*	70	35
3226	A891	3fo *Dendrocopos syriacus*	70	35
3227	A891	5fo *Upupa epops*	1.15	58
3228	A891	5fo *Merops apiaster*	1.15	58
3229	A891	10fo *Coracias garrulus*	2.25	1.10
		Nos. 3224-3229 (6)	6.65	3.31

Leucadendron tinctum pubibracteolatum A892

Flowers of the continents (Africa).

1990, Mar. 14 Litho. *Perf. 12*

3230	A892	3fo shown	70	35
3231	A892	3fo *Protea compacta*	70	35
3232	A892	3fo *Leucadendron spissifolium*	70	35
3233	A892	5fo *Protea barbigera*	1.15	58
3234	A892	5fo *Protea lepidocarpodendron*	1.15	58
3235	A892	10fo *Protea cynaroides*	2.25	1.10
		Nos. 3230-3235 (6)	6.65	3.31

Souvenir Sheet
Perf. 12½x12

3236	A892	20fo Montage of African flowers	6.75	6.75

No. 3236 contains one 27x38mm stamp.
See Nos. 3278-3283.

Kings — A893

Portraits of Hungarian kings in the Historical Portrait Gallery. King and reign: No. 3237, Janos Hunyadi (c. 1407-1409). No. 3238, Matthias Hunyadi (1443-1490).

1990, Apr. 6 Litho. *Perf. 11½x12*

3237	A893	5fo multicolored	85	42
3238	A893	5fo multicolored	85	42

Printed se-tenant.

Souvenir Sheet

Great Britain No. 1 — A894

Litho. & Engr.
1990, Apr. 17 *Perf. 12½x12*

3239	A894	20fo black & buff	6.75	6.75

Penny Black 150th anniv., Stamp World London '90.

Karoli Bible, 400th Anniv. A895

1990, Apr. 24 Litho.

3240	A895	8fo Gaspar Karoli	1.35	68

No. 3240 printed se-tenant with label picturing Bible frontispiece.

1990 World Cup Soccer Championships, Italy — A896

Various athletes.

1990, Apr. 27 *Perf. 11½x12*

3241	A896	3fo Dribble	60	30
3242	A896	5fo Heading the ball	1.00	50
3243	A896	5fo Kick	1.00	50
3244	A896	8fo Goal attempt	1.65	82
3245	A896	8fo Dribble, diff.	1.65	82
3246	A896	10fo Dribble, diff.	2.00	1.00
		Nos. 3241-3246 (6)	7.90	3.94

Souvenir Sheet
Perf. 12½

3247	A896	20fo Dribble, diff.	6.75	6.75

No. 3247 contains one 32x42mm stamp.

Kelemen Mikes (1690-1761), Writer — A897

1990, May 31 Litho. *Perf. 13½x13*

3248	A897	8fo black & gold	1.65	82

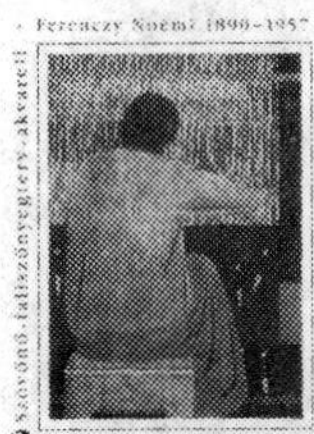

Noemi and Beni Ferenczy, Birth Cent. — A898

Designs: 3fo, Painting by Noemi Ferenczy. 5fo, Sculpture by Beni Ferenczy.

1990, June 18 Litho. *Perf. 12*

3249	A898	3fo multicolored	38	20
3250	A898	5fo multicolored	65	32

Ferenc Kazinczy (1759-1831), Hungarian Language Reformer A899

1990, July 18 Litho. *Perf. 12*

3251	A899	8fo multicolored	1.00	50

Ferenc Kolcsey (1790-1838), Poet — A900

1990, Aug. 3

3252	A900	8fo multicolored	1.00	50

New Coat of Arms A901

1990, Aug. 17 Litho. *Perf. 13½x13*

3253	A901	8fo multicolored	1.00	50

Souvenir Sheet
Perf. 11

3254	A901	20fo multicolored	2.50	1.25

No. 3254 contains one 34x50mm stamp.

Grapes and Wine Producing Areas — A902

Grapes and Growing Area: 3fo, Cabernet franc, Hajos-Vaskut. 5fo, Cabernet sauvignon, Villany-Siklos. No. 3257, Italian Riesling, Badacsony. No. 3258, Kadarka, Szekszard. No. 3259, Leanyka, Eger. 10fo, Furmint, Tokaj-Hegyalja.

1990, Aug. 31 *Perf. 13x13½*

3255	A902	3fo multicolored	38	20
3256	A902	5fo multicolored	65	32
3257	A902	8fo multicolored	1.00	50
3258	A902	8fo multicolored	1.00	50
3259	A902	8fo multicolored	1.00	50
3260	A902	10fo multicolored	1.25	65
		Nos. 3255-3260 (6)	5.28	2.67

Stamp Day — A903

Paintings by Endre Szasz: 8fo, Feast. 12fo, Message.

1990, Oct. 12 Litho. *Perf. 12*

3261	A903	8fo multicolored	1.00	50
3262	A903	12fo multicolored	1.50	75

See No. B344.

Prehistoric Animals A904

1990, Nov. 16 Litho. *Perf. 12*

3263	A904	3fo Tarbosaurus	38	20
3264	A904	5fo Brontosaurus	65	32
3265	A904	5fo Stegosaurus	65	32
3266	A904	5fo Dimorphodon	65	32
3267	A904	8fo Platybelodon	1.00	50
3268	A904	10fo Mammoth	1.25	65
		Nos. 3263-3268 (6)	4.58	2.31

Intl. Literacy Year — A905

1990, Nov. 21 ***Perf. 13x13½***
3269 A905 10fo multicolored 1.25 65

Budapest Stamp Museum, 60th Anniv. — A906

1990, Nov. 23 ***Perf. 12½***
3270 A906 5fo brn red & grn 62 30

Souvenir Sheet

Thurn & Taxis Postal System, 500th Anniv. — A907

Illustration reduced.

1990, Nov. 30 **Litho.** ***Perf. 12½x12***
3271 A907 50fo multicolored *12.00 6.00*

Antique Clocks — A908

1990, Dec. 14 ***Perf. 12***
3272 A908 3fo Travelling clock, 1576 38 20
3273 A908 5fo Table clock, 1643 65 32
3274 A908 5fo Mantel clock, 1790 65 32
3275 A908 10fo Table clock, 1814 1.25 65

Christmas — A909

Madonna with Child by Botticelli.

1990, Dec. 14 ***Perf. 12½x11½***
3276 A909 5fo multicolored 65 32

Lorand Eotvos (1848-1919) and Torsion Pendulum — A910

1991, Jan. 31 **Litho.** ***Perf. 11***
3277 A910 12fo multicolored 1.50 75

Flowers of the Continents Type

Flowers of the Americas.

1991, Feb. 28 **Litho.** ***Perf. 12***
3278 A892 5fo Mandevilla splendens 65 32
3279 A892 7fo Lobelia cardinalis 90 45
3280 A892 7fo Cobaea scandens 90 45
3281 A892 12fo Steriphoma paradoxa 1.50 75
3282 A892 15fo Beloperone guttata 1.95 1.00
Nos. 3278-3282 (5) 5.90 2.97

Souvenir Sheet
Perf. 11
3283 A892 20fo Flowers of the Americas 2.60 1.30

No. 3283 contains one 27x44mm stamp.

Post Office, Budapest A911

Designs: 7fo, Post Office, Pecs.

Perf. 11½x12½
1991, Mar. 22 **Litho.**
3284 A911 5fo multicolored 65 32
3285 A911 7fo multicolored 90 45
a. Pair, #3284-3285 1.55 78

Admission to CEPT. Nos. 3284-3285 printed in alternating pairs in sheets of 16.

Europa — A912

1991, Apr. **Litho.** ***Perf. 12½***
3286 A912 12fo Ulysses probe 1.50 75
3287 A912 30fo Cassini-Huygens probe 3.90 1.95

Budapest Zoological and Botanical Gardens, 125th Anniv. — A913

1991, May 15 ***Perf. 13½x13***
3288 A913 7fo Gorilla 90 45
3289 A913 12fo Rhinoceros 1.50 75
3290 A913 12fo Toucan 1.50 75
3291 A913 12fo Polar bear 1.50 75
3292 A913 20fo Orchid 2.50 1.25
Nos. 3288-3292 (5) 7.90 3.95

Count Pal Teleki (1879-1941), Politician — A914

1991, May 24 **Litho.** ***Perf. 12***
3293 A914 12fo multi 1.50 75

44th World Fencing Championships, Budapest — A915

1991, June 13 ***Perf. 13x13½***
3294 A915 12fo multicolored 1.50 75

Images of the Virgin and Child in Hungarian Shrines — A916

Designs: 7fo, Mariapocs. No. 3296, Mariagyud. No. 3297, Celldomolk. No. 3298, Mariaremete. 20fo, Esztergom.

1991, June 17 ***Perf. 12½***
3295 A916 7fo multicolored 90 45
3296 A916 12fo multicolored 1.50 75
3297 A916 12fo multicolored 1.50 75
3298 A916 12fo multicolored 1.50 75
3299 A916 20fo multicolored 2.50 1.25
Nos. 3295-3299 (5) 7.90 3.95

Compare with design A927.

Souvenir Sheet

Visit of Pope John Paul II, Aug. 16-20, 1991 — A917

Litho. & Engr.
1991, July 15 ***Perf. 12***
3300 A917 50fo multicolored 6.25 3.15

Karoly Marko (1791-1860), Painter — A918

1991, June 17 ***Perf. 12***
3301 A918 12fo multicolored 1.50 75

Basketball, Cent. — A919

1991, June 27 **Litho.** ***Perf. 12***
3302 A919 10fo multicolored 1.25 62

Otto Lilienthal's First Glider Flight, Cent. — A920

Aircraft of aviation pioneers.

1991, June 27
3303 A920 7fo Otto Lilienthal 90 45
3304 A920 12fo Wright Brothers 1.50 75
3305 A920 20fo Alberto Santos-Dumont 2.50 2.50
3306 A920 30fo Aladar Zselyi 3.75 1.88

3rd Intl. Hungarian Philological Congress A921

1991, Aug. 12 **Litho.** ***Perf. 13½x13***
3307 A921 12fo multicolored 1.50 75

Count Istvan Szechenyi (1791-1860), Founder of Academy of Sciences — A922

1991, Sept. 6 **Engr.** ***Perf. 12***
3308 A922 12fo dk red 1.00 50

Wolfgang Amadeus Mozart (1756-1791) A923

1991, Sept. 6 **Litho.**
3309 A923 12fo As child 1.00 50
3310 A923 20fo As adult 1.65 82

Souvenir Sheet
3311 A923 30fo +15fo, in red coat 3.75 1.85

Stamp Day. No. 3311 contains one 30x40mm stamp.

Telecom '91 A924

1991, Sept. 30 Litho. *Perf. 12*

3312 A924 12fo multicolored 1.00 50

6th World Forum and Exposition on Telecommunications, Geneva, Switzerland.

Sovereign Order of the Knights of Malta — A925

1991, Oct. 30 Litho. *Perf. 13½x13*

3313 A925 12fo multicolored 1.00 50

Early Explorers and Discovery of America, 500th Anniv. (in 1992) — A926

Explorers, territory explored: 7fo, Sebastian Cabot, Labrador Peninsula, Nova Scotia. No. 3315, Amerigo Vespucci, South American region. No. 3316, Hernando Cortez, Mexico. 15fo, Ferdinand Magellan, Straits of Magellan. 20fo, Francisco Pizarro, Peru, Andes Mountain region.30fo, Christopher Columbus and coat of arms.

1991, Oct. 30 *Perf. 12*

3314 A926 7fo multicolored 58 30
3315 A926 12fo multicolored 1.00 50
3316 A926 12fo multicolored 1.00 50
3317 A926 15fo multicolored 1.25 65
3318 A926 20fo multicolored 1.65 82
Nos. 3314-3318 (5) 5.48 2.77

Souvenir Sheet

3319 A926 30fo multicolored 2.50 1.25

No. 3319 contains one 26x37mm stamp.

No. 3021A Overprinted in Brown

1991, Oct. 22 Litho. *Perf. 12x11½*

3320 A816 12fo on #3021A 1.00 50

Anniversary of Hungarian revolution, 1956.

Christmas — A927

Images of the Virgin and Child from: 7fo, Mariapocs. 12fo, Mariaremete.

1991, Nov. 20 *Perf. 13½x13*

3322 A927 7fo multicolored 58 30
3323 A927 12fo multicolored 1.00 50

Nos. 3322-3323 issued in sheets of 20 plus 20 labels.

Fight for Human Rights — A928

1991, Nov. 20 *Perf. 12*

3324 A928 12fo multicolored 1.00 50

1992 Winter Olympics, Albertville — A929

1991, Dec. 6 *Perf. 13½x13*

3325 A929 7fo Cross-country skiing 58 30
3326 A929 12fo Slalom skiing 1.00 50
3327 A929 15fo Four-man bobsled 1.25 65
3328 A929 20fo Ski jump 1.65 82
3329 A929 30fo Hockey 2.50 1.25
Nos. 3325-3329 (5) 6.98 3.52

Souvenir Sheet

Perf. 12½x11½

3330 A929 30fo Pairs figure skating 2.50 1.25

Souvenir Sheet

First Hungarian Postage Stamp, 120th Anniv. — A930

1991, Dec. 20 Litho. *Perf. 12x12½*

3331 A930 50fo No. 6 4.25 2.10

Piarist Order in Hungary, 350th Anniv. — A931

1992, Jan. 22 *Perf. 13½x13*

3332 A931 10fo multicolored 85 42

World Heritage Village of Holloko A932

1992, Jan. 22 *Perf. 12*

3333 A932 15fo multicolored 1.25 65

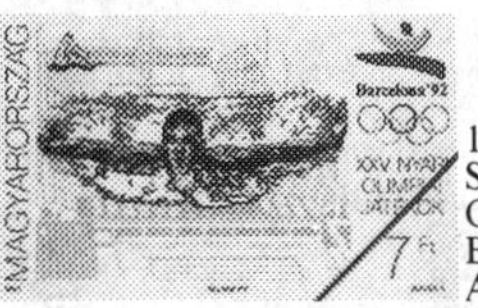

1992 Summer Olympics, Barcelona A933

1992, Feb. 26 Litho. *Perf. 13½x13*

3334 A933 7fo Swimming 58 30
3335 A933 9fo Cycling 75 38
3336 A933 10fo Gymnastics 85 42
3337 A933 15fo Running 1.25 65

Discovery of America, 500th Anniv. — A934

Designs: No. 3338, Map shaped as Indian, Columbus' fleet. No. 3339, Face-shaped map of ocean, sailing ship. No. 3340, Map shaped as European face, ship. No. 3341, Map, square, protractor, compass.

1992, Mar. 27 Litho. *Perf. 12*

3338 A934 10fo multicolored 85 42
3339 A934 10fo multicolored 85 42
3340 A934 15fo multicolored 1.25 65
3341 A934 15fo multicolored 1.25 65

Expo '92, Seville.

Jozsef Cardinal Mindszenty (1892-1975), Leader of Hungarian Catholic Church — A935

1992, Mar. 27 *Perf. 12½x11½*

3342 A935 15fo red, brn & buff 1.25 65

Comenius (Jan Amos Komensky), Writer, 400th Birth Anniv. — A936

1992, Mar. 27 *Perf. 13½x13*

3343 A936 15fo multicolored 1.25 65

SEMI-POSTAL STAMPS

Issues of the Monarchy

"Turul" and St. Stephen's Crown — SP1

Franz Josef I Wearing Hungarian Crown — SP2

Wmk. Double Cross (137)

1913, Nov. 20 Typo. *Perf. 14*

B1 SP1 1f slate 28 28
B2 SP1 2f ol yel 15 15
B3 SP1 3f orange 15 15
B4 SP1 5f emerald 15 15
B5 SP1 6f ol grn 28 22
B6 SP1 10f carmine 15 15
B7 SP1 12f vio, *yel* 52 42
B8 SP1 16f gray grn 22 15
B9 SP1 20f dk brn 1.40 90
B10 SP1 25f ultra 32 15
B11 SP1 30f org brn 52 22
B12 SP1 35f red vio 32 15
B13 SP1 50f lake, *bl* 2.75 1.25
B14 SP1 60f grn, *sal* 4.00 70
B15 SP2 1k dl red 11.50 5.25
B16 SP2 2k dl bl 35.00 24.00
B17 SP2 5k vio brn 9.25 9.25
Nos. B1-B17 (17) 66.96 43.54

Nos. B1-B17 were sold at an advance of 2f over face value, as indicated by the label at bottom. The surtax was to aid flood victims.

For overprints see Nos. 5NB1-5NB10, 6NB1-6NB11.

Semi-Postal Stamps of 1913 Surcharged in Red, Green or Brown:

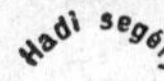

Hadi segély

Özvegyeknek és árváknak két (2) fillér

a

Özvegyeknek és árváknak két (2) fillér

b

1914

B18	SP1(a)	1f slate	24	18
B19	SP1(a)	2f ol yel	22	15
B20	SP1(a)	3f orange	22	15
B21	SP1(a)	5f emerald	15	15
B22	SP1(a)	6f ol grn	30	15
B23	SP1(a)	10f car (G)	15	15
B24	SP1(a)	12f vio, *yel*	18	15
B25	SP1(a)	16f gray grn	15	15
B26	SP1(a)	20f dk brn	22	15
B27	SP1(a)	25f ultra	48	22
B28	SP1(a)	30f org brn	60	22
B29	SP1(a)	35f red vio	1.65	75
B30	SP1(a)	50f lake, *bl*	1.25	45
B31	SP1(a)	60f grn, *sal*	3.75	75
B32	SP2(b)	1k dl red (Br)	32.50	18.00
B33	SP2(b)	2k dl bl	13.50	9.00
B34	SP2(b)	5k vio brn	8.50	6.75
		Nos. B18-B34 (17)	64.06	37.52

Regular Issue of 1913 Surcharged in Red or Green:

és árváknak Özvegyeknek Hadi segély két (2) fillér

c

Hadi segély Özvegyeknek és árváknak két (2) fillér

d

1915, Jan. 1

B35	A4(c)	1f slate	15	15
B36	A4(c)	2f ol yel	15	15
B37	A4(c)	3f orange	15	15
B38	A4(c)	5f emerald	15	15
B39	A4(c)	6f ol grn	15	15
B40	A4(c)	10f car (G)	15	15
B41	A4(c)	12f vio, *yel*	15	15
B42	A4(c)	16f gray grn	24	24
B43	A4(c)	20f dk brn	28	28
B44	A4(c)	25f ultra	15	15
B45	A4(c)	30f org brn	15	15
B46	A4(c)	35f red vio	15	15
B47	A4(c)	50f lake, *bl*	18	18
B48	A4(c)	60f grn, *sal*	35	28
B49	A5(d)	1k dl red	45	45
B50	A5(d)	2k dl bl	1.50	1.50
B51	A5(d)	5k vio brn	6.25	6.25

Surcharged as Type "c" but in Smaller Letters

B52	A4	60f grn, *sal*	1.25	1.00
		Nos. B35-B52 (18)	12.00	11.68

Nos. B18-B52 were sold at an advance of 2f over face value. The surtax to aid war widows and orphans.

Soldiers Fighting
SP3 SP4

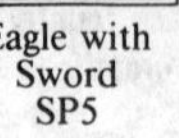

Eagle with Sword
SP5

Harvesting
SP6

1916-17 *Perf. 15*

B53	SP3	10f + 2f rose red	15	15
B54	SP4	15f + 2f dl vio	15	15
B55	SP5	40f + 2f brn car ('17)	18	18
		Set value	38	38

For overprints and surcharge see Nos. B58-B60, 1NB1-1NB3, 2NB1-2NB6, 4NJ1, 5NB11-5NB13, 6NB13-6NB15, 7NB2-7NB3, 9NB1, 10NB1-10NB4, Szeged B1-B4.

1917, Sept. 15

Surcharge in Red

B56	SP6	10f + 1k rose	25	25
B57	SP6	15f + 1k vio	25	25

Nos. B56 and B57 were issued in connection with the War Exhibition of Archduke Josef.

Issues of the Republic

Semi-Postal Stamps of 1916-17 Overprinted in Black

1918

B58	SP3	10f + 2f rose red	15	15
B59	SP4	15f + 2f dl vio	15	15
B60	SP5	40f + 2f brn car	15	15
		Set value	30	30

Nos. B58-B60 exist with inverted overprint.

Postally used copies of Nos. B69-B174 sell for more.

Issues of the Kingdom

Released Prisoner Walking Home – SP7

Prisoners of War – SP8

Homecoming of Soldier – SP9

Wmk. 137 Vert. or Horiz.

1920, Mar. 11 *Perf. 12*

B69	SP7	40f + 1k dl red	38	38
B70	SP8	60f + 2k gray brn	30	30
B71	SP9	1k + 5k dk bl	30	30

The surtax was used to help prisoners of war return home from Siberia.

Statue of Petőfi – SP10

Griffin – SP11

Sandor Petőfi – SP12

Petőfi Dying – SP13

Petőfi Addressing People – SP14

1923, Jan. 23 *Perf. 14 (10k, 40k), 12*

B72	SP10	10k sl grn	28	28
B73	SP11	15k dl bl	1.25	1.25
B74	SP12	25k gray brn	28	28
B75	SP13	40k brn vio	1.25	1.25
B76	SP14	50k vio brn	1.25	1.25
		Nos. B72-B76 (5)	4.31	4.31

Birth centenary of the Hungarian poet Sandor Petőfi. The stamps were on sale at double face value, for a limited time and in restricted quantities, after which the remainders were given to a charitable organization.

Child with Symbols of Peace – SP15

Mother and Infant – SP16

Instruction in Archery – SP17

Wmk. 133

1924, Apr. 8 **Engr.** *Perf. 12*

B77	SP15	300k dk bl	1.40	1.40
a.		Perf. 11½	10.00	10.00
B78	SP16	500k blk brn	1.40	1.40
B79	SP17	1000k blk grn	1.40	1.40

Each stamp has on the back an inscription stating that it was sold at a premium of 100 per cent over the face value.

Parade of Athletes – SP18

Skiing – SP19

Skating – SP20

Diving – SP21

Fencing
SP22

Scouts Camping
SP23

Soccer
SP24

Hurdling
SP25

Perf. 12, 12½ and Compound

1925 **Typo.** **Unwmk.**

B80	SP18	100k bl grn & brn	1.25	1.25
B81	SP19	200k lt brn & myr grn	2.00	2.00
B82	SP20	300k dk bl	2.50	2.50
B83	SP21	400k dp bl & dp grn	3.00	3.00
B84	SP22	500k pur brn	4.00	4.00
B85	SP23	1000k red brn	5.00	5.00
B86	SP24	2000k brn vio	6.00	6.00
B87	SP25	2500k ol brn	7.25	7.25
		Nos. B80-B87 (8)	31.00	31.00

These stamps were sold at double face value, plus a premium of 10 per cent on orders sent by mail. They did not serve any postal need and were issued solely to raise funds to aid athletic associations. An inscription regarding the 100 per cent premium is printed on the back of each stamp. Exist imperf.

St. Emerich
SP26

Sts. Stephen and Gisela
SP27

St. Ladislaus
SP28

Sts. Gerhardt and Emerich
SP29

1930, May 15 **Wmk. 210** *Perf. 14*

B88	SP26	8f + 2f dp grn	65	52
B89	SP27	16f + 4f brt vio	70	80
B90	SP28	20f + 4f dp rose	2.25	2.75
B91	SP29	32f + 8f ultra	3.25	4.00

900th anniv. of the death of St. Emerich, son of Stephen I, king, saint and martyr.

St. Ladislaus
SP30

Holy Sacrament
SP31

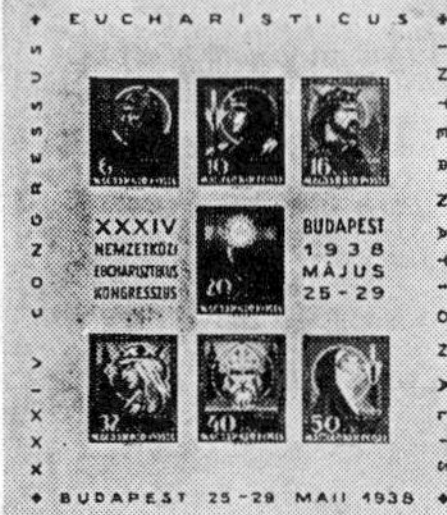

SP32

1938 May 16 Photo. *Perf. 12*

B92 SP30 16f + 16f dl sl bl		2.25	2.50
B93 SP31 20f + 20f dk car		2.25	2.50

Souvenir Sheet

B94 SP32	Sheet of seven	14.00	15.00
a.	6f + 6f St. Stephen	1.10	1.10
b.	10f + 10f St. Emerich	1.10	1.10
c.	16f + 16f slate blue (B92)	1.10	1.10
d.	20f + 20f dark car (B93)	1.10	1.10
e.	32f + 32f St. Elizabeth	1.10	1.10
f.	40f + 40f St. Maurice	1.10	1.10
g.	50f + 50f St. Margaret	1.10	1.10

Printed in sheets measuring 136½x155mm. Nos. B94c and B94d are slightly smaller than B92 and B93.

Issued in commemoration of the Eucharistic Congress in Budapest, May, 1938.

St. Stephen, Victorious Warrior SP33

St. Stephen, Offering Crown — SP34

SP35

1938, Aug. 12 *Perf. 12*

B95 SP33 10f + 10f vio brn		2.50	2.50
B96 SP34 20f + 20f red org		2.50	2.50

Souvenir Sheet

B97 SP35	Sheet of seven	15.00	16.00
a.	6f + 6f St. Stephen the Missionary	1.25	1.40
b.	10f + 10f vio brn (B95)	1.25	1.40
c.	16f + 16f Seated Upon Throne	1.25	1.40
d.	20f + 20f red org (B96)	1.25	1.40
e.	32f + 32f Receives Bishops and Monks	1.25	1.40
f.	40f + 40f St. Gisela, St. Stephen and St. Emerich	1.25	1.40
g.	50f + 50f St. Stephen on Bier	1.25	1.40

Death of St. Stephen, 900th anniversary.

No. B97 is on brownish paper, Nos. B95-B96 on white.

Statue Symbolizing Recovered Territories SP36

Admiral Horthy Entering Komarom — SP38

Cathedral of Kassa — SP39

Castle of Munkacs SP37

Girl Offering Flowers to Soldier — SP40

1939, Jan. 16

B98 SP36 6f + 3f myr grn	45	35
B99 SP37 10f + 5f ol grn	20	18
B100 SP38 20f + 10f dk red	20	18
B101 SP39 30f + 15f grnsh bl	85	60
B102 SP40 40f + 20f dk bl gray	85	60
Nos. B98-B102 (5)	2.55	1.91

The surtax was for the aid of "Hungary for Hungarians" patriotic movement.

Memorial Tablets SP41

Gaspar Karolyi, Translator of the Bible into Hungarian SP42

Albert Molnar de Szenci, Translator of the Psalms SP43

Prince Gabriel Bethlen — SP44

Susanna Lorantffy — SP45

Perf. 12x12½, 12½x12

1939 Photo. Wmk. 210

B103 SP41 6f + 3f grn	65	55
B104 SP42 10f + 5f claret	65	55
B105 SP43 20f + 10f cop red	75	75
B106 SP44 32f + 16f bister	1.10	1.00
B107 SP45 40f + 20f chlky bl	1.25	1.00
Nos. B103-B107 (5)	4.40	3.85

Souvenir Sheets

Perf. 12

B108 SP44 32f ol & vio brn	11.50	11.50

Imperf

B109 SP44 32f bl grn, cop red & gold	11.50	11.50

Issued to commemorate National Protestant Day. The surtax was used to erect an International Protestant Institute.

The souvenir sheets sold for 1.32p each.

Issue dates: Nos. B103-B107, Oct. 2. Nos. B108-B109, Oct. 27.

Boy Scout Flying Kite — SP47

Allegory of Flight — SP48

Archangel Gabriel from Millennium Monument, Budapest, and Planes — SP49

1940, Jan. 1 *Perf. 12½x12*

B110 SP47 6f + 6f yel grn	22	22
B111 SP48 10f + 10f choc	35	35
B112 SP49 20f + 20f cop red	80	80

The surtax was used for the Horthy National Aviation Fund.

SP50

Soldier Protecting Family from Floods — SP51

Souvenir Sheet

Wmk. 210

1940, May 6 Photo. *Perf. 12*

B113 SP50 20f + 1p dk bl grn	1.40	1.50

1940, May

B114 SP51 10f + 2f gray brn	15	15
B115 SP51 20f + 4f org red	18	18
B116 SP51 20f + 50f red brn	70	70

The surtax on Nos. B113-B116 was used to aid flood victims.

Hunyadi Coat of Arms — SP52

King Matthias — SP54

Hunyadi Castle — SP53

Equestrian Statue of King Matthias SP55

Corvin Codex — SP56

Equestrian Statue of King Matthias — SP57

1940 *Perf. 12½x12, 12x12½*

B117 SP52 6f + 3f bl grn	28	28
B118 SP53 10f + 5f gldn brn	22	22
B119 SP54 16f + 8f dk ol bis	28	28
B120 SP55 20f + 10f brick red	38	38
B121 SP56 32f + 16f dk gray	70	70
Nos. B117-B121 (5)	1.86	1.86

Souvenir Sheet

B122 SP57 20f + 1p dk bl grn & pale grn	1.50	1.50

Issued in commemoration of the 500th anniversary of the birth of King Matthias (1440-1490) at Kolozsvar, Transylvania. The surtax was used for war relief.

Issue dates: July 1, Nos. B117-B121. Nov. 7, No. B122.

Hungarian Soldier — SP58

Designs: 20f+50f, Virgin Mary and Szekley, symbolizing the return of transylvania. 32f+50f, Szekley Mother Offering Infant Son to the Fatherland.

1940, Dec. 2 Photo. *Perf. 12½x12*

B123 SP58 10f + 50f dk bl grn	50	50
B124 SP58 20f + 50f brn car	50	50
B125 SP58 32f + 50f yel brn	75	75

Issued in commemoration of the occupation of Transylvania. The surtax was for the Pro-Transylvania movement.

Symbol for Drama SP61

Symbol for Sculpture — SP62

Symbols: 16f+16f, Art. 20f+20f, Literature.

Perf. 12x12½, 12½x12

1940, Dec. 15

B126 SP61 6f + 6f dk grn	70	70
B127 SP62 10f + 10f ol bis	70	70
B128 SP62 16f + 16f dk vio	70	70
B129 SP61 20f + 20f fawn	70	70

Souvenir Sheet

1941, Jan. 5 *Imperf.*

B130	Sheet of 4	2.00	2.00
a.	SP61 6f + 6f olive brown	40	40
b.	SP62 10f + 10f henna brown	40	40
c.	SP62 16f + 16f dk blue green	40	40
d.	SP61 20f + 20f rose violet	40	40

Surtax on #B126-B130 was used for the Pension and Assistance Institution for Artists.

Winged Head of Pilot SP66

Designs: 10f+10f, Boy Scout with model plane. 20f+20f, Glider in flight. 32f+32f, Our Lady of Loreto, patroness of Hungarian pilots.

1941, Mar. 24 *Perf. 12x12½*

B131	SP66	6f + 6f grn ol	42	35
B132	SP66	10f + 10f dp cl	42	35
B133	SP66	20f + 20f org ver	42	35
B134	SP66	32f + 32f turq bl	80	80

The surtax was used to finance civilian and army pilot training through the Horthy National Aviation Fund.

Infantry SP70

Designs: 12f+18f, Heavy artillery. 20f+30f, Plane and tanks. 40f+60f, Cavalryman and cyclist.

1941, Dec. 1 Photo. Wmk. 266
Inscribed: "Honvedeink Karacsonyara 1941"

B135	SP70	8f + 12f dk green	18	18
B136	SP70	12f + 8f olive grn	18	18
B137	SP70	20f + 30f slate	22	22
B138	SP70	40f + 60f red brown	42	42

The surtax was for the benefit of the Army.

Soldier and Emblem SP74

1941, Dec. 1

B139	SP74	20f + 40f dk red	1.25	1.25

The surtax was for the soldiers' Christmas.

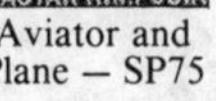
Aviator and Plane — SP75

Planes and Ghostly Band of Old Chiefs — SP76

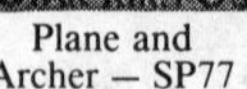
Plane and Archer — SP77

Aviators and Plane — SP78

Perf. 12½x12, 12x12½
1942, Mar. 15

B140	SP75	8f + 8f dk grn	38	38
B141	SP76	12f + 12f saph	38	38
B142	SP77	20f + 20f brn	38	38
B143	SP78	30f + 30f dk red	38	38

The surtax aided the Horthy National Aviation Fund.

Blood Transfusion — SP79

Designs: 8f+32f, Bandaging wounded soldier. 12f+50f, Radio and carrier pigeons. 20f+1p, Widows and orphans.

1942, Sept. 1 *Perf. 12½x12*

B144	SP79	3f + 18f dk ol & red	85	85
B145	SP79	8f + 32f dp brn & red	85	85
B146	SP79	12f + 50f dp cl & red	85	85
B147	SP79	20f + 1p sl bl & red	85	85

The surtax aided the Hungarian Red Cross. Sheets of 10.

Widow of Stephen Horthy — SP83

Red Cross Nurse Aiding Soldier — SP84

Magdalene Horthy Mother of Stephen Horthy — SP85

1942, Dec. 1 *Perf. 13, Imperf.*

B148	SP83	6f + 1p vio bl & red	1.75	1.75
a.		Sheet of four	20.00	20.00
B149	SP84	8f + 1p dk ol grn & red	1.75	1.75
a.		Sheet of four	20.00	20.00
B150	SP85	20f + 1p dk red brn & red	1.75	1.75
a.		Sheet of four	20.00	20.00

The surtax aided the Hungarian Red Cross.

King Ladislaus I
SP86 SP87

1942, Dec. 21 Wmk. 266 *Perf. 12*

B151	SP86	6f + 6f ol gray	35	35
B152	SP87	8f + 8f grn	35	35
B153	SP86	12f + 12f dl vio	35	35
B154	SP87	20f + 20f Prus grn	35	35
B155	SP86	24f + 24f brn	35	35
B156	SP87	30f + 30f rose car	35	35
		Nos. B151-B156 (6)	2.10	2.10

900th anniv. of the birth of St. Ladislaus (1040-95), the 700th anniv. of the beginning of the country's reconstruction by King Bela IV (1206-70) and the 600th anniv. of the accession of King Lajos the Great (1326-82).
The surtax aided war invalids and their families.

Archer on Horseback — SP92

Knight with Sword and Shield — SP93

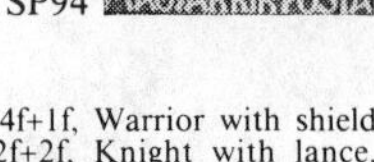
Old Magyar Arms — SP94

Designs: 3f+1f, 4f+1f, Warrior with shield and battle ax. 12f+2f, Knight with lance. 20f+2f, Musketeer. 40f+4f, Hussar. 50f+6f, Artilleryman.

1943

B157	SP92	1f + 1f dk gray	15	15
B158	SP93	3f + 1f dl vio	30	30
B159	SP93	4f + 1f lake	15	15
B160	SP93	8f + 2f grn	15	15
B161	SP92	12f + 2f bis brn	15	15
B162	SP93	20f + 2f dp claret	15	15
B163	SP92	40f + 4f gray vio	15	15
B164	SP93	50f + 6f org brn	20	15
B165	SP94	70f + 8f slate blue	20	15
		Set value	1.35	1.25

The surtax aided war invalids.

Model Glider SP101

Gliders SP102

White-tailed Sea Eagle and Planes SP103

ME-109E Fighter and Gliders SP104

1943, July 17

B166	SP101	8f + 8f green	40	40
B167	SP102	12f + 12f royal blue	40	40
B168	SP103	20f + 20f chestnut	40	40
B169	SP104	30f + 30f rose car	40	40

The surtax aided the Horthy National Aviation Fund.

Stephen Horthy SP105

1943, Aug. 16

B170	SP105	30f + 20f dp rose vio	25	25

The surtax aided the Horthy National Aviation Fund.

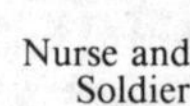

Nurse and Soldier SP106

Designs: 30f+30f, Soldier, nurse, mother and child. 50f+50f, Nurse keeping lamp alight. 70f+70f, Wounded soldier and tree shoot.

1944, Mar. 1
Cross in Red

B171	SP106	20f + 20f brown	18	18
B172	SP106	30f + 30f henna	18	18
B173	SP106	50f + 50f brn vio	18	18
B174	SP106	70f + 70f Prus bl	18	18

The surtax aided the Hungarian Red Cross.

Catalogue values for unused stamps in this section, from this point to the end of the section, are for Never Hinged items.

Issues of the Republic
Types of 1944 Surcharged in Red or Black:

a

BÉKE
3P
A NÉPFŐISKOLÁKÉRT
+9 P

b

BÉKE
4
P
A NÉP-
FŐISKOLÁKÉRT
+12P

1945, July 23 Wmk. 266 *Perf. 12*

B175	A115(a)	3p + 9p on 20f dk ol grn, *yel*	20	20
B176	A114(b)	4p + 12p on 4f yel brn, *bl* (Bk)	20	20
B177	A117(b)	8p + 24p on 50f sl bl, *yel*	20	20
B178	A115(a)	10p + 30p on 30f hn brn, *bl* (Bk)	20	20

The surtax was for the Peoples Universities. "Beke" means "peace".

Imre Sallai and Sandor Fürst — SP110

Designs: 3p+3p, L. Kabok and Illes Monus. 4p+4p, Ferenc Rozsa and Zoltan Schonerz. 6p+6p, Anna Koltai and Mrs. Paul Knurr. 10p+10p, George Sarkozi and Imre Nagy. 15p+15p, Vilmos Tartsay and Jeno Nagy. 20p+20p, Janos Kiss and Andreas Bajcsy-Zsilinszky. 40p+40p, Endre Sagvari and Otto Hoffmann.

1945, Oct. 6 **Photo.**

B179	SP110	2p + 2p yel brn	1.10	1.10
B180	SP110	3p + 3p dp red	1.10	1.10
B181	SP110	4p + 4p dk pur	1.10	1.10
B182	SP110	6p + 6p dk yel grn	1.10	1.10
B183	SP110	10p + 10p dp car	1.10	1.10
B184	SP110	15p + 15p dk sl grn	1.10	1.10
B185	SP110	20p + 20p dk brn	1.10	1.10
B186	SP110	40p + 40p dp bl	1.10	1.10
		Nos. B179-B186 (8)	8.80	8.80

The surtax was for child welfare.

Andreas Bajcsy-Zsilinszky and Eagle — SP111

1945, May 27
B187 SP111 1p + 1p dk brn vio 25 25

Issued to commemorate the 1st anniversary of the death of Andreas Bajcsy-Zsilinszky, hanged by the Nazis for anti-fascist activities.

Lion with Broken Shackles SP112

1946, May 1
B188 SP112 500ez p + 500ez p dk grn 95 95
B189 SP112 1mil p + 1mil p brn 95 95
B190 SP112 1.5mil p + 1.5mil p red 95 95
B191 SP112 2mil p + 2mil p sl bl 95 95

Issued to commemorate the 75th anniversary of Hungary's first postage stamp. The surtax was for the benefit of postal employees.

"Agriculture" Holding Wheat SP113

Physician with Syringe SP114

1946, Sept. 7 **Photo.**
B192 SP113 30f + 60f dp yel grn 3.50 3.50
B193 SP113 60f + 1.20fo rose brn 3.50 3.50
B194 SP113 1fo + 2fo dp bl 3.50 3.50

1st Agricultural Congress and Exhibition.

Perf. 12½x12
1947, May 16 **Wmk. 210**

Designs: 12f+50f, Physician examining X-ray picture. 20f+50f, Nurse and child. 60f+50f, Prisoner of war starting home.

B195 SP114 8f + 50f ultra 3.00 3.00
B196 SP114 12f + 50f choc 3.00 3.00
B197 SP114 20f + 50f dk grn 3.00 3.00
B198 SP114 60f + 50f dk red 85 85

The surtax was for charitable purposes.

Franklin D. Roosevelt and Freedom of Speech Allegory SP115

Pres. F. D. Roosevelt and Allegory: 12f+12f, Freedom of Religion. 20f+20f, Freedom from Want. 30f+30f, Freedom from Fear.

1947, June 11 Photo. ***Perf. 12x12½***
Portrait in Sepia
B198A SP115 8f + 8f dk red 2.50 2.50
B198B SP115 12f + 12f dp grn 2.50 2.50
B198C SP115 20f + 20f brn 2.50 2.50
B198D SP115 30f + 30f bl 2.50 2.50
Nos. B198A-B198D,CB1-CB1C (8) 22.00 22.00

Nos. B198A-B198D and CB1-CB1C were also printed in sheets of 4 of each denomination (size: 117x96mm). Value, set of 8, $250.

A souvenir sheet contains one each of Nos. B198A-B198D with border inscriptions and decorations in brown. Size: 161x122mm. Value $80.

Lenin SP118

XVI Century Mail Coach SP119

Designs: 60f+60f, Soviet Cenotaph, Budapest. 1fo+1fo, Joseph V. Stalin.

1947, Oct. 29 **Photo.** **Wmk. 283**
B199 SP118 40f + 40f ol grn & org brn 4.50 4.50
B200 SP118 60f + 60f red & sl bl 1.00 1.00
B201 SP118 1fo + 1fo vio & brn blk 4.50 4.50

The surtax was for the Hungarian-Soviet Cultural Association.

1947, Dec. 21 ***Perf. 12x12½***
B202 SP119 30f (+ 50f) hn brn 9.50 9.50
Sheet of 4 45.00 45.00

Issued in sheets of four stamps to commemorate Stamp Day, December 21, 1947. The surtax paid admission to a philatelic exhibition in any one of eight Hungarian towns, where the stamps were sold.

Globe and Carrier Pigeon SP120

Woman Worker SP121

1948, Oct. 17 ***Perf. 12½x12***
B203 SP120 30f (+ 1fo) grnsh bl 3.50 3.50
Sheet of 4 24.00 24.00

Issued in sheets of four stamps at the 5th National Hungarian Stamp Exhibition, Budapest. Each stamp sold for 1.30 forint, which included admission to the exhibition.

1949, Mar. 8
B204 SP121 60f + 60f mag 75 75

Issued to publicize International Woman's Day, March 8, 1949. The surtax was for the Democratic Alliance of Hungarian Women.

Aleksander S. Pushkin — SP122

SP123

1949, June 6 **Photo.**
B205 SP122 1fo + 1fo car lake 7.00 7.00

Souvenir Sheet
Perf. 12½x12, Imperf
B206 SP123 1fo + 1fo red vio & car lake 14.00 14.00

150th anniversary of the birth of Aleksander S. Pushkin. The surtax was for the Hungarian-Russian Culture Society.

Type of Regular Issue of 1951
Perf. 12½x12
1951, Oct. 6 **Engr.** **Unwmk.**
B207 A208 1fo + 1fo red 10.00 10.00
B208 A208 2fo + 2fo bl 15.00 15.00

Postwoman Delivering Mail — SP124

1953, Nov. 1 **Wmk. 106** ***Perf. 12***
B209 SP124 1fo + 1fo bl grn 1.75 1.75
B210 SP124 2fo + 2fo rose vio 1.75 1.75

Stamp Day, Nov. 1, 1953.

Stamps of 1955 Surcharged in Red or Lake

1957, Jan. 31 **Photo.** ***Perf. 12x12½***
B211 A249 20f + 20f ol grn 22 20
B212 A249 30f + 30f dk red (L) 22 25
B213 A249 40f + 40f brn 40 25
B214 A249 60f + 60f brn red (L) 60 30
B215 A249 1fo + 1fo bl 85 65
B216 A249 2fo + 2fo rose brn 1.25 1.10
Nos. B211-B216 (6) 3.54 2.75

The surtax was for the Hungarian Red Cross.

Winter Olympic Type of 1960

Design: Olympic Games emblem.

Perf. 11½x12
1960, Feb. 29 **Wmk. 106**
B217 A295 2fo + 1fo multi 1.25 50

Olympic Type of 1960

Design: 2fo+1fo, Romulus and Remus.

Perf. 11½x12
1960, Aug. 21 **Photo.** **Wmk. 106**
B218 A299 2fo + 1fo multi 95 38

Sport Club Type of 1961

Sport: 2fo+1fo, Sailboats.

1961, July 8 **Unwmk.** ***Perf. 14½***
B219 A313 2fo + 1fo multi 75 48

St. Margaret's Island and Danube SP125

Views of Budapest: No. B221, Fishermen's Bastion. No. B222, Coronation Church and Chain Bridge. No. B223, Mount Gellert.

Unwmk.
1961, Sept. 24 **Photo.** ***Perf. 12***
B220 SP125 2fo + 1fo multi 70 70
B221 SP125 2fo + 1fo multi 70 70
B222 SP125 2fo + 1fo multi 70 70
B223 SP125 2fo + 1fo multi 70 70
a. Horiz. strip of 4 3.25 3.25

Issued for Stamp Day, 1961, and to publicize the Budapest International Stamp Exhibition.

Nos. B220-B223 are printed se-tenant in sheet and show a continuous air view of Budapest. No. B223a contains one each of Nos. B220-B223.

Miniature presentation sheets, perf. and imperf., contain one each of Nos. B220-B223; size: 204x66½mm.

Soccer Type of Regular Issue, 1962

Design: Flags of Spain and Czechoslovakia.

1962, May 21 ***Perf. 11***
Flags in Original Colors
B224 A323 4fo + 1fo lt grn & bis 1.40 32

Austrian Stamp of 1850 with Pesth Postmark — SP126

Designs: No. B226, Dozsa stamp of 1919 (No. 201). No. B227, Ski stamp of 1955 (No. C164). No. B228, Butterfly stamp of 1959 (No. C208).

Lithographed and Engraved
1962, Sept. 22 **Unwmk.** ***Perf. 11***
Design and Inscription in Dark Brown
B225 SP126 2fo + 1fo yel 55 55
B226 SP126 2fo + 1fo pale pink 55 55
B227 SP126 2fo + 1fo pale bl 55 55
B228 SP126 2fo + 1fo pale yel grn 55 55
a. Horiz. strip of four, #B225-B228 2.75 2.75
b. Souv. sheet of 4, #B225-B228 6.00 6.00

Issued to commemorate the 35th Stamp Day and the 10th anniversary of Mabeosz, the Hungarian Philatelic Federation. Nos. B225-B228 are printed se-tenant in sheet.

Emblem, Cup and Soccer Ball — SP127

1962, Nov. 18 **Photo.** ***Perf. 11½x12***
B229 SP127 2fo + 1fo multi 60 50

Issued to commemorate the winning of the "Coupe de l'Europe Centrale" by the Steel Workers Sport Club (VASAS) in the Central European Soccer Championships.

Stamp Day — SP128

1963, Oct. 24 *Perf. 11½x12*
Size: 32x43mm

B230 SP128 2fo + 1fo Hyacinth 50 50
B231 SP128 2fo + 1fo Narcissus 50 50
B232 SP128 2fo + 1fo Chrysanthemum 50 50
B233 SP128 2fo + 1fo Tiger lily 50 50
a. Horiz. strip of 4, #B230-B233 3.00 3.00
b. Min. sheet of 4, #B230-B233 4.00 4.00

Nos. B230-B233 printed se-tenant. No. B233b contains four 25x32mm stamps, perf. 11.

Winter Olympic Type of 1963

Design: 4fo+1fo, Bobsledding.

1963, Nov. 11 *Perf. 12*

B234 A342 4fo + 1fo grnsh bl & bis 90 38

New Year Type of Regular Issue

Good Luck Symbols: 2.50fo+1.20fo, Horseshoe, mistletoe and clover. 3fo+1.50fo, Pigs, clover and balloon (horiz.).

Perf. 12x11½, 11½x12
1963, Dec. 12 Photo. Unwmk.
Sizes: 28x39mm (#B235); 28x22mm (#B206)

B235 A343 2.50fo + 1.20fo multi 55 25
B236 A343 3fo + 1.50fo multi 80 38

The surtax was for the modernization of the Hungarian Postal and Philatelic Museum.

Olympic Type of Regular Issue

Design: 3fo+1fo, Water polo.

1964, June 12 *Perf. 11*

B237 A352 3fo + 1fo multi 75 90

Exhibition Hall — SP129

1964, July 23 **Photo.**

B238 SP129 3fo + 1.50fo blk, red org & gray 60 35

Issued to publicize the Tennis Exhibition, Budapest Sports Museum.

Twirling Woman Gymnast SP130

1964, Sept. 4 *Perf. 11½x12*
Size: 27x38mm

B239 SP130 2fo + 1fo Lilac 45 45
B240 SP130 2fo + 1fo Mallards 45 45
B241 SP130 2fo + 1fo Gymnast 45 45
B242 SP130 2fo + 1fo Rocket & globe 45 45
a. Horiz. strip of 4, #B239-B242 2.25 2.25
b. Souv. sheet of 4, #B239-B242 3.75 3.75

37th Stamp Day and Intl. Topical Stamp Exhib., IMEX. No. B242b contains 4 20x28mm stamps, perf. 11.

13th Century Tennis SP131

History of Tennis: 40f+10f, Indoor tennis, 16th century. 60f+10f, Tennis, 18th century. 70f+30f, Tennis court and castle. 80f+40f, Tennis court, Fontainebleau (buildings). 1fo+50f, Tennis, 17th century. 1.50fo+50f, W. C. Wingfield, Wimbledon champion 1877, and Wimbledon Cup. 1.70fo+50f, Davis Cup, 1900. 2fo+1fo, Bela Kehrling (1891-1937), Hungarian champion.

Lithographed and Engraved
1965, June 15 Unwmk. *Perf. 12*

B243 SP131 30f + 10f mar, *dl org* 15 15
B244 SP131 40f + 10f blk, *pale lil* 15 15
B245 SP131 60f + 10f grn, *ol* 15 15
B246 SP131 70f + 30f lil, *brt grn* 22 15
B247 SP131 80f + 40f dk bl, *lt vio* 22 15
B248 SP131 1fo + 50f grn, *yel* 28 15
B249 SP131 1.50fo + 50f sep, *lt ol grn* 40 28
B250 SP131 1.70fo + 50f ind, *lt bl* 45 28
B251 SP131 2fo + 1fo dk red, *lt grn* 85 42
Nos. B243-B251 (9) 2.87 1.88

Flood Scene SP132

Design: 10fo+5fo, Relief commemorating 1838 flood.

1965, Aug. 14 Photo. *Perf. 12x11½*

B252 SP132 1fo + 50f org brn & bl 30 30

Souvenir Sheet

B253 SP132 10fo + 5fo gldn brn & buff 2.75 2.75

Surtax for aid to 1965 flood victims.

Geranium Stamp of 1950 (No. 909) SP133

Stamp Day: No. B255, Red deer stamp of 1953 (No. C120). No. B256, Ice skater stamp of 1963 (No. 1489). No. B257, Gagarin stamp of 1961 (No. 1382).

Perf. 12x11½
1965, Oct. 30 Photo. Unwmk.
Stamps in Original Colors

B254 SP133 2fo + 1fo gray & dk bl 65 65
B255 SP133 2fo + 1fo gray & red 65 65
B256 SP133 2fo + 1fo gray & ocher 65 65
B257 SP133 2fo + 1fo gray & vio 65 65
a. Horiz. strip of 4, #B254-B257 3.00 3.00
b. Souv. sheet of 4, #B254-B257 3.75 3.75

Nos. B254-B257 printed se-tenant. No. B254b contains 4 32x23mm stamps, perf. 11.

Soccer Type of Regular Issue

Design: 3fo+1fo, Championship emblem and map of Great Britain showing cities where matches were held.

1966, June 6 Photo. *Perf. 12x11½*

B258 A382 3fo + 1fo multi 60 50

Woman Archer and Danube at Visegrad SP134

Stamp Day: No. B260, Gloria Hungariae grapes and Lake Balaton. No. B261, Red poppies and ruins of Diosgyor Castle. No. B262, Russian space dogs Ugolek and Veterok.

1966, Sept. 16 Photo. *Perf. 12x11½*

B259 SP134 2fo + 50f multi 60 60
B260 SP134 2fo + 50f multi 60 60
B261 SP134 2fo + 50f multi 60 60
B262 SP134 2fo + 50f multi 60 60
a. Horiz. strip of 4, #B259-B262 2.75 2.75
b. Souv. sheet of 4, #B259-B262 3.25 3.25

No. B262b contains 4 29x21mm stamps, perf. 11.

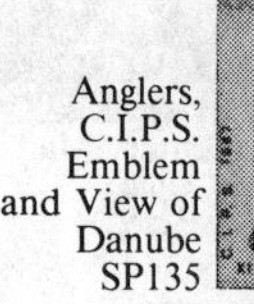

Anglers, C.I.P.S. Emblem and View of Danube SP135

1967, Aug. 22 Photo. *Perf. 12x11½*

B263 SP135 3fo + 1fo lt ultra & multi 90 45

See note after No. 1847

Olympic Type of Regular Issue

Design: 4fo+1fo, Indoor stadium and Winter Olympics emblem.

1968, Jan. 29 Photo. *Perf. 11*

B264 A402 4fo + 1fo multi 70 38

Jug, Western Hungary, 1618 — SP136

Hungarian Earthenware: No. B266, Tiszafüred vase, 1847. No. B267, Toby jug, 1848. No. B268, Decorative Baja plate, 1870. No. B269a, Jug, Northern Hungary, 1672. No. B269b, Decorative Mezöcsat plate, 1843. No. B269c, Decorative Moragy plate, 1860. No. B269d, Pitcher, Debrecen, 1793.

1968, Oct. 5 Litho. *Perf. 12*

B265 SP136 1fo + 50f ultra & multi 60 60
B266 SP136 1fo + 50f sky bl & multi 60 60
B267 SP136 1fo + 50f sep & multi 60 60
B268 SP136 1fo + 50f yel brn & multi 60 60

Miniature Sheet

B269 Sheet of 4 3.25 3.25
a. SP136 2fo + 50f ultra & multi 55 55
b. SP136 2fo + 50f yel brn & multi 55 55
c. SP136 2fo + 50f ol & multi 55 55
d. SP136 2fo + 50f brt rose & multi 55 55

Issued for 41st Stamp Day. No. B269 contains 4 25x36mm stamps. See Nos. B271-B275.

Suspension Bridge, Buda Castle and Arms of Budapest — SP137

Lithographed and Engraved
1969, May 22 *Perf. 12*

B270 SP137 5fo + 2fo sep, pale yel & gray 1.00 1.00

Budapest 71 Philatelic Exposition.

Folk Art Type of 1968

Hungarian Wood Carvings: No. B271, Stirrup cup from Okorag, 1880. No. B272, Jar with flower decorations from Felsötiszavidek, 1898. No. B273, Round jug, Somogyharsagy, 1935. No. B274, Two-legged jug, Alföld, 1740. No. B275a, Carved panel (farm couple), Csorna, 1879. No. B275b, Tankard, Okany, 1914. No. B275c, Round jar with soldiers, Sellye, 1899. No. B275d, Square box with 2 women, Lengyeltoti, 1880.

1969, Sept. 13 Litho. *Perf. 12*

B271 SP136 1fo + 50f rose cl & multi 60 60
B272 SP136 1fo + 50f dp bis & multi 60 60
B273 SP136 1fo + 50f bl & multi 60 60
B274 SP136 1fo + 50f lt bl grn & multi 60 60

Miniature Sheet

B275 Sheet of 4 3.25 3.25
a. SP136 2fo + 50f ultra & multi 60 60
b. SP136 2fo + 50f brn org & multi 60 60
c. SP136 2fo + 50f lt brn & multi 60 60
d. SP136 2fo + 50f bl grn & multi 60 60

Issued for the 42nd Stamp Day. No. B275 contains 4 stamps (size: 25x36mm).

Fishermen's Bastion, Coronation Church and Chain Bridge — SP138

Designs: No. B277, Parliament and Elizabeth Bridge. No. B278, Castle and Margaret Bridge.

1970, Mar. 7 Litho. *Perf. 12*

B276 SP138 2fo + 1fo gldn brn & multi 50 50
B277 SP138 2fo + 1fo bl & multi 50 50
B278 SP138 2fo + 1fo lt vio & multi 50 50

Budapest 71 Philatelic Exhibition, commemorating the centenary of Hungarian postage stamps.

King Matthias I Corvinus SP139

Initials and Paintings from Bibliotheca Corvina: No. B280, Letter "A." No. B281, Letter "N." No. B282, Letter "O." No. B283a, Ransanus Speaking before King Matthias. No. B283b, Scholar and letter "Q." No. B283c, Portrait of Appianus and letter "C." No. B283d, King David and letter "A."

1970, Aug. 22 Photo. *Perf. 11½x12*

B279 SP139 1fo + 50f multi 55 55
B280 SP139 1fo + 50f multi 55 55
B281 SP139 1fo + 50f multi 55 55
B282 SP139 1fo + 50f multi 55 55

Miniature Sheet

B283 Sheet of 4 3.00 3.00
a.-d. SP139 2fo + 50f, any single 55 55

Issued for the 43rd Stamp Day. No. B283 contains 4 stamps (size: 22½x32mm).

View of Buda, 1470 — SP140

Designs: No. B285, Buda, 1600. B286, Buda and Pest, about 1638. No. B287, Buda and Pest, 1770. No. B288a, Buda, 1777. No. B288b, Buda, 1850. No. B288c, Buda, 1895. No. B288d, Budapest, 1970.

1971, Feb. 26 Litho. *Perf. 12*

B284	SP140 2fo + 1fo blk & yel	60	60
B285	SP140 2fo + 1fo blk & pink	60	60
B286	SP140 2fo + 1fo blk & pale grn	60	60
B287	SP140 2fo + 1fo blk & pale sal	60	60

Souvenir Sheet

Perf. 10½

B288	Sheet of 4	3.00	3.00
a.	SP140 2fo + 1fo blk & pale sal	60	60
b.	SP140 2fo + 1fo blk & pale grn	60	60
c.	SP140 2fo + 1fo blk & lil	60	60
d.	SP140 2fo + 1fo blk & pink	60	60

Budapest 71 Intl. Stamp Exhib. for the cent. of Hungarian postage stamps, Budapest, Sept. 4-12. No. B288 contains 4 stamps (size: 39½x18mm).

Iris and No. P1 SP141

Designs: No. B290, Daisy and No. 199. No. B291, Poppy and No. 391. No. B292, Rose and No. B128. No. B293a, Carnations and No. 200. No. B292b, Dahlia and No. 1069. No. B293c, Tulips and No. C196. No. B293d, Anenomes and No. C251.

1971, Sept. 4 Photo. *Perf. 12x11½*

B289	SP141 2fo + 1fo sil & multi	70	70
B290	SP141 2fo + 1fo sil & multi	70	70
B291	SP141 2fo + 1fo sil & multi	70	70
B292	SP141 2fo + 1fo sil & multi	70	70

Souvenir Sheet

Perf. 11½

B293	Sheet of 4	3.00	3.00
a.-d.	SP141 2fo + 1fo. any single	55	55

Cent. of 1st Hungarian postage stamps and in connection with Budapest 71 Intl. Stamp Exhib., Sept. 4-12.

Miskolcz Postmark, 1818-43 SP142

Postmarks: No. B295, Szegedin, 1827-48. No. B296, Esztergom, 1848-51. No. B297, Budapest 1971 Exhibition. No. B298a, Paar family signet, 1593. No. B298b, Courier letter, 1708. No. B298c, First well-known Hungarian postmark "V. TOKAI," 1752. No. B298d, Letter, 1705.

1972, May *Perf. 12x11½*

B294	SP142 2fo + 1fo bl & blk	70	70
B295	SP142 2fo + 1fo yel & blk	70	70
B296	SP142 2fo + 1fo yel grn & blk	70	70
B297	SP142 2fo + 1fo ver & multi	70	70

Souvenir Sheet

B298	Sheet of 4	3.00	3.00
a.	SP142 2fo + 1fo yel grn & multi	60	60
b.	SP142 2fo + 1fo brn & multi	60	60
c.	SP142 2fo + 1fo ultra & multi	60	60
d.	SP142 2fo + 1fo red & multi	60	60

9th Congress of National Federation of Hungarian Philatelists (Mabeosz). No. B298 contains 4 stamps (size: 32x23mm).

Olympic Type of Regular Issue

Design: Wrestling and Olympic rings.

1972, July 15 Photo. *Perf. 11*

B299	A484 3fo + 1fo multi	55	40

Historic Mail Box, Telephone and Molnya Satellite — SP143

Design: No. B301, Post horn, Tokai postmark, and Nos. 183, 1802, 1809.

1972, Oct. 27 Litho. *Perf. 12*

B300	SP143 4fo + 2fo grn & multi	90	80
B301	SP143 4fo + 2fo bl & multi	90	80

Reopening of the Post and Philatelic Museums, Budapest.

Bird on Silver Disk, 10th Century SP144

Treasures from Hungarian Natl. Museum. No. B303, Ring with serpent's head, 11th cent. No. B304, Lovers, belt buckle, 12th cent. No. B305, Flower, belt buckle, 15th cent. No. B306a, Opal pendant, 16th cent. No. B306b, Jeweled belt buckle, 18th cent. No. B306c, Flower pin, 17th cent. No. B306d, Rosette pendant, 17th cent.

1973, Sept. 22 Litho. *Perf. 12*

B302	SP144 2fo + 50f brn & multi	65	65
B303	SP144 2fo + 50f brt rose lil & multi	65	65
B304	SP144 2fo + 50f dk bl & multi	65	65
B305	SP144 2fo + 50f grn & multi	65	65

Souvenir Sheet

B306	Sheet of 4	2.75	2.75
a.	SP144 2fo + 50f brn & multi	42	42
b.	SP144 2fo + 50f car & multi	42	42
c.	SP144 2fo + 50f ol grn & multi	42	42
d.	SP144 2fo + 50f brt bl & multi	42	42

46th Stamp Day. No. B306 contains 4 stamps (size: 25x35mm).

Gothic Wall Fountain — SP145

Visegrad Castle and Bas-reliefs — SP146

Designs: No. B308, Wellhead, Anjou period. No. B309, Twin lion-head wall fountain. B310, Fountain with Hercules riding dolphin. No. B311a, Raven panel. No. B311b, Visegrad Madonna. B311c, Lion panel. No. B311d, Visegrad Castle. Designs show artworks from Visegrad Palace of King Matthias Corvinus I, 15th century. Illustration SP146 is reduced.

1975, Sept. 13 Litho. *Perf. 12*

B307	SP145 2fo + 1fo grn & multi	2.00	2.00
B308	SP145 2fo + 1fo ver & multi	2.00	2.00
B309	SP145 2fo + 1fo bl & multi	2.00	2.00
B310	SP145 2fo + 1fo lil & multi	2.00	2.00
a.	Horizontal strip of 4	10.00	10.00

Souvenir Sheet

B311	Sheet of 4	12.00	12.00
a.	SP146 2fo + 1fo 21x32mm	1.65	1.65
b.	SP146 2fo + 1fo 47x32mm	1.65	1.65
c.	SP146 2fo + 1fo 21x32mm	1.65	1.65
d.	SP146 2fo + 1fo 99x32mm	1.65	1.65

European Architectural Heritage Year 1975 and 48th Stamp Day. Nos. B307-B310 printed se-tenant.

Knight SP147

Gothic Sculptures, Buda Castle — SP148

Designs: Gothic sculptures from Buda Castle.

1976 Photo. *Perf. 12*

B312	SP147 2.50 + 1fo shown	60	60
B313	SP147 2.50 + 1fo Armor-bearer	60	60
B314	SP147 2.50 + 1fo Apostle	60	60
B315	SP147 2.50 + 1fo Bishop	60	60
a.	Horizontal strip of 4	2.75	2.75

Souvenir Sheet

Designs: a, Man with hat. b, Woman with wimple. c, Man with cloth cap. d, Man with fur hat.

B316	Sheet of 4	3.00	3.00
a.-d.	SP148 2.50 + 1fo any single	55	55

49th Stamp Day. Nos. B312-B315 printed se-tenant.

No. B316 issued in connection with 10th Congress of National Federation of Hungarian Philatelists (Mabeosz).

Issue dates: No. B316, May 22. Nos. B312-B315, Sept. 4.

Young Runners SP149

1977, Apr. 2 Litho. *Perf. 12*

B317	SP149 3fo + 1.50fo multi	80	80

Sports promotion among young people.

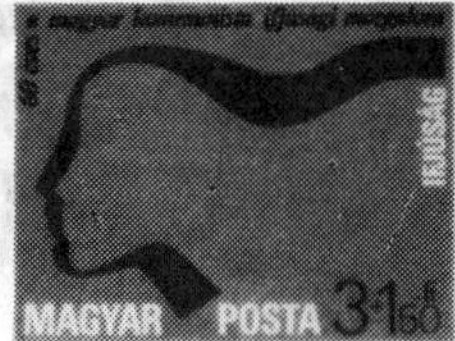

Young Man and Woman, Profiles SP150

1978, Apr. 1 Litho. *Perf. 12*

B318	SP150 3fo + 1.50fo multi	1.00	1.00

Hungarian Communist Youth Movement, 60th anniversary.

"Generations," by Gyula Derkovits SP151

1978, May 6 Litho. *Perf. 12*

B319	SP151 3fo + 1.50fo multi	1.00	1.00

Szocfilex '78, Szombathely. No. B319 printed in sheets of 3 stamps and 3 labels showing Szocfilex emblem.

Girl Reading Book, by Ferenc Kovacs — SP152

1979, Mar. 31 Litho. *Perf. 12*

B320	SP152 3fo + 1.50fo blk & ultra	50	50

Surtax was for Junior Stamp Exhibition, Bekescsaba.

Watch Symbolizing Environmental Protection SP153

1980, Apr. 3 Litho. *Perf. 12*

B321	SP153 3fo + 1.50fo multi	75	75

Surtax was for Junior Stamp Exhibition, Dunaujvaros.

Set Values

A 15-cent minimum now applies to individual stamps and sets. Where the 15-cent minimum per stamp would increase the "value" of a set beyond retail, there is a "Set Value" notation giving the retail value of the set.

International Year of the Disabled SP154

Youths and Factory SP155

1981, May 15 Litho. *Perf. 12*
B322 SP154 2fo + 1fo multi 50 50

1981, May 29 *Perf. 12x11½*
B323 SP155 4fo + 2fo multi 90 90

Young Communist League, 10th Congress, Budapest, May 29-31.

European Junior Tennis Cup, July 25-Aug. 1 — SP156

1982, Apr. 2 Litho. *Perf. 12x11½*
B324 SP156 4fo + 2fo multi 90 90

Souvenir Sheet

SP157

Perf. 12½x11½
1982, June 11 Litho.
B325 SP157 20fo + 10fo multi 4.50 4.50

PHILEXFRANCE '82 Stamp Exhibition, Paris, June 11-21.

55th Stamp Day — SP158

Budapest Architecture and Statues: No. B326, Fishermen's Bastion, Janos Hunyadi (1403-1456). No. B327, Parliament, Ferenc Rakoczi the Second (1676-1735).

1982, Sept. 10 Litho. *Perf. 12*
B326 SP158 4fo + 2fo multi 90 90
B327 SP158 4fo + 2fo shown 90 90

Souvenir Sheet

Parliament, Chain Bridge, Buda Castle, Budapest — SP159

Illustration reduced.

1982, Sept. 10 *Perf. 11½*
B328 SP159 20fo + 10fo multi 3.75 3.75

European Security and Cooperation Conference, 10th anniv.

21st Junior Stamp Exhibition, Baja, Mar. 31-Apr. 9 — SP160

1983, Mar. 31 Litho. *Perf. 12x11½*
B329 SP160 4fo + 2fo multi 1.00 1.00

Surtax was for show.

56th Natl. Stamp Day — SP161

Budapest Architecture (19th Cent. Engravings by): Rudolph Alt, H. Luders (No. B331).

1983, Sept. 9 Litho. *Perf. 12*
B330 SP161 4 + 2fo Old Natl. Theater 90 90
B331 SP161 4 + 2fo Municipal Concert Hall 90 90

Souvenir Sheet
Lithographed and Engraved
Perf. 11
B332 SP161 20 + 10fo Holy Trinity Square 4.25 4.00

No. B332 contains one stamp (28x45mm).

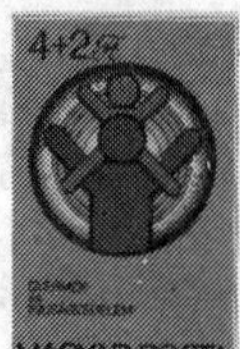

Mother and Child — SP162

1984, Apr. 2 Litho. *Perf. 12½x11½*
B333 SP162 4fo + 2fo multi 75 75

Surtax was for children's foundation.

Little Red Riding Hood, by the Brothers Grimm — SP163

1985, Apr. 2 Litho. *Perf. 11½x12*
B334 SP163 4fo + 2fo multi 75 75

Jacob (1785-1863) and Wilhelm (1786-1859) Grimm, fabulists and philologists.

Natl. SOS Children's Village Assoc., 3rd Anniv. SP164

1985, Dec. 10 Litho. *Perf. 11*
B335 SP164 4fo + 2fo multi 75 75

Surtax for natl. SOS Children's Village.

Natl. Young Pioneers Org., 40th Anniv. SP165

1986, May 30 *Perf. 11½x12½*
B336 SP165 4fo + 2fo multi 60 60

Souvenir Sheet

Budapest Natl. Theater SP166

Lithographed and Engraved
1986, Oct. 10 *Perf. 11*
B337 SP166 20fo + 10fo tan, brn & buff 4.50 4.00

Surtax benefited natl. theater construction.

Natl. Communist Youth League, 30th Anniv. — SP167

1987, Mar. 20 *Perf. 13½x13*
B338 SP167 4fo + 2fo multi 60 60

Souvenir Sheet

SOCFILEX '88, Aug. 12-21, Kecskemet — SP168

1988, Mar. 10 Litho. *Perf. 11½*
B339 SP168 20fo +10fo multi 5.50 5.00

Surtax for SOCFILEX '88.

Sky High Tree, a Tapestry by Erzsebet Szekeres SP169

1989, Apr. 12 Litho. *Perf. 12*
B340 SP169 5fo +2fo multi 1.75 1.75

Surtax to promote youth philately.

Souvenir Sheet

Battle of Solferino, by Carlo Bossoli — SP170

1989, Sept. 8 Litho. *Perf. 10½*
B341 SP170 20fo +10fo multi 7.00 7.00

Stamp Day.

Souvenir Sheet

Martyrs of Arad, Arad, Romania, 1849 — SP171

1989, Oct. 6 *Perf. 11½x12½*
B342 SP171 20fo +10fo multi 7.00 7.00

Surtax to fund production of another statue.

Teacher's Training High School, Sarospatak Municipal Arms SP172

1990, Mar. 30 Litho. *Perf. 12x11½*
B343 SP172 8fo +4fo multi 2.35 2.35

28th Youth Stamp Exhibition, Sarospatak, Apr. 6-22.

Souvenir Sheet

Yesterday, by Endre Szasz — SP173

1990, Oct. 12 Litho. *Perf. 12*

B344	SP173	20fo +10fo multi	3.75	3.75

Stamp Day. Surtax for National Federation of Hungarian Philatelists.

Tapestry, Peter and the Wolf, by Gabriella Hajnal — SP174

1991, Apr. 30 Litho. *Perf. 12*

B345	SP174	12fo +6fo multi	2.30	1.15

Surtax to promote youth philately.

AIR POST STAMPS

Issues of the Monarchy

AP1

Nos. 120, 123 Surcharged in Red or Blue

Wmk. 137

1918, July 4 Typo. *Perf. 14*

C1	AP1	1k 50f on 75f (R)	3.75	4.75
C2	AP1	4k 50f on 2k (Bl)	3.00	4.00

Counterfeits exist.

AP2

1920, Nov. 7

C3	AP2	3k on 10k (G)	1.25	1.50
C4	AP2	8k on 10k (R)	1.25	1.50
C5	AP2	12k on 10k (Bl)	1.25	1.50

Icarus — AP3

1924-25 *Perf. 14*

C6	AP3	100k red brn & red	52	52
C7	AP3	500k bl grn & yel grn	52	52
C8	AP3	1000k bis brn & brn	52	52
C9	AP3	2000k dk bl & lt bl	52	52

Wmk. 133

C10	AP3	5000k dl vio & brt vio	90	90
C11	AP3	10000k red & dl vio	1.10	1.10
		Nos. C6-C11 (6)	4.08	4.08

Issue dates: 100k-2000k, Apr. 11, 1924. Others, Apr. 20, 1925.

For surcharges see Nos. J112-J116.

Mythical "Turul" — AP4

"Turul" Carrying Messenger
AP5 AP6

1927-30 Engr. *Perf. 14*

C12	AP4	4f org ('30)	32	15
C13	AP4	12f dp grn	32	15
C14	AP4	16f red brn	32	18
C15	AP4	20f carmine	32	24
C16	AP4	32f brn vio	1.75	1.00
C17	AP4	40f dp ultra	1.75	24
C18	AP5	50f claret	1.75	75
C19	AP5	72f ol grn	1.75	52
C20	AP5	80f dp vio	1.75	60
C21	AP5	1p emer ('30)	2.75	60
C22	AP5	2p red ('30)	4.50	2.00
C23	AP5	5p dk bl ('30)	8.75	8.75
		Nos. C12-C23 (12)	26.03	15.18

1931, Mar. 27

Overprinted

C24	AP6	1p org (Bk)	27.50	25.00
C25	AP6	2p dl vio (G)	27.50	25.00

Monoplane over Danube Valley — AP7

Worker Welcoming Plane, Double Cross and Sun Rays — AP8

Spirit of Flight on Plane Wing — AP9

"Flight" Holding Propeller — AP10

Wmk. 210

1933, June 20 Photo. *Perf. 15*

C26	AP7	10f bl grn	1.00	35
C27	AP7	16f purple	1.00	55

Perf. 12½x12

C28	AP8	20f carmine	3.25	55
C29	AP8	40f blue	3.25	65
C30	AP9	48f gray blk	5.00	1.40
C31	AP9	72f bis brn	6.00	3.50
C32	AP10	1p yel grn	9.50	2.50
C33	AP10	2p vio brn	25.00	9.00
C34	AP10	5p dk gray	87.50	70.00
		Nos. C26-C34 (9)	141.50	88.50

Fokker F VII over Mail Coach — AP11

Plane over Parliament AP12

Airplane AP13

1936, May 8 *Perf. 12x12½*

C35	AP11	10f brt grn	28	16
C36	AP11	20f crimson	32	20
C37	AP11	36f brown	48	25
C38	AP12	40f brt bl	48	25
C39	AP12	52f red org	1.25	95
C40	AP12	60f brt vio	8.25	95
C41	AP12	80f dk sl grn	1.65	1.10
C42	AP13	1p dk yel grn	1.75	50
C43	AP13	2p brn car	3.75	1.65
C44	AP13	5p dk bl	12.50	9.25
		Nos. C35-C44 (10)	30.71	15.26

Catalogue values for unused stamps in this section, from this point to the end of the section, are for Never Hinged items.

Issues of the Republic

Loyalty Tower, Sopron — AP14

Designs: 20f, Cathedral of Esztergom. 50f, Liberty Bridge, Budapest. 70f, Palace Hotel, Lillafüred. 1fo, Vajdahunyad Castle, Budapest. 1.40fo, Visegrad Fortress on the Danube. 3fo, Lake Balaton. 5fo, Parliament Building, Budapest.

Perf. 12½x12

1947, Mar. 5 Photo. Wmk. 210

C45	AP14	10f rose lake	1.00	24
C46	AP14	20f gray grn	32	16
C47	AP14	50f cop brn	40	16
C48	AP14	70f ol grn	40	20
C49	AP14	1fo gray bl	75	24
C50	AP14	1.40fo brown	90	40
C51	AP14	3fo green	1.90	24
C52	AP14	5fo rose vio	4.00	1.65
		Nos. C45-C52 (8)	9.67	3.29

Johannes Gutenberg and Printing Press AP22

Designs: 2f, Columbus. 4f, Robert Fulton. 5f, George Stephenson. 6f, David Schwarz and Ferdinand von Zeppelin. 8f, Thomas A. Edison. 10f, Louis Bleriot. 12f, Roald Amundsen. 30f, Kalman Kando. 40f, Alexander S. Popov.

Perf. 12x12½

1948, May 15 Wmk. 283

C53	AP22	1f org red	15	15
C54	AP22	2f dp mag	15	15
C55	AP22	4f blue	15	15
C56	AP22	5f org brn	20	20
C57	AP22	6f green	20	20
C58	AP22	8f dp red vio	20	20
C59	AP22	10f brown	25	25
C60	AP22	12f bl grn	30	30
C61	AP22	30f brn rose	85	85
C62	AP22	40f bl vio	1.00	1.00
		Nos. C53-C62 (10)	3.45	3.45

Explorers and inventors.

See Nos. CB3-CB12.

Plane and Symbols of the UPU — AP23

1949, Nov. 1

C63	AP23	2fo org brn	52	52
a.		Bklt. pane of 6	7.50	

75th anniv. of the UPU. See No. C81.

Chain Bridge — AP24

Symbols of Labor — AP25

1949, Nov. 20

C64	AP24	1.60fo scarlet	45	45
C65	AP24	2fo olive	52	52

Souvenir Sheet

Perf. 12½x12

C66	AP25	50fo car lake	140.00	135.00

Cent. of the opening of the Chain Bridge, Budapest.

Postman and Mail Carrying Vehicles AP26

1949, Dec. 11 *Perf. 12*

C67	AP26	50f lil gray	3.25	3.25
		Sheet of 4	19.00	19.00

Stamp Day, 1949.

Plane, Globe, Stamps and Stagecoach AP27

1950, Mar. 12 *Perf. 12x12½*

C68	AP27	2fo red brn & yel	2.50	2.50

the 20th anniv. of the establishment of the Hungarian Post Office Philatelic Museum.

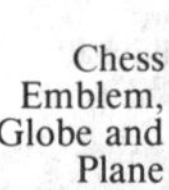

Chess Emblem, Globe and Plane AP28

1950, Apr. 9 Wmk. 106 *Perf. 12*

C69	AP28	1.60fo brown	1.75	1.00

Issued to publicize the World Chess Championship Matches, Budapest.

Globes, Parliament Building and Chain Bridge AP29

1950, May 16 ***Perf. 12x12½***
C70 AP29 1fo red brn 40 15

Issued to publicize the meeting of the World Federation of Trade Unions, Budapest, May 1950.

Statue of Liberty and View of Budapest — AP30

Designs: 30f, Crane and apartment house. 70f, Steel mill. 1fo, Stalinyec tractor. 1.60fo, Steamship. 2fo, Reaping-threshing machine. 3fo, Passenger train. 5fo, Matyas Rakosi Steel Mill, Csepel. 10fo, Budaörs Airport.

Perf. 12½x12

1950, Oct. 29 **Engr.** **Unwmk.**
C71 AP30 20f claret 48 25
C72 AP30 30f bl vio 48 20
C73 AP30 70f vio brn 25 20
C74 AP30 1fo yel brn 25 20
C75 AP30 1.60fo ultra 48 40
C76 AP30 2fo red org 52 25
C77 AP30 3fo ol blk 75 40
C78 AP30 5fo gray bl 1.50 1.20
C79 AP30 10fo chestnut 4.75 1.75
Nos. C71-C79 (9) 9.46 4.85

See Nos. C167 and C172.

Souvenir Sheet

Gen. Josef Bem and Battle at Piski — AP31

1950, Dec. 10 **Engr.** ***Imperf.***
C80 AP31 2fo dp plum 20.00 18.00

Stamp Day and Budapest Stamp Exhibition.

UPU Type of 1949

Perf. 12x12½, Imperf.

1950, July 2 **Photo.** **Wmk. 106**
C81 AP23 3fo dk car & dk brn 20.00 20.00
Sheet of 4 175.00 175.00

Volleyball AP32

Designs: 40f, Javelin-throwing. 60f, Sports badge. 70f, Soccer. 3fo, Glider meet.

1950, Dec. 2
C82 AP32 30f lil & mag 22 20
C83 AP32 40f ol & ind 45 20
C84 AP32 60f ol, dk brn & org red 80 40
C85 AP32 70f gray & dk brn 1.10 60
C86 AP32 3fo buff & dk brn 2.75 2.50
Nos. C82-C86 (5) 5.32 3.90

Mare and Foal — AP33

Designs: 70f, Sow and shoats. 1fo, Ram and ewe. 1.60fo, Cow and calf.

1951, Apr. 5 **Photo.** ***Perf. 12x12½***
C87 AP33 20f ol grn & rose brn 22 22
C88 AP33 70f red brn & ol bis 60 35
C89 AP33 1fo turq & brn 1.25 90
C90 AP33 1.60fo brn & red brn 2.00 1.40

Issued to encourage increased livestock production.

Telegraph Linemen AP34

Tank Column AP35

Designs: 1fo, Workers on vacation. 2fo, Air view of Stalin Bridge.

1951, Aug. 20
C91 AP34 70f henna brown 35 22
C92 AP34 1fo blue green 55 28
C93 AP34 2fo deep plum 1.10 45

Successful conclusion of the 1st year under Hungary's 5-year plan.

1951, Sept. 29 ***Perf. 12½x12***
C94 AP35 60f deep blue 30 20

Army Day, Sept. 29, 1951.

Souvenir Sheet

1951, Oct. 6 **Engr.** **Unwmk.**
C95 AP36 60f olive green 37.50 37.50

Stamp exhibition to commemorate the 80th anniv. of Hungary's 1st postage stamp.

Twelve hundred copies in rose lilac, perf. and imperf., were presented to exhibitors and members of the arranging committee of the exhibition. Value, each $500.

Avocet — AP37

Hungarian Birds: 30f, White stork. 40f, Golden oriole. 50f, Kentish plover. 60f, Black-winged stilt. 70f, Lesser gray shrike. 80f, Great bustard. 1fo, Redfooted falcon. 1.40fo, European bee-eater. 1.60fo, Glossy ibis. 2.50fo, Great white egret.

Perf. 13x11

1952, Mar. 16 **Photo.** **Wmk. 106**

Birds in Natural Colors

C96 AP37 20f emer, *grnsh* 16 15
C97 AP37 30f sage grn, *grysh* 16 15
C98 AP37 40f brn, *cr* 16 15
C99 AP37 50f org, *cr* 20 15
C100 AP37 60f dp car 28 16
C101 AP37 70f red org, *cr* 28 16
C102 AP37 80f olive, *cr* 38 24
C103 AP37 1fo dp bl, *bluish* 55 30
C104 AP37 1.40fo gray, *grysh* 1.25 60
C105 AP37 1.60fo org brn, *cr* 1.40 65
C106 AP37 2.50fo rose vio, *cr* 2.00 90
Nos. C96-C106 (11) 6.82 3.61

Hammer Thrower — AP38

Design: 2fo, Stadium, Budapest.

1952, May 26 ***Perf. 11***
C107 AP38 1.70fo dp red org 1.10 65
C108 AP38 2fo ol brn 1.25 95

Issued to publicize Hungary's participation in the Olympic Games, Helsinki, 1952.

Leonardo da Vinci — AP39

1952, June 15 ***Perf. 12½x12***
C109 AP39 1.60fo shown 70 60
C110 AP39 2fo Victor Hugo 80 70

Red Squirrel AP40

Hedgehog AP41

Designs: 40f, Hare. 50f, Beech marten. 60f, Otter. 70f, Red fox. 80f, Fallow deer. 1fo, Roe deer. 1.50fo, Boar. 2fo, Red deer.

1953, Mar. 4 ***Perf. 12x12½***
C111 AP40 20f yel grn & cop brn 42 18
C112 AP41 30f org brn & brn 42 18
C113 AP41 40f grn & brn blk 85 18
C114 AP40 50f lt brn & brn 55 25
C115 AP41 60f grn & brn 55 25
C116 AP41 70f ol grn & red brn 55 38
C117 AP40 80f gray grn & brn 75 45
C118 AP41 1fo yel grn & brn 90 65
C119 AP41 1.50fo ol bis & blk 1.25 1.25
C120 AP40 2fo brn org & dk brn 1.90 1.40
Nos. C111-C120 (10) 8.14 5.17

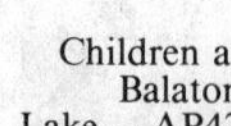

Children at Balaton Lake — AP42

Design: 1.50fo, Workers' Home at Lillafured.

1953, Apr. 19 ***Perf. 12***
C121 AP42 1fo brt grnsh bl 28 30
C122 AP42 1.50fo dp red lil 65 40

Opening of People's Stadium, Budapest — AP43

1953, Aug. 20 ***Perf. 11***
C123 AP43 80f Water polo 40 16
C124 AP43 1fo Boxing 40 20
C125 AP43 2fo Soccer 90 40
C126 AP43 3fo Track 1.50 1.00
C127 AP43 5fo Stadium 2.00 1.40
Nos. C123-C127 (5) 5.20 3.16

No. C125 Overprinted in Black

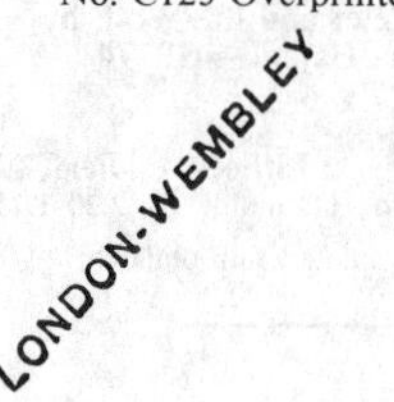

1953, Dec. 3
C128 AP43 2fo grn & brn 12.50 12.50

Issued to publicize Hungary's success in the soccer matches at Wembley, England, Nov. 25, 1953. Counterfeits exist.

Janos Bihari and Scene from Verbunkos AP44

Portraits: 40f, Ferenc Erkel. 60f, Franz Liszt. 70f, Mihaly Mosonyi. 80f, Karl Goldmark. 1fo, Bela Bartok. 2fo, Zoltan Kodaly.

1953, Dec. 5 **Photo.** ***Perf. 12***

Frames and Portraits in Brown

C129 AP44 30f bl gray 15 15
C130 AP44 40f orange 15 15
C131 AP44 60f green 15 15
C132 AP44 70f red 18 16
C133 AP44 80f gray bl 20 24
C134 AP44 1fo ol bis 52 32
C135 AP44 2fo violet 1.00 80
Nos. C129-C135 (7) 2.35 1.97

Hungarian composers.

Carrot Beetle AP45

May (or June) Beetle AP46

Designs: Various beetles. 60f, Bee.

Perf. 12½x12, 12x12½

1954, Feb. 6 Wmk. 106

C136 AP45 30f dp org & dk brn 28 18
C137 AP46 40f grn & dk brn 28 18
C138 AP46 50f rose brn & blk 52 24
C139 AP46 60f vio, dk brn & yel 28 24
C140 AP45 80f grnsh gray, pur & rose 28 24
C141 AP45 1fo ocher & blk 1.00 38
C142 AP46 1.20fo dl grn & dk brn 90 60
C143 AP46 1.50fo ol brn & dk brn 90 80
C144 AP46 2fo hn brn & dk brn 1.40 1.25
C145 AP45 3fo bl grn & dk brn 2.25 2.00
Nos. C136-C145 (10) 8.09 6.11

Lunchtime at the Nursery AP47

Designs: 1.50fo, Mother taking child from doctor. 2fo, Nurse and children.

1954, Mar. 8 ***Perf. 12***

C146 AP47 1fo ol grn 20 15
C147 AP47 1.50fo red brn 45 35
C148 AP47 2fo bl grn 90 65

Model Glider Construction — AP48

Boy Flying Model Glider AP49

Designs: 60f, Gliders. 80f, Pilot leaving plane. 1fo, Parachutists. 1.20fo, Biplane. 1.50fo, Plane over Danube. 2fo, Jet planes.

1954, June 25 ***Perf. 11***

C149 AP48 40f brn, ol & dk bl gray 15 15
C150 AP49 50f gray & red brn 15 15
C151 AP48 60f red brn & dk bl gray 15 15
C152 AP49 80f vio & sep 20 15
C153 AP48 1fo brn & dk bl gray 24 16
C154 AP49 1.20fo ol & sep 60 28
C155 AP48 1.50fo cl & dk bl gray 1.00 90
C156 AP49 2fo bl & dk brn 1.25 90
Nos. C149-C156 (8) 3.74 2.84

Souvenir Sheet

Maurus Jokai — AP50

1954, Oct. 17 Engr. ***Perf. 12½x12***

C157 AP50 1fo vio bl 15.00 15.00

Stamp Day. Exists imperforate.

Children on Sled — AP51

Skaters AP52

Designs: 50f, Ski racer. 60f, Ice yacht. 80f, Ice hockey. 1fo, Ski jumper. 1.50fo, Downhill ski racer. 2fo, Man and woman exhibition-skating.

1955 Photo. ***Perf. 12***

C158 AP51 40f multi 58 35
C159 AP52 50f multi 25 18
C160 AP51 60f multi 35 18
C161 AP52 80f multi 42 18
C162 AP51 1fo multi 70 22
C163 AP52 1.20fo multi 95 55
C164 AP51 1.50fo multi 1.65 1.10
C165 AP52 2fo multi 1.65 1.25
Nos. C158-C165 (8) 6.55 4.01

The 1.20fo and 2fo were issued Jan. 27; others Feb. 26.

Souvenir Sheet

Government Printing Plant — AP53

1955, May 28 ***Perf. 12x12½***

C166 AP53 5fo hn brn & gray grn 14.00 12.50

Cent. of the establishment of the government printing plant.

No. C78 Printed on Aluminum Foil

Perf. 12½x12

1955, Oct. 5 Engr. Unwmk.

C167 AP30 5fo gray bl 7.50 7.50

Issued to publicize the International Congress of the Light Metal Industry and to commemorate 20 years of aluminum production in Hungary. Imperfs. exist.

Bela Bartok — AP54

Wmk. 106

1955, Oct. 9 Photo. ***Perf. 12***

C168 AP54 1fo gray grn 85 85
C169 AP54 1fo vio brn 1.75 1.75
a. With ticket 12.50 12.50

Issued to commemorate the tenth anniversary of the death of Bela Bartok, composer. No. C169a was issued for the Day of the Stamp, Oct. 16, 1955. The 5fo sales price, marked on the attached ticket, was the admission fee to any one of 14 simultaneous stamp shows.

"Esperanto" AP55

Lazarus Ludwig Zamenhof — AP56

1957, June 8

C170 AP55 60f red brn 25 25
C171 AP56 1fo dk grn 30 30

10th anniversary of the death of L. L. Zamenhof, inventor of Esperanto.

Type of 1950

Design: 20fo, Budaörs Airport.

Perf. 12½x12

1957, July 18 Engr. Unwmk.

C172 AP30 20fo dk sl grn 7.00 4.50
Punched 3 holes 6.00 4.00

A few days after issuance, stocks of No. C172 were punched with three holes and used on domestic surface mail.

Courier and Fort Buda AP57

Design: No. C174, Plane over Budapest.

Wmk. 106

1957, Oct. 13 Photo. ***Perf. 12***

C173 AP57 1fo ol bis & brn, *buff* 75 75
C174 AP57 1fo ol bis & dp cl, *buff* 75 75
a. Strip of #C173-C174 + label 2.25 2.25

Printed in sheets containing 10 each of Nos. C173-C174, flanking a center label. The triptych sold for 6fo. Issued for Stamp Day, Oct. 20th.

Type of Regular Pigeon Issue

Design: 3fo, Two carrier pigeons.

1957, Dec. 14 ***Perf. 12x12½***

C175 A266 3fo red, grn, gray & blk 75 50

Hungarian Pavilion, Brussels AP58

Designs: 40f, Map, lake and local products. 60f, Parliament. 1fo, Chain Bridge, Budapest. 1.40fo, Arms of Hungary and Belgium. 2fo, Fountain, Brussels (vert.). 3fo, City Hall, Brussels (vert.). 5fo, Exposition emblem.

Perf. 14½x15

1958, Apr. 17 Litho. Wmk. 106

C176 AP58 20f red org & red brn 25 15
C177 AP58 40f lt bl & brn 25 18
C178 AP58 60f crim & sep 15 15
C179 AP58 1fo bis & red brn 20 15
C180 AP58 1.40fo dl vio & multi 30 22
C181 AP58 2fo gldn brn & dk brn 45 25
C182 AP58 3fo bl grn & sep 1.10 60
C183 AP58 5fo gray ol, blk, red, bl & yel 2.00 1.25
Nos. C176-C183 (8) 4.70 2.95

Universal and Intl. Exposition at Brussels.

View of Prague and Morse Code — AP59

1958, June 30 Photo. ***Perf. 12x12½***

C184 AP59 1fo rose brn 35 20

See No. 1194a for se-tenant pair.
Conference of Postal Ministers of Communist Countries at Prague, June 30-July 8.

Post Horn, Pigeon and Pen — AP60

Design: No. C185, Stamp under magnifying glass.

1958, Oct. 25 Wmk. 106 ***Perf. 12***

C185 AP60 1fo dp car & bis 55 55
C186 AP60 1fo yel grn & bis 55 55
a. Strip, #C185-C186 + label 1.50 1.50

Issued for the National Stamp Exhibition, Budapest, Oct. 25-Nov. 2.
#C185 inscribed: "XXXI Belyegnap 1958."

1958, Oct. 26

Designs: 60f, as No. C186. 1fo, Ship, plane, locomotive and pen surrounding letter.

C187 AP60 60f dp plum & grysh buff 30 15
C188 AP60 1fo bl & grysh buff 45 20

Issued for Letter Writing Week.

Plane over Heroes' Square Budapest — AP61

Design: 5fo, Plane over Tower of Sopron.

Perf. 12½x12

1958, Nov. 3 Engr. Wmk. 106

C189	AP61	3fo gray, rose vio & red	1.25	60
C190	AP61	5fo gray, dk bl & red	1.50	90

Issued to commemorate the 40th anniversary of Hungarian air post stamps.

Same Without Commemorative Inscription

Plane over: 20f, Szeged. 30f, Sarospatak. 70f, Gyor. 1fo, Budapest, Opera House. 1.60fo, Veszprem. 2fo, Budapest, Chain Bridge. 3fo, Sopron. 5fo, Heroes' Square, Budapest. 10fo, Budapest, Academy of Science and Parliament. 20fo, Budapest.

1958, Dec. 31 Engr. Wmk. 106
Yellow Paper and Vermilion Inscriptions

C191	AP61	20f green	15	15
C192	AP61	30f violet	15	15
C193	AP61	70f brn vio	15	15
C194	AP61	1fo blue	15	15
C195	AP61	1.60fo purple	20	15
C196	AP61	2fo Prus grn	24	15
C197	AP61	3fo brown	38	15
C198	AP61	5fo ol grn	50	20
C199	AP61	10fo dk bl	1.50	35
C200	AP61	20fo brown	3.00	90
		Nos. C191-C200 (10)	6.42	
		Set value		2.05

Transport Type of Regular Issue

Design: 3fo, Early plane.

1959, May Litho. *Perf. 14½x15*

C201	A279	3fo dl lil, blk, yel & brn	1.25	95

Tihany — AP62

Designs: 70f, Ship. 1fo, Heviz and water lily. 1.70fo, Sailboat and fisherman statue.

1959, July 15 Photo. *Perf. 11½x12*

C202	AP62	20f brt grn	15	15
C203	AP62	70f brt bl	16	15
C204	AP62	1fo ultra & car rose	24	18
C205	AP62	1.70fo red brn, *yel*	52	30

Issued to publicize Lake Balaton and the opening of the Summer University.

Moth-Butterfly Type of 1959

Butterflies: 1fo, Lycaena virgaureae. 2fo, Acherontia atropos (horiz.). 3fo, Red admiral.

Perf. 11½x12, 12x11½

1959, Nov. 20 Wmk. 106
Butterflies in Natural Colors

C206	A290	1fo blk & lt bl grn	70	24
C207	A290	2fo blk & lil	1.40	65
C208	A290	3fo dk gray & emer	2.00	1.00

Souvenir Sheet

Rockets in Orbit, Gagarin, Titov & Glenn — AP63

Perf. 11, Imperf.

1962, Mar. 29 Unwmk.

C209	AP63	10fo multi	11.00	10.00

Issued to honor astronants Yuri A. Gagarin and Gherman Titov of Russia and John H. Glenn, Jr., US.

Soccer Type of 1962

Flags of Hungary and Great Britain.

1962, May 21 Photo. *Perf. 11*
Flags in National Colors

C209A	A323	2fo grnsh & bis	70	32

Glider and Lilienthal's 1898 Design AP64

Designs: 30f, Icarus and Aero Club emblem. 60f, Light monoplane and 1912 aerobatic plane. 80f, Airship GZ-1 and Montgolfier balloon. 1fo, IL-18 Malev and Wright 1903 plane. 1.40fo, Stunt plane and Nyesterov's 1913 plane. 2fo, Helicopter and Asboth's 1929 helicopter. 3fo, Supersonic bomber and Zhukovski's turbomotor. 4fo, Space rocket and Tsiolkovsky's rocket.

1962, July 19 Unwmk. *Perf. 15*

C210	AP64	30f bl & dl yel	15	15
C211	AP64	40f yel grn & ultra	15	15
C212	AP64	60f ultra & ver	15	15
C213	AP64	80f grnsh bl & sil	15	15
C214	AP64	1fo lil, sil & bl	18	15
C215	AP64	1.40fo bl & org	18	15
C216	AP64	2fo bluish grn & brn	28	22
C217	AP64	3fo vio, sil & bl	60	28
C218	AP64	4fo grn, sil & blk	1.10	50
		Nos. C210-C218 (9)	2.94	
		Set value		1.45

Issued to show flight development: "From Icarus to the Space Rocket."

Earth, TV Screens and Rockets — AP65

Design: 2fo, Andrian G. Nikolayev, Pavel R. Popovich and rockets.

1962, Sept. 4 *Perf. 12*

C219	AP65	1fo dk bl & org brn	60	35
C220	AP65	2fo dk bl & org brn	70	55

First group space flight of Vostoks 3 and 4, Aug. 11-15, 1962. Printed in alternating horizontal rows.

John H. Glenn, Jr. — AP66

Astronauts: 40f, Yuri A. Gagarin. 60f, Gherman Titov. 1.40fo, Scott Carpenter. 1.70fo, Andrian G. Nikolayev. 2.60fo, Pavel R. Popovich. 3fo, Walter Schirra.

1962, Oct. 27 *Perf. 12x11½*
Portraits in Bister

C221	AP66	40f purple	15	15
C222	AP66	60f dk grn	15	15
C223	AP66	1fo dk bl grn	18	15
C224	AP66	1.40fo dk brn	18	15
C225	AP66	1.70fo dp bl	35	24
C226	AP66	2.60fo violet	70	35
C227	AP66	3fo red brn	1.25	60
		Nos. C221-C227 (7)	2.96	1.79

Issued to honor the first seven astronauts and in connection with the Astronautical Congress in Paris.

Eagle Owl — AP67

Birds: 40f, Osprey. 60f, Marsh harrier. 80f, Booted eagle. 1fo, African fish eagle. 2fo, Lammergeier. 3fo, Golden eagle. 4fo, Kestrel.

1962, Nov. 18 Litho. *Perf. 11½*
Birds in Natural Colors

C228	AP67	30f yel grn & blk	15	15
C229	AP67	40f org yel & blk	15	15
C230	AP67	60f bis & blk	15	15
C231	AP67	80f lt grn & blk	20	15
C232	AP67	1fo ol bis & blk	24	20
C233	AP67	2fo bluish grn & blk	35	20
C234	AP67	3fo lt vio & blk	75	38
C235	AP67	4fo dp org & blk	1.40	75
		Nos. C228-C235 (8)	3.39	2.13

Radio Mast and Albania No. 623 AP68

Designs (Communication symbols and rocket stamps of various countries): 30f, Bulgaria No. C77 (vert.). 40f, Czechoslovakia No. 1108. 50f, Communist China No. 380. 60f, North Korea. 80f, Poland No. 875. 1fo, Hungary No. 1386. 1.20fo, Mongolia No. 189 (vert.). 1.40fo, German Democratic Rep. No. 580. 1.70fo, Romania No. 1200. 2fo, Russia No. 2456 (vert.). 2.60fo, North Viet Nam.

Perf. 12x11½, 11½x12

1963, May 9 Photo. Unwmk.
Stamp Reproductions in Original Colors

C236	AP68	20f ol grn	15	15
C237	AP68	30f rose lake	15	15
C238	AP68	40f violet	15	15
C239	AP68	50f brt bl	15	15
C240	AP68	60f org brn	15	15
C241	AP68	80f ultra	15	15
C242	AP68	1fo dl red brn	20	15
C243	AP68	1.20fo aqua	20	15
C244	AP68	1.40fo olive	30	15
C245	AP68	1.70fo brn ol	30	18
C246	AP68	2fo rose lil	45	24
C247	AP68	2.60fo bluish grn	95	48
		Nos. C236-C247 (12)	3.30	
		Set value		1.65

5th Conference of Postal Ministers of Communist Countries, Budapest.

Souvenir Sheet

Globe and Spaceships — AP69

Perf. 11½x12, Imperf.

1963, July 13 Unwmk.

C248	AP69	10fo dk & lt bl	10.00	10.00

Issued to commemorate the space flights of Valeri Bykovski, June 14-19, and Valentina Tereshkova, first woman cosmonaut, June 16-19, 1963.

Souvenir Sheet

Mt. Fuji and Stadium — AP70

1964, Sept. 22 Photo. *Perf. 11½x12*

C249	AP70	10fo multi	5.50	5.00

18th Olympic Games, Tokyo, Oct. 10-24. Exists imperf.

Bridge Type of 1964 Souvenir Sheet

Design: Elizabeth Bridge.

1964, Nov. 21 Photo. *Perf. 11*

C250	A356	10fo sil & dp grn	3.75	3.50

No. C250 contains one 59x20mm stamp.

Lt. Col. Alexei Leonov in Space — AP71

Design: 2fo, Col. Pavel Belyayev, Lt. Col. Alexei Leonov and Voskhod 2.

1965, Apr. 17 Photo. *Perf. 11½x12*

C251	AP71	1fo vio & gray	48	15
C252	AP71	2fo rose cl & ocher	1.10	65

Issued to commemorate the space flight of Voskhod 2 and of Lt. Col. Alexei Leonov, the first man floating in space.

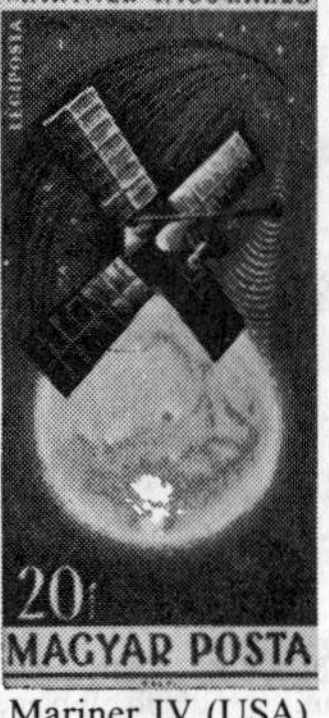

Mariner IV (USA) AP72

Plane over Helsinki AP73

New achievements in space research: 30f, San Marco satellite (Italy). 40f, Molniya satellite (USSR). 60f, Moon rocket, 1965, (USSR). 1fo, Shapir rocket (France). 2.50fo, Zond III satellite (USSR). 3fo, Syncom III satellite (USA). 10fo, Rocket sending off satellites (horiz.).

1965, Dec. 31 Photo. *Perf. 11*

C253 AP72 20f ultra, blk & org yel 15 15
C254 AP72 30f brn, vio & yel 15 15
C255 AP72 40f vio, brn & pink 15 15
C256 AP72 60f lt pur, blk & org yel 16 18
C257 AP72 1fo red lil, blk & buff 32 22
C258 AP72 2.50fo rose cl, blk & gray 80 35
C259 AP72 3fo bl grn, blk & bis 90 70
Nos. C253-C259 (7) 2.63
Set value 1.65

Souvenir Sheet

1965, Dec. 20

C260 AP72 10fo brt bl, yel & dk ol 4.50 4.00

Sport Type of Regular Issue
Souvenir Sheet

Design: 10fo, Women hurdlers and Ferihegy airport.

1966, Sept. 4 Photo. *Perf. 12x11½*

C261 A384 10fo brt bl, brn & red 4.50 4.50

1966-67 Photo. *Perf. 12x11½*

Plane over Cities Served by Hungarian Airlines: 50f, Athens. 1fo, Beirut. 1.10fo, Frankfort on the Main. 1.20fo, Cairo. 1.50fo, Copenhagen. 2fo, London. 2.50fo, Moscow. 3fo, Paris. 4fo, Prague. 5fo, Rome. 10fo, Damascus. 20fo, Budapest.

C262 AP73 20f brn org 15 15
C263 AP73 50f brown 15 15
C264 AP73 1fo blue 15 15
C265 AP73 1.10fo black 15 15
C266 AP73 1.20fo orange 15 15
C267 AP73 1.50fo bl grn 15 15
C268 AP73 2fo brt bl 24 15
C269 AP73 2.50fo brt red 20 18
C270 AP73 3fo yel grn 28 18
C271 AP73 4fo brn red 1.00 85
C272 AP73 5fo brt pur 50 24
C273 AP73 10fo vio bl ('67) 1.40 40
C274 AP73 20fo gray ol ('67) 1.25 70
Nos. C262-C274 (13) 5.77
Set value 3.00

See No. C276.

Souvenir Sheet

Icarus Falling — AP73a

1968, May 11 Photo. *Perf. 11*

C275 AP73a 10fo blk, ultra, pink & gold 3.50 3.50

Issued in memory of the astronauts Edward H. White (USA), Vladimir M. Komarov and Yuri A. Gagarin (USSR).

Type of 1966-67 without "Legiposta" Inscription

Design: 2.60fo, Malev Airlines jet over St. Stephen's Cathedral, Vienna.

1968, July 4 Photo. *Perf. 12x11½*

C276 AP73 2.60fo violet 50 18

50th anniv. of regular airmail service between Budapest and Vienna.

Women Swimmers and Aztec Calendar Stone — AP74

Aztec Calendar Stone, Olympic Rings and: 60f, Soccer. 80f, Wrestling. 1fo, Canoeing. 1.40fo, Gymnast on rings. 3fo, Fencing. 4fo, Javelin.

1968, Aug. 21 Photo. *Perf. 12*

C277 AP74 20f brt bl & multi 15 15
C278 AP74 60f grn & multi 15 15
C279 AP74 80f car rose & multi 15 15
C280 AP74 1fo grnsh bl & multi 15 15
C281 AP74 1.40fo vio & multi 24 15
C282 AP74 3fo brt lil & multi 75 35
C283 AP74 4fo grn & multi 1.10 60
Nos. C277-C283,CB31 (8) 3.07
Set value 1.70

Issued to publicize the 19th Olympic Games, Mexico City, Oct. 12-27.

Souvenir Sheet

Apollo 8 Trip Around the Moon — AP75

1969, Feb. Photo. *Perf. 12½*

C284 AP75 10fo multi 4.00 4.00

Man's 1st flight around the moon, Dec. 21-27, 1968.

Soyuz 4 and 5, and Men in Space AP76

Design: No. C286, Soyuz 4 and 5.

1969, Mar. 21 Photo. *Perf. 12x11½*

C285 AP76 2fo multi 35 35
C286 AP76 2fo dk bl, lt bl & red 35 35
a. Strip, # C285-C286 + label 85

First team flights of Russian spacecraft Soyuz 4 and 5, Jan. 16, 1969.

Nos. C285-C286 are printed with connecting label showing radar screen and astronaut; sheets of 8 contain 4 horizontal strips of Nos. C285-C286 and label.

Journey to the Moon, by Jules Verne — AP77

Designs: 60f, Tsiolkovski's space station. 1fo, Luna 1. 1.50fo, Ranger 7. 2fo, Luna 9 landing on moon. 2.50fo, Apollo 8 in orbit around moon. 3fo, Soyuz 4 and 5 docking in space. 4fo, Lunar landing module landing on moon. 10fo, Apollo 11 astronauts on moon and lunar landing module.

1969 Photo. *Perf. 12x11½*

C287 AP77 40f multi 15 15
C288 AP77 60f multi 15 15
C289 AP77 1fo multi 15 15
C290 AP77 1.50fo multi 18 15
C291 AP77 2fo multi 24 15
C292 AP77 2.50fo multi 28 24
C293 AP77 3fo multi 75 24
C294 AP77 4fo multi 1.10 60
Nos. C287-C294 (8) 3.00
Set value 1.50

Souvenir Sheet
Perf. 11

C295 AP77 10fo multi 6.50 6.50

Moon landing issue. See note after Algeria No. 427.

No. C295 contains one 74x49mm stamp. Issue dates: Nos. C287-C294, Nov. 1, No. C295, Aug. 15.

Daimler, 1886 — AP78

Automobiles: 60f, Peugeot, 1894. 1fo, Benz, 1901. 1.50fo, Cudell mail truck, 1902. 2fo, Rolls Royce, 1908. 2.50fo, Model T Ford, 1908. 3fo, Vermorel, 1912. 4fo, Csonka mail car, 1912.

1970, March Photo. *Perf. 12*

C296 AP78 40f ocher & multi 15 15
C297 AP78 60f multi 15 15
C298 AP78 1fo red & multi 15 15
C299 AP78 1.50fo bl & multi 15 15
C300 AP78 2fo multi 30 22
C301 AP78 2.50fo vio & multi 38 22
C302 AP78 3fo multi 60 42
C303 AP78 4fo multi 1.25 85
Nos. C296-C303 (8) 3.13
Set value 2.00

American Astronauts on Moon AP79

Design: No. C305, Soyuz 6, 7 and 8 in space.

1970, Mar. 20 Photo. *Perf. 11*

C304 AP79 3fo bl & multi 75 75
C305 AP79 3fo car rose & multi 75 75

Landing of Apollo 12 on the moon, Nov. 14, 1969, and group flight of Russian spacecraft Soyuz 6, 7 & 8, Oct. 11-13, 1969.

Nos. C304-C305 issued in sheets of 4. Size: 112½x78mm.

"Rain at Foot of Fujiyama," by Hokusai, and Pavilion — AP80

Design: 3fo, Sun Tower, Peace Bell and globe.

1970, Apr. 30 Photo. *Perf. 12½*

C306 AP80 2fo multi 75 75
C307 AP80 3fo multi 75 75

Issued to publicize EXPO '70 International Exhibition, Osaka, Japan, Mar. 15-Sept. 13.

Miniature Sheets

Phases of Apollo 13 Moon Flight — AP81

Designs of Vignettes of No. C308: Apollo 13 over moon; return to earth; capsule with parachutes; capsule floating, aircraft carrier and helicopter.

Designs of Vignettes of No. C309: Soyuz 9 on way to launching pad; launching of Soyuz 9 capsule in orbit; astronauts Andrian Nikolayev and Vitaly Sevastyanov.

Designs of Vignettes of No. C310: Luna 16 approaching moon; module on moon; landing; nose cone on ground.

Designs of Vignettes of No. C311: Lunokhod 1 on moon; trajectories of Luna 17 around earth and moon.

1970-71 Litho. *Perf. 11½*

C308 AP81 Sheet of 4 3.00 3.00

Photo.

C309 AP81 Sheet of 4 3.00 3.00
C310 AP81 Sheet of 4 ('71) 3.00 3.00
C311 AP81 Sheet of 4 ('71) 3.00 3.00

Nos. C308-C311 were valid for postage only as full sheets. Each contains four 2.50fo vignettes which were not valid singly.

No. C308 for the aborted moon flight and safe return of Apollo 13, American spaceship, Apr. 11-17, 1970. Issued June 10.

No. C309 for the 424-hour flight of Soyuz 9, Russian spaceship, June 1-9. Issued Sept. 4.

No. C310 for Luna 16, the unmanned, automated Russian moon mission, Sept. 12-24, 1970. Issued Jan. 15, 1971.

No. C311 for Luna 17, unmanned, automated Russian moon mission, Nov. 10-17, 1970. Issued Mar. 8, 1971.

Souvenir Sheet

American Astronauts on Moon — AP82

1971, Mar. 31 *Perf. 12½*

C312 AP82 10fo multi 3.75 3.75

Apollo 14 moon landing, Jan. 31-Feb. 9, 1971.

See Nos. C315, C326-C328.

Hunting Type of Regular Issue
Souvenir Sheet

Design: 10fo, Red deer group.

1971, Aug. 27 Photo. *Perf. 11*

C313 A460 10fo multi 3.75 3.75

No. C313 contains one 70x45mm stamp.

Astronauts Volkov, Dobrovolsky and Patsayev — AP83

Souvenir Sheet

1971, Oct. 4 Photo. *Perf. 12½*
C314 AP83 10fo multi 3.50 3.50

In memory of the Russian astronauts Vladislav N. Volkov, Lt. Col. Georgi T. Dobrovolsky and Victor I. Patsayev, who died during the Soyuz 11 space mission, June 6-30, 1971.

Apollo 14 Type of 1971
Souvenir Sheet

Design: 10fo, American Lunar Rover on moon.

1972, Jan. 20 Photo. *Perf. 12½*
C315 AP82 10fo multi 3.50 3.50

Apollo 15 moon mission, July 26-Aug. 7, 1971. Multicolored margin with Apollo 15 badge showing explorations of Lunar Rover, and names of American astronauts David Scott, Alfred Worden and James Irwin.

Soccer and Hungarian Flag — AP84

Various Scenes from Soccer and National Flags of: 60f, Romania. 80f, German Federal Republic. 1fo, Great Britain. 1.20fo, Yugoslavia. 2fo, Soviet Union. 4fo, Italy. 5fo, Belgium.

1972, Apr. 29
C316 AP84 40f gold & multi 15 15
C317 AP84 60f gold & multi 15 15
C318 AP84 80f gold & multi 15 15
C319 AP84 1fo gold & multi 15 15
C320 AP84 1.20fo gold & multi 24 15
C321 AP84 2fo gold & multi 35 18
C322 AP84 4fo gold & multi 85 45
C323 AP84 5fo gold & multi 1.25 75
a. Sheet of 8 3.75 3.75
Nos. C316-C323 (8) 3.29
Set value 1.80

European Soccer Championships for the Henri Delaunay Cup. Nos. C316-C323 printed se-tenant in sheets of 8 (2x4). Margin inscribed in black with names of event and participating countries Size: 147x197mm.

Nos. C316-C321 were later issued individually in sheets of 20 and in partly changed colors.

Souvenir Sheet

Olympic Rings and Globe — AP85

1972, June 10 Photo. *Perf. 12½*
C324 AP85 10fo multi 8.00 8.00

20th Olympic Games, Munich, Aug. 26-Sept. 11.

Olympic Type of Regular Issue
Souvenir Sheet

Design: Equestrian and Olympic Rings.

1972, July 15 Photo. *Perf. 12½*
C325 A484 10fo multi 3.75 3.75

20th Olympic Games, Munich, Aug. 26-Sept. 11. No. C325 contains one stamp (43x43mm).

Apollo 14 Type of 1971
Souvenir Sheets

Design: 10fo, Astronaut in space, Apollo 16 capsule and badge.

1972, Oct. 10 Photo. *Perf. 12½*
C326 AP82 10fo bl & multi 3.75 3.75

Apollo 16 US moon mission, Apr. 15-27, 1972.

1973, Jan. 15

Design: Astronaut exploring moon (vert.).

C327 AP82 10fo bl & multi 3.75 3.75

Apollo 17 US moon mission, Dec. 7-19, 1972. No. C327 contains one vertical stamp.

1973, Mar. 12 Photo. *Perf. 12½*
C328 AP82 10fo Venus 8 3.25 3.25

Venus 8 USSR space mission, Mar. 27-July 22, 1972.

Equestrian (Pentathlon), Olympic Rings and Medal AP86

Designs (Olympic Rings and Medals): 60f, Weight lifting. 1fo, Canoeing. 1.20fo, Swimming, women's. 1.80fo, Boxing. 4fo, Wrestling. 6fo, Fencing. 10fo, Allegorical figure lighting flame (vert.).

1973, Mar. 31
C329 AP86 40f multi 15 15
C330 AP86 60f multi 15 15
C331 AP86 1fo bl & multi 15 15
C332 AP86 1.20fo multi 18 15
C333 AP86 1.80fo multi 35 15
C334 AP86 4fo multi 75 40
C335 AP86 6fo multi 1.10 75
Nos. C329-C335 (7) 2.83
Set value 1.60

Souvenir Sheet
Perf. 11
C336 AP86 10fo bl & multi 4.50 4.50

Hungarian medalists at 20th Olympic Games. No. C336 contains one 44x71mm stamp.

Wrens — AP87

1973, Apr. 16 Litho. *Perf. 12*
C337 AP87 40f shown 15 15
C338 AP87 60f Rock thrush 15 15
C339 AP87 80f Robins 15 15
C340 AP87 1fo Firecrests 15 15
C341 AP87 1.20fo Linnets 20 15
C342 AP87 2fo Blue titmice 28 20
C343 AP87 4fo White-spotted blue throat 65 30
C344 AP87 5fo Gray wagtails 1.40 85
Nos. C337-C344 (8) 3.13
Set value 1.75

Exhibition Type of Regular Issue
Souvenir Sheet

Design: 10fo, Bavaria No. 1 with mill wheel cancellation; Munich City Hall, TV Tower and Olympic tent.

1973, May 11 Litho. *Perf. 11*
C345 A506 10fo multi 3.50 3.50

No. C345 contains one 83x45mm stamp.

Souvenir Sheet

Skylab over Earth AP88

1973, Oct. 16 Photo. *Perf. 12½*
C346 AP88 10fo dk bl, lt bl & yel 3.25 3.25

First US manned space station.

Space Type of Regular Issue

Designs: 6fo, Mars "canals" and Giovanni V. Schiaparelli. 10fo, Mars 7 spacecraft.

1974, Mar. 11 Photo. *Perf. 12½*
C347 A522 6fo gold & multi 1.10 75

Souvenir Sheet

C348 A522 10fo gold & multi 3.25 3.25

UPU Type of 1974

Designs: a, Mail coach. b, Old mail automobile. c, Jet. d, Apollo 15.

1974, May 22 Litho. *Perf. 12*
C349 A526 6fo UPU emblem and TU-154 jet 1.10 65

Souvenir Sheet

C350 Sheet of 4 3.25 3.25
a.-d. A526 2.50fo. any single 48 48

No. C350 has bister UPU emblem in center where 4 stamps meet.

Army Day Type of 1974

Designs: 2fo, Ground-to-air missiles (vert.). 3fo, Parachutist, helicopter, supersonic jets.

1974, Sept. 28 Litho. *Perf. 12*
C351 A537 2fo gold, emer & blk 24 15
C352 A537 3fo gold, bl & blk 42 18

Carrier Pigeon, Elizabeth Bridge, Mt. Gellert AP89

1975, Feb. 7 Litho. *Perf. 12*
C353 AP89 3fo multi 1.25 1.25

Carrier Pigeons' Olympics, Budapest, Feb. 7-9. No. C353 printed checkerwise with black and violet coupon showing Pigeon Olympics emblem.

Sputnik 2, Apollo-Soyuz Emblem — AP90

Spacecraft and Apollo-Soyuz Emblem: 60f, Mercury-Atlas 5. 80f, Lunokhod I on moon. 1.20fo, Lunar rover, Apollo 15 mission. 2fo, Soyuz take-off, Baikonur. 4fo, Apollo take-off, Cape Kennedy. 6fo, Apollo-Soyuz link-up. 10fo, Apollo, Soyuz, American and Russian flags over earth (horiz.).

1975, July 7 Photo. *Perf. 12x11½*
C354 AP90 40f sil & multi 15 15
C355 AP90 60f sil & multi 15 15
C356 AP90 80f sil & multi 16 15
C357 AP90 1.20fo sil & multi 20 15
C358 AP90 2fo sil & multi 25 15
C359 AP90 4fo sil & multi 50 28
C360 AP90 6fo sil & multi 1.25 55
Nos. C354-C360 (7) 2.66
Set value 1.35

Souvenir Sheet
Perf. 12½
C361 AP90 10fo bl & multi 3.50 3.50

Apollo Soyuz space test project (Russo-American cooperation), launching July 15; link-up July 17. No. C361 contains one stamp (size: 59x38mm).

Souvenir Sheet

Map of Europe and Cogwheels — AP91

1975, July 30 Litho. *Perf. 12½*
C362 AP91 10fo multi 7.00 6.50

European Security and Cooperation Conference, Helsinki, July 30-Aug. 1.

Souvenir Sheet

Hungary Nos. 1585, 1382, 2239, 2280, C81 — AP92

1975, Sept. 9 Photo. *Perf. 12½*
C363 AP92 10fo multi 3.50 3.50

30 years of stamps.

A similar souvenir sheet with blue margin, no denomination and no postal validity was released for the 25th anniversary of Filatelica Hungarica.

Souvenir Sheet

Paintings by Karoly Lotz and Janos Halapi AP93

1976, Mar. 19 Photo. *Perf. 12½*
C364 AP93 Sheet of 2 3.25 3.25
a. 5fo Horses in Storm 1.00 1.00
b. 5fo Morning at Tihany 1.00 1.00

Tourist publicity. Dark violet blue margin with view of Pest and airline emblems in gold foil. Nos. C364a and C364b se-tenant, imperf. between.

Souvenir Sheet

Montreal Olympic Stadium — AP94

1976, June 29 Litho. *Perf. 12½*

C365 AP94 20fo red, gray & blk 4.00 4.00

21st Olympic Games, Montreal, Canada, July 17-Aug. 1.

U.S. Mars Mission AP95

Designs: 60f, Viking in space. 1fo, Viking on moon. 2fo, Venus, rocket take-off. 3fo, Venyera 9 in space. 4fo, Venyera 10, separation in space. 5fo, Venyera on moon. 20fo, Viking 1 landing on Mars (vert.).

1976, Nov. 11 Photo. *Perf. 11*

C366	AP95	40f sil & multi	15	15
C367	AP95	60f sil & multi	15	15
C368	AP95	1fo sil & multi	18	15
C369	AP95	2fo sil & multi	24	18
C370	AP95	3fo sil & multi	35	20
C371	AP95	4fo sil & multi	55	28
C372	AP95	5fo sil & multi	1.00	52
		Nos. C366-C372 (7)	2.62	
		Set value		1.40

Souvenir Sheet

Perf. 12½

C373 AP95 20fo blk & multi 3.50 3.50

US-USSR space missions. No. C373 contains one stamp (size: 41x64mm).

Hungary No. CB33 — AP96

1977, Apr. Litho. *Perf. 11½x12*

C374 AP96 3fo multi 1.75 1.75

European stamp exhibitions. Issued in sheets of 3 stamps and 3 labels. Labels show exhibition emblems respectively: 125th anniversary of Brunswick stamps, Brunswick, May 5-8; Regiofil XII, Lugano, June 17-19; centenary of San Marino Stamps, Riccione, Aug. 27-29.

Space Type 1977
Souvenir Sheet

Design: 20fo, Viking on Mars.

1977, Sept. 20 Litho. *Perf. 11½*

C375 A603 20fo multi 4.00 4.00

Souvenir Sheet

"EUROPA," Map and Dove — AP97

1977, Oct. 3 *Perf. 12½*

C376 AP97 20fo multi 7.50 7.00

European Security Conference, Belgrade, Oct.-Nov.

TU-154, Malev over Europe — AP98

Planes, Airlines, Maps: 1.20fo, DC-8, Swissair, Southeast Asia. 2fo, IL-62, CSA, North Africa. 2.40fo, A 300B Airbus, Lufthansa, Northwest Europe. 4fo, Boeing 747, Pan Am, North America. 5fo, TU-144, Aeroflot, Northern Europe. 10fo, Concorde, Air France, South America. 20fo, IL-86, Aeroflot, Northeast Asia.

1977, Oct. 26 Litho. *Perf. 11½x12*

Size: 32x21mm

C377	AP98	60f org & blk	15	15
C378	AP98	1.20fo vio & blk	16	15
C379	AP98	2fo yel & blk	28	15
C380	AP98	2.40fo bl grn & blk	32	18
C381	AP98	4fo ultra & blk	55	18
C382	AP98	5fo dp rose & blk	65	25
C383	AP98	10fo bl & blk	1.40	42

Perf. 12x11½

Size: 37½x29mm

C384	AP98	20fo grn & blk	2.75	90
		Nos. C377-C384 (8)	6.26	2.38

Montgolfier Brothers and Balloon, 1783 — AP99

Designs: 60f, David Schwarz and airship, 1850. 1fo, Alberto Santos-Dumont and airship flying around Eiffel Tower, 1873. 2fo, Konstantin E. Tsiolkovsky, airship and Kremlin, 1857. 3fo, Roald Amundsen, airship Norge, Polar bears and map, 1872. 4fo, Hugo Eckener, Graf Zeppelin over Mt. Fuji, 1930. 5fo, Count Ferdinand von Zeppelin, Graf Zeppelin over Chicago, 1932. 20fo, Graf Zeppelin over Budapest, 1931.

1977, Nov. 1 Photo. *Perf. 12x11½*

C385	AP99	40f gold & multi	15	15
C386	AP99	60f gold & multi	15	15
C387	AP99	1fo gold & multi	15	15
C388	AP99	2fo gold & multi	30	18
C389	AP99	3fo gold & multi	45	28
C390	AP99	4fo gold & multi	60	35
C391	AP99	5fo gold & multi	1.10	60
		Nos. C385-C391 (7)	2.90	
		Set value		1.60

Souvenir Sheet

Perf. 12½

C392 AP99 20fo sil & multi 4.00 4.00

History of airships. No. C392 contains one 60x36mm stamp.

Moon Station — AP100

Science Fiction Paintings by Pal Varga: 60f, Moon settlement. 1fo, Spaceship near Phobos. 2fo, Exploration of asteroids. 3fo, Spaceship in gravitational field of Mars. 4fo, Spaceship and rings of Saturn. 5fo, Spaceship landing on 3rd Jupiter moon.

1978, Mar. 10 Litho. *Perf. 11*

C393	AP100	40f multi	15	15
C394	AP100	60f multi	15	15
C395	AP100	1fo multi	15	15
C396	AP100	2fo multi	30	18
C397	AP100	3fo multi	45	28
C398	AP100	4fo multi	60	35
C399	AP100	5fo multi	85	45
		Nos. C393-C399 (7)	2.65	
		Set value		1.48

Louis Bleriot and La Manche AP101

Designs: 60f, J. Alcock and R. W. Brown, Vickers Vimy, 1919. 1fo, A. C. Read and Navy Curtiss NC-4, 1919. 2fo, H. Kohl, G. Hünefeld, J. Fitzmaurice, Junkers W33, 1928. 3fo, A. Johnson, J. Mollison, Gipsy Moth, 1930. 4fo, G. Endresz, S. Magyar, Lockheed Sirius, 1931. 5fo, W. Gronau, Dornier WAL, 1932. 20fo, Wilbur and Orville Wright and their plane.

1978, May 10 Litho. *Perf. 12*

C400	AP101	40f multi	15	15
C401	AP101	60f multi	15	15
C402	AP101	1fo multi	15	15
C403	AP101	2fo multi	30	18
C404	AP101	3fo multi	45	28
C405	AP101	4fo multi	60	35
C406	AP101	5fo multi	95	50
		Nos. C400-C406 (7)	2.75	
		Set value		1.50

Souvenir Sheet

C407 AP101 20fo multi 3.50 3.50

75th anniversary of first powered flight by Wright brothers. No. C407 contains one stamp (75x25mm).

Souvenir Sheet

Jules Verne and "Voyage from Earth to Moon" — AP102

1978, Aug. 21 *Perf. 12½x11½*

C408 AP102 20fo multi 3.50 3.50

Jules Verne (1828-1905), French science fiction writer.

Vladimir Remek Postmarking Mail on Board Salyut 6 — AP103

1978, Sept. 1 Photo. *Perf. 11½x12*

C409 AP103 3fo multi 80 80

PRAGA '78 International Philatelic Exhibition, Prague, Sept. 8-17. Issued in sheets of 3 stamps and 3 labels, showing PRAGA '78 emblem and Golden Tower, Prague. FISA emblems in margin.

Ski Jump — AP104

Lake Placid '80 Emblem and: 60f, 20fo, Figure skating (diff.). 1fo, Downhill skiing. 2fo, Ice hockey. 4fo, Bobsledding. 6fo, Cross-country skiing.

1979, Dec. 15 Litho. *Perf. 12*

C410	AP104	40f multi	15	15
C411	AP104	60f multi	15	15
C412	AP104	1fo multi	18	15
C413	AP104	2fo multi	35	18
C414	AP104	4fo multi	70	35
C415	AP104	6fo multi	1.10	60
		Nos. C410-C415 (6)	2.63	
		Set value		1.32

Souvenir Sheet

C416 AP104 20fo multi 3.00 3.00

13th Winter Olympic Games, Lake Placid, N.Y., Feb. 12-24, 1980.

Soviet and Hungarian Cosmonauts AP105

1980, May 27 Litho. *Perf. 11½x12*

C417 AP105 5fo multi 75 40

Intercosmos cooperative space program.

Women's Handball, Moscow '80 Emblem, Olympic Rings — AP106

1980, June 16 Photo. *Perf. 11½x12*

C418	AP106	40f shown	15	15
C419	AP106	60f Double kayak	15	15
C420	AP106	1fo Running	15	15
C421	AP106	2fo Gymnast	28	20
C422	AP106	3fo Equestrian	42	28

C423 AP106	4fo Wrestling	60	38
C424 AP106	5fo Water polo	75	60
	Nos. C418-C424 (7)	2.50	1.91

Souvenir Sheet

C425 AP106	20fo Torch bearers	3.25	3.25

22nd Summer Olympic Games, Moscow, July 19-Aug. 3.
See No. C427

Souvenir Sheet

Cosmonauts Bertalan Farkes and Valery Kubasov, Salyut 6-Soyuz 35 and 36 — AP107

1980, July 12 **Litho.** ***Perf. 12½***

C426 AP107	20fo multi	3.25	3.25

Intercosmos cooperative space program (USSR-Hungary).

Olympic Type of 1980
Souvenir Sheet

1980, Sept. 26 **Litho.** ***Perf. 12½***

C427 AP106	20fo Greek Frieze and gold medal	3.25	3.25

Olympic Champions.

AP108

1981, Mar. 6 **Photo.** ***Perf. 11½***

C427A AP108	40f Cheetah	15	15
C427B AP108	60f Lion	15	15
C427C AP108	1fo Leopard	20	15
C427D AP108	2fo Rhinoceros	38	20
C427E AP108	3fo Antelope	60	28
C427F AP108	4fo African elephant	75	38
C427G AP108	5fo shown	95	48
	Nos. C427A-C427G (7)	3.18	
	Set value		1.50

Kalman Kittenberger (1881-1958), zoologist and explorer, birth centenary.

Graf Zeppelin over Tokyo, First Worldwide Flight, Aug. 7-Sept. 4, 1929 — AP109

Graf Zeppelin Flights (Zeppelin and): 2fo, Icebreaker Malygin, Polar flight, July 24-31, 1931. 3fo, Nine Arch Bridge, Hortobagy, Hungary, Mar. 28-30, 1931. 4fo, Holsten Tor, Lubeck, Baltic Sea, May 12-15, 1931. 5fo, Tower Bridge, England, Aug. 18-20, 1931. 6fo, Federal Palace, Chicago World's Fair, 50th crossing of Atlantic, Oct. 14-Nov. 2, 1933. 7fo, Lucerne, first flight across Switzerland, Sept. 26, 1929.

Perf. 12½x11½

1981, Mar. 16 **Litho.**

C428 AP109	1fo multi	15	15
C429 AP109	2fo multi	28	20
C430 AP109	3fo multi	42	28
C431 AP109	4fo multi	60	38
C432 AP109	5fo multi	75	45
C433 AP109	6fo multi	85	60
C434 AP109	7fo multi	95	65
	Nos. C428-C434 (7)	4.00	2.71

LURABA '81, First Aviation and Space Philatelic Exhibition, Lucerne, Switzerland, Mar. 20-29. No. C434 se-tenant with label showing exhibition emblem.

Illustrator Type of 1981

Designs: Illustrations by A. Lesznai.

1981, Dec. 29 **Litho.** ***Perf. 11½x12***

C435 A693	4fo At the End of the Village	60	55
C436 A693	5fo Dance	80	60
C437 A693	6fo Sunday	90	70

Manned Flight Bicentenary AP110

Various hot air balloons.

1983, Apr. 5 **Litho.** ***Perf. 12x11½***

C438 AP110	1fo 1811	16	15
C439 AP110	1fo 1896	16	15
C440 AP110	2fo 1904	28	15
C441 AP110	2fo 1977	28	15
C442 AP110	4fo 1981	55	28
C443 AP110	4fo 1982	55	28
C444 AP110	5fo 1981	75	40
	Nos. C438-C444 (7)	2.73	
	Set value		1.30

Souvenir Sheet
Perf. 12½

C445 AP110	20fo 1983	2.75	2.75

No. C445 contains one 39x49mm stamp.

Audubon Type of 1985

1985, June 19 **Litho.** ***Perf. 12***

C446 A778	4fo Colaptes auratus	60	35
C447 A778	6fo Richmondena cardinalis	85	50

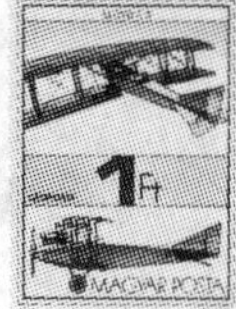

Aircraft — AP111

1988, Aug. 31 **Litho.** ***Perf. 11***

C448 AP111	1fo Lloyd CII	18	15
C449 AP111	2fo Brandenburg CI	35	20
C450 AP111	4fo UFAG CI	65	40
C451 AP111	10fo Gerle 13	1.65	1.00
C452 AP111	12fo WM 13	2.00	1.25
	Nos. C448-C452 (5)	4.83	3.00

AIR POST SEMI-POSTAL STAMPS

Catalogue values for unused stamps in this section are for Never Hinged items.

Roosevelt Type of Semipostal Stamps, 1947

F. D. Roosevelt, Plane and Place: 10f+10f, Casablanca. 20f+20f, Tehran. 50f+50f, Yalta (map). 70f+70f, Hyde Park.

Perf. 12x12½

1947, June 11 **Photo.** **Wmk. 210**

Portrait in Sepia

CB1 SP115	10f + 10f red vio	3.00	3.00
CB1A SP115	20f + 20f brn ol	3.00	3.00
CB1B SP115	50f + 50f vio	3.00	3.00
CB1C SP115	70f + 70f blk	3.00	3.00

A souvenir sheet contains one each of Nos. CB1-CB1C with border inscriptions and decorations in brown. Size: 161x122mm. Value $80.

See note below Nos. B198A-B198D.

Souvenir Sheet

Chain Bridge, Budapest — SPAP1

Perf. 12x12½

1948, May 15 **Photo.** **Wmk. 283**

CB1D SPAP1	2fo + 18fo brn car	60.00	60.00

Souvenir Sheet

Chain Bridge SPAP2

1948, Oct. 16

CB2 SPAP2	3fo + 18fo dp grnsh bl	55.00	55.00

Type of Air Post Stamps of 1948
Portraits at Right

Writers: 1f, William Shakespeare. 2f, Francois Voltaire. 4f, Johann Wolfgang von Goethe. 5f, Lord Byron. 6f, Victor Hugo. 8f, Edgar Allen Poe. 10f, Sandor Petöfi. 12f, Mark Twain. 30f, Count Leo Tolstoy. 40f, Maxim Gorky.

1948, Oct. 16 **Photo.**

CB3 AP22	1f dp ultra	15	15
CB4 AP22	2f rose car	15	15
CB5 AP22	4f dp yel grn	15	15
CB6 AP22	5f dp rose lil	15	15
CB7 AP22	6f dp bl	15	15
CB8 AP22	8f ol brn	20	20
CB9 AP22	10f red	28	28
CB10 AP22	12f dp vio	28	28
CB11 AP22	30f org brn	70	70
CB12 AP22	40f sepia	1.00	1.00
	Nos. CB3-CB12 (10)	3.21	3.21

Sold at a 50 per cent increase over face, half of which aided reconstruction of the Chain Bridge and the other half the hospital for postal employees.

Air Post Type of 1951
Souvenir Sheets
Perf. 12½x12

1951, Sept. 12 **Engr.** **Unwmk.**

CB13 AP36	1fo + 1fo red	50.00	50.00
CB14 AP36	2fo + 2fo bl	50.00	50.00

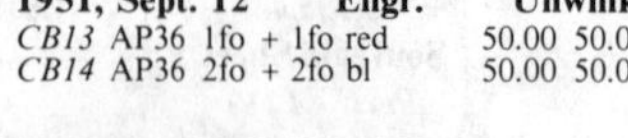

Children Inspecting Stamp Album SPAP3

Design: 2fo+2fo, Children at stamp exhibition.

Perf. 12x12½

1952, Oct. 12 **Photo.** **Wmk. 106**

CB15 SPAP3	1fo + 1fo bl	2.50	2.50
CB16 SPAP3	2fo + 2fo brn red	2.50	2.50

Stamp week, Oct. 11-19, 1952.

Globe and Mailbox SPAP4

Designs: 1fo+50f, Mobile post office. 2fo+1fo, Telegraph pole. 3fo+1.50fo, Radio. 5fo+2.50fo, Telephone. 10fo+5fo, Post horn.

1957, June 20 ***Perf. 12x12½, 12***

Cross in Red

Size: 32x21mm

CB17 SPAP4	60f + 30f bis brn	52	15
CB18 SPAP4	1fo + 50f lil	70	35
CB19 SPAP4	2fo + 1fo org ver	95	45
CB20 SPAP4	3fo + 1.50fo bl	1.25	70
CB21 SPAP4	5fo + 2.50fo gray	1.90	1.75

Size: 46x31mm

CB22 SPAP4	10fo + 5fo pale grn	4.00	4.00
	Nos. CB17-CB22 (6)	9.32	7.40

The surtax was for the benefit of hospitals for postal and telegraph employees.

Parachute of Fausztusz Verancsics, 1617 — SPAP5

History of Hungarian Aviation: No. CB24, Balloon of David Schwarz, 1897. No. CB25, Monoplane of Ernö Horvath, 1911. No. CB26, PKZ-2 helicopter, 1918.

Engraved and Lithographed

1967, May 6 ***Perf. 10½***

CB23 SPAP5	2fo + 1fo sep & yel	50	50
CB24 SPAP5	2fo + 1fo sep & lt bl	50	50
CB25 SPAP5	2fo + 1fo sep & lt grn	50	50
CB26 SPAP5	2fo + 1fo sep & pink	50	50
a.	Horiz. strip of 4, #CB23-CB26	2.75	2.75
b.	Souv. sheet of 4, #CB23-CB26	3.75	3.75

"AEROFILA 67" International Airmail Exhibition, Budapest, Sept. 3-10.

1967, Sept. 3

Aviation, 1967: No. CB27, Parachutist. No. CB28, Helicopter Mi-1. No. CB29, TU-154 jet. No. CB30, Space station Luna 12.

CB27 SPAP5	2fo + 1fo sl & lt grn	50	50
CB28 SPAP5	2fo + 1fo sl & buff	50	50
CB29 SPAP5	2fo + 1fo sl & yel	50	50
CB30 SPAP5	2fo + 1fo sl & pink	50	50
a.	Horiz. strip of 4, #CB27-CB30	2.75	2.75
b.	Souv. sheet of 4, #CB27-CB30	3.75	3.75

Issued to commemorate (in connection with AEROFILA 67) the 7th Congress of FISA (Fédération Internationale des Sociétés Aerophilatéliques) and the 40th Stamp Day.

Olympic Games Airmail Type

Design: 2fo+1fo, Equestrian.

1968, Aug. 21 **Photo.** ***Perf. 12***

CB31 AP74	2fo + 1fo multi	38	38

1st Hungarian Airmail Letter, 1918, Plane — SPAP6

Designs: No. CB33, Letter, 1931, and Zeppelin. No. CB34, Balloon post letter, 1967, and balloon. No. CB35, Letter, 1969, and helicopter.

No. CB36a, #C1. b, #C7. c, #C305. d, #C312.

1974, Oct. 19 Litho. *Perf. 12*

CB32 SPAP6 2fo + 1fo multi 95 95
CB33 SPAP6 2fo + 1fo multi 95 95
a. Pair, #CB32-CB33 2.00 2.00
CB34 SPAP6 2fo + 1fo multi 95 95
CB35 SPAP6 2fo + 1fo multi 95 95
a. Pair, #CB34-CB35 2.00 2.00

Souvenir Sheet

CB36 Sheet of 4 3.50 3.50
a. SPAP6 2fo+1fo any single 48 48

AEROPHILA, International Airmail Exhibition, Budapest, Oct. 19-27.

No. CB36 contains 4 35x25mm stamps

SPECIAL DELIVERY STAMPS

Issue of the Monarchy

SD1

SD2

1916 Typo. Wmk. 137 *Perf. 15*

E1 SD1 2f gray grn & red 15 15

For overprints and surcharges see Nos. 1NE1, 2NE1, 4N5, 5NE1, 6NE1, 7NE1, 8NE1, 10NE1, Szeged E1, J7-J8.

Issue of the Republic

Special Delivery Stamp of 1916 Overprinted

1919

E2 SD1 2f gray grn & red 15 15

General Issue

1919

E3 SD2 2f gray grn & red 15 15

REGISTRATION STAMPS

Nos. 625, 609 and 626 Overprinted in Carmine

Ajl. 1.
a

Ajánlás
b

"Ajl." or "Ajánlás" = Registered Letter.

1946 Wmk. 266 *Perf. 15*

F1 A118(a) "Ajl.1." on 20f 15 15
a. "Ajl.1." 6.00
F2 A99(a) "Ajl.2." on 12f 15 15
F3 A118(b) "Ajánlás" on 24f 15 15
Set value 15 20

POSTAGE DUE STAMPS

Issues of the Monarchy

D1

Perf. 11½, 11½x12

1903 Typo. Wmk. 135

J1 D1 1f grn & blk 30 25
J2 D1 2f grn & blk 2.00 1.25
J3 D1 5f grn & blk 9.00 5.00
J4 D1 6f grn & blk 6.00 4.50
J5 D1 10f grn & blk 45.00 3.00
J6 D1 12f grn & blk 2.00 2.00
a. Perf. 11½ 110.00 85.00
J7 D1 20f grn & blk 9.00 1.90
a. Perf. 11½ 115.00 32.50
J8 D1 50f grn & blk 12.00 12.00
a. Perf. 11½ 140.00 140.00
J9 D1 100f grn & blk 90 90
Nos. J1-J9 (9) 86.20 30.80

See Nos. J10-J26, J28-J43. For overprints and surcharges see Nos. J27, J44-J50, 1NJ1-1NJ5, 2NJ1-2NJ16, 4NJ2-4NJ3, 5NJ1-5NJ8, 6NJ1-6NJ9, 7NJ1-7NJ4, 9NJ1-9NJ3, 10NJ1-10NJ6, Szeged J1-J6.

1908-09 Wmk. 136 *Perf. 15*

J10 D1 1f green & black 45 45
J11 D1 2f green & black 30 30
J12 D1 5f green & black 2.50 1.10
J13 D1 6f green & black 50 38
J14 D1 10f green & black 1.50 38
J15 D1 12f green & black 50 38
J16 D1 20f green & black 10.00 45
c. Center inverted *4,000.*
J17 D1 50f green & black 95 95
Nos. J10-J17 (8) 16.70 4.39

1905 Wmk. 136a *Perf. 11½x12*

J12a D1 5f green & black 100.00 100.00
J13a D1 6f green & black 10.00 8.00
J14a D1 10f green & black 125.00 7.00
J15a D1 12f green & black 15.00 12.00
J17a D1 50f green & black 9.00 7.00
J18 D1 100f green & black 2.00

1906 *Perf. 15*

J11b D1 2f green & black 2.50 1.90
J12b D1 5f green & black 2.00 1.75
J13b D1 6f green & black 2.00 1.25
J14b D1 10f green & black 15.00 60
J15b D1 12f green & black 60 60
J16b D1 20f green & black 15.00 60
d. Center inverted *3,000.*
J17b D1 50f green & black 1.00 70

1914 Wmk. 137 Horiz. *Perf. 15*

J19 D1 1f green & black 18 18
J20 D1 2f green & black 18 18
J21 D1 5f green & black 40 40
J22 D1 6f green & black 60 60
J23 D1 10f green & black 70 70
J24 D1 12f green & black 35 35
J25 D1 20f green & black 35 35
J26 D1 50f green & black 40 40
Nos. J19-J26 (8) 3.16 3.16

1914 Wmk. 137 Vert.

J20a D1 2f green & black 57.50 57.50
J21a D1 5f green & black 7.50 6.25
J22a D1 6f green & black 16.00 16.00
J25a D1 20f green & black *2,750.* *1,750.*
J26a D1 50f green & black 7.50 7.50

No. J9 Surcharged in Red

20

1915 Wmk. 135

J27 D1 20f on 100f grn & blk 90 90
a. On No. J18. Wmk. 136a 20.00 20.00

1915-22 Wmk. 137

J28 D1 1f grn & red 15 15
J29 D1 2f grn & red 15 15
J30 D1 5f grn & red 20 15
J31 D1 6f grn & red 15 15
J32 D1 10f grn & red 15 15
J33 D1 12f grn & red 20 15
J34 D1 15f grn & red 18 15
J35 D1 20f grn & red 15 15
J36 D1 30f grn & red 15 15
J37 D1 40f grn & red ('20) 15 15
J38 D1 50f grn & red ('20) 15 15
a. Center inverted 60.00
J39 D1 120f grn & red ('20) 15 15
J40 D1 200f grn & red ('20) 15 15
J41 D1 2k grn & red ('22) 40 40
J42 D1 5k grn & red ('22) 15 15
J43 D1 50k grn & red ('22) 15 15
Set value 2.30 2.00

Issues of the Republic

Postage Due Stamps of 1914-18 Overprinted in Black

1918-19

On Issue of 1914

J44 D1 50f green & black 60 60

On Stamps and Type of 1915-18

J45 D1 2f grn & red 15 15
J46 D1 3f grn & red 15 15
a. "KOZTARSASAG" omitted 200.00
J47 D1 10f grn & red 15 15
J48 D1 20f grn & red 15 15
J49 D1 40f grn & red 15 15
a. Inverted overprint 4.00 4.00
J50 D1 50f grn & red 15 15
a. Center and overprint inverted 10.00 10.00
Set value 1.20 1.20

Issues of the Kingdom

D3

1919-20 Typo.

J65 D3 2f green & black 15 15
a. Inverted center 350.00
J66 D3 3f green & black 15 15
J67 D3 20f green & black 15 15
J68 D3 40f green & black 15 15
J69 D3 50f green & black 15 15
Set value 35 30

Postage Due Stamps of this type have been overprinted "Magyar Tancskztarsasag" but have not been reported as having been issued without the additional overprint "heads of wheat."

For overprints see Nos. J70-J75.

New Overprint in Black over "Magyar Tanacskoztarsasag"

1920

J70 D3 2f green & black 45 45
J71 D3 3f green & black 45 45
J72 D3 10f green & black 1.65 1.65
J73 D3 20f green & black 45 45
J74 D3 40f green & black 45 45
J75 D3 50f green & black 45 45
Nos. J70-J75 (6) 3.90 3.90

D5

D6

1921-25

Red Surcharge

J76 D5 100f on 15f vio 15 15
J77 D5 500f on 15f vio 15 15
J78 D5 2½k on 10f red vio 15 15
J79 D5 3k on 15f vio 15 15
J80 D5 6k on 1½k vio 15 15
J81 D5 9k on 40f ol grn 15 15
J82 D5 10k on 2½k grn 15 15
J83 D5 12k on 60f blk brn 15 15
J84 D5 15k on 1½k vio 15 15
J85 D5 20k on 2½k grn 15 15
J86 D5 25k on 1½k vio 15 15
J87 D5 30k on 1½k vio 15 15
J88 D5 40k on 2½k grn 15 15
J89 D5 50k on 1½k vio 15 15
J90 D5 100k on 4½k dl vio 15 15
J91 D5 200k on 4½k dl vio 15 15
J92 D5 300k on 4½k dl vio 15 15
J93 D5 500k on 2k grnsh bl 28 15
J94 D5 500k on 3k org brn 28 28
J95 D5 1000k on 2k grnsh bl 28 15
J96 D5 1000k on 3k org brn 45 18
J97 D5 2000k on 2k grnsh bl 35 15
J98 D5 2000k on 3k org brn 70 35
J99 D5 5000k on 5k brown 90 52
Set value 5.00 2.70

Year of issue: 6k, 15k, 25k, 30k, 50k, 1922. 10k, 20k, 40k, 100k-No. J93, Nos. J95, J97, 1923. 5,000k, 1924. Nos. J94, J96, J98, 1925. Others, 1921.

1926 Wmk. 133 Litho. *Perf. 14, 15*

J100 D6 1f rose red 15 15
J101 D6 2f rose red 15 15
J102 D6 3f rose red 15 15
J103 D6 4f rose red 15 15
J104 D6 5f rose red 38 22
a. Perf. 15 1.10 45
J105 D6 8f rose red 15 15
J106 D6 10f rose red 15 15
J107 D6 16f rose red 22 15
J108 D6 32f rose red 38 15
J109 D6 40f rose red 40 15
J110 D6 50f rose red 42 15
J111 D6 80f rose red 1.10 35
Set value 3.50 1.30

See Nos. J117-J123. For surcharges see Nos. J124-J129.

Air Post Stamps of 1924 Surcharged in Red or Green

1926 Wmk. 137 *Perf. 14*

J112 AP3 1f on 500k bl grn & yel grn (R) 32 22
J113 AP3 2f on 1000k bis brn & brn (G) 32 28
J114 AP3 3f on 2000k dk bl & lt bl (R) 32 18

Wmk. 133

J115 AP3 5f on 5000k dl vio & brt vio (G) 65 55
J116 AP3 10f on 1000k red & dl vio (G) 45 35
Nos. J112-J116 (5) 2.06 1.58

Type of 1926 Issue

1928-32 Wmk. 210 *Perf. 14, 15*

J117 D6 2f rose red 15 15
J118 D6 4f rose red ('32) 15 15
J119 D6 8f rose red 15 15
J120 D6 10f rose red 15 15
J121 D6 16f rose red 20 15
J122 D6 20f rose red 32 15
J123 D6 40f rose red 65 15
Nos. J117-J123 (7) 1.77
Set value 50

Postage Due Stamps of 1926 Surcharged in Black

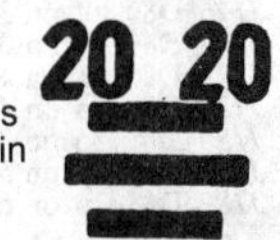

1931-33 Wmk. 133

J124 D6 4f on 5f rose red 28 18
J125 D6 10f on 16f rose red 85 80
J126 D6 10f on 80f rose red ('33) 40 20
J127 D6 12f on 50f rose red ('33) 40 20
J128 D6 20f on 32f rose red 40 28
Nos. J124-J128 (5) 2.33 1.66

Surcharged on No. J121

1931 Wmk. 210 *Perf. 15*

J129 D6 10f on 16f rose red 85 70

Figure of Value — D7

Coat of Arms and Post Horn — D8

1934 Photo. Wmk. 210

J130 D7 2f ultra 15 15
J131 D7 4f ultra 15 15
J132 D7 6f ultra 15 15
J133 D7 8f ultra 15 15
J134 D7 10f ultra 15 15
J135 D7 12f ultra 15 15
J136 D7 16f ultra 15 15
J137 D7 20f ultra 15 15

J138 D7 40f ultra 38 15
J139 D7 80f ultra 48 28
Set value 1.68 85

1941

J140 D8 2f brn red 15 15
J142 D8 4f brn red 15 15
J143 D8 6f brn red 15 15
J144 D8 8f brn red 15 15
J145 D8 10f brn red 15 15
J146 D8 12f brn red 15 15
J147 D8 16f brn red 20 20
J148 D8 20f brn red 30 20
J150 D8 40f brn red 40 25
Set value 1.50 90

1941-44 **Wmk. 266**

J151 D8 2f brn red 15 15
J152 D8 3f brn red 15 15
J153 D8 4f brn red 15 15
J154 D8 6f brn red 15 15
J155 D8 8f brn red 15 15
J156 D8 10f brn red 15 15
J157 D8 12f brn red 15 15
J158 D8 16f brn red 15 15
J159 D8 18f brn red ('44) 15 15
J160 D8 20f brn red 15 15
J161 D8 24f brn red 15 15
J162 D8 30f brn red ('44) 15 15
J163 D8 36f brn red ('44) 15 15
J164 D8 40f brn red 15 15
J165 D8 50f brn red 15 15
J166 D8 60f brn red ('44) 20 15
Set value 1.50 90

For surcharges see Nos. J167-J185.

Catalogue values for unused stamps in this section, from this point to the end of the section, are for Never Hinged items.

Issues of the Republic

Types of Hungary Postage Due Stamps, 1941-44, Surcharged in Carmine

1945
10
fillér

1945 **Wmk. 266** **Photo.** ***Perf. 15***
Blue Surface-tinted Paper

J167 D8 10f on 2f brn red 15 15
J168 D8 10f on 3f brn red 15 15
J169 D8 20f on 4f brn red 15 15
J170 D8 20f on 6f brn red 6.00 6.00
J171 D8 20f on 8f brn red 15 15
J172 D8 40f on 12f brn red 15 15
J173 D8 40f on 16f brn red 15 15
J174 D8 40f on 18f brn red 15 15
J175 D8 60f on 24f brn red 15 15
J176 D8 80f on 30f brn red 15 15
J177 D8 90f on 36f brn red 15 15
J178 D8 1p on 10f brn red 15 15
J179 D8 1p on 40f brn red 15 15
J180 D8 2p on 20f brn red 15 15
J181 D8 2p on 50f brn red 15 15
J182 D8 2p on 60f brn red 15 15

Surcharged in Black, Thicker Type

J183 D8 10p on 3f brn red 15 15
J184 D8 12p on 8f brn red 15 15
J185 D8 20p on 24f brn red 15 15
Set value 7.25 7.00

D9

1946-50 **Wmk. 210** ***Perf. 15***
Numerals in Deep Magenta

J186 D9 4f magenta 45 15
J187 D9 10f magenta 1.25 15
J188 D9 20f magenta 45 15
J189 D9 30f magenta 45 15
J190 D9 40f magenta 75 15
J191 D9 50f mag ('50) 2.10 48
J192 D9 60f magenta 1.50 15
J193 D9 1.20fo magenta 2.25 24
J194 D9 2fo magenta 3.50 30
Nos. J186-J194 (9) 12.70
Set value 1.50

1951 **Wmk. 106**
Numerals in Deep Magenta

J194A D9 4f magenta 15 15
J194B D9 10f magenta 15 15
J194C D9 20f magenta 15 15
i. "fiellr" 3.75
J194D D9 30f magenta 25 15
J194E D9 40f magenta 28 15
J194F D9 50f magenta 1.25 20
J194G D9 60f magenta 45 15
J194H D9 1.20fo magenta 75 15
J194I D9 2fo magenta 1.50 20
Nos. J194A-J194I (9) 4.93
Set value 1.00

Nos. J194A-J194I are found in both large format (about 18x22mm) and small (about 17x21mm).

D10

D11

1951 **Unwmk.** **Typo.** ***Perf. 14½x15***
Paper with Vertical Lines in Green
Blue Surcharge

J195 D10 8f dark brown 20 20
J196 D10 10f dark brown 20 20
J197 D10 12f dark brown 40 40

1951 **Wmk. 106** **Photo.** ***Perf. 14½***

J198 D11 4f brown 15 15
J199 D11 6f brown 15 15
J200 D11 8f brown 16 15
J201 D11 10f brown 15 15
J202 D11 14f brown 32 24
J203 D11 20f brown 15 15
J204 D11 30f brown 15 15
J205 D11 40f brown 15 15
J206 D11 50f brown 24 15
J207 D11 60f brown 28 15
J208 D11 1.20fo brown 28 15
J209 D11 2fo brown 48 32
Set value 2.30 1.15

D12

D13

Photo., Numeral Typo. in Black
1953
Numerals 4½mm High

J210 D12 4f dull green 15 15
J211 D12 6f dull green 15 15
J212 D12 8f dull green 15 15
J213 D12 10f dull green 15 15
J214 D12 12f dull green 15 15
J215 D12 14f dull green 24 16
J216 D12 16f dull green 24 16
J217 D12 20f dull green 15 15
J218 D12 24f dull green 24 16
J219 D12 30f dull green 16 15
J220 D12 36f dull green 24 15
J221 D12 40f dull green 15 15
J222 D12 50f dull green 16 15
J223 D12 60f dull green 20 15
J224 D12 70f dull green 20 15
J225 D12 80f dull green 28 15
J226 D12 1.20fo dull green 40 15
J227 D12 2fo dull green 65 24
a. Small "2" (3mm high) 1.00 60
Nos. J210-J227 (18) 4.06
Set value 1.50

1st Hungarian postage due stamp, 50th anniv.

Photo., Numeral Typo. in Black on Nos. J228-J243
1958 **Wmk. 106** ***Perf. 14½***
Size: 21x16½mm

J228 D13 4f red 15 15
J229 D13 6f red 15 15
J230 D13 8f red 15 15
J231 D13 10f red 15 15
J232 D13 12f red 15 15
J233 D13 14f red 15 15
J234 D13 16f red 15 15
J235 D13 20f red 15 15
J236 D13 24f red 15 15
J237 D13 30f red 15 15
J238 D13 36f red 15 15
J239 D13 40f red 15 15
J240 D13 50f red 15 15
J241 D13 60f red 18 15
J242 D13 70f red 22 15
J243 D13 80f red 30 15

Perf. 12
Size: 31x21mm

J244 D13 1.20fo dk red brn 45 18
J245 D13 2fo dk red brn 70 28
Set value 2.60 1.25

Photo., Numeral Typo. in Black on Nos. J246-J261
1965-69 **Unwmk.** ***Perf. 11½***
Size: 21x16½mm

J246 D13 4f red 15 15
J247 D13 6f red 15 15
J248 D13 8f red 15 15
J249 D13 10f red 15 15
J250 D13 12f red 15 15
J251 D13 14f red 15 15
J252 D13 16f red 15 15
J253 D13 20f red 15 15
J254 D13 24f red 15 15
J255 D13 30f red 15 15
J256 D13 36f red 15 15
J257 D13 40f red 15 15
J258 D13 50f red 15 15
J259 D13 60f red 15 15
J260 D13 70f red 16 15
J261 D13 80f red 20 15

Perf. 11½x12
Size: 31x21mm

J262 D13 1fo dk red brn ('69) 15 15
J263 D13 1.20fo dk red brn 28 15
J264 D13 2fo dk red brn 40 20
J265 D13 4fo dk red brn ('69) 65 15
Set value 2.60 1.25

Mail Plane and Truck — D14

Postal History — D15

Designs: 20f, Money order canceling machine. 40f, Scales in self-service P.O. 80f, Automat for registering parcels. 1fo, Keypunch operator. 1.20fo, Mail plane and truck. 2fo, Diesel mail train. 3fo, Mailman on motorcycle with sidecar. 4fo, Rural mail delivery. 8fo, Automatic letter sorting machine. 10fo, Postman riding motorcycle.

1973-85 **Photo.** ***Perf. 11***
Size: 21x18mm

J266 D14 20f brn & ver 15 15
J267 D14 40f dl bl & ver 15 15
J268 D14 80f vio & ver 15 15
J269 D14 1fo ol grn & ver 15 15

Perf. 12x11½
Size: 28x22mm

J270 D14 1.20fo grn & ver 18 15
J271 D14 2fo lil & ver 24 15
J272 D14 3fo brt bl & ver 35 15
J273 D14 4fo org brn & ver 45 18
J274 D14 8fo deep mag & dark red 1.50 38
J275 D14 10fo green & dark red 1.75 45
Nos. J266-J275 (10) 5.07
Set value 1.45

Issue dates: 20f-4fo, Dec. 1973. 8fo, 10fo, Dec. 16, 1985.

1987, Dec. 10 **Litho.** ***Perf. 12***

Designs: Excerpt from 18th cent. letter, innovations in letter carrying.

J276 D15 1fo Foot messenger, 16th cent. 25 15
J277 D15 4fo Post rider, 17th cent. 1.00 50
J278 D15 6fo Horse-drawn mail coach, 18th cent. 1.50 75
J279 D15 8fo Railroad mail car, 19th cent. 2.00 1.00
J280 D15 10fo Mail truck, 20th cent. 2.50 1.25
J281 D15 20fo Airplane, 20th cent. 5.00 2.50
Nos. J276-J281 (6) 12.25 6.15

OFFICIAL STAMPS

O1

1921-23 **Wmk. 137** **Typo.** ***Perf. 15***

O1 O1 10f brn vio & blk 20 15
O2 O1 20f ol brn & blk 20 15
a. Inverted center 200.00 200.00
O3 O1 60f blk brn & blk 20 15
O4 O1 100f dl rose & blk 20 15
O5 O1 250f bl & blk 20 15
O6 O1 350f gray & blk 24 15
O7 O1 500f lt brn & blk 22 15
O8 O1 1000f lil brn & blk 22 15
O9 O1 5k brn ('23) 15 15
O10 O1 10k choc ('23) 15 15
O11 O1 15k gray blk ('23) 15 15
O12 O1 25k org ('23) 15 15
O13 O1 50k brn & red ('22) 15 15
O14 O1 100k bis & red ('22) 15 15
O15 O1 150k grn & red ('23) 20 15
O16 O1 300k dl red & red ('23) 24 15
O17 O1 350k vio & red ('23) 28 15
O18 O1 500k org & red ('22) 32 15
O19 O1 600k ol bis & red ('23) 80 48
O20 O1 1000k bl & red ('22) 48 16
Nos. O1-O20 (20) 4.90
Set value 2.50

Stamps of 1921 Surcharged in Red

15 KORONA 15

1922

O21 O1 15k on 20f ol brn & blk 15 15
O22 O1 25k on 60f blk brn & blk 15 15
Set value 20 15

Stamps of 1921 Overprinted in Red

KORONA

1923

O23 O1 350k gray & blk 25 18

With Additional Surcharge of New Value in Red

O24 O1 150k on 100f dl rose & blk 22 15
O25 O1 2000k on 250f bl & blk 60 42

1923-24
Paper with Gray Moire on Face

O26 O1 500k org & red ('23) 22 15
O27 O1 1000k bl & red ('23) 28 15
O28 O1 3000k vio & red ('24) 60 28
O29 O1 5000k bl & red ('24) 70 48

1924 **Wmk. 133**

O30 O1 500k org & red 1.10 55
O31 O1 1000k blue & red 1.10 55

NEWSPAPER STAMPS

Issues of the Monarchy

St. Stephen's Crown and Post Horn
N1 N2

1871-72 **Unwmk.** **Typo.** ***Imperf.***

P1 N1 (1k) ver red 30.00 12.50
P2 N2 (1k) rose red ('72) 7.00 1.25
a. (1k) vermilion 7.00 1.25
b. Printed on both sides

Reprints of No. P2 are watermarked. Value, $450.

Letter with Crown and Post Horn — N3

N5

1874

P3 N3 1k orange 3.00 35

1881 Wmk. "kr" in Oval (132)

P4 N3 1k orange 1.25 15
a. 1k lemon yellow 14.00 2.75
b. Printed on both sides

1898 Wmk. 135

P5 N3 1k orange 1.25 20

See watermark note after No. 46.

1900 Wmk. Crown in Circle (135)

P6 N5 (2f) red orange 75 15

1905 Wmk. Crown (136a)

P7 N5 (2f) red org 1.00 15
a. Wmk. 136 ('08) 1.00 15

1914-22 Wmk. Double Cross (137)

P8 N5 (2f) orange 15 15
a. Wmk. horiz. 4.50 3.75
P9 N5 (10f) deep blue ('20) 15 15
P10 N5 (20f) lilac ('22) 15 15
Set value 27 23

For overprints and surcharges see Nos. 1NJ6-1NJ10, 1NP1, 2NP1, 5NP1, 6NP1, 8NP1, 10NP1, Szeged P1.

NEWSPAPER TAX STAMPS

Issues of the Monarchy

NT1

NT2

NT3

Wmk. 91; Unwmk. from 1871

1868 Typo. *Imperf.*

PR1 NT1 1k blue 5.50 1.50
a. Pair, one sideways
PR2 NT2 2k brown 17.50 15.00
a. 2k red brown 275.00 47.50

1868

PR2B NT3 1k blue *4,750. 4,000.*

No. PR2B was issued for the Military Border District only. All used copies are precanceled (overprinted with newspaper text). A similar 2k was not issued.

1889-90 Wmk. "kr" in Oval (132)

PR3 NT1 1k blue 2.00 80
PR4 NT2 2k brown 5.50 4.00

1898 Wmk. Crown in Oval (135)

PR5 NT1 1k blue 7.50 5.50

These stamps did not pay postage, but represented a fiscal tax collected by the postal authorities on newspapers.

Nos. PR3 and PR5 have a tall "k" in "kr."

PARCEL POST STAMPS

Stamps and Types of 1943-45 Overprinted in Black or Carmine

Cs. 5-1.
a

Csomag 5 kg.
b

"Cs." or "Csomag"=Parcel

1946 Wmk. 266 *Perf. 15*

Q1 A118 "Cs. 5-1." on 70f (#629) 15 15
Q2 A109 "Cs. 5-1." on 30f (#613) 4.00 4.00
Q3 A99 "Cs. 5-2." on 24f (#612) 15 15
Q4 A118 "Cs. 10-1." on 70f (#629) 15 15
Q5 A118 "Cs. 10-1." on 80f (#615) 4.00 4.00
Q6 A118 "Cs. 10-2." on 80f (#630) 15 15
Q7 A99 "Csomag 5kg." on 2p on 4f (#667) (C+Bk) 15 15
Q8 A118 "Csomag 10kg." on 30f cop red, *bl* 15 15
Nos. Q1-Q8 (8) 8.90 8.90

No. Q8 was not issued without overprint.

Catalogue values for unused stamps in this section, from this point to the end of the section, are for Never Hinged items.

No. 796 Surcharged with New Value in Red or Black

1954 Wmk. 210

Q9 A144 1.70fo on 1.40fo 60 20
Q10 A144 2fo on 1.40fo (Bk) 70 30
Q11 A144 3fo on 1.40fo 85 50

OCCUPATION STAMPS

Issued under French Occupation

ARAD ISSUE

Forged overprints exist.

Stamps of Hungary Overprinted in Red or Blue

Occupation
française

On Issue of 1916-18

1919 Wmk. 137 *Perf. 15, 14*

1N1 A9 2f brn org (R) 45 45
1N2 A9 3f red lil (R) 25 25
1N3 A9 5f green (R) 65 65
1N4 A9 6f grnsh bl (R) 55 55
a. Inverted overprint 1.00 1.00
1N5 A9 10f rose red 55 55
1N6 A9 15f violet (R) 45 45
a. Double overprint 3.00
1N7 A9 20f gray brn (R) 7.50 7.50
1N8 A9 35f brown (R) 9.00 9.00
1N9 A9 40f ol grn (R) 6.50 6.50
1N10 A10 50f red vio & lil 90 90
1N11 A10 75f brt bl & pale bl 80 80
1N12 A10 80f grn & pale grn 70 70
1N13 A10 1k red brn & cl 1.50 1.50
1N14 A10 2k ol brn & bis 80 80
a. Inverted overprint 3.25
1N15 A10 3k dk vio & ind 2.00 2.00
1N16 A10 5k dk brn & lt brn 2.00 2.00
1N17 A10 10k vio brn & vio 10.00 10.00
Nos. 1N1-1N17 (17) 44.60 44.60

With Additional Surcharge:

45 45 50 50
a b c d

1N18 A9 (a) 45f on 2f brn org 75 75
1N19 A9 (b) 45f on 2f brn org 1.00 1.00
1N20 A9 (c) 50f on 3f red lil 80 80
1N21 A9 (d) 50f on 3f red lil 80 80

Overprinted On Issue of 1918

1N22 A11 10f scar (Bl) 7.50 7.50
1N23 A11 20f dk brn 55 55
1N24 A11 25f brt bl 1.00 1.00
a. Inverted overprint 1.00 1.00
1N25 A12 40f ol grn 1.50 1.50

Ovptd. On Issue of 1918-19, Overprinted "Koztarsasag"

1N26 A9 2f brn org 1.50 1.50
a. Inverted overprint 2.75 2.75
1N27 A9 4f sl gray 1.50 1.50
1N28 A9 5f green 24 24
1N29 A9 6f grnsh bl 2.50 2.50
a. Inverted overprint 4.50 4.50
1N30 A9 10f rose red (Bl) 7.50 7.50
1N31 A9 20f gray brn 1.00 1.00
1N32 A11 25f brt bl 75 75
a. Inverted overprint 4.00 4.00
1N33 A9 40f ol grn 75 75
1N34 A12 40f ol grn 12.50 12.50
a. Inverted overprint 12.50
1N35 A12 50f lilac 60 60
1N36 A10 1k red brn & cl (Bl) 1.10 1.10
1N37 A10 3k dk vio & ind (Bl) 1.75 1.75
Nos. 1N26-1N37 (12) 31.69 31.69

No. 1N36 With Additional Surcharge:

10 10
e f

1N38 A10 (e) 10k on 1k 2.00 2.00
1N39 A10 (f) 10k on 1k 1.50 1.50

On Issue of 1919 Inscribed "MAGYAR POSTA"

1N40 A13 10f red (Bl) 75 75

SEMI-POSTAL STAMPS

Hungarian Semi-Postal Stamps of 1916-17 Overprinted "Occupation francaise" in Blue or Red

1919 Wmk. 137 *Perf. 15*

1NB1 SP3 10f + 2f rose red 8.00 8.00
1NB2 SP4 15f + 2f dl vio (R) 1.00 1.00
1NB3 SP5 40f + 2f brn car 1.00 1.00

SPECIAL DELIVERY STAMP

Hungarian Special Delivery Stamp of 1916 Overprinted "Occupation francaise"

1919 Wmk. 137 *Perf. 15*

1NE1 SD1 2f gray grn & red 35 35

POSTAGE DUE STAMPS

Hungarian Postage Due Stamps of 1915 Overprinted "Occupation francaise"

1919 Wmk. 137 *Perf. 15*

1NJ1 D1 2f grn & red 3.50 3.50
1NJ2 D1 10f grn & red 1.25 1.25
1NJ3 D1 12f grn & red 6.00 6.00
1NJ4 D1 15f grn & red 6.00 6.00
1NJ5 D1 20f grn & red 3.00 3.00

Hungarian Newspaper Stamp of 1914 Surcharged

Occupation
française
12 Porto 12

1NJ6 N5 12f on 2f org 80 80
1NJ7 N5 15f on 2f org 80 80
1NJ8 N5 30f on 2f org 80 80
a. Double surcharge 4.25
1NJ9 N5 50f on 2f org 4.00 4.00
1NJ10 N5 100f on 2f org 4.00 4.00
Nos. 1NJ1-1NJ10 (10) 30.15 30.15

NEWSPAPER STAMP

Hungarian Newspaper Stamp of 1914 Overprinted "Occupation francaise"

1919 Wmk. 137 *Imperf.*

1NP1 N5 (2f) orange 25 25

ISSUED UNDER ROMANIAN OCCUPATION

FIRST DEBRECEN ISSUE

The first Debrecen overprint was applied to numerous other stamps, also in other colors than are listed. These varieties were not sold to the public but to a favored few.

Excellent forgeries of this overprint are plentiful.

Hungarian Stamps of 1913-19 Overprinted in Blue, Red or Black

1919 Wmk. 137 *Perf. 15, 14½x14*

On Stamps of 1913

2N1 A4 2f ol yel *16.00 16.00*
2N2 A4 3f org *22.50 22.50*
2N3 A4 6f ol grn (R) 2.50 2.50

On Stamps of 1916

2N4 A8 10f rose 20.00 20.00
2N5 A8 15f vio (Bk) 8.00 8.00

On Stamps of 1916-18

2N6 A9 2f brn org 20 15
2N7 A9 3f red lil 16 15
2N8 A9 5f grn 80 45
2N9 A9 6f grnsh bl (R) 60 40
2N10 A9 15f vio (Bk) 80 40
2N11 A9 20f gray brn *12.50 12.50*
2N12 A9 25f dl bl (Bk) 80 40
2N13 A9 35f brn 10.00 7.50
2N14 A9 40f ol grn 80 40
2N15 A10 50f red vio & lil 1.50 80
2N16 A10 75f brt bl & pale bl (Bk) 75 35
2N17 A10 80f grn & pale grn (R) 1.00 80
2N18 A10 1k red brn & cl 1.00 80
2N19 A10 2k ol brn & bis (Bk) 80 80
2N20 A10 3k dk vio & ind (R) 2.25 1.50
a. Blue overprint *5.50 5.50*
b. Black overprint *65.00 65.00*
2N21 A10 5k dk brn & lt brn (Bk) 6.50 6.50
2N22 A10 10k vio brn & vio *40.00 40.00*

With New Value Added

2N23 A9 35f on 3f red lil 40 30
2N24 A9 45f on 2f brn org 40 40
2N25 A10 3k on 75f brt bl & pale bl (Bk) 1.25 1.25
2N26 A10 5k on 75f brt bl & pale bl (Bk) 1.25 1.25
2N27 A10 10k on 80f grn & pale grn (R) 1.10 1.10

On Stamps of 1918

2N28 A11 10f scar 4.00 4.00
2N29 A11 20f dk brn (R) 4.00 4.00
a. Black overprint 6.00 6.00
b. Blue overprint 6.50 6.50
2N30 A11 25f brt bl (R) 80 80
a. Black overprint 4.00 4.00
2N31 A12 40f ol grn 20 20
2N32 A12 50f lilac 4.00 4.00

On Stamps of 1918-19, Overprinted "Koztarsasag"

2N33 A9 2f brn org 50 25
2N34 A9 3f red lil 6.50 4.00
2N35 A9 4f sl gray (R) 65 40
2N36 A9 5f grn 20 15
2N37 A9 6f grnsh bl (R) 1.65 80
2N38 A9 10f rose red 2.00 1.10
2N39 A11 10f scar 80 40
2N40 A11 15f dp vio (Bk) 2.00 1.65
2N41 A9 20f gray brn 20 18
2N42 A11 20f dk brn (Bk) 3.50 3.50
b. Red overprint 7.00 7.00
2N43 A9 40f ol grn 4.00 4.00
2N44 A10 1k red brn & cl 40 35
2N45 A10 2k ol brn & bis (Bk) 8.00 8.00
2N46 A10 3k dk vio & ind (R) 1.10 1.10
a. Blue overprint 3.50 3.50
b. Black overprint *52.50 52.50*
2N47 A10 5k dk & lt brn (Bk) *50.00 50.00*
2N48 A10 10k vio brn & vio *80.00 80.00*
2N49 A11 25f brt bl (R) 75 65
a. Black overprint 4.00 4.00
2N50 A12 40f ol grn *10.00 10.00*
2N51 A12 50f lilac 1.00 1.00

On Stamps of 1919

2N52 A13 5f green 15 15
2N53 A13 6f grnsh bl (Bk) 1.25 80
2N54 A13 10f red 15 15
2N55 A13 20f dk brn 15 15
2N56 A13 25f dl bl (Bk) 25 16
2N57 A13 45f org 80 65
2N58 A14 5k dk brn & brn

No. 2N58 is handstamped. Counterfeits exist.

On No. 103A

2N59 A5a 10f vio brn (R) 3.25 3.25
Nos. 2N1-2N57,2N59 (58) *346.11 333.04*

SEMI-POSTAL STAMPS

Overprinted like Regular Issues in Blue or Black

1919 Wmk. 137 *Perf. 15*

2NB1 SP3 10f + 2f rose red 65 65
2NB2 SP4 15f + 2f dl vio (Bk) 1.00 1.00
2NB3 SP5 40f + 2f brn car 80 80

Same Overprint on Hungary Nos. B58-B60 (with "Köztarsasag")

1919

2NB4 SP3 10f + 2f rose red 1.50 1.50
2NB5 SP4 15f + 2f dl vio (Bk) 10.00 9.00
2NB6 SP5 40f + 2f brn car 1.75 1.75

SPECIAL DELIVERY STAMP

Hungarian Special Delivery Stamp of 1916 Overprinted like Regular Issues

1919 Wmk. 137 *Perf. 15*

2NE1 SD1 2f gray grn & red (Bl) 15 15

POSTAGE DUE STAMPS

Hungarian Postage Due Stamps of 1914-19 Overprinted in Black like Regular Issues

1919 Wmk. 137 *Perf. 15*

On Stamp of 1914

2NJ1 D1 50f grn & blk *26.00 26.00*

On Stamps of 1915

2NJ2 D1 1f grn & red 8.00 8.00
2NJ3 D1 2f grn & red 20 20
2NJ4 D1 5f grn & red *35.00 35.00*
2NJ5 D1 6f grn & red *7.50 7.50*
2NJ6 D1 10f grn & red 50 50
2NJ7 D1 12f grn & red *12.50 12.00*
2NJ8 D1 15f grn & red 90 90
2NJ9 D1 20f grn & red 1.25 1.25
2NJ10 D1 30f grn & red 1.25 1.25

On Stamps of 1918-19, Overprinted "Koztarsasag"

2NJ11 D1 2f grn & red 2.00 2.00
2NJ12 D1 3f grn & red 7.50 7.50
2NJ13 D1 10f grn & red 1.25 1.25
2NJ14 D1 20f grn & red 1.25
2NJ15 D1 40f grn & red 1.25 1.25
2NJ16 D1 50f grn & red 1.25 1.25
Nos. 2NJ1-2NJ16 (16) 107.60

NEWSPAPER STAMP

Hungarian Newspaper Stamp of 1914 Overprinted like Regular Issues

1919 Wmk. 137 *Imperf.*

2NP1 N5 (2f) orange (Bl) 25 25
a. Inverted overprint
b. Double overprint

SECOND DEBRECEN ISSUE

Counterfeits exist.

Mythical "Turul" — OS5

Throwing Lariat — OS6

Hungarian Peasant OS7

1920 Unwmk. Typo. *Perf. 11½*

3N1 OS5 2f lt brn 60 60
3N2 OS5 3f red brn 60 60
3N3 OS5 4f gray 60 60
3N4 OS5 5f lt grn 60 60
3N5 OS5 6f slate 60 60
3N6 OS5 10f scarlet 60 60
3N7 OS5 15f dk vio 60 60
3N8 OS5 20f dk brn 60 60
3N9 OS6 25f ultra 60 60
3N10 OS6 30f buff 60 60
3N11 OS6 35f claret 60 60
3N12 OS6 40f ol grn 60 60
3N13 OS6 45f salmon 60 60
3N14 OS6 50f pale vio 60 60
3N15 OS6 60f yel grn 60 60
3N16 OS6 75f Prus bl 60 60
3N17 OS7 80f gray grn 60 60
3N18 OS7 1k brn red 80 80
3N19 OS7 2k chocolate 80 80
3N20 OS7 3k brn vio 2.00 2.00
3N21 OS7 5k bis brn 2.00 2.00
3N22 OS7 10k dl vio 2.00 2.00
Nos. 3N1-3N22 (22) 17.80 17.80

Thick, Glazed Paper

3N23 OS5 2f lt brn 1.25 1.25
3N24 OS5 3f red brn 1.25 1.25
3N25 OS5 4f gray 1.25 1.25
3N26 OS5 5f lt grn 1.25 1.25
3N27 OS5 6f slate 1.25 1.25
3N28 OS5 10f scarlet 1.25 1.25
3N29 OS5 15f dk vio 1.25 1.25
3N30 OS5 20f dk brn 1.25 1.25
3N31 OS7 80f gray grn 1.50 1.50
3N32 OS7 1k brn red 1.50 1.50
3N33 OS7 1.20k orange 10.50 10.50
3N34 OS7 2k chocolate 2.25 2.25
Nos. 3N23-3N34 (12) 25.75 25.75

SEMI-POSTAL STAMPS

Carrying Wounded — SP1

1920 Unwmk. Typo. *Perf. 11½*

3NB1 SP1 20f green 1.00 1.00
3NB2 SP1 50f gray brn 1.00 1.00
3NB3 SP1 1k blue green 1.00 1.00
3NB4 SP1 2k dk grn 1.00 1.00

Colored Paper

3NB5 SP1 20f grn, *bl* 1.00 1.00
3NB6 SP1 50f brn, *rose* 1.00 1.00
3NB7 SP1 1k dk grn, *grn* 1.00 1.00
Nos. 3NB1-3NB7 (7) 7.00 7.00

POSTAGE DUE STAMPS

D1

1920 Typo. Wmk. 137 *Perf. 15*

3NJ1 D1 5f blue green 40 40
3NJ2 D1 10f blue green 40 40
3NJ3 D1 20f blue green 40 40
3NJ4 D1 30f blue green 40 40
3NJ5 D1 40f blue green 40 40
Nos. 3NJ1-3NJ5 (5) 2.00 2.00

TEMESVAR ISSUE

Issued under Romanian Occupation

OS1 OS2

OS3 OS4

1919 Wmk. 137 *Perf. 15*

4N1 OS1 30f on 2f brn org (Bl) 30 30
a. Red surcharge 65 65
b. Inverted surcharge (R)
4N2 OS2 1k on 4f sl gray (R) 25 25
4N3 OS3 150f on 3f red lil (Bk) 20 20
4N4 OS3 150f on 5f grn (Bk) 25 25
4N5 OS4 3k on 2f gray grn & red (Bk) 50 50
a. Blue surcharge 80 80
Nos. 4N1-4N5 (5) 1.50 1.50

POSTAGE DUE STAMPS

D1

D2

1919 Wmk. 137 *Perf. 15*

4NJ1 D1 40f on 15f + 2f vio (Bk) 40 40
a. Red surcharge 70 70
4NJ2 D2 60f on 2f grn & red (Bk) 70 70
a. Red surcharge 3.50 3.50
4NJ3 D2 60f on 10f grn & red (Bk) 55 55
a. Red surcharge 3.00 3.00

FIRST TRANSYLVANIA ISSUE

Issued under Romanian Occupation

Both the first and second Transylvania overprints were applied to numerous other stamps and in colors other than listed. These varieties were not sold to the public but to a favored few.

Counterfeits are plentiful.

Issued in Kolozsvar (Cluj)

Hungarian Stamps of 1916-18 Overprinted

1919 Wmk. 137 *Perf. 15, 14*

On Stamp of 1916, White Numerals

5N1 A8 15b violet 60 60

On Stamps of 1916-18

5N2 A9 2b brn org 15 15
5N3 A9 3b red lil 18 18
5N4 A9 5b green 20 20
5N5 A9 6b grnsh bl 20 20
5N6 A9 15b violet 20 20
5N7 A9 25b dl bl 18 18
5N8 A9 35b brown 18 18
5N9 A9 40b ol grn 18 18
5N10 A10 50b red vio & lil 30 30
5N11 A10 75b brt bl & pale bl 18 18
5N12 A10 80b grn & pale grn 18 18
5N13 A10 1 l red brn & cl 18 18
5N14 A10 2 l ol brn & bis 40 40
5N15 A10 3 l dk vio & ind 1.25 1.25
5N16 A10 5 l dk brn & lt brn 1.10 1.10
5N17 A10 10 l vio brn & vio 1.40 1.40

On Stamps of 1918

5N18 A11 10b scarlet 15.00 15.00
5N19 A11 15b dp vio 2.00 2.00
5N20 A11 20b dk brn 15 15
a. Gold overprint 32.50 32.50
b. Silver overprint 32.50 32.50
5N21 A11 25b brt bl 40 40
5N22 A12 40b ol grn 25 25

On No. 103A

5N23 A5a 10b vio brn 25 25
Nos. 5N1-5N23 (23) 25.11 25.11

SEMI-POSTAL STAMPS

Hungarian Semi-Postal Stamps of 1913-17 Overprinted like Regular Issues

On Issue of 1913

1919 Wmk. 137 *Perf. 14*

5NB1 SP1 1 l on 1f slate 16.00 16.00
5NB2 SP1 1 l on 2f ol yel 25.00 25.00
5NB3 SP1 1 l on 3f org 14.00 14.00
5NB4 SP1 1 l on 5f emer 80 80
5NB5 SP1 1 l on 10f car 80 80
5NB6 SP1 1 l on 12f vio,*yel* 5.00 5.00
5NB7 SP1 1 l on 16f gray grn 2.50 2.50
5NB8 SP1 1 l on 25f ultra 20.00 20.00
5NB9 SP1 1 l on 35f red vio 3.00 3.00
5NB10 SP2 1 l on 1k dl red 35.00 35.00

On Issue of 1916-17

Perf. 15

5NB11 SP3 10b + 2b rose red 15 15
5NB12 SP4 15b + 2b dl vio 15 15
5NB13 SP5 40b + 2b brn car 15 15
Nos. 5NB1-5NB13 (13) 122.55 122.55

SPECIAL DELIVERY STAMP

Hungarian Special Delivery Stamp of 1916 Overprinted like Regular Issues

1919 Wmk. 137 *Perf. 15*

5NE1 SD1 2b gray grn & red 18 18

POSTAGE DUE STAMPS

Hungarian Postage Due Stamps of 1914-18 Overprinted like Regular Issues

On Stamp of 1914

1919 Wmk. 137 *Perf. 15*

5NJ1 D1 50b grn & blk 6.50 6.50

On Stamps of 1915

5NJ2 D1 1b grn & red *75.00 75.00*
5NJ3 D1 2b grn & red 22 22
5NJ4 D1 5b grn & red 14.00 14.00
5NJ5 D1 10b grn & red 80 80
5NJ6 D1 15b grn & red 5.00 5.00
5NJ7 D1 20b grn & red 80 80
5NJ8 D1 30b grn & red 8.50 8.50
Nos. 5NJ1-5NJ8 (8) *110.82 110.82*

NEWSPAPER STAMP

Hungarian Newspaper Stamp of 1914 Overprinted like Regular Issues

1919 Wmk. 137 *Imperf.*

5NP1 N5 2b orange 1.00 1.00

SECOND TRANSYLVANIA ISSUE

Counterfeits are plentiful.

Issued in Nagyvarad (Oradea)

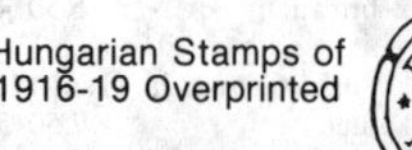

Hungarian Stamps of 1916-19 Overprinted

1919 Wmk. 137 *Perf. 15, 14*

On Stamps of 1913-16

6N1 A4 2b ol yel 1.10 1.10
6N2 A4 3b orange 2.00 2.00
6N3 A4 6b ol grn 50 50
6N4 A4 16b gray grn 18.50 18.50
6N5 A4 50b lake, *bl* 65 65
6N6 A4 70b red brn & grn 5.00 5.00

On Stamps of 1916-18

6N7 A9 2b brn org 22 22
6N8 A9 3b red lil 22 22
6N9 A9 5b green 22 22
6N10 A9 6b grnsh bl 80 80
6N11 A9 10b rose red 1.25 1.25
6N12 A9 15b violet 22 22
6N13 A9 20b gray brn 8.00 8.00
6N14 A9 25b dl bl 15 15
6N15 A9 35b brown 22 22
6N16 A9 40b ol grn 15 15
6N17 A10 50b red vio & lil 22 22
6N18 A10 75b brt bl & pale bl 15 15
6N19 A10 80b grn & pale grn 18 18
6N20 A10 1 l red brn & cl 30 30
6N21 A10 2 l ol brn & bis 15 15
6N22 A10 3 l dk vio & ind 2.00 2.00
6N23 A10 5 l dk brn & lt brn 1.25 1.25

6N24 A10 10 l vio brn & vio 80 80

On Stamps of 1918

6N25 A11 10b scarlet 1.40 1.40
6N26 A11 20b dk brn 15 15
6N27 A11 25b brt bl 30 30
6N28 A12 40b ol grn 40 40

On Stamps of 1918-19, Overprinted "Koztarsasag"

6N29 A9 2b brn org 1.75 1.75
6N30 A9 3b red lil 15 15
6N31 A9 4b sl gray 15 15
6N32 A9 5b green 18 18
6N33 A9 6b grnsh bl 1.00 1.00
6N34 A9 10b rose red 7.50 7.50
6N35 A9 20b gray brn 1.00 1.00
6N36 A9 40b ol grn 25 25
6N37 A10 1 l red brn & cl 18 18
6N38 A10 3 l dk vio & ind 32 32
6N39 A10 5 l dk brn & lt brn 1.40 1.40
6N40 A11 10b scarlet *50.00 50.00*
6N41 A11 20b dk brn 1.60 1.60
6N42 A11 25b brt bl 60 60
6N43 A12 50b lilac 18 18

On Stamps of 1919 Inscribed "MAGYAR POSTA"

6N44 A13 5b yel grn 15 15
6N45 A13 10b red 15 15
6N46 A13 20b dk brn 45 45
6N47 A13 25b dl bl 15 15
6N48 A13 40b ol grn 90 90
6N49 A14 5 l dk brn & brn 5.00 5.00

On No. 103A

6N50 A5a 10b vio brn 50 50
Nos. 6N1-6N50 (50) *120.06 120.06*

SEMI-POSTAL STAMPS

Hungarian Semi-Postal Stamps of 1913-17 Overprinted like Regular Issues

On Stamps of 1913

1919 Wmk. 137 *Perf. 14*

6NB1 SP1 1 l on 1f slate 1.00 1.00
6NB2 SP1 1 l on 2f ol yel 5.00 5.00
6NB3 SP1 1 l on 3f org 1.75 1.75
6NB4 SP1 1 l on 5f emer 60 60
6NB5 SP1 1 l on 6f ol grn 15 15
6NB6 SP1 1 l on 10f car 15 15
6NB7 SP1 1 l on 12f vio, *yel* 40.00 40.00
6NB8 SP1 1 l on 16f gray grn 1.50 1.50
6NB9 SP1 1 l on 20f dk brn 3.75 3.75
6NB10 SP1 1 l on 25f ultra 5.00 5.00
6NB11 SP1 1 l on 35f red vio 5.00 5.00

On Stamp of 1915

Wmk. 135 *Perf. 11½*

6NB12 A4 5b emerald 7.00 7.00

On Stamps of 1916-17

Wmk. 137 *Perf. 15*

6NB13 SP3 10b + 2b rose red 1.25 1.25
6NB14 SP4 15b + 2b dl vio 15 15
6NB15 SP5 40b + 2b brn car 15 15
Nos. 6NB1-6NB15 (15) 72.45 72.45

SPECIAL DELIVERY STAMP

Hungarian Special Delivery Stamp of 1916 Overprinted like Regular Issues

1919 Wmk. 137 *Perf. 15*

6NE1 SD1 2b gray grn & red 25 25

POSTAGE DUE STAMPS

Hungarian Postage Due Stamps of 1915 Overprinted like Regular Issues

1919 Wmk. 137 *Perf. 15*

6NJ1 D1 1b grn & red 13.00 13.00
6NJ2 D1 2b grn & red 18 18
6NJ3 D1 5b grn & red 25 25
6NJ4 D1 6b grn & red 1.00 1.00
6NJ5 D1 10b grn & red 1.25 1.25
6NJ6 D1 12b grn & red 80 80
6NJ7 D1 15b grn & red 80 80
6NJ8 D1 20b grn & red 15 15
6NJ9 D1 30b grn & red 80 80
Nos. 6NJ1-6NJ9 (9) 18.23 18.23

NEWSPAPER STAMP

Hungarian Newspaper Stamp of 1914 2 Overprinted like Regular Issues

1919 Wmk. 137 *Imperf.*

6NP1 N5 2b orange 28 28

FIRST BARANYA ISSUE

Issued under Serbian Occupation

Forged overprints abound.

Hungarian Stamps of 1913-18 Overprinted in Black or Red:

1919 Baranya — On A4, A9, A11, A12

1919 Baranya — On A10

1919 Wmk. 137 *Perf. 15*

On Issue of 1913-16

7N1 A4 6f ol grn (R) 65 65
7N2 A4 50f lake, *bl* 15 15
7N3 A4 60f grn, *sal* 30 30
7N4 A4 70f red brn & grn (R) 1.40 1.40
7N5 A4 70f red brn & grn (Bk) 15 15
7N6 A4 80f dl vio (R) 2.00 2.00

On Issue of 1916-18

7N7 A9 2f brn org (Bk) 2.00 2.00
7N8 A9 2f brn org (R) 20 20
7N9 A9 3f red lil (Bk) 20 20
7N10 A9 3f red lil (R) 20 20
7N11 A9 5f grn (Bk) 20 20
7N12 A9 5f grn (R) 20 20
7N13 A9 6f grnsh bl (Bk) 20 20
7N14 A9 6f grnsh bl (R) 20 20
7N15 A9 15f violet 20 20
7N16 A9 20f gray brn 15.00 15.00
7N17 A9 25f dl bl 2.00 2.00
7N18 A9 35f brown 4.00 4.00
7N19 A9 40f ol grn 15.00 15.00
7N20 A10 50f red vio & lil 1.75 1.75
7N21 A10 75f brt bl & pale bl 25 25
7N22 A10 80f grn & pale grn 25 25
7N23 A10 1k red brn & cl 25 25
7N24 A10 2k ol brn & bis 25 25
7N25 A10 3k dk vio & ind 25 25
7N26 A10 5k dk brn & lt brn 1.00 1.00
7N27 A10 10k vio brn & vio 4.00 *4.00*

OS8

7N28 OS8 45f on 2f brn org 15 15
7N29 OS8 45f on 5f grn 15 15
7N30 OS8 45f on 15f vio 15 15

On Issue of 1918

7N31 A11 10f scar (Bk) 15 15
7N32 A11 20f dk brn (Bk) 15 15
7N33 A11 20f dk brn (R) *22.50*
7N34 A11 25f dp bl (Bk) 75 75
7N35 A11 25f dp bl (R) 75 75
7N36 A12 40f ol grn (Bk) 5.00 5.00
7N37 A12 40f ol grn (R) 35.00 35.00

On Issue of 1918-19 (Koztarsasag)

7N38 A9 2f brn org (Bk) 4.00 4.00
7N39 A12 40f ol grn (Bk) *100.00 100.00*
7N40 A12 40f ol grn (R) 20.00 20.00

With New Value Added

7N41 OS8 45f on 2f brn org (Bk) 25 25
7N42 OS8 45f on 2f brn org (R) 25 25

The overprints were set in groups of 25. In each group two stamps have the figures "1" of "1919" with serifs.

No. 7N33 is considered a proof by some specialists.

SEMI-POSTAL STAMPS

Hungarian Semi-Postal Stamps Overprinted Regular Issue First Type On Stamp of 1915

1919 Wmk. 137 *Perf. 15*

7NB1 A4 50f + 2f lake, *bl* 16.00 16.00

On Stamps of 1916

7NB2 SP3 10f + 2f rose red 15 15
7NB3 SP4 15f + 2f dl vio 15 15

SPECIAL DELIVERY STAMP

SD1

1919 Wmk. 137 *Perf. 15*

7NE1 SD1 105f on 2f gray grn & red 80 80

POSTAGE DUE STAMPS

D1

1919 Wmk. 137 *Perf. 15*

7NJ1 D1 2f grn & red 2.00 2.00
7NJ2 D1 10f grn & red 1.00 1.00
7NJ3 D1 20f grn & red 1.25 1.25

With New Value Added

7NJ4 D1 40f on 2f grn & red 1.50 1.50

SECOND BARANYA ISSUE

Forged overprints exist.

Hungarian Stamps of 1916-19 Surcharged in Black and Red

1919 On Stamps of 1916-18

8N1 A9 20f on 2f brn org 1.00 1.00
8N2 A9 50f on 5f grn 40 40
8N3 A9 150f on 15f vio 1.00 1.00
8N4 A10 200f on 75f brt bl & pale bl 50 50

On Stamp of 1918-19, Overprinted "Koztarsasag"

8N5 A11 150f on 15f dp vio 25 25

On Stamps of 1919

8N6 A13 20f on 2f brn org 15 15
8N7 A13 30f on 6f grnsh bl 24 30
8N8 A13 50f on 5f yel grn 15 15
8N9 A13 100f on 25f dl bl 15 15
8N10 A13 100f on 40f ol grn 15 15
8N11 A13 100f on 45f org 35 50
8N12 A13 150f on 20f dk brn 40 60

On No. 103A

8N13 A5a 10f on 10f vio brn 24 35
Nos. 8N1-8N13 (13) 4.98 5.50

SPECIAL DELIVERY STAMP

Hungarian Special Delivery Stamp of 1916 Surcharged like Regular Issues

1919 Wmk. 137 *Perf. 15*

8NE1 SD1 10f on 2f gray grn & red 40 40

NEWSPAPER STAMP

Hungarian Newspaper Stamp of 1914 Surcharged like Regular Issues

1919 Wmk. 137 *Imperf.*

8NP1 N5 10f on 2f orange 30 30

TEMESVAR ISSUE

Issued under Serbian Occupation

Hungarian Stamps of 1916-18 Surcharged in Black, Blue or Brown:

10 filler — a

b

1919

9N1 A9(a) 10f on 2f brn org (Bl) 15 15
a. Black surcharge 25.00 25.00
9N2 A9(b) 30f on 2f brn org 15 15
a. Inverted surcharge
9N3 A11(b) 50f on 20f dk brn (Bl) 15 15
a. Inverted surcharge
9N4 A9(b) 1k 50f on 15f vio 25 25
a. Brown surcharge
b. Double surcharge (Bk)

SEMI-POSTAL STAMP

Hungarian Semi-Postal Stamp of 1916 Surcharged in Blue

45 fillér

1919 Wmk. 137 *Perf. 15*

9NB1 SP3 45f on 10f + 2f rose red 15 15

POSTAGE DUE STAMPS

Hungarian Postage Due Stamps of 1915 Surcharged

1919 Wmk. 137 *Perf. 15*

9NJ1 D1 40f on 2f grn & red 80 80
9NJ2 D1 60f on 2f grn & red 80 80
9NJ3 D1 100f on 2f grn & red 80 80

BANAT, BACSKA ISSUE

Issued under Serbian Occupation

Forged overprints exist.

Postal authorities at Temesvar applied these overprints. The stamps were available for postage, but were chiefly used to pay postal employees' salaries.

Hungarian Stamps of 1913-19 Overprinted in Black or Red:

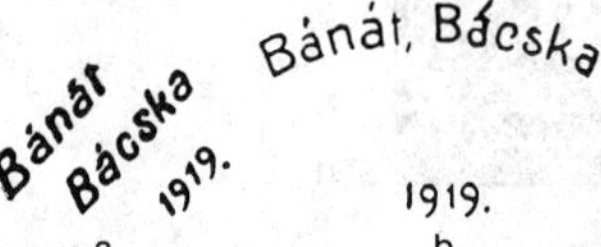

1919

Type "a" on Stamp of 1913

10N1 A4 50f lake, *bl* 5.00 5.00

Type "a" on Stamps of 1916-18

10N2 A9 2f brn org 15 15
10N3 A9 3f red lil 15 15
10N4 A9 5f green 15 15
10N5 A9 6f grnsh bl 15 15
10N6 A9 15f violet 15 15
10N7 A9 35f brown 8.50 8.50

Type "b"

10N8 A10 50f red vio & lil (R) 4.25 4.25
10N9 A10 75f brt bl & pale bl 15 15
10N10 A10 80f grn & pale grn 15 15
10N11 A10 1k red brn & cl 15 15
10N12 A10 2k ol brn & bis 15 15
a. Red overprint 6.00 6.00
10N14 A10 3k dk vio & ind 5.50 5.50
10N15 A10 5k dk brn & lt brn 32 32
10N16 A10 10k vio brn & vio 65 65

Type "a" on Stamps of 1918

10N17 A11 10f scarlet 15 15
10N18 A11 20f dk brn 15 15
10N19 A11 25f brt bl 15 15
10N20 A12 40f ol grn 15 15
10N21 A12 50f lilac 15 15

Type "a" on Stamps of 1919

Inscribed "Magyar Posta"

10N22 A13 10f red *5.50 5.50*
10N23 A13 20f dk brn *2.25 2.25*
10N24 A13 25f dl bl *7.00 7.00*

Type "a" on Stamps of 1918-19

Overprinted "Koztarsasag"

10N25 A9 4f sl gray 15 15
10N26 A9 4f sl gray (R) 5.00 5.00
10N27 A9 5f green 15 15
10N28 A9 6f grnsh bl 15 15
10N29 A9 10f rose red 2.25 2.25
10N30 A11 15f dp vio 1.65 1.65
10N31 A9 20f gray brn 2.75 2.75
10N32 A11 25f brt bl 1.00 1.00
10N33 A9 40f ol grn 15 15
10N34 A9 40f ol grn (R) 5.00 5.00

Type "b"

10N35 A10 1k red brn & cl 15 15
10N36 A10 2k ol brn & bis 2.75 2.75
10N37 A10 3k dk vio & ind 2.75 2.75
10N38 A10 5k dk brn & lt brn 2.75 2.75
10N39 A10 10k vio brn & vio 2.75 2.75

Type "a" on Temesvár Issue

10N40 A9 10f on 2f brn org (Bl & Bk) 40 40
10N41 A9 1k50f on 15f vio 40 40

OS9

10N42 OS9 50f on 10f vio brn 85 85
Nos. 10N1-10N42 (41) 72.12 72.12

SEMI-POSTAL STAMPS

Semi-Postal Stamps of 1916-17 Overprinted Type "a" in Black

1919

10NB1 SP3 10f + 2f rose red 15 15
10NB2 SP4 15f + 2f dl vio 15 15
10NB3 SP5 40f + 2f brn car 15 15

Same Overprint on Temesvar Issue

10NB4 SP3 45f on 10f + 2f rose red (Bl & Bk) 40 40

SPECIAL DELIVERY STAMP

SD1

Black Surcharge

1919

10NE1 SD1 30f on 2f gray grn & red 60 60

POSTAGE DUE STAMPS

Postage Due Stamps of 1914-15 Overprinted Type "a" in Black

1919

10NJ1 D1 2f grn & red 38 38
10NJ2 D1 10f grn & red 40 38
10NJ3 D1 15f grn & red 2.50 2.50
10NJ4 D1 20f grn & red 40 40
10NJ5 D1 30f grn & red 1.75 1.75
10NJ6 D1 50f grn & blk 2.50 2.50
Nos. 10NJ1-10NJ6 (6) 7.93 7.91

NEWSPAPER STAMP

Stamp of 1914 Overprinted Type "a" in Black

1919

10NP1 N5 (2f) orange 15 15

SZEGED ISSUE

The "Hungarian National Government, Szeged, 1919," as the overprint reads, was an anti-Bolshevist government which opposed the Soviet Republic then in control at Budapest.

Excellent counterfeits of the overprint exist.

Hungary Stamps of 1916-19 Overprinted in Green, Red and Blue

MAGYAR NEMZETI KORMÁNY Szeged, 1919.

On Stamps of 1916-18

1919 ***Perf. 15, 14***

1 A9 2f brn org (G) 80 80
2 A9 3f red lil (G) 80 80
3 A9 5f green 80 80
4 A9 6f grnsh bl 10.00 10.00
5 A9 15f violet 1.00 1.00
6 A10 50f red vio & lil 6.50 6.50
7 A10 75f brt bl & pale bl 4.00 4.00
8 A10 80f grn & pale grn 6.50 6.50
9 A10 1k red brn & cl (G) 7.50 7.50
10 A10 2k ol brn & bis 7.50 7.50
11 A10 3k dk vio & ind 8.50 8.50
12 A10 5k dk brn & lt brn 22.50 22.50
13 A10 10k vio brn & vio 22.50 22.50

With New Value Added

14 A9 45f on 3f red lil (R & G) 50 50
15 A10 10k on 1k red brn & cl (Bl & G) 6.00 6.00

On Stamps of 1918

16 A11 10f scar (G) 80 80
17 A11 20f dk brn 18 18
18 A11 25f brt bl 5.50 5.50
19 A12 40f ol grn 3.50 3.50

On Stamps of 1918-19

Overprinted "Koztarsasag"

20 A9 3f red lil (G) 12.50 12.50
21 A9 4f sl gray 3.00 3.00
22 A9 5f grn 12.50 12.50
23 A9 6f grnsh bl 2.50 2.50
24 A9 10f rose red (G) 2.50 2.50
25 A11 10f scar (G) 2.50 2.50
26 A11 15f dp vio 35 35
27 A9 20f gray brn 18.00 18.00
28 A11 20f dk brn 18.00 18.00
29 A11 25f brt bl 6.50 6.50
30 A9 40f ol grn 80 80
31 A12 50f lilac 80 80
32 A10 3k dk vio & ind 20.00 20.00

With New Value Added

33 A9 20f on 2f brn org (R & G) 50 50

On Stamps of 1919

Inscribed "Magyar Posta"

34 A13 20f dk brn 35.00 35.00
35 A13 25f dull blue 80 80
Nos. 1-35 (35) 251.63 251.63

SEMI-POSTAL STAMPS

Szeged Overprint on Semi-Postal Stamps of 1916-17 in Green or Red

1919

B1 SP3 10f + 2f rose red (G) 65 65
B2 SP4 15f + 2f dl vio (R) 2.50 2.50
B3 SP5 40f + 2f brn car (G) 6.50 6.50

With Additional Overprint "Koztarsasag"

B4 SP5 40f + 2f brn car (Bk & G) 7.50 7.50

SPECIAL DELIVERY STAMP

Szeged Overprint on Special Delivery Stamp of 1916 in Red

1919

E1 SD1 2f gray grn & red 1.50 1.50

POSTAGE DUE STAMPS

Szeged Overprint on Stamps of 1915-18 in Red

1919

J1 D1 2f green & red 1.25 1.25
J2 D1 6f green & red 4.50 4.50
J3 D1 10f green & red 1.25 1.25
J4 D1 12f green & red 3.00 3.00
J5 D1 20f green & red 3.00 3.00
J6 D1 30f green & red 3.00 3.00

D1

Red Surcharge

J7 D1 50f on 2f gray grn & red 1.50 1.50
J8 D1 100f on 2f gray grn & red 1.50 1.50
Nos. J1-J8 (8) 19.00 19.00

NEWSPAPER STAMP

Szeged Overprint on Stamp of 1914 in Green

1919 **Wmk. 137** ***Imperf.***

P1 N5 (2f) orange 40 40

ICELAND

LOCATION — Island in the North Atlantic Ocean, east of Greenland
GOVT. — Republic
AREA — 39,758 sq. mi.
POP. — 238,175 (1983)
CAPITAL — Reykjavik

Iceland became a republic on June 17, 1944. Formerly this country was united with Denmark under the government of King Christian X who, as a ruling sovereign of both countries, was assigned the dual title of king of each. Although the two countries were temporarily united in certain affairs beyond the king's person, both were acknowledged as sovereign states.

96 Skillings = 1 Rigsdaler
100 Aurar (singular "Eyrir") = 1 Krona (1876)

Catalogue values for unused stamps in this country are for Never Hinged items, beginning with Scott 324 in the regular postage section, Scott B14 in the semi-postal section.

Values of early Icelandic stamps vary according to condition. Quotations for Nos. 1-7 are for fine copies. Very fine to superb specimens sell at much higher prices, and inferior or poor copies sell at reduced prices, depending on the condition of the individual specimen.

Watermarks

Wmk. 112- Crown

Wmk. 113- Crown

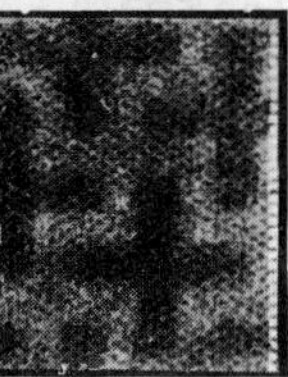

Wmk. 114- Multiple Crosses

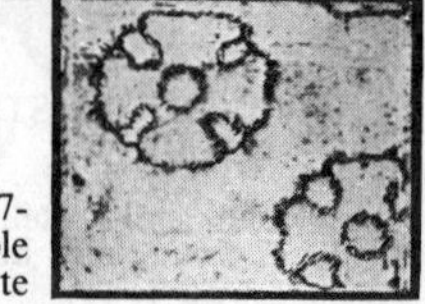

Wmk. 47- Multiple Rosette

A1

Perf. 14x13½

1873 **Typo.** **Wmk. 112**

1 A1 2s ultra 575.00 *1,150.*
a. Imperf. 525.00
2 A1 4s dk carmine 110.00 *575.00*
a. Imperf. 575.00
3 A1 8s brown 175.00 *575.00*
a. Imperf. 225.00
4 A1 16s yellow 825.00 *1,150.*
a. Imperf. 275.00

Perf. 12½

5 A1 3s gray 200.00 *725.00*
a. Imperf. 550.00
6 A1 4s carmine 700.00 *1,200.*
7 A1 16s yellow 67.50 *300.00*

False and favor cancellations are often found on Nos. 1-7. The imperforate varieties lack gum.

A2

Small "3" — A3 Large "3" — A3a

1876

8 A2 5a blue 175.00 *350.00*

Perf. 14x13½

9 A2 5a blue 240.00 *350.00*
10 A2 6a gray 52.50 10.00
11 A2 10a carmine 85.00 3.50
a. Imperf. 350.00 375.00
12 A2 16a brown 62.50 25.00
13 A2 20a dark violet 24.00 *55.00*
14 A2 40a green 62.50 *80.00*

1882-98

No.	Type	Description	Unused	Used
15	A3	3a orange	30.00	9.50
16	A2	5a green	25.00	6.25
17	A2	20a blue	140.00	18.00
a.		20a ultramarine	300.00	80.00
18	A2	40a red violet	19.00	22.50
a.		Perf. 13 ('98)	*3,600.*	
19	A2	50a bl & car ('92)	45.00	32.50
20	A2	100a brn & vio ('92)	47.50	47.50

See note after No. 68.

1896-1901 *Perf. 13*

No.	Type	Description	Unused	Used
21	A3	3a orange ('97)	45.00	4.00
22	A3a	3a yellow ('01)	2.25	*9.00*
23	A2	4a rose & gray ('99)	10.50	10.00
24	A2	5a green	1.65	1.10
25	A2	6a gray ('97)	7.00	*8.50*
26	A2	10a carmine ('97)	3.00	1.40
27	A2	16a brown	37.50	*45.00*
28	A2	20a dull blue ('98)	14.00	12.00
a.		20a dull ultramarine	200.00	13.00
29	A2	25a yel brown & blue ('00)	13.00	16.00
30	A2	50a bl & car ('98)	225.00	*400.00*

See note after No. 68.

Black and Red Surcharge

Surcharged þrír 3

1897 *Perf. 13*

No.	Type	Description	Unused	Used
31	A2	3a on 5a green	325.00	300.00
a.		Perf. 14x13½		*2,750.*
b.		Inverted surcharge	1,050.	800.00

Surcharged þrír 3

No.	Type	Description	Unused	Used
32	A2	3a on 5a green	275.00	275.00
a.		Inverted surcharge	1,000.	750.00
b.		Perf. 14x13½	*6,750.*	*1,250.*

Black Surcharge

Surcharged þrír

No.	Type	Description	Unused	Used
33	A2	3a on 5a green	425.00	375.00

Surcharged þrír

No.	Type	Description	Unused	Used
33A	A2	3a on 5a green	350.00	325.00

Excellent counterfeits are known.

King Christian IX — A4

1902-04 **Wmk. 113** *Perf. 13*

No.	Type	Description	Unused	Used
34	A4	3a orange	2.75	1.40
35	A4	4a gray & rose	2.25	45
36	A4	5a yel green	11.00	28
37	A4	6a gray brown	8.25	3.50
38	A4	10a car rose	3.75	28
39	A4	16a chocolate	3.75	3.25
40	A4	20a deep blue	1.50	2.25
a.		Inscribed "PJONUSTA"	35.00	35.00
41	A4	25a brn & grn	1.50	1.75
42	A4	40a violet	1.75	1.65
43	A4	50a gray & bl blk	3.00	*12.00*
44	A4	1k sl bl & yel brn	4.50	4.25
44A	A4	2k olive brn & brt blue ('04)	15.00	*35.00*
44B	A4	5k org brn & slate blue ('04)	82.50	*100.00*
		Nos. 34-44B (13)	141.50	*166.06*

Stamps of 1882-1901 Overprinted í GILDI '02—'03

1902-03 **Wmk. 112** *Perf. 13*

Red Overprint

No.	Type	Description	Unused	Used
45	A2	5a green	38	*4.25*
a.		Inverted overprint	8.25	
b.		"I" before Gildi omitted	15.00	
c.		'03-'03	32.50	
d.		02'-'03	32.50	
e.		Pair, one without overprint	32.50	
46	A2	6a gray	28	*3.50*
a.		Double overprint	20.00	
b.		Inverted overprint	16.00	
c.		'03-'03	60.00	
d.		02'-'03	60.00	
e.		Pair, one with invtd. ovpt.	30.00	
f.		Pair, one without overprint	25.00	
g.		As "f", inverted	40.00	
47	A2	20a dull blue	38	*4.00*
a.		Inverted overprint	16.00	16.00
b.		"I" before Gildi omitted	30.00	
c.		02'-'03	82.50	
48	A2	25a yel brn & bl	38	*8.25*
a.		Inverted overprint	11.00	11.00
b.		'03-'03	37.50	
c.		02'-'03	37.50	
d.		Double overprint	55.00	

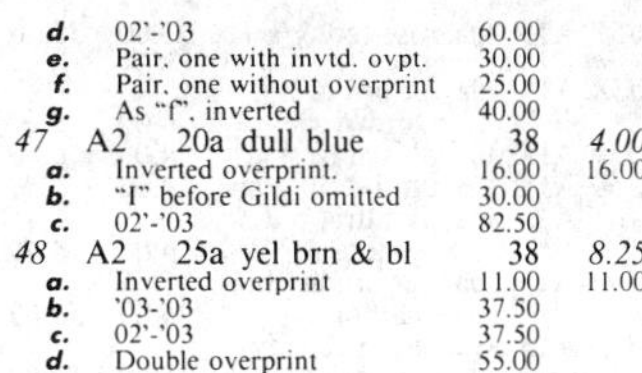

Black Overprint

No.	Type	Description	Unused	Used
49	A3	3a orange	75.00	*225.00*
b.		Inverted overprint	75.00	
c.		"I" before Gildi omitted	75.00	
d.		'03-'03	75.00	
e.		02'-'03	75.00	*235.00*
50	A3a	3a yellow	40	*90*
a.		Double overprint	35.00	
b.		Inverted overprint	6.00	
c.		"I" before Gildi omitted	50.00	
d.		'02-'03	50.00	
51	A2	4a rose & gray	17.00	*27.50*
a.		Double overprint	35.00	
b.		Inverted overprint	19.00	*30.00*
c.		Dbl. ovpt., one invtd.	60.00	
d.		"I" before Gildi omitted	24.00	
e.		'03-'03	55.00	
f.		02'-'03	55.00	60.00
g.		Pair, one with invtd. ovpt.	55.00	
52	A2	5a green	125.00	*225.00*
a.		Inverted overprint	130.00	*225.00*
b.		Pair, one without overprint	150.00	
c.		As "b", inverted	150.00	
53	A2	6a gray	275.00	*325.00*
a.		Inverted overprint	200.00	250.00
b.		Pair, one without overprint	200.00	
54	A2	10a carmine	55	*6.00*
a.		Inverted overprint	5.50	9.00
b.		Pair, one without overprint	24.00	
55	A2	16a brown	10.00	*24.00*
a.		Inverted overprint	24.00	
b.		"I" before Gildi omitted	42.50	
c.		'03-'03	67.50	
d.		02'-'03	67.50	
56	A2	20a dull blue	*4,500.*	
a.		Inverted overprint	*4,750.*	
57	A2	25a yel brn & bl	*3,750.*	
a.		Inverted overprint	*4,250.*	
58	A2	40a red vio	45	*30.00*
a.		Inverted overprint	10.00	*30.00*
59	A2	50a bl & car	2.25	*37.50*
a.		Double overprint	32.50	40.00
b.		02'-'03	32.50	
c.		'03-'03	32.50	

Perf. 14x13½

Red Overprint

No.	Type	Description	Unused	Used
60	A2	5a green	750.00	*1,250.*
a.		'03-'03	775.00	
b.		02'-'03	750.00	
61	A2	6a gray	750.00	1,250.
a.		02'-'03	750.00	
62	A2	20a blue	*2,600.*	*4,500.*

Black Overprint

No.	Type	Description	Unused	Used
63	A3	3a orange	450.00	*1,000.*
a.		Inverted overprint	475.00	
b.		02'-'03	475.00	
c.		'03-'03	475.00	
64	A2	10a carmine	*3,450.*	*3,750.*
65	A2	16a brown	450.00	*900.00*
a.		Inverted overprint	475.00	
b.		02'-'03	475.00	
d.		'03-'03	475.00	
65C	A2	20a dull blue	*3,750.*	*4,750.*
66	A2	40a red vio	10.00	*45.00*
a.		Inverted overprint	15.00	
b.		'03-'03	37.50	
c.		02'-'03	37.50	
67	A2	50a bl & car	14.00	*67.50*
a.		Inverted overprint	40.00	*70.00*
b.		'03-'03	55.00	
c.		02'-'03	55.00	
d.		As "c," inverted	105.00	
68	A2	100a brn & vio	25.00	*32.50*
a.		Inverted overprint	32.50	*37.50*
b.		02'-'03	65.00	
c.		'03-'03	65.00	

"I GILDI" means "valid."

In 1904 Nos. 20, 22-30, 45-59 (except 49, 52, 53, 56 and 57) and No. 68 were reprinted for the Postal Union. The reprints are perforated 13 and have watermark type 113. Value $50 each. Without overprint, $100 each.

Kings Christian IX and Frederik VIII — A5

Typo., Center Engr.

1907-08 **Wmk. 113** *Perf. 13*

No.	Type	Description	Unused	Used
71	A5	1e yel grn & red	70	50
72	A5	3a yel brn & ocher	1.75	50
73	A5	4a gray & red	1.00	50
74	A5	5a green	30.00	30
75	A5	6a gray & gray brn	15.00	1.25
76	A5	10a scarlet	52.50	38
77	A5	15a red & green	3.75	50
78	A5	16a brown	3.75	*12.50*
79	A5	20a blue	4.25	1.40
80	A5	25a bis brn & grn	2.50	*4.00*
81	A5	40a claret & vio	3.25	*5.00*
82	A5	50a gray & vio	3.25	*4.00*
83	A5	1k blue & brn	12.50	*26.00*
84	A5	2k dk brn & dk grn	12.50	*26.00*
85	A5	5k brn & slate	87.50	*165.00*
		Nos. 71-85 (15)	234.20	*247.83*

See Nos. 99-107.

Jon Sigurdsson — A6   Frederik VIII — A7

1911 **Typo. and Embossed**

No.	Type	Description	Unused	Used
86	A6	1e olive green	1.50	65
87	A6	3a light brown	1.75	*7.00*
88	A6	4a ultramarine	80	*1.00*
89	A6	6a gray	5.50	*10.00*
90	A6	15a violet	14.00	85
91	A6	25a orange	19.00	19.00
		Nos. 86-91 (6)	42.55	*38.50*

Jon Sigurdsson (1811-1879), statesman and author.

1912, Feb. 17

No.	Type	Description	Unused	Used
92	A7	5a green	18.00	6.75
93	A7	10a red	18.00	6.75
94	A7	20a pale blue	27.50	8.50
95	A7	50a claret	8.00	*18.00*
96	A7	1k yellow	14.00	*30.00*
97	A7	2k rose	14.00	*25.00*
98	A7	5k brown	92.50	*110.00*
		Nos. 92-98 (7)	192.00	*205.00*

Christian X — A8

Typo., Center Engr.

1915-18 **Wmk. 114** *Perf. 14x14½*

No.	Type	Description	Unused	Used
99	A5	1e yel grn & red	4.25	*8.25*
100	A5	3a bister brn	2.00	1.20
101	A5	4a gray & red	2.00	*5.00*
102	A5	5a green	42.50	55
103	A5	6a gray & gray brn	9.00	*65.00*
104	A5	10a scarlet	2.00	55
107	A5	20a blue	105.00	8.25
		Nos. 99-107 (7)	166.75	*88.80*

1920-22 **Typo.**

No.	Type	Description	Unused	Used
108	A8	1e yel grn & red	48	50
109	A8	3a bister brn	2.50	*6.25*
110	A8	4a gray & red	2.00	85
111	A8	5a green	1.25	75
112	A8	5a ol green ('22)	2.00	50
113	A8	6a dark gray	7.25	3.50
114	A8	8a dark brown	4.25	85
115	A8	10a red	75	*4.50*
116	A8	10a green ('21)	1.50	65
117	A8	15a violet	18.00	65
118	A8	20a deep blue	1.10	*7.50*
119	A8	20a choc ('22)	30.00	65
120	A8	25a brown & grn	9.25	70
121	A8	25a red ('21)	4.75	*15.00*
122	A8	30a red & green	25.00	1.25
123	A8	40a claret	25.00	1.00
124	A8	40a dk bl ('21)	35.00	5.50
125	A8	50a dk gray & cl	75.00	5.00
126	A8	1k dp bl & dk brn	55.00	70
127	A8	2k ol brn & myr green	90.00	12.50
		Revenue cancellation		1.25
128	A8	5k brn & ind	35.00	6.25
		Revenue cancellation		1.25
		Nos. 108-128 (21)	425.08	*75.05*

Revenue cancellations consisting of "TOLLUR" boxed in frame are found on stamps used to pay the tax on parcel post packages entering Iceland.

See Nos. 176-187, 202.

A9

A10

A11

1921-25 **Wmk. 113** *Perf. 13*

No.	Type	Description	Unused	Used
130	A9	5a on 16a brown	1.65	*15.00*
131	A11	5a on 16a brown	75	*3.25*
132	A10	20a on 25a brn & green	3.25	2.25
133	A11	20a on 25a bis brn & green	1.65	*2.50*
134	A9	20a on 40a violet	3.25	*7.00*
135	A11	20a on 40a cl & vio	4.50	*7.50*

137 A9 30a on 50a gray & bl blk ('25) 9.00 *12.00*
Revenue cancel 5.00
138 A9 50a on 5k org brn & sl bl ('25) 35.00 15.00
Revenue cancel 4.00
Nos. 130-138 (8) 59.05 *64.50*

No. 111 Surcharged **10 aur.**

1922 Wmk. 114 *Perf. 14x14½*
139 A8 10a on 5a green 2.75 1.25

Nos. 95-96, 44A, 85 Surcharged **Kr. 10**

1924-30 Wmk. 113 *Perf. 13*
140 A7 10k on 50a ('25) 135.00 *225.00*
Revenue cancellation 9.00
141 A7 10k on 1k 200.00 *300.00*
Revenue cancellation 22.50
142 A4 10k on 2k ('29) 40.00 15.00
Revenue cancellation 3.25
143 A5 10k on 5k ('30) 225.00 225.00
Revenue cancellation 3.00

"Tollur" is a revenue cancellation.

Landing the Mail — A12

Designs: 7a, 50a, Landing the mail. 10a, 35a, View of Reykjavik. 20a, Museum building.

Perf. 14x15
1925, Sept. 12 Typo. Wmk. 114
144 A12 7a yel green 25.00 3.00
145 A12 10a dp bl & brn 25.00 25
146 A12 20a vermilion 25.00 25
147 A12 35a deep blue 32.50 5.00
148 A12 50a yel grn & brn 32.50 60
Nos. 144-148 (5) 140.00 9.10

No. 91 Surcharged **2 krónur**

1925 Wmk. 113 *Perf. 13*
149 A6 2k on 25a orange 42.50 *70.00*
Revenue cancellation 6.00

No. 124 Surcharged in Red **EIN KRÓNA**

1926
150 A8 1k on 40a dark blue 72.50 13.00
Revenue cancellation 8.00

Parliament Building A15

Designs: 5a, Viking ship in storm. 7a, Parliament meeting place, 1690. 10a, Viking funeral. 15a, Vikings naming land. 20a, The dash for Thing. 25a, Gathering wood. 30a, Thingvalla Lake. 35a, Iceland woman in national costume. 40a, Iceland flag. 50a, First Althing, 930 A.D. 1k, Map of Iceland. 2k, Winter-bound home. 5k, Woman spinning. 10k, Viking Sacrifice to Thor.

Perf. 12½x12
1930, Jan. 1 Litho. Unwmk.
152 A15 3a dl vio & gray violet 1.75 *5.00*
153 A15 5a dk bl & sl grn 1.75 *5.00*
154 A15 7a grn & gray grn 1.75 *5.00*
155 A15 10a dk vio & lilac 5.25 *6.00*
156 A15 15a dp ultra & bl gray 1.75 *5.00*
157 A15 20a rose red & sal 23.00 *32.50*
a. Double impression 135.00
158 A15 25a dk brn & lt brown 4.00 *8.00*
159 A15 30a dk grn & sl grn 4.00 *6.00*
160 A15 35a ultra & bl gray 4.00 *8.50*
161 A15 40a dk ultra, red & slate grn 4.00 *6.00*
162 A15 50a red brn & cinnamon 35.00 *50.00*
163 A15 1k ol grn & gray green 35.00 *50.00*
164 A15 2k turq bl & gray green 42.50 *67.50*
165 A15 5k org & yellow 23.00 *50.00*
166 A15 10k mag & dl rose 23.00 *50.00*
a. Imperf., pair 60.00
Nos. 152-166 (15) 209.75 *354.50*

Millenary of the "Althing", the Icelandic Parliament, oldest in the world.

Gullfoss (Golden Falls) — A30

1931-32 Unwmk. Engr. *Perf. 14*
170 A30 5a gray 6.75 48
171 A30 20a red 5.50 18
172 A30 35a ultramarine 10.50 7.50
173 A30 60a red lil ('32) 5.50 75
174 A30 65a red brn ('32) 1.10 55
175 A30 75a grnsh bl ('32) 62.50 19.00
Revenue cancellation 1.90
Nos. 170-175 (6) 91.85 28.46

Issue dates: 5a-35a, Dec. 15. 60a-75a, May 30.

Type of 1920 Christian X Issue Redrawn

Perf. 14x14½
1931-33 Typo. Wmk. 114
176 A8 1e yel grn & red 60 *65*
177 A8 3a bister brown 3.75 *4.50*
178 A8 4a gray & red 1.00 65
179 A8 6a dark gray 1.00 *3.00*
180 A8 7a yel grn ('33) 40 70
181 A8 10a chocolate 40.00 45
182 A8 25a brn & green 9.00 1.00
183 A8 30a red & green 11.50 2.25
184 A8 40a claret 60.00 6.00
185 A8 1k dk bl & lt brn 25.00 3.50
Revenue cancellation 1.10
186 A8 2k choc & dk grn 77.50 25.00
Revenue cancellation 1.40
187 A8 10k yel grn & blk 175.00 75.00
Revenue cancellation 3.25
Nos. 176-187 (12) 404.75 122.70

On the redrawn stamps the horizontal lines of the portrait and the oval are closer together than on the 1920 stamps and are crossed by many fine vertical lines.
See No. 202.

Dynjandi Falls A31

Mount Hekla A32

Perf. 12½
1935, June 28 Engr. Unwmk.
193 A31 10a blue 10.00 15
194 A32 1k greenish gray 22.50 15

Matthias Jochumsson A33

King Christian X A34

1935, Nov. 11
195 A33 3a gray green 38 *1.75*
196 A33 5a gray 8.00 60
197 A33 7a yel green 13.00 75
198 A33 35a blue 38 *75*

Birth cent. of Matthias Jochumsson, poet.

1937, May 14 *Perf. 13x12½*
199 A34 10a green 1.50 *7.00*
200 A34 30a brown 1.50 *3.00*
201 A34 40a claret 1.50 *3.00*

Reign of Christian X, 25th anniv.

Christian X Type of 1931-33

1937 Unwmk. Typo. *Perf. 11½*
202 A8 1e yel grn & red 50 *50*

Geyser
A35 A36

1938-47 Engr. *Perf. 14*
203 A35 15a dp rose vio 2.75 *6.00*
a. Imperf., pair *1,200.*
204 A35 20a rose red 12.50 16
205 A35 35a ultra 48 48
206 A36 40a dk brn ('39) 6.00 *12.00*
207 A36 45a brt ultra ('40) 50 50
208 A36 50a dk slate grn 12.50 50
208A A36 60a brt ultra ('43) 3.75 70
c. Perf. 11½ ('47) 2.00 *2.50*
208B A36 1k indigo ('45) 1.40 24
d. Perf. 11½ ('47) 2.00 *2.50*
Nos. 203-208B (8) 39.88 *20.58*

University of Iceland A37

1938, Dec. 1 *Perf. 13½*
209 A37 25a dark grn 5.00 *7.50*
210 A37 30a brown 5.00 *7.50*
211 A37 40a brt red vio 5.00 *7.50*

20th anniversary of independence.

No. 198 Surcharged with New Value

1939, Mar. 17 *Perf. 12½*
212 A33 5a on 35a blue 1.00 *1.00*
a. Double surcharge *160.00*

Trylon and Perisphere A38

Leif Ericsson's Ship and Route to America A39

Statue of Thorfinn Karlsefni — A40

1939 Engr. *Perf. 14*
213 A38 20a crimson 2.25 3.25
214 A39 35a bright ultra 3.00 4.25
215 A40 45a bright green 2.75 5.00
216 A40 2k dark gray 32.50 *85.00*

New York World's Fair.

Codfish A41

Herring A42

Flag of Iceland — A43

1939-45 Engr. *Perf. 14, 14x13½*

217	A41	1e Prussian blue	15	*1.40*
a.		Perf. 14x13½	1.10	*2.00*
218	A42	3a dark violet	15	15
a.		Perf. 14x13½	1.00	1.00
219	A41	5a dark brown	15	15
c.		Perf. 14x13½	1.10	50
220	A42	7a dark green	3.00	*3.25*
221	A42	10a green ('40)	19.00	15
b.		Perf. 14	22.50	15
222	A42	10a sl gray ('45)	15	15
223	A42	12a dk grn ('43)	15	15
224	A41	25a brt red ('40)	9.00	15
b.		Perf. 14x13½	22.50	55
225	A41	25a hn brn ('45)	15	15
226	A42	35a carmine ('43)	40	15
227	A41	50a dk bl grn ('43)	35	15

Typo.

228	A43	10a car & ultra	1.40	50
		Nos. 217-228 (12)	34.05	*6.50*

Statue of Thorfinn Karlsefni — A44

1939-45 Engr. *Perf. 14*

229	A44	2k dark gray	1.60	15
230	A44	5k dk brn ('43)	11.00	20
231	A44	10k brn yel ('45)	10.50	1.40

1947

Perf. 11½

229a	A44	2k	4.75	90
230a	A44	5k	19.00	1.25
231a	A44	10k	14.00	*30.00*

New York World's Fair Issue of 1939 Overprinted "1940" in Black

1940, May 11 *Perf. 14*

232	A38	20a crimson	7.75	*18.00*
233	A39	35a bright ultra	7.75	*28.00*
234	A40	45a bright green	7.75	*18.00*
235	A40	2k dark gray	80.00	*200.00*

No. 195 Surcharged in Red

1941, Mar. 6 *Perf. 12½*

236	A33	25a on 3a gray grn	60	*90*

Statue of Snorri Sturluson A45

Jon Sigurdsson A46

1941, Nov. 17 Engr. *Perf. 14*

237	A45	25a rose red	65	80
238	A45	50a deep ultra	1.65	2.00
239	A45	1k dk olive grn	1.65	2.00

Snorri Sturluson, writer and historian, 700th death anniv.

Republic

1944, June 17 *Perf. 14x13½*

240	A46	10a gray black	24	*60*
241	A46	25a dk red brn	32	*60*
242	A46	50a slate grn	32	*60*
243	A46	1k blue black	32	*60*
244	A46	5k henna	6.50	*10.50*
245	A46	10k golden brn	35.00	*67.50*
		Nos. 240-245 (6)	42.70	*80.40*

Founding of Republic of Iceland, June 17, 1944.

Eruption of Hekla Volcano
A47 A48

Designs: 35a, 60a, Close view of Hekla.

Unwmk.

1948, Dec. 3 Engr. *Perf. 14*

246	A47	12a dark vio brn	15	15
247	A48	25a green	60	15
248	A47	35a carmine rose	22	15
249	A47	50a brown	65	15
250	A47	60a bright ultra	2.50	1.65
251	A48	1k orange brown	6.00	15
252	A48	10k violet black	17.50	38
		Nos. 246-252 (7)	27.62	2.78

Pack Train and UPU Monument, Bern — A49

UPU, 75th Anniv.: 35a, Reykjavik. 60a, Map. 2k, Thingvellir Road.

1949, Oct. 9

253	A49	25a dark green	20	*28*
254	A49	35a deep carmine	20	*28*
255	A49	60a blue	30	*70*
256	A49	2k orange red	1.00	70

Trawler A50

Jon Arason A51

Designs: 20a, 75a, 1k, Tractor plowing. 60a, 5k, Flock of sheep. 5a, 90a, 2k, Vestmannaeyjar harbor. 25a, 1.25k, 1.50k, Same as 10a.

1950-54 *Perf. 13*

257	A50	5a dk brn ('54)	15	15
258	A50	10a gray	15	15
259	A50	20a brown	15	15
260	A50	25a car ('54)	15	15
261	A50	60a green	5.50	*15.00*
262	A50	75a red org ('52)	42	15
263	A50	90a carmine	16	15
264	A50	1k chocolate	2.75	15
265	A50	1.25k red vio ('52)	7.00	15
266	A50	1.50k deep ultra	5.50	15
267	A50	2k purple	10.00	15
268	A50	5k dark grn	17.00	30
		Nos. 257-268 (12)	48.93	*16.80*

1950, Nov. 7 *Perf. 14*

269	A51	1.80k carmine	1.25	1.90
270	A51	3.30k green	50	*1.50*

Bishop Jon Arason, 400th anniv. of death.

Mail Delivery, 1776 — A52

Design: 3k, Airmail, 1951.

1951, May 13

271	A52	2k deep ultra	1.40	*1.10*
272	A52	3k dark purple	1.65	*1.40*

175th anniv. of Iceland's postal service.

Parliament Building — A53

1952, Apr. 1 *Perf. 13x12½*

273	A53	25k gray black	75.00	14.00

Sveinn Björnsson A54

Reykjabok A55

1952, Sept. 1 *Perf. 13½*

274	A54	1.25k deep blue	1.40	15
275	A54	2.20k deep green	35	*4.00*
276	A54	5k indigo	4.50	70
277	A54	10k brown red	16.00	19.00

Sveinn Björnsson, 1st President of Iceland.

1953, Oct. 1 *Perf. 13½x13*

Designs: 70a, Lettering manuscript. 1k, Corner of 15th century manuscript, "Stjorn." 1.75k, Reykjabok. 10k, Corner from law manuscript.

278	A55	10a black	15	15
279	A55	70a green	22	18
280	A55	1k carmine	35	15
281	A55	1.75k blue	11.00	75
282	A55	10k orange brn	7.25	35
		Nos. 278-282 (5)	18.97	1.58

No. 248 Surcharged With New Value and Bars in Black

1954, Mar. 31 *Perf. 14*

283	A47	5a on 35a car rose	15	*25*
a.		Bars omitted	35.00	
b.		Inverted surcharge	92.50	

Hannes Hafstein A56

Icelandic Wrestling A57

Portraits: 2.45k, in oval. 5k, fullface.

1954, June 1 Engr. *Perf. 13*

284	A56	1.25k deep blue	2.50	35
285	A56	2.45k dark green	9.25	*17.00*
286	A56	5k carmine	9.25	3.00

Appointment of the first native minister to Denmark, 50th anniv.

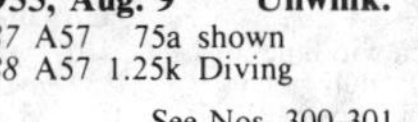
1955, Aug. 9 Unwmk. *Perf. 14*

287	A57	75a shown	20	20
288	A57	1.25k Diving	30	30

See Nos. 300-301.

Skoga Falls — A58

Ellidaar Power Plant — A59

Waterfalls: 60a, Goda. 2kr, Detti. 5kr, Gull. Electric Power Plants: 1.50kr, Sogs. 2.45kr, Andakilsar. 3kr, Laxar.

Perf. 11½, 13½x14 (A59)

1956, Apr. 4 **Unwmk.**

289	A58	15a	vio blue	20	20
290	A59	50a	dull green	32	20
291	A59	60a	brown	1.65	*3.75*
292	A59	1.50k	violet	8.00	25
293	A59	2k	sepia	1.20	25
294	A59	2.45k	gray black	4.25	4.25
295	A59	3k	dark blue	2.25	60
296	A58	5k	dark green	6.75	1.50
		Nos. 289-296 (8)		24.62	11.00

Telegraph-Telephone Emblem and Map — A60

1956, Sept. 29 **Engr.** ***Perf. 13***

297 A60 2.30k ultramarine 25 *60*

Telegraph and Telephone service in Iceland, 50th anniv.

Northern Countries Issue

Whooper Swans — A60a

1956, Oct. 30 ***Perf. 12½***

298	A60a	1.50k	rose red	65	80
299	A60a	1.75k	ultra	7.00	*10.00*

To emphasize the bonds among Denmark, Finland, Iceland, Norway and Sweden.

Sports Type of 1955

Designs: 1.50k, Icelandic wrestling. 1.75k, Diving.

1957, Apr. 1 **Engr.** ***Perf. 14***

300	A57	1.50k	carmine	60	24
301	A57	1.75k	ultramarine	42	24

Type of 1952 Air Post Stamps; Plane Omitted

Glaciers: 2k, Snaefellsjokull. 3k, Eiriksjokull. 10k, Oraefajokull.

1957, May 8 ***Perf. 13½x14***

302	AP16	2k	green	1.75	15
303	AP16	3k	dark blue	1.75	20
304	AP16	10k	reddish brn	2.75	32

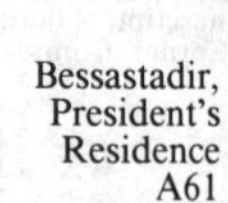

Bessastadir, President's Residence A61

1957, Aug. 1 **Engr.** **Unwmk.**

305 A61 25k gray blk 10.50 3.00

Evergreen and Volcanoes A62

Jonas Hallgrimsson A63

1957, Sept. 4 ***Perf. 13½x13***

306	A62	35a	shown	15	15
307	A62	70a	Birch	15	15

Issued to publicize a reforestation program.

1957, Nov 16

308 A63 5k grn & blk 1.10 45

150th birth anniv. of Jonas Hallgrimsson, poet.

Willow Herb — A64

Icelandic Pony — A65

1958, July 8 **Litho.** **Unwmk.**

309	A64	1k	shown	15	15
310	A64	2.50k	Wild pansy	35	35

1958, Sept. 27 **Engr.**

311	A65	10a	gray black	15	15
312	A65	2.25k	brown	50	15

See No. 324.

Flag — A66

Old Icelandic Government Building — A67

Perf. 13½x14

1958, Dec. 1 **Litho.** **Unwmk.**

Size: 17½x21mm

313 A66 3.50k brt ultra & red 1.40 65

Size: 23x26½mm

314 A66 50k brt ultra & red 6.25 5.00

40th anniversary of Icelandic flag.

1958, Dec. 9 **Photo.** ***Perf. 11½***

315	A67	2k	deep green	50	20
316	A67	4k	deep brown	50	35

See Nos. 333-334.

Jon Thorkelsson Teaching — A68

1959, May 5 **Engr.** ***Perf. 13½***

317	A68	2k	green	50	50
318	A68	3k	dull purple	50	50

Death bicentenary of Jon Thorkelsson, headmaster of Skaholt.

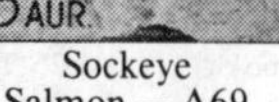

Sockeye Salmon — A69

Eider Ducks — A70

Design: 25k, Gyrfalcon.

1959-60 **Engr.** ***Perf. 14***

319	A69	25a	dark blue	15	15
320	A70	90a	chestnut & blk	15	15
321	A70	2k	olive grn & blk	22	15
322	A69	5k	gray green	4.00	65

Litho. ***Perf. 11½***

323	A70	25k	dl pur, gray & yel	12.00	10.50
		Nos. 319-323 (5)		16.52	11.60

Issue dates: 25k, Mar. 1, 1960. Others, Nov. 25.

Catalogue values for unused stamps in this section, from this point to the end of the section, are for Never Hinged items.

Pony Type of 1958

1960, Apr. 7 **Engr.** ***Perf. 13½x13***

324 A65 1k dark carmine 30 15

"The Outlaw" by Einar Jonsson A71

Wild Geranium A72

1960, Apr. 7 ***Perf. 14***

325	A71	2.50k	reddish brn	20	15
326	A71	4.50k	ultramarine	65	75

World Refugee Year, July 1, 1959-June 30, 1960.

Europa Issue, 1960

Common Design Type

1960, Sept. 18 **Photo.** ***Perf. 11½***

Size: 32½x22mm

327	CD3	3k	grn & lt grn	85	55
328	CD3	5.50k	dk bl & lt bl	65	1.50

1960-62 **Photo.** ***Perf. 11½***

Flowers: 50a, Bellflower. 2.50k, Dandelion. 3.50k, Buttercup.

329	A72	50a	gray grn, grn & violet ('62)	15	15
330	A72	1.20k	sep, vio & grn	16	16
331	A72	2.50k	brn, yel & grn	20	16
332	A72	3.50k	dl bl, yel & green ('62)	52	16

See Nos. 363-366, 393-394.

Common Design Types pictured in section at front of book.

Building Type of 1958

1961, Apr. 11 **Unwmk.** ***Perf. 11½***

333	A67	1.50k	deep blue	24	15
334	A67	3k	dark carmine	24	15

Jon Sigurdsson A73

Reykjavik A74

Typographed and Embossed

1961, June 17 ***Perf. 12½x14***

335	A73	50a	crimson	15	18
336	A73	3k	dark blue	1.10	90
337	A73	5k	deep plum	60	55

Jon Sigurdsson (1811-1879), statesman and scholar.

1961, Aug. 18 **Photo.** ***Perf. 11½***

338	A74	2.50k	blue & grn	42	25
339	A74	4.50k	lilac & vio bl	70	40

Municipal charter of Reykjavik, 175th anniv.

Europa Issue, 1961
Common Design Type

1961, Sept. 18
Size: 32x22½mm

340 CD4 5.50k multicolored 65 80
341 CD4 6k multicolored 65 80

Benedikt Sveinsson A75
University of Iceland A76

Design: 1.40k, Björn M. Olsen.

1961, Oct. 6 Photo. *Perf. 11½*
342 A75 1k red brown 15 20
343 A75 1.40k ultramarine 15 20
344 A76 10k green 1.40 75
a. Souv. sheet of 3, #342-344, imperf. 45 1.00

50th anniv. of the University of Iceland; Benedikt Sveinsson (1827-1899), statesman; and Björn M. Olsen (1850-1919), first rector.

Production Institute A77

New Buildings: 4k, Fishing Research Institute. 6k, Farm Bureau.

1962, July 6 Unwmk. *Perf. 11½*
345 A77 2.50k ultramarine 35 25
346 A77 4k dull green 45 25
347 A77 6k brown 55 30

Europa Issue, 1962
Common Design Type

1962, Sept. 17 *Perf. 11½*
Size: 32½x22½mm

348 CD5 5.50k yel, lt grn & brn 15 30
349 CD5 6.50k lt grn, grn & brn 40 65

Map Showing Submarine Telephone Cable — A78

1962, Nov. 20
Granite Paper

350 A78 5k multicolored 1.10 55
351 A78 7k grn, lt bl & red 65 45

Inauguration of the submarine telephone cable from Newfoundland, via Greenland and Iceland to Scotland.

Sigurdur Gudmundsson, Self-portrait A79
Herring Boat A80

Design: 5.50k, Knight slaying dragon, Romanesque door from Valthjofsstad Church, ca. 1200 A.D.

1963, Feb. 20 Photo. *Perf. 11½*
352 A79 4k bis brn & choc 48 35
353 A79 5.50k gray ol & brn 48 35

National Museum of Iceland, cent., and its first curator, Sigurdur Gudmundsson.

1963, Mar. 21
354 A80 5k multicolored 90 30
355 A80 7.50k multicolored 25 20

FAO "Freedom from Hunger" campaign.

View of Akureyri A81

1963, July 2 Unwmk. *Perf. 11½*
356 A81 3k gray green 22 15

Europa Issue, 1963
Common Design Type

1963, Sept. 16
Size: 32½x23mm

357 CD6 6k org brn & yel 45 45
358 CD6 7k blue & yellow 45 45

M.S. Gullfoss A82

1964, Jan. 17 Photo. *Perf. 11½*
359 A82 10k ultra, blk & gray 1.90 1.50
a. Accent on 2nd "E" omitted 25.00 20.00

Iceland Steamship Company, 50th anniv.

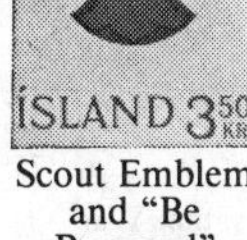

Scout Emblem and "Be Prepared" A83
Icelandic Coat of Arms A84

1964, Apr. 24
360 A83 3.50k multicolored 55 20
361 A83 4.50k multicolored 55 30

Issued to honor the Boy Scouts.

1964, June 17 *Perf. 11½*
362 A84 25k multicolored 3.00 2.00

20th anniversary, Republic of Iceland.

Flower Type of 1960-62

Flowers: 50a, Eight-petal dryas. 1k, Crowfoot (Ranunculus glacialis). 1.50k, Buck bean. 2k, Clover (trifolium repens).

1964, July 15
Flowers in Natural Colors

363 A72 50a vio bl & lt vio bl 15 15
364 A72 1k gray & dk gray 15 15
365 A72 1.50k brn & pale brn 15 15
366 A72 2k ol & pale olive 20 15
Set value 52 44

Europa Issue, 1964
Common Design Type

1964, Sept. 14 Photo. *Perf. 11½*
Granite Paper
Size: 22½x33mm

367 CD7 4.50k golden brn, yel & Prus grn 55 50
368 CD7 9k bl, yel & dk brn 60 60

Runner — A85

1964, Oct. 20 Unwmk. *Perf. 11½*
369 A85 10k lt grn & blk 1.10 75

18th Olympic Games, Tokyo, Oct. 10-25.

ITU Emblem A86

1965, May 17 Photo. *Perf. 11½*
370 A86 4.50k green 75 60
371 A86 7.50k bright ultra 15 20

ITU, centenary.

Surtsey Island, April 1964 — A87

Designs: 1.50k, Underwater volcanic eruption, November, 1963 (vert.). 3.50k, Surtsey, September, 1964.

1965, June 23 Unwmk. *Perf. 11½*
372 A87 1.50k bl, bis & blk 50 50
373 A87 2k multicolored 50 50
374 A87 3.50k bl, blk & red 75 65

Emergence of a new volcanic island off the southern coast of Iceland.

Europa Issue, 1965
Common Design Type

1965, Sept. 27 Photo. *Perf. 11½*
Size: 33x22½mm

375 CD8 5k tan, brn & brt grn 1.10 1.10
376 CD8 8k brt grn, brn & yel green 1.10 1.10

Einar Benediktsson A88

Engr. & Litho.
1965, Nov. 16 *Perf. 14*
377 A88 10k brt blue & brn 3.50 3.00

Einar Benediktsson, poet (1864-1940).

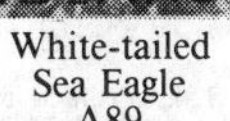

White-tailed Sea Eagle A89
National Costume A90

1965-66 Photo. *Perf. 11½*
378 A89 50k multicolored 9.75 7.50
379 A90 100k multicolored 7.75 6.25

Issue dates: No. 378, Apr. 26, 1966; No. 379, Dec. 3, 1965.

West Iceland — A91

Designs: 4k, North Iceland. 5k, East Iceland. 6.50k, South Iceland.

1966, Aug. 4 Photo. *Perf. 11½*
380 A91 2.50k multicolored 38 15
381 A91 4k multicolored 35 15
382 A91 5k multicolored 45 25
383 A91 6.50k multicolored 60 25

Europa Issue, 1966
Common Design Type

1966, Sept. 26 Photo. *Perf. 11½*
Size: 22½x33mm

384 CD9 7k grnsh bl, lt bl & red 1.25 1.25
385 CD9 8k brn, buff & red 1.25 1.25

Literary Society Emblem A92

1966, Nov. 18 Engr. *Perf. 11½*
386 A92 4k ultramarine 35 32
387 A92 10k vermilion 90 60

Icelandic Literary Society, 150th anniv.

Common Loon — A93

1967, Mar. 16 Photo. *Perf. 11½*
388 A93 20k multicolored 4.25 3.50

Europa Issue, 1967
Common Design Type

1967, May 2 Photo. *Perf. 11½*
Size: 22½x33mm

389 CD10 7k yel, brn & dk bl 1.25 1.25
390 CD10 8k emer, gray & dk bl 1.25 1.25

Old and New Maps of Iceland and North America A94

1967, June 8 Photo. *Perf. 11½*
391 A94 10k blk, tan & lt bl 35 30

EXPO '67 Intl. Exhibition, Montreal, Apr. 28-Oct. 27, 1967. The old map, drawn about 1590 by Sigurdur Stefansson, is at the Royal Library, Copenhagen.

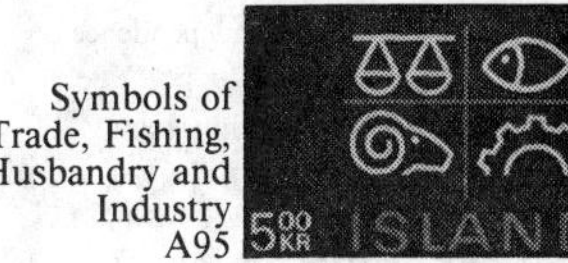

Symbols of Trade, Fishing, Husbandry and Industry A95

1967, Sept. 14 Photo. *Perf. 11½*
392 A95 5k dk bl, yel & emer 30 25

Icelandic Chamber of Commerce, 50th anniv.

Flower Type of 1960-62

Flowers: 50a, Saxifraga oppositifolia. 2.50k, Orchis maculata.

1968, Jan. 17 Photo. *Perf. 11½*
Flowers in Natural Colors

393 A72 50a green & dk brn 15 15
394 A72 2.50k dk brn, yel & grn 15 15
Set value 23 16

Europa Issue, 1968
Common Design Type

1968, Apr. 29 Photo. *Perf. 11½*
Size: 33½x23mm

395 CD11 9.50k dl yel, car rose & blk 1.00 90
396 CD11 10k brt yel grn, blk & org 1.00 90

Right-hand Driving — A96

1968, May 21 Photo. *Perf. 11½*

397 A96 4k yellow & brn 20 15
398 A96 5k lt reddish brn 20 15

Introduction of right-hand driving in Iceland, May 26, 1968.

Fridrik Fridriksson, by Sigurjon Olafsson — A97

1968, Sept. 5 Photo. *Perf. 11½*

399 A97 10k sky bl & dk gray 45 45

Rev. Fridrik Fridriksson (1868-1961), founder of the YMCA in Reykjavik and writer.

Reading Room, National Library A98

Prime Minister Jon Magnusson (1859-1926) A99

1968, Oct. 30 Photo. *Perf. 11½*
Granite Paper

400 A98 5k yellow & brn 25 15
401 A98 20k lt bl & dp ultra 85 70

Natl. Library, Reykjavik, sesquicentennial.

1968, Dec. 12
Granite Paper

402 A99 4k carmine lake 45 24
403 A99 50k dark brown 3.75 3.50

50th anniversary of independence.

Nordic Cooperation Issue

Five Ancient Ships — A99a

1969, Feb. 28 Engr. *Perf. 12½*

404 A99a 6.50k vermilion 50 50
405 A99a 10k bright blue 50 50

See footnote after Norway No. 524.

Europa Issue, 1969
Common Design Type

1969, Apr. 28 Photo. *Perf. 11½*
Size: 32½x23mm

406 CD12 13k pink & multi 1.65 1.65
407 CD12 14.50k yel & multi 75 75

Flag of Iceland and Rising Sun — A100

1969, June 17 Photo. *Perf. 11½*

408 A100 25k gray, gold, vio bl & red 1.10 70
409 A100 100k lt bl, gold, vio bl & red 5.75 5.25

25th anniversary, Republic of Iceland.

Boeing 727 A101

Design: 12k, Rolls Royce 400.

1969, Sept. 3 Photo. *Perf. 11½*

410 A101 9.50k dk bl & sky bl 50 50
411 A101 12k dk bl & ultra 50 50

50th anniversary of Icelandic aviation.

Snaefellsjökull Mountain A102

Views: 4k, Laxfoss. 5k, Hattver (vert.). 20k, Fjardargill (vert.).

1970, Jan. 6 Photo. *Perf. 11½*

412 A102 1k multicolored 15 15
413 A102 4k multicolored 25 15
414 A102 5k multicolored 25 15
415 A102 20k multicolored 70 32
Set value 62

First Meeting of Icelandic Supreme Court A103

1970, Feb. 16 Photo. *Perf. 11½*

416 A103 6.50k multicolored 25 20

Icelandic Supreme Court, 50th anniv.

Column from "Skarosbok," 1363 (Law Book) — A104

Icelandic Manuscripts: 15k, Preface to "Flateyjarbok" (History of Norwegian Kings), 1387-1394. 30k, Initial from "Flateyjarbok" showing Harald Fairhair cutting fetters of Dofri.

1970, Mar. 20 Photo. *Perf. 11½*

417 A104 5k multicolored 22 22
418 A104 15k multicolored 60 60
419 A104 30k multicolored 1.10 1.10

Europa Issue, 1970
Common Design Type

1970, May 4 Photo. *Perf. 11½*
Size: 32x22mm

420 CD13 9k brn & yellow 85 85
421 CD13 25k brt grn & bis 1.50 1.50

Nurse A105

Grimur Thomsen A106

The Rest, by Thorarinn B. Thorlaksson A107

1970, June 19 Photo. *Perf. 11½*

422 A105 7k ultra & lt bl 35 20
423 A106 10k ind & lt grnsh bl 42 30
424 A107 50k gold & multi 2.00 1.25

50th anniv. (in 1969) of the Icelandic Nursing Association (No. 422); 150th birth anniv. of Grimur Thomsen (1820-1896), poet (No. 423); Intl. Arts Festival, Reykjavik, June 1970 (No. 424).

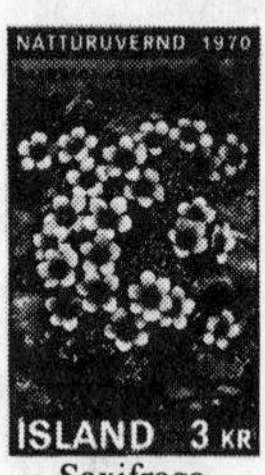

Saxifraga Oppositifolia A108

Lakagigar A109

1970, Aug. 25 Photo. *Perf. 11½*

425 A108 3k multicolored 24 24
426 A109 15k multicolored 75 75

European Nature Conservation Year.

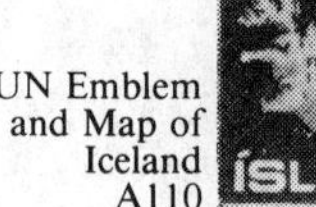

UN Emblem and Map of Iceland A110

1970, Oct. 23 Photo. *Perf. 11½*

427 A110 12k multicolored 48 48

25th anniversary of United Nations.

"Flight," by Asgrimur Jonsson A111

1971, Mar. 26 Photo. *Perf. 11½*

428 A111 10k multicolored 70 50

Joint northern campaign for the benefit of refugees.

Europa Issue, 1971
Common Design Type

1971, May 3 Photo. *Perf. 11½*
Size: 33x22mm

429 CD14 7k rose cl, yel & blk 1.10 1.10
430 CD14 15k ultra, yel & blk 1.10 1.10

Postal Checking Service Emblem A112

1971, June 22 Photo. *Perf. 11½*

431 A112 5k vio bl & lt blue 15 15
432 A112 7k dk grn & yel grn 22 20

Introduction of Postal Checking Service, Apr. 30, 1971.

Tryggvi Gunnarsson A113

Haddock Freezing Plant A114

Design: 30k, Patriotic Society emblem.

1971, Aug. 19 Photo. *Perf. 11½*

433 A113 30k lt bl & vio blk 1.25 90
434 A113 100k gray & vio blk 5.50 6.00

Icelandic Patriotic Society, cent.; Tryggvi Gunnarsson (1835-1917), founder and president.

1971, Nov. 18

Fish Industry: 7k, Cod fishing. 20k, Lobster canning plant.

435 A114 5k multicolored 18 15
436 A114 7k multicolored 15 15
437 A114 20k grn & multi 60 50

Herdubreid Mountain — A115

Engr. & Litho.

1972, Mar. 9 *Perf. 14*

438 A115 250k blue & multi 90 42

Europa Issue 1972
Common Design Type

1972, May 2 Photo. *Perf. 11½*
Size: 22x32mm

439 CD15 9k lt vio & multi 95 60
440 CD15 13k yel grn & multi 1.10 85

"United Municipalities" — A116

1972, June 14 Photo. *Perf. 11½*

441 A116 16k multicolored 18 18

Legislation for local government, cent.

Chessboard, World Map, Rook — A117

1972, July 2 Litho. *Perf. 13*
442 A117 15k lt ol & multi 38 30

World Chess Championship, Reykjavik, July-Sept. 1972.

Hothouse Tomatoes A118

Designs: 12k, Steam valve and natural steam. 40k, Hothouse roses.

1972, Aug. 23 Photo. *Perf. 11½*
443 A118 8k Prus bl & multi 15 15
444 A118 12k green & multi 15 15
445 A118 40k dk pur & multi 1.10 75

Hothouse gardening in Iceland, using natural steam and hot springs.

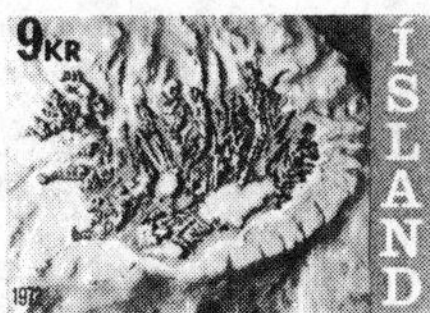

Iceland and the Continental Shelf — A119

1972, Sept. 27 Litho. *Perf. 13*
446 A119 9k blue & multi 18 15

To publicize Iceland's offshore fishing rights.

Europa Issue 1973
Common Design Type

1973, Apr. 30 Photo. *Perf. 11½*
Size: 32½x22mm
447 CD16 13k vio & multi 1.25 1.25
448 CD16 25k olive & multi 40 35

Iceland No. 1 and Messenger A120

Designs (First Issue of Iceland and): 15k, No. 5 and pony train. 20k, No. 2 and mailboat "Esja." 40k, No. 3 and mail truck. 80k, No. 4 and Beech-18 mail plane.

Litho. & Engr.
1973, May 23 *Perf. 13x13½*
449 A120 10k dl bl, blk & ultra 32 32
450 A120 15k grn, blk & gray 15 15
451 A120 20k mar, blk & car 18 18
452 A120 40k vio, blk & brn 18 18
453 A120 80k olive, blk & yel 1.00 65
Nos. 449-453 (5) 1.83 1.48

Centenary of Iceland's first postage stamps.

Nordic Cooperation Issue

Nordic House, Reykjavik A120a

1973, June 26 Engr. *Perf. 12½*
454 A120a 9k multicolored 45 22
455 A120a 10k multicolored 1.40 1.40

A century of postal cooperation among Denmark, Finland, Iceland, Norway and Sweden, and in connection with the Nordic Postal Conference, Reykjavik.

Ásgeir Ásgeirsson, (1894-1972), President of Iceland 1952-1968 — A121

1973, Aug. 1 Engr. *Perf. 13x13½*
456 A121 13k carmine 32 22
457 A121 15k blue 20 15

Islandia 73 Emblem A122

Design: 20k, Islandia 73 emblem; different arrangement.

1973, Aug. 31 Photo. *Perf. 11½*
458 A122 17k gray & multi 30 30
459 A122 20k brn, ocher & yel 30 25

Islandia 73 Philatelic Exhibition, Reykjavik, Aug. 31-Sept. 9.

Man and WMO Emblem A123

The Settlement, Tapestry by Vigdis Kristjansdottir A124

1973, Nov. 14 Photo. *Perf. 12½*
460 A123 50k sil & multi 75 45

Intl. meteorological cooperation, cent.

1974 Photo. *Perf. 11½*

Designs: 13k, Establishment of Althing, painting by Johannes Johannesson (horiz.). 15k, Gudbrandur Thorlakkson, Bishop of Holar 1571-1627. 17k, Age of Sturlungar (Fighting Vikings), drawing by Thorvaldur Skulason. 20k, Stained glass window honoring Hallgrimur Petursson (1614-74), hymn writer. 25k, Illumination from Book of Flatey, 14th century. 30k, Conversion to Christianity (altarpiece, Skalholt), mosaic by Nina Tryggvadottir. 40k, Wood carving (family and plants), 18th century. 60k, Curing the Catch, cement bas-relief. 70k, Age of Writing (Saemundur Riding Seal), sculpture by Asmundur Sveinsson. 100k, Virgin and Child with Angels, embroidered antependium, Stafafell Church, 14th century.

461 A124 10k multicolored 22 15
462 A124 13k multicolored 20 20
463 A124 15k multicolored 20 20
464 A124 17k multicolored 32 22
465 A124 20k multicolored 28 22
466 A124 25k multicolored 15 25
467 A124 30k multicolored 60 45
468 A124 40k multicolored 70 55
469 A124 60k multicolored 85 85
470 A124 70k multicolored 85 85
471 A124 100k multicolored 1.25 70
Nos. 461-471 (11) 5.62 4.64

1100th anniv. of settlement of Iceland.
Issue dates: 10k, 13k, 30k, 70k, Mar. 12; 17k, 25k, 100k, June 11; 15k, 20k, 40k, 60k, July 16.

Horseback Rider, Wood, 17th Century — A125

Europa: 20k, "Through the Sound Barrier," contemporary bronze by Asmundur Sveinsson.

1974, Apr. 29 Photo. *Perf. 11½*
472 A125 13k brn red & multi 15 15
473 A125 20k gray & multi 70 70

Clerk Selling Stamps, UPU Emblem A126

Design: 20k, Mailman delivering mail.

1974, Oct. 9 Photo. *Perf. 11½*
474 A126 17k ocher & multi 30 28
475 A126 20k olive & multi 30 28

Centenary of Universal Postal Union.

Volcanic Eruption, Heimaey, Jan. 23, 1973 — A127

Design: 25k, Volcanic eruption, night view.

1975, Jan. 23 Photo. *Perf. 11½*
476 A127 20k multicolored 40 40
477 A127 25k multicolored 20 20

Europa Issue 1975

Bird, by Thorvaldur Skulason A128

Sun Queen, by Johannes S. Kjarval — A129

1975, May 12 Photo. *Perf. 11½*
478 A128 18k multicolored 20 20
479 A129 23k gold & multi 55 42

Stephan G. Stephansson — A130

1975, Aug. 1 Engr. *Perf. 13*
480 A130 27k green & brn 55 30

Stephan G. Stephansson (1853-1927), Icelandic poet and settler in North America; centenary of Icelandic emigration to North America.

Petursson, by Hjalti Thorsteinsson A131

Einar Jonsson, Self-portrait A132

Portraits: 23k, Arni Magnusson, by Hjalti Thorsteinsson. 30k, Jon Eiriksson, sculpture by Olafur Olafsson.

1975, Sept. 18 Engr. *Perf. 13*
481 A131 18k slate grn & ind 18 18
482 A131 23k Prussian bl 18 18
483 A131 30k deep magenta 18 18
484 A132 50k indigo 18 18

Famous Icelanders: Hallgrimur Petursson (1614-1674), minister and religious poet; Arni Magnusson (1663-1730), historian, registrar and manuscript collector; Jon Eiriksson (1728-1787), professor of law and cabinet member; Einar Jonsson (1874-1954), sculptor, painter and writer.

Red Cross A133

1975, Oct. 15 Photo. *Perf. 11½x12*
485 A133 23k multicolored 32 32

Icelandic Red Cross, 50th anniversary.

Abstract Painting, by Nina Tryggvadottir — A134

1975, Oct. 15 *Perf. 12x12½*
486 A134 100k multicolored 1.25 80

International Women's Year 1975.

Thorvaldsen Statue, by Thorvaldsen A135

Saplings Growing in Bare Landscape A136

1975, Nov. 19 Photo. *Perf. 11½*
487 A135 27k lt vio & multi 70 30

Centenary of Thorvaldsen Society, a charity honoring Bertel Thorvaldsen (1768-1844), sculptor.

1975, Nov. 19 *Perf. 12x11½*
488 A136 35k multicolored 52 40

Reforestation.

Langjökull Glacier, by Asgrimur Jonsson A137

1976, Mar. 18 Photo. *Perf. 11½*
489 A137 150k gold & multi 1.65 1.00

Asgrimur Jonsson (1876-1958), painter.

Wooden Bowl — A138

Europa: 45k, Spinning wheel (vert.).

1976, May 3 Photo. *Perf. 11½*
490 A138 35k ver & multi 70 50
491 A138 45k blue & multi 95 70

No. 9 with First Day Cancel — A139

Decree Establishing Postal Service — A140

1976, Sept. 22 Photo. *Perf. 11½*
Granite Paper
492 A139 30k bis, blk & gray bl 22 22

Centenary of aurar stamps.

1976, Sept. 22 Engr. *Perf. 13*

Design: 45k, Conclusion of Decree with signatures.

493 A140 35k dark brown 40 32
494 A140 45k dark blue 40 32

Iceland's Postal Service, bicentenary.

Federation Emblem, People — A141

1976, Dec. 2 Photo. *Perf. 12½*
Granite Paper
495 A141 100k multicolored 1.00 50

Icelandic Federation of Labor, 60th anniv.

Five Water Lilies — A142

Ofaerufoss, Eldgja — A143

Photo. & Engr.
1977, Feb. 2 *Perf. 12½*
496 A142 35k brt grn & multi 85 65
497 A142 45k ultra & multi 85 80

Nordic countries cooperation for protection of the environment and 25th Session of Nordic Council, Helsinki, Feb. 19.

1977, May 2 Photo. *Perf. 12*

Europa: 85k, Kirkjufell Mountain, seen from Grundarfjord.

498 A143 45k multicolored 1.60 90
499 A143 85k multicolored 22 28

Harlequin Duck — A144

1977, June 14 Photo. *Perf. 11½*
500 A144 40k multicolored 22 22

Wetlands conservation, European campaign.

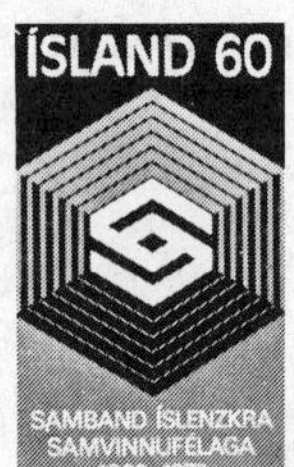

Society Emblem — A145

1977, June 14
501 A145 60k vio bl & ultra 75 42

Federation of Icelandic Cooperative Societies, 75th anniversary.

Hot Springs, Therapeutic Bath, Emblem — A146

1977, Nov. 16 Photo. *Perf. 11½*
502 A146 90k multicolored 55 38

World Rheumatism Year.

Stone Marker A147

1977, Dec. 12 Engr. *Perf. 11½*
503 A147 45k dark blue 85 50

Touring Club of Iceland, 50th anniversary.

Thorvaldur Thoroddsen, (1855-1921), Geologist, Scientist and Writer — A148

Design: 60k, Briet Bjarnhedinsdottir (1856-1940), Founder of Icelandic Women's Association and Reykjavik city councillor.

1977, Dec. 12 Engr. *Perf. 11½*
504 A148 50k brn & sl grn 28 18
505 A148 60k grn & vio brn 55 35

Bailiff's Residence, Videy Island, 1752 — A149

Europa: 120k, Husavik Church, 1906.

1978, May 2 Photo. *Perf. 11½*
506 A149 80k multicolored 48 30
507 A149 120k multi, vert. 70 60

Alexander Johannesson, Junkers Planes — A150

Design: 100k, Fokker Friendship plane over mountains.

1978, June 21 Photo. *Perf. 12½*
508 A150 60k multicolored 35 20
509 A150 100k multicolored 42 28

50th anniv. of domestic flights in Iceland.

Skeioara River Bridge A151

1978, Aug. 17 Photo. *Perf. 11½*
510 A151 70k multicolored 18 18

Lava near Mt. Hekla, by Jon Stefansson — A152

1978, Nov. 16 Photo. *Perf. 12*
511 A152 1000k multicolored 4.50 2.25

Jon Stefansson (1881-1962), Icelandic painter.

Ship to Shore Rescue A153

1978, Dec. 1 Engr. *Perf. 13*
512 A153 60k black 18 18

National Life Saving Assoc., 50th anniv.

Halldor Hermannsson (1878-1958), Historian, Librarian — A154

1978, Dec. 1
513 A154 150k indigo 48 32

Lighthouse A155

Telephone, c. 1900 A156

1978, Dec. 1 Photo. *Perf. 11½*
514 A155 90k multicolored 48 32

Centenary of Icelandic lighthouses.

1979, Apr. 30 Photo. *Perf. 11½*

Europa: 190k, Post horn and satchel.

515 A156 110k multicolored 55 48
516 A156 190k multicolored 55 55

Jon Sigurdsson and Ingibjorg Einarsdottir — A157

1979, Nov. 1 Engr. *Perf. 13x12½*
517 A157 150k black 48 38

Jon Sigurdsson (1811-1879), Icelandic statesman and leader in independence movement.

Excerpt from Olafs Saga Helga — A158

1979, Nov. 1 Photo. *Perf. 11½*
518 A158 200k multicolored 48 32

Snorri Sturluson (1178-1241), Icelandic historian and writer.

Children with Flowers ICY Emblem A159

1979, Nov. 12
519 A159 140k multicolored 60 32

International Year of the Child.

Icelandic Arms, Before 1904 and 1904-1919 — A160

1979, Nov. 12

520 A160 500k multicolored 1.65 1.10

Home rule, 75th anniversary.

Ingibjorg H. Bjarnason (1867-1941) — A161

Designs: 100k, Bjarni Porsteinsson (1861-1938), composer. 120k, Petur Gudjohnsen (1812-1877), organist. 130k, Sveinbjorn Sveinbjornson (1847-1927), composer. 170k, Torfhildur Holm (1845-1918), poet.

1979 Engr. *Perf. 13*

521 A161	80k	rose violet	15	15
522 A161	100k	black	15	15
523 A161	120k	rose carmine	15	15
524 A161	130k	sepia	22	22
525 A161	170k	carmine rose	40	30
		Nos. 521-525 (5)	1.07	97

Issue dates: 80k, 170k, Aug. 3; others, Dec. 12.

Canis Familiaris — A162

Design: 90k, Alopex lagopus.

1980, Jan. 24

526 A162	10k	black	15	15
527 A162	90k	sepia	15	15
		Set value	21	21

See Nos. 534-536, 543-545, 552, 553, 556-558, 610-612.

Jon Sveinsson Nonni (1857-1944), Writer — A163

Europa: 250k, Gunnar Gunnarsson (1889-1975), writer.

1980, Apr. 28 Photo. *Perf. 11½*
Granite Paper

528 A163	140k	dl rose & blk	55	40
529 A163	250k	tan & blk	85	65

Mountain Ash Branch and Berries — A164

1980, July 8 Photo. *Perf. 12½*

530 A164 120k multicolored 18 18

Year of the Tree.

Laugardalur Sports Complex, Reykjavik A165

1980, July 8 Engr. *Perf. 13x12½*

531 A165 300k slate green 60 60

1980 Olympic Games.

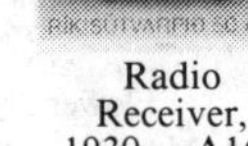

Carved and Painted Cabinet Door, 18th Cent. — A166

Radio Receiver, 1930 — A168

Nordic Cooperation Issue

Design: 180k, Embroidered cushion, 19th century.

1980, Sept. 9 Photo. *Perf. 11½*
Granite Paper

532 A166	150k	multicolored	70	50
533 A166	180k	multicolored	95	60

Animal Type of 1980

1980, Oct. 16 Engr. *Perf. 13*

Designs: 160k, Sebastes marinus. 170k, Fratercula arctica. 190k, Phoca vitulina.

534 A162	160k	rose violet	65	32
535 A162	170k	black	20	16
536 A162	190k	dark brown	20	16

1980, Nov. 20 Photo. *Perf. 12½*
Granite Paper

537 A168 400k multicolored 1.25 1.00

State Broadcasting Service, 50th anniv.

University Hospital, 50th Anniversary A169

1980, Nov. 20 *Perf. 11½*

538 A169 200k multicolored 45 35

Magnus Stephensen (1762-1833), Chief Justice — A170

Design: 190a, Finnur Magnusson (1781-1847), Privy Archives keeper.

1981, Feb. 24 Engr. *Perf. 13*

539 A170	170a	bright ultra	20	20
540 A170	190a	olive green	20	20

Europa Issue 1981

Luftur the Sorcerer — A171

1981, May 4 Photo. *Perf. 11½*
Granite Paper

541 A171	180a	shown	90	90
542 A171	220a	Sea witch	1.00	65

Animal Type of 1980

1981, Aug. 20 Engr. *Perf. 13*

Designs: 50a, Troglodytes troglodytes. 100a, Pluvialis apricaria. 200a, Corvus corax.

543 A162	50a	brown	15	15
544 A162	100a	blue	15	15
545 A162	200a	black	20	15

Intl. Year of the Disabled A173

Skyggnir Earth Satellite Station, First Anniv. A174

1981, Sept. 29 Photo. *Perf. 11½*

546 A173 200a multicolored 25 25

1981, Sept. 29 Photo. *Perf. 11½*

547 A174 500a multicolored 1.40 1.00

Hauling the Line, by Gunnlaugur Scheving (1904-1972) A175

1981, Oct. 21 Photo. *Perf. 11½*

548 A175 5000a multi 6.00 5.00

Christian Missionary Work in Iceland Millennium A176

1981, Nov. 24 Engr. *Perf. 13*

549 A176 200a dark violet 22 22

Christmas A177

1981, Nov. 24 Photo. *Perf. 12½*
Granite Paper

550 A177	200a	Leaf bread	60	52
551 A177	250a	Leaf bread, diff.	60	52

Animal Type of 1980

1982, Mar. 23 Engr. *Perf. 13*

Designs: 20a, Buccinum undatum, vert. 600a, Chlamys islandica.

552 A162	20a	copper brn	15	15
553 A162	600a	vio brown	85	50
		Set value		55

Europa Issue 1982

First Norse Settlement, 874 — A179

1982, May 3 Photo. *Perf. 11½*
Granite Paper

554 A179	350a	shown	95	75
555 A179	450a	Discovery of North America, 1000	95	75

Animal Type of 1980

1982, June 3 Engr. *Perf. 13*

Designs: 300a, Ovis aries, vert. 400a, Bos taurus, vert. 500a, Felis catus, vert.

556 A162	300a	brown	95	55
557 A162	400a	lake	30	30
558 A162	500a	gray	30	30

Kaupfelag Pingeyinga Cooperative Society Centenary A181

1982, June 3

559 A181 1000a black & red 75 75

Man Riding Iceland Pony — A182

1982, July 1 Photo. *Perf. 11½*
Granite Paper

560 A182 700a multicolored 60 60

Centenary of School of Agriculture, Holar A183

1982, July 1
Granite Paper

561 A183 1500a multi 1.10 1.10

Mount Herdubreid, by Isleifur Konradsson (1889-1972) A184

1982, Sept. 8 Photo. *Perf. 11½*
Granite Paper

562 A184 800a multicolored 85 85

UN World Assembly on Aging, July 26-Aug. 6.

Iceland stamps can be mounted in Scott's annually supplemented Scandinavia and Finland Album.

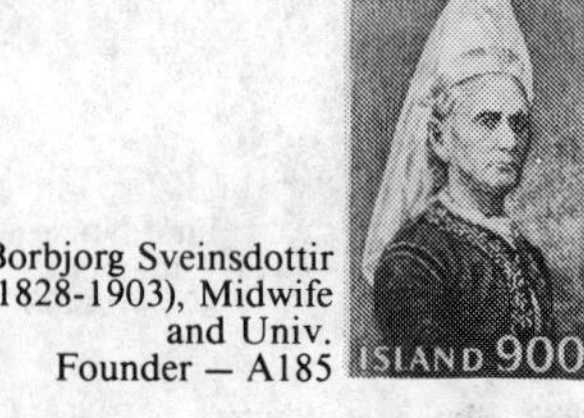

Borbjorg Sveinsdottir (1828-1903), Midwife and Univ. Founder — A185

1982, Sept. 8 Engr. *Perf. 13*
563 A185 900a red brn 70 60

Souvenir Sheet

Reynistaour Monastery Seal — A186

Photo. & Engr.
1982, Oct. 7 *Perf. 13½*
564 Sheet of 2 4.25 4.50
a. A186 400a shown 2.00 2.25
b. A186 800a Bingeyrar 2.00 2.25

NORDIA '84 Intl. Stamp Exhibition, Reykjavik, July 3-8, 1984. Sold for 18k.
See No. 581.

Christmas A187

Score from The Night was Such a Splendid One.

1982, Nov. 16 Photo. *Perf. 11½*
Granite Paper
565 A187 3k Birds 48 48
566 A187 3.50k Bells 60 60

Caltha Palustris — A188

1983, Feb. 10 Photo.
Granite Paper
567 A188 7.50k shown 48 35
568 A188 8k Lychnis alpina 1.00 90
569 A188 10k Potentilla palustris 65 48
570 A188 20k Myosotis scorpioides 2.00 1.75

See #586-587, 593-594, 602-605, 663-664.

Nordic Cooperation A189

1983, Mar. 24
Granite Paper
571 A189 4.50k Mt. Sulur 95 75
572 A189 5k Urridafossar Falls 95 75

Europa Issue, 1983

Thermal Energy Projects — A190

1983, May 5
Granite Paper
573 A190 5k shown 1.25 1.00
574 A190 5.50k multi, diff. 2.00 1.75

Fishing Industry A191

1983, June 8 Engr. *Perf. 13x12½*
575 A191 11k Fishing boats 45 45
576 A191 13k Fishermen 1.40 80

Bicentenary of Skaftareldar Volcanic Eruption A192

1983, June 8 Photo. *Perf. 11½*
Granite Paper
577 A192 15k Volcano, by Finnur Jonsson 1.10 1.10

Skiing — A193

1983, Sept. 8 Photo. *Perf. 11½*
578 A193 12k shown 80 75
579 A193 14k Running 1.25 1.25

World Communications Year — A194

1983, Sept. 8 *Perf. 12½*
580 A194 30k multi 3.00 2.75

NORDIA '84 Type of 1982
Souvenir Sheet

Bishops' Seals: 8k, Magnus Eyjolfsson of Skalholt, 1477-90. 12k, Ogmundur Palsson of Skalhot, 1521-40.

Photo. & Engr.
1983, Oct. 6 *Perf. 13½*
581 Sheet of 2 4.75 5.25
a. A186 8k violet blue & black 2.25 2.50
b. A186 12k pale green & black 2.25 2.50

Sold for 30k.

Christmas A195

Pres. Kristjan Eldjarn (1916-82) A196

1983, Nov. 10 Photo. *Perf. 11½*
Granite Paper
582 A195 6k Virgin and Child 70 55
583 A195 6.50k Angel 70 55

1983, Dec. 6
584 A196 6.50k brn carmine 1.25 1.00
585 A196 7k dark blue 48 32

Flower Type of 1983
1984, Mar. 1 Photo. *Perf. 11½*
Granite Paper
586 A188 6k Rosa pimpinellifolia 80 70
587 A188 25k Potentilla anserium 2.00 1.75

Europa 1959-84 A197

1984, May 3
588 A197 6.50k grnsh bl & blk 1.10 70
589 A197 7.50k rose & black 60 52

Souvenir Sheet

Abraham Ortelius' Map of Northern Europe, 1570 — A198

Photo. & Engr.
1984, June 6 *Perf. 14x13½*
590 A198 40k multi 6.25 6.50

NORDIA '84 Intl. Stamp Exhibition, Reykjavik, July 3-8. Sold for 60k.

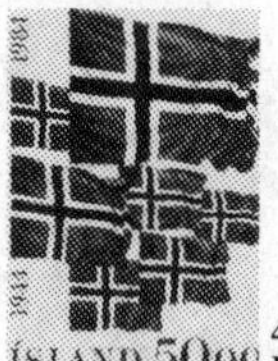

40th Anniv. of Republic — A199

1984, June 17 Photo. *Perf. 11½*
Granite Paper
591 A199 50k Flags 4.25 3.50

Good Templars Headquarters, Akureyri — A200

1984, July 18 Engr. *Perf. 13*
592 A200 10k green 75 70

Order of the Good Templars, centenary in Iceland, temperance org.

Flower Type of 1983
1984, Sept. 11 Photo. *Perf. 11½*
Granite Paper
593 A188 6.50k Loiseleuria procumbens 45 35
594 A188 7.50k Arctostaphylos uva-ursi 52 35

Christmas A201

Gudbrand's Bible, 400th Anniv. A202

1984, Nov. 29 Photo.
595 A201 600a Madonna and Child 60 36
596 A201 650a Angel, Christmas rose 80 55

1984, Nov. 29 Engr. *Perf. 12½x13*
597 A202 6.50k Text 45 42
598 A202 7.50k Illustration 52 52

First Icelandic Bible.

Confederation of Employers, 50th Anniv. A203

Bjorn Bjarnarson (1853-1918) A204

1984, Nov. 9 Photo. *Perf. 12x12½*
Granite Paper
599 A203 30k Building blocks 2.50 2.50

1984, Nov. 9 Photo. *Perf. 11½*
Granite Paper
600 A204 12k shown 80 65
601 A204 40k New gallery building, horiz. 2.50 2.25

Natl. Gallery centenary.

Flower Type of 1983
1985, Mar. 20 Photo. *Perf. 11½*
Granite Paper
602 A188 8k Rubus saxatilis 70 70
603 A188 9k Veronica fruticans 75 75
604 A188 16k Lathyrus japonicus 1.40 1.40
605 A188 17k Draba alpina 1.50 1.50

Music Year Emblem, Woman Playing the Langspil — A205

Europa: 7.50k, Man playing the Icelandic violin.

1985, May 3 Photo. *Perf. 11 ½*
Granite Paper

606 A205	6.50k	multicolored	60	60
607 A205	7.50k	multicolored	60	60

Natl. Horticulture Soc., Cent. — A206

Intl. Youth Year — A207

1985, June 20 Photo. *Perf. 12*

608 A206	20k	Sorbus intermedia	1.10	1.00

1985, June 20 Photo. *Perf. 11 ½*

609 A207	25k	Icelandic girl	1.40	1.25

Animal Type of 1980

1985, Sept. 10 Engr. *Perf. 13*

Designs: 700a, Todarodes sagittatus. 800a, Hyas araneus. 900a, Tealia felina.

610 A162	700a	brn carmine	40	40
611 A162	800a	dk brown	45	45
612 A162	900a	carmine	50	50

Hannes Stephensen (1799-1856), Cleric, Politician, Translator A209

Famous men: 30k, Jon Gudmudsson (1807-1875), editor, politician.

1985, Sept. 10 Engr.

613 A209	13k	dp magenta	75	75
614 A209	30k	deep violet	1.75	1.75

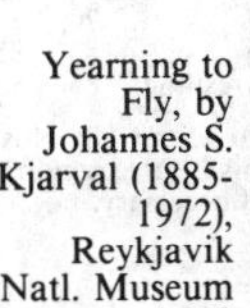

Yearning to Fly, by Johannes S. Kjarval (1885-1972), Reykjavik Natl. Museum A210

1985, Oct. 15 Photo. *Perf. 12x11 ½*

615 A210	100k	multi	5.50	5.00

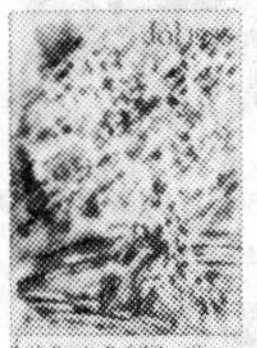

Abstract Ice Crystal Paintings, by Snorri Sveinn Fridriksson (b. 1934) — A211

1985, Nov. 14 Photo. *Perf. 11 ½*

616 A211	8k	Crucifix	45	45
617 A211	9k	Pine Trees	50	50

Christmas.

Birds — A212

1986, Mar. 19 Photo. *Perf. 11 ½*
Granite Paper

618 A212	6k	Motacilla alba	45	45
619 A212	10k	Anas acuta	70	70
620 A212	12k	Falco columbarius	85	85
621 A212	15k	Alca torda	1.00	1.00

See Nos. 642-645, 665-666, 671-672, 686-687, 721, 725.

Europa Issue 1986

Natl. Parks — A213

1986, May 5

622 A213	10k	Skaftafell	1.00	1.00
623 A213	12k	Joekulsargljufur	1.40	1.40

Nordic Cooperation Issue — A214

Sister towns.

1986, May 27 *Perf. 11 ½*

624 A214	10k	Stykkisholmur	80	80
625 A214	12k	Seydisfjordur	1.00	1.00

Natl. Bank, Cent. A215

1986, July 1 Engr. *Perf. 14*

626 A215	13k	Headquarters, Reykjavik	70	70
627 A215	250k	Banknote reverse, 1928	14.00	12.50

Reykjavik Bicent. A216

1986, Aug. 18 Engr. *Perf. 13 ½x14*

628 A216	10k	City seal, 1815	70	70
629 A216	12k	View from bank, illustration, 1856	85	85
630 A216	13k	Laugardalur hot water brook	90	90
631 A216	40k	City Theater	3.00	3.00

Introduction of the Telephone in Iceland, 80th Anniv. — A217

1986, Sept. 29 Photo. *Perf. 11 ½*
Granite Paper

632 A217	10k	Morse receiver, 1906	50	50
633 A217	20k	Handset, microchip, 1986	1.10	1.10

Souvenir Sheet

Hvita River Crossing, Loa, 1836, by Auguste Mayer — A218

Photo. & Engr.

1986, Oct. 9 *Perf. 14*

634 A218	20k	bluish black	1.90	1.90

Stamp Day. Sold for 30k to benefit philatelic organizations.

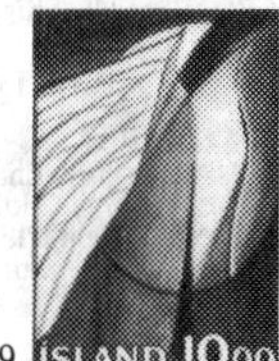

Christmas — A219

Paintings by Bjoerg Thorsteinsdottir: 10k, Christmas at Peace. 12k, Christmas Night.

1986, Nov. 13 Photo. *Perf. 12*

635 A219	10k	multicolored	60	60
636 A219	12k	multicolored	75	75

Olafsvik Trading Station, 300th Anniv. A220

1987, Mar. 26 Engr. *Perf. 14x13 ½*

637 A220	50k	Merchantman Svanur, 1777	2.40	2.40

Keflavik Intl. Airport Terminal Inauguration — A221

1987, Apr. 14 Photo. *Perf. 12x11 ½*

638 A221	100k	multi	5.00	5.00

Europa Issue 1987

Stained Glass Windows by Leifur Breidfjoerd, Fossvogur Cemetery Chapel A222

1987, May 4 Photo. *Perf. 12x11 ½*

639 A222	12k	Christ carrying the cross	60	60
640 A222	15k	Soldiers, peace dove	75	75

Rasmus Christian Rask (1787-1832), Danish Linguist — A223

1987, June 10 Engr. *Perf. 13 ½*

641 A223	20k	black	1.00	1.00

Preservation of the Icelandic language.

Bird Type of 1986

1987, Sept. 16 Photo. *Perf. 11 ½*
Granite Paper

642 A212	13k	Asio flammeus	62	62
643 A212	40k	Turdus iliacus	1.90	1.90
644 A212	70k	Haematopus ostralegus	3.35	3.35
645 A212	90k	Anas platyrhynchos	4.25	4.25

Souvenir Sheet

Trading Station of Djupivogur in 1836, by Auguste Mayer — A225

1987, Oct. 9 Engr. *Perf. 13 ½x14*

646 A225	30k	black	2.25	2.25

Stamp Day. Sold for 45k to benefit the Stamp and Postal History Fund.

Dental Protection A226

Vulture A227

1987, Oct. 9 Photo. *Perf. 11 ½x12*
Granite Paper

647 A226	12k	multi	58	58

Perf. 13 on 3 sides

1987, Oct. 9 Engr.

Guardian Spirits of the North, East, South and West.

Booklet Stamps

648 A227	13k	shown	62	62
649 A227	13k	Dragon	62	62
650 A227	13k	Bull	62	62
651 A227	13k	Giant	62	62
a.		Block of 4, #648-651	2.50	2.50
b.		Bklt. pane of 12, 3 #651a	8.50	

Legend of Heimskringla, the story of the Norse kings. Haraldur Gormsson, king of Denmark, deterred from invading Iceland after hearing of the guardian spirits.

See Nos. 656-659, 677, 688-695.

Christmas — A228

1987, Oct. 21 Photo. *Perf. 11½x12*
652 A228 13k Fir branch 62 62
653 A228 17k Candle flame 80 80

Steinn Steinarr (1908-1958) A229

Poets: 21k, David Stefansson (1895-1964).

1988, Feb. 25 Photo. *Perf. 12*
654 A229 16k multi 78 78
655 A229 21k multi 1.00 1.00

Guardian Spirit Type of 1987
Perf. 13 on 3 sides
1988, May 2 Engr.
Booklet Stamps
656 A227 16k Vulture 75 75
657 A227 16k Dragon 75 75
658 A227 16k Bull 75 75
659 A227 16k Giant 75 75
a. Block of 4, #656-659 3.00 3.00
b. Bklt. pane of 12, 3 #659a 9.00

Europa Issue, 1988

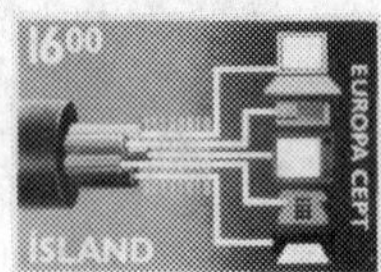

Modern Communication — A230

1988, May 2 Photo. *Perf. 12x11½*
660 A230 16k Data transmission system 88 88
661 A230 21k Facsimile machine 1.15 1.15

1988 Summer Olympics, Seoul A231

1988, June 9 Photo. *Perf. 12*
Granite Paper
662 A231 18k Handball 95 95

Flower Type of 1983
1988, June 9 *Perf. 11½*
Granite Paper
663 A188 10k Vicia cracca 52 52
664 A188 50k Thymus praecox 2.60 2.60

Bird Type of 1986
1988, Sept. 21 Photo. *Perf. 11½*
Granite Paper
665 A212 5k Limosa limosa 22 22
666 A212 30k Clangula hyemalis 1.35 1.35

Souvenir Sheet

Nupsstadur Farm, Fljotshverfi, 1836, by Auguste Mayer — A233

1988, Oct. 9 Engr. *Perf. 14*
667 A233 40k black 2.75 2.75

Stamp Day. Sold for 60k to benefit the Stamp and Postal History Fund.

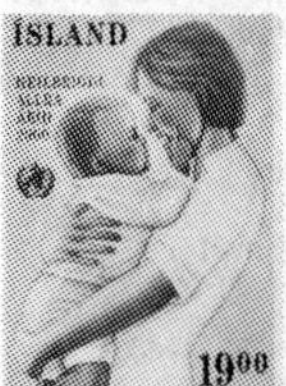

WHO, 40th Anniv. — A234

1988, Nov. 3 Photo. *Perf. 11½x12*
Granite Paper
668 A234 19k multicolored 85 85

Christmas A235

1988, Nov. 3 *Perf. 11½*
Granite Paper
669 A235 19k Fisherman at sea 85 85
670 A235 24k Ship, buoy 1.05 1.05

Bird Type of 1986
1989, Feb. 2 Photo.
671 A212 19k Phalaropus lobatus 78 78
672 A212 100k Plectrophenax nivalis 4.00 4.00

Women's Folk Costumes — A236

1989, Apr. 20 Photo. *Perf. 11½x12*
Granite Paper
673 A236 21k Peysufot 85 85
674 A236 26k Upphlutur 1.05 1.05

Nordic cooperation.

Europa 1989 — A237

Children's games.

1989, May 30 Photo. *Perf. 11½*
Granite Paper
675 A237 21k Sailing toy boats 85 85
676 A237 26k Hoop, stick pony 1.05 1.05

Guardian Spirit Type of 1987
1989, June 27 Engr. *Perf. 13*
677 A227 500k Dragon 16.00 16.00

Landscapes A238

1989, Sept. 20 Photo. *Perf. 11½*
Granite Paper
678 A238 35k Mt. Skeggi, Arnarfjord 1.35 1.35
679 A238 45k Thermal spring, Namaskard 1.70 1.70

See Nos. 713-714, 728, 737.

Agricultural College at Hvanneyri, Cent. A239

1989, Sept. 20 Engr. *Perf. 14*
680 A239 50k multi 1.90 1.90

Souvenir Sheet

NORDIA '91 — A240

Detail of *A Chart and Description of Northern Routes and Wonders to Be Found in the Nordic Countries,* 1539, by Olaus Magnus (1490-1557).

Litho. & Engr.
1989, Oct. 9 *Perf. 12½*
681 A240 Sheet of 3 4.25 4.25
a.-c. 30k any single 1.40 1.40

Stamp Day. Sold for 130k to benefit the exhibition.
See No. 715.

Natural History Soc., Cent. A241

Flowers or fish and: 21k, Stefan Stefansson (1863-1921), botanist and founder. 26k, Bjarni Saemundsson (1867-1940), chairman.

1989, Nov. 9 Photo. *Perf. 11½*
Granite Paper
682 A241 21k multi 70 70
683 A241 26k multi 85 85

Christmas — A242

Paintings like stained-glass windows by Johannes Johannesson (b. 1921): 21k, Madonna and Child. 26k, Three Wise Men.

1989, Nov. 9
Granite Paper
684 A242 21k multi 70 70
685 A242 26k multi 85 85

Bird Type of 1986
1990, Feb. 15
Granite Paper
686 A212 21k *Anas penelope* 70 70
687 A212 80k *Anser brachyrhynchus* 2.65 2.65

Guardian Spirit Type of 1987
Perf. 13 on 3 Sides
1990, Feb. 15 Engr.
688 A227 5k Vulture 17 17
689 A227 5k Dragon 17 17
690 A227 5k Bull 17 17
691 A227 5k Giant 17 17
a. Block of 4, #688-691 68 68
692 A227 21k Vulture 70 70
693 A227 21k Dragon 70 70
694 A227 21k Bull 70 70
695 A227 21k Giant 70 70
a. Block of 4, #692-695 2.80 2.80
b. Block of 8, #688-695 3.50 3.50
c. Bklt. pane, 2 each #691a, 695a 7.00 7.00

Famous Women — A243

Portraits: No. 696, Gudrun Larusdottir (1880-1938), author and politician, by Halldor Petursson. No. 697, Ragnhildur Petursdottir (1880-1961), educator, by Asgrimur Jonsson.

1990, Mar. 22 Litho. *Perf. 13½x14*
696 A243 21k multicolored 70 70
697 A243 21k multicolored 70 70

Europa 1990 A244

Old and new post offices in Reykjavik and letter scales.

1990, May 7 Photo. *Perf. 12x11½*
Granite Paper
698 A244 21k 1915 70 70
699 A244 40k 1989 1.30 1.30

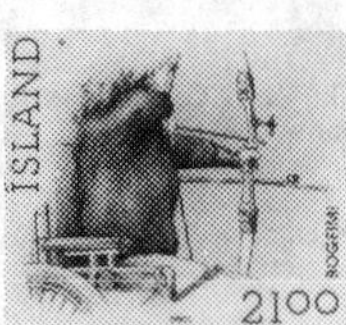

Sports — A245

1990-91 Litho. *Perf. 13x14½*
700 A245 21k Archery 70 70
701 A245 21k Soccer 70 70
706 A245 26k Golf 85 85
707 A245 26k Icelandic wrestling 85 85

Issue date: Nos. 700-701, June 28; Nos. 706-707, Aug. 14, 1991. This is an expanding set. Numbers will change if necessary.

European Tourism Year — A246

1990, Sept. 6 Litho. *Perf. 13½*
712 A246 30k multicolored 95 95

Landscape Type of 1989
1990, Sept. 6 Photo. *Perf.*
713 A238 25k Hvitserkur 80 80
714 A238 200k Lomagnupur 6.50 6.50

NORDIA '91 Map Type of 1989
Souvenir Sheet

Detail of 1539 Map by Olaus Magnus: a, Dania. b, Gothia. c, Gotlandia.

Litho. & Engr.
1990, Oct. 9 *Perf. 12½*
715 A240 Sheet of 3 6.00 6.00
a.-c. 40k any single 2.00 2.00

Stamp Day. Sold for 170k to benefit the exhibition.

Christmas A247

1990, Nov. 8 *Perf. 13½x13*

716 A247 25k shown 90 90
717 A247 30k Carolers 1.05 1.05

Bird Type of 1986

1991, Feb. 7 Photo. *Perf. 11½*

Granite Paper

721 A212 25k Podiceps auritus 95 95
725 A212 100k Sula bassana 3.75 3.75

This is an expanding set. Numbers will change if necessary.

Landscape Type of 1989

1991, Mar. 7 Photo. *Perf. 11½*

Granite Paper

728 A238 10k Vestrahorn 38 38
737 A238 300k Kverkfjoll 11.25 11.25

This is an expanding set. Numbers will change if necessary.

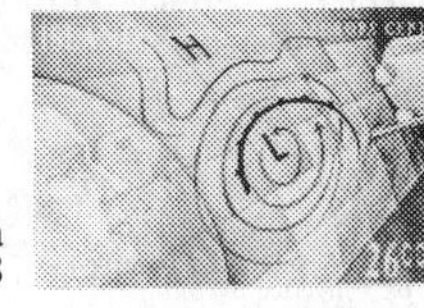

Europa A248

1991, Apr. 29 Litho. *Perf. 14*

738 A248 26k Weather map 90 90
739 A248 47k Solar panels 1.65 1.65

NORDIA '91 Map Type of 1989
Souvenir Sheet

Detail of 1539 Map by Olaus Magnus: a, Iceland's west coast. b, Islandia. c, Mare Glacial.

Litho. & Engr.

1991, May 23 *Perf. 12½*

740 A240 Sheet of 3 7.25 7.25
a.-c. 50k any single 2.42 2.42

Sold for 215k to benefit the exhibition.

Jokulsarlon Lagoon A249

Design: 31k, Strokkur hot spring.

1991, May 23 Litho. *Perf. 15x14*

741 A249 26k multicolored 85 85
742 A249 31k multicolored 1.05 1.05

Ragnar Jonsson (1904-1984), Patron of the Arts — A250

Design: 70k, Pall Isolfsson (1893-1974), musician, vert.

1991, Aug. 14 Litho. *Perf. 14*

743 A250 60k multicolored 2.00 2.00
744 A250 70k multicolored 2.30 2.00

Ships A251

Designs: a, Soloven, schooner, 1840. b, Arcturus, steamer with sails, 1858. c, Gullfoss, steamer, 1915. d, Esja II, diesel ship, 1939.

1991, Oct. 9 Litho. *Perf. 14*

745 Block or strip of 4 #745a-745d 4.20 4.20
a.-d. A251 30k any single 1.05 1.05
e. A251 Bklt. pane, 2 #745 13.00

No. 745e is distinguished from sheet of 8 by rouletted selvage at left.
Issued in sheet of 8.

College of Navigation, Reykjavik, Cent. A252

1991, Oct. 9 *Perf. 13½*

746 A252 50k multicolored 1.75 1.75

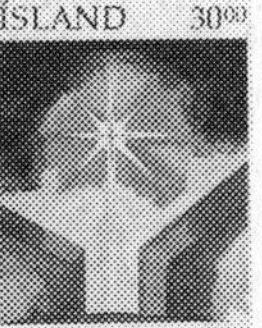

Christmas — A253

Paintings by Eirikur Smith (b. 1925): 30k, Christmas star. 35k, Star over winter landscape.

1991, Nov. 7 Litho. *Perf. 13½*

747 A253 30k multicolored 1.05 1.05
748 A253 35k multicolored 1.20 1.20

SEMI-POSTAL STAMPS

Shipwreck and Rescue by Breeches Buoy — SP1

Children Gathering Rock Plants — SP2

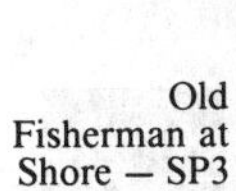

Old Fisherman at Shore — SP3

Unwmk.

1933, Apr. 28 Engr. *Perf. 14*

B1 SP1 10a + 10a red brown 1.10 *3.00*
B2 SP2 20a + 20a org red 1.10 *3.00*
B3 SP1 35a + 25a ultra 1.10 *3.00*
B4 SP3 50a + 25a blue grn 1.10 *3.00*

Receipts from the surtax were devoted to a special fund for use in various charitable works especially those indicated on the stamps: "Slysavarnir" (Rescue work), "Barnahaeli" (Asylum for scrofulous children), "Ellhaeli" (Asylum for the Aged).

Souvenir Sheets

King Christian X — SP4

1937, May 15 **Typo.**

B5 SP4 Sheet of 3 35.00 *165.00*
a. 15a violet 6.00 *35.00*
b. 25a red 6.00 *35.00*
c. 50a blue 6.00 *35.00*

Reign of Christian X, 25th anniv. Sheet sold for 2kr.

SP5

Designs: 30a, 40a, Ericsson statue, Reykjavik. 60a, Iceland's position on globe.

1938, Oct. 9 Photo. *Perf. 12*

B6 SP5 Sheet of 3 3.50 *27.50*
a. 30a scarlet 75 *6.75*
b. 40a purple 75 *6.75*
c. 60a deep green 75 *6.75*

Leif Ericsson Day, Oct. 9, 1938.

Ill Child — SP6

Red Cross Nurse and Patient — SP7

Nurse Covering Patient — SP8

Elderly Couple — SP9

Rescue at Sea — SP10

Unwmk.

1949, June 8 Engr. *Perf. 14*

B7 SP6 10a + 10a olive grn 45 *55*
B8 SP7 35a + 15a carmine 45 *55*
B9 SP8 50a + 25a choc 45 *55*
B10 SP9 60a + 25a brt ultra 45 *55*
B11 SP10 75a + 25a slate gray 45 *55*
Nos. B7-B11 (5) 2.25 *2.75*

The surtax was for charitable purposes.

Nos. 262 and 265 Surcharged in Black

Hollandshjálp 1953 +25

1953, Feb. 12 Unwmk. *Perf. 13*

B12 A50 75a + 25a red org 90 *3.25*
B13 A50 1.25k + 25a red vio 1.40 *3.25*

The surtax was for flood relief in the Netherlands.

Catalogue values for unused stamps in this section, from this point to the end of the section, are for Never Hinged items.

St. Thorlacus SP11

Cathedral at Skalholt SP12

Portrait: 1.75k+1.25k, Bishop Jon Thorkelsson Vidalin.

1956, Jan. 23 *Perf. 11½*

B14 SP11 75a + 25a car 32 45
B15 SP12 1.25k + 75a dk brn 32 45
B16 SP11 1.75k + 1.25k black 65 1.25

Bishopric of Skalholt, 900th anniv.
The surtax was for the rebuilding of Skalholt, former cultural center of Iceland.

Ambulance SP13

1963, Nov. 15 Photo. Unwmk.

B17 SP13 3k + 50a multi 22 35
B18 SP13 3.50k + 50a multi 22 35

Centenary of International Red Cross.

Rock Ptarmigan in Summer SP14

Design: #B20, Rock ptarmigan in winter.

1965, Jan. 27 Photo. *Perf. 12½*

Granite Paper

B19 SP14 3.50k + 50a multi 55 1.25
B20 SP14 4.50k + 50a blk, lt bl & gray 55 1.25

Ringed Plover's Nest — SP15

Arctic Terns — SP16

Design: 5k+50a, Rock ptarmigan's nest.

1967, Nov. 22 Photo. *Perf. 11½*

B21 SP15 4k + 50a multi 55 1.10
B22 SP15 5k + 50a multi 55 1.10

1972, Nov. 22 Litho. *Perf. 13*
B23 SP16 7k + 1k blue & multi 30 *55*
B24 SP16 9k + 1k multi 38 *55*

AIR POST STAMPS

No. 115 Overprinted 

Perf. 14x14½
1928, May 31 Wmk. 114
C1 A8 10a red 90 *7.00*

Same Overprint on No. 82
1929, June 29 Wmk. 113 *Perf. 13*
C2 A5 50a gray & violet 27.50 *42.50*

Gyrfalcon AP1

Perf. 12½x12
1930, Jan. 1 Litho. Unwmk.
C3 AP1 10a dp ultra & gray blue 11.00 *32.50*
a. Imperf., pair 300.00

Snaefellsjokull, Extinct Volcano — AP2

Parliament Millenary: 20a, Fishing boat. 35a, Iceland pony. 50a, Gullfoss (Golden Falls). 1k, Ingolfour Arnarson Statue.

Wmk. 47
1930, June 1 Typo. *Perf. 14*
C4 AP2 15a org brn & dl bl 12.00 *30.00*
C5 AP2 20a bis brn & sl bl 12.00 *30.00*
C6 AP2 35a olive grn & brn 27.50 *60.00*
C7 AP2 50a dp grn & dp bl 27.50 *60.00*
C8 AP2 1k olive grn & dk red 27.50 *60.00*
Nos. C4-C8 (5) 106.50 *240.00*

Regular Issue of 1920 Overprinted **Zeppelin 1931**

Perf. 14x14½
1931, May 25 Wmk. 114
C9 A8 30a red & green 21.00 *70.00*
C10 A8 1k dp bl & dk brn 10.00 *70.00*
C11 A8 2k ol brn & myr grn 27.50 *70.00*

Nos. 185, 128 and 187 Overprinted in Red

1933, June 16
C12 A8 1k dk bl & lt brn 85.00 *425.00*
C13 A8 5k brn & indigo 275.00 *1,100.*
C14 A8 10k yel grn & blk 550.00 *2,000.*

Excellent counterfeit overprints exist.
Visit of the Italian Flying Armada en route from Rome to Chicago; also for the payment of the charges on postal matter sent from Iceland to the US via the Italian seaplanes.

Plane over Thingvalla Lake — AP7

Designs: 10a, 20a, Plane over Thingvalla Lake. 25a, 50a, Plane and Aurora Borealis. 1k, 2k, Map of Iceland.

Perf. 12½x14
1934, Sept. 1 Engr. Unwmk.
C15 AP7 10a blue 75 *1.00*
C16 AP7 20a emerald 2.50 2.50
a. Perf. 14 5.00 3.50
C17 AP7 25a dark violet 6.00 *8.00*
a. Perf. 14 7.00 *8.00*
C18 AP7 50a red vio, perf. 14 2.00 *2.75*
C19 AP7 1k dark brown 11.00 *17.50*
C20 AP7 2k red orange 4.00 *6.00*
Nos. C15-C20 (6) 26.25 *37.75*

Thingvellir, Old Site of the Parliament AP10

Isafjörthur AP11

Eyjafjörthur AP12

Mt. Strandatindur AP13

Mt. Thyrill AP14

Aerial View of Reykjavik AP15

1947, Aug. 18 *Perf. 14*
C21 AP10 15a red orange 30 *40*
C22 AP11 30a gray black 30 *40*
C23 AP12 75a brown red 30 *40*
C24 AP13 1k indigo 30 *40*
C25 AP14 2k chocolate 85 *1.00*
C26 AP15 3k dark green 85 *1.00*
Nos. C21-C26 (6) 2.90 *3.60*

Snaefellsjokull AP16

Views: 2.50k, Eiriksjokull. 3.30k, Oracfajokull.

1952, May 2 Unwmk. *Perf. 13½x14*
C27 AP16 1.80k slate blue 5.50 *11.00*
C28 AP16 2.50k green 10.00 1.10
C29 AP16 3.30k deep ultra 4.50 4.25

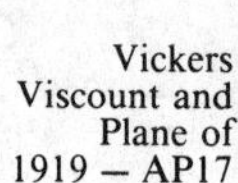

Vickers Viscount and Plane of 1919 — AP17

Design: 4.05k, Skymaster and plane of 1919.

1959, Sept. 3 Engr. *Perf. 13½*
C30 AP17 3.50k steel blue 55 55
C31 AP17 4.05k green 45 45

40th anniv. of air transportation in Iceland.

AIR POST OFFICIAL STAMPS

No. C3 Overprinted In Red **Þjónustumerki**

1930, Jan. 1 Unwmk. *Perf. 12½x12*
CO1 AP1 10a dp ultra & gray blue 20.00 *90.00*
a. Imperf.

OFFICIAL STAMPS

O1 O2 O3

Perf. 14x13½
1873 Typo. Wmk. 112
O1 O1 4s green *4,000.* *4,000.*
a. Imperf. 60.00
O2 O1 8s red lilac 225.00 240.00
a. Imperf. 225.00

Perf. 12½
O3 O1 4s green 35.00 *135.00*

The imperforate varieties lack gum.

1876-95 *Perf. 14x13½*
O4 O2 3a yellow 12.00 *27.50*
O5 O2 5a brown 3.75 *7.50*
a. Imperf. 150.00
O6 O2 10a blue 30.00 7.00
a. 10a ultramarine 165.00 35.00
O7 O2 16a carmine 7.25 *19.00*
O8 O2 20a yellow green 7.00 *12.50*
O9 O2 50a rose lilac ('95) 32.50 *42.50*

1898-1902 *Perf. 13*
O10 O2 3a yellow 6.00 *15.00*
O11 O2 4a gray ('01) 12.00 *17.50*
O12 O2 10a ultra ('02) 25.00 *55.00*

A 5a brown, perf. 13, Wmk. 112, exists. It was not regularly issued.
See note after No. O30.

1902 Wmk. 113 *Perf. 13*
O13 O3 3a buff & black 1.75 70
O14 O3 4a dp grn & blk 2.50 70
O15 O3 5a org brn & blk 1.25 *1.65*
O16 O3 10a ultra & black 1.25 *1.65*
O17 O3 16a carmine & blk 1.50 *6.00*
O18 O3 20a green & blk 6.50 3.00
O19 O3 50a violet & blk 3.00 *4.00*
Nos. O13-O19 (7) 17.75 *17.70*

Stamps of 1876-1901 Overprinted in Black **Í GILDI '02—'03**

1902-03 Wmk. 112 *Perf. 13*
O20 O2 3a yellow 70 *1.10*
a. "I" before Gildi omitted 15.00
b. Inverted overprint 5.50 6.00
c. As "a," invtd. 87.50
d. Pair, one with invtd. ovpt. 40.00
e. '03-'03 65.00
f. 02'-'03 65.00
O21 O2 4a gray 70 *1.10*
a. "I" before Gildi omitted 32.00
b. Inverted overprint 14.50 14.00
e. '03-'03 100.00 90.00
f. 02'-'03 100.00
g. Pair, one without ovpt. 32.00
h. Pair, one with invtd. ovpt. 35.00 35.00
i. "L" only of "I GILDI" inverted 160.00
O22 O2 5a brown 52 *1.00*
O23 O2 10a ultramarine 70 *1.25*
a. "I" before Gildi omitted 14.00
b. Inverted overprint 8.75 8.75
c. '03-'03 60.00
d. 02'-'03 60.00
e. "L" only of "I GILDI" 17.50
f. As "e," inverted 24.00
g. "IL" only of "I GILDI" 19.00
O24 O2 20a yel green 52 *14.00*
Nos. O20-O24 (5) 3.14 *18.45*

Perf. 14x13½
O25 O2 3a yellow 200.00 *550.00*
a. "02'-'03" 240.00
O26 O2 5a brown 6.00 *60.00*
a. Inverted overprint 12.00 *70.00*
b. '03-'03 65.00
c. 02'-'03 65.00
d. "L" only of "I GILDI" inverted 150.00
O27 O2 10a blue 225.00 *400.00*
a. "I" before Gildi omitted 275.00
b. Inverted overprint 275.00 *500.00*
c. '03-'03 275.00
d. 02'-'03 275.00
O28 O2 16a carmine 6.25 *32.50*
a. "I" before Gildi omitted 110.00
b. Double overprint 27.50 50.00
c. Dbl. ovpt., one inverted 60.00
d. Inverted overprint 30.00 45.00
e. '03-'03 110.00
O29 O2 20a yel green 5.50 *30.00*
a. Inverted overprint 45.00 45.00
b. '03-'03 87.50
c. 02'-'03 87.50
d. "I" before Gildi omitted 80.00
O30 O2 50a red lilac 5.50 *27.50*
a. "I" before Gildi omitted 14.00
b. Inverted overprint 60.00
Nos. O25-O30 (6) 448.25 *1,100.*

Nos. O10-O12, O20-O24, O28 and O30 were reprinted in 1904. They have the watermark of 1902 (type 113) and are perf. 13. Value $50 each. Without overprint $100 each.

Christian IX, Frederick VIII — O4

Christian X — O5

Engraved Center
1907-08 Wmk. 113 *Perf. 13*
O31 O4 3a yellow & gray 2.00 2.50
O32 O4 4a green & gray 1.25 *3.50*
O33 O4 5a brn org & gray 4.50 1.90
O34 O4 10a deep bl & gray 1.20 *1.50*
O35 O4 15a lt blue & gray 1.50 *2.75*
O36 O4 16a carmine & gray 1.50 *8.00*

O37 O4 20a yel grn & gray 4.50 1.00
O38 O4 50a violet & gray 3.25 2.75
Nos. O31-O38 (8) 19.70 *23.90*

1918 Wmk. 114 *Perf. 14x14½*
O39 O4 15a lt bl & gray 5.50 *15.00*

1920-30 Typo.
O40 O5 3a yellow & gray 1.50 *1.75*
O41 O5 4a dp grn & gray 48 *1.75*
O42 O5 5a orange & gray 50 *60*
O43 O5 10a dk bl & gray 1.00 55
O44 O5 15a lt blue & gray 35 55
O45 O5 20a yel grn & gray 17.50 2.00
O46 O5 50a violet & gray 20.00 85
O47 O5 1k car & gray 19.00 1.25
O48 O5 2k bl & blk ('30) 4.50 5.00
O49 O5 5k brn & blk ('30) 20.00 17.50
Nos. O40-O49 (10) 84.83 31.80

Nos. 97 and 98 Overprinted **Þjónusta.**

1922, May Wmk. 113 *Perf. 13*
O50 A7 2k rose, larger letters, no period 17.50 25.00
a. As shown 35.00 *27.50*
O51 A7 5k brown 125.00 110.00

No. 115 Surcharged **20 aur. Þjónusta**

1923 Wmk. 114 *Perf. 14x14½*
O52 A8 20a on 10a red 8.50 1.00

Parliament Millenary Issue

Nos. 152 to 166 Overprinted in Red or Blue **Þjónustumerki**

1930, Jan. 1 Unwmk. *Perf. 12½x12*
O53 A15 3a (R) 6.25 *22.50*
O54 A15 5a (R) 6.25 *22.50*
O55 A15 7a (R) 6.25 *22.50*
O56 A15 10a (Bl) 6.25 *22.50*
O57 A15 15a (R) 6.25 *22.50*
O58 A15 20a (Bl) 6.25 *22.50*
O59 A15 25a (Bl) 6.25 *22.50*
O60 A15 30a (R) 6.25 *22.50*
O61 A15 35a (R) 6.25 *22.50*
O62 A15 40a (Bl) 6.25 *22.50*
O63 A15 50a (Bl) 67.50 *110.00*
O64 A15 1k (R) 67.50 *110.00*
O65 A15 2k (R) 67.50 *110.00*
O66 A15 5k (Bl) 67.50 *110.00*
O67 A15 10k (Bl) 67.50 *110.00*
Nos. O53-O67 (15) 400.00 *775.00*

Type of 1920 Issue Redrawn

1931 Wmk. 114 Typo.
O68 O5 20a yel grn & gray 17.50 90

For differences in redrawing see note after No. 187.

No. 82 Overprinted in Black **Þjónusta**

Overprint 15mm long

1936, Dec. 7 Wmk. 113 *Perf. 13*
O69 A5 50a gray & vio 9.00 9.00

Same Overprint on Nos. 180 and 115
Perf. 14x14½
Wmk. 114
O70 A8 7a yellow green 1.40 *22.50*
O71 A8 10a red 1.50 85

IFNI

LOCATION — An enclave in southern Morocco on the Atlantic coast
GOVT. — Former Spanish possession
AREA — 580 sq. mi.
POP. — 51,517 (est. 1964)
CAPITAL — Sidi Ifni

Ifni was ceded to Spain by Morocco in 1860, but the Spanish did not occupy it until 1934. Sidi Ifni was also the administrative capital for Spanish West Africa. Spain turned Ifni back to Morocco June 30, 1969.

100 Centimos = 1 Peseta

Catalogue values for unused stamps in this country are for Never Hinged items, beginning with Scott 51 in the regular postage section, Scott B1 in the semi-postal section, and Scott C47 in the airpost section.

Stamps of Spain, 1936-40, Overprinted in Red or Blue **TERRITORIO DE IFNI**

1941-42 Unwmk. *Imperf.*
1 A159 1c green 4.00 3.75

Perf. 10 to 11
2 A160 2c org brn (Bl) 4.00 3.75
3 A161 5c gray brown 70 35
5 A161 10c dk car (Bl) 2.25 1.25
a. Red overprint 12.00 6.00
6 A161 15c light grn 55 35
7 A166 20c bright vio 55 35
8 A166 25c deep claret 55 35
9 A166 30c blue 55 50
10 A166 40c Prus green 85 30
11 A166 50c indigo 4.50 1.00
12 A166 70c blue 4.50 2.75
13 A166 1p gray blk 4.50 28
14 A166 2p dull brown 47.50 12.00
15 A166 4p dl rose (Bl) 185.00 67.50
16 A166 10p light brn 325.00 140.00
Nos. 1-16 (15) 585.00 234.48

Counterfeit overprints exist.

Nomads — A1

Alcazaba Fortress — A3

Designs: 2c, 20c, 45c, 3p, Marksman.

1943 Litho. *Perf. 12½*
17 A1 1c brn & lil rose 15 15
18 A1 2c yel grn & sl lil 15 15
19 A3 5c mag & vio 15 15
20 A1 15c sl grn & grn 15 15
21 A1 20c vio & red brn 15 15
22 A1 40c rose vio & vio 18 18
23 A1 45c brn vio & red 20 20
24 A3 75c ind & bl 20 20
25 A1 1p red & brn 1.25 1.00
26 A1 3p bl vio & sl grn 1.40 1.40
27 A3 10p blk brn & blk 13.00 11.50
Nos. 17-27 (11) 16.98 15.23

Nos. 17-27 exist imperforate.
See No. E1.

1947, Feb. *Perf. 10*
28 A1 50c vio brn & gray blk *(Nomad Family)* 6.75 50

Stamps of Spain, 1939-48, Overprinted in Carmine **Territorio de Ifni**

1948, Aug. 2 *Perf. 9½x10½, 11, 13*
29 A161 5c gray brn 1.40 35
30 A194 15c gray grn 2.75 45
31 A167 90c dk grn 8.50 2.50
32 A166 1p gray blk 24 18

Spain Nos. 769 and 770 Overprinted in Violet Blue or Carmine **Territorio de Ifni**

1949, Oct. 9 *Perf. 12½x13*
33 A202 50c red brn (VB) 1.25 70
34 A202 75c vio bl (C) 1.25 70

75th anniv. of the UPU. See No. C40.

Stamps of Spain, 1938-48, Overprinted in Blue or Carmine like Nos. 29-32

Perf. 13, 13½, 12½x13, 9½x10½
1949 Unwmk.
35 A160 2c org brn (Bl) 15 15
37 A161 10c dk car (Bl) 15 15
38 A161 15c dk grn (II) 15 15
39 A166 25c brn vio 15 15
40 A166 30c blue 15 15
41 A195 40c red brn 15 15
42 A195 45c car rose (Bl) 24 24
43 A166 50c indigo 20 15
44 A195 75c dk vio bl 30 18
47 A167 1.35p purple 2.75 2.50
48 A166 2p dl brn 2.00 1.40
49 A166 4p dl rose (Bl) 7.50 3.50
50 A166 10p lt brn 14.00 12.00
Nos. 35-50 (13) 27.89 20.87

Catalogue values for unused stamps in this section, from this point to the end of the section, are for Never Hinged items.

Gen. Francisco Franco and Desert Scene — A4

Perf. 12½x13
1951, July 18 Photo. Unwmk.
51 A4 50c dp org 50 15
52 A4 1p chocolate 4.00 1.25
53 A4 5p bl grn 32.50 11.00

Visit of Gen. Francisco Franco, 1950.

View of Granada and Globe — A5

1952, Dec. 10 *Perf. 13x12½*
54 A5 5c red org 15 15
55 A5 35c dk ol grn 15 15
56 A5 60c brown 20 15
Set value 30 15

400th anniversary of the death of Leo Africanus (c. 1485-c. 1554), Arab traveler and scholar, author of "Descrittione dell' Africa."

Musician A6

Design: 60c, Two musicians.

1953, June 1 *Perf. 12½x13*
57 A6 15c olive gray 15 15
58 A6 60c brown 15 15
Set value 15 15

Issued to promote child welfare.
See Nos. B13-B14.

Fish and Jellyfish A7

Design: 60c, Fish and seaweed.

1953, Nov. 23
59 A7 15c dark green 15 15
60 A7 60c brown 28 15
Set value 15

Colonial Stamp Day, Nov. 23, 1953.
See Nos. B15-B16.

Sea Gull — A8

Cactus — A9

Design: 25c, 60c, 2p, 5p, Salsola vermiculata.

Perf. 12½x13, 13x12½
1954, Apr. 22
61 A8 5c red org 15 15
62 A9 10c olive 15 15
63 A9 25c brn car 15 15
64 A8 35c olive gray 15 15
65 A9 40c rose lilac 15 15
66 A9 60c dk brn 15 15
67 A8 1p brown 5.75 60
68 A9 1.25p car rose 15 15
69 A9 2p darp blue 15 15
70 A9 4.50p olive grn 28 28
71 A9 5p olive blk 27.50 4.50
Nos. 61-71 (11) 34.73
Set value 5.75

Mother and Child
A10 A11

1954, June 1 *Perf. 13x12½*
72 A10 15c dk gray grn 15 15
73 A11 60c dk brn 15 15
Set value 20 15

See Nos. B17-B18.

Lobster A12

Design: 60c, Hammerhead shark.

1954, Nov. 23 *Perf. 12½x13*
74 A12 15c olive green 15 15
75 A12 60c rose brown 18 15
Set value 23 15

Issued to publicize Colonial Stamp Day.
See Nos. B19-B20.

Farmer Plowing and Statue of "Justice" A13

1955, June 1 Photo. Unwmk.
76 A13 50c gray olive 15 15

See No. B21.

Squirrel
A14

1955, Nov. 23

No.	Type	Denomination	Color	Unused	Used
77	A14	70c	yellow green	20	15

Issued to publicize Colonial Stamp Day. See Nos. B23-B24.

Senecio Antheuphorbium
A15

Design: 50c, Limoniastrum Ifniensis.

1956, June 1 ***Perf. 13x12½***

No.	Type	Denomination	Color	Unused	Used
78	A15	20c	bluish green	15	15
79	A15	50c	brown	20	15
			Set value	26	15

See Nos. B25-B26.

Arms of Sidi Ifni and Shepherd
A16

1956, Nov. 23 ***Perf. 12½x13***

No.	Type	Denomination	Color	Unused	Used
80	A16	70c	lt grn	15	15

Issued for Colonial Stamp Day.

Rock Doves — A17

1957, June 1 Photo. ***Perf. 13x12½***

No.	Type	Denomination	Color	Unused	Used
81	A17	70c	yel grn & brn	20	15

See Nos. 86, B29-B30.

Jackal
A18

Design: 70c, Jackal's head (vertical).

Perf. 12½x13, 13x12½

1957, Nov. 23

No.	Type	Denomination	Color	Unused	Used
82	A18	20c	emer & lt grn	15	15
83	A18	70c	grn & brn	30	15
			Set value		15

Issued for the Day of the Stamp, 1957. See Nos. 87, B31-B32, B41.

Basketball Players
A19

Red-legged Partridges
A20

Design: 70c, Cyclists.

1958, June 1 ***Perf. 13x12½***

No.	Type	Denomination	Color	Unused	Used
84	A19	20c	bluish green	15	15
85	A19	70c	olive green	30	15
			Set value		15

See Nos. B36-B37.

Types of 1957 inscribed "Pro-Infancia 1959"

Designs: 20c, Goat. 70c, Ewe and lamb.

1959, June 1 ***Perf. 13x12½, 12½x13***

No.	Type	Denomination	Color	Unused	Used
86	A17	20c	dull green	15	15
87	A18	70c	yellow green	20	15
			Set value		15

Issued to promote child welfare.

1960, June 10 ***Perf. 13x12½***

No.	Type	Denomination	Color	Unused	Used
88	A20	35c	shown	15	15
89	A20	80c	Camels	20	15
			Set value		15

See Nos. B46-B47.

White Stork
A21

Birds: 50c, 1.50p, 5p, European goldfinches. 75c, 2p, 10p, Skylarks (vert.).

1960 Unwmk. ***Perf. 12½x13***

No.	Type	Denomination	Color	Unused	Used
90	A21	25c	violet	15	15
91	A21	50c	olive blk	15	15
92	A21	75c	dull pur	15	15
93	A21	1p	org ver	15	15
94	A21	1.50p	brt grnsh bl	15	15
95	A21	2p	red lilac	15	15
96	A21	3p	dark blue	65	15
97	A21	5p	red brown	1.25	30
98	A21	10p	olive	5.00	1.25
			Nos. 90-98 (9)	7.80	
			Set value		2.00

Map of Ifni — A22

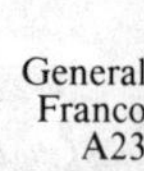

General Franco
A23

Design: 70c, Government palace.

Perf. 13x12½, 12½x13

1961, Oct. 1 Photo.

No.	Type	Denomination	Color	Unused	Used
99	A22	25c	gray vio	15	15
100	A23	50c	olive brn	15	15
101	A23	70c	brt grn	15	15
102	A23	1p	red org	15	15
			Set value	33	21

25th anniv. of the nomination of Gen. Francisco Franco as Head of State.

Admiral Jofre Tenoria
A24

Mailman
A25

Design: 50c, Cesareo Fernandez-Duro (1830-1908), writer.

1962, July 10 ***Perf. 13x12½***

No.	Type	Denomination	Color	Unused	Used
103	A24	25c	dull vio	15	15
104	A24	50c	dp bl grn	15	15
105	A24	1p	org brn	15	15
			Set value	27	15

1962, Nov. 23 Unwmk.

Stamp Day: 35c, Hands, letter and winged wheel.

No.	Type	Denomination	Color	Unused	Used
106	A25	15c	dark blue	15	15
107	A25	35c	lilac rose	15	15
108	A25	1p	rose brown	15	15
			Set value	27	15

Golden Tower, Seville
A26

Butterflies
A27

1963, Jan. 29 Photo.

No.	Type	Denomination	Color	Unused	Used
109	A26	50c	green	15	15
110	A26	1p	brn org	15	15
			Set value	20	15

Issued for flood relief in Seville.

1963, July 6 ***Perf. 13x12½***

Design: 50c, Butterfly and flower.

No.	Type	Denomination	Color	Unused	Used
111	A27	25c	deep blue	15	15
112	A27	50c	light green	15	15
113	A27	1p	carmine rose	15	15
			Set value	27	16

Issued for child welfare.

Child with Flowers and Arms
A28

1963, July 12 ***Perf. 12½x13***

No.	Type	Denomination	Color	Unused	Used
114	A28	50c	gray olive	15	15
115	A28	1p	redsh brown	15	15
			Set value	20	15

Issued for Barcelona flood relief.

Beetle (Steraspis Speciosa)
A29

Mountain Gazelle
A30

Stamp Day: 50c, Grasshopper.

1964, Mar. 6 ***Perf. 13x12½***

No.	Type	Denomination	Color	Unused	Used
116	A29	25c	violet blue	15	15
117	A29	50c	olive green	15	15
118	A29	1p	red brown	15	15
			Set value	27	18

1964, June 1 Photo.

Design: 50c, Head of roebuck.

No.	Type	Denomination	Color	Unused	Used
119	A30	25c	brt vio	15	15
120	A30	50c	slate blk	15	15
121	A30	1p	org red	15	15
			Set value	27	18

Issued for child welfare.

Bicycle Race
A31

Stamp Day: 1p, Motorcycle race.

1964, Nov. 23 ***Perf. 12½x13***

No.	Type	Denomination	Color	Unused	Used
122	A31	50c	brown	15	15
123	A31	1p	org ver	15	15
124	A31	1.50p	Prus grn	15	15
			Set value	27	18

Man — A32

Two Boys in School — A33

Cable Cars, Sidi Ifni — A34

Perf. 13x12½, 12½x13

1965, Mar. 1 Photo. Unwmk.

No.	Type	Denomination	Color	Unused	Used
125	A32	50c	dark green	15	15
126	A33	1p	org ver	15	15
127	A34	1.50p	dark blue	15	15
			Set value	27	18

25 years of peace after the Spanish Civil War.

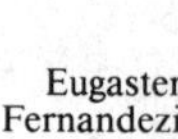

Eugaster Fernandezi
A35

Insect: 1p, Halter halteratus.

1965, June 1 Photo. Unwmk.

No.	Type	Denomination	Color	Unused	Used
128	A35	50c	purple	15	15
129	A35	1p	rose red	15	15
130	A35	1.50p	violet blue	15	15
			Set value	27	18

Issued for child welfare.

Eagle — A36

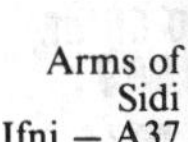

Arms of Sidi Ifni — A37

Perf. 13x12½, 12½x13

1965, Nov. 23 **Photo.**

131 A36 50c dk red brn 15 15
132 A37 1p org ver 15 15
133 A36 1.50p grnsh bl 15 15
Set value 27 18

Issued for Stamp Day 1965.

Jetliner over Sidi Ifni — A38

Syntomis Alicia — A39

Design: 2.50p, Two 1934 biplanes (horiz.).

Perf. 13x12½, 12½x13

1966, June 1 **Photo.** **Unwmk.**

134 A38 1p org brn 15 15
135 A38 1.50p brt bl 15 15
136 A38 2.50p dl vio 2.25 1.75

Issued for child welfare.

1966, Nov. 23 **Photo.** ***Perf. 13***

Designs: 40c, 4p, Danais chrysippus (butterfly).

137 A39 10c grn & red 15 15
138 A39 40c dk brn & gldn brn 15 15
139 A39 1.50p vio & yel 15 15
140 A39 4p dk pur & brt bl 25 15
Set value 42 32

Issued for Stamp Day, 1966.

Coconut Palms — A40

Designs: 40c, 4p, Cactus.

1967, June 1 **Photo.** ***Perf. 13***

141 A40 10c dp grn & brn 15 15
142 A40 40c Prus grn & ocher 15 15
143 A40 1.50p bl grn & sepia 15 15
144 A40 4p sepia & ocher 25 15
Set value 42 32

Issued for child welfare.

Sidi Ifni Harbor A41

1967, Sept. 28 **Photo.** ***Perf. 12½x13***

145 A41 1.50p grn & red brn 20 15

Modernization of harbor installations.

Needlefish (Skipper) — A42

Fish: 1.50p, John Dory (vert.). 3.50p, Gurnard (Trigla lucerna).

1967, Nov. 23 **Photo.** ***Perf. 13***

146 A42 1p bl & grn 15 15
147 A42 1.50p vio blk & yel 15 15
148 A42 3.50p brt bl & scar 30 18
Set value 42 30

Issued for Stamp Day 1967.

Zodiac Issue

Pisces — A43

Signs of the Zodiac: 1.50p, Capricorn. 2.50p, Sagittarius.

1968, Apr. 25 **Photo.** ***Perf. 13***

149 A43 1p brt mag, *lt yel* 15 15
150 A43 1.50p brn, *pink* 15 15
151 A43 2.50p dk vio, *yel* 30 15
Set value 42 27

Issued for child welfare.

Mailing a Letter A44

Designs: 1.50p, Carrier pigeon carrying letter. 2.50p, Stamp under magnifying glass.

1968, Nov. 23 **Photo.** ***Perf. 12½x13***

152 A44 1p org yel & sl grn 15 15
153 A44 1.50p brt bl & vio blk 15 15
154 A44 2.50p emer & vio blk 20 15
Set value 32 27

Issued for Stamp Day.

SEMI-POSTAL STAMPS

Catalogue values for unused stamps in this section are for Never Hinged items.

Gen. Francisco Franco — SP1

Fennec — SP2

Perf. 13x12½

1950, Oct. 19 **Unwmk.**

B1 SP1 50c + 10c sepia 60 45
B2 SP1 1p + 25c blue 20.00 6.00
B3 SP1 6.50p + 1.65p dl grn 7.50 3.25

The surtax was for child welfare.

1951, Nov. 30

B4 SP2 5c + 5c brown 15 15
B5 SP2 10c + 5c red org 15 15
B6 SP2 60c + 15c olive brn 40 15
Set value 52 22

Colonial Stamp Day, Nov. 23, 1951.

Mother and Child — SP3

Common Shag — SP4

1952, June 1

B7 SP3 5c + 5c brn 15 15
B8 SP3 50c + 10c brn blk 15 15
B9 SP3 2p + 30c dp bl 1.75 65
Set value 77

The surtax was for child welfare.

1952, Nov. 23

B10 SP4 5c + 5c brn 20 15
B11 SP4 10c + 5c brn car 20 15
B12 SP4 60c + 15c dk grn 35 15
Set value 36

Colonial Stamp Day, Nov. 23, 1952.

Musician Type of Regular Issue

1953, June 1 ***Perf. 12½x13***

B13 A6 5c + 5c As No. 57 15 15
B14 A6 10c + 5c As No. 58 15 15
Set value 16 15

The surtax was for child welfare.

Fish Type of Regular Issue

1953, Nov. 23

B15 A7 5c + 5c As No. 59 15 15
B16 A7 10c + 5c As No. 60 15 15
Set value 24 16

Colonial Stamp Day, Nov. 23, 1953.

Type of Regular Issue

1954, June 1 ***Perf. 13x12½***

B17 A10 5c + 5c org 15 15
B18 A11 10c + 5c rose vio 15 15
Set value 24 15

The surtax was for child welfare.

Type of Regular Issue

1954, Nov. 23 ***Perf. 12½x13***

B19 A12 5c + 5c As No. 74 15 15
B20 A12 10c + 5c As No. 75 15 15
Set value 15 15

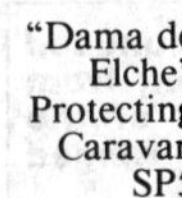

"Dama de Elche" Protecting Caravan SP5

1955, June 1 **Photo.** **Unwmk.**

B21 A13 10c + 5c rose lilac 15 15
B22 SP5 25c + 10c violet 15 15
Set value 15 15

The surtax was to help Ifni people.

Squirrel Type of Regular Issue

Design: 15c+5c, Squirrel holding nut.

1955, Nov. 23

B23 A14 5c + 5c red brown 15 15
B24 A14 15c + 5c olive bister 15 15
Set value 15 15

Type of Regular Issue

1956, June 1 ***Perf. 13x12½***

B25 A15 5c + 5c As No. 78 15 15
B26 A15 15c + 5c As No. 79 15 15
Set value 15 15

The tax was for child welfare.

Dorcas Gazelles and Arms of Spain — SP6

Design: 15c+5c, Arms of Sidi Ifni, boat and woman with drum.

1956, Nov. 23

B27 SP6 5c + 5c dark brown 15 15
B28 SP6 15c + 5c golden brn 15 15
Set value 15 15

Issued for Colonial Stamp Day.

Dove Type of Regular Issue

1957, June 1 **Photo.** ***Perf. 13x12½***

B29 A17 5c + 5c As No. 81 15 15
B30 A17 15c + 5c Stock doves 15 15
Set value 15 15

The surtax was for child welfare.

Type of Regular Issue

Perf. 12½x13, 13x12½

1957, Nov. 23 **Photo.** **Unwmk.**

B31 A18 10c + 5c As No. 82 15 15
B32 A18 15c + 5c As No. 83 15 15
Set value 15 15

Swallows and Arms of Valencia and Sidi Ifni — SP7

1958, Mar. 6 ***Perf. 12½x13***

B33 SP7 10c + 5c org brn 15 15
B34 SP7 15c + 10c bister 15 15
B35 SP7 50c + 10c brn olive 15 15
Set value 24 18

The surtax was to aid the victims of the Valencia flood, Oct. 1957.

Sport Type of Regular Issue, 1958

1958, June 1 **Photo.** ***Perf. 13x12½***

B36 A19 10c + 5c As No. 84 15 15
B37 A19 15c + 5c As No. 85 15 15
Set value 15 15

The surtax was for child welfare.

Guitarfish — SP8

Sailboats SP9

Stamp Day: 10c+5c, Spotted dogfish.

Perf. 13x12½, 12½x13

1958, Nov. 23

B38 SP9 10c + 5c brn red 15 15
B39 SP8 25c + 10c dull vio 18 15
B40 SP9 50c + 10c olive 25 15
Set value 30

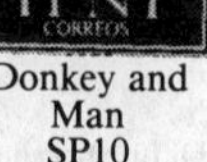

Donkey and Man SP10

Soccer SP11

Type of 1957 and SP10

Design: 10c+5c, Ewe and lamb.

Perf. 12½x13, 13x12½

1959, June 1 Photo. Unwmk.

B41 A18 10c + 5c lt red brn 15 15
B42 SP10 15c + 5c golden brn 15 15
Set value 15 15

The surtax was for child welfare.

1959, Nov. 23 ***Perf. 13x12½***

Designs: 20c+5c, Soccer players. 50c+20c, Javelin thrower.

B43 SP11 10c + 5c fawn 15 15
B44 SP11 20c + 5c slate green 15 15
B45 SP11 50c + 20c olive gray 25 15
Set value 37 18

Issued for the day of the Stamp, 1959. See Nos. B52-B54.

Type of Regular Issue, 1960

1960, June 10 ***Perf. 13x12½***

B46 A20 10c + 5c As No. 89 15 15
B47 A20 15c + 5c Wild boars 15 15
Set value 15 15

The surtax was for child welfare.

Santa Maria del Mar — SP12

Stamp Day: 20c+5c, 50c+20c, New school building (horiz.).

Perf. 13x12½, 12½x13

1960, Dec. 29 Photo.

B48 SP12 10c + 5c org brn 15 15
B49 SP12 20c + 5c dk sl grn 15 15
B50 SP12 30c + 10c red brn 15 15
B51 SP12 50c + 20c sepia 18 15
Set value 36 20

Type of 1959 inscribed: "Pro-Infancia 1961"

Designs: 10c+5c, 80c+20c, Pole vaulting (horiz.). 25c+10c, Soccer player.

Perf. 12½x13, 13x12½

1961, June 21 Unwmk.

B52 SP11 10c + 5c rose brn 15 15
B53 SP11 25c + 10c gray vio 15 15
B54 SP11 80c + 20c dk green 12 15
Set value 28 22

The surtax was for child welfare.

Camel Rider and Truck SP13

Stamp Day: 25c+10c, 1p+10c, Ship in Sidi Ifni harbor.

1961, Nov. 23 ***Perf. 12½x13***

B55 SP13 10c + 5c rose brn 15 15
B56 SP13 25c + 10c dk pur 15 15
B57 SP13 30c + 10c dk red brn 15 15
B58 SP13 1p + 10c red org 18 15
Set value 36 24

AIR POST STAMPS

Stamps formerly listed as Nos. C1-C29 were privately overprinted. These include 1936 stamps of Spain overprinted "VIA AEREA" and plane, and 1939 stamps of Spain, type AP30, overprinted "IFNI" or "Territorio de Ifni."

Oasis AP1

The Sanctuary AP2

1943 Unwmk. Litho. ***Perf. 12½***

C30 AP2 5c cer & vio brn 18 18
C31 AP1 25c yel grn & ol grn 18 18
C32 AP2 50c ind & turq grn 25 25
C33 AP1 1p pur & grnsh bl 25 25
C34 AP2 1.40p gray grn & bl 25 25
C35 AP1 2p mag & org brn 90 80
C36 AP2 5p brn & pur 1.25 1.25
C37 AP1 6p brt bl & gray grn 15.00 12.50
Nos. C30-C37 (8) 18.26 15.66

Nos. C30-C37 exist imperforate.

Type of Spain, 1939-47, Overprinted in Carmine **IFNI**

1947, Nov. 29

C38 AP30 5c dull yellow 1.75 80
C39 AP30 10c dk bl green 1.75 80

Spain No. C126 Overprinted in Carmine like Nos. 33-34

1949, Oct. 9 ***Perf. 12½x13***

C40 A202 4p dk ol grn 1.50 95

75th anniv. of the UPU.

Spain, Nos. C110 and C112 to C116, Overprinted in Blue or Carmine like Nos. 29-32

1949 ***Perf. 10***

C41 AP30 25c redsh brn (Bl) 35 15
C42 AP30 50c brown 40 18
C43 AP30 1p chalky bl 40 18
C44 AP30 2p lt gray grn 2.00 50
C45 AP30 4p gray blue 5.75 3.00
C46 AP30 10p brt pur 7.50 6.00
Nos. C41-C46 (6) 16.40 10.01

Catalogue values for unused stamps in this section, from this point to the end of the section, are for Never Hinged items.

Scott's editorial staff cannot undertake to identify, authenticate or appraise stamps and postal markings.

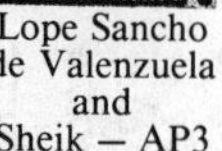

Lope Sancho de Valenzuela and Sheik — AP3

Woman Holding Dove — AP4

1950, Nov. 23 Photo. ***Perf. 13x12½***

C47 AP3 5p brown black 2.75 70

Stamp Day, Nov. 23, 1950.

1951, Apr. 22 Engr. ***Perf. 10***

C48 AP4 5p red 18.00 5.75

Issued to commemorate the 500th anniversary of the birth of Queen Isabella I of Spain.

Ferdinand the Catholic — AP5

Plane and Mountain Gazelle — AP6

Perf. 13x12½

1952, July 18 Photo. Unwmk.

C49 AP5 5p brown 24.00 6.00

500th anniv. of the birth of Ferdinand the Catholic of Spain.

1953, Apr. 1

C50 AP6 60c light grn 15 15
C51 AP6 1.20p brn car 24 15
C52 AP6 1.60p lt brown 28 15
C53 AP6 2p deep blue 2.25 20
C54 AP6 4p grnsh blk 1.25 20
C55 AP6 10p brt red vio 6.50 1.40
Nos. C50-C55 (6) 10.67
Set value 1.95

SPECIAL DELIVERY STAMPS

Type A3 inscribed "URGENTE"

1943 ***Perf. 12½***

E1 A3 25c slate grn & car 85 70

Spain, No. E20, Overprinted in Blue like Nos. 29-32

1949 Unwmk. ***Perf. 10***

E2 SD10 25c carmine 20 15

INDO-CHINA

LOCATION — French possessions on the Cambodian Peninsula in southeastern Asia, bordering on the South China Sea and the Gulf of Siam

GOVT. — Former French Colony and Protectorate

AREA — 280,849 sq. mi.

POP. — 27,030,000 (estimated 1949)

CAPITAL — Hanoi

In 1949, Indo-China was divided into Cambodia, Laos and Viet Nam each issuing its own stamps.

100 Centimes = 1 Franc
100 Cents = 1 Piaster (1918)

Stamps of French Colonies Surcharged in Black or Red:

INDO-CHINE 89 / 5 / R D — a

INDO-CHINE 1889 / 5 / R—D — b

1889 Unwmk. ***Perf. 14x13½***

1 A9(a) 5c on 35c dp vio, *org* (Bk) 3.25 2.50
a. Without date 110.00 90.00
b. Inverted surcharge 160.00 160.00
2 A9(b) 5c on 35c dp vio, *org* (R) 37.50 32.50
a. Date in smaller type 90.00 90.00
b. Inverted surcharge, #2 425.00 425.00
c. Inverted surcharge, #2a 825.00 825.00

Issue dates: No. 1, Jan. 8. No. 2, Jan. 10.

"R" is is the Colonial Governor, P. Richaud, "D" is the Saigon P.M. General P. Demars.

Navigation & Commerce A3

France A4

Name of Colony in Blue or Carmine

1892-1900 Typo. ***Perf. 14x13½***

3 A3 1c blk, *lil bl* 30 30
4 A3 2c brn, *buff* 45 35
5 A3 4c claret, *lav* 45 35
6 A3 5c grn, *grnsh* 45 25
7 A3 5c yel grn ('00) 35 20
8 A3 10c blk, *lavender* 1.90 35
9 A3 10c red ('00) 80 35
10 A3 15c blue, quadrille paper 11.00 40
11 A3 15c gray ('00) 2.25 35
12 A3 20c red, *grn* 3.00 1.50
13 A3 25c blk, *rose* 4.25 1.10
a. "INDO-CHINE" omitted *3,000. 2,500.*
14 A3 25c blue ('00) 5.75 80
15 A3 30c brn, *bis* 7.00 2.00
16 A3 40c red, *straw* 7.00 2.00
17 A3 50c car, *rose* 16.00 5.00
18 A3 50c brn, *az* ('00) 7.00 3.00
19 A3 75c dp vio, *org* 9.00 5.50
a. "INDO-CHINE" inverted *3,000. 2,500.*
20 A3 1fr brnz grn, *straw* 16.00 7.50
a. "INDO-CHINE" double 325.00 300.00
21 A3 5fr red lil, *lav* ('96) 50.00 37.50
Nos. 3-21 (19) 142.95 68.80

Perf. 13½x14 stamps are counterfeits.

Nos. 11 and 14 Surcharged in Black **5**

1903

22 A3 5c on 15c gray 38 30
23 A3 15c on 25c blue 55 30

Issue dates: No. 22, Dec. 4. No. 23, Aug. 8.

1904-06

24 A4 1c olive grn 16 15
25 A4 2c vio brn, *buff* 25 15
26 A4 4c claret, *bluish* 16 15
27 A4 5c deep green 16 15
28 A4 10c carmine 45 15
29 A4 15c org brn, *bl* 30 15
30 A4 20c red, *grn* 80 32
31 A4 25c deep blue 3.75 50
32 A4 30c pale brn 1.65 80
33 A4 35c blk, *yel* ('06) 5.25 60
34 A4 40c blk, *bluish* 1.40 40
35 A4 50c bister brn 2.00 65
36 A4 75c red, *org* 16.00 11.00
37 A4 1fr pale grn 6.00 2.25
38 A4 2fr brn, *org* 16.00 15.00
39 A4 5fr dp vio, *lil* 85.00 70.00
40 A4 10fr org brn, *grn* 80.00 65.00
Nos. 24-40 (17) 219.33 167.42

Annamite Girl — A5

Cambodian Girl — A6

Cambodian Woman A7

Annamite Women A8

Hmong Woman A9

Laotian Woman A10

Cambodian Woman — A11

1907 *Perf. 14x13½*

No.	Type	Description	Unused	Used
41	A5	1c ol brn & blk	15	15
42	A5	2c yel brn & blk	15	15
43	A5	4c blue & blk	40	35
44	A5	5c grn & blk	16	15
45	A5	10c red & blk	16	15
46	A5	15c vio & blk	55	40
47	A6	20c vio & blk	90	50
48	A6	25c bl & blk	1.90	28
49	A6	30c brn & blk	3.50	2.25
50	A6	35c ol grn & blk	55	35
51	A6	40c yel brn & blk	1.40	65
52	A6	45c org & blk	3.75	2.50
53	A6	50c car & blk	5.00	2.50

Perf. 13½x14

No.	Type	Description	Unused	Used
54	A7	75c ver & blk	4.00	3.50
55	A8	1fr car & blk	20.00	6.25
56	A9	2fr grn & blk	5.50	4.50
57	A10	5fr blue & blk	19.00	10.00
58	A11	10fr pur & blk	40.00	35.00
		Nos. 41-58 (18)	107.07	69.63

Stamps of 1904-06 Surcharged in Black or Carmine

05 **10**

1912, Nov. *Perf. 14x13½*

No.	Type	Description	Unused	Used
59	A4	5c on 4c cl, *bluish*	2.50	1.60
60	A4	5c on 15c org brn, *bl* (C)	30	30
61	A4	5c on 30c pale brn	30	30
62	A4	10c on 40c blk, *bluish* (C)	30	30
63	A4	10c on 50c bis brn (C)	32	32
64	A4	10c on 75c red, *org*	2.00	1.60
		Nos. 59-64 (6)	5.72	4.42

Two spacings between the surcharged numerals are found on Nos. 59 to 64.

Nos. 41-58 Surcharged with New Values in Cents or Piasters in Black, Red or Blue

4 CENTS

1919, Jan.

No.	Type	Description	Unused	Used
65	A5	⅖c on 1c	15	15
66	A5	⅘c on 2c	35	25
67	A5	1⅗c on 4c (R)	60	30
68	A5	2c on 5c	25	15
a.		Inverted surcharge	37.50	
69	A5	4c on 10c (Bl)	25	15
a.		Closed "4"	2.50	50
b.		Double surcharge	37.50	
70	A5	6c on 15c	70	35
a.		Inverted surcharge	42.50	
71	A6	8c on 20c	90	65
72	A6	10c on 25c	80	25
73	A6	12c on 30c	2.25	35
74	A6	14c on 35c	45	16
a.		Closed "4"	3.50	2.00
75	A6	16c on 40c	2.25	62
76	A6	18c on 45c	2.25	1.10
77	A6	20c on 50c (Bl)	3.25	45
78	A7	30c on 75c (Bl)	3.75	80
79	A8	40c on 1fr (Bl)	6.50	1.10
80	A9	80c on 2fr (R)	7.00	2.00
a.		Double surcharge	110.00	80.00
81	A10	2pi on 5fr (R)	37.50	32.50
82	A11	4pi on 10fr (R)	60.00	50.00
		Nos. 65-82 (18)	129.20	91.33

Types of 1907 Issue Surcharged with New Values in Black or Red

2 CENTS — Nos. 88-92

12 CENTS — No. 93

1922

No.	Type	Description	Unused	Used
88	A5	1c on 5c ocher & blk	35	
89	A5	2c on 10c gray grn & blk	80	
90	A6	6c on 30c lt red & blk	80	
91	A6	10c on 50c lt bl & blk	90	
92	A6	11c on 55c vio & blk, *bluish*	80	
93	A6	12c on 60c lt bl & blk, *pnksh* (R)	90	
		Nos. 88-93 (6)	4.55	

Nos. 88 to 93 were sold officially in Paris but were never placed in use in the colony.

Nos. 88-93 exist without surcharge but were not regularly issued in that condition. Value, Nos. 88-89, each $100; Nos. 90-91, each $80; Nos. 92-93, each $55.

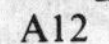

A12

A13

"CENTS" below Numerals

1922-23 *Perf. 14x13½*

No.	Type	Description	Unused	Used
94	A12	⅒c blk & sal ('23)	15	15
a.		Double impression of frame		
95	A12	⅕c blue & blk	15	15
96	A12	⅖c ol brn & blk	15	15
a.		Head and value doubled	100.00	100.00
97	A12	⅘c rose & blk, *lav*	15	15
98	A12	1c yel brn & blk	15	15
99	A12	2c gray grn & blk	25	15
100	A12	3c vio & blk	15	15
101	A12	4c org & blk	15	15
a.		Head and value doubled	50.00	50.00
102	A12	5c car & blk	15	15
a.		Head and value doubled	110.00	110.00
103	A13	6c dl red & blk	15	15
104	A13	7c grn & blk	15	15
105	A13	8c blk, *lav*	45	38
106	A13	9c ocher & blk, *grnsh*	45	38
107	A13	10c bl & blk	15	15
108	A13	11c vio & blk	15	15
109	A13	12c brn & blk	16	16
a.		Head and value double (11c+12c)	190.00	190.00
110	A13	15c org & blk	25	16
111	A13	20c bl & blk, *straw*	35	22
112	A13	40c ver & blk, *bluish*	70	45
113	A13	1pi bl grn & blk, *grnsh*	2.25	2.00
114	A13	2pi vio brn & blk, *pnksh*	3.75	2.50
		Nos. 94-114 (21)	10.41	8.20

Plowing near Tower of Confucius A14

Bay of Along A15

Angkor Wat, Cambodia A16

Carving Wood — A17

That Luang Temple, Laos — A18

Founding of Saigon A19

1927, Sept. 26

No.	Type	Description	Unused	Used
115	A14	⅒c lt olive grn	15	15
116	A14	⅕c yellow	15	15
117	A14	⅖c light blue	15	15
118	A14	⅘c dp brn	20	15
119	A14	1c orange	20	15
120	A14	2c blue grn	45	15
121	A14	3c indigo	20	15
122	A14	4c lil rose	45	32
123	A14	5c dp vio	28	15
a.		Booklet pane of 10	11.00	
124	A15	6c deep red	80	16
a.		Booklet pane of 10	11.00	
125	A15	7c lt brn	55	15
126	A15	8c gray brn	45	45
127	A15	9c red vio	55	40
128	A15	10c light blue	60	35
129	A15	11c orange	60	45
130	A15	12c myrtle grn	40	16
131	A16	15c dl rose & ol brn	3.25	3.00
132	A16	20c vio & slate	1.40	60
133	A17	25c org brn & lil rose	3.25	2.25
134	A17	30c dp bl & ol gray	1.60	1.25
135	A18	40c ver & lt bl	2.50	80
136	A18	50c lt grn & slate	3.25	1.10
137	A19	1pi dk bl, blk & yel	6.00	3.50
a.		Yellow omitted	75.00	
138	A19	2pi red, dp bl & org	7.00	5.00
		Nos. 115-138 (24)	34.43	21.14

Colonial Exposition Issue

Common Design Types Surcharged with New Values

1931, Apr. 13 **Engr.** *Perf. 12½*

Name of Country in Black

No.	Type	Description	Unused	Used
140	CD71	4c on 50c violet	90	65
141	CD72	6c on 90c red org	1.10	1.10
142	CD73	10c on 1.50fr dl bl	1.50	90

Junk — A20

Tower at Ruins of Angkor Thom — A21

Planting Rice — A22

Apsaras, Celestial Dancer — A23

1931-41 **Photo.** *Perf. 13½x13*

No.	Type	Description	Unused	Used
143	A20	⅒c Prus blue	15	15
144	A20	⅕c lake	15	15
145	A20	⅖c org red	15	15
146	A20	½c red brn	15	15
147	A20	⅘c dk vio	15	15
148	A20	1c blk brn	15	15
149	A20	2c dk grn	15	15
150	A21	3c dp brn	15	15
151	A21	3c dk grn ('34)	2.00	60
152	A21	4c dk bl	16	15
153	A21	4c dk grn ('38)	16	15
153A	A21	4c yel org ('40)	15	15
154	A21	5c dp vio	15	15
154A	A21	5c dp grn ('41)	15	15
155	A21	6c org red	15	15
a.		Bklt. pane 5 + 1 label		
156	A21	7c blk ('38)	15	15
157	A21	8c rose lake ('38)	15	15
157A	A21	9c blk, *yel* ('41)	15	15
158	A22	10c dark blue	25	15
158A	A22	10c ultra, *pink* ('41)	15	15
159	A22	15c dk brn	2.50	42
160	A22	15c dk bl ('33)	15	15
161	A22	18c blue ('38)	15	15
162	A22	20c rose	15	15
163	A22	21c olive grn	15	15
164	A22	22c dk grn ('38)	15	15
165	A22	25c dp vio	1.00	60
165A	A22	25c dk bl ('41)	15	15
166	A22	30c org brn ('32)	15	15

Perf. 13½

No.	Type	Description	Unused	Used
167	A23	50c dk brn	15	15
168	A23	60c dl vio ('32)	15	15
168A	A23	70c lt bl ('41)	20	20
169	A23	1pi yel grn	38	25
170	A23	2pi red	42	25
		Set value	9.00	4.60

Nos. 166, 167, 169 and 170 were issued without the letters "RF" in 1943, by the Vichy Government, but were not placed on sale in the colony.

Emperor Bao-Dai A24

King Sisowath Monivong A25

For Use in Annam

1936, Nov. 20 **Engr.** *Perf. 13*

No.	Type	Description	Unused	Used
171	A24	1c brown	35	35
172	A24	2c green	35	35
173	A24	4c violet	45	45
174	A24	5c red brn	45	45
175	A24	10c lil rose	62	62
176	A24	15c ultra	70	70
177	A24	20c scarlet	90	90
178	A24	30c plum	1.10	1.10
179	A24	50c slate grn	1.10	1.10
180	A24	1pi rose vio	2.00	2.00
181	A24	2pi black	2.25	2.25
		Nos. 171-181 (11)	10.27	10.27

For Use in Cambodia

No.	Type	Description	Unused	Used
182	A25	1c brown	35	35
183	A25	2c green	35	35
184	A25	4c violet	45	45
185	A25	5c red brn	45	45
186	A25	10c lil rose	1.10	1.10
187	A25	15c ultra	1.25	1.25
188	A25	20c scarlet	90	90
189	A25	30c plum	90	90
190	A25	50c slate grn	90	90
191	A25	1pi rose vio	1.20	1.20
192	A25	2pi black	2.00	2.00
		Nos. 182-192 (11)	9.85	9.85

Common Design Types pictured in section at front of book.

Paris International Exposition Issue

Common Design Types

1937, Apr. 15

No.	Type	Description	Unused	Used
193	CD74	2c dp vio	45	45
194	CD75	3c dk grn	45	45
195	CD76	4c car rose	38	38
196	CD77	6c dk brn	38	38
197	CD78	9c red	38	38
198	CD79	15c ultra	38	38
		Nos. 193-198 (6)	2.42	2.42

Colonial Arts Exhibition Issue

Souvenir Sheet

Common Design Type

1937, Apr. 15 *Imperf.*

No.	Type	Description	Unused	Used
199	CD79	30c dl vio	2.00	2.00

Governor-General Paul Doumer — A26

1938, June 8 Photo. ***Perf. 13½x13***

200	A26	5c rose car	38	25
201	A26	6c brown	38	25
202	A26	18c brt bl	38	22

Issued in commemoration of the 35th anniversary of the Trans-Indo-Chinese Railway.

New York World's Fair Issue
Common Design Type

1939, May 10 Engr. ***Perf. 12½x12***

203	CD82	13c car lake	16	16
204	CD82	23c ultra	28	28

Mot Cot Pagoda, Hanoi — A27

1939, June 12 ***Perf. 13***

205	A27	6c blk brn	35	35
206	A27	9c vermilion	35	35
207	A27	23c ultra	25	25
208	A27	39c rose vio	35	35

Golden Gate International Exposition.

Angkor Wat and Marshal Petain A27a

1941 Engr. ***Perf. 12½x12***

209	A27a	10c dk car	25
209A	A27a	25c blue	25

Nos. 209-209A were issued by the Vichy government and were not placed on sale in the colony.

King Norodom Sihanouk of Cambodia A28

Harnessed Elephant on Parade A29

Pin-perf. 12½
1941, Oct. 15 Unwmk. Litho.
Without Gum

210	A28	1c red org	30	30
211	A28	6c violet	65	65
212	A28	25c dp ultra	8.00	8.00

Coronation of Norodom Sihanouk, King of Cambodia, October, 1941.

Gum
#210-261 were issued without gum.

1942, Mar. 29

213	A29	3c redsh brn	60	45
214	A29	6c crimson	60	45

Fete of Nam-Giao in Annam.

No. 165 Surcharged in Black **10 cents** ≡

1942 ***Perf. 13***

214A	A22	10c on 25c dp vio	20	15

View of Saigon Fair — A30

1942, Dec. 20 ***Perf. 13½***

215	A30	6c car rose	15	15

Saigon Fair of 1942.

Nam-Phuong, Empress of Annam A31

Marshal Petain A32

1942, Sept. 1 ***Pin-perf. 11½***

216	A31	6c car rose	38	15

1942-44 ***Perf. 12, 13½***

217	A32	1c blk brn	15	15
218	A32	3c olive brn ('43)	15	15
219	A32	6c rose red	15	15
220	A32	10c dull grn ('43)	15	15
221	A32	40c dk blue ('43)	16	16
222	A32	40c slate bl ('44)	45	45
		Set value	85	85

Bao-Dai, Emperor of Annam A33

Norodom Sihanouk, King of Cambodia A34

1942 ***Perf. 13½***

223	A33	½c brown	16	15
224	A33	6c car rose	45	25

Issue dates: ½c, Nov. 1. 6c, Sept. 1.

1943 ***Perf. 11½***

225	A34	1c brown	30	25
226	A34	6c red	25	15

Issue dates: 1c, Mar. 10. 6c, May 10.

Sisavang-Vong, King of Laos — A35

Family, Country and Labor — A36

1943

227	A35	1c bister brown	15	15
228	A35	6c carmine rose	16	15
		Set value		22

Issue dates: 1c, Mar. 10. 6c, June 1.

1943, Nov. 5 ***Perf. 12***

229	A36	6c car rose	15	15

National revolution, 3rd anniversary.

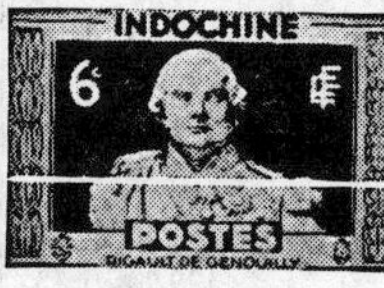

Admiral Rigault de Genouilly A37

François Chasseloup-Laubat A38

Admiral Andre A. P. Courbet A39

1943 ***Perf. 11½, 12, 12x11½***

230	A37	6c car rose	15	15
231	A38	6c car rose	15	15
232	A39	6c car rose	25	15
		Set value		29

Issue dates: Nos. 230, 232, Sept. 1. No. 231, Oct. 5.

A 5c dull brown, type A37, was not regularly issued without the Viet Nam overprint. A 3c light brown, type A39, was prepared but not issued.

Pigneau de Behaine, Bishop of Adran — A40

Alexandre Yersin — A41

1943, June 10 ***Perf. 12***

233	A40	20c dull red	45	45

1943-45 ***Perf. 12x11½***

234	A41	6c car rose	50	50
235	A41	15c vio brn ('44)	15	15
236	A41	1pi yel grn ('45)	25	25

Issued to honor Dr. Alexandre Yersin (1863-1943), the Swiss bacteriologist who introduced rubber culture into Indo-China.

Issue dates: 6c, Oct. 5. 15c, Dec. 10. 1pi, Jan. 10.

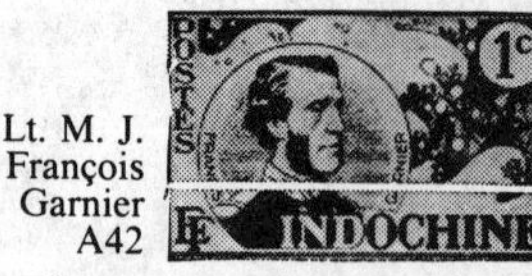

Lt. M. J. François Garnier A42

1943, Sept. ***Perf. 12***

237	A42	1c dull olive bis	40	25

A 15c brown violet was prepared but not issued.

Alexandre de Rhodes A43

1943-45 ***Pin-perf., Perf. 12***

238	A43	15c dk vio brn ('45)	15	15
239	A43	30c org brn	15	15
a.		30c yellow brown, perf. 13½	15	15

Nos. 239, 239a carry the monogram "EF."
Issue dates: 15c, Mar. 10. 30c, June 15.

Athlete Giving Olympic Salute — A44

1944, July 10 ***Perf. 12***

241	A44	10c dk vio brn & yel	1.25	1.25
242	A44	50c dl red	1.25	1.25

Adm. Pierre de La Grandiere A45

1943-45

243	A45	1c dull brn	15	15
244	A45	5c dark brn ('45)	15	15
		Set value	17	17

The upper left corner of No. 244 contains the denomination "5c" instead of "EF" monogram.

Issue dates: 1c, Aug. 5c, Jan. 10.

Auguste Pavie A46

1944 ***Perf. 12***

245	A46	4c org yel	15	15
246	A46	10c dl grn	15	15
		Set value	24	24

Issue dates: 4c, Feb. 10. 10c, Jan. 5.
A 20c dark red, type A46, was not regularly issued without the Viet Nam overprint.

Governor-General Pierre Pasquier — A47

1944

247	A47	5c brn vio	28	28
248	A47	10c dl grn	15	15

Issue dates: 5c, Nov. 1. 10c, Sept.

Joost Van Vollenhoven A48

1944, Oct. 10

249	A48	1c olive brown	15	15
250	A48	10c green	28	28

Governor-General J. M. A. de Lanessan — A49

1944

251	A49	1c dl gray brn	15	15
252	A49	15c dl rose vio	30	30

Issue dates: 1c, Dec. 10. 15c, Oct. 16.

Governor-General Paul Doumer — A50

1944

253	A50	2c red vio	15	15
254	A50	4c lt brn	15	15
255	A50	10c yel grn	15	15
		Set value	36	36

Issue dates: 2c, May 15. 4c, June 15. 10c, Jan. 5.

Admiral Charner A51

Doudart de Lagrée A52

1944

256	A51	10c green	15	15
257	A51	20c brn red	15	15
258	A51	1pi pale yel grn	30	25

Issue dates: 10c, 20c, Aug. 10. 1pi, July.

1944-45

259	A52	1c dl gray brn ('45)	15	15
260	A52	15c dl rose vio	16	16
261	A52	40c brt bl	15	15
		Set value	32	32

Issue dates: 1c, Jan. 10. 15c, 40c, Nov.

Nos. 209-209A Overprinted in Black RF

1946 Unwmk. *Perf. 12½x12*

262	A27a	10c dk car	16	16
263	A27a	25c blue	42	42

SEMI-POSTAL STAMPS

No. 45 Surcharged

5 c

1914 Unwmk. *Perf. 14x13½*

B1	A5	10c +5c red & blk	38	25

Nos. 44-46 Surcharged

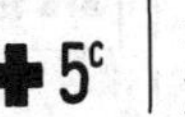

1915-17

B2	A5	5c + 5c grn & blk ('17)	25	25
a.		Double surcharge	60.00	60.00
B3	A5	10c + 5c red & blk	70	50
B4	A5	15c + 5c vio & blk ('17)	70	50
a.		Triple surcharge	70.00	70.00
b.		Quadruple surcharge	65.00	65.00

Nos. B2-B4 Surcharged with New Values in Blue or Black

1918-19

B5	A5	4c on 5c + 5c (Bl)	1.60	1.25
a.		Closed "4"	90.00	90.00
B6	A5	6c on 10c + 5c	1.50	1.25
B7	A5	8c on 15c + 5c ('19)	5.50	4.25
a.		Double surcharge	80.00	80.00

France Nos. B5-B10 Surcharged

INDOCHINE
10 CENTS

1918 (?)

B8	SP5	10c on 15c + 10c	55	55
B9	SP5	16c on 25c + 15c	1.75	1.75
B10	SP6	24c on 35c + 25c	2.75	2.75
a.		Double surcharge	250.00	
B11	SP7	40c on 50c + 50c	5.00	5.00
B12	SP8	80c on 1fr + 1fr	10.00	10.00
B13	SP8	4pi on 5fr + 5fr	100.00	75.00
		Nos. B8-B13 (6)	120.05	95.05

Curie Issue
Common Design Type
Inscription and Date in Upper Margin

1938, Oct. 24 Engr. *Perf. 13*

B14	CD80	18c + 5c brt ultra	4.50	4.50

French Revolution Issue
Common Design Type
Name and Value Typo. in Black

1939, July 5 Photo.

B15	CD83	6c + 2c green	3.50	3.50
B16	CD83	7c + 3c brown	3.50	3.50
B17	CD83	9c + 4c red org	3.50	3.50
B18	CD83	13c + 10c rose pink	3.50	3.50
B19	CD83	23c + 20c blue	3.50	3.50
		Nos. B15-B19 (5)	17.50	17.50

Common Design Type and

Tonkinese Sharpshooter SP1

Legionary SP2

1941 Photo. *Perf. 13½*

B19A	SP1	10c + 10c red	40
B19B	CD86	15c + 30c maroon	40
B19C	SP2	25c + 10c blue	40

Nos. B19A-B19C were issued by the Vichy government, and were not placed on sale in the colony.

Nos. 209-209A were surcharged "OEUVRES COLONIALES" and surtax (including change of denomination of the 25c to 5c). These were issued in 1944 by the Vichy government and not placed on sale in the colony.

Portal and Flags, City University, Hanoi — SP3

Coat of Arms and Sword — SP4

Perf. 11½

1942, June 1 Unwmk. Litho.

B20	SP3	6c + 2c car rose	20	20
B21	SP3	15c + 5c brn vio	35	35

10c +2c

No. B20 Surcharged in Black

1944, June 10

B22	SP3	10c + 2c on 6c + 2c	20	20

1942, Aug. 1 *Perf. 12*

B23	SP4	6c + 2c red & blue	16	16
B24	SP4	15c + 5c vio blk, red & bl	30	30

No. B23 Surcharged in Black Like No. B22

1944, Mar. 15

B25	SP4	10c + 2c on 6c + 2c	15	15

Aviator Do-Huu-Vi SP5

1943, Aug. 1

B26	SP5	6c + 2c car rose	20	20

No. B26 Surcharged in Black Like No. B22

1944, Feb. 10

B27	SP5	10c + 2c on 6c + 2c	15	15

Surcharge arranged to fit size of stamp.

Aviator Roland Garros — SP6

1943, Nov. 15

B28	SP6	6c + 2c rose car	15	15

No. B28 Surcharged in Black Like No. B22

1944, Feb. 10

B29	SP6	10c + 2c on 6c + 2c	15	15

Cathedral of Orleans SP7

1944, Dec. 20

B30	SP7	15c + 60c brn vio	50	40
B31	SP7	40c + 1.10pi blue	60	58

Type of France, 1945, Surcharged in Black

INDOCHINE
2 P + 2 P

1945 Unwmk. Engr. *Perf. 13*

B32	A152	50c + 50c on 2fr green	25	25
B33	A152	1pi + 1pi on 2fr hn brn	25	25
B34	A152	2pi + 2pi on 2fr Prus grn	40	40

AIR POST STAMPS

Airplane AP1

1933-41 Unwmk. Photo. *Perf. 13½*

C1	AP1	1c ol brn	15	15
C2	AP1	2c dk grn	15	15
C3	AP1	5c yel grn	15	15
C4	AP1	10c red brn	16	15
C5	AP1	11c rose car ('38)	15	15
C6	AP1	15c dp bl	16	15
C6A	AP1	16c brt pink ('41)	15	15
C7	AP1	20c grnsh gray	25	16
C8	AP1	30c org brn	15	15
C9	AP1	36c car rose	80	15
C10	AP1	37c ol grn ('38)	15	15
C10A	AP1	39c dk ol grn ('41)	15	15
C11	AP1	60c dk vio	15	15
C12	AP1	66c ol grn	25	15
C13	AP1	67c brt bl ('38)	45	45
C13A	AP1	69c brt ultra ('41)	25	25
C14	AP1	1pi black	25	15
C15	AP1	2pi yel org	50	15
C16	AP1	5pi purple	80	16
C17	AP1	10pi dp red	1.50	38
		Nos. C1-C17 (20)	6.72	
		Set value		2.60

See Nos. C27-C28.

Issue dates: 11c, 37c, June 8. 67c, Oct. 5. 16c, 39c, 69c, Feb. 5. Others, June 1, 1933.

Stamps of type AP1 without "RF" monogram were issued in 1942 and 1943 by the Vichy Government, but were not placed on sale in the colony. On the Vichy stamps, the figure of value has been moved to the lower left corner of the vignette.

Governor-General Paul Doumer — AP2

1938, June 8

C18	AP2	37c red orange	20	15

35th anniv. of the Trans-Indo-Chinese Railway.

Victory Issue
Common Design Type
Perf. 12½

1946, May 8 Unwmk. Engr.

C19	CD92	80c red org	35	25

Chad to Rhine Issue
Common Design Types

1946, June 6

C20	CD93	50c yel grn	30	30
C21	CD94	1pi violet	30	30
C22	CD95	1.50pi carmine	30	30
C23	CD96	2pi vio brn	30	30
C24	CD97	2.50pi dp bl	40	40
C25	CD98	5pi org red	60	60
		Nos. C20-C25 (6)	2.20	2.20

UPU Issue
Common Design Type

1949, July 4 *Perf. 13*

C26	CD99	3pi dp bl, dk vio, grn & red	1.50	1.10

Plane Type of 1933-41

1949, June 13 Photo. *Perf. 13½*

C27	AP1	20pi dk bl grn	4.50	2.00
C28	AP1	30pi brown	5.00	2.00

AIR POST SEMI-POSTAL STAMP

French Revolution Issue
Common Design Type
Unwmk.

1939, July 5 Photo. *Perf. 13*
Name and Value Typo. in Orange

CB1	CD83	39c + 40c brn blk	7.50	7.50

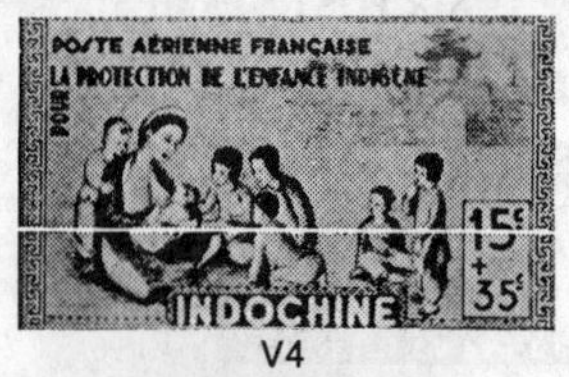

V4

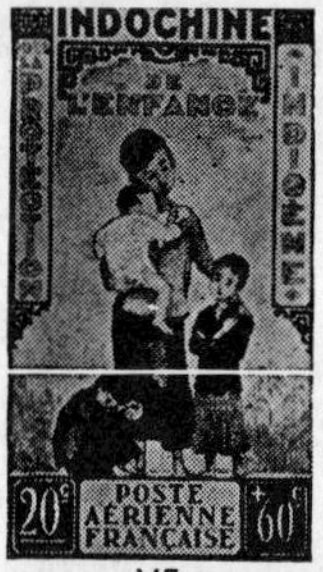

V5

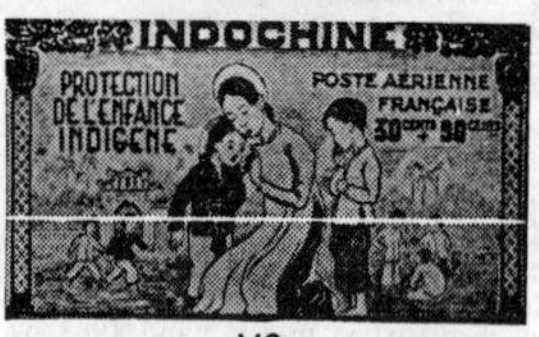

V6

Stamps of the above designs, and of Cameroun type V10 inscribed "Indochine", were issued in 1942 by the Vichy Government, but were not placed on sale in the colony.

POSTAGE DUE STAMPS

French Colonies No. J21 Surcharged **5**

1904, June 26 **Unwmk.** ***Imperf.***

J1	D1	5c on 60c brn, *buff*	4.50	3.50

French Colonies Nos. J10-J11 Surcharged in Carmine

1905, July 22

J2	D1	5c on 40c black	11.00	4.00
J3	D1	10c on 60c black	11.00	6.00
J4	D1	30c on 60c black	11.00	6.00

Dragon from Steps of Angkor Wat
D1 D2

1908 **Typo.** ***Perf. 14x13½***

J5	D1	2c black	35	35
J6	D1	4c dp bl	35	35
J7	D1	5c bl grn	35	35
J8	D1	10c carmine	1.10	35
J9	D1	15c violet	1.10	80
J10	D1	20c chocolate	35	35
J11	D1	30c ol grn	35	35
J12	D1	40c claret	3.25	2.75
J13	D1	50c grnsh bl	1.50	45
J14	D1	60c orange	4.00	3.50
J15	D1	1fr gray	7.00	5.50
J16	D1	2fr yel brn	6.00	4.00
J17	D1	5fr red	11.00	7.00
		Nos. J5-J17 (13)	36.70	26.10

Surcharged with New Values in Cents or Piasters

1919

J18	D1	4/5c on 2c blk	65	35
J19	D1	1 3/5c on 4c dp bl	60	40
J20	D1	2c on 5c bl grn	1.10	60
J21	D1	4c on 10c car	65	35
J22	D1	6c on 15c vio	2.25	1.10
J23	D1	8c on 20c choc	2.25	60
J24	D1	12c on 30c ol grn	2.25	65
J25	D1	16c on 40c cl	2.25	60
J26	D1	20c on 50c grnsh bl	4.00	2.25
J27	D1	24c on 60c org	1.00	65
a.		Closed "4"	8.00	6.25
J28	D1	40c on 1fr gray	1.25	65
a.		Closed "4"	9.00	7.00
J29	D1	80c on 20c yel brn	12.00	7.00
J30	D1	2pi on 5fr red	19.00	10.00
a.		Double surcharge	75.00	60.00
b.		Triple surch.	75.00	55.00
		Nos. J18-J30 (13)	49.25	25.20

"CENTS" below Numerals

1922, Oct.

J31	D2	2/5c black	15	15
J32	D2	4/5c red	15	15
J33	D2	1c buff	16	15
J34	D2	2c gray grn	25	16
J35	D2	3c violet	25	16
J36	D2	4c orange	20	15
a.		"4 CENTS" omitted	250.00	
b.		"4 CENTS" double	25.00	25.00
J37	D2	6c ol grn	35	25
J38	D2	8c blk, *lav*	35	15
J39	D2	10c dp bl	45	15
J40	D2	12c ocher, *grnsh*	50	35
J41	D2	20c dp bl, *straw*	62	25
J42	D2	40c red, *bluish*	62	25
J43	D2	1pi brn vio, *pnksh*	2.00	1.10
		Nos. J31-J43 (13)	6.05	
		Set value		2.90

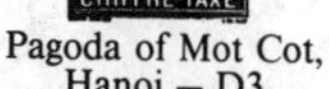

Pagoda of Mot Cot, Hanoi — D3

Dragon of Annam — D4

Perf. 14x13½, 13½x14

1927, Sept. 26

J44	D3	2/5c vio brn & org	15	15
J45	D3	4/5c vio & blk	15	15
J46	D3	1c brn red & sl	35	30
J47	D3	2c grn & brn ol	35	35
J48	D3	3c red brn & bl	35	35
J49	D3	4c ind & brn	35	35
J50	D3	6c dp red & ver	40	40
J51	D3	8c ol brn & vio	40	35
J52	D4	10c dp bl	40	25
J53	D4	12c olive	2.90	1.25
J54	D4	20c rose	1.00	40
J55	D4	40c bl grn	1.25	80
J56	D4	1pi red org	7.00	5.00
		Nos. J44-J56 (13)	15.05	10.10

D5

Value Surcharged in Black or Blue

1931-41 ***Perf. 13***

J57	D5	1/5c red, *org* ('38)	15	15
J58	D5	2/5c red, *org*	15	15
J59	D5	4/5c red, *org*	15	15
J60	D5	1c red, *org*	15	15
J61	D5	2c red, *org*	15	15
J62	D5	2.5c red, *org* ('40)	15	15
J63	D5	3c red, *org* ('38)	15	15
J64	D5	4c red, *org*	15	15
J65	D5	5c red, *org* ('38)	15	15
J66	D5	6c red, *org*	15	15
J67	D5	10c red, *org*	15	15
J68	D5	12c red, *org*	15	15
J69	D5	14c red, *org* ('38)	15	15
J70	D5	18c red, *org* ('41)	16	16
J71	D5	20c red, *org*	16	15
J72	D5	50c red, *org*	20	16
J72A	D5	1pi red, *org*	3.50	3.00
J73	D5	1pi red, *org* (Bl)	70	60
		Set value	5.65	5.00

D6

D7

Perf. 12, 13½ and Compound

1943-44 **Litho.** **Unwmk.**

J74	D6	1c red, *org*	15	15
J75	D6	2c red, *org*	15	15
J76	D6	3c red, *org*	15	15
J77	D6	4c red, *org*	15	15
J78	D6	6c red, *org*	15	15
J79	D6	10c red, *org*	15	15
J80	D7	12c blue, *pnksh*	15	15
J81	D7	20c blue, *pnksh*	15	15
J82	D7	30c blue, *pnksh*	15	15
		Set value	1.00	1.00

Issue dates: 2c, 3c, July 15, 1943. 6c-30c, Aug. 1943. 1c, 4c, June 10, 1944.

OFFICIAL STAMPS

Regular Issues of 1931-32 Overprinted in Blue or Red

Overprinted S E R V I C E

Perf. 13, 13½

1933, Feb. 27 **Unwmk.**

O1	A20	1c blk brn (Bl)	30	15
O2	A20	2c dk grn (Bl)	30	16

Overprinted **SERVICE**

O3	A21	3c dp brn (Bl)	40	28
a.		Inverted overprint	40.00	
O4	A21	4c dk bl (R)	40	30
a.		Inverted overprint	40.00	
O5	A21	5c dp vio (Bl)	65	15
O6	A21	6c org red (Bl)	65	15

Overprinted **SERVICE**

O7	A22	10c dk bl (R)	35	25
O8	A22	15c dk brn (Bl)	1.10	60
O9	A22	20c rose (Bl)	80	16
O10	A22	21c ol grn (Bl)	1.10	60
O11	A22	25c dp vio (Bl)	35	16
O12	A22	30c org brn (Bl)	80	35

Overprinted **S E R V I C E**

O13	A23	50c dk brn (Bl)	5.50	1.25
O14	A23	60c dl vio (Bl)	80	60
O15	A23	1pi yel grn (Bl)	12.00	4.00
O16	A23	2pi red (Bl)	4.25	3.50
		Nos. O1-O16 (16)	29.75	12.66

Type of Regular Issue, 1922-23

Overprinted diagonally in Black or Red "SERVICE"

1934, Oct. 4 ***Perf. 14x13***

O17	A13	1c ol grn	30	25
O18	A13	2c brn org	35	28
O19	A13	3c yel grn	30	16
O20	A13	4c cerise	50	50
O21	A13	5c yellow	25	20
O22	A13	6c org red	1.90	1.60
O23	A13	10c gray grn (R)	95	90
O24	A13	15c ultra	75	60
O25	A13	20c gray blk (R)	50	50
O26	A13	21c lt vio	3.25	2.75
O27	A13	25c rose lake	3.75	2.25
O28	A13	30c lil gray	50	40
O29	A13	50c brt vio	2.00	2.75
O30	A13	60c gray	3.75	3.50
O31	A13	1pi blue (R)	9.25	5.50
O32	A13	2pi dp red	14.00	11.00
		Nos. O17-O32 (16)	42.30	33.14

The value tablet has colorless numeral and letters on solid background.

PARCEL POST STAMPS

French Colonies No. 50 Overprinted **INDO-CHINE TIMBRE COLIS POSTAUX**

1891 **Unwmk.** ***Perf. 14x13½***

Q1	A9	10c blk, *lavender*	5.00	1.50

The overprint on No. Q1 was also handstamped in shiny ink.

Indo-China No. 8 Overprinted **Colis Postaux**

1898

Q2	A3	10c blk, *lavender*	6.00	6.25

Nos. 8 and 9 Overprinted **TIMBRE COLIS POSTAUX**

1902

Q3	A3	10c blk, *lavender*	15.00	9.00
a.		Inverted overprint	40.00	18.00
Q4	A3	10c red	15.00	7.00
a.		Inverted overprint	30.00	18.00
b.		Double overprint	30.00	18.00

INDONESIA

LOCATION — In the East Indies
GOVT. — Republic
AREA — 741,101 sq. mi.
POP. — 158,000,000 (est. 1983)
CAPITAL — Jakarta

Formerly Netherlands Indies, Indonesia achieved independence late in 1949 as the United States of Indonesia and became the Republic of Indonesia August 15, 1950. See Netherlands Indies for earlier issues.

100 Sen = 1 Rupiah

Catalogue values for all unused stamps in this country are for Never Hinged items.

Watermark

Wmk. 228

United States of Indonesia

Mountain, Palms and Flag of Republic — A49

Perf. 12½x12

1950, Jan. 17 Photo. Unwmk.

Size: 20½x26mm

333 A49 15s red		35	15

1950, June ***Perf. 11½***

Size: 18x23mm

334 A49 15s red		2.50	40

Netherlands Indies Nos. 307-315 Overprinted in Black **R I S**

1950 ***Perf. 11½, 12½***

335 A42	1s gray		20	15
336 A42	2s claret		20	15
337 A42	2½s ol brn		25	15
338 A42	3s rose pink		20	15
339 A42	4s green		25	15
340 A42	5s blue		15	15
341 A42	7½s dk grn		25	15
342 A42	10s violet		25	15
343 A42	12½s brt red		38	15

Perf. 11½, 1s, 5s. Perf. 12½, 7½s, 12½s. Others, both perfs.

Netherlands Indies Nos. 317-330 Overprinted in Black **R I S**

Perf. 11½, 12½

345 A43 20s gray blk		2.50	2.25
346 A43 25s ultra		25	15
347 A44 30s brt red		1.40	1.40
348 A44 40s gray grn		25	15
349 A44 45s claret		60	20
350 A45 50s org brn		40	15
351 A45 60s brown		1.90	1.60
352 A45 80s scarlet		1.00	20

Perf. 11½, 20s, 45s, 50s. Others, both perfs.

Overprint 12mm High

Perf. 12½

353 A46 1r purple		60	15
354 A46 2r ol grn		90.00	75.00
355 A46 3r red vio		80.00	25.00
356 A46 5r dk brn		25.00	19.00
357 A46 10r gray		45.00	15.00
358 A46 25r org brn		15.00	6.00
Nos. 335-358 (23)		266.03	147.60

For overprints see Riouw Archipelago Nos. 17-22.

Republic of Indonesia

Arms of the Republic A50

Doves in Flight A51

Perf. 12½x12

1950, Aug. 17 Photo. Unwmk.

359 A50 15s red		25	15
360 A50 25s dl grn		65	25
361 A50 1r sepia		4.50	75

5th anniv. of Indonesia's proclamation of independence.

1951, Oct. 24 Engr. ***Perf. 12***

362 A51 7½s bl grn		1.25	65
363 A51 10s violet		35	15
364 A51 20s red		1.10	40
365 A51 30s car rose		1.25	50
366 A51 35s ultra		1.25	50
367 A51 1r sepia		15.00	1.25
Nos. 362-367 (6)		20.20	3.45

6th anniv. of the UN and the 1st anniv. of the Republic of Indonesia as a member.

A52

Post Office — A53

Mythological Hero — A54

Pres. Sukarno — A55

1951-53 Photo. ***Perf. 12½***

368	A52	1s gray	15	15
369	A52	2s plum	15	15
370	A52	2½s brown	2.25	35
371	A52	5s car rose	15	15
372	A52	7½s green	15	15
373	A52	10s blue	15	15
374	A52	15s purple	15	15
375	A52	20s rose red	15	15
376	A52	25s dp grn	15	15
377	A53	30s red org	15	15
378	A53	35s purple	15	15
379	A53	40s dl grn	15	15
380	A53	45s dp claret	20	15
381	A53	50s brown	4.00	15
382	A54	60s dk brn	15	15
383	A54	70s gray	15	15
384	A54	75s ultra	15	15
385	A54	80s claret	15	15
386	A54	90s gray grn	15	15
		Set value	7.75	1.10

Perf. 12½x12

387	A55	1r purple	15	15
388	A55	1.25r dp org	15	15
389	A55	1.50r brown	15	15
390	A55	2r green	15	15
391	A55	2.50r rose brn	15	15
392	A55	3r blue	15	15
392A	A55	4r ap grn	15	15
393	A55	5r brown	15	15
394	A55	6r rose lil	15	15
395	A55	10r slate	15	15
396	A55	15r yellow	15	15
397	A55	20r sepia	15	15
398	A55	25r scarlet	15	15
399	A55	40r yel grn	15	15
400	A55	50r violet	15	15
		Set value	75	60

Nos. 368-376, 387, 390, 392, 393, 395, 398 were issued in 1951; Nos. 377-386, 388-389, 391, 392A, 394, 396-397, 399-400 in 1953.

Values are for the later Djakarta printings which have thicker numerals and a darker over-all impression. Earlier printings by Joh. Enschede and Sons, Haarlem, Netherlands, sell for more.

For surcharge see No. B68. For overprints see Riouw Archipelago Nos. 1-16, 32-40.

Melati Flowers A56

Crowd Releasing Doves A57

1953, Dec. 22 ***Perf. 12½***

401 A56 50s bl grn		3.50	25

25th anniv. of the formation of the Indonesian Women's Congress.

1955, Apr. 18 ***Perf. 13x12½***

402 A57 15s gray		42	25
403 A57 35s brown		42	25
404 A57 50s dp mag		1.10	25
405 A57 75s bl grn		48	20

Asian-African Conf., Bandung, April 18-24.

Proclamation of Independence A58

Voters A59

1955, Aug. 17 Photo. ***Perf. 12½***

406 A58 15s green		30	15
407 A58 35s ultra		30	22
408 A58 50s brown		65	15
409 A58 75s magenta		55	25

Ten years of independence.

1955, Sept. 29 ***Perf. 12***

Without gum

410 A59 15s rose vio		42	15
411 A59 35s green		42	20
412 A59 50s car rose		1.25	20
413 A59 75s lt ultra		65	25

First free elections in Indonesia.

Mas Soeharto Postmaster General A60

Helmet, Wreath and Monument A61

1955, Sept. 27 ***Perf. 12½***

414 A60 15s brown		95	45
415 A60 35s dk car		95	45
416 A60 50s ultra		3.75	90
417 A60 75s dl grn		2.50	45

Issued to mark 10 years of Indonesia's Postal, Telegraph and Telephone system.

1955, Nov. 10

418 A61 25s bluish grn		50	20
419 A61 50s ultra		1.60	40
420 A61 1r dk car rose		5.00	25

Issued in honor of the soldiers killed in the war of liberation from the Netherlands.

Torch, Book and Map A62

Lesser Malay Chevrotain A63

1956, May 26 Photo.

421 A62 25s ultra		1.40	16
422 A62 50s car rose		4.00	50
423 A62 1r dk grn		2.00	50

Issued to publicize the Asia-Africa Student Conference, Bandung, May, 1956.

1956 Unwmk. ***Perf. 12½x13½***

Animals: 5s, 10s, Lesser Malay chevrotain. 20s, 25s, Otter. 35s, Malayan pangolin. 50s, Banteng. 75s, Asiatic two-horned rhinoceros.

424 A63 5s dp ultra		15	15
425 A63 10s yel brn		15	15
426 A63 15s rose vio		15	15
427 A63 20s dl grn		15	15
428 A63 25s dp cl		15	15
429 A63 35s brt vio bl		15	15
430 A63 50s brown		15	15
431 A63 75s dk brn		15	15
Set value		40	40

See Nos. 450-456. For overprints see Riouw Archipelago Nos. 23-31.

Dancing Girl and Gate — A64

Telegraph Key — A65

1956, Oct. 7 ***Perf. 12½x12***

432 A64 15s slate grn		80	25
433 A64 35s brn vio		80	25
434 A64 50s bl blk		1.50	40
435 A64 75s dp claret		1.50	15

Issued to commemorate the 200th anniversary of the founding of the city of Jogjakarta.

1957, May 10 Unwmk.

436 A65 10s lt crim		1.40	25
437 A65 15s brt bl		32	15
438 A65 25s gray		32	15
439 A65 50s brn red		40	15
440 A65 75s lt bl grn		55	15
Nos. 436-440 (5)		2.99	
Set value			65

Indonesian telegraph system centenary.

Thrift Symbolism A66

Douglas DC-3 A67

Design: 15s, 1r, People and hands holding wreath of rice and cotton.

1957, July 12 Photo. ***Perf. 12½***

441 A66 10s blue		20	20
442 A66 15s rose car		32	20
443 A66 50s green		65	40
444 A66 1r brt vio		85	15

Cooperation Day, July 12.

1958, Apr. 9 ***Perf. 12½x12***

Aircraft: 15s, Helicopter. 30s, Miles Magister. 50s, Two-motor plane of Indonesian Airways. 75s, De Havilland Vampire.

445 A67 10s redsh brn		15	15
446 A67 15s blue		15	15
447 A67 35s orange		15	16
448 A67 50s brt grn		16	22
449 A67 75s gray		55	25
Nos. 445-449 (5)		1.16	93

Issued for National Aviation Day, April 9.

Animal Type of 1956

Animals: 30s, Otter. 40s, 45s, Malayan pangolin. 60s, 70s, Banteng 80s, 90s, Asiatic two-horned rhinoceros.

1958 Photo. *Perf. 12½x13½*

450 A63 30s orange 15 15
451 A63 40s brt yel grn 15 15
452 A63 45s rose lil 15 15
453 A63 60s dk bl 15 15
454 A63 70s org ver 15 15
455 A63 80s red 15 15
456 A63 90s yel grn 15 15
Set value 35 30

Thomas Cup — A68

1958, Aug. 15 *Perf. 13½x13*

457 A68 25s rose car 15 15
458 A68 50s orange 15 15
459 A68 1r brown 15 15
Set value 29 19

Indonesia's victory in the 1958 Thomas Cup World Badminton Championship.

Satellite Circling Globe — A69

1958, Oct. 15 Litho. *Perf. 12½x12*

460 A69 10s dk grn, pink & lt bl 35 15
461 A69 15s vio, gray & pale bluish grn 15 15
462 A69 35s brn, bl & pink 15 15
463 A69 50s bl, redsh brn & gray 15 15
464 A69 75s blk, vio & buff 15 15
Set value 75 45

International Geophysical Year, 1957-58.

Bicyclist and Map A70

1958, Nov. 15 Photo. *Perf. 13½x13*

465 A70 25s brt bl 15 15
466 A70 50s brn car 15 15
467 A70 1r gray 15 15
Set value 30

Bicycle Tour of Java, Aug. 15-30.

Man Looking into Light A71

Wild Boar (Babirusa) A72

Designs: 15s, Hands and flame. 35s, Woman holding candle. 50s, Family hailing torch. 75s, Torch and "10."

1958, Dec. 10 *Perf. 12½x12*

468 A71 10s gray brn 15 15
469 A71 15s dl red brn 15 15
470 A71 35s ultra 15 15
471 A71 50s pale brn 15 15
472 A71 75s lt bl grn 15 15
Set value 42 32

10th anniv. of the signing of the Universal Declaration of Human Rights.

1959, June 1 Photo. *Perf. 12*

Animals: 15s, Anoa (smallest buffalo). 20s, Orangutan. 50s, Javan rhinoceros. 75s, Komodo dragon (lizard). 1r, Malayan tapir.

473 A72 10s ol bis & sepia 15 15
474 A72 15s org brn & sepia 15 15
475 A72 20s lt ol grn & sepia 15 15
476 A72 50s bis brn & sepia 15 15
477 A72 75s dp rose & sepia 15 15
478 A72 1r blue grn & blk 15 15
Set value 25 25

Issued to publicize wildlife preservation.

A73

Factories — A74

1959, Aug. 17 Litho. *Perf. 12*

479 A73 20s bl & red 15 15
480 A73 50s rose red & blk 15 15
481 A73 75s brn & red 15 15
482 A73 1.50r lt grn & blk 15 15
Set value 27 20

Introduction of the constitution of 1945 embodying "guided democracy."

1959, Oct. 26 Photo. *Perf. 12*

Designs: 20s, 75s, Cogwheel and train. 1.15r, Means of transportation.

483 A74 15s brt grn & blk 15 15
484 A74 20s dl org & blk 15 15
485 A74 50s red & blk 15 15
486 A74 75s brt grnsh bl & blk 15 15
487 A74 1.15r mag & blk 15 15
Set value 36 30

11th Colombo Plan Conference, Jakarta.

Mother & Child, WRY Emblem — A75

Tea Plantation — A76

Designs: 15s, 75s, Destroyed town and fleeing family. 20s, 1.15r, World Refugee Year emblem.

1960, Apr. 7 Unwmk. *Perf. 12½x12*

488 A75 10s cl & blk 15 15
489 A75 15s bis & blk 15 15
490 A75 20s org brn & blk 15 15
491 A75 50s grn & blk 15 15
492 A75 75s dk bl & blk 15 15
493 A75 1.15r scar & blk 15 15
Set value 30 28

Issued to publicize World Refugee Year, July 1, 1959-June 30, 1960.

1960 *Perf. 12x12½*

Designs: 5s, Oil palms. 10s, Sugar cane and railroad. 15s, Coffee. 20s, Tobacco. 50s, Coconut palms. 75s, Rubber plantation. 1.15r, Rice.

494 A76 5s gray 15 15
495 A76 10s red brn 15 15
496 A76 15s plum 15 15
497 A76 20s ocher 15 15
498 A76 25s brt bl grn 15 15
499 A76 50s dp bl 15 15
500 A76 75s scarlet 15 15
501 A76 1.15r plum 15 15
Set value 35 35

For surcharges see Nos. B132-B134.

Anopheles Mosquito — A77

1960, Nov. 12 Photo. *Perf. 12x12½*

502 A77 25s car rose 15 15
503 A77 50s org brn 15 15
504 A77 75s brt grn 15 15
505 A77 3r orange 15 15
Set value 30 20

World Health Day, Nov. 12, 1960, and to promote malaria control.

Pres. Sukarno with Hoe — A78

1961, Feb. 15 *Perf. 12½x12*

506 A78 75s gray 15 15

Planned National Development.

Dayak Dancer of Borneo A79

Designs: 10s, Ambonese boat. 15s, Tangkubanperahu crater. 20s, Bull races. 50s, Toradja houses. 75s, Balinese temple. 1r, Lake Toba. 1.50r, Balinese dancer and musicians. 2r, Buffalo hole, view. 3r, Borobudur Temple, Java.

1961 *Perf. 13½x13*

507 A79 10s rose lil 15 15
508 A79 15s gray 15 15
509 A79 20s orange 15 15
510 A79 25s org ver 15 15
511 A79 50s car rose 15 15
512 A79 75s red brn 16 20
513 A79 1r brt grn 20 25
514 A79 1.50r bis brn 40 25
515 A79 2r grnsh bl 50 35
516 A79 3r gray 60 35
Set of 4 souvenir sheets 4.00 2.25
Nos. 507-516 (10) 2.61
Set value 1.75

Issued for tourist publicity.

The four souvenir sheets among them contain one each of Nos. 507-516 imperf., with two or three stamps to a sheet and English marginal inscriptions: "Visit Indonesia" and "Visit the Orient Year." Size: 139x105mm or 105x139mm.

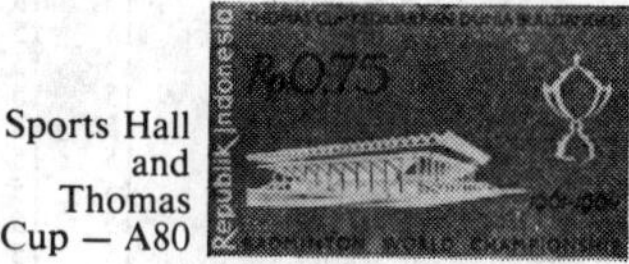

Sports Hall and Thomas Cup — A80

Perf. 13½x12½

1961, June 1 Photo.

517 A80 75s pale vio & bl 15 15
518 A80 1r citron & dk grn 15 15
519 A80 3r sal pink & dk bl 16 15
Set value 33 26

Issued to commemorate the 1961 Thomas Cup World Badminton Championship.

New Buildings and Workers A81

1961, July 6 Unwmk.

520 A81 75s vio & grnsh bl 15 15
521 A81 1.50r emer & buff 15 15
522 A81 3r dk red & sal 15 15
Set value 20 20

16th anniversary of independence.

Sultan Hasanuddin — A82

Portraits: 20s, Abdul Muis. 30s, Surjopranoto. 40s, Tengku Tjhik Di Tiro. 50s, Teuku Umar. 60s, K. H. Samanhudi. 75s, Captain Pattimura. 1r, Raden Adjeng Kartini. 1.25r, K. H. Achmad Dahlan. 1.50r, Tuanku Imam Bondjol. 2r, Si Singamangaradja XII. 2.50r, Mohammad Husni Thamrin. 3r, Ki Hadjar Dewantoro. 4r, Djenderal Sudirman. 4.50r, Dr. G. S. S. J. Ratulangie. 5r, Pangeran Diponegoro. 6r, Dr. Setyabudi. 7.50r, H. O. S. Tjokroaminoto. 10r, K. H. Agus Salim. 15r, Dr. Soetomo.

Perf. 13½x12½

1961-62 Unwmk. Photo.

Black Inscriptions; Portraits in Sepia

523 A82 20s olive 15 15
524 A82 25s gray ol 15 15
525 A82 30s brt lil 15 15
526 A82 40s brn org 15 15
527 A82 50s bluish grn 15 15
528 A82 60s grn ('62) 15 15
529 A82 75s lt red brn 15 15
530 A82 1r lt bl 15 15
531 A82 1.25r lt ol grn ('62) 15 15
532 A82 1.50r emerald 15 15
533 A82 2r org red ('62) 15 15
534 A82 2.50r rose claret 15 15
535 A82 3r gray blue 15 15
536 A82 4r olive grn 22 15
537 A82 4.50r red lil ('62) 15 15
538 A82 5r brick red 26 18
539 A82 6r bis ('62) 15 15
540 A82 7.50r vio bl ('62) 15 15
541 A82 10r green ('62) 22 15
542 A82 15r dp org ('62) 26 15
Set value 2.40 1.50

Issued to honor national heroes. The 25s, 75s, 1.50r and 5r on Aug. 17, Independence Day; 40s, 50s and 4r on Oct. 5, Army Day; 20s, 30s, 1r, 2.50r and 3r on Nov. 10, Republic Day; 60s, 2r, 7.50r and 15r on Oct. 5, 1962; 1.25r, 4.50r, 6r and 10r on Nov. 10, 1962.

Symbols of Census A83

1961, Sept. 15 *Perf. 13½x12½*

543 A83 75s rose vio 15 15

First census in Indonesia.

Djataju — A84

Scenes from Ramayana Ballet: 40s, Hanuman. 1r, Dasamuka. 1.50r, Kidang Kentiana. 3r, Dewi Sinta. 5r, Rama.

Perf. 12x12½

1962, Jan. 15 Unwmk.

544 A84 30s ocher & red brn 15 15
545 A84 40s rose lil & vio 15 15
546 A84 1r grn & cl 15 15
547 A84 1.50r sal pink & dk grn 15 15
548 A84 3r pale grn & dp bl 15 15
549 A84 5r brn org & dk brn 15 15
Set value 45 32

Asian Games Emblem — A85

Main Stadium — A86

Designs: 10s, Basketball. 15s, Main Stadium, Jakarta. 20s, Weight lifter. 25s, Hotel Indonesia. 30s, Cloverleaf intersection. 40s, Discus thrower. 50s, Woman diver. 60s, Soccer. 70s, Press House. 75s, Boxers. 1r, Volleyball. 1.25r, 2r, 3r, 5r, Asian Games emblem. 1.50r, Badminton. 1.75r, Wrestlers. 2.50r, Woman rifle shooter. 4.50r, Hockey. 6r, Water polo. 7.50r, Tennis. 10r, Table tennis. 15r, Bicyclist. 20r, Welcome Monument.

1962 Photo. *Perf. 12½*

550 A85 10s grn & yel 15 15
551 A86 15s grnsh blk & bis 15 15
552 A85 20s red lil & lt grn 15 15
553 A86 25s car & lt grn 15 15
554 A86 30s bl grn & yel 15 15
555 A85 40s ultra & pale bl 15 15
556 A85 50s choc & gray 15 15
557 A85 60s lil rose & vio gray 15 15
558 A85 70s dk brn & rose 15 15
559 A85 75s choc & org 15 15
560 A85 1r pur & lt bl 15 15
561 A85 1.25r dk bl & rose car 15 15
562 A85 1.50r red org & lil 15 15
563 A85 1.75r dk car & rose 15 15
564 A85 2r brn & yel grn 15 15
565 A85 2.50r dp bl & lt grn 15 15
566 A85 3r blk & dk red 15 15
567 A85 4.50r dk grn & red 15 15
568 A85 5r gray grn & lem 15 15
569 A85 6r brn red & dp yel 16 15
570 A85 7.50r red brn & sal 16 15
571 A85 10r dk bl & bl 16 15
572 A85 15r dl vio & pale vio 20 16
573 A85 20r dk grn & ol bis 35 25
Set value 2.50 1.75

4th Asian Games, Jakarta.

Malaria Eradication Emblem A87

Atom Diagram A88

1962, Apr. 7 *Perf. 12½x12*

574 A87 40s dl bl & vio bl 15 15
575 A87 1.50r yel org & brn 15 15
576 A87 3r grn & ind 15 15
577 A87 6r lil & blk 16 16
Set value 38 35

WHO drive to eradicate malaria. The 1.50r and 6r have Indonesian inscription on top.

1962, Sept. 24 Photo. *Perf. 12x12½*

578 A88 1.50r dk bl & yel 15 15
579 A88 4.50r brick red & yel 16 16
580 A88 6r grn & yel 22 16
Set value 45 39

Development through science.

Pacific Travel Association Emblem — A89

Mechanized Plow — A90

Designs: 1.50r, Prambanan Temple and Mount Merapi. 6r, Balinese Meru (Buildings), Pura Taman Ajun.

1963, Mar. 14 Unwmk.

581 A89 1r grn & ind 15 15
582 A89 1.50r ol & ind 15 15
583 A89 3r ocher & ind 15 15
584 A89 6r dp org & ind 15 15
Set value 22 25

Issued to publicize the 12th conference of the Pacific Area Travel Association, Bandung.

Perf. 12½x12, 12x12½
1963, Mar. 21

Design: 1r, 3r, Hand holding rice stalks (vert.).

585 A90 1r bl & yel 15 15
586 A90 1.50r brt grn & ind 15 15
587 A90 3r rose car & org 15 15
588 A90 6r org & blk 15 15
Set value 24 22

FAO "Freedom from Hunger" campaign. English inscription on 3r and 6r.

Long-Armed Lobster — A91

Fish: 1.50r, Little tuna. 3r, River roman. 6r, Chinese pompano.

1963, Apr. 6 *Perf. 12½x12*

589 A91 1r ver, blk & yel 15 15
590 A91 1.50r ultra, blk & yel 15 15
591 A91 3r Prus bl, bis & car 15 15
592 A91 6r ol grn, blk & ocher 15 15
Set value 24 22

Pen and Conference Emblem — A92

Designs: 1.50r, Pen, Emblem and map of Africa and Southeast Asia. 3r, Globe, pen and broken chain (vert.). 6r, Globe, hand holding pen and broken chain (vert.).

Perf. 12½x12, 12x12½
1963, Apr. 24 Photo. Unwmk.

593 A92 1r lt bl & dp org 15 15
594 A92 1.50r pale vio & mar 15 15
595 A92 3r ol, bl & blk 15 15
596 A92 6r brick red & blk 15 15
Set value 22 22

Asian-African Journalists' Conference.

"Indonesia's Flag from Sabang to Merauke" — A93

Designs: 4.50r, Parachutist landing in New Guinea. 6r, Bird of paradise and map of New Guinea.

1963, May 1 *Perf. 12½x12*

597 A93 1.50r org brn, blk & red 15 15
598 A93 4.50r multi 15 15
599 A93 6r multi 15 15
Set value 22 17

Issued to mark the acquisition of Netherlands New Guinea (West Irian).

Centenary Emblem — A94

Design: 1.50r, 6r, Red Cross.

1963, May 8 *Perf. 12*

600 A94 1r brt grn & red 15 15
601 A94 1.50r lt bl & red 15 15
602 A94 3r gray & red 15 15
603 A94 6r yel bis & red 15 15
Set value 24 22

Centenary of the International Red Cross.

Bank of Indonesia, Djalan A95

Daneswara, God of Prosperity A96

1963, July 5 Photo. *Perf. 12*

604 A95 1.75r lt bl & pur 15 15
605 A96 4r cit & sl grn 15 15
606 A95 6r lt grn & brn 15 15
607 A96 12r org & dk red brn 15 15
Set value 24 22

Issued for National Banking Day.

Standard Bearers — A97

Designs: 1.75r, "Pendet" dance. 4r, GANEFO building, Senajan, Jakarta. 6r, Archery. 10r, Badminton. 12r, Javelin. 25r, Sailing. 50r, Torch.

1963, Nov. 10 Unwmk. *Perf. 12½*

608 A97 1.25r gray vio & dk brn 15 15
609 A97 1.75r org & ol grn 15 15
610 A97 4r emer & dk brn 15 15
611 A97 6r rose brn & blk 15 15
612 A97 10r lt ol grn & dk brn 15 15
613 A97 12r rose car & grnsh blk 15 15
614 A97 25r bl & dk bl 15 15
615 A97 50r red & blk 15 15
Set value 45 45

1st Games of the New Emerging Forces, GANEFO, Jakarta, Nov. 10-22.

Pres. Sukarno A98

Trailer Truck A99

1964 Photo. *Perf. 12½x12*

616 A98 6r brn & dk bl 15 15
617 A98 12r bis & plum 15 15
618 A98 20r bl & org 15 15
619 A98 30r red org & bl 15 15
620 A98 40r grn & brn 15 15
621 A98 50r red & dp grn 15 15
622 A98 75r vio & red org 15 15
623 A98 100r sil & red brn 15 15
624 A98 250r dk bl & sil 15 15
625 A98 500r red & gold 15 15
Set value 45 45

See Nos. B165-B179. For surcharges see Nos. 661, 663-667.

1964 *Perf. 12x12½, 12½x12*

Designs: 1r, Oxcart. 1.75r, Freighter. 2r, Lockheed Electra plane. 2.50r, Buginese sailboat (vert.). 4r, Mailman with bicycle. 5r, Dakota plane. 7.50r, Teletype operator. 10r, Diesel train. 15r, Passenger ship. 25r, Convair Coronado Plane. 35r, Telephone switchboard operator.

626 A99 1r dl cl 15 15
627 A99 1.25r red brn 15 15
628 A99 1.75r Prus bl 15 15
629 A99 2r red org 15 15
630 A99 2.50r brt bl 15 15
631 A99 4r bluish grn 15 15
632 A99 5r ol bis 15 15
633 A99 7.50r brt grn 15 15
634 A99 10r orange 15 15
635 A99 15r dk bl 15 15
636 A99 25r vio bl 15 15
637 A99 35r red brn 15 15
Set value 50 50

For surcharges see Nos. 659-660, 662.

Ramses II — A100

Design: 6r, 18r, Kiosk of Trajan, Philae.

1964, Mar. 8 *Perf. 12½x12*

638 A100 4r ol bis & ol grn 15 15
639 A100 6r grnsh bl & ol grn 15 15
640 A100 12r rose & ol grn 15 15
641 A100 18r emer & ol grn 15 15
Set value 22 22

UNESCO world campaign to save historic monuments in Nubia.

Stamps of Netherlands Indies and Indonesia — A101

1964, Apr. 1 *Perf. 12½*

642 A101 10r gold, dk bl & red org 15 15

Centenary of postage stamps in Indonesia.

Indonesian Pavilion — A102

1964, May 16 ***Perf. 12½x12***

643	A102	25r sil, blk, red & dk bl	15	15
644	A102	50r gold, Prus bl, red & grn	15	15
		Set value	15	15

New York World's Fair, 1964-65.

Thomas Cup — A103

1964, Aug. 15 ***Perf. 12½x13½***

645	A103	25r brt grn, gold & red	15	15
646	A103	50r ultra, gold & red	15	15
647	A103	75r pur, gold & red	20	15
		Set value	40	20

Thomas Cup Badminton World Championship, 1964.

Cruisers and Map of West Irian — A104

Designs: 30r, Submarine. 40r, Torpedo boat.

Perf. 12½x12

1964, Oct. 5 **Photo.** **Unwmk.**

648	A104	20r yel & brn	15	15
649	A104	30r rose & blk	15	15
650	A104	40r brt grn & ultra	15	15
		Set value	21	21

Issued to honor the Indonesian Navy.

Map of Africa and Asia and Mosque — A105

Design: 15r, 50r, Mosque and clasped hands.

1965, Mar. 6. **Photo.** ***Perf. 12½***

651	A105	10r lt bl & pur	15	15
652	A105	15r org & red brn	15	15
653	A105	25r brt grn & brn	15	15
654	A105	50r brn red & blk	15	15
		Set value	24	20

Issued to publicize the Afro-Asian Islamic Conference, Bandung, March, 1965.

Hand Holding Scroll — A106

Design: 25r, 75r, Conference emblem (globe, cotton and grain).

1965, Apr. 18 **Unwmk.** ***Perf. 12½***

655	A106	15r sil & dp car	15	15
656	A106	25r aqua, gold & red	15	15
657	A106	50r gold & dp ultra	15	15
658	A106	75r pale vio, gold & red	15	15
		Set value	24	20

10th anniv. of the First Afro-Asian Conf.

Nos. 618-623 and Nos. 634-636 Surcharged in Revalued Currency in Orange or Black

Sen

1965, Dec. ***Perf. 12x12½, 12½x12***

659	A99	10s on 10r org (B)	15	15
660	A99	15s on 15r dk bl	15	15
661	A98	20s on 20r bl & org	15	15
662	A99	25s on 25r vio bl (B)	15	15
663	A98	30s on 30r red org & bl	15	15
664	A98	40s on 40r grn & brn	15	15
665	A98	50s on 50r red & dp grn	15	15
666	A98	75s on 75r vio & red org	15	15
667	A98	100s on 100r sil & red brn	16	15
		Set value	75	50

The surcharge on Nos. 659-660 and No. 662 is in two lines and larger.

Pres. Sukarno — A107

1966-67 **Photo.** ***Perf. 12½x12***

668	A107	1s sep & Prus grn	15	15
669	A107	3s sep & lt ol grn	15	15
670	A107	5s sep & dp car	15	15
671	A107	8s sep & Prus grn	15	15
672	A107	10s sep & vio bl	15	15
673	A107	15s sep & blk	15	15
674	A107	20s sep & dp grn	15	15
675	A107	25s sep & dk red brn	15	15
676	A107	30s sep & dp bl	15	15
677	A107	40s sep & red brn	15	15
678	A107	50s sep & brt vio	15	15
679	A107	80s sep & org	15	15
680	A107	1r sep & emer	15	15
681	A107	1.25r sep & dk gray ol	15	15
682	A107	1.50r sep & emer	15	15
683	A107	2r sep & mag	15	15
684	A107	2.50r sep & gray	15	15
685	A107	5r sep & ocher	15	15
686	A107	10r sep & ol grn	15	15
686A	A107	12r grn & org ('67)	15	15
686B	A107	25r grn & brt pur ('67)	15	15
		Set value	1.00	50

The 12r is inscribed "1967" instead of "1966."

Dockyard Workers — A108

Gen. Ahmad Yani — A109

Designs: 40s, Lighthouse. 50s, Fishermen. 1r, Maritime emblem (wheel and eagle). 1.50r, Sailboat. 2r, Loading dock. 2.50r, Diver emerging from water. 3r, Liner at pier.

1966 **Photo.** ***Perf. 12x12½***

687	A108	20s lt ultra & grn	15	15
688	A108	40s pink & dk bl	15	15
689	A108	50s grn & brn	15	15
690	A108	1r sal, bl & yel	15	15
691	A108	1.50r dl lil & dl grn	15	15
692	A108	2r gray & dp org	15	15
693	A108	2.50r rose lil & dk red	15	15
694	A108	3r brt grn & blk	15	15
a.		Souv. sheet	5.00	3.50
		Set value	50	35

Issued for Maritime Day. Nos. 687-690 issued Sept. 23; Nos. 691-694, Oct. 23.

No. 694a contains one imperf. stamp similar to No. 694.

1966, Nov. 10

Heroes of the Revolution: No. 696, Lt. Gen. R. Suprapto. No. 697, Lt. General Harjono. No. 698, Lt. Gen. S. Parman. No. 699, Maj. Gen. D. I. Pandjaitan. No. 700, Maj. Gen. Sutojo Siswomihardjo. No. 701, Brig. General Katamso. No. 702, Colonel Soegijono. No. 703, Capt. Pierre Andreas Tendean. No. 704, Adj. Insp. Karel Satsuit Tubun.

Deep Blue Frame

695	A109	5r org brn	15	15
696	A109	5r brt grn	15	15
697	A109	5r gray brn	15	15
698	A109	5r olive	15	15
699	A109	5r gray	15	15
700	A109	5r brt pur	15	15
701	A109	5r red lilac	15	15
702	A109	5r slate grn	15	15
703	A109	5r dl rose lil	15	15
704	A109	5r orange	15	15
		Nos. 695-704 (10)	1.50	
		Set value		70

Issued to honor military men killed during the Communist uprising, October, 1965.

Tjlempung, Java — A110

Aviator and MiG-21 — A111

Musical Instruments and Maps: 1r, Sasando, Timor. 1.25r, Foi doa, Flores. 1.50r, Kultjapi, Sumatra. 2r, Arababu, Sangihe and Talaud Islands. 2.50r, Drums, West New Guinea. 3r, Katjapi, Celebes. 4r, Hape, Borneo. 5r, Gangsa, Bali. 6r, Serunai, Sumatra. 8r, Rebab, Java. 10r, Trompet, West New Guinea. 12r, Totobuang, Moluccas. 15r, Drums, Nias. 20r, Kulintang, Celebes. 25r, Keledi, Borneo.

1967 **Unwmk.** **Photo.** ***Perf. 12½x12***

705	A110	50s red & gray	15	15
706	A110	1r brn & dp org	15	15
707	A110	1.25r mar & ultra	15	15
708	A110	1.50r grn & lt vio	15	15
709	A110	2r vio bl & yel bis	15	15
710	A110	2.50r ol grn & dl red	15	15
711	A110	3r brt grn & dl cl	15	15
712	A110	4r vio bl & org	15	15
713	A110	5r dl red & bl	15	15
714	A110	6r blk & brt pink	15	15
715	A110	8r red brn & brt grn	16	15
716	A110	10r lil & red	22	15
717	A110	12r ol grn & lil	25	15
718	A110	15r vio & lt ol grn	35	15
719	A110	20r gray & sep	45	15
720	A110	25r blk & grn	60	16
		Set value	2.65	1.00

Issue dates: 1.25r, 10r, 12r, 15r, 20r, 25r, Mar. 1; others Feb. 1.

For surcharges see Nos. J118-J137.

1967, Apr. 9 ***Perf. 12½***

Aviation Day: 4r, Traffic control tower and 990A Convair jetliner. 5r, Hercules transport plane.

721	A111	2.50r multi	15	15
722	A111	4r multi	15	15
723	A111	5r multi	15	15
		Set value	22	18

Thomas Cup with Victory Dates — A112

Design: 12r, Thomas Cup and globe.

1967, May 31 ***Perf. 12x12½***

724	A112	5r multi	15	15
725	A112	12r multi	20	15
		Set value	27	15

Issued to commemorate the Thomas Cup Badminton World Championship of 1967.

Balinese Girl in Front of Temple Gate — A113

1967, July 1 **Photo.** ***Perf. 12½***

726	A113	12r multi	20	15
a.		Souv. sheet of 1, imperf.	1.50	75

Intl. Tourist Year, 1967. See No. 739.

Heroes of the Revolution Monument, Lubang Buaja — A114

Designs: 5r, Full view of monument (horiz.). 7.50r, Shrine at monument.

Perf. 12x12½, 12½x12

1967, Aug. 17 **Photo.**

727	A114	2.50r pale grn & dk brn	15	15
728	A114	5r brt rose lil & pale brn	15	15
729	A114	7.50r pink & Prus grn	15	15
		Set value	27	18

Issued to publicize the "Heroes of the Revolution" Monument in Lubang Buaja.

Forest Fire, by Raden Saleh A115

Design: 50r, Fight to Death, by Raden Saleh.

1967, Oct. 30 Photo. Perf. 12½
730 A115 25r org & gray grn 30 25
a. Souv. sheet of 1 1.60 1.40
731 A115 50r vio brn & org 65 60

Indonesian painter Raden Saleh (1813-80).

Human Rights Flame — A116

1968, Jan. 1 Photo. Perf. 12½
732 A116 5r grn, lt vio bl & red 15 15
733 A116 12r grn, ol bis & red 16 15
Set value 15

International Human Rights Year 1968.

Armed Forces College Emblem — A117

1968, Jan. 29 Litho. Perf. 12½
734 A117 10r lt bl, yel & brn 16 15

Integration of the Armed Forces College.

WHO Emblem and "20" — A118

20th anniv. of WHO: 20r, WHO emblem.

1968, Apr. 7 Photo. Perf. 12½
735 A118 2r dp yel, pale yel & dk brn 15 15
736 A118 20r emer & blk 25 15
Set value 32 15

Trains of 1867 and 1967 and Railroad's Emblem — A119

1968, May 15 Photo. Perf. 12½x12
737 A119 20r multi 25 15
738 A119 30r multi 40 16

Indonesian railroad centenary (in 1967).

Tourist Type of 1967

Tourist Publicity: 30r, Butterfly dancer from West Java.

1968, July 1 Perf. 12½
739 A113 30r gray & multi 35 16
a. Souv. sheet of 1 + label 1.60 1.40

Bosscha Observatory and Andromeda Nebula — A120

Design: 30r, Observatory, globe and sky (vert.).

1968, Sept. 20 Photo. Perf. 12½x12
740 A120 15r ultra & yel 16 15
741 A120 30r vio & org 35 15
Set value 17

Bosscha Observatory, 40th anniversary.

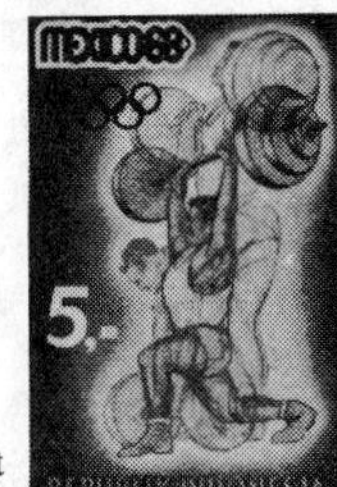

Weight Lifting — A121

Designs: 7.50r+7.50r, Sailing (horiz.). 12r, Basketball. 30r, Dove, Olympic flame and emblem (horiz.).

1968, Oct. 12 Perf. 12½
742 A121 5r ocher, blk & grn 15 15
743 A121 Pair 16 15
a. 7.50r Left half 15 15
b. 7.50r Right half 15 15
c. Souv. sheet 1.60 1.00
744 A121 12r bl & multi 15 15
745 A121 30r bl grn & multi 25 15
Set value 62 37

19th Olympic Games, Mexico City, Oct. 12-27. No. 743 is perforated vertically in the center, dividing it into two separate stamps, each inscribed "Republik Indonesia" and "7.50r." There is no gutter along the center perforation; and the design is continous over the two stamps.

No. 743c contains one No. 743 with track design surrounding the stamps.

Eugenia Aquea Burm. f. — A122

Fruits: 15r, Papaya. 30r, Durian (vert.).

Perf. 12½x12, 12x12½
1968, Dec. 20 Photo.
746 A122 7.50r multi 15 15
747 A122 15r multi 15 15
a. Souvenir sheet of 1 60 50
748 A122 30r multi 25 15
a. Souvenir sheet of 1 1.10 1.00
Set value 46 29

Issued for the 11th Social Day.

Globe, ILO and UN Emblems — A123

Designs: 7.50r, 25r, ILO and UN emblems.

1969, Feb. 1 Photo. Perf. 12½
749 A123 5r yel grn & scar 15 15
750 A123 7.50r org & dk grn 15 15
751 A123 15r lil & org 16 15
752 A123 25r bl grn & dl red 22 15
Set value 55 27

50th anniv. of the ILO.

R. Dewi Sartika — A124

Red Crosses — A125

Portraits: No. 754, Tjoet Nja Din. No. 755, Tjoet Nja Meuthia. No. 756, General Gatot Subroto. No. 757, Sutan Sjahrir. No. 758, Dr. F. L. Tobing. Nos. 753-755 show portraits of women.

1969, Mar. 1 Photo. Perf. 12½x12
753 A124 15r grn & pur 20 15
754 A124 15r red lil & grn 20 15
755 A124 15r dk bl & ver 20 15
756 A124 15r lil & dk bl 20 15
757 A124 15r lem & red 20 15
758 A124 15r pale brn & bl 20 15
Nos. 753-758 (6) 1.20
Set value 30

Heroes of Indonesian independence.

1969, May 5 Photo. Perf. 12

Design: 20r, Red Cross surrounded by arms.

759 A125 15r grn & dp red 15 15
760 A125 20r org yel & red 20 16
Set value 24

Issued to commemorate the 50th anniversary of the League of Red Cross Societies.

"Family Planning Leads to National Development and Prosperity" — A126

Design: 10r, Family, birds and factories.

1969, June 2 Photo. Perf. 12½
761 A126 10r bl grn & org 16 15
762 A126 20r gray & mag 25 15
Set value 21

Issued to publicize the Planned Parenthood Conference of Southeast Asia and Oceania, Bandung, June 1-7.

Map of Bali and Mask A127

Designs: 15r, Map of Bali and woman carrying basket with offerings on head. 30r, Map of Bali and cremation ceremony.

1969, July 1 Litho. Perf. 12½x12
763 A127 12r gray & multi 15 15
764 A127 15r lil & multi 15 15
765 A127 30r multi 22 15
a. Souv. sheet of 1 1.60 1.00
Set value 17

Issued for tourist publicity.

Agriculture A128

Radar, Djatiluhur Station A129

Designs: 5r, Religious coexistence (roofs of mosques and churches). 10r, Social welfare (house and family). 12r, Import-export (cargo and ship). 15r, Clothing industry (cloth and spindles). 20r, Education (school children). 25r, Research (laboratory). 30r, Health care (people and syringe). 40r, Fishing (fish and net). 50r, Statistics (charts).

1969 Photo. Perf. 12x12½
766 A128 5r yel grn & bl 15 15
767 A128 7.50r rose brn & yel 15 15
768 A128 10r sl & red 15 15
769 A128 12r bl & dp org 15 15
770 A128 15r sl grn & org 15 15
771 A128 20r pur & yel 15 15
772 A128 25r org & blk 15 15
773 A128 30r car rose & gray 16 15
774 A128 40r grn & org 20 15
775 A128 50r sep & org 22 15
Set value 1.15 65

Five-year Development Plan.

See No. 968a.

1969, Sept. 29 Perf. 12½

Design: 30r, Communications satellite and earth.

776 A129 15r multi 15 15
777 A129 30r multi 25 20

Vickers Vimy and Borobudur Temple A130

Design: 100r, Vickers Vimy and map of Indonesia.

1969, Nov. 1 Perf. 13½x12½
778 A130 75r dp org & dl pur 40 15
779 A130 100r yel & grn 65 20

50th anniv. of the 1st flight from England to Australia (via Java).

EXPO '70, Indonesian Pavilion — A131

Designs: 15r, Garuda, symbol of Indonesian EXPO '70 committee. 30r, like 5r.

1970, Feb. 15 Photo. Perf. 12x12½
780 A131 5r brn, yel & grn 15 15
781 A131 15r dk bl, yel grn & red 20 15
782 A131 30r red, yel & dk bl 35 15
Set value 17

Issued to publicize EXPO '70 International Exposition, Osaka, Japan, Mar. 15-Sept. 13.

Upraised Hands, Bars and Scales of Justice — A132

1970, Mar. 15 Photo. Perf. 12½
783 A132 10r red org & pur 15 15
784 A132 15r brt grn & pur 18 15
Set value 15

Rule of law and justice in Indonesia.

UPU Monument, Bern — A133

Timor Dancers — A134

Design: 30r, UPU Headquarters, Bern.

1970, May 20 Photo. *Perf. 12x12½*

785 A133 15r emer & cop red 35 15
786 A133 30r ocher & bl 60 15
Set value 17

Inauguration of the new UPU Headquarters in Bern, Switzerland.

1970, July 1 Photo. *Perf. 12*

787 A134 20r shown 30 15
788 A134 45r Bali dancers 60 18
a. Souv. sheet of 1 1.40 1.10
Set value 26

Issued for tourist publicity. No. 788a sold for 60r.

Asian Productivity Year A135

Independence Proclamation Monument A136

1970, Aug. 1 Photo. *Perf. 12*

789 A135 5r emer, org & red 25 15
790 A135 30r vio, org & red 70 15
Set value 15

1970, Aug. 17

791 A136 40r lt ultra & mag *8.00 4.00*

The 25th anniversary of independence.

Post and Telecommunications Emblems — A137

Postal Worker and Telephone Dial — A138

Perf. 12x12½, 12½x12

1970, Sept. 27 Photo.

792 A137 10r grn, ocher & yel *3.25* 15
793 A138 25r pink, blk & yel *4.25* 22

25th anniversary of the postal service.

For unused stamps, more recent issues are valued as never hinged, with the beginning point determined on a country-by-country basis. Notes to show the beginning points are prominently placed in the text.

UN Emblem A139

Education Year and UNESCO Emblems A140

1970, Oct. 10 Photo. *Perf. 12½*

794 A139 40r pur, red & yel grn *7.50 1.50*

25th anniversary of the United Nations.

1970, Nov. 16 Photo. *Perf. 12½*

Design: 50r, similar to 25r, but without oval background.

795 A140 25r yel, dk red & brn *6.00 1.50*
796 A140 50r lt bl, blk & red *9.00 2.25*

International Education Year.

Batik Worker — A141

Designs: 50r, Woman with bamboo musical instrument (angklung; vert.). 75r, Menangkabau house and family in traditional costumes.

1971, May 26 Litho. *Perf. 12½*

797 A141 20r multi 1.10 15
798 A141 50r multi 1.75 15
a. Souv. sheet of 1 3.00 1.50
799 A141 75r multi 2.25 20
Set value 37

"Visit Asian lands." No. 798a sold for 70r.

Fatahillah Park, Djakarta — A142

Designs: 30f, City Hall. 65r, Lenong Theater performance. 80r, Ismail Marzuki Cultural Center.

1971, June 19 Photo. *Perf. 12½*

800 A142 15r yel grn, brn & bl 55 25
801 A142 65r org brn, dk brn & lt grn 2.25 25
802 A142 80r ol, bl & mag 3.25 65

Souvenir Sheet

803 A142 30r bl, yel & lil rose 3.00 1.75

444th anniversary of Djakarta. No. 803 sold for 60r.

Rama and Sita — A143

Design: 100r, Rama with bow.

1971, Aug. 31

804 A143 30r yel, grn & blk 50 15
805 A143 100r bl, red & blk 1.75 25

International Ramayana Festival.

Carrier Pigeon and Conference Emblem — A144

1971, Sept. 20

806 A144 50r ocher & dp brn 75 15

5th Asian Regional Postal Conference.

Globes and UPU Monument, Berne A145

1971, Oct. 4 Photo. *Perf. 13½x13*

807 A145 40r bl & dl vio 85 15

Universal Postal Union Day.

Boy Writing, UNICEF Emblem — A146

Design: 40r, Boy with sheaf of rice and UNICEF emblem.

1971, Dec. 11 *Perf. 12½*

808 A146 20r org & multi 60 15
809 A146 40r bl & multi 70 15
Set value 21

25th anniv. UNICEF.

Lined Tang A147

Fish: 30r, Moorish goddess. 40r, Imperial angelfish.

1971, Dec. 27 Litho. *Perf. 12½*

810 A147 15r lil & multi 80 35
811 A147 30r dl grn & multi 1.75 65
812 A147 40r bl & multi 2.00 1.60

See Nos. 834-836, 859-861, 926-928, 959-961.

UN Emblem A148

Radio Tower A149

Design: 100r, Road and dam.

1972, Mar. 28 Photo. *Perf. 12½*

813 A148 40r lt grnsh bl & bl 55 15
814 A149 75r dk car, yel & grnsh bl 80 15
815 A148 100r grn, yel & blk 1.10 20

UN Economic Commission for Asia and the Far East (ECAFE), 25th anniv.

"Your Heart is your Health" — A150

Woman Weaver, Factories — A151

1972, Apr. 7

816 A150 50r multi 70 15

World Health Day.

1972, Apr. 22

817 A151 35r org, yel & pur 55 15

50th anniv. of the Textile Technology Institute.

Book Readers A152

1972, May 15 *Perf. 13½x12½*

818 A152 75r bl & multi 1.00 20

International Book Year 1972.

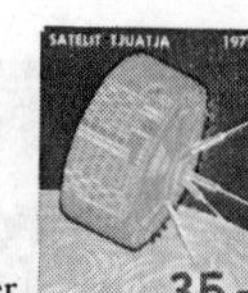

Weather Satellite — A153

1972, July 20 Photo. *Perf. 12½*

819 A153 35r shown 55 15
820 A153 50r Astronaut on moon 55 15
821 A153 60r Indonesian rocket Kartika 1 1.10 15
Set value 33

Space achievements.

Hotel Indonesia — A154

1972, Aug. 5

822 A154 50r grn, lt bl & car 80 15

Hotel Indonesia, 10th anniversary.

Silat (Self Defense) A155

Family, Houses of Worship A156

Designs (Olympic Emblems and): 35r, Running. 50r, Diving. 75r, Badminton. 100r, Olympic Stadium.

1972, Aug. 26 **Photo.**
823 A155 20r lt bl & multi 38 15
824 A155 35r multi 55 15
825 A155 50r yel grn & multi 70 16
826 A155 75r multi 1.10 20
827 A155 100r multi 1.25 25
Nos. 823-827 (5) 3.98
Set value 78

20th Olympic Games, Munich, Aug. 26-Sept. 11.

1972, Sept. 27 ***Perf. 12½x13½***

Family planning: 75r, Healthy family. 80r, Working family (national prosperity).

828 A156 30r lem & multi 35 15
829 A156 75r lil & multi 80 18
830 A156 80r multi 1.10 20

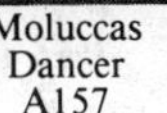

Moluccas Dancer A157

Thomas Cup, Shuttlecock A158

Designs: 60r, Man, woman and Toradja house, Celebes. 100fr, West Irian house (horiz.).

Perf. 12½x13½, 13½x12½
1972, Oct. 28 **Photo.**
831 A157 30r ol pink & brn 38 15
832 A157 60r multi 70 18
833 A157 100r lt bl, brn & dl yel 1.10 25

Fish Type of 1971

Fish: 30r, Butterflyfish. 50r, Regal angelfish. 100r, Spotted triggerfish.

1972, Dec. 4 **Litho.** ***Perf. 12½***
834 A147 30r bl & multi 45 15
835 A147 50r bl & multi 70 15
836 A147 100r bl & multi 1.50 25

1973, Jan. 2 **Litho.** ***Perf. 12½***

Designs (Thomas Cup, Shuttlecock and): 75r, National monument and Istora Sports Hall. 80r, Indonesian flag and badminton player.

837 A158 30r emer & brt bl 16 15
838 A158 75r dl grn & dk car 70 20
839 A158 80r gold & red 70 20

Thomas Cup Badminton World Championship 1973.

WMO Emblem, Anemometer, Wayang Figure — A159

Perf. 13½x12½
1973, Feb. 15 **Litho.**
840 A159 80r bl, grn & claret 80 20

Cent. of intl. meteorological cooperation.

"Health Begins at Home" — A160

1973, Apr. 7 **Photo.** ***Perf. 12½***
841 A160 80r dk grn, org & ultra 80 20

25th anniv. of WHO.

Ceremonial Mask, Java — A161

Hand Putting Coin into Bank — A162

1973, June 1 **Photo.** ***Perf. 12½***
842 A161 30r shown 40 15
843 A161 60r Mask, Kalimantan 68 16
844 A161 100r Mask, Bali 1.10 25

Tourist publicity.

1973, July 2 **Photo.** ***Perf. 12½***

Design: 30r, Symbolic coin bank and hand (horiz.).

845 A162 25r yel, lt brn & blk 30 15
846 A162 30r grn, yel & gold 42 15
Set value 18

National savings movement.

Chess A163

INTERPOL Emblem and Policemen A164

8th National Sports Week: 60r, Karate. 75r, Hurdling (horiz.).

1973, Aug. 4 **Photo.** ***Perf. 12½***
847 A163 30r red, yel & blk 50 15
848 A163 60r blk, ocher & lt grn 65 20
849 A163 75r blk, lt bl & rose 1.00 35

1973, Sept. 3

Design: 50r, INTERPOL emblem and guard statue from Sewu Prambanan Temple (vert.).

850 A164 30r yel, grn & blk 35 15
851 A164 50r yel, brn & blk 50 15
Set value 22

50th anniv. of Intl. Police Organization.

Batik Worker and Parang Rusak Pattern A165

Batik designs: 80r, Man and Pagi Sore pattern. 100r, Man and Merak Ngigel pattern.

1973, Oct. 9 **Photo.** ***Perf. 12½***
852 A165 60r multi 55 15
853 A165 80r multi 70 20
854 A165 100r multi 90 25

Farmer, Grain, UN and FAO Emblems — A166

1973, Oct. 24 **Photo.** ***Perf. 12½***
855 A166 30r lil & multi 35 15

World Food Program, 10th anniversary.

Houses of Worship — A167

Family planning: 30r, Classroom. 60r, Family and home.

1973, Nov. 10
856 A167 20r dk bl, lt bl & ver 22 15
857 A167 30r ocher, blk & yel 30 15
858 A167 60r lt grn, yel & blk 62 16
Set value 28

Fish Type of 1971

Fish: 40r, Acanthurus leucosternon. 65r, Chaetodon trifasciatus. 100r, Pomacanthus annularis.

1973, Dec. 10 **Litho.** ***Perf. 12½***
859 A147 40r multi 45 15
860 A147 65r multi 65 18
861 A147 100r multi 1.20 30

Adm. Sudarso and Battle of Arafuru — A168

1974, Jan. 15
862 A168 40r brt bl & multi 50 15

12th Navy Day.

Bengkulu Costume A169

Designs: Regional Costumes.

1974, Mar. 28 **Litho.** ***Perf. 12½***
863 A169 5r shown
864 A169 7.50r Kalimantan, Timor
865 A169 10r Kalimantan, Tengah
866 A169 15r Jambi
867 A169 20r Sulawesi, Tenggara
868 A169 25r Nusatenggara, Timor
869 A169 27.50r Maluku
870 A169 30r Lampung
871 A169 35r Sumatra, Barat
872 A169 40r Aceh
873 A169 45r Nusatenggara, Barat
874 A169 50r Riouw
875 A169 55r Kalimantan, Barat

876 A169 60r Sulawesi, Utara
877 A169 65r Sulawesi, Tengah
878 A169 70r Sumatra, Selatan
879 A169 75r Java, Barat
880 A169 80r Sumatra, Utara
881 A169 90r Yogyakarta
882 A169 95r Kalimantan, Selatan
883 A169 100r Java, Timor
884 A169 120r Irian, Java
885 A169 130r Java, Tengah
886 A169 135r Sulawesi, Selatan
887 A169 150r Bali
888 A169 160r Djakarta
Nos. 863-888 (26) 30.00 12.50

Baladewa A170

Designs (Figures from Shadow Plays): 80r, Kresna. 100r, Bima.

1974, June 1 **Photo.** ***Perf. 12½***
889 A170 40r lt vio & multi 40 15
890 A170 80r sal & multi 60 15
891 A170 100r rose 80 16
Set value 38

Pres. Suharto A171

Family and WPY Emblem A172

1974-76 **Photo.** ***Perf. 12½***
Portrait in Dark Brown
901 A171 40r lt grn & blk 15 15
903 A171 50r ultra & blk 20 15
906 A171 65r brt pink & blk 28 15
908 A171 75r yel & blk 38 15
912 A171 100r buff & blk 50 16
913 A171 150r cit & blk 75 25
914 A171 200r grn & bl 90 38
915 A171 300r brn org & car 1.40 55
916 A171 400r grn & yel 1.90 75
917 A171 500r lil & car 2.50 1.00
Nos. 901-917 (10) 8.96 3.69

Nos. 914-917 have wavy lines in background.

Issue dates: Nos. 901-913, Aug. 17, 1974. Nos. 914-917, Aug. 17, 1976.

1974, Aug. 19
918 A172 65r ultra, gray & ocher 40 15

World Population Year 1974.

"Welfare" A173

"Development" A174

"Religion"
A175

1974, Sept. 9

919 A173 25r grn & multi 16 15
920 A174 40r yel grn & multi 35 15
921 A175 65r dk vio brn & multi 50 15
Set value 27

Family planning.

Mailmen with Bicycles, UPU Emblem — A176

UPU cent.: 40r, Horse-drawn mail cart. 65r, Mailman on horseback. 100r, Sailing ship, 18th century.

1974, Oct. 9

922 A176 20r dk grn & multi 15 15
923 A176 40r dl bl & multi 20 15
924 A176 65r blk brn & yel 45 20
925 A176 100r mar & multi 75 16
Set value 46

Fish Type of 1971

Fish: 40fr, Zebrasoma veliferum. 80r, Euxiphipops navarchus. 100r, Synchiropus splendidus.

1974, Oct. 30 Photo. *Perf. 12½*

926 A147 40r bl & multi 38 15
927 A147 80r bl & multi 55 16
928 A147 100r bl & multi 62 22

Drill Team Searching for Oil — A177

Designs (Pertamina Emblem and): 75r, Oil refinery. 95r, Pertamina telecommunications and computer center. 100r, Gasoline truck and station. 120r, Plane over storage tanks. 130r, Pipes and tanker. 150r, Petro-chemical storage tanks. 200r, Off-shore drilling platform. 95r, 100r, 120r, 130r, vertical.

1974, Dec. 10 *Perf. 13½*

929 A177 40r blk & multi 22 15
930 A177 75r blk & multi 42 15
931 A177 95r blk & multi 70 18
932 A177 100r blk & multi 70 20
933 A177 120r blk & multi 90 22
934 A177 130r blk & multi 1.00 25
935 A177 150r blk & multi 1.20 30
936 A177 200r blk & multi 1.60 40
Nos. 929-936 (8) 6.74 1.85

Pertamina State Oil Enterprise, 17th anniv.

Spittoon, Sumatra — A178

Artistic Metalware: 75r, Condiment dish, Sumatra. 100r, Condiment dish, Kalimantan.

1975, Feb. 24 Photo. *Perf. 12½*

937 A178 50r red & blk 35 15
938 A178 75r grn & blk 45 16
939 A178 100r brt bl & multi 65 20

Blood Donors' Emblem
A179

Globe, Standard Meter and Kilogram
A180

1975, Apr. 7

940 A179 40r yel, red & grn 50 15

"Give blood, save lives."

1975, May 20

941 A180 65r bl, red & yel 50 15

Cent. of Intl. Meter Convention, Paris, 1875.

Farmer, Teacher, Mother, Policewoman and Nurse — A181

IWY Emblem — A182

1975, June 26 Photo. *Perf. 12½*

942 A181 40r multi 25 15
943 A182 100r multi 60 20
Set value 28

International Women's Year 1975.

Dendrobium Pakarena — A183

Stupas and Damaged Temple — A184

Orchids: 70r, Aeridachnis bogor. 85r, Vanda genta.

1975, July 21

944 A183 40r multi 25 15
945 A183 70r multi 38 15
946 A183 85r multi 65 22

See Nos. 1010-1012, 1036-1038.

1975, Aug. 10 *Perf. 12½*

Designs (UNESCO Emblem and): 40r, Buddha statues, stupas and damaged wall. 65r, Stupas and damaged wall (horiz.). 100r, Buddha statue and stupas (horiz.).

947 A184 25r yel, brn & org 22 15
948 A184 40r blk, grn & yel 35 15
949 A184 65r lem, cl & grn 70 16
950 A184 100r bis, brn & sl bl 1.00 20
Set value 48

UNESCO campaign to save Borobudur Temple, Java.

Banjarmasin Battle — A185

Battle Scenes: 40r, Batua, Sept. 8, 1946. 75r, Margarana, Nov. 20, 1946. 100r, Palembang, Jan. 1, 1947.

1975, Aug. 17

951 A185 25r yel & blk 16 15
952 A185 40r org ver & red 25 15
953 A185 75r ver & blk 55 15
954 A185 100r org & blk 80 20
Set value 48

Indonesian independence, 30th anniversary.

"Education"
A186

Heroes' Monument, Surabaya
A187

Family plannings: 25r, "Religion." 40r, "Prosperity."

1975, Oct. 20 Photo. *Perf. 12½*

955 A186 20r bl, sal & blk 15 15
956 A186 25r emer, sal & blk 15 15
957 A186 40r dp org, bl & blk 22 15
Set value 18

1975, Nov. 10

958 A187 100r mar & grn 55 22

War of independence, 30th anniversary.

Fish Type of 1971

Fish: 40r, Coris angulata. 75r, Chaetodon ephippium. 150r, Platax pinnatus (vert.).

1975, Dec. 15 Litho. *Perf. 12½*

959 A147 40r multi 30 15
960 A147 75r multi 60 15
961 A147 150r multi 1.10 30

Thomas Cup — A188

Designs: 40r, Uber Cup. 100r, Thomas and Uber Cups.

1976, Jan. 31 Photo. *Perf. 12½*

962 A188 20r bl & multi 15 15
963 A188 40r multi 22 15
964 A188 100r grn & multi 62 20
Set value 32

Indonesia, Badminton World Champions.

Refugees on Truck and New Village — A189

Designs: 50r, Neglected and restored village streets. 100r, Derelict and rebuilt houses.

1976, Feb. 28 Photo. *Perf. 12½*

965 A189 30r yel & multi 15 15
966 A189 50r bl & multi 25 15
967 A189 100r ocher & multi 50 20
Set value 36

World Human Settlements Day.

Telephones, 1876 and 1976 — A190

1976, Mar. 10 Photo. *Perf. 12½*

968 A190 100r yel, org & brn 55 20
a. Bklt. pane of 8 (4 #968, 4 #775, 2 labels) ('78) 4.25

Centenary of first telephone call by Alexander Graham Bell, Mar. 10, 1876.

Eye and WHO Emblem — A191

Design: 40r, Blind man, eye and World Health Organization emblem.

1976, Apr. 7 Photo. *Perf. 12½*

969 A191 20r yel, lt grn & blk 15 15
970 A191 40r yel, bl & blk 20 15
Set value 15

Foresight prevents blindness.

Montreal Stadium — A192

1976, May 17

971 A192 100r ultra 50 15

21st Olympic Games, Montreal, Canada, July 17-Aug. 1.

Lake Tondano, Celebes — A193

Tourist publicity: 40r, Lake Kelimutu, Flores. 75r, Lake Maninjau, Sumatra.

1976, June 1

972 A193 35r lt grn & blk 22 15
973 A193 40r gray, rose & lt grn 25 15
974 A193 75r bl & sl grn 55 15
a. Bklt. pane of 8 (7 #974, #998, 2 labels) ('78) 5.00
Set value 30

Radar Station — A194

Designs: 50r, Master control radar station. 100r, Apalata satellite.

1976, July 8 Photo. *Perf. 12½*

975 A194 20r multi 15 15
976 A194 50r grn & blk 25 15
977 A194 100r multi 50 20
a. Bklt. pane of 9 (4 #977, 5 #987, label) ('78) 6.50
Set value 35

Inauguration of domestic satellite system.

Arachnis Flos-aeris — A195

Orchids: 40r, Vanda putri serang. 100r, Coelogyne pandurata.

1976, Sept. 7

978 A195 25r multi 30 15
979 A195 40r multi 45 15
980 A195 100r multi 1.25 40
Set value 60

Tree and Mountain — A196

1976, Oct. 4

981 A196 20r grn, bl & brn 15 15

16th National Reforestation Week.

Dagger and Sheath from Timor A197

Historic Daggers and Sheaths: 40r, from Borneo. 100r, from Aceh.

1976, Nov. 1 *Perf. 12½*

982 A197 25r multi 25 15
983 A197 40r multi 40 20
a. Souv. sheet of 1 3.00 3.00
984 A197 100r grn & multi 90 40
Set value 65

No. 983a exists imperf.

Open Book A198

Children Reading A199

1976, Dec. 8 Photo. *Perf. 12½*

985 A198 20r multi 15 15
986 A199 40r multi 30 15
Set value 15

Better books for children.

UNICEF Emblem A200

Ballot Box A201

1976, Dec. 11

987 A200 40r multi 25 15

UNICEF, 30th anniv.

1977, Jan. 5 Photo. *Perf. 12½*

1977 elections: 75r, Ballot box, grain and factory. 100r, Coat of arms.

988 A201 40r multi 20 15
989 A201 75r multi 38 16
990 A201 100r multi 50 22

Camp and Flags Scout Emblems, — A202

Designs: 30r, Tent, emblems and trees. 40r, Boy and Girl Scout flags and emblems.

1977, Feb. 28

991 A202 25r multi 16 15
992 A202 30r multi 20 15
993 A202 40r multi 22 15
Set value 20

11th National Scout Jamboree.

Letter with "AOPU" — A203

Anniversary Emblem, Djakarta Arms — A204

Design: 100r, Stylized bird and letter.

1977, Apr. 1 Photo. *Perf. 12½*

994 A203 65r multi 35 15
995 A203 100r multi 50 20

Asian-Oceanic Postal Union, 15th convention.

1977, May 23 Photo. *Perf. 12½*

Designs: Anniversary emblem and arms of Djakarta in different arrangements.

996 A204 20r org & bl 15 15
997 A204 40r emer & bl 20 15
998 A204 100r sl & bl 40 22
a. Souv. sheet of 1 1.25 1.25
Set value 35

450th anniversary of Djakarta. No. 998a also issued imperf.

Rose — A205

Various Sports Emblems — A206

1977, May 26 Photo. *Perf. 12½*

999 A205 100r shown 75 30
a. Souvenir sheet 1.50 1.50
1000 A205 100r Envelope 75 30
a. Souvenir sheet of 4 2.50 2.50

Amphilex 77 Phil. Exhib., Amsterdam, May 26-June 5. Nos. 999-1000 printed se-tenant. No. 999a contains one stamp similar to No. 999 with blue background. No. 1000a contains 2 each of Nos. 999-1000.

Nos. 999a, 1000a exist imperf.

See No. 1013a.

1977, June 22

9th Natl. Sports Week: 50r, 100r, Different sports emblems.

1001 A206 40r sil & multi 30 15
1002 A206 50r sil & multi 45 20
1003 A206 100r gold & multi 1.00 45

Contest Trophy A207

Emblem A208

1977, July 20

1004 A207 40r grn & multi 45 15
1005 A208 100r yel & multi 90 30

10th Natl. Koran Reading Contest, July 20-27.

Map of ASEAN Countries, Satellite — A209

Designs: 35r, Map of ASEAN countries. 50r, Flags of founding members: Indonesia, Malaysia, Philippines, Singapore and Thailand; ship, plane and train.

1977, Aug. 8

1006 A209 25r multi 25 15
1007 A209 35r multi 30 15
1008 A209 50r multi 45 20
Set value 40

Association of South East Asian Nations (ASEAN), 10th anniversary.

Uniform, Jakarta Regiment A210

1977, Aug. 19

1009 A210 25r grn, gold & brn 15 15

Indonesia-Pakistan Economic and Cultural Organization, 1968-1977.

Orchid Type of 1975

Orchids: 25r, Taeniophyllum. 40r, Phalaenopsis violacea. 100r, Dendrobium spectabile.

1977, Oct. 28 Photo. *Perf. 12½*

1010 A183 25r org & multi 28 15
1011 A183 40r bl & multi 45 15
1012 A183 100r yel grn & multi 1.10 25
a. Souv. sheet of 1 1.90 1.90
Set value 40

No. 1012a contains one stamp similar to No. 1012 with blue background. No. 1012a exists imperf.

Child and Mosquito A211

1977, Nov. 7 *Perf. 12½*

1013 A211 40r brt grn, red & blk 22 15
a. Bklt. pane of 9+label (4 #999, 5 #1013) ('78) 4.75

Natl. Health campaign to eradicate malaria. Issue date: No. 1013a, Sept. 27, 1978.

Proboscis Monkey — A212

Designs: 40r, Indian elephant. 100r, Tiger.

1977, Dec. 22

1014 A212 20r multi 15 15
1015 A212 40r multi 30 15
1016 A212 100r multi 1.10 90
a. Souv. sheet of 1 2.00 2.00

Wildlife protection. #1016a exists imperf.

Conference Emblem A213

Mother and Child A214

1978, Mar. 27 Photo. *Perf. 12½*

1017 A213 100r lt bl & ultra 65 22

United Nations Conference on Technical Cooperation among Developing Countries.

1978, Apr. 7 Photo. *Perf. 12½*

Design: 75r, Mother and child, symbolic design.

1018 A214 40r lt grn & bl 25 15
1019 A214 75r org red & brn 42 16
Set value 24

Promotion of breast feeding.

Dome of The Rock, Jerusalem — A215

1978, May 15 Photo. *Perf. 12½*

1020 A215 100r multi 50 20

Palestinian fighters and their families.

Argentina '78 Emblem A216

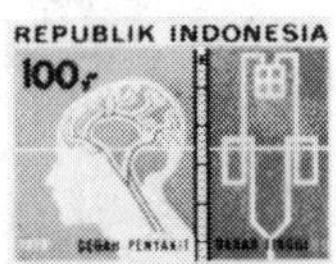

Head and "Blood Circulation" A217

1978, June 1

1021	A216	40r multi	22	15
1022	A216	100r multi	55	22
		Set value		30

11th World Cup Soccer Championships, Argentina, June 1-25.

1978, June 17 Photo. *Perf. 12½*

1023	A217	100r blk, bl & red	50	20

World Health Day and drive against hypertension.

Leather Puppets — A218

Art from Wayang Museum, Djakarta: 75r, Wooden puppets. 100r, Actors with puppet masks.

1978, July 22 Litho. *Perf. 12½*

1024	A218	40r multi	40	15
1025	A218	75r multi	85	30
1026	A218	100r multi	1.00	40

Congress Emblem A219

IAAY Emblem A220

1978, Aug. 1

1027	A219	100r slate	50	20

27th Congress of World Confederation of Organizations of Teachers (WCOTP), Djakarta, June 26-Aug. 2.

1978, Aug. 16 Photo. *Perf. 12½*

1028	A220	100r org & dk bl	50	20

International Anti-Apartheid Year.

Congress Emblem A221

Youth Pledge Emblem A222

Design: 100r, People and trees.

1978, Oct. 16 Photo. *Perf. 12½*

1029	A221	40r emer & bl	22	15
1030	A221	100r emer & blk	55	20
		Set value		28

8th World Forestry Congress, Djakarta.

1978, Oct. 28

1031	A222	40r dk brn & red	16	15
1032	A222	100r sal, brn & red	40	20
		Set value		28

50th anniv. of Youth Pledge. See No. 1044a.

Wildlife Protection — A223

1978, Nov. 1

1033	A223	40r Porcupine ant-eater	30	15
1034	A223	75r Deer	60	25
a.		Souv. sheet of 5, #1034, 4 #1035 + label	4.00	
1035	A223	100r Clouded tiger	90	30
a.		Souv. sheet of 1	1.40	

Stamps in No. 1034a are in changed colors. Souvenir sheets inscribed for Essen 2nd Intl. Stamp Fair.

Orchid Type of 1975

Orchids: 40r, Phalaenopsis sri rejeki. 75r, Dendrobium macrophilium. 100r, Cymbidium fynlaysonianum.

1978, Dec. 22 Photo. *Perf. 12½*

1036	A183	40r multi	20	15
1037	A183	75r multi	38	15
1038	A183	100r multi	55	15
a.		Souvenir sheet of 1	3.00	1.00
		Set value		20

Douglas DC-3, 1949, over Volcano — A224

Designs: 75r, Douglas DC-9 over village. 100r, Douglas DC-10 over temple.

1979, Jan. 26 Photo. *Perf. 12½*

1039	A224	40r multi	15	15
1040	A224	75r multi	25	15
1041	A224	100r multi	40	15
		Set value		22

Garuda Indonesian Airways, 30th anniv.

Badminton
A225 A226

Design: 40r, Thomas Cup and badminton player.

1979, Feb. 24 Photo. *Perf. 12½*

1042	A225	40r car & bl	15	15
1043	A225	100r car & ocher	40	15
1044	A226	100r car & ocher	50	15
a.		Blkt. pane of 9 + label (3 each #1032, 1043-1044)	4.25	
		Set value		25

11th Thomas Cup, Djakarta, May 24-June 2. Nos. 1043-1044 printed se-tenant in sheets of 100.

Paphiopedilum Lowii — A227

Orchids: 100r, Vanda limbata. 125r, Phalaenopsis gigantea.

1979, Mar. 22 Photo. *Perf. 12½*

1045	A227	60r multi	40	18
1046	A227	100r multi	65	30
1047	A227	125r multi	75	35
a.		Souvenir sheet of 1	50	
b.		Souvenir sheet of 2 (250r, 300r)	2.00	

No. 1047b, issued for Asian Phil. Exhib., Dortmund, West Germany, May 24-27, contains a 250r stamp in design of 60r and 300r stamp in design of 100r. Sold for 650r.

Family and Houses — A228

Third Five-year Plan: 60r, Pylon and fields. 100r, School and clinic. 125r, Factories and trucks. 150r, Motorized mail delivery.

1979-82

1047C	A228	12.50r Plane, food ('80)	15	15
1047D	A228	17.50r Bridge ('82)	16	15
1048	A228	35r grn & ol	16	15
1049	A228	60r bl & ol	22	15
1050	A228	100r bl & dk brn	40	20
1051	A228	125r red brn & ol	55	25
1052	A228	150r car & yel	60	32
		Nos. 1047C-1052 (7)	2.24	
		Set value		1.05

See No. 1058a.

R. A. Kartini and Girls' School
A229 A230

1979, Apr. 21 Photo. *Perf. 12½*

1053	A229	100r olive & brn	60	30
1054	A230	100r olive & brn	60	30

Mrs. R. A. Kartini, educator, birth centenary. Nos. 1053-1054 printed se-tenant.

Bureau of Education, UNESCO Emblems — A231

1979, May 25 Photo. *Perf. 12½*

1055	A231	150r multi	50	22

50th anniversary of the statutes of the International Bureau of Education.

Self Defense — A232

Cooperation Emblem — A233

Designs: 125r, Games' emblem. 150r, Senayan Main Stadium.

1979, June 21 Photo. *Perf. 12½*

1056	A232	60r multi	25	15
1057	A232	125r multi	45	25
1058	A232	150r multi	60	32
a.		Bklt. pane of 6+4 labels (#1052, 5 #1056)	5.40	

10th South East Asia Games, Djakarta, Sept. 21-30.

Issue date: No. 1058a, Sept. 27.

1979, July 12 Photo. *Perf. 12½*

1059	A233	150r multi	50	25

32nd Indonesian Cooperative Day.

IYC and Natl. IYC Emblems — A234

TELECOM 79 — A235

Design: 150r, IYC emblem.

1979, Aug. 4 Photo. *Perf. 12½*

1060	A234	60r emer & blk	25	15
1061	A234	150r bl & blk	38	25

International Year of the Child.

1979, Sept. 20 Photo. *Perf. 12½*

1062	A235	150r multi	50	25

3rd World Telecommunications Exhibition, Geneva, Sept. 20-26.

Fight Drug Abuse — A236

1979, Oct. 17 Photo. *Perf. 12½*

1063	A236	150r dp rose & black	60	32

Dolphin — A237

Wildlife Protection: 125r, Freshwater dolphin. 150r, Leatherback turtle.

1979, Nov. 24 Photo. *Perf. 12½*

1064	A237	60r multi	20	15
1065	A237	125r multi	42	22
1066	A237	150r multi	65	25

Souvenir Sheet

1066A	A237	200r like #1066	90	40

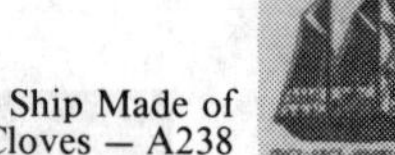

Ship Made of Cloves — A238

Spice Race, Jakarta-Amsterdam (Sailing Ships): 60r, Penisi (vert.) 150r, Madurese boat (vert.)

1980, Mar. 12 Photo. *Perf. 12½*

1067	A238	60r brt bl	16	15
1068	A238	125r red brn	35	22
1069	A238	150r red lil	50	25

1980

Souvenir Sheets

1069A	A238	300r like #1068	2.50	1.00
1069B	A238	500r like #1067	4.50	2.00

Issue dates: 300r, Mar. 12. 500r, May 6. 500r for London 1980 Intl. Stamp Exhib.

Rubber Raft in Rapids
A239

Perf. 13½x13, 13x13½

1980, Mar. 21 **Photo.**

1070	A239	60r shown	16	15
1071	A239	125r Mountain climbing, vert.	35	22
1072	A239	150r Hang gliding, vert.	50	25

Souvenir Sheet

1072A	A239	300r like #1070	1.50	65

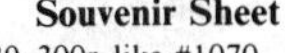

Anti-smoking Campaign — A240

1980, Apr. 15 *Perf. 12½*

1073	A240	150r multi	50	32

Flowers In Vase
A241

Conference Building
A242

1980, Apr. 21 **Photo.** *Perf. 12½*

1074	A241	125r shown	40	22
1075	A241	150r Bouquet	60	25

2nd Flower Festival, Jakarta, Apr. 19-21.
See No. 1080a-1080b.

1980, Apr. 24 *Perf. 13x13½*

1076	A242	150r gold & lil rose	50	25

Souvenir Sheet

1076A	A242	300r multi	1.50	65

1st Asian-African Conf., 25th anniv.

Taman Bali Stone Sarcophagus, 2000 B.C. — A243

1980, May 2 *Perf. 12½*

1077	A243	60r Male figure	20	15
1078	A243	125r Elephant stone	40	22
1079	A243	150r shown	55	25

Flower and Sculpture Types of 1980
Souvenir Sheet

1980 **Photo.** *Perf. 12½*

1080	Sheet of 8	6.00	3.00
a.	A241 100r like #1074	42	22
b.	A241 100r like #1074	42	22
c.	A243 200r like #1077	80	45
d.	A243 200r like #1079	80	45

London 1980 Intl. Stamp Exhib., May 6-14. No. 1080 contains 2 stamps of each design (4x2).

Draftsman in Wheelchair
A244

Discus Thrower
A245

1980, May 18 **Photo.** *Perf. 12½*

1081	A244	100r multi	35	20

Disabled Veterans Corp, 30th anniversary.

1980, May 18

1082	A245	75r dp org & sep	30	16

Olympics for the Disabled, Arnhem, Netherlands, June 21-July 5.

Pres. Suharto — A246

A246a A246b

Perf. 13½x12½, 12½

1980-83 **Photo.**

1083	A246	12.50r lt grn & grn	15	15
1084	A246	50r lt grn & bl	16	15
1084A	A246	55r red rose & red lil	15	15
1085	A246	75r lem & gldn brn	22	15
1086	A246	100r brt pink & bl	35	20
a.		Bklt pane of 8 + 2 labels (6 #1086, 2 #1088, Inscribed 1981)	4.00	
1087	A246a	110r dl org & dp red lil	15	15
1088	A246	200r dl org & brn	65	40
1088A	A246a	250r dl org & brn	1.00	50
1089	A246a	275r lt ap grn & dk grn	38	20
1090	A246	300r rose lil & gold	1.20	60
1091	A246	400r multi	1.60	80

Engr. *Perf. 12½x13*

1092	A246b	500r dk red brn	1.60	1.00
		Nos. 1083-1092 (12)	7.61	4.45

Issue dates: 12.50r, 50r, 75r, 100r, 200r, June 8. 300r, 400r, June 8, 1981. 250r, Sept. 1982. 500r, Mar. 11, 1983. 55r, July 1983. 110r, 275r, Sept. 27, 1983.
See Nos. 1257-1261, 1266, 1268.

Map of Indonesia, People — A247

1980, July 17 *Perf. 12½*

1093	A247	75r bl & pink	20	16
1094	A247	200r bl & dl yel	60	40

1980 population census.

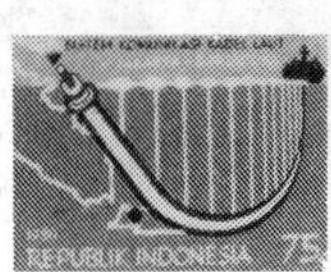

Ship Laying Cable — A248

50s Stamp of 1946 — A249

1980, Aug. 8 **Photo.** *Perf. 12½*

1095	A248	75r multi	20	16
1096	A248	200r multi	60	40

Singapore-Indonesia submarine cable opening.

1980, Aug. 17

Designs: 100r, 15s Battle of Surabaya stamp, 1946 (horiz.). 200r, 15s Independence Fund stamp, 1946.

1097	A249	75r dk brn & dp org	20	16
1098	A249	100r gold & pur	35	22
1099	A249	200r multi	60	40

Independence, 35th anniversary.

Asian Oceanic Postal Training School — A250

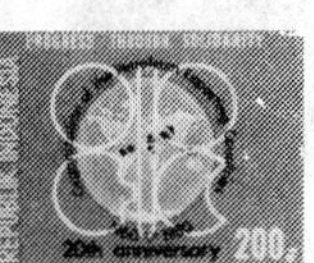

OPEC Anniv. Emblem — A251

1980, Sept. 10 **Photo.** *Perf. 12½*

1100	A250	200r multi	60	40

1980, Sept. 14

1101	A251	200r multi	60	40

Organization of Petroleum Exporting Countries, 20th anniversary.

Armed Forces, 35th Anniversary — A252

1980, Oct. 5 **Photo.** *Perf. 13½x13*

1102	A252	75r shown	20	16
1103	A252	200r Service men and emblem	60	40

Vulturine Parrot
A253

One Day Beauty Orchid
A254

Designs: Parrots.

1980, Nov. 25 **Photo.** *Perf. 13x12½*

1104	A253	75r shown	22	16
1105	A253	100r Yellow-backed lory	40	20
1106	A253	200r Red lory	65	40

Souvenir Sheet
Perf. 12½

1106A	Sheet of 3	4.00	2.50
b.	A253 250r like #1105	70	50
c.	A253 350r like #1104	1.10	70
d.	A253 400r like #1106	1.20	80

1980, Dec. 10 *Perf. 13x13½*

Designs: Orchids.

1107	A254	75r *shown*	22	16
1108	A254	100r *Dendrobium discolor*	40	20
1109	A254	200r *Dendrobium lasianthera*	65	40

Souvenir Sheet

1980 *Perf. 13x13½*

1110	Sheet of 2	2.50	1.40
a.	A254 250r like #1109	1.00	50
b.	A254 350r like #1108	1.60	80

Heinrich von Stephan (1831-1897), UPU Founder — A255

1981, Jan. 7 *Perf. 13½x12½*

1111	A255	200r brt bl & dk bl	65	40

6th Asian Pacific Scout Jamboree
A256

1981 *Perf. 13½x12½, 12½x13½*

1112	A256	75r Emblems	22	16
1113	A256	100r Scouts, vert.	35	20
1114	A256	200r Emblems, diff.	65	40

Souvenir Sheet

1115	A256	150r like #1113	80	35

Issue dates: Nos. 1112-1114, Feb. 22; No. 1115, Aug. 14.

4th Asian-Oceanian Postal Union Congress
A257

Blood Donor Campaign
A258

1981, Mar. 18 *Perf. 12½*

1116	A257	200r multi	80	40

1981, Apr. 22

1117	A258	75r Girl holding blood drop	22	16
1118	A258	100r Hands holding blood drop	35	20
1119	A258	200r Hands, blood, diff.	65	40

Intl. Family Planning Conference — A259

1981, Apr. 26

1120	A259	200r multi	80	40

The lack of a price for a listed item does not necessarily indicate rarity.

A261

A260
Natl. Education Day

Traditional Bali Paintings: Nos. 1121-1122, Song of Sritanjung. No. 1123, Birth of the Eagle.

1981, May 2

1121 A260 100r multi 35 20
1122 A261 200r multi 65 40

Souvenir Sheet

1123 Sheet of 2 4.00 2.00
a. A260 400r multi 1.60 80
b. A261 600r multi 2.50 1.25

No. 1123 has margin showing WIPA '81 emblem. Sheets exist with marginal inscription "Indonesien grusst WIPA."

ASEAN Building Jakarta, Opening — A262

1981, May 9

1124 A262 200r multi 80 40

Uber Cup '81 Badminton Championship, Tokyo — A263

1981, May 22

1125 A263 200r multi 80 40

World Environment Day — A264

Bas-reliefs, Candhi Merut Buddhist Temple, Central Java: 75r, Tree of Life. 200r, Reclining Buddha.

1981, June 5

1126 A264 75r multi 22 16
1127 A264 200r multi 65 40

12th Koran Reading Competition, June 7-14 — A265

1981, June 7 *Perf. 13½x12½*

1128 A265 200r multi 65 40

Intl. Year of the Disabled — A266

1981, July 31 *Perf. 12½*

1129 A266 75r Blind man 22 16
1130 A266 200r Speech, hearing disabilities 65 40

Soekarno-Hatta Independence Monument, Jakarta — A267

1981, Aug. 17

1131 A267 200r multi 65 40

Natl. Sports Week, Sept. 19-30 — A268

World Food Day — A268a

1981, Sept. 19

1132 A268 75r Skydiving 22 16
1133 A268 100r Skin diving, horiz. 35 20
1134 A268 200r Equestrian 65 40

See Nos. 1374-1375 for souvenir sheets containing No. 1134 in different colors.

1981, Oct. 16

1135 A268a 200r multi 65 40

Provincial Arms — A269

Natl. Arms A270

1981-83

1136 A269 100r Aceh 50 30
1137 A269 100r Bali 50 30
1138 A269 100r Bengkulu 50 30
1139 A269 100r Jakarta 50 30
1140 A269 100r West Irian 50 30
1141 A269 100r West Java ('82) 50 30
1142 A269 100r Jambi ('82) 50 30
1143 A269 100r Central Java ('82) 50 30
1144 A269 100r East Java ('82) 50 30
1145 A269 100r South Kalimantan ('82) 50 30
1146 A269 100r East Kalimantan ('82) 50 30
1147 A269 100r West Kalimantan ('82) 50 30
1148 A269 100r Lampung ('82) 50 30
1149 A269 100r Central Kalimantan ('82) 50 30
1150 A269 100r Moluccas ('82) 50 30
1151 A269 100r West Nusa Tenggara ('82) 50 30
1152 A269 100r East Nusa Tenggara ('82) 50 30
1153 A269 100r Southeast Celebes ('82) 50 30
1154 A269 100r Central Celebes ('82) 50 30
1155 A269 100r West Sumatra ('82) 50 30
1156 A269 100r North Celebes ('82) 50 30
1157 A269 100r North Sumatra ('82) 50 30
1158 A269 100r South Sumatra ('82) 50 30
1159 A269 100r Riau ('82) 50 30
1160 A269 100r South Sulawesi ('82) 50 30
1161 A269 100r Yogyakarta ('82) 50 30
1161A A269 100r Timor ('83) 20 15
1162 A270 250r shown ('82) 1.25 75
Nos. 1136-1162 (28) 14.45 8.70

Pink-crested Cockatoo — A271

1981, Dec. 10

1163 A271 75r shown 25 16
1164 A271 100r Sulphur-crested cockatoo 35 20
1165 A271 200r King cockatoo 65 40

Souvenir Sheet

1166 Sheet of 2 2.00 1.20
a. A271 150r like #1274 50 30
b. A271 350r like #1275 1.40 70

Bumiputra Mutual Life Insurance Co., 70th Anniv. — A272

1982, Feb. 12

1167 A272 75r Family 25 16
1168 A272 100r Family, diff. 35 20
1169 A272 200r Hands holding symbols 65 40

Search and Rescue Institute, 10th Anniv. A273

General Election A274

1982, Feb. 28 *Perf. 12½x13½*

1170 A273 250r multi 80 50

1982, Mar. 1 *Perf. 12½*

1171 A274 75r Ballot, houses 25 16
1172 A274 100r Farm 35 20
1173 A274 200r Arms 65 40

2nd UN Conference on Exploration and Peaceful Uses of Outer Space, Vienna, Aug. 9-21 — A275

1982, Apr. 19 *Perf. 13x13½*

1174 A275 150r Couple 50 30
1175 A275 150r Emblem 50 30

12th Thomas Badminton Cup, London, May — A276

1982, May 19

1176 A276 250r multi 80 50
a. Souvenir sheet of 2 1.60

No. 1176a also exists overprinted "INDONESIE SALUE PHILEXFRANCE" in red or black.

1982 World Cup — A277

1982, June 14

1177 A277 250r multi 80 50
a. Souvenir sheet of 2 2.00
b.-c. Souvenir sheets of 2 3.50

No. 1177b overprinted in black; No. 1177c in red.

60th Anniv. of Taman Siswa Educational System — A278

1982, July 3

1178 A278 250r multi 80 50

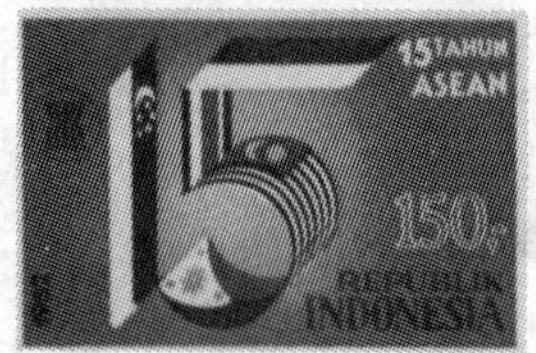

15th Anniv. of Assoc. of South East Asian Nations (ASEAN) — A279

1982, Aug. 8 **Photo.** *Perf. 12½*

1179 A279 150r Members' flags 50 30

Balinese Starling A280

Red Birds of Paradise A281

1982, Oct. 11 Photo. *Perf. 13x13½*

1180 A280 100r shown 35 20
1181 A280 250r King birds of paradise 80 50

Souvenir Sheet

1181A A280 500r Bali dove 2.00 1.00

3rd World Natl. Park Congress, Denpasar Bali.

1982, Dec. 20 *Perf. 12½x13½*

1182 A281 100r Lawe's six-wired parotia 35 20
1183 A281 150r Twelve-wired birds of paradise 50 30
1184 A281 250r shown 80 50

Souvenir Sheet

Perf. 12½x13½

1184A Sheet of 2 1.75 1.00
b. A281 200r like 100r 65 40
c. A281 300r like 250r 1.00 60

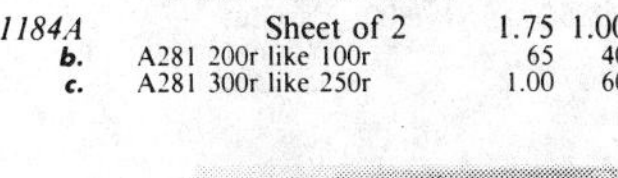

Scouting Year A282

1983, Feb. 22 Photo. *Perf. 13½x13*

1185 A282 250r multi 1.00 50

Restoration of Borobudur Temple — A283

1983, Feb. 23 *Perf. 12½*

1186 A283 100r Scaffolding, crane, vert. 25 15
1187 A283 150r Buddha statue, stupas, vert. 40 20
1188 A283 250r Statue, temple 65 35

Souvenir Sheet

1189 A283 500r Temple 2.00 1.00

Gas Plant — A284

World Communications Year — A285

1983, May 16 Photo. *Perf. 12½*

1190 A284 275r multi 80 42

7th Intl. Liquefied Natural Gas Conference and Exhibition, Jakarta, May 16-19.

1983, May 17 *Perf. 12½x13½*

1191 A285 75r Dove, ships 30 15
1192 A285 110r Satellite 40 20
1193 A285 175r Dish antenna, jet 60 30
1194 A285 275r Airmail envelope, globe 80 42

See Nos. 1215-1216.

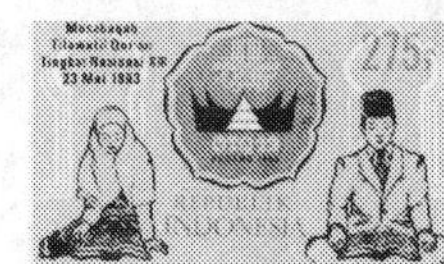

13th Natl. Koran Reading Competition, Padang, May 23-31 — A286

1983, May 23 *Perf. 13½x13*

1195 A286 275r multi 80 42

Total Solar Eclipse, June 11 — A287

1983, June 11 *Perf. 12½*

1196 A287 110r Map, eclipse 40 20
1197 A287 275r Map 80 42

Souvenir Sheet

1198 A287 500r like 275r 1.50 80

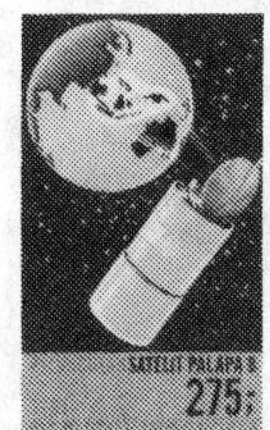

Launch of Palapa B Satellite — A288

Agricultural Census — A289

1983, June 18 *Perf. 12½x13½*

1199 A288 275r multi 80 42

1983, July 1 Photo. *Perf. 12½*

1200 A289 110r Produce 15 15
1201 A289 275r Farmer 30 15
Set value 23

15th Anniv. of Indonesia-Pakistan Economic and Cultural Cooperation Org. — A290

Weavings.

1983, Aug. 19

1202 A290 275r Indonesian, Lombok 30 15
1203 A290 275r Pakistani, Baluchistan 30 15

Krakatoa Eruption Centenary A291

1983, Aug. 26

1204 A291 110r Volcano 15 15
1205 A291 275r Map 30 15
Set value 23

CN-235, Light Air Transport — A292

1983, Sept. 10 Photo. *Perf. 12½*

1206 A292 275r multi 30 15

Tropical Fish — A293

1983, Oct. 17 Photo. *Perf. 12½*

1207 A293 110r Puntius tetrazona 15 15
1208 A293 175r Rasbora einthoveni 22 15
1209 A293 275r Toxotes jaculator 38 20

Canderawasih Birds — A294

1983, Nov. 30 Photo. *Perf. 12½*

1210 A294 110r Diphyllodes respublica 15 15
1211 A294 175r Epimachus fastuosus 22 15
1212 A294 275r Drepanornis albertisi 38 20
1213 A294 500r as #1212 65 40
a. Souvenir sheet of 1 1.50 80

Inalienable Rights of the Palestinian People A295

1983, Dec. 20 *Perf. 13½x13*

1214 A295 275r multi 38 20

WCY Type of 1983

Souvenir Sheets

1983 Photo. *Perf. 12½x13½*

1215 A285 400r like No. 1192 1.00 35
1216 A285 500r like No. 1194 1.50 50

Telecom '83 exhib., Geneva, Oct. 26-Nov. 1 (400r). Philatelic Museum opening, Jakarta (500r). Issue dates: 400r, Oct. 26; 500r, Sept. 29.

Fight Against Polio — A296

4th Five-Year Development Plan — A297

1984, Feb. 17 Photo. *Perf. 12½*

1217 A296 110r Emblem 15 15
1218 A296 275r Stylized person 38 20
Set value 28

1984, Apr. 1 Photo. *Perf. 12½*

1219 A297 55r Fertilizer industry 15 15
1220 A297 75r Aviation 15 15
1221 A297 110r Shipping 15 15
1222 A297 275r Communications 38 20
Set value 70 38

Forestry Resources A298

1984, May 17 Photo. *Perf. 12½*

1223 A298 75r Forest, paper mill 15 15
1224 A298 110r Seedling 15 15
1225 A298 175r Tree cutting 22 15
1226 A298 275r Logs 38 20
a. Souv. sheet of 2, #1225-1226 65 35
Set value 47

17th Annual Meeting of ASEAN Foreign Ministers — A299

1984, July 9 Photo. *Perf. 12½*

1227 A299 275r Flags 38 20

1984 Summer Olympics — A300

Horse Dancers, Central Java — A301

1984, July 28 Photo. *Perf. 12½*

1228 A300 75r Pole vault 15 15
1229 A300 110r Archery 15 15
1230 A300 175r Boxing 22 15
1231 A300 250r Shooting 35 20
1232 A300 275r Weight lifting 38 22
1233 A300 325r Swimming 42 25
Nos. 1228-1233 (6) 1.67
Set value 92

1984, Aug. 17 *Perf. 12½x13½*

Processions.

1234 A301 75r shown 15 15
1235 A301 110r Reyog Ponorogo, East Java 15 15
1236 A301 275r Lion Dance, West Java 38 20
1237 A301 325r Barong of Bali 42 25
Set value 58

Natl. Sports Day A302

1984, Sept. 9 Photo. *Perf. 13½x13*

1238 A302 110r Thomas Cup victory 15 15
1239 A302 275r Gymnastics 38 20
Set value 28

Postcode System Inauguration A303

1984, Sept. 27 Photo. Perf. 12½

1240 A303 110r multi 15 15
1241 A303 275r multi 38 20
Set value 28

Birds of Irian Jaya — A304

Oath of the Youth — A305

1984, Oct. 15 Perf. 12½x13½

1242 A304 75r Chlamydera lauterbachi 15 15
1243 A304 110r Sericulus aureus 15 15
1244 A304 275r Astrapia nigra 38 20
1245 A304 325r Lophorhina superba 42 25
a. Souv. sheet of 2, #1242, 1245 2.00 2.00
Set value 58

No. 1245a for PHILAKOREA '84.

1984, Oct. 28 Perf. 12½

1246 A305 275r Emblem 38 20

ICAO, 40th Anniversary — A306

1984, Dec. 7 Photo. Perf. 13½x12½

1247 A306 275r Airplane, Emblem 38 20

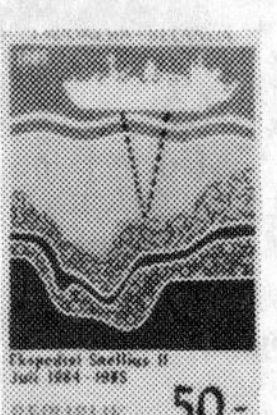

Indonesia Netherlands Marine Exped., 1984-85 — A307

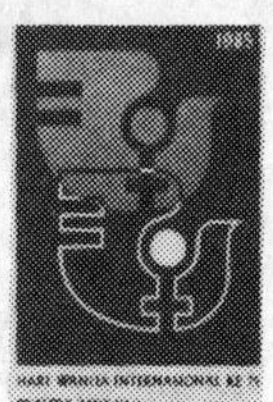

75th Intl. Women's Day — A308

Survey ship Snellius II and: 50r, Marine geological and geophysical exploration. 100r, Mapping ocean currents. 275r, Studying marine flora and fauna.

1985, Feb. 27 Photo. Perf. 13x13½

1248 A307 50r multi 15 15
1249 A307 100r multi 15 15
1250 A307 275r multi 40 22
Set value 35

1985, Mar. 8

1251 A308 100r Emblem 15 15
1252 A308 275r Silhouettes, emblem 40 22
Set value 30

Five Year Plan A309

1985, Apr. 1 Perf. 13½x13

1254 A309 75r Mecca pilgrimage program 15 15
1255 A309 140r Compulsory education 20 15
1256 A309 350r Cement industry, Padang works 50 30
Set value 48

Suharto Type of 1980-83 and

Pres. Suharto and Natl. Flag — A310

Pres. Suharto — A310a

President Suharto — A310b

Perf. 13½x12½, 12½ (A310, A310a, A310b)

1983-90 Photo.

1257 A246 10r pale grn & dk grn 15 15
1258 A246 25r pale org & dk cop red 15 15
1259 A246 50r beige & dark brown 15 15
1260 A246 55r sal rose & rose 15 15
1261 A246 100r lt blue green & ultra 15 15
1262 A310 140r rose & dp brn 20 15
1264 A310b 200r pink, bl & red 16 15
1266 A246 300r lt dull green, blue green & gold 40 20
1267 A310 350r red & brt lil 50 30
1268 A246 400r blue grn, int blue & gold 55 25
1268A A310b 700r pale grn, rose lil & grn 60 30
1269 A310a 1000r multi 1.40 70
Nos. 1257-1269 (12) 4.56
Set value 1.80

Issue dates: 10r, 25r, Mar. 11. 140r, 350r, Apr. 10, 1985. 50r, 100r, 300r, Dec. 24, 1986. 55r, 400r, Dec. 1987. 200r, Dec. 1989. 700r, Mar. 1990. 1000r, Aug. 17, 1988.

This is an expanding set. Numbers will change if necessary.

Asia-Africa Conference, 30th Anniv. — A311

1985, Apr. 24 Perf. 12½

1270 A311 350r Emblem, inscription 50 30

Intl. Youth Year — A312

UN Decade for Women — A313

1985, July 12 Perf. 12½x13½

1271 A312 75r Three youths, globe 15 15
1272 A312 140r Youths supporting globe 20 15
Set value 15

1985, July 26

1273 A313 55r Profiles of women, emblem 15 15
1274 A313 140r Globe, emblem 20 15
Set value 28 15

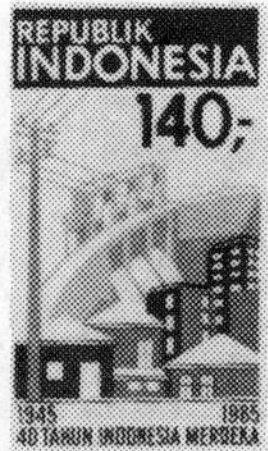

Indonesian Trade Fair — A314

1985, Aug. 1

1275 A314 140r Hydro-electric plant 20 15
1276 A314 350r Farmer, industrial plant 50 25

Republic of Indonesia, 40th anniv.

11th Natl. Sports Week, Jakarta, Sept. 9-20 A315

Perf. 13½x12½, 12½x13½

1985, Sept. 9 Photo.

1277 A315 55r Sky diving 15 15
1278 A315 100r Combat sports 15 15
1279 A315 140r High jump 20 15
1280 A315 350r Wind surfing, vert. 50 25
Set value 48

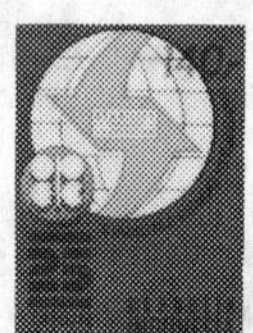

Org. of Petroleum Exporting Countries, OPEC, 25th Anniv. — A316

1985, Sept. 14 Perf. 12½

1281 A316 140r multi 20 15

Natl. Oil Industry, Cent. A317

1985, Oct. 8 Perf. 13½x13

1282 A317 140r Oil tankers 20 15
1283 A317 250r Refinery 35 16
1284 A317 350r Offshore oil rig 50 25

UN, 40th Anniv. — A318

Design: 140r, Doves, 40, emblem. 300r, Bombs transformed into plants.

1985, Oct. 24 Perf. 12½

1285 A318 140r multi 20 15
1286 A318 300r multi 40 20

Wildlife A318a

1985, Dec. 27 Photo. Perf. 14½x13

1286A A318a 75r Rhinoceros sondaicus 15 15
1286B A318a 150r Anoa depressicornis 20 15
1286C A318a 300r Varanus komodoensis 40 20
Set value 35

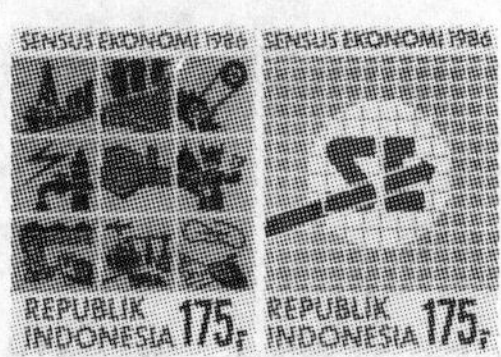

1986 Industrial Census — A319

1986, Feb. 8 Photo. Perf. 12½

1287 A319 Pair 1.10 55
a. 175r Census emblem 55 25
b. 175r Symbols of industry 55 25

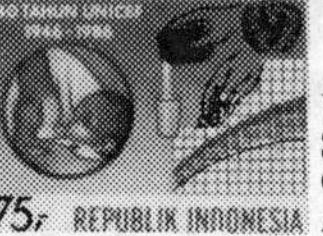

UN Child Survival Campaign A320

1986, Mar. 15 Photo. Perf. 12½

1288 A320 75r Breastfeeding 15 15
1289 A320 140r Immunization 25 15
Set value 20

UNICEF, 40th anniv.

4th 5-year Development Plan — A321

14th Thomas Cup, 13th Uber Cup, Jakarta — A322

1986, Apr. 1 Photo. Perf. 12½

1290 A321 140r Construction 28 15
1291 A321 500r Agriculture 1.00 50

1986, Apr. 22

1292 A322 55r Cup, racket 15 15
1293 A322 150r Cups, horiz. 30 15
Set value 21

EXPO '86, Vancouver — A323

1986, May 2 Perf. 12½x14½

1294 A323 75r Pinisi junk 15 15
1295 A323 150r Kentongan, satellite 30 15
1296 A323 300r Pavilion emblem 60 30

Natl. Scout Jamboree, JAMNAS '86, Cibubur Jakarta East
A324

Perf. 13½x12½, 12½x13½

1986, June 21 **Photo.**

1297 A324 100r Saluting flag 20 15
1298 A324 140r Cookout 28 15
1299 A324 210r Map-reading, vert. 42 20

Air Show '86, Jakarta, June 22-July 1
A325

1986, June 23 ***Perf. 13½x12½***

1300 A325 350r multi 70 35

Folk Dances — A326

1986, July 30 **Photo.** ***Perf. 12½***

1301 A326 140r Legong Kraton 28 15
1302 A326 350r Barong 70 35
1303 A326 500r Kecak 1.00 50

19th Congress of Intl. Society of Sugar Cane Technologists, Jakarta — A327

1986, Aug. 5 ***Perf. 12½x13½***

1304 A327 150r Planting 30 15
1305 A327 300r Sugar 60 30

Sea-Me-We Submarine Cable Inauguration — A328

1986, Sept. 8 ***Perf. 12½***

1306 A328 140r shown 28 15
1307 A328 350r Map, diff. 70 35

Southeast Asia, Middle East, Western Europe Submarine Cable.

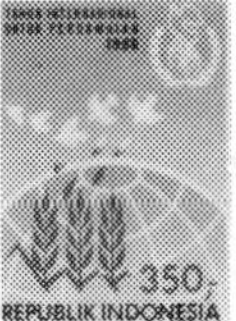

Intl. Peace Year — A329

1987 General Election — A330

1986, Dec. 17 **Photo.** ***Perf. 12½***

1308 A329 350r shown 70 35
1309 A329 500r Dove circling Earth 1.00 50

1987, Jan. 19

Designs: 75r, Tourism, party emblems, industry. 350r, Emblems, natl. eagle, ballot box.

1310 A330 75r multi 15 15
1311 A330 140r multi 28 15
1312 A330 350r multi 70 35

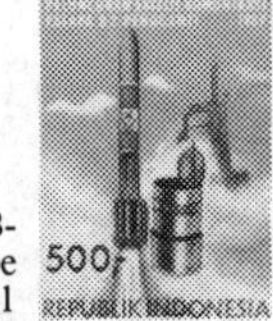

Launch of Palapa B-2P, Cape Canaveral — A331

1987, Mar. 21 **Photo.** ***Perf. 12½***

1313 A331 350r Satellite, horiz. 70 35
1314 A331 500r shown 1.00 50

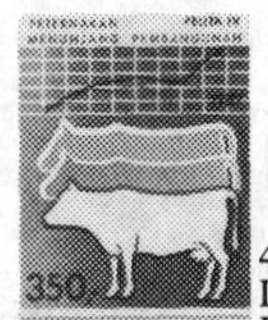

4th 5-Year Development Plan — A332

1987, Apr. 1

1315 A332 140r Boy carving figurines, horiz. 28 15
1316 A332 350r shown 70 35

Folk Costumes — A333

1987, May 25 ***Perf. 13x13½***

1317 A333 140r Kalimantan Timur 28 15
1318 A333 350r Daerah Aceh 70 35
1319 A333 400r Timor Timur 80 40

See Nos. 1358-1363, 1412-1417, 1448-1453, 1464-1469.

14th Southeast Asia Games, Jakarata, Sept. 9-20
A334

Anniv. Emblems
A335

1987, June 10 ***Perf. 12½***

1320 A334 140r Weight lifting 28 15
1321 A334 250r Swimming 50 25
1322 A334 350r Running 70 35

1987, June 20

1323 A335 75r multi, horiz. 15 15
1324 A335 100r shown 20 15
Set value 18

City of Jakarta, 460th anniv.; Jakarta Fair, 20th anniv.

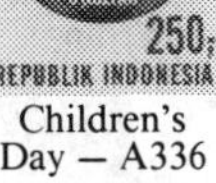

Children's Day — A336

ASEAN Headquarters, Jakarta — A337

1987, July 23

1325 A336 100r Education, horiz. 20 15
1326 A336 250r Universal immunization 50 25

1987, Aug. 8

1327 A337 350r multi 70 35

ASEAN, 20th anniv.

Assoc. of Physicians Specializing in Internal Diseases, 30th Anniv. — A338

1987, Aug. 23 **Photo.**

1328 A338 300r Stylized man, caduceus 60 30

Sand Craters, Mt. Bromo, Timur
A339

1987, Oct. 20 ***Perf. 13½x12½***

1329 A339 140r shown 28 15
1330 A339 350r Bratan (Bedugul) Lake, Bali 70 35
1331 A339 500r Sea gardens, Bunaken Is. 1.00 50

Pariwisata (tourism) 1987. See Nos. 1367-1370A, 1408-1410, 1420-1422.

Role of Women in the Fight for Independence A340

1987, Nov. 10 ***Perf. 12½***

1332 A340 75r Veteran 15 15
1333 A340 100r Soldiers, barbed wire (Laskar Wanita) 20 15
Set value 18

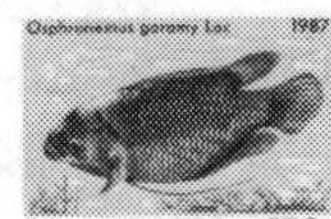

Fish — A341

1987, Dec. 30

1334 A341 150r Osphronemus goramy 30 15
1335 A341 200r Cyprinus carpio 40 20
1336 A341 500r Clarias batrachus 1.00 50

Natl. Veteran's League, 31st Anniv. — A342

1988, Jan. 2

1337 A342 250r blue grn & org 50 25

Occupational Health and Safety for Greater Efficiency and Productivity — A343

1988, Jan. 12 ***Perf. 13½x12½***

1338 A343 350r Worker using safety equipment 70 35

See No. 1419.

Natl. Craft Council, 8th Anniv. — A344

Crafts: 120r, Carved wood snake and frog. 350r, Cane rocking chair. 500r, Ornate carved bamboo containers and fan.

1988, Mar. 3 **Photo.** ***Perf. 12½***

1339 A344 120r ultra & dark brn 18 15
1340 A344 350r lt blue & dark brn 50 25
1341 A344 500r yel grn & dark brn 70 35

Pelita IV (Five-Year Development Plan) — A345

1988, Apr. 1

1342 A345 140r Oil rig, refinery 20 15
1343 A345 400r Crayfish, trawler 58 30

World Expo '88, Brisbane, Australia
A346

Intl. Red Cross and Red Crescent Organizations, 125th Annivs.
A347

Designs: 200r, Two children, Borobudur Temple in silhouette. 300r, Boy wearing armor and headdress. 350r, Girl, boy and a Tongkonan house, Toraja, South Sulawesi.

1988, Apr. 30 **Photo.** ***Perf. 12½***

1344 A346 200r multi 28 15
1345 A346 300r multi 42 20
1346 A346 350r multi 50 25
a. Souv. sheet of 3, #1344-1346 1.20 1.20

No. 1346a exists imperf.

1988, May 8

1347 A347 350r blk & red 50 25

Orchids — A348

1988, May 17 **Perf. 13x13½**
1348 A348 400r Dendrobium none 58 30
1349 A348 500r Dendrobium abang 70 35

1988 Summer Olympics, Seoul — A349

Intl. Council of Women, Cent. — A350

1988, June 15 **Photo.** **Perf. 12½**
1350 A349 75r Running 15 15
1351 A349 100r Weight lifting 15 15
1352 A349 200r Archery 28 15
1353 A349 300r Table tennis 42 20
1354 A349 400r Swimming 58 30
a. Souv. sheet of 3 + label, #1351-1352, 1354 1.00 1.00
1355 A349 500r Tennis 70 35
a. Souv. sheet of 3 + label, #1350, 1353, 1355 1.25 1.25
Nos. 1350-1355 (6) 2.28
Set value 1.12

Sheets exist imperf.

1988, June 26
1356 A350 140r brt blue & blk 20 15

7th Natl. Farmers' Week — A351

1988, July 9
1357 A351 350r lake & bister 50 25

Folk Costumes Type of 1987

Traditional wedding attire from: 55r, West Sumatra. 75p, Jambi. 100r, Bengkulu. 120r, Lampung. 200r, Moluccas. 250r, East Nusa.

1988, July 15 **Perf. 12½x14½**
1358 A333 55r multi 15 15
1359 A333 75r multi 15 15
1360 A333 100r multi 15 15
1361 A333 120r multi 18 15
1362 A333 200r multi 28 15
1363 A333 250r multi 35 18
Nos. 1358-1363 (6) 1.26
Set value 60

13th Congress of the Non-Aligned News Agencies Pool, Jakarta, Sept. 29-Oct. 1 — A352

1988, Sept. 29 **Photo.** **Perf. 12½**
1364 A352 500r multi 70 35

Intl. Letter Writing Week — A353

1988, Oct. 9
1365 A353 140r multi 20 15

Transportion and Communications Decade for Asia and the Pacific (1985-1995) A354

1988, Oct. 24
1366 A354 350r blk & lt blue 50 25

Tourism Type of 1987

Architecture: 250r, Al Mashun Mosque, Medan. 300r, Pagaruyung Palace, Batusangkar. 500r, 1000r, Keong Emas Taman Theater, Jakarta.

1988-89 **Photo.** **Perf. 13½x13**
1367 A339 250r multi 35 18
1368 A339 300r multi 42 20
1369 A339 500r multi 70 35

Souvenir Sheet
Perf. 14½x12½
1370 A339 1000r multi 1.40 70

Perf. 14½x13
1370A Sheet of 2 7.25 3.65
b. A339 1500r like No. 1367 2.75 1.35
c. A339 2500r like No. 1368 4.50 2.25

Issue dates: No. 1370A, Nov. 1989; others, Nov. 25, 1988. World Stamp Expo '89, Washington, DC. No. 1370 exists imperf.

Butterflies — A356

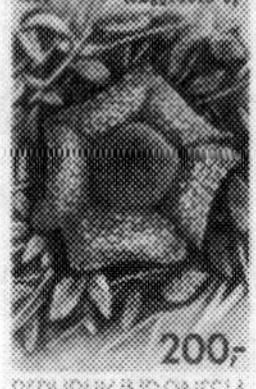

Flora — A357

1988, Dec. 20 **Perf. 12½x13½**
1371 A356 400r *Papilio gigon* 55 28
1372 A356 500r *Graphium androcles* 70 35

Souvenir Sheet
Perf. 12½x14½
1373 A356 1000r like 500r 1.40 70

No. 1373 exists imperf.

Equestrian Type of 1981
Souvenir Sheets

1988 **Perf. 12½**
1374 Sheet of 4 1.30 65
a. A268 200r blk, dark red & grn 32 16
1375 Sheet of 1 + label, dark blue, dark red & deep orange 32 15

FILACEPT '88, The Hague, Oct. 18-23, 1988. Exist imperf., same values.

1989, Jan. 7 **Photo.** **Perf. 13½x13**
1376 A357 200r *Rafflesia* 28 15
1377 A357 1000r *Amorphophallus titanum* 1.40 70

Souvenir Sheet
Perf. 13½x14½
1378 A357 1000r like No. 1377, value in black 1.40 70

Garuda Indonesia Airlines, 40th Anniv. — A358

1989, Jan. 26 **Perf. 12½**
1379 A358 350r blue grn & brt blue 50 25

World Wildlife Fund — A359

Orangutans, *Pongo pygmaeus.*

1989, Mar. 6 **Photo.** **Perf. 12½**
1380 A359 75r Adult and young 15 15
1381 A359 100r Adult hanging in tree 15 15
a. Souv. sheet of 2, #1380-1381 25 15
1382 A359 140r Adult, young in tree 20 15
1383 A359 500r Adult's head 70 35
a. Souv. sheet of 2, #1382-1383 90 45
Set value 58

Use of Postage Stamps in Indonesia, 125th Anniv. — A360

1989, Apr. 1
1384 A360 1000r grn, rose lilac & deep blue 1.40 70

5th Five-year Development Plan — A361

Industries.

1989, Apr. 1
1385 A361 55r Fertilizer 15 15
1386 A361 150r Cilegon Iron and Steel Mill 21 15
1387 A361 350r Petroleum 50 25
Set value 40

See Nos. 1427-1428, 1461-1462.

Natl. Education Day — A362

Ki Hadjar Dewantara (b. 1889), founder of Taman Siswa school and: 140r, Graduate. 300r, Pencil, globe and books.

1989, May 2
1388 A362 140r ver, lake & brt rose lil 20 15
1389 A362 300r vio & pale grn 42 20

Terbuka University (140r) and freedom from illiteracy (300r).

Asia-Pacific Telecommunity, 10th Anniv. — A363

Sudirman Cup, Flag — A364

1989, July 1 **Photo.** **Perf. 12½**
1390 A363 350r grn & vio 50 25

1989, July 3
1391 A364 100r scar, gold & dark red brn 15 15

Sudirman Cup world badminton mixed team championships, Jakarta, May 24-28.

Natl. Children's Day — A365

CIRDAP, 10th Anniv. — A366

1989, July 23
1392 A365 100r Literacy 15 15
1393 A365 250r Physical fitness 35 18
Set value 25

1989, July 29
1394 A366 140r blue & dark red brn 20 15

Center on Integrated Rural Development for Asia and the Pacific.

Paleoanthropological Discoveries in Indonesia — A367

Fossils of *Homo erectus* and *Homo sapiens* men.

1989, Aug. 31
1395 A367 100r Sangiran 17 15 15
1396 A367 150r Perning 1 21 15
1397 A367 200r Sangiran 10 28 15
1398 A367 250r Wajak 1 35 18
1399 A367 300r Sambungmacan 1 42 20
1400 A367 350r Ngandong 7 50 25
Nos. 1395-1400 (6) 1.91 1.08

Nos. 1398-1400 vert.

Interparliamentary Union, Cent. — A368

1989, Sept. 4
1401 A368 350r deep blue & yel grn 50 25

12th Natl. Sports Week — A369

1989, Sept. 18

1402	A369	75r	Tae kwando	15	15
1403	A369	100r	Tennis	15	15
1404	A369	140r	Judo	20	15
1405	A369	350r	Volleyball	50	25
1406	A369	500r	Boxing	70	35
1407	A369	1000r	Archery	1.40	70
			Nos. 1402-1407 (6)	3.10	
			Set value		1.50

Tourism Type of 1987

Structures in Miniature Park: 120r, Taman Burung. 350r, Prangko Museum. 500r, Istana Anak-Anak, vert.

Perf. 13½x12½, 12½x13½

1989, Oct. 9

1408	A339	120r	multicolored	17	15
1409	A339	350r	multicolored	50	25
1410	A339	500r	multicolored	70	35

Film Festival — A370

1989, Nov. 11 Photo. ***Perf. 12½***

1411 A370 150r yel bis & blk 15 15

Folk Costumes Type of 1987

Traditional wedding attire from: 50r, North Sumatra. 75r, South Sumatra. 100r, Jakarta. 140r, North Sulawesi. 350r, Mid Sulawesi. 500r, South Sulawesi.

1989, Dec. 11 ***Perf. 13x13½***

1412	A333	50r	multicolored	15	15
1413	A333	75r	multicolored	15	15
1414	A333	100r	multicolored	15	15
1415	A333	140r	multicolored	15	15
1416	A333	350r	multicolored	35	18
1417	A333	500r	multicolored	50	25
			Nos. 1412-1417 (6)	1.45	1.03

Health and Safety Type of 1988

1990, Jan. 12 ***Perf. 13x12½***

Size: 29x21mm

1419 A343 200r Lineman, power lines 20 15

Tourism Type of 1987

Architecture: 200r, Fort Marlborough, Bengkulu. 400r, 1000r, National Museum, Jakarta. 500r, 1500r, Mosque of Baiturrahman, Banda Aceh.

1990, Feb. 1 ***Perf. 13½x13***

1420	A339	200r	multicolored	20	15
1421	A339	400r	multicolored	45	22
1422	A339	500r	multicolored	55	28

Souvenir Sheet

1423		Sheet of 2	2.50	1.25
a.	A339	1000r multicolored	1.00	50
b.	A339	1500r multicolored	1.50	75

Flora A371

1990, Mar. 1

1424	A371	75r	Mammilaria fragilis	15	15
1425	A371	1000r	Gmelina elliptica	1.00	50

Souvenir Sheet

1426 A371 1500r like #1425 1.50 75

5th Five-year Development Plan Type of 1989

1990, Apr. 1 ***Perf. 12½***

1427	A361	200r	Road construction	20	15
1428	A361	1000r	Lighthouse, ship	1.00	50

Visit Indonesia Year, 1991 A372

Perf. 13½x12½, 12½x13½

1990, May 1

1429	A372	100r	shown	15	15
1430	A372	500r	Steps, ruin	50	25

Souvenir Sheet

Perf. 14½x12½

1430A A372 5000r like #1429 5.00 2.50

No. 1430A, Stamp World London '90.

Disabled Veterans Corps, 40th Anniv. — A373

1990, May 18 ***Perf. 12½***

1431 A373 1000r gray grn & brn org 1.00 50

World Cup Soccer Championships, Italy — A374

1990, June 8 ***Perf. 12½***

1432	A374	75r	shown	15	15
1433	A374	150r	multi, diff.	16	15
1434	A374	400r	multi, diff.	45	22

Souvenir Sheet

1435 A374 1500r multi 1.50 75

Family Planning in Indonesia, 20th Anniv. — A375

1990, June 29

1436 A375 60r brn & red 15 15

Natl. Census — A376

1990, July 1

1437 A376 90r yel grn & dk grn 15 15

Natl. Children's Day — A377

1990, July 23

1438 A377 500r multicolored 55 28

Souvenir Sheet

Traditional Lampung Wedding Costumes — A378

Perf. 12½x14½

1990, May 3 Photo.

1439 A378 2000r multicolored 2.00 1.00

Natl. Philatelic Exhibition, Stamp World London '90 and New Zealand '90.

Independence, 45th Anniv. — A379

1990, Aug. 17 ***Perf. 12½x13½***

1440	A379	200r	Soldier raising flag	35	18
1441	A379	500r	Skyscraper, highway	85	42

Souvenir Sheet

1442 A379 1000r like #1442 1.70 85

Indonesia-Pakistan Economic & Cultural Cooperation Organization — A380

Designs: 400r, Woman dancing in traditional costume, vert.

Perf. 13½x12½, 12½x13½

1990, Aug. 19 Litho.

1443	A380	75r	multicolored	20	15
1444	A380	400r	multicolored	1.00	50

Asian Pacific Postal Training Center, 20th Anniv. — A381

1990, Sept. 10 Photo. ***Perf. 12½***

1445 A381 500r vio bl, bl & ultra 85 42

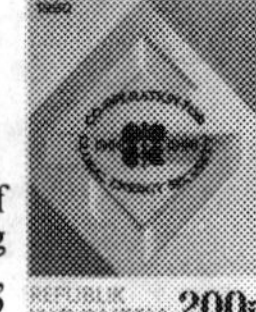

Organization of Petroleum Exporting Countries (OPEC), 30th Anniv. — A382

1990, Sept. 14

1446 A382 200r gray, blk & org 36 18

Environmental Protection Laws, 40th Anniv. — A383

1990, Oct. 24

1447 A383 1000r multicolored 1.70 85

Folk Costumes Type of 1987

Traditional wedding attire from: 75r, West Java. 100r, Central Java. 150r, Yogyakarta. 200r, East Java. 400r, Bali. 500r, West Nusa Tenggara.

1990, Nov. 1 ***Perf. 13x13½***

1448	A333	75r	multicolored	15	15
1449	A333	100r	multicolored	18	15
1450	A333	150r	multicolored	28	15
1451	A333	200r	multicolored	36	18
1452	A333	400r	multicolored	72	36
1453	A333	500r	multicolored	85	42
			Nos. 1448-1453 (6)	2.54	1.41

Visit Indonesia Year 1991 — A385

Women in traditional costumes.

1991, Jan. 1 Photo. ***Perf. 12½x13½***

1454	A385	200r	multicolored	20	15
1455	A385	500r	multicolored	55	28
1456	A385	1000r	multicolored	1.00	50

16th Natl. Koran Reading Competition, Jogjakarta — A386

1991, Feb. 4 ***Perf. 12½***

1457 A386 200r yel, grn & bl grn 20 15

Palace of Sultan Ternate, the Moluccas A387

Design: 1000r, Bari House, Palembang, South Sumatra.

1991, Mar. 1 ***Perf. 13½x12½***

1458 A387 500r multicolored 50 25
1459 A387 1000r multicolored 1.00 50

5th Five Year Development Plan Type of 1989

1991, Apr. 1 ***Perf. 12½***

1461 A361 75r Steel mill, vert. 15 15
1462 A361 200r Computers 20 15
Set value 28 15

Danger of Smoking — A388

1991, May 31 Photo. ***Perf. 12½***

1463 A388 90r multicolored 15 15

Folk Costumes Type of 1987

Traditional wedding attire from: 100r, West Kalimantan. 200r, Mid Kalimantan. 300r, South Kalimantan. 400r, Southeast Sulawesi. 500r, Riau. 1000r, Irian Jaya.

1991, June 15 ***Perf. 13x13½***

1464 A333 100r multicolored 15 15
1465 A333 200r multicolored 20 15
1466 A333 300r multicolored 30 15
1467 A333 400r multicolored 40 20
1468 A333 500r multicolored 50 25
1469 A333 1000r multicolored 1.00 50
Nos. 1464-1469 (6) 2.55
Set value 1.25

Natl. Scouting Jamboree, Cibubur A389

Monument A390

1991, June 15 ***Perf. 12½***

1470 A389 200r multicolored 20 15

1991, July 6

1471 A390 200r multicolored 20 15

Natl. Farmers' Week — A391

Indonesian Chemical Society, 4th Natl. Congress — A392

1991, July 15

1472 A391 500r brt bl, yel& grn 50 25

1991, July 28

1473 A392 400r grn, ver & dull grn 40 20

Chemindo '91.

5th Junior Men's and 4th Women's Asian Weightlifting Championships A393

1991, Aug. 24 Photo. ***Perf. 12½***

1474 A393 300r blk, red & gray 55 28

World Cup Parachuting Championships A394

1991, Aug. 30

1475 A394 500r lil & sky bl 85 42

Indonesian Red Cross, 46th Anniv. — A395

1991, Sept. 17

1476 A395 200r multicolored 36 18

Intl. Amateur Radio Union, 8th Regional Conference, Bandung — A396

1991, Oct. 6

1477 A396 300r yel & blue 55 28

Istiqlal Festival, Jakarta — A397

1991, Oct. 15

1478 A397 200r gray, blk & ver 35 18

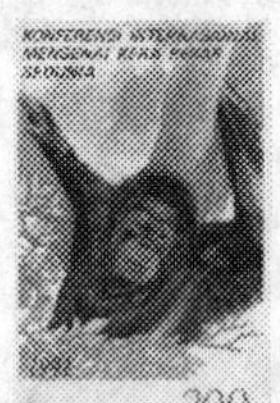

Intl. Conference on the Great Apes — A398

Pongo pygmaeus: 200r, Sitting in tree. 500r, Walking. 1000r, Sitting on ground.

1991, Dec. 18 ***Perf. 12½x13½***

1479 A398 200r multicolored 35 18
1480 A398 500r multicolored 85 42
1481 A398 1000r multicolored 1.70 85

Intl. Convention on Quality Control Circles, Bali — A399

1991, Oct. 22 ***Perf. 12½***

1482 A399 500r multicolored 85 42

SEMI-POSTAL STAMPS

Symbols of Olympic Games SP43

Wings and Flame SP44

Perf. 12½x12

1951, Jan. 2 Photo. Unwmk.

B58 SP43 5s + 3s gray grn 15 15
B59 SP43 10s + 5s dk vio bl 15 15
B60 SP43 20s + 5s org red 15 15
B61 SP43 30s + 10s dk brn 30 30
B62 SP43 35s + 10s ultra 1.25 1.25
Set value 1.70 1.70

Issued to publicize the Asiatic Olympic Games of 1951 at New Delhi, India.

1951, Oct. 15

B63 SP44 5s + 3s olive green 15 15
B64 SP44 10s + 5s dull blue 15 15
B65 SP44 20s + 5s red 15 15
B66 SP44 30s + 10s brown 15 15
B67 SP44 35s + 10s ultra 15 15
Set value 35 30

Issued to publicize the second National Games, Djakarta, October 21-28, 1951.

No. 378 Surcharged in Black

1953 BENTJANA ALAM +10s

1953, May 8 ***Perf. 12½***

B68 A53 35s + 10s purple 15 15

The surcharge reads "Natural Disaster." Surtax was for emergency relief following volcanic eruption and floods.

Merapi Erupting SP45

Young Musicians SP46

1954, Apr. 15 Litho. ***Perf. 12½x12***

B69 SP45 15s + 10s bl grn 15 15
B70 SP45 35s + 15s pur 15 15
B71 SP45 50s + 25s red 15 15
B72 SP45 75s + 25s vio bl 18 15
B73 SP45 1r + 25s car 30 22
B74 SP45 2r + 50s blk brn 60 50
B75 SP45 3r + 1r gray grn 7.75 3.75
B76 SP45 5r + 2.50r org brn 11.00 5.50
Nos. B69-B76 (8) 20.28 10.57

The surtax was for victims of the Merapi volcano eruption.

1954, Dec. 22 Photo. ***Perf. 12½***

Designs: 15s+10s, Parasol dance. 35s+15s, Girls playing dakon. 50s+15s, Boy on stilts. 75s+25s, Bamboo flute players. 1r+25s, Javanese dancer.

B77 SP46 10s + 10s dk pur 15 15
B78 SP46 15s + 10s dk grn 15 15
B79 SP46 35s + 15s car rose 15 15
B80 SP46 50s + 15s rose brn 15 15
B81 SP46 75s + 25s ultra 15 15
B82 SP46 1r + 25s red org 15 15
Set value 40 40

The surtax was for child welfare.

Scout Emblem SP47

Scout Signaling SP48

Designs: 50s+25s, Campfire. 75s+25s, Scout feeding fawn. 1r+50s, Scout saluting.

1955, June 27 Unwmk. ***Perf. 12½***

B83 SP47 15s + 10s bl grn 15 15
B84 SP48 35s + 15s ultra 15 15
B85 SP48 50s + 25s scar 15 15
B86 SP48 75s + 25s brn 15 15
B87 SP48 1r + 50s vio 15 15
Set value 38 30

First National Boy Scout Jamboree.

Blind Weaver SP49

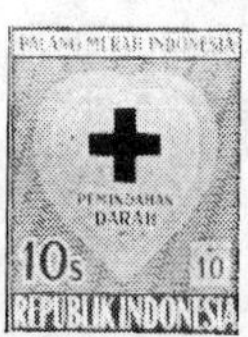

Red Cross and Heart SP50

Designs: 35s+15s, Basket weaver. 50s+25s, Boy studying map. 75s+50s, Woman reading Braille.

1956, Jan. 4

B88 SP49 15s + 10s dp grn 15 15
B89 SP49 35s + 15s yel brn 15 15
B90 SP49 50s + 25s rose car 40 25
B91 SP49 75s + 50s ultra 20 18
Set value 70 52

The surtax was for the benefit of the blind.

1956, July 26 Litho.

Designs: 35s+15s, 50s+15s, Transfusion bottle. 75s+25s, 1r+25s, Outstretched hands.

Cross in Red

B92 SP50 10s + 10s ultra 15 15
B93 SP50 15s + 10s car 15 15
B94 SP50 35s + 15s lt brn 15 15
B95 SP50 50s + 15s bl grn 15 15
B96 SP50 75s + 25s org 15 15
B97 SP50 1r + 25s brt pur 15 15
Set value 45 45

Surtax for the Indonesian Red Cross.

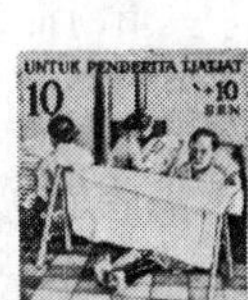

Invalids Doing Batik Work — SP51

Designs: 15s+10s, Amputee painting. 35s+15s, Lathe operator. 50s+15s, Crippled child learning to walk. 75s+25s, Treating amputee. 1r+25s, Painting with artificial hand.

1957, Mar. 26 Photo. *Perf. 12½*

B98 SP51 10s + 10s dp bl 15 15
B99 SP51 15s + 10s brn 15 15
B100 SP51 35s + 15s red 15 15
B101 SP51 50s + 15s dp vio 15 15
B102 SP51 75s + 25s grn 15 15
B103 SP51 1r + 25s dk car rose 15 15
Set value 45 45

The surtax was for rehabilitation of invalids.

Kembodja Flower SP52

Designs: 15s+10s, Michelia. 35s+15s, Sunflower. 50s+15s, Jasmine. 75s+50s, Orchid.

1957, Dec. 23 *Perf. 13½x12½*

Flowers in Natural Colors

B104 SP52 10s + 10s bl 35 20
B105 SP52 15s + 10s dp yel grn 30 20
B106 SP52 35s + 15s dk red brn 15 15
B107 SP52 50s + 15s ol & dk brn 15 15
B108 SP52 75s + 60s rose brn 15 15
Nos. B104-B108 (5) 1.10 85

Children SP53

Indonesian Scout Emblem SP54

Design: 15s+10s, 50s+25s, 1r+50s, Girl and boy.

1958, July 1 Photo. *Perf. 12½x12*

B109 SP53 10s + 10s bl 15 15
B110 SP53 15s + 10s rose brn 15 15
B111 SP53 35s + 15s gray grn 15 15
B112 SP53 50s + 25s gray ol 16 16
B113 SP53 75s + 50s brn car 20 20
B114 SP53 1r + 50s brn 25 25
Set value 85 85

The surtax was for orphans.

1959, July 17 Photo. Unwmk.

Design: 15s + 10s, 50s + 25s, 1r + 50s, Scout emblem and compass.

Emblem in Red

B115 SP54 10s + 5s bis 15 15
B116 SP54 15s + 10s bluish grn 15 15
B117 SP54 20s + 10s lil gray 15 15
B118 SP54 50s + 25s ol 15 15
B119 SP54 75s + 35s yel brn 15 15
B120 SP54 1r + 50s dk gray 15 15
Set value 45 45

10th World Scout Jamboree, Makiling National Park near Manila, July 17-26.

Palm-leaf Ribs, Gong and 5 Rings SP55

Young Couple Holding Sharpened Bamboo Weapon SP56

Design: 20s+10s, 75s+35s, Bamboo musical instrument and 5-ring emblem.

1960, Feb. 14 *Perf. 12½x12*

B121 SP55 15s + 5s bis & dk brn 15 15
B122 SP55 20s + 10s grn & blk 15 15
B123 SP55 50s + 25s bl & pur 15 15
B124 SP55 75s + 35s ol & dk grn 15 15
B125 SP56 1.15r + 50s car & blk 15 15
Set value 30 26

Issued to commemorate the All-Indonesian Youth Congress, Bandung, Feb. 14-21, 1960.

Social Emblem SP57

Pineapple SP58

Designs: 15s+15s, Rice, lotus and cotton. 20s+20s, Lotus blossom and tree. 50s+25s, Girl and boy. 75s+25s, Watering of plant in man's hand. 3r+50s, Woman nursing infant.

Perf. 12½x12

1960, Dec. 20 Photo. Unwmk.

Inscribed: "Hari Sosial Ke III"

B126 SP57 10s + 10s ocher & blk 15 15
B127 SP57 15s + 15s dp cl & blk 15 15
B128 SP57 20s + 20s bl & blk 15 15
B129 SP57 50s + 25s bis brn & blk 15 15
B130 SP57 75s + 25s emer & blk 15 15
B131 SP57 3r + 50s red & blk 15 15
Set value 45 38

3rd Social Day, Dec. 20.

Type of 1960 Overprinted: "BENTJANA ALAM 1961"

Designs: 15s+10s, Coffee. 20s+15s, Tobacco. 75s+25s, Rubber plantation.

1961, Feb. 17 *Perf. 12x12½*

B132 A76 15s + 10s plum 15 15
B133 A76 20s + 15s ocher 15 15
B134 A76 75s + 25s scar 15 15
Set value 18 15

The surtax was for flood relief.

1961, Dec. 20 *Perf. 12½x13½*

4th Social Day: 75s+25s, Mangosteen. 3r+1r, Rambutan.

B135 SP58 20s + 10s bl, yel & red 15 15
B136 SP58 75s + 25s gray, grn & dp claret 15 15
B137 SP58 3r + 1r grn, yel & red 30 15
Set value 47 25

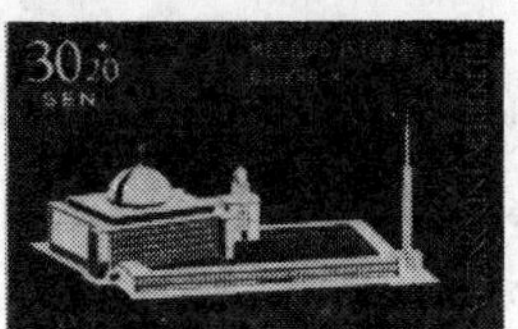
Istiqlal Mosque, Djakarta — SP59

Designs: 40s+20s, 3r+1r, Different view of mosque.

1962, Feb. 22 *Perf. 12½x12*

B138 SP59 30s + 20s Prus grn & yel 15 15
B139 SP59 40s + 20s dk red & yel 15 15
B140 SP59 1.50r + 50s brn & yel 15 15
B141 SP59 3r + 1r grn & yel 16 15
Set value 40 27

Issued for the benefit of the new Istiqlal Mosque.

National Monument, Djakarta — SP60

Design: 1.50r+50s, 6r+1.50r, Aerial view of monument.

1962, May 20 Photo. *Perf. 12x12½*

B142 SP60 1r + 50s org brn & blk 15 15
B143 SP60 1.50r + 50s ol grn & ultra 15 15
B144 SP60 3r + 1r lil rose & dk grn 15 15
B145 SP60 6r + 1.50r vio bl & red 15 15
Set value 27 27

Vanda Tricolor SP61

Orchids: 1.50r+50s, Phalaenopsis amabilis (vert.). 3fr+1fr, Dendrobium phalaenopsis (vert.). 6fr+1.50fr, Paphiopedilum praestans.

Perf. 13½x12½, 12½x13½

1962, Dec. 20 Unwmk.

Orchids in Natural Colors

B146 SP61 1r + 50s ultra & yel 15 15
B147 SP61 1.50r + 50s grnsh bl & ver 15 15
B148 SP61 3r + 1r dp bl & ocher 15 15
B149 SP61 6r + 1.50r org & dl vio 15 15
Set value 28 22

Issued for the 5th Social Day.

West Irian Monument, Djakarta — SP62

1963, Feb. 15 *Perf. 12½x13½*

B150 SP62 1r + 50s rose red & blk 15 15
B151 SP62 1.50r + 50s mag & dk brn 15 15

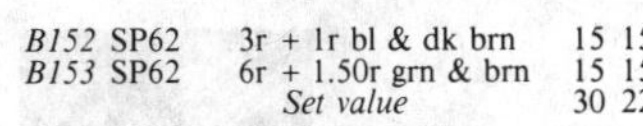
B152 SP62 3r + 1r bl & dk brn 15 15
B153 SP62 6r + 1.50r grn & brn 15 15
Set value 30 22

The surtax was for the construction of the West Irian Monument in Djakarta.

Erupting Volcano SP63

1963, June 29 Photo. *Perf. 13½x13*

B154 SP63 4r + 2r rose red 15 15
B155 SP63 6r + 3r grnsh bl 15 15
Set value 17 19

The surtax was for victims of national natural disasters.

Papilio Blumei, Celebes SP64

Malaysian Fantails SP65

Butterflies: 4r+1r, Charaxes Dehaani, Java. 6r+1.50r, Graphium, West Irian. 12r+3r, Troides Amphrysus, Sumatra.

1963, Dec. 20 *Perf. 12x12½*

B156 SP64 1.75r + 50s multi 15 15
B157 SP64 4r + 1r multi 15 15
B158 SP64 6r + 1.50r multi 15 15
B159 SP64 12r + 3r multi 15 15
Set value 25 22

Issued for the 6th Social Day.

Perf. 12½x13½

1965, Jan. 25 Photo. Unwmk.

Birds: 6r+1.50r, Zebra doves. 12r+3r, Black drongos. 20r+5r, Black-naped orioles. 30r+7.50r, Javanese sparrows.

B160 SP65 4r + 1r dl yel, lil & blk 15 15
B161 SP65 6r + 1.50 grn, blk & pink 15 15
B162 SP65 12r + 3r ol & blk 15 15
B163 SP65 20r + 5r gray, yel & red 15 15
B164 SP65 30r + 7.50r car rose, sl bl & blk 15 15
Set value 35 32

Issued for the 7th Social Day.

Type of Regular Issue, 1964, Inscribed Vertically "Conefo"

1965 *Perf. 12½x12*

B165 A98 1r + 1r org red & brn 15 15
B166 A98 1.25r + 1.25r org red & brn 15 15
B167 A98 1.75r + 1.75r org, red & brn blk 15 15
B168 A98 2r + 2r org red & sl grn 15 15
B169 A98 2.50r + 2.50r org red & red brn 15 15
B170 A98 4r + 3.50r org red & dp bl 15 15
B171 A98 6r + 4r org red & emer 15 15
B172 A98 10r + 5r org red & yel grn 15 15
B173 A98 12r + 5.50r org red & org 15 15
B174 A98 15r + 7.50r org red & bl grn 15 15
B175 A98 20r + 10r org red & dk gray 15 15
B176 A98 25r + 10r org red & pur 15 15
B177 A98 40r + 15r ver & plum 15 15
B178 A98 50r + 15r org red & dp vio 15 15
B179 A98 100r + 25r org red & dk ol gray 15 15
Set value 50 50

Conference of New Emerging Forces.

Makara Mask and Magic Rays — SP66

1965, July 17 ***Perf. 12***

B180 SP66 20r + 10r red & dk bl 15 15
B181 SP66 30r + 15r bl & dk red 15 15
Set value 15 15

Issued to publicize the fight against cancer.

Family and Produce — SP67

State Principles: 20r+10r, Humanitarianism; clasped hands, globe, flags and chain. 25r+10r, Nationalism; map of Indonesia and tree. 40r+15r, Democracy; conference and bull's head. 50r+15r, Belief in God; houses of worship and star.

1965, Aug. 17 **Photo.** ***Perf. 12½***

B182 SP67 10r + 5r fawn, yel & blk 15 15
B183 SP67 20r + 10r dp yel, red & blk 15 15
B184 SP67 25r + 10r rose red, red, grn & blk 15 15
B185 SP67 40r + 15r bl, red & blk 15 15
B186 SP67 50r + 15r lil, yel & blk 15 15
Set value 25 25

Samudra Beach Hotel and Pres. Sukarno — SP68

Designs: 25r+10r, 80r+20r, Ambarrukmo Palace Hotel and Pres. Sukarno.

1965, Dec. 1 **Photo.** ***Perf. 12½***

B187 SP68 10r + 5r dk bl & lt bl grn 15 15
B188 SP68 25r + 10r vio blk & yel grn 15 15
B189 SP68 40r + 15r dk brn & vio bl 15 15
B190 SP68 80r + 20r dk pur & org 15 15
Set value 24 24

Issued for tourist publicity.

Gloriosa — SP69

Flowers: 40r+15r, Magaguabush. 80r+20r, Balsam. 100r+25r, Crape myrtle.

1965, Dec. 20 **Photo.** ***Perf. 12***
Flowers in Natural Colors

B191 SP69 30r + 10r dp bl 15 15
B192 SP69 40r + 15r dp bl 15 15
B193 SP69 80r + 20r dp bl 15 15
B194 SP69 100r + 25r dp bl 15 15
Set value 27 22

Dated "1966"

Flowers: 10s+5s, Senna. 20s+5s, Crested barleria. 30s+10s, Scarlet ixora. 40s+10s, Rose of China (hibiscus).

1966, Feb. 10
Flowers in Natural Colors

B195 SP69 10s + 5s Prus bl 15 15
B196 SP69 20s + 5s grn 15 15
B197 SP69 30s + 10s grn 15 15
B198 SP69 40s + 10s Prus bl 15 15
Set value 22 22

Nos. B191-B198 issued for the 8th Social Day, Dec. 20, 1965. An imperf. souvenir sheet contains one No. B198. Size: 58x78mm.

Type of 1965 Inscribed: "BENTJANA ALAM / NASIONAL 1966"

Flowers: 15s+5s, Gloriosa. 25s+5s, Magaguabush. 30s+10s, Balsam. 80s+20s, Crape myrtle.

1966, May 2
Flowers in Natural Colors

B199 SP69 15s + 5s blue 15 15
B200 SP69 25s + 5s dk bl 15 15
B201 SP69 30s + 10s dk bl 15 15
B202 SP69 80s + 20s lt bl 15 15
Set value 30 28

The surtax was for victims of national natural disasters.

Reticulated Python — SP70

Reptiles: 3r+50s, Bloodsucker. 4r+75s, Salt-water crocodile. 6r+1r, Hawksbill turtle (incorrectly inscribed *chelonia mydas*, "green turtle").

1966, Dec. 20 **Photo.** ***Perf. 12½x12***

B203 SP70 2r + 25s multi 15 15
B204 SP70 3r + 50s multi 15 15
B205 SP70 4r + 75s multi 15 15
B206 SP70 6r + 1r multi 15 15
Set value 28 28

Flooded Village — SP71

Buddha & Stupa, Borobudur Temple — SP72

Designs: 2.50r+25s, Landslide. 4r+40s, Fire destroying village. 5r+50s, Erupting volcano.

1967, Dec. 20 **Photo.** ***Perf. 12½***

B207 SP71 1.25r + 10s dl vio bl & yel 15 15
B208 SP71 2.50r + 25s dl vio bl & yel 15 15
B209 SP71 4r + 40s dp org & blk 15 15
B210 SP71 5r + 50s dp org & blk 15 15
a. Souv. sheet of 2, #B209-B210 14.00 12.00
Set value 35 35

Surtax for victims of natl. natural disasters.

1968, Mar. 1 **Photo.** ***Perf. 12½***

Designs: No. B211, Musicians. No. B212, Sudhana and Princess Manohara. No. B213, Procession with elephant and horses.

B211 SP72 2.50r + 25s brt grn & gray ol 15 15
B212 SP72 2.50r + 25s brt grn & gray ol 15 15
B213 SP72 2.50r + 25s brt grn & gray ol 15 15
a. Souv. sheet of 3, #B211-B213 11.00 10.00
b. Strip of 3, #B211-B213 30 30
B214 SP72 7.50r + 75s org & gray ol 15 15
Set value 40 40

The surtax was to help save Borobudur Temple in Central Java, c. 800 A.D.

Nos. B211-B213 were printed se-tenant in same sheet. Continuous design shows a frieze from Borobudur.

Scout with Pickax — SP73

Designs: 10r+1r, Bugler. 30r+3r, Scouts singing around campfire (horiz.).

1968, June 1 **Photo.** ***Perf. 12½***
Size: 28½x44½mm

B215 SP73 5r + 50 dp org & brn 15 15
B216 SP73 10r + 1r brn & gray ol 20 15

Size: 68x28½mm

B217 SP73 30r + 3r ol gray & grn 45 42

Surtax for Wirakarya Scout Camp.

Woman with Flower SP74

1969, Apr. 21 ***Perf. 13½x12½***

B218 SP74 20r + 2r emer, red & yel 40 20

Emancipation of Indonesian women.

Noble Voluta — SP75

Sea shells: 7.50r+50s, Common hairy triton. 10r+1r, Spider conch. 15r+1.50r, Murex ternispina.

1969, Dec. 20 **Photo.** ***Perf. 12½***

B219 SP75 5r + 50s multi 15 15
B220 SP75 7.50r + 50s multi 15 15
B221 SP75 10r + 1r multi 15 15
B222 SP75 15r + 1.50r multi 18 15
Set value 42 34

Issued for the 12th Social Day, Dec. 20.

Chrysocoris Javanus SP76

Fight Against Cancer SP77

Insects: 15r+1.50r, Dragonfly. 20r+2r, Carpenter bee.

1970, Dec. 21 **Photo.** ***Perf. 12½***

B223 SP76 7.50r + 50c multi *1.25* 15
B224 SP76 15r + 1.50r multi *3.25* 15
B225 SP76 20r + 2r multi *4.00* 15
Set value 15

The 13th Social Day, Dec. 20.

1983, July 1 **Photo.** ***Perf. 12½***

Patient receiving radiation treatment, Jakarta Hospital.

B226 SP77 55r + 20r multi 15 15
B227 SP77 75r + 25r multi 15 15
Set value 24 15

Children's Day SP78

Children's Drawings. Surtax was for Children's Palace building fund.

1984, June 17 **Photo.** ***Perf. 13½x13***

B228 SP78 75r + 25r multi 15 15
B229 SP78 110r + 25r multi 18 15
B230 SP78 175r + 25r multi 25 15
B231 SP78 275r + 25r multi 40 20
a. Souv. sheet of 2, #B230-B231 80 40
b. Souv. sheet of 4 + 2 labels 1.60 80
Set value 50

AUSIPEX '84. No. B231b for FILACENTO '84, Netherlands, Sept. 6-9.

Yayasan Cancer Medical Assoc., 10th Anniv. — SP79

1987, May 12 **Photo.** ***Perf. 12½***

B232 SP79 350r +25r dark ultra & yel 50 25

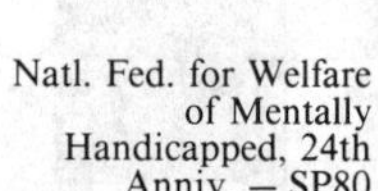

Natl. Fed. for Welfare of Mentally Handicapped, 24th Anniv. — SP80

1991, June 1 **Photo.** ***Perf. 12½***

B233 SP80 200r +25r multi 28 15

SPECIAL DELIVERY STAMPS

Garuda SD1

Perf. 13½x12½
1967 Unwmk. Photo.
E1 SD1 10r lt ultra & dl pur 16 15
E2 SD1 15r org & dl pur 40 20
Set value 27

Inscribed "1968"
1968
E3 SD1 10r lt ultra & dl pur 15 15
E4 SD1 15r org & dl pur 16 15
E5 SD1 20r yel & dl pur 18 16
E6 SD1 30r brt grn & dl pur 25 25
E7 SD1 40r lil & dl pur 35 35
Nos. E3-E7 (5) 1.09 1.06

Same Inscribed "1969"
1969
E8 SD1 20r yel & dl pur 25 15
E9 SD1 30r brt grn & dl pur 35 20
E10 SD1 40r lil & dl pur 42 25

POSTAGE DUE STAMPS

Netherlands Indies Nos. J57 to J59 Surcharged in Black
BAJAR
2½
sen
PORTO

1950 Wmk. 228 *Perf. 14½x14*
J60 D7 2½s on 50c yel 38 25
J61 D7 5s on 100c ap grn 75 65
J62 D7 10s on 75c aqua 1.00 75

D8

Wmk. 228
1951-52 Litho. *Perf. 12½*
J63 D8 2½s vermilion 15 15
J64 D8 5s vermilion 15 15
J65 D8 10s vermilion 15 15
J66 D8 20s bl ('52) 16 15
J67 D8 25s ol bis ('52) 65 50
J68 D8 50s vermilion 6.50 4.25
J69 D8 1r citron 6.50 3.75
Nos. J63-J69 (7) 14.26 9.10

1953-55 Unwmk.
J70 D8 15s lt mag ('55) 15 15
J71 D8 30s red brn 15 15
J72 D8 40s green 15 15
Set value 38 29

1958-61 *Perf. 13½x12½*
J73 D8 10s orange 15 15
J74 D8 15s org ('59) 15 15
J74A D8 20s org ('61) 15 15
J75 D8 25s org 15 15
J76 D8 30s org ('60) 15 15
J77 D8 50s orange 1.40 38
J78 D8 100s org ('60) 65 15
Set value 2.50 75

1962-65 *Perf. 13½x12½*
J79 D8 50s lt bluish grn 15 15
J80 D8 100s bister 15 15
J81 D8 250s blue 15 15
J82 D8 500s dl yel 15 15
J83 D8 750s pale lil 15 15
J84 D8 1000s salmon 15 15
J85 D8 50r red ('65) 15 15
J86 D8 100r mar ('65) 15 15
Set value 45 45

"1966" — D9

1966-67 Unwmk. Photo.
J91 D9 5s dl grn & dl yel 15 15
J92 D9 10s red & lt bl 15 15
J93 D9 20s dk bl & pink 15 15
J94 D9 30s brn & rose 15 15
J95 D9 40s plum & bis 15 15
J96 D9 50s ol grn & pale lil 15 15
J97 D9 100s dk red & yel grn 15 15
J98 D9 200s brt grn & pink ('67) 15 15
J99 D9 500s yel & lt bl ('67) 15 15
J100 D9 1000s rose lil & yel ('67) 22 15
Set value 80 60

Dated "1967"
1967
J101 D9 50s ol grn & pale lil 15 15
J102 D9 100s dk red & yel grn 15 15
J103 D9 200s brt grn & pink 15 15
J104 D9 500s yel & lt bl 15 15
J105 D9 1000s rose lil & yel 25 15
J106 D9 15r org & gray 20 16
J107 D9 25r lil & cit 35 25
Set value 1.15 80

Similar stamps inscribed "Bajar" or "Bayar", year date and "Sumbangan Ongkos Tjetak" or ". . . Cetak" are revenues.

Dated "1973" or "1974"
Inscribed "BAYAR PORTO"
1973-74
J108 D9 25r lil & cit 1.00
J109 D9 65r ol grn & bis ('74) 65 65
J110 D9 125r lil & pale pink ('74) 1.20 1.20

Dated "1975"
Inscribed "BAYAR PORTO"
1975 Photo. *Perf. 13½x12½*
J111 D9 25r lil & cit 25 25

"1976" — D10

1976
J112 D10 125r lil & pale pur 40 40

Dated "1977"
1977
J113 D10 100r dp vio & pale pink 40 40
J114 D10 200r brt bl & lt lil 80 80
J115 D10 300r choc & lt sal 1.25 1.25
J116 D10 400r brt grn & tan 1.50 1.50
J117 D10 500r red & tan 2.00 2.00
Nos. J113-J117 (5) 5.95 5.95

See Nos. J138, J139, J142.

Nos. 706, 709, 712-713, 716, 718 Surcharged in Red

BAYAR PORTO

1978 Photo. *Perf. 12½x12*
J118 A110 25r on 1r 15
J119 A110 50r on 2r 20
J120 A110 100r on 4r 60
J121 A110 200r on 5r 1.20
J122 A110 300r on 10r 1.60
J123 A110 400r on 15r 2.25
Nos. J118-J123 (6) 6.00

Surcharged in Black
J124 A110 25r on 1r 15
J125 A110 50r on 2r 20
J126 A110 100r on 4r 60
J127 A110 200r on 5r 1.20
J128 A110 300r on 10r 1.50
J129 A110 400r on 15r 2.00
Nos. J124-J129 (6) 5.65

40 1978
Nos. 710, 717 Surcharged
BAYAR PORTO

1978 Photo. *Perf. 12½x12*
J130 A110 40r on 2.50r 16
J131 A110 40r on 12r 16
J132 A110 65r on 2.50r 25
J133 A110 65r on 12r 25
J134 A110 125r on 2.50r 60
J135 A110 125r on 12r 60
J136 A110 150r on 2.50r 70
J137 A110 150r on 12r 70
Nos. J130-J137 (8) 3.42

Type of 1976 Dated "1979"
1979 *Perf. 13½x12½*
J138 D10 25r lil & cit 22 15

Type of 1976 Dated "1980" and

D11

1980 Photo. *Perf. 13½x12½*
J139 D10 25r dk lil & beige 15 15
J140 D11 50r multi 20 15
J141 D11 75r rose lake & rose 30 16
J142 D10 125r rose lil & lt pink 30 25
Set value 55

Type of 1980 Dated "1981"
Perf. 13½x13, 13½x12½ (#J149, J157-J160)
1981-83 Photo.
J144 D11 25r brt vio & pale yel grn 15 15
J145 D11 50r sl grn & lt vio 20 15
J146 D11 75r rose vio & pink 30 15
J147 D11 125r pur & yel grn 50 25
Dated "1982"
J148 D11 125r dp rose lil & pink 50 25
J149 D11 125r dp rose & lil pink 16 15
J150 D11 200r dp vio & lt bl 25 15
J151 D11 300r dk grn & cit 40 20
J152 D11 400r ol grn & brn ol 50 25
J153 D11 500r sep & beige 65 32
Dated "1988"
J157 D11 1000r dp vio & gray 36 18
J158 D11 2000r red & dp rose lil 72 36
J159 D11 3000r brn & dl org 1.10 55
J160 D11 5000r grn & bl grn 1.80 90
Nos. J144-J160 (13) 7.43 3.86

RIOUW ARCHIPELAGO

100 Sen = 1 Rupiah
(1 rupiah = 1 Malayan dollar)

Indonesia Nos. 371-386 Overprinted in Black

a

RIAU
b

Overprint "a"
1954 Unwmk. *Perf. 12½*
1 A52 5s car rose 14.00 20.00
2 A52 7½s green 50 50
3 A52 10s blue 12.00 15.00
4 A52 15s purple 50 80
5 A52 20s rose red 65 90
6 A52 25s dp grn 40.00 35.00
Overprint "b"
7 A53 30s red org 40 60
8 A53 35s purple 40 60
9 A53 40s dl grn 40 60
10 A53 45s dp cl 60 80
11 A53 50s brown 100.00 65.00
12 A54 60s dk brn 40 60
13 A54 70s gray 1.00 80
14 A54 75s ultra 1.10 1.40
15 A54 80s claret 80 1.10
16 A54 90s gray grn 80 1.40

Netherlands Indies Nos. 325-330 Overprinted Type "a" in Black
17 A46 1r purple 6.00 3.00
18 A46 2r ol grn 1.00 3.00
19 A46 3r red vio 1.50 2.25
20 A46 5r dk brn 1.50 2.25
21 A46 10r gray 2.25 3.75
22 A46 25r org brn 2.25 3.75
Nos. 1-22 (22) 188.05 163.10

Indonesia Nos. 424-428, 450 and 430 Overprinted Type "b" or RIAU

1957-64 Photo. *Perf. 12½x13½*
23 A63 (b) 5s dp ultra 20 30
24 A63 10s yel brn 3.50 50
25 A63 (b) 10s yel brn 16 22
26 A63 (b) 15s rose vio ('64) 60 1.10
27 A63 (b) 20s dl grn ('60) 16 22
28 A63 (b) 25s dp cl 16 22
29 A63 (b) 30s orange 16 22
30 A63 50s brown 3.50 4.25
31 A63 (b) 50s brown 16 20

The "b" overprint measures 12mm in this set. No. 428 also exists with this overprint.

Sukarno Type of Indonesia Overprinted Type "a"
1960 *Perf. 12½x12*
32 A55 1.25r dp org 15 45
33 A55 1.50r brown 15 45
34 A55 2.50r rose brn 22 65
35 A55 4r ap grn 22 65
36 A55 6r rose lil 30 90
37 A55 15r yellow 30 90
38 A55 20r sepia 42 1.50
39 A55 40r yel grn 75 2.50
40 A55 50r violet 90 2.50
Nos. 23-40 (18) 12.01 17.73

INHAMBANE

LOCATION — East Africa.
GOVT. — A district of Mozambique, former Portuguese colony.
AREA — 21,000 sq. mi. (approx.)
POP. — 248,000 (approx.)
CAPITAL — Inhambane

1000 Reis = 1 Milreis
100 Centavos = 1 Escudo (1913)

Stamps of Mozambique Overprinted
CENTENARIO
DE
S. ANTONIO
—
Inhambane
MDCCCXCV

On 1886 Issue
1895, July 1 Unwmk. *Perf. 12½*
Without Gum
1 A2 5r black 20.00 19.00
2 A2 10r green 19.00 15.00
a. Perf. 13½ 55.00 45.00
3 A2 20r rose 35.00 27.50
4 A2 25r lilac
5 A2 40r chocolate 35.00 27.50
6 A2 50r blue 35.00 27.50
a. Perf. 13½ 30.00 30.00
7 A2 100r yel brn
8 A2 200r gray vio 50.00 45.00
9 A2 300r orange 50.00 45.00
On 1894 Issue
Perf. 11½
10 A3 50r lt bl 30.00 24.00
a. Perf. 12½ 40.00 30.00
11 A3 75r rose 40.00 27.50
12 A3 80r yel grn 35.00 27.50
13 A3 100r brn, *buff* 67.50 45.00
14 A3 150r car, *rose* 40.00 35.00

700th anniversary of the birth of St. Anthony of Padua.
The status of Nos. 4 and 7 is questionable. No. 3 is always discolored.

King Carlos — A1

1903, Jan. 1 Typo. *Perf. 11½*
Name and Value in Black except 500r

15	A1	2½r gray	30	28
16	A1	5r orange	30	28
17	A1	10r lt grn	50	28
18	A1	15r gray grn	70	55
19	A1	20r gray vio	85	55
20	A1	25r carmine	70	55
21	A1	50r brown	1.75	1.25
22	A1	65r dl bl	10.00	6.00
23	A1	75r lilac	1.75	1.40
a.		Imperf.		
24	A1	100r dk bl, *bl*	1.75	1.25
25	A1	115r org brn, *pink*	3.75	3.75
26	A1	130r brn, *straw*	3.75	3.75
27	A1	200r red vio, *pink*	3.75	3.75
28	A1	400r dl bl, *straw*	7.50	6.00
29	A1	500r blk & red, *bl*	11.00	7.50
30	A1	700r gray blk, *straw*	10.00	11.00
		Nos. 15-30 (16)	58.35	48.14

No. 22 Surcharged in Black

50 RÉIS

1905

31	A1	50r on 65r dull blue	2.75	2.00

Nos. 15-21, 23-30 Overprinted in Carmine or Green

1911

32	A1	2½r gray	20	20
33	A1	5r orange	20	20
34	A1	10r lt grn	20	20
35	A1	15r gray grn	24	24
36	A1	20r gray vio	24	24
37	A1	25r car (G)	70	50
38	A1	50r brown	35	28
39	A1	75r lilac	38	28
40	A1	100r dk bl, *bl*	38	28
41	A1	115r org brn, *pink*	70	55
42	A1	130r brn, *straw*	70	55
43	A1	200r red vio, *pink*	85	60
44	A1	400r dl bl, *straw*	1.25	1.00
45	A1	500r blk & red, *bl*	1.25	1.00
46	A1	700r gray blk, *straw*	1.75	1.50
		Nos. 32-46 (15)	9.39	7.62

No. 31 Overprinted in Red

1914

47	A1	50r on 65r dull blue	1.75	1.25
a.		"Republica" inverted		

Vasco da Gama Issue of Various Portuguese Colonies

Common Design Types CD20-CD27 Surcharged

REPUBLICA
INHAMBANE
¼ C.

1913

On Stamps of Macao

48	CD20	¼c on ½a bl grn	1.00	1.00
49	CD21	½c on 1a red	1.00	1.00
50	CD22	1c on 2a red vio	1.00	1.00
a.		Inverted surcharge	4.50	4.50
51	CD23	2½c on 4a yel grn	1.00	1.00
52	CD24	5c on 8a dk bl	1.00	1.00
53	CD25	7½c on 12a vio brn	1.90	1.90
54	CD26	10c on 16a bis brn	1.40	1.40
55	CD27	15c on 24a bis	1.40	1.40
		Nos. 48-55 (8)	9.70	9.70

On Stamps of Portuguese Africa

56	CD20	¼c on 2½r bl grn	80	85
57	CD21	½c on 5r red	80	85
58	CD22	1c on 10r red vio	80	85
59	CD23	2½c on 25r yel grn	80	85
60	CD24	5c on 50r dk bl	80	85
61	CD25	7½c on 75r vio brn	1.75	1.75
62	CD26	10c on 100r bis brn	1.00	1.00
63	CD27	15c on 150r bis	1.00	1.00
		Nos. 56-63 (8)	7.75	8.00

On Stamps of Timor

64	CD20	¼c on ½a bl grn	1.00	1.00
a.		Inverted surch.	10.00	10.00
65	CD21	½c on 1a red	1.00	1.00
66	CD22	1c on 2a red vio	1.00	1.00
67	CD23	2½c on 4a yel grn	1.00	1.00
68	CD24	5c on 8a dk bl	1.00	1.00
69	CD25	7½c on 12a vio brn	1.90	1.90
70	CD26	10c on 16a bis brn	1.40	1.40
71	CD27	15c on 24a bis	1.40	1.40
		Nos. 64-71 (8)	9.70	9.70
		Nos. 48-71 (24)	27.15	27.40

Ceres — A2

1914 Typo. *Perf. 15x14*
Name and Value in Black

72	A2	¼c ol brn	48	40
73	A2	½c black	48	40
a.		Imperf.		
74	A2	1c bl grn	48	45
75	A2	1½c lil brn	48	45
76	A2	2c carmine	48	45
77	A2	2½c lt vio	24	20
78	A2	5c dp bl	60	45
79	A2	7½c yel brn	1.00	70
80	A2	8c slate	1.00	70
81	A2	10c org brn	85	60
82	A2	15c plum	1.25	1.00
83	A2	20c yel grn	1.25	1.00
84	A2	30c brn, *grn*	1.75	1.75
85	A2	40c brn, *pink*	1.75	1.75
86	A2	50c org, *sal*	2.75	1.90
87	A2	1e grn, *bl*	2.75	1.90
		Nos. 72-87 (16)	17.59	14.10

No. 31 Overprinted in Carmine

REPUBLICA

1915 *Perf. 11½*

88	A1	50c on 65r dull blue	3.50	3.00

Nos. 15-21, 23-30 Overprinted Locally

REPUBLICA

1917

89	A1	2½r gray	8.75	6.00
90	A1	5r orange	8.75	6.00
91	A1	15r gray grn	1.75	1.25
92	A1	20r gray vio	1.10	95
93	A1	50r brown	1.40	1.00
94	A1	75r lilac	1.40	1.00
95	A1	100r bl, *bl*	1.40	1.00
96	A1	115r org brn, *pink*	1.40	1.00
97	A1	130r brn, *straw*	1.75	1.25
98	A1	200r red vio, *pink*	1.75	1.25
99	A1	400r dl bl, *straw*	1.90	1.90
100	A1	500r blk & red, *bl*	2.00	1.90
101	A1	700r gray blk, *straw*	8.50	6.00
		Nos. 89-101 (13)	41.85	30.50

The stamps of Inhambane have been superseded by those of Mozambique.

ININI

LOCATION — In northeastern South America, adjoining French Guiana.
GOVT. — Former territory of French Guiana.
AREA — 30,301 sq. mi.
POP. — 5,024 (1946).
CAPITAL — St. Elie.

Inini was separated from French Guiana in 1930 and reunited with it in when the colony became an integral part of the Republic, acquiring the same status as the departments of Metropolitan France, under a law effective Jan. 1, 1947.

100 Centimes = 1 Franc

Used values are for canceled-to-order copies.

Stamps of French Guiana, 1929-40, Overprinted in Black, Red or Blue:

TERRITOIRE DE L'ININI
Nos. 1-9

Territoire de l'ININI
Nos. 10-26

Territoire de l'ININI
Nos. 27-40

1932-40 Unwmk. *Perf. 13½x14*

1	A16	1c gray lil & grnsh bl	15	15
2	A16	2c dk red & bl grn	15	15
3	A16	3c gray lil & grnsh bl ('40)	15	15
4	A16	4c ol brn & red vio ('38)	15	15
5	A16	5c Prus bl & red org	15	15
6	A16	10c mag & brn	15	15
7	A16	15c yel brn & red org	15	15
8	A16	20c dk bl & ol grn	15	15
9	A16	25c dk red & dk brn	22	22

Perf. 14x13½

10	A17	30c dl grn & lt grn	60	60
11	A17	30c grn & brn ('40)	15	15
12	A17	35c Prus grn & ol ('38)	28	28
13	A17	40c red brn & ol gray	15	15
14	A17	45c ol grn & lt grn ('40)	15	15
15	A17	50c dk bl & ol gray	15	15
16	A17	55c vio bl & car ('38)	1.20	1.20
17	A17	60c sal & grn ('40)	15	15
18	A17	65c sal & grn ('38)	40	40
19	A17	70c ind & sl bl ('40)	15	15
20	A17	75c ind & sl bl (Bl)	70	70
21	A17	80c blk & vio bl (R) ('38)	28	28
22	A17	90c dk red & ver	40	40
23	A17	90c red vio & brn ('39)	15	15
24	A17	1fr lt vio & brn	5.00	4.50
25	A17	1fr car & lt red ('38)	28	28
26	A17	1fr blk & vio bl ('40)	15	15
27	A18	1.25fr blk brn & bl grn ('33)	28	28
28	A18	1.25fr rose & lt red ('39)	25	25
29	A18	1.40fr ol brn & red vio ('40)	32	32
30	A18	1.50fr dk bl & lt bl	22	22
31	A18	1.60fr ol brn & bl grn ('40)	32	32
32	A18	1.75fr brn, red & blk brn ('33)	7.50	6.50
33	A18	1.75fr vio bl ('38)	40	40
34	A18	2fr dk grn & rose red	40	40
35	A18	2.25fr vio bl ('39)	35	35
36	A18	2.50fr cop red & brn ('40)	35	35
37	A18	3fr brn red & red vio	40	40
38	A18	5fr dl vio & yel grn	40	40
39	A18	10fr ol gray & dp ultra (R)	40	40
40	A18	20fr ind & ver	60	60
		Nos. 1-40 (40)	23.95	22.45

Colonial Arts Exhibition Issue
Souvenir Sheet
Common Design Type

1937 *Imperf.*

41	CD75	3fr red brown	5.00	5.00

New York World's Fair Issue
Common Design Type

1939, May 10 Engr. *Perf. 12½x12*

42	CD82	1.25fr car lake	1.60	1.60
43	CD82	2.25fr ultra	1.60	1.60

French Guiana Nos. 170A-170B Overprinted "ININI" in Green or Red

1941 Engr. *Perf. 12½x12*

44	A21a	1fr deep lilac	40	
45	A21a	2.50fr blue (R)	40	

Nos. 44-45 were issued by the Vichy government, and were not placed on sale in the territory. This is also true of four stamps of French Guiana types A16-A18 without "RF" and overprinted "TERRITOIRE DE L'ININI," released in 1944.

SEMI-POSTAL STAMPS

Common Design Type

Photo.; Name & Value Typo. in Black
1939, July 5 Unwmk. *Perf. 13*

B1	CD83	45c + 25c grn	5.50	5.50
B2	CD83	70c + 30c brn	5.50	5.50
B3	CD83	90c + 35c red org	5.50	5.50
B4	CD83	1.25fr + 1fr rose pink	5.50	5.50
B5	CD83	2.25fr + 2fr blue	5.50	5.50
		Nos. B1-B5 (5)	27.50	27.50

Common Design Type and French Guiana Nos. B9 and B11 Overprinted "ININI" in Blue or Red

1941 Photo. *Perf. 13½*

B6	SP1	1fr + 1fr red (B)	80	
B7	CD86	1.50fr + 3fr mar	60	
B8	SP2	2.50fr + 1fr bl (R)	65	

Nos. B6-B8 and Nos. 44-45 surcharged "OEUVRES COLONIALES" and surtax (including change of denomination of the 2.50fr to 50c) were issued in 1944 by the Vichy government but not placed on sale in Inini.

AIR POST SEMI-POSTAL STAMPS

Stamps of French Guiana type V6 and Cameroun type V10 inscribed "Inini" were issued in 1942 by the Vichy Government, but were not placed on sale in the territory.

POSTAGE DUE STAMPS

Postage Due Stamps of French Guiana, 1929, Overprinted in Black

TERRITOIRE DE L'ININI

1932, Apr. 7 Unwmk. *Perf. 13½x14*

J1	D3	5c indigo & Prus bl	15	15
J2	D3	10c bis brn & Prus grn	15	15
J3	D3	20c grn & rose red	15	15
J4	D3	30c ol brn & rose red	15	15
J5	D3	50c vio & ol brn	45	45
J6	D3	60c brn red & ol brn	45	45

Overprinted in Black or Red

TERRITOIRE DE L'ININI

J7	D4	1fr dp bl & org brn	55	55
J8	D4	2fr brn red & bluish grn	70	70
J9	D4	3fr vio & blk (R)	2.50	2.50
J10	D4	3fr vio & blk	1.00	1.00
		Nos. J1-J10 (10)	6.25	6.25

IONIAN ISLANDS

LOCATION — Seven Islands, of which six-Corfu, Paxos, Lefkas (Santa Maura), Cephalonia, Ithaca and Zante-are in the Ionian Sea west of Greece, and a seventh-Cerigo (Kithyra)-is in the Mediterranean south of Greece
GOVT. — Integral part of Kingdom of Greece
AREA — 752 sq. miles
POP. — 231,510 (1938)

These islands were occupied by Italian forces in 1941. The Italians withdrew in 1943 and German forces continued the occupation, using current Greek stamps without overprinting, except for Zante.

For stamps of the Italian occupation of Corfu, see Corfu.

Issued under Italian Occupation

> Values of stamps overprinted by letterpress in pairs are for unsevered pairs. Single stamps, unused, sell for one third the price of a pair; used, one half the price of a pair.
> Handstamped overprints were also applied to pairs, with "isola" instead of "isole".

Issue for Cephalonia and Ithaca

Stamps of Greece, 1937-38, Overprinted in Pairs Vertically, Reading Down, or Horizontally (H) in Black

ITALIA

Occupazione Militare Italiana isole Cefalonia e Itaca

Perf. 12½x12, 13½x12, 12x13½

1941 Wmk. 252, Unwmk.

N1	A69	5 l brn red & bl	2.00	2.00
N2	A70	10 l bl & red brn (#413) (H)	2.00	2.00
N3	A71	20 l blk & grn (H)	2.00	2.00
a.		Overprint inverted	65.00	
N4	A72	40 l grn & blk	2.00	2.00
N5	A73	50 l brn & blk	3.00	3.00
N6	A74	80 l ind & yel brn (H)	3.00	3.00
a.		Overprint inverted	75.00	80.00
N7	A67	1d grn (H)	17.50	10.00
N8	A84	1.50d grn (H)	20.00	20.00
a.		Overprint inverted	75.00	75.00
N9	A75	2d ultra	2.50	2.00
N10	A76	5d red	4.50	3.75
N11	A77	6d ol brn	5.75	4.50
N12	A78	7d dk brn	5.75	5.75
N13	A67	8d dp bl (H)	21.00	21.00
N14	A79	10d red brn	12.00	9.00
N15	A80	15d green	18.00	18.00
N16	A81	25d dk bl (H)	45.00	30.00
a.		Overprint inverted	85.00	77.50
N17	A84	30d org brn (H)	85.00	75.00
a.		Overprint inverted	125.00	125.00
		Nos. N1-N17 (17)	251.00	213.00

A variety with wrong font "C" in "Cephalonia" is found in several positions in each sheet of all denominations except those overprinted on single stamps. It sells for above three times the price of a normal pair.

Several other minor spelling errors in the overprint occur on several denominations in one of the printings.

Forgeries exist of many of the higher valued stamps and minor varieties of Nos. N1-N17, NC1-NC11 and NRA1-NRA5.

Overprint Reading Up

N1a	A69	5 l	4.00	4.00
N4a	A72	40 l	2.50	2.50
N5a	A73	50 l	5.75	5.75
N9a	A75	2d	22.50	15.00
N10a	A76	5d	25.00	27.50
N11a	A77	6d	5.75	5.75
N12a	A78	7d	7.50	7.50
N14a	A79	10d	13.00	13.00
N15a	A80	15d	22.50	22.50
		Nos. N1a-N15a (9)	108.50	103.50

General Issue

Stamps of Italy, 1929, Overprinted in Red or Black

ISOLE JONIE

1941 Wmk. 140 *Perf. 14*

N18	A90	5c ol brn (R)	22	38
N19	A92	10c dk brn (R)	22	38
N20	A91	20c rose red	22	38
N21	A94	25c dp grn	22	38
N22	A95	30c ol brn (R)	22	38
a.		"SOLE" for "ISOLE"	25.00	
N23	A95	50c pur (R)	22	38
N24	A94	75c rose red	22	38
N25	A94	1.25 l dp bl (R)	22	38
		Nos. N18-N25 (8)	1.76	3.04

The stamps overprinted "Isole Jonie" were issued for all the Ionian Islands except Cerigo which used regular postage stamps of Greece.

ISSUED UNDER GERMAN OCCUPATION

Zante Issue

Nos. N21 and N23 with Additional Handstamped Overprint in Black

1943 Wmk. 140 *Perf. 14*

N26	A94	25c deep grn	22.50	*45.00*
a.		Carmine overprint	40.00	*90.00*
N27	A95	50c purple	22.50	*45.00*
a.		Carmine overprint	40.00	*90.00*

No. N19 with this overprint is a proof. Value, black $40; carmine $85.

Nos. N26-N27 were in use 8 days, then were succeeded by stamps of Greece.

Forgeries of Nos. N26-N27, NC13 and their cancellations are plentiful.

> Greek stamps with Italian overprints for the islands of Cerigo (Kithyra), Paxos and Lefkas (Santa Maura) are fraudulent.

OCCUPATION AIR POST STAMPS

Issued under Italian Occupation

Issue for Cephalonia and Ithaca

Stamps of Greece Overprinted in Pairs Vertically, Reading Down, or Horizontally (H) in Black Like Nos. N1-N17

Perf. 13x12½, 12½x13

1941 Unwmk.

On Greece Nos. C22, C23, C25 and C27 to C30

Grayish Paper

NC1	AP16	1d dp red	12.00	12.00
NC1A	AP17	2d dl bl	42.50	
NC2	AP19	7d bl vio (H)	72.50	90.00
NC3	AP21	25d rose (H)	80.00	75.00
a.		Overprint inverted	190.00	190.00
NC4	AP22	30d dk grn	50.00	50.00
a.		Overprint reading up	55.00	55.00
b.		Horizontal overprint on single stamp	*125.00*	*125.00*
c.		As "b," inverted	*250.00*	
NC5	AP23	50d vio (H)	*325.00*	325.00
NC6	AP24	100d brown	185.00	175.00
a.		Overprint reading up	200.00	225.00

No. NC1A is known only with overprint reading up.

On Greece Nos. C31-C34

Reengraved; White Paper

NC7	AP16	1d red	5.00	4.50
NC8	AP17	2d gray bl	5.00	4.50
a.		Overprint reading up	5.00	4.50
b.		Horiz. ovpt. on pair	*90.00*	*90.00*
c.		Horizontal overprint on single stamp		
NC9	AP18	5d vio (H)	9.00	7.50
a.		Overprint inverted		
b.		Vert. ovpt. on single stamp, up or down		
NC10	AP19	7d dp ultra (H)	15.00	11.00
a.		Overprint inverted	50.00	50.00

Overprinted Horizontally on No. C36

Rouletted 13½

NC11	D3	50 l vio brn	30.00	30.00
a.		Pair, one without ovpt.	*75.00*	
b.		On No. C36a	*165.00*	

See footnote following No. N17.

General Issue

Italy No. C13 Overprinted in Red Like Nos. N18-N25

1941 Wmk. 140 *Perf. 14*

NC12	AP3	50c olive brn	22	38
a.		"SOLE" for "ISOLE"	18.50	

Used in all the Ionian Islands except Cerigo which used air post stamps of Greece.

No. NC12 with additional overprint "BOLLO" is a revenue stamp.

Issued under German Occupation

ZANTE ISSUE

No. NC12 with Additional Handstamped Overprint in Black Like Nos. N26-N27

1943 Wmk. 140 *Perf. 14*

NC13	AP3	50c olive brn	30.00	*60.00*
a.		"SOLE" for "ISOLE"	*300.00*	
b.		Carmine overprint	135.00	*250.00*

See note after No. N27.

OCCUPATION POSTAGE DUE STAMPS

General Issue

Postage Due Stamps of Italy, 1934, Overprinted in Black Like Nos. N18-N25

1941 Wmk. 140 *Perf. 14*

NJ1	D6	10c blue	22	75
NJ2	D6	20c rose red	22	75
NJ3	D6	30c red orange	22	75
NJ4	D7	1 l red orange	22	75

See footnote after No. N25.

OCCUPATION POSTAL TAX STAMPS

Issued under Italian Occupation

Issue for Cephalonia and Ithaca

Greece No. RA56 with Additional Overprint on Horizontal Pair in Black Like Nos. N1-N17

1941 Unwmk. *Serrate Roulette 13½*

NRA1	D3	10 l car (Bl+Bk)	2.50	2.50
a.		Blue overprint double	27.50	22.50
b.		Inverted overprint	37.50	37.50

Same Overprint Reading Down on Vertical Pairs of Nos. RA61-RA63

Perf. 13½x12

NRA2	PT7	10 l brt rose, *pale rose*	5.00	5.00
a.		Overprint on horiz. pair	40.00	40.00
b.		Horizontal overprint on single stamp	*100.00*	
c.		Overprint reading up	11.00	11.00
NRA3	PT7	50 l gray grn, *pale grn*	1.50	1.40
a.		Overprint reading up	5.00	5.00
b.		Ovpt. on horiz. pair	15.00	15.00
c.		Horizontal overprint on single stamp	*300.00*	
NRA4	PT7	1d dl bl, *lt bl*	12.00	12.00
a.		Overprint reading up	20.00	20.00

Same Overprint Reading Down on Vertical Pair of No. RA65

NRA5	PT7	50 l gray grn, *pale grn*	150.00	
a.		Overprint reading up	200.00	

Nos. NRA5 and NRA5a were not placed in use on any compulsory day.

See footnote following No. N17.

IRAN

(Persia)

LOCATION — Western Asia, bordering on the Persian Gulf and the Gulf of Oman

GOVT. — Islamic republic

AREA — 636,000 sq. mi.

POP. — 43,830,000 (est. 1984)

CAPITAL — Tehran

20 Shahis (or Chahis) = 1 Kran

10 Krans = 1 Toman

100 Centimes = 1 Franc = 1 Kran (1881)

100 Dinars = 1 Rial (1933)

100 Rials = 1 Pahlavi

> **Catalogue values for unused stamps in this country are for Never Hinged items, beginning with Scott 1054 in the regular postage section, Scott B36 in the semi-postal section, Scott C83 in the airpost section, Scott O72 in the officials section, Scott Q36 in the parcel post section, and Scott RA4 in the postal tax section.**

> Values of early stamps vary according to condition. Quotations for Nos. 1-20, 33-40 are for fine copies. Very fine to superb specimens sell at much higher prices, and inferior or poor copies sell at reduced prices, depending on the condition of the individual specimen.
> Cracked gum on unused stamps does not detract from the value.

Many issues have handstamped surcharges. As usual with such surcharges there are numerous inverted, double and similar varieties.

Watermarks

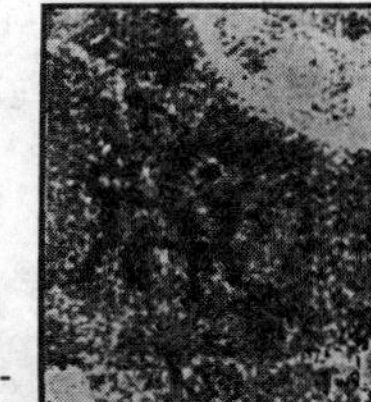

Wmk. 161- Lion

Wmk. 306- Arms of Iran

Wmk. 316- Persian Inscription

Wmk. 349 - Persian Inscription and Crown in Circle

Illustration of Wmk. 349 shown sideways. Circles in Wmk. 349 are 95mm apart.

Wmk. 353- Persian Inscription and Coat of Arms in Circle

Wmk. 381 - "Islamic Republic of Iran" in Persian (Partial Illustration)

Coat of Arms
A1 A2

Design A2 has value numeral below lion.

1868 Unwmk. Typo. *Imperf.*

1	A1 1s dull violet	65.00	
2	A1 2s green	50.00	
3	A1 4s greenish bl	50.00	
4	A1 8s red	45.00	

Values for used copies of Nos. 1-4 are omitted as postmarked copies are not known. Used copies with pen cancellation exist. Many shades exist. Printed in blocks of 4. Forgeries exist.

Printed on Both Sides

1a	A1 1s	650.	
2a	A1 2s	700.	
3a	A1 4s	1,500.	
4a	A1 8s	900.	

Vertically Rouletted 10 ½ on 1 or 2 Sides

1875 Thick Wove Paper

11	A2 1s black	90.00	50.00
a.	Imperf., pair	*400.00*	*400.00*
12	A2 2s blue	82.50	47.50
a.	Tete beche pair	*10,000.*	
b.	Imperf., pair	*575.00*	*575.00*
13	A2 4s vermilion	110.00	42.50
a.	Imperf., pair	*625.00*	*625.00*
b.	4s bright red, thin paper, imperf.	525.00	
14	A2 8s yellow green	70.00	40.00
a.	Tete beche pair	*10,000.*	*3,000.*
b.	Imperf., pair	*125.00*	*125.00*

Four varieties of each.

Nos. 11 to 14 also exist pin-perforated and perce en scie.

No. 11a has spacing of 2-3mm; No. 15, 2mm or less. Nos. 11-14 were printed in horizontal strips of four, with 3-5mm spacing.

See Nos. 15-20, 33-40.

Medium to Thin White or Grayish Paper

1876 *Imperf.*

15	A2 1s gray black	15.00	15.00
a.	Printed on both sides	500.00	
b.	Laid paper	500.00	
16	A2 2s gray blue	150.00	*250.00*
a.	Printed on both sides	600.00	
17	A2 2s black	500.00	
a.	Tete beche pair	*3,000.*	
18	A2 4s vermilion	125.00	45.00
a.	Printed on both sides	450.00	325.00
19	A2 1k rose	165.00	50.00
a.	Printed on both sides		475.00
b.	Laid paper	450.00	150.00
c.	1k yellow (error)	*5,000.*	
d.	Tete beche pair		*12,000.*
20	A2 4k yellow	500.00	70.00
a.	Printed on both sides		*500.00*
b.	Laid paper	600.00	110.00
c.	Tete beche pair	*7,000.*	

Nos. 15-16, 18-20 were printed in blocks of 4, with spacing of 2mm or less, No. 15 also in vertical strip of 4. No. 17 in a vertical strip of 4.

The 2s black and the vertical-strip printing on the 1s are on medium to thick grayish wove paper. Both printings of the 1s are found in black as well as gray black. Forgeries exist.

Official reprints of the 1s and 4s are on thick coarse white paper without gum.

Unofficial Reprints:
1875 and 1876 issues.

The reprints of the 1s and 1k stamps are readily told; the pearls of the circle are heavier, the borders of the circles containing the Persian numeral of value are wider and the figure "1" below the lion is always Roman.

The reprints of the 2s have the outer line of the frame at the left and at the bottom broken and on some specimens entirely missing.

A distinguishing mark by which to tell the 4s and 4k stamps is the frame, the outer line of which is of the same thickness as the inner line, while on the originals the inner line is very thin and the outer line thick; another feature of most of the reprints is a gash in the lower part of the circle below the figure "4."

In the reprints of the 8s stamps the small scroll nearest to the circles with Persian numerals at the bottom of the stamp touches the frame below it; the inner and outer lines of the frame are of equal thickness, while in the originals the outer line is much heavier than the inner one.

All reprints are found canceled to order.

Shah Nasr-ed-Din — A3

Perf. 10 ½, 11, 12, 13, and Compounds

1876 Typo.

27	A3 1s lilac & blk	15.00	4.50
28	A3 2s green & blk	15.00	6.50
29	A3 5s rose & blk	35.00	4.00
30	A3 10s blue & blk	40.00	8.00

Bisects of the 5s (surcharged "2 ½") and the 10s (surcharged "5 Shahi" or "5 Shahy") exist. Experts variously attribute them to local shortages, a postmaster's inventiveness or fraudulence.

1878 Typo. *Imperf.*

33	A2 1k car rose	150.00	87.50
34	A2 1k red, *yellow*	*1,000.*	70.00
a.	Tete beche pair		*4,000.*
35	A2 4k ultramarine	140.00	50.00
36	A2 5k gold	*1,000.*	175.00
37	A2 5k violet	250.00	150.00
38	A2 5k red bronze	*2,000.*	350.00
39	A2 5k vio bronze	*2,000.*	475.00
40	A2 1t bronze, *bl*	*15,000.*	*3,000.*

Four varieties of each except for 4k which has 3.

Nos. 33 and 34 are printed from redrawn cliches. They have wide colorless circles around the corner numerals.

The reprints of the 1 kran and 1 toman are printed from the same die as the reprints of the 1 shahi and 1 kran of the 1876 issue; on these and on the reprints of the 5 krans the outer frame is of irregular thickness. The impression of the reprints of this issue is better than that of the originals.

Nasr-ed-Din
A6

Sun
A7

Perf. 10 ½, 12, 13, and Compounds

1879

41	A6 1k brown & blk	40.00	3.00
a.	Imperf., pair	*275.00*	
b.	Inverted center		
42	A6 5k blue & blk	50.00	3.00
a.	Imperf., pair	*400.00*	80.00
b.	Inverted center		

1880

43	A6 1s red & black	40.00	3.00
44	A6 2s yel & black	50.00	5.00
45	A6 5s green & blk	50.00	2.00
46	A6 10s vio & black	150.00	15.00

Forgeries and official reprints exist.

The 2, 5 and 10s of this issue and the 1 and 5kr of the 1879 issue have been reprinted from a new die which resembles the 5 shahi envelope. The aigrette is shorter than on the original stamps and touches the circle above it.

Imperf., Pair

43a	A6 1s	240.00	
44a	A6 2s	400.00	*300.00*
46a	A6 10s		

1881 Litho. *Perf. 12, 13, 12x13*

47	A7 5c dull violet	15.00	5.00
48	A7 10c rose	20.00	5.00
49	A7 25c green	400.00	50.00

1882 Engr., Border Litho.

50	A7 5c blue vio & vio	15.00	3.00
51	A7 10c dp pink & rose	15.00	3.00
52	A7 25c deep grn & grn	95.00	10.00

Counterfeits of Nos. 50-52, 53, 53a are plentiful and have been used to create forgeries of Nos. 66, 66a, 70 and 70a. They usually have a strong, complete inner frameline at right. On genuine stamps that line is weak or missing.

A8

Shah Nasr-ed-Din
A9 A10

A11

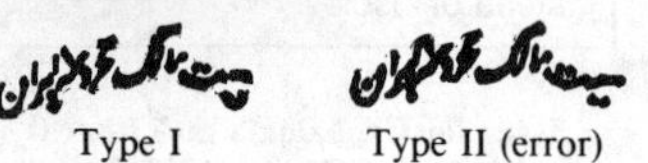

Type I Type II (error)

Type I- Three dots at right end of scroll.
Type II- Two dots at right end of scroll.

1882-84 Engr.

53	A8 5s green, type I	10.00	1.50
a.	5s green, type II	20.00	7.50
54	A9 10s buff, org & blk	20.00	3.50
55	A10 50c buff, org & blk	35.00	20.00
56	A10 50c gray & blk ('84)	35.00	10.00
57	A10 1fr blue & black	35.00	6.00
58	A10 5fr rose red & blk	40.00	5.00
59	A11 10fr buff, red & blk	35.00	7.50

Crude forgeries of Nos. 58-59 exist. Halves of the 10s, 50c and 1fr surcharged with Farsi characters in red or black are frauds. The 50c and 1fr surcharged with a large "5" surrounded by rays are also frauds.

For overprints and surcharges see #66-72.

A12

A13

1885-86 Typo.

60	A12 1c green	10.00	1.00
61	A12 2c rose	10.00	1.00
62	A12 5c dull blue	15.00	50
a.	5c violet blue	90.00	30.00
63	A13 10c brown	7.50	1.00
64	A13 1k slate	7.50	2.00
65	A13 5k dull vio ('86)	60.00	7.00

Nos. 53, 54, 56 and 58 Surcharged in Black:

OFFICIEL 6 (a) OFFICIEL 12 (b)
OFFICIEL 18 (c) OFFICIEL 1T (d)
OFFICIEL 3 (e) OFFICIEL 8 (f)

1885

66	(a) 6c on 5s grn, type I	30.00	4.00
a.	6c on 5s green, type II	55.00	20.00
67	(b) 12c on 50c gray & blk	70.00	15.00
68	(c) 18c on 10s buff, org & black	70.00	15.00
69	(d) 1t on 5fr rose red & black	60.00	15.00

1887

70	(e) 3c on 5s grn, type I	25.00	7.00
a.	3c on 5s green, type II	55.00	20.00
71	(a) 6c on 10s buff, org & black	25.00	7.50
72	(f) 8c on 50c gray & blk	75.00	20.00

The word "OFFICIEL" indicated that the surcharged stamps were officially authorized.

Surcharges on the same basic stamps of values other than those listed are believed to be bogus.

Counterfeits of Nos. 66-72 abound.

A14

A15

1889 Typo. *Perf. 11, 13½, 11x13½*

No.	Type	Description	Unused	Used
73	A14	1c pale rose	30	15
74	A14	2c pale blue	30	15
75	A14	5c lilac	30	15
76	A14	7c brown	4.00	40
77	A15	10c black	75	15
78	A15	1k red orange	1.25	15
79	A15	2k rose	7.00	1.50
80	A15	5k green	10.00	2.00
		Nos. 73-80 (8)	23.90	4.65

All values exist imperforate. Canceled to order copies of No. 76 abound.

For surcharges see Nos. 622-625.

A16

A17

1891 *Perf. 10½, 11½*

No.	Type	Description	Unused	Used
81	A16	1c black	1.00	20
82	A16	2c brown	1.00	20
83	A16	5c deep blue	50	15
84	A16	7c gray	45.00	7.00
85	A16	10c rose	1.65	20
86	A16	14c orange	2.00	20
87	A17	1k green	17.50	2.00
88	A17	2k orange	75.00	7.00
89	A17	5k ocher yellow	4.50	4.50
		Nos. 81-89 (9)	148.15	21.45

For surcharges see Nos. 626-629.

A18

Shah Nasr-ed-Din — A19

1894 *Perf. 12½*

No.	Type	Description	Unused	Used
90	A18	1c lilac	50	15
91	A18	2c blue green	50	15
92	A18	5c ultramarine	50	15
93	A18	8c brown	50	15
		Perf. 11½x11		
94	A19	10c orange	1.00	75
95	A19	16c rose	6.00	10.00
96	A19	1k red & yellow	3.00	75
97	A19	2k brn org & pale bl	3.00	1.00
98	A19	5k violet & silver	4.00	1.50
99	A19	10k red & gold	12.00	10.00
100	A19	50k green & gold	10.00	7.50
		Nos. 90-100 (11)	41.00	32.10

Canceled to order copies sell for one-third of listed values.

Reprints exist. They are hard to distinguish from the originals. Value, set $5.

See Nos. 104-112, 136-144. For overprints see Nos. 120-128, 152-167, 173-181. For surcharges see Nos. 101-103, 168, 206, 211.

Nos. 93, 98 With Violet or Magenta Surcharge

1897 *Perf. 12½, 11½x11*

No.	Type	Description	Unused	Used
101	A18	5c on 8c brown (V)	1.50	50
102	A19	1k on 5k vio & sil (V)	2.50	2.00
103	A19	2k on 5k vio & sil (M)	3.50	2.50

Lion Type of 1894 and

Shah Muzaffar-ed-Din A22

1898 Typo. *Perf. 12½*

No.	Type	Description	Unused	Used
104	A18	1c gray	45	15
105	A18	2c pale brown	45	15
106	A18	3c dull violet	50	20
107	A18	4c vermilion	50	20
108	A18	5c yellow	35	15
109	A18	8c orange	2.00	1.00
110	A18	10c light blue	2.00	20
111	A18	12c rose	1.00	1.00
112	A18	16c green	3.00	1.00
113	A22	1k ultramarine	4.00	50
114	A22	2k pink	3.00	75
115	A22	3k yellow	2.00	75
116	A22	4k gray	2.00	1.50
117	A22	5k emerald	2.00	3.00
118	A22	10k orange	7.00	7.00
119	A22	50k bright vio	15.00	15.00
		Nos. 104-119 (16)	45.25	32.55

Unauthorized reprints of Nos. 104-119 were made from original cliches. Paper shows a vertical mesh. These abound unused and canceled to order.

See Nos. 145-151. For overprints see Nos. 129-135, 182-188. For surcharges see Nos. 169, 171, 207, 209, 215.

Reprints have been used to make counterfeits of Nos. 120-135, 152-167.

Stamps of 1898 Handstamped in Violet:

1899

No.	Type	Description	Unused	Used
120	(a)	1c gray	2.00	2.00
121	(b)	2c pale brown	2.00	2.00
122	(b)	3c dull violet	3.00	2.00
123	(c)	4c vermilion	4.00	1.00
124	(c)	5c yellow	3.00	1.00
125	(d)	8c orange	3.00	1.50
126	(d)	10c light blue	3.00	1.50
127	(d)	12c rose	2.00	1.00
128	(d)	16c green	4.00	1.50
129	(e)	1k ultramarine	4.50	2.00
130	(f)	2k pink	8.00	6.00
131	(f)	3k yellow	12.50	7.50
132	(g)	4k gray	12.50	7.50
133	(g)	5k emerald	12.50	12.50
134	(h)	10k orange	30.00	30.00
135	(h)	50k brt violet	30.00	30.00
		Nos. 120-135 (16)	136.00	109.00

The handstamped control marks on Nos. 120-135 exist sideways, inverted and double. Counterfeits are plentiful.

Types of 1894-98

1899 Typo. *Perf. 12½*

No.	Type	Description	Unused	Used
136	A18	1c gray, *green*	1.00	15
137	A18	2c brown, *green*	1.00	15
138	A18	3c violet, *green*	1.75	15
139	A18	4c red, *green*	4.00	15
140	A18	5c yellow, *green*	1.00	15
141	A18	8c orange, *green*	5.00	60
142	A18	10c pale blue, *grn*	3.50	15
143	A18	12c lake, *green*	3.50	30
144	A18	16c green, *green*	7.50	60
145	A22	1k red	7.50	50
146	A22	2k deep green	12.50	1.20
147	A22	3k lilac brown	14.00	3.00
148	A22	4k orange red	14.00	3.00
149	A22	5k gray brown	22.50	3.00
150	A22	10k deep blue	60.00	10.00
151	A22	50k brown	45.00	7.00
		Nos. 136-151 (16)	203.75	30.10

Canceled to order copies abound.

Unauthorized reprints of Nos. 136-151 were made from original cliches. Paper is chalky and has white gum. The design can be seen through the back of the reprints.

For surcharges and overprints see Nos. 171, 173-188, 206-207, 209, 211, 215.

Nos. 104-111 Handstamped in Violet

(Struck once on every two stamps.)

1900

No.	Type	Description	Unused	Used
152	A18	1c gray	20.00	10.00
153	A18	2c pale brown	20.00	10.00
154	A18	3c dull violet	30.00	10.00
155	A18	4c vermilion	40.00	10.00
156	A18	5c yellow	10.00	5.00
158	A18	10c light blue	50.00	35.00
159	A18	12c rose	30.00	15.00

Pairs of Nos. 152-159 sell for three times the price of singles.

This control mark, in genuine state, was not applied to the 8c orange (Nos. 109, 125).

Same Overprint Handstamped on Nos. 120-127 in Violet

(Struck once on each block of four.)

No.	Type	Description	Unused	Used
160	A18	1c gray	40.00	10.00
163	A18	4c vermilion	40.00	25.00
164	A18	5c yellow	20.00	5.00
166	A18	10c light blue	30.00	20.00
167	A18	12c rose	20.00	15.00

Blocks of four of Nos. 160-167 sell for six times the price of singles.

Counterfeits exist of Nos. 152-167.

No. 93 Surcharged in Violet

1900

No.	Type	Description	Unused	Used
168	A18	5c on 8c brown	10.00	1.00

No. 145 Surcharged in Violet

12CH

1901

No.	Type	Description	Unused	Used
169	A22	12c on 1k red	20.00	4.00
a.		Blue surcharge	25.00	6.00

Counterfeits exist.

Some specialists state that No. 169 with black surcharge was made for collectors.

A23

1902 Violet Surcharge

No.	Type	Description	Unused	Used
171	A23	5k on 50k brown	50.00	50.00
a.		Blue surcharge	55.00	55.00

Counterfeits exist. See No. 207.

Nos. 136-151 Overprinted in Black

1902

No.	Type	Description	Unused	Used
173	A18	1c gray, *green*	3.00	2.50
174	A18	2c brown, *green*	3.00	2.50
175	A18	3c violet, *green*	4.00	2.50
176	A18	4c red, *green*	4.00	2.50

177 A18 5c yellow, *green* 3.00 1.50
178 A18 8c orange, *green* 5.00 5.00
179 A18 10c pale blue, *grn* 10.00 3.00
180 A18 12c lake, *green* 10.00 4.00
181 A18 16c green, *green* 10.00 10.00
182 A22 1k red 10.00 6.00
183 A22 2k deep green
188 A22 50k brown

Overprinted on No. 168

206 A18 5c on 8c brown 10.00 5.00

Overprinted on Nos. 171 and 171a

207 A23 5k on 50k brown 35.00 25.00
a. On #171a 40.00 35.00

Overprinted on Nos. 169 and 169a

209 A22 12c on 1k red 10.00 10.00
a. On #169a 15.00 10.00

Counterfeits of the overprint of Nos. 173-183, 188, 206-207, 209 are plentiful. Practically all examples with overprint sideways, inverted, double and double with one inverted are frauds.

Nos. 142 and 145 Surcharged in Violet

1902

211 A18 5c on 10c pale bl, *grn* 20.00 5.00
a. Blue surcharge 25.00 10.00
b. Black surcharge 35.00 10.00
c. Rose surcharge 35.00 10.00
d. Magenta surcharge 25.00 20.00
215 A22 5c on 1k red 25.00 15.00
a. Blue surcharge 25.00 15.00
b. Black surcharge 25.00 15.00
c. Rose surcharge 25.00 15.00

Initials of Victor Castaigne, Postmaster of Meshed — A24

1902 Typo. *Imperf.*

222 A24 1c black 300.00 67.50
b. Inverted center *2,750. 1,750.*
223 A24 2c black 300.00 90.00
b. "2" in right upper corner *2,250. 1,750.*
c. Frame printed on both sides 475.00
224 A24 3c black 300.00 100.00
225 A24 5c violet 300.00 90.00
a. "5" in right upper corner 325.00 225.00
b. Frame printed on both sides *1,650. 1,000.*
c. Inverted center
226 A24 5c black 190.00 52.50
a. Persian "5" in lower left corner
b. Inverted center
227 A24 12c dull blue 700.00 300.00
228 A24 1k rose 8,500. 1,000.

The design of No. 228 differs slightly from the illustration.

Pin-perforated

234 A24 12c dull blue

The post office at Meshed having exhausted its stock of stamps, the postmaster issued the above series provisionally. The center of the design is the seal of the postmaster who also wrote his initials upon the upper part, using violet ink for the 1k and red for the others.

Unauthorized reprints, including pinperforated examples of Nos. 222-226, and forgeries exist.

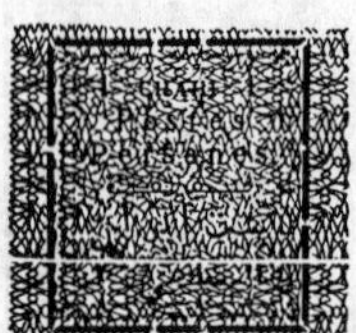

A25

TWO TYPES:
Type I - "CHAHI" or "KRANS" are in capital letters.
Type II - Only "C" of "Chahi" or "K" of "Krans" is a capital.

The 3c and 5c sometimes have a tall narrow figure in the upper left corner. The 5c is also found with the cross at the upper left broken or missing. These varieties are known with many of the overprints that were applied to type A25.

Handstamp Overprinted in Black

1902 Typeset *Imperf.*

Type I

235 A25 1c gray & buff *75.00*
236 A25 2c brown & buff *75.00*
237 A25 3c green & buff *75.00*
238 A25 5c red & buff *75.00*
239 A25 12c ultra & buff *80.00*
Nos. 235-239 (5) 380.00

Counterfeits abound.

The 3c with violet overprint is believed not to have been regularly issued.

Handstamp Overprinted in Rose

1902 Type I

247 A25 1c gray & buff 3.00 50
a. With Persian numerals "2" 25.00
248 A25 2c brown & buff 8.00 75
249 A25 3c dp grn & buff 10.00 1.00
250 A25 5c red & buff 3.00 30
251 A25 10c ol yel & buff 8.00 50
252 A25 12c ultra & buff 12.00 1.50
253 A25 1k violet & bl 35.00 3.00
254 A25 2k ol grn & bl 45.00 7.00
256 A25 10k dk bl & bl 125.00 20.00
257 A25 50k red & blue 125.00 75.00

A 5k exists with both types of overprint. Status doubtful.

Nos. 247-257 and the 12c on brown paper and on blue paper with blue quadrille lines are known without overprint but are not believed to have been regularly issued in this condition.

The 1c to 10k, A25 type I, with violet overprint are believed not to have been regularly issued. Five denominations also exist with overprint in blue, black or green.

Type II

280 A25 1c gray & yellow 20.00 20.00
a. Tete beche pair
281 A25 2c brown & yel 40.00 40.00
282 A25 3c dk grn & yel 6.50
a. "Persans" 11.50 3.25
283 A25 5c red & yellow 20.00 3.00
a. Tete beche pair
284 A25 10c ol yel & yel 20.00 5.00
285 A25 12c blue & yel 20.00 8.00
290 A25 50k org red & bl

The same overprint in violet was applied to nine denominations of the Type II stamps, but these are believed not to have been regularly issued. The overprint also exists in blue, black and green.

Reprints, counterfeits, counterfeit overprints, with or without cancellations, are plentiful for Nos. 247-257, 280-290.

Five stamps of type A25, type II, in high denominations (10, 20, 25, 50 and 100 tomans), with "Postes 1319" lion overprint in blue, were used only on money orders, not for postage. They are usually numbered on the back in red, blue or black.

Handstamp Surcharged in Black

1902

Type I

308 A25 5k on 5k ocher & bl *50.00 25.00*

Counterfeits of No. 308 abound.

This surcharge in rose, violet, blue or green is considered bogus.

This surcharge on 50k orange red and blue, and on 5k ocher and blue, type II, is considered bogus.

Handstamp Overprinted Diagonally in Black

P. L.
TEHERAN

1902

Type I

315 A25 2c brown & buff 30.00 20.00
a. Rose overprint 30.00 20.00

Type II

316 A25 2c brown & yel 30.00 20.00
a. Rose overprint 30.00 20.00

"P. L." stands for "Poste Locale."
Counterfeits of Nos. 315-316 exist.

Some specialists believe that Type II stamps were not used officially for this overprint.

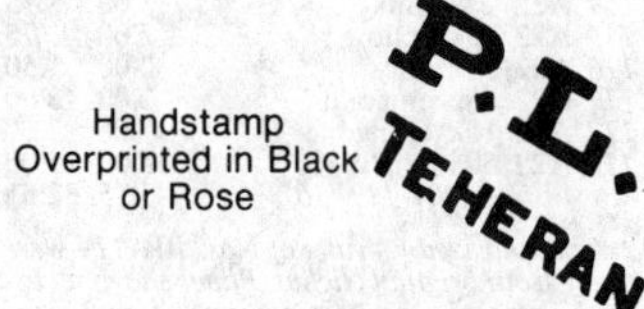

1902 Type II

317 A25 2c brn & yellow 20.00 20.00
318 A25 2c brown & yel (R) 20.00 20.00

Counterfeits of Nos. 317-318 exist.

1903

Type I

321 A25 1k violet & blue 15.00

Type II

336 A25 1c gray & yellow 10.00
337 A25 2c brown & yellow 10.00
338 A25 5c red & yellow 10.00
339 A25 10c olive yel & yel 10.00
340 A25 12c blue & yellow 15.00
Nos. 321-340 (6) 70.00

The overprint also exists in violet and black, but it is doubtful whether such items were regularly issued.

Forgeries of Nos. 321, 336-340 abound. Genuine unused examples are seldom found.

Arms of Persia A26

Shah Muzaffar-ed-Din A27

1903-04 Typo. *Perf. 12½*

351 A26 1c violet 50 15
352 A26 2c gray 50 15
353 A26 3c green 50 15
354 A26 5c rose 50 15
355 A26 10c yellow brn 50 15
356 A26 12c blue 60 15

Engr.

Perf. 11½x11

357 A27 1k violet 1.50 35
358 A27 2k ultramarine 1.50 35
359 A27 5k orange brn 2.50 60
360 A27 10k rose red 3.50 75
361 A27 20k orange ('04) 6.00 3.00
362 A27 30k green ('04) 15.00 5.00
363 A27 50k green 40.00 20.00
Nos. 351-363 (13) 73.10 30.95

No. 355 exists with blue diagonal surcharge "1 CHAHI"; its status is questioned.

See Nos. 428-433. For surcharges and overprints see Nos. 364-420, 446-447, 464-469, O8-OO28, P1.

No. 353 Surcharged in Violet or Blue

1903

364 A26 1c on 3c green (V) 10.00 5.00
365 A26 2c on 3c green (Bl) 10.00 8.50

A 2c surcharge on No. 354 exists, but its status is dubious.

No. 360 Surcharged in Blue

12CH

366 A27 12c on 10k rose red 10.00 2.00
a. Black surcharge 15.00 4.00
b. Violet surcharge 15.00 4.00

No. 363 Surcharged in Blue or Black

2 TOMANS

1903

368 A27 2t on 50k grn (Bl) 40.00 20.00
a. Rose surcharge 40.00 25.00
b. Black surcharge 50.00 30.00
370 A27 3t on 50k grn (Bk) 65.00 20.00
a. Violet surcharge 40.00 20.00
b. Rose surcharge 40.00 35.00

No. 363 Surcharged in Blue or Black

1904

372 A27 2t on 50k grn (Bl) 55.00 20.00
375 A27 3t on 50k grn (Bk) 65.00 20.00

The 2t on 50k also exists with surcharge in rose, violet, black and magenta; the 3t on 50k in rose, violet and blue. Values about the same unused; about 50 percent higher used.

No. 352 Overprinted in Violet

1904 *Perf. 12½*

393 A26 2c gray 10.00 5.00
a. Black overprint 11.50 5.00
b. Rose overprint 20.00 5.00

This overprint also exists in blue, violet blue, maroon and gray, but these were not regularly issued.

The 2c overprinted "Controle" in various types is said to be a revenue stamp.

Stamps of 1903 Surcharged in Black:

a

6
CHAHIS

b

c

9 CHAHIS

1904

400 A26(a) 3c on 5c rose 5.00 25
401 A26(b) 6c on 10c brown 10.00 25
402 A27(c) 9c on 1k violet 10.00 50

Stamps of 1903 Surcharged in Black, Magenta or Violet:

1905-06
404 A26 1c on 3c green ('06) 10.00 3.00
405 A27 1c on 1k violet 10.00 4.00
406 A27 2c on 5k orange brn 20.00 4.00
407 A26 1c on 3c grn (M) ('06) 5.00 1.00
408 A27 1c on 1k violet (M) 10.00 4.00
409 A27 2c on 5k org brn (V) 10.00 4.00
Nos. 404-409 (6) 65.00 20.00

Nos. 355 and 358 Surcharged in Violet **1 CHAI**

419 A26 1c on 10c brown 100.00 100.00
420 A27 2c on 2k ultra 125.00 125.00

Forgeries of Nos. 419-420 exist.

A28

Typeset; "Provisoire" Overprint Handstamped in Black

1906 ***Imperf.***
422 A28 1c violet 1.00 25
a. Irregular pin perf. or perf. 10½ 10.00 5.00
423 A28 2c gray 1.00 25
424 A28 3c green 1.00 25
425 A28 6c red 1.00 25
426 A28 10c brown 10.00 1.25
427 A28 13c blue 5.00 65
Nos. 422-427 (6) 19.00 2.90

Stamps of type A28 have a faint background pattern of tiny squares within squares, an ornamental frame and open rectangles for the value corners.

The 3c and 6c also exist perforated.

Nos. 422-427 are known without overprint but were probably not issued in that condition. Nearly all values are known with overprint inverted and double.

Forgeries are plentiful.

Lion Type of 1903 and

Shah Mohammed Ali
A29 A30

1907-09 **Typo.** ***Perf. 12½***
428 A26 1c vio, *blue* 30 15
429 A26 2c gray, *blue* 30 15
430 A26 3c green, *blue* 30 15
431 A26 6c rose, *blue* 30 15
432 A26 9c org, *blue* 30 15
433 A26 10c brown, *blue* 30 15

Engr.
Perf. 11, 11½
434 A29 13c dark blue 1.00 35
435 A29 1k red 1.00 35
436 A29 26c red brown 1.00 35
437 A29 2k deep grn 1.00 35
438 A29 3k pale blue 1.00 35
439 A29 4k brt yellow 60.00 10.00
440 A29 4k bister 3.00 50
441 A29 5k dark brown 3.00 50
442 A29 10k pink 3.00 1.00
443 A29 20k gray black 4.00 1.50
444 A29 30k dark violet 9.00 5.00
445 A30 50k gold, ver & black ('09) 25.00 10.00
Nos. 428-445 (18) 113.80 31.15

Frame of No. 445 lithographed. Nos. 434-444 were issued in 1908.

Forgeries of Nos. 428-445 exist.

Remainders canceled to order abound.

Nos. 428-429 Overprinted in Black

1909 ***Perf. 12½***
446 A26 1c violet, *blue* 35.00 15.00
447 A26 2c gray, *blue* 35.00 15.00

Counterfeits of Nos. 446-447 exist.

Coat of Arms — A31

1909 **Typo.** ***Perf. 12½x12***
448 A31 1c org & maroon 75 25
449 A31 2c vio & maroon 75 25
450 A31 3c yel grn & mar 75 25
451 A31 6c red & maroon 75 25
452 A31 9c gray & maroon 1.10 30
453 A31 10c red vio & mar 1.10 30
454 A31 13c dk blue & mar 2.25 45
455 A31 1k sil, vio & bis brown 10.00 60
456 A31 26c dk grn & mar 5.00 1.00
457 A31 2k sil, dk grn & bis brown 20.00 1.00
458 A31 3k sil, gray & bis brown 20.00 2.00
459 A31 4k sil, by & bis brn 25.00 3.00
460 A31 5k gold, brn & bis brown 22.50 4.00
461 A31 10k gold, org & bis brown 30.00 5.00
462 A31 20k gold, ol grn & bister brn 37.50 8.00
463 A31 30k gold, car & bis brown 57.50 10.00
Nos. 448-463 (16) 36.65

The unauthorized "reprints" of Nos. 448-463 abound. Originals have clean, bright colors, centers stand out clearly, and paper is much thinner. Nos. 460-463 originals have gleaming gold margins; reprint margins appear as blackish yellow. Centers of reprints of Nos. 448-454, 456 are brown. **Value for reprints, Nos. 448-463, $10.**

For surcharges and overprints see Nos. 541-549, 582-585, 588-594, 597, 601-606, 707-722, C1-C16, O31-O40.

Nos. 428-444, Imperf., Surcharged in Red or Black:

1910 **Blue Paper** ***Imperf.***
464 A26 1c on 1c violet 45.00 32.50
465 A26 1c on 2c gray 45.00 32.50
466 A26 1c on 3c green 45.00 32.50
467 A26 1c on 6c rose (Bk) 45.00 32.50
468 A26 1c on 9c orange 45.00 32.50
469 A26 1c on 10c brown 45.00 32.50

White Paper
470 A29 2c on 13c dp bl 52.50 37.50
471 A29 2c on 26c red brown (Bk) 52.50 37.50
472 A29 2c on 1k red (Bk) 52.50 37.50
473 A29 2c on 2k dp grn 52.50 37.50
474 A29 2c on 3k pale bl 52.50 37.50
475 A29 2c on 4k brt yel 52.50 37.50
476 A29 2c on 4k bister 52.50 37.50
477 A29 2c on 5k dk brn 52.50 37.50
478 A29 2c on 10k pink (Bk) 57.50 37.50
479 A29 2c on 20k gray blk 57.50 37.50
480 A29 2c on 30k dk vio 57.50 37.50
Nos. 464-480 (17) 862.50 607.50

Nos. 464-480 were prepared for use on newspapers, but nearly the entire printing was sold to stamp dealers. The issue is generally considered speculative. Counterfeit surcharges exist on trimmed stamps

Shah Ahmed — A32

Perf. 11½, 11½x11, 11½x12
1911-13 **Engr. center, Typo. frame**
481 A32 1c green & org 50 15
482 A32 2c red & sepia 50 15
483 A32 3c gray brn & grn 50 15
a. 3c bister brown & green 2.00 1.00
484 A32 5c brn & car ('13) 60 75
485 A32 6c gray & car 60 15
486 A32 6c grn & red brown ('13) 75 15
487 A32 9c yel brn & vio 1.00 15
488 A32 10c red & org brn 1.00 15
489 A32 12c grn & ultra ('13) 1.00 15
490 A32 13c violet & ultra 1.00 2.00
491 A32 1k ultra & car 2.00 15
492 A32 24c vio & grn ('13) 1.00 20
493 A32 26c ultra & green 2.00 7.00
494 A32 2k grn & red vio 5.00 50
495 A32 3k violet & blk 3.00 50
496 A32 4k ultramarine & gray ('13) 3.00 17.50
497 A32 5k red & ultra 5.00 1.00
498 A32 10k ol bis & cl 5.00 1.50
499 A32 20k vio brn & bis 5.00 2.00
500 A32 30k red & green 6.00 2.50
Nos. 481-500 (20) 37.80

Unauthorized "reprints" of Nos. 481-500 are ubiquitous. Perf. 11½ except 4k which is 11½x12. **Value, set of reprints, $5.**

The reprints include inverted centers for some denominations.

For surcharges and overprints see Nos. 501-540, 586-587, 595, 598, 600, 607-609, 630-634, 646-666.

Stamps of 1911 Overprinted in Black **Officiel**

1912
501 A32 1c grn & orange 3.00 75
502 A32 2c red & sepia 3.00 75
503 A32 3c gray brn & grn 3.00 75
504 A32 6c gray & carmine 3.00 75
505 A32 9c yel brn & vio 3.00 75
506 A32 10c red & org brn 3.00 75
507 A32 13c vio & ultra 25.00 5.00
508 A32 1k ultra & car 25.00 2.00
509 A32 26c ultra & green 50.00 10.00
510 A32 2k grn & red vio 30.00 1.00
511 A32 3k vio & black 40.00 1.00
512 A32 5k red & ultra 35.00 1.50
513 A32 10k ol bis & cl 65.00 3.50
514 A32 20k vio brn & bis 65.00 5.00
515 A32 30k red & green 65.00 10.00
Nos. 501-515 (15) 418.00 43.50

The "Officiel" overprint does not signify that the stamps were intended for use on official correspondence but that they were issued by authority. It was applied to the stocks in Persian post offices after a large quantity of stamps had been stolen during the Russian occupation of Tabriz.

The "Officiel" overprint has been counterfeited.

السلطان
محمد علی شاه قاجار

In 1912 this overprint, reading "Sultan Mohammed Ali Shah Kajar," was handstamped on outgoing mail in the Persian Kurdistan region occupied by the forces of the former Shah Mohammed Ali. It was applied after the stamps were on cover and is found on 8 of the Shah Ahmed stamps of 1911 (1c, 2c, 3c, 6c, 9c, 13c, 1k and 26c). Some specialists add the 10c. Forgeries are abundant.

Nos. 490 and 493 Surcharged:

a

b

1914
535 A32(a) 1c on 13c 10.00 50
536 A32(b) 3c on 26c 15.00 50

In 1914 a set of 19 stamps was prepared as a coronation issue. The 10 lower values each carry a different portrait; the 9 higher values show buildings and scenes. The same set printed with black centers was overprinted in red "SERVICE." The stamps were never placed in use, but were sold to stamp dealers in 1923.

Nos. 484 and 489 Surcharged in Black or Violet:

c

d

1915
537 A32(c) 1c on 5c brn & car 10.00 35
538 A32(c) 2c on 5c brn & carmine (V) 10.00 50
539 A32(c) 2c on 5c brn & car 40.00 15.00
540 A32(d) 6c on 12c green & ultramarine 15.00 1.00

Nos. 455, 454 Surcharged:

e f

1915 ***Perf. 12½x12***
541 A31(e) 5c on 1k multi 15.00 5.00
542 A31(f) 12c on 13c multi 18.00 5.00

Counterfeit surcharges on reprints abound.

Nos. 448-453, 455 Overprinted **۱۳۳۳**

1915
543 A31 1c org & maroon 10.00 2.00
544 A31 2c vio & maroon 10.00 2.00
545 A31 3c grn & maroon 6.00 2.00
546 A31 6c red & maroon 10.00 2.00
547 A31 9c gray & maroon 15.00 3.00
548 A31 10c red vio & mar 20.00 5.00
549 A31 1k sil, vio & bis brn 10.00 3.00
Nos. 543-549 (7) 81.00 19.00

This overprint ("1333") also exists on the 2k, 10k, 20k and 30k, but they were not issued.

Counterfeit overprints, usually on reprints, abound.

Imperial Crown
A33

King Darius, Farohar overhead
A34

Ruins of Persepolis — A35

Perf. 11, 11½ or Compound

1915 Wmk. 161 Engr., Typo.

No.	Type	Description	Unused	Used
560	A33	1c car & indigo	15	*2.00*
561	A33	2c bl & carmine	15	*2.00*
562	A33	3c dark green	15	*2.00*
a.		Inverted center	110.00	
564	A33	5c red	15	*2.50*
565	A33	6c olive grn & car	15	*2.00*
a.		Inverted center	80.00	
566	A33	9c yel brn & vio	15	*2.00*
567	A33	10c bl grn & yel brn	15	*2.00*
568	A33	12c ultramarine	15	*2.00*
569	A34	1k sil, yel brn & gray	65	*5.00*
570	A33	24c yel brn & dk brn	25	*5.00*
571	A34	2k silver, bl & rose	65	*5.00*
572	A34	3k sil, vio & brn	65	*5.00*
573	A34	5k sil, brn & green	65	*7.00*
574	A35	1t gold, pur & blk	65	*10.00*
575	A35	2t gold, grn & brn	1.00	*10.00*
576	A35	3t gold, cl & red brn	1.00	*10.00*
577	A35	5t gold, blue & ind	1.00	*10.00*
		Nos. 560-577 (17)	7.70	

Coronation of Shah Ahmed.

Nos. 560-568, 570 are engraved. Nos. 569, 571-573 are engraved except for silver margins. Nos. 574-577 have centers engraved, frames typographed.

The 3c and 6c with inverted centers are considered genuine errors. Unauthorized reprints exist of these varieties and of other denominations with inverted centers. **Values unused for Nos. 560-577 are for reprints.**

For surcharges and overprints see Nos. 610-616, 635-646, O41-O57, Q19-Q35.

Nos. 455, 461-463 Overprinted

1915 Unwmk. Typo. *Perf. 12½x12*

No.	Type	Description	Unused	Used
582	A31	1k sil, vio & bis brn	10.00	2.50
583	A31	10k multicolored	35.00	10.00
584	A31	20k multicolored	82.50	10.00
585	A31	30k multicolored	40.00	10.00

Counterfeits exist of the overprints on Nos. 582-585 and 588, and of the surcharges on Nos. 586-587.

No. 491 Surcharged

24
Chahis

1917 *Perf. 11½*

No.	Type	Description	Unused	Used
586	A32	12c on 1k multi	*350.00*	*100.00*
587	A32	24c on 1k multi	*200.00*	*125.00*

Issued during the Turkish occupation of Kermanshah.

No. 448 Overprinted "1335" in Persian Numerals

1917 *Perf. 12½x12*

No.	Type	Description	Unused	Used
588	A31	1c org & maroon	80.00	40.00

Overprint on No. 588 is similar to date in "k" and "l" surcharges.

Nos. 449, 452-453, 456 Surcharged:

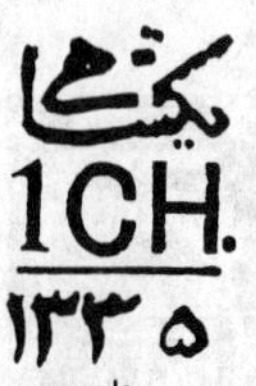

k

l

1917

No.	Type	Description	Unused	Used
589	A31(k)	1c on 2c	10.00	1.00
590	A31(k)	1c on 9c	10.00	1.00
591	A31(k)	1c on 10c	10.00	1.00
592	A31(l)	3c on 9c	10.00	1.00
593	A31(l)	3c on 10c	10.00	1.00
594	A31(l)	3c on 26c	10.00	1.00

Same Surcharge on No. 488

No.	Type	Description	Unused	Used
595	A32(k)	1c on 10c	15.00	50
596	A32(l)	3c on 10c	15.00	50

Nos. 454 & 491 Surcharged Type "e"

No.	Type	Description	Unused	Used
597	A31	5c on 13c	15.00	3.50
598	A32	5c on 1k	15.00	60

Counterfeit surcharges on "canceled" reprints of Nos. 449, 452-454, 456 abound.

No. 489 Surcharged

No.	Type	Description	Unused	Used
600	A32	6c on 12c grn & ultra	15.00	50

No. 457 Overprinted

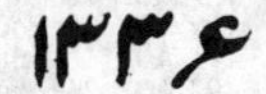

1918

No.	Type	Description	Unused	Used
601	A31	2k multi	30.00	5.00

Nos. 459-460 Surcharged:

1918

No.	Type	Description	Unused	Used
602	A31	24c on 4k multi	35.00	7.00
603	A31	10k on 5k multi	35.00	10.00

The surcharges of Nos. 602-603 have been counterfeited.

Nos. 457-463 Overprinted

1918

No.	Type	Description	Unused	Used
603A	A31	2k multicolored	70.00	8.00
604	A31	3k multicolored	30.00	10.00
604A	A31	4k multicolored	40.00	10.00
604B	A31	5k multicolored	80.00	10.00
605	A31	10k multicolored	70.00	8.00
605A	A31	20k multicolored	300.00	80.00
606	A31	30k multicolored	100.00	15.00
		Nos. 603A-606 (7)	690.00	141.00

The overprint has been counterfeited on all values.

Nos. 489, 488 and 491 Surcharged:

No.	Type	Description	Unused	Used
607	A32(m)	3c on 12c	15.00	1.00
608	A32(n)	6c on 10c	15.00	1.00
609	A32(m)	6c on 1k	15.00	1.00

Nos. 571-577 Overprinted in Black or Red

Novembre
1337-1918

1918 Wmk. 161

No.	Type	Description	Unused	Used
610	A34	2k sil, blue & rose	5.00	5.00
611	A34	3k sil, vio & brn (R)	5.00	5.00
612	A34	5k sil, brn & grn (R)	7.00	7.00
613	A35	1t gold, pur & black (R)	6.00	6.00
614	A35	2t gold, grn & brn	7.00	7.00
615	A35	3t gold, cl & red brn	10.00	10.00
616	A35	5t gold, bl & ind (R)	10.00	10.00
		Nos. 610-616 (7)	50.00	50.00

The overprint commemorates the end of World War I. Counterfeits of this overprint are plentiful.

A36

1919 Unwmk. Typo. *Perf. 11½*

No.	Type	Description	Unused	Used
617	A36	1c yel & black	2.00	20
618	A36	3c green & black	3.00	20
619	A36	5c rose & black	5.00	1.50
620	A36	6c vio & black	10.00	20
621	A36	12c blue & black	15.00	1.25
		Nos. 617-621 (5)	35.00	3.35

Nos. 617-621 exist imperf., in colors other than the originals, with centers inverted and double impressions. Some specialists call them fraudulent, others call them reprints.

Counterfeits having double line over "POSTES" abound.

Nos. 75, 85-86 Surcharged in Various Colors

دو قران
1919
2 Kr.

1919 *Perf. 10½, 11, 11½, 13½*

No.	Type	Description	Unused	Used
622	A14	2k on 5c lilac (Bk)	4.00	2.00
623	A14	3k on 5c lilac (Br)	4.00	2.00
624	A14	4k on 5c lilac (G)	4.00	2.00
625	A14	5k on 5c lilac (V)	4.00	2.00
626	A16	10k on 10c rose (Bl)	6.00	3.00
627	A16	20k on 10c rose (G)	6.00	3.00
628	A16	30k on 10c rose (Br)	6.00	3.00
629	A16	50k on 14c org (V)	6.00	3.00
		Nos. 622-629 (8)	40.00	20.00

Nos. 622-629 exist with inverted and double surcharge. Some specialists consider these fraudulent.

Nos. 486, 489 Handstamp Surcharged

1 KRAN
BENADERS

1921 *Perf. 11½, 11½x11*

No.	Type	Description	Unused	Used
630	A32	10c on 6c	45.00	10.00
631	A32	1k on 12c	45.00	10.00

Counterfeits exist.

No. 489 Surcharged

No.	Type	Description	Unused	Used
632	A32	6c on 12c	80.00	3.00

Nos. 486, 489 Surcharged in Violet:

10 Ch. 1 Kr.

1921

No.	Type	Description	Unused	Used
633	A32	10c on 6c	45.00	15.00
634	A32	1k on 12c	45.00	15.00

Counterfeits exist.

Coronation Issue of 1915 Overprinted

1921 Wmk. 161 *Perf. 11, 11½*

No.	Type	Description	Unused	Used
635	A33	3c dark grn	5.00	
a.		Center and overprint inverted	40.00	
636	A33	5c red	5.00	
637	A33	6c olive grn & car	5.00	
638	A33	10c bl grn & yel brn	6.00	
639	A33	12c ultramarine	6.00	
640	A34	1k sil, yel brn & gray	8.00	
641	A34	2k sil, blue & rose	7.00	
642	A34	5k sil, brn & green	7.00	
643	A35	2t gold, grn & brn	10.00	
644	A35	3t gold, cl & red brn	7.00	
645	A35	5t gold, blue & ind	7.00	
		Nos. 635-645 (11)	73.00	

Counterfeits of this Feb. 21, 1921, overprint are plentiful. Inverted overprints exist on all values; some specialists consider them fraudulent.

Stamps of 1911-13 Overprinted

1922 Unwmk. *Perf. 11½, 11½x11*

No.	Type	Description	Unused	Used
646	A32	1c grn & orange	3.00	20
a.		Inverted overprint	*40.00*	
647	A32	2c red & sepia	3.00	20
648	A32	3c brn & green	3.00	20
649	A32	5c brown & car	35.00	15.00
650	A32	6c grn & red brn	3.00	20
651	A32	9c yel brn & vio	3.00	20
652	A32	10c red & org brn	4.00	20
653	A32	12c green & ultra	4.00	30
654	A32	1k ultra & car	15.00	30
655	A32	24c vio & green	10.00	30
656	A32	2k grn & red vio	20.00	30
657	A32	3k vio & black	35.00	35
658	A32	4k ultra & gray	60.00	12.50
659	A32	5k red & ultra	35.00	45
660	A32	10k ol bis & cl	*140.00*	3.00
661	A32	20k vio brn & bis	*140.00*	5.00
662	A32	30k red & green	*140.00*	7.00
		Nos. 646-662 (17)	*653.00*	45.70

The status of inverted overprints on 5c and 12c is dubious. Unlisted inverts on other denominations are generally considered fraudulent. Counterfeits of this overprint exist.

Nos. 653, 655 Surcharged

3CH.

1922

No.	Type	Description	Unused	Used
663	A32	3c on 12c	20.00	1.00
664	A32	6c on 24c	35.00	1.50

Nos. 661-662 Surcharged:

دهشاهی
1o chahis

یکقران
1 Kran

1923

No.	Type	Description	Unused	Used
665	A32	10c on 20k	25.00	4.00
666	A32	1k on 30k	35.00	10.00

Shah Ahmed — A37

A38

Perf. 11½, 11x11½, 11½x11

1924-25 Engr.

No.	Type	Description	Unused	Used
667	A37	1c orange	1.00	20
668	A37	2c magenta	1.00	20
669	A37	3c orange brown	1.00	20
670	A37	6c black brown	1.00	20
671	A37	9c dark green	2.00	75
672	A37	10c dark violet	2.00	30
673	A37	12c red	2.00	30
674	A37	1k dark blue	2.50	35
675	A37	2k indigo & red	3.00	1.00
a.		Center inverted		*1,500.*
676	A37	3k dk vio & red brown	15.00	1.25
677	A37	5d red & brown	30.00	2.00
678	A37	10k choc & lilac	30.00	10.00
679	A37	20k dk grn & brn	30.00	10.00
680	A37	30k org & blk brn	55.00	10.00
		Nos. 667-680 (14)	175.50	36.75

For overprints see Nos. 703-706.

SIX CHAHIS

P.re موقتی
Type I

P.re موقتی
Type II

Surcharge in Black, "1924" etc.

1924 Typo. Perf. 11

681	A38	1c yellow brown	2.00	1.00
682	A38	2c gray	2.00	1.00
683	A38	3c deep rose	2.00	1.00
684	A38	6c orange (I)	4.00	1.50
a.		6c orange (II)	3.00	2.00

The 1c was surcharged "Chahis" by error. Later the "s" was blocked out in black.

Similar Surcharge, Dated 1925

1925

686	A38	2c yellow green	1.50	50
687	A38	3c red	1.50	50
689	A38	6c chalky blue	2.00	50
690	A38	9c light brown	2.00	75
691	A38	10c gray	5.00	1.25
694	A38	1k emerald	10.00	1.25
695	A38	2k lilac	35.00	6.00
		Nos. 686-695 (7)	57.00	10.75

Counterfeits are plentiful.

A39

Gold Overprint on Treasury Department Stamps

1925

697	A39	1c red	2.00	1.00
698	A39	2c yellow	2.00	1.50
699	A39	3c yellow green	3.00	2.00
700	A39	5c dark gray	9.00	6.00
701	A39	10c deep orange	3.00	2.00
702	A39	1k ultramarine	8.00	5.00
		Nos. 697-702 (6)	27.00	17.50

Deposition of Shah Ahmed and establishment of provisional government of Riza Khan Pahlavi.

#697-702 have same center (Persian lion in sunburst) with 6 different frames. Overprint reads: "Post / Provisional Government / of Pahlavi / 9th Abanmah / 1304 / 1925."

Nos. 667-670 Overprinted

1926 Perf. 11½, 11x11½, 11½x11

703	A37	1c orange	1.50	50
704	A37	2c magenta	1.50	50
705	A37	3c orange brown	1.50	75
706	A37	6c black brown	32.50	20.00

Overprinted to commemorate the Pahlavi government of 1925. Counterfeits exist.

Nos. 448-463 Overprinted

۱۳۰۵
سلطنت پهلوی
Règne de
Pahlavi
1926

1926 Perf. 11½, 12½x12

707	A31	1c org & maroon	75	25
a.		Inverted overprint		
708	A31	2c vio & maroon	75	25
709	A31	3c yel grn & mar	75	25
a.		Inverted overprint	16.00	
710	A31	6c red & maroon	1.00	25
711	A31	9c gray & maroon	1.90	25
712	A31	10c red vio & mar	1.50	35
713	A31	13c dk bl & mar	1.50	35
714	A31	1k multi	2.00	35
715	A31	26c dk grn & mar	3.00	35
716	A31	2k multi	7.00	50
717	A31	3k multi	7.00	50
718	A31	4k sil, bl & bis brn	45.00	5.00
719	A31	5k multi	45.00	5.00
720	A31	10k multi	75.00	7.00
721	A31	20k multi	85.00	7.00
722	A31	30k multi	85.00	7.00
		Nos. 707-722 (16)	362.15	34.65

Overprinted to commemorate the Pahlavi government in 1926.

Nos. 707-722, perf. 11½, are on thick paper, perf. 12½x12 on thin paper.

So far forgeries are perf. 12½x12 only.

Riza Shah Pahlavi
A40 A41

1926-29 Typo. Perf. 11

723	A40	1c yellow green	70	15
724	A40	2c gray violet	70	15
725	A40	3c emerald	1.00	15
727	A40	6c magenta	2.00	15
728	A40	9c rose	6.00	25
729	A40	10c bister brown	10.00	1.50
730	A40	12c deep orange	12.00	35
731	A40	15c pale ultra	15.00	50
733	A41	1k dull bl ('27)	20.00	4.50
734	A41	2k brt vio ('29)	35.00	15.00
		Nos. 723-734 (10)	102.40	22.70

1928 Redrawn

740	A40	1c yellow green	4.50	20
741	A40	2c gray violet	6.00	20
742	A40	3c emerald	4.50	20
743	A40	6c rose	4.50	20

On the redrawn stamps much of the shading of the face, throat, collar, etc., has been removed. The letters of "Postes Persanes" and those in the circle at upper right are smaller. The redrawn stamps measure 20¼x25¾mm instead of 19¾x25¼mm.

Riza Shah Pahlavi
A42 A43

Perf. 11½, 12, 12½, Compound

1929 Photo.

744	A42	1c yel grn & cer	1.00	35
745	A42	2c scar & brt blue	1.00	35
746	A42	3c mag & myr grn	1.00	35
747	A42	6c yel brn & ol grn	1.00	35
748	A42	9c Prus bl & ver	2.50	50
749	A42	10c bl grn & choc	2.50	85
750	A42	12c gray blk & pur	4.00	85
751	A42	15c citron & ultra	5.00	85
752	A42	1k dull bl & blk	20.00	1.00
753	A42	24c ol grn & red brn	7.00	1.00

Engr.

Perf. 11½

754	A42	2k brn org & dk violet	20.00	1.50
755	A42	3k dark grn & dp rose	20.00	2.00
756	A42	5k red brn & dp green	20.00	2.00
757	A42	1t ultra & dp rose	25.00	5.00
758	A42	2t carmine & blk	40.00	15.00

Engr. and Typo.

759	A43	3t gold & dp vio	40.00	15.00
		Nos. 744-759 (16)	210.00	46.95

For overprints see Nos. 810-817.

Riza Shah Pahlavi — A44

1931-32 Litho. Perf. 11

760	A44	1c ol brn & ultra	1.00	20
761	A44	2c red brn & blk	1.00	20
762	A44	3c lilac rose & ol	1.00	20
763	A44	6c red org & vio	1.00	20
764	A44	9c ultra & red org	10.00	40
765	A44	10c ver & gray	10.00	70
766	A44	11c bl & dull red	17.50	8.00
767	A44	12c turq blue & lil rose	15.00	70
768	A44	16c black & red	17.50	1.75
769	A44	1k car & turq bl	25.00	1.75
770	A44	27c dk gray & dl bl	25.00	1.75
		Nos. 760-770 (11)	124.00	15.85

For overprints see Nos. 818-826.

Riza Shah Pahlavi
A45 A46

1933-34

771	A45	5d olive brown	1.00	25
772	A45	10d blue	1.00	25
773	A45	15d gray	1.00	25
774	A45	30d emerald	1.00	25
775	A45	45d turq blue	1.50	20
776	A45	50d magenta	1.50	25
777	A45	60d green	3.00	35
778	A45	75d brown	4.00	40
779	A45	90d red	5.00	2.50
780	A46	1r dk rose & blk	5.00	35
781	A46	1.20r gray blk & rose	12.00	1.00
782	A46	1.50 citron & bl	20.00	50
783	A46	2r lt bl & choc	20.00	60
784	A46	3r mag & green	40.00	2.00
785	A46	5r dk brn & red org	75.00	20.00
		Nos. 771-785 (15)	191.00	29.15

For overprints see Nos. 795-809.

"Justice"
A47

"Education"
A49

Ruins of Persepolis
A48

Tehran Airport
A50

Sanatorium at Sakhtessar — A51

Cement Factory, Chah-Abdul-Azim — A52

Gunboat "Palang"
A53

Railway Bridge over Karun River
A54

Post Office and Customs Building, Tehran — A55

1935, Feb. 21 Photo. Perf. 12½

786	A47	5d red brn & grn	25	20
787	A48	10d red org & gray black	25	20
788	A49	15d mag & Prus bl	30	20
789	A50	30d black & green	75	55
790	A51	45d ol grn & red brn	1.25	40
791	A52	75d grn & dark brn	6.00	85
792	A53	90d blue & car rose	10.00	2.50
793	A54	1r red brn & pur	30.00	8.00
794	A55	1½r violet & ultra	15.00	5.00
		Nos. 786-794 (9)	63.80	17.90

Reign of Riza Shah Pahlavi, 10th anniv.

Stamps of 1933-34 Overprinted in Black **POSTES IRANIENNES**

1935 Perf. 11

795	A45	5d olive brown	1.00	15
796	A45	10d blue	1.00	15
797	A45	15d gray	1.00	15
798	A45	30d emerald	1.00	15
799	A45	45d turq blue	7.00	5.00
800	A45	50d magenta	2.00	30
801	A45	60d green	2.00	50
802	A45	75d brown	7.50	5.00
803	A45	90d red	20.00	15.00
804	A46	1r dk rose & blk	55.00	50.00
805	A46	1.20r gray black & rose	8.50	2.50
806	A46	1.50r citron & bl	8.50	1.50
807	A46	2r lt bl & choc	12.00	2.50
808	A46	3r mag & green	50.00	3.50
809	A46	5r dk brn & red org	100.00	80.00
		Nos. 795-809 (15)	276.50	166.40

Same Overprint on Stamps of 1929

1935 Perf. 12, 12x12½

810	A42	1c yel green & cer	175.00	
811	A42	2c scar & brt blue	80.00	40.00
812	A42	3c mag & myr grn	45.00	20.00
813	A42	6c yel brn & ol grn	25.00	20.00
814	A42	9c Prus bl & ver	20.00	20.00

Perf. 11½

815	A42	1t ultra & dp rose	25.00	10.00
816	A42	2t carmine & blk	25.00	6.50
817	A43	3t gold & dp vio	35.00	6.50
		Nos. 810-817 (8)	430.00	

No. 817 is overprinted vertically.
Forged overprints exist.

Same Ovpt. on Stamps of 1931-32

1935 Perf. 11

818	A44	1c ol brn & ultra	165.00	
819	A44	2c red brn & blk	35.00	3.00
820	A44	3c lilac rose & ol	25.00	15.00
821	A44	6c red org & vio	30.00	30.00
822	A44	9c ultra & red org	40.00	40.00
823	A44	11c bl & dl red	5.00	45
824	A44	12c turq bl & lil rose	150.00	50.00
825	A44	16c black & red	7.50	3.00
826	A44	27c dk gray & dl bl	12.00	1.50
		Nos. 818-826 (9)	469.50	

Forged overprints exist.

Riza Shah Pahlavi — A56

1935 **Photo.** ***Perf. 11***

Size: 19x27mm

No.	Type	Denom.	Color	Unused	Used
827	A56	5d	violet	1.00	15
828	A56	10d	lilac rose	1.00	15
829	A56	15d	turquoise bl	1.00	15
830	A56	30d	emerald	1.00	15
831	A56	45d	orange	1.50	15
832	A56	50d	dull lt brn	2.75	30
833	A56	60d	ultramarine	10.00	65
834	A56	75d	red orange	10.00	25
835	A56	90d	rose	12.50	65

Size: 21½x31mm

No.	Type	Denom.	Color	Unused	Used
836	A56	1r	dull lilac	15.00	50
837	A56	1.50r	blue	25.00	2.00
838	A56	2r	dk olive grn	20.00	55
839	A56	3r	dark brown	25.00	1.00
840	A56	5r	slate black	40.00	15.00
			Nos. 827-840 (14)	165.75	21.65

Riza Shah Pahlavi
A57 A58

1936-37 **Litho.** ***Perf. 11***

Size: 20x27mm

No.	Type	Denom.	Color	Unused	Used
841	A57	5d	bright vio	1.00	15
842	A57	10d	magenta	1.00	15
843	A57	15d	bright ultra	1.00	15
844	A57	30d	yellow green	1.00	15
845	A57	45d	vermilion	1.25	15
846	A57	50d	blk brn ('37)	1.25	15
847	A57	60d	brown orange	1.50	35
848	A57	75d	rose lake	1.50	15
849	A57	90d	rose red	3.00	35

Size: 23x31mm

No.	Type	Denom.	Color	Unused	Used
850	A57	1r	turq green	10.00	25
851	A57	1.50r	deep blue	10.00	35
852	A57	2r	bright blue	20.00	35
853	A57	3r	violet brown	30.00	80
854	A57	5r	slate green	40.00	1.25
855	A57	10r	dark brown & ultra ('37)	55.00	15.00
			Nos. 841-855 (15)	177.50	19.75

1938-39 ***Perf. 11***

Size: 20x27mm

No.	Type	Denom.	Color	Unused	Used
856	A58	5d	light violet	1.00	15
857	A58	10d	magenta	1.00	15
858	A58	15d	violet blue	1.00	15
859	A58	30d	bright green	1.00	15
860	A58	45d	vermilion	1.00	15
861	A58	50d	black brown	1.00	15
862	A58	60d	brown orange	1.00	15
863	A58	75d	rose lake	1.50	15
864	A58	90d	rose red ('39)	4.00	25

Size: 22½x30mm

No.	Type	Denom.	Color	Unused	Used
865	A58	1r	turq green	10.00	20
866	A58	1.50r	deep blue	15.00	30
867	A58	2r	lt blue ('39)	20.00	30
868	A58	3r	violet brown	30.00	45
869	A58	5r	gray grn ('39)	35.00	1.00
870	A58	10r	dark brown & ultra ('39)	55.00	7.50
			Nos. 856-870 (15)	177.50	11.20

A58a

1939, Mar. 15 ***Perf. 13***

No.	Type	Denom.	Color	Unused	Used
870A	A58a	5d	gray blue	60	50
870B	A58a	10d	brown	60	50
870C	A58a	30d	green	60	50
870D	A58a	60d	dark brown	80	40
870E	A58a	90d	red	1.25	30
870F	A58a	1.50r	blue	1.50	50
870G	A58a	5r	lilac	5.50	4.00
870H	A58a	10r	carmine	11.00	6.00
			Nos. 870A-870H (8)	21.85	12.70

60th birthday of Riza Shah Pahlavi. Printed in sheets of 4, perf. 13 and imperf. The imperf. sell for 50% more. The 1r violet and 2r orange were not available to the public.

Crown Prince and Princess Fawziya A59

1939, Apr. 25 **Photo.** ***Perf. 11½***

No.	Type	Denom.	Color	Unused	Used
871	A59	5d	red brown	35	20
872	A59	10d	bright violet	35	20
873	A59	30d	emerald	1.00	35
874	A59	90d	red	4.00	60
875	A59	1.50r	bright blue	8.00	1.50
			Nos. 871-875 (5)	13.70	2.85

Wedding of Crown Prince Mohammed Riza Pahlavi to Princess Fawziya of Egypt.

Bridge over Karun River A60

Veresk Bridge, North Iran — A61

Granary, Ahwaz A62

Train and Bridge A63

Museum, Side View
A64 A67

Ministry of Justice A65

School Building A66

Mohammed Riza Pahlavi
A68 A69

1942-46 **Unwmk.** **Litho.** ***Perf. 11***

No.	Type	Denom.	Color	Unused	Used
876	A60	5d	violet	30	15
877	A60	5d	red org ('44)	30	15
878	A61	10d	magenta	30	15
879	A61	10d	pck grn ('44)	30	15
880	A62	20d	lt red violet	75	25
881	A62	20d	magenta ('44)	75	25
882	A63	25d	rose carmine	3.00	50
883	A63	25d	violet ('44)	1.50	25
884	A64	35d	emerald	80	30
885	A65	50d	ultramarine	80	20
886	A65	50d	emerald ('44)	80	15
887	A66	70d	dull vio brn	60	35
888	A67	75d	rose lake	3.00	35
889	A67	75d	rose car ('46)	10.00	35
890	A68	1r	carmine	2.75	15
891	A68	1r	maroon ('45)	8.00	15
892	A68	1.50r	red	2.50	15
893	A68	2r	light blue	6.50	30
894	A68	2r	sage grn ('44)	5.00	30
895	A68	2.50r	dark blue	3.50	25
896	A68	3r	peacock grn	55.00	75
897	A68	3r	brt vio ('44)	17.50	35
898	A68	5r	sage green	65.00	7.50
899	A68	5r	lt blue ('44)	8.50	50
900	A69	10r	brn org & blk	25.00	1.00
901	A69	10r	dk org brn & black ('44)	15.00	1.00
902	A69	20r	choc & vio	175.00	25.00
903	A69	20r	orange & black ('44)	22.50	4.00
904	A69	30r	gray blk & emerald	600.00	35.00
905	A69	30r	emer & black ('44)	17.50	2.50
906	A69	50r	dl bl & brn red	50.00	15.00
907	A69	50r	brt vio & black ('45)	25.00	5.00
908	A69	100r	rose red & blk ('45)	375.00	50.00
909	A69	200r	bl & blk ('45)	250.00	40.00
			Nos. 876-909 (34)	1,752.	192.45

Sixteen denominations of this issue were handstamped at Tabriz in 1945-46 in Persian characters: "Azerbaijan National Government, Dec. 12, 1945." A rebel group did this overprinting while the Russian army held that area.

Flag of Persia A70

Designs: 50d, Docks at Bandar Shapur. 1.50r, Motor convoy. 2.50r, Gorge and railway viaduct. 5r, Map and Mohammed Riza Pahlavi.

Inscribed: "En souvenir des efforts de l'Iran pour la Victoire"

Engr. & Litho.

1949, Apr. 28 ***Perf. 12½***

No.	Type	Denom.	Color	Unused	Used
910	A70	25d	multicolored	35	30

Engr.

No.	Type	Denom.	Color	Unused	Used
911	A70	50d	purple	75	65
912	A70	1.50r	carmine rose	1.00	1.25
913	A70	2.50r	deep blue	6.00	1.50
914	A70	5r	green	10.00	2.50
			Nos. 910-914 (5)	18.10	6.20

Iran's contribution toward the victory of the Allied Nations in World War II.

Bridge over Zaindeh River A71

National Bank — A72

Former Ministry of P.T.T. A73

Mohammed Riza Pahlavi — A74

Designs: 5d-20r, Various views and buildings.

1949-50 **Unwmk.** **Litho.** ***Perf. 10½***

No.	Type	Denom.	Color	Unused	Used
915	A71	5d	rose & dk grn	35	15
916	A71	10d	ultra & brown	35	15
917	A71	20d	vio & ultra	35	25
918	A71	25d	blk brn & dp blue	40	15
919	A71	50d	grn & ultra	40	15
920	A71	75d	dk brn & red	65	15
921	A72	1r	vio & green	1.00	15
922	A72	1.50r	dk grn & ver	1.25	15
923	A72	2r	dp car & blk brn	1.00	25
924	A72	2.50r	chlky bl & bl	1.25	20
925	A72	3r	vio bl & red orange	2.50	15
926	A72	5r	dp car & vio	3.00	15
927	A73	10r	car & blue green ('50)	25.00	45
a.			Inverted center	600.00	
928	A73	20r	brown black & red ('50)	150.00	20.00
929	A74	30r	choc & deep blue ('50)	45.00	10.00
930	A74	50r	red & deep blue ('50)	55.00	10.00
			Nos. 915-930 (16)	287.50	42.50

Globes and Pigeons A75

Symbols of UPU — A76

1950, Mar. 16 **Photo.**

No.	Type	Denom.	Color	Unused	Used
931	A75	50d	brn carmine	14.00	12.50
932	A76	2.50r	deep blue	21.00	17.50

UPU, 75th anniv. (in 1949).

Riza Shah Pahlavi and his Tomb — A77

1950, May 7
933 A77 50d brown 9.00 6.25
934 A77 2r sepia 21.00 9.00

Re-burial of Riza Shah Pahlavi, May 12, 1950.

Mohammed Riza Pahlavi, 31st Birthday — A78

Various portraits.

1950, Oct. 26 Engr. *Perf. 12½*
Center in Black
935 A78 25d carmine 2.25 75
936 A78 50d orange 2.25 75
937 A78 75d brown 17.00 6.00
938 A78 1r green 14.00 1.65
939 A78 2.50r deep blue 19.00 1.65
940 A78 5r brown lake 30.00 4.50
Nos. 935-940 (6) 84.50 15.30

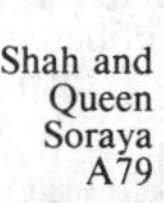

Shah and Queen Soraya A79

A80

1951, Feb. 12 Litho. *Perf. 10½*
941 A79 5d rose violet 1.10 50
942 A79 25d orange red 1.40 75
943 A79 50d emerald 4.00 2.00
944 A80 1r brown 4.50 2.00
945 A80 1.50r carmine 4.50 2.00
946 A80 2.50r blue 7.00 2.50
Nos. 941-946 (6) 22.50 9.75

Wedding of Mohammed Riza Pahlavi to Soraya Esfandiari.

Farabi — A81

1951, Feb. 20
947 A81 50d red 1.90 1.40
948 A81 2.50r blue 9.00 2.50

Death millenary of Farabi, Persian philosopher.

Mohammed Riza Pahlavi
A82 A83

1951-52 Unwmk. Photo. *Perf. 10½*
950 A82 5d brown orange 25 15
951 A82 10d violet 25 15
952 A82 20d choc ('52) 75 35
953 A82 25d blue ('52) 45 20
954 A82 50d green 65 15
955 A82 75d rose 85 30
956 A83 1r gray green 1.25 15
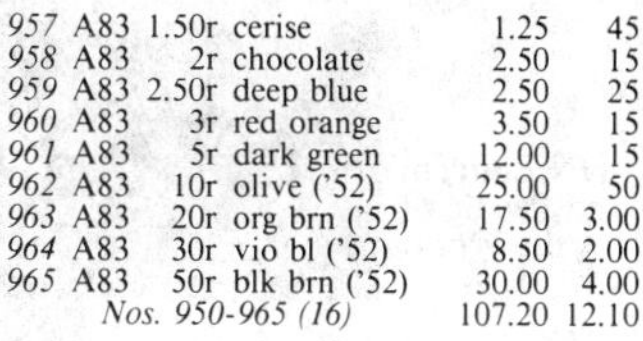
957 A83 1.50r cerise 1.25 45
958 A83 2r chocolate 2.50 15
959 A83 2.50r deep blue 2.50 25
960 A83 3r red orange 3.50 15
961 A83 5r dark green 12.00 15
962 A83 10r olive ('52) 25.00 50
963 A83 20r org brn ('52) 17.50 3.00
964 A83 30r vio bl ('52) 8.50 2.00
965 A83 50r blk brn ('52) 30.00 4.00
Nos. 950-965 (16) 107.20 12.10

See Nos. 975-977.

Oil Well and Mosque — A84

Oil Well, Mosque and Monument A85

1953, Feb. 20 Litho.
966 A84 50d green & yel 1.75 15
967 A85 1r lil rose & yel 2.00 32
968 A84 2.50r blue & yellow 3.00 80
969 A85 5r blk brn & yel 5.75 2.50

Discovery of oil at Qum.

Abadan Oil Refinery A86

Oil Wells — A87

Designs: 1r, Storage tanks. 5r, Pipe lines. 10r, Abadan refinery and wells.

1953, Mar. 20 Photo.
970 A86 50d blue green 65 45
971 A86 1r rose 1.00 45
972 A87 2.50r bright ultra 2.00 1.10
973 A86 5r red orange 4.25 1.25
974 A86 10r dark violet 6.75 1.90
Nos. 970-974 (5) 14.65 5.15

Nationalization of oil industry, 2nd anniv.

Shah Types of 1951-52

1953-54 Photo. *Perf. 10½*
975 A82 50d dark gray grn 15.00 35
976 A83 1r dk blue green 1.50 15
977 A83 1.50r cerise ('54) 1.50 15

The background has been highlighted on the 1r and 1.50r.

Gymnast — A88

Archery A89

Designs: 3r, Climbing Mt. Demavend. 5r, Ancient polo. 10r, Lion hunting.

1953, Oct. 26
978 A88 1r deep green 2.00 1.10
979 A89 2.50fr brt grnsh bl 7.25 3.00
980 A89 3r gray 20.00 3.75
981 A88 5r bister 15.00 7.50
982 A88 10r rose lilac 26.00 7.50
Nos. 978-982 (5) 70.25 22.85

Mother with Children and UN Emblem A90

1953, Oct. 24
983 A90 1r bl grn & dk grn 1.10 20
984 A90 2.50r lt bl & indigo 1.40 50

United Nations Day, Oct. 24.

Herring A91

Refrigeration Compressor A92

Processing Equipment, National Fisheries — A93

Designs: 2.50r, Sardines. 10r, Sturgeon.

1954, Jan. 31
985 A91 1r multi 3.75 90
986 A91 2.50r multi 20.00 4.50
987 A92 3r vermilion 9.00 4.50
988 A93 5r deep bl grn 13.00 8.00
989 A91 10r multi 20.00 13.00
Nos. 985-989 (5) 65.75 30.90

Nationalization of fishing industry.

Broken Shackles A94

Mother Feeding Baby A95

Designs: 3r, Torch and flag. 5r, Citizen holding flag or Iran.

1954, Aug. 19 Litho.
990 A94 2r multicolored 4.50 65
991 A94 3r multicolored 7.50 1.50
992 A94 5r multicolored 10.00 2.75

Return of the royalist government, 1st anniv.

1954, Oct. 24 Photo.
993 A95 2r red lil & org 1.75 75
994 A95 3r vio bl & org 1.75 1.25

Issued to honor the United Nations.

Woodsman Felling Tree — A96

Designs: 2.50r, Laborer carrying firewood. 5fr, Worker operating saw. 10r, Wooden galley.

1954, Dec. 11
995 A96 1r brn & grnsh black 13.00 10.00
996 A96 2.50r grnsh blk & bl 18.00 16.50
997 A96 5r lil & dk brn 52.50 21.00
998 A96 10r bl & claret 42.50 35.00

4th World Forestry Congress, Dehra Dun, India, 1954.

Mohammed Riza Pahlavi
A97 A98

1954-55 Unwmk.
999 A97 5d yellow brn 30 25
1000 A97 10d violet 30 25
1001 A97 25d scarlet 20 15
1002 A97 50d black brn 20 15
1003 A98 1r blue green 45 15
1004 A98 1.50r cerise 45 25
1005 A98 2r ocher 45 25
1006 A98 2.50r blue 1.00 20
1007 A98 3r olive 1.25 25
1008 A98 5r dk sl grn 5.00 25
1009 A98 10r lilac rose 10.00 1.00
1010 A98 20r indigo 30.00 2.00
1011 A98 30r dp yel grn 110.00 7.50
1012 A98 50r dp orange 30.00 5.00
1013 A98 100r light vio 325.00 40.00
1014 A98 200r yellow 100.00 20.00
Nos. 999-1014 (16) 614.60 77.65

See Nos. 1023-1036.

Regional Costume — A99

Regional Costumes: 1r, 2r, Men's costumes. 2.50r, 3r, 5r, Women's costumes.

Wmk. 306
1955, June 26 Photo. *Perf. 11*
1015 A99 1r bluish gray & black 1.50 90
1016 A99 2r dl rose & blk 3.75 1.75
1017 A99 2.50r buff & black 8.00 2.75
1018 A99 3r rose lil & blk 5.50 3.25
1019 A99 5r gray brn & blk 9.50 6.50
Nos. 1015-1019 (5) 28.25 15.15

Parliament Gate A100

Designs: 3r, Statue of Liberty (vertical). 5r, Old Gate of Parliament.

1955, Aug. 6 *Perf. 11*
1020 A100 2r red vio & grn 1.65 55
1021 A100 3r dk bl & aqua 5.25 1.65
1022 A100 5r Prus grn & red orange 6.50 4.25

50th anniversary of constitution.

Shah Types of 1954-55

1955-56 **Wmk. 306** *Perf. 11*
1023 A97 5d violet ('56) 50 50
1024 A97 10d carmine ('56) 50 20
1025 A97 25d brown 40 15
1026 A97 50d dk carmine 40 15
1027 A98 1r dark bl grn 50 15
1028 A98 1.50r red brn ('56) 25.00 3.00
1029 A98 2r ol grn ('56) 1.00 25
1030 A98 2.50r blue ('56) 1.50 30
1031 A98 3r bister 3.25 20
1032 A98 5r red lilac 3.00 20
1033 A98 10r brt grnsh bl 5.00 35
1034 A98 20r slate green 17.50 2.00
1035 A98 30r red org ('56) 90.00 14.00
1036 A98 50r red brn ('56) 50.00 16.50
Nos. 1023-1036 (14) 198.55 37.95

UN Emblem and Globes A101

1955, Oct. 24 *Perf. 11x12½*
1039 A101 1r dp car & org 1.40 52
1040 A101 2.50r dk bl & grnsh blue 2.25 1.25

UN, 10th anniv.Nations, Oct. 24, 1955.

Wrestlers — A102

1955, Oct. 26 **Wmk. 306** *Perf. 11*
1041 A102 2.50r multi 3.00 1.75

Victory in intl. wrestling competitions.

Garden, Nemazi Hospital A103

Soldier A105

Nemazi Hospital, Shiraz A104

Designs: 5r, Gate of the Koran. 10r, Hafiz of Shiraz.

1956, Mar. 21 *Perf. 11x12½*
1042 A103 50d multi 1.65 60
1043 A104 1r multi 3.00 1.00
1044 A105 2.50r multi 8.25 6.00
1045 A104 5r multi 7.25 4.00
1046 A105 10r multi 20.00 6.00
Nos. 1042-1046 (5) 40.15 17.60

Opening of Nemazi Hospital, Shiraz.

Arms of Iran and Olympic Rings A106

Tomb at Maragheh A107

1956, May 15 **Wmk. 306**
1047 A106 5r rose lilac 20.00 15.00

National Olympic Committee, 10th anniv.

1956, May 26 **Photo.** *Perf. 11x12½*

Designs: 2.50r, Astrolabe. 5r, Nasr-ud-Din of Tus.

1048 A107 1r orange 2.50 90
1049 A107 2.50r deep ultra 4.00 90
1050 A107 5r sepia & pur 7.75 1.10

700th death anniv. of Nasr-up-Din of Tus, mathematician.

WHO Emblem — A108

Perf. 11x12½

1956, Sept. 19 **Wmk. 306**
1051 A108 6r cerise 2.25 1.00

6th Regional Congress of the WHO.

Scout Bugler and Camp A109

Design: 5r, Scout badge and Shah in scout uniform.

1956, Aug. 5 *Perf. 12½x11*
1052 A109 2.50r ultra & blue 10.50 5.00
1053 A109 5r lil & red lil 14.00 7.50

National Boy Scout Jamboree.

Catalogue values for unused stamps in this section, from this point to the end of the section, are for Never Hinged items.

Former Telegraph Office, Tehran A110

Design: 6r, Telegraph lines and ancient monument.

1956, Oct. 26
1054 A110 2.50r brt bl & grn, *bluish* 8.50 3.50
1055 A110 6r rose car & lil 11.00 5.00

Centenary of Persian telegraph system.

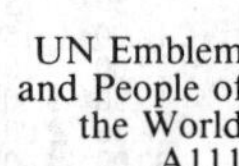

UN Emblem and People of the World A111

Design: 2.50r, UN Emblem and scales.

1956, Oct. 24
1056 A111 1r bluish green 1.40 30
1057 A111 2.50r blue & green 2.75 55

United Nations Day, Oct. 24.

Shah and Pres. Iskander Mirza of Pakistan A112

1956, Oct. 31
1058 A112 1r multicolored 2.00 60

Visit of Pres. General Iskander Mirza of Pakistan to Tehran, Oct. 31-Nov. 10.

Mohammed Riza Pahlavi A113 A114

Perf. 13½x11

1956-57 **Wmk. 306** **Photo.**

Design A113

1058A 5d brt car & red 45 1.00
1058B 10d vio bl & dl vio 45 1.00
1059 25d dk brn & brn 65 35
1059A 50d brn & ol brn 70 15
b. Inverted center
1060 1r brn & brt grn 70 20
1061 1.50r brt lil & brown 70 20
1062 2r red vio & red 70 20
1063 2.50r ultra & blue 1.00 20
1064 3r brn & dk ol bis 1.00 20
1065 5r ver & mar 1.00 20

Design A114

1066 6r dk vio & brn lil 4.50 25
1067 10r lt blue & grn 8.50 20
1068 20r green & blue 20.00 3.00
1069 30r rose red & org 25.00 5.00
1070 50r dk grn & ol grn 35.00 6.00
1071 100r lilac & cer 200.00 27.50
1072 200r dp plum & vio bl 100.00 15.00
Nos. 1058A-1072 (17) 400.35 60.65

Years of issue: 1.50r, 2r, 3r, 5r, 6r, 1956; others, 1957.
See Nos. 1082-1098.

Lord Baden-Powell A115

Railroad Tracks A116

Train and Map A117

1957, Feb. 22 *Perf. 12½*
1073 A115 10r dk grn & brn 7.00 4.00

Birth cent. of Robert Baden-Powell, founder of the Boy Scout movement.

1957, May 2 *Perf. 11x12½, 12½x11*

Design: 10r, Train and mosque.

1074 A116 2.50r grnsh blk, bl & ocher 7.25 1.00
1075 A117 5r multi 9.50 5.00
1076 A116 10r blk, yel & bl 18.00 9.00

Opening of the Tehran Meshed-Railway.

Pres. Giovanni Gronchi of Italy and Shah — A118

Design: 6r, Ruins of Persepolis and Colosseum in Rome and flags.

Wmk. 316

1957, Sept. 7 **Photo.** *Perf. 11*
1077 A118 2r sl bl, grn & red 3.25 1.00
1078 A118 6r sl bl, grn & red 6.75 2.00

Visit of Pres. Giovanni Gronchi of Italy to Iran, Sept. 7.

Queen Soraya and Hospital A119

1957, Sept. 29 **Wmk. 316** *Perf. 11*
1079 A119 2r lt bl & grn 2.50 45

Sixth Medical Congress, Ramsar.

Globes Showing Location of Iran — A120

1957, Oct. 22 **Litho.** *Perf. 12½x11*
1080 A120 10r blk, lt bl, yel & red 7.00 2.00

Intl. Cartographic Conference, Tehran.

Shah and King Faisal II — A121

1957, Oct. 18 **Photo.**
1081 A121 2r sl bl, grn & red 2.50 45

Visit of King Faisal of Iraq, Oct. 19.

Shah Types of 1956-57

1957-58 Wmk. 316 *Perf. 11*

1082 A114	5d violet & pur ('58)	25	2.00
1083 A114	10d claret & rose car ('58)	25	2.00
1084 A114	25d rose car & brick red ('58)	50	35
1085 A114	50d grn & olive grn ('58)	40	15
1086 A114	1r dk grn ('58)	40	15
1087 A114	1.50r cl & red lil	50	25
1088 A114	2r bl & grnsh blue	1.65	15
1089 A114	2.50r dk bl & blue ('58)	1.65	25
1090 A114	3r rose car & ver	1.65	20
1091 A114	5r vio bl ('58)	1.50	15
1092 A113	6r brt bl ('58)	1.60	15
1093 A113	10r dp grn ('58)	3.00	30
1094 A113	20r grn & olive grn ('58)	6.25	45
1095 A113	30r vio bl & dk brn ('58)	15.00	4.00
1096 A113	50r dk brn & lt brn ('58)	20.00	5.00
1097 A113	100r rose lil & car rose ('58)	125.00	25.00
1098 A113	200r vio & yel brn ('58)	87.50	20.00
Nos. 1082-1098 (17)		267.10	60.55

Weight Lifter A122

Modern and Old Houses, Radio Transmitter A123

1957, Nov. 8 *Perf. 11x14½*

1099 A122 10r bl, grn & red 2.50 60

Iran's victories in weight lifting.

1958, Feb. 22 Litho.

1100 A123 10r brn, ocher & bl 4.00 1.50

30th anniversary of radio in Iran.

Oil Derrick and Symbolic Flame — A124

Train on Viaduct — A125

Wmk. 316

1958, Mar. 10 Photo. *Perf. 11*

1101 A124 2r gray & multi 3.25 80
1102 A124 10r multicolored 6.00 1.00

Drilling of Iran's 1st oil well, 50th anniv.

1958, Apr. 24 Wmk. 316 *Perf. 11*

Design: 8r, Train and map.

1103 A125 6r dull purple 10.00 2.50
1104 A125 8r green 12.00 2.50

Opening of Tehran-Tabriz railway line.

Exposition Emblem A126

1958, Apr. 17 *Perf. 12½x11*

1105 A126 2.50r bl & light bl 38 15
1106 A126 6r car & salmon 60 15
Set value 22

World's Fair, Brussels, Apr. 17-Oct. 19.

Mohammed Riza Pahlavi A127

UN Emblem and Map of Iran A128

1958-59 Wmk. 316 Photo. *Perf. 11*

1107 A127	5d blue vio	50	22
1108 A127	10d light ver	50	22
1109 A127	25d crimson	50	26
1110 A127	50d bright bl	50	22
1111 A127	1r dark green	1.00	15
1113 A127	2r dark brown	30.00	22
1115 A127	3r dk red brn	15.00	18
1117 A127	6r bright blue	4.00	1.75
1118 A127	8r magenta	5.00	35
1120 A127	14r bl violet	12.00	1.75
1121 A127	20r green	15.00	45
a.	Wmk. 306	20.00	10.00
1122 A127	30r brt car rose	12.00	1.75
1123 A127	50r rose violet	45.00	3.50
1124 A127	100r red orange	20.00	4.50
1125 A127	200r slate grn	40.00	8.00
Nos. 1107-1125 (15)		201.00	23.52

See Nos. 1138-1151, 1173-1179.

1958, Oct. 24

1126 A128 6r bright blue 1.25 45
1127 A128 10r dk vio & grn 2.25 80

Issued for United Nations Day, Oct. 24.

Globe and Hands A129

1958, Dec. 10

1128 A129 6r dk red brn & brn 75 22
1129 A129 8r dk grn & gray grn 1.25 32

Universal Declaration of Human Rights, 10th anniv.

Rudagi — A130

Wrestlers, Flag and Globe — A131

Flag — A130a

Design: 5r, Rudagi, different pose.

1958, Dec. 24 Photo. Wmk. 306

1130 A130 2.50r bluish blk 6.50 90
1131 A130 5r violet 10.00 1.50
1132 A130 10r dark brown 16.00 2.75

1100th birth anniv. of Rudagi, blind Persian poet.

Perf. 14½x11

1959, May 8 Wmk. 316

1132A A130a 1r multi 75 38
1132B A130a 6r multi 2.25 50

Centenary of the Red Cross.

1959 Litho. *Perf. 11x12½*

1133 A131 6r multicolored 10.00 2.50

World Wrestling Championships, Tehran.

Globe, UN Building and Hand Holding Torch of Freedom A132

1959, Oct. 24 Photo. *Perf. 11*

1134 A132 6r gray brn, red & bis 1.50 50

Issued for United Nations Day, Oct. 24.

Shah and Pres. Ayub Khan of Pakistan — A133

1959, Nov. 9 Litho. *Perf. 11x16*

1135 A133 6r multicolored 5.00 75

Visit of Pres. Khan to Iran.

ILO Emblem A134

Uprooted Oak Emblem A136

Pahlavi Foundation Bridge, Karun River — A135

1959, Nov. 12 *Perf. 16*

1136 A134 1r blue 1.10 30
1137 A134 5r brown 1.90 45

ILO, 40th anniversary.

Shah Type of 1958-59

1959-63 Wmk. 316 Photo. *Perf. 11*

1138 A127	5d red brn ('60)	35	30
1139 A127	10d Prus green ('60)	35	30
a.	10d Prussian blue ('63)	50	50
1140 A127	25d orange	1.00	20
a.	Perf. 12x11½	10.00	10.00
1141 A127	50d scarlet	1.00	25
1142 A127	1r deep vio	1.00	15
1143 A127	3r olive	2.00	15
1144 A127	8r brn olive	1.50	15
1145 A127	10r ol blk ('60)	1.50	15
1146 A127	14r yel green	1.75	25
1147 A127	20r sl grn ('60)	3.00	35
1148 A127	30r choc ('60)	3.50	65
1149 A127	50r dp bl ('60)	3.50	60
1150 A127	100r green ('60)	110.00	10.00
1151 A127	200r cer ('60)	225.00	15.00
Nos. 1138-1151 (14)		355.45	28.50

1960, Feb. 29 Litho. *Perf. 16x11*

Design: 5r, Bridge, different view.

1152 A135 1r dk brn & brt bl 1.00 15
1153 A135 5r blue & emerald 2.00 50

Opening of Pahlavi Foundation Bridge at Khorramshahr on the Karun River.

1960, Apr. 7 *Perf. 11*

Design: 6r, Arched frame.

1154 A136 1r brt ultra 50 15
1155 A136 6r gray ol 65 18

World Refugee Year, July 1, 1959-June 30, 1960.

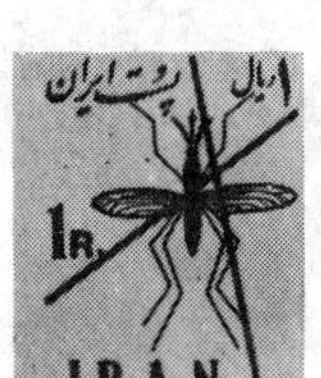

Mosquito — A137

Man with Spray Gun — A138

Design: 3r, Mosquito on water.

1960, Apr. 7 Wmk. 316

1156 A137 1r blk & red, *yel* 1.10 20
1157 A138 2r lt bl, ultra & blk 1.75 30
1158 A137 3r blk & red, *yel grn* 3.75 65

Issued to publicize malaria control.

Polo Player — A139

Design: 6r, Persian archer.

1960, June 9 Litho. Wmk. 316

1159 A139 1r deep claret 75 30
1160 A139 6r dark bl & lt bl 1.90 75

17th Olympic Games, Rome, Aug. 25-Sept. 11.

Shah and King Hussein of Jordan — A140

1960, July 6 *Perf. 11*

1161 A140 6r multicolored 5.00 65

Visit of King Hussein of Jordan to Tehran.

Iranian Scout Emblem in Flower A141

Tents and Pillars of Persepolis A142

1960, July 18

1162	A141	1r green	42	22
1163	A142	6r brn, brt bl & buff	65	45

3rd National Boy Scout Jamboree.

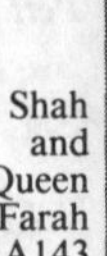

Shah and Queen Farah A143

1960, Sept. 9 **Litho.** ***Perf. 11***

1164	A143	1r green	2.25	50
1165	A143	5r blue	4.75	1.00

Marriage of Shah Mohammed Riza Pahlavi and Farah Diba.

UN Emblem and Globe — A144

1960, Oct. 24 **Wmk. 316**

1166	A144	6r bl, blk & lt brn	50	15

15th anniversary of the United Nations.

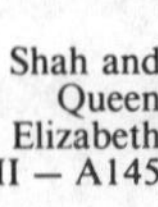

Shah and Queen Elizabeth II — A145

1961, Mar. 2 **Litho.** ***Perf. 11***

1167	A145	1r lt red brn	75	15
1168	A145	6r bright ultra	1.65	35

Visit of Queen Elizabeth II to Tehran, Feb. 1961.

Girl Playing Arganoon A146

Safiaddin Amavi A147

1961, Apr. 10 **Wmk. 316** ***Perf. 11***

1169	A146	1r dk brn & buff	65	15
1170	A147	6r greenish gray	1.40	20

International Congress of Music, Tehran.

Shah Type of 1958-59 Redrawn

1961-62 **Litho.** ***Perf. 11***

1173	A127	25d orange	1.00	50
1174	A127	50d scarlet	1.00	40
1175	A127	1r deep violet	2.00	20
1176	A127	2r chocolate	3.50	20
1177	A127	3r olive brown	4.00	50
1178	A127	6r brt bl ('62)	30.00	2.00
1179	A127	8r brn ol ('62)	16.00	2.00
		Nos. 1173-1179 (7)	57.50	5.80

On Nos. 1173-1179 (lithographed), a single white line separates the lower panel from the shah's portrait. On Nos. 1107-1125, 1138-1151 (photogravure), two lines, one in color and one in white, separate panel from portrait. Other minor differences exist.

Shah and Queen Farah Holding Crown Prince — A148

1961, June 2 **Litho.**

1186	A148	1r bright pink	1.25	75
1187	A148	6r light blue	5.00	2.25

Birth of Crown Prince Riza Cyrus Ali, Oct. 31, 1960.

Swallows and UN Emblem — A149

Planting Tree — A150

1961, Oct. 24 ***Perf. 11***

1188	A149	2r blue & car rose	75	15
1189	A149	6r blue & violet	90	28

Issued for United Nations Day, Oct. 24.

1962, Jan. 11

1190	A150	2r ol grn, cit & dk bl	60	16
1191	A150	6r ultra, grn & pale bl	75	32

Tree Planting Day.

Worker and Symbols of Labor and Agriculture A151

Map, Family and Cogwheel A152

1962, Mar. 15 **Litho.**

1192	A151	2r bl grn, brn & blk	60	15
1193	A151	6r lt ultra, brn & blk	90	28

Issued for Workers' Day.

1962, Mar. 20 ***Perf. 11***

1194	A152	2r blk, yel & lil	60	15
1195	A152	6r blk, bl & ultra	90	28

Social Insurance Week.

Sugar Refinery, Khuzistan A153

1962, Apr. 14 **Wmk. 316**

1196	A153	2r dk & lt bl & grn	65	15
1197	A153	6r ultra, buff & blue	1.00	30

Opening of sugar refinery in Khuzistan.

Karaj Dam — A154

1962, May 15

1198	A154	2r dk brn & gray grn	1.65	16
1199	A154	6r vio bl & lt blue	1.90	32

Inauguration of Karaj Dam, renamed Amir Kabir Dam.

Sefid Rud Dam A155

1962, May 19 **Litho.**

1200	A155	2r dk grn, lt bl & buff	1.25	25
1201	A155	6r red brn, sl grn & lt blue	1.75	50

Inauguration of Sefid Rud Dam.

"UNESCO" and UN Emblem — A156

1962, June 2 **Wmk. 316** ***Perf. 11***

1202	A156	2r blk, emer & red	75	15
1203	A156	6r bl, emer & red	1.50	40

15th anniv. of UNESCO.

Malaria Eradication Emblem and Sprayer — A157

Designs: 2r, Emblem and arrow piercing mosquito (horiz.). 10r, Emblem and globe (horiz.). Size: 2r and 10r, 40x25mm; 6r, 29½x34½mm.

1962, June 20

1204	A157	2r blk & bluish grn	24	15
1205	A157	6r pink & vio bl	95	15
1206	A157	10r lt bl & ultra	2.00	30

WHO drive to eradicate malaria.

Oil Field and UN Emblem — A158

1962, Sept. 1 **Photo.**

1207	A158	6r grnsh bl & brn	1.25	20
1208	A158	14r gray & sep	2.25	45

2nd Petroleum Symposium of ECAFE (UN Economic Commission for Asia and the Far East).

Mohammed Riza Pahlavi A159

Palace of Darius, Persepolis A160

Perf. 11, 10½x11

1962 **Photo.** **Wmk. 316**

1209	A159	5d green	75	25
1210	A159	10d chestnut	75	50
1211	A159	25d dark blue	50	35
1212	A159	50d Prus grn	50	15
1213	A159	1r orange	1.50	15
1214	A159	2r vio blue	1.00	15
1215	A159	5r dark brn	2.00	15
1216	A160	6r blue	9.00	2.50
1217	A160	8r yel green	4.50	1.00
1218	A160	10r grnsh bl	4.00	15
1219	A160	11r slate grn	4.50	65
1220	A160	14r purple	7.00	65
1221	A160	20r red brown	6.00	1.50
1222	A160	50r vermilion	8.00	1.50
		Nos. 1209-1222 (14)	50.00	9.65

See Nos. 1331-1344.

Hippocrates and Avicenna — A161

1962, Oct. 7 **Litho.**

1226	A161	2r brn, buff & ultra	1.40	25
1227	A161	6r grn, pale grn & ultra	1.65	38

Near and Middle East Medical Congress.

Hands Laying Bricks A162

Design: 6r, Houses and UN emblem (vert.).

1962, Oct. 24

1228	A162	6r dk bl & ultra	1.25	20
1229	A162	14r dk bl & emer	1.75	40

Issued for United Nations Day, Oct. 24.

Crown Prince Receiving Flowers A163

1962, Oct. 31

1230	A163	6r blue gray	4.25	65
1231	A163	14r dull green	8.25	1.65

Children's Day, Oct. 31; 2nd birthday of Crown Prince Riza Cyrus Ali.

Map of Iran and Persian Gulf — A164

Hilton Hotel, Tehran — A165

1962, Dec. 12 Wmk. 316 *Perf. 11*

1232 A164 6r dk & lt bl, vio bl & rose 1.00 16
1233 A164 14r dk & lt bl, pink & rose 1.50 32

The Persian Gulf Seminar.

1963, Jan. 21 Photo.

1234 A165 6r deep blue 2.75 30
1235 A165 14r dk red brn 4.25 45

Opening of the Royal Tehran Hilton Hotel.

Mohammed Riza Shah Dam — A166

1963, Mar. 14 Litho.

Center Multicolored

1236 A166 6r violet blue 3.25 30
1237 A166 14r dark brown 5.50 65

Mohammed Riza Shah Dam inauguration.

Worker with Pickax — A167

Stylized Bird over Globe — A168

1963, Mar. 15

1238 A167 2r cream & black 1.10 18
1239 A167 6r light bl & blk 2.00 32

Issued for Labor Day.

1963, Mar. 21 *Perf. 11*

Designs: 6r, Stylized globe and "FAO." 14r, Globe in space and wheat emblem.

1240 A168 2r ultra, lt bl & bis 1.50 15
1241 A168 6r lt ultra, ocher & blk 2.25 28
1242 A168 14r sl bl & ocher 3.75 85

FAO "Freedom from Hunger" campaign.

Shah and List of Bills A169

1963, Mar. 21 Wmk. 316

1243 A169 6r green & lt bl 3.75 1.10
1244 A169 14r green & dl yel 5.25 1.90

Signing of six socioeconomic bills by Shah, 1st anniv.

Shah and King of Denmark — A170

1963, May 3 Litho. *Perf. 11*

1245 A170 6r ind & dk ultra 3.00 55
1246 A170 14r dk brn & red brn 4.50 1.00

Visit of King Frederik IX of Denmark.

Flags, Shah Mosque, Isfahan, and Taj Mahal, Agra A171

1963, May 19

1247 A171 6r bl, yel grn & red 2.75 65
1248 A171 14r multi 4.00 1.25

Visit of Dr. Sarvepalli Radhakrishnan, president of India.

Chahnaz Dam — A172

Cent. Emblem with Red Lion and Sun — A173

1963, June 8 Wmk. 316 *Perf. 11*

1249 A172 6r ultra, bl & grn 2.50 38
1250 A172 14r dk grn, bl & buff 2.50 55

Inauguration of Chahnaz Dam.

1963, June 10

1251 A173 6r bl, gray & red 2.50 65
1252 A173 14r buff, gray & red 4.00 90

Centenary of International Red Cross.

Shah and Queen Juliana A174

Perf. 11x10½

1963, Oct. 3 Wmk. 349

1253 A174 6r ultra & blue 3.75 50
1254 A174 14r sl grn & dl grn 5.75 75

Visit of Queen Juliana of the Netherlands.

Literacy Corps Emblem and Soldier Teaching Village Class A175

1963, Oct. 15 Litho. *Perf. 10½*

1255 A175 6r multicolored 3.00 50
1256 A175 14r multicolored 5.00 50

Issued to publicize the Literacy Corps.

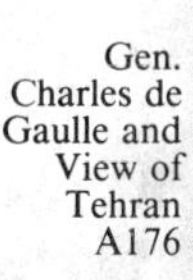

Gen. Charles de Gaulle and View of Tehran A176

1963, Oct. 16

1257 A176 6r ultra & blue 4.00 55
1258 A176 14r brn & pale brn 5.25 65

Visit of General de Gaulle of France.

Fertilizer Plant, Oil Company Emblem and Map — A177

Design: 14r, Factory and Iranian Oil Company emblem (horiz.).

Perf. 10½x11, 11x10½

1963, Oct. 18 Wmk. 316

1259 A177 6r blk, yel & red 4.00 50
1260 A177 14r blk, bl & yel 5.25 1.50

Opening of Shiraz Chemical Factory.

Pres. Heinrich Lübke of Germany and Mosque in Tehran A178

1963, Oct. 23 Wmk. 349 *Perf. 10½*

1261 A178 6r ultra & dk bl 4.25 65
1262 A178 14r gray & brn 5.00 1.65

Visit of Pres. Lubke of Germany.

UN Emblem and Iranian Flag — A179

1963, Oct. 24

1263 A179 8r multi 2.75 50

Issued for United Nations Day.

UN Emblem and Jets — A180

1963, Oct. 24

1264 A180 6r multi 2.75 50

Iranian jet fighters with UN Force in the Congo.

Crown Prince Riza — A181

Pres. Brezhnev of USSR — A182

1963, Oct. 31

1265 A181 2r brown 1.75 22
1266 A181 6r blue 4.50 48

Children's Day; Crown Prince Riza's 3rd birthday.

1963, Nov. 16 Wmk. 349 *Perf. 10½*

1267 A182 6r dk brn, yel & bl 2.25 32
1268 A182 11r dk brn, yel & red 5.00 75

Visit of Pres. Leonid I. Brezhnev.

Atatürk's Mausoleum, Ankara — A183

1963, Nov. 28 Litho.

1269 A183 4r shown 2.75 15
1270 A183 5r Kemal Ataturk 2.75 25

25th death anniv. of Kemal Atatürk, president of Turkey.

Scales and Globe — A184

1963, Dec. 10

1271 A184 6r brt yel grn, blk & ultra 2.75 30
1272 A184 14r org brn, blk & buff 3.25 35

Universal Declaration of Human Rights, 15th anniv.

Mother and Child — A185

Map of Iran, Chamber of Industry and Mines Emblem — A186

1963, Dec. 16

1273 A185 2r multi 2.25 25
1274 A185 4r multi 3.25 50

Issued for Mother's Day.

1963, Dec. 17 Litho.

1275 A186 8r bl grn, buff & dk bl 3.50 40

Chamber of Industry and Mines.

Factories and Hand Holding Bill — A187

Designs: 4r, Factories and bills on scale. 6r, Man on globe carrying torch of education. 8r, Tractor, map and yardstick. 10r, Forest. 12r, Gate of Parliament and heads of man and woman.

1964, Jan. 26 Wmk. 349 *Perf. 10½*

1276 A187 2r multicolored 3.00 75
1277 A187 4r brn & gray 3.00 75
1278 A187 6r multicolored 3.00 75
1279 A187 8r multicolored 3.00 1.00
1280 A187 10r multicolored 5.50 1.25
1281 A187 12r red org & brn 6.50 1.50
Nos. 1276-1281 (6) 24.00 6.00

2nd anniv. of six socioeconomic bills: 2r, Shareholding for factory workers. 4r, Sale of shares in government factories. 6r, Creation of Army of Education. 8r, Land reforms. 10r, Nationalization of forests. 12r, Reforms in parliamentary elections.

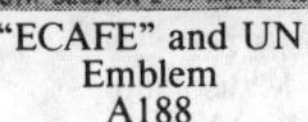

"ECAFE" and UN Emblem A188

Flowering Branch A189

1964, Mar. 2 **Wmk. 349**

1282 A188 14r brt grn & blk 2.25 45

20th session of ECAFE (Economic Commission for Asia and the Far East), Mar. 2-17.

1964, Mar. 5 ***Perf. 10½***

1283 A189 50d emer, blk & org 35 15
1284 A189 1r brt bl, blk & org 35 15
Set value 15

Novrooz, Iranian New Year, Mar. 21.

Anemometer A190

Mosque and Arches, Isfahan A191

1964, Mar. 23 **Litho.**

1285 A190 6r brt bl & vio bl 1.10 25

4th World Meteorological Day.

1964, Apr. 7 ***Perf. 10½***

Design: 11r, Griffon and winged bull, Persepolis.

1286 A191 6r lilac, grn & blk 2.00 38
1287 A191 11r org, brn & blk 2.75 55

Issued for tourist publicity.

Rudaki and Musical Instrument — A192

1964, May 16 **Photo.** **Wmk. 349**

1288 A192 6r blue 1.90 32
1289 A192 8r red brown 3.50 45

Opening of an institute for the blind. The inscription translates: "Wisdom is better than eye and sight."

Sculpture, Persepolis A193

Designs: 4r, Achaemenian horse-drawn mail cart, map of Iran (horiz.). 6r, Vessel with sculptured animals. 10r, Head of King Shapur, sculpture.

1964, June 5 **Wmk. 349** **Litho.**

1290 A193 2r gray & blue 3.25 1.00
1291 A193 4r vio bl, lt bl & bl 6.50 1.40
1292 A193 6r brown & yel 6.50 1.40
1293 A193 10r yel & ol grn 8.00 1.40

Opening of the "7000 Years of Persian Art" exhibition in Washington, D.C.

Shah and Emperor Haile Selassie A194

1964, Sept. 14 **Wmk. 349** ***Perf. 10½***

1294 A194 6r ultra & lt bl 3.00 30

Visit of Emperor Haile Selassie of Ethiopia.

Tooth and Dentists' Assoc. Emblem A195

"2 I.D.A." A196

1964, Sept. 14 **Litho.**

1295 A195 2r bl, red & dk bl 1.00 15
1296 A196 4r ultra, bl & pale brn 1.40 18
Set value 27

Iranian Dentists' Association, 2nd congress.

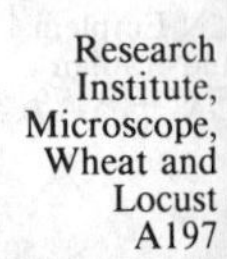

Research Institute, Microscope, Wheat and Locust A197

Beetle under Magnifying Glass A198

1964, Sept. 23 **Wmk. 349** ***Perf. 10½***

1297 A197 2r red, org & brn 1.65 22
1298 A198 6r bl, brn & indigo 2.50 40

Fight against plant diseases and damages.

Mithras (Mehr) on Ancient Seal A199

Eleanor Roosevelt (1884-1962) A200

1964, Oct. 8 **Litho.**

Size: 26x34mm

1299 A199 8r org & brn org 2.00 35

Mehragan celebration. See No. 1406.

1964, Oct. 11

1300 A200 10r vio bl & rose vio 4.00 32

Clasped Hands and UN Emblem A201

Symbolic Airplane and UN Emblem A202

1964, Oct. 24 **Wmk. 349** ***Perf. 10½***

1301 A201 6r ultra, yel, red & blk 1.50 30
1302 A202 14r org, ultra & red 2.25 50

Issued for United Nations Day.

Persian Gymnast — A203

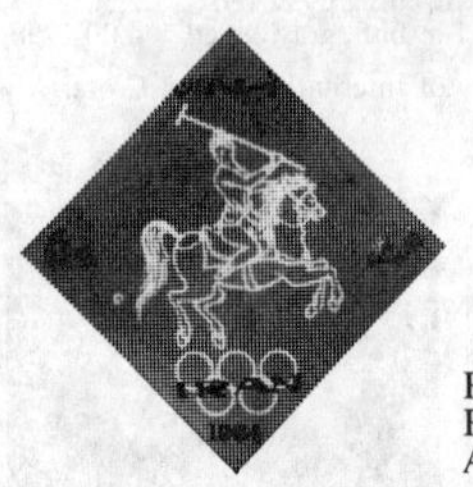

Polo Player A204

1964, Oct. 26

1303 A203 4r tan, sep & Prus bl 1.25 20
1304 A204 6r red & black 1.75 28

18th Olympic Games, Tokyo, Oct. 10-25.

Crown Prince Riza — A205

1964, Oct. 31 **Litho.**

1305 A205 1r dull grn & brn 1.40 30
1306 A205 2r dp rose & ultra 2.75 50
1307 A205 6r ultra & red 4.00 65

Children's Day; Crown Prince Riza's 4th birthday.

UN Emblem, Flame and Smokestack — A206

1964, Nov. 16 **Wmk. 349** ***Perf. 10½***

1308 A206 6r blk, lt bl & car 75 15
1309 A206 8r blk, emer & car 1.50 20

Petro-Chemical Conference and Gas Seminar, Nov.-Dec. 1964.

Shah and King Baudouin A207

1964, Nov. 17

1310 A207 6r blk, org & yel 1.10 16
1311 A207 8r blk, org & emer 1.90 28

Visit of King Baudouin of Belgium.

Rhazes — A208

1964, Dec. 27 **Wmk. 349** ***Perf. 10½***

1312 A208 2r multicolored 1.10 15
1313 A208 6r multicolored 1.90 25

1100th birth anniv. of Rhazes (abu-Bakr Muhammad ibn-Zakariya al-Razi), Persian-born Moslem physician.

Shah and King Olav V A209

1965, Jan. 7 **Litho.**

1314 A209 2r dk brn & lilac 1.10 16
1315 A209 4r brown & green 1.60 25

Visit of King Olav V of Norway.

Map of Iran and Six-pointed Star A210

1965, Jan. 26 **Wmk. 349** ***Perf. 10½***

1316 A210 2r blk, brt bl & org 1.10 20

3rd anniv. of the Shah's six socioeconomic bills.

Woman and UN Emblem A211

Green Wheat and Tulip A212

1965, Mar. 1 Wmk. 349 *Perf. 10½*
1317 A211 6r black & blue 85 15
1318 A211 8r ultra & red 1.25 20

18th session of the UN commission on the status of women.

1965, Mar. 6
1319 A212 50d multicolored 28 15
1320 A212 1r multicolored 28 15
Set value 15

Novrooz, Iranian New Year, Mar. 21.

Pres. Habib Bourguiba and Minarets of Tunis Mosque A213

1965, Mar. 14 Litho. *Perf. 10½*
1321 A213 4r multicolored 90 15

Visit of Pres. Habib Bourguiba of Tunisia.

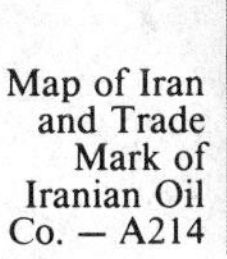

Map of Iran and Trade Mark of Iranian Oil Co. — A214

1965, Mar. 20 Litho.
1322 A214 6r multicolored 1.10 18
1323 A214 14r multicolored 1.90 35

Oil industry nationalization, 14th anniv.

ITU Emblem, Old and New Communication Equipment — A215

1965, May 17 Wmk. 349 *Perf. 10½*
1324 A215 14r dp car rose & gray 1.10 18

ITU, centenary.

ICY Emblem A216

1965, June 22 Litho. *Perf. 10½*
1325 A216 10r sl grn & gray bl 2.25 15

International Cooperation Year, 1965.

Iran Airways Emblem A217

1965, July 17 Wmk. 349 *Perf. 10½*
1326 A217 14r multicolored 2.25 30

Tenth anniversary of Iran Airways.

Hands Holding Book — A218

Map and Flags of Turkey, Iran and Pakistan A219

1965, July 21 Litho.
1327 A218 2r dk brn, org brn & buff 42 15
1328 A219 4r multicolored 70 20
Set value 30

Signing of the Regional Cooperation for Development Pact by Turkey, Iran and Pakistan, 1st anniv.

Iranian Scout Emblem and Ornament A220

1965, July 23
1329 A220 2r multicolored 70 20
a. Vert. pair, imperf. horiz. 20.00

Middle East Rover Moot (senior Boy Scout assembly).

Majlis Gate A221

1965, Aug. 5 Wmk. 349 *Perf. 10½*
1330 A221 2r lilac rose & brn 40 15

60th anniversary of Iranian constitution.

Types of Regular Issue, 1962

Wmk. 349

1964-65 Photo. *Perf. 10½*

1331	A159	5d	dk sl grn ('65)	35	30
a.			Wmk. 353	35	30
1332	A159	10d	chestnut	35	30
1333	A159	25d	dk blue ('65)	50	25
1334	A159	50d	Prus green	75	15
1335	A159	1r	orange	75	15
1336	A159	2r	vio blue	50	15
1337	A159	5r	dark brown	3.00	50
1338	A160	6r	blue ('65)	10.00	1.00
1339	A160	8r	yel grn ('65)	3.50	25
1340	A160	10r	grnsh bl ('65)	3.00	25
1341	A160	11r	sl grn ('65)	10.00	1.50
1342	A160	14r	purple ('65)	7.00	1.40
1343	A160	20r	red brn ('65)	4.50	1.00
1344	A160	50r	org ver ('65)	7.50	2.00
			Nos. 1331-1344 (14)	51.70	9.20

Perf. 11x10½

1331b	A159	5d	Wmk. 353	3.25	1.00
1332a	A159	10d		55	50
1333a	A159	25d		80	25
1334a	A159	50d		3.00	2.00
1335a	A159	1r		3.00	2.00
1337a	A159	5r		4.00	50

Dental Congress Emblem — A222

1965, Sept. 7 Litho. *Perf. 10½*
1345 A222 6r gray, ultra, & car 60 22

Iranian Dentists' Association, 3rd congress.

Classroom and Literacy Corps Emblem A223

Alphabets on Globe — A224

Designs: 6r, UNESCO emblem and open book (diamond shape). 8r, UNESCO emblem and inscription (horiz.). 14r, Shah Riza Pahlavi and inscription in six languages.

1965, Sept. 8
1346 A223 2r multi 35 20
1347 A224 5r multi 40 25

Size: 30x30mm
1348 A223 6r multi 80 30

Size: 35x23mm
1349 A223 8r dk bl, car emer & buff 80 25

Size: 34x46mm
1350 A223 14r cit, dk bl & brn 2.00 30
Nos. 1346-1350 (5) 4.35 1.30

World Congress Against Illiteracy, Tehran, Sept. 8-19.

Mohammed Riza Pahlavi — A225

1965, Sept. 16 Litho. *Perf. 10½*
1351 A225 1r crim, rose red & gray 90 15
1352 A225 2r dk red, rose red & yel 90 20

Reign of Shah, 25th anniv.

Emblem of Persian Medical Society — A226

1965, Sept. 21 Wmk. 349
1353 A226 5r ultra, dp ultra & gold 50 25

14th Medical Congress, Ramsar.

Pres. Jonas of Austria A227

1965, Sept. 30
1354 A227 6r bl, brt bl & gray 1.50 25

Visit of President Franz Jonas of Austria.

Mithras (Mehr) on Ancient Seal — A228

1965, Oct. 8 Litho. Wmk. 353
1355 A228 4r brt grn, gold, brn & blk 60 16

Mehragan celebration during month of Mehr, Sept. 23-Oct. 22. Persian inscription of watermark vertical on No. 1355.

UN Emblem — A229

1965, Oct. 24 Wmk. 353 *Perf. 10½*
1356 A229 5r bl, grn & rose car 55 15

20th anniversary of the United Nations.

Symbolic Arches A230

1965, Oct. 26
1357 A230 3r vio bl, blk, yel & red 55 15

Exhibition of Iranian Commodities.

Crown Prince Riza — A231

1965, Oct. 31
1358 A231 2r brown & yellow 1.10 45

Children's Day; Crown Prince Riza's 5th birthday.

Weight Lifters — A232

1965, Nov. 1
1359 A232 10r brt bl, vio & brt pink 60 20

World Weight Lifting Championships, Tehran.

Open Book — A233

1965, Dec. 1 Wmk. 353 *Perf. 10½*
1360 A233 8r bl, brt pink & blk 60 20

Issued for Book Week.

Shah and King Faisal A234

1965, Dec. 8 Litho.
1361 A234 4r olive bis & brn 1.50 35

Visit of King Faisal of Saudi Arabia.

Scales and Olive Branch — A235

1965, Dec. 12
1362 A235 14r multicolored 60 18

Human Rights Day (Dec. 10).

Tractor, "Land Reform" A236

Symbols of Reform Bills: 2r, Trees, nationalization of forests. 3r, Factory and gear wheel, sale of shares in government factories. 4r, Wheels, shareholding for factory workers. 5r, Parliament gate, women's suffrage. 6r, Children before blackboard, Army of Education. 7r, Caduceus, Army of Hygiene. 8r, Scales, creation of rural courts. 9r, Two girders, creation of Army of Progress.

1966, Jan. 26 Wmk. 353 *Perf. 10½*

1363	A236	1r orange & brown	20	15
1364	A236	2r dl grn & green	20	15
1365	A236	3r silver & gray	20	15
1366	A236	4r light & dk vio	30	15
1367	A236	5r rose & brown	40	15
1368	A236	6r olive & brown	60	15
1369	A236	7r bl & vio blue	85	16
1370	A236	8r ultra & dp ultra	1.00	16
1371	A236	9r brn org & dk brn	1.00	20
		Nos. 1363-1371 (9)	4.75	
		Set value		1.15

Parliamentary approval of the Shah's reform plan.

Shah A237

Ruins of Persepolis A238

Wmk. 353
1966-71 Photo. *Perf. 10½*

1372	A237	5d green	15	15
1373	A237	10d chestnut	20	15
1374	A237	25d dark blue	20	15
1375	A237	50d bl grn ('71)	50	30
a.		50d Prussian green	50	25
1376	A237	1r orange	50	15
1377	A237	2r violet	40	15
1377A	A237	4r cl brn ('68)	4.00	1.00
1378	A237	5r dark brn	1.75	25
1379	A238	6r deep blue	60	15
1380	A238	8r yellow grn	60	15
a.		8r dull green ('71)	60	15
1381	A238	10r Prus bl	95	15
1382	A238	11r slate grn	95	15
1383	A238	14r purple	1.25	25
1384	A238	20r brown	9.50	50
1385	A238	50r cop red	3.75	1.50
1386	A238	100r brt blue	12.50	1.75
1387	A238	200r chnt brn	12.50	3.25
		Nos. 1372-1387 (17)	50.30	10.15

Set, except 4r, issued Feb. 22, 1966.

Student Nurse Taking Oath A239

Narcissus A240

1966, Feb. 24 Litho.
1388 A239 5r brt pink & mag 50 15
1389 A239 5r lt bl & brt bl 50 15
Set value 24

Nurses' Day. Nos. 1388-1389 printed in sheets of 50 arranged checkerwise.

1966, Mar. 7
1390 A240 50d ultra, yel & emer 20 15
1391 A240 1r lilac, yel & emer 20 15
Set value 15

Novrooz, Iranian New Year, Mar. 21.

Oil Derricks in Persian Gulf — A241

1966, Mar. 20 *Perf. 10½*
1392 A241 14r blk, brt bl & brt rose lil 1.50 40

Formation of six offshore oil companies.

Radio Tower — A242

Designs: 2r, Radar (horiz.). 6r, Emblem and waves. 8r, Compass rose and waves. 10r, Tower and waves.

1966, Apr. 27 Litho. Wmk. 349

1393	A242	2r dark grn	16	15
1394	A242	4r ultra & dp org	20	15
1395	A242	6r gray ol & plum	28	16
1396	A242	8r brt bl & dk bl	35	20
1397	A242	10r brn & bister	52	28
		Nos. 1393-1397 (5)	1.51	94

Inauguration of the radio telecommunication system of the Central Treaty Organization of the Middle East (CENTO).

WHO Headquarters, Geneva — A243

1966, May 3 Wmk. 353
1398 A243 10r brt bl, yel & blk 50 18

Opening of the WHO Headquarters, Geneva.

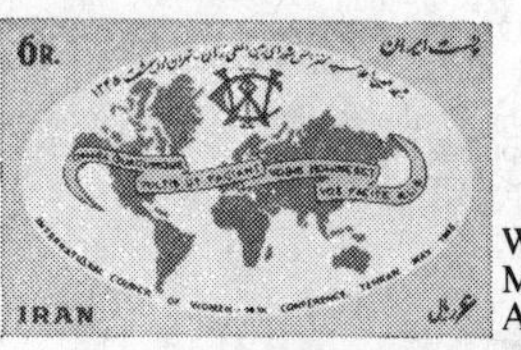

World Map A244

1966, May 14 Litho.
1399 A244 6r bl & multi 38 15
1400 A244 8r multicolored 55 15
Set value 22

Intl. Council of Women, 18th Conf., Tehran, May 1966.

Globe, Map of Iran and Ruins of Persepolis — A245

1966, Sept. 5 Wmk. 353 *Perf. 10½*
1401 A245 14r multicolored 1.00 20

International Iranology Congress, Tehran.

Emblem of Iranian Medical Society — A246

1966, Sept. 21
1402 A246 4r ultra, grnsh bl & bis 30 15

15th Medical Congress, held at Ramsar.

Gate of Parliament, Mt. Demavend and Congress Emblem — A247

Design: 8r, Senate building, Mt. Demavend and emblem.

1966, Oct. 2 Wmk. 353 *Perf. 10½*
1403 A247 6r brick red, ultra & dk grn 25 15
1404 A247 8r lt lil, ultra & dk grn 35 15
Set value 22

55th Interparliamentary Union Conf., Tehran.

Visit of President Cemal Gursel of Turkey — A248

1966, Oct. 2 Litho.
1405 A248 6r vio & dk brn 35 15

Mithras Type of 1964

1966, Oct. 8
Size: 30x40mm
1406 A199 6r olive bis & brn 45 15

Mehragan celebration.

Farmers — A249

1966, Oct. 13
1407 A249 5r olive bis & brn 1.10 50

Establishment of rural courts of justice.

UN Emblem A250

1966, Oct. 24 Wmk. 353 *Perf. 10½*
1408 A250 6r brn org & blk 35 15

21st anniversary of United Nations.

Crown Prince Riza — A251

Symbolic Woman's Face — A252

1966, Oct. 31 Litho.
1409 A251 1r ultramarine 65 15
1410 A251 2r violet 1.00 15
Set value 24

Children's Day; Crown Prince Riza's 6th birthday. Nos. 1409-1410 are printed se-tenant.

1966, Nov. 6
1411 A252 5r gold, blk & ultra 30 15

Founding of the Iranian Women's Org.

Film Strip and Song Bird A253

1966, Nov. 6
1412 A253 4r blk, red lil & vio 28 15

First Iranian children's film festival.

"Census Count" — A254

Book Cover — A255

1966, Nov. 11
1413 A254 6r dk brn & gray 28 15

National census.

1966, Nov. 15
1414 A255 8r tan, brn & ultra 35 15

Issued to publicize Book Week.

Riza Shah Pahlavi A256

Design: 2r, Riza Shah Pahlavi without kepi.

1966, Nov. 16 **Litho.**
1415 A256 1r slate blue 1.25 30
1416 A256 1r brown 1.25 30
1417 A256 2r gray green 1.25 30
1418 A256 2r violet blue 1.25 30

Riza Shah Pahlavi (1877-1944), founder of modern Iran. Stamps of same denomination printed se-tenant.

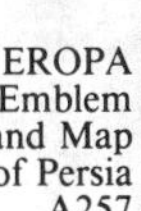

EROPA Emblem and Map of Persia A257

1966, Dec. 4 Wmk. 353 *Perf. 10½*
1419 A257 8r dk brn & emer 30 15

4th General Assembly of the Org. of Public Administrators, EROPA.

Shah Giving Land Reform Papers to Farmers A258

1967, Jan. 9 Wmk. 353 *Perf. 10½*
1420 A258 6r ol bis, yel & brn 90 15

Approval of land reform laws, 5th anniv.

Shah and 9-Star Crescent A259

Design: 2r, Torch and 9-star crescent.

1967, Jan. 26 Wmk. 353 Litho.
1421 A259 2r multicolored 70 15
1422 A259 6r multicolored 1.25 15
Set value 20

5th anniv. of Shah's reforms, the "White Revolution."

Ancient Sculpture of Bull — A260

Designs: 5r, Sculptured mythical animals. 8r, Pillar from Persepolis.

1967, Feb. 25 Wmk. 353 *Perf. 10½*
1423 A260 3r dk brn & ocher 50 15
1424 A260 5r Prus grn, brn & ocher 50 15
1425 A260 8r vio, blk & sil 1.25 25

Issued to publicize Museum Week.

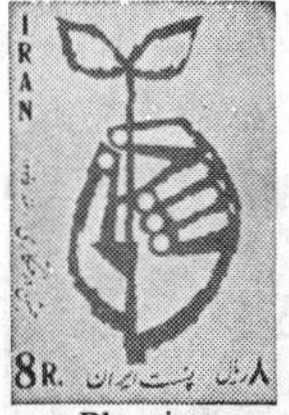
Planting Tree — A261

Goldfish — A262

1967, Mar. 6
1426 A261 8r brn org & grn 30 15

Tree Planting Day.

1967, Mar. 11
Size: 26x20mm
1427 A262 1r shown 25 15
Size: 35x27mm
1428 A262 8r Swallows 70 20
Set value 30

Issued for Novrooz, Iranian New Year.

Microscope, Animals and Emblem — A263

1967, Mar. 11 *Perf. 10½*
1429 A263 5r blk, gray & mag 35 15

Second Iranian Veterinary Congress.

Pres. Arif of Iraq, Mosque A264

1967, Mar. 14 Litho. Wmk. 353
1430 A264 6r brt bl & grn 35 15

Visit of Pres. Abdul Salam Mohammed Arif.

Fireworks A265

1967, Mar. 17
1431 A265 5r vio bl & multi 38 15

Issued for United Nations Stamp Day.

Map of Iran and Oil Company Emblem A266

1967, Mar. 20
1432 A266 6r multicolored 1.00 22

Nationalization of Iranian Oil Industry.

Fencers A267

1967, Mar. 23
1433 A267 5r vio & bister 50 15

Intl. Youth Fencing Championships, Tehran.

Shah and King of Thailand A268

1967, Apr. 23 Wmk. 353 *Perf. 10½*
1434 A268 6r brn org & dk brn 1.10 25

Visit of King Bhumibol Adulyadej.

Old and Young Couples A269

1967, Apr. 24 Litho.
1435 A269 5r ol bis & vio bl 32 15

15th anniversary of Social Insurance.

Skier and Iranian Olympic Emblem A270

Designs: 6r, Assyrian soldiers, Olympic rings and tablet inscribed "I.O.C." 8r, Wrestlers and Iranian Olympic emblem.

1967, May 5
1436 A270 3r brown & black 25 15
1437 A270 6r multicolored 35 20
1438 A270 8r ultra & brown 65 30

65th Intl. Olympic Congress, Tehran, May 2-11.

Lions International — A271

1967, May 11
Size: 41½x30½mm
1439 A271 3r shown 50 15
Size: 36x42mm
1440 A271 7r Emblem, vert. 75 25

50th anniversary of Lions International.

Visit of Pres. Chivu Stoica of Romania A272

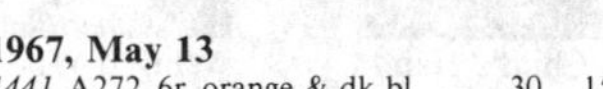

1967, May 13
1441 A272 6r orange & dk bl 30 15

International Tourist Year Emblem A273

1967, June 6 Wmk. 353 *Perf. 10½*
1442 A273 3r brick red & ultra 30 15

Iranian Pavilion and Ornament A274

1967, June 7 Litho.
1443 A274 4r dk brn, red & gold 16 15
1444 A274 10r red, dk brn & gold 28 15
Set value 23

EXPO '67, Montreal, Apr. 28-Oct. 27.

Stamp of 1870, No. 1 A275

1967, July 23 Wmk. 353 *Perf. 10½*

1445 A275 6r ultra, bl & rose claret 25 15
1446 A275 8r dk grn, lt grn & rose cl 35 15
Set value 24

Centenary of first Persian postage stamp.

World Map and School Children A276

Globe and Oriental Musician A277

1967, Sept. 8 Litho. Wmk. 353

1447 A276 3r ultra & brt & brt bl 15 15
1448 A276 5r brown & yellow 30 20
Set value 30

World campaign against illiteracy.

1967, Sept. 10 *Perf. 10½*

1449 A277 14r brn org & dk brn 75 16

Intl. Conf. on Music Education in Oriental Countries, Sept. 1967.

Child's Hand Holding Adult's — A278

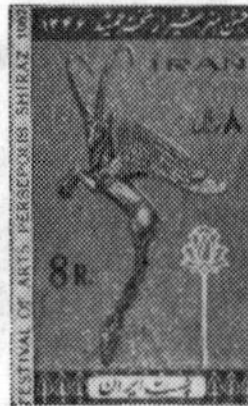
Winged Wild Goat — A279

1967, Sept. 14 Litho. Wmk. 353

1450 A278 8r dk brn & yel 3.25 2.50

Introduction of Children's Villages in Iran. (Modelled after Austrian SOS Villages for homeless children).

1967, Sept. 19

1451 A279 8r dk brn & lemon 60 25

Festival of Arts, Persepolis.

UN Emblem A280

1967, Oct. 17

1452 A280 6r ol bis & vio bl 35 15

Issued for United Nations Day.

Shah and Empress Farah — A281

1967, Oct. 26 Wmk. 353 *Perf. 10½*
Various Frames

1453 A281 2r sil, bl & brn 90 16
1454 A281 10r sil, bl & vio 90 40
1455 A281 14r lt bl, bl, gold & vio 2.25 40

Coronation of Shah Mohammed Riza Pahlavi and Empress Farah, Oct. 26, 1967.
Exist part perf., ungummed.

1967, Oct. 31 Litho.

Design: Crown Prince Riza.

1456 A281 2r silver & violet 90 15
1457 A281 8r sil & red brown 1.25 20
Set value 30

Children's Day; Crown Prince Riza's 7th birthday.

Visit of Pres. Georgi Traikov of Bulgaria — A283

1967, Nov. 20

1458 A283 10r lil & dk brn 35 15

Persian Boy Scout Emblem A284

1967, Dec. 3 Wmk. 353 *Perf. 10½*

1459 A284 8r olive & red brn 75 15

Cooperation Week of the Iranian Boy Scouts, Dec. 5-12.

Hands Holding Chain Link A285

1967, Dec. 6 Litho.

1460 A285 6r multicolored 32 15

Issued to publicize Cooperation Year.

Visit of Sheik Sabah of Kuwait — A286

1968, Jan. 10 Wmk. 353 *Perf. 10½*

1461 A286 10r lt bl & sl grn 38 20

List of Shah's 12 Reform Laws — A287

1968, Jan. 27 Litho. Wmk. 353

1462 A287 2r sl grn, brn & sal 38 15
1463 A287 8r vio, dk grn & lt grn 1.25 15
1464 A287 14r brn, pink & lt lil 1.65 20
Set value 40

"White Revolution of King and People."

Almond Blossoms A288

Haji Firooz (New Year Singer) A289

Design: 2r, Tulips.

1968, Mar. 12 Wmk. 353 *Perf. 10½*

1465 A288 1r multi 20 15
1466 A288 2r bluish gray & multi 20 15
1467 A288 2r brt rose lil & multi 20 15
1468 A289 6r multi 80 15
Set value 36

Issued for Novrooz, Iranian New Year.

Oil Worker and Derrick — A290

1968, Mar. 20 Litho.

1469 A290 14r grn, blk & org yel 60 15

Oil industry nationalization, 17th anniv.

WHO Emblem — A291

1968, Apr. 7 Wmk. 353 *Perf. 10½*

1470 A291 14r brn, bl & org 60 15

WHO, 20th anniversary.

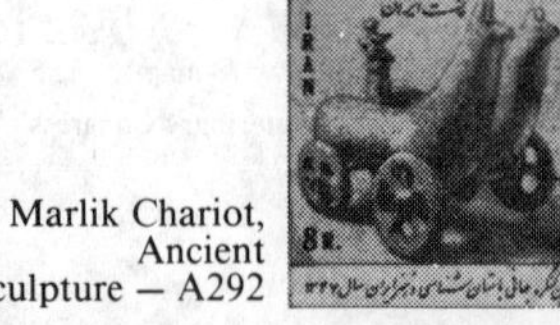
Marlik Chariot, Ancient Sculpture — A292

1968, Apr. 13

1471 A292 8r blue, brn & buff 40 15

Fifth World Congress of Persian Archaeology and Art, Tehran.

Shah and King Hassan II — A293

1968, Apr. 16

1472 A293 6r bright vio & buff 1.10 18

Visit of King Hassan II of Morocco.

Human Rights Flame — A294

Soccer Player — A295

Design: 14r, Frameline inscription reads, "International Conference on Human Rights Tehran 1968"; "Iran" at left.

1968, May 5 Wmk. 353 *Perf. 10½*

1473 A294 8r red & dk grn 25 15
1474 A294 14r vio bl & bl 50 15
Set value 24

Intl. Human Rights Year. The 8r commemorates the Iranian Human Rights Committee; the 14r, the Intl. Conference on Human Rights, Tehran, 1968.

1968, May 10 Litho.

1475 A295 8r multicolored 25 15
1476 A295 10r multicolored 50 25

Asian Soccer Cup Finals, Tehran.

Tehran Oil Refinery A296

1968, May 21 Wmk. 353 *Perf. 10½*

1477 A296 14r brt bl & multi 75 18

Opening of the Tehran Oil Refinery.

Queen Farah as Girl Guide — A297

1968, June 24 Litho. *Perf. 10½*

1478 A297 4r brt rose lil & bl green 1.25 25
1479 A297 6r car & brn 2.00 50

Great Camp of Iranian Girl Guides.

Anopheles Mosquito, Congress Emblem — A298

Winged Figure with Banner, and Globe — A299

1968, Sept. 7 Wmk. 353 Perf. 10½

1480	A298	6r brt pur & blk	30	15
1481	A298	14r dk grn & mag	45	16

8th Intl. Congress on Tropical Medicine and Malaria, Tehran, Sept. 7-15.

1968, Sept. 8 Litho.

1482	A299	6r lt vio, bis & bl	30	15
1483	A299	14r dl yel, sl grn & brn	45	16

World campaign against illiteracy.

Oramental Horse and Flower — A300

1968, Sept. 11

1484	A300	14r sl grn, org & yel grn	65	20

2nd Festival of Arts, Shiraz-Persepolis.

INTERPOL Emblem and Globe — A301

1968, Oct. 6 Wmk. 353 Perf. 10½

1485	A301	10r dk brn & bl	50	15

37th General Assembly of the Intl. Police Org. (INTERPOL) in Tehran.

Police Emblem on Iran Map in Flag Colors — A302

Peace Dove and UN Emblem — A303

1968, Oct. 7 Litho.

1486	A302	14r multicolored	1.00	20

Issued for Police Day.

1968, Oct. 24

1487	A303	14r bl & vio bl	75	20

Issued for United Nations Day.

Empress Farah — A304

Designs: 8r, Shah Mohammed Riza Pahlavi. 10fr, Shah, Empress and Crown Prince.

1968, Oct. 26

1488	A304	6r multi	4.25	1.65
1489	A304	8r multi	4.25	1.65
1490	A304	10r multi	4.25	1.65

Coronation of Shah Riza Pahlavi and Empress Farah, 1st anniv.

Shah's Crown and Bull's Head Capital A305

UNICEF Emblem and Child's Drawing A306

1968, Oct. 30

1491	A305	14r ultra, gold, sil & red	75	20

Festival of Arts and Culture.

1968, Oct. 31 Litho.

Children's Drawings and UNICEF Emblem: 3r, Boat on lake, house and trees (horiz.). 5r, Flowers (horiz.).

1492	A306	2r dk brn & multi	15	15
1493	A306	3r dk grn & multi	20	15
1494	A306	5r multicolored	30	25

Issued for Children's Day.

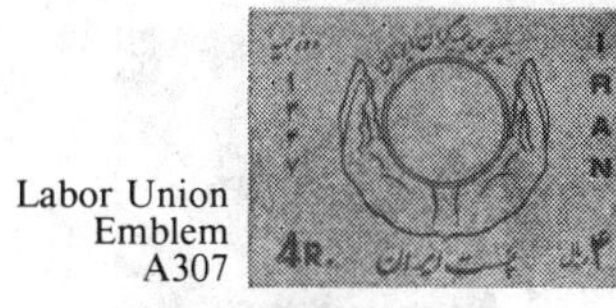
Labor Union Emblem A307

Factory and Insurance Company Emblem A308

Designs: 8r, Members of Army of Hygiene, and Insurance Company emblem. 10r, Map of Persia, Insurance Company emblem, car, train, ship and plane.

1968, Nov. 6 Wmk. 353 Perf. 10½

1495	A307	4r sil & vio bl	16	15
1496	A308	5r multicolored	16	15
1497	A308	8r ultra, gray & yel	25	15
1498	A308	10r multicolored	45	20
		Set value		50

Issued to publicize Insurance Day.

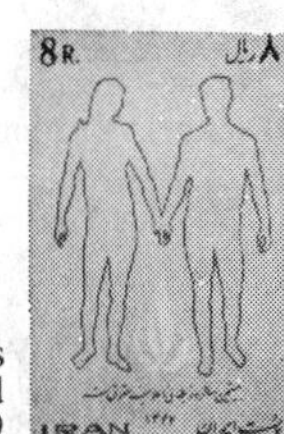
Human Rights Flame, Man and Woman — A309

1968, Dec. 10 Litho. Perf. 10½

1499	A309	8r lt bl, vio bl & car	32	15

International Human Rights Year.

Symbols of Shah's Reform Plan — A310

Design: Each stamp shows symbols of 3 of the Shah's reforms. Nos. 1500-1503 are printed se-tenant in blocks of 4. The block shows the 12 symbols in a circle with a medallion in the center picturing 3 heads and a torch.

1969, Jan. 26 Wmk. 353 Perf. 10½

1500	A310	2r ocher, grn & lil	60	15
1501	A310	4r lil, ocher & grn	60	15
1502	A310	6r lil, ocher & grn	75	25
1503	A310	8r lil, ocher & grn	1.00	25
a.		Block of four	5.50	2.50

Declaration of the Shah's Reform Plan.

Shah and Crowd A311

1969, Feb. 1 Litho.

1504	A311	6r red, bl & brn	1.50	20

10,000th day of the reign of the Shah.

European Goldfinch A312

Designs: 2r, Ring-necked pheasant. 8r, Roses.

1969, Mar. 6 Wmk. 353 Perf. 10½

1505	A312	1r multicolored	15	15
1506	A312	2r multicolored	20	15
1507	A312	8r multicolored	85	20
		Set value		36

Issued for Novrooz, Iranian New Year.

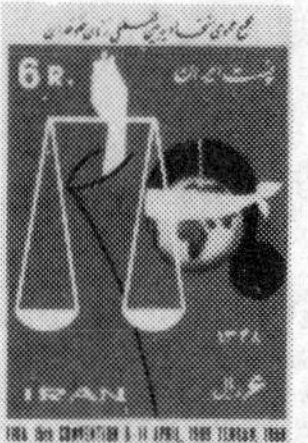
"Woman Lawyer" Holding Scales of Justice A313

Workers, ILO and UN Emblems A314

1969, Apr. 8 Litho. Perf. 10½

1508	A313	6r blk & brt bl	48	15

15th General Assembly of Women Lawyers, Tehran, Apr. 8-14.

1969, Apr. 30 Wmk. 353 Perf. 10½

1509	A314	10r bl & vio bl	55	15

ILO, 50th anniversary.

Freestyle Wrestlers and Ariamehr Cup — A315

1969, May 6 Litho.

1510	A315	10r lilac & multi	90	25

Intl. Freestyle Wrestling Championships, 3rd round.

Birds and Flower — A316

1969, June 10 Wmk. 353 Perf. 10½

1511	A316	10r vio bl & multi	75	15

Issued to publicize Handicrafts Day.

Boy Scout Symbols — A317

1969, July 9 Wmk. 353 Perf. 10½

1512	A317	6r lt bl & multi	1.00	15

Philia 1969, an outdoor training course for Boy Scout patrol leaders.

15-Cent Minimum Value

The minimum value for a single stamp is 15 cents. This value reflects the costs of the handling of inexpensive stamps.

Lady Serving Wine, Safavi Miniature, Iran — A318

Designs: No. 1514, Lady on Balcony, Mogul miniature, Pakistan. No. 1515, Sultan Suleiman Receiving Sheik Abdul Latif, 16th century miniature, Turkey.

1969, July 21 Litho.

1513 A318 25r multi 2.00 50
1514 A318 25r multi 2.00 50
1515 A318 25r multi 2.00 50

Signing of the Regional Cooperation for Development Pact by Turkey, Iran and Pakistan, 5th anniv.

Neil A. Armstrong and Col. Edwin E. Aldrin on Moon — A319

1969, July 26

1516 A319 24r bis, bl & brn 6.00 2.00

See note after Algeria No. 427.

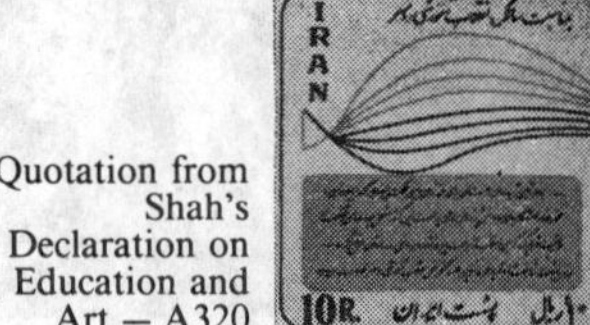

Quotation from Shah's Declaration on Education and Art — A320

1969, Aug. 6 Wmk. 353 *Perf. 10½*

1517 A320 10r car, cr & emer 60 16

Anniv. of educational and art reforms.

Offshore Oil Rig in Persian Gulf A321

1969, Sept. 1 Litho.

1518 A321 8r multicolored 1.00 16

Marine drillings by the Iran-Italia Oil Co., 10th anniv.

Dancers Forming Flower — A322

Crossed-out Fingerprint, Moon and Rocket — A323

1969, Sept. 6 Wmk. 353 *Perf. 10½*

1519 A322 6r multicolored 28 15
1520 A322 8r multicolored 35 15
Set value 20

3rd Festival of Arts, Shiraz and Persepolis, Aug. 30-Sept. 9.

1969, Sept. 8 Litho.

1521 A323 4r multicolored 30 15

World campaign against illiteracy.

Persepolis, Simulated Stamp with UPU Emblem, and Shah — A324

1969, Sept. 28

1522 A324 10r lt bl & multi 2.25 50
1523 A324 14r multicolored 2.25 50

16th Congress of the UPU, Tokyo.

Fair Emblem A325

Justice A326

Designs: 14r, like 8r, inscribed "ASIA 69." 20r, Fair emblem, world map and "ASIA 69" (horiz.).

1969, Oct. 5 Wmk. 353 *Perf. 10½*

1524 A325 8r rose & multi 30 15
1525 A325 14r blue & multi 38 18
1526 A325 20r tan & multi 55 25

2nd Asian Trade Fair, Tehran.

1969, Oct. 13 Litho.

1527 A326 8r bl grn & dk brn 60 15

Rural Courts of Justice Day.

UN Emblem A327

Emblem and Column Capital, Persepolis A328

1969, Oct. 24

1528 A327 2r lt bl & dp bl 35 15

25th anniversary of the United Nations.

1969, Oct. 28

1529 A328 2r deep bl & multi 60 15

2nd Festival of Arts and Culture. See Nos. 1577, 1681, 1735.

Child's Drawing and UNICEF Emblem A329

Children's Drawings and UNICEF Emblem: 1r, Boy and birds (vert.). 5r, Dinner.

1969, Oct. 31 Wmk. 353 *Perf. 10½*
Size: 28x40mm, 40x28mm

1530 A329 1r lt blue & multi 15 15
1531 A329 2r lt grn & multi 25 15
1532 A329 5r lt lil & multi 55 22

Children's Week. See Nos. 1578-1580.

Globe Emblem A330

1969, Nov. 6

1533 A330 8r dk brn & bl 35 15

Meeting of the Natl. Society of Parents and Educators, Tehran.

Satellite Communications Station — A331

1969, Nov. 19 Litho.

1534 A331 6r blk brn & bis 35 15

1st Iranian Satellite Communications Earth Station, Hamadan.

Mahatma Gandhi (1869-1948) — A332

1969, Dec. 29 Wmk. 353 *Perf. 10½*

1535 A332 14r gray & dk rose brn 4.25 42

Globe, Flags and Emblems A333

Design: 6r, Globe and Red Cross, Red Lion and Sun, and Red Crescent Emblems.

1969, Dec. 31

1536 A333 2r red & multi 60 15
1537 A333 6r red & multi 90 20
Set value 28

50th anniversary of the League of Red Cross Societies.

Symbols of Reform Laws and Shah A334

1970, Jan. 26 Litho. Wmk. 353

1538 A334 1r bis & multi 85 15
1539 A334 2r multicolored 85 15

Declaration of the Shah's Reform Plan.

Pansies A335

New Year's Table A336

1970, Mar. 6 Wmk. 353 *Perf. 10½*

1540 A335 1r multicolored 22 15
1541 A336 8r multicolored 1.50 30

Issued for the Iranian New Year.

Chemical Plant, Kharg Island, and Iranian Oil Company Emblem — A337

Designs (Iranian Oil Company Emblem and): 2r, Shah's portrait and quotation. 4r, Laying of gas pipe line and tractor. 8r, Tankers at pier of Kharg Island (vert.). 10r, Tehran refinery.

1970, Mar. 20 Wmk. 353 *Perf. 10½*

1542	A337	2r gray & multi	1.00	20
1543	A337	4r multicolored	1.25	25
1544	A337	6r lt bl & multi	1.40	35
1545	A337	8r multicolored	1.50	45
1546	A337	10r multicolored	1.90	55
		Nos. 1542-1546 (5)	7.05	1.80

Nationalization of the oil industry, 20th anniv.

EXPO '70 Emblem A338

Radar, Satellite and Congress Emblem A339

1970, Mar. 27 Litho.

1547	A338	4r brt rose lil & vio bl	18	15
1548	A338	10r lt bl & pur	42	15
		Set value		20

EXPO '70, Osaka, Japan, Mar. 15-Sept. 13.

1970, Apr. 20 Wmk. 353 *Perf. 10½*

1549	A339	14r multicolored	75	20

Asia-Australia Telecommunications Congress, Tehran.

UPU Headquarters, Bern — A340

1970, May 10

1550	A340	2r gray, brn & lil rose	50	15
1551	A340	4r lil, brn & lil rose	75	15
		Set value		20

Inauguration of the new UPU Headquarters, Bern.

Productivity Year Emblem — A341

1970, May 19 Wmk. 353 *Perf. 10½*

1552	A341	8r gray & multi	38	15

Asian Productivity Year, 1970.

Bird Bringing Baby A342

1970, June 15 Litho.

1553	A342	8r brn & dk blue	65	15

Iranian School for Midwives, 50th anniv.

Tomb of Cyrus the Great, Meshed-Morghab in Fars — A343

Designs: 8r, Pillars of Apadana Palace, Persepolis (vert.). 10r, Bas-relief from a Mede tomb, Iraq. 14r, Achaemenian officers, bas-relief, Persepolis.

1970, June 21 Photo. *Perf. 13*

1554	A343	6r gray, red & vio	75	18
1555	A343	8r pale rose, blk & bl grn	1.50	50
1556	A343	10r yel, red & brn	1.90	65
1557	A343	14r bl, blk & red brn	2.25	1.00

2500th anniversary of the founding of the Persian Empire by Cyrus the Great.

See Nos. 1561-1571, 1589-1596, 1605-1612.

Seeyo-Se-Pol Bridge, Isfahan — A344

Designs: No. 1559, Saiful Malook Lake, Pakistan (vert.). No. 1560, View of Fethiye, Turkey (vert.).

Wmk. 353

1970, July 21 Litho. *Perf. 10½*

1558	A344	2r multicolored	75	20
1559	A344	2r multicolored	75	20
1560	A344	2r multicolored	75	20

Signing of the Regional Cooperation for Development Pact by Iran, Turkey and Pakistan, 6th anniv.

Queen Buran, Dirhem Coin A345

Wine Goblet with Lion's Head — A346

Designs: No. 1562, Achaemenian eagle amulet. No. 1563, Mithridates I, dirhem coin. No. 1564, Sassanidae art (arch, coin, jugs). No. 1566, Shapur I, dirhem coin. No. 1567, Achaemenian courier. No. 1568, Winged deer. No. 1569, Ardashir I, dirhem coin. No. 1570, Seal of Darius I (chariot, palms, lion). 14r, Achaemenian tapestry.

1970 Wmk. 353 Photo. *Perf. 13*

1561	A345	1r gold & multi	1.00	38
1562	A346	2r gold & multi	1.00	38
1563	A345	2r gold & multi	1.25	38
1564	A346	2r lilac & multi	1.25	38
1565	A346	6r lilac & multi	1.25	38
1566	A345	6r lilac & multi	1.75	45
1567	A345	6r lilac & multi	1.75	52
1568	A346	8r lilac & multi	1.75	52
1569	A345	8r lilac & multi	1.75	52
1570	A345	8r lilac & multi	1.75	52
1571	A345	14r lt bl & multi	2.00	1.10
		Nos. 1561-1571 (11)	16.50	5.53

2500th anniversary of the founding of the Persian Empire by Cyrus the Great.

Issue dates: 1r, Nos. 1563, 1566, 1569, Aug. 22; Nos. 1562, 1565, 1568, 14r, Aug. 6; others, Sept. 22.

Candle and Globe A347

Persian Decoration A348

1970, Sept. 8 Litho. *Perf. 10½*

1572	A347	1r lt bl & multi	20	15
1573	A347	2r pale sal & multi	25	15
		Set value		20

Issued to publicize World Literacy Day.

1970, Sept. 14

1574	A348	6r multi	35	15

Isfahan Intl. Cong. of Architects, Sept. 1970.

Emblem A349

UN Emblem, Dove and Scales A350

1970, Sept. 28 *Perf. 10½*

1575	A349	2r lt bl & pur	25	15

Congress of Election Committees of Persian States and Tehran.

1970, Oct. 24 Litho. Wmk. 353

1576	A350	2r lt bl, mag & dk bl	30	15

Issued for United Nations Day.

Festival Type of 1969

1970, Oct. 28 *Perf. 10½*

1577	A328	2r org & multi	40	15

3rd Festival of Arts and Culture.

UNICEF Type of 1969

Children's Drawings and UNICEF Emblem: 50d, Herdsman and goats. 1r, Family picnic. 2r, Mosque.

1970, Oct. 31

Size: 43½x31mm

1578	A329	50d black & multi	15	15
1579	A329	1r black & multi	20	15
1580	A329	2r black & multi	40	15
		Set value		30

Issued for Children's Week.

Shah Mohammed Riza Pahlavi A351

1971, Jan. 26 Wmk. 353 *Perf. 10½*

1581	A351	2r lt bl & multi	1.65	35

Publicizing the "White Revolution of King and People" and the 12 reform laws.

Sheldrake — A352

Designs: 2r, Ruddy shelduck. 8r, Flamingo (vert.).

1971, Jan. 30 Litho.

1582	A352	1r multicolored	1.00	15
1583	A352	2r multicolored	1.25	20
1584	A352	8r multicolored	1.75	35

Intl. Wetland and Waterfowl Conf., Ramsar.

Riza Shah Pahlavi — A353

1971, Feb. 22 Wmk. 353 *Perf. 10½*

1585	A353	6r multicolored	3.25	45

50th anniversary of the Pahlavi dynasty's accession to power.

Rooster A354

Designs: 2r, Barn swallow and nest. 6r, Hoopoe.

1971, Mar. 6 Photo. *Perf. 13½x13*

1586	A354	1r multicolored	60	15
1587	A354	2r multicolored	1.00	15
1588	A354	6r multicolored	2.75	30

Novrooz, Iranian New Year.

Shapur II Hunting — A355

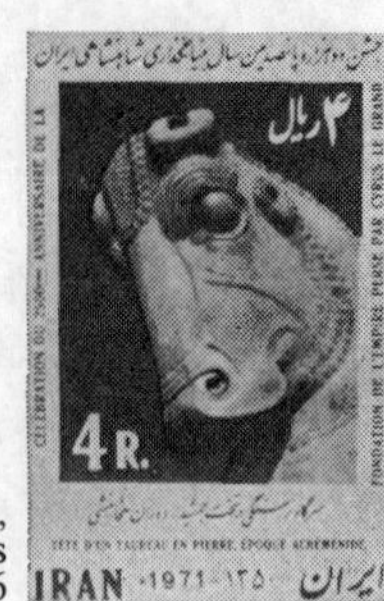

Bull's Head, Persepolis
A356

Designs: 1r, Harpist, mosaic. No. 1591, Investiture of Ardashir I, bas-relief. 5r Winged lion ornament. 6r, Persian archer, bas-relief. 8r, Royal audience, bas-relief. 10r, Bronze head of Parthian prince.

1971 Litho. *Perf. 10½*

1589	A356	1r multicolored	1.00	25
1590	A355	2r blk & brn org	1.50	25
1591	A355	2r lil, gldn brn & blk	1.50	25
1592	A356	4r pur & multi	1.50	25
1593	A356	5r multicolored	1.75	50
1594	A356	6r multicolored	1.75	50
1595	A356	8r lt bl & multi	2.25	50
1596	A356	10r dp bis, blk & sl	2.25	65
		Nos. 1589-1596 (8)	13.50	3.15

2500th anniversary of the founding of the Persian Empire by Cyrus the Great.

Issue dates: 4r, 5r, 6r, 8r, May 15; others, June 15.

Prisoners Leaving Jail
A357

1971, May 20 Litho. Wmk. 353

1597	A357	6r multicolored	1.50	15
1598	A357	8r multicolored	2.50	15
		Set value		24

Rehabilitation of Prisoners Week.

Religious School, Chaharbagh, Ispahan
A358

Designs: No. 1600, Mosque of Selim, Edirne, Turkey. No. 1601, Badshahi Mosque, Lahore, Pakistan (horiz.).

1971, July 21 Litho. *Perf. 10½*

1599	A358	2r multicolored	35	15
1600	A358	2r multicolored	35	15
1601	A358	2r multicolored	35	15
		Set value		30

7th anniversary of Regional Cooperation among Iran, Pakistan and Turkey.

"Fifth Festival of Arts" — A359

1971, Aug. 26 Litho. & Typo.

1602	A359	2r lt & dk grn, red & gold	70	15

5th Festival of Arts, Shiraz-Persepolis.

"Fight Against Illiteracy"
A360

1971, Sept. 8 Litho.

1603	A360	2r grn & multi	50	15

International Literacy Day, Sept. 8.

Kings Abdullah and Hussein II of Jordan
A361

1971, Sept. 11

1604	A361	2r yel grn, blk & red	40	15

Hashemite Kingdom of Jordan, 50th anniv.

Shahyad Aryamehr Monument — A362

Designs: 1r, Aryamehr steel mill, near Isfahan. 3r, Senate Building, Tehran. 11r, Shah Abbas Kabir Dam, Zayandeh River.

1971, Sept. 22

1605	A362	1r blue & multi	1.00	22
1606	A362	2r multicolored	1.00	36
1607	A362	3r brt pink & multi	1.00	36
1608	A362	11r org & multi	2.25	65

2500th anniversary of the founding of the Persian empire by Cyrus the Great.

Shah Mohammed Riza Pahlavi
A363

Designs: 2r, Riza Shah Pahlavi. 5r, Stone tablet with proclamation of Cyrus the Great (horiz.). 10r, Crown of present empire (erroneously inscribed *Le Couronne*).

1971, Oct. 12

1609	A363	1r gold & multi	1.65	90
1610	A363	2r gold & multi	1.65	90
1611	A363	5r gold & multi	1.65	90
1612	A363	10r gold & multi	2.75	90

2500th anniversary of the founding of the Persian empire by Cyrus the Great.

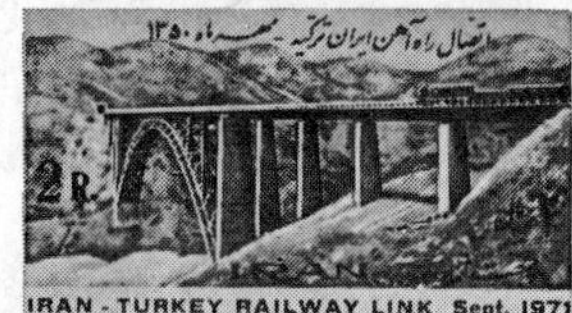

Ghatour Railroad Bridge — A364

1971, Oct. 7

1613	A364	2r multicolored	90	25

Iran-Turkey railroad.

Racial Equality Emblem
A365

Mohammed Riza Pahlavi
A366

1971, Oct. 24

1614	A365	2r lt bl & multi	20	15

Intl. Year Against Racial Discrimination.

Perf. 13½x13

1971, Oct. 26 Photo. Wmk. 353

Size: 20½x28mm

1615	A366	5d lilac	15	15
1616	A366	10d henna brown	15	15
1617	A366	50d brt bl grn	18	15
1618	A366	1r dp yel grn	26	15
1619	A366	2r brown	26	15

Size: 27x36½mm

1620	A366	6r slate grn	1.00	15
1621	A366	8r vio blue	1.50	1.00
1622	A366	10r red lilac	1.25	25
1623	A366	11r blue grn	4.50	1.00
1624	A366	14r brt blue	6.25	45
1625	A366	20r car rose	5.00	55
1626	A366	50r yel bister	6.00	1.10
		Nos. 1615-1626 (12)	26.50	5.25

See Nos. 1650-1661B, 1768-1772.

Child's Drawing and Emblem — A367

Designs: No. 1631, Ruins of Persepolis (vert.). No. 1632, Warrior, mosaic (vert.).

1971, Oct. 31 Litho. *Perf. 10½*

1630	A367	2r multicolored	25	15
1631	A367	2r multicolored	25	15
1632	A367	2r multicolored	25	15
		Set value		30

Children's Week.

UNESCO Emblem and "25" — A368

1971, Nov. 4

1633	A368	6r ultra & rose cl	40	15

25th anniversary of UNESCO.

Domestic Animals and Emblem
A369

1971, Nov. 22

1634	A369	2r gray, blk & car	40	16

4th Iranian Veterinarians' Congress.

ILO Emblem, Cog Wheels and Globe
A370

1971, Dec. 4

1635	A370	2r blk, org & bl	35	15

7th ILO Conference for the Asian Region.

UNICEF Emblem, Bird Feeding Young
A371

1971, Dec. 16 *Perf. 13x13½*

1636	A371	2r lt bl, mag & blk	35	15

25th anniversary of UNICEF.

Mohammed Riza Pahlavi — A372

1972, Jan. 26 Wmk. 353 *Perf. 10½*

1637	A372	2r lt grn & multi	2.50	20
a.		20r Souvenir sheet	7.50	5.25

"White Revolution of King and People" and the 12 reform laws. No. 1637a contains one stamp with simulated perforations.

Pintailed Sandgrouse
A373

Designs: No. 1639, Rock ptarmigan. 2r, Yellow-billed waxbill and red-cheeked cordon-bleu.

1972, Mar. 6 Litho. *Perf. 13x13½*

1638	A373	1r lt grn & multi	42	15
1639	A373	1r lt bl & multi	42	15
1640	A373	2r yellow & multi	1.40	24
		Set value		42

Iranian New Year.

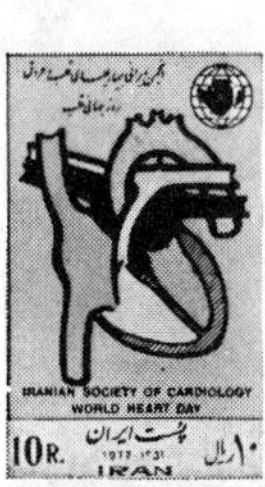

"Your Heart is your Health" A374

Film Strip and Winged Antelope A375

1972, Apr. 4 **Perf. 10½**

1641	A374	10r lem & multi	1.75	15

World Health Day; Iranian Society of Cardiology.

1972, Apr. 16 **Litho. & Engr.**

Design: 8r, Film strips and winged antelope.

1642	A375	6r ultra & gold	80	15
1643	A375	8r yel & multi	1.50	15
		Set value		24

Tehran International Film Festival.

Rose and Bud — A376

Designs: 2r, Yellow roses. 5r, Red rose.

1972, May 5 **Litho.**

1644	A376	1r lt bl & multi	32	15
1645	A376	2r multicolored	60	15
1646	A376	5r blue & multi	75	18
		Set value		35

See Nos. 1711-1713.

Persian Woman, by Behzad — A377

Paintings: No. 1648, Fisherman, by Cevat Dereli (Turkey). No. 1649, Young Man, by Abdur Rehman Chughtai (Pakistan).

1972, July 21 **Wmk. 353**

1647	A377	5r gray & multi	1.40	22
1648	A377	5r gray & multi	1.40	22
1649	A377	5r gray & multi	1.40	22

Regional Cooperation for Development Pact among Iran, Turkey and Pakistan, 8th anniv.

Shah Type of 1971

1972-73 **Photo.** ***Perf. 13½x13***

Bister Frame & Crown

Size: 20½x28mm

1650	A366	5d lilac	15	15
1651	A366	10d hn brn	15	15
1652	A366	50d brt bl grn	18	15
1653	A366	1r dp yel grn	25	15
a.		Brown frame & crown ('73)	55	15
1654	A366	2r brown	32	15

Size: 27x36½mm

1655	A366	6r slate grn	1.65	20
1656	A366	8r vio blue	1.65	20
1657	A366	10r red lilac	2.00	15
1658	A366	11r blue grn	2.75	1.00
1659	A366	14r dull blue	3.50	20
1660	A366	20r car rose	3.75	32
1661	A366	50r grnsh bl	3.75	1.00
1661A	A366	100r vio ('73)	5.00	2.00
1661B	A366	200r sl ('73)	10.00	3.50
		Nos. 1650-1661B (14)	35.10	9.32

Festival Emblem A378

1972, Aug. 31 **Litho.** ***Perf. 10½***

1662	A378	6r emer, red & blk	1.10	15
1663	A378	8r brt mag, blk & grn	1.65	25

6th Festival of Arts, Shiraz-Persepolis, Aug. 31-Sept. 8.

Pens and Emblem A379

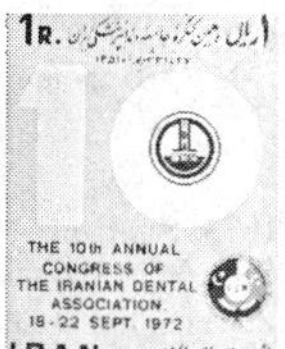

"10" and Emblems A380

1972, Sept. 8

1664	A379	1r lt bl & multi	25	15
1665	A379	2r yellow & multi	38	15
		Set value		22

World Literacy Day, Sept. 8.

1972, Sept. 18

1666	A380	1r lilac & multi	25	20
1667	A380	2r dl yel & multi	45	25

10th Congress of Iranian Dentists' Assoc., Sept. 18-22.

Asian Broadcasting Union Emblem — A381

No. 450 on Cover — A382

1972, Oct. 1

1668	A381	6r lt grn & multi	75	15
1669	A381	8r gray & multi	1.50	15
		Set value		18

9th General Assembly of Asian Broadcasting Union, Tehran, Oct. 1972.

1972, Oct. 9

1670	A382	10r lt bl & multi	2.25	25

International Stamp Day.

Chess and Olympic Rings — A383

Designs (Olympic Rings and): 2r, Hunter. 3r, Archer. 5r, Equestrians. 6r, Polo. 8r, Wrestling.

1972, Oct. 17

1671	A383	1r brown & multi	1.75	75
1672	A383	2r blue & multi	1.75	15
1673	A383	3r lilac & multi	2.25	15
1674	A383	5r bl grn & multi	2.25	22
1675	A383	6r red & multi	2.25	25
1676	A383	8r yel grn & multi	2.25	25
a.		Souv. sheet of 6, #1671-1676, imperf.	12.50	3.00
		Nos. 1671-1676 (6)	12.50	1.77

20th Olympic Games, Munich, Aug. 26-Sept. 11.

Communications Symbol, UN Emblem — A384

Children and Flowers — A385

1972, Oct. 24

1677	A384	10r multi	2.00	15

United Nations Day.

1972, Oct. 31 **Litho.** **Wmk. 353**

Children's Drawings and Emblem: No. 1679, Puppet show. 6r, Boys cutting wood (horiz.).

1678	A385	2r gray & multi	35	15
1679	A385	2r bis & multi	70	15
1680	A385	6r pink & multi	1.40	15
		Set value		26

Children's Week.

Festival Type of 1969

Design: 10r, Crown, emblems and column capital, Persepolis.

1972, Nov. 11

1681	A328	10r dp bl & multi	5.00	28

10th anniv. of White Revolution; Festival of Culture and Art.

Family Planning Emblem A386

1972, Dec. 5

1682	A386	1r blue & multi	15	15
1683	A386	2r brt pink & multi	30	15
		Set value		15

To promote family planning.

Iranian Scout Organization, 20th anniv. — A387

1972, Dec. 9

1684	A387	2r multicolored	50	15

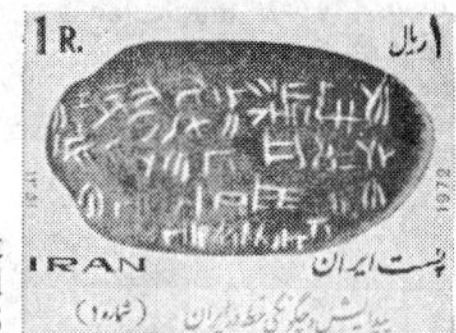

Ancient Seal A388

Designs: Various ancient seals.

1973, Jan. 5 ***Perf. 10½***

1685	A388	1r bl, red & brn	60	15
1686	A388	1r yel & multi	60	15
1687	A388	1r pink & multi	60	15
1688	A388	2r lt brick red & multi	60	15
1689	A388	2r dl org & multi	60	15
1690	A388	2r olive & multi	60	15
		Nos. 1685-1690 (6)	3.60	
		Set value		54

Development of writing.

Books and Book Year Emblem — A389

Design: 6r, Illuminated page, 10th century, from Shahnameh, by Firdousi.

1973, Jan. 10

1691	A389	2r black & multi	75	15
1692	A389	6r yellow & multi	1.10	20
		Set value		28

International Book Year.

"12 Improvements by the King" — A390

Designs: 2r, 10r, 12 circles symbolizing 12 improvements. 6r, like 1r.

1973, Jan. 26 **Litho.**

Size: 29x43mm

1693	A390	1r gold, ultra, red & yel	25	15
1694	A390	2r sil, plum, ol & yel	25	15

Size: 65x84mm

1695	A390	6r gold, ultra, red & yel	1.75	75
		Set value		86

Souvenir Sheet

Imperf

1696	A390	10r sil, plum, ol & yel	2.75	75

Introduction of the King's socioeconomic reforms, 10th anniv.

Blue Surgeonfish A391

Fish: No. 1698, Gilthead. No. 1699, Banded sergeant major. No. 1700, Porkfish. No. 1701, Black-spot snapper.

1973, Mar. 6 **Wmk. 353** ***Perf. 10½***

1697	A391	1r multicolored	65	15
1698	A391	1r multicolored	65	15
1699	A391	2r multicolored	95	18

1700 A391 2r multicolored 95 18
1701 A391 2r multicolored 95 18
Nos. 1697-1701 (5) 4.15 84

Iranian New Year.

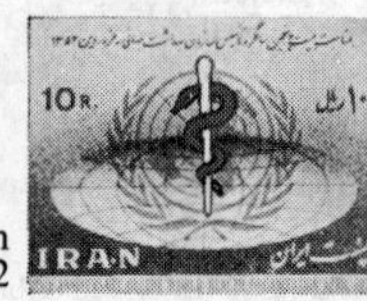

WHO Emblem A392

1973, Apr. 7 Litho. Wmk. 353
1702 A392 10r brn, grn & red 1.25 15

25th anniversary of the WHO.

Soccer — A393

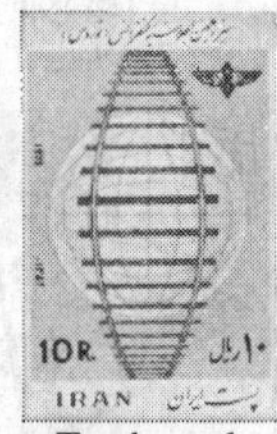

Tracks and Globe — A394

1973, Apr. 13
1703 A393 14r org & multi 1.40 25

15th Asian Youth Football (soccer) Tournament.

1973, May 10 Wmk. 353 *Perf. 10½*
1704 A394 10r dk grn, lil & vio bl 1.25 18

13th International Railroad Conference.

Clay Tablet with Aryan Script — A395

Designs: Clay tablets with various scripts.

1973, June 5 *Perf. 10½*
1705 A395 1r shown 50 15
1706 A395 1r Kharoshthi 50 15
1707 A395 1r Achaemenian 50 15
1708 A395 2r Parthian (Mianeh) 90 18
1709 A395 2r Parthian (Arsacide) 90 18
1710 A395 2r Gachtak (Dabireh) 90 15
Nos. 1705-1710 (6) 4.20 96

Development of writing.

Flower Type of 1972

Flowers: 1r, Orchid. 2r, Hyacinth. 6r, Columbine.

1973, June 20
1711 A376 1r green & multi 20 15
1712 A376 2r mag & multi 60 15
1713 A376 6r dl bl & multi 1.25 20
Set value 32

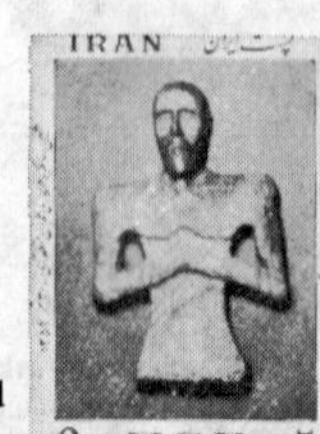

Statue, Shahdad Kerman, Persia, 4000 B.C. — A396

Designs: No. 1714, Head from mausoleum of King Antiochus I (69-34 B.C.), Turkey. No. 1716, Street, Mohenjo-Daro, Pakistan.

1973, July 21
1714 A396 2r brn & multi 35 16
1715 A396 2r grn & multi 35 16
1716 A396 2r blue & multi 35 16

Regional Cooperation for Development Pact among Iran, Turkey and Pakistan, 9th anniv. Nos. 1714-1716 printed se-tenant.

Shah, Oil Pump, Refinery and Tanker — A397

1973, Aug. 4
1717 A397 5r blue & blk 1.40 30

Nationalization of oil industry.

Soldiers and Rising Sun — A398

Gymnasts and Globe — A399

1973, Aug. 19 Litho. Wmk. 353
1718 A398 2r ultra & multi 32 15

20th anniversary of return of monarchy.

1973, Aug. 23 *Perf. 10½*
1719 A399 2r olive & multi 20 15
1720 A399 2r vio bl & multi 20 15
Set value 24

7th Intl. Congress of Physical Education and Sports for Girls and Women, Tehran, Aug. 19-25.

Shahyad Monument, Rainbow and WMO Emblem — A400

1973, Sept. 4
1721 A400 5r multicolored 75 15

Intl. meteorological cooperation, centenary.

Festival Emblem — A401

Wrestlers — A402

1973, Aug. 31
1722 A401 1r silver & multi 20 15
1723 A401 5r gold & multi 30 15
Set value 24

7th Festival of Arts, Shiraz-Persepolis.

1973, Sept. 6 Litho. Wmk. 353
1724 A402 6r lt grn & multi 70 20

World Wrestling Championships, Tehran, Sept. 6-14.

"Literacy as Light" A403

Audio-Visual Equipment A404

1973, Sept. 8
1725 A403 2r multicolored 20 15

World Literacy Day, Sept. 8.

1973, Sept. 11
1726 A404 10r yel & multi 65 20

Tehran Intl. Audio-Visual Exhib., Sept. 11-24.

Warrior Taming Winged Bull A405

1973, Sept. 16
1727 A405 8r bl gray & multi 65 15

Intl. Council of Military Sports, 25th anniv.

abu-al-Rayhan al-Biruni (973-1048), Philosopher and Mathematician A406

1973, Sept. 16
1728 A406 10r brown & blk 1.10 20

Soccer Cup A407

INTERPOL Emblem A408

1973, Oct. 2 Wmk. 353 *Perf. 10½*
1729 A407 2r lil, blk & buff 35 15

Soccer Games for the Crown Prince's Cup.

1973, Oct. 7
1730 A408 2r multicolored 25 15

50th anniversary of INTERPOL.

Symbolic Arches and Globe A409

1973, Oct. 8
1731 A409 10r orange & multi 55 15

World Federation for Mental Health, 25th anniv.

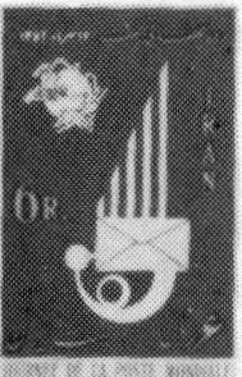
UPU Emblem, Letter, Post Horn — A410

Honeycomb — A411

1973, Oct. 9
1732 A410 6r blue & org 50 16

World Post Day, Oct. 9.

1973, Oct. 24
1733 A411 2r lt brn & multi 18 15
1734 A411 2r gray ol & multi 18 15
Set value 15

UN Volunteer Program, 5th anniv.

Festival Type of 1969

Design: 2r, Crown and column capital, Persepolis.

1973, Oct. 26
1735 A328 2r yellow & multi 40 15

Festival of Culture and Art.

Turkish Bosporus Bridge, Flag A412

Design: 8r, Kemal Ataturk and Riza Shah Pahlavi.

1973, Oct. 29 Litho. *Perf. 10½*
1736 A412 2r multicolored 75 15
1737 A412 8r multicolored 1.25 25

50th anniversary of the Turkish Republic.

Mother and Child, Emblem — A413

Children's Drawings and Emblem: No. 1739, Wagon (horiz.). No. 1740, House and garden with birds.

1973, Oct. 31

1738	A413	2r multicolored	30	15
1739	A413	2r multicolored	30	15
1740	A413	2r multicolored	30	15
		Set value		20

Children's Week.

Cow, Wheat and FAO Emblem A414

1973, Nov. 4

1741	A414	10r multicolored	1.00	20

10th anniversary of World Food Program.

Proclamation of Cyrus the Great; Red Cross, Lion and Crescent Emblems — A415

1973, Nov. 8

1742	A415	6r lt bl & multi	50	18

22nd Intl. Red Cross Conf., Tehran, 1972.

"Film Festival" A416

Globe and Travelers A417

1973, Nov. 26 Wmk. 353 *Perf. 10½*

1743	A416	2r blk & multi	20	15

2nd International Tehran Film Festival.

1973, Nov. 26 Litho.

1744	A417	10r org & multi	50	15

12th annual Congress of Intl. Assoc. of Tour Managers.

Human Rights Flame A418

Score and Emblem A419

1973, Dec. 10

1745	A418	8r lt bl & multi	40	16

Universal Declaration of Human Rights, 25th anniv.

1973, Dec. 21

Design: No. 1747, Score and emblem (diff.).

1746	A419	10r yel grn, red & blk	55	15
1747	A419	10r lt bl, ultra & red	55	15
		Set value		24

Dedicated to the art of music.

Forestry, Printing, Education — A420

Designs (Symbols of Reforms): No. 1749, Land reform, sales of shares, women's suffrage. No. 1750, Army of progress, irrigation, women's education. No. 1751, Hygiene, rural courts, housing.

1974, Jan. 26 Litho. *Perf. 10½*

1748	A420	1r lt bl & multi	20	15
1749	A420	1r lt bl & multi	20	15
1750	A420	2r lt bl & multi	25	15
1751	A420	2r lt bl & multi	25	15

Imperf

Size: 76½x102mm

1752	A420	20r multicolored	3.25	1.25

"White Revolution of King and People" and 12 reform laws.

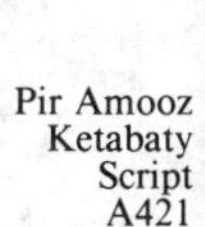

Pir Amooz Ketabaty Script A421

Various Scripts: No. 1754, Mo Eghely Ketabaty. No. 1755, Din Dabireh, Avesta script. No. 1756, Pir Amooz, Naskh style. No. 1757, Pir Amooz, decorative style. No. 1758, Decorative and architectural style.

1974, Feb. 14 Wmk. 353 *Perf. 10½*

1753	A421	1r sil, ocher & multi	75	30
1754	A421	1r gold, gray & multi	75	30
1755	A421	1r sil, yel & multi	75	30
1756	A421	2r gold, gray & multi	75	30
1757	A421	2r gold, sl & multi	75	30
1758	A421	2r gold, cl & multi	75	30
		Nos. 1753-1758 (6)	4.50	1.80

Development of writing.

Fowl, Syringe and Emblem A422

1974, Feb. 23

1759	A422	6r red brn & multi	42	15

5th Iranian Veterinary Congress.

Monarch Butterfly — A423

Designs: Various butterflies.

1974, Mar. 6 Litho. *Perf. 10½*

1760	A423	1r rose lil & multi	80	15
1761	A423	1r brt rose & multi	80	15
1762	A423	2r lt bl & multi	1.00	25
1763	A423	2r green & multi	1.00	25
1764	A423	2r bis & multi	1.00	25
		Nos. 1760-1764 (5)	4.60	1.05

Novrooz, Iranian New Year.

Jalaludin Mevlana (1207-1273), Poet — A424

1974, Mar. 12 *Perf. 13*

1765	A424	2r pale vio & multi	50	15

Shah Type of 1971

1974 Photo. *Perf. 13½x13*

Size: 20½x28mm

1768	A366	50d orange & bl	45	15
1769	A366	1r emerald & bl	50	15
1770	A366	2r red & blue	75	15

Size: 27x36½mm

1771	A366	10r lt grn & bl	6.00	15
1772	A366	20r lilac & bl	4.25	20
		Nos. 1768-1772 (5)	11.95	
		Set value		45

Palace of the Forty Columns A425

1974, Apr. 11 Litho. *Perf. 10½*

1773	A425	10r multi	50	15

9th Medical Congress of the Near and Middle East, Isfahan.

Onager — A426

Athlete and Games Emblem — A427

1974, Apr. 13

1774	A426	1r shown	40	15
1775	A426	2r Great bustard	50	20
1776	A426	6r Fawn and deer	1.25	35
1777	A426	8r Caucasian black grouse	2.00	40

Intl. Council for Game and Wildlife Preservation. Nos. 1774-1777 printed se-tenant.

1974, Apr. 30

1778	A427	1r shown	42	15
1779	A427	1r Table tennis	42	15
1780	A427	2r Wrestling	85	15
1781	A427	2r Hurdles	85	15
1782	A427	6r Weight lifting	1.25	15
1783	A427	8r Basketball	1.75	20
		Nos. 1778-1783 (6)	5.54	
		Set value		64

7th Asian Games, Tehran; first issue.

Lion of Venice — A428

Design: 8r, Audience with the Doge of Venice (painting).

1974, May 5

1784	A428	6r multicolored	55	15
1785	A428	8r multicolored	1.00	18

Safeguarding Venice.

Links and Grain — A429

1974, May 13 Litho. *Perf. 10½*

1786	A429	2r multicolored	25	15

Cooperation Day.

Military Plane, 1924 A430

1974, June 1

1787	A430	10r shown	2.00	40
1788	A430	10r Jet, 1974	2.00	40

50th anniversary of Iranian Air Force.

Swimmer and Games Emblem — A431

Bicyclists and Games Emblem — A432

1974, July 1 Wmk. 353 *Perf. 10½*

1789	A431	1r shown	65	15
1790	A431	1r Tennis, men's doubles	65	15
1791	A431	2r Wrestling	80	20
1792	A431	2r Hockey	80	20
1793	A431	4r Volleyball	1.25	40
1794	A431	10r Tennis, women's singles	2.50	50
		Nos. 1789-1794 (6)	6.65	1.60

7th Asian Games, Tehran; second issue.

1974, Aug. 1

1795	A432	2r shown	90	15
1796	A432	2r Soccer	90	15
1797	A432	2r Fencing	90	15
1798	A432	2r Small-bore rifle shooting	90	15
		Set value		48

7th Asian Games, Tehran; third issue.

Ghaskai Costume A433

Gold Winged Lion Cup A434

Regional Costumes: No. 1800, Kurdistan, Kermanshah District. No. 1801, Kurdistan, Sanandaj District. No. 1802, Mazandaran. No. 1803, Bakhtiari. No. 1804, Torkaman.

1974, July 6

1799	A433	2r lt ultra & multi	1.40	50
1800	A433	2r buff & multi	1.40	50
1801	A433	2r green & multi	1.40	50
1802	A433	2r lt bl & multi	1.40	50
1803	A433	2r gray & multi	1.40	50
1804	A433	2r dl grn & multi	1.40	50
		Nos. 1799-1804 (6)	8.40	3.00

Nos. 1799-1804 printed se-tenant.

1974, July 13

1805	A434	2r dl grn & multi	30	15

Iranian Soccer Cup.

Tabriz Rug, Late 16th Century A435

King Carrying Vases, Bas-relief A436

Designs: No. 1807, Anatolian rug, 15th century. No. 1808, Kashan rug, Lahore.

1974, July 21

1806	A435	2r brn & multi	45	15
1807	A435	2r blue & multi	45	15
1808	A435	2r red & multi	45	15
		Set value		30

Regional Cooperation for Development Pact among Iran, Turkey and Pakistan, 10th anniv. Nos. 1806-1808 printed se-tenant.

1974, Aug. 15 Litho. *Perf. 10½*

1809	A436	2r blk & multi	30	15

8th Iranian Arts Festival, Shiraz-Persepolis.

Aryamehr Stadium, Tehran — A437

Designs: No. 1811, Games' emblem and inscription. No. 1812, Aerial view of games' site.

1974

1810	A437	6r multicolored	1.00	20

Souvenir Sheets

1811	A437	10r multicolored	*2.00*	*1.00*
1812	A437	10r multicolored	*2.00*	*1.00*

7th Asian Games, Tehran; fourth and fifth issues. Nos. 1811-1812 contain one imperf. 51x38mm stamp each.

Issue dates: Nos. 1811-1812, Sept. 1; No. 1810, Sept. 16.

"Welfare" A438

"Education" A439

1974, Sept. 11

1813	A438	2r orange & multi	22	15
1814	A439	2r blue & multi	22	15
		Set value		15

Welfare and free education.

Map of Hasanlu, 1000-800 B.C. — A440

1974, Sept. 24

1815	A440	8r multicolored	42	15

2nd Intl. Congress of Architecture, Shiraz-Persepolis, Sept. 1974.

Achaemenian Mail Cart and UPU Emblem — A441

Design: 14r, UPU emblem and letters.

1974, Oct. 9 Wmk. 353 *Perf. 10½*

1816	A441	6r org, grn & blk	85	18
1817	A441	14r multicolored	1.25	18

Centenary of Universal Postal Union.

Road Through Farahabad Park — A442

1974, Oct. 16

1818	A442	1r shown	15	15
1819	A442	2r Recreation Bldg.	25	15
		Set value		15

Inauguration of Farahabad Park, Tehran.

Farahnaz Dam and Mohammed Riza Pahlavi — A443

Designs: 5d, Kharg Island petro-chemical plant. 10d, Ghatour Railroad Bridge. 1r, Tehran oil refinery. 2r, Satellite communication station, Hamadan, and Mt. Alvand. 6r, Aryamehr steel mill, Isfahan. 8r, University of Tabriz. 10r, Shah Abbas Kabir Dam. 14r, Rudagi Music Hall. 20r, Shayad Monument. 50r, Aryamehr Stadium.

1974-75 Photo. *Perf. 13x13½*

Size: 28x21mm

Frame & Shah in Brown

1820	A443	5d slate grn	50	15
1821	A443	10d orange	50	15
1822	A443	50d blue grn	50	15
1823	A443	1r ultra	50	15
1824	A443	2r deep lil	50	15

Size: 36x26½mm

Frame & Shah in Dark Blue

1825	A443	6r brown	1.75	30
1826	A443	8r grnsh blue	1.00	40
1827	A443	10r dp lilac	2.00	30
a.		Value in Persian omitted	10.00	2.50
1828	A443	14r deep grn	8.00	60
1829	A443	20r magenta	3.00	45
1830	A443	50r violet	4.00	1.25
		Nos. 1820-1830 (11)	22.25	
		Set value		3.60

Issued dates: 50d, 1r, 2r, Oct. 16, 1974; 14r, Nov. 1974; others Mar. 6, 1975.

See Nos. 1831-1841. For overprints see Nos. 2008, 2010.

1975-77

Size: 28x21mm

Frame & Shah in Green

1831	A443	5d orange ('77)	50	15
1832	A443	10d rose mag ('77)	50	15
1833	A443	50d lilac	50	15
1834	A443	1r dark blue	30	15
1835	A443	2r brown	35	15

Size: 36x26½mm

Frame & Shah in Brown

1836	A443	6r vio bl ('76)	55	35
1837	A443	8r dp org ('77)	7.50	30
1838	A443	10r dp yel grn ('76)	3.75	20
1839	A443	14r lilac	2.00	20
1840	A443	20r brt grn ('76)	3.50	40
1841	A443	50r dp blue ('76)	5.00	90
		Nos. 1831-1841 (11)	24.45	
		Set value		2.70

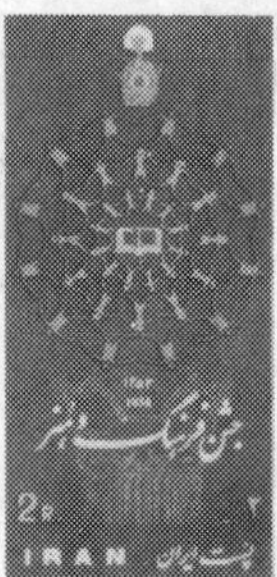
Festival Emblem, Crown and Column Capital, Persepolis — A444

1974, Oct. 26 Litho. *Perf. 10½*

1842	A444	2r multicolored	30	15

Festival of Culture and Art.

Destroyer "Palang" and Flag A445

1974, Nov. 5

1843	A445	10r multicolored	80	20

Navy Day.

Girl at Spinning Wheel A446

Designs: Children's drawings.

1974, Nov. 7 *Perf. 10½*

1844	A446	2r shown	20	15
1845	A446	2r Scarecrow, vert.	20	15
1846	A446	2r Picnic	20	15
		Set value		24

Children's Week.

Winged Ibex — A447

1974, Nov. 25 Litho. Wmk. 353

1847	A447	2r vio, org & blk	20	15

Third Tehran International Film Festival.

WPY Emblem A448

1974, Dec. 1

1848	A448	8r orange & multi	50	20

World Population Year.

Gold Bee A449

Design: 8r, Gold crown, gift of French people to Empress Farah. Bee pin was gift of the Italian people.

1974, Dec. 20

1849 A449 6r multicolored 20 15
1850 A449 8r multicolored 38 15
Set value 20

14th wedding anniv. of Shah and Empress Farah.

Angel with Banner A450

1975, Jan. 7 Litho. *Perf. 10½*

1851 A450 2r org & vio bl 22 15

International Women's Year.

Symbols of Agriculture, Industry and the Arts A451

Tourism Year 75 Emblem A452

1975, Jan. 26 Wmk. 353

1852 A451 2r multicolored 22 15

"White Revolution of King and People."

1975, Feb. 17

1853 A452 6r multicolored 26 15

South Asia Tourism Year.

"Farabi" in Shape of Musical Instrument or Alembic A453

Ornament, Rug Pattern A454

1975, Mar. 1

1854 A453 2r brn red & multi 20 15

Abu-Nasr al-Farabi (870?-950), physician, musician and philosopher, 1100th birth anniversary.

1975, Mar. 6

1855 A454 1r shown 15 15
1856 A454 1r Blossoms and cypress trees 15 15
1857 A454 1r Shah Abbasi flower 15 15
Set value 30 15

Novrooz, Iranian New Year. Nos. 1855-1857 printed se-tenant in sheets of 45 stamps and 15 labels.

Nasser Khosrov, Poet, Birth Millenary A455

Formula A456

1975, Mar. 11

1858 A455 2r blk, gold & red 25 15

1975, May 5 Litho. *Perf. 10½*

1859 A456 2r buff & multi 20 15

5th Biennial Symposium of Iranian Biochemical Society.

Charioteer, Bas-relief, Persepolis — A457

Design: 2r, Heads of Persian warriors, bas-relief from Persepolis (vert.).

1975, May 5

1860 A457 2r lt brn & multi 1.40 22
1861 A457 10r blue & multi 3.25 40

Rotary International, 70th anniversary.

Signal Fire, Persian Castle A458

Design: 8r, Communications satellite.

1975, May 17

1862 A458 6r multicolored 28 15
1863 A458 8r lil & multi 40 15
Set value 17

7th World Telecommunications Day.

Cooperation Day — A459

1975, May 13

1864 A459 2r multicolored 20 15

Jet, Shayad Monument, Statue of Liberty — A460

1975, May 29 Litho. Wmk. 353

1865 A460 10r org & multi 60 15

Iran Air's 1st flight to New York, May 1975.

Emblem — A461

1975, June 5

1866 A461 6r blue & multi 30 15

World Environment Day.

Dam A462

1975, June 10

1867 A462 10r multicolored 35 15

9th Intl. Congress on Irrigation & Drainage.

Resurgence Party Emblem A463

Girl Scout Symbols A464

1975, July 1 Wmk. 353 *Perf. 10½*

1868 A463 2r multicolored 16 15

Organization of Resurgence Party.

1975, July 16

1869 A464 2r multicolored 25 15

2nd Natl Girl Scout Camp, Tehran, July 1976.

Festival of Tus — A465

1975, July 17

1870 A465 2r gray, lil & vio 22 15

Festival of Tus in honor of Firdausi (940-1020), Persian poet born near Tus in Khorasan.

Ceramic Plate, Iran A466

Designs: No. 1872, Camel leather vase, Pakistan (vert.). No. 1873, Porcelain vase, Turkey (vert.).

1975, July 21

1871 A466 2r bister & multi 20 15
1872 A466 2r bister & multi 20 15
1873 A466 2r bister & multi 20 15
Set value 20

Regional Cooperation for Development Pact among Iran, Pakistan and Turkey.

Majlis Gate A467

1975, Aug. 5 Litho. *Perf. 10½*

1874 A467 10r multi 42 15

Iranian Constitution, 70th anniversary.

Column with Stylized Branches A468

Flags over Globe A469

1975, Aug. 21 Litho. Wmk. 353

1875 A468 8r red & multi 50 15

9th Iranian Arts Festival, Shiraz-Persepolis.

1975, Sept. 8

1876 A469 2r vio bl & multi 20 15

Intl. Literacy Symposium, Persepolis.

Stylized Globe A470

Crown, Column Capital, Persepolis A472

The Catalogue editors cannot undertake to appraise, identify or judge the genuineness or condition of stamps.

World Map and Envelope — A471

1975, Sept. 13
1877 A470 2r vio & multi 18 15

3rd Tehran International Trade Fair.

1975, Oct. 9 Litho. *Perf. 10½*
1878 A471 14r ultra & multi 60 15

World Post Day, Oct. 9.

1975, Oct. 26 Litho. Wmk. 353
1879 A472 2r ultra & multi 16 15

Festival of Culture and Art. See No. 1954.

Face and Film — A473

1975, Nov. 2
1880 A473 6r multicolored 30 15

Tehran Intl. Festival of Children's Films.

"Mother's Face" — A474

Girl — A475

Design: No. 1882, 2r, "Our House" (horiz.). All designs after children's drawings.

1975, Nov. 5
1881 A474 2r multicolored 20 15
1882 A475 2r multicolored 20 15
1883 A475 2r multicolored 20 15
Set value 24

Children's Week.

"Film" — A476

1975, Dec. 4 Wmk. 353 *Perf. 10½*
1884 A476 8r multicolored 30 15

4th Tehran International Film Festival.

Symbols of Reforms A477

People A478

1976, Jan. 26 Litho. *Perf. 10½*
1885 A477 2r shown 20 15
1886 A478 2r shown 20 15
1887 A477 2r Five reform symbols 20 15
Set value 24

"White Revolution of King and People."

Motorcycle Policeman — A479

Police Helicopter A480

1976, Feb. 16
1888 A479 2r multicolored 50 15
1889 A480 6r multicolored 85 20

Highway Police Day.

Soccer Cup A481

Candlestick A482

1976, Feb. 24 Litho. Wmk. 353
1890 A481 2r org & multi 22 15

3rd Intl. Youth Soccer Cup, Shiraz and Ahvaz.

1976, Mar. 6

Designs: No. 1892, Incense burner. No. 1893, Rose water container.

1891 A482 1r olive & multi 20 15
1892 A482 1r claret & multi 20 15
1893 A482 1r Prus bl & multi 20 15
Set value 20

Novrooz, Iranian New Year. Nos. 1891-1893 printed se-tenant.

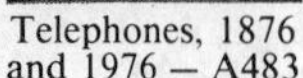

Telephones, 1876 and 1976 — A483

Eye Within Square — A484

1976, Mar. 10
1894 A483 10r multicolored 42 15

Centenary of first telephone call by Alexander Graham Bell, Mar. 10, 1876.

1976, Apr. 29 Litho. *Perf. 10½*
1895 A484 6r blk & multi 40 15
a. Perf. 12½ 6.00 4.00

World Health Day: "Foresight prevents blindness."

Nurse with Infant A485

Young Man Holding Old Man's Hand — A486

1976, May 10
1896 A485 2r shown 30 15
1897 A485 2r Engineering apprentices 30 15
1898 A486 2r shown 30 15
Set value 30

Royal Org. of Social Services, 30th anniv.

Map of Iran, Men Linking Hands A487

Waves and Ear Phones A488

1976, May 13 Wmk. 353
1899 A487 2r yel & multi 30 15

Iranian Cooperatives, 10th anniversary.

1976, May 17
1900 A488 14r gray & multi 55 15

World Telecommunications Day.

Emblem, Woman with Flag, Man with Gun — A489

1976, June 6
1901 A489 2r bister & multi 30 15

To publicize the power of stability.

Map of Iran, Columns of Persepolis, Nasser Khosrov A490

Riza Shah Pahlavi A491

1976, July 6 Litho. *Perf. 10½*
1902 A490 6r yel & multi 40 16

Tourist publicity.

1976, July 21 Litho. Wmk. 353

Designs: 6r, Mohammed Ali Jinnah. 8r, Kemal Ataturk.

1903 A491 2r gray & multi 30 15
1904 A491 6r gray & multi 60 18
1905 A491 8r gray & multi 60 22

Regional Cooperation for Development Pact among Iran, Turkey and Pakistan, 12th anniversary.

Torch, Montreal and Iranian Olympic Emblems A492

1976, Aug. 1
1906 A492 14r multicolored 75 25

21st Olympic Games, Montreal, Canada, July 17-Aug. 1.

Riza Shah Pahlavi in Coronation Robe A493

Festival Emblem A494

Designs: 2r, Shahs Riza and Mohammed Riza Pahlavi (horiz.). 14r, 20r, Shah Mohammed Riza Pahlavi in coronation robe and crown.

1976, Aug. 19 Wmk. 353 *Perf. 10½*
1907 A493 2r lilac & multi 65 15
1908 A493 6r blue & multi 1.65 18
1909 A493 14r grn & multi 1.90 30

Souvenir Sheet

1976, Oct. 8 ***Imperf.***
1910 A493 20r multi 5.00 2.00

50th anniv. of Pahlavi dynasty; 35th anniv. of reign of Shah Mohammed Riza Pahlavi. No. 1910 contains one stamp 43x62mm.

1976, Aug. 29 **Litho.** ***Perf. 10½***
1911 A494 10r multicolored 50 15

10th Iranian Arts Festival, Shiraz-Persepolis.

Iranian Scout Emblem A495

Cancer Radiation Treatment A496

1976, Oct. 2 **Litho.** ***Perf. 10½***
1912 A495 2r lt bl & multi 25 15

10th Asia Pacific Conference, Tehran 1976.

1976, Oct. 6
1913 A496 2r black & multi 30 15

Fight against cancer.

Target, Police Woman Receiving Decoration A497

1976, Oct. 7
1914 A497 2r lt bl & multi 30 15

Police Day.

UPU Emblem, No. 1907 on Cover — A498

1976, Oct. 9
1915 A498 10r multicolored 1.00 16

International Post Day.

Crown Prince Riza with Cup — A499

1976, Oct. 10
1916 A499 6r multicolored 32 15

Natl. Soc. of Village Culture Houses, anniv.

Shahs Riza and Mohammed Riza, Railroad A500

1976, Oct. 15
1917 A500 8r black & multi 2.00 30

Railroad Day.

Emblem and Column Capital, Persepolis A501

Census Emblem A502

1976, Oct. 26
1918 A501 14r blue & multi 50 15

Festival of Culture and Art.

1976, Oct. 30
1919 A502 2r gray & multi 20 15

Natl. Population & Housing Census, 1976.

Flowers and Birds — A503

Mohammed Ali Jinnah — A504

Designs: No. 1921, Flowers and bird. No. 1922, Flowers and butterfly. Designs are from covers of children's books.

1976, Oct. 31 ***Perf. 10½***
1920 A503 2r multicolored 20 15
1921 A503 2r multicolored 20 15
1922 A503 2r multicolored 20 15
Set value 30

Children's Week.

1976, Dec. 25 **Litho.** **Wmk. 353**
1923 A504 10r multicolored 45 15

Jinnah (1876-1948), 1st Governor General of Pakistan.

Development and Agriculture Corps — A505

17-Point Reform Law: 5d, Land reform. 10d, Nationalization of forests. 50d, Sale of shares of state-owned industries. 1r, Profit sharing for factory workers. 2r, Woman suffrage. 3r, Education Corps formation. 5r, Health Corps. 8r, Establishment of village courts. 10r, Nationalization of water resources. 12r, Reconstruction program, urban and rural. 14r, Administrative and educational reorganization. 20r, Sale of factory shares. 30r, Commodity pricing. 50r, Free education. 100r, Child care. 200r, Care of the aged (social security).

1977, Jan. 26 **Photo.** ***Perf. 13x13½***

Frame and Shah's Head in Gold

Size: 28x21mm

1924 A505 5d rose & green 15 15
1925 A505 10d lt grn & brn 15 15
1926 A505 50d yel & vio bl 15 15
1927 A505 1r lil & vio bl 15 15
1928 A505 2r org & green 20 15
1929 A505 3r lt bl & red 38 15
1930 A505 5r bl grn & mag 38 15

Size: 37x27mm

1931 A505 6r brn, mar & black 55 15
1932 A505 8r ultra, mar & black 55 15
1933 A505 10r lt grn, bl & black 1.50 20
1934 A505 12r vio, mar & black 1.10 15
1935 A505 14r org, red & blk 1.65 75
1936 A505 20r gray, ocher & black 3.25 50
1937 A505 30r bl, grn & blk 3.25 65
1938 A505 50r yel, brn & blk 5.50 60
1939 A505 100r multi 4.75 1.25
1940 A505 200r multi 11.00 2.50
Nos. 1924-1940 (17) 34.66
Set value 7.00

"White Revolution of King and People" reform laws.

Man in Guilan Costume A506

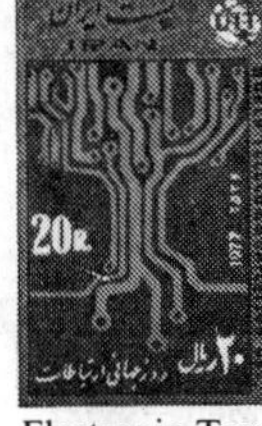

Electronic Tree A507

Design: 2r, Woman in Guilan costume (Northern Iran).

1977, Mar. 6 **Wmk. 353** ***Perf. 13***
1941 A506 1r multicolored 15 15
1942 A506 2r multicolored 20 15
Set value 18

Novrooz, Iranian New Year.

1977, May 17 **Photo.** ***Perf. 13***
1943 A507 20r multicolored 65 15

World Telecommunications Day.

Riza Shah Dam A508

1977, May 31 ***Perf. 13x13½***
1944 A508 5r multicolored 40 15

Inauguration of Riza Shah Dam.

Olympic Rings — A509

1977, June 23 **Litho.** ***Perf. 10½***
1945 A509 14r multicolored 60 15

Olympic Day.

Terra-cotta Jug, Iran — A510

Designs: No. 1947, Terra-cotta bullock cart, Pakistan. No. 1948, Terra-cotta pot with human face, Turkey.

Perf. 13x13½

1977, July 21 **Photo.** **Wmk. 353**
1946 A510 5r violet & multi 28 15
1947 A510 5r emer & multi 28 15
1948 A510 5r green & multi 28 15
Set value 24

Regional Cooperation for Development Pact among Iran, Turkey and Pakistan, 13th anniv.

Flowers with Scout Emblems, Map of Asia — A511

1977, Aug. 5 **Litho.** ***Perf. 13***
1949 A511 10r multicolored 55 16

2nd Asia-Pacific Jamboree, Nishapur.

Map of Eastern Hemisphere with Iran — A512

Tree of Learning, Symbolic Letters — A513

1977, Sept. 20 **Photo.** **Wmk. 353**
1950 A512 3r multicolored 20 15

9th Asian Electronics Conference, Tehran.

1977, Oct. 8 **Wmk. 353** ***Perf. 13***
1951 A513 10r multicolored 32 15

Honoring the teachers.

Globe, Envelope, UPU Emblem A514

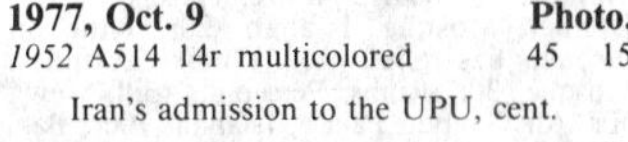

1977, Oct. 9 **Photo.**
1952 A514 14r multicolored 45 15

Iran's admission to the UPU, cent.

Folk Art — A515

1977, Oct. 16
1953 A515 5r multicolored 40 15

Festival of Folk Art.

Festival Type of 1975

Design: 20r, similar to 1975 issue, but with small crown within star.

1977, Oct. 26 ***Perf. 10½***

1954 A472 20r bis, grn, car & blk 60 15

Festival of Culture and Art.

Joust
A516

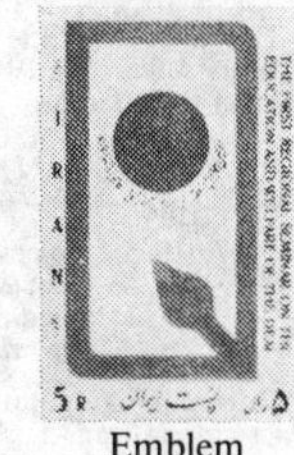

Emblem
A517

Designs: No. 1956, Rapunzel. No. 1957, Little princess with attendants.

1977, Oct. 31 **Photo.**

1955 A516 3r multicolored 20 15
1956 A516 3r multicolored 20 15
1957 A516 3r multicolored 20 15
Set value 36

Children's Week. Nos. 1955-1957 printed se-tenant.

1977, Nov. 7 **Wmk. 353** ***Perf. 13***

1958 A517 5r multicolored 30 15

First Regional Seminar on the Education and Welfare of the Deaf.

Mohammad
Iqbal
A518

African
Sculpture
A519

1977, Nov. 9 **Litho.** ***Perf. 10½***

1959 A518 5r multicolored 45 15

Iqbal (1877-1938), poet and philosopher.

1977, Dec. 14

1960 A519 20r multicolored 3.25 45

African art.

Shah Mosque,
Isfahan — A520

Designs: 1r, Ruins, Persepolis. 2r, Khajou Bridge, Isfahan. 5r, Imam Riza Shrine, Meshed. 9r, Warrior frieze, Persepolis. 10r, Djameh Mosque, Isfahan. 20r, King on throne, bas-relief. 25r, Sheik Lotfollah Mosque. 30r, Ruins, Persepolis (diff. view). 50r, Ali Ghapou Palace, Isfahan. 100r, Bas-relief, Tagh Bastan. 200r, Horseman and prisoners, bas-relief, Naqsh Rostam.

1978-79 **Photo.** ***Perf. 13x13½***

"Iran" and Head in Gold

Size: 28x21mm

1961 A520 1r deep brn 30 15
1962 A520 2r emerald 30 15
1963 A520 3r magenta 50 15
1964 A520 5r Prus blue 70 15

Size: 36x27mm

1965 A520 9r sepia ('79) 1.40 55
1966 A520 10r brt bl ('79) 5.50 70
1967 A520 20r rose 1.75 55
1968 A520 25r ultra ('79) 25.00 9.75
1969 A520 30r magenta 2.75 55
1970 A520 50r deep yel grn ('79) 4.50 3.50
1971 A520 100r dk bl ('79) 15.00 9.75
1972 A520 200r vio bl ('79) 19.00 19.00
Nos. 1961-1972 (12) 76.70 44.95

For overprints see Nos. 2009, 2011-2018.

Persian
Rug — A521

Designs: Persian rugs.

1978, Feb. 11 **Litho.** ***Perf. 10½***

1973 A521 3r sil & multi 22 15
1974 A521 5r sil & multi 45 15
1975 A521 10r sil & multi 65 30

Opening of Carpet Museum.

Iranian
Man — A522

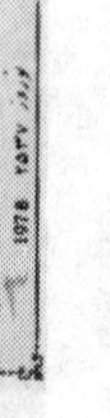

Mohammed
Riza
Pahlavi — A523

Design: 5r, Iranian woman.

1978, Mar. 6 ***Perf. 13***

1976 A522 3r yel & multi 22 15
1977 A522 5r lt bl & multi 42 15
Set value 24

Novrooz, Iranian New Year.

1978, Jan. 26

1978 A523 20r multicolored 3.75 1.00

Shah's White Revolution, 15th anniv.

Riza Shah Pahlavi and Crown Prince Inspecting Girls' School
A524

Designs (Riza Shah Pahlavi and Crown Prince Mohammed Riza Pahlavi): 5r, Inauguration of Trans-Iranian railroad. 10r, At stairs of Palace, Persepolis. 14r, Shah handing Crown Prince (later Shah) officer's diploma at Tehran Officers' Academy.

1978, Mar. 15

1979 A524 3r multicolored 35 15
1980 A524 5r multicolored 65 20
1981 A524 10r multicolored 1.10 25
1982 A524 14r multicolored 1.50 40

Riza Shah Pahlavi (1877-1944), founder of Pahlavi dynasty.

Communications Satellite over Map of Iran — A525

1978, Apr. 19 **Litho.** ***Perf. 10½***

1983 A525 20r multicolored 1.00 16

ITU, 7th meeting, Tehran; 10th anniv. of Iran's membership.

Antenna, ITU
Emblem
A526

1978, May 17 **Litho.** ***Perf. 10½***

1984 A526 15r multicolored 65 20

10th World Telecommunications Day.

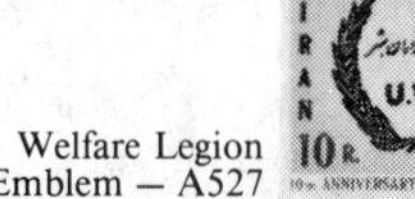

Welfare Legion
Emblem — A527

1978, June 13 **Photo.** ***Perf. 13x13½***

1985 A527 10r multicolored 60 15

Universal Welfare Legion, 10th anniversary.

Pink Roses,
Iran — A528

Designs: 10r, Yellow rose, Turkey. 15r, Red roses, Pakistan.

Perf. 13½x13

1978, July 21 **Wmk. 353**

1986 A528 5r multicolored 40 15
1987 A528 10r multicolored 65 15
1988 A528 15r multicolored 80 24

Regional Cooperation for Development Pact among Iran, Turkey and Pakistan, 14th anniversary.

Rhazes, Pharmaceutical
Tools — A529

1978, Aug. 26 **Wmk. 353** ***Perf. 13***

1989 A529 5r multicolored 40 15

Pharmacists' Day. Rhazes (850-923), chief physician of Great Hospital in Baghdad.

Girl Scouts,
Aryamehr
Arch — A530

1978, Sept. 2 ***Perf. 10½***

1990 A530 5r multicolored 35 15

23rd World Girl Scouts Conference, Tehran, Sept. 1978.

Shah
Riza
Pahlavi
A531

Design: 5r, Mohammed Riza Shah Pahlavi.

1978, Sept. 11 **Litho.** ***Perf. 10½***

1991 A531 3r multicolored 1.25 25
1992 A531 5r multicolored 1.50 35

Bank Melli Iran, 50th anniversary.

Girl and
Bird
A532

1978, Oct. 31 **Photo.** ***Perf. 13***

1993 A532 3r multicolored 35 20

Children's Week.

Envelope,
Map of Iran,
UPU
Emblem
A533

1978, Nov. 22 ***Perf. 13x13½***

1994 A533 14r gold & multi 1.25 18

World Post Day, Oct. 22.

Communications Symbols and Classroom — A534

1978, Nov. 22 ***Perf. 10½***

1995 A534 10r multicolored 1.00 18

Faculty of Communications, 50th anniv.

Human
Rights
Flame
A535

1978, Dec. 17 **Photo.** ***Perf. 13***

1996 A535 20r bl, blk & gold 3.50 26

Universal Declaration of Human Rights, 30th anniv.

Kurdistani Man — A536

Rose — A537

Design: 5r, Kurdistani woman.

1979, Mar. 17

1997	A536	3r multicolored	90	15
1998	A536	5r multicolored	1.25	15

1979, Mar. 17

1999	A537	2r multicolored	15	15

Novrooz, Iranian New Year.
See No. 2310i.

Islamic Republic

Demonstrators — A538

Islamic revolution: 3r, Demonstrators. 5r, Hands holding rose, gun and torch breaking through newspaper. 20r, Hands breaking prison bars, and dove (vert.).

1979, Apr. 20 *Perf. 10½*

2000	A538	3r multicolored	1.50	15
2001	A538	5r multicolored	1.10	15
2002	A538	10r multicolored	1.10	30
2003	A538	20r multicolored	2.50	30

Nos. 1837-1838, 1966, 1970 and Type A520 Overprinted

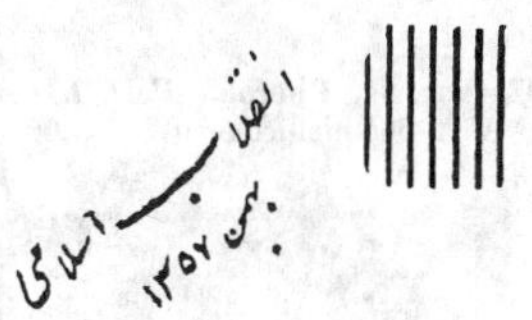

Designs: 15r, Warriors on horseback, bas-relief, Naqsh-Rostan. 19r, Chehel Sotoon Palace, Isfahan.

1979 Wmk. 353 *Perf. 13x13½*

2008	A443	8r org & brown	*3.00*	1.00
2009	A520	9r gold & dp brn	1.50	1.50
2010	A443	10r gold & dp yel grn	*50.00*	5.00
2011	A520	10r gold & brt bl	1.00	1.00
2012	A520	15r red lilac	1.00	1.00
2013	A520	19r slate green	1.00	1.00
2016	A520	50r gold & dp yel grn	2.00	2.00
2017	A520	100r gold & vio bl	10.00	4.00
2018	A520	200r gold & vio bl	12.50	8.50
		Nos. 2008-2018 (9)	*82.00*	25.00

Overprint means Islamic revolution.

Symbolic Rose — A539

1979, June 5 Photo. *Perf. 13*

2019	A539	5r multicolored	1.50	28

Potters, by Kamalel Molk A540

Paintings: No. 2021, at the Well, by Allah Baksh, Pakistan. No. 2022, Plowing, by Namik Ismail, Turkey.

1979, July 21 Litho. *Perf. 10½*

2020	A540	5r multicolored	3.25	15
2021	A540	5r multicolored	2.50	15
2022	A540	5r multicolored	2.50	15

Regional Cooperation for Development Pact among Iran, Turkey and Pakistan, 15th anniv.

"TELECOM 79" — A541

1979, Sept. 20 *Perf. 10½*

2023	A541	20r multicolored	*5.00*	25

3rd World Telecommunications Exhibition, Geneva, Sept. 20-26.

Greeting the Sunrise A542

Persian Rug Design A543

Children's Drawings and IYC Emblem: 2r, Tulip over wounded man. 2r, Children with banners.

1979, Sept. 23

2024	A542	2r multicolored	85	20
2025	A542	3r multicolored	85	20
2026	A542	5r multicolored	1.65	20

International Year of the Child.

1979 Photo. *Perf. 13½x13*

2027	A543	50d brn & pale sal	15	15
2028	A543	1r dark & lt bl	15	15
2029	A543	2r red & yellow	15	15
2030	A543	3r dk bl & lt lil	15	15
2031	A543	5r sl grn & lt grn	15	15
2032	A543	10r blk & salmon pink ('80)	28	15
2033	A543	20r brn & gray ('80)	55	15

Size: 27x37½mm

2034	A543	50r dp violet & gray ('80)	1.40	16
2035	A543	100r blk & slate grn ('80)	5.00	1.40
2036	A543	200r dk bl & cr ('80)	5.50	2.75
		Nos. 2027-2036 (10)	13.48	
		Set value		4.65

Globe in Envelope — A544

1979, Oct. 9 Litho. *Perf. 10½*

2041	A544	10r multicolored	*2.00*	25

World Post Day.

Ghyath-al-din Kashani, Astrolabe A545

1979, Dec. 5 Litho. *Perf. 10½*

2042	A545	5r ocher & blk	*1.50*	25

Kashani, mathematician, 600th death anniv.

Koran, Flame and Mosque A546

Hegira (Pilgrimage Year): 5r, Koran open over globe (vert.) 10r, Salman Farsi (follower of Mohammed), map of Iran.

1980, Jan. 19

2043	A546	3r multicolored	20	15
2044	A546	5r multicolored	25	18
2045	A546	10r multicolored	50	22

Reissued in May-June, 1980, with shiny gum and watermark position changed.

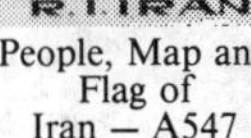

People, Map and Flag of Iran — A547

Dehkhoda, Dictionary Editor, Birth Cent. — A548

Islamic Revolution, 1st Anniversary: 3r, Blood dripping on broken sword. 5r, Window open on sun of Islam, people.

1980, Feb. 11

2046	A547	1r multicolored	18	15
2047	A547	3r multicolored	35	22
2048	A547	5r multicolored	65	30

For similar stamps measuring 24x36mm see Nos. 2310a, 2310b, 2310d.

1980, Feb. 26

2049	A548	10r multicolored	30	15

East Azerbaijani Woman A549

Mohammed Mossadegh A550

Novrooz (Iranian New Year): 5r, East Azerbaijani man.

1980, Mar. 5

2050	A549	3r multicolored	15	15
2051	A549	5r multicolored	22	15
		Set value		20

1980, Mar. 19 Photo. *Perf. 13x13½*

2052	A550	20r multi	60	16

Oil industry nationalization, 29th anniv.; Mohammed Mossadegh, prime minister who initiated nationalization, birth cent.

Ayatollah Morteza Motahhari, 1st Death Anniversary — A551

1980, May 1 Litho. *Perf. 10½*

2053	A551	10r black & red	50	16

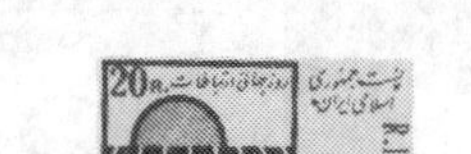

World Telecommunications Day — A552

1980, May 17 Photo. *Perf. 13x13½*

2054	A552	20r multicolored	48	15

Interior of Mosque A553

1980, June 11 Litho. *Perf. 10½*

2055	A553	50d shown	15	15
2056	A553	1r Demonstration	15	15
2057	A553	3r Avicenna, al-Biruni, Farabi	40	18
2058	A553	5r Hegira emblem	30	15
		Set value		45

Hegira, 1500th anniv.

Ali Sharyati, Educator — A554

1980, June 15 Photo. *Perf. 13x13½*

2059	A554	5r multicolored	30	15

Holy Ka'aba and Hand Waving Banner — A555

1980, June 28

2060 A555 5r multicolored 30 15

Hazrat Mehdi, 12th Imam's birth anniv.

A556

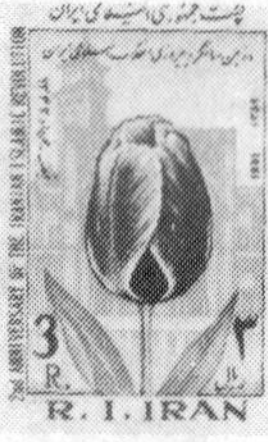

OPEC Emblem — A557

1980, Sept. 10 ***Perf. 13½x13***

2061 A556 5r multicolored 30 15

Ayatollah Seyed Mahmood Talegani, death anniv. Compare with design A829.

1980, Sept. 15

2062 A557 5r shown 30 15
2063 A557 10r Men holding OPEC emblem 60 15
Set value 20

20th anniversary of OPEC.

"Let Us Liberate Jerusalem" A558

Tulip and Fayziyye Mosque, Qum A559

1980, Oct. 9 ***Perf. 13x13½***

2064 A558 5r multicolored 18 15
2065 A558 20r multicolored 75 15
Set value 20

1981, Feb. 11 ***Perf. 13***

2066 A559 3r shown 15 15
2067 A559 5r Blood spilling on tulip 15 15
2068 A559 20r Tulip, Republic emblem 48 15
Set value 25

Islamic Revolution, 2nd anniversary.
See Nos. 2310c, 2310e, 2310j, watermark 381 (3r, unserifed "R" in denomination, 5r, bright yellow background; 20r, light blue background behind flower.)

Lorestani Man — A560

Telecommunications Day — A561

Novrooz (Iranian New Year): 10r, Lorestani woman.

1981, Mar. 11

2069 A560 5r multicolored 15 15
2070 A560 10r multicolored 30 15
Set value 20

Perf. 13½x13

1981, May 17 Photo. Wmk. 353

2071 A561 5r dk grn & org 15 15

Ayatollah Kashani Birth Centenary A562

Adult Education A563

Perf. 13x13½

1981, July 21 Wmk. 381

2072 A562 15r dk grn & dl pur 40 15

Perf. 13x13½, 13½x13 (5r, 10r, 200r)
1981, Aug.

Designs: 50d, Citizens bearing arms. 2r, Irrigation. 3r, Friday prayer service. 5r, Paasdaar emblem and members. 10r, Koran text. 20r, Hejaab (women's veil). 50r, Industrial development. 100r, Religious ceremony, Mecca. 200r, Mosque interior. 5r, 10r, 200r vert.

2073 A563 50d blk & dp bis 15 15
2074 A563 1r dl pur & grn 15 15
2075 A563 2r brn & grnsh bl 15 15

Size: 38x28mm, 28x38mm

2076 A563 3r brt yel grn & black 15 15
2077 A563 5r dk bl & brn org 15 15
2078 A563 10r dk bl & grnsh blue 22 15
2079 A563 20r red & black 45 15
2080 A563 50r lilac & blk 1.10 30
2081 A563 100r org brn & blk 2.25 60
2082 A563 200r blk & bl grn 4.50 1.25
Nos. 2073-2082 (10) 9.27
Set value 2.50

Islamic Iranian Army A564

1981, Sept. 21 Photo. *Perf. 13*

2087 A564 5r multicolored 15 15

World Post Day and 12th UPU Day — A565

Perf. 13x13½

1981, Oct. 9 Wmk. 381

2088 A565 20r black & blue 48 24

Millennium of Nahjul Balaghah (Sacred Book) — A566

1981, Oct. 17 *Perf. 13*

2089 A566 25r multicolored 60 16

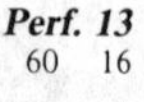

Martyrs' Memorial — A567

1981, Nov. 9 Photo. *Perf. 13*

2090 A567 3r June 28, 1981 victims 15 15
2091 A567 5r Pres. Rajai, Prime Minister Bahonar 15 15
2092 A567 10r Gen. Chamran 25 15
Set value 30

Ayatollah M. H. Tabatabaee, Scholar — A568

1981, Dec. 25 Photo. *Perf. 13*

2093 A568 5r multicolored 20 15

Literacy Campaign A569

Islamic Revolution, 3rd Anniv. A570

1982, Jan. 20 Photo. *Perf. 13x13½*

2094 A569 5r blue & gold 20 15

1982, Feb. 11 Wmk. 381 *Perf. 13*

2095 A570 5r Map 15 15
2096 A570 10r Tulip 25 15
2097 A570 20r Globe 50 20
Set value 35

Nos. 2095-2097 se-tenant.
See Nos. 2310f, 2310g, 2310k (5r, orange background, Arabian "5" 6mm above black panel. 10r, dark green background, gray dove with thick black lines around it. 20r, pink background, bright blue globe, faint latitude and longitude lines.)

Unity Week — A571

Khuzestan Man — A573

Glorification of Jesus Christ — A572

1982, Feb. 20 Photo. *Perf. 13*

2098 A571 25r multicolored 1.00 20

1982, Mar. 11 Photo. Wmk. 381

2099 A572 20r multicolored 50 20

1982, Mar. 13

2100 A573 3r shown 15 15
2101 A573 5r Khuzestan woman 15 15
Set value 20 15

Novrooz (New Year). Nos. 2100-2101 se-tenant.

3rd Anniv. of Islamic Revolution — A574

1982, Apr. 1

2102 A574 30r multicolored 90 25

Seyed Mohammad Bagher — A575

1982, Apr. 8 Photo. *Perf. 13½x13*

2103 A575 50r multicolored 1.00 40

Martyrs of Altar (Ayatollahs Madani and Dastgeyb) — A576

1982, Apr. 21 *Perf. 13*

2104 A576 50r multicolored 1.00 40

Intl. Workers' Solidarity Day — A577

Mab'as Day (Mohammad's Appointment as Prophet) — A579

14th World Telecommunications Day — A578

1982, May 1 **Photo.** ***Perf. 13½x13***
2105 A577 100r multi 2.25 80

1982, May 17 ***Perf. 13x13½***
2106 A578 100r multi 2.25 80

1982, May 21 ***Perf. 13½x13***
2107 A579 32r multicolored 90 30

1963 Islamic Rising, 19th Anniv. — A580

Lt. Islambuli, Assassin of Anwar Sadat — A581

1982, June 5 **Wmk. 381** ***Perf. 13***
2108 A580 28r multicolored 60 28

1982, June 17
2109 A581 2r multicolored 20 15

First Death Anniv. of Ayatollah Beheshti — A582

1982, June 28
2110 A582 10r multicolored 40 15
a. Missing dot in Arabic numeral 1.00 1.00

Iran-Iraq War A583

1982, July 7 ***Perf. 13x13½***
2111 A583 5r multicolored 20 15

Universal Jerusalem Day A584

1982, July 15 ***Perf. 13***
2112 A584 1r Dome of the Rock 15 15

Pilgrimage to Mecca — A585

13th World UPU Day — A586

1982, Sept. 28
2113 A585 10r multicolored 30 15

1982, Oct. 9 ***Perf. 13½x13***
2114 A586 30r multicolored 75 25

4th Anniv. of Islamic Revolution A587

4th Anniv. of Islamic Republic A588

1983, Feb. 11 **Photo.** ***Perf. 13***
2115 A587 30r multicolored 75 25

See No. 2310n for stamp with orange or orange red crowd and thick sharp lettering in black panels.

1983, Apr. 1 **Photo.** ***Perf. 13***
2116 A588 10r multicolored 30 15

Teachers' Day — A589

World Communications Year — A590

Perf. 13½x13
1983, May 1 **Wmk. 381**
2117 A589 5r multicolored 25 15

1983, May 17
2118 A590 20r multicolored 60 15

First Session of Islamic Consultative Assembly — A591

1983, May 28 ***Perf. 13***
2119 A591 5r multicolored 20 15

20th Anniv. of Islamic Movement — A592

1983, June 5 **Photo.** ***Perf. 13***
2120 A592 10r multicolored 30 15

MiG Bombing Now Rooz Oil Well A593

1983, June 11 ***Perf. 13x13½***
2121 A593 5r multicolored 50 15

Ayatollah Mohammad Sadooghi A594

1983, July 2 **Photo.** ***Perf. 13½***
2122 A594 20r blk & dl red 60 15

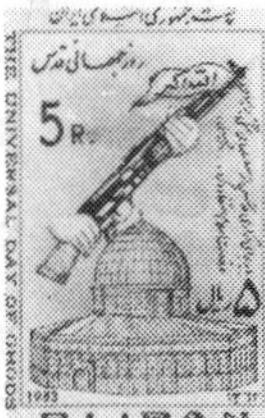

Universal Day of Jerusalem A595

Iran-Iraq War, 3rd Anniv. A597

Government Week — A596

1983, July 8
2123 A595 5r Dome of the Rock 20 15

1983, Aug. 30 **Wmk. 381** ***Perf. 13***
2124 A596 3r multicolored 15 15

Death of Pres. Rajai and Prime Minister Bahonar, 2nd anniv.

1983, Sept. 28 **Photo.** ***Perf. 13***
2125 A597 5r rose red & blk 20 15

Ayatollah Ashrafi Esphahani, Martyr of Altar — A598

Mirza Kuchik Khan — A599

1983, Oct. 15 **Photo.** ***Perf. 13***
2126 A598 5r multicolored 15 15

1983-84 **Photo.** ***Perf. 13***

Religious and Political Figures: 1r, Sheikh Mohammad Khiabani. 3r, Seyd Majtaba Navab Safavi. 5r, Seyd Jamal-ed-Din Assadabadi. 10r, Seyd Hassan Modaress. 20r, Sheikeh Fazel Assad Nouri. 30r, Mirza Mohammed Hossein Naiyni. 50r, Sheikh Mohammad Hossein Kashef. 100r, Seyd Hassan Shirazi. 200r, Mirza Reza Kermani.

2128 A599	1r	black & pink	15	15
2129 A599	2r	org & black	15	15
2130 A599	3r	brt bl & blk	15	15
2131 A599	5r	rose red & blk	15	15
2132 A599	10r	yel grn & blk	30	15
2133 A599	20r	lilac & blk	60	15
2134 A599	30r	gldn brn & blk	90	24
2135 A599	50r	blk & lt bl	1.50	50
2136 A599	100r	blk & org	3.00	1.00
2137 A599	200r	blk & bluish grn	6.00	2.00
		Nos. 2128-2137 (10)	12.90	4.64

Issue dates: 1r, 50r-200r, Feb. 1984. Others, Oct. 23, 1983.

UPU Day A600

1983, Oct. 9 **Photo.** **Wmk. 381**
2138 A600 10r multi 22 15

Takeover of the US Embassy, 4th Anniv. — A601

1983, Nov. 4 **Photo.** ***Perf. 13***
2139 A601 28r multicolored 50 50

UN Day A602

1983, Oct. 24 ***Perf. 13½***
2140 A602 32r multicolored 90 25

Protest of veto by US, Russia, People's Rep. of China.

Intl. Medical Seminar, Tehran — A603

1983, Nov. 20
2141 A603 3r Avicenna 20 15

People's Forces Preparation Day A604

1983, Nov. 26 ***Perf. 13***
2142 A604 20r multicolored 60 15

Conference on Crimes of Iraqi Pres. Saddam A605

1983, Nov. 28 ***Perf. 13½x13***
2143 A605 5r multicolored 20 15

Mohammad Mofatteh — A606

1983, Dec. 18 **Photo.** ***Perf. 13***
2144 A606 10r multicolored 30 15

A 5r stamp for the birth anniv. of the prophet Mohammed was withdrawn from sale by the Iranian Post Office because of a spelling error.

5th Anniv. of Islamic Revolution — A608

1984, Feb. 11 **Photo.** ***Perf. 13x13½***
2146 A608 10r multicolored 75 20

See No. 2310h for stamp with splotchy colors in blue background and denomination, flag colors and darker, thicker black lines around tulips. Background and denominations on No. 2146 have a screened appearance.

Nurses' Day A609

1984, Feb. 24 ***Perf. 13***
2147 A609 20r Attending wounded soldiers 45 20

Invalids' Day A610

Local Flowers A611

1984, Feb. 29
2148 A610 5r Man in wheelchair 15 15

1984, Mar. 10 ***Perf. 13½x13***
2149 A611 3r Lotus gebelia 15 15
2150 A611 5r Tulipa chrysantha 15 15
2151 A611 10r Glycyrhiza glabra 22 15
2152 A611 20r Matthiola alyssifolia 45 20
Set value 48

Novrooz (New Year) Nos. 2149-2152 se-tenant.

Islamic Republic, 5th Anniv. — A612

Sheik Ragheb Harb, Lebanese Religious Leader — A614

World Health Day A613

1984, Apr. 1 **Photo.** ***Perf. 13***
2153 A612 5r Flag, globe, map 15 15

1984, Apr. 7
2154 A613 10r Children 30 15

1984, Apr. 18
2155 A614 5r multicolored 15 15

World Red Cross Day — A615

16th World Telecommunications Day — A616

1984, May 8 **Photo.** ***Perf. 13½x13***
2156 A615 5r multicolored 15 15

1984, May 17
2157 A616 20r multicolored 45 20

Martyrdom of Seyyed Ghotb — A617

1984, May 28 ***Perf. 13***
2158 A617 10r multicolored 30 15

Struggle Against Discrimination — A618

1984, Mar. 21 **Photo.** ***Perf. 13***
2159 A618 5r multicolored 15 15

Conquest of Mecca Anniv. A619

1984, June 20
2160 A619 5r Holy Ka'aba, idol destruction 15 15

Universal Day of Jerusalem A620

Id Al-fitr Feast A621

1984, June 29
2161 A620 5r Map, Koran 15 15
2162 A621 10r Moon, praying crowd, mosque 25 15
Set value 15

Se-tenant.

Tchogha Zanbil Excavation, Susa A622

Cultural Heritage Preservation: b, Emamzadeh Hossein Shrine, Kazvin. c, Emam Mosque, Isfahan. d, Ark Fortress, Tabriz. e, Mausoleum of Daniel Nabi, Susa.

1984, Aug. 20 ***Perf. 13½***
2163 Strip of 5 75 25
a.-e. A622 5r, any single 15 15

"Eid Ul-Adha" A623

Perf. 13x13½
1984, Sept. 6 **Photo.** **Wmk. 381**
2164 A623 10r Holy Ka'aba 30 15

Feast of Sacrifices (end of pilgrimage to Mecca).

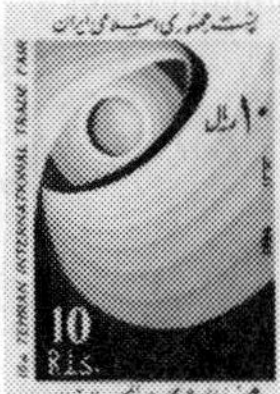
10th Tehran Intl. Trade Fair — A624

Iraq-Iran War, 4th Anniv. — A625

1984, Sept. 11
2165 A624 10r multicolored 30 15

1984, Sept. 22 **Photo.** ***Perf. 13x13½***
2166 A625 5r Flower, bullets 15 15

UPU Day A626

1984, Oct. 9 ***Perf. 13½***
2167 A626 20r Dove, UPU emblems 50 20

Haj Seyyed Mostafa Khomeini Memorial A627

1984, Oct. 23
2168 A627 5r multicolored 15 15

Ghazi Tabatabaie Memorial A628

Mohammed's Birthday, Unity Week A630

Intl. Saadi Congress A629

1984, Nov. 1 ***Perf. 13x13½***
2169 A628 5r Portrait 15 15

1984, Nov. 25 ***Perf. 13½***
2170 A629 10r Portrait, mausoleum, emblem 50 15

Saadi (c. 1213-1292), Persian poet.

1984, Dec. 6 **Photo.** ***Perf. 13x13½***
2171 A630 5r Koran, mosque 25 15

Islamic Revolution, 6th Anniv. — A631

Arbor Day — A632

1985, Feb. 11 *Perf. 13x13½*
2172 A631 40r multicolored 90 40

See No. 2310o for stamp with bright pink denomination and dove tail.

1985, Mar. 6 *Perf. 13*
2173 A632 3r Sapling, deciduous trees 15 15
2174 A632 5r Maturing trees 15 15
Set value 15

Local Flowers — A633

1985, Mar. 9 *Perf. 13½x13*
2175 A633 5r Fritillaria imperialis 15 15
2176 A633 5r Ranunculus ficarioides 15 15
2177 A633 5r Crocus sativus 15 15
2178 A633 5r Primula heterochroma stapf 15 15
Set value 48 20

Novrooz (New Year). Nos. 2175-2178 se-tenant.

Women's Day — A634

Republic of Iran, 6th Anniv. — A635

1985, Mar. 13 *Perf. 13x13½*
2179 A634 10r Procession of women 30 15

Birth anniv. of Mohammed's daughter, Fatima.

1985, Apr. 1
2180 A635 20r Tulip, ballot box 45 20

Mab'as Festival A636

1985, Apr. 18
2181 A636 10r Holy Koran 30 15

Religious festival celebrating the recognition of Mohammed as the true prophet.

Day of the Oppressed A637

World Telecommunications Day A638

1985, May 6
2182 A637 5r Koran, flag, globe 15 15

Birthday of the 12th Imam.

1985, May 17 *Perf. 13½x13*
2183 A638 20r ITU emblem 45 20

Liberation of Khorramshahr, 1st Anniv. — A639

1985, May 24
2184 A639 5r Soldier, bridge 15 15

Fist, Theological Seminary, Qum — A640

Day of Jerusalem — A642

World Handicrafts Day A641

1985, June 5 *Perf. 13x13½*
2185 A640 10r multicolored 50 15

1963 Uprising, 22nd Anniv.

1985, June 10 *Perf. 13½*
2186 A641 20r Plates, flasks 45 20

1985, June 14
2187 A642 5r multicolored 15 15

Id Al-fitr Feast — A643

Founding of the Islamic Propagation Org. — A644

1985, June 20 *Perf. 13x13½*
2188 A643 5r multicolored 15 15

1985, June 22
2189 A644 5r tan & emerald 15 15

Ayatollah Sheikh Abdolhossein Amini — A645

1985, July 3 **Photo.** *Perf. 13*
2190 A645 5r multicolored 25 15

Pilgrimage to Mecca — A646

Goharshad Mosque Uprising, 50th Anniv. — A648

Cultural Heritage Preservation — A647

1985, July 20 **Photo.** *Perf. 13½*
2191 A646 10r multicolored 30 15

1985, Aug. 20

Ceramic plates from Nishabur: a, Swords. b, Farsi script. c, Peacock. d, Four leaves.

2192 Block of 4 60 20
a.-d. A647 5r, any single 15 15

1985, Aug. 21 *Perf. 13x13½*
2193 A648 10r multicolored 20 15

Week of Government A649

Bleeding Tulips A650

Designs: a, Industry and communications. b, Industry and agriculture. c, Health care, red crescent. d, Education.

1985, Aug. 30 **Photo.** *Perf. 13x13½*
2194 Block of 4 60 20
a.-d. A649 5r, any single 15 15

1985, Sept. 8
2195 A650 10r multicolored 30 15

17th Shahrivar, Bloody Friday memorial.

OPEC, 25th Anniv. — A651

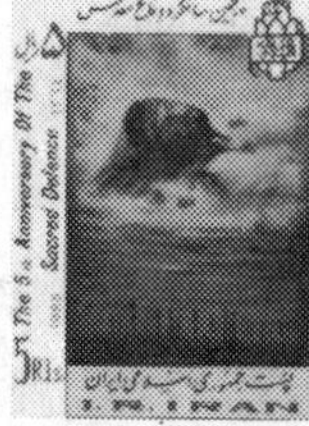
Iran-Iraq War, 5th Anniv. — A652

Design: No. 2196b, OPEC emblem and 25.

1985, Sept. 14 *Perf. 13½*
2196 Pair 50 15
a.-b. A651 5r, any single 25 15

1985, Sept. 22

Designs: a, Dead militiaman. b, Minaret and Ashura in Persian. c, Rockets descending on doves. d, Palm grove, rifle shot exploding rocket.

2197 Block of 4 60 20
a.-d. A652 5r, any single 15 15

Ashura mourning.

Ash-Sharif Ar-Radi, Writer, Death Millennium — A653

1985, Sept. 26 **Photo.** *Perf. 13x13½*
2198 A653 20r brt bl, lt bl & gold 60 20

UPU Day A654

1985, Oct. 9 *Perf. 13½*
2199 A654 20r multicolored 60 20

World Standards Day A655

1985, Oct. 14
2200 A655 20r Natl. Standards Office emblem 60 20

The indexes in each volume of the Scott Catalogue contain many listings which help to identify stamps.

Agricultural Training and Development Year — A656

Takeover of US Embassy, 6th Anniv. — A657

1985, Oct. 19 *Perf. 13x13½*
2201 A656 5r Hand, wheat 15 15

1985, Nov. 4 *Perf. 13*
2202 A657 40r multicolored 60 40

Moslem Unity Week A658

High Council of the Cultural Revolution A659

1985, Nov. 25 *Perf. 13x13½*
2203 A658 10r Holy Ka'aba 30 15

Birth of prophet Mohammed, 1015th anniv.

1985, Dec. 10
2204 A659 5r Roses 15 15

Intl. Youth Year — A660

Ezzeddin al-Qassam, 50th Death Anniv. — A661

Designs: a, Education. b, Defense. c, Construction. d, Sports.

1985, Dec. 18 Photo. *Perf. 13x13½*
2205 Block of 4 60 20
a.-d. A660 5r, any single 15 15

1985, Dec. 20 *Perf. 13½*
2206 A661 20r sil, sep & hn brn 60 20

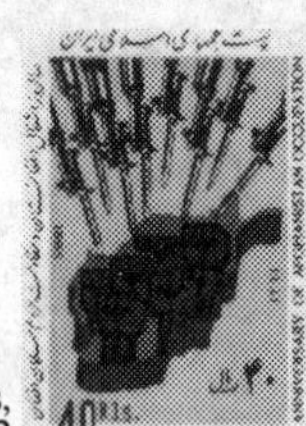
Map, Fists, Bayonets — A662

1985, Dec. 25 **Wmk. 381**
2207 A662 40r multi 1.20 40

Occupation of Afghanistan and Moslem resistance, 6th anniv.

Mirza Taqi Khan Amir Kabir (d. 1851) — A663

1986, Jan. 8 Litho. *Perf. 13*
2208 A663 5r multicolored 80 20

Students Destroying Statue of the Shah, Tulips — A664

Women's Day — A666

Sulayman Khater, 40th Death Anniv. — A665

1986, Feb. 11 Photo. *Perf. 13½*
2209 A664 20r multicolored 60 20

Iranian Revolution, 7th anniv.
See No. 2310l for 24x36mm stamp with yellow Arabic script.

1986, Feb. 15 *Perf. 13*
2210 A665 10r multicolored 30 15

1986, Mar. 3 *Perf. 13½*
2211 A666 10r multicolored 30 15

Birth anniv. of Mohammed's daughter, Fatima.

Flowers — A667

Designs: a, Papaver orientale. b, Anemone coronaria. c, Papaver bracteatum. d, Anemone biflora.

1986, Mar. 11 Photo. *Perf. 13½*
2212 Block of 4 60 20
a. A667 5r any single 15 15

Novrooz (New Year).

2000th Day of Sacred Defense A668

Intl. Day Against Racial Discrimination A669

1986, Mar. 14 Photo. *Perf. 13x13½*
2213 A668 5r scarlet & grn 15 15

1986, Mar. 21
2214 A669 5r multicolored 15 15

Islamic Republic of Iran, 7th Anniv. — A670

1986, Apr. 1 *Perf. 13*
2215 A670 10r Flag, map 30 15

Mab'as Festival — A671

1986, Apr. 7
2216 A671 40r multicolored 60 20

Army Day A672

Day of the Oppressed A673

1986, Apr. 18 *Perf. 13½*
2217 A672 5r multicolored 15 15

1986, Apr. 25 *Perf. 13x13½*
2218 A673 10r blk, gold & dk red 20 15

Helicopter Crash — A674

Teacher's Day — A675

1986, Apr. 25 **Wmk. 381**
2219 A674 40r multicolored 1.40 40

US air landing at Tabass Air Base, 6th anniv.

1986, May 2 Photo. *Perf. 13x13½*
2220 A675 5r multicolored 15 15

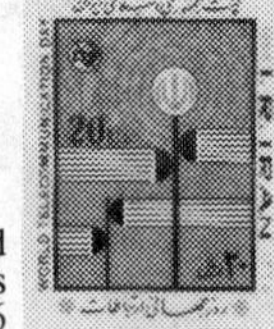
World Telecommunications Day — A676

1986, May 17 *Perf. 13½x13*
2221 A676 20r blk, sil & ultra 60 20

Universal Day of the Child — A677

1986, June 1 *Perf. 13*
2222 A677 15r Child's war drawing 45 15
2223 A677 15r Youth war casualty 45 15

Nos. 2222-2223 printed se-tenant.

1963 Uprising, 23rd Anniv. A678

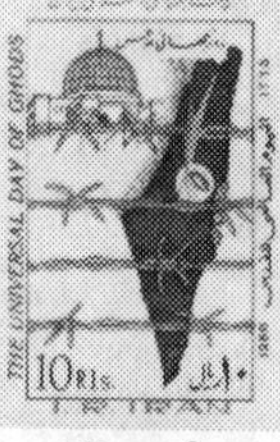
Day of Jerusalem A679

1986, June 5 *Perf. 13x13½*
2224 A678 10r Qum Theological Seminary 30 15

1986, June 6
2225 A679 10r multicolored 30 15

Id Al-Fitr Feast A680

1986, June 9 *Perf. 13*
2226 A680 10r Moslems praying 30 15

World Handicrafts Day A681

Designs: a, Baluchi cross-hatched rug. b, Craftsman. c, Qalamkar flower rug. d, Copper repousse vase.

1986, June 10 ***Perf. 13½***

2227	Block of 4	1.20	40
a.-d.	A681 10r, any single	30	15

Intl. Day for Solidarity with Black So. Africans A682

Ayatollah Beheshti A683

1986, June 26

2228 A682 10r multicolored 30 15

1986, June 28 ***Perf. 13x13½***

2229 A683 10r multicolored 30 15

Death of Beheshti and Islamic Party workers, Tehran headquarters bombing, 5th anniv.

Ayatollah Mohammad Taqi Shirazi, Map of Iraq — A684

Shrine of Imam Reza — A685

1986, June 30 **Photo.** **Wmk. 381**

2230 A684 20r multicolored 60 20

Iraqi Moslem uprising against the British.

1986, July 19 ***Perf. 13½***

2231 A685 10r multicolored 30 15

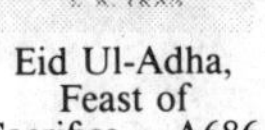

Eid Ul-Adha, Feast of Sacrifice — A686

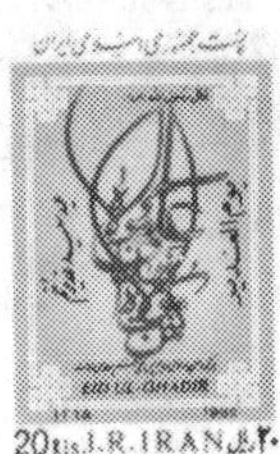

Eid Ul-Ghadir Feast — A688

Cultural Heritage Preservation — A687

1986, Aug. 17 ***Perf. 13x13½***

2232 A686 10r multicolored 30 15

1986, Aug. 20

Designs: No. 2233, Bam Fortress. No. 2234, Kabud (Blue) Mosque, Tabriz. No. 2235, Mausoleum of Sohel Ben Ali at Astenah, Arak. No. 2236, Soltanieh Mosque, Zendjan Province.

2233	A687 5r Hilltop	25	15
2234	A687 5r shown	25	15
2235	A687 5r Intact roof	25	15
2236	A687 5r Damaged roof	25	15
	Set value		40

1986, Aug. 25

2237 A688 20r multicolored 60 20

Population and Housing Census A689

Iran-Iraq War, 6th Year A690

1986, Sept. 9 ***Perf. 13½x13***

2238 A689 20r multicolored 40 15

1986, Sept. 22 ***Perf. 13***

2239	A690 10r Battleship Paykan	30	15
2240	A690 10r Susangerd	30	15
2241	A690 10r Khorramshahr	30	15
2242	A690 10r Howeizeh	30	15
2243	A690 10r Siege of Abadan	30	15
	Nos. 2239-2243 (5)	1.50	
	Set value		50

10th Asian Games, Seoul A691

1986, Oct. 2 **Photo.** **Wmk. 381**

2244	A691 15r Wrestling	40	15
2245	A691 15r Rifle shooting	40	15

World Post Day A692

1986, Oct. 9

2246 A692 20r multicolored 50 20

UNESCO, 40th Anniv. — A693

1986, Nov. 4 **Photo.** ***Perf. 13x13½***

2247 A693 45r blk, sky bl & brt rose 1.25 45

Ayatollah Tabatabaie (d. 1981) — A694

1986, Nov. 15 **Photo.** ***Perf. 13½x13***

2248 A694 10r multicolored 30 15

Unity Week — A695

1986, Nov. 20

2249 A695 10r multicolored 30 15

Birth anniv. of Mohammed.

People's Militia — A696

1986, Nov. 26 ***Perf. 13***

2250 A696 5r multicolored 15 15

Mobilization of the Oppressed Week.

Afghan Resistance Movement, 7th Anniv. — A697

1986, Dec. 27

2251 A697 40r multicolored 1.20 40

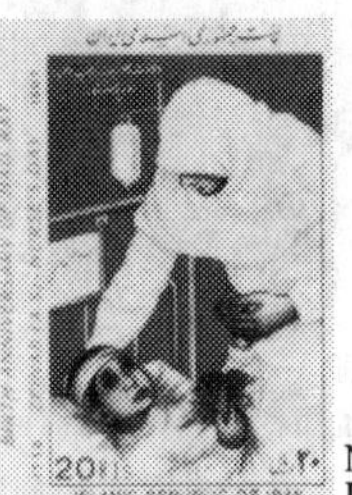

Nurses' Day — A698

1987, Jan. 12 **Photo.** ***Perf. 13***

2252 A698 20r multicolored 60 20

Hazrat Zainab birth anniv.

Fifth Islamic Theology Conference, Tehran — A699

Wmk. 381

1987, Jan. 29 **Photo.** ***Perf. 13***

2253 A699 20r multicolored 60 20

Islamic Revolution, 8th Anniv. — A700

1987, Feb. 11

2254 A700 20r multicolored 60 20

See No. 2310m for 24x36mm stamp.

Islamic Revolutionary Committees, 8th Anniv. — A701

1987, Feb. 12

2255 A701 10r brt bl, scar & yel 30 15

Women's Day — A702

1987, Feb. 19

2256 A702 10r multicolored 30 15

Birthday of Fatima, daughter of Mohammed.

> ***15-Cent Minimum Value***
> *The minimum catalogue value is 15 cents. Separating se-tenant pieces into individual stamps does not increase the "value" of the stamps... since demand for the separated stamps may be small.*

Iran Air, 25th Anniv. A703

1987, Feb. 24

2257 A703 30r multicolored 90 30

Ayatollah Mirza Mohammad Hossein Naeini, 50th Death Anniv. — A704

1987, Mar. 6 Photo. *Perf. 13*

2258 A704 10r multicolored 30 15

New Year — A705

Mab'as Festival — A706

Flowers: a, Iris persica. b, Rosa damascena. c, Iris paradoxa. d, Tulipa clusiana.

1987, Mar. 11 *Perf. 13½x13*

2259 Block of 4 1.00 50
a.-d. A705 5r. any single 25 15

See Nos. 2313, 2361, 2411.

1987, Mar. 28 *Perf. 13*

2260 A706 45r gold, dk grn & grn 1.35 45

Universal Day of the Oppressed A707

1987, Apr. 14

2261 A707 20r multicolored 60 20

Savior Mahdi's birthday.

Memorial to Lebanese Hizbollah Martyrs — A708

1987, Apr. 5

2262 A708 10r grn, gray & brt car 30 15

Revolutionary Guards Day — A709

1987, Apr. 2

2263 A709 5r multi 15 15

Imam Hossein's birthday.

8th Anniv. of Islamic Republic A710

1987, Apr. 1

2264 A710 20r multicolored 60 20

World Health Day — A711

Child survival through immunization: 3r, Intravenous. 5r, Oral. Printed se-tenant.

1987, Apr. 7 *Perf. 13x13½*

2265 A711 3r multicolored 20 15
2266 A711 5r multicolored 30 15
Set value 20

Int'l. Labor Day — A712

1987, May 1 Photo. *Perf. 13*

2267 A712 5r multicolored 15 15

Teachers' Day — A713

1987, May 2 Wmk. 381

2268 A713 5r Ayatollah Mottahari 15 15

World Telecommunications Day — A714

1987, May 17 *Perf. 13½x13*

2269 A714 20r multicoloreed 60 20

Int'l. Museum Day — A715

1987, May 18 *Perf. 13*

2270 A715 20r Sassanian silver gilt vase 60 20
2271 A715 20r Bisque pot, Rey, 12th cent. 60 20

Universal Day of Jerusalem A716

1963 Uprising, 24th Anniv. A718

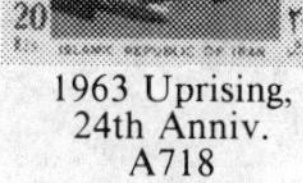

World Crafts Day A717

1987, May 22 *Perf. 13½x13*

2272 A716 20r multicolored 60 20

1987, June 10 *Perf. 13x13½*

Designs: a, Blown glass tea service. b, Stained glass window. c, Ceramic plate. d, Potter.

2273 Block of 4 60 20
a.-d. A717 5r any single 15 15

1987, June 5 Photo. *Perf. 13½*

2274 A718 20r multicolored 60 20

Tax Reform Week — A719

1987, July 10 *Perf. 13*

2275 A719 10r black, sil & gold 30 15

Welfare Week — A720

1987, July 17

2276 A720 15r multicolored 45 15

Eid Ul-adha, Feast of Sacrifice A721

1987, Aug. 6

2277 A721 12r sil, blk & Prus grn 45 15

Eid Ul-Ghadir Festival — A722

Banking Week — A723

1987, Aug. 14

2278 A722 18r black, green & gold 55 18

1987, Aug. 17 *Perf. 13½x13*

2279 A723 15r red brn, gold & pale grnsh bl 45 15

1st Cultural and Artistic Congress of Iranian Calligraphers A724

1987, Aug. 21 Photo. *Perf. 13x13½*

2280 A724 20r multicolored 60 20

Memorial to Iranian Pilgrims Killed in Mecca — A725

1987, Aug. 26 Wmk. 381 *Perf. 13*
2281 A725 8r multicolored 30 15

Assoc. of Iranian Dentists, 25th Anniv. A726

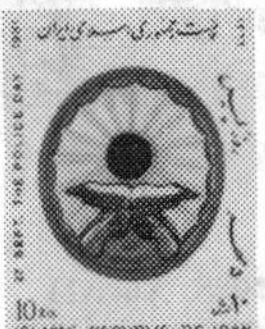
Intl. Peace Day A727

1987, Aug. 27 Photo. *Perf. 13½x13*
2282 A726 10r multicolored 30 15

1987, Sept. 1 *Perf. 13*
2283 A727 20r gold & lt ultra 60 20

Iran-Iraq War, 7th Anniv. A728

Police Day A729

1987, Sept. 22 *Perf. 13½x13*
2284 A728 25r shown 75 25
2285 A728 25r Soldier, battle scene 75 25
a. Pair. #2284-2285

1987, Sept. 28
2286 A729 10r multicolored 30 15

Intl. Social Security Week, Oct. 4-10 — A730

World Post Day — A731

1987, Oct. 4 Wmk. 381
2287 A730 15r blk, gold & brt blue 45 15

1987, Oct. 9 *Perf. 13x13½*

UPU emblem and: No. 2288, M. Ghandi, minister of the Post and Telecommunications Bureau. No. 2289, Globe, dove.

2288 A731 15r multicolored 45 15
2289 A731 15r multicolored 45 15

Importation Prohibited
Importation of stamps was prohibited effective Oct. 29, 1987.

Takeover of US Embassy, 8th Anniv. — A732

Wmk. 381
1987, Nov. 4 Photo. *Perf. 13*
2290 A732 40r multicolored

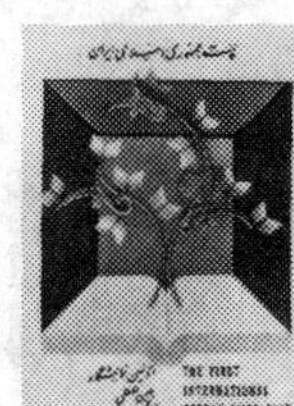
1st Intl. Tehran Book Fair — A733

1987, Nov. 5
2291 A733 20r multicolored

Mohammed's Birthday, Unity Week — A734

1987, Nov. 10
2292 A734 25r multicolored

Ayatollah Modarres Martyrdom, 50th Anniv. — A735

1987, Dec. 1
2293 A735 10r brn & bister

Agricultural Training and Extension Week — A736

1987, Dec. 6
2294 A736 10r multicolored

Afghan Resistance, 8th Anniv. — A737

1987, Dec. 27
2295 A737 40r multicolored

Mosques — A738

Various mosques.

1987-92 *Perf. 13x13½*
Silver Background
2295A A738 1r orange ('92)
2296 A738 2r red violet ('88)
2296A A738 3r olive grn ('92)
2297 A738 5r red brown
2298 A738 10r ultramarine
a. Unwatermarked
2299 A738 20r violet ('88)
a. Unwatermarked
2300 A738 30r red, vert. ('90)
2301 A738 40r blue ('90)
2302 A738 50r brown, vert. ('89)
a. Unwatermarked
2303 A738 100r blue green ('89)
2304 A738 200r black, vert. ('89)
2305 A738 500r green, vert. ('88)

Issue dates: 10r, Dec. 1. 5r, Dec. 30. 500r, Jan. 10. 20r, Jan. 14. 2r, Jan. 24. 50r, Jan. 24. 100r, Oct. 21. 200r, Oct. 28. 30r, 40r, Mar. 17. 1r and 3r values were prepared and not officially issued until Mar. 1992.

Qum Uprising, 10th Anniversary — A739

1988, Jan. 9 *Perf. 13*
2306 A739 20r multicolored

Bombing of Schools by Iraq — A740

1988, Feb. 1 *Perf. 13x13½*
2307 A740 10r multicolored

Gholamreza Takhti, World Wrestling Champion A741

1988, Feb. 4 *Perf. 13½*
2308 A741 15r multicolored

Women's Day — A742

1988, Feb. 9 *Perf. 13*
2309 A742 20r multicolored

Birth anniv. of Mohammed's daughter, Fatima.

Types of 1979-88 and

Islamic Revolution, 9th Anniv. — A743

1988, Feb. 11 Wmk. 381
2310 Souvenir sheet of 16
a. A547 1r like #2046
b. A547 3r like #2047
c. A559 3r like #2066
d. A547 5r like #2048
e. A559 5r like #2067
f. A570 5r like #2095
g. A570 10r like #2096
h. A608 10r like #2146
i. A537 18r like #1999
j. A559 20r like #2068
k. A570 20r like #2097
l. A664 20r like #2209
m. A700 20r like #2254
n. A587 30r like #2115
o. A631 40r like #2172
p. A743 40r shown

Nos. 2310a, 2310b, 2310d, 2310l, 2310m are smaller than the original issues. See original issues for distinguishing features on other stamps.
Exists imperf.

Tabriz Uprising, 10th Anniv. — A744

1988, Feb. 18 *Perf. 13*
2311 A744 25r multicolored

Arbor Day — A745

1988, Mar. 5
2312 A745 15r multicolored

New Year Festival Type of 1987

Flowers: a, Anthemis hyalina. b, Malva silvestria, Viola odorata, Echium amaenum.

1988, Mar. 10 *Perf. 13½x13*
2313 Block of 4
a.-d. A705 10r any single

Islamic Republic, 9th Anniv. — A746

1988, Apr. 1 ***Perf. 13***
2314 A746 20r multicolored

Universal Day of the Oppressed A747

1988, Apr. 3
2314 A747 20r multicolored

Saviour Mahdi's Birthday.

Cultural Heritage A748

1988, Apr. 18
2315 A748 10r Mosque
2316 A748 10r Courtyard
a. Pair, #2315-2316
2317 A748 10r Minarets, vert.
2318 A748 10r Corridor, vert.
a. Pair, #2317-2318

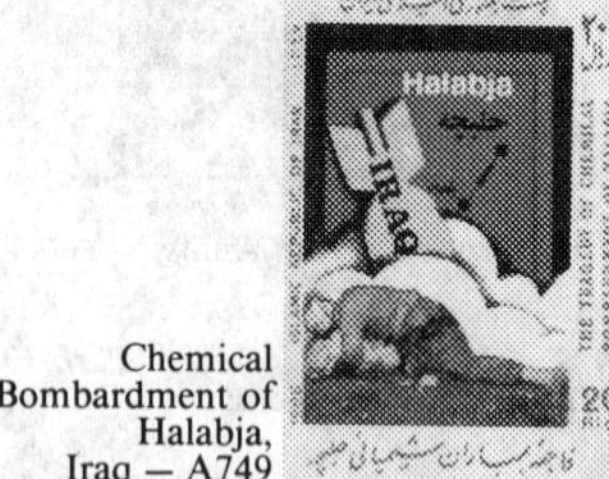

Chemical Bombardment of Halabja, Iraq — A749

1988, Apr. 26
2319 A749 20r multicolored

A750

A750a

Palestinian Uprising A750b

1988, May 13
2320 Strip of 5
a. A750 10r multi
b. A750a 10r multi
c. A750b 10r multi
d. A750b 10r multi, diff.
e. A750b 10r Rock in hand, rioters

World Telecommunications Day — A751

1988, May 17 ***Perf. 13x13½***
2321 A751 20r green & blue

Intl. Museum Day — A752

Designs: a, Ceramic vase, 1982. b, Bastan Museum, entranceway. c, Tabriz silk rug, 14th cent. d, Gold ring, 7th cent. B.C.

1988, May 18 ***Perf. 13***
2322 Block of 4
a.-d. A752 10r any single

Mining Day — A753

1988, May 22 Photo. Wmk. 381
2323 A753 20r multicolored

Intl. Day of the Child — A754

1988, June 1
2324 A754 10r multicolored

June 5th Uprising, 25th Anniv. — A755

1988, June 5
2325 A755 10r multicolored

World Crafts Day A756

1988, June 10 ***Perf. 13x13½***
2326 A756 10r Straw basket
2327 A756 10r Weaver
a. Pair, #2326-2327
2328 A756 10r Tapestry, vert.
2329 A756 10r Miniature, vert.
a. Pair, #2328-2329

Child Health Campaign A757

1988, July 6 ***Perf. 13***
2330 A757 20r blk, blue & green

Tax Reform Week — A758

1988, July 10
2331 A758 20r multicolored

Allameh Balkhi — A759

1988, July 15 ***Perf. 13½x13***
2332 A759 20r sil, blk & red

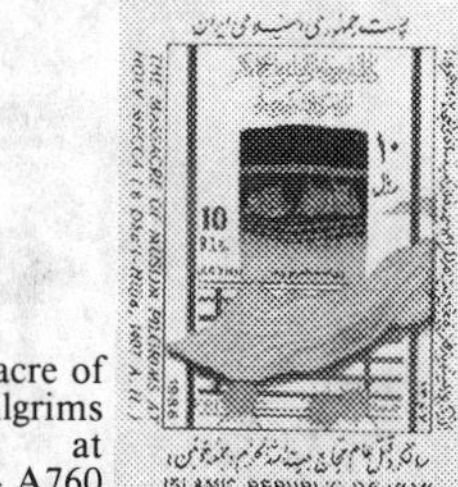

Massacre of Muslim Pilgrims at Mecca — A760

1988, July 21 ***Perf. 13***
2333 A760 10r Holy Ka'aba, dove, stars
2334 A760 10r shown

Destruction of Iranian Airliner — A761

1988, Aug. 11
2335 A761 45r multicolored

Seyyed Ali Andarzgou A762

1988, Aug. 13
2336 A762 20r multicolored

Islamic Banking Week — A763

1988, Sept. 1 ***Perf. 13½x13***
2337 A763 20r multicolored

Divine Day of 17 Shahrivar, 10th Anniv. — A764

1988, Sept. 8
2338 A764 25r multicolored

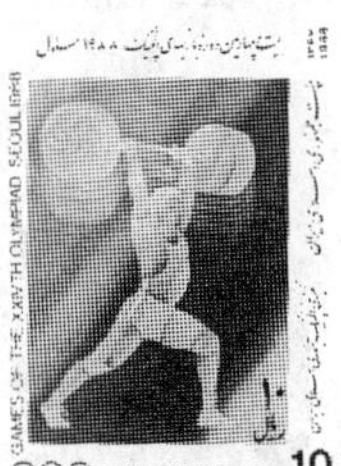
1988 Summer Olympics, Seoul — A765

Designs: a, Weightlifting. b, Pommel horse. c, Judo. d, Soccer. e, Wrestling.

1988, Sept. 10
2339 Strip of 5
a.-e. A765 10r any single

Agricultural Census — A766

1988, Sept. 17 ***Perf. 13½x13***
2340 A766 30r blk, grn & yel

Iran-Iraq War, 8th Anniv. — A767

1988, Sept. 22 ***Perf. 13x13½***
2341 A767 20r multicolored

World Post Day A768

1988, Oct. 9 ***Perf. 13***
2342 A768 20r blk, ultra & grn

Parents and Teachers Cooperation Week — A769

1988, Oct. 16
2343 A769 20r multicolored

Mohammed's Birthday, Unity Week — A770

1988, Oct. 29
2344 A770 10r multicolored

Takeover of US Embassy, 9th Anniv. — A771

1988, Nov. 4
2345 A771 45r multicolored

Insurance Day — A772

1988, Nov. 6 ***Perf. 13½x13***
2346 A772 10r multicolored

Intl. Congress on the Writings of Hafiz — A773

Illustration reduced.

1988, Nov. 19 ***Perf. 13x13½***
2347 A773 20r blue, gold & pink

Agricultural Training and Extension Week — A774

1988, Dec. 6 ***Perf. 13***
2348 A774 15r multicolored

Scientists, Artists and Writers A775

1988, Dec. 18 ***Perf. 13x13½***
2349 A775 10r Parvin E'Tessami
2350 A775 10r Jalal Al-Ahmad
2351 A775 10r Muhammad Mo'in
a. Pair, #2350-2351
2352 A775 10r Qaem Maqam Farahani
2353 A775 10r Kamal Al-Molk
a. Pair, #2352-2353

See Nos. 2398-2402.

Afghan Resistance, 9th Anniv. — A776

1988, Dec. 27 ***Perf. 13***
2354 A776 40r multicolored

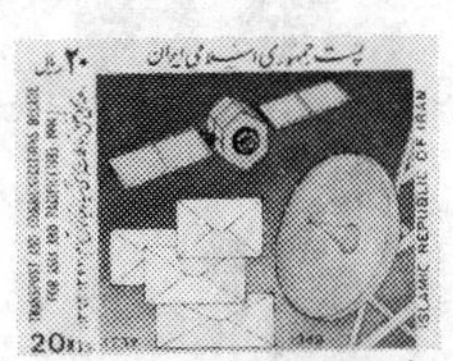
Transportion and Communication Decade — A777

Perf. 13x13½
1989, Jan. 16 **Wmk. 381**
2355 A777 20r Satellite, envelopes, microwave dish
2356 A777 20r Cargo planes
a. Pair, #2355-2356
2357 A777 20r Train, trucks
2358 A777 20r Ships
a. Pair, #2357-2358

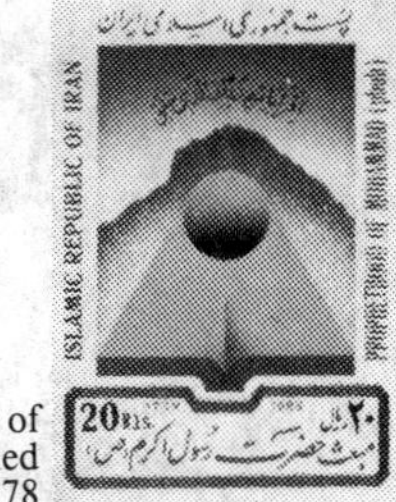
Prophethood of Mohammed A778

1989, Mar. 6 ***Perf. 13***
2359 A778 20r multicolored

Mab'as festival.

Arbor Day — A779

1989, Mar. 6
2360 A779 20r multicolored

New Year Festival Type of 1987

Flowers: a, Cephalanthera kurdica. b, Dactylorhiza romana. c, Comperia comperiana. d, Orchis mascula.

1989, Mar. 11 ***Perf. 13½x13***
2361 Block of 4
a.-d. A705 10r any single

World Meteorology Day — A780

1989, Mam. 23
2362 A780 20r shown
2363 A780 30r Meteorological devices, ship
a. Pair, #2362-2363

Islamic Republic, 10th Anniv. — A781

1989, Apr. 1 ***Perf. 13***
2364 A781 20r multicolored

Reconstruction of Abadan Refinery A782

1989, Apr. 1
2365 A782 20r multicolored

Ayatollah Morteza Motahhari, 10th Death Anniv. — A783

1989, May 2
2366 A783 20r multi

Teachers' Day.

Universal Day of Jerusalem A784

1989, May 5
2367 A784 30r multicolored

World Telecommunications Day — A785

1989, May 17 *Perf. 13½x13*
2368 A785 20r multicolored

Intl. Museum Day — A786

Gurgan pottery, 6th century.

1989, May 18 *Perf. 13x13½*
2369 A786 20r Jar
2370 A786 20r Bottle
a. Pair, #2369-2370

Nomads' Day — A787

1989, June 4 *Perf. 13*
2371 A787 20r multicolored

World Crafts Day A788

1989, July 5 *Perf. 13x13½*
2372 A788 20r Engraver
2373 A788 20r Copper vase
a. Pair, #2372-2373
2374 A788 20r Copper plate, vert.
2375 A788 20r Copper wall hanging, vert.
a. Pair, #2374-2375

Ayatollah Khomeini (1900-89) A789

1989, July 6 *Perf. 13*
2376 A789 20r multicolored

PHILEXFRANCE — A790

1989, July 7
2377 A790 30r multicolored
2378 A790 50r multicolored
a. Pair, #2377-2378

Asia-Pacific Telecommunity, 10th Anniv. — A791

1989, July 25
2379 A791 30r blk, org brn & bl

Mehdi Araghi, 10th Death Anniv. — A792

1989, Aug. 30
2380 A792 20r brn org & org brn

M.H. Shahryar, Poet — A793

1989, Sept. 17
2381 A793 20r multicolored

Iran-Iraq War, 9th Anniv. A794

1989, Sept. 22
2382 A794 20r multicolored

Ayatollah Khomeini — A795

Designs: 3r, Giving speech. 5r, Map, rifles. 10r, Khomeini, others amid flowers. 20r, Khomeini seated before microphone. 30r, Khomeini with child. 40r, Other mullahs. 50r, Khomeini gesturing with hands. 70r, On balcony before crowd. 100r, Slogan. 200r, Empty lectern. 500r, Mosque, Qum.

1989-91 Litho. Unwmk. *Perf. 13½*
2383 A795 3r grn & multi
2384 A795 5r brt vio & multi
2385 A795 10r brt bl & multi
2386 A795 20r bl & multi
2387 A795 30r pink & multi
2388 A795 40r red & multi
2389 A795 50r gray & multi
2390 A795 70r brt grn & multi
2391 A795 100r ultra & multi
2392 A795 200r red brn & multi
2393 A795 500r blk & multi

Issue dates: 3r, Mar. 16, 1990. 5r, Dec. 13. 10r, Oct. 22. 20r, 30r, 50r, Sept. 23, 1990. 40r, Feb. 9, 1990. 100, 200r, Sept. 26. 70r, 500r, June 4, 1991.

This is an expanding set. Numbers will change if necessary.

World Post Day A796

Wmk. 381

1989, Oct. 9 Photo. *Perf. 13*
2394 A796 20r multicolored

Mohammed's Birthday, Unity Week — A797

1989, Oct. 18
2395 A797 10r multi

Takeover of US Embassy, 10th Anniv. — A798

1989, Nov. 4 *Perf. 13½x13*
2396 A798 40r multicolored

Bassij of the Oppressed (Militia), 10th Anniv. — A799

1989, Nov. 27 *Perf. 13*
2397 A799 10r multicolored

Scientists, Artists and Writers Type of 1988

1989, Dec. 18 *Perf. 13x13½*
2398 A775 10r Mehdi Elahi Ghomshei
2399 A775 10r Dr. Abdulazim Gharib
2400 A775 10r Seyyed Hossein Mirkhani
a. Pair, #2399-2400
2401 A775 10r Ayatollah Seyyed Hossein Boroujerdi
2402 A775 10r Ayatollah Sheikh Abdulkarim Haeri
a. Pair, #2401-2402

Intl. Literacy Year — A800

Wmk. 381

1990, Jan. 1 Photo. *Perf. 13½*
2403 A800 20r multicolored

Cultural Heritage A801

Designs: No. 2404, Drinking vessel, 1980. No. 2405, Footed vase, 1979.

1990, Jan. 21 ***Perf. 13***
2404 A801 20r blk & deep org
2405 A801 20r blk & yel grn
a. Pair, #2404-2405

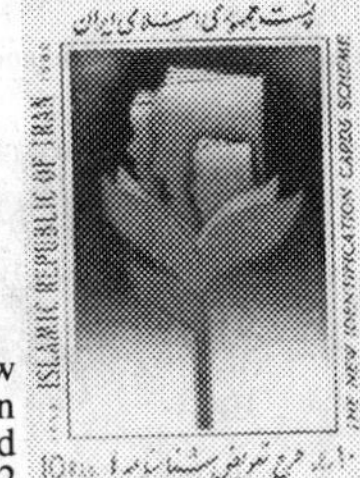

New Identification Card System — A802

1990, Feb. 9
2406 A802 10r multicolored

Islamic Revolution, 11th Anniv. — A803

1990, Feb. 11
2407 A803 50r multicolored

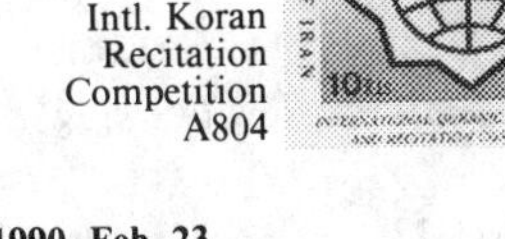

Intl. Koran Recitation Competition A804

1990, Feb. 23
2408 A804 10r blk, bl & grn

Invalids of Islamic Revolution — A805

1990, Mar. 2 ***Perf. 13½x13***
2409 A805 10r multicolored

Arbor Day — A806

1990, Mar. 6 ***Perf. 13***
2410 A806 20r multicolored

New Year Festival Type of 1987

Flowers: a, Coronilla varia. b, Astragalus cornu-caprae. c, Astragalus obtusifolius. d, Astragalus straussii.

1990, Mar. 11 ***Perf. 13½x13***
2411 Block of 4
a.-d. A705 10r any single

Islamic Republic, 11th Anniv. — A807

1990, Apr. 1 ***Perf. 13***
2412 A807 30r multicolored

World Health Day — A808

1990, Apr. 7
2413 A808 40r multicolored

Ayatollah Khomeini, 1st Death Anniv. — A809

1990, June 4 Unwmk. ***Perf. 11x10½***
2414 A809 50r multicolored

Jerusalem Day — A810

1990, Dec. 15 Litho. ***Perf. 10½***
2415 A810 100r multicolored

World Crafts Day — A811

1990, Oct. ***Perf. 13***
2416 A811 20r Turkoman jewelry
2417 A811 50r Gilded steel bird
a. Pair, #2416-2417

Intl. Day of the Child — A812

1990, Nov. 17 ***Perf. 10½***
2418 A812 20r multicolored

Aid to Earthquake Victims A813

1990, Nov. 19 ***Perf. 13x13½***
2419 A813 100r multicolored

Tribute to Former Prisoners of War — A814

1990, Nov. 21 ***Perf. 13***
2420 A814 250r multicolored

Ferdowsi Intl. Congress — A815

Illustration reduced.

1990, Dec. Litho. ***Imperf.***
Size: 60x75mm
2421 A815 100r Portrait
2422 A815 100r Statue
2423 A815 100r Monument
2424 A815 100r Slogan, diamond cartouche
2425 A815 100r Rectangular slogan
2426 A815 100r Slogan, diff.
2427 A815 200r Two riders embracing
2428 A815 200r Archer, birds
2429 A815 200r Six men
2430 A815 200r White elephant
2431 A815 200r Warrior, genie, horse
2432 A815 200r Hunting scene
2433 A815 200r Riding through fire
2434 A815 200r Four slogan tablets
2435 A815 200r Man with feet shackled
2436 A815 200r Palace scene

Conference on epic poem "Book of Kings" by Ferdowsi.

"Victory Over Iraq" — A816

1991, Feb. 25 ***Perf. 13***
2437 A816 100r multicolored

Intl. Museum Day A817

Designs: No. 2438, Gold jug with Kufric inscription, 10th cent. A.D. No. 2439, Silver-inlaid brass basin, 14th cent. A.D.

1991, Feb. 25
2438 A817 50r multicolored
2439 A817 50r multicolored
a. Pair, #2438-2439

World Telecommunications Day — A818

1991, Mar. 12 ***Perf. 10½***
2440 A818 50r multicolored

Opening of Postal Museum — A819

1991, Feb. 25 ***Perf. 13***
2441 A819 100r org brn & blk

Islamic Republic, 12th Anniv. — A825

Unwmk.

1991, Apr. 1 Photo. *Perf. 13*
2448 A825 20r blk, slate, grn & red

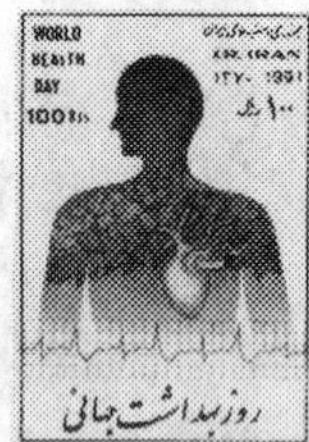
World Health Day — A826

1991, Apr. 7 *Perf. 13½x13*
2449 A826 100r multicolored

Day of Jerusalem A827

1991, Apr. 12 *Perf. 13*
2450 A827 100r bl, blk & brn

Ayatollah Borujerdi, 30th Death Anniv. — A829

Perf. 13½x13

1991, Apr. 28 Photo. Unwmk.
2452 A829 200r bl grn & blk

Teachers' Day — A830

Illustration reduced.

1991, May 2 *Perf. 13x13½*
2453 A830 50r multicolored

World Telecommunications Day — A832

Perf. 13½x13

1991, May 17 Photo. Unwmk.
2455 A832 100r multicolored

Intl. Museum Day — A833 Flags — A834

Ewers, Kashan, 13th cent.: 20r, With spout. 40r, Baluster.

1991, May 18 *Perf. 13*
2456 A833 20r multicolored
2457 A833 40r multicolored
a. Pair, #2456-2457

1991, May 24 *Perf. 13x13½*
2458 A834 30r multicolored

A835

Abol-Hassan Ali-ebne-Mosa Rreza, Birth Anniv. — A835a

Views of shrine, Meshed.

1991, May 26 *Perf. 13*
2459 A835 10r Gravestone
2460 A835a 30r Mausoleum
a. Pair, #2459-2460

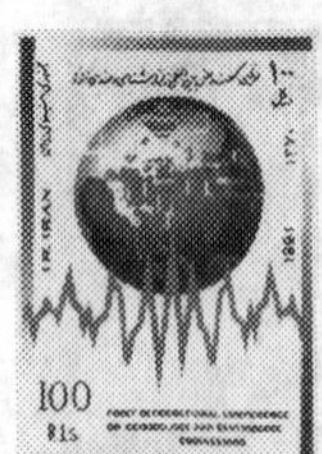
First Intl. Conf. on Seismology and Earthquake Engineering A836

1991, May 27 *Perf. 13½x13*
2461 A836 100r multicolored

Holy Shrine at Karbola, Iraq Destroyed by Invasion — A838

Unwmk.

1991, June 3 Photo. *Perf. 13*
2463 A838 70r multicolored

Ayatollah Khomeini, 2nd Death Anniv. — A839

1991, June 4
2464 A839 100r multicolored

World Handicrafts Day — A840

Designs: No. 2465, Engraved brass wares. No. 2466, Gilded samovar set.

1991, June 10 *Perf. 13½x13*
2465 A840 40r multicolored
2466 A840 40r multicolored
a. Pair #2465-2466

Intl. Congress on Poet Nezami — A841

1991, June 22 *Perf. 13*
2467 A841 50r multicolored

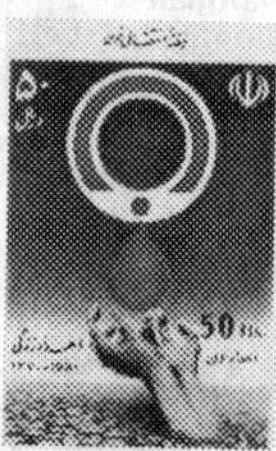
Blood Transfusion Week — A843

Unwmk.

1991, July 29 Photo. *Perf. 13*
2469 A843 50r multicolored

Return of Prisoners of War, First Anniv. — A844

Illustration reduced.

1991, Aug. 27 *Perf. 13x13½*
2470 A844 100r multicolored

Ayatollah Marashi, Death Anniv. — A845

Illustration reduced.

1991, Aug. 29 *Perf. 13½x13*
2471 A845 30r multicolored

Ayatollah-ol-Ozma Seyyed Abdol-Hossein Lary, Theologian — A846

1991, Sept. 9 *Perf. 13x13½*
2472 A846 30r multicolored

Start of Iran-Iraq War, 11th Anniv. — A847

1991, Sept. 22 *Perf. 13½x13*
2473 A847 20r multicolored

Mosque, Kaaba, Unity Week — A848

1991, Sept. 22 *Perf. 13*
2474 A848 30r multicolored

World Post Day A850

Unwmk.

1991, Oct. 9 Photo. *Perf. 13*
2476 A850 70r #2071 on cover

Khaju-ye Kermani Intl. Congress — A851

1991, Oct. 15

2477	A851	30r multicolored		

World Food Day — A852

1991, Oct. 16

2478	A852	80r multicolored		

Intl. Conference Supporting Palestinians A853

1991, Oct. 19 *Perf. 13½x13*

2479	A853	40r bl vio & gold		

Illustrators of Children's Books, 1st Asian Biennial — A854

1991, Oct. 25 *Perf. 13*

2480	A854	100r multicolored		

"Children" misspelled.

SEMI-POSTAL STAMPS

Lion and Bull, Persepolis SP1

Persian Soldier, Persepolis SP2

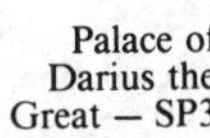

Palace of Darius the Great — SP3

Tomb of Cyrus the Great, Pasargadae SP4

King Darius on his Throne — SP5

Perf. 13x13½, 13½x13

1948, Jan. 30 **Engr.** **Unwmk.**

B1	SP1	50d + 25d emer	1.00	1.00
B2	SP2	1r + 50d red	1.00	1.00
B3	SP3	2½r + 1¼r blue	1.00	1.00
B4	SP4	5r + 2½r pur	1.75	1.75
B5	SP5	10r + 5r vio brn	1.75	1.75
		Nos. B1-B5 (5)	6.50	6.50

The surtax was for reconstruction of the tomb of Avicenna (980-1037), Arab physician and philosopher, at Hamadan.

Ardashir II — SP6

Shapur I and Valerian — SP7

Designs: 1r+50d, King Narses, Naqsh-i-Rustam. 5r+2½r, Taq-i-Kisra, Ctesiphon. 10r+5r, Ardashir I and Ahura Mazda.

1949, June 11

B6	SP6	50d + 25d green	80	80
B7	SP6	1r + 50d ver	90	90
B8	SP7	2½r + 1½r blue	90	90
B9	SP7	5r + 2½r mag	1.40	1.40
B10	SP7	10r + 5r grnsh gray	1.50	1.50
		Nos. B6-B10 (5)	5.50	5.50

The surtax was for reconstruction of Avicenna's tomb at Hamadan.

Gunbad-i-Ali SP8

Alaviyan, Hamadan SP9

Seldjukide Coin — SP10

Designs: 1r+½r, Masjid-i-Jami, Isfahan. 5r+2½r, Masjid-i-Jami, Ardistan.

1949, Dec. 22

B11	SP8	50d + 25d bl grn	50	50
B12	SP8	1r + ½r dk brn	50	50
B13	SP9	2½r + 1¼r blue	50	50
B14	SP9	5r + 2½r red	1.00	1.00
B15	SP10	10r + 5r ol gray	1.10	1.10
		Nos. B11-B15 (5)	3.60	3.60

The surtax was for reconstruction of Avicenna's tomb at Hamadan.

Book, Crescent and Flag — SP11

1950, Oct. 2 **Litho.** *Perf. 11*

B16	SP11	1.50r + 1r multi	22.50	15.00

Economic Conference of the Islamic States.

Tomb of Baba Afzal at Kashan — SP12

Gorgan Vase — SP13

Designs: 2½r+1¼r, Tower of Ghazan. 5r+2½r, Masjid-i Gawhar. 10r+5r, Mihrab of the Mosque at Rezaieh.

Perf. 13x13½, 13½x13

1950, Aug. 23 **Engr.**

B17	SP12	50d + 25d dk grn	50	50
B18	SP13	1r + ½r blue	50	50
B19	SP13	2½r + 1¼r choc	50	50
B20	SP12	5r + 2½r red	1.00	1.00
B21	SP12	10r + 5r gray	1.10	1.10
		Nos. B17-B21 (5)	3.60	3.60

The surtax was for reconstruction of Avicenna's tomb at Hamadan.

Mohammed Riza Pahlavi and Map — SP14

Monument to Fallen Liberators of Azerbaijan SP15

Designs: 1r+50d, Marching troops. 1.50r+75d, Running advance with flag. 2.50r+1.25r, Mohammed Riza Pahlavi. 3r+1.50r, Parade of victors.

1950, Dec. 12 **Litho.**

B22	SP14	10d + 5d blk brn	10.00	3.50
B23	SP15	50d + 25d blk brn	8.50	3.50
B24	SP15	1r + 50d brown lake	10.00	4.50
B25	SP14	1.50r + 75d org ver	15.00	9.00
B26	SP14	2.50r + 1.25r blue	17.50	11.00
B27	SP15	3r + 1.50r ultra	19.00	8.50
		Nos. B22-B27 (6)	80.00	40.00

Liberation of Azerbaijan Province from communists, 4th anniv.

The surtax was for families of Persian soldiers who died in the struggle.

Koran Gate at Shiraz SP16

Saadi — SP17

Design: 50d+50d, Tomb of Saadi, Shiraz.

Perf. 11x10½, 10½x11

1952, Apr. 30 **Photo.** **Unwmk.**

B28	SP16	25d + 25d dl bl grn	2.75	1.50
B29	SP16	50d + 50d brn ol	4.00	1.75
B30	SP17	1.50r + 50d vio bl	10.50	6.00

770th birthday of Saadi, Persian poet. The surtax was to help complete Saadi's tomb at Shiraz.

Three stamps of same denominations and colors, with values enclosed in tablets, were prepared but not officially issued.

View of Hamadan SP18

Avicenna SP19

Designs: 2½r+1¼r, Gonbad Qabus (tower of tomb). 5r+2½r, Old tomb of Avicenna. 10r+5r, New tomb.

Perf. 13x13½, 13½x13

1954, Apr. 21 **Engr.** **Unwmk.**

B31	SP18	50d + 25d dp grn	80	80
B32	SP19	1r + ½r vio brn	80	80
B33	SP19	2½r + 1¼r blue	80	80
B34	SP18	5r + 2½r ver	1.25	1.25
B35	SP18	10r + 5r ol gray	2.50	2.50
		Nos. B31-B35 (5)	6.15	6.15

The surtax was for reconstruction of Avicenna's tomb at Hamadan.

Catalogue values for unused stamps in this section, from this point to the end of the section, are for Never Hinged items.

Mother with Children and Ruins SP20

Wmk. 316

1963, Feb. 4 **Litho.** *Perf. 10½*

B36	SP20	14r + 6r dk bl grn & lt brn	1.75	50

The surtax was for the benefit of survivors of the Kazvin earthquake.

For overprints see Nos. C86-C88.

AIR POST STAMPS

Type of 1909 Overprinted

مخصوص پست هوائی

POSTE AÉRIENNE

1927 **Unwmk.** **Typo.** *Perf. 11½*

C1	A31	1c org & maroon	35	30
C2	A31	2c vio & maroon	40	30
C3	A31	3c grn & maroon	50	30

C4	A31	6c red & maroon	60	30
C5	A31	9c gray & mar	60	30
C6	A31	10c red vio & mar	70	30
C7	A31	13c dk bl & mar	70	50
C8	A31	1k sil, vio & bis brown	1.25	50
C9	A31	26c dk grn & mar	1.25	70
C10	A31	2k sil, dk grn & bis brown	3.00	1.25
C11	A31	3k sil, gray & bis brown	3.50	2.50
C12	A31	4k sil, bl & bis brown	6.00	3.00
C13	A31	5k gold, brn & bis brown	6.00	4.00
C14	A31	10k gold, org & bis brown	75.00	75.00
C15	A31	20k gold, ol grn & bis brn	75.00	67.50
C16	A31	30k gold, car & bis brown	75.00	72.50
		Nos. C1-C16 (16)	249.85	229.25

Counterfeit overprints are plentiful. They are found on Nos. 448-463, perf. 12½x12 instead of 11½.

Nos. C1-C16 exist without overprint. Value, set $500.

AP1

AP2

AP3

AP4

AP5

Airplane, Value and "Poste aérien" Surcharged on Revenue Stamps

1928 *Perf. 11*

C17	AP1	3k yellow brn	50.00	40.00
C18	AP2	5k dark brown	15.00	10.00
C19	AP3	1t gray vio	12.00	10.00
C20	AP4	2t olive bister	12.00	10.00
C21	AP5	3t deep green	12.00	10.00
		Nos. C17-C21 (5)	101.00	80.00

AP6

AP7

"Poste aerienne"

1928-29

C22	AP6	1c emerald	55	50
a.		1c yellow green	25	15
b.		Double overprint	16.00	
C23	AP6	2c light blue	35	15
C24	AP6	3c bright rose	65	15
C25	AP6	5c olive brn	35	15
a.		"5" omitted	400.00	650.00
b.		Horiz. pair, imperf. btwn.	*200.00*	
C26	AP6	10c dark green	35	15
a.		"10" omitted	7.00	
b.		"1" inverted	5.00	
C27	AP7	1k dull vio	50	25
a.		"1" inverted	5.00	
C28	AP7	2k orange	2.00	1.50
		Nos. C22-C28 (7)	4.75	
		Set value		1.75

Counterfeits exist.

Revenue Stamps Similar to Nos. C17 to C21, Overprinted like Nos. C22 to C28: "Poste aerienne"

1929

C29	AP1	3k yellow brn	25.00	7.00
C30	AP2	5k dark brn	9.00	3.00
C31	AP3	10k violet	9.00	5.00
C32	AP4	20k olive grn	22.00	5.00
C33	AP5	30k deep grn	15.00	10.00
		Nos. C29-C33 (5)	80.00	30.00

Riza Shah Pahlavi and Eagle AP8

1930, July 6 **Photo.** ***Perf. 12½x11½***

C34	AP8	1c ol bis & brt bl	30	30
C35	AP8	2c blue & gray blk	30	30
C36	AP8	3c ol grn & dk vio	30	30
C37	AP8	4c dk vio & pck bl	30	30
C38	AP8	5c lt grn & mag	30	30
C39	AP8	6c mag & bl grn	30	30
C40	AP8	8c dk gray & dp violet	30	30
C41	AP8	10c dp ultra & ver	1.00	1.00
C42	AP8	12c slate & org	1.00	1.00
C43	AP8	15c org brn & ol green	2.00	2.00
C44	AP8	1k Prus bl & scar	2.00	2.00
		Engr.		
C45	AP8	2k black & ultra	2.00	2.00
C46	AP8	3k dk brn & gray green	2.50	2.50
C47	AP8	5k dp red & gray black	3.50	3.50
C48	AP8	1t orange & vio	12.00	5.00
C49	AP8	2t dk grn & red brown	10.00	5.00
C50	AP8	3t brn vio & sl bl	45.00	22.00
		Nos. C34-C50 (17)	83.10	48.10

Same Overprinted in Black **Iran**

1935 **Photo.**

C51	AP8	1c ol bis & brt bl	70	60
C52	AP8	2c blue & gray blk	1.50	1.00
C53	AP8	3c ol grn & dk vio	1.90	50
C54	AP8	4c dk vio & pck bl	75	75
C55	AP8	5c lt grn & mag	75	75
C56	AP8	6c mag & bl grn	75	75
C57	AP8	8c dk gray & dp violet	1.25	1.25
C58	AP8	10c dp ultra & ver	1.40	1.50
C59	AP8	12c slate & org	1.75	2.00
C60	AP8	15c org brn & ol green	1.75	2.00
C61	AP8	1k Prus bl & scar	10.00	12.00
		Engr.		
C62	AP8	2k blk & ultra	5.00	3.00
C63	AP8	3k dk brn & gray green	8.00	4.00
C64	AP8	5k dp red & gray black	3.50	1.10
C65	AP8	1t orange & vio	50.00	30.00
C66	AP8	2t dk grn & red brown	6.00	3.00
C67	AP8	3t brn vio & sl bl	16.00	7.50
		Nos. C51-C67 (17)	111.00	71.70

Plane Over Mt. Demavend AP9

Plane above Mosque AP10

Unwmk.

1953, Jan. 21 **Photo.** ***Perf. 11***

C68	AP9	50d bl green	65	15
C69	AP10	1r car rose	65	15
C70	AP10	2r dark blue	65	15
C71	AP10	3r dark brn	65	15
C72	AP10	5r purple	1.50	15
C73	AP10	10r org ver	2.25	30
C74	AP10	20r vio blue	2.50	50
C75	AP10	30r olive	5.00	1.00
C76	AP10	50r brown	12.00	2.50
C77	AP10	100r black brn	40.00	15.00
C78	AP10	200r dk bl grn	35.00	7.00
		Nos. C68-C78 (11)	100.85	27.05

AP11

Golden Dome Mosque and Oil Well AP12

1953, May 4 **Litho.** ***Perf. 10½***

Mosque in Deep Yellow

C79	AP11	3r violet	8.00	5.00
C80	AP12	5r chocolate	12.00	5.00
C81	AP11	10r bl green	22.50	12.00
C82	AP12	20r red vio	50.00	30.00

Discovery of oil at Qum.

Catalogue values for unused stamps in this section, from this point to the end of the section, are for Never Hinged items.

Globe and UN Emblem — AP13

Perf. 10½x12½

1957, Oct. 24 **Photo.** **Wmk. 316**

C83	AP13	10r brt red lil & rose	2.25	75
C84	AP13	20r dl vio & rose vio	5.00	1.25

United Nations Day, Oct. 24, 1957.

UNESCO Emblem AP14

Wmk. 353

1966, June 20 **Litho.** ***Perf. 10½***

C85	AP14	14r multi	95	15

20th anniversary of UNESCO.

No. B36 Surcharged in Maroon, Brown or Red

1969, Dec. 4 **Wmk. 316** ***Perf. 10½***

C86	SP20	4r on 14r + 6r (M)	2.00	65
C87	SP20	10r on 14r + 6r (B)	2.00	65
C88	SP20	14r on 14r + 6r (R)	2.00	65

1st England-Australia flight, made by Capt. Ross Smith and Lt. Keith Smith, 50th anniv.

IATA Emblem and Persepolis AP15

Perf. 13x13½

1970, Oct. 27 **Photo.** **Wmk. 353**

C89	AP15	14r multi	5.00	50

26th meeting of the Intl. Air Transport Assoc. (IATA), Tehran.

"UIT" AP16

1972, May 17 **Litho.** ***Perf. 10½***

C90	AP16	14r multicolored	2.50	50

4th World Telecommunications Day.

Shah and Jet — AP17

1974, June 1 **Photo.** ***Perf. 13***

C91	AP17	4r org & black	42	15
C92	AP17	10r blue & black	1.75	15
C93	AP17	12r dull yel & blk	1.75	22
C94	AP17	14r lt green & blk	1.90	25
C95	AP17	20r red lilac & blk	2.50	32
C96	AP17	50r dull bl & blk	6.75	1.40
		Nos. C91-C96 (6)	15.07	2.49

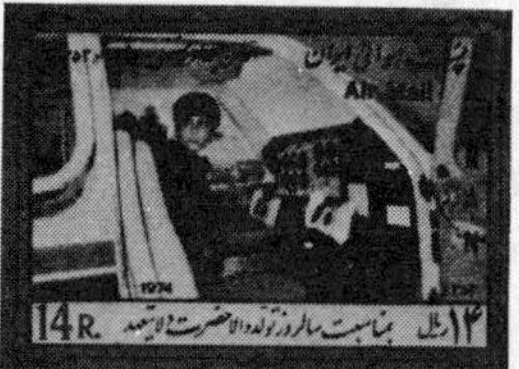

Crown Prince at Controls of Light Aircraft — AP18

1974, Oct. 31 **Litho.** ***Perf. 10½***

C97	AP18	14r gold & multi	1.25	20

Crown Prince Riza's 14th birthday.

Importation Prohibited

Importation of stamps was prohibited effective Oct. 29, 1987.

Islamic Revolution, 10th Anniv. — AP19

1989, Feb. 11 ***Perf. 13x13½***

C98	AP19	40r red vio, blk & gold		
C99	AP19	50r bl vio, blk & gold		
a.		Pair, #C98-C99		

Ayatollah Khomeini — AP20

1989, July 11 ***Perf. 13***

C100	AP20	70r multicolored		

OFFICIAL STAMPS

Four bicolored stamps of this design (1s, 2s, 5s, 10s), with centers embossed, exist, but were never issued or used in Iran. They are known imperforate and in many trial colors.

Shah Muzaffar-ed-Din — O1

No. 145 Surcharged in Black

1902 ***Perf. 12½***

O5	O1	5c on 1k red	8.50	5.00
O6	O1	10c on 1k red	8.50	5.00
O7	O1	12c on 1k red	8.50	5.00

Nos. 351-363 Overprinted in Black

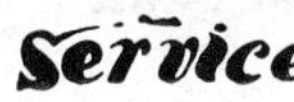

1903-06

O8	A26	1c violet	60	20
O9	A26	2c gray	60	20
O10	A26	3c green	60	20
O11	A26	5c rose	60	20
O12	A26	10c yel brown	60	20
O13	A26	12c blue	60	20

Perf. 11½x11

O14	A27	1k violet	1.50	50
O15	A27	2k ultra	3.00	50
a.		Violet overprint	6.00	5.00
O16	A27	5k org brown	6.00	75
O17	A27	10k rose red	7.50	1.00
a.		Violet overprint		12.50
O18	A27	20k orange ('06)	20.00	4.00
O19	A27	30k green ('06)	20.00	4.00
O20	A27	50k green	85.00	45.00
		Nos. O8-O20 (13)	146.60	56.95

Overprinted on Nos. 368, 370a

O21	A27	2t on 50k grn (Bl)	60.00	25.00
O22	A27	3t on 50k grn (V)	60.00	25.00

Overprinted on Nos. 372, 375, New Value Surcharged in Blue or Black

1905

O23	A27	2t on 50k grn (Bl)	60.00	25.00
O28	A27	3t on 50k grn (Bk)	60.00	25.00

The 2t on 50k also exists with surcharge in black and magenta; the 3t on 50k in violet and magenta. Values about the same.

Regular Issue of 1909 Overprinted

Service

There is a space between the word "Service" and the Persian characters.

1911 ***Perf. 12½x12***

O31	A31	1c org & maroon	6.00	3.00
O32	A31	2c vio & maroon	6.00	3.00
O33	A31	3c yel grn & mar	6.00	3.00
O34	A31	6c red & maroon	6.00	3.00
O35	A31	9c gray & maroon	12.00	5.00
O36	A31	10c multicolored	16.00	5.00
O38	A31	1k multicolored	20.00	10.00
O40	A31	2k multicolored	40.00	20.00
		Nos. O31-O40 (8)	112.00	52.00

The 13c, 26c and 3k to 30k denominations were not regularly issued with this overprint.

Dangerous counterfeits exist, usually on reprints.

Regular Issue of 1915 Overprinted

SERVICE

1915 **Wmk. 161** ***Perf. 11, 11½***

O41	A33	1c car & indigo	*2.00*	*2.00*
O42	A33	2c bl & carmine	*2.00*	*2.00*
O43	A33	3c dark green	*2.00*	*2.00*
O44	A33	5c red	*2.00*	*2.00*
O45	A33	6c ol grn & car	*2.00*	*2.00*
O46	A33	9c yel brn & vio	*2.00*	*2.00*
O47	A33	10c multicolored	*2.00*	*2.00*
O48	A33	12c ultramarine	*2.00*	*2.00*
O49	A34	1k multicolored	*5.00*	*5.00*
O50	A33	24c multicolored	*3.00*	*3.00*
O51	A34	2k sil, bl & rose	*5.00*	*5.00*
O52	A34	3k sil, vio & brn	*5.00*	*5.00*
O53	A34	5k multicolored	*5.00*	*5.00*
O54	A35	1t gold, pur & blk	*7.00*	*7.00*
O55	A35	2t gold, grn & brn	*7.00*	*7.00*
O56	A35	3t multicolored	*9.00*	*9.00*
O57	A35	5t gold, bl & ind	*10.00*	*10.00*
		Nos. O41-O57 (17)	*72.00*	*72.00*

Coronation of Shah Ahmed.

Reprints have dull rather than shiny overprint. **Value, set, $10.**

Coat of Arms
O2 O3

1941 **Unwmk.** **Litho.** ***Perf. 11***

For Internal Postage

O58	O2	5d violet	2.00	20
O59	O2	10d magenta	2.00	20
O60	O2	25d carmine	2.00	20
O61	O2	50d brown black	2.00	20
O62	O2	75d claret	3.50	45

Size: 22½x30mm

O63	O2	1r peacock grn	5.00	45
O64	O2	1½r deep blue	6.00	1.50
O65	O2	2r light blue	8.00	1.00
O66	O2	3r vio brown	15.00	1.50
O67	O2	5r gray green	20.00	2.00
O68	O2	10r dk brn & bl	55.00	5.00
O69	O2	20r chlky bl & brt pink	100.00	20.00
O70	O2	30r vio & brt grn	200.00	45.00
O71	O2	50r turq grn & dk brown	250.00	82.50
		Nos. O58-O71 (14)	670.50	160.20

Catalogue values for unused stamps in this section, from this point to the end of the section, are for Never Hinged items.

Perf. 13½x13

1974, Feb. 25 **Photo.** **Wmk. 353**

Size: 20x28mm

O72	O3	5d vio & lilac	20	25
O73	O3	10d mag & grnsh bl	20	25
O74	O3	50d org & lt green	20	20
O75	O3	1r green & gold	32	20
O76	O3	2r emerald & org	50	20

Perf. 13

Size: 23x37mm

O77	O3	6r slate grn & org	55	20
O78	O3	8r ultra & yellow	70	20
O79	O3	10r dk bl & lilac	3.00	25
O80	O3	11r pur & light bl	1.25	25
O81	O3	14r red & lt ultra	1.25	60
O82	O3	20r vio blue & org	2.50	50
O83	O3	50r dk brn & brt grn	6.50	1.75
		Nos. O72-O83 (12)	17.17	4.85

1977-79 **Wmk. 353** ***Perf. 13½x13***

Size: 20x28mm

O87	O3	1r black & lt grn	18	15
O88	O3	2r brown & gray	30	15
O89	O3	3r ultra & orange	32	15
O90	O3	5r green & rose	38	15

Perf. 13

Size: 23x37mm

O91	O3	6r dk bl & lt bl ('78)	45	45
O92	O3	8r red & bl grn ('78)	50	50
O93	O3	10r dk grn & yel grn	75	25
O94	O3	11r dk blue & brt yellow ('79)	75	50
O95	O3	14r dl grn & gray	90	50
O96	O3	15r bl & rose lil ('78)	1.00	1.00
O97	O3	20r purple & yel	1.50	40
O98	O3	30r brn & ocher ('78)	2.00	1.25
O99	O3	50r blk & gold ('78)	4.00	1.25
		Nos. O87-O99 (13)	13.03	6.70

NEWSPAPER STAMP

No. 429 Overprinted

Imprimés

1909 **Typo.** **Unwmk.** ***Perf. 12½***

P1	A26	2c gray, *blue*	*15.00*	*10.00*

PARCEL POST STAMPS

Colis Postaux

Colis Postaux

Regular issues of 1907-08 (types A26, A29) with the handstamps above in blue, black or green are of questionable status as issued stamps.

Regular Issue of 1915 Overprinted in Black

COLIS POSTAUX

1915 **Wmk. 161** ***Perf. 11, 11½***

Q19	A33	1c car & indigo	*2.00*	*2.00*
Q20	A33	2c bl & carmine	*2.00*	*2.00*
Q21	A33	3c dark green	*2.00*	*2.00*
Q22	A33	5c red	*2.00*	*2.00*
Q23	A33	6c ol green & car	*2.00*	*2.00*
Q24	A33	9c yel brn & vio	*2.00*	*2.00*
Q25	A33	10c bl grn & yel brn	*2.00*	*2.00*
Q26	A33	12c ultramarine	*2.00*	*2.00*
Q27	A34	1k multicolored	*5.00*	*5.00*
Q28	A33	24c multicolored	*3.00*	*3.00*
Q29	A34	2k multicolored	*5.00*	*5.00*
Q30	A34	3k multicolored	*5.00*	*5.00*
Q31	A34	5k multicolored	*5.00*	*5.00*
Q32	A35	1t multicolored	*7.00*	*7.00*
Q33	A35	2t gold, grn & brn	*7.00*	*7.00*
Q34	A35	3t multicolored	*9.00*	*9.00*
Q35	A35	5t multicolored	*10.00*	*10.00*
		Nos. Q19-Q35 (17)	*72.00*	*72.00*

Coronation of Shah Ahmed.

Reprints have dull rather than shiny overprint. **Value, set, $10.**

Catalogue values for unused stamps in this section, from this point to the end of the section, are for Never Hinged items.

Post Horn — PP1

Black frame and "IRAN" (reversed) are printed on back of Nos. Q36-Q65, to show through when stamp is attached to parcel.

1958 **Wmk. 306** **Typo.** ***Perf. 12½***

Q36	PP1	50d olive bis	15	15
Q37	PP1	1r carmine	15	15
Q38	PP1	2r blue	30	15
a.		Imperf., pair	32.50	
Q39	PP1	3r green	30	15
Q40	PP1	5r purple	70	15
Q41	PP1	10r orange brn	2.75	20
Q42	PP1	20r dp orange	2.75	20
Q43	PP1	30r lilac	3.75	1.40
Q44	PP1	50r dk carmine	4.50	1.75
Q45	PP1	100r yellow	11.00	2.25
Q46	PP1	200r light grn	19.00	4.50
		Nos. Q36-Q46 (11)	45.35	11.05

1961-66 **Wmk. 316**

Q51	PP1	5r purple ('66)	1.00	25
Q52	PP1	10r org brn ('62)	3.00	50
Q53	PP1	20r orange	2.75	1.00
Q54	PP1	30r red lil ('63)	4.00	1.50
Q55	PP1	50r dk car ('63)	5.00	2.50
Q56	PP1	100r yellow ('64)	24.00	5.00
Q57	PP1	200r emer ('64)	20.00	10.00
		Nos. Q51-Q57 (7)	59.75	20.75

1967-74 **Wmk. 353**

Q58	PP1	2r blue ('74)	15	15
Q59	PP1	5r dk pur ('69)	20	15
Q60	PP1	10r orange brn	40	25
Q61	PP1	20r orange ('69)	2.00	50
Q62	PP1	30r red lilac	1.50	25
Q63	PP1	50r red brn ('68)	2.00	1.25
Q64	PP1	100r yellow	3.50	1.50
Q65	PP1	200r emerald ('69)	6.00	5.00
		Nos. Q58-Q65 (8)	15.75	9.05

POSTAL TAX STAMPS

Red Lion and Sun Emblem
PT1

1950 **Unwmk.** **Litho.** ***Perf. 11***

RA1	PT1	50d grn & car rose	8.50	40
RA2	PT1	2r vio & lil rose	4.00	40

1955 **Wmk. 306**

RA3	PT1	50d emer & car rose	*50.00*	5.00

Catalogue values for unused stamps in this section, from this point to the end of the section, are for Never Hinged items.

1957-58 **Wmk. 316**

RA4	PT1	50d emer & rose lil	1.50	30
RA5	PT1	2r vio & car rose ('58)	2.50	1.00

1965 **Wmk. 349** ***Perf. 10½***

RA6	PT1	50d emer & car rose ('65)	1.50	45
RA7	PT1	2r vio & lil rose ('65)	2.00	60

A particular stamp may be scarce, but if few collectors want it, its market value may remain relatively low.

1965-66 **Wmk. 353**

RA8	PT1	50d emer & car rose (I)	1.00	15
a.		Type II	3.00	20
RA9	PT1	2r vio & car rose ('66)	3.00	35

No. RA8 was printed in two types: I. Without diagonal line before Persian "50." II. With line.

1976, Sept. **Photo.** ***Perf. 13x13½***

RA10	PT1	50d emer & red	2.50	25

No. RA10 is redrawn and has vertical watermark.

1978 **Wmk. 353** ***Perf. 13x13½***

RA11	PT1	2r sl & red ('78)	2.50	25

Nos. RA1-RA11 were obligatory on all mail. The tax was for hospitals.

The 2.25r and 2.50r of type PT1 were used only on telegrams.

IRAQ

LOCATION — In western Asia, bounded on the north by Syria and Turkey, on the east by Iran, on the south by Saudi Arabia, and on the west by Jordan
GOVT. — Republic
AREA — 167,925 sq. mi.
POP. — 12,029,700 (est. 1982)
CAPITAL — Baghdad

Iraq, formerly Mesopotamia, a province of Turkey, was mandated to Great Britain in 1920. The mandate was terminated in 1932. For earlier issues, see Mesopotamia.

16 Annas = 1 Rupee.
1000 Fils = 1 Dinar (1932)

Catalogue values for unused stamps in this country are for Never Hinged items, beginning with Scott 79 in the regular postage section, Scott C1 in the air post section, Scott CO1 in the air post official section, Scott O90 in the officials section, Scott RA1 in the postal tax section, and Scott RAC1 in the air post postal tax section.

Issues under British Mandate

Sunni Mosque — A1

Gufas on the Tigris — A2

Assyrian Winged Bull — A4

Ctesiphon Arch — A5

Motif of Assyrian Origin — A3

Colors of the Dulaim Camel Corps — A6

Golden Shiah Mosque of Kadhimain — A7

Conventionalized Date Palm or "Tree of Life" — A8

1923-25 **Engr.** **Wmk. 4** ***Perf. 12***

1	A1	½a olive grn	15	15
2	A2	1a brown	25	15
3	A3	1½a car lake	18	15
4	A4	2a brown org	20	15
5	A5	3a dp blue	20	15
6	A6	4a dull vio	25	18
7	A7	6a blue grn	30	15
8	A6	8a olive bis	50	20
9	A8	1r grn & brn	2.50	70
10	A1	2r black	15.00	12.50
11	A1	2r bis ('25)	7.00	1.50
12	A6	5r orange	22.50	12.00
13	A7	10r carmine	50.00	20.00
		Nos. 1-13 (13)	99.03	47.98

For overprints, see Nos. O1-O24, O42, O47, O51-O53.

King Faisal I — A9

1927

14	A9	1r red brown	4.00	1.00

See No. 27. For overprint and surcharges, see Nos. 43, O25, O54.

King Faisal I
A10 A11

1931

15	A10	½a green	15	15
16	A10	1a chestnut	15	15
17	A10	1½a carmine	30	25
18	A10	2a orange	20	15
19	A10	3a light blue	20	15
20	A10	4a pur brown	75	60
21	A10	6a Prus blue	1.00	18
22	A10	8a dark green	2.75	30
23	A11	1r dark brown	3.00	1.25
24	A11	2r yel brown	7.50	1.25
25	A11	5r dp orange	35.00	20.00
26	A11	10r red	70.00	70.00
27	A9	25r violet	750.00	1,000.
		Nos. 15-27 (13)	871.00	1,094.

For overprints, see Nos. O26-O41, O43-O46, O48-O50, O54.

Issues of the Kingdom

Stamps of 1923-31 Surcharged in "Fils" or "Dinars" in Red, Black or Green:

a

25Fils ٢٥ فلس
b

100Fils ١٠٠ فلس
c

1 Dinar ١ دينار
d

1932, Apr. 1

28	A10(a)	2f on ½a grn (R)	15	15
29	A10(a)	3f on ½a grn	15	15
a.		Double surcharge	250.00	
b.		Inverted surcharge	250.00	
30	A10(a)	4f on 1a chnt (G)	15	15
31	A10(a)	5f on 1a chnt	15	15
a.		Double surcharge	250.00	
b.		Inverted Arabic "5"	50.00	60.00
32	A10(a)	8f on 1½a car	30	25
a.		Inverted surcharge	200.00	
33	A10(a)	10f on 2a org	20	15
34	A10(a)	15f on 3a lt bl	40	25
35	A10(a)	20f on 4a pur brn	1.50	75
36	A6(b)	25f on 4a dull violet	75	75
a.		"Flis" for "Fils"	550.00	650.00
b.		Inverted Arabic "5"	550.00	650.00
37	A10(a)	30f on 6a Prus blue	75	75
38	A10(a)	40f on 8a dark green	1.50	1.50
39	A11(c)	75f on 1r dark brown	3.00	1.50
40	A11(c)	100f on 2r yel brown	6.00	2.00
41	A11(c)	200f on 5r dp orange	15.00	9.50
42	A11(d)	½d on 10r red	60.00	37.50
a.		Bar in "½" omitted	675.00	750.00
43	A9(d)	1d on 25r vio	125.00	125.00
		Nos. 28-43 (16)	215.00	180.50

King Faisal I
A12 A13

A14

Values in "Fils" and "Dinars"

1932, May 9 **Engr.**

44	A12	2f ultra	15	15
45	A12	3f green	15	15
46	A12	4f vio brown	15	15
47	A12	5f gray green	15	15
48	A12	8f deep red	15	15
49	A12	10f yellow	15	15
50	A12	15f deep blue	80	15
51	A12	20f orange	50	18
52	A12	25f rose lilac	1.65	15
53	A12	30f olive grn	50	15
54	A12	40f dark vio	2.25	1.00
55	A13	50f deep brown	55	25
56	A13	75f lt ultra	1.65	1.50
57	A13	100f deep green	2.75	35
58	A13	200f dark red	6.75	75
59	A14	½d gray blue	27.50	8.25
60	A14	1d claret	55.00	55.00
		Nos. 44-60 (17)	100.80	68.63

For overprints, see Nos. O55-O71.

A15

A16

King Ghazi — A17

1934-38 **Unwmk.**

61	A15	1f purple ('38)	15	15
62	A15	2f ultra	15	15
63	A15	3f green	15	15
64	A15	4f pur brown	15	15
65	A15	5f gray green	15	15
66	A15	8f deep red	18	15
67	A15	10f yellow	20	15
68	A15	15f deep blue	20	15
69	A15	20f orange	25	15
70	A15	25f brown vio	50	25
71	A15	30f olive grn	50	15
72	A15	40f dark vio	75	20
73	A16	50f deep brown	80	20
74	A16	75f ultra	1.10	30
75	A16	100f deep green	1.75	35
76	A16	200f dark red	3.75	60
77	A17	½d gray blue	12.50	7.50
78	A17	1d claret	25.00	10.00
		Nos. 61-78 (18)	48.23	20.90

For overprints, see Nos. 226, O72-O89.

Catalogue values for unused stamps in this section, from this point to the end of the section, are for Never Hinged items.

Sitt Zubaidah Mosque — A18

Mausoleum of King Faisal I — A19

Lion of Babylon A20

Malwiye of Samarra (Spiral Tower) A21

Oil Wells — A22

Mosque of the Golden Dome, Samarra — A23

Perf. 14, 13½, 12½, 12x13½, 13½x12, 14x13½

1941-42 **Engr.**

79	A18	1f dark vio ('42)	15	15
80	A18	2f chocolate ('42)	15	15
81	A19	3f brt green ('42)	15	15
82	A19	4f purple ('42)	15	15
83	A19	5f dk car rose ('42)	15	15
84	A20	8f carmine	40	25
85	A20	8f ocher ('42)	15	15
86	A20	10f ocher	8.00	40
87	A20	10f carmine ('42)	15	15
88	A20	15f dull blue	50	20
89	A20	15f black ('42)	15	15
90	A20	20f black	3.00	45
91	A20	20f dull blue ('42)	15	15
92	A21	25f dark violet	20	20
93	A21	30f deep orange	20	20
94	A21	40f brn orange	2.00	30
95	A21	40f chnt ('42)	75	15
96	A21	50f ultra	40	20
97	A21	75f rose vio	60	25
98	A22	100f ol green ('42)	1.00	30
99	A22	200f deep org ('42)	4.00	65
100	A23	½d lt bl, perf. 12x13½ ('42)	7.00	1.00
a.		Perf. 14	6.00	2.50
101	A23	1d grnsh bl ('42)	15.00	6.50
		Nos. 79-101 (23)	44.40	12.40

Nos. 92-95 measure 17¾x21½mm, Nos. 96-97 measure 21x24mm.

For overprints, see Nos. O90-O114, O165, RA5.

King Faisal II
A24 A25

Photo.; Frame Litho.

1942 *Perf. 13 x 13½*

102	A24	1f violet & brown	15	15
103	A24	2f dk blue & brown	15	15
104	A24	3f lt green & brown	15	15
105	A24	4f dull brown & brn	15	15
106	A24	5f sage green & brn	15	15
107	A24	6f red orange & brn	15	15
108	A24	10f dl rose red & lt brn	15	15
109	A24	12f yel green & brown	18	15
		Set value	77	55

For overprints, see Nos. O115-O122.

Perf. 11½x12

1948, Jan. 15 Engr. Unwmk.

Size: 17¾x20½mm

110	A25	1f slate	15	15
111	A25	2f sepia	15	15
112	A25	3f emerald	15	15
113	A25	4f purple	15	15
114	A25	5f rose lake	15	15
115	A25	6f plum	15	15
116	A25	8f ocher	1.50	15
117	A25	10f rose red	15	15
118	A25	12f dark olive	15	15
119	A25	15f black	1.50	15
120	A25	20f blue	15	15
121	A25	25f rose violet	15	15
122	A25	30f red orange	18	15
123	A25	40f orange brn	25	15

Perf. 12x11½

Size: 22x27½mm

124	A25	60f deep blue	75	15
125	A25	75f lilac rose	1.25	25
126	A25	100f olive grn	2.00	35
127	A25	200f dp orange	3.00	45
128	A25	½d blue	10.00	2.00
129	A25	1d green	25.00	10.00
		Nos. 110-129 (20)	46.93	15.30

Sheets of 6 exist, perforated and imperforate, containing Nos. 112, 117, 120 and 125-127, with arms and Arabic inscription in blue green in upper and lower margins. Value each, $25.

See Nos. 133-138. For overprints, see Nos. 188-194, O123-O142, O166-O177, O257, O272, O274, O277, O282, RA1-RA4, RA6.

Post Rider and King Ghazi — A26

Designs: 40f, Equestrian statue & Faisal I. 50f, UPU symbols & Faisal II.

1949, Nov. 1 *Perf. 13x13½*

130	A26	20f blue	32	25
131	A26	40f red orange	65	25
132	A26	50f purple	1.25	50

75th anniv. of the UPU.

Type of 1948

1950-51 Unwmk. *Perf. 11½x12*

Size: 17¾x20½mm

133	A25	3f rose lake	3.00	20
134	A25	5f emerald	5.00	28
135	A25	14f dk olive ('50)	55	15
136	A25	16f rose red	2.00	28
137	A25	28f blue	1.00	28

Perf. 12x11½

Size: 22x27½mm

138	A25	50f deep blue ('50)	1.50	35
		Nos. 133-138 (6)	13.05	1.54

For overprints, see Nos. 160, O143-O148, O258, O273, O275-O276.

King Faisal II
A27 A28

1953, May 2 Engr. *Perf. 12*

139	A27	3f deep rose car	25	15
140	A27	14f olive	50	15
141	A27	28f blue	1.00	30
b.		Souv. sheet of 3, #139-141	60.00	40.00
		Set value		50

Coronation of King Faisal II, May 2, 1953.

1954-57 *Perf. 11½x12*

Size: 18x20½mm

141A	A28	1f blue ('56)	15	15
142	A28	2f chocolate	15	15
143	A28	3f rose lake	15	15
144	A28	4f violet	15	15
145	A28	5f emerald	15	15
146	A28	6f plum	15	15
147	A28	8f ocher	15	15
148	A28	10f blue	15	15
149	A28	15f black	15	15
149A	A28	16f brt rose ('57)	2.25	1.00
150	A28	20f olive	20	15
151	A28	25f rose vio ('55)	35	15
152	A28	30f ver ('55)	50	15
153	A28	40f orange brn	30	15

Size: 22x27½mm

154	A28	50f blue	75	15
155	A28	75f pink	1.25	35
156	A28	100f olive green	1.50	75
157	A28	200f orange	6.00	1.00
		Nos. 141A-157 (18)	14.45	
		Set value		4.00

For overprints, see Nos. 158-159, 195-209, 674, 676, 678, O148A-O161A, O178-O191, O259-O260, O283-O291.

No. 143, 148 and 137 Overprinted in Black

1955, Apr. 6 *Perf. 11½x12*

158	A28	3f rose lake	15	15
159	A28	10f blue	25	15
160	A25	28f blue	45	30

Abrogation of Anglo-Iraq treaty of 1930.

King Faisal II — A29

1955, Nov. 26 *Perf. 13½x13*

161	A29	3f rose lake	15	15
162	A29	10f light ultra	20	15
163	A29	28f blue	55	45

6th Arab Engineers' Conf., Baghdad, 1955.
For surcharge, see No. 227.

Faisal II and Globe — A30

1956, Mar. 3 *Perf. 13x13½*

164	A30	3f rose lake	15	15
165	A30	10f light ultra	25	15
166	A30	28f blue	50	20
		Set value		35

Arab Postal Conf., Baghdad, Mar. 3.
For overprint, see No. 173. For surcharge, see No. 251.

Mechanical Loom A31

Designs: 3f, Dam. 5f, Modern city development. 10f, Pipeline. 40f, Tigris Bridge.

1957, Apr. 8 Photo. *Perf. 11½*

Granite Paper

167	A31	1f Prus bl & org yel	15	15
168	A31	3f multicolored	15	15
169	A31	5f multicolored	15	15
170	A31	10f lt bl, ocher & red	28	15
171	A31	40f lt bl, blk & ocher	60	15
		Set value	1.10	45

Development Week, 1957. See #185-187.

Fair Emblem — A32

1957, June 1 Unwmk.

Granite Paper

172	A32	10f brown & buff	25	15

Agricultural and Industrial Exhibition, Baghdad, June 1.

No. 166 Overprinted in Red

1957, Nov. 14 *Perf. 13x13½*

173	A30	28f blue	1.00	1.00
a.		Double overprint	200.00	225.00

Iraqi Red Crescent Soc., 25th anniv.

King Faisal II — A33

Perf. 11½x12

1957-58 Unwmk. Engr.

174	A33	1f blue	15	15
175	A33	2f chocolate	15	15
176	A33	3f dark car ('57)	15	15
177	A33	4f dull violet	15	15
177A	A33	5f emerald	1.00	1.50
178	A33	6f plum	15	20
179	A33	8f ocher	35	30
180	A33	10f blue	15	15
		Nos. 174-180 (8)	2.25	2.75

Higher denominations exist without Republic overprint. They were probably not regularly issued.

See note below No. 225.

For overprints, see Nos. 210-225, 675, O162-O164, O192-O199, O292-O294. For types overprinted, see #677, 679, O261, O295.

Tanks — A34

King Faisal II — A35

Army Day, Jan. 6: 10f, Marching soldiers. 20f, Artillery and planes.

1958, Jan. 6 *Perf. 13x13½*

181	A34	8f green & black	30	15
182	A34	10f brown & black	40	20
183	A34	20f blue & red brown	50	15
184	A35	30f car & purple	80	30

Type of 1957

Designs: 3f, Sugar beet, bag and refining machinery (vert.). 5f, Farm. 10f, Dervendi Khan dam.

1958, Apr. 26 Photo. *Perf. 11½*

Granite Paper

185	A31	3f gray vio, grn & lt gray	15	15
186	A31	5f multicolored	18	15
187	A31	10f multicolored	35	25

Development Week, 1958.

Republic

Stamps of 1948-51 Overprinted

الجمهورية
العراقية

Perf. 11½x12, 12x11½

1958 Engr. Unwmk.

Size: 17¾x20½mm

188	A25	12f dark olive	20	15
189	A25	14f olive	30	20
190	A25	16f rose red	3.50	2.25
191	A25	28f blue	1.00	45

Size: 22x27½mm

192	A25	60f deep blue	1.25	45
193	A25	½d blue	10.00	3.25
194	A25	1d green	22.50	11.00
		Nos. 188-194 (7)	38.75	17.75

Other denominations of type A25 exist with this overprint, but these were probably not regularly issued.

Same Overprint on Stamps of 1954-57

Size: 18x20½mm

195	A28	1f blue	15	15
196	A28	2f chocolate	15	15
196A	A28	4f violet	15	15
196B	A28	5f emerald	18	18
197	A28	6f plum	18	15
198	A28	8f ocher	20	20
199	A28	10f blue	24	15
200	A28	15f black	28	15
201	A28	16f bright rose	1.10	35
202	A28	20f olive	40	40
203	A28	25f rose violet	24	18
204	A28	30f vermilion	40	25
205	A28	40f orange brn	48	20

Size: 22½x27½mm

206	A28	50f blue	2.75	2.00
207	A28	75f pink	1.50	1.50
208	A28	100f olive green	2.25	2.00
209	A28	200f orange	7.25	4.00
		Nos. 195-209 (17)	17.90	12.16

The lines of this overprint are found transposed on Nos. 195, 196 and 199.

Same Overprint on Stamps and Type of 1957-58

Size: 18x20mm

210	A33	1f blue	15	15
211	A33	2f chocolate	15	15
212	A33	3f dark carmine	18	18
213	A33	4f dull violet	15	15
214	A33	5f emerald	15	15
215	A33	6f plum	15	15
216	A33	8f ocher	15	15
217	A33	10f blue	18	15
218	A33	20f olive	18	15
219	A33	25f rose violet	55	55
220	A33	30f vermilion	70	15
221	A33	40f orange brn	2.25	90

Size: 22x27½mm

222	A33	50f rose violet	1.75	50
223	A33	75f olive	4.50	90
224	A33	100f orange	3.75	90
225	A33	200f blue	6.50	1.40
		Nos. 210-225 (16)	21.44	6.68

#218-225 were not issued without overprint.

The lines of this overprint are found transposed on Nos. 210 and 214.

Many errors of overprint exist of #188-226.

For overprint, see No. O198.

Same Overprint on No. 78

Perf. 12

226	A17	1d claret	17.50	14.00

No. 163 Surcharged in Red

الجمهورية العراقية
المؤتمر الرابع للمحامين العرب
بغداد ١٩٥٨
10 FILS ١٠ فلوس

1958, Nov. 26 *Perf. 13x13½*
227 A29 10f on 28f blue 50 25

Arab Lawyers' Conf., Baghdad, Nov. 26.

Soldier and Flag — A36

1959, Jan. 6 **Photo.** *Perf. 11½*
228 A36 3f bright blue 15 15
229 A36 10f olive green 15 15
230 A36 40f purple 1.00 35
Set value 50

Issued for Army Day, Jan. 6.

Orange Tree A37

Emblem of Republic A38

1959, Mar. 21 **Unwmk.** *Perf. 11½*
231 A37 10f green, dk grn & org 50 15

Issued for Arbor Day.

1959-60 **Litho. & Photo.** *Perf. 11½*
Granite Paper
Emblem in Gold, Red and Blue; Blue Inscriptions

232 A38 1f gray 15 15
233 A38 2f salmon 15 15
234 A38 3f pale violet 15 15
235 A38 4f bright yel 15 15
236 A38 5f light blue 15 15
237 A38 10f bright pink 15 15
238 A38 15f light green 15 15
239 A38 20f bister brn 15 15
240 A38 30f light gray 20 15
241 A38 40f orange yel 25 15
242 A38 50f yel green 1.75 15
243 A38 75f pale grn ('60) 60 20
244 A38 100f orange ('60) 1.40 30
245 A38 200f lilac ('60) 2.25 60
246 A38 500f bister ('60) 7.25 1.75
247 A38 1d brt grn ('60) 7.25 3.50
Nos. 232-247 (16) 22.15
Set value 7.00

See Nos. 305A-305B. For overprints, see Nos. 252, 293-295, O200-O221.

Worker and Buildings — A39

Victorious Fighters A40

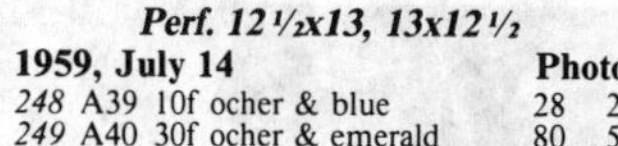

Perf. 12½x13, 13x12½
1959, July 14 **Photo.**
248 A39 10f ocher & blue 28 20
249 A40 30f ocher & emerald 80 50

1st anniv. of the Revolution of July 14 (1958), which overthrew the kingdom.

Harvest — A41

1959, July 14 *Perf. 11½*
250 A41 10f lt grn & dk grn 25 15

No. 166 Surcharged in Dark Red

الجمهورية العراقية
يوم الطفل العالمي
١ حزيران ١٩٥٩
10 FILS ١٠ فلوس

1959, June 1 **Engr.** *Perf. 13x13½*
251 A30 10f on 28f blue 40 28

Issued for Children's Day, 1959.

No. 237 Overprinted

اسبوع
الصحة والنظافة

Litho. and Photo.
1959, Oct. 23 *Perf. 11½*
252 A38 10f brt pink, gold, red & bl 65 35

Health and Sanitation Week.

Abdul Karim Kassem and Army Band — A42

Abdul Karim Kassem and: 16f, Field maneuvers (horiz.). 30f, Antiaircraft. 40f, Troops at attention, flag and bugler. 60f, Fighters and flag (horiz.).

1960, Jan. 6 **Photo.** *Perf. 11½*
253 A42 10f blue, grn & mar 15 15
254 A42 16f brt blue & red 45 15
255 A42 30f ol grn, yel & brn 45 20
256 A42 40f deep vio & buff 60 25
257 A42 60f dk brown & buff 1.40 40
Nos. 253-257 (5) 3.05 1.15

Issued for Army Day, Jan. 6.

Prime Minister Abdul Karim Kassem — A43

Maroof el Rasafi — A44

1960, Feb. 1 **Engr.** *Perf. 12½*
258 A43 10f lilac 35 15
259 A43 30f emerald 70 18
Set value 24

Issued to honor Prime Minister Kassem on his recovery from an assassination attempt.

1960, May 10 **Photo.** *Perf. 13½x13*
260 A44 10f maroon & blk 65 65
a. Inverted overprint 75.00 60.00

Exists without overprint.

Symbol of the Republic A45

Unknown Soldier's Tomb and Kassem with Freedom Torch A46

1960, July 14 *Perf. 11½*
261 A45 6f ol grn, red & gold 15 15
262 A46 10f green, blue & red 15 15
263 A46 16f vio, blue & red 15 15
264 A45 18f ultra, red & gold 18 15
265 A45 30f brown, red & gold 30 20
266 A46 60f dk brn, bl & red 1.00 40
Nos. 261-266 (6) 1.93
Set value 95

2nd anniv. of the July 14, 1958 revolution.

Gen. Kassem and Marching Troops — A47

Gen. Kassem and Arch — A48

1961, Jan. 6 *Perf. 11½*
Granite Paper
267 A47 3f gray ol, emer, yel & gold 15 15
268 A47 6f pur, emer, yel & gold 15 15
269 A47 10f sl, emer, yel & gold 15 15
270 A48 20f bl grn, blk & buff 18 15
271 A48 30f bis brn, blk & buff 35 20
272 A48 40f ultra, black & buff 65 25
Set value 1.30 70

Issued for Army Day, Jan. 6.

Gen. Kassem and Children A49

1961, June 1 **Photo.** **Unwmk.**
Granite Paper
273 A49 3f yellow & brown 15 15
274 A49 6f blue & brown 15 15
275 A49 10f pink & brown 15 15
276 A49 30f yellow & brown 65 20
277 A49 50f lt grn & brown 65 35
Nos. 273-277 (5) 1.75
Set value 70

Issued for World Children's Day.

Gen. Kassem and Flag — A50

Design: 5f, 30f, 40f, Gen. Kassem saluting and flags.

1961, July 14 *Perf. 11½*
Granite Paper
278 A50 1f multicolored 15 15
279 A50 3f multicolored 15 15
280 A50 5f multicolored 15 15
281 A50 6f multicolored 15 15
282 A50 10f multicolored 15 15
283 A50 30f multicolored 42 18
284 A50 40f multicolored 60 22
285 A50 50f multicolored 30 25
286 A50 100f multicolored 4.25 1.65
Nos. 278-286 (9) 6.32
Set value 2.50

3rd anniv. of the July 14, 1958 revolution.

Gen. Kassem and Flag — A51

Gen. Kassem and Symbol of Republic A52

Perf. 11½
1962, Jan. 6 **Unwmk.** **Photo.**
Granite Paper
287 A51 1f multicolored 15 15
288 A51 3f multicolored 15 15
289 A51 6f multicolored 15 15
290 A52 10f blk, lilac & gold 15 15
291 A52 30f black, org & gold 40 18
292 A52 50f blk, pale grn & gold 75 30
Set value 1.35 65

Issued for Army Day, Jan. 6.

Nos. 234, 237 and 240 Overprinted

مؤتمر
العالم الاسلامي
بغداد
١٣٨١هـ-١٩٦٢م

Litho. & Photo.
1962, May 29 *Perf. 11½*
Emblem in Gold, Red and Blue; Blue Inscriptions
293 A38 3f pale violet 15 15
294 A38 10f bright pink 20 15
295 A38 30f light gray 80 25
Set value 40

Fifth Islamic Congress.

Hands Across Map of Arabia and North Africa — A53

1962, July 14 **Photo.**
296 A53 1f brn, org, grn & gold 15 15
297 A53 3f brn, yel grn, grn & gold 15 15
298 A53 6f blk, lt brn, grn & gold 15 15
299 A53 10f brn, lil, grn & gold 15 15
300 A53 30f brn, rose, grn & gold 40 20
301 A53 50f brn, gray, grn & gold 75 35
Set value 1.45 75

Revolution of July 14, 1958, 4th anniv.

al-Kindi A54

Emblem of Republic A54a

Designs: 3f, Horsemen with standards and trumpets. 10f, Old map of Baghdad and Tigris. 40f, Gen. Kassem, modern building and flag.

Perf. 14x13½

1962, Dec. 1 Litho. Unwmk.

302	A54	3f multicolored	15	15
303	A54	6f multicolored	15	15
304	A54	10f multicolored	32	15
305	A54	40f multicolored	90	75
		Set value		92

9th century Arab philosopher al-Kindi; millenary of the Round City of Baghdad.

1962, Dec. 20 ***Perf. 13½x14***

305A	A54a	14f brt green & blk	1.10	25
305B	A54a	35f ver & black	1.65	35

Nos. 305A-305B were originally sold affixed to air letter sheets, obliterating the portrait of King Faisal II. They were issued in sheets for general use in 1966.

For overprints, see Nos. RA15-RA16.

Tanks on Parade and Gen. Kassem — A55

Malaria Eradication Emblem — A56

1963, Jan. 6 Photo. ***Perf. 11½***

306	A55	3f black & yellow	15	15
307	A55	5f brown & plum	15	15
308	A55	6f blk & lt green	15	15
309	A55	10f blk & lt blue	18	15
310	A55	10f black & pink	18	15
311	A55	20f black & ultra	38	15
312	A55	40f blk & rose lilac	55	25
313	A55	50f brn & brt ultra	75	40
		Set value	2.15	1.05

Issued for Army Day, Jan. 6.

1962, Dec. 31 ***Perf. 14***

Republic Emblem in Red, Blue & Gold

314	A56	3f yel grn, blk & dk grn	15	15
315	A56	10f org, blk & dark blue	20	15
316	A56	40f lilac, black & blue	50	30
		Set value		45

WHO drive to eradicate malaria.

Gufas on the Tigris A57

Shepherd and Sheep A58

Designs: 2f, 500f, Spiral tower, Samarra. 4f, 15f, Ram's head harp, Ur. 5f, 75f, Map and Republic emblem. 10f, 50f, Lion of Babylon. 20f, 40f, Baghdad University. 30f, 200f, Kadhimain mosque. 100f, 1d, Winged bull, Khorsabad.

Engr.; Engr. and Photo. (bicolored)

1963, Feb. 16 Unwmk. ***Perf. 12x11***

317	A57	1f green	15	15
318	A57	2f purple	15	15
319	A57	3f black	15	15
320	A57	4f black & yel	15	15
321	A57	5f lil & lt grn	15	15
322	A57	10f rose red	15	15
323	A57	15f brn & buff	20	15
324	A57	20f violet blue	20	15
325	A57	30f orange	24	15
326	A57	40f brt green	32	15
327	A57	50f dark brown	3.25	15
328	A57	75f blk & lt grn	1.50	25
329	A57	100f brt lilac	1.50	25
330	A57	200f brown	3.25	75
331	A57	500f blue	5.50	1.75
332	A57	1d dp claret	8.00	3.50
		Nos. 317-332 (16)	24.86	
		Set value		7.00

For overprints, see Nos. RA7-RA12.

1963, Mar. 21 Litho. ***Perf. 13½x14***

Designs: 10f, Man holding sheaf. 20f, Date palm grove.

333	A58	3f emerald & gray	15	20
334	A58	10f dp brn & lil rose	15	25
335	A58	20f dk bl & red brn	60	42
a.		Souv. sheet of 3, #333-335	3.00	

FAO "Freedom from Hunger" campaign. No. 335a sold for 50f.

No. 335a was overprinted in 1970 in black to commemorate the UN 25th anniv. Denominations on the 3 stamps were obliterated, leaving "Price 50 Fils" in the margin.

Cent. Emblem — A59

Rifle, Helmet and Flag — A60

Design: 30f, Iraqi Red Crescent Society Headquarters (horiz.).

Perf. 11x11½, 11½x11

1963, Dec. 30 Photo.

336	A59	3f violet & red	15	15
337	A59	10f gray & red	15	15
338	A59	30f blue & red	50	20
		Set value		35

Centenary of International Red Cross.

1964, Jan. 6 Unwmk. ***Perf. 11½***

Granite Paper

339	A60	3f brn, blue & emer	15	15
340	A60	10f brn, pink & emer	25	15
341	A60	30f brown, yel & emer	50	15
		Set value		35

Issued for Army Day, Jan. 6.

Flag and Soldiers Storming Government Palace — A61

1964-67 ***Perf. 11½***

Granite Paper

342	A61	10f pur, red, grn & blk	15	15
343	A61	30f red brn, red, grn & blk	40	18
a.		Souv. sheet of 2	4.25	2.75
b.		Souv. sheet of 2 (4th anniv.) ('67)	4.25	2.75
		Set value		24

1st anniv. of the Revolution of Ramadan 14. No. 343a contains 2 imperf. stamps similar to Nos. 342-343 in changed colors (10f olive, red, green & black; 30f ultramarine, red, green & black). Sold for 50f. Nos. 342-343, 343a issued Feb. 8, 1964.

No. 343b consists of various block-outs and overprints on No. 343a. It commemorates the 4th anniv. of the Revolution of Ramadan 14. Sold for 70f. Issued Feb. 8, 1967.

Hammurabi and a God from Stele in Louvre — A62

Design: 10f, UN emblem and scales.

1964, June 10 Litho. ***Perf. 13½***

344	A62	6f lilac & pale grn	15	15
345	A62	10f org & vio blue	20	15
346	A62	30f blue & pale grn	70	25
		Set value		45

15th anniv. (in 1963) of the Universal Declaration of Human Rights.

"Industrialization of Iraq" — A63

Soldier Planting New Flag — A64

1964, July 14 ***Perf. 11***

347	A63	3f gray, org & black	15	15
348	A64	10f rose red, blk & emer	15	15
349	A64	20f rose red, blk & emer	35	15
350	A63	30f gray, org & black	70	20
		Set value		46

6th anniv. of the July 14, 1958 revolution.

Star and Fighters A65

1964, Nov. 18 Photo. ***Perf. 11½***

351	A65	5f sepia & orange	15	15
352	A65	10f lt bl & orange	15	15
353	A65	50f vio & red orange	65	30

Revolution of Nov. 18, 1963, 1st anniv.

Musician with Lute — A66

Perf. 13x13½

1964, Nov. 28 Litho. Unwmk.

354	A66	3f bister & multi	65	45
355	A66	10f dl grn & multi	65	45
356	A66	30f dl rose & multi	90	65

International Arab Music Conference.

Map of Arab Countries and Emblem A67

1964, Dec. 13 ***Perf. 12½x14***

357	A67	10f lt grn & rose lilac	35	15

9th Arab Engineers' Conference, Baghdad.

Arab Postal Union Emblem A67a

Soldier, Flag and Rising Sun A68

1964, Dec. 21 Photo. ***Perf. 11***

358	A67a	3f sal pink & blue	15	15
359	A67a	10f brt red lil & brn	15	15
360	A67a	30f orange & blue	75	25
		Set value		36

10th anniv. of Permanent Office of Arab Postal Union.

For overprint, see No. 707.

Perf. 14x12½

1965, Jan. 6 Litho. Unwmk.

361	A68	5f dull grn & multi	15	15
362	A68	15f henna brn & multi	15	15
363	A68	30f black brn & multi	60	20
		Set value		36

Issued for Army Day, Jan. 6.

An imperf. souvenir sheet carries a revised No. 363 with "30 FILS" omitted, and a portrait of Pres. Abdul Salam Arif. Violet inscriptions including "PRICE 60 FILS."

Symbols of Agriculture and Industry A69

1965, Jan. 8 ***Perf. 12½x14***

364	A69	10f ultra, brn & blk	25	15

Arab Labor Ministers' Conference.

Tanker A70

1965, Jan. 30 ***Perf. 14***

365	A70	10f multicolored	25	15

Inauguration (in 1962) of the deep sea terminal for oil tankers.

Demand, as well as supply, determines a stamp's market value. One is as important as the other.

Soldier with Flag and Rifle — A71

Tree Week — A72

1965, Feb. 8 Litho. *Perf. 13½*
366 A71 10f multicolored 25 15

Revolution of Ramadan 14, 2nd anniv.

1965, Mar. 6 Unwmk. *Perf. 13*
367 A72 6f multicolored 15 15
368 A72 20f multicolored 75 15
Set value 20

Federation Emblem A73

Dagger in Map of Palestine A74

1965, Mar. 24 Unwmk. *Perf. 14*
369 A73 3f lt bl, vio bl & gold 15 15
370 A73 10f gray, black & gold 15 15
371 A73 30f rose, car & gold 30 30
Set value 41 41

Arab Federation of Insurance.

1965, Apr. 9 Litho. *Perf. 14x12½*
372 A74 10f gray & black 15 15
373 A74 20f lt brn & dk blue 25 15
Set value 18

Deir Yassin massacre, Apr. 9, 1948.

Smallpox Attacking People — A75

1965, Apr. 30 Litho. *Perf. 14*
374 A75 3f multicolored 15 15
375 A75 10f multicolored 22 15
376 A75 20f multicolored 65 25

WHO's fight against smallpox. Exist imperf. Value $2.

ITU Emblem, Old and New Telecommunication Equipment — A76

1965, May 17 *Perf. 14, Imperf.*
377 A76 10f multicolored 30 18
378 A76 20f multicolored 75 15
a. Souv. sheet of 2, #377-378 5.00 5.75

ITU, centenary. No. 378a sold for 40 and exists imperf.

Map of Arab Countries and Banner — A77

1965, May 26 Litho. *Perf. 14x12½*
379 A77 10f multicolored 25 15

Anniversary of the treaty with the UAR.

Library Aflame and Lamp A78

1965, June Photo. *Perf. 11*
380 A78 5f black, grn & red 25 15
381 A78 10f blk, green & red 40 15
Set value 15

Burning of the Library of Algiers, June 2, 1962.

Revolutionist with Torch, Cannon and Flames — A79

1965, June 30 Litho. *Perf. 13*
382 A79 5f multicolored 15 15
383 A79 10f multicolored 20 15
Set value 15

45th anniversary, Revolution of 1920.

Mosque — A80

1965, July 12 Photo. *Perf. 12*
384 A80 10f multicolored 25 15

Prophet Mohammed's birthday. A souvenir sheet contains one imperf. stamp similar to No. 384. Sold for 50f. Value $5

Factories and Grain — A81

Arab Fair Emblem — A82

1965, July 14 Litho. *Perf. 13*
385 A81 10f multicolored 15 15

7th anniv. of the July 14, 1958 Revolution.

1965, Oct. 22 Unwmk. *Perf. 13*
386 A82 10f multicolored 15 15

Second Arab Fair, Baghdad.

Pres. Abdul Salam Mohammed Arif — A83

1965, Nov. 18 Photo. *Perf. 11½*
Granite Paper
387 A83 5f org, buff & dk blue 22 15
388 A83 10f lt ultra, gray & dk brn 30 15
389 A83 50f lil, pale pink & sl blk 1.40 60

Revolution of Nov. 18, 1963, 2nd anniv.

Census Chart and Adding Machine — A84

1965, Nov. 29 Litho. *Perf. 13*
390 A84 3f gray & plum 28 15
391 A84 5f brown red & brn 35 15
392 A84 15f olive bis & dl bl 70 15
Set value 24

Issued to publicize the 1965 census.

Date Palms A85

Soldiers' Monument A86

1965, Dec. 27 Litho. *Perf. 13½x14*
393 A85 3f olive bis & multi 16 15
394 A85 10f car rose & multi 32 20
395 A85 15f blue & multi 80 30

2nd FAO Intl. Dates Conference, Baghdad, Dec. 1965.
For surcharges, see Nos. 694, 695.

1966, Jan. 6 Photo. *Perf. 12*
396 A86 2f car rose & multi 15 15
397 A86 5f multicolored 20 15
398 A86 40f yel grn & multi 1.10 75
Set value 85

Issued for Army Day.

Eagle and Flag of Iraq — A87

Perf. 12½
1966, Feb. 8 Photo. Unwmk.
399 A87 5f dl bl & multi 20 15
400 A87 10f orange & multi 40 15
Set value 15

3rd anniv. of the Revolution of Ramadan 14, which overthrew the Kassem government.

Arab League Emblem — A88

Soccer Players — A89

1966, Mar. 22 *Perf. 11x11½*
401 A88 5f org, brn & brt grn 15 15
402 A88 15f ol, rose lil & ultra 40 15

Arab Publicity Week.

1966, Apr. 1 *Perf. 12*

Designs: 5f, Player and goal post. 15f, As 2f. 50f, Legs of player, ball and emblem (horiz.).

403 A89 2f multicolored 28 15
404 A89 5f multicolored 15 15
405 A89 15f multicolored 90 45

Miniature Sheet
Imperf
406 A89 50f vio & multi 4.25 10.50

3rd Arab Soccer Cup, Baghdad, Apr. 1-10.

Steam Shovel Within Cogwheel A90

1966, May 1 Litho. *Perf. 13½*
407 A90 15f multicolored 15 15
408 A90 25f red, blk, & sil 25 15
Set value 18

Issued for Labor Day, May 1, 1966.

Queen Nefertari — A91

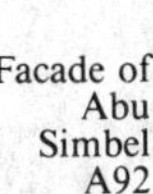

Facade of Abu Simbel A92

Perf. 12½x13, 13½

1966, May 20 **Litho.**

409	A91	5f olive, yel & blk	15	15
410	A91	15f blue, yel & brn	18	15
411	A92	40f bis brn, red & blk	1.25	1.00

UNESCO world campaign to save historic monuments in Nubia.

President Arif and Flag — A93

1966, July 14 **Photo.** ***Perf. 11½***

412	A93	5f multicolored	15	15
413	A93	15f multicolored	25	15
414	A93	50f multicolored	75	25
		Set value		42

8th anniv. of the July 14, 1958 revolution.

A94

1966, July 22 **Litho.** ***Perf. 12***
Multicolored Vignette

415	A94	5f lt olive green	15	15
416	A94	15f lt greenish blue	15	15
417	A94	30f lt yellow green	25	18
		Set value	40	30

Mohammed's 1,396th birthday.

Iraqi Museum, Baghdad A95

Designs: 50f, Golden headdress, Ur. 80f, Carved Sumerian head (vert.).

1966, Nov. 9 **Litho.** ***Perf. 14***

418	A95	15f multicolored	22	15
419	A95	50f lt bl, blk, gold & pink	90	50
420	A95	80f crim, blk, bl & gold	2.25	75

Opening of New Iraqi Museum, Baghdad.

UNESCO Emblem — A96

Iraqi Citizens — A97

1966, Dec. ***Perf. 13½***

421	A96	5f blue, black & tan	15	15
422	A96	15f brt org brn, blk & gray	15	15
		Set value	15	15

20th anniv. of UNESCO.

1966, Nov. 18 ***Perf. 13½x13***

423	A97	15f multicolored	40	35
424	A97	25f multicolored	65	85

3rd anniv. of the Revolution of Nov. 18, 1963.

Rocket Launchers and Soldier A98

1967, Jan. 6 **Photo.** ***Perf. 11½***

425	A98	15f cit, dk brn & dp bis	20	15
426	A98	20f brt lil, dk brn & dp bis	40	20

Issued for Army Day, Jan. 6.

Oil Derrick, Pipeline, Emblem — A99

Design: 15f, 50f, Refinery and emblem (horiz.).

1967, Mar. 6 **Litho.** ***Perf. 14***

427	A99	5f ol grn, pale yel & blk	15	15
428	A99	15f multicolored	15	15
429	A99	40f vio, yel & blk	20	16
430	A99	50f multicolored	40	30
		Set value	75	58

6th Arab Petroleum Congress, Baghdad, Mar. 1967.

New Year's Emblem and Spider's Web A100

1967, Apr. 11 **Litho.** ***Perf. 13½***

431	A100	5f multicolored	15	15
432	A100	15f multicolored	15	15
		Set value	15	15

Issued for the Hajeer Year (New Year)

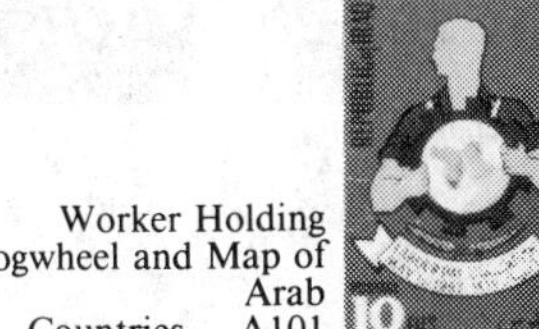
Worker Holding Cogwheel and Map of Arab Countries — A101

1967, May 1 ***Perf. 12½x13***

433	A101	10f gray & multi	15	15
434	A101	15f lt ultra & multi	15	15
		Set value	16	15

Issued for Labor Day.

A102

1967, June 20 **Litho.** ***Perf. 14***

435	A102	5f multicolored	15	15
436	A102	15f blue & multi	25	15
		Set value		15

Mohammed's 1,397th birthday.

Flag, Hands with Clubs — A103

1967, July 7 ***Perf. 13x13½***

437	A103	5f multicolored	15	15
438	A103	15f multicolored	15	15
		Set value	15	15

47th anniversary of Revolution of 1920.

Um Qasr Harbor A104

Designs: 10f, 15f, Freighter loading in Um Qasr harbor.

1967, July 14 **Litho.** ***Perf. 14x13½***

439	A104	5f multicolored	15	15
440	A104	10f multicolored	15	15
441	A104	15f multicolored	45	15
442	A104	40f multicolored	1.65	18
		Set value		36

9th anniv. of the July 14, 1958 revolution and the inauguration of the port of Um Qasr.

Iraqi Man — A105

President Arif — A106

Iraqi Costumes: 5f, 15f, 25f, Women's costumes. 10f, 20f, 30f, Men's costumes.

1967, Nov. 10 **Litho.** ***Perf. 13***

443	A105	2f pale brn & multi	15	15
444	A105	5f ver & multi	15	15
445	A105	10f multicolored	20	15
446	A105	15f ultra & multi	26	15
447	A105	20f lilac & multi	52	18
448	A105	25f lemon & multi	52	20
449	A105	30f fawn & multi	52	26
		Nos. 443-449,C19-C21 (10)	6.07	
		Set value		2.00

For overprints, see Nos. 597-599, RA17.

Perf. 11x11½, 11½x11

1967, Nov. 18

Design: 15f, Pres. Arif and map of Iraq (horiz.).

450	A106	5f bl, vio blk & yel	15	15
451	A106	15f rose & multi	50	25

4th anniversary of Nov. 18th revolution.

Ziggurat of Ur — A107

Designs: 5f, Gate with Nimrod statues. 10f, Gate, Babylon. 15f, Minaret of Mosul (vert.). 25f, Arch and ruins of Ctesiphon.

1967, Dec. 1 **Litho.** ***Perf. 13***

452	A107	2f orange & multi	15	15
453	A107	5f lilac & multi	15	15
454	A107	10f orange & multi	15	15
455	A107	15f rose red & multi	28	15
456	A107	25f vio bl & multi	40	15
		Nos. 452-456,C22-C26 (10)	32.58	15.87

International Tourist Year.
For overprints, see Nos. 593, 680, RA18.

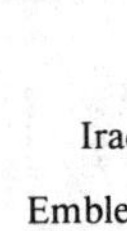

Iraqi Girl Scout Emblem and Sign — A108

Designs: 5f, Girl Scouts at campfire and Girl Scout emblem. 10f, Boy Scout emblem and Boy Scout sign. 15f, Boy Scouts pitching tent and Boy Scout sign.

1967, Dec. 15

457	A108	2f orange & multi	85	20
458	A108	5f blue & multi	1.00	25
459	A108	10f green & multi	1.10	40
460	A108	15f blue & multi	1.10	50
a.		Souv. sheet of 4	5.50	5.50

Issued to honor the Scout movement.
No. 460a contains 4 stamps similar to Nos. 457-460 with simulated perforations. Sold for 50f.
For overprint, see No. RA19.

Soldiers on Maneuvers A109

1968, Jan. 6 **Photo.** ***Perf. 11½***

461	A109	5f lt bl, brn & brt grn	15	15
462	A109	15f lt bl, ind & olive	40	15
		Set value		15

Issued for Army Day 1968.

White-cheeked Bulbul — A110

Birds: 10f, Hoopoe. 15f, Eurasian jay. 25f, Peregrine falcon. 30f, White stork. 40f, Black partridge. 50f, Marbled teal.

1968, Jan. **Litho.** ***Perf. 14***

463	A110	5f org & black	20	15
464	A110	10f blue, blk & brn	25	15
465	A110	15f pink & multi	50	20

466 A110 25f dl org & multi 60 40
467 A110 30f emer, blk & brn 65 20
468 A110 40f rose lil & multi 1.90 20
469 A110 50f multicolored 2.00 45
Nos. 463-469 (7) 6.10 1.75

Fighting Soldiers A111

1968, Feb. 8 ***Perf. 11½***
470 A111 15f blk, org & brt bl 1.90 20

Revolution of Ramadan 14, 5th anniv.

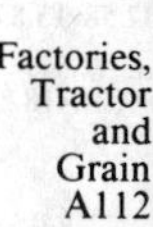

Factories, Tractor and Grain A112

1968, May 1 **Litho.** ***Perf. 13***
471 A112 15f lt bl & multi 15 15
472 A112 25f multicolored 25 15
Set value 18

Issued for Labor Day.

Soccer A113

Designs: 5f, 25f, Goalkeeper holding ball (vert.).

1968, June 14 ***Perf. 13½***
473 A113 2f multicolored 15 15
474 A113 5f multicolored 15 15
475 A113 15f multicolored 22 15
476 A113 25f multicolored 1.50 50
a. Souv. sheet, 70f, imperf. 5.00 8.50
Set value 75

23rd C.I.S.M. (Conseil Internationale du Sports Militaire) Soccer Championships.

No. 476a shows badge of Military Soccer League.

Soldier, Flag, Chain and Rising Sun – A114

1968, July 14 **Photo.** ***Perf. 13½x14***
478 A114 15f multicolored 25 15

10th anniv. of the July 14, 1958 revolution.

World Health Organization Emblem – A115

Design: 5f, 10f, Staff of Aesculapius over emblem (vert.).

1968, Nov. 29 **Litho.** ***Perf. 13½***
479 A115 5f multicolored 15 15
480 A115 10f multicolored 15 15
481 A115 15f blue, red & black 25 15
482 A115 25f yel grn, red & blk 50 15
Set value 30

WHO, 20th anniv. Exist imperf.

Human Rights Flame – A116

Mother and Children – A117

1968, Dec. 22 **Litho.** ***Perf. 13½***
483 A116 10f lt bl, yel & car 15 15
484 A116 25f lt yel grn, yel & car 25 15
a. Souv. sheet, 100f, imperf. 3.00 3.00
Set value 17

International Human Rights Year.

1968, Dec. 31 **Litho.** ***Perf. 13½***
485 A117 15f multi 25 15
486 A117 25f bl & multi 75 15
a. Souv. sheet, 100f, imperf. 5.00 3.25
Set value 23

UNICEF. For overprints, see Nos. 624-625.

Tanks A118

1969, Jan. 6 **Photo.**
487 A118 25f vio, car & brn 2.00 1.00

Issued for Army Day, Jan. 6.

Harvester A119

1969, Feb. **Photo.** ***Perf. 13½***
488 A119 15f yel brn & multi 22 15

6th anniv. of the Revolution of Ramadan 14.

Mosque A119a

1969, Mar. 19 **Photo.** ***Perf. 13x13½***
488A A119a 15f multicolored 15 15

Issued for Hajeer (pilgrimage) Year.

Emblem A120

1969, Apr. 12 **Litho.** ***Perf. 12½x12***
489 A120 10f yel grn & multi 40 15
490 A120 15f orange & multi 60 15

1st conference of the Arab Veterinary Union, Baghdad, Apr. 1969.

Barbus Grypus A121

Fish: 3f, Barbus puntius sharpeyi. 10f, Pampus argenteus. 100f, Barbus esocinus.

1969, May 9 ***Perf. 14***
491 A121 2f multicolored 85 15
492 A121 3f multicolored 85 15
493 A121 10f multicolored 1.00 15
494 A121 100f multicolored 3.25 2.00

Holy Kaaba, Mecca A122

1969, May 28 **Photo.** ***Perf. 12***
495 A122 15f blue & multi 15 15

Mohammed's 1,399th birthday.

ILO Emblem A123

1969, June 6 **Litho.** ***Perf. 13x12½***
496 A123 5f lt vio, yel & blk 15 15
497 A123 15f grnsh gray, yel & black 20 15
498 A123 50f rose, yel & blk 70 50
a. Souv. sheet, 100f, imperf. 3.00 5.00

ILO, 50th anniv.

Weight Lifting A124

Coat of Arms, Symbols of Industry A125

Design: 5f, 35f, High jump.

1969, June 20 ***Perf. 13½x13***
500 A124 3f org yel & multi 15 15
501 A124 5f blue & multi 15 15
502 A124 10f rose pink & multi 20 15

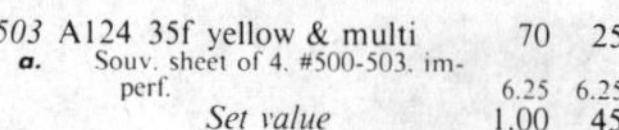

503 A124 35f yellow & multi 70 25
a. Souv. sheet of 4, #500-503, imperf. 6.25 6.25
Set value 1.00 45

19th Olympic Games, Mexico City, Oct. 12-27, 1968. No. 503a sold for 100f.

1969, July 14 **Photo.** ***Perf. 13***
504 A125 10f brn org & multi 20 15
505 A125 15f multicolored 30 15
Set value 15

11th anniv. of the July 14, 1958 revolution.

Street Fighting A126

Pres. Ahmed Hassan al-Bakr A127

Wheat and Fair Emblem A128

Design: 20f, Baghdad International Airport.

1969, July 17 ***Perf. 13½***
506 A126 10f yel & multi 28 15
507 A126 15f blue & multi 28 15
508 A126 20f blue & multi 90 25
509 A127 200f gold & multi 9.00 5.00

1st anniv. of the coup of July 17, 1968. No. 508 also commemorates the inauguration of Baghdad Intl. Airport.

1969, Oct. 1 **Photo.** ***Perf. 13½***
510 A128 10f brt grn, gold & dl red 15 15
511 A128 15f ultra, gold & red 15 15
Set value 20 15

6th International Fair, Baghdad. For overprints, see Nos. 567A-567B.

Motor Ship Al-Waleed A129

Designs: 15f, Floating crane Antara. 30f, Pilot ship Al-Rasheed. 35f, Suction dredge Hillah. 50f, Survey ship Al-Fao.

1969, Oct. 8 **Litho.** ***Perf. 12½***
512 A129 15f black & multi 24 18
513 A129 20f black & multi 28 24
514 A129 30f black & multi 48 28
515 A129 35f black & multi 95 55
516 A129 50f black & multi 2.75 1.40
Nos. 512-516 (5) 4.70 2.65

50th anniversary of Basrah Harbor.

Radio Tower and Map of Palestine A130

"Search for Knowledge" A131

1969, Nov. 9 Litho. *Perf. 12½x13*
517 A130 15f multicolored 60 16
518 A130 50f multicolored 1.65 40

10th anniversary of Iraqi News Agency.
For overprints, see Nos. 698-699.

1969, Nov. 21 Photo. *Perf. 13*
519 A131 15f blue & multi 15 15
520 A131 20f green & multi 20 15
Set value 18

Campaign against illiteracy.

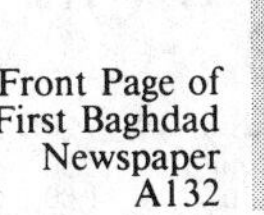

Front Page of First Baghdad Newspaper A132

1969, Dec. 26 Litho. *Perf. 13½*
521 A132 15f yel, org & black 50 30

Centenary of the Iraqi press.
For overprint, see No. 552.

Soldier, Map of Iraq and Plane — A133

1970, Jan. 6 Photo. *Perf. 13*
522 A133 15f lt vio & multi 40 15
523 A133 20f yellow & multi 80 30

Issued for Army Day 1970.

Soldier, Farmer and Worker Shoring up Wall in Iraqi Colors A134

Poppies A135

1970, Feb. 8 Photo. *Perf. 13*
524 A134 10f multicolored 25 15
525 A134 15f brick red & multi 50 25

7th anniv. of the Revolution of Ramadan 14.

1970, June 12 Litho. *Perf. 13*

Flowers: 3f, Poet's narcissus. 5f, Tulip. 10f, 50f, Carnations. 15f, Rose.

526 A135 2f emer & multi 15 15
527 A135 3f blue & multi 15 15
528 A135 5f multicolored 15 15
529 A135 10f lt grn & multi 15 15
530 A135 15f pale sal & multi 75 15
531 A135 50f lt grn & multi 1.50 75
Nos. 526-531 (6) 2.85
Set value 1.00

The overprinted sets Nos. 532-543 were released before Nos. 526-531.
For overprints, see Nos. 621-623, RA20. For surcharge, see No. 726.

Nos. 526-531 Overprinted in Ultramarine
عيد نوروز
1970

1970, Mar. 21
532 A135 2f emer & multi 15 15
533 A135 3f lt bl & multi 15 15
534 A135 5f multicolored 15 15
535 A135 10f lt grn & multi 40 15
536 A135 15f pale sal & multi 80 15
537 A135 50f lt grn & multi 3.25 1.50
Nos. 532-537 (6) 4.90
Set value 1.80

Issued for Novrooz (New Year).

Nos. 526-531 Overprinted in Black
مهرجان الربيع
الموصل
1970

1970, Apr. 18
538 A135 2f emer & multi 15 15
539 A135 3f lt bl & multi 15 15
540 A135 5f multicolored 15 15
541 A135 10f lt grn & multi 25 15
542 A135 15f pale sal & multi 45 15
543 A135 50f lt grn & multi 2.25 75
Nos. 538-543 (6) 3.40
Set value 1.00

Issued for the Spring Festival, Mosul.

Map of Arab Countries, Slogans — A136

Design: 35f, like 15f. 50f, 150f, People, flag, sun and map of Iraq.

1970, Apr. 7 *Perf. 13x12½*
544 A136 15f gold & multi 15 15
545 A136 35f sil & multi 25 20
546 A136 50f red & multi 50 30
a. Souv. sheet, 150f, imperf. 3.00 3.00

23rd anniversary of Al-Baath Party.

Workers and Cogwheel A137

1970, May 1
547 A137 10f silver & multi 20 15
548 A137 15f silver & multi 24 15
549 A137 35f silver & multi 80 40

Issued for Labor Day.

Kaaba, Mecca, and Koran A138

1970, May 17 Photo. *Perf. 13*
550 A138 15f brt bl & multi 15 15
551 A138 20f orange & multi 15 15
Set value 18

Mohammed's 1,400th birthday.

No. 521 Overprinted "1970" and Arabic Inscription in Prussian Blue

1970, June 15 Litho. *Perf. 13½*
552 A132 15f yel, org & black 20 20

Day of Iraqi press.

Revolutionists and Guns — A139

Designs: 35f, Revolutionist and rising sun.

1970, June 30 Litho. *Perf. 13*
553 A139 10f blk & apple grn 15 15
554 A139 15f black & gold 15 15
555 A139 35f blk & red org 50 20
a. Souv. sheet, 100f, imperf. 2.25 2.25
Set value 66 32

50th anniversary, Revolution of 1920.

Broken Chain and New Dawn — A140

1970, July 14 *Perf. 13x13½*
557 A140 15f vio bl, org, yel & gold 15 15
558 A140 20f emer, org, yel & gold 15 15
Set value 17

12th anniv. of the July 14, 1958 revolution.

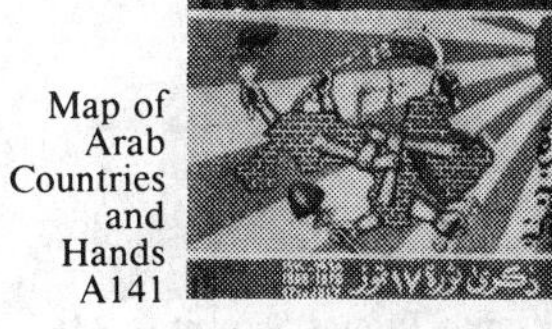
Map of Arab Countries and Hands A141

1970, July 17 *Perf. 13*
559 A141 15f gold & multi 15 15
560 A141 25f gold & multi 20 15
Set value 22

2nd anniversary of coup of July 17, 1968.

Pomegranates A142

1970, Aug. 21 *Perf. 14*
561 A142 3f shown 15 15
562 A142 5f Grapefruit 15 15
563 A142 10f Grapes 15 15
564 A142 15f Oranges 45 15
565 A142 35f Dates 90 30
Nos. 561-565 (5) 1.80
Set value 50

The Latin inscriptions on the 5f and 10f have been erroneously transposed.
For overprints, see Nos. 613-615. For surcharge, see No. 725.

Kaaba, Mecca, Moon over Mountain and Spider Web — A143

1970, Sept. 4 Photo. *Perf. 13*
566 A143 15f blk, grn, gold & brn 15 15
567 A143 25f blk, vio bl, gold & brn 20 15
Set value 22

Issued for Hajeer (Pilgrimage) Year.

Nos. 510-511 Overprinted in Red
الثورة السابعة
970 - ٩٧٠

1970, Sept. Photo. *Perf. 13½*
567A A128 10f multi 1.10 1.10
567B A128 15f multi 1.65 2.00

7th International Fair, Baghdad.

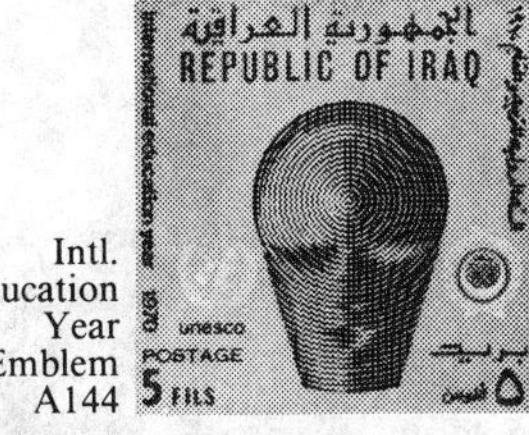
Intl. Education Year Emblem A144

1970, Nov. 13 Photo. *Perf. 13*
568 A144 5f yel green & multi 15 15
569 A144 15f brick red & multi 15 15
Set value 20 15

Flag and Map of Arab League Countries A145

1970 *Perf. 11*
570 A145 15f olive & multi 15 15
571 A145 35f gray & multi 25 20
Set value 27

25th anniversary of the Arab League.

Baghdad Hospital and Emblem A146

1970, Dec. 7 Litho. *Perf. 12*
572 A146 15f yellow & multi 15 15
573 A146 40f lt green & multi 50 25
Set value 32

Iraqi Medical Society, 50th anniv.

Sugar Beet — A147

Designs: 15f, Sugar factory (horiz.). 30f, like 5f.

Perf. 13x13½, 13½x13
1970, Dec. 25 Photo.
574 A147 5f ocher, grn & blk 15 15
575 A147 15f black & multi 15 15
576 A147 30f org ver, grn & blk 18 15
Set value 32 27

Publicity for Mosul sugar factory.

OPEC Emblem A148

1970, Dec. 30 Litho. *Perf. 13x13½*

577 A148 10f rose cl, bis & bl	40	20
578 A148 40f emer, bis & blue	1.65	70

OPEC, 10th anniversary.

Soldiers — A149

Soldiers, Maps of Arab Countries and Israel A150

Perf. 13½x14, 11½x12½

1971, Jan. 6

579 A149 15f blk, brt pink & gold	30	15
580 A150 40f red org & multi	1.75	50
a. Souvenir sheet of 2, #579-580, imperf.	4.00	6.25

Army Day, 50th anniversary. No. 580a sold for 100f.

Marchers and Map of Arab Countries A151

1971, Feb. 8 Litho. *Perf. 11½x12½*

581 A151 15f yellow & multi	25	15
582 A151 40f pink & multi	75	30

Revolution of Ramadan 14, 8th anniversary.

Spider Web, Pilgrims A152

1971, Feb. 26 Photo. *Perf. 13*

583 A152 10f pink & multi	15	15
584 A152 15f buff & multi	15	15
Set value		15

Hajeer (New) Year.

President al-Bakr A153

1971, Mar. 11 Litho. *Perf. 14*

585 A153 15f orange & multi	50	15
586 A153 100f emer & multi	2.75	85

First anniversary of Mar. 11th Manifesto.

Marshland A154

Tourist Publicity: 10f, Stork flying over Baghdad. 15f, "Summer Resorts." 100f, Return of Sindbad the Sailor.

1971, Mar. 15 *Perf. 13*

587 A154 5f multicolored	24	15
588 A154 10f lt grn & multi	32	15
589 A154 15f pink & multi	70	50
590 A154 100f multicolored	4.75	3.00

Blacksmith Taming Serpent — A155

1971, Mar. 21 *Perf. 11½x12*

591 A155 15f multicolored	48	15
592 A155 25f yel & multi	1.00	40

Novrooz Festival.

No. 455 Overprinted يوم الأنواء W.M. DAY 1971

1971, Mar. 23 Litho. *Perf. 13*

593 A107 15f rose red & multi	3.75	2.50

World Meteorological Day. See No. C39.

Workers, Soldier, Map of Arab Countries A156

1971, Apr. 7

594 A156 15f yel & multi	60	15
595 A156 35f multicolored	1.10	45
596 A156 250f multicolored	9.00	5.50

24th anniv. of the Al Baath Party. No. 596 has circular perforation around vignette set within a white square of paper, perforated on 4 sides. The design of No. 596 is similar to Nos. 594-595, but with denomination within the circle and no inscriptions in margin.

Nos. 443-444, 448 Overprinted مهرجان الربيع 1971

1971, Apr. 14

597 A105 2f pale brn & multi	45	15
598 A105 5f ver & multi	45	15
599 A105 25f lemon & multi	1.75	1.00

Mosul Festival.

Worker, Farm Woman with Torch A157

1971, May 1 Litho. *Perf. 13*

600 A157 15f ocher & multi	15	15
601 A157 40f olive & multi	75	20
Set value		27

Labor Day.

Muslim Praying in Mecca A158

1971, May 7

602 A158 15f yellow & multi	22	15
603 A158 100f pink & multi	2.75	1.00

Mohammed's 1,401st birthday.

People, Fists, Map of Iraq A159

1971, July 14 Photo. *Perf. 14*

604 A159 25f green & multi	20	15
605 A159 50f lt bl & multi	40	25

13th anniv. of the July 14, 1958 revolution.

Surveyor, Preacher, Rising Sun A160

1971, July 17 *Perf. 13*

606 A160 25f multicolored	25	15
607 A160 70f orange & multi	75	45

3rd anniversary of July 17, 1968, coup.

Rafidain Bank Emblem A161

1971, Sept. 24 Photo. *Perf. 13½*

Diameter: 27mm

608 A161 10f org, green & multi	40	80
609 A161 15f multicolored	80	80
610 A161 25f multicolored	1.50	2.50

Diameter: 32mm

611 A161 65f multicolored	8.00	4.00
612 A161 250f multicolored	20.00	12.00
Nos. 608-612 (5)	30.70	20.10

30th anniversary of Rafidain Bank. Nos. 608-612 have circular perforation around design within a white square of paper, perforated on 4 sides.

Nos. 561, 564-565 Overprinted التعداد الزراعي العام ١٩٧١/١٠/١٥

1971, Oct. 15 Litho. *Perf. 14*

613 A142 3f bl grn & multi	30	15
614 A142 15f red & multi	1.00	50
615 A142 35f orange & multi	2.00	75

Agricultural census, Oct. 15, 1971.

Soccer A162

Designs: 25f, Track and field. 35f, Table tennis. 75f, Gymnastics. 95f, Volleyball and basketball.

1971, Nov. 17 Litho. *Perf. 13½*

616 A162 15f green & multi	28	15
617 A162 25f pink & multi	50	30
618 A162 35f lt bl & multi	75	70
619 A162 70f lt grn & multi	3.25	1.00
620 A162 95f yel grn & multi	5.25	2.00
a. Souvenir sheet of 5	11.00	5.50
Nos. 616-620 (5)	10.03	4.15

4th Pan-Arab Schoolboys Sports Games, Baghdad. No. 620a contains 5 stamps similar to Nos. 616-620 with simulated perforations. Sold for 200f.

Nos. 527-528, 530 Overprinted and Surcharged 70 Fils  يوم الطالب ٢٣ تشرين الثاني ٩٦١ – ٩٧١ ٧٠ فلسا

1971, Nov. 23 Litho. *Perf. 13*

621 A135 15f multicolored	80	25
622 A135 25f on 5f multi	1.50	75
623 A135 70f on 3f multi	5.50	2.00

Students' Day. The 15f has only first 3 lines of Arabic overprint.

Nos. 485-486 Overprinted 25th Anniversary 971

1971, Dec. 11 Litho. *Perf. 13½*

624 A117 15f multicolored	2.00	75
625 A117 25f blue & multi	4.75	2.00

25th anniv. of UNICEF.

Children Crossing Street A162a

1971, Dec. 17 Litho. *Perf. 13x12½*

625A A162a 15f yel & multi	1.00	50
625B A162a 25f brt rose & multi	2.00	1.00

2nd Traffic Week. For overprints, see Nos. 668-669.

Arab Postal Union Emblem A163

1971, Dec. 24 Photo. *Perf. 11 1/2*

626	A163 25f emer, yel & brn	30	15
627	A163 70f vio bl, yel & red	1.10	45

25th anniv. of the Conf. of Sofar, Lebanon, establishing Arab Postal Union.

Racial Equality Emblem — A164

1971, Dec. 31 *Perf. 13 1/2x14*

628	A164 25f brt grn & multi	25	15
629	A164 70f orange & multi	65	35

Intl. Year Against Racial Discrimination.

Soldiers with Flag and Torch — A165 Workers — A166

1972, Jan. 6 Photo. *Perf. 14x13 1/2*

630	A165 25f blue & multi	70	40
631	A165 70f brt grn & multi	2.75	1.50

Army Day, Jan. 6.

1972, Feb. 8

632	A166 25f brt grn & multi	80	40
633	A166 95f lilac & multi	5.75	1.50

Revolution of Ramadan 14, 9th anniv.

Mosque, Minaret, Crescent and Caravan A167

1972, Feb. 26 Litho. *Perf. 12 1/2x13*

634	A167 25f bl grn & multi	25	15
635	A167 35f purple & multi	35	18

Hajeer (Pilgrimage) Year.

Peace Symbols and "11" — A168

1972, Mar. 11 Photo. *Perf. 11x12 1/2*

636	A168 25f lt blue & blk	85	25
637	A168 70f brt lil & blk	2.50	75

2nd anniversary of Mar. 11 Manifesto.

Mountain Range and Flowers — A169

1972, Mar. 21 *Perf. 11 1/2x11*

638	A169 25f vio blue & multi	90	20
639	A169 70f vio blue & multi	2.75	1.00

Novrooz, New Year Festival.

Party Emblem A170

Symbolic Design — A171

Perf. 14 (A170), 13 (A171)

1972 Litho.

640	A170 10f brn org & multi	15	15
641	A171 25f bister & multi	24	25
642	A170 35f brn org & multi	40	50
643	A171 70f red & multi	2.50	75

25th anniv. of the Iraqi Arab Baath Socialist Party.

Issue dates: 25f, 70f, Mar. 23; 10f, 35f, Apr. 7.

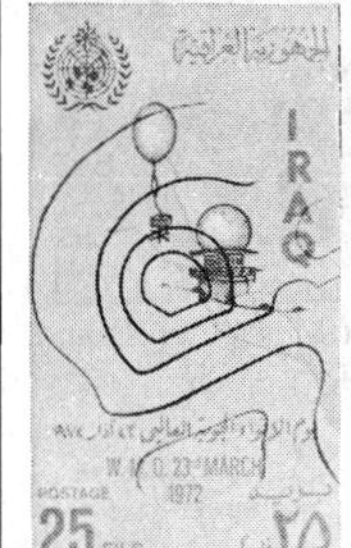
Emblem, Map, Weather Balloons and Chart — A172

Cogwheel and Ship — A173

1972, Mar. 23 Photo. *Perf. 14x13 1/2*

644	A172 25f multicolored	65	15
645	A172 35f yel & multi	95	25

12th World Meteorological Day.

1972, Mar. 25 *Perf. 11x11 1/2*

646	A173 25f ocher & multi	25	15
647	A173 35f pink & multi	40	15

Arab Chamber of Commerce.

Derrick and Flame A174

Quill Pens, Map of Arab Countries A175

1972, Apr. 7 *Perf. 13x13 1/2*

648	A174 25f multicolored	50	25
649	A174 35f multicolored	75	30

Opening of North Rumaila (INOC, North Iraq Oil Fields).

1972, Apr. 17 Photo. *Perf. 11x11 1/2*

650	A175 25f orange & multi	30	15
651	A175 35f blue & multi	55	18

3rd Congress of Arab Journalists.

Women's Federation Emblem A176

1972, Apr. 22 Litho. *Perf. 13 1/2*

652	A176 25f green & multi	30	15
653	A176 35f lilac & multi	55	18

Iraqi Women's Federation, 4th anniversary.

Hand Holding Globe-shaped Wrench — A177

1972, May 1 Photo. *Perf. 11 1/2*

654	A177 25f yel grn & multi	30	15
655	A177 35f orange & multi	55	18

Labor Day.

Kaaba, Mecca, and Crescent — A178

1972, May 26

656	A178 25f green & multi	30	15
657	A178 35f purple & multi	55	18

Mohammed's 1,402nd birthday.

Soldier, Civilian and Guns — A179

1972, July 14 Photo. *Perf. 13 1/2x14*

658	A179 35f multicolored	60	25
659	A179 70f lil & multi	1.90	75

14th anniv. of July 14, 1958, revolution.

Dome of the Rock, Arab Countries' Map, Fists — A180

1972, July 17 *Perf. 13*

660	A180 25f citron & multi	60	15
661	A180 95f blue & multi	1.90	75

4th anniv. of July 17, 1968 coup.

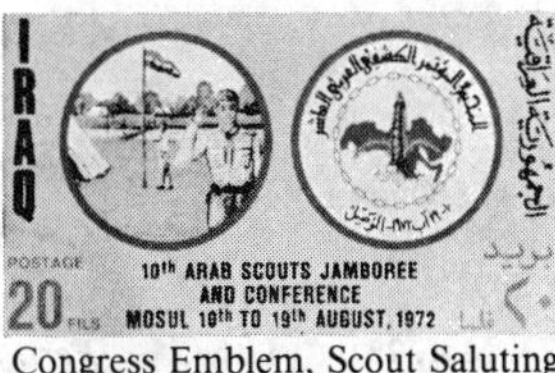
Congress Emblem, Scout Saluting Iraqi Flag — A182

1972, Aug. 12 Photo. *Perf. 13 1/2x14*

664	A182 20f multicolored	1.00	55
665	A182 25f lilac & multi	2.00	80

10th Arab Boy Scouts Jamboree and Conference, Mosul, Aug. 10-19.

1972, Aug. 24

Design: Congress emblem and Girl Guide in camp.

666	A182 10f yellow & multi	1.00	45
667	A182 45f multicolored	3.00	90

4th Arab Guides Camp and Conference, Mosul, Aug. 24-30.

No. 625A Overprinted and Surcharged, No. 625B Overprinted with New Date:

1972 ١٩٧٢

●● 70 Fils ٧٠ ●●

1972, Oct. 4 Photo. *Perf. 13x12 1/2*

668	A162a 25f brt rose & multi	3.75	1.75
669	A162a 70f on 15f multi	5.00	4.50

Third Traffic Week.

Central Bank of Iraq — A183

1972, Nov. 16 Photo. *Perf. 13*

670 A183 25f lt blue & multi 35 30
671 A183 70f lt green & multi 1.00 70

25th anniversary, Central Bank of Iraq.

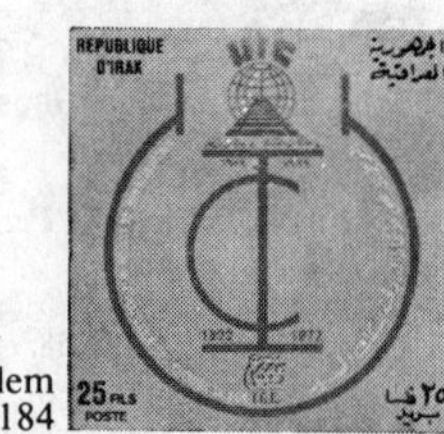

UIC Emblem A184

1972, Dec. 29

672 A184 25f dp rose & multi 65 20
673 A184 45f brt vio & multi 1.40 50

50th anniv., Intl. Railroad Union (UIC).

Nos. 148-149, 151, 180 and Type of 1957-58 Overprinted with 3 Bars

1973, Jan. 29 Engr. *Perf. 11½x12*

674 A28 10f blue 40 20
675 A33 10f blue 40 20
676 A28 15f black 80 35
677 A33 15f black 80 35
678 A28 25f rose violet 1.50 50
679 A33 25f rose violet 1.50 50
Nos. 674-679 (6) 5.40 2.10

The size and position of the bottom bar of overprint differs; the bar can be same size as 2 top bars, short and centered or moved to the right.

No. 455 Overprinted المؤتمر الدولي للتاريخ/١٩٧٣

1973, Mar. 25 Litho. *Perf. 13*

680 A107 15f rose red & multi 6.00 2.50

Intl. History Cong. See Nos. C52-C53.

Workers and Oil Wells A185

Ram's-head Harp A186

1973, June 1 Litho. *Perf. 13*

681 A185 25f yel & multi 1.25 50
682 A185 70f rose & multi 5.50 2.00

1st anniv. of nationalization of oil industry.

1973, June Litho. *Perf. 13x12½*

Designs: 25f, 35f, 45f, Minaret, Mosul, 50f, 70f, 95f, Statue of goddess. 10f, 20f, like 5f.

683 A186 5f orange & blk 15 15
684 A186 10f bister & blk 15 15
685 A186 20f brt rose & blk 15 15
686 A186 25f ultra & blk 18 15
687 A186 35f emer & blk 25 18
688 A186 45f blue & black 32 23
689 A186 50f olive & yel 35 25
690 A186 70f violet & yel 50 36
691 A186 95f brown & yel 65 48
Nos. 683-691 (9) 2.70
Set value 1.82

For overprint, see No. RA21.

People with Flags, Grain A187

1973, July 14

692 A187 25f multicolored 20 25
693 A187 35f multicolored 40 30

July Festivals.

Nos. 393 and 395 Surcharged مهرجان النخيل وعيد التمور ١٩٧٢ 25 Fils ٢٥

1973 Litho. *Perf. 13½x14*

694 A85 25f on 3f multi 2.50 1.50
695 A85 70f on 15f multi 6.75 4.00

Festival of Date Trees.

INTERPOL Headquarters A188

1973, Sept. 20 Litho. *Perf. 12*

696 A188 25f multicolored 30 15
697 A188 70f brt bl & multi 65 35

50th anniv. of Intl. Criminal Police Org.

Nos. 517-518 Overprinted in Silver

I.O.J.
SEPTEMBER
26-29. 1973

1973, Sept. 29 Litho. *Perf. 12½x13*

698 A130 15f multicolored 3.50 1.00
699 A130 50f multicolored 6.00 3.00

Meeting of Intl. Org. of Journalists' Executive Committee, Sept. 26-29.

Flags and Fair Emblem A189

WMO Emblem A190

1973, Oct. 10 Photo. *Perf. 11*

700 A189 10f brt grn & dk brn 15 15
701 A189 20f ocher & multi 32 15
702 A189 65f blue & multi 80 55
Set value 74

10th International Baghdad Fair, Oct. 1-21.

1973, Nov. 15 Litho. *Perf. 12*

703 A190 25f org, blk & green 50 20
704 A190 35f brt rose, blk & grn 70 25

Intl. meteorological cooperation, cent.

Flags of Arab League and Iraq, Maghreb Emblem A191

1973, Dec. 1 Photo. *Perf. 14*

705 A191 20f dl org & multi 25 15
706 A191 35f blue & multi 35 18

11th session of Civil Aviation Council of Arab States, Baghdad, Dec. 1973.

المجلس التنفيذي

No. 360 Overprinted

بغداد/١٩٧٣

1973, Dec. 12 Photo. *Perf. 11*

707 A67a 30f orange & blue 3.00 2.25

6th Executive Council Meeting of APU.

Human Rights Flame — A192

1973, Dec. 25 *Perf. 11½*

708 A192 25f multicolored 20 15
709 A192 70f ultra & multi 60 35

25th anniversary of Universal Declaration of Human Rights.

Military College Crest and Cadets A193

1974, Jan. 6 *Perf. 12x11½*

710 A193 25f ocher & multi 20 15
711 A193 35f ultra & multi 28 18

50th anniversary of the Military College.

UPU and Arab Postal Union Emblems — A194

1974, May 28 Photo. *Perf. 11½x12*

712 A194 25f gold & multi 45 15
713 A194 35f gold & multi 45 30
714 A194 70f gold & multi 90 75

Centenary of the Universal Postal Union.

Symbols of Ancient Mesopotamia and Oil Industry — A195

1974, June 1 Litho. *Perf. 12½*

715 A195 10f blue & multi 15 15
716 A195 25f ocher & multi 28 25
717 A195 70f rose & multi 1.10 75

Nationalization of the oil industry, 2nd anniv.

Festival — A196

1974, July 17 *Perf. 11½x12*

718 A196 20f lilac & multi 20 15
719 A196 35f dull org & multi 35 18

July Festivals.

National Front Emblem and People A197

1974, July 17 *Perf. 12x11½*

720 A197 25f blue & multi 25 15
721 A197 70f brt grn & multi 65 36

1st anniv. of Progressive National Front.

Cement Plant and Brick Wall — A198

1974, Oct. 19 *Perf. 11½x12*

722 A198 20f gray bl & multi 22 15
723 A198 25f red & multi 28 15
724 A198 70f emerald & multi 90 55

25th anniversary of Iraqi Cement Plant.

Nos. 561 and 527 Surcharged

١٠ فلوس
10 Fils
a

٢٥ فلسا
25 Fils
b

1975, Jan. 9 Litho. *Perf. 13, 14*

725 A142 (a) 10f on 3f multi 2.50 1.50
726 A135 (b) 25f on 3f multi 7.75 5.00

Globe and WPY Emblem — A199

1975, Jan. 30 *Perf. 11½x12*

727	A199	25f dull bl & blk	35	15
728	A199	35f brt pink & ind	75	25
729	A199	70f yel grn & vio	2.00	75

World Population Year 1974.

Festival Symbols — A200

1975, July 17 **Litho.** *Perf. 12x11½*

730	A200	5f lt brn & multi	15	15
731	A200	10f lt brn & multi	15	15
732	A200	35f lt brn & multi	1.00	75
		Set value		90

Festivals, July 1975.

Map of Arab Countries A201

1975, Aug. 5 **Photo.** *Perf. 13*

733	A201	25f rose & multi	30	15
734	A201	35f multicolored	32	25
735	A201	45f multicolored	52	35

Arab Working Org., 10th anniv.

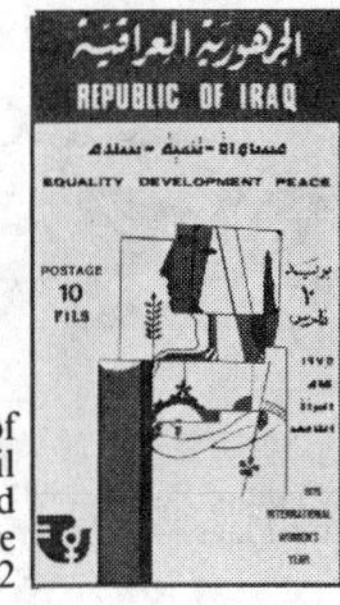

Symbols of Women, Oil Industry and Agriculture A202

1975, Aug. 15 *Perf. 14*

736	A202	10f lilac & multi	32	15
737	A202	35f multicolored	65	50
738	A202	70f bl & multi	2.75	1.00
a.		Souv. sheet. 100f. imperf.	9.50	11.00

International Women's Year.

Euphrates Dam and Causeway A203

1975, Sept. 5 **Litho.** *Perf. 12x11½*

739	A203	3f orange & multi	15	15
740	A203	25f purple & multi	38	15
741	A203	70f rose red & multi	2.00	50
		Set value		70

Intl. Commission on Irrigation and Drainage, 25th anniv.

National Insurance Co. Seal — A204

1975, Oct. 11 **Photo.** *Perf. 13*

742	A204	20f brt bl & multi	55	15
743	A204	25f crim & multi	70	30
a.		Souv. sheet. 100f. imperf.	7.00	8.50

Natl. Insurance Co., Baghdad, 25th anniv.

Musician Entertaining King — A205

1975, Nov. 21 *Perf. 14*

744	A205	25f silver & multi	30	15
745	A205	45f gold & multi	55	22

Baghdad Intl. Music Conf., Nov. 1975.

Telecommunications Center — A206

1975, Dec. 22 **Litho.** *Perf. 12½*

746	A206	5f lil rose & multi	15	15
747	A206	10f blue & multi	18	15
748	A206	60f green & multi	1.10	50
		Set value		65

Inauguration of Telecommunications Center Building during July 1975 Festival.

Diesel Locomotive — A207

Conference Emblem and: 30f, Diesel passenger locomotive #511. 35f, 0-3-0 steam tank locomotive with passenger train. 50f, 2-3-0 German steam locomotive, c. 1914.

1975, Dec. 22 **Photo.** *Perf. 14*

749	A207	25f tan & multi	2.25	38
750	A207	30f tan & multi	3.00	75
751	A207	35f yel grn & multi	4.00	1.50
752	A207	50f yel grn & multi	6.00	4.00

15th Taurus Railway Conference, Baghdad.

Soldier on Guard — A208

1976, Jan. 6 *Perf. 13*

753	A208	5f silver & multi	15	15
754	A208	25f silver & multi	30	15
755	A208	50f gold & multi	90	40
		Set value		58

55th Army Day.

Fingerprint Crossed Out, Arab World — A209

1976, Jan. 8 **Photo.** *Perf. 13½x13*

756	A209	5f violet & multi	15	15
757	A209	15f blue & multi	35	15
758	A209	35f green & multi	1.10	75

Statue of Goddess A210

Iraq Earth Station A211

Designs: 10f, 15f, like 5f. 20f, 25f, 30f, Two female figures forming column. 35f, 50f, 75f, Head of bearded man.

1976, Jan. 1 **Litho.** *Perf. 13x12½*

759	A210	5f lilac & multi	15	15
760	A210	10f rose & multi	15	15
761	A210	15f yellow & multi	15	15
762	A210	20f bister & multi	16	15
763	A210	25f lt grn & multi	18	15
764	A210	30f blue & multi	20	15
765	A210	35f lil rose & multi	20	18
766	A210	50f citron & multi	32	25
767	A210	75f violet & multi	48	40
		Nos. 759-767 (9)	1.99	
		Set value		1.35

1976, Feb. 8 *Perf. 13x13½*

768	A211	10f silver & multi	25	15
769	A211	25f silver & multi	80	30
770	A211	75f gold & multi	3.25	1.25

Revolution of Ramadan 14, 13th anniv.

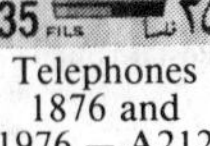

Telephones 1876 and 1976 — A212

Map of Maghreb, ICATU Emblem — A213

1976, Mar. 17 **Litho.** *Perf. 12x12½*

771	A212	35f multicolored	80	30
772	A212	50f multicolored	1.65	50
773	A212	75f multicolored	2.50	75

Centenary of first telephone call by Alexander Graham Bell, Mar. 10, 1876.

1976, Mar. 24 **Photo.** *Perf. 13½*

774	A213	5f green & multi	15	15
775	A213	10f multicolored	25	15
		Set value	30	20

20th Intl. Conference of Arab Trade Unions. See No. C54.

Map of Iraq, Family, Torch and Wreath — A214

1976, Apr. 1 *Perf. 12½*

776	A214	5f multicolored	15	15
777	A214	15f lilac & multi	24	15
778	A214	35f multicolored	50	25
		Set value		40

Police Day.

Pipeline, Map of Iraq — A215

Pres. A. H. al-Bakr Embracing Vice Pres. Saddam Hussein — A216

1976, June 1 **Photo.** *Perf. 13*

779	A215	25f multicolored	1.50	75
780	A215	75f multicolored	4.50	2.00

Souvenir Sheet

Imperf

781	A216	150f multicolored	19.00	22.50

4th anniversary of oil nationalization.

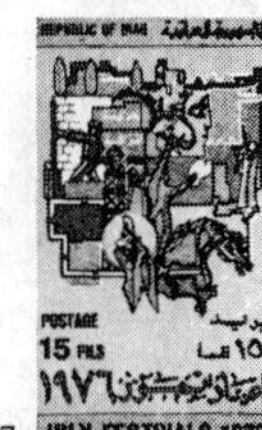

"Festival" — A217

1976, July 17 *Perf. 14*

782	A217	15f orange & multi	25	15
783	A217	35f orange & multi	75	50

Festivals, July 1976.

Archbishop Capucci, Map of Palestine A218

1976, Aug. 18 **Litho.** *Perf. 12*

784	A218	25f multicolored	45	18
785	A218	35f multicolored	70	18
786	A218	75f multicolored	2.25	1.00

Detention of Archbishop Hilarion Capucci in Israel, Aug. 18, 1974.

Common Kingfisher A219

"15" A220

Birds: 10f, Turtle dove. 15f, Pin-tailed sandgrouse. 25f, Blue rock thrush. 50f, Purple and gray herons.

1976, Sept. 15 Litho. *Perf. 13½x14*

787 A219 5f multicolored 15 15
788 A219 10f multicolored 16 15
789 A219 15f multicolored 28 15
790 A219 25f multicolored 40 25
791 A219 50f multicolored 1.50 35
Nos. 787-791 (5) 2.49 1.05

1976, Nov. 23 Photo. *Perf. 13½*

792 A220 30f multicolored 1.00 50
793 A220 70f multicolored 3.00 75

15th anniv. of National Students Union.

Oil Tanker and Emblems A221

Designs: 15f, like 10f. 25f, 50f, Pier, refinery, pipeline.

1976, Dec. 25 *Perf. 12½x12*

794 A221 10f multicolored 48 15
795 A221 15f multicolored 75 24
796 A221 25f multicolored 2.00 48
797 A221 50f multicolored 2.75 70

1st Iraqi oil tanker (10f, 15f) and Nationalization of Basrah Petroleum Co. Ltd., 1st anniv. (25f, 50f).

Happy Children A222

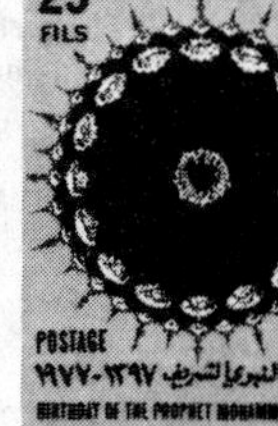

Ornament A223

UNESCO Emblem and: 25f, Children with flowers and butterflies. 75f, Children planting flowers around flagpole.

1976, Dec. 25 *Perf. 12x12½*

798 A222 10f multicolored 15 15
799 A222 25f multicolored 1.50 25
800 A222 75f multicolored 2.50 75

30th anniv. of UNESCO, and Books for Children Campaign.

1977, Mar. 2 Photo. *Perf. 13½*

801 A223 25f gold & multi 48 20
802 A223 35f gold & multi 70 25

Birthday of Mohammed (570-632).

Peace Dove — A224

Dahlia — A225

1977, Mar. 11 *Perf. 14x13½*

803 A224 25f lt bl & multi 30 15
804 A224 30f buff & multi 35 15

Peace Day.

1977, Mar. 21 Litho. *Perf. 12½*

Flowers: 10f, Sweet peas. 35f, Chrysanthemums. 50f, Verbena.

805 A225 5f multicolored 20 15
806 A225 10f multicolored 24 15
807 A225 35f multicolored 80 25
808 A225 50f multicolored 1.50 50
Set value 90

Spring Festivals, Baghdad.

Emblem with Doves A226

Designs: 75f, Emblem with flame. 100f, Dove with olive branch.

1977, Apr. 7 Photo. *Perf. 13*

809 A226 25f yel & multi 60 15
810 A226 75f yel & multi 2.25 40

Souvenir Sheet

Imperf

811 A226 100f multicolored 4.75 6.50

Al Baath Party, 30th anniversary. No. 811 contains one 49x35mm stamp.

APU Emblem, Members' Flags — A227

1977, Apr. 12 Litho. *Perf. 14*

812 A227 25f orange & multi 35 15
813 A227 35f gray & multi 45 18

25th anniversary of Arab Postal Union.

Cogwheel, Globe and "1" — A228

1977, May 1 Litho. *Perf. 14½x14*

814 A228 10f multicolored 15 15
815 A228 30f multicolored 35 15
816 A228 35f multicolored 42 18
Set value 38

Labor Day.

Weight Lifting A229

Designs: 75f, Weight lifter, standing up. 100f, Symbolic weight lifter with Iraqi coat of arms, laurel wreath.

1977, May 8 Photo. *Perf. 14*

817 A229 25f multicolored 60 60
818 A229 75f multicolored 1.25 85

Souvenir Sheet

Imperf

819 A229 100f multicolored 6.50 7.50

8th Asian Weight Lifting Championship, Baghdad, May 1977. No. 819 contains one 42x52mm stamp.

Arabian Garden — A230

Grain and Dove — A231

Arab Tourist Year: 10f, View of town with minarets (horiz.). 30f, Landscape with bridge and waterfall. 50f, Hosts welcoming tourists, and drum (horiz.).

Perf. 11½x12, 12x11½

1977, June 15 Litho.

820 A230 5f multicolored 15 15
821 A230 10f multicolored 15 15
822 A230 30f multicolored 75 20
823 A230 50f multicolored 2.00 1.25

1977, July 17 Photo. *Perf. 14*

824 A231 25f multicolored 28 15
825 A231 30f multicolored 35 15

Festivals, July 1977.

Map of Arab Countries A232

1977, Sept. 9 Photo. *Perf. 13½x14*

826 A232 30f multicolored 38 25
827 A232 70f multicolored 1.65 50

UN Conference on Desertification, Nairobi, Kenya, Aug. 29-Sept. 9.

Census Emblem A233

Festival Emblem A234

1977, Oct. 17 Litho. *Perf. 14x14½*

828 A233 20f ultra & multi 22 15
829 A233 30f brown & multi 35 15
830 A233 70f gray & multi 70 35

Population Census Day, Oct. 17.

1977, Nov. 1 Photo. *Perf. 14*

831 A234 25f silver & multi 30 15
832 A234 50f gold & multi 60 24

Al Mutanabby Festival, Nov. 1977.

Junblatt, Caricatures of Britain, USA, Israel — A235

1977, Nov. 16 Photo. *Perf. 14*

833 A235 20f multicolored 24 15
834 A235 30f multicolored 35 15
835 A235 70f multicolored 80 35

Kemal Junblatt, Druse leader, killed in Lebanese war.

Ornament — A236

1977, Dec. 12 Photo. *Perf. 14*

836 A236 30f gold & multi 40 15
837 A236 35f silver & multi 50 18

Hajeer (Pilgrimage) Year.

Young People and Flags — A237

Coins and Coin Bank — A238

1978, Apr. 7 Photo. *Perf. 11½x11*

838 A237 10f multicolored 15 15
839 A237 15f multicolored 25 15
840 A237 35f multicolored 55 18
Set value 30

Youth Day.

1978, Apr. 15

841 A238 15f multicolored 15 15
842 A238 25f multicolored 30 15
843 A238 35f multicolored 42 18
Set value 38

6th anniversary of postal savings law.

Microwave Transmission and Receiving A239

Emblems and Flags of Participants A240

1978, May 17 Photo. *Perf. 14*
844 A239 25f org & multi 20 15
845 A239 35f lilac & multi 28 18
846 A239 75f emer & multi 60 35

10th World Telecommunications Day and 1st anniversary of commissioning of national microwave network.

Perf. 12½x11½
1978, June 19 Litho.
847 A240 25f multicolored 55 15
848 A240 35f multicolored 85 18

Conference of Postal Ministers of Arabian Gulf Countries, Baghdad (Saudi Arabia, United Arab Emirates, Qatar, Bahrain, Kuwait, Oman, People's Republic of Yemen).

Ancient Coin — A241

Designs: Ancient Iraqi coins. 75f vertical.

Perf. 11½x12½
1978, June 25 Photo.
849 A241 1f citron & multi 15 15
850 A241 2f blue & multi 15 15
851 A241 3f salmon & multi 15 15
852 A241 4f salmon & multi 15 15
853 A241 75f bl grn & multi 2.25 40
Nos. 849-853 (5) 2.85
Set value 60

Festival Emblem — A242

Festival Poster — A243

1978, July 17 *Perf. 13½x13*
854 A242 25f multicolored 20 15
855 A242 35f multicolored 28 18

Souvenir Sheet
Perf. 13x13½
856 A243 100f multicolored 4.25 5.00

Festivals, July 1978.

WHO Emblem, Nurse, Hospital, Sick Child A244

1978, Aug. 18 Photo. *Perf. 14*
857 A244 25f multicolored 24 15
858 A244 35f multicolored 32 18
859 A244 75f multicolored 70 35

Eradication of smallpox.

Maritime Union Emblem A245

1978, Aug. 30 Photo. *Perf. 11½x12*
860 A245 25f multicolored 30 15
861 A245 75f multicolored 90 35

1st World Maritime Day.

Workers A246

1978, Sept. 12 *Perf. 14*
862 A246 10f multicolored 18 15
863 A246 25f multicolored 40 15
864 A246 35f multicolored 70 18
Set value 35

10th anniv. of People's Work Groups.

Fair Emblem with Atom Symbol — A247

Map of Iraq, Ruler and Globe — A248

1978, Oct. 1
865 A247 25f multicolored 24 15
866 A247 35f multicolored 32 18
867 A247 75f multicolored 70 35

15th International Fair, Baghdad, Oct. 1-15.

1978, Oct. 14
868 A248 25f multicolored 24 15
869 A248 35f multicolored 32 18
870 A248 75f multicolored 70 35

World Standards Day.

Altharthar-Euphrates Dam — A249

1978 Photo. *Perf. 11½*
871 A249 5f multicolo. 15 15
872 A249 10f multicolored 15 15
873 A249 15f multicolored 15 18
874 A249 25f multicolored 28 15
875 A249 35f multicolored 40 18
876 A249 50f multicolored 60 25
Nos. 871-876 (6) 1.73
Set value 82

Arab Summit Conference A250

Surgeons' Conference Emblem A251

1978, Nov. 2 Photo. *Perf. 14*
890 A250 25f multicolored 22 15
891 A250 35f multicolored 45 25
892 A250 75f multicolored 90 50

9th Arab Summit Conference, Baghdad, Nov. 2-5.

1978, Nov. 8 Litho. *Perf. 12x11½*
893 A251 25f multicolored 25 15
894 A251 75f multicolored 80 35

4th Congress of the Association of Thoracic and Cardiovascular Surgeons of Asia, Baghdad, Nov. 6-10.

Pilgrims at Mt. Arafat and Holy Kaaba A252

1978, Nov. 9 Photo. *Perf. 14*
895 A252 25f multicolored 25 15
896 A252 35f multicolored 35 18

Pilgrimage to Mecea.

Atom Symbol, Map of South America, Africa, Arabia — A253

1978, Nov. 11 *Perf. 13½*
897 A253 25f multicolored 65 15
898 A253 50f multicolored 55 25
899 A253 75f multicolored 80 35

Technical Cooperation Among Developing Countries Conference, Buenos Aires, Argentina, Sept. 1978.

Hands Holding Emblem — A254

Globe and Flame Emblem — A255

1978, Nov. 30 Litho. *Perf. 13½x13*
900 A254 25f multicolored 30 15
901 A254 50f multicolored 60 25
902 A254 75f multicolored 95 35

Anti-Apartheid Year.

1978, Dec. 20 *Perf. 14*
903 A255 25f multicolored 20 15
904 A255 75f multicolored 60 35

Declaration of Human Rights, 30th anniv.

Candle and Emblem — A256

Book, Pencil and Flame — A257

1979, Jan. 9 Photo. *Perf. 14*
905 A256 10f multicolored 15 15
906 A256 25f multicolored 20 15
907 A256 35f multicolored 28 18
Set value 36

Police Day.

1979, Feb. 15 Photo. *Perf. 14*
908 A257 15f multicolored 25 15
909 A257 25f multicolored 35 15
910 A257 35f multicolored 65 18
Set value 36

Application of Compulsory Education Law, anniversary.

Pupils, School and Teacher — A258

1979, Mar. 1 *Perf. 13*
911 A258 10f multicolored 15 15
912 A258 15f multicolored 20 15
913 A258 50f multicolored 80 25
Set value 38

Teacher's Day.

Pupils, Flag, Pencil — A259

1979, Mar. 10 *Perf. 13½x13*
914 A259 15f multicolored 15 15
915 A259 25f multicolored 25 15
916 A259 35f multicolored 50 18
Set value 38

National Comprehensive Compulsory Literacy Campaign.

Book, World Map, Arab Achievements A260

1979, Mar. 22 *Perf. 13*
917 A260 35f multicolored 28 18
918 A260 75f multicolored 60 38

Achievements of the Arabs.

Girl Playing Flute — A261

1979, Apr. 15 Litho. *Perf. 13½*
919 A261 15f multicolored 22 15
920 A261 25f multicolored 35 15
921 A261 35f multicolored 75 30

Mosul Spring Festival.

Iraqi Flag, Globe, UPU Emblem A262

1979, Apr. 22 Photo. *Perf. 13x13½*
922 A262 25f multicolored 40 15
923 A262 35f multicolored 45 18
924 A262 75f multicolored 1.00 50

50th anniv. of Iraq's admission to the UPU.

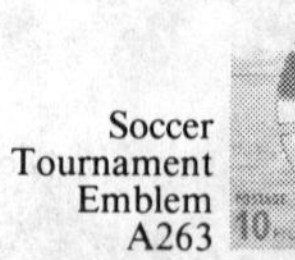
Soccer Tournament Emblem A263

1979, May 4 Photo. *Perf. 13*

925 A263 10f multicolored	15	15
926 A263 15f multicolored	30	15
927 A263 50f multicolored	1.00	50
Set value		64

5th Arabian Gulf Soccer Championship.

Child With Globe and Candle A264

Design: 100f, IYC emblem, boy and girl reaching for U.S. emblem, vert.

1979, June 1 Photo. *Perf. 13x13½*

928 A264 25f multicolored	38	18
929 A264 75f multicolored	1.25	65

Souvenir Sheet

930 A264 100f multicolored	21.00	17.50

International Year of the Child. No. 930 contains one stamp 30x42mm.

Leaf and Flower — A265

1979, July 17 Litho. *Perf. 12½*

931 A265 15f multicolored	15	15
932 A265 25f multicolored	20	15
933 A265 35f multicolored	28	18
Set value		38

July festivals.

Students Holding Globe, UNESCO Emblem A266

1979, July 25

934 A266 25f multicolored	40	15
935 A266 40f multicolored	70	25
936 A266 100f multicolored	2.00	50

Intl. Bureau of Education, Geneva, 50th anniv.

S. al Hosari, Philosopher A267

Designs: No. 938, Mustapha Jawad, historian. No. 939, Jawad Selim, sculptor.

1979, Oct. 15 Litho. *Perf. 12½*

937 A267 25f multicolored	30	15
938 A267 25f multicolored	30	15
939 A267 25f multicolored	30	15
Set value		36

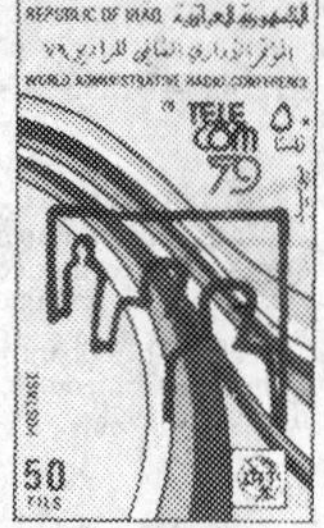

Pilgrimage to Mecca A268

1979, Oct. 25 Litho. *Perf. 12½*

940 A268 25f multicolored	30	15
941 A268 50f multicolored	60	24

Iraqi News Agency, 20th Anniversary A269

Telecom 79 A270

1979, Nov. 9 Photo. *Perf. 11½*

942 A269 25f multicolored	20	15
943 A269 50f multicolored	40	25
944 A269 75f multicolored	60	35

1979, Nov. 20 Litho. *Perf. 11½*

945 A270 25f multicolored	25	15
946 A270 50f multicolored	50	35
947 A270 75f multicolored	75	50

3rd World Telecommunications Exhibition, Geneva, Sept. 20-26.

International Palestinian Solidarity Day — A271

1979, Nov. 29 Photo. *Perf. 11½x12*

948 A271 25f multicolored	60	15
949 A271 50f multicolored	1.10	35
950 A271 75f multicolored	1.50	50

Ahmad Hassan Al-Bakr — A272

1979, Dec. 1 Photo. *Perf. 13x13½*

951 A272 25f shown	20	15
952 A272 35f Pres. Saddam Hussain	28	18
953 A272 75f Like No. 951	60	28
954 A272 100f Like No. 952	2.50	1.50

Vanguard Emblem — A273

Vanguard Emblem and: 10f, Boy and violin. 15f, Children, map of Iraq. 25f, Youths.

1979, Dec. 10 *Perf. 14*

955 A273 10f multicolored	15	15
956 A273 15f multicolored	16	15
957 A273 25f multicolored	25	15
958 A273 35f multicolored	35	18
Set value		42

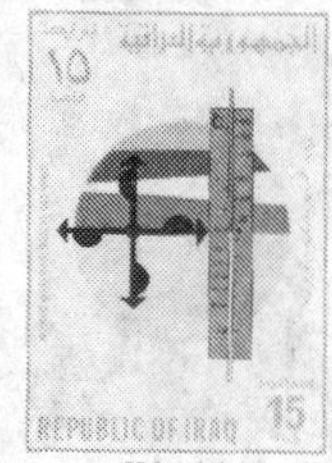
World Meteorological Day — A274

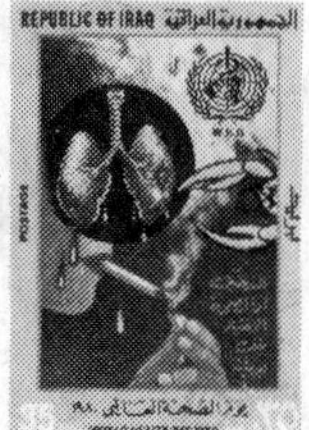
World Health Day — A275

1980, Mar. 23 Photo. *Perf. 14*

959 A274 15f multicolored	16	15
960 A274 25f multicolored	25	15
961 A274 35f multicolored	35	18
Set value		38

1980, Apr. 7 Photo. *Perf. 14*

962 A275 25f multicolored	24	15
963 A275 35f multicolored	35	18
964 A275 75f multicolored	1.25	38

Festivals Emblem — A276

Pres. Hussein — A277

1980, July 17 Photo. *Perf. 13½x13*

965 A276 25f multicolored	22	15
966 A276 35f multicolored	30	18

Souvenir Sheet

Perf. 13½

967 A277 100f multicolored	3.75	3.75

July Festivals.

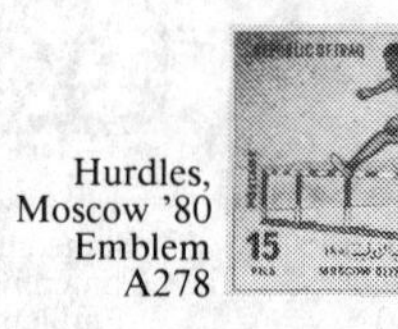
Hurdles, Moscow '80 Emblem A278

1980, July 30 Photo. *Perf. 14*

968 A278 15f shown	18	15
969 A278 20f Weight lifting, vert.	28	25
970 A278 30f Boxing	55	35
971 A278 35f Soccer, vert.	1.10	55

Souvenir Sheet

972 A278 100f Wrestling	4.75	4.75

22nd Summer Olympic Games, Moscow, July 19-Aug. 3.

Fruits — A279

1980, Aug. 15

973 A279 5f Blackberries	15	15
974 A279 15f Apricots	20	15
975 A279 20f Pears	35	15
976 A279 25f Apples	50	15
977 A279 35f Plums	1.00	25
Nos. 973-977 (5)	2.20	
Set value		70

World Tourism Conference, Manila, Sept. 27 — A279a

1980, Aug. 30 Litho. *Perf. 12½*

978 A279a 25f multicolored	28	15
979 A279a 50f multicolored	55	25
980 A279a 100f multicolored	1.10	55

Postal Union Emblem, Posthorn, Map of Arab States — A280

1980, Sept. 8 *Perf. 12*

981 A280 10f multicolored	15	15
982 A280 30f multicolored	35	16
983 A280 35f multicolored	40	18
Set value		38

Arab Postal Union, 11th Congress, Baghdad.

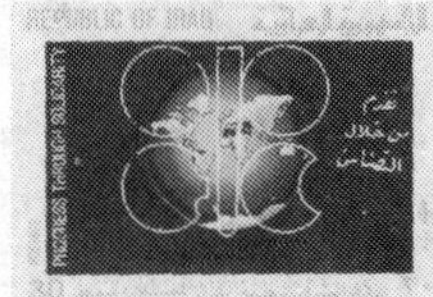
20th Anniversary of OPEC — A281

1980, Sept. 30

984 A281 30f multicolored	1.00	25
985 A281 75f multicolored	1.50	50

Papilio Machaon A282

1980, Oct. 20 Photo. *Perf. 13½x14*

987 A282 10f shown	35	15
988 A282 15f Danaus chrysippus	45	20
989 A282 20f Vanessa atalanta	60	25
990 A282 30f Colias croceus	1.00	25

Hegira, 1,500th Anniv. A283

1980, Nov. 9 Litho. *Perf. 11½x12*

991 A283 15f multicolored 18 15
992 A283 25f multicolored 30 15
993 A283 35f multicolored 40 18
Set value 38

International Palestinian Solidarity Day — A284

1980, Nov. 29

994 A284 25f multicolored 30 15
995 A284 35f multicolored 40 18
996 A284 75f multicolored 80 38

Army Day A285

February Revolution, 18th Anniversary A286

1981, Jan. 6 Photo. *Perf. 14x13½*

997 A285 5f multicolored 15 15
998 A285 30f multicolored 35 16
999 A285 75f multicolored 90 38
Set value 58

1981, Feb. 8 *Perf. 12*

1000 A286 15f multicolored 18 15
1001 A286 30f multicolored 30 16
1002 A286 35f multicolored 40 18

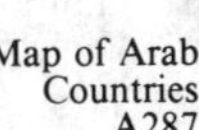
Map of Arab Countries A287

1981, Mar. 22 Litho. *Perf. 12½*

1003 A287 5f multicolored 15 15
1004 A287 25f multicolored 30 15
1005 A287 35f multicolored 40 18
Set value 34

Battle of Qadisiya — A288

1981, Apr. 7 Photo. *Perf. 13½x13*

1006 A288 30f multicolored 35 16
1007 A288 35f multicolored 40 18
1008 A288 75f multicolored 80 38

Souvenir Sheet

1009 A288 100f multicolored 4.50 5.50

No. 1009 contains one horiz. stamp.

Helicopters and Tank A289

1981, June 1 Photo.

1010 A289 5f shown 15 15
1011 A289 10f Plane 25 15
1012 A289 15f Rocket 50 15
Set value 30

Air Force, 50th anniv. See No. C66.

Natl. Assembly Election, First Anniv. — A290

1981, June 20 *Perf. 12½*

1013 A290 30f multicolored 35 16
1014 A290 35f multicolored 40 18
1015 A290 45f multicolored 55 24

July Festivals A291

1981, July 17 Photo.

1016 A291 15f multicolored 15 15
1017 A291 25f multicolored 30 15
1018 A291 35f multicolored 40 18
Set value 40

Pottery Maker — A292

Designs: Popular industries.

1981, Aug. 15 *Perf. 14*

1019 A292 5f Straw weaver 15 15
1020 A292 30f Metal worker 35 16
1021 A292 35f shown 40 18
1022 A292 50f Rug maker, horiz. 1.00 28

Islamic Pilgrimage A293

1981, Oct. 7 Photo. *Perf. 12x11½*

1023 A293 25f multicolored 30 15
1024 A293 45f multicolored 55 24
1025 A293 50f multicolored 60 30

World Food Day A294

1981, Oct. 16 Photo. *Perf. 14*

1026 A294 30f multicolored 35 16
1027 A294 45f multicolored 50 24
1028 A294 75f multicolored 80 45

Intl. Year of the Disabled — A295

1981, Nov. 15

1029 A295 30f multicolored 30 16
1030 A295 45f multicolored 50 24
1031 A295 75f multicolored 70 45

5th Anniv. of United Arab Shipping Co. — A296

1981, Dec. 2 *Perf. 13x13½*

1032 A296 50f multicolored 75 30
1033 A296 120f multicolored 2.25 75

Saddam Hussein Gymnasium A297

1981, Sept. 26 Litho. *Perf. 12x12½*

1034 A297 45f shown 48 24
1035 A297 50f Palace of Conferences 52 30
1036 A297 120f like #1035 1.25 75
1037 A297 150f like #1034 1.40 90

For surcharges, see Nos. 1097-1099.

35th Anniv. of Al Baath Party — A298

Mosul Spring Festival — A299

1982, Apr. 7 Photo. *Perf. 13½x13*

1038 A298 25f Pres. Hussein, flowers 22 15
1039 A298 30f "7 7 7" 26 16
1040 A298 45f like 25f 40 24
1041 A298 50f like 30f 45 30

Souvenir Sheet

Imperf

1042 A298 150f multicolored 1.75 1.25

1982, Apr. 15 Litho. *Perf. 11½x12*

1043 A299 25f Birds 30 15
1044 A299 30f Girl 35 16
1045 A299 45f like 25f 55 24
1046 A299 50f like 30f 60 30

Intl. Workers' Day A300

1982, May 1 *Perf. 12½*

1047 A300 25f multicolored 20 15
1048 A300 45f multicolored 36 24
1049 A300 50f multicolored 40 30

14th World Telecommunications Day — A301

1982, May 17 Photo. *Perf. 13x13½*

1050 A301 5f multicolored 15 15
1051 A301 45f multicolored 36 24
1052 A301 100f multicolored 80 60

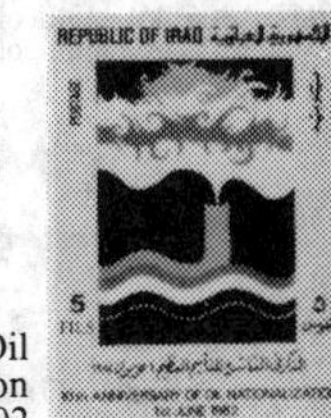
10th Anniv. of Oil Nationalization A302

1982, June 1 Litho. *Perf. 12½*

1053 A302 5f Oil gusher 15 15
1054 A302 25f like 5f 60 15
1055 A302 45f Statue 1.25 24
1056 A302 50f like 45f 1.40 30
Set value 72

Martyrs' Day — A303

Women's Day — A304

1981, Dec. 1 Photo. *Perf. 14*

1057 A303 45f multicolored 36 24
1058 A303 50f multicolored 40 30
1059 A303 120f multicolored 1.00 75
Nos. 1057-1059,O339A-O339C (6) 3.48 2.47

1982, Mar. 4 Litho. *Perf. 12½x13*

1060 A304 25f multicolored 30 15
1061 A304 45f multicolored 55 24
1062 A304 50f multicolored 60 30

Arab Postal Union, 30th Anniv. — A305

1982, Apr. 12 *Perf. 12½*

1063 A305 25f multicolored 30 15
1064 A305 45f multicolored 55 24
1065 A305 50f multicolored 60 30

First Anniv. of Attack on Nuclear Power Reactor — A305a

1982, June 7 Photo. *Perf. 14*

1065A A305a 30f Nuclear power emblem, lion 50 20
1065B A305a 45f shown 75 30
1065C A305a 50f like 30f 90 40
1065D A305a 120f like 45f 2.00 1.00

July Festivals — A306

1982, July 17 Photo. *Perf. 14½x14*

1066 A306 25f multicolored 40 15
1067 A306 45f multicolored 55 24
1068 A306 50f multicolored 60 30

Lacerta Viridis A307

1982, Aug. 20 Litho. *Perf. 12½*

1069 A307 25f shown 30 15
1070 A307 30f Vipera aspis 35 16
1071 A307 45f Lacerta virdis, diff. 55 24
1072 A307 50f Natrix tessellata 60 30

7th Non-aligned Countries Conference, Baghdad, Sept. — A308

Designs: No. 1073, Tito. No. 1074, Nehru. No. 1075, Nasser. No. 1076, Kwame Nkrumah. No. 1077, Pres. Hussein.

1982, Sept. 6 Photo. *Perf. 13x13½*

1073 A308 50f multicolored 55 40
1074 A308 50f multicolored 55 40
1075 A308 50f multicolored 55 40
1076 A308 50f multicolored 55 40
1077 A308 100f multicolored 1.10 55
Nos. 1073-1077 (5) 3.30 2.15

TB Bacillus Centenary A309

1982, Oct. 1 *Perf. 14x14½*

1078 A309 20f multicolored 20 15
1079 A309 50f multicolored 55 30
1080 A309 100f multicolored 1.10 40

1982 World Cup — A310

Designs: Various soccer players. 150f horiz.

1982, July 1 Litho. *Perf. 11½x12*

1081 A310 5f multicolored 15 15
1082 A310 45f multicolored 50 24
1083 A310 50f multicolored 55 30
1084 A310 100f multicolored 1.10 60

Souvenir Sheet

Perf. 12½

1085 A310 150f multicolored 1.75 1.25

13th UPU Day A311

1982, Oct. 9 *Perf. 12x11½*

1086 A311 5f multicolored 15 15
1087 A311 45f multicolored 40 24
1088 A311 100f multicolored 90 60

Musical Instruments A312

1982, Nov. 15 *Perf. 12½x13*

1089 A312 5f Drums 15 15
1090 A312 10f Zither 20 15
1091 A312 35f Stringed instrument 65 35
1092 A312 100f Lute 1.75 85

Birth Anniv. of Mohammed A313

Mecca Mosque views.

1982, Dec. 27 Litho. *Perf. 12x11½*

1093 A313 25f multicolored 20 15
1094 A313 30f multicolored 28 22
1095 A313 45f multicolored 36 24
1096 A313 50f multicolored 40 30

Nos. 1034-1036 Surcharged

1983, May 15 Litho. *Perf. 12x12½*

1097 A297 60f on 50f multi 75 32
1098 A297 70f on 45f multi 90 45
1099 A297 160f on 120f multi 2.00 90

July Festivals A314

1983, July 17 Litho. *Perf. 14½x14*

1100 A314 30f multicolored 35 16
1101 A314 60f multicolored 75 32
1102 A314 70f multicolored 90 45

Local Flowers — A315

1983, June 15 Photo. *Perf. 15x14*

Border Color

1103 A315 10f shown, light blue 15 15
1104 A315 20f Flowers, diff., pale yellow 16 15
1105 A315 30f like 10f, yellow 25 16
1106 A315 40f like 20f, gray 35 25
1107 A315 50f like 10f, pale green 40 30
1108 A315 100f like 20f, pink 80 60
a. Bklt. pane of 6, #1103-1108 3.00
Nos. 1103-1108 (6) 2.11 1.61

Nos. 1103-1108 issued in booklets only.

Battle of Thi Qar A316 A317

1983, Oct. 30 Photo. *Perf. 12½x13*

1109 A316 20f silver & multi 24 15
1110 A317 50f silver & multi 60 30
1111 A316 60f gold & multi 70 32
1112 A317 70f gold & multi 1.10 40

World Communications Year — A318

Design: 25f, 70f show emblem and hexagons.

1983, Oct. 20 Photo. *Perf. 11½x12*

1113 A318 5f brt yel grn & multi 15 15
1114 A318 25f rose lil & multi 30 15
1115 A318 60f brt org yel & multi 70 34
1116 A318 70f brt bl vio & multi 1.10 40

Souvenir Sheet

1117 A318 200f ap grn & multi 3.75 3.75

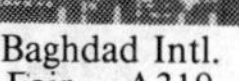

Baghdad Intl. Fair — A319

Symbolic "9" — A320

1983, Nov. 1 Photo. *Perf. 12½*

1118 A319 60f multicolored 48 32
1119 A319 70f multicolored 56 40
1120 A319 160f multicolored 1.30 90

1983, Nov. 10 Photo. *Perf. 14*

9th Natl. Congress of Arab Baath Socialist Party: 30f, 70f, Symbols of development. 60f, 100f, Torch, eagle, globe, open book.

1121 A320 30f multicolored 24 16
1122 A320 60f multicolored 48 32
1123 A320 70f multicolored 56 40
1124 A320 100f multicolored 80 55

Festival Crowd — A321

Various Paintings.

1983, Nov. 20 Litho. *Perf. 12½*

1125 A321 60f shown 48 32
1126 A321 60f Men hauling boat, vert. 48 32
1127 A321 60f Decorations 48 32
1128 A321 70f Village 56 40
1129 A321 70f Crowd 56 40
Nos. 1125-1129 (5) 2.56 1.76

Sabra and Shattela Palestinian Refugee Camp Massacre — A322

Various Victims.

1983, Nov. 29 *Perf. 11½x12*

1130 A322 10f multicolored 15 15
1131 A322 60f multicolored 1.00 32
1132 A322 70f multicolored 1.10 40
1133 A322 160f multicolored 2.00 92

Pres. Hussein, Map — A323

1983 Photo. *Perf. 13½x13*

1134 A323 60f multicolored 60 32
1135 A323 70f multicolored 70 40
1136 A323 250f multicolored 2.50 1.65

Pres. Hussein as head of Al Baath Party, 4th anniv.

Modern Building — A324

Various buildings.

1983, Dec. 31 Litho. *Perf. 14*

1137 A324 60f multicolored 48 32
1138 A324 70f multicolored 56 40
1139 A324 160f multicolored 1.30 92
1140 A324 200f multicolored 1.60 1.10
Nos. 1137-1140,O340-O341 (6) 4.98 3.46

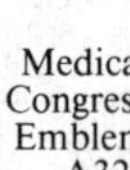

Medical Congress Emblem A325

1984, Mar. 10 *Perf. 13x12½*

1141 A325 60f multicolored 60 32
1142 A325 70f multicolored 70 40
1143 A325 200f multicolored 2.00 1.10

25th Intl. Congress of Military Medicine and Pharmacy, Baghdad, Mar. 10-15.

Pres. Hussein's Birthday — A326

Various portraits of Hussein.

1984, Apr. 28 Litho. *Perf. 12½x13*

1144 A326 60f multicolored 48 32
1145 A326 70f multicolored 56 40
1146 A326 160f multicolored 1.30 92
1147 A326 200f multicolored 1.60 1.10

Souvenir Sheet

Imperf

1148 A326 250f multicolored 2.00 1.75

Gold ink on Nos. 1144-1147 and dark green ink in "margin" of No. 1148 was applied by a thermographic process, producing a raised effect. No. 1148 has perf. 12½x13 label picturing Pres. Hussein.

1984 Summer Olympics, Los Angeles A327

1984, Aug. 12 Litho. *Perf. 12x11½*

1149 A327 50f Boxing 32 22
1150 A327 60f Weight lifting 38 25
1151 A327 70f like 50f 45 30
1152 A327 100f like 60f 65 45

Size: 80x60mm

Imperf

1153 A327 200f Soccer 1.40 95
Nos. 1149-1153 (5) 3.20 2.17

Nos. 1153 contains one 32x41mm perf. 12½ label within the stamp.

Pres. Hussein, Flaming Horses Heads, Map — A328

Designs: 50f, 70f, Shown. 60f, 100f, Abstract of woman, sapling, rifle. 200f, Shield, heraldic eagle.

1984, Sept. 22 *Perf. 11½x12*

1154 A328 50f multicolored 32 22
1155 A328 60f multicolored 38 25
1156 A328 70f multicolored 45 30
1157 A328 100f multicolored 65 45

Size: 80x60mm

Imperf

1158 A328 200f multicolored 1.40 95
Nos. 1154-1158 (5) 3.20 2.17

Battle of Qadisiya. No. 1158 contains one 32x41mm perf. 12½ label within the stamp.

Martyrs' Day — A329

Designs: 50f, 70f, Natl. flag as flame. 60f, 100f, Woman holding rifle, medal.

1984, Dec. 1 *Perf. 13½*

1159 A329 50f multicolored 32 22
1160 A329 60f multicolored 38 25
1161 A329 70f multicolored 45 30
1162 A329 100f multicolored 65 45

Pres. Hussein's Visit to Al-Mustansiriyah University, 5th Anniv. — A330

1985, Apr. 2 Photo. *Perf. 12x11½*

1163 A330 60f dk bl gray & dk pink 38 25
1164 A330 70f myr grn & dk pink 45 30
1165 A330 250f blk & dk pink 1.75 1.15

Iraqi Air Force, 54th Anniv. — A331

Pres. Hussein, 48th Birthday — A332

Designs: 10f, 160f, Pres. Hussein, fighter planes, pilot's wings. 60f, 70f, 200f, Planes, flag, "54," horiz.

Perf. 13x12½, 13½ (60f, 70f)

1985, Apr. 22 Litho.

1166 A331 10f multicolored 15 15
1167 A331 60f multicolored 38 25
1168 A331 70f multicolored 45 30
1169 A331 160f multicolored 1.05 70

Souvenir Sheet

Perf. 12½

1170 A331 200f multicolored 1.40 95

1985, Apr. 28 *Perf. 13½*

Designs: 30f, 70f, Pres. Hussein, sunflower. 60f, 100f, Pres., candle and flowers. 200f, Flowers and text.

1171 A332 30f multicolored 20 15
1172 A332 60f multicolored 38 25
1173 A332 70f multicolored 45 30
1174 A332 100f multicolored 65 45

Souvenir Sheet

Perf. 13x12½

1175 A332 200f multicolored 1.40 95

Posts and Telecommunications Development Program — A333

Designs: 20f, 60f, Graph, woman in modern office. 50f, 70f, Satellite dish and graphs.

1985, June 30 *Perf. 12½*

1176 A333 20f multicolored 15 15
1177 A333 50f multicolored 32 22
1178 A333 60f multicolored 38 25
1179 A333 70f multicolored 45 30

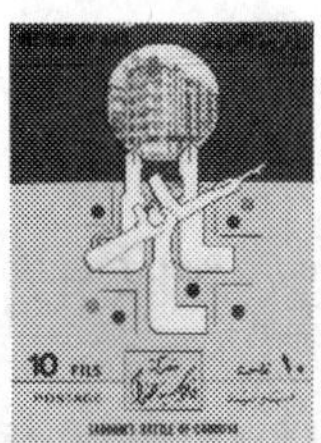

Battle of Qadisiya — A334

Designs: 10f, 60f, Shown. 20f, 70f, Pres. Hussein, Al-Baath Party emblem. 200f, Dove, natl. flag as shield, soldier.

1985, Sept. 4 *Perf. 11½x12*

1180 A334 10f multicolored 15 15
1181 A334 20f multicolored 15 15
1182 A334 60f multicolored 38 25
1183 A334 70f multicolored 45 30

Souvenir Sheet

Perf. 12x12½

1184 A334 200f multicolored 1.40 95

No. 1184 contains one stamp 30x45mm.

Solar Energy Research Center A335

1985, Sept. 19 *Perf. 13½*

1185 A335 10f multicolored 15 15
1186 A335 50f multicolored 32 22
1187 A335 100f multicolored 65 45

UN Child Survival Campaign A336

Al Sharif, Poet, Death Millennium A337

Designs: 10f, 50f, Stop Polio Campaign. 15f, 100f, Girl, infant.

1985, Oct. 10

1188 A336 10f multicolored 15 15
1189 A336 15f multicolored 15 15
1190 A336 50f multicolored 32 22
1191 A336 100f multicolored 65 45
Set value 80

1985, Oct. 20

1192 A337 10f multicolored 15 15
1193 A337 50f multicolored 32 22
1194 A337 100f multicolored 65 45

UN, 40th Anniv. A338

1985, Oct. 24

1195 A338 10f multicolored 15 15
1196 A338 40f multicolored 28 18
1197 A338 100f multicolored 65 45

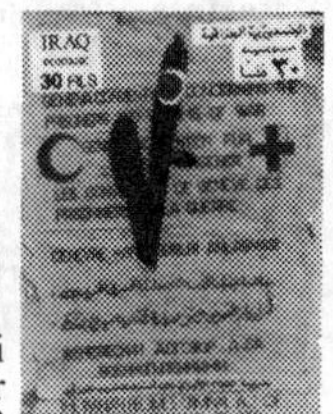

Death of Iraqi Prisoners of War in Iran — A339

Designs: 30f, 100f, Knife, Geneva Convention declaration, red crescent, red cross. 70f, 200f, POWs, gun shell, natl. flag, cherub and dove.

1985, Nov. 10 *Perf. 14*

1198 A339 30f multicolored 20 15
1199 A339 70f multicolored 45 30
1200 A339 100f multicolored 65 45
1201 A339 200f multicolored 1.40 95

Size: 110x80mm

Imperf

1202 A339 250f multicolored 2.75 1.15
Nos. 1198-1202 (5) 5.45 3.00

No. 1202 contains 2 perf. 14 labels similar to 100f and 200f designs within the stamp.

Intl. Palestinian Solidarity Day — A341

1985, Nov. 29 Litho. *Perf. 13½*

1207 A341 10f multicolored 15 15
1208 A341 50f multicolored 50 25
1209 A341 100f multicolored 1.00 50

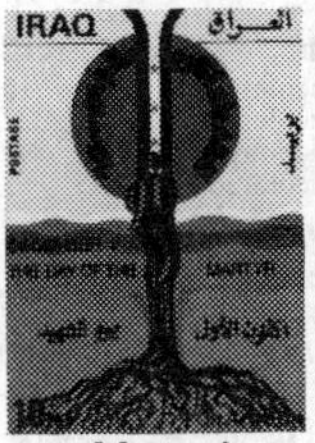

Martyrs' Day — A342

Intl. Youth Year — A343

1985, Dec. 1 *Perf. 11½x12*

1210 A342 10f multicolored 15 15
1211 A342 40f multicolored 28 18
1212 A342 100f multicolored 70 50

1985, Dec. 12 Litho. *Perf. 11½x12*

IYY emblem and: 40f, 100f, Soldier holding flag. 50f, 200f, Youths, flag. 250f, Flag, cogwheel, rifle muzzle, symbols of industry.

1213 A343 40f multicolored 40 18
1214 A343 50f multicolored 45 22
1215 A343 100f multicolored 90 45
1216 A343 200f multicolored 2.00 95

Souvenir Sheet

Perf. 12x12½

1217 A343 250f multicolored 2.50 1.15

No. 1217 contains one stamp 30x45mm. Exists imperf.

Army Day A344

Pres. Hussein, "6" and: 10f, 50f, Soldier, flowers, vert. 40f, 100f, Flag, cogwheel, rockets. 200f, Al-Baath Party emblem, rifle, waves.

1986, Jan. 6 *Perf. 11½x12, 12x11½*

1218 A344 10f multicolored 15 15
1219 A344 40f multicolored 40 18
1220 A344 50f multicolored 45 22
1221 A344 100f multicolored 90 45

Miniature Sheet

Perf. 12½x11½

1222 A344 200f multicolored 2.00 95

No. 1222 contains one stamp 52x37mm.

Women's Day A345

Designs: 30f, 100f, Women in traditional and modern occupations, vert. 50f, 150f, Emblem, green flag, battle scene, grapes.

Perf. 11½x12, 12x11½

1986, Mar. 8 **Litho.**

1223	A345	30f multicolored	22	15
1224	A345	50f multicolored	35	24
1225	A345	100f multicolored	70	48
1226	A345	150f multicolored	1.05	70

Pres. Hussein, 49th Birthday — A346

Designs: 30f, 100f, Children greeting Pres. 50f, 150f, Portrait. 250f, Portrait, flag, flowers.

1986, Apr. 28 **Litho.** ***Perf. 11½x12***

1227	A346	30f multicolored	28	15
1228	A346	50f multicolored	45	22
1229	A346	100f multicolored	90	45
1230	A346	150f multicolored	1.25	65

Size: 80x60mm

Imperf

1231	A346	250f multicolored	2.50	1.15
		Nos. 1227-1231 (5)	5.38	2.62

Oil Nationalization Day, June 1 — A347

Labor Day — A348

Designs: 10f, 100f, Symbols of industry, horiz. 40f, 150f, Oil well, pipeline to refinery.

Perf. 12x11½, 11½x12

1986, July 25 **Litho.**

1232	A347	10f multicolored	15	15
1233	A347	40f multicolored	45	18
1234	A347	100f multicolored	85	45
1235	A347	150f multicolored	1.25	65

1986, July 28 ***Perf. 11½x12***

Designs: 10f, 100f, Laborer, cog wheel. 40f, 150f, May Day emblem.

1236	A348	10f multicolored	15	15
1237	A348	40f multicolored	28	18
1238	A348	100f multicolored	65	45
1239	A348	150f multicolored	95	65

Iraqi Air Force, 55th Anniv. A349

Designs: 30f, 100f, Fighter plane, pilot's wings, natl. flag. 50f, 150f, Fighter planes. 250f, Medal, aircraft in flight.

1986, July 28 ***Perf. 12x11½***

1240	A349	30f multicolored	30	15
1241	A349	50f multicolored	42	22
1242	A349	100f multicolored	85	45
1243	A349	150f multicolored	1.25	65

Size: 81x61mm

Imperf

1244	A349	250f multicolored	2.50	1.10
		Nos. 1240-1244 (5)	5.32	2.57

No. 1244 also exists perf.

July Festivals — A350

Pres. Hussein and: 20f, 100f, Flag. 30f, 150f, "17." 250f, Inscription, portrait inside medal of honor.

1986, July 29 ***Perf. 11½x12***

1245	A350	20f multicolored	15	15
1246	A350	30f multicolored	22	15
1247	A350	100f multicolored	65	45
1248	A350	150f multicolored	95	65

Size: 81x61mm

Imperf

1249	A350	250f multicolored	1.60	1.10
		Nos. 1245-1249 (5)	3.57	2.50

1st Qadisiya Battle — A351

Designs: 20f, 70f, Warrior, shield, vert. 60f, 100f, Pres. Hussein, star, battle scene.

Perf. 13x13½, 13½x13

1986, Sept. 4 **Litho.**

1250	A351	20f multicolored	15	15
1251	A351	60f multicolored	42	28
1252	A351	70f multicolored	50	35
1253	A351	100f multicolored	70	48

Battle between the Arabs and Persian Empire.

Hussein's Battle of Qadisiya — A352

Designs: 30f, 100f, Pres. Hussein, soldiers saluting peace, vert. 40f, 150f, Pres., armed forces. 250f, Pres., soldiers, flags, military scenes.

Perf. 11½x12½, 12½x11½

1986, Sept. 4

1254	A352	30f multicolored	22	15
1255	A352	40f multicolored	28	20
1256	A352	100f multicolored	70	48
1257	A352	150f multicolored	1.05	70

Size: 80x60mm

Imperf

1258	A352	250f multicolored	1.75	1.15
		Nos. 1254-1258 (5)	4.00	2.68

Intl. Peace Year — A353

1986, Nov. 15 **Litho.** ***Perf. 11½x12***

1259	A353	50f Dove, flag, G clef	32	24
1260	A353	100f Globe, dove, rifle	65	48
1261	A353	150f like 50f	1.00	70
1262	A353	250f like 100f	1.60	1.10

Size: 80x69mm

Imperf

1263	A353	200f Emblem, flag, map, fist	1.30	1.00
		Nos. 1259-1263 (5)	4.87	3.52

Pres. Hussein
A354 A355

1986 ***Perf. 12½x12***

1264	A354	30f multicolored	20	15
1265	A355	30f multicolored	20	15
1266	A354	50f multicolored	32	22
1267	A355	50f multicolored	32	22
1268	A354	100f multicolored	65	45
1269	A355	100f multicolored	65	45
1270	A354	150f multicolored	1.00	68
1271	A355	150f multicolored	1.00	68
1272	A354	250f multicolored	1.60	1.05
1273	A354	350f multicolored	2.25	1.50
		Nos. 1264-1273 (10)	8.19	5.55

For overprints, see Nos. 1347-1348.

Army Day — A356

1987, Jan. 6 **Litho.** ***Perf. 12x12½***

1274	A356	20f shown	15	15
1275	A356	40f Hussein, armed forces	25	25
1276	A356	90f like 20f	58	58
1277	A356	100f like 40f	65	65

United Arab Shipping Co., 10th Anniv. (in 1986) A357

1987, Apr. 3 **Litho.** ***Perf. 12½***

1278	A357	50f Cargo ship	32	22
1279	A357	100f Container ship Chaleb Ibn Al Waleeb	65	45
1280	A357	150f like 50f	1.00	68
1281	A357	250f like 100f	1.60	1.05

Size: 102x91mm

Imperf

1282	A357	200f Loading cargo aboard the Waleeb	1.30	1.00

Arab Baath Socialist Party, 40th Anniv. — A358

1987, Apr. 7 **Litho.** ***Perf. 12x12½***

1283	A358	20f shown	15	15
1284	A358	40f Hussein, "7," map	25	25
1285	A358	90f like 20f	58	58
1286	A358	100f like 40f	65	65

Pres. Hussein's 50th Birthday A359

1987, Apr. 28 ***Perf. 12½x12***

1287	A359	20f shown	15	15
1288	A359	40f Portrait	25	25
1289	A359	90f like 20f	58	58
1290	A359	100f like 40f	65	65

July Festivals — A360

UNICEF, 40th Anniv. — A361

Perf. 12½x12, 12x12½

1987, July 17

1291	A360	20f Hussein, star, flag, horiz.	15	15
1292	A360	40f shown	25	25
1293	A360	90f like 20f, horiz.	58	58
1294	A360	100f like 40f	65	65

1987, Oct. 4 ***Perf. 12x12½, 12½x12***

1295	A361	20f shown	15	15
1296	A361	40f "40," horiz.	25	25
1297	A361	90f like 20f	58	58
1298	A361	100f like 40f, horiz.	65	65

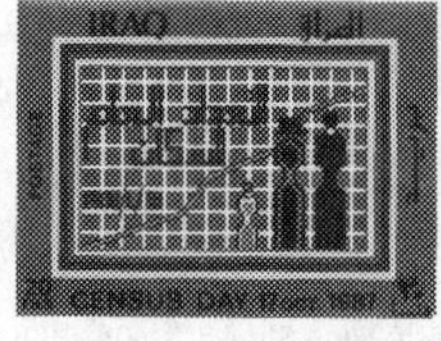

Census Day A362

1987, Nov. 1 ***Perf. 12x11½***

1299	A362	20f shown	15	15
1300	A362	30f Graph, Arabs, diff.	20	20
1301	A362	50f like 30f	35	35
1302	A362	500f like 20f	3.25	3.25

Army Day A363

Perf. 11½x12, 12x11½

1988, Jan. 6 **Litho.**

1303	A363	20f "6," Hussein, troops, vert.	15	15
1304	A363	30f shown	20	15
1305	A363	50f like 20f, vert.	35	15
1306	A363	150f like 30f	1.00	38
		Set value		60

Art Day — A364

A365

1988, Jan. 8 Litho. ***Perf. 11½x12***

1307 A364 20f shown 15 15
1308 A364 30f Hussein, rainbow, gun barrel, music 22 15
1309 A364 50f like 20f 38 15
1310 A364 100f like 30f 75 25

Size: 60x80mm

Imperf

1311 A364 150f Notes, instruments, floral ornament 1.20 80
Set value 1.30

1988, Feb. 8 ***Perf. 11½x12, 12x11½***

1312 A365 20f "8," troops, Hussein, horiz. 15 15
1313 A365 30f "8," Hussein, eagle 22 15
1314 A365 50f like 20f, horiz. 38 15
1315 A365 150f like 30f 1.20 40
Set value 65

Popular Army, 18th anniv. (20f, 50f); Feb. 8th Revolution, 25th anniv. (30f, 150f).

Al-Baath Arab Socialist Party, 50th Anniv. A366

President Hussein's 50th Birthday A367

1988, Apr. 7 ***Perf. 12x12½, 12½x12***

1316 A366 20f Flag, grain, convention, horiz. 15 15
1317 A366 30f shown 22 15
1318 A366 50f like 20f, horiz. 38 15
1319 A366 150f like 30f 1.20 40
Set value 65

1988, Apr. 28 ***Perf. 12x12½***

1320 A367 20f shown 15 15
1321 A367 30f Hussein, 3 hands, flowers 22 15
1322 A367 50f like 20f 38 15
1323 A367 100f like 50f 75 25

Size: 90x99mm

Imperf

1324 A367 150f Sun, Hussein, heart, flowers 1.20 80
Set value 1.30

World Health Organization, 40th Anniv. — A368

Regional Marine Environment Day, Apr. 24 — A369

1988, June 1 ***Perf. 12½x12, 12x12½***

1325 A368 20f WHO anniv. emblem, horiz. 15 15
1326 A368 40f shown 30 15
1327 A368 90f like 20f, horiz. 68 22
1328 A368 100f like 40f 75 25
Set value 60

Perf. 12x12½, 12½x12

1988, Apr. 24

1329 A369 20f shown 15 15
1330 A369 40f Flag in map, fish, horiz. 30 15
1331 A369 90f like 20f 68 22
1332 A369 100f like 40f, horiz. 75 25
Set value 60

Shuhada School Victims Memorial A370

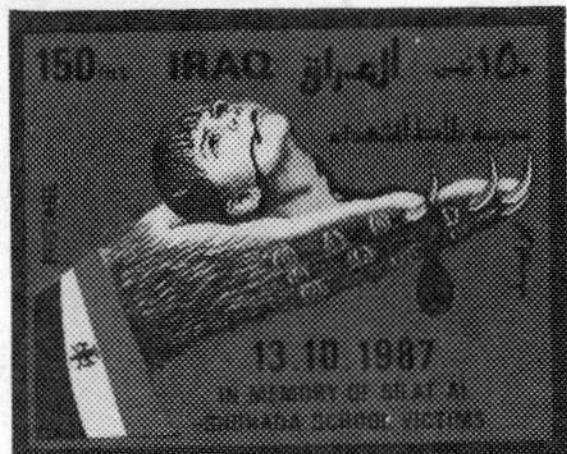

A371

1988, June 1 ***Perf. 11½x12, 12x11½***

1333 A370 20f shown 15 15
1334 A370 40f Girl caught in explosion, horiz. 30 15
1335 A370 90f like 20f 68 22
1336 A370 100f like 40f, horiz. 75 25
Set value 60

Souvenir Sheet

Perf. 12½

1337 A371 150f red, blk & brt grn 1.15 75

Pilgrimage to Mecca — A372

1988, July 24 Litho. ***Perf. 13½***

1338 A372 90f multicolored 70 22
1339 A372 100f multicolored 80 28
1340 A372 150f multicolored 1.20 40

Basra, 1350th Anniv. A373

1988, Oct. 22 ***Perf. 12x11½***

1341 A373 100f multicolored 75 25

Natl. Flag, Grip on Lightning — A374

Pres. Hussein, Natl. Flag — A375

1988, July 17 ***Perf. 12x12½***

1342 A374 50f shown 38 15
1343 A374 90f Map, Hussein, desert 68 22
1344 A374 100f like 50f 75 25
1345 A374 150f like 90f 1.15 35

Size: 90x70mm

Imperf

1346 A375 250f shown 1.90 65

July Festivals and 9th anniv. of Pres. Hussein's assumption of office.

Nos. 1272-1273 Overprinted انتصر العراق ١٩٨٨/٨/٨

1988, Aug. 7 Litho. ***Perf. 12½x12***

1347 A354 250f multicolored 2.90 95
1348 A354 350f multicolored 4.00 1.35

Victory.

Navy Day — A376

1988, Aug. 12 ***Perf. 12x12½***

1349 A376 50f shown 58 20
1350 A376 90f Map, boats 1.05 35
1351 A376 100f like 50f 1.15 38
1352 A376 150f like 90f 1.75 58

Size: 91x70mm

Imperf

1353 A376 250f Emblem, Pres. Hussein decorating officers 3.50 1.15

1988 Summer Olympics, Seoul — A377

1988, Sept. 19 ***Perf. 12x12½***

1354 A377 100f Boxing, character trademark 1.15 38
1355 A377 150f Flag, emblems 1.75 58

Size: 101x91mm

Imperf

1356 A377 500f Emblem, trademark, Hussein, trophy 7.00 2.35

Liberation of Fao A378

1988, Sept. 1 ***Perf. 12x11½***

1357 A378 100f multicolored 1.15 38
1358 A378 150f multicolored 1.75 58

Size: 60x80mm

Imperf

1359 A378 500f Hussein, text 7.00 2.35

Mosul A379

Baghdad — A380

Ancient cities.

Perf. 12x11½, 11½x12

1988, Oct. 22

1360 A379 50f Fortress 58 20
1361 A380 150f Astrolabe, modern architecture 1.75 58

Al-Hussein Missile — A381

1988, Sept. 10 ***Perf. 11½x12***

1362 A381 100f multicolored 80 28
1363 A381 150f multicolored 1.20 40

Size: 80x60mm

Imperf

1364 A381 500f Hussein, map, missile 3.75 1.25

2nd Intl. Festival, Babylon — A382

1988, Sept. 30 ***Perf. 11½x12***

1365 A382 100f multicolored 78 25
1366 A382 150f multicolored 1.15 38

Size: 60x80mm

Imperf

1367 A382 500f Medallions 3.75 1.25

Victorious Iraq A383

1988, Aug. 8 Litho. *Perf. 12x11½*

1368	A383	50f multicolored	40	15
1369	A383	100f multicolored	80	28
1370	A383	150f multicolored	1.20	40

Birthday of Mohammed A384

1988, Oct. 23 Litho. *Perf. 11½x12*

1371	A384	100f multicolored	75	25
1372	A384	150f multicolored	1.10	38
1373	A384	1d multicolored	7.50	2.50

Martyrs' Day — A385

1988, Dec. 1 Litho. *Perf. 13½*

1374	A385	100f multicolored	75	25
1375	A385	150f multicolored	1.10	38
1376	A385	500f multicolored	3.75	1.25

Police Day A386

1989, Jan. 9 Litho. *Perf. 12x11½*

1377	A386	50f multicolored	38	15
1378	A386	100f multicolored	75	25
1379	A386	150f multicolored	1.10	38

Postal Savings Bank — A387

بريد
a

1988 Litho. *Perf. 11½x12*

1380 A387 50f shown

Size: 23½x25mm

Perf. 13½x13

1381 A387(a) 100f multi
1382 A387(a) 150f multi

Nos. 1381-1382 without overprint are postal savings stamps.

Arab Cooperation Council — A388

1989, Feb. 12 Litho. *Perf. 12x11½*

1383	A388	100f shown	78	26
1384	A388	150f Statesmen, diff.	1.15	38

52nd Birthday of Pres. Hussein A392

1989, Apr. 28 Litho. *Perf. 12x11½*

1392	A392	100f multicolored	68	22
1393	A392	150f multicolored	1.00	32

Size: 60x81mm

Imperf

1394	A392	250f Hussein, diff.	1.70	58

Fao Liberation, 1st Anniv. — A393

1989, Apr. 18 *Perf. 12x11½*

1395	A393	100f multi	68	22
1396	A393	150f multi	1.00	32

Size: 60x81mm

Imperf

1397	A393	250f Calendar	1.70	58

Gen. Adnan Khairalla — A394

Reconstruction of Basra — A395

1989, May 6 Litho. *Perf. 13½*

1398	A394	50h gold & multi	48	16
1399	A394	100h cop & multi	95	32
1400	A394	150h sil & multi	1.45	48

Gen. Adnan Khairalla (1940-1989), deputy commander-in-chief of the armed forces and minister of defense.

1989, June 14

1401	A395	100h multi	95	32
1402	A395	150h multi	1.45	48

Reconstruction of Fao — A396

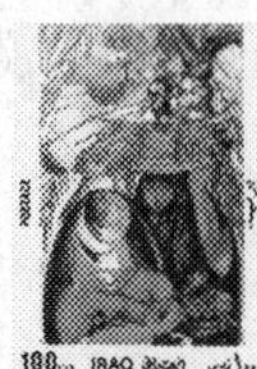

Women — A397

1989, June 25

1403	A396	100h multi	95	32
1404	A396	150h multi	1.45	48

1989, June 25 Litho. *Perf. 11½x12*

1405	A397	100f yel & multi	58	20
1406	A397	150f brt pink & multi	88	30
1407	A397	1d brt blue & multi	5.75	2.00
1408	A397	5d white & multi	28.75	9.50

July Festivals — A398

1989, July 17 Litho. *Perf. 12x12½*

1409	A398	50f multicolored	40	15
1410	A398	100f multicolored	78	26
1411	A398	150f multicolored	1.20	40

Election of Pres. Hussein, 10th anniv.

Family A399

1989, July 19 *Perf. 13½*

1412	A399	50f multicolored	40	15
1413	A399	100f multicolored	78	26
1414	A399	150f multicolored	1.20	40

A400

Victory Day — A401

1989, Aug. 8 *Perf. 12x12½*

1415	A400	100f multicolored	78	26
1416	A400	150f multicolored	1.20	40

Size: 71x91mm

Imperf

1417	A401	250f multicolored	2.00	68

Interparliamentary Union, Cent. — A402

1989, Sept. 15 *Perf. 12½x12*

1418	A402	25f multicolored	20	15
1419	A402	100f multicolored	78	26
1420	A402	150f multicolored	1.20	40

Ancient Cities A403

1989, Oct. 15 *Perf. 11½x12½*

1421	A403	100f Dhi Qar-ur	78	26
1422	A403	100f Erbil	78	26
1423	A403	100f An Najaf	78	26

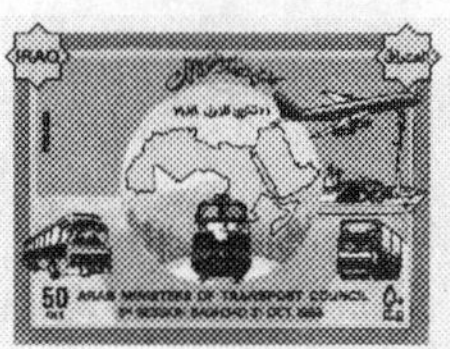

5th Session of the Arab Ministers of Transport Council, Baghdad, Oct. 21 A404

Designs: 100f, Land, air and sea transport, diff. 150f, Modes of transport, flags, vert.

Perf. 12x11½, 11½x12

1989, Oct. 21

1424	A404	50f shown	40	15
1425	A404	100f multicolored	78	26
1426	A404	150f multicolored	1.20	40

Iraqi News Agency, 30th Anniv. A405

1989, Nov. 9 *Perf. 13½*

1427	A405	50f multicolored	40	15
1428	A405	100f multicolored	78	26
1429	A405	150f multicolored	1.20	40

Declaration of Palestinian State, 1st Anniv. — A406

Flowers — A407

1989, Nov. 15 *Perf. 12x12½*

1430 A406 25f shown 20 15
1431 A406 50f Palestinian uprising 40 15
1432 A406 100f like 25f 78 26
1433 A406 150f like 50f 1.20 40

1989, Nov. 20 *Perf. 13½x13*

1434 A407 25f *Viola sp.* 20 15
1435 A407 50f *Antirrhinum majus* 40 15
1436 A407 100f *Hibiscus trionum* 78 26
1437 A407 150f *Mesembryanthemum sparkles* 1.20 40

Miniature Sheet

Perf. 12½x11½

1438 Sheet of 4 4.00 4.00
a. A407 25f like No. 1434 1.00 1.00
b. A407 50f like No. 1435 1.00 1.00
c. A407 100f like No. 1436 1.00 1.00
d. A407 150f like No. 1437 1.00 1.00

Nos. 1438a-1438d printed in a continuous design. No. 1438 sold for 500f.

Reconstruction of Fao — A408

1989, Oct. 25 **Litho.** *Perf. 13½*

1439 A408 100f multicolored 78 26
1440 A408 150f multicolored 1.15 38

Martyrs' Day — A409

1989, Dec. 4 **Litho.** *Perf. 13½*

1441 A409 50f multicolored 38 16
1442 A409 100f multicolored 78 26
1443 A409 150f multicolored 1.15 38

Iraqi Red Crescent Soc. — A410

1989, Dec. 10 **Litho.** *Perf. 13½*

1444 A410 100f multicolored 38 16
1445 A410 150f multicolored 1.15 38
1446 A410 500f multicolored 3.75 1.25

AIR POST STAMPS

Catalogue values for unused stamps in this section are for Never Hinged items.

Basra Airport — AP1

Diyala Railway Bridge — AP2

Vickers Viking over: 4f, 20f, Kut Dam. 5f, 35f, Faisal II Bridge.

Perf. 11½, 11½x12

1949, Feb. 1 **Engr.** **Unwmk.**

C1 AP1 3f blue green 15 15
C2 AP1 4f red violet 15 15
C3 AP1 5f red brown 15 15
C4 AP1 10f carmine 15 15
C5 AP1 20f blue 15 15
C6 AP1 35f red orange 25 15
C7 AP2 50f olive 1.50 18
C8 AP2 100f violet 2.00 25
Nos. C1-C8 (8) 4.50
Set value 1.00

Sheets exist, perf. and imperf., containing one each of Nos. C1-C8, with arms and Arabic inscription in blue green in upper and lower margin. Value (2 sheets) $40.

Republic

ICY Emblem — AP3

1965, Aug. 13 **Litho.** *Perf. 13½*

C9 AP3 5f brn org & black 42 15
C10 AP3 10f citron & dk brn 60 15
C11 AP3 30f ultra & black 1.65 50

International Cooperation Year.

Trident 1E Jet Plane — AP4

1965, Dec. 1 **Photo.** *Perf. 11½*

Granite Paper

C12 AP4 5f multicolored 15 15
C13 AP4 10f multicolored 20 15
C14 AP4 40f multicolored 2.50 50
Set value 62

Introduction by Iraqi Airways of Trident 1E jet planes.

Arab International Tourist Union Emblem — AP5

Travelers on Magic Carpet AP6

1966, Dec. 3 **Litho.** *Perf. 13½, 14*

C15 AP5 2f multicolored 15 15
C16 AP6 5f yellow & multi 18 15
C17 AP5 15f blue & multi 22 15
C18 AP6 50f multicolored 90 35
Set value 55

Meeting of the Arab Intl. Tourist Union, Baghdad.

For overprint, see No. RAC1.

Costume Type of Regular Issue

Iraqi Costumes: 40f, Woman's head. 50f, Woman's costume. 80f, Man's costume.

1967, Nov. 10 **Litho.** *Perf. 13*

C19 A105 40f multicolored 30 15
C20 A105 50f blue & multi 45 24
C21 A105 80f green & multi 3.00 60

International Tourist Year Type of Regular Issue

Designs: 50f, Female statue, Temples of Hatra. 80f, Spiral Tower (Malwiye of Samarra). 100f, Adam's Tree. 200f, Aladdin's Cave. 500f, Golden Shiah Mosque of Kadhimain. (50f, 80f, 100f and 200f are vertical)

1967, Dec. 1 **Litho.**

C22 A107 50f multicolored 60 24
C23 A107 80f multicolored 1.10 40
C24 A107 100f multicolored 2.25 48
C25 A107 200f ver & multi 3.50 2.00
C26 A107 500f brn & multi 24.00 12.00
Nos. C22-C26 (5) 31.45 15.12

For overprints, see Nos. C39, C52, C53.

Arabian AP7

Animals: 2f, Striped hyena. 3f, Leopard. 5f, Mountain gazelle. 200f, Arabian stallion.

1969, Sept. 1 **Litho.** *Perf. 14*

C27 AP7 2f multicolored 15 15
C28 AP7 3f multicolored 15 15
C29 AP7 5f multicolored 15 15
C30 AP7 10f multicolored 25 18
C31 AP7 200f multicolored 6.50 3.50
Nos. C27-C31 (5) 7.20 4.13

Ross Smith's Vickers Vimy AP8

1969, Dec. 4 **Litho.** *Perf. 14*

C32 AP8 15f dk bl & multi 80 35
C33 AP8 35f multicolored 1.65 50
a. Souv. sheet of 2, #C32-C33, imperf. 7.50 6.00

50th anniv. of the first England to Australia flight of Capt. Ross Smith and Lt. Keith Smith. No. C33a sold for 100f.

View Across Euphrates — AP9

Iraqi Banknotes and Pres. Hassan al-Bakr AP10

1970, Oct. 30 **Litho.** *Perf. 13*

C34 AP9 10f brt bl & multi 75 15
C35 AP9 15f multicolored 75 15
C36 AP10 1d multicolored 18.00 7.50

National Development Plan.

For overprints, see Nos. C42-C43.

Telecommunications Emblem — AP11

1970, Dec. 15 **Litho.** *Perf. 14x13½*

C37 AP11 15f gray & multi 25 15
C38 AP11 25f lt bl & multi 50 35

Tenth Conference of Arab Telecommunications Union.

No. C23 Overprinted **يوم الأنواء W.M. DAY 1971**

1971, Apr. 23 *Perf. 13*

C39 A107 80f multicolored 5.50 4.00

World Meteorological Day.

Iraqi Philatelic Society Emblem — AP12

1972, Feb. 25 **Litho.** *Perf. 13*

C40 AP12 25f multicolored 80 50
C41 AP12 70f pink & multi 2.50 1.50

Iraqi Philatelic Society, 20th anniversary.

Nos. C34-C35 Overprinted

المؤتمر التاسع للاتحاد الوطني
لطلبة العراق
٢٥ شباط – ٢ آذار / ١٩٧٢

1972, Feb. 25

C42 AP9 10f brt bl & multi 1.00 25
C43 AP9 15f multicolored 2.00 1.00

9th Cong. of Natl. Union of Iraqi Students.

Soccer and C.I.S.M. Emblem AP13

Designs: 20f, 35f, Players, soccer ball, C.I.S.M. emblem. 100f, Winged lion, Olympic and C.I.S.M. emblems.

1972, June 9 **Litho.** *Perf. 13½*

C46 AP13 10f lt bl & multi 35 15
C47 AP13 20f dp bl & multi 70 15
C48 AP13 25f green & multi 70 20
C49 AP13 35f brt bl & multi 2.75 50
a. Souv. sheet, 100f, imperf. 8.00 8.00

25th Military Soccer Championships (C.I.S.M.), Baghdad, June 9-19.

Statue of Athlete — AP14

Design: 70f, Mesopotamian archer on horseback, ancient and modern athletes.

1972, Nov. 15 Photo. *Perf. 14x13½*

No.	Type	Description	Unused	Used
C50	AP14	25f multicolored	75	50
C51	AP14	70f multicolored	2.25	1.50

Cong. of Asian and World Body Building Championships, Baghdad, Nov. 15-23, 1972.

Nos. C23, C26 Overprinted

المؤتمر الدولي
للتاريخ/١٩٧٣

1973, Mar. 25 Litho. *Perf. 13*

No.	Type	Description	Unused	Used
C52	A107	80f multi	11.00	4.50
C53	A107	500f multi	37.50	*52.50*

International History Congress.

ICATU Type of 1976

1976, Mar. 24 Photo. *Perf. 13½*

No.	Type	Description	Unused	Used
C54	A213	75f blue & multi	4.00	2.00

Symbolic Eye
AP15

Basketball
AP16

1976, June 20 Photo. *Perf. 14*

No.	Type	Description	Unused	Used
C55	AP15	25f ultra & dk brn	20	15
C56	AP15	35f brt grn & dk brn	25	18
C57	AP15	50f orange & multi	40	25

World Health Day: Foresight prevents blindness.

1976, July 30 Litho. *Perf. 12x12½*

Montreal Olympic Games Emblem and: 35f, Volleyball. 50f, Wrestling. 75f, Boxing. 100f, Target shooting (horiz.).

No.	Type	Description	Unused	Used
C58	AP16	25f yel & multi	50	15
C59	AP16	35f blue & multi	75	25
C60	AP16	50f ver & multi	1.00	50
C61	AP16	75f yel grn & multi	1.50	70

Souvenir Sheet

Imperf

No.	Type	Description	Unused	Used
C62	AP16	100f grn & multi	6.00	6.00

21st Olympic Games, Montreal, Canada, July 17-Aug. 1.

13th World Telecommunications Day — AP17

1981, May 17 Photo. *Perf. 12½*

No.	Type	Description	Unused	Used
C63	AP17	25f multicolored	20	15
C64	AP17	50f multicolored	40	25
C65	AP17	75f multicolored	60	38

Air Force Type of 1981

1981, June 1 Photo. *Perf. 14x13½*

No.	Type	Description	Unused	Used
C66	A289	120f Planes, vert.	1.00	75

AIR POST OFFICIAL STAMP

Catalogue values for all unused stamps in this section are for Never Hinged items.

Nos. C19-C22 Overprinted

Official رسمي

1971 Litho. *Perf. 13*

No.	Type	Description	Unused	Used
CO1	A105	40f multicolored	3.25	1.00
CO2	A105	50f multicolored	4.25	1.00
CO3	A105	80f multicolored	4.00	1.00

"Official" Reading Down

No.	Type	Description	Unused	Used
CO4	A107	50f multicolored	3.50	2.25

Nos. C27-C28, C30 Overprinted or Surcharged

Official رسمي

25 Fils ٢٥

1971 *Perf. 14*

No.	Type	Description	Unused	Used
CO5	AP7	10f multicolored	55	25
CO6	AP7	15f on 3f multi	80	50
CO7	AP7	25f on 2f multi	1.65	1.00

No bar and surcharge on No. CO5.

OFFICIAL STAMPS

British Mandate

Regular Issue of 1923 Overprinted:

ON STATE SERVICE
k

ON
STATE
SERVICE
l

1923 Wmk. 4 *Perf. 12*

No.	Type	Description	Unused	Used
O1	A1(k)	½a ol grn	15	15
O2	A2(k)	1a brown	15	15
O3	A3(l)	1½a car lake	35	15
O4	A4(k)	2a brn org	25	15
O5	A5(k)	3a dp blue	35	15
O6	A6(l)	4a dl vio	25	15
O7	A7(k)	6a blue grn	30	25
O8	A6(l)	8a ol bis	35	35
O9	A8(l)	1r grn & brn	5.00	85
O10	A1(k)	2r blk (R)	11.00	1.50
O11	A6(l)	5r orange	32.50	15.00
O12	A7(k)	10r carmine	57.50	40.00
		Nos. O1-O12 (12)	108.15	58.85

Regular Issue of 1923-25 Overprinted:

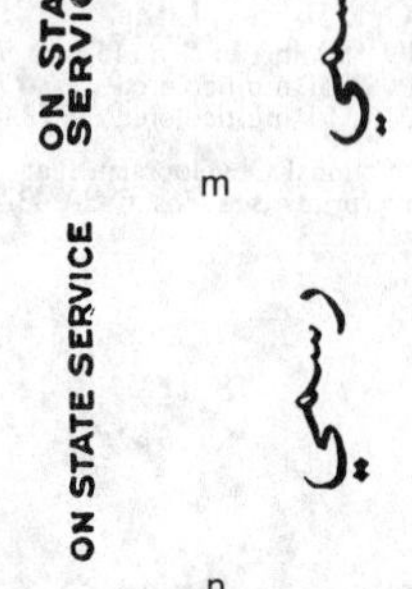

m

n

1924-25

No.	Type	Description	Unused	Used
O13	A1(m)	½a olive grn	15	15
O14	A2(m)	1a brown	15	15
O15	A3(n)	1½a car lake	15	15
O16	A4(m)	2a brn org	15	15
O17	A5(m)	3a dp blue	20	15
O18	A6(n)	4a dull vio	30	15
O19	A7(m)	6a blue grn	35	15
O20	A6(n)	8a olive bis	50	15
O21	A8(n)	1r grn & brn	3.00	75
O22	A1(m)	2r bis ('25)	10.00	5.00
O23	A6(n)	5r orange	32.50	20.00
O24	A7(m)	10r brn red	57.50	30.00
		Nos. O13-O24 (12)	104.95	56.95

For overprint, see Nos. O42, O47, O51-O53.

No. 14 Overprinted Type "n"

1927

No.	Type	Description	Unused	Used
O25	A9	1r red brown	3.00	60

Regular Issue of 1931 Overprinted Vertically

ON STATE SERVICE رسمي
o

1931

No.	Type	Description	Unused	Used
O26	A10	½a green	15	15
O27	A10	1a chestnut	15	15
O28	A10	1½a carmine	13.00	5.00
O29	A10	2a orange	25	15
O30	A10	3a light blue	30	15
O31	A10	4a purple brn	50	15
O32	A10	6a Prussian bl	16.00	1.25
O33	A10	8a dark green	12.00	1.50

Overprinted Horizontally

ON STATE SERVICE

p

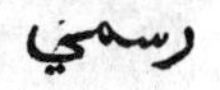

No.	Type	Description	Unused	Used
O34	A11	1r dark brown	3.25	1.10
O35	A11	2r yel brown	6.00	6.00
O36	A11	5r deep org	30.00	30.00
O37	A11	10r red	50.00	50.00
		Nos. O26-O37 (12)	131.60	95.60

Overprinted Vertically Reading Up

No.	Type	Description	Unused	Used
O38	A9(p)	25r violet	1,000.	1,050.

For overprints, see Nos. O39-O41, O43-O46, O48-O50, O54.

Kingdom

Official Stamps of 1924-31 Surcharged with New Values in Fils and Dinars, like Nos. 28 to 43

1932, Apr. 1

No.	Type	Description	Unused	Used
O39	A10	3f on ½a green	35	35
O40	A10	4f on 1a chnt (G)	15	15
O41	A10	5f on 1a chnt	18	15
a.		Inverted Arabic "5"	*40.00*	*35.00*
O42	A3	8f on 1½a car lake	70	15
O43	A10	10f on 2a org	25	15
O44	A10	15f on 3a lt bl	40	15
O45	A10	20f on 4a pur brn	45	15
O46	A10	25f on 4a pur brn	50	25
O47	A7	30f on 6a bl grn	60	35
O48	A10	40f on 8a dk grn	1.10	35
a.		"Flis" for "Fils"	*300.00*	*450.00*
O49	A11	50f on 1r dk brn	1.75	80
O50	A11	75f on 1r dk brn	3.00	2.75
O51	A1	100f on 2r bis	6.00	1.00
O52	A6	200f on 5r org	12.00	8.00
O53	A7	½d on 10r brn red	35.00	32.50
a.		Bar in "½" omitted	*700.00*	
O54	A9	1d on 25r vio	87.50	80.00
		Nos. O39-O54 (16)	149.93	127.25

Regular Issue of 1932 Overprinted Vertically like Nos. O26 to O33

1932, May 9

No.	Type	Description	Unused	Used
O55	A12	2f ultramarine	15	15
O56	A12	3f green	15	15
O57	A12	4f vio brown	15	15
O58	A12	5f gray	15	15
O59	A12	8f deep red	15	15
O60	A12	10f yellow	15	15
O61	A12	15f deep blue	1.40	15
O62	A12	20f orange	25	15
O63	A12	25f rose lilac	3.50	40
O64	A12	30f olive grn	75	40
O65	A12	40f dark vio	1.40	40

Overprinted Horizontally Like Nos. O34 to O37

No.	Type	Description	Unused	Used
O66	A13	50f deep brown	1.40	50
O67	A13	75f lt ultra	2.00	25
O68	A13	100f deep green	5.25	50
O69	A13	200f dark red	14.00	2.75

Overprinted Vertically like No. O38

No.	Type	Description	Unused	Used
O70	A14	½d gray blue	14.00	3.50
O71	A14	1d claret	35.00	50.00
		Nos. O55-O71 (17)	79.85	59.90

Regular Issue of 1934-38 Overprinted Type "o" Vertically Reading up in Black

1934-38 Unwmk.

No.	Type	Description	Unused	Used
O72	A15	1f purple ('38)	80	15
O73	A15	2f ultramarine	30	15
O74	A15	3f green	15	15
O75	A15	4f purple brn	15	15
O76	A15	5f gray green	15	15
O77	A15	8f deep red	80	15
O78	A15	10f yellow	15	15
O79	A15	15f deep blue	4.00	15
O80	A15	20f orange	25	15
O81	A15	25f brn violet	8.00	1.65
O82	A15	30f olive green	45	18
O83	A15	40f dark violet	1.00	18

Overprinted Type "p"

No.	Type	Description	Unused	Used
O84	A16	50f deep brown	45	20
O85	A16	75f ultramarine	65	52
O86	A16	100f deep green	1.65	45
O87	A16	200f dark red	3.25	65

Overprinted Type "p" Vertically Reading Up

No.	Type	Description	Unused	Used
O88	A17	½d gray blue	12.00	6.25
O89	A17	1d claret	24.00	12.50
		Nos. O72-O89 (18)	58.20	23.93

Catalogue values for unused stamps in this section, from this point to the end of the section, are for Never Hinged items.

Stamps of 1941-42 Overprinted in Black or Red:

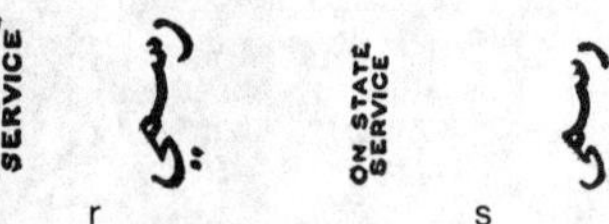

r s

Perf. 11½x13½, 13 to 14 and Compound

1941-42

No.	Type	Description	Unused	Used
O90	A18(r)	1f dk vio ('42)	15	15
O91	A18(r)	2f choc ('42)	15	15
O92	A19(r)	3f brt grn ('42)	15	15
O93	A19(r)	4f pur (R) ('42)	15	15
O94	A19(r)	5f dk car rose ('42)	15	15
O95	A20(s)	8f carmine	50	15
O96	A20(s)	8f ocher ('42)	15	15
O97	A20(s)	10f ocher	2.00	15
O98	A20(s)	10f car ('42)	20	15
O99	A20(s)	15f dull blue	5.50	35
O100	A20(s)	15f blk (R) ('42)	20	15
O101	A20(s)	20f black (R)	1.00	20
O102	A20(s)	20f dl bl ('42)	40	15
O103	A21(s)	25f dark vio	1.50	18
O104	A21(r)	25f dk vio ('42)	30	15
O105	A21(s)	30f dp orange	1.10	15
O106	A21(r)	30f dk org ('42)	25	15
O107	A21(s)	40f brown org	1.10	25
O108	A21(r)	40f chnt ('42)	50	25
O109	A21(s)	50f ultra	1.00	18
O110	A21(r)	75f rose vio	40	30
O111	A22(s)	100f ol grn ('42)	60	40
O112	A22(s)	200f dp org ('42)	1.65	1.65
O113	A23(r)	½d blue ('42)	8.00	5.00
O114	A23(r)	1d grnsh bl ('42)	13.00	10.00
		Nos. O90-O114 (25)	40.10	20.86

The space between the English and Arabic on overprints "r" and "s" varies with the size of the stamps.

For overprints, see Nos. O165, RA5.

Stamps of 1942 Overprinted in Black

1942 Unwmk. *Perf. 13x13½*

No.	Type	Description	Unused	Used
O115	A24	1f violet & brown	15	15
O116	A24	2f dark blue & brn	15	15
O117	A24	3f lt green & brn	15	15

O118 A24 4f dl brown & brn 15 15
O119 A24 5f sage green & brn 15 15
O120 A24 6f red orange & brn 15 15
O121 A24 10f dl rose red & brn 15 15
O122 A24 12f yel green & brn 20 15
Set value 90 45

Stamps of 1948 Overprinted in Black — ON STATE SERVICE

1948, Jan. 15 ***Perf. 11½x12***

Size: 17¾x20½mm

O123 A25 1f slate 15 15
O124 A25 2f sepia 15 15
O125 A25 3f emerald 15 15
O126 A25 4f purple 15 15
O127 A25 5f rose lake 15 15
O128 A25 6f plum 15 15
O129 A25 8f ocher 15 15
O130 A25 10f rose red 15 15
O131 A25 12f dark olive 15 15
O132 A25 15f black 25 75
O133 A25 20f blue 15 15
O134 A25 25f rose violet 18 15
O135 A25 30f red orange 20 15
O136 A25 40f orange brn 25 15

Perf. 12x11½

Size: 22x27½mm

O137 A25 60f deep blue 35 25
O138 A25 75f lilac rose 40 40
O139 A25 100f olive grn 55 35
O140 A25 200f dp orange 1.15 1.00
O141 A25 ½d blue 5.00 2.75
O142 A25 1d green 10.00 5.50
Nos. O123-O142 (20) 19.83 12.95

For overprints, see Nos. O166-O177, O257, O272, O274, O277, O282, RA1, RA3, RA4.

Same Overprint on Nos. 133-138

1949-51 ***Perf. 11½x12***

Size: 17¾x20½mm

O143 A25 3f rose lake ('51) 80 35
O144 A25 5f emerald ('51) 80 35
O145 A25 14f dk olive ('50) 80 15
O146 A25 16f rose red ('51) 80 35
O147 A25 28f blue ('51) 80 25

Perf. 12x11½

Size: 22x27½mm

O148 A25 50f deep blue 1.25 50
Nos. O143-O148 (6) 5.25 1.95

For overprints, see Nos. O258, O273, O275, O276.

Same Overprint in Black on Stamps and Type of 1954-57

1955-59 ***Perf. 11½x12***

O148A A28 1f blue ('56) 15 15
O149 A28 2f chocolate 15 15
O150 A28 3f rose lake 15 15
O151 A28 4f violet 15 15
O152 A28 5f emerald 15 15
O153 A28 6f plum ('56) 15 15
O154 A28 8f ocher ('56) 15 15
O155 A28 10f blue 15 15
O155A A28 16f brt rose ('57) 12.50 11.00
O156 A28 20f olive 15 15
O157 A28 25f rose violet 80 45
O158 A28 30f vermilion 20 15
O159 A28 40f orange brn 30 20

Size: 22½x27½mm

O160 A28 50f blue 2.00 30
O161 A28 60f pale pur 7.00 3.00
O161A A28 100f ol grn ('59) 15.00 3.00
Nos. O148A-O161A (16) 39.15 19.45

Dates of issue for Nos. O155A and O161A are suppositional.

For overprints, see Nos. O178-O191, O259-O260, O283-O291.

Same Ovpt. on Stamps of 1957-58

O162 A33 1f blue 2.50 60
O162A A33 2f chocolate 3.00 1.00
O162B A33 3f dk carmine 3.75 1.50
O162C A33 4f dull violet 4.50 80
O162D A33 5f emerald 2.50 80
O163 A33 6f plum 2.50 80
O164 A33 10f blue 2.50 80
Nos. O162-O164 (7) 21.25 6.30

For overprints, see #O192-O199, O292-O293.

Republic

Official Stamps of 1942-51 with Additional Overprint — الجمهورية العراقية

Perf. 13½x14

1958-59 **Engr.** **Unwmk.**

O165 A22 200f dp orange 3.25 2.50

Perf. 11½x12, 12x11½

O166 A25 12f dk olive 60 45
O167 A25 14f olive 60 55
O168 A25 15f black 35 25
O169 A25 16f rose red 1.40 1.40
O170 A25 25f rose vio 2.00 1.25
O171 A25 28f blue 1.00 1.00
O172 A25 40f orange brn 60 60
O173 A25 60f deep blue 1.50 1.40
O174 A25 75f lilac rose 1.25 1.00
O175 A25 200f dp orange 1.50 1.50
O176 A25 ½d blue 10.00 3.50
O177 A25 1d green 16.00 7.25
Nos. O166-O177 (12) 36.80 20.15

Other denominations of types A22 and A25 exist with this overprint, but these were probably not regularly issued.

Same Ovpt. on Nos. O148A-O161A

O178 A28 1f blue 15 15
O179 A28 2f chocolate 15 15
O180 A28 3f rose lake 15 15
O181 A28 4f violet 15 15
O181A A28 5f emerald 40 15
O182 A28 6f plum 15 15
O183 A28 8f ocher 30 15
O183A A28 10f blue 80 25
O184 A28 16f bright rose 3.25 2.00
O185 A28 20f olive 30 15
O186 A28 25f rose violet 30 20
O187 A28 30f vermilion 40 20
O188 A28 40f orange brn 50 25
O189 A28 50f blue 60 40
O190 A28 60f pale purple 75 55
O191 A28 100f olive grn 80 50
Nos. O178-O191 (16) 9.15 5.55

Same Ovpts. on #O162-O164, 216

O192 A33 1f blue 15 15
O193 A33 2f chocolate 15 15
O194 A33 3f dark carmine 15 15
O195 A33 4f dull violet 15 15
O196 A33 5f emerald 15 15
O197 A33 6f plum 15 15
O198 A33 8f ocher 15 15
O199 A33 10f blue 15 15
Set value 92 55

Nos. 232-233, 235-237, 242 Overprinted — On State Service

Litho. & Photo.

1961, Apr. 1 **Unwmk.** ***Perf. 11½***

O200 A38 1f multi 15 15
O201 A38 2f multi 15 15
O202 A38 4f multi 18 15
O203 A38 5f multi 25 15
O204 A38 10f multi 45 35
O205 A38 50f multi 5.00 2.00
Nos. O200-O205 (6) 6.18 2.95

Nos. 232-247 Overprinted — ON STATE SERVICE

1961

Emblem in Gold, Red and Blue; Blue Inscriptions

O206 A38 1f gray 15 15
O207 A38 2f salmon 15 15
O208 A38 3f pale violet 15 15
O209 A38 4f bright yel 15 15
O210 A38 5f light blue 15 15
O211 A38 10f bright pink 15 15
O212 A38 15f lt green 15 15
O213 A38 20f bister brn 15 15
O214 A38 30f light gray 25 15
O215 A38 40f orange yel 24 15
O216 A38 50f yel green 30 15
O217 A38 75f pale green 45 25
O218 A38 100f orange 55 40
O219 A38 200f lilac 1.10 55
O220 A38 500f bister 7.50 3.75
O221 A38 1d brt green 15.00 7.50
Nos. O206-O221 (16) 26.59 14.10

Nos. 480-482 Overprinted — Official رسمي

1971 **Litho.** ***Perf. 13½***

O222 A115 10f multicolored 50 1.00
O223 A115 15f blue & multi 5.00 1.00
O224 A115 25f multicolored 5.00 2.00

Overprint lines are spaced 16mm on No. O222, 32½mm on Nos. O223-O224.

Same Overprint on Nos. 453, 455-456

1971 ***Perf. 13***

O225 A107 5f lilac & multi 4.75 18
O226 A107 15f rose red & multi 4.75 35
O227 A107 25f vio bl & multi 7.50 1.00

Overprint horizontal on Nos. O225 and O227; vertical, reading down on No. O226. Distance between English and Arabic words: 8mm.

Nos. 446, 448-449 Overprinted — Official

1971 **Litho.** ***Perf. 13***

O228 A105 15f multicolored 1.00 50
O229 A105 15f multicolored 45.00 5.00
O230 A105 25f multicolored 8.00 2.00
O231 A105 30f multicolored 8.00 2.00

No. O229 overprinted "Official" horizontally

Same Overprint on Nos. 483-486

1972 ***Perf. 13½***

O232 A116 10f multicolored 1.50 50
O233 A116 25f multicolored 3.00 1.00

1972

O234 A117 15f multicolored 2.00 50
O235 A117 25f multicolored 3.00 1.00

Same Overprint, "Official" Reading Down on Nos. 562-565

1972

O240 A142 5f multicolored 50 25
O241 A142 10f multicolored 2.00 50
O242 A142 15f multicolored 5.00 50
O243 A142 35f multicolored 6.00 1.00

Latin inscription on Nos. O240-O241 obliterated with heavy bar.

No. 487 Overprinted "Official" like No. CO5

1972 **Photo.** ***Perf. 13½***

O244 A118 25f multicolored 20 15

#O134, O148 Ovptd. with 3 Bars

Perf. 11½x12, 12x11½

1973, Jan. 29 **Engr.**

O257 A25 25f rose violet 6.00 2.00
O258 A25 50f deep blue 6.00 5.00

Same on Nos. O157 and O160

O259 A28 25f rose violet 6.00 6.00
O260 A28 50f blue 6.00 6.00

Type of 1957 Overprinted with 3 Bars and — ON STATE SERVICE

Size: 22x27½mm

O261 A33 50f rose violet 6.00 6.00

See note after No. 679. No. O261 not issued without overprints.

King Faisal Issues Overprinted — Official

Two sizes of overprint: Arabic 6½mm or 9mm.

1973

O263 A28 15f black (#149) 6.00 6.00
O264 A33 15f black 6.00 1.00
O265 A25 25f rose vio (#121) 8.50 2.00
O266 A28 25f rose vio (#151) 8.50 2.00
O267 A33 25f rose violet 8.50 2.00

Same Overprint on Nos. 674-677

O268 A28 10f blue 1.50 50
O269 A33 10f blue 1.50 50
O270 A28 15f black 6.00 1.00
O271 A33 15f black 6.00 1.00

Official Stamps of 1948-51 Overprinted

Overprint design faces left or right.

1973

O272 A25 12f (#O131) 75 20
O273 A25 14f (#O145) 75 30
O274 A25 15f (#O132) 75 30
O275 A25 16f (#O146) 2.00 50
O276 A25 28f (#O147) 4.00 75
O277 A25 30f (#O135) 4.00 50
O278 A25 40f (#O136) 4.00 90
O279 A25 60f (#O137) 4.00 3.00
O280 A25 100f (#O139) 13.00 5.00
O281 A25 ½d (#O141) 32.50 13.00
O282 A25 1d (#O142) 67.50 67.50
Nos. O272-O282 (11) 133.25 91.95

Same Overprint on Official Stamps of 1955-59

O283 A28 3f (#O150) 20 15
O284 A28 6f (#O153) 20 15
O285 A28 8f (#O154) 20 15
O286 A28 16f (#O155A) *10.00 10.00*
O287 A28 20f (#O156) 1.00 32
O288 A28 30f (#O158) 1.00 50
O289 A28 40f (#O159) 1.00 1.00
O290 A28 60f (#O161) 8.75 2.00
O291 A28 100f (#O161A) *17.50 5.00*

Same Overprint on 1957-58 Issues

O292 A33 3f dk car (#O162B) 20 20
O293 A33 6f plum (#O163) 20 20
O294 A33 8f ocher (#179) 20 20
O295 A33 30f red orange 1.00 1.00

The overprint on Nos. O294-O295 includes the "On State Service" overprint; No. O295 was not issued without overprints. The overprint leaf design faces left or right and varies in size.

Nos. 403, 497, 681 Overprinted — رسمي Official

Perf. 12½, 13x12½, 13½

1974 (?) **Photo., Litho.**

O296 A89 2f multicolored 1.00
O297 A123 15f multicolored 1.00 50
O298 A185 25f multicolored 3.00 1.00

Size of "Official" on Nos. O297-O298 9mm.

Nos. 683-691 Overprinted — OFFICIAL

1974 **Litho.** ***Perf. 13x12½***

O299 A186 5f orange & blk 15 15
O300 A186 10f bister & blk 15 15
O301 A186 20f brt rose & blk 35 20
O302 A186 25f ultra & blk 75 75
O303 A186 35f emerald & blk 75 28
O304 A186 45f blue & black 75 35
O305 A186 50f olive & yel 1.00 40
O306 A186 70f violet & yel 1.00 55
O307 A186 95f brown & yel 1.50 75
Nos. O299-O307 (9) 6.40 3.58

Nos. 455 and 467 Overprinted — رسمي Official

1975 **Litho.** ***Perf. 13, 14***

O308 A107 15f multicolored 1.00 35
O311 A110 30f multicolored 4.00 60

Space between Arabic and English lines of overprint is 4mm on No. O308, 13mm on No. O311.

Nos. 491-493 Overprinted or Surcharged like Nos. CO5-CO7

1975 ***Perf. 14***

O312 A121 10f multicolored 1.50 70
O312A A121 15f on 3f multi 6.00 1.00
O313 A121 25f on 2f multi 5.00 1.00

Nos. 322-325 Overprinted — رسمي Official

Engr.; Engr. & Photo.

1975 ***Perf. 12x11***

O314 A57 10f rose red 8.00 60
O315 A57 15f brown & buff 8.00 75
O316 A57 20f violet blue 8.00 75
O317 A57 30f orange 15.00 80

Arms of Iraq — O1

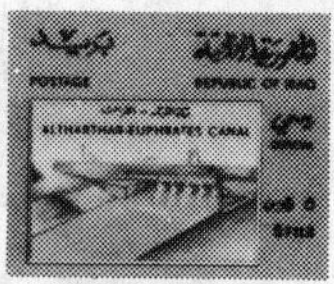

Altharthar - Euphrates Canal — O2

1975 Photo. *Perf. 14*

O318 O1 5f multicolored 15 15
O319 O1 10f blue & multi 15 15
O320 O1 15f yel & multi 24 24
O321 O1 20f ultra & multi 32 32
O322 O1 25f org & multi 40 40
O323 O1 30f rose & multi 50 50
O324 O1 50f multicolored 80 80
O325 O1 100f multicolored 1.65 1.65
Nos. O318-O325 (8) 4.21 4.21

Nos. 787-791 Overprinted "OFFICIAL" in English and Arabic

1976 Litho. *Perf. 13½x14*

O327 A219 5f multicolored 15 15
O328 A219 10f multicolored 15 15
O329 A219 15f multicolored 80 15
O330 A219 25f multicolored 1.00 35
O331 A219 50f multicolored 2.25 75
Nos. O327-O331 (5) 4.35 1.55

1978 Photo. *Perf. 11½*

O332 O2 5f multicolored 15 15
O333 O2 10f multicolored 15 15
O334 O2 15f multicolored 15 15
O335 O2 25f multicolored 40 20
Set value 68 45

Baghdad University Entrance — O3

1981, Oct. 21 Litho. *Perf. 12x12½*

O336 O3 45f multicolored 36 24
O337 O3 50f multicolored 40 30

Nos. O336-O337 Surcharged

1983, May 15 Litho. *Perf. 12x12½*

O338 O3 60f on 45f multi 50 32
O339 O3 70f on 50f multi 60 45

Martyrs Type of 1981

1981 Photo. *Perf. 14*

O339A A303 45f silver border 36 24
O339B A303 50f gold border 40 30
O339C A303 120f metallic bl border 96 64

Building Type of 1983

1982, Dec. 31 Litho. *Perf. 14*

O340 A324 60f multicolored 48 32
O341 A324 70f multicolored 56 40

Martyr Type of 1984

1984, Dec. 1

O342 A329 20f multicolored 15 15
O343 A329 30f multicolored 20 15
O344 A329 50f multicolored 32 22
O345 A329 60f multicolored 38 25

No. RA22 Overprinted بريد رسمي

1985 (?) Litho. *Perf. 13x12½*

O346 PT2 5f bister, blk & yel 30 30

POSTAL TAX STAMPS

Catalogue values for unused stamps in this section are for Never Hinged items.

Nos. O125 and 115 Surcharged in Carmine or Black

مالية
فلسان
انقاذ فلسطين

1949 Unwmk. *Perf. 11½x12*

RA1 A25 2f on 3f emer (C) 9.25 5.75
RA2 A25 2f on 6f plum 24.00 3.75

Similar Overprint in Carmine or Black on Nos. O124, O127 and O94 Middle Arabic Line Omitted

Perf. 11½x12

RA3 A25 2f sepia (C) 8.75 1.75
RA4 A25 5f rose lake 25.00 3.75

Perf. 12x13½, 14

RA5 A19 5f dark car rose 6.25 1.90

Larger overprint on #RA5, 20½mm wide.

No. 115 Surcharged in Black

مالية
٥ فلوس
انقاذ فلسطين

Perf. 11½x12

RA6 A25 5f on 6f plum 27.50 10.50

The tax on Nos. RA1 to RA6 was to aid the war in Palestine.

Nos. 317, 322-326 Surcharged

دفاع وطني
٥ فلوس

Engr.; Engr. & Photo.

1963 *Perf. 12x11*

RA7 A57 5f on 1f green 60 60
RA8 A57 5f on 10f rose red 60 60
RA9 A57 5f on 15f brn & buff 60 60
RA10 A57 5f on 20f vio blue 60 60
RA11 A57 5f on 30f orange 60 60
RA12 A57 5f on 40f brt green 60 60
Nos. RA7-RA12 (6) 3.60 3.60

Surtax was for the Defense Fund.

PT1

دفاع
وطني
b

1967, Aug. Photo. *Perf. 13½*

RA13 PT1 5f brown 35 15

Surtax was for flood victims.

Same Overprinted "b"

1967, Nov.

RA14 PT1 5f brown 1.00 1.00

Surtax was for Defense Fund.

Nos. 305A-305B with Surcharge Similar to Nos. RA7-RA12

1972 Litho. *Perf. 13½x14*

RA15 A54a 5f on 14f 5.25 3.75
RA16 A54a 5f on 35f 5.25 3.75

Surtax was for the Defense Fund. The 2 disks obliterating old denominations are on one line at the bottom. Size of Arabic inscription: 17x12mm.

No. 452 with Surcharge Similar to Nos. RA7-RA12 and Nos. 443, 457 and 526 Surcharged:

دفاع وطني
٥ فلوس

1973 Litho. *Perf. 13*

RA17 A105 5f on 2f multi 5.75 40
RA18 A107 5f on 2f multi 5.75 40
RA19 A108 5f on 2f multi 5.75 40
RA20 A135 5f on 2f multi 5.75 40

Surtax was for the Defense Fund. Surcharges on Nos. RA17-RA20 are adjusted to fit shape of stamps and to obliterate old denominations.

No 683 Overprinted

دفاع
وطني

1974 Litho. *Perf. 13x12½*

RA21 A186 5f orange & blk 2.50 2.50

Soldier PT2

Dome of the Rock, Jerusalem PT3

1974

RA22 PT2 5f bister, blk & yel 50 30

Surtax of Nos. RA21-RA22 was for the Defense Fund.
For overprint, see No. O346.

1977 Photo. *Perf. 14*

RA23 PT3 5f multicolored 2.00 15

Surtax was for families of Palestinians.

AIR POST POSTAL TAX STAMPS

Catalogue values for unused stamps in this section are for Never Hinged items.

#C15 Surcharged Like #RA17-RA20

1973 Litho. *Perf. 13½*

RAC1 AP5 5f on 2f multi 5.00 5.00

Surtax was for the Defense Fund.

ISRAEL

LOCATION — Western Asia, bordering on the Mediterranean Sea
GOVT. — Republic
AREA — 8,017 sq. mi.
POP. — 4,150,000 (est. 1984)
CAPITAL — Jerusalem

When the British mandate of Palestine ended in May 1948, the Jewish state of Israel was proclaimed by the Jewish National Council in Palestine.

1000 Mils = 1 Pound
1000 Prutot = 1 Pound (1949)
100 Agorot = 1 Pound (1960)
100 Agorot = 1 Shekel (1980)

Catalogue values for all unused stamps in this country are for Never Hinged items.

Tabs

Stamps of Israel are printed in sheets with tabs (labels) usually attached below the bottom row, sometimes at the sides. Stamps with tab attached are valued by issue or separately through No. 86. From No. 87 onward, stamps with tab attached sell for 10 to 100 per cent higher values than those quoted, except where noted otherwise.

Tabs of the following numbers are in two parts, perforated between: 9, 15, 23-37, 44, 46-47, 50, 55, 62-65, 70-72, 74-77, 86-91, 94-99, 104-118, 123-126, 133-136B, 138-141, 143-151, 160-161, 165-167, 178-179, 182, 187-189, 203, 211-213, 222-223, 228-237, 243-244, 246-250, 256-258, 269-270, 272-273, 275, 294-295, 312, 337-339, 341-344, 346-347, 353-354, C1-C13, C22-C30.

Watermarks

Wmk. 301- ISRAEL in Hebrew

Wmk. 302- Multiple Stag

Ancient Judean Coins
A1 A2

Designs: Nos. 1-6, Various coins.

Perf. 10, 11 and Compound

1948, May 16 Typo. Unwmk.

1 A1 3m orange 40 15
2 A1 5m yellow grn 40 15
3 A1 10m red violet 70 15
4 A1 15m red 1.40 15
5 A1 20m bright ultra 3.50 15
6 A1 50m orange brown 6.50 15
Nos. 1-6 (6) 12.90 90
Nos. 1-6 (6) with tabs 250.00

Size: 34½x22mm

7 A2 250m dark sl grn 50.00 13.00
8 A2 500m red brn, *cr* 170.00 55.00

Size: 36 ½x24mm

9 A2 1000m blk bl, *pale bl* 225.00 85.00
Nos. 7-9 (3) 445.00 153.00
Nos. 7-9 with tabs *4,500.*

Nos. 1-9 exist imperf.
See type A6. For overprints see Nos. J1-J5.

Rouletted

1a A1 3m 90 15
2b A1 5m 2.75 20
3b A1 10m 6.25 65
With tabs 300.00

Flying Scroll — A3

1948, Sept. 26 Litho. *Perf. 11 ½*
10 A3 3m brn red & ultra 40 15
11 A3 5m dl grn & ultra 70 22
12 A3 10m dp car & ultra 80 40
13 A3 20m dp ultra & ultra 1.65 65
14 A3 65m brown & red 10.00 3.50
Nos. 10-14 (5) 13.55 4.92
With tabs 260.00

Jewish New Year, 5709.

Flag of Israel — A4

1949, Mar. 31
15 A4 20m bright blue 52 20
With tab 45.00

Appointment of the government by the Knesset.

Souvenir Sheet

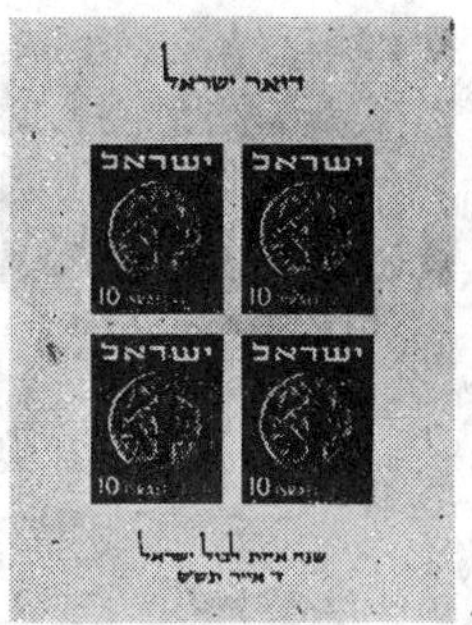
A5

1949, May 1 *Imperf.*
16 A5 Sheet of 4 100.00 22.50
a. 10m dark carmine rose 25.00 2.75

1st anniv. of Israeli postage stamps.
The sheet was sold at "TABUL," First National Stamp Exhibition, in Tel Aviv, May 1-6, 1949. Tickets, costing 100 mils, covered the entrance fee and one sheet.

Bronze Half-Shekel of 67 A.D. — A6

Approach to Jerusalem — A8

Hebrew University, Jerusalem A7

"The Negev" by Reuven Rubin — A9

1949-50 Unwmk. *Perf. 11 ½, 14*
17 A6 3p gray black 28 15
18 A6 5p purple 15 15
19 A6 10p green 18 15
20 A6 15p deep rose 25 15
21 A6 30p dark blue 32 15
22 A6 50p brown 1.25 18
23 A7 100p Prus grn ('50) 32 15
With tab 25.00
24 A8 250p org brn & gray 1.10 65
With tab 40.00
25 A9 500p dp org & brown ('50) 6.25 5.00
With tab 250.00
Nos. 17-25 (9) 10.10 6.73
Nos. 17-22 with tabs (6) 85.00
Tete beche pairs, Nos. 18-21 72.50 72.50

Each of Nos. 17-22 portrays a different coin. For other stamps of coin design, see Nos. 38-43, 56-61, 80-83, and type A1. For overprints see Nos. O1-O4.
25th anniv. of the Hebrew University in Jerusalem (No. 23).

Well at Petah Tikva — A10

1949, Aug. 10 *Perf. 11*
27 A10 40p dk grn & brn 6.50 30
With tab 80.00

70th anniv. of Petah Tikva.

Arms and Service Insignia: Air Force A11

1949, Sept. 20 *Perf. 11 ½*
28 A11 5p dark blue 42 20
29 A11 10p dl grn *(Navy)* 1.10 32
30 A11 35p dl redsh brn *(Army)* 4.75 2.00
With tabs 450.00

Jewish New Year, 5710.

Running Stag — A12

1950, Mar. 26
31 A12 40p purple 75 15
a. Booklet pane of 4 3.50
32 A12 80p rose red 75 18
a. Booklet pane of 4 7.00
b. Nos. 31 and 32 tete beche 45.00 25.00
With tabs 72.50

75th anniv. (in 1949) of the UPU.

Struggle for Free Immigration A13

Arrival of Immigrants A14

1950, Apr. 23
33 A13 20p dull brown 2.75 1.25
34 A14 40p dull green 5.25 3.25
With tabs 400.00

Independence Day, Apr. 22, 1950.

Fruit and Star of David — A15

1950, Aug. 31 Litho. *Perf. 14*
35 A15 5p vio blue & org 15 15
36 A15 15p red brn & grn 35 15
Set value 15
With tabs 45.00

Jewish New Year, 5711.

Runner and Track — A16

1950, Oct. 1
37 A16 80p olive & sl blk 1.65 48
With tab 55.00

3rd Maccabiah, Ramat Gan, Sept. 27, 1950.

Coin Type of 1949 Redrawn

Designs: Various coins.

1950
38 A6 3p gray black 15 15
39 A6 5p purple 15 15
a. Tete beche pair 3.00 3.00
40 A6 10p green 15 15
a. Tete beche pair 1.25 1.00
41 A6 15p deep rose 15 15
a. Tete beche pair 2.00 1.75
42 A6 30p dark blue 15 15
a. Tete beche pair 4.00 4.00
43 A6 50p brown 15 15
Set value 35 30
With tabs 2.50

Inscription at left measures 11mm on Nos. 38-43; 9mm on Nos. 17-22.

Detail from Tablet, "Founding of Tel Aviv" A17

1951, Mar. 22
44 A17 40p dark brown 28 15
With tab 18.00

40th anniversary of Tel Aviv.

Young Man Holding Outline Map of Israel — A18

1951, Apr. 30 Litho.
45 A18 80p red brown 18 15
With tab 4.00

Issued to promote the sale of Independence Bonds.

Metsudat Yesha A19

Hakastel A20

1951, May 9 Unwmk.
46 A19 15p red brown 15 15
47 A20 40p deep blue 50 20
Set value 25
With tabs 45.00

Proclamation of State of Israel, 3rd anniv.

Tractor and Wheat A21

Tree A22

Plower and National Fund Stamp of 1902 — A23

1951, June 24 *Perf. 14*
48 A21 15p red brown 15 15
49 A22 25p Prussian green 15 15
50 A23 80p dull blue 45 15
Set value 62 28
With tabs 100.00

Jewish National Fund, 50th anniversary.

Theodor Zeev Herzl — A24

Carrier Pigeons — A25

1951, Aug. 14
51 A24 80p gray green 16 15
With tab 4.25

23rd Zionist Congress, Jerusalem.

1951, Sept. 16

Designs: 15p, Girl holding dove and fruit. 40p, Scrolls of the law.

52 A25 5p blue 15 15
53 A25 15p cerise 15 15
54 A25 40p rose violet 15 15
Set value 20 18
With tabs 2.50

Jewish New Year, 5712.

Menorah and Emblems of Twelve Tribes — A26

1952, Feb. 27

55 A26 1000p dk bl & gray 15.00 6.25
With tab 250.00

Redrawn Coin Type of 1950

Designs: Various coins.

1952, Mar. 30

56 A6 20p orange 15 15
a. Tete beche pair 2.50 2.50
57 A6 35p olive green 15 15
58 A6 40p orange brown 15 15
59 A6 45p red violet 15 15
a. Tete beche pair 4.50 4.50
60 A6 60p carmine 15 15
61 A6 85p aquamarine 15 15
Set value 40 30
With tabs 12.00

Thistle and Yad Mordecai Battlefield A27

Battlefields: 60p, Cornflower and Deganya. 110p, Anemone and Safed.

1952, Apr. 29

62 A27 30p lil rose & vio brn 15 15
63 A27 60p ultra & gray blk 15 15
64 A27 110p crimson & gray 35 24
Set value 56 42
With tabs 22.50

Proclamation of State of Israel, 4th anniv.

Manhattan Skyline and American Zionists' House A28

1952, May 13

65 A28 220p dark bl & gray 38 20
With tab 14.00

Opening of American Zionists' House, Tel Aviv.

Figs — A29

Designs: 40p, Lily. 110p, Dove. 220p, Nut cluster.

Unwmk.

1952, Sept. 3 Litho. *Perf. 14*

66 A29 15p shown 15 15
67 A29 40p Lily 15 15
68 A29 110p Dove 20 15
69 A29 220p Nut cluster 30 16
Set value 66 45
With tabs 24.00

Jewish New Year, 5713.

Pres. Chaim Weizmann (1874-1952) and Presidential Standard A30

1952, Dec. 9

70 A30 30p slate 15 15
71 A30 110p black 25 15
Set value 16
With tabs 10.00

Weizmann, president of Israel 1948-52.

Numeral Incorporating Agricultural Scenes — A31

1952, Dec. 31

72 A31 110p brn, buff & emer 18 15
With tab 9.00

70th anniversary of B.I.L.U. (Bet Yaakov Lechu Venelcha) immigration.

Five Anemones and State Emblem — A32

1953, Apr. 19

73 A32 110p grnsh bl, bl blk & red 18 15
With tab 4.50

5th anniversary of State of Israel.

Rabbi Moshe ben Maimon (Maimonides) A33

Holy Ark, Jerusalem A34

1953, Aug. 3 Wmk. 301 *Perf. 14x13*

74 A33 110p brown 35 35
With tab 8.00

7th International Congress of History of Science, Jerusalem, Aug. 4-11.

1953, Aug. 11

Holy Arks: 45p, Petah Tikva. 200p, Safed.

75 A34 20p sapphire 15 15
76 A34 45p brown red 15 15
77 A34 200p purple 15 15
Set value 28 18
With tabs 8.50

Jewish New Year, 5714.

Combined Ball-Globe A35

Desert Rose A36

Unwmk.

1953, Sept. 20 Litho. *Perf. 14*

78 A35 110p bl & dark brn 15 15
With tab 4.50

4th Maccabiah, Sept. 20-29, 1953.

1953, Sept. 22

79 A36 200p multicolored 15 15
With tab 4.50

Conquest of the Desert Exhibition, Sept. 22-Oct. 14.

Redrawn Type of 1950

Designs: Various coins.

1954, Jan. 5

80 A6 80p olive bister 15 15
81 A6 95p blue green 15 15
82 A6 100p fawn 15 15
83 A6 125p violet blue 15 15
Set value 26 20
With tabs 2.50

Marigold and Ruins at Yehiam — A37

Design: 350p, Narcissus and bridge at Gesher.

1954, May 5 Litho.

84 A37 60p dk bl, mag & ol gray 15 15
85 A37 350p dk brn, grn & yel 15 15
Set value 17 15
With tabs 2.00

Memorial Day and 6th anniversary of proclamation of State of Israel.

Theodor Zeev Herzl (1860-1904), Founder of Zionist Movement A38

1954, July 21 Wmk. 302

86 A38 160p dk bl, dk brn & cr 15 15
With tab 85

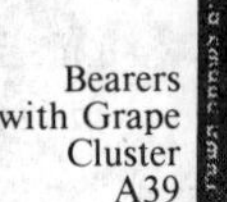

Bearers with Grape Cluster A39

1954, Sept. 8 *Perf. 13x14*

87 A39 25p dark brown 15 15

Jewish New Year, 5715.

19th Century Mail Coach and Jerusalem Post Office A40

Design: 200p, Mail truck and present G.P.O., Jerusalem.

1954, Oct. 13 *Perf. 14*

88 A40 60p blue, blk & yel 15 15
89 A40 200p dk grn, blk & red 15 15
Set value 18 15
With tabs 3.25

TABIM, National Stamp Exhibition, Jerusalem, Oct. 13-18.

Baron Edmond de Rothschild (1845-1934) and Grape Cluster A41

1954, Nov. 23 *Perf. 13x14*

90 A41 300p dark blue grn 15 15
With tab 85

Lighted Oil Lamp A42

1955, Jan. 13 *Perf. 13x14*

91 A42 250p dark blue 15 15
With tab 75

Teachers' Association, 50th anniversary.

Parachutist and Barbed Wire — A43

Lighted Menorah — A44

1955, Mar. 31 Litho. *Perf. 14*

92 A43 120p dk Prussian grn 15 15
With tab 42

Jewish volunteers from Palestine who served in British army in World War II.

1955, Apr. 26

93 A44 150p dk grn, blk & org 15 15
With tab 32

Proclamation of State of Israel, 7th anniv.

Immigration by Ship — A45

Designs: 10p, Immigration by plane. 25p, Agricultural training. 30p, Gardening. 60p, Vocational training. 750p, Scientific education.

1955, May 10 Unwmk. *Perf. 14*

94 A45 5p brt blue & black 15 15
95 A45 10p red & black 15 15
96 A45 25p deep grn & black 15 15
97 A45 30p orange & black 15 15
98 A45 60p lilac rose & blk 15 15
99 A45 750p olive bis & blk 22 15
With tab 1.75
Set value 45 35

20th anniversary of Israel's Youth Immigration Institution.

Musicians with Tambourine and Cymbals — A46

Mandrake, Reuben — A48

Ambulance A47

Musician with: 60p, Ram's Horn. 120p, Loud Trumpet. 250p, Harp.

1955, Aug. 25 Photo. Wmk. 302

100	A46	25p dark green & org	15	15

Unwmk.

101	A46	60p dk gray & orange	15	15
102	A46	120p dark blue & yel	15	15
103	A46	250p red brn & org	15	15
		Set value	36	40

Jewish New Year, 5716.

See Nos. 121-123.

1955, Nov. 1 Wmk. 301 *Perf. 14*

104	A47	160p grn, red & blk	15	15

25th anniversary of Magen David Adom (Israeli Red Cross).

1955-57 Wmk. 302 *Perf. 13x14*

Twelve Tribes: 20p, Gates of Sechem, Simeon. 30p, Ephod, Levi. 40p, Lion, Judah. 50p, Scales, Dan. 60p, Stag, Naphtali. 80p, Tents, Gad. 100p, Tree, Asher. 120p, Sun and stars, Issachar. 180p, Ship, Zebulon. 200p, Sheaf of wheat, Joseph. 250p, Wolf, Benjamin.

105	A48	10p bright green	15	15
106	A48	20p red lilac ('56)	15	15
107	A48	30p bright ultra	15	15
108	A48	40p brown ('56)	15	15
109	A48	50p grnsh bl ('56)	15	15
110	A48	60p lemon	15	15
111	A48	80p deep vio ('56)	15	15
112	A48	100p vermilion	15	15
113	A48	120p olive ('56)	15	15
114	A48	180p lil rose ('56)	15	15
115	A48	200p green ('56)	15	15
116	A48	250p gray ('56)	15	15
		Set value	60	50
		With tabs	2.00	

See Nos. 133-136B.

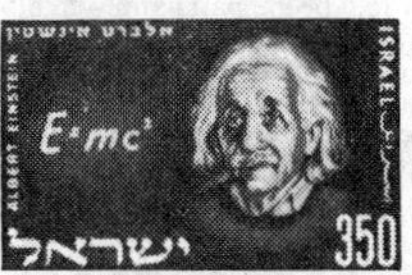

Albert Einstein (1879-1955) and Equation of his Relativity Theory A49

1956, Jan. 3 *Perf. 13x14*

117	A49	350p brown	15	15
		With tab	60	

Technion, Haifa — A50

1956, Jan. 3 Wmk. 302

118	A50	350p lt ol grn & blk	15	15

Israel Institute of Technology, 30th anniv.

"Eight Years of Israel" — A51

Jaffa Oranges — A52

1956, Apr. 12 Litho. *Perf. 14*

119	A51	150p multicolored	15	15

Proclamation of State of Israel, 8th anniv.

1956, May 20 Wmk. 302 *Perf. 14*

120	A52	300p bl grn & orange	15	15

4th Intl. Congress of Mediterranean Citrus Growers.

New Year Type of 1955

Musician with: 30p, Lyre. 50p, Cymbals. 150p, Double oboe, horiz.

1956, Aug. 14 Photo. *Perf. 14x13*

121	A46	30p brown & brt blue	15	15

Perf. 14

122	A46	50p purple & orange	15	15
123	A46	150p dk bl grn & org	15	15
		Set value	16	15

Jewish New Year, 5717.

Haganah Insignia A54

Bezalel Museum and Antique Lamp A55

1957, Jan. 1 *Perf. 13x14*

124	A54	20p + 80p brt grn	15	15
125	A54	50p + 150p car rose	15	15
126	A54	50p + 350p ultra	15	15
		Set value	18	15

Defense issue. Divided denomination used to show increased postal rate.

1957, Apr. 29 Litho. *Perf. 14*

127	A55	400p multicolored	15	15

Bezalel Natl. Museum, Jerusalem, 50th anniv.

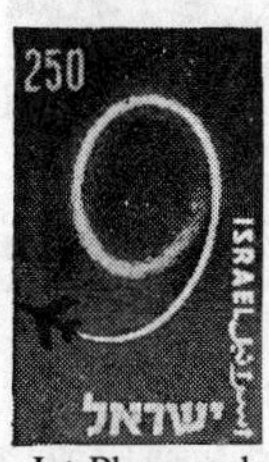

Jet Plane and "9" — A56

Horse and Seal — A57

1957, Apr. 29

128	A56	250p deep bl & blk	15	15

Proclamation of State of Israel, 9th anniv.

1957, Sept. 4 Wmk. 302 *Perf. 14*

Ancient Seals: 160p, Lion. 300p, Gazelle.

129	A57	50p ocher & blk, *lt bl*	15	15

Perf. 14x13

Photo. Unwmk.

130	A57	160p grn & blk, *bis brn*	15	15
131	A57	300p dp car & blk, *pink*	15	15
		Set value	15	15

Jewish New Year, 5718.

TABIL

Souvenir Sheet

Bet Alpha Synagogue Mosaic — A58

1957, Sept. 17 Litho. *Roulette 13*

132	A58	Sheet of four	25	20
a.		100p multicolored	15	15
b.		200p multicolored	15	15
c.		300p multicolored	15	15
d.		400p multicolored	15	15

1st Intl. stamp exhibition in Israel, Tel Aviv, Sept. 17-23.

Tribes Type of 1955-57

Perf. 13x14

1957-59 Unwmk. Photo.

133	A48	10p brt grn ('58)	15	15
133A	A48	20p red lilac	15	15
133C	A48	40p brown ('59)	75	45
134	A48	50p greenish bl	15	15
135	A48	60p lemon	15	15
136	A48	100p vermilion	18	15
136B	A48	120p olive ('58)	20	15
		Set value	1.45	85
		With tabs	37.50	

Hammer Thrower — A59

Menorah and Olive Branch — A61

Ancient Ship — A60

1958, Jan. 20 *Perf. 14x13*

137	A59	500p bister & car	16	15

Maccabiah Games, 25th anniversary.

Wmk. 302

1958, Jan. 27 Litho. *Perf. 14*

Ships: 20p, Three-master used for "illegal immigration." 30p, Cargo ship "Shomron." 1000p, Passenger ship "Zion."

Size: 36½x22½mm

138	A60	10p ocher, red & blk	15	15

Photo. *Perf. 13x14*

139	A60	20p brt grn, blk & brn	15	15
140	A60	30p red, blk & grnsh bl	15	15

Size: 56½x22½mm

141	A60	1000p brt bl, blk & grn	15	15
		Set value	28	20

Issued to honor Israel's merchant fleet.

Unwmk.

1958, Apr. 21 Litho. *Perf. 14*

142	A61	400p gold, blk & grn	15	15

Memorial Day and 10th anniversary of proclamation of State of Israel.

Dancing Youths Forming "10" — A62

1958, July 2

143	A62	200p dk org & dk grn	15	15

First World Conference of Jewish Youth, Jerusalem, July 28-Aug. 1.

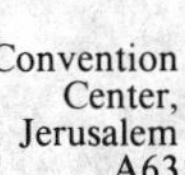

Convention Center, Jerusalem A63

1958, July 2

144	A63	400p vio & org, *yellow*	15	15

10th Anniversary of Independence Exhibition, Jerusalem, June 5-Aug. 21.

Wheat — A64

Designs: 60p, Barley. 160p, Grapes. 300p, Figs.

1958, Aug. 27 Photo. *Perf. 14x13*

145	A64	50p bister & brn	15	15
146	A64	60p citron & blk	15	15
147	A64	160p vio & red lilac	15	15
148	A64	300p yel grn & dk grn	15	15
		Set value	28	18

Jewish New Year, 5719.

"Love Thy Neighbor . . ." — A65

1958, Dec. 10 Litho. *Perf. 14*

149	A65	750p yel, gray & grn	15	15
		With tab	90	

Universal Declaration of Human Rights, 10th anniversary.

Designing and Printing Stamps A66

Radio and Telephone — A67

Designs: 120p, Mobile post office. 500p, Teletype.

1959, Feb. 25 Wmk. 302 *Perf. 14*

150	A66	60p olive, blk & red	15	15
151	A66	120p olive, blk & red	15	15
152	A67	250p olive, blk & red	15	15
153	A67	500p olive, blk & red	15	15
		Set value	28	18

Decade of postal activities in Israel.

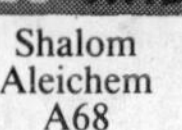

Shalom Aleichem A68

Cyclamen A69

Portraits: No. 155, Chaim Nachman Bialik. No. 156, Eliezer Ben-Yehuda.

1959 Unwmk. Photo. *Perf. 14x13*

154 A68 250p yel grn & red brn 15 15
155 A68 250p ocher & ol gray 15 15
Set value 24 20

Litho. *Perf. 14*

156 A68 250p bl & vio bl 15 15
With tab 50

Birth cent. of Aleichem (Solomon Rabinowitz), Yiddish writer (No. 154); 25th death anniv. of Bialik, Hebrew poet (No. 155); birth cent. of Ben-Yehuda, father of modern Hebrew (No. 156).

1959, May 11 Wmk. 302 *Perf. 14*

Flowers: 60p, Anemone. 300p, Narcissus.

Flowers in Natural Colors

157 A69 60p deep green 15 15
158 A69 120p deep plum 15 15
159 A69 300p blue 15 15
Set value 22 20

Memorial Day and 11th anniversary of proclamation of State of Israel.

Buildings, Tel Aviv A70

1959, May 4

160 A70 120p multicolored 15 15

50th anniversary of Tel Aviv.

Bristol Britannia and Windsock A71

1959, July 22

161 A71 500p multicolored 16 15
With tab 35

Civil Aviation in Israel, 10th anniversary.

Pomegranates — A72

Perf. 14x13

1959, Sept. 9 Photo. Unwmk.

162 A72 60p shown 15 15
163 A72 200p Olives 15 15
164 A72 350p Dates 18 15
Set value 32 20
With tabs 2.25

Jewish New Year, 5720.

Merhavya A73

Judean Coin (66-70 A.D.) A74

Settlements: 120p, Yesud Ha-Maala. 180p, Deganya.

1959, Nov. 25 Photo. *Perf. 13x14*

165 A73 60p citron & dk grn 15 15
166 A73 120p red brn & ocher 15 15
167 A73 180p blue & dk grn 15 15
Set value 28 18
With tabs 2.75

Settlements of Merhavya and Deganya, 50th anniv.; Yesud Ha-Maala, 75th anniv.

1960 Unwmk. *Perf. 13x14*

Denominations in Black

168 A74 1a brn, *pinkish* 15 15
a. On surface colored paper 15 15
As "a," with tab 75
b. Black overprint omitted
169 A74 3a brt red, *pinkish* 15 15
170 A74 5a gray, *pinkish* 15 15
171 A74 6a brt grn, *lt bl* 15 15
171A A74 7a gray, *bluish* 15 15
172 A74 8a mag, *lt blue* 15 15
173 A74 12a grnsh bl, *lt bl* 15 15
a. Black overprint omitted
174 A74 18a orange 15 15
175 A74 25a blue 15 15
176 A74 30a carmine 15 15
177 A74 50a bright lilac 15 15
Set value 55 50
With tabs 1.75

Issue dates: 7a, July 6. Others, Jan. 6.

Operation "Magic Carpet" A75

Design: 50a, Resettled family in front of house, grapes and figs.

1960, Apr. 7 Unwmk. *Perf. 13x14*

178 A75 25a red brown 15 15
179 A75 50a green 15 15
Set value 16 16
With tabs 40

World Refugee Year, July 1, 1959-June 30, 1960.

Sand Lily — A76

Design: 32a, Evening primrose.

1960, Apr. 27 Litho. *Perf. 14*

180 A76 12a multicolored 15 15
181 A76 32a brn, yel & grn 15 15
Set value 16 15
With tabs 55

Memorial Day; proclamation of State of Israel, 12th anniv. See #204-206, 238-240.

Atom Diagram and Atomic Reactor A77

1960, July 6 Wmk. 302 *Perf. 14*

182 A77 50a blue, red & blk 15 15
With tab 60

Installation of Israel's first atomic reactor.

Theodor Herzl and Rhine at Basel — A78

King Saul — A79

1960, Aug. 31 Litho. *Perf. 14*

183 A78 25a gray brown 15 15
With tab 40

1960, Aug. 31 Wmk. 302

Designs: 25a, King David. 40a, King Solomon.

Kings in Multicolor

184 A79 7a emerald 15 15

Unwmk.

185 A79 25a brown 15 15
186 A79 40a blue 25 15
Set value 35 20
With tabs 1.25

Jewish New Year, 5721. See Nos. 208-210.

Jewish Postal Courier, Prague, 18th Century A80

Perf. 13x14

1960, Oct. 9 Photo. Unwmk.

187 A80 25a olive blk, *gray* 22 15
With tab 2.50
a. Souvenir sheet 13.00 6.00

TAVIV Natl. Stamp Exhibition, Tel Aviv, Oct. 9-19.

No. 187a sold only at Exhibition for 50a.

Henrietta Szold and Hadassah Medical Center A81

1960, Dec. 14 *Perf. 13x14*

188 A81 25a turq bl & vio gray 15 15
With tab 32

Birth cent. of Henrietta Szold, founder of Hadassah, American Jewish women's organization.

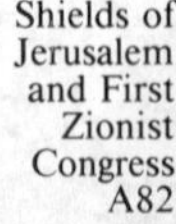

Shields of Jerusalem and First Zionist Congress A82

1960, Dec. 14 Unwmk. *Perf. 14*

189 A82 50a vio bl & turq blue 15 15
With tab 1.10

25th Zionist Congress, Jerusalem, 1960.

Ram A83

Signs of Zodiac A84

Signs of the Zodiac: 2a, Bull. 6a, Twins. 7a, Crab. 8a, Lion. 10a, Virgin. 12a, Scales. 18a, Scorpion. 20a, Archer. 25a, Goat. 32a, Water bearer. 50a, Fishes.

1961, Feb. 27 Photo. *Perf. 13x14*

190 A83 1a emerald 15 15
191 A83 2a red 15 15
192 A83 6a ultramarine 15 15
193 A83 7a brown 15 15
194 A83 8a green 15 15
a. Booklet pane of 6 ('65) 42
195 A83 10a orange 15 15
196 A83 12a violet 15 15
a. Booklet pane of 6 ('65) 42
197 A83 18a lilac rose 15 15
198 A83 20a olive 15 15
199 A83 25a red lilac 15 15
200 A83 32a gray 15 15
201 A83 50a greenish blue 15 15

Perf. 14

Litho.

202 A84 £1 dk bl, gold & lt bl 22 15
Set value 1.00 65
With tabs 3.75

Booklet pane sheets (Nos. 194a, 196a) of 36 (9x4) contain 6 panes of 6, with gutters dividing the sheet in four sections. Each sheet yields 4 tete beche pairs and 4 tete beche gutter pairs, or strips. See Nos. 215-217.

Vertical strips of 6 of the 1a, 10a and No. 216 (5a) are from larger sheets from which coils were produced. Regular sheets of 50 are arranged 10x5.

Javelin Thrower and "7" — A85

1961, Apr. 18 Litho. *Perf. 14*

203 A85 25a multicolored 15 15
With tab 42

7th Intl. Congress of the Hapoel Sports Org., Ramat Gan, May 1961.

Flower Type of 1960

Flowers: 7a, Myrtle. 12a, Sea onion. 32a, Oleander.

1961, Apr. 18 Unwmk.

Flowers in Natural Colors

204 A76 7a green 15 15
205 A76 12a rose carmine 15 15
206 A76 32a brt greenish bl 15 15
Set value 30 18
With tabs 1.00

Memorial Day; proclamation of State of Israel, 13th anniv.

Scaffold Around "10" and Sapling — A86

1961, June 14 Photo. *Perf. 14*

207 A86 50a Prussian blue 15 15
With tab 55

Israel bond issue 10th anniv.

Type of 1960

Designs: 7a, Samson. 25a, Judas Maccabaeus. 40a, Bar Cocheba.

1961, Aug. 21 Litho. *Perf. 14*
Multicolored Designs

208 A79 7a red orange 15 15
209 A79 25a gray 15 15
210 A79 40a lilac 20 15
Set value 32 22
With tabs 1.25

Jewish New Year, 5722.

Bet Hamidrash Synagogue, Medzibozh A87

1961, Aug. 21 Photo. *Perf. 13x14*

211 A87 25a dk brn & yel 15 15
With tab 38

Bicentenary of death of Rabbi Israel Baal-Shem-Tov, founder of Hasidism.

Pine Cone — A88

Design: 30a, Symbolic trees.

1961, Dec. 26 Unwmk. *Perf. 13x14*

212 A88 25a green, yel & blk 15 15
213 A88 30a org, green & ind 15 15
Set value 24 15
With tabs 2.00

Achievements of afforestation program.

Cello, Harp, French Horn and Kettle Drum — A89

1961, Dec. 26 Litho. *Perf. 14*

214 A89 50a multicolored 25 25
With tab 2.00

Israel Philharmonic Orchestra, 25th anniv.

Zodiac Type of 1961 Surcharged with New Value

1962, Mar. 18 Photo. *Perf. 13x14*

215 A83 3a on 1a lt lilac 15 15
a. Without overprint 80.00
216 A83 5a on 7a gray 15 15
217 A83 30a on 32a emerald 15 15
Set value 18 16
a. Without overprint 32.50

See note after No. 202.

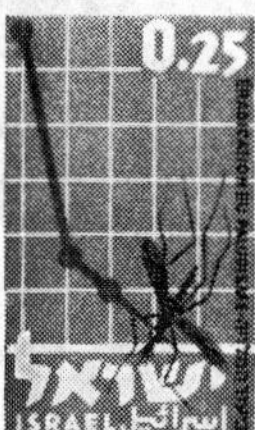

Anopheles Maculipennis and Chart Showing Decline of Malaria in Israel — A90

View of Rosh Pinna — A91

1962, Apr. 30 *Perf. 14x13*

218 A90 25a ocher, red & blk 16 15
With tab 48

WHO drive to eradicate malaria.

1962, Apr. 30 Unwmk.

219 A91 20a yel, green & brn 18 18
With tab 48

Rosh Pinna agricultural settlement, 80th anniv.

Flame ("Hear, O Israel . . .") A92

Yellow Star of David and Six Candles A93

1962, Apr. 30 Photo.

220 A92 12a black, org & red 15 15

Perf. 14

221 A93 55a multicolored 22 15
Set value 30 18
With tabs 1.40

Heroes and Martyrs Day, in memory of the 6,000,000 Jewish victims of Nazi persecution.

Vautour Fighter-Bomber — A94

Design: 30a, Fighter-Bombers in formation.

1962, Apr. 30 *Perf. 13x14*

222 A94 12a blue 15 15
223 A94 30a olive green 15 15
Set value 18 18
With tabs 1.75

Memorial Day; proclamation of the state of Israel, 14th anniv.

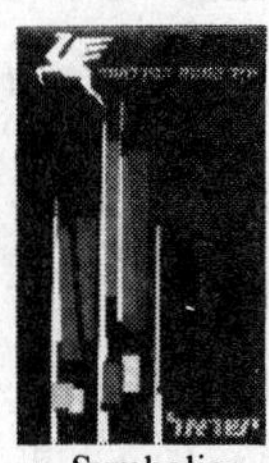

Symbolic Flags — A95

Wolf and Lamb, Isaiah 11:6 — A96

1962, June 5 *Perf. 14*

224 A95 55a multicolored 18 18
With tab 1.00

Near East Intl. Fair, Tel Aviv, June 5-July 5.

1962, Sept. 5

Designs: 28a, Leopard and kid, Isaiah 11:6. 43a, Child and asp, Isaiah 11:8.

225 A96 8a buff, red & black 15 15
226 A96 28a buff, lilac & black 15 15
227 A96 43a buff, org & black 22 15
Set value 38 22
With tabs 3.00

Jewish New Year, 5723.

Boeing 707 — A97

1962, Nov. 7 *Perf. 13x14*

228 A97 55a bl, dk bl & rose lil 28 15
With tab 1.10
a. Souvenir sheet 2.50 1.25

El Al Airlines; El Al Philatelic Exhibition, Tel Aviv, Nov. 7-14. Issued in sheets of 15.

No. 228a contains one stamp in greenish blue, dark blue & rose lilac with greenish blue color continuing into margin design (No. 228 has white perforations). Sold for £1 for one day at philatelic counters in Jerusalem, Haifa and Tel Aviv and for one week at the El Al Exhibition.

Cogwheel Symbols of UJA Activities A98

1962, Dec. 26 Unwmk. *Perf. 13x14*

229 A98 20a org red, sil & bl 18 15
With tab 50

25th anniv. of the United Jewish Appeal (United States) and its support of immigration, settlement, agriculture and care of the aged and sick.

Janusz Korczak A99

1962, Dec. 26 Photo.

230 A99 30a olive grn & blk 15 15
With tab 45

Dr. Janusz Korczak (Henryk Goldszmit, 1879-1942), physician, teacher and writer, killed in Treblinka concentration camp.

Pennant Coral Fish — A100

Red Sea fish: 6a, Orange butterflyfish. 8a, Lionfish. 12a, Zebra-striped angelfish.

1962, Dec. 26 Litho. *Perf. 14*
Fish in Natural Colors

231 A100 3a green 15 15
232 A100 6a purple 15 15
233 A100 8a brown 15 15
234 A100 12a dark blue 15 15
Set value 28 25
With tabs 60

See Nos. 246-249.

Stockade at Dawn A101

Design: 30a, Completed stockade at night.

1963, Mar. 21 Unwmk. *Perf. 14*

235 A101 12a yel brn, blk & yel 15 15
236 A101 30a dp plum, blk & lt bl 18 15
With tab 1.10
Set value 15

25th anniv. of the "Stockade and Tower" villages.

Hand Offering Food to Bird — A102

1963, Mar. 21 Photo. *Perf. 13x14*

237 A102 55a gray & blk 22 15
With tab 1.00
a. Booklet pane of 4 32.50

FAO "Freedom from Hunger" campaign.

Issued in sheets of 15 (5x3) with 5 tabs. The booklet pane sheet of 16 (4x4) is divided into 2 panes of 8 (4x2) by horizontal gutter. The 4 stamps at left in each pane are inverted in relation to the 4 at right, making 4 horizontal tete beche pairs down the center of the sheet.

Flower Type of 1960

Flower: 8a, White lily. 30a, Hollyhock. 37a, Tulips.

1963, Apr. 25 Litho. *Perf. 14*
Flowers in Natural Colors

238 A76 8a slate 15 15
239 A76 30a yellow green 22 15
240 A76 37a sepia 28 15
Set value 35
With tabs 3.25

Memorial Day; proclamation of the State of Israel, 15th anniv.

Typesetter, 19th Century — A103

1963, June 19 Photo. *Perf. 14x13*

241 A103 12a tan & vio brn 65 38
With tab 2.00
a. Sheet of 16 55.00 65.00

Hebrew press in Palestine, cent. Printed in sheets of 16; the background of the sheet shows page of first issue of "Halbanon" newspaper, giving each stamp different background.

"The Sun Beat upon the Head of Jonah" A104

Hoe Clearing Thistles A105

Designs: 30a, "There was a mighty tempest in the sea." 55a, "Jonah was in the belly of the fish" (30a, 55a, horiz.).

1963, Aug. 21 *Perf. 14x13, 13x14*

242 A104 8a org, lil & blk 15 15
243 A104 30a multicolored 15 15
244 A104 55a multicolored 16 18
Set value 30 32
With tabs 2.75

Jewish New Year, 5724.

1963, Aug. 21 *Perf. 14*

245 A105 37a multicolored 15 15
With tab 90

80 years of agricultural settlements in Israel; "Year of the Pioneers."

Fish Type of 1962

Red Sea Fish: 2a, Undulate triggerfish. 6a, Radiate turkeyfish. 8a, Bigeye. 12a, Imperial angelfish.

1963, Dec. 16 Litho. *Perf. 14*
Fish in Natural Colors

246 A100 2a violet blue 15 15
247 A100 6a green 15 15
248 A100 8a orange 15 15
249 A100 12a olive green 15 15
Set value 35 25
With tabs 90

S.S. Shalom, Sailing Vessel and Ancient Map of Coast Line — A106

1963, Dec. 16 Photo. *Perf. 13x14*

250 A106 £1 ultra, brt grn & lil 85 45
With tab 9.00

Maiden voyage of S.S. Shalom.

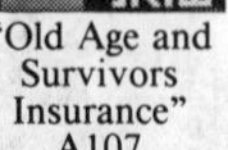

"Old Age and Survivors Insurance" A107

Pres. Izhak Ben-Zvi (1884-1963) A108

Designs (Insurance): 25a, Maternity. 37a, Large family. 50a, Workers' compensation.

1964, Feb. 24 Litho. *Perf. 14*

251 A107 12a multicolored 15 15
252 A107 25a multicolored 15 15
253 A107 37a multicolored 28 20
254 A107 50a multicolored 40 30
Set value 82 65
With tabs 8.75

Natl. Insurance Institute 10th anniv.

1964, Apr. 13 Photo. *Perf. 14x13*

255 A108 12a dark brown 15 15

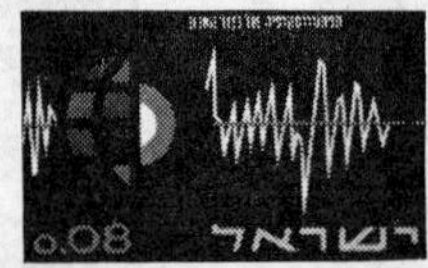

Terrestrial Spectroscopy — A109

Designs: 35a, Macromolecules of the living cell. 70a, Electronic computer.

1964, Apr. 13 *Perf. 14*

256 A109 8a multicolored 15 15
257 A109 35a multicolored 15 15
258 A109 70a multicolored 22 15
Set value 38 28
With tabs 3.50

Proclamation of the State of Israel, 16th anniv.; Israel's contribution to science.

Basketball Players A110

Serpent of Aesculapius and Menorah A111

Designs: 8a, Runner. 12a, Discus thrower. 50a, Soccer.

1964, June 24 *Perf. 14x13*

259 A110 8a brt brick red & dk brown 15 15
260 A110 12a rose lil & dk brn 15 15
261 A110 30a bl, car & dk brn 15 15
262 A110 50a yel grn, org red & dk brown 22 18
Set value 45 40
With tabs 90

Israel's participation in the 18th Olympic Games, Tokyo, Oct. 10-25.

1964, Aug. 5 Unwmk.

263 A111 £1 ol bis & slate grn 55 28
With tab 95

6th World Congress of the Israel Medical Association, Haifa, Aug. 3-13.

Ancient Glass Vase — A112

Designs: Different glass vessels, 1st to 3rd centuries.

1964, Aug. 5 Litho.

264 A112 8a vio, brn & org 15 15
265 A112 35a ol, grn & bl grn 15 15
266 A112 70a brt car rose, blue & violet blue 16 15
Set value 30 18
With tabs 1.15

Jewish New Year, 5725.

Steamer Bringing Immigrants A113

Eleanor Roosevelt (1884-1962) A114

1964, Nov. 2 Litho. *Perf. 14*

267 A113 25a sl bl, bl grn & blk 15 15
With tab 32

30th anniv. of the blockade runners bringing immigrants to Israel.

1964, Nov. 2 Photo. *Perf. 14x13*

268 A114 70a dull purple 18 15
With tab 45

Chess Board, Knight and Emblem of Chess Olympics — A115

1964, Nov. 2 *Perf. 13x14*

269 A115 12a shown 15 15
270 A115 70a Rook 32 32
Set value 40
With tabs 1.90

16th Chess Olympics, Tel Aviv, Nov. 1964.

"Africa-Israel Friendship" — A116

1964, Nov. 30 Photo. *Perf. 14x13*

271 A116 57a ol, blk, gold & red brown 35 20
With tab 2.75
a. Souvenir sheet 1.75 1.50

TABAI, Natl. Stamp Exhibition, dedicated to African-Israel friendship, Haifa, Nov. 30-Dec. 6. No. 271a contains one imperf. stamp. Sold for £1.

View of Masada from West A117

Designs: 36a, Northern Palace, lower terrace. £1, View of Northern Palace (vert.).

1965, Feb. 3 Photo. *Perf. 13x14*

272 A117 25a dull green 15 15
273 A117 36a bright blue 16 15
274 A117 £1 dark red brn 28 22
Set value 38
With tabs 1.75

Ruins of Masada, the last stronghold in the war against the Romans, 66-73 A.D.

Book Fair Emblem A118

Arms of Ashdod A119

1965, Mar. 24 Photo. *Perf. 13x14*

275 A118 70a gray ol, brt bl & blk 15 15

2nd Intl. Book Fair, Jerusalem, April.

1965-66 *Perf. 13x14*

Town Emblems: 1a, Lydda (Lod). 2a, Qiryat Shemona. 5a, Petah Tikva. 6a, Nazareth. 8a, Beersheba. 10a Bet Shean. 12a, Tiberias. 20a, Elat. 25a, Acre (Akko). 35a, Dimona. 37a, Zefat. 50a, Rishon Leziyyon. 70a, Jerusalem. £1, Tel Aviv-Jaffa. £3, Haifa.

Size: 17x22½mm

276 A119 1a brown 15 15
277 A119 2a lilac rose 15 15
278 A119 5a gray 15 15
279 A119 6a violet 15 15
280 A119 8a orange 15 15
a. Booklet pane of 6 42
281 A119 10a emerald 15 15
282 A119 12a dark purple 15 15
a. Booklet pane of 6 50
283 A119 15a green 15 15
284 A119 20a rose red 15 15
285 A119 25a ultramarine 15 15
286 A119 35a magenta 15 15
287 A119 37a olive 15 15
288 A119 50a greenish bl 15 15

Perf. 14x13

Size: 22x27mm

289 A119 70a dark brown 20 15
290 A119 £1 dark green 25 15
291 A119 £3 dk carmine rose 52 15
Set value 2.00 1.00
With tabs 10.00

Dates of issue: Nos. 283-286, Mar. 24, 1965. No. 290, Nov. 24, 1965. No. 291, Mar. 14, 1966. Others, Feb. 2, 1966.

The uncut booklet pane sheets of 36 are divided into 4 panes (2 of 6 stamps, 2 of 12) by horizontal and vertical gutters. Half of the stamps in the 2 panes of 12 are inverted, causing 4 horizontal tete beche pairs and 4 horizontal tete beche gutter pairs.

Vertical strips of 6 of the 1a, 5a and 10a are from larger sheets, released Jan. 10, 1967, from which coils were produced. Regular sheets of 50 are arranged 10x5.

No. 290 also comes tagged (1975).

See Nos. 334-336, 386-393.

Hands Reaching for Hope, and Star of David A120

"Irrigation of the Desert" A121

1965, Apr. 27 Unwmk. *Perf. 14x13*

292 A120 25a gray, black & yel 15 15
With tab 50

Liberation of Nazi concentration camps, 20th anniv.

1965, Apr. 27 Photo.

293 A121 37a olive bis & bl 15 15

Memorial Day; proclamation of the state of Israel, 17th anniv.

Telegraph Pole and Syncom Satellite A122

1965, July 21 Unwmk. *Perf. 13x14*

294 A122 70a vio, blk & grnsh bl 15 15
With tab 48

ITU, centenary.

Symbol of Cooperation and UN Emblem — A123

1965, July 21 Litho. *Perf. 14*

295 A123 36a gray, dp claret, bl, red & bis 15 15
With tab 30

International Cooperation Year.

Dead Sea Extraction Plant A124

"Let There be Light . . ." A125

1965, July 21

296 A124 12a Crane 15 15
297 A124 50a shown 15 15
Set value 20 15
With tabs 1.00

Dead Sea chemical industry.

1965, Sept. 7 Photo. *Perf. 13x14*

Genesis 1, The Creation: 8a, Firmament and Waters. 12a, Dry land and vegetation. 25a, Heavenly lights. 35a, Fish and fowl. 70a, Man.

298	A125	6a dk pur, lil & gold	15	15
299	A125	8a brt grn, dk bl & gold	15	15
300	A125	12a red brn, blk & gold	15	15
301	A125	25a dk pur, pink & gold	15	15
302	A125	35a lt & dk bl & gold	18	15
303	A125	70a dp cl, car & gold	52	35
		Set value	95	65
		With tabs	1.90	

Jewish New Year, 5726. Sheets of 20 (10x2).

Charaxes Jasius A126

Flags over Rooftops A127

Butterflies: 6a, Papilio alexanor maccabaeus. 8a, Daphnis nerii. 12a, Zegris eupheme uarda.

1965, Dec. 15 Litho. *Perf. 14*

Butterflies in Natural Colors

304	A126	2a lt olive green	15	15
305	A126	6a lilac	15	15
306	A126	8a ocher	15	15
307	A126	12a blue	15	15
		Set value	35	24

1966, Apr. 20 Litho. *Perf. 14*

Designs: 30a, Fireworks over Tel Aviv. 80a, Warships and Super Mirage jets, Haifa.

308	A127	12a multi	15	15
309	A127	30a multi	15	15
310	A127	80a multi	20	15
		Set value	35	25

Proclamation of state of Israel, 18th anniv.

Memorial, Upper Galilee — A128

1966, Apr. 20 Photo. *Perf. 14x13*

311	A128	40a olive gray	18	15

Issued for Memorial Day.

Knesset Building, Jerusalem — A129

1966, June 22 Photo. *Perf. 13x14*

312	A129	£1 dp bl	28	15
		With tab	60	

Inauguration of the Knesset Building (Parliament). Sheets of 12.

Road Sign and Motorcyclist A130

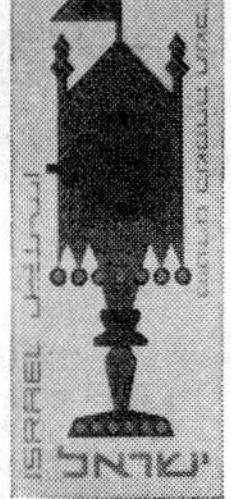
Spice Box A131

Designs (Road Signs and): 5a, Bicyclist. 10a, Pedestrian. 12a, Child playing ball. 15a, Automobile.

1966, June 22 *Perf. 14*

313	A130	2a sl, red brn & lil rose	15	15
314	A130	5a ol bis, sl & lil rose	15	15
315	A130	10a vio, lt bl & lil rose	15	15
316	A130	12a bl, grn & lil rose	15	15
317	A130	15a grn, red & lil rose	15	15
		Set value	28	25

Issued to publicize traffic safety.

1966, Aug. 24 Photo. *Perf. 13x14*

Ritual Art Objects: 15a, Candlesticks. 35a, Kiddush cup. 40a, Torah pointer. 80a, Hanging lamp.

318	A131	12a sil, gold, blk & bl	15	15
319	A131	15a sil, gold, blk & lil	15	15
320	A131	35a sil, gold, blk & emer	15	15
321	A131	40a sil, gold, blk & vio bl	15	15
322	A131	80a sil, gold, blk & red	18	18
		Set value	45	45

Jewish New Year, 5727.

Bronze Panther, Avdat, 1st Century, B.C. — A132

Designs: 30a, Stone menorah, Tiberias, 2nd Century. 40a, Phoenician ivory sphinx, 9th century, B.C. 55a, Gold earring (calf's head), Ashdod, 6th-4th centuries B.C. 80a, Miniature gold capital, Persia, 5th century, B.C. £1.15, Gold drinking horn (ram's head), Persia, 5th century, B.C. (vert.).

1966, Oct. 26 Litho. *Perf. 14*

323	A132	15a dp bl & yel brn	15	15
324	A132	30a vio brn & bister	15	15
325	A132	40a sepia & yel bis	15	15
326	A132	55a Prus grn, dp yel & brown	28	16
327	A132	80a lake, dp yel & brown	42	22

Perf. 13x14

328	A132	£1.15 vio, gold & brn	90	55
		Nos. 323-328 (6)	2.05	
		Set value		1.20
		With tabs	6.50	

Israel Museum, Jerusalem. Sheets of 12.

Coach and Mailman of Austrian Levant A133

Microscope and Cells A134

Designs: 15a, Turkish mailman and caravan. 40a, Palestinian mailman and locomotive. £1, Israeli mailman and jet liner.

1966, Dec. 14 Photo. *Perf. 14*

329	A133	12a ocher & green	15	15
330	A133	15a lt grn, brn & dp car	15	15
331	A133	40a brt rose & dk blue	15	15
332	A133	£1 grnsh bl & brown	22	15
		Set value	48	35
		With tabs	95	

Issued for Stamp Day.

1966, Dec. 14 *Perf. 14x13*

333	A134	15a red & dark sl grn	15	15

Campaign against cancer.

Arms Type of 1965-66

Town Emblems: 40a, Mizpe Ramon. 55a, Ashkelon. 80a, Rosh Pinna.

1967, Feb. 8 Unwmk. *Perf. 13x14*

334	A119	40a dark olive	15	15
335	A119	55a dk carmine rose	15	15
336	A119	80a red brown	24	15
		Set value	42	20
		With tabs	2.25	

Port of Acre A135

Ancient Ports: 40a, Caesarea. 80a, Jaffa.

1967, Mar. 22 Photo. *Perf. 13x14*

337	A135	15a dark brown	15	15
338	A135	40a dark blue grn	15	15
339	A135	80a deep blue	25	15
		Set value	45	26
		With tabs	1.25	

Page of Shulhan Aruk and Crowns — A136

1967, Mar. 22 *Perf. 13½x13*

340	A136	40a dk & lt bl, gray & gold	18	15

400th anniv. of the publication (in 1565) of the Shulhan Aruk, a compendium of Jewish religious and civil law, by Joseph Karo (1488-1575).

War of Independence Memorial — A137

1967, May 10 Unwmk. *Perf. 13x14*

341	A137	55a lt bl, ind & sil	18	15
		With tab	42	

Issued for Memorial Day, 1967.

Auster Plane over Convoy on Jerusalem Road A138

Military Aircraft: 30a, Mystere IV jet fighter over Dead Sea area. 80a, Mirage jet fighters over Masada.

1967, May 10 Photo.

342	A138	15a lt ol grn & dk bl grn	15	15
343	A138	30a ocher & dark brn	15	15
344	A138	80a grnsh bl & vio bl	20	15
		Set value	35	24
		With tabs	1.10	

Issued for Independence Day, 1967.

Israeli Ships in Straits of Tiran A139

Torah, Scroll of the Law A140

Designs: 15a, Star of David, sword and olive branch (vert.). 80a, Wailing (Western) Wall, Jerusalem.

1967, Aug. 16 *Perf. 14x13, 13x14*

345	A139	15a dk red, blk & yel	15	15
346	A139	40a Prussian green	15	15
347	A139	80a deep violet	20	15
		Set value	32	28

Victory of the Israeli forces, June, 1967.

1967, Sept. 13 *Perf. 13x14*

Designs: Various ancient, decorated Scrolls of the Law.

348	A140	12a gold & multi	15	15
349	A140	15a silver & multi	15	15
350	A140	35a gold & multi	15	15
351	A140	40a silver & multi	15	15
352	A140	80a gold & multi	20	16
		Set value	50	40

Jewish New Year, 5728. Sheets of 20 (10x2).

Chaim Weizmann A141

Design: 40a, Lord Balfour.

1967, Nov. 2 Photo. *Perf. 13x14*

353	A141	15a dark green	15	15
354	A141	40a brown	15	15
		Set value	17	17

50th anniv. of the Balfour Declaration, which established the right to a Jewish natl. home in Palestine. Issued in sheets of 15.

Emblem and Doll — A142

Nubian Ibex — A143

Designs: 30a, Hebrew inscription. 40a, French inscription.

1967, Nov. 2 Litho. *Perf. 14*

355	A142	30a yellow & multi	15	15
356	A142	40a brt bl & multi	15	15
357	A142	80a brt grn & multi	16	15
		Set value	30	24

Intl. Tourist Year. Issued in sheets of 15.

1967, Dec. 27 Litho. *Perf. 13*

Designs: 18a, Caracal lynx. 60a, Dorcas gazelles.

Animal in Ocher & Brown

358	A143	12a dull purple	15	15
359	A143	18a bright green	15	15
360	A143	60a bright blue	15	15
		Set value	26	20

Flags Forming Soccer Ball — A144

1968, Mar. 11 Photo. *Perf. 13*

361	A144	80a ocher & multi	15	15

Pre-Olympic soccer tournament.

Welcoming Immigrants A145

Resistance Fighter A146

Design: 80a, Happy farm family.

1968, Apr. 24 Litho. *Perf. 14*

362	A145	15a lt green & multi	15	15
363	A145	80a cream & multi	15	15
		Set value	15	15

Issued for Independence Day, 1968.

1968, Apr. 24 Photo. *Perf. 14x13*

364	A146	60a brown olive	15	15

Warsaw Ghetto Uprising, 25th anniv. Design from Warsaw Ghetto Memorial.

The Scott Catalogue value is a retail price, what you could expect to pay for the stamp in a grade of Fine-Very Fine. The value listed is a reference which reflects recent actual dealer selling price.

Sword and Laurel A147

Rifles and Helmet A148

1968, Apr. 24 Litho. *Perf. 14*

365	A147	40a gold & multi	15	15
366	A148	55a black & multi	15	15
		Set value	24	24

Zahal defense army, Independence Day, No. 365; Memorial Day, No. 366.

Candle and Prison Window A149

Prime Minister Moshe Sharett (1894-1965) A150

1968, June 5 Photo. *Perf. 14x13*

367	A149	80a blk, gray & sepia	18	15

Issued to honor those who died for freedom.

1968, June 5 Unwmk.

368	A150	£1 deep brown	18	15

27th Zionist Congress.

Knot Forming Star of David — A151

Dome of the Rock and Absalom's Tomb — A152

1968, Aug. 21 Litho. *Perf. 13*

369	A151	30a multi	15	15

50 years of Jewish Scouting. Sheets of 15 (5x3).

1968, Aug. 21 Photo. *Perf. 14x13*

Views of Jerusalem: 15a, Church of the Resurrection. 35a, Tower of David and City Wall. 40a, Yemin Moshe District and Mount of Olives. 60a, Israel Museum and "Shrine of the Book."

370	A152	12a gold & multi	15	15
371	A152	15a gold & multi	15	15
372	A152	35a gold & multi	15	15
373	A152	40a gold & multi	15	15
374	A152	60a gold & multi	15	15
		Set value	40	35

Jewish New Year, 5729. Sheets of 15 (5x3).

Detail from Lions' Gate, Jerusalem (St. Stephen's Gate) A153

1968, Oct. 8 Unwmk. *Perf. 13x14*

375	A153	£1 brown org	15	15
a.		Souvenir sheet	35	30

TABIRA Natl. Philatelic Exhibition. No. 375a contains one imperf. stamp. Sold only at exhibition for £1.50. No. 375 Issued in sheets of 15 (5x3).

Abraham Mapu A154

Handicapped Boys Playing Basketball A155

1968, Oct. 8 Photo. *Perf. 14x13*

376	A154	30a dark olive grn	15	15

Mapu (1808-1867), novelist and historian.

1968, Nov. 6 Photo. *Perf. 14x13*

377	A155	40a green & yel grn	15	15

17th Stoke-Mandeville Games for the Paralyzed, Nov. 4-13. Sheets of 15 (5x3).

Port of Elat — A156

Ports of Israel: 60a, Ashdod. £1, Haifa.

1969, Feb. 19 Unwmk. *Perf. 13x14*

378	A156	30a deep magenta	15	15
379	A156	60a brown	16	15
380	A156	£1 dull green	24	15
		Set value	46	34
		With tabs	2.50	

Gun Carrier A157

1969, Apr. 16 Photo. *Perf. 13x14*

381	A157	15a shown	15	15
382	A157	80a Destroyer	15	15
		Set value	22	18

Issued for Independence Day 1969.

Israel's Flag at Half-mast A158

Worker and ILO Emblem A159

1969, Apr. 16

383	A158	55a vio, gold & bl	15	15

Issued for Memorial Day.

1969, Apr. 16

384	A159	80a dark blue grn	15	15

ILO, 50th anniversary.

Hand Holding Torch A160

Arms of Hadera A161

1969, July 9 Photo. *Perf. 14x13*

385	A160	60a gold & multi	15	15
		With tab	60	

Issued to publicize the 8th Maccabiah.

1969-73 *Perf. 13x14*

Town Emblems: 3a, Hertseliya. 5a, Holon. 15a, Bat Yam. 18a, Ramla. 20a, Kefar Sava. 25a, Giv'atayim. 30a, Rehovot. 40a, Netanya. 50a, Bene Beraq. 60a, Nahariyya. 80a, Ramat Gan.

386	A161	2a green	15	15
387	A161	3a deep magenta	15	15
388	A161	5a orange	15	15
389	A161	15a bright rose	15	15
c.		Bklt. pane of 6 (2 #389 + 4 #389A) ('71)	65	
389A	A161	18a ultra ('70)	15	15
d.		Bklt. pane of 6 ('71)	70	
e.		Bklt. pane of 6 (1 #281 + 5 #389A) ('73)	65	
389B	A161	20a brown ('70)	15	15
f.		Bklt. pane of 5 + label ('73)	90	
390	A161	25a dark blue	15	15
390A	A161	30a brt pink ('70)	15	15
391	A161	40a purple	15	15
392	A161	50a greenish bl	18	15
392A	A161	60a olive ('70)	20	15
393	A161	80a dark green	22	15
		Set value	1.20	70
		With tabs	3.75	

Nos. 389c and 389d were also sold in uncut sheets of 36. No. 389e in uncut sheet of 18. See note after No. 291 about similar sheets.

Noah Building the Ark — A162

The Story of the Flood: 15a, Animals boarding the Ark. 35a, The Ark during the flood. 40a, Noah sending out the dove. 60a, Noah and the rainbow.

1969, Aug. 13 Unwmk. *Perf. 14*

394	A162	12a multicolored	15	15
395	A162	15a multicolored	15	15
396	A162	35a multicolored	15	15

397 A162 40a multicolored 15 15
398 A162 60a multicolored 25 15
Set value 66 50

Jewish New Year, 5730. Sheets of 15 (5x3).

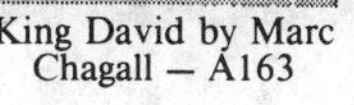

King David by Marc Chagall — A163

Atom Diagram and Test Tube — A164

1969, Sept. 24 Photo. *Perf. 14*
399 A163 £3 multicolored 80 55
With tab 1.40

1969, Nov. 3 *Perf. 14x13*
400 A164 £1.15 vio bl & multi 60 45
With tab 2.50

Weizmann Institute of Science, 25th anniv.

Joseph Trumpeldor A165

Dum Palms, Emeq Ha-Arava A166

1970, Jan. 21 Photo. *Perf. 14x13*
401 A165 £1 dark purple 25 15

50th anniv. of the defense of Tel Hay under the leadership of Joseph Trumpeldor.

1970, Jan. 21

Views: 3a, Tahana Waterfall. 5a, Nahal Baraq Canyon, Negev. 6a, Cedars in Judean Hills. 30a, Soreq Cave, Judean Hills.

402 A166 2a olive 15 15
403 A166 3a deep blue 15 15
404 A166 5a orange red 15 15
405 A166 6a slate green 15 15
406 A166 30a brt purple 22 15
Set value 40 25

Issued to publicize nature reserves.

Magic Carpet Shaped as Airplane A167

Prime Minister Levi Eshkol (1895-1969) A168

1970, Jan. 21 Litho. *Perf. 13*
407 A167 30a multicolored 15 15

20th anniv. of "Operation Magic Carpet" which airlifted the Yemeni Jews to Israel.

1970, Mar. 11 Litho. *Perf. 14*
408 A168 15a bl & multi 15 15

Mania Shochat A169

Camel and Train A170

Portrait: 80a, Ze'ev Jabotinsky (1880-1940), writer and Zionist leader.

1970, Mar. 11 Photo. *Perf. 14x13*
409 A169 40a dp plum & buff 16 16
410 A169 80a green & cream 18 18
With tabs 1.10

Ha-Shomer (Watchmen defense organization), 60th anniv. (No. 409); defense of Jerusalem, 50th anniv. (No. 410)

1970, Mar. 11 Litho. *Perf. 13*
411 A170 80a orange & multi 38 25
With tab 1.00

Opening of Dimona-Oron Railroad.

Scene from "The Dibbuk" — A171

1970, Mar. 11 Photo. *Perf. 14x13*
412 A171 £1 multicolored 22 15
With tab 70

Habimah Natl. Theater, 50th anniv.

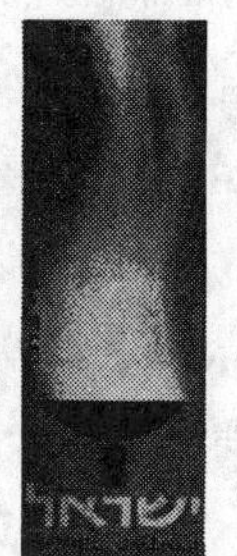

Memorial Flame A172

Orchis Laxiflorus A173

1970, May 6 Photo. *Perf. 13x14*
413 A172 55a vio, pink & blk 18 15

Issued for Memorial Day, 1970.

1970, May 6 Litho. *Perf. 14*

Flowers: 15a, Iris mariae. 80a, Lupinus pilosus.

414 A173 12a pale gray, plum & grn 15 15
415 A173 15a multicolored 15 15
416 A173 80a pale bl & multi 30 30
Set value 46 42
With tabs 1.10

Issued for Independence Day, 1970.

Charles Netter A174

420 Class Yachts A175

Design: 80a, Agricultural College (Mikwe Israel) and garden.

1970, May 6 Photo. *Perf. 14x13*
417 A174 40a lt grn, dk brn & gold 15 15
418 A174 80a gold & multi 22 15
Set value 21
With tabs 1.40

Centenary of first agricultural college in Israel; its founder, Charles Netter.

1970, July 8 Photo. *Perf. 14x13*

Designs: Various 420 Class yachts.

419 A175 15a grnsh bl, blk & sil 15 15
420 A175 30a ol, red, blk & sil 15 15
421 A175 80a ultra, blk & silver 28 15
Set value 42 22
With tabs 1.10

World "420" Class Sailing Championships.

Hebrew Letters Shaped Like Ship and Buildings A176

1970, July 8 *Perf. 13x14*
422 A176 40a gold & multi 15 15

Keren Hayesod, a Zionist Fund to maintain schools and hospitals in Palestine, 50th anniv.

Arava Plane A177

1970, July 8
423 A177 £1 brt blue, blk & sil 22 15

First Israeli designed and built aircraft.

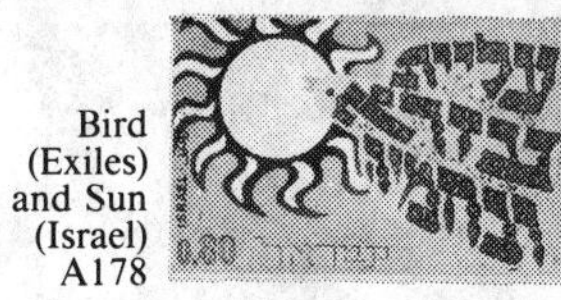

Bird (Exiles) and Sun (Israel) A178

1970, Sept. 7 Litho. *Perf. 14*
424 A178 80a yel & multi 18 15

Issued to commemorate "Operation Ezra and Nehemiah," the exodus of Iraqi Jews.

Old Synagogue, Cracow — A179

Historic Synagogues: 15a, Great Synagogue, Tunis. 35a, Portuguese Synagogue, Amsterdam. 40a, Great Synagogue, Moscow. 60a, Shearith Israel Synagogue, New York.

Perf. 14, 13 (15a)

1970, Sept. 7 Photo.
425 A179 12a gold & multi 15 15
426 A179 15a gold & multi 15 15
427 A179 35a gold & multi 15 15
428 A179 40a gold & multi 15 15
429 A179 60a gold & multi 15 15
Set value 42 35

Jewish New Year, 5731.

Tel Aviv Post Office, 1920 — A180

1970, Oct. 18 Photo. *Perf. 14*
430 A180 £1 multicolored 18 15
a. Souvenir sheet 1.25 1.50

TABIT Natl. Stamp Exhibition, Tel Aviv, Oct. 18-29. No. 430a contains an imperf. stamp similar to No. 430. Sold for £1.50.

Mother and Child A181

1970, Oct. 18 *Perf. 13x14*
431 A181 80a dp grn, yel & gray 18 15
With tab 48

WIZO, Women's Intl. Zionist Org., 50th anniv.

Paris Quai, by Camille Pissarro — A182

Paintings from Tel Aviv Museum: 85a, The Jewish Wedding, by Josef Israels. £2, Flowers in a Vase, by Fernand Leger.

1970, Dec. 22 Litho. *Perf. 14*
432 A182 85a black & multi 15 15
433 A182 £1 black & multi 16 15
434 A182 £2 black & multi 52 30
With tabs 2.00

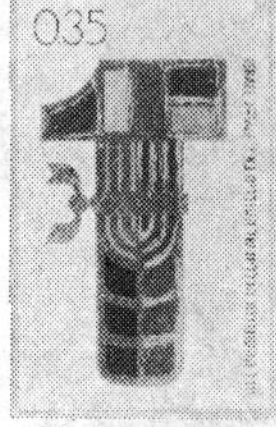

Hammer and Menorah Emblem A183

Persian Fallow Deer A184

1970, Dec. 22
435 A183 35a gold & multi 15 15

General Federation of Labor in Israel (Histadrut), 50th anniversary.

1971, Feb. 16 Litho. *Perf. 13*

Animals of the Bible: 3a, Asiatic wild ass. 5a, White oryx. 78a, Cheetah.

436	A184	2a multicolored	15	15
437	A184	3a multicolored	15	15
438	A184	5a multicolored	15	15
439	A184	78a multicolored	15	15
		Set value	25	22

"Samson and Dalila," Israel National Opera — A185

Theater Art in Israel: No. 441, Inn of the Ghosts, Cameri Theater. No. 442, A Psalm of David, Inbal Dance Theater.

1971, Feb. 16 *Perf. 14x13*

440	A185	50a bister & multi	15	15
441	A185	50a lt grn & multi	15	15
442	A185	50a blue & multi	15	15
		Set value		30

Basketball A186

Defense Forces Emblem A187

Designs: No. 444, Runner. No. 445, Athlete on rings.

1971, Apr. 13 Litho. *Perf. 14*

443	A186	50a green & multi	15	15
444	A186	50a ocher & multi	15	15
445	A186	50a lt vio & multi	15	15
		Set value	36	20

9th Hapoel Games.

1971, Apr. 13 Photo. *Perf. 14x13*

446	A187	78a multicolored	18	15

Memorial Day, 1971, and the war dead.

Jaffa Gate, Jerusalem — A188

Gates of Jerusalem: 18c, New Gate. 35c, Damascus Gate. 85c, Herod's Gate.

1971, Apr. 13 *Perf. 14*
Size: 41x41mm

447	A188	15a gold & multi	15	15
448	A188	18a gold & multi	15	15
449	A188	35a gold & multi	25	18
450	A188	85a gold & multi	60	45
a.		Souvenir sheet of 4	3.50	3.50

Independence Day, 1971. No. 450a contains 4 stamps similar to Nos. 447-450, but smaller (27x27mm). Sold at the Jerusalem Exhibition for £2.

See Nos. 488-491.

"He Wrote . . . Words of the Covenant" A189

"You shall rejoice in your feast" A190

Designs: 85a, "First Fruits . . ." Exodus 23:19. £1.50, ". . . Feast of Weeks" Exodus 34:22. The quotation on 50a is from Exodus 34:28. The quotations are in English on the tabs.

1971, May 25 Photo. *Perf. 14x13*

451	A189	50a yellow & multi	15	15
452	A189	85a yellow & multi	28	20
453	A189	£1.50 yellow & multi	45	30
		With tabs	1.75	

For the Feast of Weeks (Shabuoth).

1971, Aug. 24 Photo. *Perf. 14x13*

Designs: 18a, "You shall dwell in booths for seven days . . ." Leviticus 23:42. 20a, "That I made the people of Israel dwell in booths . . ." Lev. 23:43. 40a, ". . . when you have gathered in the produce of the land" Lev. 23:39. 65a, ". . . then I will give you your rains in their season" Lev. 26:4. The quotation on 15a is from Deuteronomy 16:14. The quotations are in English on tabs.

454	A190	15a yellow & multi	15	15
455	A190	18a yellow & multi	15	15
456	A190	20a yellow & multi	15	15
457	A190	40a yellow & multi	15	15
458	A190	65a yellow & multi	15	15
		Set value	32	32
		With tabs	80	

For the Feast of Tabernacles (Sukkoth).

Sun Shining on Fields A191

1971, Aug. 24 *Perf. 14*

459	A191	40a gold & multi	15	15

1st cooperative settlement in Israel, at Emeq (Valley of Israel), 50th anniv.

Retort and Grain — A192

Negev — A193

1971, Oct. 25 Litho. *Perf. 14*

460	A192	£1 grn & multi	18	15

50th anniversary of Volcani Institute of Agricultural Research.

> **Tagging**
> Starting in 1975, vertical luminescent bands were overprinted on various regular and commemorative stamps.
> In the 1971-75 regular series, values issued both untagged and tagged are: 20a, 25a, 30a, 35a, 45a, 50a, 65a, £1.10, £1.30, £2 and £3. Also No. 290 was re-issued with tagging in 1975.
> Regular issues from 1975 onward, including the £1.70, are tagged unless otherwise noted.
> Tagged commemoratives include Nos. 562-563 and all from Nos. 567-569 onward unless otherwise noted.

1971-75 Photo. *Perf. 13x14*

Landscapes: 3a, Judean desert. 5a, Gan Ha-Shelosha. 18a, Kinneret. 20a, Tel Dan. 22a, Fishermen, Yafo. 25a, Arava. 30a, En Avedat. 35a, Brekhat Ram, Golan Heights. 45a, Grazing sheep, Mt. Hermon. 50a, Rosh Pinna. 55a, Beach and park, Netanya. 65a, Plain of Zebulun. 70a, Shore, Engedi. 80a, Beach at Elat. 88a, Boats in Akko harbor. 95a, Hamifratz Hane'elam (lake). £1.10, Aqueduct near Akko. £1.30, Zefat. £1.70, Upper Nazareth. £2, Coral Island. £3, Haifa.

461	A193	3a dp bl ('72)	20	15
462	A193	5a green ('72)	15	15
463	A193	15a dp orange	16	15
464	A193	18a bright mag	65	15
464A	A193	20a dk grn ('73)	15	15
465	A193	22a brt bl ('72)	1.00	25
465A	A193	25a org red ('74)	15	15
466	A193	30a brt rose ('72)	15	15
466A	A193	35a plum ('73)	15	15
467	A193	45a dull vio blue ('73)	15	15
468	A193	50a green	15	15
469	A193	55a olive ('72)	16	15
469A	A193	65a black ('73)	16	15
470	A193	70a dp car ('72)	20	15
470A	A193	80a dp ultra ('74)	15	15
471	A193	88a greenish bl	1.00	16
472	A193	95a org ver ('73)	80	15
472A	A193	£1.10 olive ('73)	16	15
472B	A193	£1.30 dp bl ('74)	16	15
472C	A193	£1.70 dk brn ('75)	40	15
473	A193	£2 brown ('73)	40	15
474	A193	£3 dp vio ('72)	55	15
		Nos. 461-474 (22)	7.20	
		Set value		1.90
		With tabs	14.00	

See No. 592.

"Get Wisdom" Proverbs 4:7 — A194

Abstract Designs: 18a, Mathematical and scientific formula. 20a, Tools and engineering symbols. 40a, Abbreviations of various college degrees.

1972, Jan. 4 Litho. *Perf. 14*

475	A194	15a brt grn & multi	15	15
476	A194	18a multicolored	15	15
477	A194	20a multicolored	15	15
478	A194	40a red, blk & gold	15	15
		Set value	32	25

The Scribe, Sculpture by Boris Schatz A195

Works by Israeli Artists: 55a, Young Girl (Sarah), by Abel Pann. 70a, Zefat (landscape), by Menahem Shemi (horiz.). 85a, Old Jerusalem, by Jacob Steinhardt. £1, Resurrection (abstract), by Aharon Kahana.

Perf. 13x14 (40a, 85a), 14

1972, Mar. 7

479	A195	40a black & tan	15	15
480	A195	55a red brn & multi	15	15
481	A195	70a lt grn & multi	16	15
482	A195	85a blk & yellow	32	18
483	A195	£1 blk & multi	35	28
		Nos. 479-483 (5)	1.13	
		Set value		75

Exodus — A196

"Let My People Go" — A197

Passover: 45a, Baking unleavened bread. 95a, Seder.

1972, Mar. 7 Litho. *Perf. 13*

484	A196	18a buff & multi	15	15
485	A196	45a buff & multi	20	15
486	A196	95a buff & multi	32	20
		Set value		35
		With tabs	1.40	

1972, Mar. 7 *Perf. 14*

487	A197	55a blk, bl & yel grn	45	30
		With tab	4.00	

No. 487 inscribed in Hebrew, Arabic, Russian and English.

Gate Type of 1971

Gates of Jerusalem: 15a, Lions' Gate. 18a, Golden Gate. 45a, Dung Gate. 55a, Zion Gate.

1972, Apr. 17 Photo. *Perf. 14*
Size: 40x40mm

488	A188	15a gold & multi	15	15
489	A188	18a gold & multi	15	15
490	A188	45a gold & multi	28	25
491	A188	55a gold & multi	35	35
a.		Souvenir sheet of 4	3.50	3.50
		Set value		75
		With tabs	3.00	

Independence Day. #491a contains 4 27x27mm stamps similar to #488-491. Sold for £2.

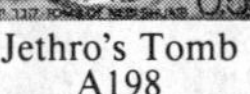
Jethro's Tomb A198

Flowers A199

1972, Apr. 17 **Litho.** ***Perf. 13***
492 A198 55a multicolored 18 15

1972, Apr. 17 ***Perf. 14***
493 A199 55a multicolored 18 15

Memorial Day.

Hebrew Words Emerging from Opened Ghetto — A200

Printed Page — A201

1972, June 6 ***Perf. 13***
494 A200 70a blue & multi 45 35
With tab 2.00

400th anniversary of the death of Rabbi Isaac ben Solomon Ashkenazi Luria ("Ari") (1534-1572), Palestinian cabalist.

1972, June 6 ***Perf. 14x13***
495 A201 95a blk, red & blue 28 15

International Book Year.

Satellite Earth Station, Satellite and Rainbow — A202

1972, June 6 ***Perf. 13***
496 A202 £1 tan & multi 20 15

Opening of satellite earth station in Israel.

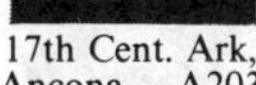
17th Cent. Ark, Ancona — A203

Menorah and "25" — A204

Holy Arks from: 45a, Padua, 1729. 70a, Parma, 17th century. 95a, Reggio Emilia, 1756. Arks moved to Israel from Italian synagogues.

1972, Aug. 8 **Photo.** ***Perf. 14x13***
497 A203 15a deep brn & yel 15 15
498 A203 45a dp grn, yel grn & gold 15 15
499 A203 70a brn red, yel & bl 22 15

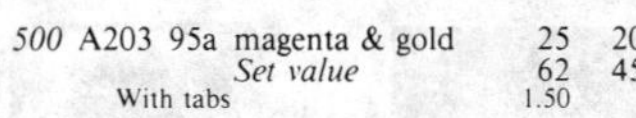
500 A203 95a magenta & gold 25 20
Set value 62 45
With tabs 1.50

Jewish New Year, 5733.

1972, Aug. 8
501 A204 £1 silver, bl & mag 15 15

25th anniversary of the State of Israel.

Brass Menorah, Morocco, 18th-19th Century A205

Menorahs: 25a, Brass, Poland, 18th century. 70a, Silver, Germany, 17th century.

1972, Nov. 7 **Litho.** ***Perf. 14x13***
502 A205 12a emer, blk & bl grn 15 15
503 A205 25a lil rose, blk & org 15 15
504 A205 70a blue, blk & vio 15 15
Set value 32 25

Hanukkah (Festival of Lights), 1972.

Child's Drawing A206

Pendant A207

Designs: Children's drawings.

1973, Jan. 16 **Litho.** ***Perf. 14***
Sizes: 22½x37mm (2a, 55a); 17x48mm (3a)
505 A206 2a blk & multi 15 15
506 A206 3a multicolored 15 15
507 A206 55a multicolored 15 15
Set value 15 15

Youth Wing of Israel Museum, Jerusalem (2a, 3a) and Youth Workshops, Tel Aviv Museum (55a).

1973, Jan. 16 **Photo.** ***Perf. 14x13***
508 A207 18a silver & multi 15 15

Immigration of North African Jews.

Levi, by Marc Chagall A208

Tribes of Israel: No. 510, Simeon. No. 511, Reuben. No. 512, Issachar. No. 513, Zebulun. No. 514, Judah. No. 515, Dan. No. 516, Gad. No. 517, Asher. No. 518, Naphtali. No. 519, Joseph. No. 520, Benjamin.

1973 **Litho.** ***Perf. 14***
509 A208 £1 multicolored 32 32
510 A208 £1 gray grn & multi 32 32
511 A208 £1 olive & multi 32 32
512 A208 £1 gray bl & multi 32 32
513 A208 £1 lemon & multi 32 32
514 A208 £1 gray & multi 32 32
515 A208 £1 bl grn & multi 32 32
516 A208 £1 gray & multi 32 32
517 A208 £1 yel grn & multi 32 32
518 A208 £1 sepia & multi 32 32
519 A208 £1 olive & multi 32 32
520 A208 £1 tan & multi 32 32
Nos. 509-520 (12) 3.84 3.84

Designs from stained glass windows by Marc Chagall, Hadassah-Hebrew University Medical Center Synagogue, Jerusalem.
Issue dates: Nos. 509-514, Mar. 27; Nos. 515-520, Aug. 21.

Israel's Declaration of Independence — A209

1973, May 4 **Photo.** ***Perf. 14***
521 A209 £1 ocher & multi 16 15
a. Souvenir sheet 65 75

25 years of Independence. No. 521a sold for £1.50.

Star of David and Runners A210

1973, May 4 **Litho.**
522 A210 £1.10 multicolored 15 15

9th Maccabiah.

Prison-cloth Hand — A211

1973, May 4 **Photo.**
523 A211 55a blue black 15 15

Heroes and martyrs of the Holocaust, 1933-1945.

Flame A212

Prophet Isaiah A213

1973, May 4 **Litho.**
524 A212 65a multicolored 16 15

Memorial Day.

1973, Aug. 21 **Photo.** ***Perf. 13x14***

Prophets: 65a, Jeremiah. £1.10, Ezekiel.

525 A213 18a multicolored 15 15
526 A213 65a multicolored 15 15
527 A213 £1.10 ultra & multi 15 15
Set value 32 20

Jewish New Year, 5734.

Torch of Learning, Cogwheel A214

Rescue Boat and Danish Flag A215

1973, Oct. 24 ***Perf. 14x13***
528 A214 £1.25 slate & multi 15 15

50th anniversary of the Technion, Israel Institute of Technology.

1973, Oct. 24 ***Perf. 13x14***
529 A215 £5 bister, red & blk 55 30

30th anniversary of the rescue by the Danes of the Jews in Denmark.

Spectators at Stamp Show — A216

Design: £1, Spectators, different design.

1973, Dec. 19 **Litho.** ***Perf. 13***
530 A216 20a brown & multi 15 15
531 A216 £1 brown & multi 15 15
Set value 15 15

JERUSALEM '73 Philatelic Exhibition, Mar. 25-Apr. 2, 1974.

Souvenir Sheets

Israel No. 7 — A217

Designs (First Issue): £2, No. 8. £3, No. 9.

1974, Feb. 19 **Photo.** ***Perf. 14x13***
532 A217 £1 sil & dk slate grn 15 18
533 A217 £2 silver & red brn 22 28
534 A217 £3 sil & blk blue 42 55

Jerusalem '73 Philatelic Exhibition, Mar. 25-Apr. 2, 1974 (postponed from Dec. 1973), 25th anniv. of State of Israel. Each sheet was sold with a 50 per cent surcharge.

The only foreign revenue stamps listed in this Catalogue are those authorized for prepayment of postage.

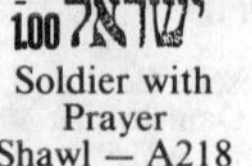

Soldier with Prayer Shawl — A218

Quill and Inkwell with Hebrew Letters — A219

1974, Apr. 23 *Perf. 13x14*
535 A218 £1 blk & light bl 15 15

Memorial Day.

1974, Apr. 23 *Perf. 14x13*
536 A219 £2 gold & black 15 15

50th anniversary of Hebrew Writers Assn.

Lady in Blue, by Moshe Kisling A220

Designs: £2, Mother and Child, Sculpture by Chana Orloff. £3, Girl in Blue, by Chaim Soutine.

1974, June 11 **Litho.** *Perf. 14*
537 A220 £1.25 multicolored 15 15
538 A220 £2 multicolored 18 15
539 A220 £3 multicolored 38 30

Art works from Tel Aviv, En Harod and Jerusalem Museums.

Wrench A221

1974, June 11
540 A221 25a multicolored 15 15

50th anniv. of Working Youth Movement.

Istanbuli Synagogue, Jerusalem — A222

Designs: Interiors of restored synagogues in Jerusalem's Old City.

1974, Aug. 6 **Photo.** *Perf. 13x14*
541 A222 25a shown 15 15
542 A222 70a Emtzai Synagogue 15 15
543 A222 £1 Rabbi Yohanan Synagogue 15 15
Set value 22 20

Jewish New Year, 5735.

Lady Davis Technical Center "AMAL," Tel Aviv — A223

Designs: 60a, Elias Sourasky Library, Tel Aviv University. £1.45, Mivtahim Rest Home, Zikhron Yaaqov.

1974, Aug. 6 *Perf. 13½x14*
544 A223 25a violet black 15 15
545 A223 60a dark blue 15 15
546 A223 £1.45 maroon 15 15
Set value 28 22

Modern Israeli architecture.

David Ben-Gurion — A224

1974, Nov. 5 *Perf. 14*
547 A224 25a brown 15 15
548 A224 £1.30 slate green 15 15
Set value 18 16

David Ben-Gurion (1886-1973), first Prime Minister and Minister of Defense of Israel.

Arrows on Globe — A225

Dove Delivering Letter — A226

1974, Nov. 5 **Litho.** *Perf. 14*
549 A225 25a black & multi 15 15

Photo.
550 A226 £1.30 gold & multi 15 15
Set value 18 18

Centenary of Universal Postal Union.

Hebrew University, Mount Scopus, Jerusalem — A227

1975, Jan. 14 **Litho.** *Perf. 13*
551 A227 £2.50 multicolored 18 15

Hebrew University, 50th anniv.

Girl Carrying Plant — A228

Welder — A229

Arbor Day: 35a, Bird singing in tree. £2, Boy carrying potted plant.

1975, Jan. 14 *Perf. 14*
552 A228 1a multicolored 15 15
553 A228 35a multicolored 15 15
554 A228 £2 multicolored 15 15
Set value 18 16

1975, Jan. 14 **Photo.** *Perf. 14x13*

Designs: 80a, Tractor driver. £1.20, Electrical lineman.

555 A229 30a multicolored 15 15
556 A229 80a multicolored 15 15
557 A229 £1.20 ultra & multi 15 15
Set value 18 18

Occupational safety and publicity for the Institute for Safety and Hygiene.

Hebrew University Synagogue, Jerusalem — A230

Modern Israeli architecture: £1.30, Yad Mordecai Museum. £1.70, Bat Yam City Hall.

Perf. 14, 13½x14 (#559)
1975, Mar. 5 **Photo.**
558 A230 80a brown 15 15
559 A230 £1.30 slate green 15 15
560 A230 £1.70 brown olive 18 15
Set value 38 26

US President Harry S Truman (1884-1972) — A231

1975, Mar. 5 **Engr.** *Perf. 14*
561 A231 £5 dk brn 35 15

Eternal Flame over Soldier's Grave — A232

Memorial Tablet — A233

1975, Apr. 10 **Photo.** *Perf. 14x13*
562 A232 £1.45 black & multi 16 15

Memorial Day.

1975, Apr. 10
563 A233 £1.45 black, red & gray 16 15

In memory of soldiers missing in action.

Hurdling A234

1975, Apr. 10 *Perf. 13x14*
564 A234 25a shown 15 15
565 A234 £1.70 Bicycling 15 15
566 A234 £3 Volleyball 20 16
Set value 35 30

10th Hapoel Games; 50th anniv. of Hapoel Org.

Hanukkah, by Mortiz D. Oppenheim A235

Paintings: £1.40, The Purim Players, by Jankel Adler (horiz.). £4, Yom Kippur, by Maurycy Gottlieb.

1975, June 17 **Litho.** *Perf. 14*
567 A235 £1 multicolored 15 15
568 A235 £1.40 multicolored 15 15
569 A235 £4 multicolored 32 24
Set value 48 38

Paintings of religious holidays.

Old Couple A236

1975, June 17 **Photo.** *Perf. 13x14*
570 A236 £1.85 multicolored 15 15

International Gerontological Association, 10th triennial conference, Jerusalem.

Pres. Zalman Shazar (1889-1974) A237

Pioneer Women's Emblem A238

1975, Aug. 6 **Photo.** *Perf. 14x13*
571 A237 35a silver & blk 15 15

1975, Aug. 6 *Perf. 14½*
572 A238 £5 multicolored 30 15

Pioneer Women, 50th anniversary.

Judges of Israel — A239

1975, Aug. 6 *Perf. 13x14*

573	A239	35a	Gideon	15	15
574	A239	£1	Deborah	15	15
575	A239	£1.40	Jephthah	15	15
			Set value	34	26

Jewish New Year, 5736.

Hebrew University, Mt. Scopus — A240

1975, Oct. 14 **Photo.** *Perf. 14x13*

576	A240	£4	multicolored	30	15

Return of Hadassah to Mt. Scopus, Jerusalem.

Collared Pratincoles A241

Protected Birds: £1.70, Spur-winged plover. £2, Black-winged stilts.

1975, Oct. 14 **Litho.** *Perf. 13*

577	A241	£1.10	pink & multi	15	15
578	A241	£1.70	lem & multi	15	15
579	A241	£2	multicolored	15	15
			Set value	34	26

Butterfly and Factory (Air Pollution) — A242

Designs: 80a, Fish and tanker (water pollution). £1.70, Ear and jet (noise pollution).

1975, Dec. 9 **Photo.** *Perf. 14*

580	A242	50a	car & multi	15	15
581	A242	80a	green & multi	15	15
582	A242	£1.70	orange & multi	16	15
			Set value	30	22

Environmental protection.

Star of David — A243

1975-80 *Perf. 13x14*

583	A243	75a	vio bl & carmine ('77)	15	15
584	A243	£1.80	violet bl & gray ('79)	15	15
585	A243	£1.85	vio bl & lt brn	24	22
586	A243	£2.45	vio bl & brt green ('76)	30	18
587	A243	£2.70	vio bl & purple ('80)	15	15
588	A243	£4.30	ultra & red ('80)	15	15
589	A243	£5.40	vio bl & ol ('78)	52	18
590	A243	£8	vio bl & bl ('79)	75	24
			Nos. 583-590 (8)	2.41	
			Set value		1.05

Landscape Type of 1971-75

Design: £10, View of Elat and harbor.

1976, Aug. 17 **Photo.** *Perf. 14x14½*

592	A193	£10	Prussian bl	90	15

No. 592 issued both tagged and untagged.

"In the days of Ahasuerus." — A247

Designs (from Book of Esther): 80a, "He set the royal crown on her head." £1.60, "Thus shall it be done to the man whom the king delights to honor."

1976, Feb. 17 **Photo.** *Perf. 14*

593	A247	40a	multicolored	15	15
594	A247	80a	multicolored	15	15
595	A247	£1.60	multicolored	15	15
a.			Souvenir sheet of 3, #593-595, perf. 13x14	45	35
			Set value	32	30

Purim Festival. No. 595a sold for £4.

Border Settlement, Barbed Wire — A248

1976, Feb. 17

596	A248	£1.50	olive & multi	15	15

Border settlements, part of Jewish colonization of Holy Land.

Symbolic Key A249

1976, Feb. 17

597	A249	£1.85	multicolored	15	15

Bezalel Academy of Arts and Design, Jerusalem, 70th anniv.

"200" US Flag A250

1976, Apr. 25 **Photo.** *Perf. 13x14*

598	A250	£4	gold & multi	38	22

American Bicentennial.

Dancers of Meron, by Reuven Rubin A251

1976, Apr. 25 **Litho.** *Perf. 14*

599	A251	£1.30	multicolored	15	15

Lag Ba-Omer festival.

8th Brigade Monument, Ben-Gurion Airport — A252

1976, Apr. 25 **Photo.** *Perf. 14x13*

600	A252	£1.85	multicolored	24	15

Memorial Day.

Souvenir Sheet

Tourism, Sport and Industry — A253

1976, Apr. 25

601	A253		Sheet of 3	75	50
a.			£1 multicolored	15	15
b.			£2 multicolored	20	15
c.			£4 multicolored	45	28

No. 601 sold for £10.

High Jump A254

1976, June 23 *Perf. 13x14*

602	A254	£1.60	shown	15	15
603	A254	£2.40	Diving	16	16
604	A254	£4.40	Gymnastics	35	30

21st Olympic Games, Montreal, Canada, July 17-Aug. 1.

Tents and Suns — A255

1976, June 23 *Perf. 14*

605	A255	£1.50	green & multi	15	15

Israel Camping Union.

"Truth" A256

Pawn A257

Design: £1.50, "Judgment" (scales). £1.90, "Peace" (dove and olive branch).

1976, Aug. 17 **Photo.** *Perf. 14x13*

Tagged

606	A256	45a	gold & multi	15	15
607	A256	£1.50	gold & multi	15	15
608	A256	£1.90	gold & multi	15	15
			Set value	28	25

Festivals 5737.

1976, Oct. 19 **Litho.** *Perf. 14*

609	A257	£1.30	shown	15	15
610	A257	£1.60	Rook	15	15
			Set value		15

22nd Men's and 7th Women's Chess Olympiad, Haifa, Oct. 24-Nov. 11.

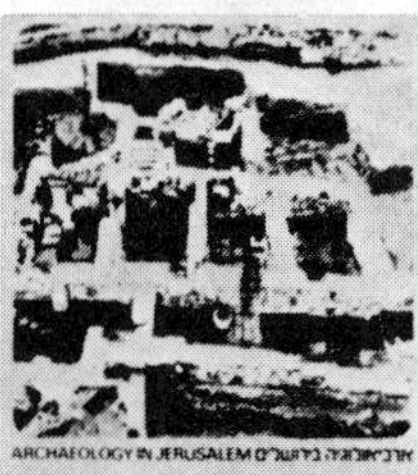

Byzantine Building, 6th Century A258

Designs: 70a, City wall, 7th century B.C. £2.40, Robinson's Arch. £2.80, Steps to Gate of Hulda. Both from area leading to 2nd Temple, 1st century B.C. £5, Wall, Omayyad Palace, 8th century A.D.

1976 **Litho.** *Perf. 14*

611	A258	70a	multicolored	15	15
612	A258	£1.30	multicolored	15	15
613	A258	£2.40	multicolored	20	15
614	A258	£2.80	multicolored	35	20
615	A258	£5	multicolored	48	42
			Nos. 611-615 (5)	1.33	1.07

Excavations in Old Jerusalem.

Issue dates: Nos. 612-614, Oct. 19; Nos. 611, 615, Dec. 14.

Clearing the Land, 1890 A259

Designs: 10a, Building harbor wall. 60a, Road building (vert.). £1.40, Plower and horse-drawn plow. £1.80, Planting trees.

1976, Dec. 14 **Photo.** *Perf. 13*

616	A259	5a	brown & gold	15	15
617	A259	10a	purple & gold	15	15
618	A259	60a	gold & car	15	15
619	A259	£1.40	gold & blue	15	15
620	A259	£1.80	green & gold	15	15
			Set value	40	35

Work of the pioneers.

"Let's Pull up Grandfather's Carrot" — A260

1977, Feb. 15 **Litho.** ***Perf. 14***

621 A260 £2.60 multicolored 25 18

Voluntary service.

Doves, Jew and Arab Shaking Hands A261

Designs: £1.40, Arab and Jew holding hands, and flowers. £2.70, Peace dove, Arab and Jew dancing. Illustrations for the book "My Shalom-My Peace."

1977, Feb. 15

622 A261 50a multicolored 15 15
623 A261 £1.40 multicolored 19 15
624 A261 £2.70 multicolored 32 25
Set value 45

Children's drawings for peace.

"By the Rivers of Babylon . . ." — A262

Drawings by Efraim Moshe Lilien: £1.80, Abraham (vert.). £2.10, "May our eyes behold thee when thou returnest to Zion in compassion."

Perf. 14x13, 13x14

1977, Feb. 15 **Photo.**

625 A262 £1.70 gray, brn & blk 24 18
626 A262 £1.80 yel, blk & brn 25 18
627 A262 £2.10 lt grn & dk grn 30 22

Souvenirs for 5th Zionist Congress, 1902.

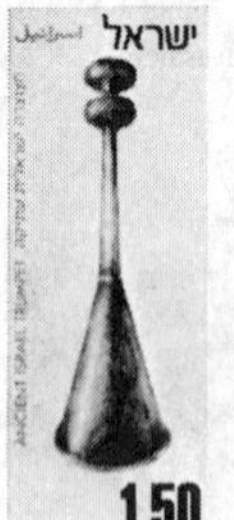
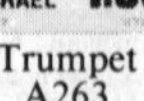

Trumpet A263

Embroidered Sabbath Cloth A264

1977, Apr. 17 **Litho.** ***Perf. 14***

628 A263 £1.50 shown 15 15
629 A263 £2 Lyre 15 15
630 A263 £5 Cymbals 32 24
Set value 42

Ancient musical instruments, Haifa Music Museum and Amli Library.

1977, Apr. 17 ***Perf. 13x14***

631 A264 £3 buff & multi 26 15

Importance of Sabbath observation in Jewish life.

Parachutists' Memorial, Bilu-Gedera, Tel Aviv A265

1977, Apr. 17 ***Perf. 13x14***

632 A265 £3.30 gray, blk & grn 38 28

Memorial Day.

10th Maccabiah A266

ZOA Convention Emblem A267

1977, June 23 **Photo.** ***Perf. 14x13***

633 A266 £1 Fencing 16 15
634 A266 £2.50 Shot put 20 15
635 A266 £3.50 Judo 28 20

1977, June 23 ***Perf. 14***

636 A267 £4 sil & multi 32 20

Convention of Zionist Organization of America (ZOA), Jerusalem, June 1977.

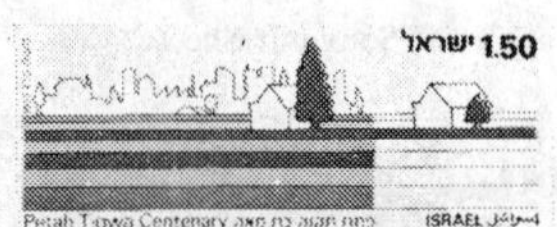

Petah Tikva Centenary — A268

1977, June 23 ***Perf. 14x13***

637 A268 £1.50 multicolored 15 15

Matriarchs of the Bible — A269

1977, Aug. 16 **Photo.** ***Perf. 14***

638 A269 70a Sarah 15 15
639 A269 £1.50 Rebekah 15 15
640 A269 £2 Rachel 15 15
641 A269 £3 Leah 20 20
Set value 48 46

Jewish New Year, 5738.

Police — A270

Illuminated Page — A271

1977, Aug. 16 **Litho.** ***Perf. 14***

642 A270 £1 shown 15 15
643 A270 £1 Fronteir Guards 15 15
644 A270 £1 Civil Guard 15 15
Set value 30 20

Israel Police Force, established Mar. 26, 1948.

1977, July 21 **Photo.** ***Perf. 14x13***

645 A271 £4 multicolored 28 15

4th cent. of Hebrew printing at Safad.

Farm Growing from Steel Helmet A272

Koffler Accelerator A273

1977, Oct. 18 **Litho.** ***Perf. 14***

646 A272 £3.50 multicolored 28 15

Fighting Pioneer Youth (NAHAL), established 1949.

1977, Oct. 18 **Photo.** ***Perf. 14x13***

647 A273 £8 blk & blue 65 42

Inauguration of Koffler accelerator at Weizmann Institute of Science, Rehovot. Untagged.

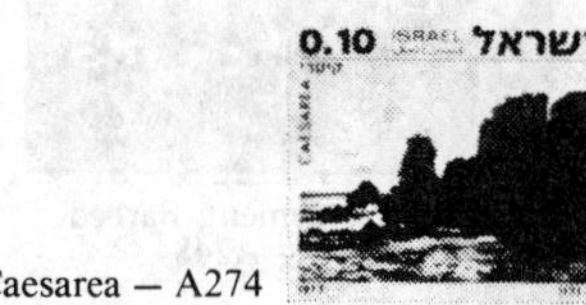

Caesarea — A274

Scenes: £1, Arava on the Dead Sea. £20, Rosh Pinna.

1977-78 ***Perf. 13½x14***

Size: 27x22mm

649 A274 10a violet blue 15 15
664 A274 £1 ol bister 15 15

Perf. 14½x14

Size: 27½x26½mm

672 A274 £20 org & dk grn ('78) 1.10 15
Set value 22

The 10a and £20 are untagged.

First Holy Land Locomotive — A276

Locomotives: £1.50, Jezreel Valley train. £2, British Mandate period. £2.50, Israel Railways.

1977, Dec. 13 **Photo.** ***Perf. 13x14***

674 A276 65a multicolored 15 15
675 A276 £1.50 multicolored 18 15
676 A276 £2 multicolored 28 22
677 A276 £2.50 multicolored 32 28
a. Souvenir sheet of 4, #674-677 1.40 1.40
Set value 68

Railways in the Holy Land. No. 677a sold for £10.

Cypraea Isabella — A277

Designs: Red Sea shells.

1977, Dec. 13 **Litho.** ***Perf. 14***

678 A277 £2 shown 15 15
679 A277 £2 Lioconcha castrensis 15 15
680 A277 £2 Gloripallium pallium 15 15
681 A277 £2 Malea pomum 15 15
Set value 48 40

Street in Jerusalem, by Haim Glicksberg (1904-1970) A278

Paintings: £3.80, Thistles, by Leopold Krakauer (1890-1954). £4.40, An Alley in Zefat, by Mordekhai Levanon (1901-1968).

1978, Feb. 14

682 A278 £3 multicolored 16 15
683 A278 £3.80 multicolored 24 20
684 A278 £4.40 multicolored 28 24

Marriage Contract, Netherlands, 1648 — A279

Marriage Contracts (Ketubah): £3.90, Morocco, 1897. £6, Jerusalem, 1846.

1978, Feb. 14

685 A279 75a multicolored 15 15
686 A279 £3.90 multicolored 15 16
687 A279 £6 multicolored 25 20
Set value 45 40

Eliyahu Golomb — A280

Designs: Portraits.

1978, Apr. 23 **Photo.** ***Perf. 14x13***

688 A280 £2 shown 15 15
689 A280 £2 Dr. Moshe Sneh 15 15
690 A280 £2 David Raziel 15 15
691 A280 £2 Yitzhak Sadeh 15 15
692 A280 £2 Abraham Stern 15 15
Nos. 688-692 (5) 75 75

Heroes of underground movement. Nos. 688-692 issued in sheets of 15.

See Nos. 695-696, 699-700, 705-706, 712-714, 740-742.

Souvenir Sheet

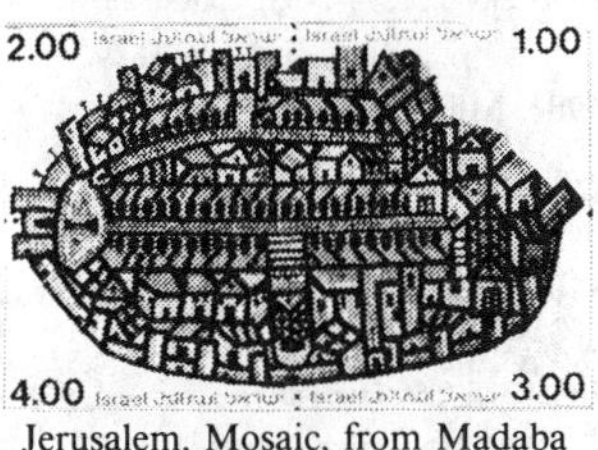

Jerusalem, Mosaic, from Madaba Map — A281

1978, Apr. 23 Litho. *Perf. 14*

693 A281 Sheet of 4 1.75 1.50
a. £1 multicolored 15 15
b. £2 multicolored 35 28
c. £3 multicolored 50 42
d. £4 multicolored 65 55

Tabir '78 National Stamp Exhibition, Jerusalem, Apr. 23. No. 693 sold for £15.

Flowers A282

Design: Flowers, after children's paintings on Memorial Wall in Yad-Lebanim Museum, Petah Tikva. Each stamp shows different flowers.

1978, Apr. 23 *Perf. 14*

694 Sheet of 15, multi 2.25 1.75
a.-o. A282 £1.50 single stamp 15 15

Memorial Day.

Heroes Type

Designs: No. 695, Theodor Herzl. No. 696, Chaim Weizmann.

1978, July 5 Photo. *Perf. 14x13*

695 A280 £2 gray & gray ol 15 15
696 A280 £2 buff & vio bl 15 15
Set value 15

Herzl, founder of Zionism; Weizmann, 1st President of Israel.

Hatiqwa, 1st Verse A285

YMCA Building, Jerusalem A286

1978, July 4 *Perf. 13x14*

697 A285 £8.40 multicolored 48 38

Centenary of Israeli National Anthem, Hatiqwa, by poet Naftali Herz Imber.

1978, July 4 Litho. *Perf. 13*

698 A286 £5.40 multicolored 28 20

Centenary of YMCA in Jerusalem.

Heroes Type

Designs: No. 699, Rabbi Kook (1865-1935). No. 700, Rabbi Ouziel (1880-1963).

1978, Aug. 22 Photo. *Perf. 14x13*

699 A280 £2 pale gray & sl grn 15 15
700 A280 £2 pale gray & dk pur 15 15
Set value 15

Patriarchs A288

1978, Aug. 22 *Perf. 14*

701 A288 £1.10 Abraham & Isaac 15 15
702 A288 £5.20 Isaac 28 26
703 A288 £6.60 Jacob 35 32
Set value 62

Festivals 5739.

Families and Houses A289

1978, Aug. 22 *Perf. 13x14*

704 A289 £5.10 multicolored 32 20

Social welfare.

Heroes Type

Designs: No. 705, David Ben-Gurion. No. 706, Ze'ev Jabotinsky.

1978, Oct. 31 Photo. *Perf. 14x13*

705 A280 £2 buff & vio brn 16 15
706 A280 £2 gray & indigo 16 15
Set value 15

30 years of independence. Ben-Gurion, first Prime Minister, and Ze'ev Vladimir Jabotinsky (1880-1940), leader of World Union of Zionist Revisionists.

Star of David and Growing Tree — A291

1978, Oct. 31 Litho. *Perf. 14*

707 A291 £8.40 multicolored 55 38

United Jewish Appeal, established 1939 in US to help Israel.

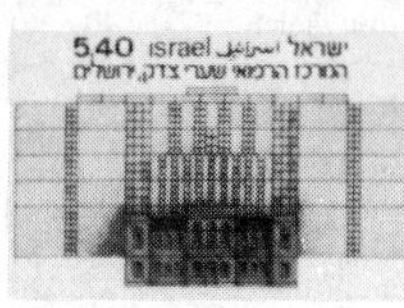

Old and New Hospital Buildings A292

1978, Oct. 31

708 A292 £5.40 multicolored 28 22

Opening of new Shaare Zedek Medical Center, Jerusalem.

Silver and Enamel Vase, India A293

Iris Lortetii A295

Designs: £3, Elephant with howdah, Persia, 13th century. £4, Mosque lamp, glass and enamel, Syria, 14th century.

1978, Oct. 31

709 A293 £2.40 multicolored 15 15
710 A293 £3 multicolored 20 15
711 A293 £4 multicolored 22 18

Leo Arie Mayer Memorial Museum for Islamic Art, Jerusalem.

Heroes Type

Portraits: No. 712, Menachem Ussishkin (1863-1941). No. 713, Berl Katzenelson (1878-1944). No. 714, Max Nordau (1849-1923).

1978, Dec. 26 Photo. *Perf. 14x13*

712 A280 £2 citron & sl grn 15 15
713 A280 £2 gray & vio blue 15 15
714 A280 £2 buff & black 15 15
Set value 36 26

30th anniversary of independence.

1978, Dec. 26 Litho. *Perf. 14*

Protected Wild Flowers: £5.40, Iris haynei. £8.40, Iris nazarena.

715 A295 £1.10 multicolored 15 15
716 A295 £5.40 multicolored 32 25
717 A295 £8.40 multicolored 48 35
Set value 65

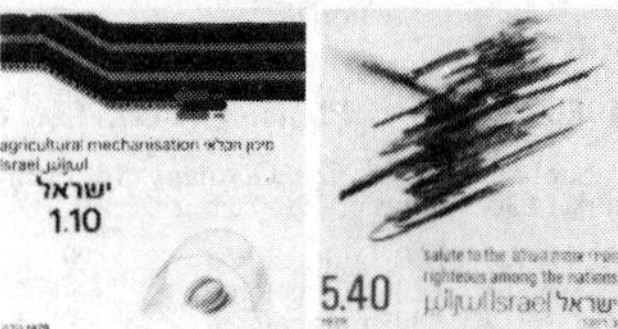

Agricultural Mechanization A296

"Hope from Darkness" A297

Symbolic Designs: £2.40, Seawater desalination. £4.30, Electronics. £5, Chemical fertilizers.

1979, Feb. 13 Litho. *Perf. 13*

718 A296 £1.10 multicolored 15 15
719 A296 £2.40 multicolored 20 15
720 A296 £4.30 multicolored 22 20
721 A296 £5 multicolored 25 25
Set value 62

Technological Achievements.

1979, Feb. 13

722 A297 £5.40 multicolored 38 25

Salute to "the Righteous among Nations," an award to those who helped during Nazi period.

Jewish Brigade Flag — A298

Paper (Prayer for Peace) in Crevice of Western Wall — A299

1979, Feb. 13 Photo. *Perf. 14*

723 A298 £5.10 blue, yel & blk 28 24

Jewish Brigade served with British Armed Forces during WWII.

1979, Mar. 26 Photo. *Perf. 14x13*

724 A299 £10 multicolored 45 24
a. Souv. sheet of 1, imperf. 50 60

Signing of peace treaty between Israel and Egypt, Mar. 26.

11th Hapoel Games A300

"50" and Rotary Emblem A301

1979, Apr. 23 Litho. *Perf. 13*

725 A300 £1.50 Weightlifting 15 15
726 A300 £6 Tennis 32 22
727 A300 £11 Gymnastics 65 42

1979, Apr. 23 Photo. *Perf. 14x13*

728 A301 £7 multicolored 38 25

Rotary Intl. in Israel, 50th anniv.

Navy Memorial, Ashdod A302

1979, Apr. 23

729 A302 £5.10 multicolored 32 32

Memorial Day.

Rabbi Yehoshua ben Hananya A303

Flag Colors as Search Light A304

Craftsmen-Sages: £8.50, Rabbi Meir Baal Ha-Ness, scribe. £13, Rabbi Johanan, sandal maker.

1979, Aug. 14 Photo. *Perf. 14x13*

730 A303 £1.80 multicolored 15 15
731 A303 £8.50 multicolored 22 22
732 A303 £13 multicolored 40 42

Jewish New Year 5740.

1979, Aug. 14

733 A304 £10 multicolored 28 20

Jewish Agency, 50th anniversary.

Hot Springs, Tiberias A305

Boy Riding Rainbow A306

Design: £12, Dead Sea health resorts.

1979, Aug. 14 Litho. *Perf. 14*

734	A305	£8 multicolored	20	22
735	A305	£12 multicolored	38	35

1979, Nov. 6 Photo. *Perf. 13x14*

736	A306	£8.50 multicolored	28	28

International Year of the Child.

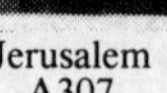

Jerusalem A307

Sorek Cave A308

Children's Drawings of Jerusalem: £4, People of different nationalities (horiz.). £5, Praying at the Western Wall (horiz.).

1979 *Perf. 14*

737	A307	£1.80 multicolored	15	15
738	A307	£4 multicolored	15	15
739	A307	£5 multicolored	15	15
		Set value	26	20

Heroes Type

Designs: £7, Arthur Ruppin (1876-1943). £9, Joseph Trumpeldor (1880-1920). £13, Aaron Aaronsohn (1876-1919).

1979, Nov. 6 Photo. *Perf. 14x13*

740	A280	£7 gray & magenta	18	18
741	A280	£9 pale grn & Prus bl	25	25
742	A280	£13 pale yel & dk ol	38	38

1980, Jan. 15 Litho. *Perf. 13x14*

743	A308	£50 multi	1.10	52

Star of David in Cogwheel A309

Scolymus Maculatus A310

1980, Jan. 15 *Perf. 14*

744	A309	£13 multicolored	42	40

Organization for Rehabilitation through Training (ORT), centenary.

1980, Jan. 15

Thistles: £5.50, Echinops viscosus. £8.50, Cynara syriaca.

745	A310	50a multicolored	15	15
746	A310	£5.50 multicolored	15	15
747	A310	£8.50 multicolored	24	20
		Set value	44	36

Men and Drop of Blood — A311

Mobile Intensive Care Unit — A312

1980, Apr. 15 Photo. *Perf. 14x13*

748	A311	£2.70 multicolored	15	15
749	A312	£13 multicolored	32	32
a.		Souv. sheet of 4, 2 each #748-749	1.10	1.10
		Set value	38	36

Magen David Adom (Red Star of David), 50th anniv.

Road of Courage Monument A313

Sabbath Lamp, Netherlands, 18th Century A314

1980, Apr. 15 Litho. *Perf. 14*

750	A313	£12 multicolored	38	38

Memorial Day.

1980, Aug. 5 Photo. *Perf. 13x14*

Sabbath Lamps: £20, Germany, 18th century. £30, Morocco, 19th century.

751	A314	£4.30 multicolored	15	15
752	A314	£20 multicolored	45	45
753	A314	£30 multicolored	65	65

Yizhak Gruenbaum A315

Renewal of Jewish Settlement in Gush Etzion A316

1980, Aug. 5 *Perf. 14x13*

754	A315	£32 sepia	90	85

Yizhak Gruenbaum (1879-1970), first minister of the interior.

1980, Aug. 5

755	A316	£19 multicolored	45	38

NATIONAL STAMP EXHIBITION HAIFA 80

View of Haifa and Mt. Carmel, 17th Century — A317

1980, Sept. 28 Litho. *Perf. 14x13*

756	A317	Sheet of 2	1.75	2.00
a.		2s multicolored	60	70
b.		3s multicolored	90	1.05

Haifa 80 National Stamp Exhibition, Haifa, Sept. 28-Oct. 7.

A318

1980-81 Photo. *Perf. 13x14*

757	A318	5a brt yel grn & green	15	15
758	A318	10a red & brt mag	15	15
759	A318	20a grnsh bl & dk blue	15	15
760	A318	30a lil & dp vio	15	15
761	A318	50a red org & red brown	15	15
762	A318	60a brt yel grn & dk brown	15	15
762A	A318	70a Prus bl & black	15	15
763	A318	1s brt mag & dk green	20	15
764	A318	2s dk bl grn & brn red	32	16
765	A318	2.80s brown & grn	40	24
766	A318	3.20s gray & red	45	26
767	A318	4.20s ultra & dk pur	52	32
768	A318	5s green & blk	70	42
769	A318	10s brn org & brn	1.40	70
		Nos. 757-769 (14)	5.04	
		Set value		2.50

Issue dates: 70a, May 5, 1981; others, Dec. 16, 1980.

See Nos. 784-786, 807-808

Prime Minister Golda Meir (1898-1978) A319

Hand Putting Coin in Light Bulb A321

View of Jerusalem, by Mordechai Ardon — A320

1981, Feb. 10 Photo. *Perf. 14x13*

770	A319	2.60s rose violet	40	40

1981, Feb. 10 Litho. *Perf. 14*

Paintings of Jerusalem by: 50a, Anna Ticho. 1.50s, Joseph Zaritsky (vert.).

771	A320	50a multicolored	15	15
772	A320	1.50s multicolored	22	20
773	A320	2.50s multicolored	38	35

1981, Mar. 17 Photo. *Perf. 14*

774	A321	2.60s shown	25	24
775	A321	4.20s Hand squeezing solar energy	40	38

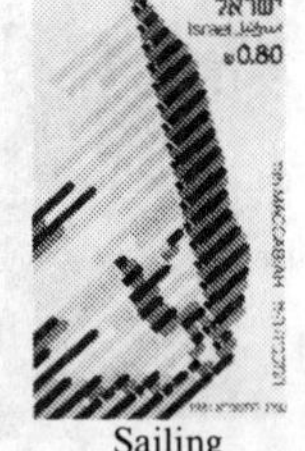

Shmuel Yosef Agnon (1880-1970), Writer A322

Sailing A323

Designs: 2.80s, Moses Montefiore (1784-1885), first knighted English Jew. 3.20s, Abba Hillel Silver (1893-1963), statesman.

Perf. 14x13, 14 (3.20s)

1981, Mar. 17

776	A322	2s dk blue & blk	25	25
777	A322	2.80s dk bl grn & blk	35	40
778	A322	3.20s deep bis & blk	38	42

1981, May 5 *Perf. 14x13*

779	A323	80a shown	15	15
780	A323	4s Basketball	55	52
781	A323	6s High jump	80	95

11th Maccabiah Games, July 8-16.

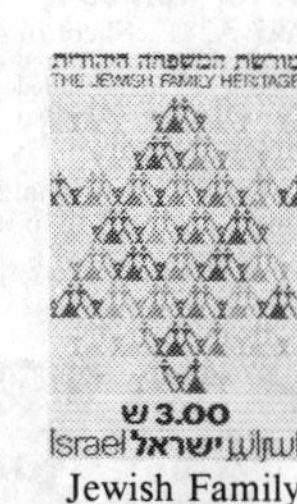

Biq'at Hayarden Memorial A324

Jewish Family Heritage A325

1981, May 5 *Perf. 13x14*

782	A324	1s red & black	22	15

1981, May 5 Litho. *Perf. 14*

783	A325	3s multicolored	42	38

Type of 1980

1981, Aug. 25 Photo. *Perf. 13x14*

784	A318	90a dp vio & brn org	15	15
785	A318	3s red & dk blue	45	32
786	A318	4s dk brn vio & dp lil rose	58	35

The Burning Bush — A326

Roses — A327

Festivals 5742 (Book of Exodus): 1s "Let my people go . . ." 3s, Crossing of the Red Sea. 4s, Moses with Tablets.

1981, Aug. 25

787	A326	70a multicolored	15	15
788	A326	1s multicolored	16	15
789	A326	3s multicolored	38	38
790	A326	4s multicolored	45	42

1981, Oct. 22 Litho. *Perf. 14*

791	A327	90a Rosa damascena	16	16
792	A327	3.50s Rosa phoenicia	40	38
793	A327	4.50s Rosa hybrida	50	45

Ha-Shiv'a Interchange, Morasha-Ashod Highway — A328

1981, Oct. 22 Photo. *Perf. 14x13*

794	A328	8s multicolored	95	95

Elat Stone — A329

Wild Strawberry Tree — A330

1981, Dec. 29 Litho. *Perf. 14*

795 A329	2.50s	shown	25	25
796 A329	5.50s	Star sapphire	55	55
797 A329	7s	Emerald	70	70

1981, Dec. 29

798 A330	3s	shown	38	38
799 A330	3s	Judas tree	38	38
800 A330	3s	Balonea oak	38	38

Issued in sheets of 9 (se-tenant vert. and horiz.).

Road Safety — A331

1982, Mar. 2 Photo. *Perf. 14x13*

801 A331 7s multicolored		70	70
a.	Souvenir sheet	1.25	1.25

No. 801a sold for 10s.

Joseph Gedalyah Klausner (1874-1958), Historian and Philosopher — A331a

Designs: 7s, Perez Bernstein (1890-1971), writer and editor. 8s, Rabbi Arys Levin (1885-1969).

1982, Mar. 2

802 A331a	7s	multi	65	65
803 A331a	8s	multi	70	70
804 A331a	9s	cream & dk bl	80	80

Type of 1980 and

Produce — A332

1982-83 Photo. *Perf. 13 x 14*

805 A332	40a	Prus bl & grn ('83)	15	15
806 A332	80a	lt bl & pur ('83)	15	15
807 A318	1.10s	ol & red	15	15
808 A318	1.20s	bl & red	15	15
809 A332	1.40s	ol grn & red	15	15
810 A332	6s	red vio & brn org ('83)	26	18
811 A332	7s	brn org & ol ('83)	16	15
812 A332	8s	brt grn & red brn ('83)	22	15
813 A332	9s	ol & brn ('83)	25	18
814 A332	15s	ver & brt grn ('83)	40	26
		Set value	1.50	1.10

See Nos. 876-879.

Tel Aviv Landscape, by Aryeh Lubin (d. 1980) — A333

Landscapes by: 8s, Sionah Tagger (vert.). 15s, Israel Paldi (1892-1979).

1982, Apr. 22 Litho. *Perf. 14*

815 A333	7s	multicolored	42	45
816 A333	8s	multicolored	48	52
817 A333	15s	multicolored	1.00	1.00

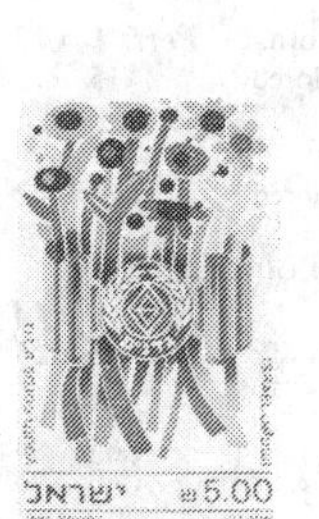
Gedudei Nouar Youth Corps A334

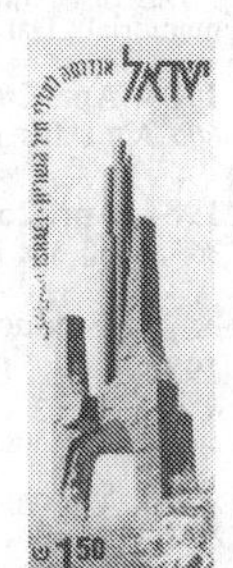
Armour Memorial, En Zetim A335

1982, Apr. 22 Photo. *Perf. 14x13*

818 A334 5s multicolored		42	38

1982, Apr. 22 Litho. *Perf. 14*

819 A335 1.50s multicolored		16	16

Memorial Day.

Joshua Addressing Crowd — A336

Hadassah, 70th Anniv. — A337

Festivals 5743 (Book of Joshua): 5.50s, Crossing River Jordan. 7.50s, Blowing down walls of Jericho. 9.50s, Battle with five kings of Amorites.

1982, Aug. 10 *Perf. 14*

820 A336	1.50s	multicolored	15	15
821 A336	5.50s	multicolored	32	32
822 A336	7.50s	multicolored	45	48
823 A336	9.50s	multicolored	55	55

1982, Aug. 10 Litho.

824 A337 12s multicolored		85	70

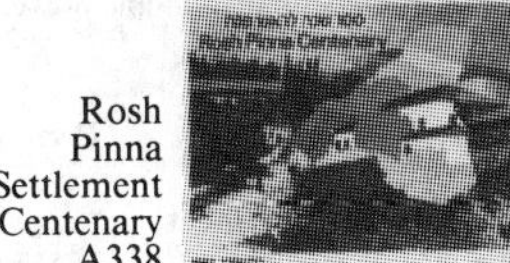
Rosh Pinna Settlement Centenary A338

1982 Photo. *Perf. 13x14*

825 A338	2.50s	shown	20	16
826 A338	3.50s	Rishon Leziyyon	24	20
827 A338	6s	Zikhron Yaaqov	38	32
828 A338	9s	Mazkeret Batya	70	60

Issue dates: 2.50s, 3.50s, Aug. 10; others, Oct. 5.

See Nos. 849-850.

Olive Branch A339

Emblem of Council for a Beautiful Israel A340

1982, Sept. 12

829 A339 multicolored		15	15
a.	Booklet pane of 8 + 8 ('84)	2.75	

Sold at various values.

1982, Oct. 5 Litho. *Perf. 14*

830 A340 17s multicolored		95	95
a.	Souv. sheet of 1, imperf.	1.50	1.50

No. 830a was for Beer Sheva '82 National Stamp Exhibition. Sold for 25s.

Eliahu Bet Tzuri — A341

Anti-Smoking Campaign — A342

Independence Martyrs: b, Hannah Szenes. c, Shlomo Ben Yosef. d, Yosef Lishanski. e, Naaman Belkind. f, Eliezer Kashani. g, Yechiel Dresner. h, Dov Gruner. i, Mordechai Alkachi. j, Eliahu Hakim. k, Meir Nakar. l, Avshalom Haviv. m, Yaakov Weiss. n, Meir Feinstein. o, Moshe Barazani. p, Eli Cohen. q, Samuel Azaar. r, Moshe Marzouk. s, Shalom Salih. t, Yosef Basri.

1982, Dec. *Perf. 14x13½*

831	Sheet of 20	4.75	4.25
a.-t.	A341 3s multicolored	15	16

1983, Feb. 15 Litho. *Perf. 13*

832 A342 7s Candy in ash tray		38	42

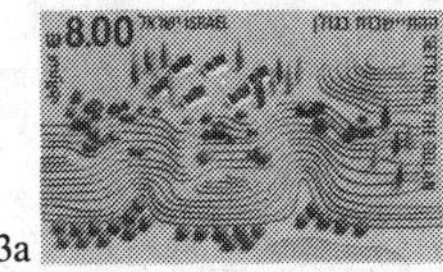
Beekeeping A343

1983, Feb. 15 Photo. *Perf. 13x14*

833 A343 30s multi		1.65	1.50

A343a

1983, Feb. 15 Litho. *Perf. 14*

834 A343a	8s	Golan	32	30
835 A343a	15s	Galil	65	55
836 A343a	20s	Yehuda and Shomeron	90	70

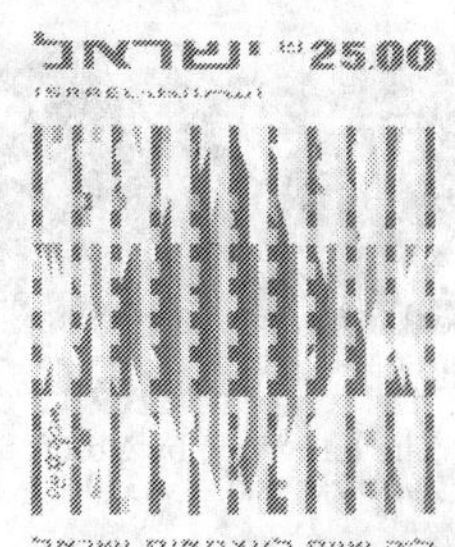
Memorial Day (Apr. 17) — A344

1983, Apr. 12 *Perf. 13*

837 A344 3s Division of Steel Memorial, Besor Region		15	15

Independence Day — A345

1983, Apr. 12 *Perf. 14*

838 A345 25s multicolored		1.25	1.00
a.	Souvenir sheet, imperf.	2.25	1.90

No. 838a sold for 35s.

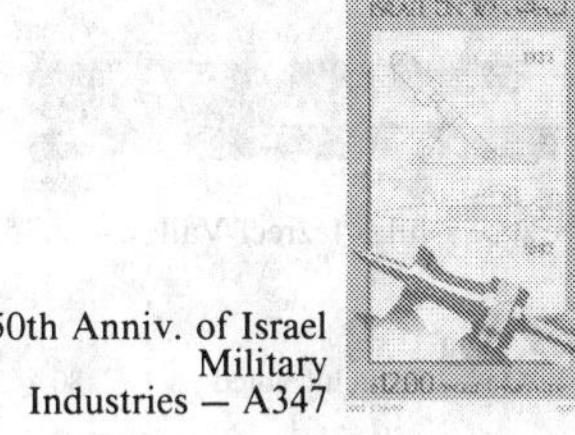
12th Hapoel Games — A346

1983, Apr. 12 *Perf. 14x13*

839 A346 6s multicolored		28	25

50th Anniv. of Israel Military Industries — A347

1983, Apr. 12

840 A347 12s multicolored		55	55

Souvenir Sheet

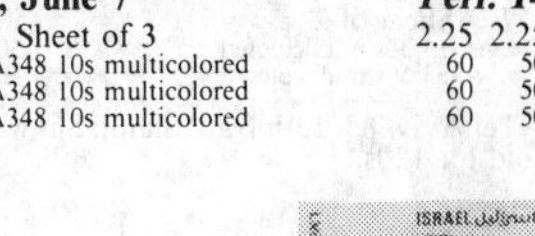
WWII Uprising Leaders — A348

Designs: a, Yosef Glazman (1908-1943), Founder of United Partisans Org. b, Text. c, Mordechai Anilewicz (1919-1943), leader of Warsaw Ghetto revolt. No. 841 sold for 45s.

1983, June 7 *Perf. 14*

841	Sheet of 3	2.25	2.25
a.	A348 10s multicolored	60	50
b.	A348 10s multicolored	60	50
c.	A348 10s multicolored	60	50

Raoul Wallenberg (1912-1945), Swedish Diplomat — A349

1983, June 7 *Perf. 14x13*

842 A349 14s multicolored		80	65

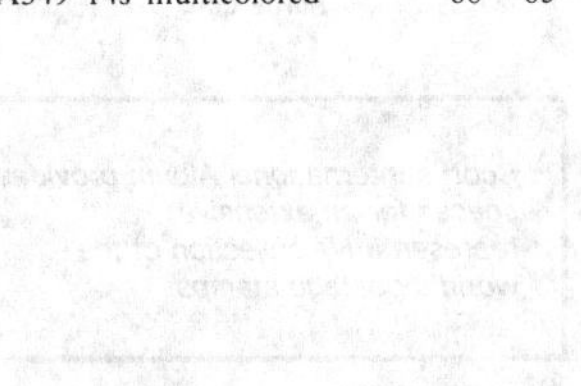

The Last Way, by Yosef Kuzkovski — A350

1983, June 7 *Perf. 14*

843 A350 35s multicolored 1.50 1.50

Ohel Moed Synagogue, Tel Aviv A351

1983, Aug. 23

844 A351 3s shown 15 15
845 A351 12s Yeshurun Society, Jerusalem 38 42
846 A351 16s Ohel Aharon, Haifa 50 50
847 A351 20s Eliyahu Khakascni, Beer Sheva 60 60

View of Afula, Jezreel Valley — A352

1983, Aug. 23

848 A352 15s multicolored 80 55

Settlement Type of 1982

1983, Aug. 23

849 A338 11s Yesud Ha-Maala 55 42
850 A338 13s Nes Ziyyona 60 48

Souvenir Sheet

Tel Aviv Seashore Promenade — A353

1983, Sept. 25 *Perf. 14x13*

851 Sheet of 2 5.50 4.75
a. A353 30s multicolored 1.50 1.75
b. A353 50s multicolored 2.50 2.75

Tel Aviv '83, 13th Natl. Stamp Show, Sept. Sold for 120s.

KFIR-C2 Tactical Fighter — A354

1983, Dec. 13 **Photo.** *Perf. 14*

852 A354 8s shown 15 16
853 A354 18s Reshef class missile boat 35 35
854 A354 30s Merkava-MK1 battle tank 60 60

Scott's International Album provides spaces for an extensive representative collection of the world's postage stamps.

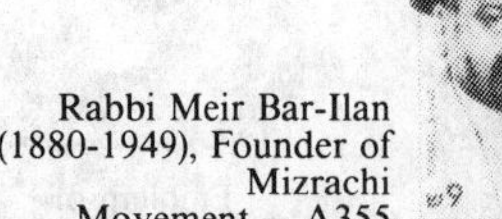

Rabbi Meir Bar-Ilan (1880-1949), Founder of Mizrachi Movement — A355

1983, Dec. 13 **Photo.** *Perf. 14x13*

855 A355 9s multicolored 15 15

Jewish Immigration from Germany, 50th Anniv. A356

1983, Dec. 13 **Photo.** *Perf. 13x14*

856 A356 14s multicolored 60 35

Michael Halperin (1860-1919), Zionist — A357

Uri Zvi Grinberg (1896-1981), Poet — A358

Design: 15s, Yigal Allon (1918-1980), military commander, founder of Israel Labor Party.

1984, Mar. 15 **Photo.** *Perf. 14x13*

857 A357 7s multicolored 15 15

Litho.

Perf. 14

858 A357 15s multicolored 28 25

Perf. 13

859 A358 16s multicolored 30 28

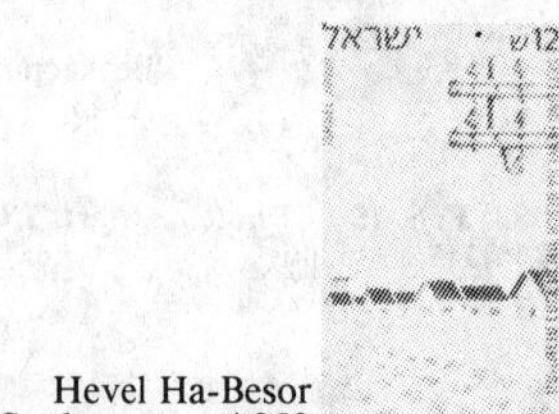

Hevel Ha-Besor Settlement — A359

1984, Mar. 15 *Perf. 14*

860 A359 12s shown 22 15
861 A359 17s Arava 30 24
862 A359 40s Gaza Strip 75 52

Monument of Alexander Zaid, by David Polus A360

Monuments: No. 864, Tel Hay Defenders (seated lion), by Abraham Melnikov (1892-1960). No. 865, Dov Gruner, by Chana Orloff (1888-1968).

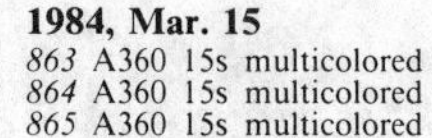

1984, Mar. 15 *Perf. 13x14*

863 A360 15s multicolored 35 26
864 A360 15s multicolored 35 26
865 A360 15s multicolored 35 26

Memorial Day — A361

Natl. Labor Fed., 50th Anniv. — A362

Design: Oliphant House (Druse military memorial), Dalyat Al Karmil.

1984, Apr. 26 **Photo.** *Perf. 14x13*

866 A361 10s multicolored 15 15

1984, Apr. 26

867 A362 35s multicolored 38 42

Produce Type of 1982-83

1984 **Photo.** *Perf. 13x14*

876 A332 30s vio brn & red 48 25
877 A332 50s dp bis & rose magenta 80 40
878 A332 100s gray & green 1.65 80
879 A332 500s dp org & bl blk 1.40 90

Leon Pinsker (1821-91), A363

Gen. Charles O. Wingate (1903-44) A364

1984, July 3 *Perf. 14x13*

880 A363 20s Hovevei Zion founder 22 24
881 A364 20s British soldier 22 24

Hearts, Stars — A365

1984 Summer Olympics — A366

1984, July 3

882 A365 30s multicolored 28 28

70th anniv. of American Jewish Joint Distribution Committee (philanthropic org. created during World War I).

1984, July 3 **Litho.** *Perf. 14*

883 A366 80s Dove 70 70

Souvenir Sheet

884 A366 240s like 80s 3.75 3.25

No. 884 contains one stamp (23x32mm., perf. 14x13). Sold for 350s.

Biblical Women A367

David Wolffsohn (1856-1914), Jewish Colonial Trust Founder A368

1984, Sept. 4 **Photo.** *Perf. 13x14*

885 A367 15s Hannah 15 15
886 A367 70s Ruth 38 38
887 A367 100s Huldah 60 60

1984, Sept. 4 *Perf. 14x14½*

888 A368 150s multicolored 1.25 90

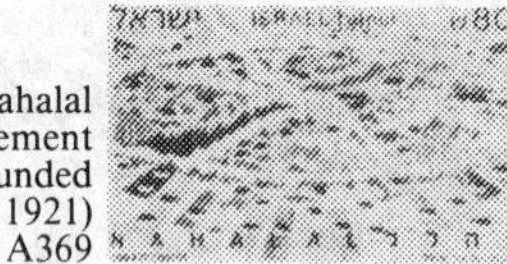

Nahalal Settlement (Founded 1921) A369

1984, Sept. 4 *Perf. 14*

889 A369 80s multicolored 65 48

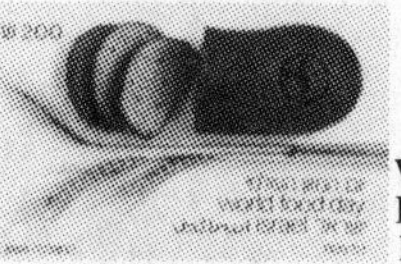

World Food Day, Oct. 16 — A370

1984, Nov. **Litho.**

891 A370 200s Bread, wheat 70 65

Rabbi Isaac Herzog (1888-1959), Statesman and Scholar — A371

1984, Nov. **Photo.** *Perf. 14½*

892 A371 400s multicolored 1.65 1.40

Children's Book Illustrations — A372

Authors and their books: 20s, Apartment to Let, by Leah Goldberg (1911-70). 30s, Why is the Zebra Wearing Pajamas, by Omer Hillel (b. 1926) (30x30mm.). 50s, Across the Sea, by Haim Nahman Bialik (1873-1934).

1984, Nov. **Litho.** *Perf. 14, 13 (30s)*

893 A372 20s multicolored 15 15
894 A372 30s multicolored 15 15
895 A372 50s multicolored 25 22
Set value 42

Birds of Prey — A373

1985, Feb. 5 Litho. *Perf. 14*

896	A373 100s Lappet faced vulture	28	28
897	A373 200s Bonelli's eagle	55	55
898	A373 300s Sooty falcon	80	85
899	A373 500s Griffon vulture	1.40	1.40

Souvenir Sheet

899A	Sheet of 4	4.00	3.75
b.	A373 100s like #896	32	32
c.	A373 200s like #897	65	65
d.	A373 300s like #898	1.00	1.00
e.	A373 500s like #899	1.50	1.50

No. 899A sold for 1650s.

Aviation in the Holy Land A374

1985, Apr. 2 Litho. *Perf. 14*

900	A374 50s Bleriot XI, 1913	20	16
901	A374 150s Scipio-Short S-17 Kent, 1931	50	40
902	A374 250s Tiger Moth DH-82, 1934	80	70
903	A374 300s Scion-Short S-16, 1937	85	1.00

Natl. Assoc. of Nurses — A375

1985, Apr. 2 Litho. *Perf. 14*

904	A375 400s multi	1.00	95

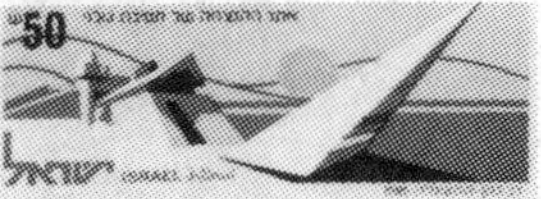

Golani Brigade Memorial and Museum — A376

1985, Apr. 2 Photo. *Perf. 14x13*

905	A376 50s multicolored	24	20

Zivia (1914-1978) and Yitzhak (1915-1981) Zuckerman, Resistasnce Heroes, Warsaw Ghetto A377

1985, Apr. 2 Photo. *Perf. 13x14*

906	A377 200s multi	65	52

Souvenir Sheets

Dome of the Rock A378

16th Cent. Bas-relief, Ottoman Period A379

Adam, Eve and the Serpent (detail) — A380

Designs: No. 907b, The Western Wall. No. 907c, Church of the Holy Sepulchre. No. 908b, Hand, 18th cent. bas-relief, Jewish Quarter. No. 908c, Rosette carving, 12th-13th cent. Crusader capital. No. 909, Frontispiece and detail, Schocken Bible, South Germany, ca. 1290.

1985, May 14 Litho. *Perf. 13x14*

907	Sheet of 3	2.25	2.00
a.-c.	A378 200s any single	70	65

Sold for 900s.

Perf. 14x13

908	Sheet of 3	3.50	3.50
a.-c.	A379 350s any single	1.00	1.00

Sold for 1500s.

Perf. 14

909	A380 800s multi	3.00	3.00

Sold for 1200s.

The Israeli postal administration authorized the International Philatelic Federation (FIP) to overprint a limited number of these souvenir sheets for sale exclusively at ISRAPHIL '85 to raise funds. The FIP overprints have control numbers and are inscribed "Under the Patronage of the Philatelic Federation" in the sheet margin. The sheets remained valid for postage but were not sold by the post office.

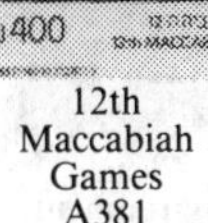

12th Maccabiah Games A381

1985 Festivals A382

1985, July 16 Litho. *Perf. 14*

910	A381 400s Basketball	75	75
911	A381 500s Tennis	90	90
912	A381 600s Windsurfing	1.10	1.10

1985, July 16 Litho. *Perf. 14*

Tabernacle utensils: 100sh, Ark of the Covenant. 150sh, Acacia showbread table. 200sh, Menora. 300sh, Incense altar.

913	A382 100s multi	15	15
914	A382 150s multi	30	30
915	A382 200s multi	35	35
916	A382 300s multi	52	52

Intl. Youth Year — A383

1985, July 16 Litho. *Perf. 14*

917	A383 150s Emblem, badges	48	25

Leon Yehuda Recanati (1890-1945), Financier and Philanthropist A384

1985, Nov. 5 Litho. *Perf. 14*

918	A384 200s multi	80	26

Meir Dizengoff (1861-1936), Founder and Mayor of Tel Aviv — A385

1985, Nov. 5

919	A385 500s multi	1.00	65

Gedera Settlement, Cent. A386

1985, Nov. 5 Photo. *Perf. 13x14*

920	A386 600s multi	1.10	80

The Kibbutz — A387

1985, Nov. 5 Litho. *Perf. 14*

921	A387 900s multi	1.25	1.10

Theodor Herzl — A388

Capital, Second Temple, Jerusalem — A389

Designs: 1s, Corinthian, A.D. 1st cent. 3s, Ionic, 1st cent. B.C.

1986, Jan. 1 Photo. *Perf. 13x14*

922	A388 1a red & ultra	15	15
923	A388 2a green & ultra	15	15
924	A388 3a brown & ultra	15	15
925	A388 5a blue & ultra	15	15
926	A388 10a org & ultra	15	15
927	A388 20a pink & ultra	24	18
928	A388 30a lemon & ultra	35	26
929	A388 50a pur & ultra	55	42
930	A389 1s multi	1.25	95
931	A389 3s multi	3.25	2.75
	Nos. 922-931 (10)	6.39	5.31

1s and 3s designs with 1000a and 1500a values were not issued.

See Nos. 1014-1020.

Red Sea Coral A390

1986, Mar. 14 Litho. *Perf. 14*

932	A390 30a Balanophyllia	52	52
933	A390 40a Goniopora	70	70
934	A390 50a Dendronephthya	90	90

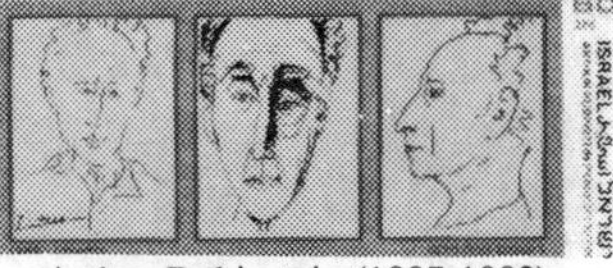

Arthur Rubinstein (1887-1982), Pianist — A391

1986, Mar. 4 Photo. *Perf. 13x14*

935	A391 60a Picasso portraits	90	80

Broadcasting from Jerusalem, 50th Anniv. — A392

1986, Mar. 4 Litho. *Perf. 14*

936	A392 70a Map and microphone, 1936	90	90

Negev Brigade Memorial, Beer Sheva — A393

Al Jazzar Mosque, Akko — A394

1986, May 4 Litho. *Perf. 13*

937	A393 20a multicolored	30	30

Memorial Day.

1986, May 4 Photo. *Perf. 14x13*

938	A394 30a multicolored	38	38

Id Al-Fitr Feast.

Institutes of Higher Learning in the US — A395

Designs: No. 939, 942a, Hebrew Union College, Jewish Institute of Religion, 1875,

Cincinnati. No. 940, 942b, Yeshiva University, 1886, NYC. No. 941, 942c, Jewish Theological Seminary of America, 1886, NYC.

1986, May 4 Litho. *Perf. 14*

939 A395 50a multicolored	60	60
940 A395 50a multicolored	60	60
941 A395 50a multicolored	60	60

Souvenir Sheet

942 Sheet of 3 + label	4.00	4.00
a.-c. A395 75a any single	1.25	1.25

AMERIPEX '86. Size of Nos. 942a-942c: 36x23mm. No. 942 sold for 3s.

Ben Gurion Airport, 50th Anniv. A396

1986, July 22 *Perf. 14x13*

943 A396 90a Terminal from aircraft	1.10	1.10

"No to Racism" in Graffiti — A397

1986, July 22 *Perf. 14*

944 A397 60a multicolored	80	70

Druze Feast of Prophet Nabi Sabalan A398

1986, July 22 Photo. *Perf. 14*

945 A398 40a Tomb, Hurfeish	52	52

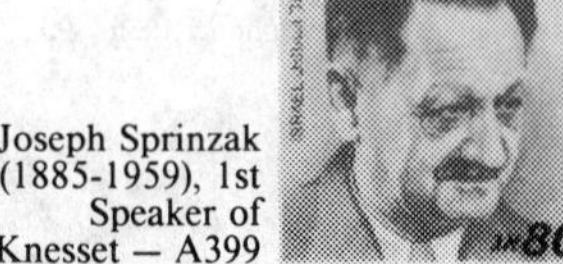

Joseph Sprinzak (1885-1959), 1st Speaker of Knesset — A399

1986, July 22 Litho. *Perf. 13*

946 A399 80a multicolored	1.05	1.05

Worms Illuminated Mahzor, 13th Cent. — A400

1986, Sept. 23 Litho. *Perf. 13x14*

947 A400 20a Gates of Heaven	24	24
948 A400 40a Sheqalim, prayer	48	48
949 A400 90a Rose flower prayer introduction	1.10	1.10

David Ben-Gurion (1886-1973) A401

1986, Oct. 19 Litho. *Perf. 14x13*

950 A401 1s multicolored	1.30	1.30

Souvenir Sheet

Map of the Holyland, by Gerard de Jode, 1578 — A402

1986, Oct. 19 *Perf. 14½*

951 A402 2s multi	3.25	3.25

NATANYA '86 Stamp Exhibition; Organized philately in Natanya, 50th anniv. Sold for 3s.

Israel Meteorological Service, 50th Anniv. A403

Basilica of the Annunciation, Nazareth A404

1986, Dec. 18 Litho. *Perf. 13*

952 A403 50a multicolored	70	70

1986, Dec. 18 Litho. *Perf. 14*

953 A404 70a multicolored	90	90

Israel Philharmonic Orchestra, 50th Anniv. — A405

1986, Dec. 18

954 A405 1.50s Bronislaw Huberman, violinist	1.90	1.65
955 A405 1.50s Arturo Toscanini, conductor	1.90	1.65
a. Pair, Nos. 954-955	4.00	3.50

Owls A406

1987, Feb. 17 Litho. *Perf. 14x13*

956 A406 30a Bubo bubo	42	42
957 A406 40a Otus brucei	55	55
958 A406 50a Tyto alba	70	70
959 A406 80a Strix butleri	1.15	1.15

Souvenir Sheet

960 Sheet of 4	4.25	4.25
a. A406 30a like #956	65	65
b. A406 40a like #957	85	85
c. A406 50a like #958	1.05	1.05
d. A406 80a like #959	1.70	1.70

Sold for 3s.

Ammunition Hill Memorial, Jerusalem — A407

1987, Apr. 16 Litho. *Perf. 14*

961 A407 30a multi	40	40

Memorial Day.

13th Hapoel Games A408

1987, Apr. 16

962 A408 90a multi	1.25	1.25

Souvenir Sheet

HAIFA '87 Stamp Exhibition — A409

1987, Apr. 16 *Perf. 14x13*

963 A409 2.70s No. C8	5.25	5.25

Sold for 4s.

Amateur Radio Operators — A410

1987, June 14 Litho. *Perf. 14*

964 A410 2.50s multi	3.00	3.00

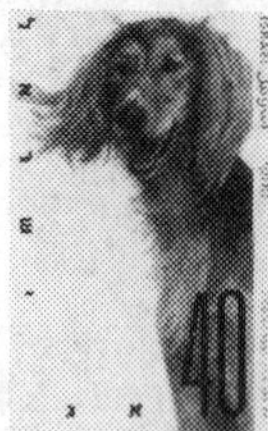

World Dog Show, June 23-27 A411

Clean Environment A412

1987, June 14

965 A411 40a Saluki	48	48
966 A411 50a Sloughi	60	60
967 A411 2s Canaan	2.50	2.50

1987, June 14 *Perf. 13*

968 A412 40a multicolored	48	48

Rabbi Moshe Avigdor Amiel (1883-1945), Founder of Yeshivas — A413

1987, Sept. 10 Litho. *Perf. 14*

969 A413 1.40s multi	1.40	1.40

Synagogue Models, Nahum Goldmann Museum, Tel Aviv A414

Kupat Holim Health Insurance Institute, 75th Anniv. A415

1987, Sept. 10 *Perf. 13x14*

970 A414 30a Altneuschul, Prague, 13th cent.	40	40
971 A414 50a Aleppo, Syria, 9th cent.	65	65
972 A414 60a Florence, Italy, 19th cent.	78	78

See Nos. 996-998.

1987, Sept. 10 *Perf. 14*

973 A415 1.50s multi	1.50	1.50

Pinhas Rosen (1887-1978), First Minister of Justice — A416

1987, Nov. 24 Litho. *Perf. 13*

974 A416 80a multicolored	90	90

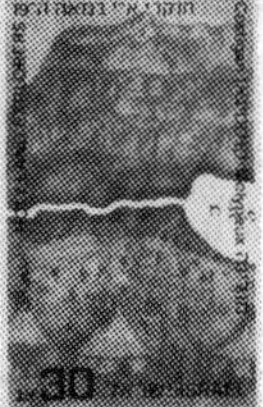

Exploration of the Holy Land, 19th Cent. — A417

Explorations by: 30a, Thomas Howard Molyneux (1847) and Christopher Costigan (1835). 50a, William Francis Lynch (1848). 60a, John MacGregor (1868-1869).

1987, Nov. 24 *Perf. 14*

975 A417 30a multi	40	40
976 A417 50a multi	65	65
977 A417 60a multi	78	52

Souvenir Sheet

978 Sheet of 3	3.25	3.25
a. A417 40a like #975	75	75
b. A417 50a like #976	95	95
c. A417 80a like #977	1.55	1.55

No. 978 sold for 2.50s.

Industrialization of Israel, Cent. — A418

1988, Jan. 26

979 A418 10a Computer technology 15 15
980 A418 80a Genetic engineering 95 95
981 A418 1.40s Medical engineering 1.65 1.65

Water Conservation — A419

1988, Jan. 26

982 A419 40a multicolored 52 52

Australia Bicentennial A420

1988, Jan. 26 ***Perf. 14***

983 A420 1s multi 1.30 1.30

Sunflower A421

Anne Frank (1929-1945), Amsterdam House Where She Hid A422

1988, Mar. 9 Photo. ***Perf. 13x14***

984 A421 (30a) dk yel grn & yel 25 25

1988, Apr. 19 **Litho.**

985 A422 60a multicolored 55 55

Modern Jerusalem — A423

1988, Apr. 19

986 A423 1s shown 1.10 1.10

Souvenir Sheet

987 A423 2s like 1s 3.25 3.25

Independence 40 Stamp Exhibition, Jerusalem. No. 987 sold for 3s.

Memorial Day — A424

1988, Apr. 19 ***Perf. 14x13***

988 A424 40a multicolored 35 35
a. Souvenir sheet of one 75 75

Natl. independence, 40th anniv. No. 988a contains one stamp like No. 988 but without copyright inscription LR. Sold for 60a.

Souvenir Sheet

Israel's 40th Anniv. Exhibition, Tel Aviv — A425

Stamps on stamps: a, No. 245. b, No. 297. c, No. 120. d, No. 96. e, Like No. 794. f, No. 252. g, No. 333. h, No. 478.

1988, June 9 Litho. ***Perf. 14***

989 Sheet of 8 + label 3.50 3.50
a.-h. A425 20a any single 38 38

Sold for 2.40s. Center label pictures Israel 40 emblem.

B'nai B'rith in Jerusalem, Cent. — A426

1988, June 27 ***Perf. 14***

990 A426 70a multicolored 88 88

Nature Reserves in the Negev A427

1988, June 27

991 A427 40a Ein Zin 42 42
992 A427 60a She'Zaf 60 60
993 A427 70a Ramon 75 75

Agents Executed During World War II — A428

Portraits: 40a, Havivah Reik (1914-1944). 1.65s, Enzo Hayyim Sereni (1905-1944).

1988, Sept. 1 **Litho.**

994 A428 40a multicolored 48 48
995 A428 1.65s multicolored 1.90 1.90

Synagogue Models Type of 1987

Models in the Nahum Goldmann Museum, Tel Aviv: 35a, Kai-Feng Fu Synagogue, 12th cent., China. 60a, Zabludow Synagogue, 17th cent., Poland. 70a, Touro Synagogue, 1763, Newport, Rhode Island, designed by Peter Harrison.

1988, Sept. 1 ***Perf. 13x14***

996 A414 35a multicolored 40 40
997 A414 60a multicolored 70 70
998 A414 70a multicolored 82 82

Kristallnacht, Nazi Pogrom in Germany, 50th Anniv. — A429

1988, Nov. 9 ***Perf. 14***

999 A429 80a multicolored 85 85

Moshe Dayan (1915-1981), Foreign Minister and Minister of Defense — A430

1988, Nov. 9 ***Perf. 13***

1000 A430 40a multicolored 48 48

Jewish Legion, 70th Anniv. A431

1988, Nov. 9 ***Perf. 14***

1001 A431 2s yel brn, sepia & lem 2.35 2.35

Agricultural Achievements — A433

Designs: 50a, Avocado (fruit-growing). 60a, Lilium longiflorum (horticulture). 90a, Irrigation.

1988, Dec. 22 ***Perf. 14***

1004 A433 50a multicolored 58 58
1005 A433 60a multicolored 70 70
1006 A433 90a multicolored 1.05 1.05

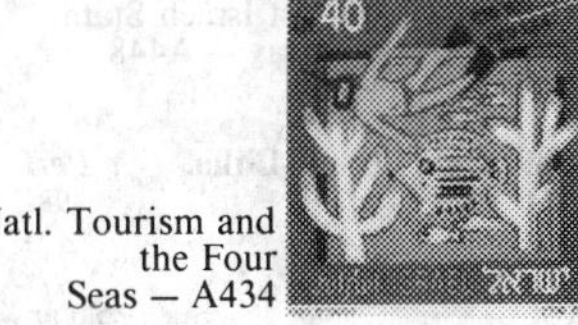

Natl. Tourism and the Four Seas — A434

1989, Mar. 12 Litho. ***Perf. 13***

1007 A434 40a Red Sea 45 30
1008 A434 60a Dead Sea 65 45
1009 A434 70a Mediterranean Sea 75 50
1010 A434 1.70s Sea of Galilee 1.85 1.25

Rabbi Judah Leib Maimon (1875-1962), Religious Scholar — A435

1989, Mar. 12 ***Perf. 14***

1011 A435 1.70s multi 1.85 1.25

Rashi, Rabbi Solomon Ben Isaac (b. 1039), Talmudic Commentator A436

1989, Mar. 12

1012 A436 4s buff & black 4.35 2.90

Memorial Day — A437

Design: Fallen Airmen's Memorial at Har Tayassim.

1989, Apr. 30 Litho. ***Perf. 14***

1013 A437 50a multi 60 45

Archaeology Type of 1986

Gates of Huldah, Temple Compound, Mt. Moriah: 40a, Rosettes and rhomboids, frieze and columns, facade of the eastern gate, 1st cent. B.C. 60a, Corinthian capital, 6th cent.

70a, Bas-relief from the Palace of Umayade Caliphs, 8th cent. 80a, Corinthian capital from the Church of Ascension on the Mount of Olives, 12-13th cent. 90a, Star of David, limestone relief, northern wall, near the new gate, Suleiman's Wall. 2s, Mamluk relief, 14th century. 10s, Carved frieze from a sepulcher entrance, end of the Second Temple Period.

1988-90 Litho. ***Perf. 14***

1014 A389 40a multi 48 48
1015 A389 60a multi 70 70
1016 A389 70a multi 78 58
1017 A389 80a multi 90 68
1018 A389 90a multi 88 65
1019 A389 2s multi 2.00 1.30
1020 A389 10s multi 12.00 8.00
Nos. 1014-1020 (7) 17.74 12.39

Issue dates: 40a, 60a, Dec. 22, 1988. 70a, 80a, June 11, 1989. 10s, Apr. 30, 1989. 90a, Oct. 17, 1989. 2s, June 12, 1990.

UNICEF — A438

1989, Apr. 30 ***Perf. 14***

1022 A438 90a multi 1.10 82

Moshe Smoira (1888-1961), 1st Pres. of Israeli Supreme Court — A439

1989, June 11 Litho. ***Perf. 13***

1023 A439 90a deep blue 1.05 78

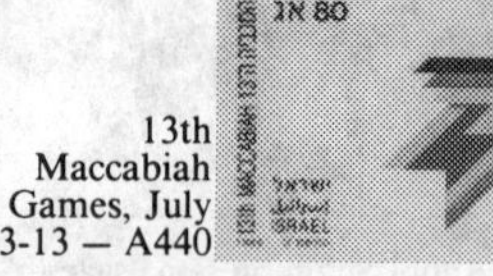
13th Maccabiah Games, July 3-13 — A440

1989, June 11 *Perf. 13x14*
1024 A440 80a multi 90 68

Ducks A441

Designs: a, Garganey. b, Mallard. c, Teal. d, Shelduck.

1989, July 18 **Litho.** *Perf. 14*
1025 Strip of 4 3.40 2.40
a.-d. A441 80a any single 80 60

Souvenir Sheet

1989, Nov. 17
1025E Sheet of 4 4.75 4.75
f. A441 80a like No. 1025d 1.15 1.15
g. A441 80a like No. 1025b 1.15 1.15
h. A441 80a like No. 1025a 1.15 1.15
i. A441 80a like No. 1025c 1.15 1.15

World Stamp Expo '89. No. 1025E contains four 29x33mm stamps. Sold for 5s.

Graphic Design Industry — A442

1989, July 18
1026 A442 1s multi 1.00 75

Souvenir Sheet

French Revolution, Bicent. — A443

1989, July 18
1027 A443 3.50s multi 5.00 5.00

Sold for 5s.

Hebrew Language Council, Cent. — A444

Rabbi Yehuda Hai Alkalai (1798-1878), Zionist — A445

1989, Sept. 3 **Litho.** *Perf. 13x14*
1028 A444 1s multi 95 72

1989, Sept. 3 *Perf. 14*
1029 A445 2.50s multi 2.40 1.80

Mizrah Festival A446

Paper cutouts: 50a, Menorah and lions, by Gadoliahu Neminsky, Holbenisk, Ukraine, 1921. 70a, Menorah and hands, Morocco, 19th-20th cent. 80a, "Misrah," hunting scene and deer, Germany, 1818.

1989, Sept. 3 *Perf. 14x13*
1030 A446 50a multi 48 36
1031 A446 70a multi 68 50
1032 A446 80a multi 78 58

Tevel '89 Youth Stamp Exhibition, Oct. 15-21 A447

1989, Oct. 12 **Photo.** *Perf. 13x14*
1033 A447 50a multi 48 36

1st Israeli Stamp Day — A448

1989, Oct. 17 **Litho.** *Perf. 14*
1034 A448 1s multi 98 75

Special Occasions A449

1989, Nov. 17 **Photo.** *Perf. 13½x14*
1035 A449 (50a) Good luck 48 35
1036 A449 (50a) With love 48 35
a. Bklt. pane of 10 5.15
1037 A449 (50a) See you again 48 35

No. 1036a contains 5 tete-beche pairs. Issued Aug. 7, 1990.
See Nos. 1059-1061, 1073-1075.

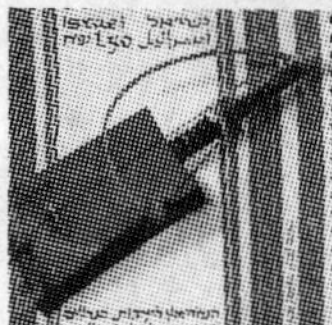
Tapestry and Rebab, a Stringed Instrument, from the Museum of Bedouin Culture — A450

1990, Feb. 13 **Litho.** *Perf. 13*
1038 A450 1.50s multicolored 1.45 1.05

Circassian Folk Dancers — A451

1990, Feb. 13 **Photo.** *Perf. 14x13*
1039 A451 1.50s multicolored 1.45 1.05

The Circassians in Israel.

Rehovot City, Cent. A452

1990, Feb. 13 *Perf. 14*
1040 A452 2s multicolored 1.90 1.40

Souvenir Sheet

Isaiah's Vision of Eternal Peace, by Mordecai Ardon — A453

Series of 3 stained-glass windows, The Hall of Eternal Jewishness and Humanism, Hebrew University Library, Jerusalem: a, "Roads to Jerusalem" (inscription at L). b, Isaiah's prophecy of broken guns beaten into ploughshares (inscription at R).

1990, Apr. 17 **Litho.** *Perf. 14*
1041 Sheet of 2 4.30 4.30
a.-b. A453 1.50s any single 2.15 2.15

Stamp World London '90. Sold for 4.50s.
Also exists imperf.

Architecture — A454

Design: 75a, School, Deganya Kibbutz, 1930. 1.10s, Dining hall, Kibbutz Tel Yosef by Leopold Krakauer, 1933. 1.20s, Engel House by Ze'ev Rechter, 1933. 1.40s, Home of Dr. Chaim Weizmann, Rehovot by Erich Mendelsohn, 1936.

1990-91 **Photo.** *Perf. 14x13½*
1044 A454 75a black, pale grn & buff 72 55
1046 A454 1.10s blk, yel & grn 1.05 1.05
1047 A454 1.20s blk, bl & yel 1.15 1.15
1049 A454 1.40s blk, lt lil & buff 1.35 1.35

Issue dates: 75a, Apr. 17. 1.10s, 1.20s, Dec. 12, 1.40s, Apr. 9, 1991.
This is an expanding set. Numbers will change if necessary.

Nature Reserves A455

1990, Apr. 17 **Litho.** *Perf. 14*
1052 A455 60a Gamla, Yehudiyya 58 45
1053 A455 80a Huleh 78 58
1054 A455 90a Mt. Meron 88 65

Memorial Day A456

1990, Apr. 17 **Photo.** *Perf. 13x14*
1055 A456 60a Artillery Corps Memorial 58 45

Intl. Folklore Festival, Haifa
A457 A458

1990, June 12 **Litho.** *Perf. 14*
1056 A457 1.90s multicolored 1.80 1.80
1057 A458 1.90s multicolored 1.80 1.80
a. Pair, #1056-1057 3.60 3.60

Hagana, 70th Anniv. — A459

1990, June 12
1058 A459 1.50s multicolored 1.50 1.50

Special Occasions Type of 1989

1990, June 12 *Perf. 13½x14*
1059 A449 55a Good luck 52 35
1060 A449 80a See you again 75 50
1061 A449 1s With love 95 62

Austro-Hungarian Spice Box, 19th Cent. — A460

Spice Boxes: 80a, Italian, 19th cent. 1s, German, 18th cent.

1990, Sept. 4 Litho. *Perf. 13x14*

1062 A460 55a sil, gray & blk 52 52
1063 A460 80a sil, gray & blk 75 75
1064 A460 1s multicolored 95 95
a. Bklt. pane of 6 (3 #1062, 2 #1063, #1064) 4.05 4.05

Aliya Absorption A461

1990, Sept. 4 *Perf. 13*

1065 A461 1.10s multicolored 1.10 1.10

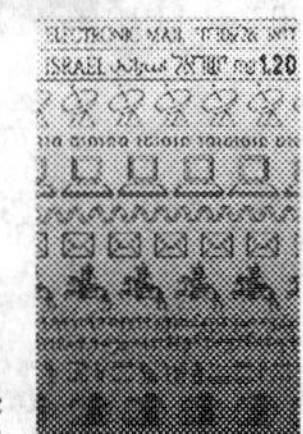

Electronic Mail — A462

1990, Sept. 4 *Perf. 14x13*

1066 A462 1.20s blk & grn 1.25 1.25

Souvenir Sheet

Beersheba '90 Stamp Exhibition — A463

1990, Sept. 4 *Perf. 13x14*

1067 A463 3s multicolored 4.00 4.00

Sold for 4s.

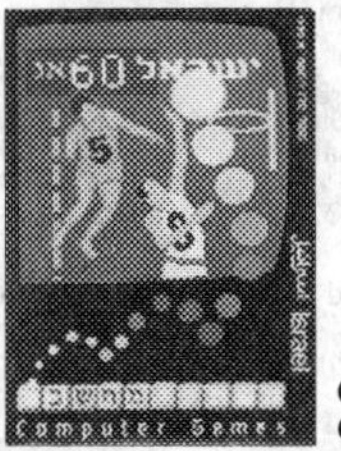

Computer Games — A464

1990, Dec. 12 Litho. *Perf. 13x14*

1068 A464 60a Basketball 60 60
1069 A464 60a Chess 60 60
1070 A464 60a Auto racing 60 60

Ze'ev Jabotinsky (1880-1940), Zionist Leader — A465

1990, Dec. 12 Litho. *Perf. 13x14*

1071 A465 1.90s multicolored 1.80 1.80

Philately Day — A466

1990, Dec. 12 *Perf. 14*

1072 A466 1.20s P.O., Yafo, #5 1.15 1.15

Special Occasions Type of 1989

1991, Feb. 19 Photo. *Perf. 13½x14*

1073 A449 (60a) Happy birthday 58 38
1074 A449 (60a) Keep in touch 58 38
1075 A449 (60a) Greetings 58 38

Famous Women A467

Designs: No. 1076, Sarah Aaronsohn (1890-1917), World War I heroine. No. 1077, Rahel Bluwstein (1890-1931), poet. No. 1078, Lea Goldberg (1911-1970), poet.

1991, Feb. 19 *Perf. 14*

1076 A467 1.30s multicolored 1.25 1.25
1077 A467 1.30s multicolored 1.25 1.25
1078 A467 1.30s multicolored 1.25 1.25

See Nos. 1096-1097.

Hadera, Cent. — A468

1991, Feb. 19 *Perf. 13*

1079 A468 2.50s multicolored 2.45 2.45

Intelligence Services Memorial, G'lilot — A469

1991, Apr. 9 Litho. *Perf. 14*

1080 A469 65a multicolored 60 60

14th Hapoel Games A470

1991, Apr. 9

1081 A470 60a multicolored 58 38
1082 A470 90a multicolored 85 55
1083 A470 1.10s multicolored 1.05 70

Electrification A471

Designs: 70a, First power station, Tel Aviv, 1923. 90a, Yarden Power Station, Naharayim, 1932. 1.20s, Rutenberg Power Station, Ashqelon, 1991.

1991, June 11 Litho. *Perf. 13*

1084 A471 70a multicolored 70 45
1085 A471 90a multicolored 85 65
1086 A471 1.20s multicolored 1.15 85

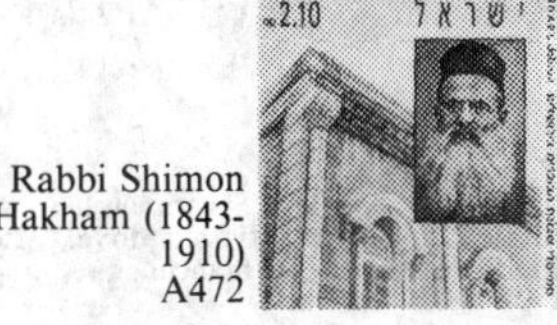

Rabbi Shimon Hakham (1843-1910) A472

1991, June 11

1087 A472 2.10s multicolored 2.00 1.50

Souvenir Sheet

Postal and Philatelic Museum, Tel Aviv — A473

Design: Israel No. 5, Palestine No. 70, and Turkey No. 133.

1991, June 11 *Perf. 14x13*

1088 A473 3.40s multicolored 4.90 4.90

No. 1088 sold for 5s. Exists imperf.

Jewish Festivals — A474

Designs: 65a, Man blowing ram's horn, Rosh Hashanah. 1s, Father blessing children, Yom Kippur. 1.20s, Family seated at harvest table, Sukkot.

1991, Aug. 27 Litho. *Perf. 14*

1089 A474 65a multicolored 55 55
1090 A474 1s multicolored 85 85
1091 A474 1.20s multicolored 1.00 1.00

Jewish Chronicle, 150th Anniv. — A475

1991, Aug. 27

1092 A475 1.50s multicolored 2.65 2.65

Baron Maurice De Hirsch (1831-1896), Founder of Jewish Colonization Assoc. — A476

1991, Aug. 27 ***Perf. 14***

1093 A476 1.60s multicolored 2.70 2.70

Souvenir Sheet

Haifa, by Gustav Bauernfeind — A477

1991, Aug. 27 ***Perf. 14x13***

1094 A477 3s multicolored 3.50 3.50

Haifa '91, Israeli-Polish Philatelic Exhibition. Sold for 4s.

Philately Day — A478

1991, Dec. 2 **Litho.** ***Perf. 13***

1095 A478 70a #2 on piece 60 60

Famous Women Type of 1991

Designs: 1s, Rahel Yanait Ben-Zvi (1886-1979), politician. 1.10s, Dona Gracia (Nasi, 1510?-1569), philanthropist.

1991, Dec. 2 **Litho.** ***Perf. 14***

1096 A467 1s multicolored 80 80
1097 A467 1.10s multicolored 85 85

1992 Summer Olympics, Barcelona — A479

1991, Dec. 2

1098 A479 1.10s multicolored 85 85

Lehi — A480

Etzel — A481

1991, Dec. 2 ***Perf. 14***

1099 A480 1.50s multicolored 1.30 1.30

1991, Dec. 2

1100 A481 1.50s blk & red 1.30 1.30

Wolfgang Amadeus Mozart, Death Bicent. — A482

1991, Dec. 2 ***Perf. 13***

1101 A482 2s multicolored 1.70 1.70

AIR POST STAMPS

Doves Pecking at Grapes AP1

Marisa Eagle AP2

Designs: 30p, Beth Shearim eagle. 40p, Mosaic bird. 50p, Stylized dove. 250p, Mosaic dove and olive branch.

Perf. 11½

1950, June 25 **Unwmk.** **Litho.**

C1	AP1	5p brt grnsh bl	70	38
C2	AP1	30p gray	22	22
C3	AP1	40p dark green	60	38
C4	AP1	50p henna brown	95	38
C5	AP2	100p rose car	10.00	8.50
C6	AP2	250p dk gray bl	2.75	1.40
		Nos. C1-C6 (6)	15.22	11.26
		With tabs	250.00	

Haifa Bay and City Seal — AP3

Design: 120p, Haifa, Mt. Carmel and city seal.

1952, Apr. 13 ***Perf. 14***

Seal in Gray

C7	AP3	100p ultramarine	25	16
C8	AP3	120p purple	32	20
		With tabs	18.00	

Stamps were available only on purchase of a ticket to the National Stamp Exhibition, Haifa. Price, including ticket, 340p.

Olive Tree — AP4

Tanur Cascade AP5

Coast at Tel Aviv-Jaffa AP6

Designs: 70p, En Gev, Sea of Galilee. 100p, Road to Jerusalem. 150p, Lion Rock. 350p, Bay of Elat, Red Sea. 750p, Lake Hule. 3000p, Tomb of Rabbi Meir Baal Haness, Tiberias.

1953-56 **Litho.**

C9	AP4	10p olive grn	15	15
C10	AP4	70p violet	15	15
C11	AP4	100p green	15	15
C12	AP4	150p orange brn	15	15
C13	AP4	350p car rose	15	15
C14	AP5	500p dull & dk bl	15	15
C15	AP6	750p brown	15	15
C16	AP6	1000p deep bl grn	1.90	75
		With tab	95.00	
C17	AP6	3000p claret	18	15
		Set value	2.60	1.25
		Nos. C9-C15, C17 with tabs	5.50	

Issue dates: 1000p, Mar. 16, 1953; 10p, 100p, 500p, Mar. 2, 1954; 70p, 150p, 350p, Apr. 6, 1954; 750p, Aug. 21, 1956; 3000p, Nov. 13, 1956.

Old Town, Zefat — AP7

Houbara Bustard — AP9

Port of Elat ('Aqaba) — AP8

Designs: 20a, Ashkelon, Afridar Center. 25a, Acre, tower and boats. 30a, Haifa, view from Mt. Carmel. 35a, Capernaum, ancient synagogue (horiz.). 40a, Jethro's tomb (horiz.). 50a, Jerusalem (horiz.). 65a, Tiberias, tower and lake (horiz.). £1, Jaffa (horiz.).

1960-61 **Photo.** ***Perf. 13x14, 14x13***

C18	AP7	15a light lil & blk	15	15
C19	AP7	20a brt yel grn & blk	15	15
C20	AP7	25a orange & blk ('61)	15	15
C21	AP7	30a grnsh bl & blk ('61)	22	15
C22	AP7	35a yel grn & blk ('61)	24	15
C23	AP7	40a lt vio & blk ('61)	25	15
C24	AP7	50a olive & blk ('61)	20	15
C25	AP7	65a lt ultra & black	24	15
C26	AP7	£1 pink & blk ('61)	50	30
		Set value	1.80	1.00
		With tabs	14.00	

Issue dates: Nos. C18, C19, C25, Feb. 24, 1960. Nos. C20-C22, June 14, 1961. Nos. C23, C24, C26, Oct. 26, 1961.

Wmk. 302

1962, Feb. 21 **Litho.** ***Perf. 14***

C27	AP8	£3 multicolored	1.65	1.10
		With tab	11.00	

Perf. 13x14, 14x13

1963 **Unwmk.** **Photo.**

Birds: 5a, Sinai rose finch (horiz.). 20a, White-breasted kingfisher (horiz.). 28a, Mourning wheatear (horiz.). 30a, Blue-cheeked bee eater. 40a, Graceful prinia. 45a, Palestine sunbird. 70a, Scops owl. £1, Purple heron. £3, White-tailed Sea eagle.

C28	AP9	5a dp vio & multi	15	15
C29	AP9	20a red & multi	15	15
C30	AP9	28a emerald & multi	15	15
C31	AP9	30a orange & multi	15	15
C32	AP9	40a multicolored	15	15
C33	AP9	45a yellow & multi	18	18
C34	AP9	55a multicolored	22	22
C35	AP9	70a black & multi	24	24
C36	AP9	£1 multicolored	32	32
C37	AP9	£3 ultra & multi	1.10	1.10
		Nos. C28-C37 (10)	2.81	2.81
		With tabs	6.00	

Issue dates: #C28-C30, Apr. 15. #C31-C33, June 19. #C34-C36, Feb. 13. #C37, Oct. 23.

Diamond and Boeing 707 — AP10

Designs (Boeing 707 and): 10a, Textiles. 30a, Symbolic stamps. 40a, Vase and jewelry. 50a, Chick and egg. 55a, Melon, avocado and strawberries. 60a, Gladioli. 80a, Electronic equipment and chart. £1, Heavy oxygen isotopes (chemical apparatus). £1.50, Women's fashions.

1968 **Photo.** ***Perf. 13x14***

C38	AP10	10a ultra & multi	15	15
C39	AP10	30a gray & multi	15	15
C40	AP10	40a multicolored	15	15
C41	AP10	50a multicolored	15	15
C42	AP10	55a multicolored	16	15
C43	AP10	60a sl grn, lt grn & red	18	15
C44	AP10	80a yel, brn & lt bl	22	15
C45	AP10	£1 dark bl & org	28	15
C46	AP10	£1.50 multicolored	35	20
C47	AP10	£3 pur & lt bl	70	38
		Nos. C38-C47 (10)	2.49	
		Set value		1.20
		With tabs	4.75	

Israeli exports. Sheets of 15 (5x3).

Issue dates: Nos. C38-C41, Mar. 11; No. C47, Feb. 7; Nos. C42-C43, C45, Nov. 6; Nos. C44, C46, Dec. 23.

POSTAGE DUE STAMPS

Types of Regular Issue Overprinted in Black **דמי דאר**

Designs: Various coins, as on postage denominations.

Unwmk.

1948, May 28 **Typo.** ***Perf. 11***

Yellow Paper

J1	A1	3m orange	2.00	1.50
J2	A1	5m yellow grn	2.75	2.00
J3	A1	10m red violet	8.25	4.75
J4	A1	20m ultramarine	21.00	15.00
J5	A1	50m orange brn	55.00	42.50
		Nos. J1-J5 (5)	89.00	65.75
		With tabs (blank)	*1,500.*	

The 3m, 20m and 50m are known with overprint omitted.

Nos. J1-J5 exist imperf.

D1

Running Stag — D2

1949, Dec. 18 **Litho.** ***Perf. 11½***

J6	D1	2p orange	15	15
J7	D1	5p purple	15	15
J8	D1	10p yellow grn	15	15
J9	D1	20p vermilion	22	15
J10	D1	30p vio blue	40	20
J11	D1	50p orange brn	70	28
		Set value	1.45	80
		With tabs (blank)	125.00	

1952, Nov. 30 Unwmk. *Perf. 14*

No.	Type	Description	Unused	Used
J12	D2	5p orange brown	15	15
J13	D2	10p Prussian blue	15	15
J14	D2	20p magenta	15	15
J15	D2	30p gray black	15	15
J16	D2	40p green	15	15
J17	D2	50p brown	15	15
J18	D2	60p purple	15	15
J19	D2	100p red	15	15
J20	D2	250p blue	15	15
		Set value	50	45
		With tabs (blank)	5.50	

OFFICIAL STAMPS

Redrawn Type of 1950 Overprinted in Black בול שרות

1951, Feb. 1 Unwmk. *Perf. 14*

No.	Type	Description	Unused	Used
O1	A6	5p bright red vio	15	15
O2	A6	15p vermilion	15	15
O3	A6	30p ultramarine	15	15
O4	A6	40p orange brown	15	15
		Set value	30	20
		With tabs	16.00	

ITALIAN COLONIES

General Issues for all Colonies

100 Centesimi = 1 Lira

Watermark

Wmk. 140

Type of Italy, Dante Alighieri Society Issue, in New Colors and Overprinted in Red or Black

COLONIE ITALIANE

1932, July 11 Wmk. 140 *Perf. 14*

No.	Type	Description	Unused	Used
1	A126	10c gray blk	25	40
2	A126	15c olive brn	25	40
3	A126	20c slate grn	25	30
4	A126	25c dk grn	25	30
5	A126	30c red brn (Bk)	25	50
6	A126	50c bl blk	25	25
7	A126	75c car rose (Bk)	50	85
8	A126	1.25 l dk bl	50	85
9	A126	1.75 l violet	60	1.10
10	A126	2.75 l org (Bk)	60	1.10
11	A126	5 l + 2 l ol grn	60	1.10
12	A126	10 l + 2.50 l dp bl	60	1.10
		Nos. 1-12,C1-C6 (18)	9.80	16.75

Types of Italy, Garibaldi Issue, in New Colors and Inscribed: "POSTE COLONIALI ITALIANE"

1932, July 1 Photo.

No.	Type	Description	Unused	Used
13	A138	10c green	1.25	2.50
14	A138	20c car rose	1.25	2.50
15	A138	25c green	1.25	2.50
16	A138	30c green	1.25	2.50
17	A138	50c car rose	1.25	2.50
18	A141	75c car rose	1.25	2.50
19	A141	1.25 l deep blue	1.25	2.50
20	A141	1.75 l + 25c dp bl	3.00	7.50
21	A144	2.55 l + 50c ol brn	3.00	7.50
22	A145	5 l + 1 l dp bl	3.00	7.50
		Nos. 13-22,C8-C12 (15)	29.75	67.50

See Nos. CE1-CE2.

Plowing with Oxen — A1

Pack Camel — A2

Lioness — A3

1933, Mar. 27 Wmk. 140

No.	Type	Description	Unused	Used
23	A1	10c ol brn	1.90	3.00
24	A2	20c dl vio	1.90	3.00
25	A3	25c green	1.90	2.00
26	A1	50c purple	1.90	2.00
27	A2	75c carmine	1.90	3.00
28	A3	1.25 l blue	1.90	3.00
29	A1	2.75 l red orange	3.25	6.00
30	A2	5 l + 2 l gray grn	7.00	14.00
31	A3	10 l + 2.50 l org brn	7.00	14.00
		Nos. 23-31,C13-C19 (16)	57.45	101.50

Annexation of Eritrea by Italy, 50th anniv.

Agricultural Implements A4

Arab and Camel — A5

"Eager with New Life" — A7

Steam Roller A6

1933 Photo. *Perf. 14*

No.	Type	Description	Unused	Used
32	A4	5c orange	2.00	2.50
33	A5	25c green	2.00	2.50
34	A6	50c purple	2.00	2.50
35	A4	75c carmine	2.00	3.75
36	A5	1.25 l deep blue	2.00	3.75
37	A6	1.75 l rose red	2.00	4.50
38	A4	2.75 l dark blue	2.00	6.00
39	A5	5 l brnsh blk	3.50	8.75
40	A6	10 l bluish blk	3.50	8.75
41	A7	25 l gray black	5.50	12.00
		Nos. 32-41,C20-C27 (18)	55.25	127.00

10th anniversary of Fascism. Each denomination bears a different inscription.
Issue dates: 25 l, Dec. 26. Others, Oct. 5.

Mercury and Fasces — A8

Soccer Kickoff — A10

Scoring a Goal — A9

1934, Apr. 18

No.	Type	Description	Unused	Used
42	A8	20c red orange	50	1.25
43	A8	30c slate green	50	1.25
44	A8	50c indigo	50	1.25
45	A8	1.25 l blue	50	1.25

15th annual Trade Fair, Milan.

1934, June 5

No.	Type	Description	Unused	Used
46	A9	10c olive green	8.00	10.00
47	A9	50c purple	8.00	7.50
48	A9	1.25 l blue	17.50	27.50
49	A10	5 l brown	21.00	27.50
50	A10	10 l gray blue	25.00	27.50
		Nos. 46-50,C29-C35 (12)	160.50	222.50

2nd World Soccer Championship.

SEMI-POSTAL STAMPS

Many issues of Italy and Italian Colonies include one or more semi-postal denominations. To avoid splitting sets, these issues are generally listed as regular postage, airmail, etc., unless all values carry a surtax.

AIR POST STAMPS

Italian Air Post Stamps for Dante Alighieri Society Issue in New Colors and Overprinted in Red or Black Like Nos. 1-12

1932, July 11 Wmk. 140 *Perf. 14*

No.	Type	Description	Unused	Used
C1	AP10	50c gray blk (R)	45	75
C2	AP11	1 l indigo (R)	45	75
C3	AP11	3 l gray (R)	1.00	1.75
C4	AP11	5 l ol brn (R)	1.00	1.75
C5	AP10	7.70 l + 2 l car rose	1.00	1.75
C6	AP11	10 l + 2.50 l org	1.00	1.75
		Nos. C1-C6 (6)	4.90	8.50

Leonardo da Vinci — AP1

1932, Sept. 7 Photo. *Perf. 14½*

No.	Type	Description	Unused	Used
C7	AP1	100 l dp grn & brn	10.00	12.00

Types of Italian Air Post Stamps, Garibaldi Issue, in New Colors and Inscribed: "POSTE AEREA COLONIALE ITALIANA"

1932, July 1

No.	Type	Description	Unused	Used
C8	AP13	50c car rose	1.50	2.50
C9	AP14	80c green	1.50	2.50
C10	AP13	1 l + 25c ol brn	3.00	7.50
C11	AP13	2 l + 50c ol brn	3.00	7.50
C12	AP14	5 l + 1 l ol brn	3.00	7.50
		Nos. C8-C12 (5)	12.00	27.50

Eagle AP2

Savoia Marchetti 55 — AP3

Savoia Marchetti 55 over Map of Eritrea AP4

1933 *Perf. 14*

No.	Type	Description	Unused	Used
C13	AP2	50c org brn	1.65	2.50
C14	AP2	1 l blk vio	1.65	2.50
C15	AP3	3 l carmine	2.25	3.75
C16	AP3	5 l olive brn	2.25	3.75
C17	AP2	7.70 l + 2 l slate	7.00	13.00
C18	AP3	10 l + 2.50 l dp bl	7.00	13.00
C19	AP4	50 l dk vio	7.00	13.00
		Nos. C13-C19 (7)	28.80	51.50

50th anniv. of Italian Government of Eritrea.

Issue dates: 50 l, June 1. Others, Mar. 27.

Macchi-Costoldi Seaplane — AP5

Savoia S73 — AP6

Winding Propeller AP7

"More Efficient Machinery" AP8

1933-34

No.	Type	Description	Unused	Used
C20	AP5	50c org brn	2.50	4.50
C21	AP6	75c red vio	2.50	4.50
C22	AP5	1 l bis brn	2.50	4.50
C23	AP6	3 l olive gray	2.50	9.50
C24	AP5	10 l dp vio	2.50	9.50
C25	AP6	12 l bl grn	2.50	9.50
C26	AP7	20 l gray blk	6.00	15.00
C27	AP8	50 l blue ('34)	7.75	15.00
		Nos. C20-C27 (8)	28.75	72.00

Tenth anniversary of Fascism.
Issue dates: 50l, Dec. 26. Others, Oct. 5.

Natives Hailing Dornier Wal — AP9

1934, Apr. 24

No.	Type	Description	Unused	Used
C28	AP9	25 l brown olive	13.00	37.50

Issued in honor of Luigi Amadeo, Duke of the Abruzzi (1873-1933).

Airplane over Stadium AP10

Goalkeeper Leaping — AP11

Seaplane and Soccer Ball AP12

1934, June

C29	AP10	50c yel brn	5.50	*6.25*
C30	AP10	75c dp vio	5.50	*6.25*
C31	AP11	5 l brn blk	14.00	*22.00*
C32	AP11	10 l red org	14.00	*22.00*
C33	AP11	15 l car rose	14.00	*22.00*
C34	AP11	25 l green	14.00	*22.00*
C35	AP12	50 l bl grn	14.00	*22.00*
		Nos. C29-C35 (7)	81.00	*122.50*

World Soccer Championship Games, Rome. Issue dates: 50 l, June 21. Others, June 5.

AIR POST SPECIAL DELIVERY STAMPS

Garibaldi Type of Italy

Wmk. 140

1932, Oct. 6 Photo. *Perf. 14*

CE1	APSD1	2.25 l + 1 l dk vio & sl	3.50	*7.50*
CE2	APSD1	4.50 l + 1.50 l dk brn & grn	3.50	*7.50*

ITALIAN E. AFRICA

LOCATION — In eastern Africa, bordering on the Red Sea and Indian Ocean
GOVT. — Former Italian Colony
AREA — 665,977 sq. mi. (estimated)
POP. — 12,100,000 (estimated)
CAPITAL — Asmara

This colony was formed in 1936 and included Ethiopia and the former colonies of Eritrea and Italian Somaliland. For previous issues see listings under these headings.

100 Centesimi = 1 Lira

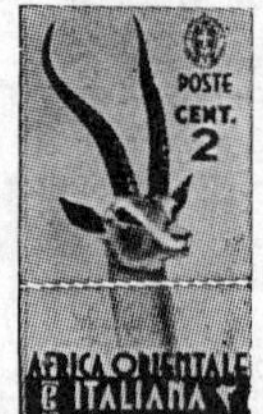
Grant's Gazelle — A1

Eagle and Lion — A2

Victor Emmanuel III — A3

Fascist Legionary — A5

Statue of the Nile — A4

Desert Road — A6

Wmk. 140

1938, Feb. 7 Photo. *Perf. 14*

1	A1	2c red org	35	*45*
2	A2	5c brown	35	35
3	A3	7½c dk vio	65	*75*
4	A4	10c olive brn	35	20
5	A5	15c slate grn	35	42
6	A3	20c crimson	35	20
7	A6	25c green	35	20
8	A1	30c olive brn	45	55
9	A2	35c sapphire	85	*1.25*
10	A3	50c purple	35	20

Engr.

11	A5	75c car lake	65	28
12	A6	1 l ol grn	55	20
13	A3	1.25 l dp bl	65	24
14	A4	1.75 l orange	6.75	20
15	A2	2 l cerise	75	30
16	A6	2.55 l dk brn	2.75	*4.00*
17	A1	3.70 l purple	17.50	5.50
18	A5	5 l purple	1.90	45
19	A2	10 l henna brn	3.75	1.40
20	A4	20 l dull grn	3.75	1.50
		Nos. 1-20,C1-C11,CE1-CE2 (33)	70.20	29.89

Augustus Caesar (Octavianus) A7

Goddess Abundantia A8

1938, Apr. 25 Photo. *Perf. 14*

21	A7	5c bis brn	15	35
22	A8	10c copper red	15	35
23	A7	25c deep grn	30	24
24	A8	50c purple	30	24
25	A7	75c crimson	30	*90*
26	A8	1.25 l deep blue	30	*90*
		Nos. 21-26,C12-C13 (8)	2.20	*4.68*

Bimillenary of the birth of Augustus Caesar (Octavianus), first Roman emperor.

Native Boat — A9

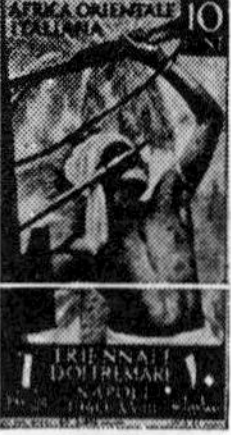
Native Soldier A10

Statue Suggesting Italy's Conquest of Ethiopia A11

1940, May 11 Wmk. 140

27	A9	5c ol brn	15	*28*
28	A10	10c red org	15	*28*
29	A11	25c green	38	*70*
30	A9	50c purple	38	*70*
31	A10	75c rose red	38	*1.10*
32	A11	1.25 l dark blue	38	*1.10*
33	A10	2 l + 75c car	38	*1.65*
		Nos. 27-33,C14-C17 (11)	3.38	

Issued in connection with the first Triennial Overseas Exposition held at Naples.

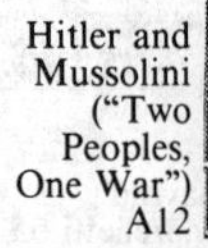

Hitler and Mussolini ("Two Peoples, One War") A12

1941, June 19

34	A12	5c ocher	15	
35	A12	10c chestnut	15	
36	A12	20c black	28	
37	A12	25c turq grn	28	
38	A12	50c rose lilac	28	
39	A12	75c rose car	28	
40	A12	1.25 l brt ultra	28	
		Nos. 34-40,C18-C19 (9)	15.70	

Rome-Berlin Axis.

Four stamps of type AP8, without "Posta Aerea," were prepared in 1941, but not issued. Value, each $1500.

SEMI-POSTAL STAMPS

Many issues of Italy and Italian Colonies include one or more semi-postal denominations. To avoid splitting sets, these issues are generally listed as regular postage, airmail, etc., unless all values carry a surtax.

AIR POST STAMPS

Plane Flying over Mountains AP1

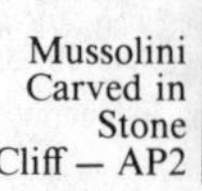

Mussolini Carved in Stone Cliff — AP2

Airplane over Lake Tsana AP3

Bataleur Eagle AP4

Eagle Attacking Serpent AP5

Wmk. Crowns (140)

1938, Feb. 7 Photo. *Perf. 14*

C1	AP1	25c slate grn	70	*1.40*
C2	AP2	50c olive brn	15.00	15
C3	AP3	60c red org	70	*1.50*
C4	AP1	75c org brn	1.50	90
C5	AP4	1 l slate blue	18	15

Engr.

C6	AP2	1.50 l violet	42	28
C7	AP3	2 l slate blue	42	42
C8	AP1	3 l car lake	55	60
C9	AP4	5 l red brown	90	60
C10	AP2	10 l vio brn	2.50	1.40
C11	AP1	25 l slate blue	3.25	1.90
		Nos. C1-C11 (11)	26.12	9.30

1938, Apr. 25 Photo.

C12	AP5	50c bister brn	35	45
C13	AP5	1 l purple	35	*1.25*

Bimillenary of the birth of Augustus Caesar (Octavianus), first Roman emperor.

Tractor — AP6

Plane over City — AP7

1940, May 11

C14	AP6	50c olive gray	24	*1.25*
C15	AP7	1 l purple	24	*1.25*
C16	AP6	2 l + 75c gray blue	35	*1.50*
C17	AP7	5 l + 2.50 l red brn	35	*1.50*

Issued in connection with the first Triennial Overseas Exposition held at Naples.

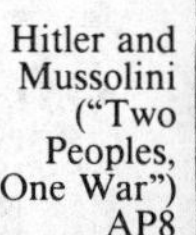

Hitler and Mussolini ("Two Peoples, One War") AP8

AP9

1941, Apr. 24

C18	AP8	1 l slate blue	12.00	
C19	AP9	1 l slate blue	2.00	

Issued in commemoration of the Rome-Berlin Axis.

AIR POST SPECIAL DELIVERY STAMPS

Plow and Airplane — APSD1

Wmk. 140

1938, Feb. 7 Engr. *Perf. 14*

CE1	APSD1	2 l slate blue	30	*70*
CE2	APSD1	2.50 l dark brown	38	*1.25*

SPECIAL DELIVERY STAMPS

Victor Emmanuel III — SD1

Wmk. 140

1938, Apr. 16 Engr. *Perf. 14*

E1	SD1	1.25 l dark green	30	45
E2	SD1	2.50 l dark car	38	*2.25*

POSTAGE DUE STAMPS

Italy, Nos. J28 to J40, Overprinted in Black **A.O.I.**

1941	**Wmk. 140**		*Perf. 14*
J1	D6	5c brown	55
J2	D6	10c blue	55
J3	D6	20c rose red	1.10
J4	D6	25c green	1.10
J5	D6	30c red org	2.00
J6	D6	40c blk brn	2.50
J7	D6	50c violet	2.50
J8	D6	60c slate blk	3.75
J9	D7	1 l red org	20.00
J10	D7	2 l green	20.00
J11	D7	5 l violet	20.00
J12	D7	10 l blue	20.00
J13	D7	20 l car rose	20.00
		Nos. J1-J13 (13)	114.05

In 1943 a set of 11 "Segnatasse" stamps, picturing a horse and rider and inscribed "A. O. I.," was prepared but not issued. Value, $4.

ITALIAN STATES

Watermarks

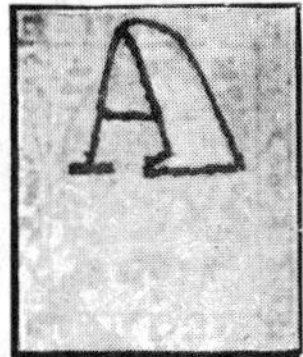

Wmk. 157- Large Letter "A"

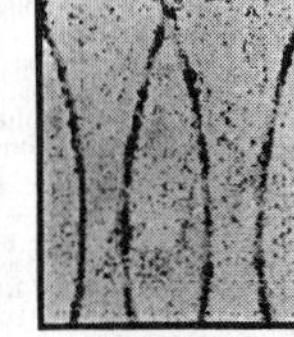

Wmk. 184- Interlaced Wavy Lines

Wmk. 184 has double lined letters diagonally across the sheet readiing: "II R R POSTE TOSCANE."

Wmk. 185- Crowns in the sheet

The watermark consists of twelve crowns, arranged in four rows of three, with horizontal and vertical lines between them. Only parts of the watermark appear on each stamp. (Reduced illustration.)

Wmk. 186- Fleurs-de-Lis in Sheet

MODENA

LOCATION — In northern Italy
GOVT. — Former Duchy
AREA — 1,003 sq. mi.
POP. — 448,000 (approx.)
CAPITAL — Modena

In 1852, when the first postage stamps were issued, Modena was under the rule of Duke Francis V of the House of Este-Lorraine. In June, 1859, he was overthrown and the Duchy was annexed to the Kingdom of Sardinia which on March 17, 1861, became the Kingdom of Italy.

100 Centesimi = 1 Lira

Values of Modena stamps vary according to condition. Quotations are for fine copies, the unused with original gum. Very fine to superb specimens sell at much higher prices, and inferior to poor copies sell at reduced prices, depending on the condition of the individual specimens.

Coat of Arms
A1 A2

1852 Unwmk. Typo. ***Imperf.***

Without Period After Figures of Value

1	A1 5c blk, *green*	90.00	6.00
a.	Pair, one with period	180.00	*500.00*
2	A1 10c blk, *rose*	75.00	8.00
a.	"EENT. 10"	*1,800.*	*800.00*
b.	"1" of "10" inverted	*1,800.*	*800.00*
c.	"CNET"	*120.00*	*240.00*
d.	No period after "CENT"	*500.00*	260.00
e.	Pair, #2, 7	225.00	*600.00*
3	A1 15c blk, *yellow*	8.50	8.00
a.	"CETN 15."	*2,250.*	*350.00*
b.	No period after "CENT"	75.00	*180.00*
4	A1 25c blk, *buff*	9.00	6.50
a.	No period after "CENT"	200.00	*400.00*
b.	"ENT.25" omitted	*325.00*	
5	A1 40c blk, *blue*	55.00	35.00
a.	40c black, *pale blue*	*1,500.*	160.00
b.	No period after "CENT"	*600.00*	*400.00*
c.	As "a," no period after "CENT"		*1,300.*
d.	Pair, #5, 8	*140.00*	*700.00*

Unused examples of No. 5a lack gum.

With Period After Figures of Value

6	A1 5c blk, *green*	6.00	12.00
a.	5c black, *olive green*	40.00	20.00
	As "a," without gum	6.00	
b.	"ENT"	*1,400.*	*800.00*
c.	"CNET"	*1,400.*	*1,200.*
d.	As "a," "CNET"	*600.00*	*600.00*
e.	"E" of "CENT" sideways	*2,250.*	*1,600.*
f.	As "a," "CEN1"	*600.00*	*600.00*
g.	As "a," no period after "5"	140.00	*140.00*
h.	Double impression	*300.00*	
i.	As "a," double impression	*260.00*	
7	A1 10c blk, *rose*	20.00	24.00
a.	"CENE"	300.00	*500.00*
b.	"CNET"	150.00	*260.00*
c.	"CE6T"	300.00	*500.00*
d.	"N" of "CENT" sideways	*1,600.*	*1,100.*
e.	Double impression	240.00	*1,200.*
8	A1 40c blk, *blue*	8.00	*45.00*
a.	"CNET"	80.00	*300.00*
b.	"CENE"	160.00	*600.00*
c.	"CE6T"	160.00	*600.00*
d.	"49"	80.00	*300.00*
e.	"4C"	160.00	*600.00*
f.	"CEN.T"	*6,000.*	

Wmk. 157

9	A1 1 l black	10.00	*500.00*
a.	With period after "LIRA"	50.00	*1,400.*

Provisional Government

1859 **Unwmk.**

10	A2 5c green	90.00	*170.00*
a.	5c emerald	110.00	*200.00*
b.	5c dark green	100.00	*180.00*
11	A2 15c brown	40.00	*800.00*
a.	15c gray brown	35.00	
b.	15c black brown	*60.00*	675.00
c.	No period after "15"	*200.00*	*1,600.*
d.	Period after "CENT"	*200.00*	*1,600.*
e.	Double impression	*180.00*	
12	A2 20c lilac	10.00	*150.00*
a.	20c violet	60.00	27.50
b.	20c blue violet	130.00	37.50
c.	No period after "20"	12.00	*260.00*
d.	"ECNT"	67.50	*800.00*
e.	"N" inverted	37.50	*400.00*
f.	Double impression		*700.00*
13	A2 40c carmine	10.00	*300.00*
a.	40c brown rose	10.00	*300.00*
b.	No period after "40"	80.00	*1,000.*
c.	Period before "CENT"	80.00	*1,000.*
d.	Inverted "5" before the "C"	*5,500.*	*5,500.*
14	A2 80c buff	14.00	*4,000.*
a.	80c brown orange	16.00	*4,500.*
b.	"CENT 8"	160.00	
c.	"CENT 0"	70.00	
d.	No period after "80"	70.00	
e.	"N" inverted	70.00	

The reprints of the 1859 issue have the word "CENT" and the figures of value in different type from the originals. There is no frame line at the bottom of the small square in the lower right corner.

NEWSPAPER TAX STAMPS

NT1 NT2

B. G. CEN. 9 B. G. CEN. 9.
Type I Type II

1853 Unwmk. Typo. ***Imperf.***

PR1	NT1 9c blk, *violet* (I)	*2,250.*	*650.00*
PR2	NT1 9c blk, *violet* (II)	50.00	12.00
a.	No period after "9"	*180.00*	90.00

All known unused examples of No. PR1 lack gum.

1855-57

PR3	A1 9c blk, *violet*	1.50	
a.	No period after "9"	2.50	
PR4	A1 10c blk, *gray vio* ('57)	9.00	*60.00*
a.	"CEN1"	70.00	*775.00*

No. PR3 was never placed in use.

1859

PR5	NT2 10c black	120.00	*480.00*

These stamps did not pay postage, but were a fiscal tax collected by the postal authorities on newspapers arriving from foreign countries.

The stamps of Modena were superseded by those of Sardinia in February, 1860.

PARMA

LOCATION — Comprising the present provinces of Parma and Piacenza in northern Italy.
GOVT. — A former independent Duchy
AREA — 2,750 sq. mi. (1860)
POP. — 500,000 (1860)
CAPITAL — Parma

Parma was annexed to Sardinia in 1860.

100 Centesimi = 1 Lira

Values of Parma stamps vary according to condition. Quotations are for fine copies. Very fine to superb specimens sell at much higher prices, and inferior or poor copies sell at reduced prices, depending on the condition of the individual specimen.

Values for unused are for copies with gum except No. 8 which is known only without gum. Copies of other stamps without gum sell for about a third less.

Crown and Fleur-de-lis
A1 A2

1852	Unwmk.	Typo.		*Imperf.*
1	A1	5c blk, *yellow*	7.50	8.00
2	A1	10c blk, *white*	7.50	8.00
3	A1	15c blk, *pink*	300.00	14.00
a.		Tete beche pair		*25,000.*
b.		Double impression		*1,000.*
4	A1	25c blk, *violet*	*1,300*	16.00
5	A1	40c blk, *blue*	300.00	75.00
a.		40c black, *pale blue*	*600.00*	80.00

1854-55				
6	A1	5c org yel	*600.00*	160.00
a.		5c lemon yellow	*1,600.*	160.00
b.		Double impression		*4,000.*
7	A1	15c red	*800.00*	37.50
8	A1	25c red brn ('55)	*2,600.*	55.00
a.		Double impression		*8,000.*

No. 8 unused is without gum.

1857-59				
9	A2	15c red ('59)	26.00	*120.00*
10	A2	25c red brown	30.00	25.00
11	A2	40c bl, wide "0" ('58)	8.00	*110.00*
a.		Narrow "0" in "40"	12.00	*120.00*

Provisional Government

A3

1859				
12	A3	5c yel grn	75.00	*3,500.*
a.		5c blue green	160.00	*900.00*
13	A3	10c brown	40.00	*140.00*
a.		10c deep brown	40.00	*140.00*
b.		"1" of "10" inverted	110.00	*1,600.*
c.		Thick "0" in "10"	55.00	*170.00*
14	A3	20c pale blue	30.00	24.00
a.		20c deep blue	45.00	35.00
b.		Thick "0" in "20"	90.00	60.00
15	A3	40c red	67.50	*1,300.*
a.		40c brown red	*1,500.*	*1,300.*
b.		Thick "0" in "40"	85.00	*1,300.*
16	A3	80c org yel	*850.00*	
a.		80c olive yellow	*575.00*	
d.		Thick "0" in "80"	*900.00*	

Nos. 12-16 exist in two other varieties: with spelling "CFNTESIMI" and with small "A" in "STATI." These are valued about 50 per cent more than normal stamps.

See Nos. PR1-PR2.

NEWSPAPER TAX STAMPS

Type of 1859

1853-57	Unwmk.	Typo.		*Imperf.*
PR1	A3	6c blk, *rose* ('57)	10.00	
a.		6c black, *deep rose*	75.00	70.00
PR2	A3	9c black, *blue*	6.50	*5,000.*

These stamps belong to the same class as the Newspaper Tax Stamps of Modena, Austria, etc. No. PR1 was not regularly issued.

Note following No. 16 also applies to Nos. PR1-PR2.

The stamps of Parma were superseded by those of Sardinia in 1860.

ROMAGNA

LOCATION — Comprised the present Italian provinces of Forli, Ravenna, Ferrara and Bologna.
GOVT. — Formerly one of the Roman States
AREA — 5,626 sq. mi.
POP. — 1,341,091 (1853)
CAPITAL — Ravenna

Postage stamps were issued when a provisional government was formed pending the unification of Italy. In 1860 Romagna was annexed to Sardinia and since 1862 the postage stamps of Italy have been used.

100 Bajocchi = 1 Scudo

Values of Romagna stamps vary according to condition. Quotations are for fine copies. Very fine to superb specimens sell at much higher prices, and inferior or poor copies sell at reduced prices, depending on the condition of the individual specimen.

A1

1859	Unwmk.	Typo.		*Imperf.*
1	A1	½b blk, *straw*	7.00	*110.00*
2	A1	1b blk, *drab*	7.00	*50.00*
3	A1	2b blk, *buff*	12.50	*50.00*
4	A1	3b blk, *dk grn*	14.00	*130.00*
5	A1	4b blk, *fawn*	90.00	60.00
6	A1	5b blk, *gray vio*	12.00	60.00
7	A1	6b blk, *yel grn*	70.00	*2,600.*
8	A1	8b blk, *rose*	50.00	*425.00*
9	A1	20b blk, *gray grn*	24.00	*800.00*

These stamps have been reprinted several times. The reprints usually resemble the originals in the color of the paper but there are impressions on incorrect colors and also in colors on white paper. They often show broken letters and other injuries. The Y shaped ornaments between the small circles in the corners are broken and blurred and the dots outside the circles are often missing or joined to the circles.

Forged cancellations are plentiful.

The stamps of Romagna were superseded by those of Sardinia in February, 1860.

ROMAN STATES

LOCATION — Comprised most of the central Italian Peninsula, bounded by the former Kingdom of Lombardy-Venetia and Modena on the north, Tuscany on the west, and the Kingdom of Naples on the southeast.
GOVT. — Formerly under the direct government of the See of Rome.
AREA — 16,000 sq. mi.
POP. — 3,124,758 (1853)
CAPITAL — Rome

Upon the formation of the Kingdom of Italy, the area of the Roman States was greatly reduced and in 1870 they disappeared from the political map of Europe. Postage stamps of Italy have been used since that time.

100 Bajocchi = 1 Scudo
100 Centesimi = 1 Lira (1867)

Values of Roman States stamps vary according to condition. Quotations are for fine copies. Very fine to superb specimens sell at much higher prices, and inferior or poor copies sell at reduced prices depending on the condition of the individual specimen.

Values for unused are for copies with original gum.

Papal Arms
A1 A2

A3 A4

A5 A6

A7 A8

A9 A10

A11

1852	Unwmk.	Typo.		*Imperf.*
1	A1	½b blk, *dl vio*	12.00	*24.00*
a.		½b black, *gray blue*	45.00	18.00
b.		½b black, *gray lilac*	30.00	26.00
c.		½b black, *gray*	60.00	18.00
d.		½b black, *reddish violet*	350.00	180.00
e.		½b black, *dark violet*	57.50	60.00
f.		Tete beche pair		*4,400.*
i.		Double impression		*1,600.*
j.		Impression on both sides		*3,500.*
2	A2	1b blk, *bl grn*	14.00	5.00
a.		1b black, *gray green*	24.00	2.50
c.		Grayish greasy ink	140.00	8.00
d.		Double impression		*1,600.*
e.		Impression on both sides		*3,400.*

3	A3	2b blk, *grnsh white*	1.25	*5.00*
a.		2b black, *yellow green*	26.00	1.60
d.		Grayish greasy ink	180.00	8.00
e.		No period after "BAJ"	60.00	10.00
f.		As "a" and "e"	67.50	6.00
g.		Double impression		*1,200.*
4	A4	3b blk, *brown*	26.00	7.25
a.		3b black, *light brown*	24.00	8.00
b.		3b black, *yellow brown*	40.00	10.00
c.		3b black, *yellow buff*	3.25	*22.50*
g.		Grayish greasy ink		30.00
h.		Impression on both sides		*3,400.*
i.		Double impression		*1,600.*
5	A5	4b blk, *lemon*	26.00	7.00
a.		4b black, *yellow*	26.00	7.00
b.		4b black, *rose brown*	400.00	7.00
c.		4b black, *gray brown*	350.00	7.00
f.		Impression on both sides		*3,400.*
g.		Ribbed paper	30.00	7.00
h.		Grayish greasy ink	*1,000*	40.00
6	A6	5b blk, *rose*	24.00	1.90
a.		5b black, *pale rose*	40.00	2.00
c.		Impression on both sides		*2,600.*
d.		Double impression		*2,000.*
e.		Grayish greasy ink	200.00	12.00
7	A7	6b blk, *grnsh grn*	45.00	6.75
a.		6b black, *gray*	120.00	7.50
b.		6b black, *grayish lilac*	70.00	22.50
c.		Grayish greasy ink	325.00	35.00
d.		Double impression		*1,600.*
8	A8	7b blk, *blue*	80.00	13.00
b.		Double impression		*1,000.*
c.		Grayish greasy ink	360.00	35.00
9	A9	8b black	20.00	6.75
c.		Double impression		
d.		Grayish greasy ink	*450.00*	45.00
10	A10	50b dull blue	*975.00*	160.00
a.		50b deep blue (worn impression)	*1,400.*	575.00
11	A11	1sc rose	*325.00*	*600.00*

Counterfeits exist of Nos. 10-11. Fraudulent cancellations are found on No. 11.

A12 A13

A14 A15

A16 A17

A18

1867				*Imperf.*
		Glazed Paper		
12	A12	2c blk, *green*	20.00	*45.00*
a.		No period after "Cent"	24.00	*50.00*
13	A13	3c blk, *gray*	37.50	*1,800.*
a.		3c black, *lilac gray*	240.00	*575.00*
14	A14	5c blk, *lt bl*	16.00	*20.00*
a.		No period after "5"	40.00	*150.00*
15	A15	10c blk, *vermilion*	40.00	9.00
a.		Double impression		*1,600.*
16	A16	20c blk, *cop red* (unglazed)	20.00	8.00
a.		No period after "20"	90.00	45.00
b.		No period after "CENT"	90.00	45.00
17	A17	40c blk, *yellow*	12.00	*40.00*
a.		No period after "40"	12.00	*60.00*
18	A18	80c blk, *lil rose*	12.00	*40.00*
a.		No period after "80"	20.00	*120.00*

Imperforate stamps on unglazed paper, or in colors other than listed, are unfinished remainders of the 1868 issue.

Fraudulent cancellations are found on Nos. 13, 14, 17, 18.

1868	Glazed Paper			*Perf. 13*
19	A12	2c blk, *green*	1.25	*9.00*
a.		No period after "CENT"	1.10	*55.00*
20	A13	3c blk, *gray*	5.00	*750.00*
a.		3c black, *lilac gray*	*550.00*	*3,000.*
21	A14	5c blk, *lt bl*	2.00	*4.00*
a.		No period after "5"	3.00	*9.00*
b.		No period after "Cent"	12.00	*50.00*
c.		5c black, *lt bl* (unglazed, imperf., without gum)	7.50	

22 A15 10c blk, *org ver* 40 *1.75*
a. 10c black, *vermilion* 50.00 2.50
b. 10c black, *ver* (unglazed) 80
c. 10c black, *ver* (unglazed, imperf., without gum) 15
23 A16 20c blk, *dp crim* 60 *3.25*
a. 20c black, *magenta* 1.25 *4.00*
b. 20c blk, *mag* (unglazed) 1.25 *4.00*
c. 20c blk, *mag* (imperf., without gum) 15
d. 20c blk, *cop red* (unglazed) 110.00 3.75
e. 20c blk, *dp crim* (imperf., without gum) 15
f. No period after "20" *(copper red)* *200.00* 14.00
g. No period after "20" *(mag)* 3.00 *12.00*
h. No period after "20" *(deep crimson)* 3.00 *12.00*
i. No period after "CENT" *(copper red)* *200.00* 14.00
j. No period after "CENT" *(magenta)* 3.00 *14.00*
k. No period after "CENT" *(deep crimson)* 3.00 *14.00*
24 A17 40c blk, *grnsh yel* 80 *24.00*
a. 40c black, *yellow* 80 *24.00*
b. 40c black, *orange yel* 18.00 *140.00*
c. No period after "40" 2.50 *32.50*
25 A18 80c blk, *rose lil* 3.00 *50.00*
a. 80c black, *bright rose* *400.00* *4,750.*
b. 80c blk, *rose* (unglazed) 6.00
c. No period after "80" *(rose lilac)* 20.00

All values except the 3c are known imperforate vertically or horizontally.

Double impressions are known of the 5c, 10c, 20c (all three colors), 40c and 80c.

Fraudulent cancellations are found on Nos. 20, 24 and 25.

The stamps of the 1867 and 1868 issues have been privately reprinted; many of these reprints are well executed and it is difficult to distinguish them from the originals. Most reprints show more or less pronounced defects of the design. On the originals the horizontal lines between stamps are unbroken, while on most of the reprints these lines are broken. Most of the perforated reprints gauge 11½.

Roman States stamps were replaced by those of Italy in 1870.

SARDINIA

LOCATION — An island in the Mediterranean Sea off the west coast of Italy and a large area in northwestern Italy, including the cities of Genoa, Turin and Nice.
GOVT. — A former Kingdom

As a result of war and revolution, most of the former independent Italian States were joined to the Kingdom of Sardinia in 1859 and 1860. On March 17, 1861, the name was changed to the Kingdom of Italy.

100 Centesimi = 1 Lira

Values of Sardinia stamps vary according to condition. Quotations for Nos. 1-9 are for fine copies. Very fine to superb specimens sell at much higher prices, and inferior or poor copies sell at reduced prices, depending on the condition of the individual specimen.
Values for unused are for copies with original gum.

King Victor Emmanuel II
A1 A2

A3

A4

1851 Unwmk. Litho. *Imperf.*

1 A1 5c gray blk 325.00 325.00
a. 5c black 325.00 325.00
2 A1 20c blue 450.00 16.00
a. 20c deep blue 500.00 24.00
3 A1 40c rose 160.00 *425.00*
a. 40c violet rose 375.00 *500.00*

1853 Embossed

4 A2 5c blk, *bl grn* 450.00 120.00
a. Double embossing *1,000.*
5 A2 20c blk, *dl bl* 300.00 37.50
a. Double embossing 200.00
6 A2 40c blk, *pale rose* 450.00 80.00
a. Double embossing *1,000.*

1854 Lithographed and Embossed

7 A3 5c yel grn *3,600.* 140.00
a. Double embossing *675.00*
b. 5c green 40.00
8 A3 20c blue *900.00* 40.00
a. Double embossing *200.00*
b. 20c indigo 20.00
9 A3 40c rose *6,000.* 700.00
a. Double embossing *2,400.*
b. 40c brown rose 16.00

Nos. 7b, 8b and 9b, differing in shade from the original stamps, were prepared but not issued.

Typographed Frame in Color, Colorless Embossed Center
1855-63 Unwmk. *Imperf.*

Stamps of this issue vary greatly in color, paper and sharpness of embossing as between the early (1855-59) printings and the later (1860-63) ones. Year dates after each color name indicate whether the stamp falls into the Early or Late printing group.

As a rule, early printings are on smooth thick paper with sharp embossing, while later printings are usually on paper varying from thick to thin and of inferior quality with embossing less distinct and printing blurred. The outer frame shows a distinct design on the early printings, while this design is more or less blurred or even a solid line on the later printings.

10 A4 5c grn ('62-63) 2.00 *2.50*
a. 5c yellow grn ('62-63) 2.00 *2.50*
b. 5c olive grn ('60-61) 35.00 12.00
c. 5c yellow grn ('55-59) *140.00* 24.00
d. 5c myrtle grn ('57) *800.00* 50.00
e. 5c emerald ('55-57) *650.00* 55.00
f. Head inverted *750.00*
g. Double head, one inverted *900.00*
11 A4 10c bis ('63) 80 *1.65*
a. 10c ocher ('62) 60.00 4.00
b. 10c olive bister ('62) 6.00 4.00
c. 10c olive green ('61) 16.00 4.00
d. 10c reddish brown ('61) 70.00 8.00
e. 10c gray brown ('61) 16.00 8.00
f. 10c olive gray ('60-61) 18.00 14.00
g. 10c gray ('60) 24.00 18.00
h. 10c green ('59) 12.00 16.00
i. 10c violet brown ('59) 90.00 40.00
j. 10c dark brown ('58) *120.00* 50.00
k. Head inverted *800.00*
l. Double head, one inverted *675.00*
12 A4 20c indigo ('62) 8.00 1.50
a. 20c blue ('61) 11.00 3.75
b. 20c light blue ('60-61) 14.00 3.75
c. 20c Prussian bl ('59-60) 45.00 5.75
d. 20c indigo ('57-58) 50.00 6.00
e. 20c sky blue ('55-56) *700.00* 18.00
f. 20c cobalt ('55) *550.00* 22.50
g. Head inverted *300.00*
h. Double head, one inverted *450.00*
13 A4 40c red ('63) 1.00 *7.50*
a. 40c rose ('61-62) 6.00 7.00
b. 40c carmine ('60) 40.00 24.00
c. 40c light red ('58-59) 60.00 30.00
d. 40c vermilion ('55-57) *300.00* 20.00
e. Head inverted *1,250.*
f. Double head, one inverted *1,000.*
14 A4 80c org yel ('62) 2.00 *25.00*
a. 80c yellow ('60-61) 10.00 *24.00*
b. 80c yellow ocher ('59) *65.00* 45.00
c. 80c ocher ('58) 20.00 *40.00*
d. 80c brown oanreg ('58) 35.00 *57.50*
e. Head inverted *4,500.*
15 A4 3 l bronze ('61) 50.00 *325.00*

Forgeries of the inverted and double head varieties have been made by applying a faked head embossing to printer's waste without head. These forgeries are plentiful.

Fraudulent cancellations are found on Nos. 13-15.

The 5c, 20c and 40c have been reprinted; the embossing of the reprints is not as sharp as that of the originals, the colors are dull and blurred.

NEWSPAPER STAMPS

N1

Typographed and Embossed
1861 Unwmk. *Imperf.*

P1 N1 1c black 20 *1.00*
a. Numeral "2" 35.00 *300.00*
b. Figure of value inverted 225.00 *5,500.*
c. Double impression *450.00*
P2 N1 2c black 6.75 8.00
a. Numeral "1" *1,200.* *5,500.*
b. Figure of value inverted *225.00* *5,500.*

Forgeries of the varieties of the embossed numerals have been made from printer's waste without numerals.

See Italy No. P1 for 2c buff.

The stamps of Sardinia were superseded in 1862 by those of Italy, which were identical with the 1855 issue of Sardinia, but perforated. Until 1863, imperforate and perforated stamps were issued simultaneously.

TUSCANY

LOCATION — In the north central part of the Apennine Peninsula.
GOVT. — A former Grand Duchy, now a department of Italy.
AREA — 8,890 sq. mi.
POP. — 2,892,000 (approx.)
CAPITAL — Florence

Tuscany was annexed to Sardinia in 1860.

60 Quattrini = 20 Soldi = 12 Crazie = 1 Lira
100 Centesimi = 1 Lira (1860)

Values of Tuscany stamps vary according to condition. They were narrowly spaced. Quotations are for fine copies. Very fine to superb copies with margins all around sell at much higher prices. Inferior specimens with designs partly cut away sell at greatly reduced prices, depending on the individual specimen.
Values for unused stamps are for copies with original gum. Copies without gum sell for about 40 per cent less.

Lion of Tuscany — A1

1851-52 Typo. Wmk. 185 *Imperf.*
Blue, Grayish Blue or Gray Paper

1 A1 1q blk ('52) 500.00 80.00
2 A1 1s ocher 850.00 160.00
a. 1s orange 1,100. 140.00
b. 1s yellow 1,200. 140.00
3 A1 2s scarlet *3,250.* 700.00
4 A1 1cr carmine 400.00 6.50
a. 1cr brown carmine 450.00 6.50
5 A1 2cr blue 120.00 8.50
a. 2cr greenish blue 120.00 12.50
6 A1 4cr green 400.00 12.00
a. 4cr bluish green 400.00 12.50
7 A1 6cr blue 400.00 14.00
a. 6cr slate blue 500.00 14.00
b. 6cr indigo 525.00 14.00
8 A1 9cr gray lil 1,100. 26.00
a. 9cr deep violet 1,100. 26.00
9 A1 60cr red ('52) *6,000.* *2,400.*

The first paper was blue, later paper more and more grayish. Stamps on distinctly blue paper sell about 20 percent higher, except Nos. 3 and 9 which were issued on blue paper only. Examples without watermark are proofs.

Reprints of Nos. 3 and 9 have re-engraved value labels, color is too brown and impressions blurred and heavy. Paper same as originals.

1857-59 Wmk. 184
White Paper

10 A1 1q black 85.00 130.00
11 A1 1s yellow *2,400.* 450.00
12 A1 1cr carmine 550.00 50.00
13 A1 2cr blue 160.00 12.00
14 A1 4cr bl grn 500.00 26.00
15 A1 6cr deep blue *675.00* 20.00
16 A1 9cr gray lil ('59) *180.00* *500.00*

Provisional Government

Coat of Arms — A2

1860

17 A2 1c brn lilac 120.00 80.00
a. 1c red lilac 120.00 80.00
b. 1c gray lilac 120.00 80.00
18 A2 5c green 550.00 24.00
a. 5c olive green 550.00 24.00
b. 5c yellow green 550.00 24.00
19 A2 10c gray brn 72.50 5.00
a. 10c deep brown 72.50 5.00
b. 10c purple brown 72.50 5.00
20 A2 20c blue 300.00 14.00
a. 20c deep blue 300.00 14.00
b. 20c gray blue 300.00 14.00
21 A2 40c rose 400.00 26.00
a. 40c carmine 400.00 26.00
22 A2 80c pale red brn *1,000.* 37.50
a. 80c brown orange *1,000.* 37.50
23 A2 3 l ocher *12,000.* *6,500.*

Dangerous counterfeits exist of #1-PR1c.

NEWSPAPER TAX STAMP

NT1

A little time given to the study of the arrangement of the Scott Catalogue can make it easier to use effectively.

1854 Unwmk. Typo. *Imperf.*
Yellowish Pelure Paper

PR1 NT1 2s black 2.00
a. Tete beche pair 60.00
b. Tete beche pair, one stamp on back 60.00
c. Double impression 40.00

This stamp represented a fiscal tax on newspapers coming from foreign countries. It was not canceled when used.

The stamps of Tuscany were superseded by those of Sardinia in 1861.

TWO SICILIES

LOCATION — Formerly comprised the island of Sicily and the lower half of the Apennine Peninsula.
GOVT. — A former independent Kingdom
CAPITAL — Naples

The Kingdom was annexed to Sardinia in 1860.

200 Tornesi = 100 Grana = 1 Ducat

> Values of Two Sicilies stamps vary according to condition. Quotations for Nos. 1-18 are for fine copies. Very fine to superb specimens sell at much higher prices, and inferior or poor copies sell at reduced prices, depending on the condition of the individual specimen.
> Values for unused are for copies with original gum.

Naples

Coat of Arms
A1 A2

A3 A4

A5 A6

A7

1858 Engr. Wmk. 186 *Imperf.*

1 A1 ½g pale lake 40.00 16.00
a. ½g rose lake 180.00 55.00
b. ½g lake 160.00 75.00
c. ½g carmine lake 160.00 70.00
2 A2 1g pale lake 60.00 6.75
a. 1g rose lake 70.00 8.00
b. 1g brown lake 60.00 8.00
c. 1g carmine lake 60.00 9.00
d. Printed on both sides 275.00
e. Double impression 60.00
3 A3 2g pale lake 24.00 2.00
a. 2g rose lake 26.00 2.00
b. 2g lake 50.00 5.25
c. 2g carmine lake 60.00 6.00
d. Impression of 1g on reverse 500.00
e. Double impression 67.50 12.00
f. Printed on both sides 500.00
4 A4 5g rose lake 160.00 10.00
a. 5g brown lake 175.00 14.00
b. 5g carmine lake 290.00 18.00
c. Double impression 190.00 20.00
d. Printed on both sides 2,000.
5 A5 10g rose lake 300.00 10.00
a. 10g lake 300.00 26.00
b. 10g carmine lake 325.00 26.00
c. Printed on both sides 5,000.
d. Double impression 600.00 100.00
6 A6 20g rose lake 375.00 30.00
a. 20g lake 375.00 30.00
b. Double impression 650.00 140.00
7 A7 50g rose lake 3,000. 750.00
a. 50g lake 3,250. 1,500.
b. Double impression 4,000.

As a secret mark, the engraver, G. Masini, placed a minute letter of his name just above the lower outer line of each stamp. There were three plates of the 2g, one plate of the 50g, and two plates of each of the other values.

Nos. 1 to 7, except No. 3, have been reprinted in bright rose and Nos. 1 and 7 in dull brown. The reprints are on thick unwatermarked paper. Value $8 each.

Provisional Government

A8 A9

1860

8 A8 ½t deep blue 26,000. 2,250.
9 A9 ½t blue 4,500. 400.00
a. ½t deep blue 4,500. 1,000.

100 varieties of each.

No. 8 was made from the plate of No. 1, which was altered by changing the "G" to "T".

No. 9 was made from the same plate after a second alteration erasing the coat of arms and inserting the Cross of Savoy. Dangerous counterfeits exist of Nos. 8-9.

Sicily

Ferdinand II — A10

1859 Unwmk. Engr. *Imperf.*

10 A10 ½g orange 100.00 250.00
a. ½g yellow 1,500. 675.00
b. ½g olive yellow 6,000.
c. Printed on both sides 9,000.
11 A10 1g dk brn 4,000. 300.00
a. 1g olive brown (I) 7,000. 300.00
12 A10 1g ol grn 32.50 50.00
a. 1g grysh olive grn (II) 60.00 32.50
b. 1g olive brown (II) 160.00 30.00
c. Double impression 1,100. 1,300.
13 A10 2g blue 26.00 22.50
a. 2g deep blue 1,000. 80.00
b. Printed on both sides 6,750.
14 A10 5g carmine 175.00 140.00
a. 5g deep rose 180.00 130.00
b. 5g brick red 260.00 120.00
15 A10 5g vermilion 65.00 450.00
a. 5g orange vermilion 60.00 500.00
16 A10 10g dark blue 110.00 70.00
a. 10g indigo 120.00 80.00
17 A10 20g dk gray vio 110.00 130.00
18 A10 50g dk brn red 100.00 1,25

There were three plates each for the 1g and 2g, two each for the ½g and 5g and one plate each for the other values.

Nos. 10a, 10b, 11, 11a, 14, 14a, 14b and 15 are printed from Plate I on which the stamps are 2 to 2½mm apart. On almost all stamps from Plate I, the S and T of POSTA touch.

Nos. 12a, and 15a are from Plate II and No. 12 is from Plate III. On both Plates II and III stamps are spaced 1½mm apart. Most stamps from Plate II have a white line about 1mm long below the beard.

The ½g blue is stated to be a proof of which two copies are known used on cover.

Fraudulent cancellations are known on Nos. 10, 15, 15a and 18.

Neapolitan Provinces

King Victor Emmanuel II — A11

Lithographed, Center Embossed
1861 Unwmk. *Imperf.*

19 A11 ½t green 1.65 18.00
a. ½t yellow green 1.65 18.00
b. ½t emerald 500.00 60.00
c. ½t black (error) 3,500. 5,000.
d. Head inverted (green) 24.00
e. Head inverted (yel grn) 2,000.
f. Printed on both sides 5,000.
20 A11 ½g bister 30.00 35.00
a. ½g brown 26.00 35.00
b. ½g gray brown 500.00 37.50
c. Head inverted 35.00
21 A11 1g black 30.00 35.00
a. Head inverted 350.00
22 A11 2g blue 14.00 2.00
a. 2g deep blue 14.00 2.00
b. Head inverted 60.00 120.00
c. 2g black (error) 7,500.
23 A11 5g car rose 20.00 12.00
a. 5g vermilion 22.50 19.00
b. 5g lilac rose 37.50 24.00
c. Head inverted 160.00 1,200.
e. Printed on both sides 2,400.
25 A11 10g orange 12.00 22.50
a. 10g ocher 240.00 75.00
b. 10g bister 18.00 37.50
26 A11 20g yellow 70.00 160.00
a. Head inverted 3,500.
27 A11 50g gray 2.00 1,600.
a. 50g slate 3.50 1,600.
b. 50g slate blue 5.00 1,700.

Counterfeits of the inverted head varieties of this issue are plentiful. See note on forgeries after Sardinia No. 15.

Fraudulent cancellations are found on Nos. 19-20, 23-27.

Stamps similar to those of Sardinia 1855-61, type A4 but with inscriptions in larger, clearer lettering, were prepared in 1861 for the Neapolitan Provinces. They were not officially issued although a few are known postally used. Denominations: 5c, 10c, 20c, 40c and 80c.

Stamps of Two Sicilies were replaced by those of Italy in 1862.

ITALY

LOCATION — Southern Europe
GOVT. — Republic
AREA — 119,764 sq. mi.
POP. — 56,929,101 (est. 1983)
CAPITAL — Rome

Formerly a kingdom, Italy became a republic in June 1946

100 Centesimi = 1 Lira

See Sardinia for stamps formerly listed as Italy Nos. 1-16 and black 1c and 2c newspaper stamps, type N1.

> **Catalogue values for unused stamps in this country are for Never Hinged items, beginning with Scott 691 in the regular postage section, Scott C129 in the airpost section, Scott D21 in the pneumatic post section, Scott E32 in the special delivery section, Scott EY11 in the authorized delivery section, Scott J83 in the postage due section, Scott Q77 in the parcel post section, Scott QY5 in the parcel post authorized delivery section, Scott 1N1 in the A.M.G. section, Scott 1LN1 in the Venezia Giulia section, 1LNC1 in the occupation air post section, 1LNE1 in the occupation special delivery section, and all of the items in the Italian Social Republic area.**

> Values of Italy Nos. 17-91, J1-J27, O1-O8 and Q1-Q6 are for specimens in fine condition with original gum. Very fine to superb stamps sell at higher prices. Copies without gum or with perforations cutting into the design sell at much lower prices.

Watermarks

Wmk. 87-Honeycomb

Wmk. 140-Crown

Wmk. 277-Winged Wheel

Wmk. 303-Multiple Stars

King Victor Emmanuel II
A4 A5

Typographed; Head Embossed
1862 Unwmk. *Perf. 11½x12*

17 A4 10c bister 2,400. 80.00
a. 10c yel brn 2,400. 80.00
b. 10c brown 7,250. 120.00
19 A4 20c dark blue 5.50 9.00
20 A4 40c red 110.00 60.00
21 A4 80c orange 19.00 900.00

The outer frame shows a distinct design on the early printings, while this design is more or less blurred, or even a solid line, on the later printings.

The 20c and 40c exist perf. 11½. These are remainders of Sardinia with forged perforations.

Counterfeit cancellations are often found on No. 21.

Lithographed; Head Embossed
1863 *Imperf.*

22 A4 15c blue 30.00 17.50
a. Head inverted 15,000.
b. Double head 45.00 24.00

See note after Sardinia No. 15.

Two types of No. 23:

Type I- First "C" in bottom line nearly closed. Type II- "C" open. Line broken below "Q."

1863 Litho.

23 A5 15c blue, Type II 1.00 2.00
a. Type I 300.00 5.50
Without gum 11.00

A6 A7

A8

A13

1863-77 Typo. Wmk. 140 *Perf. 14*

No.	Type	Description	Unused	Used
24	A6	1c gray grn	1.40	40
a.		Imperf., pair		4,250.
25	A7	2c org brn ('65)	4.50	38
a.		Imperf., pair	52.50	135.00
26	A8	5c slate grn	210.00	40
27	A8	10c buff	375.00	45
a.		10c org brn	375.00	45
28	A8	10c bl ('77)	850.00	90
29	A8	15c blue	300.00	55
a.		Imperf., pair		3,600.
30	A8	30c brown	5.50	1.10
a.		Imperf., pair		4,250.
31	A8	40c carmine	725.00	75
a.		40c rose	725.00	75
32	A8	60c lilac	5.50	5.50
33	A13	2 l vermilion	12.50	30.00

Nos. 26 to 32 have the head of type A8 but with different corner designs for each value.

Early printings of Nos. 24-27, 29-33 were made in London, later printings in Turin. Values are for Turin printings. London printings of 1c, 2c, 30c, 60c and 2 l sell for more.

No. 29 Surcharged in Brown

1865

Type I- Dots flanking stars in oval, and dot in eight check-mark ornaments in corners.
Type II- Dots in oval, none in corners.
Type III- No dots.

No.	Type	Description	Unused	Used
34	A8	20c on 15c bl (I)	135.00	60
a.		Type II	1,500.	3.00
b.		Type III	425.00	38
c.		Inverted surcharge (I)		18,000.
d.		Double surcharge (I)		
e.		Double surcharge (III)		5,750.

A15

1867-77 Typo.

No.	Type	Description	Unused	Used
35	A15	20c blue	135.00	24
36	A15	20c org ('77)	450.00	45

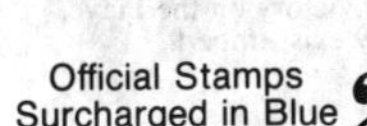
Official Stamps Surcharged in Blue

1877

No.	Type	Description	Unused	Used
37	O1	2c on 2c lake	27.50	3.00
38	O1	2c on 5c lake	27.50	4.00
39	O1	2c on 20c lake	165.00	1.25
40	O1	2c on 30c lake	52.50	1.65
41	O1	2c on 1 l lake	120.00	1.40
42	O1	2c on 2 l lake	125.00	2.00
43	O1	2c on 5 l lake	165.00	3.00
44	O1	2c on 10 l lake	95.00	3.75

Inverted Surcharge

No.	Type	Description	Unused	Used
37a	O1	2c on 2c		450.00
38a	O1	2c on 5c		350.00
39a	O1	2c on 20c	5,500.	350.00
40a	O1	2c on 30c		275.00
41a	O1	2c on 1 l	5,500.	350.00
42a	O1	2c on 2 l	5,500.	350.00
43a	O1	2c on 5 l		350.00
44a	O1	2c on 10 l		350.00

King Humbert I — A17

1879 Typo. *Perf. 14*

No.	Type	Description	Unused	Used
45	A17	5c bl grn	6.00	30
46	A17	10c claret	65.00	24
47	A17	20c orange	60.00	24
48	A17	25c blue	85.00	55
49	A17	30c brown	52.50	900.00
50	A17	50c violet	7.25	2.00
51	A17	2 l vermilion	22.50	75.00

Nos. 45 to 51 have the head of type A17 with different corner designs for each value.

Arms of Savoy — A24

Humbert I — A25

A26

A27

A28

A29

1889

No.	Type	Description	Unused	Used
52	A24	5c dk grn	100.00	75
53	A25	40c brown	4.50	1.00
54	A26	45c gray grn	400.00	1.00
55	A27	60c violet	4.50	3.75
56	A28	1 l brn & yel	5.00	1.00
a.		1 l brn & org	5.00	1.25
57	A29	5 l grn & cl	6.75	210.00

Forged cancellations exist on Nos. 49, 51 and 57.

Parcel Post Stamps of 1884-86 Surcharged in Black

Valevole per le stampe

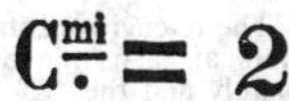

1890

No.	Type	Description	Unused	Used
58	PP1	2c on 10c ol gray	1.10	1.25
a.		Inverted surcharge	45.00	150.00
59	PP1	2c on 20c blue	1.40	1.00
60	PP1	2c on 50c claret	9.00	4.50
a.		Inverted surcharge		4,750.
61	PP1	2c on 75c bl grn	1.10	75
62	PP1	2c on 1.25 l org	9.50	4.25
a.		Inverted surcharge	6,000.	4,750.
63	PP1	2c on 1.75 l brn	5.00	7.50

Stamps of 1879 Surcharged

C.mi 2

1890-91

No.	Type	Description	Unused	Used
64	A17	2c on 5c bl grn ('91)	7.50	12.50
a.		"2" with thin tail	55.00	90.00
65	A17	20c on 30c brn	100.00	1.90
66	A17	20c on 50c vio	105.00	6.00

On Nos. 65-66 the period is omitted in the surcharge.

Arms of Savoy — A33

Humbert I — A34

A35 A36 A37 A38

1891-96 Typo.

No.	Type	Description	Unused	Used
67	A33	5c green	100.00	45
68	A34	10c claret ('96)	4.00	28
69	A35	20c org ('95)	4.00	28
70	A36	25c blue	4.00	40
71	A37	45c ol grn ('95)	4.00	60
72	A38	5 l blue & rose	27.50	37.50

Arms of Savoy — A39

A40

A41

1896-97

No.	Type	Description	Unused	Used
73	A39	1c brown	1.90	90
74	A40	2c orange brown	2.75	22
75	A41	5c green ('97)	5.00	24

A42

Coat of Arms
A43 A44

Victor Emmanuel III
A45 A46

1901-26

No.	Type	Description	Unused	Used
76	A42	1c brown	15	15
a.		Imperf., pair	225.00	400.00
77	A43	2c org brn	15	15
a.		Double impression	18.00	67.50
b.		Imperf., pair	37.50	67.50
78	A44	5c bl grn	15.00	15
a.		Imperf., pair		
79	A45	10c claret	18.00	15
a.		Imperf., pair		4,500.
80	A45	20c orange	4.25	15
81	A45	25c dp bl	20.00	15
a.		25c ultra	20.00	15
82	A46	25c grn & pale grn ('26)	24	15
83	A45	40c brown	120.00	1.50
84	A45	45c ol grn	2.25	15
a.		Imperf., pair	90.00	165.00
85	A45	50c violet	120.00	2.50
86	A46	75c dk red & rose ('26)	75	15
87	A46	1 l brn & grn	1.25	15
a.		Imperf., pair	22.50	37.50
88	A46	1.25 l bl & ultra ('26)	1.40	15
89	A46	2 l dk grn & org ('23)	5.50	55
90	A46	2.50 l dk grn & org ('26)	12.50	48
91	A46	5 l bl & rose	7.50	85
		Nos. 76-91 (16)	328.94	7.53

The borders of Nos. 79-81, 83-85, 87, 89 and 91 differ slightly for each denomination.
On Nos. 82, 86, 88 and 90, the value is expressed as "Cent. 25," etc.
See No. 87b following No. 174G.

No. 80 Surcharged in Black **C. 15**

1905

92	A45 15c on 20c org	30.00	28
a.	Double surcharge		*1,200.*

A47 No. 93 No. 111 No. 123

1906 Unwmk. Engr. *Perf. 12*

93	A47 15c slate	16.00	24
a.	Imperf. horiz. or vert., pair	67.50	90.00
b.	Booklet pane of 6	210.00	

A48

A49

1906-19 Wmk. 140 Typo. *Perf. 14*

94	A48 5c green	15	15
a.	Imperf., pair	17.00	24.00
b.	Printed on both sides	45.00	
95	A48 10c claret	15	15
a.	Imperf., pair	17.00	24.00
96	A48 15c slate ('19)	45	15
a.	Imperf., pair	55.00	67.50
	Set value	60	15

The frame of #95 differs in several details.
See Nos. 96b-96d following No. 174G.

1908-27

97	A49 20c brn org ('25)	24	15
98	A49 20c grn ('25)	22	15
99	A49 20c lil brn ('26)	45	15
100	A49 25c blue	35	15
a.	Imperf., pair	27.50	40.00
b.	Printed on both sides	67.50	100.00
101	A49 25c lt grn ('27)	2.25	2.50
102	A49 30c org brn ('22)	70	18
a.	Imperf., pair	45.00	67.50
103	A49 30c gray ('25)	45	15
104	A49 40c brown	55	15
a.	Imperf., pair	40.00	60.00
105	A49 50c violet	45	15
a.	Imperf., pair	32.50	47.50
106	A49 55c dl vio ('20)	1.50	1.50
107	A49 60c car ('17)	45	15
108	A49 60c blue ('23)	2.75	*9.00*
109	A49 60c brn org ('26)	1.40	15
110	A49 85c red brn ('20)	1.65	52
	Nos. 97-110 (14)	13.41	*15.05*

The upper panels of Nos. 104 and 105 are in solid color with white letters. A body of water has been added to the background.
See Nos. 100c-105j following No. 174G.

A50

A51

Redrawn

Perf. 13x13½, 13½x14

1909-17 Typo. Unwmk.

111	A50 15c slate blk	135.00	40
112	A50 20c brn org ('16)	9.75	75

No. 111 is similar to No. 93, but the design has been redrawn and the stamp is 23mm high instead of 25mm. There is a star at each side of the coat collar, but one is not distinct. See illustrations next to A47.

Wmk. 140 *Perf. 14*

113	A50 20c brn org ('17)	70	15
a.	Imperf., pair	3.75	5.50

Stamps overprinted "Prestito Nazionale, 1917", or later dates, are Thrift or Postal Savings Stamps.

1910, Nov. 1

114	A51 10 l gray grn & red	27.50	4.50

Giuseppe Garibaldi
A52 A53

Perf. 14x13½

1910, Apr. 15 Unwmk.

115	A52 5c green	4.00	7.50
116	A52 15c claret	9.50	12.50

50th anniversary of freedom of Sicily.

1910, Dec. 1

117	A53 5c claret	30.00	27.50
118	A53 15c green	67.50	45.00

50th anniversary of the plebiscite of the southern Italian provinces in 1860.

Symbols of Rome and Turin — A54

Symbol of Valor — A55

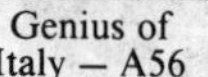

Genius of Italy — A56

Glory of Rome — A57

1911, May 1 Engr. *Perf. 14x13½*

119	A54 2c brown	38	*1.10*
120	A55 5c deep green	1.50	*4.00*
121	A56 10c carmine	2.00	*4.75*
122	A57 15c slate	1.50	*4.75*

50th anniv. of the union of Italian States to form the Kingdom of Italy.
Nos. 115 to 122 were sold at a premium over their face value.

Victor Emmanuel III — A58

Campanile, Venice — A59

1911, Oct. Re-engraved *Perf. 13½*

123	A58 15c slate	8.50	18
a.	Imperf., pair	22.50	55.00
b.	Printed on both sides	100.00	150.00
c.	Bklt. pane of 6	70.00	

The re-engraved stamp is 24mm high. The stars at each side of the coat collar show plainly and the "C" of "Cent" is nearer the frame than in No. 93. See illustrations next to A47.

1912, Apr. 25 *Perf. 14x13½*

124	A59 5c indigo	70	*1.25*
125	A59 15c dk brn	3.00	*5.75*

Issued to commemorate the re-erection of the Campanile at Venice.

Nos. 120-121 Surcharged in Black **2 2**

1913, Mar. 1

126	A55 2c on 5c dp grn	28	55
127	A56 2c on 10c car	38	60

No. 122 Surcharged in Violet **2 2**

128	A57 2c on 15c slate	28	60

No. 123 Surcharged **CENT 20**

1916

129	A58 20c on 15c slate	3.00	18
a.	Bklt. pane of 6	30.00	
b.	Inverted surcharge	47.50	90.00
c.	Double surcharge	30.00	55.00

Old Seal of Republic of Trieste
A60

Allegory of Dante's Divine Comedy
A61

Italy Holding Laurels for Dante
A62

Dante Alighieri
A63

Wmk. 140

1921, June 5 Litho. *Perf. 14*

130	A60 15c blk & rose	55	*5.50*
131	A60 25c bl & rose	55	*5.50*
132	A60 40c brn & rose	55	*5.50*

Reunion of Venezia Giulia with Italy.

1921, Sept. 28 Typo.

133	A61 15c vio brn	45	*3.75*
a.	Imperf., pair	14.00	27.50
134	A62 25c gray grn	45	*3.75*
a.	Imperf., pair	14.00	27.50
135	A63 40c brown	45	*3.75*
a.	Imperf., pair	14.00	27.50

600th anniversary of the death of Dante.
A 15c gray was not issued. Value, $22.50
Nos. 133-135 exist in part perforate pairs.

"Victory" — A64

Perf. 14, 14x13½

1921, Nov. 1 Engr.

136	A64 5c olive grn	24	*38*
137	A64 10c red	35	*48*
138	A64 15c slate grn	70	*1.50*
139	A64 25c ultra	35	*90*

3rd anniv. of the victory on the Piave.
Nos. 136-137, 139 exist imperf.

Flame of Patriotism Tempering Sword of Justice
A65

Giuseppe Mazzini
A66

Mazzini's Tomb
A67

1922, Sept. 20 Typo. *Perf. 14*

No.	Type	Description	Unused	Used
140	A65	25c maroon	90	*9.00*
141	A66	40c vio brn	1.00	*9.00*
142	A67	80c dk bl	90	*9.00*

Issued to commemorate the 50th anniversary of the death of Giuseppe Mazzini (1805-1872), patriot and writer.

Nos. 95, 96, 100 and 104 Overprinted in Black

IX CONGRESSO FILATELICO ITALIANO TRIESTE 1922

1922, June 4 Wmk. 140 *Perf. 14*

No.	Type	Description	Unused	Used
142A	A48	10c claret	135.00	90.00
142B	A48	15c slate	105.00	75.00
142C	A49	25c blue	105.00	75.00
142D	A49	40c brown	150.00	90.00

9th Italian Philatelic Congress, Trieste. Counterfeits exist.

Christ Preaching The Gospel — A68

Portrait at upper right and badge at lower right differ on each value. Portrait at upper left is of Pope Gregory XV. Others: 20c, St. Theresa. 30c, St. Dominic. 50c, St. Francis of Assisi. 1 l, St. Francis Xavier.

1923, June 11

No.	Type	Description	Unused	Used
143	A68	20c ol grn & brn org	75	*15.00*
144	A68	30c cl & brn org	75	*15.00*
145	A68	50c vio & brn org	60	*14.00*
146	A68	1 l bl & brn org	60	*14.00*

300th anniv. of the Propagation of the Faith. Practically the entire issue was delivered to speculators.

Nos. 143-146 exist imperf. and part perf.

Stamps of Previous Issues, Surcharged:

Cent. 7½
a

10 CENTESIMI
b

DIECI
c

Cent. 25
d

Lire 1,75
e

1923-25

No.	Type	Description	Unused	Used
147	A49(a)	7½c on 85c choc	15	35
a.		Double surcharge	150.00	*450.00*
148	A42(b)	10c on 1c brn	15	15
a.		Inverted surcharge	3.50	*6.75*
149	A43(b)	10c on 2c org brn	15	15
a.		Inverted surcharge	9.00	*18.00*
150	A48(c)	10c on 15c sl	15	15
151	A49(a)	20c on 25c bl	15	15
152	A45(d)	25c on 45c ol grn	18	*1.50*
153	A49(a)	25c on 60c bl	70	35
154	A49(a)	30c on 50c vio	15	15
155	A49(a)	30c on 55c dl vio	24	18
156	A49(a)	50c on 40c brn	15	15
a.		Inverted surcharge	45.00	*90.00*
b.		Double surcharge	30.00	55.00
157	A49(a)	50c on 55c dl vio	9.50	3.25
a.		Inverted surcharge	*375.00*	*675.00*
158	A51(e)	1.75 l on 10 l gray grn & red	4.50	5.50
		Nos. 147-158 (12)	16.17	12.03

Years of issue: Nos. 148-149, 156-157, 1923; Nos. 147, 152-153, 1924; others, 1925.

Emblem of the New Government A69

Wreath of Victory, Eagle and Fasces A70

Symbolical of Fascism and Italy — A71

Unwmk.

1923, Oct. 24 Engr. *Perf. 14*

No.	Type	Description	Unused	Used
159	A69	10c dk grn	80	1.40
a.		Imperf., pair	60.00	115.00
160	A69	30c dk vio	90	1.40
161	A69	50c brn car	1.25	*2.25*

Wmk. 140 Typo.

No.	Type	Description	Unused	Used
162	A70	1 l blue	80	1.40
163	A70	2 l brown	1.25	*2.75*
164	A71	5 l blk & bl	4.00	*11.00*
a.		Imperf., pair	75.00	
		Nos. 159-164 (6)	9.00	*20.20*

Issued in commemoration of the anniversary of the March of the Fascisti on Rome.

Fishing Scene A72

Designs: 15c, Mt. Resegone. 30c, Fugitives bidding farewell to native mountains. 50c, Part of Lake Como. 1 l, Manzoni's home, Milan. 5 l, Alessandro Manzoni. The first four designs show scenes from Manzoni's work "I Promessi Sposi."

1923, Dec. 29 *Perf. 14*

No.	Type	Description	Unused	Used
165	A72	10c brn red & blk	32	*6.00*
166	A72	15c bl grn & blk	32	*6.00*
167	A72	30c blk & sl	32	*6.00*
a.		Imperf., pair	*1,800.*	
168	A72	50c org brn & blk	32	*6.00*
169	A72	1 l bl & blk	5.50	*40.00*
a.		Imperf., pair	180.00	*450.00*
170	A72	5 l vio & blk	175.00	*400.00*
a.		Imperf., pair	600.00	
		Nos. 165-170 (6)	181.78	*464.00*

50th anniv. of the death of Alessandro Manzoni.

Nos. 136-139 Surcharged

1924, Feb.

No.	Type	Description	Unused	Used
171	A64	1 l on 5c ol grn	6.75	*30.00*
172	A64	1 l on 10c red	4.50	*30.00*
173	A64	1 l on 15c sl grn	6.75	*30.00*
174	A64	1 l on 25c ultra	4.50	*30.00*

Surcharge forgeries exist.

Perf. 14x13½

No.	Type	Description	Unused	Used
171a	A64	1 l on 5c	14.00	*42.50*
172a	A64	1 l on 10c	9.00	*42.50*
173a	A64	1 l on 15c	14.00	*42.50*
174b	A64	1 l on 25c	9.00	*42.50*

Nos. 95, 102, 105, 108, 110, 87 and 89 Overprinted in Black or Red

CROCIERA ITALIANA 1924

1924, Feb. 16

No.	Type	Description	Unused	Used
174A	A48	10c claret	55	*4.25*
174B	A49	30c org brn	55	*4.25*
174C	A49	50c violet	55	*4.25*
174D	A49	60c bl (R)	5.00	*12.50*
174E	A49	85c choc (R)	1.75	*12.50*
174F	A46	1 l brn & grn	21.00	*75.00*
174G	A46	2 l dk grn & org	14.00	*75.00*
		Nos. 174A-174G (7)	43.40	*187.75*

These stamps were sold on an Italian warship which made a cruise to South American ports in 1924.

Overprint forgeries exist of #174D-174G.

Stamps of 1901-22 with Advertising Labels Attached

Perf. 14 all around, Imperf. between

1924-25

No.	Type	Description	Unused	Used
96b	A48	15c + Bitter Campari	60	2.25
96c	A48	15c + Cordial Campari	60	2.25
96d	A48	15c + Columbia	5.00	5.50
100c	A49	25c + Abrador	20.00	14.00
100d	A49	25c + Coen	45.00	6.75
100e	A49	25c + Piperno	375.00	80.00
100f	A49	25c + Reinach	20.00	9.50
100g	A49	25c + Tagliacozzo	160.00	70.00
102a	A49	30c + Columbia	5.50	5.50
105b	A49	50c + Coen	375.00	9.00
105c	A49	50c + Columbia	2.25	70
105d	A49	50c + De Montel	45	1.65
105e	A49	50c + Piperno	400.00	20.00
105f	A49	50c + Reinach	45.00	7.75
105g	A49	50c + Siero Casali	2.75	5.50
105h	A49	50c + Singer	45	28
105i	A49	50c + Tagliacozzo	*600.00*	47.50
105j	A49	50c + Tantal	47.50	17.00
87b	A46	1 l + Columbia	180.00	95.00
		Nos. 96b-87b (19)	*2,285.*	400.13

No. 113 with Columbia label and No. E3 with Cioccolato Perugina label were prepared but not issued. Values $9, $1.40.

King Victor Emmanuel III — A78

Perf. 11, 13½ (No. 177)

1925-26 Engr. Unwmk.

No.	Type	Description	Unused	Used
175	A78	60c brn car	15	15
a.		Perf. 13½	1.50	28
b.		Imperf., pair	37.50	55.00
176	A78	1 l dk bl	15	15
a.		Perf. 13½	70	24
b.		Imperf., pair	37.50	55.00
177	A78	1.25 l dk bl ('26)	1.35	38
a.		Perf. 11	42.50	11.00
b.		Imperf., pair	135.00	200.00
		Set value		52

25th year of the reign of Victor Emmanuel III.

Nos. 175 to 177 exist with sideways watermark of fragments of letters or a crown, which are normally on the sheet margin.

St. Francis and His Vision A79

Monastery of St. Damien A80

Assisi Monastery A81

1226 VII CENTENARIO FRANCESCANO 1926
LIRE POSTE ITALIANE 1.25

St. Francis' Death A82

St. Francis — A83

1926, Jan. 30 Wmk. 140 *Perf. 14*

No.	Type	Description	Unused	Used
178	A79	20c gray grn	15	15
179	A80	40c dk vio	15	15
180	A81	60c red brn	15	15
a.		Imperf., pair	110.00	110.00

Unwmk. *Perf. 11*

No.	Type	Description	Unused	Used
181	A83	30c slate blk	15	15
a.		Perf. 13½	5.50	1.25
182	A82	1.25 l dark blue	15	18
a.		Perf. 13½	180.00	5.50

Perf. 13½

No.	Type	Description	Unused	Used
183	A83	5 l + 2.50 l dk brn	3.50	*37.50*
		Nos. 178-183 (6)	4.25	*38.28*

700th anniv. of the death of St. Francis of Assisi.

Alessandro Volta — A84

1927 Wmk. 140 Typo. *Perf. 14*

No.	Type	Description	Unused	Used
188	A84	20c dk car	18	15
189	A84	50c grnsh blk	75	15
190	A84	60c chocolate	70	60
191	A84	1.25 l ultra	75	60

Cent. of the death of Alessandro Volta.

The 20c in purple is Cyrenaica No. 25 with overprint omitted.

A85

A86

1927-29 Size: 17½x22mm *Perf. 14*

No.	Type	Description	Unused	Used
192	A85	50c brn & slate	45	15
a.		Imperf., pair	90.00	160.00

Unwmk.

Engr. *Perf. 11*

Size: 19x23mm

No.	Type	Description	Unused	Used
193	A85	1.75 l dp brn	1.40	15
a.		Perf. 13½ ('29)	*6,000.*	400.00
b.		Perf. 11x13½ ('29)		600.00
c.		Perf. 13½x11 ('29)		600.00
194	A85	1.85 l black	18	18
195	A85	2.55 l brn car	1.40	1.50
196	A85	2.65 l dp vio	1.65	*15.00*
		Nos. 192-196 (5)	5.08	*16.98*

1928-29 Wmk. 140 Typo. *Perf. 14*

No.	Type	Description	Unused	Used
197	A86	7½c lt brn	45	*1.25*
198	A86	15c brn org ('29)	55	15
199	A86	35c gray blk ('29)	75	*2.75*
200	A86	50c dl vio	90	15

Emmanuel Philibert, Duke of Savoy — A87

Statue of Philibert, Turin — A88

Philibert and Italian Soldier of 1918 — A89

1928 ***Perf. 11, 14***

201	A87	20c red brn & ultra	24	40
a.		Perf. 13½	9.00	9.50
202	A87	25c dp red & bl grn	24	40
a.		Perf. 13½	6.75	3.75
203	A87	30c bl grn & red brn	35	45
a.		Center inverted	*10,000.*	*2,500.*
b.		Perf. 13½	2.00	2.00
204	A89	50c org brn & bl	18	15
205	A89	75c dp red	28	18
206	A88	1.25 l bl & blk	40	30
207	A89	1.75 l bl grn	70	75
208	A87	5 l vio & bl grn	2.75	*21.00*
209	A89	10 l blk & pink	5.00	*57.50*
210	A88	20 l vio & blk	7.75	*180.00*
		Nos. 201-210 (10)	17.89	*261.13*

400th anniv. of the birth of Emmanuel Philibert, Duke of Savoy; 10th anniv. of the victory of 1918; Turin Exhibition.

She-wolf Suckling Romulus and Remus
A90 A95a

Julius Caesar — A91

Augustus Caesar — A92

"Italia" — A93

A94

A95

1929-42 Wmk. 140 Photo. ***Perf. 14***

213	A90	5c ol brn	15	15
214	A91	7½c dp vio	15	15
215	A92	10c dk brn	15	15
216	A93	15c sl grn	15	15
217	A91	20c rose red	15	15
218	A94	25c dp grn	15	15
219	A95	30c ol brn	15	15
a.		Imperf., pair	225.00	
220	A93	35c dp bl	15	15
221	A95	50c purple	15	15
a.		Imperf., pair	75.00	115.00
222	A94	75c rose red	15	15
222A	A91	1 l dk pur ('42)	15	15
223	A94	1.25 l dp bl	15	15
224	A92	1.75 l red org	15	15
225	A93	2 l car lake	15	15
226	A95a	2.55 l slate grn	15	15
226A	A95a	3.70 l pur ('30)	15	15
227	A95a	5 l rose red	15	15
228	A93	10 l purple	15	24
229	A91	20 l lt grn	60	*2.25*
230	A92	25 l bluish sl	1.25	*7.75*
231	A94	50 l dp vio	1.90	*14.00*
		Set value	4.75	

See Nos. 427-438, 441-459.

Stamps of the 1929-42 issue overprinted "G.N.R." are 1943 local issues of the Guardia Nazionale Repubblicana.

Courtyard of Monte Cassino A96

Monks Laying Cornerstone A98

St. Benedict of Nursia — A100

Designs: 25c, Fresco, "Death of St. Benedict." 75c+15c, 5 l+1 l, Monte Cassino Abbey.

1929, Aug. 1 Photo. Wmk. 140

232	A96	20c red org	24	15
233	A96	25c dk grn	24	15
234	A98	50c + 10c ol brn	70	*3.00*
235	A98	75c + 15c crim	75	*4.50*
236	A96	1.25 l + 25c saph	90	*5.75*
237	A98	5 l + 1 l dk vio	1.00	*18.00*

Unwmk. Engr.

238	A100	10 l + 2 l sl grn	1.50	*32.50*
		Nos. 232-238 (7)	5.33	*64.05*

14th cent. of the founding of the Abbey of Monte Cassino by St. Benedict in 529 A.D. The premium on some of the stamps was given to the committee for the celebration of the centenary.

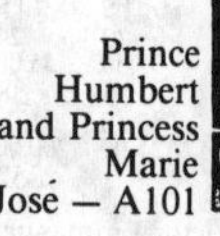

Prince Humbert and Princess Marie José — A101

1930, Jan. 8 Photo. Wmk. 140

239	A101	20c org red	20	15
240	A101	50c + 10c ol brn	60	90
241	A101	1.25 l + 25c dp bl	85	*3.00*

Marriage of Prince Humbert of Savoy with Princess Marie Jose of Belgium.

The surtax on Nos. 240 and 241 was for the benefit of the Italian Red Cross Society.

The 20c in green is Cyrenaica No. 35 with overprint omitted.

Ferrucci Leading His Army A102

Fabrizio Maramaldo Killing Ferrucci A103

Francesco Ferrucci — A104

1930, July 10

242	A102	20c rose red	15	18
243	A103	25c dp grn	15	18
244	A103	50c purple	15	15
245	A103	1.25 l dp bl	35	75
246	A104	5 l + 2 l org red	1.90	*32.50*
		Nos. 242-246 (5)	2.70	*33.76*

4th cent. of the death of Francesco Ferrucci, Tuscan warrior.

See Nos. C20-C22.

Helenus and Aeneas A106

Designs: 20c, Anchises and Aeneas watch passing of Roman Legions. 25c, Aeneas feasting in shade of Albunea. 30c, Ceres and her children with fruits of Earth. 50c, Harvesters at work. 75c, Woman at loom, children and calf. 1.25 l, Anchises and his sailors in sight of Italy. 5 l+1.50 l, Shepherd piping by fireside. 10 l+2.50 l, Aeneas leading his army.

1930, Oct. 21 Photo. ***Perf. 14***

248	A106	15c ol brn	18	20
249	A106	20c orange	18	20
250	A106	25c green	22	18
251	A106	30c dl vio	28	22
252	A106	50c violet	18	15
253	A106	75c rose red	45	55
254	A106	1.25 l blue	55	45

Unwmk. Engr.

255	A106	5 l +1.50 l red brn	13.00	*50.00*
256	A106	10 l +2.50 l gray grn	13.00	*50.00*
		Nos. 248-256 (9)	28.04	*101.95*

Bimillenary of the birth of Virgil. Surtax on Nos. 255-256 was for the National Institute Figli del Littorio.

See Nos. C23-C26.

Arms of Italy (Fascist Emblems Support House of Savoy Arms) — A115

1930, Dec. 16 Photo. Wmk. 140

257	A115	2c deep orange	15	15

St. Anthony being Installed as a Franciscan A116

Olivares Hermitage, Portugal A118

St. Anthony Freeing Prisoners A120

St. Anthony's Death A121

St. Anthony Succoring the Poor — A122

Designs: 25c, St. Anthony preaching to the fishes. 50c, Basilica of St. Anthony, Padua.

Wmk. 140

1931, Mar. 9 Photo. ***Perf. 14***

258	A116	20c dl vio	24	18
259	A116	25c gray grn	35	18
260	A118	30c brown	45	24
261	A118	50c violet	24	15
262	A120	1.25 l blue	1.50	70

Unwmk. Engr.

263	A121	75c brn red	2.00	1.25
a.		Perf. 12	50.00	57.50
264	A122	5 l + 2.50 l ol grn	9.00	*47.50*
		Nos. 258-264 (7)	13.78	*50.20*

Issued to commemorate the seventh centenary of the death of Saint Anthony of Padua.

Tower of Meloria — A123

Training Ship "Amerigo Vespucci" A124

Cruiser "Trento" A125

1931, Nov. 29 Photo. Wmk. 140

265	A123	20c rose red	24	18
266	A124	50c purple	28	15
267	A125	1.25 l dk bl	1.10	55

50th anniv. of the Royal Naval Academy at Leghorn (Livorno) in 1881.

Giovanni Boccaccio A126

Designs: 15c, Niccolo Machiavelli. 20c, Paolo Sarpi. 25c, Count Vittorio Alfieri. 30c, Ugo Foscolo. 50c, Count Giacomo Leopardi. 75c, Giosue Carducci. 1.25 l, Carlo Giuseppe Botta. 1.75 l, Torquato Tasso. 2.75 l, Francesco Petrarca. 5 l+2 l, Ludovico Ariosto. 10 l+2.50 l, Dante Alighieri.

1932, Mar. 14 ***Perf. 14***

268	A126	10c ol brn	22	28
269	A126	15c sl grn	28	18
270	A126	20c rose red	22	15
271	A126	25c dp grn	30	18
272	A126	30c ol brn	42	18
273	A126	50c violet	15	15
274	A126	75c car rose	1.00	1.00
275	A126	1.25 l dp bl	65	65
276	A126	1.75 l orange	1.00	1.00
277	A126	2.75 l gray	5.00	*9.00*
278	A126	5 l + 2 l car rose	7.75	*45.00*
279	A126	10 l + 2.50 l ol grn	9.00	*55.00*
		Nos. 268-279 (12)	25.99	*112.77*

Dante Alighieri Society, a natl. literary association founded to promote development of the Italian language and culture. The surtax was added to the Society funds to help in its work.

See Nos. C28-C34.

View of Caprera A138

Garibaldi Carrying His Dying Wife
A141

Garibaldi Memorial
A144

Giuseppe Garibaldi
A145

Designs: 20c, 30c, Garibaldi meeting Victor Emmanuel II. 25c, 50c, Garibaldi at Battle of Calatafimi. 1.25 l, Garibaldi's tomb. 1.75 l+25c, Rock of Quarto.

1932, Apr. 6

280	A138	10c gray blk	28	18
281	A138	20c ol brn	28	18
282	A138	25c dl grn	55	28
283	A138	30c orange	65	28
284	A138	50c violet	32	15
285	A141	75c rose red	1.75	1.00
286	A141	1.25 l dp bl	1.50	70
287	A141	1.75 l + 25c bl gray	6.50	*24.00*
288	A144	2.55 l + 50c red brn	8.25	*30.00*
289	A145	5 l + 1 l cop red	9.25	*35.00*
		Nos. 280-289 (10)	29.33	*91.77*

50th anniv. of the death of Giuseppe Garibaldi, patriot.
See Nos. C35-C39, CE1-CE2.

Plowing with Oxen and Tractor
A146

Designs: 10c, Soldier guarding mountain pass. 15c, Marine, battleship and seaplane. 20c, Head of Facist youth. 25c, Hands of workers and tools. 30c, Flags, Bible and altar. 35c, "New roads for the new Legions." 50c, Mussolini statue, Bologna. 60c, Hands with spades. 75c, Excavating ruins. 1 l, Steamers and galleons. 1.25 l, Italian flag, map and points of compass. 1.75 l, Flag, athlete and stadium. 2.55 l, Mother and child. 2.75 l, Emblems of drama, music, art and sport. 5 l+2.50 l, Roman emperor.

1932, Oct. 27 **Photo.**

290	A146	5c dk brn	16	15
291	A146	10c dk brn	22	15
292	A146	15c dk gray grn	28	18
293	A146	20c car rose	22	15
294	A146	25c dp grn	28	15
295	A146	30c dk brn	32	45
296	A146	35c dk bl	90	*1.90*
297	A146	50c purple	16	15
298	A146	60c org brn	1.00	1.25
299	A146	75c car rose	55	40
300	A146	1 l blk vio	70	65
301	A146	1.25 l dp bl	52	35
302	A146	1.75 l orange	70	35
303	A146	2.55 l dk gray	8.50	*12.00*
304	A146	2.75 l slate grn	8.50	*13.00*
305	A146	5 l + 2.50 l car rose	14.00	*57.50*
		Nos. 290-305 (16)	37.01	*88.78*

10th anniv. of the Fascist government and the March on Rome.
See Nos. C40-C41, E16-E17.

Statue of Athlete
A162

Cross in Halo, St. Peter's Dome
A163

1933, Aug. 16 ***Perf. 14***

306	A162	10c dk brn	15	18
307	A162	20c rose red	15	24
308	A162	50c purple	20	18
309	A162	1.25 l blue	85	1.25

Issued in connection with the International University Games at Turin, September, 1933.

1933, Oct. 23

Designs: 25c, 50c, Angel with cross. 1.25 l, as 20c. 2.55 l, + 2.50 l, Cross with doves.

310	A163	20c rose red	35	18
311	A163	25c green	45	24
312	A163	50c purple	35	15
313	A163	1.25 l dp bl	65	65
314	A163	2.55 l + 2.50 l blk	1.90	*32.50*
		Nos. 310-314 (5)	3.70	*33.72*

Issued at the solicitation of the Order of the Holy Sepulchre of Jerusalem to mark the Holy Year.
See Nos. CB1-CB2.

Anchor of the "Emanuele Filiberto"
A166

Antonio Pacinotti
A172

Designs: 20c, Anchor. 50c, Gabriele d'Annunzio. 1.25 l, St. Vito's Tower. 1.75 l, Symbolizing Fiume's annexation. 2.55 l+2 l, Victor Emmanuel III arriving aboard "Brindisi." 2.75 l+2.50 l, Galley, gondola and battleship.

1934, Mar. 12

315	A166	10c dk brn	1.90	28
316	A166	20c rose red	18	18
317	A166	50c purple	18	15
318	A166	1.25 l blue	24	*90*
319	A166	1.75 l + 1 l ind	35	*12.00*
320	A166	2.55 l + 2 l dl vio	35	*16.00*
321	A166	2.75 l + 2.50 l ol grn	35	*18.00*
		Nos. 315-321 (7)	3.55	*47.51*

10th anniversary of annexation of Fiume. See Nos. C56-C61, CE5-CE7.

1934, May 23

322	A172	50c purple	45	15
323	A172	1.25 l sapphire	45	90

75th anniversary of invention of the dynamo by Antonio Pacinotti (1841-1912), scientist.

Guarding the Goal — A173

Players — A175

Soccer Players
A174

1934, May 23

324	A173	20c red org	1.90	1.25
325	A174	25c green	1.90	60
326	A174	50c purple	1.90	18
327	A174	1.25 l blue	6.50	3.25
328	A175	5 l + 2.50 l brn	22.50	*67.50*
		Nos. 324-328 (5)	34.70	*72.78*

2nd World Soccer Championship. See Nos. C62-C65.

Luigi Galvani — A176

1934, Aug. 16

329	A176	30c brn, *buff*	70	24
330	A176	75c car, *rose*	70	1.25

Intl. Congress of Electro-Radio-Biology.

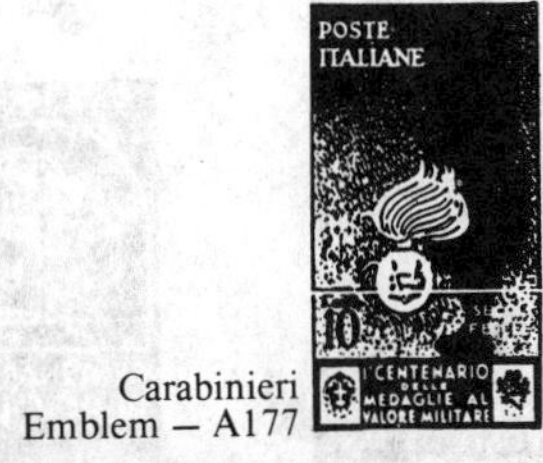

Carabinieri Emblem — A177

Cutting Barbed Wire
A178

Designs: 20c, Sardinian Grenadier and soldier throwing grenade. 25c, Alpine Infantry. 30c, Military courage. 75c, Artillery. 1.25 l, Acclaiming the Service. 1.75 l+1 l, Cavalry. 2.55 l+2 l, Sapping Detail. 2.75 l+2 l, First aid.

1934, Sept. 6 **Photo.** **Wmk. 140**

331	A177	10c dk brn	28	28
332	A178	15c ol grn	40	60
333	A178	20c rose red	35	24
334	A177	25c green	45	24
335	A178	30c dk brn	75	75
336	A178	50c purple	75	18
337	A178	75c car rose	1.65	1.40
338	A178	1.25 l dk bl	1.40	1.00
339	A177	1.75 l + 1 l red org	5.50	*20.00*
340	A178	2.55 l + 2 l dp cl	6.25	*22.50*
341	A178	2.75 l + 2 l vio	7.25	*24.00*
		Nos. 331-341 (11)	25.03	*71.19*

Centenary of Military Medal of Valor. See Nos. C66-C72.

Man Holding Fasces
A187

Standard Bearer, Bayonet Attack
A188

Design: 30c, Eagle and soldier.

1935, Apr. 23 ***Perf. 14***

342	A187	20c rose red	18	18
343	A187	30c dk brn	75	1.10
344	A188	50c purple	15	15

Issued in honor of the University Contests.

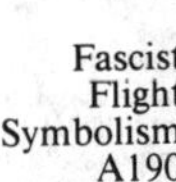

Fascist Flight Symbolism
A190

Leonardo da Vinci — A191

1935, Oct. 1

345	A190	20c rose red	75	35
346	A190	30c brown	6.00	90
347	A191	50c purple	14.00	24
348	A191	1.25 l dk bl	4.50	1.00

International Aeronautical Salon, Milan.

Vincenzo Bellini — A192

Bellini's Villa — A194

Bellini's Piano
A193

1935, Oct. 15

349	A192	20c rose red	52	30
350	A192	30c brown	85	45
351	A192	50c violet	52	22
352	A192	1.25 l dk bl	1.90	1.40
353	A193	1.75 l + 1 l red org	9.25	*30.00*
354	A194	2.75 l + 2 l ol blk	13.00	*35.00*
		Nos. 349-354 (6)	26.04	*67.37*

Bellini (1801-35), operatic composer.
See Nos. C79-C83.

Map of Italian Industries
A195

Designs: 20c, 1.25l, Map of Italian Industries. 30c, 50c, Cogwheel and plow.

1936, Mar. 23

355	A195	20c red	15	15
356	A195	30c brown	18	18
357	A195	50c purple	15	15
358	A195	1.25 l blue	38	40

The 17th Milan Trade Fair.

Flock of Sheep
A197

Ajax Defying the Lightning
A199

Bust of Horace
A200

Designs: 20c, 1.25 l+1 l, Countryside in Spring. 75c, Capitol. 1.75 l+1 l, Pan piping. 2.55 l+1 l, Dying warrior.

Wmk. Crowns (140)

1936, July 1 Photo. *Perf. 14*

359	A197	10c dp grn	48	22
360	A197	20c rose red	42	22
361	A199	30c ol brn	48	35
362	A200	50c purple	42	15
363	A197	75c rose red	80	70
364	A197	1.25 l + 1 l dk bl	5.50	*15.00*
365	A199	1.75 l + 1 l car rose	6.50	*30.00*
366	A197	2.55 l + 1 l sl blk	11.00	*37.50*
		Nos. 359-366 (8)	25.60	*84.14*

2000th anniv. of the birth of Quintus Horatius Flaccus (Horace), Roman poet. See Nos. C84-C88.

Child Holding Wheat A204

Child Giving Salute A205

Child and Fasces A206

"Il Bambino" by della Robbia A207

1937, June 28

367	A204	10c yel brn	28	24
368	A205	20c car rose	28	24
369	A204	25c green	35	28
370	A206	30c dk brn	60	40
371	A205	50c purple	35	18
372	A207	75c rose red	1.65	75
373	A205	1.25 l dk bl	2.00	1.00
374	A206	1.75 l + 75c org	9.00	*30.00*
375	A207	2.75 l + 1.25 l dk bl grn	6.00	*32.50*
376	A205	5 l + 3 l bl gray	6.00	*35.00*
		Nos. 367-376 (10)	26.51	*100.59*

Issued to commemorate the Summer Exhibition for Child Welfare. The surtax on Nos. 374 to 376 was used to support summer camps for children.

See Nos. C89-C94.

Rostral Column — A208

Designs: 15c, Army Trophies. 20c, Augustus Caesar (Octavianus) offering sacrifice. 25c, Cross and Roman Standards. 30c, Julius Caesar and Julian Star. 50c, Augustus receiving acclaim. 75c, Augustus Caesar. 1.25 l, Symbolizing maritime glory of Rome. 1.75 l+1 l, Sacrificial Altar. 2.55 l+2 l, Capitol.

1937, Sept. 23

377	A208	10c myr grn	32	20
378	A208	15c ol grn	32	28
379	A208	20c red	32	22
380	A208	25c green	32	20
381	A208	30c ol bis	50	28
382	A208	50c purple	32	18
383	A208	75c scarlet	65	70
384	A208	1.25 l dk bl	85	70
385	A208	1.75 l + 1 l plum	10.00	*22.50*
386	A208	2.55 l + 2 l sl blk	12.50	*24.00*
		Nos. 377-386 (10)	26.10	*49.26*

Bimillenary of the birth of Emperor Augustus Caesar (Octavianus) on the occasion of the exhibition opened in Rome by Mussolini, Sept. 22, 1937.

See Nos. C95-C99.

Gasparo Luigi Pacifico Spontini A218

Antonius Stradivarius A219

Count Giacomo Leopardi A220

Giovanni Battista Pergolesi A221

Giotto di Bondone — A222

1937, Oct. 25

387	A218	10c dk brn	15	20
388	A219	20c rose red	15	20
389	A220	25c dk grn	15	18
390	A221	30c dk brn	15	28
391	A220	50c purple	15	18
392	A221	75c crimson	38	75
393	A222	1.25 l dp bl	40	90
394	A218	1.75 l dp org	40	90
395	A219	2.55 l + 2 l gray grn	3.25	*22.50*
396	A222	2.75 l + 2 l red brn	3.25	*24.00*
		Nos. 387-396 (10)	8.43	*50.09*

Centennials of Spontini, Stradivarius, Leopardi, Pergolesi and Giotto.

Guglielmo Marconi A223

Romulus Plowing A224

1938, Jan. 24

397	A223	20c rose pink	45	15
398	A223	50c purple	15	15
399	A223	1.25 l blue	30	60

Guglielmo Marconi (1874-1937), electrical engineer, inventor of wireless telegraphy.

1938, Oct. 28

Designs: 20c, Augustus Caesar (Octavianus). 25c, Dante. 30c, Columbus. 50c, Leonardo da Vinci. 75c, Victor Emmanuel II and Garibaldi. 1.25 l, Tomb of Unknown Soldier, Rome. 1.75 l, Blackshirts' March on Rome, 1922. 2.75 l, Map of Italian East Africa and Iron Crown of Monza. 5 l, Victor Emmanuel III.

400	A224	10c brown	18	15
401	A224	20c car rose	18	15
402	A224	25c dk grn	18	15
403	A224	30c ol brn	18	18
404	A224	50c lt vio	18	15
405	A224	75c rose red	35	28
406	A224	1.25 l dp bl	45	28
407	A224	1.75 l vio blk	60	28
408	A224	2.75 l sl grn	2.75	*7.75*
409	A224	5 l lt red brn	3.25	*9.25*
		Nos. 400-409 (10)	8.30	*18.62*

Issued to commemorate the proclamation of the Empire. See Nos. C100-C105.

Wood-burning Engine and Streamlined Electric Engine — A234

1939, Dec. 15 Photo. *Perf. 14*

410	A234	20c rose red	15	15
411	A234	50c brt vio	15	15
412	A234	1.25 l dp bl	24	60

Centenary of Italian railroads.

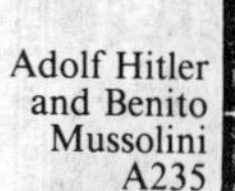

Adolf Hitler and Benito Mussolini A235

Hitler and Mussolini A236

1941 Wmk. 140

413	A235	10c dp brn	15	15
414	A235	20c red org	15	15
415	A235	25c dp grn	15	15
416	A236	50c violet	15	15
417	A236	75c rose red	18	18
418	A236	1.25 l dp bl	18	28
		Nos. 413-418 (6)	96	1.06

Rome-Berlin Axis.

Stamps of type A236 in the denominations and colors of Nos. 413 to 415 were prepared but not issued. They were sold for charitable purposes in 1948. Value $4 each.

Galileo Teaching Mathematics at Padua — A237

Designs: 25c, Galileo presenting telescope to Doge of Venice. 50c, Galileo Galilei (1564-1642). 1.25 l, Galileo studying at Arcetri.

1942, Sept. 28

419	A237	10c dk org & lake	15	18
420	A237	25c gray grn & grn	15	22
421	A237	50c brn vio & vio	15	22
a.		Frame missing		*400.00*
422	A237	1.25 l Prus bl & ultra	15	45
		Set value		42

Statue of Rossini — A241

Gioacchino Rossini — A242

1942, Nov. 23 Photo.

423	A241	25c dp grn	15	15
424	A241	30c brown	15	18
425	A242	50c violet	15	15
426	A242	1 l blue	15	35
		Set value		36

150th anniv. of the birth of Gioacchino Antonio Rossini (1792-1868), operatic composer.

"Victory for the Axis" A243

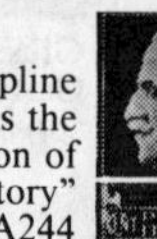

"Discipline is the Weapon of Victory" A244

"Everything and Everyone for Victory" A245

"Arms and Hearts Must Be Stretched Out Towards the Goal" A246

Perf. 14 all around, Imperf. between

1942 Photo. Wmk. 140

427	A243	25c dp grn	15	18
428	A244	25c dp grn	15	18
429	A245	25c dp grn	15	18
430	A246	25c dp grn	15	18
431	A243	30c ol brn	15	*55*
432	A244	30c ol brn	15	*55*
433	A245	30c ol brn	15	*55*
434	A246	30c ol brn	15	*55*
435	A243	50c purple	15	18
436	A244	50c purple	15	18
437	A245	50c purple	15	18
438	A246	50c purple	15	18
		Set value		80

Issued in honor of the Italian Army.

The left halves of Nos. 431-438 are type A95.

She-Wolf Suckling Romulus and Remus — A247

Perf. 10½x11½, 11x11½, 11½, 14

1944, Jan. Litho. Wmk. 87

Without Gum

439	A247	50c rose vio & bis rose	28	40

Unwmk.

440	A247	50c rose vio & pale rose	15	18

Nos. 439-440 exist imperf., part perf.

Types of 1929

1945, May Unwmk. *Perf. 14*

441	A93	15c slate green	15	15
442	A93	35c deep blue	15	15
443	A91	1 l deep violet	15	15
		Set value	25	36

Types of 1929 Redrawn
Fasces Removed

Victor Emmanuel III
A248

Julius Caesar
A249

1944-45 Wmk. 140 Photo. *Perf. 14*

No.	Type	Description	Unused	Used
444	A248	30c dk brn	15	15
445	A248	50c purple	18	60
446	A248	60c slate grn ('45)	15	18
447	A249	1 l dp bl ('45)	15	15
		Set value		48

Augustus Caesar
A250

"Italia"
A251

A252

1945 Unwmk. *Perf. 14*

No.	Type	Description	Unused	Used
448	A250	10c dk brn	15	15
448A	A249	20c rose red	15	15
449	A251	50c dk vio	15	15
450	A248	60c sl grn	15	15
451	A251	60c red org	15	15
452	A249	1 l dp vio	15	15
452A	A249	1 l dp vio, redrawn	15	15
452B	A251	2 l dp car	15	15
452C	A251	10 l purple	60	1.25
		Set value	1.35	2.00

1945 Wmk. 277

No.	Type	Description	Unused	Used
453	A249	20c rose red	15	15
454	A248	60c slate grn	15	15
455	A249	1 l dp vio	15	15
456	A251	1.20 l dk brn	15	15
457	A251	2 l dk red	15	15
458	A252	5 l dk red	15	15
459	A251	10 l purple	70	1.25
		Set value	1.25	1.75

Nos. 452A and 457 are redrawings of types A249 and A251. In the redrawn 1 l, the "L" of "LIRE" extends under the "IRE" and the letters of "POSTE ITALIANE" are larger. In the original the "L" extends only under the "I."

In the redrawn 2 l, the "2" is smaller and thinner, and the design is less distinct.

No. 224 Surcharged in Black

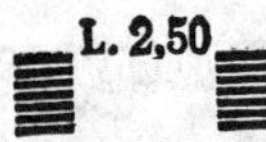

1945, Mar. Wmk. 140

No.	Type	Description	Unused	Used
460	A92	2.50 l on 1.75 l red org	15	15
a.		Six bars at left	70	90

Loggia dei Mercanti, Bologna
A253

Basilica of San Lorenzo, Rome
A254

Stamps of Italian Social Republic Surcharged in Black

1945, May 2 Photo. *Perf. 14*

No.	Type	Description	Unused	Used
461	A253	1.20 l on 20c crim	15	15
462	A254	2 l on 25c green	15	15
a.		2½ mm between "2" and "LIRE"	45	70
		Set value	15	24

Breaking Chain — A255

United Family and Scales — A256

Planting Tree — A257

Tying Tree — A258

Torch
A259

"Italia" and Sprouting Oak Stump
A260

1945-47 Wmk. 277 Photo. *Perf. 14*

No.	Type	Description	Unused	Used
463	A255	10c rose brn	15	15
464	A256	20c dk brn	15	15
464A	A256	25c brt bl grn ('46)	15	15
465	A257	40c slate	15	15
465A	A255	50c dp vio ('46)	15	15
466	A258	60c dk grn	15	15
467	A255	80c car rose	15	15
468	A257	1 l dk grn	15	15
469	A259	1.20 l chestnut	15	15
470	A258	2 l dk cl brn	15	15
471	A259	3 l red	15	15
471A	A259	4 l red org ('46)	24	15
472	A256	5 l deep blue	15	15
472A	A257	6 l dp vio ('47)	42	15
473	A255	10 l slate	15	15
473A	A257	15 l dp bl ('46)	90	15
474	A259	20 l dk red vio	18	15
475	A260	25 l dk grn	1.90	15
476	A260	50 l dk vio brn	75	15
		Set value	5.25	90

See Nos. 486-488.

United Family and Scales
A261

1946 Engr. *Perf. 14*

No.	Type	Description	Unused	Used
477	A261	100 l car lake	50.00	1.25
a.		Perf. 14x13½	55.00	1.50

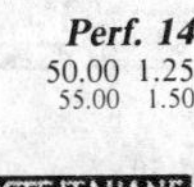

Cathedral of St. Andrea, Amalfi
A262

Church of St. Michael, Lucca
A263

"Peace" from Fresco at Siena
A264

Signoria Palace, Florence
A265

View of Cathedral Domes, Pisa — A266

Republic of Genoa
A267

"Venice Crowned by Glory," by Paolo Veronese
A268

Oath of Pontida
A269

1946, Oct. 30

No.	Type	Description	Unused	Used
478	A262	1 l brown	15	15
479	A263	2 l dk bl	15	15
480	A264	3 l dk bl grn	15	15
481	A265	4 l dp org	15	15
482	A266	5 l dp vio	15	15
483	A267	10 l car rose	15	15
484	A268	15 l dp ultra	22	28
485	A269	20 l red brn	15	15
		Set value	65	65

Proclamation of the Republic.

Types of 1945

1947-48 Wmk. 277 Photo. *Perf. 14*

No.	Type	Description	Unused	Used
486	A255	8 l dk grn ('48)	25	15
487	A256	10 l red org	2.25	15
488	A259	30 l dk bl ('48)	42.50	15
		Set value		17

St. Catherine Giving Mantle to Beggar — A270

Designs: 5 l, St. Catherine carrying cross. 10 l, St. Catherine, arms outstretched. 30 l, St. Catherine and scribe.

1948, Mar. 1 Photo.

No.	Type	Description	Unused	Used
489	A270	3 l yel grn & gray grn	18	18
490	A270	5 l vio & bl	28	32
491	A270	10 l red brn & vio	35	40
492	A270	30 l bis & gray brn	1.75	2.25
		Nos. 489-492,C127-C128 (6)	29.81	31.90

600th anniv. of the birth of St. Catherine of Siena, Patroness of Italy.

"Constitutional Government" — A271

1948, Apr. 12

No.	Type	Description	Unused	Used
493	A271	10 l rose vio	18	35
494	A271	30 l blue	85	70

Issued to commemorate the proclamation of the constitution of January 1, 1948.

Uprising at Palermo, Jan. 12, 1848
A272

Designs (Revolutionary scenes): 4 l, Rebellion at Padua. 5 l, Proclamation of statute, Turin. 6 l, "Five Days of Milan." 8 l, Daniele Manin proclaming the Republic of Venice. 10 l, Defense of Vicenza. 12 l, Battle of Curtatone. 15 l, Battle of Gioto. 20 l, Insurrection at Bologna. 30 l, "Ten Days of Brescia." 50 l, Garibaldi in Rome fighting. 100 l, Death of Goffredo Mameli.

1948, May 3

No.	Type	Description	Unused	Used
495	A272	3 l dk brn	15	15
496	A272	4 l red vio	15	15
497	A272	5 l dp bl	15	15
498	A272	6 l dp yel grn	15	35
499	A272	8 l brown	15	28
500	A272	10 l org red	24	15
501	A272	12 l dk gray grn	40	*1.00*
502	A272	15 l gray blk	1.10	48
503	A272	20 l car rose	3.00	3.25
504	A272	30 l brt ultra	1.40	28
505	A272	50 l violet	22.50	1.25
506	A272	100 l bl blk	27.50	9.50
		Nos. 495-506 (12)	56.89	16.99

Centenary of the Risorgimento, uprisings of 1848-49 which led to Italian unification.
See No. E26.

Alpine Soldier and Bassano Bridge
A273

1948, Oct. 1 Wmk. 277 *Perf. 14*

No.	Type	Description	Unused	Used
507	A273	15 l dk grn	65	75

Issued to commemorate the re-opening of the Bridge of Bassano, October 3, 1948.

Gaetano Donizetti — A274

1948, Oct. 23 Photo.

No.	Type	Description	Unused	Used
508	A274	15 l dk brn	65	75

Issued to commemorate the centenary of the death of Gaetano Donizetti, composer.

Fair Buildings
A275

1949, Apr. 12

No.	Type	Description	Unused	Used
509	A275	20 l dk brn	1.50	1.10

27th Milan Trade Fair, April 1949.

Standard of Doges of Venice — A276

Designs: 15 l, Clock strikers, Lion Tower and Campanile of St. Mark's. 20 l, Lion standard and Venetian galley. 50 l, Lion tower and gulls.

1949, Apr. 12

Buff Background

510 A276	5 l red brn	15	15
511 A276	15 l dk grn	90	60
512 A276	20 l dp red brn	1.10	15
513 A276	50 l dk bl	7.25	60

Issued to commemorate 50th anniversary of the Biennial Art Exhibition of Venice.

"Transportation" and Globes — A277

1949, May 2 Wmk. 277 *Perf. 14*

514 A277 50 l brt ultra 7.50 2.00

75th anniv. of the UPU.

Workman and Ship — A278

1949, May 30 Photo.

515 A278	5 l dk grn	1.75	3.00
516 A278	15 l violet	4.75	7.25
517 A278	20 l brown	27.50	8.25

European Recovery Program.

The Vascello, Rome A279

1949, May 18

518 A279 100 l brown 60.00 35.00

Centenary of Roman Republic.

Giuseppe Mazzini A280

Vittorio Alfieri A281

1949, June 1

519 A280 20 l gray 1.90 85

Issued to commemorate the erection of a monument to Giuseppe Mazzini (1805-1872), Italian patriot and revolutionary.

1949, June 4 Photo.

520 A281 20 l brown 2.25 85

200th anniv. of the birth of Vittorio Alfieri, tragic dramatist.

Values quoted in this catalogue are for stamps graded at Fine-Very Fine and with no faults. An illustrated guide to grade is provided in introductory material, beginning on Page 1A.

Basilica of St. Just, Trieste A282

1949, June 8

521 A282 20 l brn red 4.00 5.50

Trieste election, June 12, 1949.

Staff of Aesculapius, Globe — A283

1949, June 13 Wmk. 277 *Perf. 14*

522 A283 20 l violet 6.00 6.00

2nd World Health Cong., Rome, 1949.

Lorenzo de Medici A284

Andrea Palladio A285

1949, Aug. 4

523 A284 20 l vio bl 2.00 75

Issued to commemorate the 500th anniversary of the birth of Lorenzo de Medici.

1949, Aug. 4

524 A285 20 l violet 4.00 3.00

Andrea Palladio (1518-1580), architect.

Tartan and Fair Buildings A286

1949, Aug. 16

525 A286 20 l red 1.25 75

133th Levant Fair, Bari, September, 1949.

Voltaic Pile — A287

Alessandro Volta — A288

1949, Sept. 14 Engr. *Perf. 14*

526 A287	20 l rose car	1.00	85
a.	Perf. 13x14	15.00	2.50
527 A288	50 l deep blue	15.00	6.75
a.	Perf. 13x14	150.00	50.00

Issued to commemorate the 150th anniversary of the invention of the Voltaic Pile.

Holy Trinity Bridge — A289

1949, Sept. 19 Photo.

528 A289 20 l dp grn 4.00 75

Issued to publicize plans to reconstruct Holy Trinity Bridge, Florence.

Gaius Valerius Catullus A290

Domenico Cimarosa A291

1949, Sept. 19 Wmk. 277 *Perf. 14*

529 A290 20 l brt bl 3.00 75

2000th anniversary of the death of Gaius Valerius Catullus, Lyric poet.

1949, Dec. 28

530 A291 20 l vio blk 3.00 75

Issued to commemorate the bicentenary of the birth of Domenico Cimarosa, composer.

Milan Fair Scene A292

1950, Apr. 12 Photo.

531 A292 20 l brown 1.10 75

The 28th Milan Trade Fair.

Flags and Italian Automobile A293

1950, Apr. 29

532 A293 20 l vio gray 2.75 70

Issued to publicize the 32nd International Auto Show, Turin, May 4-14, 1950.

Pitti Palace, Florence A294

"Perseus" by Cellini A295

Composite of Italian Cathedrals and Churches A296

1950, May 22

533 A294	20 l ol grn	1.00	45
534 A295	55 l blue	14.00	2.00

5th General Conf. of UNESCO.

1950, May 29

535 A296	20 l violet	75	28
536 A296	55 l blue	8.75	75

Holy Year, 1950.

Gaudenzio Ferrari A297

Radio Mast and Tower of Florence A298

1950, July 1 Wmk. 277 *Perf. 14*

537 A297 20 l gray grn 3.00 1.00

Issued to honor Gaudenzio Ferrari.

1950, July 15 Photo.

538 A298	20 l purple	3.75	4.00
539 A298	55 l blue	67.50	67.50

Issued to commemorate the International Shortwave Radio Conference, Florence, 1950.

Ludovico A. Muratori A299

Guido d'Arezzo A300

1950, July 22

540 A299 20 l brown 1.40 75

Issued to commemorate the 200th anniversary of the death of Ludovico A. Muratori, writer.

1950, July 29

541 A300 20 l dk grn 3.00 75

Issued to commemorate the 900th anniversary of the death of Guido d'Arezzo, music teacher and composer.

Tartan and Fair Buildings A301

1950, Aug. 21

542 A301 20 l chestnut brn 2.50 60

Levant Fair, Bari, September, 1950.

SS1
SS2
SS3
SS4
SS5
SS6
Collect the Scott way with
Scott StockPages
SS9
SS7
SS8
9 different page formats,
8½" x 11", hold every size stamp.

G. Marzotto and A. Rossi — A302

Tobacco Plant — A303

1950, Sept. 11

543	A302	20 l indigo	30	18

Issued to honor the pioneers of the Italian wool industry.

1950, Sept. 11

Designs: 20 l, Mature plant, different background. 55 l, Girl holding tobacco plant.

544	A303	5 l dp cl & grn	48	1.10
545	A303	20 l brn & grn	2.00	20
546	A303	55 l dp ultra & brn	27.50	7.25

Issued to publicize the European Tobacco Conference, Rome, 1950.

Arms of the Academy of Fine Arts A304

Augusto Righi A305

1950, Sept. 16

547	A304	20 l ol brn & red brn	1.90	1.00

200th anniv. of the founding of the Academy of Fine Arts, Venice.

1950, Sept. 16

548	A305	20 l cr & gray blk	1.40	1.00

Issued to commemorate the centenary of the birth of Augusto Righi, physicist.

Blacksmith, Aosta Valley A306

1851 Stamp of Tuscany A307

Designs: 1 l, Auto mechanic. 2 l, Mason. 5 l, Potter. 6 l, Lace-making. 10 l, Weaving. 12 l, Sailor steering boat. 15 l, Shipbuilding. 20 l, Fisherman. 25 l, Sorting oranges. 30 l, Woman carrying grapes. 35 l, Olive picking. 40 l, Wine cart. 50 l, Shepherd and flock. 55 l, Plowing. 60 l, Grain cart. 65 l, Girl worker in hemp field. 100 l, Husking corn. 200 l, Woodcutter.

1950, Oct. 20 Wmk. 277 *Perf. 14*

549	A306	50c vio bl	15	15
550	A306	1 l dk bl vio	15	15
551	A306	2 l sepia	15	15
552	A306	5 l dk gray	15	15
553	A306	6 l chocolate	15	15
554	A306	10 l dp grn	70	15
555	A306	12 l dp bl grn	20	15
556	A306	15 l dk gray bl	30	15
557	A306	20 l bl vio	1.50	15
558	A306	25 l brn org	80	15
559	A306	30 l magenta	30	15
560	A306	35 l crimson	90	15
561	A306	40 l brown	15	15

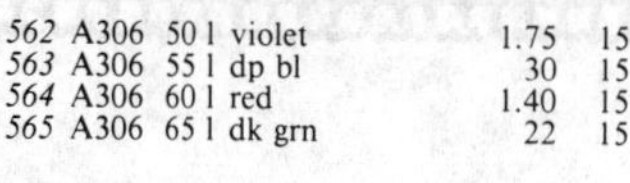

562	A306	50 l violet	1.75	15
563	A306	55 l dp bl	30	15
564	A306	60 l red	1.40	15
565	A306	65 l dk grn	22	15

Perf. 13x14, 14x13
Engr.

566	A306	100 l brn org	13.00	15
a.		Perf. 13	14.00	15
b.		Perf. 14	15.00	15
567	A306	200 l ol brn	3.25	38
a.		Perf. 14	3.25	45
		Nos. 549-567 (19)	25.52	
		Set value		1.60

See Nos. 668-673A.

1951, Mar. 27 Photo. *Perf. 14*

Design: 55 l, Tuscany 6cr.

568	A307	20 l red vio & red	1.00	85
569	A307	55 l ultra & bl	12.00	13.00

Centenary of Tuscany's first stamps.

Italian Automobile A308

1951, Apr. 2

570	A308	20 l dk grn	3.00	1.00

33rd International Automobile Exhibition, Turin, April 4-15, 1951.

Altar of Peace, Medea A309

1951, Apr. 11

571	A309	20 l bl vio	1.90	1.00

Issued to publicize the consecration of the Altar of Peace at Redipuglia Cemetery, Medea.

Helicopter over Leonardo da Vinci Heliport — A310

P. T. T. Building, Milan Fair — A311

1951, Apr. 12 Photo.

572	A310	20 l brown	1.90	70
573	A311	55 l dp bl	17.00	20.00

29th Milan Trade Fair.

Symbols of the International Gymnastic Festival A312

Statue of Diana, Spindle and Turin Tower A313

Wmk. 277
1951, May 18 Photo. *Perf. 14*
Fleur-de-lis in Red

574	A312	5 l dk brn	12.00	*100.00*
575	A312	10 l Prus grn	12.00	*100.00*
576	A312	15 l vio bl	12.00	*100.00*

International Gymnastic Festival and Meet, Florence, 1951.

Fake cancellations exist on Nos. 574-576.

1951, Apr. 26

577	A313	20 l purple	3.75	1.40

Tenth International Exhibition of Textile Art and Fashion, Turin, May 2-16.

Landing of Columbus A314

1951, May 5

578	A314	20 l Prus grn	3.50	1.40

500th anniversary of birth of Columbus.

Reconstructed Abbey of Montecassino — A315

Design: 55 l, Montecassino Ruins.

1951, June 18

579	A315	20 l violet	1.00	70
580	A315	55 l brt bl	13.00	14.00

Issued to commemorate the reconstruction of the Abbey of Montecassino.

Pietro Vannucci (Il Perugino) A316

Stylized Vase A317

Cartouche of Amenhotep III and Pitcher A318

1951, July 23

581	A316	20 l brn & red brn	1.40	1.50

Issued to commemorate the 500th anniversary (in 1950) of the birth of Pietro Vannucci, painter.

1951, July 23

582	A317	20 l grnsh gray & blk	1.40	1.25
583	A318	55 l vio bl & pale sal	10.00	11.00

Triennial Art Exhibition, Milan, 1951.

Cyclist — A319

1951, Aug. 23

584	A319	25 l gray blk	1.25	1.40

Issued to publicize the World Bicycle Championship Races, Milan, Aug.-Sept. 1951.

Tartan and Globes A320

1951, Sept. 8 Photo.

585	A320	25 l deep blue	1.90	1.10

15th Levant Fair, Bari, September 1951.

"La Figlia di Jorio" by Michetti A321

1951, Sept. 15 Wmk. 277 *Perf. 14*

586	A321	25 l dk brn	1.50	1.10

Issued to commemorate the centenary of the birth of Francesco Paolo Michetti, painter.

Sardinia Stamps of 1851 A322

1951, Oct. 5

587	A322	10 l shown	1.00	1.90
588	A322	25 l 20c stamp	1.40	1.40
589	A322	60 l 40c stamp	4.75	5.75

Centenary of Sardinia's 1st postage stamp.

Mercury — A323

Roman Census A324

1951, Oct. 31

590	A323	10 l green	50	85
591	A324	25 l vio gray	1.00	70

Issued to publicize the 3rd Industrial and the 9th General Italian Census.

Winter Scene A325

Trees A326

1951, Nov. 21

592 A325 10 l ol & dl grn 60 95
593 A326 25 l dl grn 1.50 75

Issued to publicize the Festival of Trees.

Giuseppe Verdi A327

Designs: Portraits of Verdi, various backgrounds.

1951, Nov. 19 **Engr.**

594 A327 10 l vio brn & dk grn 40 1.25
595 A327 25 l red brn & dk brn 2.00 85
596 A327 60 l dp grn & ind 4.50 4.25

Issued to commemorate the 50th anniversary of the death of Giuseppe Verdi, composer.

Vincenzo Bellini — A328

Wmk. 277

1952, Jan. 28 **Photo.** ***Perf. 14***

597 A328 25 l gray & gray blk 1.00 55

Issued to commemorate the 150th anniversary of the birth of Vincenzo Bellini, composer.

Palace of Caserta and Statuary A329

1952, Feb. 1

598 A329 25 l dl grn & ol bis 1.00 50

Issued to honor Luigi Vanvitelli, architect.

Statues of Athlete and River God Tiber — A330

1952, Mar. 22

599 A330 25 l brn & sl blk 32 45

Issued on the occasion of the first International Exhibition of Sports Stamps.

Milan Fair Buildings A331

1952, Apr. 12 **Engr.**

600 A331 60 l ultra 6.00 4.00

30th Milan Trade Fair.

Leonardo da Vinci A332

Virgin of the Rocks A332a

1952 **Wmk. 277** **Photo.** ***Perf. 14***

601 A332 25 l dp org 15 15

Unwmk.

Engr. ***Perf. 13***

601A A332a 60 l ultra 95 3.00

Wmk. 277

601B A332 80 l brn car 4.00 15
c. Perf. 14x13 3.25 38

Issued to commemorate the 500th anniversary of the birth of Leonardo da Vinci.

First Stamps and Cathedral Bell Towers of Modena and Parma A333

1952, May 29 ***Perf. 14***

602 A333 25 l blk & red brn 70 35
603 A333 60 l blk & ultra 3.50 3.75

Cent. of the 1st postage stamps of Modena and Parma.

Globe and Torch A334

Lion of St. Mark A335

1952, June 7

604 A334 25 l brt bl 75 40

Issued to honor the Overseas Fair at Naples and Italian labor throughout the world.

1952, June 14

605 A335 25 l blk & yel 50 40

26th Biennial Art Exhibition, Venice.

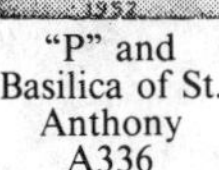

"P" and Basilica of St. Anthony A336

Flag and Basilica of St. Just A337

1952, June 19

606 A336 25 l bl gray, red & dk bl 1.00 40

30th International Sample Fair of Padua.

1952, June 28

607 A337 25 l dp grn, dk brn & red 65 38

4th International Sample Fair of Trieste.

Fair Entrance and Tartan A338

1952, Sept. 6 **Wmk. 277** ***Perf. 14***

608 A338 25 l dk grn 38 38

16th Levant Fair, Bari, Sept. 1952.

Girolamo Savonarola A339

Mountain Peak and Climbing Equipment A340

1952, Sept. 20

609 A339 25 l purple 65 40

Issued to commemorate the 500th anniversary of the birth of Girolamo Savonarola.

1952, Oct. 4

610 A340 25 l gray 38 28

Issued to publicize the National Exhibition of the Alpine troops, Oct. 4, 1952.

Colosseum and Plane A341

1952, Sept. 29

611 A341 60 l vio bl & dk bl 6.75 5.50

Issued to publicize the first International Civil Aviation Conference, Rome, Sept. 1952.

Guglielmo Cardinal Massaia and Map A342

1952, Nov. 21 **Engr.** ***Perf. 13***

612 A342 25 l brn & dk brn 70 40

Issued to commemorate the centenary of the establishment of the first Catholic mission in Ethiopia.

Symbols of Army, Navy and Air Force — A343

Sailor, Soldier and Aviator — A344

Design: 60 l, Boat, plane and tank.

1952, Nov. 3 **Photo.** ***Perf. 14***

613 A343 10 l dk grn 15 15
614 A344 25 l blk & dk brn 40 15
615 A344 60 l blk & bl 1.50 1.50

Armed Forces Day, Nov. 4, 1952.

Antonio Mancini A345

Vincenzo Gemito A346

1952, Dec. 6

616 A345 25 l dk grn 38 35
617 A346 25 l brown 38 28

Issued to commemorate the birth centenaries of Antonio Mancini, painter, and Vincenzo Gemito, sculptor.

Martyrs, Jailer and Artist Boldini A347

1952, Dec. 31

618 A347 25 l gray blk & dk bl 1.00 45

Issued to commemorate the centenary of the deaths of the five Martyrs of Belfiore.

Antonello da Messina — A349

1953, Feb. 21 **Photo.** ***Perf. 14***

621 A349 25 l car lake 85 38

Issued to commemorate the Messina Exhibition of the paintings of Antonello and his 15th century contemporaries.

Racing Cars — A350

1953, Apr. 24

622 A350 25 l violet 85 30

20th 1,000-mile auto race.

Decoration "Knights of Labor" Bee and Honeycomb
A351

Arcangelo Corelli
A352

1953, Apr. 30

623	A351	25 l violet	50	30

1953, May 30

624	A352	25 l dk brn	38	30

Issued to commemorate the 300th anniversary of the birth of Arcangelo Corelli, composer.

St. Clare of Assisi and Convent of St. Damien — A353

"Italia" after Syracusean Coin — A354

1953, June 27

625	A353	25 l brn & dl red	25	18

Issued to commemorate the 700th anniversary of the death of St. Clare of Assisi.

1953-54 Wmk. 277 *Perf. 14*
Size: 17x21mm

626	A354	5 l gray	15	15
627	A354	10 l org ver	15	15
628	A354	12 l dl grn	15	15
628A	A354	13 l brt lil rose ('54)	15	15
629	A354	20 l brown	75	15
630	A354	25 l purple	65	15
631	A354	35 l rose car	24	15
632	A354	60 l blue	2.00	15
633	A354	80 l org brn	12.50	15
		Nos. 626-633 (9)	16.74	
		Set value		50

See Nos. 661-662, 673B-689, 785-788, 998A-998W, 1288-1295.

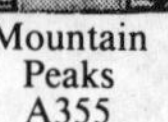

Mountain Peaks
A355

Tyche, Goddess of Fortune
A356

1953, July 11

634	A355	25 l bl grn	75	18

Festival of the Mountain.

1953, July 16

635	A356	25 l dk brn	35	15
636	A356	60 l dp bl	1.25	75

Issued to publicize the International Exposition of Agriculture, Rome, 1953.

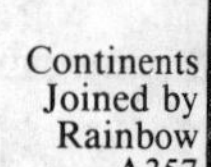

Continents Joined by Rainbow
A357

1953, Aug. 6

637	A357	25 l org & Prus bl	2.75	15
638	A357	60 l lil rose & dk vio bl	6.00	1.40

4th anniversary of the signing of the North Atlantic Treaty.

Luca Signorelli
A358

Agostino Bassi
A359

1953, Aug. 13

639	A358	25 l dk brn & dl grn	28	20

Issued to publicize the opening of an exhibition of the works of Luca Signorelli, painter.

1953, Sept. 5

640	A359	25 l dk gray & brn	24	18

6th International Microbiology Congress, Rome, Sept. 6-12, 1953.

Siena
A360

Rapallo
A361

Views: 20 l, Seaside at Gardone. 25 l, Mountain, Cortina d'Ampezzo. 35 l, Roman ruins, Taormina. 60 l, Rocks and sea, Capri.

1953, Dec. 31 *Perf. 14*

641	A360	10 l dk brn & red brn	15	15
642	A361	12 l lt bl & gray	15	15
643	A361	20 l brn org & dk brn	15	15
644	A360	25 l dk grn & pale bl	15	15
645	A361	35 l cream & brn	28	18
646	A361	60 l bl grn & ind	48	32
		Set value	1.05	75

Lateran Palace, Rome
A362

Television Screen and Aerial
A363

1954, Feb. 11

647	A362	25 l dk brn & choc	24	15
648	A362	60 l bl & ultra	1.00	1.00

Issued to commemorate the 25th anniversary of the signing of the Lateran Pacts.

1954, Feb. 25

649	A363	25 l purple	50	15
650	A363	60 l dp bl grn	2.00	1.75

Issued to commemorate the introduction of regular national television service.

"Italia" and Quotation from Constitution
A364

194, Mar. 20

651	A364	25 l purple	70	15

Propaganda for the payment of taxes.

Vertical Flight Trophy
A365

Eagle Perched on Ruins
A366

1954, Apr. 24

652	A365	25 l gray black	50	50

Issued to publicize the experimental transportation of mail by helicopter, April 1954.

1954, June 1

653	A366	25 l gray, org brn & blk	18	18

Issued to commemorate the 10th anniversary of Italy's resistance movement.

Alfredo Catalani, Composer, Birth Centenary — A367

1954, June 19 *Perf. 14*

654	A367	25 l dk grnsh gray	15	15

Marco Polo, Lion of St. Mark and Dragon
A368

1954, July 8 Engr. *Perf. 14*

655	A368	25 l red brn	24	15

Perf. 13

656	A368	60 l gray grn	1.50	1.75
a.		Perf. 13x12	7.50	4.00

Issued to commemorate the 700th anniversary of the birth of Marco Polo.

Automobile and Cyclist
A369

1954, Sept. 6 Photo. *Perf. 14*

657	A369	25 l dp grn & red	18	15

60th anniv. of the founding of the Italian Touring Club.

St. Michael Overpowering the Devil
A370

Pinocchio and Group of Children
A371

1954, Oct. 9

658	A370	25 l rose red	28	15
659	A370	60 l blue	85	1.10

23rd general assembly of the International Criminal Police, Rome 1954.

1954, Oct. 26

660	A371	25 l rose red	15	15

Carlo Lorenzini, creator of Pinocchio.

Italia Type of 1953-54

1954, Dec. 28 Engr. *Perf. 13*
Size: 22 ½x27 ½mm

661	A354	100 l brown	15.00	15
662	A354	200 l dp bl	2.75	20

Madonna, Perugino
A372

Amerigo Vespucci and Map
A373

Design: 60 l, Madonna of the Pieta, Michelangelo.

1954, Dec. 31 Photo. *Perf. 14*

663	A372	25 l brn & bis	22	15
664	A372	60 l blk & cr	70	1.10

Issued to mark the end of the Marian Year.

1954, Dec. 31 Engr. *Perf. 13*

665	A373	25 l dp plum	24	15
a.		Perf. 13x14	2.25	50
666	A373	60 l bl blk	85	1.10
a.		Perf. 13x14	45	1.10

500th anniv. of the birth of Amerigo Vespucci, explorer, 1454-1512.

Silvio Pellico (1789-1854), Dramatist — A374

Wmk. 277

1955, Jan. 24 Photo. *Perf. 14*

667	A374	25 l brt bl & vio	28	15

Italy at Work Type of 1950

1955-57 Wmk. 303

668	A306	50c vio bl	15	15
669	A306	1 l dk bl vio	15	15
670	A306	2 l sepia	15	15
671	A306	15 l dk gray bl	22	15
672	A306	30 l magenta	15.00	25
673	A306	50 l violet	9.50	15
673A	A306	65 l dk grn ('57)	5.50	18.00
		Nos. 668-673A (7)	30.67	19.00

Italia Type of 1953-54 and

St. George, by Donatello A374a

1955-58 Wmk. 303 Photo. *Perf. 14*
Size: 17x21mm

673B	A354	1 l gray ('58)	15	15
674	A354	5 l slate	15	15
675	A354	6 l ocher ('57)	15	15
676	A354	10 l org ver	15	15
677	A354	12 l dl grn	15	15
678	A354	13 l brt lil rose	15	15
679	A354	15 l gray vio ('56)	15	15
680	A354	20 l brown	15	15
681	A354	25 l purple	15	15
682	A354	35 l rose car	15	15
683	A354	50 l olive ('58)	22	15
685	A354	60 l blue	15	15
686	A354	80 l brn org	15	15
687	A354	90 l lt red brn ('58)	15	15

Engr. *Perf. 13½*
Size: 22½x28mm

688	A354	100 l brn ('56)	3.00	15
a.		Perf. 13½x12	3.00	18
b.		Perf. 13½x14	300.00	15.00
689	A354	200 l gray bl ('57)	3.00	15
690	A374a	500 l grn ('57)	75	15
b.		Perf. 14x13½	60	15
690A	A374a	1000 l rose car ('57)	95	15
c.		Perf. 14x13½	1.25	15
		Set value, #673B-690A	8.75	1.00

Nos. 690-690A were printed on ordinary and fluorescent paper.

See Nos. 785-788. See Nos. 998A-998W for small-size set.

Catalogue values for unused stamps in this section, from this point to the end of the section, are for Never Hinged items.

"Italia" A375

Oil Derrick and Old Roman Aqueduct A376

1955, Mar. 15 Photo. *Perf. 14*

691	A375	25 l rose vio	2.00	15

Issued as propaganda for the payment of taxes.

1955, June 6

Design: 60 l, Marble columns and oil field on globe.

692	A376	25 l ol grn	50	15
693	A376	60 l henna brn	1.10	1.25

Issued to publicize the fourth World Petroleum Congress, Rome, June 6-15, 1955.

Antonio Rosmini, Philosopher, Death Centenary A377

1955, July 1 Wmk. 303 *Perf. 14*

694	A377	25 l sepia	75	15

Girolamo Fracastoro and Stadium at Verona A378

1955, Sept. 1

695	A378	25 l gray blk & brn	70	15

International Medical Congress, Verona, Sept. 1-4.

Basilica of St. Francis, Assisi A379

1955, Oct. 4

696	A379	25 l blk & cr	40	15

Issued in honor of St. Francis and to commemorate the 7th centenary (in 1953) of the Basilica in Assisi.

Young Man at Drawing Board — A380

1955, Oct. 15

697	A380	25 l Prus grn	40	15

Centenary of technical education in Italy.

Harvester — A381

FAO Headquarters, Rome — A382

1955, Nov. 3

698	A381	25 l rose red & brn	30	15
699	A382	60 l blk & brt pur	1.25	75

50th anniv. of the Intl. Institute of Agriculture and 10th anniv. of the FAO, successor to the Institute.

An enhanced introduction to the Scott Catalogue begins on Page 1A. A thorough understanding of the material presented there will greatly aid your use of the catalogue itself.

Giacomo Matteotti A383

Battista Grassi A384

1955, Nov. 10

700	A383	25 l rose brn	1.10	15

70th anniversary of the birth of Giacomo Matteotti, Italian socialist leader.

1955, Nov. 19

701	A384	25 l dk grn	55	15

Issued to commemorate the 30th anniversary of the death of Battista Grassi, zoologist.

"St. Stephen Giving Alms" — A385

"St. Lorenzo Giving Alms" A386

1955, Nov. 26

702	A385	10 l blk & cr	15	18
703	A386	25 l ultra & cr	45	15

Issued to commemorate the 500th anniversary of the death of Fra Angelico, painter.

Giovanni Pascoli A387

1955, Dec. 31

704	A387	25 l gray blk	50	15

Issued to commemorate the centenary of the birth of Giovanni Pascoli, poet.

Ski Jump "Italia" A388

Stadiums at Cortina: 12 l, Skiing. 25 l, Ice skating. 60 l, Ice racing, Lake Misurina.

1956, Jan. 26 Photo.

705	A388	10 l bl grn & org	15	15
706	A388	12 l yel & blk	15	20
707	A388	25 l vio blk & org brn	30	15
708	A388	60 l saph & org	1.50	1.00

VII Winter Olympic Games at Cortina d'Ampezzo, Jan. 26-Feb. 5, 1956.

Mail Coach and Tunnel Exit — A389

1956, May 19 Wmk. 303 *Perf. 14*

709	A389	25 l dk bl grn	1.75	15

50th anniv. of the Simplon Tunnel.

Arms of Republic and Symbols of Industry A390

1956, June 2

710	A390	10 l gray & sl bl	18	15
711	A390	25 l pink & rose red	30	15
712	A390	60 l lt bl & brt bl	1.90	1.40
713	A390	80 l org & brn	4.75	15

Tenth anniversary of the Republic.

Amedeo Avogadro A391

1956, Sept. 8

714	A391	25 l blk vio	30	15

Issued to commemorate the centenary of the death of Amedeo Avogadro, physicist.

Europa Issue

"Rebuilding Europe" — A392

1956, Sept. 15

715	A392	25 l dk grn	90	15
716	A392	60 l blue	8.00	32
		Set value		38

Issued to symbolize the cooperation among the six countries comprising the Coal and Steel Community.

Globe and Satellites A393

1956, Sept. 22

717	A393	25 l int bl	30	15

7th International Astronautical Congress, Rome, Sept. 17-22.

Globe — A394

1956, Dec. 29 Litho. Unwmk.

718 A394 25 l red & bl grn, *pink* 15 15
719 A394 60 l bl grn & red, *pale bl grn* 48 18
Set value 22

Italy's admission to the United Nations.
The design, viewed through red and green glasses, becomes three-dimensional.

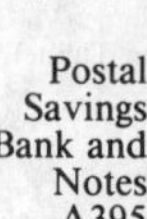

Postal Savings Bank and Notes
A395

1956, Dec. 31 Photo. Wmk. 303

720 A395 25 l sl bl & dp ultra 20 15

80th anniversary of Postal Savings.

Ovid
A396

Antonio Canova
A397

Paulina Borghese as Venus
A398

1957, June 10 ***Perf. 14***

721 A396 25 l ol grn & blk 18 15

2000th anniversary of the birth of the poet Ovid (Publius Ovidius Naso).

1957, July 15 Engr.

Design: 60 l, Sculpture: Hercules and Lichas.

722 A397 25 l brown 15 15
723 A397 60 l gray 24 55
724 A398 80 l vio bl 24 15
Set value 72

Issued to commemorate the bicentenary of the birth of Antonio Canova, sculptor.

Traffic Light — A399

"United Europe" — A400

Wmk. 303

1957, Aug. 7 Photo. ***Perf. 14***

725 A399 25 l grn, blk & red 20 15

Campaign for careful driving.

1957, Sept. 16 Litho. ***Perf. 14***

Flags in Original Colors

726 A400 25 l light blue 15 15

Perf. 13

727 A400 60 l violet blue 1.40 15
Set value 17

Issued to publicize a united Europe for peace and prosperity.

Giosue Carducci
A401

Filippino Lippi
A402

1957, Oct. 14 Engr. ***Perf. 14***

728 A401 25 l brown 20 15

Issued to commemorate the 50th anniversary of the death of the poet Giosue Carducci.

1957, Nov. 25 Wmk. 303 ***Perf. 14***

729 A402 25 l redsh brn 20 15

Issued to commemorate the 500th anniversary of the birth of Filippino Lippi, painter.

2000th Anniv. of the Death of Marcus Tullius Cicero, Roman Statesman and Writer — A403

1957, Nov. 30 Photo.

730 A403 25 l brown red 20 15

St. Domenico Savio and Students of Various Races
A404

1957, Dec. 14

731 A404 15 l brt lil & blk 18 15

Cent. of the death of St. Domenico Savio.

St. Francis of Paola
A405

Giuseppe Garibaldi
A406

1957, Dec. 21 Engr.

732 A405 25 l black 25 15

450th anniv. of the death of St. Francis of Paola, patron saint of seafaring men.

1957, Dec. 14 ***Perf. 14x13, 13x14***

Design: 110 l, Garibaldi monument (horiz.).

733 A406 15 l slate grn 15 15
734 A406 110 l dull pur 38 15
Set value 20

Issued to commemorate the 150th anniversary of the birth of Giuseppe Garibaldi.

Peasant, Dams and Map of Sardinia
A407

1958, Feb. 1 Engr. ***Perf. 14***

738 A407 25 l bluish grn 15 15

Issued to commemorate the completion of the Flumendosa-Mulargia irrigation system.

Immaculate Conception Statue, Rome, and Lourdes Basilica — A408

1958, Apr. 16 Wmk. 303 ***Perf. 14***

739 A408 15 l rose claret 15 15
740 A408 60 l blue 15 15
Set value 15

Centenary of the apparition of the Virgin Mary at Lourdes.

Book and Symbols of Labor Industry and Agriculture
A409

Designs: 60 l, "Tree of Freedom" (vert.). 110 l, Montecitorio Palace.

1958, May 9 Photo. ***Perf. 14***

741 A409 25 l bl grn & ocher 15 15
742 A409 60 l blk brn & bl 15 15
743 A409 110 l ol bis & blk brn 35 15
Set value 56 25

10th anniversary of the constitution.

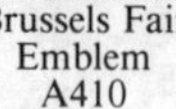
Brussels Fair Emblem
A410

Prologue from Pagliacci
A411

1958, June 12

744 A410 60 l bl & yel 15 15

Issued for the International and Universal Exposition at Brussels.

1958, July 10

745 A411 25 l dk bl & dk red 15 15

Issued to commemorate the centenary of the birth of Ruggiero Leoncavallo, composer.

Scene from La Boheme
A412

1958, July 10 Engr. Unwmk.

746 A412 25 l dk bl 15 15

Issued to commemorate the centenary of the birth of Giacomo Puccini, composer.

Giovanni Fattori, Self-portrait
A413

"Ave Maria on the Lake" by Giovanni Segantini
A414

1958, Aug. 7 Wmk. 303 ***Perf. 13x14***

747 A413 110 l redsh brn 35 15

Issued to commemorate the 50th anniversary of the death of Giovanni Fattori, painter.

1958, Aug. 7 ***Perf. 14***

748 A414 110 l slate, *buff* 15 18

Issued to commemorate the centenary of the birth of Giovanni Segantini, painter.

Map of Brazil, Plane and Arch of Titus
A415

1958, Aug. 23 Photo. ***Perf. 14***

749 A415 175 l Prus grn 60 1.25

Italo-Brazilian friendship on the occasion of Pres. Giovanni Gronchi's visit to Brazil.

Europa Issue, 1958

Common Design Type

1958, Sept. 13

Size: 20½x35½mm

750 CD1 25 l red & bl 15 15
751 CD1 60 l bl & red 15 18
Set value 20

Issued to show the European Postal Union at the service of European integration.

½g Stamp of Naples
A416

Evangelista Torricelli
A417

Design: 60 l, 1g Stamp of Naples.

Perf. 14x13½, 13½

1958, Oct. 4 Engr. Unwmk.

752 A416 25 l brn red 15 15
753 A416 60 l blk & red brn 15 15
Set value 21 17

Centenary of the stamps of Naples.

1958, Oct. 20 Wmk. 303 ***Perf. 14***

754 A417 25 l rose claret 40 28

350th anniv. of the birth of Evangelista Torricelli, mathematician and physicist.

"The Triumph of Caesar," Montegna
A418

Persian Style Bas-relief, Sorrento
A419

Designs: 25 l, Coats of Arms of Trieste, Rome and Trento (horiz). 60 l, War memorial bell of Rovereto.

1958, Nov. 3 Engr. *Perf. 14x13½*

755 A418 15 l green 15 15
756 A418 25 l gray 15 15
757 A418 60 l rose claret 18 20
Set value 32 30

Issued to commemorate the 40th anniversary of Italy's victory in World War I.

1958, Nov. 27 Photo.

758 A419 25 l sepia, *bluish* 16 15
759 A419 60 l vio bl, *bluish* 45 60
Set value 65

Visit of the Shah of Iran to Italy.

Eleonora Duse — A420

Dancers and Antenna — A421

Unwmk.

1958, Dec. 11 Engr. *Perf. 14*

760 A420 25 l brt ultra 15 15

Issued to commemorate the centenary of the birth of Eleonora Duse, actress.

1958, Dec. 29 Photo. Wmk. 303

Design: 60 l, Piano, dove and antenna.

761 A421 25 l red, bl & blk 15 15
762 A421 60 l ultra & blk 15 15
Set value 20 20

10th anniv. of the Prix Italia (International Radio and Television Competitions).

Stamp of Sicily — A422

Design: 60 l, Stamp of Sicily, 5g.

Perf. 14x13½

1959, Jan. 2 Engr. Unwmk.

763 A422 25 l Prus grn 15 15
764 A422 60 l dp org 15 15
Set value 18 15

Centenary of the stamps of Sicily.

Dome of St. Peter's and Tower of Lateran Palace
A423

Wmk. 303

1959, Feb. 11 Photo. *Perf. 14*

765 A423 25 l ultra 15 15

Issued to commemorate the 30th anniversary of the Lateran Pacts.

Common Design Types pictured in section at front of book.

Map of North Atlantic and NATO Emblem
A424

1959, Apr. 4

766 A424 25 l dk bl & ocher 15 15
767 A424 60 l dk bl & grn 18 22
Set value 26 28

10th anniv. of NATO.

Arms of Paris and Rome
A425

1959, Apr. 9

768 A425 15 l bl & red 15 15
769 A425 25 l bl & red 15 15
Set value 16 17

Issued to publicize the cultural ties between Rome and Paris.

"A Gentle Peace Has Come"
A426

Statue of Lord Byron
A427

1959, Apr. 13 Engr. Unwmk.

770 A426 25 l olive green 15 15

International War Veterans Association convention, Rome.

1959, Apr. 21

771 A427 15 l black 15 15

Issued to commemorate the unveiling in Rome of a statue of Lord Byron by Bertel Thorvaldson, Danish sculptor.

Camillo Prampolini — A428

1959, Apr. 27 Unwmk. *Perf. 14*

772 A428 15 l car rose 1.65 15

Camillo Prampolini, socialist leader and reformer, birth centenary.

Fountain of Dioscuri and Olympic Rings — A429

Baths of Carcalla
A430

Designs: 25 l, Capitoline tower. 60 l, Arch of Constantine. 110 l, Ruins of Basilica of Massentius.

1959, June 23 Photo. Wmk. 303

Designs in Dark Sepia

773 A429 15 l red orange 15 15
774 A429 25 l blue 15 15
775 A430 35 l bister 15 15
776 A430 60 l rose lilac 22 18
777 A430 110 l yellow 25 15
Set value 75 48

1960 Olympic Games in Rome.

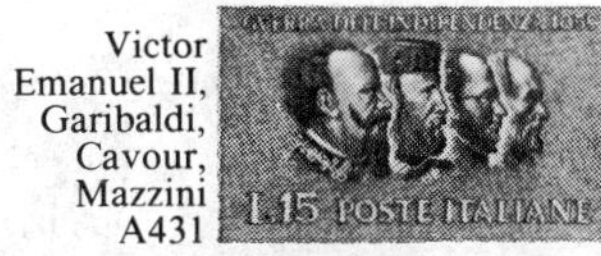

Victor Emanuel II, Garibaldi, Cavour, Mazzini
A431

Battle of San Fermo
A432

Designs: 25 l, "After the Battle of Magenta" by Fattori and Red Cross (vert.). 60 l, Battle of Palestro. 110 l, "Battle of Magenta" by Induno (vert.).

Engr., Cross Photo. on 25 l

1959, June 27 Unwmk.

778 A431 15 l gray 15 15
779 A431 25 l brn & red 15 15
780 A432 35 l dk vio 15 15
781 A432 60 l ultra 15 15
782 A432 110 l magenta 15 15
Set value 32 30

Issued to commemorate the centenary of the war of independence. No. 779 commemorates the centenary of the Red Cross idea.

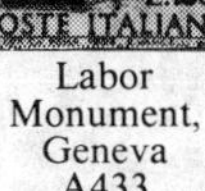

Labor Monument, Geneva
A433

Stamp of Romagna
A434

1959, July 20 *Perf. 14x13, 14*

783 A433 25 l violet 15 15
784 A433 60 l brown 15 15
Set value 20 16

40th anniv. of the ILO.

Italia Type of 1953-54

Photo.; Engr. (100 l, 200 l)

1959-66 Wmk. 303 *Perf. 14*

Size: 17x21mm

785 A354 30 l bis brn ('60) 38 15
786 A354 40 l lil rose ('60) 1.65 15
786A A354 70 l Prus grn ('60) 48 15
787 A354 100 l brown 60 15

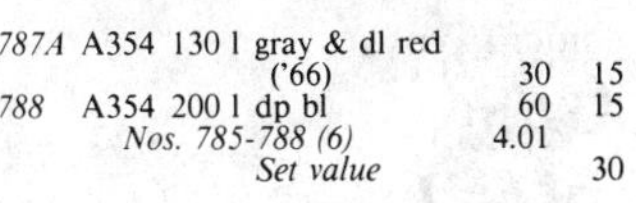

787A A354 130 l gray & dl red ('66) 30 15
788 A354 200 l dp bl 60 15
Nos. 785-788 (6) 4.01
Set value 30

1959, Sept. 1 Photo.

Design: 60 l, Stamp of Romagna, 20b.

789 A434 25 l pale brn & blk 15 15
790 A434 60 l gray grn & blk 15 15
Set value 22 17

Centenary of the stamps of Romagna.

Europa Issue, 1959

Common Design Type

1959, Sept. 19

Size: 22x27½mm

791 CD2 25 l olive green 15 15
792 CD2 60 l blue 22 15
Set value 21

Stamp of 1953 with Facsimile Cancellation
A435

Aeneas Fleeing with Father and Son, by Raphael
A436

1959, Dec. 20 Wmk. 303 *Perf. 14*

793 A435 15 l gray, rose car & blk 15 15

Italy's first Stamp Day, Dec. 20, 1959.

1960, Apr. 7 Engr. Unwmk.

794 A436 25 l lake 15 15
795 A436 60 l gray vio 15 15
Set value 25 21

Issued to publicize World Refugee Year, July 1, 1959-June 30, 1960. Design is detail from "The Fire in the Borgo."

Garibaldi's Proclamation to the Sicilians — A437

King Victor Emmanuel and Garibaldi Meeting at Teano — A438

Design: 60 l, Volunteers embarking, Quarto, Genoa.

Wmk. 303

1960, May 5 Photo. *Perf. 14*

796 A437 15 l brown 15 15

Perf. 13x14, 14x13

Engr. Unwmk.

797 A438 25 l rose claret 15 15
798 A437 60 l ultramarine 15 15
Set value 22 20

Cent. of the liberation of Southern Italy (Kingdom of the Two Sicilies) by Garibaldi.

Emblem of 17th Olympic Games — A439

Olympic Stadium A440

Statues: 15 l, Roman Consul on way to the games. 35 l, Myron's Discobolus. 110 l, Seated boxer. 200 l, Apoxyomenos by Lysippus.
Stadia: 25 l, Velodrome. 60 l, Sports palace. 150 l, Small sports palace.

Photogravure, Engraved
Perf. 14x13½, 13½x14

1960 Wmk. 303, Unwmk.

799 A439 5 l yel brn 15 15
800 A440 10 l dp org & dk bl 15 15
801 A439 15 l ultra 15 15
802 A440 25 l lt vio & brn 15 15
803 A439 35 l rose cl 15 15
804 A440 60 l bluish grn & brn 15 15
805 A439 110 l plum 15 15
806 A440 150 l bl & brn 55 55
807 A439 200 l green 22 15
Set value 1.40 1.00

17th Olympic Games, Rome, Aug. 25-Sept. 11.

The photo. denominations (5, 10, 25, 60, 150-lire) are wmkd.; the engraved (15, 35, 110, 200-lire) are unwmkd.

Bottego Statue, Parma A441

Michelangelo da Caravaggio A442

1960 Unwmk. Engr. *Perf. 14*

808 A441 30 l brown 15 15

Issued to commemorate the centenary of the birth of Vittorio Bottego, explorer.

Europa Issue, 1960
Common Design Type

1960 Photo. Wmk. 303
Size: 37x27mm

809 CD3 30 l dk grn & bis brn 15 15
810 CD3 70 l dk bl & sal 15 15
Set value 22 15

1960 Unwmk. Engr. *Perf. 13x13½*

811 A442 25 l org brn 15 15

350th anniv. of the death of Michelangelo da Caravaggio (Merisi), painter.

Mail Coach and Post Horn A443

1960 Wmk. 303 Photo. *Perf. 14*

812 A443 15 l blk brn & org brn 15 15

Issued for Stamp Day, Dec. 20.

Slave, by Michelangelo — A444

Designs from Sistine Chapel by Michelangelo: 5 l, 10 l, 115 l, 150 l, Heads of various "slaves." 15 l, Joel. 20 l, Libyan Sybil. 25 l, Isaiah. 30 l, Eritrean Sybil. 40 l, Daniel. 50 l, Delphic Sybil. 55 l, Cumaean Sybil. 70 l, Zachariah. 85 l, Jonah. 90 l, Jeremiah. 100 l, Ezekiel. 200 l, Self-portrait. 500 l, Adam. 1000 l, Eve.

Wmk. 303
1961, Mar. 6 Photo. *Perf. 14*
Size: 17x21mm

813 A444 1 l gray 15 15
814 A444 5 l brn org 15 15
815 A444 10 l red org 15 15
816 A444 15 l brt lil 15 15
817 A444 20 l Prus grn 15 15
818 A444 25 l brown 30 15
819 A444 30 l purple 15 15
820 A444 40 l rose red 15 15
821 A444 50 l olive 42 15
822 A444 55 l red brn 15 15
823 A444 70 l blue 16 15
824 A444 85 l slate grn 18 15
825 A444 90 l lil rose 40 15
826 A444 100 l vio gray 55 15
827 A444 115 l ultra 25 15

Engr.

828 A444 150 l chocolate 55 15
829 A444 200 l dark blue 1.65 15
a. Perf. 13½ 1.65 15

Perf. 13½
Size: 22x27mm

830 A444 500 l bl grn 1.00 15
831 A444 1000 l brn red 1.10 52
Nos. 813-831 (19) 7.76
Set value 1.50

Map Showing Flight from Italy to Argentina A445

Designs: 185 l, Italy to Uruguay. 205 l, Italy to Peru.

1961, Apr. Photo. *Perf. 14*

832 A445 170 l ultra 4.50 4.50
833 A445 185 l dl grn 4.50 4.50
834 A445 205 l vio blk 9.00 9.00
a. 205 l rose lilac 600.00

Issued to commemorate the visit of President Gronchi to South America, April 1961.

Nos. 832-833 and 834a were issued Apr. 4, to become valid on Apr. 6. The map of Peru on No. 834a was drawn incorrectly and the stamp was therefore withdrawn on Apr. 4. A corrected design in new color (No. 834) was issued Apr. 6.

Statue of Pliny, Como Cathedral A446

Ippolito Nievo (1831-61), Writer A447

1961, May 27

835 A446 30 l brown 15 15

Issued to commemorate the 1900th anniversary of the birth of Pliny the Younger, Roman consul and writer.

1961, June 8 Wmk. 303 *Perf. 14*

836 A447 30 l multi 15 15

St. Paul Aboard Ship — A448

1961, June 28

837 A448 30 l multi 15 15
838 A448 70 l multi 32 40

1,900th anniversary of St. Paul's arrival in Rome. The design is after a miniature from the Bible of Borso D'Este.

Cavalli Gun and Gaeta Fortress A449

Cent. of Italian unity: 30 l, Carignano palace, Turin. 40 l, Montecitorio palace, Rome. 70 l, Palazzo Vecchio, Florence. 115 l, Villa Madama, Rome. 300 l, Steel construction, Italia '61 Exhibition, Turin.

1961, Aug. 12 Photo.

839 A449 15 l dk bl & redsh brn 15 15
840 A449 30 l dk bl & red brn 15 15
841 A449 40 l bl & brn 24 24
842 A449 70 l brn & pink 35 15
843 A449 115 l org brn & dk bl 1.25 15
844 A449 300 l brt grn & red 3.75 4.00
Nos. 839-844 (6) 5.89 4.84

Europa Issue, 1961
Common Design Type

1961, Sept. 18 Wmk. 303 *Perf. 14*
Size: 36½x21mm

845 CD4 30 l carmine 15 15
846 CD4 70 l yel grn 15 15
Set value 16 15

Giandomenico Romagnosi — A450

Perf. 13½
1961, Nov. 28 Unwmk. Engr.

847 A450 30 l green 15 15

Issued to commemorate the bicentenary of the birth of Giandomenico Romagnosi, jurist and philosopher.

Design from 1820 Sardinia Letter Sheet A451

Wmk. 303
1961, Dec. 3 Photo. *Perf. 14*

848 A451 15 l lil rose & blk 15 15

Issued for Stamp Day 1961.

Family Scene "I am the Lamp that Glows so Gently . . ." A452

1962, Apr. 6 Wmk. 303 *Perf. 14*

849 A452 30 l red 15 15
850 A452 70 l blue 24 30

Issued to commemorate the 50th anniversary of the death of Giovanni Pascoli, poet.

Pacinotti's Dynamo A453

1962, June 12

851 A453 30 l rose & blk 15 15
852 A453 70 l ultra & blk 24 30

50th anniv. of the death of Antonio Pacinotti (1841-1912), physicist and inventor of the ring winding dynamo.

St. Catherine of Siena, by Andrea Vanni A454

Lion of St. Mark A455

Design: 70 l, St. Catherine, 15th century woodcut.

1962, June 26 Photo.

853 A454 30 l black 15 15

Engraved and Photogravure

854 A454 70 l red & blk 24 40

500th anniversary of the canonization of St. Catherine of Siena, Patroness of Italy.

1962, Aug. 25 Photo.

Design: 30 l, Stylized camera eye.

855 A455 30 l bl & blk 20 15
856 A455 70 l red org & blk 20 24
Set value 32

Issued to mark the 30th anniversary of the International Film Festival in Venice.

Motorcyclist and Bicyclist A456

Designs: 70 l, Group of cyclists. 300 l, Bicyclist.

1962, Aug. 30

857 A456 30 l grn & blk 35 15
858 A456 70 l bl & blk 15 15
859 A456 300 l dp org & blk 2.25 2.50

World Bicycle Championship Races.

Europa Issue, 1962
Common Design Type

1962, Sept. 17
Size: 37x21mm

860 CD5 30 l carmine 55 15
861 CD5 70 l blue 55 28

Swiss and Italian Flags, Eugenio and Angela Lina Balzan Medal A457

1962, Oct. 25 Wmk. 303 *Perf. 14*

862 A457 70 l rose red, grn & brn 30 15

1st distribution of the Balzan Prize by the International Balzan Foundation for Italian-Swiss Cooperation.

Malaria Eradication Emblem A458

Stamps of 1862 and 1961 A459

1962, Oct. 31 **Photo.**
863 A458 30 l light violet 15 15
864 A458 70 l light blue 24 30

WHO drive to eradicate malaria.

1962, Dec. 2
865 A459 15 l pur, buff & bis 15 15

Issued for Stamp Day and to commemorate the centenary of Italian postage stamps.

Holy Spirit Descending on Apostles — A460

1962, Dec. 8
866 A460 30 l org & dk bl grn, *buff* 15 15
867 A460 70 l dk bl grn & org, *buff* 15 18
Set value 25 26

21st Ecumenical Council of the Roman Catholic Church, Vatican II. The design is an illumination from the Codex Syriacus.

Statue of Count Camillo Bensi di Cavour — A461

1962, Dec. 10 **Engr.** **Unwmk.**
868 A461 30 l dk grn 15 15

Centenary of Court of Accounts.

Count Giovanni Pico della Mirandola A462

Gabriele D'Annunzio A463

Wmk. 303
1963, Feb. 25 **Photo.** ***Perf. 14***
869 A462 30 l gray blk 15 15

Mirandola (1463-94), Renaissance scholar.

1963, Mar. 12 **Engr.** **Unwmk.**
870 A463 30 l dk grn 15 15

Issued to commemorate the centenary of the birth of Gabriele d'Annunzio, author and soldier.

Sower — A464

Design: 70 l, Harvester typing sheaf, sculpture from Maggiore Fountain, Perugia.

1963, Mar. 21 **Photo.** **Wmk. 303**
871 A464 30 l rose car & brn 15 15
872 A464 70 l bl & brn 30 30
Set value 38

FAO "Freedom from Hunger" campaign.

Mt. Viso, Alpine Club Emblem, Ax and Rope — A465

Map of Italy and "INA" Initials — A466

1963, Mar. 30 **Wmk. 303** ***Perf. 14***
873 A465 115 l dk brn & brt bl 15 15

Issued to commemorate the centenary of the founding of the Italian Alpine Club.

1963, Apr. 4
874 A466 30 l grn & blk 15 15

Issued to commemorate the 50th anniversary of the National Insurance Institute.

Globe and Stamp A467

1963, May 7 **Photo.** ***Perf. 14***
875 A467 70 l bl & grn 15 15

Cent. of the 1st Intl. Postal Conf., Paris, 1863.

Crosses and Centenary Emblem on Globe — A468

1963, June 8 **Wmk. 303** ***Perf. 14***
876 A468 30 l dk gray & red 15 15
877 A468 70 l dl bl & red 22 30

Issued to commemorate the centenary of the founding of the International Red Cross.

Roman Column, Globe and Highways A469

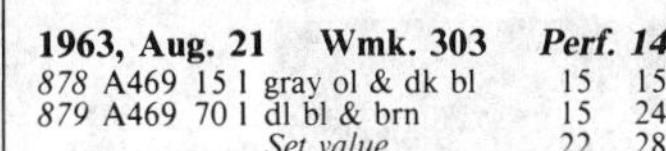

1963, Aug. 21 **Wmk. 303** ***Perf. 14***
878 A469 15 l gray ol & dk bl 15 15
879 A469 70 l dl bl & brn 15 24
Set value 22 28

UN Tourist Conf., Rome, Aug. 21-Sept. 5.

Europa Issue, 1963
Common Design Type
1963, Sept. 16
Size: 27½x23mm
880 CD6 30 l rose & brn 15 15
881 CD6 70 l brn & grn 15 15
Set value 22 18

Bay of Naples, Vesuvius and Sailboats — A470

Athlete on Greek Vase — A471

1963, Sept. 21 **Wmk. 303** ***Perf. 14***
882 A470 15 l bl & org 15 15
883 A471 70 l dk grn & org brn 15 15
Set value 18 17

Issued to commemorate the 4th Mediterranean Games, Naples, Sept. 21-29.

Giuseppe Gioachino Belli (1791-1863), Poet A472

Stamps Forming Flower A473

1963, Nov. 14 **Wmk. 303** ***Perf. 14***
884 A472 30 l red brn 15 15

1963, Dec. 1
885 A473 15 l bl & car 15 15

Issued for Stamp Day.

Pietro Mascagni and Old Costanzi Theater, Rome — A474

Design: No. 886, Giuseppe Verdi and La Scala, Milan.

1963 **Photo.**
886 A474 30 l gray grn & yel brn 15 15
887 A474 30 l yel brn & gray grn 15 15
Set value 16 15

Verdi (1813-1901), and Mascagni (1863-1945), composers. Dates of issue: No. 886, Oct. 10; No. 887, Dec. 7.

Galileo Galilei A475

Nicodemus by Michelangelo A476

1964, Feb. 15 **Wmk. 303** ***Perf. 14***
888 A475 30 l org brn 15 15
889 A475 70 l black 15 15
Set value 19 15

Issued to commemorate the 400th anniversary of the birth of Galileo Galilei (1564-1642), astronomer and physicist.

1964, Feb. 18 **Photo.**
890 A476 30 l brown 15 15

Michelangelo Buonarroti (1475-1564), artist. Head of Nicodemus (self-portrait?) from the Pieta, Florence Cathedral. See No. C137.

Carabinieri A477

Design: 70 l, Charge of Pastrengo, 1848, by De Albertis.

1964, June 5 **Wmk. 303** ***Perf. 14***
891 A477 30 l vio bl & red 15 15
892 A477 70 l brown 15 15
Set value 16 15

Issued to commemorate the 150th anniversary of the Carabinieri (police corps).

Giambattista Bodoni — A478

Perf. 14x13
1964, July 30 **Engr.** **Unwmk.**
893 A478 30 l carmine 15 15
a. Perf. 13 18 15

150th anniversary of the death of Giambattista Bodoni (1740-1813), printer and type designer (Bodoni type).

Europa Issue, 1964
Common Design Type
Wmk. 303
1964, Sept. 14 **Photo.** ***Perf. 14***
Size: 21x37mm
894 CD7 30 l brt rose lil 15 15
895 CD7 70 l bl grn 15 15
Set value 20 15

Walled City — A479

Left Arch of Victor Emmanuel Monument, Rome — A480

1964, Oct. 15 **Photo.** ***Perf. 14***
896 A479 30 l emer & dk brn 15 15
897 A479 70 l bl & dk brn 18 15

Unwmk. **Engr.**
898 A479 500 l red 90 50
Set value 66

7th Congress of European Towns. The buildings in design are: Big Ben, London; Campodoglio, Rome; Town Hall, Bruges; Römer, Frankfurt; Town Hall, Paris; Belfry, Zurich; Gate, Kampen (Holland).

1964, Nov. 4 Photo. Wmk. 303

899	A480	30 l dk red brn	15	15
900	A480	70 l blue	15	15
		Set value	18	16

Issued to commemorate the pilgrimage to Rome of veterans living abroad.

Giovanni da Verrazano and Verrazano-Narrows Bridge, New York Bay — A481

1964, Nov. 21 Wmk. 303 *Perf. 14*

901	A481	30 l blk & brn	15	15

Issued to commemorate the opening of the Verrazano-Narrows Bridge connecting Staten Island and Brooklyn, New York, and to honor Giovanni da Verrazano (1485-1528), discoverer of New York Bay. See No. C138.

Italian Sports Stamps, 1934-63 — A482

1964, Dec. 6 Photo. *Perf. 14*

902	A482	15 l gldn brn & dk brn	15	15

Issued for Stamp Day.

Italian Soldiers in Concentration Camp — A483

Victims Trapped by Swastika A484

Designs: 15 l, Italian soldier, sailor and airman fighting for the Allies. 70 l, Guerrilla fighters in the mountains. 115 l, Marchers with Italian flag. 130 l, Ruins of city and torn Italian flag.

1965, Apr. 24 Photo. Wmk. 303

903	A483	10 l black	15	15
904	A483	15 l grn & rose car	15	15
905	A484	30 l plum	15	15
906	A483	70 l dp bl	15	15
907	A484	115 l rose car	15	15
908	A484	130 l grn, sep & red	15	15
		Set value	40	35

20th anniversary of the Italian resistance movement during World War II.

Antonio Meucci, Guglielmo Marconi and ITU Emblem A485

1965, May 17 *Perf. 14*

909	A485	70 l red & dk grn	15	15

Cent. of the ITU.

Sailboats of Flying Dutchman Class A486

Designs: 70 l, Sailboats of 5.5-meter class (vert.). 500 l, Sailboats, Lightning class.

1965, May 31 Photo. Wmk. 303

910	A486	30 l blk & dl rose	15	15
911	A486	70 l blk & ultra	15	15
912	A486	500 l blk & gray bl	38	32
		Set value	55	45

Issued to publicize the World Yachting Championships, Naples and Alassio.

Mont Blanc and Tunnel A487

1965, June 16 Wmk. 303 *Perf. 14*

913	A487	30 l black	15	15

Issued to commemorate the opening of the Mont Blanc Tunnel connecting Entrayes, Italy, and Le Polerins, France.

Alessandro Tassoni and Scene from "Seccia Rapita" — A488

Unwmk.

1965, Sept. 20 Photo. *Perf. 14*

914	A488	40 l blk & multi	15	15

400th anniv. of the birth of Alessandro Tassoni (1565-1635), poet. Design is from 1744 engraving by Bartolomeo Soliani.

Europa Issue, 1965

Common Design Type

1965, Sept. 27 Wmk. 303

Size: 36½x27mm

915	CD8	40 l ocher & ol grn	15	15
916	CD8	90 l ultra & ol grn	15	15
		Set value	21	18

Dante, 15th Century Bust A489

House under Construction A490

Designs (from old Manuscripts): 40 l, Dante in Hell. 90 l, Dante in Purgatory led by Angel of Chastity. 130 l, Dante in Paradise interrogated by St. Peter on faith (horiz.).

Perf. 13½x14, 14x13½

1965, Oct. 21 Photo. Unwmk.

917	A489	40 l multi	15	15
918	A489	90 l multi	15	15
919	A489	130 l multi	15	15
		Set value	28	20

Wmk. 303 *Perf. 14*

920	A489	500 l slate grn	38	32

700th anniversary of the birth of Dante Alighieri (1265-1321), poet.

1965, Oct. 31 Wmk. 303 *Perf. 14*

921	A490	40 l buff, blk & org brn	15	15

Issued for Savings Day.

Jet Plane, Moon and Airletter Border A491

Design: 40 l, Control tower and plane.

1965, Nov. 3

922	A491	40 l dk Prus bl & red	15	15

Unwmk.

923	A491	90 l red, grn, dp bl & buff	15	15
		Set value	15	15

Night air postal network.

Map of Italy with Milan-Rome Highway — A492

Two-Man Bobsled — A493

1965, Dec. 5 Photo. *Perf. 13x14*

924	A492	20 l bl, blk, ocher & gray	15	15

Issued for Stamp Day.

1966, Jan. 24 Wmk. 303 *Perf. 14*

Design: 90 l, Four-man bobsled.

925	A493	40 l dl bl, gray & red	15	15
926	A493	90 l vio & bl	15	15
		Set value	15	15

Issued to commemorate the International Bobsled Championships, Cortina d'Ampezzo.

Woman Skater — A494

Benedetto Croce — A495

Winter University Games: 40 l, Skier holding torch (horiz.). 500 l, Ice hockey.

1966, Feb. 5 Photo.

927	A494	40 l blk & red	15	15
928	A494	90 l vio & red	15	15
929	A494	500 l brn & red	38	32
		Set value	55	45

1966, Feb. 25 Wmk. 303 *Perf. 14*

930	A495	40 l brown	15	15

Issued to commemorate the centenary of the birth of Benedetto Croce (1866-1952), philosopher, statesman and historian.

Arms of Venice and Other Cities in Venezia — A496

1966, Mar. 22 Photo. Unwmk.

932	A496	40 l gray & multi	15	15

Centenary of Venezia's union with Italy.

Battle of Bezzecca — A497

1966, July 21 Wmk. 303 *Perf. 14*

933	A497	90 l ol grn	15	15

Centenary of the unification of Italy and of the Battle of Bezzecca.

Umbrella Pine A498

Carnations A499

Designs: 25 l, Apples. 50 l, Florentine iris. 55 l, Cypresses. 90 l, Daisies. 170 l, Olive tree. 180 l, Juniper.

1966-68 Unwmk. *Perf. 13½x14*

934	A498	20 l multi	15	15
934A	A498	25 l multi ('67)	15	15
935	A499	40 l multi	15	15
935A	A498	50 l multi ('67)	15	15
935B	A498	55 l multi ('68)	15	15
936	A499	90 l multi	15	15
937	A498	170 l multi	24	15
937A	A498	180 l multi ('68)	24	15
		Set value	1.05	45

Tourist Attractions A500

"I" in Flag Colors A501

1966, May 28 Wmk. 303 *Perf. 14*
938 A500 20 l yel, org & blk 15 15

Issued for tourist publicity and in connection with the National Conference on Tourism, Rome.

Perf. 13½x14
1966, June 2 Photo. Unwmk.
939 A501 40 l multi 15 15
940 A501 90 l multi 15 15
Set value 15 15

20th anniversary of the Republic of Italy.

Singing Angels, by Donatello A502

Madonna, by Giotto A503

Perf. 13½x14
1966, Sept. 24 Photo. Unwmk.
941 A502 40 l multi 15 15

Issued to commemorate the centenary of the death of Donatello (1386-1466), sculptor.

Europa Issue, 1966
Common Design Type

1966, Sept. 26 Wmk. 303 *Perf. 14*
Size: 22x38mm
942 CD9 40 l brt pur 15 15
943 CD9 90 l brt bl 15 15
Set value 21 15

Perf. 13½x14
1966, Oct. 20 Photo. Unwmk.
944 A503 40 l multi 15 15

700th anniversary of the birth of Giotto di Bondone (1266?-1337), Florentine painter.

Italian Patriots A504

1966, Nov. 3 Wmk. 303 *Perf. 14*
945 A504 40 l gray & dl grn 15 15

Issued to commemorate the 50th anniversary of the execution by Austrians of four Italian patriots: Fabio Filzi, Cesare Battisti, Damiano Chiesa and Nazario Sauro.

Postrider — A505

Perf. 14x13½
1966, Dec. 4 Photo. Unwmk.
946 A505 20 l multi 15 15

Issued for Stamp Day.

Globe and Compass Rose A506

1967, Mar. 20 Photo. Wmk. 303
947 A506 40 l dull blue 15 15

Centenary of Italian Geographical Society.

Arturo Toscanini (1867-1957), Conductor A507

1967, Mar. 25 *Perf. 14*
948 A507 40 l dp vio & cream 15 15

Seat of Parliament on Capitoline Hill, Rome A508

1967, Mar. 25 *Perf. 14*
949 A508 40 l sepia 15 15
950 A508 90 l rose lil & blk 15 15
Set value 23 15

10th anniv. of the Treaty of Rome, establishing the European Common Market.

Europa Issue, 1967
Common Design Type

1967, Apr. 10 Wmk. 303 *Perf. 14*
Size: 22x28mm
951 CD10 40 l plum & pink 15 15
952 CD10 90 l ultra & pale gray 24 15
Set value 32 15

Alpine Ibex, Grand Paradiso Park — A509

National Parks: 40 l, Brown bear, Abruzzi Apennines (horiz.). 90 l, Red deer, Stelvio Pass, Ortler Mountains (horiz.). 170 l, Oak and deer, Circeo.

Perf. 13½x14, 14x13½
1967, Apr. 22 Photo.
953 A509 20 l multi 15 15
954 A509 40 l multi 15 15
955 A509 90 l multi 15 15
956 A509 170 l multi 24 15
Set value 50 32

Claudio Monteverdi and Characters from "Orfeo" A510

1967, May 15 *Perf. 14*
957 A510 40 l bis brn & brn 15 15

Issued to commemorate the 4th centenary of the birth of Claudio Monteverdi (1567-1643), composer.

Bicyclists and Mountains A511

50th Bicycle Tour of Italy: 90 l. Three bicyclists on the road. 500 l, Group of bicyclists.

Perf. 14x13½
1967, May 15 Photo. Unwmk.
958 A511 40 l multi 15 15
959 A511 90 l brt bl & multi 15 15
960 A511 500 l yel grn & multi 70 45
Set value 58

Luigi Pirandello and Stage A512

1967, June 28 *Perf. 14x13*
961 A512 40 l blk & multi 15 15

Issued to commemorate the centenary of the birth of Luigi Pirandello (1867-1936), novelist and dramatist.

Stylized Mask A513

1967, June 30 Wmk. 303 *Perf. 14*
962 A513 20 l grn & blk 15 15
963 A513 40 l car rose & blk 15 15
Set value 15 15

10th "Festival of Two Worlds," Spoleto.

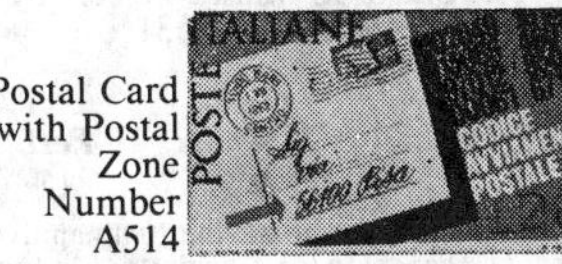
Postal Card with Postal Zone Number A514

Design: 40 l, 50 l, Letter addressed with postal zone number.

Wmk. 303, Unwmkd, (20 l, 40 l)
1967-68
964 A514 20 l multi 15 15
965 A514 25 l multi ('68) 15 15
966 A514 40 l multi 15 15
967 A514 50 l multi ('68) 15 15
Set value 30 20

Issued to publicize the introduction of postal zone numbers, July 1, 1967.

Pomilio PC-1 Biplane and 1917 Airmail Postmark A515

1967, July 18 Photo. Wmk. 303
968 A515 40 l blk & lt bl 15 15

Issued to commemorate the 50th anniversary of the first airmail stamp, Italy No. C1.

St. Ivo Church, Rome A516

Umberto Giordano and "Improvisation" from Opera Andrea Chenier A517

1967, Aug. 2 Unwmk. *Perf. 14*
969 A516 90 l multi 15 15

Francesco Borromini (1599-1667), architect.

1967, Aug. 28 Wmk. 303
970 A517 20 l blk & org brn 15 15

Umberto Giordano (1867-1948), composer.

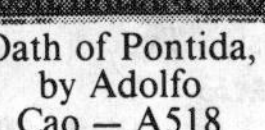
Oath of Pontida, by Adolfo Cao — A518

ITY Emblem — A519

1967, Sept. 2
971 A518 20 l dk brn 15 15

800th anniv. of the Oath of Pontida, which united the Lombard League against Emperor Frederick I.

Perf. 13½x14
1967, Oct. 23 Photo. Unwmk.
972 A519 20 l blk, cit & brt bl 15 15
973 A519 50 l blk, org & brt bl 15 15
Set value 15 15

Issued for International Tourist Year, 1967.

Lions Emblem A520

Soldier at the Piave A521

1967, Oct. 30 *Perf. 14x13½*
974 A520 50 l multi 15 15

50th anniversary of Lions International.

1967, Nov. 9 *Perf. 13x14*
975 A521 50 l multi 15 15

50th anniversary of Battle of the Piave.

Enrico Fermi at Los Alamos and Model of 1st Atomic Reactor — A522

"Day and Night" and Pigeon Carrying Italy No. 924 — A523

Wmk. 303

1967, Dec. 2 Photo. *Perf. 14*

976 A522 50 l org brn & blk 15 15

Issued to commemorate the 25th anniversary of the first atomic chain reaction under Enrico Fermi (1901-1954), Chicago, Ill.

1967, Dec. 3 Unwmk. *Perf. 13½x14*

977 A523 25 l multi 15 15

Issued for Stamp Day, 1967.

Scouts at Campfire — A524

St. Aloysius Gonzaga, by Pierre Legros — A525

1968, Apr. 23 *Perf. 13x14*

978 A524 50 l multi 15 15

Issued to honor the Boy Scouts.

Europa Issue, 1968
Common Design Type
Perf. 14x13

1968, Apr. 29 Wmk. 303

Size: 36½x26mm

979 CD11 50 l blk, rose & sl grn 15 15
980 CD11 90 l blk, bl & brn 15 15
Set value 18

Perf. 13½x14

1968, May 28 Photo. Wmk. 303

981 A525 25 l red brn & dl vio 15 15

Aloysius Gonzaga (1568-1591), Jesuit priest who ministered to victims of the plague.

Arrigo Boito and Mephistopheles — A526

1968, June 10 Unwmk. *Perf. 14*

982 A526 50 l multi 15 15

Issued to commemorate the 50th anniversary of the death of Arrigo Boito (1842-1918), composer and librettist.

The first price column gives the catalogue value of an unused stamp, the second that of a used stamp.

Francesco Baracca and "Planes," by Giacomo Balla A527

1968, June 19

983 A527 25 l multi 15 15

Issued to commemorate the 50th anniversary of the death of Major Francesco Baracca (1888-1918), World War I aviator.

Giambattista Vico — A528

Bicycle Wheel and Velodrome, Rome — A529

Designs: No. 985, Tommaso Campanella. No. 986, Gioacchino Rossini.

Perf. 14x13½

1968 Engr. Wmk. 303

984 A528 50 l ultra 15 15
985 A528 50 l black 15 15
a. Perf. 13½ 90 18
986 A528 50 l car rose 15 15
Set value 32 18

Vico (1668-1744), philosopher; Campanella (1568-1639), Dominican monk, philosopher, poet and teacher; Rossini (1792-1868), composer.

Issue dates: No. 984, June 24; No. 985, Sept. 5; No. 986, Oct. 25.

Perf. 13x14

1968, Aug. 26 Photo. Unwmk.

Design: 90 l, Bicycle and Sforza Castle, Imola.

987 A529 25 l sl, rose & brn 15 15
988 A529 90 l sl, bl & ver 15 15
Set value 18 15

Issued to publicize the Bicycling World Championships. The 25 l commemorates the track championships at the Velodrome in Rome, the 90 l, the road championships at Imola.

"The Small St. Mark's Place," by Canaletto — A531

1968, Sept. 30 Unwmk. *Perf. 14*

989 A531 50 l pink & multi 15 15

Issued to commemorate the 200th anniversary of the death of Canaletto (Antonio Canale, 1697-1768), Venetian painter.

"Mobilization" — A533

Symbolic Designs: 25 l, Trench war. 40 l, The Navy. 50 l, The Air Force. 90 l, The Battle of Vittorio Veneto. 180 l, The Unknown Soldier.

1968, Nov. 2 Photo. Unwmk.

990 A533 20 l brn & multi 15 15
991 A533 25 l bl & multi 15 15
992 A533 40 l multi 15 15
993 A533 50 l multi 15 15
994 A533 90 l grn & multi 15 15
995 A533 180 l bl & multi 15 15
Set value 62 48

50th anniv. of the Allies' Victory in WW I.

Emblem — A534

1968, Nov. 20 *Perf. 14x13½*

996 A534 50 l blk, bl grn & red 15 15

Issued to commemorate the 50th anniversary of the Postal Checking Service.

Parabolic Antenna, Fucino A535

1968, Nov. 25 Photo. *Perf. 14*

997 A535 50 l multi 15 15

Issued to publicize the expansion of the space communications center at Fucino.

Development of Postal Service — A536

1968, Dec. 1 Wmk. 303

998 A536 25 l car & yel 15 15

Issued for the 10th Stamp Day.

Fluorescent Paper was introduced in 1968 for regular and special delivery issues. These stamps are about 1mm. smaller each way than the non-fluorescent ones they replaced, except Nos. 690-690A which remained the same size.

Commemorative or nonregular stamps issued only on fluorescent paper are Nos. 935B, 937A, 965, 967 and from 981 onward unless otherwise noted.

Italia Type of 1953-54
Small Size: 16x19½-20mm

Photo.; Engr. (100, 150, 200-400 l)

1968-76 Wmk. 303 *Perf. 14*

998A A354 1 l dk gray 15 15
998B A354 5 l slate 15 15
998C A354 6 l ocher 15 15
998D A354 10 l org ver 15 15
998E A354 15 l gray vio 15 15
998F A354 20 l brown 15 15
998G A354 25 l purple 15 15
998H A354 30 l bis brn 15 15
998I A354 40 l lil rose 15 15
998J A354 50 l olive 15 15
998K A354 55 l vio ('69) 15 15
998L A354 60 l blue 15 15
998M A354 70 l Prus grn 15 15
998N A354 80 l brn org 15 15
998O A354 90 l lt red brn 15 15
998P A354 100 l redsh brn 15 15
998Q A354 125 l ocher & lil ('74) 15 15
998R A354 130 l gray & dl red 15 15
998S A354 150 l vio ('76) 15 15
998T A354 180 l gray & vio brn ('71) 22 15
998U A354 200 l slate bl 15 15
998V A354 300 l Prus grn ('72) 28 15
998W A354 400 l dl red ('76) 28 15
Set value 2.50 1.25

Memorial Medal — A537

Unwmk.

1969, Apr. 22 Photo. *Perf. 14*

999 A537 50 l pink & blk 15 15

Centenary of the State Audit Bureau.

Europa Issue, 1969
Common Design Type

1969, Apr. 28 *Perf. 14x13*

Size: 35½x25½mm

1000 CD12 50 l mag & multi 15 15
1001 CD12 90 l bl & multi 15 15
Set value 19

Niccolo Machiavelli A538

ILO Emblem A539

1969, May 3 *Perf. 14x13½*

1002 A538 50 l bl & multi 15 15

Niccolo Machiavelli (1469-1527), statesman and political philosopher.

Wmk. 303

1969, June 7 Photo. *Perf. 14*

1003 A539 50 l grn & blk 15 15
1004 A539 90 l car & blk 15 15
Set value 22 15

50th anniv. of the ILO.

Federation Emblem, Tower of Superga Basilica and Matterhorn A540

1969, June 26 Unwmk. *Perf. 14*

1005 A540 50 l gold, bl & car 15 15

50th anniversary of the Federation of Italian Philatelic Societies.

Sondrio-Tirano Stagecoach, 1903 — A541

1969, Dec. 7 Engr. Wmk. 303

1006 A541 25 l vio bl 15 15

Issued for the 11th Stamp Day.

Downhill Skier — A542

Design: 90 l, Sassolungo and Sella Group, Dolomite Alps.

Perf. 13x14

1970, Feb. 6 Unwmk. Photo.

1007 A542 50 l bl & multi 15 15
1008 A542 90 l bl & multi 15 15
Set value 22 15

Issued to publicize the World Alpine Ski Championships, Val Gardena, Bolzano Province, Feb. 6-15.

Galatea, by Raphael A543

Painting: 50 l, Madonna with the Goldfinch (detail), by Raphael.

1970, Apr. 6 Photo. *Perf. 14x13*

1009 A543 20 l multi 15 15
1010 A543 50 l multi 15 15
Set value 18 15

Issued to commemorate the 450th anniversary of the death of Raphael (1483-1520).

Symbol of Flight, Colors of Italy and Japan A544

1970, May 2 Unwmk. *Perf. 14*

1011 A544 50 l multi 15 15
1012 A544 90 l multi 15 15
Set value 22 15

50th anniv. of Arturo Ferrarin's flight from Rome to Tokyo, Feb. 14-May 31, 1920.

Europa Issue, 1970

Common Design Type

1970, May 4 Wmk. 303

Size: 36x20mm

1013 CD13 50 l red & org 15 15
1014 CD13 90 l bl grn & org 20 15
Set value 18

Gattamelata, Bust by Donatello — A545

1970, May 30 Engr. *Perf. 14x13*

1015 A545 50 l slate grn 15 15

Issued to commemorate the 6th centenary of the birth of Erasmo de' Narni, called Il Gattamelata (1370-1443), condottiere.

Runner A546

Unwmk.

1970, Aug. 26 Photo. *Perf. 14*

1016 A546 20 l shown 15 15
1017 A546 180 l Swimmer 18 15
Set value 27 15

Issued to publicize the 1970 World University Games, Turin, Aug. 26-Sept. 6.

Dr. Maria Montessori and Children A547

1970, Aug. 31 *Perf. 14x13*

1018 A547 50 l multi 15 15

Montessori (1870-1952), educator & physician.

Map of Italy and Quotation of Count Camillo Cavour — A548

1970, Sept. 19 Unwmk. *Perf. 14*

1019 A548 50 l multi 15 15

Issued to commemorate the centenary of the union of the Roman States with Italy.

Loggia of St. Mark's Campanile, Venice A549

Perf. 14x13½

1970, Sept. 26 Engr. Wmk. 303

1020 A549 50 l red brown 15 15

Iacopo Tatti "Il Sansovino" (1486-1570), architect.

Garibaldi at Battle of Dijon A550

1970, Oct. 15 Photo. *Perf. 14*

1021 A550 20 l gray & dk bl 15 15
1022 A550 50 l brt rose lil & dk bl 15 15
Set value 15 15

Centenary of Garibaldi's participation in the Franco-Prussian War during Battle of Dijon.

Tree and UN Emblem — A551

1970, Oct. 24 Unwmk. *Perf. 13x14*

1023 A551 25 l blk, sep & grn 15 15
1024 A551 90 l blk, brt bl & yel grn 15 15
Set value 22 15

25th anniversary of the United Nations.

Rotary Emblem A552

1970, Nov. 12 Wmk. 303 *Perf. 14*

1025 A552 25 l bluish vio & org 15 15
1026 A552 90 l bluish vio & org 15 15
Set value 22 15

Rotary International, 65th anniversary.

Telephone Dial and Trunk Lines A553

1970, Nov. 24

1027 A553 25 l yel grn & dk red 15 15
1028 A553 90 l ultra & dk red 15 15
Set value 22 15

Issued to publicize the completion of the automatic trunk telephone dialing system.

"Man Damaging Nature" — A554

Virgin and Child, by Fra Filippo Lippi — A556

Mail Train A555

1970, Nov. 28 Wmk. 303 *Perf. 14*

1029 A554 20 l car lake & grn 15 15
1030 A554 25 l dk bl & emer 15 15
Set value 24 18

For European Nature Conservation Year.

1970, Dec. 6 Engr.

1031 A555 25 l black 15 15

For the 12th Stamp Day.

1970, Dec. 12 Photo. Unwmk.

1032 A556 25 l multi 15 15

Christmas 1970. See No. C139.

Saverio Mercadante (1795-1870), Composer A557

1970, Dec. 17 Wmk. 303

1033 A557 25 l vio & gray 15 15

Mercury, by Benvenuto Cellini A558

Bramante's Temple, St. Peter in Montorio A559

1971, Mar. 20 Photo. *Perf. 14*

1034 A558 50 l Prus bl 15 15

400th anniversary of the death of Benvenuto Cellini (1500-1571), sculptor.

Photogravure and Engraved

1971, Apr. 8 *Perf. 13x14*

1035 A559 50 l ocher & blk 15 15

Honoring Bramante (Donato di Angelo di Antonio, 1444-1514), architect.

Adenauer, Schuman, De Gasperi A560

Perf. 14x13½

1971, Apr. 28 Photo. Wmk. 303

1036 A560 50 l blk & lt grnsh bl 15 15
1037 A560 90 l blk & lil rose 15 15
Set value 22 15

20th anniversary of the European Coal and Steel Community.

Europa Issue, 1971

Common Design Type

1971, May 3 *Perf. 14*

1038 CD14 50 l ver & dk red 15 15
1039 CD14 90 l brt rose lil & dk lil 15 15
Set value 18

Giuseppe Mazzini, Italian Flag — A561

Perf. 14x13½

1971, June 12 Unwmk.

1040 A561 50 l multi 15 15
1041 A561 90 l multi 15 15
Set value 17

25th anniversary of the Italian Republic.

Kayak Passing Between Poles A562

Design: 90 l, Kayak in free descent.

1971, June 16 Photo. *Perf. 14*

1042 A562 25 l multi 15 15
1043 A562 90 l multi 15 15
Set value 22 15

Canoe Slalom World Championships, Merano.

Skiing, Basketball, Volleyball — A563

Design: 50 l, Gymnastics, cycling, track and swimming.

Perf. 13½x14

1971, June 26 Photo. Unwmk.

1044 A563 20 l emer, ocher & blk 15 15
1045 A563 50 l dl bl, org & blk 15 15
Set value 15 15

Youth Games.

Plane Circling Globe and "A" — A564

Designs: 50 l, Ornamental "A." 150 l, Tail of B747 in shape of "A."

1971, Sept. 16 ***Perf. 14x13½***

1046 A564 50 l multi 15 15
1047 A564 90 l multi 15 15
1048 A564 150 l multi 15 15
Set value 30

25th anniversary of the founding of ALITALIA, Italian airlines.

Grazia Deledda (1871-1936), Novelist A565

Child in Barrel Made of Banknote A566

Photogravure and Engraved

Perf. 13½x14

1971, Sept. 28 Wmk. 303

1049 A565 50 l blk & sal 15 15

Perf. 13x14

1971, Oct. 27 Photo. Unwmk.

1050 A566 25 l blk & multi 15 15
1051 A566 50 l multi 15 15
Set value 18 15

Publicity for postal savings bank.

UNICEF Emblem and Children A567

Design: 90 l, Children hailing UNICEF emblem.

1971, Nov. 26 ***Perf. 14x13***

1052 A567 25 l pink & multi 15 15
1053 A567 90 l multi 15 15
Set value 22 15

25th anniv. of UNICEF.

Packet Tirrenia and Postal Ensign A568

1971, Dec. 5 Wmk. 303 ***Perf. 14***

1054 A568 25 l slate green 15 15

Stamp Day.

Nativity A569

Christmas: 90 l, Adoration of the Kings. Both designs are from miniatures in Evangelistary of Matilda in Nonantola Abbey, 12th-13th centuries.

Perf. 14x13

1971, Dec. 10 Photo. Unwmk.

1055 A569 25 l gray & multi 15 15
1056 A569 90 l gray & multi 15 15
Set value 22 15

Giovanni Verga and Sicilian Cart — A570

1972, Jan. 27

1057 A570 25 l org & multi 15 15
1058 A570 50 l multi 15 15
Set value 15 15

Verga (1840-1922), writer & playwright.

Giuseppe Mazzini (1805-1872), Patriot and Writer — A571

Wmk. 303

1972, Mar. 10 Engr. ***Perf. 13***

1059 A571 25 l blk & Prus grn 15 15
1060 A571 90 l black 15 15
1061 A571 150 l blk & rose red 15 15
Set value 32 24

Flags, Milan Fair — A572

Designs: 50 l, 90 l, Different abstract views.

Perf. 14x13½

1972, Apr. 14 Photo. Unwmk.

1062 A572 25 l emer & blk 15 15
1063 A572 50 l dp org & blk 15 15
1064 A572 90 l bl & blk 15 15
Set value 30 22

50th anniversary of the Milan Sample Fair.

Europa Issue 1972

Common Design Type

1972, May 2 ***Perf. 13x14***

Size: 26x36mm

1065 CD15 50 l multi 15 15
1066 CD15 90 l multi 15 15
Set value 18

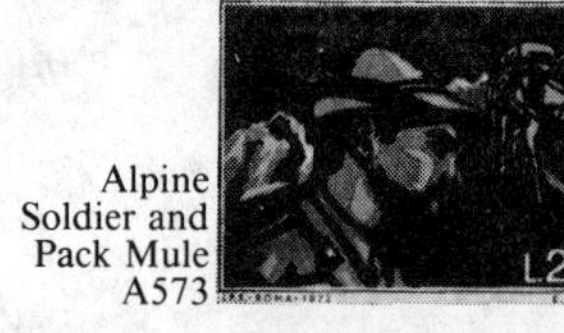

Alpine Soldier and Pack Mule A573

Designs: 50 l, Mountains, Alpinist's hat, pick and laurel. 90 l, Alpine soldier and mountains.

1972, May 10 ***Perf. 14x13***

1067 A573 25 l ol & multi 15 15
1068 A573 50 l bl & multi 15 15
1069 A573 90 l grn & multi 15 15
Set value 32 20

Centenary of the Alpine Corps.

Brenta Mountains, Society Emblem A574

Designs (Emblem and): 50 l, Mountain climber and Brenta Mountains. 180 l, Sunset over Mt. Crozzon.

Perf. 14x13

1972, Sept. 2 Photo. Unwmk.

1070 A574 25 l multi 15 15
1071 A574 50 l multi 15 15
1072 A574 180 l multi 15 15
Set value 35 18

Tridentine Alpinist Society centenary.

Conference Emblem, Seating Diagram A575

1972, Sept. 21

1073 A575 50 l multi 15 15
1074 A575 90 l multi 15 15
Set value 22 15

60th Conference of the Inter-Parliamentary Union, Montecitorio Hall, Rome.

St. Peter Damian, by Giovanni di Paoli, c. 1445 — A576

1972, Sept. 21 Photo.

1075 A576 50 l multi 15 15

St. Peter Damian (1007-72), church reformer, cardinal, papal legate.

The Three Graces, by Antonio Canova (1757-1822), Sculptor — A577

1972, Oct. 13 Engr. Wmk. 303

1076 A577 50 l black 15 15

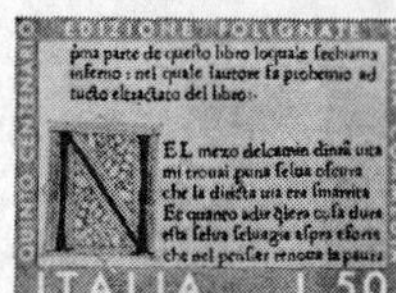

Page from Divine Comedy, Foligno Edition A578

Designs (Illuminated First Pages): 90 l, Mantua edition (vert.). 180 l, Jesina edition.

Perf. 14x13½, 13½x14

1972, Nov. 23 Photo. Unwmk.

1077 A578 50 l ocher & multi 15 15
1078 A578 90 l multi 15 15
1079 A578 180 l multi 18 15
Set value 28

500th anniversary of three illuminated editions of Dante's Divine Comedy.

Angel — A579

Christmas: 25 l, Christ Child in cradle (horiz.). 150 l, Angel. All designs from 18th century Neapolitan creche.

Perf. 13x14, 14x13

1972, Dec. 6 Photo.

1080 A579 20 l multi 15 15
1081 A579 25 l multi 15 15
1082 A579 150 l multi 15 15
Set value 32 24

Passenger and Mail Autobus A580

1972, Dec. 16 Engr. Wmk. 303

1083 A580 25 l magenta 15 15

Stamp Day.

Leon Battista Alberti A581

Lorenzo Perosi A582

1972, Dec. 16 ***Perf. 14***

1084 A581 50 l ultra & ocher 15 15

Leon Battista Alberti (1404-1472), architect, painter, organist and writer.

1972, Dec. 20 Photo. Unwmk.

1085 A582 50 l dk vio brn & org 15 15
1086 A582 90 l blk & yel grn 15 15
Set value 22 15

Centenary of the birth of Lorenzo Perosi (1872-1956), priest and composer.

Luigi Orione and Boys — A583

Ship Exploring Ocean Floor — A584

1972, Dec. 30

1087 A583 50 l lt bl & dk bl 15 15
1088 A583 90 l ocher & sl grn 15 15
Set value 22 15

Centenary of the birth of Luigi Orione (1872-1940), founder of CARITAS; Catholic Welfare Organization.

1973, Feb. 15 Photo. *Perf. 13x14*

1089 A584 50 l multi 15 15

Cent. of the Naval Hydrographic Institute.

Palace Staircase, Caserta A585

1973, Mar. 1 Engr. *Perf. 14x13½*

1090 A585 25 l gray ol 15 15

Luigi Vanvitelli (1700-1773), architect.

Schiavoni Shore — A586

The Tetrarchs, 4th Century Sculpture — A587

Designs: 50 l, "Triumph of Venice," by Vittore Carpaccio. 90 l, Bronze horses from St. Mark's. 300 l, St. Mark's Square covered by flood.

1973 Photo. *Perf. 14*

1091 A586 20 l ultra & multi 15 15
1092 A587 25 l ultra & multi 15 15
1093 A586 50 l ultra & multi 15 15
1094 A587 90 l ultra & multi 15 15
1095 A586 300 l ultra & multi 38 28
Set value 72 50

Save Venice campaign. Issue dates: No. 1091, Mar. 5; others Apr. 10.

Verona Fair Emblem — A588

Title Page for Book about Rosa — A589

1973, Mar. 10 *Perf. 13x14*

1096 A588 50 l multi 15 15

75th International Fair, Verona.

1973, Mar. 15 *Perf. 14*

1097 A589 25 l org & blk 15 15

300th anniversary of death of Salvator Rosa (1615-1673), painter and poet.

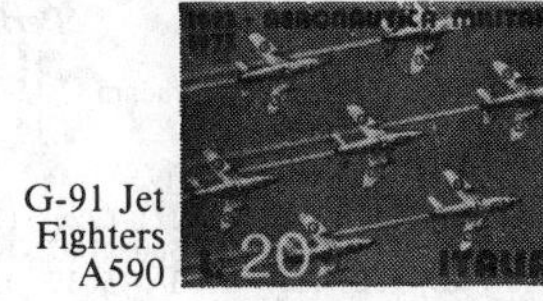

G-91 Jet Fighters A590

Designs: 25 l, Formation of S-55 seaplanes. 50 l, G-91Y fighters. 90 l, Fiat CR-32's flying figure 8. 180 l, Camprini-Caproni jet, 1940.

1973, Mar. 28 *Perf. 14x13½*

1098 A590 20 l multi 15 15
1099 A590 25 l multi 15 15
1100 A590 50 l multi 15 15
1101 A590 90 l multi 15 15
1102 A590 180 l multi 18 15

Set value, #1098-1102, C140 80 50

50th anniversary of military aviation.

Soccer Field and Ball — A591

Design: 90 l, Soccer players and goal.

1973, May 19 Photo. *Perf. 14x13½*

1103 A591 25 l ol, blk & lt grn 15 15
1104 A591 90 l grn & multi 15 15
Set value 20 15

75th anniv. of Italian Soccer Federation.

Alessandro Manzoni, by Francisco Hayez A592

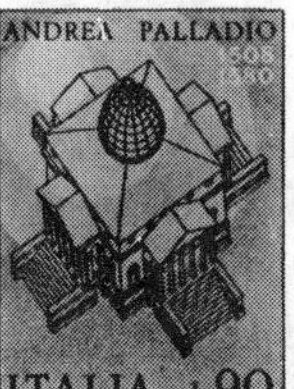

Villa Rotunda, by Andrea Palladio (1508-80), Architect. A593

1973, May 22 Engr.

1105 A592 25 l blk & brn 15 15

Centenary of the death of Alessandro Manzoni (1785-1873), novelist and poet.

1973, May 30 Photo. Unwmk.
Perf. 13x14

1106 A593 90 l blk, yel & lem 15 15

Spiral and Cogwheels A594

1973, June 20 *Perf. 14x13*

1107 A594 50 l gold & multi 15 15

50th anniversary of the State Supply Office.

Europa Issue 1973
Common Design Type

1973, June 30 Litho. *Perf. 14*
Size: 36x20mm

1108 CD16 50 l lil, gold & yel 15 15
1109 CD16 90 l lt bl grn, gold & yel 15 15
Set value 22 18

Catcher and Diamond A595

Design: 90 l, Diamond and batter.

1973, July 21 Photo. *Perf. 14x13½*

1110 A595 25 l multi 15 15
1111 A595 90 l multi 15 15
Set value 20 15

International Baseball Cup.

Viareggio by Night A596

Gaetano Salvemini A598

Assassination of Minzoni A597

1973, Aug. 10 Photo. *Perf. 13x14*

1112 A596 25 l blk & multi 15 15

Viareggio Carnival.

1973, Aug. 23 *Perf. 14x13*

1113 A597 50 l multi 15 15

Giovanni Minzoni (1885-1923), priest and social worker.

1973, Sept. 8 *Perf. 14x13½*

1114 A598 50 l pink & multi 15 15

Gaetano Salvemini (1873-1957), historian, anti-Fascist.

Palazzo Farnese, Caprarola, by Vignola A599

1973, Sept. 21 Engr. *Perf. 14x13½*

1115 A599 90 l choc & yel 15 15

400th anniversary of the death of Giacomo da Vignola (real name, Giacomo Barocchio), 1507-1573, architect.

St. John the Baptist, by Caravaggio A600

Lithographed & Engraved

1973, Sept. 28 *Perf. 14*

1116 A600 25 l blk & dl yel 15 15

400th anniversary of the birth of Michelangelo da Caravaggio (1573-1610?), painter.

Tower of Pisa — A601

1973, Oct. 8 Photo.

1117 A601 50 l multi 15 15

8th century of Leaning Tower of Pisa.

Sandro Botticelli A602

Trevi Fountain, Rome A603

1973-74 Photo. *Perf. 14x13½*

1118 A602 50 l shown 15 15
1119 A602 50 l Giambattista Piranesi 15 15
1120 A602 50 l Paolo Veronese 15 15
1121 A602 50 l Andrea del Verrocchio 15 15
1122 A602 50 l Giovanni Battista Tiepolo 15 15
1123 A602 50 l Francesco Borromini 15 15
1124 A602 50 l Rosalba Carriera 15 15
1125 A602 50 l Giovanni Bellini 15 15
1126 A602 50 l Andrea Mantegna 15 15
1127 A602 50 l Raphael 15 15
Set value 90 45

Famous artists.

Issue dates: Nos. 1118-1122, Nov. 5, 1973. Nos. 1123-1127, May 25, 1974.

Photogravure and Engraved

1973, Nov. 10 *Perf. 13½x14*

Designs: No. 1129, Immacolatella Fountain, Naples. No. 1130, Pretoria Fountain, Palermo.

1128 A603 25 l blk & multi 15 15
1129 A603 25 l blk & multi 15 15
1130 A603 25 l blk & multi 15 15
Set value 24 15

See Nos. 1166-1168, 1201-1203, 1251-1253, 1277-1279, 1341-1343, 1379-1381.

Angels, by Agostino di Duccio A604

Map of Italy, Rotary Emblems A605

Sculptures by Agostino di Duccio: 25 l, Virgin and Child. 150 l, Angels with flute and trumpet.

1973, Nov. 26

1131 A604 20 l yel grn & blk 15 15
1132 A604 25 l lt bl & blk 15 15
1133 A604 150 l yel & blk 15 15
Set value 30 18

Christmas 1973.

1973, Nov. 28 Photo.

1134 A605 50 l red, grn & dk bl 15 15

50th anniv. of Rotary International of Italy.

Caravelle
A606

Wmk. 303

1973, Dec. 2 Engr. *Perf. 14*
1135 A606 25 l Prus bl 15 15

15th Stamp Day.

Medal of Valor — A607

Enrico Caruso — A608

Perf. 13½x14

1973, Dec. 10 Photo. Unwmk.
1136 A607 50 l gold & multi 15 15

Gold Medal of Valor, 50th anniversary.

1973, Dec. 15 Engr.

Design: 50 l, Caruso as Duke in Rigoletto.

1137 A608 50 l magenta 15 15

Enrico Caruso (1873-1921), operatic tenor.

Christ Crowning King Roger
A609

Luigi Einaudi
A610

Design: 50 l, King William II offering model of church to the Virgin, mosaic from Monreale Cathedral. The design of 20 l, is from a mosaic in Martorana Church, Palermo.

Lithographed and Engraved

1974, Mar. 4 *Perf. 13½x14*
1138 A609 20 l ind & buff 15 15
1139 A609 50 l red & lt grn 15 15
Set value 15 15

Norman art in Sicily.

1974, Mar. 23 Engr. *Perf. 14x13½*
1140 A610 50 l green 15 15

Luigi Einaudi (1874-1961), Pres. of Italy.

Guglielmo Marconi (1874-1937), Italian Inventor and Physicist
A611

Design: 90 l, Marconi and world map.

1974, Apr. 24 Photo. *Perf. 14x13½*
1141 A611 50 l bl grn & gray 15 15
1142 A611 90 l vio & multi 15 15
Set value 22 15

David, by Giovanni L. Bernini — A612

Europa: 90 l, David, by Michelangelo.

1974, Apr. 29 Photo. *Perf. 13½x14*
1143 A612 50 l sal, ultra & gray 15 15
1144 A612 90 l grn, ultra & buff 15 15
Set value 22 18

Customs Frontier Guards, 1774, 1795, 1817 — A613

Uniforms of Customs Service: 50 l, Lombardy Venetia, 1848, Sardinia, 1815, Tebro Battalion, 1849. 90 l, Customs Guards, 1866, 1880 and Naval Marshal, 1892. 180 l, Helicopter pilot, Naval and Alpine Guards, 1974. All bordered with Italian flag colors.

1974, June 21 Photo. *Perf. 14*
1145 A613 40 l multi 15 15
1146 A613 50 l multi 15 15
1147 A613 90 l multi 15 15
1148 A613 180 l multi 18 15
Set value 46 30

Customs Frontier Guards bicentenary.

Sprinter
A614

1974, June 28 Photo. *Perf. 14x13*
1149 A614 40 l shown 15 15
1150 A614 50 l Pole vault 15 15
Set value 18 15

European Athletic Championships, Rome.

Sharpshooter
A615

Design: 50 l, Bersaglieri emblem.

1974, June 27
1151 A615 40 l multi 15 15
1152 A615 50 l grn & multi 15 15
Set value 18 15

50th anniversary of the Bersaglieri Veterans Association.

View of Portofino — A616

1974, July 10 *Perf. 14*
1153 A616 40 l shown 15 15
1154 A616 40 l View of Gradara 15 15
Set value 18 15

Tourist publicity.

See Nos. 1190-1192, 1221-1223, 1261-1265, 1314-1316, 1357-1360, 1402-1405, 1466-1469, 1520-1523, 1563A-1563D, 1599-1602, 1630-1633, 1708-1711, 1737-1740, 1803-1806, 1830-1833.

Petrarch (1304-74), Poet — A617

Design: 50 l, Petrarch at his desk (from medieval manuscript).

Lithographed and Engraved

1974, July 19 *Perf. 13½x14*
1155 A617 40 l ocher & multi 15 15
1156 A617 50 l ocher, yel & bl 15 15
Set value 18 15

Tommaseo Statue, by Ettore Ximenes, Shibenik
A618

Giacomo Puccini (1858-1924), Composer
A619

1974, July 19
1157 A618 50 l grn & pink 15 15

Niccolo Tommaseo (1802-1874), writer, Venetian education minister.

1974, Aug. 16 Photo.
1158 A619 40 l multi 15 15

King Roland, Woodcut — A620

1974, Sept. 9 Engr. *Perf. 14x13½*
1159 A620 50 l car & vio bl 15 15

500th anniversary of the birth of Lodovico Ariosto (1474-1533), poet. The design is from a contemporary illustration of Ariosto's poem "Orlando Furioso."

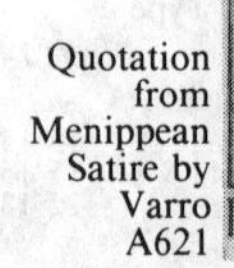

Quotation from Menippean Satire by Varro
A621

1974, Sept. 21
1160 A621 50 l ocher & dk red 15 15

Marcus Terentius Varro (116-27 BC), Roman scholar and writer.

"October," 15th Century Mural
A622

1974, Sept. 28 Photo. *Perf. 14*
1161 A622 50 l multi 15 15

14th International Wine Congress, Trento.

"UPU" and Emblem
A623

Design: 90 l, Letters, "UPU" and emblem.

1974, Oct. 19 Photo. *Perf. 14*
1162 A623 50 l multi 15 15
1163 A623 90 l multi 15 15
Set value 22 15

Centenary of Universal Postal Union.

St. Thomas Aquinas, by Francesco Traini — A624

Bas-relief from Ara Pacis — A625

1974, Oct. 25 *Perf. 13x14*
1164 A624 50 l multi 15 15

St. Thomas Aquinas (1225-1274), scholastic philosopher, 700th death anniversary.

1974, Oct. 26
1165 A625 50 l multi 15 15

Centenary of the Ordini Forensi (Bar Association).

Fountain Type of 1973

Designs: No. 1166, Oceanus Fountain, Florence. No. 1167, Neptune Fountain, Bologna. No. 1168, Fontana Maggiore, Perugia.

Photogravure and Engraved

1974, Nov. 9 *Perf. 13x14*
1166 A603 40 l blk & multi 15 15
1167 A603 40 l blk & multi 15 15
1168 A603 40 l blk & multi 15 15
Set value 24 15

St. Francis Adoring Christ Child, by Presepe di Greccio
A626

Photogravure and Engraved

1974, Nov. 26 *Perf. 14x13½*
1169 A626 40 l multi 15 15

Christmas 1974.

Masked Dancers — A627

1974, Dec. 1 Photo. *Perf. 13½x14*
1170 A627 40 l Pulcinella 15 15
1171 A627 50 l shown 15 15
1172 A627 90 l Pantaloon 15 15
Set value 30 18

16th Stamp Day 1974.

God Admonishing Adam, by Jacopo della Quercia — A628

Courtyard, Uffizi Gallery, Florence, by Giorgio Vasari A629

1974, Dec. 20 Engr. *Perf. 14*
1173 A628 90 l dk vio bl 15 15

Lithographed and Engraved
1174 A629 90 l multi 15 15
Set value 18

Italian artists: Jacopo della Quercia (1374-c. 1438), sculptor, and Giorgio Vasari (1511-1574), architect, painter and writer.

Angel with Tablet — A630

Angel with Cross — A632

Angels' Bridge, Rome A631

Holy Year 1975: 50 l, Angel holding column. 150 l, Angel holding Crown of Thorns. The angels are statues by Giovanni Bernini on the Angels' Bridge (San Angelo).

1975, Mar. 25 Photo. *Perf. 14*
1175 A630 40 l multi 15 15
1176 A630 50 l bl & multi 15 15
1177 A631 90 l bl & multi 15 15
1178 A630 150 l vio & multi 15 15
1179 A632 180 l multi 18 15
Set value 62 40

Pitti Madonna, by Michelangelo A633

Flagellation of Jesus, by Caravaggio A634

Designs (Works of Michelangelo): 50 l, Niche in Vatican Palace. 90 l, The Flood, detail from Sistine Chapel.

1975, Apr. 18 Engr. *Perf. 13½x14*
1180 A633 40 l dl grn 15 15
1181 A633 50 l sepia 15 15
1182 A633 90 l red brn 15 15
Set value 28 18

500th birth anniversary of Michelangelo Buonarroti (1475-1564), sculptor, painter and architect.

1975, Apr. 29 Photo. *Perf. 13x14*

Europa: 150 l, Apparition of Angel to Hagar and Ishmael, by Tiepolo (detail).

1183 A634 100 l multi 15 15
1184 A634 150 l multi 15 15
Set value 18

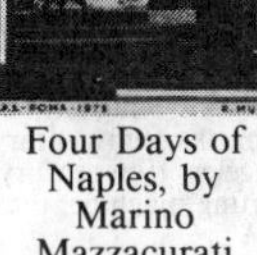
Four Days of Naples, by Marino Mazzacurati A635

Resistance Fighters of Cuneo, by Umberto Mastroianni A636

Design: 100 l, Martyrs of Ardeatine Caves, by Francesco Coccia.

1975, Apr. 23
1185 A635 70 l multi 15 15
1186 A636 100 l ol & multi 15 15
1187 A636 150 l multi 15 15
Set value 38 26

30th anniversary of victory of the resistance movement.

Globe and IWY Emblem A637

1975, May *Perf. 14x13½*
1188 A637 70 l multi 15 15

International Women's Year 1975.

Satellite, San Rita Launching Platform — A638

1975, May 28 *Perf. 13½x14*
1189 A638 70 l multi 15 15

San Marco satellite project.

Tourist Type of 1974

Paintings: No. 1190, View of Isola Bella. No. 1191, Baths of Montecatini. No. 1192, View of Cefalu.

1975, June 16 Photo. *Perf. 14*
1190 A616 150 l grn & multi 18 15
1191 A616 150 l bl grn & multi 18 15
1192 A616 150 l red brn & multi 18 15
Set value 27

Artist and Model, Armando Spadini A640

Painting: No. 1194, Flora, by Guido Reni.

1975, June 20 Engr. *Perf. 14*
1193 A640 90 l blk & multi 15 15
1194 A640 90 l multi 15 15
Set value 18

50th death anniv. of Armando Spadini and 400th birth anniv. of Guido Reni.

Giovanni Pierluigi da Palestrina (1525-94), Composer of Sacred Music — A641

1975, June 27 Engr. *Perf. 13½x14*
1195 A641 100 l mag & tan 15 15

Emmigrants and Ship A642

1975, June 30 Photo. *Perf. 14x13½*
1196 A642 70 l multi 15 15

Italian emigration centenary.

Emblem of United Legal Groups A643

Perf. 14x13½
1975, July 25 Photo. Engr.
1197 A643 100 l yel, grn & red 15 15

Centenary of unification of Italian legal organizations.

Locomotive Wheels A644

1975, Sept. 15 Photo. *Perf. 14x13½*
1198 A644 70 l multi 15 15

Intl. Railroad Union, 21st cong., Bologna.

Salvo D'Acquisto, by Vittorio Pisano A645

1975, Sept. 23
1199 A645 100 l multi 15 15

D'Acquisto died in 1943 saving 22 people.

Stylized Syracusean Italia — A646

1975, Sept. 26 Photo. *Perf. 13½x14*
1200 A646 100 l org & multi 15 15

Cent. of unification of the State Archives.

Fountain Type of 1973

Designs: No. 1201, Rosello Fountain, Sassari. No. 1202, Fountain of the 99 Faucets, Aquila. No. 1203, Piazza Fontana, Milan.

Photogravure and Engraved
1975, Oct. 20 *Perf. 13x14*
1201 A603 70 l blk & multi 15 15
1202 A603 70 l blk & multi 15 15
1203 A603 70 l blk & multi 15 15
Set value 36 24

Antonio Vivaldi — A647

1975, Nov. 14 Photo. *Perf. 14x13½*
1204 A647 100 l Alessandro Scarlatti 15 15
1205 A647 100 l shown 15 15
1206 A647 100 l Gaspare Spontini 15 15
1207 A647 100 l F. B. Busoni 15 15
1208 A647 100 l Francesco Cilea 15 15
1209 A647 100 l Franco Alfano 15 15
Nos. 1204-1209 (6) 90
Set value 48

Famous musicians.
See Nos. 1243-1247, 1266-1270.

Annunciation to the Shepherds A648

"The Magic Orchard" A649

Christmas: 100 l, Nativity. 150 l, Annunciation to the Kings. Designs from painted wood panels, portal of Alatri Cathedral, 14th century.

Lithographed and Engraved

1975, Nov. 25 ***Perf. 13½x14***

1210 A648 70 l grn & multi 15 15
1211 A648 100 l ultra & multi 15 15
1212 A648 150 l brn & multi 15 15
Set value 26

Perf. 14x13½, 13½x14

1975, Dec. 7 **Photo.**

Designs (Children's Drawings): 70 l, Children on Horseback, horiz. 150 l, Village and procession, horiz.

1213 A649 70 l multi 15 15
1214 A649 100 l multi 15 15
1215 A649 150 l multi 15 15

17th Stamp Day.

Boccaccio, by Andrea del Castagno — A650

State Advocate's Office, Rome — A651

Design: 150 l, Frontispiece for "Fiammetta," 15th century woodcut.

Engraved and Lithographed

1975, Dec. 22 ***Perf. 13½x14***

1216 A650 100 l yel grn & blk 15 15
1217 A650 150 l buff & multi 18 15
Set value 18

Giovanni Boccaccio (1313-1375), writer, 600th death anniversary.

1976, Jan. 30 **Photo.** ***Perf. 13½x14***

1218 A651 150 l multi 18 15

State Advocate's Office, centenary.

ITALIA 76 Emblem — A652

Majolica Plate, Deruta — A653

Design: 180 l, Milan Fair pavilion.

1976, Mar. 27 **Photo.** ***Perf. 13½x14***

1219 A652 150 l blk, red & grn 15 15
1220 A652 180 l blk, red, grn & bl 18 15
Set value 22

ITALIA 76 International Philatelic Exhibition, Milan, Oct. 14-24.

Tourist Type of 1974

Tourist publicity: No. 1221, Fenis Castle. No. 1222, View of Ischia. No. 1223, Itria Valley.

1976, May 21 **Photo.** ***Perf. 14***

1221 A616 150 l grn & multi 20 15
1222 A616 150 l plum & multi 20 15
1223 A616 150 l yel & multi 20 15
Set value 27

1976, May 22 ***Perf. 13½x14***

Europa: 180 l, Ceramic vase in shape of woman's head, Caltagirone.

1224 A653 150 l multi 15 15
1225 A653 180 l brn & multi 25 15
Set value 18

Italian Flags A654

Italian Presidents A655

1976, June 1

1226 A654 100 l multi 15 15
1227 A655 150 l multi 18 15
Set value 18

30th anniversary of Italian Republic.

Fortitude, by Giacomo Serpotta, 1656-1732 A656

Paintings: No. 1229, Woman at Table, by Umberto Boccioni, 1882-1916. No. 1230, The Gunner's Letter, by F. T. Marinetti, 1876-1944.

1976, July 26 **Engr.** ***Perf. 14***

1228 A656 150 l blue 20 15

Lithographed and Engraved

1229 A656 150 l multi 20 15
1230 A656 150 l blk & red 20 15
Set value 27

Italian art.

St. George, by Vittore Carpaccio A657

Design: No. 1231, Dragon, by Vittore Carpaccio, after painting in Church of St. George Schiavoni, Venice.

1976, July 30 **Engr.** ***Perf. 14x13½***

1231 A657 150 l rose lake 20 15
1232 A657 150 l rose lake 20 15
a. Pair, #1231-1232 + label 40 20
Set value 15

Carpaccio (1460-1526), Venetian painter.

Flora, by Titian A658

1976, Sept. 15 **Engr.** ***Perf. 14***

1233 A658 150 l carmine 20 15

Titian (1477-1576), Venetian painter.

St. Francis, 13th Century Fresco — A659

1976, Oct. 2 **Engr.** ***Perf. 14***

1234 A659 150 l brown 20 15

St. Francis of Assisi, 750th death anniv.

Cart, from Trajan's Column A660

Designs: 100 l, Emblem of Kingdom of Sardinia. 150 l, Marble mask, 19th century mail box. 200 l, Hand canceler, 19th century. 400 l, Automatic letter sorting machine.

1976, Oct. 14 **Photo.** ***Perf. 14x13½***

1235 A660 70 l multi 15 15
1236 A660 100 l multi 15 15
1237 A660 150 l multi 18 15
1238 A660 200 l multi 20 15
1239 A660 400 l multi 40 22
Nos. 1235-1239 (5) 1.08
Set value 64

ITALIA 76 International Philatelic Exhibition, Milan, Oct. 14-24.

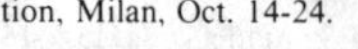

Girl and Animals — A661

Designs (Children' Drawings): 100 l, Trees, rabbit and flowers. 150 l, Boy healing tree.

1976, Oct. 17 ***Perf. 13½x14***

1240 A661 40 l multi 15 15
1241 A661 100 l multi 15 15
1242 A661 150 l multi 15 15
Set value 38 18

18th Stamp Day and nature protection.

Vivaldi Type of 1975

1976, Nov. 22 **Photo.** ***Perf. 14x13½***

1243 A647 170 l Lorenzo Ghiberti 20 15
1244 A647 170 l Domenico Ghirlandaio 20 15
1245 A647 170 l Sassoferrato 20 15
1246 A647 170 l Carlo Dolci 20 15
1247 A647 170 l Giovanni Piazzetta 20 15
Nos. 1243-1247 (5) 1.00
Set value 25

Famous painters.

The Visit, by Silvestro Lega A662

1976, Dec. 7 **Photo.** ***Perf. 14x13½***

1248 A662 170 l multi 25 15

Silvestro Lega (1826-1895), painter, sesquicentennial of birth.

Adoration of the Kings, by Bartolo di Fredi — A663

Christmas: 120 l, Nativity, by Taddeo Gaddi.

1976, Dec. 11 ***Perf. 13½x14***

1249 A663 70 l multi 15 15
1250 A663 120 l multi 15 15
Set value 15

Fountain Type of 1973

Designs: No. 1251, Antique Fountain, Gallipoli. No. 1252, Madonna Fountain, Verona. No. 1253, Silvio Cosini Fountain, Palazzo Doria, Genoa.

Lithographed and Engraved

1976, Dec. 21 ***Perf. 13½x14***

1251 A603 170 l blk & multi 22 15
1252 A603 170 l blk & multi 22 15
1253 A603 170 l blk & multi 22 15
Set value 18

Snakes Forming Net — A664

Design: 170 l, Drug addict and poppy.

1977, Feb. 28 **Photo.** ***Perf. 14x13½***

1254 A664 120 l multi 16 15
1255 A664 170 l multi 22 15
Set value 15

Fight against drug abuse.

Micca Setting Fire — A665

1977, Mar. 5

1256 A665 170 l multi 24 15

Pietro Micca (1677-1706), patriot who set fire to the powder magazine of Turin Citadel, 300th birth anniversary.

Globe with Cross in Center — A666

Design: 120 l, People of the World united as brothers by St. John Bosco.

1977, Mar. 29 Photo. Perf. 13x13½
1257 A666 70 l multi 15 15
1258 A666 120 l multi 15 15
Set value 15

Honoring the Salesian missionaries.

Italian Constitution, Article 53 — A667

1977, Apr. 14 Photo. Perf. 14
1259 A667 120 l bis, brn & blk 15 15
1260 A667 170 l lt grn, grn & blk 20 15
Set value 15

"Pay your taxes."

Tourist Type of 1974

Europa (Europa Emblem and): 170 l, Taormina. 200 l, Castle del Monte.

1977, May 2
1261 A616 170 l multi 20 15
1262 A616 200 l multi 30 15
Set value 17

Tourist Type of 1974

Paintings: No. 1263, Canossa Castle. No. 1264, Fermo. No. 1265, Castellana Caves.

1977, May 30 Photo. Perf. 14
1263 A616 170 l brn & multi 22 15
1264 A616 170 l vio & multi 22 15
1265 A616 170 l gray & multi 22 15
Set value 15

Vivaldi Type of 1975

1977, June 27 Perf. 14x13½
1266 A647 70 l Filippo Brunelleschi 15 15
1267 A647 70 l Pietro Aretino 15 15
1268 A647 70 l Carlo Goldoni 15 15
1269 A647 70 l Luigi Cherubini 15 15
1270 A647 70 l Eduardo Bassini 15 15
Set value 60 30

Famous artists, writers and scientists.

Justice, by Andrea Delitio A669

Painting: No. 1272, Winter, by Giuseppe Arcimboldi, 1527-c.1593.

Engraved and Lithographed

1977, Sept. 5 Perf. 14
1271 A669 170 l multi 25 15
1272 A669 170 l multi 25 15
Set value 18

Corvette Caracciolo — A670

Italian Ships: No. 1274, Hydrofoil gunboat Sparviero. No. 1275, Paddle steamer Ferdinando Primo. No. 1276, Passenger liner Saturnia.

Photogravure and Engraved

1977, Sept. 23 Perf. 14x13½
1273 A670 170 l multi 32 15
1274 A670 170 l multi 32 15
1275 A670 170 l multi 32 15
1276 A670 170 l multi 32 15
a. Block of 4, #1273-1276 + 2 labels 1.50
Set value 32

See #1323-1326, 1382-1385, 1435-1438.

Fountain Type of 1973

Designs: No. 1277, Pacassi Fountain, Gorizia. No. 1278, Fraterna Fountain, Isernia. No. 1279, Palm Fountain, Palmi.

Lithographed and Engraved

1977, Oct. 18 Perf. 13x14
1277 A603 120 l blk & multi 15 15
1278 A603 120 l blk & multi 15 15
1279 A603 120 l blk & multi 15 15
Set value 18

Volleyball — A671

Designs (Children's Drawings): No. 1281, Butterflies and net. No. 1282, Flying kites.

1977, Oct. 23 Photo. Perf. 13x14
1280 A671 120 l multi 15 15
1281 A671 120 l multi 15 15
1282 A671 120 l multi 15 15
a. Block of 3, #1280-1282 + label 50 30
Set value 24

19th Stamp Day.

Symbolic Blood Donation A672

Design: 70 l, Blood donation symbolized.

1977, Oct. 26 Perf. 14x13½
1283 A672 70 l multi 15 15
1284 A672 120 l multi 15 15
Set value 15

Blood donors.

Quintino Sella and Italy No. 24 — A673

1977, Oct. 23 Perf. 13½x14
1285 A673 170 l ol & blk brn 22 15

Quintino Sella (1827-1884), statesman, engineer, mineralogist, birth sesquicentenary.

Italia Type of 1953-54 and

Italia — A674

1977-87 Wmk. 303 Perf. 14
Size: 16x20mm
Photo.
1288 A354 120 l dk bl & emer 18 15
Photo. & Engr.
1292 A354 170 l grn & ocher 35 15
Litho. & Engr.
1295 A354 350 l red, ocher & pur 55 15

Perf. 14x13½
Engr. Unwmk.

1304 A674 1500 l multi 1.50 15
1305 A674 2000 l multi 1.90 15
1306 A674 3000 l multi 3.00 15
1307 A674 4000 l multi 3.75 15
1308 A674 5000 l multi 5.00 38
1308A A674 10,000 l multi 9.50 1.40
1308B A674 20,000 l multi 22.50 12.00
Nos. 1288-1308B (10) 48.23 14.83

Issue dates: Nos. 1288, 1292, 1295, Nov. 22. No. 1308, Dec. 4, 1978. No. 1307, Feb. 12, 1979. No. 1306, Mar. 12, 1979. No. 1305, Apr. 12, 1979. No. 1304, May 14, 1979. No. 1308A, June 27, 1983. No. 1308B, Jan. 5, 1987.

This is an expanding set. Numbers will change if necessary.

Dina Galli — A675

La Scala — A677

Adoration of the Shepherds, by Pietro Testa — A676

Perf. 13½x14
1977, Dec. 2 Photo. Unwmk.
1309 A675 170 l multi 22 15

Dina Galli (1877-1951), actress, birth centenary.

Lithographed and Engraved

1977, Dec. 13 Perf. 14

Christmas: 120 l, Adoration of the Shepherds, by Gian Jacopo Caraglio.

1310 A676 70 l blk & ol 15 15
1311 A676 120 l blk & bl grn 15 15
Set value 15

1978, Mar. 15 Litho. Perf. 13½x14

Design: 200 l, La Scala, auditorium.

1312 A677 170 l multi 22 15
1313 A677 200 l multi 28 15
Set value 17

La Scala Opera House, Milan, bicentenary.

Tourist Type of 1974

Paintings: 70 l, Gubbio. 200 l, Udine. 600 l, Paestum.

1978, Mar. 30 Photo. Perf. 14
1314 A616 70 l multi 15 15
1315 A616 200 l multi 22 15
1316 A616 600 l multi 70 38
Set value 52

Giant Grouper A678

Designs (outline of "Amerigo Vespucci" in background): No. 1318, Leatherback turtle. No. 1319, Mediterranean monk seal. No. 1320, Audouin's gull.

1978, Apr. 3 Perf. 14x13
1317 A678 170 l multi 25 15
1318 A678 170 l multi 25 15
1319 A678 170 l multi 25 15
1320 A678 170 l multi 25 15
a. Strip of 4, #1317-1320 + label 1.25 1.00
Set value 32

Endangered species in Mediterranean.

Castel Nuovo, Angevin Fortifications, Naples — A679

Europa: 200 l, Pantheon, Rome.

1978, Apr. 29 Litho. Perf. 14x13½
1321 A679 170 l multi 20 15
1322 A679 200 l multi 30 15
Set value 15

Ship Type of 1977

Designs: No. 1323, Cruiser Benedetto Brin. No. 1324, Frigate Lupo. No. 1325, Ligurian brigantine Fortuna. No. 1326, Container ship Africa.

1978, May 8 Litho. & Engr.
1323 A670 170 l multi 60 15
1324 A670 170 l multi 60 15
1325 A670 170 l multi 60 15
1326 A670 170 l multi 60 15
a. Block of 4, #1323-1326 + 2 labels 2.50
Set value 36

Matilde Serao A680 Constitution A681

Designs: Portraits of famous Italians.

1978, May 10 Engr. Perf. 14x13½
1327 A680 170 l shown 22 15
1328 A680 170 l Vittorino da Feltre 22 15
1329 A680 170 l Victor Emmanuel II 22 15
1330 A680 170 l Pope Pius IX 22 15
1331 A680 170 l Marcello Malpighi 22 15
1332 A680 170 l Antonio Meucci 22 15
a. Block of 6, #1327-1332 1.50
Nos. 1327-1332 (6) 1.32
Set value 48

1978, June 2 Litho. Perf. 13½x14
1333 A681 170 l multi 24 15

30th anniversary of Constitution.

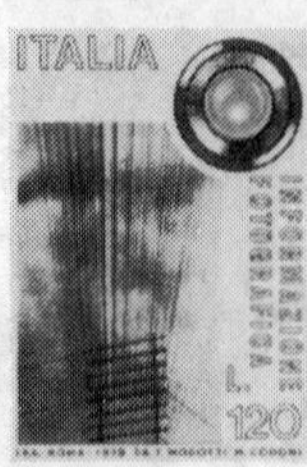

Telegraph Wires and Lens — A682

1978, June 30 **Photo.**
1334 A682 120 l lt bl & gray 18 15

Photographic information.

The Lovers, by Tranquillo Cremona (1837-1878) A683

Design: 520 l, The Cook (woman with goose), by Bernardo Strozzi (1581-1644).

Engraved and Lithographed

1978, July 12 ***Perf. 14***
1335 A683 170 l multi 1.40 15
1336 A683 520 l multi 4.00 75

Holy Shroud of Turin, by Giovanni Testa, 1578 — A684

1978, Sept. 8 **Photo.** ***Perf. 14***
1337 A684 220 l yel, red & blk 30 15

400th anniversary of the transfer of the Holy Shroud from Savoy to Turin.

Volleyball A685

Mother and Child, by Masaccio A686

Design: 120 l, Volleyball (diff.).

1978, Sept. 20
1338 A685 80 l multi 18 15
1339 A685 120 l multi 30 15
Set value 15

Men's Volleyball World Championship.

1978, Oct. 18 **Engr.** ***Perf. 13½x14***
1340 A686 170 l indigo 24 15

Masaccio (real name Tommaso Guidi; 1401-1428), painter, 550th death anniversary.

Fountain Type of 1973

Designs: No 1341, Neptune Fountain, Trent. No. 1342, Fortuna Fountain, Fano. No. 1343, Cavallina Fountain, Genzano di Lucania.

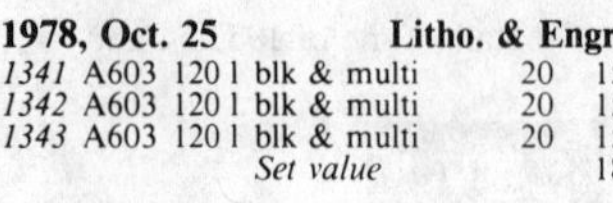
1978, Oct. 25 **Litho. & Engr.**
1341 A603 120 l blk & multi 20 15
1342 A603 120 l blk & multi 20 15
1343 A603 120 l blk & multi 20 15
Set value 18

Virgin and Child, by Giorgione — A687

Adoration of the Kings, by Giorgione — A688

1978, Nov. 8 **Engr.** ***Perf. 13x14***
1344 A687 80 l dk red 15 15

Photo. ***Perf. 14x13½***
1345 A688 120 l multi 15 15

Christmas 1978.

Flags as Flowers — A689

Designs: No. 1347, European flags. No. 1348, "People hailing Europe."

1978, Nov. 26 **Photo.** ***Perf. 13x14***
1346 A689 120 l multi 18 15
1347 A689 120 l multi 18 15
1348 A689 120 l multi 18 15
Set value 18

20th Stamp Day on theme "United Europe."

State Printing Office, Stamps A690

Design: 220 l, Printing press and stamps.

1979, Jan. 6 **Photo.** ***Perf. 14x13½***
1349 A690 170 l multi 18 15
1350 A690 220 l multi 28 15
Set value 17

50th anniversary of first stamps printed by State Printing Office.

St. Francis Washing Lepers, 13th Century Painting A691

1979, Jan. 22
1351 A691 80 l multi 15 15

Leprosy relief.

Bicyclist Carrying Bike — A692

1979, Jan. 27 ***Perf. 13½x14***
1352 A692 170 l multi 18 15
1353 A692 220 l multi 28 15
Set value 17

World Crosscountry Bicycle Championships.

Virgin Mary, by Antonello da Messina A693

Painting: 520 l, Haystack, by Ardengo Soffici (1879-1964).

1979, Feb. 15 **Engr.** ***Perf. 14***
1354 A693 170 l multi 30 15
1355 A693 520 l multi 70 45

Albert Einstein (1879-1955), Theoretical Physicist and his Equation — A694

Lithographed and Engraved

1979, Mar. 14 ***Perf. 13x14***
1356 A694 120 l multi 18 15

Tourist Type of 1974

Paintings: 70 l, Asiago. 90 l, Castelsardo. 170 l, Orvieto. 220 l, Scilla.

1979, Mar. 30 **Photo.** ***Perf. 14***
1357 A616 70 l grn & multi 15 15
1358 A616 90 l car & multi 15 15
1359 A616 170 l ultra & multi 22 15
1360 A616 220 l gray & multi 32 15
Set value 38

Carlo Maderno (1556-1629), Architect — A695

Famous Italians: No. 1362, Lazzaro Spallanzani (1729-1799), physiologist. No. 1363, Ugo Foscolo (1778-1827), writer. No. 1364 Massimo Bontempelli (1878-1960), journalist. No. 1365, Francesco Severi (1879-1961), mathematician.

1979, Apr. 23 **Engr.** ***Perf. 14x13½***
1361 A695 170 l multi 24 15
1362 A695 170 l multi 24 15
1363 A695 170 l multi 24 15
1364 A695 170 l multi 24 15
1365 A695 170 l multi 24 15
Nos. 1361-1365 (5) 1.20
Set value 30

Telegraph A696

Europa: 220 l, Carrier pigeons.

1979, Apr. 30 **Photo.** ***Perf. 14***
1366 A696 170 l multi 30 15
1367 A696 220 l multi 40 15
Set value 17

Flags and "E" — A697

1979, May 5 ***Perf. 14x13½***
1368 A697 170 l multi 20 15
1369 A697 220 l multi 30 15
Set value 15

European Parliament, first direct elections, June 7-10.

Exhibition Emblem, Dome of Milan A698

1979, June 22 **Photo.** ***Perf. 14***
1370 A698 170 l multi 20 15
1371 A698 220 l multi 30 15
Set value 17

3rd World Machine Tool Exhibition, Milan, Oct. 10-18.

Aeneas and Rotary Emblem A699

Basket A700

1979, June 9 ***Perf. 13½x14***
1372 A699 220 l multi 30 15

70th World Rotary Cong., Rome, June 1979.

1979, June 13 ***Perf. 14***

Design: 120 l, Basketball players.

1373 A700 80 l multi 20 15
1374 A700 120 l multi 30 15
Set value 16

21st European Basketball Championship, June 9-20.

Set Values
A 15-cent minimum now applies to individual stamps and sets. Where the 15-cent minimum per stamp would increase the "value" of a set beyond retail, there is a "Set Value" notation giving the retail value of the set.

Patient and Physician, 16th Century Woodcut — A701

1979, June 16 **Photo. & Engr.**
1375 A701 120 l multi 18 15

Digestive Ailments Study Week.

Ottorino Respighi (1879-1936), Composer, Roman Landscape A702

Lithographed and Engraved

1979, July 9 ***Perf. 13x14***
1376 A702 120 l multi 18 15

Woman Making Phone Call A703

Design: 200 l, Woman with old-fashioned phone.

1979, Sept. 20 **Photo.** ***Perf. 14***
1377 A703 170 l red & gray 20 15
1378 A703 220 l grn & slate 30 15
Set value 21

3rd World Telecommunications Exhibition, Geneva, Sept. 20-26.

Fountain Type of 1973

Designs: No. 1379, Great Fountain, Viterbo. No. 1380, Hot Springs, Acqui Terme. No. 1381, Pomegranate Fountain, Issogne Castle.

Lithographed and Engraved

1979, Sept. 22 ***Perf. 13x14***
1379 A603 120 l multi 22 15
1380 A603 120 l multi 22 15
1381 A603 120 l multi 22 15
Set value 18

Ship Type of 1977

Designs: No. 1382, Cruiser Enrico Dandolo. No. 1383, Submarine Carlo Fecia. No. 1384, Freighter Cosmos. No. 1385, Ferry Deledda.

1979, Oct. 12 ***Perf. 14x13½***
1382 A670 170 l multi 32 15
1383 A670 170 l multi 32 15
1384 A670 170 l multi 32 15
1385 A670 170 l multi 32 15
a. Block of 4, #1382-1385 + 2 labels 1.50
Set value 36

Penny Black, Rowland Hill — A704

1979, Oct. 25 **Photo.**
1386 A704 220 l multi 30 15

Sir Rowland Hill (1795-1879), originator of penny postage.

Minstrels and Church A705

1979, Nov. 7 **Photo.** ***Perf. 14x13½***
1387 A705 120 l multi 18 15

Christmas 1979.

Black and White Boys Holding Hands A706

Children's Drawings: 120 l, Children of various races under umbrella map (vert.). 150 l, Children and red balloons.

Perf. 14x13½, 13½x14

1979, Nov. 25 **Photo.**
1388 A706 70 l multi 15 15
1389 A706 120 l multi 15 15
1390 A706 150 l multi 20 15
Set value 18

21st Stamp Day.

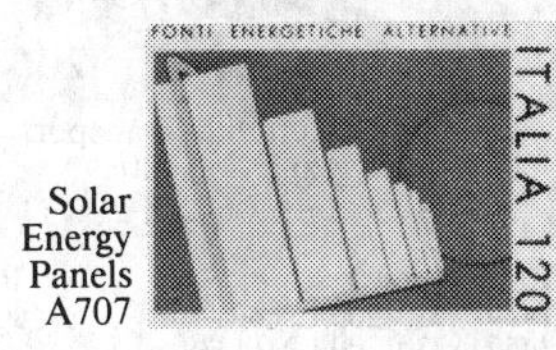

Solar Energy Panels A707

Energy Conservation: 170 l, Sun and pylon.

1980, Feb. 25 **Photo.** ***Perf. 14x13½***
1391 A707 120 l multi 15 15
1392 A707 170 l multi 24 15
Set value 18

St. Benedict of Nursia, 1500th Birth Anniversary A708

1980, Mar. 21 **Engr.** ***Perf. 13½x14***
1393 A708 220 l dark blue 30 15

Royal Palace, Naples — A709

Lithographed and Engraved

1980, Apr. 16 ***Perf. 13½x14***
1394 A709 220 l multi 30 15

20th International Philatelic Exhibition, Europa '80, Naples, Apr. 26-May 4.

Antonio Pigafetta, Caravel A710

Europa: 220 l, Antonio Lo Surdo (1880-1949) geophysicist.

1980, Apr. 28 **Litho.** ***Perf. 14x13½***
1395 A710 170 l multi 25 15
1396 A710 220 l multi 35 15
Set value 17

St. Catherine, Reliquary Bust — A711

1980, Apr. 29 **Photo.**
1397 A711 170 l multi 25 15

St. Catherine of Siena (1347-1380).

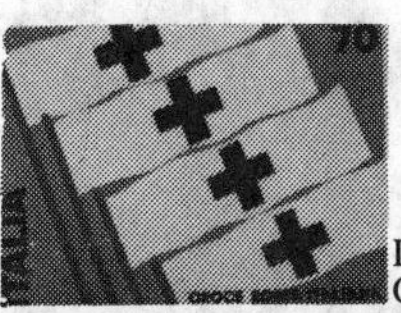

Italian Red Cross — A712

1980, May 15 **Photo.** ***Perf. 14x13½***
1398 A712 70 l multi 15 15
1399 A712 80 l multi 15 15
Set value 24 17

Temples of Philae, Egypt — A713

1980, May 20
1400 Pair + label 60 15
a. A713 220 l shown 25 15
b. A713 220 l Temple of Philae, diff. 25 15

Italian civil engineering achievements (Temples of Philae saved from ruin by Italian engineers).

Soccer Player A714

1980, June 11
1401 A714 80 l multi 20 15

European Soccer Championships, Milan, Turin, Rome, Naples, June 9-22.

Tourist Type of 1974

Paintings: 80 l, Erice. 150 l, Villa Rufolo, Ravello. 200 l, Roseto degli Abruzzi. 670 l, Public Baths, Salsomaggiore Terme.

1980, June 28 ***Perf. 14***
1402 A616 80 l multi 18 15
1403 A616 150 l multi 28 15
1404 A616 200 l multi 35 15
1405 A616 670 l multi 70 40
Set value 67

Cosimo I with his Artists, by Giorgio Vasari — A715

1980, July 2 ***Perf. 13½x14***
1406 Pair + label 50 50
a. A715 170 l shown 20 15
b. A715 170 l Armillary sphere 20 15

The Medici in Europe of the 16th Century Exhibition, Florence.

Fonte Avellana Monastery Millennium A716

1980, Sept. 3 **Engr.** ***Perf. 14x13½***
1407 A716 200 l grn & brn 30 15

St. Angelo Castle, Rome — A717

Designs: Castles.

Perf. 14x13½

1980, Sept. 22 **Wmk. 303**

Design A717

1408 5 l shown 15 15
1409 10 l Sforzesco, Milan 15 15
1410 20 l Del Monte, Andria 15 15
1411 40 l Ursino, Catania 15 15
1412 50 l Rocca di Calascio 15 15
1413 60 l Norman Tower, St. Mauro Fort 15 15
1414 90 l Isola Capo Rizzuto 18 15
1415 100 l Aragonese, Ischia 18 15
1416 120 l Estense, Ferrara 18 15
1417 150 l Miramare, Trieste 20 15
1418 170 l Ostia, Rome 24 15
1419 180 l Gavone, Savona 24 15
1420 200 l Cerro al Volturno, Isernia 24 15
1421 250 l Rocca di Mondavio 35 15
1422 300 l Svevo, Bari 40 15
1423 350 l Mussomeli, Caltanissetta 45 15
1424 400 l Imperatore-Prato, Florence 52 15
1425 450 l Bosa, Nuoro 60 15
1426 500 l Rovereto, Trento 70 15

1427 600 l Scaligero, Sirmione 75 15
1428 700 l Ivrea, Turin 1.00 15
1429 800 l Rocca Maggiore, Assisi 1.10 15
1430 900 l St. Pierre, Aosta 1.25 15
1431 1000 l Montagnana, Padua 1.25 15
Nos. 1408-1431 (24) 10.73
Set value 1.40

Coil Stamps

Engr. ***Perf. 14 Vert.***
Size: 16x21mm

1432 30 l St. Severna, Rome 15 15
1433 120 l Lombardia, Enna 22 15
a. Pair, Nos. 1432-1433 40 18
1434 170 l Serralunga d'Alba, Cuneo 30 15
a. Pair, Nos. 1432, 1434 75 75
Set value 18

See Nos. 1475-1484, 1657-1666.

Ship Type of 1977

Designs: No. 1435, Corvette Gabbiano. No. 1436, Torpedo boat Audace. No. 1437, Sailing ship Italia. No. 1438, Floating dock Castoro Sei.

Lithographed and Engraved
1980, Oct. 11 ***Perf. 14x13½***
1435 A670 200 l multi 1.50 15
1436 A670 200 l multi 1.50 15
1437 A670 200 l multi 1.50 15
1438 A670 200 l multi 1.50 15
a. Block of 4, #1435-1438 + 2 labels
Set value 36

Philip Mazzei (1730-1816), Political Writer in United States — A718

1980, Oct. 18 Photo. ***Perf. 13½x14***
1439 A718 320 l multi 45 15

Villa Foscari Malcontenta, Venezia — A719

Villas: 150 l, Barbaro Maser, Treviso. 170 l, Godi Valmarana, Vicenza.

Lithographed and Engraved
1980, Oct. 31 ***Perf. 14x13½***
1440 A719 80 l multi 20 15
1441 A719 150 l multi 25 15
1442 A719 170 l multi 30 15
Set value 25

See Nos. 1493-1495, 1528-1530, 1565-1568, 1606-1609, 1646-1649, 1691-1695.

St. Barbara, by Palma the Elder (1480-1528) A720

Design: No. 1444, Apollo and Daphne, by Gian Lorenzo Bernini (1598-1680).

1980, Nov. 20 ***Perf. 14***
1443 A720 520 l multi 70 42
1444 A720 520 l multi 70 42

Nativity Sculpture by Federico Brandini, 16th Cent. — A721

1980, Nov. 22 **Engr.**
1445 A721 120 l brn org & blk 20 15

Christmas 1980.

View of Verona A722

22nd Stamp Day: Views of Verona drawings by school children.

1980, Nov. 30 Photo. ***Perf. 14x13½***
1446 A722 70 l multi 15 15
1447 A722 120 l multi 20 15
1448 A722 170 l multi 25 15
Set value 18

Daniele Comboni (1831-1881), Savior of the Africans — A723

1981, Mar. 14 **Engr.**
1449 A723 80 l multi 15 15

Alcide de Gasperi (1881-1954), Statesman A724

International Year of the Disabled A725

1981, Apr. 3 ***Perf. 13½x14***
1450 A724 200 l ol grn 30 15

1981, Apr. 11 **Photo.**
1451 A725 300 l multi 50 15

Roses — A726

1981, Apr. 27 Photo. ***Perf. 13½x14***
1452 A726 200 l shown 30 15
1453 A726 200 l Anemones 30 15
1454 A726 200 l Oleanders 30 15
Set value 18

See Nos. 1510-1512, 1555-1557.

Europa Issue 1981

Chess Game with Human Pieces, Marostica — A727

1981, May 4
1455 A727 300 l shown 40 15
1456 A727 300 l Horse race, Siena 40 15
Set value 16

St. Rita Offering Thorn A728

Ciro Menotti (1798-1831), Patriot A729

1981, May 22
1457 A728 600 l multi 80 35

St. Rita of Cascia, 600th birth anniversary.

1981, May 26 Engr. ***Perf. 14x13½***
1458 A729 80 l brn & blk 15 15

G-222 Aeritalia Transport Plane — A730

1981, June 1 **Photo.**
1459 A730 200 l shown 30 15
1460 A730 200 l MB-339 Aermacchi jet 30 15
1461 A730 200 l A-109 Agusta helicopter 30 15
1462 A730 200 l P-68 Partenavia transport plane 30 15
a. Block of 4, #1459-1462 + 2 labels 1.35
Set value 36

See Nos. 1505-1508, 1550-1553.

Hydro-geological Research — A731

1981, June 8 ***Perf. 13½x14***
1463 A731 80 l multi 15 15

Sao Simao Dam and Power Station, Brazil — A732

Civil Engineering Works Abroad: No. 1465, High Island Power Station, Hong Kong.

1981, June 26 Engr. ***Perf. 14x13½***
1464 A732 300 l dark blue 50 15
1465 A732 300 l red 50 15
a. Pair, #1464-1465 + label 1.10 30
Set value 16

See Nos. 1516-1517, 1538-1539.

Tourist Type of 1974

1981, July 4 Photo. ***Perf. 14***
1466 A616 80 l View of Matera 15 15
1467 A616 150 l Lake Garda 32 15
1468 A616 300 l St. Teresa di Gallura beach 48 15
1469 A616 900 l Tarquinia 2.50 45
Set value 68

Naval Academy, Livorno and Navy Emblem A735

Naval Academy of Livorno Centenary: 150 l, View. 200 l, Cadet with sextant, training ship Amerigo Vespucci.

1981, July 24 ***Perf. 14x13½***
1472 A735 80 l multi 15 15
1473 A735 150 l multi 20 15
1474 A735 200 l multi 28 15
Set value 22

Castle Type of 1980

Perf. 14x13½
1981-84 Photo. Wmk. 303
1475 A717 30 l Aquila 15 15
1476 A717 70 l Aragonese, Reggio Calabria 15 15
1477 A717 80 l Sabbionara, Avio 16 15

Perf. 13½
1478 A717 550 l Rocca Sinibalda 65 15
1479 A717 1400 l Caldorosco, Vasto 2.00 60
Nos. 1475-1479 (5) 3.11
Set value 85

Issue dates: Nos. 1475-1477, Aug. 20, 1981. Nos. 1478-1479, Feb. 14, 1984.

Coil Stamps

Size: 16x21mm

1981-85 Engr. ***Perf. 14 Vert.***
1480 A717 50 l Scilla 15 15
1481 A717 200 l Angionia, Lucera *2.00 2.00*
1482 A717 300 l Norman Castle, Melfi 60 15
1483 A717 400 l Venafro 45 15
1484 A717 450 l Piobbico Pesaro 40 15
a. Pair, #1480, 1484 60 24
Nos. 1480-1484 (5) *3.60 2.60*

Issue dates: Nos. 1481-1482, Sept. 30. No. 1483, June 25, 1983. Nos. 1480, 1484, July 25, 1985.

Palazzo Spada, Rome (Council Seat) A736

1981, Aug. 31 Engr. Unwmk.
1485 A736 200 l multi 30 15

State Council sesquicentennial.

World Cup Races — A737

1981, Sept. 4 Photo. ***Perf. 13½x14***
1486 A737 300 l multi 45 15

Harbor View, by Carlo Carra (1881-1966) — A738

Paintings: No. 1478, Castle, by Guiseppe Ugonia (1881-1944).

Lithographed and Engraved

1981, Sept. 7 ***Perf. 14***
1487 A738 200 l multi 30 15
1488 A738 200 l multi 30 15

See Nos. 1532-1533, 1638-1639, 1697-1698, 1732.

Riace Bronze, 4th Cent. B.C. — A739

1981, Sept. 9 Photo. ***Perf. 13½x14***
1489 A739 200 l shown 30 15
1490 A739 200 l Statue, diff. 30 15
a. Pair, #1489-1490 65 30
Set value 18

Greek statues found in 1972 in sea near Reggio di Calabria.

Virgil, Mosiac, Treviri A740

1981, Sept. 19 ***Perf. 14***
1491 A740 600 l multi 80 42

Virgil's death bimillennium.

Food and Wine, by Gregorio Sciltian A741

1981, Oct. 16 Litho. ***Perf. 14***
1492 A741 150 l multi 20 15

World Food Day.

Villa Type of 1980

Lithographed and Engraved

1981, Oct. 17 ***Perf. 14x13½***
1493 A719 100 l Villa Campolieto, Ercolano 20 15
1494 A719 200 l Cimbrone, Ravello 40 15
1495 A719 300 l Pignatelli, Naples 55 15
Set value 24

Adoration of the Magi, by Giovanni de Campione d'Italia (Christmas 1981) — A743

1981, Nov. 21 Engr. ***Perf. 14***
1496 A743 200 l multi 35 15

Pope John XXIII (1881-1963) A744

Stamp Day A745

1981, Nov. 25 Photo. ***Perf. 13½x14***
1497 A744 200 l multi 30 15

Photogravure, Photogravure and Engraved (200 l)

Perf. 14x13½, 13½x14

1981, Nov. 29
1498 A745 120 l Letters, horiz. 25 15
1499 A745 200 l Angel, letter chest 40 15
1500 A745 300 l Letter seal 60 18
Set value 40

St. Francis Receiving the Stigmata, by Pietro Cavaro — A746

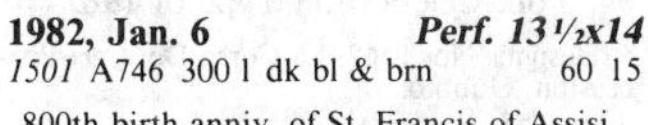

1982, Jan. 6 ***Perf. 13½x14***
1501 A746 300 l dk bl & brn 60 15

800th birth anniv. of St. Francis of Assisi.

Niccolo Paganini (1782-1840), Composer and Violinist — A748

1982, Feb. 19 Photo. ***Perf. 13½x14***
1503 A748 900 l multi 1.40 70

Anti-smoking Campaign — A749

1982, Mar. 2 Photo. ***Perf. 14x13½***
1504 A749 300 l multi 45 15

Aircraft Type of 1981

1982, Mar. 27 Litho. ***Perf. 14x13½***
1505 A730 300 l Aeritalia MRCA 45 15
1506 A730 300 l SIAI 260 Turbo 45 15
1507 A730 300 l Piaggio 166-dl3 Turbo 45 15
1508 A730 300 l Nardi NH-500 45 15
a. Block of 4, #1505-1508 + 2 labels 2.00

Sicilian Vespers, 700th Anniv. — A750

1982, Mar. 31 Engr. ***Perf. 13½x14***
1509 A750 120 l multi 28 15

Flower Type of 1981

1982, Apr. 10 **Photo.**
1510 A726 300 l Cyclamens 45 15
1511 A726 300 l Camellias 45 15
1512 A726 300 l Carnations 45 15
Set value 36

Europa 1982 — A751

Photogravure and Engraved

1982, May 3 ***Perf. 13½x14***
1513 A751 200 l Coronation of Charlemagne, 799 30 15
1514 A751 450 l Treaty of Rome signatures, 1957 70 15
Set value 24

Engineering Type of 1981

1982, May 29 Photo. ***Perf. 14x13½***
1516 A732 450 l Microwaves across Red Sea 70 18
1517 A732 450 l Automatic letter sorting 70 18
a. Pair, #1516-1517 + label 1.50 60

Giuseppe Garibaldi (1807-82) — A753

Game of the Bridge, Pisa — A754

1982, June 2 ***Perf. 13½x14***
1518 A753 200 l multi 30 15

1982, June 5
1519 A754 200 l multi 30 15

See Nos. 1562, 1603, 1628-1629, 1655, 1717, 1749, 1807.

Tourist Type of 1974

1982, June 28 ***Perf. 14***
1520 A616 200 l Frasassi Caves 30 15
1521 A616 200 l Paganella Valley 30 15
1522 A616 450 l Temple of Agrigento 70 18
1523 A616 450 l Rodi Garganico Beach 70 18

World Junior Canoeing Championship — A755

1982, Aug. 4 Photo. ***Perf. 14***
1524 A755 200 l multi 30 15

Duke Federico da Montefeltro (1422-1482) A756

Photogravure and Engraved

1982, Sept. 10 ***Perf. 14x13½***
1525 A756 200 l Urbino Palace, Gubbio Council House 30 15

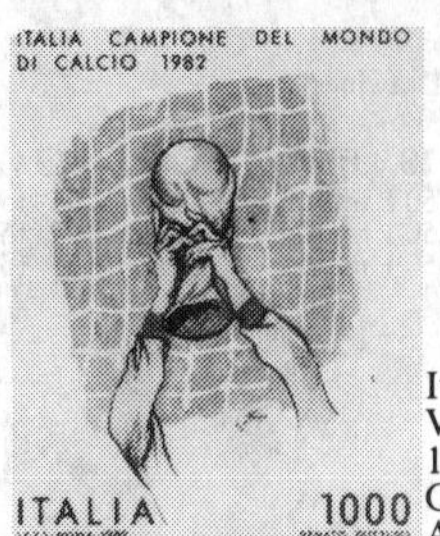

Italy's Victory in 1982 World Cup A757

1982, Sept. 12 Photo. ***Perf. 14***
1526 A757 1000 l World Cup 1.50 75

Canceled-to-order stamps are often from remainders. Most collectors of canceled stamps prefer postally used specimens.

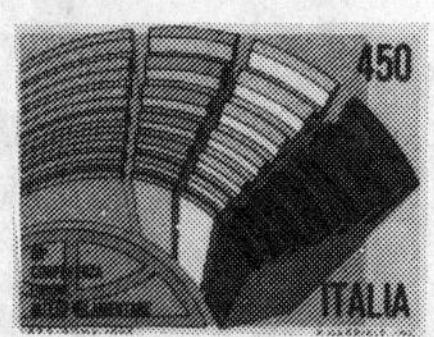

69th Inter-Parliamentary Conference, Rome — A758

1982, Sept. 14 *Perf. 14x13½*
1527 A758 450 l multi 70 15

Villa Type of 1980

Designs: 150 l, Temple of Aesculapius, Villa Borghese, Rome. 250 l, Villa D'Este, Tivoli, Rome. 350 l, Villa Lante, Bagnaia, Viterbo.

Photogravure and Engraved

1982, Oct. 1 *Perf. 14x13½*
1528 A719 150 l multi 25 15
1529 A719 250 l multi 40 15
1530 A719 350 l multi 55 15

Thurn and Taxis Family Postal Service — A759

1982, Oct. 23 Engr. *Perf. 13½x14*
1531 A759 300 l Franz von Taxis (1450-1517) 45 15

Art Type of 1981

Paintings: No. 1532, The Fortune Teller by G.B. Piazzetta (1682-1754). No. 1533, Antonietta Negroni Prati Morosini as a Little Girl by Francesco Hayez (1791-1882).

Lithographed and Engraved

1982, Nov. 3 *Perf. 14*
1532 A738 300 l multi 45 15
1533 A738 300 l multi 45 15

24th Stamp Day A761

Children's Drawings.

1982, Nov. 28 Photo. *Perf. 14x13½*
1534 A761 150 l multi 25 15
1535 A761 250 l multi 42 15
1536 A761 350 l multi 55 15

Cancer Research — A762

1983, Jan. 14 Photo. *Perf. 13½x14*
1537 A762 400 l multi 45 15

Engineering Type of 1981

1983, Jan. 20 *Perf. 13½*
1538 A732 400 l Globe, factories 45 15
1539 A732 400 l Automated assembly line 45 15
a. Pair, #1538-1539 1.00 60

Crusca Academy, 400th Anniv. — A763

1983, Jan. 25 Engr. *Perf. 14x13½*
1540 A763 400 l Emblem 45 15

World Biathlon Championship — A764

1983, Feb. 5 Photo. *Perf. 14*
1541 A764 200 l multi 22 15

Gabriele Rossetti (1783-1854), Writer — A765

1983, Feb. 28 Engr. *Perf. 14x13½*
1542 A765 300 l dk brn & dk bl 35 15

Francesco Guicciardini (1483-1540), Historian — A766

1983, Mar. 5 Engr. *Perf. 13½x14*
1543 A766 450 l sepia 55 15

Umberto Saba (1883-1957), Poet — A767

1983, Mar. 9 Photo. *Perf. 14x13½*
1544 A767 600 l multi 70 15

Pope Pius XII (1876-1958) A768

Holy Year A769

1983, Mar. 21 Engr. *Perf. 13½x14*
1545 A768 1400 l dark blue 1.65 30

1983, Mar. 25 Photo. *Perf. 14*
1546 A769 250 l St. Paul's Basilica 30 15
1547 A769 300 l St. Maria Maggiore Church 35 15
1548 A769 400 l San Giovanni Church 45 15
1549 A769 500 l St. Peter's Church 60 15

Aircraft Type of 1981

1983, Mar. 28 Litho. *Perf. 14x13½*
1550 A730 400 l Caproni C22J glider 45 15
1551 A730 400 l Aeritalia Macchi jet fighter 45 15
1552 A730 400 l SIAI-211 jet trainer 45 15
1553 A730 400 l A-129 Agusta helicopter 45 15
a. Block of 4, #1550-1553 + 2 labels 2.00

Intl. Workers' Day (May 1) — A770

1983, Apr. 29 Engr. *Perf. 14x13½*
1554 A770 1200 l blue 1.75 38

Flower Type of 1981

1983, Apr. 30 Photo. *Perf. 13½x14*
1555 A726 200 l Mimosa 22 15
1556 A726 200 l Rhododendron 22 15
1557 A726 200 l Gladiolus 22 15
Set value 36

Europa 1983 A771

Perf. 14x13½

1983, May 2 Litho. Engr.
1558 A771 400 l Galileo, telescope, 1601 65 15
1559 A771 500 l Archimedes and his screw 85 15

Ernesto T. Moneta (1833-1918), Nobel Peace Prize Winner, 1907 A772

1983, May 5 Engr. *Perf. 14x13½*
1560 A772 500 l multi 55 15

Monument, Globe, TV Screen A773

20th Natl. Eucharistic Congress A775

1983, May 9 Photo. *Perf. 13½x14*
1561 A773 500 l multi 55 15

3rd Intl. Congress of Jurisdicial Information.

Folk Celebration Type of 1982

Design: No. 1562, La Corsa Dei Ceri Procession, Gubbio.

1983, May 13 *Perf. 13½*
1562 A754 300 l multi 35 15

1983, May 14 *Perf. 14*
1563 A775 300 l multi 35 15

Tourist Type of 1974

1983, July 30 Photo. *Perf. 14*
1563A A616 250 l Alghero 40 20
1563B A616 300 l Bardonecchia 48 24
1563C A616 400 l Riccione 64 32
1563D A616 500 l Taranto 80 40

Girolamo Frescobaldi (1583-1643), Composer — A776

1983, Sept. 14 Engr. *Perf. 13½x14*
1564 A776 400 l brn & grn 50 25

Villa Type of 1980

Designs: 250 l, Fidelia, Spello. 300 l, Imperiale, Pesaro. 400 l, Michetti Convent, Francavilla al Mare. 500 l, Riccia.

Photogravure and Engraved

1983, Oct. 10 *Perf. 14x13½*
1565 A719 250 l multi 30 15
1566 A719 300 l multi 40 20
1567 A719 400 l multi 50 25
1568 A719 500 l multi 60 30

Francesco de Sanctis (1817-1883), Writer A777

1983, Oct. 28 **Photo.**
1569 A777 300 l multi 40 20

Christmas 1983 — A778

25th Stamp Day, World Communications Year — A779

Raphael Paintings: 250 l, Madonna of the Chair. 400 l, Sistine Madonna. 500 l, Madonna of the Candelabra.

1983, Nov. 10 *Perf. 13½x14*
1570 A778 250 l multi 30 15
1571 A778 400 l multi 50 25
1572 A778 500 l multi 60 30

Perf. 14x13½, 13½x14

1983, Nov. 27

Children's Drawings. 200 l, 400 l horiz.

1573 A779 200 l Letters holding hands 25 15
1574 A779 300 l Spaceman 40 20
1575 A779 400 l Flag train, globe 50 25

Road Safety A780

Perf. 13½x14, 14x13½

1984, Jan. 20 **Photo.**
1576 A780 300 l Bent road sign, vert. 40 20
1577 A780 400 l Accident 55 28

Promenade in Bois de Boulogne, by Giuseppe de Nittis (1846-1884) A781

Design: 400 l, Portrait of Paul Guillaume, 1916, by Amedeo Modigliani (1884-1920).

Lithographed and Engraved

1984, Jan. 25 *Perf. 14*

1578 A781 300 l multi 40 20
1579 A781 400 l multi 50 25

Galaxy-Same Tractor — A782

Italian-made vehicles.

1984, Mar. 10 Photo. *Perf. 14x13½*

1580 A782 450 l shown 55 28
1581 A782 450 l Alfa-33 car 55 28
1582 A782 450 l Maserati Biturbo car 55 28
1583 A782 450 l Iveco 190-38 truck 55 28
a. Block of 4, #1580-1583 + 2 labels 2.25 1.50

See Nos. 1620-1623, 1681-1684.

Glass Blower — A783

1984, Apr. 10

1584 A783 300 l Mosaic, furnace 40 20
1585 A783 300 l shown 40 20
a. Pair, #1584-1585 + label 85 45

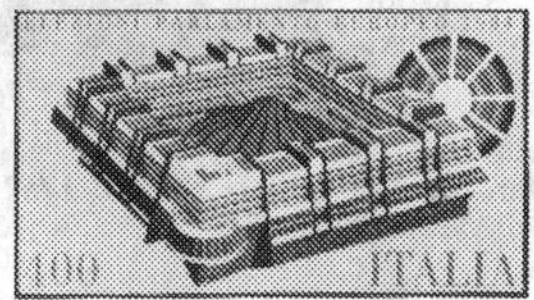
2nd European Parliament Elections — A784

1984, Apr. 16

1586 A784 400 l Parliament Strasbourg 48 24

Forest Preservation A785

1984, Apr. 24 Photo. *Perf. 14x13½*

1587 A785 450 l Helicopter fire patrol 55 28
1588 A785 450 l Hedgehog, squirrel, badger 55 28
1589 A785 450 l Riverside waste dump 55 28
1590 A785 450 l Plant life, animals 55 28
a. Block of 4, #1587-1590 2.25 1.50

Italia '85 A786

1984, Apr. 26 *Perf. 14*

1591 A786 450 l Ministry of Posts, Rome 55 28
1592 A786 550 l Via Appia Antiqua, Rome 68 34

Rome Pacts, 40th Anniv. A787

Trade Unionists: Giuseppe di Vittorio, Bruno Buozzi, Achille Grandi.

1984, Apr. 30 *Perf. 14x13½*

1593 A787 450 l multi 55 28

Europa (1959-84) A788

1984, May 5

1594 A788 450 l multi 55 28
1595 A788 550 l multi 68 34

Intl. Telecommunications Symposium, Florence, May — A789

1984, May 7 *Perf. 14*

1596 A789 550 l multi 68 34

Italian Derby Centenary A790

Lithographed and Engraved

1984, May 12 *Perf. 14x13½*

1597 A790 250 l Racing 28 15
1598 A790 400 l Racing, diff. 48 24

Tourist Type of 1974

1984, May 19 Photo. *Perf. 14*

1599 A616 350 l Campione d'Italia 45 22
1600 A616 400 l Chianciano Terme baths 48 24
1601 A616 450 l Padula 55 28
1602 A616 550 l Greek ampitheater, Syracuse 68 34

Folk Celebration Type of 1982

Design: La Macchina Di Santa Rosa.

1984, Sept. 3 Photo. *Perf. 13½x14*

1603 A754 400 l multi 45 22

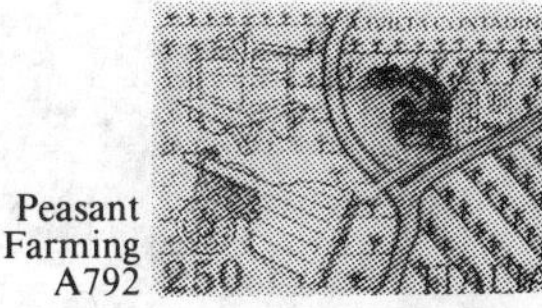
Peasant Farming A792

1984, Oct. 1 Photo. *Perf. 14x13½*

1604 A792 250 l Grain harvester, thresher 28 15
1605 A792 350 l Cart, hand press 40 20

Villa Type of 1980

Designs: 250 l, Villa Caristo, Stignano. 350 l, Villa Doria Pamphili, Genoa. 400 l, Villa Reale, Stupinigi. 450 l, Villa Mellone, Lecce.

Lithographed and Engraved

1984, Oct. 6 *Perf. 14x13½*

1606 A719 250 l multi 28 15
1607 A719 350 l multi 40 20
1608 A719 400 l multi 45 22
1609 A719 450 l multi 50 25

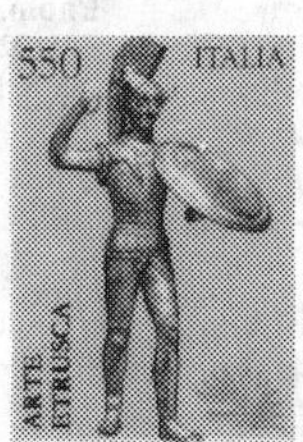
Italia '85 — A793

1984, Nov. 9 *Perf. 13½x14*

1610 A793 550 l Etruscan bronze statue 60 30
1611 A793 550 l Italia '85 emblem 60 30
1612 A793 550 l Etruscan silver mirror 60 30
a. Strip of 3, #1610-1612 2.00 1.50

Journalistic Information A794

Modern Problems A795

1985, Jan. 15 Photo. *Perf. 13½x14*

1613 A794 350 l Globe, paper tape, microwave dish 40 20

1985, Jan. 23 Photo. *Perf. 13½x14*

1614 A795 250 l Aging 28 15

The Hunt, by Raphael (1483-1520) A796

Italia '85. No. 1616, Emblem. No. 1617, Detail from fresco by Baldassare Peruzzi (1481-1536) in Bishop's Palace, Ostia Antica.

Photo. and Engr., Photo. (#1616)

1985, Feb. 13 *Perf. 13½x14*

1615 A796 600 l multi 60 30
1616 A796 600 l multi 60 30
1617 A796 600 l multi 60 30
a. Strip of 3, #1615-1617 2.00 1.50

Faience Tiles, Plate, Flask and Covered Bowl — A797

Italian ceramics: No. 1619, Tile mural, gladiators in combat.

1985, Mar. 2 Photo. *Perf. 14x13½*

1618 A797 600 l multi 60 30
1619 A797 600 l multi 60 30
a. Pair, #1618-1619 + label 1.25 75

Italian Vehicle Type of 1984

1985, Mar. 21

1620 A782 450 l Lancia Thema 45 24
1621 A782 450 l Fiat Abarth 45 24
1622 A782 450 l Fiat Uno 45 24
1623 A782 450 l Lamborghini 45 24
a. Block of 4, #1620-1623 + 2 labels 2.00 1.50

Church of St. Mary of Peace, Rome, by Pietro de Cortona (1596-1669) A799

Italia '85: No. 1625, Exhibition emblem. No. 1626, Church of St. Agnes, Rome, fountain and obelisk.

Photo. and Engr., Photo. (#1625)

1985, Mar. 30 *Perf. 13½x14*

1624 A799 250 l multi 25 15
1625 A799 250 l multi 25 15
1626 A799 250 l multi 25 15
a. Strip of 3, #1624-1626 85 50

Pope Sixtus V, (1520-1590), 400th Anniv. of Papacy — A800

Design: Sixtus V, dome of St. Peter's Basilica, Rome.

1985, Apr. 24 **Litho. and Engr.**

1627 A800 1500 l multi 1.75 90

Folk Celebration Type of 1982

Folktales: No. 1628, The March of the Turks, Potenza. No. 1629, San Marino Republican Regatta, Amalti.

1985, May 29 **Photo.**

1628 A754 250 l multi 28 15
1629 A754 350 l multi 38 20

Tourist Type of 1974

Scenic views: 350 l, Bormio town center. 400 l, Mt. Vesuvius from Castellamare di Stabia. 450 l, Stromboli Volcano from the sea. 600 l, Beach, old town at Termoli.

1985, June 1 *Perf. 14*

1630 A616 350 l multi 38 20
1631 A616 400 l multi 42 22
1632 A616 450 l multi 48 24
1633 A616 600 l multi 65 35

Nature Conservation A803

1985, June 5 *Perf. 13½x14*

1634 A803 500 l European beaver 52 28
1635 A803 500 l Primula 52 28
1636 A803 500 l Nebrodi pine 52 28
1637 A803 500 l Italian sandpiper 52 28
a. Block of 4, #1634-1637 2.25 1.50

Art Type of 1981

Designs: No. 1638, Madonna bu Il Sassoferrato, G.B. Salvi, 1609-1685. No. 1639, Pride of the Work by Mario Sironi, 1885-1961.

Lithographed and Engraved

1985, June 15 ***Perf. 14***

1638 A738 350 l multi 38 20
1639 A738 400 l multi 42 22

Europa 1985 — A805

Tenors and composers: 500 l, Aureliano Pertile (1885-1969) and Giovanni Martinelli (1885-1962). 600 l, Johann Sebastian Bach (1685-1750) and Vincenzo Bellini (1801-1835).

1985, June 20 Photo. ***Perf. 13½x14***

1640 A805 500 l multi 85 30
1641 A805 600 l multi 1.00 35

San Salvatore Abbey, Monte Amiata, 950th Anniv. A806

Lithographed and Engraved

1985, Aug. 1 ***Perf. 14x13½***

1642 A806 450 l multi 50 25

World Cycling Championships — A807

1985, Aug. 21 **Photo.**

1643 A807 400 l multi 45 22

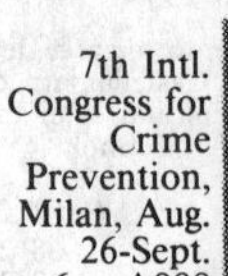

7th Intl. Congress for Crime Prevention, Milan, Aug. 26-Sept. 6 — A808

1985, Aug. 26

1644 A808 600 l multi 68 35

Intl. Youth Year — A809

1985, Sept. 3

1645 A809 600 l multi 68 35

Villa Type of 1980

Designs: 300 l, Nitti, Maratea. 400 l, Aldrovandi Mazzacorati, Bologna. 500 l, Santa Maria, Pula. 600 l, De Mersi, Villazzano.

Lithographed and Engraved

1985, Oct. 1 ***Perf. 14x13½***

1646 A719 300 l multi 35 18
1647 A719 400 l multi 42 22
1648 A719 500 l multi 58 30
1649 A719 600 l multi 68 35

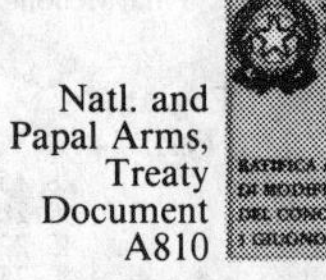

Natl. and Papal Arms, Treaty Document A810

1985, Oct. 15 **Photo.**

1650 A810 400 l multi 45 22

Ratification of new Concordat with the Vatican.

Souvenir Sheets

Parma No. 10, View of Parma A812

Switzerland No. 3L1 A813

Sardinia #1, Great Britain #1 (illustration reduced) — A814

No. 1651b, Two Sicilies No. 3, Naples. c, Two Sicilies No. 10, Palermo. d, Modena No. 3, Modena. e, Roman States No. 8, Rome. f, Tuscany No. 5, Florence. g, Sardinia No. 15, Turin. h, Romagna No. 7, Bologna. i, Lombardy-Venetia No. 4, Milan.

No. 1652b, Japan No. 1. c, US No. 2. d, Western Australia No. 1. e, Mauritius No. 4.

Lithographed and Engraved

1985, Oct. 25 ***Perf. 14***

1651 Sheet of 9 3.25 1.75
a.-i. A812 300 l, any single 35 18

Perf. 14x13½

1652 Sheet of 5 + label 3.00 1.50
a.-e. A813 500 l, any single 60 30

Imperf

1653 A814 4000 l multi 4.75 2.50

Italia '85, Rome, Oct. 25-Nov. 3.

Long-distance Skiing — A815

1986, Jan. 25 Photo. ***Perf. 14x13½***

1654 A815 450 l multi 55 28

Folk Celebration Type of 1982

Design: Procession of St. Agnes, Le Candelore Folk Festival, Catania.

1986, Feb. 3 ***Perf. 13½x14***

1655 A754 450 l multi 55 28

Amilcare Ponchielli (1834-1886), Composer A816

Photogravure and Engraved

1986, Mar. 8 ***Perf. 14x13½***

1656 A816 2000 l Scene from La Giaconda 2.50 1.25

Castle Type of 1980

Design: 380 l, Vignola, Modena. 650 l, Montecchio Castle, Castiglion Fiorentino. 750 l, Rocca di Urbisaglia.

Perf. 14x13½

1986-90 Photo. Wmk. 303

1657 A717 380 l multi ('87) 60 30
1658 A717 650 l multi 65 32

Engr.

1659 A717 750 l multi ('90) 1.50 75

Issue date: 750 l, Sept. 20.

Coil Stamps

Perf. 14 Vert.

1988 Engr. Wmk. 303

Size: 16x21mm

1660 A717 50 l Scilla 15 15
1661 A717 100 l St. Severa 16 15
1662 A717 450 l Piobicco, Pesaro 75 38
1663 A717 500 l Norman Castle, Melfi 82 40
1663A A717 600 l Scaligero, Sirmione 1.15 58
1664 A717 650 l Serralunga D'Alba 1.05 52
1665 A717 750 l Venafro 1.25 60
1666 A717 800 l Rocca Maggiore, Assisi 1.50 75
Nos. 1660-1666 (8) 6.83 3.53

Issue dates: 600 l, 800 l, Feb. 20, 1991; others, Mar. 1.

Giovanni Battista Pergolesi (1710-1736), Musician — A817

Perf. 13½x14

1986, Mar. 15 Photo. Unwmk.

1667 A817 2000 l multi 2.50 1.25

The Bay, Acitrezza — A818

1986, Mar. 24 ***Perf. 14***

1668 A818 350 l shown 45 22
1669 A818 450 l Piazzetta, Capri 58 30
1670 A818 550 l Kursaal, Merano 70 35
1671 A818 650 l Lighthouse, San Benedetto del Tronto 85 42

Europa 1986 — A819

Trees in special shapes: a, Heart (life). b, Star (poetry). c, Butterfly (color). d, Sun (energy).

1986, Apr. 28 Photo. ***Perf. 13x14***

1672 Block of 4 3.60 1.80
a.-d. A819 650 l, any single 90 45

25th Intl. Opthalmological Congress, Rome, May 4-10 — A820

1986, May 3 Photo. ***Perf. 14***

1673 A820 550 l multi 75 38

Police in Uniform — A821

1986, May 10

1674 A821 550 l multi 75 38
1675 A821 650 l multi 90 45

European Police Conference, Chianciano Terme, May 10-12. Nos. 1674-1675 printed se-tenant with labels picturing male or female police.

Battle of Bezzecca, 120th Anniv. A822

1986, May 31 ***Perf. 14x13½***

1676 A822 550 l multi 72 35

Memorial Day for Independence Martyrs — A823

1986, May 31 ***Perf. 14***

1677 A823 2000 l multi 2.60 1.30

Bersaglieri Corps of Mountain Troops, 150th Anniv. — A824

1986, June 1 *Perf. 13½x14*
1678 A824 450 l multi 60 30

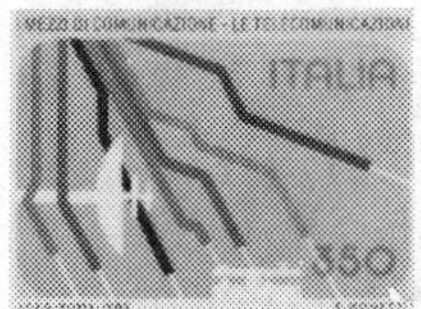

Telecommunications — A825

1986, June 16 *Perf. 14x13½*
1679 A825 350 l multi 48 24

Sacro Monte di Varallo Monastery — A826

1986, June 28 **Engr.** *Perf. 14*
1680 A826 2000 l Prus bl & sage grn 2.70 1.35

Italian Vehicle Type of 1984

1986, July 4 **Photo.** *Perf. 14x13½*
1681 A782 450 l Alfa Romeo AR8 Turbo 62 30
1682 A782 450 l Innocenti 650 SE 62 30
1683 A782 450 l Ferrari Testarossa 62 30
1684 A782 450 l Fiatallis FR 10B 62 30
a. Block of 4, #1681-1684 + 2 labels 2.50

Ladies' Fashions — A827

Breda Heavy Industry — A828

Olivetti Computer Technology — A829

1986, July 14
1685 A827 450 l shown 62 30
1686 A827 450 l Men's fashions 62 30
a. Pair, #1685-1686 + label 1.30 75
1687 A828 650 l shown 90 45
1688 A829 650 l shown 90 45

Alitalia, Italian Airlines, 40th Anniv. A830

1986, Sept. 16 **Photo.** *Perf. 14x13½*
1689 A830 550 l Anniv. emblem 82 40
1690 A830 650 l Jet, runway lights 98 50

Villa Type of 1980

1986, Oct. 1 **Photo. & Engr.**
1691 A719 350 l Necker, Trieste 52 25
1692 A719 350 l Borromeo, Cassano D'Adda 52 25
1693 A719 450 l Palagonia, Bagheria 68 35
1694 A719 550 l Medicea, Poggio a Caiano 82 40
1695 A719 650 l Castello d'Issogne, Issogne 98 50
Nos. 1691-1695 (5) 3.52 1.75

Christmas — A831

Madonna and Child, bronze sculpture by Donatello, Basilica del Santo, Padua.

1986, Oct. 10 **Engr.** *Perf. 14*
1696 A831 450 l brown olive 68 35

Art Type of 1981

Designs: 450 l, Seated Woman Holding a Book, drawing by Andrea del Sarto, Uffizi, Florence, vert. 550 l, Daphne at Pavarola, painting by Felice Casorati, Museum of Modern Art, Turin, vert.

1986, Oct. 11 **Litho. & Engr.**
1697 A738 450 l blk & pale org 68 35
1698 A738 550 l multi 82 40

Memorial, Globe, Plane — A832

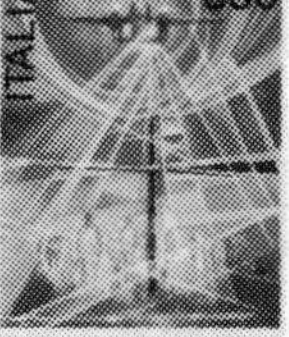

Plane, Cross, Men — A833

1986, Nov. 11 **Photo.** *Perf. 13½x14*
1699 A832 550 l multi 80 40
1700 A833 650 l multi 95 48

Intl. Peace Year, memorial to Italian airmen who died at Kindu, Zaire, while on a peace mission.

Stamp Day A834

1986, Nov. 29 *Perf. 14x13½*
1701 A834 550 l Die of Sardinia No. 2 85 42

Francesco Matraire, printer of first Sardinian stamps.

A835

Industries — A836

Perf. 14½x13½
1987, Feb. 27 **Photo.**
1702 A835 700 l Marzotto Textile, 1836 1.05 52
1703 A836 700 l Italgas Energy Corp., 1837 1.05 52

See No. 1755-1757.

Environmental Protection — A837

Designs: a, Volturno River. b, Garda Lake. c, Trasimeno Lake. d, Tirso River.

1987, Mar. 6 **Litho.** *Perf. 14x13½*
1704 Block of 4 3.15 1.60
a.-d. A837 500 l, any single 78 40

Antonio Gramsci (1891-1937), Author and Artist — A838

1987, Apr. 27 **Litho.** *Perf. 14x13½*
1705 A838 600 l scar & gray black 95 48

Europa 1987 A839

Modern architecture: 600 l, Church of Sun Motorway, Florence, designed by Michelucci. 700 l, Railway station, Rome, designed by Nervi.

1987, May 4 **Photo.**
1706 A839 600 l multi 95 48
1707 A839 700 l multi 1.10 55

Tourist Type of 1974

1987, May 9 *Perf. 14*
1708 A616 380 l Verbania Pallanza 60 30
1709 A616 400 l Palmi 65 32
1710 A616 500 l Vasto 80 40
1711 A616 600 l Villacidro 95 48

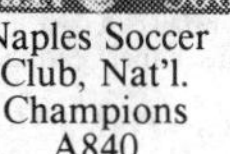

Naples Soccer Club, Nat'l. Champions A840

The Absinthe Drinkers, by Degas A841

1987, May 18 **Litho.** *Perf. 13½x14*
1712 A840 500 l multi 78 40

1987, May 29
1713 A841 380 l multi 60 30

Fight against alcoholism.

St. Alfonso M. de Liguori (1696-1787) and Gulf of Naples A842

1987, Aug. 1 *Perf. 14x13½*
1714 A842 400 l multi 62 30

Events A843

Emblems and natl. landmarks: No. 1715, OLYMPHILEX '87, Intl. Olympic Committee Building, Foro Italico, Rome. No. 1716, World Athletics Championships, Olympic Stadium, Rome.

1987, Aug. 29 **Photo.** *Perf. 14x14½*
1715 A843 700 l multi 1.10 55
1716 A843 700 l multi 1.10 55

Folk Celebration Type of 1982

Design: Quintana Joust, Foligno.

Perf. 13½x14½
1987, Sept. 12 **Photo.**
1717 A754 380 l multi 60 30

Piazzas A844

Designs: 380 l, Piazza del Popolo, Ascoli Piceno. 500 l, Piazza Giuseppe Verdi, Palermo. 600 l, Piazza San Carlo, Turin. 700 l, Piazza dei Signori, Verona.

Litho. & Engr.
1987, Oct. 10 *Perf. 14x13½*
1718 A844 380 l multi 60 30
1719 A844 500 l multi 80 40
1720 A844 600 l multi 95 48
1721 A844 700 l multi 1.10 55

See Nos. 1747-1748, 1765-1766.

Christmas A845

Paintings by Giotto: 500 l, Adoration in the Manger, Basilica of St. Francis, Assisi. 600 l, The Epiphany, Scrovegni Chapel, Padua.

1987, Oct. 15 Photo. *Perf. 13½x14*
1722 A845 500 l multi 80 40
1723 A845 600 l multi 95 48

Battle of Mentana, 120th Anniv. A846

Litho. & Engr.

1987, Nov. 3 *Perf. 14x13½*
1724 A846 380 l multi 65 32

Il Pantocrator (Christ), Mosaic, Monreale Cathedral — A847

Coat of Arms and San Carlo Theater, Naples, from an 18th Cent. Engraving — A848

1987, Nov. 4 *Perf. 14*
1725 A847 500 l multi 85 42
1726 A848 500 l multi 85 42

Artistic heritage.

Nunziatella Military School, 200th Anniv. A849

1987, Nov. 14 *Perf. 14x13½*
1727 A849 600 l multi 1.00 50

Buying Sets
Frequently it is less expensive to purchase complete sets rather than the individual stamps that make up the set. "Set Values" are provided for many such sets.

Stamp Day — A850

Design: Philatelist Marco DeMarchi (d. 1936) holding magnifying glass and stamp album, Milan Cathedral.

1987, Nov. 20 Photo. *Perf. 13½x14*
1728 A850 500 l multi 85 42

Homo Aeserniensis (Flint Knapper) — A851

Photo. & Engr.

1988, Feb. 6 *Perf. 13½x14*
1729 A851 500 l multi 85 42

Remains of Isernia Man, c. 736,000 years-old, discovered near Isernia.

E. Quirino Visconti School, Rome A852

Litho. & Engr.
Perf. 14x13½

1988, Mar. 1 Unwmk.
1730 A852 500 l multi 82 40

See Nos. 1764, 1824, 1842.

St. John Bosco (1815-1888), Educator — A853

1988, Apr. 2 Photo. *Perf. 13½x14*
1731 A853 500 l multi 82 40

Art Type of 1981

Painting: *Gli Archeologi*, by Giorgio de Chirico (1888-1978).

1988, Apr. 7 Engr. *Perf. 14*
1732 A738 650 l multi, vert. 1.05 52

1st Printed Hebrew Bible, 500th Anniv. A854

Soncino Bible excerpt, 15th cent.

1988, Apr. 22 Photo. *Perf. 14x13½*
1733 A854 550 l multi 90 45

Epilepsy Foundation A855

Design: St. Valentine, electroencephalograph readout, epileptic in seizure and medieval crest.

1988, Apr. 23
1734 A855 500 l multi 82 40

Europa 1988 A856

Transport and communication: 650 l, ETR 450 locomotive. 750 l, Electronic mail, map of Italy.

1988, May 2
1735 A856 650 l multi 1.05 52
1736 A856 750 l multi 1.25 62

Tourist Type of 1974

Scenic views: 400 l, Castiglione della Pescaia. 500 l, Lignano Sabbiadoro. 650 l, Noto. 750 l, Vieste.

1988, May 7 Photo. *Perf. 14*
1737 A616 400 l multi 62 30
1738 A616 500 l multi 78 40
1739 A616 650 l multi 1.00 50
1740 A616 750 l multi 1.15 58

Golf — A858

1988, May 16
1741 A858 500 l dull grn, yel & blk 78 40

1990 World Cup Soccer Championships — A859

1988, May 16 Litho. *Perf. 14x13½*
1742 A859 3150 l blk, grn & dark red 4.75 2.40

1988 Natl. Soccer Championships, Milan — A860

1988, May 23 *Perf. 13½x14*
1743 A860 650 l multi 1.00 50

Bronze Sculpture, Pergola — A861

1988, June 4 Engr. *Perf. 14*
1744 A861 500 l Horse 75 38
1745 A861 650 l Woman 95 48

Bologna University, 900th Anniv. — A862

1988, June 10 Engr. *Perf. 13½x14*
1746 A862 500 l vio 75 38

Piazza Type of 1987

Designs: 400 l, Piazza del Duomo, Pistoia. 550 l, Piazza del Unita d'Italia, Trieste.

Litho. & Engr.

1988, July 2 *Perf. 14x13½*
1747 A844 400 l multi 60 30
1748 A844 550 l multi 82 40

Folk Celebration Type of 1982

Discesa Dei Candelieri, Sassari: Man wearing period costume, column and bearers.

1988, Aug. 13 Photo. *Perf. 13½x14*
1749 A754 550 l multi 80 40

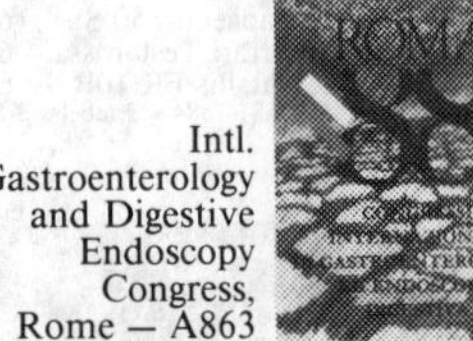

Intl. Gastroenterology and Digestive Endoscopy Congress, Rome — A863

1988, Sept. 5
1750 A863 750 l multi 1.10 55

Surrealistic Films A864

Italian films amd directors: 500 l, *Ossessione*, 1942, by Luchino Visconti. 650 l, *Ladri di Biciclette*, 1948, by Vittorio DeSica. 2400 l, *Roma Citta Aperta*, 1945, by Roberto Rossellini. 3050 l, *Riso Amaro*, 1949, by Giuseppe DeSantis.

1988, Oct. 13 Litho. *Perf. 14x13½*
1751 A864 500 l multi 80 40
1752 A864 650 l multi 1.05 52
1753 A864 2400 l multi 3.75 1.90
1754 A864 3050 l multi 4.75 2.40

Elsag
A865

Aluminia — A866

State Mint and Polygraphic Insitute — A867

Italian Industries.

1988, Oct. 19 **Photo.**
1755 A865 750 l multi 1.30 65
1756 A866 750 l multi 1.30 65

Photo. & Engr.
1757 A867 750 l multi 1.30 65

Christmas: *Nativity,* by Roseto Degli Abruzzi, Church of the Virgin's Assumption
A868

1988, Oct. 29 **Photo.** ***Perf. 13½x14***
1758 A868 650 l multi 1.05 52

Christmas
A869

Photo. & Engr.
1988, Nov. 12 ***Perf. 14x13½***
1759 A869 500 l dark blue grn & chest brn 78 40

St. Charles Borromeo (1538-1584), Ecclesiastical Reformer — A870

1988, Nov. 4 **Litho. & Engr.**
1760 A870 2400 l multi 3.75 1.85

Stamp Day — A871

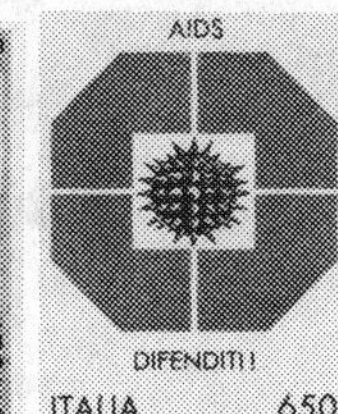

Campaign Against AIDS — A872

Design: Japan No. 69 and stamp designer Edoardo Chiossone.

1988, Dec. 9 **Photo.** ***Perf. 13½x14***
1761 A871 500 l multi 75 38

1989, Jan. 13
1762 A872 650 l multi 98 50

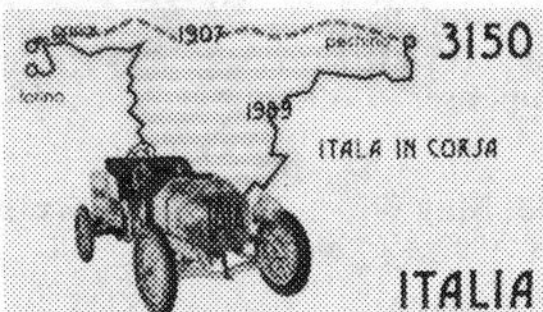

Paris-Peking Rally — A873

1989, Jan. 21 ***Perf. 14½x13½***
1763 A873 3150 l Map, Itala race car 4.65 2.30

School Type of 1988

1989 **Photo. & Engr.** ***Perf. 14x13½***
1764 A852 650 l multi 1.00 50

Piazza Type of 1987

Designs: No. 1765, Piazza Del Duomo, Catanzaro. No. 1766, Piazza Di Spagna, Rome.

Litho. & Engr.
1989, Apr. 10 ***Perf. 14x13½***
1765 A844 400 l multi 60 30
1766 A844 400 l multi 60 30

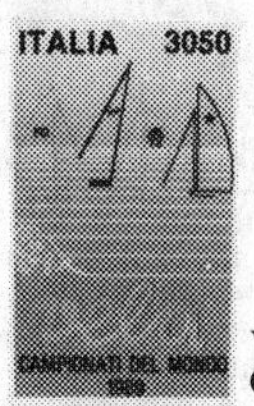

Velo World Yachting Championships
A875

1989, Apr. 8 **Photo.** ***Perf. 14***
1767 A875 3050 l multi 4.60 2.30

Artistic Heritage Type of 1987

Art and architecture: 500 l, King with scepter and orb, Palazzo Della Ragione, Padova, vert. 650 l, Crypt of St. Nicolas, St. Nicolas Basilica, Bari, vert.

1989, Apr. 8 **Litho. & Engr., Engr.**
1768 A847 500 l multi 75 38
1769 A847 650 l indigo 1.00 50

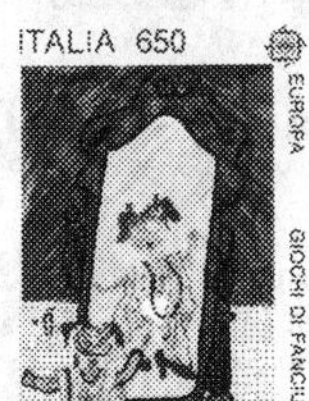

Europa 1989 — A876

European Parliament 3rd Elections — A877

Children's games.

Perf. 14x13½, 13½x14
1989, May 8 **Photo.**
1770 A876 500 l Leapfrog, horiz. 72 35
1771 A876 650 l shown 92 45
1772 A876 750 l Sack race, horiz. 1.05 52

1989, June 3 ***Perf. 13½x14***
1773 A877 500 l multi 72 35

No. 1773 also inscribed in European Currency Units "ECU 0,31."

Pisa University — A878

1989, May 29 **Engr.** ***Perf. 14x13½***
1774 A878 500 l violet 72 35

Folk Celebration Type of 1982

Design: Priest and Flower Feast street scene.

1989, May 27 **Photo.** ***Perf. 13½x14***
1775 A754 400 l multi 58 30

Landscape Type of 1981

1989, June 10 **Photo.** ***Perf. 14***
1776 A733 500 l Naxos Gardens 70 35
1777 A733 500 l Spotorno 70 35
1778 A733 500 l Pompei 70 35
1779 A733 500 l Grottammare 70 35

Ministry of Posts, Cent.
A879

1989, June 24 ***Perf. 14x13½***
1780 A879 500 l Posthorn, No. 52 70 35
1781 A879 2400 l Posthorn, Earth 3.25 1.65

INTER Soccer Championships — A880

1989, June 26
1782 A880 650 l multi 90 45

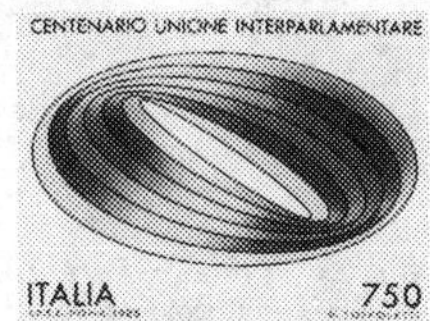

Interparliamentary Union, Cent. — A881

1989, June 28
1783 A881 750 l multi 1.05 52

French Revolution, Bicent. — A882

1989, July 7 **Photo.** ***Perf. 14***
1784 A882 3150 l multi 4.75 2.35

Fortified Walls of Corinaldo, by Francesco di Giorgio Martini (1439-1502)
A883

Litho. & Engr.
1989, Sept. 2 ***Perf. 14***
1785 A883 500 l multi 75 38

Charlie Chaplin (1889-1977)
A884

1989, Sept. 23 **Engr.** ***Perf. 14x13½***
1786 A884 750 l black & sepia 1.10 55

Naples-Portici Railway, 150th Anniv.
A885 A886

Illustration reduced.

1989, Oct. 3 **Litho. & Engr.**
1787 A885 550 l multicolored 82 40
1788 A886 550 l multicolored 82 40
a. Pair, #1787-1788 1.75 1.00

Adoration of the Kings, by Correggio
A887 A888

1989, Oct. 21 **Photo.** ***Perf. 13½x14***
1789 A887 500 l multicolored 75 38
1790 A888 500 l multicolored 75 38
a. Pair, #1789-1790 1.65 90

Christmas.

Footnotes often refer to other stamps of the same design.

Fidardo Castle, the Stradella, Accordion — A889

Industries.

1989, Oct. 14 Photo. *Perf. 14x13½*
1791 A889 450 l Music 70 35
1792 A889 450 l Arnoldo World Publishing 70 35

Stamp Day — A890

1989, Nov. 24 *Perf. 13½x14*
1793 A890 500 l Emilio Diena 78 38

1990 World Soccer Championships, Italy — A891

1989, Dec. 9 Engr. *Perf. 13½x14*
1794 A891 450 l multicolored 75 36

Columbus's First Voyage, 1474-1484
A892 A893

1990, Feb. 24 Photo.
1795 A892 700 l multicolored 1.15 58
1796 A893 700 l multicolored 1.15 58
a. Pair, #1795-1796 2.50 1.50

Souvenir Sheets

1990 World Cup Soccer Championships, Italy — A894

Soccer club emblems and stadiums in Italy.

No. 1797: a, Italy. b, US. c, Olympic Stadium, Rome. d, Municipal Stadium, Florence. e, Austria. f, Czechoslovakia.

No. 1798: a, Argentina. b, Russia. c, St. Paul Stadium, Naples. d, New Stadium, Bari. e, Cameroun. f, Romania.

No. 1799: a, Brazil. b, Costa Rica. c, Alps Stadium, Turin. d, Ferraris Stadium, Genoa. e, Sweden. f, Scotland.

No. 1800: a, UAE. b, West Germany. c, Dall'ara Stadium, Bologna. d, Meazza Stadium, Milan. e, Colombia. f, Yugoslavia.

No. 1801: a, Belgium. b, Uruguay. c, Bentegodi Stadium, Verona. d, Friuli Stadium, Udine. e, South Korea. f, Spain.

No. 1802: a, England. b, Netherlands. c, Sant'elia Stadium, Cagliari. d, La Favorita Stadium, Palermo. e, Ireland. f, Egypt.

1990, Mar. 24 *Perf. 14x13½*
1797 Sheet of 6 4.50 2.20
a.-f. A894 450 l any single .75 .36
1798 Sheet of 6 5.90 2.90
a.-f. A894 600 l any single .98 .48
1799 Sheet of 6 6.30 3.15
a.-f. A894 650 l any single 1.05 .52
1800 Sheet of 6 6.90 3.50
a.-f. A894 700 l any single 1.15 .58
1801 Sheet of 6 7.80 3.90
a.-f. A894 800 l any single 1.30 .65
1802 Sheet of 6 11.70 5.90
a.-f. A894 1200 l any single 1.95 .98

See No. 1819.

Tourist Type of 1974

1990, Mar. 30 Photo. *Perf. 14*
1803 A616 600 l Sabbioneta 98 50
1804 A616 600 l Montepulciano 98 50
1805 A616 600 l Castellammare del Golfo 98 50
1806 A616 600 l San Felice Circeo 98 50

Folk Celebration Type of 1982

Design: Horse race, Merano.

1990, Apr. 9 *Perf. 13½x14*
1807 A754 600 l multicolored 98 50

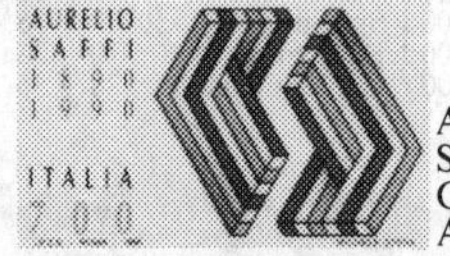

Aurelio Saffi, Death Cent. A895

1990, Apr. 10 *Perf. 14*
1808 A895 700 l multicolored 1.15 58

Giovanni Giorgi (1871-1950) A896

1990, Apr. 23 *Perf. 14x13½*
1809 A896 600 l multicolored 1.15 58

Metric System in Italy, 55th. anniv.

Labor Day, Cent. — A897

1990, Apr. 28 Photo. *Perf. 13½x14*
1810 A897 600 l multicolored 1.15 58

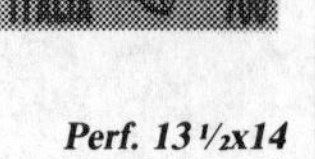

Naples Soccer Club, Italian Champions A898

1990, Apr. 30 *Perf. 13½x14*
1811 A898 700 l multicolored 1.30 65

Europa A899

Post Offices: 700 l, San Silvestro Piazza, Rome. 800 l, Fondaco Tedeschi, Venice.

1990, May 7 *Perf. 14x13½*
1812 A899 700 l multicolored 1.30 65
1813 A899 800 l multicolored 1.50 75

Giovanni Paisiello (1740-1816), Composer — A900

1990, May 9 *Perf. 14x13½*
1814 A900 450 l multicolored 82 40

Dante Alighieri (1265-1321), Poet A901

1990, May 12 *Perf. 14x13½*
1815 A901 700 l multicolored 1.25 62

Dante Alighieri Soc., cent.

Mosaic (Detail) — A902

Sculpture — A903

Photo. (#1816), Litho. & Engr. (#1817)

1990, May 19 *Perf. 13½x14*
1816 A902 450 l multicolored 82 40
1817 A903 700 l multicolored 1.25 62

Malatestiana Music Festival, Rimini, 40th Anniv. — A904

1990, June 15 Photo. *Perf. 14*
1818 A904 600 l multicolored 1.15 58

World Cup Soccer Type of 1990 Inscribed "Campione Del Mondo"

1990, July 9 Litho. *Perf. 14x13½*
1819 A894 600 l like No. 1800b 1.15 58

Still Life, by Giorgio Morandi (1890-1964) A905

1990, July 20 Engr. *Perf. 14*
1820 A905 750 l black 1.45 75

Greco-Roman Wrestling, World Championships — A906

1990, Oct. 11 Litho. *Perf. 14x13½*
1821 A906 3200 l multicolored 6.50 3.25

Christmas — A907

Paintings of the Nativity by: 600 l, Emidio Vangelli. 750 l, Pellegrino.

1990, Oct. 26 *Perf. 14*
1822 A907 600 l multicolored 1.25 65
1823 A907 750 l multicolored 1.60 80

School Type of 1988 and

Italian Schools A908

Designs: 600 l, Bernardino Telesio gymnasium, Cosenza. 750 l, University of Catania.

Litho. & Engr.

1990, Nov. 5 *Perf. 14x13½*
1824 A852 600 l multicolored 1.25 65

Engr.

Size: 47½x27mm

1825 A908 750 l multicolored 1.60 80

Self-portrait, Corrado Mezzana (1890-1952) A909

1990, Nov. 16 Litho. *Perf. 13½x14*
1826 A909 600 l multicolored 1.25 65

Stamp day.

The Nativity — A910

Genoa Flower Show — A911

1991, Jan. 5 Litho. *Perf. 13½x14*
1827 A910 600 l multicolored 1.25 65

1991, Jan. 10 *Perf. 14*
1828 A911 750 l multicolored 1.60 80

Seal of the Univ. of Siena — A912

1991, Jan. 15 Photo. *Perf. 13½x14*
1829 A912 750 l multicolored 1.60 80

Tourist Type of 1974

1991 Photo.
1830 A616 600 l San Remo 1.25 65
1831 A616 600 l Roccaraso 1.25 65
1832 A616 600 l La Maddalena 1.25 65
1833 A616 600 l Calgi 1.25 65

United Europe — A913

Perf. 14x13½
1991, Mar. 12 Photo. Unwmk.
1834 A913 750 l multi 1.45 90

#1834 also carries .48 ECU denomination.

A914

Discovery of America, 500th Anniv. (in 1992) A915

1991, Mar. 22 Litho.
1835 A914 750 l Ships leaving port 1.45 70
1836 A915 750 l Columbus, Queen's court 1.45 70
a. Pair, #1835-1836 2.90 1.50

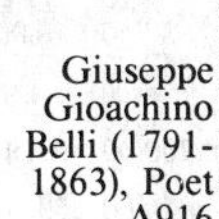

Giuseppe Gioachino Belli (1791-1863), Poet A916

1991, Apr. 15 Litho. *Perf. 14x13½*
1837 A916 600 l bl & gray blk 1.15 60

Church of St. Gregory, Rome — A917

1991, Apr. 20 Photo. *Perf. 14x13½*
1838 A917 3200 l multicolored 6.00 3.00

Europa A918

1991, Apr. 29 Photo. *Perf. 14x13½*
1839 A918 750 l DRS satellite 1.40 70
1840 A918 800 l Hermes space shuttle 1.50 75

Santa Maria Maggiore Church, Lanciano — A919

1991, May 2 Engr. *Perf. 13½x14*
1841 A919 600 l brown 1.10 55

Schools Type of 1988

Design: D. A. Azuni school, Sassari.

Litho. & Engr.
1991, May 3 *Perf. 14x13½*
1842 A852 600 l multicolored 1.10 55

Team Genoa, Italian Soccer Champions, 1990-91 — A920

1991, May 27 Photo. *Perf. 13½x14*
1843 A920 3000 l multicolored 5.25 2.60

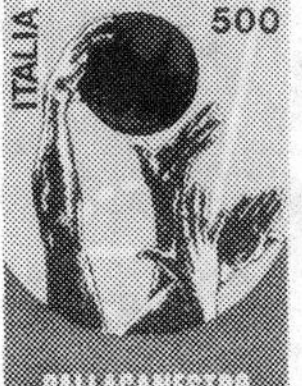

Basketball, Cent. — A921

Children's Rights — A922

1991, June 5
1844 A921 500 l multicolored 90 45

1991, June 14
1845 A922 600 l shown 1.05 52
1846 A922 750 l Man, child with balloon 1.30 65

Art and Culture A923

Designs: 600 l, Sculpture by Pericle Fazzini (b. 1913). 3200 l, Exhibition Hall, Turin, designed by Pier Luigi Nervi (1891-1979).

Litho. & Engr.
1991, June 21 *Perf. 14*
1847 A923 600 l multicolored 1.05 52
1848 A923 3200 l multicolored 5.60 2.80

Egyptian Museum, Turin — A924

1991, Aug. 31 Litho. *Perf. 13½x14*
1849 A924 750 l grn, yel & gold 1.35 65

Luigi Galvani (1737-1798), Electrophysicist — A925

1991, Sept. 24 *Perf. 14x13½*
1850 A925 750 l multicolored 1.35 65

Radio, cent. (in 1995).

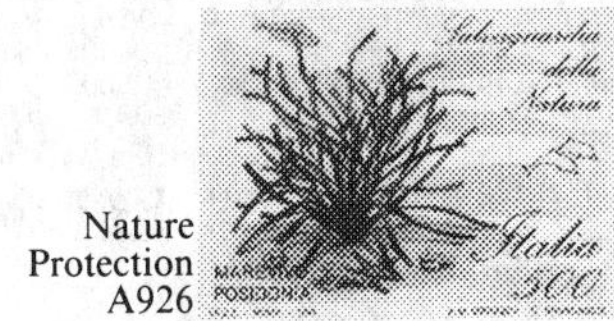

Nature Protection A926

1991, Oct. 10 Photo. *Perf. 14x13½*

1851 A926 500 l Marevivo posidonia 90 45
1852 A926 500 l Falco pellegrino 90 45
1853 A926 500 l Cervo sardo 90 45
1854 A926 500 l Orso marsicano 90 45

World Wildlife Fund.

Wolfgang Amadeus Mozart, Death Bicent. — A927

1991, Oct. 7 *Perf. 13½x14*

1855 A927 800 l multicolored 1.50 75

Christmas — A928

1991, Oct. 18

1856 A928 600 l multicolored 1.15 58

Giulio and Alberto Bolaffi, Philatelists — A929

1991, Oct. 25 *Perf. 14*

1857 A929 750 l multicolored 1.45 70

Stamp Day.

Pietro Nenni (1891-1980), Politician — A930

1991, Oct. 30

1858 A930 750 l multicolored 1.45 70

SEMI-POSTAL STAMPS

Many issues of Italy and Italian Colonies include one or more semi-postal denominations. To avoid splitting sets, these issues are generally listed as regular postage, airmail, etc., unless all values carry a surtax.

Italian Flag — SP1

Italian Eagle Bearing Arms of Savoy — SP2

1915-16 Typo. Wmk. 140 *Perf. 14*

B1 SP1 10c + 5c rose 1.25 1.75
B2 SP2 15c + 5c slate 90 1.75
B3 SP2 20c + 5c orange 1.65 5.50

No. B2 Surcharged **20**

1916

B4 SP2 20c on 15c + 5c sl 2.00 6.75
a. Double overprint 200.00
b. Inverted overprint 200.00 300.00

Regular Issues of 1906-16 Overprinted in Blue or Red **B.L.P.**

1921

B5 A48 10c claret (Bl) 350.00 65.00
B6 A50 20c brn org (Bl) 400.00 25.00
B7 A49 25c blue (R) 37.50 5.00
B8 A49 40c brn (Bl) 12.00 75
a. Inverted overprint 12.00 15.00

Regular Issues of 1901-22 Overprinted in Black, Blue, Brown or Red **B.L.P.**

1922-23

B9 A48 10c cl ('23) (Bk) 25.00 5.00
a. Blue overprint 30.00 7.50
b. Brown overprint 30.00 7.50
B10 A48 15c sl (Bl) 90.00 25.00
a. Red overprint 100.00 30.00
B11 A50 20c brn org (Bk) 90.00 25.00
a. Blue overprint 200.00 30.00
B12 A49 25c bl ('23) (Bk or Bl) 25.00 7.50
b. Red overprint 90.00 25.00
B12A A49 30c org brn (Bk) 37.50 10.00
B13 A49 40c brn (Bl) 40.00 7.50
a. Black overprint 40.00 8.50
b. As "a." invtd. ovpt. 30.00
B14 A49 50c vio ('23) (Bk) 200.00 32.50
a. Blue overprint
B15 A49 60c car (Bk) 850.00 250.00
B15A A49 85c choc (Bk) 80.00 22.50
B16 A46 1 l brn & grn ('23) (Bk) 1,250. 450.00
a. Inverted overprint 600.00

The stamps overprinted "B. L. P." were sold by the Government below face value to the National Federation for Assisting War Invalids. Most of them were affixed to special envelopes (Buste Lettere Postali) which bore advertisements. The Federation was permitted to sell these envelopes at a reduction of 5c from the face value of each stamp. The profits for the war invalids were derived from the advertisements.

Values of Nos. B5-B16 unused are for stamps with original gum. Most copies without gum or with part gum sell for about a quarter of values quoted. Uncanceled stamps affixed to the special envelopes usually sell for about half value.

The overprint on Nos. B9-B16 is wider (13½mm) than that on Nos. B5-B8 (11mm). The 1922-23 overprint exists both typo. and litho. on 10c, 15c, 20c and 25c; only litho. on 40c, 50c, 60c and 1 l; and only typo. on 30c and 85c.

Counterfeits of the B.L.P. overprints exist.

Administering Fascist Oath — SP3

1923, Oct. 29 *Perf. 14x14½*

B17 SP3 30c + 30c brn 7.00 17.50
B18 SP3 50c + 50c vio 11.50 17.50
B19 SP3 1 l + 1 l gray 7.00 17.50

The surtax was given to the Benevolent Fund of the Black Shirts (the Italian National Militia).

Anniv. of the March of the Fascisti on Rome.

St. Maria Maggiore SP4

Pope Opening Holy Door SP8

Designs: 30c+15c, St. John Lateran. 50c+25c, St. Paul's Church. 60c+30c, St. Peter's Basilica. 5 l+2.50 l, Pope closing Holy Door.

1924, Dec. 24 *Perf. 12*

B20 SP4 20c + 10c dk grn & brn 80 3.75
B21 SP4 30c + 15c dk brn & brn 80 3.75
B22 SP4 50c + 25c vio & brn 80 3.75
B23 SP4 60c + 30c dp rose & brn 80 9.00
B24 SP8 1 l + 50c dp bl & vio 80 7.50
B25 SP8 5 l + 2.50 l org brn & vio 1.00 19.00
Nos. B20-B25 (6) 5.00 46.75

The surtax was contributed toward the Holy Year expenses.

Castle of St. Angelo — SP10

Victor Emmanuel II — SP14

Designs: 50c+20c, 60c+30c, Aqueduct of Claudius. 1.25 l+50c, 1.25 l+60c, Capitol, Roman Forum. 5 l+2 l, 5 l+2.50 l, People's Gate.

Unwmk.

1926, Oct. 26 Engr. *Perf. 11*

B26 SP10 40c + 20c dk brn & blk 55 2.75
B27 SP10 60c + 30c brn red & ol brn 55 2.75
B28 SP10 1.25 l + 60c bl grn & blk 55 7.75
B29 SP10 5 l + 2.50 l dk bl & blk 1.00 24.00

1928, Mar. 1

B30 SP10 30c + 10c dl vio & blk 1.65 5.50
B31 SP10 50c + 20c ol grn & sl 1.65 3.75
B32 SP10 1.25 l + 50c dp bl & blk 2.50 12.50
B33 SP10 5 l + 2 l brn red & blk 5.75 35.00

The tax on Nos. B26 to B33 was devoted to the charitable work of the Voluntary Militia for National Defense.

See Nos. B35-B38.

1929, Jan. 4 Photo. *Perf. 14*

B34 SP14 50c + 10c ol grn 75 1.50

50th anniv. of the death of King Victor Emmanuel II. The surtax was for veterans.

Type of 1926 Issue

Designs in same order.

1930, July 1 Engr.

B35 SP10 30c + 10c dk grn & vio 25 3.00
B36 SP10 50c + 10c dk grn & bl grn 25 1.50
B37 SP10 1.25 l + 30c ind & grn 35 6.50
B38 SP10 5 l + 1.50 l blk brn & ol brn 2.25 27.50

The surtax was for the charitable work of the Voluntary Militia for National Defense.

Militiamen at Ceremonial Fire with Quotation from Leonardo da Vinci SP15

Symbolical of Pride for Militia SP16

Symbolical of Militia Guarding Immortality of Italy SP17

Militia Passing Through Arch of Constantine SP18

1935, July 1 Photo. Wmk. 140

B39	SP15	20c + 10c rose red	2.00	*3.00*
B40	SP16	25c + 15c green	2.00	*3.50*
B41	SP17	50c + 30c purple	2.00	*4.25*
B42	SP18	1.25 l + 75c blue	2.00	*4.50*
		Nos. B39-B42,CB3 (5)	10.00	*21.00*

The surtax was for the Militia.

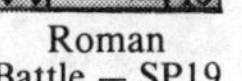

Roman Battle — SP19

Roman Warriors — SP20

1941, Dec. 13

B43	SP19	20c + 10c rose red	20	55
B44	SP19	30c + 15c brown	20	70
B45	SP20	50c + 25c violet	22	85
B46	SP20	1.25 l + 1 l blue	28	90

2,000th anniv. of the birth of Livy (59 B.C.-17 A.D.), Roman historian.

AIR POST STAMPS

Special Delivery Stamp No. E1 Overprinted

ESPERIMENTO POSTA AEREA
MAGGIO 1917
TORINO-ROMA • ROMA-TORINO

1917, May Wmk. 140 *Perf. 14*

C1 SD1 25c rose red 3.00 *5.75*

Type of SD3 Surcharged in Black

IDROVOLANTE

NAPOLI - PALERMO - NAPOLI

25 CENT. 25

1917, June 27

C2 SD3 25c on 40c vio 4.50 *6.00*

Type SD3 was not issued without surcharge.

AP2

1926-28 Typo.

C3	AP2	50c rose red ('28)	1.25	*2.00*
C4	AP2	60c gray	90	*1.50*
C5	AP2	80c brn vio & brn ('28)	5.00	*12.50*
C6	AP2	1 l blue	60	*1.50*
C7	AP2	1.20 l brn ('27)	5.00	*20.00*
C8	AP2	1.50 l buff	4.00	5.50
C9	AP2	5 l gray grn	9.25	*15.00*
		Nos. C3-C9 (7)	26.00	*58.00*

Nos. C4 and C6 Surcharged

Cent. 50

1927, Sept. 16

C10	AP2	50c on 60c gray	1.25	*5.75*
a.		Pair, one without surcharge	400.00	
C11	AP2	80c on 1 l blue	4.75	*27.50*

Pegasus AP3

Wings AP4

Spirit of Flight AP5

Arrows AP6

1930-32 Photo. Wmk. 140

C12	AP4	25c dk grn ('32)	15	15
C13	AP3	50c ol brn	15	15
C14	AP5	75c org brn ('32)	15	15
C15	AP4	80c org red	15	30
C16	AP5	1 l purple	15	15
C17	AP6	2 l deep blue	15	18
C18	AP3	5 l dk grn	15	30
C19	AP3	10 l dp car	20	60
		Set value	70	

The 50c, 1 l and 2 l were reprinted in 1942 with labels similar to those of Nos. 427-438, but were not issued. Value, set of 3, $100.

Statue of Ferrucci — AP7

1930, July 10

C20	AP7	50c purple	50	*2.50*
C21	AP7	1 l org brn	50	*5.00*
C22	AP7	5 l + 2 l brn vio	1.65	*37.50*

400th anniv. of the death of Francesco Ferrucci, Tuscan warrior.

Jupiter Sending Forth his Eagle AP8

1930, Oct. 21 Photo. Wmk. 140

C23	AP8	50c lt brn	1.75	*3.00*
C24	AP8	1 l orange	2.25	*4.50*

Engr.
Unwmk.

C25	AP8	7.70 l + 1.30 l vio brn	10.00	*35.00*
C26	AP8	9 l + 2 l indigo	11.00	*35.00*

Bimillenary of the birth of Virgil.
The surtax on Nos. C25 and C26 was for the National Institute Figli del Littorio.

Trans-Atlantic Squadron — AP9

1930, Dec. 15 Photo. Wmk. 140

C27	AP9	7.70 l Prus bl & gray	105.00	*325.00*
a.		Seven stars instead of six	325.00	*2,000.*

Issued in connection with the flight by Italian aviators from Rome to Rio de Janeiro, Dec., 1930-Jan. 12, 1931.

Leonardo da Vinci's Flying Machine AP10

Leonardo da Vinci AP11

Leonardo da Vinci — AP12

1932

C28	AP10	50c olive brn	70	*1.50*
C29	AP11	1 l violet	70	*2.00*
C30	AP11	3 l brn red	1.65	*6.50*
C31	AP11	5 l dp grn	1.75	*8.00*
C32	AP10	7.70 l + 2 l dk bl	2.50	*27.50*
C33	AP11	10 l + 2.50 l blk brn	2.50	*30.00*
		Nos. C28-C33 (6)	9.80	*75.50*

Engr.
Unwmk.

C34	AP12	100 l brt bl & grnsh blk	20.00	*100.00*
a.		Thin paper	37.50	*150.00*

Dante Alighieri Soc. and especially Leonardo da Vinci, to whom the invention of a flying machine has been attributed. Surtax was for the benefit of the Society.

Inscription on No. C34: "Man with his large wings by beating against the air will be able to dominate it and lift himself above it".

Issue dates: Nos. C28-C33, Mar. 14; No. C34, Aug. 6.

Garibaldi's Home at Caprera — AP13

Farmhouse where Anita Garibaldi Died — AP14

Designs: 50c, 1 l+25c, Garibaldi's home, Caprera. 2 l+50c, Anita Garibaldi. 5 l+1 l, Giuseppe Garibaldi.

1932, Apr. 6 Photo. Wmk. 140

C35	AP13	50c copper red	55	*1.50*
C36	AP14	80c deep green	90	*2.25*
C37	AP13	1 l + 25c red brn	1.50	*7.50*
C38	AP13	2 l + 50c dp bl	2.50	*12.50*
C39	AP14	5 l + 1 l dp grn	2.75	*15.00*
		Nos. C35-C39 (5)	8.20	*38.75*

50th anniv. of the death of Giuseppe Garibaldi, patriot. The surtax was for the benefit of the Garibaldi Volunteers.

Eagle Sculpture and Airplane AP17

Design: 75c, Italian buildings from the air.

1932, Oct. 27 *Perf. 14*

C40	AP17	50c dk brn	7.00	*2.75*
C41	AP17	75c org brn	1.65	*6.50*

10th anniversary of the Fascist government and the March on Rome.

Graf Zeppelin Issue

Zeppelin over Pyramid of Caius Cestius AP19

Designs: 5 l, Tomb of Cecilia Metlella. 10 l, Stadium of Mussolini. 12 l, St. Angelo Castle and Bridge. 15 l, Roman Forum. 20 l, Imperial Avenue.

1933, Apr. 24

C42	AP19	3 l blk & grn	5.00	*7.50*
C43	AP19	5 l grn & brn	3.25	*7.50*
C44	AP19	10 l car & dl bl	3.25	*20.00*
C45	AP19	12 l dk bl & red org	3.25	*25.00*
C46	AP19	15 l dk brn & gray	3.25	*32.50*
C47	AP19	20 l org brn & bl	3.25	*37.50*
a.		Vertical pair, imperf. btwn.	1,850.	
		Nos. C42-C47 (6)	21.25	*130.00*

Balbo's Trans-Atlantic Flight Issue

Italian Flag

King Victor Emmanuel III

Allegory "Flight" — AP25

Design: No. C49, Colosseum at Rome, Chicago skyline. Nos. C48-C49 consist of three parts; Italian flag, Victor Emmanuel III, and scene arranged horizontally.

1933, May 20

C48	AP25	5.25 l + 19.75 l red, grn & ultra	42.50	*325.00*
a.		Left stamp without ovpt.	*950.00*	
C49	AP25	5.25 l + 44.75 l grn, red & ultra	42.50	*325.00*

Transatlantic Flight, Rome-Chicago, of 24-seaplane squadron led by Gen. Italo Balbo. Center and right sections paid postage. At left is registered air express label overprinted "APPARECCHIO" and abbreviated pilot's name. Twenty triptychs of each value differ in name overprint.

No. C49 overprinted "VOLO DI RITORNO/ NEW YORK-ROMA" was not issued; flight canceled.

Type of Air Post Stamp of 1930 Surcharged in Black

1934, Jan. 18

C52	AP6	2 l on 2 l yel	1.25	*19.00*
C53	AP6	3 l on 2 l yel grn	1.25	*22.50*
C54	AP6	5 l on 2 l rose	1.25	*27.50*
C55	AP6	10 l on 2 l vio	1.25	*37.50*

For use on mail carried on a special flight from Rome to Buenos Aires.

View of Fiume Harbor — AP28

Designs: 50c, 1 l+50c, Monument to the Dead. 2 l+1.50 l, Venetian Lions. 3 l+2 l, Julian wall.

1934, Mar. 12

C56	AP28	25c green	18	*55*
C57	AP28	50c brown	18	*38*
C58	AP28	75c org brn	18	*95*
C59	AP28	1 l + 50c dl vio	18	*5.50*
C60	AP28	2 l + 1.50 l dl bl	18	*6.50*
C61	AP28	3 l + 2 l blk brn	18	*7.50*
		Nos. C56-C61 (6)	1.08	*21.38*

Annexation of Fiume, 10th anniversary.

Airplane and View of Stadium AP32

For unused stamps, more recent issues are valued as never hinged, with the beginning point determined on a country-by-country basis. Notes to show the beginning points are prominently placed in the text.

Soccer Player and Plane — AP33

Airplane and Stadium Entrance — AP35

Airplane over Stadium AP34

1934, May 24

C62	AP32	50c car rose	2.00	*3.00*
C63	AP33	75c gray blue	3.25	*4.50*
C64	AP34	5 l + 2.50 l ol grn	9.25	*40.00*
C65	AP35	10 l + 5 l brn blk	12.00	*45.00*

2nd World Soccer Championships.

Zeppelin under Fire — AP36

Air Force Memorial — AP40

Designs: 25c, 80c, Zeppelin under fire. 50c, 75c, Motorboat patrol. 1 l+50c, Desert infantry. 2 l+1 l, Plane attacking troops.

1934, Apr. 24

C66	AP36	25c dk grn	38	*95*
C67	AP36	50c gray	38	*1.25*
C68	AP36	75c dk brn	50	*1.50*
C69	AP36	80c slate blue	75	*2.00*
C70	AP36	1 l + 50c red brn	2.00	*8.00*
C71	AP36	2 l + 1 l brt bl	2.50	*9.00*
C72	AP40	3 l + 2 l brn blk	3.00	*10.50*
		Nos. C66-C72 (7)	9.51	*33.20*

Cent. of the institution of the Military Medal of Valor.

King Victor Emmanuel III — AP41

1934, Nov. 5

C73	AP41	1 l purple	50	*5.50*
C74	AP41	2 l brt bl	50	*6.50*
C75	AP41	4 l red brn	80	*27.50*
C76	AP41	5 l dl grn	80	*37.50*
C77	AP41	8 l rose red	4.50	*50.00*
C78	AP41	10 l brown	5.00	*60.00*
		Nos. C73-C78 (6)	12.10	*187.00*

65th birthday of King Victor Emmanuel III and the nonstop flight from Rome to Mogadiscio.

Muse Playing Harp AP42

Angelic Dirge for Bellini AP43

Scene from Bellini Opera, La Sonnambula — AP44

1935, Sept. 24

C79	AP42	25c dl yel	45	*1.00*
C80	AP42	50c brown	45	*95*
C81	AP42	60c rose car	70	*1.75*
C82	AP43	1 l + 1 l pur	3.25	*30.00*
C83	AP44	5 l + 2 l grn	5.00	*37.50*
		Nos. C79-C83 (5)	9.85	*71.20*

Vincenzo Bellini, (1801-35), operatic composer.

Seaplane in Flight AP45

Designs: 50c, 1 l+1 l, Monoplane over valley. 60c, Oak and eagle. 5 l+2 l, Ruins of ancient Rome.

1936, July 1

C84	AP45	25c dp grn	50	*1.10*
C85	AP45	50c dk brn	60	*1.10*
C86	AP45	60c scarlet	75	*2.00*
C87	AP45	1 l + 1 l vio	3.50	*30.00*
C88	AP45	5 l + 2 l sl bl	5.50	*45.00*
		Nos. C84-C88 (5)	10.85	*79.20*

Issued to commemorate the 2000th anniversary of the birth of Quintus Horatius Flaccus (Horace).

Child of the Balilla AP49

Heads of Children AP50

1937, June 28

C89	AP49	25c dk bl grn	1.10	*2.00*
C90	AP50	50c brown	1.50	*2.00*
C91	AP49	1 l purple	1.10	*3.00*
C92	AP50	2 l + 1 l dk bl	4.00	*27.50*
C93	AP49	3 l + 2 l org	5.50	*32.50*
C94	AP50	5 l + 3 l rose lake	7.00	*37.50*
		Nos. C89-C94 (6)	20.20	*104.50*

Issued to commemorate the Summer Exhibition for Child Welfare. The surtax on Nos. C92-C94 was used to support summer camps for poor children.

Prosperous Italy AP51

Designs: 50c, Prolific Italy. 80c, Apollo's steeds. 1 l+1 l, Map and Roman Standard. 5 l+1 l, Augustus Caesar.

1937, Sept. 23

C95	AP51	25c red vio	1.25	*2.00*
C96	AP51	50c olive brn	1.25	*1.50*
C97	AP51	80c org brn	2.50	*3.50*
C98	AP51	1 l + 1 l dk bl	6.00	*19.00*
C99	AP51	5 l + 1 l dl vio	9.25	*30.00*
		Nos. C95-C99 (5)	20.25	*56.00*

Bimillenary of the birth of Augustus Caesar (Octavianus) on the occasion of the exhibition opened in Rome by Mussolini on Sept. 22nd, 1937.

King Victor Emmanuel III — AP56

Designs: 25c, 3 l, King Victor Emmanuel III. 50c, 1 l, Dante Alighieri. 2 l, 5 l, Leonardo da Vinci.

1938, Oct. 28

C100	AP56	25c dl grn	48	*70*
C101	AP56	50c dk yel brn	48	*70*
C102	AP56	1 l violet	52	*95*
C103	AP56	2 l ryl bl	90	*3.75*
C104	AP56	3 l brn car	1.25	*7.50*
C105	AP56	5 l dp grn	1.75	*9.00*
		Nos. C100-C105 (6)	5.38	*22.60*

Proclamation of the Empire.

Plane and Clasped Hands AP59

Swallows in Flight AP60

1945-46 Wmk. 277 Photo. *Perf. 14*

C106	AP59	1 l slate bl	15	15
C107	AP60	2 l dk bl	15	15
C108	AP59	3.20 l red org	15	15
C109	AP60	5 l dk grn	15	15
C110	AP59	10 l car rose	15	15
C111	AP60	25 l dk bl ('46)	3.50	2.75
C112	AP59	50 l dk grn ('46)	5.25	6.00
		Nos. C106-C112 (7)	9.50	9.50

1947, Apr. 21

C113	AP60	25 l brown	15	15
C114	AP59	50 l violet	15	15

See No. C130-C131.

No. C108 Surcharged in Black

LIRE 6–

1947, July 1

C115	AP59	6 l on 3.20 l	15	15
a.		Pair, one without surch.	*975.00*	
b.		Inverted surcharge		*5,500.*

Radio on Land AP61

Plane over Capitol Bell Tower AP65

Designs: 6 l, 25 l, Radio on land. 10 l, 35 l, Radio at sea. 20 l, 50 l, Radio in the skies.

1947, Sept. 1 Photo. *Perf. 14*

C116	AP61	6 l dp vio	15	15
C117	AP61	10 l dk car rose	15	20
C118	AP61	20 l dp org	75	20
C119	AP61	25 l aqua	45	20

C120 AP61 35 l brt bl 45 40
C121 AP61 50 l lil rose 95 1.00
Nos. C116-C121 (6) 2.90 2.15

50th anniv. of radio.

1948

C123 AP65 100 l green 3.00 15
C124 AP65 300 l lil rose 30 20
C125 AP65 500 l ultra 38 30

Engr.

C126 AP65 1000 l dk brn 1.40 85
a. Vert. pair, imperf. btwn. *250.00 250.00*
b. Perf. 14x13 1.90 1.40

See No. C132-C135.

St. Catherine Carrying Cross AP66

Design: 200 l, St. Catherine with outstretched arms.

1948, Mar. 1 **Photo.**

C127 AP66 100 l bl vio & brn org 20.00 21.00
C128 AP66 200 l dp bl & bis 7.25 7.75

600th anniversary of the birth of St. Catherine of Siena, patroness of Italy.

Catalogue values for unused stamps in this section, from this point to the end of the section, are for Never Hinged items.

Giuseppe Mazzini (1805-1872), Patriot — AP67

1955, Dec. 31 **Wmk. 303** ***Perf. 14***

C129 AP67 100 l Prus grn 1.50 75

Types of 1945-46, 1948

1955-62 **Wmk. 303** ***Perf. 14***

C130 AP60 5 l grn ('62) 15 15
C131 AP59 50 l vio ('57) 15 15
C132 AP65 100 l green 75 15
C133 AP65 300 l lil rose 85 55
C134 AP65 500 l ultra ('56) 1.00 90

Engr.

Perf. 13½

C135 AP65 1000 l mar ('59) 1.50 1.40
Nos. C130-C135 (6) 4.40 3.30

Fluorescent Paper

See note below No. 998.

No. C132 was issued on both ordinary and fluorescent paper.

Airmail stamps issued only on fluorescent paper are Nos. C139-C140.

Type of 1945-46 Surcharged in Ultramarine

1956

L 120

Visita
del Presidente
della Repubblica
negli U.S.A.
e nel Canada

1956, Feb. 24

C136 AP59 120 l on 50 l mag 1.50 1.25

Visit of Pres. Giovanni Gronchi to the US and Canada.

Madonna of Bruges, by Michelangelo — AP68

Wmk. 303

1964, Feb. 18 **Photo.** ***Perf. 14***

C137 AP68 185 l black 28 30

400th anniversary of the death of Michelangelo Buonarroti (1475-1564), artist.

Verrazano Type of Regular Issue

1964, Nov. 21 **Wmk. 303** ***Perf. 14***

C138 A481 130 l blk & dl grn 18 15

See note after No. 901.

Adoration of the Kings, by Gentile da Fabriano — AP69

1970, Dec. 12 **Photo.** **Unwmk.**

C139 AP69 150 l multi 30 18

Christmas 1970.

Aviation Type of Regular Issue

Design: F-140S Starfighter over Aeronautical Academy, Pozzuoli.

1973, Mar. 28 **Photo.** ***Perf. 14x13½***

C140 A590 150 l multi 28 18

AIR POST SEMI-POSTAL STAMPS

Holy Year Issue

Dome of St. Peter's, Dove with Olive Branch, Church of the Holy Sepulcher SPAP1

Wmk. 140

1933, Oct. 23 **Photo.** ***Perf. 14***

CB1 SPAP1 50c + 25c org brn 70 *3.00*
CB2 SPAP1 75c + 50c brn vio 85 *4.50*

Symbolical of Military Air Force — SPAP2

1935, July 1

CB3 SPAP2 50c + 50c brown 2.00 *5.75*

The surtax was for the Militia.

AIR POST SPECIAL DELIVERY STAMPS

Garibaldi, Anita Garibaldi, Plane APSD1

Wmk. 140

1932, June 2 **Photo.** ***Perf. 14***

CE1 APSD1 2.25 l + 1 l dp red & gray vio 3.00 *11.50*
CE2 APSD1 4.50 l + 1.50 l dp grn & ol brn 3.25 *12.50*

50th anniversary of the death of Giuseppe Garibaldi.

Airplane and Sunburst APSD2

1933-34

CE3 APSD2 2 l gray blk ('34) 15 *45*
CE4 APSD2 2.25 l gray blk 1.50 *45.00*

Flag Raising before Fascist Headquarters APSD3

1934, Mar. 12

CE5 APSD3 2 l + 1.25 l dp bl 1.10 *11.50*
CE6 APSD3 2.25 l + 1.25 l ol grn 18 *6.50*
CE7 APSD3 4.50 l + 2 l car rose 18 *7.50*

10th anniv. of the annexation of Fiume.

Triumphal Arch in Rome APSD4

1934, Aug. 31

CE8 APSD4 2 l + 1.25 l brn 2.00 *8.75*
CE9 APSD4 4.50 l + 2 l cop red 2.25 *11.00*

Centenary of the institution of the Military Medal of Valor.

AIR POST OFFICIAL STAMPS

Balbo Flight Type of Air Post Stamp of 1933 Overprinted

SERVIZIO DI STATO

1933 **Wmk. 140** ***Perf. 14***

CO1 AP25 5.25 l + 44.75 l red, grn & red vio 900.00 *6,750.*

Type of Air Post Stamp of 1934 Overprinted in Gold Crown and "SERVIZIO DI STATO"

1934

CO2 AP41 10 l bl blk 250.00 *5,250.*

65th birthday of King Victor Emmanuel III and the non-stop flight from Rome to Mogadiscio.

PNEUMATIC POST STAMPS

PN1

1913-28 **Wmk. 140** **Typo.** ***Perf. 14***

D1 PN1 10c brown 1.00 *5.25*
D2 PN1 15c brn vio ('28) 80 *3.25*
a. 15c dl vio ('21) 2.00 *8.00*
D3 PN1 15c rose red ('28) 2.25 *5.25*
D4 PN1 15c claret ('28) 80 *3.25*
D5 PN1 20c brn vio ('25) 2.75 *10.50*
D6 PN1 30c blue ('23) 2.00 *17.50*
D7 PN1 35c rose red ('27) 4.75 *40.00*
D8 PN1 40c dp red ('26) 5.75 *47.50*
Nos. D1-D8 (8) 20.10 *132.50*

Stamps of 1913-26 Surcharged Like Nos. C10-C11

1924-27

D9 PN1 15c on 10c brn 1.25 *7.00*
D10 PN1 15c on 20c brn vio ('27) 2.25 *7.75*
D11 PN1 20c on 10c brn ('25) 2.00 *11.00*
D12 PN1 20c on 15c dl vio ('25) 1.25 *5.50*
D13 PN1 35c on 40c dp red ('27) 4.00 *37.50*
D14 PN1 40c on 30c bl ('25) 2.00 *27.50*
Nos. D9-D14 (6) 12.75 *96.25*

Dante Alighieri PN2

Galileo Galilei PN3

1933, Mar. 29 **Photo.**

D15 PN2 15c dk vio 15 *50*
D16 PN3 35c rose red 15 *50*
Set value 16

Dante Alighieri PN4

Galileo Galilei PN5

1945, Oct. 22 **Wmk. 277**

D17 PN4 60c dl brn 15 15
D18 PN5 1.40 l dull blue 15 15
Set value 15 16

Minerva — PN6

1947, Nov. 15

D19 PN6 3 l rose lilac 5.00 9.00
D20 PN6 5 l aqua 15 15

Catalogue values for unused stamps in this section, from this point to the end of the section, are for Never Hinged items.

1958-66 **Wmk. 303**

D21 PN6 10 l rose red 15 15
D22 PN6 20 l saph ('66) 20 15
Set value 18

SPECIAL DELIVERY STAMPS

Victor Emmanuel III — SD1

1903-26 **Typo.** **Wmk. 140** ***Perf. 14***

E1 SD1 25c rose red 4.50 20
a. Imperf., pair 75.00 150.00
E2 SD1 50c dl red ('20) 75 30
E3 SD1 60c dl red ('22) 75 28
E4 SD1 70c dl red ('25) 15 18
E5 SD1 1.25 l dp bl ('26) 15 15
Nos. E1-E5 (5) 6.30 1.11

Victor Emmanuel III — SD2

1908-26

E6 SD2 30c bl & rose 28 80
E7 SD2 2 l bl & red ('25) 38 *14.00*
E8 SD2 2.50 l bl & red ('26) 75 *1.25*

The 1.20 lire blue and red (see No. E12) was prepared in 1922, but not issued. Value $60.

SD3

1917, Nov.

E9 SD3 25c on 40c violet 5.50 *18.00*

Type SD3 not issued without surcharge.

No. E6 Surcharged

1921, Oct.

E10 SD2 1.20 l on 30c 38 *4.25*
a. Comma in value omitted 1.65 *18.00*
b. Double surcharge 32.50

No. E2 Surcharged **Cent. 60**

1922, Jan. 9

E11 SD1 60c on 50c dl red 4.50 40
a. Inverted surcharge 27.50 55.00
b. Double surcharge 350.00
c. Imperf., pair 110.00 250.00

Type of 1908 Surcharged

Lire 1,60

1924, May

E12 SD2 1.60 l on 1.20 l bl & red 38 *15.00*
a. Double surch., one inverted 27.50 *60.00*

No. E3 Surcharged like No. E11

1925, Apr. 11

E13 SD1 70c on 60c dl red 15 40
a. Inverted surcharge 32.50 65.00

Victor Emmanuel III — SD4

1932-33 **Photo.**

E14 SD4 1.25 l green 15 15
E15 SD4 2.50 l dp org ('33) 15 *1.00*
Set value 22

Ancient Pillars and Entrenchments — SD5

Design: 2.50 l, Head of Mussolini, trophies of flags, etc.

1932, Oct. 27

E16 SD5 1.25 l dp grn 15 *90*
E17 SD5 2.50 l dp org 1.65 *60.00*

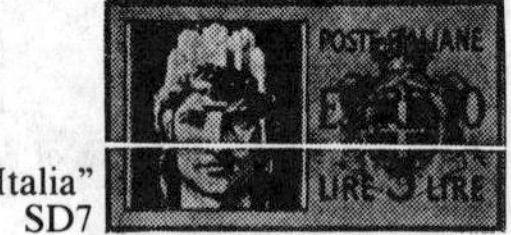

"Italia" SD7

1945, Aug. **Wmk. 277** ***Perf. 14***

E18 SD7 5 l rose carmine 15 15

Winged Foot — SD8

Rearing Horse and Torch-Bearer SD9

1945-51

E19 SD8 5 l henna brn 15 15
E20 SD9 10 l deep blue 15 15
E21 SD9 15 l dk car rose ('47) 1.25 20
E22 SD8 25 l brt red org ('47) 5.75 20
E23 SD8 30 l dp vio ('46) 1.40 20
E24 SD8 50 l lil rose ('51) 7.00 15
E25 SD9 60 l car rose ('48) 4.50 20
Nos. E19-E25 (7) 20.20 1.25

See No. E32.

Type of Regular Issue of 1948
Inscribed: "Espresso"

1948, Sept. 18 **Photo.** ***Perf. 14***

E26 A272 35 l vio *(Naples)* 6.75 6.25

Catalogue values for unused stamps in this section, from this point to the end of the section, are for Never Hinged items.

Type of 1945-51

1955, July 7 **Wmk. 303** ***Perf. 14***

E32 SD8 50 l lilac rose 4.00 15

Etruscan Winged Horses SD10

1958-76 **Photo.**

Size: 36½x20¼mm

E33 SD10 75 l magenta 20 15

Size: 36x20mm

E34 SD10 150 l dl bl grn ('68) 25 15
a. Size: 36½x20¼mm ('66) 1.25 15
E35 SD10 250 l blue ('74) 50 15
E36 SD10 300 l brown ('76) 50 15
Set value 22

Nos. E34-E36 are fluorescent.

AUTHORIZED DELIVERY STAMPS

For the payment of a special tax for the authorized delivery of correspondence privately instead of through the post office.

AD1

Coat of Arms — AD2

1928 **Wmk. 140** **Typo.** ***Perf. 14***

EY1 AD1 10c dull blue 38 15
a. Perf. 11 1.75 60

1930 **Photo.** ***Perf. 14***

EY2 AD2 10c dark brown 15 15

No. EY2 Surcharged in Black

1945

EY3 AD2 40c on 10c dark brown 15 15

Coat of Arms — AD3

"Italia" — AD4

1945-46 **Photo.** **Wmk. 277**

EY4 AD3 40c dark brown 15 25
EY5 AD3 1 l dk brn ('46) 40 40

1947-52

Size: 27½x22½mm

EY6 AD4 1 l brt grnsh bl 15 15
EY7 AD4 8 l brt red ('48) 5.25 15

Size: 20½x16½mm

EY8 AD4 15 l violet ('49) 15.00 20
EY9 AD4 20 l rose vio ('52) 1.25 20

Catalogue values for unused stamps in this section, from this point to the end of the section, are for Never Hinged items.

Italia Type of 1947

1955-90 **Wmk. 303** **Photo.** ***Perf. 14***

Size: 20½x16½mm

EY11 AD4 20 l rose vio 20 20
EY12 AD4 30 l Prus grn ('65) 20 20
EY13 AD4 35 l ocher ('74) 20 20
EY14 AD4 110 l lt ultra ('77) 20 20
EY15 AD4 270 l brt pink ('84) 50 20

Size: 19½x16½mm

EY16 AD4 300 l rose & green ('87) 60 20
EY17 AD4 370 l tan & brn vio 78 40
Nos. EY11-EY17 (7) 2.68 1.60

Issue date: 370 l, Sept. 24, 1990.

POSTAGE DUE STAMPS

Unused values for Postage Due stamps are for examples with full original gum. Stamps without gum, with part gum or privately gummed sell for much less.

D1

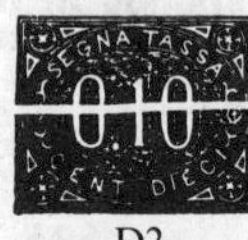

D2

1863 **Unwmk.** **Litho.** ***Imperf.***

J1 D1 10c yellow 450.00 50.00
a. 10c yellow orange 500.00 50.00
Without gum 30.00

1869 **Wmk. 140** **Typo.** ***Perf. 14***

J2 D2 10c buff 750.00 10.00

D3

D4

1870-1925

J3 D3 1c buff & mag 90 1.00
J4 D3 2c buff & mag 5.50 6.00
J5 D3 5c buff & mag 30 15
J6 D3 10c buff & mag ('71) 30 15
b. Imperf., pair *1,100.*
J7 D3 20c buff & mag ('94) 40 15
a. Imperf., pair 37.50 45.00
J8 D3 30c buff & mag 75 22
b. Imperf., pair *3,750.*
J9 D3 40c buff & mag 90 24
J10 D3 50c buff & mag 75 15
b. Imperf., pair *750.00*
J11 D3 60c buff & mag 37.50 45
J12 D3 60c buff & brn ('25) 7.50 1.75
J13 D3 1 l lt bl & brn 1,000. 3.00
J14 D3 1 l bl & mag ('94) 28 18
a. Imperf., pair 37.50 37.50
J15 D3 2 l lt bl & brn 900.00 4.00
J16 D3 2 l bl & mag ('03) 9.00 45
J17 D3 5 l bl & brn ('74) 90.00 3.00
J18 D3 5 l bl & mag ('03) 30.00 1.00
J19 D3 10 l bl & brn ('74) *1,800.* 6.00
J20 D3 10 l bl & mag ('94) 45.00 38

Early printings of 5c, 10c, 30c, 40c, 50c and 60c were in buff and magenta, later ones (1890-94) in stronger shades. The earlier, paler shades and their inverted-numeral varieties sell for considerably more than those of the later shades. Values are for the later shades.

Numeral Inverted

J3a	D3	1c	1,300.	600.00
J4a	D3	2c	*3,500.*	750.00
J5a	D3	5c	85	85
J6a	D3	10c	1.50	1.50
J7b	D3	20c	7.50	9.00
J8a	D3	30c	2.00	2.75
J9a	D3	40c	125.00	125.00
J10a	D3	50c	9.00	9.00
J11a	D3	60c	67.50	90.00
J13a	D3	1 l		*7,500.*
J14b	D3	1 l	900.00	450.00
J15a	D3	2 l		*550.00*
J16a	D3	2 l	*750.00*	*900.00*
J17a	D3	5 l		250.00
J19a	D3	10 l		140.00

1884-1903

J21	D4	50 l green	11.00	5.50
J22	D4	50 l yellow ('03)	19.00	6.00
J23	D4	100 l claret	12.00	4.25
J24	D4	100 l blue ('03)	12.50	3.00

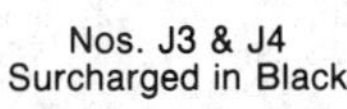

Nos. J3 & J4 Surcharged in Black

1890-91

J25	D3	10c on 2c	20.00	6.00
J26	D3	20c on 1c	85.00	4.50
a.		Inverted surcharge		*1,500.*
J27	D3	30c on 2c	275.00	2.50
a.		Inverted surcharge		*575.00*

Coat of Arms
D6 D7

1934 **Photo.**

J28	D6	5c brown	15	15
J29	D6	10c blue	15	15
J30	D6	20c rose red	15	15
J31	D6	25c green	15	15
J32	D6	30c red org	15	15
J33	D6	40c blk brn	15	*24*
J34	D6	50c violet	15	15
J35	D6	60c slate blk	22	*50*
J36	D7	1 l red org	15	15
J37	D7	2 l green	15	15
J38	D7	5 l violet	35	15
J39	D7	10 l blue	75	22
J40	D7	20 l car rose	85	50
		Set value	2.60	2.10

D8

D9

1945-46 **Unwmk.** ***Perf. 14***

J41	D8	5c brn ('46)	15	18
J42	D8	10c blue	15	15
J43	D8	20c rose red ('46)	15	15
J44	D8	25c dk grn	15	15
J45	D8	30c red org	15	15
J46	D8	40c blk brn	15	18
J47	D8	50c violet	15	15
J48	D8	60c black	15	15
J49	D9	1 l red org	28	15
J50	D9	2 l green	15	15
J51	D9	5 l violet	15	15
J52	D9	10 l blue	15	15
J53	D9	20 l car rose	18	15
		Set value	1.20	1.68

Nos. J41 and J43 are printed on grayish paper and have yellow gum.

Wmk. 277

J54	D8	10c dark blue	15	15
J55	D8	25c dk grn	35	45
J56	D8	30c red org	35	60
J57	D8	40c blk brn	15	15
J58	D8	50c vio ('46)	1.50	45
J59	D8	60c bl blk ('46)	1.75	1.25
J60	D9	1 l red org	15	15
J61	D9	2 l dk grn	15	15
J62	D9	5 l violet	4.00	28
J63	D9	10 l dark blue	5.75	4.00
J64	D9	20 l car rose	8.25	75
		Nos. J54-J64 (11)	22.55	8.38

D10

1947-54 **Photo.** ***Perf. 14***

J65	D10	1 l red org	15	15
J66	D10	2 l dk grn	15	15
J67	D10	3 l carmine	15	45
J68	D10	4 l brown	22	24
J69	D10	5 l violet	35	15
J70	D10	6 l vio bl	75	24
J71	D10	8 l rose vio	1.65	60
J72	D10	10 l deep blue	55	15
J73	D10	12 l golden brn	1.00	60
J74	D10	20 l lil rose	17.00	15
J75	D10	25 l dk red ('54)	22.50	45
J76	D10	50 l aqua	13.50	15
J77	D10	100 l org yel ('52)	1.40	15

Engr.
Perf. 13½x14

J78	D10	500 l dp bl & dk car ('52)	2.50	18
a.		Perf. 11x13	4.50	24
b.		Perf. 13	4.50	18
		Nos. J65-J78 (14)	61.87	
		Set value		3.00

1955-91 **Wmk. 303** **Photo.** ***Perf. 14***

J83	D10	5 l violet	15	15
J85	D10	8 l rose vio	140.00	140.00
J86	D10	10 l deep blue	15	15
J87	D10	20 l lil rose	15	15
J88	D10	25 l dk red	15	15
J89	D10	30 l gray brn ('61)	15	15
J90	D10	40 l dl brn ('66)	15	15
J91	D10	50 l aqua	15	15
J92	D10	100 l org yel ('58)	18	15

Engr.

J93	D10	500 l dp bl & dk car ('61)	90	18
J94	D10	900 l dp car & gray grn ('84)	80	22
J95	D10	1500 l brown & orange ('91)	3.00	1.60
		Set value, #J83, J86-J95	5.45	2.35

Issue date: 1500 l, Feb. 20.

MILITARY STAMPS

Regular Stamps, 1929-42, Overprinted

P.M.

1943 **Wmk. 140** ***Perf. 14***

M1	A90	5c ol brn	15	24
M2	A92	10c dk brn	15	24
M3	A93	15c slate grn	15	24
M4	A91	20c rose red	15	24
M5	A94	25c dp grn	15	24
M6	A95	30c ol brn	15	24
M7	A95	50c purple	15	15
M8	A91	1 l dk pur	15	*3.00*
M9	A94	1.25 l deep blue	15	*35*
M10	A92	1.75 l red org	15	24
M11	A93	2 l car lake	18	35
M12	A95a	5 l rose red	24	*45*
M13	A93	10 l purple	28	*70*
		Set value	1.75	

Due to a shortage of regular postage stamps during 1944-45, this issue was used for ordinary mail. "P. M." stands for "Posta Militare."

MILITARY AIR POST STAMPS

Air Post Stamps, 1930 Overprinted Like Nos. M1-M13 in Black

1943 **Wmk. 140** ***Perf. 14***

MC1	AP3	50c ol brn	15	24
MC2	AP5	1 l purple	15	*45*
MC3	AP6	2 l dp bl	15	*1.25*
MC4	AP3	5 l dk grn	18	*3.00*
MC5	AP3	10 l dp car	24	*5.50*
		Set value	70	

MILITARY AIR POST SPECIAL DELIVERY STAMP

No. CE3 Overprinted Like Nos. M1-M13 in Black

1943 **Wmk. 140** ***Perf. 14***

MCE1	APSD2	2 l gray black	18	*5.50*

MILITARY SPECIAL DELIVERY STAMP

No. E14 Overprinted Like Nos. M1-M13 in Black

1943 **Wmk. 140** ***Perf. 14***

ME1	SD4	1.25 l green	15	*70*

OFFICIAL STAMPS

O1

1875 **Wmk. 140** **Typo.** ***Perf. 14***

O1	O1	2c lake	70	70
O2	O1	5c lake	70	70
O3	O1	20c lake	18	18
O4	O1	30c lake	18	24
O5	O1	1 l lake	1.50	2.75
O6	O1	2 l lake	10.50	9.00
O7	O1	5 l lake	47.50	42.50
O8	O1	10 l lake	85.00	22.50
		Nos. O1-O8 (8)	146.26	78.57

Nos. O1-O8 surcharged "2 C" are listed as Nos. 37-44.

Stamps inscribed "Servizio Commissioni" were used in connection with the postal service but not for the payment of postage.

NEWSPAPER STAMP

N1

Typographed, Numeral Embossed
1862 **Unwmk.** ***Imperf.***

P1	N1	2c buff	15.00	30.00
a.		Numeral double	85.00	*500.00*

Black 1c and 2c stamps of similar type are listed under Sardinia.

PARCEL POST STAMPS

King Humbert I — PP1

1884-86 **Wmk. 140** **Typo.** ***Perf. 14***
Various Frames

Q1	PP1	10c olive gray	32.50	8.00
Q2	PP1	20c blue	50.00	15.00
Q3	PP1	50c claret	3.00	1.75
Q4	PP1	75c blue grn	3.00	1.75
Q5	PP1	1.25 l orange	5.00	5.50
Q6	PP1	1.75 l brown	6.50	16.00

Nos. Q1-Q6 overprinted "Valevole per le stampe" and surcharged "Cmi. 2" are listed as Nos. 58-63.

Parcel Post stamps from No. Q7 onward were used by affixing them to the waybill so that one half remained on it following the parcel, the other half staying on the receipt given the sender. Most used halves are right halves. Complete stamps were and are obtainable canceled, probably to order.

Both unused and used values are for complete stamps.

PP2

1914-22 **Wmk. 140** ***Perf. 13***

Q7	PP2	5c brown	15	28
Q8	PP2	10c deep blue	15	28
Q9	PP2	20c black ('17)	15	28
Q10	PP2	25c red	15	28
Q11	PP2	50c orange	15	45
Q12	PP2	1 l violet	20	18
Q13	PP2	2 l green	45	22
Q14	PP2	3 l bister	65	45
Q15	PP2	4 l slate	75	45
Q16	PP2	10 l rose lil ('22)	8.75	1.25
Q17	PP2	12 l red brn ('22)	35.00	75.00
Q18	PP2	15 l ol grn ('22)	35.00	75.00
Q19	PP2	20 l brn vio ('22)	35.00	67.50
		Nos. Q7-Q19 (13)	116.55	221.62

Halves Used

Q7-Q15	15
Q16	18
Q17-Q19	75

Imperfs exist. Value per pair: 20c, 25c, 50c, 2 l, 4 l, 10 l, $50 each; 3 l, $60; 12 l, 15 l, 20 l, $200 each.

No. Q7 Surcharged

60 CENT. 60

Q20	PP2	30c on 5c brown	25	*2.75*
		Half stamp		15
Q21	PP2	60c on 5c brown	38	*2.75*
		Half stamp		15
Q22	PP2	1.50 l on 5c brown	1.00	*18.00*
		Half stamp		25
a.		Double surcharge	25.00	

No. Q16 Surcharged

LIRE 3 LIRE 3

Q23	PP2	3 l on 10 l rose lilac	1.00	*10.00*
		Half stamp		20

PP3

1927-39 **Wmk. 140**

Q24	PP3	5c brn ('38)	15	25
Q25	PP3	10c dp bl ('39)	15	25
Q26	PP3	25c red ('32)	15	25
Q27	PP3	30c ultra	15	45
Q28	PP3	50c org ('32)	15	25
Q29	PP3	60c red	15	45
Q30	PP3	1 l lilac ('31)	15	25
Q31	PP3	1 l brn vio ('36)	10.00	10.00
Q32	PP3	2 l grn ('32)	15	45
Q33	PP3	3 l bister	15	45
a.		Printed on both sides	15.00	
Q34	PP3	4 l gray	15	45
Q35	PP3	10 l rose lil ('34)	20	*1.40*
Q36	PP3	20 l lil brn ('33)	24	*2.75*
		Nos. Q24-Q36 (13)	11.94	17.65

Value of used halves, Nos. Q24-Q36, each 15 cents.

Nos. Q24-Q30, Q32-Q36 Overprinted Between Halves in Black

1945 **Wmk. 140** ***Perf. 13***

Q37	PP3	5c brown	15	45
Q38	PP3	10c dp bl	15	45
Q39	PP3	25c red	15	45
Q40	PP3	30c ultra	1.40	1.90
Q41	PP3	50c orange	15	18
Q42	PP3	60c red	15	18
Q43	PP3	1 l lilac	15	18
Q44	PP3	2 l green	15	18
Q45	PP3	3 l bister	15	28
Q46	PP3	4 l gray	15	22
Q47	PP3	10 l rose lil	70	*3.75*
Q48	PP3	20 l lil brn	1.90	*8.00*
		Nos. Q37-Q48 (12)	5.35	*16.22*

Halves Used

Q37-Q39, Q41-Q47	15
Q40	18
Q48	15

Type of 1927
With Fasces Removed

1946 **Typo.**

Q55 PP3	1 l lilac	45	15
Q56 PP3	2 l green	35	15
Q57 PP3	3 l yel org	60	28
Q58 PP3	4 l gray	90	18
Q59 PP3	10 l rose lil	17.00	3.00
Q60 PP3	20 l lil brn	22.50	9.75
	Nos. Q55-Q60 (6)	41.80	13.51

Halves Used

Q55-Q58	15
Q59	25
Q60	30

PP4

PP5

Perf. 13, 13x14, 12½x13

1946-54 **Photo.** **Wmk. 277**

Q61 PP4	25c dl vio bl ('48)	15	15
Q62 PP4	50c brn ('47)	15	15
Q63 PP4	1 l golden brn ('47)	15	15
Q64 PP4	2 l lt bl grn ('47)	18	18
Q65 PP4	3 l red org ('47)	15	15
Q66 PP4	4 l gray blk ('47)	90	1.40
Q67 PP4	5 l lil rose ('47)	15	15
a.	Perf. 13	15	15
Q68 PP4	10 l violet	1.25	15
a.	Perf. 13	1.65	90
Q69 PP4	20 l lil brn	70	24
a.	Perf. 13	4.50	45
Q70 PP4	30 l plum ('52)	1.10	1.25
a.	Perf. 13	70	90
Q71 PP4	50 l rose red	3.50	55
a.	Perf. 13	3.50	70
Q72 PP4	100 l sapphire	11.50	7.00
a.	Perf. 13	70.00	11.00
Q73 PP4	200 l grn ('48)	14.00	14.00
a.	Perf. 13	18.00	18.00
Q74 PP4	300 l brn car ('48)	200.00	180.00
a.	Perf. 13	200.00	180.00
Q75 PP4	500 l brn ('48)	40.00	35.00

Engr.

Perf. 13

Q76 PP5	1000 l ultra ('54)	900.00	975.00
	Nos. Q61-Q76 (16)	1,173.	1,215.

Halves Used

Q61-Q69, Q70, Q71, Q72	15
Q69a, Q70a, Q71a	15
Q72a	15
Q73,Q75	18
Q73a	25
Q74	30
Q74a	40
Q76	1.25

Catalogue values for unused stamps in this section, from this point to the end of the section, are for Never Hinged items.

Perf. 12½x13

1955-59 **Wmk. 303** **Photo.**

Without Imprint

Q77 PP4	25c vio bl	28	38
Q77A PP4	50c brn ('56)	8.00	11.50
Q78 PP4	5 l lil rose ('59)	15	15
Q79 PP4	10 l violet	15	15
Q80 PP4	20 l lil brn	15	15
Q81 PP4	30 l plum ('56)	15	15
Q82 PP4	40 l dl vio ('57)	15	15
Q83 PP4	50 l rose red	15	15
Q84 PP4	100 l sapphire	16	15
Q85 PP4	150 l org brn ('57)	22	22
Q86 PP4	200 l grn ('56)	28	22
Q87 PP4	300 l brn car ('58)	48	38
Q88 PP4	400 l gray blk ('57)	55	45
Q89 PP4	500 l brn ('57)	1.00	60

Engr.

Perf. 13

Q90 PP5	1000 l ultra ('57)	1.25	95
Q91 PP5	2000 l red brn & car ('57)	3.25	1.90
	Nos. Q77-Q91 (16)	16.37	17.65

Halves Used

Q77-Q89	15
Q90-Q91	40

1960-66 **Photo.** ***Perf. 12½x13***

Q92 PP4	60 l brt lil	15	15
Q93 PP4	140 l dl red	22	30
Q94 PP4	280 l yellow	60	45
Q95 PP4	600 l olive bister	70	75
Q96 PP4	700 l bl ('66)	1.10	75
Q97 PP4	800 l dp org ('66)	1.25	95
	Nos. Q92-Q97 (6)	4.02	3.35

Halves Used

Q92-Q93	15
Q94	18
Q95	40
Q96-Q97	25

Imprint: "I.P.S.-Off. Carte Valori-Roma"

1973, Mar. **Photo.** **Wmk. 303**

Q98 PP4	20 l lilac brown	20	15
Q99 PP4	30 l plum	20	15
	Set value		15

PARCEL POST AUTHORIZED DELIVERY STAMPS

For the payment of a special tax for the authorized delivery of parcels privately instead of through the post office.

PAD1

1953 **Wmk. 277** **Photo.** ***Perf. 13***

QY1 PAD1	40 l org red	1.50	2.25
QY2 PAD1	50 l ultra	52.50	72.50
QY3 PAD1	75 l brown	32.50	45.00
QY4 PAD1	110 l lil rose	32.50	50.00

Halves Used

QY1	30
QY2	60
QY3	1.50
QY4	1.90

Catalogue values for unused stamps in this section, from this point to the end of the section, are for Never Hinged items.

1956-58 **Wmk. 303** ***Perf. 12½x13***

QY5 PAD1	40 l org red	1.10	90
QY6 PAD1	50 l ultra	2.25	2.25
QY7 PAD1	60 l brt vio bl ('58)	6.00	5.25
QY8 PAD1	75 l brown	175.00	150.00
QY9 PAD1	90 l lil ('58)	22	18
QY10 PAD1	110 l lil rose	165.00	125.00
QY11 PAD1	120 l grnsh bl ('58)	22	18
	Nos. QY5-QY11 (7)	349.79	283.76

Halves Used

QY5-QY6	15
QY7	90
QY8,QY10	4.00
QY9	30
QY11	22

1960-79

QY12 PAD1	70 l grn ('66)	37.50	37.50
QY13 PAD1	80 l brown	28	35
QY14 PAD1	110 l org yel	28	35
QY15 PAD1	140 l black	30	50
QY16 PAD1	150 l car rose ('68)	30	50
QY17 PAD1	180 l red ('66)	38	60
QY18 PAD1	240 l dk bl ('66)	45	70

Perf. 13½

QY19 PAD1	500 l ocher ('76)	1.40	1.40
QY20 PAD1	600 l bl grn ('79)	1.40	1.40
QY21 PAD1	900 l ultra ('81)	1.10	1.40
	Nos. QY12-QY21 (10)	43.39	44.70

Halves Used

QY12	4.00
QY13-QY15, QY18, QY21	20
QY16, QY17, QY19	25
QY20	35

PAD2

Perf. 14x13½

1984 **Photo.** **Wmk. 303**

QY22 PAD2	3000 l multi	3.75	3.75

OCCUPATION STAMPS

Issued under Austrian Occupation

Emperor Karl of Austria
OS1 OS2

1918 **Unwmk.** ***Perf. 12½***

N1 OS1	2c on 1h grnsh bl	18	40
N2 OS1	3c on 2h red org	18	40
N3 OS1	4c on 3h ol gray	18	40
N4 OS1	6c on 5h ol grn	18	40
N5 OS1	7c on 6h vio	18	40
a.	Perf. 12½x11½	14.00	27.50
N6 OS1	11c on 10h org brn	18	40
N7 OS1	13c on 12h blue	18	40
N8 OS1	16c on 15h brt rose	18	40
N9 OS1	22c on 20h red brn	18	40
a.	Perf. 11½	6.75	14.00
N10 OS1	27c on 25h ultra	45	40
N11 OS1	32c on 30h slate	24	40
N12 OS1	43c on 40h ol bis	18	40
a.	Perf. 11½	6.75	14.00
N13 OS1	53c on 50h dp grn	18	40
N14 OS1	64c on 60h rose	18	40
N15 OS1	85c on 80h dl bl	18	40
N16 OS1	95c on 90h dk vio	18	40
N17 OS1	2 l 11c on 2k rose, *straw*	28	40
N18 OS1	3 l 16c on 3k grn, *bl*	1.00	2.00
N19 OS1	4 l 22c on 4k rose, *grn*	1.00	2.00
	Nos. N1-N19 (19)	5.49	10.80

Emperor Karl — OS3

1918

N20 OS3	2c on 1h grnsh bl	2.50
N21 OS3	3c on 2h orange	2.50
N22 OS3	4c on 3h ol gray	2.50
N23 OS3	6c on 5h yel grn	2.50
N24 OS3	11c on 10h dk brn	2.50
N25 OS3	22c on 20h red	2.50
N26 OS3	27c on 25h blue	2.50
N27 OS3	32c on 30h bister	2.50
N28 OS3	48c on 45h dk sl	2.50
N29 OS3	53c on 50h dp grn	2.50
N30 OS3	64c on 60h violet	2.50
N31 OS3	85c on 80h rose	2.50
N32 OS3	95c on 90h brn vio	2.50
N33 OS3	1 l 6c on 90h brn vio	2.50
	Nos. N20-N33 (14)	35.00

Nos. N20 to N33 inclusive were never placed in use in the occupied territory. They were, however, on sale at the Post Office in Vienna for a few days before the Armistice.

OCCUPATION SPECIAL DELIVERY STAMPS

Special Handling Stamps of Bosnia Surcharged **3 Centesimi**

1918 **Unwmk.** ***Perf. 12½***

NE1 SH1	3c on 2h ver	5.50	11.00
NE2 SH1	6c on 5h dp grn	5.50	11.00

Nos. NE1-NE2 are on yellowish paper. Reprints on white paper sell for about 70 cents a set.

OCCUPATION POSTAGE DUE STAMPS

Postage Due Stamps of Bosnia Surcharged Like Nos. NE1-NE2

1918 **Unwmk.** ***Perf. 12½***

NJ1 D2	6c on 5h red	1.90	3.75
a.	Perf. 11½	5.50	11.00
NJ2 D2	11c on 10h red	1.90	3.75
a.	Perf. 11½	5.50	11.00
NJ3 D2	16c on 15h red	90	1.90
NJ4 D2	27c on 25h red	90	1.90
NJ5 D2	32c on 30h red	90	1.90
NJ6 D2	43c on 40h red	90	1.90
NJ7 D2	53c on 50h red	90	1.90
	Nos. NJ1-NJ7 (7)	8.30	17.00

OCCUPATION NEWSPAPER STAMPS

Austrian Military Newspaper Stamps Surcharged **3 Centesimi**

1918 **Unwmk.** ***Perf. 12½***

NP1 MN1	3c on 2h blue	15	24
a.	Perf. 11½	2.75	5.50
NP2 MN1	7c on 6h org	45	90
NP3 MN1	11c on 10h car	45	90
NP4 MN1	22c on 20h brn	35	70
a.	Perf. 11½	15.00	30.00

A.M.G.

Issued jointly by the Allied Military Government of the United States and Great Britain, for civilian use in areas under Allied occupation.

Catalogue values for unused stamps in this section are for Never Hinged items.

OS4

Offset Printing
"Italy Centesimi" (or "Lira") in Black

1943 **Unwmk.** ***Perf. 11***

1N1 OS4	15c pale org	65	60
1N2 OS4	25c pale citron	65	60
1N3 OS4	30c lt gray	65	60
1N4 OS4	50c lt vio	65	60
1N5 OS4	60c org yel	65	90
1N6 OS4	1 l lt yel grn	65	60
1N7 OS4	2 l dp rose	65	90
1N8 OS4	5 l lt blue	65	*1.75*
1N9 OS4	10 l buff	85	*3.50*
	Nos. 1N1-1N9 (9)	6.05	*10.05*

Italy Nos. 217, 220 and 221 Overprinted in Blue, Vermilion, Carmine or Orange **GOVERNO MILITARE ALLEATO**

1943, Dec. 10 **Wmk. 140** ***Perf. 14***

1N10 A91	20c rose red (Bl)	1.25	2.25
1N11 A93	35c deep bl (C)	8.50	*15.00*
a.	35c deep blue (V)	24.00	*30.00*
1N13 A95	50c pur (C)	30	1.00
a.	50c purple (O)	65	1.25

Nos. 1N1-1N9 were for use in Sicily, Nos. 1N10-1N13 for use in Naples.

VENEZIA GIULIA

Catalogue values for unused stamps in this section are for Never Hinged items.

Stamps of Italy, 1929 to 1945 Overprinted in Black:

On Stamps of 1929

1945-47 **Wmk. 140** ***Perf. 14***

1LN1	A92 (a) 10c dk brn	28	28
1LN1A	A91 (a) 20c rose red ('47)	42	42

On Stamps of 1945

1945	Wmk. 277	Perf. 14	
1LN2	A249 (a) 20c rose red	30	30
1LN3	A248 (a) 60c sl grn	30	25
1LN4	A249 (a) 1 l dp vio	35	25
1LN5	A251 (a) 2 l dk red	40	25
1LN6	A252 (b) 5 l dk red	75	35
1LN7	A251 (a) 10 l purple	1.00	55
	Nos. 1LN2-1LN7 (6)	3.10	1.95

On Stamps of 1945

1945-46	Unwmk.		
1LN7A	A250(a) 10c dk brn ('46)	30	25
1LN7B	A249(a) 20c rose red ('46)	30	25
1LN8	A251(a) 60c red org	30	25

On Air Post Stamp of 1930

1945	Wmk. 140	Perf. 14	
1LN9	AP3 (a) 50c ol brn	30	35

On Stamp of 1929

1946			
1LN10	A91 (a) 20 l lt grn	2.00	2.50

On Stamps of 1945

Wmk. 277

1LN11	A260 (a) 25 l dk grn	3.25	4.00
1LN12	A260 (a) 50 l dk vio brn	4.25	5.25

Italy No. 477 Overprinted in Black

A.M.G.
V.G.

1LN13	A261 100 l car lake	16.00	17.00

Stamps of Italy, 1945-47 Overprinted Type "a" in Black

1947			
1LN14	A259 25c brt bl grn	30	25
1LN15	A258 2 l dk cl brn	60	65
1LN16	A259 3 l red	50	25
1LN17	A259 4 l red org	75	35
1LN18	A257 6 l dp vio	1.75	1.65
1LN19	A259 20 l dk red vio	16.00	1.00
	Nos. 1LN14-1LN19 (6)	19.90	4.15

Some denominations of the Venezia Giulia A.M.G. issues exist with inverted overprint; several values exist in horizontal and vertical pairs, one stamp without overprint.

OCCUPATION AIR POST STAMPS

Catalogue values for unused stamps in this section are for Never Hinged items.

Italy Nos. C106-C107 and C109-C113 Overprinted Like 1LN13 in Black

1946-47	Wmk. 277	Perf. 14	
1LNC1	AP59 1 l sl bl ('47)	28	35
1LNC2	AP60 2 l dk bl ('47)	28	35
1LNC3	AP60 5 l dk grn ('47)	1.75	*2.00*
1LNC4	AP59 10 l car rose ('47)	1.75	*2.00*
1LNC5	AP60 25 l dk bl	1.75	*2.00*
1LNC6	AP60 25 l brn ('47)	8.75	*15.00*
1LNC7	AP59 50 l dk grn	3.50	*4.25*
	Nos. 1LNC1-1LNC7 (7)	18.06	*25.95*

Nos. 1LNC5 and 1LNC7 exist with inverted overprint; No. 1LNC5 with double overprint, one inverted.

OCCUPATION SPECIAL DELIVERY STAMPS

Catalogue values for unused stamps in this section are for Never Hinged items.

Italy Nos. E20 and E23 Overprinted Like 1LN13 in Black

1946	Wmk. 277	Perf. 14	
1LNE1	SD9 10 l dp bl	1.40	1.75
1LNE2	SD8 30 l dp vio	5.75	7.50

ITALIAN SOCIAL REPUBLIC

On Sept. 15, 1943, Mussolini proclaimed the establishment of a Republican fascist party and a new fascist government. This government's authority covered only the Northern Italy area occupied by the Germans.

Catalogue values for unused stamps in this section are for Never Hinged items.

Italy Nos. 218, 219, 221 to 223 and 231 Overprinted in Black or Red:

1944	Wmk. 140	Perf. 14	
1	A94(a) 25c dp grn	22	15
2	A95(b) 30c ol brn (R)	22	15
3	A95(c) 50c pur (R)	22	15
4	A94(a) 75c rose red	22	15
5	A94(b) 1.25 l dp bl (R)	22	15
5A	A94(b) 50 l dp vio (R)	200.00	*675.00*

Nos. 1 to 5 exist with overprint inverted. No. 1 exists with overprint "b." Counterfeits of No. 5A exist.

Italy Nos. 427 to 438 Overprinted Same in Black or Red

6	A243(a) 25c dp grn	35	*55*
7	A244(a) 25c dp grn	35	*55*
8	A245(a) 25c dp grn	35	*55*
9	A246(a) 25c dp grn	35	*55*
10	A243(b) 30c ol brn (R)	42	*75*
11	A244(b) 30c ol brn (R)	42	*75*
12	A245(b) 30c ol brn (R)	42	*75*
13	A246(b) 30c ol brn (R)	42	*75*
14	A243(c) 50c pur (R)	35	*55*
15	A244(c) 50c pur (R)	35	*55*
16	A245(c) 50c pur (R)	35	*55*
17	A246(c) 50c pur (R)	35	*55*
	Nos. 6-17 (12)	4.48	*7.40*

Loggia dei Mercanti, Bologna — A1

Basilica of San Lorenzo, Rome — A2

Drummer Boy — A3

1944	Photo.	Perf. 14	
18	A1 20c crimson	15	15
19	A2 25c green	15	15
20	A3 30c brown	15	15
21	A3 75c dk red	15	15
	Set value	48	20

Church of St. Ciriaco, Ancona — A4

Monte Cassino Abbey — A5

Loggia dei Mercanti, Bologna — A6

Basilica of San Lorenzo, Rome — A7

Statue of "Rome" A8

Basilica of St. Maria delle Grazie, Milan A9

1944		Unwmk.	
22	A4 5c brown	15	15
23	A5 10c brown	15	15
24	A6 20c rose red	15	15
25	A7 25c dp grn	15	15
26	A3 30c brown	15	15
27	A8 50c purple	18	15
28	A3 75c dk red	15	15
29	A5 1 l purple	15	15
30	A9 1.25 l blue	15	*30*
31	A9 3 l dp grn	15	*15.00*
	Set value	1.15	

Bandiera Brothers — A10

1944, Dec. 6			
32	A10 25c dp grn	15	*22*
33	A10 1 l purple	15	*22*
34	A10 2.50 l rose red	15	*2.75*
	Set value	34	

Cent. of the execution of Attilio (1811-44) and Emilio Bandiera (1819-44), revolutionary patriots who were shot at Cosenza, July 23, 1844, by Neapolitan authorities after an unsuccessful raid.

This set was overprinted in 1945 by the committee of the National Philatelic Convention to publicize that gathering at Venice.

SPECIAL DELIVERY STAMPS

Catalogue values for unused stamps in this section are for Never Hinged items.

Italy Nos. E14 and E15 Overprinted in Red or Black

1944	Wmk. 140	Perf. 14	
E1	SD4 1.25 l green (R)	15	*22*
E2	SD4 2.50 l deep orange	15	*1.25*
	Set value	24	

Cathedral, Palermo SD1

1944		Photo.	
E3	SD1 1.25 l green	24	55

AUTHORIZED DELIVERY STAMP

Catalogue values for unused stamps in this section are for Never Hinged items.

Italy No. EY2 Overprinted

1944	Wmk. 140	Perf. 14	
EY1	AD2 10c dark brown	30	15

POSTAGE DUE STAMPS

Catalogue values for unused stamps in this section are for Never Hinged items.

Italy Nos. J28 to J40 Overprinted Like No. EY1

1944	Wmk. 140	Perf. 14	
J1	D6 5c brown	15	*38*
J2	D6 10c blue	15	*38*
J3	D6 20c rose red	15	*38*
J4	D6 25c green	15	*38*
J5	D6 30c red org	15	*1.10*
J6	D6 40c blk brn	15	*1.50*
J7	D6 50c violet	15	*22*
J8	D6 60c sl blk	1.00	*4.50*
J9	D7 1 l red org	15	*22*
J10	D7 2 l green	1.50	*3.00*
J11	D7 5 l violet	20.00	*25.00*
J12	D7 10 l blue	40.00	*55.00*
J13	D7 20 l car rose	40.00	*55.00*
	Nos. J1-J13 (13)	103.70	*147.06*

PARCEL POST STAMPS

Both unused and used values are for complete stamps.

Catalogue values for unused stamps in this section are for Never Hinged items.

Italian Parcel Post Stamps and Types of 1927-39 Overprinted Like No. EY1

1944	Wmk. 140	Perf. 13	
Q1	PP3 5c brown	2.25	1.75
Q2	PP3 10c deep blue	2.25	1.75
Q3	PP3 25c carmine	2.25	1.75
Q4	PP3 30c ultra	2.25	1.75
Q5	PP3 50c orange	2.25	1.75
Q6	PP3 60c red	2.25	1.75
Q7	PP3 1 l lilac	2.25	1.75
Q8	PP3 2 l green	165.00	165.00
Q9	PP3 3 l yel grn	4.50	4.75
Q10	PP3 4 l gray	4.50	4.75
Q11	PP3 10 l rose lil	120.00	120.00
Q12	PP3 20 l lil brn	285.00	285.00
	Nos. Q1-Q12 (12)	594.75	591.75

No parcel post service existed in 1944. Nos. Q1-Q12 were used undivided, for regular postage.

ITALIAN OFFICES ABROAD

Stamps listed under this heading were issued for use in the Italian Post Offices which, for various reasons, were maintained from time to time in foreign countries.

100 Centesimi = 1 Lira

GENERAL ISSUE

Values of early Italian Offices Abroad vary according to condition. Quotations for Nos. 1-11 are for fine copies. Very fine to superb specimens sell at much higher prices, and inferior or poor copies sell at reduced prices, depending on the condition of the individual specimen.

Italian Stamps with Corner Designs Slightly Altered and Overprinted

1874-78	Wmk. 140	Perf. 14	
1	A6 1c gray grn	35	*2.75*
a.	Inverted overprint	5,000.	
c.	2 dots in lower right corner	5.50	*27.50*

d. Three dots in upper right corner 67.50 160.00
e. Without overprint 450.00
2 A7 2c org brn 45 3.50
a. Without overprint 375.00
3 A8 5c sl grn 45.00 2.75
a. Lower right corner not altered 3,000. 450.00
4 A8 10c buff 135.00 6.75
a. Upper left corner not altered 2,750. 225.00
b. None of the corners altered 13,000. 13,500.
c. Lower corners not altered 5,000. 800.00
5 A8 10c bl ('78) 27.50 1.90
6 A15 20c blue 125.00 3.50
7 A15 20c org ('78) 350.00 1.50
8 A8 30c brown 52 1.80
a. None of the corners altered 5,500.
b. Right lower corner not altered
c. Double overprint 3,000.
9 A8 40c rose 45 2.00
10 A8 60c lilac 60 11.50
11 A13 2 l vermilion 16.00 85.00

1881

12 A17 5c green 1.00 1.65
13 A17 10c claret 60 90
14 A17 20c orange 60 90
a. Double overprint 900.00
15 A17 25c blue 60 1.25
16 A17 50c violet 75 9.75
17 A17 2 l vermilion 3.00

The "Estero" stamps were used in various parts of the world, South America, Africa, Turkey, etc.

Forged cancellations exist on Nos. 1-2, 9-11, 16.

OFFICES IN CHINA

100 Cents = 1 Dollar

PEKING

Italian Stamps of 1901-16 Handstamped PECHINO 2 CENTS

Wmk. 140, Unwmk.

1917 *Perf. 12, 13 1/2, 14*

1 A48 2c on 5c grn 16.00 11.50
c. 4c on 5c green 750.00
3 A48 4c on 10c claret (No. 95) 42.50 20.00
c. 4c on 10c claret (No. 79)
5 A58 6c on 15c slate 80.00 50.00
b. 8c on 15c slate 500.00 375.00
7 A58 8c on 20c on 15c slate 600.00 275.00
8 A50 8c on 20c brn org (No. 112) 1,000. 350.00
9 A49 20c on 50c vio 6,000. 3,750.
b. 40c on 50c violet 1,400. 1,400.
11 A46 40c on 1 l brn & grn 37,500. 4,250.

Inverted surcharges are found on Nos. 1, 3, 3c, 5, 7-9; values same. Double surcharge one inverted exist on Nos. 1, 3; value about double.

Excellent forgeries exist of the higher valued stamps of Offices in China.

Italian Stamps of 1901-16 Overprinted Pechino

1917-18

12 A42 1c brown 70 1.65
13 A43 2c org brn 70 1.65
a. Double overprint 42.50
14 A48 5c green 15 35
a. Double overprint 22.50
15 A48 10c claret 15 35
16 A50 20c brn org (No.112) 6.75 9.00
17 A49 25c blue 18 45
18 A49 50c violet 28 70
19 A46 1 l brn & grn 40 1.00
20 A46 5 l bl & rose 45 2.00
21 A51 10 l gray grn & red 6.75 14.00
Nos. 12-21 (10) 16.51 31.15

Italy No. 113, the watermarked 20c brown orange, was also overprinted "Pechino," but not issued. Value $1.40.

Italian Stamps of 1901-16 Surcharged:

1 CENT Pechino (a) — 2 dollari Pechino (b)

TWO DOLLARS:

Type I- Surcharged "2 dollari" as illustration "b".

Type II- Surcharged "2 DOLLARI".

Type III- Surcharged "2 dollari". "Pechino" measures 11 1/2mm wide, instead of 13mm.

1918-19 *Perf. 14*

22 A42 1/2c on 1c brn 7.25 11.50
a. Surcharged "1 cents" 55.00 67.50
23 A43 1c on 2c org brn 15 45
a. Surcharged "1 cents" 27.50 35.00
24 A48 2c on 5c grn 15 45
25 A48 4c on 10c claret 15 45
26 A50 8c on 20c brn org (No. 112) 60 1.40
27 A49 10c on 25c blue 35 90
28 A49 20c on 50c vio 45 1.25
29 A46 40c on 1 l brn grn 9.00 16.00
30 A46 $2 on 5 l bl & rose (type I) 42.50 60.00
a. Type II 10,000. 10,000.
b. Type III 1,500. 1,150.

Italy No. 100 Surcharged 10 CENTS Pechino

1919

32 A49 10c on 25c blue 24 70

PEKING SPECIAL DELIVERY STAMPS

Italian Special Delivery Stamp 1908 Overprinted Like Nos. 12-21

1917 **Wmk. 140** *Perf. 14*

E1 SD2 30c blue & rose 70 1.50

No. E1 Surcharged 12 CENTS

1918

E2 SD2 12c on 30c bl & rose 6.75 16.00

PEKING POSTAGE DUE STAMPS

Italian Postage Due Stamps Overprinted Like Nos. 12-21

1917 **Wmk. 140** *Perf. 14*

J1 D3 10c buff & mag 38 90
J2 D3 20c buff & mag 38 90
J3 D3 30c buff & mag 38 90
J4 D3 40c buff & mag 48 90

Nos. J1-J4 Surcharged Like No. E2

1918

J5 D3 4c on 10c 11,000. 8,250.
J6 D3 8c on 20c 70 1.50
J7 D3 12c on 30c 4.50 10.00
J8 D3 16c on 40c 18.00 37.50

In 1919, the same new values were surcharged on Italy Nos. J6-J9 in a different style: four lines to cancel the denomination, and "-PECHINO-4 CENTS." These were not issued. Value 90 cents each.

TIENTSIN

Italian Stamps of 1906 Handstamped TIENTSIN 2 CENTS

Wmk. 140, Unwmk.

1917 *Perf. 12, 13 1/2, 14*

1 A48 2c on 5c grn 42.50 35.00
c. 4c on 5c green 1,400.
2 A48 4c on 10c claret 70.00 57.50
4 A58 6c on 15c slate 150.00 115.00
b. 4c on 15c slate 500.00 375.00

Italian Stamps of 1901-16 Overprinted Tientsin

1917-18

5 A42 1c brown 70 1.65
a. Inverted overprint 27.50 35.00
6 A43 2c org brn 70 1.65
7 A48 5c green 15 35
8 A48 10c claret 15 35
9 A50 20c brn org (No.112) 6.75 9.00
10 A49 25c blue 18 45
11 A49 50c violet 28 70
12 A46 1 l brn & grn 40 1.00
13 A46 5 l bl & rose 75 2.00
14 A51 10 l gray grn & red 6.75 14.00
Nos. 5-14 (10) 16.81 31.15

Italy No. 113, the watermarked 20c brown orange was also overprinted "Tientsin," but not issued. Value $1.40.

Italian Stamps of 1901-16 Surcharged:

1 CENT Tientsin (a) — 2 Dollari Tientsin (b)

TWO DOLLARS:

Type I- Surcharged "2 Dollari" as illustration "b".

Type II- Surcharged "2 dollari".

Type III- Surcharged "2 Dollari". "Tientsin" measures 10mm wide instead of 13mm.

1918-21 *Perf. 14*

15 A42 1/2c on 1c brn 6.75 11.50
a. Inverted surcharge 27.50 35.00
b. Surcharged "1 cents" 55.00 70.00
16 A43 1c on 2c org brn 15 45
a. Surcharged "1 cents" 27.50 35.00
b. Inverted surcharge 27.50 35.00
17 A48 2c on 5c grn 15 45
18 A48 4c on 10c claret 15 45
19 A50 8c on 20c brn org (No.112) 60 1.40
20 A49 10c on 25c blue 35 90
21 A49 20c on 50c vio 45 1.25
22 A46 40c on 1 l brn & grn 9.00 16.00
23 A46 $2 on 5 l bl & rose (type I) 42.50 70.00
a. Type II 1,600. 1,250.
b. Type III ('21) 1,500. 1,050.
Nos. 15-23 (9) 60.10 102.40

SPECIAL DELIVERY STAMPS

Italian Special Delivery Stamp of 1908 Overprinted Tientsin

1917 **Wmk. 140** *Perf. 14*

E1 SD2 30c blue & rose 70 1.50

No. E1 Surcharged 12 CENTS

1918

E2 SD2 12c on 30c bl & rose 6.75 16.00

POSTAGE DUE STAMPS

Italian Postage Due Stamps Overprinted Tientsin

1917 **Wmk. 140** *Perf. 14*

J1 D3 10c buff & mag 38 90
a. Double overprint 27.50
J2 D3 20c buff & mag 38 90
J3 D3 30c buff & mag 38 90
a. Double overprint 27.50
J4 D3 40c buff & mag 48 90

Nos. J1-J4 Surcharged 8 CENTS

1918

J5 D3 4c on 10c 275.00 500.00
J6 D3 8c on 20c 70 1.50
J7 D3 12c on 30c 4.50 9.75
J8 D3 16c on 40c 18.00 37.50

In 1919, the same new values were surcharged on Italy Nos. J6-J9 in a different style: four lines to cancel the denomination, and "-TIENTSIN-4 CENTS." These were not issued. Value 90 cents each.

OFFICES IN CRETE

40 Paras = 1 Piaster
100 Centesimi = 1 Lira (1906)

Italy Nos. 70 and 81 Surcharged in Red or Black

LA CANEA — 1 PIASTRA 1 (a) — 1 PIASTRA 1 (b)

1900-01 **Wmk. 140** *Perf. 14*

1 A36(a) 1pi on 25c blue 1.25 3.50
2 A45(b) 1pi on 25c dp bl (Bk) ('01) 1.25 1.50

Italian Stamps Overprinted LA CANEA

1906

On Nos. 76-79, 92, 81, 83-85, 87, 91

3 A42 1c brown 15 28
a. Pair, one without ovpt. 75.00
4 A43 2c org brn 15 28
a. Imperf., pair 180.00
b. Double overprint 45.00
5 A44 5c bl grn 18 38
6 A45 10c claret 30.00 22.50
7 A45 15c on 20c org 24 45
8 A45 25c blue 1.25 1.25
9 A45 40c brown 70 1.25
10 A45 45c ol grn 70 1.25
11 A45 50c violet 75 1.40
12 A46 1 l brn & grn 4.50 5.50
13 A46 5 l bl & rose 18.00 30.00
Nos. 3-13 (11) 56.62 64.54

On Nos. 94-95, 100, 104-105

1907-10

14 A48 5c green 15 28
a. Inverted overprint 57.50
15 A48 10c claret 15 28
16 A49 25c blue 35 70
17 A49 40c brown 2.25 4.50
18 A49 50c violet 35 70
Nos. 14-18 (5) 3.25 6.46

On No. 111 in Violet

1912 **Unwmk.** *Perf. 13x13 1/2*

19 A50 15c slate black 24 45

SPECIAL DELIVERY STAMP

Special Delivery Stamp of Italy Overprinted LA CANEA

1906 **Wmk. 140** *Perf. 14*

E1 SD1 25c rose red 70 1.40

OFFICES IN AFRICA

40 Paras = 1 Piaster
100 Centesimi = 1 Lira (1910)

BENGASI

Italy No. 81 Surcharged in Black BENGASI 1 PIASTRA 1

1901 **Wmk. 140** *Perf. 14*

1 A45 1pi on 25c dp bl 8.00 18.00

Same Surcharge on Italy No. 100

1911

2 A49 1pi on 25c blue 8.00 18.00

TRIPOLI

Italian Stamps of 1901-09 Overprinted in Black or Violet Tripoli di Barberia

1909 **Wmk. 140**

2 A42 1c brown 45 70
a. Inverted overprint 27.50
3 A43 2c org brn 24 45
4 A48 5c green 7.25 2.25
a. Double overprint 55.00
5 A48 10c claret 28 55
a. Double overprint 27.50 35.00
6 A49 25c blue 35 70
7 A49 40c brown 70 1.40
8 A49 50c violet 75 1.50

Perf. 13½x14
Unwmk.

9 A50 15c slate blk (V) 45 90
Nos. 2-9 (9) 18.47 26.45

Italian Stamps of 1901 Overprinted TRIPOLI DI BARBERIA

1909 Wmk. 140 *Perf. 14*
10 A46 1 l brn & grn 24.00 16.00
11 A46 5 l bl & rose 10.00 32.50

Same Overprint on Italy Nos. 76-77

1915
12 A42 1c brown 45
13 A43 2c org brn 35

Nos. 12-13 were prepared but not issued.

SPECIAL DELIVERY STAMPS

Italy Nos. E1, E6 Overprinted Like Nos. 10-11

1909 Wmk. 140 *Perf. 14*
E1 SD1 25c rose red 70 1.40
E2 SD2 30c blue & rose 1.40 2.75

Tripoli was ceded by Turkey to Italy in Oct., 1912, and became known as the Colony of Libya. Later issues will be found under Libya.

OFFICES IN TURKISH EMPIRE

40 Paras = 1 Piaster

Various powers maintained post offices in the Turkish Empire before World War I by authority of treaties which ended with the signing of the Treaty of Lausanne in 1923. The foreign post offices were closed Oct. 27, 1923.

GENERAL ISSUE

Italian Stamps of 1906-08 Surcharged 10 Parà 10

Printed at Turin

1908 Wmk. 140
1 A48 10pa on 5c green 15 35
2 A48 20pa on 10c claret 15 35
3 A49 40pa on 25c blue 30 38
4 A49 80pa on 50c violet 38 55

See Janina Nos. 1-4.

Surcharged in Violet 30 Parà 30

Unwmk.
5 A47 30pa on 15c slate 24 35
Nos. 1-5 (5) 1.22 1.98

Nos. 1, 2, 3 and 5 were first issued in Janina, Albania, and subsequently for general use. They can only be distinguished by the cancellations.

Italian Stamps of 1901-08 Surcharged:

10 PARA Nos. 6-8 — 1 PIASTRA No. 9 — 2 PIASTRE Nos. 10-12

Printed at Constantinople

1908 First Printing
6 A48 10pa on 5c grn 32.50 30.00
7 A48 20pa on 10c cl 32.50 30.00
8 A47 30pa on 15c slate 105.00 90.00
9 A49 1pi on 25c blue 115.00 105.00
a. "PIASTRE" 120.00 115.00
10 A49 2pi on 50c vio 300.00 225.00
11 A46 4pi on 1 l brn & grn 1,350. 850.00
12 A46 20pi on 5 l bl & rose 4,250. 2,900.

On Nos. 8, 9 and 10 the surcharge is at the top of the stamp. No. 11 has the "4" closed at the top. No. 12 has the "20" wide.

Second Printing
Surcharged:

10 PARA Nos. 13-15 — 1 PIASTRA No. 16 — 2 PIASTRE Nos. 17-19

13 A48 10pa on 5c grn 45 70
14 A48 20pa on 10c cl 45 70
15 A47 30pa on 15c slate 2.25 2.75
a. Double surcharge 14.00 14.00
16 A49 1pi on 25c blue 60 75
a. "PIPSTRA" 14.00 14.00
b. "1" omitted 14.00 14.00
17 A49 2pi on 50c vio 6.75 9.00
a. Surcharged "20 PIASTRE" 135.00 135.00
b. "20" with "0" scratched out 57.50 57.50
c. "2" 5mm from "PIASTRE" 27.50 27.50
18 A46 4pi on 1 l brn & grn 180.00 160.00
19 A46 20pi on 5 l bl & rose 750.00 550.00
Nos. 13-19 (7) 940.50 723.90

On No. 18 the "4" is open at the top.

Third Printing

Surcharged in Red 30 PARA

20 A47 30pa on 15c slate 35 60
a. Double surcharge 27.50 27.50

Fourth Printing
Surcharged:

4 4 PIASTRE — 20 20 PIASTRE

20B A46 4pi on 1 l brn & grn 6.75 9.00
c. Inverted "S" 18.00 18.00
20D A46 20pi on 5 l bl & rose 27.50 42.50
i. Inverted "S" 120.00 120.00

Fifth Printing
Surcharged

4 4 PIASTRE — 20 20 PIASTRE

20E A46 4pi on 1 l brn & grn 6.75 8.00
f. Surch. "20 PIASTRE" 275.00
20G A46 20pi on 5 l bl & rose 6.75 8.00
h. Double surcharge 225.00 275.00

Italian Stamps of 1906-19 Surcharged 2 PIASTRE

1921
21 A48 1pi on 5c grn 37.50 80.00
22 A48 2pi on 15c slate 45 60
23 A50 4pi on 20c brn org (No. 113) 3.75 5.50
24 A49 5pi on 25c blue 3.75 5.50
a. Double surcharge 45.00
25 A49 10pi on 60c car 24 35
Nos. 21-25 (5) 45.69 91.95

On No. 25 the "10" is placed above "PIASTRE."

Italian Stamps of 1901-19 Surcharged

PARA 30 n — PIASTRE 1 PARA 20 o

1922
26 A42(n) 10pa on 1c brn 24 45
27 A43(n) 20pa on 2c org brn 24 45
28 A48(n) 30pa on 5c grn 35 60
29 A48(o) 1pi20pa on 15c sl 35 60
30 A50(n) 3pi on 20c brn org (#113) 1.35 2.25
31 A49(o) 3pi30pa on 25c bl 35 60
32 A49(o) 7pi20pa on 60c car 45 70
33 A46(n) 15pi on 1 l brn & grn 2.25 3.75
Nos. 26-33 (8) 5.58 9.40

Italy No. 100 Surcharged Piastre 3,75

34 A49 3.75pi on 25c blue 28 28

Italian Stamps of 1901-20 Surcharged:

PIASTRE — 30 PARÀ q — 3,75 r

1922
35 A48 30pa on 5c grn 90 1.50
36 A49 1.50pi on 25c blue 35 90
37 A49 3.75pi on 40c brn 35 1.00
38 A49 4.50pi on 50c vio 70 1.25
39 A49 7.50pi on 60c car 70 1.25
40 A49 15pi on 85c red brn 1.35 2.50
41 A46 18.75pi on 1 l brn & grn 90 2.00

On No. 40 the numerals of the surcharge are above "PIASTRE."

Surcharged 45 PIASTRE

42 A46 45pi on 5 l bl & rose 37.50 60.00
43 A51 90pi on 10 l gray grn & red 50.00 90.00

Italian Stamps of 1901-17 Surcharged Type "q" or: 1,50 PIASTRE

44 A43 30pa on 2c org brn 18 60
45 A50 1.50pi on 20c brn org (#113) 24 60
Nos. 35-45 (11) 93.17 161.60

Italian Stamps of 1901-20 Surcharged in Black or Red 1½ PIASTRE

46 A48 30pa on 5c grn 15 24
47 A48 1½pi on 10c claret 18 38
48 A49 3pi on 25c blue 1.25 75
49 A49 3¾pi on 40c brn 24 35
50 A49 4½pi on 50c vio 5.50 5.50
51 A49 7½pi on 85c red brn 90 1.90
a. "PIASIRE" 9.00 14.00
52 A46 7½pi on 1 l brn & grn (R) 1.25 2.00
a. Double surcharge 27.50 27.50
b. "PIASIRE" 11.00 17.00
53 A46 15pi on 1 l brn & grn 15.00 18.00
54 A46 45pi on 5 l bl & rose 9.00 14.00
55 A51 90pi on 10 l gray grn & red 8.00 14.00
Nos. 46-55 (10) 41.47 57.12

Italian Stamps of 1901-20 Surcharged Type "o" or:

4 PIASTRE 20 PARA No. 58 — 15 PIASTRE No. 59 — 45 PIASTRE Nos. 61-62

1923
56 A49 1pi20pa on 25c bl 1.90
57 A49 3pi30pa on 40c brn 1.90
58 A49 4pi20pa on 50c vio 1.90
58A A49 7pi20pa on 60c car 6.75
59 A49 15pi on 85c red brn 1.90
60 A46 18pi30pa on 1 l brn & grn 1.90
61 A46 45pi on 5 l bl & rose 4.50
62 A51 90pi on 10 l gray grn & red 2.25
Nos. 56-62 (8) 23.00

Nos. 56-62 were not issued.

SPECIAL DELIVERY STAMPS

Italian Special Delivery Stamps Surcharged

Surcharged LEVANTE 1 PIASTRA 1

1908 Wmk. 140 *Perf. 14*
E1 SD1 1pi on 25c rose red 20 35

Surcharged LEVANTE 60 Parà 60

1910
E2 SD2 60pa on 30c bl & rose 38 75

Surcharged 15 PIASTRE

1922
E3 SD2 15pi on 1.20 l on 30c bl & rose 2.75 6.75

On No. E3, lines obliterate the first two denominations.

Surcharged 15 PIASTRE

E4 SD2 15pi on 30c bl & rose 42.50 90.00

Surcharged 15 PIASTRE

1924
E5 SD2 15pi on 1.20 l bl & red 1.90

No. E5 was not regularly issued.

ALBANIA

Stamps of Italy Surcharged in Black ALBANIA 10 Parà 10

1902 Wmk. 140 *Perf. 14*
1 A44 10pa on 5c green 35 38
2 A45 35pa on 20c org 75 1.00
3 A45 40pa on 25c blue 1.25 90

1907
4 A48 10pa on 5c green 12.50 27.50
5 A48 20pa on 10c claret 1.25 2.25
6 A45 80pa on 50c vio 1.50 3.25

CONSTANTINOPLE

Stamps of Italy Surcharged in Black or Violet Costantinopoli 10 Parà 10

Wmk. 140, Unwmk. (#3)

1909-11 *Perf. 14, 12*
1 A48 10pa on 5c grn 15 24
2 A48 20pa on 10c claret 15 24
3 A47 30pa on 15c sl (V) 15 24
4 A49 1pi on 25c blue 15 24
a. Double surcharge 27.50 35.00
5 A49 2pi on 50c vio 18 35

Surcharged COSTANTINOPOLI 4 PIASTRE 4

6 A46 4pi on 1 l brn & grn 28 45
7 A46 20pi on 5 l bl & rose 1.65 1.90
8 A51 40pi on 10 l gray grn & red 1.00 2.25
Nos. 1-8 (8) 3.71 5.91

Italian Stamps of 1901-19 Surcharged:

COSTANTINOPOLI PIASTRE 1 PARA 20 Nos. 10, 12-13 — COSTANTINOPOLI PIASTRE 3 Nos. 9, 11

1922
9 A48 20pa on 5c grn 1.90 3.75
10 A48 1pi20pa on 15c slate 24 35
11 A49 3pi on 30c org brn 24 60
12 A49 3pi30pa on 40c brn 24 45
13 A46 7pi20pa on 1 l brn & grn 24 45
Nos. 9-13 (5) 2.86 5.60

COSTANTINOPOLI

Italian Stamps of 1901-20 Surcharged — PIASTRE 1 PARÀ 20

1923

14	A48	30pa on 5c green	30	50
15	A49	1pi20pa on 25c blue	30	50
16	A49	3pi30pa on 40c brn	30	50
17	A49	4pi20pa on 50c vio	30	50
18	A49	7pi20pa on 60c car	30	50
19	A49	15pi on 85c red brn	30	50
20	A46	18pi30pa on 1 l brn & grn	45	75
21	A46	45pi on 5 l bl & rose	60	1.00
22	A51	90pi on 10 l gray grn & red	60	1.25
		Nos. 14-22 (9)	3.45	6.00

CONSTANTINOPLE SPECIAL DELIVERY STAMP

King Victor Emmanuel III — SD1

Type of Italian Special Delivery Stamp of 1909 Surcharged in Black

1923 Wmk. 140 *Perf. 14*

E1 SD1 15pi on 1.20 l bl & red 75 2.25

CONSTANTINOPLE POSTAGE DUE STAMPS

Italian Postage Due Stamps of 1870-1903 Overprinted — Costantinopoli

1922 Wmk. 140 *Perf. 14*

J1	D3	10c buff & mag	60	1.25
J2	D3	30c buff & mag	75	1.25
J3	D3	60c buff & mag	75	1.25
J4	D3	1 l bl & mag	60	1.25
J5	D3	2 l bl & mag	275.00	425.00
J6	D3	5 l bl & mag	70.00	90.00
		Nos. J1-J6 (6)	347.70	520.00

A circular control mark, having the appearance of a cancellation, was applied to each block of four of these stamps.

DURAZZO

Stamps of Italy Surcharged in Black or Violet — Durazzo 10 Parà 10

Wmk. 140, Unwmk. (#3)

1909-11 *Perf. 14, 12*

1	A48	10pa on 5c grn	15	35
2	A48	20pa on 10c clar	15	35
3	A47	30pa on 15c sl (V)	1.40	1.40
4	A49	1pi on 25c bl	15	35
5	A49	2pi on 50c vio	18	45

Surcharged — DURAZZO 4 PIASTRE 4

6	A46	4pi on 1 l brn & grn	30	70
7	A46	20pi on 5 l bl & rose	12.00	18.00
8	A51	40pi on 10 l gray grn & red	3.75	*12.50*
		Nos. 1-8 (8)	18.08	34.10

No. 3 Surcharged — CENT 20

1916 Unwmk. *Perf. 12*

9 A47 20c on 30pa on 15c sl 60 *3.50*

JANINA

Stamps of Italy Surcharged — 10 Parà 10

1902-07 Wmk. 140 *Perf. 14*

1	A44	10pa on 5c grn	1.25	60
2	A45	35pa on 20c org	60	75
3	A45	40pa on 25c bl	3.50	1.40
4	A45	80pa on 50c vio ('07)	5.25	8.50

Surcharged in Black or Violet — Janina 10 Parà 10

Wmk. 140, Unwmk. (#7)

1909-11 *Perf. 14, 12*

5	A48	10pa on 5c green	15	35
6	A48	20pa on 10c claret	15	35
7	A47	30pa on 15c sl (V)	15	45
8	A49	1pi on 25c blue	15	45
9	A49	2pi on 50c vio	15	60

Surcharged — JANINA 4 PIASTRE 4

10	A46	4pi on 1 l brn & grn	18	70
11	A46	20pi on 5 l bl & rose	18.00	32.50
12	A51	40pi on 10 l gray grn & red	3.75	11.50
		Nos. 5-12 (8)	22.68	46.90

JERUSALEM

Stamps of Italy Surcharged in Black or Violet — Gerusalemme 10 Parà 10

Wmk. 140, Unwmk. (#3)

1909-11 *Perf. 14, 12*

1	A48	10pa on 5c grn	24	*1.25*
2	A48	20pa on 10c claret	24	*1.25*
3	A47	30pa on 15c sl (V)	24	*1.25*
4	A49	1pi on 25c blue	24	*1.25*
5	A49	2pi on 50c vio	70	*2.25*

Surcharged — GERUSALEMME 4 PIASTRE 4

6	A46	4pi on 1 l brn & grn	1.25	*4.50*
7	A46	20pi on 5 l bl & rose	45.00	*75.00*
8	A51	40pi on 10 l gray grn & red	9.00	*35.00*
		Nos. 1-8 (8)	56.91	

Forged cancellations exist on Nos. 1-8.

SALONIKA

Stamps of Italy Surcharged in Black or Violet — Salonicco 10 Parà 10

Wmk. 140, Unwmk. (#3)

1909-11 *Perf. 14, 12*

1	A48	10pa on 5c green	15	35
2	A48	20pa on 10c claret	15	35
3	A47	30pa on 15c sl (V)	15	35
4	A49	1pi on 25c blue	15	35
5	A49	2pi on 50c vio	22	70

Surcharged — SALONICCO 4 PIASTRE 4

6	A46	4pi on 1 l brn & grn	24	75
7	A46	20pi on 5 l bl & rose	42.50	60.00
8	A51	40pi on 10 l gray grn & red	4.50	14.00
		Nos. 1-8 (8)	48.06	76.85

SCUTARI

Stamps of Italy Surcharged in Black or Violet — Scutari di Albania 10 Parà 10

Wmk. 140, Unwmk. (#3)

1909-11 *Perf. 14, 12*

1	A48	10pa on 5c grn	15	35
2	A48	20pa on 10c claret	15	35
3	A47	30pa on 15c sl (V)	2.25	1.50
4	A49	1pi on 25c blue	15	45
5	A49	2pi on 50c vio	15	60

Surcharged — SCUTARI DI ALBANIA 4 PIASTRE 4

6	A46	4pi on 1 l brn & grn	28	75
7	A46	20pi on 5 l bl & rose	1.25	3.50
8	A51	40pi on 10 l gray grn & red	11.00	22.50
		Nos. 1-8 (8)	15.38	30.00

Surcharged like Nos. 1-5

1915

9 A43 4pa on 2c org brn 24 45

No. 3 Surcharged — CENT 20

1916 Unwmk. *Perf. 12*

10 A47 20c on 30pa on 15c sl 90 3.50

SMYRNA

Stamps of Italy Surcharged in Black or Violet — Smirne 10 Parà 10

Wmk. 140, Unwmk. (#3)

1909-11 *Perf. 14, 12*

1	A48	10pa on 5c grn	15	35
2	A48	20pa on 10c claret	15	35
3	A47	30pa on 15c sl (V)	15	35
4	A49	1pi on 25c blue	15	45
5	A49	2pi on 50c vio	15	45

Surcharged — SMIRNE 4 PIASTRE 4

6	A46	4pi on 1 l brn & grn	22	60
7	A46	20pi on 5 l bl & rose	4.25	6.75
8	A51	40pi on 10 l gray grn & red	6.50	14.00
		Nos. 1-8 (8)	11.72	23.30

Italian Stamps of 1901-22 Surcharged:

SMIRNE PIASTRE 1 PARÀ 20 — Nos. 10, 12-13

SMIRNE PIASTRE 3 — Nos. 9, 11

1922

9	A48	20pa on 5c grn	2.75	
10	A48	1pi20pa on 15c sl	15	
11	A49	3pi on 30c org brn	15	
12	A49	3pi30pa on 40c brn	15	
13	A46	7pi20pa on 1 l brn & grn	15	
		Nos. 9-13 (5)	3.35	

Nos. 9-13 were not issued.

VALONA

Stamps of Italy Surcharged in Black or Violet — Valona 10 Parà 10

Wmk. 140, Unwmk. (#3)

1909-11 *Perf. 14, 12*

1	A48	10pa on 5c grn	15	35
2	A48	20pa on 10c claret	15	35
3	A47	30pa on 15c sl (V)	2.25	1.50
4	A49	1pi on 25c blue	15	45
5	A49	2pi on 50c vio	15	60

Surcharged — VALONA 4 PIASTRE 4

6	A46	4pi on 1 l brn & grn	28	75
7	A46	20pi on 5 l bl & rose	1.50	*5.00*
8	A51	40pi on 10 l gray grn & red	14.00	27.50
		Nos. 1-8 (8)	18.63	36.50

Italy No. 123 Surcharged in Violet or Red Violet — VALONA 30 PARA 30

1916

9	A58	30pa on 15c sl (V)	45	1.40
a.		Red violet surcharge	70	3.50

No. 9 Surcharged — CENT 20

10 A58 20c on 30pa on 15c sl 24 1.90

AEGEAN ISLANDS

(Dodecanese)

A group of islands in the Aegean Sea off the coast of Turkey. They were occupied by Italy during the Tripoli War and were ceded to Italy by Turkey in 1924 by the Treaty of Lausanne. Stamps of Italy overprinted with the name of the island were in use at the post offices maintained in the various islands.

Rhodes, on the island of the same name, was capital of the entire group.

100 Centesimi = 1 Lira

GENERAL ISSUE

Italian Stamps of 1907-08 Overprinted — EGEO

1912 Wmk. 140 *Perf. 14*

1	A49	25c blue	2.75	5.50
a.		Inverted overprint	35.00	57.50
2	A49	50c violet	2.75	5.50
a.		Inverted overprint	35.00	57.50

Virgil Issue

Types of Italian Stamps of 1930 Overprinted in Red or Blue — ISOLE ITALIANE DELL'EGEO

1930 Photo. Wmk. 140 *Perf. 14*

3	A106	15c vio blk	24	*1.40*
4	A106	20c org brn	24	*1.40*
5	A106	25c dk grn	24	*1.40*
6	A106	30c lt brn	24	*1.40*
7	A106	50c dl vio	24	*1.40*
8	A106	75c rose red	24	*1.40*
9	A106	1.25 l gray bl	24	*1.40*

Engr.

Unwmk.

10	A106	5 l + 1.50 l dk vio	1.00	*3.50*
11	A106	10 l + 2.50 l ol brn	1.00	*3.50*
		Nos. 3-11,C4-C7 (13)	7.48	

St. Anthony of Padua Issue

Types of Italian Stamps of 1931 Overprinted in Blue or Red — ISOLE ITALIANE DELL'EGEO

1932 Photo. Wmk. 140 *Perf. 14*

12	A116	20c blk brn	4.50	5.50
13	A116	25c dl grn	4.50	3.50
14	A118	30c brn org	4.50	5.50
15	A118	50c dl vio	4.50	3.50
16	A120	1.25 l gray bl	4.50	5.50

Engr.

Unwmk.

17	A121	75c lt red	4.50	5.50
18	A122	5 l + 2.50 l dp org	4.50	*18.00*
		Nos. 12-18 (7)	31.50	47.00

Dante Alighieri Society Issue

Types of Italian Stamps of 1932 Overprinted

ISOLE DELL' — ITALIANE EGEO

1932 Photo. Wmk. 140

19	A126	10c grnsh gray	38	60
20	A126	15c blk vio	38	60
21	A126	20c brn org	38	60
22	A126	25c dp grn	38	35
23	A126	30c dp org	38	60

24 A126 50c dl vio 38 35
25 A126 75c rose red 38 60
26 A126 1.25 l blue 38 60
27 A126 1.75 l ol brn 50 90
28 A126 2.75 l car rose 50 90
29 A126 5 l + 2 l dp vio 75 1.50
30 A126 10 l + 2.50 l dk brn 75 1.50
Nos. 19-30 (12) 5.54 9.10

See Nos. C8-C14.

Soccer Issue

Types of Italy, "Soccer" Issue, Overprinted in Black or Red

ISOLE ITALIANE DELL'EGEO

1934

31 A173 20c brn rose (Bk) 8.00 *9.00*
32 A174 25c grn (R) 8.00 *9.00*
33 A174 50c vio (R) 35.00 6.75
34 A174 1.25 l gray bl (R) 8.00 *16.00*
35 A175 5 l +2.50 l bl (R) 8.00 *50.00*
Nos. 31-35 (5) 67.00 *90.75*

See Nos. C28-C31.

Same Overprint on Types of Medal of Valor Issue of Italy, in Red or Black

1935

36 A177 10c sl gray (R) 10.00 *22.50*
37 A178 15c brn (Bk) 10.00 *22.50*
38 A178 20c red org (Bk) 10.00 *22.50*
39 A177 25c dp grn (R) 10.00 *22.50*
40 A178 30c lake (Bk) 10.00 *22.50*
41 A178 50c ol grn (Bk) 10.00 *22.50*
42 A178 75c rose red (Bk) 10.00 *22.50*
43 A178 1.25 l dp bl (R) 10.00 *22.50*
44 A177 1.75 l + 1 l pur (R) 8.00 *22.50*
45 A178 2.55 l + 2 l dk car (Bk) 8.00 *22.50*
46 A178 2.75 l + 2 l org brn (Bk) 8.00 *22.50*
Nos. 36-46 (11) 104.00 *247.50*

See Nos. C32-C38, CE3-CE4.

Types of Italy, 1937, Overprinted in Blue or Red — ISOLE ITALIANE DELL'EGEO

1938 Wmk. 140 *Perf. 14*

47 A208 10c dk brn (Bl) 75 80
48 A208 15c pur (R) 75 80
49 A208 20c yel bis (Bl) 75 80
50 A208 25c myr grn (R) 75 80
51 A208 30c dp cl (Bl) 75 80
52 A208 50c sl grn (R) 75 80
53 A208 75c rose red (Bl) 75 85
54 A208 1.25 l dk bl (R) 75 85
55 A208 1.75 l + 1 l dp org (Bl) 1.00 1.25
56 A208 2.55 l + 2 l ol brn (R) 1.00 1.25
Nos. 47-56 (10) 8.00 9.00

Bimillenary of birth of Augustus Caesar (Octavianus), first Roman emperor.
See Nos. C39-C43.

Same Overprint of Type of Italy, 1937, in Red

1938

57 A222 1.25 l deep blue 60 70
58 A222 2.75 l + 2 l brown 75 *2.75*

600th anniversary of the death of Giotto di Bondone, Italian painter.

Statue of Roman Wolf — A1

Arms of Rhodes — A2

Dante's House, Rhodes A3

1940 Photo.

59 A1 5c lt brn 15 15
60 A2 10c pale org 15 15
61 A3 25c bl grn 40 40
62 A1 50c rose vio 40 40
63 A2 75c dl ver 40 40
64 A3 1.25 l dl bl 40 40
65 A2 2 l + 75c rose 40 40
Nos. 59-65,C44-C47 (11) 4.70 4.70

Triennial Overseas Exposition, Naples.

AIR POST STAMPS

Ferrucci Issue

Types of Italian Air Post Stamps of 1930 Overprinted in Blue or Red Like Nos. 12-18

1930 Wmk. 140 *Perf. 14*

C1 AP7 50c brn vio (Bl) 3.00 *4.50*
C2 AP7 1 l dk bl (R) 3.00 *4.50*
C3 AP7 5 l + 2 l dp car (Bl) 6.00 *11.50*

Nos. C1 to C3 were sold at Rhodes only.

Virgil Issue

Types of Italian Air Post Stamps of 1930 Overprinted in Red or Blue Like Nos. 3-11

Photo.

C4 AP8 50c dp grn (R) 90 *2.25*
C5 AP8 1 l rose red (Bl) 90 *2.25*

Engr.

Unwmk.

C6 AP8 7.70 l + 1.30 l dk brn (R) 1.00 *4.50*
C7 AP8 9 l + 2 l gray (R) 1.00 *4.50*

Dante Alighieri Society Issue

Types of Italian Air Post Stamps of 1932 Overprinted Like Nos. 19-30

1932 Wmk. 140

C8 AP10 50c car rose 70 90
C9 AP11 1 l dp grn 45 90
C10 AP11 3 l dl vio 45 90
C11 AP11 5 l dp org 45 90
C12 AP10 7.70 l + 2 l ol brn 75 1.65
C13 AP11 10 l + 2.50 l dk bl 75 1.65
Nos. C8-C13 (6) 3.55 6.90

Leonardo da Vinci — AP12

1932 Photo. *Perf. 14½*

C14 AP12 100 l dp bl & grnsh gray 6.75 *14.00*

Garibaldi Types of Italian Air Post Stamps of 1932 Overprinted in Red or Blue Like Nos. 12-18

1932

C15 AP13 50c dp grn 10.00 *20.00*
C16 AP14 80c copper red 10.00 *20.00*
C17 AP13 1 l + 25c dl bl 10.00 *20.00*
C18 AP13 2 l + 50c red brn 10.00 *20.00*
C19 AP14 5 l + 1 l bluish sl 10.00 *20.00*
Nos. C15-C19 (5) 50.00 *100.00*

See Nos. CE1-CE2.

Graf Zeppelin over Rhodes AP17

1933 *Perf. 14*

C20 AP17 3 l ol brn 22.50 *50.00*
C21 AP17 5 l dp vio 14.00 *50.00*
C22 AP17 10 l dk grn 14.00 *100.00*
C23 AP17 12 l dk bl 14.00 *100.00*
C24 AP17 15 l car rose 14.00 *100.00*
C25 AP17 20 l gray blk 14.00 *100.00*
Nos. C20-C25 (6) 92.50 *500.00*

Balbo Flight Issue

Types of Italian Air Post Stamps of 1933 Overprinted

ISOLE ITALIANE DELL EGEO

1933 Wmk. 140 *Perf. 14*

C26 AP25 5.25 l + 19.75 l grn, red & bl gray 17.00 35.00
C27 AP26 5.25 l + 44.75 l red, grn & bl gray 17.00 35.00

Soccer Issue

Types of Italian Air Post Stamps of 1934 Overprinted in Black or Red Like Nos. 31-35

1934

C28 AP32 50c brn (R) 2.50 *6.00*
C29 AP33 75c rose red) 2.50 *6.00*
C30 AP34 5 l + 2.50 l red org 5.00 *10.00*
C31 AP35 10 l + 5 l grn (R) 5.00 *10.00*

Types of Medal of Valor Issue of Italy Overprinted in Red or Black Like Nos. 31-35

1935

C32 AP36 25c dp grn 14.00 *30.00*
C33 AP36 50c blk brn (R) 14.00 *30.00*
C34 AP36 75c rose 14.00 *30.00*
C35 AP36 80c dk brn 14.00 *30.00*
C36 AP36 1 l + 50c ol grn 10.00 *30.00*
C37 AP36 2 l + 1 l dp bl (R) 10.00 *30.00*
C38 AP40 3 l + 2 l vio (R) 10.00 *30.00*
Nos. C32-C38 (7) 86.00 *210.00*

Types of Italy Air Post Stamps, 1937, Overprinted in Blue or Red Like Nos. 47-56

1938 Wmk. 140 *Perf. 14*

C39 AP51 25c dl gray vio (R) 1.25 1.25
C40 AP51 50c grn (R) 1.25 1.25
C41 AP51 80c brt bl (R) 1.25 1.25
C42 AP51 1 l + 1 l rose lake 1.50 1.90
C43 AP51 5 l + 1 l rose red 1.50 2.75
Nos. C39-C43 (5) 6.75 8.40

Bimillenary of the birth of Augustus Caesar (Octavianus).

Statues of Stag and Roman Wolf AP18

Plane over Government Palace, Rhodes — AP19

1940 Photo.

C44 AP18 50c olive blk 60 60
C45 AP19 1 l dk vio 60 60
C46 AP18 2 l + 75c dk bl 60 60
C47 AP19 5 l + 2.50 l cop brn 60 60

Triennial Overseas Exposition, Naples.

AIR POST SPECIAL DELIVERY STAMPS

Type of Italian Garibaldi Air Post Special Delivery Stamps Overprinted in Blue or Ocher Like Nos. 12-18

1932 Wmk. 140 *Perf. 14*

CE1 APSD1 2.25 l + 1 l bl & rose & (Bl) 12.50 *20.00*
CE2 APSD1 4.50 l + 1.50 l ocher & gray (O) 12.50 *20.00*

Type of Medal of Valor Issue of Italy, Overprinted in Black Like Nos. 31-35

1935

CE3 APSD4 2 l + 1.25 l dp bl 10.00 *30.00*
CE4 APSD4 4.50 l + 2 l grn 10.00 *30.00*

ISSUES FOR THE INDIVIDUAL ISLANDS

Italian Stamps of 1901-20 Overprinted with Names of Various Islands as

Caso (a) — CASO (b) — **CASO** (c)

The 1912-22 issues of each island have type "a" overprint in black on all values except 15c (type A58) and 20c on 15c, which have type "b" overprint in violet.

The 1930-32 Ferruci and Garibaldi issues are types of the Italian issues overprinted type "c."

CALCHI

Overprinted "Karki" in Black or Violet

1912-22 Wmk. 140 *Perf. 13½, 14*

1 A43 2c org brn 90 1.40
a. Double overprint 57.50
2 A48 5c green 15 *1.40*
a. Double overprint 42.50
3 A48 10c claret 15 *1.40*
4 A48 15c slate ('22) 90 *10.00*
a. Double overprint 57.50
5 A50 20c brn org ('21) 70 *10.00*
6 A49 25c blue 15 *1.40*
7 A49 40c brown 15 *1.40*
8 A49 50c violet 15 *1.40*

Unwmk.

9 A58 15c slate (V) 5.75 1.40
10 A50 20c brn org ('17) 15.00 *24.00*
Nos. 1-10 (10) 24.00 *53.80*

No. 9 Surcharged ≡ CENT 20 ≡

1916 *Perf. 13½*

11 A58 20c on 15c slate 35 5.00

Ferrucci Issue

Overprinted in Red or Blue

1930 Wmk. 140 *Perf. 14*

12 A102 20c vio (R) 24 *60*
13 A103 25c dk grn (R) 24 *60*
14 A103 50c blk (R) 24 *60*
15 A103 1.25 l dp bl (R) 24 *60*
16 A104 5 l + 2 l dp car (Bl) 1.25 *1.90*
Nos. 12-16 (5) 2.21 *4.30*

Garibaldi Issue

Overprinted "CARCHI" in Red or Blue

1932

17 A138 10c brown 1.50 *3.50*
18 A138 20c red brn (Bl) 1.50 *3.50*
19 A138 25c dp grn 1.50 *3.50*
20 A138 30c bluish sl 1.50 *3.50*
21 A138 50c red vio (Bl) 1.50 *3.50*
22 A141 75c cop red (Bl) 1.50 *3.50*
23 A141 1.25 l dl bl 1.50 *3.50*
24 A141 1.75 l + 25c brn 1.50 *3.50*
25 A144 2.55 l + 50c org (Bl) 1.50 *3.50*
26 A145 5 l + 1 l dl vio 1.50 *3.50*
Nos. 17-26 (10) 15.00 *35.00*

CALINO

Overprinted "Calimno" in Black or Violet

1912-21 Wmk. 140 *Perf. 13½, 14*

1 A43 2c org brn 90 1.40
2 A48 5c green 24 *1.40*
3 A48 10c claret 15 *1.40*
4 A48 15c slate ('21) 70 *10.00*
5 A50 20c brn org ('21) 70 *10.00*
6 A49 25c blue 60 *1.40*
7 A49 40c brown 15 *1.40*
8 A49 50c violet 15 *1.40*

Unwmk.

9 A58 15c slate (V) 5.50 1.40
10 A50 20c brn org ('17) 13.00 *24.00*
Nos. 1-10 (10) 22.09 *53.80*

No. 9 Surcharged Like Calchi No. 11

1916 *Perf. 13½*

11 A58 20c on 15c slate 3.25 *5.00*

Ferrucci Issue
Overprinted in Red or Blue

1930 Wmk. 140 Perf. 14
12 A102 20c vio (R) 24 60
13 A103 25c dk grn (R) 24 60
14 A102 50c blk (R) 24 60
15 A102 1.25 l dp bl (R) 24 60
16 A104 5 l + 2 l dp car (Bl) 1.25 1.90
Nos. 12-16 (5) 2.21 4.30

Garibaldi Issue
Overprinted in Red or Blue

1932
17 A138 10c brown 1.50 3.50
18 A138 20c red brn (Bl) 1.50 3.50
19 A138 25c dp grn 1.50 3.50
20 A138 30c bluish sl 1.50 3.50
21 A138 50c red vio (Bl) 1.50 3.50
22 A141 75c cop red (Bl) 1.50 3.50
23 A141 1.25 l dl bl 1.50 3.50
24 A141 1.75 l + 25c brn 1.50 3.50
25 A144 2.55 l + 50c org (Bl) 1.50 3.50
26 A145 5 l + 1 l dl vio 1.50 3.50
Nos. 17-26 (10) 15.00 35.00

CASO

Overprinted "Caso" in Black or Violet

1912-21 Wmk. 140 Perf. 13½, 14
1 A43 2c org brn 90 1.40
2 A48 5c green 15 1.40
3 A48 10c claret 15 1.40
4 A48 15c slate ('21) 70 10.00
5 A50 20c brn org ('20) 60 10.00
6 A49 25c blue 15 1.40
7 A49 40c brown 15 1.40
8 A49 50c violet 15 1.40

Unwmk.
9 A58 15c slate (V) 5.50 1.40
10 A50 20c brn org ('17) 13.00 24.00
Nos. 1-10 (10) 21.45 53.80

No. 9 Surcharged Like Calchi No. 11

1916 Perf. 13½
11 A58 20c on 15c slate 24 5.00

Ferrucci Issue
Overprinted in Red or Blue

1930 Wmk. 140 Perf. 14
12 A102 20c vio (R) 24 60
13 A103 25c dk grn (R) 24 60
14 A103 50c blk (R) 24 60
15 A103 1.25 l dp bl (R) 24 60
16 A104 5 l + 2 l dp car (Bl) 1.25 1.90
Nos. 12-16 (5) 2.21 4.30

Garibaldi Issue
Overprinted in Red or Blue

1932
17 A138 10c brown 1.50 3.50
18 A138 20c red brn (Bl) 1.50 3.50
19 A138 25c dp grn 1.50 3.50
20 A138 30c bluish sl 1.50 3.50
21 A138 50c red vio (Bl) 1.50 3.50
22 A141 75c cop red (Bl) 1.50 3.50
23 A141 1.25 l dl bl 1.50 3.50
24 A141 1.75 l + 25c brn 1.50 3.50
25 A144 2.55 l + 50c org (Bl) 1.50 3.50
26 A145 5 l + 1 l dl vio 1.50 3.50
Nos. 17-26 (10) 15.00 35.00

COO

(Cos, Kos)

Overprinted "Cos" in Black or Violet

1912-22 Wmk. 140 Perf. 13½, 14
1 A43 2c org brn 90 1.40
2 A48 5c green 5.50 1.40
3 A48 10c claret 15 1.40
4 A48 15c slate ('22) 70 10.00
5 A50 20c brn org ('21) 90 10.00
6 A49 25c blue 3.75 1.40
7 A49 40c brown 15 1.40
8 A49 50c violet 15 1.40

Unwmk.
9 A58 15c slate (V) 5.50 1.40
10 A50 20c brn org ('17) 7.25 24.00
Nos. 1-10 (10) 24.95 53.80

No. 9 Surcharged Like Calchi No. 11

1916 Perf. 13½
11 A58 20c on 15c slate 3.25 5.00

Ferrucci Issue
Overprinted in Red or Blue

1930 Wmk. 140 Perf. 14
12 A102 20c vio (R) 24 60
13 A103 25c dk grn (R) 24 60
14 A103 50c blk (R) 24 60
15 A103 1.25 l dp bl (R) 24 60
16 A104 5 l + 2 l dp car (Bl) 1.25 1.90
Nos. 12-16 (5) 2.21 4.30

Garibaldi Issue
Overprinted in Red or Blue

1932
17 A138 10c brown 1.50 3.50
18 A138 20c red brn (Bl) 1.50 3.50
19 A138 25c dp grn 1.50 3.50
20 A138 30c bluish sl 1.50 3.50
21 A138 50c red vio (Bl) 1.50 3.50
22 A141 75c cop red (Bl) 1.50 3.50
23 A141 1.25 l dl bl 1.50 3.50
24 A141 1.75 l + 25c brn 1.50 3.50
25 A144 2.55 l + 50c org (Bl) 1.50 3.50
26 A145 5 l + 1 l dl vio 1.50 3.50
Nos. 17-26 (10) 15.00 35.00

LERO

Overprinted "Leros" in Black or Violet

1912-22 Wmk. 140 Perf. 13½, 14
1 A43 2c org brn 90 1.40
2 A48 5c green 28 1.40
3 A48 10c claret 15 1.40
4 A48 15c slate ('22) 70 10.00
5 A50 20c brn org ('21) 15.00 10.00
6 A49 25c blue 7.25 1.40
7 A49 40c brown 15 1.40
8 A49 50c violet 15 1.40

Unwmk.
9 A58 15c slate (V) 6.00 1.40
10 A50 20c brn org ('17) 7.25 24.00
Nos. 1-10 (10) 37.83 53.80

No. 9 Surcharged Like Calchi No. 11

1916 Perf. 13½
11 A58 20c on 15c slate 3.25 5.00

Ferrucci Issue
Overprinted in Red or Blue

1930 Perf. 14
12 A102 20c vio (R) 24 60
13 A103 25c dk grn (R) 24 60
14 A103 50c blk (R) 24 60
15 A103 1.25 l dp bl (R) 24 60
16 A104 5 l + 2 l dp car (Bl) 1.25 1.90
Nos. 12-16 (5) 2.21 4.30

Garibaldi Issue
Overprinted in Red or Blue

1932
17 A138 10c brown 1.50 3.50
18 A138 20c red brn (Bl) 1.50 3.50
19 A138 25c dp grn 1.50 3.50
20 A138 30c bluish sl 1.50 3.50
21 A138 50c red vio (Bl) 1.50 3.50
22 A141 75c cop red (Bl) 1.50 3.50
23 A141 1.25 l dl bl 1.50 3.50
24 A141 1.75 l + 25c brn 1.50 3.50
25 A144 2.55 l + 50c org (Bl) 1.50 3.50
26 A145 5 l + 1 l dl vio 1.50 3.50
Nos. 17-26 (10) 15.00 35.00

LISSO

Overprinted "Lipso" in Black or Violet

1912-22 Wmk. 140 Perf. 13½, 14
1 A43 2c org brn 90 1.40
2 A48 5c green 15 1.40
3 A48 10c claret 15 1.40
4 A48 15c slate ('22) 70 10.00
5 A50 20c brn org ('21) 70 10.00
6 A49 25c blue 15 1.40
7 A49 40c brown 15 1.40
8 A49 50c violet 15 1.40

Unwmk.
9 A58 15c slate (V) 5.50 1.40
10 A50 20c brn org ('17) 7.25 24.00
Nos. 1-10 (10) 15.80 53.80

No. 9 Surcharged Like Calchi No. 11

1916 Perf. 13½
11 A58 20c on 15c slate 24 5.00

Ferrucci Issue
Overprinted in Red or Blue

1930 Wmk. 140 Perf. 14
12 A102 20c vio (R) 24 60
13 A103 25c dk grn (R) 24 60
14 A103 50c blk (R) 24 60
15 A103 1.25 l dp bl (R) 24 60
16 A104 5 l + 2 l dp car (Bl) 1.25 1.90
Nos. 12-16 (5) 2.21 4.30

Garibaldi Issue
Overprinted "LIPSO" in Red or Blue

1932
17 A138 10c brown 1.50 3.50
18 A138 20c red brn (bl) 1.50 3.50
19 A138 25c dp grn 1.50 3.50
20 A138 30c bluish sl 1.50 3.50
21 A138 50c red vio (Bl) 1.50 3.50
22 A141 75c cop red (Bl) 1.50 3.50
23 A141 1.25 l dl bl 1.50 3.50
24 A141 1.75 l + 25c brn 1.50 3.50
25 A144 2.55 l + 50c org (Bl) 1.50 3.50
26 A145 5 l + 1 l dl vio 1.50 3.50
Nos. 17-26 (10) 15.00 35.00

NISIRO

Overprinted "Nisiros" in Black or Violet

1912-22 Wmk. 140 Perf. 13½, 14
1 A43 2c org brn 90 1.40
2 A48 5c green 15 1.40
3 A48 10c claret 15 1.40
4 A48 15c slate ('22) 2.75 10.00
5 A50 20c brn org ('21) 15.00 10.00
6 A49 25c blue 15 1.40
7 A49 40c brown 15 1.40
8 A49 50c violet 15 1.40

Unwmk.
9 A58 15c slate (V) 5.50 1.40
10 A50 20c brn org ('17) 13.00 24.00
Nos. 1-10 (10) 37.90 53.80

No. 9 Surcharged Like Calchi No. 11

1916 Perf. 13½
11 A58 20c on 15c slate 24 5.00

Ferrucci Issue
Overprinted in Red or Blue

1930 Wmk. 140 Perf. 14
12 A102 20c vio (R) 24 60
13 A103 25c dp grn (R) 24 60
14 A103 50c blk (R) 24 60
15 A103 1.25 l dp bl (R) 24 60
16 A104 5 l + 2 l dp car (Bl) 1.25 1.90
Nos. 12-16 (5) 2.21 4.30

Garibaldi Issue
Overprinted in Red or Blue

1932
17 A138 10c brown 1.50 3.50
18 A138 20c red brn (Bl) 1.50 3.50
19 A138 25c dp grn 1.50 3.50
20 A138 30c bluish slate 1.50 3.50
21 A138 50c red vio (Bl) 1.50 3.50
22 A141 75c cop red (Bl) 1.50 3.50
23 A141 1.25 l dull blue 1.50 3.50
24 A141 1.75 l + 25c brn 1.50 3.50
25 A144 2.55 l + 50c org (Bl) 1.50 3.50
26 A145 5 l + 1 l dl vio 1.50 3.50
Nos. 17-26 (10) 15.00 35.00

PATMO

Overprinted "Patmos" in Black or Violet

1912-22 Wmk. 140 Perf. 13½, 14
1 A43 2c org brn 90 1.40
2 A48 5c green 15 1.40
3 A48 10c claret 15 1.40
4 A48 15c slate ('22) 70 10.00
5 A50 20c brn org ('21) 20.00 10.00
6 A49 25c blue 15 1.40
7 A49 40c brown 15 1.40
8 A49 50c violet 15 1.40

Unwmk.
9 A58 15c slate (V) 7.25 1.40
10 A50 20c brn org ('17) 7.25 24.00
Nos. 1-10 (10) 36.85 53.80

No. 9 Surcharged Like Calchi No. 11

1916 Perf. 13½
11 A58 20c on 15c slate 2.75 5.00

Ferrucci Issue
Overprinted in Red or Blue

1930 Wmk. 140 Perf. 14
12 A102 20c vio (R) 24 60
13 A103 25c dk grn (R) 24 60
14 A103 50c blk (R) 24 60
15 A103 1.25 l dp bl (R) 24 60
16 A104 5 l + 2 l dp car (Bl) 1.25 1.90
Nos. 12-16 (5) 2.21 4.30

Garibaldi Issue
Overprinted in Red or Blue

1932
17 A138 10c brown 1.50 3.50
18 A138 20c red brn (Bl) 1.50 3.50
19 A138 25c dp grn 1.50 3.50
20 A138 30c bluish slate 1.50 3.50
21 A138 50c red vio (Bl) 1.50 3.50
22 A141 75c cop red (Bl) 1.50 3.50
23 A141 1.25 l dl bl 1.50 3.50
24 A141 1.75 l + 25c brn 1.50 3.50
25 A144 2.55 l + 50c org (Bl) 1.50 3.50
26 A145 5 l + 1 l dl vio 1.50 3.50
Nos. 17-26 (10) 15.00 35.00

PISCOPI

Overprinted "Piscopi" in Black or Violet

1912-21 Wmk. 140 Perf. 13½, 14
1 A43 2c org brn 90 1.40
2 A48 5c green 15 1.40
3 A48 10c claret 15 1.40
4 A48 15c slate ('21) 1.50 10.00
5 A50 20c brn org ('21) 7.25 10.00
6 A49 25c blue 15 1.40
7 A49 40c brown 15 1.40
8 A49 50c violet 15 1.40

Unwmk.
9 A58 15c slate (V) 5.50 1.40
10 A50 20c brn org ('17) 7.25 24.00
Nos. 1-10 (10) 23.15 53.80

No. 9 Surcharged Like Calchi No. 11

1916 Perf. 13½
11 A58 20c on 15c slate 24 5.00

Ferrucci Issue
Overprinted in Red or Blue

1930 Wmk. 140 Perf. 14
12 A102 20c vio (R) 24 60
13 A103 25c dk grn (R) 24 60
14 A103 50c blk (R) 24 60
15 A103 1.25 l dp bl (R) 24 60
16 A104 5 l + 2 l dp car (Bl) 1.25 1.90
Nos. 12-16 (5) 2.21 4.30

Garibaldi Issue
Overprinted in Red or Blue

1932
17 A138 10c brown 1.50 3.50
18 A138 20c red brn (Bl) 1.50 3.50
19 A138 25c dp grn 1.50 3.50
20 A138 30c bluish sl 1.50 3.50
21 A138 50c red vio (Bl) 1.50 3.50
22 A141 75c cop red (Bl) 1.50 3.50
23 A141 1.25 l dl bl 1.50 3.50
24 A141 1.75 l + 25c brn 1.50 3.50
25 A144 2.55 l + 50c org (Bl) 1.50 3.50
26 A145 5 l + 1 l dl vio 1.50 3.50
Nos. 17-26 (10) 15.00 35.00

RHODES

(Rodi)

Overprinted "Rodi" in Black or Violet

1912-24 Wmk. 140 Perf. 13½, 14
1 A43 2c org brn 15 90
2 A48 5c green 15 60
a. Double overprint 57.50
3 A48 10c claret 15 60
4 A48 15c slate ('21) 20.00 11.50
5 A45 20c org ('16) 15 1.00
6 A50 20c brn org ('19) 24 45
a. Double overprint 11.50
7 A49 25c blue 15 75
8 A49 40c brown 15 90
9 A49 50c violet 15 90
10 A49 85c red brn ('22) 4.25 14.00
11 A46 1 l brn & grn ('24) 24

No. 11 was not regularly issued.

Unwmk.
12 A58 15c slate (V) 6.75 90
13 A50 20c brn org ('17) 30.00 24.00
Nos. 1-13 (13) 62.53

No. 12 Surcharged Like Calchi No. 11

1916 Perf. 13½
14 A58 20c on 15c slate 20.00 32.50

Windmill, Rhodes — A1

Medieval Galley — A2

Christian Knight — A3

Crusader Kneeling in Prayer — A4

Crusader's Tomb — A5

No Imprint

1929 Unwmk. Litho. Perf. 11

15	A1	5c magenta	70	18
16	A2	10c ol brn	70	18
17	A3	20c rose red	70	18
18	A3	25c green	70	15
19	A4	30c dk bl	70	30
20	A5	50c dk brn	1.10	15
21	A5	1.25 l dk bl	70	28
22	A4	5 l magenta	4.50	9.00
23	A4	10 l ol brn	9.00	*22.50*
		Nos. 15-23 (9)	18.80	*32.92*

Visit of the King and Queen of Italy to the Aegean Islands. The stamps are inscribed "Rodi" but were available for use in all the Aegean Islands.

Nos. 15-23 and C1-C4 were used in eastern Crete in 1941-42 with Greek postmarks.

See Nos. 55-63.

Ferrucci Issue

Overprinted in Red or Blue

1930 Wmk. 140 Perf. 14

24	A102	20c vio (R)	24	*60*
25	A103	25c dk grn (R)	24	*60*
26	A103	50c blk (R)	24	*60*
27	A103	1.25 l dp bl (R)	24	*60*
28	A104	5 l + 2 l dp car (Bl)	1.25	*1.90*
		Nos. 24-28 (5)	2.21	*4.30*

Hydrological Congress Issue

Rhodes Issue of 1929 Overprinted

XXI Congresso Idrologico

1930 Unwmk. Perf. 11

29	A1	5c magenta	70	1.90
30	A2	10c ol brn	70	1.40
31	A3	20c rose red	1.25	1.40
32	A3	25c green	1.40	1.40
33	A4	30c dk bl	70	1.90
34	A5	50c dk brn	110.00	13.00
35	A5	1.25 l dk bl	85.00	17.00
36	A4	5 l magenta	17.00	27.50
37	A4	10 l ol grn	17.00	27.50
		Nos. 29-37 (9)	233.75	93.00

Rhodes Issue of 1929 Overprinted in Blue or Red

1931 CONGRESSO EUCARISTICO ITALIANO

1931

38	A1	5c mag (Bl)	24	1.40
39	A2	10c ol brn (R)	24	1.40
40	A3	20c rose red (Bl)	24	1.40
41	A3	25c grn (R)	24	1.40
42	A4	30c dk bl (R)	24	1.40
43	A5	50c dk brn (R)	16.00	11.00
44	A5	1.25 l dk bl (R)	12.00	15.00
		Nos. 38-44 (7)	29.20	33.00

Italian Eucharistic Congress, 1931.

Garibaldi Issue

Overprinted in Red or Blue

1932 Wmk. 140 Perf. 14

45	A138	10c brown	1.50	*3.50*
46	A138	20c red brn (Bl)	1.50	*3.50*
47	A138	25c dp grn	1.50	*3.50*
48	A138	30c bluish sl	1.50	*3.50*
49	A138	50c red vio (Bl)	1.50	*3.50*
50	A141	75c cop red (Bl)	1.50	*3.50*
51	A141	1.25 l dl bl	1.50	*3.50*
52	A141	1.75 l + 25c brn	1.50	*3.50*
53	A144	2.55 l + 50c org (Bl)	1.50	*3.50*
54	A145	5 l + 1 l dl vio	1.50	*3.50*
		Nos. 45-54 (10)	15.00	*35.00*

Types of Rhodes Issue of 1929

Imprint: "Officina Carte-Valori Roma"

1932

55	A1	5c rose lake	15	15
56	A2	10c dk brn	15	15
57	A3	20c red	15	15
58	A3	25c dl grn	15	15
59	A4	30c dl bl	15	15
60	A5	50c blk brn	15	15
61	A5	1.25 l dp bl	15	15
62	A4	5 l rose lake	15	15
63	A4	10 l ol brn	15	15
		Set value	55	75

Aerial View of Rhodes — A6

Map of Rhodes — A7

Deer and Palm — A8

1932 Wmk. 140 Litho. Perf. 11

Shield in Red

64	A6	5c blk & grn	90	1.40
65	A6	10c blk & vio bl	90	1.40
66	A6	20c blk & dl yel	90	1.40
67	A6	25c lil & blk	90	1.40
68	A6	30c blk & pink	90	1.40

Shield and Map Dots in Red

69	A7	50c blk & gray	90	1.40
70	A7	1.25 l red brn & gray	90	1.40
71	A7	5 l dk bl & gray	5.50	9.00
72	A7	10 l dk grn & gray	12.50	18.00
73	A7	25 l choc & gray	350.00	*525.00*
		Nos. 64-73 (10)	374.30	*561.80*

20th anniv. of the Italian occupation and 10th anniv. of Fascist rule.

1935, Apr. Photo. Wmk. 140

74	A8	5c orange	1.65	*5.50*
75	A8	10c brown	1.65	*5.50*
76	A8	20c car rose	1.65	*5.50*
77	A8	25c green	1.65	*5.50*
78	A8	30c purple	1.65	*5.50*
79	A8	50c red brn	1.65	*5.50*
80	A8	1.25l blue	1.65	*5.50*
81	A8	5 l yellow	37.50	*80.00*
		Nos. 74-81 (8)	49.05	*118.50*

Holy Year.

WEIHNACHTEN 1944 WEIHNACHTEN 1944

The above overprints on No. 55 are stated to have been prepared locally for use on German military correspondence, but banned by postal authorities in Berlin.

RHODES SEMI-POSTAL STAMPS

Rhodes Nos. 55 to 62 Surcharged in Black or Red

CENT. 5 PRO ASSISTENZA EGEO

1943 Wmk. 140 Perf. 14

B1	A1	5c + 5c rose lake	24	28
B2	A2	10c + 10c dk brn	24	28
B3	A3	20c + 20c red	24	28
B4	A3	25c + 25c dl grn	24	28
B5	A4	30c + 30c dl bl (R)	35	35
B6	A5	50c + 50c blk brn	45	45
B7	A5	1.25 l + 1.25 l dp bl (R)	60	60
B8	A4	5 l + 5 l rose lake	22.50	22.50
		Nos. B1-B8 (8)	24.86	25.02

The surtax was for general relief.

Rhodes Nos. 55 to 58, 60 and 61 Surcharged in Black or Red

1944

B9	A1	5c + 3 l rose lake	35	*90*
B10	A2	10c + 3 l dk brn (R)	35	*90*
B11	A3	20c + 3 l red	35	*90*
B12	A3	25c + 3 l dl grn (R)	35	*90*
B13	A5	50c + 3 l blk brn (R)	35	*90*
B14	A5	1.25 l + 5 l dp bl (R)	5.50	9.00
		Nos. B9-B14 (6)	7.25	13.50

The surtax was for war victims.

Rhodes Nos. 62 and 63 Surcharged in Red

+ 10 FEBBRAIO 1945

1945

B17	A4	5 l + 10 l rose lake	2.25	4.50
B18	A4	10 l + 10 l ol brn	2.25	4.50

The surtax was for the Red Cross.

RHODES AIR POST STAMPS

Symbolical of Flight — AP18

1934 Typo. Wmk. 140 Perf. 14

C1	AP18	50c blk & yel	15	15
C2	AP18	80c blk & mag	35	*1.25*
C3	AP18	1 l blk & grn	15	15
C4	AP18	5 l blk & red vio	35	*2.00*

RHODES AIR POST SEMI-POSTAL STAMPS

Rhodes Nos. C1 to C4 Surcharged in Silver

PRO SINISTRATI DI GVERRA £. 2

1944 Wmk. 140 Perf. 14

CB1	AP18 50c + 2 l	1.90	2.00
CB2	AP18 80c + 2 l	2.25	2.75
CB3	AP18 1 l + 2 l	2.75	3.50
CB4	AP18 5 l + 2 l	14.00	20.00

The surtax was for war victims.

RHODES SPECIAL DELIVERY STAMPS

Stag — SD1

1936 Photo. Wmk. 140 Perf. 14

E1	SD1	1.25 l green	24	24
E2	SD1	2.50 l vermilion	35	35

Nos. 58 and 57 Surcharged in Black

LIRE 1,25 ESPRESSO

1943

E3	A3	1.25 l on 25c dl grn	15	*45*
E4	A3	2.50 l on 20c red	15	*45*
		Set value	16	

RHODES SEMI-POSTAL SPECIAL DELIVERY STAMPS

Rhodes Nos. E1 and E2 Surcharged in Red or Black

LIRE 1,25 PRO ASSISTENZA EGEO

1943 Wmk. 140 Perf. 14

EB1	SD1	1.25 l + 1.25 l (R)	6.75	6.75
EB2	SD1	2.50 l + 2.50 l	9.00	9.00

The surtax was for general relief.

RHODES POSTAGE DUE STAMPS

Maltese Cross PD1

Immortelle PD2

1934 Photo. Wmk. 140 Perf. 13

J1	PD1	5c vermilion	15	15
J2	PD1	10c carmine	15	15
J3	PD1	20c dk grn	15	15
J4	PD1	30c purple	15	15
J5	PD1	40c dk bl	15	15
J6	PD2	50c vermilion	15	15
J7	PD2	60c carmine	15	15
J8	PD2	1 l dk grn	15	15
J9	PD2	2 l purple	15	15
		Set value	80	

RHODES PARCEL POST STAMPS

Both unused and used values are for complete stamps.

PP1

PP2

1934 Photo. Wmk. 140 Perf. 13

Q1	PP1	5c vermilion	24	18
Q2	PP1	10c carmine	24	18
Q3	PP1	20c dk grn	24	18
Q4	PP1	25c purple	24	18
Q5	PP1	50c dk bl	24	18
Q6	PP1	60c black	24	18

No.	Type	Description	Unused	Used
Q7	PP2	1 l vermilion	24	18
Q8	PP2	2 l carmine	24	18
Q9	PP2	3 l dk grn	24	18
Q10	PP2	4 l purple	24	18
Q11	PP2	10 l dk bl	24	18
		Nos. Q1-Q11 (11)	2.64	1.98

Value of used halves, Nos. Q1-Q11, each 15 cents.

See note preceding No. Q7 of Italy.

SCARPANTO

Overprinted "Scarpanto" in Black or Violet

1912-22 Wmk. 140 *Perf. 13½, 14*

No.	Type	Description	Unused	Used
1	A43	2c org brn	90	1.40
2	A48	5c green	15	*1.40*
3	A48	10c claret	15	*1.40*
4	A48	15c slate ('22)	1.90	*10.00*
5	A50	20c brn org ('21)	7.25	10.00
6	A49	25c blue	70	*1.40*
7	A49	40c brown	15	*1.40*
8	A49	50c violet	15	*1.40*

Unwmk.

No.	Type	Description	Unused	Used
9	A58	15c slate (V)	5.50	1.40
10	A50	20c brn org ('17)	18.00	24.00
		Nos. 1-10 (10)	34.85	53.80

No 9 Surcharged Like Calchi No. 11

1916 *Perf. 13½*

No.	Type	Description	Unused	Used
11	A58	20c on 15c slate	24	*5.00*

Ferrucci Issue

Overprinted in Red or Blue

1930 Wmk. 140 *Perf. 14*

No.	Type	Description	Unused	Used
12	A102	20c vio (R)	24	*60*
13	A103	25c dk grn (R)	24	*60*
14	A103	50c blk (R)	24	*60*
15	A103	1.25 l dp bl (R)	24	*60*
16	A104	5 l + 2 l dp car (Bl)	1.25	*1.90*
		Nos. 12-16 (5)	2.21	*4.30*

Garibaldi Issue

Overprinted in Red or Blue

1932

No.	Type	Description	Unused	Used
17	A138	10c brown	1.50	*3.50*
18	A138	20c red brn (Bl)	1.50	*3.50*
19	A138	25c dp grn	1.50	*3.50*
20	A138	30c bluish sl	1.50	*3.50*
21	A138	50c red vio (Bl)	1.50	*3.50*
22	A141	75c cop red (Bl)	1.50	*3.50*
23	A141	1.25 l dl bl	1.50	*3.50*
24	A141	1.75 l + 25c brn	1.50	*3.50*
25	A144	2.55 l + 50c org (Bl)	1.50	*3.50*
26	A145	5 l + 1 l dl vio	1.50	*3.50*
		Nos. 17-26 (10)	15.00	*35.00*

SIMI

Overprinted "Simi" in Black or Violet

1912-21 Wmk. 140 *Perf. 13½, 14*

No.	Type	Description	Unused	Used
1	A43	2c org brn	90	1.40
2	A48	5c green	2.50	1.40
3	A48	10c claret	15	*1.40*
4	A48	15c slate ('21)	20.00	10.00
5	A50	20c brn org ('21)	7.25	10.00
6	A49	25c blue	28	*1.40*
7	A49	40c brown	15	*1.40*
8	A49	50c violet	15	*1.40*

Unwmk.

No.	Type	Description	Unused	Used
9	A58	15c slate (V)	6.00	1.40
10	A50	20c brn org ('17)	13.00	*24.00*
		Nos. 1-10 (10)	50.38	*53.80*

No. 9 Surcharged Like Calchi No. 11

1916 *Perf. 13½*

No.	Type	Description	Unused	Used
11	A58	20c on 15c slate	3.25	*5.00*

Ferrucci Issue

Overprinted in Red or Blue

1930 Wmk. 140 *Perf. 14*

No.	Type	Description	Unused	Used
12	A102	20c vio (R)	24	*60*
13	A103	25c dk grn (R)	24	*60*
14	A103	50c blk (R)	24	*60*
15	A103	1.25 l dp bl (R)	24	*60*
16	A104	5 l + 2 l dp car (Bl)	1.25	*1.90*
		Nos. 12-16 (5)	2.21	*4.30*

Garibaldi Issue

Overprinted in Red or Blue

1932

No.	Type	Description	Unused	Used
17	A138	10c brown	1.50	*3.50*
18	A138	20c red brn (Bl)	1.50	*3.50*
19	A138	25c dp grn	1.50	*3.50*
20	A138	30c bluish sl	1.50	*3.50*
21	A138	50c red vio (Bl)	1.50	*3.50*
22	A141	75c cop red (Bl)	1.50	*3.50*
23	A141	1.25 l dl bl	1.50	*3.50*
24	A141	1.75 l + 25c brn	1.50	*3.50*
25	A144	2.55 l + 50c org (Bl)	1.50	*3.50*
26	A145	5 l + 1 l dl vio	1.50	*3.50*
		Nos. 17-26 (10)	15.00	*35.00*

STAMPALIA

Overprinted "Stampalia" in Black or Violet

1912-21 Wmk. 140 *Perf. 13½, 14*

No.	Type	Description	Unused	Used
1	A43	2c org brn	90	1.40
2	A48	5c green	15	*1.40*
3	A48	10c claret	15	*1.40*
4	A48	15c slate ('21)	1.50	*10.00*
5	A50	20c brn org ('21)	5.00	*10.00*
6	A49	25c blue	15	*1.40*
7	A49	40c brown	15	*1.40*
8	A49	50c violet	15	*1.40*

Unwmk.

No.	Type	Description	Unused	Used
9	A58	15c slate (V)	5.75	1.40
10	A50	20c brn org ('17)	17.00	*24.00*
		Nos. 1-10 (10)	30.90	*53.80*

No. 9 Surcharged Like Calchi No. 11

1916 *Perf. 13½*

No.	Type	Description	Unused	Used
11	A58	20c on 15c slate	24	*5.00*

Ferrucci Issue

Overprinted in Red or Blue

1930 Wmk. 140 *Perf. 14*

No.	Type	Description	Unused	Used
12	A102	20c vio (R)	24	*60*
13	A103	25c dk grn (R)	24	*60*
14	A103	50c blk (R)	24	*60*
15	A103	1.25 l dp bl (R)	24	*60*
16	A104	5 l + 2 l dp car (Bl)	1.25	*1.90*
		Nos. 12-16 (5)	2.21	*4.30*

Garibaldi Issue

Overprinted in Red or Blue

1932

No.	Type	Description	Unused	Used
17	A138	10c brown	1.50	*3.50*
18	A138	20c red brn (Bl)	1.50	*3.50*
19	A138	25c dp grn	1.50	*3.50*
20	A138	30c bluish sl	1.50	*3.50*
21	A138	50c red vio (Bl)	1.50	*3.50*
22	A141	75c cop red (Bl)	1.50	*3.50*
23	A141	1.25 l dull blue	1.50	*3.50*
24	A141	1.75 l + 25c brn	1.50	*3.50*
25	A144	2.55 l + 50c org (Bl)	1.50	*3.50*
26	A145	5 l + 1 l dl vio	1.50	*3.50*
		Nos. 17-26 (10)	15.00	*35.00*

TRIESTE

A free territory (1947-1954) on the Adriatic Sea between Italy and Yugoslavia. In 1954 the territory was divided, Italy acquiring the northern section and seaport, Yugoslavia the southern section (Zone B).

Catalogue values for all unused stamps in this country are for Never Hinged items.

ZONE A

Issued jointly by the Allied Military Government of the United States and Great Britain

Stamps of Italy 1945-47 Overprinted:

A.M.G. F.T.T. (a)

A.M.G. F.T.T. (b)

A.M.G. F.T.T. (c)

1947, Oct. 1 Wmk. 277 *Perf. 14*

No.	Type	Description	Unused	Used
1	A259(a)	25c brt bl grn	15	25
2	A255(a)	50c dp vio	15	25
3	A257(a)	1 l dk grn	15	15
4	A258(a)	2 l dk cl brn	15	15
5	A259(a)	3 l red	15	15
6	A259(a)	4 l red org	15	15
7	A256(a)	5 l dp bl	22	15
8	A257(a)	6 l dp vio	28	15
9	A255(a)	10 l slate	28	15
10	A257(a)	15 l dp bl	50	15
11	A259(a)	20 l dk red vio	28	15
12	A260(b)	25 l dk grn	2.00	1.65
13	A260(b)	50 l dk vio brn	3.25	1.25

Perf. 14x13½

No.	Type	Description	Unused	Used
14	A261(c)	100 l car lake	12.50	5.00
		Nos. 1-14 (14)	20.21	9.75

The letters "F. T. T." are the initials of "Free Territory of Trieste."

Italy Nos. 486-488 Ovptd. Type "a"

1948, Mar. 1 *Perf. 14*

No.	Type	Description	Unused	Used
15	A255	8 l dk grn	2.00	1.50
16	A256	10 l red org	6.25	15
17	A259	30 l dk bl	75.00	1.25

Italy Nos. 495 to 506 Overprinted

A.M.G.- F. T. T. (d)

1948, July 1

No.	Type	Description	Unused	Used
18	A272	3 l dk brn	24	15
19	A272	4 l red vio	15	15
20	A272	5 l dp bl	18	15
21	A272	6 l dp yel grn	35	24
22	A272	8 l brown	24	20
23	A272	10 l org red	35	15
24	A272	12 l dk gray grn	45	*1.10*
25	A272	15 l gray blk	7.75	*6.75*
26	A272	20 l car rose	12.00	6.75
27	A272	30 l brt ultra	75	1.10
28	A272	50 l violet	6.00	*10.50*
29	A272	100 l bl blk	30.00	*45.00*
		Nos. 18-29 (12)	58.46	*72.24*

Italy, Nos. 486 to 488, Overprinted in Carmine

1948, Sept. 8

No.	Type	Description	Unused	Used
30	A255	8 l dk grn	30	24
31	A256	10 l red org	30	24
32	A259	30 l dk bl	1.65	2.25
		Nos. 30-32,C17-C19 (6)	4.00	*4.88*

The overprint is embossed.

Italy, No. 507, Overprinted Type "d" in Carmine

1948, Oct. 15

No.	Type	Description	Unused	Used
33	A273	15 l dk grn	1.25	1.10

Italy, No. 508, Overprinted in Green

A.M.G. F.T.T. (e)

1948, Nov. 15

No.	Type	Description	Unused	Used
34	A274	15 l dk brn	1.25	1.10

Italy, No. 509, Overprinted Type "d" in Red

1949, May 2 Wmk. 277 *Perf. 14*

No.	Type	Description	Unused	Used
35	A275	20 l dk brn	5.75	1.90

Italy, Nos. 510 to 513, Overprinted

A.M.G. F.T.T. (f)

1949, May 2 Buff Background

No.	Type	Description	Unused	Used
36	A276	5 l red brn	45	*85*
37	A276	15 l dk grn	11.00	12.00
38	A276	20 l dp red brn	4.00	1.25
39	A276	50 l dk bl	17.50	11.50

Italy, No. 514, Overprinted Type "d" in Red

1949, May 2

No.	Type	Description	Unused	Used
40	A277	50 l brt ultra	4.00	5.00

Italy, No. 518, Overprinted Type "d" in Red

1949, May 30

No.	Type	Description	Unused	Used
41	A279	100 l brown	57.50	*87.50*

Italy, Nos. 515-517, Ovptd. Type "f"

1949, June 15

No.	Type	Description	Unused	Used
42	A278	5 l dk grn	7.00	*8.25*
43	A278	15 l violet	8.00	*12.00*
44	A278	20 l brown	12.50	15.00

Italy, Nos. 519 and 520, Overprinted Type "e" in Carmine

1949, July 16

No.	Type	Description	Unused	Used
45	A280	20 l gray	8.75	3.75
46	A281	20 l brown	7.25	3.75

Italy, No. 521 Overprinted in Green

AMG-FTT (g)

1949, June 8

No.	Type	Description	Unused	Used
47	A282	20 l brn red	3.50	2.00

Italy, No. 522, Overprinted Type "f" in Carmine

1949, July 8

No.	Type	Description	Unused	Used
49	A283	20 l violet	17.50	5.00

Italy, No. 523 Overprinted Type "e", without Periods, in Black

1949, Aug. 27

No.	Type	Description	Unused	Used
50	A284	20 l vio bl	6.25	3.25

Italy, No. 524 Ovptd. Type "f"

1949, Aug. 27

No.	Type	Description	Unused	Used
51	A285	20 l violet	17.50	13.00

Italy, No. 525, Overprinted Type "d" in Green

1949, Sept. 10

No.	Type	Description	Unused	Used
52	A286	20 l red	6.25	3.75

Italy Nos. 526 and 527 Overprinted

AMG-FTT (h)

Wmk. 277

1949, Nov. 7 Photo. *Perf. 14*

No.	Type	Description	Unused	Used
53	A287	20 l rose car	3.00	2.50
54	A288	50 l dp bl	9.00	7.50

Same Overprint on No. 528

1949, Nov. 7

No.	Type	Description	Unused	Used
55	A289	20 l dp grn	3.25	2.75

Same Overprint on No. 529

1949, Nov. 7

No.	Type	Description	Unused	Used
56	A290	20 l brt bl	3.25	2.75

Same Overprint in Red on No. 530

1949, Dec. 28

No.	Type	Description	Unused	Used
57	A291	20 l vio blk	3.25	2.00

Same Overprint in Black on Italian Stamps of 1945-48

1949-50 Photo.

No.	Type	Description	Unused	Used
58	A257	1 l dk grn	16	15
59	A258	2 l dk cl brn	16	15
60	A259	3 l red	16	15
61	A256	5 l dp bl	20	15
62	A257	6 l dp vio	16	15
63	A255	8 l dk grn	5.75	*8.00*
64	A256	10 l red org	26	15
65	A257	15 l dp bl	1.10	30
66	A259	20 l dk red vio	42	15
67	A260	25 l dk grn ('50)	11.50	1.65
68	A260	50 l dk vio brn ('50)	22.50	80

Engr.

No.	Type	Description	Unused	Used
69	A261	100 l car lake	45.00	5.25
		Nos. 58-69 (12)	87.37	*17.05*

Issue dates: 3 l, 20 l, Oct. 21. 5 l, Nov. 5. 10 l, Nov. 7. 100 l, Nov. 23. 15 l, Nov. 28. 1 l, 2 l, 6 l, 8 l, Dec. 28. 50 l, Jan. 19. 25 l, Feb. 25.

Italy, No. 531, Overprinted Type "g" in Carmine

1950, Apr. 12

No.	Type	Description	Unused	Used
70	A292	20 l brown	1.75	1.40

Same Overprint in Carmine on Italy, No. 532

1950, Apr. 29

No.	Type	Description	Unused	Used
71	A293	20 l vio gray	1.75	1.60

Same Overprint in Carmine on Italy, Nos. 533 and 534

1950, May 22

No.	Type	Description	Unused	Used
72	A294	20 l ol grn	1.90	1.65
73	A295	55 l blue	6.75	*12.00*

Italy, Nos. 535 and 536, Overprinted Type "h" in Black

1950, May 29

No.	Type	Description	Unused	Used
74	A296	20 l violet	2.00	1.65
75	A296	55 l blue	7.00	*12.00*

Italy, No. 537, Overprinted Type "g" in Carmine

1950, July 10

No.	Type	Description	Unused	Used
76	A297	20 l gray grn	2.75	2.00

Same Overprint in Carmine on Italy, Nos. 538-539

1950, July 15
77 A298 20 l purple 5.75 5.00
78 A298 55 l blue 18.00 25.00

Italy, No. 540, Overprinted Type "h"

1950, July 22
79 A299 20 l brown 2.75 2.00

Italy, No. 541 Overprinted in Carmine

i AMG
FTT

1950, July 29
80 A300 20 l dk grn 2.75 2.00

Italy, No. 542, Overprinted Type "g"

1950, Aug. 21
81 A301 20 l chnt brn 2.50 2.00

AMG
FTT
fiera di trieste
1950

Italy, Nos. 473A and 474, Overprinted

1950, Aug. 27
82 A257 15 l dp bl 1.75 1.65
83 A259 20 l dk red vio 1.75 60

Trieste Fair.

Italy, No. 543, Overprinted Type "i" in Carmine

1950, Sept. 11
84 A302 20 l indigo 1.25 1.10

Italy Nos. 544-546, Ovptd. Type "h"

1950, Sept. 16 Wmk. 277 *Perf. 14*
85 A303 5 l dp cl & grn 80 2.25
86 A303 20 l brn & grn 3.50 2.25
87 A303 55 l dp ultra & brn 24.00 27.50

Same, in Black, on Italy No. 547

1950, Sept. 16
88 A304 20 l ol brn & red brn 2.50 1.65

Same, in Black, on Italy No. 548

1950, Sept. 16
89 A305 20 l cr & gray blk 2.25 1.65

Italy, Nos. 549 to 565, Overprinted Type "g" in Black

1950, Oct. 20
90 A306 50c vio bl 15 15
91 A306 1 l dk bl vio 15 15
92 A306 2 l sepia 15 15
93 A306 5 l dk gray 15 15
94 A306 6 l chocolate 25 15
95 A306 10 l dp grn 25 15
96 A306 12 l dp bl grn 35 90
97 A306 15 l dk gray bl 1.00 15
98 A306 20 l bl vio 1.00 15
99 A306 25 l brn org 2.00 15
100 A306 30 l magenta 75 55
101 A306 35 l crimson 2.00 1.40
102 A306 40 l brown 1.25 75
103 A306 50 l violet 25 30
104 A306 55 l dp bl 25 55
105 A306 60 l red 6.75 3.50
106 A306 65 l dk grn 25 50

Italy Nos. 566 and 567 Overprinted

k AMG-FTT

Perf. 14, 14x13½
Engr.
107 A306 100 l brn org 2.50 15
108 A306 200 l ol brn 2.50 5.50
Nos. 90-108 (19) 21.95 15.45

Italy Nos. 568 and 569 Overprinted Type "k" in Black

1951, Mar. 27 Photo. *Perf. 14*
109 A307 20 l red vio & red 2.00 2.50
110 A307 55 l ultra & bl 30.00 37.50

Italy No. 570 Overprinted Type "g"

1951, Apr. 2
111 A308 20 l dk grn 1.75 2.00

Same, on Italy No. 571

1951, Apr. 11
112 A309 20 l bl vio 1.65 2.00

Italy Nos. 572 and 573 Overprinted

1951, Apr. 12
113 A310(h) 20 l brown 1.65 2.75
114 A311(g) 55 l dp bl 3.25 4.75

Italy Nos. 574 to 576 Overprinted Type "h" in Black

1951, May 18 Fleur-de-Lis in Red
115 A312 5 l dk brn 5.75 11.00
116 A312 10 l Prus grn 5.75 11.00
117 A312 15 l vio bl 5.75 11.00

Italy No. 577 Overprinted

m AMG-FTT

1951, Apr. 26
118 A313 20 l purple 1.65 2.00

Italy No. 578 Overprinted Type "h"

1951, May 5
119 A314 20 l Prus grn 2.75 3.25

Italy Nos. 579-580 Ovptd. Type "g"

1951, June 18
120 A315 20 l violet 60 1.25
121 A315 55 l brt bl 1.90 3.50

FIERA
di
TRIESTE
1951

Nos. 94, 98 and 104 Overprinted

1951, June 24
122 A306 6 l chocolate 42 75
123 A306 20 l bl vio 55 60
124 A306 55 l dp bl 70 1.20

Issued to publicize the Trieste Fair, 1951.

Italy No. 581 Overprinted

AMG
n
FTT

1951, July 23
125 A316 20 l brn & red brn 1.00 1.10

Italy Nos. 582 and 583 Overprinted Types "n" and "h" in Red

1951, July 23
126 A317(n) 20 l grnsh gray & blk 1.10 1.25
127 A318(h) 55 l vio bl & pale sal 2.50 3.75

Italy No. 584 Overprinted Type "g" in Carmine

1951, Aug. 23
128 A319 25 l gray blk 1.00 1.10

Overprint "g" on Italy No. 585

1951, Sept. 8
129 A320 25 l deep blue 1.00 1.10

Italy No. 586 Overprinted Type "h" in Red

1951, Sept. 15
130 A321 25 l dk brn 1.00 1.10

Italy Nos. 587-589 Overprinted in Blue

o AMG FTT

1951, Oct. 11
131 A322 10 l dk brn & gray 40 75
132 A322 25 l rose red & bl grn 75 75
133 A322 60 l vio bl & red org 1.10 1.50

Italy Nos. 590-591 Overprinted

p AMG FTT

1951, Oct. 31 Photo.
Overprint Spaced to Fit Design
134 A323 10 l green 75 90
135 A324 25 l vio gray 75 90

Italy Nos. 592-593 Ovptd. Type "k"

1951, Nov. 21
136 A325 10 l ol & dl grn 80 1.25
137 A326 25 l dl grn 1.00 80

Italy Nos. 594-596 Overprinted Types "k" or "p" in Black

1951, Nov. 23
Overprint "p" Spaced to Fit Design
138 A327(p) 10 l vio brn & dk grn 52 90
139 A327(k) 25 l red brn & dk brn 90 90
140 A327(p) 60 l dp grn & ind 1.40 1.90

Italy No. 597 Overprinted Type "p"

1952, Jan. 28 Wmk. 277 *Perf. 14*
Overprint Spaced to Fit Design
141 A328 25 l gray & gray blk 1.00 70

Italy No. 598 Overprinted Type "k"

1952, Feb. 2
142 A329 25 l dl grn & ol bis 1.00 70

Same on Italy No. 599

1952, Mar. 26
143 A330 25 l brn & sl blk 85 70

Same on Italy No. 600

1952, Apr. 12
144 A331 60 l ultra 2.50 3.25

Same on Italy No. 601

1952, Apr. 16
145 A332 25 l dp org 75 15

Stamps of Italy Overprinted "AMG FTT" in Various Sizes and Arrangements

On Nos. 602-603

1952, June 14 Wmk. 277 *Perf. 14*
146 A333 25 l blk & red brn 65 60
147 A333 60 l blk & ultra 1.10 1.75

On No. 604

1952, June 7
148 A334 25 l brt bl 90 70

On No. 605

1952, June 14
149 A335 25 l blk & yel 90 70

On No. 606

1952, June 19
150 A336 25 l bl gray, red & dk bl (R) 90 70

On No. 607

1952, June 28
151 A337 25 l dp grn, dk brn & red 90 70

On No. 608

1952, Sept. 6
152 A338 25 l dk grn 90 70

On No. 609 in Bronze

1952, Sept. 20
153 A339 25 l purple 90 70

On No. 610

1952, Oct. 4
154 A340 25 l gray 90 70

On No. 611

1952, Oct. 1
155 A341 60 l vio bl & dk bl 2.25 3.25

On No. 612

1952, Nov. 21 *Perf. 13*
156 A342 25 l brn & dk brn 90 70

On Nos. 613-615

1952, Nov. 3 *Perf. 14*
157 A343 10 l dk grn 20 35
158 A344 25 l blk & dk brn 80 30
159 A344 60 l blk & bl 80 1.50

On No. 616

1952, Dec. 6
160 A345 25 l dk grn 90 70

On No. 617

1952, Dec. 6
161 A346 25 l brown 90 70

On No. 618

1953, Jan. 5
162 A347 25 l gray blk & dk bl (Bl) 90 70

On Nos. 601A-601B

1952, Dec. 31
163 A332a 60 l ultra (G) 75 1.25
164 A332 80 l brn car 1.65 50

On No. 621

1953, Feb. 21
165 A349 25 l car lake 90 70

On No. 622

1953, Apr. 24
166 A350 25 l violet 90 70

On No. 623

1953, Apr. 30
167 A351 25 l violet 90 70

On No. 624

1953, May 30
168 A352 25 l dk brn 90 70

On No. 625

1953, June 27
169 A353 25 l brn & dl red 90 70

On Nos. 626-633

1953-54
170 A354 5 l gray 15 15
171 A354 10 l org ver 25 15
172 A354 12 l dl grn 25 18
172A A354 13 l brt lil rose ('54) 25 18
173 A354 20 l brown 25 15
174 A354 25 l purple 25 15
175 A354 35 l rose car 50 90
176 A354 60 l blue 60 1.25
177 A354 80 l org brn 65 1.40
Nos. 170-177 (9) 3.15 4.51

Issue dates: 13 l, Feb. 1. Others, June 16.

FIERA DI TRIESTE

Italy, Nos. 554, 558 and 564 Overprinted in Red or Green

AMG FTT 1953

1953, June 27
178 A306 10 l dp grn (R) 40 *65*
179 A306 25 l brn org 50 40
180 A306 60 l red 60 1.00

5th International Sample Fair of Trieste.

On No. 634

1953, July 11
181 A355 25 l bl grn 90 70

On Nos. 635-636

1953, July 16
182 A356 25 l dk brn 45 50
183 A356 60 l dp bl 70 1.00

On Nos. 637-638

1953, Aug. 6
184 A357 25 l org & Prus bl 1.00 70
185 A357 60 l lil rose & dk vio bl 3.00 3.25

On No. 639

1953, Aug. 13
186 A358 25 l dk brn & dl grn 90 70

On No. 640

1953, Sept. 5
187 A359 25 l dk gray & brn 90 70

On Nos. 641-646

1954, Jan. 26
188 A360 10 l dk brn & red brn 25 32
189 A361 12 l lt bl & gray 30 50
190 A361 20 l brn org & dk brn 40 35
191 A360 25 l dk grn & pale bl 40 18
192 A361 35 l cream & brn 40 *80*
193 A361 60 l bl grn & ind 55 *1.00*
Nos. 188-193 (6) 2.30 *3.15*

On Nos. 647-648

1954, Feb. 11
194 A362 25 l dk brn & choc 45 52
195 A362 60 l bl & ultra 65 1.00

On Nos. 649-650

1954, Feb. 25
196 A363 25 l purple 42 35
197 A363 60 l dp bl grn 95 *1.50*

On No. 651

1954, Mar. 20
198 A364 25 l purple 90 48

On No. 652

1954, Apr. 24
199 A365 25 l gray blk 90 70

On No. 653

1954, June 1
200 A366 25 l gray, org brn & blk 90 70

On No. 654

1954, June 19
201 A367 25 l dk grnsh gray 90 70

On Nos. 655-656

1954, July 8
202 A368 25 l red brn 42 55
203 A368 60 l gray grn 95 1.25

Nos. 644, 646 With Additional Overprint

FIERA DI TRIESTE 1954

1954, June 17
204 A360 25 l dk grn & pale bl 45 52
205 A361 60 l bl grn & ind 65 1.00

International Sample Fair of Trieste.

On No. 657

1954, Sept. 6
206 A369 25 l dp grn & red 90 70

On Nos. 658-659

1954, Oct. 30
207 A370 25 l rose red 32 42
208 A370 60 l blue 55 65

OCCUPATION AIR POST STAMPS

Air Post Stamps of Italy, 1945-47, Overprinted Type "c" in Black

1947, Oct. 1 Wmk. 277 *Perf. 14*
C1 AP59 1 l slate bl 20 30
C2 AP60 2 l dk bl 25 30
C3 AP60 5 l dk grn 1.00 *1.50*
C4 AP59 10 l car rose 1.00 *1.50*
C5 AP60 25 l brown 1.25 *2.00*
C6 AP59 50 l violet 5.75 2.25
Nos. C1-C6 (6) 9.45 *7.85*

Italy, Nos. C116 to C121, Overprinted Type "b" in Black

1947, Nov. 19
C7 AP61 6 l dp vio 60 *1.00*
C8 AP61 10 l dk car rose 60 *1.00*
C9 AP61 20 l dp org 3.50 2.75
C10 AP61 25 l aqua 60 *1.65*
C11 AP61 35 l brt bl 60 *1.65*
C12 AP61 50 l lilac rose 3.50 1.65
Nos. C7-C12 (6) 9.40 *9.70*

Italy, Nos. C123 to C126, Overprinted Type "f" in Black

1948
C13 AP65 100 l green 27.50 2.75
C14 AP65 300 l lil rose 15.00 *15.00*
C15 AP65 500 l ultra 20.00 *20.00*
C16 AP65 1000 l dk brn 150.00 *190.00*

Issue date: Nos. C13-C15, Mar. 1.

Italy, No. C110, C113 and C114, Overprinted in Black

(Reduced Illustration) A.M.G. F.T.T. 1948 TRIESTE

1948, Sept. 8
C17 AP59 10 l carmine rose 35 35
C18 AP60 25 l brown 70 *90*
C19 AP59 50 l violet 70 *90*

The overprint is embossed.

Italy Air Post Stamps of 1945-48 Overprinted Type "h" in Black

1949-52
C20 AP59 10 l car rose 30 15
C21 AP60 25 l brn ('50) 30 30
C22 AP59 50 l violet 30 32
C23 AP65 100 l green 55 30
C24 AP65 300 l lil rose ('50) 7.25 *9.00*
C25 AP65 500 l ultra ('50) 6.75 *12.00*
C26 AP65 1000 l dk brn ('52) 20.00 *22.50*
Nos. C20-C26 (7) 35.45 *44.57*

No. C26 is found in two perforations: 14 and 14x13.

Issue dates: 100 l, Nov. 7. 50 l, Dec. 5. 10 l, Dec. 28. 25 l, Jan. 23. 300 l, 500 l, Nov. 25. 1000 l, Feb. 18.

OCCUPATION SPECIAL DELIVERY STAMPS

Special Delivery Stamps of Italy 1946-48 Overprinted Type "c"

1947-48 Wmk. 277 *Perf. 14*
E1 SD9 15 l dk car rose 28 30
E2 SD8 25 l brt red org ('48) 10.50 5.50
E3 SD8 30 l dp vio 65 *90*
E4 SD9 60 l car rose ('48) 10.50 *10.00*

Issue dates: Oct. 1, 1947. Mar. 1, 1948.

Italy No. E26, Overprinted Type "d"

1948, Sept. 24
E5 A272 35 l violet 5.00 *3.50*

Italy No. E25, Overprinted Type "h"

1950, Sept. 27
E6 SD9 60 l car rose 1.75 1.40

Italy No. E32 Overprinted Type "k"

1952, Feb. 4
E7 SD8 50 l lil rose 1.65 1.40

OCCUPATION AUTHORIZED DELIVERY STAMPS

Authorized Delivery Stamp of Italy, 1946 Overprinted Type "a" in Black

1947, Oct. 1 Wmk. 277 *Perf. 14*
EY1 AD3 1 l dk brn 24 15

Italy, No. EY7 Overprinted in Black

A.M.G. F.T.T.

1947, Oct. 29
EY2 AD4 8 l brt red 2.50 65

Italy, No. EY8, Overprinted Type "a" in Black

1949, July 30
EY3 AD4 15 l violet 10.00 1.90

Same, Overprinted Type "h" in Black

1949, Nov. 7
EY4 AD4 15 l violet 90 15

Italy No. EY9 Overprinted Type "h" in Black

1952, Feb. 4
EY5 AD4 20 l rose vio 1.40 15

OCCUPATION POSTAGE DUE STAMPS

Postage Due Stamps of Italy, 1945-47, Overprinted Type "a"

1947, Oct. 1 Wmk. 277 *Perf. 14*
J1 D9 1 l red org 25 28
J2 D10 2 l dk grn 30 15
J3 D9 5 l violet 1.90 28
J4 D9 10 l dk bl 2.25 90
J5 D9 20 l car rose 9.75 90
J6 D10 50 l aqua 1.75 15
Nos. J1-J6 (6) 16.20 2.66

Same Overprint on Postage Due Stamps of Italy, 1947

1949
J7 D10 1 l red org 32 25
J8 D10 3 l carmine 85 *1.25*
J9 D10 4 l brown 5.50 *7.00*
J10 D10 5 l violet 30.00 *7.00*
J11 D10 6 l vio bl 12.00 *14.00*
J12 D10 8 l rose vio 17.00 *22.50*
J13 D10 10 l dp bl 37.50 2.75
J14 D10 12 l golden brn 13.00 *14.00*
J15 D10 20 l lil rose 9.25 80
Nos. J7-J15 (9) 125.42 69.55

Issue dates: 3 l, 4 l, 6 l, 8 l, 12 l, Jan. 24. Others, Apr. 15.

Postage Due Stamps of Italy, 1947-54, Overprinted Type "h"

1949-54
J16 D10 1 l red org 18 15
J17 D10 2 l dk grn 18 15
J18 D10 3 l car ('54) 30 70
J20 D10 5 l violet 38 20
J21 D10 6 l vio bl ('50) 30 15
J22 D10 8 l rose vio ('50) 30 15
J23 D10 10 l deep blue 38 15
J24 D10 12 l gldn brn ('50) 90 70
J25 D10 20 l lil rose 1.50 48
J26 D10 25 l dk red ('54) 3.75 6.50
J27 D10 50 l aqua ('50) 2.50 15
J28 D10 100 l org yel ('52) 4.25 48
J29 D10 500 l dp bl & dk car ('52) 25.00 12.00
Nos. J16-J29 (13) 39.92 21.96

Issue dates: 5 l, 10 l, Nov. 7. 1 l, Nov. 22. 2 l, 20 l, Dec. 28. 6 l, 8 l, 12 l, May 16. 50 l, Nov. 25. 100 l, Nov. 11. 500 l, June 19. 3 l, Jan. 24. 25 l, Feb. 1.

OCCUPATION PARCEL POST STAMPS

See note preceding Italy No. Q7.

Parcel Post Stamps of Italy, 1946-48, Overprinted:

A.M.G. F.T.T. A.M.G. F.T.T.

1947-48 Wmk. 277 *Perf. 13½*
Q1 PP4 1 l gldn brn 24 *38*
Q2 PP4 2 l lt bl grn 35 *48*
Q3 PP4 3 l red org 40 *60*
Q4 PP4 4 l gray blk 50 *75*
Q5 PP4 5 l lil rose ('48) 1.40 *2.00*
Q6 PP4 10 l violet 2.75 *4.00*
Q7 PP4 20 l lil brn 4.00 *6.00*
Q8 PP4 50 l rose red 6.50 *9.00*
Q9 PP4 100 l sapphire 8.00 *12.00*
Q10 PP4 200 l grn ('48) 325.00 *450.00*
Q11 PP4 300 l brn car ('48) 160.00 *225.00*
Q12 PP4 500 l brn ('48) 95.00 *140.00*
Nos. Q1-Q12 (12) 604.14 *850.21*

Halves Used

Q1-Q4 15
Q5 15
Q6-Q7 15
Q8 15
Q9 22
Q10 5.75
Q11 4.50
Q12 1.90

Issue dates: Nos. Q1-Q4, Q6-Q9, Oct. 1. Others, Mar. 1.

Parcel Post Stamps of Italy, 1946-54, Overprinted:

AMG-FTT AMG-FTT

1949-54
Q13 PP4 1 l gldn brn ('50) 1.10 *1.25*
Q14 PP4 2 l lt bl grn ('51) 25 *28*
Q15 PP4 3 l red org ('51) 25 *28*
Q16 PP4 4 l gray blk ('51) 32 30
Q17 PP4 5 l lil rose 35 *40*
Q18 PP4 10 l violet 45 28
Q19 PP4 20 l lil brn 48 28
Q20 PP4 30 l plum ('52) 65 *70*
Q21 PP4 50 l rose red ('50) 80 28
Q22 PP4 100 l saph ('50) 2.50 *3.00*
Q23 PP4 200 l green 22.50 *32.50*
Q24 PP4 300 l brn car ('50) 67.50 *85.00*
Q25 PP4 500 l brn ('51) 42.50 *50.00*

Perf. 13x13½
Q26 PP5 1000 l ultra ('54) 110.00 *150.00*
Nos. Q13-Q26 (14) 249.65 *324.55*

Halves Used

Q13-Q18, Q20 15
Q19, Q22 15
Q21 15
Q23 15
Q24 60
Q25 70
Q26 1.40

Pairs of Q18 exist with 5mm between overprints instead of 11mm. Value $800.

Issue dates: 20 l, 200 l, Nov. 22. 5 l, 10 l, Nov. 28. 300 l, Jan. 19. 50 l, Mar. 10. 1 l, Oct. 7. 100 l, Nov. 9. 500 l, Nov. 25. 2 l, 3 l, 4 l, Aug. 1. 30 l, Mar. 6. 1000 l, Aug. 12.

PARCEL POST AUTHORIZED DELIVERY STAMPS

For the payment of a special tax for the authorized delivery of parcels privately instead of through the post office. Both unused and used values are for complete stamps.

Parcel Post Authorized Delivery Stamps of Italy 1953 Overprinted in Black like Nos. Q13-Q26

1953, July 8 Wmk. 277
QY1 PAD1 40 l org red 2.50 *1.00*
QY2 PAD1 50 l ultra 2.50 *1.00*
QY3 PAD1 75 l brown 2.50 *1.00*
QY4 PAD1 110 l lil rose 2.50 *1.00*

Halves Used

QY1 15
QY2 20
QY3-QY4 35

IVORY COAST

LOCATION — West coast of Africa, bordering on Gulf of Guinea
GOVT. — Republic
AREA — 127,520 sq. mi.
POP. — 8,500,000 (est. 1984)
CAPITAL — Abidjan

The former French colony of Ivory Coast became part of French West Africa and used its stamps, starting in 1945. On December 4, 1958, Ivory Coast became a republic, with full independence on August 7, 1960.

100 Centimes = 1 Franc

Catalogue values for unused stamps in this country are for Never Hinged items, beginning with Scott 167 in the regular postage section, Scott B15 in the semi-postal section, Scott C14 in the airpost section, Scott J19 in the postage due section, Scott M1 in the military section, and Scott O1 in the official section.

Navigation and Commerce — A1

Perf. 14x13½

1892-1900 Typo. Unwmk.

Name of Colony in Blue or Carmine

No.	Type	Description	Unused	Used
1	A1	1c black, *lil bl*	60	60
2	A1	2c brown, *buff*	85	85
3	A1	4c claret, *lav*	1.50	1.25
4	A1	5c green, *grnsh*	4.50	2.75
5	A1	10c blk, *lavender*	5.25	3.75
6	A1	10c red ('00)	47.50	42.50
7	A1	15c blue, quadrille paper	7.00	4.25
8	A1	15c gray ('00)	3.75	1.25
9	A1	20c red, *green*	7.00	6.00
10	A1	25c black, *rose*	7.00	1.25
11	A1	25c bl ('00)	13.00	8.50
12	A1	30c brn, *bister*	10.50	8.50
13	A1	40c red, *straw*	8.00	7.00
14	A1	50c car, *rose*	37.50	24.00
15	A1	50c brn, *azure* ('00)	7.50	4.75
16	A1	75c deep vio, *org*	15.00	8.50
17	A1	1fr brnz grn, *straw*	17.50	15.00
		Nos. 1-17 (17)	193.95	140.70

Perf. 13½x14 stamps are counterfeits.
For surcharges see Nos. 18-20, 37-41.

Nos. 12, 16-17 Surcharged in Black

0,05

1904

No.	Type	Description	Unused	Used
18	A1	0,05c on 30c brn, *bis*	32.50	32.50
19	A1	0,10c on 75c vio, *org*	6.25	6.25
20	A1	0,15c on 1fr brnz grn, *straw*	6.50	6.50

Gen. Louis Faidherbe — A2

Oil Palm — A3

Dr. N. Eugene Ballay — A4

1906-07

Name of Colony in Red or Blue

No.	Type	Description	Unused	Used
21	A2	1c slate	60	60
22	A2	2c chocolate	60	60
23	A2	4c choc, *gray bl*	75	75
a.		Name double	75.00	75.00
24	A2	5c green	75	75
25	A2	10c carmine (B)	2.50	1.90
26	A3	20c black, *azure*	3.25	2.75
27	A3	25c bl, *pinkish*	2.50	1.90
28	A3	30c choc, *pnksh*	5.25	2.75
30	A3	35c black, *yel*	5.25	1.75
31	A3	45c choc, *grnsh*	6.00	4.50
32	A3	50c deep violet	6.00	4.50
33	A3	75c blue, *org*	6.75	4.50
34	A4	1fr black, *azure*	15.00	11.50
35	A4	2fr blue, *pink*	22.50	15.00
36	A4	5fr car, *straw* (B)	37.50	32.50
		Nos. 21-36 (15)	115.20	86.25

Stamps of 1892-1900 Surcharged in Carmine or Black

05 10

1912

No.	Type	Description	Unused	Used
37	A1	5c on 15c gray (C)	32	32
38	A1	5c on 30c brn, *bis* (C)	60	60
39	A1	10c on 40c red, *straw*	60	60
a.		Pair, one without surcharge	62.50	
40	A1	10c on 50c brn, *az* (C)	70	70
41	A1	10c on 75c dp vio, *org*	4.00	4.00
		Nos. 37-41 (5)	6.22	6.22

Two spacings between the surcharged numerals are found on Nos. 37 to 41.

River Scene — A5

1913-35

No.	Type	Description	Unused	Used
42	A5	1c vio brn & vio	15	15
43	A5	2c brown & blk	15	15
44	A5	4c vio & vio brn	15	15
45	A5	5c yel grn & bl grn	15	15
46	A5	5c choc & ol brn ('22)	15	15
47	A5	10c red org & rose	35	30
48	A5	10c yel grn & bl grn ('22)	15	15
49	A5	10c car rose, *bluish* ('26)	15	15
50	A5	15c org & rose ('17)	32	15
51	A5	20c black & gray	25	15
52	A5	25c ultra & bl	2.75	1.90
53	A5	25c blk & vio ('22)	15	15
54	A5	30c choc & brn	60	40
55	A5	30c red org & rose ('22)	60	60
56	A5	30c lt bl & rose red ('26)	15	15
57	A5	30c dl grn & grn ('27)	15	15
58	A5	35c vio & org	25	15
59	A5	40c gray & bl grn	60	32
60	A5	45c red org & choc	25	18
61	A5	45c dp rose & mar ('34)	2.50	2.25
62	A5	50c black & vio	1.40	1.25
63	A5	50c ultra & bl ('22)	25	25
64	A5	50c ol grn & bl ('25)	15	15
65	A5	60c vio, *pnksh* ('25)	15	15
66	A5	65c car rose & ol grn ('26)	60	60
67	A5	75c brn & rose	25	22
68	A5	75c ind & ultra ('34)	1.25	1.10
69	A5	85c red vio & blk ('26)	60	60
70	A5	90c brn red & rose ('30)	5.00	5.00
71	A5	1fr org & black	55	50
72	A5	1.10fr dl grn & dk brn ('28)	2.50	2.50
73	A5	1.50fr lt bl & dp bl ('30)	3.25	2.50
74	A5	1.75fr lt ultra & mag ('35)	4.50	2.75
75	A5	2fr brn & blue	1.50	75
76	A5	3fr red vio ('30)	3.25	2.75
77	A5	5fr dk bl & choc	3.25	1.90
		Nos. 42-77 (36)	38.42	30.87

Nos. 45, 47, 50 and 58 exist on both ordinary and chalky paper.
For surcharges see Nos. 78-91, B1.

Stamps and Type of 1913-34 Surcharged

60 60

1922-34

No.	Type	Description	Unused	Used
78	A5	50c on 45c dp rose & maroon ('34)	1.40	75
79	A5	50c on 75c indigo & ultra ('34)	75	75
80	A5	50c on 90c brn red & rose ('34)	75	75
81	A5	60c on 75c vio, *pnksh*	16	16
82	A5	65c on 15c orange & rose ('25)	50	50
83	A5	85c on 75c brown & rose ('25)	50	50
		Nos. 78-83 (6)	4.06	3.41

Stamps and Type of 1913 Surcharged with New Value and Bars

1924-27

No.	Type	Description	Unused	Used
84	A5	25c on 2fr brown & blue (R)	40	35
85	A5	25c on 5fr dk bl & choc	40	35
86	A5	90c on 75c brn red & cer ('27)	50	40
87	A5	1.25fr on 1fr dk bl & ultra (R) ('26)	30	22
88	A5	1.50fr on 1fr lt bl & dk blue ('27)	60	50
89	A5	3fr on 5fr brn red & bl grn ('27)	1.25	1.25
90	A5	10fr on 5fr dl red & rose lil ('27)	6.75	6.25
91	A5	20fr on 5fr bl grn & ver ('27)	7.50	7.25
		Nos. 84-91 (8)	17.70	16.57

Colonial Exposition Issue

Common Design Types

Name of Country in Black

1931 Engr. *Perf. 12½*

No.	Type	Description	Unused	Used
92	CD70	40c deep green	1.25	1.25
93	CD71	50c violet	2.50	2.50
94	CD72	90c red orange	1.10	1.10
95	CD73	1.50fr dull blue	2.50	2.50

Côte d'Ivoire

Stamps of Upper Volta 1928, Overprinted

1933 *Perf. 13½x14*

No.	Type	Description	Unused	Used
96	A5	2c brown & lilac	15	15
97	A5	4c blk & yellow	15	15
98	A5	5c ind & gray bl	22	18
99	A5	10c indigo & pink	25	22
100	A5	15c brown & blue	30	25
101	A5	20c brown & green	30	30
102	A6	25c brn & yellow	75	60
103	A6	30c dp grn & brn	90	75
104	A6	45c brown & blue	3.75	3.00
105	A6	65c indigo & bl	1.25	90
106	A6	75c black & lilac	1.50	1.10
107	A6	90c brn red & lil	1.25	1.10

Common Design Types pictured in section at front of book.

Overprinted

Côte d'Ivoire

No.	Type	Description	Unused	Used
108	A7	1fr brown & green	1.25	1.10
109	A7	1.50fr ultra & grysh	1.25	1.10

Surcharged

Côte d'Ivoire 1F.25

No.	Type	Description	Unused	Used
110	A6	1.25fr on 40c blk & pink	1.10	75
111	A6	1.75fr on 50c blk & green	1.25	80
		Nos. 96-111 (16)	15.62	12.45

Baoule Woman — A6

Rapids on Comoe River — A9

Mosque at Bobo-Dioulasso — A7

Coastal Scene — A8

1936-44 *Perf. 13*

No.	Type	Description	Unused	Used
112	A6	1c carmine rose	15	15
113	A6	2c ultramarine	15	15
114	A6	3c dp grn ('40)	15	15
115	A6	4c chocolate	15	15
116	A6	5c violet	15	15
117	A6	10c Prussian bl	15	15
118	A6	15c copper red	15	15
119	A7	20c ultramarine	15	15
120	A7	25c copper red	15	15
121	A7	30c blue green	15	15
122	A7	30c brown ('40)	15	15
123	A6	35c dp grn ('38)	15	15
124	A7	40c carmine rose	15	15
125	A7	45c brown	25	22
126	A7	45c blue grn ('40)	15	15
127	A7	50c plum	15	15
128	A7	55c dark vio ('38)	15	15
129	A8	60c car rose ('40)	15	15
130	A8	65c red brown	15	15
131	A8	70c red brn ('40)	22	22
132	A8	75c dark violet	25	15
133	A8	80c blk brn ('38)	30	30
134	A8	90c carmine rose	3.75	2.25
135	A8	90c dk grn ('39)	22	22
136	A8	1fr dark green	1.25	60
137	A8	1fr car rose ('38)	22	15
138	A8	1fr dk vio ('40)	15	15
139	A8	1.25fr copper red	22	15
140	A8	1.40fr ultra ('40)	15	15
141	A8	1.50fr ultramarine	15	15
141A	A8	1.50fr grnsh blk ('44)	16	16
142	A8	1.60fr blk brn ('40)	35	35
143	A9	1.75fr carmine rose	16	15
144	A9	1.75fr dull bl ('38)	25	22
145	A9	2fr ultramarine	25	15
146	A9	2.25fr dark bl ('39)	35	35
147	A9	2.50fr rose red ('40)	40	40
148	A9	3fr green	35	22
149	A9	5fr chocolate	40	35
150	A9	10fr violet	52	45
151	A9	20fr copper red	1.25	90
		Set value	12.50	9.25

Stamps of types A7-A9 without "RF" were issued in 1944, but were not placed on sale in the colony.
For surcharges see Nos. B8-B11.

Paris International Exposition Issue

Common Design Types

1937 *Perf. 13*

No.	Type	Description	Unused	Used
152	CD74	20c deep vio	45	45
153	CD75	30c dark grn	45	45
154	CD76	40c car rose	60	60
155	CD77	50c dk brn & bl	45	45
156	CD78	90c red	45	45
157	CD79	1.50fr ultra	60	60
		Nos. 152-157 (6)	3.00	3.00

Colonial Arts Exhibition Issue
Souvenir Sheet
Common Design Type

1937 ***Imperf.***
158 CD76 3fr sepia 2.00 2.00

Louis Gustave Binger — A10

1937 ***Perf. 13***
159 A10 65c red brown 15 15

Death of Governor General Binger; 50th anniv. of his exploration of the Niger.

Caillie Issue
Common Design Type

1939 **Engr.** ***Perf. 12½x12***
160 CD81 90c org brn & org 32 32
161 CD81 2fr bright violet 50 50
162 CD81 2.25fr ultra & dk bl 50 50

New York World's Fair Issue
Common Design Type

1939
163 CD82 1.25fr carmine lake 65 65
164 CD82 2.25fr ultramarine 65 65

Ebrié Lagoon and Marshal Petain A11

1941
165 A11 1fr green 40
166 A11 2.50fr deep blue 40

It is doubtful whether Nos. 165-166 were placed in use.

Catalogue values for unused stamps in this section, from this point to the end of the section, are for Never Hinged items.

Republic

Elephant A12

President Felix Houphouet-Boigny A13

1959, Oct. 1 **Engr.** ***Perf. 13***
167 A12 10fr black & emerald 16 15
168 A12 25fr vio brn & olive 32 20
169 A12 30fr ol blk & grnsh bl 35 25

Imperforates

Most Ivory Coast stamps from 1959 onward exist imperforate in issued and trial colors, and also in small presentation sheets in issued colors.

1959, Dec. 4 **Unwmk.**
170 A13 25fr violet brown 30 20

Proclamation of the Republic, 1st anniv.

Bété Mask — A14

Designs: Masks of 5 tribes: Bété, Gueré, Baoule, Senufo and Guro. Nos. 174-176 are horizontal.

1960 ***Perf. 13***
171 A14 50c pale brn & vio brn 15 15
172 A14 1fr violet & mag 15 15
173 A14 2fr ultra & bl grn 15 15
174 A14 4fr dk grn & org 15 15
175 A14 5fr ver & brown 15 15
176 A14 6fr dark brn & vio 15 15
177 A14 45fr dk grn & brn vio 60 22
178 A14 50fr dk brn & grnsh bl 65 25
179 A14 85fr car & slate grn 1.10 60
Set value 2.70 1.35

C.C.T.A. Issue
Common Design Type

1960, May 16 **Engr.** ***Perf. 13***
180 CD106 25fr grnsh bl & vio 40 38

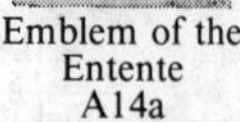

Emblem of the Entente A14a

Blood Lilies A16

Young Couple with Olive Branch and Globe — A15

1960, May 29 **Photo.** ***Perf. 13x13½***
181 A14a 25fr multicolored 42 42

1st anniv. of the Entente (Dahomey, Ivory Coast, Niger and Upper Volta).

1961, Aug. 7 **Engr.** ***Perf. 13***
182 A15 25fr emer, bis & blk 30 20

First anniversary of Independence.

1961-62

Designs: Various Local Plants & Orchids.

183 A16 5fr dk grn, red & orange ('62) 15 15
184 A16 10fr ultra, cl & yel 15 15
185 A16 15fr org, rose lil & green ('62) 20 15
186 A16 20fr brn, dk red & yel 25 16
187 A16 25fr grn, red brn & yel 38 20
188 A16 30fr blk, car & green 40 25
189 A16 70fr green, ver & yel 90 40
190 A16 85fr brn, lil, yel & grn 1.20 75
Nos. 183-190 (8) 3.63 2.21

Early Letter Carrier and Modern Mailman — A17

1961, Oct. 14 **Unwmk.** ***Perf. 13***
191 A17 25fr choc, emer & bl 35 25

Issued for Stamp Day.

Ayamé Dam — A18

1961, Nov. 18 **Engr.**
192 A18 25fr grnsh bl, blk & grn 30 18

Swimming Race — A19

1961, Dec. 23 **Unwmk.** ***Perf. 13***
193 A19 5fr shown 15 15
194 A19 20fr Basketball 20 15
195 A19 25fr Soccer 25 15
Set value 50 35

Abidjan Games, Dec. 24-31. See No. C17.

Palms — A20

1962, Feb. 5 **Photo.** ***Perf. 12x12½***
196 A20 25fr brn, blue & org 30 18

Commission for Technical Co-operation in Africa South of the Sahara, 17th session, Abidjan, Feb. 5-16.

Fort Assinie and Assinie River — A21

1962, May 26 **Engr.** ***Perf. 13***
197 A21 85fr Prus grn, grn & dl red brn 1.00 55

Centenary of the Ivory Coast post.

African and Malagasy Union Issue
Common Design Type

1962, Sept. 8 **Photo.** ***Perf. 12½x12***
198 CD110 30fr multicolored 75 55

African and Malagasy Union, 1st anniv.

Fair Emblem, Cotton and Spindles — A22

1963, Jan. 26 **Engr.** ***Perf. 13***
199 A22 50fr grn, brn org & sep 45 25

Bouake Fair, Jan. 26-Feb. 4.

Stylized Map of Africa A23

1963, May 25 **Photo.** ***Perf. 12½x12***
200 A23 30fr ultra & emerald 40 40

Conference of African heads of state for African unity, Addis Ababa.

Hartebeest A24

UNESCO Emblem, Scales and Globe A25

Designs: 1fr, Yellow-backed duiker (horiz). 2fr, Potto. 4fr, Beecroft's hyrax (horiz.). 5fr, Water chevrotain. 15fr, Forest hog (horiz.). 20fr, Wart hog (horiz.). 25fr, Bongo (antelope). 45fr, Cape hunting dogs, or hyenas (horiz.). 50fr, Black-and-white colobus (monkey).

1963-64 **Engr.** ***Perf. 13***
201 A24 1fr choc, grn & yellow ('64) 15 15
202 A24 2fr blk, dk bl, gray ol & brown ('64) 15 15
203 A24 4fr red brn, dk bl, brn & black ('64) 15 15
204 A24 5fr sl grn, brn & citron ('64) 15 15
205 A24 10fr ol grn & ocher 16 15
206 A24 15fr red brn, grn & black ('64) 25 15
207 A24 20fr red org grn & blk 40 16
208 A24 25fr red brn & green 42 16
209 A24 45fr choc, bl grn & yel green 75 42
210 A24 50fr red brn, grn & blk 80 40
a. Min. sheet of 4, #205, 207, 209-210 1.75 1.75
Nos. 201-210 (10) 3.38
Set value 1.55

See Nos. 218-220.

1963, Dec. 10 **Unwmk.**
211 A25 85fr dk bl, blk & org 80 50

Universal Declaration of Human Rights, 15th anniv.

Sun Radiating from Ivory Coast over Africa A26

Weather Station and Balloon A27

1964, Mar. 17 Photo. *Perf. 12x12½*
212 A26 30fr grn, dl vio & red 35 20

Inter-African Conference of Natl. Education Ministers.

1964, Mar. 23 *Perf. 13x12½*
213 A27 25fr multicolored 30 22

World Meteorological Day, Mar. 23.

Physician Vaccinating Child — A28

1964, May 8 Engr. *Perf. 13*
214 A28 50fr dk brn, bl & red 55 35

Issued to honor the National Red Cross.

Wrestlers, Globe and Torch — A29

1964, June 27 Unwmk. *Perf. 13*
215 A29 35fr Globe, torch, athletes, vert. 45 35
216 A29 65fr shown 80 65

18th Olympic Games, Tokyo, Oct. 10-25.

Europafrica Issue, 1964
Common Design Type

Design: 30fr, White man and black man beneath tree of industrial symbols.

1964, July 20 Photo. *Perf. 12x13*
217 CD116 30fr multicolored 30 20

Animal Type of 1963-64

Designs: 5fr, Manatee (horiz.). 10fr, Pygmy hippopotamus (horiz.). 15fr, Royal antelope.

1964, Oct. 17 Engr. *Perf. 13*
218 A24 5fr yel grn, sl grn & brn 15 15
219 A24 10fr sep, Prus grn & dp cl 20 15
220 A24 15fr lil rose, grn & org brn 35 20
Set value 35

Co-operation Issue
Common Design Type

1964, Nov. 7 Unwmk. *Perf. 13*
221 CD119 25fr grn, dk brn & red 30 22

Korhogo Mail Carriers with Guard, 1914 — A30

1964, Nov. 28 Engr.
222 A30 85fr blk, brn, bl & brn red 80 60

Issued for Stamp Day.

Potter — A31

Artisans: 10fr, Wood carvers. 20fr, Ivory carver. 25fr, Weaver.

1965, Mar. 27 Engr. *Perf. 13*
223 A31 5fr mag, green & blk 15 15
224 A31 10fr red lil, grn & blk 15 15
225 A31 20fr bis, dp bl & dk brn 20 15
226 A31 25fr brn, olive & car 25 16
Set value 64 38

Unloading Mail, 1900 — A32

1965, Apr. 24 Unwmk. *Perf. 13*
227 A32 30fr multicolored 35 22

Issued for Stamp Day.

ITU Emblem, Old and New Telecommunication Equipment — A32a

1965, May 17
228 A32a 85fr mar, brt grn & dk bl 90 60

ITU, centenary.

Abidjan Railroad Station A33

1965, June 12 Engr. *Perf. 13*
229 A33 30fr mag, bl & brn ol 35 22

Pres. Felix Houphouet-Boigny and Map of Ivory Coast — A34

1965, Aug. 7 Photo. *Perf. 12½x13*
230 A34 30fr multicolored 35 22

Fifth anniversary of Independence.

Hammerhead Stork — A35

Baoulé Mother and Child, Carved in Wood — A37

Mail Train, 1906 — A36

Birds: 1fr, Bruce's green pigeon (horiz.). 2fr, Spur-winged goose (horiz.). 5fr, Stone partridge. 15fr, White-breasted guinea fowl. 30fr, Namaqua dove (horiz.). 50fr, Lizard buzzard (horiz.). 75fr, Yellow-billed stork. 90fr, Forest (or Latham's) francolin.

1965-66 Engr. *Perf. 13*
231 A35 1fr yel grn, pur & yellow ('66) 15 15
232 A35 2fr slate grn, blk & red ('66) 15 15
233 A35 5fr dk ol, dk brn & brn red ('66) 15 15
234 A35 10fr red lil, blk & red brown 15 15
235 A35 15fr sl grn, gray & ver 20 15
236 A35 30fr sl grn, mar & red brown 40 20
237 A35 50fr brn, blk & chlky bl 60 35
238 A35 75fr org, mar & sl grn 80 40
239 A35 90fr emerald, blk & brown ('66) 1.25 65
Nos. 231-239 (9) 3.85 2.35

1966, Mar. 26 Engr. *Perf. 13*
240 A36 30fr grn, blk & mar 38 22

Issued for Stamp Day.

1966, Apr. 9 Unwmk.

Designs: 10fr, Unguent vessel, Wamougo mask lid. 20fr, Atie carved drums. 30fr, Bete female ancestral figure.

241 A37 5fr blk & emerald 15 15
242 A37 10fr purple & blk 16 15
243 A37 20fr orange & blk 35 22
244 A37 30fr red & black 45 25
Set value 66

Intl. Negro Arts Festival, Dakar, Senegal, Apr. 1-24.

Hotel Ivoire — A38

1966, Apr. 30 Engr. *Perf. 13*
245 A38 15fr bl, grn, red & ol 20 15

Farm Tractor A39

1966, Aug. 7 Photo. *Perf. 12½x12*
246 A39 30fr multicolored 30 22

6th anniversary of independence.

Uniformed Teacher and Villagers A40

1966, Sept. 1 Engr. *Perf. 13*
247 A40 30fr dk red, ind & dk brn 30 22

National School of Administration.

Veterinarian Treating Cattle A41

1966, Oct. 22 Engr. *Perf. 13*
248 A41 30fr ol, bl & dp brn 35 25

Campaign against cattle plague.

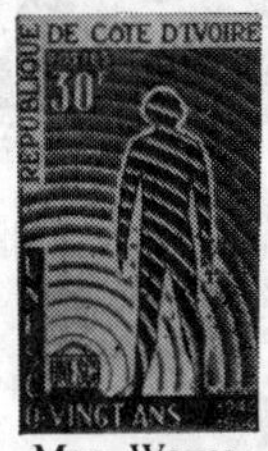

Man, Waves, UNESCO Emblem — A42

Delivery of Gift Parcels — A43

1966, Nov. 14 Engr. *Perf. 13*
249 A42 30fr dp bl & vio brn 35 25

UNESCO, 20th anniv.

1966, Dec. 11 Engr. *Perf. 13*
250 A43 30fr dk bl, brn & blk 35 25

UNICEF, 20th anniv.

Bouaké Hospital and Red Cross — A44

1966, Dec. 20
251 A44 30fr red brn, red & lil 35 25

Sikorsky S-43 Seaplane and Boats — A45

1967, Mar. 25 Engr. *Perf. 13*
252 A45 30fr ind, bl grn & brn 40 25

Stamp Day; 30th anniv. of the Sikorsky S-43 flying boat route.

Pineapple Harvest A46

1967 **Engr.** ***Perf. 13***
253 A46 20fr shown 20 15
254 A46 30fr Cabbage tree 30 15
255 A46 100fr Bananas 1.10 60

Issue dates: 30fr, June 24; others, Mar. 25.

Genie, Protector of Assamlangangan A47

1967, July 31 **Engr.** ***Perf. 13***
256 A47 30fr grn, blk & mar 30 15

Intl. PEN Club (writers' organization), 25th Congress, Abidjan, July 31-Aug. 5.

Old and New Houses A48

1967, Aug. 7 **Photo.** ***Perf. 12½x12***
257 A48 30fr multicolored 30 16

7th anniversary of independence.

Lions Emblem and Elephant's Head — A49

1967, Sept. 2 **Photo.** ***Perf. 12½x13***
258 A49 30fr lt bl & multi 40 30

50th anniversary of Lions International.

Monetary Union Issue
Common Design Type

1967, Nov. 4 **Engr.** ***Perf. 13***
259 CD125 30fr car, sl grn & blk 25 20

Allegory of French Recognition of Ivory Coast — A50

Tabou Radio Station — A51

1967, Nov. 17 **Photo.** ***Perf. 13x12½***
260 A50 90fr multicolored 80 50

Days of Recognition, 20th anniv. See No. 298.

1968, Mar. 9 **Engr.** ***Perf. 13***
261 A51 30fr dk grn, brn & brt grn 35 20

Issued for Stamp Day.

Cotton Mill — A52

Designs: 5fr, Palm oil extraction plant. 15fr, Abidjan oil refinery. 20fr, Unloading raw cotton and spinning machine (vert.). 30fr, Flour mill. 50fr, Cacao butter extractor. 70fr, Instant coffee factory (vert.). 90fr, Saw mill and timber.

1968 **Engr.** ***Perf. 13***
262 A52 5fr ver, sl grn & blk 15 15
263 A52 10fr dk grn, gray & olive bister 15 15
264 A52 15fr ver, lt ultra & blk 20 15
265 A52 20fr Prus blue & choc 20 15
266 A52 30fr dk grn, brt bl & brown 35 16
267 A52 50fr red, brt grn & blk 45 22
268 A52 70fr dk brn, bl & brn 65 40
269 A52 90fr dp bl, blk & brn 90 42
Nos. 262-269 (8) 3.05
Set value 1.50

Issue dates: 5fr, 15fr, June 8. 10fr, 20fr, 90fr, Mar. 23. Others, Oct. 5.

Canoe Race — A53

1968, Apr. 6 **Engr.** ***Perf. 13***
270 A53 30fr shown 35 20
271 A53 100fr Runners 1.00 60

19th Olympic Games, Mexico City, Oct. 12-27.

Queen Pokou Sacrificing her Son — A54

1968, Aug. 7 **Photo.** ***Perf. 12½x12***
272 A54 30fr multicolored 30 16

8th anniversary of independence.

Vaccination, WHO Emblem and Elephant's Head — A55

1968, Sept. 28 **Engr.** ***Perf. 13***
273 A55 30fr choc, brt bl & mar 35 20

WHO, 20th anniversary.

Antelope in Forest — A56

1968, Oct. 26 **Engr.** ***Perf. 13***
274 A56 30fr ultra, brn & olive 40 20

Protection of fauna and flora.

Abidjan Anthropological Museum and Carved Screen — A57

1968, Nov. 2
275 A57 30fr vio bl, ol & rose mag 30 16

Human Rights Flame and Statues of "Justitia" A58

1968, Nov. 9 **Engr.** ***Perf. 13***
276 A58 30fr sl, org & dk brn 35 20

International Human Rights Year.

"Ville de Maranhao" at Grand Bassam A59

1969, Mar. 8 **Engr.** ***Perf. 13***
277 A59 30fr brn, brt bl & grn 38 20

Issued for Stamp Day.

Opening of Hotel Ivoire, Abidjan — A60

1969, Mar. 29
278 A60 30fr ver, bl & grn 30 16

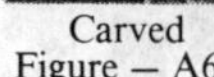

Carved Figure — A61

Mountains and Radio Tower, Man — A62

1969, July 5 **Engr.** ***Perf. 13***
279 A61 30fr red lil, blk & red org 30 16

Ivory Coast art exhibition, Fine Arts Museum, Vevey, Switzerland, July 12-Sept. 22.

1969, Aug. 7 **Engr.** ***Perf. 13***
280 A62 30fr dl brn, sl & grn 35 20

9th anniversary of independence.

Development Bank Issue
Common Design Type

Design: Development Bank emblem and Ivory Coast coat of arms.

1969, Sept. 6
281 CD130 30fr ocher, grn & mar 30 16

Arms of Bouake A63

Sport Fishing and SKAL Emblem A64

Coats of Arms: 15fr, Abidjan. 30fr, Ivory Coast.

1969 **Photo.** ***Perf. 13***
282 A63 10fr multicolored 15 15
283 A63 15fr multicolored 15 15
284 A63 30fr multicolored 22 15
Set value 18

Issue dates: 10fr, Oct. 25; 15fr, Dec. 27; 30fr, Dec. 20.

See Nos. 335-336, designs A113, A297.

1969, Nov. 22 **Engr.** ***Perf. 13***
285 A64 30fr shown 35 20
286 A64 100fr Vacation village, SKAL emblem 1.00 50

1st Intl. Congress in Africa of the SKAL Tourist Assoc., Abidjan, Nov. 23-28.

ASECNA Issue
Common Design Type

1969, Dec. 13 **Engr.** ***Perf. 13***
287 CD132 30fr vermilion 30 16

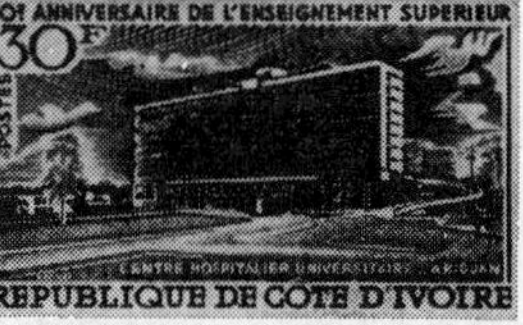

University Center, Abidjan — A65

1970, Feb. 26 **Engr.** ***Perf. 13***
288 A65 30fr indigo & yel grn 25 15

Higher education in Ivory Coast, 10th anniv.

Gabriel Dadie and Telegraph Operator A66

1970, Mar. 7 **Engr.** ***Perf. 13***
289 A66 30fr dk red, sl grn & blk 25 15

Stamp Day; Gabriel Dadié (1891-1953) 1st native-born postal administrator.

University of Abidjan — A67

1970, Mar. 21 **Photo.**
290 A67 30fr Prus bl, dk pur & dk yel grn 25 15

3rd General Assembly of the Assoc. of French-language Universities (A.U.P.E.L.F.).

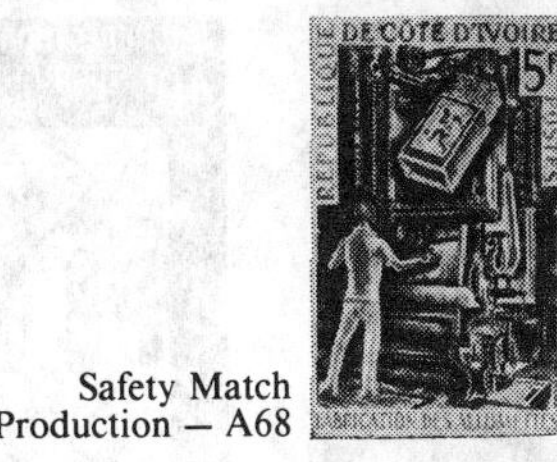
Safety Match Production — A68

1970, May 9 Engr. *Perf. 13*

291 A68 5fr shown	15	15
292 A68 20fr Textile industry	16	15
293 A68 50fr Shipbuilding	40	20
Set value	60	30

Radar, Classroom with Television — A69

1970, May 17
294 A69 40fr red, grn & gray ol 40 35

Issued for World Telecommunications Day.

UPU Headquarters Issue
Common Design Type

1970, May 20
295 CD133 30fr lil, brt grn & ol 35 16

UN Emblem, Lion, Antelopes and Plane A70

1970, June 27 Engr. *Perf. 13*
296 A70 30fr dk red brn, ultra & dk green 38 25

25th anniversary of the United Nations.

Coffee Branch and Bags Showing Increased Production — A71

1970, Aug. 7 Engr. *Perf. 13*
297 A71 30fr org, bluish grn & gray 25 15

Tenth anniversary of independence.

Type of 1967

1970, Oct. 29 Photo. *Perf. 12x12½*
298 A50 40fr multicolored 38 20

Ivory Coast Democratic Party, 5th Congress.

Power Plant at Uridi — A73

1970, Nov. 21 Engr. *Perf. 13*
299 A73 40fr multicolored 38 16

Postal Service Autobus, 1925 — A74

1971, Mar. 6 Engr. *Perf. 13*
300 A74 40fr dp grn, dk brn & gldn brn 35 16

Stamp Day.

Marginella Desjardini A75

Marine Life: 1fr, Aporrhaispes gallinae. 5fr, Neptunus validus. 10fr, Hermodice carunculata (vert.). No. 305, Natica fanel (vert.). No. 306, Goniaster cuspidatus (vert.). No. 307, Xenorhora digitata. 25fr, Conus prometheus. 35fr, Polycheles typhlops (vert.). No. 310, Conus genuanus. No. 311, Chlamys flabellum. 45fr, Strombus bubonius. 50fr, Enoplometopus callistus (vert.). 65fr, Cypraea stercoraria.

1971-72 Engr. *Perf. 13*

301 A75 1fr olive & multi	15	15
302 A75 5fr red & multi	15	15
303 A75 10fr emer & multi	15	15
304 A75 15fr brt bl & multi	16	15
305 A75 15fr dp car & multi ('72)	16	15
306 A75 20fr ocher & car	20	15
307 A75 20fr ver & multi ('72)	22	15
308 A75 25fr dk car, rose brn & black ('72)	22	15
309 A75 35fr yel & multi	30	16
310 A75 40fr emer & multi	45	25
311 A75 40fr brown & multi	38	20
312 A75 45fr multi ('72)	40	25
313 A75 50fr green & multi	60	38
314 A75 65fr bl, rose brn & sl grn ('72)	60	40
Nos. 301-314 (14)	4.14	
Set value		2.30

Issue dates: Nos. 304, 306, 310, Apr. 24, 1971; 5fr, 35fr, 50fr, June 5, 1971; 1fr, 10fr, No. 311, Oct. 23, 1971; 25fr, 65fr, Jan. 29, 1972; Nos. 305, 307, 45fr, June 3, 1972.

Submarine Cable Station, 1891 — A76

1971, May 17
315 A76 100fr bl, ocher & olive 75 45

3rd World Telecommunications Day.

Apprentice and Lathe — A77

1971, June 19 Engr. *Perf. 13*
316 A77 35fr grn, sl & org brn 30 16

Technical instruction and professional training.

Map of Africa and Telecommunications System — A78

1971, June 26 *Perf. 13x12½*
317 A78 45fr magenta & multi 38 20

Pan-African Telecommunications system.

Bondoukou Market — A79

1971, Aug. 7 Engr. *Perf. 13*
Size: 48x27mm
318 A79 35fr ultra, brn & sl 30 16

11th anniv. of independence. See No. C46.

White, Black and Yellow Girls — A80

1971, Oct. 10 Photo. *Perf. 13*
319 A80 40fr shown 35 16
320 A80 45fr Boys around globe 38 20

Intl. Year Against Racial Discrimination.

Gaming Table and Lottery Tickets A81

1971, Nov. 13 *Perf. 12½*
321 A81 35fr green & multi 25 16

National lottery.

Electric Power Installations — A82

1971, Dec. 18 *Perf. 13*
322 A82 35fr red brn & multi 35 16

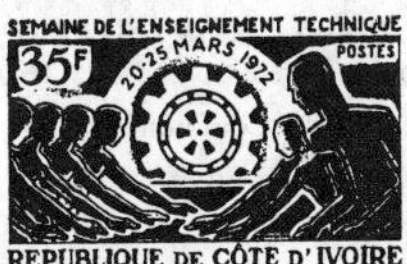
Cogwheel and Workers A83

1972, Mar. 18 Engr. *Perf. 13*
323 A83 35fr org, bl & dk brn 25 15

Technical Cooperation Week.

"Your Heart is Your Health" — A84

Girls Reading, Book Year Emblem — A85

1972, Apr. 7 Photo. *Perf. 12½x13*
324 A84 40fr bl, olive & red 35 20

World Health Day.

Perf. 12½x13, 13x12½
1972, Apr. 22 Engr.
325 A85 35fr Boys reading, horiz. 25 15
326 A85 40fr shown 35 20

International Book Year.

Postal Sorting Center, Abidjan A86

1972, May 13 *Perf. 13*
327 A86 40fr dk grn, rose lil & bis 35 15

Stamp Day.

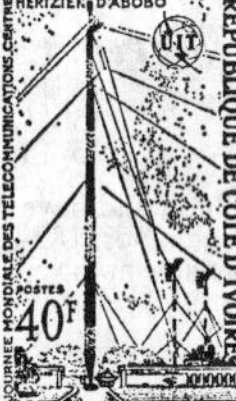
Radio Tower, Abobo, and ITU Emblem — A87

1972, May 17 Engr. *Perf. 13*
328 A87 40fr blue, red & grn 35 16

4th World Telecommunications Day.

Computer Operator, Punch Card — A88

1972, June 24
329 A88 40fr brt grn, bl & red 35 16

Development of computerized information.

View of Odienné — A89

1972, Aug. 7 Engr. *Perf. 13*
330 A89 35fr bl, grn & brn 25 16

12th anniversary of independence.

West African Monetary Union Issue
Common Design Type

1972, Nov. 2 Engr. *Perf. 13*
331 CD136 40fr brn, gray & red lil 30 15

Diamond and Diamond Mine — A90

1972, Nov. 4
332 A90 40fr Prus bl, sl & org brn 35 16

Pasteur Institute, Louis Pasteur A91

1972, Nov. 21
333 A91 35fr vio bl, grn & brn 30 20

Pasteur (1822-1895), chemist and bacteriologist.

Children at Village Pump — A92

1972, Dec. 9 **Engr.** ***Perf. 13***
334 A92 35fr dk red, grn & blk 25 15

Water campaign. See No. 360.

Arms Type of 1969

1973 **Photo.** ***Perf. 12***
335 A63 5fr Daloa 15 15
336 A63 10fr Gagnoa 15 15
Set value 15 15

Nos. 335-336 are 16½-17x22mm and have "DELRIEU" below design at right. Nos. 282-284 are 17x23mm and have no name at lower right.

Dr. Armauer G. Hansen — A93

1973, Feb. 3 **Engr.** ***Perf. 13***
342 A93 35fr lil, dp bl & brn 30 16

Centenary of the discovery of the Hansen bacillus, the cause of leprosy.

Lake Village Bletankoro — A94

1973, Mar. 10 **Engr.** ***Perf. 13***
343 A94 200fr choc, bl & grn 1.50 80

Balistes Capriscus A95

Fish: 20fr, Pseudupeneus prayensis. 25fr, Cephalopholis taeniops. 35fr, Priacanthus arenatus. 50fr, Xyrichthys novacula.

1973-74 **Engr.** ***Perf. 13***
344 A95 15fr ind & slate grn 15 15
345 A95 20fr lilac & multi 18 15
346 A95 25fr sl grn & rose ('74) 15 15
347 A95 35fr rose red & sl grn 30 16
348 A95 50fr blk, ultra & rose red 42 30
Nos. 344-348 (5) 1.20
Set value 70

Issue dates: 50fr, Mar. 24; 15fr, 20fr, July 7; 35fr, Dec. 1. 25fr, Mar. 2, 1974.

Children A96

1973, Apr. 7 **Engr.** ***Perf. 13***
354 A96 40fr grn, blk & dl red 35 16

Establishment of first children's village in Africa (SOS villages for homeless children).

Parliament, Abidjan — A97

1973, Apr. 24 **Photo.** ***Perf. 13x12½***
355 A97 100fr multicolored 70 40

112th session of the Inter-parliamentary Council.

Teacher and PAC Store — A98

1973, May 12 **Photo.** ***Perf. 13x12½***
356 A98 40fr multicolored 25 15

Commercial Action Program (PAC).

Mother, Typist, Dress Form and Pot — A99

1973, May 26
357 A99 35fr multicolored 22 15

Technical instruction for women.

Farmers, African Scout Emblem A100

1973, July 16 **Photo.** ***Perf. 13x12½***
358 A100 40fr multicolored 25 16

24th Boy Scout World Conference, Nairobi, Kenya, July 16-21.

Party Headquarters, Yamoussokro — A101

1973, Aug. 7 **Photo.** ***Perf. 13***
359 A101 35fr multicolored 22 15

Children at Dry Pump A102

1973, Aug. 16 **Engr.**
360 A102 40fr multicolored 25 15

African solidarity in drought emergency.

African Postal Union Issue
Common Design Type

1973, Sept. 12 **Engr.** ***Perf. 13***
361 CD137 100fr pur, blk & red 65 40

Decorated Arrow Heads, Abidjan Museum — A103

1973, Sept. 15 **Photo.** ***Perf. 12½x13***
362 A103 5fr blk, brn red & brn 15 15

Ivory Coast No. 1 — A104

1973, Oct. 9 **Engr.** ***Perf. 13***
363 A104 40fr emer, blk & org 30 20

Stamp Day.

Highway Intersection A105

1973, Oct. 13
364 A105 35fr bl, blk & grn 22 15

Indenie-Abidjan intersection.

Map of Africa, Federation Emblem A106

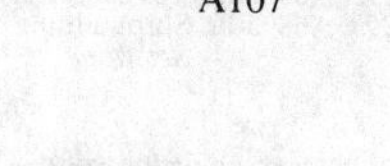

Elephant Emblem A107

1973, Oct. 26 **Photo.** ***Perf. 13***
365 A106 40fr ultra, red brn & vio bl 22 15

Intl. Social Security Federation, 18th General Assembly, Abidjan, Oct. 26-Nov. 3.

1973, Nov. 19
366 A107 40fr blk & bister 22 15

7th World Congress of the Universal Federation of World Travel Agents' Associations, Abidjan.

Kong Mosque — A108

1974, Mar. 9
367 A108 35fr bl, grn & brn 20 15

People and Sun — A109

1974, Apr. 20 **Photo.** ***Perf. 13***
368 A109 35fr multicolored 20 15

Permanent Mission to UN.

Grand Lahou Post Office — A110

1974, May 17 **Engr.** ***Perf. 13***
369 A110 35fr multicolored 20 15

Stamp Day.

Map and Flags of Members A110a

1974, May 29 **Photo.** ***Perf. 13x12½***
370 A110a 40fr blue & multi 22 15

15th anniversary of the Council of Accord.

Pres. Houphouet-Boigny
A111 A112

1974-76 Engr. *Perf. 13*

371 A111 25fr grn, org & brn 15 15
a. Booklet pane of 10 1.60
b. Booklet pane of 20 3.50
373 A112 35fr org, grn & brn 20 15
a. Booklet pane of 10 2.25
b. Booklet pane of 20 4.50
374 A112 40fr grn, org & brn 22 15
a. Booklet pane of 10 2.50
375 A112 60fr bl, car & brn ('76) 35 15
376 A112 65fr car, bl & brn ('76) 35 15
Nos. 371-376 (5) 1.27
Set value 36

See Nos. 783-792.

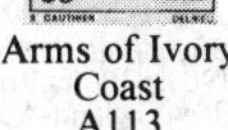

Arms of Ivory Coast A113 WPY Emblem A114

1974, June 29 Photo. *Perf. 12*

377 A113 30fr emer, brn & gold
378 A113 35fr brn, emer & gold 20 15
a. Booklet pane of 10 2.25
b. Booklet pane of 20 4.50
379 A113 40fr vio, bl, emer & gold 20 15
a. Booklet pane of 10 2.50
b. Booklet pane of 20 5.50

1976, Jan.
Inscribed: "COTE D'IVOIRE"

380 A113 60fr car, gold & emer 30 16
381 A113 65fr grn, gold & emer 35 20
382 A113 70fr bl, gold & emer 38 22
Nos. 378-382 (5) 1.43
Set value 72

1974, Aug. 19 Engr. *Perf. 13*

383 A114 40fr emer & bl 22 15

World Population Year.

Cotton Harvest — A115

1974, Sept. 21 Litho. *Perf. 12½x13*

384 A115 50fr multicolored 25 15

UPU Centenary A116

1974, Oct. 9 Engr. *Perf. 13*

385 A116 40fr multicolored 22 15

See Nos. C59-C60.

Plowing Farmer, Service Emblem A117

1974, Dec. 7 Photo. *Perf. 13*

386 A117 35fr multicolored 20 15

14th anniversary of independence.

National Library, First Anniv. — A118

1975, Jan. 9 Photo. *Perf. 13*

387 A118 40fr multicolored 22 15

Raoul Follereau and Blind Students — A119

1975, Jan. 26 Engr. *Perf. 13*

388 A119 35fr multicolored 20 15

Follereau, educator of the blind and lepers.

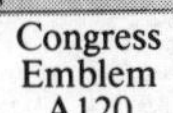

Congress Emblem A120 Coffee Cultivation A121

1975, Mar. 4 Photo. *Perf. 12½x13*

389 A120 40fr blk & emerald 22 15

52nd Congress of the Intl. Assoc. of Seed Crushers, Abidjan, Mar. 2-7.

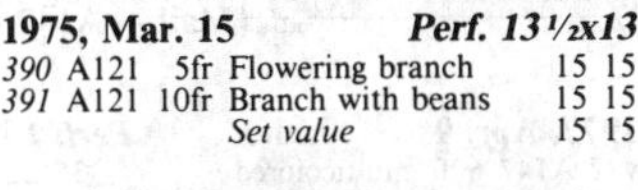

1975, Mar. 15 *Perf. 13½x13*

390 A121 5fr Flowering branch 15 15
391 A121 10fr Branch with beans 15 15
Set value 15 15

Sassandra Wharf — A122

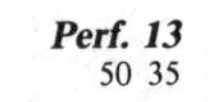

1975, Apr. 19 Engr. *Perf. 13*

392 A122 100fr multicolored 50 35

Letter Sorting A123

1975, Apr. 26 Photo. *Perf. 13*

393 A123 40fr multicolored 22 16

Stamp Day.

Cotton Flower — A124 Cotton Bolls — A125

1975, May 3 Photo. *Perf. 13*

394 A124 5fr multicolored 15 15
395 A125 10fr multicolored 15 15
Set value 15 15

Cotton cultivation.

Marie Kore, Women's Year Emblem — A126

1975, May 19 Engr. *Perf. 13*

396 A126 45fr lt bl, yel grn & brn 25 20

International Women's Year.

Fort Dabou — A127

1975, June 7 Engr. *Perf. 13*

397 A127 50fr multicolored 25 20

Abidjan Harbor — A128

Designs: 40fr, Grand Bassam wharf, 1906 (vert.). 100fr, Planned harbor expansion on Locodjro.

1975, July 1 Photo. *Perf. 13*

398 A128 135fr multicolored 20 15

Miniature Sheet

399 Sheet of 3 1.10 1.10
a. A128 40fr multicolored 20 20
b. A128 100fr multicolored 50 50

25th anniversary of Abidjan Harbor. No. 399 contains Nos. 398, 399a, 399b.

Cacao Pods on Tree — A129

1975, Aug. 2

400 A129 35fr multicolored 20 15

Farm Workers A130

1975, Oct. 4 Photo. *Perf. 13x12½*

401 A130 50fr multicolored 25 16

Natl. Org. for Rural Development.

Railroad Bridge, N'zi River — A131

1975, Dec. 7 Photo. *Perf. 13*

402 A131 60fr multicolored 35 20

15th anniversary of independence.

Baoulé Mother and Child, Carved in Wood — A132

1976, Jan. 24 Litho. *Perf. 13*

403 A132 65fr black & multi 38 22

Baoulé Mask — A133

1976, Feb. 7 Photo. *Perf. 12½*

404 A133 20fr shown 15 15
405 A133 150fr Chief Abron's chair 80 50

Scott's editorial staff cannot undertake to identify, authenticate or appraise stamps and postal markings.

Senufo Statuette — A134

Telephones 1876 and 1976 — A135

1976, Feb. 21 *Perf. 13x13½*
406 A134 25fr ocher & multi 15 15

1976, Mar. 10 Litho. *Perf. 12*
407 A135 70fr multicolored 38 25

Centenary of first telephone call by Alexander Graham Bell, Mar. 10, 1876.

Ivory Coast Map, Pigeon, Carving A136

1976, Apr. 10 Photo. *Perf. 12½*
408 A136 65fr multicolored 35 25

20th Stamp Day.

Smiling Trees and Cat — A137

Children with Books — A138

1976, June 5 Litho. *Perf. 12½*
409 A137 65fr multicolored 35 20

Nature protection.

1976, July 3 Photo. *Perf. 12½x13*
410 A138 65fr multicolored 35 22

Runner, Maple Leaf, Olympic Rings — A139

1976, July 17 Litho. *Perf. 12*
411 A139 60fr Javelin, vert. 35 22
412 A139 65fr shown 35 25

21st Olympic Games, Montreal, Canada, July 17-Aug. 1.

Cashew A140

1976, Sept. 18 *Perf. 12½*
413 A140 65fr blue & multi 35 20

Highway and Conference Emblem — A141

1976, Oct. 25 Litho. *Perf. 12½x12*
414 A141 60fr multicolored 35 22

3rd African Highway Conference, Abidjan, July 25-30.

Pres. Houphouet-Boigny A142

1976-77 Photo. *Perf. 13½x12½*
415 A142 35fr brn, red lil & blk ('77)
416 A142 40fr brt grn, ocher & brn blk 20 15
a. Bklt. pane of 12 (8#416, 4#417) 7.50
417 A142 45fr ocher, brt grn & brn blk 22 15
418 A142 60fr brn, mag & brn blk 35 15
419 A142 65fr grn, org & brn blk 35 15
Set value, #416-419 26

The 40fr and 45fr issued in booklet and coil; 35fr, 60fr and 65fr in coil only.
Stamps from booklets are imperf. on one side or two adjoining sides. Coils have control number on back of every 10th stamp.

John Paul Jones, American Marine and Ship — A143

American Bicentennial: 125fr, Count de Rochambeau and grenadier of Touraine Regiment. 150fr, Admiral Count Jean Baptiste d'Estaing and French marine. 175fr, Marquis de Lafayette and grenadier of Soissons Regiment. 200fr, Thomas Jefferson, American soldier, Declaration of Independence. 500fr, George Washington, US flag, Continental officer.

1976, Nov. 27 Litho. *Perf. 11*
421 A143 100fr multicolored 60 28
422 A143 125fr multicolored 80 35
423 A143 150fr multicolored 1.00 40
424 A143 175fr multicolored 1.10 42
425 A143 200fr multicolored 1.25 50
Nos. 421-425 (5) 4.75 1.95

Souvenir Sheet

426 A143 500fr multicolored 3.00 1.40

"Development and Solidarity" — A144

1976, Dec. 7 Photo. *Perf. 13*
427 A144 60fr multicolored 35 20

16th anniversary of independence.

Benin Head, Ivory Coast Arms — A145

1977, Jan. 15 Photo. *Perf. 13*
428 A145 65fr gold, dk brn & grn 35 20

2nd World Black and African Festival, Lagos, Nigeria, Jan. 15-Feb. 12.

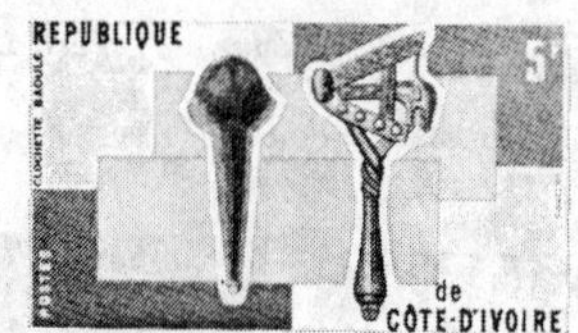

Musical Instruments — A146

1977, Mar. 5 Engr. *Perf. 13*
429 A146 5fr Baoule bells 15 15
430 A146 10fr Senufo balafon 15 15
431 A146 20fr Dida drum 15 15
Set value 24 16

Air Afrique Plane Unloading Mail — A147

1977, Apr. 9 Litho. *Perf. 13*
432 A147 60fr multicolored 35 22

Stamp Day.

Sassenage Castle, Grenoble — A148

1977, May 21 Litho. *Perf. 12½*
433 A148 100fr multicolored 50 35

Intl. French Language Council, 10th anniv.

Orville and Wilbur Wright, "Wright Flyer," 1903 — A149

History of Aviation: 75fr, Louis Bleriot crossing English Channel, 1909. 100fr, Ross Smith and Vickers-Vimy (flew England-Australia, 1919). 200fr, Charles A. Lindbergh and "Spirit of St. Louis" (flew New York-Paris, 1927). 300fr, Supersonic jet Concorde, 1976. 500fr, Lindbergh in flying suit and "Spirit of St. Louis."

1977, June 27 Litho. *Perf. 14*
434 A149 60fr multi 40 16
435 A149 75fr multi 50 20
436 A149 100fr multi 65 20
437 A149 200fr multi 1.25 40
438 A149 300fr multi 2.00 60
Nos. 434-438 (5) 4.80 1.56

Souvenir Sheet

439 A149 500fr multi 3.25 1.40

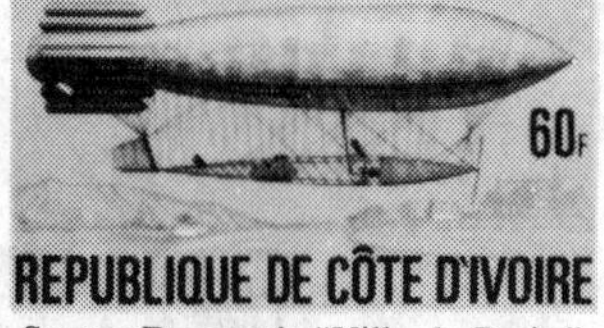

Santos Dumont's "Ville de Paris," 1907 — A150

Designs: 65fr, LZ 1 at takeoff. 150fr, "Schwaben" LZ 10 over Germany. 200fr, "Bodensee" LZ 120, 1919. 300fr, LZ 127 over Sphinx and pyramids.

1977, Sept. 3 Litho. *Perf. 11*
440 A150 60fr multi 38 16
441 A150 65fr multi 40 16
442 A150 150fr multi 90 38
443 A150 200fr multi 1.20 50
444 A150 300fr multi 1.75 75
Nos. 440-444 (5) 4.63 1.95

History of the Zeppelin. Exist imperf.
See No. C63.

Congress Emblem — A151

1977, Sept. 12 Photo. *Perf. 12½*
445 A151 60fr lt & dk grn 35 22

17th Intl. Congress of Administrative Sciences in Africa, Abidjan, Sept. 12-16.

Yamoussoukro, First Ivory Coast Container Ship — A152

1977, Nov. 12 Photo. *Perf. 13½x14*
446 A152 65fr multicolored 35 22

Hand Holding Produce, Generators, Factories — A153

1977, Dec. 7 Photo. *Perf. 13½*
447 A153 60fr multicolored 35 22

17th anniversary of independence.

Presidents Giscard d'Estaing and Houphouet-Boigny — A154

1978, Jan. 11 *Perf. 13*
448 A154 60fr multicolored 35 22
449 A154 65fr multicolored 35 22
450 A154 100fr multicolored 50 38
a. Souvenir sheet, 500fr 3.25 1.40

Visit of Pres. Valery Giscard d'Estaing. No. 450a contains one stamp.

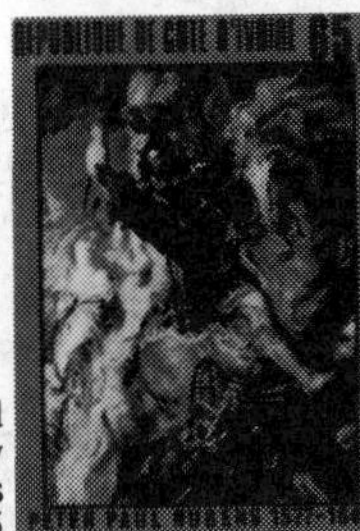
St. George and the Dragon, by Rubens A155

Paintings by Peter Paul Rubens (1577-1640): 150fr, Child's head. 250fr, Annunciation. 300fr, The Birth of Louis XIII. 500fr, Virgin and Child.

1978, Mar. 4 Litho. *Perf. 13½*
451 A155 54fr gold & multi 40 20
452 A155 150fr gold & multi 90 38
453 A155 250fr gold & multi 1.60 55
454 A155 300fr gold & multi 1.90 70

Souvenir Sheet

455 A155 500fr gold & multi 3.25 1.40

Royal Guards — A156

1978, Apr. 1 Litho. *Perf. 12½*
456 A156 60fr shown 30 16
457 A156 65fr Cosmological figures 35 20

Rural Postal Center — A157

1978, Apr. 8
458 A157 60fr multicolored 30 16

Stamp Day.

Antenna, ITU Emblem A158

1978, May 17 *Perf. 13*
459 A158 60fr multicolored 30 16

10th World Telecommunications Day.

Svante August Arrhenius, Electrolytic Apparatus — A159

Nobel Prize Winners: 75fr, Jules Bordet, child, mountains, eagle and Petri dish. 100fr, André Gide, and St. Peter's, Rome. 200fr, John Steinbeck and horse farm. 300fr, Children with flowers and UNICEF emblem. 500fr, Max Planck, rockets and earth.

1978, May 27 Litho. *Perf. 13½*
460 A159 60fr multi 38 16
461 A159 75fr multi 45 22
462 A159 100fr multi 60 30
463 A159 200fr multi 1.40 60
464 A159 300fr multi 1.90 90
Nos. 460-464 (5) 4.73 2.18

Souvenir Sheet

465 A159 500fr multi 3.25 1.40

Soccer Ball, Player and Argentina '78 Emblem — A160

Soccer Ball, Argentina '78 Emblem and: 65fr, Player (vert.). 100fr, Player (diff.). 150fr, Goalkeeper. 300fr, Ball as sun, and player (vert.). 500fr, Ball as globe with Argentina on map of South America.

1978, June 17
466 A160 60fr multi 40 16
467 A160 65fr multi 42 20
468 A160 100fr multi 60 30
469 A160 150fr multi 90 42
470 A160 300fr multi 1.90 90
Nos. 466-470 (5) 4.22 1.98

Souvenir Sheet

471 A160 500fr multi 2.50 1.40

11th World Cup Soccer Championship, Argentina, June 1-25.

Miniodes Discolor A161

Butterflies: 65fr, Charaxes lactetinctus. 100fr, Papilio zalmoxis. 200fr, Papilio antimachus.

1978, July 8 Photo. *Perf. 14x13*
472 A161 60fr multicolored 30 16
473 A161 65fr multicolored 35 20
474 A161 100fr multicolored 50 30
475 A161 200fr multicolored 1.00 60

Cricket A162

Insects: 20fr, 60fr, Various hemiptera. 65fr, Goliath beetle.

1978, Aug. 26 Litho. *Perf. 12½*
476 A162 10fr multicolored 15 15
477 A162 20fr multicolored 15 15
478 A162 60fr multicolored 30 16
479 A162 65fr multicolored 35 35
Set value 80 62

Stylized Figures Emerging from TV Screen A163

Design: 65fr, Passengers on train made up of TV sets.

1978, Sept. 18 *Perf. 13*
480 A163 60fr multicolored 30 16
481 A163 65fr multicolored 35 22

Educational television programs.

Map of Ivory Coast, Mobile Drill Platform Ship A164

Map of Ivory Coast, Ram at Discovery Site and: 65fr, Gold goblets. 500fr, Pres. Houphouet-Boigny holding gold goblets.

1978, Oct. 18 Litho. *Perf. 12½x12*
482 A164 60fr multicolored 30 16
483 A164 65fr multicolored 35 22

Souvenir Sheet

484 A164 500fr multicolored 2.50 1.40

Announcement of oil discovery off the coast of Ivory Coast, 1st anniv.

National Assembly, Paris, UPU Emblem A165

1978, Dec. 2 Litho. *Perf. 13½*
485 A165 200fr multicolored 1.25 60

Congress of Paris, centenary.

Drummer A166

Poster A167

1978, Dec. 7 Photo. *Perf. 12½x13*
486 A166 60fr multicolored 30 16

18th anniversary of independence.

1978, Dec. 12

Design: 65fr, Arrows made of flags, and television screen.

487 A167 60fr multicolored 30 16
488 A167 65fr multicolored 35 22

Technical cooperation among developing countries with the help of educational television.

Plowing — A168

1979, Jan. 27 Photo. *Perf. 13*
489 A168 100fr multicolored 50 30

King Hassan II, Pres. Houphouet-Boigny, Flags and Map of Morocco and Ivory Coast — A169

1979, Jan. 27 Photo. Perf. 13

490 A169 60fr multicolored 30 20
491 A169 65fr multicolored 35 22
492 A169 500fr multicolored 2.50 1.50

Visit of King Hassan of Morocco to Ivory Coast.

Horus — A170

1979, Feb. 17 Litho. Perf. 12½

493 A170 200fr multi 1.00 60
494 A170 500fr Vulture with ankh, cartouches 2.50 1.50

UNESCO drive to save Temples of Philae.

Flowers — A171

1979, Feb. 24

495 A171 30fr Locranthus 15 15
496 A171 60fr Vanda Josephine 30 20
497 A171 65fr Renanthera storiei 35 22

Wildlife Protection A172

1979, Mar. 24 Photo. Perf. 13x13½

498 A172 50fr Hippopotamus 35 25

Globe and Emblem A173

Child Riding Dove A174

1979, Apr. 1 Litho. Perf. 12x12½

499 A173 60fr multicolored 40 32
500 A174 65fr multicolored 42 35
501 A173 100fr multicolored 65 55
502 A174 500fr multicolored 3.50 2.50

International Year of the Child.

15-Cent Minimum Value
The minimum value for a single stamp is 15 cents. This value reflects the costs of the handlling of inexpensive stamps.

Rural Mail Delivery — A175

1979, Apr. 7 Perf. 12½

503 A175 60fr multicolored 40 32

Stamp Day.

Korhogo Cathedral — A176

1979, Apr. 9 Perf. 13

504 A176 60fr multicolored 40 32

Arrival of Catholic missionaries, 75th anniv.

Crying Child — A177

1979, May 17 Litho. Perf. 12½

505 A177 65fr multicolored 42 35

10th anniv. of SOS Village (for homeless children).

Euphaedra Xypete A178

Butterflies: 65fr, Pseudacraea bois duvali. 70fr, Auchenisa schausi.

1979, May 26 Perf. 13x13½

506 A178 60fr multicolored 40 25
507 A178 65fr multicolored 42 25
508 A178 70fr multicolored 45 28

Endangered Animals A179

1979, June 2

509 A179 5fr Antelopes 15 15
510 A179 20fr Duikerbok 15 15
511 A179 60fr Aardvark 40 25
Set value 58 38

UPU Emblem, Radar, Truck and Ship — A180

Design: No. 513, Ancestral figure and antelope (vert.).

1979, June 8 Engr. Perf. 13

512 A180 70fr multi 45 28

Photo.

513 A180 70fr multi 45 28

Philexafrique II, Libreville, Gabon, June 8-17. Nos. 512, 513 each printed in sheets of 10 with 5 labels showing exhibition emblem.

Rowland Hill, Steam Locomotive, Great Britain No. 75 — A181

Rowland Hill, Locomotives and: 75fr, Ivory Coast No. 125. 100fr, Hawaii No. 4. 150fr, Japan No. 17. 300fr, France No. 2. 500fr, Ivory Coast No. 123.

1979, July 7 Litho. Perf. 13½

514 A181 60fr multi 40 25
515 A181 75fr multi 50 30
516 A181 100fr multi 65 40
517 A181 150fr multi 1.00 60
518 A181 300fr multi 2.00 1.20
Nos. 514-518 (5) 4.55 2.75

Souvenir Sheet

519 A181 500fr multi 3.50

Sir Rowland Hill (1795-1879), originator of penny postage.

"TELECOM 79" — A182

Culture Day — A183

1979, Sept. 20 Litho. Perf. 13x12½

520 A182 60fr multicolored 40 25

3rd World Telecommunications Exhibition, Geneva, Sept. 20-26.

1979, Oct. 13 Perf. 12½

521 A183 65fr multicolored 42 25

Boxing — A184

1979, Oct. 27 Litho. Perf. 14x13½

522 A184 60fr shown 40 25
523 A184 65fr Running 42 25
524 A184 100fr Soccer 65 40
525 A184 150fr Bicycling 1.00 65
526 A184 300fr Wrestling 2.00 1.40
Nos. 530-534 (5) 4.55 3.02

Souvenir Sheet

527 A184 500fr Gymnastics 3.50 2.00

Pre-Olympic Year.

Wildlife Fund Emblem and Jentink's Duiker — A185

Wildlife Protection: 60fr, Colobus Monkey. 75fr, Manatees. 100fr, Epixerus ebii. 150fr, Hippopotamus. 300fr, Chimpanzee.

1979, Nov. 3 Litho. Perf. 14½

528 A185 40fr multi 25 16
529 A185 60fr multi 40 22
530 A185 75fr multi 50 35
531 A185 100fr multi 65 40
532 A185 150fr multi 1.00 65
533 A185 300fr multi 2.00 1.40
Nos. 528-533 (6) 4.80 3.18

Raoul Follerau Institute, Adzope — A186

1979, Dec. 6 Litho. Perf. 12½

534 A186 60fr multi 40 22

Independence, 19th Anniversary A187

1979, Dec. 7 Litho. Perf. 14x13½

535 A187 60fr multicolored 40 22

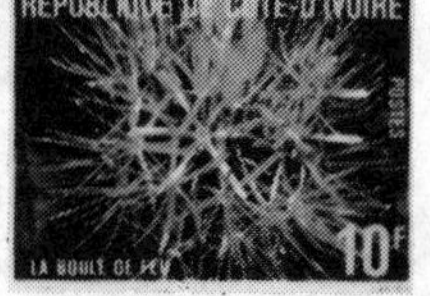

Fireball A188

Local Flora: 5fr, Clerodendron thomsonae (vert.). 50fr, Costus incanusiamus (vert.). 60fr, Ficus elastica abidjan (vert.).

1980 Litho. Perf. 12½

536 A188 5fr multicolored 15 15
537 A188 10fr multicolored 15 15
538 A188 50fr multicolored 35 20
539 A188 60fr multicolored 40 22
Set value 86 50

Issue dates: 5fr, 10fr, Jan. 26; 50fr, 60fr, Feb. 16.

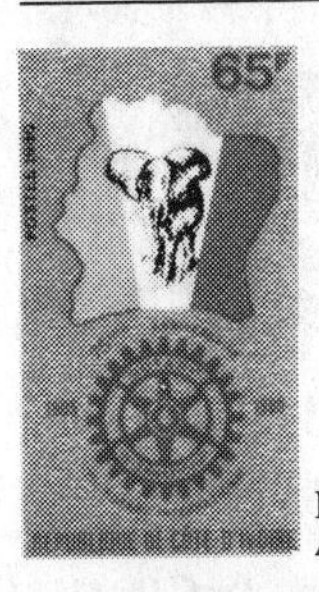

Rotary Intl., 75th Anniv. — A189

1980, Feb. 23 **Photo.** ***Perf. 13½***
540 A189 65fr multicolored 42 30

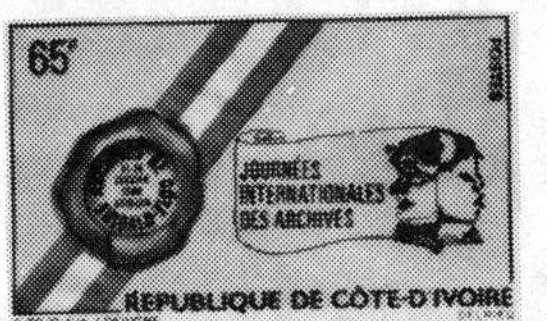

International Archives Day — A190

1980, Feb. 26 **Litho.**
541 A190 65fr multicolored 42 30

Astronaut Shaking Hands with Boy — A191

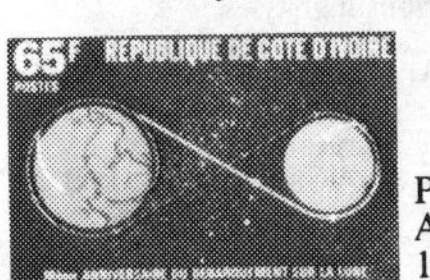

Path of Apollo 11 — A192

1980, July 6 **Photo.**
542 A191 60fr multicolored 40 25
543 A192 65fr multicolored 42 30
544 A191 70fr multicolored 45 35
545 A192 150fr multicolored 1.00 65

Apollo 11 moon landing, 10th anniv. (1979).

Jet and Map of Africa A193

1980, Mar. 22 ***Perf. 12½***
546 A193 60fr multicolored 40 22

ASECNA (Air Safety Board), 20th anniv.

Boys and Stamp Album, Globe — A194

1980, Apr. 12 **Litho.** ***Perf. 12½***
547 A194 65fr bl grn & red brn 42 25

Stamp Day; Youth philately.

Missionary and Church, Aboisso A195

1980, Apr. 26 **Photo.** ***Perf. 13x13½***
548 A195 60fr multicolored 40 22

Settlement of the Holy Fathers at Aboisso, 75th anniversary.

Fight Against Cigarette Smoking A196

1980, May 3 ***Perf. 12½***
549 A196 60fr multicolored 40 22

Pope John Paul II, Pres. Houphouet-Boigny — A197

1980, May 10 **Photo.** ***Perf. 13***
550 A197 65fr multicolored 42 30

Visit of Pope John Paul II to Ivory Coast.

Le Belier Locomotive A198

1980, May 17 **Litho.** ***Perf. 13***
551 A198 60fr shown 40 22
552 A198 65fr Abidjan Railroad Station, 1904 42 30
553 A198 100fr Passenger car, 1908 65 40
554 A198 150fr Steam locomotive, 1940 1.00 60

Central Bank of West African States, 1st Anniversary A199

1980, May 26 **Litho.** ***Perf. 12x12½***
555 A199 60fr multicolored 40 22

Lujtanus Sebae — A200

1980, Apr. 19 **Photo.** ***Perf. 14***
556 A200 60fr shown 40 22
557 A200 65fr Monodactylus sebae, vert. 42 30
558 A200 100fr Colisa fasciata 65 42

Snake — A201

1980, July 12 **Litho.** ***Perf. 12½***
559 A201 60fr shown 40 22
560 A201 150fr Toad 1.00 55

Tourists in Village, by K. Ehouman Pierre A202

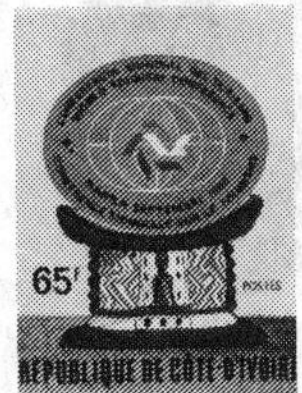

Conference Emblem — A203

1980, Aug. 9
561 A202 60fr multicolored 40 22
562 A203 65fr multicolored 42 25

National Tourist Office, Abidjan; World Tourism Conference, Manila.

Forticula Auricularia A204

Perf. 14x13, 13x14
1980, Sept. 6 **Photo.**
563 A204 60fr shown 40 22
564 A204 65fr Praying mantis, vert. 42 25

Perf. 13½x13, 13x13½
1980, Oct. 11 **Photo.**

Designs: 60fr, 200fr, Various grasshoppers.

565 A204 60fr multi, vert. 40 22
566 A204 200fr multi 1.40 70

Hands Free from Chain, Map of Ivory Coast, Pres. Houphouet-Boigny — A205

Pres. Houphouet-Boigny, Symbols of Development — A206

Perf. 12½x13, 14x14½ (A206)
1980, Oct. 18
567 A205 60fr shown 40 22
578 A206 65fr shown 42 25
569 A205 70fr Map, colors, document 45 25
570 A205 150fr like #567 1.00 55
571 A206 300fr like #568 2.00 1.10
Nos. 567-571 (5) 4.27 2.37

Pres. Houphouet-Boigny, 75th birthday.

7th PDCI and RDA Congress A207

1980, Oct. 25 ***Perf. 12½***
572 A207 60fr multicolored 40 22
573 A207 65fr multicolored 42 25

River Cruise Boat Sotra A208

1980, Dec. 6 **Litho.** ***Perf. 13x13½***
574 A208 60fr multicolored 40 22

View of Abidjan — A209

1980, Dec. 7 ***Perf. 13x12½***
575 A209 60fr multicolored 40 22

20th anniversary of independence.

Universities Association Emblem A210

African Postal Union, 5th Anniversary A211

1980, Dec. 16 *Perf. 12½*
576 A210 60fr multicolored 40 22

African Universities Assoc., 5th General Conference.

1980, Dec. 24 Photo. *Perf. 13½*
577 A211 150fr multi 1.00 55

Herichtys Cyanoguttatum — A212

1981, Mar. 14 Litho. *Perf. 12½*
578 A212 60fr shown 40 22
579 A212 65fr Labeo bicolor 42 25
580 A212 200fr Tetraodon fluviatilis 1.40 1.80

Post Office, Grand Lahou A213

25th Anniv. of Ivory Coast Philatelic Club — A214

1981, May 2 Litho. *Perf. 12½*
581 A213 60fr multicolored 40 22
582 A214 65fr multicolored 42 25

Stamp Day.

13th World Telecommunications Day — A215

1981, May 17
583 A215 30fr multicolored 20 15
584 A215 60fr multicolored 40 22

Viking Satellite Landing, 1976 — A216

Space Conquest: Columbia space shuttle.

1981, June 13 Litho. *Perf. 13½*
585 A216 60fr multi 40 22
586 A216 75fr multi 50 30
587 A216 125fr multi 80 50
588 A216 300fr multi 2.00 1.10

Souvenir Sheet

589 A216 500fr multi 3.50 1.50

Local Flowers — A217

Elephant on Flag and Map — A219

Prince Charles and Lady Diana, Coach — A218

1981, July 4 Photo. *Perf. 14½x14*
590 A217 50fr Amorphophallus 35 20
591 A217 60fr Sugar Cane 40 22
592 A217 100fr Heliconia ivoirea 65 38

1981, Aug. 8 Litho. *Perf. 12½*

Royal Wedding: Couple and coaches.

593 A218 80fr multi 55 30
594 A218 100fr multi 65 38
595 A218 125fr multi 80 42

Souvenir Sheet

596 A218 500fr multi 3.50 1.50

For overprints see Nos. 642-645.

1981, Sept. Litho. *Perf. 12½*
597 A219 80fr multicolored 55 30
598 A219 100fr multicolored 65 38
599 A219 125fr multicolored 80 42

See Nos. 662-666, 833.

Soccer Players A220

Designs: Soccer players. 70fr, 80fr, 500fr, horiz.

1981, Sept. 19 *Perf. 14*
600 A220 70fr multi 45 25
601 A220 80fr multi 55 30
602 A220 100fr multi 65 38
603 A220 150fr multi 1.00 60
604 A220 350fr multi 2.25 1.40
Nos. 600-604 (5) 4.90 2.93

Souvenir Sheet

605 A220 500fr multi 3.50 1.50

ESPANA '82 World Cup Soccer Championship.
For overprints see Nos. 651-656.

West African Rice Development Assoc., 10th Anniv. A221

1981, Oct. 3 *Perf. 12½*
606 A221 80fr multicolored 55 30

World Food Day A222

1981, Oct. 18
607 A222 100fr multicolored 65 38

Post Day A223

1981, Oct. 9 Litho. *Perf. 12½*
608 A223 70fr multicolored 45 25
609 A223 80fr multicolored 55 30
610 A223 100fr multicolored 65 38

75th Anniv. of Grand Prix — A224

Designs: Winners and their cars.

1981, Nov. 21 *Perf. 14*
611 A224 15fr Felice Nazarro, 1907 15 15
612 A224 40fr Jim Clark, 1962 25 15
613 A224 80fr Fiat, 1907 55 30
614 A224 100fr Auto Union, 1936 65 38
615 A224 125fr Ferrari, 1961 80 42
Nos. 611-615 (5) 2.40 1.40

Souvenir Sheet

616 A224 500fr 1933 car 3.50 1.90

21st Anniv. of Independence — A225

1981, Dec. 7 *Perf. 13x12½*
617 A225 50fr multicolored 35 20
618 A225 80fr multicolored 55 30

Traditional Hairstyle — A226

Rotary Emblem on Map of — A228

Stamp Day Africa — A227

Designs: Various hairstyles.

1981, Dec. 19 Photo. *Perf. 14½x14*
619 A226 80fr multicolored 55 30
620 A226 100fr multicolored 65 40
621 A226 125fr multicolored 80 50

1982, Apr. 3 Litho. *Perf. 12½x12*
622 A227 100fr Bingerville P.O., 1902 65 40

1982, Apr. 13 *Perf. 12½*
623 A228 100fr ultra & gold 65 40

Pres. Houphouet-Boigny's Rotary Goodwill Conference, Abidjan, Apr. 13-15.

250th Birth Anniv. of George Washington — A229

Anniversaries: 100fr, Auguste Piccard (1884-1962), Swiss physicist. 350fr, Goethe (1749-1832). 450fr, 500fr, Princess Diana, 21st birthday (portraits).

1982, May 15 Litho. *Perf. 13*
624 A229 80fr multi 55 30
625 A229 100fr multi 65 40
626 A229 350fr multi 2.25 1.25
627 A229 450fr multi 3.00 1.90

Souvenir Sheet

628 A229 500fr multi 3.50 2.00

Visit of French Pres. Mitterand, May 21-24 — A230

1982, May 21 Photo. ***Perf. 13½***

629	A230	100fr multicolored	65	40

14th World Telecommunications Day — A231

1982, May 29 Litho. ***Perf. 13***

630	A231	80fr multicolored	55	30

Scouting Year — A232

Designs: Scouts sailing. 80fr, 150fr, 350fr, 500fr vert.

1982, May 29 ***Perf. 12½***

631	A232	80fr multi	55	30
632	A232	100fr multi	65	40
633	A232	150fr multi	1.00	60
634	A232	350fr multi	2.25	1.25

Souvenir Sheet

635	A232	500fr multi	3.50	2.00

TB Bacillus Centenary A233

1982, June 5 Photo. ***Perf. 13x13½***

636	A233	30fr brown & multi	20	15
637	A233	80fr lt grn & multi	55	30

UN Conference on Human Environment, 10th Anniv. A234

League of Ivory Coast Secretaries, First Congress A235

1982, July Photo. ***Perf. 13½x13***

638	A234	40fr multicolored	25	15
639	A234	80fr multicolored	55	30

1982, Aug. 9 Litho. ***Perf. 12½x13***

640	A235	80fr tan & multi	55	30
641	A235	100fr silver & multi	65	40

593-596 Overprinted in Blue: "NAISSANCE / ROYALE 1982"

1982, Aug. 21 ***Perf. 12½***

642	A218	80fr multi	55	30
643	A218	100fr multi	65	40
644	A218	125fr multi	80	50

Souvenir Sheet

645	A218	500fr multi	3.50	2.00

Birth of Prince William of Wales, June 21.

La Colombe de l'Avenir, 1962, by Pablo Picasso (1881-1973) — A236

Picasso Paintings: 80fr, Child with Dove, 1901. 100fr, Self-portrait, 1901. 185fr, Les Demoiselles d'Avignon, 1907. 350fr, The Dream, 1932. Nos. 646-649 vert.

1982, Sept. 4 Litho. ***Perf. 13***

646	A236	80fr multi	55	30
647	A236	100fr multi	65	40
648	A236	185fr multi	1.25	70
649	A236	350fr multi	2.25	1.40
650	A236	500fr multi	3.50	2.00
		Nos. 646-650 (5)	8.20	4.80

Nos. 600-605 Overprinted with World Cup Winners 1966-1982 in Black on Silver

1982, Oct. 9 Litho. ***Perf. 14***

651	A220	70fr multi	45	25
652	A220	80fr multi	55	30
653	A220	100fr multi	65	38
654	A220	150fr multi	75	45
655	A220	350fr multi	2.25	1.40
		Nos. 651-655 (5)	4.65	2.78

Souvenir Sheet

656	A220	500fr multi	2.75	1.50

Italy's victory in 1982 World Cup.

13th World UPU Day — A237

Designs: 80fr, P.O. counter. 100fr, Postel-2001 building, Abidjan, vert. 350fr, Postal workers. 500fr, Postel-2001 interior.

1982, Oct. 23 ***Perf. 12½***

657	A237	80fr multi	55	30
658	A237	100fr multi	65	38
659	A237	350fr multi	2.25	1.40

Size: 48x37mm

Perf. 13

660	A237	500fr multi	3.50	1.50

22nd Anniv. of Independence — A238

1982, Dec. 7 ***Perf. 13***

661	A238	100fr multicolored	65	38

Elephant Type of 1981

1982-84

662	A219	5fr multicolored	15	15
662A	A219	10fr multi ('84)	15	15
662B	A219	20fr multicolored	15	15
663	A219	25fr multicolored	16	15
664	A219	30fr multicolored	20	15
665	A219	40fr multicolored	25	15
666	A219	50fr multicolored	35	20
		Set value	1.10	70

Man Waterfall A238a

1982 Photo. ***Perf. 15x14***

666A	A238a	80fr shown	55	30
666B	A238a	80fr Boisee Savanna	55	30
666C	A238a	500fr like #666A	3.50	1.90

Issue dates: No. 666B, Dec. 18; others, Nov. 27.

20th Anniv. of West African Monetary Union A239

1982, Dec. 21 Litho. ***Perf. 12½***

667	A239	100fr Emblem	65	38

Abouissa Children's Village A240

1983, Mar. 5 Photo. ***Perf. 13½x13***

668	A240	125fr multicolored	80	42

Anteater A241

1983, Mar. 12 Litho. ***Perf. 12½x13***

669	A241	35fr Pangolin, vert.	22	15
670	A241	90fr shown	60	35
671	A241	100fr Colobus monkey, vert.	65	38
672	A241	125fr Buffalo	80	42

Stamp Day A242

1983, Mar. 19 Litho. ***Perf. 12½***

673	A242	100fr Grand Bassam P.O., 1903	65	38

Easter 1983 — A243

Paintings by Rubens (1577-1640). 100fr, 400fr, 500fr vert.

1983, Apr. 9 ***Perf. 13***

674	A243	100fr Descent from the Cross	65	38
675	A243	125fr Resurrection	80	42
676	A243	350fr Crucifixion	2.25	1.40
677	A243	400fr Piercing of the Sword	2.50	1.50
678	A243	500fr Descent, diff.	3.50	1.90
		Nos. 674-678 (5)	9.70	5.60

25th Anniv. of UN Economic Commission for Africa A244

1983, Apr. 29 Litho. ***Perf. 13x12½***

679	A244	100fr multicolored	65	38

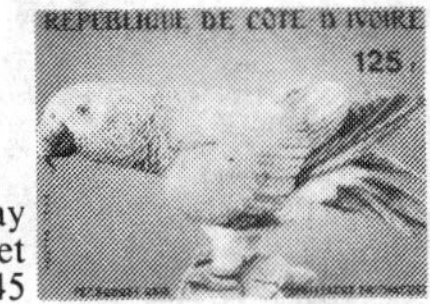

Gray Parakeet A245

1983, June 11

680	A245	100fr Fish eagle, vert.	65	38
681	A245	125fr shown	80	42
682	A245	150fr Touracoes	1.00	50

Traditional Dances — A246

1983, Sept. 3 Litho. ***Perf. 12½***

683	A246	50fr Flali, Gouro	35	20
684	A246	100fr Masked dancer, Guere	65	38
685	A246	125fr Stilt dancer, Yacouba	80	45

20th Anniv. of the Ivory Hotel, Abidjan — A249

1983, Sept. 7 ***Perf. 13***

693	A249	100fr multicolored	65	38

Ecology in Action A250

1983, Oct. 24 **Litho.**
694 A250 25fr Forest after fire 15 15
695 A250 100fr Animals fleeing 32 20
696 A250 125fr Animals grazing 40 22
Set value 47

Raphael (1483-1520), 500th Birth Anniv. — A252

Paintings: 100fr, Christ and St. Peter. 125fr, Study for St. Joseph (vert.). 350fr, Virgin of the House of Orleans (vert.). 500fr, Virgin with the Blue Diadem (vert.).

1983, Nov. 5 **Litho.** ***Perf. 13***
698 A252 100fr multi 32 20
699 A252 125fr multi 40 22
700 A252 350fr multi 1.10 62
701 A252 500fr multi 1.60 1.00

Auto Race — A253

1983, Oct. 24 **Litho.** ***Perf. 12½***
702 A253 100fr Car, map 32 20

23rd Anniv. of Independence — A255

1983, Dec. 7
706 A255 100fr multicolored 32 20

First Audio-visual Forum, Abidjan A256

1984, Jan. 25 **Litho.** ***Perf. 13x12½***
707 A256 100fr Screen, arrow 30 16

14th African Soccer Cup — A257

1984, Mar. 4 **Photo.** ***Perf. 12½***
708 A257 100fr Emblem 30 16
709 A257 200fr Maps shaking hands 60 35

Local Insects A258

1984, Mar. 24 **Litho.** ***Perf. 13***
710 A258 100fr Argiope, vert. 30 16
711 A258 125fr Polistes gallicus 38 20

Stamp Day A259

1984, Apr. 7 **Litho.** ***Perf. 12½***
712 A259 100fr Abidjan P.O., 1934 32 20

Lions Emblem A260

1984, Apr. 27 ***Perf. 13½x13***
713 A260 100fr multicolored 32 20
714 A260 125fr multicolored 40 22

3rd Convention of Multi-district 403, Abidjan, Apr. 27-29.

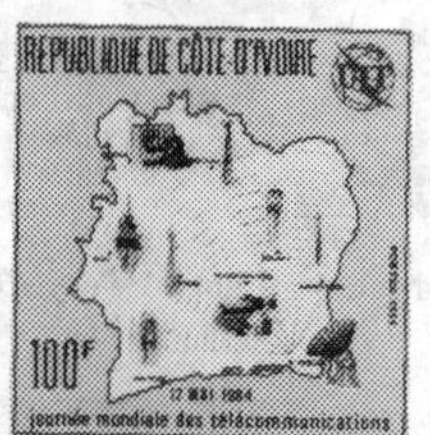

16th World Telecommunications Day — A261

1984, May 17 ***Perf. 12½***
715 A261 100fr multi 32 20

Council of Unity, 25th Anniv. — A262

1984, May 29
716 A262 100fr multicolored 32 20
717 A262 125fr multicolored 40 22

First Governmental Palace, Grand-Bassam — A263

1984, July 14 **Litho.** ***Perf. 12½***
718 A263 100fr shown 32 16
719 A263 125fr Palace of Justice, Grand-Bassam 38 20

Men Playing Eklan — A264

1984, Aug. 11 ***Perf. 13***
720 A264 100fr Board 30 16
721 A264 125fr shown 38 20

Locomotive "Gazelle" — A265

1984 ***Perf. 12½***
722 A265 100fr shown 30 16
723 A265 100fr Cargo ship 30 16
724 A265 125fr Superpacific 38 20
725 A265 125fr Cargo ship, diff. 38 20
726 A265 350fr Pacific type 10 1.10 62
727 A265 350fr Ocean liner 1.10 62
728 A265 500fr Mallet class GT2 1.50 90
729 A265 500fr Ocean liner, diff. 1.50 90
Nos. 722-729 (8) 6.56 3.76

Issue dates: trains, Aug. 25; ships, Sept. 1.

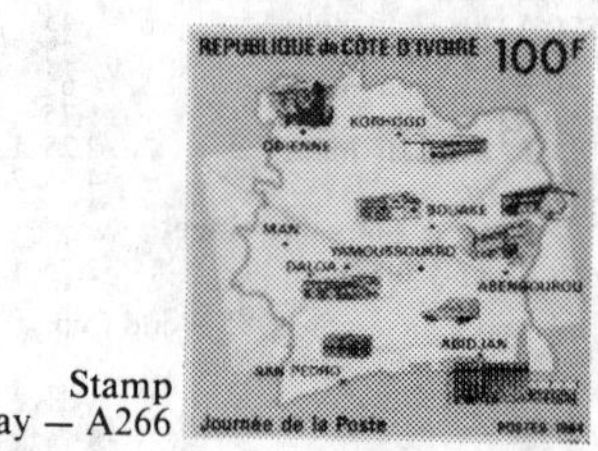

Stamp Day — A266

1984, Oct. 20 **Litho.** ***Perf. 12½***
730 A266 100fr Map, post offices 25 16

10th Anniv., West African Union A267

1984, Oct. 27 **Litho.** ***Perf. 13½***
731 A267 100fr Map, member nations 25 16

90th Anniv., Ivory Coast Postage Stamps A268

1984, Nov. 23 **Litho.** ***Perf. 12½***
732 A268 125fr Book cover 35 20

24th Anniv. of Independence — A269

1984, Dec. 7 **Litho.** ***Perf. 12½***
733 A269 100fr Citizens, outline map 25 16

Rotary Intl. Conf. — A270 Traditional Costumes — A271

1985, Jan. 16 **Litho.** ***Perf. 12½x13***
734 A270 100fr multicolored 25 16
735 A270 125fr multicolored 35 20

1985, Feb. 16 **Litho.** ***Perf. 13½***
736 A271 90fr Dan le Babou 22 15
737 A271 100fr Post-natal gown 25 15

Stamp Day — A272

1985, Apr. 13 **Litho.** ***Perf. 12½***
738 A272 100fr Riverboat Adjame 25 15

18th District of Zonta Intl., 7th Conference, Abidjan, Apr. 25-27 A273

1985, Apr. 25 **Litho.** ***Perf. 13½***
739 A273 125fr Zonta Intl. emblem 35 16

PHILEXAFRICA '85, Lome — A274

1985, May 15 ***Perf. 13***
740 A274 200fr Factory, jet, van 55 25
741 A274 200fr Youth sports, farming 55 25

Nos. 740-741 printed se-tenant with center label picturing map of Africa or the UAPT emblem.

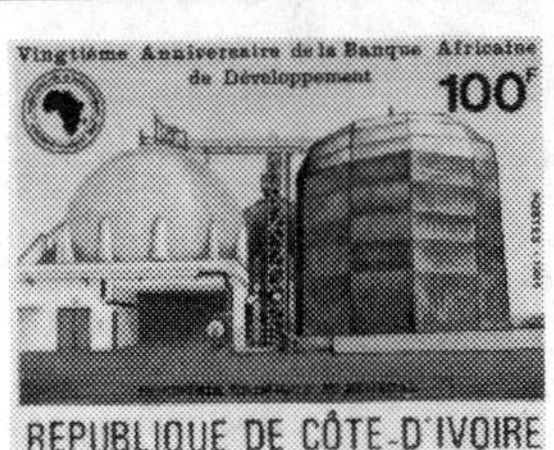
African Development Bank, 20th Anniv. — A275

1985, June 18
742 A275 100fr Senegal chemical industry 25 15
743 A275 125fr Gambian tree nursery 35 16

Intl. Youth Year — A276

1985, July 20 *Perf. 12½*
744 A276 125fr Map, profiles, dove 38 20

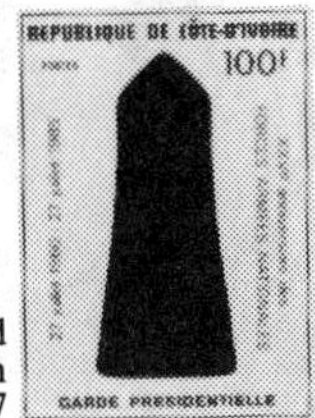
Natl. Armed Forces, 25th Anniv. — A277

Emblems: No. 745, Presidential Guard. No. 746, F.A.N.C.I. 125fr, Air Transport & Liaison Group, G.A.T.L. 200fr, National Marines. 350fr, National Gendarmerie.

1985, July 27 *Perf. 12½x13*
745 A277 100fr dp rose lil & gold 30 15
746 A277 100fr dark bl & gold 30 15
747 A277 125fr blk brn & gold 38 20
748 A277 200fr blk brn & gold 60 30
749 A277 350fr brt ultra & sil 1.00 50
Nos. 745-749 (5) 2.58 1.30

1986 World Cup Soccer Preliminaries, Mexico — A279

1985, Aug. *Perf. 13*
751 A279 100fr Heading the ball 30 15
752 A279 150fr Tackle 42 20
753 A279 200fr Dribbling 60 30
754 A279 350fr Passing 1.00 50

Souvenir Sheet
755 A279 500fr Power shot 1.40 65

Ivory Coast - Sovereign Military Order of Malta Postal Convention, Dec. 19, 1984 — A280

1985, Aug. 31 *Perf. 13x12½*
756 A280 125fr Natl. arms 38 20
757 A280 350fr S.M.O.M. arms 1.00 50

Visit of Pope John Paul II A281

1985, Sept. 24 *Perf. 13*
758 A281 100fr Portrait, St. Paul's Cathedral, Abidjan 30 15

UN Child Survival Campaign A282

1985, Oct. 5 **Litho.** *Perf. 13½x14*
759 A282 100fr Breast-feeding 35 16
760 A282 100fr Oral rehydration therapy 35 16
761 A282 100fr Mother and child 35 16
762 A282 100fr Vaccination 35 16

UN 40th Anniv. — A283

1985, Oct. 31 *Perf. 13*
763 A283 100fr multicolored 35 16

Admission to UN, 25th anniv.

World Wildlife Fund — A284

Striped antelopes.

1985, Nov. 30
764 A284 50fr multicolored 16 15
765 A284 60fr multicolored 20 15
766 A284 75fr multicolored 25 15
767 A284 100fr multicolored 35 16
Set value 46

City Skyline — A285

1985, Nov. 21 **Litho.** *Perf. 13*
768 A285 125fr multicolored 42 20

Expo '85 national industrial exhibition.

Return to the Land Campaign A286

Handicrafts A287

1985, Dec. 7 *Perf. 12½*
769 A286 125fr multicolored 42 20

Natl. independence, 25th anniv.

1986, Jan. *Perf. 13½*
770 A287 125fr Spinning thread 65 32
771 A287 155fr Painting 80 40

Flora — A288

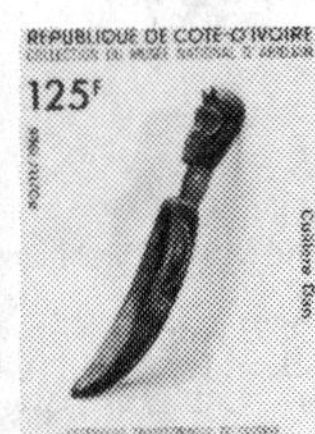
Cooking Utensils, Natl. Museum, Abidjan — A289

1986, Feb. 22 **Litho.** *Perf. 13½*
772 A288 40fr Omphalocarpum elatum 22 15
773 A288 50fr Momordica charantia 28 15
774 A288 125fr Millettia takou 68 35
775 A288 200fr Costus afer 1.10 55

1986, Mar. 6 *Perf. 13x12½, 12½x13*
776 A289 20fr We bowl 15 15
777 A289 30fr Baoule bowl 18 15
778 A289 90fr Baoule platter 50 25
779 A289 125fr Dan scoop 68 35
780 A289 440fr Baoule lidded pot 2.50 1.25
Nos. 776-780 (5) 4.01 2.15

Nos. 776-778 horiz.

Natl. Pedagogic and Vocational School, 10th Anniv. — A290

1986, Mar. 20 *Perf. 13½*
781 A290 125fr multicolored 68 35

Cable Ship Stephan, 1910 — A291

1986, Apr. 12 **Litho.** *Perf. 12½*
782 A291 125fr multicolored 68 35

Stamp Day.

Houphouet-Boigny Type of 1974-76

1986, Apr. **Engr.** *Perf. 13*
783 A112 5fr dk red, dp rose lil & brn 15 15
784 A112 10fr gray grn, brt bl & brn 15 15
785 A112 20fr brt ver, blk brn & brn 15 15
786 A112 25fr bl, dp rose lil & brn 15 15
787 A112 30fr brt ver, blk brn & brn 16 15
789 A112 50fr lake, dk vio & brn 28 15
790 A112 90fr dk brn vio, rose lake & brn 50 25
791 A112 125fr brt lil rose, brt ver & brn 68 35
792 A112 155fr dk brn vio, Prus bl & brn 85 42
Nos. 783-792 (9) 3.07
Set value 1.45

The 1986 printing of the 40fr is in slightly darker colors.

Natl. Youth and Sports Institute, 25th Anniv. — A293

1986, May 9 **Litho.** *Perf. 12½*
793 A293 125fr brt org & dk yel grn 68 35

Fish A294

Designs: 5fr, Polypterus endlicheri. 125fr, Synodontis punctifer. 150fr, Protopterus annectens. 155fr, Synodontis koensis. 440fr, Malapterurus electricus.

1986, July 5 **Litho.** *Perf. 14½x13½*
794 A294 5fr multi 15 15
795 A294 125fr multi 75 38
796 A294 150fr multi 90 45
797 A294 155fr multi 95 48
798 A294 440fr multi 2.75 2.00
Nos. 794-798 (5) 5.50 3.46

Enthronement of a Chief, Agni District — A295

1986, July 19 *Perf. 13½x14½*
799 A295 50fr Drummer, vert. 28 15
800 A295 350fr Chief in litter 2.00 1.00
801 A295 440fr Royal entourage 2.75 2.00

Rural Houses A296

1986, Aug. 2 **Litho.** *Perf. 14x15*
802 A296 125fr Baoule aoulo 75 38
803 A296 155fr Upper Antiam eva 95 48
804 A296 350fr Lobi soukala 2.00 1.00

Coat of Arms A297

Coastal Landscapes A298

1986-87 **Engr.** ***Perf. 13***
807 A297 50fr bright org 28 15
810 A297 125fr dark green 75 38
813 A297 155fr crimson 95 48
815 A297 195fr blue ('87) 1.10 55

Issue dates: 50fr, 125fr, 155fr, Aug. 23.
This is an expanding set. Numbers will change if necessary.

Perf. 14x15, 15x14
1986, Aug. 30 **Litho.**
820 A298 125fr Grand Bereby 75 38
821 A298 155fr Sableux Boubele, horiz. 95 48

Oceanographic Research Center — A299

Perf. 14½x13½
1986, Sept. 13 **Litho.**
822 A299 125fr Fishing grounds 68 35
823 A299 155fr Net fishing 85 42

Intl. Peace Year — A300

1986, Oct. 16 **Litho.** ***Perf. 14x13½***
824 A300 155fr multicolored 85 42

Research and Development — A301

1986, Nov. 15 ***Perf. 13½x14***
825 A301 125fr Bull 68 35
826 A301 155fr Wheat 85 42

Natl. Independence, 26th Anniv. — A302

1986, Dec. 6 **Litho.** ***Perf. 13½x14***
827 A302 155fr multicolored 85 42

Rural Housing A303

1987, Mar. 14 **Litho.** ***Perf. 13½x14***
828 A303 190fr Guesseple Dan 1.05 52
829 A303 550fr M'Bagui Senoufo 3.00 1.50

Stamp Day A304

Jean Mermoz College, 25th Anniv. A305

1987, Apr. 4 ***Perf. 13x13½***
830 A304 155fr Mailman, 1918 85 42

1987, Apr. 9 ***Perf. 13***
831 A305 40fr Cock, elephant 22 15
832 A305 155fr Dove, children 85 42

Elephant Type of 1981
1987, Apr. 9
833 A219 35fr multicolored 20 15

This is an expanding set. Numbers will change if necessary.

Fouilles, by Krah N'Guessan A306

Paintings by local artists: 500fr, Cortege Ceremonial, by Santoni Gerard.

1987, Aug. 14 **Litho.** ***Perf. 14½x15***
841 A306 195fr multi 1.35 68
842 A306 500fr multi 3.50 1.75

World Post Day, Express Mail Service A307

1987, Oct. 9 ***Perf. 13½***
843 A307 155fr multi 1.05 52
844 A307 195fr multi 1.30 65

Intl. Trade Cent. A308

1987, Oct. 24
845 A308 155fr multi 1.05 52

Natl. Independence, 27th Anniv. — A309

1987, Dec. 5 **Litho.** ***Perf. 14x13½***
846 A309 155fr multicolored 1.05 52

Lions Club for Child Survival — A310

1988, Feb. 20 **Litho.** ***Perf. 14x13½***
847 A310 155fr multicolored 1.10 55

The Modest Canary, by Monne Bou A311

Paintings by local artists: 20fr, The Couple, by K.J. Houra, vert. 150fr, The Eternal Dance, by Bou, vert. 155fr, La Termitiere, by Mathilde Moro, vert. 195fr, The Sun of Independence, by Michel Kodjo, vert.

Perf. 12½x13, 13x12½
1988, Jan. 30
848 A311 20fr multi 15 15
849 A311 30fr shown 20 15
850 A311 150fr multi 1.05 52
851 A311 155fr multi 1.10 55
852 A311 195fr multi 1.35 68
Nos. 848-852 (5) 3.85 2.05

Stamp Day — A312

1988, Apr. 4 **Litho.** ***Perf. 13***
853 A312 155fr Bereby P.O., c. 1900 1.05 52

15th French-Language Nations Cardiology Congress, Abidjan, Apr. 18-20 — A313

1988, Apr. 18 **Litho.** ***Perf. 15x14***
854 A313 195fr blk & dark red 1.30 65

Intl. Fund for Agricultural Development (IFAD), 10th Anniv. — A314

1988, May 21 **Litho.** ***Perf. 12x13***
855 A314 195fr multicolored 1.35 68

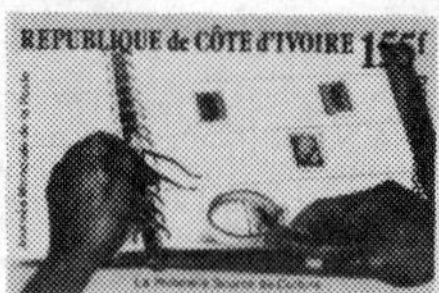
1st Intl. Day for the Campaign Against Drug Abuse and Drug Trafficking A315

1988, Aug. 27 **Litho.** ***Perf. 13½***
856 A315 155fr multi 1.05 52

Stone Heads — A316

Natl. Independence 28th Anniv. — A318

World Post Day — A317

Various stone heads from the Niangoran-Bouah Archaeological Collection.

Litho. & Engr.
1988, July 9 ***Perf. 13x14½***
857 A316 5fr beige & sep 15 15
858 A316 10fr buff & sep 15 15
859 A316 30fr pale grn & sep 20 15
860 A316 155fr pale yel & sep 1.05 52
861 A316 195fr pale yel grn & sep 1.20 60
Nos. 857-861 (5) 2.75
Set value 1.30

1988, Oct. 15 **Litho.** ***Perf. 14***
862 A317 155fr multi 1.00 50

1988, Dec. 6 ***Perf. 11½x12***

Year of the Forest: 40fr, Healthy trees. No. 864, Stop forest fires. No. 865, Planting trees.

863 A318 40fr multi 25 15
864 A318 155fr multi 1.00 50
865 A318 155fr multi 1.00 50

History of Money A319

1989, Feb. 25 Litho. *Perf. 12x11½*
Granite Paper

866 A319 50fr shown 32 16
867 A319 195fr Senegal bank notes, 1854, 1901 1.25 62

See Nos. 885-886, 896-898, 915. For surcharges see Nos. 904-905.

"Valeur d'echange 0fr.25" on 25c Type A5, 1920 A320

1989, Apr. *Perf. 12½*

868 A320 155fr multi 1.00 50

Stamp Day.

Jewelry from the National Museum Collection A321

1989, Mar. 25 Litho. *Perf. 14*

869 A321 90fr Voltaic bracelets 55 28
870 A321 155fr Anklets 95 48

Sculptures by Christian Lattier A322

Perf. 11½x12, 12x11½
1989, May 13 Granite Paper

871 A322 40fr *The Old Man and the Infant*, vert. 25 15
872 A322 155fr *The Saxophone Player*, vert. 95 48
873 A322 550fr *The Panther* 3.25 1.65

For surcharge see No. 903.

Council for Rural Development, 30th Anniv. — A323

1989, May 29 *Perf. 15x14*

874 A323 75fr Flags, well, tractor, field 45 22

See Togo No. 1526.

Intl. Peace Congress — A324

1989, June Litho. *Perf. 13*

875 A324 195fr multi 1.15 58

Rural Habitat A325

1989, June 10 Litho. *Perf. 14*

876 A325 155fr Hut, Sirikukube Dida 1.00 50

For surcharge see No. 902.

Sekou Watara, King of Kong (1710-1745) — A326

Designs: No. 878, Bastille, Declaration of Human Rights and Citizenship.

1989, July 7 Litho. *Perf. 13*

877 A326 200fr shown 1.20 60
878 A326 200fr multi 1.20 60

PHILEXFRANCE '89, French revolution bicent. Nos. 877-878 printed se-tenant with center label picturing exhibition emblem.

Endangered Species — A327

1989, Sept. 16 *Perf. 12x11½*
Granite Paper

879 A327 25fr *Varanus niloticus* 16 15
880 A327 100fr *Crocodylus niloticus* 65 32

World Post Day A328

1989, Oct. 9 Litho. *Perf. 12½x13*

881 A328 195fr multi 1.30 65

CAPTEAO, 30th Anniv. A329

1989, Oct. 28 Litho. *Perf. 12½*

882 A329 155fr multicolored 1.10 55

Conference of Postal and Telecommunication Administrations of West African Nations.

Natl. Independence, 29th Anniv. — A330

1989, Dec. 7 *Perf. 13*

883 A330 155fr multicolored 1.10 55

Pan-African Union, 10th Anniv. — A331

1990, Jan. 18 Litho. *Perf. 13*

884 A331 155fr multicolored 1.10 55

History of Money Type of 1989

1990, Mar. 17 Litho. *Perf. 12x11½*
Granite Paper

885 A319 155fr 1923 25fr note 1.25 62
886 A319 195fr 1, 2, 5fr notes 1.50 75

Stamp Day — A332

1990, Apr. 21 Litho. *Perf. 13x12½*

887 A332 155fr Packet Africa 1.25 62

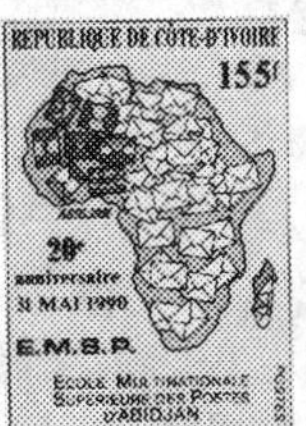

Multinational Postal School, 20th Anniv. — A333

1990, May 31 *Perf. 12½*

888 A333 155fr multicolored 1.25 62

Rural Village A334

1990, June 30 *Perf. 14*

889 A334 155fr multicolored 1.25 62

Intl. Literacy Year A335

1990, July 28 *Perf. 15x14*

890 A335 195fr multicolored 1.50 75

Dedication of Basilica of Notre Dame of Peace, Yamoussoukro — A336

1990, Sept. 8 *Perf. 14½x13½*

891 A336 155fr shown 1.25 62
892 A336 195fr Basilica, diff. 1.50 75

Visit of Pope John Paul II — A337

1990, Sept. 9 *Perf. 13*

893 A337 500fr multicolored 4.00 2.00

World Post Day — A338

1990, Oct. 9 Litho. *Perf. 14x15*

894 A338 195fr multicolored 1.75 88

Independence, 30th Anniv. — A339

1990, Dec. 6 Litho. *Perf. 13½x14½*

895 A339 155fr multicolored 1.35 70

History of Money Type of 1989

1991, Mar. 1 Litho. *Perf. 11½*
Granite Paper

896 A319 40fr French West Africa 1942 5fr, 100fr notes 30 15
897 A319 155fr like #896 1.10 55

898 A319 195fr French West Africa & Togo 50fr, 500fr notes 1.40 70

For surcharges see Nos. 904-905.

Stamp Day A340

1991, May 18 Litho. *Perf. 13½*
899 A340 150fr multicolored 1.10 55

Miniature Sheets

French Open Tennis Championships, Cent. — A341

Tennis Players: No. 900a, Henri Cochet. b, Rene Lacoste. c, Jean Borotra. d, Don Budge. e, Marcel Bernard. f, Ken Rosewall. g, Rod Laver. h, Bjorn Borg. i, Yannick Noah.

No. 901a, Suzanne Lenglen. b, Helen Wills Moody. c, Simone Mathieu. d, Maureen Connolly. e, Francoise Durr. f, Margaret Court. g, Chris Evert. h, Martina Navratilova. i, Steffi Graf.

1991, May 24 Litho. *Perf. 13½*
900 A341 200fr Sheet of 9, #900a-900i 13.50 6.75
901 A341 200fr Sheet of 9, #901a-901i 13.50 6.75

Nos. 872, 876, 897-898 Surcharged

 150F

Perfs. as Before
1991, July 15 Litho.
902 A325 150fr on 155fr #876 1.10 55

Granite Paper
903 A322 150fr on 155fr #872 1.10 55
904 A319 150fr on 155fr #897 1.10 55
905 A319 200fr on 195fr #898 1.50 75

Location of obliterator and surcharge varies.

Packet Boats A342

1991, June 28 Litho. *Perf. 12x11½*
Granite Paper
906 A342 50fr Europe 40 20
907 A342 550fr Asia 4.30 2.15

World Post Day — A343

1991, Oct. 9 *Perf. 13*
908 A343 50fr shown 40 20
909 A343 100fr SIPE, globe 80 40

Tribal Drums — A344

1991 Litho. *Perf. 14x15*
910 A344 5fr We 15 15
911 A344 25fr Krou, Soubre region 20 15
912 A344 150fr Sinematiali 1.20 60
913 A344 200fr Akye, Alepe region 1.60 80

Independence, 31st Anniv. — A345

1991, Dec. 7 Litho. *Perf. 13½x14½*
914 A345 150fr multicolored 1.25 65

History of Money Type of 1989
1991, Dec. 8 *Perf. 12x11½*
Granite Paper
915 A319 100fr like #898 88 45

Flowers A346

Various flowers.

1991, Dec. 20 Engr. *Perf. 13*
916 A346 150fr grn, blk & mag, vert. 1.25 65
917 A346 200fr grn, olive & rose car 1.65 85

SEMI-POSTAL STAMPS

No. 47 Surcharged in Red ✚5c

1915 Unwmk. *Perf. 14x13½*
B1 A5 10c + 5c red org & rose 35 35
a. Double surcharge 27.50 27.50

Issued on ordinary and chalky paper.

Curie Issue
Common Design Type
1938 *Perf. 13*
B2 CD80 1.75fr + 50c brt ultra 3.75 3.75

French Revolution Issue
Common Design Type
1939 Photo.
Name and Value Typo. in Black
B3 CD83 45c + 25c grn 3.00 3.00
B4 CD83 70c + 30c brn 3.00 3.00
B5 CD83 90c + 35c red org 3.00 3.00
B6 CD83 1.25fr + 1fr rose pink 3.00 3.00
B7 CD83 2.25fr + 2fr bl 3.00 3.00
Nos. B3-B7 (5) 15.00 15.00

Stamps of 1936-38 Surcharged in Red or Black

SECOURS + 1 fr. NATIONAL

1941
B8 A7 50c + 1fr plum (Bk) 65 65
B9 A8 80c + 2fr blk brn (R) 5.00 5.00
B10 A8 1.50fr + 2fr ultra (R) 5.00 5.00
B11 A9 2fr + 3fr ultra (Bk) 5.00 5.00

Common Design Type and

Native Engineer SP1

Senegalese Light Artillery SP2

1941 Photo. *Perf. 13½*
B12 SP1 1fr + 1fr red 45
B13 CD86 1.50fr + 3fr claret 45
B14 SP2 2.50fr + 1fr blue 45

It is doubtful whether Nos. B12-B14 were placed in use. They were issued by the Vichy government.

Nos. 165-166 were surcharged "OEUVRES COLONIALES" and surtax (including change of denomination of the 2.50fr to 50c). These were issued in 1944 by the Vichy government and not placed on sale in the colony.

Catalogue values for unused stamps in this section, from this point to the end of the section, are for Never Hinged items.

Republic
Anti-Malaria Issue
Common Design Type
1962, Apr. 7 Engr. *Perf. 12½x12*
B15 CD108 25fr + 5fr ol grn 65 65

Freedom from Hunger Issue
Common Design Type
1963, Mar. 21 *Perf. 13*
B16 CD112 25fr + 5fr red lil, dk vio & brn 80 80

Red Cross - Red Crescent Soc., Child Survival Campaign — SP3

1987, May 8 Litho. *Perf. 13½*
B17 SP3 195fr +5fr multi 1.15 1.15

No. B17 surcharged "+5fr" in red. Not issued without surcharge. Surtax for the Red Cross - Red Crescent Soc.

Organization of African Unity, 25th Anniv. SP4

1988, Nov. 19 Litho. *Perf. 12½x13*
B18 SP4 195fr +5fr multi 1.40 1.40

Marie Therese Houphouet-Boigny and N'Daya Intl. Emblem — SP5

1988, Dec. 9 Litho. *Perf. 13*
B19 SP5 195fr +5fr multi 1.35 1.35

N'Daya Intl., 1st anniv.

AIR POST STAMPS

Common Design Type
1940 Unwmk. Engr. *Perf. 12½x12*
C1 CD85 1.90fr ultramarine 16 16
C2 CD85 2.90fr dark red 16 16
C3 CD85 4.50fr dk gray grn 22 22
C4 CD85 4.90fr yel bister 28 28
C5 CD85 6.90fr deep orange 65 65
Nos. C1-C5 (5) 1.47 1.47

Common Design Types
1942
C6 CD88 50c car & blue 15
C7 CD88 1fr brn & black 25
C8 CD88 2fr dk grn & red brn 28
C9 CD88 3fr dk blue & scar 32
C10 CD88 5fr vio & dk red 35

Frame Engraved, Center Typographed
C11 CD89 10fr multicolored 42
C12 CD89 20fr multicolored 50
C13 CD89 50fr multicolored 60 90
Nos. C6-C13 (8) 2.87

There is doubt whether Nos. C6-C12 were officially placed in use.

Catalogue values for unused stamps in this section, from this point to the end of the section, are for Never Hinged items.

Republic

Lapalud Place and Post Office, Abidjan — AP1

Designs: 200fr, Houphouet-Boigny Bridge. 500fr, Ayame dam.

1959, Oct. 1 Engr. *Perf. 13*
C14 AP1 100fr multicolored 1.10 38
C15 AP1 200fr multicolored 1.50 1.10
C16 AP1 500fr multicolored 5.25 2.25

Sports Type of 1961
1961, Dec. 23
C17 A19 100fr High jump 90 65

Air Afrique Issue
Common Design Type
1962, Feb. 17 Unwmk. *Perf. 13*
C18 CD107 50fr Prus bl, choc & org brn 65 50

Village in Man Region — AP2

1962, June 23 Engr. *Perf. 13*
C19 AP2 200fr Street in Odienne, vert. 2.25 90
C20 AP2 500fr shown 4.50 2.00

UN Headquarters, New York — AP3

1962, Sept. 20 *Perf. 13*
C21 AP3 100fr multi 1.10 70

Admission to the UN, 2nd anniv.

Sassandra Bay — AP4

1963 Unwmk. *Perf. 13*
C22 AP4 50fr Moossou bridge 50 25
C23 AP4 100fr shown 1.10 65
C24 AP4 200fr Comoe River 2.00 1.00

African Postal Union Issue
Common Design Type

1963, Sept. 8 Photo. *Perf. 12½*
C25 CD114 85fr org brn, ocher & red 90 75

1963 Air Afrique Issue
Common Design Type

1963, Nov. 19 Unwmk. *Perf. 13x12*
C26 CD115 25fr crim, gray, blk & grn 35 25

Ramses II and Queen Nefertari — AP5

President John F. Kennedy (1917-63) — AP7

Arms of Republic — AP6

1964, Mar. 7 Engr. *Perf. 13*
C27 AP5 60fr car, blk & red brn 80 65

UNESCO campaign to save historic monuments in Nubia.

1964, June 13 Photo.
C28 AP6 200fr ultra, yel grn & gold 1.75 75

1964, Nov. 14 Unwmk. *Perf. 12½*
C29 AP7 100fr gray, cl brn & blk 1.20 80
a. Souvenir sheet of 4 4.00 4.00

Liana Bridge, Lieupleu — AP8

1965, Dec. 4 Engr. *Perf. 13*
C30 AP8 100fr ol grn, dk grn & dk red brn 1.00 65

Street in Kong — AP9

1966, Mar. 5 Engr. *Perf. 13*
C31 AP9 300fr brt bl, bis brn & vio brn 3.25 1.60

Air Afrique Issue, 1966
Common Design Type

1966, Aug. 20 Photo. *Perf. 13*
C32 CD123 30fr dk grn, blk & gray 35 20

Air Afrique Headquarters AP10

1967, Feb. 4 Engr. *Perf. 13*
C33 AP10 500fr emer, ind & ocher 5.00 2.00

Opening of Air Afrique headquarters in Abidjan.

African Postal Union Issue, 1967
Common Design Type

1967, Sept. 9 Engr. *Perf. 13*
C34 CD124 100fr blk, vio & car lake 1.10 65

Senufo Village — AP11

1968 Engr. *Perf. 13*
C35 AP11 100fr shown 1.10 70
C36 AP11 500fr Tiegba village 4.50 2.00

Issue dates: 100fr, Feb. 17; 500fr, Apr. 27.

PHILEXAFRIQUE Issue

Street in Grand Bassam, by Achalme — AP12

1969, Jan. 11 Photo. *Perf. 12x12½*
C37 AP12 100fr grn & multi 1.10 1.10

PHILEXAFRIQUE Phil. Exhib., Abidjan, Feb. 14-23. Printed with alternating green label.

2nd PHILEXAFRIQUE Issue
Common Design Type

Designs: 50fr, Ivory Coast No. 130 and view of San Pedro. 100fr, Ivory Coast No. 149 and man wearing chief's garments (vert.). 200fr, Ivory Coast No. 77 and Exhibition Hall, Abidjan.

1969, Feb. 14 Engr. *Perf. 13*
C38 CD128 50fr grn, brn red & deep bl 50 50
C39 CD128 100fr brn, org & dp blue 1.00 1.00
C40 CD128 200fr brn, gray & dp blue 1.75 1.75
a. Min. sheet of 3, #C38-C40 3.50 3.50

Opening of PHILEXAFRIQUE.

Man Waterfall — AP13

Mount Niangbo — AP14

1970 Engr. *Perf. 13*
C41 AP13 100fr ocher, sl grn & vio bl 75 45
C42 AP14 200fr hn brn, grn & lt ol 1.75 75

Issue dates: 100fr, Jan. 6; 200fr, July 18.

San Pedro Harbor — AP15

1971, Mar. 21 Engr. *Perf. 13*
C43 AP15 100fr sl grn, red brn & brt bl 80 45

The lack of a price for a listed item does not necessarily indicate rarity.

Treichville Swimming Pool — AP16

1971, May 29 Photo. *Perf. 12½*
C44 AP16 100fr multicolored 80 50

Aerial View of Coast Line — AP17

1971, July 3 Engr. *Perf. 13*
C45 AP17 500fr multi 4.25 2.00

Tourist publicity for the African Riviera.

Bondoukou Market Type of Regular Issue

Design: 200fr, Similar to No. 318, but without people at left and in center.

Embossed on Gold Paper

1971, Aug. 7 *Perf. 12½*
Size: 36x26mm
C46 A79 200fr gold, ultra & blk 1.90 1.50

African Postal Union Issue, 1971
Common Design Type

Design: 100fr, Ivory Coast coat of arms and UAMPT building, Brazzaville, Congo.

1971, Nov. 13 Photo. *Perf. 13x13½*
C47 CD135 100fr bl & multi 80 45

Lion of St. Mark AP18

1972, Feb. 5 Photo. *Perf. 12½*
C48 AP18 100fr shown 1.00 65
C49 AP18 200fr Waves, St. Mark's Basilica, Venice 2.25 1.50

UNESCO campaign to save Venice.

Kawara Mosque — AP19

1972, Apr. 29 Engr. *Perf. 13*
C50 AP19 500fr bl, brn & ocher 4.00 1.90

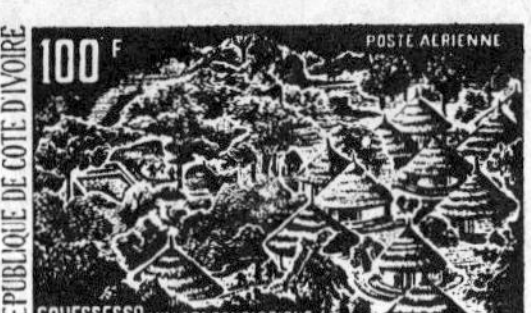

View of Gouessesso — AP20

1972 Engr. *Perf. 13*

C51	AP20	100fr shown	80	45
C52	AP20	200fr Jacqueville Lake	2.00	80
C53	AP20	500fr Kossou Dam	4.00	2.00

Issue dates: 100fr, June 10; 200fr, Oct. 28; 500fr, Nov. 17.

Akakro Radar Earth Station — AP21

1972, Nov. 27 Engr. *Perf. 13*

C54	AP21	200fr brt bl, sl grn & choc	1.75	90

The Judgment of Solomon, by Nandjui Legue — AP22

1973, Aug. 26 Photo. *Perf. 13*

C55	AP22	500fr multi	3.75	2.00

6th World Peace Conference for Justice.

Sassandra River Bridge — AP23

1974, May 4 Engr. *Perf. 13*

C56	AP23	100fr blk & yel grn	55	30
C57	AP23	500fr sl grn & brn	2.50	1.50

Vridi Soap Factory, Abidjan — AP24

1974, July 6 Photo. *Perf. 13*

C58	AP24	200fr multi	1.10	65

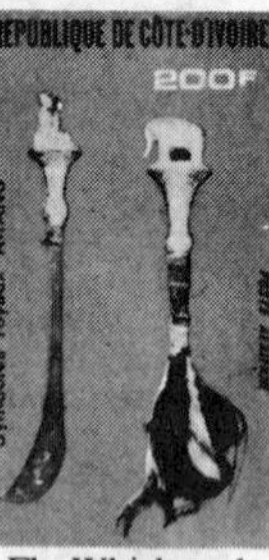

UPU Emblem, Ivory Coast Flag, Post Runner and Jet — AP25

Fly Whisk and Panga Knife, Symbols of Akans Royal Family — AP26

1974, Oct. 9 Photo. *Perf. 13*

C59	AP25	200fr multi	1.10	90
C60	AP25	300fr multi	1.75	1.25

Centenary of Universal Postal Union.

1976, Apr. 3 Photo. *Perf. 12½x13*

C61	AP26	200fr brt bl & multi	1.10	65

Tingrela Mosque — AP27

1977, May 7 Engr. *Perf. 13*

C62	AP27	500fr multi	2.50	1.50

Zeppelin Type of 1977
Souvenir Sheet

Design: "Graf Zeppelin" LZ 127 over New York.

1977, Sept. 3 Litho. *Perf. 11*

C63	A150	500fr multi	3.25	1.40

Exists imperf.

Philexafrique II - Essen Issue
Common Design Types

Designs: No. C64, Elephant and Ivory Coast No. 239. No. C65, Pheasant and Bavaria No. 1. Printed se-tenant.

1978, Nov. 1 Litho. *Perf. 13x12½*

C64	CD138	100fr multi	50	30
C65	CD139	100fr multi	50	30

Gymnast, Olympic Rings — AP28

Designs: Various gymnasts. 75fr, 150fr, 350fr, vert.

1980, July 24 Litho. *Perf. 14½*

C66	AP28	75fr multi	50	30
C67	AP28	150fr multi	1.00	60
C68	AP28	250fr multi	1.60	1.00
C69	AP28	350fr multi	2.25	1.25

Souvenir Sheet

C70	AP28	500fr multi	3.50	2.00

22nd Summer Olympic Games, Moscow, July 19-Aug. 3.

Manned Flight Bicentenary — AP29

Various balloons. 100fr, 125fr, 350fr vert.

1983, Apr. 2 Litho. *Perf. 13*

C71	AP29	100fr Montgolfier, 1783	65	38
C72	AP29	125fr Hydrogen, 1783	80	42
C73	AP29	150fr Mail transport, 1870	1.00	55
C74	AP29	350fr Double Eagle II, 1978	2.25	1.40
C75	AP29	500fr Dirigible	3.50	1.75
		Nos. C71-C75 (5)	8.20	4.50

Pre-Olympic Year — AP30

Various swimming events.

1983, July 9 Litho. *Perf. 14*

C76	AP30	100fr Crawl	25	16
C77	AP30	125fr Diving	35	20
C78	AP30	350fr Backstroke	90	55
C79	AP30	400fr Butterfly	1.10	62

Souvenir Sheet

C80	AP30	500fr Water polo	1.40	80

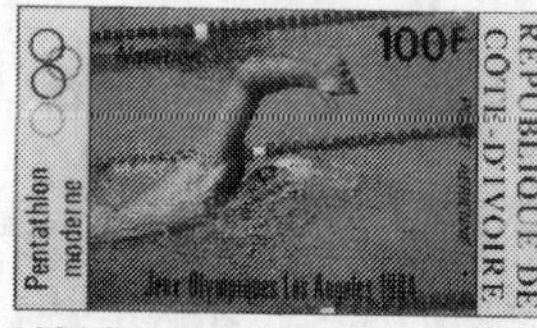

1984 Summer Olympics — AP31

Pentathlon.

1984, Mar. *Perf. 12½*

C81	AP31	100fr Swimming	30	16
C82	AP31	125fr Running	40	22
C83	AP31	185fr Shooting	55	35
C84	AP31	350fr Fencing	1.10	70

Souvenir Sheet

C85	AP31	500fr Equestrian	1.50	70

Los Angeles Olympics Winners AP32

1984, Dec. 15 Litho. *Perf. 13*

C86	AP32	100fr Tiacoh, silver	25	16
C87	AP32	150fr Lewis, gold	40	22
C88	AP32	200fr Babers, gold	65	35
C89	AP32	500fr Cruz, gold	1.40	80

Christmas AP33

Paintings: 100fr, Virgin and Child, by Correggio. 200fr, Holy Family with Angels, by Andrea del Sarto. 400fr, Virgin and Child, by Bellini.

1985, Jan. 12 *Perf. 13*

C90	AP33	100fr multi	25	16
C91	AP33	200fr multi	60	35
C92	AP33	400fr multi	1.10	65

Nos. C91-C92 have incorrect frame inscriptions.

Audubon Birth Bicentenary — AP34

Birds: 100fr, Mergus serrator. 150fr, Pelecanus erythrorhynchos. 200fr, Mycteria americana. 350fr, Melanitta deglandi.

1985, June 8 Litho. *Perf. 13*

C93	AP34	100fr multi	25	15
C94	AP34	150fr multi, vert.	40	20
C95	AP34	200fr multi, vert.	55	25
C96	AP34	350fr multi	90	45

PHILEXAFRICA '85, Lome, Togo — AP35

1985, Nov. 16 Litho. *Perf. 13*

C97	AP35	250fr shown	65	35
C98	AP35	250fr Soccer, boys and deer	65	35

Nos. C97-C98 printed se-tenant with center labels picturing a map of Africa or the UAPT emblem.

Edmond Halley, Computer Drawing of Comet — AP36

Return of Halley's Comet: 155fr, Sir William Herschel, Uranus. 190fr, Space probe, comet. 350fr, MS T-5 probe, comet. 440fr, Skylab, Kohoutek comet.

1986, Jan. Litho. *Perf. 13*

C99	AP36	125fr shown	50	25
C100	AP36	155fr multi	62	30
C101	AP36	190fr multi	75	38
C102	AP36	350fr multi	1.40	70
C103	AP36	440fr multi	1.75	85
		Nos. C99-C103 (5)	5.02	2.48

1986 World Cup Soccer Championships, Mexico — AP37

Various soccer plays.

1986, Apr. 26 Litho. *Perf. 13*

C104	AP37	90fr multi	50	25
C105	AP37	125fr multi	68	35
C106	AP37	155fr multi	85	42
C107	AP37	440fr multi	2.40	1.20
C108	AP37	500fr multi	2.75	1.40
		Nos. C104-C108 (5)	7.18	3.62

Souvenir Sheet
Perf. 13½x13

C109 AP37 600fr multi		3.25	1.75

AP38

1988 Summer Olympics, Seoul — AP39

Sailing sports.

1987, May 23 **Litho.** ***Perf. 12½***

C110 AP38 155fr	Soling Class	85	42
C111 AP38 195fr	Windsurfing	1.10	55
C112 AP38 250fr	470 Class	1.40	70
C113 AP38 550fr	Windsurfing, diff.	3.00	1.50

Souvenir Sheet

C114 AP39 650fr	470 Class, diff.	3.75	2.00

1988 Summer Olympics, Seoul — AP40

1988, June 18 **Litho.** ***Perf. 13***

C115 AP40 100fr	Gymnastic rings	65	32
C116 AP40 155fr	Women's handball	1.00	50
C117 AP40 195fr	Boxing	1.25	62
C118 AP40 500fr	Parallel bars	3.25	1.65

Souvenir Sheet

C119 AP40 500fr	Horizontal bar	3.25	1.65

1990 World Cup Soccer Championships, Italy — AP41

Italian monuments and various athletes.

1989, Nov. 25 **Litho.** ***Perf. 13***

C120 AP41 195fr	Milan Cathedral	1.40	70
C121 AP41 300fr	Columbus Monument, Genoa	2.10	1.05
C122 AP41 450fr	Turin	3.20	1.60
C123 AP41 550fr	Bologna	3.85	3.85

World Cup Soccer Championships, Italy — AP32

Various plays.

1990, May 31 **Litho.** ***Perf. 13***

C124 AP32 155fr	multicolored	1.25	62
C125 AP32 195fr	multicolored	1.50	75
C126 AP32 500fr	multicolored	3.75	1.90
C127 AP32 600fr	multicolored	4.75	2.40

AIR POST SEMI-POSTAL STAMPS

Stamps of Dahomey types V1, V2, V3 and V4 inscribed "Cote d'Ivoire" were issued in 1942 by the Vichy Government, but were not placed on sale in the colony.

POSTAGE DUE STAMPS

Natives — D1

D2

Perf. 14x13½

1906-07 **Unwmk.** **Typo.**

J1 D1	5c grn, *greenish*	1.25	1.25
J2 D1	10c red brown	1.40	1.40
J3 D1	15c dark blue	2.25	2.25
J4 D1	20c blk, *yellow*	3.25	3.25
J5 D1	30c red, *straw*	3.25	3.25
J6 D1	50c violet	2.50	2.50
J7 D1	60c black, *buff*	12.50	12.50
J8 D1	1fr blk, *pinkish*	15.00	15.00
	Nos. J1-J8 (8)	41.40	41.40

1914

J9 D2	5c green	15	15
J10 D2	10c rose	15	15
J11 D2	15c gray	15	15
J12 D2	20c brown	15	15
J13 D2	30c blue	25	25
J14 D2	50c black	40	40
J15 D2	60c orange	50	50
J16 D2	1fr violet	60	60
	Set value	2.00	2.00

Type of 1914 Issue Surcharged **2F.**

1927

J17 D2	2fr on 1fr lilac rose	60	60
J18 D2	3fr on 1fr org brown	60	60

Catalogue values for unused stamps in this section, from this point to the end of the section, are for Never Hinged items.

Republic

Gueré Mask — D3

Mask — D4

1960 **Engr.** ***Perf. 14x13***
Denomination Typographed in Black

J19 D3	1fr purple	15	15
J20 D3	2fr bright green	15	15
J21 D3	5fr orange yellow	25	25
J22 D3	10fr ultramarine	50	50
J23 D3	20fr lilac rose	80	80
	Nos. J19-J23 (5)	1.85	1.85

1962, Nov. 3 **Typo.** ***Perf. 13½x14***

Designs: Various masks and heads, Bingerville school of art.

J24 D4	1fr org & brt blue	15	15
J25 D4	2fr black & red	15	15
J26 D4	5fr red & dark grn	15	15
J27 D4	10fr green & lil	45	45
J28 D4	20fr dark pur & blk	80	80
	Nos. J24-J28 (5)	1.70	1.70

Baoulé Weight — D5

Gold Weight — D6

Designs: Various Baoulé weights.

1968, May 18 **Photo.** ***Perf. 13***

J29 D5	5fr cit, brn & bl grn	15	15
J30 D5	10fr lt bl, brn & bl grn	15	15
J31 D5	15fr sal, brn & bl grn	40	40
J32 D5	20fr gray, car & bl grn	60	60
J33 D5	30fr bis, brn & bl grn	70	70
	Nos. J29-J33 (5)	2.00	2.00

1972, May 27 **Engr.**

Designs: Various gold weights.

J34 D6	20fr vio bl & org red	42	42
J35 D6	40fr ver & ocher	65	65
J36 D6	50fr orange & choc	90	90
J37 D6	100fr sl grn & ocher	2.00	2.00

MILITARY STAMP

The catalogue value for the unused stamp in this section is for Never Hinged.

Coat of Arms — M1

Perf. 13x14

1967, Jan. 1 **Unwmk.** **Typo.**

M1 M1	multi	1.60	1.60

OFFICIAL STAMPS

Catalogue values for unused stamps in this section are for Never Hinged items.

Ivory Coast Coat of Arms — O1

1974, Jan. 1 **Photo.** ***Perf. 12***

O1 O1	(35fr) green & multi	42	22
O2 O1	(75fr) orange & multi	65	35
O3 O1	(100fr) lil rose & multi	90	60
O4 O1	(250fr) violet & multi	2.50	1.20

PARCEL POST STAMPS

Postage Due Stamps of French Colonies Overprinted

Overprinted in Black

Côte d'Ivoire
COLIS
Postaux

1903 **Unwmk.** ***Imperf.***

Q1 D1	50c lilac	17.50	17.50
Q2 D1	1fr rose, *buff*	17.50	17.50

Overprinted in Black

Colis
Postaux

Q3 D1	50c lilac	*2,000.*	*2,000.*
Q4 D1	1fr rose, *buff*	*2,000.*	*2,000.*

Accents on "C" of "COTE"

Nos. Q7-Q8, Q11-Q12, Q15, Q17-Q18, Q21-Q22, Q24-Q25 exist with or without accent.

Overprinted

Côte d'Ivoire
Colis Postaux

Red Overprint

Q5 D1	50c lilac	50.00	50.00
a.	Inverted overprint	175.00	175.00

Blue Black Overprint

Q6 D1	1fr rose, *buff*	30.00	30.00
a.	Inverted overprint	175.00	175.00

Surcharged in Black

Cote d Ivoire

Colis Postaux

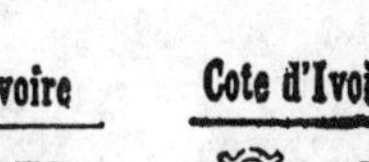

Cote d'Ivoire
1 FR
Colis Postaux
a

Cote d'Ivoire
1 FR
Colis Postaux
b

Cote d'Ivoire
fr 1 fr
Colis Postaux
c

Cote d'Ivoire
fr 1 fr
Colis Postaux
d

Cote d'Ivoire
fr 1 fr
Colis Postaux
e

Cote d'Ivoire
fr 1 fr
Colis Postaux
f

Côte d'Ivoire
UN FR
Colis Postaux
g

Côte d'Ivoire
UN FR
Colis Postaux
h

1903

Q7 D1 50c on 15c pale grn 5.00 5.00
a. Inverted surcharge 75.00 75.00
Q8 D1 50c on 60c brn, *buff* 17.50 15.00
a. Inverted surcharge 75.00 75.00

Q9 (a) 1fr on 5c blue *2,000.* *2,000.*
Q10 (b) 1fr on 5c blue *2,000.* *1,400.*
Q11 (c) 1fr on 5c blue 6.00 5.25
a. Inverted surcharge 125.00 125.00
Q12 (d) 1fr on 5c blue 8.75 8.00
Q13 (e) 1fr on 5c blue *2,250.* *2,250.*
Q14 (f) 1fr on 5c blue *5,500.* *5,500.*
Q15 (g) 1fr on 5c blue 50.00 50.00
Q16 (h) 1fr on 5c blue *1,800.* *1,800.*
Q17 (c) 1fr on 10c gray brn 8.50 6.00
a. Inverted surcharge 100.00 100.00
Q18 (d) 1fr on 10c gray brn 9.00 9.00
a. Inverted surcharge 100.00 100.00
Q19 (g) 1fr on 10c gray brn *1,500.* *1,500.*
Q20 (h) 1fr on 10c gray brn *22,500.*

Some authorities regard Nos. Q9 and Q10 as essays. A sub-type of type "a" has smaller, bold "XX" without serifs.

Surcharged in Black:

Côte d'Ivoire
fr 4 fr
Colis Postaux
i

Cote d Ivoire
fr 4 fr
Colis Postaux
k

Côte d'Ivoire
fr 4 fr
Colis Postaux
l

Q21 (i) 4fr on 60c brn, *buff* 60.00 42.50
a. Double surcharge *110.00*
Q22 (k) 4fr on 60c brn, *buff* 160.00 125.00
Q23 (l) 4fr on 60c brn, *buff* 525.00 425.00

Surcharged in Black

Colis Postaux

Côte d'Ivoire

Q24 D1 4fr on 15c green 60.00 42.50
a. One large star 275.00 175.00
b. Two large stars 90.00 75.00
Q25 D1 4fr on 30c rose 60.00 42.50
a. One large star 275.00 175.00
b. Two large stars 90.00 75.00

Overprinted in Black

C. P.
Cote d'Ivoire

1904

Q26 D1 50c lilac 15.00 15.00
a. Inverted overprint
Q27 D1 1fr rose, *buff* 15.00 15.00
a. Inverted overprint

Overprinted in Black

Cote d'Ivoire
C. P.

Q28 D1 50c lilac 15.00 15.00
a. Inverted overprint 70.00 70.00
Q29 D1 1fr rose, *buff* 16.00 16.00
a. Inverted overprint 70.00 70.00

Surcharged in Black

Colis Postaux
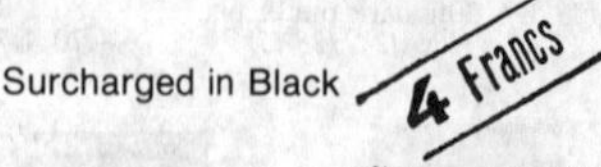

Cote d'Ivoire

Q30 D1 4fr on 5c blue 75.00 75.00
Q31 D1 8fr on 15c green 110.00 110.00

Overprinted in Black

Cote d'Ivoire
C.
P.

1905

Q32 D1 50c lilac 17.50 17.50
Q33 D1 1fr rose, *buff* 17.50 17.50

Surcharged in Black

Cote d'Ivoire
2 Francs
C. P.

Q34 D1 2fr on 1fr rose, *buff* 110.00 110.00
Q35 D1 4fr on 1fr rose, *buff* 120.00 120.00
a. Italic "4" 750.00 750.00
Q36 D1 8fr on 1fr rose, *buff* 275.00 275.00

Nearly all the Parcel Post stamps are to be found without the circumflex accent on the "o" of "Cote".

JAPAN

LOCATION — North Pacific Ocean, east of China
GOVT. — Constitutional monarchy
AREA — 142,726 sq. mi.
POP. — 120,020,000 (est. 1984)
CAPITAL — Tokyo

1000 Mon = 10 Sen
100 Sen = 1 Yen (or En)
10 Rin = 1 Sen

Catalogue values for unused stamps in this country are for Never Hinged items, beginning with Scott 362 in the regular postage section, Scott B8 in the semi-postal section, and Scott C9 in the airpost section.

Watermarks

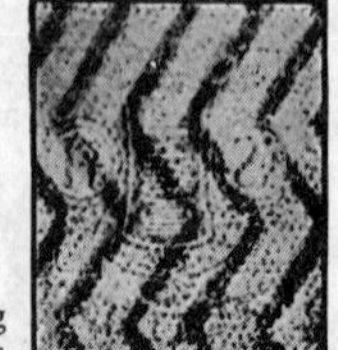
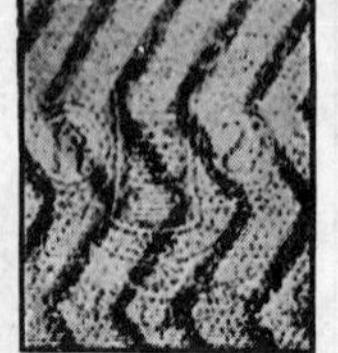

Wmk. 141- Zigzag Lines

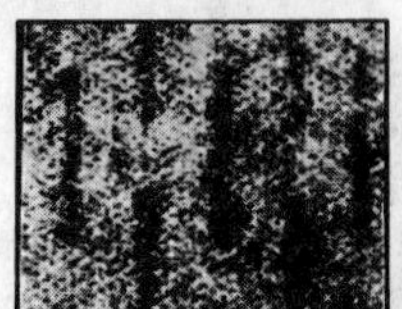

Wmk. 142- Parallel Lines

Wmk. 257- Curved Wavy Lines

After 1945, Wmk. 257 exists also in a narrow spacing on a small number of issues.

Counterfeits of Nos. 1-71 are plentiful. Some are excellent and deceive many collectors.

Nos. 1-54A were printed from hand engraved plates of 40. Each stamp in the sheet is slightly different.

Pair of Dragons Facing Characters of Value — A1

Plate I Plate II

48 mon:
Plate I- Solid dots in inner border.
Plate II- Tiny circles replace dots.

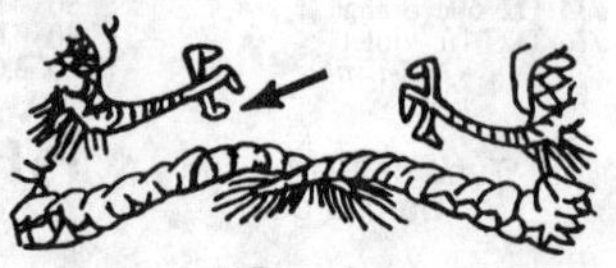

Plate I

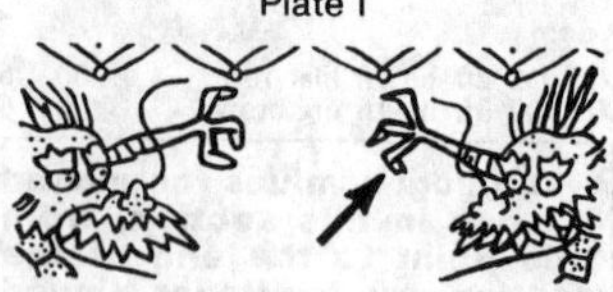
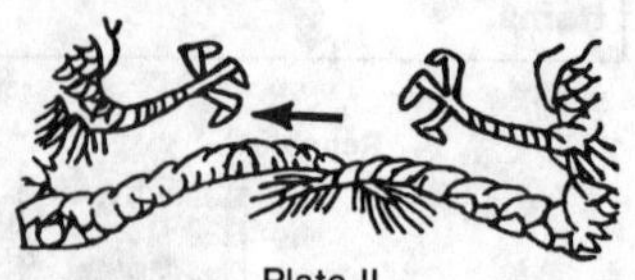

Plate II

100 mon:
Plate I- Lowest dragon claw at upper right and at lower left point upward.
Plate II- Same two claws point downward.

Plate I

Plate II

200 mon:
Plate I- Dot in upper left corner.
Plate II- No dot. (Some Plate I copies show dot faintly; these can be mistaken for Plate II.)

Plate I Plate II

500 mon:
Plate I- Lower right corner of Greek-type border incomplete
Plate II- Short horizontal line completes corner border pattern.

Unwmk.

1871, Apr. 20 Engr. *Imperf.*

Native Laid Paper Without Gum
Denomination in Black

1 A1 48m brn (I) 225.00 210.00
a. 48m red brown (I) 225.00 210.00
b. Wove paper (I) 230.00 240.00
c. 48m brown (II) 250.00 260.00
d. Wove paper (II) 260.00 260.00
2 A1 100m blue (I) 200.00 195.00
a. Wove paper (I) 220.00 220.00
b. Plate II 500.00 425.00
c. Wove paper (II) 600.00 600.00
3 A1 200m ver (I) 300.00 210.00
a. Wove paper (I) 315.00 275.00
b. Plate II 2,000. 1,200.
c. Wove paper (II) 3,000.
4 A1 500m bl grn (I) 375.00 350.00
a. 500m greenish blue (I) 360.00 340.00
b. 500m green (I) 800.00 800.00
c. 500m yellow green (I) 850.00 825.00
d. Wove paper (I) 360.00 360.00
e. 500m blue green (II) 400.00 *2,100.*
f. 500m greenish blue (II) 400.00 *2,100.*
g. Wove paper (II) 1,650. *3,000.*
h. Denomination inverted (I) *95,000.*

Perforations

Values are for copies with damaged perfs. on Nos. 5-8 because of the perforating equipment used and the quality of the paper. The perfs. also touch the design.

Dragons and Denomination — A1a

½ sen:
Plate I- Same as 48m Plate II. Measures not less than 19.8x19.8mm. Some subjects on this plate measure 20.3x20.2mm.
Plate II- Same as 48m Plate II. Measures not more than 19.7x19.3mm. Some subjects measure 19.3x18.7mm.

Plates I & II

Plate III

1 sen:
Plate I- Same as 100m Plate I. Narrow space between frameline and Greek-type border.
Plate II- Same as 100m Plate II. Same narrow space between frameline and border.
Plate III- Space between frameline and border is much wider. Frameline thinner. Shading on dragon heads heavier than on Plates I and II.

Native Laid Paper
With or Without Gum

1872 *Perf. 9-12 & compound*

Denomination in Black

5 A1a ½s brn (II) 77.50 85.00
a. ½s red brown (II) 77.50 85.00
b. ½s gray brown (II) 77.50 85.00
c. Wove paper (II) 675.00 600.00
d. ½s brown (I) 95.00 130.00
e. ½s red brown (I) 95.00 130.00
f. ½s gray brown (I) 95.00 130.00
g. Wove paper (I) 130.00 200.00
6 A1a 1s bl (II) 195.00 195.00
a. Wove paper (II) 380.00 400.00
b. Plate I 850.00 *1,900.*
c. Wove paper (I) *3,750.*
d. Plate III *6,500.* 1,300.
e. Wove paper (III) *3,000.*
7 A1a 2s vermilion 300.00 300.00
a. Wove paper 315.00 315.00

8 A1a 5s bl grn 400.00 400.00
a. 5s yellow green 400.00 400.00
b. Wove paper 775.00 775.00

In 1896 the government made imperforate imitations of Nos. 6-7 to include in a presentation book.

Perforations on Nos. 9-52 frequently are very rough and irregular. Values are for copies that have perfs. touching the design.

Imperial Crest and Branches of Kiri Tree — A2

Dragons and Chrysanthemum Crest — A3

Imperial Chrysanthemum Crest — A4

Imperial Crest and Branches of Kiri Tree — A5

1872-73 ***Perf. 9 to 13 and Compound***
Native Wove or Laid Paper of Varying Thickness

9 A2 ½s brown, *wove* 18.00 18.00
a. Upper character in left label has 2 diagonal top strokes missing 1,800. 1,400.
b. Laid paper 60.00
c. As "a," laid paper 2,000.

Nos. 9, 9a are on stiff, brittle wove paper. Nos. 9b, 9c on a soft, fibrous paper. Nos. 9b and 9c probably were never put in use.

10 A2 1s blue, *wove* 45.00 27.50
a. Laid paper 45.00 27.50
11 A2 2s ver, *wove* 110.00 45.00
12 A2 2s dl rose, *laid* 72.50 27.50
a. Wove paper 100.00 37.50
13 A2 2s yel, *laid* ('73) 72.50 18.00
a. Wove paper ('73) 190.00 24.00
14 A2 4s rose, *laid* ('73) 60.00 20.00
a. Wove paper ('73) 190.00 27.50
15 A3 10s bl grn, *wove* 225.00 150.00
16 A3 10s yel grn, *laid* 465.00 300.00
a. Wove paper ('73) 600.00 550.00
17 A4 20s lil, *wove* 360.00 250.00
a. 20s violet, *wove* 360.00 250.00
b. 20s red violet, *laid*
18 A5 30s gray, *wove* 500.00 400.00

See Nos. 24-25, 30-31, 37-39, 51-52.

1874
Foreign Wove Paper

24 A2 4s rose 525.00 180.00
25 A5 30s gray *5,250.*

A6

A7

A8

Type A6 differs from A2 by the addition of a syllabic character in a box covering crossed kiri branches above SEN. Stamps of type A6 differ for each value in border and spandrel designs.

In type A7, the syllabic character appears just below the buckle. In type A8, it appears in an oval frame at bottom center below SE of SEN.

With Syllabic Characters

イ	ロ	ハ	ニ	ホ	ヘ	ト	チ
i	ro	ha	ni	ho	he	to	chi
1	2	3	4	5	6	7	8
リ	ヌ	ル	ヲ	ワ	カ	ヨ	タ
ri	nu	ru	wo	wa	ka	yo	ta
9	10	11	12	13	14	15	16
レ	ソ	ツ	子	ナ	ラ	ム	
re	so	tsu	ne	na	ra	mu	
17	18	19	20	21	22	23	

Perf. 9½ to 12½ and Compound
1874
Native Laid or Wove Paper

28 A6 2s yellow 210.00 300.00

Unused value is for copies with syll. 16, used value for copies with syll. 1.

29 A7 6s vio brn (Syll. 1) 1,000. 340.00
Syllabic 2 1,250. 360.00
Syllabic 3 900.00
Syllabic 4,5,7 465.00
Syllabic 6 550.00
Syllabic 8 425.00
Syllabic 9 500.00
Syllabic 10 3,000.
Syllabic 11 2,750.
Syllabic 12 1,600.
30 A4 20s red vio (Syll. 3) *7,250.*
Syllabic 2 *7,500.*
31 A5 30s gray (Syll. 1) 2,500. 3,000.
a. Very thin laid paper 2,500. 3,000.

No. 30, syll. 1, comes only with specimen dot. Value $22,500.

1874 ***Perf. 11 to 12½ and Compound***
Foreign Wove Paper

32 A6 ½s brn (Syll. 1) 19.00 16.00
Syllabic 2 35.00 35.00
33 A6 1s bl (Syll. 4,6,9) 125.00 27.50
Syllabic 1,2,3 140.00 27.50
Syllabic 5 450.00 105.00
Syllabic 7 200.00 27.50
Syllabic 8 125.00 27.50
Syllabic 10 150.00 40.00
Syllabic 11 150.00 40.00
Syllabic 12 165.00 40.00
34 A6 2s yel (Syll. 2-4, 9, 15, 17, 20) 125.00 25.00
Syllabic 1 250.00 25.00
Syllabic 5 305.00 25.00
Syllabic 6 1,800. 35.00
Syllabic 7 1,750. 20.00
Syllabic 8 125.00 27.50
Syllabic 10 *2,500.* 37.50
Syllabic 11 125.00 20.00
Syllabic 12,22 *2,500.* 20.00
Syllabic 13 *2,000.* 20.00
Syllabic 14 *2,500.* 27.50
Syllabic 16 *2,100.* 20.00
Syllabic 18,19 125.00 20.00
Syllabic 21 200.00 20.00
Syllabic 23 210.00 20.00
35 A6 4s rose (Syll. 1) 2,000. 315.00
36 A7 6s vio brn (Syll. 16) 125.00 42.50
Syllabic 10 475.00 500.00
Syllabic 11 425.00
Syllabic 13 *4,750.*
Syllabic 14 250.00 200.00
Syllabic 15 *2,500.*
Syllabic 17 150.00 65.00
Syllabic 18 225.00 87.50
37 A3 10s yel grn (Syll. 2) 75.00 45.00
Syllabic 1 250.00 80.00
Syllabic 3 550.00 315.00
38 A4 20s vio (Syll. 5) 210.00 60.00
Syllabic 4 210.00 60.00
39 A5 30s gray (Syll. 1) 175.00 57.50

1875 ***Perf. 9 to 13 and Compound***

40 A6 ½s gray (Syll. 2, 3) 16.00 14.00
Syllabic 4 24.00
41 A6 1s brn (Syll. 15-17) 30.00 16.00
Syllabic 5 315.00 40.00
Syllabic 7,8 225.00
Syllabic 12 525.00 150.00
Syllabic 13 37.50 16.00
Syllabic 14 40.00 16.00
42 A6 4s grn (Syll. 1) 87.50 18.00
Syllabic 2 135.00 18.00
Syllabic 3 110.00 18.00
43 A7 6s org (Syll. 16,17) 72.50 16.00
Syllabic 10 150.00 40.00
Syllabic 11 130.00 30.00
Syllabic 13 135.00 27.50
Syllabic 14 175.00 30.00
Syllabic 15
44 A8 6s org (Syll. 20) 72.50 16.00
Syllabic 19 80.00 14.00
Syllabic 21 100.00 18.00
Syllabic 22 3,750. 1,500.

Dragons — A9

Wild Goose — A10

Wagtail — A11

Imperial Crest — A11a

Kiri Branches — A11b

Goshawk — A12

45 A9 10s ultra (Syll. 4) 105.00 16.00
Syllabic 5 *3,350.* 300.00
46 A10 12s rose (Syll. 1) 230.00 105.00
Syllabic 2 235.00 130.00
Syllabic 3 *3,250.* 425.00
47 A11 15s lil (Syll. 1) 210.00 140.00
Syllabic 2 220.00 125.00
Syllabic 3 250.00 140.00
48 A11a 20s rose (Syll. 8) 57.50 14.00
49 A11b 30s vio (Syll. 2-4) 110.00 45.00
50 A12 45s lake (Syll. 1) 250.00 130.00
Syllabic 2 1,350. 425.00
Syllabic 3 1,250. 380.00

Issue dates: No. 46, syll. 2, 1882. No. 46, syll. 3, 1883. Others, 1875.

The 1s brown on laid paper, type A6, formerly listed as No. 50A, is one of several stamps of the preceding issue which exist on a laid type paper. They are difficult to identify and mainly of interest to specialists.

Without Syllabic Characters
1875

51 A2 1s brown *5,750.* 600.00
52 A2 4s green 235.00 60.00

Branches of Kiri Tree Tied with Ribbon — A13

Imperial Crest and Kiri Branches — A14

1875-76

53 A13 1s brown 40.00 11.00
54 A13 2s yellow 65.00 11.00
54A A14 5s grn ('76) 160.00 80.00

A15

A16

Imperial Crest, Star and Kiri Branches — A17

Sun, Kikumon and Kiri Branches — A18

Imperial Crest and Kiri Branches — A19

Kikumon — A20

Perf. 8 to 14 and Compound
1876-77 **Typo.**

55 A15 5r slate 15.00 12.00
56 A16 1s black 32.50 4.50
a. Horiz. pair, imperf. btwn.
57 A16 2s brn ol 47.50 3.00
58 A16 4s bl grn 40.00 4.00
a. 4s green 40.00 4.00

59	A17	5s brown	60.00	24.00
60	A17	6s org ('77)	125.00	45.00
61	A17	8s vio brn ('77)	60.00	6.00
62	A17	10s bl ('77)	47.50	2.50
63	A17	12s rose ('77)	210.00	150.00
64	A18	15s yel grn ('77)	130.00	3.00
65	A18	20s dk bl ('77)	155.00	12.50
66	A18	30s vio ('77)	200.00	100.00
a.		30s red violet	195.00	90.00
67	A18	45s car ('77)	550.00	525.00

1879

68	A16	1s maroon	12.00	1.10
69	A16	2s dk vio	27.50	1.40
70	A16	3s orange	47.50	22.50
71	A18	50s car	150.00	13.00

1883

72	A16	1s green	8.75	50
73	A16	2s car rose	11.00	20
74	A17	5s ultra	18.00	50

1888-92

75	A15	5r gray blk ('89)	4.75	42
76	A16	3s lil rose ('92)	14.00	42
77	A16	4s ol bis	12.00	42
78	A17	8s bl lil	18.00	1.65
79	A17	10s brn org	16.00	42
80	A18	15s purple	50.00	45
81	A18	20s orange	70.00	1.65
a.		20s yellow	70.00	1.65
82	A19	25s bl grn	125.00	1.75
83	A18	50s brown	100.00	3.50
84	A20	1y carmine	150.00	4.50

Stamps of types A16-A18 differ for each value, in backgrounds and ornaments.

Nos. 58, 61-62, 65, 71-84 are found with telegraph or telegraph office cancellations. These sell at considerably lower prices than postally used copies.

Cranes and Imperial Crest — A21

Perf. 11½ to 13 and Compound

1894, Mar. 9

85	A21	2s carmine	22.50	2.75
86	A21	5s ultra	37.50	12.50

25th wedding anniv. of Emperor Meiji (Mutsuhito) and Empress Haru.

Gen. Yoshihisa Kitashirakawa
A22 A23

Field Marshal Akihito Arisugawa
A24 A25

1896, Aug. 1 **Engr.**

87	A22	2s rose	24.00	2.50
88	A23	5s deep ultra	55.00	2.25
89	A24	2s rose	24.00	2.50
90	A25	5s deep ultra	55.00	2.25

Victory in Chinese-Japanese War (1894-95).

A26

A27

A28

A29

Perf. 11½ to 14 and Compound

1899-1907 **Typo.**

91	A26	5r gray	5.00	60
92	A26	½s gray ('01)	2.75	15
93	A26	1s lt red brn	3.50	15
94	A26	1½s ultra ('00)	12.50	90
95	A26	1½s vio ('06)	8.75	20
96	A26	2s lt grn	8.75	16
97	A26	3s vio brn	8.75	20
a.		Double impression		
98	A26	3s rose ('06)	5.00	20
99	A26	4s rose	5.50	95
a.		4s pink ('06)	5.50	1.00
100	A26	5s org yel	18.00	20
101	A27	6s mar ('07)	27.50	3.50
102	A27	8s ol grn	30.00	3.75
103	A27	10s dp bl	10.50	15
104	A27	15s purple	42.50	1.40
105	A27	20s red org	22.50	15
106	A28	25s bl grn	60.00	90
107	A28	50s red brn	60.00	1.10
108	A29	1y carmine	70.00	1.25
		Nos. 91-108 (18)	401.50	15.91

For overprints see Nos. M1, Offices in China, 1-18, Offices in Korea, 1-14.

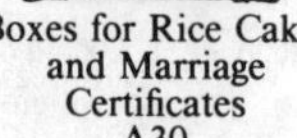

Boxes for Rice Cakes and Marriage Certificates
A30

Symbols of Korea and Japan
A31

Perf. 11½ to 12½ and Compound

1900, May 10

109	A30	3s carmine	19.00	75

Wedding of the Crown Prince Yoshihito and Princess Sadako.

For overprints see Offices in China No. 19, Offices in Korea, 15.

1905, July 1

110	A31	3s rose red	90.00	20.00

Issued to commemorate the amalgamation of the postal services of Japan and Korea. Korean stamps were withdrawn from sale June 30, 1905, but remained valid until Aug. 31. No. 110 was used in the Korea and China Offices of Japan, as well as in Japan proper.

Field-piece and Japanese Flag
A32

Empress Jingo
A33

1906, Apr. 29

111	A32	1½s blue	30.00	3.75
112	A32	3s car rose	62.50	17.50

Triumphal military review following the Russo-Japanese War.

1908 **Engr.**

113	A33	5y green	575.00	3.50
114	A33	10y dk vio	750.00	5.75

The frame of No. 114 differs slightly from the illustration.

For overprints see Offices in China Nos. 20-21, 48-49.

A34

A35

A36

Perf. 12, 12x13, 13x13½

1913 **Typo.** **Unwmk.**

115	A34	½s brown	6.00	75
116	A34	1s orange	7.25	75
117	A34	1½s lt bl	7.25	1.10
a.		Bklt. pane of 6	210.00	
118	A34	2s green	9.00	75
119	A34	3s rose	10.50	38
a.		Bklt. pane of 6	210.00	
120	A35	4s red	18.00	9.00
121	A35	5s violet	22.50	1.10
122	A35	10s dp bl	60.00	75
123	A35	20s claret	97.50	1.25
124	A35	25s olive grn	100.00	2.25
125	A36	1y yel grn & mar	575.00	20.00
		Nos. 115-125 (11)	913.00	38.08

1914-25 **Wmk. 141** **Granite Paper**

Size: 19x22½mm ("Old Die")

127	A34	½s brown	1.90	15
128	A34	1s orange	2.00	15
129	A34	1½s blue	2.00	15
a.		Bklt. pane of 6	85.00	
d.		As "a," imperf.		
130	A34	2s green	3.25	15
a.		Bklt. pane of 6	85.00	
131	A34	3s rose	1.50	15
a.		Bklt. pane of 6	72.50	
132	A35	4s red	10.50	1.25
a.		Bklt. pane of 6	85.00	
133	A35	5s violet	10.00	52
134	A35	6s brn ('19)	14.00	2.75
136	A35	8s gray ('19)	13.00	10.50
137	A35	10s dp bl	7.00	15
a.		Bklt. pane of 6	85.00	
138	A35	13s ol brn ('25)	25.00	2.25
139	A35	20s claret	35.00	70
140	A35	25s ol grn	11.00	1.00
141	A36	30s org brn ('19)	12.50	60
143	A36	50s dk brn ('19)	19.00	1.00
145	A36	1y yel grn & mar	77.50	1.00
b.		Imperf., pair		
146	A33	5y green	350.00	2.75
147	A33	10y violet	500.00	5.25
		Nos. 127-147 (18)	1,095.	30.47

1924-33

"New Die" Size: 18½x22mm (Flat Plate) or 18½x22½mm (Rotary)

127a	A34	½s brown	2.00	1.00
128a	A34	1s orange	2.00	1.00
129b	A34	1½s blue	3.25	28
c.		Bklt. pane of 6 ('30)	21.00	
131b	A34	3s rose	1.40	15
c.		Bklt. pane of 6 ('28)	50.00	
133a	A35	5s violet	17.50	15
135	A35	7s red org ('30)	8.75	15
138a	A35	13s bis brn ('25)	7.00	15
140a	A35	25s ol grn	50.00	16
142	A36	30s org & grn ('29)	19.00	28
144	A36	50s yel brn & dk bl ('29)	13.00	55
145a	A36	1y yel grn & mar	80.00	60
		Nos. 127a-145a (11)	203.90	4.47

See Nos. 212-213, 239-241, 243, 245, 249-252, 255. For overprints see Nos. C1-C2, M2-M5, Offices in China, 22-47.

Ceremonial Cap — A37

Imperial Throne — A38

Enthronement Hall, Kyoto — A39

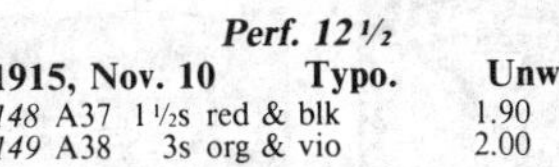

Perf. 12½

1915, Nov. 10 Typo. Unwmk.

148	A37	1½s red & blk	1.90	50
149	A38	3s org & vio	2.00	60

Engr.

Perf. 12x12½

150	A39	4s car rose	11.00	9.25
151	A39	10s ultra	22.50	17.00

Enthronement of Emperor Yoshihito.

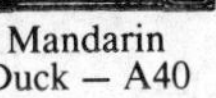

Mandarin Duck — A40

Ceremonial Cap — A41

1916, Nov. 3 Typo. ***Perf. 12½***

152	A40	1½s grn, red & yel	1.65	80
153	A40	3s red & yel	3.00	1.00
154	A41	10s ultra & dk bl	525.00	240.00

Nomination of the Prince Heir Apparent, later Emperor Hirohito.

Dove and Olive Branch
A42 A43

Perf. 12, 12½, 13½x13

1919, July 1 Engr.

155	A42	1½s dk brn	1.90	65
156	A43	3s gray grn	2.25	95
157	A42	4s rose	5.25	3.00
158	A43	10s dk bl	21.00	11.00

Restoration of peace after World War I.

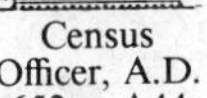

Census Officer, A.D. 652 — A44

Meiji Shrine, Tokyo — A45

Perf. 12½

1920, Sept. 25 Typo. Unwmk.

159	A44	1½s red vio	7.00	3.00
160	A44	3s vermilion	7.75	3.00

Taking of the 1st modern census in Japan. Not available for foreign postage except to China.

1920, Nov. 1 Engr.

161	A45	1½s dull violet	2.50	1.25
162	A45	3s rose	2.50	1.25

Dedication of the Meiji Shrine. Not available for foreign postage except to China.

National and Postal Flags — A46

Ministry of Communications Building, Tokyo — A47

Typographed (A46), Engraved (A47)

1921, Apr. 20 ***Perf. 12½, 13x13½***

163	A46	1½s gray grn & red	1.50	90
164	A47	3s vio brn	2.00	1.10
165	A46	4s rose & red	32.50	15.00
166	A47	10s dk bl	175.00	125.00

50th anniv. of the establishment of postal service and Japanese postage stamps.

Battleships "Katori" and "Kashima" — A48

1921, Sept. 3 Litho. ***Perf. 12½***

167	A48	1½s violet	2.00	90
168	A48	3s ol grn	2.75	90
169	A48	4s rose red	37.50	18.00
170	A48	10s dp bl	42.50	21.00

Return of Crown Prince Hirohito from his European visit.

Mount Fuji — A49

Mt. Niitaka, Taiwan — A50

Perf. 13x13½

1930-37 Typo. Wmk. 141

Granite Paper

Size: 18½x22mm ("New Die")

171	A49	4s grn ('37)	2.75	32
172	A49	4s orange	6.50	25
174	A49	8s ol grn	10.00	15
175a	A49	20s blue ('37)	20.00	25.00
176	A49	20s brn vio	30.00	20
		Nos. 171-176 (5)	69.25	25.92

1922-29

Size: 19x22½mm ("Old Die")

171a	A49	4s green	9.00	3.00
172a	A49	4s org ('29)	90.00	9.00
173	A49	8s rose	18.00	6.00
174a	A49	8s ol grn ('29)	250.00	80.00
175	A49	20s dp bl	20.00	60
176a	A49	20s brn vio ('29)	90.00	1.50
		Nos. 171a-176a (6)	477.00	100.10

See Nos. 242, 246, 248.

Perf. 12½

1923, Apr. 16 Unwmk. Engr.

177	A50	1½s orange	10.00	8.00
178	A50	3s dk vio	15.00	7.00

1st visit of Crown Prince Hirohito to Taiwan. The stamps were sold only in Taiwan, but were valid throughout the empire.

Cherry Blossoms A51

Sun and Dragonflies A52

Empress Jingo — A53

1923 Wmk. 142 Litho. ***Imperf.***

Without Gum; Granite Paper

179	A51	½s gray	2.00	2.00
180	A51	1½s lt bl	2.75	1.00
181	A51	2s red brn	2.50	1.00
182	A51	3s brt rose	1.75	70
183	A51	4s gray grn	17.50	14.00
184	A51	5s dl vio	8.50	1.00
185	A51	8s red org	30.00	25.00
186	A52	10s dp brn	17.50	1.00
187	A52	20s dp bl	21.00	1.40
		Nos. 179-187 (9)	103.50	47.10

#179-187 exist rouletted and with various perforations. These were made privately.

Perf. 12, 13x13½

1924 Engr. Wmk. 141

Granite Paper

188	A53	5y gray grn	165.00	2.00
189	A53	10y dl vio	275.00	1.50

See Nos. 253-254.

Cranes — A54

Phoenix — A55

Perf. 10½ to 13½ and Compound

1925, May 10 Litho. Unwmk.

190	A54	1½s gray vio	1.50	75
191	A55	3s sil & brn org	2.50	1.50
a.		Vert. pair, imperf. btwn.	500.00	
192	A54	8s lt red	20.00	9.75
193	A55	20s sil & gray grn	50.00	24.00

25th wedding anniv. of the Emperor Yoshihito (Taisho) and Empress Sadako.

Mt. Fuji — A56

Yomei Gate, Nikko — A57

Nagoya Castle — A58

Perf. 13½x13

1926-37 Typo. Wmk. 141

Granite Paper

194	A56	2s green	1.90	15
195	A57	6s carmine	6.75	15
196	A58	10s dk bl	8.25	15
197	A58	10s car ('37)	8.00	6.00

See Nos. 244, 247. For surcharges see People's Republic of China No. 2L5-2L6.

Baron Hisoka Maejima — A59

Map of World on Mollweide's Projection — A60

Perf. 12½, 13x13½

1927, June 20 **Unwmk.**

198	A59	1½s lilac	2.25	90
199	A59	3s olive grn	2.25	90
200	A60	6s car rose	65.00	40.00
201	A60	10s blue	80.00	40.00

50th anniv. of Japan's joining the UPU. Baron Maejima (1835-1919) organized Japan's modern postal system and was postmaster general.

Phoenix — A61

Enthronement Hall, Kyoto — A62

1928, Nov. 10 **Engr.** ***Perf. 12½***
Yellow Paper

202	A61	1½s dp grn	90	50
203	A62	3s red vio	90	50
204	A61	6s car rose	2.75	2.00
205	A62	10s dp bl	3.50	2.50

Enthronement of Emperor Hirohito.

Great Shrines of Ise — A63

Map of Japanese Empire — A64

1929, Oct. 2 ***Perf. 12½***

206	A63	1½s gray vio	1.25	1.00
207	A63	3s carmine	1.75	1.25

58th rebuilding of the Ise Shrines.

1930, Sept. 25 **Unwmk.**

208	A64	1½s dp vio	2.50	1.25
209	A64	3s dp red	2.75	1.65

2nd census in the Japanese Empire.

Meiji Shrine — A65

1930, Nov. 1 **Litho.**

210	A65	1½s green	1.75	1.00
211	A65	3s brn org	2.25	1.25

10th anniv. of dedication of Meiji Shrine.

Coil Stamps

Wmk. Zigzag Lines (141)

1933 **Typo.** ***Perf. 13 Horiz.***

212	A34	1½s lt bl	13.00	18.00
213	A34	3s rose	15.00	22.00

Japanese Red Cross Badge — A66

Red Cross Building, Tokyo — A67

Perf. 12½

1934, Oct. 1 **Engr.** **Unwmk.**

214	A66	1½s grn & red	1.65	1.10
215	A67	3s dl vio & red	1.90	1.25
216	A66	6s dk car & red	9.00	5.50
217	A67	10s bl & red	12.00	8.50

15th International Red Cross Congress. Sheets of 20 with commemorative marginal inscription. One side of sheet is perf. 13.

White Tower of Liaoyang and Warship "Hiei" — A68

Akasaka Detached Palace, Tokyo — A69

1935, Apr. 2

218	A68	1½s olive grn	1.10	75
219	A69	3s red brown	1.65	1.00
220	A68	6s carmine	7.25	3.75
221	A69	10s blue	10.00	6.00

Visit of Emperor Kang Teh of Manchukuo (Henry Pu-yi) to Tokyo, April 6, 1935. Sheets of 20 with commemorative marginal inscription. One side of sheet is perf. 13.

Mt. Fuji — A70

1935 **Typo.** ***Perf. 13x13½***
Granite Paper

222	A70	1½s rose car	10.00	25
a.		Miniature sheet of 20	475.00	450.00

Issued to pay postage on New Year's cards from Dec. 1-31, 1935. After Jan. 1, 1936, used for ordinary letter postage. No. 222 was issued in sheets of 100.

Mt. Fuji A71

Fuji from Lake Ashi A72

Fuji from Lake Kawaguchi — A73

Fuji from Mishima A74

1936, July 10 **Photo.** **Wmk. 141**
Granite Paper

223	A71	1½s red brn	2.75	2.25
224	A72	3s dk grn	5.00	3.75
225	A73	6s car rose	11.00	9.00
226	A74	10s dk bl	13.00	11.00

Fuji-Hakone National Park.

Dove, Map of Manchuria and Kwantung A75

Shinto Shrine, Port Arthur A76

Headquarters of Kwantung Government A77

1936, Sept. 1 **Litho.** ***Perf. 12½***
Granite Paper

227	A75	1½s gray vio	17.00	12.00
228	A76	3s red brn	12.50	12.50
229	A77	10s dull grn	165.00	165.00

30th anniv. of Japanese administration of Kwantung Leased Territory and the South Manchuria Railway Zone. Sold only in Kwantung Territory and South Manchuria Railway Zone, but valid throughout Japan.

Imperial Diet Building A78

Grand Staircase A79

1936, Nov. 7 **Engr.** ***Perf. 13***

230	A78	1½s green	1.50	1.00
231	A79	3s brn vio	1.75	1.25
232	A79	6s car	4.75	4.00
233	A78	10s blue	7.25	5.25

Opening of the new Diet Building, Tokyo.

"Wedded Rocks," Futamigaura — A80

1936, Dec. 10 **Photo.**

234	A80	1½s rose car	4.25	20

Issued to pay postage on New Year's greeting cards.

Types of 1913-26

Perf. 13½x13, 13x13½

1937 **Typo.** **Wmk. 257**

239	A34	½s brown	1.65	1.10
240	A34	1s org yel	2.50	1.50
241	A34	3s rose	95	15
242	A49	4s green	3.50	22
243	A35	5s violet	4.50	15
244	A57	6s crimson	6.75	1.10
245	A35	7s red org	6.75	15
246	A49	8s ol bis	7.50	55
247	A58	10s carmine	6.00	15
248	A49	20s blue	11.00	30
249	A35	25s ol grn	30.00	1.25
250	A36	30s org & grn	18.00	25
251	A36	50s brn org & dk bl	95.00	1.10
252	A36	1y yel grn & mar	52.50	45
		Nos. 239-252 (14)	246.60	8.42

Engr.

253	A53	5y gray grn	300.00	4.00
254	A53	10y dl vio	350.00	3.50

For overprint see People's Republic of China No. 2L6.

Coil Stamp

1938 **Typo.** ***Perf. 13 Horiz.***

255	A34	3s rose	3.75	3.75

New Year's Decoration — A81

1937, Dec. 15	Photo.		*Perf. 13*	
256 A81	2s scarlet		8.00	20

Issued to pay postage on New Year's cards, later for ordinary use.

Trading Ship — A82

Rice Harvest — A83

Gen. Maresuke Nogi — A84

Power Plant — A85

Admiral Heihachiro Togo — A86

Mount Hodaka — A87

Garambi Lighthouse, Taiwan — A88

Diamond Mountains, Korea — A89

Meiji Shrine, Tokyo — A90

Yomei Gate, Nikko — A91

Plane and Map of Japan — A92

Kasuga Shrine, Nara — A93

Mount Fuji and Cherry Blossoms — A94

Horyu Temple, Nara — A95

Miyajima Torii, Itsukushima Shrine — A96

Golden Pavilion, Kyoto — A97

Great Buddha, Kamakura — A98

Kamatari Fujiwara — A99

Plum Blossoms — A100

Typographed or Engraved

1937-45	Wmk. 257	*Perf. 13*	
257 A82	½s purple	60	28
258 A83	1s fawn	1.75	24
259 A84	2s crimson	42	15
a.	Bklt. pane of 20	50.00	
b.	2s pink, perf. 12 ('45)	1.50	1.00
c.	2s ver ('44)	2.50	2.00
260 A85	3s grn ('39)	42	15
261 A86	4s dk grn	90	15
a.	Bklt. pane of 20	15.00	
262 A87	5s dk ultra ('39)	90	15
263 A88	6s org ('39)	1.75	70
264 A89	7s dp grn ('39)	52	15
265 A90	8s dk pur & pale vio ('39)	50	20
266 A91	10s lake ('38)	2.75	15
267 A92	12s ind ('39)	52	35
268 A93	14s rose lake & pale rose ('38)	52	24
269 A94	20s ultra ('40)	55	15
270 A95	25s dk brn & pale brn ('38)	52	15
271 A96	30s pck bl ('39)	1.40	15
a.	Imperf., pair	375.00	
272 A97	50s ol & pale ol ('39)	70	15
a.	Pale olive (forest) omitted		
273 A98	1y brn & pale brn ('39)	2.75	35
274 A99	5y dp gray grn ('39)	20.00	1.40
275 A100	10y dk brn vio ('39)	13.00	1.00
	Nos. 257-275 (19)	50.47	6.26

Nos. 257 to 261, 265, 268, 270, 272 and 273 are typographed; the others are engraved.

Coil Stamps

1938-39	Typo.	*Perf. 13 Horiz.*	
276 A82	½s pur ('39)	3.00	3.75
277 A84	2s crimson	3.25	4.00
278 A86	4s dk grn	3.25	4.00
279 A93	14s rose lake & pale rose	85.00	60.00

See Nos. 329, 331, 333, 341, 351, 360 and 351. For surcharges see Nos. B4-B5, Burma 2N4-2N27, China-Taiwan, 8-9, People's Republic of China 2L3, 2L7, 2L9-2L10, 2L39, Korea 55-56. For overprints see Ryukyu Islands (US Specialized) Nos. 2X1-2X2, 2X4-2X7, 2X10, 2X13-2X14, 2X17, 2X20, 2X23, 2X27, 2X29, 2X33-2X34, 3X2-3X7, 3X10-3X11, 3X14, 3X17, 3X19, 3X21, 3X23, 3X26-3X30, 5X1-5X3, 5X5-5X8, 5X10.

Mount Nantai A101

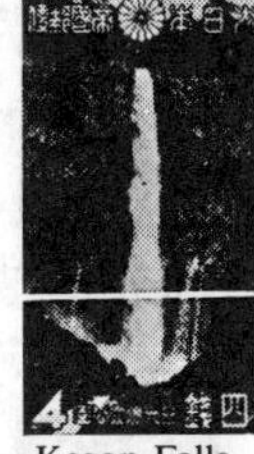
Kegon Falls A102

Sacred Bridge, Nikko A103

Mount Hiuchi A104

Unwmk.

1938, Dec. 25	Photo.	*Perf. 13*	
280 A101	2s brn org	70	60
281 A102	4s ol grn	70	60
282 A103	10s dp rose	5.50	4.50
283 A104	20s dk bl	5.50	4.50
a.	Souvenir sheet of 4, #280-283	40.00	45.00

Nikko National Park.
No. 283a sold for 50s.

Mount Daisen A106

Yashima Plateau, Inland Sea A107

Abuto Kwannon Temple A108

Tomo Bay, Inland Sea A109

1939, Apr. 20			
285 A106	2s lt brn	65	60
286 A107	4s yel grn	1.25	1.25
287 A108	10s dl rose	5.75	4.75
288 A109	20s blue	5.75	4.75
a.	Souvenir sheet of 4, #285-288	20.00	22.50

Daisen and Inland Sea National Parks.
No. 288a sold for 50s.

View from Kuju Village, Kyushu A111

Mount Naka A112

Crater of Mount Naka A113

Volcanic Cones of Mt. Aso A114

1939, Aug. 15			
290 A111	2s ol brn	85	50
291 A112	4s yel grn	2.75	1.90
292 A113	10s carmine	17.50	10.00
293 A114	20s sapphire	25.00	11.00
a.	Souvenir sheet of 4, #290-293	75.00	70.00

Aso National Park.
No. 293a sold for 50s.

Globe — A116

Tsunetami Sano — A117

1939, Nov. 15 *Perf. 12½*

Cross in Carmine

295	A116	2s brown	1.25	90
296	A117	4s yel grn	1.40	1.00
297	A116	10s crimson	8.50	7.75
298	A117	20s sapphire	8.50	7.75

75th anniv. of the founding of the Intl. Red Cross Society.

Sacred Golden Kite A118

Mount Takachiho A119

Five Ayu Fish and Sake Jar — A120

Kashiwara Shrine — A121

1940 **Engr.** *Perf. 12*

299	A118	2s brn org	80	80
300	A119	4s dk grn	60	48
301	A120	10s dk car	3.75	3.50
302	A121	20s dk ultra	80	80

2,600th anniv. of the legendary date of the founding of Japan.

Mt. Hokuchin, Hokkaido A122

Mt. Asahi, Hokkaido A123

Sounkyo Gorge — A124

Tokachi Mountain Range A125

1940, Apr. 20 **Photo.** *Perf. 13*

303	A122	2s brown	75	75
304	A123	4s yel grn	2.75	2.00
305	A124	10s carmine	7.50	6.00
306	A125	20s sapphire	7.50	6.50
a.		Souvenir sheet of 4, #303-306	200.00	200.00

Daisetsuzan National Park.
No. 306a sold for 50s.

Mt. Karakuni, Kyushu A127

Mt. Takachiho A128

Torii of Kirishima Shrine A129

Lake of the Six Kwannon A130

1940, Aug. 21

308	A127	2s brown	80	55
309	A128	4s green	1.75	1.40
310	A129	10s carmine	6.00	4.50
311	A130	20s dp ultra	7.25	5.50
a.		Souvenir sheet of 4, #308-311	185.00	185.00

Kirishima National Park.
No. 311a sold for 50s.

Education Minister with Rescript on Education A132

Characters Signifying Loyalty and Filial Piety A133

1940, Oct. 25 **Engr.** *Perf. 12½*

313	A132	2s purple	75	75
314	A133	4s green	90	90

50th anniv. of the imperial rescript on education, given by Emperor Meiji to clarify Japan's educational policy.

Mt. Daiton, Taiwan A134

Central Peak of Mt. Niitaka A135

Buddhist Temple on Mt. Kwannon A136

View from Mt. Niitaka A137

1941, Mar. 10 **Photo.** *Perf. 13*

315	A134	2s brown	60	52
316	A135	4s brt grn	1.00	85
317	A136	10s rose red	3.50	2.00
318	A137	20s bril ultra	4.50	2.00
a.		Souv. sheet of 4, #315-318	30.00	32.50

Daiton and Niitaka-Arisan National Parks.
#318a sold with #323a in same folder for 90s.

Seisui Precipice, East Taiwan Coast — A139

Taroko Gorge — A141

Mt. Tsugitaka A140

Upper River Takkiri District A142

1941, Mar. 10

320	A139	2s brown	70	52
321	A140	4s brt grn	1.00	90
322	A141	10s rose red	3.25	1.50
323	A142	20s bril ultra	4.50	2.25
a.		Souv. sheet of 4, #320-323	55.00	25.00

Tsugitaka-Taroko National Park.
See note after No. 318.

War Factory Girl — A144

Building of Wooden Ship — A145

Hyuga Monument and Mt. Fuji — A146

War Worker and Planes — A147

Palms and Map of "Greater East Asia" A148

"Enemy Country Surrender" A149

Aviator Saluting and Japanese Flag — A150

Torii of Yasukuni Shrine — A151

Mt. Fuji and Cherry Blossoms — A152

Torii of Miyajima — A153

Garambi Lighthouse, Taiwan — A154

Typographed; Engraved

1942-45 **Wmk. 257** *Perf. 13*

325	A144	1s org brn ('43)	15	15
328	A145	2s green	28	25
329	A84	3s brn ('44)	45	20
330	A146	4s emerald	15	15
331	A86	5s brn lake	16	15
332	A147	6s lt ultra ('44)	28	24
a.		Imperf., pair		
333	A86	7s org ver ('44)	16	15
334	A148	10s crim & dl rose	35	15
a.		Dull rose (map) omitted	350.00	350.00
335	A149	10s lt gray ('45)	2.00	2.00
336	A150	15s dl bl	1.40	85
337	A151	17s gray vio ('43)	42	32
338	A152	20s bl ('44)	42	15
339	A151	27s rose brn ('45)	45	35
340	A153	30s bluish grn ('44)	1.40	52
341	A88	40s dl vio	35	15
342	A154	40s dk vio ('44)	1.00	85
		Nos. 325,328-342 (16)	9.42	6.63

Nos. 325-335, 337-340 and 342 are typo. Nos. 336 and 341 are engr. Nos. 329, 331, 333, 334 and 342 were issued with and without gum. No. 335 was issued only without gum.

#328, 342 exist with watermark sideways. #328 exists printed on gummed side.

Most stamps of the above series exist in numerous shades.

For overprints and surcharges see North Borneo Nos. N34, N37, N41-N42, People's Republic of China 2L4, 2L8, Korea 57-60, Ryukyu Islands (US Specialized) Nos. 2X3, 2X9, 2X12, 2X15-2X16, 2X18-2X19, 2X21-2X22, 2X24-2X26, 2X28, 3X1, 3X8-3X9, 3X12-3X13, 3X15-3X16, 3X18, 3X20, 3X25, 3X31, 4X1-4X2, 5X4.

Kenkoku Shrine, Hsinking — A155

Boys of Japan and Manchukuo A156

Orchid Crest of Manchukuo A157

1942 **Unwmk.** **Engr.** *Perf. 12*

343	A155	2s brown	90	90
344	A156	5s olive	50	35
345	A155	10s red	80	80
346	A157	20s dk bl	2.00	2.00

The 2s and 10s were issued Mar. 1 for the 10th anniv. of the creation of Manchukuo; 5s and 20s on Sept. 15 for the 10th anniv. of Japanese diplomatic recognition of Manchukuo.

C-59 Locomotive
A158

Yasukuni Shrine, Tokyo
A159

1942, Oct. 14 **Photo.**
347 A158 5s Prus grn 3.50 3.50

70th anniv. of Japan's 1st railway.

1944, June 29 ***Perf. 13***
348 A159 7s Prus grn 60 60

75th anniversary of Yasukuni Shrine.

Kwantung Shrine and Map of Kwantung Peninsula — A160

1944, Oct. 1
349 A160 3s red brn 3.00 5.25
350 A160 7s gray vio 3.25 5.25

Dedication of Kwantung Shrine, Port Arthur.

Sun and Cherry Blossoms — A161

Sunrise at Sea and Plane — A162

Coal Miners — A163

Yasukuni Shrine — A164

Lithographed, Typographed
1945-47 **Wmk. 257** ***Imperf.***
Without Gum

351 A84 2s rose red 35 35
352 A161 3s rose car 20 30
353 A162 5s green 20 20
a. 5s blue 8.00 8.00
354 A149 10s lt gray 9.00 9.00
354A A149 10s blue 22.50
355 A152 10s red org 20 15
356 A152 20s ultra ('46) 40 15
357 A153 30s brt bl ('46) 1.50 90
358 A163 50s dk brn ('46) 30 15
a. Souvenir sheet of 5 ('47) 11.00 13.00
359 A164 1y dp ol grn ('46) 90 90
360 A99 5y dp gray grn 5.00 80
361 A100 10y dk brn vio 35.00 90
Nos. 351-354,355-361 (11) 53.05 13.80

Nos. 351 and 354 are typographed. The other stamps in this set are printed by offset lithography.

No. 358a was issued with marginal inscriptions to commemorate the Sapporo (Hokkaido) Philatelic Exhibition, Nov., 1947.

Nos. 351 to 361 are on grayish paper, and Nos. 355 to 361 also exist on white paper.

Most stamps of the above series exist in numerous shades and with private perforation or roulette.

See No. 404. For overprints see Ryukyu Islands (US Specialized) Nos. 2X8, 2X11, 2X30, 3X22, 4X3, 5X9.

Catalogue values for unused stamps in this section, from this point to the end of the section, are for Never Hinged items.

Baron Hisoka Maejima — A165

Horyu Temple Pagoda — A166

"Thunderstorm below Fuji," by Hokusai — A167

"First Geese," Print by Hokusai — A168

Kintai Bridge, Iwakuni — A169

Kiyomizu Temple, Kyoto — A170

Goldfish — A171

Noh Mask — A172

Plum Blossoms — A173

Characters Read Right to Left
1946-47 **Wmk. 257** **Litho.** ***Imperf.***
Without Gum

362 A165 15s dk grn 38 25
363 A166 30s dl lil 50 15
364 A167 1y dp ultra 1.90 15
a. 1y ultramarine 65 18
b. 1y light blue 75 15
365 A168 1.30y ol bis 2.25 52
366 A169 1.50y dk gray 2.25 38
367 A170 2y vermilion 2.00 15
a. Souvenir sheet of 5 ('47) 22.50 21.00
368 A171 5y lil rose 7.25 48
Nos. 362-368 (7) 16.53 2.08

Nos. 363, 368 exist with and without gum.

No. 367a was issued in sheets measuring 113x71mm, with marginal inscriptions and ornaments, to commemorate the "Know Your Stamps" exhibition, Kyoto, Aug. 19-24, 1947.

#362, 369 exist with watermark horizontal.

See Nos. 384-387, 512A. For overprints see Ryukyu Islands (US Specialized) Nos. 2X32, 3X24, 4X4.

Engr.
369 A172 50y bis brn 70.00 75
370 A173 100y brn car ('47) 70.00 75

Perf. 13
371 A172 50y bis brn, with gum ('47) 70.00 75
372 A173 100y brn car, with gum ('47) 70.00 38

Litho.
Perf. 13x13½, 12, 12x12½
373 A166 30s dull lilac 2.75 2.75

Rouletted in Colored Lines
Typo. **Unwmk.**
With Gum
374 A166 30s deep lilac 1.00 1.50

Medieval Postman's Bell
A175

Baron Hisoka Maejima
A176

Design of First Japanese Stamp — A177

Communication Symbols — A178

Perf. 12½, 13½x13
1946, Dec. 12 **Engr.** **Unwmk.**
With Gum

375 A175 15s orange 4.50 3.25
376 A176 30s dp grn 5.25 4.25
377 A177 50s carmine 2.25 2.25
378 A178 1y dp bl 2.25 2.25
a. Souvenir sheet of 4, #375-378, imperf. 125.00 110.00

75th anniversary of government postal service in Japan.

No. 378a measures 183x125mm and is ungummed. There were 2 printings: I - The 4 colors were printed simultaneously. Arched top inscription in high relief (2,000 sheets). II - Stamps were printed in one step, sheet inscriptions in another. Top inscription flat, almost level with paper's surface (49,000 sheets). 1st printing value $700.

Mother and Child, Diet Building
A180

Bouquet of Japanese May Flowers
A181

Wmk. 257
1947, May 3 **Litho.** ***Perf. 12½***
380 A180 50s rose brn 25 30
381 A181 1y brt ultra 52 42
a. Souvenir sheet of 2, #380-381, imperf. 11.00 6.00
b. As "a," 50s omitted 1,000.
c. As "a," 1y omitted 1,000.

Issued to commemorate the inauguration of the constitution of May 3, 1947.

A182

1947, Aug. 15 **Photo.** ***Perf. 12½***
382 A182 1.20y brown 2.25 1.10
383 A182 4y brt ultra 4.50 1.50

Issued to commemorate the reopening of foreign trade on a private basis.

The ornaments on No. 383 differ from those shown in the illustration.

Types of 1946 Redrawn
Characters Read Left to Right
1947-48 **Wmk. 257** **Typo.** ***Perf. 13***
384 A166 30s dp lil 1.50 1.40
385 A166 1.20y lt ol grn 95 35
a. Souvenir sheet of 15 125.00 135.00
386 A170 2y ver ('48) 3.75 20
387 A168 4y lt ultra 2.50 28

No. 385a was issued with marginal inscriptions to commemorate the "Know Your Stamps" Exhibition, Tokyo, May, 1947.

On No. 386, the chrysanthemum crest has been eliminated and the top inscription centered.

Plum Blossoms — A183

1947 **Typo.** ***Imperf.***
388 A183 10y dk brn vio 25.00 80

This stamp is similar to type A100 but with new inscription "Nippon Yubin" (Japan Post), reading from left to right. The characters for the denomination are likewise transposed.

A184

A185

Baron Hisoka Maejima
A186

Whaling
A187

National Art, Imperial Treasure House, Nara — A188

1947 **Typo.** ***Perf. 13x13½***
389 A184 35s green 40 30

Litho.
390 A185 45s lil rose 55 55
a. Imperf., pair 700.00
b. Perf. 11x13½ 4.50 4.50
391 A186 1y dl brn 2.50 40

Typo.
392 A187 5y blue 6.00 15
a. Imperf., pair 600.00
b. Perf. 11x13½ 22.50 2.75

Engr.
Perf. 13½x13
393 A188 10y lilac 13.00 15
a. Imperf., pair
Nos. 389-393 (5) 22.45 1.55

No. 389 was produced on both rotary and flat press. Sheets of the rotary press printing have a border. Those of the flat press printing have none.

Lily of the Valley — A188a

1947, Sept. 13 **Unwmk.** ***Perf. 12½***
394 A188a 2y dk Prus grn 3.25 1.40

Relief of Ex-convicts Day, Sept. 13, 1947.

Souvenir Sheet

A189

1947 Wmk. 257 Litho. *Imperf.*
Without Gum

395 A189 Sheet of 5, ultra 2.75 3.00

Issued in connection with Stamp Hobby Week, November 1-7, 1947. Sheet size: 113½x71½mm, on white or grayish paper.

"Benkei," 1880 Locomotive — A190

1947, Oct. 14 Unwmk. Engr.

396 A190 4y dp ultra 15.00 15.00

75th anniv. of railway service in Japan.

Hurdling
A191

Diving
A192

Discus
Throwing
A193

Volleyball
A194

1947, Oct. 25 Photo. *Perf. 12½*
With Gum

397	A191 1.20y red vio		7.00	6.50
398	A192 1.20y red vio		7.00	6.50
399	A193 1.20y red vio		7.00	6.50
400	A194 1.20y red vio		7.00	6.50
a.	Block of 4, #397-400		37.50	30.00

2nd Natl. Athletic Meet, held in Kanazawa, Oct. 30-Nov. 3.

Souvenir Sheets

A195

1948 Wmk. 257 Litho. *Imperf.*
Without Gum

401 A195 Sheet of 2, #368 12.00 14.00

Same, Inscribed with Three instead of Two Japanese Characters at Bottom Center

402 A195 Sheet of 2, #368 13.00 14.00

Philatelic exhibitions at Osaka (No. 401) and Nagoya (No. 402).

Stylized
Tree — A196

National Art
Treasure,
Nara — A197

Perf. 12½

1948, Apr. 1 Unwmk. Photo.

403 A196 1.20y dp yel grn 80 60

Forestation movement. Sheets of 30, marginal inscription.

Coal Miners Type of 1946, and Type A197

1948 Wmk. 257 Litho. *Perf. 13*
With Gum

404 A163 50s dk brn 1.00 50

Typo.

405 A197 10y rose vio 10.00 15

See No. 515A.

School
Children — A198

Perf. 12½

1948, May 3 Unwmk. Photo.

406 A198 1.20y dk car 75 60

Reorganization of Japan's educational system. Sheets of 30, marginal inscription.

Souvenir Sheets

No. 402 Overprinted at Top, Bottom and Sides with Japanese Characters and Flowers in Green

1948, Apr. 3 Wmk. 257 *Imperf.*

407	A195 Sheet of 2	50.00	35.00
a.	Overprint inverted	250.00	
b.	Overprint on No. 401	175.00	

Mishima Philatelic Exhibition, Apr. 3-9.

No. 395 Overprinted at Top and Bottom With Japanese Characters in Plum

1948, Apr. 18

408 A189 Sheet of 5, ultra 16.00 17.50

Issued to commemorate the centenary of the death of Katsushika Hokusai, painter.

Sampans on Inland Sea, Near
Suma — A199

Engr. & Litho.

1948, Apr. 22 Unwmk. *Imperf.*
Without Gum

409 A199 Sheet of two 10.50 5.50

Communications Exhib., Tokyo, Apr. 27-May 3, 1948. Sheet contains two 2y deep carmine stamps.

Sheet exists with green border omitted.

1948, May 20

410 A199 Sheet of 2, ultra border 12.00 12.00

Aomori Newspaper and Stamp Exhibition. Border design of apples and apple blossoms.

Type A199 With Altered Border and Inscriptions

1948, May 23

411 A199 Sheet of 2, blue border 12.00 12.00

Fukushima Stamp Exhibition. Border design of cherries and crossed lines.

Horse
Race — A200

1948, June 6 Photo. *Perf. 12½*
With Gum

412 A200 5y brown 2.10 60

25th anniv. of the enforcement of Japan's horse racing laws. Each sheet contains 30 stamps and 2 labels, with marginal inscription.

A201

A202

Wmk. 257

1948, Sept. 10 Litho. *Perf. 13*

413	A201 1.50y blue	1.20	45
414	A202 3.80y lt brn	4.50	3.50

Souvenir Sheet
Imperf

415 Sheet of 4 22.50 22.50

Kumamoto Stamp Exhibition, Sept. 20. Souvenir sheet, issued Sept. 20, contains two each of 1.50y deep blue (A201) and 3.80y brown (A202).

Rectifying
Tower — A203

Perf. 12½

1948, Sept. 14 Photo. Unwmk.

416 A203 5y dk ol bis 2.50 1.25

Government alcohol monopoly.

Swimmer — A204

Runner — A205

Designs: No. 419, High jumper. No. 420, Baseball players. No. 421, Bicycle racers.

1948

417	A204 5y blue	3.00	1.50
418	A205 5y green	7.00	3.00
419	A205 5y green	7.00	3.00
420	A205 5y green	7.00	3.00
421	A205 5y green	7.00	3.00
a.	Block of 4, #418-421	35.00	15.00
	Nos. 417-421 (5)	31.00	13.50

3rd Natl. Athletic Meet. Swimming matches held at Yawata, Sept. 16-19, field events, Fukuoka, Oct. 29-Nov. 3.

"Beauty Looking Back," Print by Moronobu — A206

1948, Nov. 29 *Perf. 13*

422	A206 5y brown	47.50	40.00
a.	Sheet of five	275.00	175.00

Philatelic Week, Nov. 29-Dec. 5. Sheets of 5 with marginal inscriptions.

Souvenir Sheet

1948, Dec. 3 *Imperf.*
Without Gum

423 A206 5y brn, sheet of 1 30.00 21.00

Kanazawa and Takaoka stamp exhibitions.

Child Playing Hane-tsuki — A207

1948, Dec. 13 Litho. *Perf. 13*

424 A207 2y scarlet 3.50 2.00

Issued to pay postage on New Year's cards, later for ordinary use.

Farm
Woman
A208

Whaling
A209

Miner
A210

Tea Picking
A211

Girl Printer
A212

Factory Girl with
Cotton Bobbin
A213

Mt.
Hodaka
A214

Planting A215

Postman A216

Blast Furnace A217

Locomotive Assembly A218

Typographed, Engraved

1948-49 Wmk. 257 *Perf. 13x13½*

425 A208 2y green 1.00 15
a. Overprinted with 4 characters in frame 50 60
b. As "a," ovpt. inverted *150.00*
426 A209 3y lt grnsh bl ('49) 5.00 15
427 A210 5y ol bis 14.00 15
a. Booklet pane of 20 65.00
428 A211 5y bl grn ('49) 27.50 4.50
429 A212 6y red org ('49) 5.50 15
430 A210 8y brn org ('49) 5.50 15
a. Booklet pane of 20 *100.00*
431 A213 15y blue 2.25 15
432 A214 16y ultra ('49) 6.00 3.00
433 A215 20y dk grn ('49) 22.50 15
434 A216 30y vio bl ('49) 30.00 15
435 A217 100y car lake ('49) 250.00 80
436 A218 500y dp bl ('49) 240.00 1.40
Nos. 425-436 (12) 609.25 10.90

No. 425a has a red control overprint of four characters ("Senkyo Jimu", or "Election Business") arranged vertically in a rectangular frame. Each candidate received 1,000 copies.

Nos. 432, 435-436 are engraved.

See Nos. 511-512, 514-515, 518, 520, 521A-521B.

Souvenir Sheets

Typo. and Litho.

1948, Oct. 16 *Imperf.*

437 A213 15y bl, sheet of 1 30.00 32.50

Nagano Stamp Exhibition, Oct. 16.

1948, Nov. 2 *Imperf.*

438 A210 5y ol bis, sheet of 2 32.50 32.50

Shikoku Traveling Stamp Exhib., Nov. 1948.

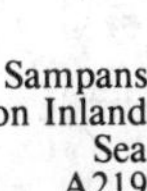

Sampans on Inland Sea A219

Perf. 13x13½

1949 Wmk. 257 Engr.

439 A219 10y rose lake 27.50 10.50
440 A219 10y car rose 20.00 8.50
441 A219 10y org ver 20.00 9.50
442 A214 16y brt bl 9.25 4.25

Issued in sheets of 20 stamps with marginal inscription publicizing expositions at Takamatsu (#439), Okayama (#440) and Matsuyama (#441), Nagano Peace Exposition, Apr. 1-May 31, 1949 (#442).

Ice Skater A221

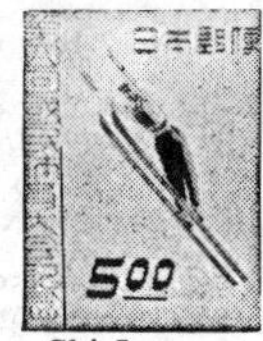
Ski Jumper A222

1949 Unwmk. Photo. *Perf. 12*

444 A221 5y violet 1.90 1.00
445 A222 5y ultra 2.25 1.00

Issued for the winter events of the 4th National Athletic Meet - skating at Suwa Jan. 27-30 and skiing at Sapporo Mar. 3-6. Issue dates: No. 444, Jan. 27; No. 445, Mar. 3.

Steamer in Beppu Bay — A223

1949, Mar. 10 Engr. *Perf. 13x13½*

446 A223 2y carmine & ultra 85 60
447 A223 5y green & ultra 3.25 80

Scene at Fair — A224

Stylized Trees — A225

1949, Mar. 15 Photo. *Perf. 13*

448 A224 5y brt rose 2.50 1.00
a. Imperf. 1.75 90
b. Sheet of 20, imperf. 55.00 55.00

Issued to publicize the Japan Foreign Trade Fair, Yokohama, 1949.

No. 448 was printed in sheets of 50 (10x5); No. 448a in sheets of 20 (4x5) with marginal inscriptions (No. 448b).

1949, Apr. 1 Unwmk. *Perf. 12*

449 A225 5y brt grn 8.00 90

Issued to publicize the forestation movement.

Lion Rock A226

Daiho-zan (Mt. Ohmine) A227

Doro Gorge A228

Bridge Pier Rocks A229

1949, Apr. 10 Photo. *Perf. 13*

450 A226 2y brown 1.00 50
451 A227 5y yel grn 2.50 1.00
452 A228 10y scarlet 11.00 4.00
453 A229 16y blue 5.00 1.50
a. Souv. sheet of 4, #450-453, no gum 22.50 22.50
b. As "a," 10y omitted

Yoshino-Kumano National Park.

No. 453a sold for 40y.

Boy — A230

Radio Tower and Star — A231

1949, May 5 *Perf. 12*

455 A230 5y rose brn & org 4.00 1.25
a. Orange omitted 200.00

Children's Day, May 5, 1949.

Souvenir Sheets

1949, May 5 *Imperf.*

456 A230 5y rose brn & org, sheet of 10 225.00 250.00

Children's Exhib., Inuyama, Apr. 1-May 31.

1949, May 11 *Perf. 13*

457 A231 20y dp bl, sheet of one 100.00 80.00

Electrical Communication Week, May 11-18.

Symbols of Communication A232

Central Meteorological Observatory, Tokyo A233

Wmk. 257

1949, June 1 Engr. *Perf. 12*

458 A232 8y brt ultra 3.50 1.10

Establishment of the Post Ministry and the Ministry of Electricity and Communication.

1949, June 1 Unwmk. *Perf. 12½*

459 A233 8y dp grn 3.50 1.10

57th anniv. of the establishment of the Central Meteorological Observatory.

Mt. Fuji in Autumn A234

Lake Kawaguchi A235

Fiji from Mt. Shichimen — A236

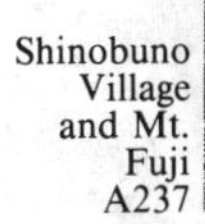

Shinobuno Village and Mt. Fuji A237

1949, July 15 Photo. *Perf. 13*

460 A234 2y yel brn 1.50 65
461 A235 8y yel grn 2.75 1.00
462 A236 14y car lake 1.50 40
463 A237 24y blue 2.25 60
a. Souvenir sheet of 4, #460-463 26.00 30.00

Fuji-Hakone National Park.

No. 463a sold for 55y.

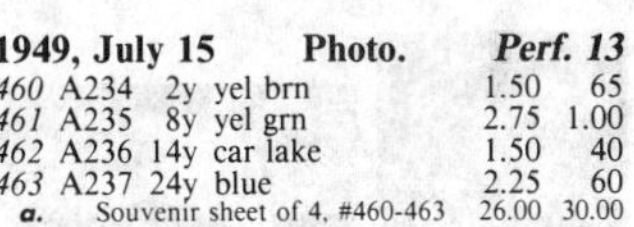

Allegory of Peace A238

Doves over Nagasaki — A239

Perf. 13x13½, 13½x13

1949 Photo. Unwmk.

465 A238 8y yel brn 4.75 1.50
466 A239 8y green 3.50 1.25

Issued to publicize the establishment of Hiroshima as the City of Eternal Peace and of Nagasaki as the International City of Culture. Issue dates: No. 465, Aug. 6; No. 466, Aug. 9.

Boy Scout A240

Pen Nib of Newspaper Stereotype Matrix A241

1949, Sept. 22 *Perf. 13x13½*

467 A240 8y brown 5.25 2.00

Natl. Boy Scout Jamboree.

1949, Oct. 1 *Perf. 13½x13*

468 A241 8y dp bl 3.25 1.50

Natl. Newspaper Week.

Racing Swimmer Poised for Dive — A242

Javelin Thrower — A243

1949 *Perf. 13½*

469 A242 8y dl bl 2.50 1.10

Perf. 12

470 A243 8y shown 3.50 1.90
471 A243 8y Yacht Racing 3.50 1.90
472 A243 8y Relay Race 3.50 1.90
473 A243 8y Tennis 3.50 1.90
a. Block of 4, #470-473 19.00 9.50
Nos. 469-473 (5) 16.50 8.70

Nos. 469-473 commemorate the 4th Natl. Athletic Meet. The swimming matches were held at Yokohama, Sept. 15-18 and the fall events at Tokyo, Oct. 30.

Issue dates: No. 469, Sept. 15; Nos. 470-473, Oct. 30.

Map and Envelopes Forming "75" — A244

Symbols of UPU — A245

1949, Oct. 10 Engr. *Perf. 12, 13½*

474 A244 2y dl grn 1.75 48
475 A245 8y maroon 2.00 48
a. Souv. sheet of 2, #474-475, imperf. 3.25 4.00
476 A244 14y carmine 6.75 2.50
477 A245 24y aqua 10.00 2.50
a. Imperf., pair

75th anniv. of the UPU.

Floating Zenith Telescope A246

"Moon and Geese," Print by Hiroshige A247

1949, Oct. 30 Photo. *Perf. 12*

478 A246 8y dk bl grn 2.25 1.00

50th anniv. of the Mizusawa Latitudinal Observatory.

1949, Nov. 1 *Perf. 13x13½*

479 A247 8y purple 75.00 27.50
a. Sheet of 5 475.00 165.00

Postal Week, Nov. 1-7. Sheets of 5, inscribed in top margin.

Dr. Hideyo Noguchi A248

Yukichi Fukuzawa A249

Soseki Natsume A250

Shoyo Tsubouchi A251

Danjuro Ichikawa A252

Joseph Hardy Niijima A253

Hogai Kano A254

Kanzo Uchimura A255

Ichiyo Higuchi A256

Ogai Mori A257

Shiki Masaoka A258

Shunso Hishida A259

Amane Nishi — A260

Kenjiro Ume — A261

Hisashi Kimura A262

Inazo Nitobe A263

Torahiko Terada A264

Tenshin Okakura A265

1949-52 Unwmk. Engr. *Perf. 12½*

480 A248 8y green 7.75 80
481 A249 8y dp ol ('50) 3.25 80
a. Imperf., pair
482 A250 8y dk Prus grn ('50) 3.25 80
483 A251 8y Prus grn ('50) 3.25 80
484 A252 8y dk vio ('50) 8.50 2.25
485 A253 8y vio brn ('50) 3.25 80
486 A254 8y dk grn ('51) 6.50 1.50
487 A255 8y dp pur ('51) 6.50 1.50
488 A256 8y car ('51) 11.00 2.00
489 A257 8y vio brn ('51) 20.00 2.50
490 A258 8y choc ('51) 11.00 2.50
491 A259 8y dk bl ('51) 8.75 2.50
492 A260 10y dk grn ('52) 55.00 4.00
493 A261 10y brn vio ('52) 8.75 1.00
494 A262 10y car ('52) 3.25 1.00
495 A263 10y dk grn ('52) 3.25 1.00
496 A264 10y choc ('52) 3.25 1.25
497 A265 10y dk bl ('52) 4.50 1.00
Nos. 480-497 (18) 171.00 28.00

Tiger — A266

Microphones of 1925 and 1950 — A267

1950, Feb. 1 Photo. *Perf. 12*

498 A266 2y dk red 5.00 1.25

6th prize (lottery), sheet of 5, value $120.

1950, Mar. 21 *Perf. 13*

499 A267 8y ultra 2.75 1.00

25th anniversary of broadcasting in Japan. Sheets of 20 with marginal inscription.

Dove and Olive Twig on Letter Box — A268

1950, Apr. 20 *Perf. 12*

500 A268 8y dp yel grn 2.25 1.00

Day of Posts, Apr. 20.

Lake Akan and Mt. Akan A269

Lake Kutcharo, Hokkaido A270

Mt. Akan-Fuji A271

Lake Mashu A272

1950, July 15 Unwmk. *Perf. 13*

501 A269 2y yel brn 1.50 50
502 A270 8y dp yel grn 1.90 1.00
503 A271 14y rose car 8.25 3.00
504 A272 24y brt bl 10.50 4.00
a. Souvenir sheet of 4, #501-504 27.50 30.00

Akan National Park.
No. 504a sold for 55y.

Gymnast on Rings — A273

Designs: No. 506, Pole vault. No. 507, Soccer. No. 508, Equestrian.

1950, Oct. 28 *Perf. 13½x13*

505 A273 8y rose brn 20.00 6.00
506 A273 8y rose brn 20.00 6.00
507 A273 8y rose brn 20.00 6.00
508 A273 8y rose brn 20.00 6.00
a. Strip of 4, Nos. 505-508 95.00
b. Block of 4, Nos. 505-508 150.00

5th National Athletic Meet. Sheets of 20 stamps in which each horizontal row contains all four designs.

Types of 1947-49 and

Ishiyama-dera Pagoda — A274

Hisoka Maejima — A275

Long-tailed Cock of Tosa — A276

Goddess Kannon — A277

Himeji Castle — A278

Nyoirin Kannon of Chuguji — A280

Phoenix Hall, Byodoin Temple Temple A279

Perf. 13x13½, 13½x13 (14y)

1950-52 Typo. Unwmk.

509 A274 80s car ('51) 1.25 1.25
a. Sheet of 1 5.50 6.50

Photo.

510 A275 1y dk brn ('51) 1.75 30
a. Souvenir sheet of 4 9.25 9.00

Typo.

511 A208 2y grn ('51) 1.65 15
512 A209 3y lt grnsh bl ('51) 40.00 1.00
512A A168 4y lt ultra ('52) 32.50 80
513 A276 5y dp grn & org brn ('51) 4.75 15
a. Orange brown omitted 175.00
514 A212 6y red org ('51) 4.50 25
515 A210 8y dk org brn ('51) 35.00 40
515A A197 10y rose vio ('51) 57.50 4.50
516 A277 10y red brn & lil ('51) 12.00 15

Engr.

517 A278 14y brn & car ('51) 37.50 20.00
a. Sheet of 1 45.00 50.00

Typo.

518 A215 20y dk grn ('51) 40.00 70

Engr.

519 A279 24y dp ultra 26.00 10.00
a. Sheet of 1 27.50 32.50

Typo.

520 A216 30y vio bl ('52) 92.50 1.00

Photo.

521 A280 50y dk brn ('51) 92.50 90
c. Sheet of 1 175.00 195.00

Engr.

521A A217 100y car lake ('52) 250.00 1.00
521B A218 500y dp bl ('52) 225.00 1.50
Nos. 509-521B (17) 954.40 44.05

No. 510a for the 80th anniv. of Japan's postal service. On No. 512A, characters read from left to right.

See Nos. 557-559, 580, 623, 636-636A, 672, 879A, 885, 916, 1244, 1256.

Girl and Rabbit — A281

1951, Jan. 1 **Photo.** ***Perf. 12***

522 A281 2y rose pink 4.25 60

9th prize (lottery), sheet of 5, value $32.50.

Scenic Spots Issue

Mt. Zao

Skiers on Mt. Zao
A282 A283

1951, Feb. 15 ***Perf. 13***

523 A282 8y olive 12.00 1.40
524 A283 24y blue 14.00 3.50

Nihon-daira Plateau

Tea Picking A284

Mt. Fuji Seen from Nihon Plateau A285

1951, Apr. 2

525 A284 8y ol grn 14.00 3.00
526 A285 24y brt bl 60.00 12.00

Hakone Hot Springs

Hot Springs, Hakone A286

Lake Ashi, Hakone A287

1951, May 25

527 A286 8y chnt brn 7.75 1.75
528 A287 24y dp bl 6.00 2.00

Akame 48 Waterfalls

Senju Waterfall A288

Ninai Waterfall A289

1951, June 1

529 A288 8y dp grn 6.00 2.00
530 A289 24y dp bl 9.00 1.40

Wakanoura & Tomogashima

Pavilion, Wakanoura Bay — A290

Wakanoura Bay — A291

1951, June 25

531 A290 8y brown 5.50 1.10
532 A291 24y brt bl 5.00 1.25

Uji River

Uji River — A292

View from Uji Bridge — A293

Perf. 13x13½, 13½x13

1951, Aug. 1 **Engr.**

533 A292 8y brown 5.50 1.50
534 A293 24y dp bl 5.00 1.75

Nagasaki

Oura Catholic Church, Nagasaki A294

Sofuku Temple A295

1951, Sept. 15 **Photo.** ***Perf. 13½***

535 A294 8y car rose 8.50 90
536 A295 24y dl bl 6.25 1.50

Marunuma & Sugenuma Lakes

Marunuma A296

Sugenuma A297

1951, Oct. 1

537 A296 8y rose vio 8.50 1.00
538 A297 24y dl bl grn 4.75 1.25

Shosenkyo Gorge

Kakuenpo (peak) — A298

Nagatoro Bridge — A299

1951, Oct. 15

539 A298 8y brn red 7.25 1.00
540 A299 24y dp Prus grn 6.75 1.25
Nos. 523-540 (18) 191.75 39.55

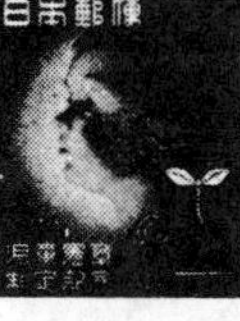

Boy's Head and Seedling — A300

1951, May 5 ***Perf. 13½***

541 A300 8y org brn 17.00 1.75

Issued to publicize Children's Day, May 5, 1951.

Oirase River A301

Lake Towada A302

View from Kankodai A303

Mt. Hakkoda from Mt. Yokodake A304

1951, July 20 **Photo.** ***Perf. 13x13½***

542 A301 2y brown 1.65 50
543 A302 8y green 7.00 85
544 A303 14y dk red 5.00 2.00
545 A304 24y blue 5.75 3.00
a. Souv. sheet of 4, #542-545 22.50 25.50

Towada National Park.
No. 545a sold for 55y.

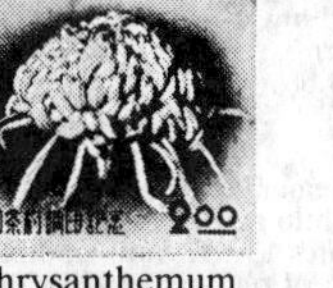

Chrysanthemum A305

National Flag A306

1951, Sept. 9 ***Perf. 13½***

546 A305 2y org brn 1.75 60
547 A306 8y sl bl & red 4.25 1.25
548 A305 24y bl grn 9.50 3.25

Signing of the peace treaty of 1951.

Putting the Shot A307

Hockey A308

1951, Oct. 27

549 A307 2y org brn 2.75 1.25
550 A308 2y gray bl 2.75 1.25
a. Pair, #549-550 6.00 3.00

6th Natl. Athletic Meet, Hiroshima, Oct. 27-31.

Okina Mask — A309

1952, Jan. 16 **Photo.** ***Perf. 13½x13***

551 A309 5y crim rose 6.75 40

Sheets reproducing four of these stamps with Japanese inscriptions and floral ornament at left were awarded as sixth prize in the national lottery. Value $62.50.

Southern Cross from Ship A310

Earth and Big Dipper A311

1952, Feb. 19

552 A310 5y purple 5.50 60
553 A311 10y dk grn 11.00 1.25

75th anniv. of Japan's admission to the UPU.

Red Cross and Lilies — A312

Red Cross Nurse — A313

1952, May 1

554 A312 5y rose red & dk red 4.00 65
555 A313 10y dk grn & red 9.25 1.25
a. Red cross omitted

75th anniv. of the formation of the Japanese Red Cross Society.

Goldfish — A314 A314a

A314b A314c

Japanese Serow — A315

1952 ***Perf. 13x13½***

556 A314 35y red org 8.00 15

Types of 1951
Redrawn; Zeros Omitted
Unwmk.

557 A314a 1y dk brn 22 15
558 A314b 50y dk brn 3.25 15

Typo.

559 A314c 4y dp cl & pale rose 1.10 15
a. Background (pale rose) omitted

Ornamental frame and background added, denomination at upper left, Japanese characters at upper right.

Photo.

560 A315 8y brown 15 15
Set value, #556-560 25

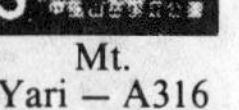

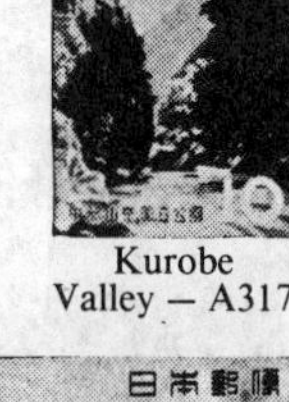

Mt. Yari — A316

Kurobe Valley — A317

Mt. Shirouma A318

Mt. Norikura A319

1952, July 5 ***Perf. 13½x13, 13x13½***

561 A316 5y brown 3.75 32
562 A317 10y bl grn 17.00 1.25
563 A318 14y brt red 5.50 1.10
564 A319 24y brt bl 11.00 2.00
a. Souv. sheet of 4, #561-564, imperf. 40.00 45.00

Japan Alps (Chubu-Sangaku) National Park.
No. 564a sold for 60y.

Yasuda Hall, Tokyo University A320

Yomei Gate, Nikko A321

1952, Oct. 1 **Engr.** ***Perf. 13***

565 A320 10y dl grn 12.00 1.25

75th anniversary of the founding of Tokyo University.

1952, Oct. 15 **Photo.** ***Perf. 13x13½***

566 A321 45y blue 3.00 15

Mountain Climber — A322

1952, Oct. 18

Dated "1952"

567 A322 5y shown 4.00 1.50
568 A322 5y Wrestlers 4.00 1.50
a. Pair, #567-568 17.00 4.00

7th National Athletic Meet, Fukushima, Oct. 18-22.

Mt. Azuma A323

Mt. Asahi A324

Mt. Bandai A325

Mt. Gatsun A326

Unwmk.

1952, Oct. 18 **Photo.** ***Perf. 13***

569 A323 5y brown 2.25 45
570 A324 10y ol grn 9.50 1.25
571 A325 14y rose red 5.00 1.65
572 A326 24y blue 7.75 3.25
a. Souv. sheet of 4, #569-572, imperf. 50.00 55.00

Bandai-Asahi National Park.
No. 572a sold for 60y.

Kirin — A327

Flag of Crown Prince — A328

Engr. and Photo.

1952, Nov. 10 ***Perf. 13½***

573 A327 5y red org & pur 2.25 32
574 A327 10y red org & dk grn 2.75 50
575 A328 24y dp bl 11.00 4.00
a. Souv. sheet of 3, #573-575, imperf. 62.50 125.00

Issued to commemorate the nomination of Crown Prince Akihito as Heir Apparent.

No. 575a measures 130x129mm, and has a background design of phoenix and clouds in violet brown and blue. Sold for 50y.

Sambaso Doll — A329

First Electric Lamp in Japan — A330

Perf. 13½x13

1953, Jan, 1 **Photo.** **Unwmk.**

576 A329 5y carmine 5.00 40

For postage on New Year's cards, later for ordinary use.

Sheets of 4 were awarded as 6th prize in the natl. lottery. Value $45.

1953, Mar. 25

577 A330 10y brown 5.25 1.25

75th anniv. of electric lighting in Japan.

"Kintai Bridge," Print by Hiroshige A331

Kintai Bridge as Rebuilt in 1953 A332

1953, May 3 ***Perf. 13***

578 A331 10y chestnut 5.75 2.00
579 A332 24y blue 5.75 2.25

Kannon Type of 1951
Redrawn; Zeros Omitted

A332a

1953-54 **Typo.**

580 A332a 10y red brn & lil 3.25 15
a. Booklet pane 10 + 2 labels (souvenir) ('54) 150.00 150.00
b. Bklt. pane 10 + 2 labels ('54) 50.00

No. 580a was issued in honor of Philatelic Week 1954. The inscriptions on the two labels are arranged in two rows of boldface characters.

On No. 580b, the label inscriptions are arranged in three rows of mixed heavy and thin characters.

See Nos. 611a and 672.

Lake Shikotsu, Hokkaido A333

Mt. Yotei A334

1953, July 25 **Photo.** ***Perf. 13***

581 A333 5y ultra 1.45 45
582 A334 10y green 4.00 1.00
a. Souv. sheet of 2, #581-582, imperf., no gum 25.00 27.50

Shikotsu-Toya National Park.
No. 582a sold for 20 yen.

Akita Dog A335

Cormorant Fishing A336

1953 **Unwmk.**

583 A335 2y gray 15 15

Engr.

584 A336 100y dk red 27.50 15
a. Imperf., pair 600.00
Set value 15

See No. 1621A.

Futamigaura Beach — A337

Namikiri Coast A338

1953, Oct. 2 **Photo.**

585 A337 5y red 1.50 50
586 A338 10y blue 3.50 75
a. Souv. sheet of 2, #585-586, imperf., no gum 16.00 16.00

Ise-Shima National Park.

Phoenix — A339

Design: 10y, Japanese crane in flight.

1953, Oct. 12 **Engr.** ***Perf. 12½***

587 A339 5y brn car 2.00 1.00

Photo.

588 A339 10y dark blue 5.00 1.75

Nos. 587-588 were issued on the occasion of the return of Crown Prince Akihito from his visit to Europe and America. Issued in sheets of 20 with marginal inscription.

Rugby Match — A340

Judo — A341

1953, Oct. 22 ***Perf. 13½***

589 A340 5y black 3.00 1.00
590 A341 5y bl grn 3.00 1.00
a. Pair, #589-590 14.00 3.00

8th National Athletic Meet, Matsuyama, Oct. 22-26.

Sky and Top of Observatory A342

1953, Oct. 29

591 A342 10y dk gray bl 8.00 1.00

75th anniversary of the Tokyo Astronomical Observatory.

Mt. Unzen from Golf Course A343

Mt. Unzen from Chijiwa Beach A344

1953, Nov. 20 ***Perf. 13***

592 A343 5y red 1.45 32
593 A344 10y blue 3.75 50
a. Souv. sheet of 2, #592-593, imperf., no gum 16.00 17.50

Unzen National Park.

Toy Horse — A345

Racing Skaters — A346

1953, Dec. 25 *Perf. 13½x13*
594 A345 5y rose 5.50 40

Issued to pay postage on New Year's cards, later for ordinary use. A sheet reproducing four of these stamps was awarded as sixth prize in the national lottery. Value $40.

1954, Jan. 16
595 A346 10y blue 4.00 1.00

World Speed Skating Matches for Men, Sapporo City, Jan. 16-17, 1954.

Golden Hall, Chusonji Temple — A347

Thread, Pearls, Gears, Buttons and Globe — A348

1954, Jan. 20
596 A347 20y ol grn 85 15

1954, Apr. 10
597 A348 10y dk red 3.00 65

International Trade Fair, Osaka, Apr. 10-23.

Little Cuckoo A349

Wrestlers A350

1954, May 10 *Perf. 13x13½*
598 A349 3y bl grn 15 15
a. Imperf., pair 350.00

1954, May 22 **Engr.**
599 A350 10y dp grn 2.25 65

World Free Style Wrestling Championship Matches, Tokyo, 1954.

Mt. Asama A351

Mt. Tanikawa A352

1954, June 25 *Perf. 13*
600 A351 5y dk gray brn 1.65 40
601 A352 10y dk bl grn 3.25 90
a. Souvenir sheet of 2, #600-601, no gum 16.00 16.00

Jo-Shin-etsu National Park.

Table Tennis — A353

Archery — A354

1954, Aug. 22 **Engr.** *Perf. 12*
602 A353 5y dl brn 3.00 70
603 A354 5y gray grn 3.00 70
a. Se-tenant pair, #602-603 7.00

9th Natl. Athletic Meet, Sapporo, Aug. 22-26.

Morse Telegraph Instrument A355

ITU Monument A356

Perf. 13x13½, 13½x13
1954, Oct. 13
604 A355 5y dk pur brn 1.75 35
605 A356 10y dp bl 4.00 60

75th anniv. of Japanese membership in the ITU.

Daruma Doll — A357

1954, Dec. 20 **Photo.** *Perf. 13½x13*
606 A357 5y blk & red 3.50 35

Sheets reproducing four of these stamps with Japanese inscriptions and ornaments were awarded as fifth prize in the national lottery. Value $35.

Mountain Stream, Tama Gorge — A358

Chichibu Mountains — A359

1955, Mar. 1 **Engr.** *Perf. 13*
607 A358 5y blue 1.25 35
608 A359 10y red brn 1.65 42
a. Souv. sheet of 2, #607-608, imperf., no gum 12.00 13.00

Chichibu-Tama National Park.

The Catalogue editors cannot undertake to appraise, identify or judge the genuineness or condition of stamps.

Bridge and Iris — A360

1955, Mar. 15 *Perf. 13x13½*
609 A360 500y dp plum 75.00 25

Paper Carp as Flown on Boys' Day A361

Mandarin Ducks A362

Unwmk.
1955, May 16 **Photo.** *Perf. 13*
610 A361 10y multi 3.75 70

15th congress of the International Chamber of Commerce, Tokyo, May 16-21, 1955.

1955-64
611 A362 5y lt bl & red brn 25 15
a. Bklt. pane of 12 (4 No. 611 + 8 No. 580) ('59) 20.00
b. Bklt. pane of 12 (4 No. 611 + 8 No. 725) ('63) 18.00
c. Bklt. pane of 4 ('64) 7.00
d. Imperf., pair 650.00

See Nos. 738, 881d, 914b.

Benten Cape — A363

Jodo Beach A364

1955, Sept. 30
612 A363 5y dp grn 1.25 22
613 A364 10y rose lake 1.75 40
a. Souv. sheet of 2, #612-613, imperf., no gum 16.00 12.00

Rikuchu-Kaigan National Park. No. 613a sold for 20y.

Girl Athletes A365

Runners A366

1955, Oct. 30 **Engr.**
614 A365 5y brn lake 1.00 40
615 A366 5y bluish blk 1.00 40
a. Se-tenant pair, #614-615 3.50

10th National Athletic Meet, Kanagawa Prefecture.
See Nos. 639-640, 657.

"A Girl Blowing Glass Toy," by Utamaro A367

1955, Nov. 1 **Photo.**
616 A367 10y multi 9.50 4.00

150th anniv. of the death of Utamaro, woodcut artist, and to publicize Philatelic Week, Nov., 1955. Issued in sheets of 10.

Kokeshi Dolls A368

Table Tennis A369

1955, Dec. 30 **Unwmk.** *Perf. 13*
617 A368 5y ol grn & red 1.75 18

Sheets reproducing four of these stamps, were awarded as fifth prize in the New Year's lottery. Value $22.50.

1956, Apr. 2 *Perf. 13x13½*
618 A369 10y red brn 1.10 35

International Table Tennis Championship, Tokyo, Apr. 2-11.

Judo — A370

1956, May 2 *Perf. 13*
619 A370 10y grn & lil 1.50 35

Issued to publicize the first World Judo Championship Meet, Tokyo, May 3, 1956.

Boy and Girl with Paper Carp A371

1956, May 5
620 A371 5y lt bl & blk 90 25

Issued to commemorate the establishment of World Children's Day, May 5, 1956.

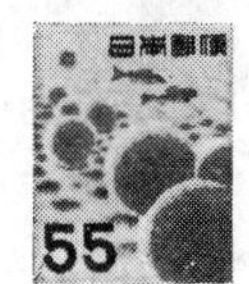
Water Plants, Lake Akan A372

Big Purple Butterfly A373

1956 **Unwmk.** *Perf. 13*
621 A372 55y lt bl, grn & blk 13.00 15
622 A373 75y multi 7.75 25

See Nos. 887A, 917.

Castle Type of 1951
Redrawn; Zeros Omitted

A373a

1956 Engr. *Perf. 13½x13*

623 A373a 14y gray olive 5.50 1.00

Osezaki Promontory — A374

Kujuku Island A375

1956, Oct. 1 Photo.

624 A374 5y red brn 85 30

Engr. & Photo.

625 A375 10y lt bl & ind 1.10 40
a. Souv. sheet of 2, #624-625, imperf., no gum 15.00 16.00

Saikai National Park.
No. 625a sold for 20y.

Palace Moat and Modern Tokyo A376

1956, Oct. 1 Engr.

626 A376 10y dl pur 2.00 40

500th anniv. of the founding of Tokyo.

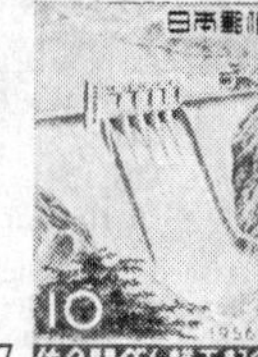

Sakuma Dam — A377

1956, Oct. 15 Unwmk. *Perf. 13*

627 A377 10y dk bl 2.00 50

Completion of Sakuma Dam.

Long Jump A378

Basketball A379

1956, Oct. 28 *Perf. 13½x13*

628 A378 5y brn vio 75 30
629 A379 5y steel bl 75 30
a. Pair, #628-629 2.25

11th Natl. Athletic Meet, Hyogo Prefecture.
See No. 658.

Kabuki Actor Ebizo Ichikawa by Sharaku A380

1956, Nov. 1 Photo. *Perf. 13*

630 A380 10y multi 9.50 4.25

Stamp Week. Sheets of 10.

Mount Manaslu A381

1956, Nov. 3

631 A381 10y multi 3.00 1.25

Issued in honor of the Japanese expedition which climbed Mount Manaslu in the Himalayas on May 9 and 11, 1956.

Electric Locomotive and Hiroshige's "Yui Stage" — A382

1956, Nov. 19 Unwmk. *Perf. 13*

632 A382 10y dk ol bis, blk & grn 3.75 1.00

Electrification of Tokaido Line.

Cogwheel, Vacuum Tube and Ship — A383

1956, Dec. 18 Engr.

633 A383 10y ultra 75 35

Japanese Machinery Floating Fair.

Toy Whale — A384

United Nations Emblem — A385

1956, Dec. 20 Photo.

634 A384 5y multi 1.00 15
a. Imperf., pair

Sheets reproducing four of these stamps, with inscriptions and ornaments, were awarded as sixth prize in the national lottery. Value $12.

Photogravure and Engraved
Perf. 13½x13

1957, Mar. 8 Unwmk.

635 A385 10y lt bl & dk car 65 40

Japan's admission to the UN, Dec. 18, 1956.

Temple Type of 1950
Redrawn; Zeros Omitted

A385a

1957-59 Engr. *Perf. 13x13½*

636 A385a 24y violet 16.00 2.00
636A A385a 30y rose lil ('59) 37.50 35
b. Imperf., pair

IGY Emblem, Penguin and "Soya" A386

Atomic Reactor A387

1957, July 1 Photo. *Perf. 13*

637 A386 10y bl, yel & blk 60 35

International Geophysical Year.

1957, Sept. 18 Engr. *Perf. 13*

638 A387 10y dk pur 38 15

Completion of Japan's atomic reactor at Tokai-Mura, Ibaraki Prefecture.

Sports Type of 1955

Designs: No. 639, Girl on parallel bars. No. 640, Boxers.

1957, Oct. 26 Unwmk. *Perf. 13*

639 A366 5y ultra 35 15
640 A366 5y dk red 35 15
a. Pair, #639-640 1.00
Set value 20

12th Natl. Athletic Meet, Shizuoka Prefecture.

"Girl Bouncing Ball," by Suzuki Harunobu A388

1957, Nov. 1 Photo.

641 A388 10y multi 2.50 1.00

1957 Stamp Week. Issued in sheets of 10. See Nos. 646, 671, 728, 757.

Lake Okutama and Ogochi Dam — A389

1957, Nov. 26 Engr. *Perf. 13½*

642 A389 10y ultra 30 15

Completion of Ogochi Dam, part of the Tokyo water supply system.

Modern and First Japanese Blast Furnaces A390

Toy Dog (Inu-hariko) A391

1957, Dec. 1 Photo. Unwmk.

643 A390 10y org & dk pur 25 15

Centenary of Japan's iron industry.

1957, Dec. 20 *Perf. 13½x13*

644 A391 5y multi 28 15

Issued for New Year 1958. Sheets reproducing four of No. 644, with inscriptions and ornaments, were awarded as fifth prize in the New Year lottery. Value $4.75.

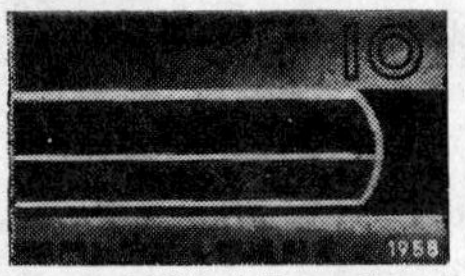

Shimonoseki-Moji Tunnel — A392

1958, Mar. 9 *Perf. 13x13½*

645 A392 10y multi 30 15

Issued to commemorate the completion of the Kan-Mon Underwater Highway connecting Honshu and Kyushu Islands.

Stamp Week Type of 1957

Design: 10y, Woman with Umbrella, woodcut by Kiyonaga.

1958, Apr. 20 Unwmk. *Perf. 13*

646 A388 10y multi 80 20

Stamp Week, 1958. Sheets of 10.

Statue of Ii Naosuke and Harbor A393

Unwmk.

1958, May 10 Engr. *Perf. 13*

647 A393 10y gray bl & car 18 15

Issued to commemorate the centenary of the opening of the ports of Yokohama, Nagasaki and Hakodate to foreign powers.

National Stadium — A394

3rd Asian Games, Tokyo: 10y, Torch and emblem. 14y, Runner. 24y, Woman diver.

1958, May 24 Photo.

648 A394 5y bl grn, bis & pink 15 15
649 A394 10y multi 25 15
650 A394 14y multi 32 15
651 A394 24y multi 40 15
Set value 42

Kasato Maru, Map and Brazilian Flag A395

1958, June 18
652 A395 10y multi 18 15

50 years of Japanese emigration to Brazil.

Sado Island and Local Dancer A396

Mt. Yahiko and Echigo Plain — A397

1958, Aug. 20 Unwmk. *Perf. 13*
653 A396 10y multi 60 15
654 A397 10y multi 60 15
Set value 24

Sado-Yahiko Quasi-National Park.

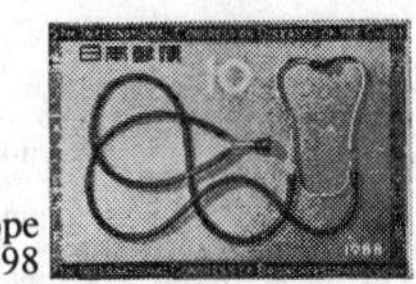
Stethoscope A398

1958, Sept. 7 Photo. *Perf. 13*
655 A398 10y Prus grn 30 15

5th Intl. Cong. on Diseases of the Chest and the 7th Intl. Cong. of Bronchoesophagology.

"Kyoto" (Sanjo Bridge), Print by Hiroshige A399

1958, Oct. 5
656 A399 24y multi 2.75 40

Issued for International Letter Writing Week, Oct. 5-11. See No. 679.

Sports Types of 1955-56

Designs: No. 657, Weight lifter. No. 658, Girl badminton player.

1958, Oct. 19 Engr.
657 A365 5y gray blue 35 15
658 A379 5y claret 35 15
a. Pair, #657-658 1.00

13th Natl. Athletic Meet, Toyama Prefecture.

Keio University and Yukichi Fukuzawa — A400

1958, Nov. 8 Engr. *Perf. 13½*
659 A400 10y magenta 28 15

Centenary of Keio University.

Globe and Playing Children A401

1958, Nov. 23 Photo. *Perf. 13*
660 A401 10y dp grn 28 15

Issued to publicize the 9th International Conference of Social Work and the 2nd International Study Conference on Child Welfare.

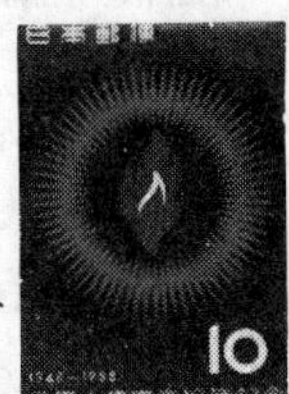
Flame: Symbol of Human Rights — A402

1958, Dec. 10 Unwmk. *Perf. 13*
661 A402 10y multi 32 15

10th anniv. of the signing of the Universal Declaration of Human Rights.

Toy of Takamatsu (Tai-Ebisu) A403

Tractor and Map of Kojima Bay A404

1958, Dec. 20 *Perf. 13½*
662 A403 5y multi 38 15

Issued for New Year 1959. Sheets reproducing four of No. 662, with inscriptions and ornaments, were awarded as prizes in the New Year lottery. Size: 103x89mm. Value $4.

1959, Feb. 1 *Perf. 12½*
663 A404 10y claret & bis brn 30 15

Completion of the embankment closing Kojima Bay for reclamation.

Karst Plateau — A405

Akiyoshi Cave — A406

1959, Mar. 16 Photo. *Perf. 13½*
664 A405 10y grn, bl & ocher 1.00 15
665 A406 10y multi 1.60 15
Set value 24

Akiyoshidai Quasi-National Park.

Map of Southeast Asia — A407

1959, Mar. 27
666 A407 10y dp car 28 15

Asian Cultural Cong., Tokyo, Mar. 27-31, marking the 2,500th anniv. of the death of Buddha.

Ceremonial Fan — A408

Prince Akihito and Princess Michiko A409

Photogravure; Portraits Engraved

1959, Apr. 10
667 A408 5y mag & vio 16 15
668 A409 10y red brn & dl pur 50 15
a. Souv. sheet of 2, #667-668, imperf. 3.00 3.00
669 A408 20y org brn & brn 60 15
670 A409 30y yel grn & dk grn 1.25 25

Wedding of Crown Prince Akihito and Princess Michiko, Apr. 10, 1959.

Type of 1957

Design: 10y, Women Reading Poetry Print by Eishi Fujiwara.

1959, May 20 Photo. *Perf. 13*
671 A388 10y multi 3.50 1.25

Issued to publicize Stamp Week, 1959. Issued in sheets of 10.

Redrawn Kannon Type of 1953
Coil Stamp
Perf. 13 Horiz.

1959, Jan. 20 Typo. Unwmk.
672 A332a 10y red brn & lil 22.50 22.50

Measuring Glass, Tape Measure and Scales — A410

Nurses Carrying Stretcher — A411

1959, June 5 Photo. *Perf. 13*
673 A410 10y lt bl & blk 30 15

Adoption of the metric system.

1959, June 24
674 A411 10y ol grn & red 28 15

Centenary of the Red Cross idea.

Mt. Fuji and Lake Motosu A412

1959, July 21 Engr. *Perf. 13*
675 A412 10y grn, bl & sep 52 15

Establishment of Natural Park Day and 1st Natural Park Convention, Yumoto, Nikko, July 21, 1959.

Ao Cave Area of Yabakei A413

Hita, Mt. Hiko and Great Cormorant A414

1959, Sept. 25 Photo. *Perf. 13*
676 A413 10y multi 1.25 15
677 A414 10y multi 1.25 15

Yaba-Hita-Hiko Quasi National Park.

Golden Dolphin, Nagoya Castle — A415

Japanese Crane, IATA Emblem — A416

1959, Oct. 1
678 A415 10y brt bl, gold & blk 60 15

350th anniversary of Nagoya.

Hiroshige Type of 1958

Design: 30y, "Kuwana," the 7-ri Crossing Point, print by Hiroshige.

1959, Oct. 4 Unwmk.
679 A399 30y multi 5.25 1.00

Intl. Letter Writing Week, Oct. 4-10.

1959, Oct. 12 Engr.
680 A416 10y brt grnsh bl 32 15

15th General Meeting of the International Air Transport Association.

Shoin Yoshida and PTA Symbol — A417

Throwing the Hammer — A418

1959, Oct. 27 Photo. *Perf. 13*
681 A417 10y brown 32 15

Centenary of the death of Shoin Yoshida, educator, and in connection with the Parent-Teachers Association convention.

1959, Oct. 25 Engr.

Design: No. 683, Woman Fencer.

682 A418 5y gray bl 52 15
683 A418 5y ol bis 52 15
a. Pair, #682-683 1.25
Set value 24

14th National Athletic Meet, Tokyo.

Globes A419

1959, Nov. 2 Photo.
684 A419 5y brn red 38 15

15th session of GATT (General Agreement on Tariffs & Trade), Tokyo, Oct. 12-Nov. 21.

Toy Mouse of Kanazawa — A420

1959, Dec. 19 Unwmk. *Perf. 13½*
685 A420 5y gold, red, grn & blk 60 15

Issued for New Year 1960. Sheets reproducing four of No. 685, with marginal inscription and ornaments, were awarded as prizes in national lottery. Value $4.75.

Yukio Ozaki and Clock Tower, Ozaki Memorial Hall — A421

Nara Period Artwork, Shosoin Treasure House — A422

1960, Feb. 25 **Photo.** ***Perf. 13½***

686	A421 10y red brn & dk brn	28	15

Issued to commemorate the completion of Ozaki Memorial Hall, erected in memory of Yukio Ozaki (1858-1954), statesman.

1960, Mar. 10

687	A422 10y ol gray	32	15

1250th anniversary of the transfer of the capital to Nara.

Scenic Trio Issue

Bay of Matsushima A423

Ama-no-hashidate (Heavenly Bridge) — A424

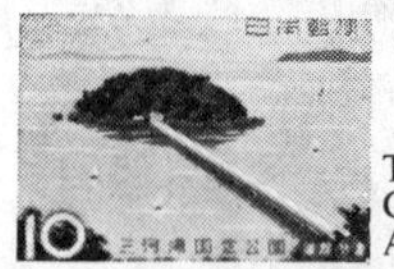

Miyajima from the Sea — A425

1960 **Engr.**

688	A423 10y mar & bl grn	1.25	40
689	A424 10y grn & lt bl	1.50	40
690	A425 10y vio blk & bl grn	1.50	40

Issue dates: No. 688, Mar. 15. No. 689, July 15. No. 690, Nov. 15.

Takeshima, off Gamagori A426

1960, Mar. 20 **Photo.** ***Perf. 13½***

691	A426 10y multi	75	15

Mikawa Bay Quasi-National Park.

Poetess Ise, 13th Century Painting — A427

1960, Apr. 20 **Unwmk.** ***Perf. 13***

692	A427 10y multi	2.50	1.25

Stamp Week, 1960.

Kanrin Maru — A428

Design: 30y, Pres. Buchanan receiving first Japanese diplomatic mission.

1960, May 17 **Engr.**

693	A428 10y bl grn & brn	65	20
694	A428 30y car & indigo	1.00	20

Cent. of the Japan-US Treaty of Amity and Commerce. Nos. 694 and 693 form pages of an open book when placed next to each other. Souvenir sheet is No. 703.

Crested Ibis (Toki) — A429

Radio Waves Encircling Globe — A430

1960, May 24 **Photo.** ***Perf. 13½***

695	A429 10y gray, pink & red	52	20

12th Intl. Congress for Bird Preservation.

1960, June 1 **Engr.**

696	A430 10y car rose	28	15

25th anniv. of the Intl. Radio Program by the Japanese Broadcasting Corporation.

Flower Garden (Gensei Kaen) — A431

1960, June 15 **Photo.**

697	A431 10y multi	1.00	20

Abashiri Quasi-National Park.

Cape Ashizuri A432

1960, Aug. 1 **Unwmk.**

698	A432 10y multi	1.00	20

Ashizuri Quasi-National Park.

Rainbow Spanning Pacific, Cherry Blossoms and Pineapples A433

Henri Farman's Biplane and Jet A434

1960, Aug. 20 ***Perf. 13½***

699	A433 10y multi	60	25

75th anniversary of Japanese contract emigration to Hawaii.

1960, Sept. 20 ***Perf. 13***

700	A434 10y brn & chlky bl	48	15

50th anniversary of Japanese aviation.

Seat Plan of Diet — A435

"Red Fuji" by Hokusai and Diet Building — A436

1960, Sept. 27

701	A435 5y ind & org	28	15
702	A436 10y bl & red brn	65	15
	Set value		24

49th Inter-Parliamentary Conference.

Souvenir Sheet
Type A428

1960, Sept. 27 **Engr.**

703	Sheet of 2, #693-694	15.00	15.00

Visit of Prince Akihito and Princess Michiko to the US.

"Night Snow at Kambara," by Hiroshige A437

1960, Oct. 9 **Photo.**

704	A437 30y multi	10.50	2.00

Issued for International Letter Writing Week, Oct. 9-15. See Nos. 735, 769.

Japanese Fencing (Kendo) A438

Okayama Astrophysical Observatory A439

Design: No. 706, Girl gymnast and vaulting horse.

1960, Oct. 23 **Engr.** ***Perf. 13½***

705	A438 5y dull blue	55	15
706	A438 5y rose vio	55	15
a.	Pair, #705-706	1.25	

15th National Athletic Meet, Kumamoto.

1960, Oct. 19

707	A439 10y brt vio	60	15

Issued to commemorate the opening of the Okayama Astrophysical Observatory.

Lt. Naoshi Shirase and Map of Antarctica A440

Little Red Calf of Aizu, Gold Calf of Iwate A441

1960, Nov. 29 **Photo.**

708	A440 10y fawn & blk	38	15

50th anniv. of the 1st Japanese Antarctic expedition.

1960, Dec. 20 **Unwmk.** ***Perf. 13½***

709	A441 5y multi	60	15

Issued for New Year 1961. Sheets reproducing four of No. 709, with ornamental side panels, one inscribed, were awarded as prizes in the New Year lottery. Size: 102x89mm. Value $6.

Diet Building at Night — A442

Opening of First Session — A443

1960, Dec. 24 **Photo.; Engr. (10y)**

710	A442 5y gray & dk bl	45	15
711	A443 10y carmine	45	15
	Set value		24

70th anniversary of the Japanese Diet.

Narcissus A444

Nojima Cape Lighthouse and Fisherwomen A445

Designs: No. 713, Plum blossoms. No. 714, Camellia japonica. No. 715, Cherry blossoms. No. 716, Peony. No. 717, Iris. No. 718, Lily. No. 719, Morning glory. No. 720, Bellflower. No. 721, Gentian. No. 722, Chrysanthemum. No. 723, Camellia sasanqua.

1961 **Photo.** ***Perf. 13½***

712	A444 10y lil, yel & grn	2.25	60
713	A444 10y brn, grn & yel	1.50	60
714	A444 10y lem, grn, pink & yel	1.10	50
715	A444 10y gray, brn, pink, yel & blk	1.10	65
716	A444 10y blk, grn, pink & yel	1.10	65
717	A444 10y gray, pur, grn & yel	75	45
718	A444 10y gray grn, yel & brn	55	25
719	A444 10y lt bl, grn & lil	55	25
720	A444 10y lt yel grn, vio & grn	55	25
721	A444 10y org, vio bl & grn	55	25
722	A444 10y bl, yel & grn	55	25
723	A444 10y sl, pink, yel & grn	55	25
	Nos. 712-723 (12)	11.10	4.95

1961, Mar. 15

724	A445 10y multi	52	10

South Boso Quasi-National Park.

Cherry Blossoms A446

Hisoka Maejima A447

Unwmk.

1961, Apr. 1 **Photo.** ***Perf. 13***

725	A446 10y lil rose & gray	18	15
a.	Lilac rose omitted	350.00	
b.	Imperf., pair	500.00	
c.	Booklet pane of 4	7.50	
d.	Gray omitted	300.00	

See No. 611b.

Coil Stamp

1961, Apr. 25 ***Perf. 13 Horiz.***

726	A446 10y lil rose & gray	4.50	1.65

1961, Apr. 20 ***Perf. 13***

727	A447 10y ol & blk	65	15

90th anniv. of Japan's modern postal service from Tokyo to Osaka, inaugurated by Deputy Postmaster General Hisoka Maejima.

Type of 1957

Design: "Dancing Girl" from a "Screen of Dancers."

1961, Apr. 20 *Perf. 13½*
728 A388 10y multi 1.25 65

Stamp Week, 1961. Sheets of 10 (5x2).

Lake Biwa — A448

1961, Apr. 25
729 A448 10y blk, dk bl & yel grn 60 15

Lake Biwa Quasi-National Park.

Rotary Emblem and People of Various Races — A449

1961, May 29 Engr. *Perf. 13*
730 A449 10y gray & org 22 15

52nd convention of Rotary Intl., Tokyo, May 29-June 1, 1961.

Faucet, Wheat, Insulator & Cogwheel A450

Sun, Earth and Meridian A451

1961, July 7 Photo. *Perf. 13½*
731 A450 10y vio & aqua 30 15

Aichi irrigation system, Kiso river.

1961, July 12
732 A451 10y yel, red & blk 28 15

75th anniv. of Japanese standard time.

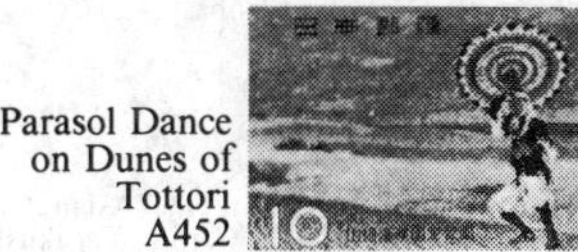
Parasol Dance on Dunes of Tottori A452

1961, Aug. 15
733 A452 10y multi 60 18

San'in Kaigan Quasi-National Park.

Onuma Lake and Komagatake Volcano — A453

Gymnast on Horizontal Bar — A454

1961, Sept. 15
734 A453 10y grn, red brn & bl 60 18

Onuma Quasi-National Park.

Hiroshige Type of 1960

1961, Oct. 8 *Perf. 13*

Design: 30y, "Hakone," print by Hiroshige from the 53 Stages of the Tokaido.

735 A437 30y multi 5.50 2.25

Intl. Letter Writing Week, Oct. 8-14.

1961, Oct. 8 Engr. *Perf. 13½*

Design: No. 737, Women rowing.

736 A454 5y bl grn 45 15
737 A454 5y ultra 45 15
a. Pair, #736-737 1.00
Set value 24

16th National Athletic Meet, Akita. See Nos. 770-771, 816-817, 852-853.

Duck Type of 1955
Coil Stamp

1961, Oct. 2 Photo. *Perf. 13 Horiz.*
738 A362 5y lt bl & red brn 3.00 3.00

National Diet Library and Book — A455

Papier Mache Tiger — A456

1961, Nov. 1 *Perf. 13½*
739 A455 10y dp ultra & gold 32 15

Issued to commemorate the opening of the new National Diet Library, Tokyo.

1961, Dec. 15 *Perf. 13½*
740 A456 5y multi 38 15

Issued for New Year 1962. Sheets reproducing four of No. 740, with marginal decorations and inscriptions, were awarded as fifth prize in the New Year lottery. Size: 102x90. Value $5.50.

Mt. Fuji from Lake Ashi — A457

Minokake-Iwa at Irozaki — A458

Mt. Fuji from Mitsu Pass — A459

Mt. Fuji from Cape of Ose — A460

1962, Jan. 16 Unwmk. Photo.
741 A457 5y dp grn 70 15
742 A458 5y dk bl 45 15
743 A459 10y red brn 1.75 20
744 A460 10y black 1.50 25

Fuji-Hakone-Izu National Park

Omishima A461

1962, Feb. 15 *Perf. 13½*
745 A461 10y ultra, red & yel 48 15

Kitanagato-Kaigan Quasi-National Park.

Perotrochus Hirasei — A462

Sacred Bamboo — A463

Shari-den of Engakuji — A464

Yomei Gate, Nikko — A465

Noh Mask A466

Copper Pheasant A466a

Wind God, Fujin, by Sotatsu — A467

Japanese Crane — A468

Mythical Winged Woman, Chusonji — A469

1962-65 Unwmk. *Perf. 13*
746 A462 4y dk brn & red ('63) 15 15
747 A463 6y gray grn & car 15 15
748 A464 30y vio blk 3.25 15
749 A465 40y rose red 3.25 15
750 A466 70y yel brn & blk ('65) 1.95 15
751 A466a 80y crim & brn ('65) 1.25 15
752 A467 90y brt bl grn 30.00 20
753 A468 100y pink & blk ('63) 8.75 15
754 A469 120y purple 7.75 15
Nos. 746-754 (9) 56.50
Set value 90

See Nos. 888, 888A, 890, 1076, 1079, 1257.

Coil Stamp

755 A464 30y dl vio ('63) 3.50 1.25

Hinamatsuri, Doll Festival — A470

1962, Mar. 3 *Perf. 13½*
756 A470 10y brn, blk, bl & car 1.25 35

The Doll Festival is celebrated Mar. 3 in honor of young girls.

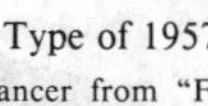

Type of 1957

Design: Dancer from "Flower Viewing Party" by Naganobu Kano.

1962, Apr. 20 Photo. *Perf. 13½*
757 A388 10y multi 1.40 90

Stamp Week, 1962. Sheets of 10.

Sakurajima Volcano and Kagoshima Bay — A471

1962, Apr. 30
758 A471 10y multi 42 15

Kinkowan Quasi-National Park.

Mount Kongo — A472

1962, May 15 *Perf. 13½*
759 A472 10y gray bl, dk grn & sal 42 15

Kongo-Ikoma Quasi-National Park.

Suigo Park Scene and Iris — A473

1962, June 1 *Perf. 13½*
760 A473 10y multi 52 15

Suigo Quasi-National Park.

Train Emerging from Hokuriku Tunnel — A474

1962, June 10 **Photo.**
761 A474 10y olive gray 80 15

Opening of Hokuriku Tunnel between Tsuruga and Imajo, Fukui Prefecture.

Star Festival (Tanabata Matsuri) A475

Boy Scout Hat on Map of Southeast Asia A476

1962, July 7 Unwmk. *Perf. 13½*
762 A475 10y multi 42 15

The Tanabata festival is celebrated on the evening of July 7.

1962, Aug. 3
763 A476 10y red org, blk & bis 22 15

Issued to commemorate the Asian Boy Scout Jamboree, Mt. Fuji, Aug. 3-7.

Ozegahara Swampland and Mt. Shibutsu A477

Fumes on Mt. Chausu, Nasu — A478

Lake Chuzenji and Mt. Nantai — A479

Senryu-kyo Narrows, Shiobara A480

1962, Sept. 1

764 A477	5y greenish blue	25	15
765 A478	5y maroon	25	15
766 A479	10y purple	38	15
767 A480	10y olive	38	15
	Set value		32

Nikko National Park.

Wakato Suspension Bridge — A481

Perf. 13½x13

1962, Sept. 26 Engr. Unwmk.

768 A481 10y rose red 75 25

Opening of Wakato Bridge over Dokai Bay in North Kyushu.

Hiroshige Type of 1960

Design: 40y, "Nihonbashi," print by Hiroshige from the 53 Stages of the Tokaido.

1962, Oct. 7 Photo. *Perf. 13*

769 A437 40y multi 4.50 1.65

Intl. Letter Writing Week, Oct. 7-13.

Sports Type of 1961

Design: No. 770, Woman softball pitcher. No. 771, Rifle shooting.

1962, Oct. 21 Engr. *Perf. 13½*

770 A454	5y bluish blk	25	15
771 A454	5y brn vio	25	15
a.	Pair, #770-771	60	
	Set value		16

17th National Athletic Meeting, Okayama.

Japan stamps can be mounted in Scott's annually supplemented Japan Album.

Shichi-go-san Festival A482

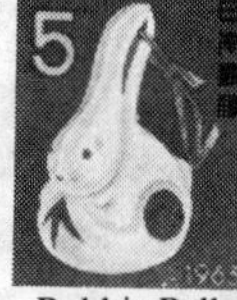
Rabbit Bell A483

1962, Nov. 15 Photo. *Perf. 13½*

772 A482 10y multi 40 15

This festival for 7 and 3-year-old girls and 5-year-old boys is celebrated on Nov. 15.

1962, Dec. 15

773 A483 5y multi 22 15

Issued for New Year 1963. Sheets reproducing four of No. 773 with marginal decorations and inscriptions were awarded as prizes in the New Year lottery. Value $6.25.

Mt. Ishizuchi A484

1963, Jan. 11 Unwmk. *Perf. 13½*

774 A484 10y multi 28 15

Ishizuchi Quasi-National Park.

Setsubun, Spring Festival, Bean Scattering Ceremony — A485

Map of City, Birds, Ship and Factory — A486

1963, Feb. 3 Photo.

775 A485 10y multi 30 15

1963, Feb. 10

776 A486 10y chocolate 18 15

Consolidation of the communities of Moji, Kokura, Wakamatsu, Yawata and Tobata into Kita-Kyushu City.

"Frost Flowers" on Mt. Fugen — A487

Amakusa Island and Mt. Unzen — A488

1963, Feb. 15

777 A487	5y gray blue	25	15
778 A488	10y carmine rose	25	15
	Set value		16

Unzen-Amakusa National Park.

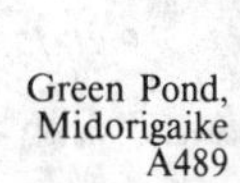

Green Pond, Midorigaike A489

Hakusan Range — A490

Perf. 13½

1963, Mar. 1 Unwmk. Photo.

779 A489	5y vio brn	20	15
780 A490	10y dk grn	20	15
	Set value		16

Hakusan National Park.

Keya-no-Oto Rock — A491

1963, Mar. 15

781 A491 10y multi 22 15

Genkai Quasi-National Park.

Wheat Emblem and Globe — A492

1963, Mar. 21

782 A492 10y dk grn 18 15

FAO "Freedom from Hunger" campaign.

"Girl Reading Letter," Yedo Screen — A493

1963, Apr. 20 *Perf. 13½*

783 A493 10y multi 65 65

Issued to publicize Stamp Week, 1963.

World Map and Centenary Emblem A494

1963, May 8

784 A494 10y multi 15 15

Centenary of the International Red Cross.

Globe and Leaf with Symbolic River System — A495

1963, May 15 Photo.

785 A495 10y blue 15 15

5th Congress of the Intl. Commission on Irrigation and Drainage.

Ito-dake, Asahi Range — A496

Lake Hibara and Mt. Bandai A497

1963, May 25 Unwmk. *Perf. 13½*

786 A496	5y green	20	15
787 A497	10y red brn	20	15
	Set value		16

Bandai-Asahi National Park.

Lidth's Jay — A498

Designs: No. 789, Rock ptarmigan. No. 790, Eastern turtle dove. No. 791, Japanese white stork. No. 792, Bush warbler. No. 792A, Meadow bunting.

1963-64 *Perf. 13½*

Design and Inscription

788	A498	10y lt grn	85	55
789	A498	10y blue	24	15
790	A498	10y pale yel	24	15
791	A498	10y grnsh bl ('64)	24	15
792	A498	10y grn ('64)	24	15
792A	A498	10y lt rose brn ('64)	22	15
		Nos. 788-792A (6)	2.03	
		Set value		95

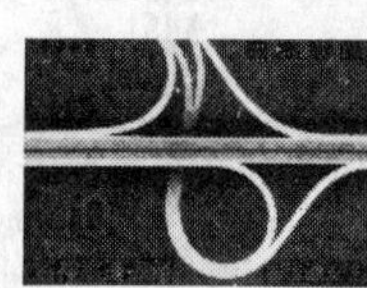
Intersection at Ritto, Shiga — A499

Girl Scout and Flag — A500

1963, July 15 Unwmk. *Perf. 13½*

793 A499 10y bl grn, blk & org 15 15

Issued to commemorate the opening of the Nagoya-Kobe expressway, linking Nagoya with Kyoto, Osaka and Kobe.

1963, Aug. 1 Photo.

794 A500 10y multi 15 15

Issued to commemorate the Asian Girl Scout and Girl Guides Camp, Togakushi Heights, Nagano, Aug. 1-7.

View of Nashu — A501

Whirlpool at Naruto A502

1963, Aug. 20

795 A501	5y ol bis	18	15
796 A502	10y dk grn	18	15
	Set value		16

Inland Sea National Park.

Lake Shikaribetsu, Hokkaido A503

Mt. Kurodake from Sounkyo Valley — A504

1963, Sept. 1 Unwmk. *Perf. 13½*

797	A503	5y dp Prus bl	18	15
798	A504	10y rose vio	18	15
		Set value		16

Daisetsuzan National Park.

Parabolic Antenna for Space Communications A505

1963, Sept. 9 Photo.

799 A505 10y multi 15 15

Issued to publicize the 14th General Assembly of the International Scientific Radio Union, Tokyo.

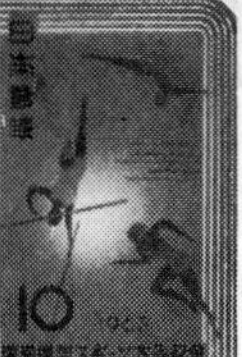
"Great Wave off Kanagawa," by Hokusai A506

1963, Oct. 10 *Perf. 13*

800 A506 40y gray, dk bl & yel 2.50 55

Issued for International Letter Writing Week, Oct. 6-12. Design from Hokusai's "36 Views of Fuji." Printed in sheets of 10 (5x2).

Diver, Pole Vaulter and Relay Runner A507

Woman Gymnast A508

1963, Oct. 11 *Perf. 13½*

801 A507 10y bl, ocher, blk & red 15 15

Tokyo Intl. (Pre-Olympic) Sports Meet, Tokyo, Oct. 11-16.

Perf. 13½

1963, Oct. 27 Unwmk. Engr.

Design: #803, Japanese wrestling (sumo).

802	A508	5y slate green	15	15
803	A508	5y brown	15	15
a.		Pair, #802-803	40	
		Set value		15

18th National Athletic Meet, Yamaguchi.

Phoenix Tree and Hachijo Island A509

Toy Dragons of Tottori and Yamanashi A510

1963, Dec. 10 Photo.

804 A509 10y multi 18 15

Izu Islands Quasi-National Park.

1963, Dec. 16

805	A510	5y gold, pink, aqua, indigo & red	15	15
a.		Aqua omitted		

Issued for New Year 1964. Sheets containing four of No. 805 were awarded as fifth prize in the New Year lottery. Value $3.75.

Wakasa-Fuji from Takahama A511

1964, Jan 25 *Perf. 13½*

806 A511 10y multi 18 15

Wakasa Bay Quasi-National Park.

Agave and View from Horikiri Pass — A512

1964, Feb. 20 Unwmk.

807 A512 10y multi 18 15

Nichinan-Kaigan Quasi-National Park.

Uji Bridge — A513

View of Toba — A514

1964, Mar. 15 Photo.

808	A513	5y sepia	15	15
809	A514	10y red lilac	15	15
		Set value		15

Ise-Shima National Park.

Takayama Festival Float and Mt. Norikura — A515

Design: No. 811, Yamaboko floats and Gion Shrine, Kyoto.

1964 Photo. *Perf. 13½*

810	A515	10y lt grn & multi	20	15
811	A515	10y grnsh bl & multi	20	15
		Set value		15

No. 810 issued for the annual Takayama spring and autumn festivals, Takayama City, Gifu Prefecture. No. 811 for the annual Gion festival of Kyoto, July 10-30.

Issue dates: #810, Apr. 15. #811, July 15.

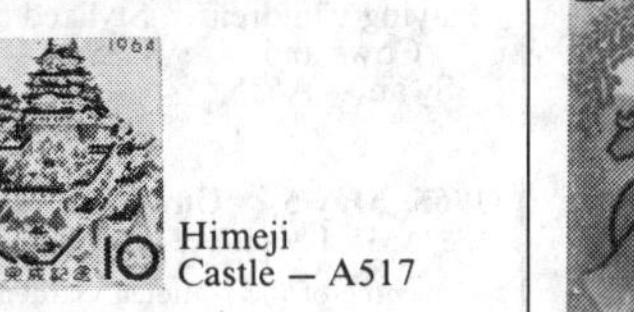
Yadorigi Scene from Genji Monogatari Scroll — A516

1964, Apr. 20

814 A516 10y multi 32 15

Stamp Week, 1964. Sheets of 10 (2x5).

Himeji Castle — A517

1964, June 1 *Perf. 13½*

815 A517 10y dk brn 15 15

Restoration of Himeji Castle.

Sports Type of 1961

1964, June 6 *Perf. 13½*

816	A454	5y Handball	15	15
817	A454	5y Woman on beam	15	15
a.		Pair, #816-817	40	
		Set value	24	20

19th National Athletic Meeting, Niigata.

Cable Cross Section, Map of Pacific Ocean A518

Tokyo Expressway Crossing Nihonbashi A519

1964, June 19

818 A518 10y gray grn, dp mag & yel 15 15

Opening of the transpacific cable.

1964, Aug. 1 Photo.

819 A519 10y grn, sil & blk 15 15

Opening of the Tokyo Expressway.

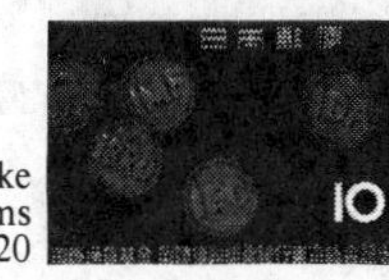
Coin-like Emblems A520

1964, Sept. 7 Unwmk. *Perf. 13½*

820 A520 10y scar, gold & blk 15 15

Annual general meeting of the Intl. Monetary Fund, Intl. Bank for Reconstruction and Development, Intl. Financial Corporation and the Intl. Development Assoc., Tokyo, Sept. 7-11.

Athletes, Olympic Flame and Rings — A521

National Stadium, Tokyo — A522

Designs: 30y, Nippon Bodokan (fencing hall). 40y, National Gymnasium. 50y, Komazawa Gymnasium.

1964

821	A521	5y multi	15	15
822	A522	10y multi	15	15
823	A522	30y multi	40	15
824	A522	40y multi	40	15
825	A522	50y multi	52	18
a.		Souvenir sheet of 5, #821-825	2.75	3.00
		Nos. 821-825 (5)	1.62	
		Set value		45

18th Olympic Games, Tokyo, Oct. 10-25. Issue dates: 5y, Sept. 9. Others, Oct. 10.

Hand with Grain, Cow and Fruit — A523

Express Train — A524

1964, Sept. 15 *Perf. 13½*

826 A523 10y vio brn & gold 15 15

Draining of Hachirogata Lagoon, providing new farmland for the future.

1964, Oct. 1

827 A524 10y bl & blk 20 15

Opening of the new Tokaido railroad line.

Mt. Fuji Seen from Tokaido, by Hokusai A525

1964, Oct. 4 *Perf. 13*

828 A525 40y multi 1.25 35

Issued for International Letter Writing Week, Oct. 4-10. Issued in sheets of 10 (5x2). See Nos. 850, 896, 932, 971, 1016.

"Straw Snake" Mascot — A526

1964, Dec. 15 Photo. *Perf. 13½*

829 A526 5y crim, blk & yel 15 15

Issued for New Year 1965. Sheets containing four of No. 829 were awarded as prizes in the New Year lottery (issued Jan. 20, 1965). Value $2.25.

Mt. Daisen — A527

Paradise Cove, Oki Islands
A528

1965, Jan. 20 Unwmk. *Perf. 13½*

830 A527 5y dk bl 15 15
831 A528 10y brn org 15 15
Set value 15

Daisen-Oki National Park.

Niseko-Annupuri — A529

1965, Feb. 15 Photo.

832 A529 10y multi 15 15

Niseko-Shakotan-Otarukaigan Quasi-Natl. Park.

Meteorological Radar Station on Mt. Fuji — A530

1965, Mar. 10 Photo. *Perf. 13½*

833 A530 10y multi 15 15

Completion of the Meteorological Radar Station on Kengamine Heights of Mt. Fuji.

Kiyotsu Gorge — A531

Lake Nojiri and Mt. Myoko — A532

1965, Mar. 15

834 A531 5y brown 15 15
835 A532 10y magenta 15 15
Set value 15

Jo-Shin-etsu Kogen National Park.

Communications Museum, Tokyo — A533

1965, Mar. 25 Unwmk. *Perf. 13½*

836 A533 10y green 15 15

Philatelic Exhibition celebrating the completion of the Communications Museum.

"The Prelude" by Shoen Uemura
A534

1965, Apr. 20 Photo.

837 A534 10y gray & multi 35 15

Issued for Stamp Week, 1965.

Playing Children, Cows and Swan — A535

Stylized Tree and Sun — A536

1965, May 5 Unwmk. *Perf. 13½*

838 A535 10y pink & multi 15 15

Opening of the National Garden for Children, Tokyo-Yokohama.

1965, May 9

839 A536 10y multi 15 15

Issued to publicize the forestation movement and the forestation ceremony, Tottori Prefecture.

Globe, Old and New Communication Equipment — A537

1965, May 17

840 A537 10y brt bl, yel & blk 15 15

Cent. of the ITU.

Crater of Mt. Naka, Kyushu
A538

Five Central Peaks of Aso and Mountain Road — A539

1965, June 15 Photo. *Perf. 13½*

841 A538 5y car rose 15 15
842 A539 10y dp grn 15 15
Set value 15

Aso National Park.

ICY Emblem and Doves
A540

1965, June 26 Unwmk.

843 A540 40y multi 50 15

Intl. Cooperation Year, 1965, and 20th anniv. of the UN.

Horse Chase, Soma
A541

Chichibu Festival Scene
A542

1965 Photo. *Perf. 13x13½*

844 A541 10y multi 18 15
845 A542 10y multi 20 15
Set value 20

No. 844 issued to publicize the ancient Soma Nomaoi Festival, Fukushima Prefecture; No. 845, to publicize the festival dedicated to the Chichibu Myoken Shrine (built 1584).

Issue dates: #844, July 16. #845, Dec. 3.

Meiji Maru, Black-tailed Gulls — A543

1965, July 20 *Perf. 13½*

846 A543 10y grn, gray, blk & yel 15 15

25th Maritime Day, July 20.

Drop of Blood, Girl's Face and Bloodmobile
A544

1965, Sept. 1 *Perf. 13½*

847 A544 10y yel, grn, blk & red 15 15

Issued to publicize the national campaign for blood donations, Sept. 1-30.

Tokai Atomic Power Station and Structure of Alpha Uranium — A545

1965, Sept. 21 Photo.

848 A545 10y multi 15 15

Issued to publicize the Ninth General Conference of the International Atomic Energy Agency, IAEA, Tokyo, Sept. 21-30.

People and Flag — A546

1965, Oct. 1

849 A546 10y multi 15 15

Tenth national census.

Hokusai Type of 1964

Design: No. 850, "Waters at Misaka" by Hokusai (Mt. Fuji seen across Lake Kawaguchi).

1965, Oct. 6 Unwmk. *Perf. 13*

850 A525 40y multi 75 20

Issued for International Letter Writing Week, Oct. 6-12. Issued in sheets of 10 (5x2).

Emblems and Diagram of Seats in National Diet — A547

1965, Oct. 15 *Perf. 13½*

851 A547 10y multi 15 15

75th anniv. of natl. suffrage, 40th anniv. of universal suffrage and 20th anniv. of women's suffrage.

Sports Type of 1961

Designs: No. 852, Gymnast on vaulting horse. No. 853, Walking race.

1965, Oct. 24 Engr. *Perf. 13½*

852 A454 5y red brn 15 15
853 A454 5y yel grn 15 15
Set value 15
a. Pair, #852-853 30 20

20th National Athletic Meeting, Gifu.

Profile and Infant
A548

1965, Oct. 30 Photo. *Perf. 13*

854 A548 30y car lake, yel & lt bl 35 15

8th Intl. Conf. of Otorhinolaryngology and the 11th Intl. Conf. of Pediatrics.

Mt. Iwo from Shari Coast, Hokkaido
A549

Rausu Lake and Mt. Rausu
A550

1965, Nov. 15 *Perf. 13½*

855 A549 5y Prus grn 15 15
856 A550 10y brt bl 15 15
Set value 15

Shiretoko National Park.

Aurora Australis, Map of Antarctica and "Fuji" — A551

1965, Nov. 20

857	A551	10y bl, yel & dk bl	15	15

Issued to publicize the Antarctic expedition, which left on the observation ship "Fuji," Nov. 20, 1965.

"Secret Horse" Straw Toy, Iwate Prefecture A552

Telephone Dial and 1890 Switchboard A553

1965, Dec. 10

858	A552	5y lt bl & multi	15	15

Issued for New Year 1966. Sheets containing four of No. 858 were awarded as prizes in the New Year lottery (issued Jan. 20, 1966). Value $1.75.

1965, Dec. 16

859	A553	10y multi	15	15

Issued to commemorate the 75th anniversary of telephone service in Japan.

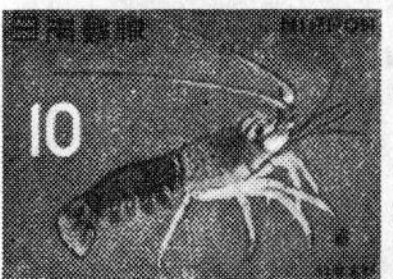

Japanese Spiny Lobster A554

Carp — A555

1966-67 Photo. *Perf. 13*

Multicolored; Background in Colors Indicated

860	A554	10y grn & ultra	16	15
861	A555	10y bl grn	16	15
862	A555	10y dk bl *(Bream)*	16	15
863	A555	10y dk ultra *(Skipjack tuna)*	16	15
864	A555	10y bis & dk grn *(3 Ayu)*	16	15
865	A555	15y grnsh bl & yel *(Eel)*	25	15
866	A555	15y brt grn *(Jack mackerel)*	25	15
867	A555	15y brt grn & bl *(Chum salmon)*	25	15
868	A555	15y lt bl grn *(Yellow-tail)* ('67)	30	15
869	A555	15y brt grn *(Tiger puffer)* ('67)	32	15
870	A554	15y ultra & grn *(Squid)* ('67)	42	15
871	A554	15y chlky bl *(Turbo cornutus)* ('67)	42	15
		Nos. 860-871 (12)	3.01	
		Set value		1.00

Famous Gardens Issue

Kobuntei Pavilion and Plum Blossoms, Kairakuen Garden, Ibaragi A556

Japanese Cranes and Okayama Castle, Korakuen Garden, Okayama A557

Kenrokuen Garden in the Snow — A558

1966-67 *Perf. 13½*

872	A556	10y gold, blk & grn	20	15
873	A557	15y bl, blk & mag	22	15
874	A558	15y sil, grn & dk brn	22	15
		Set value		24

Dates of issue: 10y, Feb. 25; No. 873, Nov. 3; No. 874, Jan. 25, 1967.

Crater Lake, Zao — A559

1966, Mar. 15

875	A559	10y multi	16	15

Zao Quasi-National Park.

Muroto Cape — A560

Senba Cliffs, Anan Coast — A561

1966, Mar. 22 *Perf. 13½*

876	A560	10y multi	16	15
877	A561	10y multi	16	15
		Set value		15

Muroto-Anan Coast Quasi-National Park.

AIPPI Emblem A562

1966, Apr. 11 *Perf. 13*

878	A562	40y multi	50	15

26th General Assembly of the Intl. Association for the Protection of Industrial Properties, Tokyo, Apr. 11-16.

"Butterflies" by Takeji Fujishima — A563

Photogravure and Engraved

1966, Apr. 20 *Perf. 13½*

879	A563	10y gray & multi	32	15

Stamp Week, 1966. Sheets of 10 (2x5). See No. 907.

Hisoka Maejima A563a

Goldfish A564

Chrysanthemums A565

Wistaria A565a

Hydrangea A565b

Golden Hall, Chusonji A565c

Yomei Gate, Nikko A565d

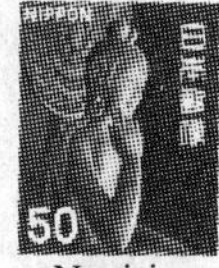

Nyoirin Kannon of Chuguji A565f

Central Hall, Enryakuji Temple A566

Ancient Clay Horse (Haniwa) A567

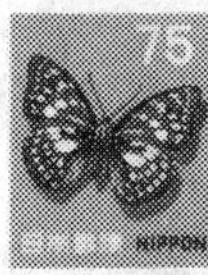

A567a

A567b

A567c

Katsura Palace Garden — A568

A569

Bodhisattva Playing Flute (from Todaiji Lantern) — A570

Designs: 20y, Wistaria. 25y, Hydrangea. 35y, Luminescent squid. 45y, Lysichiton camtschatsense (white flowers). 500y, Deva King statue, South Gate, Todaiji.

1966-69 Photo. *Perf. 13*

879A	A563a	1y ol bis ('68)	15	15
880	A564	7y ol & dp org	1.00	15
881	A565	15y bl & yel (bl "15")	90	15
b.		Bklt. pane of 2 + label ('67)	3.25	
c.		Bklt. pane of 4 ('67)	2.25	
d.		Bklt. pane of 4 (2 #881 + 2 #611) ('67)	6.00	
e.		Imperf., pair	350.00	
881A	A565a	20y vio & multi ('67)	1.65	1.00
882	A565b	25y grn & lt ultra	50	15
882A	A565c	30y dp ultra & gold ('68)	60	15
883	A564	35y bl, gray & blk	85	15
883A	A565d	40y bl grn & brn ('68)	60	15
884	A565	45y bl & multi ('67)	60	15
885	A565f	50y dk car rose	10.50	15
		Engr.		
886	A566	60y sl grn	1.40	15
		Photo.		
887	A567	65y org brn	13.00	15
887A	A567a	75y rose, blk, yel & pur	1.40	15
888	A567b	90y gold & brn	2.50	15
888A	A567c	100y ver & blk ('68)	1.65	15
		Engr.		
889	A568	110y brown	1.90	15
890	A569	120y red	3.25	15
891	A570	200y Prus grn (22x33mm)	6.50	15
891A	A570	500y dl pur ('69)	9.50	15
		Nos. 879A-891A (19)	58.45	
		Set value		1.60

Nos. 880-881 were also issued with fluorescent frame on July 18, 1966.

See Nos. 913-916, 918, 926, 1072, 1081.

UNESCO Emblem A571

Map of Pacific Ocean A572

1966, July 2 Photo. *Perf. 13*

892	A571	15y multi	22	15

20th anniv. of UNESCO.

1966, Aug. 22 *Perf. 13*

893	A572	15y bis brn, dl bl & rose	22	15

11th Pacific Science Congress, Tokyo, Aug. 22-Sept. 10.

The Scott Catalogue value is a retail price, what you could expect to pay for the stamp in a grade of Fine-Very Fine. The value listed is a reference which reflects recent actual dealer selling price.

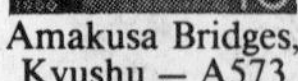

Amakusa Bridges, Kyushu — A573

Emblem of Post Office Life Insurance and Family — A574

1966, Sept. 24 **Photo.** ***Perf. 13***
894 A573 15y multi 22 15

Issued to commemorate the completion of five bridges linking Misumi Harbor, Kyushu, with Amakusa islands.

1966, Oct. 1
895 A574 15y yel grn & multi 22 15

50th anniversary of post office life insurance service.

Hokusai Type of 1964

Design: 50y, "Sekiya on the Sumida" (horseback riders and Mt. Fuji) from Hokusai's "36 Views of Fuji."

1966, Oct. 6
896 A525 50y multi 1.00 40

Intl. Letter Writing Week, Oct. 6-12. Printed in sheets of 10 (5x2).

Sharpshooter — A575

Design: No. 898, Hop, skip and jump.

1966, Oct. 23 **Engr.** ***Perf. 13½***
897 A575 7y ultra 15 15
898 A575 7y car rose 15 15
a. Se-tenant pair, #897-898 40
Set value 15

21st Natl. Athletic Meet, Oita, Oct. 23-28.

National Theater A576

Kabuki Scene — A577

Bunraku Puppet Show — A578

1966, Nov. 1 ***Perf. 13, 13½***
899 A576 15y multi 20 15
900 A577 25y multi 52 20
901 A578 50y multi 52 25
Set value 50

Inauguration of first National Theater in Japan. Nos. 900-901 issued in sheets of 10.

Rice Year Emblem A579

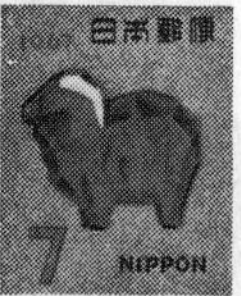

Ittobori Carved Sheep, Nara Prefecture A580

1966, Nov. 21 ***Perf. 13½***
902 A579 15y red, blk & ocher 18 15

FAO International Rice Year.

1966, Dec. 10 **Photo.** ***Perf. 13½***
903 A580 7y bl, gold, blk & pink 15 15

Issued for New Year 1967. Sheets containing four of No. 903 were awarded as prizes in the New Year lottery. Value $1.25.

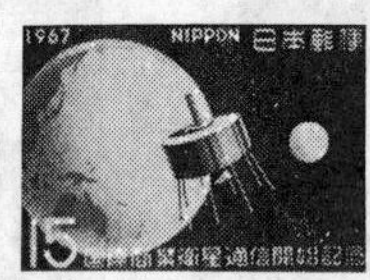

International Communications Satellite, Lani Bird 2 — A581

1967, Jan. 27 ***Perf. 13½***
904 A581 15y dk Prus bl & sep 18 15

Inauguration in Japan of International commercial communications service via satellite.

Around the World Air Route and Jet Plane — A582

1967, Mar. 6 **Photo.** ***Perf. 13½***
905 A582 15y multi 18 15

Issued to publicize the inauguration of Japan Air Lines Tokyo-London service via New York, which completes the around the world air route.

Library of Modern Japanese Literature A583

1967, Apr. 11
906 A583 15y grnsh bl, lt & dk brn 18 15

Issued to commemorate the opening of the Library of Modern Japanese Literature, Komaba Park, Meguro-ku, Tokyo.

Painting Type of 1966

Design: 15y, Lakeside (seated woman), by Seiki (Kiyoteru) Kuroda.

1967, Apr. 20
907 A563 15y multi 60 20

Stamp Week, 1967. Sheets of 10 (2x5).

Kobe Harbor A584

1967, May 8 **Photo.** ***Perf. 13x13½***
908 A584 50y multi 70 18

5th Cong. of the Intl. Association of Ports and Harbors, Tokyo, May 8-13.

Welfare Commissioner's Emblem A585

Traffic Light, Automobile and Children A586

1967, May 12 ***Perf. 13½***
909 A585 15y dk brn & gold 18 15

50th anniversary of the Welfare Commissioner System.

1967, May 22 ***Perf. 13x13½***
910 A586 15y emer, red, blk & yel 18 15

Issued to publicize traffic safety.

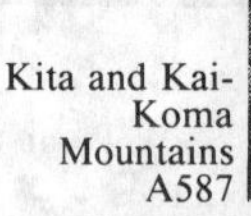

Kita and Kai-Koma Mountains A587

Akaishi and Hijiri Mountains A588

1967, July 10
911 A587 7y Prus bl 15 15
912 A588 15y rose lil 24 15
Set value 15

South Japan Alps National Park.

Types of 1966-69 Redrawn and

A588a

Original 20y No. 881A

Redrawn 20y No. 915

1967-69 **Photo.** ***Perf. 13***
913 A564 7y brt yel grn & dp org 22 15
914 A565 15y bl & yel (white "15") 35 15
a. Pane of 10 (5x2) ('68) 2.75
b. Bklt. panes of 4 with gutter (6 #914 + 2 #611) ('68) 3.25
c. Imperf., pair 225.00
d. Blue shading omitted
e. Bklt. panes of 2 & 4 with gutter ('68) 17.50
915 A565 20y vio & multi ('69) 1.50 15
916 A565f 50y brt car 1.10 15
917 A588a 55y lt bl, grn & blk ('69) 1.25 15
918 A567 65y dp org 1.50 15
Nos. 913-918 (6) 5.92
Set value 30

Issued for use in facer-canceling machines. Issue dates: 7y, Aug. 1; 15y, 50y, July 1; 65y, July 20, 1967; 20y, Apr. 1, 1969; 55y, Sept. 1, 1969.

On No. 913 the background has been lightened and a frame line of shading added at top and right side.

No. 914a is imperf. on four sides.

The two panes of Nos. 914b and 914e are connected by a vertical creased gutter 21mm wide. The left pane of No. 914b consists of 2 No. 914 and 2 No. 611; the right pane, 4 of No. 914. The left pane of 2 of No. 914e includes a 4-line inscription.

On No. 915 the wistaria leaves do not touch frame at left and top. On No. 881A they do.

Coil Stamp

1968, Jan. 9 ***Perf. 13 Horiz.***
926 A565 15y bl & yel (white "15") 80 45

Mitochondria and Protein Model — A589

1967, Aug. 19 **Photo.** ***Perf. 13***
927 A589 15y gray & multi 20 15

7th Intl. Biochemistry Cong., Tokyo, Aug. 19-25.

Gymnast on Horizontal Bar — A590

Universiade Emblem — A591

1967, Aug. 26
928 A590 15y red & multi 24 15
929 A591 50y yel & multi 65 24
Set value 28

World University Games, Universiade 1967, Tokyo, Aug. 26-Sept. 4.

Paper Lantern, ITY Emblem — A592

"Sacred Mt. Fuji" by Taikan Yokoyama — A593

1967, Oct. 2 **Photo.** ***Perf. 13***
930 A592 15y ultra & multi 22 15
931 A593 50y multi 1.75 1.10

International Tourist Year, 1967. No. 931 issued in sheets of 10.

Hokusai Type of 1964

Design: 50y, "Kajikazawa, Koshu" (fisherman and waves) from Hokusai's "36 Views of Fuji."

1967, Oct. 6
932 A525 50y multi 1.75 50

Issued for International Letter Writing Week, Oct. 6-12. Sheets of 10 (5x2).

Athlete, Wild Primrose and Chichibu Mountains
A594

1967, Oct. 22 **Photo.** ***Perf. 13***
933 A594 15y gold & multi 30 15

22nd Natl. Athletic Meet, Saitama, Oct. 22-27.

Miroku Bosatsu, Koryuji Temple, Kyoto — A595

Kudara Kannon, Horyuji Temple, Nara — A596

Golden Hall and Pagoda, Horyuji Temple, Nara — A597

1967, Nov. 1 **Photo.**
934 A595 15y multi 32 24

Engr.

935 A596 15y pale grn, blk & red 32 24

Photo. & Engr.

936 A597 50y multi 2.00 65

National treasures of Asuka Period (6th-7th centuries). No. 936 issued in sheets of 10.

Highway and Congress Emblem
A598

1967, Nov. 5 **Photo.** ***Perf. 13***
937 A598 50y multi 65 15

Issued to publicize the 13th World Road Congress, Tokyo, Nov. 5-11.

Mt. Kumotori
A599

Lake Chichibu
A600

1967, Nov. 27

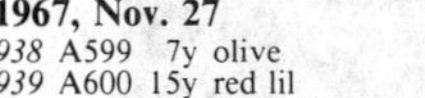

938 A599 7y olive 15 15
939 A600 15y red lil 25 15
Set value 15

Chichibu-Tama National Park

Climbing Monkey Toy (Noborizaru), Miyazaki Prefecture — A601

1967, Dec. 11 **Photo.** ***Perf. 13***
940 A601 7y multi 15 15

Issued for New Year 1968. Sheets containing four of No. 940 were awarded as prizes in the New Year lottery. Value $1.25.

Mt. Sobo — A602

Takachiho Gorge — A603

1967, Dec. 20
941 A602 15y multi 22 15
942 A603 15y multi 22 15
Set value 20

Sobo Katamuki Quasi-National Park.

Girl, Boy and Sakura Maru — A604

1968, Jan. 19 **Photo.** ***Perf. 13***
943 A604 15y ultra, ocher & blk 18 15

Cent. of the Meiji Era, and 1st Japanese Youth Good Will Cruise in celebration of the centenary.

Ashura, Kofukuji Temple, Nara — A605

Gakko Bosatsu, Todaiji Temple, Nara — A606

Kichijo Ten, Yakushiji Temple, Nara — A607

1968, Feb. 1 **Engr.** ***Perf. 13***
944 A605 15y sep & car 28 30

Engr. & Photo.

945 A606 15y dk brn, pale grn & org 50 35

Photo.

946 A607 50y multi 1.50 70

Issued to show National Treasures of the Nara Period (710-784).

Grazing Cows and Mt. Yatsugatake
A608

Mt. Tateshina
A609

1968, Mar. 21 **Photo.** ***Perf. 13***
947 A608 15y multi 24 15
948 A609 15y multi 24 15
Set value 24

Yatsugatake-Chushin-Kogen Quasi-Natl. Park.

Young Dancer (Maiko) in Tenjuan Garden, by Bakusen Tsuchida
A610

1968, Apr. 20 **Photo.** ***Perf. 13***
949 A610 15y multi 45 15

Stamp Week, 1968. Sheets of 10 (5x2).

Rishiri Isl. Seen from Rebun Isl. — A611

1968, May 10 **Photo.** ***Perf. 13***
950 A611 15y multi 18 15

Rishiri-Rebun Quasi-National Park.

Gold Lacquer and Mother-of-Pearl Box — A612

"The Origin of Shigisan" Painting from Chogo-sonshiji, Nara — A613

Bodhisattva Samantabhadra
A614

1968, June 1 **Engr. & Photo.**
951 A612 15y lt bl & multi 45 20

Photo.

952 A613 15y tan & multi 45 35
953 A614 50y sep & multi 3.25 1.00

Issued to show national treasures of the Heian Period (8-12th centuries).

Memorial Tower and Badge of Hokkaido — A615

1968, June 14
954 A615 15y grn, vio bl, bis & red 22 15

Centenary of development of Hokkaido.

Sunrise over Pacific and Fan Palms — A616

1968, June 26 **Photo.** ***Perf. 13***
955 A616 15y blk, org & red org 22 15

Return of Bonin Islands to Japan by US.

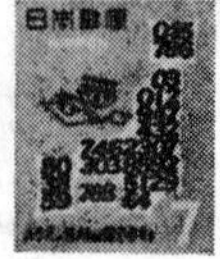

Map of Japan Showing Postal Codes — A617

Two types of inscription:
Type I (enlarged)

あなたの住所にも郵便番号を

"Postal code also on your address"

Type II (enlarged)

あて名に郵便番号を

"Don't omit postal code on the address"

1968, July 1
956 A617 7y yel grn & red (I) 1.40 35
957 A617 7y yel grn & red (II) 1.40 35
a. Pair, #956-957 4.50

958 A617 15y sky bl & car (I) 1.00 15
a. Bklt. panes of 4 with gutter (3 #958 + 3 #959 + 2 #611) 35.00
959 A617 15y sky bl & car (II) 1.00 15
a. Pair. #958-959 3.00

Issued to publicize the introduction of the postal code system.

The double booklet pane, No. 958a, comes in two forms, the positions of the Postal Code types being transposed.

Coil Stamps
Perf. 13 Horiz.

959A A617 15y sky bl & car (I) 1.10 65
959B A617 15y sky bl & car (II) 1.10 65
a. Pair. #959A-959B 2.25 1.59

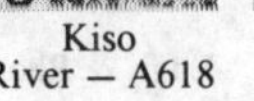

Kiso River — A618

Inuyama Castle — A619

1968, July 20 ***Perf. 13½***

960 A618 15y multi 20 15
961 A619 15y multi 20 15
Set value 15

Hida-Kisogawa Quasi-National Park.

Youth Hostel Emblem, Trees and Sun — A620

1968, Aug. 6 **Photo.** ***Perf. 13***

962 A620 15y cit & multi 22 15

Issued to publicize the 27th International Youth Hostel Congress, Tokyo, Aug. 6-20.

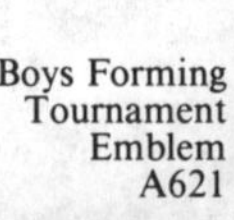

Boys Forming Tournament Emblem A621

Pitcher and Tournament Flag — A622

1968, Aug. 9

963 A621 15y yel grn, yel, blk & red 30 15
964 A622 15y red, yel & blk 30 15
a. Pair. #963-964 65 30
Set value 24

Issued to commemorate the 50th All-Japan High School Baseball Championship Tournament, Koshi-en Baseball Grounds, Aug. 9. Nos. 963-964 printed checkerwise.

Minamoto Yoritomo, Jingoji, Kyoto — A623

Heiji Monogatari Scroll Painting — A624

Red-threaded Armor, Kasuga Shrine, Nara — A625

1968, Sept. 16 **Photo.** ***Perf. 13***

965 A623 15y blk & multi 55 30
966 A624 15y tan & multi 65 35

Photo. & Engr.

967 A625 50y multi 2.00 1.35

National treasures of Kamakura period (1180-1192 to 1333).

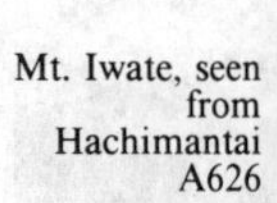

Mt. Iwate, seen from Hachimantai A626

Lake Towada, seen from Mt. Ohanabe A627

1968, Sept. 16 **Photo.**

968 A626 7y red brn 15 15
969 A627 15y green 24 15
Set value 15

Towada-Hachimantai National Park.

Gymnast, Tojimbo Cliff and Narcissus — A628

1968, Oct. 1 **Photo.** ***Perf. 13***

970 A628 15y multi 30 15

23rd National Athletic Meet, Fukui Prefecture, Oct. 1-6.

Hokusai Type of 1964

Design: 50y, "Fujimihara in Owari Province" (cooper working on a barrel) from Hokusai's "36 Views of Fuji."

1968, Oct. 7

971 A525 50y multi 1.25 45

Issued for International Letter Writing Week, Oct. 7-13. Sheets of 10 (5x2).

Centenary Emblem, Sun and First Western Style Warship — A629

Imperial Carriage Arriving in Tokyo (1868), by Tomone Kobori A630

1968, Oct. 23

972 A629 15y vio bl, red, gold & gray 20 15
973 A630 15y multi 24 15
Set value 15

Meiji Centenary Festival.

Old and New Lighthouses A631

1968, Nov. 1 **Photo.** ***Perf. 13***

974 A631 15y multi 22 15

Issued to commemorate the centenary of the first western style lighthouse in Japan.

Ryo'o Court Dance and State Hall, Imperial Palace — A632

1968, Nov. 14

975 A632 15y multi 22 15

Completion of the new Imperial Palace.

Mt. Takachiho A633

Mt. Motobu, Yaku Island — A634

1968, Nov. 20

976 A633 7y purple 15 15
977 A634 15y orange 24 15
Set value 15

Kirishima-Yaku National Park.

Carved Toy Cock of Yonezawa, Yamagata Prefecture — A635

Human Rights Flame, Dancing Children and Globe — A636

1968, Dec. 5 **Photo.** ***Perf. 13***

978 A635 7y lt bl & multi 15 15

Issued for New Year 1969. Sheets containing 4 of No. 978 were awarded as prizes in the New Year lottery. Value $1.25.

1968, Dec. 10

979 A636 50y org & multi 75 15

International Human Rights Year.

Striped Squirrel A637

Kochomon Cave and Road A638

1968, Dec. 14

980 A637 15y emer & blk 30 15

Issued to promote saving.

1969, Jan. 27 **Photo.**

981 A638 15y multi 30 15

Echizen-Kaga-Kaigan Quasi-National Park.

Silver Pavilion, Jishoji Temple, Kyoto — A639

Pagoda, Anrakuji Temple, Nagano — A640

Winter Landscape by Sesshu — A641

1969, Feb. 10 **Photo.** ***Perf. 13***

982 A639 15y multi 30 15

Photo. & Engr.

983 A640 15y lt grn & multi 30 15

Photo.

984 A641 50y tan, blk & ver 1.50 1.20

Issued to show national treasures of the Muromachi Period (1333-1572).

Mt. Chokai, seen from Tobishima Island — A642

1969, Feb. 25 **Photo.**
985 A642 15y brt bl & multi 22 15

Chokai Quasi-National Park.

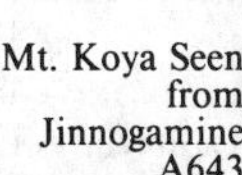

Mt. Koya Seen from Jinnogamine A643

Mt. Gomadan and Rhododendron A644

1969, Mar. 25 **Photo.** ***Perf. 13***
986 A643 15y multi 20 15
987 A644 15y multi 20 15
Set value 15

Koya-Ryujin Quasi-National Park.

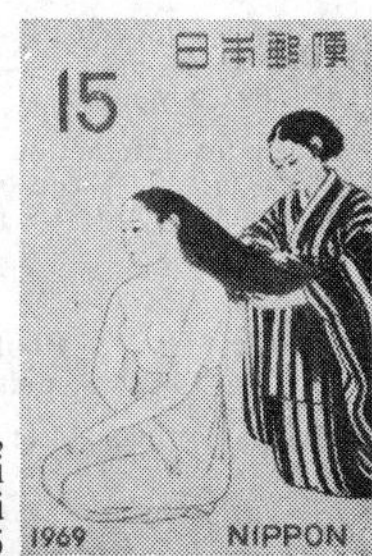

Hair (Kami), by Kokei Kobayashi A645

1969, Apr. 20 **Photo.** ***Perf. 13***
988 A645 15y multi 40 22

Issued for Philatelic Week.

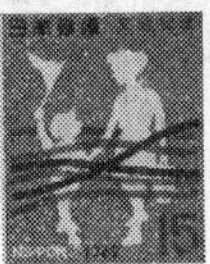

Mother, Son Crossing Street — A646

Tokyo-Nagoya Expressway and Sakawagawa Bridge — A647

1969, May 10 **Photo.** ***Perf. 13***
989 A646 15y lt bl, red & grn 22 15

National traffic safety campaign.

1969, May 26
990 A647 15y multi 22 15

Completion of Tokyo-Nagoya Expressway.

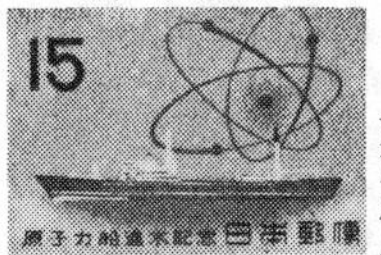

Nuclear Ship Mutsu and Atom Diagram A648

1969, June 12
991 A648 15y gray, blk, pink & bl 22 15

Issued to publicize the launching of the first Japanese nuclear ship, Mutsu.

Museum of Modern Art and Palette — A649

1969, June 11 **Photo.** ***Perf. 13½***
992 A649 15y lt bl, brn, yel & blk 22 15

Opening of the new National Museum of Modern Art, Tokyo.

Cable Ship KKD Maru and Map of Japan Sea — A650

1969, June 25
993 A650 15y lt bl, blk & ocher 22 15

Completion of the Japan sea cable between Naoetsu, Japan, and Nakhodka, Russia.

Postcards, Postal Code Symbol — A651

Mailbox, Postal Code Symbol — A652

1969, July 1 **Photo.** ***Perf. 13***
997 A651 7y yel grn & car 40 15
998 A652 15y sky bl & car 40 15
Set value 24

1st anniv. of the postal code system and to promote its use.

Lions Emblem and Rose — A653

1969, July 2
999 A653 15y bl, blk, rose & gold 22 15

Issued to publicize the 52nd Convention of Lions International, Tokyo, July 2-5.

Hotoke-ga-ura on Shimokita Peninsula, Northern Honshu A654

1969, July 15
1000 A654 15y multi 22 15

Shimokita Hanto Quasi-National Park.

Himeji Castle, Hyogo Prefecture A655

"Pine Forest" (Detail), by Tohaku Hasegawa — A656

"Cypresses," Attributed to Eitoku Kano — A657

1969, July 21 **Photo. & Engr.**
1001 A655 15y lt bl & multi 28 20

Photo.

1002 A656 15y pale brn & blk 28 20
1003 A657 50y gold & multi 1.25 80

Issued to show national treasures of the Momoyama period (1573-1614). The 50y is in sheets of 10 (2x5); Nos. 1001-1002 in sheets of 20 (5x4).

Harano-fudo Waterfall A658

Mt. Nagisan A659

1969, Aug. 20
1004 A658 15y multi 20 15
1005 A659 15y multi 20 15
Set value 15

Hyobosen-Ushiroyama-Nagisan Quasi-Natl. Park.

Mt. O-akan, Hokkaido A660

Mt. Iwo A661

1969, Aug. 25 **Photo.** ***Perf. 13***
1006 A660 7y bright blue 15 15
1007 A661 15y sepia 20 15
Set value 15

Akan National Park.

Angling, by Taiga Ikeno — A662

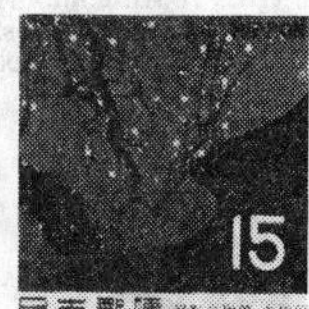

The Red Plum, by Korin Ogata — A663

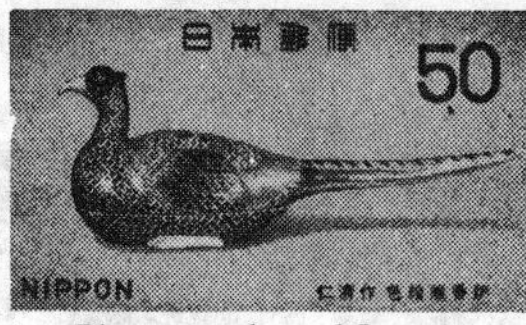

Pheasant-shaped Incense Burner — A664

Design: No. 1010, The White Plum, by Korin Ogata.

1969, Sept. 25 **Photo.** ***Perf. 13x13½***
1008 A662 15y multi 30 15

Perf. 13

1009 A663 15y gold & multi 35 15
1010 A663 15y gold & multi 35 15
a. Pair, #1009-1010 75 25

Photo. & Engr.

1011 A664 50y multi 1.00 35
Set value 58

Natl. treasures, Edo Period (1615-1867).

Birds Circling Globe and UPU Congress Emblem A665

Woman Reading Letter, by Utamaro A666

Designs (UPU Congress Emblem and): 50y, Two Women Reading a Letter, by Harunobu. 60y, Man Reading a Letter (Miyako Dennai), by Sharaku.

1969, Oct. 1 **Photo.** ***Perf. 13***
1012 A665 15y red & multi 22 15
1013 A666 30y multi 55 38
1014 A666 50y multi 65 48
1015 A666 60y multi 95 65

16th Congress of the UPU, Tokyo, Oct. 1-Nov. 16. 15y issued in sheets of 20, others in sheets of 10.

Hokusai Type of 1964

Design: 50y, "Passing through Koshu down to Mishima" from Hokusai's 36 Views of Fuji.

1969, Oct. 7 **Photo.** ***Perf. 13***
1016 A525 50y multi 1.00 55

Issued for International Letter Writing Week Oct. 7-13. Sheets of 10 (5x2).

Rugby Player, Camellia and Oura Catholic Church — A667

1969, Oct. 26
1017 A667 15y lt ultra & multi 22 15

24th National Athletic Meet, Nagasaki, Oct. 26-31.

Cape Kitayama
A668

Goishi Coast
A669

1969, Nov. 20 **Photo.** ***Perf. 13***

1018 A668 7y gray & dk bl 15 15
1019 A669 15y sal & dk red 24 15
Set value 32 15

Rikuchu Coast National Park Issue

Worker in Hard Hat — A670

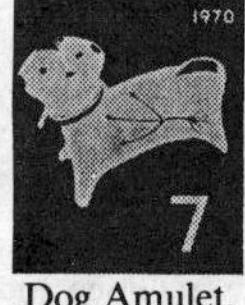

Dog Amulet, Hokkeji, Nara — A671

1969, Nov. 26

1020 A670 15y ultra, blk yel & brn 22 15

50th anniv. of the ILO.

1969, Dec. 10

1021 A671 7y org & multi 15 15

Issued for New Year 1970. Sheets containing 4 of No. 1021 were awarded as prizes in the New Year lottery. Value $1.25.

Aso Bay and Tsutsu Women with Horse — A672

1970, Feb. 25 **Photo.** ***Perf. 13***

1022 A672 15y multi 22 15

Iki-Tsushima Quasi-National Park.

Fireworks over EXPO '70 — A673

Cherry Blossoms Around Globe — A674

Irises, by Korin Ogata (1658-1716) — A675

1970, Mar. 14 **Photo.** ***Perf. 13***

1023 A673 7y red & multi 15 15
1024 A674 15y gold & multi 15 15
1025 A675 50y gold & multi 65 65
a. Souv. sheet of 3, #1023-1025 1.40 1.40
b. Bklt. pane of 4 & 3 with gutter 3.00
Set value 75

EXPO '70 Intl. Exposition, Senri, Osaka, Mar. 15-Sept. 13.

No. 1025b contains a pane of 4 No. 1023 and a pane with Nos. 1023-1025. A 35mm gutter separates the panes.

Woman with Hand Drum, by Saburosuke Okada — A676

1970, Apr. 20 **Photo.** ***Perf. 13***

1026 A676 15y multi 45 15

Issued for Stamp Week, Apr. 20-26.

Mt. Yoshino
A677

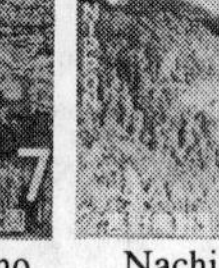

Nachi Waterfall
A678

1970, Apr. 30 **Photo.** ***Perf. 13***

1027 A677 7y gray & pink 15 15
1028 A678 15y pale bl & grn 24 15
Set value 32 15

Yoshino-Kumano National Park.

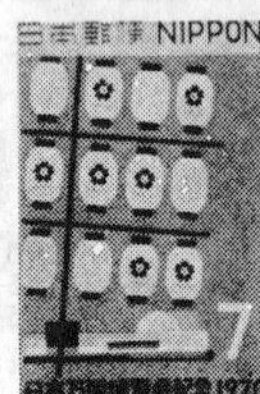

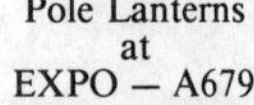

Pole Lanterns at EXPO — A679

View of EXPO Within Globe — A680

Grass in Autumn Wind, by Hoitsu Sakai (1761-1828) — A681

1970, June 15 **Photo.** ***Perf. 13***

1029 A679 7y red & multi 15 15
1030 A680 15y bl & multi 24 15
1031 A681 50y sil & multi 60 15
a. Souv. sheet of 3, #1029-1031 1.40
b. Bklt. panes of 4 & 3 with gutter 3.00
Set value 20

EXPO '70, 2nd issue.

No. 1031b contains a pane of 4 No. 1029 and a pane with Nos. 1029-1031. A 35mm gutter separates the panes.

Buildings and Postal Code Symbol — A682

1970, July 1 **Photo.** ***Perf. 13***

1032 A682 7y emer & vio 35 15
1033 A682 15y brt bl & choc 48 15
Set value 20

Postal code system.

"Maiden at Dojo Temple"
A683

Scene from "Sukeroku"
A684

"The Subscription List" (Kanjincho) — A685

1970, July 10

1034 A683 15y multi 24 15
1035 A684 15y multi 24 16
1036 A685 50y multi 65 40

Issued to publicize the Kabuki Theater.

Girl Scout — A686

1970, July 26

1037 A686 15y multi 18 15

50th anniversary of Japanese Girl Scouts.

Kinoura Coast and Festival Drum — A687

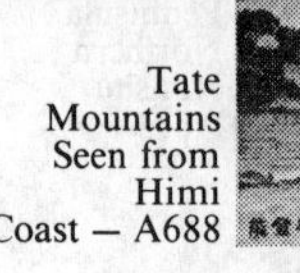

Tate Mountains Seen from Himi Coast — A688

1970, Aug. 1

1038 A687 15y multi 20 15
1039 A688 15y multi 20 15
Set value 15

Noto Hanto Quasi-National Park

Sunflower and UN Emblem — A689

1970, Aug. 17

1040 A689 15y lt bl & multi 22 15

Issued to publicize the 4th United Nations Congress on the Prevention of Crime and the Treatment of Offenders, Kyoto, Aug. 17-26.

Mt. Myogi — A690

Mt. Arafune
A691

1970, Sept. 11 **Photo.** ***Perf. 13***

1041 A690 15y multi 20 15
1042 A691 15y multi 20 15
Set value 15

Myogi-Arafune-Sakukogen Quasi-Natl. Park.

G.P.O., Tokyo, by Hiroshige III
A692

Equestrian, Mt. Iwate and Paulownia
A693

1970, Oct. 6

1043 A692 50y multi 70 30

Issued for International Letter Writing Week, Oct. 6-12. Sheets of 10 (5x2). Design from wood block series, "Noted Places in Tokyo."

1970, Oct. 10 **Photo.** ***Perf. 13***

1044 A693 15y sil & multi 22 15

25th Natl. Athletic Meet, Morioka, Oct. 10-16.

Hodogaya Stage, by Hiroshige III — A694

Tree and UN Emblem — A695

1970, Oct. 20

1045 A694 15y silver & multi 22 15

Centenary of telegraph service in Japan.

1970, Oct. 24

Design: 50y, UN emblem and Headquarters with flags.

1046 A695 15y ol, ap grn & gold 20 15
1047 A695 50y multi 60 15
Set value 20

25th anniversary of United Nations.

Vocational Training Competition Emblem A696

Diet Building and Doves A697

1970, Nov. 10 **Photo.** ***Perf. 13***
1048 A696 15y multi 22 15

The 19th International Vocational Training Competition, Chiba City, Nov. 10-19.

1970, Nov. 29
1049 A697 15y multi 22 15

80th anniversary of Japanese Diet.

Wild Boar, Folk Art, Arai City, Niigata Prefecture — A698

1970, Dec. 10
1050 A698 7y multi 15 15

New Year 1971. Sheets containing 4 of No. 1050 were awarded as prizes in the New Year lottery. Value $1.25.

Gen-jo-raku A699

Ko-cho A700

Tai-hei-raku — A701

1971, Apr. 1 **Photo.** ***Perf. 13***
1051 A699 15y multi 24 15
1052 A700 15y multi 24 15
1053 A701 50y multi 65 15
Set value 24

Gagaku, classical Japanese court entertainment.

Woman Voter and Parliament A702

Pines and Maple Leaves A703

1971, Apr. 10 **Photo.** ***Perf. 13***
1054 A702 15y org & multi 22 15

25th anniversary of woman suffrage.

1971, Apr. 18
1055 A703 7y emer & vio 15 15

National forestation campaign.

Woman of Tokyo, by Kiyokata Kaburagi — A704

1971, Apr. 19
1056 A704 15y gray & multi 32 15

Philatelic Week, Apr. 19-25.

Mailman A705

Mailbox A706

Railroad Post Office — A707

1971, Apr. 20
1057 A705 15y blk & org brn 20 15
1058 A706 15y multi 20 15
1059 A707 15y multi 20 15
Set value 15

Centenary of Japanese postage stamps.

Titmouse A708

Penguins A709

1971, May 10 **Photo.** ***Perf. 13***
1060 A708 15y emer, blk & bis 22 15

25th Bird Week.

1971, June 23 **Photo.** ***Perf. 13***
1061 A709 15y dk bl, yel & grn 25 15

Tenth anniversary of the Antarctic Treaty pledging peaceful uses of and scientific co-operation in Antarctica.

Goto Wakamatsu Seto Region A710

Kujukushima ("99 Islands"), Kyushu A711

1971, June 26 **Photo.** ***Perf. 13***
1062 A710 7y dk grn 15 15
1063 A711 15y dp brn 22 15
Set value 15

Saikai National Park.

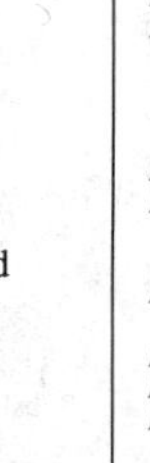

Arabic Numerals and Postal Code Symbol — A712

1971, July 1
1064 A712 7y emer & red 20 15
1065 A712 15y bl & car 28 15
Set value 22

Promotion for postal code system.

Inscribed "NIPPON" Types of 1962-67 and

Little Cuckoo — A713

Mute Swan — A714

Sika Deer — A715

Beetle — A716

Pine — A717

Noh Mask — A717a

Pheasant A717b

Golden Eagle A717c

Bronze Phoenix, Uji — A718

Burial Statue of Warrior, Ota — A718a

Buddha, Sculpture, 685 — A718b

Tentoki Sculpture, 11th Century — A718c

Bazara-Taisho, c. 710-794 — A718d

Goddess Kissho — A718e

Designs: 25y, Hydrangea. No. 1076, Wind God Fujin. 120y, Mythical winged woman. 1081, Bodhisattva.

1971-75 **Photo.** ***Perf. 13***
1067 A713 3y emerald 15 15
a. Bklt. pane of 20 ('72) 2.00
1068 A714 5y brt bl 15 15
1069 A715 10y yel grn & sep ('72) 16 15
a. Bklt. pane of 6 (2 #1069, 4 #1071 with gutter btwn.) ('72) 1.40
1070 A716 12y dp brn 16 15
1071 A717 20y grn & sep ('72) 25 15
a. Pane of 10 (5x2) ('72) 2.75
1072 A565 25y emer & lt ultra ('72) 30 15
1074 A717a 70y dp org & blk 95 15
1075 A717b 80y crim & brn 1.25 15
1076 A467 90y org & dk brn 1.40 15
1077 A717c 90y org & brn ('73) 1.40 15
1079 A469 120y dk brn & lt grn ('72) 1.65 15
1080 A718 150y lt & dk grn 1.90 15
1081 A570 200y dp car (18x22mm; '72) 3.00 15
1082 A718a 200y red brn ('74) 3.00 15
1083 A718b 300y dk bl ('74) 3.75 15
1084 A718c 400y car rose ('74) 5.25 15
1085 A718d 500y grn ('74) 6.25 25
1087 A718e 1000y multi ('75) 14.00 1.00
a. Miniature sheet of 1 14.00 9.00
Nos. 1067-1087 (18) 44.97
Set value 2.25

No. 1071a is imperf. on four sides.
See Nos. 1249-1250, 1254, 1631.

Coil Stamp
Perf. 13 Horiz.
1088 A717 20y grn & sep ('72) 42 30

Boy Scout Bugler — A719

Rose and Rings — A720

1971, Aug. 2
1090 A719 15y lt bl & multi 22 15

13th World Boy Scout Jamboree, Asagiri Plain, Aug. 2-10.

1971, Oct. 1
1091 A720 15y ultra & multi 22 15

50th anniv. of Japanese Conciliation System.

Tokyo Horsedrawn Streetcar, by Yoshimura A721

1971, Oct. 6
1092 A721 50y multi 75 30

Intl. Letter Writing Week. Sheets of 10 (5x2).

Emperor's Flag, Chrysanthemums and Phoenix — A722

"Beyond the Sea," by Empress Nagako A723

1971, Oct. 14

1093	A722	15y gold, vio, red & bl	24	15
1094	A723	15y gold, vio, red & bl	24	15
a.		Souvenir sheet of 2, #1093-1094, imperf.	85	85
b.		Pair, #1093-1094	50	25
		Set value		15

European trip of Emperor Hirohito and Empress Nagako, Sept. 28-Oct. 15. No. 1094a has violet map of Asia, Africa and Europe in background.

Tennis, Cape Shiono-misaki, Plum Blossoms — A724

Child's Face and "100" — A725

1971, Oct. 24 Photo. *Perf. 13*

1095	A724	15y org & multi	22	15

26th National Athletic Meet, Wakayama Prefecture, Oct. 24-29.

1971, Oct. 27

1096	A725	15y pink, car & blk	22	15

Centenary of Japanese Family Registration System.

Tiger, by Gaho Hashimoto A726

Design: No. 1098, Dragon, from "Dragon and Tiger," by Gaho Hashimoto.

1971, Nov. 1 Engr. *Perf. 13*

1097	A726	15y ol & multi	28	15
1098	A726	15y ol & multi	28	15
a.		Pair, #1097-1098	75	
		Set value		15

Centenary of Government Printing Works. Nos. 1097-1098 printed checkerwise.

Mt. Yotei from Lake Toya — A727

Mt. Showa-Shinzan A728

Treasure Ship A729

1971, Dec. 6

1099	A727	7y sl grn & yel	15	15
1100	A728	15y pink & vio bl	24	15
		Set value		16

Shikotsu-Toya National Park.

1971-72

1101	A729	7y emer, gold & org	15	15
1102	A729	10y lt bl, org & gold ('72)	16	15
		Set value		16

New Year 1972. Sheets containing 3 of No. 1102 were awarded as prizes in the New Year lottery. Value $1.75.

Issue dates: 7y, Dec. 10, 1971; 10y, Jan. 11, 1972.

Downhill Skiing — A730

Designs (Olympic Rings and): No. 1104, Bobsledding. 50y, Figure skating, pairs.

1972, Feb. 3 Photo. *Perf. 13*

Size: 24x34mm

1103	A730	20y ultra & multi	25	15
1104	A730	20y ultra & multi	25	15

Size: 49x34mm

1105	A730	50y ultra & multi	65	22
a.		Souv. sheet of 3, #1103-1105	1.50	1.40
		Set value		34

11th Winter Olympic Games, Sapporo, Feb. 3-13. No. 1105a has continuous design extending into margin.

Bunraku, Ningyo Jyoruri Puppet Theater

A731 A732

A733

1972, Mar. 1 Photo. *Perf. 13½*

1106	A731	20y gray & multi	32	15

Perf. 12½x13

1107	A732	20y multi	32	15

Lithographed and Engraved

Perf. 13½x13

1108	A733	50y multi	65	18
		Set value		28

Japanese classical entertainment.

Express Train on New Sanyo Line — A734

Taishaku-kyo Valley — A735

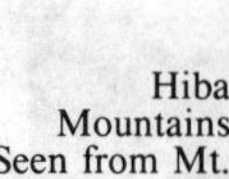

Hiba Mountains Seen from Mt. Dogo — A736

1972, Mar. 15 Photo. *Perf. 13*

1109	A734	20y multi	30	15

Centenary of first Japanese railroad.

1972, Mar. 24

1110	A735	20y gray & multi	25	15
1111	A736	20y grn & multi	25	15
		Set value		15

Hiba-Dogo-Taishaku Quasi-National Park.

Heart and UN Emblem A737

1972, Apr. 15

1112	A737	20y gray, red & blk	30	15

"Your heart is your health," World Health Day.

"A Balloon Rising," by Gakuryo Nakamura — A738

1972, Apr. 20

1113	A738	20y vio bl & multi	32	15

Philatelic Week, Apr. 20-26.

Shurei Gate, Okinawa A739

Camellia A740

1972, May 15

1114	A739	20y ultra & multi	30	15

Ratification of the Reversion Agreement with US under which the Ryukyu Islands were returned to Japan.

1972, May 20

1115	A740	20y brt grn, vio bl & yel	30	15

National forestation campaign and 23rd Arbor Day, May 21.

Mt. Kurikoma and Kijiyama Kokeshi Doll — A741

Naruko-kyo Gorge and Naruko Kokeshi Doll — A742

1972, June 20 Photo. *Perf. 13*

1116	A741	20y bl & multi	25	15
1117	A742	20y red & multi	25	15
		Set value		24

Kurikoma Quasi-National Park.

Envelope, Postal Code Symbol — A743

Mailbox, Postal Code Symbol — A744

1972, July 1

1118	A743	10y bl, blk & gray	22	15
1119	A744	20y emer & org	40	15
		Set value		20

Publicity for the postal code system.

Mt. Hodaka A745

Mt. Tate — A746

1972, Aug. 10 Photo. *Perf. 13*

1120	A745	10y rose & vio	15	15
1121	A746	20y bl & buff	28	15
		Set value		20

Chubu Sangaku National Park.

Ghost in "Tamura" A747

Lady Rokujo in "Lady Hollyhock" A748

"Hagoromo" (Feather Robe) — A749

1972, Sept. 20 Engr.

1122	A747	20y multi	30	15

Photo.

1123	A748	20y multi	30	15

Perf. 13½x13

1124	A749	50y multi	75	15
		Set value		30

Noh, classical public entertainment.

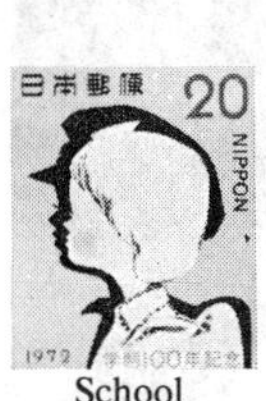
School Children A750

Eitai Bridge, Tokyo, by Hiroshige III A751

1972, Oct. 5 Photo. *Perf. 13*
1125 A750 20y lt ultra, vio bl & car 28 15

Centenary of modern education system.

1972, Oct. 9
1126 A751 50y multi 70 15

Intl. Letter Writing Week, Oct. 9-15.

Inauguration of Railway Service, by Hiroshige III — A752

Locomotive, Class C62 — A753

1972, Oct. 14
1127 A752 20y multi 32 15
1128 A753 20y multi 32 15
Set value 15

Centenary of Japanese railroad system.

Kendo (Fencing) and Sakurajima Volcano — A754

1972, Oct. 22
1129 A754 10y yel & multi 18 15

27th National Athletic Meet, Kagoshima Prefecture, Oct. 22-27.

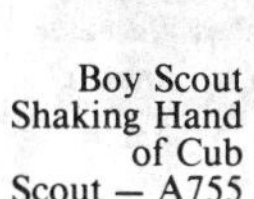

Boy Scout Shaking Hand of Cub Scout — A755

1972, Nov. 4
1130 A755 20y yel & multi 28 15

50th anniversary of the Boy Scouts of Japan.

US Ship, Yokohama Harbor A756

"Clay Plate with Plum Blossoms" A757

1972, Nov. 28 Photo. *Perf. 13*
1131 A756 20y multi 30 15

Centenary of Japanese customs. Wood block by Hiroshige III (d. 1896).

1972, Dec. 11
1132 A757 10y bl & multi 15 15

New Year 1973. Art work by Kenzan Ogata (1663-1743). Sheets containing 3 of No. 1132 were awarded as prizes in the New Year lottery. Value $1.75.

Mt. Tsurugi A758

Oboke Valley — A759

1973, Feb. 20 Photo. *Perf. 13*
1133 A758 20y multi 25 15
1134 A759 20y multi 25 15
Set value 15

Mt. Tsurugi Quasi-National Park.

Mt. Takao — A760

Minoo Falls — A761

1973, Mar. 12 Photo. *Perf. 13*
1135 A760 20y multi 25 15
1136 A761 20y multi 25 15
Set value 15

Meiji Forests Quasi-National Park.

Phoenix Tree A762

Sumiyoshi Shrine Visitor A763

1973, Apr. 7 Photo. *Perf. 13*
1137 A762 20y brt grn, yel & dk bl 30 15

National forestation campaign.

1973, Apr. 20
1138 A763 20y multi 30 15

Philatelic Week, Apr. 20-26. Design from painting by Ryusei Kishida (1891-1929) of his daughter, "A Portrait of Reiko Visiting Sumiyoshi Shrine."

Mt. Kamagatake A764

Mt. Haguro A765

1973, May 25 Photo. *Perf. 13*
1139 A764 20y multi 25 15
1140 A765 20y multi 25 15
Set value 20

Suzuka Quasi-National Park.

Chichijima Beach — A766

Coral Reef on Minami Island — A767

1973, June 26
1141 A766 10y grnsh bl & Prus bl 16 15
1142 A767 20y lil & dk pur 24 15
Set value 15

Ogasawara National Park.
5th anniversary of the return of the Bonin (Ogasawara Islands) to Japan.

Tree, Postal Code Symbol — A768

Mailman, Postal Code Symbol — A769

1973, July 1 Photo. *Perf. 13*
1143 A768 10y brt grn & gold 20 15
1144 A769 20y bl, pur & car 30 15
Set value 20

Postal code system, 5th anniversary.

Sandan Gorge — A770

Mt. Shinnyu — A771

1973, Aug. 28 Photo. *Perf. 13*
1145 A770 20y multi 25 15
1146 A771 20y multi 25 15
Set value 15

Nishi-Chugoku-Sanchi Quasi-National Park.

Tenryu Valley A772

Mt. Horaiji A773

1973, Sept. 18 Photo. *Perf. 13*
1147 A772 20y lil & multi 25 15
1148 A773 20y vio bl, lt bl & sil 25 15
Set value 15

Tenryu-Okumikawa Quasi-National Park.

Cock, by Jakuchu Ito (1716-1800) — A774

Woman Runner at Start — A775

1973, Oct. 6
1149 A774 50y gold & multi 70 25

International Letter Writing Week, Oct. 7-13. Sheets of 10.

1973, Oct. 14
1150 A775 10y sil & multi 20 15

28th National Athletic Meet, Chiba Prefecture, Oct. 14-19.

Kan Mon Bridge A776

1973, Nov. 14 Engr. *Perf. 13*
1151 A776 20y blk, rose & yel 28 15

Opening of Kan Mon Bridge connecting Honshu and Kyushu.

Old Man and Dog — A777

Designs: No. 1153, Old man and wife pounding rice mortar, which yields gold. No. 1154, Old man sitting in tree and landlord admiring tree.

1973, Nov. 20 **Photo.**
1152 A777 20y multi 24 15
1153 A777 20y multi 24 15
1154 A777 20y multi 24 15
Set value 15

Folk tale "Hanasaka-jijii" (The Old Man Who Made Trees Bloom).

Bronze Lantern, Muromachi Period — A778

1973, Dec. 10
1155 A778 10y emer, blk & org 20 15

New Year 1974. Sheets containing 3 of No. 1155 were awarded as prizes in the New Year lottery. Value $1.50.

Nijubashi, Tokyo A779

Imperial Palace, Tokyo A780

1974, Jan. 26 **Photo.** ***Perf. 13***
1156 A779 20y gold & multi 25 15
1157 A780 20y gold & multi 25 15
a. Souv. sheet of 2, #1156-1157 90 40
Set value 15

50th anniversary of the wedding of Emperor Hirohito and Empress Nagako.

Young Wife — A781

Crane Weaving A782

Cranes in Flight A783

1974, Feb. 20 **Photo.** ***Perf. 13***
1158 A781 20y multi 25 15
1159 A782 20y multi 25 15
1160 A783 20y multi 25 15
Set value 15

Folk tale "Tsuru-nyobo" (Crane becomes wife of peasant).

Marudu Falls — A784

Marine Scene — A785

1974, Mar. 15
1161 A784 20y multi 25 15
1162 A785 20y multi 25 15
Set value 15

Iriomote National Park.

"Finger," by Ito Shinsui — A786

Nambu Red Pine Sapling & Mt. Iwate — A787

1974, Apr. 20 **Photo.** ***Perf. 13***
1163 A786 20y multi 30 15

Philatelic Week, Apr. 20-27.

1974, May 18
1164 A787 20y multi 30 15

National forestation campaign.

Supreme Court Building A788

1974, May 23 **Engr.**
1165 A788 20y redsh brn 30 15

Completion of Supreme Court Building, Tokyo.

Midget Using Bowl as Boat — A789

Designs: No. 1167, Midget fighting demon. No. 1168, Princess and midget changed into prince with magic hammer.

1974, June 10 **Photo.** ***Perf. 13***
1166 A789 20y yel & multi 25 15
1167 A789 20y bis & multi 25 15
1168 A789 20y bis & multi 25 15
Set value 15

Folk tale "Issun Hoschi" (The Story of the Mini-mini Boy).

"Police," by Kunimasa Baido — A790

1974, June 17 ***Perf. 13***
1169 A790 20y multi 30 15

Centenary of the Tokyo Metropolitan Police Department.

Iriomote Wildcat A791

Japanese Otter A792

Ogasawara Flying Fox — A793

Litho. and Engr.; Photo. and Engr. (Nos. 1172-1173)

1974
1170 A791 20y shown 30 15
1171 A792 20y shown 30 15
1172 A792 20y Black hare 30 15
1173 A793 20y shown 30 15
Set value 40

Nature conservation.
Issue dates: #1170, Mar. 25; #1171, June 25; #1172, Aug. 30; #1173, Nov. 15.

Transfusion Bottle, Globe, Doves — A794

1974, July 1 **Photo.**
1174 A794 20y brt bl & multi 30 15

Intl. Red Cross Blood Donations Year.

Discovery of Kaguya Hime in Shining Bamboo A795

Kaguya Hime as Grown-up Beauty A796

Kaguya Hime and Escorts Returning to Moon A797

1974, July 29 **Photo.** ***Perf. 13***
1175 A795 20y multi 25 15
1176 A796 20y multi 25 15
1177 A797 20y multi 25 15
Set value 15

Folk tale "Kaguya Hime" or "Tale of the Bamboo Cutter."

Rich and Poor Men with Wens A798

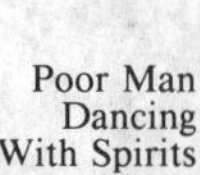

Poor Man Dancing With Spirits A798a

Design: No. 1180, Rich man with two wens, poor man without wen, spirits.

1974, Sept. 9 **Photo.** ***Perf. 13***
1178 A798 20y multi 25 15
1179 A798a 20y multi 25 15
1180 A798 20y multi 25 15
Set value 15

Folk tale "Kobutori Jiisan," or "The Old Man who had his Wen Taken by Spirits."

Goode's Projection and Diet — A799

"Aizen" by Ryushi Kawabata — A800

1974, Oct. 1 **Photo.** ***Perf. 13***
1181 A799 20y multi 25 15
1182 A800 50y multi 60 15
Set value 24

Interparliamentary Union, 61st Meeting, Tokyo, Nov. 2-11.

Pine and Hawk, by Sesson A801

UPU Emblem A802

Tending Cow, Fan by Sotatsu Tawaraya — A803

1974, Oct. 7
1183 A801 50y sep, blk & dk brn 65 15

Intl. Letter Writing Week, Oct. 6-12.

1974, Oct. 9
1184 A802 20y multi 25 15
1185 A803 50y multi 60 15
Set value 15

Centenary of Universal Postal Union.

Soccer Players and Sailboat A804

Various Mushrooms A805

1974, Oct. 20 **Photo.**
1186 A804 10y multi 18 15

29th National Athletic Meet, Ibaraki Prefecture, Oct. 20-25.

1974, Nov. 2
1187 A805 20y multi 30 15

9th International Congress on the Cultivation of Edible Fungi, Japan, Nov. 4-13.

Steam Locomotive Class D51 — A806

Class C57 — A807

Class 8620 — A808

Class C11 — A809

Designs: Steam locomotives.

1974, Nov. 26 **Photo.** ***Perf. 13***
1188 A806 20y shown 40 15
1189 A807 20y shown 40 15
a. Pair, #1188-1189 80 15

1975, Feb. 25
1190 A806 20y Class D52 40 15
1191 A807 20y Class C58 40 15
a. Pair, #1190-1191 80 15

1975, Apr. 3
1192 A808 20y shown 40 15
1193 A809 20y shown 40 15
a. Pair, #1192-1193 80 15

1975, May 15
1194 A806 20y Class 9600 40 15
1195 A807 20y Class C51 40 15
a. Pair, #1194-1195 80 15

1975, June 10 **Photo. & Engr.**
1196 A806 20y Class 7100 40 15
1197 A806 20y Class 150 40 15
a. Pair, #1196-1197 80 15
Nos. 1188-1197 (10) 4.00
Set value 50

Japanese National Railways.

Ornamental Nail Cover, Katsura Palace — A810

1974, Dec. 10
1198 A810 10y bl & multi 20 15

New Year 1975. Sheets containing 3 of No. 1198 were awarded as prizes in the New Year Lottery. Value $1.50.

Short-tailed Albatrosses — A811

Bonin Island Honey-eater A812

Temminck's Robin A813

Ryukyu-Yamagame Tortoise — A814

Design: No. 1200, Japanese cranes.

1975-76 **Photo. & Engr.** ***Perf. 13***
1199 A811 20y multi 28 15
1200 A811 20y multi 28 15
1201 A812 20y multi 28 15
1202 A813 50y multi 65 15
1203 A814 50y multi 65 15
Nos. 1199-1203 (5) 2.14
Set value 35

Nature conservation.
Issue dates: No. 1199, Jan. 16; No. 1200, Feb. 13; No. 1201, Aug. 8; No. 1202, Feb. 27, 1976; No. 1203, Mar. 25, 1976.

Taro Urashima Releasing Turtle A815

Palace of the Sea God and Fish — A816

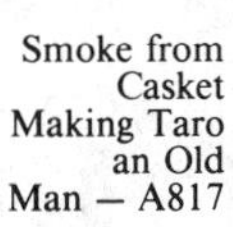

Smoke from Casket Making Taro an Old Man — A817

1975, Jan. 28 **Photo.** ***Perf. 13***
1204 A815 20y multi 25 15
1205 A816 20y multi 25 15
1206 A817 20y multi 25 15
Set value 15

Folk tale "Legend of Taro Urashima."

Kan-mon-sho (Seeing and Hearing), by Shiko Munakata — A818

1975, Mar. 20 **Photo.** ***Perf. 13***
1207 A818 20y brn & multi 30 15

Japan Broadcasting Corporation, 50th anniversary.

Old Man Feeding Mouse A819

Man Following Mouse Underground A820

Mice Entertaining and Bringing Gifts A821

1975, Apr. 15 **Photo.** ***Perf. 13***
1208 A819 20y multi 25 15
1209 A820 20y multi 25 15
1210 A821 20y multi 25 15
Set value 15

Folk tale "Paradise for the Mice."

Matsuura Screen (detail), 16th Century
A822 A823

1975, Apr. 21
1211 A822 20y gold & multi 30 15
1212 A823 20y gold & multi 30 15
a. Pair, #1211-1212 60 15
Set value 15

Philatelic Week, Apr. 21-27.

15-Cent Minimum Value
The minimum catalogue value is 15 cents. Separating se-tenant pieces into individual stamps does not increase the "value" of the stamps... since demand for the separated stamps may be small.

Oil Derricks, Congress Emblem — A824

1975, May 10 **Photo.** ***Perf. 13***
1213 A824 20y multi 30 15

9th World Petroleum Congress, Tokyo, May 11-16.

Trees and River A825

IWY Emblem, Sun and Woman A826

1975, May 24
1214 A825 20y grn & multi 30 15

National forestation campaign.

1975, June 23
1215 A826 20y org & multi 30 15

International Women's Year 1975.

Okinawan Dancer, EXPO 75 Emblem A827

Birds in Flight (Bingata) A828

Aquapolice and Globe — A829

1975, July 19 **Photo.** ***Perf. 13***
1216 A827 20y ultra & multi 25 15
1217 A828 30y bl grn & multi 35 15
1218 A829 50y ultra & multi 60 15
a. Souv. sheet of 3, #1216-1218 1.50 90
Set value 24

Oceanexpo 75, 1st Intl. Ocean Exposition, Okinawa, July 20, 1975-Jan. 18, 1976.

Historic Ship Issue

Kentoshi-sen 7th-9th Centuries A830

Ships: No. 1220, Kenmin-sen, 7th-9th centuries. No. 1221, Goshuin-sen, merchant ship, 16th-17th centuries. No. 1222, Tenchi-maru, state barge, built 1630. No. 1223, Sengoku-bune (cargo ship) and fishing vessel. No. 1224, Shoheimaru, 1852, European-type sailing ship. No. 1225, Taisei-maru, four-mast bark training ship, 1903. No. 1226, Tenyomaru, first Japanese passenger liner, 1907. No. 1227, Asama-maru, passenger

liner. No. 1228, Kinai-maru, transpacific freighter and Statue of Liberty. No. 1229, Container ship. No. 1230, Tanker.

1975-76 Engr. *Perf. 13*

1219	A830	20y rose red	28	15
1220	A830	20y sepia	28	15
a.		Pair, #1219-1220	56	15
1221	A830	20y lt ol	28	15
1222	A830	20y dk bl	28	15
a.		Pair, #1221-1222	56	15
1223	A830	50y vio bl	65	15
1224	A830	50y lilac	65	15
a.		Pair, #1223-1224	1.30	25
1225	A830	50y gray	65	15
1226	A830	50y dk brn	65	15
a.		Pair, #1225-1226	1.30	25
1227	A830	50y ol grn	65	15
1228	A830	50y ol brn	65	15
a.		Pair, #1227-1228	1.30	25
1229	A830	50y ultra	65	15
1230	A830	50y vio bl	65	15
a.		Pair, #1229-1230	1.30	25
		Nos. 1219-1230 (12)	6.32	
		Set value		1.00

Printed checkerwise in sheets of 20.

Issue dates: Nos. 1219-1220, Aug. 30; Nos. 1221-1222, Sept. 25, 1975; Nos. 1223-1224, Mar. 11; Nos. 1225-1226, Apr. 12; Nos. 1227-1228, June 1, 1976; Nos. 1229-1230, Aug. 18, 1976.

Apple and Apple Tree — A831

Peacock, by Korin Ogata — A832

1975, Sept. 17 Photo. *Perf. 13*

1231 A831 20y gray, blk & red 30 15

Centenary of apple cultivation in Japan.

1975, Oct. 6 Photo. *Perf. 13*

1232 A832 50y gold & multi 70 15

Intl. Letter Writing Week, Oct. 6-12.

American Flag and Cherry Blossoms A833

Japanese Flag and Dogwood A834

1975, Oct. 14

1233	A833	20y ultra & multi	25	15
1234	A834	20y grn & multi	25	15
a.		Souv. sheet of 2, #1233-1234	90	60
		Set value		15

Visit of Emperor Hirohito and Empress Nagako to the United States, Oct. 1-14.

Savings Box and Coins — A835

Weight Lifter — A836

1975, Oct. 24

1235 A835 20y multi 30 15

Japan's Postal Savings System, centenary.

1975, Oct. 25

1236 A836 10y multi 20 15

30th National Athletic Meet, Mie Prefecture, Oct. 26-31.

Papier-mache Dragon, Fukushima Prefecture — A837

1975, Dec. 13 Photo. *Perf. 13*

1237 A837 10y multi 18 15

New Year 1976. Sheets containing 3 of No. 1237 were awarded as prizes in the New Year Lottery. Value $1.50.

Inscribed "NIPPON"
Types of 1951-1974 and

Japanese Narcissus — A841

Noh Mask, Old Man — A843

Guardian Dog, Katori Shrine — A845

Sho-Kannon, Yakushiji Temple — A846

Designs: 50y, Nyoirin Kannon, Chuguji Temple. 150y, Bronze phoenix, Uji. 200y, Clay burial figure of warrior, Ota.

1976-79 Photo. *Perf. 13*

1244	A280	50y emerald	80	15
a.		Bklt. panes of 2 & 4 with gutter	5.00	
1245	A841	60y multi	1.00	15
1248	A843	140y lil rose & lil	2.00	15
1249	A718	150y red org & brn	2.00	15
1250	A718a	200y red org	2.75	15
1251	A845	250y blue	3.50	15
1253	A846	350y dk vio brn	4.25	15
		Nos. 1244-1253 (7)	16.30	
		Set value		50

Coil Stamps

Perf. 13 Horiz.

1254	A715	10y yel grn & sep ('79)	20	15
1256	A280	50y emerald	1.25	15
1257	A468	100y ver & blk ('79)	1.50	30
		Set value		50

See No. 1635.

Hikone Folding Screen (detail), 17th Century
A850 A851

1976, Apr. 20 Photo. *Perf. 13*

1258	A850	50y gold & multi	75	15
1259	A851	50y gold & multi	75	15
a.		Pair, #1258-1259	1.75	
		Set value		20

Philatelic Week, Apr. 20-26.

Plum Blossoms, Cedars, Mt. Tsukuba — A852

1976, May 22

1260 A852 50y multi 70 15

National forestation campaign.

Green Tree Frog — A853

Bitterlings A854

Sticklebacks A855

1976 Photo. & Engr. *Perf. 13*

1261	A853	50y multi	60	15
1262	A854	50y multi	60	15
1263	A855	50y multi	60	15
		Set value		30

Nature conservation.

Issue dates: No. 1261, July 20; No. 1262, Aug. 26; No. 1263, Sept. 16.

Crows, by Yosa Buson A856

Gymnasts and Stadium A857

1976, Oct. 6 Photo. *Perf. 13*

1264 A856 100y gray, blk & buff 1.25 20

Intl. Letter Writing Week, Oct. 6-12.

1976, Oct. 23 Photo. *Perf. 13*

1265 A857 20y multi 30 15

31st National Athletic Meet, Saga Prefecture, Oct. 24-29.

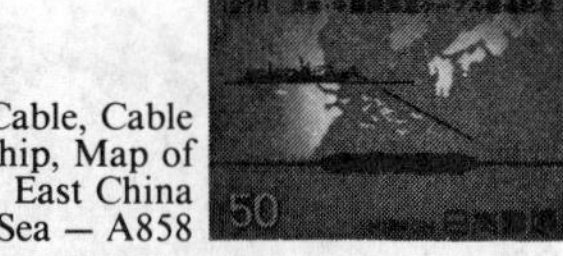

Cable, Cable Ship, Map of East China Sea — A858

1976, Oct. 25

1266 A858 50y bl, blk & sil 65 15

Opening of Sino-Japanese cable between Shanghai and Reihoku-cho, Kumamoto Prefecture.

Classical Court Dance A859

Imperial Coach A860

1976, Nov. 10 Photo. *Perf. 13*

1267	A859	50y multi	65	15
1268	A860	50y multi	65	15
a.		Souv. sheet of 2, #1267-1268	1.40	80
		Set value		20

Emperor Hirohito's accession to the throne, 50th anniversary.

Kindergarten Class — A861

1976, Nov. 16

1269 A861 50y multi 60 15

Centenary of first Kindergarten in Japan.

Healthy Family A862

Bamboo Toy Snake A863

1976, Nov. 24
1270 A862 50y multi 60 15

Natl. Health Insurance, 50th anniv.

1976, Dec. 1 Photo. *Perf. 13*
1271 A863 20y multi 30 15

New Year 1977. Sheets containing two of No. 1271 were awarded as prizes in the New Year lottery. Value $1.65.

National Treasures

East Pagoda, Yakushiji Temple, c. 730 — A864

Deva King in Armor Holding Spear, Nara Period — A865

1976, Dec. 9 Photo. *Perf. 13*
1272 A864 50y multi 60 15

Engr.
1273 A865 100y grn & multi 1.25 20

Golden Pavilion, Toshodai-ji Temple, 8th Century — A866

Praying Women, from Heike Nokyo Sutra, 12th Century A867

Photogravure and Engraved
1977, Jan. 20 *Perf. 13*
1274 A866 50y multi 65 15

Photo.
1275 A867 100y multi 1.40 20

Comic Picture Scroll, Attributed to Toba Sojo Kakuyu (1053-1140) — A868

Saint on Cloud, 11th Century Wood Carving, Byodoin Temple A869

1977, Mar. 25 Photo. *Perf. 13*
1276 A868 50y multi 65 15

Engr.
1277 A869 100y multi 1.40 20

Noblemen on Way to Court, from Picture Scroll, Heian Period — A870

Statue of Seitaka-doji, Messenger, Kamakura Period A871

1977, June 27 Photo. *Perf. 13*
1278 A870 50y multi 65 15

Engr.
1279 A871 100y multi 1.40 20

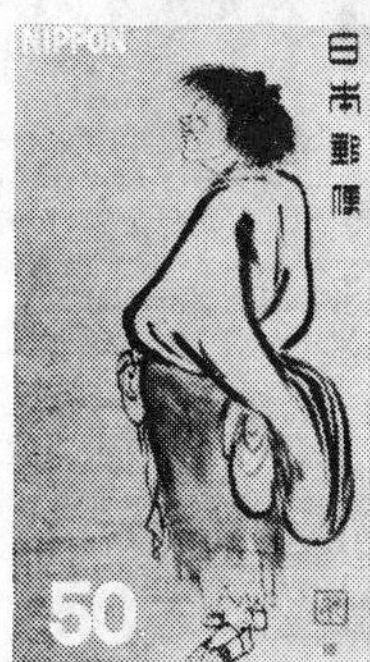
The Recluse Han Shan, 14th Century Painting A872

Tower, Matsumoto Castle, 16th Century — A873

1977, Aug. 25 Photo. *Perf. 13*
1280 A872 50y multi 65 15

Photogravure and Engraved
1281 A873 100y blk & multi 1.40 20

Pine and Flowers, Chishakuin Temple, Kyoto, 1591 — A874

Main Hall, Kiyomizu Temple, 1633 — A875

1977, Nov. 16 Photo. *Perf. 13*
1282 A874 50y multi 65 15

Engr.
1283 A875 100y multi 1.40 20

Scene from Tale of Genji, by Sotatsu Tawaraya — A876

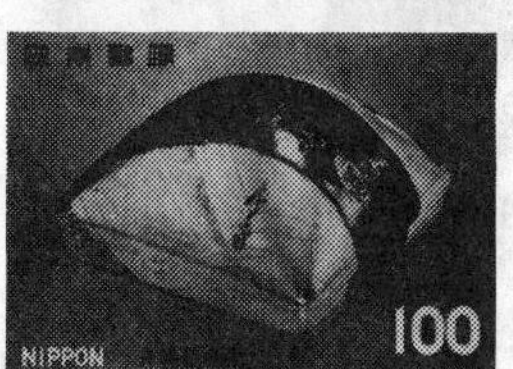
Inkstone Case, by Koetsu Honami — A877

1978, Jan. 26 Photo. *Perf. 13*
1284 A876 50y multi 65 15

Photogravure and Engraved
1285 A877 100y blk & multi 1.40 25

Family Enjoying Cool Evening, by Morikage Kusumi — A878

Yomeimon, Toshogu Shrine, 1636 — A879

1978, Mar. 3 Photo. *Perf. 13*
1286 A878 50y gray & multi 65 15

Photogravure and Engraved
1287 A879 100y multi 1.40 25

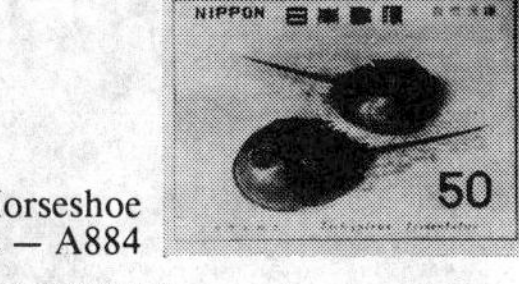
Horseshoe Crabs — A884

Graphium Doson Albidum — A885

Firefly A886

Cicada A887

Dragonfly A888

1977 Photo. *Perf. 13*
1292 A884 50y multi 60 15

Photogravure and Engraved
1293 A885 50y multi 60 15
1294 A886 50y multi 60 15
1295 A887 50y multi 60 15

Photo.
1296 A888 50y multi 60 15
Nos. 1292-1296 (5) 3.00
Set value 50

Issue dates: No. 1292, Feb. 18; No. 1293, May 18; No. 1294, July 22; No. 1295, Aug. 15; No. 1296, Sept. 14.

Figure Skating — A889

Figure Skating Pair — A890

1977, Mar. 1
1297 A889 50y sil & multi 65 15
1298 A890 50y sil & multi 65 15
Set value 20

World Figure Skating Championships, National Yoyogi Stadium, March 1-6.

Sun Shining on Forest — A891

1977, Apr. 16 Photo. *Perf. 13*
1299 A891 50y grn & multi 65 15

National forestation campaign.

Weavers and Dyers (Detail from Folding Screen)
A892 A893

1977, Apr. 20

1300 A892 50y gold & multi		65	15
1301 A893 50y gold & multi		65	15
a. Pair, #1300-1301		1.50	
Set value			20

Philatelic Week, Apr. 20-26.

Nurses
A894

1977, May 30 Photo. *Perf. 13*

1302 A894 50y multi 65 15

16th Quadrennial Congress of the Intl. Council of Nurses, Tokyo, May 30-June 3.

Fast Breeder Reactor, Central Part — A895

1977, June 6

1303 A895 50y multi 65 15

Experimental fast breeder reactor "Joyo," which began operating Apr. 24, 1977.

Workers and Safety Emblems
A896

Work on High-rise Buildings
A897

Cargo Unloading
A898

Machinery Work
A899

1977, July 1

1304 A896 50y multi	70	15
1305 A897 50y multi	70	15
1306 A898 50y multi	70	15
1307 A899 50y multi	70	15
a. Strip of 4, #1304-1307	3.00	
Set value		40

National Safety Week, July 1-July 7.

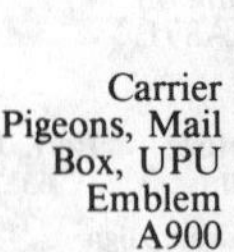

Carrier Pigeons, Mail Box, UPU Emblem
A900

Design: 100y, UPU emblem, Postal Service flag of Meiji era, world map.

1977, June 20 Photo. *Perf. 13*

1308 A900 50y multi	60	15
1309 A900 100y multi	1.25	20
a. Souv. sheet of 2, #1308-1309	2.00	1.00

Cent. of Japan's admission to the UPU.

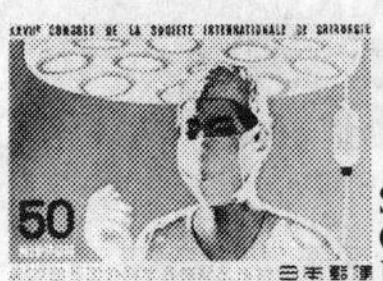

Surgeon in Operating Room — A901

1977, Sept. 3 Photo. *Perf. 13*

1310 A901 50y multi 65 15

27th Congress of the International Surgeon's Society on the 75th anniversary of its founding, Kyoto, Sept. 3-8.

Child Using Telephone, Map of New Cable Route — A902

1977, Aug. 26

1311 A902 50y multi 65 15

Inauguration of underwater telephone cable linking Okinawa, Luzon and Hong Kong.

Early Speaker, Waves and Telegraph Key — A903

1977, Sept. 24 Photo. *Perf. 13*

1312 A903 50y multi 65 15

50th anniversary of amateur radio in Japan.

Bicyclist, Mt. Iwaki and Iwaki River — A904

Flowers and Ducks, Attributed to Hasegawa Tohaku — A905

1977, Oct. 1

1313 A904 20y multi 30 15

32nd National Athletic Meet, Aomori Prefecture, Oct. 2-7.

1977, Oct. 6

1314 A905 100y multi 1.40 20

Intl. Letter Writing Week, Oct. 6-12.

Dinosaur, Stars, Museum
A906

1977, Nov. 2 Photo. *Perf. 13*

1315 A906 50y multi 65 15

Centenary of National Science Museum.

Decorated Horse, Fushimi Toy — A907

Tokyo Subway, 1927 — A908

1977, Dec. 1 Photo. *Perf. 13*

1316 A907 20y multi 30 15

New Year 1978. Sheets containing two of No. 1316 were awarded as prizes in the New Year lottery. Value $1.50.

1977, Dec. 6

1317 A908 50y shown	65	15
1318 A908 50y Subway, 1977	65	15
a. Pair, #1317-1318	1.50	
Set value		20

Tokyo Subway, 50th anniversary.

Primrose
A909

Pinguicula Ramosa
A910

Dicentra — A911

1978 Photo. & Engr. *Perf. 13*

1319 A909 50y multi	65	15
1320 A910 50y multi	65	15
1321 A911 50y multi	65	15
Set value		36

Nature protection.
Issue dates: No. 1319, Apr. 12. No. 1320, June 8. No. 1321, July 25.

Kanbun Bijinzu Folding Screen, Edo Period
A912 A913

1978, Apr. 20 Photo. *Perf. 13*

1322 A912 50y multi	65	15
1323 A913 50y multi	65	15
a. Pair, #1322-1323	1.50	
Set value		24

Philatelic Week, Apr. 16-22.

Rotary Emblem, Mt. Fuji
A914

Congress Emblem, by Taro Okamoto
A915

1978, May 13 Photo. *Perf. 13*

1324 A914 50y multi 65 15

69th Rotary International Convention, Tokyo, May 14-18.

1978, May 15

1325 A915 50y multi 65 15

23rd International Ophthalmological Congress, Kyoto, May 14-20.

Narita International Airport, Tokyo — A916

1978, May 20

1326 A916 50y multi 65 15

Opening of Tokyo International Airport.

Rainbow, Japanese Cedars, Cape Ashizuri
A917

Lion, by Sotatsu Tawaraya, Lions Emblem
A918

1978, May 20

1327 A917 50y multi 65 15

National forestation campaign.

1978, June 21 Photo. *Perf. 13*

1328 A918 50y multi 65 15

61st Lions International Convention, Tokyo, June 21-24.

Sumo Print Issues

Grand Champion Hidenoyama with Sword Bearer and Herald, by Kunisada I (Toyokuni III)
A919 A920

Ekoin Drum Tower, Ryogoku, by Hiroshige — A921

Photogravure and Engraved

1978, July 1 *Perf. 13*

1329 A919 50y multi 70 15
1330 A920 50y multi 70 15
a. Pair, #1329-1330 1.40 30

Photo.

1331 A921 50y multi 70 15
Set value 36

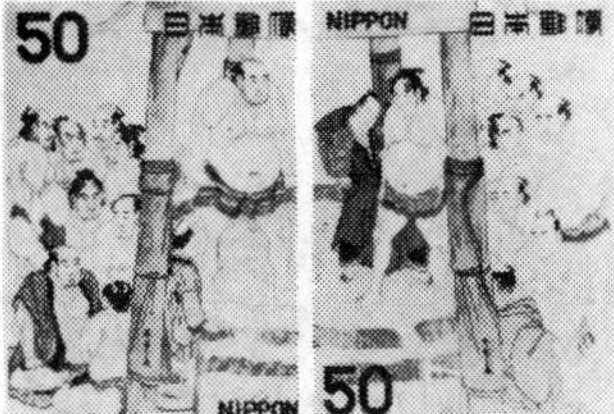

Champions Tanikaze and Onogawa in Ring-entry Ceremony, 1782, by Shunsho
A922 A923

Jimmaku, Raiden and Referee Shonosuke, 1791 Bout, by Shun'ei — A924

Photogravure and Engraved

1978, Sept. 9 *Perf. 13*

1332 A922 50y multi 70 15
1333 A923 50y multi 70 15
a. Pair, #1332-1333 1.40 30
1334 A924 50y multi 70 15
Set value 36

Referee Shonosuke and Champion Onomatsu, by Kunisada I
A925 A926

Children's Sumo Play, by Utamaro — A927

1978, Nov. 11 *Perf. 13*

1335 A925 50y multi 70 15
1336 A926 50y multi 70 15
a. Pair, #1335-1336 1.40 30
1337 A927 50y multi 70 15
Set value 36

Wrestlers on Ryogoku Bridge, by Kunisada I
A928 A929

Bow-receiving Ceremony at Tournament, by Kunisada II — A930

1979, Jan. 13 *Perf. 13*

1338 A928 50y multi 70 15
1339 A929 50y multi 70 15
a. Pair, #1338-1339 1.40 30
1340 A930 50y multi 70 15
Set value 36

Takekuma and Iwamigata (Hidenoyama) Wrestling, by Kuniyoshi
A931 A932

Daidozan (Great Child Mountain) in Ring-entry Ceremony, by Sharaku — A933

1979, Mar. 10 *Perf. 13*

1341 A931 50y multi 70 15
1342 A932 50y multi 70 15
a. Pair, #1341-1342 1.40 30
1343 A933 50y multi 70 15
Set value 36

Radio Gymnastics Emblem — A934

1978, Aug. 1 **Photo.** *Perf. 13*

1344 A934 50y multi 65 15

Radio gymnastics program exercises, 50th anniversary.

Chamber of Commerce and Industry A935

1978, Aug. 28 **Photo.** *Perf. 13*

1345 A935 50y multi 65 15

Tokyo Chamber of Commerce, centenary.

Symbolic Sculptures, Tokyo Stock Exchange A936

Flowering Plum with Pheasant, from Screen, Tenkyuin Temple A937

1978, Sept. 14 **Engr.** *Perf. 13*

1346 A936 50y lil, grn & brn 65 15

Centenary of the Tokyo and Osaka Stock Exchanges.

1978, Oct. 6 **Photo.** *Perf. 13*

1347 A937 100y multi 1.40 25

Intl. Letter Writing Week, Oct. 6-12.

Softball and Mt. Yarigatake A938

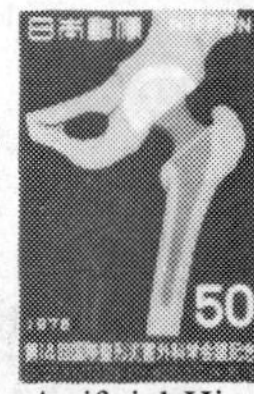

Artificial Hip, Orthopedists' Emblem A939

1978, Oct. 14

1348 A938 20y multi 30 15

33rd National Athletic Meet, Nagano Prefecture, Oct. 15-20.

1978, Oct. 16

1349 A939 50y multi 65 15

14th World Congress of International Society of Orthopedic Surgeons (50th anniversary), Kyoto, Oct. 15-20.

Telescope and Stars — A940

Sheep Bell, Nakayama Toy — A941

1978, Dec. 1 **Photo.**

1350 A940 50y multi 65 15

Tokyo Astronomical Observatory, cent.

1978, Dec. 4

1351 A941 20y multi 30 15

New Year 1979. Sheets containing two of No. 1351 were awarded as prizes in the New Year Lottery. Value $1.50.

Family, Human Rights Emblem — A942

Hands Shielding Children — A943

1978, Dec. 4

1352 A942 50y multi 65 15

Human Rights Week, Dec. 4-10.

1979, Feb. 16 **Photo.** *Perf. 13*

1353 A943 50y multi 65 15

Education of the handicapped, centenary.

Telephone Dials — A944

Sketch of Man, by Leonardo da Vinci — A945

1979, Mar. 14 **Photo.** *Perf. 13*

1354 A944 50y multi 65 15

Completion of nation-wide telephone automatization.

Photogravure and Engraved

1979, Apr. 7 *Perf. 13*

1355 A945 50y multi 65 15

Centenary of, promulgation of State Medical Act, initiating modern medicine.

Standing Beauties, Middle Edo Period
A946 A947

1979, Apr. 20 **Photo.**

1356 A946 50y multi 65 15
1357 A947 50y multi 65 15
a. Pair, #1356-1357 1.50
Set value 24

Philatelic Week, Apr. 16-22.

Mt. Horaiji and Maple — A948

1979, May 26 **Photo.** *Perf. 13*

1358 A948 50y multi 65 15

National forestation campaign.

A particular stamp may be scarce, but if few collectors want it, its market value may remain relatively low.

Modern Japanese Art Issue

Merciful Mother Goddess, by Kano Hogai — A949

Sea God's Princess, by Aoki Shigeru — A950

1979, May 30 **Photo.** ***Perf. 13***

1359 A949 50y multi 70 15
1360 A950 50y multi 70 15
Set value 24

Fire Dance, by Gyoshu Hayami — A951

Leaning Figure, by Tetsugoro Yorozu — A952

1979, June 25 **Photo.** ***Perf. 13***

1361 A951 50y red & multi 65 15

Photogravure and Engraved

1362 A952 50y red & multi 65 15
Set value 24

The Black Cat, by Shunso Hishida A953

Kinyo, by Sotaro Yasui A954

1979, Sept. 21 **Photo.** ***Perf. 13***

1363 A953 50y multi 65 15
1364 A954 50y multi 65 15
Set value 24

Nude, by Kagaku Murakami A955

Harvest, by Asai Chu — A956

Photogravure and Engraved

1979, Nov. 22 ***Perf. 13***

1365 A955 50y multi 65 15
1366 A956 50y multi 65 15
Set value 24

Salmon — A956a

Hall of the Supreme Buddha — A956b

Photogravure and Engraved

1980, Feb. 22 ***Perf. 13½***

1367 A956a 50y multi 65 15

Photo.

1368 A956b 50y multi 65 15
Set value 24

Quarantine Officers, Ships, Plane, Microscope A957

1979, July 14 **Photo.**

1369 A957 50y multi 65 15

Centenary of Japanese Quarantine system.

Girl Mailing Letter A958

Hakata Doll with Letter-paper Roll A959

1979, July 23

1370 A958 20y multi 32 15
1371 A959 50y multi 65 15
Set value 17

Letter Writing Day.

Pitcher, Baseball with Black Lion Emblem — A960

1979, July 27

1372 A960 50y multi 65 15

50th National Inter-city Amateur Baseball Tournament, Tokyo, August.

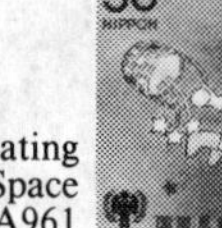

Girl Floating in Space A961

Design: No. 1374, Boy floating in space.

1979, Aug. 1

1373 A961 50y mag & multi 65 15
1374 A961 50y bl & multi 65 15
a. Souv. sheet of 2, #1373-1374 1.50
Set value 24

International Year of the Child.

Japanese Song Issue

Moon over Castle, by Rentaro Taki A962

Evening Glow, by Shin Kusakawa A963

Maple Leaves, by Teiichi Okano A964

The Birthplace, by Teiichi Okano — A965

Winter Landscape A966

Mt. Fuji — A967

Spring Brook — A968

Cherry Blossoms A969

1979, Aug. 24 **Photo. & Engr.**

1375 A962 50y multi 65 15
1376 A963 50y multi 65 15
Set value 24

1979, Nov. 26

1377 A964 50y multi 65 15
1378 A965 50y multi 65 15
Set value 24

1980, Jan. 28 ***Perf. 13***

1379 A966 50y multi 65 15
1380 A967 50y multi 65 15
Set value 24

1980, Mar. 21 ***Perf. 13***

1381 A968 50y multi 65 15
1382 A969 50y multi 65 15
Set value 24

Great Owl, by Okyo Maruyama — A970

1979, Oct. 8 **Photo.** ***Perf. 13***

1383 A970 100y multi 1.25 24

Intl. Letter Writing Week, Oct. 8-14.

Runner — A971

"ITU," Globe — A972

1979, Oct. 13

1384 A971 20y multi 32 15

34th National Athletic Meet, Miyazaki, Oct. 4-19.

1979, Oct. 13 **Litho.** ***Perf. 13½***

1385 A972 50y multi 65 15

Admission to ITU, cent.

Woman and Fetus — A973

1979, Nov. 12 **Photo.**

1386 A973 50y multi 65 15

9th World Congress of Gynecology and Obstetrics, Tokyo, Oct. 25-31.

Happy Monkeys, Osaka Toy — A974

Government Auditing Centenary — A975

1979, Dec. 1 **Photo.** ***Perf. 13x13½***

1387 A974 20y multi 30 15

New Year 1980.
Sheets of two No. 1387 were New Year Lottery prizes. Value $1.40.

1980, Mar. 5 **Photo.** ***Perf. 13½***

1388 A975 50y multi 65 15

Scenes of Outdoor Play in Spring, by Sukenobu Nishikawa
A976 A977

1980, Apr. 21 **Photo.** ***Perf. 13½***

1389 A976 50y multi	65	15
1390 A977 50y multi	65	15
a. Pair, #1389-1390	1.30	50
Set value		24

Philatelic Week, Apr. 21-27. Sheets of 10.

Japanese Song Issue

The Sea — A978

The Night of the Hazy Moon — A979

Memories of Summer — A981

The Sun Flag — A980

1980 **Photo. & Engr.** ***Perf. 13***

1391 A978 50y multi	70	15
1392 A979 50y multi	70	15
1393 A980 50y multi	70	15
1394 A981 50y multi	70	15
Set value		48

Issue dates: Nos. 1391-1392, Apr. 28; Nos. 1393-1394, June 16.

Song by the Sea — A982

The Red Dragonfly — A983

1980, Sept. 18 ***Perf. 13***

1395 A982 50y multi	65	15
1396 A983 50y multi	65	15
Set value		24

Lullaby
A984

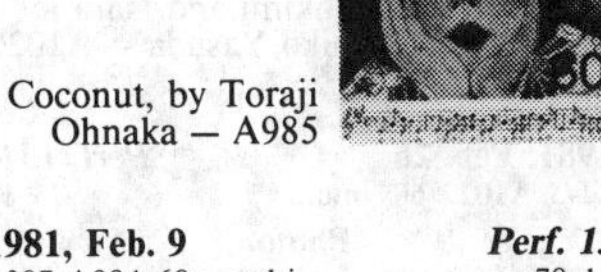

Coconut, by Toraji Ohnaka — A985

1981, Feb. 9 ***Perf. 13***

1397 A984 60y multi	70	15
1398 A985 60y multi	70	15
Set value		20

Spring Has Come, by Tatsuyuki Takano — A986

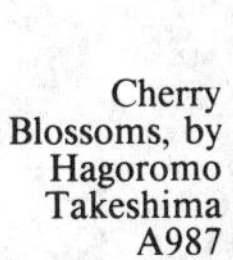

Cherry Blossoms, by Hagoromo Takeshima
A987

1981, Mar. 10 ***Perf. 13***

1399 A986 60y multi	70	15
1400 A987 60y multi	70	15
Set value		20

Modern Japanese Art Issue

Dancers, by Seiki Kuroda — A988

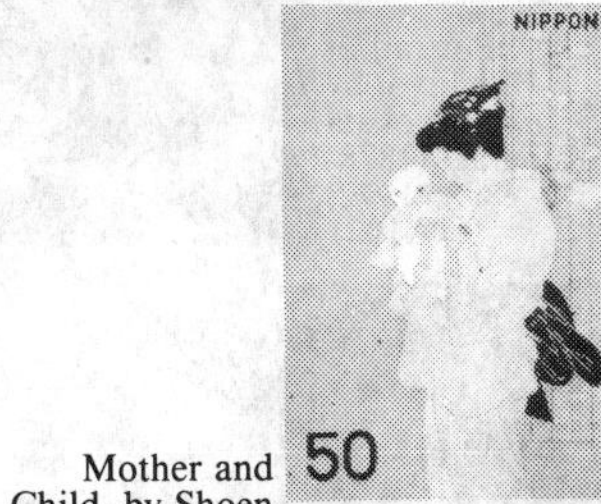

Mother and Child, by Shoen Uemura — A989

1980, May 12 **Photo.** ***Perf. 13½***

1401 A988 50y multi	70	15
1402 A989 50y multi	70	15
Set value		24

The Black Fan, by Takeji Fujishima
A990

Dear Me . . . It's a Shower, by Seiho Takeuchi
A991

1980, July 7 **Photo.** ***Perf. 13½***

1403 A990 50y multi	70	15
1404 A991 50y multi	70	15
Set value		24

Woman, by Morie Ogiwara — A992

Kurofuneya, by Yumeji Takehisa — A993

1980, Oct. 27 **Photo.** ***Perf. 13½***

1405 A992 50y multi	70	15
1406 A993 50y multi	70	15
Set value		24

Nippon Maru, Institute Emblem — A994

1980, May 17

1407 A994 50y multi	65	15

Institute for Nautical Training, training ships Nippon Maru and Kaio Maru, 50th anniversary.

Mt. Gozaisho-dake, Cedars, Flowers — A995

1980, May 24 ***Perf. 13x13½***

1408 A995 50y multi	65	15

National forestation campaign.

Yayosu Fire Brigade Review, by Hiroshige III
A996

Teddy Bear Holding Letter
A997

1980, May 31

1409 A996 50y multi	65	15

Fire fighting centenary.

Perf. 13x13½, 13½x13

1980, July 23

Letter Writing Day: 50y, Folded and tied letter of good wishes (horiz).

1410 A997 20y multi	30	15
1411 A997 50y multi	60	15
Set value		18

Lühdorfla Japonica
A998

1980, Aug. 2 ***Perf. 13½***

1412 A998 50y multi	65	15

16th Intl. Congress of Entomology, Kyoto, Aug. 3-9.

Three-dimensional World Map — A999

1980, Aug. 25 **Photo.**

1413 A999 50y multi	65	15

24th International Geographic Congress and 10th International Cartographic Conference, Tokyo, August.

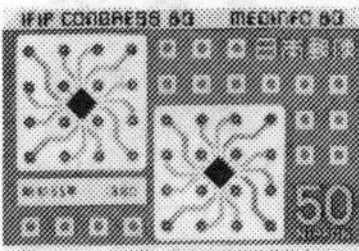

Integrated Circuit
A1000

Camellia
A1001

1980, Sept. 29

1414 A1000 50y multi	65	15

International Federation for Information Processing Congress '80, Tokyo, Oct. 6-9 and World Conference on Medical Informatics '80, Tokyo, Sept. 29-Oct. 4.

1980, Oct. 1

1415 A1001 30y shown	42	15
1416 A1001 40y Rape flower, cabbage butterflies	50	15
1417 A1001 50y Cherry blossoms	70	15
Set value		24

See No. 1437.

Cranes, by Motooki Watanabe A1002

Archery, Mt. Nantai A1003

1980, Oct. 6 ***Perf. 13***

1418 A1002 100y multi 1.25 24

24th Intl. Letter Writing Week, Oct. 6-12.

1980, Oct. 11

1419 A1003 20y multi 32 15

35th Natonal Athletic Meet, Tochigi, Oct.

Globe, Jaycee Emblem A1004

Diet Building and Doves A1005

1980, Nov. 8 ***Perf. 13***

1420 A1004 50y multi 65 24

35th Jaycee (International Junior Chamber of Commerce) World Congress, Osaka, Nov. 9-15.

1980, Nov. 29 ***Perf. 13½***

1421 A1005 50y multi 65 15

90th anniversary of Japanese Diet.

Type of 1980 and:

Amur Adonis — A1006

White Trumpet Lily — A1007

Hanging Bell, Byodoin Temple — A1008

Bronze Buddhist Ornament, 7th Century — A1009

Writing Box Cover — A1010

Mirror with Figures — A1011

Heart-shaped Figurine — A1012

Silver Crane — A1013

Maitreya, Horyuji Temple — A1014

Ichiji Kinrin, Chusonji Temple — A1015

Komokuten, Todaiji Temple — A1016

Lady Maya — A1017

Enamel Jar, by Ninsei Nonomura A1018

Miroku Bosatsu, Koryuji Temple A1019

1980-82 **Photo.** ***Perf. 13x13½***

1422 A1006 10y multi 25 15
1423 A1007 20y multi 30 15
1424 A1008 60y multi 90 15
a. Bklt. pane (#1424, 4 #1424 with gutter btwn.) ('81) 4.00
1425 A1009 70y multi 1.10 20
1426 A1010 70y multi 1.10 15
1427 A1011 80y multi 1.25 15
1428 A1012 90y multi 1.40 16
1429 A1013 100y multi 1.50 18
1430 A1014 170y multi 2.50 25
1431 A1015 260y multi 3.75 40
1432 A1016 310y multi 4.50 65
1433 A1017 410y multi 5.75 1.15
1434 A1018 410y multi 5.75 1.15
1435 A1019 600y multi 8.50 1.40
Nos. 1422-1435 (14) 38.55 6.29

Coil Stamps

Perf. 13 Horiz.

1436 A1006 10y multi ('82) 25 15
1437 A1001 40y as #1416 60 15
1438 A1008 60y multi ('82) 90 15
1439 A1013 100y multi ('82) 1.50 18
Set value 42

See Nos. 1627, 1629.

Clay Chicken, Folk Toy — A1026

1980, Dec. 1 ***Perf. 13 Horiz.***

1442 A1026 20y multi 30 15

New Year 1981.
Sheets of two were New Year Lottery Prizes. Value $1.25.

Modern Japanese Art Issue

Snow-Covered Power Station, by Shikanosuke Oka — A1027

NuKada-no-Ohkimi and Nara in Spring, by Yukihiko Yasuda — A1028

1981, Feb. 26 ***Perf. 13½***

1443 A1027 60y multi 75 15

Photo.

1444 A1028 60y multi 75 15
Set value 20

Artist's Family, by Narashige Koide — A1029

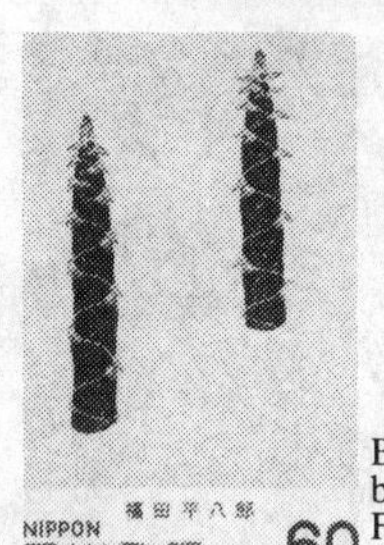

Bamboo Shoots, by Heihachiro Fukuda A1030

Photo. & Engr., Photo.

1981, June 18 ***Perf. 13½***

1445 A1029 60y multi 75 15
1446 A1030 60y multi 75 15
Set value 20

Portrait of Ichiyo, by Kiyokata Kaburagi (1878-1972) A1031

Portrait of Reiko, by Ryusei Kishida (1891-1929) A1032

Photo., Photo. and Engr.

1981, Nov. 27 **Engr.** ***Perf. 13½***

1447 A1031 60y multi 75 15
1448 A1032 60y multi 75 15
Set value 20

Yoritomo in a Cave, by Seison Maeda — A1033

Advertisement of a Terrace, by Yuzo Saeki — A1034

1982, Feb. 25 **Photo.** ***Perf. 13½***

1449 A1033 60y multi 75 15
1450 A1034 60y multi 75 15
Set value 20

Emblem, Port Island A1035

1981, Mar. 20 ***Perf. 13***

1451 A1035 60y multi 70 15

Portopia '81, Kobe Port Island Exhibition, Mar. 20-Sept. 15.

Agriculture, Forestry and Fishery Promotion Centenary A1036

1981, Apr. 7

1452 A1036 60y multi 70 15

Moonflower, by Harunobu Suzuki A1037 A1038

1981, Apr. 20 **Photo.** ***Perf. 13½***

1453 A1037 60y multi 75 15
1454 A1038 60y multi 75 15
a. Pair, #1453-1454 1.50 30
Set value 20

Philatelic Week, Apr. 21-27.

Cherry Blossoms A1039

Cargo Ship and Crane A1040

1981, May 23 Photo. *Perf. 13x13½*
1455 A1039 60y multi 70 15

1981, May 25 *Perf. 13*
1456 A1040 60y multi 70 15

International Port and Harbor Association, 12th Convention, Nagoya, May 23-30.

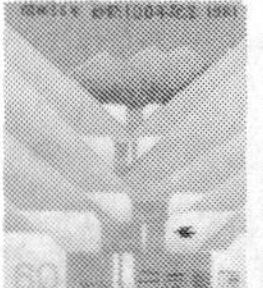
Land Erosion Control Cent. A1041

Stylized Man and Spinal Cord Dose Response Curve A1042

1981, June 27 *Perf. 13½*
1457 A1041 60y multi 70 15

1981, July 18 Photo. *Perf. 13*
1458 A1042 60y multi 70 15

8th Intl. Pharmacology Congress, Tokyo, July 19-24.

Girl Writing Letter A1043

Japanese Crested Ibis A1044

1981, July 23
1459 A1043 40y shown 48 15
1460 A1043 60y Boy, stamp 70 15
Set value 16

Letter Writing Day (23rd of each month).

1981, July 27 Litho.
1461 A1044 60y multi 70 15

Energy Conservation A1045

1981, Aug. 1 Photo.
1462 A1045 40y Plug, faucet 48 15
1463 A1045 60y shown 70 15
Set value 16

Western Architecture Issue

Oura Cathedral — A1046

Hyokei Hall, Tokyo A1047

Photogravure and Engraved

1981, Aug. 22
1464 A1046 60y multi 70 15
1465 A1047 60y multi 70 15
Set value 20

Old Kaichi School, Nagano A1048

Doshisha University Chapel, Kyoto A1049

1981, Nov. 9 *Perf. 13*
1466 A1048 60y multi 70 15
1467 A1049 60y multi 70 15
Set value 20

St. John's Church, Meiji-mura A1050

Military Exercise Hall (Former Sapporo Agricultural School), Sapporo A1051

1982, Jan. 29 *Perf. 13*
1468 A1050 60y multi 70 15
1469 A1051 60y multi 70 15
Set value 20

Former Kyoto Branch of Bank of Japan A1052

Main Building, Former Saiseikan Hospital — A1053

1982, Mar. 10 *Perf. 13*
1470 A1052 60y multi 70 15
1471 A1053 60y multi 70 15
Set value 20

Oyama Shrine Gate, Kanazawa A1054

Former Iwasaki Family Residence, Tokyo A1055

1982, June 12 *Perf. 13*
1472 A1054 60y multi 70 15
1473 A1055 60y multi 70 15
Set value 20

Hokkaido Prefectural Govt. Building, Sapporo A1056

Former Residence of Tsugumichi Saigo A1057

1982, Sept. 10 *Perf. 13*
1474 A1056 60y multi 70 15
1475 A1057 60y multi 70 15
Set value 20

Old Mutsuzawa School — A1058

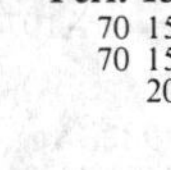

Sakuranomiya Public Hall — A1059

1983, Feb. 15
1476 A1058 60y multi 70 15
1477 A1059 60y multi 70 15
Set value 20

Globe on Brain A1060

1981, Sept. 12 Photo.
1478 A1060 60y multi 70 15

Intl. medical conferences, Kyoto: 12th Neurology, Sept. 20-25; 10th Brainwaves and Clinical Neurophysiology, Sept. 13-17; 1981 Intl. Epilepsy Conference, Sept. 17-21.

Congress Emblem — A1061

1981, Sept. 16
1479 A1061 60y multi 70 15

24th World PTTI (Post, Telegraph and Telephone Intl. Labor Federation) Congress, Tokyo, Sept. 16-22.

Plum Trees and Fowl, by Sanraku Kano A1062

No. 1, Philatokyo '81 Emblem A1063

1981, Oct. 6 Photo.
1480 A1062 130y multi 1.75 18

25th Intl. Letter Writing Week, Oct. 6-12.

1981, Oct. 9 Photo. & Engr.
1481 A1063 60y shown 85 15
1482 A1063 60y No. 2 85 15
1483 A1063 60y No. 3 85 15
1484 A1063 60y No. 4 85 15
a. Strip or block of 4, #1481-1484 3.50 1.00

Philatokyo '81 Intl. Stamp Exhibition, Tokyo, Oct. 9-18.

36th Natl. Athletic Meet, Oct. 13-18 — A1064

1981, Oct. 13 Photo.
1485 A1064 40y multi 50 15

New Year of 1982 (Year of the Dog) — A1065

1981, Dec. 1 Photo. *Perf. 13x13½*
1486 A1065 40y multicolored 48 15

Sheets of 2 were lottery prizes. Value $1.50.

Ueno Zoo Centenary — A1066

Designs: a, Gorilla, flamingo. b, Penguins, lion. c, Panda, elephants. d, Zebras, giraffe.

1982, Mar. 20 **Photo.**
1487 Strip of 4 3.25 1.40
a.-d. A1066 60y any single 70 32

Views of the Snow on Matsuchiyama, by Kiyonago Torii
A1067 A1068

1982, Apr. 20 **Photo.** ***Perf. 13½***
1488 A1067 60y multi 75 35
1489 A1068 60y multi 75 35
a. Pair, #1488-1489 1.50 70

Philatelic Week.

Shisa (Lion-shaped Guard Dog)
A1069

Natl. Forestation Campaign
A1070

1982, May 15 **Photo.**
1490 A1069 60y multi 70 32

10th anniv. of Reversion Agreement returning Ryukyu Islands.

1982, May 22 ***Perf. 13x13½***
1491 A1070 60y multi 70 32

16th Intl. Dermatology Conference Tokyo, May 23-28 — A1071

1982, May 24 ***Perf. 13***
1492 A1071 60y Noh mask 70 32

Tohoku-Shinkansen Railroad Line Opening — A1072

1982, June 23
1493 A1072 60y Diesel locomotive 70 32
1494 A1072 60y Steam model 1290 70 32
a. Pair, #1493-1494 1.50

Letter Writing Day — A1073

Perf. 13x13½, 13½x13
1982, July 23
1495 A1073 40y Sea gull, letter 50 15
1496 A1073 60y Fairy, letter, horiz. 75 35

Modern Japanese Art Issue

Kimono Patterned with Irises, by Saburosuke Okada (1869-1939)
A1074

Bodhisattva Kuan-yin on Potalaka Island, by Tessai Tomioka (1837-1924)
A1075

1982, Aug. 5 **Photo.** ***Perf. 13½***
1497 A1074 60y multi 70 32
1498 A1075 60y multi 70 32

The Sarasvati, by Shiko Munakata (1903-1975)
A1076

Saltim- banque, by Seiji Togo (1897-1978)
A1077

1982, Nov. 24
1499 A1076 60y multi 70 32
1500 A1077 60y multi 70 32

Snowstorm, by Shinsui Ito — A1078

Spiraeas and Callas with Persian Pot, by Zenzaburo Kojima — A1079

1983, Jan. 24 **Photo.**
1501 A1078 60y multi 70 32
1502 A1079 60y multi 70 32

Muga, by Taikan Yokoyama (1868-1958)
A1080

Roen, by Koun Takamura (1852-1934)
A1081

Photo., Photo. and Engr.
1983, Mar. 10 ***Perf. 13½***
1503 A1080 60y multi 70 32
1504 A1081 60y multi 70 32

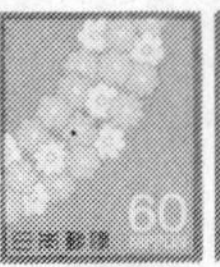

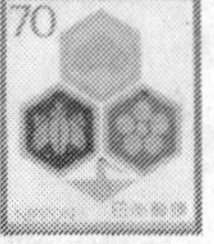

A1082 A1083 A1084

1982, Aug. 23 ***Perf. 13x13½***
1505 A1082 60y Wreath 75 35
1506 A1083 60y Crane 75 35
1507 A1084 70y Tortoise 85 38

For use on greeting (Nos. 1506-1507) and condolence (No. 1505) cards.

See Nos. 1555-1556, 1836-1839 and footnote after No. 1765.

400th Anniv. of Boys' Delegation to Europe, Tensho Era — A1085

1982, Sept. 20 **Photo.** ***Perf. 13***
1508 A1085 60y 16th cent. ship, map 70 32

10th Anniv. of Japanese-Chinese Relations Normalization — A1086

Design: Hall of Prayer for Good Harvests, Temple of Heaven, Peking, by Ryuzaburo Umehara.

1982, Sept. 29
1509 A1086 60y multi 70 32

Table Tennis — A1087

"Amusement," Doll by Goyo Hirata — A1088

1982, Oct. 2
1510 A1087 40y multi 50 25

37th Natl. Athletic Meet, Matsue, Oct. 3-8.

1982, Oct. 6
1511 A1088 130y multi 1.65 60

Intl. Letter Writing Week, Oct. 6-12.

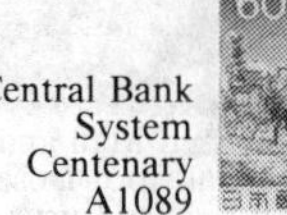

Central Bank System Centenary
A1089

Design: The Bank of Japan near Eitaibashi in Snow, by Yasuji Inoue.

Photogravure and Engraved
1982, Oct. 12 ***Perf. 13½***
1512 A1089 60y multi 70 32

A1090

A1091

Opening of Joetsu Shinkansen Railroad Line

1982, Nov. 15
1513 A1090 60y Locomotive, 1982 70 32
1514 A1091 60y Locomotive, 1931 70 32
a. Pair, #1513-1514 1.50

New Year 1983
A1092

Natl. Museum of History and Folklore Opening
A1093

1982, Dec. 1 ***Perf. 13x13½***
1515 A1092 40y Kintaro on Wild Boar 50 15

Sheets of 2 were lottery prizes. Value, $1.50.

1983, Mar. 16 **Photo.** ***Perf. 13½x13***
1516 A1093 60y multi 70 32

Women Working in the Kitchen, by Utamaro Kitagawa (1753-1806)
A1094 A1095

1983, Apr. 20 **Photo.** ***Perf. 13***

1517 A1094 60y multi 70 32
1518 A1095 60y multi 70 32
a. Pair, #1517-1518 1.40 70

Philatelic Week.

Natl. Forestation Campaign — A1096
50th Nippon Derby — A1097

1983, May 21 ***Perf. 13***

1519 A1096 60y Hakusan Mountains, black lily, forest 70 32

1983, May 28

1520 A1097 60y Colt, racing horse 70 32

Islands Cleanup Campaign — A1098

1983, June 13 **Photo.** ***Perf. 13½***

1521 A1098 60y multi 70 32

Western Architecture Series

Hohei Hall Sapporo A1099

Old Glover House, Nagasaki A1100

Gojyuku Bank, Hirosaki A1101

Gakushuin Elementary School, Tokyo A1102

Bank of Japan, Tokyo A1103

Old Hunter House, Kobe A1104

Photogravure and Engraved

1983, June 23 ***Perf. 13***

1522 A1099 60y multi 75 35
1523 A1100 60y multi 75 35

1983, Aug. 15 ***Perf. 13***

1524 A1101 60y multi 75 35
1525 A1102 60y multi 75 35

1984, Feb. 16 ***Perf. 13***

1526 A1103 60y multi 75 35
1527 A1104 60y multi 75 35

Official Gazette Centenary A1107
Letter Writing Day A1108

Design: First issue, Drawing of the Government Bulletin Board at Nihonbashi, by Hiroshige Ando III.

1983, July 2 **Photo.** ***Perf. 13***

1530 A1107 60y multi 70 32

Perf. 13x13½, 13½x13

1983, July 23

1531 A1108 40y Boy writing letter 50 22
1532 A1108 60y Fairy bringing letter, horiz. 75 35

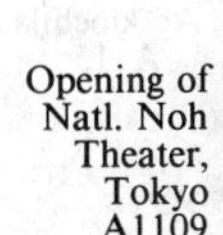

Opening of Natl. Noh Theater, Tokyo A1109

1983, Sept. 14 **Photo.** ***Perf. 13***

1533 A1109 60y Masked actor, theater 70 32

Endangered Birds Issue

Rallus Okinawae — A1110

Ketupa Blakistoni A1111

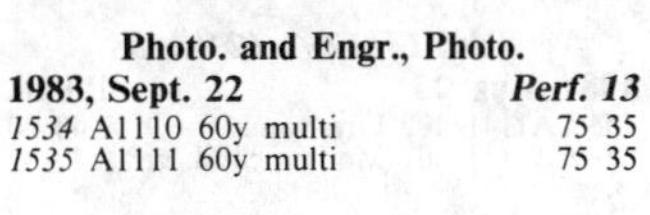

Photo. and Engr., Photo.

1983, Sept. 22 ***Perf. 13***

1534 A1110 60y multi 75 35
1535 A1111 60y multi 75 35

Photo., Photo. & Engr.

1983, Nov. 25 ***Perf. 13***

1536 A1110 60y Sapheopipo noguchii 75 35
1537 A1111 60y Branta canadensis leucopareia 75 35

Photo., Photo. and Engr.

1984, Jan. 26 ***Perf. 13***

1538 A1111 60y Megalurus pryeri pryeri 75 35
1539 A1110 60y Spilornis cheela perplexus 75 35

1984, Mar. 15 **Photo.** ***Perf. 13***

1540 A1110 60y Columba janthina nitens 75 35
1541 A1111 60y Tringa guttifer 75 35

1984, June 22 **Photo.** ***Perf. 13***

1542 A1110 60y Falco peregrinus frutti 75 35

Photo. and Engr.

1543 A1111 60y Dendrocopus leucutus austoni 75 35

Souvenir Sheet

1984, Dec. 10 **Photo. & Engr.**

1544 Sheet of 3 2.75 1.10
a. A1111 60y Prus grn, engr., #1535 80 35
b. A1110 60y vio brn, engr., #1539 80 35
c. A1110 60y ol blk, engr., #1542 80 35

Intl. Letter Writing Week — A1124
38th Natl. Athletic Meet — A1125

Design: Chikyu Doll by Juzo Kagoshima (1898-1982).

1983, Oct. 6 **Photo.** ***Perf. 13***

1548 A1124 130y multi 1.75 70

1983, Oct. 15 ***Perf. 13***

1549 A1125 40y Naginata event 50 26

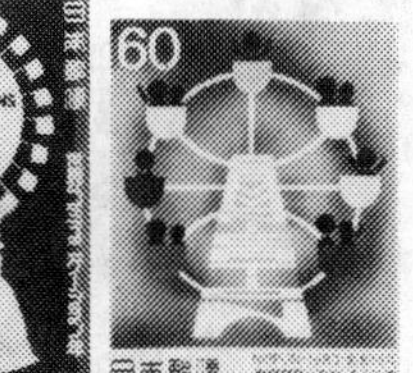

World Communications Year
A1126 A1127

1983, Oct. 17 **Photo.** ***Perf. 13***

1550 A1126 60y multi 70 32
1551 A1127 60y multi 70 32

Showa Memorial National Park Opening A1128

1983, Oct. 26 **Photo.** ***Perf. 13***

1552 A1128 60y multi 70 32

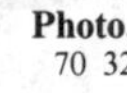

71st World Dentistry Congress — A1129

1983, Nov. 14 **Photo.**

1553 A1129 60y multi 70 32

Shirase, Antarctic Observation Ship, Maiden Voyage — A1130

1983, Nov. 14 **Photo.** ***Perf. 13***

1554 A1130 60y multi 70 32

Type of 1982

1983, Nov. 22 **Photo.** ***Perf. 12½***

1555 A1082 40y Wreath 60 26
1556 A1083 40y Crane 60 26

For use on condolence and greeting cards.

New Year 1984 — A1131

1983, Dec. 1 **Photo.** ***Perf. 13x13½***

1557 A1131 40y Rat riding hammer 50 26

Sheets of 2 were lottery prizes. Value, $1.45.

Universal Declaration of Human Rights, 35th Anniv. — A1132

1983, Dec. 5 **Photo.** ***Perf. 13½***

1558 A1132 60y Emblem 70 32

20th Grand Confectionery Fair, Tokyo, Feb. 24-Mar. 12 — A1133

1984, Feb. 24 **Photo.**

1559 A1133 60y Confection, tea whisk 70 32

Natl. Bunraku Theater Opening, Osaka A1134

1984, Apr. 6 **Photo.** ***Perf. 13***

1560 A1134 60y Bunraku puppet 70 32

A1135

A1136

Philatelic Week (Sharaku Prints): No. 1561, Hanshiro Iwai IV Playing Shigenoi. No. 1562, Oniji Otani Playing Edobe.

Photogravure and Engraved

1984, Apr. 20 ***Perf. 13½***

1561 A1135 60y multi 70 32
1562 A1136 60y multi 70 32
a. Pair, #1561-1562 1.40 70

Natl. Forestation Campaign A1137

Weather Forecasting Centenary A1138

1984, May 19 **Photo.**

1563 A1137 60y Cedar Forest, Sakurajima 70 32

1984, June 1 ***Perf. 13x13½***

1564 A1138 60y Himawari satellite, map 70 32

UNESCO Emblem, Doves A1139

Letter Writing Day A1140

1984, July 16 **Photo.**

1565 A1139 60y multi 70 32

UNESCO Clubs and Associations World Congress, July 16-24.

Perf. 13x13½, 13½x13

1984, July 23

1566 A1140 40y Birds in tree 48 20
1567 A1140 40y Bird holding letter, horiz. 70 32

Disaster Relief A1141

Perf. 13x12½, 12½x13

1984, Aug. 23 **Photo.**

1568 A1141 40y Fire, wind 48 20
1569 A1141 60y Mother, child, vert. 70 32

Alpine Plant Series

Leontopodium Fauriei — A1142

Lagotis Glauca A1143

Photogravure and Engraved

Perf. 12½x13, 13x12½

1984, Aug. 27

1570 A1142 60y multi 75 35
1571 A1143 60y multi 75 35

Trollius Riederianus A1144

Primula Cuneifolia A1145

1984, Sept. 21 ***Perf. 13***

1572 A1144 60y multi 75 35
1573 A1145 60y multi 75 35

Rhododendron Aureum — A1146

Oxytropis Nigrescens Var. Japonica A1147

1985, Jan. 25 ***Perf. 13***

1574 A1146 60y multi 75 35
1575 A1147 60y multi 75 35

Draba Japonica — A1148

Dryas Octopetala A1149

1985, Feb. 28

1576 A1148 60y multi 75 35
1577 A1149 60y multi 75 35

Callianthemum Insigne Var. Miyabeanum A1150

Gentiana Nipponica A1151

1985, July 31 ***Perf. 13***

1578 A1150 60y multi 75 35
1579 A1151 60y multi 75 35

Campanula Chamissonis A1152

Viola Crassa A1153

1985, Sept. 27

1580 A1152 60y multi 75 35
1581 A1153 60y multi 75 35

Deapensia Lapponica A1154

Pedicularis Apodochila A1155

1986, Feb. 13 ***Perf. 13***

1582 A1154 60y multi 75 35
1583 A1155 60y multi 75 35

Basho's Street, Sendai — A1156

1984, Sept. 1 **Photo.** ***Perf. 13***

1584 A1156 60y multi 70 32

Intl. Microbiological Association's 6th Intl. Congress of Virology, Sendai, Sept. 1-7.

Demand, as well as supply, determines a stamp's market value. One is as important as the other.

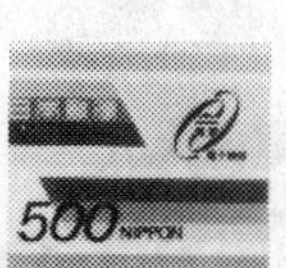
Electronic Mail — A1157

28th Intl. Letter Writing Week, Oct. 6-12 — A1158

1984, Oct. 1 **Photo.**

1585 A1157 500y multi 10.00 4.00

1984, Oct. 6

1586 A1158 130y Wooden doll 1.65 70

17th Intl. Internal Medicine Congress, Kyoto, Oct. 7-12 — A1159

1984, Oct. 8

1587 A1159 60y Ginkakuji Temple 70 32

39th Natl. Athletic Meet, Nara City, Oct. 12-17 — A1160

1984, Oct. 12

1588 A1160 40y Field hockey 50 25

Traditional Crafts Series

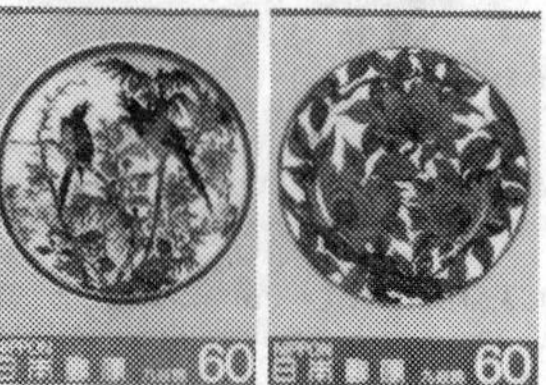
Kutaniyaki Plates
A1161 A1162

Nishijinori Weavings
A1163 A1164

1984, Nov. 2 **Photo.** ***Perf. 12½x13***

1589 A1161 60y Birds 75 35
1590 A1162 60y Flowers 75 35
a. Pair, #1589-1590 1.50 75
1591 A1163 60y Flowers 75 35
1592 A1164 60y Leaves 75 35
a. Pair, #1591-1592 1.50 75

Edokimekomi Dolls
A1165 A1166

Ryukyubingata Cloth
A1167 A1168

1985, Feb. 15 Photo. *Perf. 13*

1593 A1165 60y Adult figures 75 35
1594 A1166 60y Child and pet 75 35
a. Pair, #1593-1594 1.50 75
1595 A1167 60y Bird and branch 75 35
1596 A1168 60y Birds 75 35
a. Pair, #1595-1596 1.50 75

Ichii-ittobori Carved Birds
A1169 A1170

Imariyaki & Aritayaki Ceramic Ware
A1171 A1172

Kamakurabori Wood Carvings
A1173 A1174

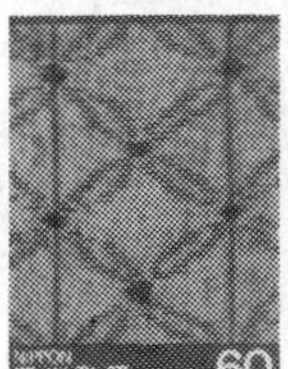

Ojiyachijimi Weavings
A1175 A1176

Hakata Ningyo Clay Figures
A1177 A1178

Nanbu Tekki Iron Ware
A1179 A1180

1985, May 23 Photo. *Perf. 13*

1597 A1169 60y Bird 75 35
1598 A1170 60y Birds 75 35
a. Pair, #1597-1598 1.50 75
1599 A1171 60y Bowl 75 35
1600 A1172 60y Plate 75 35
a. Pair, #1599-1600 1.50 75

1985, June 24 Photo. & Engr.

1601 A1173 60y Bird and flower panel 75 35
1602 A1174 60y Round flower panel 75 35
a. Pair, #1601-1602 1.50 75

Litho.

1603 A1175 60y Hemp star pattern 75 35
1604 A1176 60y Hemp linear pattern 75 35
a. Pair, #1603-1604 1.50 75

1985, Aug. 8 Photo.

1605 A1177 60y Man 75 38
1606 A1178 60y Woman and child 75 38
a. Pair, #1605-1606 1.50 80

Photogravure and Engraved

1607 A1179 60y Silver kettle 75 38
1608 A1180 60y Black kettle 75 38
a. Pair, #1607-1608 1.50 80

Wajimanuri Lacquerware
A1181 A1182

Izumo-ishidoro Sandstone Sculptures
A1183 A1184

Photo., Photo. & Engr. (#1611-1612)
1985, Nov. 15

1609 A1181 60y Bowl on table 75 38
1610 A1182 60y Bowl 75 38
1611 A1183 60y Columnar lantern 75 38
1612 A1184 60y Lantern on four legs 75 38

Kyo-sensu Silk Fans
A1185 A1186

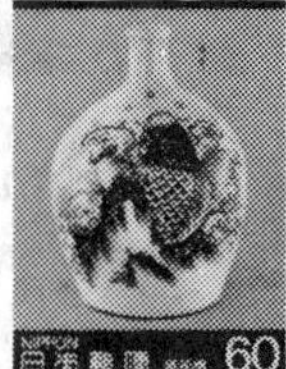

Tobeyaki Porcelain
A1187 A1188

1986, Mar. 13 Photo. *Perf. 13*

1613 A1185 60y Flower bouquets 75 38
1614 A1186 60y Sun and trees 75 38
1615 A1187 60y Jug 75 38
1616 A1188 60y Jar 75 38

Japanese Professional Baseball, 50th Anniv. — A1189

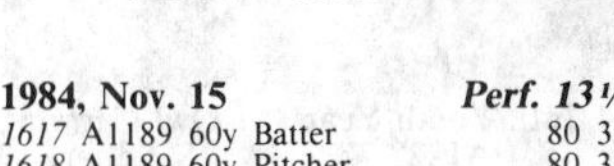

1984, Nov. 15 *Perf. 13½*

1617 A1189 60y Batter 80 35
1618 A1189 60y Pitcher 80 35
1619 A1189 60y Matsutaro Shoriki 80 35

Industrial Education Centenary — A1190

New Year 1984 — A1191

1984, Nov. 20 *Perf. 13x12½*

1620 A1190 60y Workers, symbols 70 32

1984, Dec. 1 Photo. *Perf. 13½x13*

1621 A1191 40y Sakushu Cattle Folk Toy 50 25

Sheets of 2 were lottery prizes. Value, $1.25.

A1191a

Ivory Shell — A1192

Hiougi-gai (Bivalve) A1192a

Rinbo Shell A1193

Ooitokake-gai (Conch) — A1194

A1196

A1198

A1200

Keiki-doji Statue, Kongobuki A1203

Temple A1205

1984-89 Photo. *Perf. 13x13½*

1621A A1191a 2y turq blue ('89) 15 15
1622 A1192 40y multi ('88) 52 15
1622A A1192a 41y multi ('89) 62 15
b. Imperf., self-adhesive 62 15
1623 A1193 60y multi ('88) 80 15
a. Bklt. pane, 5 each #1622-1623 6.75
1624 A1194 62y multi ('89) 92 15
a. Bklt. pane, 2 #1622A, 4 #1624 5.00
b. Imperf., self-adhesive 92 15
c. Bklt. pane, 2 #1622b, 4 #1624b ('89) 5.00
1627 A1196 72y dark vio, blk & org yel ('89) 1.10 20
1629 A1198 175y multi ('89) 2.65 25
1631 A1200 210y multi ('89) 3.15 30

Engr.

1633 A1203 300y dk red brn 4.25 1.40
1635 A1205 360y ('89) 5.50 80
Nos. 1621A-1635 (10) 19.66
Set value 3.10

Coil Stamps
Perf. 13 Horiz.

1636 A1192a 41y multi ('89) 62 15
1637 A1194 62y multi ('89) 92 15
Set value 15

No. 1621A inscribed "Nippon," unlike No. 583.

No. 1624c is adhered to the booklet cover, made of peelable paper, folded in half and rouletted down the center fold.

Issue dates: 40y, 60y, Apr. 1. 300y, Apr. 3. 2y, 72y, Apr. 1; 42y, Nos. 1624, 1624a, 41y, No. 1637, Mar. 24; 175y, 210y, 360y, June 1. No. 1624d, July 3.

This is an expanding set. Numbers will change if necessary.

A1210

EXPO '85 — A1211

1985, Mar. 16 Photo. *Perf. 13*

1640 A1210 40y multi 50 22
1641 A1211 60y multi 75 35
a. Souv. sheet of 2, #1640-1641 1.65

University of the Air — A1212

1985, Apr. 1 Photo. *Perf. 13½*

1642 A1212 60y University broadcast tower 70 35

Inauguration of adult education through broadcasting.

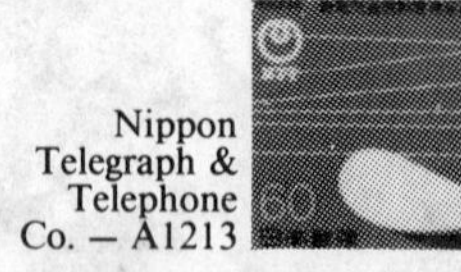

Nippon Telegraph & Telephone Co. — A1213

1985, Apr. 1
1643 A1213 60y Satellite receiver 70 35

Inauguration of Japan's new telecommunications system.

World Import Fair, Nagoya A1214

1985, Apr. 5 Photo. *Perf. 13*
1644 A1214 60y 16th century map of Japan 70 35

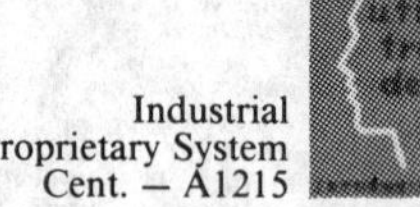

Industrial Proprietary System Cent. — A1215

Design: Portrait of Korekiyo Takashashi, system promulgator, inscriptions in English.

1985, Apr. 18 Photo. *Perf. 13½*
1645 A1215 60y multi 70 35

Winter in the North — A1216

To the Morning Light — A1217

Paintings by Yumeji Takehisa (1884-1934).

1985, Apr. 20 *Perf. 13*
1646 A1216 60y multi 70 35
1647 A1217 60y multi 70 35

Philatelic Week. Printed in sheets of 10.

Natl. Land Forestation Project — A1218

Intl. Year of the Forest: Autumn bellflower, camphor tree, cattle and Mt. Aso.

1985, May 10 *Perf. 13½*
1648 A1218 60y multi 70 35

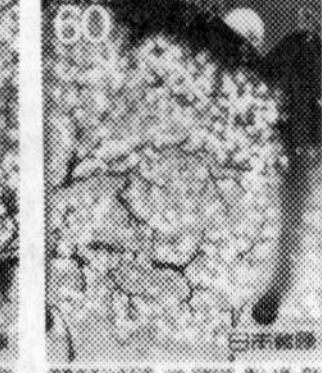

Radio Japan, 50th Anniv. — A1219

Painting: Cherry Blossoms at Night, by Taikan Yokoyama.

1985, June 1 Photo. *Perf. 13*
1649 A1219 60y multi (Left) 75 35
1650 A1219 60y multi (Right) 75 35
a. Pair, #1649-1650 1.60

Hisoko Maejima, 1st Postmaster General — A1220

1985, June 5 Photo. *Perf. 13*
1651 A1220 60y Portrait, former P.O. building 70 35

Oonaruto Bridge Opening A1221

1985, June 7 *Perf. 13½*
1652 A1221 60y multi 70 35

Intl. Youth Year A1222

Owl Carrying Letter A1223

1985, July 20 Photo. *Perf. 13*
1653 A1222 60y Emblem, silhouette 70 35

Perf. 13½x13, 13x13½
1985, July 23 Photo.
1654 A1223 40y shown 60 28
1655 A1223 60y Girl, cat, bird, letter 75 45

Letter Writing Day (23rd of each month).

Electronic Mail A1224

Meson Theory, 50th Anniv. A1225

1985, Aug. 1 Photo. *Perf. 13x13½*
1656 A1224 500y multi 7.00 3.00

1985, Aug. 15 Photo. *Perf. 13*
1657 A1225 60y Portrait, nuclear particles 70 35

Dr. Hideki Yukawa was presented the Nobel Prize for Physics for the Meson Theory in 1949, which is the foundation for high-energy physics.

Universiade 1985, Kobe — A1226

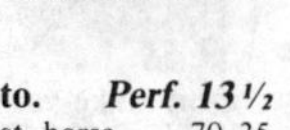

1985, Aug. 24 Photo. *Perf. 13½*
1658 A1226 60y Gymnast, horse 70 35

28th Intl. Vocational Training Competition, Oct. 21-27 — A1227

1985, Sept. 13 Photo.
1659 A1227 40y Emblem, competitor 50 25

Rose of Sharon — A1228

1985, Sept. 18
1660 A1228 60y multi 70 30

Normalization of diplomatic relations between Japan and the Republic of Korea, 20th anniv.

Kan-Etsu Tunnel Opening A1229

1985, Oct. 2 *Perf. 13*
1661 A1229 60y Mountains, diagram, cross sections 70 35

Seisen Doll by Goyo Hirata (1903-1981) A1230

1985, Oct. 7
1662 A1230 130y multi 1.75 85

Intl. Letter Writing Week, Oct. 6-12.

30th Intl. Apicultural Congress, Oct. 10-16, Nagoya A1231

1985, Oct. 9
1663 A1231 60y Honeybee, strawberry plants 70 35

Japanese Overseas Cooperation Volunteers, 20th Anniv. A1232

1985, Oct. 9 Litho.
1664 A1232 60y Planting crop 70 35

40th Natl. Athletic Meet, Oct. 20-25, Tottori City Sports Arena — A1233

1985, Oct. 19 Photo.
1665 A1233 40y Handball player, Mt. Daisen 50 25

New Year 1986 A1234

Natl. Ministerial System of Government, Cent. A1235

1985, Dec. 2 Photo. *Perf. 13x13½*
1666 A1234 40y Shinno papier-mache tiger 50 25

Sheets of 2 were lottery prizes. Value, $1.40.

1985, Dec. 20 Litho. *Perf. 13½*
1667 A1235 60y Official seal, Cabinet emblem 70 35

Building Institute, Cent. — A1236

Philately Week — A1237

1986, Apr. 9 Photo. *Perf. 13*
1668 A1236 60y multi 70 42

1986, Apr. 15

Southern Hateroma (details), by Keigetsu Kikuchi.

1669 A1237 60y Woman standing 75 42
1670 A1237 60y Seated woman 75 42
a. Pair, #1669-1670 1.60

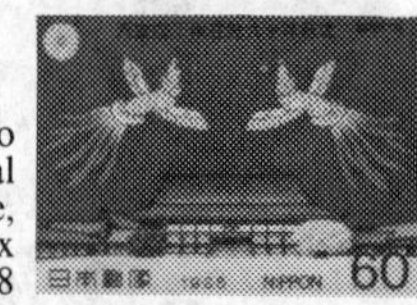

Kyoto Imperial Palace, Phoenix A1238

Designs: No. 1672, Imperial chrysanthemum crest and partridges.

1986, Apr. 28
1671 A1238 60y multi 75 42
1672 A1238 60y multi 75 42
a. Souv. sheet of 2, #1671-1672 1.65 1.25

Reign of Emperor Hirohito, 60th anniv.

6th Intl. Summit, Tokyo A1239

1986, May 2
1673 A1239 60y Mt. Fuji 70 42

Shrike on Reed, Emperor Nintoku's Mausoleum
A1240

1986, May 9 *Perf. 13½*
1674 A1240 60y multi 70 42

Natl. Land Afforestation Campaign.

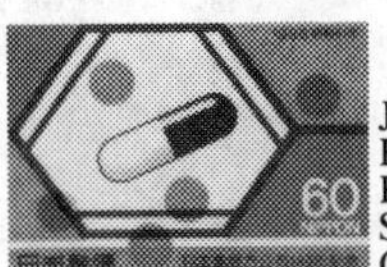
Japanese Pharmaceutical Regulatory Syst., Cent. — A1241

1986, June 25 Photo. *Perf. 13½*
1675 A1241 60y multi 70 45

Japanese Standard Time, Cent.
A1242

Letter Writing Day
A1243

1986, July 11 Litho. *Perf. 13*
1676 A1242 60y Meridian, clock 70 45

1986, July 23 Photo. *Perf. 13x13½*
1677 A1243 40y Bird 55 35
1678 A1243 60y Girl, rabbit, birds 80 52
a. Bklt. pane, 5 each #1677-1678 7.50

Sheets of 2 were lottery prizes. Value, *$50.*

Merchant Marine Education, 110th Anniv.
A1244

Design: Training ship Nihonmaru and navigation training institute founders Makoto Kondo, Yataro Iwasaki.

1986, July 26 *Perf. 13*
1679 A1244 60y multi 75 48

Insects

Parnassius Eversmanni
A1245

Photogravure and Engraved

1986, July 30 *Perf. 13*
1680 A1245 60y shown 80 48
1681 A1245 60y Poecilocoris Lewisi 80 48
a. Pair, #1680-1681 1.60 1.00
1682 A1245 60y Rasalia Batesi 80 48
1683 A1245 60y Epiophlebia Superstes 80 48
a. Pair, #1682-1683 1.60 1.00

1986, Sept. 26 *Perf. 13*
1684 A1245 60y Dorcus hopei 80 55
1685 A1245 60y Thermo-zephyrus ataxus 80 55
a. Pair, #1684-1685 1.60 1.10
1686 A1245 60y Sympetrum pedemontanum 80 55
1687 A1245 60y Damaster blaptoides 80 55
a. Pair, #1686-1687 1.60 1.10

1986, Nov. 21 *Perf. 13*
1688 A1245 60y Elcysma westwoodii 80 52
1689 A1245 60y Rhyothemis variegata 80 52
a. Pair, #1688-1689 1.60 1.10
1690 A1245 60y Tibicen japonicus 80 52
1691 A1245 60y Chrysochroa holstii 80 52
a. Pair, #1690-1691 1.60 1.10

1987, Jan. 23 *Perf. 13*
1692 A1245 60y Parantica sita 80 55
1693 A1245 60y Cheirotonus jambar 80 55
a. Pair, #1692-1693 1.60 1.10
1694 A1245 60y Lucanus maculifemoratus 80 55
1695 A1245 60y Anotogaster sieboldii 80 55
a. Pair, #1694-1695 1.60 1.10

1987, Mar. 12 *Perf. 13*
1696 A1245 60y Ascaraphus ramburi 80 55
1697 A1245 60y Polyphylla laticollis 80 55
a. Pair, #1696-1697 1.60 1.10
1698 A1245 60y Kallima inachus 80 55
1699 A1245 60y Calopteryx cornelia 80 55
a. Pair, #1698-1699 1.60 1.10

Miniature Sheet

1699A Sheet of 4 (#1680, 1692, 1699b-1699c) 3.50 2.75
b. A1245 40y Anthocaris cardamines 75 55
c. A1245 40y Sasakia charonda 75 55
d. Bklt. pane, 5 #1680, 5 #1699b 8.50
e. Bklt. pane, 5 #1692, 5 #1699c 8.50

Booklet panes are perf. 13x13½ on 2 or 3 sides.

Folkways in Twelve Months (Detail), by Shunsho Katsukawa
A1265

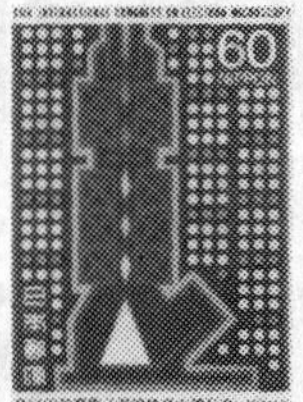
Electron Microscope
A1266

1986, Aug. 23 Photo. *Perf. 13*
1700 A1265 60y multi 70 48

52nd conference of the Intl. Federation of Library Associations, Tokyo, Aug. 24-29.

1986, Aug. 30
1701 A1266 60y multi 70 48

11th Int. Congress of Electron Microscopy, Kyoto, Aug. 31-Sept. 7.

23rd Intl. Conference on Social Welfare, Tokyo, Aug. 31-Sept. 5 — A1267

1986, Aug. 30 **Litho.**
1702 A1267 60y multi 70 48

Ohmorimiyage Doll, by Juzoh Kagoshima
A1268

41st Natl. Athletic Meet, Oct. 12-17, Kofu
A1269

1986, Oct. 6 **Photo.**
1703 A1268 130y multi 1.75 1.10

Intl. Letter Writing Week.

1986, Oct. 9
1704 A1269 40y multi 52 38

5th World Ikebana Convention
A1270

Painting: Flower in Autumn and a Girl in Rakuhoku.

1986, Oct. 17 Photo. *Perf. 13½x13*
1705 A1270 60y multi 70 48

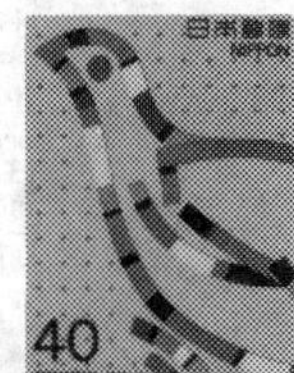
A1271

Intl. Peace Year — A1272

Lithographed, Photogravure (#1707)

1986, Nov. 28
1706 A1271 40y multi 55 35
1707 A1272 60y multi 80 52

New Year 1987 (Year of the Hare) — A1273

Design: A Couple of Rabbits Making Rice Cake, Nagoya clay figurine.

1986, Dec. 1 Photo. *Perf. 13x13½*
1708 A1273 40y multi 52 32

Sheets of two containing one each of Nos. 1506 and 1708 were lottery prizes. Value, $1.75.

Real Estate Registry System, Cent.
A1274

1987, Jan. 30 Photo. *Perf. 13½*
1709 A1274 60y multi 70 48

Literature Series

Basho — A1275

Verse from Basho's Haiku — A1276

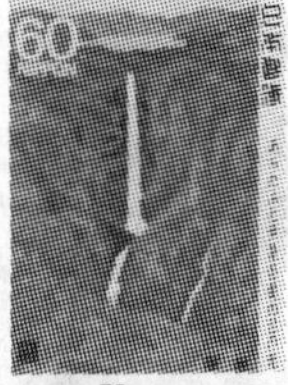
Kegon Falls — A1277

Haiku Verse — A1278

Cuckoo — A1279

Horse and Verse — A1280

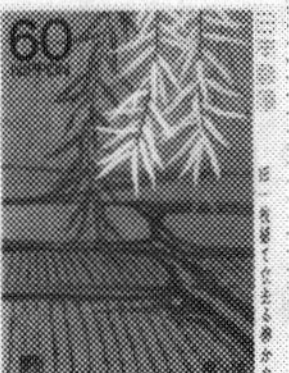
Willow Tree — A1281

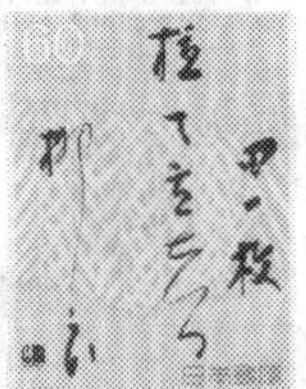
Rice Paddy and Verse — A1282

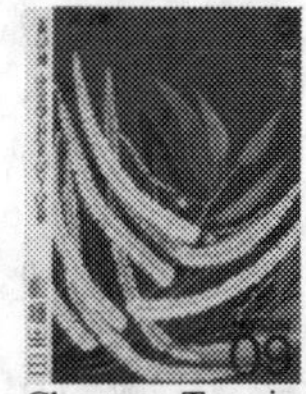
Chestnut Tree in Bloom — A1283

Chestnut Leaves and Verse — A1284

Planting Rice Paddy — A1285

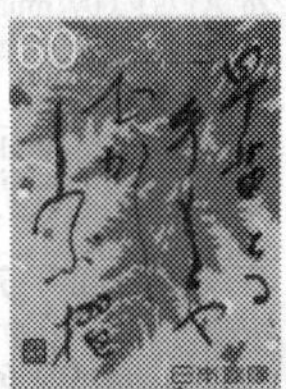
Fern Leaves and Verse — A1286

Sweetflags
A1287

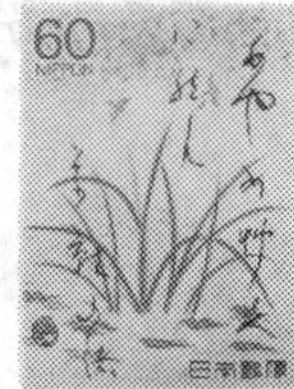
Sweetflags and Verse
A1288

Prosperous Man, 17th Cent. — A1289

Summer Grass and Verse — A1290

Safflowers in Bloom — A1291

Verse — A1292

Yamadera (Temple) A1293

Forest and Verse A1294

1987-89 Photo. *Perf. 13x13½*

1710	A1275 60y multi		90	60
1711	A1276 60y multi		90	60
a.	Sheet of 2, #1710-1711, imperf. ('89)		1.80	
b.	Pair, #1710-1711		1.80	1.25
1712	A1277 60y multi		90	60
1713	A1278 60y multi		90	60
a.	Sheet of 2, #1712-1713, imperf. ('89)		1.80	
b.	Pair, #1712-1713		1.80	1.25
1714	A1279 60y multi		90	60
1715	A1280 60y multi		90	60
a.	Sheet of 2, #1714-1715, imperf. ('89)		1.80	
b.	Pair, #1714-1715		1.80	1.25
1716	A1281 60y multi		90	60
1717	A1282 60y multi		90	60
a.	Sheet of 2, #1716-1717, imperf. ('89)		1.80	
b.	Pair, #1716-1717		1.80	1.25
1718	A1283 60y multi		90	60
1719	A1284 60y multi		90	60
a.	Sheet of 2, #1718-1719, imperf. ('89)		1.80	
b.	Pair, #1718-1719		1.80	1.25
1720	A1285 60y multi		90	60
1721	A1286 60y multi		90	60
a.	Sheet of 2, #1720-1721, imperf. ('89)		1.80	
b.	Pair, #1720-1721		1.80	1.25
1722	A1287 60y multi ('88)		90	60
1723	A1288 60y multi ('88)		90	60
a.	Sheet of 2, #1722-1723, imperf. ('89)		1.80	
b.	Pair, #1722-1723		1.80	1.25
1724	A1289 60y multi ('88)		90	60
1725	A1290 60y multi ('88)		90	60
a.	Sheet of 2, #1724-1725, imperf. ('89)		1.80	
b.	Pair, #1724-1725		1.80	1.25
1726	A1291 60y multi ('88)		90	60
1727	A1292 60y multi ('88)		90	60
a.	Sheet of 2, #1726-1727, imperf. ('89)		1.80	
b.	Pair, #1726-1727		1.80	1.25
1728	A1293 60y multi ('88)		90	60
1729	A1294 60y multi ('88)		90	60
a.	Sheet of 2, #1728-1729, imperf. ('89)		1.80	
b.	Pair, #1728-1729		1.80	1.25
	Nos. 1710-1729 (20)		18.00	12.00

Illustrations and text from Oku-no hosomichi, 1694, a travel description haiku written by Munefus "Basho" Matsuo (1644-1694), poet.

Issue dates: #1710-1713, Feb. 26. #1714-1717, June 23. #1718-1721, Aug. 25. #1722-1725, Jan. 3. #1726-1729, Mar. 26.

12th World Orchid Congress, Tokyo
A1295 A1296

1987, Mar. 19 Photo. *Perf. 13*

1730	A1295 60y multi	80	60
1731	A1296 60y multi	80	60

Railway Post Office Termination, Oct. 1, 1986 A1297

1987, Mar. 26 Litho. *Perf. 13½*

1732	A1297 60y Mail car	80	60
1733	A1297 60y Loading mail on car	80	60
a.	Pair, #1732-1733	1.60	1.25

Privatization of Japan Railways A1298

1987, Apr. 1 Photo. *Perf. 13½*

1734	A1298 60y Locomotive No. 137, c. 1900	80	60
1735	A1298 60y Linear induction train, 1987	80	60

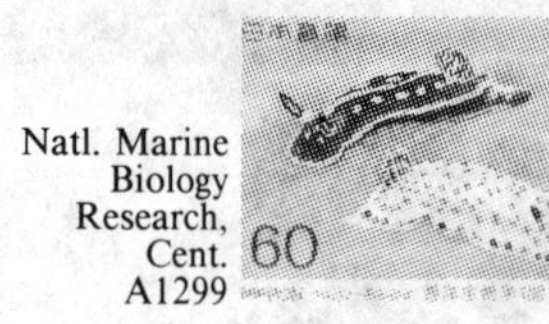

Natl. Marine Biology Research, Cent. A1299

1987, Apr. 2 *Perf. 13*

1736	A1299 60y Sea slugs	80	60

Philately Week
A1300 A1301

1987, Apr. 14

1737	A1300 60y multi	80	60
1738	A1301 60y multi	80	60
a.	Pair, #1737-1738	1.60	1.25

Map of Asia and Oceania A1302

1987, Apr. 27 Photo. *Perf. 13½*

1739	A1302 60y multi	80	60

20th annual meeting of the Asian Development Bank.

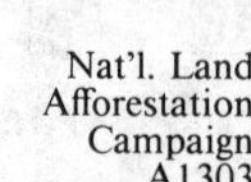

Nat'l. Land Afforestation Campaign A1303

1987, May 23

1740	A1303 60y Magpie, seashore	80	60

National Treasures Series

A1304

A1305

Golden Turtle Sharito A1306

Imuyama Dastle Donjon, 1469 A1307

Kongo Sanmai in Tahotoh Temple, Kamakura Era — A1308

Wood Ekoh-Dohji Statue in the Likeness of Kongobuji Fudodo, Kamakura Era, by Unkei — A1309

Itsukushima Shrine, Heian Period A1310

Kozakura-gawa, Braided Armor Worn by Minamoto-no-Yoshimitsu, Heian Period War Lord, Kai Province — A1311

Statue of *Nakatsu-hime-no-mikoto,* a Hachiman Goddess, Heian Period, Yakushiji Temple — A1312

Murou-ji Temple Pagoda, 9th Cent. — A1313

Designs: No. 1741, Yatuhashi gold inkstone box, by Kohrin Ogata. No. 1742, Donjon of Hikone Castle, c. 1573-1592.

1987, May 26 Photo. *Perf. 13*

1741	A1304 60y multi	90	60

Photo. & Engr.
Perf. 13½

1742	A1305 110y multi	1.65	1.15

1987, July 17 Photo. *Perf. 13*

1743	A1306 60y multi	90	62

Photo. & Engr.
Perf. 13½

1744	A1307 110y multi	1.65	1.15

1988, Feb. 12 Photo. *Perf. 13*

1745	A1308 60y multi	90	62

Photo. & Engr.
Perf. 13½

1746	A1309 110y multi	1.65	1.15

1988, June 23 Photo. *Perf. 13*

1747	A1310 60y multi	90	68

Photo. & Engr.
Perf. 13½

1748	A1311 100y multi	1.50	1.15

1988, Sept. 26 Photo. *Perf. 13*

1749	A1312 60y multi	92	70

Photo. & Engr.
Perf. 13½

1750	A1313 100y multi	1.50	1.15
	Nos. 1741-1750 (10)	12.47	8.97

Letter Writing Day — A1314

1987, July 23 Photo. *Perf. 13x13½*

1751	A1314 40y Flowers, envelope	55	42
1752	A1314 60y Elephant	82	62
a.	Bklt. pane, 5 each #1751-1752	7.00	

Sheets of 2, Nos. 1751-1752, were lottery prizes. Value, *$20.*

Kiso Three Rivers Flood Control, Cent. A1315

1987, Aug. 7 Photo. *Perf. 13½*

1753	A1315 60y Kiso, Nagara and Ibi Rivers	82	62

Japan - Thailand Diplomatic Relations, Cent. A1316

Design: Temple of the Emerald Buddha and cherry blossoms.

1987, Sept. 26 ***Perf. 13***
1754 A1316 60y multi 85 65

Intl. Letter Writing Week — A1317

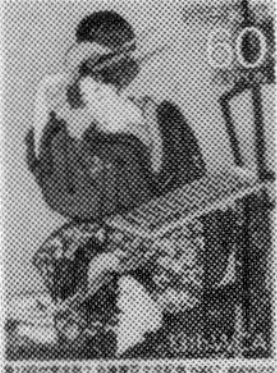
13th World Congress of Certified Public Accountants, Tokyo, Oct. 11-15 — A1318

Dolls by Goyo Hirata: 130y, Gensho Kanto, by Royojo Hori (1898-1984). 150y, Utage-no-Hana (Fair Woman at the Party).

1987, Oct. 6 **Photo.** ***Perf. 13***
1755 A1317 130y multi 1.85 1.40
1756 A1317 150y multi 2.10 1.60

1987, Oct. 9 ***Perf. 13***

Design: Three Beauties (adaptation), by Toyokuni Utagawa (1769-1825).

1757 A1318 60y multi 85 65

Modern Waterworks, Cent. A1319

Shurei Gate, Okinawa, Basketball Players A1320

Design: Lion's head public fountain, 1887, Waterworks Museum, Yokohama.

1987, Oct. 16 **Engr.**
1758 A1319 60y multi 88 65

1987, Oct. 24 **Photo.**
1759 A1320 40y multi 88 65

42nd Natl. Athletic Meet, Okinawa.

6th World Cong. on Smoking & Health, Nov. 9-12, Tokyo — A1321

World Telecommunications Conf., Nov. 15-18, Tokyo — A1322

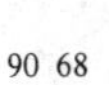

1987, Nov. 9
1760 A1321 60y multi 90 68

1987, Nov. 13 ***Perf. 13½***

Design: Microwave dish antenna at Kashima Station Radio Research Laboratory.

1761 A1322 60y multi 90 68

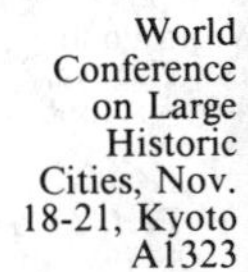

World Conference on Large Historic Cities, Nov. 18-21, Kyoto A1323

Design: Nijo Castle guardhouse roof and Ninomaru Hall, 17th cent.

1987, Nov. 18 ***Perf. 13***
1762 A1323 60y multi 90 68

Intl. Year of Shelter for the Homeless A1324

Prize-winning illustrations by: 40y, Takahiro Nahahama. 60y, Yoko Sasaki.

1987, Nov. 25
1763 A1324 40y multi 60 45
1764 A1324 60y multi 90 68

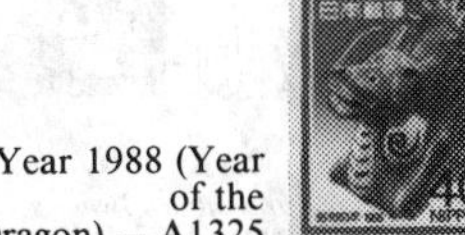
New Year 1988 (Year of the Dragon) — A1325

Design: Kurashiki papier-mache dragon, 1869, by Tajuro Omizu.

1987, Dec. 1 ***Perf. 13x13½***
1765 A1325 40y multi 60 45

Sheets of 2, Nos. 1506, 1765, were lottery prizes. Value, $2.25.

Seikan Tunnel Opening A1326

1988, Mar. 11 **Engr.** ***Perf. 13½***
1766 A1326 60y ED 79 locomotive, map 95 72

Opening of Seto-Oohashi Bridge

Kagawa Side
A1327 A1328

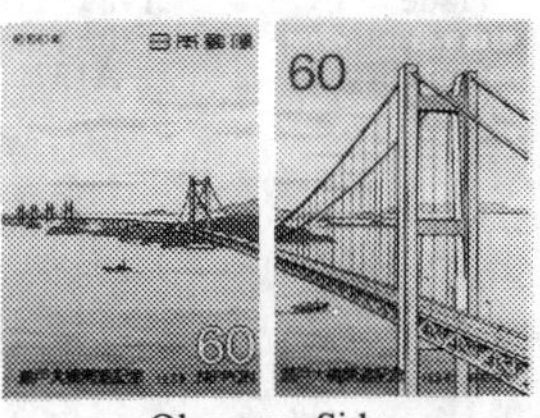
Okayama Side
A1329 A1330

1988, Apr. 8 **Engr.** ***Perf. 13½***
1767 A1327 60y multi 98 75
1768 A1328 60y multi 98 75
1769 A1329 60y multi 98 75
1770 A1330 60y multi 98 75
a. Strip of 4, #1767-1770 4.00 3.00

Nos. 1767-1768 and 1769-1770 have continuous designs.

Philately Week
A1331 A1332

Prints by Kotondo Torii (b. 1900): No. 1771, Long Undergarment. No. 1772, Kimono Sash.

1988, Apr. 19 **Photo.** ***Perf. 13***
1771 A1331 60y multi 98 75
1772 A1332 60y multi 98 75
a. Pair, #1771-1772 2.00

Souv. sheet of 2 exists. Value $9.

Silk Road Exposition, Apr. 24-Oct. 23, Nara — A1333

Design: Plectrum guard playing the biwa, detail of Raden-Shitan-no-Gogen-Biwa, a five-panel work of gold lacquer nacre on sandalwood preserved at Shosoin.

1988, Apr. 23 **Photo. & Engr.**
1773 A1333 60y multi 98 75

Natl. Afforestation Campaign A1334

Design: Yahsima, site of the Genji-Heike war, and cuckoo on olive tree branch.

1988, May 20 **Photo.** ***Perf. 13½***
1774 A1334 60y multi 98 75

Literature Series

Mogami River — A1335

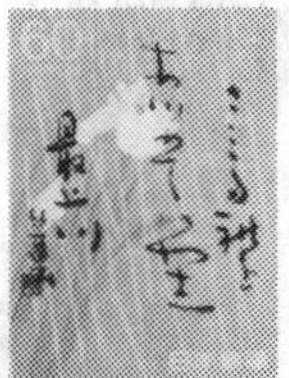
Verse and Flower — A1336

Mt. Gassan A1337

Verse and Mountain A1338

Mimosa in Bloom — A1339

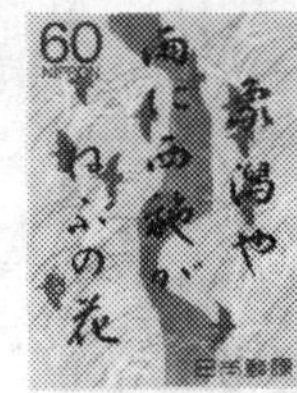
Verse, Birds, Kisagata Inlet — A1340

Ocean Waves — A1341

Verse and Current — A1342

Rice — A1343

Birds in Flight, Verse — A1344

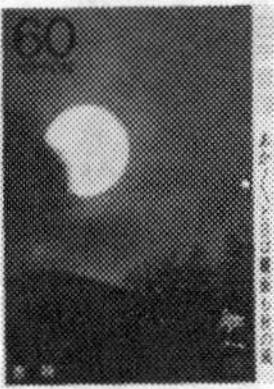
Sun Glow — A1345

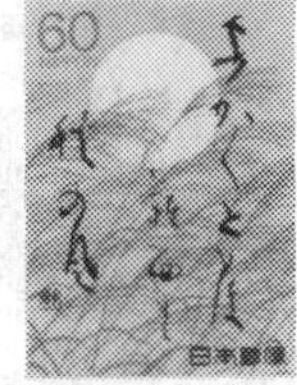
Rice, Verse — A1346

Nata-dera Temple — A1347

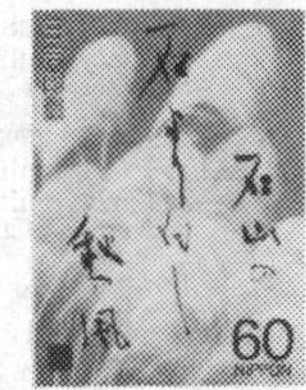
Verse, White Grass — A1348

Trees — A1349

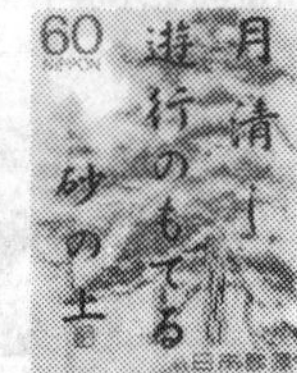
Verse, Moonlit Forest — A1350

Autumn on the Beach — A1351

Verse — A1352

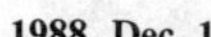

Clams — A1353

Verse — A1354

1988, May 30 Photo. *Perf. 13x13½*

1775 A1335 60y multi 98 75
1776 A1336 60y multi 98 75
a. Souv. sheet of 2, #1775-1776, imperf. ('89) 2.00
b. Pair, #1775-1776 2.00 1.50
1777 A1337 60y multi 98 75
1778 A1338 60y multi 98 75
a. Souv. sheet of 2, #1777-1778, imperf. ('89) 2.00
b. Pair, #1777-1778 2.00 1.50

1988, Aug. 23

1779 A1339 60y multi 92 70
1780 A1340 60y multi 92 70
a. Souv. sheet of 2, #1779-1780, imperf ('89) 2.00
b. Pair, #1779-1780 1.90 1.50
1781 A1341 60y multi 92 70
1782 A1342 60y multi 92 70
a. Souv. sheet of 2, #1781-1782, imperf. ('89) 2.00
b. Pair, #1781-1782 1.90 1.50

1988, Nov. 11

1783 A1343 60y multi 92 70
1784 A1344 60y multi 92 70
a. Souv. sheet of 2, #1783-1784, imperf. ('89) 2.00
b. Pair, #1783-1784 1.90 1.50
1785 A1345 60y multi 92 70
1786 A1346 60y multi 92 70
a. Souv. sheet of 2, #1785-1786, imperf. ('89) 2.00
b. Pair, #1785-1786 1.90 1.50

1989, Feb. 13

1787 A1347 60y multi 95 72
1788 A1348 60y multi 95 72
a. Souv. sheet of 2, #1787-1788, imperf. 2.00
b. Pair, #1787-1788 2.00 1.50
1789 A1349 60y multi 95 72
1790 A1350 60y multi 95 72
a. Souv. sheet of 2, #1789-1790, imperf. 2.00
b. Pair, #1789-1790 2.00 1.50

1989, May 12

1791 A1351 62y multi 92 68
1792 A1352 62y multi 92 68
a. Souv. sheet of 2, #1791-1792, imperf. 2.00
b. Pair, #1791-1792 1.90 1.40
1793 A1353 62y multi 92 68
1794 A1354 62y multi 92 68
a. Souv. sheet of 2, #1793-1794, imperf. 2.00
b. Pair, #1793-1794 1.90 1.40

Illustrations and text from *Oku-no-hosomichi,* "Narrow Road to a Far Province," 1694, a travel description written in haiku by munefus "Basho" Matsuo (1644-94), poet.

Issue date: Nos. 1776a-1794a, Aug. 1, 1989.

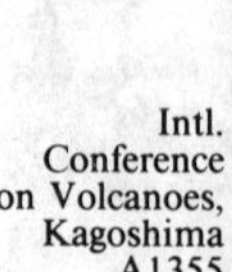

Intl. Conference on Volcanoes, Kagoshima A1355

1988, July 19 Photo. *Perf. 14*

1795 A1355 60y multi 92 70

A1356

A1357

A1358

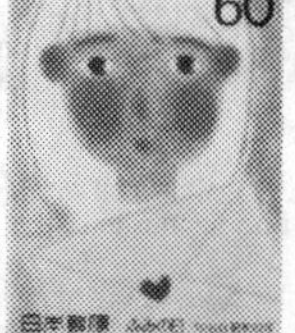

Letter Writing Day, 10th Anniv. — A1359

Designs and contest-winning children's drawings: No. 1796, Cat and letter. No. 1797, *Crab and Letter,* by Katsuyuki Yamada. No. 1798, Fairy and letter. No. 1799, *Girl and Letter,* by Takashi Ukai.

Photo., Litho. (Nos. 1797, 1799)

1988, July 23 *Perf. 13x13½*

1796 A1356 40y multi 62 48
a. Imperf., self-adhesive 62 48
1797 A1357 40y multi 62 48
1798 A1358 60y multi 92 70
a. Bklt. pane, 5 each #1796, 1798 7.75
b. Imperf., self-adhesive 92 70
c. Bklt. pane, 3 each #1796a, 1798b 4.65
1799 A1359 60y multi 92 70

No. 1798c is adhered to the booklet cover, made of peelable paper, folded in half and rouletted down the center fold, with No. 1796a at left and No. 1798b at right of the roulette.

Sheets of 2 containing Nos. 1796, 1798 were lottery prizes. Value, $9.

A1360 A1361

A1362 A1363

15th World Puppetry Festival, July 27-Aug. 11

Puppets: No. 1800, *Ohana,* string puppet from the film *Spring and Fall in the Meiji Era,* by Kinosuke Takeda (1923-1979), Japan. No. 1801, Girl, stick puppet from the Natl. Radost Puppet Theater, Brno, Czechoslovakia. No. 1802, Woman, shadow puppet from China. No. 1803, Knight, a marionette from Sicily.

1988, July 27 Photo. *Perf. 13*

1800 A1360 60y multi 92 70
1801 A1361 60y multi 92 70
1802 A1362 60y multi 92 70
1803 A1363 60y multi 92 70
a. Block of 4, #1800-1803 4.00 3.00

Japan-China Treaty, 10th Anniv.
A1364 A1365

1988, Aug. 12 Photo.

1804 A1364 60y Peony 92 70
1805 A1365 60y Panda 92 70

18th World Poultry Congress, Nagoya, Sept. 4-9 — A1366

1988, Sept. 3 *Perf. 13½*

1806 A1366 60y multi 92 70

Rehabilitation Intl. 16th World Congress, Tokyo, Sept. 5-9 — A1367

Photo. & Embossed

1988, Sept. 5 *Perf. 13*

1807 A1367 60y multi 92 70

Intl. Letter-Writing Week — A1368

Prints: 80y, *Kumesaburo Iwai as Chiyo,* by Kunimasa Utagawa (1773-1810), late Edo Period. 120y, *Komazo Ichikawa III as Ganryu Sasaki,* by Toyokuni Utagawa (1769-1825).

1988, Oct. 6 Photo.

1808 A1368 80y multi 1.30 1.00
1809 A1368 120y multi 2.00 1.50

43rd Natl. Athletic Meet, Kyoto — A1369

Design: Gymnast on parallel bars and "Kinkakuji," Temple of the Golden Pavilion.

1988, Oct. 14

1810 A1369 40y multi 65 50

Japan-Mexico Trade Agreement, Cent. A1370

New Year 1989 (Year of the Snake) A1371

1988, Nov. 30 Photo.

1811 A1370 60y multi 98 75

1988, Dec. 1

Design: Clay bell snake by Masanobu Ogawa.

1812 A1371 40y multi 65 50

Sheets of two containing Nos. 1506, 1812 were lottery prizes. Value, $2.50.

UN Declaration of Human Rights, 40th Anniv. — A1372

1988, Dec. 5 Litho. *Perf. 13½*

1813 A1372 60y multi 98 75

National Treasures Series

Votive Silver Lidded Bowl Used in Todai-ji Temple Ground-Breaking Ceremony, 8th Cent. — A1373

Bronze Yakusi-nyorai Buddha, Asuka Period, 7th Cent. — A1374

Kondo-Sukashibori-Kurakanagu, Bronze Saddle from Ohjin Imperial Mausoleum — A1375

Tamamushi-no-Zushi, Buddhist Altar in Lacquered Cypress from the Azuka Era — A1376

Kin-in, a Gokan Era Gold Seal Given to the King of Na by Emperor Kobutai — A1377

Shinninshaba-gazokyo, a 5th Cent. European Bronze Plate — A1378

Photo., Photo & Engr. (100y)

1989, Jan. 20 *Perf. 13, 13½ (100y)*

1814 A1373 60y multi 95 72
1815 A1374 100y multi 1.60 1.20

1989, June 30

1816 A1375 62y multi 88 65
1817 A1376 100y multi 1.40 1.05

1989, Aug. 15

1818 A1377 62y multi 88 65
1819 A1378 100y multi 1.40 1.05

Asian-Pacific Expo, Fukuoka, Mar. 17-Sept. 3 — A1383

1989 **Photo.** *Perf. 13*

1822 A1383 60y multicolored 95 72
1823 A1383 62y multicolored 1.25 95

Issue dates: 60y, Mar. 16. 62y, Apr. 18.

Yokohama Exposition (Space and Children), Yokohama City, Mar. 25 to Oct. 1 — A1384

Design: Detail of *Russian Lady Sight-seeing at the Port,* by Yoshitora, and entrance to the Yokohama City Art Museum.

1989, Mar. 24 **Litho.**

1824 A1384 60y multicolored 95 72
1825 A1384 62y multicolored 95 72

World Bonsai Convention, Omiya, Apr. 6-9 — A1385

1989, Apr. 6 **Photo.** *Perf. 13*

1826 A1385 62y multi 92 68

Awa-odori, by Tsunetomi Kitano (b. 1880)

A1386 A1387

1989, Apr. 18 *Perf. 13*

1827 A1386 62y multi 92 68
1828 A1387 62y multi 92 68
a. Pair, #1827-1828 2.00

Philately Week.

Holland Festival 1989 — A1388

1989, Apr. 19 *Perf. 13½*

1829 A1388 62y Ship 92 68

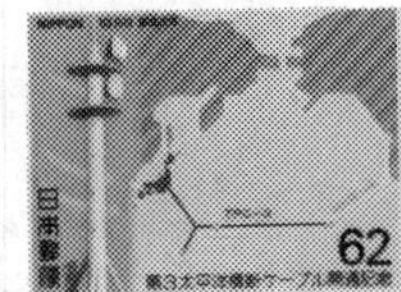

Fiber-optic Cable, the 3rd Transpacific Line Relay Linking Japan and the US — A1389

1989, May 10 *Perf. 13½x13*

1830 A1389 62y Station tower, map 92 68

Natl. Afforestation Campaign — A1390

1989, May 19 *Perf. 13½*

1831 A1390 62y Bayberry, lime, Mt. Tsurugi 92 68

World Design Exposition, Nagoya, July 15-Nov. 26

A1391 A1392

1989, July 14

1832 A1391 41y multi 58 42
1833 A1392 62y multi 88 65

Letter Writing Day

A1393 A1394

1989, July 21 *Perf. 13x13½*

1834 A1393 41y multi 58 42
1835 A1394 62y multi 88 65
a. Bklt. pane, 5 each #1834-1835 7.30

Sheets of 2 containing Nos. 1834-1835 were lottery prizes. Value, $5.25.

Congratulations and Condolences Types of 1982

1989, Aug. 10 **Photo.** *Perf. 13x13½*

1836 A1082 41y Wreath 58 42
1837 A1083 41y Crane 58 42
1838 A1083 62y Crane 88 65
1839 A1084 72y Tortoise 1.05 78

6th Interflora World Congress, Tokyo, Aug. 27-30 — A1395

1989, Aug. 25 **Photo.** *Perf. 13½*

1840 A1395 62y multi 88 65

Prefecture Issues

Nos. 1841-1990 have been reserved for issues for Japan's 47 prefectures (political subdivisions). These stamps were available only in the prefecture for which they were issued, except for No. 1909a, which was available nationwide. All of the stamps were valid throughout Japan. Prefecture stamps are distinguishable from other Japanese issues by the calligraphic style of the four characters which represent the country name.

Monkeys (Nagano) A1396

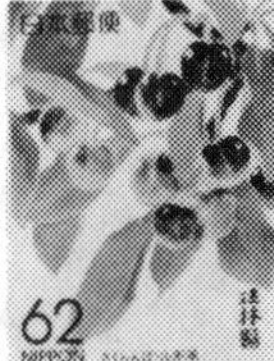

Cherries on Tree (Yamagata) A1397

Shurei-mon, Gate of Courtesy (Okinawa) A1398

Dogo Hot Spa (Ehime) A1399

Blue-eyed Doll (Kanagawa) A1400

Seto Inland Sea (Hiroshima)

A1401 A1402

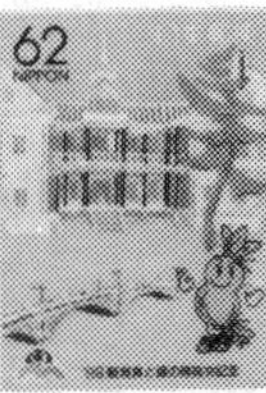

Memorial Hall and Mandai Bridge (Niigata) — A1403

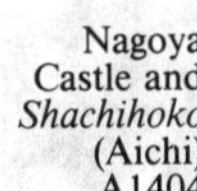

Nagoya Castle and *Shachihoko* (Aichi) A1404

Mt. Takasaki Monkey Holding Perilla Leaf, Fruit (Oita) A1405

City Hall, 1888 (Hokkaido) A1406

Runner, Flower (Hokkaido) A1407

Kumamoto Castle (Kumamoto) A1408

Stone Lantern, Kenroku-en Park (Ishikawa) A1409

Bunraku Puppets and Theater (Osaka) A1410

Shigaraki Ware Raccoon Dog and Lake Biwa (Shiga) A1411

Apples and Blossoms (Aomori) A1412

Raccoon Dogs Dancing (Chiba) A1413

Blowfish Lanterns (Yamaguchi) A1414

Tokyo Station (Tokyo) A1415

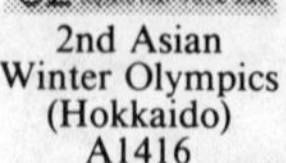

2nd Asian Winter Olympics (Hokkaido)
A1416

Waterfalls (Toyama)
A1417

Perf. 13, 13½ (#1844, 1851, 1860), 13x13½ (#1852-1859)
Photo., Litho. (#1856-1857)

1989-90

No.	Type	Value	Description	Unused	Used
1841	A1396	62y	multi	88	65
1842	A1397	62y	multi	88	65
1843	A1398	62y	multi	88	65
1844	A1399	62y	multi	88	65
1845	A1400	62y	multi	88	65
1846	A1401	62y	multi	88	65
1847	A1402	62y	multi	88	65
a.			Pair, #1846-1847	2.00	1.50
1848	A1403	62y	multi	88	65
1849	A1404	62y	multi	88	65
1850	A1405	62y	multi	88	65
1851	A1406	62y	multi	88	65
1852	A1407	62y	multi	88	65
1853	A1408	62y	multi	88	65
1854	A1409	62y	multi	88	65
1855	A1410	62y	multi	88	65
1856	A1411	62y	multi	88	65
1857	A1412	62y	multi	88	65
1858	A1413	62y	multi	88	65
1859	A1414	62y	multi	88	65
1860	A1415	62y	multi	88	65
1861	A1416	62y	multi	88	65
1862	A1417	62y	multi	82	62

Sheets containing 4 of Nos. 1841, 1842, 1844, 1851 or 3 No. 1859 + label were lottery prizes. Value of set, unattached in booklet, $35.

Issue dates: Nos. 1841-1842, Apr. 1; No. 1843, May 15; No. 1844, June 1; No. 1845, June 2; Nos. 1846-1847, July 7; No. 1848, July 14. No. 1849, Aug. 1; Nos. 1850-1851, Aug. 15. No. 1852, Sept. 1; No. 1853, Sept. 29; Nos. 1854-1857, Oct. 2; No. 1858, Oct. 27; Nos. 1859-1860, Nov. 1; No. 1861, Mar. 1, 1990; No. 1862, Apr. 18, 1990.

Nos. 1863-1909 were issued as one set. It is broken into sections for ease of reference.

Hokkaido
A1418

Aomori
A1419

Iwate
A1420

Miyagi
A1421

Akita
A1422

Yamagata
A1423

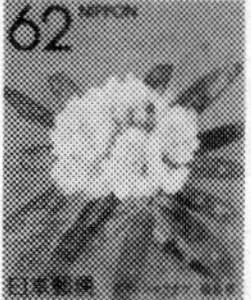

Fukushima
A1424

Ibaraki
A1425

Flowers of the Prefectures.

1990, Apr. 27 Litho. *Perf. 13½*

No.	Type	Value	Description	Unused	Used
1863	A1418	62y	Sweet briar	82	62
1864	A1419	62y	Apple blossom	82	62
1865	A1420	62y	Paulowina	82	62
1866	A1421	62y	Japanese bush clover	82	62
1867	A1422	62y	Butterbur flower	82	62
1868	A1423	62y	Safflower	82	62
1869	A1424	62y	Alpine rose	82	62
1870	A1425	62y	Rose	82	62

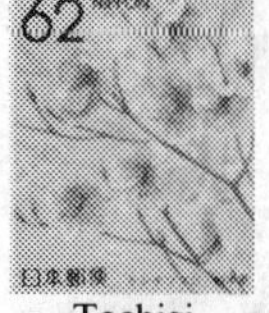

Tochigi
A1426

Gunma
A1427

Saitama
A1428

Chiba
A1429

Kanagawa
A1430

Yamanashi
A1431

Tokyo
A1432

Nagano
A1433

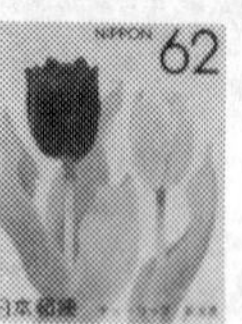
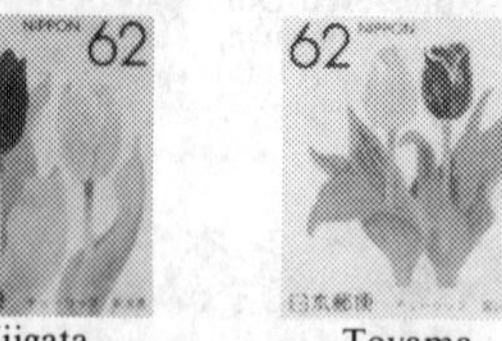

Niigata
A1434

Toyama
A1435

No.	Type	Value	Description	Unused	Used
1871	A1426	62y	Yashio azalea	82	62
1872	A1427	62y	Japanese azalea	82	62
1873	A1428	62y	Primrose	82	62
1874	A1429	62y	Rape blossom	82	62
1875	A1430	62y	Gold-banded lily	82	62
1876	A1431	62y	Cherry blossom	82	62
1877	A1432	62y	Cherry blossom	82	62
1878	A1433	62y	Autumn bell-flower	82	62
1879	A1434	62y	Tulip	82	62
1880	A1435	62y	Tulip	82	62

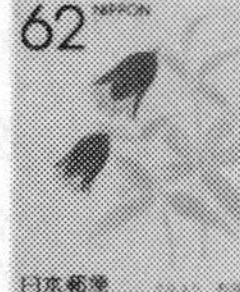

Ishikawa
A1436

Fukui
A1437

Gifu
A1438

Shizuoka
A1439

Aichi
A1440

Mie
A1441

Shiga
A1442

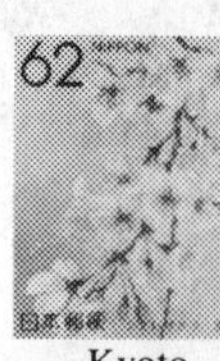

Kyoto
A1443

Osaka
A1444

Hyogo
A1445

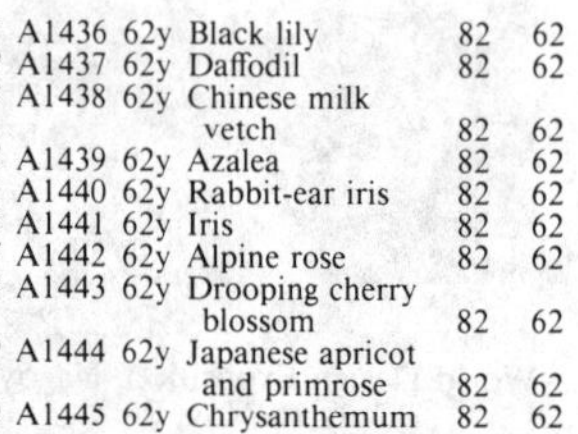

No.	Type	Value	Description	Unused	Used
1881	A1436	62y	Black lily	82	62
1882	A1437	62y	Daffodil	82	62
1883	A1438	62y	Chinese milk vetch	82	62
1884	A1439	62y	Azalea	82	62
1885	A1440	62y	Rabbit-ear iris	82	62
1886	A1441	62y	Iris	82	62
1887	A1442	62y	Alpine rose	82	62
1888	A1443	62y	Drooping cherry blossom	82	62
1889	A1444	62y	Japanese apricot and primrose	82	62
1890	A1445	62y	Chrysanthemum	82	62

Nara
A1446

Wakayama
A1447

Tottori
A1448

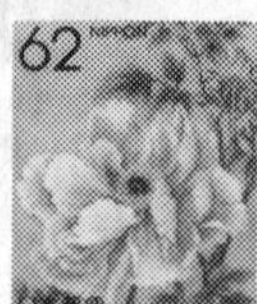

Shimane
A1449

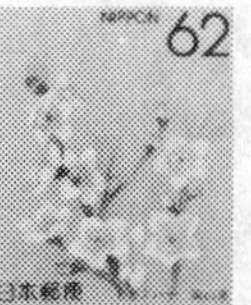

Okayama
A1450

Hiroshima
A1451

Yamaguchi
A1452

Tokushima
A1453

Kagawa
A1454

Ehime
A1455

No.	Type	Value	Description	Unused	Used
1891	A1446	62y	Double cherry blossom	82	62
1892	A1447	62y	Japanese apricot	82	62
1893	A1448	62y	Pear blossom	82	62
1894	A1449	62y	Peony	82	62
1895	A1450	62y	Peach blossom	82	62
1896	A1451	62y	Japanese Mmple	82	62
1897	A1452	62y	Summer orange blossom	82	62
1898	A1453	62y	Sudachi orange blossom	82	62
1899	A1454	62y	Olive blossom	82	62
1900	A1455	62y	Mandarin orange blossom	82	62

Kochi
A1456

Fukuoka
A1457

Saga
A1458

Nagasaki
A1459

Kumamoto
A1460

Oita
A1461

Miyazaki
A1462

Kagoshima
A1463

Okinawa — A1464

1901	A1456	62y	Myrica	82	62
1902	A1457	62y	Japanese apricot	82	62
1903	A1458	62y	Laurel	82	62
1904	A1459	62y	Unzen azalea	82	62
1905	A1460	62y	Autumn bellflower	82	62
1906	A1461	62y	Japanese apricot of bungo	82	62
1907	A1462	62y	Crinum	82	62
1908	A1463	62y	Rosebay	82	62
1909	A1464	62y	Coral tree	82	62
a.			Sheet of 47 + 3 labels, #1863-1909	39.00	

Nos. 1863-1909 were issued in sheets of 20.

Seven Baby Crows (Ibaraki) — A1465

Inns of Tsumago & Magome (Nagano)
A1466 A1467

Mt. Fuji and Tea Picking (Shizuoka) A1468

Two Peaches (Fukushima) A1469

Mt. Sakurajima (Kagoshima) A1470

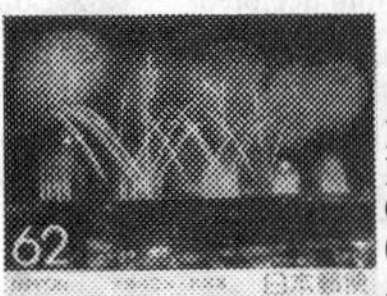
Fireworks Festival of Omagari (Akita) A1471

Travel Expo '90, Nagasaki (Nagasaki) A1472

Tokyo Shin Post Office (Tokyo) A1473

Yasukibushi Folk Song (Shimane) A1474

Ryukyu Dancer (Okinawa) A1475

Litho., Litho. & Engr. (#1911-1912)

1990 ***Perf. 13***

1910	A1465	62y	multicolored	82	62
1911	A1466	62y	blk & buff	82	62
1912	A1467	62y	blk & pale grn	82	62
a.			Pair, #1911-1912	1.65	1.25
1913	A1468	62y	multicolored	82	62
1914	A1469	62y	multicolored	95	72
1915	A1470	62y	multicolored	95	72
1916	A1471	62y	multicolored	95	72
1917	A1472	62y	multicolored	95	72
1918	A1473	62y	multicolored	95	72
1919	A1474	62y	multicolored	95	72
1920	A1475	62y	multicolored	95	72

Issue dates: Nos. 1910-1912, May 1. No. 1913, May 2. No. 1914, June 1. Nos. 1915-1916, July 2. No. 1917, Aug. 1. No. 1918, Aug. 6. Nos. 1919-1920, Aug. 15.

Sheets of 3 + label of Nos. 1910, 1913, 1920 were lottery prizes. Value, each $3.25.

Dancing Girl (Kyoto) A1476

Old Path of Kumano (Wakayama) A1477

45th Natl. Athletic Meet (Fukuoka) A1478

Izu Swamp, Swans (Miyagi) A1479

Spring (Gifu) — A1480

Summer (Gifu) — A1481

Autumn (Gifu) — A1482

Winter (Gifu) — A1483

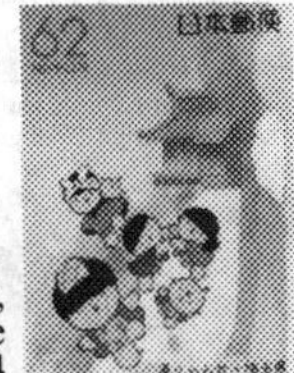
Nursery Rhyme, Toryanse (Saitama) — A1484

Japanese Cranes (Hokkaido) A1485

1990

1921	A1476	62y	multicolored	95	72
1922	A1477	62y	multicolored	95	72
1923	A1478	62y	multicolored	95	72
1924	A1479	62y	multicolored	1.00	75
1925	A1480	62y	multicolored	1.00	75
1926	A1481	62y	multicolored	1.00	75
1927	A1482	62y	multicolored	1.00	75
1928	A1483	62y	multicolored	1.00	75
a.			Strip of 4, #1925-1928	4.00	3.00
1929	A1484	62y	multicolored	1.00	75
1930	A1485	62y	multicolored	1.00	75

Issue dates: Nos. 1921-1923, Sept. 3. No. 1924, Oct. 1. Nos. 1925-1928, Oct. 9. No. 1929, Oct. 12. No. 1930, Oct. 30.

Bizen Ware (Okayama)
A1487 A1488

Battle of Yashima (Kagawa) A1486

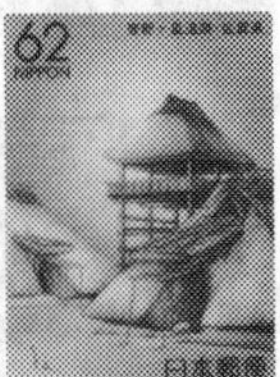
Yoshinogari Ruins (Saga) A1489

Bride Under Cherry Blossoms (Yamanashi) A1490

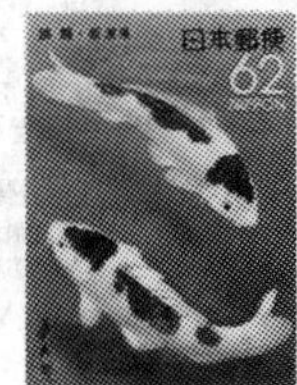
Carp (Niigata) A1491

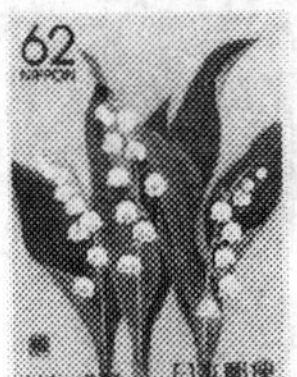
Lily Bell (Hokkaido) A1492

Lilac (Hokkaido) A1493

Day Lily (Hokkaido) A1494

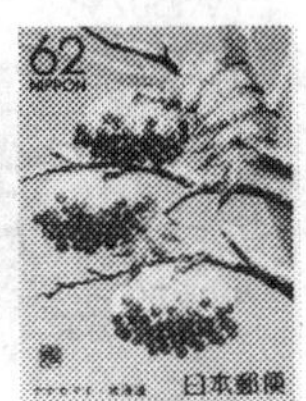
Rowanberry (Hokkaido) A1495

Litho., Photo. (#1934-1935)

1991 ***Perf. 13***

1931	A1486	62y	multicolored	1.00	75
1932	A1487	62y	multicolored	95	70
1933	A1488	62y	multicolored	95	70
a.			Pair, #1932-1933	1.90	1.50
1934	A1489	62y	multicolored	95	70
1935	A1490	62y	multicolored	95	70
1936	A1491	62y	multicolored	95	70
1937	A1492	62y	multicolored	95	70
1938	A1493	62y	multicolored	95	70
1939	A1494	62y	multicolored	95	70
1940	A1495	62y	multicolored	95	70
a.			Strip of 4, #1937-1940	3.80	2.50

Issue dates: No. 1931, Feb. 19. Nos. 1932-1933, Apr. 5. No. 1934, Apr. 12. No. 1935, Apr. 18. No. 1936, May 1. Nos. 1937-1940, May 31.

Nikkou Mountains (Tochigi) A1496

Mt. Iwate by Yaoji Hashimoto (Iwate) A1497

Wooden Puppet (Tokushima) A1498

Whales (Kochi) A1499

Fringed Orchids (Tokyo) A1500

Cape Toi, Horses (Miyazaki) A1501

The only foreign revenue stamps listed in this Catalogue are those authorized for prepayment of postage.

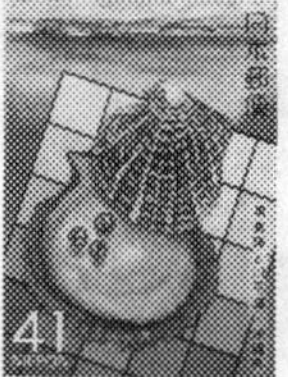

Black Pearls of Kabira Bay (Okinawa)
A1502

Japanese Pears (Tottori)
A1504

Tsujun-kyo Bridge (Kumamoto)
A1503

1991 **Photo.**

1941 A1496 62y multicolored	95	70
1942 A1497 62y multicolored	95	70
a. Booklet pane of 10	9.50	
1943 A1498 62y multicolored	95	70
a. Booklet pane of 10	9.50	
1944 A1499 62y multicolored	95	70
a. Booklet pane of 10	9.50	
1945 A1500 41y multicolored	68	50
a. Booklet pane of 10	15.00	
1946 A1501 62y multicolored	95	70
a. Booklet pane of 10	15.00	
1947 A1502 41y multicolored	68	50
1948 A1503 62y multicolored	95	70
a. Bklt. pane of 10	15.00	
1949 A1504 62y multicolored	95	70

Issue dates: No. 1941, May 29. No. 1942, June 10. Nos. 1943-1944, June 26. Nos. 1945-1946, July 1. Nos. 1947-1948, Aug. 1. No. 1949, Aug. 26.

Ninja, Iga Ueno Castle (Mie)
A1506

46th Natl. Athletic Meet (Ishikawa)
A1505

Eyeglass Industry (Fukui)
A1507

Nursery Rhyme, Tortoise and the Hare — A1508

Kobe City Weathervane (Hyogo) — A1509

Spring (Nara)
A1510

Autumn (Nara) (Gunma)
A1511

Litho., Photo. (#1950, 1952)

1991 ***Perf. 13, 13½ (#1950)***

1950 A1505 41y multicolored	68	50
1951 A1506 62y multicolored	95	70
a. Bklt. pane of 10	14.00	
1952 A1507 62y multicolored	1.00	75
a. Booklet pane of 10	14.00	10.50
1953 A1508 62y multicolored	1.00	75
a. Booklet pane of 10	14.00	
1954 A1509 62y multicolored	1.00	75
a. Booklet pane of 10	14.00	
1955 A1510 62y multicolored	1.00	75
1956 A1511 62y multicolored	1.00	75
a. Pair, #1955-1956	2.00	1.50
b. Bklt. pane of 5 #1956a	14.00	

Issue dates: No. 1950, Sept. 2. No. 1951, Sept. 10. No. 1952, Oct. 1. Nos. 1953-1956, Oct.

This is an expanding set. Format and numbers will change if necessary.

Far East and South Pacific Games for the Disabled (FESPIC), Kobe, Sept. 15-20
A1546

1989, Sept. 14 **Photo.** ***Perf. 13½***

1991 A1546 62y multicolored	88	65

Okuni Kabuki Screen
A1547 A1548

1989, Sept. 18 ***Perf. 13***

1992 A1547 62y multicolored	88	65
1993 A1548 70y multicolored	98	75

EUROPALIA '89, Japan.

A1549

A1550

Scenes from the Yadori and Takekawa Chapters of the Tales of the Genji picture scroll, attributed to Fujiwara-no-Takeyoshi, late Heian Period (897-1185).

1989, Oct. 6 **Photo.** ***Perf. 13½***

1994 A1549 80y multicolored	1.15	88
1995 A1550 120y multicolored	1.70	1.25

Intl. Letter Writing Day.

Intl. Conference on Irrigation and Drainage
A1551

100th Tenno Sho Horse Race
A1552

1989, Oct. 13

1996 A1551 62y Rice	90	68

1989, Oct. 27 ***Perf. 13***

1997 A1552 62y Jockey riding Shinzan	90	68

9th Hot Air Balloon World Championships, Saga — A1553

1989, Nov. 17 **Photo.** ***Perf. 13x13½***

1998 A1553 62y multicolored	88	65

Copyright Control System, 50th Anniv.
A1554

1989, Nov. 17 ***Perf. 13***

1999 A1554 62y Conductor	88	65

New Year 1990 (Year of the Horse)
A1555 A1556

1989, Dec. 1 ***Perf. 13x13½, 13½***

2000 A1555 41y *Yawata-Uma* festival horse	58	42
2001 A1556 62y *Kazari-Uma,* Meiji Period	88	65

No. 2001 was sold through Jan. 10, 1990, serving as a lottery ticket.

Sheets of two containing Nos. 1838, 2000 were lottery prizes. Value, $2.

Electric Locomotives

10,000
A1557

Photo. & Engr., Photo.

1990 ***Perf. 13***

2002 A1557 62y shown	88	65
2003 A1557 62y EF58	88	65
2004 A1557 62y ED40	88	65
2005 A1557 62y EH10	88	65
2006 A1557 62y EF53	88	65
2007 A1557 62y ED70	88	65
2008 A1557 62y EF55	82	62
2009 A1557 62y ED61	82	62
2010 A1557 62y EF57	82	62
2011 A1557 62y EF30	82	62
Nos. 2002-2011 (10)	8.56	6.38

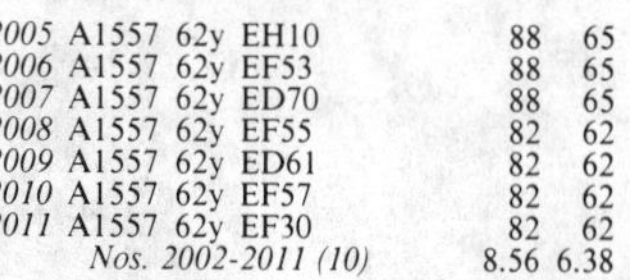

Issued two stamps at a time, the first photo. & engr., the second photo.

Issue dates: Nos. 2002-2003, Jan. 31; Nos. 2004-2005, Feb. 28; Nos. 2006-2007, Apr. 23; Nos. 2008-2009, May 23; Nos. 2010-2011, July 18.

Intl. Garden and Greenery Exposition, Osaka
A1558

1990, Mar. 30 **Photo.** ***Perf. 13***

2021 A1558 62y multicolored	88	65

See No. B45.

Philately Week — A1559

Painting: *Women Gazing at the Stars,* by Chou Ohta.

1990, Apr. 20 **Photo.** ***Perf. 13***

2022 A1559 62y multicolored	88	65
a. Souvenir sheet of 1	88	

Natl. Land Afforestation Campaign
A1560

1990, May 18 **Photo.** ***Perf. 13½***

2023 A1560 62y Azalea, Mt. Unzen	82	62

Flower, Butterfly
A1561

Designs: 70y, Abstract art.

1990, June 1 **Photo.** ***Perf. 13***

2024 A1561 62y multicolored	82	62
2025 A1561 70y multicolored	88	66

Japan-Turkey Relations, Cent. — A1562

1990, June 13

2026 A1562 62y multicolored	82	62

Horses Series

Horse at Stable from Umaya-zu Byobu — A1563

Ponies — A1564

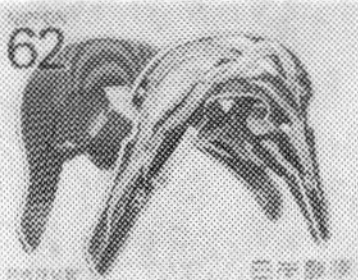

Lacquered Saddle, 16th Cent. — A1565

Lacquered Stirrups, 16th Cent. — A1566

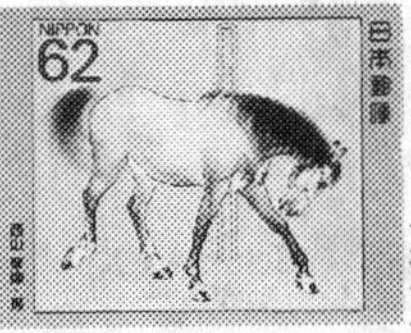

Horse by S. Nishiyama A1567

"Kamo-Kurabeuma-Monyo-Kosode" A1568

Kettei A1569

Postal Carriages
A1569a A1569b

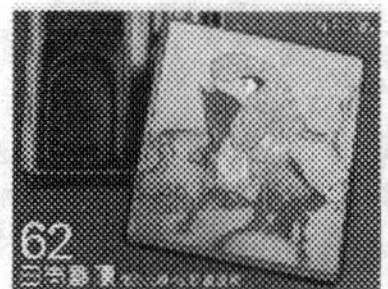

Inkstone Case "Sano-no-Watashi" — A1570

"Bushu-Senju-zu" by Hokusai — A1571

"Shudan" by Kogetsu Saigo A1571a

Designs: Nos. 2027-2031 each show a panel of folding screen with a different horse tied up at a stable.

Perf. 13x13½, 13

1990, June 20 **Litho. & Engr.**

Color of Horse

2027 A1563 62y red brown 82 62
2028 A1563 62y gray 82 62
2029 A1563 62y beige 82 62
2030 A1563 62y tan 82 62
2031 A1563 62y mottled 82 62
a. Strip of 5, #2027-2031 4.10

Photo.

2032 A1564 62y shown 82 62

Photo. & Engr.

2033 A1565 62y shown 82 62
2034 A1566 62y shown 82 62
a. Pair, #2033-2034 1.65 1.25

Photo.

2035 A1567 62y multicolored 82 62
2036 A1568 62y multicolored 82 62
2037 A1569 62y multicolored 82 62

Photo. & Engr., photo. (#2040, 2042)

1991 *Perf. 12½x13*

2038 A1569a 62y multicolored 1.00 75
2039 A1569b 62y multicolored 1.00 75
a. Pair, #2038-2039 2.00 1.50

Perf. 13½x13

2040 A1570 62y multicolored 1.00 75
2041 A1571 62y multicolored 1.00 75
2042 A1571a 62y multicolored 1.00 75
Nos. 2027-2037 (11) 9.02 6.82

Issue dates: Nos. 2038-2040, Jan. 31. Nos. 2041-2042, Feb. 28.

38th Intl. Youth Hostel Fed. Conference A1573

1990, June 25 **Litho.** *Perf. 13*

2057 A1573 62y multicolored 82 62

Letter Writing Day
A1574 A1575

1990, July 23 **Photo.** *Perf. 13½*

2058 A1574 41y multicolored 54 40
2059 A1575 62y multicolored 82 62
a. Souv. sheet of 1 90 70
b. Bklt. pane, 5 each #2058-2059 7.50

See No. 2117.

21st Intl. Congress of Mathematicians — A1576

1990, Aug. 17 **Photo.** *Perf. 13*

2060 A1576 62y multicolored 82 62

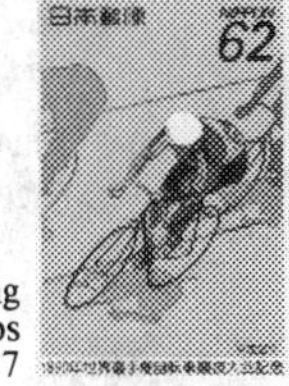

World Cycling Championships A1577

1990, Aug. 20 **Litho.** *Perf. 13½*

2061 A1577 62y multicolored 82 62

Ogai Mori, Educator A1578

1990, Aug. 27 **Photo.**

2062 A1578 62y multicolored 82 62

Intl. Assoc. for Germanic Studies (IVG), 8th Congress.

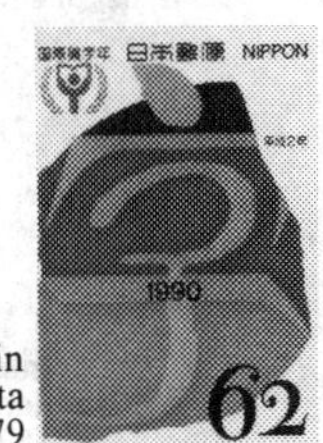

Character "Ji" in Shape of Rosetta Stone — A1579

1990, Sept. 7 *Perf. 13*

2063 A1579 62y multicolored 82 62

Intl. Literacy Year.

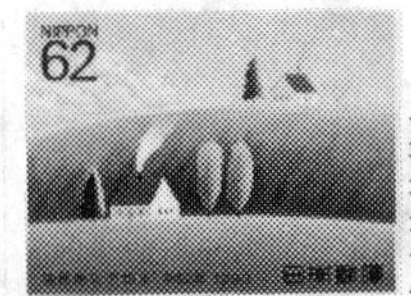

Decade for Natural Disaster Reduction A1580

1990, Sept. 27 **Photo.**

2064 A1580 62y multicolored 82 62

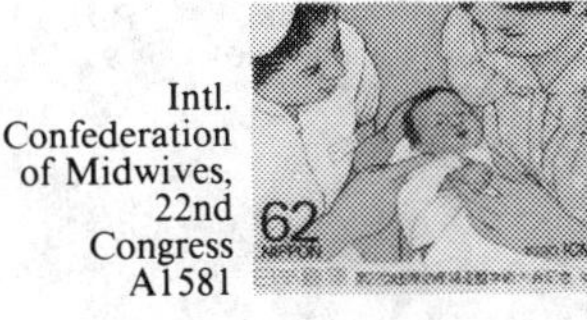

Intl. Confederation of Midwives, 22nd Congress A1581

1990, Oct. 5 **Photo.**

2065 A1581 62y multicolored 90 65

A1582

"Choju-Jinbutsu-Giga" — A1583

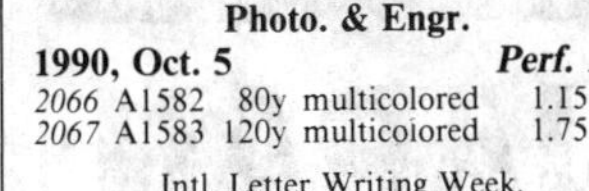

Photo. & Engr.

1990, Oct. 5 *Perf. 13½*

2066 A1582 80y multicolored 1.15 90
2067 A1583 120y multicolored 1.75 1.30

Intl. Letter Writing Week.

"Fumizukai-zu" by Harunobu Suiendo A1584

1990, Oct. 16 **Photo.**

2068 A1584 100y multicolored 1.45 1.10
a. Souv. sheet of 1 1.45 1.10

No. 2068a exists with surcharge which paid admission to PHILANIPPON '91. These were not sold by the post office.

Court System, Cent. — A1585

1990, Nov. 1 **Photo.** *Perf. 13x13½*

2069 A1585 62y "Justice" 90 65

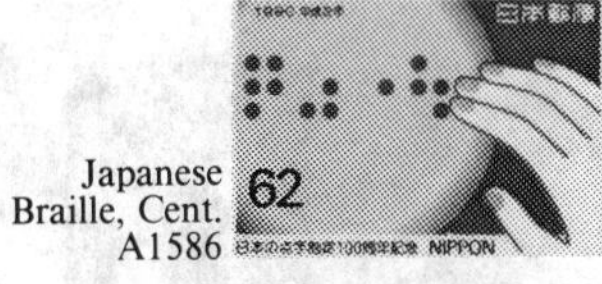

Japanese Braille, Cent. A1586

Photo & Embossed

1990, Nov. 1 *Perf. 13½*

2070 A1586 62y multicolored 90 65

Enthronement of Akihito — A1587

Designs: No. 2071, Chinese phoenix depicted on Emperor's chair. No. 2072, Diamond pattern for costume worn at banquet ceremony.

1990, Nov. 9 **Photo.** *Perf. 13*

2071 A1587 62y multicolored 90 65
2072 A1587 62y multicolored 90 65
a. Souv. sheet of 2, #2071-2072 1.80 1.30

Japanese Diet, Cent. — A1588

1990, Nov. 29 **Litho.**

2073 A1588 62y multicolored 90 65

New Year 1991 (Year of the Sheep)
A1589 A1590

1990, Dec. 3 Photo. *Perf. 13x13½*
2074 A1589 41y multicolored 62 42

Photo. & Engr.
Perf. 13½
2075 A1590 41y multicolored 62 42
2076 A1590 62y multi, diff. 90 65

Sheets of 2 No. 2074 were lottery prizes. Value, $1.50.

Dr. Yoshio Nishina, Physicist
A1591

Telephone Service, Cent.
A1592

1990, Dec. 6 Photo. *Perf. 13*
2077 A1591 62y multicolored 90 65

Use of radio isotopes in Japan, 50th anniv.

1990, Dec. 14
2078 A1592 62y multicolored 90 65

1991 Winter Universiade
A1593

1991, Mar. 1 Photo. *Perf. 13½*
2079 A1593 41y Figure skating 60 45
Perf. 13½x13
2080 A1593 62y Speed skating, horiz. 1.00 75

Postal Life Insurance System — A1594

1991, Apr. 1 Photo. *Perf. 13*
2081 A1594 62y multicolored 95 70

Philately Week
A1595 A1596

Designs: No. 2082, Beauty Looking Back by Moronobu. No. 2083, Opening Dance by Shuho Yamakawa.

1991, Apr. 19
2082 A1595 62y multicolored 95 70
2083 A1596 62y multicolored 95 70
a. Souv. sheet of 2, #2082-2083 1.90 1.50

Postal Service, 120th anniv.
Pairs of Nos. 2082-2083 with label between are available from sheets of 20.

Ceramic World Shigaraki '91 — A1597

1991, Apr. 19 *Perf. 13½*
2084 A1597 62y multicolored 95 70

Natl. Land Afforestation Campaign — A1598

1991, May 24 Photo. *Perf. 13½*
2085 A1598 41y multicolored 65 48

Standard Datum of Leveling, Cent. — A1599

1991, May 30 Photo. *Perf. 13*
2086 A1599 62y mutlicolored 95 70

Flowers — A1600

Couple in Ethnic Dress
A1601

1991, May 31 Photo. *Perf. 13*
2087 A1600 41y shown 62 30
2088 A1601 62y shown 95 70
2089 A1600 70y World peace 1.05 80
2090 A1601 100y Butterfly 1.50 1.15

Intl. Stamp Design Contest winning entries.

Kabuki Series

Kagamijishi
A1602

Yaegakihime
A1603

Koshiro Matsumoto VII
A1604

Baigyoku Nakamura III
A1606

Danjuro Ichikawa XI
A1605

Ganjiro Nakamura II
A1607

Perf. 13 (62y), 13½ (100y)
1991 Photo.
2091 A1602 62y dp bl grn & gold 95 70
2092 A1603 100y multicolored 1.50 1.15
2093 A1604 62y multicolored 1.00 75
2094 A1605 100y multicolored 1.60 1.20
2095 A1606 62y multicolored 1.00 75
2096 A1607 100y multicolored 1.60 1.20
Nos. 2091-2096 (6) 7.65 5.75

Issue dates: #2091-2092, June 28. #2093-2094, Sept. 27. #2095-2096, Nov. 20.

Waterbird Series

Gallinago Hardwickii (Latham's Snipe)
A1614

1991 Photo. *Perf. 13½*
2103 A1614 62y shown 95 70
2104 A1614 62y Sula leucogaster 95 70
2105 A1614 62y Larus crassirostris 1.00 75
2106 A1614 62y Podiceps ruficollis 1.00 75

Nos. 2103-2104 printed in blocks of 12 with gutter between in sheet of 24.
Issue dates: Nos. 2103-2104, June 28. Nos. 2105-2106, Sept. 27.

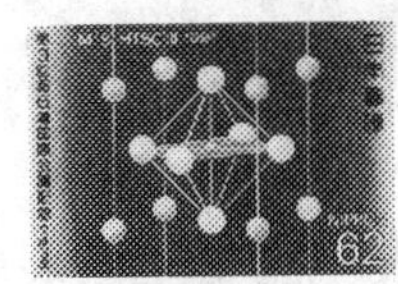

Intl. Conf. on Superconductivity — A1620

1991, July 19 Litho. *Perf. 13½*
2115 A1620 62y multicolored 95 70

Type of Letter Writing Day of 1990 and

A1621

1991, July 23 Photo. *Perf. 13x13½*
2116 A1621 41y multicolored 68 50
2117 A1575 62y multicolored 95 70
a. Souvenir sheet of 1 95 70
b. A1621 Bklt. pane, 5 each #2116-2117 8.00

Nos. 2117, 2117a have light blue frameline and inscription and violet denomination.

3rd IAAF World Track & Field Championships, Tokyo — A1622

1991, Aug. 23 *Perf. 13*
2118 A1622 41y High jump 68 50
2119 A1622 62y Shot put 95 70

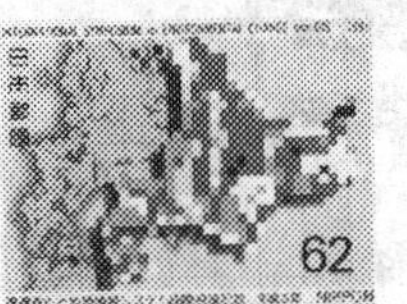

Intl. Symposium on Environmental Change and Geographical Information Systems — A1623

1991, Aug. 23
2120 A1623 62y multicolored 95 70

Intl. Letter Writing Week A1624

Bandainagon-emaki picture scroll probably by Mitsunaga Tokiwa: 80y, Crowd of people. 120y, People, house.

Photo. & Engr.
1991, Oct. 7 *Perf. 13½*
2121 A1624 80y multicolored 1.30 95
2122 A1624 100y multicolored 1.60 1.20

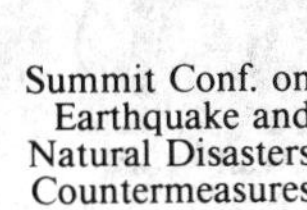

Summit Conf. on Earthquake and Natural Disasters Countermeasures A1625

Design: 62y, Breezy Fine Weather by Hokusai.

1991, Oct. 8 Photo. *Perf. 13*
2123 A1625 62y multicolored 1.00 75

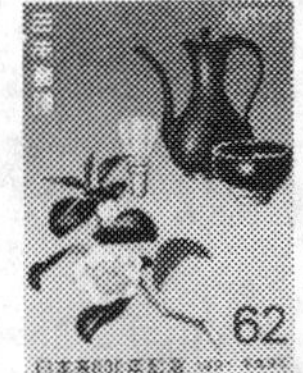

Japanese Green Tea, 800th Anniv. — A1626

1991, Oct. 31 Litho. *Perf. 13*
2124 A1626 62y multicolored 1.00 75

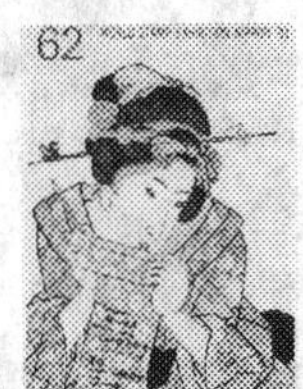

Koshaku-Musume by Kunisada Utagawa — A1627

Photo. & Engr.
1991, Nov. 15 *Perf. 13*
2125 A1627 62y multicolored 1.05 80
a. Sheet of 2 2.10 1.60

World Stamp Exhibition, Nippon '91.

Administrative Counselors System, 30th Anniv. — A1628

1991, Nov. 20 Photo.
2126 A1628 62y multicolored 1.05 80

A1629

A1630

New Year 1992 (Year of the Monkey)
A1631 A1632

1991, Dec. 2 Photo. *Perf. 13½*
2127 A1629 41y multicolored 70 52
2128 A1630 62y multicolored 1.00 75
2129 A1631 41y +3y, multi 75 58
2130 A1632 62y +3y, multi 1.05 80

SEMI-POSTAL STAMPS

Douglas Plane over Japan Alps — SP1

Wmk. Zigzag Lines (141)
1937, June 1 Photo. *Perf. 13*
B1 SP1 2s + 2s rose carmine 1.75 80
B2 SP1 3s + 2s purple 1.75 1.40
B3 SP1 4s + 2s green 2.75 1.15

The surtax was for the Patriotic Aviation Fund to build civil airports.

Nos. 259 and 261 Surcharged in Blue or Red

1942, Feb. 16 Wmk. 257 *Perf. 13*
B4 A84 2s + 1s crim (Bl) 1.00 1.00
B5 A86 4s + 2s dk grn (R) 1.50 1.50

Fall of Singapore to Japanese forces.

Tank Corps Attack, Bataan — SP2

Pearl Harbor under Japanese Attack — SP3

Unwmk.
1942, Dec. 8 Photo. *Perf. 12*
B6 SP2 2s + 1s rose brn 1.50 1.10
B7 SP3 5s + 2s saph 2.00 1.65

1st anniv. of the "Greater East Asia War."

The surtax was for national defense.

Catalogue values for unused stamps in this section, from this point to the end of the section, are for Never Hinged items.

SP4

1947, Nov. 25 Wmk. 257 *Perf. 12½*
B8 SP4 1.20y + 80s dk rose red 1.25 1.00

Japan's 1st Community Chest drive. The surtax was for charitable purposes.

Nurse — SP5

Bird Feeding Young — SP6

1948, Oct. 1 Unwmk. *Perf. 12½*
B9 SP5 5y + 2.50y brt red 8.50 8.50
B10 SP6 5y + 2.50y emer 8.50 8.50

Souvenir Sheet
Wmk. 257
Imperf

B11 SP7 Sheet of 2 40.00 45.00

The surtax on Nos. B9-B11 was divided between the Red Cross and Community Chest organizations.

No. B11 contains Nos. B9-B10, imperf.

Javelin Thrower SP8

Designs: No. B13, Wrestlers. No. B14, Diver. No. B15, Water polo. No. B16, Woman gymnast. No. B17, Judo. No. B18, Fencing. No. B19, Basketball. No. B20, Rowing. No. B21, Sailing. No. B22, Boxing. No. B23, Volleyball. No. B24, Bicyclist. No. B25, Equestrian. No. B26, Field hockey. No. B27, Pistol shooting. No. B28, Modern pentathlon. No. B29, Weight lifter. No. B30, Women's kayak doubles. No. B31, Soccer.

Perf. 13½

1961, Oct. 11 Unwmk. Engr.
B12 SP8 5y + 5y bister 1.00 52
B13 SP8 5y + 5y dk grn 1.00 52
B14 SP8 5y + 5y car 1.00 52
a. Souv. sheet of 3 ('64) 4.50 5.00

1962, June 23
B15 SP8 5y + 5y green 52 28
B16 SP8 5y + 5y dk pur 52 28
B17 SP8 5y + 5y dk car 52 28
a. Souv. sheet of 3 ('64) 3.00 3.50

1962, Oct. 10
B18 SP8 5y + 5y brick red 35 28
B19 SP8 5y + 5y slate grn 35 28
B20 SP8 5y + 5y vio 35 28
a. Souv. sheet of 3 ('64) 2.50 2.75

1963, June 23
B21 SP8 5y + 5y blue 45 28
B22 SP8 5y + 5y dk brn 45 28
B23 SP8 5y + 5y brown 45 28
a. Souv. sheet of 3 ('64) 4.00 4.25

1963, Nov. 11
B24 SP8 5y + 5y dk bl 20 15
B25 SP8 5y + 5y olive 20 15
B26 SP8 5y + 5y blk 20 15
B27 SP8 5y + 5y claret 20 15
a. Souv. sheet of 4 ('64) 4.00 4.25

1964, June 23
B28 SP8 5y + 5y bluish vio 24 15
B29 SP8 5y + 5y dp olive 24 15
B30 SP8 5y + 5y grnsh bl 24 15
B31 SP8 5y + 5y rose claret 24 15
a. Souv. sheet of 4 ('64) 4.00 4.25
Nos. B12-B31 (20) 8.72 5.28

Issued to raise funds for the 1964 Olympic Games in Tokyo.

The souvenir sheets were issued Aug. 20, 1964. Each contains one each of the stamps in the set it follows. Nos. B14a, B20a, B23a and B27a, exist imperf.

Cobalt Treatment Unit SP9

Early Cancer Detection with X-rays SP10

1966, Oct. 21 Photo. *Perf. 13*
B32 SP9 7y + 3y yel org & blk 22 15
B33 SP10 15y + 5y multi 42 20

9th Intl. Anticancer Congress, Tokyo, Oct. 23-29. The surtax was for the fight against cancer and for research.

EXPO '70 Emblem and Globe — SP11

Cherry Blossoms, Screen, Chishakuin Temple — SP12

1969, Mar. 15 Photo. *Perf. 13*
B34 SP11 15y + 5y bl, ocher & ver 80 80
B35 SP12 50y + 10y gold, brn & grn 1.50 1.50

Issued to publicize EXPO '70, International Exhibition, Osaka, 1970.

Ice Hockey, Sapporo Olympic Emblem SP13

Design: No. B37, Ski jump and Sapporo Olympic Games emblem (vert.).

1971, Feb. 6 Photo. *Perf. 13*
B36 SP13 15y + 5y multi 35 15
B37 SP13 15y + 5y multi 35 15

To promote the 11th Winter Olympic Games, Sapporo, Japan, 1972.

Blue Dragon, East Wall — SP14

Murals from ancient tomb mound: No. B39, Two men, east wall (vert.). 50y+10y, Four women, west wall (vert.).

1973, Mar. 26 Photo. *Perf. 13*
Size: 48x27mm, 27x48mm
B38 SP14 20y + 5y multi 35 15
B39 SP14 20y + 5y multi 35 15

Photogravure and Engraved
Size: 33x48mm
B40 SP14 50y + 10y multi 75 25

Surtax was for restoration work on the murals of the Takamatsu-zuka tomb mound, discovered in March, 1972, and excavated in Nara Prefecture.

Reefs, by Hyakusui Hirafuku — SP15

1974, Mar. 2 Photo. *Perf. 13*
B41 SP15 20y + 5y multi 30 15

The surtax was for the International Ocean Exposition, Okinawa, 1975.

Intl. Year of the Disabled — SP16

Photogravure and Embossed
1981, Sept. 1 *Perf. 13½*
B42 SP16 60y + 10y multi 1.00 20

Surtax was for education of the disabled.

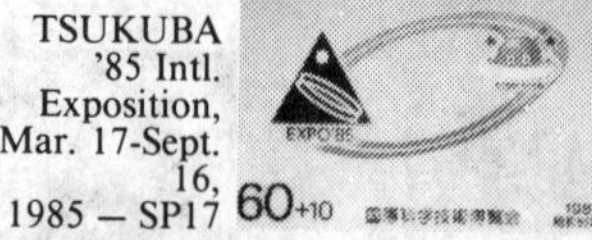
TSUKUBA '85 Intl. Exposition, Mar. 17-Sept. 16, 1985 — SP17

1984, Feb. 19 Photo. *Perf. 13½*
B43 SP17 60y + 10y multi 1.10 45

Intl. Garden and Greenery Exposition, Osaka — SP18

1989, June 1 Photo. *Perf. 13*
B44 SP18 62y +10y multi 1.10 82

Surtax for the preparation and management of the exposition.

Intl. Garden and Greenery Exposition, Osaka — SP19

1990, Mar. 30
B45 SP19 41y +4y multi 60 45

11th World Congress of the World Federation of the Deaf — SP20

1991, July 5 Photo. *Perf. 13*
B46 SP20 62y +10y multi 1.20 90

AIR POST STAMPS

Regular Issue of 1914 Overprinted in Red or Blue

Wmk. Zigzag Lines (141)
1919, Oct. 3 *Perf. 13x13½*
Granite Paper
C1 A34 1½s blue (R) 250.00 85.00
C2 A34 3s rose (Bl) 450.00 250.00

Excellent counterfeits exist.

Passenger Plane over Lake Ashi — AP1

1929-34 Engr. *Perf. 13½x13*
Granite Paper
C3 AP1 8½s org brn 22.50 13.50
C4 AP1 9½s rose ('34) 6.75 3.50
C5 AP1 16½s yel grn 7.75 4.25
C6 AP1 18s ultra 8.25 3.50
C7 AP1 33s gray 16.00 3.00
Nos. C3-C7 (5) 61.25 27.75

Souvenir Sheet
C8 AP1 Sheet of 4, #C4-C7 900.00 1,200.

Issue dates: 9½s, Mar. 1, 1929; No. C8, Apr. 20, 1934; others, Oct. 6, 1929. No. C8 for Communications Commemoration Day (1st observance of establishment of the postal service and issuance of Nos. 1-4). Sold only at Phil. Exhib. p.o., Tokyo, Apr. 20-27. Size: 110x100mm.

Catalogue values for unused stamps in this section, from this point to the end of the section, are for Never Hinged items.

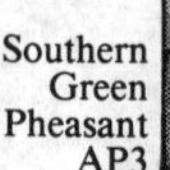

Southern Green Pheasant AP3

Perf. 13x13½
1950, Jan. 10 Engr. Unwmk.
C9 AP3 16y gray 14.00 5.50
C10 AP3 34y brn vio 35.00 10.00
C11 AP3 59y carmine 50.00 8.00

C12 AP3 103y org yel 37.50 14.00
C13 AP3 144y olive 42.50 14.00
Nos. C9-C13 (5) 179.00 51.50

Pagoda and Plane — AP4

Plane and Mt. Tsurugi-dake — AP5

1951-52 **Photo.**
C14 AP4 15y purple 2.50 2.75
C15 AP4 20y blue 22.50 90
C16 AP4 25y yel grn 20.00 32
C17 AP4 30y brn red 15.00 32
C18 AP4 40y gray blk 5.75 40
C19 AP5 55y brt bl 150.00 42.50
C20 AP5 75y brnsh red 110.00 17.00
C21 AP5 80y magenta 17.50 3.00
C22 AP5 85y black 12.00 6.00
C23 AP5 125y ol bis 12.00 3.50
C24 AP5 160y Prus grn 25.00 4.25
Nos. C14-C24 (11) 392.25 80.94

Issue dates: 25y, 30y, Dec. 20. 15y, 20y, 40y, Sept. 1. 55y-160y, Feb. 11, 1952.

Redrawn; Underlined Zeros Omitted

1952-62
C25 AP4 15y pur ('62) 95 60
C26 AP4 20y blue 30.00 70
C27 AP4 25y yel grn ('53) 60 15
C28 AP4 30y brn red 3.75 15
C29 AP4 40y gray blk ('53) 2.50 15
C30 AP5 55y brt bl 37.50 4.00
C32 AP5 75y brnsh red 77.50 10.00
C33 AP5 80y magenta 60.00 4.00
C34 AP5 85y black 3.00 1.40
C36 AP5 125y ol bis 4.75 1.50
C38 AP5 160y Prus grn 19.00 2.00
Nos. C25-C38 (11) 239.55 24.65

See No. C43.

Great Buddha of Kamakura — AP6

1953, Aug. 15 ***Perf. 13½***
C39 AP6 70y red brn 3.00 15
C40 AP6 80y blue 4.50 15
C41 AP6 115y olive grn 2.75 40
C42 AP6 145y Prus grn 11.00 1.40

Coil Stamp
Redrawn Type of 1952-62

1961, Oct. 2 ***Perf. 13 Horiz.***
C43 AP4 30y brn red 30.00 22.50

MILITARY STAMPS

Nos. 98, 119, 131 Overprinted

事

1910-14 Unwmk. ***Perf. 11½ to 13½***
M1 A26 3s rose 175.00 35.00
M2 A34 3s rose ('13) 250.00 160.00

Wmk. 141

M3 A34 3s rose ('14) 30.00 17.50

Nos. M1-M3 overprint type I has 3.85mm between characters; type II, 4-4.5mm (movable type).

1921 On Offices in China No. 37
M4 A34 3s rose *6,000. 5,000.*

No. M4 is a provisional military stamp issued at the Japanese Post Office, Tsingtao, China. The overprint differs from the illustration, being 12mm high with thicker characters. Counterfeits are plentiful.

Overprint 16mm High

1924 **On No. 131**
M5 A34 3s rose 80.00 70.00
a. 3s rose (#131b) 85.00 75.00

Excellent forgeries exist of Nos. M1-M5.

JAPANESE OFFICES ABROAD

Offices in China

Regular Issues of Japan Overprinted in Red or Black 支那

Perf. 11½, 12, 12½, 13½, 13x13½

1900-06 **Unwmk.**
1 A26 5r gray (R) 3.50 3.25
2 A26 ½s gray (R) ('01) 2.00 85
3 A26 1s lt red brn (R) 2.00 85
4 A26 1½s ultra 9.00 2.50
5 A26 1½s vio ('06) 5.00 1.15
6 A26 2s lt grn (R) 5.00 85
7 A26 3s vio brn 5.50 85
8 A26 3s rose ('06) 4.00 60
9 A26 4s rose 4.50 1.50
10 A26 5s org yel (R) 9.00 1.50
11 A27 6s mar ('06) 16.00 12.00
12 A27 8s ol grn (R) 8.00 7.00
13 A27 10s dp bl 8.00 70
14 A27 15s purple 18.50 1.50
15 A27 20s red org 16.50 70
16 A28 25s bl grn (R) 35.00 4.00
17 A28 50s red brn 37.50 2.25
18 A29 1y carmine 55.00 2.25
Nos. 1-18 (18) 244.00 44.30

No. 6 with black overprint is bogus.

1900
19 A30 3s carmine 25.00 16.00

Wedding of Crown Prince Yoshihito and Princess Sadako.

1908
20 A33 5y green 375.00 40.00
21 A33 10y dk vio 700.00 100.00

On #20-21 the space between characters of the overprint is 6½mm instead of 1½mm.

1913 ***Perf. 12, 12x13, 13x13½***
22 A34 ½s brown 14.00 14.00
23 A34 1s orange 15.00 15.00
24 A34 1½s lt bl 40.00 17.50
a. Bklt. pane of 6 350.00
25 A34 2s green 45.00 20.00
26 A34 3s rose 22.50 7.50
a. Bklt. pane of 6 350.00
27 A35 4s red 60.00 60.00
28 A35 5s violet 60.00 45.00
29 A35 10s dp bl 60.00 18.00
30 A35 20s claret 240.00 130.00
31 A35 25s ol grn 90.00 20.00
32 A36 1y yel grn & mar 750.00 500.00
Nos. 22-32 (11) 1,396. 847.00

1914-21 **Wmk. 141**

Granite Paper

33 A34 ½s brown 2.50 85
34 A34 1s orange 2.75 85
35 A34 1½s blue 3.00 85
a. Booklet pane of 6 250.00
36 A34 2s green 2.00 1.00
a. Booklet pane of 6 250.00
37 A34 3s rose 1.75 85
a. Booklet pane of 6 250.00
38 A35 4s red 7.50 5.00
a. Booklet pane of 6 250.00
39 A35 5s violet 14.00 1.85
40 A35 6s brn ('20) 25.00 20.00
41 A35 8s gray ('20) 28.50 22.50
42 A35 10s dp bl 10.00 1.40
a. Booklet pane of 6
43 A35 20s claret 32.50 3.50
44 A35 25s ol grn 40.00 3.75
45 A36 30s org brn ('20) 70.00 30.00
46 A36 50s dk brn ('20) 75.00 35.00
47 A36 1y yel grn & mar ('18) 110.00 7.00
48 A33 5y green 1,200. 500.00
49 A33 10y vio ('21) 1,800. 1,100.
Nos. 33-49 (17) 3,424. 1,734.

On Nos. 48-49 the space between characters of overprint is 4½mm, instead of 6½mm on Nos. 20-21 and 1½mm on all lower values. See No. M4.

Counterfeit overprints exist of Nos. 1-49.

Offices in Korea

Regular Issue of Japan Overprinted in Red or Black 朝鮮

1900 Unwmk. ***Perf. 11½, 12, 12½***
1 A26 5r gray (R) 17.50 10.00
2 A26 1s lt red brn (R) 18.50 5.50
3 A26 1½ ultra 225.00 160.00
4 A26 2s lt grn (R) 17.50 11.00
5 A26 3s vio brn 15.00 5.00
6 A26 4s rose 57.50 30.00
7 A26 5s org yel (R) 60.00 30.00
8 A27 8s ol grn (R) 225.00 160.00
9 A27 10s dp bl 30.00 10.00
10 A27 15s purple 75.00 6.50
11 A27 20s red org 75.00 5.50
12 A28 25s bl grn (R) 200.00 60.00
13 A28 50s red brn 150.00 20.00
14 A29 1y carmine 425.00 15.00
Nos. 1-14 (14) 1,591. 528.50

1900
15 A30 3s carmine 85.00 35.00

Wedding of Crown Prince Yoshihito and Princess Sadako. 1-15.

Counterfeit overprints exist of Nos. 1-15.

Taiwan (Formosa)

Numeral of Value and Imperial Crest — A1

1945 Unwmk. Litho. ***Imperf.***
1 A1 3s carmine 25.00 25.00
2 A1 5s blue green 20.00 20.00
3 A1 10s pale blue 30.00 30.00

Additional values, prepared, but not issued, were: 30s, 40s, 50s, 1y, 5y and 10y. The entire set of nine was overprinted by Chinese authorities after World War II and issued for use in Taiwan.

For overprints see China-Taiwan Nos. 1-7.

JORDAN

Trans-Jordan

LOCATION — In the Near East, separated from the Mediterranean Sea by Israel
GOVT. — Kingdom
AREA — 38,400 sq. mi.
POP. — 3,750,000 (est. 1982)
CAPITAL — Amman

The former Turkish territory was mandated to Great Britain following World War I. It became an independent state in 1946.

10 Milliemes = 1 Piaster
1000 Mils = 1 Palestine Pound (1930)
1000 Fils = 1 Jordan Dinar (1951)

Catalogue values for unused stamps in this country are for Never Hinged items, beginning with Scott 221 in the regular postage section, Scott C1 in the air post section, Scott J47 in the postage due section, Scott RA1 in the postal tax section, Scott N1 in the occupation section, Scott NJ1 in the occupation postage due section, and Scott NRA1 in the occupation postal tax section.

Watermarks

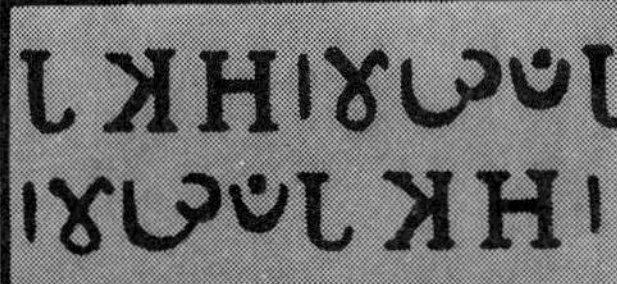
Wmk. 305 - Roman and Arabic Initials

Wmk. 328 - UAR

British Mandate

Stamps and Type of Palestine 1918 Overprinted in Black or Silver

شرقي الاردن

Perf. 14, 15x14

1920, Nov. **Wmk. 33**
1 A1 1m dark brown 15 28
a. Inverted overprint 87.50 87.50
b. Perf. 15x14 25 38
c. As "b," inverted overprint 75.00 65.00
2 A1 2m blue green 15 20
a. Perf. 15x14 1.90 2.25
3 A1 3m light brown 20 30
a. Perf. 14 2.75 3.25
4 A1 4m scarlet 30 38
a. Perf. 14 5.00 6.25
5 A1 5m orange 30 25
a. Perf. 15x14 50 65
6 A1 1pi dark blue (S) 35 45
a. Perf. 15x14
7 A1 2pi olive green 90 90
a. Perf. 15x14 1.10 1.25
8 A1 5pi plum 1.00 2.00
a. Perf. 15x14 7.50 10.00
9 A1 9pi bister 2.50 3.50
a. Perf. 15x14 875.00 875.00
10 A1 10pi ultramarine 2.75 5.00
11 A1 20pi gray 4.25 6.25
Nos. 1-11 (11) 12.85 19.51

The overprint reads "Sharqi al-ardan" (East of Jordan).

For overprints, see Nos. 12-63, 83A.

Stamps of 1920 Issue Handstamp Surcharged "Ashir el qirsh" (tenth of piaster) and numeral in Black, Red or Violet

عشر القرش ١

1922
12 A1 1/10pi on 1m dk brn 17.50 20.00
13 A1 1/10pi on 1m dk brn (R) 67.50 67.50
13A A1 1/10pi on 1m dk brn (V) 67.50 67.50
14 A1 2/10pi on 2m bl grn 17.50 20.00
a. 3/10pi on 2m bl grn (error) 75.00 75.00
15 A1 2/10pi on 2m bl grn (R) 75.00 60.00
16 A1 2/10pi on 2m bl grn (V) 75.00 75.00
17 A1 3/10pi on 3m lt brn 6.25 6.25

17A A1 3/10pi on 3m lt brn (V) 165.00 165.00
18 A1 4/10pi on 4m scar 32.50 35.00
19 A1 5/10pi on 5m org 100.00 87.50
c. Perf. 15x14 140.00 140.00
19A A1 5/10pi on 5m dp org (R) 225.00
19B A1 5/10pi on 5m org (V) 250.00

For overprint, see No. 83B.

Handstamp Surcharged "El qirsh" (piaster) and numeral in Black, Red or Violet

20 A1 1pi dk bl (R) 87.50 42.50
20A A1 1pi dk bl (V) 180.00 175.00
21 A1 2pi ol grn (Bk) 150.00 22.50
22 A1 2pi ol grn (R) 150.00 42.50
22A A1 2pi ol grn (V) 165.00 55.00
23 A1 5pi plum (Bk) 30.00 32.50
23A A1 5pi plum (V) *250.00*
24 A1 9pi bister (Bk) 150.00 145.00
25 A1 9pi bister (R) 60.00 62.50
a. Perf. 14 175.00 175.00
26 A1 10pi ultra (Bk) 750.00 750.00
27 A1 20pi gray (Bk) 600.00 600.00
27A A1 20pi gray (V) 625.00 625.00

Same Surcharge in Black on Palestine Nos. 13-14

28 A1 10pi on 10pi ultra *1,900.*
29 A1 20pi on 20pi gray *1,900.*

For overprints, see Nos. 86, 88, 94, 97, 98.

Stamps of 1920 Handstamped in Violet, Black or Red

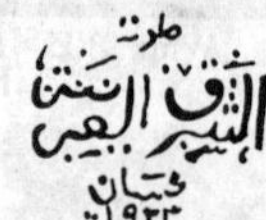

1922, Dec. ***Perf. 15x14, 14***

30 A1 1m dk brn (V) 15.00 15.00
31 A1 1m dk brn (Bk) 15.00 15.00
32 A1 1m dk brn (R) 6.00 6.00
33 A1 2m bl grn (V) 3.00 3.00
34 A1 2m bl grn (Bk) 4.50 4.50
35 A1 2m bl grn (R) 15.00 15.00
36 A1 3m lt brn (V) 3.75 3.75
37 A1 3m lt brn (Bk) 4.50 4.50
38 A1 3m lt brn (R) 17.50 17.50
39 A1 4m scar (V) 32.50 32.50
39A A1 4m scar (Bk) 32.50 32.50
40 A1 4m scar (R) 32.50 32.50
41 A1 5m orange (V) 8.25 8.25
42 A1 5m orange (R) 22.50 19.00
a. Perf. 14 225.00 55.00
43 A1 1pi dk blue (V) 8.25 8.25
44 A1 1pi dk blue (R) 14.00 14.00
45 A1 2pi ol grn (V) 14.00 11.50
a. Perf. 14 47.50 47.50
46 A1 2pi ol grn (Bk) 7.50 7.50
47 A1 2pi ol grn (R) 40.00 40.00
48 A1 5pi plum (V) 37.50 37.50
a. Perf. 14 67.50 67.50
49 A1 5pi plum (R) 60.00 60.00
50 A1 9pi bister (V) 150.00 150.00
50A A1 9pi bister (Bk) 45.00 45.00
50B A1 9pi bister (R) 225.00 225.00
51 A1 10pi ultra (V) 950.00 950.00
51A A1 10pi ultra (R) *1,750. 1,750.*
52 A1 20pi gray (V) 950.00 950.00
52A A1 20pi gray (R) *2,000. 2,000.*

The overprint reads "Hukumat al Sharqi al Arabia" (Arab Government of the East) and date, 1923. The surcharges or overprints on Nos. 12 to 52A inclusive are handstamped and, as usual, are found inverted and double.

Ink pads of several colors were in use at the same time and the surcharges and overprints frequently show a mixture of two colors.

For overprints, see Nos. 84, 87, 89, 92-93, 95-96.

Stamps of 1920 Overprinted in Gold

حكومة الشرق
العربية
نيسان سنة ٩٢١

1923, Mar. 1 ***Perf. 14, 15x14***

53 A1 1m dark brn (G) 8.75 10.00
a. Perf. 15x14 1,000. 1,000.
54 A1 2m blue grn (G) 10.00 15.00
a. Double overprint 200.00
b. Inverted overprint 200.00
55 A1 3m lt brn (G) 6.00 7.00
a. Black overprint 50.00 50.00
56 A1 4m scarlet (Bk) 6.00 6.00
57 A1 5m orange (Bk) 6.00 6.00
a. Perf. 15x14 25.00 25.00
58 A1 1pi dk blue (G) 6.00 6.00
a. Double overprint 300.00 300.00
b. Black overprint *300.00 300.00*
59 A1 2pi ol grn (G) 7.50 7.50
a. Black overprint 200.00
b. Overprint on back 175.00
60 A1 5pi plum (G) 27.50 30.00
a. Inverted overprint 225.00 175.00
b. "922" for "921"
61 A1 9pi bister (Bk) 32.50 40.00
a. Perf. 15x14 *200.00 200.00*
62 A1 10pi ultra (G) 40.00 42.50
63 A1 20pi gray (G) 40.00 42.50
a. Inverted overprint 300.00
b. Double overprint 350.00
c. Double ovpt., one inverted 450.00

The overprint reads "Hukumat al Sharqi al Arabia, Nissan Sanat 921" (Arab Government of the East, April, 1921).

For overprints, see Nos. 85, 99, 100, 102.

Stamps of Hejaz, 1922, Overprinted in Black

Coat of Arms (Hejaz A7)

حكومة
الشرق العربية
٩ شعبان ١٣٤١

1923, Apr. **Unwmk.** ***Perf. 11½***

64 A7 ⅛pi orange brn 1.40 1.50
a. Double overprint 100.00
65 A7 ½pi red 1.40 50
a. Inverted overprint 100.00
66 A7 1pi dark blue 28 28
a. Inverted overprint 105.00
67 A7 1½pi violet 45 50
a. Double overprint 125.00
68 A7 2pi orange 45 50
a. Inverted overprint
b. Pair, one without overprint
69 A7 3pi olive brn 1.10 1.40
a. Inverted overprint 125.00
b. Double overprint 150.00
c. Pair, one without overprint *300.00*
70 A7 5pi olive green 1.90 2.25
Nos. 64-70 (7) 6.98 6.93

The overprint is similar to that on the preceding group but is differently arranged. There are numerous varieties in the Arabic letters.

For overprints, see Nos. 71-72, 91, J1-J5.

With Additional Surcharge of New Value in Arabic:

71 A7(a) ¼pi on ⅛pi 2.50 2.75
a. Inverted surcharge 175.00
72 A7(b) 10pi on 5pi 5.00 6.25

Independence Issue

Palestine Stamps and Type of 1918 Overprinted Vertically in Black or Gold

1923, May **Wmk. 33** ***Perf. 15x14***

73 A1 1m dark brn (Bk) 7.00 8.00
a. Double ovpt., one reversed 425.00 425.00
73B A1 1m dark brn (G) 225.00 225.00
c. Double ovpt., one reversed 625.00 625.00
74 A1 2m blue grn 22.50 24.50
75 A1 3m lt brown 5.00 5.50
76 A1 4m scarlet 5.00 5.50
77 A1 5m orange 37.50 40.00
78 A1 1pi dk blue (G) 37.50 40.00
a. Double overprint *550.00 550.00*
79 A1 2pi olive grn 37.50 40.00
80 A1 5pi plum (G) 37.50 40.00
a. Double overprint *360.00*
81 A1 9pi bis, perf. 14 37.50 40.00
82 A1 10pi ultra, perf. 14 37.50 40.00
83 A1 20pi gray 37.50 40.00

The overprint reads, "Arab Government of the East (abbreviated), Souvenir of Independence, 25th, May, 1923 ('923')".

There were printed 480 complete sets and a larger number of the 1, 2, 3 and 4m. A large number of these sets were distributed to high officials. The overprint was in a setting of twenty-four and the error "933" instead of "923" occurs once in the setting.

The overprint exists reading downward on all values, as illustrated, and reading upward on all except the 5m and 2pi.

Forged overprints exist.

For overprint, see No. 101.

Stamps of Preceding Issues, Handstamp Surcharged

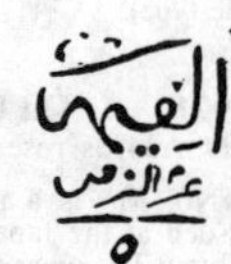

83A A1 2½/10pi on 5m dp org 175.00 190.00
83B A1 5/10pi on 3m (#17) *8,000.*
84 A1 5/10pi on 3m (#36) 20.00 20.00
85 A1 5/10pi on 3m (#55) 8.75 8.75
86 A1 5/10pi on 5pi (#23) 42.50 42.50
87 A1 5/10pi on 5pi (#48) 4.00 4.00
88 A1 1pi on 5pi (#23) 42.50 42.50
89 A1 1pi on 5pi (#48) *1,500.*

Same Surcharge on Palestine Stamp of 1918

90 A1 5/10pi on 3m lt brn *6,500.*

As is usual with handstamped surcharges these are found double, inverted, etc.

No. 67 Surcharged by Handstamp

نصف قرش

Unwmk. ***Perf. 11½***

91 A7 ½pi on 1½pi vio 3.50 3.75
a. Surcharge typographed 30.00 32.50

The surcharge reads: "Nusf el qirsh" (half piastre). See note after No. 90.

Stamps of Preceding Issues Surcharged by Handstamp

Perf. 14, 15x14

1923, Nov. **Wmk. 33**

92 A1 ½pi on 2pi (#45) 45.00 45.00
93 A1 ½pi on 2pi (#47) 87.50 87.50
94 A1 ½pi on 5pi (#23) 27.50 27.50
95 A1 ½pi on 5pi (#48) 2,250. 2,000.
96 A1 ½pi on 5pi (#49) 1,800. 1,750.
97 A1 ½pi on 9pi (#24) *6,500.*
98 A1 ½pi on 9pi (#25) 87.50 87.50
99 A1 ½pi on 9pi (#61) 165.00 165.00

Surcharged by Handstamp

100 A1 1pi on 10pi (#62) *2,000. 2,000.*
101 A1 1pi on 10pi (#82) *3,000. 3,000.*
102 A1 2pi on 20pi (#63) 22.50 24.00

Of the 25 copies made of No. 100, a few were handstamped in violet.

Stamp of Hejaz, 1922, Overprinted by Handstamp

1923, Dec. **Unwmk.** ***Perf. 11½***

103 A7 ½pi red 3.00 3.25

Stamp of Hejaz, 1922, Overprinted

1924

104 A7 ½pi red 3.25 3.75

King Hussein Issue

Stamps of Hejaz, 1922, Overprinted

1924

Gold Overprint

105 A7 ½pi red 1.25 1.25
106 A7 1pi dark blue 1.75 1.75
107 A7 1½pi violet 1.50 1.50
108 A7 2pi orange 2.00 2.00

Black Overprint

109 A7 ½pi red 65 65
110 A7 1pi dark blue 75 75
111 A7 1½pi violet 90 90
112 A7 2pi orange 1.00 1.00
Nos. 105-112 (8) 9.80 9.80

The overprint reads: "Arab Government of the East. In commemoration of the visit of H. M. the King of the Arabs, 11 Jemad el Than i 1342 (17th Jan. 1924)." The overprint was in a setting of thirty-six and the error "432" instead of "342" occurs once in the setting and is found on all values.

Stamps of Hejaz, 1922-24, Overprinted in Black or Red

Coat of Arms (Hejaz A8)

حكومة الشرق
العربي
١٣٤٢

1924

113 A7 ⅛pi red brown 20 15
114 A7 ¼pi yellow green 15 15
a. Tete beche pair 2.00 2.00
115 A7 ½pi red 15 15
116 A7 1pi dark blue 2.50 2.50
117 A7 1½pi violet 1.40 1.40
118 A7 2pi orange 75 75
119 A7 3pi red brown 50 50
120 A7 5pi olive green 75 75
121 A8 10pi vio & dk brn (R) 1.10 1.40
a. Pair, one without overprint
Nos. 113-121 (9) 7.50 7.75

The overprint reads: "Hukumat al Sharqi al Arabia, 1342." (Arab Government of the East, 1924).

Stamps of Hejaz, 1925, Overprinted in Black or Red

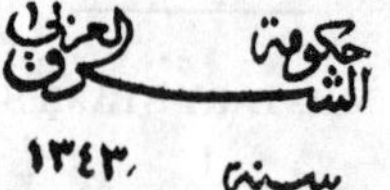

(Hejaz A9)

(Hejaz A10)

(Hejaz A11)

1925, Aug.

122	A9	1/8pi	chocolate	15	15
123	A9	1/4pi	ultramarine	15	15
124	A9	1/2pi	carmine rose	15	15
125	A10	1pi	yellow green	15	15
126	A10	1 1/2pi	orange	20	20
127	A10	2pi	deep blue	25	25
128	A11	3pi	dark green (R)	38	38
129	A11	5pi	orange brn	75	75
			Nos. 122-129 (8)	2.18	2.18

The overprint reads: "Hukumat al Sharqi al Arabi. 1343 Sanat." (Arab Government of the East, 1925). Nos. 122-129 exist imperforate, and with overprint inverted or double.

Type of Palestine, 1918, Overprinted in Black

شرق الاردن

1925, Nov. 1 Wmk. 4 *Perf. 14*

130	A1	1m	dark brown	15	15
131	A1	2m	yellow	15	15
132	A1	3m	Prussian bl	15	15
133	A1	4m	rose	15	15
134	A1	5m	orange	15	15
135	A1	6m	blue green	15	15
136	A1	7m	yel brown	15	15
137	A1	8m	red	20	20
138	A1	1pi	gray	28	16
139	A1	13m	ultramarine	28	30
140	A1	2pi	olive green	40	48
141	A1	5pi	plum	85	1.00
142	A1	9pi	bister	3.25	2.75
143	A1	10pi	light blue	2.75	2.00
144	A1	20pi	violet	6.50	5.50
			Nos. 130-144 (15)	15.56	13.44

This overprint reads: "Sharqi al-ardan" (East of Jordan).

For overprints, see Nos. J12-J23.

Perf. 15x14

142a	A1	9pi	600.00	400.00
143a	A1	10pi	50.00	55.00
144a	A1	20pi	825.00	500.00

Amir Abdullah ibn Hussein
A1 A2

1927-29 Engr. *Perf. 14*

145	A1	2(m)	Prus blue	15	15
146	A1	3(m)	rose	15	15
147	A1	4(m)	green	25	22
148	A1	5(m)	orange	15	15
149	A1	10(m)	red	15	18
150	A1	15(m)	ultra	30	15
151	A1	20(m)	olive grn	50	65
152	A2	50(m)	claret	1.00	1.10
153	A2	90(m)	bister	3.00	3.00
154	A2	100(m)	lt blue	3.00	2.25
155	A2	200(m)	violet	6.50	5.00
156	A2	500(m)	dp brn ('29)	30.00	20.00
157	A2	1000(m)	gray ('29)	75.00	10.00
			Nos. 145-157 (13)	120.15	43.00

For overprints, see Nos. 158-168, B1-B12, J24-J29.

Stamps of 1927 Overprinted in Black

1928, Sept. 1

158	A1	2(m)	Prus blue	25	25
159	A1	3(m)	rose	25	25
160	A1	4(m)	green	28	28
161	A1	5(m)	orange	15	15
162	A1	10(m)	red	30	30
163	A1	15(m)	ultra	1.00	65
164	A1	20(m)	olive grn	2.00	2.00
165	A2	50(m)	claret	3.75	3.75
166	A2	90(m)	bister	7.50	7.50
167	A2	100(m)	lt blue	10.00	10.00
168	A2	200(m)	violet	25.00	25.00
			Nos. 158-168 (11)	50.48	50.13

The overprint is the Arabic word "Dastour," meaning "Constitution." The stamps were in commemoration of the enactment of the law setting forth the Constitution.

A3

"MILS" or "L. P." at lower right and Arabic equivalents at upper left.

1930-36 Engr. *Perf. 14*

Size: 17 1/4x21mm

169	A3	1m	red brn ('34)	15	15
170	A3	2m	Prus blue	15	15
171	A3	3m	rose	15	15
172	A3	3m	green ('34)	42	15
173	A3	4m	green	15	15
174	A3	4m	rose ('34)	55	15
175	A3	5m	orange	15	15
a.			Perf. 13 1/2x14 (coil) ('36)	2.00	55
176	A3	10m	red	15	15
177	A3	15m	ultra	25	16
a.			Perf. 13 1/2x14 (coil) ('36)	2.00	70
178	A3	20m	olive grn	38	15

Size: 19 1/4x23 1/2mm

179	A3	50m	red violet	38	32
180	A3	90m	bister	55	50
181	A3	100m	light blue	1.10	1.00
182	A3	200m	violet	1.90	1.50
183	A3	500m	deep brown	8.75	4.00
184	A3	£1	gray	20.00	7.50
			Nos. 169-184 (16)	35.18	16.33

See Nos. 199-220, 230-235. For overprint, see No. N15a.

1939 *Perf. 13 1/2x13*

Size: 17 1/4x21mm

169a	A3	1m	red brown	25	15
170a	A3	2m	Prussian bl	25	15
172a	A3	3m	green	65	25
174a	A3	4m	rose	3.00	2.50
175b	A3	5m	orange	5.00	35
176a	A3	10m	red	20.00	1.00
177b	A3	15m	ultramarine	65	30
178a	A3	20m	olive green	9.00	3.00
			Nos. 169a-178a (8)	38.80	7.70

For overprint, see No. N3a.

Mushetta — A4

Nymphaeum, Jerash — A5

Kasr Kharana — A6

Kerak Castle — A7

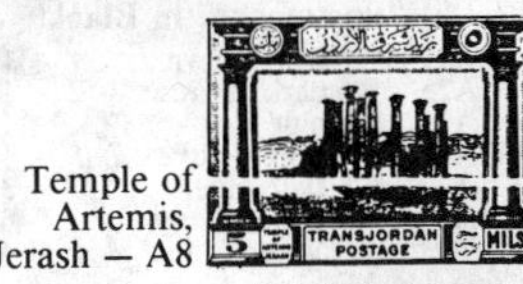

Temple of Artemis, Jerash — A8

Aijalon Castle — A9

Khazneh, Rock-hewn Temple, Petra — A10

Allenby Bridge, River Jordan — A11

Amir Abdullah ibn Hussein — A13

Ancient Threshing Floor — A12

1933, Feb. 1 *Perf. 12*

185	A4	1m	dk brn & blk	22	28
186	A5	2m	claret & blk	30	32
187	A6	3m	blue green	55	42
188	A7	4m	bister & blk	55	50
189	A8	5m	orange & blk	55	52
190	A9	10m	brown red	70	65
191	A10	15m	dull blue	1.50	85
192	A11	20m	ol grn & blk	1.75	1.00
193	A12	50m	brn vio & blk	3.00	2.25
194	A6	90m	yel & black	4.75	3.50
195	A8	100m	blue & blk	5.75	4.25
196	A9	200m	dk vio & blk	26.00	30.00
197	A10	500m	brn & ver	70.00	72.50
198	A13	£1	green & blk	325.00	350.00
			Nos. 185-198 (14)	440.62	467.04

Nos. 194-197 are larger than the lower values in the same designs.

Amir Abdullah ibn Hussein — A14

Perf. 13x13 1/2

1942, May 18 Litho. Unwmk.

199	A14	1m	dull red brn	15	15
200	A14	2m	dull green	15	15
201	A14	3m	dp yel green	18	15
202	A14	4m	rose pink	26	15
203	A14	5m	orange yel	30	18
204	A14	10m	dull ver	45	30
205	A14	15m	deep blue	60	30
206	A14	20m	dull ol grn	1.00	75
			Nos. 199-206 (8)	3.09	2.13

Type A14 differs from A3 in the redrawn inscription above the head and in the form of the "millieme" character at upper left.

For overprint, see No. N1.

Abdullah Type of 1930-39
White Paper

1943-44 Engr. Wmk. 4 *Perf. 12*

Size: 17 3/4x21 1/2mm

207	A3	1m	red brown	15	15
208	A3	2m	Prussian grn	15	15
209	A3	3m	blue green	15	15
210	A3	4m	deep rose	15	15
211	A3	5m	orange	15	15
212	A3	10m	scarlet	15	15
213	A3	15m	blue	15	15
214	A3	20m	olive ('44)	18	15

Size: 20x24mm

215	A3	50m	red lil ('44)	22	20
216	A3	90m	ocher	50	50
217	A3	100m	dp bl ('44)	75	42
218	A3	200m	dk vio ('44)	1.50	1.00
219	A3	500m	dk brn ('44)	5.00	1.75
220	A3	£1	black ('44)	12.50	2.50
			Nos. 207-220 (14)	21.70	7.57

See Nos. 230-235. For overprints, see Nos. 255-256, 259, 264-269, RA23, N2-N4, N7, N12-N17.

Catalogue values for unused stamps in this section, from this point to the end of the section, are for Never Hinged items.

Independent Kingdom

Symbols of Peace and Liberty — A15

Perf. 11 1/2

1946, May 25 Unwmk. Litho.

221	A15	1m	sepia	15	15
222	A15	2m	yel orange	15	15
223	A15	3m	dl ol grn	15	15
224	A15	4m	lt violet	15	15
225	A15	10m	orange brn	15	15
226	A15	12m	rose red	15	15
227	A15	20m	dark blue	15	15
228	A15	50m	ultra	55	45
229	A15	200m	green	1.00	1.00
			Set value	2.15	2.00

Independence of the Kingdom of Trans-Jordan.

Nos. 221 to 229 exist imperforate.

Abdullah Type of 1930-39

1947 Wmk. 4 Engr. *Perf. 12*

230	A3	3m	rose carmine	15	15
231	A3	4m	deep yel green	15	15
232	A3	10m	violet	15	15
233	A3	12m	deep rose	65	65
234	A3	15m	dull olive grn	16	16
235	A3	20m	deep blue	20	20
			Set value	1.20	1.20

For overprints, see Nos. 257-258, 260-263, RA24-RA25, N5-N6, N8-N11.

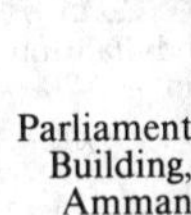

Parliament Building, Amman A16

1947, Nov. 1 Engr. Unwmk.

236	A16	1m	purple	15	15
237	A16	3m	red orange	15	15
238	A16	4m	yel green	15	15
239	A16	10m	dk vio brn	15	15
240	A16	12m	carmine	15	15
241	A16	20m	deep blue	15	15
242	A16	50m	red vio	20	20
243	A16	100m	rose	35	35
244	A16	200m	dark green	75	75
			Set value	1.70	1.70

Founding of the new Trans-Jordan parliament, 1947.

Nos. 236 to 244 exist imperforate.

Symbols of the UPU A17

King Abdullah ibn Hussein A18

1949, Aug. 1 Wmk. 4 *Perf. 13*

245	A17	1m	brown	15	15
246	A17	4m	green	15	15
247	A17	10m	red	15	15
248	A17	20m	ultramarine	16	16
249	A18	50m	dull green	28	28
			Set value	64	62

75th anniv. of the UPU. For overprints, see Nos. N18-N22.

Nos. 207-208, 211, 215-220, 230-235 Surcharged in Carmine, Black or Green

FILS

1952 **Wmk. 4** ***Perf. 12***

Size: 17¾x21½mm

255 A3 1f on 1m red brn (Bk) 15 15
256 A3 2f on 2m Prus grn 15 15
257 A3 3f on 3m rose car (Bk) 15 15
258 A3 4f on 4m dp yel grn 20 15
259 A3 5f on 5m org (G) 65 20
260 A3 10f on 10m vio 48 48
261 A3 12f on 12m dp rose (Bk) 48 48
262 A3 15f on 15m dl ol grn 52 30
263 A3 20f on 20m dp bl 75 45

Size: 20x24mm

264 A3 50f on 50m red lil (G) 1.10 65
265 A3 90f on 90m ocher (G) 5.75 5.50
266 A3 100f on 100m dp bl 3.50 1.10
267 A3 200f on 200m dk vio 4.75 1.00
268 A3 500f on 500m dk brn 10.00 2.75
269 A3 1d on £1 black 21.00 4.75
Nos. 255-269 (15) 49.63 18.26

This surcharge also exists on Nos. 199-203, 205, 209-210, 212-214. Numerous inverted, double and wrong color surcharges exist.

Relief Map — A19

Amir Abdullah ibn Hussein — A20

Perf. 13½x13

1952, Apr. 1 **Engr.** **Wmk. 4**

270 A19 1f red brn & yel grn 15 15
271 A19 2f dk bl grn & red 15 15
272 A19 3f car & gray blk 15 15
273 A19 4f green & orange 15 15
274 A19 5f choc & rose vio 15 15
275 A19 10f violet & brown 15 15
276 A19 20f dark bl & blk 20 20
277 A19 100f dp blue & brn 1.10 80
278 A19 200f purple & orange 1.40 1.40
Nos. 270-278 (9) 3.60 3.30

Unity of Jordan, Apr. 24, 1950.
For overprints, see Nos. 297-305.

1952 **Wmk. 4** ***Perf. 11½***

279 A20 5f orange 15 15
280 A20 10f violet 15 15
281 A20 12f carmine 35 35
282 A20 15f olive 15 15
283 A20 20f deep blue 20 15

Size: 20x24½mm

Perf. 12x12½

284 A20 50f plum 48 48
285 A20 90f brn orange 1.40 1.10
286 A20 100f deep blue 1.10 52
Nos. 279-286 (8) 3.98 3.05

Nos. RA5-RA7 Overprinted in Black or Carmine

Perf. 11½x12½

1953 **Unwmk.** **Engr.**

286A PT1 10m carmine 27.50 27.50
286B PT1 15m gray (C) 2.75 1.25
286C PT1 20m dark brown 35.00 35.00

Same Overprint on Nos. NRA4-NRA7

286D PT1 5m plum 35.00 35.00
286E PT1 10m carmine 35.00 35.00
286F PT1 15m gray (C) 35.00 35.00
286G PT1 20m dk brn (C) 35.00 35.00

In addition a few sheets of Nos. RA9, NRA1, NRA3, NRA8-NRA9 and RA37-RA41 have been reported with this overprint. It is doubtful whether they were regularly issued. See Nos. 344-347.

Same Overprint on Nos. RA28 to RA31 in Black or Carmine

1953 **Wmk. 4** ***Perf. 11½x12½***

287 PT1 5f plum 15 15
288 PT1 10f carmine 18 18
289 PT1 15f gray (C) 35 25
290 PT1 20f dark brown (C) 55 40

King Hussein A21

Unwmk.

1953, Oct. 1 **Engr.** ***Perf. 12***

Portrait in Black

291 A21 1f dark green 15 15
292 A21 4f deep plum 15 15
293 A21 15f deep ultra 20 15
294 A21 20f dark purple 24 15
295 A21 50f dark blue grn 75 35
296 A21 100f dark blue 1.10 70
Nos. 291-296 (6) 2.59
Set value 1.40

Accession of King Hussein, May 2, 1953.

Nos. 270 to 278 Overprinted in Black with Two Bars Through Center Inscription

1953 **Wmk. 4** ***Perf. 13½x13***

297 A19 1f red brn & yel grn 15 15
298 A19 2f dk bl grn & red 15 15
299 A19 3f car & gray blk 15 15
300 A19 4f green & orange 15 15
301 A19 5f choc & rose vio 18 18
302 A19 10f violet & brown 45 20
303 A19 20f dark bl & blk 45 38
304 A19 100f dp blue & brn 2.00 1.00
305 A19 200f purple & org 3.75 1.65
Nos. 297-305 (9) 7.43 4.01

Two main settings of the bars exist on Nos. 297-300 and 304—the "normal" 1½mm spacing, and the "narrow" ½mm spacing.

El Deir Temple, Petra — A22

Dome of the Rock — A23

Designs: 2f, 4f, 500f, 1d, King Hussein. 3f, 5f, Treasury Bldg., Petra. 12f, 50f, 100f, 200f, Al Aqsa Mosque. 20f, as 10f.

1954 **Unwmk.** **Engr.** ***Perf. 12½***

306 A22 1f dk bl grn & red brn 15 15
307 A22 2f red & black 15 15
308 A22 3f dp plum & vio bl 15 15
309 A22 4f org brn & dk grn 15 15
310 A22 5f vio & dk grn 1.25 15
311 A23 10f pur & dk grn 25 15
312 A23 12f car rose & sep 60 40
313 A23 20f dp bl & dk grn 25 15
314 A23 50f dk bl & dp rose 2.25 2.25
315 A23 100f dk grn & dp bl 1.10 45
316 A23 200f dp cl & pck bl 3.50 75
317 A22 500f choc & purple 9.00 4.50
318 A22 1d dk ol grn & rose brn 17.50 10.00
Nos. 306-318 (13) 36.30 19.40

See Nos. 324-337. For overprint, see No. 425.

Globe — A23a

Perf. 13½x13

1955, Jan. 1 **Photo.** **Wmk. 195**

319 A23a 15f green 15 15
320 A23a 20f violet 15 15
321 A23a 25f yellow brown 18 15
Set value 35

Founding of the APU, July 1, 1954.

Princess Dina Abdul Hamid and King Hussein — A24

1955, Apr. 19 ***Perf. 11x11½***

322 A24 15f ultramarine 18 15
323 A24 100f rose brown 75 75

Marriage of King Hussein and Princess Dina Abdul Hamid.

Types of 1954

Design: 15f, Dome of the Rock.

Wmk. 305

1955-64 **Engr.** ***Perf. 12½***

324 A22 1f dk bl grn & red brn ('57) 15 15
325 A22 2f red & blk ('57) 15 15
326 A22 3f dp plum & vio bl ('56) 15 15
327 A22 4f org brn & dk grn ('56) 15 15
328 A22 5f vio & dk grn ('56) 15 15
329 A23 10f pur & grn ('57) 15 15
330 A23 12f car rose & sep 15 15
331 A23 15f dp brn & rose red 15 15
332 A23 20f dp bl & dk grn ('57) 15 15
333 A23 50f dk bl & dp rose 30 18
334 A23 100f dk grn & dp bl ('62) 60 35
335 A23 200f dp cl & pck bl ('65) 2.00 50
336 A22 500f choc & pur ('65) 7.50 3.00
337 A22 1d dk ol grn & rose brn ('65) 20.00 4.00
Nos. 324-337 (14) 31.75 9.38

Envelope A25

Wmk. 305

1956, Jan. 15 **Engr.** ***Perf. 14***

"Postmarks" in Black

338 A25 1f light brown 15 15
339 A25 4f dark car rose 15 15
340 A25 15f blue 15 15
341 A25 20f yellow olive 15 15
342 A25 50f slate blue 38 20
343 A25 100f vermilion 65 38
Set value 1.40 90

1st Arab Postal Congress in Amman.

Nos. RA1, RA3, RA8 and RA33 Overprinted in Carmine or Black

Perf. 11½x12½

1956, Jan. 5 **Unwmk.**

344 PT1 1m ultramarine 15 15
345 PT1 3m emerald 15 15
346 PT1 50m purple 30 18

Wmk. 4

347 PT1 100f orange (Bk) 1.00 55
Set value 1.40 80

Numerous inverted, double and wrong color surcharges exist.

Torch of Liberty — A26

King Hussein — A27

1958 **Wmk. 305** **Engr.** ***Perf. 12½***

348 A26 5f blue & red brown 15 15
349 A26 15f bister brn & blk 15 15
350 A26 35f blue grn & plum 20 16
351 A26 45f car & olive grn 28 20
Set value 65 55

10th anniv. of the Universal Declaration of Human Rights.

Perf. 12x11½

1959 **Wmk. 305** **Engr.**

Centers in Black

352 A27 1f deep green 15 15
353 A27 2f violet 15 15
354 A27 3f deep carmine 15 15
355 A27 4f brown black 15 15
356 A27 7f dark green 15 15
357 A27 12f deep carmine 15 15
358 A27 15f dark red 15 15
359 A27 21f green 32 28
360 A27 25f ocher 20 15
361 A27 35f dark blue 20 15
362 A27 40f olive green 28 15
363 A27 50f red 35 16
364 A27 100f blue green 80 20
365 A27 200f rose lake 1.20 40
366 A27 500f gray blue 3.00 1.40
367 A27 1d dark purple 7.25 3.50
Nos. 352-367 (16) 14.65 7.44

For overprints, see Nos. 423-424, 425a, 426-427.

Arab League Center, Cairo, and King Hussein A28

Perf. 13x13½

1960, Mar. 22 **Photo.** **Wmk. 328**

368 A28 15f dull green & blk 15 15

Opening of the Arab League Center and the Arab Postal Museum in Cairo.

World Refugee Year Emblem A29

Wmk. 305

1960, Apr. 7 **Litho.** ***Perf. 13½***

369 A29 15f pale blue & red 16 15
370 A29 35f bister & blue 26 26

World Refugee Year, July 1, 1959-June 30, 1960.
For overprints, see Nos. 377-378.

Shah of Iran, King Hussein and Flags A30

Perf. 13x13½

1960, May 15 Wmk. 305

Flags in Green, Red & Black

371	A30	15f yellow & black	15	15
372	A30	35f blue & black	18	15
373	A30	50f salmon & black	26	15
		Set value		34

Visit of Mohammed Riza Pahlavi, Shah of Iran, to Jordan, Nov. 2, 1959.

Oil Refinery, Zarka A31

1961, May 1 Engr. *Perf. 14x13*

374	A31	15f dull vio & blue	15	15
375	A31	35f dl vio & brick red	20	15
		Set value		21

Opening of oil refinery at Zarka.

Urban and Nomad Families and Chart A32

Perf. 13x13½

1961, Oct. 15 Photo. Unwmk.

376	A32	15f org brown	20	15

First Jordanian census, 1961.

Nos. 369-370 Overprinted in English and Arabic, "In Memorial of Dag Hammarskjoeld 1904-1961," and Laurel Leaf Border

1961 Wmk. 305 Litho. *Perf. 13½*

377	A29	15f pale bl & red	2.75	1.40
378	A29	35f bister & blue	2.75	1.40

Issued in memory of Dag Hammarskjold, Secretary General of the United Nations, 1953-1961.

Malaria Eradication Emblem — A33

Perf. 11x11½

1962, Apr. 15 Unwmk.

379	A33	15f bright pink	15	15
380	A33	35f blue	22	22

WHO drive to eradicate malaria. A souvenir sheet exists with one each of Nos. 379-380. Value $2.

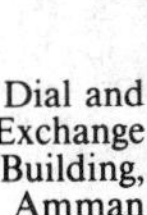

Dial and Exchange Building, Amman A34

1962, Dec. 11 Engr. Wmk. 305

381	A34	15f blue & lilac	15	15
382	A34	35f lilac & emer	22	22

Telephone automation in Amman (in 1960).

Opening of the Port of 'Aqaba A35

1962, Dec. 11

383	A35	15f lil & blk	16	16
384	A35	35f vio bl & blk	25	25
a.		Souvenir sheet of 2, #383-384	75	75

No. 384a imperf., same value.

Dag Hammarskjold and UN Headquarters, NY — A36

Perf. 14x14½

1963, Jan. 24 Photo. Unwmk.

385	A36	15f ultra, ol grn & brn red	20	16
386	A36	35f ol, brn red & ultra	42	40
387	A36	50f brn red, ol & ultra	65	65

17th anniv. of the UN and in memory of Dag Hammarskjold, Secretary General of the UN, 1953-61. An imperf. souvenir sheet contains one each of Nos. 385-387 with simulated perforations. Value $5.

Imperforates
Starting with No. 385, imperforates exist of many Jordanian stamps.

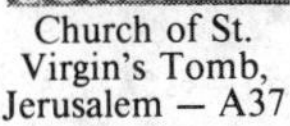

Church of St. Virgin's Tomb, Jerusalem — A37

Arab League Building, Cairo — A38

Designs: No. 389, Basilica of the Agony, Gethsemane. No. 390, Church of the Holy Sepulcher, Jerusalem. No. 391, Church of the Nativity, Bethlehem. No. 392, Haram el-Khalil (tomb of Abraham), Hebron. No. 393, Dome of the Rock, Jerusalem. No. 394, Mosque of Omar el-Khatab, Jerusalem. No. 395, Al Aqsa Mosque, Jerusalem.

1963, Feb. 5 *Perf. 14½x14*

Center Multicolored

388	A37	50f blue	45	38
389	A37	50f dull red	45	38
390	A37	50f bright blue	45	38
391	A37	50f olive green	45	38
a.		Vert. strip of 4, #388-391	1.90	
392	A37	50f gray	60	38
393	A37	50f purple	60	38
394	A37	50f dull red	60	38
395	A37	50f light purple	60	38
a.		Vert. strip of 4, #392-395	2.50	
		Nos. 388-395 (8)	4.20	3.04

Nos. 388-391 and 392-395 printed in sheets of 16 (4x4), each design in a horizontal row of 4 stamps.

1963, July 16 Photo. *Perf. 13½x13*

396	A38	15f slate blue	15	15
397	A38	35f orange red	22	15
		Set value		20

Arab League.

Wheat and UN Emblem — A39

Perf. 11½x12½

1963, Sept. Litho. Wmk. 305

398	A39	15f lt bl, grn & black	15	15
399	A39	35f lt grn, grn & blk	18	15
a.		Souv. sheet of 2, #398-399	75	75
		Set value		24

FAO "Freedom from Hunger" campaign. No. 399a imperf., same value.

East Ghor Canal, Pylon, Gear Wheel and Wheat A40

1963, Sept. 20 *Perf. 14½x14*

400	A40	1f dull yel & black	15	15
401	A40	4f blue & black	15	15
402	A40	5f lilac & black	15	15
403	A40	10f brt yel grn & blk	15	15
404	A40	35f orange & black	15	15
		Set value	35	32

East Ghor Canal Project.

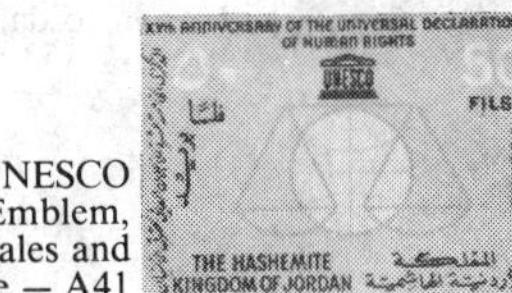

UNESCO Emblem, Scales and Globe — A41

Perf. 13½x13

1963, Dec. 10 Unwmk.

405	A41	50f pale vio bl & red	32	32
406	A41	50f rose red & blue	32	32

15th anniv. of the Universal Declaration of Human Rights.

Red Crescent and King Hussein — A42

1963, Dec. 24 Photo. *Perf. 14x14½*

407	A42	1f red & red lilac	15	15
408	A42	2f red & bl green	15	15
409	A42	3f red & dk blue	15	15
410	A42	4f red & dk green	15	15
411	A42	5f red & dk brown	15	15
412	A42	85f red & dp green	95	95

Design: Red Cross at right, no portrait

413	A42	1f red lilac & red	15	15
414	A42	2f blue grn & red	15	15
415	A42	3f dk blue & red	15	15
416	A42	4f dk green & red	15	15
417	A42	5f dk brown & red	15	15
418	A42	85f dp green & red	3.75	3.75
		Set value, #407-418	5.00	5.00

Centenary of the Intl. Red Cross. Two 100f imperf. souvenir sheets, red and red lilac, exist in the Red Crescent and Red Cross designs. Value $15.

Hussein ibn Ali and King Hussein A43

Perf. 11x11½

1963, Dec. 25 Litho. Unwmk.

419	A43	15f yellow & multi	15	15
420	A43	25f multicolored	16	15
421	A43	35f brt pink & multi	35	28
422	A43	50f lt blue & multi	50	50

Arab Renaissance Day, June 10, 1916. Perf. and imperf. souvenir sheets exist containing one each of Nos. 419-422. Value for both, $3.

Nos. 359, 312, 357 and 361 Surcharged

1 Fils ١ فلس

Wmk. 305, Unwmk.

Perf. 12x11½, 12½

1963, Dec. 16 Engr.

423	A27	1f on 21f grn & blk	15	15
424	A27	2f on 21f grn & blk	15	*1.00*
425	A23	4f on 12f car rose & sepia	15	15
a.		4f on 12f dp car & blk (#357)	6.50	5.00
426	A27	5f on 21f grn & blk	16	15
427	A27	25f on 35f dk bl & blk	35	15
		Set value	75	

Pope Paul VI, King Hussein and Al Aqsa Mosque, Jerusalem — A44

Portraits and: 35f, Dome of the Rock. 50f, Church of the Holy Sepulcher. 80f, Church of the Nativity, Bethlehem.

1964, Jan. 4 Litho. *Perf. 13x13½*

428	A44	15f emerald & blk	15	15
429	A44	35f car rose & blk	25	25
430	A44	50f brown & black	45	45
431	A44	80f vio bl & blk	75	75

Visit of Pope Paul VI to the Holy Land, Jan. 4-6. An imperf. souvenir sheet contains 4 stamps similar to Nos. 428-431. Value $3.

A45

Crown Prince Abdullah ben Al-Hussein — A46

Design: 5f, Crown Prince standing (vert.).

1964, Mar. 30 Photo. *Perf. 14*

432	A46	5f multicolored	15	15
433	A45	10f multicolored	15	15
434	A46	35f multicolored	25	25
		Set value	35	35

2nd birthday of Crown Prince Abdullah ben Al-Hussein (b. Jan. 30, 1962).

A47

Mercury Astronauts, Spacecraft — A48

Designs: b, M. Scott Carpenter. c, Entering space. d, Alan Shepard. e, At launch pad. f, Virgil Grissom. g, After separation. h, Walter Schirra. i, Lift-off. j, John Glenn. Stamp has point down on b, d, f, h, j.

1964, Mar. 25 Photo. *Perf. 14*

435	A47	20f Block of 10, #435a-435j	5.00	5.00

Imperf

Size: 111x80mm

436	A48	100f multicolored	6.50	6.50

Table Tennis A49

Designs: 1f, 2, 3f, 5f vertical.

Perf. 14½x14, 14x14½

1964, June 1 Litho. Unwmk.

446	A49	1f Basketball	15	15
447	A49	2f Volleyball	15	15
448	A49	3f Soccer	15	15
449	A49	4f shown	15	15
450	A49	5f Running	15	15
451	A49	35f Bicycling	70	70
452	A49	50f Fencing	1.00	1.00
453	A49	100f High jump	1.75	1.75
		Nos. 446-453 (8)	4.20	4.20

1964 Olympic Games, Tokyo, Oct. 10-25. An imperf. 200f greenish blue souvenir sheet in design of 100f exists. Value $6.

Mother and Child — A50

1964, June 1 Wmk. 305 *Perf. 14*

454	A50	5f multicolored	15	15
455	A50	10f multicolored	15	15
456	A50	25f multicolored	16	15
		Set value	28	20

Social Studies Seminar, fourth session.

Pres. John F. Kennedy — A51

1964, July 15 Unwmk.

457	A51	1f brt violet	15	15
458	A51	2f carmine rose	15	15
459	A51	3f ultramarine	15	15
460	A51	4f orange brn	15	15
461	A51	5f bright green	15	15
462	A51	85f rose red	2.50	2.50
		Set value	2.75	2.75

President John F. Kennedy (1917-1963). An imperf. 100f brown souvenir sheet exists. Size of stamp: 58x83mm. Value $5.

Ramses II — A52

Perf. 14½x14

1964, July Litho. Wmk. 305

463	A52	4f lt blue & dark brn	15	15
464	A52	15f yellow & violet	15	15
465	A52	25f lt yel grn & dk red	15	15
		Set value	28	22

UNESCO world campaign to save historic monuments in Nubia.

King Hussein and Map of Jordan and Israel — A53

1964, Sept. 5 Unwmk. *Perf. 12*

466	A53	10f multicolored	15	15
467	A53	15f multicolored	15	15
468	A53	25f multicolored	16	15
469	A53	50f multicolored	35	26
470	A53	80f multicolored	50	45
		Set value	1.15	90

Council of the Heads of State of the Arab League (Arab Summit Conference), Cairo, Jan. 13, 1964. An imperf. souvenir sheet contains Nos. 466-470 with simulated perforations. Value $1.

Pope Paul VI, King Hussein and Patriarch Athenagoras; Church of St. Savior, Church of the Holy Sepulcher and Dome of the Rock — A54

1964, Aug. 17 Litho.

471	A54	10f dk grn, sep & org	15	15
472	A54	15f claret, sep & org	15	15
473	A54	25f choc, sepia & org	20	18
474	A54	50f blue, sepia & org	42	38
475	A54	80f brt grn, sep & org	60	52
		Nos. 471-475 (5)	1.52	1.38

Meeting between Pope Paul VI and Patriarch Athenagoras of the Greek Orthodox Church in Jerusalem, Jan. 5, 1964. An imperf. souvenir sheet contains Nos. 471-475 with simulated perforations. Value $3.

A two-line bilingual overprint, "Papa Paulus VI World Peace Visit to United Nations 1965", was applied to Nos. 471-475 and the souvenir sheet. These overprints were issued Apr. 27, 1966.

Pagoda, Olympic Torch and Emblem — A55

1964, Nov. 21 Litho. *Perf. 14*

476	A55	1f dark red	15	15
477	A55	2f bright vio	15	15
478	A55	3f blue green	15	15
479	A55	4f brown	15	15
480	A55	5f henna brown	15	15
481	A55	35f indigo	45	45
482	A55	50f olive	65	65
483	A55	100f violet bl	1.40	1.40
		Set value	2.75	2.75

18th Olympic Games, Tokyo, Oct. 10-25. An imperf. 100f carmine rose souvenir sheet exists. Size of stamp: 82mm at the base. Value $7.

Scouts Crossing Stream on Log Bridge — A56

Designs: 2f, First aid. 3f, Calisthenics. 4f, Instruction in knot tying. 5f, Outdoor cooking. 35f, Sailing. 50f, Campfire.

1964, Dec. 7 Unwmk.

484	A56	1f brown	25	15
485	A56	2f bright vio	25	15
486	A56	3f ocher	25	15
487	A56	4f maroon	25	15
488	A56	5f yel green	25	15
489	A56	35f bright blue	1.00	1.00
490	A56	50f dk slate grn	1.75	1.50
		Nos. 484-490 (7)	4.00	3.25

Jordanian Boy Scouts. An imperf. 100f dark blue souvenir sheet in campfire design exists. Size of stamp: 104mm at the base. Value $8.

Yuri A. Gagarin — A57

Russian Cosmonauts: No. 492, Gherman Titov. No. 493, Andrian G. Nikolayev. No. 494, Pavel R. Popovich. No. 495, Valeri Bykovski. No. 496, Valentina Tereshkova.

1965, Jan. 20 Litho. *Perf. 14*

491	A57	40f sepia & vio bl	40	40
492	A57	40f pink & dk grn	40	40
493	A57	40f lt bl & vio blk	40	40
494	A57	40f olive & dk vio	40	40
495	A57	40f lt grn & red brn	40	40
496	A57	40f chlky bl & blk	40	40
		Nos. 491-496 (6)	2.40	2.40

Issued to honor Russian cosmonauts. A blue 100f souvenir sheet exists showing portraits of the 6 astronauts and space-ship circling globe. This sheet received later an additional overprint honoring the space flight of Komarov, Feoktistov and Yegorov. Value $10 each.

For overprints see Nos. 527-527E.

UN Headquarters and Emblem — A58

1965, Feb. 15 *Perf. 14x15*

497	A58	30f yel brn, pur & lt bl	15	15
498	A58	70f vio, lt bl & yel brn	35	35

19th anniv. of the UN (in 1964). A souvenir sheet contains Nos. 497-498, imperf. Value $9.

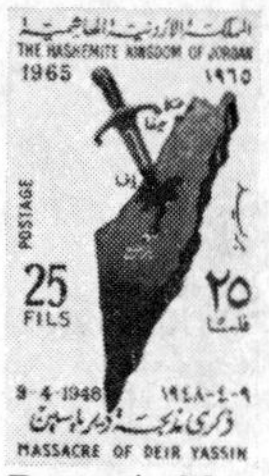

Dagger in Map of Palestine A59

Volleyball Player and Cup A60

1965, Apr. 9 Photo. *Perf. 11x11½*

499	A59	25f red & olive	65	20

Deir Yassin massacre, Apr. 9, 1948.

1965, June Litho. *Perf. 14½x14*

500	A60	15f lemon	15	15
501	A60	35f rose brown	22	18
502	A60	50f greenish blue	32	26

Arab Volleyball Championships. An imperf. 100f orange brown souvenir sheet exists. Size of stamp: 33x57mm. Value $7.

Cavalry Horsemanship A61

Army Day: 10f, Tank. 35f, King Hussein and aides standing in army car.

1965, May 24

503	A61	5f green	15	15
504	A61	10f violet blue	15	15
505	A61	35f brown red	32	24
		Set value	42	34

John F. Kennedy — A62

1965, June 1 Wmk. 305 *Perf. 14*

506	A62	10f blk & brt green	15	15
507	A62	15f vio & orange	30	20
508	A62	25f brn & lt blue	30	30
509	A62	50f deep cl & emer	1.00	60

John F. Kennedy (1917-63). An imperf. 50f salmon and dark blue souv. sheet exists. Value $8.

Pope Paul VI, King Hussein and Dome of the Rock — A63

Perf. 13½x14

1965, June 15 Litho. Wmk. 305

510	A63	5f brown & rose lil	15	15
511	A63	10f vio brn & lt yel grn	22	15
512	A63	15f ultra & salmon	22	18
513	A63	50f black & rose	75	52

1st anniversary of the visit of Pope Paul VI to the Holy Land. An imperf. 50f violet and light blue souvenir sheet exists with simulated perforations. Value $7.50.

Jordan's Pavilion and Unisphere — A64

Perf. 14x13½

1965, Aug. Unwmk. Photo.

514	A64	15f silver & multi	15	15
515	A64	25f bronze & multi	15	15
516	A64	50f gold & multi	30	26
a.		Souvenir sheet of 1, 100f	1.00	1.00
		Set value		42

New York World's Fair, 1964-65.
No. 516a contains a 100f gold and multicolored stamp, type A64, imperf.

Library Aflame and Lamp A64a

1965, Aug. Wmk. 305 *Perf. 11½x11*

517	A64a	25f black, grn & red	15	15

Burning of the Library of Algiers, June 2, 1962.

ITU Emblem, Old and New Telecommunication Equipment — A65

1965, Aug. Litho. *Perf. 14x13½*

518	A65	25f lt blue & dk bl	15	15
519	A65	45f grnsh gray & blk	26	22

ITU, centenary. An imperf. 100f salmon and carmine rose souvenir sheet exists with carmine rose border. Size of stamp: 39x32mm. Value $1.

Syncom Satellite over Pagoda — A66

Designs: 10f, 20f, Rocket in space. 15f, Astronauts in cabin.

1965, Sept. *Perf. 14*

521	A66	5f brt ultra, org & grnsh blk	15	15
521A	A66	10f multicolored	20	15
521B	A66	15f multicolored	30	25
521C	A66	20f multicolored	38	30
521D	A66	50f brt ultra, brt & dp yel grn	1.00	75
		Nos. 521-521D (5)	2.03	
		Set value		1.35

Achievements in space research. A 50f multicolored imperf. souvenir sheet shows earth and Syncom satellite. Value $5.

Dead Sea A66a

Designs: b, Qumran Caves. c, Dead Sea. d, Dead Sea Scrolls.

1965, Sept. 23 Photo. *Perf. 14*

522	A66a	35f Strip of 4, #a.-d.	

Visit of King Hussein to France and US — A66b

Wmk. 305

1965, Oct. 5 Litho. *Perf. 14*

523	A66b	5f shown	15	15
523A	A66b	10f With Charles DeGaulle	18	18
523B	A66b	20f With Lyndon Johnson	35	35
523C	A66b	50f like #523	90	90

No. 523C exists in a 50f imperf. souvenir sheet.

Intl. Cooperation Year — A66c

1965, Oct. 24 *Perf. 14x13½*

524	A66c	5f brt org & dk org	15	15
524A	A66c	10f brt bl & dk bl	22	22
524B	A66c	45f brt grn & dk violet	1.00	1.00

Arab Postal Union, 10th Anniv. — A66d

1965, Nov. 5 *Perf. 15x14*

525	A66d	15f violet bl & blk	20	20
525A	A66d	25f brt yel grn & blk	35	35

Dome of the Rock A66e

1965, Nov. 20 *Perf. 14x15*

526	A66e	15f multicolored	
526A	A66e	25f multicolored	

Nos. 491-496 with Spaceship and Bilingual Ovpt. in Blue "Alexei Leonov / Pavel Belyaev / 18-3-65"

1966, Jan. 15 Litho. *Perf. 14*

527	A57	40f on No. 491	2.25	2.25
527A	A57	40f on No. 492	2.25	2.25
527B	A57	40f on No. 493	2.25	2.25
527C	A57	40f on No. 494	2.25	2.25
527D	A57	40f on No. 495	2.25	2.25
527E	A57	40f on No. 496	2.25	2.25

Both souvenir sheets mentioned after No. 496 exist overprinted in red violet.

King Hussein — A67

Perf. 14½x14

1966, Jan. 15 Photo. Unwmk.

Portrait in Slate Blue

528	A67	1f orange	15	15
528A	A67	2f ultramarine	15	15
528B	A67	3f dk purple	15	15
528C	A67	4f plum	15	15
528D	A67	7f brn orange	15	15
528E	A67	12f cerise	15	15
528F	A67	15f olive brn	15	15

Portrait in Violet Brown

528G	A67	21f green	22	15
528H	A67	25f greenish bl	26	15
528I	A67	35f yel bister	38	22
528J	A67	40f orange yel	45	26
528K	A67	50f olive grn	55	15
528L	A67	100f lt yel grn	1.10	32
528M	A67	150f violet	1.90	75
		Nos. 528-528M,C43-C45 (17)	18.66	9.55

Anti-tuberculosis Campaign — A67a

1966, May 17 Photo. *Perf. 14x15*

Blue Overprint

529	A67a	15f multicolored	25	25
529A	A67a	35f multicolored	60	60
529B	A67a	50f multicolored	85	85

Unissued Freedom from Hunger stamps overprinted. Two imperf. souvenir sheets exist, one with simulated perforations.

Nos. 529-529B with Added Surcharge Obliterated with Black Bars

1966, May 17 Photo. *Perf. 14x15*

530	A67a	15f on 15f + 15f	25	25
530A	A67a	35f on 35f + 35f	60	60
530B	A67a	50f on 50f + 50f	85	85

Stations of the Cross — A67b

Designs: Stations on Jesus' walk to Calvary along Via Dolorosa. Denominations expressed in Roman numerals.

1966, Sept. 14 Photo. *Perf. 15x14*

531	A67b	1f Condemned to death	15	15
531A	A67b	2f Takes up cross	15	15
531B	A67b	3f Falls the 1st time	16	16
531C	A67b	4f Meets His mother	22	22
531D	A67b	5f Simon helps carry cross	28	28
531E	A67b	6f Woman wipes Jesus' brow	32	32
531F	A67b	7f Falls 2nd time	38	38
531G	A67b	8f Tells women not to weep	45	45
531H	A67b	9f Falls 3rd time	50	50
531I	A67b	10f Stripped of His garment	55	55
531J	A67b	11f Nailed to cross	60	60
531K	A67b	12f Death on cross	65	65
531L	A67b	13f Removal from cross	70	70
531M	A67b	14f Burial	75	75
		Nos. 531-531M (14)	5.86	5.86

Souvenir Sheet

Imperf

531N	A67b	100f like #551	*13.00*	*13.00*

Gemini Astronauts, Spacecraft — A67c

Astronauts and spacecraft from Gemini Missions 6-8.

1966, Nov. 15 Photo. *Perf. 15x14*

532	A67c	1f Walter M. Schirra	15	15
532A	A67c	2f Thomas P. Stafford	15	15
532B	A67c	3f Frank Borman	15	15
532C	A67c	4f James A. Lovell	15	15
532D	A67c	30f Neil Armstrong	60	60
532E	A67c	60f David R. Scott	1.25	1.25
		Set value	2.00	2.00

Imperf

Size: 119x89mm

532F A67c 100f Gemini 6-8 astronauts *12.00 12.00*

Christmas — A67d

Perf. 14x15, 15x14

1966, Dec. 21 Photo.

533 A67d 5f Magi following star 15 15
533A A67d 10f Adoration of the Magi 20 20
533B A67d 35f Flight to Egypt, vert. 70 70

Souvenir Sheet

Imperf

533C A67d 50f like #533A *12.50 12.50*

King Hussein — A67e

Builders of World Peace: No. 534, Dag Hammarskjold. No. 534A, U Thant. No. 534B, Jawaharlal Nehru. No. 534C, Charles DeGaulle. No. 534D, John F. Kennedy. No. 534E, Lyndon B. Johnson. No. 534F, Pope John XXIII. No. 534G, Pope Paul VI. No. 534H, King Abdullah of Jordan.

1967, Jan. 5 Photo. Perf. 15x14

Background Color

534 A67e 5f gray 15 15
534A A67e 5f brt yel grn 15 15
534B A67e 10f rose lilac 18 18
534C A67e 10f red brown 18 18
534D A67e 35f olive green 60 60
534E A67e 35f orange 60 60
534F A67e 50f rose claret 85 85
534G A67e 50f yel bister 85 85
534H A67e 100f brt blue 1.75 1.75
534I A67e 100f dull blue 1.75 1.75

Imperf

Size: 99x64mm

534J A67e 100f Kennedy, etc. *12.50 12.50*
534K A67e 100f DeGaulle, etc. *12.50 12.50*

King Hussein A67f

Photo. & Embossed

1967, Feb. 7 Imperf.

Gold Portrait and Border

Diameter: 50f, 100f, 48mm; 200f, 54mm

Portrait of King Hussein

535 A67f 5f dk bl & salmon 15 15
535A A67f 10f purple & salmon 15 15
535B A67f 50f blk brn & vio 75 75
535C A67f 100f dk ol grn & pink 1.50 1.50
535D A67f 200f dp bl & bl 3.00 3.00

Portrait of Crown Prince Hassan

536 A67f 5f brt yel grn & blk 15 15
536A A67f 10f vio & blk 15 15
536B A67f 50f bl & blk 75 75
536C A67f 100f bister & blk 1.50 1.50
536D A67f 200f brt pink & blk 3.00 3.00

Portrait of John F. Kennedy

537 A67f 5f brt bl & lt grn 15 15
537A A67f 10f dp grn & pink 15 15
537B A67f 50f brt rose & org yel 75 75
537C A67f 100f brn & apple grn 1.50 1.50
537D A67f 200f dk purple & pale grn 3.00 3.00
Nos. 535-537D (15) 16.65 16.65

1968 Summer Olympic Games, Mexico — A67g

Olympic torch and: 1f, Natl. University Library with O'Gormans mosaics, statue, Mexico City. 2f, Fishermen on Lake Patzcuaro. 3f, Natl. University buildings. 4f, Paseo de la Reforma, Mexico City. 30f, Guadalajara Cathedral. 60f, 100f, Palace of Fine Arts, Mexico City.

Perf. 14x15

1967, Mar. Photo. Unwmk.

538 A67g 1f lake, dk bl vio & blk 15 15
538A A67g 2f blk, lake & dk bl vio 15 15
538B A67g 3f dark bl vio, blk & lake 15 15
538C A67g 4f bl, grn & brn 15 15
538D A67g 30f grn, brn & bl 45 45
538E A67g 60f brn, bl & grn 90 90
Set value 1.50 1.50

Souvenir Sheet

Imperf

538F A67g 100f brn, dark bl & grn

Symbolic Water Cycle — A68

Perf. 14½x14

1967, Mar. 1 Litho. Wmk. 305

539 A68 10f dp org, blk & gray 15 15
540 A68 15f grnsh bl, blk & gray 15 15
541 A68 25f brt rose lil, blk & gray 18 18
Set value 35 35

Hydrological Decade (UNESCO), 1965-74.

UNESCO Emblem — A69

1967, Mar. 16

542 A69 100f multicolored 65 65

20th anniv. of UNESCO.

Dromedary — A70

Animals: 2f, Karakul. 3f, Angora goat.

Perf. 14x15

1967, Feb. 11 Photo. Unwmk.

543 A70 1f dark brn & multi 15 15
544 A70 2f yellow & multi 15 15
545 A70 3f lt blue & multi 15 15
Set value, #543-545, C46-C48 85 65

A souvenir sheet exists with a 100f in design and colors of No. C47, simulated perforation and marginal animal design. Value $6.

Inauguration of WHO Headquarters, Geneva — A71

1967, Apr. 7 Wmk. 305

546 A71 5f emerald & blk 15 15
547 A71 45f dl orange & blk 32 32
Set value 36 36

Arab League Emblem and Hands Reaching for Knowledge — A72

1968, May 5 Unwmk. Perf. 11

548 A72 20f org & slate grn 15 15
549 A72 20f brt pink & dk bl 15 15
Set value 20 20

Issued to publicize the literacy campaign.

"20" and WHO Emblem A73

Perf. 14½x14

1968, Aug. 10 Wmk. 305

550 A73 30f multicolored 22 18
551 A73 100f multicolored 75 60

20th anniv. of the WHO.

European Goldfinch A74

Protected Game: 10f, Rock partridge (vert.). 15f, Ostriches (vert.). 20f, Sand partridge. 30f, Dorcas gazelle. 40f, Oryxes. 50f, Houbara bustard.

1968, Oct. 5 Unwmk. Perf. 13½

552 A74 5f multicolored 15 15
553 A74 10f multicolored 18 15
554 A74 15f multicolored 20 15
555 A74 20f multicolored 32 15
556 A74 30f multicolored 45 18
557 A74 40f multicolored 60 25
558 A74 50f multicolored 85 30
Nos. 552-558,C49-C50 (9) 4.90 3.48

Human Rights Flame — A75

1968, Dec. 10 Litho. Perf. 13

559 A75 20f dp org, lt org & blk 18 15
560 A75 60f grn, lt blue & blk 50 45

International Human Rights Year.

Dome of the Rock, Jerusalem A76

Designs: 5f, 45f, Holy Kaaba, Mecca, and Dome of the Rock.

1969, Oct. 8 Photo. Perf. 12

Size: 56x25mm

561 A76 5f dull vio & multi 15 15

Size: 36x25mm

562 A76 10f vio blue & multi 18 15
563 A76 20f Prus bl & multi 38 15

Size: 56x25mm

564 A76 45f Prus bl & multi 75 22
Set value 44

ILO Emblem A77

1969, June 10 Perf. 13½x14

565 A77 10f blue & black 15 15
566 A77 20f bister brn & blk 15 15
567 A77 25f lt olive & black 15 15
568 A77 45f lil rose & black 26 25
569 A77 60f orange & black 38 32
Nos. 565-569 (5) 1.09
Set value 84

ILO, 50th anniversary.

Horses A78

Designs: 20f, White stallion. 45f, Mare and foal.

1969, July 6 Unwmk. Perf. 13½

570 A78 10f dark bl & multi 15 15
571 A78 20f dl green & multi 18 15
572 A78 45f red & multi 45 30
Set value 46

Prince Hassan and Princess Tharwat
A79

Designs: 60f, 100f, Prince Hassan and bride in western bridal gown.

1969, Dec. 2 Photo. *Perf. 12½*

573 A79 20f gold & multi 15 15
573A A79 60f gold & multi 45 38
573B A79 100f gold & multi 75 75
c. Strip of 3, #573-573B 1.50

Wedding of Crown Prince Hassan, Nov. 14, 1968.

The Tragedy and the Flight of the Refugees
A79a

Different design on each stamp. Each strip of 5 has five consecutive denominations.

Perf. 14½x13½

1969, Dec. 10 Photo.

574 A79a 1f-5f multi
574A A79a 6f-10f multi
574B A79a 11f-15f multi
574C A79a 16f-20f multi
574D A79a 21f-25f multi
574E A79a 26f-30f multi

For surcharges see Nos. 870-875.

Inscribed: Tragedy in the Holy Lands

Different design on each stamp. Each strip of 5 has five consecutive denominations.

Perf. 14½x13½

1969, Dec. 10 Photo.

575 A79a 1f-5f multi
575A A79a 6f-10f multi
575B A79a 11f-15f multi
575C A79a 16f-20f multi
575D A79a 21f-25f multi
575E A79a 26f-30f multi

For surcharges see Nos. 876-881.

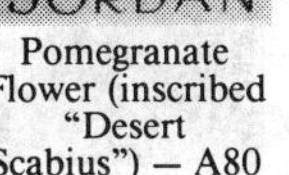

Pomegranate Flower (inscribed "Desert Scabius") — A80

Oranges — A81

Black Bush Robin — A82

Designs: 15f, Wattle flower ("Caper"). 20f, Melon. 25f, Caper flower ("Pomegranate"). 30f, Lemons. 35f, Morning glory. 40f, Grapes. 45f, Desert scabius ("Wattle"). 50f, Olive-laden branch. 75f, Black iris. 100f, Apples. 180f, Masked shrike. 200f, Palestine sunbird. (Inscriptions incorrect on 5f, 15f, 25f and 45f.)

Perf. 14x13½ (flowers), 12 (fruit), 13½x14 (birds)

1969-70 Photo.

576 A80 5f yel & multi ('70) 15 15
577 A81 10f blue & multi 15 15
578 A80 15f tan & multi ('70) 20 15
579 A81 20f sepia & multi 30 15
580 A80 25f multi ('70) 38 15
581 A81 30f vio bl & multi 42 15
582 A80 35f multi ('70) 45 15
583 A81 40f dull yel & multi 52 15
584 A80 45f gray & multi ('70) 55 15
585 A81 50f car rose & multi 60 15
586 A80 75f multi ('70) 1.00 22
587 A81 100f dk gray & multi 1.25 38
588 A82 120f org & multi ('70) 1.90 45
589 A82 180f multi ('70) 2.25 1.00
590 A82 200f multi ('70) 2.75 1.25
Nos. 576-590 (15) 12.87
Set value 4.10

Issue dates: Fruits, Nov. 22; flowers, Mar. 21; birds, Sept. 1.

Soccer — A83

Designs: 10f, Diver. 15f, Boxers. 50f, Runner. 100f, Bicyclist (vert.). 150f, Basketball (vert.).

1970, Aug. *Perf. 13½x14, 14x13½*

651 A83 5f green & multi 15 15
652 A83 10f lt bl & multi 15 15
653 A83 15f gray & multi 15 15
654 A83 50f gray & multi 38 30
655 A83 100f yellow & multi 75 60
656 A83 150f multicolored 1.10 1.00
Nos. 651-656 (6) 2.68 2.35

Boy Fetching Water, UNICEF and Refugee Emblems — A84

UNICEF and Refugee Emblems and: 5f, Refugee children (horiz.). 15f, Girl and tents. 20f, Boy in front of tent.

1970, Aug.

657 A84 5f multicolored 15 15
658 A84 10f multicolored 30 20
659 A84 15f multicolored 42 20
660 A84 20f multicolored 60 20
Set value 65

Issued for Childhood Day.

Nativity Grotto, Bethlehem
A85

Church of the Nativity, Bethlehem: 10f, Manger. 20f, Altar. 25f, Interior.

1970, Dec. 25 Photo. *Perf. 13½*

661 A85 5f blue & multi 15 15
662 A85 10f scarlet & multi 15 15
663 A85 20f rose lilac & multi 15 15
664 A85 25f green & multi 20 15
Set value 45 30

Christmas.

Flag and Map of Arab League Countries
A85a

1971, May 10 Photo. *Perf. 11½x11*

665 A85a 10f orange & multi 15 15
666 A85a 20f lt blue & multi 15 15
667 A85a 30f olive & multi 20 15
Set value 40 25

25th anniversary of the Arab League.

Emblem and Doves — A86

Designs: 5f, Emblem and 4 races (vert.). 10f, Emblem as flower (vert.).

1971, July

668 A86 5f green & multi 15 15
669 A86 10f brick red & multi 15 15
670 A86 15f dk blue & multi 20 15
Set value 40 18

Intl. Year Against Racial Discrimination.

Dead Sea — A87

Views of the Holy Land: 30f, Excavated building, Petra. 45f, Via Dolorosa, Jerusalem (vert.). 60f, Jordan River. 100f, Christmas bell, Bethlehem (vert.).

1971, Aug. *Perf. 14x13½, 13½x14*

671 A87 5f blue & multi 15 15
672 A87 30f pink & multi 38 20
673 A87 45f blue & multi 50 38
674 A87 60f gray & multi 75 50
675 A87 100f gray & multi 1.25 90
Nos. 671-675 (5) 3.03 2.13

Tourist publicity.

Opening of UPU Headquarters, Bern in 1970 — A88

1971, Oct. *Perf. 11*

676 A88 10f brn, brn & yel grn 15 15
677 A88 20f dk vio, grn & yel grn 28 15
Set value 17

Avicenna (980-1037)
A89

Child Learning to Write
A90

Arab Scholars: 10f, Averroes (1126-1198). 20f, ibn-Khaldun (1332-1406). 25f, ibn-Tufail (?-1185). 30f, Alhazen (965?-1039?).

1971, Sept. *Perf. 12*

678 A89 5f gold & multi 15 15
679 A89 10f gold & multi 15 15
680 A89 20f gold & multi 28 15
681 A89 25f gold & multi 30 15
682 A89 30f gold & multi 40 20
Nos. 678-682 (5) 1.28
Set value 52

1972, Feb. 9 Photo. *Perf. 11*

683 A90 5f ultra, brn & grn 15 15
684 A90 15f mag, brn & blue 15 15
685 A90 20f grn, brn & blue 20 15
686 A90 30f org, brn & blue 30 20
Set value 50

International Education Year.

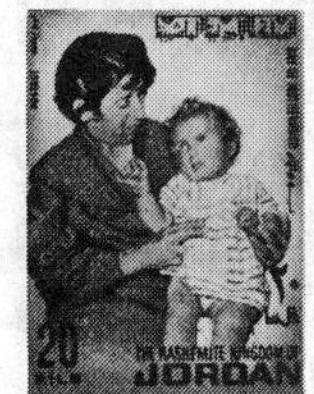

Mother and Child
A91

Pope Paul VI and Holy Sepulcher
A92

Mother's Day: 10f, Mothers and children (horiz.). 30f, Arab mother and child.

1972, Mar. *Perf. 14x13½*

687 A91 10f lt grn & multi 15 15
688 A91 20f red brown & blk 16 15
689 A91 30f blue, brn & blk 25 16
Set value 32

1972, Apr. Photo. *Perf. 14x13½*

690 A92 30f black & multi 20 15

Easter. See Nos. C51-C52.

UNICEF Emblem, Children
A93

UNICEF Emblem and: 20f, Child playing with blocks spelling "UNICEF" (vert.). 30f, Mother and child.

1972, May *Perf. 11½x11, 11x11½*

691 A93 10f bl, vio bl & blk 15 15
692 A93 20f multicolored 16 15
693 A93 30f blue & multi 25 16
Set value 30

25th anniv. (in 1971) of UNICEF.

UN Emblem, Dove and Grain — A94

1972, July *Perf. 11x11½*

694 A94 5f vio & multi 15 15
695 A94 10f multicolored 15 15
696 A94 15f black & multi 16 15
697 A94 20f green & multi 20 15
698 A94 30f multicolored 35 20
Nos. 694-698 (5) 1.01
Set value 50

25th anniv. (in 1970) of the UN.

Al Aqsa Mosque, Jerusalem — A95

Designs: 60f, Al Aqsa Mosque on fire. 100f, Al Aqsa Mosque, interior.

1972, Aug. 21 Litho. *Perf. 14½*

No.	Type	Description	Unused	Used
699	A95	30f green & multi	25	20
700	A95	60f blue & multi	50	35
701	A95	100f ocher & multi	80	52

3rd anniversary of the burning of Al Aqsa Mosque, Jerusalem.

House in Desert — A96

1972, Nov. *Perf. 14x13½, 13½x14*

No.	Type	Description	Unused	Used
702	A96	5f Falconer (vert.)	15	15
703	A96	10f shown	15	15
704	A96	15f Man on camel	20	15
705	A96	20f Pipe line construction	28	15
706	A96	25f Shepherd	30	15
707	A96	30f Camels at water trough	48	20
708	A96	35f Chicken farm	52	20
709	A96	45f Irrigation canal	75	35
		Nos. 702-709 (8)	2.83	
		Set value		1.15

Life in the Arab desert.

Wasfi el Tell and Dome of the Rock A97

Wasfi el Tell, Map of Palestine and Jordan — A98

Perf. 13x13½, 13½x13

1972, Dec. Photo.

No.	Type	Description	Unused	Used
710	A97	5f citron & multi	15	15
711	A98	10f red & multi	15	15
712	A97	20f dl blue & multi	25	18
713	A98	30f green & multi	45	25
		Set value	86	52

In memory of Prime Minister Wasfi el Tell, who was assassinated in Cairo by Black September terrorists.

Trapshooting A99

Designs: 75f, Trapshooter facing right (horiz.). 120f, Trapshooter facing left (horiz.).

1972, Dec. *Perf. 14x13½, 13½x14*

No.	Type	Description	Unused	Used
714	A99	25f multicolored	15	15
715	A99	75f multicolored	42	35
716	A99	120f multicolored	75	50

World Trapshooting Championships.

Aero Club Emblem A100

1973, Jan. Photo. *Perf. 13½x14*

No.	Type	Description	Unused	Used
717	A100	5f blue, blk & yel	15	15
718	A100	10f blue, blk & yel	20	15
		Nos. 717-718,C53-C55 (5)	1.06	
		Set value		52

Royal Jordanian Aero Club.

Peace Dove and Jordanian Flag — A101

Designs: 10f, Emblem. 15f, King Hussein. 30f, Map of Jordan.

1973, Mar. *Perf. 11½*

No.	Type	Description	Unused	Used
719	A101	5f blue & multi	15	15
720	A101	10f pale grn & multi	15	15
721	A101	15f olive & multi	18	15
722	A101	30f yel grn & multi	35	30
		Set value	70	45

Hashemite Kingdom of Jordan, 50th anniv.

Battle, Flag and Map of Palestine — A102

Designs: 10f, Two soldiers in combat, map of Palestine. 15f, Map of Palestine, olive branch, soldier on tank.

1973, Apr. 10 Photo. *Perf. 11*

No.	Type	Description	Unused	Used
723	A102	5f crimson & multi	16	15
724	A102	10f crimson & multi	30	16
725	A102	15f grn, blue & brn	50	20
		Set value		40

5th anniversary of Karama Battle.

Father and Child — A103

Father's Day: 20f, Father and infant. 30f, Family.

1973, Apr. 20 *Perf. 13½*

No.	Type	Description	Unused	Used
726	A103	10f citron & multi	15	15
727	A103	20f lt blue & multi	15	15
728	A103	30f multicolored	22	15
		Set value		30

Phosphate Mine — A104

1973, June 25 Litho. *Perf. 13½x14*

No.	Type	Description	Unused	Used
729	A104	5f shown	15	15
730	A104	10f Cement factory	16	15
731	A104	15f Sharmasil Dam	25	15
732	A104	20f Kafrein Dam	30	20
		Set value		50

Development projects.

Camel Racer — A105

Designs: Camel racing.

1973, July 21

No.	Type	Description	Unused	Used
733	A105	5f multicolored	15	15
734	A105	10f multicolored	15	15
735	A105	15f multicolored	15	15
736	A105	20f multicolored	16	15
		Set value	35	22

Book Year Emblem — A106

1973, Aug. 25 Photo. *Perf. 13x13½*

No.	Type	Description	Unused	Used
737	A106	30f dk grn & multi	32	15
738	A106	60f purple & multi	65	25

Intl. Book Year. For overprints, see Nos. 781-782.

Family A107

Family Day: 30f, Family around fire. 60f, Large family outdoors.

1973, Sept. 18 Litho. *Perf. 13½*

No.	Type	Description	Unused	Used
739	A107	20f multicolored	15	15
740	A107	30f multicolored	20	15
741	A107	60f multicolored	42	25
		Set value		46

Kings of Iran and Jordan, Tomb of Cyrus the Great and Mosque of Omar — A108

1973, Oct. Litho. *Perf. 13*

No.	Type	Description	Unused	Used
742	A108	5f ver & multi	15	15
743	A108	10f brown & multi	20	15
744	A108	15f gray & multi	32	18
745	A108	30f blue & multi	60	35
		Set value		70

2500th anniversary of the founding of the Persian Empire by Cyrus the Great.

Palestine Week Emblem A109

Palestine Week: 10f, Torch and laurel. 15f, Refugee family behind barbed wire (vert.). 30f, Children, Map of Palestine, globe. Sizes: 5f, 10f, 30f; 38½x22mm. 15f, 25x46mm.

1973, Nov. 17 Photo. *Perf. 11*

No.	Type	Description	Unused	Used
746	A109	5f multicolored	15	15
747	A109	10f dl bl & multi	25	15
748	A109	15f yel grn & multi	30	15
749	A109	30f brt grn & multi	65	25
		Set value		50

Traditional Harvest A110

Designs: Traditional and modern agricultural methods.

1973, Dec. 25 *Perf. 13½*

No.	Type	Description	Unused	Used
750	A110	5f shown	15	15
751	A110	10f Harvesting machine	15	15
752	A110	15f Traditional seeding	15	15
753	A110	20f Seeding machine	18	15
754	A110	30f Ox plow	25	22
755	A110	35f Plowing machine	30	22
756	A110	45f Pest control	38	32
757	A110	60f Horticulture	55	50
		Nos. 750-757,C56 (9)	2.76	2.31

Red Sea Fish A111

Designs: Various Red Sea fishes.

1974, Feb. 15 Photo. *Perf. 14*

No.	Type	Description	Unused	Used
758	A111	5f multicolored	15	15
759	A111	10f multicolored	15	15
760	A111	15f multicolored	18	15
761	A111	20f multicolored	22	15
762	A111	25f multicolored	25	15
763	A111	30f multicolored	30	18
764	A111	35f multicolored	32	22
765	A111	40f multicolored	38	25
766	A111	45f multicolored	45	30
767	A111	50f multicolored	52	38
768	A111	60f multicolored	75	48
		Nos. 758-768 (11)	3.67	2.56

Battle of Muta, 1250 A112

1974, Mar. 15 Photo. *Perf. 13½*

No.	Type	Description	Unused	Used
769	A112	10f shown	30	15
770	A112	20f Yarmouk Battle, 636	60	30
771	A112	30f Hitteen Battle, 1187	90	45

Clubfooted Boy, by Murillo — A113

Paintings: 10f, Praying Hands, by Dürer. 15f, St. George and the Dragon, by Paolo Uccello. 20f, Mona Lisa, by Da Vinci. 30f, Hope, by Frederic Watts. 40f, Angelus, by Jean F. Millet (horiz.). 50f, The Artist and her Daughter, by Angelica Kauffmann. 60f, Portrait of my Mother, by James Whistler (horiz.). 100f, Master Hare, by Reynolds.

Perf. 14x13½, 13½x14

1974, Apr. 15 Litho.

No.	Type	Description	Unused	Used
772	A113	5f black & multi	15	15
773	A113	10f black & gray	15	15
774	A113	15f black & multi	15	15
775	A113	20f black & multi	15	15
776	A113	30f black & multi	20	15
777	A113	40f black & multi	25	15

778	A113	50f black & multi	32	22
779	A113	60f black & multi	42	25
780	A113	100f black & multi	65	45
		Nos. 772-780 (9)	2.44	
		Set value		1.40

Nos. 737-738 Overprinted

المؤتمر الدولي لتاريخ بلاد الشام
٢٠ – ١٩٧٤/٤/٢٥
الجامعة الاردنية

1974, Apr. 20 Photo. *Perf. 13x13½*

781	A106	30f dk grn & multi	35	20
782	A106	60f purple & multi	75	50

International Conference for Damascus History, Apr. 20-25.

UPU Emblem — A114

1974 *Perf. 13x12½*

783	A114	10f yel grn & multi	15	15
784	A114	30f blue & multi	30	15
785	A114	60f multicolored	60	30
		Set value		48

Centenary of Universal Postal Union.

Camel Caravan at Sunset A115

Designs: 3f, 30f, Palm at shore of Dead Sea. 4f, 40f, Hotel at shore. 5f, 50f, Jars from Qumran Caves. 6f, 60f, Copper scrolls (vert.). 10f, 100f, Cracked cistern steps (vert.). 20f, like 2f.

1974, June 25 Photo. *Perf. 14*

786	A115	2f multicolored	15	15
787	A115	3f multicolored	15	15
788	A115	4f multicolored	15	15
789	A115	5f multicolored	15	15
790	A115	6f multicolored	15	15
791	A115	10f multicolored	15	15
792	A115	20f multicolored	18	15
793	A115	30f multicolored	26	15
794	A115	40f multicolored	38	18
795	A115	50f multicolored	42	25
796	A115	60f multicolored	62	32
797	A115	100f multicolored	1.00	50
		Set value	3.10	1.70

WPY Emblem — A116

Water Skiing — A117

1974, Aug. 20 Photo. *Perf. 11*

798	A116	5f lt green, blk & pur	15	15
799	A116	10f lt green, blk & car	15	15
800	A116	20f lt green, blk & org	20	15
		Set value	35	20

World Population Year.

Perf. 14x13½, 13½x14

1974, Sept. 20

Water Skiing: 10f, 100f, Side view (horiz.). 20f, 200f, Turning (horiz.). 50f, like 5f.

801	A117	5f multicolored	15	15
802	A117	10f multicolored	15	15
803	A117	20f multicolored	15	15
804	A117	50f multicolored	35	20
805	A117	100f multicolored	65	40
806	A117	200f multicolored	1.40	80
		Nos. 801-806 (6)	2.85	
		Set value		1.55

Holy Kaaba, Mecca, and Pilgrims — A118

1974, Nov. Photo. *Perf. 11*

807	A118	10f blue & multi	15	15
808	A118	20f yellow & multi	25	15
		Set value		20

Pilgrimage season.

Amrah Palace A119

Ruins: 20f, Hisham Palace. 30f, Kharraneh Castle.

1974, Nov. 25 Photo. *Perf. 14x13½*

809	A119	10f black & multi	25	15
810	A119	20f black & multi	50	30
811	A119	30f black & multi	75	50

Jordanian Woman — A120

Designs: Various women's costumes.

1975, Feb. 1 Photo. *Perf. 12*

812	A120	5f lt green & multi	15	15
813	A120	10f yellow & multi	15	15
814	A120	15f lt blue & multi	15	15
815	A120	20f ultra & multi	15	15
816	A120	25f green & multi	18	15
		Set value	50	35

Treasury, Petra — A121

Ommayyad Palace, Amman A122

Designs: 30f, Dome of the Rock, Jerusalem. 40f, Columns, Forum of Jerash.

Perf. 14x13½, 13½x14

1975, Mar. 1 Photo.

824	A121	15f lt blue & multi	15	15
825	A122	20f pink & multi	18	15
826	A122	30f yellow & multi	30	15
827	A122	40f lt blue & multi	38	18
		Nos. 824-827,C59-C61 (7)	2.27	1.47

King Hussein — A123

1975, Apr. 8 Photo. *Perf. 14*

Size: 19x23mm

831	A123	5f green & ind	15	15
832	A123	10f vio & indigo	15	15
833	A123	15f car & indigo	15	15
834	A123	20f brn ol & ind	15	15
835	A123	25f vio bl & ind	15	15
836	A123	30f brown & ind	15	15
837	A123	35f vio & indigo	16	15
838	A123	40f orange & ind	18	15
839	A123	45f red lil & ind	20	15
840	A123	50f bl green & ind	22	15
		Nos. 831-840,C62-C68 (17)	8.61	5.84

Globe, "alia" and Plane — A125

Designs: 30f, Boeing 727 connecting Jordan with world (horiz.). 60f, Globe and "alia."

1975, June 15 Photo. *Perf. 11*

853	A125	10f multicolored	15	15
854	A125	30f multicolored	26	18
855	A125	60f multicolored	55	38
		Set value	85	60

Royal Jordanian Airline, 30th anniversary.

Satellite Transmission System, Map of Mediterranean — A126

1975, Aug. 1 Photo. *Perf. 11*

856	A126	20f vio bl & multi	25	15
857	A126	30f green & multi	32	18

Opening of satellite earth station.

Chamber of Commerce Emblem — A127

1975, Oct. 15 Photo. *Perf. 11*

858	A127	10f yellow & blue	15	15
859	A127	15f yel, red & blue	15	15
860	A127	20f yel, grn & blue	16	15
		Set value	38	18

Amman Chamber of Commerce, 50th anniv.

Hand Holding Wrench, Wall and Emblem — A128

1975, Nov. Photo. *Perf. 11½*

861	A128	5f green, car & blk	15	15
862	A128	10f car, green & blk	15	15
863	A128	20f blk, green & car	20	15
		Set value	35	20

Three-year development plan.

Family and IWY Emblem A129

Salt Industry A130

IWY Emblem and: 25f, Woman scientist with microscope. 60f, Woman graduate.

1976, Apr. 27 Litho. *Perf. 14x13½*

864	A129	5f multicolored	15	15
865	A129	25f multicolored	15	15
866	A129	60f multicolored	38	25
		Set value	58	40

International Women's Year.

1976, June 1 Litho. *Perf. 13½x14*

Arab Labor Organization Emblem and: 30f, Welders. 60f, Ship at 'Aqaba.

867	A130	10f gray & multi	15	15
868	A130	30f bister & multi	18	15
869	A130	60f brown & multi	38	25
		Set value	60	40

Arab Labor Organization.

Nos. 574-574E Surcharged

Perf. 14½x13½

1976, July 18 Photo.

Strips of 5

870	A79a	25f on 1f-5f
871	A79a	25f on 6f-10f
872	A79a	40f on 11f-15f
873	A79a	50f on 16f-20f
874	A79a	75f on 21f-25f
875	A79a	125f on 26f-30f

Nos. 575-575E Surcharged

876	A79a	25f on 1f-5f
877	A79a	25f on 6f-10f
878	A79a	40f on 11f-15f
879	A79a	50f on 16f-20f
880	A79a	75f on 21f-25f
881	A79a	125f on 26f-30f

Tennis — A132

Designs: 10f, Athlete and wreath. 15f, Soccer. 20f, Equestrian and Jordanian flag. 30f, Weight lifting. 100f, Stadium, Amman.

1976, Nov. 1 Litho. *Perf. 14x13½*

990	A132	5f buff & multi	15	15
991	A132	10f lt bl & multi	15	15
992	A132	15f green & multi	15	15
993	A132	20f green & multi	16	15
994	A132	30f green & multi	25	15
995	A132	100f multicolored	80	48
		Nos. 990-995 (6)	1.66	
		Set value		88

Sports and youth.

Dam — A133

Telephones, 1876 and 1976 — A134

Designs: Various dams.

1976, Dec. 7 Litho. *Perf. 14x13½*

996	A133	30f multicolored	22	15
997	A133	60f multicolored	45	32
998	A133	100f multicolored	75	50

1977, Feb. 17 Litho. *Perf. 11½x12*

Design: 125f, 1876 telephone and 1976 receiver.

999	A134	75f rose & multi	60	45
1000	A134	125f blue & multi	90	75

Centenary of first telephone call by Alexander Graham Bell, Mar. 10, 1876.

Street Crossing, Traffic Light — A135

Designs: 75f, Traffic circle and light. 125f, Traffic light and signs, motorcycle policeman.

1977, May 4 Litho. *Perf. 11x12*

1001	A135	5f rose & multi	15	15
1002	A135	75f black & multi	60	45
1003	A135	125f yellow & multi	1.00	75

International Traffic Day.

Plane over Ship — A136

Child with Toy Bank — A137

Coat of Arms and: 25f, Factories and power lines. 40f, Fertilizer plant and trucks. 50f, Ground to air missile. 75f, Mosque and worshippers. 125f, Radar station and TV emblem.

1977, Aug. 11 Photo. *Perf. 11½x12*

1004	A136	10f sil & multi	15	15
1005	A136	25f sil & multi	20	15
1006	A136	40f sil & multi	30	24
1007	A136	50f sil & multi	42	30
1008	A136	75f sil & multi	60	45
1009	A136	125f sil & multi	1.10	75
		Nos. 1004-1009 (6)	2.77	2.04

Imperf

Size: 100x70mm

1009A	A136	100f multicolored		

25th anniv. of the reign of King Hussein.

1977, Sept. 1 Litho. *Perf. 11½x12*

Postal Savings Bank: 25f, Boy with piggy bank. 50f, Postal Savings Bank emblem. 75f, Boy talking to teller.

1010	A137	10f multicolored	15	15
1011	A137	25f multicolored	22	15
1012	A137	50f multicolored	45	30
1013	A137	75f multicolored	65	45

King Hussein and Queen Alia — A138

Queen Alia — A139

1977, Nov. 1 Litho. *Perf. 11½x12*

1014	A138	10f lt grn & multi	15	15
1015	A138	25f rose & multi	15	15
1016	A138	40f yellow & multi	28	16
1017	A138	50f blue & multi	35	20
		Set value		50

1977, Dec. 1 Litho. *Perf. 11½x12*

1018	A139	10f green & multi	15	15
1019	A139	25f brown & multi	20	15
1020	A139	40f blue & multi	35	20
1021	A139	50f yellow & multi	42	25
		Set value		60

Queen Alia, died in 1977 air crash.

Jinnah, Flags of Pakistan and Jordan A140

APU Emblem, Members' Flags A141

1977, Dec. 20 *Perf. 11½*

1022	A140	25f multicolored	20	15
1023	A140	75f multicolored	60	40

Mohammed Ali Jinnah (1876-1948), 1st Governor General of Pakistan.

1978, Apr. 12 Litho. *Perf. 12x11½*

1024	A141	25f yellow & multi	45	30
1025	A141	40f buff & multi	75	50

25th anniv. (in 1977), of Arab Postal Union.

Copper Coffee Set — A142

Roman Amphitheater, Jerash — A143

Handicraft: 40f, Porcelain plate and ashtray. 75f, Vase and jewelry. 125f, Pipe holder.

1978, May 30 Photo. *Perf. 11½x12*

1026	A142	25f olive & multi	20	15
1027	A142	40f lilac & multi	32	20
1028	A142	75f ultra & multi	60	40
1029	A142	125f orange & multi	1.00	65

1978, July 30 Litho. *Perf. 12*

Tourist Views: 20f, Roman Columns, Jerash. 40f, Goat, grapes and man, Roman mosaic, Madaba. 75f, Rock formations, Rum, and camel rider.

1030	A143	5f multicolored	15	15
1031	A143	20f multicolored	16	15
1032	A143	40f multicolored	32	20
1033	A143	75f multicolored	60	40
		Set value		75

King Hussein and Pres. Sadat — A144

Designs: No. 1035, King Hussein and Pres. Assad, Jordanian and Syrian flags (horiz.). No. 1036, King Hussein, King Khalid, Jordanian and Saudi Arabian flags (horiz.).

1978, Aug. 20 *Perf. 11½x12*

1034	A144	40f multicolored	32	20
1035	A144	40f multicolored	32	20
1036	A144	40f multicolored	32	20

Visits of Arab leaders to Jordan.

Cement Factory A145

Designs: 10f, Science laboratory. 25f, Printing press. 75f, Artificial fertilizer plant.

1978, Sept. 25 Litho. *Perf. 12*

1037	A145	5f multicolored	15	15
1038	A145	10f multicolored	15	15
1039	A145	25f multicolored	30	20
1040	A145	75f multicolored	90	60

Industrial development.

"UNESCO" Scales and Globe — A146

1978, Dec. 5 Litho. *Perf. 12x11½*

1041	A146	40f multicolored	40	30
1042	A146	75f multicolored	90	65

30th anniversary of UNESCO.

1976-1980 Development Plan — A147

1979, Oct. 25 Litho. *Perf. 12½x12*

1043	A147	25f multicolored	22	15
1044	A147	40f multicolored	36	24
1045	A147	50f multicolored	45	25

IYC Emblem, Flag of Jordan — A148

1979, Nov. 15 Litho. *Perf. 12x12½*

1046	A148	25f multicolored	20	15
1047	A148	40f multicolored	32	20
1048	A148	50f multicolored	40	24

International Year of the Child.

1979 Population and Housing Census — A149

1979, Dec. 25 Litho. *Perf. 12½x12*

1049	A149	25f multicolored	22	15
1050	A149	40f multicolored	38	24
1051	A149	50f multicolored	45	30

King Hussein — A150

1980 Litho. *Perf. 13½x13*

1052	A150	5f multicolored	15	15
1053	A150	10f multicolored	15	15
1055	A150	20f multicolored	16	15
1056	A150	25f multicolored	20	15
a.		Inscribed 1979	20	15
1058	A150	40f multicolored	32	20
a.		Inscribed 1979	32	20
1059	A150	50f multicolored	40	25
1060	A150	75f multicolored	55	32
1061	A150	125f multicolored	1.00	65
		Nos. 1052-1061 (8)	2.93	
		Set value		1.70

The 5f, 10f, 20f, 25f and 40f also come inscribed 1981.

International Nursing Day — A151

El Deir Temple, Petra — A152

1980, May 12 Litho. *Perf. 12x12½*

1062	A151	25f multicolored	22	15
1063	A151	40f multicolored	35	22
1064	A151	50f multicolored	40	25

1980 Litho. *Perf. 14½*

1065	A152	25f multicolored	24	16
1066	A152	40f multicolored	35	24
1067	A152	50f multicolored	45	30

World Tourism Conf., Manila, Sept. 27.

Hegira (Pilgrimage Year) — A153

1980, Nov. 11 Litho. *Perf. 14½*

1068	A153	25f multicolored	22	15
1069	A153	40f multicolored	40	22
1070	A153	50f multicolored	50	28
1071	A153	75f multicolored	90	42
1072	A153	100f multicolored	90	55
		Nos. 1068-1072 (5)	2.92	1.62

Souvenir Sheet

Imperf

1073	A153	290f multicolored	4.25	2.75

#1073 contains designs of #1068-1071.

11th Arab Summit Conference, Amman — A153a

1980, Nov. 25 Litho. *Perf. 14½*

1073A A153a 25f multi 20 15
1073B A153a 40f multi 30 25
1073C A153a 50f multi 45 32
1073D A153a 75f multi 75 45
1073E A153a 100f multi 90 65
f. Souv. sheet of 5, #1073A-1073E, imperf. 4.00 4.00
Nos. 1073A-1073E (5) 2.60 1.82

Red Crescent Society — A154

1981, May 8 Litho. *Perf. 14½*

1074 A154 25f multicolored 25 15
1075 A154 40f multicolored 40 28
1076 A154 50f multicolored 45 35

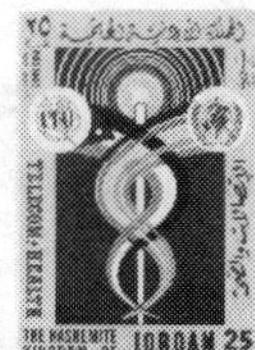
13th World Telecommunications Day — A155

1981, June 17 Litho. *Perf. 14x14½*

1077 A155 25f multicolored 25 15
1078 A155 40f multicolored 32 28
1079 A155 50f multicolored 45 32

Nos. 174 and 832 — A156

Perf. 13½x14½, 14½x13½

1981, July 1 Litho.

1080 A156 25f shown 25 18
1081 A156 40f Nos. 313, 189, vert. 45 30
1082 A156 50f Nos. 272, 222 50 38

Postal Museum opening.

Khawla Bint El-Azwar, Ancient Warrior — A157

Arab Women: 40f, El-Khansa (d.645), writer. 50f, Rabia El-Adawiyeh, religious leader.

1981, Aug. 25 Litho. *Perf. 14½x14*

1083 A157 25f multicolored 22 15
1084 A157 40f multicolored 36 24
1085 A157 50f multicolored 45 30

World Food Day — A158

1981, Oct. 16 Litho. *Perf. 14x14½*

1086 A158 25f multicolored 22 15
1087 A158 40f multicolored 36 24
1088 A158 50f multicolored 45 30

Intl. Year of the Disabled A159

Hands Reading Braille A160

1981, Nov. 14 Litho. *Perf. 14½x14*

1089 A159 25f multicolored 22 15
1090 A159 40f multicolored 36 24
1091 A159 50f multicolored 45 30

1981, Nov. 14 *Perf. 14x14½*

1092 A160 25f multicolored 22 15
1093 A160 40f multicolored 36 24
1094 A160 50f multicolored 45 30

Hand Holding Jug and Stone Tablet — A161

1982, Mar. 10 Litho. *Perf. 14x14½*

1095 A161 25f multicolored 32 22
1096 A161 40f multicolored 55 35
1097 A161 50f multicolored 70 45

Nos. 1095-1097 inscribed 1981.

30th Anniv. of Arab Postal Union — A162

1982, Apr. 12 Litho. *Perf. 14x14½*

1098 A162 10f multicolored 15 15
1099 A162 25f multicolored 22 15
1100 A162 40f multicolored 36 24
1101 A162 50f multicolored 45 30
1102 A162 100f multicolored 90 60
Nos. 1098-1102 (5) 2.08 1.44

King Hussein and Rockets A163

1982, May 25 Litho. *Perf. 14½x14*

1103 A163 10f shown 15 15
1104 A163 25f Tanks crossing bridge 22 15
1105 A163 40f Jet 36 24
1106 A163 50f Tanks, diff. 45 30
1107 A163 100f Raising flag 90 60
Nos. 1103-1107 (5) 2.08 1.44

Independence and Army Day; 30th anniv. of King Hussein's accession to the throne.

Salt Secondary School — A164

1982, Sept. 12 Litho. *Perf. 14½x14*

1108 A164 10f multicolored 15 15
1109 A164 25f multicolored 22 15
1110 A164 40f multicolored 36 24
1111 A164 50f multicolored 45 30
1112 A164 100f multicolored 90 60
Nos. 1108-1112 (5) 2.08 1.44

International Heritage of Jerusalem — A165

1982, Nov. 14 Litho. *Perf. 14x14½*

1113 A165 10f Gate to Old City 20 15
1114 A165 25f Minaret 55 30
1115 A165 40f Al Aqsa 90 50
1116 A165 50f Dome of the Rock 1.10 60
1117 A165 100f Dome of the Rock, diff. 2.25 1.25
Nos. 1113-1117 (5) 5.00 2.80

Yarmouk Forces — A166

1982, Nov. 14 *Perf. 14½x14*

1118 A166 10f multicolored 15 15
1119 A166 25f multicolored 30 20
1120 A166 40f multicolored 48 30
1121 A166 50f multicolored 60 40
1122 A166 100f multicolored 1.20 90

Size: 71x51mm

Imperf

1123 A166 100f Armed Forces emblem 11.50 11.50

2nd UN Conf. on Peaceful Uses of Outer Space, Vienna, Aug. 9-21 — A167

1982, Dec. 1 *Perf. 14½x14*

1124 A167 10f multicolored 15 15
1125 A167 25f multicolored 22 15
1126 A167 40f multicolored 36 24
1127 A167 50f multicolored 45 30
1128 A167 100f multicolored 90 60
Nos. 1124-1128 (5) 2.08 1.44

Birth Centenary of Amir Abdullah ibn Hussein — A168

1982, Dec. 13 Litho. *Perf. 14½*

1129 A168 10f multicolored 15 15
1130 A168 25f multicolored 25 15
1131 A168 40f multicolored 40 30
1132 A168 50f multicolored 60 50
1133 A168 100f multicolored 1.40 90
Nos. 1129-1133 (5) 2.80 2.00

Roman Ruins of Jerash A169

1982, Dec. 29 Litho. *Perf. 15*

1134 A169 10f Temple colonnade 15 15
1135 A169 25f Arch 22 15
1136 A169 40f Columns 36 24
1137 A169 50f Ampitheater 45 30
1138 A169 100f Hippodrome 90 60
Nos. 1134-1138 (5) 2.08 1.44

King Hussein — A170

1983 Litho. *Perf. 14½x14*

1139 A170 10f multicolored 15 15
1140 A170 25f multicolored 25 15
1141 A170 40f multicolored 40 30
1142 A170 60f multicolored 60 40
1143 A170 100f multicolored 1.00 65
1144 A170 125f multicolored 1.25 70
Nos. 1139-1144 (6) 3.65 2.35

Issue dates: 10f, 60f, Feb. 1; 40f, Feb. 8; 25f, 100f, 125f, Mar. 3. Inscribed 1982.

Massacre at Shatilla and Sabra Palestinian Refugee Camps A171

Designs: 10f, 25f, 50f, No. 1149, Various victims. 40f, Children. No. 1150, Wounded child.

1983, Apr. 9 Litho. *Perf. 14½*

1145 A171 10f multicolored *25* *20*
1146 A171 25f multicolored *45* *40*
1147 A171 40f multicolored *70* *50*
1148 A171 50f multicolored *85* *70*
1149 A171 100f multicolored *1.25* *1.00*
Nos. 1145-1149 (5) *3.50* *2.80*

Souvenir Sheet

Imperf

1150 A171 100f multicolored *15.00*

Opening of Queen Alia Intl. Airport A172

1983, May 25 Litho. *Perf. 12½*

1151 A172 10f Aerial view 15 15
1152 A172 25f Terminal buildings 22 15
1153 A172 40f Hangar 36 24
1154 A172 50f Terminal buildings, diff. 45 30
1155 A172 100f Embarkation Bridge 90 60
Nos. 1151-1155 (5) 2.08 1.44

Royal Jordanian Radio Amateurs' Society A173

1983, Aug. 11 Litho. *Perf. 12*

1156 A173 10f multicolored 15 15
1157 A173 25f multicolored 22 15
1158 A173 40f multicolored 36 24
1159 A173 50f multicolored 45 30
1160 A173 100f multicolored 90 60
Nos. 1156-1160 (5) 2.08 1.44

Royal Academy for Islamic Cultural Research A174

1983, Sept. 16 Litho. *Perf. 12*

1161 A174 10f Academy Bldg. 20 16
1162 A174 25f Silk carpet 45 30
1163 A174 40f Mosque, Amman 65 45
1164 A174 50f Dome of the Rock 85 55

1165 A174 100f Islamic city views 1.75 1.10
Nos. 1161-1165 (5) 3.90 2.56

A 100f souvenir sheet shows letter from Mohammed.

World Food Day — A175

1983, Oct. 16 Litho. *Perf. 12*
1166 A175 10f Irrigation canal 15 15
1167 A175 25f Greenhouses 25 15
1168 A175 40f Light-grown crops 40 24
1169 A175 50f Harvest 50 30
1170 A175 100f Sheep farm 1.00 60
Nos. 1166-1170 (5) 2.30 1.44

World Communications Year — A176

1983, Nov. 14
1171 A176 10f Radio switch-board operators 15 15
1172 A176 25f Earth satellite station 28 15
1173 A176 40f Symbols of communication 42 28
1174 A176 50f Emblems 52 32
1175 A176 100f Airmail letter 1.10 65
Nos. 1171-1175 (5) 2.47 1.55

Intl. Palestinian Solidarity Day — A177

Dome of the Rock, Jerusalem.

1983, Nov. 29 *Perf. 12*
1176 A177 5f multicolored 35 15
1177 A177 10f multicolored 65 30

35th Anniv. of UN Declaration of Human Rights A178

1983, Dec. 10
1178 A178 10f multicolored 15 15
1179 A178 25f multicolored 25 15
1180 A178 40f multicolored 32 25
1181 A178 50f multicolored 45 30
1182 A178 100f multicolored 1.00 60
Nos. 1178-1182 (5) 2.17 1.45

Anti-Paralysis — A179

1984, Apr. 7 *Perf. 13½x11½*
1183 A179 40f multicolored 40 24
1184 A179 60f multicolored 60 36
1185 A179 100f multicolored 1.00 60

Anti-Polio Campaign.

Israeli Bombing of Iraq Nuclear Reactor A180

Various designs.

1984, June 7 Litho. *Perf. 13½x11½*
1186 A180 40f multicolored 60 24
1187 A180 60f multicolored 80 35
1188 A180 100f multicolored 1.25 60

Independence and Army Day — A181

King Hussein and various armed forces.

1984, June 10
1189 A181 10f multicolored 15 15
1190 A181 25f multicolored 25 15
1191 A181 40f multicolored 40 24
1192 A181 60f multicolored 60 35
1193 A181 100f multicolored 1.00 60
Nos. 1189-1193 (5) 2.40 1.49

1984 Summer Olympics, Los Angeles A182

1984, July 28
1194 A182 25f shown 25 15
1195 A182 40f Swimming 40 24
1196 A182 60f Shooting, archery 60 35
1197 A182 100f Gymnastics 1.00 60

An imperf. 100f souvenir sheet exists picturing pole vaulting.

Water and Electricity Year A183

1984, Aug. 11
1198 A183 25f Power lines, factory 25 15
1199 A183 40f Amman Power Station 40 24
1200 A183 60f Irrigation 60 35
1201 A183 100f Hydro-electric dam 1.00 60

Coins A184

1984, Sept. 26 Photo. *Perf. 13*
1202 A184 40f Omayyad gold dinar 40 24
1203 A184 60f Abbasid gold dinar 60 35
1204 A184 125f Hashemite silver dinar 1.25 75

Royal Society for the Conservation of Nature — A185

1984, Oct. 18
1205 A185 25f Four antelopes 25 15
1206 A185 40f Grazing 40 24
1207 A185 60f Three antelopes 60 35
1208 A185 100f King Hussein, Queen Alia, Duke of Edinburgh 1.00 60

Natl. Universities — A186

Designs: 40f, Mu'ta Military University, Karak. 60f, Yarmouk University, Irbib. 125f, Jordan University, Amman.

1984, Nov. 14 *Perf. 13x13½*
1209 A186 40f multicolored 40 24
1210 A186 60f multicolored 60 35
1211 A186 125f multicolored 1.25 75

Al Sahaba Tombs A187

Designs: 10f, El Harath bin Omier el-Azdi and Derer bin El-Azwar. 25f, Sharhabil bin Hasna and Abu Obaidah Amer bin el-Jarrah. 40f, Muath bin Jabal. 50f, Zaid bin Haretha and Abdullah bin Rawaha. 60f, Amer bin Abi Waqqas. 100f, Jafar bin Abi Taleb.

1984, Dec. 5 Litho. *Perf. 13½x11½*
1212 A187 10f multicolored 15 15
1213 A187 25f multicolored 25 15
1214 A187 40f multicolored 40 24
1215 A187 50f multicolored 50 30
1216 A187 60f multicolored 60 35
1217 A187 100f multicolored 1.00 60
Nos. 1212-1217 (6) 2.90 1.79

Independence and Army Day — A188

Designs: 25f, King Hussein, soldier descending mountain. 40f, Hussein, Arab revolt flag, globe, King Abdullah. 60f, Flag, natl. arms, equestrian. 100f, Natl. flag, arms, King Abdullah.

1985, June 10 *Perf. 13x13½*
1218 A188 25f multicolored 25 15
1219 A188 40f multicolored 40 24
1220 A188 60f multicolored 60 35
1221 A188 100f multicolored 1.00 60

Men in Postal History A189

1985, July 1
1222 A189 40f Sir Rowland Hill 40 24
1223 A189 60f Heinrich von Stephan 60 35
1224 A189 125f Yacoub al-Sukkar 1.25 75

1st Convention of Jordanian Expatriates A190

Various designs.

1985, July 20 Photo.
1225 A190 40f multicolored 40 24
1226 A190 60f multicolored 60 35
1227 A190 125f multicolored 1.25 75

Intl. Youth Year — A191

Various designs.

1985, Aug. 11 Litho. *Perf. 13½x13*
1228 A191 10f multicolored 15 15
1229 A191 25f multicolored 25 15
1230 A191 40f multicolored 40 24
1231 A191 60f multicolored 60 35
1232 A191 125f multicolored 1.25 75
Nos. 1228-1232 (5) 2.65 1.64

World Tourism Organization, 10th Anniv. — A192

1985, Sept. 13 *Perf. 13½x13*
1233 A192 10f Ruins of the Treasury, Petra 15 15
1234 A192 25f Jerash Temple 25 15
1235 A192 40f Roman baths 40 24
1236 A192 50f Jordanian valley town 50 30
1237 A192 60f Aqaba Bay 60 35
1238 A192 125f Roman amphitheater 1.25 75
Nos. 1233-1238 (6) 3.15 1.94

An imperf. 100f souvenir sheet exists picturing flower, 10 and natl. flag.

UN Child Survival Campaign A193

Various designs.

1985, Oct. 7
1239 A193 25f multicolored 25 15
1240 A193 40f multicolored 40 24
1241 A193 60f multicolored 60 35
1242 A193 125f multicolored 1.25 75

An imperf. 100f souvenir sheet exists picturing campaign emblem and the faces of healthy children.

5th Jerash Festival A194

1985, Oct. 21

1243 A194 10f Opening ceremony, 1980 15 15
1244 A194 25f Folk dancers 25 15
1245 A194 40f Dancers 40 24
1246 A194 60f Choir, Roman theater 60 35
1247 A194 100f King and Queen 1.00 60
Nos. 1243-1247 (5) 2.40 1.49

UN, 40th Anniv. A195

1985, Oct. 25 Photo. *Perf. 13x13½*

1248 A195 60f multicolored 60 35
1249 A195 125f multicolored 1.25 75

King Hussein, 50th Birthday A196

Various photos of King.

1985, Nov. 14 Litho. *Perf. 14½*

1250 A196 10f multicolored 15 15
1251 A196 25f multicolored 25 15
1252 A196 40f multicolored 40 24
1253 A196 60f multicolored 60 35
1254 A196 100f multicolored 1.00 60
Nos. 1250-1254 (5) 2.40 1.49

An imperf. 200f souvenir sheet exists picturing flags, King Hussein and Dome of the Rock.

Restoration of Al Aqsa Mosque, Jerusalem A196a

1985, Nov. 25 Litho. *Perf. 13x13½*

1254A A196a 5f multicolored *65 65*
1254B A196a 10f multicolored *1.40 1.00*

Police A197

1985, Dec. 18

1255 A197 40f Patrol car 30 20
1256 A197 60f Crossing guard 42 28
1257 A197 125f Police academy 90 60

Launch of ARABSAT-1, 1st Anniv. — A198

1986, Feb. 8 Litho. *Perf. 13½x13*

1258 A198 60f Satellite in orbit 32 20
1259 A198 100f Over map of Arab countries 55 32

Arabization of the Army, 30th Anniv. — A199

Designs: 40f, King Hussein presenting flag. 60f, Greeting army sergeant. 100f, Hussein addressing army.

1986, Mar. 1 *Perf. 11½x12½*

1260 A199 40f multicolored 22 15
1261 A199 60f multicolored 32 20
1262 A199 100f multicolored 55 32

An imperf. souvenir sheet exists with design of 100f.

Natl. Independence, 40th Anniv. — A200

Design: King Abdullah decorating soldier.

1986, May 25 *Perf. 12½x11½*

1263 A200 160f multicolored 88 52

Arab Revolt against Turkey, 70th Anniv. — A201

Unattributed paintings (details): 40f, The four sons of King Hussein, Prince of Mecca, vert. 60f, Abdullah, retainers and bodyguard. 160f, Abdullah and followers on horseback.

Perf. 12½x11½, 11½x12½

1986, June 10

1264 A201 40f multicolored 22 15
1265 A201 60f multicolored 32 20
1266 A201 160f multicolored 88 52

An imperf. 200f souvenir sheet exists picturing the Arab Revolt flag, King Abdullah and text from independence declaration.

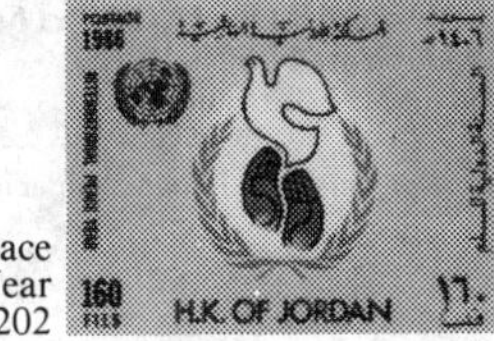

Intl. Peace Year A202

1986, July 1 Litho. *Perf. 13½x13*

1267 A202 160f multicolored 90 55
1268 A202 240f multicolored 1.35 80

King Hussein Medical City Cardiac Center A203

1986, Aug. 11

1269 A203 40f Cardiac Center 22 15
1270 A203 60f Surgery 35 22
1271 A203 100f Surgery, diff. 55 32

UN, 40th Anniv. — A204

Excerpts from King Hussein's speech: 40f, In Arabic. 80f, Arabic, diff. 100f, English.

1986, Sept. 27 *Perf. 12½x11½*

1272 A204 40f multicolored 22 15
1273 A204 80f multicolored 45 28
1274 A204 100f multicolored 55 32

An imperf. 200f stamp 90x70mm exists picturing speech in Arabic and English, King Hussein at podium.

Arab Postal Union, 35th Anniv. A205

1987, Apr. 12 Litho. *Perf. 13½x13*

1275 A205 80f Old post office 45 28
1276 A205 160f New post office 90 55

Chemical Soc. Emblem and Chemists — A206

Designs: 60f, Jaber ibn Hayyan al-Azdi (720-813). 80f, Abu-al-Qasem al-Majreeti (950-1007). 240f, Abu-Bakr al-Razi (864-932).

1987, Apr. 24

1277 A206 60f multicolored 35 22
1278 A206 80f multicolored 45 28
1279 A206 240f multicolored 1.35 80

SOS Children's Village — A207

1987, May 7

1280 A207 80f Village in Amman 45 28
1281 A207 240f Child, bird mural 1.35 80

4th Brigade, 40th Anniv. A208

1987, June 10

1282 A208 60f shown 35 22
1283 A208 80f Soldiers in armored vehicle 45 28

Size: 70x91mm

Imperf

1284 A208 160f Four veterans 90 55

Indigenous Birds A209

1987, June 24

1285 A209 10f Hoopoe 15 15
1286 A209 40f Palestine sunbird 30 20
1287 A209 50f Black-headed bunting 38 25
1288 A209 60f Spur-winged plover 45 30
1289 A209 80f Greenfinch 60 40
1290 A209 100f Black-winged stilt 75 50
Nos. 1285-1290 (6) 2.63 1.80

King Hussein — A210

1987, June 24 Litho. *Perf. 13x13½*

1291 A210 60f multicolored 45 30
1292 A210 80f multicolored 60 40
1293 A210 160f multicolored 1.20 80
1294 A210 240f multicolored 1.80 1.20

Battle of Hittin, 800th Anniv. A211

Dome of the Rock and Saladin (1137-1193), Conqueror of Jerusalem — A212

1987, July 4

1295 A211 60f Battle, Jerusalem 35 24

1296 A211 80f Horseman, Jerusalem, Dome of the Rock 45 30

1297 A211 100f Saladin 75 50

Souvenir Sheet

Perf. 12x12½

1298 A212 100f shown 75 50

No. 1298 exists imperf.

Natl. Coat of Arms — A213

Perf. 11½x12½

1987, Aug. 11 **Litho.**

1299 A213 80f multicolored 60 40

1300 A213 160f multicolored 1.20 80

Amman Industrial Park at Sahab — A214

1987, Aug. 11 ***Perf. 13½x13***

1301 A214 80f multicolored 60 40

University Crest A215

University Entrance — A216

Perf. 11½x11, 12½x11½

1987, Sept. 2

1302 A215 60f multicolored 45 30

1303 A216 80f multicolored 60 40

University of Jordan, 25th anniv.

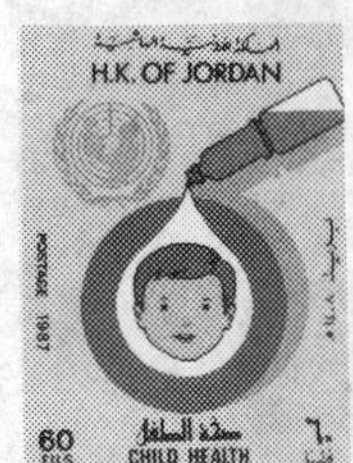

UN Child Survival Campaign A217

1987, Oct. 5 **Litho.** ***Perf. 13x13½***

1304 A217 60f Oral vaccine 45 30

1305 A217 80f Natl. flag, child 60 40

1306 A217 160f Growth monitoring 1.20 80

Parliament, 40th Anniv. — A218

1987, Oct. 20 ***Perf. 13½x13***

1307 A218 60f Opening ceremony, 1947 45 30

1308 A218 80f In session, 1987 60 40

A219

Special Arab Summit Conference, Amman — A220

1987, Nov. 8

1309 A219 60f multicolored 45 30

1310 A219 80f multicolored 60 40

1311 A219 160f multicolored 1.20 80

1312 A219 240f multicolored 1.80 1.20

Size: 90x66mm

Imperf

1313 A220 100f multicolored

King Hussein, Dag Hammarskjold Peace Prize Winner for 1987 — A221

1988, Feb. 6 **Litho.** ***Perf. 12½***

1314 A221 80f Hussein, woman, vert. 60 40

1315 A221 160f shown 1.20 80

Natl. Victory at the 1987 Arab Military Basketball Championships — A222

1988, Mar. 1 ***Perf. 13½x13***

1316 A222 60f Golden Sword Award 45 30

1317 A222 80f Hussein congratulating team 60 40

1318 A222 160f Jump ball 1.20 80

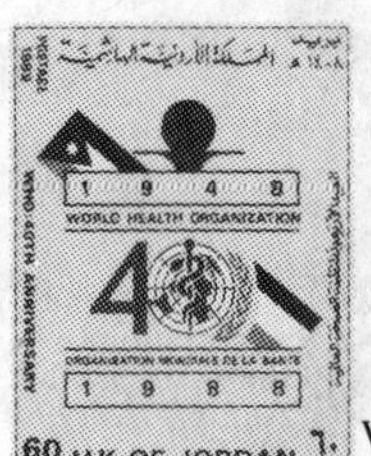

WHO, 40th Anniv. — A223

1988, Apr. 7 **Photo.** ***Perf. 13x13½***

1319 A223 60f multicolored 55 38

1320 A223 80f multicolored 72 48

Arab Scouts, 75th Anniv. — A224

1988, July 2 **Litho.** ***Perf. 13x13½***

1321 A224 60f multicolored 45 35

1322 A224 80f multicolored 60 45

Birds A225

1988, July 21 **Litho.** ***Perf. 11½x12***

1323 A225 10f Crested lark 15 15

1324 A225 20f Stone curlew 15 15

1325 A225 30f Redstart 20 15

1326 A225 40f Blackbird 28 22

1327 A225 50f Rock dove 35 28

1328 A225 160f Smyrna kingfisher 1.10 82

Size: 71x90mm

Imperf

1328A A225 310f Six species 3.75 2.75

Nos. 1323-1328A (7) 5.98 4.52

Restoration of San'a, Yemen Arab Republic A226

1988, Aug. 11 **Litho.** ***Perf. 12x11½***

1329 A226 80f multicolored 60 45

1330 A226 160f multicolored 1.20 90

Historic Natl. Sites A227

1988, Aug. 11 ***Perf. 13½x13***

1331 A227 60f Umm Al-rasas 45 35

1332 A227 80f Umm Qais 60 45

1333 A227 160f Iraq Al-amir 1.20 90

An imperf. souvenir sheet of 3 exists containing one each Nos. 1331-1333.

1988 Summer Olympics, Seoul — A228

1988, Sept. 17 **Litho.** ***Perf. 13x13½***

1334 A228 10f Tennis 15 15

1335 A228 60f Character trademark 45 35

1336 A228 80f Running, swimming 60 45

1337 A228 120f Basketball 90 68

1338 A228 160f Soccer 1.20 90

Nos. 1334-1338 (5) 3.30 2.53

Size: 70x91mm

Imperf

1339 A228 100f Emblems

Royal Jordanian Airlines, 25th Anniv. — A229

1988, Dec. 15 **Litho.** ***Perf. 11½x12***

1340 A229 60f Ruins of Petra 42 32

1341 A229 80f Aircraft, world map 55 42

UN Declaration of Human Rights, 40th Anniv. — A230

1988, Dec. 10

1342 A230 80f multicolored 55 42

1343 A230 160f multicolored 1.10 82

Arab Cooperation Council, Feb. 16 — A231

1989 Litho. *Perf. 13½x13*
1344 A231 10f shown 15 15
1345 A231 30f multi, diff. 15 15
1346 A231 40f multi, diff. 20 15
1347 A231 60f multi, diff. 30 22
Set value 54

Martyrs of Palestine and Their Families A232

1989 *Perf. 14½*
1348 A232 5f multi 15 15
1349 A232 10f multi 15 15
Set value 20 16

Interparliamentary Union, Cent. — A233

1989 Litho. *Perf. 12*
1350 A233 40f multicolored 22 16
1351 A233 60f multicolored 35 25

Arab Housing Day and World Refuge Day — A234

Designs: 5f, Housing complex, emblems, vert. 60f, Housing complex, emblem.

1989
1352 A234 5f multicolored 15 15
1353 A234 40f shown 22 16
1354 A234 60f multicolored 35 25
Set value 60 55

Ministry of Agriculture, 50th Anniv. A235

1989 Litho. *Perf. 12*
1355 A235 5f shown 15 15
1356 A235 40f Tree, anniv. emblem 17 15
1357 A235 60f Fruit tree, emblem, apiary 25 16
Set value 46 30

Arabian Horse Festival — A236

1989 *Perf. 12*
1358 A236 5f shown 15 15
1359 A236 40f Horse, building facade 17 15
1360 A236 60f Horse's head, vert. 25 16

Size: 90x70mm

Imperf
1361 A236 100f Mare and foal 7.50 5.00

Natl. Library Assoc. A237

1989 *Perf. 12*
1362 A237 40f multicolored 15 15
1363 A237 60f multicolored 22 15
Set value 24

Mosque of the Martyr King Abdullah — A238

1989 *Perf. 12*
1364 A238 40f multicolored 15 15
1365 A238 60f multicolored 22 15

Size: 90x70mm

Imperf
1366 A238 100f multicolored 5.25 5.25

Mosaics A239

1989, Dec. 23 Litho. *Perf. 12*
1367 A239 5f Man with Basket 15 15
1368 A239 10f Building 15 15
1369 A239 40f Deer 42 28
1370 A239 60f shown 62 40
1371 A239 80f Town, horiz. 82 55

Size: 90x70mm

Imperf
1372 A239 100f like #1371, horiz. 6.00 4.00

Arab Cooperation Council, 1st Anniv. — A240

1990, Feb. 16 *Perf. 13*
1373 A240 5f multicolored 15 15
1374 A240 20f multicolored 18 15
1375 A240 60f multicolored 55 36
1376 A240 80f multicolored 72 48

Nature Conservation — A241

1990, Apr. 22
1377 A241 40f Horses 20 15
1378 A241 60f Mountain 30 15
1379 A241 80f Oasis 40 25

Prince Abdullah's Arrival in Ma'an, 70th Anniv. — A243

1990 Litho. *Perf. 13½x13*
1382 A243 40f org & multi 15 15
1383 A243 60f grn & multi 22 15

Size: 90x70mm

Imperf
1384 A243 200f multicolored 2.75 1.80

UN Development Program, 40th Anniv. — A244

1990 *Perf. 13*
1385 A244 60f multicolored 22 15
1386 A244 80f multicolored 30 20

King Hussein — A245

1991 Litho. *Perf. 12x13½*
1387 A245 5f yel org & multi 15 15
1393 A245 60f blue & multi 30 15
1395 A245 80f pink & multi 45 22
Set value 42

This is an expanding set. Numbers will change if necessary.

Endangered Animals A246

1991, Sept. 1 Litho. *Perf. 13x13½*
1401 A246 5f Nubian ibex 15 15
1402 A246 40f Onager 18 15
1403 A246 80f Arabian gazelle 35 18
1404 A246 160f Arabian oryx 70 25
Set value 60

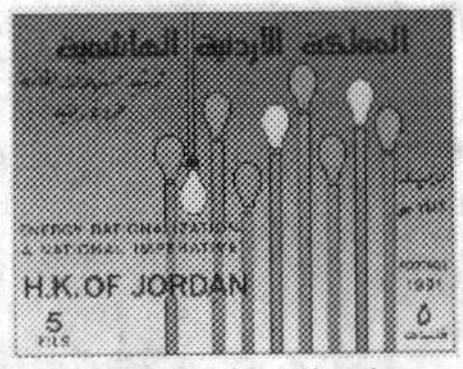

Energy Rationalization Program — A247

Designs: 5f, Light bulbs. 40f, Solar panels, sun, vert. 80f, Electric table lamp, vert.

Perf. 13½x13, 13x13½
1991, Oct. 3 Litho.
1405 A247 5f multicolored 15 15
1406 A247 40f multicolored 18 15
1407 A247 80f multicolored 35 18
Set value 56 28

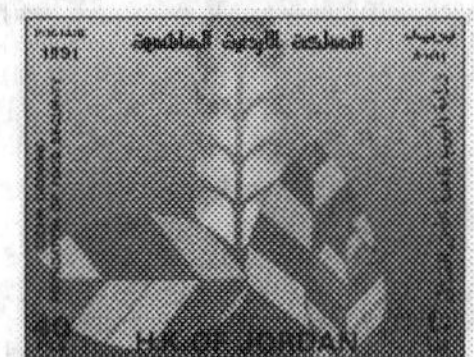

Grain Production for Food Security — A248

1991, Oct. 16 *Perf. 13½x13*
1408 A248 5f Different grains 15 15
1409 A248 40f shown 18 15
1410 A248 80f Wheat stalk, kernels 35 18
Set value 56 28

Palestinian Uprising — A249

1991 Litho. *Perf. 11*
1411 A249 20f multicolored 68 35

SEMI-POSTAL STAMPS

Locust Campaign Issue

Nos. 145-156 Overprinted مكافحة الجراد LOCUST CAMPAIGN

1930, Apr. 1 Wmk. 4 *Perf. 14*
B1 A1 2(m) Prus blue 1.00 1.10
a. Inverted overprint 175.00
B2 A1 3(m) rose 1.25 1.40
B3 A1 4(m) green 18 20

B4 A1 5(m) orange 5.00 5.25
a. Double overprint 250.00
B5 A1 10(m) red 25 30
B6 A1 15(m) ultra 30 32
a. Inverted overprint 150.00
B7 A1 20(m) olive grn 35 40
B8 A2 50(m) claret 1.40 1.50
B9 A2 90(m) bister 5.00 5.50
B10 A2 100(m) lt blue 3.50 3.50
B11 A2 200(m) violet 15.00 15.00
B12 A2 500(m) brown 40.00 40.00
a. "C" of "Locust" omitted 600.00
Nos. B1-B12 (12) 73.23 74.47

These stamps were issued to raise funds to help combat a plague of locusts.

AIR POST STAMPS

Catalogue values for unused stamps in this section are for Never Hinged items.

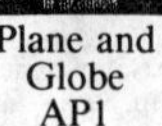

Plane and Globe
AP1

Temple of Artemis, Jerash
AP2

Perf. 13½x13

1950, Sept. 16 Engr. Wmk. 4

C1 AP1 5f org & red vio 15 15
C2 AP1 10f pur & brown 16 16
C3 AP1 15f ol grn & rose car 20 20
C4 AP1 20f deep blue & blk 30 30
C5 AP1 50f rose pink & dl grn 40 30
C6 AP1 100f blue & brown 70 70
C7 AP1 150f blk & red org 1.00 1.00
Nos. C1-C7 (7) 2.91 2.81

1954 Unwmk. *Perf. 12*

C8 AP2 5f blue blk & org 15 15
C9 AP2 10f vio brn & ver 15 15
C10 AP2 25f bl grn & ultra 15 15
C11 AP2 35f dp plum & grnsh bl 18 15
C12 AP2 40f car rose & blk 22 15
C13 AP2 50f dp ultra & org yel 25 25
C14 AP2 100f dk bl & vio brn 45 45
C15 AP2 150f stl bl & red brn 60 60
Nos. C8-C15 (8) 2.15 2.05

1958-59 Wmk. 305 *Perf. 12*

C16 AP2 5f blue blk & org 15 15
C17 AP2 10f vio brn & ver 15 15
C18 AP2 25f bl grn & ultra 20 15
C19 AP2 35f dp plum grnsh bl 20 20
C20 AP2 40f car rose & blk 25 25
C21 AP2 50f dp ultra & org yel ('59) 60 60
Set value 1.30 1.25

Stadium and Torch
AP3

Perf. 11x11½

1964, July 12 Litho. Wmk. 305

C22 AP3 1f yellow & multi 15 15
C23 AP3 4f red & multi 15 15
C24 AP3 10f blue & multi 15 15
C25 AP3 35f yel grn & multi 42 42
a. Souvenir sheet of 4, #C22-C25 1.00 1.00
Set value 65 65

Opening of Hussein Sports City. No. C25a also exists imperf.

Gorgeous Bush-Shrike — AP4

Birds: 500f, Ornate hawk-eagle (vert.). 1d, Gray-headed kingfisher (vert.).

Perf. 14x14½

1964, Dec. 18 Photo. Unwmk.

Birds in Natural Colors

C26 AP4 150f lt grn, blk & car 1.65 40
C27 AP4 500f brt bl, blk & grn 8.25 2.75
C28 AP4 1d lt ol grn & blk 16.00 8.25

Pagoda, Olympic Torch and Emblem — AP5

1965, Mar. 5 Litho. *Perf. 14*

C29 AP5 10f deep rose 15 15
C30 AP5 15f violet 15 15
C31 AP5 20f blue 15 15
C32 AP5 30f green 18 18
C33 AP5 40f brown 25 25
C34 AP5 60f carmine rose 38 38
Set value 1.05 1.05

18th Olympic Games, Tokyo, Oct. 10-25, 1964. An imperf. 100f violet blue souvenir sheet exists. Size of stamp: 60x60mm. Value $9.

For overprints see Nos. C42A-C42F.

Forum, Jerash
AP6

Antiquities of Jerash: No. C36, South Theater. No. C37, Triumphal arch. No. C38, Temple of Artemis. No. C39, Cathedral steps. No. C40, Artemis Temple, gate. No. C41, Columns. No. C42, Columns and niche, South Theater. Nos. C39-C42 are vertical.

1965, June 22 Photo. *Perf. 14x15*

Center Multicolored

C35 AP6 55f bright pink 45 45
C36 AP6 55f light blue 45 45
C37 AP6 55f green 45 45
C38 AP6 55f black 45 45
C39 AP6 55f light green 45 45
C40 AP6 55f carmine rose 45 45
C41 AP6 55f gray 45 45
C42 AP6 55f blue 45 45
Nos. C35-C42 (8) 3.60 3.60

Nos. C35-C38 are printed in horizontal rows of four; Nos. C39-C42 in vertical rows of four; sheets of 16.

Nos. C29-C34 with Bilingual Ovpt. "James McDivitt / Edward White / 2-6-1965" and Rocket

1965, Sept. 25 Litho. *Perf. 14*

C42A AP5 10f deep rose 30 30
C42B AP5 15f violet 45 45
C42C AP5 20f blue 60 60
C42D AP5 30f green 90 90
C42E AP5 40f brown 1.25 1.25
C42F AP5 60f carmine rose 1.75 1.75

The imperf. 100f blue souvenir sheet exists overprinted.

King Hussein Type of Regular Issue

1966, Jan. 15 Photo. *Perf. 14½x14*

Portrait in Brown

C43 A67 200f brt blue grn 1.50 75
C44 A67 500f light green 3.75 2.00
C45 A67 1d light ultra 7.50 3.75

Animal Type of Regular Issue, 1967

Animals: 4f, Striped hyena. 30f, Arabian stallion. 60f, Persian gazelle.

1967, Feb. 11 Photo. *Perf. 14x15*

C46 A70 4f dk brn & multi 15 15
C47 A70 30f lt bl & multi 22 15
C48 A70 60f yellow & multi 45 30
Set value 70 50

Game Type of Regular Issue, 1968

Protected Game: 60f, Nubian ibex (vert.). 100f, Wild ducks.

1968, Oct. 5 Litho. *Perf. 13½*

C49 A74 60f multicolored 75 75
C50 A74 100f multicolored 1.40 1.40

Easter Type of Regular Issue

Designs: 60f, Altar, Holy Sepulcher. 100f, Feet Washing, Holy Gate, Jerusalem.

1972, Apr. Photo. *Perf. 14x13½*

C51 A92 60f dk bl & multi 45 45
C52 A92 100f multicolored 75 75

Aero Club Type of Regular Issue

Designs: 15f, Two Piper 140s. 20f, R.J.A.C. Beechcraft. 40f, Aero Club emblem with winged horse.

1973, Jan. Photo. *Perf. 13½x14*

C53 A100 15f blue, blk & red 15 15
C54 A100 20f blue, blk & red 18 15
C55 A100 40f mag, blk & yel 38 22
Set value 38

Agriculture Type of Regular Issue

Design: 100f, Soil conservation.

1973, Dec. 25 *Perf. 13½*

C56 A110 100f multicolored 65 45

King Hussein Driving Car — AP7

1974, Dec. 20 *Perf. 12*

C57 AP7 30f multicolored 20 15
C58 AP7 60f multicolored 45 32

Royal Jordanian Automobile Club.

Building Type of Regular Issue

Designs: 50f, Palms, Aqaba. 60f, Obelisk tomb. 80f, Fort of Wadi Rum.

1975, Mar. 1 Photo. *Perf. 13½x14*

C59 A121 50f pink & multi 32 22
C60 A121 60f lt bl & multi 42 30
C61 A121 80f yellow & multi 52 32

Hussein Type of Regular Issue

1975, Apr. 8 Photo. *Perf. 14x13½*

Size: 22x27mm

C62 A123 60f dk grn & brn 28 18
C63 A123 100f org brn & brn 42 30
C64 A123 120f dp bl & brn 50 36
C65 A123 180f brt mag & brn 85 50
C66 A123 200f grnsh bl & brn 90 50
C67 A123 400f pur & brown 1.75 1.10
C68 A123 500f orange & brn 2.25 1.40
Nos. C62-C68 (7) 6.95 4.34

POSTAGE DUE STAMPS

Stamps of Regular Issue (Nos. 69, 66-68) Surcharged with New Value like No. 91) Overprinted

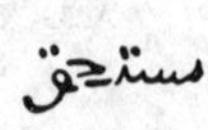

This overprint reads: "Mustahaq" (Tax or Due)

1923 Unwmk. *Perf. 11½*

Typo. Ovpt. "Mustahaq" 10mm long

J1 A7 ½pi on 3pi ol brn 62.50 65.00
a. Inverted overprint 120.00 120.00
b. Double overprint 160.00 150.00

Handstamped Overprints "Mustahaq" 12mm long

J2 A7 ½pi on 3pi ol brn 24.00 25.00
J3 A7 1pi dark blue 12.00 12.50
J4 A7 1½pi violet 12.00 12.50
J5 A7 2pi orange 12.00 12.50

These overprints are found double, inverted, etc. as is usual with handstamps.

Stamps of Hejaz Handstamped

J6 A7 ½pi red 45 45
J7 A7 1pi dark blue 52 52
J8 A7 1½pi violet 65 65
J9 A7 2pi orange 85 85
J10 A7 3pi olive brown 1.40 1.40
J11 A7 5pi olive green 1.90 1.90
Nos. J6-J11 (6) 5.77 5.77

Type of Palestine, 1918, Overprinted

1925 Wmk. 4 *Perf. 14*

J12 A1 1m dark brown 25 38
J13 A1 2m yellow 30 60
J14 A1 4m rose 45 75
J15 A1 8m red 52 75
J16 A1 13m ultramarine 75 80
J17 A1 5pi plum 1.25 1.50
a. Perf. 15x14 5.00 5.50
Nos. J12-J17 (6) 3.52 4.78

The overprint reads: "Mustahaq. Sharqi al'Ardan." (Tax. Eastern Jordan).

Stamps of Palestine, 1918, Surcharged

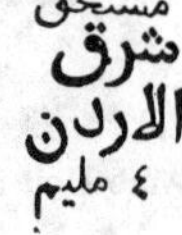

1926

J18 A1 1m on 1m dk brn 65 80
J19 A1 2m on 1m dk brn 65 80
J20 A1 4m on 3m Prus bl 1.25 1.40
J21 A1 8m on 3m Prus bl 1.00 1.25
J22 A1 13m on 13m ultra 1.40 1.90
J23 A1 5pi on 13m ultra 1.40 1.90
Nos. J18-J23 (6) 6.35 8.05

The surcharge reads "Tax—Eastern Jordan" and New Value.

Stamps of Regular Issue, 1927, Overprinted

1929

J24 A1 2m Prussian bl 38 25
J25 A1 10m red 90 45
J26 A2 50m claret 1.65 1.25

With Additional Surcharge

J27 A1 4(m) on 3(m) rose 25 25
J28 A1 4(m) on 15(m) ultra 65 42
a. Inverted surch. and ovpt. 90.00
J29 A2 20(m) on 100(m) lt bl 1.40 1.20

D1

D2

1929 Engr. *Perf. 14*

Size: 17¼x21mm

J30 D1 1m brown 15 15
a. Perf. 13½x13 90.00 45.00
J31 D1 2m orange 20 20
J32 D1 4m green 20 20
J33 D1 10m carmine 40 40

J34 D1 20m olive green 40 40
J35 D1 50m blue 65 65
Nos. J30-J35 (6) 2.00 2.00

See Nos. J39-J43. For surcharge, see No. J52. For overprints, see Nos. NJ1a, NJ3, NJ5a, NJ6-NJ7.

1942 Unwmk. Litho. *Perf. 13x13½*
J36 D2 1m dull red brn 15 15
J37 D2 2m dl orange yel 25 25
J38 D2 10m dark carmine 50 50

For overprints, see Nos. NJ8-NJ10.

Type of 1929

1943-44 Engr. Wmk. 4 *Perf. 12*
Size: 17¾x21¼mm
J39 D1 1m orange brn 15 15
J40 D1 2m yel orange 15 15
J41 D1 4m yel green 15 15
J42 D1 10m rose carmine 15 15
J43 D1 20m olive green 4.50 4.50
Nos. J39-J43 (5) 5.10 5.10

For overprints, see Nos. J47-J51, NJ1-NJ2, NJ3a, NJ5, NJ6a.

Catalogue values for unused stamps in this section, from this point to the end of the section, are for Never Hinged items.

Nos. J39-J43, J35 Surcharged "FILS" and its Arabic Equivalent in Black, Green or Carmine

1952 Wmk. 4 *Perf. 12*
J47 D1 1f on 1m org brn (Bk) 15 15
J48 D1 2f on 2m yel org (G) 15 15
J49 D1 4f on 4m yel grn 15 15
J50 D1 10f on 10m rose car (Bk) 40 35
J51 D1 20f on 20m ol grn 50 50

Perf. 14
J52 D1 50f on 50m blue 65 65
Nos. J47-J52 (6) 2.00 1.95

This overprint exists on Nos. J34, J36-J38. Exists inverted, double and in wrong color.

D3

Inscribed: "The Hashemite Kingdom of the Jordan"

1952 Engr. *Perf. 11½*
J53 D3 1f orange brown 15 15
J54 D3 2f yel orange 15 15
J55 D3 4f yel green 15 15
J56 D3 10f rose carmine 15 15
J57 D3 20f yel brown 15 15
J58 D3 50f blue 52 30
Set value 90 60

Type of 1952 Redrawn

Inscribed: "The Hashemite Kingdom of Jordan"

1957 Wmk. 305 *Perf. 11½*
J59 D3 1f orange brown 15 15
J60 D3 2f yel orange 15 15
J61 D3 4f yel green 15 15
J62 D3 10f rose carmine 18 15
J63 D3 20f yel brown 35 25
Set value 70 50

OFFICIAL STAMP

Saudi Arabia No. L34 Overprinted

(حكومة)
الشرق العربي
١٣٤٢

1924, Jan. Typo. *Perf. 11½*
O1 A7 ½pi red 45.00

Overprint reads: "(Government) the Arabian East 1342."

POSTAL TAX STAMPS

Catalogue values for unused stamps in this section are for Never Hinged items.

Mosque at Hebron — PT1

Designs: 10m, 15m, 20m, 50m, Dome of the Rock. 100m, 200m, 500m, £1, Acre.

Perf. 11½x12½
1947 Unwmk. Engr.
RA1 PT1 1m ultra 20 15
RA2 PT1 2m carmine 20 20
RA3 PT1 3m emerald 28 28
RA4 PT1 5m plum 38 20
RA5 PT1 10m carmine 40 30
RA6 PT1 15m gray 60 30
RA7 PT1 20m dk brn 75 45
RA8 PT1 50m purple 1.90 1.10
RA9 PT1 100m org red 3.75 2.50
RA10 PT1 200m dp blue 9.00 7.50
RA11 PT1 500m green 15.00 12.50
RA12 PT1 £1 dk brn 25.00 25.00
Nos. RA1-RA12 (12) 57.46 50.48

Issued to help the Welfare Fund for Arabs in Palestine. Required on foreign-bound letters to the amount of half the regular postage.
For surcharges, see Nos. RA37-RA46. For Overprints, see Nos. 286A-286C, 344-346, NRA1-NRA12.

اغاثة

Nos. 211, 232 and 234 Overprinted in Black

Aid

1950 Wmk. 4 *Perf. 12*
RA23 A3 5m orange 6.50
RA24 A3 10m violet 10.00
RA25 A3 15m dull ol grn 12.00

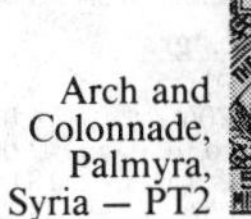

Arch and Colonnade, Palmyra, Syria — PT2

Two types of 5m:
Type I - "A" with serifs. Arabic ovpt. 8mm wide.
Type II - "A" without serifs. Arabic ovpt. 5mm wide.

Black or Carmine Overprint

1950-51 Engr. *Perf. 13½x13*
RA26 PT2 5m org (I) 6.55
a. Type II ('51) 27.50
RA27 PT2 10m vio (C) 6.50

The overprint on No. RA27 is similar to that on RA23-RA25 but slightly bolder.

Type of 1947

Designs: 5f, Hebron Mosque. 10f, 15f, 20f, Dome of the Rock. 100f, Acre.

1951 Wmk. 4 *Perf. 11½x12½*
RA28 PT1 5f plum 15 15
RA29 PT1 10f carmine 15 15
RA30 PT1 15f gray 16 16
RA31 PT1 20f dk brown 22 22
RA33 PT1 100f orange 1.50 1.50
Nos. RA28-RA33 (5) 2.18 2.18

The tax on Nos. RA1-RA33 was for Arab aid in Palestine.
For overprints, see Nos. 287-290.

Postal Tax Stamps of 1947 Surcharged "FILS" or "J.D." and Their Arabic Equivalents and Bars in Carmine or Black

1952 Unwmk.
RA37 PT1 1f on 1m ultra 25 15
RA38 PT1 3f on 3m emer 25 15
RA39 PT1 10f on 10m car 40 28
RA40 PT1 15f on 15m gray 55 40
RA41 PT1 20f on 20m dk brown 80 55
RA42 PT1 50f on 50m pur 2.00 1.40
RA43 PT1 100f on 100m org red 5.50 3.50
RA44 PT1 200f on 200m dp blue 14.00 4.25
RA45 PT1 500f on 500m grn 22.50 9.00
RA46 PT1 1d on £1 dk brn 37.50 21.00
Nos. RA37-RA46 (10) 83.75 40.68

"J.D." stands for Jordanian Dinar.

OCCUPATION STAMPS

Catalogue values for unused stamps in this section are for Never Hinged items.

For Use in Palestine

Stamps of Jordan Overprinted in Red, Black, Dark Green, Green or Orange Red

فلسطين
PALESTINE

On No. 200

1948 Unwmk. *Perf. 13x13½*
N1 A14 2m dull green (R) 75 75

On Nos. 207 to 209, 211, 230 to 235 and 215 to 220

1948 Wmk. 4 *Perf. 12, 13½x13, 14*
N2 A3 1m red brown 20 20
N3 A3 2m Prus green (R) 30 30
a. 2m Prussian blue, perf. 13½x13 (R) (#170a) 30 50
N4 A3 3m blue green (R) 50 50
N5 A3 3m rose carmine 25 25
N6 A3 4m dp yel grn (R) 25 25
N7 A3 5m orange (G) 60 25
N8 A3 10m violet (OR) 75 35
N9 A3 12m deep rose 60 60
N10 A3 15m dl ol grn (R) 70 50
N11 A3 20m dp blue (R) 60 60
N12 A3 50m red lil (Dk G) 1.25 1.25
N13 A3 90m ocher (Dk G) 4.00 3.50
N14 A3 100m dp blue (R) 4.50 4.00
N15 A3 200m dk vio (R) 8.00 7.00
a. 200m vio, perf. 14 (R) (#182) 15.00 15.00
N16 A3 500m dk brn (R) 13.00 5.00
N17 A3 £1 black (R) 20.00 10.00
Nos. N2-N17 (16) 55.50 34.55

The first overprinting of these stamps include Nos. N1-N6, N9-N17. The second overprinting includes Nos. N1, N3, N5-N17, in inks differing in shade from the originals.
Many values exist with inverted or double overprint.

فلسطين

Jordan, Nos. 245 to 249, Overprinted in Black or Red

PALESTINE

1949, Aug. Wmk. 4 *Perf. 13*
N18 A17 1m brown (Bk) 15 15
N19 A17 4m green 18 18
a. "PLAESTINE" 20.00
N20 A17 10m ultra 28 28
N21 A17 20m ultra 28 28
N22 A18 50m dull green 70 70
a. "PLAESTINE" 20.00
Nos. N18-N22 (5) 1.59 1.59

The overprint is in one line on No. N22.
UPU, 75th anniversary.

OCCUPATION POSTAGE DUE STAMPS

Catalogue values for unused stamps in this section are for Never Hinged items.

فلسطين

Jordan Nos. J39, J30a, J40, J32, J41-J43, J34 and J35 Overprinted in Black, Red or Carmine

PALESTINE

1948-49 Wmk. 4 *Perf. 12, 14*
NJ1 D1 1m org brn, perf. 12 15 15
a. Perf. 13½x13 (#J30a) 15.00 10.00
NJ2 D1 2m yel orange 15 15
NJ3 D1 4m grn (R) (#J32) 50 50
a. 4m yel grn (C) (#J41) 3.75
NJ5 D1 10m rose car (#J42) ('49) 80 80
a. Perf. 14 (#J33) 80.00
NJ6 D1 20m ol grn (R), perf. 14 50 50
a. Perf. 12 (R) (#J43) 20.00
NJ7 D1 50m blue (R) 50 50
Nos. NJ1-NJ3,NJ5-NJ7 (6) 2.60 2.60

The second overprinting of these stamps includes Nos. NJ1-NJ3, NJ3a and NJ5-NJ7, in inks differing in shade from the originals.
Double and inverted overprints exist.

Same Overprint in Black on Jordan Nos. J36-J38

1948-49 Unwmk. *Perf. 13x13½*
NJ8 D2 1m dl red brn 100.00 100.00
NJ9 D2 2m dl org yel ('49) 5.00 5.00
NJ10 D2 10m dark car 2.00 2.00

OCCUPATION POSTAL TAX STAMPS

Catalogue values for unused stamps in this section are for Never Hinged items.

Postal Tax Stamps of 1947 Overprinted in Red or Black

فلسطين
PALESTINE

1950
NRA1 PT1 1m ultra (R) 20 16
NRA2 PT1 2m carmine 20 16
NRA3 PT1 3m emer (R) 28 20
NRA4 PT1 5m plum 40 28
NRA5 PT1 10m carmine 90 40
NRA6 PT1 15m gray (R) 1.40 60
NRA7 PT1 20m dk brn (R) 2.00 75
NRA8 PT1 50m pur (R) 2.75 1.40
NRA9 PT1 100m org red 3.50 1.75
NRA10 PT1 200m dp bl (R) 10.00 4.00
NRA11 PT1 500m green (R) 20.00 10.00
NRA12 PT1 £1 dk brn (R) 37.50 20.00
Nos. NRA1-NRA12 (12) 79.13 39.70

For overprints, see Nos. 286D-286G.

KARELIA

LOCATION — In northwestern Soviet Russia.
GOVT. — An autonomous republic of the Soviet Union.
AREA — 55,198 sq. mi. (approx.).
POP. — 270,000 (approx.).
CAPITAL — Petrozavodsk (Kalininsk).

In 1921 the Karelians rebelled and for a short period a form of sovereignty independent of Russia was maintained.

100 Pennia = 1 Markka

Bear — A1

1922 Unwmk. Litho. *Perf. 11½, 12*
1 A1 5p dk gray 8.00 *27.50*
2 A1 10p lt bl 8.00 *27.50*
3 A1 20p rose red 8.00 *27.50*
4 A1 25p yel brn 8.00 *27.50*
5 A1 40p magenta 8.00 *27.50*
6 A1 50p gray grn 8.00 *27.50*
7 A1 75p org yel 8.00 *27.50*
8 A1 1m pink & gray 8.00 *27.50*
9 A1 2m yel grn & gray 20.00 *35.00*
10 A1 3m lt bl & gray 25.00 *35.00*
11 A1 5m red lil & gray 25.00 *65.00*
12 A1 10m lt brn & gray 25.00 *90.00*
13 A1 15m grn & car 25.00 *90.00*

14	A1	20m rose & grn	25.00	*90.00*
15	A1	25m yel & bl	25.00	*90.00*
		Nos. 1-15 (15)	234.00	

Nos. 1-15 were valid Jan. 31-Feb. 16, 1922. Counterfeits abound.

OCCUPATION STAMPS

Issued under Finnish Occupation

Issued in the Russian territory of Eastern Karelia under Finnish military administration.

Types of Finland Stamps, 1930 Overprinted in Black:

ITÄ-KARJALA Sot.hallinto On A26 — **ITÄ-KARJALA Sot.hallinto** On A27-A28

1941		**Unwmk.**		***Perf. 14***
N1	A26	50p brt yel grn	35	*85*
N2	A26	1.75m dk gray	75	*1.25*
N3	A26	2m dp org	1.50	*2.25*
N4	A26	2.75m yel org	70	*1.25*
N5	A26	3½m lt ultra	1.50	*2.25*
N6	A27	5m rose vio	3.50	*6.75*
N7	A28	10m pale brn	3.50	*7.75*
		Nos. N1-N7 (7)	11.80	*22.35*

Types of Finland Stamps, 1930 Overprinted in Green:

ITÄ-KARJALA Sot. hallinto On A26 — **ITÄ-KARJALA Sot. hallinto** On A27-A29

N8	A26	50p brt yel grn	35	*65*
N9	A26	1.75m dk gray	52	*70*
N10	A26	2m dp org	70	*1.10*
N11	A26	2.75m yel org	52	*70*
N12	A26	3½m lt ultra	70	*1.25*
N13	A27	5m rose vio	1.50	*3.25*
N14	A28	10m pale brn	3.50	*6.00*
N15	A29	25m green	3.50	*6.00*
		Nos. N8-N15 (8)	11.29	*19.65*

Mannerheim Type of Finland Overprinted **ITÄ-KARJALA Sot.hallinto**

1942				
N16	A48	50p dk yel grn	60	*1.40*
N17	A48	1.75m slate bl	60	*1.40*
N18	A48	2m red org	60	*1.40*
N19	A48	2.75m brn org	48	*1.25*
N20	A48	3.50m brt ultra	48	*1.25*
N21	A48	5m brn vio	48	*1.25*
		Nos. N16-N21 (6)	3.24	*7.95*

Same Overprint on Ryti Type of Finland

N22	A49	50p dk yel grn	48	*1.24*
N23	A49	1.75m slate bl	48	*1.24*
N24	A49	2m red org	48	*1.24*
N25	A49	2.75m brn org	60	*1.40*
N26	A49	3.50m brt ultra	60	*1.40*
N27	A49	5m brn vio	60	*1.40*
		Nos. N22-N27 (6)	3.24	*7.92*

The overprint translates, "East Karelia Military Administration."

OCCUPATION SEMI-POSTAL STAMP

Arms of East Karelia — SP1

1943		**Unwmk.**	**Engr.**	***Perf. 14***
NB1	SP1	3.50m + 1.50m dk ol	60	*2.50*

This surtax aided war victims in East Karelia.

KATANGA

Katanga province seceded from the Congo (ex-Belgian) Republic in July, 1960, but established nations did not recognize it as an independent state. The United Nations declared the secession ended in September, 1961. During the secession, Congo stamps were overprinted "KATANGA" at Elisabethville, and a few were surcharged. Also a set of Katanga stamps in new designs was released. These stamps were tolerated in the international mails, but the government authorizing them was not recognized.

KIAUCHAU

(Kiautschou)

LOCATION — A district of China on the south side of the Shantung peninsula.
GOVT. — A former German colony.
AREA — 200 sq. mi.
POP. — 192,000 (approx. 1914).

The area was seized by Germany in 1897 and through negotiations that followed was leased to Germany by China.

100 Pfennig = 1 Mark
100 Cents = 1 Dollar (1905)

Tsingtau Issues

Stamps of Germany, Offices in China 1898, with Additional Surcharge:

5 Pfg. *a* **5 Pfg.** *b* **5 Pfg.** *c*

1900

"China" Overprint at 56 degree Angle

1	A10(a)	5pfg on 10pf car	35.00	35.00
c.		Dbl. surch., one inverted	300.00	
2	A10(b)	5pfg on 10pf car	35.00	35.00
c.		Dbl. surch., one inverted	300.00	
3	A10(c)	5pfg on 10pf car	37.50	40.00
c.		Dbl. surch., one inverted	350.00	

"China" Overprint at 48 degree Angle

1a	A10(a)	5pfg on 10pf car	110.00	125.00
b.		Double surcharge	450.00	575.00
2a	A10(b)	5pfg on 10pf car	110.00	125.00
b.		Double surcharge	450.00	575.00
3a	A10(c)	5pfg on 10pf car	125.00	140.00
b.		Double surcharge	500.00	600.00

Surcharged:

5 Pf. *d* **5 Pf.** *e* **5 Pf.** *f*

"China" Overprint at 48 degree Angle on Nos. 4-9

4	A10(d)	5pf on 10pf car	*2,500.*	*2,750.*
a.		Double surcharge		
5	A10(e)	5pf pn 10pf car	*2,500.*	*2,750.*
a.		Double surcharge		
6	A10(f)	5pf on 10pf car	*3,000.*	*3,650.*
a.		Double surcharge		
b.		5fP		
c.		As "b." double surcharge		

With Additional Handstamp **5**

7	A10(d)	5pf on 10pf car	*30,000.*	*37,500.*
8	A10(f)	5pf on 10pf car	*30,000.*	*37,500.*
a.		On No. 6b		

With Additional Handstamp **5 Pf.**

9	A10(f)	5pf on 10pf car	*4,000.*	*6,000.*
a.		Double surcharge	*9,500.*	*10,500.*
b.		On No. 6a		
c.		On No. 6b		
d.		On No. 6c		

On Nos. 1-9, a blue or violet line is drawn through "PF. 10 PF." All exist without this line. All copies of Nos. 1b, 2b and 3b lack the colored line.

Kaiser's Yacht "Hohenzollern"
A1 A2

1900		**Unwmk.**	**Typo.**	***Perf. 14***
10	A1	3pf brown	1.90	1.75
11	A1	5pf green	1.50	65
12	A1	10pf carmine	2.50	1.50
13	A1	20pf ultra	6.50	7.25
14	A1	25pf org & blk, *yel*	13.00	16.00
15	A1	30pf org & blk, *sal*	13.00	16.00
16	A1	40pf lake & blk	15.00	20.00
17	A1	50pf pur & blk, *sal*	15.00	20.00
18	A1	80pf lake & blk, *rose*	25.00	45.00
		Engr.		***Perf. 14½x14***
19	A2	1m carmine	45.00	62.50
20	A2	2m blue	62.50	90.00
21	A2	3m blk vio	62.50	*160.00*
22	A2	5m sl & car	205.00	*500.00*
		Nos. 10-22 (13)	468.40	*940.65*

A3 A4

1905				**Typo.**
23	A3	1c brown	1.10	1.10
24	A3	2c green	1.75	90
25	A3	4c carmine	3.75	85
26	A3	10c ultra	9.00	4.00
27	A3	20c lake & blk	25.00	16.00
28	A3	40c lake & blk, *rose*	70.00	100.00
		Engr.		
29	A4	$½ carmine	62.50	95.00
30	A4	$1 blue	125.00	95.00
31	A4	$1½ blk vio	675.00	*1,300.*
32	A4	$2½ sl & car	1,100.	*3,500.*

1905-09		**Wmk. 125**		**Typo.**
33	A3	1c brown ('06)	65	90
34	A3	2c green ('09)	65	70
35	A3	4c car ('09)	90	90
36	A3	10c ultra ('09)	90	*1.90*
37	A3	20c lake & blk ('08)	1.75	*14.00*
38	A3	40c lake & blk, *rose*	3.00	*57.50*
		Engr.		
39	A4	$½ car ('07)	4.25	*60.00*
40	A4	$1 blue ('06)	6.00	*62.50*
41	A4	$1½ blk vio	7.00	*150.00*
42	A4	$2½ slate & car	18.00	*400.00*
		Nos. 33-42 (10)	43.10	

KIONGA

LOCATION — Southeast Africa and northeast Mozambique, on Indian Ocean south of Rovuma River
GOVT. — Formerly part of German East Africa
AREA — 400 sq. mi.

This territory, occupied by Portuguese troops during World War I was allotted to Portugal by the Treaty of Versailles. Later it became part of Mozambique.

100 Centavos = 1 Escudo

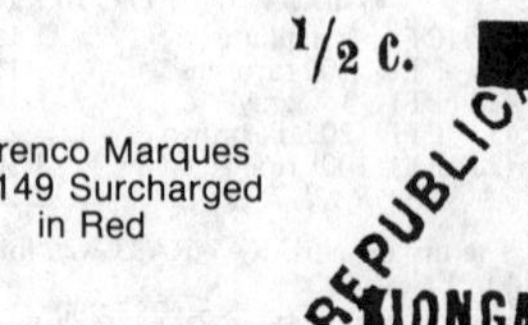

Lourenco Marques No. 149 Surcharged in Red

1916, May 29		**Unwmk.**		***Perf. 11½***
1	A2	½c on 100r bl, *bl*	17.50	12.50
2	A2	1c on 100r bl, *bl*	17.50	12.50
3	A2	2½c on 100r bl, *bl*	17.50	12.50
4	A2	5c on 100r bl, *bl*	17.50	12.50

Most of the stock of Lourenço Marques No. 149 used for these surcharges lacked gum.

KOREA

(Corea)

(Chosen, Tyosen, Tae Han)

LOCATION — Peninsula extending from Manchuria between the Yellow Sea and the Sea of Japan
GOVT. — Republic
AREA — 38,221 sq. mi.
POP. — 39,950,743 (1983)
CAPITAL — Seoul

Korea (or Corea) an independent monarchy for centuries under Chinese influence, came under Japanese influence in 1895. Japanese stamps were used there as early as 1875. Administrative control was assumed by Japan in 1904 and annexation followed in 1910. Postage stamps of Japan were used in Korea from 1905 to early 1946.

At the end of World War II, American forces occupied South Korea and Russian forces occupied North Korea, with the 38th parallel of latitude as the dividing line. A republic was established in 1948 following an election in South Korea. North Korea issues its own stamps. See note following air post listings.

100 Mon = 1 Tempo
5 Poon = 1 Cheun
100 Sen = 1 Yen
1000 Re = 100 Cheun = Weun
100 Weun = 1 Hwan (1953)
100 Chun = 1 Won (1962)

Catalogue values for unused stamps in this country are for Never Hinged items, beginning with Scott 283 in the regular postage section, Scott B5 in the semi-postal section, and Scott C23 in the airpost section.

Watermarks

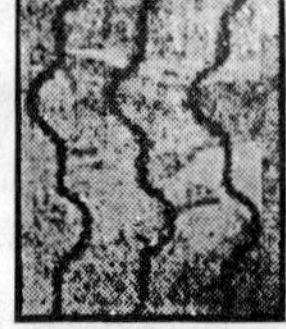

Wmk. 257- Curved Wavy Lines

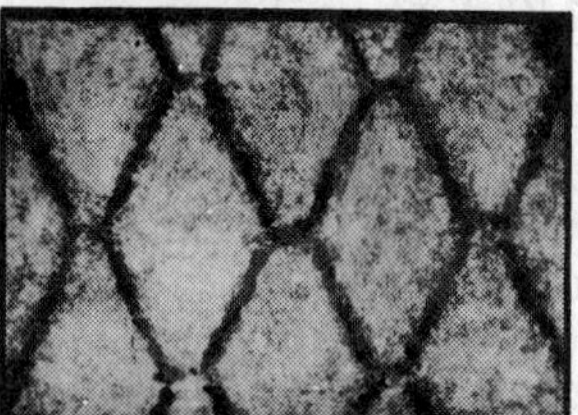

Wmk. 312- Zigzag Lines

Wmk. 317- Communications Department Emblem

Karelia stamps can be mounted in Scott's Scandinavia and Finland Part I and Soviet Republics Part I Albums.

Stylized Yin Yang
A1 A2

Perf. 8½ to 11½

1884 Typo. Unwmk.

1 A1 5m rose 30.00
2 A2 10m blue 9.00

Reprints of Nos. 1-2 exist.

A3

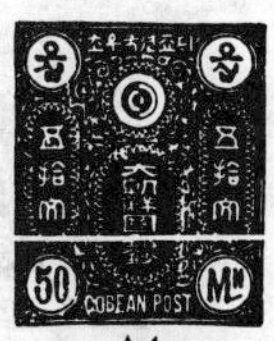
A4

A5

1885

3 A3 25m orange 5.00
4 A4 50m green 5.00
5 A5 100m bl & pink 8.00

Nos. 3 to 5 were never placed in use. Many counterfeits of Nos. 1-5 exist.

Yin Yang — A6

Two types of 50p:
I- No period after "50."
II- Period after "50."

Perf. 11½, 12, 12½, 13 and Compound

1895 Litho.

6 A6 5p green 17.00 12.00
a. 5p pale yellow green 24.00 15.00
b. Vert. pair, imperf horiz. 50.00 50.00
c. Horiz. pair, imperf. vert. 50.00 50.00
d. Vertical pair, imperf. between 55.00 55.00
e. Horiz. pair, imperf. btwn. 55.00 55.00
7 A6 10p deep blue 17.00 12.00
a. Horiz. pair, imperf. between 50.00 50.00
b. Vert. pair, imperf. horiz. 40.00 40.00
8 A6 25p maroon 25.00 19.00
a. Horiz. pair, imperf. between 65.00 65.00
b. Vert. pair, imperf. horiz. 60.00 60.00
9 A6 50p purple (II) 15.00 12.00
a. Horiz. pair, imperf. between 70.00 70.00
b. Vert. pair, imperf. horiz. 40.00 40.00
c. Horiz. pair, imperf. vert. 40.00 40.00
d. Type I 20.00 14.00

For overprints and surcharges see Nos. 10-17C, 35-38.
Counterfeits exist.

Overprinted "Tae Han" in Korean and Chinese Characters

1897

Red Overprint

10 A6 5p green 15.00 10.00
a. 5p pale yellow green 40.00 35.00
b. Inverted overprint 35.00 35.00
c. Without ovpt. at bottom 30.00 30.00
d. Without overprint at top 30.00 30.00

f. Double overprint at top 35.00 35.00
g. Overprint at bottom in blk 40.00 40.00
h. Pair, one without overprint 125.00 125.00
i. Double overprint at top, inverted at bottom 150.00
11 A6 10p deep blue 20.00 15.00
a. Without ovpt. at bottom 32.50 32.50
b. Without overprint at top 32.50 32.50
c. Double overprint at top 37.50 37.50
d. Bottom overprint inverted 32.50 32.50
e. Top ovpt. dbl., one in blk 65.00 65.00
f. Top overprint omitted, bottom overprint inverted 150.00
12 A6 25p maroon 24.00 17.00
a. Overprint at bottom invtd. 37.50 37.50
b. Overprint at bottom in blk 55.00 55.00
c. Bottom overprint omitted 30.00 30.00
e. Top ovpt. dbl., one in blk 65.00 65.00
f. Top and bottom overprints double, one of each in blk 80.00 80.00
g. Pair, one without overprint 130.00 130.00
13 A6 50p purple 25.00 12.00
a. Without ovpt. at bottom 45.00 45.00
b. Without overprint at top 45.00 45.00
c. Bottom overprint double 40.00 40.00
e. Pair, one without overprint 135.00 135.00

1900

Black Overprint

13F A6 5p green 150.00 100.00
13G A6 10p deep blue 150.00 100.00
h. Without ovpt. at bottom 200.00
14 A6 25p maroon 160.00 100.00
a. Without ovpt. at bottom 175.00 120.00
b. Without overprint at top 175.00 120.00
c. Double overprint at bottom 175.00 120.00
15 A6 50p purple 130.00 100.00
a. Without ovpt. at bottom 165.00 110.00

These stamps with black overprint, also No. 16A, are said not to have been officially authorized.

Nos. 6, 6a and 8 Surcharged in Red or Black

1900

15B A6 1ch on 5p grn (R) *750.00 350.00*
c. Yellow green
16 A6 1ch on 25p mar 80.00 55.00

Same Surcharge in Red or Black on Nos. 10, 12, 12c and 14

16A A6 1ch on 5p grn (R) 250.00 125.00
b. 1ch on 5p pale yel grn 250.00 125.00
17 A6 1ch on 25p mar 25.00 17.50
a. Figure "1" omitted 65.00
b. Overprint at bottom omitted (No. 12c) 55.00 55.00
17C A6 1ch on 25p mar (on No. 14) 200.00 160.00

Counterfeit overprints and surcharges of Nos. 10-17C exist.

A8

A9

A10

A11

A12

A13

A14

A15

A16

A17

1900 Typo. *Perf. 11*

18 A8 2re gray 6.00 3.00
19 A9 1ch yel grn 7.00 3.50
21 A11 3ch org red 8.00 4.00
a. Imperf. horiz. 85.00 85.00
22 A12 4ch carmine 22.50 12.50
23 A13 5ch pink 10.00 5.00
24 A14 6ch dp bl 11.00 5.50
25 A15 10ch purple 15.00 7.50
26 A16 15ch gray vio 14.00 7.50
27 A17 20ch red brn 17.50 9.00
Nos. 18-27 (9) 111.00 57.50

Nos. 22, 23, 25, 26 exist imperf.

Reprints of No. 24 were made in light blue, perf. 12x13, in 1905 for a souvenir booklet. See note after No. 54.

Perf. 10

18a A8 2re 9.00 3.00
19a A9 1ch 8.00 4.00
20 A10 2ch blue 30.00 14.00
a. Horiz. pair, imperf. btwn. 150.00
21b A11 3ch 9.00 4.00
22a A12 4ch 30.00 15.00
23a A13 5ch 12.50 7.00
24a A14 6ch 13.00 8.50
26a A16 15ch 135.00 100.00
27a A17 20ch 185.00 150.00

A18

A19

A20

A21

1901 *Perf. 11*

30 A18 2ch pale blue 12.00 7.00
a. Perf. 10 35.00 27.50
31 A19 50ch ol grn & pink 125.00 55.00
32 A20 1wn rose, blk & bl 350.00 125.00
33 A21 2wn pur & yel grn 475.00 140.00

No. 33 exists imperf.

See Nos. 52-54.

Emperor's Crown — A22

1902, Oct. 18 *Perf. 11½*

34 A22 3ch orange 27.50 15.00

40th year of the reign of Emperor Kojong. An imperf. single was part of the 1905 souvenir booklet. See note following No. 54.
Counterfeits exist.

Nos. 8 and 9 Surcharged in Black

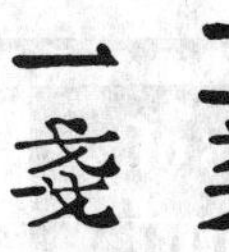
1ch

2ch

3ch

Perf. 11½, 12, 12½, 13 and Compound

1902

35 A6 1ch on 25p mar 8.00 5.00
a. Inverted surcharge 100.00
b. Horiz. pair, imperf. btwn. 80.00
c. Imperf. 35.00
d. Vert. pair, imperf. horiz. 35.00
e. On No. 12 90.00 70.00
36 A6 2ch on 25p mar 11.00 6.00
a. Inverted surcharge 65.00 50.00
b. Imperf. 30.00
c. Double surcharge 100.00 100.00
d. On No. 12 90.00 70.00
e. 2ch on 50p pur 165.00 125.00
f. As "e," character "cheun" unabbreviated (in two rows instead of one) 250.00 150.00

37	A6 3ch on 50p pur		12.00	6.00
a.	Inverted surcharge		60.00	60.00
b.	With character "cheun" unabbreviated (in two rows instead of one)		100.00	75.00
c.	As "b," inverted		135.00	110.00
d.	Horiz. pair, imperf. btwn.		60.00	
e.	Vert. pair, imperf. btwn.		60.00	
f.	Double surcharge			60.00
g.	On No. 13		50.00	50.00
38	A6 3ch on 25p mar		60.00	45.00

There are several sizes of these surcharges. Counterfeit surcharges exist.

Falcon — A23

1903 *Perf. 13½x14*

39	A23	2re slate	7.50	3.50
40	A23	1ch vio brn	7.50	3.50
41	A23	2ch green	7.50	3.50
42	A23	3ch orange	12.50	3.50
43	A23	4ch rose	15.00	6.00
44	A23	5ch yel brn	15.00	7.00
45	A23	6ch lilac	15.00	7.00
46	A23	10ch blue	15.00	7.00
47	A23	15ch red, *straw*	40.00	16.00
48	A23	20ch vio brn, *straw*	40.00	15.00
49	A23	50ch red, *grn*	95.00	50.00
50	A23	1wn vio, *lav*	150.00	75.00
51	A23	2wn vio, *org*	160.00	110.00
		Nos. 39-51 (13)	580.00	307.00

Types of 1901

1903 *Perf. 12½*

Thin, Semi-Transparent Paper

52	A19	50ch pale ol grn & pale pink	*150.00*	*125.00*
53	A20	1wn rose, blk & bl	*250.00*	*160.00*
54	A21	2wn lt vio & lt grn	*250.00*	*160.00*

No. 24, perf. 12x13, No. 34 imperf. and most examples of Nos. 52-54 unused are from souvenir booklets made up in 1905 when the Japanese withdrew all Korean stamps from circulation.

Nos. 1-54 Watermarked In 1957 the Ministry of Communications issued 4000 presentation booklets containing Nos, 1-54 reproduced on watermark 312 paper.

Issued under US Military Rule

Stamps of Japan Nos. 331, 268, 342, 332, 339 and 337 Surcharged in Black

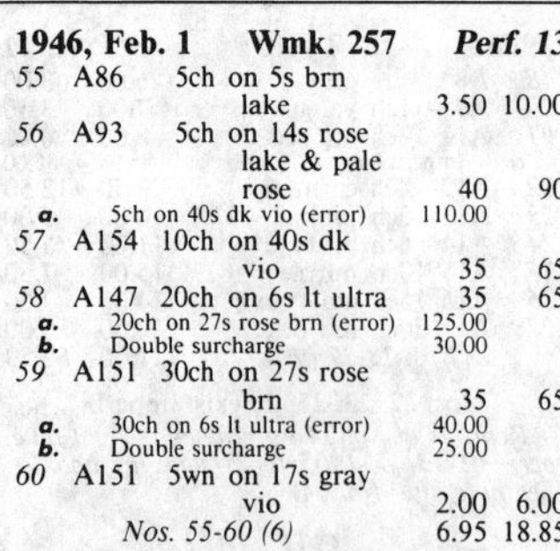

1946, Feb. 1 **Wmk. 257** *Perf. 13*

55	A86	5ch on 5s brn lake	3.50	10.00
56	A93	5ch on 14s rose lake & pale rose	40	90
a.		5ch on 40s dk vio (error)	110.00	
57	A154	10ch on 40s dk vio	35	65
58	A147	20ch on 6s lt ultra	35	65
a.		20ch on 27s rose brn (error)	125.00	
b.		Double surcharge	30.00	
59	A151	30ch on 27s rose brn	35	65
a.		30ch on 6s lt ultra (error)	40.00	
b.		Double surcharge	25.00	
60	A151	5wn on 17s gray vio	2.00	6.00
		Nos. 55-60 (6)	6.95	18.85

Five essays for this provisional issue exist both with and without additional overprint of two Chinese characters ("specimen") in vermilion. The essays are: 20ch on Japan No. 269; 50ch on No. 272; 1wn on No. 336; 1wn on No. 273; 10wn on No. 265.

Korean Family and Flag — A24

Arms of Korea — A25

Wmk. 257

1946, May 1 **Litho.** *Perf. 10½*

61	A24	3ch org yel	15	30
62	A24	5ch green	15	20
63	A24	10ch carmine	15	20
64	A24	20ch dk bl	18	25
65	A25	50ch brn vio	28	50
66	A25	1wn lt brn	38	75
		Nos. 61-66 (6)	1.29	2.20

Liberation from Japan.

Imperfs., Part Perfs.

Imperforate and part-perforate examples of a great many Korean stamps from No. 61 onward exist.

The imperfs. include Nos. 61-90, 93-97, 116-117, 119-126, 132-173, 182-186, 195, 197-199, 202A, 203, 204-205, 217, etc.

The part-perfs. include Nos. 62-65, 69, 72-73, 109, 111-113, 132, etc.

Printers waste includes printed on both sides, etc.

As the field is so extensive, the editors believe that they belong more properly in a specialized catalogue.

Dove — A26

1946, Aug. 15 **Unwmk.**

67	A26	50ch dp vio	1.25	2.50

First anniversary of liberation.

Perforations often are rough on stamps issued between Aug. 1946 and the end of 1954.

Flags of US and Korea A27

1946, Sept. 9 *Perf. 11*

68	A27	10wn carmine	1.75	1.75

Issued to commemorate the resumption of postal communication with the United States.

Astronomical Observatory, Kyongju — A28

Hibiscus with Rice — A29

Map of Korea — A30

Gold Crown of Silla Dynasty — A31

Admiral Li Sun-sin — A32

1946 *Rouletted 12*

69	A28	50ch dk bl	24	40
70	A29	1wn buff	20	40
71	A30	2wn indigo	50	50
72	A31	5wn magenta	2.00	3.00
73	A32	10wn emerald	3.00	2.25
		Nos. 69-73 (5)	5.94	6.55

Perf. 11

70a	A29	1wn	1.00	1.00
71a	A30	2wn	20.00	20.00
72a	A31	5wn	15.00	20.00

Korean Phonetic Alphabet — A33

1946, Oct. 9 *Perf. 11*

74	A33	50ch deep blue	60	1.25

500th anniv. of the introduction of the Korean phonetic alphabet (Hangul).

Li Jun A34

Admiral Li Sun-sin A35

Perf. 11½x11, 11½

1947, Aug. 1 **Litho.** **Wmk. 257**

75	A34	5wn lt bl grn	2.00	3.50
76	A35	10wn light blue	2.00	3.50

Presentation Sheets

Starting in 1947 with No. 75, nearly 100 Korean stamps were printed in miniature or souvenir sheets and given to government officials and others. These sheets were released in quantities of 300 to 4,000. In 1957 the Ministry of Communications began to sell the souvenir sheets at post offices at face value to be used for postage. They are listed from No. 244a onward.

Letter-encircled Globe — A36

1947, Aug. 1 *Perf. 11½x11*

77	A36	10wn light blue	2.00	3.50

Resumption of international mail service between Korea and all countries of the world.

Granite Paper

Starting with No. 77, most Korean stamps, except those on Laid Paper, are on Granite Paper. Granite Paper is noted above listing if the issue was printed on both ordinary and Granite Paper, such as Nos. 360a-374A.

Arch of Independence, Seoul — A37

Tortoise Ship, First Ironclad War Vessel — A38

1948, Apr.

78	A37	20wn rose	5.50	6.00
79	A38	50wn dl red brn	5.50	7.50

Republic

Flag and Ballot — A39

Woman and Man Casting Ballots — A40

Perf. 11x11½

1948, May 10 **Litho.** **Wmk. 257**

80	A39	2wn orange	1.40	60
81	A39	5wn lil rose	2.75	1.50
82	A39	10wn lt vio	7.00	4.00
83	A40	20wn carmine	9.50	8.00
84	A40	50wn blue	14.00	12.50
		Nos. 80-84 (5)	34.65	26.60

South Korea election of May 10, 1948.

Korean Flag and Olive Branches A41

Olympic Torchbearer and Map of Korea — A42

1948, June 1 ***Perf. 11x11½, 11½x11***

85 A41 5wn green 37.50 32.50
86 A42 10wn purple 12.50 8.00

Issued to commemorate Korea's participation in the 1948 Olympic Games.

National Assembly A43

1948, July 1 **Wmk. 257** ***Perf. 11½***

87 A43 4wn org brn 6.00 6.00

Opening of the Assembly July 1, 1948.

Exists without period between "5" and "31."

Korean Family and Capitol — A44

Pres. Syngman Rhee — A46

Flag of Korea A45

1948, Aug. 1 **Litho.**

88 A44 4wn emerald 19.00 5.00
89 A45 10wn org brn 8.75 5.00

Issued to commemorate the signing of the new constitution, July 17, 1948.

1948, Aug. 5

90 A46 5wn deep blue 25.00 6.00

Inauguration of Korea's first president, Syngman Rhee.

Dove — A47

Hibiscus — A48

Two types of 5wn:

I- "1948" 3mm wide; top inscription 9mm wide; periods in "8.15." barely visible.

II- "1948" 4mm wide; top inscription 9½mm; periods in "8.15." bold and strong.

1948 ***Perf. 11, 11x11½***

91 A47 4wn blue 15.00 15.00
92 A48 5wn rose lil (II) 11.00 12.50
a. Type I 50.00 60.00

Issued to commemorate the establishment of Korea's republican government.

Li Jun A49

Observatory, Kyongju A50

1948, Oct. 1 ***Perf. 11½x11***

93 A49 4wn rose car 20 20
94 A50 14wn deep blue 38 30
a. 14wn light blue 60.00 30.00

For surcharges see Nos. 127, 174, 176.

Doves over UN Emblem — A51

Korean Citizen and Census Date — A52

1949, Feb. 12 **Wmk. 257** ***Perf. 11***

95 A51 10wn blue *9.00* 12.50

Arrival of the UN Commission on Korea, Feb. 12, 1949.

1949, Apr. 25

96 A52 15wn purple 10.00 9.00

Census of May 1, 1949.

Korean Boy and Girl — A53

1949, May 5

97 A53 15wn purple 6.00 8.00

20th anniversary of Children's Day, May 5, 1949.

Postman — A54

Worker and Factory — A55

Rice Harvesting — A56

Japanese Cranes — A57

Diamond Mountains — A58

Ginseng Plant — A59

South Gate, Seoul — A60

Tabo Pagoda, Kyongju — A61

1949 **Litho.** ***Perf. 11***

98 A54 1wn rose 1.90 1.50
99 A55 2wn dk bl gray 45 30
100 A56 5wn yel grn 1.10 1.50
101 A57 10wn bl grn 45 50
102 A58 20wn org brn 38 35
103 A59 30wn bl grn 70 50
104 A60 50wn vio bl 55 50
105 A61 100wn dl yel grn 55 50
Nos. 98-105 (8) 6.08 5.65

For surcharges see Nos. 129-131, 175, 177B-179, 181.

Phoenix and Yin Yang — A62

1949, Aug. 25

106 A62 15wn deep blue 6.00 7.00

1st anniv. of Korea's independence.

Express Train "Sam Chun Li" — A63

1949, Sept. 18 ***Perf. 11½x12***

107 A63 15wn vio bl 20.00 15.00

50th anniversary of Korean railroads.

Korean Flag — A64

Perf. 11½x11

1949, Oct. 15 **Wmk. 257**

108 A64 15wn red org, yel & dk bl 6.00 8.50

75th anniv. of the UPU.

No. 108 exists unwatermarked. These are counterfeit.

Hibiscus A65

Magpies and Map of Korea A66

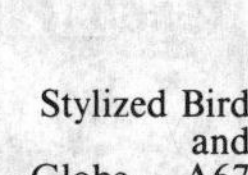

Stylized Bird and Globe — A67

Diamond Mountains A68

Admiral Li Sun-sin — A69

1949 **Wmk. 257** **Litho.** ***Perf. 11***

109 A65 15wn vermilion 16 25
110 A66 65wn dp bl 16 25
111 A67 200wn green 20 25
112 A68 400wn brown 20 35
113 A69 500wn dp bl 20 25
Nos. 109-113 (5) 92 1.35

For surcharges see Nos. 128, 177, 180.

Canceled to Order

More than 100 Korean stamps and souvenir sheets were canceled to order, the cancellation incorporating the date "67.9.20." These include 81 stamps between Nos. 111 and 327, 18 airmail stamps between Nos. C6 and C26, and 5 souvenir sheets between Nos. 313 and 332, etc.

Ancient Postal Medal (Ma-Pae) A70

1950, Jan. 1

114 A70 15wn yel grn 5.50 5.00
115 A70 65wn red brn 4.50 4.00

50th anniv. of Korea's entrance into the UPU.

Revolutionists — A71

1950, Mar. 10 ***Perf. 11½***

116 A71 15wn olive 6.00 4.00
117 A71 65wn lt vio 4.00 4.00

41st anniversary of Korea's declaration of Independence.

Korean Emblem and National Assembly — A72

1950, May 30

118 A72 30wn bl, red, brn & grn 4.50 5.00

2nd natl. election of the Korean Republic.

Syngman Rhee
A73

Korean Flag and White Mountains
A74

Flags of UN and Korea, Map of Korea — A75

1950, Nov. 20 Wmk. 257 *Perf. 11*

119 A73 100wn blue 75 1.00
120 A74 100wn green 1.00 1.00
121 A75 200wn dk grn 1.00 1.00

Crane — A76

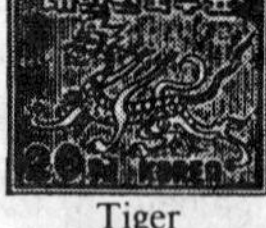
Tiger Mural — A77

Dove and Flag
A78

Postal Medal
A79

Mural from Ancient Tomb — A80

1951 Unwmk. *Perf. 11*
Ordinary Paper

122 A76 5wn org brn 55 75
123 A77 20wn purple 40 75
124 A78 50wn green 55 1.00
125 A79 100wn dp bl 2.50 2.00
126 A80 1000wn green 7.25 2.50
Nos. 122-126 (5) 11.25 7.00

Rouletted 12

122a A76 5wn org brn 45 75
123a A77 20wn purple 70 1.50
124a A78 50wn green 85 75
125a A79 100wn blue 1.10 2.00

No. 126 also exists perforated 12½. See Nos. 187-189.

No. 93 Surcharged with New Value and Wavy Lines in Blue

1951 Wmk. 257 *Perf. 11½x11*

127 A49 100wn on 4wn rose car 70 60
a. Inverted surcharge 35.00

Nos. 109, 101, 102 and 104 Surcharged in Blue or Brown

Perf. 11

128 A65 200wn on 15wn 1.00 75
a. Inverted surcharge 10.00 10.00
129 A57 300wn on 10wn (Br) 2.00 2.00
a. Inverted surcharge 17.50
130 A58 300wn on 20wn 1.40 1.50
a. Inverted surcharge 17.50
131 A60 300wn on 50wn (Br) 2.75 2.50
Nos. 127-131 (5) 7.85 7.35

Size of surcharge varies. Numeral upright on Nos. 129 and 131; numeral slanted on Nos. 175 and 179. See Nos. 174-181.

On No. 130, the zeros in "300" are octagonal; on No. 177B they are oval.

Flags of US and Korea and Statue of Liberty — A81

Design (blue stamps): Flag of same country as preceding green stamp, UN emblem and doves.

1951-52 Wmk. 257 *Perf. 11*
Flags in Natural Colors, Participating Country at Left

132 A81 500wn green 6.50 5.00
133 A81 500wn blue 6.50 5.00
134 A81 500wn grn *(Australia)* 5.25 4.00
135 A81 500wn blue 6.50 5.00
136 A81 500wn grn *(Belgium)* 5.25 4.00
137 A81 500wn blue 5.25 4.00
138 A81 500wn grn *(Britain)* 6.50 5.00
139 A81 500wn blue 6.50 5.00
140 A81 500wn grn *(Canada)* 6.50 5.00
141 A81 500wn blue 5.25 4.00
142 A81 500wn grn *(Colombia)* 5.25 4.00
143 A81 500wn blue 6.50 5.00
144 A81 500wn grn *(Denmark)* 10.00 15.00
145 A81 500wn blue 10.50 15.00
146 A81 500wn grn *(Ethiopia)* 5.25 4.00
147 A81 500wn blue 6.50 5.00
148 A81 500wn grn *(France)* 5.25 4.00
149 A81 500wn blue 6.50 5.00
150 A81 500wn grn *(Greece)* 6.50 5.00
151 A81 500wn blue 6.50 5.00
152 A81 500wn grn *(India)* 8.00 6.00
153 A81 500wn blue 8.00 6.00
154 A81 500wn grn *(Italy)* 8.00 6.00
a. Flag without crown ('52) 9.00
155 A81 500wn blue 8.00 6.00
a. Flag without crown ('52) 9.00
156 A81 500wn grn *(Luxembourg)* 8.00 6.00
157 A81 500wn blue 6.50 5.00
158 A81 500wn grn *(Netherlands)* 5.25 4.00
159 A81 500wn blue 5.25 4.00
160 A81 500wn grn *(New Zealand)* 6.50 5.00
161 A81 500wn blue 6.50 5.00
162 A81 500wn grn *(Norway)* 8.00 6.00
163 A81 500wn blue 8.00 6.00
164 A81 500wn grn *(Philippines)* 6.50 5.00
165 A81 500wn blue 6.50 5.00
166 A81 500wn grn *(Sweden)* 5.25 4.00
167 A81 500wn blue 6.50 5.00
168 A81 500wn grn *(Thailand)* 5.25 4.00
169 A81 500wn blue 6.50 5.00
170 A81 500wn grn*(Turkey)* 6.50 5.00
171 A81 500wn blue 6.50 5.00
172 A81 500wn grn *(Union of So. Africa)* 6.50 5.00
173 A81 500wn blue 6.50 5.00
Nos. 132-173 (42) 277.25 226.00

Twenty-two imperf. souvenir sheets of two, containing the green and the blue stamps for each participating country (including both types of Italy) were issued. Size: 140x90mm. Value, set $400.

Nos. 93-94, 101-105, 109-110 Surcharged Like Nos. 128-131 in Blue or Brown

1951 Wmk. 257 *Perf. 11½x11, 11*

174 A49 300wn on 4wn 1.25 90
a. Inverted surcharge 70.00 50.00
175 A57 300wn on 10wn (Br) 90 75
a. Inverted surcharge 50.00 40.00
176 A50 300wn on 14wn (Br) 1.50 1.25
a. 300wn on 14wn lt bl 600.00 125.00
b. Inverted surcharge 50.00 50.00
177 A65 300wn on 15wn 1.25 90
a. Inverted surcharge 40.00 40.00
177B A58 300wn on 20wn 3.50 3.50
178 A59 300wn on 30wn (Br) 1.25 90
a. Inverted surcharge 42.50 40.00
179 A60 300wn on 50wn (Br) 1.25 90
180 A66 300wn on 65wn (Br) 90 75
a. Inverted monad 52.50 50.00
181 A61 300wn on 100wn 1.50 1.25
a. Inverted surcharge 50.00 40.00
Nos. 174-181 (9) 13.30 11.10

"300" slanted on Nos. 175, 177B and 179; "300" upright on Nos. 129 and 131. The surcharge exists double on several of these stamps.

No. 177B differs from No. 130 in detail noted after No. 131.

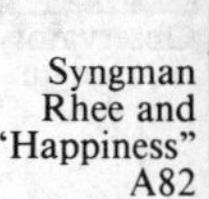

Syngman Rhee and "Happiness"
A82

1952, Sept. 10 Litho. *Perf. 12½*

182 A82 1000wn dk grn 1.25 1.00

Second inauguration of President Syngman Rhee, Aug. 15, 1952.

Sok Kul Am, Near Kyongju — A83

Bool Gook Temple, Kyongju — A84

Tombstone of Mu Yal Wang
A85

Choong Yul Sa Shrine, Tongyung
A86

1952 Wmk. 257 Typo. *Perf. 12½*

183 A83 200wn hn brn 45 15
184 A84 300wn green 45 15
185 A85 500wn carmine 65 60
186 A86 2000wn dp bl 75 15

Rough Perf. 10-11, 11½x11 and Compound
Litho.

186A A83 200wn hn brn 75 50
186B A84 300wn green 1.25 60
Nos. 183-186B (6) 4.30 2.15

Types of 1951
(Designs Slightly Smaller)

1952-53 *Rough Perf. 10-11*

187 A77 20wn purple 2.25 90
187A A78 50wn green 4.50 30
187B A79 100wn dp bl 1.75 40
187C A80 1000wn green 52.50 4.00

(Designs Slightly Larger)

187D A78 50wn green 1.00 50
188 A79 100wn dp bl 1.00 50
189 A80 1000wn grn ('53) 3.25 75

Type of 1952

1953

189A A85 500wn deep blue 11.00 *50.00*

All copies of No. 189A were affixed to postal cards before sale.

See Nos. 191-192, 203B, 248.

Types of 1952 and

Planting Trees — A87

Wmk. 257
1953, Apr. 5 Litho. *Perf. 12½*

190 A87 1h aqua 25 28
191 A85 2h aqua 25 32
192 A85 5h brt grn 45 32
193 A87 10h brt grn 65 18
194 A86 20h brown 1.40 65
Nos. 190-194 (5) 3.00 1.75

See Nos. 203A, 247.

Map and YMCA Emblem — A88

1953, Oct. 25 *Perf. 13½*

195 A88 10h dk sl bl & red 1.25 1.25

50th anniv. of the Korean YMCA.

Tombstone of Mu Yal Wang — A88a

Sika Deer
A89 A90

1954, Apr. *Perf. 12½*

196 A88a 5h dk grn 38 15
197 A89 100h brn car 7.00 50
198 A90 500h brn org 19.00 1.25
199 A90 1000h bis brn 32.50 1.50

See Nos. 203C, 203D, 238-239, 248A, 250-251, 259, 261-262, 269-270, 279, 281-282.

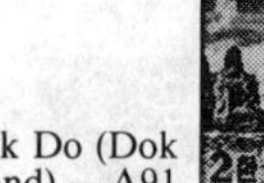
Dok Do (Dok Island) — A91

Design: 10h, Dok Do, lateral view.

1954, Sept. 15

200 A91 2h claret 20 15
201 A91 5h blue 42 20
202 A91 10h blue green 60 25

Moth and Flag
A92

Pagoda Park, Seoul
A92a

1954, Apr. 16 Wmk. 257 *Perf. 12½*

202A A92 10h brown 80 50
203 A92a 30h dk bl 1.00 50

See Nos. 203E, 260, 280.

Types of 1952-54

1955-56 Unwmk. *Perf. 12½*
Laid Paper

203A A87 1h aqua ('56) 25 20
203B A85 2h aqua ('56) 25 20
203C A88a 5h brt grn ('56) 25 20
203D A89 100h brn car 2.50 75
203E A92a 200h violet 2.50 1.00
Nos. 203A-203E (5) 5.75 2.35

On No. 203C the right hand character is redrawn as in illustration above No. 212D.

Nos. 203A and 203C are found on horizontally and vertically laid paper.

Erosion Control on Mountainside
A93

1954, Dec. 12 **Wmk. 257**
204 A93 10h dk grn & yel grn 38 20
205 A93 19h dk grn & yel grn 60 40

Issued to publicize the 1954 forestation campaign.

Presidents Rhee and Eisenhower Shaking Hands — A94

1954, Dec. 25 ***Perf. 13½***
206 A94 10h vio bl 40 25
207 A94 19h brown 60 40
208 A94 71h dl grn 1.40 75

Issued to publicize the adoption of the United States-Korea mutual defense treaty.

"Reconstruction"
A95

Wmk. 257
1955, Feb. 10 **Litho.** ***Perf. 12½***
209 A95 10h brown 80 50
210 A95 15h violet 60 50
211 A95 20h blue 350.00 7.50
212 A95 50h plum 1.90 40

Issued to publicize Korea's industrial reconstruction.

1955, Oct. 19 **Unwmk.** ***Perf. 12½***
Laid Paper
212A A95 15h violet 70 35
212B A95 20h blue 95 60
212C A95 50h plum 1.40 35

No. 212B is found on horizontally and vertically laid paper.

Same with Right Character at Top Redrawn

Original

Redrawn

1956, June 5 **Unwmk.** ***Perf. 12½***
Laid Paper
212D A95 10h brown 1.25 35
212E A95 15h violet 80 35
212F A95 20h blue 80 30
a. Bklt. pane of 6 22.50

Nos. 212D-212F are found on horizontally and vertically laid paper. See Nos. 248B, 256, 272, 276.

Rotary Emblem — A96

Syngman Rhee — A98

1955, Feb. 23 **Wmk. 257** ***Perf. 13½***
213 A96 20h violet 55 35
214 A96 25h dl grn 70 50
215 A96 71h magenta 95 85

Rotary International, 50th anniversary.

1955, Mar. 26
217 A98 20h deep blue 2.75 1.75

80th birthday of Pres. Syngman Rhee, Apr. 26.

Flag and Arch of Independence
A99

1955, Aug. 15 **Litho.** ***Perf. 13½***
218 A99 40h Prus grn 85 60
219 A99 100h lake 1.25 90

Tenth anniversary of independence.

UN Emblem in Circle of Clasped Hands — A100

Olympic Torch and Runners — A101

1955, Oct. 24
221 A100 20h bluish grn 95 60
222 A100 55h aqua 1.40 1.00

United Nations, 10th anniversary.

1955, Oct. 23
223 A101 20h claret 1.00 60
224 A101 55h dk grn 1.50 1.00

36th National Athletic Meet.

Adm. Li Sun-sin, Navy Flag and Tortoise Ship
A102

Perf. 13x13½
1955, Nov. 11 **Unwmk.**
Laid Paper
225 A102 20h vio bl 1.50 1.75

Korean Navy, 10th anniversary.

Rhee Monument near Seoul — A103

Syngman Rhee — A104

1956 ***Perf. 13½x13***
226 A103 20h dl grn 1.40 1.25

81st birthday of Pres. Syngman Rhee.

No. 226 is found on horizontally and vertically laid paper.

1956, Aug. 15 ***Perf. 13x13½***
227 A104 20h brown 7.50 1.10
228 A104 55h vio bl 7.50 1.50

Third inauguration of Pres. Syngman Rhee.

Olympic Rings and Torch — A105

1956, Nov. 1 **Litho.** ***Perf. 12½***
Laid Paper
229 A105 20h red org 1.10 1.00
230 A105 55h brt grn 1.90 1.75

16th Olympic Games in Melbourne, Nov. 22-Dec. 8, 1956.

Central Post Office, Seoul — A107

Stamp of 1884 — A108

Mail Delivered by Donkey
A109

1956, Dec. 4 **Laid Paper** **Unwmk.**
232 A107 20h lt bl grn 85 60
233 A108 50h lt car 1.10 90
234 A109 55h green 1.40 1.25

Issued to commemorate Postal Day.

Types of 1954 Redrawn and

Hibiscus
A110

King Sejong
A111

Kyongju Observatory — A112

No Hwan Symbol; Redrawn Character

1956, Dec. 4 **Unwmk.** ***Perf. 12½***
Laid Paper
235 A110 10h lilac rose 75 20
236 A111 20h lilac 1.25 20
237 A112 50h violet 1.50 20
238 A89 100h brn car 1.75 50
239 A90 500h brn org 7.50 75
Nos. 235-239 (5) 12.75 1.85

On Nos. 238-239, the character after numeral has been omitted and the last character of the inscription has been redrawn as illustrated above No. 212D.

Nos. 235-236 are found on horizontally and vertically laid paper.

See Nos. 240-242, 253, 255, 258, 273, 275, 278, 291d, 291f, B3-B4.

Types of 1956

1957, Jan. 21 **Wmk. 312** ***Perf. 12½***
240 A110 10h lilac rose 45 30
241 A111 20h red lilac 55 60
242 A112 50h violet 1.10 30

Telecommunication Symbols — A117

1957, Jan. 31 ***Perf. 13½***
243 A117 40h lt ultra 65 50
244 A117 55h brt grn 85 75
a. Souv. sheet of 2, #243-244, imperf. 375.00

5th anniv. of Korea's joining the ITU.

Boy Scout and Emblem
A118

1957, Feb. 27 **Wmk. 312**
245 A118 40h pale pur 65 60
246 A118 55h lt mag 1.40 1.00
a. Souv. sheet of 2, #245-246, imperf. 1,500.

50th anniversary of Boy Scout movement.

Types of 1953-56
Top Right Character Redrawn; Hwan Symbol Retained

1957 **Wmk. 312** ***Perf. 12½***
247 A87 1h aqua 35 20
248 A85 2h aqua 26 25
248A A88a 5h brt grn 70 25
248B A95 15h violet 1.25 40

Redrawn Types of 1954, 1956 and

Planting Trees
A119

South Gate, Seoul
A120

Tiger
A121

Diamond Mountains
A122

No Hwan Symbol; Redrawn Character

1957 **Wmk. 312** **Litho.** ***Perf. 12½***
249 A119 2h aqua 18 20
250 A88a 4h aqua 18 20
251 A88a 5h emerald 22 20
252 A120 10h green 22 20
253 A110 20h lil rose 42 20
254 A121 30h pale lil 42 25
255 A111 40h red lil 65 25
a. Booklet pane of 6 45.00
256 A95 50h lake 1.10 30
257 A122 55h vio brn 2.25 1.50
258 A112 100h violet 1.75 40
259 A89 200h brn car 5.25 40
260 A92a 400h brt vio 7.75 1.25
261 A90 500h ocher 19.00 3.50
262 A90 1000h dk ol bis 26.00 8.00
Nos. 249-262 (14) 65.39 16.85

The "redrawn character" is illustrated above No. 212D.

See Nos. 268, 271, 274, 277, 291c, 291e.

Miniature Sheet of 1, Imperf.

249a	A119	2h	17.00
250a	A88a	4h	17.00
252a	A120	10h	17.00
253a	A110	20h	17.00
254a	A121	30h	21.00
255b	A111	40h	17.00
257a	A122	55h	21.00
258a	A112	100h	72.50
259a	A89	200h	13.00
260a	A92a	400h	27.50

Mercury and Flags of Korea and US A123

1957, Nov. 7 Wmk. 312 *Perf. 13½*

263 A123 40h dp org	45	35
264 A123 205h emerald	1.40	90
a. Souv. sheet of 2, #263-264, imperf.	600.00	

Treaty of friendship, commerce and navigation between Korea and the US.

Star of Bethlehem and Pine Cone — A124

Designs: 25h, Christmas tree and tassel. 30h, Christmas tree, window and dog.

1957, Dec. 11 Litho. *Perf. 12½*

265 A124 15h org, brn & grn	95	75
a. Souv. sheet of 1, imperf.	400.00	
266 A124 25h lt grn, yel & red	1.10	1.00
a. Souv. sheet of 1, imperf.	400.00	
267 A124 30h bl, lt grn & yel	1.50	1.25
a. Souv. sheet of 1, imperf.	400.00	

Issued for Christmas and the New Year.

Redrawn Types of 1954-57

Wmk. 317

1957-59 Litho. *Perf. 12½*

268	A119	2h aqua	26	15
269	A88a	4h aqua	26	15
270	A88a	5h emerald ('58)	32	20
271	A120	10h green	42	20
272	A95	15h violet ('58)	35	20
273	A110	20h lil rose	42	20
274	A121	30h pale lilac ('58)	52	20
275	A111	40h red lilac	1.10	25
276	A95	50h lake ('58)	2.25	20
277	A122	55h vio brn ('59)	3.25	2.25
278	A112	100h violet	3.25	60
279	A89	200h brn car ('59)	5.25	75
280	A92a	400h brt vio ('59)	13.00	4.50
281	A90	500h ocher ('58)	16.00	2.50
282	A90	1000h dk ol bis ('58)	26.00	3.00
		Nos. 268-282 (15)	72.65	15.35

Nos. 268-282 have no hwan symbol, and final character of inscription is the redrawn one illustrated above No. 212D.

See No. 291B.

Catalogue values for unused stamps in this section, from this point to the end of the section, are for Never Hinged items.

Winged Envelope — A125

1958, May 20 Wmk. 317

283 A125 40h dk bl & red	1.00	60
a. Souv. sheet of 1, imperf.	*1,100.*	

Issued for the Second Postal Week.

Children Looking at Industrial Growth A126

Design: 40h, Hibiscus forming "10".

1958, Aug. 15 *Perf. 13½*

284 A126 20h gray	75	30
285 A126 40h dk car	1.00	45
a. Souv. sheet of 2, # 284-285, imperf.	275.00	

10th anniversary of Republic of Korea.

UNESCO Building, Paris A127

1958, Nov. 3 Wmk. 317

286 A127 40h org & grn	75	60
a. Souv. sheet of 1, imperf.	60.00	

Opening of UNESCO. headquarters in Paris, Nov. 3.

Children Flying Kites — A128

Christmas Tree and Fortune Screen — A129

Children in Costume — A130

1958, Dec. 11 Litho. *Perf. 12½*

287 A128 15h yel grn	75	60
a. Souv. sheet of 1, imperf.	30.00	
288 A129 25h bl, red & yel	75	60
a. Souv. sheet of 1, imperf.	30.00	
289 A130 30h yel, ultra & red	1.25	85
a. Souv. sheet of 1, imperf.	30.00	

Issued for Christmas and the New Year.

Flag and Pagoda Park A131

1959, Mar. 1 *Perf. 13½*

290 A131 40h rose lil & brn	90	50
a. Souv. sheet of 1, imperf.	15.00	

40th anniv. of Independence Movement Day.

Korean Marines Landing A132

1959, Apr. 15

291 A132 40h ol grn	90	50
a. Souv. sheet of 1, imperf.	7.00	

Korean Marine Corps, 10th anniversary.

Souvenir Sheet

Types of 1956-57

Wmk. 317

1959, May 20 Litho. *Imperf.*

291B Sheet of 4	7.00	7.50
c. A120 10h green	90	50
d. A110 20h lilac rose	90	50
e. A121 30h pale lilac	90	50
f. A111 40h red lilac	90	50

3rd Postal Week, May 20-26.

WHO Emblem and Family A133

1959, Aug. 17 Wmk. 317 *Perf. 13½*

292 A133 40h pink & rose vio	65	35
a. Souv. sheet of 1, imperf.	7.00	

10th anniv. of Korea's joining the WHO.

Diesel Train A134

1959, Sept. 18 Litho.

293 A134 40h brn & bis	80	50
a. Souv. sheet of 1, imperf.	7.00	

60th anniversary of Korean railroads.

Relay Race and Emblem A135

1959, Oct. 3

294 A135 40h lt bl & red brn	80	60
a. Souv. sheet of 1, imperf.	7.00	

40th National Athletic Meet.

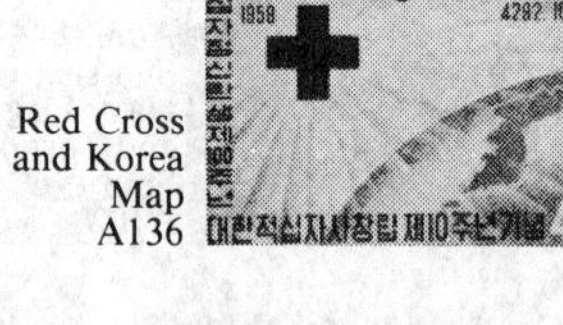

Red Cross and Korea Map A136

Design: 55h, Red Cross superimposed on globe.

1959, Oct. 27 *Perf. 13½*

295 A136 40h red & bl grn	50	20
296 A136 55h pale lil & red	75	30
a. Souv. sheet of 2, #295-296, imperf.	15.00	

Centenary of the Red Cross idea.

Old Postal Flag and New Communications Flag — A137

1959, Dec. 4

297 A137 40h bl & red	80	50
a. Souv. sheet of 1, imperf.	7.00	

75th anniv. of the Korean postal system.

Mice and Chinese Happy New Year Character — A138

Designs: 25h, Children singing Christmas hymns. 30h, Red-crested crane.

1959, Dec. 15 *Perf. 12½*

298 A138 15h gray, vio bl & pink	50	30
a. Souv. sheet of 1, imperf.	6.50	
299 A138 25h bl, red & emer	60	30
a. Souv. sheet of 1, imperf.	6.50	
300 A138 30h lt lil, blk & red	75	30
a. Souv. sheet of 1, imperf.	6.50	

Issued for Christmas and the New Year.

UPU Monument and Means of Transportation — A139

Wmk. 317

1960, Jan. 1 Litho. *Perf. 13½*

301 A139 40h grnsh bl & brn	65	35
a. Souv. sheet of 1, imperf.	7.00	

60th anniv. of Korean membership in the UPU.

Bee, Honeycomb and Clover — A140

Snail and Money Bag — A141

1960, Apr. 1 Wmk. 317 *Perf. 12½*

302 A140 10h emer, brn & org	20	15
303 A141 20h pink, bl & brn	40	25

Issued to encourage systematic saving by children. See No. 313, souvenir sheet.

See Nos. 377-380.

Uprooted Oak Emblem and Yin Yang A142

Dwight D. Eisenhower A143

1960, Apr. 7 Wmk. 312 *Perf. 13½*

304 A142 40h emer, car & ultra	65	35
a. Souv. sheet of 1, imperf.	15.00	

Issued to publicize World Refugee Year, July 1, 1959-June 30, 1960.

1960, June 19 Litho. Wmk. 317

305 A143 40h bl, red & bluish grn	1.40	75
a. Souv. sheet of 1, imperf.	8.50	

Pres. Eisenhower's visit to Korea, June 19.

Children in School and Ancient Home Teaching A144

1960, Aug. 3 Wmk. 317 *Perf. 13½*
306 A144 40h cit, cl & org brn 65 35
a. Souv. sheet of 1, imperf. 3.00

75th anniv. of the modern educational system.

Hibiscus and House of Councilors A145

1960, Aug. 8
307 A145 40h blue 65 35
a. Souv. sheet of 1, imperf. 3.00

Inaugural session, House of Councilors.

Woman Holding Torch and Man with Flag — A146

1960, Aug. 15
308 A146 40h bis, lt bl & brn 55 35
a. Souv. sheet of 1, imperf. 2.75

15th anniversary of liberation.

Weight Lifter A147

Design: 40h, South Gate, Seoul, and Olympic emblem.

1960, Aug. 25 Litho.
309 A147 20h brn, lt bl & sal 42 25
310 A147 40h brn, lt bl & dk bl 80 40
a. Souv. sheet of 2, #309-310, imperf. 6.00

Issued to commemorate the 17th Olympic Games, Rome, Aug. 25-Sept. 11.

Swallow and Telegraph Pole — A148

1960, Sept. 28 *Perf. 13½*
311 A148 40h lt bl, lil & gray 65 35
a. Souv. sheet of 1, imperf. 2.00

75th anniv. of the establishment of telegraph service.

Students and Sprout A149

1960, Oct. 1 Wmk. 317
312 A149 40h bl, sal pink & emer 65 35
a. Souv. sheet of 1, imperf. 2.00

Rebirth of the Republic.

Souvenir Sheet
Savings Types of 1960

1960, Oct. 7 *Imperf.*
313 Sheet of two 1.75 1.75
a. A140 10h emer, brn & org 75 75
b. A141 20h pink, bl & brn 75 75

4th Postal Week, Oct. 7-13, and Intl. Letter Writing Week, Oct. 3-9.

Torch — A150

1960, Oct. 15 *Perf. 13½*
314 A150 40h dk bl, lt bl & yel 65 35
a. Souv. sheet of 1, imperf. 2.00

Cultural Month (October).

UN Flag, Globe and Laurel A151

UN Emblem and Grave Markers A152

1960, Oct. 24 Litho.
315 A151 40h rose lil, bl & grn 65 35
a. Souv. sheet of 1, imperf. 2.75

15th anniversary of United Nations.

1960, Nov. 1 Wmk. 317
316 A152 40h sal & brn 65 35
a. Souv. sheet of 1, imperf. 2.50

Establishment of the UN Memorial Cemetery, Tanggok, Pusan, Korea.

"Housing, Agriculture, Population" — A153

1960, Nov. 15 *Perf. 13½*
317 A153 40h multi 65 35
a. Souv. sheet of 1, imperf. 2.00

Issued to publicize the 1960 census.

Boy and Head of Ox — A154

Star of Bethlehem and Korean Sock — A155

Girl Giving New Year's Greeting — A156

1960, Dec. 15 Litho. *Perf. 12½*
318 A154 15h gray, brn & org yel 40 30
a. Souv. sheet of 1, imperf. 4.00
319 A155 25h vio bl, red & grn 50 30
a. Souv. sheet of 1, imperf. 4.00
320 A156 30h red, vio bl & yel 60 40
a. Souv. sheet of 1, imperf. 4.00

Issued for Christmas and the New Year.

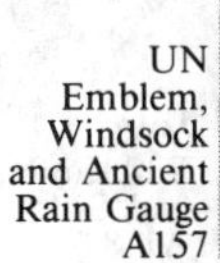

UN Emblem, Windsock and Ancient Rain Gauge A157

1961, Mar. 23 *Perf. 13½*
321 A157 40h lt bl & ultra 65 35
a. Souv. sheet of 1, imperf. 1.40

1st World Meteorological Day.

Children, Globe and UN Emblem A158

1961, Apr. 7 Wmk. 317
322 A158 40h sal & brn 65 35
a. Souv. sheet of 1, imperf. 1.40

10th World Health Day.

Students Demonstrating — A159

1961, Apr. 19 Litho.
323 A159 40h red, grn & ultra 75 40
a. Souv. sheet of 1, imperf. 2.00

1st anniv. of the Korean April revolution.

Workers — A160

1961, May 6
324 A160 40h brt grn 60 35
a. Souv. sheet of 1, imperf. 2.00

International Conference on Community Development, Seoul.

Girl Scout A161

1961, May 10
325 A161 40h brt grn 75 50
a. Souv. sheet of 1, imperf. 6.00

15th anniversary of Korea's Girl Scouts.

Soldier's Grave — A162

Soldier with Torch — A163

Wmk. 317
1961, June 6 Litho. *Perf. 13½*
326 A162 40h blk & ol gray 75 35
a. Souv. sheet of 1, imperf. 2.00

6th National Mourning Day.

1961, June 16
327 A163 40h brn & yel 75 50
a. Souv. sheet of 1, imperf. 2.00

Military Revolution of May 16, 1961.

Map of Korea, Torch and Broken Chain — A164

1961, Aug. 15 Wmk. 317 *Perf. 13½*
328 A164 40h dk bl, ver & aqua 75 50
a. Souv. sheet of 1, imperf. 1.40

16th anniv. of liberation.

Flag and Servicemen A165

1961, Oct. 1 Litho.
329 A165 40h vio bl, red & brn 65 50
a. Souv. sheet of 1, imperf. 1.40

Issued for Armed Forces Day.

Kyongbok Palace Art Museum — A166

1961, Nov. 1 Wmk. 317 *Perf. 13½*
330 A166 40h beige & dk brn 65 35
a. Souv. sheet of 1, imperf. 1.40

10th Natl. Exhibition of Fine Arts.

"UNESCO," Candle and Laurel A167

1961, Nov. 4

331 A167 40h lt grn & dk bl 65 35
a. Souv. sheet of 1, imperf. 1.40

15th anniv. of UNESCO.

Mobile X-Ray Unit A168

1961, Nov. 16

332 A168 40h rose beige & red brn 65 35
a. Souv. sheet of 1, imperf. 1.40

Tuberculosis Prevention Week.

Ginseng A169

King Sejong and Hangul Alphabet A170

Tristram's Woodpecker A171

Rice Farmer A172

Ancient Drums — A173

1961-62 Unwmk. Litho. *Perf. 12½*

338 A169 20h rose brn ('62) 1.00 25
339 A170 30h pale pur 1.25 25
340 A171 40h dk bl & red 1.25 25
341 A172 40h dk grn ('62) 1.50 25
342 A173 100h red brn 1.50 60
Nos. 338-342 (5) 6.50 1.60

See Nos. 363-366, 368, 388-392, 517-519, B5-B7.

Globe with Map of Korea and ITU Emblem A175

1962, Jan. 31 Unwmk. *Perf. 13½*

348 A175 40h ver & dk bl 75 35
a. Souv. sheet of 1, imperf. 2.00

10th anniv. of Korea's joining the ITU.

Korea stamps can be mounted in Scott's annual Korea Supplement.

Atomic Reactor and Atom Symbol A176

1962, Mar. 30 Litho. *Perf. 13½*

349 A176 40h lt bl, sl grn & ol gray 50 35

Issued to commemorate the inauguration of the Triga Mark II atomic reactor.

Malaria Eradication Emblem and Mosquito A177

1962, Apr. 7 Unwmk.

350 A177 40h grn & red org 65 40
a. Souv. sheet of 1, imperf. 1.50

WHO drive to eradicate malaria.

YWCA Emblem and Girl A178

1962, Apr. 20 *Perf. 13½*

351 A178 40h pink & dk bl 65 40

40th anniv. of the Korean Young Women's Christian Association.

South Gate and FPA Emblem A179

1962, May 12 Wmk. 317

352 A179 40h lt bl, dk vio & red 60 35

Meeting of the Federation of Motion Picture Producers in Asia, May 12-16.

Men Pushing Cogwheel A180

Soldiers on Hang Kang Bridge — A181

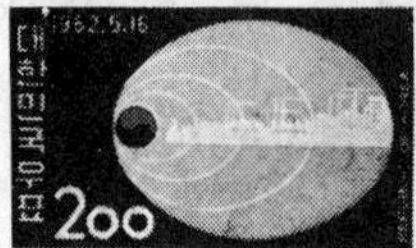

Yin Yang and Factory A182

Wmk. 317

1962, May 16 Litho. *Perf. 13½*

353 A180 30h brn & pale ol 1.20 50
a. Souv. sheet of 1, Korean text 4.00
b. Souv. sheet of 1, English text 7.00
354 A181 40h brn, lt bl & cit 1.20 50
a. Souv. sheet of 1, Korean text 4.00
b. Souv. sheet of 1, English text 7.00
355 A182 200h ultra, yel & red 2.50 75
a. Souv. sheet of 1, Korean text 4.00
b. Souv. sheet of 1, English text 7.00

1st anniv. of the May 16th Revolution.
The souvenir sheets are imperf.
The sheets with English text also exist with "E" in "POSTAGE" omitted. The English-text sheets are not watermarked except those with "E" omitted. Value, each $17.

Tortoise Warship, 16th Century A183

Design: 4w, Tortoise ship, heading right.

1962, Aug. 14 Unwmk. *Perf. 13½*

356 A183 2w dk bl & pale bl 1.00 75
357 A183 4w blk, bluish grn & lil 1.75 1.25

370th anniv. of Korea's victory in the naval battle with the Japanese off Hansan Island.

Flag, Scout Emblem and Tents — A184

Wmk. 312

1962, Oct. 5 Litho. *Perf. 13½*

358 A184 4w brn, bl & red 75 40
a. Souv. sheet of 1, imperf., unwmkd. 1.75

Wmk. 317

359 A184 4w grn, bl & red 75 40
a. Souv. sheet of 1, imperf., unwmkd. 1.75

40th anniv. of Korean Boy Scouts.

Types of 1961-62 and

Hanabusaya Asiatica A185

Miruk Bosal A186

Long-horned Beetle A186a

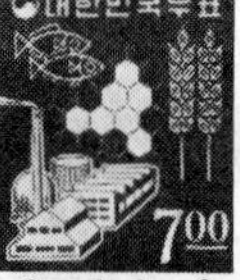

Symbols of Thrift and Development A186b

Meesun Blossoms and Fruit A186c

Library of Early Buddhist Scriptures A186d

Sika Deer — A186e

King Songdok Bell, 8th Cent. — A186f

Bodhisattva in Cavern Temple, Silla Dynasty A187

Tile of Silla Dynasty A187a

Designs: 20ch, Jin-Do dog. 1w, Folk dancers. 1.50w, Miruk Bosal. 2w, Ginseng. 3w, King Sejong. 4w, Rice farmer. 5w, Dragon waterpot. 10w, Ancient drums. 500w, Blue dragon fresco, Koguryo dynasty.

1962-66 Unwmk. Litho. *Perf. 12½*

Ordinary Paper

Size: 22x25mm, 25x22mm

360 A186 20ch gldn brn 1.00 65
361 A185 40ch blue 1.00 65
362 A186 50ch cl brn 1.00 65
363 A169 1w brt bl ('63) 1.25 65
364 A169 2w red brn 1.25 65
365 A170 3w vio brn 1.50 65
366 A172 4w green 2.00 75
367 A186 5w grnsh bl 2.00 1.00
368 A173 10w red brn 10.00 1.50
369 A186c 20w lil rose ('63) 6.00 3.00
370 A186d 40w dl pur ('63) 15.00 5.00
Nos. 360-370 (11) 42.00 15.15

1964-66

Granite Paper

360a A186 20ch org brn 1.00 40
361a A185 40ch blue 1.00 40
362a A186 50ch cl brn 1.00 40
362B A186a 60ch blk ('66) 1.00 40
363a A169 1w brt bl 1.00 40
363B A186 1.50w dk sl grn ('66) 1.00 40
364a A169 2w red brn 1.00 40
365a A170 3w vio brn 1.00 40
366a A172 4w green 1.00 40
367a A186 5w grnsh bl 1.00 40
367B A186b 7w lil rose ('66) 2.00 75
368a A173 10w red brn 2.50 75
369a A186c 20w lil rose 2.50 75
370a A186d 40w vio brn 8.50 1.50
371 A186e 50w red brn 7.00 1.50
372 A186f 100w sl grn 14.00 1.50
373 A187 200w dk & lt grn ('65) 8.50 2.00
374 A187a 300w sl grn & buff ('65) 15.00 3.50
374A A187a 500w dk & lt bl ('65) 17.50 5.00
Nos. 360a-374A (19) 87.50 21.25

The paper of Nos. 360a to 374A contains a few colored fibers; the paper of Nos. 385-396 contains many fibers.

Counterfeits exist of Nos. 369a, 370a and 371.

See Nos. 385-396, 516, 521-522, 582-584, 1076-1079, B8.

Map, Mackerel and Trawler A188

1962, Oct. 10 *Perf. 13½*

375 A188 4w dk bl & grnsh bl 52 40

10th anniv. of the Pacific Fishery Council.

ICAO Emblem and Plane A189

1962, Dec. 11 ***Perf. 13½***

376	A189 4w bl & brn	65	40
a.	Souv. sheet of 1, imperf.	1.75	

10th anniv. of Korea's joining the ICAO.

Savings Types of 1960

1962-64 **Unwmk.** ***Perf. 12½***

377	A140 1w emer, brn & org ('63)	75	50
a.	Granite paper	3.00	65
378	A141 2w pink, bl & brn	1.00	75
a.	Granite paper	1.50	75

Wmk. 317

379	A140 1w emer, brn & org ('64)	6.50	4.00
380	A141 2w pink, bl & brn ('64)	3.00	1.25

Wheat Emblem A190

Wmk. 317

1963, Mar. 21 **Litho.** ***Perf. 13½***

381	A190 4w emer, dk bl & ocher	52	30
a.	Souv. sheet of 1, imperf.	1.20	

FAO "Freedom from Hunger" campaign.

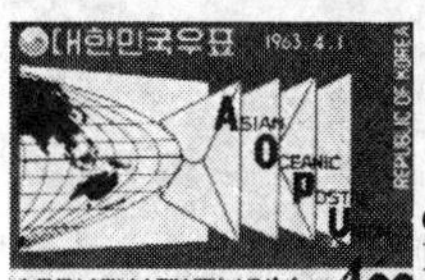

Globe and Letters A191

1963, Apr. 1

382	A191 4w rose lil, ol & dk bl	52	30
a.	Souv. sheet of 1, imperf.	1.20	

1st anniv. of the formation of the Asian-Oceanic Postal Union, AOPU.

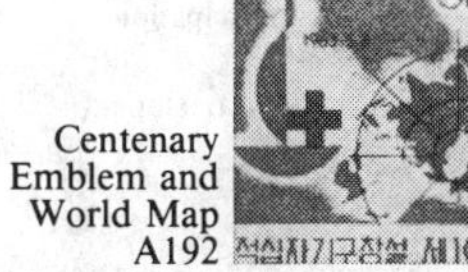

Centenary Emblem and World Map A192

1963, May 8 **Litho.**

383	A192 4w org, red & gray	70	30
384	A192 4w lt bl, red & gray	70	30
a.	Souv. sheet of 2, #383-384, imperf.	2.00	

Cent. of the Intl. Red Cross.

Types of 1961-63

Designs: 20ch, Jin-Do dog. 40ch, Hanabusaya. 50ch, Miruk Bosal. 1w, Folk dancers. 2w, Ginseng. 3w, King Sejong. 4w, Rice farmer. 10w, Ancient drums. 20w, Meesun blossoms and fruit. 40w, Library of early Buddhist scriptures. 50w, Deer. 100w, King Songdok bell, 8th century.

1963-64 **Wmk. 317** ***Perf. 12½***

Granite Paper

Size: 22x25mm, 25x22mm

385	A186	20ch gldn brn ('64)	38	25
386	A185	40ch blue	38	25
387	A186	50ch cl brn ('64)	38	25
388	A169	1w brt bl	55	35
389	A169	2w red brn	55	35
390	A170	3w vio brn	1.10	35
391	A172	4w green	1.10	60
392	A173	10w red brn	2.25	60
393	A186c	20w lil rose ('64)	2.75	1.75
394	A186d	40w dl pur	9.00	1.50
395	A186e	50w brown	9.00	2.00
396	A186f	100w sl grn	17.50	4.00
		Nos. 385-396 (12)	44.94	12.25

Hibiscus and "15" A193

1963, Aug. 15 **Wmk. 317** ***Perf. 13½***

398	A193 4w vio bl, pale bl & red	75	35

15th anniversary of the Republic.

Army Nurse and Corps Emblem A194

1963, Aug. 26 **Litho.**

399	A194 4w cit, grn & blk	65	35

Army Nurses Corps, 15th anniversary.

First Five-Year Plan Issue

Transformer and Power Transmission Tower A195

Irrigated Rice Fields — A196

Designs: No. 402, Cement factory. No. 403, Coal Miner. No. 404, Oil refinery. No. 405, Fishing industry (ships). No. 406, Cargo ship and cargo. No. 407, Fertilizer plant and grain. No. 408, Radar and telephone. No. 409, Transportation (plane, train, ship and map).

1962-66 **Unwmk.** ***Perf. 12½***

400	A195 4w org & dk vio	70	35
401	A196 4w lt bl & vio bl	70	35

Wmk. 317

402	A195 4w dk bl & gray	70	35
403	A196 4w buff & brn	70	35
404	A195 4w yel & ultra	55	28
405	A196 4w lt bl & blk	55	28

Unwmk.

406	A195 4w pale pink & vio bl	52	28
407	A196 4w bis brn & blk	52	28
408	A195 7w yel bis & blk	60	28
409	A196 7w vio bl & lt bl	60	28
	Nos. 400-409 (10)	6.14	3.08

Issued to publicize the Economic Development Five-Year Plan.

Issue dates: Nos. 400-401, Dec. 28, 1962. Nos. 402-403, Sept. 1, 1963. Nos. 404-405, June 15, 1964. Nos. 406-407, June 1, 1965. Nos. 408-409, June 1, 1966.

Ramses Temple, Abu Simbel
A197 A198

Wmk. 317

1963, Oct. 1 **Litho.** ***Perf. 13½***

410	A197 3w gray & ol gray	75	30
411	A198 4w gray & ol gray	90	50
a.	Souv. sheet of 2, #410-411, imperf.	2.50	
b.	Pair, #410-411	1.75	1.25

UNESCO world campaign to save historic monuments in Nubia.

Rugby and Torch Bearer A199

1963, Oct. 4 **Wmk. 317** ***Perf. 13½***

412	A199 4w pale bl, red brn & dk grn	75	40

44th National Athletic Games.

Nurse & Mobile X-Ray Unit A200

Eleanor Roosevelt A201

1963, Nov. 6 ***Perf. 13½***

413	A200 4w org & bluish blk	60	35

10h anniv. of the Korean Natl. Tuberculosis Association.

1963, Dec. 10 **Litho.** **Wmk. 317**

Design: 4w, Hands holding torch and globe.

414	A201 3w lt red brn & dk bl	45	25
415	A201 4w dl org, ol & dk bl	70	40
a.	Souv. sheet of 2, 414-415, imperf.	1.75	

Issued to honor Eleanor Roosevelt on the 15th anniv. of the Universal Declaration of Human Rights.

Korean Flag and UN Headquarters A202

Tang-piri (Recorder) A203

1963, Dec. 12 **Wmk. 317** ***Perf. 13½***

416	A202 4w grnsh bl, ol & blk	65	35
a.	Souv. sheet of 1, imperf.	1.75	

15th anniv. of Korea's recognition by the UN.

1963, Dec. 17 **Unwmk.**

Musical Instruments: No. 418, Pyen-kyeng (chimes). No. 419, Chang-ko (drums). No. 420, Tai-keum (large flute). No. 421, Taipyeng-so (Chinese oboe). No. 422, Na-bal (brass trumpet). No. 423, Hyang-pipa (Chinese short lute). No. 424, Wul-keum (banjo). No. 425, Kaya-ko (zither, horiz.). No. 426, Wa-kong-hu (harp, horiz.).

417	A203 4w pink, blk & car	80	35
418	A203 4w bl, bl grn & blk	80	35
419	A203 4w rose, vio bl & brn	80	35
420	A203 4w tan, dk grn & brn	80	35
421	A203 4w yel, vio bl & brn	80	35
422	A203 4w gray, brn & vio	80	35
423	A203 4w pink, vio bl & red brn	80	35
424	A203 4w grnsh bl, blk & bl	80	35
425	A203 4w rose, red brn & blk	80	35
426	A203 4w lil, blk & bl	80	35
	Nos. 417-426 (10)	8.00	3.50

Pres. Park and Capitol A204

1963, Dec. 17 **Wmk. 317**

427	A204 4w blk & brt grn	3.75	1.00

Inauguration of Pres. Park Chung Hee.

Symbols of Metric System A205

1964, Jan. 1 **Litho.**

428	A205 4w multi	52	35
a.	Imperf., pair	*75.00*	

Introduction of the metric system.

UNESCO Emblem and Yin Yang — A206

1964, Jan. 30 **Wmk. 317** ***Perf. 13½***

429	A206 4w red, lt bl & ultra	52	30

10th anniversary of the Korean National Commission for UNESCO.

Industrial Census A207

1964, Mar. 23 **Wmk. 317** ***Perf. 13½***

430	A207 4w gray, blk & red brn	60	35

National Mining and Industrial Census.

YMCA Emblem and Head A208

1964, Apr. 12 **Litho.**

431	A208 4w ap grn, dk bl & red	60	35

50th anniv. of the Korean YMCA.

Unisphere, Ginseng and Cargo Ship A209

Design: 100w, Korean pavilion and globe.

1964, Apr. 22 **Wmk. 317** ***Perf. 13½***

432	A209 40w buff, red brn & grn	1.75	60
433	A209 100w bl red brn & ultra	2.75	1.75
a.	Souv. sheet of 1, imperf.	4.50	

New York World's Fair, 1964-65.

Secret Garden, Changdok Palace, Seoul A210

Views: 2w, Whahong Gate, Suwon. 3w, Uisang Pavilion, Yangyang-gun. 4w, Maitreya Buddha, Bopju Temple at Mt. Songni. 5w, Paekma River and Rock of Falling Flowers. 6w, Anab Pond, Kyongju. 7w, Choksok Pavilion, Chinju. 8w, Kwanghan Pavilion. 9w, Whaom Temple, Mt. Chiri. 10w, Chonjeyon Falls, Soguipo.

1964, May 25 Wmk. 317 *Perf. 13½*

Light Blue Background

434	A210	1w green	25	15
435	A210	2w gray	25	15
436	A210	3w dk grn	45	25
437	A210	4w emerald	45	25
438	A210	5w violet	65	25
439	A210	6w vio bl	95	30
a.		Souv. sheet of 2 (5w, 6w)	1.65	
440	A210	7w dk brn	95	30
a.		Souv. sheet of 2 (4w, 7w)	1.65	
441	A210	8w brown	95	35
a.		Souv. sheet of 2 (3w, 8w)	1.65	
442	A210	9w lt vio	1.65	50
a.		Souv. sheet of 2 (2w, 9w)	1.65	
443	A210	10w sl grn	1.65	60
a.		Souv. sheet of 2 (1w, 10w)	1.65	
		Nos. 434-443 (10)	8.20	3.10
		Nos. 439a-443a (5)	8.25	

The five souvenir sheets are imperf.

Globe and Wheel A211

1964, July 1 Litho. *Perf. 13½*

444	A211	4w lt ol grn, dl brn & ocher	65	35
a.		Souv. sheet of 1, imperf.	1.40	

Issued to honor the Colombo Plan for cooperative economic development of south and southeast Asia.

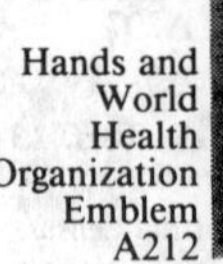

Hands and World Health Organization Emblem A212

1964, Aug. 17 Wmk. 317 *Perf. 13½*

445	A212	4w brt yel grn, yel grn & blk	65	35
a.		Souv. sheet of 1, imperf.	1.40	

15th anniv. of Korea's joining the UN.

Runner A213

1964, Sept. 3

446	A213	4w red lil, grn & pink	75	35

45th Natl. Athletic Meet, Inchon, Sept. 3-8.

UPU Monument, Bern — A214

1964, Sept. 15

447	A214	4w pink, red brn & bl	65	40
a.		Souv. sheet of 1, imperf.	1.40	

90th anniv. of the 1st Intl. Cong. for establishing the UPU.

Crane Hook and Emblem — A215

1964, Sept. 29 Wmk. 317 *Perf. 13½*

448	A215	4w red brn & dl grn	52	35

5th Convention of the Intl. Federation of Asian and Western Pacific Contractors' Assoc. (IFAWPCA), Seoul, Sept. 29-Oct. 7.

Marathon Runners A216

Design: No. 453, "V," Olympic rings, laurel and track, vert.

1964, Oct. 10 Litho.

449	A216	4w shown	65	25
450	A216	4w Equestrian	65	25
451	A216	4w Gymnast	65	25
452	A216	4w Rowing	65	25
453	A216	4w multi	65	25
		Nos. 449-453 (5)	3.25	1.25

18th Olympic Games, Tokyo, Oct. 10-25.

Souvenir Sheets of 1, Imperf., Unwmk.

449a	A216	4w	90
450a	A216	4w	90
451a	A216	4w	90
452a	A216	4w	90
453a	A216	4w	90
		Nos. 449a-453a (5)	4.50

Stamp of 1885 — A217

Yong Sik Hong — A218

1964, Dec. 4 Unwmk. *Perf. 13½*

454	A217	3w lil, vio & dl bl grn	60	35
455	A218	4w gray, vio bl & blk	80	50

80th anniv. of the Korean postal system. Yong Sik Hong (1855-84) was Korea's 1st general postmaster.

Pine Branch and Cones — A219

Designs: No. 457, Plum Blossoms. No. 458, Forsythia. No. 459, Azalea. No. 460, Lilac. No. 461, Sweetbrier. No. 462, Garden balsam. No. 463, Hibiscus. No. 464, Crape myrtle. No. 465, Chrysanthemum lucidum. No. 466, Paulownia coreana. No. 467, Bamboo.

1965 Litho. *Perf. 13½*

456	A219	4w pale grn, dp grn & brn	40	18
457	A219	4w gray, blk, rose & yel	40	18
458	A219	4w lt bl, yel & brn	40	18
459	A219	4w brt grn, lil rose & sal	55	18
460	A219	4w red lil & brt grn	40	15
461	A219	4w yel grn, grn, car & brn	40	18
462	A219	4w bl, grn & red	40	18
463	A219	4w bluish gray, rose red & grn	40	18
464	A219	4w multi	45	15
465	A219	4w pale grn, dk brn, grn & car rose	55	15
466	A219	4w buff, ol grn & brn	55	15
467	A219	4w ultra & emer	45	15
		Nos. 456-467 (12)	5.35	2.01

Souvenir Sheets of 1, Imperf.

456a	A219	4w	75
457a	A219	4w	75
458a	A219	4w	75
459a	A219	4w	75
460a	A219	4w	75
461a	A219	4w	75
462a	A219	4w	75
463a	A219	4w	75
464a	A219	4w	75
465a	A219	4w	75
466a	A219	4w	75
467a	A219	4w	75
		Nos. 456a-467a (12)	9.00

Dancing Women, PATA Emblem and Tabo Tower A220

1965, Mar. 26

468	A220	4w lt bl grn, dk brn & dk vio bl	65	35
a.		Souv. sheet of 1, imperf.	1.10	

14th conf. of the Pacific Travel Association, Seoul, Mar. 26-Apr. 2.

Map of Viet Nam and Flag of Korean Assistance Group A221

1965, Apr. 20 *Perf. 13½*

469	A221	4w blk, lt yel grn & grnsh bl	65	35
a.		Souv. sheet of 1, imperf.	1.10	

Issued to honor the Korean military assistance group in Viet Nam.

Symbols of 7-Year Plan — A222

1965, May 1 Litho.

470	A222	4w emer, dk grn & dk brn	40	25

Issued to publicize the 7-year plan for increased food production.

Scales with Families and Homes A223

1965, May 8

471	A223	4w lt & dk grn & gray	45	30
a.		Souv. sheet of 1, imperf.	1.10	

May as Month of Family Planning.

ITU Emblem, Old and New Communication Equipment — A224

1965, May 17

472	A224	4w lt bl, car & blk	45	30
a.		Souv. sheet of 1, imperf.	1.10	

Cent. of the ITU.

UN Emblem and Flags of Australia, Belgium, Great Britain, Canada and Colombia A225

Gen. Douglas MacArthur and Flags of Korea, UN and US — A226

UN Emblem and Flags: No. 474, Denmark, Ethiopia, France, Greece and India. No. 475, Italy, Luxembourg, Netherlands, New Zealand and Norway. No. 476, Philippines, Sweden, Thailand, Turkey and South Africa.

1965, June 25

Flags in Original Colors

473	A225	4w gray & vio bl	40	15
474	A225	4w grnsh bl & vio bl	40	15
475	A225	4w grnsh bl & vio bl	40	15
476	A225	4w grnsh bl & vio bl	40	15
477	A226	10w lt bl, blk, vio bl & red	75	45
		Nos. 473-477 (5)	2.35	1.05

15th anniv. of the participation of UN Forces in the Korean war.

Souvenir Sheets of 1, Imperf.

473a	A225	4w	50
474a	A225	4w	50
475a	A225	4w	50
476a	A225	4w	50
477a	A226	10w	1.10
		Nos. 473a-477a (5)	3.10

Flag, Factories and "20" — A227

South Gate, Seoul, Fireworks and Yin Yang — A228

1965, Aug. 15 Litho.

478	A227	4w lt bl, vio bl & red	30	20
479	A228	10w vio bl, lt bl & red	75	40

Issued to commemorate the 20th anniversary of liberation from the Japanese.

Factory, Leaf and Ants — A229

1965, Sept. 20 ***Perf. 13½***

480 A229 4w brt yel grn, brn & bis 52 30

Issued to publicize the importance of saving.

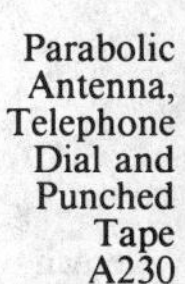

Parabolic Antenna, Telephone Dial and Punched Tape A230

Telegraph Operator, 1885 A231

1965, Sept. 28

481 A230 3w lt bl, blk & ol 30 20
482 A231 10w cit, Prus bl & blk 60 35

80th anniv. of telegraph service between Seoul and Inchon.

Korean Flag and Capitol, Seoul — A232

1965, Sept. 28

483 A232 3w org, sl grn & bl grn 65 25

15th anniversary of recapture of Seoul.

Pole Vault A233

1965, Oct. 5

484 A233 3w blk, lil & sal 55 25

Issued to publicize the 46th National Athletic Meet, Kwangju, Oct. 5-10.

ICY Emblem A234

UN Flag and Headquarters, NY — A235

1965, Oct. 24 **Litho.**

485 A234 3w lt & dk grn & org brn 40 25
 a. Souv. sheet of 1, imperf. 95
486 A235 10w lt bl, vio bl & grn 70 40
 a. Souv. sheet of 1, imperf. 1.10

ICY, 1965, and 20th anniv. of the UN.

Child Posting Letter A236

Design: 10w, Airmail envelope, telephone.

1965, Dec. 4 ***Perf. 13½***

487 A236 3w bl grn, blk, grn & red 40 20
488 A236 10w ol, dk bl & red 70 35

Tenth Communications Day.

Children with Sled — A237

Children and South Gate — A238

1965, Dec. 11 **Litho.** ***Perf. 12½***

489 A237 3w pale grn, vio bl & red 35 25
490 A238 4w lt bl, grn, vio bl & red 85 60
 a. Souv.r sheet of 2, #489-490, imperf. 1.25

Issued for Christmas and the New Year.

Freedom House — A239

1966, Feb. 15 **Unwmk.** ***Perf. 12½***

491 A239 7w brt grn, blk & cit 55 30
492 A239 39w lil, blk & pale grn 1.25 65
 a. Souv. sheet of 1, imperf. 2.50

Opening of "Freedom House" at Panmunjom.

Wildlife Issue

Mandarin Ducks A240

Alaska Pollack A241

Firefly — A242

Badger A243

Birds: 5w, Japanese cranes. 7w, Ringnecked pheasants.

1966, Mar. 15 **Litho.** ***Perf. 12½***

493 A240 3w multi 35 25
494 A240 5w multi 50 30
495 A240 7w multi 60 35

1966, June 15

Fish: 5w, Manchurian trout. 7w, Yellow corvina.

496 A241 3w bl, dk brn & yel 35 20
497 A241 5w grnsh bl, blk & mag 45 25
498 A241 7w brt grnsh bl, blk & yel 60 30

1966, Sept. 15

Insects: 5w, Grasshopper. 7w, Silk butterfly (sericinus telamon).

499 A242 3w multi 30 20
500 A242 5w dp yel & multi 40 25
501 A242 7w lt bl & multi 60 30

1966, Dec. 15

Animals: 5w, Asiatic black bear. 7w, Tiger.

502 A243 3w multi 30 20
503 A243 5w multi 40 25
504 A243 7w multi 50 30
 Nos. 493-504 (12) 5.35 3.15

Souvenir Sheets of 1, Imperf.

493a A240 3w 60
494a A240 5w 75
495a A240 7w 90
496a A241 3w 52
497a A241 5w 75
498a A241 7w 90
499a A242 3w 52
500a A242 5w 65
501a A242 7w 90
502a A243 3w 52
503a A243 5w 65
504a A243 7w 90
 Nos. 493a-504a (12) 8.56

Hwansung-gun and Kwangnung Forests — A244

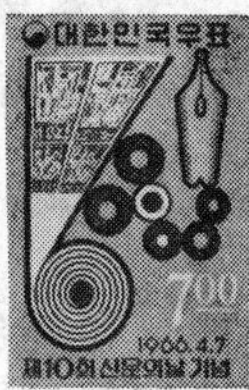

Symbolic Newspaper Printing and Pen — A245

1966, Apr. 5 **Unwmk.** ***Perf. 12½***

505 A244 7w grn & brn 40 20

Forestation Movement.

1966, Apr. 7 **Litho.**

506 A245 7w lt bl, vio brn & yel 40 20

Tenth Newspaper Day.

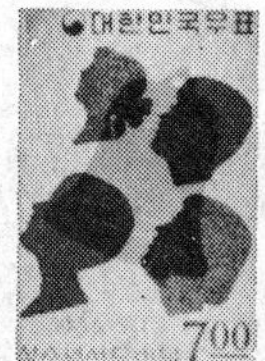

Children and Bell — A246

1966, May 1 **Unwmk.** ***Perf. 12½***

507 A246 7w org, grn & bl 40 20

Proper guidance of young people.

WHO Headquarters, Geneva — A247

1966, May 3 **Litho.**

508 A247 7w lt bl, blk & yel 45 15
 a. Souv. sheet of 1, imperf. 1.25
509 A247 39w bluish gray, yel & red 1.40 45

Inauguration of the WHO Headquarters, Geneva.

Girl Scout and Flag — A248

1966, May 10

510 A248 7w yel, emer & dk bl 70 40

Girl Scouts of Korea, 20th anniversary.

Pres. Park and Flags of Korea, Malaysia, Thailand and China — A249

1966, May 10

511 A249 7w multi 75 50

State visit of President Chung Hee Park to Malaysia, Thailand and China.

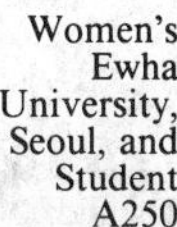

Women's Ewha University, Seoul, and Student A250

1966, May 31

512 A250 7w lt bl, vio bl & dp org 60 30

80th anniv. of modern education for women.

Types of 1961-66 Inscribed "Republic of Korea," and

Porcelain Incense Burner, 11th-12th Centuries A253

Celadon Vessel, 12th Century A254

Unjin Miruk Buddha, Kwanchok Temple — A255

Designs: 60ch, Long-horned beetle. 1w, Folk dancers. 2w, Ginseng. 3w, King Sejong. 5w, Dragon waterpot. 7w, Symbols of thrift and development.

Perf. 12½

1966, Aug. 20 **Unwmk.** **Litho.**

Size: 22x19mm, 19x22mm

Granite Paper

516 A186a 60ch gray grn 20 15
517 A169 1w green 25 15
518 A169 2w bl grn 25 15
519 A170 3w dl red brn 25 15
521 A186 5w gray grn 30 15

522 A186b 7w grnsh bl 50 15

Size: 22x25mm

523 A253 13w vio bl 75 15
524 A254 60w green 2.00 30
525 A255 80w sl grn 3.50 40
Nos. 516-525 (9) 8.00
Set value 1.40

Souvenir Sheet

Carrier Pigeons — A258

1966, July 13 Wmk. 317 *Imperf.*
Red Brown Surcharge

534 A258 7w on 40h emer & dk grn 1.00 50

6th Intl. Letter Writing Week, June 13-19. No. 534 was not issued without surcharge.

Children and World Map Projection A259

1966, July 28 Unwmk. *Perf. 12½*

535 A259 7w lt & dk vio bl & gray 40 20
a. Souv. sheet of 1, imperf. 1.10

15th annual assembly of WCOTP (World Conf. of Teaching Profession), Seoul, July 28-Aug. 9.

Factory, Money Bag and Honeycomb A260

1966, Sept. 1 Unwmk. *Perf. 12½*

536 A260 7w multi 40 20

Issued to publicize systematic saving.

Map of Korea, and People — A261

1966, Sept. 1 Litho.

537 A261 7w multi 40 20

Ninth national census.

CISM Emblem and Round-Table Conference A262

1966, Sept. 29 Unwmk. *Perf. 12½*

538 A262 7w multi 40 20
a. Souv. sheet of 1, imperf. 1.00

21st General Assembly of the Intl. Military Sports Council (CISM), Seoul, Sept. 29-Oct. 9.

Flags of Korea and Viet Nam and Korean Soldiers A263

1966, Oct. 1

539 A263 7w multi 70 40

Issued to commemorate the first anniversary of Korean combat troops in Viet Nam.

Wrestlers A264

1966, Oct. 10

540 A264 7w red brn, buff & blk 60 30

47th Natl. Athletic Meet, Seoul, Oct. 10-15.

Lions Emblem and Map of Southeast Asia — A265

1966, Oct. 15

541 A265 7w multi 48 20
a. Souv. sheet of 1, imperf. 1.25

5th East and Southeast Asia Lions Convention, Seoul, Oct. 15-17.

Seoul University Emblem A266

1966, Oct. 15 Litho.

542 A266 7w multi 40 25

20th anniversary of Seoul University.

Anticommunist League Emblem — A267

1966, Oct. 31 Unwmk. *Perf. 12½*

543 A267 7w multi 40 25
a. Souv. sheet of 1, imperf. 90

12th Conf. of the Asian Anticommunist League, Seoul, Oct. 31-Nov. 7.

Presidents Park and Johnson, Flags of US and Korea A268

1966, Oct. 31 Litho. *Perf. 12½*

544 A268 7w multi 70 30
545 A268 83w multi 1.40 1.20
a. Souv. sheet of 2, #544-545, imperf. 4.50

Visit of Pres. Lyndon B. Johnson to Korea.

UNESCO Emblem and Symbols of Learning — A269

1966, Nov. 4

546 A269 7w multi 40 30
a. Souv. sheets 1.10

20th anniv. of UNESCO.

Good Luck Bag and "Joy" A270

Ram and "Completion" A271

Perf. 12½x13, 13x12½

1966, Dec. 10

547 A270 5w multi 30 20
a. Souv. sheet of 1, imperf. 75
548 A271 7w multi 40 30
a. Souv. sheet of 1, imperf. 1.00

Issued for Christmas and the New Year.

Syncom Satellite over Globe — A272

1967, Jan. 31 Litho. *Perf. 12½*

549 A272 7w dk bl & multi 55 25
a. Souv. sheet of 1, imperf. 1.25

15th anniv. of Korea's membership in the ITU.

Presidents Park and Lübke — A273

Perf. 12½

1967, Mar. 2 Litho. Unwmk.

550 A273 7w multi 90 50
a. Souv. sheet of 1, imperf. 3.00

Issued to commemorate the visit of Pres. Heinrich Lübke of Germany, March 2-6.

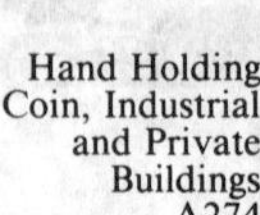

Hand Holding Coin, Industrial and Private Buildings A274

1967, Mar. 3

551 A274 7w lt grn & blk brn 40 25

1st anniv. of the Natl. Taxation Office.

Folklore Series

Okwangdae Clown — A275

Perfect Peace Dance — A276

Girls on Seesaw A277

Korean Shuttlecock A278

Designs: 5w, Sandi mask and dance (horiz.). 7w, Hafoe mask.

1967, Mar. 15 Litho. *Perf. 12½*

552 A275 4w gray, blk & yel 32 15
553 A275 5w multi 45 20
554 A275 7w multi 60 30

1967, June 15

Designs: 4w, Sword dance (horiz.). 7w, Buddhist Monk dance.

555 A276 4w multi 32 15
556 A276 5w multi 45 20
557 A276 7w multi 60 30

1967, Sept. 15

Designs: 4w, Girls on swing (horiz.). 7w, Girls dancing in the moonlight.

558 A277 4w multi 32 15
559 A277 5w multi 45 20
560 A277 7w multi 60 30

1967, Dec. 15

Designs: 5w, Girls celebrating full moon (horiz.). 7w, Archery.

561 A278 4w multi 32 15
562 A278 5w multi 45 20
563 A278 7w multi 60 30
Nos. 552-563 (12) 5.48 2.60

Souvenir Sheets of 1, Imperf.

552a A275 4w 55
553a A275 5w 70
554a A275 7w 1.10
555a A276 4w 50
556a A276 5w 65
557a A276 7w 1.10
558a A277 4w 50
559a A277 5w 65
560a A277 7w 1.10
561a A278 4w 50
562a A278 5w 65
563a A278 7w 1.10
Nos. 552a-563a (12) 9.10

JCI Emblem and Kyunghoe Pavilion A279

1967, Apr. 13 Litho. *Perf. 12½*

564 A279 7w dk brn, brt grn, bl & red 40 30
a. Souv. sheet of 1, imperf. 1.40

Intl. Junior Chamber of Commerce Conf., Seoul, Apr. 13-16.

Emblem, Map of Far East — A280

1967, Apr. 24 Unwmk. *Perf. 12½*
565 A280 7w vio bl & multi 40 25
a. Souv. sheet of 1, imperf. 1.40

Issued to publicize the 5th Asian Pacific Dental Congress, Seoul, Apr. 24-28.

EXPO '67 Korean Pavilion A281

1967, Apr. 28
566 A281 7w yel, blk & red 70 50
567 A281 83w lt bl, blk & red 2.00 1.10
a. Souv. sheet of 1, imperf. 3.25

EXPO '67, Intl. Exhibition, Montreal, Apr. 28-Oct. 27, 1967.

Worker, Soldier, Emblem and Buildings — A282

1967, May 1
568 A282 7w multi 40 25

Veterans' Day, May 1.

Second Five-Year Plan Issue

Nut and Arrows A283

Designs: No. 570, Iron wheel and rail. No. 571, Express highway. No. 572, Cloverleaf intersection. No. 573, Rising income for fishermen and farmers (oysters, silk worm, mushrooms and bull's head). No. 574, Machine industry (cogwheels, automobile, wrench and motor). No. 575, Harbor. No. 576, Housing projects plans. No. 577, Atomic power plant. No. 578, Four Great River Valley development.

1967-71 Litho. *Perf. 12½*
569 A283 7w blk, red brn & dl org 70 35
570 A283 7w dl org, yel & blk 70 35
571 A283 7w grn, bl & ol 50 30
572 A283 7w dk brn, yel & grn 50 30

Perf. 13x12½
573 A283 7w brn, grn, yel & org 42 25
574 A283 7w dk bl, lil rose & buff 42 25
575 A283 10w dk bl, bl, yel & grn 40 25
576 A283 10w lt bl, bl, grn & red 40 25

Photo. *Perf. 13*
577 A283 10w blk, car & bl 40 15
578 A283 10w blk, grn & brn 40 15
Nos. 569-578 (10) 4.84 2.60

Issued to publicize the Second Economic Development Five-Year Plan.
Issue dates: Nos. 569-570, June 1, 1967. Nos. 571-572, Dec. 5, 1968. Nos. 573-574, Dec. 5, 1969. Nos. 575-576, Dec. 5, 1970. Nos. 577-578, Dec. 5, 1971.

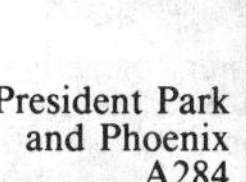

President Park and Phoenix A284

1967, July 1 Unwmk. *Perf. 12½*
579 A284 7w multi 2.25 1.00
a. Souv. sheet of 1, imperf. 8.00

Inauguration of President Park Chung Hee for a 2nd term, July 1, 1967.

Korean Boy Scout, Emblem and Tents — A285

Design: 20w, Korean Boy Scout emblem, bridge and tents.

1967, Aug. 10 Litho. *Perf. 12½*
580 A285 7w multi 40 25
a. Souv. sheet of 1, imperf. 80
581 A285 20w multi 75 60
a. Souv. sheet of 1, imperf. 1.65

3rd Korean Boy Scout Jamboree, Hwarangdae, Seoul, Aug. 10-15.

Types of 1962-66 Redrawn (Inscribed "Republic of Korea")

Designs: 20w, Meesun blossoms and fruit. 40w, Library of early Buddhist scriptures. 50w, Deer.

1967, Aug. 25
Granite Paper
582 A186c 20w grn & lt bl grn 2.00 20
583 A186d 40w dk grn & lt ol 3.00 30
584 A186e 50w dk brn & bis 4.00 50

The printing of redrawn designs of the regular issue of 1962-66 became necessary upon discovery of large quantities of counterfeits, made to defraud the post. The position of the denominations was changed and elaborate fine background tracings were added.

Freedom Center and Emblem — A286

Hand Breaking Chain — A287

Boxing — A288

1967, Sept. 25 Litho. *Perf. 12½*
586 A286 5w multi 30 15
a. Souv. sheet of 1, imperf. 50
587 A287 7w multi 40 25
a. Souv. sheet of 1, imperf. 1.25

1st Conf. of the World Anti-Communist League, WACL, Taipei, China, Sept. 25-29.

1967, Oct. 5

Design: 7w, Women's basketball.

588 A288 5w tan & multi 40 35
589 A288 7w pale rose & multi 75 50

48th Natl. Athletic Meet, Seoul, Oct. 5-10.

Students' Memorial, Kwangjoo — A289

Symbolic Water Cycle — A290

1967, Nov. 3 Litho. *Perf. 12½*
590 A289 7w lt grn & multi 40 25

Issued for Student Day commemorating 1929 students' uprising against Japan.

1967, Nov. 20
591 A290 7w multi 40 25

Hydrological Decade (UNESCO), 1965-74.

Children Spinning Top A291

Monkey and Oriental Zodiac A292

1967, Dec. 10
592 A291 5w sal, org & vio bl 30 20
a. Souv. sheet of 1, imperf. 60
593 A292 7w yel bis, brn & vio bl 48 35
a. Souv. sheet of 1, imperf. 1.25

Issued for Christmas and New Year.

Parabolic Antenna and Electric Waves — A293

1967, Dec. 21
594 A293 7w lt bl, blk & yel 48 25
a. Souv. sheet of 1, imperf. 1.10

Opening of the natl. microwave communications network, Dec. 21.

Carving from King Songdok Bell — A294

Earrings, 6th Cent. — A295

Flag — A296

Perf. 13x12½
1968, Feb. 1 Litho. Unwmk.
Granite Paper
595 A294 1w yel & brn 28 15
596 A295 5w dk grn & yel 32 15
597 A296 7w dk bl & red 55 20

WHO Emblem A297

EATA Emblem and Korean Buildings A298

1968, Apr. 7 Unwmk. *Perf. 12½*
598 A297 7w multi 40 25
a. Souv. sheet of 1, imperf. 1.40

20th anniv. of the WHO.

1968, Apr. 9 Litho.
599 A298 7w multi 40 25
a. Souv. sheet of 1, imperf. 1.40

2nd General Meeting of the East Asia Travel Association (EATA), Seoul, Apr. 9-13.

Door Knocker, Factories and Emblem A299

1968, May 6 Unwmk. *Perf. 12½*
600 A299 7w multi 50 30
a. Souv. sheet of 1, imperf. 1.40

2nd Conf. of the Confederation of Asian Chambers of Commerce and Industry, Seoul.

Pres. Park and Emperor Haile Selassie A300

1968, May 18 Litho.
601 A300 7w multi 90 50
a. Souv. sheet of 1, imperf. 2.75

Visit of Haile Selassie I, May 18-20.

Mailman's Pouch — A301

Mailman A302

1968, May 31 Unwmk. *Perf. 12½*
602 A301 5w multi 30 15
603 A302 7w multi 45 25

First Postman's Day, May 31, 1968.

Atom Diagram and Symbols of Development A303

1968, June 1 Litho.
604 A303 7w dk bl, cit & ver 45 25

Issued to promote science and technology.

Kyung Hee University and Conference Emblem A304

1968, June 18 **Unwmk.**

605 A304 7w bl, pink & blk	45	35
a. Souv. sheet of 1, imperf.	3.50	

2nd Conf. of the Intl. Association of University Presidents.

Liberated People A305

1968, July 1 **Litho.** ***Perf. 12½***

606 A305 7w multi	40	25

Issued to publicize the movement to liberate people under communist rule.

Peacock and Industrial Plant — A306

1968, Aug. 15 **Unwmk.** ***Perf. 12½***

607 A306 7w multi	40	30

Republic of Korea, 20th anniversary.

Fair Entrance A307

1968, Sept. 9 **Unwmk.** ***Perf. 12½***

608 A307 7w lil & multi	50	25

Issued to publicize the first Korean Trade Fair, Seoul, Sept. 9-Oct. 18.

Assembly Emblem and Pills — A308

Soldier, Insigne and Battle Scene — A309

1968, Sept. 16 **Litho.**

609 A308 7w multi	40	25

Issued to commemorate the 3rd General Assembly of the Federation of Asian Pharmaceutical Associations, Seoul, Sept. 16-21.

1968, Oct. 1

Designs: No. 611, Sailor, insigne and ship's guns. No. 612, Servicemen and flags. No. 613, Aviator, insigne and planes. No. 614, Marine, insigne and landing group.

610 A309 7w grn & org	1.00	35
611 A309 7w lt & dk bl	1.00	35
612 A309 7w dk bl & org	1.00	35
613 A309 7w dk bl & lt bl	1.00	35
614 A309 7w org & grn	1.00	35
a. Vert. strip of 5, #610-614	5.00	2.50
Nos. 610-614 (5)	5.00	1.75

20th anniv. of the Korean armed forces.

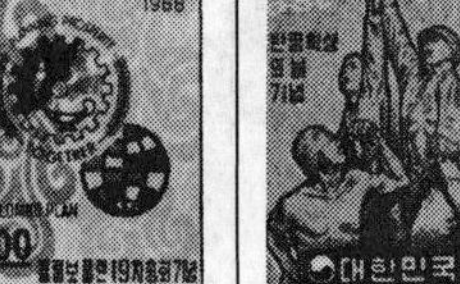
Colombo Plan Emblem and Globe — A310

1968, Oct. 8 **Litho.** ***Perf. 12½***

615 A310 7w dk brn, pale sal & grn	40	25

Issued to commemorate the 19th meeting of the Consultative Committee of the Colombo Plan, Seoul, Oct. 8-28.

Bicycling (Type I) — A311

Type II (2nd line flush left)

Designs (Olympic Rings and): No. 617, Bicycling, Type II. Nos. 618-619, Wrestling. Nos. 620-621, Boxing. Nos. 622-623, Olympic flame, "68" and symbols of various sports events.

1968, Oct. 12 **Unwmk.** ***Perf. 12½***

616 A311 7w pink & multi (I)	85	30
617 A311 7w pink & multi (II)	85	30
a. Souv. sheet of 2, #616-617, imperf.	1.75	
b. Pair, #616-617	1.75	75
618 A311 7w ol & multi (I)	85	30
619 A311 7w ol & multi (II)	85	30
a. Souv. sheet of 2, #618-619, imperf.	1.75	
b. Pair, #618-619	1.75	75
620 A311 7w org & multi (I)	85	30
621 A311 7w org & multi (II)	85	30
a. Souv. sheet of 2, #620-621, imperf.	1.75	
b. Pair, #620-621	1.75	75
622 A311 7w bluish grn & multi (I)	85	30
623 A311 7w bluish grn & multi (II)	85	30
a. Souv. sheet of 2, #622-623, imperf.	1.75	
b. Pair, #622-623	1.75	75
Nos. 616-623 (8)	6.80	2.40

Issued to commemorate the 19th Olympic Games, Mexico City, Oct. 12-27.

The position of the "7" is reversed on Nos. 619, 621 and 623 as are the designs of Nos. 619 and 621.

"Search for Knowledge" and School Girls — A312

1968, Oct. 15

624 A312 7w multi	35	25

60th anniv. of public secondary education for women.

Coin and Statistics A313

1968, Nov. 1

625 A313 7w multi	35	25

National Wealth Survey.

Memorial to Students' Uprising — A314

1968, Nov. 23

626 A314 7w gray & multi	35	25

Issued to commemorate the anti-communist students' uprising, Nov. 23, 1945.

Men With Banners Declaring Human Rights — A315

1968, Dec. 10

627 A315 7w multi	40	30

Issued for the 20th anniversary of the Declaration of Human Rights.

Christmas Decorations A316

Cock and Good Luck Characters A317

1968, Dec. 11

628 A316 5w sal & multi	90	60
a. Souv. sheet of 1, imperf.	1.50	
629 A317 7w multi	90	60
a. Souv. sheet of 1, imperf.	1.50	

Issued for Christmas and the New Year.

UN Emblems and Korean House — A318

1968, Dec. 12

630 A318 7w lt bl & multi	40	25

20th anniv. of the recognition of the Republic of Korea by the UN.

Boy Scout Emblem — A319

1968, Sept. 30 **Litho.** ***Perf. 12½***

631 A319 7w blk & multi	50	25

Regional Boy Scout conference.

Torch, Map and Students Demonstrating against Japan, 1919 — A320

1969, Mar. 1 **Unwmk.** ***Perf. 12½***

632 A320 7w multi	40	25

50th anniversary of Sam-il movement.

Hyun Choong Sa Shrine and Tortoise Ships — A321

1969, Apr. 28 **Unwmk.** ***Perf. 12½***

633 A321 7w dp bl, grn & brn	50	40

Issued to commemorate the completion of the Hyun Choong Sa Shrine at Onyang, dedicated to the memory of Adm. Li Sun-sin.

Pres. Park and Tuanku Nasiruddin of Malaysia A322

1969, Apr. 29 **Litho.**

634 A322 7w yel & multi	85	40
a. Souv. sheet of 1, imperf.	3.50	

Visit of Tuanku Ismail Nasiruddin, ruler of Malaysia, Apr. 29, 1969.

Hanabusaya Asiatica — A323

Flag of Korea — A324

Ancient Drums — A325

Red-crested Cranes — A326

Highway and Farm — A327

Pitcher (12-13th Centuries) — A328

Ceramic Duck (Water Jar) — A329

Library of Early Buddhist Scriptures — A330

Miruk Bosal — A333

Designs: 1w, Old man's mask. No. 637, Stone lamp, 8th century. No. 638, Chipmunk. No. 644, Tiger lily. No. 649, Bee. No. 651, Vase, Yi dynasty, 17th-18th centuries. No. 653, Gold crown, Silla Dynasty.

Zeros Omitted except 7w, No. 639

Perf. 13x12, 12x13 (Litho.); 13½x12½, 12½x13½ (Photo.)

Litho. (40ch, Nos. 641, 650); Photo.

1969-74 Unwmk.

Granite Paper (Lithographed); Ordinary Paper (Photogravure)

635 A323 40ch green 15 15
636 A326 1w dk rose brn ('74) 15 15
637 A328 5w brt plum 15 15
638 A326 5w mar ('74) 15 15
639 A324 7w bl ("7.00") 15 15
640 A324 7w bl ("7") 15 15
641 A325 10w ultra 25 15
642 A324 10w ultra ("10") ('70) 20 15
643 A326 10w bl & dk bl ('73) 15 15
644 A323 10w grn & multi ('73) 15 15
645 A327 10w grn, red & gray ('73) 15 15
647 A328 20w green 50 15
648 A329 30w dl grn ('70) 60 18
649 A326 30w yel & dk brn ('74) 50 15
650 A330 40w vio bl & pink 1.25 25
651 A328 40w ultra & lil 1.25 20
652 A333 100w dp cl & yel 7.00 90
653 A333 100w brn & yel ('74) 3.00 60
Nos. 635-653 (18) 15.90
Set value 3.10

See No. 1090. For surcharge see No. B18.

Red Cross, Faces and Doves — A336

1969, May 5 Litho. *Perf. 12½*

654 A336 7w multi 40 25
a. Souv. sheet of 1, imperf. 1.35

50th anniv. of the League of Red Cross Societies.

Savings Bank, Factories and Highway — A337

1969, May 20 Unwmk. *Perf. 12½*

655 A337 7w yel grn & multi 40 20

Second Economy Drive.

Pres. Park, Pres. Thieu and Flags of Korea and Viet Nam — A338

1969, May 27 Litho.

656 A338 7w pink & multi 80 40
a. Souv. sheet of 1, imperf. 2.50

Issued to commemorate the visit of Pres. Nguyen Van Thieu of Viet Nam, May 27.

"Reforestation and Parched Fields" — A339

Growing and Withering Plants — A340

1969, June 10

657 A339 7w multi 40 20
658 A340 7w multi 40 20

Issued to publicize the need for prevention of damages from floods and droughts.

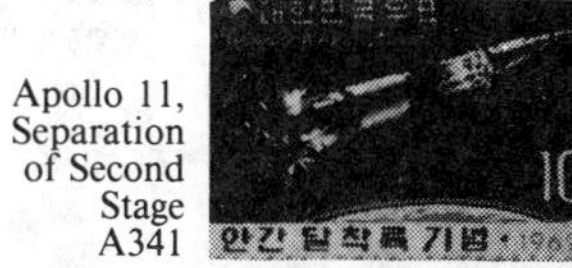

Apollo 11, Separation of Second Stage A341

Designs: No. 660, Apollo 11, separation of 3rd Stage. No. 661, Orbits of command and landing modules around moon. No. 662, Astronauts gathering rock samples on moon. 40w, Spacecraft splashdown.

1969, Aug. 15 Unwmk. *Perf. 12½*

659 A341 10w ind, bl & red 30 20
660 A341 10w ind, bl & red 30 20
661 A341 20w ind, bl, red & lem 60 30
662 A341 20w ind, bl, red & lem 60 30
663 A341 40w ind, bl & red 1.25 60
a. Souv. sheet of 5, #659-663, imperf. 2.50
b. Strip of 5, #659-663 3.25 2.00
Nos. 659-663 (5) 3.05 1.60

Man's 1st landing on the moon, July 20, 1969. US astronauts Neil A. Armstrong and Col. Edwin E. Aldrin, Jr., with Lieut. Col. Michael Collins piloting Apollo 11.

Fable Issue

Girl and Stepmother A342

The Sick Princess A343

Mother Meeting Tiger — A344

Woodcutter Stealing Fairy's Clothes A345

Heungbu and Wife Release Healed Swallow A346

Kongji and Patji (Cinderella): 7w, Sparrows help Kongji separate rice. 10w, Ox helps Kongji to weed a field. 20w, Kongji in a sedan chair on the way to the palace.

1969, Sept. 1 Litho. *Perf. 12½*

664 A342 5w ap grn & multi 20 15
665 A342 7w yel & multi 25 15
666 A342 10w lt vio & multi 35 20
667 A342 20w lt grn & multi 60 35

1969, Nov. 1 *Perf. 13x12½*

"The Hare's Liver": 7w, Hare riding to the palace on back of turtle. 10w, Hare telling a lie to the King to save his life. 20w, Hare mocking the turtle.

668 A343 5w yel & multi 20 15
669 A343 7w lt vio & multi 20 15
670 A343 10w lt grnsh bl & multi 35 20
671 A343 20w lt yel grn & multi 60 35

1970, Jan. 5

"The Sun and the Moon": 7w, Tiger disguised as mother at children's house. 10w, Tiger, and children on tree. 20w, Children safe on cloud, and tiger falling to his death.

672 A344 5w org & multi 20 15
673 A344 7w gray grn & multi 25 15
674 A344 10w lt grn & multi 35 20
675 A344 20w gray & multi 60 35

1970, Mar. 5

Designs: No. 677, Woodcutter with wife and children. No. 678, Wife taking children to heaven. No. 679, Husband joining family in heaven.

676 A345 10w dl bl grn & multi 35 20
677 A345 10w buff & multi 35 20
678 A345 10w lt grnsh bl & multi 35 20
679 A345 10w pink & multi 35 20

1970, May 5 *Perf. 12½*

Designs: No. 681, Heungbu and wife finding gold treasure in gourd. No. 682, Nolbu and wife with large gourd. No. 683, Demon emerging from gourd punishing evil Nolbu and wife.

680 A346 10w lt grnsh bl & multi 35 20
681 A346 10w org & multi 35 20
682 A346 10w ap grn & multi 35 20
683 A346 10w tan & multi 35 20
Nos. 664-683 (20) 6.95 4.15

Souvenir Sheets of 1, Imperf.

664a A342 5w 28
665a A342 7w 35
666a A342 10w 45
667a A342 20w 95
668a A343 5w 25
669a A343 7w 35
670a A343 10w 50
671a A343 20w 90
672a A344 5w 25
673a A344 7w 35
674a A344 10w 50
675a A344 20w 85
676a A345 10w 50
677a A345 10w 50
678a A345 10w 50
679a A345 10w 50
680a A346 10w 50
681a A346 10w 50
682a A346 10w 50
683a A346 10w 50
Nos. 664a-683a (20) 9.98

1869 Locomotive and Diesel Train — A347

Design: No. 685, Early locomotive.

Perf. 12½

1969, Sept. 18 Litho. Unwmk.

684 A347 7w yel & multi 40 20
685 A347 7w grn & multi 40 20

70th anniversary of Korean Railroads.

Formation of F-5A Planes — A348

Design: No. 687, F-4D Phantom.

1969, Oct. 1 Photo. *Perf. 13½x13*

686 A348 10w bl, blk & car 50 25

Litho. *Perf. 13x12½*

687 A348 10w multi 50 25

20th anniversary of Korean Air Force.

Cha-jun Game — A349

1969, Oct. 3

688 A349 7w ap grn, dk bl & blk 40 25

10th National Festival of Traditional Skills.

Institute of Science and Technology A350

1969, Oct. 23

689 A350 7w bis, grn & choc 40 25

Completion of the Korean Institute of Science and Technology, Hongnung, Seoul.

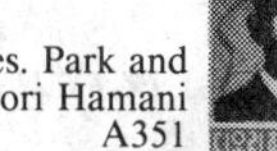

Pres. Park and Diori Hamani A351

1969, Oct. 27

690 A351 7w yel grn & multi 70 25
a. Souv. sheet of 1, imperf. 2.00

Visit of Diori Hamani, Pres. of Niger, Oct. 27.

Korean Wrestling A352

Sports: No. 692, Fencing. No. 693, Korean karate (taekwondo). No. 694, Volleyball (vert.). No. 695, Soccer (vert.).

Perf. 13x12½, 12½x13

1969, Oct. 28

691 A352 10w yel grn & multi 45 20
692 A352 10w bl & multi 45 20
693 A352 10w grn & multi 45 20
694 A352 10w ol & multi 45 20
695 A352 10w ultra & multi 45 20
Nos. 691-695 (5) 2.25 1.00

Issued to commemorate the 50th National Athletic Meet, Seoul, Oct. 28-Nov. 2.

Allegory of National Education Charter — A353

1969, Dec. 5 Litho. *Perf. 12½x13*

696 A353 7w dl yel & multi 40 25

1st anniv. of the proclamation of the Natl. Education Charter.

Toy Dogs and Lattice Pattern A354

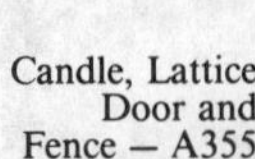

Candle, Lattice Door and Fence — A355

1969, Dec. 11 Photo. *Perf. 13½*

697 A354 5w grn & multi 30 15
698 A355 7w bl & multi 40 25

Issued for New Year 1970.

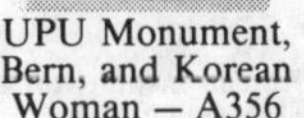

UPU Monument, Bern, and Korean Woman — A356

Education Year Emblem and Book — A357

1970, Jan. 1 Photo. *Perf. 13x13½*

699 A356 10w multi 95 25

70th anniv. of Korea's admission to the UPU.

1970, Mar. 10 Litho. *Perf. 12½x13*

700 A357 10w pink & multi 75 25

International Education Year 1970.

EXPO '70 Emblem, Seated Buddha, Korean Pavilion A358

1970, Mar. 15 *Perf. 13x12½*

701 A358 10w multi 60 25

Issued to publicize EXPO '70 International Exhibition, Osaka, Japan, March 15-Sept. 13.

Korean Youths and 4-H Club Emblem — A359

1970, Mar. 28 *Perf. 12½x13*

702 A359 10w yel & multi 40 25

Issued to publicize the 15th Korean 4-H Club Central Contest, Suwon, March 28.

Money and Bank Emblem A360

1970, Apr. 9 Litho. *Perf. 13x12½*

703 A360 10w yel & multi 40 25

Issued to commemorate the 3rd annual Board of Governors' meeting of the Asian Development Bank, Seoul, Apr. 9-11.

Royal Palanquin A361

1899 Streetcar A362

Historic Means of Transportation: No. 706, Emperor Sunjong's Cadillac, 1903. No. 707, Nieuport biplane, 1922.

Perf. 13x13½, 13½x13

1970, May 20 Photo.

704 A361 10w cit & multi 45 15
705 A362 10w yel & multi 45 15
706 A362 10w ocher & multi 45 15
707 A362 10w aqua & multi 45 15

UPU Headquarters A363

1970, May 30 *Perf. 13½x13*

708 A363 10w multi 40 25

New UPU Headquarters in Bern, Switzerland.

Map, Radar and Satellite — A364

1970, June 2 *Perf. 13x13½*

709 A364 10w sky bl, vio bl & blk 60 25

Issued to commemorate the completion of the Kum San Earth Station of the International Satellite Consortium (INTELSAT).

"PEN" and Manuscript Paper — A365

1970, June 28 Photo. *Perf. 13x13½*

710 A365 10w bl grn, bl & car 35 25

37th Intl. P.E.N. Cong. (Poets, Playwrights, Editors, Essayists and Novelists), Seoul, June 28-July 4.

Seoul-Pusan Expressway — A366

1970, June 30

711 A366 10w multi 65 30

Opening of Seoul-Pusan Expressway.

Postal Code Symbol and Number A367

Mail Sorting Machine A368

1970, July 1

712 A367 10w multi 40 20

Issued to publicize the introduction of postal zone numbers, July 1, 1970.

1970, July 2

713 A368 10w lt vio & multi 40 20
a. Souv. sheet of 4, 2 each #712-713 7.00

Mechanization of Korean postal system.

Boy and Children's Hall — A369

1970, July 25

714 A369 10w pink & multi 40 25

Paintings Issue

Jongyangsa Temple and Mt. Kumgang, by Chong Son (1676-1759) — A370

The Fierce Tiger, by Shim Sa-yung (1707-1769) A371

Paintings: No. 716, Mountains and Rivers, by Yi In-moon (1745-1821). No. 717, Mountains and Rivers in Moonlight, by Kim Doo-ryang (1696-1763).

Perf. 13x13½, 13½x13

1970, Aug. 31 Photo.

715 A370 10w bl & multi 65 35
716 A370 10w buff & multi 65 35
717 A371 10w multi 65 35

1970, Oct. 30

Paintings: No. 719, Cats and Sparrows, by Pyun Sang-byuk (18th century). No. 720, Dog with puppies, by Yi Am (1499-?).

718 A371 30w multi 1.65 65
719 A371 30w multi 1.65 65
720 A371 30w multi 1.65 65

Nos. 718-720 exist imperf., same values.

1970, Dec. 30

Paintings: No. 721, Cliff and Boat, by Kim Hong-do (1745-?). No. 722, Cock, Hens and Chick, by Pyun Sang-byuk (early 18th century). No. 723, Woman Playing Flute, by Shin Yun-bok (late 18th century).

721 A371 10w yel brn, blk & red 65 35
722 A371 10w pale rose, blk & grn 65 35
723 A371 10w multi 65 35
Nos. 715-723 (9) 8.85 4.05

Souvenir Sheets of 2

715a A370 10w 2.00
716a A370 10w 2.00
717a A371 10w 2.00
718a A371 30w 5.00
719a A371 30w 5.00
720a A371 30w 5.00
721a A371 10w 2.50
722a A371 10w 2.50
723a A371 10w 2.50
Nos. 715a-723a (9) 28.50

Nos. 715a-717a have simulated perforations. Background color of stamps on No. 717a is yellow instead of greenish gray as on No. 717.

Nos. 718a-720a exist imperf., same values. Nos. 721a-723a exist imperf.

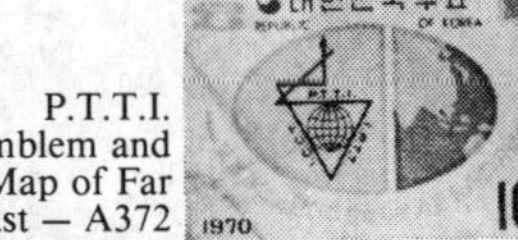

P.T.T.I. Emblem and Map of Far East — A372

1970, Sept. 6 Litho. *Perf. 13x12½*

724 A372 10w lt yel grn, bl & dk bl 35 25

Issued to publicize the opening of the Councillors' Meeting of the Asian Chapter of the Postal, Telegraph and Telephone International Organization, Sept. 6-12.

Korean WAC and Emblem — A373

1970, Sept. 6 Photo. *Perf. 13x13½*

725 A373 10w bl & multi 45 25

20th anniv. of the founding of the Korean Women's Army Corps.

Pres. Park, Korean Flag and Means of Transportation — A374

Pres. Park, Highways, Factories A375

1970 *Perf. 13x13½, 13½x13*

726 A374 10w vio bl, blk & car 1.00 40
727 A375 10w dk bl, grnsh bl & blk 95 40

Presidents Park and Hernandez, Flags of Korea, Salvador A376

1970, Sept. 28 Litho. *Perf. 13x12½*
728 A376 10w dk bl, red & blk 90 25
a. Souv. sheet of 1, imperf. 9.50

Visit of Gen. Fidel Sanchez Hernandez, President of El Salvador.

People and Houses A377

1970, Oct. 1 Litho. *Perf. 13x12½*
729 A377 10w lil & multi 35 20

Issued to publicize the national census of population and housing, Oct. 1.

Diver A378

1970, Oct. 6 Photo. *Perf. 12½x13½*
730 A378 10w shown 60 20
a. Souv. sheet of 2, imperf. 1.50
731 A378 10w Field hockey 60 20
a. Souv. sheet of 2, imperf. 1.50
732 A378 10w Baseball 60 20
a. Souv. sheet of 2, imperf. 1.50

51st Natl. Athletic Games, Seoul, Oct. 6-11.

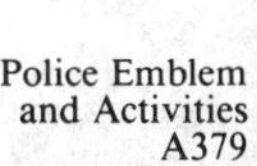

Police Emblem and Activities A379

1970, Oct. 21 Litho. *Perf. 12½*
733 A379 10w ultra & multi 45 25

The 25th Policemen's Day.

Freedom Bell, UN Emblem over Globe — A380

1970, Oct. 24 Photo. *Perf. 13x13½*
734 A380 10w bl & multi 40 25

25th anniversary of United Nations.

Kite and Holly — A380a

Boar — A381

1970, Dec. 1 Litho. *Perf. 13*
735 A380a 10w lt bl & multi 30 18
a. Souvenir sheet of 3 1.25
736 A381 10w grn & multi 30 18
a. Souvenir sheet of 3 1.25

New Year 1971.

Pres. Park Quotation, Globe and Telecommunications Emblems — A382

1970, Dec. 4 Photo.
737 A382 10w multi 40 25

For the 15th Communications Day.

Power Dam — A383

Coal Mining A384

Highway Intersection A385

Designs: No. 739, Crate wrapped in world map, and ships. No. 740, Irrigation project and farm (vert.). No. 742, Cement factory (vert.). No. 743, Fertilizer factory. No. 744, Increased national income (scales). No. 745, Increased savings (factories, bee and coins).

1971 *Perf. 13x13½, 13½x13*

738	A383 10w bl & multi	25	15
739	A383 10w pale lil & multi	25	15
740	A383 10w grn & multi	25	15
741	A384 10w bl grn, lt bl & blk	25	15
742	A384 10w lt bl, vio & brt mag	25	15
743	A384 10w vio, grn & bis	25	15
744	A384 10w pink & multi	25	15
745	A384 10w lt bl grn & multi	25	15
746	A385 10w vio & multi	25	15
	Nos. 738-746 (9)	2.25	1.35

Economic Development.

Souvenir Sheets of 1, Imperf.

738a	A383	10w	50
739a	A383	10w	50
740a	A383	10w	50

Souvenir Sheets of 2, Imperf.

741a	A384	10w	60
742a	A384	10w	60
743a	A384	10w	60
744a	A384	10w	60
745a	A384	10w	60
746a	A385	10w	60
	Nos. 738a-746a (9)		5.10

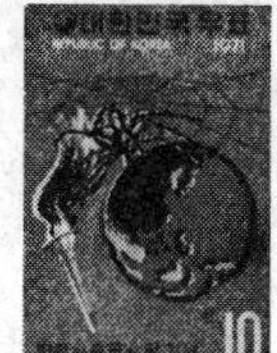

Torch, Globe and Spider — A386

1971, Mar. 1 Litho. *Perf. 12½x13*
747 A386 10w gray & multi 35 25

March, the month for anti-espionage and victory over communism.

Reservist, Reserve Forces Emblem A387

1971, Apr. 3 Photo. *Perf. 13½x13*
748 A387 10w lt ultra & multi 35 25

Home Reserve Forces Day, Apr. 3.

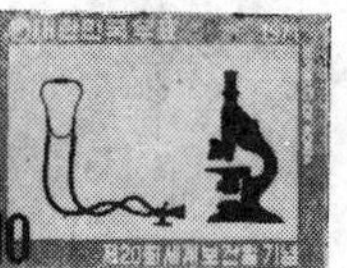

WHO Emblem, Stethoscope, Microscope A388

1971, Apr. 7
749 A388 10w lt bl, pur & yel 35 25

20th World Health Day, Apr. 7.

Subway Tunnel and Train — A389

Soccer Player — A390

1971, Apr. 12 Litho. *Perf. 12½x13*
750 A389 10w multi 40 25

Seoul subway construction start.

1971, May 2
751 A390 10w grn, dk brn & blk 40 30

First Asian Soccer Games, Seoul, May 2-13.

Veterans Flag and Veterans A391

Girl Scouts and Emblem A392

1971, May 8 Photo. *Perf. 13x13½*
752 A391 10w ultra & multi 40 25

20th Korean Veterans Day.

1971, May 10
753 A392 10w lilac & multi 40 30

25th anniversary of the Korean Federation of Girl Scouts.

Torch and Development A393

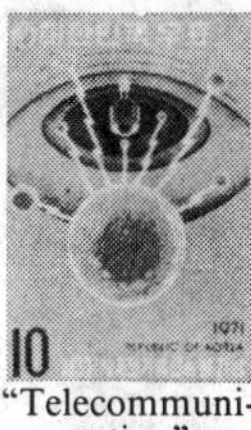

"Telecommunication" A394

1971, May 16
754 A393 10w lt bl & multi 35 25

10th anniversary of May 16th revolution.

1971, May 17
755 A394 10w bl & multi 35 25

3rd World Telecommunications Day.

Security Council A395

Korean Flag — A396

UN Organizations: No. 756, ILO. No. 757, FAO. No. 758, General Assembly (UN Headquarters). No. 759, UNESCO. No. 760, WHO. No. 761, World Bank. No. 762, Intl. Development Association (IDA). No. 763, Security Council. No. 764, Intl. Finance Corp. (IFC). No. 765, Intl. Monetary Fund. No. 766, ICAO. No. 767, Economic and Social Council. No. 768, Korean Flag. No. 769, Trusteeship Council. No. 770, UPU. No. 771, ITU. No. 772, World Meteorological Org. (WMO). No. 773, Intl. Court of Justice. No. 774, Intl. Maritime Consultative Org. No. 775, UNICEF. No. 776, Intl. Atomic Energy Agency. No. 777, UN Industrial Development Org. No. 778, UN Commission for the Unification and Rehabilitation of Korea. No. 779, UN Development Program. No. 780, UN Conf. on Trade and Development.

1971, May 30 *Perf. 13½x13*

756	A395 10w grn, blk & pink	65	25
757	A395 10w pink, blk & bl	65	25
758	A395 10w bl, blk, grn & pink	65	25
759	A395 10w pink, blk & bl	65	25
760	A395 10w grn, blk & pink	65	25
761	A395 10w pink, blk & bl	65	25
762	A395 10w bl, blk & pink	65	25
763	A395 10w grn, blk & pink	65	25
764	A395 10w bl, blk & pink	65	25
765	A395 10w pink, blk & bl	65	25
766	A395 10w bl, blk & pink	65	25
767	A395 10w grn, blk & pink	65	25
768	A396 10w bl, blk & pink	65	25
769	A395 10w grn, blk & pink	65	25
770	A395 10w bl, blk & pink	65	25
771	A395 10w pink, blk & bl	65	25
772	A395 10w bl, blk & pink	65	25
773	A395 10w grn, blk & pink	65	25
774	A395 10w bl, blk & pink	65	25
775	A395 10w pink, blk & bl	65	25
776	A395 10w grn, blk & pink	65	25
777	A395 10w pink, blk & bl	65	25
778	A395 10w bl, blk & pink	65	25
779	A395 10w pink, blk & bl	65	25
780	A395 10w grn, blk & pink	65	25
	Nos. 756-780 (25)	16.25	6.25

Sheet of 50 incorporates 2 each of #756-780.

Boat Ride, by Shin Yun-bok — A397

Man and Boy under Pine Tree — A398

Paintings by Shin Yun-bok: No. 782, Greeting travelers. No. 783, Tea ceremony. No. 784, Lady traveling with servants. No. 785, Man and woman on the road.

Perf. 13x13½, 13½x13

1971, June 20 **Photo.**

781 A397 10w multi 80 20
782 A397 10w multi 80 20
783 A397 10w multi 80 20
784 A397 10w multi 80 20
785 A397 10w multi 80 20
786 A398 10w multi 80 20
b. Vert. strip of 5, #781-785 5.00 3.00
Nos. 781-786 (6) 4.80 1.20

Souvenir Sheets of 2

781a A397 10w 1.75
782a A397 10w 1.75
783a A397 10w 1.75
784a A397 10w 1.75
785a A397 10w 1.75
786a A398 10w 1.75
Nos. 781a-786a (6) 10.50

Types A397-A398 with Inscription at Left

1971, July 20

Paintings: No. 787, Farmyard scene, by Kim Deuk-shin. No. 788, Family living in valley, by Lee Chae-kwan. No. 789, Man reading book under pine tree, by Lee Chae-kwan.

787 A397 10w pale grn & multi 60 25
788 A398 10w pale grn & multi 60 25
789 A398 10w lt yel grn & multi 60 25

Souvenir Sheets of 2

787a A397 10w 1.40
788a A398 10w 1.40
789a A398 10w 1.40

Teacher and Students, by Kim Hong-do A399

Paintings by Kim Hong-do (Yi Dynasty): No. 791, Wrestlers. No. 792, Dancer and musicians. No. 793, Weavers. No. 794, At the Well.

1971, Aug. 20 ***Perf. 13½x13***

790 A399 10w blk, lt grn & rose 90 25
791 A399 10w blk, lt grn & rose 90 25
792 A399 10w blk, lt grn & rose 90 25
793 A399 10w blk, lt grn & rose 90 25
794 A399 10w blk, lt grn & rose 90 25
b. Horiz. strip of 5, #790-794 4.50 2.50
Nos. 790-794 (5) 4.50 1.25

Souvenir Sheets of 2

790a A399 10w 1.90
791a A399 10w 1.90
792a A399 10w 1.90
793a A399 10w 1.90
794a A399 10w 1.90
Nos. 790a-794a (5) 9.50

Pres. Park, Highway and Phoenix A400

1971, July 1 ***Perf. 13½x13***

795 A400 10w grn, blk & org 1.40 50
a. Souvenir sheet of 2 4.75

Inauguration of President Park Chung Hee for a third term, July 1.

Campfire and Tents — A401

1971, Aug. 2 Photo. ***Perf. 13x13½***

796 A401 10w bl grn & multi 40 25

13th Boy Scout World Jamboree, Asagiri Plain, Japan, Aug. 2-10.

Symbol of Conference A402

1971, Sept. 27 ***Perf. 13***

797 A402 10w multi 40 25
a. Souvenir sheet of 2 5.00

Asian Labor Ministers' Conference, Seoul, Sept. 27-30.

Archers — A403

1971, Oct. 8 Photo. ***Perf. 13x13½***

798 A403 10w shown 60 20
a. Souvenir sheet of 3 2.50
799 A403 10w Judo 60 20
a. Souvenir sheet of 3 2.50

52nd National Athletic Meet.

Taeguk on Palette — A404

1971, Oct. 11 ***Perf. 13½x13***

800 A404 10w yel & multi 35 25

20th National Fine Arts Exhibition.

Physician, Globe and Emblem A405

1971, Oct. 13

801 A405 10w multi 35 25

7th Congress of the Confederation of Medical Associations in Asia and Oceania.

Symbols of Contest Events — A406

1971, Oct. 20 Photo. ***Perf. 13x13½***

802 A406 10w multi 35 25
a. Souvenir sheet of 2 4.00

2nd National Skill Contest for High School Students.

Slide Caliper and KS Emblem A407

1971, Nov. 11 ***Perf. 13x13½***

803 A407 10w multi 35 25

10th anniversary of industrial standardization in Korea.

Rats — A408

Japanese Crane — A409

1971, Dec. 1

804 A408 10w multi 35 18
a. Souvenir sheet of 3 1.25
805 A409 10w multi 35 18
a. Souvenir sheet of 3 1.25

New Year 1972.

Emblem of Hangul Hakhoe and Hangul Letters — A410

1971, Dec. 3 **Photo.**

806 A410 10w dk bl & multi 35 20

50th anniversary of Korean Language Research Society (Hangul Hakhoe).

Red Cross Headquarters and Map of Korea — A411

1971, Dec. 31 ***Perf. 13½x13***

807 A411 10w multi 40 20
a. Souvenir sheet of 2 1.65

First South and North Korean Red Cross Conference, Panmunjom, Aug. 20, 1971.

Globe and Book — A412

1972, Jan. 5 ***Perf. 13x13½***

808 A412 10w multi 45 30
a. Souvenir sheet of 2 2.00

International Book Year 1972.

Intelsat 4 Sending Signals to Korea — A413

1972, Jan. 31 ***Perf. 13½x13***

809 A413 10w dk bl & multi 35 25

Korea's entry into ITU, 20th anniv.

Figure Skating, Sapporo '72 Emblem A414

Map of Korea with Forest Sites A415

Design: No. 811, Speed skating.

1972, Feb. 3 ***Perf. 13x13½***

810 A414 10w lt & dk bl & car 35 15
811 A414 10w lt & dk bl & car 35 15
a. Souv. sheet of 2, #810-811 3.50

11th Winter Olympic Games, Sapporo, Japan, Feb. 3-13.

1972, Mar. 10 Photo. ***Perf. 13x13***

812 A415 10w buff, bl grn & red 35 20

Publicity for forests planted to mark hope for re-unification of Korea.

Junior Chamber of Commerce Emblem and Beetles A416

1972, Mar. 19 ***Perf. 13½x13***

813 A416 10w pink & multi 35 20

Junior Chamber of Commerce, 20th anniversary.

U.N. Emblem, Agriculture and Industry — A417

1972, Mar. 28 ***Perf. 13x13½***

814 A417 10w vio, grn & car 35 20

Economic Commission for Asia and the Far East (ECAFE), 25th anniversary.

Flags — A418

1972, Apr. 1 ***Perf. 13½x13***

815 A418 10w bl & multi 35 20

Asian-Oceanic Postal Union, 10th anniv.

Korean Flag — A419

YWCA Emblem, Butterflies — A420

1972, Apr. 1 Photo. ***Perf. 13x13½***
816 A419 10w yel & multi 35 25

Homeland Reserve Forces Day, Apr. 1.

1972, Apr. 20
817 A420 10w vio & multi 40 20

50th anniv. of the YWCA of Korea.

Community Projects A421

Korean Flag & Inscription A422

1972, May 1 ***Perf. 13x13½***
818 A421 10w pink & multi 35 20

Rural rehabilitation and construction movement.

1972, May 1
819 A422 10w grn & multi 35 20

Anti-espionage and victory over communism month.

Children with Balloons A423

1972, May 5 ***Perf. 13½x13***
820 A423 10w yel & multi 35 20

Children's Day, May 5.

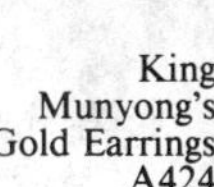

King Munyong's Gold Earrings A424

Design: No. 822, Gold ornament from King's crown (vert.).

Perf. 13½x13, 13x13½
1972, May 10
821 A424 10w grn & multi 30 20
822 A424 10w grn & multi 30 20

National treasures from tomb of King Munyong of Paekche, who reigned 501-523.

Kojo Island — A425

National parks: No. 823, Crater Lake.

1972, May 30 ***Perf. 13½x13***
823 A425 10w bl grn & multi 30 20
824 A425 10w grn & multi 30 20

Daisy, Environment Emblem — A426

1972, May 30 Litho. ***Perf. 13x13½***
825 A426 10w grn & multi 35 20
a. Souvenir sheet of 2 1.90

UN Conference on Human Environment, Stockholm, June 5-16.

Gwanghwa Gate, Flags of Participants — A427

1972, June 14
826 A427 10w yel & multi 35 20

7th Meeting of Asian-Pacific Council (ASPAC).

Farm and Fish Hatchery A428

Weight Lifting A429

Third Five-Year Plan Issue

1972, July 1 Photo. ***Perf. 13½x13***
827 A428 10w shown 30 15
828 A428 10w Steel industry and products 30 15
829 A428 10w Globe and cargo 30 15

3rd Economic Development Five-Year Plan.

1972, Aug. 26 Photo. ***Perf. 13x13½***
830 A429 20w shown 30 15
831 A429 20w Judo 30 15
a. Souv. sheet of 2, #830-831 1.40
b. Pair, #830-831 65 35
832 A429 20w Boxing 30 15
833 A429 20w Wrestling 30 15
a. Souv. sheet of 2, #832-833 1.40
b. Pair, #832-833 65 35

20th Olympic Games, Munich, Aug. 26-Sept. 11. Nos. 831b, 833b each printed checkerwise.

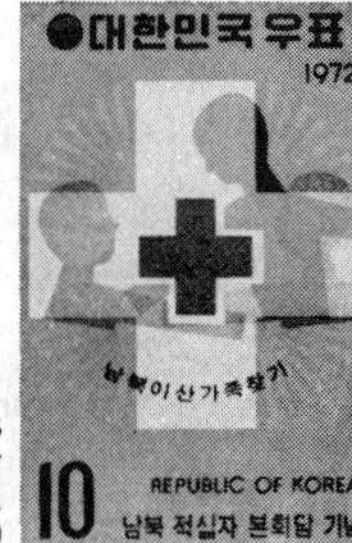

Families Reunited by Red Cross — A430

1972, Aug. 30 Photo. ***Perf. 13½x13***
834 A430 10w lt bl & multi 48 20
a. Souv. sheet of 2 2.50

Plenary meeting of the South-North Red Cross Conference, Pyongyang, Aug. 30, 1972.

Bulkuk-sa Temple, Kyongju Park — A431

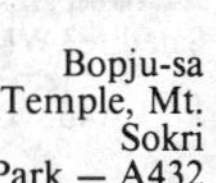

Bopju-sa Temple, Mt. Sokri Park — A432

1972, Sept. 20 Photo. ***Perf. 13½x13***
835 A431 10w brn & multi 30 20
836 A432 10w bl & multi 30 20

National parks.

"5" and Conference Emblem — A433

1972, Sept. 25 ***Perf. 13x13½***
837 A433 10w vio bl & multi 35 15

Fifth Asian Judicial Conference, Seoul, Sept. 25-29.

Lions Emblem, Taeguk Fan — A434

1972, Sept. 28 ***Perf. 13½x13***
838 A434 10w multi 35 15

11th Orient and Southeast Asian Lions Convention, Seoul, Sept. 28-30.

Scout Taking Oath, Korean Flag and Scout Emblem A435

1972, Oct. 5
839 A435 10w yel & multi 35 15

Boy Scouts of Korea, 50th anniversary.

Children and Ox A436

Children in Balloon A437

1972, Dec. 1 Photo. ***Perf. 13x13½***
840 A436 10w grn & multi 30 15
a. Souvenir sheet of 2 1.25
841 A437 10w bl & multi 30 15
a. Souvenir sheet of 2 1.25
Set value 24

New Year 1973.

Mt. Naejang Park and Temple — A438

Mt. Sorang and Madeungryong Pass — A439

Perf. 13x13½, 13½x13
1972, Dec. 10
842 A438 10w multi 25 20
843 A439 10w multi 25 20

National parks.

Pres. Park, Korean Flag and Modern Landscape — A440

1972, Dec. 27 ***Perf. 13x13½***
844 A440 10w multi 90 20
a. Souvenir sheet of 2 2.75

Inauguration of Park Chung Hee for a 4th term as president of Korea.

Tourism Issue

Kyongbok Palace (National Museum) A441

Mt. Sorak and Kejo-am Temple — A442

Palmi Island and Beach — A443

Sain-am Rock, Mt. Dokjol A444

Shrine for Adm. Li Sun-sin A445

Values quoted in this catalogue are for stamps graded at Fine-Very Fine and with no faults. An illustrated guide to grade is provided in introductory material, beginning on Page 1A.

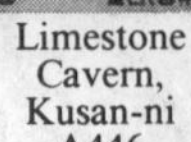

Limestone Cavern, Kusan-ni
A446

Namhae Bridge
A447

Hongdo Island — A448

Mt. Mai — A449

Tangerine Orchard, Cheju Island — A450

1973, Feb. 20 Photo. ***Perf. 13½x13***
845 A441 10w multi 25 15
846 A442 10w multi 25 15

1973, Apr. 20 ***Perf. 13x13½***
847 A443 10w multi 25 15
848 A444 10w multi 25 15

1970, June 20
849 A445 10w multi 25 15
850 A446 10w multi 25 15

1970, Aug. 20 ***Perf. 13½x13***
851 A447 10w multi 25 15
852 A448 10w multi 25 15

1973, Oct. 20
853 A449 10w multi 25 15
854 A450 10w multi 25 15
Nos. 845-854 (10) 2.50 1.50

Praying Family
A451

Flags of Korea and South Viet Nam, Victory Sign
A452

1973, Mar. 1 ***Perf. 13x13½***
855 A451 10w yel & multi 25 15

Prayer for national unification.

1973, Mar. 1
856 A452 10w vio & multi 25 15

Return of Korean Expeditionary Force from South Viet Nam.

A little time given to the study of the arrangement of the Scott Catalogue can make it easier to use effectively.

Workers, Factory, Cogwheel
A453

Satellite, WMO Emblem
A454

1973, Mar. 10 **Unwmk.**
857 A453 10w bl & multi 25 15

10th Labor Day.

1973, Mar. 23
858 A454 10w bl & multi 25 15
a. Souvenir sheet of 2 1.50

Cent. of Intl. Meteorological Cooperation.

King's Ceremonial Robe — A455

Traditional Korean Costumes (Yi dynasty): No. 860, Queen's ceremonial dress. No. 861, King's robe. No. 862, Queen's robe. No. 863, Crown Prince. No. 864, Princess. No. 865, Courtier. No. 866, Royal bridal gown. No. 867, Official's wife. No. 868, Military official.

1973 Photo. ***Perf. 13½x13***

859	A455	10w ocher & multi	35	15
860	A455	10w sal & multi	35	15
861	A455	10w rose lil & multi	35	15
862	A455	10w ap grn & multi	35	15
863	A455	10w lt bl & multi	35	15
864	A455	10w lil rose & multi	35	15
865	A455	10w yel & multi	35	15
866	A455	10w lt bl & multi	35	15
867	A455	10w ocher & multi	35	15
868	A455	10w lil rose & multi	35	15
		Nos. 859-868 (10)	3.50	
		Set value		1.20

Issue dates: #859-860, Mar. 30. #861-862, May 30. #863-864, July 30. #865-866, Sept. 30. #867-868, Nov. 30.

Souvenir Sheets of 2

859a	A455	10w (#1)	75
860a	A455	10w (#2)	75
861a	A455	10w (#3)	75
862a	A455	10w (#4)	75
863a	A455	10w (#5)	75
864a	A455	10w (#6)	75
865a	A455	10w (#7)	75
866a	A455	10w (#8)	75
867a	A455	10w (#9)	75
868a	A455	10w (#10)	75
		Nos. 859a-868a (10)	7.50

Parenthetical numbers after souvenir sheet listings appear in top marginal inscriptions.

Nurse Holding Lamp — A456

Homeland Reservists and Flag — A457

1973, Apr. 1 ***Perf. 13½x13***
869 A456 10w rose & multi 25 15

50th anniv. of Korean Nurses Association.

1973, Apr. 7 ***Perf. 13x13½***
870 A457 10w yel & multi 35 15

Homeland Reserve Forces Day on 5th anniversary of their establishment.

Table Tennis Player, and Globe — A458

1973, May 23 ***Perf. 13x13½***
871 A458 10w pink & multi 42 15

Victory of Korean women's table tennis team, 32nd Intl. Table Tennis Championships, Sarajevo, Yugoslavia, Apr. 5-15.

World Vision Children's Choir — A459

1973, June 25 ***Perf. 13x13½***
872 A459 10w multi 38 15

20th anniversary of World Vision International, a Christian service organization.

Converter, Pohang Steel Works — A460

1973, July 3 ***Perf. 13x13½***
873 A460 10w bl & multi 25 15

Inauguration of Pohang iron and steel plant.

INTERPOL Emblem
A461

1973, Sept. 3 ***Perf. 13½x13***
874 A461 10w lt vio & multi 25 15

50th anniversary of the International Criminal Police Organization (INTERPOL).

Children with Stamp Albums
A462

1973, Oct. 12 ***Perf. 13½x13***
875 A462 10w dp grn & multi 25 15
a. Souvenir sheet of 2 1.50

Philatelic Week, Oct. 12-18.

Woman Hurdler — A463

1973, Oct. 12 ***Perf. 12½x13½***
876 A463 10w shown 25 15
877 A463 10w Tennis player 25 15
Set value 24

54th Natl. Athletic Meet, Pusan, Oct. 12-17.

Soyang River Dam, Map Showing Location
A464

1973, Oct. 15 ***Perf. 13½x13***
878 A464 10w bl & multi 30 15

Inauguration of Soyang River Dam and hydroelectric plant.

Fire from Match and Cigarette — A465

1973, Nov. 1 ***Perf. 13x13½***
879 A465 10w multi 30 15

10th Fire Prevention Day.

Tiger and Candles
A466

Toys
A467

1973, Dec. 1 Photo. ***Perf. 13x13½***
880 A466 10w emer & multi 25 15
a. Souvenir sheet of 2 60

881 A467 10w bl & multi 25 15
a. Souvenir sheet of 2 60
Set value 24

New Year 1974.

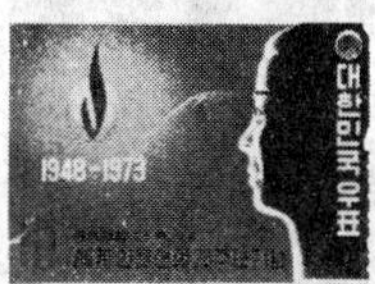

Human Rights Flame, and Head — A468

1973, Dec. 10 ***Perf. 13½x13***
882 A468 10w org & multi 25 15

25th anniversary of Universal Declaration of Human Rights.

Musical Instruments Issue

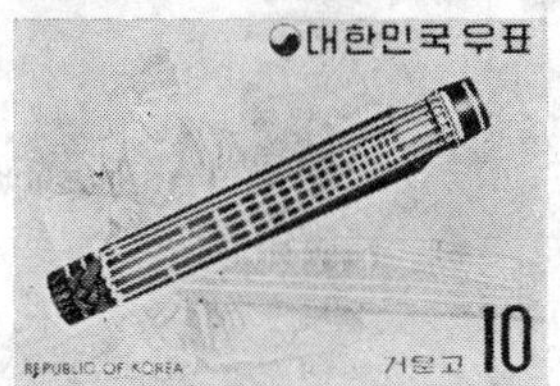

Komunko, Six-stringed Zither — A469

Design: 30w, Nagak, shell trumpet.

1974, Feb. 20 Photo. ***Perf. 13x13½***
883 A469 10w lt bl, blk & brn 20 15
884 A469 30w org & multi 30 20

1974, Apr. 20

Designs: 10w, Tchouk; wooden hammer in slanted box, used to start orchestra. 30w, Eu; crouching tiger, used to stop orchestra.

885 A469 10w brt bl & multi 15 15
886 A469 30w lt grn & multi 30 20

1974, June 20

Designs: 10w, A-chaing, 7-stringed instrument. 30w, Kyobang-ko, drum.

887 A469 10w dl yel & multi 15 15
888 A469 30w sal pink & multi 30 20

1974, Aug. 20

Designs: 10w, So, 16-pipe ritual instrument. 30w, Kaikeum, 2-stringed fiddle.

889 A469 10w lt bl & multi 15 15
890 A469 30w brt pink & multi 30 20

1974, Oct. 20

Designs: 10w, Pak (clappers). 30w, Pyenchong (bell chimes).

891 A469 10w lt lil & multi 15 15
892 A469 30w lem & multi 30 20
Nos. 883-892 (10) 2.30 1.75

Souvenir Sheets of 2

883a A469 10w (#1) 50
884a A469 30w (#2) 75
885a A469 10w (#3) 35
886a A469 30w (#4) 70
887a A469 10w (#5) 35
888a A469 30w (#6) 70
889a A469 10w (#7) 35
890a A469 30w (#8) 70
891a A469 10w (#9) 35
892a A469 30w (#10) 70
Nos. 883a-892a (10) 5.45

Fruit Issue

Apricots — A470

1974, Mar. 30 Photo. ***Perf. 13x13½***
893 A470 10w shown 15 15
894 A470 30w Strawberries 30 20

1974, May 30
895 A470 10w Peaches 15 15
896 A470 30w Grapes 30 20

1974, July 30
897 A470 10w Pears 15 15
898 A470 30w Apples 30 20

1974, Sept. 30
899 A470 10w Cherries 15 15
900 A470 30w Persimmons 30 20

1974, Nov. 30
901 A470 10w Tangerines 15 15
902 A470 30w Chestnuts 30 20
Nos. 893-902 (10) 2.25 1.75

Souvenir Sheets of 2

893a A470 10w (#1) 35
894a A470 30w (#2) 70
895a A470 10w (#3) 30
896a A470 30w (#4) 60
897a A470 10w (#5) 30
898a A470 30w (#6) 60
899a A470 10w (#7) 30
900a A470 30w (#8) 60
901a A470 10w (#9) 30
902a A470 30w (#10) 60
Nos. 893a-902a (10) 4.65

Reservist and Factory A471

1974, Apr. 6 Photo. ***Perf. 13½x13***
903 A471 10w yel & multi 25 15

Homeland Reserve Forces Day.

WPY Emblem and Scales — A472

1974, Apr. 10 ***Perf. 13x13½***
904 A472 10w sal & multi 20 15
a. Souvenir sheet of 2 75

World Population Year 1974.

Train and Communications Emblem — A473

1974, Apr. 22 ***Perf. 13½x13***
905 A473 10w multi 20 15

19th Communications Day.

Emblem and Stylized Globe — A474

1974, May 6 Photo. ***Perf. 13***
906 A474 10w red lil & multi 20 15

22nd Session of Intl. Chamber of Commerce (Eastern Division), Seoul, May 6-8.

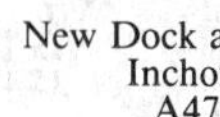

New Dock at Inchon A475

1974, May 10
907 A475 10w yel & multi 20 15

Dedication of dock, Inchon.

UNESCO Emblem, "20" and Yin Yang — A476

1974, June 14 Photo. ***Perf. 13***
908 A476 10w org yel & multi 20 15

20th anniversary of the Korean National Commission for UNESCO.

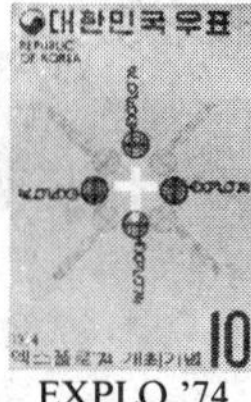

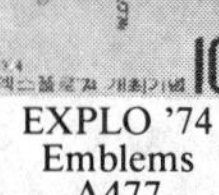

EXPLO '74 Emblems A477

Subway, Bus and Plane A478

Design: No. 910, EXPLO emblem rising from map of Korea.

1974, Aug. 13 Photo. ***Perf. 13***
909 A477 10w org & multi 25 15
910 A477 10w bl & multi 25 15
Set value 20

EXPLO '74, International Christian Congress, Yoido Islet, Seoul, Aug. 13-18.

1974, Aug. 15
911 A478 10w grn & multi 25 15

Inauguration of Seoul subway (first in Korea), Aug. 15, 1974.

Target Shooting — A479

1974, Oct. 8 Photo. ***Perf. 13x13½***
912 A479 10w shown 25 15
913 A479 30w Rowing 30 15

55th National Athletic Meet.

UPU Emblem A480

1974, Oct. 9 ***Perf. 13***
914 A480 10w yel & multi 25 15
a. Souvenir sheet of 2 75

Cent. of UPU. See No. C43.

International Landmarks — A481

1974, Oct. 11
915 A481 10w multi 25 15

International People to People Conference, Seoul, Oct. 11-14.

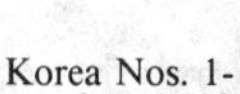

Korea Nos. 1-2 — A482

1974, Oct. 17
916 A482 10w lil & multi 25 15
a. Souvenir sheet of 2 1.00

Philatelic Week, Oct. 17-23 and 90th anniversary of first Korean postage stamps.

Taekwondo and Kukkiwon Center — A483

1974, Oct. 18
917 A483 10w yel grn & multi 25 15

First Asian Taekwondo (self-defense) Games, Seoul, Oct. 18-20.

Presidents Park and Ford, Flags and Globe — A484

1974, Nov. 22 Photo. ***Perf. 13***
918 A484 10y multi 60 20
a. Souvenir sheet of 2 2.75

Visit of Pres. Gerald R. Ford to South Korea.

Yook Young Soo — A485

1974, Nov. 29
919 A485 10w green 45 20
920 A485 10w orange 45 20
921 A485 10w lilac 45 20
922 A485 10w blue 45 20
a. Souv. sheet of 4, #919-922 4.50
b. Block of 4, #919-922 1.80 1.00

Yook Young Soo (1925-1974), wife of Pres. Park.

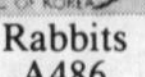

Rabbits
A486

Good-luck
Purse
A487

1974, Dec. 1 Litho. *Perf. 12½x13*

923 A486 10w multi 22 15
a. Souvenir sheet of 2 65
924 A487 10w multi 22 15
a. Souvenir sheet of 2 65
Set value 24

New Year 1975.

Good-luck Key and Pigeon — A488

1975, Jan. 1 Photo. *Perf. 13*

925 A488 10w lt bl & multi 22 15

Introduction of National Welfare Insurance System.

UPU Emblem and "75" — A489

UPU Emblem and Paper Plane — A490

1975, Jan. 1

926 A489 10w yel & multi 15 15
927 A490 10w lt bl & multi 15 15
Set value 20

75th anniv. of Korea's membership in UPU.

Dr. Schweitzer, Map of Africa, Hypodermic Needle
A491

1975, Jan. 14

928 A491 10w olive 15 15
929 A491 10w brt rose 15 15
930 A491 10w orange 15 15
931 A491 10w brt grn 15 15
a. Block of 4, #928-931 50 40
Set value 40 32

Dr. Albert Schweitzer (1875-1965), medical missionary, birth centenary.

Folk Dance Issue

Dancer — A492

Bupo
Nori — A492a

Designs: No. 933, Dancer with fan. No. 934, Woman with butterfly sleeves. No. 935, Group of Women. No. 936, Pongsan mask dance. No. 937, Pusan mask dance. No. 938, Buddhist drum dance. No. 939, Bara (cymbals) dance. No. 940, Sogo dance.

1975, Feb. 20 Photo. *Perf. 13*

932 A492 10w emer & multi 15 15
933 A492 10w brt bl & multi 15 15

1975, Apr. 20

934 A492 10w yel grn & multi 15 15
935 A492 10w yel & multi 15 15

1975, June 20

936 A492 10w pink & multi 15 15
937 A492 10w bl & multi 15 15

1975, Aug. 20

938 A492 20w yel & multi 20 15
939 A492 20w sal & multi 20 15

1975, Oct. 20

940 A492 20w bl & multi 20 15
941 A492a 20w yel & multi 20 15
Nos. 932-941 (10) 1.70
Set value 1.00

Souvenir Sheets of 2

932a A492 10w (#1) 30
933a A492 10w (#2) 30
934a A492 10w (#3) 30
935a A492 10w (#4) 30
936a A492 10w (#5) 30
937a A492 10w (#6) 30
938a A492 20w (#7) 40
939a A492 20w (#8) 40
940a A492 20w (#9) 40
941a A492 20w (#10) 40
Nos. 932a-941a (10) 3.40

Globe and Rotary Emblem
A493

1975, Feb. 23

942 A493 10w multi 15 15

Rotary International, 70th anniversary.

Women and IWY Emblem
A494

1975, Mar. 8

943 A494 10w multi 15 15

International Women's Year 1975.

Flower Issue

Violets
A495

Anemones
A496

Clematis
Patens — A496a

Broad-bell
Flowers — A496b

Designs: No. 946, Rhododendron. No. 948, Thistle. No. 949, Iris. No. 951, Bush clover. No. 952, Camellia. No. 953, Gentian.

1975, Mar. 15

944 A495 10w org & multi 15 15
945 A496 10w yel & multi 15 15

1975, May 15

946 A495 10w dk grn & multi 15 15
947 A496a 10w yel grn & multi 15 15

1975, July 15

948 A495 10w emer & multi 15 15
949 A495 10w bl & multi 15 15

1975, Sept. 15

950 A496b 20w yel & multi 15 15
951 A495 20w bl grn & multi 15 15

1975, Nov. 15

952 A495 20w yel & multi 15 15
953 A496 20w sal & multi 15 15
Nos. 944-953 (10) 1.50
Set value 1.00

Forest and Water Resources — A497

Reduced illustration.

1975, Mar. 20

954 A497 Strip of 4 40 30
a. 10w Saemaeul forest 15 15
b. 10w Dam and reservoir 15 15
c. 10w Green forest 15 15
d. 10w Timber industry 15 15

Natl. Tree Planting Month, Mar. 21-Apr. 20.

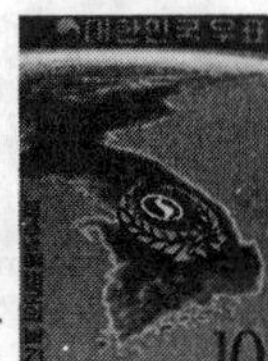

Map of Korea, HRF Emblem — A498

1975, Apr. 12 Photo. *Perf. 13*

955 A498 10w bl & multi 40 20

Homeland Reserve Forces Day.

Lily — A499

Ceramic
Jar — A500

Ceramic Vase
A501

Adm. Li
Sun-sin
A502

1975, Oct. 10 Photo. *Perf. 13½x13*

957 A499 6w grn & bl grn 20 15
964 A500 50w gray grn & brn 45 30
965 A501 60w brn & yel 54 52
969 A502 100w carmine 60 40

Metric System Symbols
A507

1975, May 20 *Perf. 13*

975 A507 10w sal & multi 15 15

Centenary of International Meter Convention, Paris, 1875.

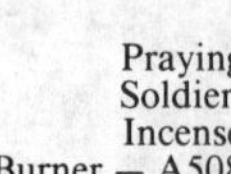

Praying Soldier, Incense Burner — A508

1975, June 6 Photo. *Perf. 13*

976 A508 10w multi 15 15

20th Memorial Day.

Flags of Korea, UN and US — A509

Designs (Flags of): No. 978, Ethiopia, France, Greece, Canada, South Africa. No. 979, Luxembourg, Australia, Great Britain, Colombia, Turkey. No. 980, Netherlands, Belgium, Philippines, New Zealand, Thailand.

1975, June 25 Photo. *Perf. 13*

977 A509 10w dk bl & multi 15 15
978 A509 10w dk bl & multi 15 15
979 A509 10w dk bl & multi 15 15
980 A509 10w dk bl & multi 15 15
a. Strip of 4, #977-980 45 40
Set value 40 24

25th anniv. of beginning of Korean War.

Presidents Park and Bongo, Flags of Korea and Gabon — A510

1975, July 5

981 A510 10w bl & multi 15 15
a. Souvenir sheet of 2 75

Visit of Pres. Albert Bongo of Gabon, July 5-8.

Scout Emblem, Tents and Neckerchief — A511

1975, July 29 Photo. *Perf. 13*

982 A511 10w shown 15 15
983 A511 10w Pick and oath 15 15
984 A511 10w Tents 15 15
985 A511 10w Ax, rope and tree 15 15
986 A511 10w Campfire 15 15
a. Strip of 4, #982-986 65 45
Set value 60 30

Nordjamb 75, 14th Boy Scout Jamboree, Lillehammer, Norway, July 29-Aug. 7.

Flame and Broken Chain — A512

Balloons with Symbols of Development over Map — A513

1975, Aug. 15 ***Perf. 13½x13***

987 A512 20w gold & multi	15	15
988 A513 20w sil & multi	15	15
Set value		20

30th anniversary of liberation.

Taekwondo — A514

1975, Aug. 26 ***Perf. 13***

989 A514 20w multi 15 15

2nd World Taekwondo Championships, Seoul, Aug. 25-Sept. 1.

National Assembly and Emblem A515

1975, Sept. 1 Photo. ***Perf. 13½x13***

990 A515 20w multi 15 15

Completion of National Assembly Building.

Convention Emblem and Dump Truck — A516

1975, Sept. 7 Photo. ***Perf. 13½x13***

991 A516 20w ultra & multi 15 15

14th Convention of the Intl. Fed. of Asian and Western Pacific Contractors.

Cassegrainian Telescope and Morse Key — A517

1975, Sept. 28

992 A517 20w red lil, org & blk 15 15

90th anniversary of Korean telecommunications system.

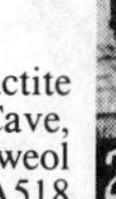

Stalactite Cave, Yeongweol A518

View of Mt. Sorak — A519

1975, Sept. 28

993 A518 20w multi	15	15
994 A519 20w multi	15	15
Set value		20

International Tourism Day.

Armed Forces Flag and Missiles — A519a

1975, Oct. 1 Photo. ***Perf. 13***

994A A519a 20w multi 15 15

Armed Forces Day.

Gymnastics A520

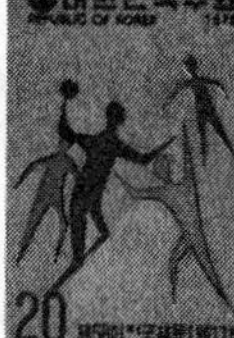

Handball A521

1975, Oct. 7 Photo. ***Perf. 13***

995 A520 20w yel & multi	15	15
996 A521 20w multi	15	15
Set value		20

56th Natl. Athletic Meet, Taegu, Oct. 7-12.

An enhanced introduction to the Scott Catalogue begins on Page 1A. A thorough understanding of the material presented there will greatly aid your use of the catalogue itself.

Stamp Collecting Kangaroo A522

Hands and UN Emblem A523

1975, Oct. 8

997 A522 20w multi 15 15

Philatelic Week, Oct. 8-14.

1975, Oct. 24

998 A523 20w multi 15 15

United Nations, 30th anniversary.

Red Cross and Activities A524

Emblem and Dove A525

1975, Oct. 30

999 A524 20w org, red & brn 15 15

Korean Red Cross, 70th anniversary.

1975, Nov. 30 Photo. ***Perf. 13***

1000 A525 20w multi 15 15

Asian Parliamentary Union, 10th anniv.

Children Playing A526

Dragon A527

1975, Dec. 1

1001 A526 20w multi	15	15
a. Souvenir sheet of 2	30	
1002 A527 20w multi	15	15
a. Souvenir sheet of 2	30	
Set value		20

New Year 1976.

Inchong-Bukpyong Railroad — A528

1975, Dec. 5 Photo. ***Perf. 13***

1003 A528 20w multi 15 15

Opening of electric cross-country railroad.

Butterfly Issue

Dilipa Fenestra A529

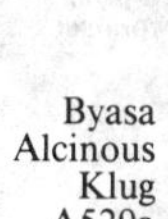

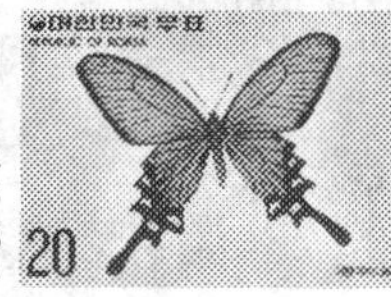

Byasa Alcinous Klug A529a

Graphium Sarpedon A529b

Fabriciana Nerippe A529c

Nymphalis Xanthomelas A529d

Butterflies: No. 1005, Luehdorfia puziloi. No. 1006, Papilio xuthus linne. No. 1007, Parnassius bremeri. No. 1008, Colias erate esper. No. 1010, Hestina assimilis.

1976, Jan. 20 Photo. ***Perf. 13***

1004 A529 20w dp rose & multi	15	15
1005 A529 20w dp bl & multi	15	15

1976, Mar. 20

1006 A529 20w yel & multi	15	15
1007 A529 20w yel grn & multi	15	15

1976, June 20

1008 A529 20w lt vio & multi	15	15
1009 A529a 20w cit & multi	15	15

1976, Aug. 20

1010 A529 20w tan & multi	15	15
1011 A529b 20w lt gray & multi	15	15

1976, Oct. 20

1012 A529c 20w lt grn & multi	15	15
1013 A529d 20w lil & multi	15	15
Nos. 1004-1013 (10)	1.50	
Set value		1.00

Emblems of Science, Industry and KIST — A530

1976, Feb. 10 Photo. ***Perf. 13***

1014 A530 20w multi 15 15

Korean Institute of Science and Technology (KIST), 10th anniversary.

Siberian Bustard — A531

White-naped Crane — A532

1976, Feb. 20 Photo. ***Perf. 13x13½***

1015 A531 20w shown	15	15
1016 A532 20w shown	15	15

1976, May 20
1017 A531 20w Blue-winged pitta 15 15
1018 A532 20w Tristam's woodpecker 15 15

1976, July 20
1019 A531 20w Wood pigeon 15 15
1020 A532 20w Oyster catcher 15 15

1976, Sept. 20
1021 A531 20w Black-faced spoonbill 15 15
1022 A532 20w Black stork 15 15

1976, Nov. 20
1023 A531 20w Whooper swan 15 15
1024 A532 20w Black vulture 15 15
Nos. 1015-1024 (10) 1.50
Set value 1.00

1876 and 1976 Telephones, Globe — A533

1976, Mar. 10
1025 A533 20w multi 15 15

Centenary of first telephone call by Alexander Graham Bell, Mar. 10, 1876.

Homeland Reserves A534

1976, Apr. 3 Photo. *Perf. 13½x13*
1026 A534 20w multi 15 15

8th Homeland Reserve Forces Day.

"People and Eye" — A535

1976, Apr. 7 *Perf. 13x13½*
1027 A535 20w multi 15 15

World Health Day; "Foresight prevents blindness."

Pres. Park, Village Movement Flag A536

Intellectual Pursuits A537

1976, Apr. 22
1028 A536 20w shown 15 15
1029 A537 20w shown 15 15
1030 A537 20w Village improvement 15 15
1031 A537 20w Agriculture 15 15
1032 A537 20w Income from production 15 15
a. Strip of 5, #1028-1032 80
Set value 50

6th anniv. of Pres. Park's New Village Movement for National Prosperity.

Mohenjo-Daro A538

1976, May 1 *Perf. 13½x13*
1033 A538 20w multi 15 15

UNESCO campaign to save the Mohenjo-Daro excavations in Pakistan.

13-Star and 50-Star Flags A539

Girl Scouts, Campfire and Emblem A540

Designs (Bicentennial Emblem and): No. 1035, Statue of Liberty. No. 1036, Map of U.S. and Mt. Rushmore monument. No. 1037, Liberty Bell. No. 1038, First astronaut on moon.

1976, May 8 *Perf. 13x13½*
1034 A539 100w blk, dp bl & red 50 30
a. Souvenir sheet of 1 1.50
1035 A539 100w blk, dp bl & red 50 30
1036 A539 100w blk, dp bl & red 50 30
1037 A539 100w blk, dp bl & red 50 30
1038 A539 100w blk, dp bl & red 50 30
Nos. 1034-1038 (5) 2.50 1.50

American Bicentennial.

1976, May 10
1039 A540 20w org & multi 15 15

Korean Federation of Girl Scouts, 30th anniversary.

Stupas, Buddha of Borobudur A541

"Life Insurance" A542

1976, June 10
1040 A541 20w multi 15 15

UNESCO campaign to save the Borobudur Temple, Java.

1976, July 1 Photo. *Perf. 13x13½*
1041 A542 20w multi 15 15

National Life Insurance policies: "Over 100 billion-won," Apr. 30, 1976.

Volleyball — A543

1976, July 17
1042 A543 20w shown 15 15
1043 A543 20w Boxing 15 15
Set value 20

21st Olympic Games, Montreal, Canada, July 17-Aug. 1.

Children and Books — A544

1976, Aug. 10 *Perf. 13½x13*
1044 A544 20w brn & multi 15 15

Books for children.

Civil Defense Corps, Flag and Members — A545

1976, Sept. 15 *Perf. 13x13½*
1045 A545 20w multi 15 15

Civil Defense Corps, first anniversary.

Chamsungdan, Mani Mountain A546

Front Gate, Tongdosa Temple A547

1976, Sept. 28 *Perf. 13½x13*
1046 A546 20w multi 15 15
1047 A547 20w multi 15 15
Set value 20

International Tourism Day.

Cadets and Academy A548

1976, Oct. 1
1048 A548 20w multi 15 15

Korean Military Academy, 30th anniversary.

Leaves and Stones, by Cheong Ju — A549

1976, Oct. 5 *Perf. 13x13½*
1049 A549 20w blk, gray & red 15 15
a. Souvenir sheet of 2 60

Philatelic Week, Oct. 5-11.

Snake-headed Figure, Bas-relief A550

Door-pull and Cranes A551

1976, Dec. 1 Photo. *Perf. 13x13½*
1050 A550 20w multi 20 15
a. Souvenir sheet of 2 50
1051 A551 20w multi 20 15
a. Souvenir sheet of 2 50
Set value 20

New Year 1977.

Arrows, Cogwheels, Worker at Lathe — A552

Design: No. 1053, Arrows, Cogwheels, ship in dock.

1977, Jan. 20 Photo. *Perf. 13½x13*
1052 A552 20w multi 15 15
1053 A552 20w multi 15 15
Set value 20

4th Economic Development Five-Year Plan.

Satellite Antenna and Microwaves — A553

1977, Jan. 31 *Perf. 13x13½*
1054 A553 20w multi 15 15

Membership in ITU, 25th anniv.

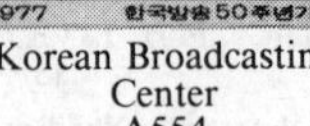
Korean Broadcasting Center A554

Parents and Two Children A555

1977, Feb. 16 *Perf. 13½x13*
1055 A554 20w multi 15 15

50th anniversary of broadcasting in Korea.

1977, Apr. 1 Photo. *Perf. 13½x13*
1056 A555 20w brt grn & org 15 15

Family planning.

Reservist on Duty A556 — Head with Symbols A557

1977, Apr. 2 *Perf. 13x13½*
1057 A556 20w multi 15 15

9th Homeland Reserve Forces Day.

1977, Apr. 21 Photo. *Perf. 13x13½*
1058 A557 20w dp lil & multi 15 15

10th anniversary of Science Day.

Book, Map, Syringe A558

1977, Apr. 25
1059 A558 20w bl & multi 15 15

35th International Meeting on Military Medicine.

Boy with Flowers and Dog — A559 — Veteran's Emblem and Flag — A560

1977, May 5
1060 A559 20w multi 15 15

Proclamation of Children's Charter, 20th anniversary.

1977, May 8
1061 A560 20w multi 15 15

25th anniversary of Korean Veterans' Day.

Buddha, 8th Century, Sokkulam Grotto — A561

1977, May 25 Photo. *Perf. 13x13½*
1062 A561 20w sep & ol 15 15
a. Souvenir sheet of 2 45

"2600th" anniversary of birth of Buddha.

Ceramic Issues

Jar with Grape Design, 17th Century A562 — Celadon Vase, Bamboo Design, 12th Century A563

1977, Mar. 15 Photo. *Perf. 13x13½*
1063 A562 20w vio brn & multi 15 15
1064 A563 20w gray, grn & bis 15 15
Set value 20

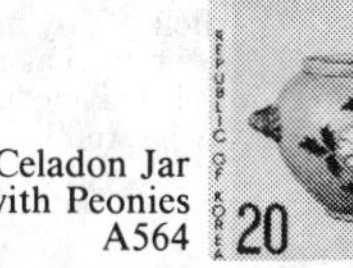

Celadon Jar with Peonies A564

Vase with Willow Reed Peony Pattern — A565

Perf. 13x13½, 13½x13

1977, June 15 **Photo.**
1065 A564 20w multi 15 15
1066 A565 20w multi 15 15
Set value 20

Celadon Manshaped Wine Jug — A566 — Celadon Melon-shaped Vase — A567

1977, July 15
1067 A566 20w multi 15 15
1068 A567 20w multi 15 15
Set value 20

1977, Aug. 15

Designs: No. 1069, White porcelain bowl with inlaid lotus vine design. No. 1070, Black Koryo ware vase with plum blossom vine.

1069 A564 20w multi 15 15
1070 A565 20w multi 15 15
Set value 20

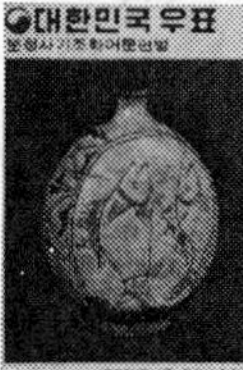

Punch'ong Jar — A568 — Celadon Cylindrical Vase — A569

1977, Nov. 15
1071 A568 20w multi 15 15
1072 A569 20w multi 15 15
Set value 20

Ceramic, national treasures.

Types of 1962-66
Designs as Before

1976-77 Litho. *Perf. 12½*
Granite Paper
1076 A187 200w brn & lt grn
1077 A187a 300w sl grn & sal ('76)
1078 A187a 300w brn & sal
1079 A187a 500w pur & lt grn

Magpie A570 — Nature Protection A571

"Family Planning" A572 — Children on Swing A573

Ceramic Horseman A574 — Muryangsu Hall, Busok Temple A575

Pagoda, Pobjusa Temple A576 — Gold Crown, from Chonmachong Mound A577

Monster Mask Tile, 6th or 7th Century A578 — Flying Angels from Bronze Bell from Sangwon-sa, 725 A.D. A579

Perf. 12½x13½, 13½x12½

1977-79 **Photo.**
1088 A570 3w lt bl & blk 15 15
1090 A326 10w emer & blk 15 15
1091 A571 20w multi 15 15
1092 A572 20w emer & blk ('78) 15 15
1093 A573 20w grn & org ('79) 15 15
1097 A574 80w lt brn & sep 48 40
1099 A575 200w sal & brn 1.00 50
1100 A576 300w brn pur 1.50 60
1101 A577 500w multi 2.75 1.00

Perf. 13½x13
1102 A578 500w brn & pur 2.50 1.00

Perf. 13
1103 A579 1000w sl grn ('78) 5.00 2.00
Nos. 1088-1103 (11) 13.98 6.25

Ulleung Island — A580 — Armed Forces — A581

Design: No. 1105, Haeundae Beach.

1977, Sept. 28 Photo. *Perf. 13*
1104 A580 20w multi 15 15
1105 A580 20w multi 15 15
Set value 20

World Tourism Day.

1977, Oct. 1 Photo. *Perf. 13*
1106 A581 20w grn & multi 15 15

Armed Forces Day.

Mt. Inwang after the Rain, by Chung Seon (1676-1759)
A582 A583

1977, Oct. 4
1107 A582 20w multi 15 15
1108 A583 20w multi 15 15
a. Souvenir sheet of 2 75
Set value 20

Philatelic Week, Oct. 4-10.

Rotary Emblem on Bronze Bell, Koryo Dynasty — A584

1977, Nov. 10 Photo. *Perf. 13*
1109 A584 20w multi 15 15

Korean Rotary Club, 50th anniversary.

Korean Flag on Mt. Everest A585

1977, Nov. 11
1110 A585 20w multi 15 15

Korean Mt. Everest Expedition, reached peak, Sept. 15, 1977.

Children and Kites A586 — Horse-headed Figure, Bas-relief A587

1977, Dec. 1 **Photo.** ***Perf. 13***
1111 A586 20w multi 22 15
a. Souvenir sheet of 2 42
1112 A587 20w multi 22 15
a. Souvenir sheet of 2 42
Set value 20

New Year 1978.

Clay Pigeon Shooting A588

Designs: No. 1114, Air pistol shooting. No. 1115, Air rifle shooting and target.

1977, Dec. 3
1113 A588 20w multi 15 15
a. Souvenir sheet of 2 ('78) 55
1114 A588 20w multi 15 15
a. Souvenir sheet of 2 ('78) 55
1115 A588 20w multi 15 15
a. Souvenir sheet of 2 ('78) 55
Set value 30

42nd World Shooting Championships, Seoul, 1978.

Boeing 727 over Globe, ICAO Emblem A589

1977, Dec. 11
1116 A589 20w multi 15 15

25th anniv. of Korea's membership in the ICAO.

Plane, Cargo, Freighter and Globe — A590

1977, Dec. 22 **Photo.** ***Perf. 13***
1117 A590 20w multi 15 15

Korean exports.

Ships and World Map — A591

1978, Mar. 13 **Photo.** ***Perf. 13***
1118 A591 20w multi 15 15

Maritime Day.

Stone Pagoda Issue

Four Lions Pagoda, Hwaom-sa — A592

Punhwang-sa Temple A593

Kyongch'on sa Temple A594

Design: No. 1120, Seven-storied pagoda, T'appyongri.

1978, Mar. 20 **Photo.** ***Perf. 13***
1119 A592 20w lt grn & multi 15 15
1120 A592 20w ocher & multi 15 15

1978, May 20

Design: No. 1122, Miruk-sa Temple.

1121 A593 20w lt grn & blk 15 15
1122 A593 20w grn, brn & yel 15 15

1978, June 20

Designs: #1123, Tabo Pagoda, Pulguk-sa. #1124, Three-storied pagoda, Pulguk-sa.

1123 A592 20w gray, lt grn & blk 15 15
1124 A592 20w lil & blk 15 15

1978, July 20 ***Perf. 13½x12½***

Design: No. 1126, Octagonal Pagoda, Wolchong-sa Temple.

1125 A594 20w gray & brn 15 15
1126 A594 20w lt grn & blk 15 15

1978, Nov. 20 ***Perf. 13x13½***

Designs: No. 1127, 13-storied pagoda, Jeonghye-sa. No. 1128, Three-storied pagoda, Jinjeon-sa.

1127 A592 20w pale grn & multi 15 15
1128 A592 20w lil & multi 15 15
Nos. 1119-1128 (10) 1.50
Set value 1.00

Ants and Coins — A595

Reservist with Flag — A596

1978, Apr. 1
1129 A595 20w multi 15 15

Importance of saving.

1978, Apr. 1
1130 A596 20w multi 15 15

10th Homeland Reserve Forces Day.

Seoul Cultural Center A597

1978, Apr. 1
1131 A597 20w multi 15 15

Opening of Seoul Cultural Center.

National Assembly in Plenary Session A598

1978, May 31
1132 A598 20w multi 15 15

30th anniversary of National Assembly.

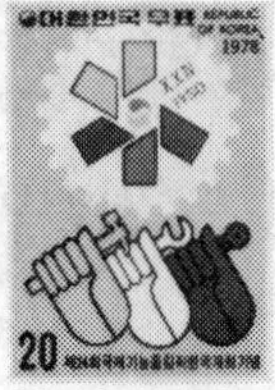

Hands Holding Tools, Competition Emblem A599

Bell of Joy and Crater Lake, Mt. Baegdu A600

1978, Aug. 5 **Photo.** ***Perf. 13***
1133 A599 20w multi 15 15
a. Souvenir sheet of 2 60

24th World Youth Skill Olympics, Busan, Aug. 30-Sept. 15.

1978, Aug. 15
1134 A600 20w multi 15 15

Founding of republic, 30th anniversary.

Nurse, Badge and Flowers A601

Sobaeksan Observatory A602

1978, Aug. 26
1135 A601 20w multi 15 15

Army Nurse Corps, 30th anniversary.

1978, Sept. 13 **Photo.** ***Perf. 13***
1136 A602 20w multi 15 15

Opening of Sobaeksan Natl. Observatory.

Kyunghoeru Pavilion, Kyongbok Palace, Seoul — A603

Design: No. 1138, Baeg Do (island).

1978, Sept. 28
1137 A603 20w multi 15 15
1138 A603 20w multi 15 15
Set value 20

Tourist publicity.

Customs Flag and Officers A604

1978, Sept. 28
1139 A604 20w multi 15 15

Cent. of 1st Korean Custom House, Busan.

Armed Forces A605

1978, Oct. 1 **Photo.** ***Perf. 13***
1140 A605 20w multi 15 15

Armed Forces, 30th anniversary.

Clay Figurines, Silla Dynasty A606

Portrait of a Lady, by Shin Yoon-bok A607

1978, Oct. 1
1141 A606 20w lt grn & blk 15 15

Culture Month, October 1978.

1978, Oct. 24
1142 A607 20w multi 15 15
a. Souvenir sheet of 2 40

Philatelic Week, Oct. 24-29.

Young Men, YMCA Emblem A608

1978, Oct. 28
1143 A608 20w multi 15 15

75th anniv. of founding of Korean YMCA.

Hand Protecting Against Fire — A609

1978, Nov. 1 **Photo.** ***Perf. 13***
1144 A609 20w multi 15 15

Fire Prevention Day, Nov. 1.

Winter Landscape A610

Ram-headed Figure, Bas-relief A611

1978, Dec. 1 Photo. ***Perf. 13x13½***
1145 A610 20w multi 15 15
a. Souvenir sheet of 2 30
1146 A611 20w multi 15 15
a. Souvenir sheet of 2 30
Set value 20

New Year 1979.

Hibiscus, Students, Globe — A612

President Park — A613

1978, Dec. 5
1147 A612 20w multi 15 15

Proclamation of National Education Charter, 10th anniversary.

1978, Dec. 27
1148 A613 20w multi 15 15
a. Souvenir sheet of 2 30

Inauguration of Park Chung Hee for fifth term as president.

Nature Conservation Issue

Golden Mandarinfish A614

Lace-bark Pines A615

Mandarin Ducks — A616

Neofinettia Orchid — A617

Goral — A618

Lilies of the Valley — A619

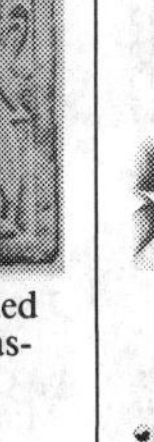
Rain Frog A620

Asian Polypody A621

Firefly — A622

Meesun Tree — A623

1979, Feb. 20 Photo. ***Perf. 13x13½***
1149 A614 20w multi 15 15
1150 A615 20w multi 15 15

1979, May 20
1151 A616 20w multi 15 15
1152 A617 20w multi 15 15

1979, June 20
1153 A618 20w multi 15 15
1154 A619 20w multi 15 15

1979, Nov. 25
1155 A620 20w multi 15 15
1156 A621 20w multi 15 15

1980, Jan. 20
1157 A622 30w multi 18 15
1158 A623 30w multi 18 15
Nos. 1149-1158 (10) 1.56
Set value 90

Samil Monument — A624

1979, Mar. 1 Photo. ***Perf. 13x13½***
1159 A624 20w multi 15 15

60th anniversary of Samil independence movement.

Worker and Bulldozer A625

1979, Mar. 10 ***Perf. 13½x13***
1160 A625 20w multi 15 15

Labor Day.

Hand Holding Tools, Gun and Grain A626

Tabo Pagoda, Pulguk-sa Temple A627

Women, Silk Screen — A628

1979, Apr. 1 ***Perf. 13x13½***
1161 A626 20w multi 15 15

Strengthening national security.

1979, Apr. 1

Art Treasures: No. 1163, Statue. No. 1164, Crown. No. 1165, Celadon Vase.

1162 A627 20w gray bl & multi 15 15
1163 A627 20w bis & multi 15 15
1164 A627 20w vio & multi 15 15
1165 A627 20w brt grn & multi 15 15
1166 A628 60w multi 35 30
a. Souvenir sheet of 2 1.00
Set value 82 70

5000 years of Korean art.
See Nos. 1175-1179, 1190.

Pulguk-sa Temple and PATA Emblem A629

1979, Apr. 16 ***Perf. 13½x13***
1167 A629 20w multi 15 15

28th Pacific Area Travel Association (PATA) Conference, Seoul, Apr. 16-18, and Gyeongju, Apr. 20-21.

Presidents Park and Senghor A630

1979, Apr. 22 ***Perf. 13½x13***
1168 A630 20w multi 15 15
a. Souvenir sheet of 2 42

Visit of Pres. Leopold Sedar Senghor of Senegal.

Basketball — A631

1979, Apr. 29 ***Perf. 13x13½***
1169 A631 20w multi 15 15

8th World Women's Basketball Championship, Seoul, Apr. 29-May 13.

Children and IYC Emblem A632

1979, May 5 Photo. ***Perf. 13½x13***
1170 A632 20w multi 15 15
a. Souvenir sheet of 2 60

International Year of the Child.

Traffic Pollution — A633

1979, June 5 Photo. ***Perf. 13x13½***
1171 A633 20w grn & dk brn 15 15

Pollution control.

Flags, Presidents Park and Carter A634

1979, June 29 ***Perf. 13½x13***
1172 A634 20w multi 15 15
a. Souvenir sheet of 2 60

Visit of Pres. Jimmy Carter.

Korean Exhibition Center — A635

1979, July 3
1173 A635 20w multi 15 15

Opening of Korean Exhibition Center.

Jet, Globe, Pagoda A636

1979, Aug. 1 Photo. ***Perf. 13½x13***
1174 A636 20w multi 15 15

10th anniversary of Korean airlines.

Art Treasure Types

Designs: No. 1175, Porcelain jar, 17th century. No. 1176, Man on horseback, ceremonial pitcher (horiz.). No. 1177, Sword Dance, by Shin Yuk-bok. No. 1178, Golden Amitabha with halo, 8th century. No. 1179, Hahoe ritual mask.

1979 Photo. ***Perf. 13x13½, 13½x13***
1175 A627 20w lil & multi 15 15
1176 A627 20w multi 15 15
1177 A628 60w multi 35 30
a. Souvenir sheet of 2 1.00
Set value 50

Issue dates: No. 1177, Sept. 1. Nos. 1175-1176, Oct. 15.

1979, Nov. 15
1178 A627 20w dp grn & multi 15 15
1179 A627 20w multi 15 15
Set value 24 20

Yongdu Rock — A637

1979, Sept. 28
1180 A637 20w shown 15 15
1181 A637 20w Mt. Mai, vert. 15 15
Set value 24 20

World Tourism Day.

People, Blood and Heart — A637a

1979, Oct. 1 *Perf. 13½x13*

1182 A637a 20w multi	15	15

Blood Banks, 4th anniversary.

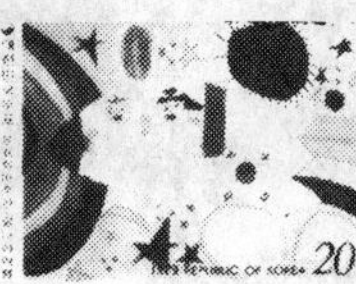

"My Life in the Year 2000" A638

1979, Oct. 30 *Perf. 13½x13*

1183 A638 20w multi	15	15
a. Souvenir sheet of 2	50	

Philatelic Week, Oct. 30-Nov. 4.

Monkey-headed Figure, Bas-relief A639

Children Playing Yut A640

1979, Dec. 1

1184 A639 20w multi	15	15
a. Souvenir sheet of 2	42	
1185 A640 20w multi	15	15
a. Souvenir sheet of 2	42	
Set value	24	20

New Year 1980.

Inauguration of Pres. Choi Kyu-hah A641

1979, Dec. 21

1186 A641 20w multi	15	15
a. Souvenir sheet of 2	60	

President Park — A642

1980, Feb. 2 Photo. *Perf. 13x13½*

1187 A642 30w org brn	18	15
1188 A642 30w dl pur	18	15
a. Souvenir sheet of 2	52	

President Park Chung Hee (1917-1979) memorial. Nos. 1187-1188 se-tenant.

The first price column gives the catalogue value of an unused stamp, the second that of a used stamp.

Art Treasure Type of 1979 and

Dragon-shaped Kettle — A643

Design: 60w, Landscape, by Kim Hong-do.

Perf. 13½x13, 13x13½

1980, Feb. 20 **Photo.**

1189 A643 30w multi	18	15
1190 A628 60w multi	35	30
a. Souvenir sheet of 2	90	

Art Treasure Issue

Heavenly Horse, Saddle A644

Dragon Head, Banner Staff — A645

Tiger, Granite Sculpture — A647

Mounted Nobleman Mural — A646

Human Face, Roof Tile — A648

Deva King Sculpture — A650

White Tiger Mural — A649

Earthenware Ducks A651 A652

Tiger, Folk Painting — A653

1980 Photo. *Perf. 13½x13, 13x13½*

1191 A644 30w multi	18	15
1192 A645 30w multi	18	15
1193 A646 30w multi	18	15
1194 A647 30w multi	18	15
1195 A648 30w multi	18	15
1196 A649 30w multi	18	15

Engr. *Perf. 12½x13*

1197 A650 30w black	18	15
1198 A650 30w red	18	15
Nos. 1191-1198 (8)	1.44	
Set value		40

Issue dates: Nos. 1191-1192, Apr. 20. Nos. 1193-1194, May 20; Nos. 1195-1196, Aug. 20; Nos. 1197-1198, Nov. 20.

1983 Litho. Engr. *Perf. 13*

1199 A651 1000w bis brn & red brn	3.75	75
1200 A652 1000w bis brn & red brn	3.75	75
1201 A653 5000w dp bis & multi	17.50	4.00
a. Souvenir sheet, perf. 13½x13, imperf.	20.00	

Issue dates: Nos. 1199-1200, Nov. 25. No. 1201, Dec. 1. Nos. 1199-1200 se-tenant. No. 1201a for PHILAKOREA '84.

Lotus Blossoms and Ducks — A656

Tiger and Magpie — A657

Perf. 13x13½, 13½x13

1980, Mar. 10

1203 A656 30w multi	18	15
1204 A657 60w multi	35	30

Red Phoenix (in Form of Rooster) — A658

Moon Over Mt. Konryun — A659

Design: No. 1207, Sun over Mt. Konryun. Nos. 1206-1207 se-tenant in continuous design.

1980, May 10 *Perf. 13x13½*

1205 A658 30w multi	18	15
1206 A659 60w multi	35	30
1207 A659 60w multi	35	30
a. Souvenir sheet of 2, #1206-1207	75	
Set value		65

Rabbits Pounding Grain in a Mortar — A660

Dragon in the Clouds — A661

1980, July 10 Photo. *Perf. 13x13½*

1208 A660 30w multi	18	15
1209 A661 30w multi	18	15
Set value		15

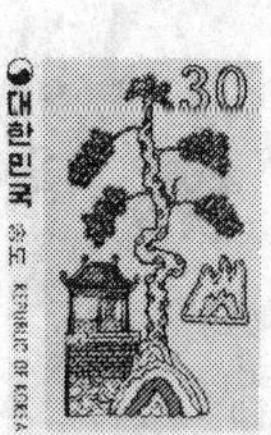

Pine Tree, Pavilion, Mountain A662

Flowers and Birds, Bridal Room Screen A663

1980, Aug. 9 Photo. *Perf. 13x13½*

1210 A662 30w multi	18	15
1211 A663 30w multi	18	15
Set value		15

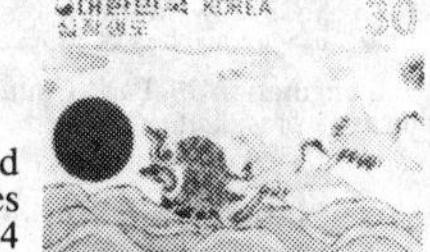

Tortoises and Cranes A664

Designs: Symbols of longevity.

1980, Nov. 10 Photo. *Perf. 13½x13*

1212 Strip of 4	75	20
a. A664 30w any single	18	15

New Community Movement, 10th Anniv. — A668

Freighters at Sea — A669

1980, Apr. 22 *Perf. 13x13½*

1216 A668 30w multi	18	15

1980, Mar. 13

1217 A669 30w multi	18	15

Increase of Korea's shipping tonnage to 5 million tons.

Soccer — A670

1980, Aug. 23 *Perf. 13x13½*
1218 A670 30w multi 18 15

10th President's Cup Soccer Tournament, Aug. 23-Sept. 5.

Mt. Sorak — A671

Paikryung Island — A672

Perf. 12½x13½
1980, Apr. 10 **Photo.**
1219 A671 15w multi 15 15
1220 A672 90w multi 60 15
Set value 16

Flag — A673

1980 *Perf. 13½x13*
1221 A673 30w multicolored 18 15

Coil Stamp
Perf. Vert.
1221A A673 30w multicolored 18 15

UN Intervention, 30th Anniv. — A674

Election of Miss World in Seoul — A675

1980, June 25 *Perf. 13x13½*
1222 A674 30w multi 18 15

1980, July 8
1223 A675 30w multi 18 15

Women's Army Corps, 30th Anniversary A676

1980, Sept. 6 *Perf. 13½x13*
1224 A676 30w multi 18 15

Baegma River — A677

Three Peaks of Dodam A678

1980, Sept. 28
1225 A677 30w multi 18 15
1226 A678 30w multi 18 15
Set value 15

Inauguration of Pres. Chun Doo-hwan A679

1980, Sept. 1
1227 A679 30w multi 18 15
a. Souvenir sheet of 2 75

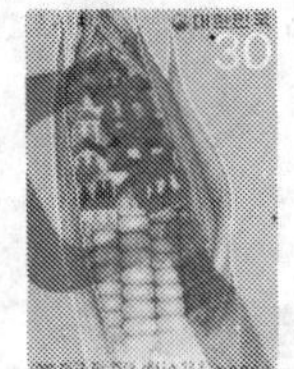
Ear of Corn — A680

Symbolic Tree — A681

1980, Oct. 20 *Perf. 13x13½*
1228 A680 30w multi 18 15

12th population and housing census.

1980, Oct. 27
1229 A681 30w multi 18 15

National Red Cross, 75th anniversary.

"Mail-Delivering Angels" — A682

1980, Nov. 6 *Perf. 13½x13*
1230 A682 30w multi 18 15
a. Souvenir sheet of 2 45

Philatelic Week, Nov. 6-11.

Korea-Japan Submarine Cable System Inauguration A683

1980, Nov. 28 *Perf. 13x13½*
1231 A683 30w multi 18 15

Rooster — A684

Cranes — A685

1980, Dec. 1
1232 A684 30w multi 22 15
a. Souvenir sheet of 2 45
1233 A685 30w multi 22 15
a. Souvenir sheet of 2 45
Set value 15

New Year 1981.

Second Inauguration of Pres. Chun Doo-hwan A686

1981, Mar. 3 **Photo.** *Perf. 13½x13*
1234 A686 30w multi 18 15
a. Souvenir sheet of 2 55

Ship Issue

Oil Tanker — A687

Cargo Ship — A688

Oil Tanker A689

Cargo Ship — A690

Tug Boat — A691

Stern Trawler A692

Log Carrier — A693

Auto Carrier A694

Chemical Carrier A695

Passenger Boat A696

Perf. 13½x13, 13x13½
1981, Mar. 13
1235 A687 30w multi 18 15
1236 A688 90w multi 55 15

5th Maritime Day.

1981, May 10 **Photo.** *Perf. 13½x13*
1237 A689 30w multi 18 15
1238 A690 90w multi 55 15

1981, July 10 *Perf. 13½x13*
1239 A691 40w multi 24 15
1240 A692 100w multi 60 18

1981, Aug. 10
1241 A693 40w multi 24 15
1242 A694 100w multi 60 18

1981, Nov. 10 **Engr.** *Perf. 13x12½*
1243 A695 40w black 24 15
1244 A696 100w dk bl 60 18
Nos. 1235-1244 (10) 3.98
Set value 1.05

11th Natl. Assembly Opening Session A697

1981, Apr. 17 **Photo.** *Perf. 13½x13*
1245 A697 30w gold & dk brn 18 15

Hand Reading Braille, Helping Hands — A698

1981, Apr. 30 **Photo.** *Perf. 13x13½*
1246 A698 30w shown 18 15
1247 A698 90w Man in wheelchair 55 15
Set value 20

International Year of the Disabled.

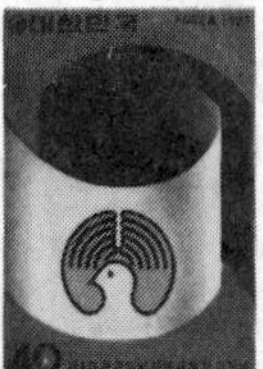
Ribbon and Council Emblem A699

Clena River and Mountains A700

1981, June 5 **Photo.** *Perf. 13x13½*
1248 A699 40w multi 24 15

Advisory Council on Peaceful Unification Policy (North and South Korea) anniv.

1981, June 5
1249 A700 30w shown 18 15
1250 A700 90w Seagulls 55 15
Set value 20

10th World Environment Day.

Pres. Chun and Pres. Suharto of Indonesia A701

Pres. Chun Visit to Asia: b, King of Malaysia. c, Korean, Singapore flags. d, King Bhumibol Adulyadej of Thailand. e, Pres. Marcos of Philippines.

1981, June 25 *Perf. 13½x13*

1251	Strip of 5	1.25	25
a.-e.	A701 40w any single	24	15
f.	Souvenir sheet of 5, imperf.	1.25	

Size: 49x33mm

Perf. 13x13½

1252	A701 40w multi	24	15
a.	Souvenir sheet of 2, imperf.	60	
	Set value		30

36th Anniv. of Liberation — A702

1981, Aug. 15 Photo. *Perf. 13x13½*

1253 A702 40w multi 24 15

Tolharubang, "Stone Grandfather" A704

Rose of Sharon A705

Porcelain Jar, 17th Cent. — A706

Chomsongdae Observatory, 7th Cent. — A707

Mounted Warrior, Earthenware Jug, 5th Cent. A708

Family Planning A709

Walking Stick — A710

Ryu Kwan-soon (1904-20), Martyr — A711

"Tasan" Chung Yak-yong, Lee Dynasty Scholar — A712

Ahn Joong-guen (1879-1910), Martyr — A713

Ahn Chang-ho (1878-1938), Independence Fighter — A714

Koryo Celadon Incense Burner — A715

Kim Ku (1876-1949), Statesman A716

Mountain Landscape Brick Bas-relief A717

Mandarin Duck, Celadon Incense Burner — A718

Perf. 13½x12½ (Nos. 1256, 1257, 1266), 13, 13½x13, 13x13½

1981-89 **Photo., Engr.**

1255	A704	20w	multi ('86)	15	15
1256	A705	40w	multi	24	15
1257	A706	60w	multi	36	15
1258	A707	70w	multi	42	15
1259	A708	80w	multi ('83)	48	15
1260	A709	80w	multi ('86)	25	15
1261	A710	80w	multi ('89)	24	15
1262	A711	100w	lilac	65	15
1263	A712	100w	gray blk ('86)	30	15
1264	A713	200w	lt ol grn & ol	1.25	25
1265	A714	300w	dl lil ('83)	1.10	22
1266	A715	400w	multi	2.75	50
1267	A715	400w	pale grn & multi ('83)	2.40	40
1268	A716	450w	dk vio brn ('86)	1.20	40
1269	A717	500w	multi	3.00	75
1270	A718	700w	multi ('83)	4.25	80
			Nos. 1255-1270 (16)	19.04	
			Set value		3.95

Inscription and denomination of No. 1267, colorless, No. 1267, dark brown.

See No. 1449.

Coil Stamp

Photo. *Perf. 13 Horiz.*

1271 A707 70w multi 18 15

Girl Flying Model Plane — A721

Air Force Chief of Staff Cup, 3rd Aeronautic Competition: Various model planes.

1981, Sept. 20 *Perf. 13½x13*

1272	Strip of 5	1.25	30
a.	A721 10w multi	15	15
b.	A721 20w multi	15	15
c.	A721 40w multi	24	15
d.	A721 50w multi	30	15
e.	A721 80w multi	50	15

WHO Emblem, Citizens A722

World Tourism Day A723

1981, Sept. 22 *Perf. 13x13½*

1273 A722 40w multi 24 15

WHO, 32nd Western Pacific Regional Committee Meeting, Seoul, Sept. 22-28.

1981, Sept. 28

1274	A723 40w Seoul Tower	24	15
1275	A723 40w Ulreung Isld.	24	15
	Set value		15

Bicycle Racing A724

1981, Oct. 10 *Perf. 13½x13*

1276	A724 40w shown	24	15
1277	A724 40w Swimming	24	15
	Set value		15

62nd Natl. Sports Festival, Seoul, Oct. 10-15.

Flags, Presidents Chun and Carazo A725

1981, Oct. 12 *Perf. 13½x13*

1278 A725 40w multi 24 15

Visit of Pres. Rodrigo Carazo Odio of Costa Rica, Oct. 12-14.

World Food Day — A726

First Natl. Aviation Day — A727

1981, Oct. 16 *Perf. 13x13½*

1279 A726 40w multi 24 15

1981, Oct. 30 *Perf. 13½x13*

1280 A727 40w multi 24 15

1988 Olympic Games, Seoul — A728

9th Philatelic Week, Nov. 18-24 — A729

1981, Oct. 30 *Perf. 13x13½*

1281 A728 40w multi 24 15

1981, Nov. 18 *Perf. 13½x13*

1282	A729 40w multi	24	15
a.	Souvenir sheet of 2	50	

Camellia and Dog — A730

Children Flying Kite — A731

1981, Dec. 1 *Perf. 13x13½*

1283	A730 40w multi	24	15
a.	Souvenir sheet of 2	50	
1284	A731 40w multi	24	15
a.	Souvenir sheet of 2	50	
	Set value		15

New Year 1982 (Year of the Dog).

Hangul Hakhoe Language Society, 60th Anniv. A732

1981, Dec. 3 *Perf. 13½x13*

1285 A732 40w multi 24 15

Telecommunications Authority Inauguration A733

Scouting Year A734

1982, Jan. 4 Photo. *Perf. 13x13½*

1286 A733 60w multi 36 15

1982, Feb. 22

1287 A734 60w multi 36 15

60th Anniv. of YWCA in Korea — A735

Intl. Polar Year Centenary — A736

1982, Apr. 20 Photo. *Perf. 13x13½*

1288 A735 60w multi 36 15

1982, Apr. 21 *Perf. 13½x13*

1289 A736 60w multi 36 15

60th Children's Day — A737

1982, May 5 *Perf. 13½x13*

1290 A737 60w multi 36 15

Visit of Liberian Pres. Samuel K. Doe, May 9-13 A738

1982, May 9 Litho. *Perf. 13x12½*

1291	A738 60w multi	36	15
a.	Souvenir sheet of 2, imperf.	75	

Centenary of US-Korea Treaty of Amity — A739

1982, May 18 Photo. *Perf. 13½x13*

1292	A739 60w Statue of Liberty, pagoda	36	15
1293	A739 60w Emblem	36	15
a.	Souvenir sheet of 2	75	
	Set value		15

Nos. 1292-1293 se-tenant.

Visit of Zaire Pres. Mobutu Sese Seko, June 7-10
A740

1982, June 7 Litho. *Perf. 13x12½*

1294 A740 60w multi	36	15
a. Souvenir sheet of 2, imperf.	75	

Historical Painting Issue

Gen. Kwon Yul's Victory at Haengju, by Oh Seung-woo — A747

Designs: No. 1295, Territorial Expansion by Kwanggaeto the Great, by Lee Chong-sang, 1975. No. 1296, Gen. Euljimunduck's Victory at Salsoo, by Park Kak-soon, 1975. No. 1297, Shilla's Repulse of Tang's Army, by Oh Seung-woo. No. 1298, Gen. Kang Kam-chan's Victory at Kyiju, by Lee Yong-hwan. No. 1299, Admiral Yi Sun-sin's Victory at Hansan, 1592, by Kim Hyung-ku. No. 1300, Gen. Kim Chwa-jin's Battle at Chungsanri, by Sohn Soo-kwang. No. 1302, Kim Chong-suh's Exploitation of Yukjin, 1434, by Kim Tae.

1982 Photo. *Perf. 13x13½*

1295 A747 60w multi	36	24
1296 A747 60w multi	36	24
1297 A747 60w multi	36	24
1298 A747 60w multi	36	24
1299 A747 60w multi	36	15
1300 A747 60w multi	36	15
1301 A747 60w multi	36	15
1302 A747 60w multi	36	15
Nos. 1295-1302 (8)	2.88	
Set value		1.20

Issue dates: Nos. 1295-1296, June 15; Nos. 1297-1298, July 15; Nos. 1299-1300, Oct. 15, Nos. 1301-1302, Dec. 15.

55th Intl. YMCA Convention, Seoul, July 20-23 — A749

Flags, Presidents Chun and Arap Moi — A750

1982, July 20

1303 A749 60w multi	36	24

1982, Aug. 17 *Perf. 13½x13*

Pres. Chun's Visit to Africa and Canada: No. 1304, Kenya (Pres. Daniel T. Arap Moi), Aug. 17-19. No. 1305, Nigeria (Pres. Alhaji Shehe Shagari), Aug. 19-22. No. 1306, Gabon (Pres. El Hadj Omar Bongo), Aug. 22-24. No. 1307, Senegal (Pres. Abdou Diouf), Aug. 24-26. No. 1308, Canada, Aug. 28-31.

1304 A750 60w multi	36	24
1305 A750 60w multi	36	24
1306 A750 60w multi	36	24
1307 A750 60w multi	36	24
1308 A750 60w multi	36	24
Nos. 1304-1308 (5)	1.80	1.20

Souvenir Sheets of 2

1304a A750 60w	75
1305a A750 60w	75
1306a A750 60w	75
1307a A750 60w	75
1308a A750 60w	75
Nos. 1304a-1308a (5)	3.75

Natl. Flag Centenary
A751

1982, Aug. 22

1309 A751 60w multi	36	24
a. Souvenir sheet of 2	75	

2nd Seoul Open Intl. Table Tennis Championship, Aug. 25-31 — A752

1982, Aug. 25

1310 A752 60w multi	36	24

27th World Amateur Baseball Championship Series, Seoul, Sept. 4-18 — A753

1982, Sept. 4 Engr. *Perf. 13*

1311 A753 60w red brn	36	15

Seoul Intl. Trade Fair (SITRA '82), Sept. 24-Oct. 18 — A754

1982, Sept. 17 Photo. *Perf. 13½x13*

1312 A754 60w multi	36	15

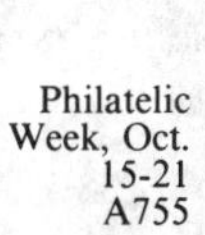

Philatelic Week, Oct. 15-21
A755

Design: Miners reading consolatory letters.

1982, Oct. 15

1313 A755 60w multi	36	15
a. Souvenir sheet of 2	75	

Visit of Indonesian Pres. Suharto, Oct. 16-19
A756

1982, Oct. 16 Litho. *Perf. 13x12½*

1314 A756 60w multi	36	15
a. Souvenir sheet of 2, imperf.	75	

37th Jaycee (Intl. Junior Chamber of Commerce) World Congress, Seoul, Nov. 3-18 — A757

1982, Nov. 3 *Perf. 13½x13*

1315 A757 60w multi	36	15

2nd UN Conference on Peaceful Uses of Outer Space, Vienna, Aug. 9-21 — A758

1982, Nov. 20 *Perf. 13x13½*

1316 A758 60w multi	36	15

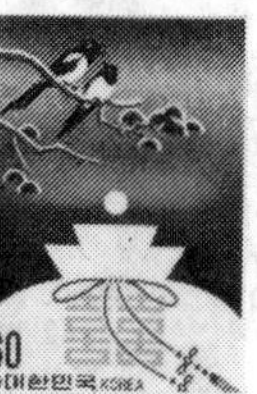

New Year 1983 (Year of the Boar) — A759

Flags of Korea and Turkey — A760

1982, Dec. 1

1317 A759 60w Magpies, money bag	36	15
a. Souvenir sheet of 2	75	
1318 A759 60w Boar, bas-relief	36	15
a. Souvenir sheet of 2	75	
Set value		15

1982, Dec. 20 *Perf. 13*

1319 A760 60w multi	36	15
a. Souvenir sheet of 2, imperf.	75	

Visit of Pres. Kenan Evren of Turkey, Dec. 20-23.

Letter Writing Campaign
A761

First Intl. Customs Day
A762

1982, Dec. 31 Photo. *Perf. 13x13½*

1320 A761 60w multi	36	15

1983, Jan. 26 *Perf. 13½x13*

1321 A762 60w multi	36	15

Korean-made Vehicle Issue

Hyundai Pony-2
A764

Daewoo Maepsy
A765

Super Titan Truck — A768

Flat-bed Truck — A770

1983 Photo. *Perf. 13½x13*

1322 A764 60w Keohwa Jeep	36	15
1323 A764 60w shown	36	15
a. Pair, #1322-1323	75	30
1324 A765 60w shown	36	15
1325 A764 60w Kia minibus	36	15
a. Pair, #1324-1325	75	30
1326 A764 60w Highway bus	36	15
1327 A768 60w shown	36	15
1328 A764 70w Dump truck	42	15
1329 A770 70w shown	42	15
1330 A764 70w Cement mixer	42	15
1331 A764 70w Oil truck	42	15
Nos. 1322-1331 (10)	3.84	
Set value		68

Issue dates: Nos. 1322-1323, Feb. 25; Nos. 1324-1325, Mar. 25; Nos. 1326-1327, May 25; Nos. 1328-1329, July 25; Nos. 1330-1331, Aug. 25.

Visit of Malaysian Seri Paduka Baginda, Mar. 22-26 — A773

1983, Mar. 22

1332 A773 60w multi	36	15
a. Souvenir sheet of 2	75	

Postal Service Issue

General Bureau of Postal Administration Building
A774

Mailman, 1884 — A776

Ancient Mail Carrier
A778

Nos. 1-2 — A780

Pre-modern Period Postal Symbol, Mailbox
A782

Designs: #1334, Seoul Central PO. #1336, Mailman on motorcycle, 1983. #1338, Modern mail transport. #1340, No. 1201. #1342, Current postal symbol, mailbox.

1983, Apr. 22 Photo. *Perf. 13½x13*

1333 A774 60w multi	36	15
1334 A774 60w multi	36	15
1335 A776 70w multi	42	15
1336 A776 70w multi	42	15
1337 A778 70w multi	42	15
1338 A778 70w multi	42	15
1339 A780 70w multi ('84)	25	15
1340 A780 70w multi ('84)	25	15
1341 A782 70w multi ('84)	25	15
1342 A782 70w multi ('84)	25	15
Nos. 1333-1342 (10)	3.40	
Set value		64

PHILAKOREA '84, Seoul, Oct. 22-31, 1984.
Issue dates: #1333-1334, Apr. 22; #1335-1336, June 10; #1337-1338, Aug. 10; #1339-1340, Feb. 10; #1341-1342, Mar. 10.

Teachers' Day — A784

1983, May 15 Photo. *Perf. 13x13½*

1343 A784 60w Village schoolhouse, score 36 15
a. Souvenir sheet of 2 75

World Communications Year — A785

1983, June 20

1344 A785 70w multi 42 15
a. Souvenir sheet of 2 1.00

Communications Life Insurance Inauguration — A786

1983, July 1 Photo. *Perf. 13½x13*

1345 A786 70w multi 42 15

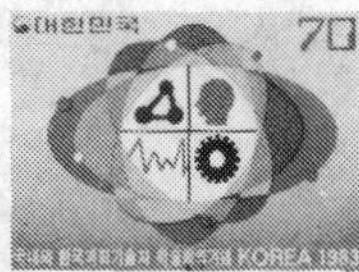
Science and Technology Symposium, Seoul, July 4-8 — A787

1983, July 4

1346 A787 70w multi 42 15

Visit of Jordan's King Hussein, Sept. 10-13
A788

1983, Sept. 10 Litho. *Perf. 13x12½*

1347 A788 70w Pres. Hwan, King Hussein, flags 42 15
a. Souvenir sheet of 2, imperf. 85

ASTA, 53rd World Travel Congress, Seoul — A789

1983, Sept. 25 Photo. *Perf. 13*

1348 A789 70w multi 42 15

70th Inter-Parliamentary Union Conference — A790

1983, Oct. 4 Photo. *Perf. 13*

1349 A790 70w multi 42 15
a. Souvenir sheet of 2 85

64th National Sports Festival — A791

1983, Oct. 6 Photo. *Perf. 13*

1350 A791 70w Gymnastics 42 15
1351 A791 70w Soccer 42 15
Set value 16

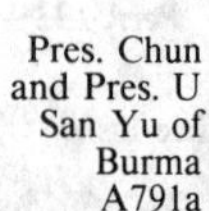

Pres. Chun and Pres. U San Yu of Burma
A791a

Pres. Chun's Curtailed Visit to Southwest Asia: No. 1351B, India. No. 1351C, Pres. Junius R. Jayawardene, Sri Lanka. No. 1351D, Australia, flag. No. 1351E, New Zealand, flag. Withdrawn after one day due to political assassination.

1983, Oct. 8 Photo. *Perf. 13½x13*

1351A A791a 70w multi 1.50
1351B A791a 70w multi 1.50
1351C A791a 70w multi 1.50
1351D A791a 70w multi 1.50
1351E A791a 70w multi 1.50
Nos. 1351A-1351E (5) 7.50

Souvenir Sheets of 2

1351f A791a 70w 2.25
1351g A791a 70w 2.25
1351h A791a 70w 2.25
1351i A791a 70w 2.25
1351j A791a 70w 2.25
Nos. 1351f-1351j (5) 11.25

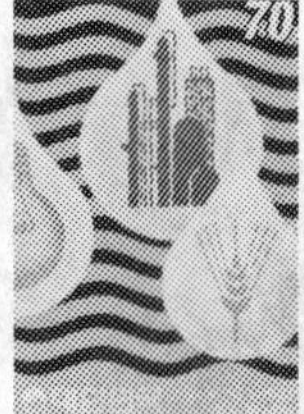
Water Resource Development
A792

Newspaper Publication Cent.
A793

1983, Oct. 15 Litho. *Perf. 13*

1352 A792 70w multi 42 15

1983, Oct. 31 Litho. *Perf. 13*

1353 A793 70w multi 25 15

Natl. Tuberculosis Assoc., 30th Anniv. — A794

1983, Nov. 6 Photo. *Perf. 13*

1354 A794 70w multi 25 15

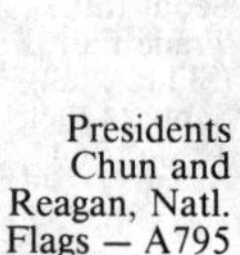

Presidents Chun and Reagan, Natl. Flags — A795

1983, Nov. 12 Photo. *Perf. 13*

1355 A795 70w multi 25 15
a. Souvenir sheet of 2 50

Visit of Pres. Ronald Reagan, Nov. 12-14.

11th Philatelic Week — A796

1983, Nov. 18 Photo. *Perf. 13*

1356 A796 70w multi 25 15
a. Souvenir sheet of 2 50

New Year 1984
A797 A798

1983, Dec. 1 Photo. *Perf. 13*

1357 A797 70w Mouse, stone wall relief 25 15
a. Souvenir sheet of 2 50
1358 A798 70w Cranes, pine tree 25 15
a. Souvenir sheet of 2 50
Set value 15

Bicentenary of Catholic Church in Korea — A799

1984, Jan. 4 Photo. *Perf. 13x13½*

1359 A799 70w Cross 25 15
a. Souvenir sheet of 2 50

Visit of Brunei's Sultan Bolkiah-Apr. 7-9 — A800

1984, Apr. 7 Litho. *Perf. 13x12½*

1360 A800 70w multi 18 15
a. Souvenir sheet of 2, imperf. 50

Visit of Qatar's Sheik Khalifa, Apr. 20-22
A801

1984, Apr. 20

1361 A801 70w multi 18 15
a. Souvenir sheet of 2, imperf. 50

Girl Mailing Letter — A802

Mailman in City — A803

1984, Apr. 22 Photo. *Perf. 13½x13*

1362 A802 70w multi 18 15
a. Souvenir sheet of 2 50
1363 A803 70w multi 18 15
a. Souvenir sheet of 2 50
Set value 15

Korean postal service.

Visit of Pope John Paul II, May 3-7 — A808

Engraved, Photogravure and Engraved

1984, May 3 *Perf. 12½*

1368 A808 70w dk brn 18 15
1369 A808 70w multi 18 15
a. Souvenir sheet of 2, #1368-1369, perf. 13½ 50
Set value 15

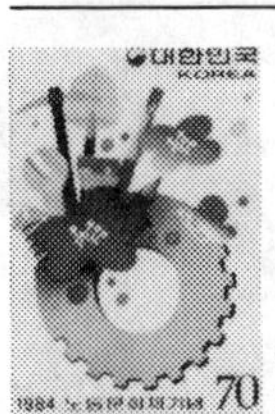

Workers' Cultural Festival — A809

1984, May 11 Photo. *Perf. 13x13½*

1370 A809 70w Tools, brushes, flower 18 15

Customs Cooperation Council 63rd-64th Sessions, Seoul, May 21-25 — A810

1984, May 21 Photo. *Perf. 13x13½*

1371 A810 70w Jet, ship, Asia map 18 15

Visit of Sri Lanka's Pres. Jayewardene, May 27-30 — A811

1984, May 27 *Perf. 13½x13*

1372 A811 70w Asia map, flags, flowers 18 15
a. Souvenir sheet of 2 50

Advertising Congress Emblem A812

'88 Olympic Expressway Opening A813

1984, June 18 Photo. *Perf. 13x13½*

1373 A812 70w ADASIA '84 emblem 18 15

14th Asian Advertising Congress, Seoul, June 18-21.

1984, June 22

1374 A813 70w multi 18 15

Intl. Olympic Committee, 90th Anniv. — A814

1984, June 23

1375 A814 70w multi 18 15

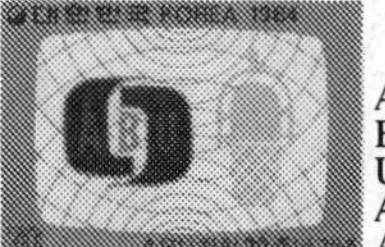

Asia-Pacific Broadcasting Union, 20th Anniv. A815

1984, June 30 *Perf. 13½x13*

1376 A815 70w Emblem, microphone 18 15

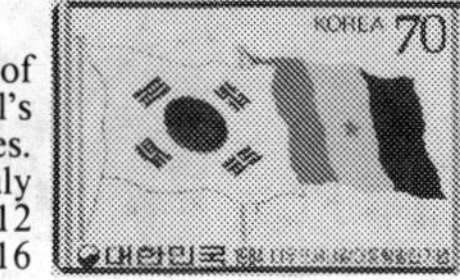

Visit of Senegal's Pres. Diouf, July 9-12 A816

1984, July 9 Litho. *Perf. 13x12½*

1377 A816 70w Flags of Korea & Senegal 18 15
a. Souvenir sheet of 2, imperf. 50

1984 Summer Olympics A817

Lithographed and Engraved

1984, July 28 *Perf. 12½*

1378 A817 70w Archery 18 15
1379 A817 440w Fencing 1.15 25
Set value 30

Korean Protestant Church Cent. A818

Groom on Horseback A819

Stained glass windows. Se-tenant.

1984, Aug. 16 *Perf. 13*

1380 A818 70w Crucifixion 18 15
1381 A818 70w Cross, dove 18 15
a. Souvenir sheet of 2 50
Set value 15

1984, Sept. 1 Photo. *Perf. 13x13½*

Wedding Procession: a, Lantern carrier. b, Groom. c, Musician. d, Bride in sedan chair (52x33mm).

1382 Strip of 4 75 20
a.-d. A819 70w any single 18 15
e. Souvenir sheet 25

No. 1382e contains No. 1382d.

Pres. Chun's Visit to Japan, Sept. 6-8 A820

1984, Sept. 6 Litho. *Perf. 13x12½*

1383 A820 70w Chun, flag, Mt. Fuji 18 15
a. Souvenir sheet of 2, imperf. 50

Visit of Gambia's Pres. Jawara, Sept. 12-17 A821

1984, Sept. 12

1384 A821 70w Flags of Korea & Gambia 18 15
a. Souvenir sheet of 2, imperf. 50

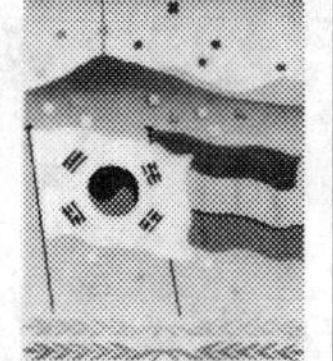

Visit of Gabon's Pres. Bongo, Sept. 21-23 — A822

1984, Sept. 21 *Perf. 13*

1385 A822 70w Flags of Korea & Gabon 18 15
a. Souvenir sheet of 2, imperf. 50

Seoul Intl. Trade Fair — A823

1984, Sept. 18 Photo. *Perf. 13x13½*

1386 A823 70w Products 18 15

65th Natl. Sports Festival, Taegu, Oct. 11-16 — A824

1984, Oct. 11 Photo. *Perf. 13½x13*

1387 A824 70w Badminton 18 15
1388 A824 70w Wrestling 18 15
Set value 15

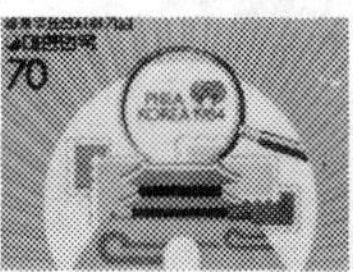

Philakorea '84 Stamp Show, Seoul, Oct. 22-31 — A825

Perf. 13½x13, 13x13½

1984, Oct. 22

1389 A825 70w South Gate, stamps 18 15
a. Souvenir sheet of 4 75
1390 A825 70w Emblem under magnifier, vert. 18 15
a. Souvenir sheet of 4 75
Set value 15

Visit of Maldives Pres. Maumoon Abdul Gayoom, Oct. 29-Nov. 1 — A826

1984, Oct. 29 Litho. *Perf. 13x12½*

1392 A826 70w multi 18 15
a. Souvenir sheet of 2, imperf. 50

Chamber of Commerce and Industry Cent. A827

Children Playing Jaegi-chagi A828

1984, Oct. 31 Photo. *Perf. 13x13½*

1393 A827 70w "100" 18 15

1984, Dec. 1 Photo. *Perf. 13x13½*

New Year 1985 (Year of the ox).

1394 A828 70w Ox, bas-relief 18 15
a. Souvenir sheet of 2 36
1395 A828 70w shown 18 15
a. Souvenir sheet of 2 36
Set value 15

Intl. Youth Year — A829

1985, Jan. 25 Photo. *Perf. 13½x13*

1396 A829 70w IYY emblem 18 15

Folkways — A830

1985, Feb. 19 Photo. *Perf. 13x13½*

1397 A830 70w Pounding rice 18 15
1398 A830 70w Welcoming full moon 18 15
Set value 15

1985, Aug. 20

1399 A830 70w Wrestling 18 15
1400 A830 70w Janggi, Korean chess 18 15
Set value 15

Modern Art Series

Rocky Mountain in the Early Spring, 1915, by Shimjoen, (Ahn Jung-shik) A831

Still-life with a Doll, 1927, by Suhlcho, (Lee Chong-woo) A832

Spring Day on a Farm, 1961, by Eijai, (Huh Paik-ryun, 1903-1977) A833

The Exorcist, 1941, by Chulma, (Kim Chung-hyun, 1901-1953) — A834

Chunhyang-do, by Kim Un-ho — A835

Flowers, by Lee Sang-bum — A836

Image of A Friend, by Ku Bon-wung A837

Woman in a Ski Suit, by Son Ung-seng A838

Valley of the Peach Blossoms, 1964, by Pyen Kwan-Sik (1899-1976) A839

Rural Landscape, 1940, by Lee Yong-Wu (1904-1952) A840

Male, 1932, by Lee Ma-Dong A841

Woman with a Water Jar on Her Head, 1944, by Yun Hyo-Chung (1917-1967) A842

Photo.; Litho. & Engr. (#1411-1412)

1985-87 ***Perf. 13½x13, 13x13½***

1401	A831	70w multi	18	15
1402	A832	70w multi	18	15
1403	A833	70w multi	18	15
1404	A834	70w multi	18	15
1405	A835	80w multi ('86)	22	15
1406	A836	80w multi ('86)	22	15
1407	A837	80w multi ('86)	22	15
1408	A838	80w multi ('86)	22	15
1409	A839	80w multi ('87)	28	15
1410	A840	80w multi ('87)	28	15
1411	A841	80w multi ('87)	28	15
1412	A842	80w multi ('87)	28	15
		Nos. 1401-1412 (12)	2.72	
		Set value		84

Issue dates: Nos. 1401-1402, Apr. 10. Nos. 1403-1404, July 5. Nos. 1405-1408, Dec. 1. Nos. 1409-1412, June 12.

State Visit of Pres. Chun to the US — A843

Photo. & Engr.

1985, Apr. 24 ***Perf. 13***

1413	A843	70w multi	20	15
a.		Souvenir sheet of 2	40	

Coastal and Inland Fish Series

Gak-si- Bung-eo (silver carp) — A844

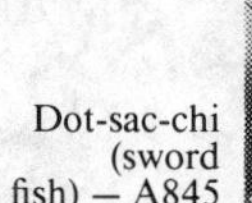

Dot-sac-chi (sword fish) — A845

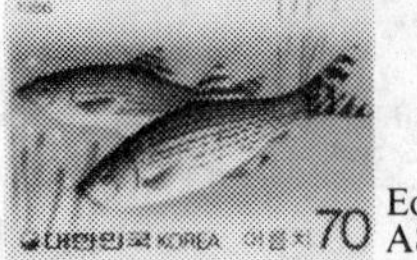

Eoreumchi A846

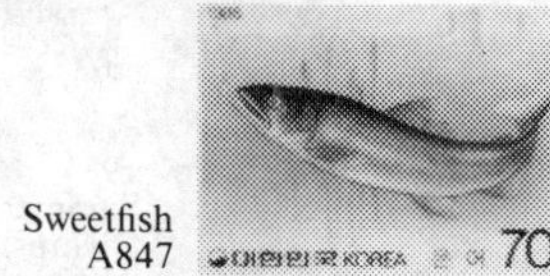

Sweetfish A847

Sardine A848

Hammerhead Shark — A849

Cham-jung-go-ji — A850

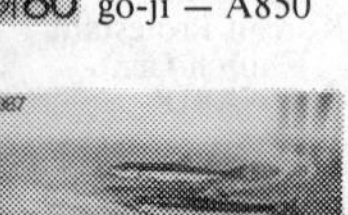

Swi-ri — A851

Oar Fish — A852

Devil-ray A853

1985-87 **Photo.** ***Perf. 13½x13***

1414	A844	70w multi	18	15
1415	A845	70w multi	18	15
1416	A846	70w multi ('86)	20	15
1417	A847	70w multi ('86)	20	15
1418	A848	70w multi ('86)	20	15
1419	A849	70w multi ('86)	20	15
1420	A850	80w multi ('87)	30	15
1421	A851	80w multi ('87)	30	15
1422	A852	80w multi ('87)	30	15
1423	A853	80w multi ('87)	30	15
		Nos. 1414-1423 (10)	2.36	
		Set value		65

Issue dates: Nos. 1414-1415, May 30. Nos. 1416-1423, July 25.

Yonsei University and Medical School, Cent. A854

Photogravure and Engraved

1985, May 6 ***Perf. 13***

1424	A854	70w Underwood Hall	20	15

State Visit of Pres. Mohammad Zia-Ul-Haq of Pakistan, May 6-10 — A855

State Visit of Pres. Luis Alberto Monge of Costa Rica, May 19-23 — A856

1985, May 6 **Photo.** ***Perf. 13x13½***

1425	A855	70w multi	20	15
a.		Souvenir sheet of 2	40	

1985, May 18 ***Perf. 13½x13***

1426	A856	70w multi	20	15
a.		Souvenir sheet of 2	40	

State Visit of Pres. Hussain Muhammad Eshrad of Bangladesh, June 15-19 — A857

1985, June 15

1427	A857	70w multi	20	15
a.		Souvenir sheet of 2, imperf.	40	

State Visit of Pres. Joao Bernardo Vieira of Guinea-Bissau, June 25-28 — A858

1985, June 25

1428	A858	70w multi	20	15
a.		Souvenir sheet of 2, imperf.	40	

Liberation from Japanese Occupation Forces, 40th Anniv. A859

Design: Heavenly Lake, Mt. Paektu, natl. flower.

1985, Aug. 14 **Litho.** ***Perf. 13x12½***

1429	A859	70w multi	20	15

Folk Music Series

The Spring of My Home, Music by Hong Nan-pa and Lyrics by Lee Won-su A860

A Leaf Boat, Music by Yun Yong-ha and Lyrics by Park Hong-Keun A861

Half Moon, 1924, by Yun Keuk-Young A862

Let's Go and Pick the Moon, by Yun Seok-Jung and Park Tae Hyun A863

Korean Farm Music — A864

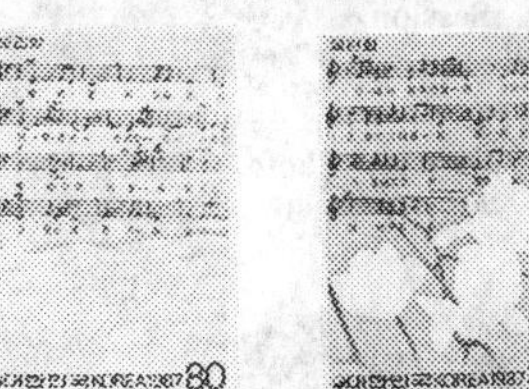

Barley Field, by Park Wha-mok and Yun Yong-ha — A865

Magnolia, by Cho Young-Shik and Kim Dong-jin — A866

Chusok, Harvest Moon Festival — A867

1985, Sept. 10 Photo. *Perf. 13x13½*

1430 A860 70w multi	20	15
1431 A861 70w multi	20	15
Set value		15

1986, June 25 Photo. *Perf. 13x13½*

1432 A862 70w multi	20	15
1433 A863 70w multi	20	15
Set value		15

1986, Aug. 26 Photo. *Perf. 13½x13*

Musicians with: a, Flag, hand gong. b, Drum flute. c, Drum, hand gong. d, Taborets, ribbons. e, Taboret, sun, woman, child. Printed se-tenant in a continuous design.

1434 Strip of 5	1.00	32
a.-e. A864 70w any single	20	15

1987, Mar. 25 Photo. *Perf. 13x13½*

1435 A865 80w multi	24	15
1436 A866 80w multi	24	15
Set value		16

1987, Sept. 10 Photo. *Perf. 13x13½*

Harvest moon dance: No. 1437a, Eight dancers, harvest moon. No. 1437b, Four dancers, festival wheels, balloons. No. 1437c, Three dancers, children on see-saw. No. 1437d, Four dancers, women preparing meal.

1437 Strip of 4	1.20	32
a.-d. A867 80w any single	30	15

Folklore Series

Tano, Spring Harvest Festival — A868

Sick for Home, by Lee Eun-sang and Kim Kong-jin A869

Pioneer, by Yoon Hae-young and Cho Doo-nam A870

Mask Dance (Talchum) — A871

Designs: a, Woman on shore, riding a swing. b, Sweet flag coiffures. c, Boy picking flowers, girl on swing. d, Boys wrestling.
Illustration reduced.

1988, Aug. 25 Photo. *Perf. 13x13½*

1438 A868 Strip of 4	88	24
a.-d. 80w multi	22	15

1988, Nov. 15

1439 A869 80w multi	24	15
1440 A870 80w multi	24	15
Set value		15

1989, Feb. 25

Designs: a, Two mask dancers with scarves. b, Dancers with fans. c, Dancers with scarf and laurel or fan. d, Three dancers, first as an animal and two more carrying fan and bells or torch.

1441 Strip of 4	96	24
a.-d. A871 80w any single	24	15

Korean Telecommunications, Cent. — A872

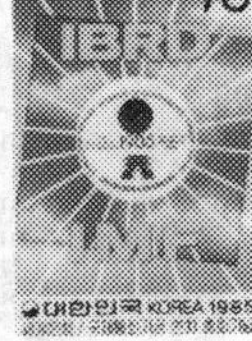

World Bank Conference, Seoul, Oct. 8-11 — A873

1985, Sept. 28 *Perf. 13½x13*

1442 A872 70w Satellite, emblem, dish receiver	20	15

1985, Oct. 8 *Perf. 13x13½*

1443 A873 70w Emblem	20	15

Intl. Bank for Reconstruction & Development, 40th Anniv.

UN, 40th Anniv. — A874

1985, Oct. 24 *Perf. 13½x13*

1444 A874 70w Emblem, doves	20	15

Natl. Red Cross, 80th Anniv. — A875

1985, Oct. 26

1445 A875 70w red, blk & bl	20	15

Segment of Canceled Cover — A876

New Year 1986 — A877

1985, Nov. 18 Photo. *Perf. 13½x13*

1446 A876 70w multi	20	15

12th Philatelic Week, Nov. 18-23.

Lithographed and Engraved

1985, Dec. 2 *Perf. 13x13½*

1447 A877 70w multi	20	15

Mt. Fuji, Korean Airlines Jet — A878

1985, Dec. 18 Photo.

1448 A878 70w brt bl, blk & red	20	15

Normalization of diplomatic relations between Korea and Japan, 20th anniv.
See No. C44.

Statesman Type of 1986 and Types of 1981-86

Engr., Photo. (40w)

1986-87 *Perf. 13*

1449 A716 550w indigo	2.00	68

Coil Stamps

Perf. 13 Vert.

1449A A704 20w multicolored	15	15
1449B A705 40w multicolored	20	15
1449C A708 80w multicolored	48	15
Set value, #1449A-1449C		16

Issue dates: 550w, Dec. 10; others, 1987.

Intl. Peace Year — A879

State Visits of Pres. Chun — A880

1986, Jan. 15 Photo. *Perf. 13x13½*

1450 A879 70w multi	20	15
1451 A879 400w multi	1.15	35
a. Souvenir sheet of 4	4.60	
Set value		40

1986, Apr. 4 Litho. *Perf. 12½x13*

Portrait, natl. flags and: No. 1452, Parliament, Brussels. No. 1453, Eiffel Tower, Paris. No. 1454, Cathedral, Cologne. No. 1455, Big Ben, London.

1452 A880 70w multi	16	15
1453 A880 70w multi	16	15
1454 A880 70w multi	16	15
1455 A880 70w multi	16	15
Set value		20

Souvenir Sheets of 2

Perf. 13½

1452a A880 70w	35
1453a A880 70w	35
1454a A880 70w	35
1455a A880 70w	35

Science Series

Chomsongdae Observatory, Satellites — A881

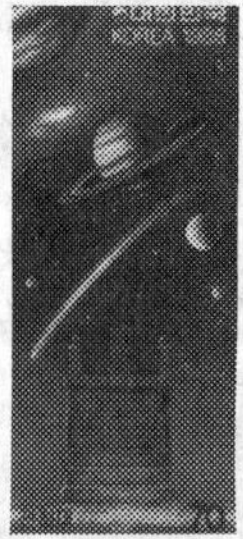

Kwanchondae Observatory, Halley's Comet — A882

Weather

A883 A884

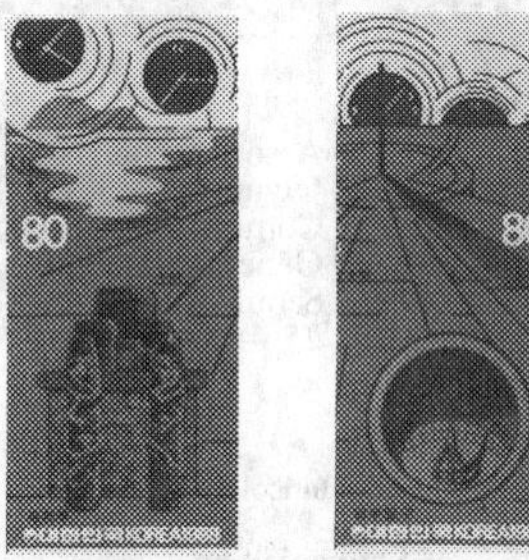

Clocks

A885 A886

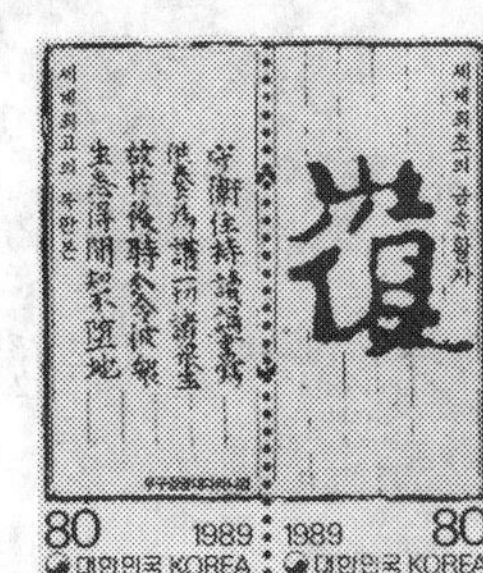

Early Printing Methods

A887 A888

A889 A890

1986, Apr. 21 *Perf. 13½x13*

1456 A881 70w multi	16	15
1457 A882 70w multi	16	15
a. Pair, #1456-1457	32	15

1987, Apr. 21 Photo. *Perf. 13½*

Designs: No. 1458, Wind observatory stone foundation, Chosun Dynasty. No. 1459, Rain gauge, Sejong Period to Chosun Dynasty.

1458 A883 80w multi 28 15
1459 A884 80w multi 28 15
a. Pair, #1458-1459 56 20

1988, Apr. 21 Photo. *Perf. 13½x13*

Designs: No. 1460, *Chagyokru*, water clock invented by Chang Yongshil and Kim Bin in 1434. No. 1461, *Angbuilgu*, sundial completed during King Sejong's reign (1418-1450).

1460 A885 80w multi 26 15
1461 A886 80w multi 26 15
a. Pair, #1460-1461 52 18

Designs: No. 1462, Sutra manuscript (detail) printed from wood type, Shila Dynasty, c.704-751. No. 1463, Character from a manuscript printed from metal type, Koryo, c.1237.

1989, Apr. 21

1462 A887 80w buff & sepia 24 15
1463 A888 80w buff & sepia 24 15
a. Pair, #1462-1463 48 16

Designs: No. 1464, 7th century gilt bronze Buddha. No. 1465, Bronze Age dagger, spear molds.

1990, Apr. 21

1464 A889 100w multicolored 45 15
1465 A890 100w multicolored 45 15
a. Pair, #1464-1465 90 30
Set value 24

Pairs have continuous designs.

Assoc. of Natl. Olympic Committees, 5th General Assembly, Seoul, Apr. 21-25 — A891

1986, Apr. 21 *Perf. 13x13½*

1466 A891 70w multicolored 16 15

Souvenir Sheet

Butterflies A892

1986, May 22 Litho. *Perf. 13½*

1467 Sheet of 6 6.05 2.10
a. A892 70w multicolored 20 15
b. A892 370w multicolored 1.00 35
c. A892 400w multicolored 1.10 38
d. A892 440w multicolored 1.20 42
e. A892 450w multicolored 1.25 42
f. A892 470w multicolored 1.30 45

AMERIPEX '86, Chicago, May 22-June 1. No. 1467 contains stamps of different sizes (370w, 42x41mm; 400w, 42x33mm; 440w, 39x45mm; 450w, 32x42mm; 470w, 33x44mm); margin continues the designs.

Women's Education, Cent. A893

1986, May 31 *Perf. 13x12½*

1468 A893 70w multicolored 20 15

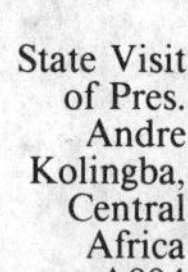

State Visit of Pres. Andre Kolingba, Central Africa A894

1986, June 10 *Perf. 13*

1469 A894 70w multicolored 20 15
a. Souvenir sheet of 2, imperf. 40

Completion of Han River Development Project — A895

1986, Sept. 10 Litho. *Perf. 13*

1470 Strip of 3 58 22
a. A895 30w Bridge 15 15
b. A895 60w Buildings 20 15
c. A895 80w Seoul Tower, buildings 28 15

Printed in a continuous design.

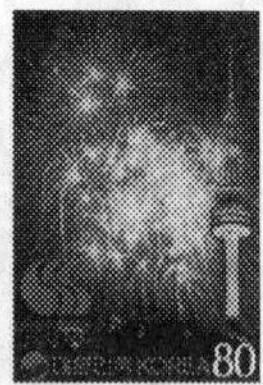

Fireworks, Seoul Tower A896

Games Emblem A897

10th Asian Games, Seoul, Sept. 20-Oct. 5 — A898

1986, Sept. 20 Photo. *Perf. 13x13½*

1471 A896 80w multi 25 15
a. Souvenir sheet of 2 50
1472 A897 80w multi 25 15
a. Souvenir sheet of 2 50
Set value 16

Souvenir Sheet

1986, Oct. 31

1473 A898 550w multi 1.60

Juan Antonio Samaranch, Korean IOC Delegation, 1981 — A899

1986, Sept. 30

1474 A899 80w multi 25 15

Intl. Olympic Committee decision to hold 24th Olympic Games in Seoul, 5th anniv.

Philatelic Week — A900

1986, Nov. 18 Photo. *Perf. 13½x13*

1475 A900 80w Boy fishing for stamp 22 15

New Year 1987 (Year of the Hare) — A901

Birds — A902

1986, Dec. 1 Photo. *Perf. 13x13½*

1476 A901 80w multi 22 15

1986, Dec. 20 *Perf. 13x14*

1477 A902 80w Waxwing 22 15
1478 A902 80w Oriole 22 15
1479 A902 80w Kingfisher 22 15
1480 A902 80w Hoopoe 22 15
1481 A902 80w Roller 22 15
a. Strip of 5, #1477-1481 1.10 40
Set value 40

Coil Stamps
Perf. 14 Horiz.

1481B A902 80w like No. 1479 22 15
1481C A902 80w like No. 1480 22 15
1481D A902 80w like No. 1481 22 15
1481E A902 80w like No. 1477 22 15
1481F A902 80w like No. 1478 22 15
g. Strip of 5, #1481B-1481F 1.10 40
Set value 40

Wildlife Conservation A903

Endangered species: No. 1482, Panthera tigris altaica. No. 1483, Felis bengalensis. No. 1484, Vulpes vulpes. No. 1485, Sus scrofa.

1987, Feb. 25 Photo. *Perf. 13½x13*

1482 A903 80w multi 22 15
1483 A903 80w multi 22 15
1484 A903 80w multi 22 15
1485 A903 80w multi 22 15
a. Strip of 4, #1482-1485 88 32
Set value 32

Flowers — A904

1987, Mar. 20 Photo. *Perf. 14x13*

1486 A904 550w Dicentra spectabilis 1.65 55
1487 A904 550w Hanabusaya asiatica 1.65 55
1488 A904 550w Erythronium japonicum 1.65 55
1489 A904 550w Dianthus chinensis 1.65 55
1490 A904 550w Chrysanthemum zawadskii coreanum 1.65 55
a. Strip of 5, #1486-1490 8.25 2.75

Coil Stamps
Perf. 13 Vert.

1490B A904 550w like No. 1486 1.65 55
1490C A904 550w like No. 1487 1.65 55
1490D A904 550w like No. 1488 1.65 55
1490E A904 550w like No. 1489 1.65 55
1490F A904 550w like No. 1490 1.65 55
g. Strip of 5, #1490B-1490F 8.25 2.75

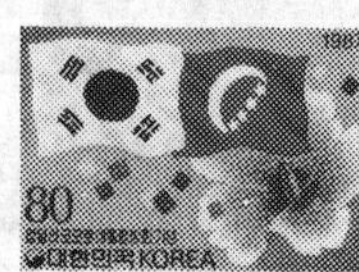

State Visit of Pres. Ahmed Abdallah Abderemane of the Comoro Isls., Apr. 6-9 — A905

1987, Apr. 6 Litho. *Perf. 13½x13*

1491 A905 80w multi 28 15
a. Souvenir sheet of 2 60

Electrification of Korea, Cent. — A906

1987, Apr. 10 Photo.

1492 A906 80w multi 28 15

Int'l. Assoc. of Ports and Harbors, 15th General Session, Seoul — A907

1987, Apr. 25 Photo. *Perf. 13½x13*

1493 A907 80w multi 28 15

State Visit of Pres. U San Yu of Burma A908

1987, June 8 Litho. *Perf. 13½x13*

1494 A908 80w multi 28 15
a. Souvenir sheet of 2 60

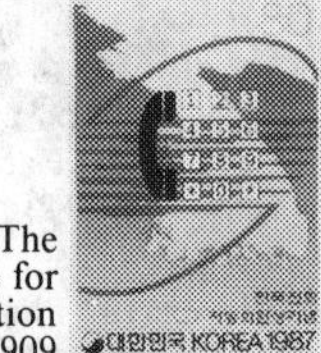

Year of The Communications for Information Society — A909

1987, June 30 *Perf. 13x13½*

1495 A909 80w Map, digital telephone 28 15
1496 A909 80w Emblem 28 15
Set value 16

Introduction of automatic switching telephone system.

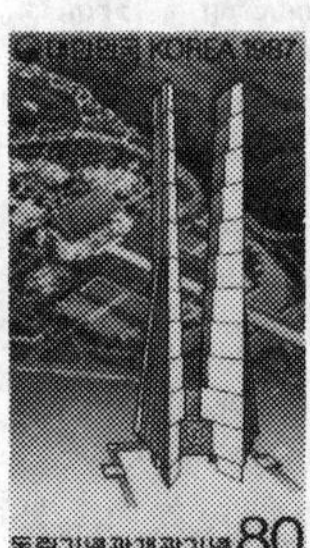

Independence Hall, Monument to the Nation — A910

Statue of Indomitable Koreans, Nat'l. Flag — A911

1987, Aug. 14 Photo. *Perf. 13½x13*

1497 A910 80w multi 30 15
a. Souvenir sheet of 2 60
1498 A911 80w multi 30 15
a. Souvenir sheet of 2 60
Set value 16

Opening of Independence Hall, Aug. 15.

16th Pacific Science Congress, Seoul, Aug. 20-30 — A912

1987, Aug. 20 ***Perf. 13x13½***
1499 A912 80w multi 30 15
a. Souvenir sheet of 2 60

State Visit of Pres. Virgilio Barco of Colombia A913

1987, Sept. 8 Litho. ***Perf. 13½x13***
1500 A913 80w multicolored 30 15
a. Souvenir sheet of 2 60

Installation of 10-millionth Telephone A914

1987, Sept. 28 ***Perf. 13½x13***
1501 A914 80w multi 30 15

Servicemen, Flags of Three Military Services — A915

1987, Sept. 30 Litho. ***Perf. 13***
1502 A915 80w multi 30 15

Armed Forces Day, Armed Forces 39th Anniv.

14th Philatelic Week, Nov. 18-24 — A916

Signing of the Antarctic Treaty by Korea, 1st Anniv. — A917

1987, Nov. 18 Photo. ***Perf. 13½***
1503 A916 80w Boy playing the nalrali 30 15

1987, Nov. 28 Litho.
1504 A917 80w multi 30 15

New Year 1988 (Year of the Dragon) — A918

1987, Dec. 1 Photo.
1505 A918 80w multi 30 15

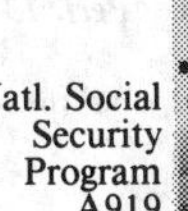

Natl. Social Security Program A919

1988, Jan. 4 Litho. ***Perf. 13½x13***
1506 A919 80w multi 26 15

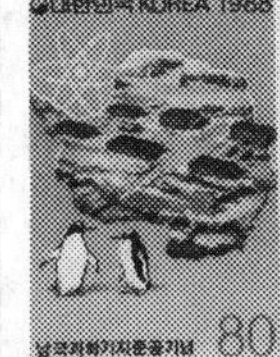

Completion of the Korean Antarctic Base — A919a

1988, Feb. Photo. ***Perf. 13x13½***
1506A A919a 80w multi 26 15

Inauguration of Roh Tae-Woo, 13th President A920

1988, Feb. 24 Photo. ***Perf. 13½x13***
1507 A920 80w multi 26 15
a. Souv. sheet of 2 55

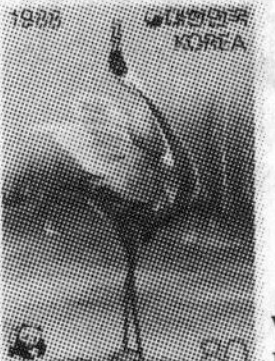

World Wildlife Fund — A921

White-naped crane *(Grus vipio)* displaying various behaviors: a, Calling (1). b, Running (2). c, Spreading wings (3). d, Flying (4).

1988, Apr. 1 ***Perf. 13x13½***
1508 Strip of 4 1.05 25
a.-d. A921 80w any single 26 15

Intl. Red Cross & Red Crescent Organizations, 125th Annivs. A922

Telepress Medium, 1st Anniv. A923

1988, May 7 Photo. ***Perf. 13x13½***
1509 A922 80w multi 28 15

1988, June 1 Litho.
1510 A923 80w multi 28 15

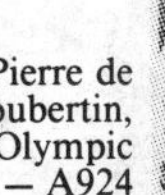

Pierre de Coubertin, Olympic Flag — A924

Olympic Temple A925

View of Seoul A926

Folk Dancers A927

Litho. & Engr.

1988, Sept. 16 ***Perf. 13½x13***
1511 A924 80w multi 25 15
1512 A925 80w multi 25 15

Photo.

Perf. 13x13½
1513 A926 80w multi 25 15
1514 A927 80w multi 25 15
Set value 24

1988 Summer Olympics, Seoul.

Souvenir Sheets of 2

1511a A924 80w 50
1512a A925 80w 50
1513a A926 80w 50
1514a A927 80w 50

Margin inscriptions on Nos. 1511a-1512a are photo.

OLYMPHILEX '88, Sept. 19-28, Seoul — A928

1988, Sept. 19 Photo. ***Perf. 13x13½***
1515 A928 80w multi 25 15
a. Souv. sheet of 2 50

22nd Congress of the Intl. Iron and Steel Institute, Seoul — A929

1988, Oct. 8 ***Perf. 13½x13***
1516 A929 80w multi 25 15

1988 Natl. Special Olympics (Paralympics), Seoul — A930

1988, Oct. 15 ***Perf. 13x13½***
1517 A930 80w shown 25 15
1518 A930 80w Archer seated in wheelchair 25 15
Set value 15

New Year 1989 (Year of the Snake) — A931

1988, Dec. 1 Photo. ***Perf. 13x13½***
1519 A931 80w multi 24 15

Souvenir Sheet

Successful Completion of the 1988 Summer Olympics, Seoul — A932

1988, Dec. 20 Litho. ***Perf. 13x12½***
1520 A932 550w Opening ceremony 1.75

Folklore Series

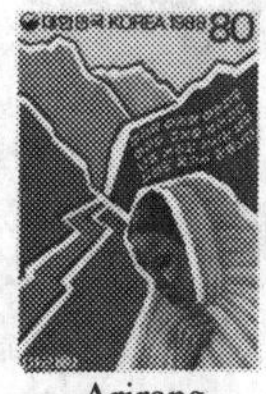

Arirang A933

Doraji A934

Pakyon Falls A935

Chonan-Samkori A936

Willowing Bow — A937

Spinning Wheel A938

Treating Threads A939

Weaving Fabric A940

Orchard Avenue
A941

In Flower Garden
A942

Natl. ballads.

1989, Mar. 27 Photo. *Perf. 13x13½*
1521 A933 80w multi 24 15
1522 A934 80w multi 24 15

1990, Feb. 26 Litho.
1523 A935 80w multicolored 42 15
1524 A936 80w multicolored 42 15

Litho. & Engr.
1990, Sept. 25 *Perf. 13½x13*
1525 A937 100w multicolored 45 15
1526 A938 100w multicolored 45 15
1527 A939 100w multicolored 45 15
1528 A940 100w multicolored 45 15
a. Strip of 4, #1525-1528 1.80 60

1991, Mar. 27 Litho. *Perf. 13x13½*
1529 A941 100w multicolored 42 15
1530 A942 100w multicolored 42 15

14th Asian-Pacific Dental Congress — A945

1989, Apr. 26 Photo. *Perf. 13x13½*
1533 A945 80w multi 24 15

Rotary Intl. Convention, Seoul, May 21-25 — A946

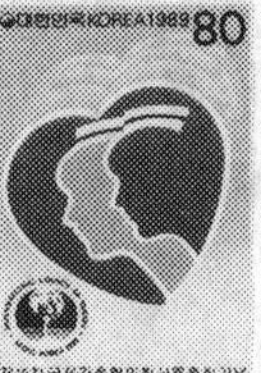
19th Cong. of the Intl. Council of Nurses, Seoul, May 28-June 2 — A947

1989, May 20 Photo. *Perf. 13x13½*
1534 A946 80w multi 24 15

1989, May 27
1535 A947 80w multi 24 15

Information Industry Month — A948

World Environment Day — A949

1989, June 1
1536 A948 80w multi 24 15

1989, June 5
1537 A949 80w multi 24 15

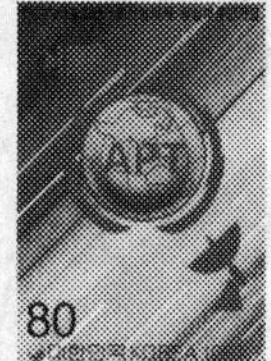
Asia-Pacific Telecommunity, 10th Anniv. — A950

1989, July 1 Photo. *Perf. 13x13½*
1538 A950 80w multi 24 15

French Revolution, Bicent.
A951

1989, July 14 Litho. *Perf. 13½x13*
1539 A951 80w multi 24 15

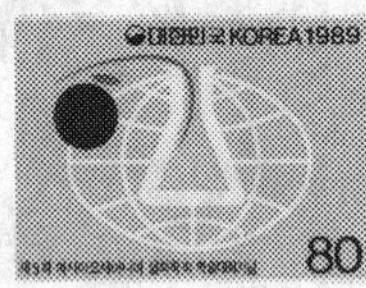
Federation of Asian and Oceanian Biochemists 5th Congress
A952

1989, Aug. 12 Photo.
1540 A952 80w multi 24 15

Modern Art Series

A White Ox, by Lee Joong-Sub — A953

A Street Stall, by Park Lae-hyun
A954

A Little Girl, by Lee Bong-Sang
A955

An Autumn Scene, by Oh Ji-ho — A956

Litho. & Engr.; Photo. (#1542, 1544)
1989, Sept. 4 *Perf. 13x13½, 13½x13*
1541 A953 80w multi 24 15
1542 A954 80w multi 24 15
1543 A955 80w multi 24 15
1544 A956 80w multi 24 15
Set value 24

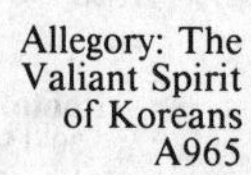

Allegory: The Valiant Spirit of Koreans
A965

1989, Sept. 12 Litho. *Perf. 13½x13*
1553 A965 80w multi 24 15

1988 Seoul Olympics and the World Korean Sports Festival.

Personification of Justice and Ancient Codex — A966

1989, Sept. 18
1554 A966 80w multi 24 15

Constitutional Court, 1st anniv.

Fish

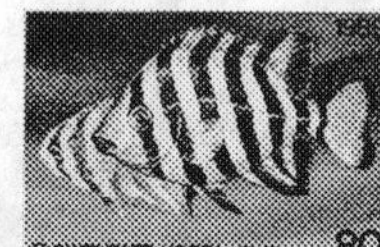
A967

A968

A969

A970

A971

A972

A973

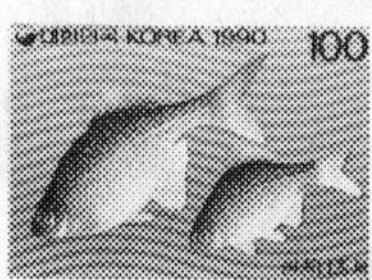
A974

A975

A976

A977

A978

1989, Sept. 30 Photo. *Perf. 13½x13*
1555 A967 80w Oplegnathus fasciatus 24 15
1556 A968 80w Cobitis multifasciata 24 15
1557 A969 80w Liobagrus mediadiposalis 24 15
1558 A970 80w Monocentris japonicus 24 15

1990, July 2
1559 A971 100w Hapalogenys mucronatus 45 15
1560 A972 100w Fugu niphobles 45 15
1561 A973 100w Oncorhynchus masou 45 15
1562 A974 100w Rhodeus ocellatus 45 15

1991, June 8
1563 A975 100w Microphysogobio longidorsalis 42 15
1564 A976 100w Gnathopogon majimae 42 15
1565 A977 100w Therapon oxyrhnchus 42 15
1566 A978 100w Psettina ijimae 42 15
Nos. 1555-1566 (12) 4.44 1.80

Light of Peace Illuminating the World
A979

1989, Oct. 4
1567 A979 80w multi 24 15

44th Intl. Eucharistic Cong., Seoul, Oct. 4-8.

29th World Congress of the Intl. Civil Airports Assoc., Seoul, Oct. 17-19 — A980

1989, Oct. 17
1568 A980 80w multi 24 15

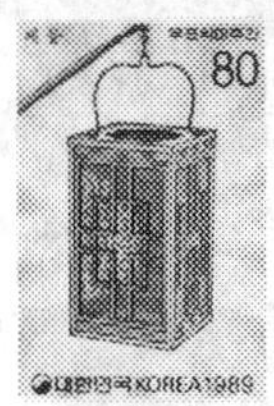

Philatelic Week — A981

Two Cranes — A982

Folk Festival Customs A983

1989, Nov. 18 Photo. ***Perf. 13x13½***

1569 A981 80w Lantern		24	15
a. Souv. sheet of 2		60	

1989, Dec. 1 ***Perf. 13x13½, 13½x13***

1570 A982 80w multicolored	24	15
a. Souv. sheet of 2	60	
1571 A983 80w multicolored	24	15
a. Souv. sheet of 2	60	
Set value		15

New Year 1990.

World Meteorological Day — A984

1990, Mar. 23 ***Perf. 13½x13***

1572 A984 80w multicolored 42 15

UNICEF in Korea, 40th Anniv. — A985

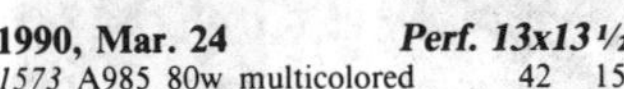

1990, Mar. 24 ***Perf. 13x13½***

1573 A985 80w multicolored 42 15

Cheju-Kohung Fiber Optic Submarine Cable — A986

1990, Apr. 21 ***Perf. 13½x13***

1574 A986 80w multicolored 42 15

Saemaul Movement, 20th Anniv. A987

1990, Apr. 21

1575 A987 100w multicolored 45 15

Youth Month A988

1990, May 1

1576 A988 100w multicolored 45 15

Cart-shaped Earthenware A992

Fire Safety A995

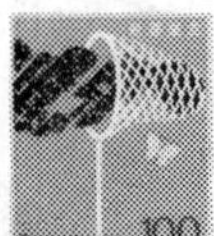

Environmental Protection A996

Traffic Safety A997

Waiting One's Turn A997a

Saving Energy A997b

Ginger Jar — A998

Hong Yung Sik — A1004

Dragon Head, Banner Staff — A1006

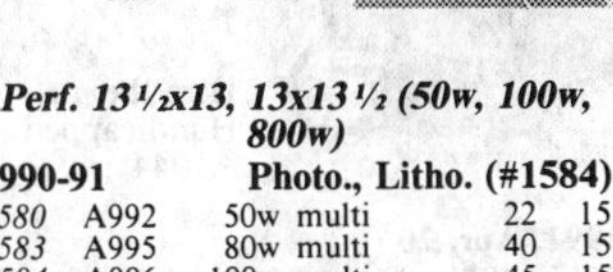

Perf. 13½x13, 13x13½ (50w, 100w, 800w)

1990-91 Photo., Litho. (#1584)

1580	A992	50w multi	22	15
1583	A995	80w multi	40	15
1584	A996	100w multi	45	15
1585	A997	100w multi	42	15
1585A	A997a	100w multi	42	15
1585B	A997b	100w multi	42	15
1586	A998	150w multi	65	22
1592	A1004	600w multi	2.55	85
1594	A1006	800w multi	3.00	1.00
	Nos. 1580-1594 (9)		8.53	2.97

Issue dates: No. 1584, June 5. 600w, June 25. 150w, July 2. 800w, July 10. No. 1585, July 25. 50w, Sept. 28. 80w, Nov. 1. 1585A, June 26, 1991. No. 1585B, Nov. 1, 1991.

This is an expanding set. Numbers will change if necessary.

Coil Stamp

1990 Litho. ***Perf. 13 Vert.***

1594A A996 100w multicolored 45 15

Seoul Mail Center A1007

1990, July 4 Litho. ***Perf. 13½x13***

1595 A1007 100w multicolored 45 15

8th Korean Boy Scout Jamboree — A1008

1990, Aug. 8 ***Perf. 13x13½***

1596 A1008 100w multicolored 45 15

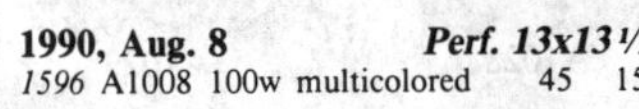

Wild Flowers

A1009

A1010

A1011

A1012

A1013

1990, Aug. 25 **Photo.**

1597 A1009 370w Lilium		1.65	55
1598 A1010 400w Aster		1.80	60
1599 A1011 440w Adonis		2.00	65
1600 A1012 470w Scabiosa		2.10	70

1991, July 26

1601 A1013 100w Aerides japonicum	35	15
1602 A1013 100w Heloniopsis orientalis	35	15
1603 A1013 370w Aquilegia buergeriana	1.15	40
1604 A1013 440w Gentiana zollingeri	1.40	50

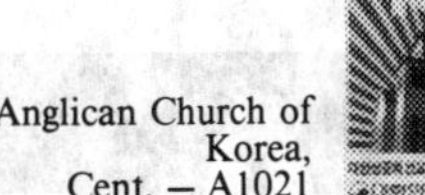

Anglican Church of Korea, Cent. — A1021

1990, Sept. 29 Litho. ***Perf. 13x13½***

1609 A1021 100w 42 15

Opening of Seoul Tower, 10th Anniv. — A1022

1990, Oct. 15

1610 A1022 100w blk, red & bl 42 15

National Census — A1023

1990, Oct. 20 ***Perf. 13x13½***

1611 A1023 100w multicolored 42 15

UN Development Program, 40th Anniv. A1024

1990, Oct. 24

1612 A1024 100w multicolored 42 15

Philatelic Week — A1025

Litho. & Engr.

1990, Nov. 16 ***Perf. 13x13½***

1613 A1025 100w multicolored	42	15
a. Souv. sheet of 2	85	

New Year 1991 (Year of the Sheep) A1026

Two Cranes A1027

1990, Dec. 1 Litho. *Perf. 13x13½*
1614 A1026 100w multicolored 42 15
1615 A1027 100w multicolored 42 15
a. Souv. sheet of 2, #1614-1615 84

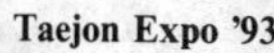
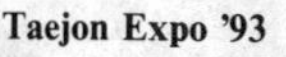

Taejon Expo '93

A1028

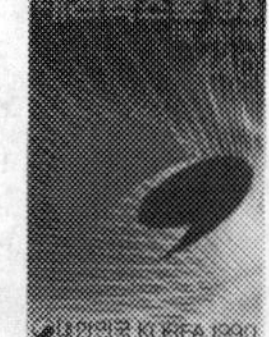

A1029

A1030

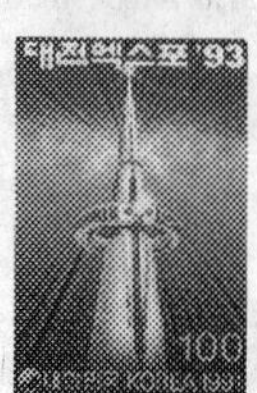
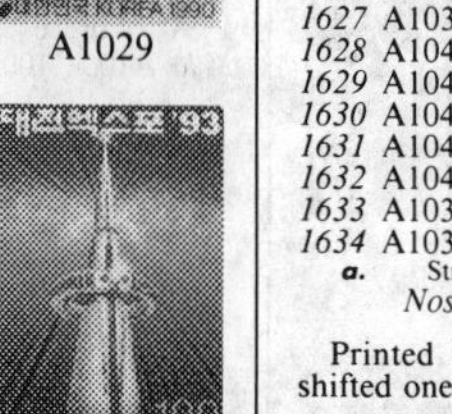
A1031

1990, Dec. 12
1616 A1028 100w multicolored 42 15
a. Souv. sheet of 2 84
1617 A1029 440w multicolored 1.85 65
a. Souv. sheet of 2 3.75

1991, Mar. 23
1618 A1030 100w multicolored 42 15
a. Souv. sheet of 2 84
1619 A1031 100w multicolored 42 15
a. Souv. sheet of 2 84

Saemaul Minilibrary, 30th Anniv. A1036

1991, Jan. 2 Litho. *Perf. 13½x13*
1624 A1036 100w multicolored 42 15

Moth A1037

Beetle A1038

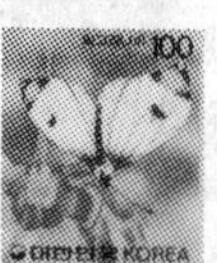
Butterfly A1039

Beetle A1040

Cicada — A1041

1991, Apr. 8 Photo. *Perf. 13½x13*
1625 A1037 100w shown 42 15
1626 A1038 100w shown 42 15
1627 A1039 100w shown 42 15
1628 A1040 100w shown 42 15
1629 A1041 100w shown 42 15
1630 A1040 100w Water beetle 42 15
1631 A1040 100w Bee 42 15
1632 A1040 100w Lady bug 42 15
1633 A1037 100w Dragonfly 42 15
1634 A1037 100w Grasshopper 42 15
a. Strip of 10, #1625-1634 4.25 2.00
Nos. 1625-1634 (10) 4.20 1.50

Printed in sheets of 100 with each row shifted one design.

Traditional Performing Arts Center, 40th Anniv. — A1042

1991, Apr. 10 *Perf. 13x13½*
1635 A1042 100w multicolored 42 15

Provisional Government, 72nd Anniv. A1043

1991, Apr. 13 *Perf. 13½x13*
1636 A1043 100w multicolored 42 15

Hire the Handicapped A1044

1991, Apr. 20
1637 A1044 100w multicolored 42 15

Teachers' Day, 10th Anniv. A1045

1991, May 15 Litho. *Perf. 13½x13*
1638 A1045 100w multicolored 42 15

17th World Scouting Jamboree — A1046

1991, Aug. 8 Litho. *Perf. 13x13½*
1639 A1046 100w multicolored 42 15
a. Souvenir sheet of 2 1.15 40

YMCA World Assembly — A1047

1991, Aug. 22 Litho. *Perf. 13x13½*
1640 A1047 100w multicolored 42 15

Natl. Desire for Reunification A1048

1991, Sept. 11 Litho. *Perf. 13x13½*
1641 A1048 100w multicolored 42 15

Admission to UN — A1049

1991, Sept. 18 *Perf. 13½x13*
1642 A1049 100w multicolored 42 15

Musical Instruments

Deerskin Drum (Galgo) A1050

Mouth Organ (Saenghwang) A1051

Designs: No. 1645, Brass chimes (Unra). No. 1646, Large gong (Jing).

1991, Sept. 26 Photo. *Perf. 13x13½*
Background color
1643 A1050 100w gray 42 15
1644 A1051 100w tan 42 15
1645 A1050 100w violet 42 15
1646 A1050 100w pale green 42 15

Month of Culture A1056

Telecom '91 A1057

1991, Oct. 1 Litho. *Perf. 13x13½*
1655 A1056 100w multicolored 42 15

1991, Oct. 7 Photo.
1656 A1057 100w multicolored 42 15

Sixth World Telecommunication Exhibition & Forum, Geneva, Switzerland.

Beauty Series

A1058

A1059

Kottam Architectural Patterns
A1060 A1061

1991, Oct. 18

1657	A1058 100w multicolored		42	15
1658	A1059 100w multicolored		42	15
1659	A1060 100w multicolored		42	15
1660	A1061 100w multicolored		42	15
a.	Block or strip of 4, #1657-1660		1.70	60

Philatelic Week — A1070

1991, Nov. 16 Photo. *Perf. 13x13½*

1669	A1070 100w multicolored	42	15
a.	Souvenir sheet of 2	85	30

New Year 1992, Year of the Monkey
A1071 A1072

1991, Dec. 2 Photo. & Engr.

1670	A1071 100w multicolored	42	15
a.	Souvenir sheet of 2	85	30
1671	A1072 100w multicolored	42	15
a.	Souvenir sheet of 2	85	30

SEMI-POSTAL STAMPS

Field Hospital SP1

Nurses Supporting Patient — SP2

Perf. 13½x14, 14x13½

1953, Aug. 1 Litho. Wmk. 257

Crosses in Red

B1	SP1 10h + 5h bl grn	2.00	1.25
B2	SP2 10h + 5h blue	2.00	1.25

The surtax was for the Red Cross. Nos. B1-B2 exist imperf.

Type of Regular Issue, 1956, with Added inscription at Upper Left

1957, Sept. 1 Wmk. 312 *Perf. 12½*

Granite Paper

B3	A111 40h + 10h lt bl grn	80	60

Wmk. 317

B4	A111 40h + 10h lt bl grn	80	60

The surtax was for flood relief.

Catalogue values for unused stamps in this section, from this point to the end of the section, are for Never Hinged items.

Rice Farmer Type of Regular Issue, 1961-62

1963, July 10 Wmk. 317 *Perf. 12½*

B5	A172 4w + 1w dk bl	65	35

The surtax was for flood victims in southern Korea.

1965, Oct. 1 Unwmk. *Perf. 12½*

B6	A172 4w + 2w indigo	60	35

The surtax was for flood relief.

1965, Oct. 11

B7	A172 4w + 2w magenta	52	30

The surtax was for a scholarship fund.

Type of Regular Issue 1964-66

1966, Nov. 10 Litho. *Perf. 12½*

Granite Paper

B8	A186b 7w + 2w car rose	60	30

The surtax was to help the needy.

Soldier with Wife and Child SP3

Reservist SP4

1967, June 20 *Perf. 12½x13*

B9	SP3 7w + 3w rose lil & blk	65	30

The surtax was for veterans of the war in Viet Nam and their families.

1968, Aug. 1 Litho. *Perf. 13x12½*

B10	SP4 7w + 3w grn & blk	2.00	1.50

Issued for the fund-raising drive to arm reservists.

Flag — SP5

"Pin of Love" — SP6

1968, Nov. 1 Litho. Unwmk.

B11	SP5 7w + 3w dk bl & red	5.25	2.50

The surtax was for disaster relief.

1969, Feb. 15

B12	SP5 7w + 3w lt grn, dk bl & red	2.25	85

Surtax for military helicopter fund.

Flag Type of 1968 Redrawn
Zeros Omitted

1969, Nov. 1 Litho. *Perf. 13x12½*

B13	SP5 7w + 3w dk bl & red	1.65	75

The surtax was for the searchlight fund.

Perf. 13½x12½

1972, Aug. 1 Photo.

B14	SP6 10w + 5w bl & car	60	25

Disaster relief.

"Pin of Love" — SP7

Paddle and Ball — SP8

1973, July 1 Photo. *Perf. 12½x13½*

B15	SP7 10w + 5w multi	60	25

Disaster relief.

Perf. 13½x12½

1973, Aug. 1 Photo.

B16	SP8 10w + 5w multi	60	25

Surtax was for gymnasium to be built to commemorate the victory of the Korean women's table tennis team at the 32nd World Table Tennis Championships.

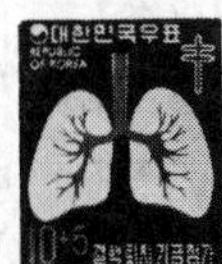

Lungs — SP9

1974, Nov. 1 *Perf. 13½x12½*

B17	SP9 10w + 5w grn & red	60	25

Surtax was for tuberculosis control.

No. 647 Surcharged 수해구제 +10

Perf. 13½x12½

1977, July 25 Photo.

B18	A328 20w + 10w grn	*2.50*	*2.00*

Surtax was for flood relief.

Seoul 1988 Olympic Games Series

'88 Seoul Games Emblem SP10

Korean Tiger, Mascot SP11

Track and Field — SP12

1985, Mar. 20 Photo. *Perf. 13x13½*

B19	SP10 70w + 30w blk & multi	35	30
B20	SP11 70w + 30w blk & multi	35	30
a.	Souvenir sheet of 2, #B19-20	75	

1985, June 10

B21	SP12 70w + 30w shown	35	30
B22	SP12 70w + 30w Rowing	35	30
a.	Souvenir sheet of 2, #B21-B22	75	

1985, Sept. 16

B23	SP12 70w + 30w Boxing	35	30
B24	SP12 70w + 30w Women's basketball	35	30
a.	Souvenir sheet of 2, #B23-B24	75	

1985, Nov. 1

B25	SP12 70w + 30w Canoeing	35	25
B26	SP12 70w + 30w Cycling	35	25
a.	Souvenir sheet of 2, #B25-B26	75	

Surtax for the 24th Summer Olympic Games, Sept. 17-Oct. 2, 1988.

Equestrian — SP18

Designs: No. B28, Fencing. No. B29, Soccer. No. B30, Gymnastic rings.

1986, Mar. 25 Photo. *Perf. 13x13½*

B27	SP18 70w + 30w multi	25	20
B28	SP18 70w + 30w multi	25	20
B29	SP18 70w + 30w multi	25	20
B30	SP18 70w + 30w multi	25	20

Souvenir Sheets

B31	Sheet of 4	4.25	1.25
a.	SP18 370w + 100w like #B27	1.05	32
B32	Sheet of 4	4.75	1.50
a.	SP18 400w + 100w like #B28	1.15	35
B33	Sheet of 4	5.00	1.50
a.	SP18 440w + 100w like #B29	1.25	38
B34	Sheet of 4	5.25	1.60
a.	SP18 470w + 100w like #B30	1.30	40

1986 Photo. *Perf. 13x13½*

B35	SP18 80w +50w Weight lifting	50	30
B36	SP18 80w +50w Team handball	50	30
B37	SP18 80w +50w Judo	50	30
B38	SP18 80w +50w Field hockey	50	30

Souvenir Sheets

B39	Sheet of 4	5.40	
a.	SP18 370w + 100w like #B35	1.35	1.00
B40	Sheet of 4	5.80	
a.	SP18 400w + 100w like #B36	1.45	1.10
B41	Sheet of 4	6.20	
a.	SP18 440w + 100w like #B37	1.55	1.25
B42	Sheet of 4	6.60	
a.	SP18 470w + 100w like #B38	1.65	1.35

Issue dates: Nos. B35-B36, B39-B40, Oct. 10; others, Nov. 1.

1987, May 25 Photo. *Perf. 13x13½*

B43	SP18 80w +50w Women's tennis	50	35
B44	SP18 80w +50w Wrestling	50	35
B45	SP18 80w +50w Dressage	50	35
B46	SP18 80w +50w Diving	50	35

1987, Oct. 10

B47	SP18 80w +50w Table Tennis	42	32
B48	SP18 80w +50w Men's shooting	42	32
B49	SP18 80w +50w Women's archery	42	32
B50	SP18 80w +50w Women's volleyball	42	32

1988, Mar. 5 Photo. *Perf. 13x13½*

B51	SP18 80w +20w Sailing	35	25
B52	SP18 80w +20w Taekwondo	35	25

1988, May 6 Photo. *Perf. 13½x13*

B53	SP18 80w +20w Torch relay, horiz.	35	25

Litho. & Engr.

B54	SP18 80w +20w Olympic Stadium, horiz.	35	25

See Greece No. 1627.

Souvenir Sheets of 2

B43a	SP18	80w +50w	1.00
B44a	SP18	80w +50w	1.00
B45a	SP18	80w +50w	1.00
B46a	SP18	80w +50w	1.00
B47a	SP18	80w +50w	85
B48a	SP18	80w +50w	85
B49a	SP18	80w +50w	85
B50a	SP18	80w +50w	85
B51a	SP18	80w +20w	70

B52a SP18 80w +20w 70
B53a SP18 80w +20w 70
B54a SP18 80w +20w 70

AIR POST STAMPS

Four-motor Plane and Globe — AP1

Perf. 11½x11

1947-50 Litho. Wmk. 257

C1 AP1 50wn car rose 1.75 1.50
a. Horiz. pair, imperf. btwn. 55.00

Perf. 11

C2 AP1 150wn blue ('49) 45 1.25
a. "KORFA" 14.00 10.00
C3 AP1 150wn grn ('50) 1.25

Nos. C2-C3 are redrawn. Issue date: 50wn, Oct. 1.

For surcharge see No. C5.

Plane and Korea Map — AP2

Douglas C-47 and Ship — AP3

1950, Jan. 1

C4 AP2 60wn light blue 2.75 4.50

No. C2 Surcharged with New Value and Wavy Lines in Black

1951, Oct. 10

C5 AP1 500wn on 150wn bl 65 1.00
a. "KORFA" 15.00 12.50
b. Surcharge inverted 100.00

Perf. 13x12½

1952, Oct. 15 Litho. Wmk. 257

C6 AP3 1200wn red brn 15 15
C7 AP3 1800wn lt bl 18 15
C8 AP3 4200wn purple 30 25

Nos. C6-C8 exist imperf.

1953, Apr. 5

C9 AP3 12h dp bl 15 30
C10 AP3 18h purple 25 30
C11 AP3 42h Prus grn 50 42

Douglas DC-7 over East Gate, Seoul — AP4

1954, June 15 *Perf. 12½*

C12 AP4 25h brown 20 15
C13 AP4 35h dp pink 30 20
C14 AP4 38h dk grn 45 20
C15 AP4 58h ultra 50 25
C16 AP4 71h dp bl 50 35
Nos. C12-C16 (5) 1.95 1.15

Nos. C12-C16 exist imperf.

Type of 1954 Redrawn

1956, July 20 Unwmk.

Laid Paper

C17 AP4 70h brt bluish grn 50 60
C18 AP4 110h brown 85 1.00
C19 AP4 205h magenta 1.00 1.00

Nos. C18-C19 are found on horizontally and vertically laid paper.

1957, July Wmk. 312 *Perf. 12½*

Granite Paper

C20 AP4 70h brt bluish grn 50 50
C21 AP4 110h brown 75 65
C22 AP4 205h magenta 1.25 1.00

On the redrawn stamps, Nos. C17-C22, the lines of the entire design are lighter, and the colorless character at right end of bottom row has been redrawn as in illustration above No. 212D.

Catalogue values for unused stamps in this section, from this point to the end of the section, are for Never Hinged items.

Girl on Palace Balcony AP5

Designs: 100h, Suwon Castle. 200h, Songnyu Gate, Tuksu Palace. 400h, Kyunghoeru Pavilion.

Perf. 12½

1961, Dec. 1 Unwmk. Litho.

C23 AP5 50h lt bl & vio 1.00 20
C24 AP5 100h pale grn & sep 1.90 25
C25 AP5 200h pale grn & brn 3.75 50
C26 AP5 400h grn & pale bl 4.50 85

Values in Won; Same Designs; Underlined Zeros Added

1962-63

C27 AP5 5w lt bl & vio ('63) 4.00 15
C28 AP5 10w pale grn & sep 6.50 25
C29 AP5 20w pale grn & brn ('63) 8.50 50
C30 AP5 40w grn & pale bl ('63) 16.00 80

1964, May 10 Wmk. 317 *Perf. 12½*

Granite Paper

C32 AP5 10w pale grn & sep 1.50 25
C33 AP5 20w pale grn & brn 2.50 50
C34 AP5 40w pale bl & grn 4.00 1.00

1964, Oct. Unwmk. *Perf. 12½*

Designs: 39w, Girl on palace balcony. 64w, Suwon Castle. 78w, Songnyu Gate, Tuksu Palace. 112w, Kyunghoeru Pavilion.

Granite Paper

C35 AP5 39w vio bl & gray ol 90 25
C36 AP5 64w bl & grnsh gray 1.25 35
C37 AP5 78w grnsh bl & ultra 1.50 45
C38 AP5 112w bl & grn 2.25 65

World Map and Plane — AP6

Designs: 135w, Plane over eastern hemisphere. 145w, Plane over world map. 180w, Plane over world map.

1973, Dec. 30 Photo. *Perf. 13x12½*

C39 AP6 110w pink & multi 65 50
C40 AP6 135w yel grn & red 80 60
C41 AP6 145w lt bl & rose 90 65
C42 AP6 180w lil & yel 1.10 75

UPU Type of 1974

1974, Oct. 9 Photo. *Perf. 13*

C43 A480 110w bl & multi 85 50
a. Souvenir sheet of 2 1.75

Mt. Fuji, Korean Airlines Jet Type

1985, Dec. 18 Photo. *Perf. 13x13½*

C44 A878 370w brt bl, blk & red 1.05 32

North Korea

Stamps issued by the Korean People's Republic have not been listed because the US Treasury Department (Foreign Assets Control Section) has prohibited their purchase abroad and importation.

LAOS

LOCATION — In northwestern Indo-China
GOVT. — Republic
AREA — 89,320 sq. mi.
POP. — 3,460,000 (est. 1977)
CAPITAL — Vientiane

Before 1949, Laos was part of the French colony of Indo-China and used its stamps until 1951. The kingdom was replaced by the Lao Peoples Democratic Republic Dec. 2, 1975.

100 Cents = 1 Piaster
100 Cents = 1 Kip (1955)

Imperforates

Most Laos stamps exist imperforate in issued and trial colors, and also in small presentation sheets in issued colors.

Catalogue values for all unused stamps in this country are for Never Hinged items.

Boat on Mekong River — A1

King Sisavang-Vong A2

Laotian Woman A3

Designs: 50c, 60c, 70c, Luang Prabang. 1pi, 2pi, 3pi, 5pi, 10pi, Temple at Vientiane.

1951-52 Unwmk. Engr. *Perf. 13*

1 A1 10c dk grn & emer 15 15
2 A1 20c dk car & car 15 15
3 A1 30c ind & dp ultra 55 15
4 A3 30c ind & pur ('52) 15 15
5 A1 50c dark brown 15 15
6 A1 60c red & red org 15 15
7 A1 70c ultra & bl grn 15 15
8 A3 80c brt grn & dk bl green ('52) 15 15
9 A1 1pi dk pur & pur 20 18
10 A3 1.10pi dark plum & carmine ('52) 28 15
11 A2 1.50pi blk brn & vio brown 32 18
12 A3 1.90pi indigo & dp blue ('52) 45 35
13 A1 2pi dk grn & gray green 8.75 1.10
14 A1 3pi dk car & red 35 25
15 A3 3pi choc & black brown ('52) 70 32
16 A1 5pi ind & dp ultra 50 32
17 A1 10pi blk brn & vio brown 1.40 50
Nos. 1-17 (17) 14.55 4.55

A booklet containing 26 souvenir sheets was issued in 1952 on the anniversary of the first issue of Laos stamps. Each sheet contains a single stamp in the center (Nos. 1-17, C2-C4, J1-J6). Value $100.

See No. 223.

UPU Monument and King Sisavang-Vong — A4

1952, Dec. 7

18 A4 80c ind, blue & pur 25 22
19 A4 1pi dk car, car & org brown 25 22
20 A4 1.20pi dk pur, purple & ultra 25 22
21 A4 1.50pi dk grn, bl grn & dk brn 25 22
22 A4 1.90pi blk brn, vio brn & dk Prus grn 25 22
Nos. 18-22,C5-C6 (7) 5.25 3.90

Laos' admission to the UPU, May 13, 1952.

Court of Love — A5

1953, July 14

23 A5 4.50pi indigo & bl grn 42 40
24 A5 6pi gray & dark brn 60 40

Composite of Laotian Temples — A6

1954, Mar. 4

25 A6 2pi indigo & purple 17.00 12.00
26 A6 3pi blk brn & dk red 18.00 15.00

Accession of King Sisavang-Vong, 50th anniv. See No. C13.

Buddha Statue and Monks — A7

1956, May 24 Engr. *Perf. 13*

27 A7 2k reddish brown 1.40 1.00
28 A7 3k black 1.40 1.00
29 A7 5k chocolate 1.75 1.40
Nos. 27-29,C20-C21 (5) 24.55 19.40

2500th anniversary of birth of Buddha.

UN Emblem — A8

1956, Dec. 14 *Perf. 13½x13*

30	A8	1k black	30	24
31	A8	2k blue	42	42
32	A8	4k bright red	48	45
33	A8	6k purple	65	55
		Nos. 30-33,C22-C23 (6)	6.10	5.91

Admission of Laos to the UN, 1st anniv.

Khouy Player — A9

Khene Player — A10

Musical Instrument: 8k, Ranat.

1957, Mar. 25 **Unwmk.** *Perf. 13*

34	A9	2k multicolored	75	55
35	A10	4k multicolored	75	65
36	A9	8k org, bl & red brn	75	65
		Nos. 34-36,C24-C26 (6)	5.40	4.10

See No. 224.

Harvesting Rice — A11

Drying Rice — A12

1957, July 22 **Engr.** *Perf. 13*

37	A11	3k shown	50	35
38	A12	5k shown	65	40
39	A12	16k Winnowing rice	1.10	80
40	A11	26k Polishing rice	2.00	1.25

Elephants — A13

Various Elephants: 30c, 5k, 10k, 13k, vert.

1958, Mar. 17

41	A13	10c multi	16	15
42	A13	20c multi	16	15
43	A13	30c multi	16	15
44	A13	2k multi	16	15
45	A13	5k multi	60	50
46	A13	10k multi	65	60
47	A13	13k multi	1.00	80
		Nos. 41-47 (7)	2.89	2.50

For surcharge see No. B5.

Globe and Goddess — A14

UNESCO Building and Mother with Children — A15

Designs: 70c, UNESCO building, globe and mother with children. 1k, UNESCO building and Eiffel tower.

1958, Nov. 3 **Engr.** *Perf. 13*

48	A14	50c multi	15	15
49	A15	60c emer, vio & maroon	15	15
50	A15	70c ultra, rose red & brn	15	15
51	A14	1k ol bis, cl & grnsh bl	15	15
		Set value	40	30

Opening of UNESCO Headquarters in Paris, Nov. 3.

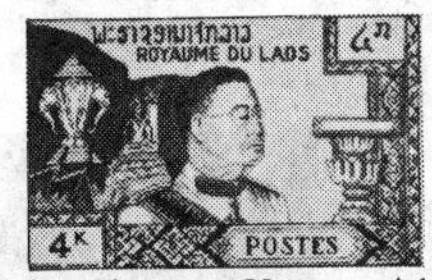
King Sisavang-Vong — A16

1959, Sept. 16 **Unwmk.**

52	A16	4k rose claret	15	15
53	A16	6.50k orange red	15	15
54	A16	9k bright pink	15	15
55	A16	13k green	15	15

For surcharges see Nos. 112-113, B4.

Dancers A17

Student and Torch of Learning — A18

Portal of Wat Phou, Pakse — A19

Education and Fine Arts: 3k, Globe, key of knowledge and girl student. 5k, Dancers and temple.

1959, Oct. 1 **Engr.** *Perf. 13*

56	A17	1k vio blk, ol & bl	15	15
57	A18	2k maroon & black	15	15
58	A17	3k slate grn & vio	15	15
59	A18	5k rose vio, yel & brt grn	20	20
		Set value	50	48

1959, Nov. 2 **Unwmk.** *Perf. 13*

Historic Monuments: 1.50k, That Inghang, Savannakhet, horiz. 2.50k, Phou Temple, Pakse, horiz. 7k, That Luang, Vientiane. 11k, That Luang, Vientiane, horiz. 12.50k, Phousi, Luang Prabang.

60	A19	50c sep, grn & org	15	15
61	A19	1.50k multi	15	15
62	A19	2.50k pur, vio bl & ol	15	15
63	A19	7k vio, olive & cl	15	15
64	A19	11k brn, car & grn	15	15
65	A19	12.50k bl, vio & bis	15	15
		Set value	42	42

Funeral Urn and Monks A20

King Sisavang-Vong A21

Designs: 6.50k, Urn under canopy. 9k, Catafalque on 7-headed dragon carriage.

1961, Apr. 29 **Engr.** *Perf. 13*

66	A20	4k black, bis & org	16	16
67	A20	6.50k black & bister	16	16
68	A20	9k black & bister	16	16
69	A21	25k black	42	42

Issued in memory of King Sisavang-Vong (1885-1959) and to commemorate the funeral, Apr. 23-29, 1961.

King Savang Vatthana — A22

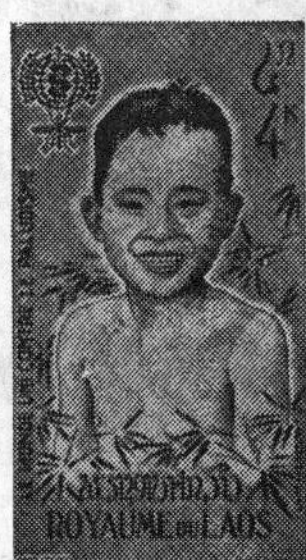
Boy and Malaria Eradication Emblem — A23

1962, Apr. 16 *Perf. 13*

Portrait in Brown and Carmine

70	A22	1k ultramarine	15	15
71	A22	2k lilac rose	15	15
72	A22	5k greenish blue	15	15
73	A22	10k olive	22	22
		Set value	45	45

1962, July 19 **Engr.**

Designs: 9k, Girl. 10k, Malaria eradication emblem.

74	A23	4k bluish grn, blk & buff	15	15
75	A23	9k lt bl, blk & lt brn	16	15
76	A23	10k ol, bis & rose red	30	25
		Set value	52	45

WHO drive to eradicate malaria. A souvenir sheet exists.

Stamp Day — A24

Royal Messenger — A25

Designs: 50c, Modern mail service (truck, train, plane). 1k, Ancient mail service (messenger on elephant).

1962, Nov. 15 **Unwmk.** *Perf. 13*

77	A24	50c multi	15	15
78	A24	70c multi	15	15
79	A25	1k dp cl, grn & blk	16	16
80	A25	1.50k multi	16	16

Souvenir sheets exist. One contains the 50c and 70c; the other, the 1k and 1.50k. The sheets exist both perf. and imperf.

Fishermen with Nets — A26

Threshing Rice — A27

Designs: 5k, Plowing and planting in rice paddy. 9k, Woman with infant harvesting rice.

1963, Mar. 21 *Perf. 13*

81	A26	1k grn, bister & pur	15	15
82	A27	4k bister, bl & grn	15	15
83	A26	5k grn, bis & indigo	15	15
84	A27	9k grn, vio bl & ocher	20	20
a.		Min. sheet of 4, #81-84, imperf.	2.00	1.75
		Set value	50	50

FAO "Freedom from Hunger" campaign.

Queen Khamphouy Handing out Gifts — A28

1963, Oct. 10 **Engr.**

85	A28	4k brn, dp car & blue	15	15
86	A28	6k grn, red, yel & bl	15	15
87	A28	10k bl, dp car & dk brn	16	16
a.		Miniature sheet of 3, #85-87	1.25	1.10

Centenary of the International Red Cross.

Man Holding UN Emblem A29

1963, Dec. 10 Unwmk. *Perf. 13*

88 A29 4k dk bl, dp org & vio brn 25 15

15th anniv. of the Universal Declaration of Human Rights.

Temple of That Luang, Map of Nubia and Ramses II — A30

1964, Mar. 8 Engr.

89	A30	4k multicolored	15	15
90	A30	6k multicolored	15	15
91	A30	10k multicolored	16	16
a.		Miniature sheet of 3, #89-91	1.00	90

UNESCO world campaign to save historic monuments in Nubia. No. 91a sold for 25k.

Ceremonial Chalice A31

Designs: 15k, Buddha. 20k, Soldier leading people through Mekong River Valley. 40k, Royal Palace, Luang Prabang.

1964, July 30 Unwmk. *Perf. 13*

92	A31	10k multicolored	15	15
93	A31	15k multicolored	15	15
94	A31	20k multicolored	20	16
95	A31	40k multicolored	35	30
a.		Miniature sheet of 4, #92-95	2.00	1.75

"Neutral and Constitutional Laos." When the stamps are arranged in a block of four with 40k and 15k in first row and 10k and 20k in second row, the map of Laos appears.

Prince Vet and Wife Mathie — A32

Lao Women — A33

Scenes from Buddhist Legend of Phra Vet Sandone: 32k, God of the Skies sending his son to earth. 45k, Phaune's daughter with beggar husband. 55k, Beggar cornered by guard and dogs.

1964, Nov. 17 Photo. *Perf. 13x12½*

96	A32	10k multicolored	18	18
97	A32	32k multicolored	22	22
98	A32	45k multicolored	35	35
99	A32	55k multicolored	45	45
a.		Miniature sheet of 4	2.25	2.00

No. 99a contains 4 imperf. stamps similar to Nos. 96-99.

1964, Dec. 15 Engr. *Perf. 13*

100 A33 25k blk, org brn & pale ol 22 22

See Nos. C43-C45, C45a.

Butterflies A34

1965, Mar. 13 Unwmk. *Perf. 13*

Size: 36x36mm

101	A34	10k Cethosia biblis	38	16
102	A34	25k Precis cebrene	42	25

Size: 48x27mm

103 A34 40k Dysphania militaris 70 38

See No. C46.

Teacher and School, American Aid — A35

Designs: 25k, Woman at Wattay Airport, French aid, horiz. 45k, Woman bathing child and food basket, Japanese aid. 55k, Musicians broadcasting, British aid, horiz.

1965, Mar. 30 Engr. *Perf. 13*

104	A35	25k bl grn, brn & car rose	15	15
105	A35	45k ol grn & brn	30	30
106	A35	55k brt bl & bis	35	35
107	A35	75k multicolored	45	45

Issued to publicize foreign aid to Laos.

Hophabang Temple A36

1965, Apr. 23 Unwmk. *Perf. 13*

108 A36 10k multicolored 25 16

Telewriter, Map of Laos and Globe A37

Designs: 30k, Communication by satellite and map of Laos. 50k, Globe, map of Laos and radio.

1965, June 15 Engr. *Perf. 13*

109	A37	5k vio bl, brn & red lil	15	15
110	A37	30k bl, org brn & sl grn	22	20
111	A37	50k crim, lt bl & bis	35	30
a.		Miniature sheet of 3, #109-111	2.75	2.50

ITU, centenary.

Nos. 52-53 Surcharged in Dark Blue with New Value and Bars

1965, July 5 Unwmk. *Perf. 13*

112	A16	1k on 4k rose claret	15	15
113	A16	5k on 6.50k org red	16	15
		Set value		16

Mother and Child, UNICEF and WHO Emblems — A38

Map of Laos and UN Emblem — A39

1965, Sept. 1 Engr. *Perf. 13*

114	A38	35k lt ultra & dk red	50	25
a.		Miniature sheet	3.00	1.75

Mother and Child Protection movement, 6th anniv.

1965, Nov. 3 *Perf. 12½x13*

115	A39	5k emer, gray & vio bl	15	15
116	A39	25k lil rose, gray & vio bl	16	15
117	A39	40k bl, gray & vio bl	25	25

UN, 20th anniv. Although first day covers were canceled "Oct. 24," the actual day of issue is reported to have been Nov. 3.

Tikhy (Hockey) A40

Pastimes: 10k, Two bulls fighting. 25k, Canoe race. 50k, Rocket festival.

1965, Dec. 23 Engr. *Perf. 13*

118	A40	10k org, brn & gray	15	15
119	A40	20k grn, ver & dk bl	16	16
120	A40	25k brt blue & multi	16	15
121	A40	50k orange & multi	35	35

Slaty-headed Parakeet A41

Birds: 15k, White-crested laughing thrush. 20k, Osprey. 45k, Bengal roller.

1966, Feb. 10 Engr. *Perf. 13*

122	A41	5k car rose, ol & brn	16	15
123	A41	15k bluish grn, brn & blk	22	15
124	A41	20k dl bl, sep & bis	30	15
125	A41	45k vio, Prus bl & sep	60	38
		Set value		70

WHO Headquarters, Geneva — A42

1966, May 3 Engr. *Perf. 13*

126	A42	10k bl grn & indigo	15	15
127	A42	25k car & dk green	20	16
128	A42	50k ultra & black	40	40
a.		Miniature sheet of 3, #126-128	2.25	2.00

Inauguration of the WHO Headquarters, Geneva. No. 128a sold for 150k.

Ordination of Buddhist Monk — A43

Folklore: 25k, Women building ceremonial sand hills. 30k, Procession of the Wax Pagoda, vert. 40k, Wrist-tying ceremony (3 men, 3 women), vert.

1966, May 20 *Perf. 13*

129	A43	10k multicolored	15	15
130	A43	25k multicolored	20	16
131	A43	30k multicolored	22	22
132	A43	40k multicolored	25	25

UNESCO Emblem A44

1966, July 7 Engr. *Perf. 13*

133	A44	20k ocher & gray	15	15
134	A44	30k brt blue & gray	20	16
135	A44	40k brt green & gray	25	16
136	A44	60k crimson & gray	38	20
a.		Miniature sheet, #133-136	3.25	3.25

UNESCO, 20th anniv. No. 136a sold for 250k.

Addressed Envelope Carrier Pigeon, Globe and Hand with Quill Pen — A45

1966, Sept. 7 Engr. *Perf. 13*

137	A45	5k red, brn & bl	15	15
138	A45	20k bl grn, blk & lil	16	15
139	A45	40k bl, red brn & dk ol bister	22	20
140	A45	45k brt rose lil, bl grn & black	25	22
a.		Miniature sheet #137-140	2.00	2.00

Intl. Letter Writing Week, Oct. 6-12. No. 140a sold for 250k.

Sculpture from Siprapouthbat Temple — A46

Sculptures: 20k, from Visoun Temple. 50k, from Xiengthong Temple. 70k, from Visoun Temple.

1967, Feb. 21 Engr. *Perf. 12½x13*

141	A46	5k olive grn & grn	15	15
142	A46	20k brn ol & gray bl	15	15
143	A46	50k dk brn & dp cl	20	20
144	A46	70k dk brn & dk mag	28	28
		Set value	65	65

General Post Office A47

1967, Apr. 6 Engr. Perf. 13

145 A47 25k brn, grn & vio brn 15 15
146 A47 50k ind, brt blue & grn 25 20
147 A47 70k dk red, grn & brn 35 25

Inauguration of the new Post and Telegraph Headquarters.

Snakehead A48

Fish: 35k, Giant catfish. 45k, Spiny eel. 60k, Knifefish.

1967, June 8 Engr. Perf. 13x12½

148 A48 20k dl bl, bis & blk 15 15
149 A48 35k aqua, bis & gray 22 15
150 A48 45k pale grn, bis & ol brn 38 18
151 A48 60k sl grn, bis & blk 42 20

Drumstick Tree Flower — A49

Blossoms: 55k, Turmeric. 75k, Peacock flower. 80k, Pagoda tree.

1967, Aug. 10 Engr. Perf. 12½x13

152 A49 30k red lil, yel & grn 15 15
153 A49 55k org, mag & lt grn 40 20
154 A49 75k bl, red & lt grn 42 20
155 A49 80k brt grn, mag & yel 55 28

Banded Krait — A50

Reptiles: 40k, Marsh crocodile. 100k, Malayan moccasin. 200k, Water monitor.

1967, Dec. 7 Engr. Perf. 13

156 A50 5k emer, ind & yel 20 15
157 A50 40k sep, lt grn & yel 25 15
158 A50 100k lt grn, brn & ocher 55 35
159 A50 200k grn, blk & bister 80 80

Human Rights Flame — A51

1968, Feb. 8 Engr. Perf. 13

160 A51 20k brt grn, red & grn 15 15
161 A51 30k brn, red & grn 20 16
162 A51 50k brt bl, red & grn 38 28
a. Souv. sheet of 3, #160-162 1.50 1.50

Intl. Human Rights Year. No. 162a sold for 250k.

WHO Emblem — A52

1968, July 5 Engr. Perf. 12½x13

163 A52 15k rose vio, ver & ocher 15 15
164 A52 30k brt bl, brt grn & ocher 15 15
165 A52 70k ver, plum & ocher 35 15
166 A52 110k brn, brt rose lil & ocher 55 38
167 A52 250k brt grn, brt bl & ocher 1.60 70
a. Souv. sheet of 5, #163-167 4.50 3.50
Nos. 163-167 (5) 2.80 1.53

WHO, 20th anniv. No. 167a sold for 500k.

Parade and Memorial Arch — A53

Designs: 20k, Armored Corps with tanks. 60k, Three soldiers with Laotian flag.

1968, July 15 Perf. 13

168 A53 15k multicolored 15 15
169 A53 20k multicolored 15 15
170 A53 60k multicolored 30 16
Nos. 168-170,C52-C53 (5) 2.25 1.56

Laotian Army. For souvenir sheet see No. C53a.

Chrysochroa Mnizechi A54

Mangoes A55

Insects: 50k, Aristobia approximator. 90k, Eutaenia corbetti.

1968, Aug. 28 Engr. Perf. 13

171 A54 30k vio bl, grn & yel 22 15
172 A54 50k lil, blk & ocher 38 25
173 A54 90k bis, blk & org 55 40
Nos. 171-173,C54-C55 (5) 2.60 1.57

1968, Oct. 3 Engr. Perf. 13

Fruits: 50k, Tamarind. 180k, Jackfruit, horiz. 250k, Watermelon, horiz.

174 A55 20k ind, lt bl & emer 15 15
175 A55 50k lt bl, emer & brn 25 20
176 A55 180k sep, org & yel grn 70 60
177 A55 250k sep, bis & emer 1.00 70

Hurdling — A56

1968, Nov. 15 Engr. Perf. 13

178 A56 15k shown 15 15
179 A56 80k Tennis 50 22
180 A56 100k Soccer 60 30
181 A56 110k High jump 65 35

19th Olympic Games, Mexico City, Oct. 12-27.

Wedding of Kathanam and Nang Sida — A57

Design: 200k, Thao Khathanam battling the serpent Ngou Xouang and the giant bird Phanga Houng. Design from panels of the central gate of Ongtu Temple, Vientiane. Design of 150k is from east gate.

1969, Feb. 28 Photo. Perf. 12x13

182 A57 150k blk, gold & red 80 40
183 A57 200k blk, gold & red 1.20 60

Soukhib Ordered to Attack — A58

Scenes from Royal Ballet: 15k, Pharak pleading for Nang Sita. 20k, Thotsakan reviewing his troops. 30k, Nang Sita awaiting punishment. 40k, Pharam inspecting troops. 60k, Hanuman preparing to rescue Nang Sita.

1969 Photo. Perf. 14

184 A58 10k multicolored 15 15
185 A58 15k blue & multi 15 15
186 A58 20k lt bl & multi 15 15
187 A58 30k salmon & multi 16 15
188 A58 40k salmon & multi 20 16
189 A58 60k pink & multi 35 25
Nos. 184-189,C56-C57 (8) 3.81 2.53

For surcharges see Nos. B12-B17, CB1-CB2.

ILO Emblem and Basket Weavers at Vientiane Vocational Center A59

1969, May 7 Engr. Perf. 13

190 A59 30k claret & violet 20 15
191 A59 60k sl grn & vio brn 40 25

ILO, 50th anniv. See No. C58.

Chinese Pangolin — A60

1969, Nov. 6 Photo. Perf. 13x12

192 A60 15k multicolored 15 15
193 A60 30k multicolored 15 15
Nos. 192-193,C59-C61 (5) 1.14 1.08

That Luang, Luang Prabang A61

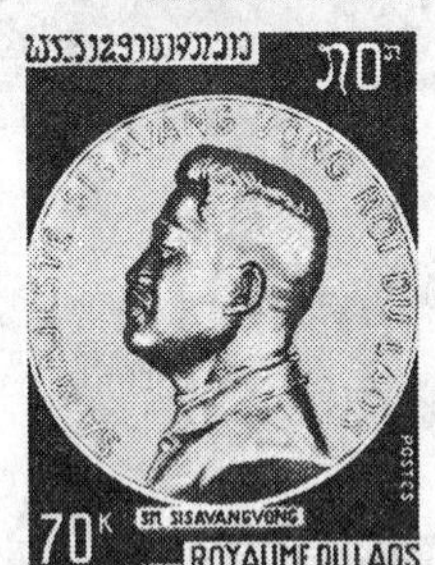
King Sisavang-Vong — A62

1969, Nov. 19 Engr. Perf. 13

194 A61 50k dk brn, bl & bis 35 15
195 A62 70k maroon & buff 45 22

Death of King Sisavang-Vong, 10th anniv. Nos. 194-195 are printed se-tenant with connecting label with dark green commemorative inscription.

Carved Capital from Wat Xiengthong A63

1970, Jan. 10 Photo. Perf. 12x13

196 A63 70k multicolored 45 45

See Nos. C65-C66.

Kongphene (Midday) Drum — A64

Designs: 55k, Kongthong (bronze) drum.

1970, Mar. 30 **Engr.** ***Perf. 13***

197 A64 30k bl gray, ol & org 38 15
198 A64 55k ocher, blk & yel grn 70 40

See No. C67.

Lenin Explaining Electrification Plan, by L. Shmatko — A65

1970, Apr. 22 **Litho.** ***Perf. 12½x12***

199 A65 30k blue & multi 16 15
200 A65 70k rose red & multi 45 28

Lenin (1870-1924), Russian communist leader.

Silk Weaver and EXPO Emblem A66

1970, July 7 **Engr.** ***Perf. 13***

201 A66 30k shown 15 15
202 A66 70k Woman winding thread 35 35

Laotian silk industry; EXPO '70 Intl. Exposition, Osaka, Japan, Mar. 15-Sept. 13. See No. C69.

Wild Boar — A67

1970, Sept. 7 **Engr.** ***Perf. 13***

203 A67 20k green & dp brn 15 15
204 A67 60k dp brn & ol bis 20 20
Set value 27 27

See Nos. C70-C71.

Buddha, UN Headquarters and Emblem — A68

1970, Oct. 24

Size: 22x36mm

205 A68 30k ultra, brn & rose red 20 15
206 A68 70k brt grn, sep & vio 38 22

UN, 25th anniv. See No. C75.

> ***Set Values***
> *A 15-cent minimum now applies to individual stamps and sets. Where the 15-cent minimum per stamp would increase the "value" of a set beyond retail, there is a "Set Value" notation giving the retail value of the set.*

Nakhanet, Symbol of Arts and Culture — A69

1971, Feb. 5

207 A69 70k shown 55 30
208 A69 85k Rahu swallowing the moon 65 40

See No. C76.

Silversmithing — A70

1971, Apr. 12 **Engr.** ***Perf. 13***

Size: 36x36mm

209 A70 30k shown 16 15
210 A70 50k Pottery 25 20

Size: 47x36mm

211 A70 70k Boat building 40 22

Laotian and African Children, UN Emblem — A71

Design: 60k, Women musicians, elephants and UN emblem.

1971, May 1 **Engr.** ***Perf. 13***

212 A71 30k lt grn, brn & blk 16 15
213 A71 60k yel, pur & dl red 38 25

Intl. year against racial discrimination.

Miss Rotary, Wat Ho Phrakeo A72

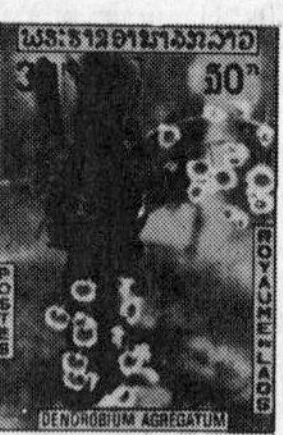

Dendrobium Aggregatum A73

Design: 30k, Monk on roof of That Luang and Rotary emblem, horiz.

1971, June 28 **Engr.** ***Perf. 13***

214 A72 30k purple & ocher 35 15
215 A72 70k gray ol, dk bl & rose 65 25

Rotary International, 50th anniversary.

Perf. 12½x13, 13x12½

1971, July 7 **Photo.**

Size: 26x36, 36x26mm

216 A73 30k shown 15 15
217 A73 50k Asocentrum ampullaceum, horiz. 20 15
218 A73 70k Trichoglottis fasciata, horiz. 30 15
Set value 36

See Nos. 230-232, C79, C89.

Palm Civet — A74

Animals: 40k, like 25k. 50k, Lesser Malay chevrotain. 85k, Sika deer.

1971, Sept. 16 **Engr.** ***Perf. 13***

219 A74 25k pur, dk bl & blk 15 15
220 A74 40k grn, ol bis & blk 15 15
221 A74 50k brt grn & ocher 15 15
222 A74 85k sl grn, grn & brn orange 20 20
Nos. 219-222,C83 (5) 1.45 1.05

Types of 1952-57 with Ornamental Panels and Inscriptions

Designs: 30k, Laotian woman. 40k, So player (like #C25). 50k, Rama (like #C19).

1971, Nov. 2

223 A3 30k brn vio & brn 15 15
a. Souvenir sheet of 3 1.75 1.75
224 A10 40k sep, blk & ver 15 15
225 AP7 50k ultra, blk & sal 20 20

20th anniv. of Laotian independent postal service. All stamps inscribed: "Vingtieme Anniversaire de la Philatelie Lao," "Postes" and "1971." No. 223a contains No. 223 and 60k and 85k in design of 30k, sold for 250k. See No. C84.

Children Learning to Read — A75

1972, Jan. 30 **Engr.** ***Perf. 13***

Size: 36x22mm

226 A75 30k shown 15 15
227 A75 70k Scribe writing on palm leaves 22 22

Intl. Book Year. See No. C87.

Nam Ngum Hydroelectric Dam, Monument and ECAFE Emblem — A76

1972, Mar. 28 **Engr.** ***Perf. 13***

228 A76 40k grn, ultra & lt brn 15 15
229 A76 80k grn, brn ol & dk bl 22 22

25th anniv. of the Economic Commission for Asia and the Far East (ECAFE), which helped build the Nam Ngum Hydroelectric Dam. See No. C88.

Orchid Type of 1971

Orchids: 40k, Rynchostylis giganterum. 60k, Paphiopedilum exul. 80k, Cattleya (horiz.).

1972, May 1 **Photo.** ***Perf. 13***

Size: 26x36mm, 36x26mm

230 A73 40k lt bl & multi 16 15
231 A73 60k multicolored 20 15
232 A73 80k lt bl & multi 30 15
Set value 32

Woman Carrying Water, UNICEF Emblem — A77

Children's drawings: 80k, Child learning bamboo-weaving, UNICEF emblem.

1972, July 20 **Engr.** ***Perf. 13***

233 A77 50k blue & multi 15 15
234 A77 80k brown & multi 22 22

25th anniv. (in 1971) of UNICEF. See No. C90.

Attopeu Costume, Religious Ceremony A78

Lion from Wat That Luang and Lions Emblem A79

Design: 90k, Phongsaly festival costume.

1973, Feb. 16 **Engr.** ***Perf. 13***

235 A78 40k mar & multi 15 15
236 A78 90k multicolored 16 16
Set value 24 24

See Nos. C101-C102.

1973, Mar. 30 **Engr.** ***Perf. 13***

237 A79 40k vio bl, rose cl & lil 16 15
238 A79 80k pur, org brn & yel 25 16

Lions International of Laos. See No. C103.

Dr. Hansen, Map of Laos, "Dok Hak" Flowers — A80

1973, June 28 **Engr.** ***Perf. 13***

239 A80 40k multicolored 16 15
240 A80 80k multicolored 35 20

Centenary of the discovery by Dr. Armauer G. Hansen of the Hansen bacillus, the cause of leprosy.

Wat Vixun, Monk Blessing Girl Scouts — A81

1973, Sept. 1 **Engr.** ***Perf. 13***

241	A81	70k	ocher & brown	22	22

25th anniv. of Laotian Scout Movement. See Nos. C106-C107.

INTERPOL Headquarters A82

1973, Dec. 22 **Engr.** ***Perf. 13x12½***

242	A82	40k	greenish bl	15	15
243	A82	80k	brown	22	22

50th anniv. of Intl. Criminal Police Org. See No. C110.

Boy Mailing Letter A83

Eranthemum Nervosum A84

1974, Apr. 30 **Engr.** ***Perf. 13***

244	A83	70k	bl, lt grn & ocher	15	15
245	A83	80k	lt grn, bl & ocher	20	20

UPU, cent. See Nos. C114-C115.

1974, May 31
Size: 26x36mm, 36x26mm

246	A84	30k	grn & vio	15	15
247	A84	50k	Water lilies, horiz.	15	15
248	A84	80k	Scheffler's kapokier, horiz.	15	20
			Set value	26	32

See No. C116.

Mekong River Ferry — A85

Design: 90k, Samlo (passenger tricycle; vert.).

1974, July 31 **Engr.** ***Perf. 13***

249	A85	25k	red brn & choc	15	15
250	A85	90k	brown ol & lt ol	16	16
			Set value	20	20

See No. C117.

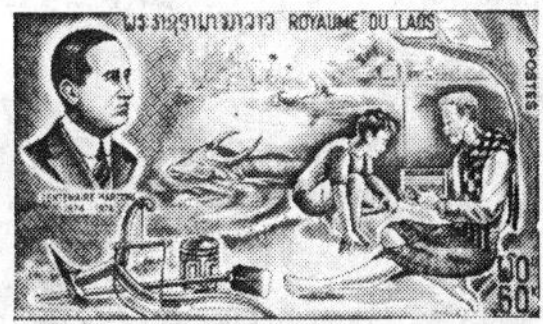

Marconi, Indigenous Transmission Methods, Transistor Radio — A86

1974, Aug. 28 **Engr.** ***Perf. 13***

251	A86	60k	multicolored	15	15
252	A86	90k	multicolored	16	16

Guglielmo Marconi (1874-1937), Italian electrical engineer and inventor. See No. C118.

Diastocera Wallichi Tonkinensis A87

1974, Oct. 23 **Engr.** ***Perf. 13***

253	A87	50k	shown	15	15
254	A87	90k	Macrochenus isabellunus	20	20
255	A87	100k	Purpuricenus malaccensis	22	22

See No. C119.

Temple, Houeisai, and Sapphire A88

1975, Feb. 12 **Engr.** ***Perf. 13x12½***

256	A88	100k	bl, brn & grn	22	22
257	A88	110k	Sapphire panning at Attopeu	30	30

King Sisavang-Vong, Princes Souvanna Phouma and Souphanou-Vong — A89

1975, Feb. 21 **Engr.** ***Perf. 13***

258	A89	80k	ol & multi	25	20
259	A89	300k	multicolored	60	45
260	A89	420k	multicolored	70	70

1st anniv. of Peace Treaty of Vientiane.

Fortuneteller Working on Forecast for New Year (Size of pair: 100x27mm)
A90 A91

New Year Riding Rabbit, and Tiger (Old Year) — A92

1975, Apr. 14 **Engr.** ***Perf. 13***

261	A90	40k	bister & red brn	15	15
262	A91	200k	bis, red brn & sl	35	25
263	A92	350k	blue & multi	62	50

New Year 1975, Year of the Rabbit. Nos. 261-262 printed se-tenant.

UN Emblem, "Equality" — A93

Design: 200k, IWY emblem, man and woman.

1975, June 19 **Engr.**

264	A93	100k	dl bl & vio bl	20	20
265	A93	200k	multi	40	40
a.			Miniature sheet of 2, #264-265	80	80

International Women's Year.

UPU, Cent. — A93a

Designs: 15k, Runner, rocket reaching orbit, vert. 30k, Docked Soyuz capsules, chariot, vert. 40k, Biplane, Concorde. 1000k, Apollo spacecraft in orbit. 1500k, Apollo spacecraft, astronaut, vert. No. 266G, Mail truck, Concorde. No. 266H, Stagecoach. No. 266I, Zeppelin, locomotive.

Perf. 13x14, 14x13
1975, July 7 **Litho.**

266	A93a	10k	multicolored		
266A	A93a	15k	multicolored		
266B	A93a	30k	multicolored		
266C	A93a	40k	multicolored		
266D	A93a	1000k	multicolored		
266E	A93a	1500k	multicolored		

Litho. & Embossed
Perf. 13½

266G	A93a	3000k	gold & multi		

Souvenir Sheets

266H	A93a	2500k	gold & multi		
266I	A93a	3000k	gold & multi		

Nos. 266D-266E, 266G-266I are airmail.

Apollo-Soyuz Mission — A93b

Designs: 125k, Astronauts, Thomas Stafford, Vance D. Brand, Donald Slayton. 150k, Cosmonauts Alexei Leonov, Valery Koubasov. 200k, Apollo-Soyuz link-up. 300k, Handshake in space. 450k, Preparation for re-entry. 700k, Apollo splashdown.

1975, July 7 **Litho.** ***Perf. 14x13***

267	A93b	125k	multicolored		
267A	A93b	150k	multicolored		
267B	A93b	200k	multicolored		
267C	A93b	300k	multicolored		
267D	A93b	450k	multicolored		
267E	A93b	700k	multicolored		

Nos. 267D-267E are airmail.

Scene from Vet Sandone Legend — A94

Designs: Scenes from Buddhist legend of Prince Vet Sandone.

1975, July 22 **Photo.** ***Perf. 13***

268	A94	80k	multicolored	22	16
268A	A94	110k	multicolored	30	22
268B	A94	120k	multicolored	35	25
268C	A94	130k	multicolored	38	28

American Revolution, Bicent. — A94a

Presidents: 10k, Washington, J. Adams, Jefferson, Madison. 15k, Monroe, J.Q. Adams, Jackson, Van Buren. 40k, Harrison, Tyler, Polk, Taylor. 1000k, Truman, Eisenhower, Kennedy. 1500k, L. Johnson, Nixon, Ford.

1975, July 30 **Litho.** ***Perf. 13½***

269	A94a	10k	multicolored		
269A	A94a	15k	multicolored		
269B	A94a	40k	multicolored		
269C	A94a	1000k	multicolored		
269D	A94a	1500k	multicolored		

Nos. 269C-269D are airmail. Stamps of similar design in denominations of 50k, 100k, 125k, 150k, and 200k exist but were not available in Laotian post offices.

Buddha, Stupas of Borobudur — A95

Design: 200k, Borobudur sculptures and UNESCO emblem.

1975, Aug. 20 **Engr.** ***Perf. 13***

270	A95	100k	ind & multi	18	15
271	A95	200k	multicolored	35	22
a.			Miniature sheet of 2, #270-271	1.25	90

UNESCO campaign to save Borobudur Temple, Java.

Coat of Arms of Republic A96

Thathiang Pagoda, Vientiane A97

1976, Dec. 2 Litho. *Perf. 14*

No.	Type	Value	Color	Unused	Used
272	A96	1k	blue & multi	15	15
273	A96	2k	rose & multi	15	15
274	A96	5k	brt grn & multi	15	15
275	A96	10k	lilac & multi	15	15
276	A96	200k	orange & multi	80	80
a.			Min. sheet of 5, #272-276	3.00	2.75
			Set value	1.00	1.00

1976, Dec. 18 *Perf. 13½*

Designs: 2k, 80k, 100k, Phonsi Pagoda, Luang Prabang. 30k, 300k, like 1k.

No.	Type	Value	Color	Unused	Used
277	A97	1k	multicolored	15	15
278	A97	2k	multicolored	15	15
279	A97	30k	multicolored	15	15
280	A97	80k	multicolored	25	25
281	A97	100k	multicolored	35	35
282	A97	300k	multicolored	1.00	1.00
			Nos. 277-282 (6)	2.05	2.05

Silversmith A98

Perf. 13x12½, 12½x13

1977, Apr. 1 Litho.

No.	Type	Value	Design	Unused	Used
283	A98	1k	shown	15	15
284	A98	2k	Weaver	15	15
285	A98	20k	Potter	15	15
286	A98	50k	Basket weaver, vert.	20	20
			Set value	40	40

Miniature sheets of 2 exist, perf. and imperf.

Cosmonauts A.A. Gubarev, G.M. Grechko — A99

Government Palace, Vientiane, Kremlin, Moscow — A100

Designs: 20k, 50k, Lenin speaking on Red Square. 60k, like 5k. 250k, like 100k.

Perf. 12x12½, 12½x12

1977, Oct. 25 Litho.

No.	Type	Value	Color	Unused	Used
287	A99	5k	multicolored	15	15
288	A99	20k	multicolored	15	15
289	A99	50k	multicolored	15	15
290	A99	60k	multicolored	15	15
291	A100	100k	multicolored	25	25
a.			Souv. sheet of 3, #288, 290-291	1.25	1.00
292	A100	250k	multicolored	70	70
a.			Souv. sheet of 3, #287, 289, 292	2.00	1.75
			Set value	1.30	1.30

60th anniv. of Russian October Revolution.

Natl. Arms — A101

1978, May 26 Litho. *Perf. 12½*

No.	Type	Value	Color	Unused	Used
293	A101	5k	dull org & blk	15	15
294	A101	10k	tan & black	15	15
295	A101	50k	brt pink & blk	15	15
296	A101	100k	yel grn & blk	25	25
297	A101	250k	violet & blk	65	65
			Set value	1.10	1.10

Soldiers with Flag — A102

Army Day: 40k, Fighters and burning house, horiz. 300k, Anti-aircraft battery.

Perf. 12½x12, 12x12½

1978, Sept. 15 Litho.

No.	Type	Value	Color	Unused	Used
298	A102	20k	multicolored	15	15
299	A102	40k	multicolored	15	15
300	A102	300k	multicolored	70	70
			Set value	80	80

Marchers with Banner — A103

1978, Dec. 2 Litho. *Perf. 11½*

No.	Type	Value	Design	Unused	Used
301	A103	20k	shown	15	15
302	A103	50k	Women with flag	15	15
303	A103	400k	Dancer	80	80
a.			Sheet of 3, #301-303, imperf.		

National Day. A second printing in slightly different colors and with rough perforation exists. Stamps in souvenir sheet are in reverse order.

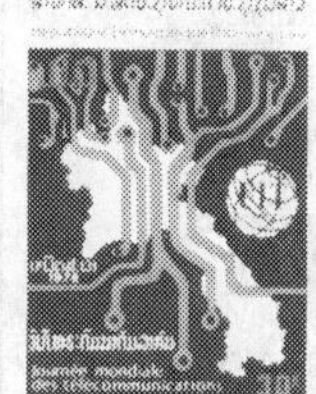

Electronic Tree, Map of Laos, ITU Emblem — A104

Design: 250k, Electronic tree, map of Laos and broadcast tower.

1979, Jan. 18 Litho. *Perf. 12½*

No.	Type	Value	Color	Unused	Used
304	A104	30k	multicolored	15	15
305	A104	250k	multicolored	55	55

World Telecommunications Day, 1978.

Woman Mailing Letter A105

Designs: 10k, 80k, Processing mail. 100k, like 5k.

1979, Jan. 18

No.	Type	Value	Color	Unused	Used
306	A105	5k	multicolored	15	15
307	A105	10k	multicolored	15	15
308	A105	80k	multicolored	20	20
309	A105	100k	multicolored	25	25
			Set value	50	50

Asian-Oceanic Postal Union, 15th anniv.

Intl. Year of the Child A106

1979 Litho. *Perf. 11*

Without Gum

No.	Type	Value	Design	Unused
310	A106	20k	Playing with ball, vert.	15
311	A106	50k	Studying	18
312	A106	100k	Playing musical instruments	35
313	A106	200k	Breast-feeding, vert.	70
314	A106	200k	Map, globe, vert.	70
315	A106	500k	Immunization, vert.	1.75
316	A106	600k	Girl dancing, vert.	2.25
			Nos. 310-316 (7)	6.08

Issue dates: Nos. 310-311, 313, 315, Aug. 1. Others, Dec. 25. Imperf. sheets of 4 containing Nos. 310-311, 313, 315 issued Aug. 1; imperf. sheet of 3 containing Nos. 312, 314, 316 issued on Dec. 25.

Traditional Modes of Transportation — A107

1979, Oct. 9 *Perf. 12½x13*

No.	Type	Value	Design	Unused
317	A107	5k	Elephants, buffalo, pirogues	15
318	A107	10k	Buffalo, carts	15
319	A107	70k	like 10k	25
320	A107	500k	like 5k	1.75

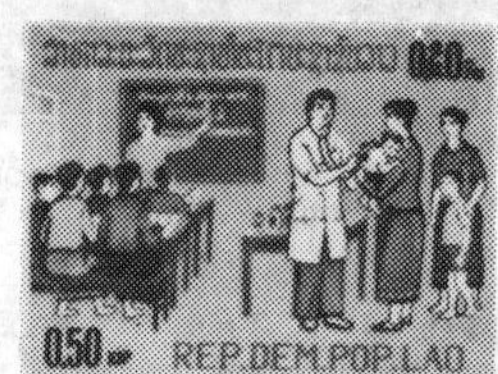

5th Anniv. of the Republic — A108

1980, May 30 *Perf. 11*

No.	Type	Value	Design	Unused
321	A108	30c	Agriculture, vert.	15
322	A108	50c	Education, health services	15
323	A108	1k	Three women, vert.	60
324	A108	2k	Hydroelectric energy	1.25

Imperf. souvenir sheet of 4 exists.

Lenin, 110th Birth Anniv. A109

1980, July 5 *Perf. 12x12½, 12½x12*

No.	Type	Value	Design	Unused
325	A109	1k	Lenin reading	15
326	A109	2k	Writing	30
327	A109	3k	Lenin, red flag, vert.	50
328	A109	4k	Orating, vert.	65

Imperf. souvenir sheet of 4 exists.

5th Anniv. of the Republic — A110

1980, Dec. 2 *Perf. 11*

Without Gum

No.	Type	Value	Design	Unused
329	A110	50c	Threshing rice	15
330	A110	1.60k	Logging	25
331	A110	4.60k	Veterinary medicine	60
332	A110	5.40k	Rice paddy	70

Imperf. souvenir sheet of 4 exists.

26th Communist Party (PCUS) Congress A111

1981, June 26 *Perf. 12x12½*

Without Gum

No.	Type	Value	Design	Unused
333	A111	60c	shown	15
334	A111	4.60k	Globe, broken chains	60
335	A111	5.40k	Grain, cracked bomb	70
a.			Souv. sheet of 3, Nos. 333-335, imperf.	4.00

No. 335a sold for 15k.

Souvenir Sheet

PHILATOKYO '81 — A112

1981, Sept. 20 *Perf. 13*

Without Gum

No.	Type	Value	Design	Unused
336	A112	10k	Pandas	2.25

1982 World Cup Soccer Championships, Spain — A113

Intl. Year of the Disabled — A114

1981, Oct. 15 *Perf. 12½*

Without Gum

No.	Type	Value	Design	Unused
337	A113	1k	Heading ball	22
338	A113	2k	Dribble	45
339	A113	3k	Kick	65
340	A113	4k	Goal, horiz.	85
341	A113	5k	Dribble, diff.	1.10
342	A113	6k	Kick, diff.	1.35
			Nos. 337-342 (6)	4.62

1981 *Perf. 13*

Without Gum

343 A114 3k Office worker 70
344 A114 5k Teacher 1.10
345 A114 12k Weaver, fishing net 2.75

Wildcats A115

1981 *Perf. 12½*

Without Gum

346 A115 10c Felis silvestris ornata 15
347 A115 20c Felis viverrinus 15
348 A115 30c Felis caracal 15
349 A115 40c Neofelis nebulosa 15
350 A115 50c Felis planiceps 15
351 A115 9k Felis chaus 2.50
Nos. 346-351 (6) 3.25

6th Anniv. of the Republic A116

1981, Dec. *Perf. 13*

Without Gum

352 A116 3k Satellite dish, flag 50
353 A116 4k Soldier, flag 65
354 A116 5k Map, flag, women, soldier 85

Indian Elephants A117

1982, Jan. 23 *Perf. 12½x13*

Without Gum

355 A117 1k Head 25
356 A117 2k Carrying log in trunk 50
357 A117 3k Transporting people 75
358 A117 4k In trap 1.00
359 A117 5k Adult and young 1.25
360 A117 5.50k Herd 1.40
Nos. 355-360 (6) 5.15

Laotian Wrestling — A118

Various moves.

1982, Jan. 30 *Perf. 13*

Without Gum

361 A118 50c multicolored 15
362 A118 1.20k multi, diff. 25
363 A118 2k multi, diff. 42
364 A118 2.50k multi, diff. 55
365 A118 4k multi, diff. 85
366 A118 5k multi, diff. 1.10
Nos. 361-366 (6) 3.32

Water Lilies A119

1982, Feb. 10 *Perf. 12½x13*

Without Gum

367 A119 30c Nymphaea zanzibariensis 15
368 A119 40c Nelumbo nucifera gaertn rose 15
369 A119 60c Nymphaea rosea 15
370 A119 3k Nymphaea nouchali 65
371 A119 4k Nymphaea white 85
372 A119 7k Nelumbo nucifera gaertn white 1.50
Nos. 367-372 (6) 3.45

Birds A120

1982, Mar. 9 *Perf. 13*

Without Gum

373 A120 50c Hirundo rustica, vert. 15
374 A120 1k Upupa epops, vert. 25
375 A120 2k Alcedo atthis, vert. 50
376 A120 3k Hypothymis azurea 75
377 A120 4k Motacilla cinerea 1.00
378 A120 10k Orthotomus sutorius 2.50
Nos. 373-378 (6) 5.15

A121

1982 World Cup Soccer Championships, Spain — A122

Various match scenes.

1982, Apr. 7

Without Gum

379 A121 1k multicolored 25
380 A121 2k multicolored 50
381 A121 3k multicolored 75
382 A121 4k multicolored 1.00
383 A121 5k multicolored 1.25
384 A121 6k multicolored 1.50
Nos. 379-384 (6) 5.25

Souvenir Sheet

385 A122 15k multicolored 5.75

Butterflies A123

1982, May 5 *Perf. 12½x13*

Without Gum

386 A123 1k Herona marathus 25
387 A123 2k Neptis paraka 50
388 A123 3k Euripus halitherses 75
389 A123 4k Lebadea martha 1.00

Size: 42x26mm

Perf. 12½

390 A123 5k Iton semamora 1.25

Size: 54x36½mm

Perf. 13x12½

391 A123 6k Elymnias hypermnestra 1.50
Nos. 386-391 (6) 5.25

Souvenir Sheet

PHILEXFRANCE '82 — A124

1982, June 9 *Perf. 13*

Without Gum

392 A124 10k Temple, Vientiane 3.00

River Vessels A125

1982, June 24

Without Gum

393 A125 50c Raft 15
394 A125 60c River punt 18
395 A125 1k Houseboat 28
396 A125 2k Passenger steamer 55
397 A125 3k Ferry 85
398 A125 8k Self-propelled barge 2.00
Nos. 393-398 (6) 4.01

Pagodas A126

1982, Aug. 2

Without Gum

399 A126 50c Chanh 15
400 A126 60c Inpeng 18
401 A126 1k Dong Mieng 28
402 A126 2k Ho Tay 55
403 A126 3k Ho Pha Keo 85
404 A126 8k Sisaket 2.25
Nos. 399-404 (6) 4.26

Dogs A127

1982, Oct. 13

Without Gum

405 A127 50c Poodle 15
406 A127 60c Samoyed 18
407 A127 1k Boston terrier 30
408 A127 2k Cairn terrier 60
409 A127 3k Chihuahua 90
410 A127 8k Bulldog 2.50
Nos. 405-410 (6) 4.63

World Food Day — A128

1982, Oct. 16

Without Gum

411 A128 7k Watering seedlings 2.00
412 A128 8k Planting rice 2.25

Classic Automobiles — A129

1982, Nov. 7

Without Gum

413 A129 50c 1925 Fiat 15
414 A129 60c 1925 Peugeot 18
415 A129 1k 1925 Berliet 30
416 A129 2k 1925 Ballot 60
417 A129 3k 1926 Renault 90
418 A129 8k 1925 Ford 2.50
Nos. 413-418 (6) 4.63

7th Anniv. of the Republic A130

1982, Dec. 2

Without Gum

419 A130 50c Souphanouvong, vert. 15
420 A130 1k Tractors, field, industry 25
421 A130 2k Cows, farm 50
422 A130 3k Truck, microwave dish 75
423 A130 4k Nurse, child, vert. 1.00
424 A130 5k Education 1.25
425 A130 6k Folk dancer, vert. 1.50
Nos. 419-425 (7) 5.40

For unused stamps, more recent issues are valued as never hinged, with the beginning point determined on a country-by-country basis. Notes to show the beginning points are prominently placed in the text.

Bulgarian Flag, Coat of Arms and George Dimitrov (1882-1949), Bulgarian Statesman — A131

1982, Dec. 15 *Perf. 12½*

Without Gum

426 A131 10k multicolored 2.75

Constitution of the USSR, 60th Anniv. — A132

1982, Dec. 30

Without Gum

427 A132 3k shown 90
428 A132 4k Maps 1.25

Souvenir Sheet

Perf. 13½x13

428A Sheet of 2 4.00
b. A132 5k like 3k 1.25
c. A132 10k like 4k 2.50

Nos. 428b-428c not inscribed in Laotian at top; buff and gold decorative margin contains the inscription.

1984 Summer Olympics, Los Angeles — A133

1983, Jan. 25 *Perf. 13*

Without Gum

429 A133 50c Hurdling 15
430 A133 1k Women's javelin 25
431 A133 2k Basketball 50
432 A133 3k Diving 75
433 A133 4k Gymnastics 1.00
434 A133 10k Weight lifting 2.50
Nos. 429-434 (6) 5.15

Souvenir Sheet

435 A133 15k Soccer 4.00

No. 435 contains one stamp 32x40mm.

Horses A134

Various breeds.

1983, Feb. 1

Without Gum

436 A134 50c multicolored 15
437 A134 1k multi, diff. 25
438 A134 2k multi, diff. 50
439 A134 3k multi, diff. 75
440 A134 4k multi, diff. 1.00
441 A134 10k multi, diff. 2.50
Nos. 436-441 (6) 5.15

A135

Raphael, 500th Birth Anniv. A136

Paintings (details) by Raphael: 50c, St. Catherine of Alexandra, Natl. Gallery, London. 1k, Adoration of the Kings (spectators), Vatican. 2k, Granduca Madonna, Pitti Gallery, Florence. 3k, St. George and the Dragon, The Louvre, Paris. 4k, Vision of Ezekiel, Pitti Gallery. No. 447, Adoration of the Kings (Holy Family), Vatican. No. 448, Coronation of the Virgin, Vatican.

1983, Mar. 9 *Perf. 12½x13*

Without Gum

442 A135 50c multicolored 15
443 A135 1k multicolored 28
444 A135 2k multicolored 55
445 A135 3k multicolored 85
446 A135 4k multicolored 1.10
447 A135 10k multicolored 2.75
Nos. 442-447 (6) 5.68

Souvenir Sheet

Perf. 13x13½

448 A136 10k multicolored 2.75

INTERCOSMOS Space Cooperation Program — A137

Cosmonaut and flags of USSR and participating nations.

1983, Apr. 12 *Perf. 12½*

449 A137 50c Czechoslovakia 15
450 A137 50c Poland 15
451 A137 1k East Germany 25
452 A137 1k Bulgaria 25
453 A137 2k Hungary 50
454 A137 3k Mongolia 80
455 A137 4k Romania 1.10
456 A137 6k Cuba 1.65
457 A137 10k France 2.50
Nos. 449-457 (9) 7.35

Souvenir Sheet

Perf. 13½x13

458 A137 10k Vietnam 3.00

No. 458 contains one stamp 32x40mm.

A138

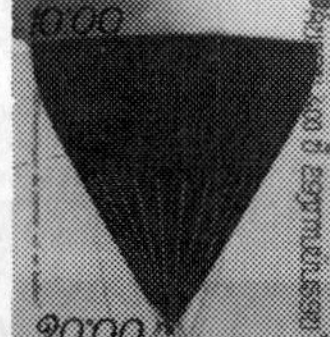

First Manned Balloon Flight, Bicent. — A139

Various balloons.

1983, May 4 *Perf. 12½x13*

459 A138 50c shown 15
460 A138 1k multi, diff. 25
461 A138 2k multi, diff. 50
462 A138 3k multi, diff. 75
463 A138 4k multi, diff. 1.00
464 A138 10k multi, diff. 2.50
Nos. 459-464 (6) 5.15

Souvenir Sheet

Perf. 13½x13

465 A139 10k shown 3.50

Souvenir Sheet

TEMBAL '83, Basel — A140

1983, May 21 *Perf. 13x13½*

Without Gum

466 A140 10k German Maybach 3.00

Flora A141

1983, June 10 *Perf. 13*

Without Gum

467 A141 1k Dendrobium sp. 25
468 A141 2k Aerides odoratum 50
469 A141 3k Dendrobium aggregatum 75
470 A141 4k Dendrobium 1.00
471 A141 5k Moschatum 1.25
472 A141 6k Dendrobium sp., diff. 1.50
Nos. 467-472 (6) 5.25

1984 Winter Olympics, Sarajevo A142

1983, July 2

Without Gum

473 A142 50c Downhill skiing 15
474 A142 1k Slalom 30
475 A142 2k Ice hockey 60
476 A142 3k Speed skating 90
477 A142 4k Ski jumping 1.25
478 A142 10k Luge 3.00
Nos. 473-478 (6) 6.20

Souvenir Sheet

Perf. 13x13½

479 A142 15k 2-Man bobsled 4.50

No. 479 contains one 40x32mm stamp.

Souvenir Sheet

BANGKOK '83 — A143

1983, Aug. 4 *Perf. 13½x13*

480 A143 10k Boats on river 2.50

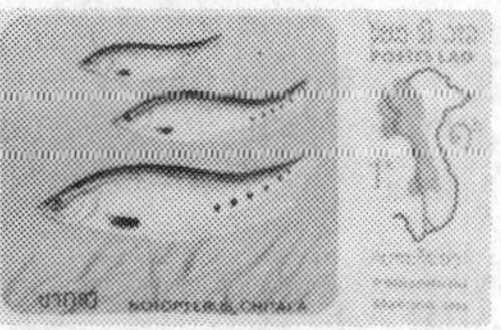

Mekong River Fish — A144

1983, Sept. 5 *Perf. 12½*

Without Gum

481 A144 1k Notopterus chitala 25
482 A144 2k Cyprinus carpio 50
483 A144 3k Pangasius sp. 75
484 A144 4k Catlocarpio siamensis 1.00
485 A144 5k Morulius sp. 1.25
486 A144 6k Tilapia nilotica 1.50
Nos. 481-486 (6) 5.25

Explorers and Their Ships — A145

1983, Oct. 8 *Perf. 13x12½*

Without Gum

487 A145 1k Victoria, Magellan 25
488 A145 2k Grand Hermine, Cartier 50
489 A145 3k Santa Maria, Columbus 75
490 A145 4k Cabral and caravel 1.00
491 A145 5k Endeavor, Capt. Cook 1.25
492 A145 6k Pourquoi-Pas, Charcot 1.50
Nos. 487-492 (6) 5.25

No. 492 incorrectly inscribed "CABOT".

Domestic Cats A146

1983, Nov. 9 *Perf. 12½x13*

Without Gum

493 A146 1k Tabby 25
494 A146 2k Long-haired Persian 50
495 A146 3k Siamese 75
496 A146 4k Burmese 1.00
497 A146 5k Persian 1.25
498 A146 6k Tortoiseshell 1.50
Nos. 493-498 (6) 5.25

Karl Marx (1818-1883) — A147

1983, Nov. 30 *Perf. 13*

Without Gum

499 A147 1k shown 25
500 A147 4k Marx, 3 flags, diff., vert. 1.00
501 A147 6k Marx, flag of Laos 1.50

8th Anniv. of the Republic — A148

1983, Dec. 2 *Perf. 12½x13, 13x12½*

Without Gum

502 A148 1k Elephant dragging log, vert. 28
503 A148 4k Oxen, pig 1.10
504 A148 6k Produce, vert. 1.75
a. Souv. sheet of 6 with gutter between 5.55

World Communications Year — A149

1983, Dec. 15 *Perf. 13*

505 A149 50c Teletype 15
506 A149 1k Telephone 25
507 A149 4k Television 1.00
508 A149 6k Satellite, dish receiver 1.50

1984 Winter Olympics, Sarajevo — A150

1984, Jan. 16

509 A150 50c Women's figure skating 15
510 A150 1k Speed skating 25
511 A150 2k Biathlon 50
512 A150 4k Luge 1.00
513 A150 5k Downhill skiing 1.25
514 A150 6k Ski jumping 1.50
515 A150 7k Slalom 1.75
Nos. 509-515 (7) 6.40

Souvenir Sheet

Perf. 13½x13

516 A150 10k Ice hockey 2.75

Nos. 509-511, 514-515 vert. No. 516 contains one stamp 32x40mm.

World Wildlife Fund A151

Panthera tigris.

1984, Feb. 1 *Perf. 13*

517 A151 25c Adult, vert. 15
518 A151 25c shown 15
519 A151 3k Nursing cubs 75
520 A151 4k Two cubs, vert. 1.00

1984 Summer Olympics, Los Angeles — A152

Gold medals awarded during previous games, and athletes. 50c, Athens 1896, women's diving. 1k, Paris 1900, women's volleyball. 2k, St. Louis 1904, running. 4k, London 1908. basketball. 5k, Stockholm 1912, judo. 6k, Antwerp 1920, soccer. 7k, Paris 1924, gymnastics. 10k, Moscow 1980, wrestling.

1984, Mar 26

521 A152 50c multicolored 15
522 A152 1k multicolored 25
523 A152 2k multicolored 50
524 A152 4k multicolored 1.00
525 A152 5k multicolored 1.25
526 A152 6k multicolored 1.50
527 A152 7k multicolored 1.75
Nos. 521-527 (7) 6.40

Souvenir Sheet

Perf. 12½

528 A152 10k multicolored 3.00

No. 528 contains one stamp 32x40mm.

Musical Instruments — A153

1984, Mar. 27 *Perf. 13*

529 A153 1k Tuned drums 25
530 A153 2k Xylophone 55
531 A153 3k Pair of drums 80
532 A153 4k Hand drum 1.10
533 A153 5k Barrel drum 1.40
534 A153 6k Pipes, string instrument 1.65
Nos. 529-534 (6) 5.75

Natl. Day — A154 Chess — A155

1984, Mar. 30 *Perf. 12½*

535 A154 60c Natl. flag 15
536 A154 1k Natl. arms 18
537 A154 2k like 1k 38

1984, Apr. 14 *Perf. 12½x13*

Illustrations of various medieval and Renaissance chess games.

538 A155 50c multi 15
539 A155 1k multi, diff. 28
540 A155 2k multi, red brn board, diff. 55
541 A155 2k multi, blk board, diff. 55
542 A155 3k multi, diff. 65
543 A155 4k multi, diff. 1.10
544 A155 8k multi, diff. 2.25
a. Souv. sheet of 6 with gutter between 5.55
Nos. 538-544 (7) 5.53

Souvenir Sheet

Perf. 13½x13

545 A155 10k Royal game, human chessmen 3.00

World Chess Federation, 60th anniv. No. 545 contains one stamp 32x40mm.

ESPANA '84, Madrid — A156

Woodland Flowers — A157

Paintings: 50c, Cardinal Nino de Guevara, by El Greco. 1k, Gaspar de Guzman, Duke of Olivares, on Horseback, by Velazquez. No. 548, The Annunciation, by Murillo. No. 549, Portrait of a Lady, by Francisco de Zurburan (1598-1664). 3k, The Family of Charles IV, by Goya. 4k, Two Harlequins, by Picasso. 8k, Abstract, by Miro. 10k, Burial of the Count of Orgaz, by El Greco.

1984, Apr. 27 *Perf. 12½*

546 A156 50c multicolored 15
547 A156 1k multicolored 25
548 A156 2k multicolored 50
549 A156 2k multicolored 50
550 A156 3k multicolored 75
551 A156 4k multicolored 1.00
552 A156 8k multicolored 2.00
Nos. 546-552 (7) 5.15

Souvenir Sheet

Perf. 13½x13

553 A156 10k multicolored 3.00

No. 553 contains one stamp 32x40mm.

1984, May 11 *Perf. 13*

554 A157 50c Adonis aestivalis 15
555 A157 1k Alpinia speciosa 25
556 A157 2k Aeschynanthus speciosus 50
557 A157 2k Cassia lechenaultiana 50
558 A157 3k Datura meteloides 75
559 A157 4k Quamoclit pennata 1.00
560 A157 8k Commelina benghalensis 2.00
Nos. 554-560 (7) 5.15

A158

19th UPU Congress, Hamburg — A159

Classic sport and race cars.

1984, June 19

561 A158 50c Nazzaro 15
562 A158 1k Daimler 25
563 A158 2k Delage 50
564 A158 2k Fiat S 57/14B 50
565 A158 3k Bugatti 75
566 A158 4k Itala 1.00
567 A158 8k Blitzen Benz 2.00
Nos. 561-567 (7) 5.15

Souvenir Sheet

Perf. 12½

568 A159 10k Winton Bullet 2.75

Paintings by Corregio (1494-1534) A160

Designs: 50c, Madonna and Child (Holy Family). 1k, Madonna and Child (spectators). No. 571, Madonna and Child (Holy Family, diff.). No. 572, Mystical Marriage of St. Catherine (Catherine, child, two women). 3k, The Four Saints. 4k, Noli Me Tangere. 8k, Christ Bids Farewell to the Virgin Mary. 10k, Madonna and Child, diff.

1984, June 26 *Perf. 13*

569 A160 50c multicolored 15
570 A160 1k multicolored 16
571 A160 2k multicolored 32
572 A160 2k multicolored 32
573 A160 3k multicolored 50
574 A160 4k multicolored 65
575 A160 8k multicolored 1.40
Nos. 569-575 (7) 3.50

Souvenir Sheet

Perf. 13½x13

576 A160 10k multicolored 4.00

No. 576 contains one stamp 32x40mm.

Space Exploration — A161

1984, July 12 *Perf. 13*

577 A161 50c Luna 1 15
578 A161 1k Luna 2 22
579 A161 2k Luna 3 45
580 A161 2k Sputnik 2, Kepler 45
581 A161 3k Lunokhod 2, Newton 65
582 A161 4k Luna 13, Jules Verne 90
583 A161 8k Space station, Copernicus 1.75
Nos. 577-583 (7) 4.57

Reptiles A162

1984, Aug. 20

584 A162 50c Malaclemys terrapin 15
585 A162 1k Bungarus fasciatus 25
586 A162 2k Python reticulatus 50
587 A162 2k Python molurus, vert. 50
588 A162 3k Gekko gecko 75
589 A162 4k Natrix subminiata 1.00
590 A162 8k Eublepharis macumiliaris 2.00
Nos. 584-590 (7) 5.15

Marsupials — A163

1984, Sept. 21

591 A163 50c Schoinobates volans 15
592 A163 1k Ornithorhynchus anatinus 25
593 A163 2k Sarcophilus harrisii 55
594 A163 2k Lasiorhinus latifrons 55
595 A163 3k Thylacinus cynocephalus 80
596 A163 4k Dasyurops maculatus 1.00
597 A163 8k Wallabia isabelinus 2.00
Nos. 591-597 (7) 5.30

Souvenir Sheet

Perf. 12½

598 A163 10k Macropus rufus 3.00

AUSIPEX '84, Melbourne. No. 598 contains one stamp 32x40mm.

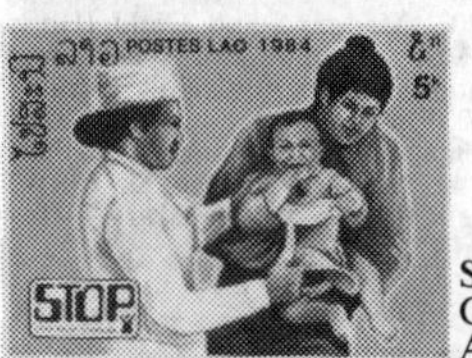

Stop Polio Campaign A164

1984, Sept. 29 ***Perf. 13***

599 A164 5k shown 1.25
600 A164 6k Vaccinating child 1.50

Art A165

1984, Oct. 26

601 A165 50c Dragon (hand rail) 15
602 A165 1k Capital 28
603 A165 2k Oval panel 55
604 A165 2k Deity 55
605 A165 3k Leaves 80
606 A165 4k Floral pattern 1.00
607 A165 8k Lotus flower (round panel) 2.00
Nos. 601-607 (7) 5.33

Nos. 601-604 and 607 vert.

9th Anniv. of the Republic A166

1984, Dec. 17

608 A166 1k River boats 25
609 A166 2k Aircraft 50
610 A166 4k Bridge building 1.00
611 A166 10k Surveying, construction 2.50

1986 World Cup Soccer Championships, Mexico — A167

Various match scenes and flag of Mexico.

1985, Jan. 18

612 A167 50c multicolored 15
613 A167 1k multi, diff. 25
614 A167 2k multi, diff. 50
615 A167 3k multi, diff. 75
616 A167 4k multi, diff. 1.00
617 A167 5k multi, diff. 1.25
618 A167 6k multi, diff. 1.50
Nos. 612-618 (7) 5.40

Souvenir Sheet

Perf. 12½

619 A167 10k multi, diff. 2.75

No. 619 contains one stamp 32x40mm.

Motorcycle, Cent. — A168

1985, Feb. 25 ***Perf. 12½***

620 A168 50c shown 15
621 A168 1k 1920 Gnome Rhone 25
622 A168 2k 1928 F.N. M67C 50
623 A168 3k 1930 Indian Chief 75
624 A168 4k 1914 Rudge Multi 1.00
625 A168 5k 1953 Honda Benly J 1.25
626 A168 6k 1938 CZ 1.50
Nos. 620-626 (7) 5.40

Mushrooms A169

Lenin, 115th Birth Anniv. A170

1985, Apr. 8 ***Perf. 13***

627 A169 50c Amanita muscaria 15
628 A169 1k Boletus edulis 25
629 A169 2k Coprinus comatus 50
630 A169 2k Amanita rubescens 50
631 A169 3k Xerocomus subtomentosus 75
632 A169 4k Lepiota procera 1.00
633 A169 8k Paxillus involutus 2.00
Nos. 627-633 (7) 5.15

End of World War II, 40th Anniv. A169a

Designs: 1k, Battle of Kursk. 2k, Red Army parade, Moscow. 4k, Battle of Stalingrad. 5k, Battle for Berlin. 6k, Victory parade through Brandenburg Gate.

1985, May **Litho.** ***Perf. 12½x12***

633A A169a 1k multicolored 28
633B A169a 2k multicolored 55
633C A169a 4k multicolored 1.10
633D A169a 5k multicolored 1.40
633E A169a 6k multicolored 1.65

1985, June 28 ***Perf. 12½***

634 A170 1k Reading Pravda, horiz. 30
635 A170 2k shown 60
636 A170 10k Addressing revolutionaries 2.00

Orchids — A171 Fauna — A172

1985, July 5 ***Perf. 13***

637 A171 50c Cattleya percivaliana 15
638 A171 1k Odontoglossum luteo-purpureum 25
639 A171 2k Cattleya lueddemanniana 50
640 A171 2k Maxillaria sanderiana 50
641 A171 3k Miltonia vexillaria 75
642 A171 4k Oncidium varicosum 1.00
643 A171 8k Cattleya dowiana aurea 2.00
Nos. 637-643 (7) 5.15

Souvenir Sheet

Perf. 13½x13

644 A171 10k Catasetum fimbriatum 3.00

ARGENTINA '85, Buenos Aires. No. 644 contains one stamp 32x40mm.

1985, Aug. 15 ***Perf. 13***

645 A172 2k Macaca mulatta 45
646 A172 3k Bos sauveli 65
647 A172 4k Hystrix leucura, horiz. 90
648 A172 5k Selenarctos thibotanus, horiz. 1.10
649 A172 10k Manis pentadactyla 2.25
Nos. 645-649 (5) 5.35

Apollo-Soyuz Flight, 10th Anniv. — A173

1985, Sept. 6

650 A173 50c Apollo launch pad, vert. 15
651 A173 1k Soyuz launch pad, vert. 25
652 A173 2k Apollo approaching Soyuz 50
653 A173 2k Soyuz approaching Apollo 50
654 A173 3k Apollo, astronauts 75
655 A173 4k Soyuz, cosmonauts 1.00
656 A173 8k Docked spacecrafts 2.00
Nos. 650-656 (7) 5.15

Aircraft A174

1985, Oct. 25

657 A174 50c Fiat 15
658 A174 1k Cant z.501 30
659 A174 2k MF-5 60
660 A174 3k Macchi Castoldi 90
661 A174 4k Anzani 1.20
662 A174 5k Ambrosini 1.50
663 A174 6k Piaggio 1.75
Nos. 657-663 (7) 6.40

Souvenir Sheet

Perf. 13x13½

664 A174 10k MF-4 6.50

ITALIA '85, Rome. No. 664 contains one stamp 40x32mm.

Miniature Sheet

Columbus's Fleet — A175

1985, Oct. 25 ***Perf. 13***

665 Sheet of 5 + 4 labels 3.00
a. A175 1k Pinta 18
b. A175 2k Nina 35
c. A175 3k Santa Maria 55
d. A175 4k Columbus 75
e. A175 5k Map of 1st voyage 90

ITALIA '85.

UN, 40th Anniv. — A176 Health — A177

1985, Oct.

666 A176 2k UN and natl. flag 65
667 A176 3k Coats of arms 1.00
668 A176 10k Map, globe 3.00

1985, Nov. 15

669 A177 1k Mother feeding child 25
670 A177 3k Immunization, horiz. 75
671 A177 4k Hospital care, horiz. 1.00
672 A177 10k Breast-feeding 2.50

10th Anniv. of the Republic A178

1985, Dec. 2

673 A178 3k shown 90
674 A178 10k multi, diff. 3.00

People's Revolutionary Party, 30th Anniv. — A179

1985, Dec. 30

675 A179 2k shown 70
676 A179 8k multi, diff. 2.75

1986 World Cup Soccer Championships, Mexico — A180

Flowering Plants — A181

Various match scenes.

1986, Jan. 20

677 A180 50c multicolored 15
678 A180 1k multi, diff. 22
679 A180 2k multi, diff. 45
680 A180 3k multi, diff. 60
681 A180 4k multi, diff. 80
682 A180 5k multi, diff. 1.00
683 A180 6k multi, diff. 1.25
Nos. 677-683 (7) 4.47

Souvenir Sheet

Perf. 13x13½

684 A180 10k multi, diff. 2.30

No. 684 contains one stamp 40x32mm.

27th Congress of the Communist Party of the Soviet Union A180a

1986, Jan. Litho. ***Perf. 12x12½***

684A A180a 4k Cosmonaut, spacecraft 85
684B A180a 20k Lenin 4.25

1986, Feb. 28 ***Perf. 13***

685 A181 50c Pelargonium grandiflorum 15
686 A181 1k Aquilegia vulgaris 24
687 A181 2k Fuchsia globosa 48
688 A181 3k Crocus aureus 70
689 A181 4k Althaea rosea 92
690 A181 5k Gladiolus purpureo 1.15
691 A181 6k Hyacinthus orientalis 1.40
Nos. 685-691 (7) 5.04

Butterflies A182

1986, Mar. 30

692 A182 50c Aporia hippia 15
693 A182 1k Euthalia irrubescens 20
694 A182 2k Japonica lutea 40
695 A182 3k Pratapa ctesia 60
696 A182 4k Kallina inachus 80
697 A182 5k Ixias pyrene 1.00
698 A182 6k Parantica sita 1.20
Nos. 692-698 (7) 4.35

A183

First Man in Space, 25th Anniv. — A184

Designs: 50c, Launch, Baikonur Space Center, vert. 1k, Molniya communications satellite, vert. 2k, Salyut space station. 3k, Yuri Gagarin, Sputnik 1 disengaging stage. 4k, Luna 3, the Moon, vert. 5k, Komarov on first space walk, vert. 6k, Luna 16 lifting off Moon, vert. 10k, Spacecrafts docking.

1986, Apr. 12

699 A183 50c multicolored 15
700 A183 1k multicolored 25
701 A183 2k multicolored 50
702 A183 3k multicolored 75
703 A183 4k multicolored 98
704 A183 5k multicolored 1.25
705 A183 6k multicolored 1.40
Nos. 699-705 (7) 5.28

Souvenir Sheet

Perf. 13x13½

706 A184 10k multicolored 3.00

Fauna — A185

AMERIPEX '86, Chicago — A186

Perf. 12½x13, 13x12½

1986, May 22

707 A185 50c Giraffa camelopardalis 15
708 A185 1k Panthera leo 20
709 A185 2k Loxodonta africana africana 42
710 A185 3k Macropus rufus 62
711 A185 4k Gymnobelideus leadbeateri 85
712 A185 5k Phoenicopterus ruber 1.05
713 A185 6k Ailuropoda melanoleucus 1.25
Nos. 707-713 (7) 4.54

Souvenir Sheet

Perf. 13½x13

714 A186 10k Bison 3.00

Nos. 707-712 vert.

Pheasants — A187

1986, June 29 ***Perf. 12½x13***

715 A187 50c Argusianus argus 15
716 A187 1k Cennaeus nycthemerus 24
717 A187 2k Phasianus colchicus 48
718 A187 3k Chrysolophus amherstiae 70
719 A187 4k Symaticus reevesii 92
720 A187 5k Chrysolophus pictus 1.15
721 A187 6k Syrmaticus soemmerringii 1.40
Nos. 715-721 (7) 5.04

Snakes — A188

Perf. 12½x13, 13x12½

1986, July 21

722 A188 50c Elaphe guttata 15
723 A188 1k Thalerophis richardi 20
724 A188 1k Lampropeltis doliata annulata 20
725 A188 2k Diadophis amabilis 40
726 A188 4k Boiga dendrophila 80
727 A188 5k Python molurus 1.00
728 A188 8k Naja naja 1.60
Nos. 722-728 (7) 4.35

Nos. 722-723 and 728 vert.

Halley's Comet — A189

1986, Aug. 22 ***Perf. 12½x13***

729 A189 50c Acropolis, Athens 15
730 A189 1k Bayeux Tapestry 24
731 A189 2k Edmond Halley 48
732 A189 3k Vega space probe 68
733 A189 4k Galileo 95
734 A189 5k Comet 1.20
735 A189 6k Giotto probe 1.90
Nos. 729-735 (7) 5.60

Souvenir Sheet

Perf. 13x13½

736 A189 10k Comet, diff. 3.00

Nos. 730-731, 732-733 and 734-735 printed se-tenant in continuous designs. Size of Nos. 730, 732 and 735: 46x25mm. Size of Nos. 731, 733-734: 23x25mm. No. 736 contains one stamp 40x32mm.

Dogs — A190 Cacti — A191

1986, Aug. 28 ***Perf. 13***

737 A190 50c Keeshond 15
738 A190 1k Elkhound 20
739 A190 2k Bernese 42
740 A190 3k Pointing griffon 62
741 A190 4k Sheep dog (border collie) 85
742 A190 5k Irish water spaniel 1.05
743 A190 6k Briard 1.25
Nos. 737-743 (7) 4.54

Souvenir Sheet

Perf. 13x13½

744 A190 10k Brittany spaniels 2.00

STOCKHOLMIA '86. Nos. 738-743 horiz. No. 744 contains one stamp 40x32mm.

1986, Sept. 28 ***Perf. 13***

Designs: 50c, Mammillaria matudae. 1k, Mammillaria theresae. 2k, Ariocarpus trigonus. 3k, Notocactus crassigibbus. 4k, Astrophytum asterias hybridum. 5k, Melocactus manzanus. 6k, Astrophytum ornatum hybridum.

745 A191 50c multicolored 15
746 A191 1k multicolored 20
747 A191 2k multicolored 42
748 A191 3k multicolored 62
749 A191 4k multicolored 85
750 A191 5k multicolored 1.05
751 A191 6k multicolored 1.25
Nos. 745-751 (7) 4.54

Intl. Peace Year — A192

UNESCO Programs in Laos — A193

1986, Oct. 24

752 A192 3k Natl. arms, dove, globe 68
753 A192 5k Dove, shattered bomb 1.10
754 A192 10k Emblem held aloft 2.20

1986, Nov. 4

755 A193 3k Vat Phu Champasak ruins 60
756 A193 4k Satellite dish, map, globe 80
757 A193 9k Laotians learning to read, horiz. 1.75

1988 Winter Olympics, Calgary — A194

1987, Jan. 14

758 A194 50c Speed skating 15
759 A194 1k Biathlon 20
760 A194 2k Pairs figure skating 40
761 A194 3k Luge 60
762 A194 4k 4-Man bobsled 80
763 A194 5k Ice hockey 1.00
764 A194 6k Ski jumping 1.20
Nos. 758-764 (7) 4.35

Souvenir Sheet

Perf. 13½x13

765 A194 10k Slalom 2.50

Nos. 758-760 vert. No. 765 contains one stamp 32x40mm.

1988 Summer Olympics, Seoul — A195

1987, Feb. 2 *Perf. 12½x13, 13x13½*

766 A195 50c Women's gymnastics 15
767 A195 1k Women's discus 22
768 A195 2k Running 45
769 A195 3k Equestrian 68
770 A195 4k Women's javelin 90
771 A195 5k High jump 1.10
772 A195 6k Wrestling 1.35
Nos. 766-772 (7) 4.85

Souvenir Sheet

Perf. 12½

773 A195 10k Runners leaving start 2.25

Nos. 766, 768, 770 and 772 vert. No. 773 contains one stamp 40x32mm.

Dogs A196

1987, Mar. 5 *Perf. 12½x13*

774 A196 50c Great Dane 15
775 A196 1k Labrador retriever 22
776 A196 2k St. Bernard 45
777 A196 3k Schippercke 68
778 A196 4k Alsatian (German shepherd) 90
779 A196 5k Beagle 1.10
780 A196 6k Spaniel 1.35
Nos. 774-780 (7) 4.85

Manned Space Flight, 30th Anniv. A197

1987, Apr. 12 *Perf. 13*

781 A197 50c Sputnik 1 15
782 A197 1k Sputnik 2 18
783 A197 2k Cosmos 87 35
784 A197 3k Cosmos 55
785 A197 4k Mars 75
786 A197 5k Luna 1 90
787 A197 9k Luna 3, vert. 1.65
Nos. 781-787 (7) 4.53

Packet Ships and Stampless Packet Letters — A198

Canada No. 282 A199

1987, May 12

788 A198 50c "Montreal" 15
789 A198 1k "Paid Montreal" 20
790 A198 2k "Paid" and "Montreal Nov 24" 40
791 A198 3k "Williamsbvrg" and "Forwarded" 60
792 A198 4k "Montreal Fe 18 1844" 80
793 A198 5k "Paid" and "Montreal Jy 10 1848" 1.00
794 A198 6k "Paid" and "Montreal Paid Ap 16 1861 Canada" 1.20
Nos. 788-794 (7) 4.35

Souvenir Sheet

Perf. 12½

795 A199 10k multicolored 2.50

CAPEX '87.

Orchids — A200

1987, Aug. 10 **Litho.** *Perf. 13*

796 A200 3k *Vanda teres* 15
796A A200 7k *Laeliocattleya* 16
796B A200 10k *Paphiopedilum hibrido* 22
796C A200 39k *Sobralia* 88
796D A200 44k *Paphiopedilum hibrido*, diff. 1.00
796E A200 47k *Paphiopedilum hibrido*, diff. 1.10
796F A200 50k *Cattleya trianaei* 1.15
Nos. 796-796F (7) 4.66

Souvenir Sheet

Perf. 12½

796G A200 95k *Vanda tricolor* 2.50

No. 796G contains one 32x40mm stamp.

Automobiles A201

1987, July 2 **Litho.** *Perf. 12½*

797 A201 50c Toyota 480 15
798 A201 1k Alfa 33 22
799 A201 2k Ford Fiesta 45
800 A201 3k Datsun 68
801 A201 4k Vauxhall Cavalier 90
802 A201 5k Renault 5 1.10
803 A201 6k Rover-800 1.35
Nos. 797-803 (7) 4.85

Miniature Sheet

Perf. 13

804 A201 10k Talbot 2.25

HAFNIA '87, Denmark A202

Various Indian elephants.

1987, Sept. 2 *Perf. 13*

805 A202 50c Adult, calf 15
806 A202 1k Two adults, calf 22
807 A202 2k Adult eating grass 45
808 A202 3k Adult, diff. 68
809 A202 4k Adult, calf drinking 90
810 A202 5k Adult, diff. 1.10
811 A202 6k Adult, vert. 1.35
Nos. 805-811 (7) 4.85

Souvenir Sheet

812 A202 10k Herd, diff. 2.50

No. 812 contains one stamp 40x32mm.

Horses — A203

Perf. 13x12½, 12½x13

1987, June 3 **Litho.**

813 A203 50c multicolored 15
814 A203 1k multi, diff. 28
815 A203 2k multi, diff. 55
816 A203 3k multi, diff. 85
817 A203 4k multi, diff. 1.15
818 A203 5k multi, diff. 1.40
819 A203 6k multi, diff. 1.70
Nos. 813-819 (7) 6.08

Nos. 814-819 vert.

Fish A204

Designs: 3k, Botia macracantha. 7k, Oxymocanthus longirostris. 10k, Adioryx caudimaculatus. 39k, Synchiropus splendidus. 44k, Cephalopolis miniatus. 47k, Dendrochirus zebra. 50k, Pomacantus semicirculatus.

1987, Oct. 14 **Litho.** *Perf. 13x12½*

820 A204 3k multicolored 15
821 A204 7k multicolored 16
822 A204 10k multicolored 22
823 A204 39k multicolored 88
824 A204 44k multicolored 1.00
825 A204 47k multicolored 1.05
826 A204 50k multicolored 1.15
Nos. 820-826 (7) 4.61

World Food Day A205

1987, Oct. 16 *Perf. 13*

827 A205 1k Tending crops 15
828 A205 3k Harvesting corn, vert. 15
829 A205 5k Harvesting wheat 15
830 A205 63k Youths, fish, vert. 1.45
831 A205 142k Tending pigs, chickens 3.25
Nos. 827-831 (5) 5.15

Cultivation of Rice in Mountainous Regions — A206

1987, Nov. 9 *Perf. 13*

832 A206 64k Tilling soil 1.50
833 A206 100k Rice paddy 2.30

October Revolution, Russia, 70th Anniv. A207

Paintings: 1k, Wounded soldier on battlefield. 2k, Mother and child. 4k, Storming the Winter Palace. 8k, Lenin and revolutionaries. 10k, Rebuilding Red Square.

1987, Nov. *Perf. 12x12½*

834 A207 1k multicolored 20
835 A207 2k multicolored 40
836 A207 4k multicolored 75
837 A207 8k multicolored 1.50
838 A207 10k multicolored 2.00
Nos. 834-838 (5) 4.85

Women Wearing Regional Costumes A208

1987, Dec. 2

839 A208 7k Mountain 16
840 A208 38k Urban 88
841 A208 144k Mountain, diff. 3.35

A209

1988 Winter Olympics, Calgary — A210

1988, Jan.10 *Perf. 13x12½*

842 A209 1k Bobsled 15
843 A209 4k Biathlon 15
844 A209 20k Skiing 48
845 A209 42k Ice hockey 1.00

846 A209 63k Speed skating 1.50
847 A209 70k Slalom 1.65
Nos. 842-847 (6) 4.93

Souvenir Sheet
Perf. 13

848 A210 95k Slalom, diff. 2.50

No. 848 contains one stamp 40x32mm.

ESSEN '88 — A211

Locomotives: 6k, Nonpareil, vert. 15k, Rocket, vert. 20k, Royal George. 25k, Trevithick. 30k, Novelty. 100k, Tom Thumb. 95k, Locomotion.

1988 ***Perf. 12½x13, 13x12½***
849 A211 6k multicolored 15
850 A211 15k multicolored 35
851 A211 20k multicolored 48
852 A211 25k multicolored 58
853 A211 30k multicolored 70
854 A211 100k multicolored 2.30
Nos. 849-854 (6) 4.56

Souvenir Sheet
Perf. 13

855 A211 95k multicolored 2.50

No. 855 contains one stamp 40x32mm.

Intl. Year of Shelter for the Homeless A212

1988 **Litho.** ***Perf. 13***
856 A212 1k Building frame of house 15
857 A212 27k Cutting lumber 62
858 A212 46k Completed house 1.15
859 A212 70k Community 1.75

Dinosaurs — A213

Perf. 13x12½, 12½x13
1988, Mar. 3 **Litho.**
860 A213 3k Tyrannosaurus 15
861 A213 7k Ceratosaurus nasicornis 16
862 A213 39k Iguanodon bernissartensis 88
863 A213 44k Scolosaurus 1.00
864 A213 47k Phororhacus 1.10
865 A213 50k Trachodon 1.15
Nos. 860-865 (6) 4.44

Souvenir Sheet
Perf. 12½

866 A213 95k Pteranodon 2.50

JUVALUX '88. Nos. 861-864 vert.
Identifications on Nos. 860 and No. 865 are switched.
No. 866 contains one 40x32mm stamp.

WHO, 40th Anniv. A214

1988, Apr. 8 ***Perf. 12½***
867 A214 5k Students, teacher 15
868 A214 27k Pest control 62
869 A214 164k Public water supply, vert. 3.75

Flowers — A215   Birds — A216

1988 ***Perf. 13x12½***
870 A215 8k *Plumieria rubra* 18
871 A215 9k *Althaea rosea* 22
872 A215 15k *Ixora coccinea* 40
873 A215 33k *Cassia fistula* 78
874 A215 64k *Dahlia coccinea* (pink) 1.50
875 A215 69k *Dahlia coccinea* (yellow) 1.65
Nos. 870-875 (6) 4.73

Souvenir Sheet
Perf. 13

876 A215 95k Plumieria, Althaea, Ixora 2.50

FINLANDIA '88. No. 876 contains one 32x40mm stamp.

1988 ***Perf. 13***
877 A216 6k *Pelargopsis capensis* 15
878 A216 10k *Coturnix japonica* 24
879 A216 13k *Psittacula roseata* 32
880 A216 44k *Treron bicincta* 1.05
881 A216 63k *Pycnonotus melanicterus* 1.50
882 A216 64k *Ducula badia* 1.55
Nos. 877-882 (6) 4.81

1988 Summer Olympics, Seoul — A217

1988 ***Perf. 12½x12***
883 A217 2k Javelin 15
884 A217 5k Long jump 15
885 A217 10k Horizontal bar 24
886 A217 12k Canoeing 30
887 A217 38k Balance beam 90
888 A217 46k Fencing 1.10
889 A217 100k Wrestling 2.35
Nos. 883-889 (7) 5.19

Souvenir Sheet
Perf. 13

889A A217 95k Horizontal bar, diff. 2.25

No. 889A contains one 40x32mm stamp.

Decorative Stencils — A218

1988 ***Perf. 13***
890 A218 1k Scarf 15
891 A218 2k Pagoda entrance, vert. 15
892 A218 3k Pagoda wall, vert. 15
893 A218 25k Pagoda pillar 60
894 A218 163k Skirt 4.00
Nos. 890-894 (5) 5.05

Completion of the 5-Year Plan (1981-85) — A219

1988 **Litho.** ***Perf. 13***
895 A219 20k Health care 45
896 A219 40k Literacy 88
897 A219 50k Irrigation 1.10
898 A219 100k Communication, transport 2.20

Intl. Red Cross and Red Crescent Organizations, 125th Annivs. — A220

Designs: 4k, Dove, 3 stylized figures representing mankind, vert. 52k, Giving aid to the handicapped, vert. 144k, Child immunization.

1988
899 A220 4k multi 15
900 A220 52k multi 1.15
901 A220 144k multi 3.20

Chess Champions — A220a

1988 **Litho.** ***Perf. 13***
901A A220a 1k R. Segura 15
901B A220a 2k Adolph Anderssen 15
901C A220a 3k P. Morphy 15
901D A220a 6k W. Steinitz 15
901E A220a 7k E. Lasker 16
901F A220a 12k J.R. Capablanca 28
901G A220a 172k A. Alekhine 3.90
Nos. 901A-901G (7) 4.94

Nos. 901C is incorrectly inscribed "Murphy."

1990 World Cup Soccer Championships, Italy — A221

Various plays.

1989 ***Perf. 13x12½***
902 A221 10k multi 22
903 A221 15k multi, diff. 35
904 A221 20k multi, diff. 45
905 A221 25k multi, diff. 58
906 A221 45k multi, diff. 1.00
907 A221 105k multi, diff. 2.40
Nos. 902-907 (6) 5.00

Souvenir Sheet
Perf. 13

907A A221 95k multi, diff. 2.25

No. 907A contains one 40x32mm stamp.

INDIA '89 A222

Cats.

1989, Jan. 7 ***Perf. 12½***
908 A222 5k multi 15
909 A222 6k multi, diff. 15
910 A222 10k multi, diff. 22
911 A222 20k multi, diff. 45
912 A222 50k multi, diff. 1.15
913 A222 172k multi, diff. 3.90
Nos. 908-913 (6) 6.02

Souvenir Sheet
Perf. 13

914 A222 95k multi, diff. 2.25

No. 914 contains one 32x40mm stamp.

1992 Winter Olympics, Albertville — A223

Various figure skaters.

1989, May 1 ***Perf. 13***
915 A223 9k multi, vert. 20
916 A223 10k shown 22
917 A223 15k multi, diff., vert. 32
918 A223 24k multi, diff., vert. 55
919 A223 29k multi, diff., vert. 65
920 A223 114k multi, diff., vert. 2.55
Nos. 915-920 (6) 4.49

Souvenir Sheet
Perf. 12½

921 A223 95k Pairs figure skating 2.25

No. 921 contains one 32x40mm stamp.

People's Army, 40th Anniv. A224

1989, Jan. 20 ***Perf. 13***
922 A224 1k shown 15
923 A224 2k Military school, vert. 15
924 A224 3k Health care 15
925 A224 250k Ready for combat 5.50

1992 Summer Olympics, Barcelona — A225

Perf. 12x12½, 12½x12

1989, June 1 **Litho.**

926 A225 5k Pole vault, vert. 15
927 A225 15k Gymnastic rings, vert. 35
928 A225 20k Cycling 45
929 A225 25k Boxing 58
930 A225 70k Archery, vert. 1.60
931 A225 120k Swimming, vert. 2.70
Nos. 926-932 (7) 8.08

Souvenir Sheet

Perf. 13

932 A225 95k Baseball 2.25

No. 932 contains one 32x40mm stamp.

PHILEXFRANCE '89 — A226

Paintings by Picasso: 5k, *Beggars by the Edge of the Sea.* 7k, *Maternity.* 8k, *Portrait of Jaime S. Le Bock.* 9k, *Harlequins.* 105k, *Dog with Boy.* 114k, *Girl Balancing on Ball.*

1989, July 17 ***Perf. 12½x13***

933 A226 5k multi 15
934 A226 7k multi 15
935 A226 8k multi 18
936 A226 9k multi 20
937 A226 105k multi 2.35
938 A226 114k multi 2.55
Nos. 933-938 (6) 5.58

Souvenir Sheet

Perf. 12½

939 A226 95k shown 2.25

No. 939 contains one 32x40mm stamp.

Cuban Revolution, 30th Anniv. — A227

1989, Apr. 20 **Litho.** ***Perf. 13***

940 A227 45k shown 1.00
941 A227 50k Flags 1.15

Fight the Destruction of Forests — A228

1989, Mar. 30 **Litho.** ***Perf. 13***

942 A228 4k Planting saplings 15
943 A228 10k Fight forest fires 22
944 A228 12k Do not chop down trees 28
945 A228 200k Map of woodland 4.50

Nos. 944-945 are vert.

Jawaharlal Nehru (1889-1964), Indian Statesman A229

1989, Nov. 9 **Litho.** ***Perf. 12½***

946 A229 1k multicolored 15
947 A229 60k multi, horiz. 1.35
948 A229 200k multi, diff. 4.50

Mani Ikara Zapota — A230

A231

1989, Sept. 18 ***Perf. 12½x13***

949 A230 5k shown 15
950 A230 20k Psidium guajava 45
951 A230 20k Annona sguamosa 45
952 A230 30k Durio zibethinus 68
953 A230 50k Punica granatum 1.15
954 A230 172k Moridica charautia 4.00
Nos. 949-954 (6) 6.88

1989, Oct. 19 **Litho.** ***Perf. 12½***

Historic Monuments: No. 955, That Sikhotabong, Khammouane. No. 956, That Dam, Vientiane. No. 957, That Ing Hang, Savannakhet. No. 958, Ho Vay Phra Thatluang, Vientiane.

955 A231 5k multicolored 15
956 A231 15k multicolored 35
957 A231 61k multicolored 1.40
958 A231 161k multicolored 3.70

1992 Summer Olympics, Barcelona A232

1990, Mar. 5 **Litho.** ***Perf. 12½x13***

959 A232 10k Basketball 24
960 A232 30k Hurdles 70
961 A232 45k High jump 1.03
962 A232 50k Cycling 1.15
963 A232 60k Javelin 1.40
964 A232 90k Tennis 2.00
Nos. 959-964 (6) 6.52

Souvenir Sheet

965 A232 95k Rhythmic gymnastics 2.20

1992 Winter Olympics, Albertville — A233

1990, June 20 ***Perf. 13***

966 A233 10k Speed skating 24
967 A233 25k Cross country skiing, vert. 60
968 A233 30k Slalom skiing 70
969 A233 35k Luge 80
970 A233 80k Ice dancing, vert. 1.85
971 A233 90k Biathlon 2.00
Nos. 966-971 (6) 6.19

Souvenir Sheet

972 A233 95k Hockey, vert. 2.20

New Zealand Birds A234

Designs: 10k, Prosthemadera novaeseelandie. 15k, Alauda arvensis. 20k, Haemotopus unicolor. 50k, Phalacrocorax carbo. 50k, Demigretta sacra. 100k Apteryx australis mantelli. 95k, Phalacrocorax corunculatus.

1990, Aug. 24 ***Perf. 12½***

973 A234 10k multicolored 24
974 A234 15k multicolored 35
975 A234 20k multicolored 45
976 A234 50k multicolored 1.15
977 A234 60k multicolored 1.40
978 A234 100k multicolored 2.30
Nos. 973-978 (6) 5.89

Souvenir Sheet

979 A234 95k multicolored 2.20

World Stamp Expo, New Zealand '90. No. 979 contains one 32x40mm stamp.

That Luang Temple, 430th Anniv. A235

Perf. 13x12½, 12½x13

1990, July 25

980 A235 60k 1867 1.40
981 A235 70k 1930 1.60
982 A235 130k 1990, vert. 3.00

Ho Chi Minh (1890-1969), Vietnamese Leader — A236

1990, May 11 ***Perf. 13***

983 A236 40k Addressing people 90
984 A236 60k With Laotian President 1.40
985 A236 160k Waving, vert. 3.65

UN Development Program, 40th Anniv. — A237

1990, Oct. 24 **Litho.** ***Perf. 13***

986 A237 30k Surgeons 68
987 A237 45k Fishermen 1.00
988 A237 80k Flight controller, vert. 1.80
989 A237 90k Power plant 2.00

15th Anniv. of the Republic A238

Designs: 15k, Placing flowers at monument. 20k, Celebratory parade. 80k, Visiting sick. 120k, Women marching with banner.

1990, Dec. 2 **Litho.** ***Perf. 13***

990 A238 15k multicolored 35
991 A238 20k multicolored 45
992 A238 80k multicolored 1.80
993 A238 120k multicolored 2.75

New Year's Day A239

1990, Nov. 20

994 A239 5k shown 15
995 A239 10k Parade 25
996 A239 50k Ceremony 1.15

Size: 40x29mm

997 A239 150k Ceremony, diff. 3.35

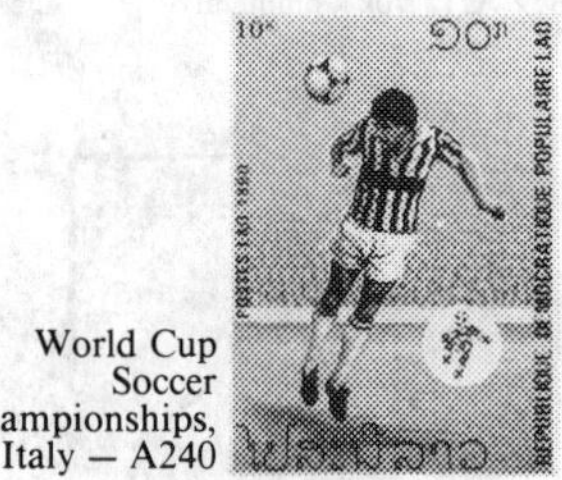

World Cup Soccer Championships, Italy — A240

Various soccer players in action.

1990 **Litho.** ***Perf. 13***

998 A240 10k multicolored 25
999 A240 15k multicolored 35
1000 A240 20k multicolored 50
1001 A240 25k multicolored 60
1002 A240 45k multicolored 1.05
1003 A240 105k multicolored 2.50
Nos. 998-1003 (6) 5.25

Souvenir Sheet

Perf. 12½

1004 A240 95k multi, horiz. 2.25

No. 1004 contains one 39x31mm stamp.

Intl. Literacy Year A241

1990, Feb. 27 Litho. *Perf. 12½*

1005 A241 10k shown 50
1006 A241 50k Woman with child, vert. 2.40
1007 A241 60k Monk teaching class 2.85
1008 A241 150k Two women, man reading 7.00

Stamp World London '90 — A242

Stamps, modes of mail transport: 15k, Great Britain #1, stagecoach. 20k, US #1, train. 40k, France #3, balloons. 50k, Sardinia #1, post rider. 60k, Indo-China #3, elephant. 95k, Laos #272, jet. 100k, Spain #1, sailing ship.

1990, Apr. 26 Litho. *Perf. 13x12½*

1009 A242 15k multicolored 42
1010 A242 20k multicolroed 58
1011 A242 40k multicolored 1.15
1012 A242 50k multicolored 1.40
1013 A242 60k multicolored 1.70
1014 A242 100k multicolored 2.90
Nos. 1009-1014 (6) 8.15

Souvenir Sheet

Perf. 13

1015 A242 95k multicolored 2.85

No. 1015 contains one 40x32mm stamp.

A243

1992 Olympics, Barcelona and Albertville A244

Perf. 12½x12, 12x12½, 13 (A244)

1991, Jan. 25

1016 A243 22k 2-man canoe 15
1017 A243 32k 1-man kayak 15
1018 A244 32k Bobsled, vert. 15
1019 A244 135k Cross country skiing 42
1020 A244 250k Ski jumping 78
1021 A244 275k Biathlon 85
1022 A243 285k Diving, vert. 90
1023 A243 330k Sailing, vert. 1.05
1024 A244 900k Speed skating 2.75
1025 A243 1000k Swimming 3.10
Nos. 1016-1025 (10) 10.30

Souvenir Sheets

Perf. 12½, 13½x13

1026 A243 700k 2-man kayak 2.20
1027 A244 700k Slalom skiing, vert. 2.20

No. 1026 contains one 40x32mm stamp. No. 1027 contains one 32x40mm stamp.

Tourism — A245

Designs: 155k, Rapids, Champassak. 220k, Vangvieng. 235k, Waterfalls, Saravane, vert. 1000k Plain of Jars, Xieng Khouang, vert.

1991 *Perf. 13x12½, 12½x13*

1028 A245 155k multicolored 50
1029 A245 220k multicolored 70
1030 A245 235k multicolored 75
1031 A245 1000k multicolored 3.10

1994 World Cup Soccer Championships — A246

Various players in action.

1991 Litho. *Perf. 13*

1032 A246 32k multicolored 15
1033 A246 330k multicolored 1.00
1034 A246 340k multi, vert. 1.05
1035 A246 400k multicolored 1.25
1036 A246 500k multicolored 1.55
Nos. 1032-1036 (5) 5.00

Souvenir Sheet

Perf. 13½x13

1037 A246 700k multi, vert. 2.15

No. 1037 contains one 32x40mm stamp.

SEMI-POSTAL STAMPS

Laotian Children — SP1

Unwmk.

1953, July 14 Engr. *Perf. 13*

B1 SP1 1.50pi + 1pi multi 90 65
B2 SP1 3pi + 1.50pi multi 90 65
B3 SP1 3.90pi + 2.50pi multi 90 65

The surtax was for the Red Cross.

Nos. 52 and 46 Surcharged: "1k ANNEE MONDIALE DU REFUGIE 1959-1960"

1960, Apr. 7

B4 A16 4k + 1k rose claret 35 40
B5 A13 10k + 1k multicolored 35 40

World Refugee Year, July 1, 1959-June 30, 1960. The surcharge was for aid to refugees.

Flooded Village SP2

Designs: 40k+10k, Flooded market place and truck. 60k+15k, Flooded airport and plane.

1967, Jan. 18 Engr. *Perf. 13*

B6 SP2 20k + 5k multi 16 16
B7 SP2 40k + 10k multi 25 25
B8 SP2 60k + 15k multi 38 38
a. Miniature sheet of 3 1.50 1.50

The surtax was for victims of the Mekong Delta flood. No. B8a contains one each of Nos. B6-B8. Size: 148x99mm. Sold for 250k.

Women Working in Tobacco Field — SP3

1967, Oct. 5 Engr. *Perf. 13*

B9 SP3 20k + 5k multi 15 15
B10 SP3 50k + 10k multi 25 25
B11 SP3 60k + 15k multi 35 35
a. Souv. sheet of 3, #B9-B11 1.50 1.50

Laotian Red Cross, 10th anniv. No. B11a sold for 250k+30k.

Nos. 184-189 Surcharged: "Soutien aux Victimes / de la Guerre / + 5k"

1970, May 1 Photo. *Perf. 14*

B12 A58 10k + 5k multi 16 15
B13 A58 15k + 5k multi 16 15
B14 A58 20k + 5k multi 20 15
B15 A58 30k + 5k multi 25 16
B16 A58 40k + 5k multi 35 20
B17 A58 60k + 5k multi 45 25
Nos. B12-B17,CB1-CB2 (8) 3.97 2.76

AIR POST STAMPS

Weaving — AP1

Design: 3.30pi, Wat Pra Keo.

Unwmk.

1952, Apr. 13 Engr. *Perf. 13*

C1 AP1 3.30pi dk pur & pur 55 25
C2 AP1 10pi ultra & bl grn 1.10 70
C3 AP1 20pi deep cl & red 1.75 1.25
C4 AP1 30pi blk brn & dk brn violet 2.75 1.90

See note following No. 17.

UPU Monument and King Sisavang-Vong — AP2

1952, Dec. 7

C5 AP2 25pi vio bl & indigo 2.00 1.40
C6 AP2 50pi dk brn & vio brn 2.00 1.40

Laos' admission to the UPU, May 13, 1952.

AP3

AP4

Designs: Various Buddha statues.

1953, Nov. 18

C7 AP3 4pi dark green 16 15
C8 AP4 6.50pi dk bl green 15 15
C9 AP4 9pi blue green 30 15
C10 AP3 11.50pi red, yel & dk vio brn 32 15
C11 AP4 40pi purple 60 45
C12 AP4 100pi olive 1.75 1.40
Nos. C7-C12 (6) 3.28 2.45

Great Oath of Laos ceremony.

Composite of Laotian Temples — AP5

1954, Mar. 4 Unwmk.

C13 AP5 50pi ind & bl grn 47.50 47.50

Accession of King Sisavang-Vong, 50th anniv.

Ravana — AP6

Sita and Rama — AP7

Scenes from the Ramayana: 4k, Hanuman, the white monkey. 5k, Ninh Laphath, the black monkey. 20k, Lucy with a friend of Ravana. 30k, Rama.

1955, Oct. 28 Engr. *Perf. 13*

C14 AP6 2k bl grn, emer & ind 25 24
C15 AP6 4k red brn, dk red brn & ver 35 35
C16 AP6 5k scar, sep & ol 52 45
C17 AP7 10k blk, org & brn 95 80
C18 AP7 20k vio, dk grn & ol 1.25 1.10
C19 AP7 30k ultra, blk & sal 1.65 1.65
Nos. C14-C19 (6) 4.97 4.59

See No. 225.

Buddha Type of Regular Issue, 1956

1956, May 24

C20 A7 20k carmine rose 10.00 8.00
C21 A7 30k ol & ol bis 10.00 8.00

2500th anniversary of birth of Buddha.

UN Emblem AP8

1956, Dec. 14

C22 AP8 15k light blue	1.75	1.75
C23 AP8 30k deep claret	2.50	2.50

Admission of Laos to the UN, 1st anniv.

Types of Regular Issue, 1957

Musical Instruments: 12k, Khong vong. 14k, So. 20k, Kong.

1957, Mar. 25 Unwmk. *Perf. 13*

C24 A9 12k multicolored	95	65
C25 A10 14k multicolored	95	65
C26 A10 20k bl grn, yel grn & pur	1.25	95

Monk Receiving Alms — AP9

Monks Meditating in Boat — AP10

Designs: 18k, Smiling Buddha. 24k, Ancient temple painting (horse and mythological figures.)

1957, Nov. 5

C27 AP9 10k dk pur, pale brn & dk grn	35	35
C28 AP10 15k dk vio brn, brn org & yel	35	35
C29 AP9 18k sl grn & ol	50	48
C30 AP10 24k cl, org yel & blk	80	70

No. C28 measures 48x27mm. No. C30, 48x36mm. See No. C84.

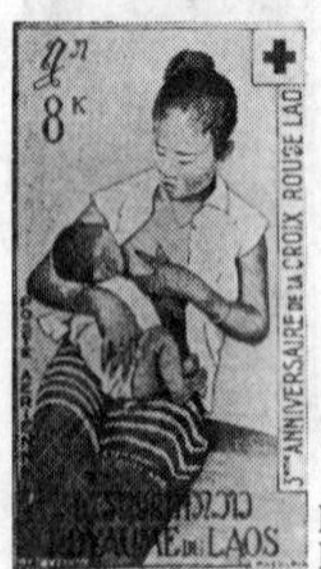

Mother Nursing Infant — AP11

1958, May 2

Cross in Red

C31 AP11 8k lil gray & dk gray	70	45
C32 AP11 12k red brn & brn	1.00	62
C33 AP11 15k sl grn & bluish green	1.25	70
C34 AP11 20k bister & vio	1.50	80

3rd anniversary of Laotian Red Cross.

Plain of Stones, Xieng Khouang — AP12

Papheng Falls, Champassak — AP13

Natl. Tourism Industry: 15k, Buffalo cart. 19k, Buddhist monk and village.

1960, July 1 Engr. *Perf. 13*

C35 AP12 9.50k bl, ol & cl	16	16
C36 AP13 12k vio bl, red brn & gray	22	22
C37 AP13 15k yel grn, ol gray & cl	25	25
C38 AP12 19k multicolored	35	35

Pou Gneu Nha Gneu Legend — AP14

Garuda — AP15

Hanuman, the White Monkey — AP16

Nang Teng One Legend AP17

1962, Feb. 19 Unwmk. *Perf. 13*

C39 AP14 11k grn, car & ocher	20	20
C40 AP15 14k ultra & org	20	20
C41 AP16 20k multicolored	30	30
C42 AP17 25k multicolored	30	30

Makha Bousa festival.

Yao Hunter — AP18

Phayre's Flying Squirrel — AP19

1964, Dec. 15 Engr. *Perf. 13*

C43 AP18 5k shown	15	15
C44 AP18 10k Kha hunter	15	15
C45 AP18 50k Meo woman	50	50
a. Min. sheet of 4, #100, C43-C45	4.00	3.50

No. C45a exists imperf.

Butterfly Type of 1965

1965, Mar. 13

Size: 48x27mm

C46 A34 20k Atlas moth	50	30

1965, Oct. 7 Engr. *Perf. 13*

Designs: 25k, Leopard cat. 75k, Javan mongoose. 100k, Crestless porcupine. 200k, Binturong.

C47 AP19 25k dk brn, yel grn & ocher	30	16
C48 AP19 55k brown & blue	50	25
C49 AP19 75k brt grn & brn	65	35
C50 AP19 100k ocher, brn & blk	80	55
C51 AP19 200k red & black	1.60	1.20
Nos. C47-C51 (5)	3.85	2.51

Army Type of Regular Issue

Design: 200k, 300k, Parading service flags before National Assembly Hall.

1968, July 15 Engr. *Perf. 13*

C52 A53 200k multicolored	65	45
C53 A53 300k multicolored	1.00	65
a. Souvenir sheet of 3, #168-170, C52-C53	4.00	3.50

No. C53a sold for 600k.

Insect Type of Regular Issue

Insects: 120k, Dorysthenes walkeri, horiz. 160k, Megaloxantha bicolor, horiz.

1968, Aug. 28 Engr. *Perf. 13*

C54 A54 120k brn, org & blk	65	35
C55 A54 160k rose car, Prus bl & yel	80	42

Ballet Type of Regular Issue

Designs: 110k, Sudagnu battling Thotsakan. 300k, Pharam dancing with Thotsakan.

1969 Photo. *Perf. 14*

C56 A58 110k multicolored	65	42
a. Souv. sheet of 4, #184-186, C57, imperf.	2.75	1.75
C57 A58 300k multicolored	2.00	1.10
a. Souv. sheet of 4, #187-189, C56, imperf.	9.00	6.50

No. C56a sold for 480k; No. C57a for 650k.

For surcharges see Nos. CB1-CB2.

Timber Industry, Paksane AP20

1969, May 7 Engr. *Perf. 13*

C58 AP20 300k ol bis & blk	2.00	1.50

ILO, 50th anniversary.

Animal Type of Regular Issue

Animals: 70k, Asiatic black bear. 120k, White-handed gibbon, vert. 150k, Tiger.

1969, Nov. 6 Photo. *Perf. 12x13*

C59 A60 70k multicolored	16	15
C60 A60 120k multicolored	30	25
C61 A60 150k multicolored	38	38

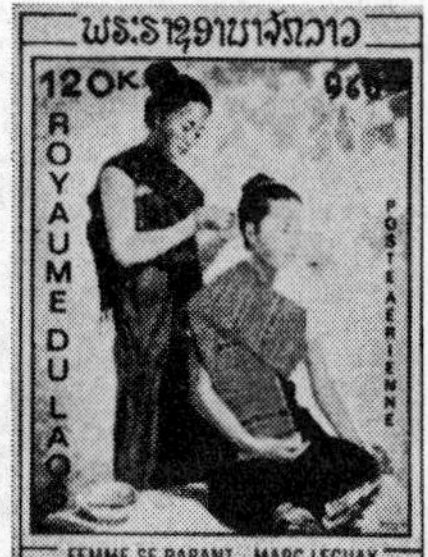

Hairdressing, by Marc Leguay — AP21

Paintings: No. C63, Village Market, by Marc Leguay, horiz. No. C64, Tree on the Bank of the Mekong, by Marc Leguay, horiz.

1969-70 Photo. *Perf. 12x13, 13x12*

C62 AP21 120k multicolored	70	40
C63 AP21 150k multicolored	1.10	62
C64 AP21 150k multi ('70)	1.10	62

See Nos. C72-C74.

Wat Xiengthong, Luang Prabang — AP22

1970, Jan. 10 *Perf. 12x13, 13x12*

C65 AP22 100k Library, Wat Sisaket, vert.	62	40
C66 AP22 120k shown	70	55

Drum Type of 1970

1970, Mar. 30 Engr. *Perf. 13*

C67 A64 125k Pong wooden drum, vert.	2.00	1.20

Franklin D. Roosevelt (1882-1945) AP23

1970, Apr. 12

C68 AP23 120k olive & slate	1.00	65

EXPO '70 Type of Regular Issue

Design: 125k, Woman boiling cocoons in kettle, and spinning silk thread.

1970, July 7 Engr. *Perf. 13*

C69 A66 125k ol & multi	55	55

See note after No. 202.

Animal Type of Regular Issue

1970, Sept. 7 Engr. *Perf. 13*

C70 A67 210k Leopard	35	55
C71 A67 500k Gaur	2.25	2.00

Painting Type of 1969-70

Paintings by Marc Leguay: 100k, Village Foot Path. 120k, Rice Field in Rainy Season, horiz. 150k, Village Elder.

Perf. 11½x13, 13x11½

1970, Dec. 21 **Photo.**

C72 AP21 100k multicolored 40 40
C73 AP21 120k multicolored 35 35
C74 AP21 150k multicolored 50 50

UN Type of Regular Issue

Design: 125k, Earth Goddess Nang Thorani wringing her hair; UN Headquarters and emblem.

1970, Oct. 24
Size: 26x36mm

C75 A68 125k brt bl, pink & dk grn 50 50

Hanuman and Nang Matsa — AP24

1971, Feb. 5

C76 AP24 125k multicolored 1.00 60

Orchid Type of Regular Issue

Design: 125k, Brasilian cattleya.

1971, July **Photo.** ***Perf. 13x12½***
Size: 48x27mm

C79 A73 125k Brasilian cattleya 60 30

Laotian and French Women, That Luang Pagoda and Arms AP25

1971, Aug. 6 **Engr.** ***Perf. 13***

C80 AP25 30k brn & dl red 22 15
C81 AP25 70k vio & lilac 40 35
C82 AP25 100k sl grn & grn 60 45

Kinship between the cities Keng Kok, Laos, and Saint Astier, France.

Animal Type of Regular Issue

1971, Sept. 16

C83 A74 300k Javan rhinoceros 80 40

Type of 1957 with Ornamental Panel and Inscription

Design: 125k, Monk receiving alms (like No. C27).

1971, Nov. 2 **Engr.** ***Perf. 13***

C84 AP9 125k dk pur, pale brn & dk grn 35 35

20th anniv. of Laotian independent postal service. No. C84 inscribed: "Vingtième Anniversaire de la Philatelie Lao," "Poste Aerienne" and "1971."

Sunset Over the Mekong, by Chamnane Prisayane — AP26

Design: 150k, "Quiet Morning" (village scene), by Chamnane Prisayane.

1971, Dec. 20 **Photo.** ***Perf. 13x12***

C85 AP26 125k black & multi 35 35
C86 AP26 150k black & multi 42 42

Book Year Type of Regular Issue

Design: 125k, Father teaching children to read palm leaf book.

1972, Jan. 30 **Engr.** ***Perf. 13***
Size: 48x27mm

C87 A75 125k brt purple 35 35

Dam Type of Regular Issue

Design: 145k, Nam Ngum Hydroelectric Dam and ECAFE emblem.

1972, Mar. 28 **Engr.** ***Perf. 13***

C88 A76 145k brn, bl & grn 42 42

Orchid Type of Regular Issue 1971

1972, May 1 **Photo.** ***Perf. 13x12½***
Size: 48x27mm

C89 A73 150k Vanda trees, horiz. 55 28

UNICEF Type of Regular Issue

Design: 120k, Boy riding buffalo to water hole (child's drawing).

1972, July **Engr.** ***Perf. 13***

C90 A77 120k multicolored 35 35

Nakharath, Daughter of the Dragon King — AP27

Wood carvings from Wat Sikhounvieng Dongmieng, Vientiane: 120k, Nang Kinnali, Goddess from Mt. Kailath. 150k, Norasing, Lion King from Himalayas.

1972, Sept. 15 **Engr.** ***Perf. 13***

C91 AP27 100k blue green 20 20
C92 AP27 120k violet 22 22
C93 AP27 150k brn orange 30 30

That Luang Religious Festival — AP28

1972, Nov. 18 **Engr.** ***Perf. 13***

C94 AP28 110k Presentation of wax castles 42 42
C95 AP28 125k Procession 55 55

Workers in Rice Field, by Leguay AP29

Paintings by Mark Leguay: No. C97, Women and water buffalo in rice field. Nos. C98, Rainy Season in Village (Water buffalo in water). No. C99, Rainy Season in Village (Water buffalo on land) 120k, Mother and Child.

1972, Dec. 23 **Photo.** ***Perf. 13***

C96 AP29 50k multicolored 16 16
C97 AP29 50k multicolored 16 16
C98 AP29 70k multicolored 22 22
C99 AP29 70k multicolored 22 22
C100 AP29 120k yel & multi 35 35
Nos. C96-C100 (5) 1.11 1.11

Nos. C97, C99 have denomination and frame at right.

Costume Type of Regular Issue

Women's Costumes: 120k, Luang Prabang marriage costume. 150k, Vientiane evening costume.

1973, Feb. 16 **Engr.** ***Perf. 13***

C101 A78 120k multicolored 22 22
C102 A78 150k brn & multi 28 28

Lions Club Emblems, King Sayasettha-Thirath — AP30

1973, Mar. 30 **Engr.** ***Perf. 13***

C103 AP30 150k rose & multi 38 25

Lions Club of Vientiane.

Rahu with Rockets and Sputnik — AP31

Space achievements: 150k, Laotian festival rocket and US lunar excursion module.

1973, May 11 **Engr.** ***Perf. 13***

C104 AP31 80k ultra & multi 25 16
C105 AP31 150k buff & ultra 45 25

Dancing Around Campfire — AP32

Design: 125k, Boy Scouts helping during Vientiane Flood, 1966.

1973, Sept. 1 **Engr.** ***Perf. 13***

C106 AP32 110k vio & orange 45 20
C107 AP32 125k Prus grn & bis 55 22

Laotian Scout Movement, 25th anniv.

Sun Chariot and WMO Emblem — AP33

Design: 90k, Nang Mekhala, the weather goddess, and WMO emblem, vert.

1973, Oct. 24 **Engr.** ***Perf. 13***

C108 AP33 90k vio, red & ocher 35 20
C109 AP33 150k ocher, red & brn ol 40 30

Intl. meteorological cooperation, cent.

Woman in Poppy Field, INTERPOL Emblem — AP34

1973, Dec. 22 **Engr.** ***Perf. 13***

C110 AP34 150k vio, yel grn & red 1.00 40

Intl. Criminal Police Org., 50th anniv.

Phra Sratsvady, Wife of Phra Phrom AP35

Designs: 110k, Phra Indra on 3-headed elephant Erawan. 150k, Phra Phrom, the Creator, on phoenix. Designs show giant sculptures in park at Thadeua.

1974, Mar. 23 **Engr.** ***Perf. 13***

C111 AP35 100k lilac, red & blk 42 25
C112 AP35 110k car, vio & brn 50 40
C113 AP35 150k ocher, vio & sep 65 45

UPU Emblem, Women Reading Letter — AP36

1974 **Engr.** ***Perf. 13***

C114 AP36 200k lt brn & car 60 55
C115 AP36 500k lil & red 1.40 1.10
a. Souvenir sheet 5.00 5.00

Centenary of Universal Postal Union.
Issue dates: 200k, Apr. 30; 500k, Oct. 9.

Flower Type of 1974

1974, May 31
Size: 36x36mm

C116 A84 500k Pitcher plant 1.10 80

Transportation Type of Regular Issue

1974, July 31 **Engr.** ***Perf. 13***

C117 A85 250k Sampan 40 30

Marconi Type of 1974

Design: Old and new means of communications.

1974, Aug. 28 **Engr.** ***Perf. 13***

C118 A86 200k vio bl & brn 40 35

Insect Type of 1974

1974, Oct. 23 **Engr.** ***Perf. 13***

C119 A87 110k Sternocera multipunctata 38 22

Boeing 747 AP37

1986, June 2	Litho.	Perf. 12½	
C120 AP37 20k shown		3.00	
C121 AP37 50k IL86		7.00	

AIR POST SEMI-POSTAL STAMPS

Nos. C56-C57 Surcharged: "Soutien aux Victimes / de la Guerre / + 5k"

1970, May 1	Photo.	Perf. 13	
CB1 A58 110k + 5k multi		80	60
CB2 A58 300k + 5k multi		1.60	1.10

The surtax was for war victims.

POSTAGE DUE STAMPS

Vat-Sisaket Monument D1

Boat and Raft D2

Perf. 13½x13

1952-53	Unwmk.	Engr.	
J1 D1 10c dark brown		15	15
J2 D1 20c purple		15	15
J3 D1 50c carmine		15	15
J4 D1 1pi dark green		15	15
J5 D1 2pi deep ultra		15	15
J6 D1 5pi rose violet		45	45
J7 D2 10pi indigo ('53)		60	60
Set value		1.50	1.50

Serpent — D3

1973, Oct. 31	Photo.	Perf. 13	
J8 D3 10k yellow & multi		15	15
J9 D3 15k emerald & multi		15	15
J10 D3 20k blue & multi		15	15
J11 D3 50k scarlet & multi		15	15
Set value		30	30

LATAKIA

LOCATION — A division of Syria in Western Asia
GOVT. — French Mandate
AREA — 2,500 sq. mi.
POP. — 278,000 (approx. 1930)
CAPITAL — Latakia

This territory, included in the Syrian Mandate to France under the Versailles Treaty, was formerly known as Alaouites. The name Latakia was adopted in 1930. See Alaouites and Syria.

100 Centimes = 1 Piaster

Stamps of Syria Overprinted in Black or Red

LATTAQUIE

or

Perf. 12x12½, 13½

1931-33		Unwmk.	
1 A6 10c red vio		25	25
2 A6 10c vio brn ('33)		30	30
3 A7 20c dk bl (R)		25	25
4 A7 20c brn org ('33)		30	30
5 A8 25c gray grn (R)		25	25
6 A8 25c dk bl gray (R) ('33)		50	50
7 A9 50c violet		60	60
8 A15 75c org red ('32)		60	60
9 A10 1p grn (R)		60	60
10 A11 1.50p bis brn (R)		90	90
11 A11 1.50p dp grn ('33)		1.00	1.00
12 A12 2p dk vio (R)		1.00	1.00
13 A13 3p yel grn (R)		1.75	1.75
14 A14 4p orange		1.75	1.75
15 A15 4.50p rose car		1.75	1.75
16 A16 6p grnsh blk (R)		1.75	1.75
17 A17 7.50p dl bl (R)		1.75	1.75
18 A18 10p dp brn (R)		2.50	2.50
19 A19 15p dp grn (R)		3.75	3.75
20 A20 25p vio brn		7.00	7.00
21 A21 50p dk brn (R)		6.50	6.50
22 A22 100p red org		20.00	20.00
Nos. 1-22 (22)		55.05	55.05

AIR POST STAMPS

Air Post Stamps of Syria, 1931, Overprinted in Black or Red

LATTAQUIE

1931-33	Unwmk.	Perf. 13½	
C1 AP2 50c ocher		35	35
a. Inverted overprint		300.00	300.00
C2 AP2 50c blk brn (R) ('33)		45	45
C3 AP2 1p chnt brn		80	80
C4 AP2 2p Prus bl (R)		1.10	1.10
C5 AP2 3p bl grn (R)		1.40	1.40
C6 AP2 5p red vio		3.25	3.25
C7 AP2 10p sl grn (R)		4.00	4.00
C8 AP2 15p org red		4.75	4.75
C9 AP2 25p org brn		9.00	9.00
C10 AP2 50p black (R)		14.00	14.00
C11 AP2 100p magenta		14.00	14.00
Nos. C1-C11 (11)		53.10	53.10

POSTAGE DUE STAMPS

Postage Due Stamps of Syria, 1931, Overprinted like Regular Issue

1931	Unwmk.	Perf. 13½	
J1 D7 8p blk, *gray bl* (R)		9.00	9.00
J2 D8 15p blk, *dl rose* (R)		7.00	7.00

Stamps of Latakia were superseded in 1937 by those of Syria.

LATVIA

(Lettonia, Lettland)

LOCATION — Northern Europe, bordering on the Baltic Sea and the Gulf of Riga
GOVT. — Independent Republic
AREA — 25,395 sq. mi.
POP. — 1,994,506 (estimated 1939)
CAPITAL — Riga

Latvia was created a sovereign state following World War I and was admitted to the League of Nations in 1922. In 1940 it became a republic in the Union of Soviet Socialist Republics. Latvian independence was recognized by the Soviet Union on Sept. 6, 1991.

100 Kapeikas = 1 Rublis
100 Santims = 1 Lat (1923)
100 Kopecks = 1 Ruble (1991)

Catalogue values for unused stamps in this country are for Never Hinged items, beginning with Scott 300 in the regular postage section.

Watermarks

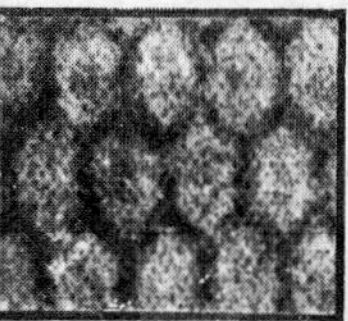
Wmk. 108- Honeycomb

Wmk. 145- Wavy Lines

Wmk. 181- Wavy Lines

Wmk. 197- Star and Triangles

Wmk. 212- Multiple Swastikas

Wmk. 265- Multiple Waves

Arms — A1

Printed on the Backs of German Military Maps

Unwmk.

1918, Dec. 18	Litho.	Imperf.	
1 A1 5k carmine		38	38
Perf. 11½			
2 A1 5k carmine		38	38

Stamps from outer rows of the sheets sometimes have no printing on the back.

Redrawn
Paper with Ruled Lines

1919		Imperf.	
3 A1 5k carmine		50	50
4 A1 10k dk bl		50	50
5 A1 15k green		50	50
Perf. 11½			
6 A1 5k carmine		1.00	1.00
7 A1 10k dk bl		1.00	1.00
8 A1 15k dp grn		1.50	1.50
Nos. 3-8 (6)		5.00	5.00

In the redrawn design the wheat heads are thicker, the ornament at lower left has five points instead of four, and there are minor changes in other parts of the design.

The sheets of this and subsequent issues were usually divided in half by a single line of perforation gauging 10. Thus stamps are found with this perforation on one side.

1919	Pelure Paper	Imperf.	
9 A1 3k lilac		3.75	3.75
10 A1 5k carmine		15	15
11 A1 10k dp bl		15	15
12 A1 15k dk grn		15	15
13 A1 20k orange		15	15
13A A1 25k gray		25.00	25.00
14 A1 35k dk brn		15	15
15 A1 50k purple		18	18
16 A1 75k emerald		3.00	4.00
Nos. 9-16 (9)		32.68	33.68
Perf. 11½, 9½			
17 A1 3k lilac		15.00	15.00
18 A1 5k carmine		90	90
19 A1 10k dp bl		1.90	1.90
20 A1 15k dk grn		1.90	1.90
21 A1 20k orange		1.80	1.90
22 A1 35k dk brn		2.50	2.50
23 A1 50k purple		3.75	3.75
24 A1 75k emerald		7.25	7.25
Nos. 17-24 (8)		35.00	35.10

Nos. 17 to 24 are said to be unofficially perforated varieties of Nos. 9 to 16.

1919	Wmk. 108	Imperf.	
25 A1 3k lilac		15	15
26 A1 5k carmine		15	15
27 A1 10k dp bl		15	15
28 A1 15k dp grn		15	15
29 A1 20k orange		18	18
30 A1 25k gray		45	45
31 A1 35k dk brn		45	45
32 A1 50k purple		30	30
33 A1 75k emerald		60	60
Nos. 25-33 (9)		2.58	2.58

The variety "printed on both sides" exists for 3k, 10k, 15k, 20k and 35k.

See Nos. 57-58, 76-82.

Liberation of Riga — A2

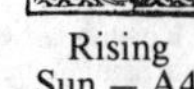

Rising Sun — A4

1919		Wmk. 108	
43 A2 5k carmine		30	30
44 A2 15k dp grn		30	30
45 A2 35k brown		45	45
Unwmk.			
Pelure Paper			
49 A2 5k carmine		9.00	12.00
50 A2 15k dp grn		9.00	12.00
51 A2 35k brown		9.00	12.00

1919		Imperf.	
55 A4 10k gray blue		18	18
Perf. 11½			
56 A4 10k gray blue		50	50

Type of 1918

1919 Laid Paper		Perf. 11½	
57 A1 3r slate & org		85	85
58 A1 5r gray brn & org		75	52

Independence Issue

Allegory of One Year of Independence
A5

1919, Nov. 18 **Unwmk.**

Wove Paper

Size: 33x45mm

59 A5 10k brn & rose 60 60

Laid Paper

60 A5 10k brn & rose 85 85

Size: 28x38mm

61 A5 10k brn & rose 26 26
a. Imperf.
62 A5 35k ind & grn 22 22
a. Vertical pair, imperf. between 20.00 20.00

There are two types of Nos. 59 and 60. In type I the trunk of the tree is not outlined. In type II it has a distinct white outline.

Wmk. 197

Thick Wove Paper

Blue Design on Back

63 A5 1r grn & red 60 60
Nos. 59-63 (5) 2.53 2.53

No. 63 was printed on the backs of unfinished 5r bank notes of the Workers and Soldiers Council, Riga.

Warrior Slaying Dragon — A6

1919-20 **Unwmk.** ***Perf. 11½***

Wove Paper

64 A6 10k brn & car 20 20
a. Horiz. pair, imperf. btwn. 10.00 10.00
65 A6 25k ind & yel grn 30 30
a. Pair, imperf. between 20.00 20.00
66 A6 35k blk & bl ('20) 30 30
a. Horiz. pair, imperf. btwn. 20.00 20.00
67 A6 1r dk grn & brn ('20) 60 60
a. Horiz. pair, imperf. vert. 20.00 20.00
b. Horiz. pair, imperf. btwn. 20.00 20.00

Issued in honor of the liberation of Kurzeme (Kurland). The paper sometimes shows impressed quadrille lines.

Latgale Relief Issue

Latvia Welcoming Home Latgale Province — A7

1920, Mar.

Brown and Green Design on Back

68 A7 50k dk grn & rose 38 38
a. Horiz. pair, imperf. vert. 20.00
69 A7 1r sl grn & brn 38 38
a. Horiz. pair, imperf. vert. 20.00

No. 68-69 were printed on the backs of unfinished bank notes of the government of Colonel Bermondt-Avalov and on the so-called German "Ober-Ost" money.

First National Assembly Issue

Latvia Hears Call to Assemble — A8

1920

70 A8 50k rose 35 20
a. Imperf., pair 6.00 6.00
71 A8 1r blue 35 20
a. Vertical pair, imperf. between 15.00 15.00
b. Imperf., pair 6.00 6.00
72 A8 3r dk brn & grn 60 60
73 A8 5r sl & vio brn 75 60

Type of 1918 Issue
Wove Paper

1920-21 **Unwmk.** ***Perf. 11½***

76 A1 5k carmine 15 15
78 A1 20k orange 15 15
79 A1 40k lilac ('21) 18 15
80 A1 50k violet 18 15
81 A1 75k emerald 18 15
82 A1 5r gray brn & org ('21) 1.40 20
Nos. 76-82 (6) 2.24 95

No. 63 Surcharged in Black, Brown or Blue

1920, Sept. 1

83 A5 10r on 1r grn & red (Bk) 1.40 1.10
84 A5 20r on 1r grn & red (Br) 4.00 3.50
85 A5 30r on 1r grn & red (Bl) 5.25 4.25

Types of 1919 Surcharged

2
DIWI
RUBLI

1920-21 **Wmk. 108** ***Perf. 11½***

86 A1 2r on 10k dp bl 1.10 85
87 A2 2r on 35k brown 55 55

No. 62 Surcharged in Red

DIWI
RUBLI
2

Unwmk.

88 A5 2r on 35k ind & grn 48 48

No. 70 Surcharged in Blue

DIVI
2 RUB. 2

1921

90 A8 2r on 50k rose 48 48

Nos. 64-66 Surcharged in Red or Blue

WEENS
1
RUBLIS

1920-21

91 A6 1r on 35k blk & bl (R) 42 28
92 A6 2r on 10k brn & rose (Bl) 42 28
93 A6 2r on 25k ind & grn (R) 55 20
a. Imperf.

On Nos. 92 and 93 the surcharge reads "DIVI 2 RUBLI."

No. 83 with Added Surcharge

1921 **Wmk. 197**

94 A5 10r on 10r on 1r 1.40 1.00

Latgale Relief Issue of 1920 Surcharged in Black or Blue

10
DESMIT RBL.

1921, May 31 **Unwmk.**

95 A7 10r on 50k grn & rose 1.00 80
a. Imperf.
96 A7 20r on 50k grn & rose 3.75 3.00
97 A7 30r on 50k grn & rose 3.00 2.00
98 A7 50r on 50k grn & rose 6.00 4.75
99 A7 100r on 50k grn & rose (Bl) 12.50 11.00
Nos. 95-99 (5) 26.25 21.55

Excellent counterfeits exist.

Arms and Stars for Vidzeme, Kurzeme & Latgale — A10

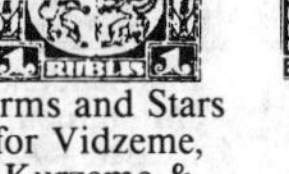

Coat of Arms — A11

Perf. 10, 11½ and Compound

Wmk. Similar to 181

1921-22 **Typo.**

Type I, slanting cipher in value.
Type II, upright cipher in value.

101 A10 50k vio (II) 38 15
102 A10 1r org yel 38 20
103 A10 2r dp grn 38 15
104 A10 3r brt grn 20 20
105 A10 5r rose 65 15
106 A10 6r dp claret 1.25 30
107 A10 9r orange 75 25
108 A10 10r blue (I) 75 15
109 A10 15r ultra 1.75 85
a. Printed on both sides 25.00
110 A10 20r dl lil (II) 7.50 2.25

1922, Aug. 21 ***Perf. 11½***

111 A11 50r dk brn & pale brn (I) 17.00 3.50
112 A11 100r dk bl & pale bl (I) 19.00 4.50
Nos. 101-112 (12) 49.99 12.65

Nos. 101 to 131 sometimes show letters of a paper maker's watermark "PACTIEN LIGAT MILLS".
See Nos. 126-131, 152-154.

A12

1923-25 ***Perf. 10, 11, 11½***

2 SANTIMS
Type A, tail of "2" ends in an upstroke.
Type B, tail of "2" is nearly horizontal.

113 A12 1s violet 42 15
114 A12 2s org yel (A) 42 15
115 A12 4s dk grn 55 15
a. Horiz. pair, imperf. btwn. 20.00 20.00
116 A12 5s lt grn ('25) 1.10 15
117 A12 6s grn, *yel* ('25) 2.25 15
118 A12 10s rose red (I) 85 15
a. Horiz. pair, imperf. btwn. 20.00 20.00
119 A12 12s claret 15 15
120 A12 15s brn, *sal* 1.90 15
a. Horiz. pair, imperf. btwn. 20.00 20.00
121 A12 20s dp bl (II) 1.40 15
122 A12 25s ultra ('25) 15 15
123 A12 30s pink (I) ('25) 2.50 15
124 A12 40s lilac (I) 1.10 15
125 A12 50s lil gray (II) 2.25 18
126 A11 1 l dk brn & pale brn 6.75 50
127 A11 2 l dk bl & bl 11.00 1.00
130 A11 5 l dp grn & pale grn 37.50 6.00
131 A11 10 l car rose & pale rose (I) 3.25 3.00
Nos. 113-131 (17) 73.54 12.48

Value in "Santims" (1s); "Santimi" (2s-6s) or "Santimu" (others).
See note after No. 110.
See Nos. 135-151, 155-157.

Stamps of 1920-21 Surcharged

15
SANTIMU

1927 **Unwmk.** ***Perf. 11½***

132 A1 15s on 40k lilac 55 42
133 A1 15s on 50k violet 85 85

Stamp of 1920 Surcharged

1 Ls

134 A8 1 l on 3r brn & grn 4.75 4.75

Types of 1923-25 Issue

1927-33 **Wmk. 212** ***Perf. 10, 11½***

135 A12 1s dl vio 18 15
136 A12 2s org yel (A) 18 15
137 A12 2s org yel (B) ('33) 15 15
138 A12 3s org red ('31) 18 15
139 A12 4s dk grn ('29) 2.00 1.25
140 A12 5s lt grn ('31) 60 15
141 A12 6s grn, *yel* 15 15
142 A12 7s dk grn ('31) 60 22
143 A12 10s red (I) 1.50 15
144 A12 10s grn, *yel* (I) ('32) 6.00 15
145 A12 15s brn, *sal* 3.75 15
146 A12 20s pink (I) 4.25 15
147 A12 20s pink (II) 3.00 15
148 A12 30s lt bl (I) 1.50 15
149 A12 35s dk bl ('31) 1.25 15
150 A12 40s dl lil (I) ('29) 1.50 15
151 A12 50s gray (II) 2.25 15
152 A11 1 l dk brn & pale brn 6.50 28
153 A11 2 l dk bl & bl ('31) 15.00 1.10
154 A11 5 l grn & pale grn ('33) 125.00 21.00
Nos. 135-154 (20) 175.54 26.10

The paper of Nos. 141, 144 and 145 is colored on the surface only.
See note above No. 113 for types A and B, and note above No. 101 for types I and II.

Type of 1927-33 Issue
Paper Colored Through

1931-33 ***Perf. 10***

155 A12 6s grn, *yel* 15 15
156 A12 10s grn, *yel* (I) ('33) 19.00 18
157 A12 15s brn, *sal* 3.50 15

View of Rezekne — A13

Designs (Views of Cities): 15s, Jelgava. 20s, Cesis (Wenden). 30s, Liepaja (Libau). 50s, Riga. 1 l, Riga Theater.

1928, Nov. 18 **Litho.** ***Perf. 10, 11½***

158 A13 6s dp grn & vio 75 30
159 A13 15s dk brn & ol grn 75 30
160 A13 20s cer & bl grn 1.25 38
161 A13 30s ultra & vio brn 1.25 50
162 A13 50s dk gray & plum 1.50 1.25
163 A13 1 l blk brn & brn 2.50 1.50
Nos. 158-163 (6) 8.00 4.23

10th anniv. of Latvian Independence.

Riga Exhibition Issue

Stamps of 1927-33 Overprinted

Latvijas ražojumu
Izstāde Rīgā,
1932.g.10.—18.IX.

1932, Aug. 30 ***Perf. 10, 11***

164 A12 3s orange 1.90 90
165 A12 10s grn, *yel* 1.90 1.25
166 A12 20s pink (I) 1.90 60
167 A12 35s dk bl 2.50 1.40

Riga Castle — A19

Arms and Shield — A20

Allegory of Latvia — A21

Ministry of Foreign Affairs — A22

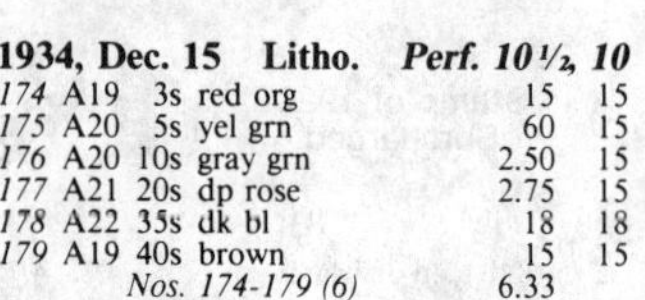

1934, Dec. 15 Litho. *Perf. 10½, 10*

No.	Type	Description	Unused	Used
174	A19	3s red org	15	15
175	A20	5s yel grn	60	15
176	A20	10s gray grn	2.50	15
177	A21	20s dp rose	2.75	15
178	A22	35s dk bl	18	18
179	A19	40s brown	15	15
		Nos. 174-179 (6)	6.33	
		Set value		78

Atis Kronvalds — A23

A. Pumpurs — A24

Juris Maters — A25

Mikus Krogzemis (Auseklis) — A26

1936, Jan. 4 Wmk. 212 *Perf. 11½*

No.	Type	Description	Unused	Used
180	A23	3s vermilion	2.75	2.75
181	A24	10s green	2.75	2.75
182	A25	20s rose pink	2.75	2.75
183	A26	35s dk bl	2.75	2.75

President Karlis Ulmanis — A27

1937, Sept. 4 Litho. *Perf. 10, 11½*

No.	Type	Description	Unused	Used
184	A27	3s org red & brn org	65	52
185	A27	5s yel grn	65	52
186	A27	10s dk sl grn	65	52
187	A27	20s rose lake & brn lake	1.00	52
188	A27	25s blk vio	1.25	65
189	A27	30s dk bl	1.25	65
190	A27	35s indigo	2.00	2.00
191	A27	40s lt brn	1.50	1.50
192	A27	50s ol blk	2.00	1.75
		Nos. 184-192 (9)	10.95	8.63

60th birthday of President Ulmanis.

Independence Monument, Rauna (Ronneburg) A28

Independence Monument, Jelgava A30

Monument Entrance to Cemetery at Riga — A29

War Memorial, Valka — A31

Independence Monument, Iecava — A32

Independence Monument, Riga — A33

Tomb of Col. Kalpaks — A34

Unwmk.

1937, July 12 Litho. *Perf. 10*

Thick Paper

No.	Type	Description	Unused	Used
193	A28	3s vermilion	55	80
194	A29	5s yel grn	55	80
195	A30	10s dp grn	55	80
196	A31	20s carmine	2.00	1.90
197	A32	30s lt bl	1.65	2.25

Wmk. 212

Engr. *Perf. 11½*

Thin Paper

No.	Type	Description	Unused	Used
198	A33	35s dk bl	1.65	2.25
199	A34	40s brown	2.50	2.75
		Nos. 193-199 (7)	9.45	11.55

View of Vidzeme — A35

General J. Balodis A37

President Karlis Ulmanis A38

Views: 5s, Latgale. 30s, Riga waterfront. 35s, Kurzeme. 40s, Zemgale.

1938, Nov. 17 *Perf. 10, 10½x10*

No.	Type	Description	Unused	Used
200	A35	3s brn org	15	15
a.		Booklet pane of 4	*20.00*	
201	A35	5s yel grn	28	15
a.		Booklet pane of 4	*20.00*	
202	A37	10s dk grn	40	15
a.		Booklet pane of 2	*20.00*	
203	A38	20s red lil	55	15
a.		Booklet pane of 2	*15.00*	
204	A35	30s dp bl	95	20
205	A35	35s indigo	70	20
a.		Booklet pane of 2	*20.00*	
206	A35	40s rose vio	1.10	28
		Nos. 200-206 (7)	4.13	
		Set value		1.05

The 20th anniversary of the Republic.

School, Riga — A42

Independence Monument, Riga — A45

President Karlis Ulmanis — A49

Designs: 5s, Castle of Jelgava. 10s, Riga Castle. 30s, Symbol of Freedom. 35s, Community House Daugavpils. 40s, Powder Tower and War Museum, Riga.

1939, May 13 Photo. *Perf. 10*

No.	Type	Description	Unused	Used
207	A42	3s brn org	70	55
208	A42	5s dp grn	70	55
209	A42	10s dk sl grn	85	55
210	A45	20s dk car rose	1.10	70
211	A42	30s brt ultra	1.25	55
212	A42	35s dk bl	1.40	1.40
213	A45	40s brn vio	1.65	1.10
214	A49	50s grnsh blk	2.00	1.10
		Nos. 207-214 (8)	9.65	6.50

5th anniv. of National Unity Day.

Harvesting Wheat A50

Apple A51

1939, Oct. 8

No.	Type	Description	Unused	Used
215	A50	10s slate green	65	65
216	A51	20s rose lake	85	85

8th Agricultural Exposition held near Riga.

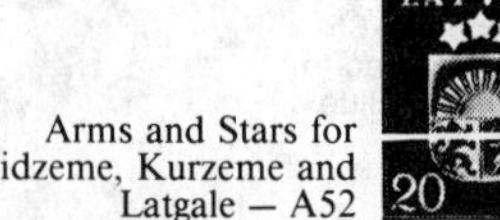

Arms and Stars for Vidzeme, Kurzeme and Latgale — A52

1940

No.	Type	Description	Unused	Used
217	A52	1s dk vio brn	15	15
218	A52	2s ocher	15	15
219	A52	3s red org	15	15
220	A52	5s dk ol brn	15	15
221	A52	7s dk grn	15	15
222	A52	10s dk bl grn	65	15
224	A52	20s rose brown	65	15
225	A52	30s dp red brn	70	22
226	A52	35s brt ultra	22	55
228	A52	50s dk slate grn	65	42
229	A52	1 l olive green	1.40	1.10
		Nos. 217-229 (11)	5.02	
		Set value		2.70

Catalogue values for unused stamps in this section, from this point to the end of the section, are for Never Hinged items.

Natl. Arms — A70

1991, Oct. 19 Litho. *Perf. 13x12½*

No.	Type	Description	Unused	Used
300	A70	5k multicolored	25	15
301	A70	10k multicolored	50	15
302	A70	15k multicolored	75	15
303	A70	20k multicolored	1.00	20
304	A70	40k multicolored	2.00	40
305	A70	50k multicolored	2.50	50

Size: 28x32mm

Perf. 13½x14

No.	Type	Description	Unused	Used
306	A70	100k sil & multi	5.00	1.00
307	A70	200k gold & multi	10.00	2.00
		Nos. 300-307 (8)	22.00	4.55

SEMI-POSTAL STAMPS

"Mercy" Assisting Wounded Soldier — SP1

1920 Unwmk. Typo. *Perf. 11½*

Brown and Green Design on Back

No.	Type	Description	Unused	Used
B1	SP1	20(30)k dk brn & red	30	50
B2	SP1	40(55)k dk bl & red	30	50
B3	SP1	50(70)k dk grn & red	30	50
B4	SP1	1(1.30)r dl sl & red	30	75

Wmk. Star and Triangles (197)

Blue Design on Back

No.	Type	Description	Unused	Used
B5	SP1	20(30)k dk brn & red	50	75
B6	SP1	40(55)k dk bl & red	50	75
a.		Vert. pair, imperf. btwn.	20.00	
B7	SP1	50(70)k dk grn & red	50	1.00
B8	SP1	1(1.30)r dk sl & red	50	1.00

Wmk. Similar to 145

Pink Paper *Imperf.*

Brown, Green and Red Design on Back

No.	Type	Description	Unused	Used
B9	SP1	20(30)k dk brn & red	50	1.40
B10	SP1	40(55)k dk bl & red	50	1.40
B11	SP1	50(70)k dk grn & red	50	1.40
B12	SP1	1(1.30)r dk sl & red	50	1.40
		Nos. B1-B12 (12)	5.20	11.35

These semi-postal stamps were printed on the backs of unfinished bank notes of the Workers and Soldiers Council, Riga, and the Bermondt-Avalov Army.

Nos. B1-B8 Surcharged **RUB. 2 RUB.**

1921 Unwmk. *Perf. 11½*

Brown and Green Design on Back

No.	Type	Description	Unused	Used
B13	SP1	20k + 2r dk brn & red	1.00	1.65
B14	SP1	40k + 2r dk bl & red	1.00	1.65
B15	SP1	50k + 2r dk grn & red	1.00	1.65
B16	SP1	1r + 2r dk sl & red	1.00	1.65

Wmk. Star and Triangles (197)

Blue Design on Back

No.	Type	Description	Unused	Used
B17	SP1	20k + 2r dk brn & red	7.50	6.00
B18	SP1	40k + 2r dk bl & red	7.50	6.00
B19	SP1	50k + 2r dk grn & red	7.50	6.00
B20	SP1	1r + 2r dk sl & red	7.50	6.00
		Nos. B13-B20 (8)	34.00	30.60

Regular Issue of 1923-25 Surcharged in Blue

1923 Wmk. Similar to 181 *Perf. 10*

B21	A12	1s + 10s vio	65	75
B22	A12	2s + 10s yel	65	75
B23	A12	4s + 10s dk grn	65	75

The surtax benefited the Latvian War Invalids Society.

Lighthouse and Harbor, Liepaja (Libau) — SP2

Church at Liepaja — SP5

Coat of Arms of Liepaja — SP6

Designs: 15s (25s), City Hall, Liepaja. 25s (35s), Public Bathing Pavilion, Liepaja.

1925, May 29 *Perf. 11½*

B24	SP2	6s (12s) red brn & dp bl	1.40	65
B25	SP2	15s (25s) dk bl & brn	75	1.00
B26	SP2	25s (35s) vio & dk grn	1.25	1.00
B27	SP5	30s (40s) dk bl & lake	2.75	3.75
B28	SP6	50s (60s) dk grn & vio	4.00	6.00
		Nos. B24-B28 (5)	10.15	12.40

Tercentenary of Liepaja (Libau). The surtax benefited that city. Exist imperf.

President Janis Cakste — SP7

1928, Apr. 18 Engr.

B29	SP7	2s (12s) red org	1.65	2.00
B30	SP7	6s (16s) dp grn	1.65	2.00
B31	SP7	15s (25s) red brn	1.65	2.00
B32	SP7	25s (35s) dp bl	2.25	2.75
B33	SP7	30s (40s) claret	1.65	2.00
		Nos. B29-B33 (5)	8.85	10.75

The surtax helped erect a monument to Janis Cakste, 1st pres. of the Latvian Republic.

Venta River — SP8

Allegory, "Latvia" — SP9

View of Jelgava — SP10

National Theater, Riga — SP11

View of Cesis (Wenden) SP12

Riga Bridge and Trenches SP13

Perf. 11½, Imperf.

1928, Nov. 18 Wmk. 212 Litho.

B34	SP8	6s (16s) grn	1.65	1.65
B35	SP9	10s (20s) scar	1.65	1.65
B36	SP10	15s (25s) mar	1.90	1.90
B37	SP11	30s (40s) ultra	2.25	2.25
B38	SP12	50s (60s) dk gray	2.25	2.25
B39	SP13	1 l (1.10 l) choc	3.25	3.25
		Nos. B34-B39 (6)	12.95	12.95

The surtax was given to a committee for the erection of a Liberty Memorial.

Z. A. Meierovics — SP14

1929, Aug. 22 *Perf. 11½, Imperf.*

B46	SP14	2s (4s) org	1.75	1.50
B47	SP14	6s (12s) dp grn	1.75	2.50
B48	SP14	15s (25s) red brn	1.75	2.50
B49	SP14	25s (35s) dp bl	2.25	2.50
B50	SP14	30s (40s) ultra	2.25	2.50
		Nos. B46-B50 (5)	9.75	11.50

The surtax was used to erect a monument to Z. A. Meierovics, Latvian statesman.

Tuberculosis Cross — SP15

Allegory of Hope for the Sick — SP16

Gustavs Zemgals SP17

Riga Castle SP18

Daisies and Double-barred Cross — SP20

Tuberculosis Sanatorium, near Riga — SP22

Cakste, Kviesis and Zemgals SP23

Designs: No. B61, Janis Cakste, 1st pres. of Latvia. No. B63, Pres. Alberts Kviesis.

1930, Dec. 4 Typo. *Perf. 10, 11½*

B56	SP15	1s (2s) dk vio & red org	1.00	1.00
B57	SP15	2s (4s) org & red org	1.00	1.00
a.		Cliché of 1s (2s) in plate of 2s (4s)	*450.00*	*600.00*
B58	SP16	4s (8s) dk grn & red	1.25	1.25
B59	SP17	5s (10s) brt grn & dk brn	1.25	1.25
B60	SP18	6s (12s) ol grn & bis	1.25	1.65
B61	SP17	10s (20s) dp red & blk	1.50	1.50
B62	SP20	15s (30s) mar & dl grn	1.40	1.90
B63	SP17	20s (40s) rose lake & ind	1.90	1.90
B64	SP22	25s (50s) multi	3.00	3.00
B65	SP23	30s (60s) multi	3.75	4.50
		Nos. B56-B65 (10)	17.30	18.95

The surtax was for the Latvian Anti-Tuberculosis Society.

J. Rainis and New Buildings, Riga SP24

Character from Play and Rainis SP25

Characters from Plays SP26

Rainis and Lyre SP27

Flames, Flag and Rainis SP28

1930, May 23 Wmk. 212 *Perf. 11½*

B66	SP24	1s (2s) dl vio	65	65
B67	SP25	2s (4s) yel org	65	65
B68	SP26	4s (8s) dp grn	65	65
B69	SP27	6s (12s) yel grn & red brn	65	65
B70	SP28	10s (20s) dk red	6.25	14.00
B71	SP27	15s (30s) red brn & yel grn	6.25	12.50
		Nos. B66-B71 (6)	15.10	29.10

Sold at double face value, surtax going to memorial fund for J. Rainis (Jan Plieksans, 1865-1929), writer and politician.

Exist imperf. Value twice that of perf. stamps.

Nos. B56 to B65 Surcharged in Black

1931, Aug. 19 *Perf. 10, 11½*

B72	SP18	9s on 6s (12s)	60	1.10
B73	SP15	16s on 1s (2s)	9.00	8.00
B74	SP15	17s on 2s (4s)	1.25	1.40
B75	SP16	19s on 4s (8s)	3.00	3.25
B76	SP17	20s on 5s (10s)	1.75	2.25
B77	SP20	23s on 15s (30s)	1.25	1.10
B78	SP17	25s on 10s (20s)	2.50	2.75
B79	SP17	35s on 20s (40s)	3.50	3.25
B80	SP22	45s on 25s (50s)	11.00	14.00
B81	SP23	55s on 30s (60s)	11.00	14.00
		Nos. B72-B81 (10)	44.85	51.10

The surcharge replaces the original total price, including surtax.

Nos. B73 to B81 have no bars in the surcharge. The surtax aided the Latvian Anti-Tuberculosis Society.

Lacplesis, the Deliverer SP29

Designs: 1s, Kriva telling stories under Holy Oak. 2s, Enslaved Latvians building Riga under knight's supervision. 4s, Death of Black Knight. 5s, Spirit of Lacplesis over freed Riga.

Inscribed: "AIZSARGI" (Army Reserve)

1932, Feb. 10 *Perf. 10½, Imperf.*

B82	SP29	1s (11s) vio brn & bluish	1.50	1.75
B83	SP29	2s (17s) ocher & ol grn	1.50	1.75
B84	SP29	3s (23s) red brn & org brn	1.50	2.00
B85	SP29	4s (34s) dk grn & grn	1.75	2.25
B86	SP29	5s (45s) grn & emer	2.50	3.25
		Nos. B82-B86 (5)	8.75	11.00

Surtax aided the Militia Maintenance Fund.

Marching Troops SP30

Infantry in Action SP31

Nurse Binding Soldier's Wound SP32

Army Soup Kitchen SP33

Gen. J. Balodis — SP34

1932, May ***Perf. 10½, Imperf.***

B87 SP30 6s (25s) ol brn & red vio 2.75 3.00
B88 SP31 7s (35s) dk bl grn & dk bl 2.75 3.00
B89 SP32 10s (45s) ol grn & blk brn 2.75 3.00
B90 SP33 12s (55s) lake & ol grn 3.00 3.75
B91 SP34 15s (75s) red org & brn vio 4.50 5.00
Nos. B87-B91 (5) 15.75 17.75

The surtax aided the Latvian Home Guards.

Symbolical of Unified Latvia — SP35

Aid to the Sick — SP37

Symbolical of the Strength of the Latvian Union SP36

"Charity" SP38

Wmk. Multiple Swastikas (212)

1936, Dec. 28 **Litho.** ***Perf. 11½***

B92 SP35 3s org red 1.50 2.00
B93 SP36 10s green 1.50 2.00
B94 SP37 20s rose pink 1.50 2.00
B95 SP38 35s blue 1.50 2.00

Souvenir Sheets

SP39

1938, May 12 **Wmk. 212** ***Perf. 11***

B96 SP39 Sheet of 2 5.50 12.00
a. 35s Justice Palace, Riga 1.50 2.00
b. 40s Power Station, Kegums 1.50 2.00

Sold for 2 l. The surtax of 1.25 l was for the National Reconstruction Fund.

Overprinted in Blue with Dates 1934 1939 and "15" over "V"

1939

B97 SP39 Sheet of 2 7.50 15.00

5th anniv. of Natl. Unity Day. Sold for 2 lats. Surtax for the Natl. Reconstruction Fund.

AIR POST STAMPS

Blériot XI — AP1

Wmk. Wavy Lines Similar to 181

1921, July 30 **Litho.** ***Perf. 11½***

C1 AP1 10r emerald 1.75 1.25
a. Imperf. 7.50 10.50
C2 AP1 20r dark blue 1.75 1.25
a. Imperf. 7.50 10.50

1928, May 1

C3 AP1 10s dp grn 1.50 1.10
C4 AP1 15s red 1.50 1.10
C5 AP1 25s ultra 2.00 3.50
a. Pair, imperf. between 22.50

Nos. C1 to C5 sometimes show letters of a paper maker's watermark "PACTIEN LIGAT MILLS".

1931-32 **Wmk. 212** ***Perf. 11, 11½***

C6 AP1 10s dp grn 1.25 90
C7 AP1 15s red 1.90 1.40
C8 AP1 25s dp bl ('32) 2.50 1.65

Type of 1921 Overprinted or Surcharged in Black

LATVIJA-AFRIKA
1933.

1933, May 26 **Wmk. 212** ***Imperf.***

C9 AP1 10s dp grn 5.75 8.00
C10 AP1 15s red 5.75 8.00
C11 AP1 25s dp bl 10.50 16.00
C12 AP1 50s on 15s red 72.50 92.50
C13 AP1 100s on 25s dp bl 82.50 92.50
Nos. C9-C13 (5) 177.00 217.00

Issued to commemorate and finance a flight from Riga to Bathurst, Gambia. The plane crashed at Neustettin, Germany.

Counterfeits exist of Nos. C1-C13.

AIR POST SEMI-POSTAL STAMPS

Durbes Castle, Rainis Birthplace — SPAP1

Wmk. 212

1930, May 26 **Litho.** ***Perf. 11½***

CB1 SPAP1 10s (20s) red & ol grn 3.75 5.00
CB2 SPAP1 15s (30s) dk yel grn & cop red 3.75 5.00

Surtax for the Rainis Memorial Fund.

Imperf.

CB1a SPAP1 10s (20s) 7.00 15.00
CB2a SPAP1 15s (30s) 7.00 15.00

Nos. C6-C8 Surcharged in Magenta, Blue or Red

1931, Dec. 5

CB3 AP1 10s + 50s dp grn (M) 4.50 7.75
CB4 AP1 15s + 1 l red (Bl) 4.50 7.75
CB5 AP1 25s + 1.50 l dp bl 4.50 7.75

Surtax for the Latvian Home Guards.

Imperf.

CB3a AP1 10s + 50s 7.75 7.75
CB4a AP1 15s + 1 l 7.75 7.75
CB5a AP1 25s + 1.50 l 7.75 7.75

SPAP2

1932, June 17 ***Perf. 10½***

CB6 SPAP2 10s (20s) dk sl grn & grn 11.00 14.00
CB7 SPAP2 15s (30s) brt red & buff 11.00 14.00
CB8 SPAP2 25s (50s) dp bl & gray 11.00 14.00

Surtax for the Latvian Home Guards.

Imperf.

CB6a SPAP2 10s (20s) 14.00 16.00
CB7a SPAP2 15s (30s) 14.00 16.00
CB8a SPAP2 25s (50s) 14.00 16.00

Icarus SPAP3

Leonardo da Vinci SPAP4

Charles Balloon — SPAP5

Wright Brothers Biplane SPAP6

Bleriot Monoplane SPAP7

1932, Dec. ***Perf. 10, 11½***

CB9 SPAP3 5s (25s) ol bis & grn 8.50 8.50
CB10 SPAP4 10s (50s) ol brn & gray grn 8.50 8.50
CB11 SPAP5 15s (75s) red brn & gray grn 7.75 8.50
CB12 SPAP6 20s (1 l) gray grn & lil rose 6.50 7.50
CB13 SPAP7 25s (1.25 l) brn & bl 6.50 7.50
Nos. CB9-CB13 (5) 37.75 40.50

Issued to honor pioneers of aviation. The surtax of four times the face value was for wounded Latvian aviators.

Imperf.

CB9a SPAP3 5s (25s) 12.00 13.00
CB10a SPAP4 10s (50s) 12.00 13.00
CB11a SPAP5 15s (75s) 12.00 11.00
CB12a SPAP6 20s (1 l) 9.25 11.00
CB13a SPAP7 25s (1.25 l) 9.25 11.00
Nos. CB9a-CB13a (5) 54.50 59.00

Latvia German Occupation Stamps can be mounted in Scott's Germany Part II Album.

Icarus Falling SPAP8

Monument to Aviators SPAP9

Proposed Tombs for Aviators SPAP10 SPAP11

1933, Mar. 15 ***Perf. 11½***

CB14 SPAP8 2s (52s) blk & ocher 8.25 15.00
CB15 SPAP9 3s (53s) blk & red org 8.25 15.00
CB16 SPAP10 10s (60s) blk & dk yel grn 8.25 12.00
CB17 SPAP11 20s (70s) blk & cer 8.25 15.00

50s surtax for wounded Latvian aviators.

Imperf.

CB14a SPAP8 2s (52s) 11.00 14.00
CB15a SPAP9 3s (53s) 11.00 14.00
CB16a SPAP10 10s (60s) 11.00 14.00
CB17a SPAP11 20s (70s) 11.00 14.00

Monoplane Taking Off SPAP12

Designs: 7s (57s), Biplane under fire at Riga. 35s (1.35 l), Map and planes.

1933, June 15 **Wmk. 212** ***Perf. 11½***

CB18 SPAP12 3s (53s) org & sl bl 14.00 17.00
CB19 SPAP12 7s (57s) sl bl & dk brn 14.00 17.00
CB20 SPAP12 35s (1.35 l) dp ultra & ol blk 14.00 17.00

Surtax for wounded Latvian aviators. Counterfeits exist.

Imperf.

CB18a SPAP12 3s (53s) 17.50 21.00
CB19a SPAP12 7s (57s) 17.50 21.00
CB20a SPAP12 35s (1.35 l) 17.50 21.00

American Gee-Bee SPAP13

English Seaplane S6B SPAP14

Graf Zeppelin over Riga SPAP15

DO-X SPAP16

1933, Sept. 5 *Perf. 11½*

CB21	SPAP13	8s (68s) brn & gray blk	40.00	50.00
CB22	SPAP14	12s (1.12 l) brn car & ol grn	40.00	50.00
CB23	SPAP15	30s (1.30 l) bl & gray blk	40.00	50.00
CB24	SPAP16	40s (1.90 l) brn vio & ind	40.00	50.00

Surtax for wounded Latvian aviators.

Imperf.

CB21a	SPAP13	8s (68s)	40.00	55.00
CB22a	SPAP14	12s (1.12 l)	40.00	55.00
CB23a	SPAP15	30s (1.30 l)	40.00	55.00
CB24a	SPAP16	40s (1.90 l)	40.00	55.00

OCCUPATION STAMPS

Issued under German Occupation

German Stamps of 1905-18 Handstamped

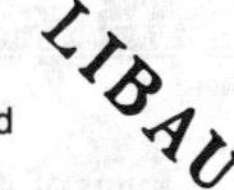

1919 **Wmk. 125** *Perf. 14, 14½*

Red Overprint

1N1	A22	2½pf gray	225.00	225.00
1N2	A16	5pf green	180.00	90.00
1N3	A22	15pf dk vio	275.00	90.00
1N4	A16	20pf bl vio	110.00	37.50
1N5	A16	25pf org & blk, *yel*	375.00	275.00
1N6	A16	50pf pur & blk, *buff*	375.00	275.00

Blue Overprint

1N7	A22	2½pf gray	225.00	225.00
1N8	A16	5pf green	110.00	57.50
1N9	A16	10pf carmine	92.50	27.50
1N10	A22	15pf dk vio	275.00	150.00
1N11	A16	20pf bl vio	110.00	27.50
1N12	A16	25pf org & blk, *yel*	375.00	275.00
1N13	A16	50pf pur & blk, *buff*	375.00	275.00

Inverted and double overprints exist, as well as counterfeit overprints.

Some experts believe that Nos. 1N1-1N7 were not officially issued. All used copies are canceled to order.

LATVIJA
1941.
1. VII

Russia Nos. 734, 616, 735, 617, 736 and 619A were overprinted in black or dark green with the three lines above in 1941. They were used in Latvia under the German occupation in July-September, 1941, and were replaced by German stamps in October, 1941.

Kurland

Four stamps of Germany were surcharged for use in Kurzeme in April, 1945, during World War II. Those are Germany Nos. 509, 511A and 516 (5pf, 10pf, 20pf with Hitler's head), surcharged "KURLAND" and "6", and No. MQ1 (red brown military parcel post stamp) surcharged "Kurland" and "12". After the Germans capitulated to the Russians May 8, 1945, in the territory of Latvia, these surcharged stamps were replaced by stamps of Russia.

Issued under Russian Occupation

The following stamps were issued at Mitau during the occupation of Kurland by the West Russian Army under Colonel Bermondt-Avalov.

Latvia Russian Occupation stamps can be mounted in Scott's Soviet Republics Part I Album.

Stamps of Latvia Handstamped

1919 **Wmk. 108** *Imperf.*

On Stamps of 1919

2N1	A1	3k lilac	12.50	17.50
2N2	A1	5k carmine	12.50	17.50
2N3	A1	10k dp bl	67.50	92.50
2N4	A1	20k orange	12.50	17.50
2N5	A1	25k gray	12.50	17.50
2N6	A1	35k dk brn	12.50	17.50
2N7	A1	50k purple	12.50	17.50
2N8	A1	75k emerald	15.00	22.50

On Riga Liberation Stamps

2N9	A2	5k carmine	7.50	12.50
2N10	A2	15k dp grn	7.50	12.50
2N11	A2	35k brown	7.50	12.50

Stamps of Latvia Overprinted

On Stamps of 1919

2N12	A1	3k lilac	5.00	7.50
2N13	A1	5k carmine	5.00	7.50
2N14	A1	10k dp bl	60.00	92.50
2N15	A1	20k orange	10.00	15.00
2N16	A1	25k gray	17.50	32.50
2N17	A1	35k dk brn	12.50	17.50
2N18	A1	50k purple	12.50	17.50
2N19	A1	75k emerald	12.50	17.50

On Riga Liberation Stamps

2N20	A2	5k carmine	4.00	5.00
2N21	A2	15k dp grn	4.00	5.00
2N22	A2	35k brown	4.00	5.00
a.		Inverted overprint	*115.00*	

The letters "Z. A." are the initials of "Zapadnaya Armiya"-i.e. Western Army.

Russian Stamps of 1909-17 Surcharged Like Illustration

Perf. 14, 14½x15

Unwmk.

On Stamps of 1909-12

2N23	A14	10k on 2k grn	4.00	5.00
a.		Inverted surcharge	*25.00*	
2N24	A15	30k on 4k car	3.50	4.50
2N25	A14	40k on 5k cl	3.50	4.50
2N26	A15	50k pn 10k dk bl	3.50	4.50
2N27	A11	70k on 15k red brn & bl	3.50	4.50
a.		Inverted surcharge	*50.00*	
2N28	A8	90k on 20k bl & car	3.50	4.50
2N29	A11	1r on 25k grn & vio	3.50	4.50
2N30	A11	1½r on 35k red brn & grn	22.50	37.50
2N31	A8	2r on 50k vio & grn	4.50	6.50
a.		Inverted surcharge	*30.00*	
2N32	A11	4r on 70k brn & org	12.50	15.00

Perf. 13½

2N33	A9	6r on 1r pale brn, brn & org	12.50	15.00

On Stamps of 1917

Imperf

2N34	A14	20k on 3k red	4.50	5.00
2N35	A14	40k on 5k cl	32.50	42.50
2N36	A12	10r on 3.50r mar & lt grn	32.50	42.55
a.		Inverted surcharge	*100.00*	
		Nos. 2N1-2N36 (36)	473.50	676.05

Eight typographed stamps of this design were prepared in 1919, but never placed in use. They exist both perforated and imperforate. Value, set, imperf. $1, perf. $2.

Arms of Soviet Latvia — OS1

1940 **Typo.** **Wmk. 265** *Perf. 10*

2N45	OS1	1s dk vio	15	15
2N46	OS1	2s org yel	15	15
2N47	OS1	3s org ver	15	15
2N48	OS1	5s dk ol grn	15	15
2N49	OS1	7s turq grn	15	15
2N50	OS1	10s slate grn	38	15
2N51	OS1	20s brn lake	65	15
2N52	OS1	30s light blue	75	25
2N53	OS1	35s brt ultra	15	15
2N54	OS1	40s chocolate	50	15
2N55	OS1	50s lt gray	65	15
2N56	OS1	1 l brn	1.25	25
2N57	OS1	5 l brt grn	10.00	4.50
		Nos. 2N45-2N57 (13)	15.08	6.50

Used values of 2N45-2N57 are for CTOs.

LEBANON

(Grand Liban)

LOCATION — Asia Minor, bordering on the Mediterranean Sea
GOVT. — Republic
AREA — 4,036 sq. mi.
POP. — 3,500,000 (est. 1984)
CAPITAL — Beirut

Formerly a part of the Syrian province of Turkey, Lebanon was occupied by French forces after World War I. It was mandated to France after it had been declared a separate state. Limited autonomy was granted in 1927 and full independence achieved in 1941. The French issued two sets of occupation stamps (with T.E.O. overprint) for Lebanon in late 1919. The use of these and later occupation issues (of 1920-24, with overprints "O.M.F." and "Syrie-Grand Liban") was extended to Syria, Cilicia, Alaouites and Alexandretta. By custom, these are all listed under Syria.

100 Centimes = 1 Piaster
100 Piasters = 1 Pound

Catalogue values for unused stamps in this country are for Never Hinged items, beginning with Scott 177 in the regular postage section, Scott B13 in the semi-postal section, Scott C97 in the airpost section, Scott CB5 in the airpost semi-postal section, Scott J37 in the postage due section, and Scott RA11 in the postal tax section.

Issued under French Mandate

Stamps of France 1900-21 Surcharged

GRAND
LIBAN
50
CENTIEMES

1924 **Unwmk.** *Perf. 14x13½*

1	A16	10c on 2c vio brn	35	35
a.		Inverted surcharge	9.00	9.00
2	A22	25c on 5c orange	35	16
3	A22	50c on 10c green	25	15
4	A20	75c on 15c sl grn	65	65
5	A22	1pi on 20c red brn	40	22
a.		Double surcharge	9.00	9.00
b.		Inverted surcharge	9.00	9.00
6	A22	1.25pi on 25c blue	1.00	80
7	A22	1.50pi on 30c org	50	50
8	A22	1.50pi on 30c red	50	50
9	A20	2.50pi on 50c dl bl	50	35
a.		Inverted surcharge	9.00	9.00

Surcharged

GRAND LIBAN
2 PIASTRES

10	A18	2pi on 40c red & pale bl	1.40	80
a.		Inverted surcharge	12.00	12.00
11	A18	3pi on 60c violet & ultra	2.50	2.25
12	A18	5pi on 1fr cl & ol green	2.50	2.25
13	A18	10pi on 2fr org & pale bl	4.50	4.00
a.		Inverted surcharge	18.00	18.00
14	A18	25pi on 5fr dk bl & buff	7.50	6.50
a.		Inverted surcharge	35.00	35.00
		Nos. 1-14 (14)	22.90	19.48

Broken and missing letters and varieties of spacing are numerous in these surcharges.

Stamps of France, 1923, (Pasteur) Surcharged "GRAND LIBAN" and New Values

15	A23	50c on 10c green	38	25
a.		Inverted surcharge	11.00	11.00
16	A23	1.50pi on 30c red	50	42
17	A23	2.50pi on 50c blue	38	25
a.		Inverted surcharge	11.00	11.00

Commemorative Stamps of France, 1924, (Olympic Games) Surcharged "GRAND LIBAN" and New Values

18	A24	50c on 10c gray grn & yel grn	14.00	14.00
a.		Inverted surcharge	100.00	
19	A25	1.25pi on 25c rose & dk rose	14.00	14.00
a.		Inverted surcharge	100.00	
20	A26	1.50pi on 30c brn red & blk	14.00	14.00
a.		Inverted surcharge	100.00	
21	A27	2.50pi on 50c ultra & dk bl	14.00	14.00
a.		Inverted surcharge	100.00	

Stamps of France, 1900-24, Surcharged

Gd Liban
0, P. 25
لبنان الكبير
٤/١ القرش

c

1924-25

22	A16	0p10 on 2c vio brn	15	15
23	A22	0p25 on 5c orange	25	25
24	A22	0p50 on 10c green	35	35
25	A20	0p75 on 15c gray grn	25	25
26	A22	1pi on 20c red brn	20	20
27	A22	1p25 on 25c blue	40	40
28	A22	1p50 on 30c red	35	35
29	A22	1p50 on 30c orange	25.00	22.50
30	A22	2pi on 35c vio ('25)	45	45
31	A20	3pi on 60c lt vio ('25)	55	55
32	A20	4pi on 85c ver	80	80

Surcharged

Grand Liban
2 Piastres
لبنان الكبير
غرش ٢

33	A18	2pi on 40c red & pale bl	20	20
a.		Second line of Arabic reads "2 Piastre" (singular)	50	50
34	A18	2pi on 45c green & blue ('25)	10.00	10.00
35	A18	3pi on 60c violet & ultra	55	55
36	A18	5pi on 1fr cl & ol green	80	80
37	A18	10pi on 2fr org & pale bl	2.50	2.50
38	A18	25pi on 5fr dk bl & buff	4.00	3.50
		Nos. 22-38 (17)	46.80	43.80

Last line of surcharge on No. 33 has four characters, with a 9-like character between the third and fourth in illustration. Last line on No. 33a is as illustrated.

The surcharge may be found inverted on most of Nos. 22-38, and double on some values.

Stamps of France 1923-24 (Pasteur) Surcharged Type "c"

39	A23 0p50 on 10c green	25	22
a.	Inverted surcharge	7.00	7.00
b.	Double surcharge	6.00	6.00
40	A23 0p75 on 15c green	35	30
41	A23 1p50 on 30c red	40	35
a.	Inverted surcharge	9.00	9.00
42	A23 2pi on 45c red	75	65
a.	Inverted surcharge	8.00	8.00
43	A23 2p50 on 50c blue	25	22
a.	Inverted surcharge	8.00	8.00
b.	Double surcharge	7.00	7.00
44	A23 4pi on 75c blue	62	55
	Nos. 39-44 (6)	2.62	2.29

France Nos. 198 to 201 (Olympics) Surcharged Type "c"

45	A24 0p50 on 10c gray grn & yel grn	12.00	12.00
46	A25 1p25 on 25c rose & dk rose	12.00	12.00
47	A26 1p50 on 30c brn red & black	12.00	12.00
48	A27 2p50 on 50c ultra & dk bl	12.00	12.00

France No. 219 (Ronsard) Surcharged Type "c"

49	A28 4pi on 75c bl, *bluish*	62	62
a.	Inverted surcharge	18.00	18.00

Cedar of Lebanon A1

Crusader Castle, Tripoli A3

View of Beirut — A2

Designs: 50c, Crusader Castle, Tripoli. 75c, Beit-ed-Din Palace. 1p, Temple of Jupiter, Baalbek. 1.25p, Mouktara Palace. 1.50p, Harbor of Tyre. 2p, View of Zahle. 2.50p, Ruins at Baalbek. 3p, Square at Deir-el-Kamar. 5p, Castle at Sidon. 25p, Square at Beirut.

1925 Litho. *Perf. 12½, 13½*

50	A1 0p10 dark violet	15	15

Photo.

51	A2 0p25 olive black	28	20
52	A2 0p50 yellow grn	15	15
53	A2 0p75 brn orange	20	15
54	A2 1pi magenta	40	30
55	A2 1p25 deep green	55	50
56	A2 1p50 rose red	20	15
57	A2 2pi dark brown	32	15
58	A2 2p50 peacock bl	40	30
59	A2 3pi orange brn	60	40
60	A2 5pi violet	60	50
61	A3 10pi violet brn	1.25	80
62	A2 25pi ultramarine	5.00	4.50
	Nos. 50-62 (13)	10.10	8.25

Stamps of 1925 with Bars and Surcharged — 3P·50

1926

63	A2 3p50 on 0p75 brn org	25	25
64	A2 4pi on 0p25 ol blk	40	40
65	A2 6pi on 2p50 pck bl	35	35
66	A2 12pi on 1p25 dp grn	40	40
67	A2 20pi on 1p25 dp grn	1.40	1.40

Stamps of 1925 with Bars and Surcharged — 4P·50

68	A2 4p50 on 0p75 brn org	50	50
69	A2 7p50 on 2p50 pck bl	50	50
70	A2 15pi on 25pi ultra	60	60
	Nos. 63-70 (8)	4.40	4.40

No. 51 with Bars and Surcharged — 4P.

1927

71	A2 4pi on 0p25 ol blk	65	65

Issues of Republic under French Mandate

Stamps of 1925 Issue Overprinted in Black or Red — République Libanaise

1927

72	A1 0p10 dark vio (R)	15	15
a.	Black overprint	11.00	11.00
73	A2 0p50 yellow grn	15	15
74	A2 1pi magenta	15	15
75	A2 1p50 rose red	20	20
76	A2 2pi dark brown	80	20
77	A2 3pi orange brn	32	15
78	A2 5pi violet	60	30
79	A3 10pi violet brn	85	30
80	A2 25pi ultramarine	3.75	65
	Nos. 72-80 (9)	6.97	
	Set value		1.90

On Nos. 72 and 79 the overprint is set in two lines. On all stamps the double bar obliterates GRAND LIBAN.

Same Overprint on Provisional Issues of 1926-27

15 PIASTERS ON 25 PIASTERS

TYPE I - "Republique Libanaise" at foot of stamp.

TYPE II - "République Libanaise" near top of stamp.

81	A2 4pi on 0p25 ol blk	15	15
82	A2 4p50 on 0p75 brn org	22	15
83	A2 7p50 on 2p50 pck bl	32	15
84	A2 15pi on 25pi ultra (I)	2.75	1.40
a.	Type II	3.50	2.00

Most of Nos. 72-84 are known with overprint double, inverted or on back as well as face.

Stamps of 1927 Overprinted in Black or Red — الجمهورية اللبنانية

1928

86	A1 0p10 dark vio (R)	16	16
a.	French overprint omitted	4.00	4.00
87	A2 0p50 yel grn (Bk)	45	45
a.	Arabic overprint inverted	2.00	2.00
88	A2 1pi magenta (Bk)	20	20
a.	Inverted overprint	10.00	10.00
89	A2 1p50 rose red (Bk)	65	50
90	A2 2pi dark brown (R)	80	80
90A	A2 2pi dk brn (Bk+R)	40.00	40.00
91	A2 3pi org brown (Bk)	35	35
92	A2 5pi violet (Bk+R)	80	80
93	A2 5pi violet (R)	6.00	6.00
a.	French ovpt. above Arabic	6.50	6.50
94	A3 10pi vio brn (Bk)	1.40	1.40
a.	Double overprint	7.00	7.00
b.	Double overprint inverted		
c.	Inverted overprint	25.00	25.00
95	A2 25pi ultra (Bk+R)	3.50	2.50
95A	A2 25pi ultra (R)	5.00	4.00
	Nos. 86-95A (12)	59.31	57.16

On all stamps the double bar with Arabic overprint obliterates Arabic inscription.

Same Overprint on Nos. 81-84

96	A2 4pi on 0p25 (Bk+R)	35	35
97	A2 4p50 on 0p75 (Bk)	65	50
98	A2 7p50 on 2p50 (Bk+R)	80	80
99	A2 7p50 on 2p50 (R)	4.00	4.00
100	A2 15pi on 25pi (II) (Bk+R)	2.50	2.50
a.	Arabic overprint inverted		
101	A2 15pi on 25pi (I) (R)	4.00	4.00
	Nos. 96-101 (6)	12.30	12.15

The new values are surcharged in black. The initials in ( ) refer to the colors of the overprints.

Stamps of 1925 Surcharged in Red or Black

1928-29 *Perf. 13½*

102	A2 0p50 on 0p75 brn org (Bk) ('29)	38	38
103	A2 2pi on 1p25 dp grn	38	38
104	A2 4pi on 0p25 ol blk	38	38
a.	Double surcharge	9.00	9.00
105	A2 7p50 on 2p50 pck bl	60	60
a.	Double surcharge	9.00	9.00
b.	Inverted surcharge	9.00	9.00
106	A2 15pi on 25pi ultra	5.25	5.25
	Nos. 102-106 (5)	6.99	6.99

On Nos. 103, 104 and 105 the surcharged numerals are 3¼mm high, and have thick strokes.

No. 86 Surcharged in Red — 05

1928

107	A1 (0p)05 on 0p10 dk vio	16	16

Silkworm, Cocoon and Moth — A4

1930, Feb. 11 Typo. *Perf. 11*

108	A4 4pi black brown	5.50	5.25
109	A4 4½pi vermilion	5.50	5.25
110	A4 7½pi dark blue	5.50	5.25
111	A4 10pi dk violet	5.50	5.25
112	A4 15pi dark green	5.50	5.25
113	A4 25pi claret	5.50	5.25
	Nos. 108-113 (6)	33.00	31.50

Sericultural Congress, Beirut. Presentation imperfs exist.

Pigeon Rocks, Ras Beirut — A5

View of Bickfaya — A8

Beit-ed-Din Palace — A10

Crusader Castle, Tripoli A11

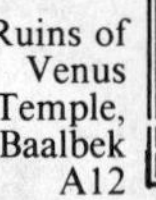

Ruins of Venus Temple, Baalbek A12

Ancient Bridge, Dog River — A13

Belfort Castle — A14

Afka Falls — A19

Designs: 0p20, Cedars of Lebanon. 0p25, Ruins of Bacchus Temple, Baalbek. 1pi, Crusader Castle, Sidon Harbor. 5pi, Arcade of Beit-ed-Din Palace. 6pi, Tyre Harbor. 7.50pi, Ruins of Sun Temple, Baalbek. 10pi, View of Hasbeya. 25pi, Government House, Beirut. 50pi, View of Deir-el-Kamar. 0p75, 100pi, Ruins at Baalbek.

1930-35 Litho. *Perf. 12½, 13½*

114	A5 0p10 brn orange	15	15
115	A5 0p20 yellow brn	15	15
116	A5 0p25 deep blue	15	15

Photo.

117	A8 0p50 orange brn	42	30
118	A11 0p75 ol brn ('32)	15	15
119	A8 1pi deep green	30	20
120	A8 1pi brn vio ('35)	30	20
121	A10 1.50pi violet brn	50	30
122	A10 1.50pi dp grn ('32)	1.40	25
123	A11 2pi Prussian bl	80	30
124	A12 3pi black brown	60	30
125	A13 4pi orange brn	60	15
126	A14 4p50 carmine	60	40
127	A14 5pi greenish blk	40	20
128	A13 6pi brn violet	1.60	45
129	A10 7.50pi deep blue	60	25
130	A10 10pi dk ol grn	2.00	25
131	A19 15pi blk violet	1.90	42
132	A19 25pi blue green	2.50	55
133	A8 50pi apple grn	10.00	2.50
134	A11 100pi black	10.00	7.00
	Nos. 114-134 (21)	35.12	14.62

See Nos. 135, 144, 152-155.

Pigeon Rocks Type of 1930-35 Redrawn

1934 Litho. *Perf. 12½x12*

135	A5 0p10 dull orange	1.75	1.00

Lines in rocks and water more distinct. Printer's name "Helio Vaugirard, Paris," in larger letters.

Cedar of Lebanon A23 — President Emile Edde A24

Dog River Panorama A25

1937-40 Typo. *Perf. 14x13½*

137 A23 0p10 rose car 15 15
137A A23 0p20 aqua ('40) 15 15
137B A23 0p25 pale rose lilac ('40) 15 15
138 A23 0p50 magenta 15 15
138A A23 0p75 brown ('40) 16 15

Engr.
Perf. 13

139 A24 3pi dark vio 1.20 30
140 A24 4pi black brown 16 15
141 A24 4p50 carmine 25 15
142 A25 10pi brn carmine 65 20
142A A25 12½pi dp ultra ('40) 22 15
143 A25 15pi dk grn ('38) 1.00 30
143A A25 20pi chestnut ('40) 30 22
143B A25 25pi crimson ('40) 35 25
143C A25 50pi dk vio ('40) 2.00 65
143D A25 100pi sepia ('40) 1.20 90
Nos. 137-143D (15) 8.09 4.02

Nos. 137A, 137B, 138A, 142A, 143A, 143B, 143C, and 143D exist imperforate.

View of Bickfaya A26

Type A8 Redrawn

1937 Photo. *Perf. 13½*

144 A26 0p50 org brown 5.00 3.50

Arabic inscriptions more condensed.

Stamps of 1930-37 Surcharged in Black or Red

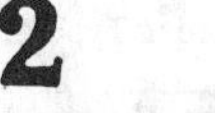

1937-42 *Perf. 13, 13½*

145 A24 2pi on 3pi dk vio 25 25
146 A24 2½pi on 4pi blk brn 25 25
146A A24 2½pi on 4pi black brown (R) ('42) 25 25
147 A10 6pi on 7.50pi deep blue (R) 1.00 42

Stamps of 1930-35 and Type of 1937-40 Surcharged in Black or Red

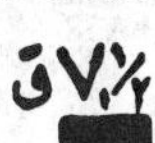

Perf. 13½, 13

148 A8 7.50pi on 50pi ap grn 60 60
149 A11 7.50pi on 100pi black (R) 60 60
150 A25 12.50pi on 7.50pi dark blue (R) 1.40 1.40

Type of 1937-40 Surcharged in Red with Bars and

12½ 

1939 Engr. *Perf. 13*

151 A25 12½pi on 7.50pi dk bl 40 35
Nos. 145-151 (8) 4.75 4.12

Type of 1930-35 Redrawn
Imprint: "Beiteddine-Imp.-Catholique-Beyrouth-Liban."

1939 Litho. *Perf. 11½*

152 A10 1pi dk slate grn 40 15
153 A10 1.50pi brn violet 42 35
154 A10 7.50pi carmine lake 45 40

Bridge Type of 1930-35
Imprint: "Degorce" instead of "Hélio Vaugirard"

1940 Engr. *Perf. 13*

155 A13 5pi grnsh blue 22 15

Exists imperforate.

Independent Republic

Amir Beshir Shehab — A27

1942, Sept. 18 Litho. *Perf. 11½*

156 A27 0p50 emerald 1.25 1.25
157 A27 1.50pi sepia 1.25 1.25
158 A27 6pi rose pink 1.25 1.25
159 A27 15pi dull blue 1.25 1.25

1st anniv. of the Proclamation of Independence, Nov. 26, 1941.
Nos. 156-159 exist imperforate.

Nos. 140, 154 and 142A Surcharged in Blue, Green or Black

10 P.

1943 *Perf. 13, 11½*

160 A24 2pi on 4pi (Bl) 2.50 2.00
161 A10 6pi on 7.50pi (G) 40 20
162 A25 10pi on 12½pi (Bk) 40 30

The surcharge is arranged differently on each value.

Parliament Building A28

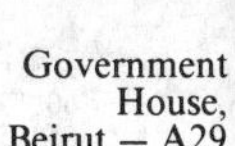

Government House, Beirut — A29

1943 Litho. *Perf. 11½*

163 A28 25pi salmon rose 5.00 5.00
164 A29 50pi bluish green 5.00 5.00
165 A28 150pi light ultra 5.00 5.00
166 A29 200pi dull vio brn 5.00 5.00

2nd anniv. of Proclamation of Independence. Nos. 163-166 exist imperforate. See Nos. C82-C87.

Quarantine Station, Beirut — A30

1943, July 8 Photo.
Black Overprint

167 A30 10pi cerise 2.00 2.00
168 A30 20pi light blue 2.00 2.00
Nos. 167-168,C88-C90 (5) 8.50 8.50

Arab Medical Congress, Beirut.

Nos. 163 to 166 Overprinted in Blue, Violet, Red or Black

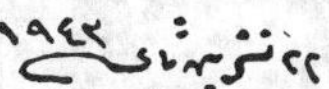

1944

169 A28 25pi sal rose (Bl) 5.00 5.00
170 A29 50pi bluish green (V) 5.00 5.00
171 A28 150pi lt ultra (R) 5.00 5.00
172 A29 200pi dull vio brn (Bk) 7.00 7.00
Nos. 169-172,C91-C96 (10) 83.00 83.00

Return to office of the president and his ministers, Nov. 22, 1943.

Type of 1930 and No. 142A Surcharged in Violet, Black or Carmine

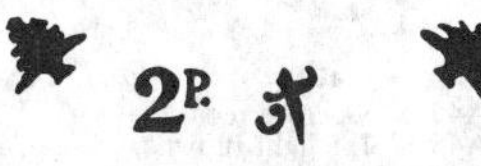

1945 Unwmk. Engr. *Perf. 13*

173 A13 2pi on 5pi dk bl grn (V) 30 16
174 A13 3pi on 5pi dk bl grn (Bk) 30 22
175 A25 6pi on 12½pi deep ultra (Bk) 38 25
176 A25 7½pi on 12½pi deep ultra (C) 65 65

Trees at bottom on Nos. 175 and 176.

Catalogue values for unused stamps in this section, from this point to the end of the section, are for Never Hinged items.

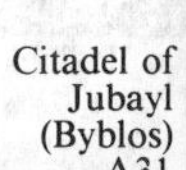

Citadel of Jubayl (Byblos) A31

Crusader Castle, Tripoli A32

1945 Litho. *Perf. 11½*

177 A31 15pi violet brown 1.25 1.10
178 A31 20pi deep green 1.25 1.10
179 A32 25pi deep blue 1.25 1.10
180 A32 50pi dp carmine 2.25 1.25

See Nos. 229-233.

Soldiers and Flag of Lebanon A33

1946 Litho.
Stripes of Flag in Red Orange

181 A33 7.50pi red & pale lil 40 15
182 A33 10pi lil & pale lilac 50 15
183 A33 12.50pi choc & yel grn 60 15
184 A33 15pi sepia & pink 1.25 15
185 A33 20pi ultra & pink 1.10 15
186 A33 25pi dk grn & yel green 1.90 25
187 A33 50pi dk bl & pale bl 3.00 90
188 A33 100pi gray blk & pale bl 5.00 2.25
Nos. 181-188 (8) 13.75 4.15

Type of 1946 Overprinted in Red

1946, May 8
Stripes of Flag in Red

189 A33 7.50pi choc & pink 30 15
190 A33 10pi dk vio & pink 42 15
191 A33 12.50pi brn red & pale lilac 50 38
192 A33 15pi lt grn & yel green 1.00 50
193 A33 20pi sl grn & yel green 85 55
194 A33 25pi sl bl & pale bl 1.40 75
195 A33 50pi ultra & gray 2.50 70
196 A33 100pi blk & pale bl 4.00 1.75
Nos. 189-196 (8) 10.97 4.93

See Nos. C101-C106, note after No. C106.

Cedar of Lebanon A34

Night Herons over Mt. Sanin A35

1946-47 Unwmk. *Perf. 10½*

197 A34 50c red brn ('47) 24 15
198 A34 1pi purple ('47) 24 15
199 A34 2.50pi violet 45 15
200 A34 5pi red 75 15
201 A34 6pi gray ('47) 75 15

Perf. 11½

202 A35 12.50pi deep car 5.50 15
Nos. 197-202,C107-C110 (10) 24.93 4.64

See Nos. C107-C110. For surcharge, see No. 246.

A36

Crusader Castle, Tripoli — A37

1947 Litho. *Perf. 14x13½*

203 A36 50c dark brown 35 15
204 A36 2.50pi bright green 65 15
205 A36 5pi car rose 75 15

Perf. 11½

206 A37 12.50pi rose pink 2.00 15
207 A37 25pi ultramarine 3.00 18
208 A37 50pi turq green 9.00 35
209 A37 100pi violet 12.50 2.25
Nos. 203-209 (7) 28.25 3.38

A38

Zebaide Aqueduct — A39

1948 *Perf. 14x13½*

210 A38 50c blue 15 15
211 A38 1pi yel brown 18 15
212 A38 2.50pi rose violet 38 15
213 A38 3pi emerald 65 15
214 A38 5pi crimson 75 15

Perf. 11½

215 A39 7.50pi rose red 3.00 15
216 A39 10pi dl violet 1.65 15
217 A39 12.50pi blue 4.50 15
218 A39 25pi blue vio 5.50 25
219 A39 50pi green 12.00 1.75
Nos. 210-219 (10) 28.76
Set value 2.45

See Nos. 227A-228A, 234-237. For surcharge, see No. 245.

The Scott Catalogue value is a retail price, what you could expect to pay for the stamp in a grade of Fine-Very Fine. The value listed is a reference which reflects recent actual dealer selling price.

Europa
A40

Avicenna
A41

1948 **Litho.**

220	A40	10pi	dk red & org red	1.50	1.40
221	A40	12.50pi	pur & rose	2.00	1.90
222	A40	25pi	ol grn & pale green	2.50	1.50
223	A41	30pi	org brn & buff	3.50	1.50
224	A41	40pi	Prus grn & buff	4.50	1.50
			Nos. 220-224 (5)	14.00	7.80

UNESCO. Nos. 220 to 224 exist imperforate (see note after No. C145).

Camel Post Rider — A42

1949, Aug. 16 **Unwmk.** ***Perf. 11½***

225	A42	5pi	violet	50	40
226	A42	7.50pi	red	70	60
227	A42	12.50pi	blue	1.20	1.00
			Nos. 225-227,C148-C149 (5)	8.90	5.25

UPU, 75th anniv. See note after No. C149.

Cedar Type of 1948 Redrawn and Jubayl Type of 1945

1949 **Litho.** ***Perf. 14x13½***

227A	A38	50c	blue	35	15
228	A38	1pi	red orange	50	15
228A	A38	2.50pi	rose lilac	3.75	35
			Perf. 11½		
229	A31	7.50pi	rose red	90	15
230	A31	10pi	violet brn	1.60	15
231	A31	12.50pi	deep blue	3.75	20
232	A31	25pi	violet	7.00	40
233	A31	50pi	green	15.00	1.90
			Nos. 227A-233 (8)	32.85	3.45

On No. 227A in left numeral tablet, top of "P" stands higher than flag of the 1¼mm high "5." On No. 210, tops of "P" and the 2mm "5" are on same line.

On No. 228, "1 P." is smaller than on No. 211, and has no line below "P."

On No. 228A, the "O" does not touch tablet frame; on No. 212, it does. No. 228A exists on gray paper.

Cedar Type of 1948 Redrawn and

Ancient Bridge across Dog River — A43

1950 **Litho.** ***Perf. 14x13½***

234	A38	50c	rose red	15	15
235	A38	1pi	salmon	25	15
236	A38	2.50pi	violet	50	15
237	A38	5pi	claret	1.00	15

Cedar slightly altered and mountains eliminated.

			Perf. 11½		
238	A43	7.50pi	rose red	55	15
239	A43	10pi	rose vio	1.00	15
240	A43	12.50pi	light blue	1.40	15
241	A43	25pi	deep blue	3.25	38
242	A43	50pi	emerald	7.50	1.65
			Nos. 234-242 (9)	15.60	
			Set value		2.40

See Nos. 251-255, 310-312.

Flags and Building
A44

Cedar
A45

1950, Aug. 8 ***Perf. 11½***

243	A44	7.50pi	gray	30	20
244	A44	12.50pi	lilac rose	30	20
			Nos. 243-244,C150-C153 (6)	3.57	2.40

Conference of Emigrants, 1950. See note after No. C153.

Nos. 213 and 201 Surcharged with New Value and Bars in Carmine

1950 **Unwmk.** ***Perf. 14x13½, 10½***

245	A38	1pi	on 3pi emerald	18	15
246	A34	2.50pi	on 6pi gray	80	15
			Set value		15

1951 **Litho.** ***Perf. 14x13½***

247	A45	50c	rose red	15	15
248	A45	1pi	light brown	25	15
249	A45	2.50pi	slate gray	1.20	15
250	A45	5pi	rose lake	1.10	15

Bridge Type of 1950, Redrawn

Typo. ***Perf. 11½***

251	A43	7.50pi	red	1.20	16
252	A43	10pi	dl rose vio	2.00	15
253	A43	12.50pi	blue	3.50	20
254	A43	25pi	dull blue	4.50	50
255	A43	50pi	green	10.00	3.50
			Nos. 247-255 (9)	23.90	5.11

Nos. 238-242 are lithographed from a fine-screen halftone; "P" in the denomination has serifs. Nos. 251-255 are typographed and much coarser; "P" without serifs.

Cedar
A46

Ruins at Baalbek
A47

Design: 50pi, 100pi, Beaufort Castle.

1952 **Litho.** ***Perf. 14x13½***

256	A46	50c	emerald	25	15
257	A46	1pi	orange brn	25	15
258	A46	2.50pi	greenish bl	40	15
259	A46	5pi	car rose	55	15
			Perf. 11½		
260	A47	7.50pi	red	80	20
261	A47	10pi	bright vio	1.65	22
262	A47	12.50pi	blue	1.65	22
263	A47	25pi	violet bl	2.25	45
264	A47	50pi	dk bl grn	6.00	90
265	A47	100pi	chocolate	12.00	2.50
			Nos. 256-265 (10)	25.80	5.09

Cedar of Lebanon
A48

Postal Administration Building
A49

1953 ***Perf. 14x13½***

266	A48	50c	blue	32	15
267	A48	1pi	rose lake	32	15
268	A48	2.50pi	lilac	45	15
269	A48	5pi	emerald	80	15
			Perf. 11½		
270	A49	7.50pi	car rose	1.25	16
271	A49	10pi	dp yel grn	1.65	25
272	A49	12.50pi	aquamarine	2.75	30
273	A49	25pi	ultra	3.75	40
274	A49	50pi	violet brn	6.50	1.00
			Nos. 266-274 (9)	17.79	2.71

See No. 306.

A50

Gallery, Beit-ed-Din Palace — A51

1954 ***Perf. 14x13½***

275	A50	50c	blue	15	15
276	A50	1pi	dp orange	15	15
277	A50	2.50pi	purple	25	15
278	A50	5pi	blue green	60	15
			Perf. 11½		
279	A51	7.50pi	dp carmine	1.20	20
280	A51	10pi	dl ol grn	1.50	20
281	A51	12.50pi	blue	3.00	25
282	A51	25pi	vio blue	3.75	80
283	A51	50pi	aqua	5.50	1.40
284	A51	100pi	black brn	12.00	2.50
			Nos. 275-284 (10)	28.10	5.95

Arab Postal Union Issue

Globe — A52

1955, Jan. 1 **Litho.** ***Perf. 13½x13***

285	A52	12.50pi	blue green	20	20
286	A52	25pi	violet	25	25

Founding of the APU, July 1, 1954. See No. C197.

Cedar
A53

Jeita Cave
A54

1955 ***Perf. 14x13½***

287	A53	50c	violet blue	15	15
288	A53	1pi	vermilion	15	15
289	A53	2.50pi	purple	18	15
290	A53	5pi	emerald	30	15
			Perf. 11½		
291	A54	7.50pi	deep orange	40	15
292	A54	10pi	yellow grn	60	15
293	A54	12.50pi	blue	65	15
294	A54	25pi	dp vio blue	1.60	15
295	A54	50pi	dk gray grn	2.25	25
			Nos. 287-295 (9)	6.28	
			Set value		70

See Nos. 308-309, 315-318, 341-343A.

Cedar of Lebanon
A55

Globe and Columns
A56

1955 **Unwmk.** ***Perf. 13x13½***

296	A55	50c	dark blue	15	15
297	A55	1pi	deep orange	15	15
298	A55	2.50pi	deep violet	16	15
299	A55	5pi	green	16	15
300	A56	7.50pi	yel org & cop red	25	15
301	A56	10pi	emer & sal	35	15
302	A56	12.50pi	ultra & bl grn	50	15
303	A56	25pi	dp ultra & brt pink	1.00	15
304	A56	50pi	dk grn & lt bl	1.40	16
305	A56	100pi	dk brn & sal	2.00	40
			Nos. 296-305 (10)	6.12	
			Set value		90

For surcharge, see No. 333.

Cedar Type of 1953 Redrawn

1956 **Litho.** ***Perf. 13x13½***

306	A48	2.50pi	violet	2.75	1.40

No. 306 measures 17x20½mm. The "2p.50" is in Roman (upright) type face.

Cedar Type of 1955 Redrawn and Bridge Type of 1950, Second Redrawing

1957 **Litho.** ***Perf. 13x13½***

308	A53	50c	light ultra	15	15
309	A53	2.50pi	claret	35	22
			Perf. 11½		
310	A43	7.50pi	vermilion	50	35
311	A43	10pi	brn orange	70	40
312	A43	12.50pi	blue	90	50
			Nos. 308-312 (5)	2.60	1.62

On Nos. 308 and 309 numerals are slanted and clouds slightly changed.

Nos. 310-312 inscribed "Liban" instead of "Republique Libanaise," and different Arabic characters.

Runners — A57

1957, Sept. 12 **Litho.** ***Perf. 13***

313	A57	2.50pi	shown	20	20
314	A57	12.50pi	Soccer players	35	35

Second Pan-Arab Games, Beirut. See Nos. C243-C244.

A souvenir sheet of four contains one each of Nos. 313-314, C243-C244.

Cedar Type of 1955 Redrawn and

Workers
A58

Ancient Potter
A59

1957 **Unwmk.** ***Perf. 13x13½***

315	A53	50c	light blue	15	15
316	A53	1p	light brown	15	15
317	A53	2.50p	bright vio	25	15
318	A53	5p	light green	60	15
			Perf. 11½, 13½x13 (A59)		
319	A58	7.50p	crim rose	50	15
320	A58	10p	dull red brn	65	15
321	A58	12.50p	bright blue	1.00	15
322	A59	25p	dull blue	70	10
323	A59	50p	yellow grn	1.50	16
324	A59	100p	sepia	2.25	60
			Nos. 315-324 (10)	7.75	
			Set value		1.20

The word "piaster" is omitted on No. 315; on Nos. 316 and 318 there is a line below "P"; on No. 317 there is a period between "2" and "50."

Nos. 315-318 are 16mm wide and have three shading lines above tip of cedar. See No. 343A and footnote.

For surcharges, see Nos. 334-335.

Cedar of Lebanon
A60

Soldier and Flag
A61

1958 Litho. Perf. 13
325 A60 50c blue 15 15
326 A60 1p dull orange 15 15
327 A60 2.50p violet 15 15
328 A60 5p yellow grn 18 15
329 A61 12.50p bright blue 35 15
330 A61 25p dark blue 40 15
331 A61 50p orange brn 60 15
332 A61 100p black brn 1.25 25
Nos. 325-332 (8) 3.23
Set value 75

مؤتمر المحامين العرب
من ١ الى ٥ ايلول ١٩٥٩

No. 304 Surcharged

30P. ٣٠ق
= =

1959, Sept. 1
333 A56 30p on 50p dk grn & lt bl 40 25

Arab Lawyers Congress. See No. C265.

= =

No. 323 Surcharged مؤتمر المغتربين
صيف - ١٩٥٩
30P. ٣٠ق

1959 Perf. 13½x13
334 A59 30p on 50p yel grn 28 22
335 A59 40p on 50p yel grn 42 35

Convention of the Assoc. of Arab Emigrants in the United States.

Nos. 329-330 and 323 Surcharged with New Value and Bars

1959 Perf. 13, 13½x13
336 A61 7.50p on 12.50p brt bl 15 15
337 A61 10p on 12.50p brt bl 15 15
338 A61 15p on 25p dark blue 16 15
339 A59 40p on 50p yel grn 40 16
Nos. 336-339,C271 (5) 1.66
Set value 60

Arab League Center, Cairo — A62

1960 Unwmk. Litho. Perf. 13x13½
340 A62 15p light blue grn 20 15

Opening of the Arab League Center and the Arab Postal Museum in Cairo.

Cedar Type of 1955, Second Redrawing

1960 Litho. Perf. 13x13½
341 A53 50c light violet 15 15
342 A53 1p rose claret 15 15
343 A53 2.50p ultramarine 15 15
343A A53 5p light green 15 15
Set value 44 22

Nos. 341-343A are 16½-17mm wide and have two shading lines above cedar. In other details they resemble the redrawn A53 type of 1957 (Nos. 315-318).

President Fuad Chehab
A63 A64

1960 Photo. Perf. 13½
344 A63 50c deep green 15 15
345 A63 2.50p olive 15 15
346 A63 5p green 15 15
347 A63 7.50p rose brown 15 15
348 A63 15p bright blue 15 15
349 A63 50p lilac 35 15
350 A63 100p brown 60 18
Set value 1.30 55

Nos. 343A and 340 Overprinted in Red

1960, Nov. Litho. Perf. 13x13½
351 A53 5p light green 15 15
352 A62 15p lt blue green 20 18
Set value 26 24

Arabian Oil Conference, Beirut.

1961, Feb. Litho. Perf. 13½x13
353 A64 2.50p blue & light bl 15 15
354 A64 7.50p dark vio & pink 15 15
355 A64 10p red brn & yel 15 15
Set value 22 20

Cedar
A65

Post Office, Beirut
A66

1961 Unwmk. Litho. Perf. 13
356 A65 2.50p green 15 15

Redrawn

357 A65 2.50p orange 50 25
358 A65 5p maroon 15 15
359 A65 10p black 15 15

Nos. 357-359 have no clouds.

Perf. 11½

361 A66 2.50p rose carmine 15 15
362 A66 5p bright green 38 15
363 A66 15p dark blue 22 15
Nos. 356-363 (7) 1.70
Set value 65

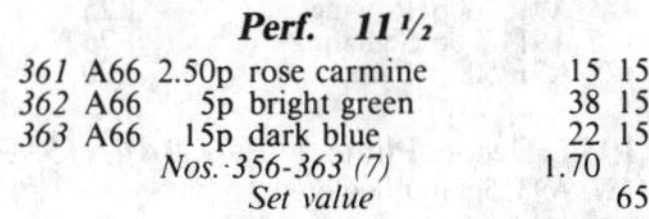

Cedars — A67

Design: 10p, 15p, 50p, 100p, View of Zahle.

1961 Litho. Perf. 13
365 A67 50c yellow green 15 15
366 A67 1p brown 15 15
367 A67 2.50p ultramarine 15 15
368 A67 5p carmine 15 15
369 A67 7.50p violet 15 15
370 A67 10p dark brown 40 15
371 A67 15p dark blue 45 15
372 A67 50p dark green 70 22
373 A67 100p black 85 35
Set value 2.75 90

See Nos. 381-384.

Unknown Soldier Monument — A68

1961, Dec. 30 Unwmk. Perf. 12
374 A68 10p shown 18 15
375 A68 15p Soldier & flag 25 18

Anniv. of Lebanon's independence; evacuation of foreign troops, Dec. 31, 1946.
See Nos. C329-C330.

Bugler — A69

Scout Carrying Flag and Scout Emblem
A70

Designs: 2.50p, First aid. 6p, Lord Baden-Powell. 10p, Scouts building campfire.

1962, Mar. 1 Litho. Perf. 12
376 A69 50c yel grn, blk & yel 15 15
377 A70 1p multicolored 15 15
378 A70 2.50p dk red, blk & grn 15 15
379 A69 6p multicolored 15 15
380 A70 10p dp bl, blk & yel 15 15
Set value, #376-380, C331-C333 1.10 80

50th anniversary of Lebanese Boy Scouts.

Type of 1961 Redrawn

Designs as before.

1962 Unwmk. Perf. 13
381 A67 50c yellow green 15 15
382 A67 1p brown 15 15
383 A67 2.50p ultramarine 15 15
384 A67 15p dark blue 1.00 20
Nos. 381-384,C341-C342 (6) 4.80
Set value 84

Temple of Nefertari, Abu Simbel — A71

Cherries — A72

1962, Aug. 1 Unwmk. Perf. 13
390 A71 5p light ultra 16 15
391 A71 15p brn lake & mar 22 15

Campaign to save the historic monuments in Nubia. See Nos. C351-C352.

1962 Litho.

Designs: 50c, 2.50p, 7.50p, Cherries. 1p, 5p, Figs. 10p, 17.50p, 30p, Grapes. 50p, Oranges. 100p, Pomegranates.

Vignette Multicolored
392 A72 50c violet blue 15 15
393 A72 1p gray blue 15 15
394 A72 2.50p brown 15 15
395 A72 5p bright blue 15 15
396 A72 7.50p lilac rose 15 15
397 A72 10p chocolate 15 15
398 A72 17.50p slate 22 15
399 A72 30p slate grn 38 15
400 A72 50p green 55 16
401 A72 100p brown blk 1.40 50
Nos. 392-401,C359-C366 (18) 6.90
Set value 2.40

Elementary Schoolboy — A73

1962, Oct. 1 Litho. Perf. 12
404 A73 30p multicolored 20 18

Students' Day, Oct. 1. See No. C355.

Cedar of Lebanon
A74 A75

1963-64 Unwmk. Perf. 13x13½
405 A74 50c green 15 15
406 A75 50c gray grn ('64) 15 15
407 A75 2.50p ultra ('64) 15 15
408 A75 5p brt pink ('64) 15 15
409 A75 7.50p orange ('64) 18 15
410 A75 17.50p rose lil ('64) 32 18
Nos. 405-410 (6) 1.10
Set value 66

Bicyclist — A76

Hyacinth — A77

1964, Feb. 11 Litho. Perf. 13
415 A76 2.50p shown 15 15
416 A76 5p Basketball 15 15
417 A76 10p Track 15 15
Set value, #415-417, C385-C387 88 58

4th Mediterranean Games, Naples, Sept. 21-29, 1963.

1964 Unwmk. Perf. 13x13½

Size: 26x27mm

418 A77 50c shown 15 15
419 A77 1p Hyacinth 15 15
420 A77 2.50p Hyacinth 15 15
421 A77 5p Cyclamen 15 15
422 A77 7.50p Cyclamen 15 15

Perf. 13

Size: 26x37mm

423 A77 10p Poinsettia 15 15
424 A77 17.50p Anemone 38 15
425 A77 30p Iris 55 22
426 A77 50p Poppy 1.25 45
Set value 2.55 1.00

See Nos. C391-C397.

Temple of the Sun, Baalbek
A78

1965, Jan. 11 Litho. *Perf. 13x13½*
429 A78 2.50p blk & red org 15 15
430 A78 7.50p black & bl 16 15
Nos. 429-430,C420-C423 (6) 2.01 1.50

International Festival at Baalbek.

Swimmer
A79

1965, Jan. 23 Engr. *Perf. 13*
431 A79 2.50p shown 15 15
432 A79 7.50p Fencer 20 15
433 A79 10p Basketball, vert. 25 22
Nos. 431-433,C424-C426 (6) 1.30
Set value 78

18th Olympic Games, Toyko, Oct. 10-25, 1964.

Golden Oriole
A80

1965 Engr. *Perf. 13*
434 A80 5p Bullfinch 15 15
435 A80 10p European goldfinch 25 15
436 A80 15p Hoopoe 15 15
437 A80 17.50p Rock partridge 20 15
438 A80 20p shown 25 15
439 A80 32.50p European bee-eater 38 15
Nos. 434-439 (6) 1.38
Set value 40

For surcharge, see No. 459.

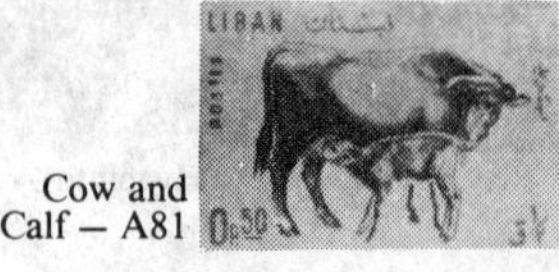

Cow and Calf – A81

1965 Photo. *Perf. 11x12*
440 A81 50c shown 15 15
441 A81 1p Rabbit 15 15
442 A81 2.50p Ewe & lamb 16 15
Set value 36 32

Hippodrome, Beirut – A82

Designs: 1p, Pigeon Rocks. 2.50p, Tabarja. 5p, Ruins, Beit-Mery. 7.50p, Statue and ruins, Anjar.

1966 Unwmk. *Perf. 12x11½*
443 A82 50c gold & multi 15 15
444 A82 1p gold & multi 15 15
445 A82 2.50p gold & multi 15 15
446 A82 5p gold & multi 15 15
447 A82 7.50p gold & multi 18 15
Set value 63 40

See Nos. C486-C492. For surcharge, see No. 460.

ITY Emblem and Cedars – A83

1967 Photo. *Perf. 11x12*
448 A83 50c lem, blk & brt bl 15 15
449 A83 1p sal, blk & brt bl 15 15
450 A83 2.50p gray, blk & brt bl 15 15
451 A83 5p lt rose lil, blk & brt bl 15 15
452 A83 7.50p yel, blk & brt bl 15 15
Set value 60 40

Intl. Tourist Year; used as a regular issue. See Nos. C515-C522. For surcharge, see No. 461.

Goat and Kid – A84

1968, Feb. Photo. *Perf. 12x11½*
453 A84 50c shown 15 15
454 A84 1p Cattle 15 15
455 A84 2.50p Sheep 15 15
456 A84 5p Camels 15 15
457 A84 10p Donkey 18 15
458 A84 15p Horses 25 15
Set value 82 30

See Nos. C534-C539.

No. 439 Surcharged

25P. ٢٥ق

1972, Apr. Engr. *Perf. 13*
459 A80 25p on 32.50p multi 18 15

Nos. 447 and 452 Surcharged with New Value and Bars

Perf. 12x11½, 11x12

1972, May Photo.
460 A82 5p on 7.50p multi 15 15
461 A83 5p on 7.50p multi 15 15
Set value 24 16

Cedar – A85

Army Badge – A86

1974 Litho. *Perf. 11*
462 A85 50c org & olive 50 25

1980, Dec. 28 Litho. *Perf. 11½*
463 A86 25p multicolored 15 15

Army Day. See Nos. C792-C793.

Pres. Elias Sarkis – A87

World Communications Year – A89

World Food Day, Oct. 16, 1981
A88

1981, Sept. 23 Photo. *Perf. 14x13½*
464 A87 125p multicolored 1.00 50
465 A87 300p multicolored 1.00 1.00
466 A87 500p multicolored 2.50 1.50

1982, Nov. 23 Photo. *Perf. 12x11½*
467 A88 50p Stork carrying food packages 38 25
468 A88 75p Wheat, globe 50 38
469 A88 100p Produce 75 50

1983, Dec. 19 Photo. *Perf. 14*
470 A89 300p multicolored 1.25

Illustrations from Khalil Gibran's The Prophet
A90

1983, Dec. 19 *Perf. 13½x14*
471 A90 200p The Soul Is Back 1.00
472 A90 300p The Family 1.50
473 A90 500p Self-portrait 2.50
474 A90 1000p The Prophet 5.00
a. Souv. sheet. Nos. 471-474 12.50

No. 474a sold for £25.

Scouting Year – A91

Cedar of Lebanon – A93

1983, Dec. 19 *Perf. 14*
475 A91 200p Rowing 1.25
476 A91 300p Signaling 1.75
477 A91 500p Camp 3.00

1984, Dec. Photo. *Perf. 14½x13½*
481 A93 5p multicolored 50

Flowers – A94

Defense – A95

1984, Dec. Photo. *Perf. 14½x13½*
482 A94 10p Iris of Sofar 15
483 A94 25p Periwinkle 28
484 A94 50p Flowering thorn 50

1984, Dec. Photo. *Perf. 14½x13½*
485 A95 75p Dove over city 30
486 A95 150p Soldier, cedar 65
487 A95 300p Olive wreath, cedar 1.25

Temple Ruins
A96

1985 Photo. *Perf. 13½x14½*
488 A96 100p Fakra 38
489 A96 200p Bziza 65
490 A96 500p Tyre 1.40

Pres. Gemayel, Map of Lebanon, Dove, Text – A97

Pres. Gemayel, Military Academy Graduate – A98

1988, Feb. 1 Litho. *Perf. 14*
491 A97 £50 multicolored 2.25

1988, Mar. 9
492 A98 £25 multicolored 1.75

Arab Scouts, 75th Anniv. – A99

1988, Mar. 9 *Perf. 13½x14½*
493 A99 £20 multicolored 1.75

UN Child Survival Campaign – A100

1988, Mar. 9 *Perf. 14½x13½*
494 A100 £15 multicolored 1.00

Prime Minister Rashid Karame (1921-1987), Satellite, Flags, Earth – A101

1988, Mar. 9 *Perf. 13½x14½*
495 A101 £10 multicolored 70

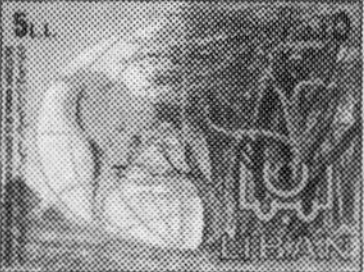

1st World Festival for Youths of Lebanese Descent in Uruguay
A102

1988, Mar. 9
496 A102 £5 multicolored 70

Cedar — A103

1989 Photo. *Perf. 13x13½*

497	A103	£50 dark grn & vio		
498	A103	£70 dark grn & brn		
499	A103	£100 dark grn & brt yel		
500	A103	£200 dark grn & bluish grn		
501	A103	£500 dark grn & brt yel grn		

SEMI-POSTAL STAMPS

Regular Issue of 1925 Surcharged in Red or Black

Secours aux Réfugiés
اعانات للاجئين
Afft الاجرة
0P.25 ١/٤ غ

1926 Unwmk. *Perf. 14x13½*

B1	A2	0p25 + 0p25 ol blk	1.40	1.40
B2	A2	0p50 + 0p25 yellow green (B)	1.40	1.40
B3	A2	0p75 + 0p25 brown orange (B)	1.40	1.40
B4	A2	1pi + 0p50 mag	1.40	1.40
B5	A2	1pi25 + 0p50 dp grn	1.60	1.60
B6	A2	1p50 + 0p50 rose red (B)	1.60	1.60
a.		Double surcharge	14.00	14.00
B7	A2	2pi + 0p75 dk brn	1.40	1.40
B8	A2	2p50 + 0p75 pck bl	1.60	1.60
B9	A2	3pi + 1pi org brn	1.60	1.60
B10	A2	5pi + 1pi vio (B)	1.60	1.60
B11	A3	10pi + 2pi violet brown (B)	1.60	1.60
B12	A2	25pi + 5pi ultra	1.60	1.60
		Nos. B1-B12 (12)	18.20	18.20

On No. B11 the surcharge is set in six lines to fit the shape of the stamp. All values of this series exist with inverted surcharge. Value each, $14.

See Nos. CB1-CB4.

Catalogue values for unused stamps in this section, from this point to the end of the section, are for Never Hinged items.

Boxing — SP1

1961, Jan. 12 Litho. *Perf. 13*

B13	SP1	2.50p + 2.50p shown	15	15
B14	SP1	5p + 5p Wrestling	15	15
B15	SP1	7.50p + 7.50p Shot put	25	20
		Nos. B13-B15,CB12-CB14 (6)	3.55	3.50

17th Olympic Games, Rome, Aug. 25-Sept. 11, 1960.

Nos. B13-B15 with Arabic and French Overprint in Black, Blue or Green and two Bars through Olympic Inscription: "CHAMPIONNAT D'EUROPE DE TIR, 2 JUIN 1962"

1962, June 2

B16	SP1	2.50p + 2.50p blue & brown (Bk)	16	15
B17	SP1	5p + 5p orange & brown (G)	30	16
B18	SP1	7.50p + 7.50p violet & brown (Bl)	42	42
		Nos. B16-B18,CB15-CB17 (6)	3.43	3.28

European Marksmanship Championships held in Lebanon.

Red Cross — SP2

1988, June 8 Litho. *Perf. 14*

B19	SP2	£10 + £1 shown		
B20	SP2	£20 + £2 Stylized profile		
B21	SP2	£30 + £3 Globe, emblems, dove		

AIR POST STAMPS

Nos. 10 to 13 with Additional Overprint

Poste par Avion

1924 Unwmk. *Perf. 14x13½*

C1	A18	2pi on 40c	2.75	*4.00*
a.		Double surcharge	10.00	
C2	A18	3pi on 60c	2.75	*4.00*
C3	A18	5pi on 1fr	2.75	*4.00*
a.		Dbl. surch. and ovpt.	12.00	
C4	A18	10pi on 2fr	2.75	*4.00*
a.		Invtd. surch. and ovpt.	35.00	35.00

Nos. 33, 35-37 Overprinted

Avion طيارة

C5	A18	2pi on 40c	4.00	4.00
C6	A18	3pi on 60c	4.00	4.00
C7	A18	5pi on 1fr	4.00	4.00
a.		Overprint reversed	14.00	
C8	A18	10pi on 2fr	4.00	4.00
a.		Overprint reversed	14.00	
b.		Double surcharge	14.00	

Nos. 57, 59-61 Overprinted in Green

AVION
طيارة

1925

C9	A2	2pi dark brown	1.25	1.25
C10	A2	3pi orange brown	1.25	1.25
C11	A2	5pi violet	1.25	1.25
a.		Inverted overprint	6.00	
C12	A3	10pi violet brown	1.25	1.25

Nos. 57, 59-61 Overprinted in Red

c

1926

C13	A2	2pi dark brown	1.25	1.25
C14	A2	3pi orange brown	1.25	1.25
C15	A2	5pi violet	1.25	1.25
C16	A3	10pi violet brown	1.25	1.25

Exist with inverted overprint. Value, each $14.

Issues of Republic under French Mandate

Nos. C13-C16 Overprinted

République Libanaise
d

1927

C17	A2	2pi dark brown	1.25	1.25
C18	A2	3pi orange brown	1.25	1.25
C19	A2	5pi violet	1.25	1.25
C20	A3	10pi violet brown	1.25	1.25

Overprint set in two lines on No. C20.

Nos. C17-C20 with Additional Overprint

الجمهورية اللبنانية
e

1928

Black Overprint

C21	A2	2pi dark brown	3.00	3.00
a.		Double overprint	10.00	
b.		Inverted overprint	10.00	
C22	A2	3pi orange brown	3.00	3.00
a.		Double overprint	10.00	
C23	A2	5pi violet	3.00	3.00
a.		Double overprint	6.50	
C24	A3	10pi violet brown	3.00	3.00
a.		Double overprint	6.50	

Red Overprint

C25	A2	2pi dark brown	65	65
C26	A2	3pi orange brown	65	65
C27	A2	5pi violet	65	65
C28	A3	10pi violet brown	1.00	65
		Nos. C21-C28 (8)	14.95	14.60

On Nos. C21-C28 the airplane is always in red.

The red overprint of a silhouetted plane and "Republique Libanaise," as on Nos. C25-C27, was also applied to Nos. C9-C12. These are believed to have been essays, and were not regularly issued.

Nos. 52, 54 and 62 Overprinted Type "e" in Red or Black

1929

C33	A2	0p50 yel green (R)	35	35
a.		Inverted overprint	14.00	14.00
C34	A2	1pi magenta (Bk)	42	42
a.		Inverted overprint	14.00	14.00
C35	A2	25pi ultra (R)	65.00	65.00
a.		Inverted overprint	190.00	190.00

No. 62 with Surcharge Added in Red

Two types of surcharge:

I- The "5" of "15 P." is italic. The "15" is 4mm high. Arabic characters for "Lebanese Republic" and for "15 P." are on same line in that order.

II- The "5" is in Roman type (upright) and smaller; "15" is 3½mm high. Arabic for "Lebanese Republic" is centered on line by itself, with Arabic for "15 P." below right end of line.

C36	A2	15pi on 25pi ultra (I)	100.00	100.00
a.		Type II (#106)	*500.00*	*500.00*

Nos. 102 Overprinted Type "c" in Blue

C37	A2	0p50 on 0p75	22	22
a.		Airplane inverted	14.00	
b.		French and Arabic surcharge inverted	14.00	
c.		"P" omitted	6.50	
d.		Airplane double	14.00	

No. 55 Surcharged in Red

1930

C38	AP2	2pi on 1p25 dp grn	42	42
a.		Inverted surcharge	14.00	14.00

Airplane over Racheya AP2

Designs: 1pi, Plane over Broumana. 2pi, Baalbek. 3pi, Hasroun. 5pi, Byblos. 10pi, Kadicha River. 15pi, Beirut. 25pi, Tripoli. 50pi, Kabeljas. 100pi, Zahle.

1930-31 Photo. *Perf. 13½*

C39	AP2	50c dk vio ('31)	15	15
C40	AP2	1pi yel grn ('31)	15	15
C41	AP2	2pi dp org ('31)	30	30
C42	AP2	3pi magenta ('31)	30	30
C43	AP2	5pi indigo	30	30
C44	AP2	10pi orange red	75	50
C45	AP2	15pi orange brn	40	40
C46	AP2	25pi gray vio ('31)	65	65
C47	AP2	50pi dp claret	2.50	2.25
C48	AP2	100pi olive brown	3.00	2.75
		Nos. C39-C48 (10)	8.50	7.75

Nos. C39 to C48 exist imperforate.

Tourist Publicity Issue

Skiing in Lebanon AP12

Bay of Jounie AP13

1936, Oct. 12

C49	AP12	50c slate grn	1.00	1.00
C50	AP13	1pi red orange	1.20	1.20
C51	AP12	2pi blk violet	1.20	1.20
C52	AP13	3pi yellow grn	1.20	1.20
C53	AP12	5pi brown car	1.20	1.20
C54	AP13	10pi orange brn	1.20	1.20
C55	AP13	15pi dk carmine	16.00	16.00
C56	AP12	25pi green	45.00	45.00
		Nos. C49-C56 (8)	68.00	68.00

Nos. C49 to C56 exist imperforate.

Lebanese Pavilion at Exposition AP14

1937, July 1 *Perf. 13½*

C57	AP14	50c olive blk	50	50
C58	AP14	1p yellow grn	50	50
C59	AP14	2pi dk red org	50	50
C60	AP14	3pi dk ol grn	50	50
C61	AP14	5pi dp green	65	65
C62	AP14	10pi car lake	3.50	3.50
C63	AP14	15pi rose lake	3.75	3.75
C64	AP14	25pi orange brn	6.50	6.50
		Nos. C57-C64 (8)	16.40	16.40

Paris International Exposition.

Arcade of Beit-ed-Din Palace AP15

Ruins of Baalbek AP16

1937-40 Engr. *Perf. 13*

C65	AP15	50c ultra ('38)	15	15
C66	AP15	1pi hn brn ('40)	16	16
C67	AP15	2pi sepia ('40)	15	15
C68	AP15	3pi rose ('40)	65	35
C69	AP15	5pi lt grn ('40)	16	15
C70	AP16	10pi dull vio	16	15
C71	AP16	15pi turq bl ('40)	55	50
C72	AP16	25pi violet ('40)	1.40	1.40

C73 AP16 50pi yel grn ('40) 2.50 2.00
C74 AP16 100pi brown ('40) 1.40 1.00
Nos. C65-C74 (10) 7.28 6.01

Nos. C65-C74 exist imperforate.

Medical College of Beirut AP17

1938, May 9 Photo. *Perf. 13*

C75 AP17 2pi green 80 1.00
C76 AP17 3pi orange 80 1.00
C77 AP17 5pi lilac gray 1.60 2.00
C78 AP17 10pi lake 4.00 5.50

Medical Congress.

Maurice Nogues and View of Beirut — AP18

1938, July 15 *Perf. 11*

C79 AP18 10pi brn carmine 1.25 1.25
a. Souv. sheet of 4, perf. 13½ 16.00 16.00
b. Perf. 13½ 2.50 2.50

10th anniversary of first Marseille-Beirut flight, by Maurice Nogues.

No. C79a has marginal inscriptions in French and Arabic. Exists imperf.; value $165.

Independent Republic

Plane Over Mt. Lebanon AP19

1942, Sept. 18 Litho. *Perf. 11½*

C80 AP19 10pi dk brown vio 1.60 2.00
C81 AP19 50pi dk gray grn 1.60 2.00

1st anniv. of the Proclamation of Independence, Nov. 26, 1941.

Nos. C80 and C81 exist imperforate.

Bechamoun AP20

Rachaya Citadel AP21

Air View of Beirut AP22

1943, May 1 *Perf. 11½*

C82 AP20 25pi yellow grn 1.10 1.00
C83 AP20 50pi orange 1.65 1.25
C84 AP21 100pi buff 1.65 1.10
C85 AP21 200pi blue vio 2.25 1.90
C86 AP22 300pi sage green 7.25 6.25
C87 AP22 500pi sepia 15.00 13.00
Nos. C82-C87 (6) 28.90 24.50

2nd anniv. of the Proclamation of Independence. Nos. C82-C87 exist imperforate.

Bhannes Sanatorium AP23

1943, July 8 Photo.

Black Overprint

C88 AP23 20pi orange 1.25 1.25
C89 AP23 50pi steel blue 1.25 1.25
C90 AP23 100pi rose violet 2.00 2.00

Arab Medical Congress, Beirut.

Nos. C82 to C87 Overprinted in Red, Blue or Violet

1944, Nov. 23

C91 AP20 25pi yel grn (R) 2.50 2.50
C92 AP20 50pi orange (Bl) 4.50 4.50
C93 AP21 100pi buff (V) 5.00 5.00
C94 AP21 200pi blue vio (R) 10.00 10.00
C95 AP22 300pi sage grn (R) 14.00 14.00
C96 AP22 500pi sepia (Bl) 25.00 25.00
Nos. C91-C96 (6) 61.00 61.00

Return to office of the President and his ministers, Nov. 22, 1943.

Catalogue values for unused stamps in this section, from this point to the end of the section, are for Never Hinged items.

Falls of Litani AP24

The Cedars AP25

1945, July Unwmk. Litho.

C97 AP24 25pi gray brown 75 60
C98 AP24 50pi rose violet 1.10 80
C99 AP25 200pi violet 4.25 1.50
C100 AP25 300pi brown black 8.00 3.00

Lebanese Soldiers at Bir Hacheim AP26

1946, May 8

C101 AP26 15pi bl blk, org & red org 35 22
C102 AP26 20pi red, lil & bl 35 30
C103 AP26 25pi brt bl, org & red 40 20
C104 AP26 50pi gray blk, bl & red 60 25
C105 AP26 100pi pur, pink & red 1.90 60
C106 AP26 150pi brn, pink & red 2.25 1.90
Nos. C101-C106 (6) 5.85 3.47

Victory of the Allied Nations in WWII, 1st anniv.

Three imperf. souvenir sheets of 14 exist. They contain one each of Nos. C101-C106 and 189-196 in changed colors. One has sepia inscriptions, and one on thin white card has blue inscriptions. Value $30 each. The third, with blue inscriptions, is on thick honeycombed chamois card. Value $110.

Night Herons Type

1946, Sept. 11

C107 A35 10pi orange 1.50 42
C108 A35 25pi ultra 1.75 20
C109 A35 50pi blue green 5.50 62
C110 A35 100pi dk vio brn 8.25 2.50

Symbols of Communications — AP28

1946, Nov. 22

C111 AP28 25pi deep blue 40 40
C112 AP28 50pi green 60 50
C113 AP28 75pi orange red 1.10 1.00
C114 AP28 150pi brn black 2.00 1.60

Arab Postal Congress, Sofar, 1946.

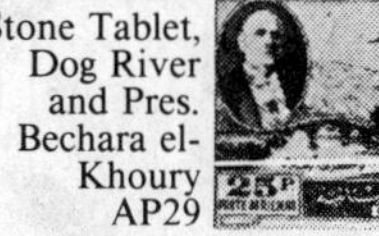

Stone Tablet, Dog River and Pres. Bechara el-Khoury AP29

1947, Feb. 11

C115 AP29 25pi ultra 40 40
C116 AP29 50pi dull rose 60 60
C117 AP29 75pi gray black 80 65
C118 AP29 150pi blue green 1.60 1.40

Evacuation of foreign troops from Lebanon, Dec. 31, 1946.

Bay of Jounie AP30

Government House, Beirut AP31

1947, Feb. 11

Grayish Paper

C119 AP30 5pi dp blue grn 15 15
C120 AP30 10pi rose vio 16 15
C121 AP30 15pi vermilion 35 15
C122 AP30 20pi orange 42 15
a. 20pi red org, white paper 45 15
C123 AP30 25pi deep blue 50 15
C124 AP30 50pi henna brn 90 15
C125 AP30 100pi chocolate 2.25 25
C126 AP31 150pi dk vio brn 4.25 45
C127 AP31 200pi slate 6.00 2.00
C128 AP31 300pi black 10.00 5.00
Nos. C119-C128 (10) 24.98 8.60

See Nos. C145A-C147B.

Post Horn and Letter AP32

Phoenician Galley AP33

1947, June 17 Litho.

C129 AP32 10pi brt ultra 40 35
C130 AP32 15pi rose car 45 35
C131 AP32 25pi bright blue 65 60
C132 AP33 50pi dark sl grn 1.90 65
C133 AP33 75pi purple 2.50 1.40
C134 AP33 100pi dark brown 3.50 1.90
Nos. C129-C134 (6) 9.40 5.25

Lebanon's participation in the 12th UPU congress, Paris.

Lebanese Village AP34

1948, Sept. 1 *Perf. 11½*

C135 AP34 5pi dp orange 20 15
C136 AP34 10pi rose lilac 42 15
C137 AP34 15pi orange brn 1.10 16
C138 AP34 20pi slate 1.60 15
C139 AP34 25pi Prussian bl 4.00 55
C140 AP34 50pi gray black 6.50 80
Nos. C135-C140 (6) 13.82 1.96

Apollo AP35

Minerva AP36

1948, Nov. 23 Unwmk.

C141 AP35 7.50pi bl & lt bl 1.20 80
C142 AP35 15pi blk & gray 1.40 1.00
C143 AP35 20pi rose brn & rose 2.25 1.50
C144 AP36 35pi car rose & rose 4.00 2.00
C145 AP36 75pi bl grn & lt green 8.00 4.00
Nos. C141-C145 (5) 16.85 9.30

UNESCO. Nos. C141-C145 exist imperforate, and combined with Nos. 220-224 in an imperforate souvenir sheet on thin buff cardboard, with black inscriptions in top margin in Arabic and at bottom in French. Value $125.

Bay Type of 1947 Redrawn

1949

White Paper

C145A AP30 10pi rose lilac 2.25 42
C146 AP30 15pi dark green 3.00 50
C147 AP30 20pi orange 6.50 3.50
C147A AP30 25pi dark blue 18.00 1.25
C147B AP30 50pi brick red 82.50 14.00
Nos. C145A-C147B (5) 112.25 19.67

In the redrawn designs, Nos. C145A, C147 and C147B have zeros with broader centers than in the 1947 issue (Nos. C120, C122 and C124).

Helicopter Mail Delivery — AP37

1949, Aug. 16 Unwmk. *Perf. 11½*

C148 AP37 25pi deep blue 2.50 1.50
C149 AP37 50pi green 4.00 1.75
a. Souvenir sheet of 5, #225-227, C148-C149 11.00 11.00

UPU, 75th anniv. No. 149a exists on thin cardboard.

Homing Birds AP38

Pres. Bechara el-Khoury AP39

1950, Aug. 8 Litho.

C150 AP38 5pi violet blue 50 35
C151 AP38 15pi rose vio 75 40
C152 AP39 25pi chocolate 62 50
C153 AP39 35pi gray green 1.10 75
a. Souvenir sheet of 6, #243-244, C150-C153, chamois paper 20.00 20.00

Conference of Emigrants, 1950.

Crusader Castle, Sidon Harbor AP40

1950, Sept. 7

C154	AP40	10pi chocolate	20	16
C155	AP40	15pi dark green	42	15
C156	AP40	20pi crimson	1.10	20
C157	AP40	25pi ultra	1.90	50
C158	AP40	50pi gray black	3.00	1.40
		Nos. C154-C158 (5)	6.62	2.41

1951, June 9 Redrawn Typo.

C159	AP40	10pi grnsh black	20	15
C160	AP40	15pi black brown	38	15
C161	AP40	20pi vermilion	38	15
C162	AP40	25pi deep blue	50	15
C163	AP40	35pi lilac rose	1.40	1.00
C164	AP40	50pi indigo	2.25	1.00
		Nos. C159-C164 (6)	5.11	2.60

Nos. C154-C158 are lithographed from a fine-screen halftone; Nos. C159-C164 are typographed and much coarser, with larger plane and many other differences.

Khaldé International Airport, Beirut — AP41

Design: 50pi to 300pi, Amphitheater, Byblos.

1952 Litho. *Perf. 11½*

C165	AP41	5pi crimson	15	15
C166	AP41	10pi dark gray	15	15
C167	AP41	15pi rose lilac	20	15
C168	AP41	20pi brown org	32	16
C169	AP41	25pi grnsh blue	35	20
C170	AP41	35pi violet bl	45	20
C171	AP41	50pi blue green	3.00	22
C172	AP41	100pi deep blue	16.00	1.00
C173	AP41	200pi dk bl grn	8.50	1.60
C174	AP41	300pi black brn	13.00	3.25
		Nos. C165-C174 (10)	42.12	7.08

Lockheed Constellation — AP42

1953, Oct. 1

C175	AP42	5pi yel green	15	15
C176	AP42	10pi deep plum	16	15
C177	AP42	15pi scarlet	25	15
C178	AP42	20pi aqua	35	15
C179	AP42	25pi blue	80	15
C180	AP42	35pi orange brn	1.25	15
C181	AP42	50pi vio blue	2.50	25
C182	AP42	100pi black brn	4.25	2.00
		Nos. C175-C182 (8)	9.71	
		Set value		2.65

Ruins at Baalbek AP43

Irrigation Canal, Litani AP44

1954, Mar.

C183	AP43	5pi yel green	15	15
C184	AP43	10pi dl purple	15	15
C185	AP43	15pi carmine	16	15
C186	AP43	20pi brown	20	15
C187	AP43	25pi dull blue	25	15
C188	AP43	35pi black brn	42	16
C189	AP44	50pi dk ol grn	2.00	25
C190	AP44	100pi deep car	4.00	35
C191	AP44	200pi dark brown	6.00	65
C192	AP44	300pi dk gray bl	11.00	1.50
		Nos. C183-C192 (10)	24.33	3.66

Khaldé International Airport, Beirut — AP45

1954, Apr. 23 *Perf. 11½*

C193	AP45	10pi pink & rose red	22	20
C194	AP45	25pi dp bl & gray bl	60	35
C195	AP45	35pi dl brn & yel brn	80	60
C196	AP45	65pi dp grn & grn	1.90	1.20

Opening of Beirut's International Airport. Exist imperf.

Arab Postal Union Type of Regular Issue, 1955

1955, Jan. 1 *Perf. 13½x13*

C197	A52	2.50pi yellow brn	22	20

Rotary Emblem AP47

1955, Feb. 23 *Perf. 11½*

C198	AP47	35pi dull green	50	42
C199	AP47	65pi dull blue	90	55

Rotary International, 50th anniversary.

Skiing Among the Cedars AP48

1955, Feb. 24 Litho.

C200	AP48	5pi blue green	20	15
C201	AP48	15pi crimson	30	15
C202	AP48	20pi lilac	50	15
C203	AP48	25pi blue	1.00	15
C204	AP48	35pi olive brn	1.50	22
C205	AP48	50pi chocolate	3.00	32
C206	AP48	65pi deep blue	4.75	75
		Nos. C200-C206 (7)	11.25	1.89

See Nos. C233-C235.

Tourist — AP49

1955, Sept. 10 Unwmk. *Perf. 13*

C207	AP49	2.50pi brn vio & lt bl	15	15
C208	AP49	12.50pi ultra & lt bl	20	15
C209	AP49	25pi ind & lt bl	50	16
C210	AP49	35pi ol grn & lt bl	60	22
a.		Sheet of 4, #C207-C210, imperf.	6.50	6.50
		Set value		55

Tourist Year. No. C210a is printed on cardboard.

Oranges AP50

Designs: 25pi, 35pi, 50pi, Grapes, vert. 65pi, 100pi, 200pi, Apples.

1955, Oct. 15

C211	AP50	5pi yel grn & yel	15	15
C212	AP50	10pi dk grn & dp orange	20	15
C213	AP50	15pi yel grn & red orange	25	15
C214	AP50	20pi ol & yel org	42	15
C215	AP50	25pi bl & vio bl	60	15
C216	AP50	35pi green & cl	80	15
C217	AP50	50pi blk brn & dl yellow	80	15
C218	AP50	65pi grn & lemon	1.90	16
C219	AP50	100pi yel grn & dp orange	2.50	42
C220	AP50	200pi green & car	4.00	2.00
		Nos. C211-C220 (10)	11.62	
		Set value		3.00

For surcharge, see No. C265.

United Nations Emblem AP52

1956, Jan. 23 *Perf. 11½*

C221	AP52	35pi violet blue	2.00	1.50
C222	AP52	65pi green	2.25	1.75

UN, 10th anniv. (in 1955).

An imperf. souvenir sheet contains one each of Nos. C221 and C222. Value $20.

Temple of the Sun Colonnade, Masks and Lion's Head — AP53

Temple of Bacchus, Baalbek AP54

Design: 35pi, 65pi, Temple of the Sun colonnade, masks and violincello.

1956, Dec. 10 Litho. *Perf. 13*

C223	AP53	2.50pi dark brown	18	15
C224	AP53	10pi green	25	18
C225	AP54	12.50pi light blue	25	22
C226	AP54	25pi brt vio bl	40	35
C227	AP53	35pi red lilac	75	45
C228	AP53	65pi slate blue	1.10	90
		Nos. C223-C228 (6)	2.93	2.25

International Festival at Baalbek.

Skiing Type of 1955 Redrawn and

Irrigation Canal, Litani AP55

1957 Litho. *Perf. 11½*

C229	AP55	10pi bright vio	15	15
C230	AP55	15pi orange	18	15
C231	AP55	20pi yel green	20	15
C232	AP55	25pi slate bl	30	15
C233	AP48	35pi gray grn	90	15
C234	AP48	65pi dp claret	1.25	22
C235	AP48	100pi brown	2.25	50
		Nos. C229-C235 (7)	5.23	
		Set value		1.00

Different Arabic characters used for the country name; letters in "Liban" larger.

For surcharge, see No. C271.

Pres. Camille Chamoun and King Saud AP56

King Saud, Pres. Chamoun, King Hussein, Pres. Kouatly, King Faisal, Pres. Nasser — AP57

Pres. Chamoun and: No. C237, King Hussein. No. C238, Pres. Kouatly. No. C239, King Faisal. No. C240, Pres. Nasser. 25pi, Map of Lebanon.

1957, July 15 Litho. *Perf. 13*

C236	AP56	15pi green	22	20
C237	AP56	15pi blue	22	20
C238	AP56	15pi red lilac	22	20
C239	AP56	15pi red orange	22	20
C240	AP56	15pi claret	22	20
C241	AP56	25pi blue	22	20
C242	AP57	100pi dl red brn	1.90	1.40
		Nos. C236-C242 (7)	3.22	2.60

Issued to commemorate the Congress of Arab Leaders, Beirut, Nov. 12-15, 1956.

Fencing AP58

Design: 50pi, Pres. Chamoun and stadium with flags.

1957, Sept. 12 Unwmk. *Perf. 13*

C243	AP58	35pi claret	75	60
C244	AP58	50pi light grn	1.00	90

2nd Pan-Arab Games, Beirut. See note on souvenir sheet below No. 314.

Symbols of Communications — AP59

Power Plant, Chamoun AP60

1957 *Perf. 13x13½, 11½ (AP60)*

C245	AP59	5p bright grn	15	15
C246	AP59	10p yel orange	15	15
C247	AP59	15p brown	15	15
C248	AP59	20p maroon	20	15
C249	AP59	25p vio blue	20	15
C250	AP60	35p violet brn	40	15
C251	AP60	50p green	65	18
C252	AP60	65p sepia	85	18
C253	AP60	100p dark gray	1.25	50
		Nos. C245-C253 (9)	4.00	
		Set value		1.40

Plane at Airport AP61

Cogwheel AP62

1958-59 **Unwmk.** ***Perf. 13***

C254	AP61	5p green	15	15
C255	AP61	10p magenta	15	15
C256	AP61	15p dull violet	20	15
C257	AP61	20p orange ver	30	15
C258	AP61	25p dk vio bl	35	16
C259	AP62	35p grnsh gray	50	16
C260	AP62	50p aquamarine	60	16
C261	AP62	65p pale brown	1.10	25
C262	AP62	100p brt ultra	1.40	15
		Nos. C254-C262 (9)	4.75	
		Set value		1.00

Nos. C259 and C261 Surcharged in Black or Dark Blue

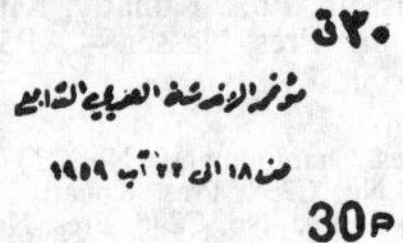

1959 **Unwmk.** **Litho.** ***Perf. 13***

C263	AP62	30p on 35p grnsh gray	25	22
C264	AP62	40p on 65p pale brn (Bl)	40	38

Arab Engineers Congress.

No. C217 Overprinted as Illustrated and Surcharged with New Value and Bars

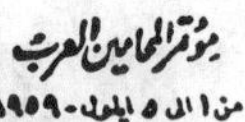

1959, Sept. 1

C265	AP50	40p on 50p blk brn & dl yellow	35	32

Arab Lawyers Congress.

Myron's Discobolus — AP63

Wreath and Hand Holding Torch AP64

1959, Oct. 11 **Litho.** ***Perf. 11½***

C266	AP63	15p shown	18	15
C267	AP63	30p Weight lifter	30	20
C268	AP64	40p shown	55	30

3rd Mediterranean Games, Beirut.

A souvenir sheet on white cardboard contains one each of Nos. C266-C268, imperf. Sold for 100p. Value $5.

Soldiers and Flag — AP65

Hands Planting Tree — AP66

1959, Nov. 25 ***Perf. 13½x13***

C269	AP65	40p sep, brick red & sl	32	28
C270	AP65	60p sep, dk grn & brick red	48	32

Lebanon's independence, 1941-1959.

No. C234 Surcharged with New Value and Bars

1959, Dec. 15 ***Perf. 11½***

C271	AP48	40p on 65p deep cl	80	22

1960, Jan. 18 **Litho.** ***Perf. 11½***

C272	AP66	20p rose vio & grn	28	20
C273	AP66	40p dk brn & green	40	32

Friends of the Tree Society, 25th anniv.

Postal Administration Building — AP67

1960, Feb. **Unwmk.** ***Perf. 13***

C274	AP67	20p green	22	15

President Fuad Chehab AP68

Uprooted Oak Emblem AP69

1960, Mar. 12 **Photo.** ***Perf. 13½***

C275	AP68	5p green	15	15
C276	AP68	10p Prussian bl	15	15
C277	AP68	15p orange brn	15	15
C278	AP68	20p brown	15	15
C279	AP68	30p olive	15	15
C280	AP68	40p dull red	18	15
C281	AP68	50p blue	20	15
C282	AP68	70p red lilac	38	15
C283	AP68	100p dark green	70	32
		Set value	1.75	90

1960, Apr. 7 **Litho.** ***Perf. 13½x13***

Size: 20½x36½mm

C284	AP69	25p yellow brn	28	20
C285	AP69	40p green	40	28
a.		Souv. sheet of 2, #C284-C285, imperf.	6.50	6.50

Size: 20x36mm

C284b	AP69	25p yellow brn	40	40
C285b	AP69	40p green	60	60

World Refugee Year, July 1, 1959-June 30, 1960.

No. C285a sold for 150p.

Nos. C284b-C285b appear fuzzy and pale when compared to the bolder, clear-cut printing of Nos. C284-C285.

Nos. C284b-C285b exist with carmine surcharges of "30P.+15P." (on C284b) and "20P.+10P." (on C285b), repeated in Arabic, with ornaments covering original denominations.

Martyrs' Monument — AP70

Martyrs of May 6th: 70p, Statues from Martyrs' monument, vert.

1960, May 6 ***Perf. 13x13½, 13½x13***

C286	AP70	20p rose lilac & grn	18	15
C287	AP70	40p Prus grn & dk grn	25	22
C288	AP70	70p gray olive & blk	60	50

Pres. Chehab and King of Morocco AP71

1960, June 1 ***Perf. 13x13½***

C289	AP71	30p choc & dk brn	32	28
C290	AP71	70p blk, dk brn & buff	65	35

Visit of King Mohammed V of Morocco.

A souvenir sheet of 2 on white cardboard contains Nos. C289-C290, imperf.

Child Learning to Walk — AP72

Bird, Ribbon of Flags and Map of Beirut — AP73

1960, Aug. 16 **Litho.** ***Perf. 13½x13***

C291	AP72	20p shown	18	16
C292	AP72	60p Mother & child	50	42

Day of Mother and Child, Mar. 21-22. See Nos. CB10-CB11.

Perf. 13½x13, 13x13½

1960, Sept. 20 **Unwmk.**

Designs: 40p, Cedar and birds. 70p, Globes and cedar, horiz.

C293	AP73	20p multicolored	15	15
C294	AP73	40p vio, bl & grn	25	15
C295	AP73	70p multicolored	40	20
		Set value		40

Union of Lebanese Emigrants in the World. A souvenir sheet of 3 contains Nos. C293-C295, imperf., printed on cardboard. Sold for 150p. Value $4.

Pres. Chehab and Map of Lebanon — AP74

1961, Feb. **Litho.** ***Perf. 13½x13***

C296	AP74	5p bl grn & yel grn	15	15
C297	AP74	10p brown & bister	15	15
C298	AP74	70p vio & rose lilac	48	25
		Set value	62	35

Casino, Maameltein AP75

1961 ***Perf. 13x13½***

C299	AP75	15p rose claret	20	15
C300	AP75	30p greenish blue	28	15
C301	AP75	40p brown	35	15
C302	AP75	200p bis brn & dl bl	2.00	1.00
		Nos. C296-C302 (8)	4.23	
		Set value		1.70

On Nos. C299-C301, the denomination, inscription and trees differ from type AP75.

UN Headquarters, New York — AP76

Designs: 20p, UN Emblem and map of Lebanon. 30p, UN Emblem and symbolic building. 20p, 30p are vertical.

1961, May 5 ***Perf. 13½x13, 13x13½***

C306	AP76	20p lake & lt blue	18	15
C307	AP76	30p green & beige	24	15
C308	AP76	50p vio bl & grnsh bl	40	20
a.		Souv. sheet of 3	4.00	4.00
		Set value		36

UN, 15th anniv. (in 1960).

No. C308a contains one each of Nos. C306-C308, imperf., against a light blue background showing UN emblem. Sold for 125p.

Pottery Workers AP77

1961, July 11 **Litho.** ***Perf. 13x13½***

C309	AP77	30p shown	38	18
C310	AP77	70p Weaver	18	15

Issued for Labor Day, 1961.

Fireworks — AP78

Water Skiing AP79

Design: 70p, Tourists on boat ride through cave.

1961, Aug. 8 ***Perf. 13½x13, 13x13½***

C311	AP78	15p lt pur & dk bl	40	28
C312	AP79	40p blue & pink	60	42
C313	AP79	70p dl brn & pink	20	15

Issued to publicize tourist month.

Highway Circle at Dora, Beirut Suburb AP80

1961, Aug. ***Perf. 11½***

C314	AP80	35p yellow green	35	18
C315	AP80	50p orange brown	48	28
C316	AP80	100p gray	48	32

Beach at Tyre — AP81

Afka Falls — AP82

1961, Sept. **Litho.** ***Perf. 13***

C317	AP81	5p carmine rose	15	15
C318	AP81	10p bright vio	15	15
C319	AP81	15p bright blue	15	15
C320	AP81	20p orange	15	15
C321	AP81	30p bright grn	19	15
C322	AP82	40p dp claret	22	15
C323	AP82	50p ultramarine	32	16

C324 AP82 70p yellow grn 40 24
C325 AP82 100p dark brown 75 35
Nos. C317-C325 (9) 2.48
Set value 1.20

See Nos. C341-C342.

Entrance to UNESCO Building AP83

"UNESCO" and Cedar — AP84

Design: 50p, UNESCO headquarters, Paris.

1961, Nov. 20 Unwmk. *Perf. 12*
C326 AP83 20p bl, buff & blk 16 15
C327 AP84 30p lt grn, blk & mag 20 15
C328 AP83 50p multicolored 42 20
Set value 40

UNESCO, 15th anniv.

Emir Bechir and Fakhr-el-Din El Maani — AP85

Design: 25p, Cedar emblem.

1961, Dec. 30 Litho.
C329 AP85 25p Cedar emblem 16 15
C330 AP85 50p shown 32 28

See note after No. 375.

Scout Types of Regular Issue, 1962

Designs: 15p, Trefoil and cedar emblem. 20p, Hand making Scout sign. 25p, Lebanese Scout emblem.

1962, Mar. 1 Unwmk. *Perf. 12*
C331 A70 15p grn, blk & red 16 15
C332 A69 20p lil, blk & yel 22 16
C333 A70 25p multicolored 38 24

Arab League Building, Cairo — AP86

1962, Mar. 22 *Perf. 13*
C334 AP86 20p ultra & lt bl 15 15
C335 AP86 30p red brn & pink 20 16
C336 AP86 50p grn & grnsh bl 32 28

Arab League Week, Mar. 22-28. See Nos. C372-C375.

Blacksmith — AP87

Farm Tractor AP88

Perf. 13½x13, 13x13½

1962, May 1 Litho.
C337 AP87 5p green & lt blue 15 15
C338 AP87 10p blue & pink 15 15
C339 AP88 25p brt vio & pink 25 15
C340 AP88 35p car rose & blue 35 18
Set value 40

Issued for Labor Day.

Types of 1961 Redrawn with Large Numerals Similar to Redrawn Regular Issue of 1962

1962 *Perf. 13*
C341 AP81 5p carmine rose 35 15
C342 AP82 40p deep claret 3.00 35
Set value 40

Hand Reaching for Malaria Eradication Emblem — AP89

Bas-relief of Isis, Kalabsha Temple, Nubia — AP90

Design: 70p, Malaria eradication emblem.

1962, July 1 Litho. *Perf. 13½x13*
C349 AP89 30p tan & brown 35 20
C350 AP89 70p bluish lil & vio 50 40

WHO drive to eradicate malaria.

1962, Aug. 1 Unwmk. *Perf. 13*
C351 AP90 30p yellow green 62 25
C352 AP90 50p slate 1.10 60

Campaign to save historic monuments in Nubia.

Spade, Heart, Diamond, Club — AP91

College Student — AP92

1962, Sept.
C353 AP91 25p car rose, blk & red 1.10 80
C354 AP91 40p multicolored 1.20 80

European Bridge Championship Tournament.

1962, Oct. 1 *Perf. 12*
C355 AP92 45p multicolored 40 20

Issued for Students' Day, Oct. 1.

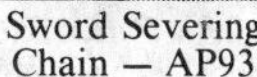

Sword Severing Chain — AP93

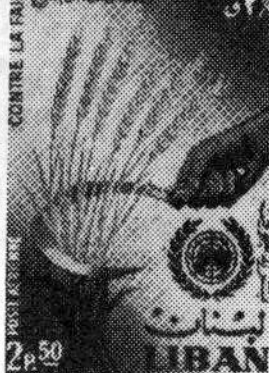

Harvest — AP94

1962, Nov. 22 Litho. *Perf. 13*
C356 AP93 25p vio, lt bl & red 42 25
C357 AP93 25p bl, lt bl & red 42 25
C358 AP93 25p grn, lt bl & red 42 25

19th anniversary of independence.

Fruit Type of Regular Issue, 1962

Designs: 5p, Apricots. 10p, 30p, Plums. 20p, 40p, Apples. 50p, Pears. 70p, Medlar. 100p, Lemons.

1962

Vignette Multicolored

C359 A72 5p orange brown 15 15
C360 A72 10p black 15 15
C361 A72 20p brown 22 15
C362 A72 30p gray 28 16
C363 A72 40p dark gray 35 16
C364 A72 50p light brown 45 20
C365 A72 70p gray olive 65 28
C366 A72 100p blue 1.20 45
Nos. C359-C366 (8) 3.45
Set value 1.40

1963, Mar. 21 Litho. *Perf. 13*

Design: 15p, 20p, UN Emblem and hand holding Wheat Emblem, horiz.

C367 AP94 2.50p ultra & yel 15 15
C368 AP94 5p gray grn & yel 15 15
C369 AP94 7.50p rose lil & yel 15 15
C370 AP94 15p rose brn & pale grn 22 15
C371 AP94 20p rose & pale grn 30 16
Set value 78 42

FAO "Freedom from Hunger" campaign.

Redrawn Type of 1962, Dated "1963"

Design: Arab League Building, Cairo.

1963, Mar. Unwmk. *Perf. 12*
C372 AP86 5p vio & light bl 15 15
C373 AP86 10p green & lt bl 15 15
C374 AP86 15p claret & lt bl 16 16
C375 AP86 20p gray & lt blue 28 25
Set value 60 56

Issued for Arab League Week.

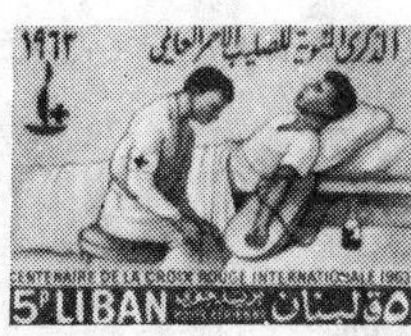

Blood Transfusion AP95

Design: 35p, 40p, Nurse and infant, vert.

1963, Oct. 5 Unwmk. *Perf. 13*
C376 AP95 5p green & red 15 15
C377 AP95 20p grnsh bl & red 15 15
C378 AP95 35p org, red & blk 25 16
C379 AP95 40p purple & red 38 20
Set value 80 48

Centenary of International Red Cross.

Lyre Player and Columns — AP96

Lebanon Flag, Rising Sun — AP97

1963, Nov. 7 Unwmk. *Perf. 13*
C380 AP96 35p lt bl, org & blk 40 28

International Festival at Baalbek.

1964, Jan. 8 Litho.
C381 AP97 5p bluish grn, ver & yel 15 15
C382 AP97 10p yel grn, ver & yel 15 16
C383 AP97 25p ultra, ver & yel 25 25
C384 AP97 40p gray, ver & yel 40 40

20th anniversary of Independence.

Sports Type of Regular Issue, 1964

1964, Feb. 11 Unwmk. *Perf. 13*
C385 A76 15p Tennis 15 15
C386 A76 17.50p Swimming, horiz. 20 15
C387 A76 30p Skiing, horiz. 35 20
a. Souv. sheet of 3 5.50 5.50
Set value 40

No. C387a contains three imperf. stamps similar to Nos. C385-C387 with simulated orange brown perforations and green marginal inscription. Sold for 100p.

Anemone AP98

Flame and UN Emblem AP100

Girls Jumping Rope AP99

1964, June 9 Unwmk. *Perf. 13*
C391 AP98 5p Lily 15 15
C392 AP98 10p Ranunculus 16 15
C393 AP98 20p shown 25 15
C394 AP98 40p Tuberose 38 20
C395 AP98 45p Rhododendron 40 20
C396 AP98 50p Jasmine 45 20
C397 AP98 70p Yellow broom 70 30
Nos. C391-C397 (7) 2.49 1.35

1964, Apr. 8

Children's Day: 20p, 40p, Boy on hobbyhorse, vert.

C398 AP99 5p emer, org & red 15 15
C399 AP99 10p yel brn, org & red 15 15
C400 AP99 20p dp ultra, lt bl & org 18 16
C401 AP99 40p lil, lt bl & yel 35 30
Set value 62

1964, May 15 Litho. Unwmk.

Design: 40p, Flame, UN emblem and broken chain.

C402 AP100 20p salmon, org & brn 15 15
C403 AP100 40p lt bl, gray bl & org 25 16
Set value 24

15th anniv. (in 1963) of the Universal Declaration of Human Rights.

Arab League Conference — AP101

1964, Apr. 20 *Perf. 13x13½*

C404	AP101	5p blk & pale sal	30	20
C405	AP101	10p black	50	35
C406	AP101	15p green	65	50
C407	AP101	20p dk brn & pink	1.00	65

Arab League meeting.

Child in Crib — AP102

Beit-ed-Din Palace and Children — AP103

1964, July 20 *Perf. 13½x13, 13½*

C408	AP102	2.50p multi	15	15
C409	AP102	5p multi	15	15
C410	AP102	15p multi	15	15
C411	AP103	17.50p multi	20	15
C412	AP103	20p multi	25	15
C413	AP103	40p multi	30	16
		Set value	1.00	55

Ball of the Little White Beds, Beirut, for the benefit of children's hospital beds.

Clasped Hands and Map of Lebanon — AP104

1964, Oct. 16 **Litho.** *Perf. 13½x13*

C414	AP104	20p yel grn, yel & gray	25	16
C415	AP104	40p slate, yel & gray	40	35

Issued to publicize the Congress of the International Lebanese Union.

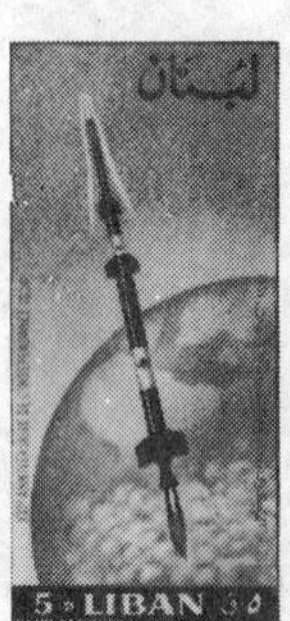
Rocket Leaving Earth AP105

Woman in Costume AP107

Battle Scene — AP106

1964, Nov. 24 **Unwmk.** *Perf. 13½*

C416	AP105	5p multicolored	15	15
C417	AP105	10p multicolored	15	15
C418	AP106	40p sl bl & blk	40	28
C419	AP106	70p dp cl & blk	60	50

21st anniversary of independence.

1965, Jan. 11 **Litho.** *Perf. 13½*

Design: 10p, 15p, Man in costume.

C420	AP107	10p multicolored	20	15
C421	AP107	15p multicolored	35	20
C422	AP107	25p grn & multi	50	35
C423	AP107	40p brn & multi	65	50

International Festival at Baalbek.

Equestrian AP108

1965, Jan. 23 **Engr.** *Perf. 13*

C424	AP108	15p shown	15	15
C425	AP108	25p Target shooting, vert.	20	15
C426	AP108	40p Gymnast on rings	35	20
a.		Souvenir sheet of 3, #C424-C426, imperf.	5.00	5.00
		Set value		40

18th Olympic Games, Tokyo, Oct. 10-25, 1964. No. 426a sold for 100p.

Heliconius Cybria AP109

Designs: 30p, Pericallia matronula. 40p, Red admiral. 45p, Satyrus semele. 70p, Machaon. 85p, Aurore. 100p, Morpho cypris. 200p, Erasmia sanguiflua. 300p, Papilio crassus. 500p, Charaxes ameliae.

1965 **Unwmk.** *Perf. 13*

Size: 36x22mm

C427	AP109	30p ver, yel & dk brown	15	15
C428	AP109	35p ol bis, dk bl & red	16	15
C429	AP109	40p sl grn, org & brown	18	15
C430	AP109	45p blk, Prus bl & yellow	25	16
C431	AP109	70p multicolored	35	25
C432	AP109	85p blk, grn & orange	50	25
C433	AP109	100p dk pur & bl	70	25
C434	AP109	200p dl pur, blk & blue	1.50	42
C435	AP109	300p brn, sl grn & yellow	2.00	80

Engr. and Litho.
Perf. 12
Size: 35x25mm

C436	AP109	500p lt ultra & blk	4.25	2.00
		Nos. C427-C436 (10)	10.04	4.58

For surcharges, see Nos. C654-C656.

Pope Paul VI and Pres. Chehab — AP110

1965, June 28 **Photo.** *Perf. 12*

C437	AP110	45p gold & brt vio	1.50	80
a.		Souv. sheet of 1, imperf.	25.00	25.00

Visit of Pope Paul VI to Lebanon. No. C437a sold for 50p.

Cedars of Friendship AP111

1965, Oct. 16 **Photo.** *Perf. 13x12½*

C438	AP111	40p multicolored	35	15

Cocoon, Spindle and Silk — AP112

Design: 15p, 30p, 40p, 50p, Silk weaver at loom.

1965, Oct. 16 *Perf. 12½x13*

Design in Buff and Bright Green

C439	AP112	2.50p brown	15	15
C440	AP112	5p dk ol green	15	15
C441	AP112	7.50p Prussian bl	15	15
C442	AP112	15p deep ultra	15	15
C443	AP112	30p deep claret	16	15
C444	AP112	40p brown	25	20
C445	AP112	50p rose brown	50	25
		Set value	1.15	70

Parliament Building AP113

1965, Oct. 26 *Perf. 13x12½*

C446	AP113	35p red, buff & brn	20	15
C447	AP113	40p emer, buff & brn	30	16

Centenary of the Lebanese parliament.

UN Headquarters, NYC, UN Emblem and Lebanese Flags — AP114

1965, Nov. 10 **Engr.** *Perf. 12*

C448	AP114	2.50p dull blue	15	15
C449	AP114	10p magenta	15	15
C450	AP114	17.50p dull vio	15	15
C451	AP114	30p green	16	15
C452	AP114	40p brown	25	20
		Set value	60	45

UN, 20th anniv. A souvenir sheet contains one 40p imperf. stamp in bright rose lilac. Sold for 50p. Value $8.

Playing Card King, Laurel and Cedar AP115

Dagger in Map of Palestine AP116

1965, Nov. 15 **Photo.** *Perf. 12½x13*

C453	AP115	2.50p multi	15	15
C454	AP115	15p multi	15	15
C455	AP115	17.50p multi	20	15
C456	AP115	40p multi	40	20
		Set value		40

Intl. Bridge Championships. A souvenir sheet contains two imperf. stamps similar to Nos. C454 and C456. Sold for 75p. Value $8.

1965, Dec. 13 *Perf. 12½x11*

C457	AP116	50p multi	1.00	50

Deir Yassin massacre, Apr. 9, 1948.

ITU Emblem, Old and New Communication Equipment and Syncom Satellite — AP117

1966, Apr. 13 *Perf. 13x12½*

C458	AP117	2.50p multi	15	15
C459	AP117	15p multi	15	15
C460	AP117	17.50p multi	16	15
C461	AP117	25p multi	35	15
C462	AP117	40p multi	40	20
		Nos. C458-C462 (5)	1.21	
		Set value		55

ITU, centenary (in 1965).

Folk Dancers Before Temple of Bacchus — AP118

Designs: 7.50p, 15p, Dancers before Temple of Jupiter, vert. 30p, 40p, Orchestra before Temple of Bacchus.

1966, July 20 **Unwmk.** *Perf. 12*

Gold Frame

C463	AP118	2.50p brn vio, bl & orange	15	15
C464	AP118	5p mag, bl & org	15	15
C465	AP118	7.50p vio bl, bl & pink	15	15
C466	AP118	15p pur, bl & pink	15	15
C467	AP118	30p dk grn, org & blue	20	15
C468	AP118	40p vio, org & bl	38	20
		Set value	95	55

11th International Festival at Baalbek.

Opening of WHO Headquarters, Geneva — AP119

1966, Aug. 25 Engr. *Perf. 12*

C469 AP119 7.50p dp yel grn 15 15
C470 AP119 17.50p car rose 15 15
C471 AP119 25p blue 16 15
Set value 32 24

Skier AP120

Designs: 5p, Children on toboggan. 17.50p, Cedar in snow. 25p, Ski lift.

1966, Sept. 15 Photo. *Perf. 12x11½*

C472 AP120 2.50p multi 15 15
C473 AP120 5p multi 15 15
C474 AP120 17.50p multi 15 15
C475 AP120 25p multi 30 16
Set value 60 35

International Festival of Cedars.

Sarcophagus of King Ahiram with Early Alphabet — AP121

Designs: 15p, Phoenician ship. 20p, Map of the Mediterranean Sea showing Phoenician travel routes, and ship. 30p, Phoenician with alphabet tablet.

Litho. & Engr.

1966, Sept. 25 *Perf. 12*

C476 AP121 10p dl grn, blk & lt brn 15 15
C477 AP121 15p rose lil, brn & ocher 15 15
C478 AP121 20p tan, dk brn & bl 16 15
C479 AP121 30p org, dk brn & yel 35 20
Set value 68 46

Invention of alphabet by Phoenicians.

Child in Bathtub and UNICEF Emblem AP122

UNICEF Emblem and: 5p, Boy in rowboat. 7.50p, Girl skier. 12p, Girl feeding bird. 20p, Boy doing homework. 50p, Children of various races, horiz.

1966, Oct. 10 Photo. *Perf. 11½x12*

C480 AP122 2.50p multi 15 15
C481 AP122 5p multi 15 15
C482 AP122 7.50p multi 15 15
C483 AP122 15p multi 15 15
C484 AP122 20p multi 22 16
Set value 56 36

Miniature Sheet

Imperf

C485 AP122 50p dl yellow & multi 1.90 1.90

UNICEF; World Children's Day. No. C485 contains one horizontal stamp 43x33mm.

Scenic Type of Regular Issue, 1966

Designs: 10p, Waterfall, Djezzine. 15p, Castle of the Sea, Saida. 20p, Amphitheater, Jubayl (Byblos). 30p, Temple of the Sun, Baalbek. 50p, Beit-ed-Din Palace. 60p, Church of Christ the King, Nahr-el-Kalb. 75p, Abu Bakr Mosque, Tripoli.

1966, Oct. 12 *Perf. 12x11½*

C486 A82 10p gold & multi 15 15
C487 A82 15p gold & multi 15 15
C488 A82 20p gold & multi 15 15
C489 A82 30p gold & multi 16 15
C490 A82 50p gold & multi 35 15
C491 A82 60p gold & multi 45 15
C492 A82 75p gold & multi 62 18
Nos. C486-C492 (7) 2.03
Set value 58

Symbolic Water Cycle — AP123

Daniel Bliss — AP124

Designs: 15p, 20p, Different wave pattern without sun.

1966, Nov. 15 Photo. *Perf. 12½*

C493 AP123 5p red, bl & vio bl 15 15
C494 AP123 10p org, bl & brn 15 15
C495 AP123 15p org, emer & dk brn 15 15
C496 AP123 20p org, emer & grnsh blue 15 15
Set value 36 30

Hydrological Decade (UNESCO), 1965-74.

1966, Dec. 3

Designs: 30p, Chapel, American University, Beirut. 50p, Daniel Bliss, D.D., and American University, horiz.

C497 AP124 20p grn, yel & brn 16 15
C498 AP124 30p red brn, grn & blue 20 15
Set value 20

Souvenir Sheet

Imperf

C499 AP124 50p grn, brn & org brown 1.00 1.00

Cent. of American University, Beirut, founded by the Rev. Daniel Bliss (1823-1916). Nos. C497-C498 are printed each with alternating labels showing University emblem.

No. C499 contains one stamp 59x37mm.

Flags of Arab League Members, Hand Signing Scroll — AP125

1967, Aug. 2 Photo. *Perf. 12x11½*

C500 AP125 5p brn & multi 15 15
C501 AP125 10p multicolored 15 15
C502 AP125 15p blk & multi 15 15
C503 AP125 20p multicolored 16 16
Set value 38 38

Signing of Arab League Pact in 1945.

Veteran's War Memorial Building, San Francisco — AP126

Design: 10p, 20p, 30p, Scroll, flags of Lebanon and United Nations.

1967, Sept. 1 Photo. *Perf. 12x11½*

C504 AP126 2.50p bl & multi 15 15
C505 AP126 5p multicolored 15 15
C506 AP126 7.50p multicolored 15 15
C507 AP126 10p bl & multi 15 15
C508 AP126 20p multicolored 15 15
C509 AP126 30p multicolored 22 15
Set value 60 40

22nd anniv. of the San Francisco Pact, the United Nations Charter.

Ruins at Baalbek — AP127

Intl. Tourist Year: 10p, Ruins at Anjar. 15p, Bridge over Ibrahim River and ruins. 20p, Boat on underground lake, Jaita cave. 50p, St. George's Bay, Beirut.

1967, Sept. 25 *Perf. 12½*

C510 AP127 5p multi 15 15
C511 AP127 10p multi 15 15
C512 AP127 15p vio & multi 15 15
C513 AP127 20p brn & multi 20 15
Set value 50 25

Souvenir Sheet

Imperf

C514 AP127 50p multi *20.00 20.00*

View of Tabarja AP128

Views: 15p, Pigeon Rock and shore, Beirut. 17.50p, Beit-ed-Din Palace. 20p, Ship at Sidon. 25p, Tripoli. 30p, Beach at Byblos. 35p, Ruins, Tyre. 40p, Temple of Bacchus, Baalbek.

1967, Oct. *Perf. 12x11½*

C515 AP128 10p multi 15 15
C516 AP128 15p multi 16 15
C517 AP128 17.50p multi 22 15
C518 AP128 20p multi 22 15
C519 AP128 25p multi 22 15
C520 AP128 30p multi 35 15
C521 AP128 35p multi 40 15
C522 AP128 40p multi 65 16
Nos. C515-C522 (8) 2.37
Set value 1.00

Intl. Tourist Year; used as a regular airmail issue.

India Day AP129

1967, Oct. 30 Engr. *Perf. 12*

C523 AP129 2.50p orange 15 15
C524 AP129 5p magenta 15 15
C525 AP129 7.50p brown 15 15
C526 AP129 10p blue 15 15
C527 AP129 15p green 20 15
Set value 42 26

Globe and Arabic Inscription — AP130

Design: 10p, 20p, 30p, UN emblem.

1967, Nov. 25 Engr. *Perf. 12*

C528 AP130 2.50p rose 15 15
C529 AP130 5p gray blue 15 15
C530 AP130 7.50p green 15 15
C531 AP130 10p bright car 15 15
C532 AP130 20p vio blue 15 15
C533 AP130 30p dark green 20 15
Set value 55 32

Lebanon's admission to the UN. A 100p rose red souvenir sheet in the globe design exists. Value $2.50.

Basking Shark AP131

Fish: 30p, Needlefish. 40p, Pollack. 50p, Cuckoo wrasse. 70p, Red mullet. 100p, Rainbow trout.

1968, Feb. Photo. *Perf. 12x11½*

C534 AP131 20p multi 22 15
C535 AP131 30p multi 22 15
C536 AP131 40p multi 42 15
C537 AP131 50p multi 55 15
C538 AP131 70p multi 1.10 15
C539 AP131 100p multi 1.50 15
Nos. C534-C539 (6) 4.01
Set value 45

Ski Jump — AP132

Designs: 5p, 7.50p, 10p, Downhill skiers (various). 25p, Congress emblem (skis and cedar).

1968 *Perf. 12½x11½*

C540 AP132 2.50p multicolored 15 15
C541 AP132 5p multicolored 15 15
C542 AP132 7.50p multicolored 15 15
C543 AP132 10p multicolored 15 15
C544 AP132 25p multicolored 18 15
Set value 42 32

26th Intl. Ski Congress, Beirut. A 50p imperf. souvenir sheet exists in design of the 25p. Value $4.50.

Emir Fakhr al-Din II — AP133

Designs: 2.50p, Emira Khaskiah. 10p, Citadel of Sidon, horiz. 15p, Citadel of Chekif and grazing sheep, horiz. 17.50p, Citadel of Beirut and harbor, horiz.

Perf. 11½x12, 12x11½

1968, Feb. 20 **Litho.**

C546	AP133	2.50p	multicolored	15	15
C547	AP133	5p	multicolored	15	15
C548	AP133	10p	multicolored	15	15
C549	AP133	15p	multicolored	22	15
C550	AP133	17.50p	multicolored	22	15
			Set value	60	35

In memory of the Emir Fakhr al-Din II. A 50p imperf. souvenir sheet exists showing the Battle of Anjar. Value $5.50.

Roman Bust — AP134

Ruins of Tyre: 5p, Colonnade, horiz. 7.50p, Arch, horiz. 10p, Banquet, bas-relief.

Litho. & Engr.

1968, Mar. 20 ***Perf. 12***

C552	AP134	2.50p	pink, brn & buff	16	15
C553	AP134	5p	yel, brn & lt bl	20	15
C554	AP134	7.50p	lt grnsh bl, brn & yel	25	15
C555	AP134	10p	sal, brn & lt bl	35	15
a.			Souvenir sheet	11.00	11.00
			Set value		40

No. C555a contains one dark brown and light blue stamp, perf. 10½x11½. Sold for 50p. Exists imperf.

For surcharge, see No. C657.

Emperor Justinian AP135

Design: 15p, 20p, Justinian and map of the Mediterranean, horiz.

Perf. 11½x12, 12x11½

1968, May 10 **Photo.**

C556	AP135	5p	blue & multi	15	15
C557	AP135	10p	blue & multi	15	15
C558	AP135	15p	red & multi	15	15
C559	AP135	20p	blue & multi	15	15
			Set value	32	24

Beirut, site of one of the greatest law schools in antiquity; Emperor Justinian (483-565), who compiled and preserved the Roman law.

Arab League Emblem — AP136

1968, June 6 **Photo.** ***Perf. 12x11½***

C560	AP136	5p	org & multi	15	15
C561	AP136	10p	multicolored	15	15
C562	AP136	15p	pink & multi	15	15
C563	AP136	20p	multicolored	16	15
			Set value	35	22

Issued for Arab League Week.

Cedar and Globe Emblem — AP137

1968, July 10

C564	AP137	2.50p	sal pink, brn & green	16	15
C565	AP137	5p	gray, brn & grn	20	15
C566	AP137	7.50p	brt bl, brn & grn	22	15
C567	AP137	10p	yel grn, brn & green	35	15
			Set value		40

3rd Congress of Lebanese World Union.

Temple of Jupiter, Baalbek AP138

Designs: 10p, Fluted pilasters, cella of Bacchus Temple. 15p, Corniche, south peristyle of Jupiter Temple, horiz. 20p, Gate, Bacchus Temple. 25p, Ceiling detail, south peristyle of Bacchus Temple.

1968, Sept. 25 **Photo.** ***Perf. 12½***

C568	AP138	5p	gold & multi	15	15
C569	AP138	10p	gold & multi	15	15
C570	AP138	15p	gold & multi	15	15
C571	AP138	20p	gold & multi	16	15
C572	AP138	25p	gold & multi	25	16
			Set value	60	42

13th Baalbek International Festival.

Broad Jump and Phoenician Statue — AP139

Designs: 10p, High jump and votive stele, Phoenician, 6th century B.C. 15p, Fencing and Olmec jade head, 500-400 B.C. 20p, Weight lifting and axe in shape of human head, Vera Cruz region. 25p, Aztec stone calendar and Phoenician ship.

1968, Oct. 19 **Photo.** ***Perf. 12x11½***

C573	AP139	5p	lt ultra, yel & gray	15	15
C574	AP139	10p	mag, lt ultra & blk	15	15
C575	AP139	15p	cit, ocher & brn	15	15
C576	AP139	20p	dp org, brn & ocher	16	15
C577	AP139	25p	light brown	25	18
			Set value	62	45

19th Olympic Games, Mexico City, Oct. 12-27.

Human Rights Flame and Tractor — AP140

Human Rights Flame and: 15p, People. 25p, Boys of 3 races placing hands on globe.

1968, Dec. 10 **Litho.** ***Perf. 11½***

C578	AP140	10p	multicolored	15	15
C579	AP140	15p	yel & multi	16	15
C580	AP140	25p	lil & multi	35	15
			Set value		20

International Human Rights Year.

Minshiya Stairs, Deir El-Kamar AP141

Views in Deir El-Kamar: 15p, The Seraglio Kiosk. 25p, Old paved city road.

1968, Dec. 26

C581	AP141	10p	multicolored	15	15
C582	AP141	15p	multicolored	15	15
C583	AP141	25p	multicolored	15	15
			Set value	24	20

1st Municipal Council in Lebanon, established in Deir El-Kamar by Daoud Pasha, cent.

Nurse Treating Child, and UN Emblem — AP142

Designs: 10p, Grain, fish, grapes and jug. 15p, Mother and children. 20p, Reading girl and Phoenician alphabet. 25p, Playing children.

1969, Jan. 20 **Litho.** ***Perf. 12***

C584	AP142	5p	blk, lt bl & sep	15	15
C585	AP142	10p	blk, brt yel & grn	15	15
C586	AP142	15p	blk, red lil & ver	15	15
C587	AP142	20p	blk, cit & bl	15	15
C588	AP142	25p	blk, pink & bis brn	16	15
			Set value	44	30

UNICEF, 22nd anniversary.

Silver Coin from Byblos, 5th Century B.C. — AP143

Designs (National Museum, Beirut): 5p, Gold dagger, Byblos, 18th century B.C. 7.50p, King Dining in the Land of the Dead, sarcophagus of Ahiram, 13-12th century B.C. 30p, Breastplate with cartouche of Amenemhat III (1849-1801 B.C.). 40p, Phoenician bird vase from Khalde, 8th century B.C.

Photogravure; Gold Impressed

1969, Feb. 20 ***Perf. 12***

C589	AP143	2.50p	grn, yel & lt bl	16	15
C590	AP143	5p	vio, brn & yel	22	15
C591	AP143	7.50p	dl yel, brn & pink	30	15
C592	AP143	30p	blue & multi	42	15
C593	AP143	40p	multicolored	55	20
			Nos. C589-C593 (5)	1.65	
			Set value		45

Intl. Congress of Museum Councils; 20th anniv. of the Intl. Council of Museums.

Water Skier AP144

Designs: 5p, Water ballet. 7.50p, Parachutist, vert. 30p, Yachting, vert. 40p, Regatta.

1969, Mar. 3 **Litho.** ***Perf. 11½***

C594	AP144	2.50p	multicolored	15	15
C595	AP144	5p	multicolored	15	15
C596	AP144	7.50p	multicolored	15	15
C597	AP144	30p	multicolored	18	18
C598	AP144	40p	multicolored	28	28
			Set value	62	62

Tomb of Unknown Soldier at Military School — AP145

Designs: 2.50p, Frontier guard. 7.50p, Soldiers doing forestry work. 15p, Army engineers building road. 30p, Ambulance and helicopter. 40p, Ski patrol.

1969, Aug. 1 **Litho.** ***Perf. 12x11½***

C599	AP145	2.50p	multicolored	15	15
C600	AP145	5p	multicolored	15	15
C601	AP145	7.50p	multicolored	15	15
C602	AP145	15p	multicolored	15	15
C603	AP145	30p	multicolored	15	15
C604	AP145	40p	multicolored	18	18
			Set value	52	50

25th anniversary of independence.

Crosses and Circles — AP146

1971, Jan. 6 **Photo.** ***Perf. 11½x12***

C605	AP146	15p	shown	15	15
C606	AP146	85p	Crosses, cedar	60	45

Lebanese Red Cross, 25th anniversary.

Foil Fencing AP147

Designs: 10p, Flags of participating Arab countries. 15p, Flags of participating non-Arab countries. 40p, Sword fencing. 50p, Saber fencing.

1971, Jan. 15 Litho. *Perf. 12*

C607	AP147 10p yel & multi		15	15
C608	AP147 15p yel & multi		15	15
C609	AP147 35p yel & multi		18	16
C610	AP147 40p yel & multi		25	20
C611	AP147 50p yel & multi		30	25
	Set value		84	72

10th World Fencing Championships, held in Lebanon.

Agricultural Workers, Arab Painting, 12th Century — AP148

1971, Feb. 1

C612	AP148 10p silver & multi	35	15
C613	AP148 40p gold & multi	65	15
	Set value		17

International Labor Organization.

UPU Building and Monument, Bern — AP149

1971, Feb. 15 Litho. *Perf. 12*

C614	AP149 15p yel, blk & dp org	55	16
C615	AP149 35p dp org, yel & blk	1.00	35

Opening of new UPU Headquarters in Bern, Switzerland.

Ravens Burning Owls — AP150

Children's Day: 85p, Jackal and lion. Designs of the 15p and 85p are after 13th-14th century paintings, illustrations for the "Kalila wa Dumna."

1971, Mar. 1 Photo. *Perf. 11*
Size: 30x30mm

C616	AP150 15p gold & multi	15	15

Perf. 12x11½
Size: 38½x29mm

C617	AP150 85p gold & multi	60	30
	Set value		36

Map and Flag of Arab League AP151

1971, Mar. 20 *Perf. 12x11½*

C618	AP151 30p org & multi	16	15
C619	AP151 70p yel & multi	42	25

Arab League, 25th anniv.

Kahlil Gibran AP152

Famous Lebanese Men: No. C620, Symbolic design for Imam al Ouzai. No. C621, Bechara el Khoury. No. C622, Hassan Kamel al Sabbah.

1971, Apr. 10

C620	AP152 25p lt grn, gold & brn	16	15
C621	AP152 25p yel, gold & brn	22	15
C622	AP152 25p yel, gold & brn	22	15
C623	AP152 25p lt grn, gold & brn	22	15
	Set value		32

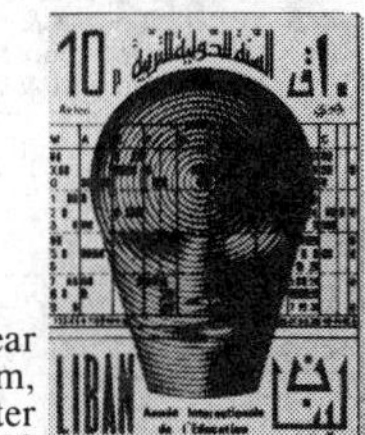

Education Year Emblem, Computer Card — AP153

1971, Apr. 30 Photo. *Perf. 11½x12*

C624	AP153 10p blk, vio & bl	16	15
C625	AP153 40p blk, org & yel	35	15
	Set value		18

Intl. Education Year.

Jamhour Substation AP154

Designs: 10p, Maameltein Bridge. 15p, Hotel Management School. 20p, Litani Dam. 25p, Television set wiring. 35p, Temple of Bziza. 40p, Jounieh Port. 45p, Airport radar. 50p, Flower. 70p, New School of Sciences. 85p, Oranges. 100p, Arbanieh earth satellite station.

1971, May Litho. *Perf. 12*

C626	AP154 5p multi	15	15
C627	AP154 10p multi	15	15
C628	AP154 15p multi	15	15
C629	AP154 20p multi	15	15
C630	AP154 25p multi	15	15
C631	AP154 35p multi	20	15
C632	AP154 40p multi	20	15
C633	AP154 45p multi	22	15
C634	AP154 50p multi	35	15
C635	AP154 70p multi	50	15
C636	AP154 85p multi	65	20
C637	AP154 100p multi	80	38
	Nos. C626-C637 (12)	3.67	
	Set value		1.35

For stamps overprinted with overall patterns, see Nos. C758-C787.

Dahr-el-Bacheq Sanatorium AP155

1971, June 1

C638	AP155 50p shown	35	16
C639	AP155 100p multi, diff.	50	35

Campaign against tuberculosis.

Solar Wheel (Festival Emblem) AP156

1971, July 1 Photo. *Perf. 11*

C640	AP156 15p ultra & org	15	15
C641	AP156 85p Corinthian capital	50	30
	Set value		36

16th Baalbek International Festival.

155mm Cannon AP157

Army Day: 25p, Mirage fighters flying over Baalbek ruins. 40p, Army Headquarters. 70p, Naval patrol boat.

1971, Aug. 1 *Perf. 12x11½*

C642	AP157 15p gold & multi	22	15
C643	AP157 25p gold & multi	35	15
C644	AP157 40p gold & multi	50	16
C645	AP157 70p gold & multi	80	25
	Set value		58

Wooden Console, Al Aqsa Mosque — AP158

1971, Aug. 21 *Perf. 12*

C646	AP158 15p dk brn & ocher	40	15
C647	AP158 35p dk brn & ocher	60	16
	Set value		24

2nd anniversary of the burning of Al Aqsa Mosque in Jerusalem.

Lenin (1870-1924) AP159

1971, Oct. 1 *Perf. 12x11½*

C648	AP159 30p gold & multi	30	15
C649	AP159 70p multicolored	65	30

UN Emblem, World Map AP160

1971, Oct. 24 *Perf. 13x12½*

C650	AP160 15p multicolored	15	15
C651	AP160 85p multicolored	65	25
	Set value		30

UN, 25th anniv. (in 1970).

The Rape of Europa, Mosaic from Byblos AP161

1971, Nov 20 Litho. *Perf. 12*

C652	AP161 10p slate & multi	15	15
C653	AP161 40p gold & multi	50	16
	Set value		20

Publicity for World Lebanese Union (ULM).

Nos. C435-C436 Surcharged

100P. ق١٠٠

Engr.; Engr. & Litho.

1972, May *Perf. 13, 12*

C654	AP109 100p on 300p multi	80	40
C655	AP109 100p on 500p multi	80	40
C656	AP109 200p on 300p multi	1.25	80

The numerals on No. C655 are taller (5mm) and bars spaced 1½mm apart.

No. C554 Surcharged

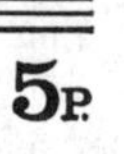

(Reduced)

1972, June Litho. & Engr. *Perf. 12*

C657	AP134 5p on 7.50p multi	16	16

Hibiscus AP162

Lebanese House AP163

1973 Litho. *Perf. 12*

C658	AP162 2.50p shown	15	15
C659	AP162 5p Roses	15	15
C660	AP162 15p Tulips	15	15
C661	AP162 25p Lilies	35	15
C662	AP162 40p Carnations	40	15
C663	AP162 50p Iris	55	15
C664	AP162 70p Apples	45	15
C665	AP162 75p Grapes	50	16
C666	AP162 100p Peaches	65	35
C667	AP162 200p Pears	2.25	25
C668	AP162 300p Cherries	2.50	55
C669	AP162 500p Oranges	4.00	90
	Nos. C658-C669 (12)	12.10	
	Set value		2.70

For stamps overprinted with overall patterns, see Nos. C758-C787.

1973 *Perf. 14*

Designs: Old Lebanese houses.

C670	AP163 35p yel & multi	1.00	16
C671	AP163 50p lt bl & multi	1.40	20
C672	AP163 85p buff & multi	2.25	28
C673	AP163 100p multicolored	3.00	40

For stamps overprinted with overall patterns, see Nos. C758-C787.

Woman with Rose — AP164

Lebanese Costumes: 10p, Man. 20p, Man on horseback. 25p, Woman playing mandolin.

1973, Sept. 1 Litho. *Perf. 14*

C674 AP164	5p yel & multi		15	15
C675 AP164	10p yel & multi		25	15
C676 AP164	20p yel & multi		40	15
C677 AP164	25p yel & multi		55	15
	Set value			25

For stamps overprinted with overall patterns, see Nos. C758-C787.

Swimming, Temple at Baalbek — AP165

Designs: 10p, Running and portal. 15p, Woman athlete and castle. 20p, Women's volleyball and columns. 25p, Basketball and aqueduct. 50p, Women's table tennis and buildings. 75p, Handball and building. 100p, Soccer and cedar.

1973, Sept. 25 Photo. *Perf. 11½x12*

C678 AP165	5p multicolored	15	15
C679 AP165	10p multicolored	15	15
C680 AP165	15p grn & multi	16	15
C681 AP165	20p multicolored	16	15
C682 AP165	25p ultra & multi	22	15
C683 AP165	50p org & multi	50	30
C684 AP165	75p vio & multi	65	40
C685 AP165	100p multicolored	1.10	80
a.	Souvenir sheet	1.25	1.25
	Nos. C678-C685 (8)	3.09	2.25

5th Pan-Arabic Scholastic Games, Beirut. No. C685a contains one stamp with simulated perforations similar to No. C685; gold inscription and denomination.

View of Brasilia AP166

Designs: 20p, Old Salvador (Bahia). 25p, Lebanese sailing ship enroute from the Old World to South America. 50p, Dom Pedro I and Emir Fakhr al-Din II.

1973, Nov. 15 Litho. *Perf. 12*

C686 AP166	5p gold & multi	15	15
C687 AP166	20p gold & multi	50	35
C688 AP166	25p gold & multi	50	35
C689 AP166	50p gold & multi	1.00	65

Sesquicentennial of Brazil's independence.

Inlay Worker AP167

1973, Dec. 1

C690 AP167	10p shown	40	15
C691 AP167	20p Weaver	65	25
C692 AP167	35p Glass blower	1.00	35
C693 AP167	40p Potter	1.40	50
C694 AP167	50p Metal worker	1.60	50
C695 AP167	70p Cutlery maker	2.50	65
C696 AP167	85p Lace maker	3.50	1.00
C697 AP167	100p Handicraft Museum	4.00	1.40
	Nos. C690-C697 (8)	15.05	4.80

Lebanese handicrafts.

For stamps overprinted with overall patterns, see Nos. C758-C787.

Camp Site, Log Fire and Scout Emblem — AP168

Designs: 5p, Lebanese Scout emblem and map. 7½p, Lebanese Scout emblem and map of Middle East. 10p. Lord Baden-Powell, ruins of Baalbek. 15p, Girl Guide, camp and emblem. 20p, Lebanese Girl Guide and Scout emblems. 25p, Scouts around camp fire. 30p, Symbolic globe with Lebanese flag and Scout emblem. 35p, Flags of participating nations. 50p, Old man, and Scout chopping wood.

1974, Aug. 24 Litho. *Perf. 12*

C698 AP168	2.50p multi	25	25
C699 AP168	5p multi	25	25
C700 AP168	7.50p multi	55	25
C701 AP168	10p multi	55	25
C702 AP168	15p multi	65	55
C703 AP168	20p multi	90	65
C704 AP168	25p multi	1.20	65
C705 AP168	30p multi	1.50	65
C706 AP168	35p multi	2.00	90
C707 AP168	50p multi	2.50	1.40
	Nos. C698-C707 (10)	10.35	5.80

11th Arab Boy Scout Jamboree, Smar-Jubeil, Aug. 1974. Nos. C702-C703 are for the 5th Girl Guide Jamboree, Deir-el-Kamar. Nos. C698-C702 and C703-C707 printed vertically se-tenant.

Mail Train and Postman Loading Mail, UPU Emblem — AP169

UPU Emblem and: 20p, Postal container hoisted onto ship. 25p, Postal Union Congress Building, Lausanne, and UPU Headquarters, Bern. 50p, Fork-lift truck loading mail on plane.

1974, Nov. 4 Photo. *Perf. 11½x12*

C708 AP169	5p multicolored	15	15
C709 AP169	20p multicolored	35	25
C710 AP169	25p multicolored	50	22
C711 AP169	50p ultra & multi	1.00	70

Centenary of Universal Postal Union.

Congress Building, Sofar — AP170

Arab Postal Union Emblem and: 20p, View of Sofar. 25p, APU Headquarters, Cairo. 50p, Ministry of Post, Beirut.

1974, Dec. 4 Litho. *Perf. 13x12½*

C712 AP170	5p org & multi	15	15
C713 AP170	20p yel & multi	30	20
C714 AP170	25p bl & multi	42	22
C715 AP170	50p multicolored	1.90	1.00

Arab Postal Union, 25th anniversary.

Mountain Road, by Omar Onsi — AP171

Paintings by Lebanese artists: No. C717, Clouds, by Moustapha Farroukh. No. C718, Woman, by Gebran Kahlil Gebran. No. C719, Embrace, by Cesar Gemayel. No. C720, Self-portrait, by Habib Serour. No. C721, Portrait of a Man, by Daoud Corm.

1974, Dec. 6 Litho. *Perf. 13x12½*

C716 AP171	50p lil & multi	1.00	50
C717 AP171	50p bl & multi	1.00	50
C718 AP171	50p grn & multi	1.00	50
C719 AP171	50p lt vio & multi	1.00	50
C720 AP171	50p brn & multi	1.00	50
C721 AP171	50p gray brn & multi	1.00	50
	Nos. C716-C721 (6)	6.00	3.00

Hunter Spearing Lion — AP172

Excavations at Hermel: 10p, Statue of Astarte. 25p, Dogs hunting boar, tiled panel. 35p, Greco-Roman tomb.

1974, Dec. 13

C722 AP172	5p bl & multi	15	15
C723 AP172	10p lil & multi	20	15
C724 AP172	25p multicolored	50	22
C725 AP172	35p multicolored	65	38
	Set value		76

UNESCO Emblems and Globe AP173

1974, Dec. 16 *Perf. 12½x13*

C726 AP173	5p vio & multi	15	15
C727 AP173	10p bis & multi	20	15
C728 AP173	25p blue & multi	50	30
C729 AP173	35p multicolored	60	40

International Book Year.

Symbolic Stamp under Magnifying Glass — AP174

Designs (Symbolic): 10p, Post horns. 15p, Stamp printing. 20p, Mounted stamp.

1974, Dec. 20 *Perf. 13x12½*

C730 AP174	5p blue & multi	15	15
C731 AP174	10p olive & multi	15	15
C732 AP174	15p brown & multi	22	22
C733 AP174	20p lilac & multi	30	22
	Set value	70	62

Georgina Rizk — AP175

Designs: 5p, 25p, Georgina Rizk in Lebanese costume. 50p, Like 20p.

1974, Dec. 21

C734 AP175	5p multicolored	15	15
C735 AP175	20p vio & multi	15	15
C736 AP175	25p yel & multi	15	15
C737 AP175	50p blue & multi	30	20
a.	Souvenir sheet of 4	80	80
	Set value	60	40

Georgina Rizk, Miss Universe 1971. No. C737a contains 4 stamps similar to Nos. C734-C737 with simulated perforations.

UNICEF Emblem, Helicopter, Camel, Supplies — AP176

UNICEF Emblem and: 25p, Child welfare clinic. 35p, Kindergarten class. 70p, Girls in chemistry laboratory.

1974, Dec. 28 Litho. *Perf. 12½x13*

C738 AP176	20p multi	15	15
C739 AP176	25p multi	16	15
C740 AP176	35p blue & multi	25	15
C741 AP176	70p blue & multi	55	15
a.	Souvenir sheet of 4	1.90	1.90
	Set value		45

UNICEF, 25th anniv. No. C741a contains 4 stamps similar to Nos. C738-C741 with simulated perforations. Sold for 200p.

Discus and Olympic Rings — AP177

1974, Dec. 30 *Perf. 13x12½*

C742 AP177	5p shown	15	15
C743 AP177	10p Shot put	15	15
C744 AP177	15p Weight lifting	15	15
C745 AP177	35p Running	30	22
C746 AP177	50p Wrestling	42	22
C747 AP177	85p Javelin	70	35
a.	Souvenir sheet of 6	2.00	2.00
	Nos. C742-C747 (6)	1.87	
	Set value		90

20th Olympic Games, Munich, Aug. 26-Sept. 11, 1972. No. C747a contains 6 stamps similar to Nos. C742-C747 with simulated perforations.

Clouds and Environment Emblem AP178

1975

C748	AP178	5p shown	15	15
C749	AP178	25p Landscape	16	15
C750	AP178	30p Flowers and tree	16	15
C751	AP178	40p Waves	25	20
a.		Souvenir sheet of 4	1.40	1.40
		Set value	60	40

UN Conf. on Human Environment, Stockholm, June 5-16, 1972. No. C751a contains four stamps similar to Nos. C748-C751 with simulated perforations. Sold for 150p.

Archaeology — AP179

Designs (Symbols of): 25p, Science and medicine. 35p, Justice and commerce. 70p, Industry and commerce.

1975, Aug. Litho. *Perf. 12½x13*

C752	AP179	20p multi	30	20
C753	AP179	25p multi	42	22
C754	AP179	35p blue & multi	60	38
C755	AP179	70p buff & multi	1.40	70

Beirut, University City.

Stamps of 1971-73 Overprinted with Various Overall Patterns Including Cedars in Blue, Red, Orange, Lilac, Brown or Green

1978 Litho. *Perf. 12, 14*

C758	AP162	2.50p (#C658;B)	15	15
C759	AP162	5p (#C659;R)	15	15
C760	AP164	5p (#C674;B)	15	15
C761	AP164	10p (#C675;B)	15	15
C762	AP167	10p (#C690;O)	15	15
C763	AP162	15p (#C660;R)	30	15
C764	AP164	20p (#C676;B)	20	15
C765	AP167	20p (#C691;B)	20	15
C766	AP162	25p (#C661;L)	20	15
C767	AP164	25p (#C677;B)	42	15
C768	AP163	35p (#C670;Br)	50	15
C769	AP162	40p (#C662;L)	50	16
C770	AP167	40p (#C693;G)	50	16
C771	AP154	45p (#C633;L)	50	20
C772	AP162	50p (#C663;L)	70	20
C773	AP163	50p (#C671;L)	70	20
C774	AP167	50p (#C694;Br)	70	20
C775	AP154	70p (#C635;L)	80	30
C776	AP162	70p (#C664;L)	80	30
C777	AP167	70p (#C695;B)	80	30
C778	AP162	75p (#C665;B)	1.25	30
C779	AP154	85p (#C636;R)	1.00	35
C780	AP163	85p (#C672;B)	1.00	35
C781	AP167	85p (#C696;G)	1.00	35
C782	AP162	100p (#C666;O)	1.50	42
C783	AP163	100p (#C673;B)	1.50	42
C784	AP167	100p (#C697;L)	1.50	42
C785	AP162	200p (#C667;O)	3.00	1.60
C786	AP162	300p (#C668;O)	4.25	3.00
C787	AP162	500p (#C669;O)	6.50	4.25
		Nos. C758-C787 (30)	31.07	15.13

Heart and Arrow — AP180

1978, Apr. 7 Litho. *Perf. 12*

C788	AP180	50p bl, blk & red	1.00	65

World Health Day; drive against hypertension.

Poet Mikhail Naimy and Sannine Mountains — AP181

Designs: 50p, Naimy and view of Al Chakhroub Baskinta. 75p, Naimy portrait in sunburst, vert.

1978, May 17

C789	AP181	25p gold & multi	55	24
C790	AP181	50p gold & multi	1.00	55
C791	AP181	75p gold & multi	1.60	80

Mikhail Naimy Festival.

Army Day Type of 1980

Designs: 50p, Emir Fakhr al-Din statue, vert. 75p, Soldiers and flag.

1980, Dec. 28 Litho. *Perf. 11½*

C792	A86	50p multicolored	50	25
C793	A86	75p multicolored	65	40

28th UPU Congress, Rio de Janeiro, 1979 AP182

1981, Feb. 17 Photo. *Perf. 12x11½*

C794	AP182	25p multicolored	22	15
C795	AP182	50p multicolored	55	30
C796	AP182	75p multicolored	1.00	45

Intl. Year of the Child (1979) AP183

1981, Mar. 25 Litho. *Perf. 12x11½*

C797	AP183	100p multi	1.20	65

1974 Chess Championships — AP184

Designs: Various chess pieces. Nos. C799-C802 vert.

Perf. 12x11½, 11½x12

1980-81 Photo.

C798	AP184	50p multi	1.40	50
C799	AP184	75p multi	1.50	65
C800	AP184	100p multi	1.90	1.00
C801	AP184	150p multi	3.00	1.90
C802	AP184	200p multi	4.25	2.50
		Nos. C798-C802 (5)	12.05	6.55

Makassed Islamic Institute Centenary (1978) AP185

1981 Photo. *Perf. 13½x14*

C803	AP185	50p Children	30	15
C804	AP185	75p Institute	50	20
C805	AP185	100p Makassed	65	38

AIR POST SEMI-POSTAL STAMPS

Nos. C13-C16 Surcharged Like Nos. B1-B12

1926 *Perf. 13½*

CB1	A2	2pi + 1pi dark brn	2.25	2.25
CB2	A2	3pi + 2pi org brown	2.25	2.25
CB3	A2	5pi + 3pi violet	2.25	2.25
CB4	A3	10pi + 5pi vio brown	2.25	2.25

These stamps were sold for their combined values, original and surcharged. The latter represented their postal franking value and the former was a contribution to the relief of refugees from the Djebel Druze War.

Catalogue values for unused stamps in this section, from this point to the end of the section, are for Never Hinged items.

Independent Republic

Natural Bridge, Faraya SPAP1

Bay of Jounie SPAP2

Perf. 11½

1947, June 27 Unwmk. Litho.

Cross in Carmine

CB5	SPAP1	12.50 + 25pi brt bl grn	3.50	3.00
CB6	SPAP1	25 + 50pi bl	4.00	3.50
CB7	SPAP2	50 + 100pi choc	5.00	4.00
CB8	SPAP2	75 + 150pi brt pur	10.00	8.00
CB9	SPAP2	100 + 200pi sl	15.00	11.00
		Nos. CB5-CB9 (5)	37.50	29.50

The surtax was for the Red Cross.

Mother & Child Type of Air Post Stamps, 1960

1960, Aug. 16 *Perf. 13½x13*

CB10	AP72	20p + 10p dk red & buff	35	16
CB11	AP72	60p + 15p bl & lt bl	90	50

Olympic Games Type of Semi-Postal Issue, 1961

1961, Jan. 12 Unwmk. *Perf. 13*

CB12	SP1	15p + 15p Fencing	1.00	1.00
CB13	SP1	25p + 25p Bicycling	1.00	1.00
CB14	SP1	35p + 35p Swimming	1.00	1.00

An imperf. souvenir sheet exists, containing one each of Nos. CB12-CB14. Value $22.50.

Nos. CB12-CB14 with Arabic and French Overprint in Green, Red or Maroon and two Bars through Olympic Inscription: "CHAMPIONNAT D'EUROPE DE TIR, 2 JUIN 1962"

1962, June 2

CB15	SP1	15p + 15p (G)	45	45
CB16	SP1	25p + 25p (M)	90	90
CB17	SP1	35p + 35p (R)	1.20	1.20

European Marksmanship Championships held in Lebanon.

POSTAGE DUE STAMPS

Postage Due Stamps of France, 1893-1920, Surcharged like Regular Issue

1924 Unwmk. *Perf. 14x13½*

J1	D2	50c on 10c choc	1.60	1.60
J2	D2	1pi on 20c ol grn	1.60	1.60
J3	D2	2pi on 30c red	1.60	1.60
J4	D2	3pi on 50c vio brn	1.60	1.60
J5	D2	5pi on 1fr red brn, *straw*	1.60	1.60
		Nos. J1-J5 (5)	8.00	8.00

Postage Due Stamps of France, 1893-1920, Surcharged

Gd Liban
2 Piastres
لبنان الكبير
غرش ٢

1924

J6	D2	0p50 on 10c choc	1.90	1.60
J7	D2	1pi on 20c ol grn	1.90	1.60
J8	D2	2pi on 30c red	1.90	1.60
J9	D2	3pi on 50c vio brn	1.90	1.60
J10	D2	5pi on 1fr red brn, *straw*	1.90	1.60
		Nos. J6-J10 (5)	9.50	8.00

Ancient Bridge across Dog River — D3

Designs: 1p, Village scene. 2p, Pigeon Rocks, near Beirut. 3p, Belfort Castle. 5p, Venus Temple at Baalbek.

1925 Photo. *Perf. 13½*

J11	D3	0p50 brown, *yellow*	16	16
J12	D3	1pi violet, *rose*	25	25
J13	D3	2pi black, *blue*	42	42
J14	D3	3pi black, *red org*	80	80
J15	D3	5pi black, *bl grn*	1.40	1.40
		Nos. J11-J15 (5)	3.03	3.03

Nos. J11 to J15 Overprinted

République Libanaise

1927

J16	D3	0p50 brown, *yellow*	22	22
J17	D3	1pi violet, *rose*	35	35
J18	D3	2pi black, *blue*	50	50
J19	D3	3pi black, *red org*	1.40	1.40
J20	D3	5pi black, *bl grn*	1.60	1.60
		Nos. J16-J20 (5)	4.07	4.07

Nos. J16 to J20 with Additional Overprint

= =

الجمهورية اللبنانية

1928

J21	D3	0p50 brn, *yel* (Bk+R)	50	50
J22	D3	1pi vio, *rose* (Bk)	50	50
J23	D3	2pi blk, *bl* (Bk+R)	1.00	1.00
J24	D3	3pi blk, *red org* (Bk)	2.00	2.00
J25	D3	5pi blk, *bl grn* (Bk+R)	2.25	2.25
		Nos. J21-J25 (5)	6.25	6.25

No. J23 has not the short bars in the upper corners.

Postage Due Stamps of 1925 Overprinted in Red like Nos. J21-J25

1928

J26	D3	0p50 brn, *yel* (R)	22	22
J27	D3	2pi blk, *bl* (R)	1.40	1.40
J28	D3	5pi blk, *bl grn* (R)	4.00	4.00

No. J28 has not the short bars in the upper corners.

D4

Bas-relief of a Ship — D5

D6

D7

D8

Bas-relief from Sarcophagus of King Ahiram — D9

D10

1930-40 Photo.; Engr. (No. J35)

J29 D4	0p50	black, *rose*	16	16
J30 D5	1pi	blk, *gray bl*	35	35
J31 D6	2pi	blk, *yellow*	50	50
J32 D7	3pi	blk, *bl grn*	50	50
J33 D8	5pi	blk, *orange*	2.25	2.25
J34 D9	8pi	blk, *lt rose*	1.50	1.50
J35 D8	10pi	dk grn ('40)	2.50	2.00
J36 D10	15pi	black	2.00	1.40
		Nos. J29-J36 (8)	9.76	8.66

Nos. J29-J36 exist imperf.

Catalogue values for unused stamps in this section, from this point to the end of the section, are for Never Hinged items.

Independent Republic

National Museum, Beirut D11

1945 Unwmk. Litho. *Perf. 11 ½*

J37 D11	2pi	brn black, *yel*	1.40	1.40
J38 D11	5pi	ultra, *rose*	2.00	1.60
J39 D11	25pi	blue, *bl green*	3.00	2.50
J40 D11	50pi	dark bl, *blue*	3.25	2.50

D12

1947

J41 D12	5pi	black, *green*	2.00	50
J42 D12	25pi	blk, *yellow*	20.00	1.40
J43 D12	50pi	black, *blue*	10.00	2.00

Hermel Monument D13

1948

J44 D13	2pi	blk, *yellow*	1.40	35
J45 D13	3pi	black, *pink*	2.50	1.25
J46 D13	10pi	black, *blue*	6.50	2.25

D14

1950

J47 D14	1pi	carmine rose	60	15
J48 D14	5pi	violet blue	2.25	35
J49 D14	10pi	gray green	4.50	65

D15

1952

J50 D15	1pi	dp rose lilac	15	15
J51 D15	2pi	bright violet	15	15
J52 D15	3pi	dark blue grn	25	15
J53 D15	5pi	blue	35	15
J54 D15	10pi	chocolate	50	20
J55 D15	25pi	black	4.25	65
		Nos. J50-J55 (6)	5.65	
		Set value		1.20

D16

D17

1953

J56 D16	1pi	carmine rose	15	15
J57 D16	2pi	blue green	15	15
J58 D16	3pi	orange	15	15
J59 D16	5pi	lilac rose	16	15
J60 D16	10pi	brown	35	15
J61 D16	15pi	deep blue	65	35
		Set value	1.35	75

1955 Unwmk. *Perf. 13*

J62 D17	1pi	orange brown	15	15
J63 D17	2pi	yellow green	15	15
J64 D17	3pi	blue green	15	15
J65 D17	5pi	carmine lake	15	15
J66 D17	10pi	gray green	15	15
J67 D17	15pi	ultramarine	20	15
J68 D17	25pi	red lilac	42	25
		Set value	1.00	60

Cedar of Lebanon D18

Emir Fakhr al-Din II D19

1966 Photo. *Perf. 11 ½*

J69 D18	1p	bright green	15	15
J70 D18	5p	rose lilac	15	15
J71 D18	15p	ultramarine	16	15
		Set value	36	24

1968 Litho. *Perf. 11*

J72 D19	1p	dk & light gray	16	15
J73 D19	2p	dk & lt blue grn	16	15
J74 D19	3p	deep org & yel	16	15
J75 D19	5p	brt rose lil & pink	16	15
J76 D19	10p	olive & lemon	16	15
J77 D19	15p	vio & pale violet	20	15
J78 D19	25p	brt bl & lt blue	35	20
		Nos. J72-J78 (7)	1.35	
		Set value		65

POSTAL TAX STAMPS

Fiscal Stamp Surcharged in Violet

R1

Wmk. A T 39 Multiple

1945 *Perf. 13 ½*

RA1 R1	5pi on 30c red brn		16.50	1.40

The tax was for the Lebanese Army.

No. RA1 Overprinted in Black

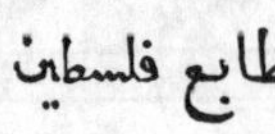

1948

RA2 R1	5pi on 30c red brn		16.50	1.40

Fiscal Stamps Surcharged in Various Colors

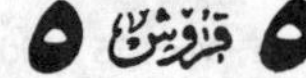

RA3 R1	5pi on 15pi dk vio bl (R)		14.00	1.60
a.	Brown surcharge		18.00	2.25
RA4 R1	5pi on 25c dk blue green (R)		14.00	1.60
RA5 R1	5pi on 30c red brn (Bl)		16.00	1.60
RA6 R1	5pi on 60c lt ultra (Br)		22.50	1.60
RA7 R1	5pi on 3pi salmon rose (Ult)		14.00	1.60

Same With Additional Overprint طابع قضائي

RA8 R1	5pi on 10pi red		*65.00*	5.00

Fiscal Stamp Surcharged Like Nos. RA3-RA7 with Top Arabic Characters Replaced by

ضريبة فلسطين

RA9 R1	5pi on 3pi rose (Bk+V)		16.50	1.60

Fiscal Stamp Surcharged in Black and Violet

RA10 R1	5pi on 3pi sal rose		*190.00*	15.00

The tax was to aid the war in Palestine.

Catalogue values for unused stamps in this section, from this point to the end of the section, are for Never Hinged items.

Family among Ruins — R2

Building a House — R3

1956 Unwmk. Litho. *Perf. 13*

RA11 R2	2.50pi brown		1.00	16

The tax was for earthquake victims. These stamps were obligatory on all inland mail and all mail going to Arab countries.

1957 *Perf. 13 ½x13*

RA12 R3	2.50p brown		65	15

1958

RA13 R3	2.50p dark blue grn		42	15

Type of 1957 Redrawn

1959

RA14 R3	2.50p light brown		1.00	16

On No. RA14 the denomination is on top and the Arabic lines are at the bottom of design.

Building a House

R4 R5

1961 Unwmk. *Perf. 13 ½x13*

RA15 R4	2.50p yellow brown		50	15

1962 *Perf. 13 ½x14*

RA16 R5	2.50p blue green		45	15

The tax was for the relief of earthquake victims.

LIBERIA

LOCATION — West coast of Africa, between Ivory Coast and Sierra Leone
GOVT. — Republic
AREA — 43,000 sq. mi.
POP. — 1,900,000 (est. 1984)
CAPITAL — Monrovia

100 Cents = 1 Dollar

Catalogue values for unused stamps in this country are for Never Hinged items, beginning with Scott 330 in the regular postage section, Scott B19 in the semi-postal section, Scott C67 in the airpost section, and Scott CB4 in the airpost semi-postal section.

Watermarks

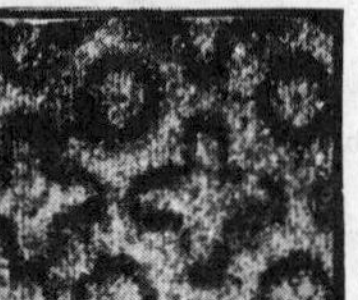

Wmk. 116- Crosses and Circles

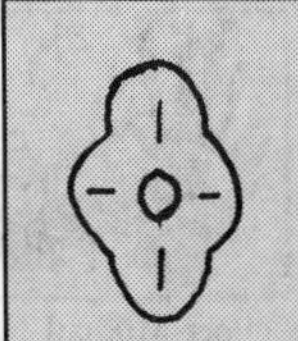

Wmk. 143

"Liberia" — A1

1860 Unwmk. Litho. *Perf. 12*

Thick Paper

No.	Type	Description	Unused	Used
1	A1	6c red	100.00	100.00
a.		Imperf.	125.00	
2	A1	12c deep blue	22.50	30.00
a.		Imperf.	90.00	
3	A1	24c green	22.50	30.00
a.		Imperf.	90.00	

Stamps set very close together. Margins small and perforation close to or touching the design. Copies of the 12c occasionally show traces of a frame line around the design.

Medium to Thin Paper

With a single-line frame around each stamp, about 1mm from the border

1864 *Perf. 11, 12*

No.	Type	Description	Unused	Used
7	A1	6c red	52.50	57.50
a.		Imperf.	90.00	
8	A1	12c blue	52.50	57.50
a.		Imperf.	90.00	
9	A1	24c lt grn	52.50	57.50
a.		Imperf.	90.00	

Stamps set about 5mm apart. Margins large and perforation usually outside the frame line.

Without Frame Line

1866-69

No.	Type	Description	Unused	Used
13	A1	6c lt red	17.50	25.00
14	A1	12c lt bl	15.00	25.00
15	A1	24c lt yel grn	15.00	25.00

Stamps set 2-2½mm apart with small margins. Stamps are usually without frame line but those from one transfer show broken and irregular parts of a frame.

With Frame Line

1880 *Perf. 10½*

No.	Type	Description	Unused	Used
16	A1	1c ultra	3.25	5.00
17	A1	2c rose	3.25	3.00
a.		Imperf., pair	100.00	
18	A1	6c violet	3.25	3.00
19	A1	12c yellow	3.25	3.00
20	A1	24c rose red	3.25	3.50

Unused values for Nos. 16-20 are for copies without gum.

For surcharges see Nos. 157-159.

From Arms of Liberia — A2

1881

No.	Type	Description	Unused	Used
21	A2	3c black	3.50	3.50

Unused value is for copies without gum.

A3

A4

1882 *Perf. 11½, 12, 14*

No.	Type	Description	Unused	Used
22	A3	8c blue	25.00	4.00
23	A4	16c red	4.00	2.50

On No. 22 the openings in the figure "8" enclose a pattern of slanting lines. Compare with No. 32.

Canceled to Order

Beginning with the issue of 1885, values in the used column are for "canceled to order" stamps. Postally used copies sell for much more.

A5

A6

From Arms of Liberia — A7

A8

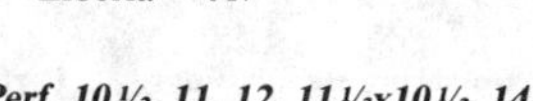

Perf. 10½, 11, 12, 11½x10½, 14, 14½

1885

No.	Type	Description	Unused	Used
24	A5	1c carmine	1.00	1.00
a.		1c rose	1.00	1.00
25	A5	2c green	1.00	1.00
26	A5	3c violet	1.00	1.00
27	A5	4c brown	1.00	1.00
28	A5	6c olive gray	1.00	1.00
29	A6	8c bluish gray	2.50	2.50
a.		lilac	2.50	2.50
30	A6	16c yellow	3.50	3.50
31	A7	32c deep blue	12.00	12.00
		Nos. 24-31 (8)	23.00	23.00

In the 1885 printing, the stamps are spaced 2mm apart and the paper is medium. In the 1892 printing, the stamps are 4½mm apart.

For surcharges see Nos. J1-J2.

Imperf., Pair

No.	Type	Description	Unused	Used
24b	A5	1c	2.50	
25a	A5	2c	3.50	
26a	A5	3c	4.00	
27a	A5	4c	4.00	
28a	A5	6c	3.50	3.50
29b	A6	8c	10.00	
30a	A6	16c	12.50	
31a	A7	32c	25.00	

Imperf. pairs with 2mm spacing sell for higher prices.

1889 *Perf. 12, 14*

No.	Type	Description	Unused	Used
32	A8	8c blue	3.50	3.50
a.		Imperf., pair	15.00	

The openings in the figure "8" are filled with network. See No. 22.

A9

Elephant — A10

Oil Palm — A11

Pres. Hilary R. W. Johnson — A12

Vai Woman in Full Dress — A13

Coat of Arms — A14

Liberian Star — A15

Coat of Arms — A16

Hippopotamus A17

Liberian Star A18

President Johnson — A19

1892-96 Wmk. 143 Engr. *Perf. 15*

No.	Type	Description	Unused	Used
33	A9	1c vermilion	32	24
a.		1c blue (error)	30.00	
34	A9	2c blue	32	24
a.		2c ver (error)	30.00	
35	A10	4c grn & blk	1.25	60
a.		Center inverted	75.00	75.00
36	A11	6c bl grn	50	35
37	A12	8c brn & blk	60	60
a.		Center inverted	225.00	225.00
38	A12	10c chrome yel & indigo ('96)	60	45
39	A13	12c rose red	60	45
40	A13	15c slate ('96)	60	45
41	A14	16c lilac	1.75	1.25
42	A14	20c ver ('96)	1.75	1.25
43	A15	24c ol grn, *yel*	1.00	75
44	A15	25c yel grn ('96)	1.25	90
45	A16	30c steel bl ('96)	4.25	3.00
46	A16	32c grnsh bl	2.50	1.75
47	A17	$1 ultra & blk	4.75	3.25
a.		$1 blue & black	5.25	4.00
48	A18	$2 brn, *yel*	2.75	2.50
49	A19	$5 car & blk	5.00	4.25
a.		Center inverted	225.00	225.00
		Nos. 33-49 (17)	29.79	22.28

Many misperforated and part-perforated varieties exist.

The 1c, 2c and 4c were issued in sheets of 60; 6c, sheet of 40; 8c, 10c, sheets of 30; 12c, 15c, 24c, 25c, sheets of 20; 16c, 20c, 30c, sheets of 15; $1, $2, $5, sheets of 10.

For overprints see Nos. 64B-64F, 66, 71-77, 79-81, 85-90, O1-O12, O15-O25, O37-O41. For surcharges see Nos. 50, 91-93, 95-100, 160, O13, O44-O45.

No. 36 Surcharged:

5 5	5 5
Five Cents	Five Cents
a	b

1893

No.	Type	Description	Unused	Used
50	A11 (a)	5c on 6c bl grn	1.50	90
a.		"5" with short flag	4.00	4.00
b.		Both 5's with short flags	2.00	2.00
c.		"i" dot omitted	15.00	15.00
d.		Surcharge "b"	25.00	25.00

"Commerce," Globe and Krumen — A22

1894 Unwmk. Engr. *Imperf.*

No.	Type	Description	Unused	Used
52	A22	5c car & blk	2.50	1.75

Rouletted

No.	Type	Description	Unused	Used
53	A22	5c car & blk	4.00	2.75

For overprints see Nos. 69, O26-O27.

Oil Palm A23

Hippopotamus A24

Elephant A25

Liberty A26

1897-1905 Wmk. 143 *Perf. 14 to 16*

No.	Type	Description	Unused	Used
54	A23	1c lil rose	65	38
a.		1c violet	65	40
55	A23	1c dp grn ('00)	80	52
56	A23	1c lt grn ('05)	1.40	70
57	A24	2c bis & blk	1.65	95
58	A24	2c org red & blk ('00)	2.25	95
59	A24	2c rose & blk ('05)	1.65	95
60	A25	5c lake & blk	1.65	95
a.		5c lil rose & blk	1.65	95
61	A25	5c gray bl & blk ('00)	3.25	1.50
62	A25	5c ultra & blk ('05)	2.50	1.50
a.		Center inverted	400.00	
63	A26	50c red brn & blk	2.25	1.50
		Nos. 54-63 (10)	18.05	9.90

For overprints see Nos. 65, 66A-68, 70, 78, 82-84, O28-O36, O42. For surcharges see Nos. M1, O92.

A27

Two types:
I - 13 pearls above "Republic Liberia."
II - 10 pearls.

1897 Unwmk. Litho. *Perf. 14*

64 A27 3c red & grn (I) 20 40
  a. Type II *10.00* 15

No. 64a is considered a reprint, unissued. "Used" copies are CTO.
For surcharge see No. 128.

Official Stamps Handstamped in Black **ORDINARY**

1901-02 Wmk. 143

On Nos. O7-O8, O10-O12

64B A14 16c lilac *325.00 325.00*
64C A15 24c ol grn, *yel* *300.00 300.00*
64D A17 $1 bl & blk *1,350. 1,350.*
64E A18 $2 brn, *yel*
64F A19 $5 car & blk

On Stamps with "O S" Printed

65 A23 1c green 27.50 32.50
66 A9 2c blue 77.50 82.50
66A A24 2c bis & blk 60.00
67 A24 2c org red & blk 27.50 32.50
68 A25 5c gray bl & blk 22.50 27.50
69 A22 5c vio & grn (No. O26) 225.00 235.00
70 A25 5c lake & blk 150.00 155.00
71 A12 10c yel & bl blk 27.50 32.50
  a. "O S" omitted
72 A13 15c slate 27.50 32.50
73 A14 16c lilac 225.00 235.00
74 A14 20c vermilion 32.50 37.50
75 A15 24c ol grn, *yel* 32.50 37.50
76 A15 25c yel grn 32.50 37.50
  a. "O S" omitted
77 A16 30c stl bl 27.50 32.50
78 A26 50c red brn & blk 37.50 42.50
79 A17 $1 ultra & blk 225.00 225.00
  a. "O S" omitted
80 A18 $2 brn, *yel* *1,200. 1,200.*
81 A19 $5 car & blk *1,500. 1,500.*
  a. "O S" omitted *2,250. 2,250.*

On Stamps with "O S" Handstamped

82 A23 1c dp grn 50.00
83 A24 2c org red & blk 60.00
84 A25 5c lake & blk 100.00
85 A12 10c yel & bl blk 90.00
86 A14 20c vermilion 100.00
87 A15 24c ol grn, *yel* 100.00
88 A15 25c yel grn 125.00
89 A16 30c steel bl 250.00
90 A16 32c grnsh bl 140.00

Varieties of Nos. 65-90 include double and inverted overprints.

Nos. 47, O10, O23a Surcharged in Carmine **75c.**

1902

91 A17 75c on $1 ultra & blk, #47 8.50 7.50
  a. Thin "C" and comma 15.00 15.00
  b. Inverted surcharge 50.00 50.00
  c. As "a." inverted
92 A17 75c on $1 bl & blk, #O10 *1,750.*
  a. Thin "C" and comma *2,500.*
93 A17 75c on $1 ultra & blk, #O23a *1,900.*
  a. Thin "C" and comma *2,500.*

Liberty — A29

1903 Unwmk. Engr. *Perf. 14*

94 A29 3c black 30 15
  a. Printed on both sides 45.00
  b. Perf. 12 5.00 3.00

For overprint see No. O43.

Stamps of 1892 Surcharged in Blue

TEN Cents. a **FIFTEEN Cents.** b

1903 Wmk. 143

95 A14 (a) 10c on 16c lil 2.50 3.25
96 A15 (b) 15c on 24c ol grn, *yel* 3.50 4.50
97 A16 (b) 20c on 32c grnsh bl 5.00 6.25

Nos. 50, O3 and 45 Surcharged in Black or Red

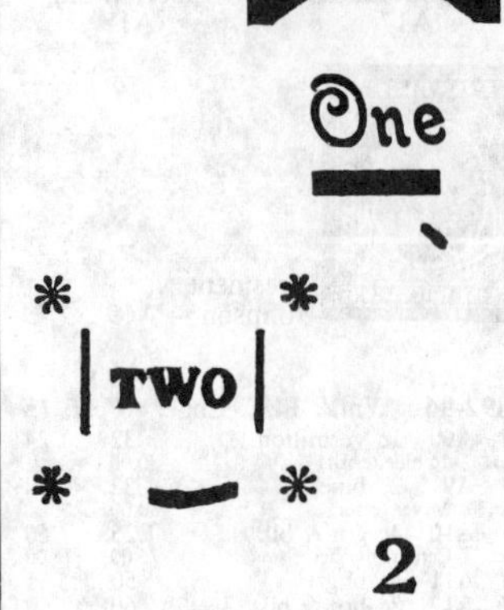

1904

98 A11 1c on 5c on 6c bl grn 50 45
  a. "5" with short flag 3.50 3.50
  b. Both 5's with short flags 7.00 7.00
  c. "i" dot omitted
  d. Surcharge on #50d 10.00 10.00
  e. Inverted surcharge 5.50 5.50
99 A10 2c on 4c grn & blk 1.25 2.25
  a. Pair, one without surcharge 27.50
  b. Double surcharge
  c. Double surcharge, red and blk 50.00
  d. Surcharged on back also 15.00
  e. "Official" overprint missing 25.00
100 A16 2c on 30c stl bl (R) 7.00 11.00

African Elephant A33

Mercury A34

Chimpanzee A35

Great Blue Touraco A36

Agama — A37

Egret — A38

Head of Liberty From Coin — A39

A40

Liberian Flag A41

Pygmy Hippopotamus A42

Liberty with Star of Liberia on Cap A43

Mandingos A44

Executive Mansion and Pres. Arthur Barclay — A45

1906 Unwmk. Engr. *Perf. 14*

101 A33 1c grn & blk 65 30
102 A34 2c car & blk 15 15
103 A35 5c ultra & blk 1.40 45
104 A36 10c red brn & blk 2.00 45
105 A37 15c pur & dp grn 5.00 1.65
106 A38 20c org & blk 4.25 1.40
107 A39 25c dl bl & gray 45 15
108 A40 30c dp vio 50 15
109 A41 50c dp grn & blk 50 15
110 A42 75c brn & blk 5.00 1.40
111 A43 $1 rose & gray 1.40 18
112 A44 $2 dp grn & blk 2.00 20
113 A45 $5 red brn & blk 4.00 30
  Nos. 101-113 (13) 27.30 6.93

For surcharges see Nos. 114, 129, 130, 141, 145-149, 161, M2, M5, O72-O73, O82-O85, O96. For overprints see Nos. O46-O58.

Center Inverted

101a A33 1c 32.50 32.50
102a A34 2c 25.00 25.00
103a A35 5c 110.00 110.00
104a A36 10c 50.00 50.00
105a A37 15c 110.00 110.00
106b A38 20c 110.00 110.00
107a A39 25c 47.50 47.50
109b A41 50c 47.50 47.50
110b A42 75c 80.00 80.00
111a A43 $1 65.00 65.00
112a A44 $2 62.50 62.50

Imperf., Pairs

101b A33 1c 10.00
102b A34 2c 4.00
106a A38 20c 15.00
107b A39 25c 40.00 40.00
109a A41 50c 15.00
110a A42 75c 15.00
113a A45 $5 20.00

No. 104 Surcharged in Black *Inland 3Cents*

1909

114 A36 3c on 10c red brn & blk 4.00 4.00

Coffee Plantation — A46

Pres. Barclay — A47

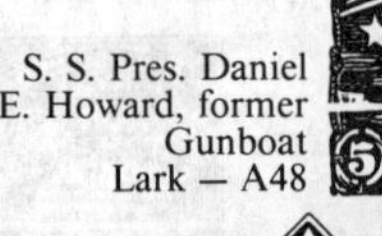
S. S. Pres. Daniel E. Howard, former Gunboat Lark — A48

Commerce with Caduceus — A49

Vai Woman Spinning Cotton — A50

Blossom and Fruit of Pepper Plant — A51

Circular House — A52

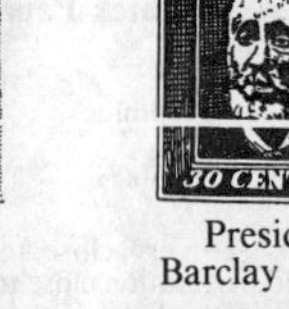
President Barclay — A53

Men in Canoe — A54

Liberian Village — A55

1909-12 *Perf. 14*

115 A46 1c yel grn & blk 30 30
116 A47 2c lake & blk 30 30
117 A48 5c ultra & blk 30 30
118 A49 10c plum & blk, perf. 12½ ('12) 30 30
  a. Imperf., pair 10.00
119 A50 15c ind & blk 40 35
120 A51 20c rose & grn 1.90 35
  b. Imperf.
121 A52 25c dk brn & blk 55 35
  a. Imperf.
122 A53 30c dk brn 1.90 35
123 A54 50c grn & blk 1.50 35
124 A55 75c red brn & blk 1.10 35
  Nos. 115-124 (10) 8.55 3.30

Rouletted

125 A49 10c plum & blk 60 38

For surcharges see Nos. 126-127E, 131-133, 136-140, 142-144, 151-156, 162, B1-B2, M3-M4, M6-M7, O70-O1, O74-O81, O86-O91, O97.
For overprints see Nos. O59-O69.

Center Inverted

116a A47 2c 60.00 52.50
117a A48 5c 55.00 47.50
119a A50 15c 42.50 42.50
120a A51 20c 62.50 47.50
121b A52 25c 42.50 37.50
123a A54 50c 65.00 55.00

Stamps and Types of 1909-12 Surcharged in Blue or Red

3 CENTS INLAND POSTAGE

1910-12 *Rouletted*

126 A49 3c on 10c plum & blk (Bl) 35 20
  a. "3" inverted
126B A49 3c on 10c blk & ultra (R) 20.00 2.50

No. 126B is roulette 7. It also exists in roulette 13.

Perf. 12½, 14, 12½x14

127 A49 3c on 10c plum & blk (Bl) ('12) 35 20
  a. Imperf., pair 20.00
  b. Double surcharge, one invtd. 20.00
  c. Double vertical surcharge
127E A49 3c on 10c blk & ultra (R) ('12) 12.00 50

Nos. 64, 64a Surcharged in Dark Green

1913

128 A27 8c on 3c red & grn (I) 25 15
  a. Surcharge on No. 64a 2.50 15
  b. Double surcharge 5.00
  c. Imperf., pair 16.00
  d. Inverted surcharge 20.00

Stamps of Preceding Issues Surcharged

1914 2 CENTS — a 5 — b

1914

On Issue of 1906

129	A39 (a)	2c on 25c dl bl & gray	7.50	2.00
130	A40 (b)	5c on 30c dp vio	7.50	2.00

On Issue of 1909

131	A52 (a)	2c on 25c brn & blk	7.50	2.00
132	A53 (b)	5c on 30c dk brn	7.50	2.00
133	A54 (a)	10c on 50c grn & blk	7.50	2.00
		Nos. 129-133 (5)	37.50	10.00

Liberian House — A57

Providence Island, Monrovia Harbor — A58

1915 Engr. Wmk. 116 *Perf. 14*

134	A57	2c red	15	15
135	A58	3c dull violet	15	15
		Set value		16

For overprints see Nos. 196-197, O113-O114, O128-O129.

Nos. 109, 111-113, 119-124 Surcharged with New Values in Dark Blue, Black or Red:

c d e f g

1915-16 Unwmk.

136	A50 (c)	2c on 15c (R)	80	80
137	A52 (d)	2c on 25c (R)	6.00	6.00
138	A51 (e)	5c on 20c (Bk)	1.00	5.00
139	A53 (f)	5c on 30c (R)	4.00	4.00
a.		Double surcharge	12.00	12.00
140	A53 (g)	5c on 30c (R)	35.00	35.00

h i

141	A41 (h)	10c on 50c (R)	7.00	7.00
a.		Double surch., one invtd.		
142	A54 (i)	10c on 50c (R)	12.50	12.50
a.		Double surcharge red & blk	30.00	30.00
b.		Blue surcharge	30.00	30.00
143	A54 (i)	10c on 50c (Bk)	12.50	12.50

j k

144	A55 (j)	20c on 75c (Bk)	3.00	5.00
145	A43 (k)	25c on $1 (Bk)	37.50	37.50

l m

146	A44 (l)	50c on $2 (R)	10.00	10.00
a.		"Ceuts"	15.00	15.00
147	A44 (m)	50c on $2 (R)	550.00	550.00

n

148	A45	$1 on $5 (Bk)	50.00	50.00
a.		Double surcharge	75.00	75.00

o

149	A45	$1 on $5 (R)	45.00	45.00

The color of the red surcharge varies from light dull red to almost brown.

Handstamped Surcharge, Type "i"

150	A54	10c on 50c (Dk Bl)	12.50	12.50

No. 119 Surcharged in Black

151	A50	2c on 15c	325.00	325.00

No. 119 Surcharged in Red

152	A50	2c on 15c	40.00	35.00
a.		Double surcharge	80.00	

Nos. 116-117 Surcharged in Black or Red

a1 b1 c1 d1 e1 f1 g1 h1 i1 j1 k2 l2 m2 n2 o2 p2 q2 r2 s2 t2

153	A47	1c on 2c lake & blk	2.25	2.25
a.		Strip of 10 types	30.00	
154	A48	2c on 5c ultra & blk (R)	2.25	2.25
a.		Black surcharge	12.00	12.00
b.		Strip of 10 types (R)	30.00	
c.		Strip of 10 types (Bk)	140.00	

The 10 types of surcharge are repeated in illustrated sequence on 1c on 2c in each horiz. row and on 2c on 5c in each vert. row of sheets of 100 (10x10).

No. 116 and Type of 1909 Surcharged:

155	A47	1c on 2c lake & blk	85.00	85.00

156	A48	2c on 5c turq & blk	80.00	80.00

Nos. 18-20 Surcharged

1916

157	A1	3c on 6c vio	35.00	35.00
a.		Inverted surcharge	60.00	60.00
158	A1	5c on 12c yel	2.50	2.50
a.		Inverted surcharge	10.00	10.00
b.		Surcharge sideways	10.00	
159	A1	10c on 24c rose red	2.25	2.50
a.		Inverted surcharge	12.00	12.00
b.		Surcharge sideways		

Unused values for Nos. 157-159 are for copies without gum.

Nos. 44 and 108 Surcharged

p r

1917 Wmk. 143

160	A15 (p)	4c on 25c yel grn	9.00	9.00
a.		"OUR"	20.00	20.00
b.		"FCUR"	20.00	20.00

Unwmk.

161	A40 (r)	5c on 30c dp vio	70.00	70.00

No. 118 Surcharged in Red 3 CENTS

1918

162	A49	3c on 10c plum & blk	2.00	2.00
a.		"3" inverted	8.00	8.00

Bongo Antelope — A59

Symbols of Liberia — A61

Two-spot Palm Civet — A60

A62

Palm-nut Vulture — A66

Oil Palm — A63

Mercury — A64

Traveler's Tree — A65

"Mudskipper" or Bommi Fish — A67

Footnotes often refer to other stamps of the same design.

Mandingos
A68

"Liberia"
A71

Coast
Scene — A69

Liberia
College
A70

1918 Engr. *Perf. 12½, 14*

163	A59	1c dp grn & blk	48	15
164	A60	2c rose & blk	60	15
165	A61	5c gray bl & blk	15	15
166	A62	10c dk grn	16	15
167	A63	15c blk & dk grn	2.25	15
168	A64	20c claret & blk	25	15
169	A65	25c dk grn & grn	2.50	15
170	A66	30c red vio & blk	7.50	42
171	A67	50c ultra & blk	12.00	70
172	A68	75c ol bis & blk	65	15
173	A69	$1 yel brn & bl	4.00	15
174	A70	$2 lt vio & blk	4.75	15
175	A71	$5 dk brn	5.00	30
		Nos. 163-175 (13)	40.29	2.92

For surcharges see Nos. 176-177, 228-229, 248-270, B3-B15, O111-O112, O155-O157.
For overprints see Nos. O98-O110.

Nos. 163-164, F10-F14 Surcharged

1920

THREE
CENTS

1920

1920
FOUR CENTS

1920

176	A59	3c on 1c grn & blk	85	85
a.		"CEETS"	15.00	15.00
b.		Double surcharge	6.00	6.00
c.		Triple surcharge	7.50	7.50
177	A60	4c on 2c rose & blk	85	85
a.		Inverted surcharge	12.00	12.00
b.		Double surcharge	4.75	4.75
c.		Double surcharge, one invtd.	12.00	
d.		Triple surcharge, one inverted	12.00	12.00
e.		Quadruple surcharge	15.00	15.00
f.		Typewritten surcharge		
g.		Same as "f" but inverted		
h.		Printed and typewritten surcharges, both inverted		
178	R6	5c on 10c bl & blk	2.25	2.25
a.		Inverted surcharge	4.50	4.50
b.		Double surcharge	7.25	7.25
c.		Double surcharge, one invtd.	7.25	7.25
d.		Typewritten surcharge ("five")		62.50
e.		Printed and typewritten surcharges	62.50	
179	R6	5c on 10c org red & blk	2.25	2.25
a.		5c on 10c org & blk	3.50	2.50
b.		Inverted surcharge	7.25	
c.		Double surcharge	7.25	
d.		Double surcharge, one invtd.	9.00	8.50
e.		Typewritten surch. in violet	62.50	62.50
f.		Typewritten surch. in black		
g.		Printed and typewritten surcharges	62.50	
180	R6	5c on 10c grn & blk	2.25	2.25
a.		Double surcharge	7.25	7.25
b.		Double surcharge, one invtd.	11.00	11.00
c.		Inverted surcharge		11.00
d.		Quadruple surcharge	18.50	18.50
e.		Typewritten surcharge		62.50
f.		Printed and typewritten surcharges		
181	R6	5c on 10c vio & blk (Monrovia)	3.50	3.50
a.		Double surcharge, one invtd.	11.00	11.00

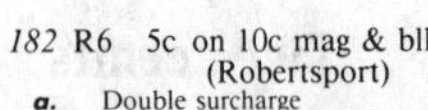

182	R6	5c on 10c mag & blk (Robertsport)	1.75	1.75
a.		Double surcharge	11.00	11.00
b.		Double surcharge, one invtd.	11.00	11.00
c.		Double surcharge, both invtd.	18.50	
		Nos. 176-182 (7)	13.70	13.70

Cape
Mesurado
A75

Pres. Daniel E.
Howard — A76

Arms of
Liberia — A77

Crocodile
A78

Pepper
Plant — A79

Leopard
A80

Village
Scene — A81

Krumen in
Dugout — A82

Rapids in St.
Paul's
River — A83

Bongo
Antelope
A84

Hornbill
A85

Elephant
A86

1921 Wmk. 116 *Perf. 14*

183	A75	1c green	15	15
184	A76	5c dp bl & blk	15	15
185	A77	10c red & dl bl	15	15
186	A78	15c dl vio & grn	3.25	25
187	A79	20c rose red & grn	1.40	15
188	A80	25c org & blk	3.75	25
189	A81	30c grn & dl vio	20	15
190	A82	50c org & ultra	26	15
191	A83	75c red & blk brn	40	15
a.		Center inverted		32.50
192	A84	$1 red & blk	16.00	90
193	A85	$2 yel & ultra	5.25	38
194	A86	$5 car rose & vio	16.00	50
		Nos. 183-194 (12)	46.96	
		Set value		2.75

For overprints see Nos. 195, 198-208, O115-O127, O130-O140.

Nos. 134-135, 183-194 Overprinted "1921"

195	A75	1c green	13.00	22
196	A57	2c red	13.00	22
197	A58	3c dl vio	17.50	22
198	A76	5c dp bl & blk	2.75	22
199	A77	10c red & dl bl	27.50	22
200	A78	15c dl vio & grn	13.00	70
201	A79	20c rose red & grn, ovpt. invtd.	5.75	48
202	A80	25c org & blk	13.00	70
203	A81	30c grn & dl vio	2.00	22
204	A82	50c org & ultra	2.75	22
205	A83	75c red & blk brn	3.75	22
206	A84	$1 red & blk	37.50	1.10
207	A85	$2 yel & ultra	13.00	1.10
208	A86	$5 car rose & vio	35.00	1.40
		Nos. 195-208 (14)	199.50	7.24

Overprint exists inverted in Nos. 195-208 and normal on No. 201.

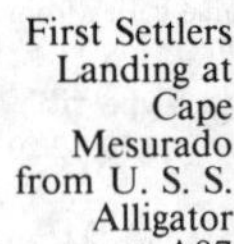

First Settlers Landing at Cape Mesurado from U. S. S. Alligator
A87

1923 Litho.

209	A87	1c lt bl & blk	12.00	20
210	A87	2c cl & ol gray	17.50	20
211	A87	5c ol grn & ind	17.50	20
212	A87	10c bl grn & vio	65	20
213	A87	$1 rose & brn	2.25	20
		Nos. 209-213 (5)	49.90	1.00

Centenary of founding of Liberia.

Memorial to J. J.
Roberts, 1st
Pres. — A88

Liberian
Star — A90

Hall of Representatives,
Monrovia — A89

Pres. Charles Dunbar Burgess King
A91 A92

Hippopotamus — A93

Antelope
A94

West African
Buffalo — A95

Grebos
Making
Dumboy
A96

Pineapple — A97

Carrying Ivory
Tusk — A98

Rubber Planter's House — A99

Stockton Lagoon — A100

Grebo Houses — A101

1923 *Perf. 13½x14½, 14½x13½*
White Paper

214	A88	1c yel grn & dp grn	3.50	15
215	A89	2c cl & brn	3.50	15
216	A90	3c lil & blk	25	15
217	A91	5c bl vio & blk	30.00	15
218	A92	10c slate & brn	25	15

219 A93 15c bister & bl 17.50 25
220 A94 20c bl grn & vio 2.00 25
221 A95 25c org red & brn 50.00 30

White, Buff or Brownish Paper

222 A96 30c dk brn & vio 50 15
223 A97 50c dl vio & org 1.00 15
224 A98 75c gray & bl 1.50 32
225 A99 $1 dp red & dk vio 3.50 50
a. White paper 25.00
226 A100 $2 org & bl 4.00 45
a. Buff or brownish paper
227 A101 $5 dp grn & brn 10.00 45
a. White paper 25.00
Nos. 214-227 (14) 127.50
Set value 3.00

Nos. 222-224 on buff or brownish paper sell for about 10% more.
For overprints see Nos. O141-O154.

No. 163 Surcharged

Two Cents

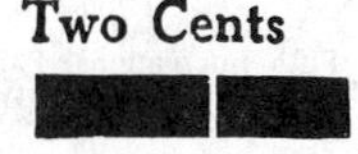

1926 Unwmk. *Perf. 14*

228 A59 2c on 1c dp grn & blk 2.25 2.25
a. Surch. with ornamental design as on #O155 9.00

No. 163 Surcharged in Red

Two Cents

1927

229 A59 2c on 1c dp grn & blk 6.00 6.00
a. "Ceuts" 8.50
b. "Vwo" 8.50
c. "Twc" 8.50
d. Double surcharge 17.00
e. Wavy lines omitted 11.00

Palms A102

Map of Africa — A103

President King — A104

1928 Engr. *Perf. 12*

230 A102 1c green 20 15
231 A102 2c dk vio 30 22
232 A102 3c bis brn 30 22
233 A103 5c ultra 75 38
234 A104 10c ol gray 1.00 38
235 A103 15c dl vio 4.00 1.50
236 A103 $1 red brn 40.00 15.00
Nos. 230-236 (7) 46.55 17.85

For surcharges see Nos. 288A, 289A, 290A-291, 292A, C1-C3, O165. For overprints see Nos. O158-O164.

Nos. 164-168, 170-175 Surcharged in Various Colors and Styles, "1936" and New Values

1936 *Perf. 12½, 14*

248 A60 1c on 2c (Bl) 22 22
249 A61 3c on 5c (Bl) 15 15
250 A62 4c on 10c (Br) 15 15
251 A63 6c on 15c (Bl) 22 22
252 A64 8c on 20c (V) 15 15
253 A66 12c on 30c (V) 40 40
254 A67 14c on 50c (Bl) 45 45
255 A68 16c on 75c (Br) 24 24
256 A69 18c on $1 (Bk) 24 24
a. 22c on $1 yel brn & bl 3.25
257 A70 22c on $2 (V) 32 32
258 A71 24c on $5 (Bk) 40 40
Nos. 248-258 (11) 2.94 2.94

Official Stamps, Nos. O99-O110, Surcharged or Overprinted in various colors and styles with 6 pointed star and "1936"

1936

259 A60 1c on 2c (Bl) 16 16
260 A61 3c on 5c (Bl) 15 15
261 A62 4c on 10c (Bl) 15 15
262 A63 6c on 15c (Bl) 16 16
263 A64 8c on 20c (V) 15 15
264 A66 12c on 30c (V) 32 32
a. "193" instead of "1936" 8.25
265 A67 14c on 50c (Bl) 42 42
266 A68 16c on 75c (Bk) 22 22
267 A69 18c on $1 (Bk) 22 22
268 A70 22c on $2 (Bl) 28 28
269 A71 24c on $5 (Bk) 32 32
270 A65 25c (Bk) 38 38
Nos. 259-270 (12) 2.93 2.93

Hornbill — A106

Designs: 2c, Bushbuck. 3c, West African dwarf buffalo. 4c, Pygmy hippopotamus. 5c, Lesser egret. 6c, Pres. E. J. Barclay.

Perf. Compound of 11½, 12, 12½, 14

1937, Apr. 10 Engr. Unwmk.

271 A106 1c grn & blk 50 25
272 A106 2c car & blk 50 18
273 A106 3c vio & blk 50 25
274 A106 4c org & blk 75 42
275 A106 5c bl & blk 75 30
276 A106 6c grn & blk 25 15
Nos. 271-276 (6) 3.25 1.55

Coast Line of Liberia, 1839 A107

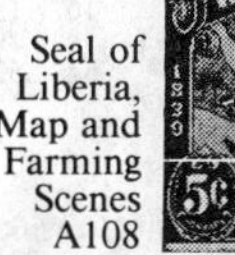
Seal of Liberia, Map and Farming Scenes A108

Thomas Buchanan and Residence at Bassa Cove A109

1940, July 29 Engr. *Perf. 12*

277 A107 3c dk bl 15 15
278 A108 5c dl red brn 15 15
279 A109 10c dk grn 15 15
Set value 26 20

100th anniv. of the founding of the Commonwealth of Liberia.
For overprints see Nos. 280-282, B16-B18, C14-C16. For surcharges see Nos. CB1-CB3, CE1, CF1, E1, F35.

Nos. 277-279 Overprinted in Red or Blue

1941, Feb. 21

280 A107 3c dk bl (R) 1.25 1.25
281 A108 5c dl red brn (Bl) 1.25 1.25
282 A109 10c dk grn (R) 1.25 1.25
Nos. 280-282,C14-C16 (6) 7.05 7.05

Royal Antelope A110

Bay-thighed Diana Monkey A115

Designs: 2c, Water chevrotain. 3c, White-shouldered duiker. 4c, Bushbuck. 5c, Zebra antelope.

1942 Engr.

283 A110 1c vio & fawn 25 15
284 A110 2c brt ultra & yel brn 25 15
285 A110 3c brt grn & yel brn 48 24
286 A110 4c blk & red org 60 48
287 A110 5c ol & fawn 75 48
288 A115 10c red & blk 1.25 60
Nos. 283-288 (6) 3.58 2.10

Nos. 231, 233-234, 271-276 Surcharged with New Values and Bars or X's in Violet, Black, Red Brown or Blue

Perf. 12, 12x12½, 14

1944-46 Unwmk.

288A A102 1c on 2c (Bk) 7.00 5.00
289 A106 1c on 4c (Bk) 37.50 35.00
289A A104 1c on 10c (R Br) 9.50 6.50
290 A106 2c on 3c 45.00 37.50
290A A103 2c on 5c (Bk) 2.00 2.00
290B A103 2c on 5c (Bl) 16.00 7.00
291 A102 3c on 2c 22.50
292 A106 4c on 5c 8.00 5.25
292A A104 4c on 10c (Bk) 2.50 2.50
b. Double surch., one inverted
293 A106 5c on 1c (Bk) 60.00 37.50
294 A106 6c on 2c (Bk) 8.00 7.00
295 A106 10c on 6c 8.00 7.00

Surcharges on Nos. 289, 290, 293, 294 are found inverted. Values same as normal.

Pres. Franklin D. Roosevelt Reviewing Troops — A116

1945, Nov. 26 Engr. *Perf. 12½*

Grayish Paper

296 A116 3c brt vio & blk 15 15
297 A116 5c dk bl & blk 25 25

In memory of Pres. Franklin D. Roosevelt (1882-1945).
See No. C51.

Monrovia Harbor A117

1947, Jan. 2

298 A117 5c deep blue 15 15

Opening of the Monrovia Harbor Project, Feb. 16, 1946. See No. C52.

Without Inscription at Top

1947, May 16

299 A117 5c violet 15 15

See No. C53.

1st US Postage Stamps and Arms of Liberia A118

1947, June 6

300 A118 5c car rose 15 15

Cent. of US postage stamps and the 87th anniv. of Liberian postal issues.
See Nos. C54-C56, C56a.

Matilda Newport Firing Cannon A119

1947, Dec. 1 Engr. & Photo.

Center in Gray Black

301 A119 1c brt bl grn 15 15
302 A119 3c brt red vio 16 15
303 A119 5c brt ultra 32 15
304 A119 10c yellow 1.65 42
Nos. 301-304,C57 (5) 3.38
Set value 90

125th anniv. of Matilda Newport's defense of Monrovia, Dec. 1, 1822.

Liberian Star — A120

Cent. of Independence: 2c, Liberty. 3c, Liberian Arms. 5c, Map of Liberia.

1947, Dec. 22 Engr.

305 A120 1c dk grn 15 15
306 A120 2c brt red vio 15 15
307 A120 3c brt pur 15 15
308 A120 5c dk bl 15 15
Set value, #305-308, C58-C60 1.15 85

Centenary of independence.

Natives Approaching Village — A124

Rubber Tapping and Planting A125

Landing of First Colonists A126

Jehudi Ashmun and Defenders A127

1949, Apr. 4 Litho. *Perf. 11½*

309	A124	1c multi	25	45
310	A125	2c multi	25	45
311	A126	3c multi	25	45
312	A127	5c multi	25	45
		Nos. 309-312,C63-C64 (6)	1.64	3.00

Nos. 309-312 exist perf. 12½ and sell at a much lower price. The status of the perf. 12½ set is indefinite.

Pres. Joseph J. Roberts A128

Designs (Liberian Presidents): 2c, Stephen Benson. 3c, Daniel B. Warner. 4c, James S. Payne. 5c, Executive mansion. 6c, Edward J. Roye. 7c, A. W. Gardner and A. F. Russell. 8c, Hilary R. W. Johnson. 9c, Joseph J. Cheeseman. 10c, William D. Coleman. 15c, Garretson W. Gibson. 20c, Arthur Barclay. 25c, Daniel E. Howard. 50c, Charles D. B. King. $1, Edwin J. Barclay.

1948-50 Unwmk. Engr. *Perf. 12½*

Caption and Portrait in Black

313	A128	1c grn ('48)	1.25	*3.75*
314	A128	2c sal pink	28	*40*
315	A128	3c rose vio	28	*40*
a.		"1876-1878" added	6.50	*19.00*
316	A128	4c lt ol grn	28	*60*
317	A128	5c ultra	32	*60*
318	A128	6c red org	42	*1.00*
319	A128	7c lt bl ('50)	55	*1.40*
320	A128	8c carmine	55	*1.65*
321	A128	9c red vio	80	*1.25*
322	A128	10c yel ('50)	55	35
323	A128	15c yel org	65	45
324	A128	20c blue gray	95	80
325	A128	25c cerise	1.25	1.25
326	A128	50c aqua	2.50	85
327	A128	$1 rose lilac	4.00	80
		Nos. 313-327,C65 (16)	15.18	*16.15*

Issue dates: 1c, Nov. 18. 7c, 10c, 1950. Others, July 21, 1949.

See Nos. 328, 371-378, C118.

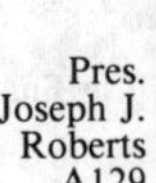

Pres. Joseph J. Roberts A129

1950

328	A129	1c grn & blk	15	15

Hand Holding Book — A130

1950, Feb. 14

329	A130	5c deep blue	28	15

National Literacy Campaign. See No. C66.

Catalogue values for unused stamps in this section, from this point to the end of the section, are for Never Hinged items.

UPU Monument — A131

First UPU Building, Bern A132

1950, Apr. 21 Engr. Unwmk.

330	A131	5c grn & blk	15	15
331	A132	10c red vio & blk	18	18

UPU, 75th anniv. (in 1949).

Nos. 330-331 exist imperf., same value.

See Nos. C67, C67a.

Jehudi Ashmun and Seal of Liberia — A133

John Marshall, Ashmun and Map of Town of Marshall A134

Designs (Map or View and Two Portraits): 2c, Careysburg, Gov. Lott Carey (1780-1828), freed American slave, and Jehudi Ashmun (1794-1828), American missionary credited as founder of Liberia. 3c, Town of Harper, Robert Goodlow Harper (1765-1825), American statesman, and Ashmun. 5c, Upper Buchanan, Gov. Thomas Buchanan and Ashmun. 10c, Robertsport, Pres. Joseph J. Roberts and Ashmun.

1952, Apr. 10 *Perf. 10½*

332	A133	1c dp grn	15	15
333	A133	2c scar & ind	15	15
334	A133	3c pur & grn	15	15
335	A134	4c brn & grn	15	15
336	A133	5c ultra & org red	15	15
337	A134	10c org red & dk bl	15	15
		Set value, #332-337, C68-C69	1.00	95

Nos. 332-337 exist imperf. Value about two and one-half times that of the perf. set.

See No. C69a.

UN Headquarters Building — A135

Scroll and Flags A136

Design: 10c, Liberia arms, letters "UN" and emblem.

1952, Dec. 20 Unwmk. *Perf. 12½*

338	A135	1c ultra	15	15
339	A136	4c car & ultra	15	15
340	A136	10c red brn & yel	15	15
a.		Souv. sheet of 3, #338-340	1.25	1.25
		Set value	25	25

See No. C70.

Nos. 338-340 and 340a exist imperforate. Same values as above.

Pepper Bird — A137

Roller A138

1953, Nov. 18 *Perf. 10½*

341	A137	1c shown	15	15
342	A138	3c shown	15	15
343	A137	4c Hornbill	15	15
344	A137	5c Kingfisher	15	15
345	A138	10c Jacana	24	15
346	A138	12c Weaver	38	15
		Set value	1.00	30

Exist imperf. Value, set unused $2.75.

Tennis A139

Callichilia Stenosepala A140

1955, Jan. 26 Litho. *Perf. 12½*

347	A139	3c shown	15	15
348	A139	5c Soccer	15	15
349	A139	25c Boxing	16	15
		Set value, #347-349, C88-C90	54	52

See No. C90a.

1955, Sept. 28 Unwmk.

Various Native Flowers: 7c, Gomphia subcordata. 8c, Listrostachys caudata. 9c, Musaenda isertiana.

350	A140	6c yel grn, org & yel	15	15
351	A140	7c emer, yel & car	15	15
352	A140	8c yel grn, buff & bl	15	15
353	A140	9c org & grn	15	15
		Set value, #350-353, C91-C92	55	55

Rubber Tapping A141

1955, Dec. 5 *Perf. 12½*

354	A141	5c emer & yel	15	15

50th anniv. of Rotary Intl. No. 354 exists printed entirely in emerald. See Nos. C97-C99.

Statue of Liberty — A142

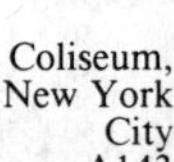

Coliseum, New York City A143

Design: 6c, Globe inscribed FIPEX.

1956, Apr. 28 *Perf. 12*

355	A142	3c brt grn & dk red brn	15	15
356	A143	4c Prus grn & bis brn	15	15
357	A143	6c gray & red lil	15	15
		Set value, #355-357, C100-C102	72	40

Fifth International Philatelic Exhibition (FIPEX), New York City, Apr. 28-May 6, 1956.

Kangaroo and Emu A144

Discus Thrower — A145

Designs: 8c, Goddess of Victory and Olympic symbols. 10c, Classic chariot race.

1956, Nov. 15 Litho. Unwmk.

358	A144	4c lt ol grn & gldn brn	15	15
359	A145	6c emer & gray	15	15
360	A144	8c lt ultra & redsh brn	15	15
361	A144	10c rose red & blk	15	15
		Set value, #358-361, C104-C105	64	35

16th Olympic Games at Melbourne, Nov. 22-Dec. 8, 1956.

Idlewild Airport, New York A146

Design: 5c, Roberts Field, Liberia, plane and Pres. Tubman.

Lithographed and Engraved

1957, May 4 *Perf. 12*

362	A146	3c org & dk bl	15	15
363	A146	5c red lil & blk	15	15
		Set value, #362-363, C107-C110	1.00	50

1st anniv. of direct air service between Roberts Field, Liberia, and Idlewild (Kennedy), NY.

Orphanage Playground — A147

Orphanage and: 5c, Teacher and pupil. 6c, Singing boys and natl. anthem. 10c, Children and flag.

1957, Nov. 25 Litho. *Perf. 12*

364 A147 4c grn & red 15 15
365 A147 5c bl grn & red brn 15 15
366 A147 6c brt vio & bis 15 15
367 A147 10c ultra & rose car 15 15
Set value, #364-367, C111-C112 62 42

Founding of the Antoinette Tubman Child Welfare Foundation.

Windmill and Dutch Flag A148

Designs: No. 369, German flag and Brandenburg Gate. No. 370, Swedish flag, palace and crowns.

Engraved and Lithographed
1958, Jan. 10 Unwmk. *Perf. 10½*
Flags in Original Colors

368 A148 5c redsh brn 15 15
369 A148 5c blue 15 15
370 A148 5c lil rose 15 15
Set value, #368-370, C114-C117 58 40

European tour of Pres. Tubman in 1956.

Presidential Types of 1948-50

Designs as before.

1958-60 Engr. *Perf. 12*
Caption and Portrait in Black

371 A129 1c sal pink 25 20
372 A128 2c brt yel 25 20
373 A128 10c bl gray 28 28
374 A128 15c brt bl & blk ('59) 15 15
375 A128 20c dk red 35 32
376 A128 25c blue 35 32
377 A128 50c red lil & blk ('59) 38 32
378 A128 $1 bis brn ('60) 2.50 40
Nos. 371-378,C118 (9) 4.89 2.47

Many shades of 1c.

Open Globe Projection A149

Designs: 5c, UN Emblem and building. 10c, UN Emblem. 12c, UN Emblem and initials of agencies.

1958, Dec. 10 Litho. *Perf. 12*

379 A149 3c gray, bl & blk 15 15
380 A149 5c bl & choc 15 15
381 A149 10c blk & org 16 16
382 A149 12c blk & car 22 22
Set value 52 52

10th anniv. of the Universal Declaration of Human Rights. See No. C119.

People of Africa on the March A150

Symbols of UNESCO A151

1959, Apr. 15

383 A150 20c org & brn 24 24

African Freedom Day, Apr. 15. See No. C120.

1959, May 11 Unwmk.

384 A151 25c dp plum & emer 30 35

Opening of UNESCO Headquarters in Paris, Nov. 3, 1958.
See Nos. C121, C121a.

Abraham Lincoln — A152

1959, Nov. 20 Engr. *Perf. 12*

385 A152 10c ultra & blk 15 15
386 A152 15c org & blk 18 18
a. Souv. sheet of 3, Nos. 385-386, C122, imperf. 90 1.50

150th anniv. of the birth of Abraham Lincoln. See No. C122.

Touré, Tubman and Nkrumah A153

1960, Jan. 27 Litho. Unwmk.

387 A153 25c crim & blk 30 30

1959 "Big Three" conference of Pres. Sékou Toure of Guinea, Pres. William V. S. Tubman of Liberia and Prime Minister Kwame Nkrumah of Ghana at Saniquellie, Liberia. See No. C123.

World Refugee Year Emblem A154

Map of Africa A155

1960, Apr. 7 *Perf. 11½*

388 A154 25c emer & blk 30 45

World Refuge Year, July 1, 1959-June 30, 1960. See No. C124, C124a.

1960, May 11 Litho. *Perf. 11½*

389 A155 25c grn & blk 30 30

10th anniv. of the Commission for Technical Cooperation in Africa South of the Sahara (C.C.T.A.). See No. C125.

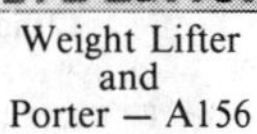

Weight Lifter and Porter — A156

Liberian Stamps of 1860 — A157

Designs: 10c, Rower and canoeists (horiz.). 15c, Walker and porter.

1960, Sept. 6 Unwmk.

390 A156 5c dk brn & emer 15 15
391 A156 10c brn & red lil 15 18
392 A156 15c brn & org 25 30

17th Olympic Games, Rome, Aug. 25-Sept. 11. See Nos. C126-C127.

1960, Dec. 1 Litho. *Perf. 11½*

393 A157 5c multi 15 15
394 A157 20c multi 32 32

Cent. of Liberian postage stamps. See Nos. C128-C129.

Laurel Wreath — A158

1961, May 19 Unwmk. *Perf. 11½*

395 A158 25c red & dk bl 26 38

Liberia's membership in the UN Security Council. Exists imperf. See Nos. C130-C131 and note after No. C131.

Anatomy Class — A159

1961, Sept. 8 *Perf. 11½*

396 A159 25c grn & brn 35 35

15th anniv. of UNESCO. See #C132-C133.

Joseph J. Roberts Monument, Monrovia — A160

Design: 10c, Pres. Roberts and old and new presidential mansions (horiz.).

1961, Oct. 25 Litho.

397 A160 5c org & sep 15 15
398 A160 10c ultra & sep 15 15
Set value 20 20

150th anniv. of the birth of Joseph J. Roberts, 1st pres. of Liberia.
See No. C134, C134a.

Boy Scout — A161

Design: Insignia and Scouts camping.

1961, Dec. 4 Unwmk. *Perf. 11½*

399 A161 5c lil & sep 15 15
400 A161 10c ultra & bis 25 25
Set value 28 28

Issued to honor the Boy Scouts of Liberia. Exist imperf. See Nos. C135-C136.

Dag Hammarskjold and UN Emblem — A162

1962, Feb. 1 *Perf. 12*

401 A162 20c blk & ultra 26 26

Issued in memory of Dag Hammarskjold, Secretary General of the United Nations, 1953-61. See Nos. C137-C138.

Malaria Eradication Emblem — A163

1962, Apr. 7 Litho. *Perf. 12½*

402 A163 25c dk grn & red 32 22

WHO drive to eradicate malaria. See Nos. C139-C140.

United Nations Emblem A164

1962, Oct. 22 *Perf. 12x12½*

403 A164 20c grn & yel bis 24 24

Issued to mark the observance of United Nations Day, Oct. 24, as a national holiday.
See Nos. C144-C145.

Treasury Department Building, Monrovia A165

Buildings: 1c, 80c, Executive Mansion, Monrovia. 10c, Information Service. 15c, Capitol.

1962-64

403A A165 1c vio bl & dp org ('64) 15 15
404 A165 5c lt bl & pur 15 15
405 A165 10c bis & brn 15 15
406 A165 15c sal & dk bl 18 18
406A A165 80c brn & yel ('64) 1.00 1.00
Nos. 403A-406A,C146-C148 (9) 4.58 3.68

"FAO" Emblem and Food Bowl — A166

1963, Mar. 21 *Perf. 12½*

407 A166 5c aqua & dk car 15 15

FAO "Freedom from Hunger" campaign. See Nos. C149-C150.

Rocket in Space A167

Design: 15c, Space capsule and globe.

1963, May 27 **Litho.** *Perf. 12½*

408 A167 10c dp vio bl & yel 15 15
409 A167 15c bl & red brn 22 22

Achievements in space exploration for peaceful purposes. See Nos. C151-C152.

Red Cross — A168

Design: 10c, Centenary emblem and torch (vert.).

1963, Aug. 26 **Unwmk.** *Perf. 11½*

410 A168 5c bl grn & red 15 15
411 A168 10c gray & red 15 15
Set value 15 15

Cent. of the Intl. Red Cross. See Nos. C153-C154.

Palm Tree and Scroll — A169

Ski Jump — A170

1963, Oct. 28 *Perf. 12½*

412 A169 20c brn & grn 25 25

Issued to commemorate the conference of African heads of state for African Unity, Addis Ababa, May, 1963. See No. C156.

1963, Dec. 11 **Unwmk.** *Perf. 12½*

413 A170 5c rose red & dk vio bl 15 15

Issued to publicize the 9th Winter Olympic Games, Innsbruck, Austria, Jan. 29-Feb. 9, 1964. See Nos. C157-C159.

Scott's editorial staff cannot undertake to identify, authenticate or appraise stamps and postal markings.

John F. Kennedy A171

1964, Apr. 6 **Litho.**

414 A171 20c blk & brt bl 26 26

Issued in memory of John F. Kennedy (1917-63). See Nos. C160-C161.

Syncom Satellite A172

Designs (Satellites): 15c, Relay I (vert.). 25c, Mariner II.

1964, June 22 **Unwmk.** *Perf. 12½*

415 A172 10c org & emer 15 15
416 A172 15c brt car rose & vio 15 15
417 A172 25c bl, org & blk 32 32

Issued to publicize progress in space communications and the peaceful uses of outer space. See No. C162.

Mt. Fuji — A173

Designs: 15c, Torii and Olympic flame. 25c, Cherry blossoms and stadium.

1964, Sept. 15 **Litho.**

418 A173 10c org yel & emer 15 15
419 A173 15c lt red & pur 18 18
420 A173 25c ocher & red 45 45

Issued for the 18th Olympic Games, Tokyo, Oct. 10-25, 1964. See No. C163.

Boy Scout Emblem and Scout Sign — A174

"Emancipation" by Thomas Ball — A175

Design: 10c, Bugle and Liberian Scout emblem (horiz.).

1965, Mar. 8 **Litho.** *Perf. 12½*

421 A174 5c lt bl & brn 15 15
422 A174 10c dk grn & ocher 20 20
Set value 28 28

Issued to honor the Liberian Boy Scouts. See Nos. C164-C165.

1965, May 3 **Unwmk.** *Perf. 12½*

Designs: 20c, Abraham Lincoln and John F. Kennedy (horiz.). 25c, Lincoln by Augustus St. Gaudens, Lincoln Park, Chicago.

423 A175 5c dk gray & brn org 15 15
424 A175 20c emer & lt gray 28 28
425 A175 25c mar & bl 35 35

Centenary of the death of Abraham Lincoln. See No. C166.

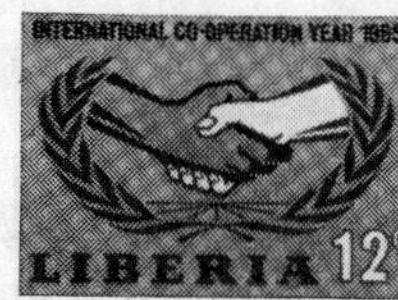

ICY Emblem A176

1965, June 21 **Litho.** *Perf. 12½*

426 A176 12c org & brn 15 15
427 A176 25c vio bl & brn 28 28
428 A176 50c emer & brn 60 60

Intl. Cooperation Year. See No. C167.

ITU Emblem, Old and New Communication Equipment — A177

1965, Sept. 21 **Unwmk.** *Perf. 12½*

429 A177 25c brt grn & red brn 25 25
430 A177 35c blk & car rose 35 35

Cent. of the ITU. See No. C168.

Pres. Tubman and Liberian Flag — A178

1965, Nov. 29 **Litho.**

431 A178 25c red, ultra & brn 40 40

Pres. William V. S. Tubman's 70th birthday. See No. C169, C169a.

Churchill in Admiral's Uniform A179

Pres. Joseph J. Roberts A180

Designs: 15c, Churchill giving "V" sign (vert.).

1966, Jan. 18 **Litho.** *Perf. 12½*

432 A179 15c org & blk 18 15
433 A179 20c blk & brt grn 26 15

Issued in memory of Sir Winston Spencer Churchill (1874-1965), statesman and World War II leader. See Nos. C170-C171.

1966-69 **Litho.** *Perf. 12½*

Presidents: 2c, Stephen Benson. 3c, Daniel Bashiel Warner. 4c, James S. Payne. 5c, Edward James Roye. 10c, William D. Coleman. 25c, Daniel Edward Howard. 50c, Charles Dunbar Burgess King. 80c, Hilary R. W. Johnson. $1, Edwin J. Barclay. $2, Joseph James Cheeseman ("Cheesman" on stamp).

434 A180 1c blk & brick red 15 15
435 A180 2c blk & yel 15 15
436 A180 3c blk & lil 15 15
437 A180 4c ap grn & blk ('67) 15 15
438 A180 5c blk & dl org 15 15
439 A180 10c pale grn & blk ('67) 15 15
440 A180 25c blk & lt bl 30 15
441 A180 50c blk & brt lil rose 60 48
442 A180 80c dp rose & blk ('67) 1.00 65
443 A180 $1 blk & ocher 1.25 15

Perf. 11½x11

443A A180 $2 blk & dp red lil ('69) 2.50 1.75
Nos. 434-443A,C182 (12) 6.95
Set value 3.60

Soccer Players and Globe A181

Designs: 25c, World Championships Cup, ball and shoes (vert.). 35c, Soccer player dribbling (vert.).

1966, May 3 **Litho.** *Perf. 12½*

444 A181 10c brt grn & dk brn 15 15
445 A181 25c brt pink & brn 30 20
446 A181 35c brn & org 42 26

Issued to publicize the World Cup Soccer Championships, Wembley, England, July 11-30. See No. C172.

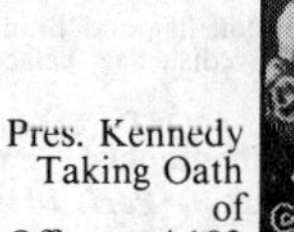

Pres. Kennedy Taking Oath of Office — A182

Designs: 20c, 1964 Kennedy stamps, Nos. 414 and C160.

1966, Aug. 16 **Litho.** *Perf. 12½*

447 A182 15c red & blk 18 15
448 A182 20c brt bl & red lil 22 15
Set value 16

3rd anniv. of Pres. Kennedy's death (Nov. 22). See Nos. C173-C175.

Children on Seesaw and UNICEF Emblem A183

Design: 80c, Boy playing doctor.

1966, Oct. 25 **Unwmk.** *Perf. 12½*

449 A183 5c brt bl & red 15 15
450 A183 80c org brn & yel grn 75 75

20th anniv. of UNICEF.

Giraffe — A184

Jamboree Badge — A185

Designs: 3c, Lion. 5c, Slender-nosed crocodile (horiz.). 10c, Baby chimpanzees. 15c, Leopard (horiz.). 20c, Black rhinoceros (horiz.). 25c, Elephant.

1966, Dec. 20

451 A184 2c multi 15 15
452 A184 3c multi 15 15
453 A184 5c multi 15 15
a. Black omitted ("5c LIBERIA" and imprint) 8.25
454 A184 10c multi 15 15
455 A184 15c multi 25 15
456 A184 20c multi 32 16
457 A184 25c multi 45 20
Set value 1.30 70

1967, Mar. 23 Litho. *Perf. 12½*

Designs: 25c, Boy Scout emblem and various sports (horiz.). 40c, Scout at campfire and vision of moon landing (horiz.).

458 A185 10c brt lil rose & grn	15	15
459 A185 25c brt red & bl	32	24
460 A185 40c brt grn & brn org	45	35

Issued to publicize the 12th Boy Scout World Jamboree, Farragut State Park, Idaho, Aug. 1-9. See No. C176.

Pre-Hispanic Sculpture of Mexico — A186

Designs: 25c, Aztec Calendar and Olympic rings. 40c, Mexican pottery, sombrero and guitar (horiz.).

1967, June 20 Litho. *Perf. 12½*

461 A186 10c ocher & vio	15	15
462 A186 25c lt bl, org & blk	30	24
463 A186 40c yel grn & car	45	38

Issued to publicize the 19th Olympic Games, Mexico City. See No. C177.

WHO Office for Africa — A187

Design: 5c, WHO Office for Africa (horiz.).

1967, Aug. 28 Litho. *Perf. 12½*

464 A187 5c bl & yel	15	15
465 A187 80c brt grn & yel	1.00	1.00

Inauguration of the WHO Regional Office for Africa in Brazzaville, Congo.

Boy Playing African Rattle — A188

Africans Playing Native Instruments: 3c, Tom-tom and soko violin (horiz.). 5c, Mang harp (horiz.). 10c, Alimilim. 15c, Xylophone drums. 25c, Large tom-toms. 35c, Large harp.

1967, Oct. 16 Litho. *Perf. 14*

466 A188 2c vio & multi	15	15
467 A188 3c bl & multi	15	15
468 A188 5c lil rose & multi	15	15
469 A188 10c yel grn & multi	18	15
470 A188 15c vio & multi	24	15
471 A188 25c ocher & multi	52	22
472 A188 35c dp rose & multi	75	35
Nos. 466-472 (7)	2.14	
Set value		1.00

Ice Hockey A189

Pres. William Tubman A190

Designs: 25c, Ski jump. 40c, Bobsledding.

1967, Nov. 20 Litho. *Perf. 12½*

473 A189 10c emer & vio bl	15	15
474 A189 25c grnsh bl & dp plum	24	20
475 A189 40c ocher & org brn	35	32

10th Winter Olympic Games, Grenoble, France, Feb. 6-18, 1968. See No. C178.

1967, Dec. 22 Litho. *Perf. 12½*

476 A190 25c ultra & brn	40	24

Souvenir Sheet

Imperf

477 A190 50c ultra & brn	80	80

Inauguration of President Tubman, Jan. 1, 1968. No. 477 contains one stamp with simulated perforations and picture frame.

Human Rights Flame — A191

Martin Luther King, Jr. — A192

1968, Apr. 26 Litho. *Perf. 12½*

478 A191 3c ver & dp bl	15	15
479 A191 80c brn & emer	75	75

Issued for International Human Rights Year. See No. C179.

1968, July 11 Unwmk. *Perf. 12½*

Designs: 15c, Mule-drawn hearse and Dr. King. 35c, Dr. King and Lincoln monument by Daniel Chester French (horiz.).

480 A192 15c brt bl & brn	18	15
481 A192 25c ind & brn	26	18
482 A192 35c ol & blk	40	22

Issued in memory of the Rev. Dr. Martin Luther King, Jr. (1929-1968). American civil rights leader. See No. C180.

Javelin and Diana Statue, Mexico City — A193

Designs: 25c, Discus, pyramid and serpent god Quetzalcoatl. 35c, Woman diver and Xochicalco from ruins near Cuernavaca.

1968, Aug. 22 Litho. *Perf. 12½*

483 A193 15c dp vio & org brn	15	15
484 A193 25c red & brt bl	22	18
485 A193 35c brn & emer	32	24

19th Olympic Games, Mexico City, Oct. 12-27. See No. C181.

Pres. Wm. V. S. Tubman — A194

Unification Monument, Voinjama-Lofa County — A195

1968, Dec. 30 Unwmk. *Perf. 12½*

486 A194 25c sil, blk & brn	70	32

Souvenir Sheet

Imperf

487 A195 80c sil, ultra & red	1.65	1.25

25th anniv. of Pres. Tubman's administration.

"ILO" with Cogwheel and Wreath A196

1969, Apr. 16 Litho. *Perf. 12½*

488 A196 25c lt bl & gold	40	25

50th anniv. of the ILO. See No. C183.

Red Roofs, by Camille Pisarro — A197

Paintings: 3c, Prince Balthasar Carlos on Horseback, by Velazquez (vert.). 10c, David and Goliath, by Caravaggio. 12c, Still Life, by Jean Baptiste Chardin. 15c, The Last Supper, by Leonardo da Vinci. 20c, Regatta at Argenteuil, by Claude Monet. 25c, Judgment of Solomon, by Giorgione. 35c, Sistine Madonna, by Raphael.

1969, June 26 Litho. *Perf. 11*

489 A197 3c gray & multi	15	15
490 A197 5c gray & multi	15	15
491 A197 10c lt bl & multi	15	15
492 A197 12c gray & multi	20	15
493 A197 15c gray & multi	22	15
494 A197 20c gray & multi	32	15
495 A197 25c gray & multi	42	18
496 A197 35c gray & multi	55	25
Nos. 489-496 (8)	2.16	
Set value		90

See Nos. 502-509.

African Development Bank Emblem — A198

1969, Aug. 12 Litho. *Perf. 12½*

497 A198 25c bl & brn	35	30
498 A198 80c yel grn & red	1.10	60

5th anniversary of the African Development Bank.

Moon Landing and Liberia No. C174 — A199

Designs: 15c, Memorial tablet left on moon, rocket, earth and moon (horiz.). 35c, Take-off from moon.

1969, Oct. 15 Litho. *Perf. 12½*

499 A199 15c bl & bis	32	15
500 A199 25c dk vio bl & org	48	16
501 A199 35c gray & red	70	22

Man's 1st landing on the moon, July 20, 1969. US astronauts Neil A. Armstrong and Col. Edwin E. Aldrin, Jr., with Lieut. Col. Michael Collins piloting Apollo 11. See No. C184.

Painting Type of 1969

1969, Nov. 18 Litho. *Perf. 11*

Paintings: 3c, The Gleaners, by Francois Millet. 5c, View of Toledo, by El Greco (vert.). 10c, Heads of Negroes, by Rubens. 12c, The Last Supper, by El Greco. 15c, Dancing Peasants, by Brueghel. 20c, Hunters in the Snow, by Brueghel. 25c, Detail from Descent from the Cross, by Rogier van der Weyden (vert.). 35c, The Ascension, by Murillo (vert., inscribed "The Conception").

502 A197 3c lt bl & multi	15	15
503 A197 5c lt bl & multi	15	15
504 A197 10c lt bl & multi	15	15
505 A197 12c gray & multi	18	15
506 A197 15c gray & multi	22	15
507 A197 20c lt bl & multi	32	16
508 A197 25c gray & multi	40	22
509 A197 35c lt bl & multi	55	25
Nos. 502-509 (8)	2.12	
Set value		1.00

Peace Dove, UN Emblem and Atom — A200

1970, Apr. 16 Litho. *Perf. 12½*

510 A200 5c grn & sil	15	15

25th anniv. of the UN. See No. C185.

Official Emblem A201

Designs: 10c, Statue of rain god Tlaloc (vert.). 25c, Jules Rimet cup and sculptured wall (vert.). 35c, Sombrero and soccer ball. 55c, Two soccer players.

1970, June 10 Litho. *Perf. 12½*

511 A201	5c pale bl & brn	15	15
512 A201	10c emer & ocher	15	15
513 A201	25c dp rose lil & gold	35	18
514 A201	35c ver & ultra	50	24
	Set value		55

Souvenir Sheet

Perf. 11½

515 A201	55c brt bl, yel & grn	1.25	60

9th World Soccer Championships for the Jules Rimet Cup, Mexico City, May 30-June 21, 1970.

EXPO '70 Emblem, Japanese Singer and Festival Plaza — A202

Designs (EXPO '70 Emblem and): 3c, Male Japanese singer, EXPO Hall and floating stage. 5c, Tower of the Sun and view of exhibition. 7c, Tanabata Festival. 8c, Awa Dance Festival. 25c, Sado-Okesa Dance Festival. 50c, Ricoh Pavilion with "eye," and Mt. Fuji (vert.).

1970, July Litho. *Perf. 11*

516 A202	2c multi	15	15
517 A202	3c multi	15	15
518 A202	5c multi	20	15
519 A202	7c multi	32	15
520 A202	8c multi	38	15
521 A202	25c multi	95	24
	Nos. 516-521 (6)	2.15	
	Set value		60

Souvenir Sheet

522 A202	50c multi	2.00	65

Issued to publicize EXPO '70 International Exhibition, Osaka, Japan, Mar. 15-Sept. 13.

UPU Headquarters and Monument, Bern — A203

Design: 80c, Like 25c (vert.).

1970, Aug. 25 *Perf. 12½*

523 A203	25c bl & multi	28	28
524 A203	80c multi	70	70

Inauguration of the new UPU Headquarters in Bern.

Napoleon as Consul, by Joseph Marie Vien, Sr. — A204

Paintings of Napoleon: 5c, Visit to a School, by unknown painter. 10c, Napoleon Bonaparte, by François Pascal Gerard. 12c, The French Campaign, by Ernest Meissonier. 20c, Napoleon Signing Abdication at Fontainebleau, by François Bouchot. 25c, Napoleon Meets Pope Pius VII, by Jean-Louis Demarne. 50c, Napoleon's Coronation, by Jacques Louis David.

1970, Oct. 20 Litho. *Perf. 11*

525 A204	3c bl & multi	15	15
526 A204	5c bl & multi	15	15
527 A204	10c bl & multi	24	15
528 A204	12c bl & multi	30	15
529 A204	20c bl & multi	48	15
530 A204	25c bl & multi	60	18
	Nos. 525-530 (6)	1.92	
	Set value		62

Souvenir Sheet

Imperf

531 A204	50c bl & multi	1.25	48

200th anniv. of the birth of Napoleon Bonaparte (1769-1821). No. 531 contains one stamp with simulated perforations.

Pres. Tubman A205

1970, Nov. 20 Litho. *Perf. 13½*

532 A205	25c multi	70	35

Souvenir Sheet

Imperf

533 A205	50c multi	1.00	70

Pres. Tubman's 75th birthday. No. 533 contains one imperf. stamp with simulated perforations.

Adoration of the Kings, by Rogier van der Weyden — A206

Paintings (Adoration of the Kings, by): 5c, Hans Memling. 10c, Stefan Lochner. 12c, Albrecht Altdorfer (vert.). 20c, Hugo van der Goes, Adoration of the Shepherds. 25c, Hieronymus Bosch (vert.). 50c, Andrea Mantegna (triptych).

Perf. 13½x14, 14x13½

1970, Dec. 21 Litho.

534 A206	3c multi	15	15
535 A206	5c multi	15	15
536 A206	10c multi	18	15
537 A206	12c multi	24	15
538 A206	20c multi	35	15
539 A206	25c multi	48	15
	Nos. 534-539 (6)	1.55	
	Set value		50

Souvenir Sheet

Imperf

540 A206	50c multi	1.65	40

Christmas 1970.
No. 540 contains one 60x40mm stamp.

Dogon Tribal Mask A207

African Tribal Ceremonial Masks: 2c, Bapende. 5c, Baoule. 6c, Dedougou. 9c, Dan. 15c, Bamileke. 20c, Bapende mask and costume. 25c, Bamileke mask and costume.

1971, Feb. 24 Litho. *Perf. 11*

541 A207	2c lt grn & multi	15	15
542 A207	3c pink & multi	15	15
543 A207	5c lt bl & multi	15	15
544 A207	6c lt grn & multi	15	15
545 A207	9c lt bl & multi	15	15
546 A207	15c pink & multi	22	15
547 A207	20c lt grn & multi	50	35
548 A207	25c pink & multi	26	18
	Set value	1.35	90

Astronauts on Moon — A208

Designs: 5c, Astronaut and lunar transport vehicle. 10c, Astronaut with U.S. flag on moon. 12c, Space capsule in Pacific Ocean. 20c, Astronaut leaving capsule. 25c, Astronauts Alan B. Shepard, Stuart A. Roosa and Edgar D. Mitchell.

1971, May 20 Litho. *Perf. 13½*

549 A208	3c vio bl & multi	15	15
550 A208	5c vio bl & multi	15	15
551 A208	10c vio bl & multi	24	15
552 A208	12c vio bl & multi	32	15
553 A208	20c vio bl & multi	45	20
554 A208	25c vio bl & multi	60	25
	Nos. 549-554 (6)	1.91	
	Set value		70

Apollo 14 moon landing, Jan. 31-Feb. 9. See No. C186.

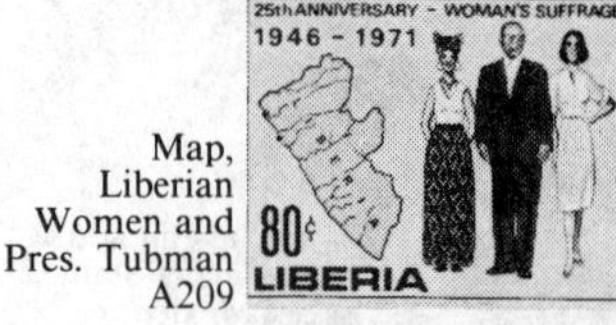

Map, Liberian Women and Pres. Tubman A209

Design: 3c, Pres. Tubman and women at ballot box (vert.).

1971, May 27 *Perf. 12½*

555 A209	3c ultra & brn	15	15
556 A209	80c grn & brn	1.25	1.25

25th anniversary of women's suffrage.

Hall of Honor, Munich, and Olympic Flag — A210

Munich Views and Olympic Flag: 5c, General view. 10c, National Museum. 12c, Max Joseph's Square. 20c, Propylaeum on King's Square. 25c, Liesel-Karlstadt Fountain.

1971, June 28 Litho. *Perf. 11*

557 A210	3c multi	15	15
558 A210	5c multi	15	15
559 A210	10c multi	18	15
560 A210	12c multi	25	15
561 A210	20c multi	35	20
562 A210	25c multi	45	28
	Nos. 557-562 (6)	1.53	
	Set value		80

Publicity for the 20th Summer Olympic Games, Munich, Germany, 1972. See No. C187.

Boy Scout, Emblem and U. S. Flag — A211

Designs (Boy Scout, National Flag and Boy Scout Emblem of): 5c, German Federal Republic. 10c, Australia. 12c, Great Britain. 20c, Japan. 25c, Liberia.

1971, Aug. 6 Litho. *Perf. 13½*

563 A211	3c multi	15	15
564 A211	5c multi	15	15
565 A211	10c multi	18	15
566 A211	12c multi	25	15
567 A211	20c multi	38	15
568 A211	25c multi	50	20
	Nos. 563-568 (6)	1.61	
	Set value		55

13th Boy Scout World Jamboree, Asagiri Plain, Japan, Aug. 2-10. See No. C188.

Pres. Tubman (1895-1971) A212

1971, Aug. 23 *Perf. 12½*

569 A212	3c blk, ultra & brn	15	15
570 A212	25c blk, brt rose lil & brn	42	42

Zebra and UNICEF Emblem — A213

Animals (UNICEF Emblem and Animals with their Young): 7c, Koala. 8c, Llama. 10c, Red fox. 20c, Monkey. 25c, Brown bear.

1971, Oct. 1 *Perf. 11*

571 A213	5c multi	20	15
572 A213	7c multi	28	15
573 A213	8c multi	32	15
574 A213	10c multi	38	15
575 A213	20c multi	80	28
576 A213	25c multi	1.00	38
	Nos. 571-576 (6)	2.98	
	Set value		1.05

25th anniv. of UNICEF. See No. C189.

Sapporo 72 Emblem, Long-distance Skiing, Sika Deer — A214

Designs (Sapporo 72 Emblem and): 3c, Sledding and black woodpecker. 5c, Ski Jump and brown bear. 10c, Bobsledding and murres. 15c, Figure skating and pikas. 25c, Downhill skiing and Japanese cranes.

1971, Nov. 4 — *Perf. 13x13½*

577	A214	2c multi	15	15
578	A214	3c multi	15	15
579	A214	5c multi	15	15
580	A214	10c multi	26	15
581	A214	15c multi	32	15
582	A214	25c multi	75	20
		Set value	1.30	55

11th Winter Olympic Games, Sapporo, Japan, Feb. 3-13, 1972. See No. C190.

Dove Carrying Letter, APU Emblem A215

1971, Dec. 9 — *Perf. 12½*

583	A215	25c ultra & dp org	38	32
584	A215	80c gray & dp brn	1.10	95

10th anniversary of African Postal Union.

Pioneer Fathers' Monument, Monrovia A216

Pres. William R. Tolbert, Jr. A217

Designs: 3c, 25c, Sailing ship "Elizabeth," Providence Island (horiz.). 35c, as 20c.

1972, Jan. 1

585	A216	3c bl & brt grn	15	15
586	A216	20c org & bl	60	42
587	A216	25c org & pur	65	55
588	A216	35c lil rose & brt grn	1.10	75

Sesquicentennial of founding of Liberia. See No. C191.

1972, Jan. 1

Design: 25c, Pres. Tolbert and map of Liberia (horiz.).

589	A217	25c emer & brn	40	22
590	A217	80c bl & brn	1.40	45

Inauguration of William R. Tolbert, Jr. as 19th president of Liberia.

Soccer and Swedish Flag — A218

Designs (Olympic Rings, "Motion" Symbol and): 5c, Swimmers at start and Italian flag. 10c, Equestrian and British flag. 12c, Bicycling and French flag. 20c, Long jump and American flag. 25c, Running and Liberian flag.

1972, May 19 Litho. — *Perf. 11*

591	A218	3c lem & multi	15	15
592	A218	5c lt lil & multi	15	15
593	A218	10c multi	30	15
594	A218	12c gray & multi	40	15
595	A218	20c lt bl & multi	55	24
596	A218	25c pink & multi	75	30
		Nos. 591-596 (6)	2.30	
		Set value		90

20th Olympic Games, Munich, Aug. 26-Sept. 10. See No. C192.

Y's Men's Club Emblem, Map — A219

Design: 90c, Y's Men's Club emblem and globe; inscribed "fifty and forward."

1972, June 12 — *Perf. 13½*

597	A219	15c pur & gold	22	18
598	A219	90c vio bl & emer	1.25	1.10

Intl. Y's Men's Club, 50th anniv.

Astronaut and Lunar Rover — A220

Designs: 5c, Moon scene reflected in astronaut's helmet. 10c, Astronauts with cameras. 12c, Astronauts placing scientific equipment on moon. 20c, Apollo 16 badge. 25c, Astronauts riding lunar rover.

1972, June 26

599	A220	3c lt bl & multi	15	15
600	A220	5c red org & multi	15	15
601	A220	10c pink & multi	18	15
602	A220	12c yel & multi	28	15
603	A220	20c lt vio & multi	42	15
604	A220	25c emer & multi	50	20
		Nos. 599-604 (6)	1.68	
		Set value		60

Apollo 16 U.S. moon mission, Apr. 15-27, 1972. See No. C193.

Emperor Haile Selassie — A221

1972, July 21 — *Perf. 14x14½*

605	A221	20c ol grn & yel	45	45
606	A221	25c mar & yel	55	55
607	A221	35c brn & yel	80	80

80th birthday of Emperor Haile Selassie of Ethiopia.

Ajax, 1809, and Figurehead — A222

1972, Sept. 6 — *Perf. 11*

608	A222	3c *shown*	15	15
609	A222	5c *Hogue, 1811*	15	15
610	A222	7c *Ariadne, 1816*	20	15
611	A222	15c *Royal Adelaide, 1828*	40	15
612	A222	20c *Rinaldo, 1860*	55	16
613	A222	25c *Nymphe, 1888*	65	22
		Nos. 608-613 (6)	2.10	
		Set value		65

Famous sailing ships and their figureheads. See No. C194.

Pres. Tolbert Taking Oath, Richard A. Henries A223

1972, Oct. 23 Litho. — *Perf. 13½*

614	A223	15c grn & multi	55	55
615	A223	25c vio bl & multi	85	85

Pres. William R. Tolbert, Jr. sworn in as 19th President of Liberia, July 23, 1971. See No. C195.

Klaus Dibiasi, Italy, Diving — A224

Designs (Flag, Olympic Emblems and): 8c, Valery Borzov, USSR, running. 10c, Hideaki Yanagida, Japan, wrestling. 12c, Mark Spitz, USA, swimming. 15c, Kipchoge Keino, Kenya, 3000-meter steeplechase. 25c, Richard Meade, Great Britain, equestrian. 55c, Hans Winkler, Germany, grand prix jumping.

1973, Jan. 5 Litho. — *Perf. 11*

616	A224	5c lt bl & multi	15	15
617	A224	8c vio & multi	15	15
618	A224	10c multi	18	15
619	A224	12c grn & multi	22	15
620	A224	15c org & multi	30	20
621	A224	25c pale sal & multi	40	26
		Nos. 616-621 (6)	1.40	
		Set value		90

Souvenir Sheet

622	A224	55c multi	1.25	65

Gold medal winners in 20th Olympic Games.

Astronaut on Moon and Apollo 17 Badge — A225

Designs (Apollo 17 Badge and): 3c, Astronauts on earth in lunar rover. 10c, Astronauts collecting yellow lunar dust. 15c, Astronauts in lunar rover exploring moon crater. 20c, Capt. Eugene A. Cernan, Dr. Harrison H. Schmitt and Comdr. Ronald E. Evans on launching pad. 25c, Astronauts on moon with scientific equipment.

1973, Mar. 28 Litho. — *Perf. 11*

623	A225	2c bl & multi	15	15
624	A225	3c bl & multi	15	15
625	A225	10c bl & multi	15	15
626	A225	15c bl & multi	24	16
627	A225	20c bl & multi	35	24
628	A225	25c bl & multi	48	32
		Set value	1.25	90

Apollo 17 US moon mission, Dec. 7-19, 1972. See No. C196.

Locomotive, England — A226

Designs: Locomotives, 1895-1905.

1973, May 4

629	A226	2c shown	15	15
630	A226	3c Netherlands	15	15
631	A226	10c France	24	15
632	A226	15c United States	32	15
633	A226	20c Japan	50	20
634	A226	25c Germany	65	26
		Nos. 629-634 (6)	2.01	
		Set value		75

See No. C197.

OAU Emblem and Flags — A227

1973, May 24 Litho. — *Perf. 13½*

635	A227	3c multi	15	15
636	A227	5c multi	15	15
637	A227	10c multi	16	15
638	A227	15c multi	24	20
639	A227	25c multi	30	26
640	A227	50c multi	60	50
		Nos. 635-640 (6)	1.60	
		Set value		1.20

10th anniv. of the Organization for African Unity.

WHO Emblem, Edward Jenner and Roses — A228

Designs (WHO Emblem and): 4c, Sigmund Freud and pansies. 10c, Jonas E. Salk and chrysanthemums. 15c, Louis Pasteur and scabiosa caucasia. 20c, Emil von Behring and rhododendron. 25c, Alexander Fleming and tree mallows.

1973, June 26 Litho. — *Perf. 11*

641	A228	1c gray & multi	15	15
642	A228	4c org & multi	15	15
643	A228	10c lt bl & multi	15	15
644	A228	15c rose & multi	22	15
645	A228	20c bl & multi	30	18
646	A228	25c yel grn & multi	38	24
		Set value	1.10	65

25th anniv. of WHO. See No. C198.

Stanley Steamer, 1910 — A229

Designs: Classic automobiles.

1973, Sept. 11 Litho. *Perf. 11*

No.	Type	Value	Description	Unused	Used
647	A229	2c	shown	15	15
648	A229	3c	Cadillac, 1903	15	15
649	A229	10c	Clement-Bayard, 1904	24	15
650	A229	15c	Rolls Royce, 1907	35	15
651	A229	20c	Maxwell, 1905	45	20
652	A229	25c	Chadwick, 1907	60	28
			Nos. 647-652 (6)	1.94	
			Set value		78

See No. C199.

Copernicus, Armillary Sphere, Satellite Communication — A230

Portraits of Copernicus and: 4c, Eudoxus solar system. 10c, Aristotle, Ptolemy, Copernicus and satellites. 15c, Saturn and Apollo spacecraft. 20c, Orbiting astronomical observatory. 25c, Satellite tracking station.

1973, Dec. 14 Litho. *Perf. 13½*

No.	Type	Value	Description	Unused	Used
653	A230	1c	yel & multi	15	15
654	A230	4c	lt vio & multi	15	15
655	A230	10c	lt bl & multi	20	15
656	A230	15c	yel grn & multi	30	15
657	A230	20c	bis & multi	40	18
658	A230	25c	pink & multi	50	24
			Nos. 653-658 (6)	1.70	
			Set value		65

Nicolaus Copernicus (1473-1543), Polish astronomer. See No. C200.

Radio Tower, Map of Africa A231

Designs: 15c, 25c, Map of Liberia, Radio tower and man listening to broadcast. 17c, like 13c.

1974, Jan. 16 Litho. *Perf. 13½*

No.	Type	Value	Description	Unused	Used
659	A231	13c	multi	35	35
660	A231	15c	yel & multi	35	28
661	A231	17c	lt gray & multi	42	32
662	A231	25c	brt grn & multi	55	42

20th anniv. of Radio ELWA, Monrovia.

Thomas Courts, 1817; Aureal, 1974; UPU Emblem — A232

Designs (UPU Emblem and): 3c, Jet, satellite, Post Office, Monrovia, ship. 10c, US and USSR telecommunication satellites. 15c, Mail runner and jet. 20c, Futuristic mail train and mail truck. 25c, American Pony Express rider.

1974, Mar. 4 Litho. *Perf. 13½*

No.	Type	Value	Description	Unused	Used
663	A232	2c	ocher & multi	15	15
664	A232	3c	lt grn & multi	15	15
665	A232	10c	lt bl & multi	20	15
666	A232	15c	pink & multi	30	15
667	A232	20c	gray & multi	38	20
668	A232	25c	lt lil & multi	50	26
			Set value	1.20	75

Cent. of UPU. See No. C201.

Fox Terrier — A233

1974, Apr. 16 Litho. *Perf. 13½*

No.	Type	Value	Description	Unused	Used
669	A233	5c	shown	15	15
670	A233	10c	Boxer	15	15
671	A233	16c	Chihuahua	30	15
672	A233	19c	Beagle	35	15
673	A233	25c	Golden retriever	42	15
674	A233	50c	Collie	90	24
			Nos. 669-674 (6)	2.27	
			Set value		62

See No. C202.

Soccer Game, West Germany and Chile — A234

Designs: Games between semi-finalists, and flags of competing nations.

1974, June 4 Litho. *Perf. 11*

No.	Type	Value	Description	Unused	Used
675	A234	1c	shown	15	15
676	A234	2c	Australia and East Germany	15	15
677	A234	5c	Brazil and Yugoslavia	15	15
678	A234	10c	Zaire and Scotland	16	15
679	A234	12c	Netherlands and Uruguay	20	15
680	A234	15c	Sweden and Bulgaria	24	15
681	A234	20c	Italy and Haiti	32	18
682	A234	25c	Poland and Argentina	40	25
			Set value	1.45	80

World Cup Soccer Championship, Munich, June 13-July 7. See No. C203.

Chrysiridia Madagascariensis — A235

Tropical Butterflies: 2c, Catagramma sorana. 5c, Erasmia pulchella. 17c, Morpho cypris. 25c, Agrias amydon. 40c, Vanessa cardui.

1974, Sept. 11 Litho. *Perf. 13½*

No.	Type	Value	Description	Unused	Used
683	A235	1c	gray & multi	15	15
684	A235	2c	gray & multi	15	15
685	A235	5c	gray & multi	15	15
686	A235	17c	gray & multi	40	15
687	A235	25c	gray & multi	55	22
688	A235	40c	gray & multi	90	38
			Set value	1.70	85

See No. C204.

Pres. Tolbert and Medal — A236

Design: $1, Pres. Tolbert, medal and Liberian flag (vert.).

1974, Dec. 10 Litho. *Perf. 13½*

No.	Type	Value	Description	Unused	Used
689	A236	3c	multi	15	15
690	A236	$1	multi	1.65	1.25

Pres. William R. Tolbert, Jr., recipient of 1974 Family of Man Award.

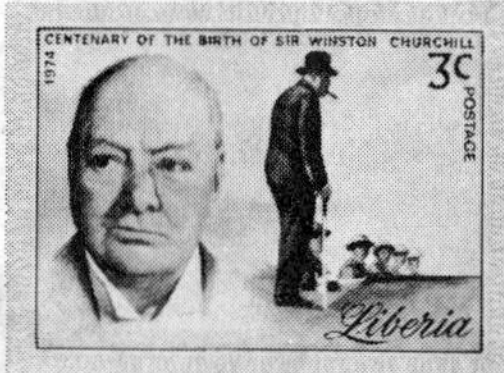

Winston Churchill, 1940 — A237

Designs (Churchill and): 10c, RAF planes in dog fight. 15c, In naval launch on way to Normandy. 17c, In staff car reviewing troops in desert. 20c, Aboard landing craft crossing Rhine. 25c, In conference with Pres. Roosevelt.

1975, Jan. 17 Litho. *Perf. 13½*

No.	Type	Value	Description	Unused	Used
691	A237	3c	multi	15	15
692	A237	10c	multi	15	15
693	A237	15c	multi	18	15
694	A237	17c	multi	22	15
695	A237	20c	multi	24	15
696	A237	25c	multi	30	22
			Nos. 691-696 (6)	1.24	
			Set value		70

Sir Winston Churchill (1874-1965), birth centenary. See No. C205.

Women's Year Emblem and Marie Curie A238

Designs (Women's Year Emblem and): 3c, Mahalia Jackson with microphone. 5c, Joan of Arc. 10c, Eleanor Roosevelt and children. 25c, Matilda Newport firing cannon. 50c, Valentina Tereshkova in space suit.

1975, Mar. 14 Litho. *Perf. 14½*

No.	Type	Value	Description	Unused	Used
697	A238	2c	cit & multi	15	15
698	A238	3c	dl org & multi	15	15
699	A238	5c	lil rose & multi	15	15
700	A238	10c	yel & multi	18	15
701	A238	25c	yel grn & multi	42	16
702	A238	50c	lil & multi	85	32
			Set value	1.60	65

Intl. Women's Year 1975. See No. C206.

Old State House, Boston, US No. 627 — A239

Designs: 10c, George Washington, US #644. 15c, Town Hall and Court House, Philadelphia, US #798. 20c, Benjamin Franklin, US #835. 25c, Paul Revere's Ride, US #618. 50c, Santa Maria, US #231.

1975, Apr. 25 Litho. *Perf. 13½*

No.	Type	Value	Description	Unused	Used
703	A239	5c	multi	15	15
704	A239	10c	multi	24	15
705	A239	15c	multi	35	15
706	A239	20c	multi	45	15
707	A239	25c	multi	60	15
708	A239	50c	multi	1.25	24
			Nos. 703-708 (6)	3.04	
			Set value		70

American Revolution Bicentennial. See No. C207.

Dr. Schweitzer, Hospital and Baboon Mother — A240

Designs (Dr. Schweitzer and): 3c, Elephant, and tribesmen poling boat. 5c, Water buffalo, egret, man and woman paddling canoe. 6c, Antelope and dancer. 25c, Lioness, woman cooking outdoors. 50c, Zebra and colt, doctor's examination at clinic.

1975, June 26 Litho. *Perf. 13½*

No.	Type	Value	Description	Unused	Used
709	A240	1c	multi	15	15
710	A240	3c	multi	15	15
711	A240	5c	multi	15	15
712	A240	6c	multi	15	15
713	A240	25c	multi	60	16
714	A240	50c	multi	1.25	38
			Set value	1.80	70

Dr. Albert Schweitzer (1875-1965), medical missionary, birth centenary. See No. C208.

American-Russian Handshake in Space — A241

Designs (Apollo-Soyuz Emblem and): 5c, Apollo. 10c, Soyuz. 20c, Flags and maps of US and USSR. 25c, A. A. Leonov, and V. N. Kubasov. 50c, D. K. Slayton, V. D. Brand, T. P. Stafford.

1975, Sept. 18 Litho. *Perf. 13½*

No.	Type	Value	Description	Unused	Used
715	A241	5c	multi	15	15
716	A241	10c	multi	16	15
717	A241	15c	multi	24	15
718	A241	20c	multi	32	15
719	A241	25c	multi	40	15
720	A241	50c	multi	80	30
			Nos. 715-720 (6)	2.07	
			Set value		65

Apollo Soyuz space test project (Russo-American cooperation), launching July 15; link-up, July 17. See No. C209.

Presidents Tolbert, Siaka Stevens; Treaty Signing; Liberia and Sierra Leone Maps — A242

1975, Oct. 3 Litho. *Perf. 13½*

No.	Type	Value	Description	Unused	Used
721	A242	2c	gray & multi	15	15
722	A242	3c	gray & multi	15	15
723	A242	5c	gray & multi	15	15
724	A242	10c	gray & multi	16	15
725	A242	25c	gray & multi	38	24
726	A242	50c	gray & multi	80	50
			Set value	1.50	1.00

Mano River Union Agreement between Liberia and Sierra Leone, signed Oct. 3, 1973.

Figure Skating — A243

Designs (Winter Olympic Games Emblem and): 4c, Ski jump. 10c, Slalom. 25c, Ice hockey. 35c, Speed skating. 50c, Two-man bobsled.

1976, Jan. 23 Litho. *Perf. 13½*

727	A243	1c lt bl & multi	15	15
728	A243	4c lt bl & multi	15	15
729	A243	10c lt bl & multi	16	15
730	A243	25c lt bl & multi	42	15
731	A243	35c lt bl & multi	55	18
732	A243	50c lt bl & multi	80	28
		Nos. 727-732 (6)	2.23	
		Set value		72

12th Winter Olympic Games, Innsbruck, Austria, Feb. 4-15. See No. C210.

Pres. Tolbert Taking Oath of Office — A244

Designs: 25c, Pres. Tolbert at his desk (vert.). $1, Seal and flag of Liberia, $400 commemorative gold coin.

1976, Apr. 5 Litho. *Perf. 13½*

733	A244	3c multi	15	15
734	A244	25c multi	26	26
735	A244	$1 multi	1.25	1.25

Inauguration of President William R. Tolbert, Jr., Jan. 5, 1976.

Weight Lifting and Olympic Rings — A245

Designs (Olympic Rings and): 3c, Pole vault. 10c, Hammer and shot put. 25c, Yachting. 35c, Women's gymnastics. 50c, Hurdles.

1976, May 4 Litho. *Perf. 13½*

736	A245	2c gray & multi	15	15
737	A245	3c org & multi	15	15
738	A245	10c lt vio & multi	16	15
739	A245	25c lt grn & multi	42	16
740	A245	35c yel & multi	60	25
741	A245	50c pink & multi	85	25
		Nos. 736-741 (6)	2.33	
		Set value		80

21st Olympic Games, Montreal, Canada, July 17-Aug. 1. See No. C211.

A. G. Bell, Telephone and Receiver, 1876, UPU Emblem — A246

UPU Emblem and: 4c, Horsedrawn mail coach and ITU emblem. 5c, Intelsat IV satellite, radar and ITU emblem. 25c, A. G. Bell, ship laying underwater cable, 1976 telephone. 40c, A. G. Bell, futuristic train, telegraph and telephone wires. 50c, Wright brothers' plane, Zeppelin and Concorde.

1976, June 4 Litho. *Perf. 13½*

742	A246	1c grn & multi	15	15
743	A246	4c ocher & multi	15	15
744	A246	5c org & multi	15	15
745	A246	25c grn & multi	32	15
746	A246	40c lil & multi	50	18
747	A246	50c bl & multi	65	25
		Set value	1.60	65

Cent. of 1st telephone call by Alexander Graham Bell, Mar. 10, 1876. See No. C212.

Gold Nugget on Chain, Gold Panner A247

1976-81 Litho. *Perf. 14½*

749	A247	1c Mano River Bridge	15	15
750	A247	3c shown	15	15
751	A247	5c "V" ring	15	15
752	A247	7c like 5c ('81)	18	15
753	A247	10c Rubber tire, tree	24	15
754	A247	15c Harvesting	38	32
755	A247	17c like 55c ('81)	42	35
756	A247	20c Hydroelectric plant	50	42
757	A247	25c Mesurado shrimp	60	15
758	A247	27c Woman tie-dying cloth	65	55
759	A247	55c Lake Piso, barracuda	1.25	35
760	A247	$1 Train hauling iron ore	2.50	2.00
		Nos. 749-760 (12)	7.17	4.89

See Nos. 944-953.

Rhinoceros — A249

African Animals: 3c, Zebra antelope. 5c, Chimpanzee (vert.). 15c, Pigmy hippopotamus. 25c, Leopard. $1, Gorilla (vert.).

1976, Sept. 1 Litho. *Perf. 13½*

763	A249	2c org & multi	15	15
764	A249	3c gray & multi	15	15
765	A249	5c bl & multi	15	15
766	A249	15c brt bl & multi	25	15
767	A249	25c ultra & multi	45	22
768	A249	$1 multi	1.65	75
		Nos. 763-768 (6)	2.80	
		Set value		1.20

See No. C213.

Maps of US and Liberia; Statue of Liberty, Unification Monument, Voinjama and Liberty Bell — A250

Designs: $1, George Washington, Gerald R. Ford, Joseph J. Roberts (1st Pres. of Liberia), William R. Tolbert, Jr., Bicentennial emblem, US and Liberian flags.

1976, Sept. 21 Litho. *Perf. 13½*

769	A250	25c multi	45	25
770	A250	$1 multi	1.65	60

American Bicentennial and visit of Pres. William R. Tolbert, Jr. to the US, Sept. 21-30. See No. C214.

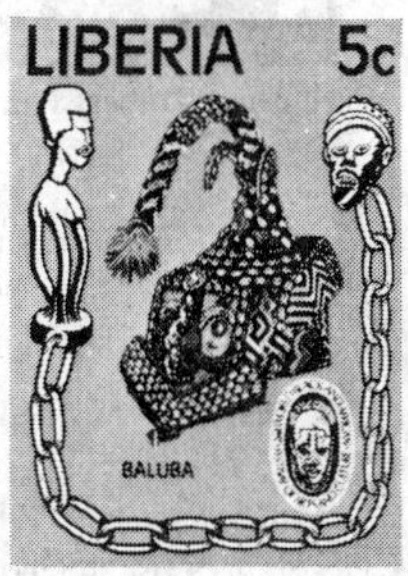

Baluba Masks and Festival Emblem A251

Tribal Masks: 10c, Bateke. 15c, Basshilele. 20c, Igungun. 25c, Masai. 50c, Kifwebe.

1977, Jan. 20 Litho. *Perf. 13½*

771	A251	5c yel & multi	15	15
772	A251	10c grn & multi	16	15
773	A251	15c sal & multi	25	15
774	A251	20c lt bl & multi	32	15
775	A251	25c vio & multi	40	18
776	A251	50c lem & multi	80	28
		Nos. 771-776 (6)	2.08	
		Set value		80

FESTAC '77, 2nd World Black and African Festival, Lagos, Nigeria, Jan. 15-Feb. 12. See No. C215.

Latham's Francolin — A252

Birds of Liberia: 10c, Narina trogon. 15c, Rufous-crowned roller. 20c, Brown-cheeked hornbill. 25c, Common bulbul. 50c, Fish eagle. 80c, Gold Coast touraco.

1977, Feb. 18 Litho. *Perf. 14*

777	A252	5c multi	15	15
778	A252	10c multi	20	15
779	A252	15c multi	30	15
780	A252	20c multi	40	15
781	A252	25c multi	50	18
782	A252	50c multi	1.00	28
		Nos. 777-782 (6)	2.55	
		Set value		80

Souvenir Sheet

783	A252	80c multi	1.50	1.10

Edmund Coffin, Military Dressage, USA — A253

Designs: 15c, Alwin Schockemohle, single jump, Germany (vert.). 20c, Christine Stuckelberger, Switzerland, single dressage. 25c, Prize of the Nations (team), France.

1977, Apr. 22 Litho. *Perf. 13½*

784	A253	5c ocher & multi	15	15
785	A253	15c ocher & multi	28	15
786	A253	20c ocher & multi	32	16
787	A253	25c ocher & multi	42	24
		Nos. 784-787,C216 (5)	2.17	1.20

Equestrian gold medal winners in Montreal Olympic Games. See No. C217.

Elizabeth II Wearing Crown — A254

Designs: 25c, Elizabeth II Prince Philip, Pres. and Mrs. Tubman. 80c, Elizabeth II, Prince Philip, royal coat of arms.

1977, May 23 Litho. *Perf. 13½*

788	A254	15c sil & multi	28	15
789	A254	25c sil & multi	45	15
790	A254	80c sil & multi	1.40	45

25th anniversary of the reign of Queen Elizabeth II. See No. C218.

Jesus Blessing Children A255

Christmas: 25c, The Good Shepherd. $1, Jesus and the Samaritan Woman. Designs after stained-glass windows, Providence Baptist Church, Monrovia.

1977, Nov. 3 Litho. *Perf. 13½*

791	A255	20c lt bl & multi	40	25
792	A255	25c lt bl & multi	52	28
793	A255	$1 lt bl & multi	1.75	95

Dornier DOX, 1928 — A256

Progress of Aviation: 3c, Piggyback space shuttle, 1977. 5c, Eddie Rickenbacker and Douglas DC 3. 25c, Charles A. Lindbergh and Spirit of St. Louis. 35c, Louis Bleriot and Bleriot XI. 50c, Orville and Wilbur Wright and flying machine, 1903. 80c, Concorde landing at night at Dulles Airport, Washington, DC.

1978, Jan. 6 Litho. *Perf. 13½*

794	A256	2c multi	15	15
795	A256	3c multi	15	15
796	A256	5c multi	15	15
797	A256	25c multi	45	24
798	A256	35c multi	65	30
799	A256	50c multi	95	42
		Nos. 794-799 (6)	2.50	
		Set value		1.10

Souvenir Sheet

800	A256	80c multi	1.40	1.10

Baladeuse by Santos-Dumont, 1903 — A257

Airships: 3c, Baldwin's, 1908, and US flag. 5c, Tissandier brothers', 1883. 25c, Parseval

PL VII, 1912. 40c, Nulli Secundus II, 1908. 50c, R34 rigid airship, 1919.

1978, Mar. 9 Litho. *Perf. 13½*

801	A257	2c multi	15	15
802	A257	3c multi	15	15
803	A257	5c multi	15	15
804	A257	25c multi	35	15
805	A257	40c multi	55	16
806	A257	50c multi	75	20
		Set value	1.75	55

75th anniv. of the Zeppelin. See No. C219.

Soccer, East Germany and Brazil — A258

Soccer Games: 2c, Poland and Argentina (vert.). 10c, West Germany and Netherlands. 25c, Yugoslavia and Brazil. 35c, Poland and Italy (vert.). 50c, Netherlands and Uruguay.

1978, May 16 Litho. *Perf. 13½*

807	A258	2c multi	15	15
808	A258	3c multi	15	15
809	A258	10c multi	22	15
810	A258	25c multi	55	28
811	A258	35c multi	75	38
812	A258	50c multi	1.10	55
		Nos. 807-812 (6)	2.92	
		Set value		1.40

11th World Cup Soccer Championships, Argentina, June 1-25. See No. C220.

Coronation Chair — A259

Designs: 25c, Imperial state crown. $1, Buckingham Palace (horiz.).

1978, June 12

813	A259	5c multi	15	15
814	A259	25c multi	45	15
815	A259	$1 multi	1.65	65
		Set value		80

25th anniversary of coronation of Queen Elizabeth II. See No. C221.

Jinnah, Liberian and Pakistani Flags — A260

1978, June Litho. *Perf. 13*

816	A260	30c multi	*25.00*	5.00

Mohammed Ali Jinnah (1876-1948), first Governor General of Pakistan.

> ***15-Cent Minimum Value***
> *The minimum value for a single stamp is 15 cents. This value reflects the costs of the handling of inexpensive stamps.*

Carter and Tolbert Families — A261

Designs: 25c, Pres. Tolbert, Rosalynn Carter and Pres. Carter at microphone, Robertsfield Airport. $1, Jimmy Carter and William R. Tolbert, Jr. in motorcade from airport.

1978, Oct. 26 Litho. *Perf. 13½*

817	A261	5c multi	15	15
818	A261	25c multi	42	42
819	A261	$1 multi	1.75	1.75

Pres. Carter's visit to Liberia, Apr. 1978.

Soccer Game: Italy-France A262

Soccer Games: 1c, Brazil-Spain (horiz.). 10c, Poland-West Germany (horiz.). 27c, Peru-Scotland. 35c, Austria-West Germany. 50c, Argentina the victor.

1978, Dec. 8 Litho. *Perf. 13½*

820	A262	1c multi	15	15
821	A262	2c multi	15	15
822	A262	10c multi	22	16
823	A262	27c multi	60	38
824	A262	35c multi	75	52
825	A262	50c multi	1.10	75
		Nos. 820-825 (6)	2.97	2.11

1978 World Cup Soccer winners. See No. C222.

Liberian Lumbermen — A263

Designs: 10c, Hauling timber by truck (vert.). 25c, Felling trees with chain saw. 50c, Moving logs.

1978, Dec. 15 Litho. *Perf. 13½x14*

826	A263	5c multi	15	15
827	A263	10c multi	25	16
828	A263	25c multi	55	38
829	A263	50c multi	1.10	75

8th World Forestry Congress, Djakarta, Indonesia.

"25" and Waves — A264

Design: $1, Radio tower and waves.

1979, Apr. 6 Litho. *Perf. 14x13½*

830	A264	35c multi	65	65
831	A264	$1 multi	1.90	1.90

25th anniversary of Radio ELWA.

Emblems of IYC, African Child's Decade and SOS Village — A265

Designs: 25c, $1, like 5c, with UNICEF emblem replacing SOS emblem. 35c, like 5c.

1979, Apr. 6 *Perf. 13½x14*

832	A265	5c multi	15	15
833	A265	25c multi	38	38
834	A265	35c multi	52	52
835	A265	$1 multi	1.50	1.50

IYC and Decade of the African Child.

Presidents Gardner and Tolbert, and Post Office, Monrovia — A266

Design: 35c, Anthony W. Gardner, William R. Tolbert, Jr. and UPU emblem.

1979, Apr. 2 Litho. *Perf. 13½x14*

836	A266	5c multi	15	15
837	A266	35c multi	80	80

Cent. of Liberia's joining UPU.

Unity Problem, Map of Africa, Torches — A267

Designs: 27c, Masks. 35c, Elephant, giraffe, lion, antelope, leopard and map of Africa. 50c, Huts, pepper birds and map of Africa.

1979, July 6 Litho. *Perf. 14x13½*

838	A267	5c multi	15	15
839	A267	27c multi	52	52
840	A267	35c multi	65	65
841	A267	50c multi	95	95

Organization for African Unity, 16th anniversary, and OAU Summit Conference.

Liberia No. 666, Rowland Hill — A268

Rowland Hill and: 10c, Pony Express rider, 1860. 15c, British mail coach, 1800. 25c, Mail steamship John Penn, 1860. 27c, Stanier Pacific train, 1939. 50c, Concorde. $1, Curtiss Jenny, 1916.

1979, July 20

842	A268	3c multi	15	15
843	A268	10c multi	15	15
844	A268	15c multi	24	24
845	A268	25c multi	38	38
846	A268	27c multi	42	42
847	A268	50c multi	75	75
		Nos. 842-847 (6)	2.09	2.09

Souvenir Sheet

848	A268	$1 multi	1.50	1.25

Sir Rowland Hill (1795-1879), originator of penny postage.

Red Cross, Pres. Tolbert Donating Blood — A269

Design: 50c, Red Cross, Pres. Tolbert.

1979, Aug. 15 Litho. *Perf. 13½*

849	A269	30c multi	55	55
850	A269	50c multi	95	95

National Red Cross, 30th anniversary and blood donation campaign.

M.S. World Peace A270

Design: $1, M.S. World Peace (diff.).

1979, Aug. 15

851	A270	5c multi	15	15
852	A270	$1 multi	1.90	1.90

2nd World Maritime Day, March 16; Liberia Maritime Program, 30th anniversary.

A Good Turn, by Norman Rockwell A271

Paintings: Scouting through the eyes of Norman Rockwell, 1925-1976. Each denomination in 10 different designs.

1979, Sept. 1 Litho. *Perf. 11*

853	A271	5c any single	15	15
854	A271	10c any single	15	15
855	A271	15c any single	18	16
856	A271	25c any single	35	24
857	A271	35c any single	50	40
		Nos. 853-857 (50)	12.10	9.30

Mrs. Tolbert, Children, Children's Village Emblem — A272

Design: 40c, Mrs. Tolbert, children, emblem (vert.).

1979, Nov. 14 Litho. *Perf. 14*

No.	Type	Description	Unused	Used
858	A272	25c multi	50	50
859	A272	40c multi	80	80

SOS Children's Village in Monrovia, Liberia.

Rotary International Headquarters, Evanston, Ill., Emblem — A273

Rotary Emblem and: 5c, Vocational services. 17c, Man in wheelchair, nurse (vert.). 27c, Flags of several nations. 35c, People of various races holding hands around globe. 50c, Pres. Tolbert, map of Africa (vert.). $1, "Gift of Life."

1979, Dec. 28 *Perf. 11*

No.	Type	Description	Unused	Used
860	A273	1c multi	15	15
861	A273	5c multi	15	15
862	A273	17c multi	22	22
863	A273	27c multi	45	45
864	A273	35c multi	55	55
865	A273	50c multi	85	85
		Nos. 860-865 (6)	2.37	2.37

Souvenir Sheet

No.	Type	Description	Unused	Used
866	A273	$1 multi	1.65	1.65

Rotary International, 75th anniversary.

Ski Jump, Lake Placid '80 Emblem — A274

Lake Placid '80 Emblem and: 5c, Figure skating. 17c, Bobsledding. 27c, Cross-country skiing. 35c, Women's speed skating. 50c, Ice hockey. $1, Slalom.

1980, Jan. 21

No.	Type	Description	Unused	Used
867	A274	1c multi	15	15
868	A274	5c multi	15	15
869	A274	17c multi	35	35
870	A274	27c multi	70	70
871	A274	35c multi	70	70
872	A274	50c multi	1.00	1.00
		Nos. 867-872 (6)	3.05	3.05

Souvenir Sheet

No.	Type	Description	Unused	Used
873	A274	$1 multi	1.75	1.75

13th Winter Olympic Games, Lake Placid, NY, Feb. 12-24.

Pres. Tolbert, Pres. Stevens, Maps of Liberia and Sierra Leone, Mano River — A275

1980, Mar. 6 Litho. *Perf. 14x13½*

No.	Type	Description	Unused	Used
874	A275	8c multi	16	16
875	A275	27c multi	55	55
876	A275	35c multi	70	70
877	A275	80c multi	1.60	1.60

Mano River Agreement, 5th anniversary; Mano River Postal Union, 1st anniversary.

Sgt. Doe and Soldiers, Clenched Hands Angel — A276

1981 Litho. *Perf. 14*

No.	Type	Description	Unused	Used
878	A276	1c Redemption horn, vert.	15	15
879	A276	6c like 1c	15	15
880	A276	10c shown	15	15
881	A276	14c Citizens, map, Flag	20	20
882	A276	23c like 10c	32	32
883	A276	31c like 14c	45	45
884	A276	41c like $2	60	60
885	A276	$2 Sgt. Samuel Doe, vert.	3.00	3.00
		Nos. 878-885 (8)	5.02	5.02

Establishment of new government under the People's Redemption Council, Apr. 12, 1980.

Soccer Players, World Cup, Flags of 1930 and 1934 Finalists — A277

Soccer Players, Cup, Flags of Finalists from: 5c, 1938, 1950. 20c, 1954, 1958. 27c, 1962, 1966. 40c, 1970, 1974. 55c. 1978. $1, Spanish team.

1981, Mar. 4 Litho. *Perf. 14*

No.	Type	Description	Unused	Used
886	A277	3c multi	15	15
887	A277	5c multi	15	15
888	A277	20c multi	32	32
889	A277	27c multi	45	45
890	A277	40c multi	65	65
891	A277	55c multi	95	95
		Nos. 886-891 (6)	2.67	2.67

Souvenir Sheet

No.	Type	Description	Unused	Used
892	A277	$1 multi	1.65	1.65

ESPANA '82 World Cup Soccer Championship.

Sgt. Samuel Doe and Citizens — A278

1981, Apr. 7 Litho. *Perf. 14*

No.	Type	Description	Unused	Used
893	A278	22c shown	38	38
894	A278	27c Doe, Liberian flag	45	45
895	A278	30c Clasped arms	50	50
896	A278	$1 Doe, soldiers, Justice	1.65	1.65

People's Redemption Council government, first anniversary.

Royal Wedding — A279

1981, Aug. 12 Litho. *Perf. 14x13½*

No.	Type	Description	Unused	Used
897	A279	31c Couple	40	40
898	A279	41c Initials, roses	50	50
899	A279	62c St. Paul's Cathedral	1.00	1.00

Souvenir Sheet

No.	Type	Description	Unused	Used
900	A279	$1 Couple	1.50	1.50

John Adams, US President, 1797-1801 A280

Washington Crossing the Delaware A281

1981, July 4 *Perf. 11*

No.	Type	Description	Unused	Used
901	A280	4c shown	*15*	*15*
902	A280	5c William H. Harrison	*15*	*15*
903	A280	10c Martin Van Buren	*16*	*15*
904	A280	17c James Monroe	*30*	*24*
905	A280	20c John Q. Adams	*35*	*28*
906	A280	22c James Madison	*40*	*32*
907	A280	27c Thomas Jefferson	*45*	*38*
908	A280	30c Andrew Jackson	*50*	*40*
909	A280	40c John Tyler	*70*	*55*
910	A280	80c George Washington	*1.40*	*1.10*
		Nos. 901-910 (10)	*4.56*	*3.72*

Souvenir Sheet

No.	Type	Description	Unused	Used
911	A281	$1 multi	*1.65*	*1.65*

1981, Nov. 26 Litho. *Perf. 11*

No.	Type	Description	Unused	Used
912	A280	6c Rutherford B. Hayes	*15*	*15*
913	A280	12c Ulysses S. Grant	*22*	*18*
914	A280	14c Millard Fillmore	*22*	*18*
915	A280	15c Zachary Taylor	*25*	*20*
916	A280	20c Abraham Lincoln	*35*	*28*
917	A280	27c Andrew Johnson	*45*	*38*
918	A280	31c James Buchanan	*50*	*40*
919	A280	41c James A. Garfield	*75*	*60*
920	A280	50c James K. Polk	*90*	*70*
921	A280	55c Franklin Pierce	*1.00*	*75*
		Nos. 912-921 (10)	*4.79*	*3.82*

Souvenir Sheet

No.	Type	Description	Unused	Used
922	A281	$1 Washington at Valley Forge	*1.65*	*1.65*

1982, Apr. 7 Litho. *Perf. 11*

No.	Type	Description	Unused	Used
923	A280	4c William H. Taft	*15*	*15*
924	A280	5c Calvin Coolidge	*15*	*15*
925	A280	6c Benjamin Harrison	*15*	*15*
926	A280	10c Warren G. Harding	*16*	*15*
927	A280	22c Grover Cleveland	*40*	*32*
928	A280	27c Chester Arthur	*45*	*38*
929	A280	31c Woodrow Wilson	*50*	*40*
930	A280	41c William McKinley	*75*	*60*
931	A280	80c Theodore Roosevelt	*1.40*	*1.10*
		Nos. 923-931 (9)	*4.11*	*3.40*

Souvenir Sheet

No.	Type	Description	Unused	Used
932	A281	$1 Signing Constitution, horiz.	*1.65*	*1.65*

1982, July 15 Litho. *Perf. 11*

No.	Type	Description	Unused	Used
933	A280	4c Jimmy Carter	*15*	*15*
934	A280	6c Gerald Ford	*15*	*15*
935	A280	14c Harry Truman	*22*	*18*
936	A280	17c Franklin D. Roosevelt	*30*	*24*
937	A280	23c Lyndon B. Johnson	*40*	*32*
938	A280	27c Richard Nixon	*45*	*38*
939	A280	31c John F. Kennedy	*50*	*40*
940	A280	35c Ronald Reagan	*60*	*48*
941	A280	50c Herbert Hoover	*90*	*70*
942	A280	55c Dwight D. Eisenhower	*1.00*	*75*
		Nos. 933-942 (10)	*4.67*	*3.75*

Souvenir Sheet

Perf. 14x13½

No.	Type	Description	Unused	Used
943	A281	$1 Battle of Yorktown	*1.65*	*1.65*

See No. 1113.

Type of 1976

1981-83 Litho. *Perf. 14½x13½*

Size: 34x20mm

No.	Type	Description	Unused	Used
944	A247	1c like #749	15	15
945	A247	3c like #750	15	15
947	A247	6c like #753	15	15
948	A247	15c like #754	32	32
949	A247	25c like #757	52	52
950	A247	31c like #756	65	65
951	A247	41c like #758	85	85
952	A247	80c like #759	1.75	1.75
953	A247	$1 like #760	2.00	2.00
		Nos. 944-953 (9)	6.54	6.54

Issue dates: Nos. 945, 947, 949, 950, Nov. 27, 1981; Nos. 944, 953, Oct. 12, 1982; Nos. 948, 951, Dec. 10, 1982. No. 952, Nov. 3, 1983.

Intl. Year of the Disabled (1981) — A282

Designs: Various disabled people.

1982, Mar. 24 Litho. *Perf. 14*

No.	Type	Description	Unused	Used
954	A282	23c multi, vert.	38	38
955	A282	62c multi	1.00	1.00

30th Anniv. of West African Examinations Council — A283

1982, Mar. 24

No.	Type	Description	Unused	Used
956	A283	6c multi	15	15
957	A283	31c multi	50	50

21st Birthday of Princess Diana — A284

Designs: 31c, 41c, 62c, Diana portraits. $1, Wedding.

1982, July 1 *Perf. 14x13½*

No.	Type	Description	Unused	Used
958	A284	31c multi	50	50
959	A284	41c multi	65	65

960 A284 62c multi 1.00 1.00

Souvenir Sheet

961 A284 $1 multi 1.65 1.65

Nos. 958-961 Overprinted in Silver: "ROYAL BABY / 21-6-82 / PRINCE WILLIAM"

1982, Aug. 30 Litho. *Perf. 14x13½*

962 A284 31c multi 50 50
963 A284 41c multi 65 65
964 A284 62c multi 1.00 1.00

Souvenir Sheet

965 A284 $1 multi 1.65 1.65

Birth of Prince William of Wales, June 21.

3rd Natl. Redemption Day — A285

1983, Apr. 5 Litho. *Perf. 13½*

966 A285 3c Fallah Varney 15 15
967 A285 6c Samuel Doe 15 15
968 A285 10c Jlatoh N. Podier, Jr. 16 16
969 A285 15c Jeffry S. Gbatu 25 25
970 A285 31c Thomas G. Quiwonkpa 50 50
971 A285 41c Abraham D. Kollie 65 65
Nos. 966-971 (6) 1.86 1.86

Souvenir Sheet

972 A285 $1 like 6c 1.90 1.90

Natl. Archives Opening — A286

Building views.

1983, Apr. 5

973 A286 6c multi 15 15
974 A286 31c multi 50 50

Christmas 1983 — A287

Raphael Paintings: 6c, Circumcision of Christ. 15c, Adoration of the Magi. 25c, Announcement to Mary. 31c, Madonna with Baldachin. 41c, Holy Family. 62c, Detail of Madonna with Child Surrounded by Five Saints. $1.25 Madonna of Foligno.

1983, Dec. 14 Litho. *Perf. 13½*

975 A287 6c multi 15 15
976 A287 15c multi 25 25
977 A287 25c multi 40 40
978 A287 31c multi 50 50
979 A287 41c multi 65 65
980 A287 62c multi 1.00 1.00
Nos. 975-980 (6) 2.95 2.95

Souvenir Sheet

981 A287 $1.25 multi 2.00 2.00

Mano River Union, 10th Anniv. (1983) — A288

1984, Apr. 6 Litho. *Perf. 14x13½*

982 A288 6c Training school graduates 15 15
983 A288 25c Emblem 42 42
984 A288 31c Maps, leaders 50 50
985 A288 41c Guinea's accession 65 65

Souvenir Sheet

986 A288 75c Guinea's accession, diff. 1.25 1.25

4th Natl. Redemption Day — A289

1984, Apr. 12 *Perf. 14½*

987 A289 3c Hospital, New Kru Town 15 15
988 A289 10c Ganta-Harper Highway construction 16 16
989 A289 20c Constitution Assembly opening 32 32
990 A289 31c Doe at highway construction 50 50
991 A289 41c Draft Constitution presentation 65 65
Nos. 987-991 (5) 1.78 1.78

Adoration of the Wise Men, by Rubens (1577-1640) A290

1984, June 1 Litho. *Perf. 13½*

992 A290 6c shown 15 15
993 A290 15c Crowning of Katharina 25 25
994 A290 25c Mother and Child Adored by Wise Men 40 40
995 A290 31c Madonna and Child with Halo 50 50
996 A290 41c Adoration of the Shepherds 65 65
997 A290 62c Madonna and Child with Saints 1.00 1.00
Nos. 992-997 (6) 2.95 2.95

Souvenir Sheet

998 A290 $1.25 Madonna Adored by Saints 2.00 2.00

1984 Summer Olympics A291

1984, July 2 *Perf. 13½x14*

999 A291 3c Jesse Owens, 1936 15 15
1000 A291 4c Rafer Johnson, 1960 15 15
1001 A291 25c Miruts Yifter, 1980 50 50
1002 A291 41c Kipchoge Keino, 1968, 1972 80 80
1003 A291 62c Muhammad Ali, 1960 1.25 1.25
Nos. 999-1003 (5) 2.85 2.85

Souvenir Sheet

Perf. 14x13½

1004 A291 $1.25 Wilma Rudolph, 1960, horiz. 2.50 2.50

1984 Louisiana Expo — A292

1984, July 24 *Perf. 14½*

1005 A292 6c Water birds 15 15
1006 A292 31c Ship, Buchanan Harbor 55 55
1007 A292 41c Fish 70 70
1008 A292 62c Train carrying iron ore 1.10 1.10

Pygmy Hippopotamus, World Wildlife Fund Emblem — A293

Various pygmy hippopotomi.

1984, Nov. 22 Litho. *Perf. 14½*

1009 A293 6c multi 15 15
1010 A293 10c multi 24 24
1011 A293 20c multi 48 48
1012 A293 31c multi 75 75

Indigent Children Home, Bensonville — A294

First Lady Mrs. Nancy Doe and various children.

1984, Dec. 14

1013 A294 6c multi 15 15
1014 A294 31c multi 50 50

Natl. Redemption Day, Apr. 12 — A295

1985, Apr. 5 Litho. *Perf. 14½*

1015 A295 6c Army barracks, Monrovia 15 15
1016 A295 31c Pan-African Plaza, Monrovia 50 50

Liberian Revolution, fifth anniv.

Audubon Birth Bicentenary — A296

Illustrations by artist/naturalist J. J. Audubon.

1985, Apr. 5

1017 A296 1c Bohemian waxwing 15 15
1018 A296 3c Bay-breasted warbler 15 15
1019 A296 6c White-winged crossbill 15 15
1020 A296 31c Red phalarope 62 62
1021 A296 41c Eastern bluebird 80 80
1022 A296 62c Northern cardinal 1.25 1.25
Nos. 1017-1022 (6) 3.12 3.12

Venus and Mirror A297

Paintings (details) by Rubens: 15c, Adam & Eve in Paradise. 25c, Andromeda. 31c, The Three Graces. 41c, Venus & Adonis. 62c, The Daughters of Leucippus. $1.25, The Judgement of Paris.

1985, Nov. 14 Litho. *Perf. 14*

1023 A297 6c multi 15 15
1024 A297 15c multi 25 25
1025 A297 25c multi 40 40
1026 A297 31c multi 50 50
1027 A297 41c multi 60 60
1028 A297 62c multi 1.00 1.00
Nos. 1023-1028 (6) 2.90 2.90

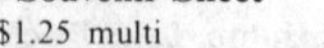

Souvenir Sheet

1029 A297 $1.25 multi 2.00 2.00

1986 World Cup Soccer Championships, Mexico — A298

1985, Nov. 14

1030 A298 6c Germany-Morocco, 1970 15 15
1031 A298 15c Zaire-Brazil, 1974 25 25
1032 A298 25c Tunisia-Germany, 1978 40 40
1033 A298 31c Cameroun-Peru, 1982, vert. 50 50
1034 A298 41c Algeria-Germany, 1982 60 60
1035 A298 62c 1986 Senegal team 1.00 1.00
Nos. 1030-1035 (6) 2.90 2.90

Souvenir Sheet

1036 A298 $1.25 Liberia-Nigeria 2.00 2.00

Queen Mother, 85th Birthday — A299

World Food Day — A300

1985, Dec. 12 Litho. *Perf. 14½*

1037 A299 31c Elizabeth in garter robes 28 28
1038 A299 41c At the races 75 75
1039 A299 62c In garden, waving 1.10 1.10

Souvenir Sheet

1040 A299 $1.25 Wearing diadem 2.00 2.00

1985, Dec. 12

1041 A300 25c multi 40 40
1042 A300 31c multi 50 50

AMERIPEX '86 — A301

Statue of Liberty, Cent. — A302

1986, June 10 Litho. *Perf. 14½*

1043 A301 25c The Alamo 50 50
1044 A301 31c Liberty Bell 62 62
1045 A301 80c Nos. 344, 802, C102 1.60 1.60

1986, June 10

1046 A302 20c Unveiling, 1886 40 40
1047 A302 31c Frederic A. Bartholdi 62 62
1048 A302 $1 Statue close-up 2.00 2.00

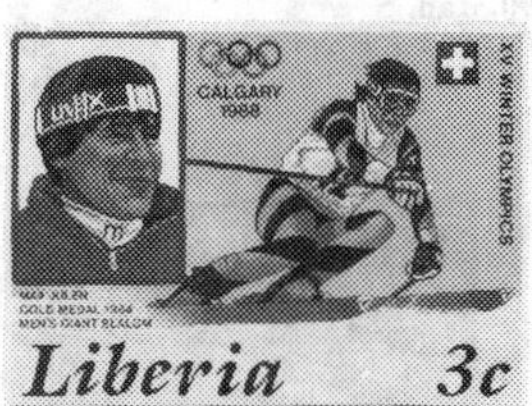

1988 Winter Olympics, Calgary — A303

1984 Gold medalists: 3c, Max Julen, Switzerland, men's giant slalom. 6c, Debbie Armstrong, US, women's giant slalom. 31c, Peter Angerer, West Germany, biathlon. 60c, Bill Johnson, US, men's downhill. 80c, East Germany, 4-man bobsled. $1.25, H. Stangassinger, F. Wembacher, West Germany, 2-man luge.

1987, Aug. 21 Litho. *Perf. 14*

1049 A303 3c multi 15 15
1050 A303 6c multi 15 15
1051 A303 31c multi 62 62
1052 A303 60c multi 1.20 1.20
1053 A303 80c multi 1.60 1.60
Nos. 1049-1053 (5) 3.72 3.72

Souvenir Sheet

1054 A303 $1.25 multi 2.50 2.50

City of Berlin, 750th Anniv. — A304

Designs: 6c, State (Royal) Theater in the Gendarmenmarkt, c. 1820, architect Schinkel. 31c, Kaiser Friedrich Museum, Museum Is. on River Spree. 60c, Charlottenburg Castle, 17th cent. 80c, Modern church bell tower and Kaiser Wilhelm Gedachteinskirche. $1.50, MIRAK rocket development, Spaceship Society Airfield, Reinickendorf, 1930.

1987, Sept. 4

1055 A304 6c multi 15 15
1056 A304 31c multi 62 62
1057 A304 60c multi 1.20 1.20
1058 A304 80c multi 1.60 1.60

Souvenir sheet

Perf. 11½

1059 A304 $1.50 buff & dk brn 3.00 3.00

No. 1059 contains one 25x61mm stamp.

Shakespearean Plays — A305

1987, Nov. 6 Litho. *Perf. 14*

1060 Sheet of 8 8.10 8.10
a. A305 3c Othello 15 15
b. A305 6c Romeo & Juliet 15 15
c. A305 10c The Merry Wives of Windsor 20 20
d. A305 15c Henry IV 30 30
e. A305 31c Hamlet 62 62
f. A305 60c Macbeth 1.20 1.20
g. A305 80c King Lear 1.60 1.60
h. A305 $2 Shakespeare and the Globe Theater, 1598 4.00 4.00

Amateur Radio Association, 25th Anniv. — A306

1987, Nov. 23 Litho. *Perf. 14*

1061 A306 10c Emblem 25 25
1062 A306 10c Village 25 25
1063 A306 35c On-the-Air certificate 85 85
1064 A306 35c Globe, flags 85 85

Miniature Sheets

Statue of Liberty, Cent. (in 1986) A307

No. 1065a, Torch, southern view of NYC. b, Overhead view of crown and scaffold. c, 4 workmen repairing crown. d, 5 workmen, crown. e, Statue's right foot.

No. 1066a, Tall ship, statue. b, Bay Queen ferry. c, Statue on poster at a construction site, NYC. d, Tug boat, tall ship. e, Building frieze.

No. 1067a, Statue flanked by fireworks. b, Lighting of the statue. c, Crown observatory illuminated. d, Statue surrounded by fireworks. e, Crown and torch observatories illuminated.

No. 1068a, Liberty "Happy Birthday" poster at a construction site. b, Ships in NY Harbor. c, Woman renovating statue nose. d, Man and woman renovating nose. e, Man, nose. Nos. 1068a-1068e vert.

1987, Dec. 10 *Perf. 13½*

1065 Sheet of 5 + label 60
a.-e. A307 6c any single 15 15
1066 Sheet of 5 + label 1.50
a.-e. A307 15c any single 30 30
1067 Sheet of 5 + label 3.10
a.-e. A307 31c any single 62 62
1068 Sheet of 5 + label 6.00
a.-e. A307 60c any single 1.20 1.20

Nos. 1065-1068 contain label inscribed "CENTENARY OF THE STATUE OF LIBERTY" in two or five lines.

Second Republic, 2nd Anniv. A308

Design: Natl. flag, coat of arms, hand grip, Pres. Doe and Vice Pres. Moniba.

1988, Jan. 6 *Perf. 14½*

1069 A308 10c multi 20 20
1070 A308 35c multi 70 70

U.N. Child Survival Campaign A309

Perf. 13x13½, 13½x13

1988, Jan. 15

1071 A309 3c Breast-feeding 15 15
1072 A309 6c Oral rehydration therapy, vert. 15 15
1073 A309 31c Immunization 62 62
1074 A309 $1 Growth monitoring, vert. 2.00 2.00

Inauguration of the Second Republic — A310

Design: Pres. Doe greeting Chief Justice Emmanuel N. Gbalazeh.

1988, Jan. 15 *Perf. 13x13½*

1075 A310 6c multi 15 15

Samuel Kanyon Doe Sports Complex, Opened Apr. 12, 1986 A311

1988, Jan. 15

1076 A311 31c multi 62 62

Green (Agricultural) Revolution — A312

1988, Apr. 4 *Perf. 15*

1077 A312 10c multi 20 20
1078 A312 35c multi 70 70

US Peace Corps in Liberia, 25th Anniv. A313

1988, Apr. 4

1079 A313 10c multi 20 20
1080 A313 35c multi 70 70

Souvenir Sheet

1988 Summer Olympics, Seoul — A314

1988, Apr. 14 *Perf. 14*

1081 A314 $3 multi 6.00 6.00

Organization of African Unity, 25th Anniv. — A315

1988, May 25

1082 A315 10c multi 20 20
1083 A315 35c multi 70 70
1084 A315 $1 multi 2.00 2.00

Rail Transport A316

1988, July 30 Litho. *Perf. 14½*

1085 A316 10c GP10 at Nimba 20 20
1086 A316 35c Triple-headed iron ore train 70 70

Souvenir Sheets

Perf. 11

1087 A316 $2 King Edward II, 1930 3.50 3.50
1088 A316 $2 GWR 57 No. 3697, 1941 3.50 3.50
1089 A316 $2 GWR 0-4-2T No. 1408, 1932 3.50 3.50
1090 A316 $2 GWR No. 7034 Ince Castle, 1950 3.50 3.50

Nos. 1087-1090 contain one stamp each, size: 64x44mm.

1988 Summer Olympics, Seoul — A317

1988, Sept. 13 **Litho.**

1091 A317 10c Baseball 20 20
1092 A317 35c Hurdles 70 70
1093 A317 45c Fencing 90 90
1094 A317 80c Synchronized swimming 1.60 1.60
1095 A317 $1 Yachting 2.00 2.00
Nos. 1091-1095 (5) 5.40 5.40

Souvenir Sheet

1096 A317 $1.50 Tennis 3.00 3.00

Intl. Tennis Federation, 75th anniv. ($1.50).

St. Joseph's Catholic Hospital, 25th Anniv. A318

1988, Aug. 26 **Litho.** ***Perf. 14½***

1097 A318 10c shown 20 20
1098 A318 10c Hospital, 4 staff members 20 20
1099 A318 35c St. John of God 70 70
1100 A318 $1 Doctor, nurse, map 2.00 2.00

Lloyds of London, 300th Anniv.
Common Design Type

CD341

Designs: 10c, Royal Exchange destroyed by fire, 1838, vert. 35c, Air Liberia BN2A aircraft. 45c, Supertanker *Chevron Antwerp.* $1, *Lakonia* on fire off Madeira, 1963, vert.

1988, Oct. 31 **Litho.** ***Perf. 14***

1101 CD341 10c multi 20 20
1102 CD341 35c multi 70 70
1103 CD341 45c multi 90 90
1104 CD341 $1 multi 2.00 2.00

Sasa Players A319

Perf. 14x14½, 14½x14
1988, Sept. 30 **Litho.**

1105 A319 10c Monkey bridge, vert. 20 20
1106 A319 35c shown 70 70
1107 A319 45c Snake dancers, vert. 90 90

Intl. Fund for Agricultural Development, 10th Anniv. — A320

1988, Oct. 7 **Litho.** ***Perf. 14x14½***

1108 A320 10c Crops 20 20
1109 A320 35c Spraying crops, livestock 70 70

3rd Anniv. of the 2nd Republic — A321

1989, Jan. 6 **Litho.** ***Perf. 14***

1110 A321 10c Pres. Doe, officials 20 20
1111 A321 35c like 10c 70 70
1112 A321 50c Pres. Doe, doctor 1.00 1.00

US Presidents Type of 1981-82

1989, Jan. 20 ***Perf. 13½x14***

1113 A280 $1 George Bush 2.00 2.00

Rissho Kosei-Kai Buddhist Assoc., Tokyo, 50th Anniv. — A322

Natl. flags and: No. 1114, "Harmony" in Japanese. No. 1115, Organization headquarters, Tokyo. No. 1116, Nikkyo Niwano, founder. 50c, Statue of Buddha in the Great Sacred Hall.

1989, Feb. 28 **Litho.** ***Perf. 14x14½***

1114 A322 10c multi 25 25
1115 A322 10c multi 25 25
1116 A322 10c multi 25 25
1117 A322 50c multi 1.25 1.25

Liberian-Japanese friendship.

Souvenir Sheet

Emperor Hirohito of Japan (1901-1989) — A323

Commemorative coins: a, Silver. b, Gold.

1989, Feb. 28 **Unwmk.** ***Perf. 14½***

1118 A323 Sheet of 2 3.00 3.00
a.-b. 75c any single 1.50 1.50

For overprint see No. 1147.

Mano River Union, 15th Anniv. A324

Natl. flag, crest and: 10c, Union Glass Factory, Gardnersville, Monrovia. 35c, Pres. Doe, Momoh of Sierra Leone and Conte of Guinea. 45c, Monrovia-Freetown Highway. 50c, Sierra Leone-Guinea land postal services. $1, Communique, 1988 summit.

Unwmk.
1989, May 8 **Litho.** ***Perf. 14***

1119 A324 10c multi 20 20
1120 A324 35c multi 70 70
1121 A324 45c multi 90 90
1122 A324 50c multi 1.00 1.00
1123 A324 $1 multi 2.00 2.00
Nos. 1119-1123 (5) 4.80 4.80

World Telecommunications Day — A325

1989, May 17 **Litho.** ***Perf. 12½***

1124 A325 50c multi 1.00 1.00

Moon Landing, 20th Anniv.
Common Design Type

CD342

Apollo 11: 10c, Recovery ship USS *Okinawa.* 35c, Buzz Aldrin, Neil Armstrong and Michael Collins. 45c, Mission emblem. $1, Aldrin steps on the Moon. $2, Aldrin preparing to conduct experiments on the Moon's surface.

Perf. 14x13½, 14 (35c, 45c)
1989, July 20 **Litho.** **Wmk. 384**
Size of Nos. 1126-1127: 29x29mm

1125 CD342 10c multi 20 20
1126 CD342 35c multi 70 70
1127 CD342 45c multi 90 90
1128 CD342 $1 multi 2.00 2.00

Souvenir Sheet

1129 CD342 $2 multi 4.00 4.00

Souvenir Sheet

The Women's March on Versailles — A326

1989, July 7 **Wmk. 384** ***Perf. 14***

1130 A326 $1.50 multi 3.00 3.00

French revolution, bicent., PHILEXFRANCE '89.

Souvenir Sheet

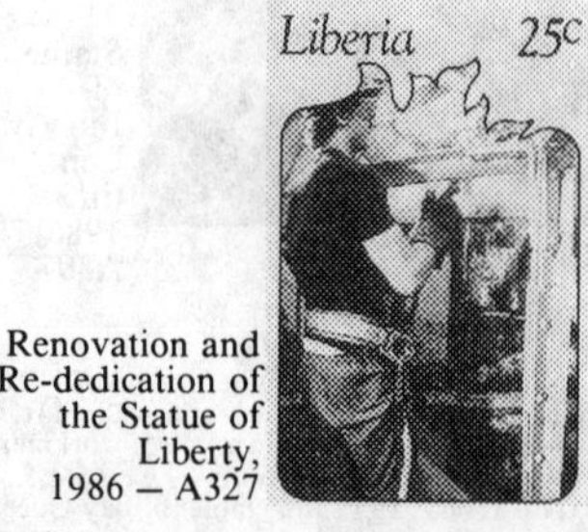

Renovation and Re-dedication of the Statue of Liberty, 1986 — A327

Photographs: a, Workman. b, French dignitary, US flag. c, Dignitaries at ceremony, statue.

Perf. 14x13½
1989, Oct. 2 **Litho.** **Wmk. 373**

1131 Sheet of 3 1.50 1.50
a.-c. A327 25c any single 50 50

World Stamp Expo '89 and PHILEXFRANCE '89.

Souvenir Sheet

World Stamp Expo '89, Washington, DC — A328

1989, Nov. 17 **Unwmk.** ***Perf. 14½***

1132 A328 $2 black 4.00 4.00

Jawaharlal Nehru, 1st Prime Minister of Independent India — A329

1989, Dec. 22 **Unwmk.** ***Perf. 14***

1133 A329 45c Nehru, signature, flag 90 90
1134 A329 50c Nehru, signature 1.00 1.00

New Standard-A Earth Satellite Station — A330

1990, Jan. 5

1135 A330 10c shown 20 20
1136 A330 35c multi, diff. 70 70

US Educational & Cultural Foundation in Liberia, 25th Anniv. (in 1989) — A331

1990, Jan. 5

1137 A331 10c multicolored 20 20
1138 A331 45c multicolored 90 90

Pan-African Postal Union, 10th Anniv. — A332

1990, Jan. 18 ***Perf. 13x12½***

1139 A332 35c multicolored 70 70

Flags of Liberian Counties — A333

Designs: a, Bomi. b, Bong. c, Grand Bassa. d, Grand Cape Mount. e, Grand Gedeh. f, Grand Kru. g, Lofa. h, Margibi. i, Maryland. j, Montserrado. k, Nimba. l, Rivercess. m, Sinoe.

Perf. 14x13½

1990, Mar. 2 **Litho.** **Unwmk.**

1140	Strip of 13	2.60	2.60
a.-m.	A333 10c any single	20	20
1141	Strip of 13	9.10	9.10
a.-m.	A333 35c any single	70	70
1142	Strip of 13	11.70	11.70
a.-m.	A333 45c any single	90	90
1143	Strip of 13	13.00	13.00
a.-m.	A333 50c any single	1.00	1.00
1144	Strip of 13	26.00	26.00
a.-m.	A333 $1 any single	2.00	2.00
	Nos. 1140-1144 (5)	62.40	62.40

Queen Mother, 90th Birthday

Common Design Types

At Age 6 — CD343

At Age 22 — CD344

Perf. 14x15

1991, Oct. 28 **Wmk. 384**

1145	CD343	10c multicolored	20	20

Perf. 14½

1146	CD344	$2 brn & blk	4.00	4.00

Souvenir Sheet

No. 1118 Overprinted

Perf. 14½

1991, Nov. 16 **Litho.** **Unwmk.**

1147	A323 Sheet of 2	3.00	3.00
a.-b.	75c any single	1.50	1.50

National Unity — A334

Designs: 35c, Hands clasp over map of Liberia. 45c, Liberian flag, hands, African map. 50c, All Liberia conference, March 1991, conferees, flag, map.

1991, Dec. 30 ***Perf. 13½***

1148	A334	35c multicolored	70	70
1149	A334	45c multicolored	90	90
1150	A334	50c multicolored	1.00	1.00

SEMI-POSTAL STAMPS

No. 127 Surcharged in Red

+ 2c

1915 **Unwmk.** ***Perf. 14***

B1	A49	2c + 3c on 10c plum & blk	75	2.50
a.		Double red surcharge		
b.		Double blue surcharge		
c.		Both surcharges double		
d.		Pair, one without "2c"		

Same Surcharge On Official Stamp of 1912

B2	A49	2c + 3c on 10c blk & ultra	75	2.50
a.		Double surcharge		

Regular Issue of 1918 Surcharged in Black and Red

1918 ***Perf. 12½, 14***

B3	A59	1c + 2c dp grn & blk	35	35
B4	A60	2c + 2c rose & blk	35	35
a.		Double surch., one inverted		
b.		Invtd. surch., cross double		
c.		Invtd. surch., cross omitted	15.00	
B5	A61	5c + 2c gray bl & blk	15	15
a.		Imperf., pair	8.00	
B6	A62	10c + 2c dk grn	15	15
a.		Inverted surcharge	5.00	5.00
B7	A63	15c + 2c blk & dk grn	15	15
B8	A64	20c + 2c cl & blk	28	28
B9	A65	25c + 2c dk grn & grn	50	50
B10	A66	30c + 2c red vio & blk	35	35
B11	A67	50c + 2c ultra & blk	50	50
B12	A68	75c + 2c ol bis & blk	1.00	1.00
B13	A69	$1 + 2c yel brn & bl	1.65	1.65
B14	A70	$2 + 2c lt vio & blk	2.00	2.00
B15	A71	$5 + 2c dk brn	8.25	8.25
		Nos. B3-B15 (13)	15.68	15.68

Nos. 277-279 Surcharged in Red or Blue

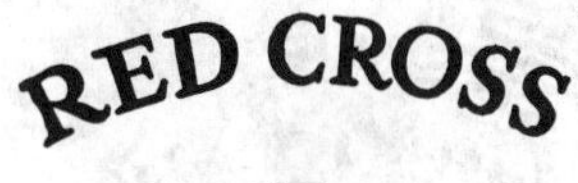

1941 **Unwmk.** ***Perf. 12***

B16	A107	3c + 2c dk bl (R)	1.10	1.25
B17	A108	5c + 2c dl red brn	1.10	1.25
B18	A109	10c + 2c dk grn (R)	1.10	1.25

Catalogue values for unused stamps in this section, from this point to the end of the section, are for Never Hinged items.

Research SP1

Lithographed and Engraved

1954 **Unwmk.** ***Perf. 12½***

B19	SP1	5c + 5c rose lil & blk	15	15

The surtax was for the Liberian Government Hospital. No. B19 exists imperforate.

AIR POST STAMPS

Regular Issue of 1928 Surcharged in Black "AIR MAIL" and New Values

1936, Feb. 28 **Unwmk.** ***Perf. 12***

C1	A102	6c on 2c vio	150.00	90.00
C2	A102	6c on 3c bis brn	150.00	90.00

Same Surcharge on Official Stamp of 1928

C3	A102	6c on 1c grn	150.00	90.00
m.		On No. 230 (error)	*600.00*	

Many counterfeits exist.

Waco Plane AP1

1936, Sept. 30 **Engr.** ***Perf. 14***

C3A	AP1	1c yel grn & blk	15	15
C3B	AP1	2c car & blk	15	15
C3C	AP1	3c pur & blk	15	15
C3D	AP1	4c org & blk	15	15
C3E	AP1	5c bl & blk	15	15
C3F	AP1	6c grn & blk	15	15
		Set value	74	36

Liberia's 1st air mail service of Feb. 28, 1936.

Nos. C3A-C3F exist in pairs imperf. between (value, $50 each) and in pairs imperf. (value $15 each).

Eagle in Flight — AP2

Sikorsky Amphibian — AP5

Trimotor Plane AP3

Egrets — AP4

Designs: 3c, 30c, Albatross.

1938, Sept. 12 **Photo.** ***Perf. 12½***

C4	AP2	1c green	15	15
C5	AP3	2c red org	15	15
C6	AP3	3c ol grn	15	15
C7	AP4	4c orange	15	15
C8	AP4	5c brt bl grn	16	15
C9	AP3	10c violet	16	15
C10	AP5	20c magenta	22	15
C11	AP3	30c gray blk	32	15
C12	AP2	50c brown	45	15
C13	AP5	$1 blue	85	15
		Nos. C4-C13 (10)	2.76	
		Set value		75

For surcharges see Nos. C17-C36, C45-C46, C46-C48, C50.

Nos. 280-282 Overprinted in Red or Dark Blue

1941, Feb. 25 ***Perf. 12***

C14	A107	3c dk bl (R)	1.10	1.10
C15	A108	5c dl red brn (DB)	1.10	1.10
C16	A109	10c dk grn (R)	1.10	1.10

Nos. C4-C13 Surcharged in Black

First Flight
LIBERIA · U.S.
1941

—— 50c

1941 ***Perf. 12½***

C17	AP2	50c on 1c grn	*1,650.*	190.00
C18	AP3	50c on 2c red org	110.00	70.00
C19	AP3	50c on 3c ol grn	110.00	70.00
C20	AP4	50c on 4c org	42.50	27.50
C21	AP4	50c on 5c brt bl grn	42.50	27.50
C22	AP3	50c on 10c vio	42.50	27.50
C23	AP5	50c on 20c mag	*1,350.*	45.00
C24	AP3	50c on 30c gray blk	37.50	21.00
C25	AP2	50c brown	37.50	21.00
C26	AP5	$1 blue	42.50	21.00

Nos. C17 to C26 with Additional Overprint of Two Bars, Obliterating "1941"

1942

C27	AP2	50c on 1c grn	4.74	4.75
C28	AP3	50c on 2c red org	4.75	4.00
C29	AP3	50c on 3c ol grn	4.25	4.00
C30	AP4	50c on 4c org	3.50	4.25
C31	AP4	50c on 5c brt bl grn	2.00	2.00
C32	AP3	50c on 10c vio	3.00	3.00
C33	AP5	50c on 20c mag	3.00	3.00
C34	AP3	50c on 30c gray blk	3.50	3.50
C35	AP2	50c brown	3.50	3.50
C36	AP5	$1 blue	3.00	3.00
		Nos. C27-C36 (10)	35.24	35.00

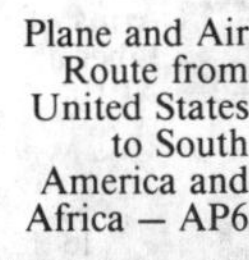

Plane and Air Route from United States to South America and Africa — AP6

Plane over House AP7

1942-44 **Engr.** ***Perf. 12***

C37	AP6	10c rose	15	15
C38	AP7	12c brt ultra ('44)	15	15
C39	AP7	24c turq grn ('44)	15	15
C40	AP6	30c brt grn	15	15
C41	AP6	35c red lil ('44)	15	15
C42	AP6	50c violet	15	15
C43	AP6	70c ol gray ('44)	25	15
C44	AP6	$1.40 scar ('44)	65	30
		Nos. C37-C44 (8)	1.80	
		Set value		86

No. C3A-C3C, C5-C8, C12 Surcharged with New Values and Large Dot, Bar or Diagonal Line in Violet, Blue, Black or Violet and Black

1944-45 ***Perf. 12½***

C45	AP3	10c on 2c (V+Bk)	22.50	17.50
C46	AP4	10c on 5c (V+Bk) ('45)	8.00	8.00
C46A	AP1	30c on 1c (Bk)	85.00	42.50
C47	AP3	30c on 3c (V)	95.00	42.50
C48	AP4	30c on 4c (V+Bk)	8.00	8.00
C48A	AP1	50c on 3c (Bk)	19.00	19.00
C48B	AP1	70c on 2c (Bk)	37.50	37.50
C49	AP3	$1 on 3c (Bl)	15.00	15.00
C50	AP2	$1 on 50c (V)	22.50	17.50
		Nos. C45-C50 (9)	312.50	207.50

These surcharges were handstamped with the possible exception of the large "10 CTS." of No. C46 and the "30 CTS." of No. C48. On No. C47, the new value was created by handstamping a small, violet, broken "O" beside the large "3" of the basic stamp.

Surcharges on Nos. C46A, C48A, C48B are found inverted. Values same as normal.

Franklin D. Roosevelt Reviewing Troops — AP8

1945, Nov. 26 **Engr.**

C51	AP8	70c brn & blk, *grysh*	1.10	1.25

In memory of Pres. Franklin D. Roosevelt (1882-1945).

Copies on thick white paper appeared later on the stamp market at reduced prices.

Opening Monrovia Harbor Project AP9

1947, Jan. 2

C52 AP9 24c brt bluish grn 1.10 1.20

Issued to commemorate the opening of the Monrovia Harbor Project, February 16, 1946.

Without Inscription at Top

1947, May 16

C53 AP9 25c dk car 35 40

1st US Postage Stamps and Arms of Liberia AP10

1947, June 6

C54 AP10 12c green 15 15

C55 AP10 25c brt red vio 15 15

C56 AP10 50c brt bl 15 15

a. Souv. sheet of 4, #300, C54-C56 35.00

Set value 32 32

Cent. of US postage stamps and 87th anniv. of Liberian stamps.

No. C56a exists imperf., same value.

Matilda Newport Firing Cannon AP11

1947, Dec. 1 **Engr. & Photo.**

C57 AP11 25c scar & gray blk 1.10 28

See note after No. 304.

Monument to Joseph J. Roberts AP12

Centenary Monument AP14

Design: 25c, Flag of Liberia.

1947, Dec. 22 **Engr.**

C58 AP12 12c brick red 16 15

C59 AP12 25c carmine 26 15

C60 AP14 50c red brn 55 42

Centenary of independence.

L. I. A. Plane in Flight AP15

1948, Aug. 17 ***Perf. 11½***

C61 AP15 25c red 90 60

C62 AP15 50c deep blue 45 60

1st flight of Liberian Intl. Airways, Aug. 17, 1948.

Map and Citizens AP16

Farm Couple, Arms and Agricultural Products — AP17

1949, Apr. 12 **Litho.** ***Perf. 11½***

C63 AP16 25c multi 32 60

C64 AP17 50c multi 32 60

Nos. C63-C64 exist perf. 12½. Definite information concerning the status of the perf. 12½ set has not reached the editors. The set also exists imperf.

Type of Regular Issue of 1948-50

Design: William V. S. Tubman.

1949, July 21 **Engr.** ***Perf. 12½***

C65 A128 25c blue & black 55 60

See No. C118.

Sun and Open Book — AP18

UPU Monument — AP19

1950, Feb. 14 **Engr.** ***Perf. 12½***

C66 AP18 25c rose car 1.00 50

a. Souv. sheet of 2, #329, C66, imperf. 1.65 1.65

Campaign for National Literacy.

Catalogue values for unused stamps in this section, from this point to the end of the section, are for Never Hinged items.

1950, Apr. 21

C67 AP19 25c org & vio 1.75 1.75

a. Souv. sheet of 3, #330-331, C67, imperf. 4.50 4.50

UPU, 75th anniv. (in 1949).

No. C67 exists imperf.

Map of Monrovia, James Monroe and Ashmun AP20

Design: 50c, Jehudi Ashmun, President Tubman and map.

1952, Apr. 1 ***Perf. 10½***

C68 AP20 25c lil rose & blk 20 20

C69 AP20 50c dk bl & car 40 40

a. Souvenir sheet of 8 12.00

Nos. C68-C69 exist imperf. Value about two and one half times that of the perf. set.

Nos. C68-C69 exist with center inverted. Value $50 each.

No. C69a contains one each of Nos. 332 and C68, and types of Nos. 333-337 and C69 with centers in black; imperf.

The 25c exists in colors of the 50c and vice versa. Value, each $3.50.

Flags of Five Nations AP21

1952, Dec. 10 ***Perf. 12½***

C70 AP21 25c ultra & car 40 32

a. Souvenir sheet 1.65 1.65

Nos. C70 and C70a exist imperforate.

Road Building AP22

Designs: 25c, Ships in Monrovia harbor. 35c, Diesel locomotive. 50c, Free port, Monrovia. 70c, Roberts Field. $1, Wm. V. S. Tubman bridge.

1953, Aug. 3 **Litho.**

C71 AP22 12c org brn 15 15

C72 AP22 25c lil rose 25 15

C73 AP22 35c purple 35 15

C74 AP22 50c orange 40 18

C75 AP22 70c dl grn 68 20

C76 AP22 $1 blue 90 30

Nos. C71-C76 (6) 2.73 1.13

See Nos. C82-C87.

Flags, Emblem and Children — AP23

1954, Sept. 27

Size: 51x39mm

C77 AP23 $5 bl, red, vio bl & blk 15.00 17.50

A reproduction of No. C77, size 63x49mm, was prepared for presentation purposes. Value $15.

Half the proceeds from the sale of No. C77 was given to the UNICEF.

UN Technical Assistance Agencies AP24

Designs: 15c, Printing instruction. 20c, Sawmill maintenance. 25c, Geography class.

1954, Oct. 25

C78 AP24 12c blk & bl 15 15

C79 AP24 15c dk brn & yel 18 15

C80 AP24 20c blk & yel grn 25 15

C81 AP24 25c vio bl & red 32 20

Set value 50

UN Technical Assistance program.

Type of 1953 Inscribed: "Commemorating Presidential Visit U. S. A.-1954"

Designs as before.

1954, Nov. 19

C82 AP22 12c vermilion 15 15

C83 AP22 25c blue 20 15

C84 AP22 35c car rose 28 15

C85 AP22 50c rose vio 40 15

C86 AP22 70c org brn 55 26

C87 AP22 $1 dl grn 80 32

Nos. C82-C87 (6) 2.38

Set value 98

Visit of Pres. William V.S. Tubman to the US. Exist imperforate.

Baseball AP25

Designs: 12c, Swimming. 25c, Running.

1955, Jan. 26 **Litho.** ***Perf. 12½***

C88 AP25 10c ultra & pink 15 15

C89 AP25 12c choc & bl 15 15

C90 AP25 25c cer & lt grn 15 15

a. Souvenir sheet 12.00 12.00

Set value 28 28

No. C90a contains one each of Nos. 349 and C90 with colors transposed. Exists imperf.; same value.

Costus AP26

Design: 25c, Barteria nigritiana.

1955, Sept. 28 **Unwmk.** ***Perf. 12½***

C91 AP26 20c vio, grn & yel 15 15

C92 AP26 25c grn, red & yel 16 16

Set value 25 25

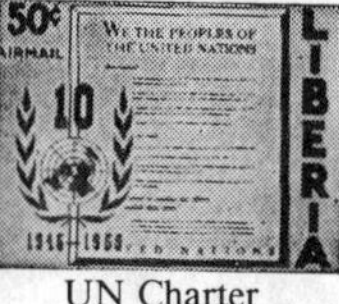

UN Emblem AP27

UN Charter AP28

Designs: 15c, General Assembly. 25c, Gabriel L. Dennis signing UN Charter for Liberia.

1955, Oct. 24 **Unwmk.** ***Perf. 12***

C93 AP27 10c ultra & red 15 15

C94 AP27 15c vio & blk 20 15

C95 AP27 25c grn & red brn 32 15

C96 AP28 50c brick red & grn 70 18

Set value 38

10th anniv. of the UN, Oct. 24, 1955.

Rotary International Headquarters, Evanston, Ill. — AP29

Design: 15c, View of Monrovia.

1955, Dec. 5 **Litho.** ***Perf. 12½***

C97 AP29 10c dp ultra & red 18 15

C98 AP29 15c redsh brn, red & bis 28 22

Souvenir Sheet

C99 AP29 50c dp ultra & red 95 95

No. C99 design as C97, but redrawn and with leaves omitted.

50th anniversary of Rotary International.

Nos. C97-C99 exist without Rotary emblem; No. C97 printed entirely in deep ultramarine; No. C98 with bister impression omitted.

New York Coliseum AP30

Statue of Liberty — AP31

Design: 12c, Globe inscribed FIPEX.

1956, Apr. 28 Unwmk. *Perf. 12*

C100 AP30 10c rose red & ultra	15	15
C101 AP30 12c org & pur	18	15
C102 AP31 15c aqua & red lil	22	15
Set value		21

Souvenir Sheet

C103 AP31 50c lt grn & brn 1.00 1.00

FIPEX, NYC, Apr. 28-May 6, 1956.

Olympic Park, Melbourne — AP32

Designs: 20c, 40c, Map of Australia and Olympic torch.

1956, Nov. 15 Unwmk. *Perf. 12*

C104 AP32 12c emer & vio	15	15
C105 AP32 20c multi	18	15
Set value		15

Souvenir Sheet

C106 AP32 40c multi 1.00 1.00

Issued to commemorate the 16th Olympic Games, Melbourne, Nov. 22-Dec. 8.

Type of Regular Issue, 1957.

Designs: 12c, 25c, Idlewild airport, New York. 15c, 50c, Roberts Field, Liberia, plane and Pres. Tubman.

Lithographed and Engraved

1957, May 4 *Perf. 12*

C107 A146 12c brt grn & dk bl	15	15
C108 A146 15c red brn & blk	15	15
C109 A146 25c car & dk bl	24	15
C110 A146 50c lt ultra & blk	45	15
Set value		40

Type of Regular Issue, 1957

Orphanage and: 15c, Nurse inoculating boy. 35c, The Kamara triplets. 70c, Children and flag.

1957, Nov. 25 Litho. *Perf. 12*

C111 A147 15c lt bl & brn	15	15
C112 A147 35c mar & lt gray	22	15
Set value		21

Souvenir Sheet

C113 A147 70c ultra & rose car 95 85

Type of Regular Issue, 1958

Designs: 10c, Italian flag and Colosseum. No. C115, French flag and Arc de Triomphe. No. C116, Swiss flag and chalet. No. C117, Vatican flag and St. Peter's.

Engr. and Litho.

1958, Jan. 10 *Perf. 10½*

Flags in Original Colors

C114 A148 10c dk gray	15	15
C115 A148 15c dp yel grn	15	15
C116 A148 15c ultra	15	15
C117 A148 15c purple	15	15
Set value	44	25

Type of Regular Issue, 1948-50

Design: William V. S. Tubman.

1958 Engr. *Perf. 12*

C118 A128 25c lt grn & blk 38 28

Souvenir Sheet

Preamble to Declaration of Human Rights — AP33

1958, Dec. 10 Litho. *Perf. 12*

C119 AP33 20c bl & red 1.75 1.75

10th anniv. of the signing of the Universal Declaration of Human Rights.

Liberians Reading Proclamation — AP34

1959, Apr. 15 Unwmk.

C120 AP34 25c bl & brn 26 26

African Freedom Day, Apr. 15.

UNESCO Building, Paris — AP35

1959, May 1

C121 AP35 25c ultra & red	30	24
a. Souvenir sheet	1.40	1.40

Opening of UNESCO Headquarters in Paris, Nov. 3, 1958.

Lincoln Type of Regular Issue

1959, Nov. 20 Engr. *Perf. 12*

C122 A152 25c emer & blk 38 38

For souvenir sheet see No. 386a.

Touré, Tubman and Nkrumah AP36

1960, Jan. 27 Litho. Unwmk.

C123 AP36 25c beige, vio bl & blk 30 30

See note after No. 387.

WRY Type of Regular Issue, 1960

1960, Apr. 7 *Perf. 11½*

C124 A154 25c ultra & blk	42	35
a. Souv. sheet of 2, #388, C124, imperf.	2.00	2.00

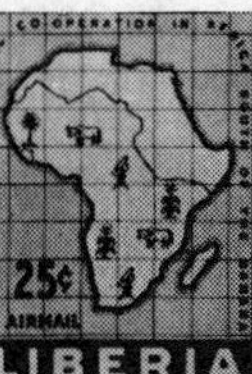
Map of Africa — AP37

1960, May 11 *Perf. 11½*

C125 AP37 25c ultra & brn 35 35

See note after No. 389.

Olympic Games Type of 1960

Designs: 25c, Javelin thrower and hunter (horiz.). 50c, Runner and stadium (horiz.).

1960, Sept. 6 *Perf. 11½*

C126 A156 25c brn & brt ultra 50 38

Souvenir Sheet

Imperf

C127 A156 50c lil & brn 2.75 2.75

Stamp Centenary Type of 1960

1960, Dec. 1 Litho. *Perf. 11½*

C128 A157 25c multi 32 32

Souvenir Sheet

C129 A157 50c multi 1.25 1.25

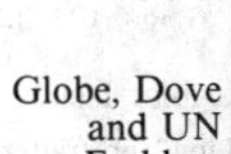
Globe, Dove and UN Emblem AP38

Design: 50c, Globe and dove.

1961, May 19 Unwmk. *Perf. 11½*

C130 AP38 25c ind & red 22 22

Souvenir Sheet

C131 AP38 50c red brn & emer 1.25 1.25

Liberia's membership in the UN Security Council.

A second souvenir sheet contains one each of Nos. 395, C130 and the 50c from No. C131, imperf. Size: 133x83mm.

No. C130 exists imperf.

Science Class — AP39

Design: 50c, Science class, different design.

1961, Sept. 8 Litho.

C132 AP39 25c pur & brn 28 20

Souvenir Sheet

C133 AP39 50c bl & brn 1.00 1.00

15th anniv. of UNESCO.

Joseph J. Roberts and Providence Island — AP40

1961, Oct. 25 Litho. *Perf. 11½*

C134 AP40 25c emer & sep	30	30
a. Souv. sheet of 3	1.00	1.00

150th anniv. of the birth of Joseph J. Roberts, 1st pres. of Liberia.

No. C134a contains three imperf. stamps similar to Nos. 397-398 and C134, but printed in different colors; 5c, emerald & sepia. 10c, orange & sepia. 25c, ultramarine & sepia.

Scout Type of Regular Issue and

Boy Scout — AP41

1961, Dec. 4 Unwmk. *Perf. 11½*

C135 AP41 25c emer & sepia 65 65

Souvenir Sheet

Design: Like No. 399.

C136 A161 35c dl bl & sepia 80 80

Dag Hammarskjold Type of 1962

1962, Feb. 1 Unwmk. *Perf. 12*

C137 A162 25c blk & red lil 32 32

Souvenir Sheet

Imperf

C138 A162 50c blk & ultra 1.00 1.00

Malaria Eradication Emblem AP42

1962, Apr. 7 *Perf. 12½*

C139 AP42 25c pur & org 32 20

Souvenir Sheet

Imperf

C140 AP42 50c dk red & ultra 80 80

Pres. Tubman, Statue of Liberty, New York Skyline and Flags of US and Liberia AP43

1962, Sept. 17 Litho. *Perf. 11½x12*

C141 AP43 12c multi	16	15
C142 AP43 25c multi	32	26
C143 AP43 50c multi	65	48

Pres. Tubman's visit to the US in 1961.

United Nations Emblem and Flags — AP44

Design: 50c, UN emblem.

1962, Oct. 22 *Perf. 12x12½*

C144 AP44 25c lt ultra & dk bl 30 30

Souvenir Sheet

Imperf

C145 AP44 50c brt grnsh bl & blk 50 50

Observance of UN Day, Oct. 24, as a national holiday.

Building Type of Regular Issue

Buildings: 12c, 70c, Capitol. 50c, Information Service. $1, Treasury Department Building, Monrovia.

1962-63 *Perf. 12x12½, 12 (70c)*

C146 A165 12c brt yel grn & mar	15	15
C147 A165 50c org & ultra	65	65
C147A A165 70c brt pink & dk bl ('63)	90	90
C148 A165 $1 sal & blk ('63)	1.25	35

"FAO" Emblem and Globe — AP45

Design: 50c, "FAO" and UN Emblems.

1963, Mar. 21 Unwmk. *Perf. 12½*
C149 AP45 25c dk grn & yel 30 30

Souvenir Sheet
Perf. 12
C150 AP45 50c emer & ultra 1.00 1.00

FAO "Freedom from Hunger" campaign.

Type of Regular Issue, 1963

Designs: 25c, Telstar satellite (vert.). 50c, Telstar and rocket (vert.).

1963, May 27 Litho. *Perf. 12½*
C151 A167 25c Prus bl & org 30 30

Souvenir Sheet
Perf. 12
C152 A167 50c dp vio & yel 1.00 52

Red Cross Type of Regular Issue

Design: 25c, Red Cross and globe. 50c, Centenary emblem and globe.

1963, Aug. 26 Unwmk. *Perf. 12*
C153 A168 25c pur & red 22 22
C154 A168 50c dp ultra & red 42 42

Map of Africa — AP46

1963, Oct. 28 *Perf. 12½*
C156 AP46 25c red org & grn 22 22

See note after No. 412.

Olympic Type of Regular Issue

Designs: 10c, Torch and mountains. 25c, Mountains (horiz.). 50c, Torch, background like No. 413.

1963, Dec. 11 Litho. *Perf. 12½*
C157 A170 10c vio bl & red 15 15
C158 A170 25c grn & org 32 32

Souvenir Sheet
Perf. 12
C159 A170 50c gray & red 1.00 1.00

Kennedy Type of Regular Issue, 1964

Designs: 25c, John F. Kennedy (vert.). 50c, John F. Kennedy (like No. 414).

1964, Apr. 6 Unwmk. *Perf. 12½*
C160 A171 25c blk & red lil 35 30

Souvenir Sheet
Perf. 12
C161 A171 50c blk & red lil 1.00 80

An imperf. miniature sheet containing one of No. C160 exists. No marginal inscription.

Satellite Type of Regular Issue
Souvenir Sheet

Design: Launching rocket separating from booster in space (vert.).

1964, June 22 Litho.
C162 A172 50c vio bl & red 1.00 1.00

Olympic Type of Regular Issue
Souvenir Sheet

Design: 50c, Runner and Olympic rings.

1964, Sept. 15 Unwmk. *Perf. 12*
C163 A173 50c grnsh bl & red 1.00 45

Scout Type of Regular Issue, 1965

Designs: 25c, Liberian flag and fleur-delis. 50c, Globe and Scout emblem.

1965, Mar. 8 Litho. *Perf. 12½*
C164 A174 25c crim & ultra 45 45

Souvenir Sheet
Perf. 12
C165 A174 50c yel & lil 60 60

Lincoln Type of Regular Issue
Souvenir Sheet

Design: 50c, Lincoln and John F. Kennedy (horiz.).

1965, May 3 Unwmk. *Perf. 12*
C166 A175 50c dp plum & lt gray 1.25 1.25

ICY Type of Regular Issue, 1965
Souvenir Sheet

1965, June 21 Litho.
C167 A176 50c car rose & brn 1.25 1.25

ITU Type of Regular Issue, 1965

1965, Sept. 21 Unwmk. *Perf. 12½*
C168 A177 50c red org & vio bl 50 45

Tubman Type of Regular Issue

Design: 25c, Pres. Tubman and coat of arms.

1965, Nov. 29 Litho. *Perf. 12½*
C169 A178 25c ultra, red & brn 40 40
a. Souv. sheet of 2, #431, C169, imperf. 1.25 1.25

Churchill Type of Regular Issue

Designs: 25c, "Angry Lion" portrait by Karsh and Parliament, London. 50c, "Williamsburg Award Dinner" portrait by Karsh and map of Europe.

1966, Jan. 18 Litho. *Perf. 12½*
C170 A179 25c blk & vio bl 30 24

Souvenir Sheet
Perf. 12
C171 A179 50c blk & red lil 1.25 1.25

Soccer Type of Regular Issue
Souvenir Sheet

Design: 50c, Soccer match in stadium.

1966, May 3 Litho. *Perf. 11½*
C172 A181 50c ultra & red brn 1.25 1.25

Kennedy Type of Regular Issue

Designs: 25c, UN General Assembly and Pres. Kennedy. 35c, Pres. Kennedy and rocket on launching pad, Cape Kennedy. 40c, Flame on grave at Arlington.

1966, Aug. 16 Litho. *Perf. 12½*
C173 A182 25c ultra, blk & ocher 28 15
C174 A182 35c dk vio bl & pink 35 20

Souvenir Sheet
Perf. 11½
C175 A182 40c dk vio bl & multi 1.25 1.25

Boy Scout Type of Regular Issue
Souvenir Sheet

Design: 50c, Scout at campfire and vision of moon landing.

1967, Mar. 23 Litho. *Perf. 12½*
C176 A185 50c brt red lil & scar 1.25 1.25

Olympic Type of Regular Issue
Souvenir Sheet

Design: 50c, Pre-Hispanic sculpture, serape and Olympic rings (horiz.).

1967, June 20 Litho. *Perf. 12½*
C177 A186 50c vio & car 1.25 50

Winter Olympic Games Type of Regular Issue
Souvenir Sheet

Design: 50c, Woman skater.

1967, Nov. 20 Litho. *Perf. 11½*
C178 A189 50c ver & blk 1.25 40

Human Rights Type of Regular Issue
Souvenir Sheet

1968, Apr. 26 Litho. *Perf. 11½*
C179 A191 80c bl & red 1.50 55

M. L. King Type of Regular Issue
Souvenir Sheet

Design: 55c, Pres. Kennedy congratulating Dr. King.

1968, July 11 Litho. *Perf. 11½*
C180 A192 55c brn & blk 1.25 40

Olympic Type of Regular Issue
Souvenir Sheet

Design: 50c, Steeplechase and ancient sculpture.

1968, Aug. 22 Litho. *Perf. 11½*
C181 A193 50c brt bl & org brn 1.00 65

President Type of Regular Issue 1966-69

Design: 25c, Pres. William V. S. Tubman.

1969, Feb. 18 Litho. *Perf. 11½x11*
C182 A180 25c blk & emer 40 30

ILO Type of Regular Issue

Design: 80c, "ILO" surrounded by cogwheel and wreath (vert.).

1969, Apr. 16 Litho. *Perf. 12½*
C183 A196 80c emer & gold 1.25 60

Apollo 11 Type of Regular Issue
Souvenir Sheet

Design: 65c, Astronauts Neil A. Armstrong, Col. Edwin E. Aldrin, Jr., and Lieut. Col. Michael Collins (horiz.).

1969, Oct. 15 Litho. *Perf. 11½*
C184 A199 65c dk vio bl & brt red 1.25 52

UN Type of 1970

Design: $1, UN emblem, olive branch and plane as symbols of peace and progress (vert.).

1970, Apr. 16 Litho. *Perf. 12½*
C185 A200 $1 ultra & sil 1.40 80

Apollo 14 Type of Regular Issue
Souvenir Sheet

Design: 50c, Moon, earth and star.

1971, May 20 Litho. *Imperf.*
C186 A208 50c multi 1.60 1.60

Souvenir Sheet

Olympic Yachting Village, Kiel, and Yachting — AP47

Illustration reduced.

1971, June 28 Litho. *Perf. 14½x14*
C187 AP47 Sheet of 2 1.25 1.25
a. 25c multi 50 50
b. 30c multi 60 60

Publicity for the 20th Summer Olympic Games, and the yachting races in Kiel, Germany, 1972.

Boy Scout Type of Regular Issue
Souvenir Sheet

Design: 50c, Boy Scouts of various nations cooking (horiz.).

1971, Aug. 6 Litho. *Perf. 15*
C188 A211 50c multi 1.00 40

UNICEF Type of Regular Issue
Souvenir Sheet

Design: 50c, UNICEF emblem and Bengal tigress with cubs.

1971, Oct. 1 *Imperf.*
C189 A213 50c multi 1.25 1.25

Souvenir Sheet

Japanese Royal Family — AP48

1971, Nov. 4 *Perf. 15*
C190 AP48 50c multi 2.00 80

11th Winter Olympic Games, Sapporo, Japan, Feb. 3-13, 1972.

Sesquicentennial Type of Regular Issue
Souvenir Sheet

Design: 50c, Sailing ship "Elizabeth" between maps of America and Africa (horiz.).

1972, Jan. 1 Litho. *Imperf.*
C191 A216 50c car & vio bl 1.50 1.50

Olympic Type of Regular Issue
Souvenir Sheet

Design: 55c, View of Olympic Stadium and symbol of "Motion."

1971, May 19 Litho. *Perf. 15*
C192 A218 55c multi 1.50 65

Apollo 16 Type of Regular Issue
Souvenir Sheet

Design: 55c, Lt. Comdr. Thomas K. Mattingly, 2nd, Capt. John W. Young and Lt. Col. Charles M. Duke, Jr.

1972, June 26 Litho. *Perf. 15*
C193 A220 55c pink & multi 1.00 1.00

Ship Type of 1972
Souvenir Sheet

Design: Lord Nelson's flagship Victory, and her figurehead (1765).

1972, Sept. 6 Litho. *Perf. 15*
C194 A222 50c multi 1.50 1.50

Pres. Tolbert Type of 1972.
Souvenir Sheet

1972, Oct. 23 Litho. *Perf. 15*
C195 A223 55c multi 1.10 1.10

Apollo 17 Type of Regular Issue
Souvenir Sheet

Design: 55c, Apollo 17 badge, moon and earth.

1973, Mar. 28 Litho. *Perf. 11*
C196 A225 55c bl & multi 1.10 1.10

Locomotive Type of Regular Issue
Souvenir Sheet

Design: 55c, Swiss locomotive.

1973, May 4 Litho. *Perf. 11*
C197 A226 55c multi 1.10 1.10

WHO Type of Regular Issue 1973
Souvenir Sheet

Design: 55c, WHO emblem, Paul Ehrlich and poppy anemones.

1973, June 26 Litho. *Perf. 11*
C198 A228 55c lt vio & multi 1.00 1.00

Automobile Type of Regular Issue
Souvenir Sheet

Design: Franklin 10 HP cross-engined 1904-1905 models.

1973, Sept. 11 Litho. *Perf. 11*
C199 A229 55c multi 1.50 1.50

Copernicus Type of Regular Issue
Souvenir Sheet

Design: 55c, Copernicus and concept of orbiting station around Mars.

1973, Dec. 14 Litho. *Perf. 13½*
C200 A230 55c gray & multi 1.25 1.25

UPU Type of Regular Issue
Souvenir Sheet

Design: 55c, UPU emblem and English coach, 1784.

1974, Mar. 4 Litho. *Perf. 13½*
C201 A232 55c multi 1.25 60

Dog Type of Regular Issue
Souvenir Sheet

Design: Hungarian sheepdog (kuvasz).

1974, Apr. 16 Litho. *Perf. 13½*
C202 A233 75c multi 1.25 1.25

Soccer Type of Regular Issue
Souvenir Sheet

Design: 60c, World Soccer Championship Cup and Munich Stadium.

1974, June 4 Litho. *Perf. 11*
C203 A234 60c multi 1.25 1.25

Butterfly Type of Regular Issue
Souvenir Sheet

Tropical butterfly: 60c, Pierella nereis.

1974, Sept. 11 Litho. *Perf. 13½*
C204 A235 60c gray & multi 1.25 1.25

Churchill Type of 1974
Souvenir Sheet

Design: 60c, Churchill at easel painting landscape.

1975, Jan. 17 Litho. *Perf. 13½*
C205 A237 60c multi 1.25 1.25

Women's Year Type of 1975
Souvenir Sheet

Design: 75c, Vijaya Lakshmi Pandit, Women's Year emblem and dais of UN General Assembly.

1975, Mar. 14 Litho. *Perf. 13*
C206 A238 75c gray & multi 1.40 1.40

American Bicentennial Type
Souvenir Sheet

Design: 75c, Mayflower and US No. 548.

1975, Apr. 25 Litho. *Perf. 13½*
C207 A239 75c multi 2.00 65

Dr. Schweitzer Type, 1975
Souvenir Sheet

Design: 60c, Dr. Schweitzer as surgeon in Lambarene Hospital.

1975, June 26 Litho. *Perf. 13½*
C208 A240 60c multi 1.25 1.25

Apollo-Soyuz Type, 1975
Souvenir Sheet

Design: 75c, Apollo-Soyuz link-up and emblem.

1975, Sept. 18 Litho. *Perf. 13½*
C209 A241 75c multi 1.40 1.40

Winter Olympic Games Type, 1976
Souvenir Sheet

Design: 75c, Downhill skiing and Olympic Games emblem.

1976, Jan. 23 Litho. *Perf. 13½*
C210 A243 75c multi 1.40 1.40

Olympic Games Type, 1976
Souvenir Sheet

Design: 75c, Dressage and jumping.

1976, May 4 Litho. *Perf. 13½*
C211 A245 75c multi 1.40 1.40

Bell Type
Souvenir Sheet

Design: 75c, A. G. Bell making telephone call, UPU and ITU emblems.

1976, June 4 Litho. *Perf. 13½*
C212 A246 75c ocher & multi 1.40 1.40

Animal Type of 1976
Souvenir Sheet

Design: 50c, Elephant (vert.).

1976, Sept. 1 Litho. *Perf. 13½*
C213 A249 50c org & multi 1.50 1.50

Bicentennial Type of 1976
Souvenir Sheet

Design: 75c, Like No. 770.

1976, Sept. 21 Litho. *Perf. 13½*
C214 A250 75c multi 1.50 1.50

Mask Type of 1977
Souvenir Sheet

Design: 75c, Ibo mask and Festival emblem.

1977, Jan. 20 Litho. *Perf. 13½*
C215 A251 75c lil & multi 1.00 1.00

Equestrian Type of 1977

Designs: 55c, Military dressage (team), USA. 80c, Winners receiving medals (vert.).

1977, Apr. 22 Litho. *Perf. 13½*
C216 A253 55c ocher & multi 1.00 50

Souvenir Sheet

C217 A253 80c ocher & multi 1.50 1.50

Elizabeth II Type of 1977
Souvenir Sheet

Design: 75c, Elizabeth II, laurel and crowns.

1977, May 23 Litho. *Perf. 13½*
C218 A254 75c sil & multi 1.75 1.25

Zeppelin Type of 1978
Souvenir Sheet

Design: 75c, Futuristic Goodyear aerospace airship.

1978, Mar. 9 Litho. *Perf. 13½*
C219 A257 75c multi 1.40 1.40

Soccer Type of 1978
Souvenir Sheet

Design: 75c, Soccer game Netherlands and Uruguay (vert.).

1978, May 16 Litho. *Perf. 13½*
C220 A258 75c multi 1.40

Coronation Type of 1978
Souvenir Sheet

Design: 75c, Coronation coach (horiz.).

1978, June 12
C221 A259 75c multi 1.40

Soccer Winners' Type of 1978
Souvenir Sheet

Design: 75c, Argentine team (horiz.).

1978, Dec. 8 Litho. *Perf. 13½*
C222 A262 75c multi 1.40

AIR POST SEMI-POSTAL STAMPS

Nos. C14-C16 Overprinted in Red or Blue Like Nos. B16-B18

1941 Unwmk. *Perf. 12*
CB1 A107 3c +2c dk bl (R) 1.10 1.10
CB2 A108 5c +2c dl red brn (Bl) 1.10 1.10
CB3 A109 10c +2c dk grn (R) 1.10 1.10

Catalogue values for unused stamps in this section, from this point to the end of the section, are for Never Hinged items.

Nurses Taking Oath SPAP1

Designs: 20c+5c, Liberian Government Hospital. 25c+5c, Medical examination.

1954, June 21 Litho. & Engr.
Size: 39½x28½mm
CB4 SPAP1 10c +5c car & blk 15 15
CB5 SPAP1 20c +5c emer & blk 18 15
Size: 45x34mm
CB6 SPAP1 25c +5c ultra, car & blk 20 15
Set value 26

Surtax for the Liberian Government Hospital. Nos. CB4-CB6 exist imperf. No. CB6 exists with carmine omitted.

AIR POST SPECIAL DELIVERY STAMP

No. C15 Overprinted in Dark Blue Like No. E1

1941 Unwmk. *Perf. 12*
CE1 A108 10c on 5c dl red brn 1.25 1.00

AIR POST REGISTRATION STAMP

No. C15 Overprinted in Dark Blue Like No. F35

1941 Unwmk. *Perf. 12*
CF1 A108 10c on 5c dl red brn 1.25 1.00

SPECIAL DELIVERY STAMP

No. 278 Surcharged in Dark Blue

SPECIAL DELIVERY
10 CENTS 10

1941 Unwmk. *Perf. 12*
E1 A108 10c on 5c dl red brn 1.25 1.00

REGISTRATION STAMPS

R1

1893 Unwmk. Litho. *Perf. 14, 15*
Without Value Surcharged
F1 R1 (10c) blk (Buchanan) 210.00 210.00
F2 R1 (10c) blk (Greenville) *1,750.* *1,750.*
F3 R1 (10c) blk (Harper) *1,750.* *1,750.*
F4 R1 (10c) blk (Monrovia) 25.00 25.00
F5 R1 (10c) blk (Robertsport) 800.00 800.00

Types of 1893 Surcharged in Black

10 CENTS 10

10 CENTS 10

1894 *Perf. 14*
F6 R1 10c bl, *pink* (Buchanan) 4.00 4.25
F7 R1 10c grn, *buff* (Harper) 4.00 4.25
F8 R1 10c red, *yel* (Monrovia) 4.00 4.25
F9 R1 10c rose, *bl* (Robertsport) 4.00 4.25

Exist imperf or missing one 10. Value, each $7.50.

President Garretson W. Gibson — R6

1903 Engr. *Perf. 14*
F10 R6 10c bl & blk (Buchanan) 1.00 15
 a. Center inverted 90.00
F11 R6 10c org red & blk ("Grenville") 1.00
 a. Center inverted 90.00
 b. 10c orange & black 1.60 15
F12 R6 10c grn & blk (Harper) 1.00 15
 a. Center inverted 90.00
F13 R6 10c vio & blk (Monrovia) 1.00 15
 a. Center inverted 90.00
 b. 10c lilac & black 1.60
F14 R6 10c mag & blk (Robertsport) 1.00 15
 a. Center inverted 90.00
 Nos. F10-F14 (5) 5.00
 Nos. F10, F11b, F12-F14 75

For surcharges see Nos. 178-182.

S.S. Quail on Patrol R7

1919 Litho. *Serrate Roulette 12*
F15 R7 10c blk & bl (Buchanan) 50 1.00
Serrate Roulette 12, Perf. 14
F16 R7 10c ocher & blk ("Grenville") 50 1.00
F17 R7 10c grn & blk (Harper) 50 1.00
F18 R7 10c vio & bl (Monrovia) 50 1.00
F19 R7 10c rose & blk (Robertsport) 50 1.00
 Nos. F15-F19 (5) 2.50 5.00

Gabon Viper R8

Wmk. Crosses and Circles (116)
1921 Engr. *Perf. 13x14*
F20 R8 10c cl & blk (Buchanan) 22.50 1.25
F21 R8 10c red & blk (Greenville) 14.00 1.25
F22 R8 10c ultra & blk (Harper) 18.00 1.25
F23 R8 10c org & blk (Monrovia) 14.00 1.25
 a. Imperf., pair 120.00

F24 R8 10c grn & blk (Robertsport) 14.00 1.25
a. Imperf., pair 120.00
Nos. F20-F24 (5) 82.50 6.25

Preceding Issue Overprinted "1921"

F25 R8 10c (Buchanan) 16.00 2.50
F26 R8 10c (Greenville) 17.00 2.50
F27 R8 10c (Harper) 16.00 2.50
F28 R8 10c (Monrovia) 15.00 2.50
F29 R8 10c (Robertsport) 16.00 2.50
Nos. F25-F29 (5) 80.00 12.50

Nos. F25-F29 exist with "1921" inverted. Value same as normal.

Passengers Going Ashore from Ship — R9

Designs: No. F31, Transporting merchandise, shore to ship (Greenville). No. F32, Sailing ship (Harper). No. F33, Ocean liner (Monrovia). No. F34, Canoe in surf (Robertsport).

1924 **Litho.** ***Perf. 14***

F30 R9 10c gray & car 3.00 25
F31 R9 10c gray & bl grn 3.00 25
F32 R9 10c gray & org 3.00 25
F33 R9 10c gray & bl 3.00 25
F34 R9 10c gray & vio 3.00 25
Nos. F30-F34 (5) 15.00 1.25

No. 278 Surcharged in Dark Blue

1941 **Unwmk.** ***Perf. 12***

F35 A108 10c on 5c dl red brn 1.00 1.00

POSTAGE DUE STAMPS

Nos. 26, 28 Surcharged

1892 **Unwmk.** ***Perf. 11***

J1 A5 3c on 3c vio 1.00 80
a. Imperf., pair 10.00
b. Inverted surcharge 30.00 30.00
c. As "a," inverted surcharge 75.00

Perf. 12

J2 A5 6c on 6c ol gray 5.00 4.00
a. Imperf., pair 15.00
b. Inverted surcharge 35.00 35.00

D2

Engr.; Figures of Value Typographed in Black

1893 **Wmk. 143** ***Perf. 14, 15***

J3 D2 2c org, *yel* 1.00 52
J4 D2 4c rose, *rose* 1.00 52
J5 D2 6c brown, *buff* 1.00 70
J6 D2 8c blue, *blue* 1.00 70
J7 D2 10c grn, *lil rose* 1.35 90
J8 D2 20c vio, *gray* 1.35 90
a. Center inverted 90.00 90.00
J9 D2 40c ol brn, *grnsh* 2.35 1.65
Nos. J3-J9 (7) 9.05 5.89

All values of the above set exist imperforate.

MILITARY STAMPS

"LFF" are the initials of "Liberian Frontier Force." Nos. M1-M7 were issued for the use of troops sent to guard the frontier.

Issues of 1905, 1906 and 1909 Surcharged **L F F 1c**

1916 **Wmk. 143**

M1 A23 1c on 1c lt grn 135.00 135.00
a. 2nd "F" inverted 175.00 175.00
b. "FLF" 175.00 175.00
c. Inverted surcharge 175.00 175.00

Unwmk.

M2 A33 1c on 1c grn & blk 425.00 425.00
a. 2nd "F" inverted 450.00 450.00
b. "FLF" 450.00 450.00
M3 A46 1c on 1c yel grn & blk 3.25 2.25
a. 2nd "F" inverted 6.50 6.50
b. "FLF" 6.50 6.50
M4 A47 1c on 2c lake & blk 3.25 2.25
a. 2nd "F" inverted 6.50 6.50
b. "FLF" 6.50 6.50

Surcharge exists sideways on Nos. M2, M5; double on Nos. M1-M4; inverted on Nos. M2-M4.

Nos. O46, O59-O60 Surcharged **L F F 1c**

M5 A33 1c on 1c 325.00 325.00
a. 2nd "F" inverted 450.00 450.00
b. "FLF" 450.00 450.00
M6 A46 1c on 1c 3.25 2.25
a. 2nd "F" inverted 6.50 6.50
b. "FLF" 6.50 6.50
c. "LFF 1c" inverted 8.50 8.50
d. As "a" and "1c" inverted 12.00
e. "FLF 1c" inverted 12.00
M7 A47 1c on 2c 2.50 1.90
a. 2nd "F" inverted 5.00 5.00
b. "FLF" 5.00 5.00
c. Pair, one without "LFF 1c"

OFFICIAL STAMPS

Types of Regular Issues Overprinted "OFFICIAL" in Various Colors

Perf. 12½ to 15 and Compound

1892 **Wmk. 143**

O1 A9 1c vermilion 40 40
O2 A9 2c blue 40 40
O3 A10 4c grn & blk 40 40
O4 A11 6c bl grn 40 40
O5 A12 8c brn & blk 40 40
O6 A13 12c rose red 1.00 1.00
O7 A14 16c red lil 1.00 1.00
a. "OFFICSL"
O8 A15 24c ol grn, *yel* 1.00 1.00
O9 A16 32c grnsh bl 1.00 1.00
a. "OFFICSL"
O10 A17 $1 bl & blk 20.00 7.75
O11 A18 $2 brn, *yel* 8.50 5.75
O12 A19 $5 car & blk 12.00 5.25
Nos. O1-O12 (12) 46.50 24.75

1893

O13 A11 (a) 5c on 6c bl grn (No. 50) 75 75
a. "5" with short flag 4.00 4.00
b. Both 5's with short flags 4.00 4.00
c. "i" dot omitted 15.00 15.00
d. Overprinted on #50d 37.50 37.50

1894

Overprinted "O S" in Various Colors

O15 A9 1c vermilion 40 20
O16 A9 2c blue 60 25
a. Imperf.
O17 A10 4c grn & blk 75 32
O18 A12 8c brn & blk 75 32
O19 A13 12c rose red 1.00 38
O20 A14 16c red lil 1.00 38
O21 A15 24c ol grn, *yel* 1.00 42
O22 A16 32c grnsh bl 1.50 50
O23 A17 $1 bl & blk 12.00 12.00
a. $1 ultra & black 12.00 12.00
O24 A18 $2 brn, *yel* 12.00 12.00
O25 A19 $5 car & blk 75.00 50.00
Nos. O15-O25 (11) 106.00 76.77

Unwmk.

Imperf

O26 A22 5c vio & grn 2.50 1.50

Rouletted

O27 A22 5c vio & grn 2.50 1.50

Regular Issue of 1896-1905 Overprinted "O S" in Black or Red

1898-1905 **Wmk. 143** ***Perf. 14, 15***

O28 A23 1c lil rose 42 42
O29 A23 1c dp grn ('00) 42 42
O30 A23 1c lt grn (R) ('05) 42 42
O31 A24 2c bis & blk 75 25
a. Pair, one without overprint 50.00
O32 A24 2c org red & blk ('00) 1.25 60
O33 A24 2c rose & blk ('05) 1.90 1.25
O34 A25 5c lake & blk 1.25 60
O35 A25 5c gray bl & blk ('00) 1.65 60
O36 A25 5c ultra & blk (R) ('05) 1.65 70
O37 A12 10c chr yel & ind 75 75
O38 A13 15c slate 75 75
O39 A14 20c vermilion 1.25 90
O40 A15 25c yel grn 75 75
O41 A16 30c steel blue 1.90 1.25
O42 A26 50c red brn & blk 1.90 1.25
Nos. O28-O42 (15) 17.01 10.91

For surcharge see No. O92.

Official stamps overprinted "ORDINARY" or with a bar with an additional surcharge are listed as Nos. 64B-90, 92-93, 99.

O1

Red Overprint

1903 **Unwmk.** ***Perf. 14***

O43 O1 3c green 16 15
a. Overprint omitted 5.00
b. Inverted overprint

Two overprint types: I - Thin, sharp, dark red. II - Thick, heavier, orange red. Same value.

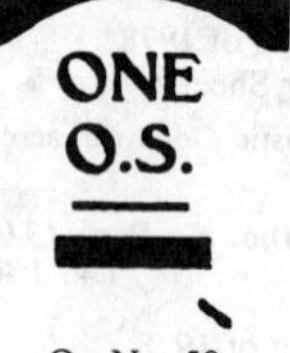

On No. 50

O3

1904 **Black Surcharge** **Wmk. 143**

O44 A11 1c on 5c on 6c bl grn 1.00 1.20
a. "5" with short flag 3.50
b. Both "5s" with straight flag 6.50 6.50

Red Surcharge

O45 O3 2c on 30c steel blue 6.50 6.00
a. Double surcharge, red and blk
b. Surcharge also on back

Types of Regular Issue Overprinted in Various Colors — a

1906 **Unwmk.**

O46 A33 1c grn & blk (R) 40 26
O47 A34 2c car & blk (Bl) 15 15
a. Center and overprint inverted 14.00 10.00
b. Inverted overprint 4.00
O48 A35 5c ultra & blk (Bk) 40 26
a. Inverted overprint 4.00 4.00
b. Center and overprint invtd. 25.00
O49 A36 10c dl vio & blk (R) 50 35
a. Inverted overprint
b. Center and overprint invtd. 27.50
O50 A37 15c brn & blk (Bk) 2.00 35
a. Inverted overprint 4.00
b. Overprint omitted
c. Center and overprint invtd. 35.00
O51 A38 20c dp grn & blk (R) 50 35
a. Overprint omitted
O52 A39 25c plum & gray (Bl) 30 15
a. With 2nd ovpt. in blue, invtd.
O53 A40 30c dk brn (Bk) 35 15
O54 A41 50c org brn & dp grn (G) 50 15
a. Inverted overprint 2.50
O55 A42 75c ultra & blk (Bk) 90 60
a. Inverted overprint 8.25 5.00
b. Overprint omitted 20.00
O56 A43 $1 dp grn & gray (R) 55 15
a. Inverted overprint
O57 A44 $2 plum & blk (Bl) 1.60 15
a. Overprint omitted 20.00
O58 A45 $5 org & blk (Bk) 3.50 15
a. Overprint omitted 10.00
b. Inverted overprint 5.50 3.50
Nos. O46-O58 (13) 11.65 3.22

Nos. O52, O54, O55, O56 and O58 are known with center inverted.

For surcharges see Nos. O72, O82-O85, O96.

1909-12

O59 A46 1c emer & blk (R) 22 16
O60 A47 2c car rose & brn (Bl) 22 16
a. Overprint omitted
O61 A48 5c turq & blk (Bk) 25 16
a. Double overprint, one inverted 6.50
O62 A49 10c blk & ultra (R) ('12) 35 16
O63 A50 15c cl & blk (Bl) 35 26
O64 A51 20c bis & grn (Bk) 65 30
O65 A52 25c ultra & grn (Bk) 65 32
a. Double overprint 4.25 4.25
O66 A53 30c dk bl (R) 50 16
O67 A54 50c brn & grn (Bk) 80 20
a. Center inverted 25.00
b. Inverted overprint 3.50 2.50
O68 A55 75c pur & blk (R) 90 18
Nos. O59-O68 (10) 4.89 2.06

Nos. O63, O64, O67 and O68 are known without overprint and with center inverted.

For surcharges see Nos. O74-O81, O86-O90, O97.

Rouletted

O69 A49 10c blk & ultra (R) 60 60

Nos. 126B and 127E Overprinted type "a" ("OS") in Red

1910-12 ***Rouletted***

O70 A49 3c on 10c blk & ultra 60 1.00

Perf. 12½, 14, 12½x14

O71 A49 3c on 10c blk & ultra ('12) 60 30
a. Pair, one without surch., the other with dbl. surch., one invtd.
b. Double surcharge, one inverted 3.75

Stamps of Preceding Issues Surcharged with New Values like Regular Issue and

c **CENTS 20 OFFICIAL**

1914

On Nos. O52 and 110

O72 A39 (a) 2c on 25c plum & gray 15.00 6.00
O73 A42 (c) 20c on 75c brn & blk 5.00 3.00

On Nos. O66 and O68

O74 A53 (b) 5c on 30c dk bl 5.00 3.00
O75 A55 (c) 20c on 75c pur & blk (R) 7.50 3.00

Official Stamps of 1906-09 Surcharged Like Regular Issues of Same Date

1915-16

O76 A50 (c) 2c on 15c (Bk) 65 45
O77 A52 (d) 2c on 25c (Bk) 3.75 3.75
O78 A51 (e) 5c on 20c (Bk) 65 45
O79 A53 (g) 5c on 30c (R) 5.00 5.00
O80 A54 (i) 10c on 50c (Bk) 4.00 2.50
O81 A55 (j) 20c on 75c (R) 2.00 2.00
O82 A43 (k) 25c on $1 (R) 12.50 12.50
a. "25" double 20.00
b. "OS" inverted 20.00
O83 A44 (l) 50c on $2 (Bk) 35.00 35.00
a. "Cents" 60.00 60.00
O84 A44 (m) 50c on $2 (Br) 15.00 15.00
O85 A45 (n) $1 on $5 (Bk) 13.00 13.00

Handstamped Surcharge

O86 A54 (i) 10c on 50c (Bk) 7.50 7.50

Nos. O60-O61 Surcharged like Nos. 153-154 in Black or Red

O87 A47 1c on 2c 2.00 2.00
Strip of 10 types 22.50
O88 A48 2c on 5c (R) 2.00 2.00
Strip of 10 types (R) 22.50
a. Black surcharge 7.50 7.50
Strip of 10 types (Bk) 110.00

See note following Nos. 153-154.

#O60-O61 Surcharged like #155-156

O90 A47 1c on 2c 35.00 35.00
O91 A48 2c on 5c 30.00 30.00

No. O42 Surcharged

10

O92 A26 10c on 50c (Bk) 10.00 10.00

No. O53 Surcharged like No. 161

1917

O96 A40 5c on 30c dk brn 13.00 15.00
a. "FIV" 25.00 25.00

The editors consider the 1915-17 issues unnecessary and speculative.

#O62 Surcharged in Red like #162

1918

O97 A49 3c on 10c blk & ultra 1.65 1.65

Types of Regular Issue of 1918 Overprinted Type "a" ("OS") in Black, Blue or Red

1918 Unwmk. *Perf. 12½, 14*

O98 A59 1c dp grn & red brn (Bk) 35 16
O99 A60 2c red & blk (Bl) 35 16
O100 A61 5c ultra & blk (R) 65 15
O101 A62 10c ultra (R) 35 15
O102 A63 15c choc & dk grn (Bl) 1.60 38
O103 A64 20c gray lil & blk (R) 50 15
O104 A65 25c choc & grn (Bk) 3.00 40
O105 A66 30c brt vio & blk (R) 3.75 40
O106 A67 50c mar & blk (Bl) 4.50 40
a. Overprint omitted 10.00
O107 A68 75c car brn & blk (Bl) 1.75 16
O108 A69 $1 ol bis & turq bl (Bk) 3.50 16
O109 A70 $2 ol bis & blk (R) 5.50 16
O110 A71 $5 yel grn (Bk) 7.00 20
Nos. O98-O110 (13) 32.80 3.03

For surcharges see Nos. 259-269, O111-O112, O155-O157. For overprint see No. 270.

Official Stamps of 1918 Surcharged like Regular Issue

1920

O111 A59 3c on 1c grn & red brn 75 50
a. "CEETS" 8.25
b. Double surcharge 2.50 2.50
c. Double surch., one invtd. 5.00 5.00
d. Triple surcharge 4.00 4.00
O112 A60 4c on 2c red & blk 50 50
a. Inverted surcharge 4.00 4.00
b. Double surcharge 4.00 4.00
c. Double surch., one invtd. 6.00 6.00
d. Triple surcharge 6.00 6.00

Types of Regular Issues of 1915-21 Overprinted **OFFICIAL**

1921 Wmk. 116 *Perf. 14*

O113 A57 2c rose red 4.50 15
O114 A58 3c brown 85 15
O115 A79 20c brn & ultra 1.25 22

Same, Overprinted "O S"

O116 A75 1c dp grn 85 15
O117 A76 5c dp bl & brn 85 15
O118 A77 10c red vio & blk 45 15
O119 A78 15c blk & grn 2.50 32
a. Double overprint
O120 A80 25c org & grn 3.50 32
O121 A81 30c brn & red 85 15
O122 A82 50c grn & blk 85 15
a. Overprinted "S" only
O123 A83 75c bl & vio 1.90 15
O124 A84 $1 bl & blk 12.00 35
O125 A85 $2 grn & org 6.50 55
O126 A86 $5 grn & bl 7.25 1.10
Nos. O113-O126 (14) 44.10
Set value 3.50

Preceding Issues Overprinted "1921"

1921

O127 A75 1c dp grn 3.50 15
O128 A57 2c rose red 3.50 15
O129 A58 3c brown 3.50 15
O130 A76 5c dp bl & brn 2.00 15
O131 A77 10c red vio & blk 3.50 15
O132 A78 15c blk & grn 4.00 15
O133 A79 20c brn & ultra 4.00 22
O134 A80 25c org & grn 4.50 42
O135 A81 30c brn & red 3.50 15
O136 A82 50c grn & blk 4.25 15
O137 A83 75c bl & vio 2.50 15
O138 A84 $1 bl & blk 7.00 1.00
O139 A85 $2 org & grn 9.00 1.10
O140 A86 $5 grn & bl 7.00 1.65
Nos. O127-O140 (14) 61.75 5.74

Types of Regular Issue of 1923 Overprinted "O S"

1923 *Perf. 13½x14½, 14½x13½*

White Paper

O141 A88 1c bl grn & blk 5.00 15
O142 A89 2c dl red & yel brn 5.00 15
O143 A90 3c gray bl & blk 5.00 15
O144 A91 5c org & dk grn 5.00 15
O145 A92 10c ol bis & dk vio 5.00 15
O146 A93 15c yel grn & bl 65 20
O147 A94 20c vio & ind 65 20
O148 A95 25c brn & red brn 10.00 20

White, Buff or Brownish Paper

O149 A96 30c dp ultra & brn 65 15
a. Overprint omitted
O150 A97 50c dl bis & red brn 65 20
O151 A98 75c gray & grn 65 15
O152 A99 $1 red org & grn 1.40 40
a. Overprint omitted 10.00
O153 A100 $2 red lil & ver 2.00 60
O154 A101 $5 bl & brn vio 3.50 50
Nos. O141-O154 (14) 45.15 3.35

No. O98 Surcharged in Red Brown

Two Cents

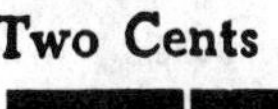

1926 Unwmk. *Perf. 14*

O155 A59 2c on 1c 2.00 2.00
a. "Gents" 6.25
b. Surcharged in black 5.00
c. As "b," "Gents" 8.25

No. O98 Surcharged in Black

Two Cents

1926

O156 A59 2c on 1c 75 75
a. Inverted surcharge
b. "Gents" 5.00

No. O98 Surcharged in Red

Two Cents

1927

O157 A59 2c on 1c 20.00 20.00
a. "Ceuts" 35.00
b. "Vwo" 35.00
c. "Twc" 35.00

Regular Issue of 1928 Overprinted in Red or Black

OFFICIAL SERVICE

1928 *Perf. 12*

O158 A102 1c grn (R) 75 35
O159 A102 2c gray vio (R) 1.40 55
O160 A102 3c bis brn (Bk) 1.40 35
O161 A103 5c ultra (R) 75 35
O162 A104 10c ol gray (R) 2.25 1.10
O163 A103 15c dl vio (R) 1.40 55
O164 A103 $1 red brn (Bk) 27.50 14.00
Nos. O158-O164 (7) 35.45 17.25

For surcharges see Nos. C3, O165.

No. O162 Surcharged with New Value and Bar in Black

1945 Unwmk. *Perf. 12*

O165 A104 4c on 10c (Bk) 6.00 6.00

LIBYA

(Libia)

LOCATION — North Africa, bordering on the Mediterranean Sea
GOVT. — Republic
AREA — 679,358 sq. mi.
POP. — 3,500,000 (est. 1982)
CAPITAL — Tripoli

In 1939, the four northern provinces of Libya, a former Italian colony, were incorporated in the Italian national territory. Included in the territory is the former Turkish Vilayet of Tripoli, annexed in 1912. Libya became a kingdom on Dec. 24, 1951. The Libyan Arab Republic was established Sept. 1, 1969. "People's Socialist . . ." was added to its name in 1977. See Cyrenaica and Tripolitania.

100 Centesimi = 1 Lira
Military Authority Lira (1951)
Franc (1951)
1,000 Milliemes = 1 Pound (1952)
1,000 Dirhams = 1 Dinar (1972)

Catalogue values for unused stamps in this country are for Never Hinged items, beginning with Scott 102 in the regular postage section, Scott C51 in the airpost section, Scott E13 in the special delivery section, Scott J25 in the postage due section, Scott O1 in the official section, Scott N1 in the Fezzan-Ghadames section, Scott 2N1 in the Fezzan section, Scott 2NB1 in the Fezzan semi-postal section, Scott 2NC1 in the Fezzan airpost section, Scott 2NJ1 in the Fezzan postage due section, Scott 3N1 in the Ghadames section, and Scott 3NC1 in the Ghadames airpost section.

Watermarks

Wmk. 195- Multiple Crown and Arabic F

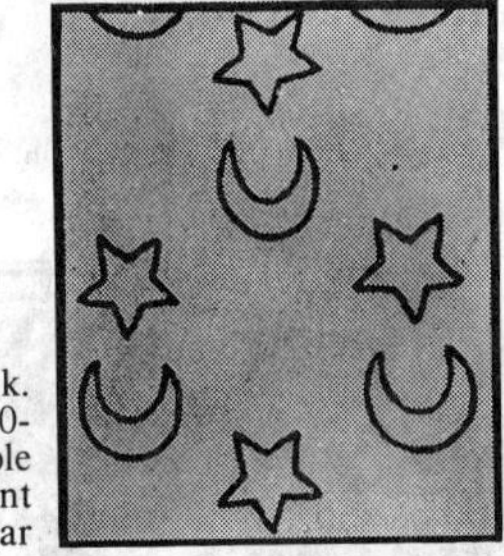

Wmk. 310- Multiple Crescent and Star

Stamps of Italy Overprinted in Black **Libia**

1912-22 Wmk. 140 *Perf. 14*

1 A42 1c brown ('15) 15 50
a. Double overprint 70.00 110.00
2 A43 2c orange brn 15 25
3 A48 5c green 15 15
a. Double overprint 16.00 25.00
b. Imperf., pair 35.00 50.00
c. Inverted overprint 900.00
d. Pair, one without overprint 45.00 65.00
4 A48 10c claret 15 15
a. Pair, one without overprint 60.00 90.00
b. Double overprint 30.00 45.00
5 A48 15c slate ('22) 80 2.00
6 A45 20c orange ('15) 25 25
a. Double overprint 45.00 65.00
b. Pair, one without overprint 125.00
7 A50 20c brn org ('18) 38 1.00
8 A49 25c blue 38 30
9 A49 40c brown 50 62
10 A45 45c ol grn ('17) 2.00 5.50
a. Inverted overprint 70.00
11 A49 50c violet 1.25 62
12 A49 60c brn car ('18) 2.00 5.50
13 A46 1 l brown & green ('15) 22.50 1.25
14 A46 5 l bl & rose ('15) 50.00 80.00
15 A51 10 l gray green & red ('15) 6.00 18.00
Nos. 1-15 (15) 86.66 116.09

Overprinted in Violet **LIBIA**

1912 Unwmk.

16 A58 15c slate 10.00 80
a. Blue black overprint 1,800. 3.75

No. 16 Surcharged CENT 20

1916, Mar. Unwmk.

19 A58 20c on 15c slate 10.00 2.00

Roman Legionary A1

Diana of Ephesus A2

Ancient Galley Leaving Tripoli A3

"Victory" A4

1921 Engr. Wmk. 140 *Perf. 14*

20 A1 1c blk & gray brn 25 70
21 A1 2c blk & red brn 25 70
22 A1 5c black & green 38 38
a. 5c blk & red brn (error) 625.00
b. Center inverted 15.00 21.00
c. Imperf., pair 50.00 70.00
23 A2 10c blk & rose 38 25
a. Center inverted 15.00 21.00
24 A2 15c blk brn & brn orange 2.50 50
a. Center inverted 25.00 37.50
25 A2 25c dk bl & bl 38 20
a. Center inverted 3.75 6.00
b. Imperf., pair 100.00 150.00
26 A3 30c blk & blk brn 2.00 50
a. Center inverted 550.00 500.00
27 A3 50c blk & ol grn 1.50 15
a. 50c blk & brn (error) 125.00
b. Center inverted *1,300.* *825.00*
28 A3 55c black & vio 1.00 2.50
29 A4 1 l dk brn & brn 1.25 16
30 A4 5 l blk & dk blue 5.00 3.75
31 A4 10 l dk bl & ol grn 12.50 25.00
Nos. 20-31 (12) 27.39 34.79

Nos. 20-31 also exist perf. 14x13, with values somewhat higher.
See Nos. 47-61.

Italy Nos. 136-139 Overprinted **LIBIA**

1921, Apr.

33 A64 5c olive green 38 *1.50*
a. Double overprint 70.00 90.00
34 A64 10c red 38 *1.50*
a. Double overprint 70.00 90.00
b. Inverted overprint 70.00 90.00
35 A64 15c slate green 50 *2.50*
36 A64 25c ultramarine 50 *2.00*

3rd anniv. of the victory of the Piave.

Nos. 11, 8 Surcharged **C. 40**

1922, June 1

37 A49 40c on 50c violet 62 70
38 A49 80c on 25c blue 80 *3.00*

Libyan Sibyl — A6

1924-31 Unwmk. *Perf. 14½x14*

39 A6 20c deep green 25 15
40 A6 40c brown 65 35
41 A6 60c deep blue 25 15
42 A6 1.75 l orange ('31) 15 15
43 A6 2 l carmine 80 60
44 A6 2.55 l violet ('31) 70 1.60
Nos. 39-44 (6) 2.80 3.00

1926-29 *Perf. 11*

No.	Type	Denomination	Unused	Used
39a	A6	20c	10.00	20
40a	A6	40c	6.00	1.25
41a	A6	60c	2.00	15
43a	A6	2 l ('29)	7.00	2.00

Type of 1921

1924-40 Unwmk. *Perf. 13½ to 14*

No.	Type	Description	Unused	Used
47	A1	1c blk & gray brown	25	1.00
48	A1	2c blk & red brn	38	1.00
49	A1	5c blk & green	50	38
50	A1	7½c blk & brown ('31)	30	1.00
51	A2	10c blk & dl red	15	15
b.		Center inverted	25.00	
52	A2	15c blk brn & org	80	42
b.		Center inverted, perf. 11	550.00	
53	A2	25c dk bl & bl	3.00	15
a.		Center inverted	25.00	37.50
54	A3	30c blk & blk brn	22	30
55	A3	50c blk & ol grn	15	15
b.		Center inverted	650.00	650.00
56	A3	55c black & vio	60.00	100.00
57	A4	75c violet & red ('31)	15	15
58	A4	1 l dk brn & brn	4.00	15
59	A3	1.25 l indigo & ultra ('31)	15	15
60	A4	5 l blk & dark blue ('40)	11.00	10.00
		Nos. 47-60 (14)	81.05	115.00

Perf. 11

No.	Type	Denomination	Unused	Used
47a	A1	1c	45.00	
48a	A1	2c	45.00	
49a	A1	5c	13.00	2.50
51a	A2	10c	6.00	50
52a	A2	15c	25.00	3.25
54a	A3	30c	18.00	50
55a	A3	50c	250.00	15
58a	A4	1 l	2.50	20
60a	A4	5 l ('37)	*650.00*	45.00
61	A4	10 l dk bl & olive grn ('37)	150.00	80.00

Italy #197 and 88 Overprinted Like #1-15

1929 Wmk. 140 *Perf. 14*

No.	Type	Description	Unused	Used
62	A86	7½c light brown	5.00	*13.50*
63	A46	1.25 l blue & ultra	22.50	5.00

Italy #193 Overprinted Like #33-36

1929 Unwmk. *Perf. 11*

No.	Type	Description	Unused	Used
64	A85	1.75 l deep brown	20.00	1.50

Water Carriers A7

Man of Tripoli — A8

Designs: 25c, Minaret. 30c, 1.25 l, Tomb of Holy Man near Tagiura. 50c, Statue of Emperor Claudius at Leptis. 75c, Ruins of gardens.

1934, Feb. 17 Photo. *Perf. 14*

No.	Type	Description	Unused	Used
64A	A7	10c brown	2.00	*5.00*
64B	A8	20c carmine rose	2.00	*5.00*
64C	A8	25c green	2.00	*5.00*
64D	A7	30c dark brown	2.00	*5.00*
64E	A8	50c purple	2.00	*5.00*
64F	A7	75c rose	2.00	*5.00*
64G	A7	1.25 l blue	19.00	*32.50*
		Nos. 64A-64G (7)	31.00	*62.50*

8th Sample Fair, Tripoli. See #C14-C18.

Bedouin Woman — A15

Highway Memorial Arch — A16

1936, May 11 Wmk. 140 *Perf. 14*

No.	Type	Description	Unused	Used
65	A15	50c purple	50	75
66	A15	1.25 l deep blue	65	2.25

10th Sample Fair, Tripoli.

1937, Mar. 15

No.	Type	Description	Unused	Used
67	A16	50c copper red	1.00	*2.50*
68	A16	1.25 l sapphire	1.00	*5.00*

Opening of a coastal road to the Egyptian frontier. See #C28-C29.

Nos. 67-68 Overprinted in Black

XI FIERA DI TRIPOLI

1937, Apr. 24

No.	Type	Description	Unused	Used
69	A16	50c copper red	3.50	*7.00*
70	A16	1.25 l sapphire	3.50	*7.00*

11th Sample Fair, Tripoli. See #C30-C31.

Roman Wolf and Lion of St. Mark — A17

View of Fair Buildings A18

1938, Mar. 12

No.	Type	Description	Unused	Used
71	A17	5c brown	15	38
72	A18	10c olive brown	15	38
73	A17	25c green	25	38
74	A18	50c purple	25	25
75	A17	75c rose red	30	*1.00*
76	A18	1.25 l dark blue	38	*1.10*
		Nos. 71-76,C32-C33 (8)	2.36	*6.01*

12th Sample Fair, Tripoli.

Augustus Caesar (Octavianus) A19

Goddess Abundantia A20

1938, Apr. 25

No.	Type	Description	Unused	Used
77	A19	5c olive brown	22	50
78	A20	10c brown red	22	50
79	A19	25c dk yel green	28	38
80	A20	50c dk violet	28	38
81	A19	75c orange red	59	*1.10*
82	A20	1.25 l dull blue	50	*1.10*
		Nos. 77-82,C34-C35 (8)	2.89	*5.96*

Birth bimillenary of Augustus Caesar (Octavianus), first Roman emperor.

Desert City — A21

View of Ghadames A22

1939, Apr. 12 Photo.

No.	Type	Description	Unused	Used
83	A21	5c olive brown	15	38
84	A22	20c red brown	15	38
85	A21	50c rose violet	22	38
86	A22	75c scarlet	22	*62*
87	A21	1.25 l gray blue	25	*70*
		Nos. 83-87,C36-C38 (8)	1.74	*4.41*

13th Sample Fair, Tripoli.

Modern City — A23

Oxen and Plow — A24

Mosque — A25

1940, June 3 Wmk. 140 *Perf. 14*

No.	Type	Description	Unused	Used
88	A23	5c brown	15	38
89	A24	10c red orange	15	38
90	A25	25c dull green	35	*70*
91	A23	50c dark violet	35	*70*
92	A24	75c crimson	35	*1.10*
93	A25	1.25 l ultramarine	35	*1.10*
94	A24	2 l + 75c rose lake	35	*1.50*
		Nos. 88-94,C39-C42 (11)	3.31	*11.56*

Triennial Overseas Exposition, Naples.

"Two Peoples, One War," Hitler and Mussolini A26

1941, May 16

No.	Type	Description	Unused	Used
95	A26	5c orange	15	*2.50*
96	A26	10c brown	15	*2.50*
97	A26	20c dull violet	30	*2.50*
98	A26	25c green	30	*2.50*
99	A26	50c purple	38	*2.50*
100	A26	75c scarlet	38	*5.00*
101	A26	1.25 l sapphire	38	*5.00*
		Nos. 95-101,C43 (8)	2.29	*32.50*

The Rome-Berlin Axis.

Catalogue values for unused stamps in this section, from this point to the end of the section, are for Never Hinged items.

United Kingdom of Libya

Stamps of Cyrenaica 1950 Surcharged in Black

— ليبيا —

2 MAL. LIBYA

For Use in Tripolitania

1951, Dec. 24 Unwmk. *Perf. 12½*

No.	Type	Description	Unused	Used
102	A2	1mal on 2m rose car	15	20
103	A2	2mal on 4m dk grn	15	20
104	A2	4mal on 8m red org	15	25
105	A2	5mal on 10m pur	20	38
106	A2	6mal on 12m red	25	*65*
a.		Inverted surcharge	25.00	25.00
107	A2	10mal on 20m dp bl	35	*60*
a.		Arabic "20" for "10"	20.00	20.00
108	A3	24mal on 50m choc & ultra	1.10	*2.50*
109	A3	48mal on 100m bl blk & car rose	4.25	*8.00*
110	A3	96mal on 200m vio & pur	9.00	*19.00*
111	A3	240mal on 500m dk grn & org	20.00	*42.50*
		Nos. 102-111 (10)	35.60	*74.28*

The surcharge is larger on Nos. 108 to 111.

Same Surcharge in Francs

For Use in Fezzan

No.	Type	Description	Unused	Used
112	A2	2fr on 2m rose car	15	22
113	A2	4fr on 4m dk grn	15	22
114	A2	8fr on 8m red org	20	28
115	A2	10fr on 10m pur	20	28
116	A2	12fr on 12m red	70	1.10
117	A2	20fr on 20m dp bl	1.10	*1.60*
118	A3	48fr on 50m choc & ultra	11.00	*16.00*
119	A3	96fr on 100m bl blk & car rose	14.00	*21.00*
120	A3	192fr on 200m vio & pur	32.50	*50.00*
121	A3	480fr on 500m dk grn & org	25.00	*40.00*
		Nos. 112-121 (10)	85.00	*130.70*

The surcharge is larger on Nos. 118-121.

A second printing of Nos. 118-121 has an elongated first character in second line of Arabic surcharge.

ليبيا

Cyrenaica Nos. 65-77 Overprinted in Black

LIBYA

For Use in Cyrenaica

No.	Type	Description	Unused	Used
122	A2	1m dark brown	15	25
123	A2	2m rose carmine	15	25
124	A2	3m orange	15	38
125	A2	4m dark green	9.50	7.00
126	A2	5m gray	40	*70*
127	A2	8m red orange	40	*80*
128	A2	10m purple	45	*70*
129	A2	12m red	45	*1.00*
130	A2	20m deep blue	45	*70*
131	A3	50m choc & ultra	4.00	*7.00*
132	A3	100m bl blk & car rose	7.00	*12.00*
133	A3	200m violet & pur	19.00	*30.00*
134	A3	500m dk grn & org	50.00	*90.00*
		Nos. 122-134 (13)	92.10	*150.78*

Wider spacing between the two lines on Nos. 131-134.

King Idris

A27 A28

1952, Apr. 15 Engr. *Perf. 11½*

No.	Type	Description	Unused	Used
135	A27	2m yellow brown	15	15
136	A27	4m gray	15	15
137	A27	5m blue green	10.00	16
138	A27	8m vermilion	16	15
139	A27	10m purple	9.25	15
140	A27	12m lilac rose	16	15
141	A27	20m deep blue	9.25	20
142	A27	25m chocolate	10.00	25
143	A28	50m brown & blue	90	35
144	A28	100m gray blk & car rose	1.40	40
145	A28	200m dk blue & pur	2.75	2.25
146	A28	500m dk grn & brn orange	13.00	7.50
		Nos. 135-146 (12)	57.17	11.86

Globe — A29

Perf. 13½x13

1955, Jan. 1 Photo. Wmk. 195

No.	Type	Value	Color	Unused	Used
147	A29	5m	yellow brown	40	38
148	A29	10m	green	80	65
149	A29	30m	violet	2.25	1.25

Arab Postal Union founding, July 1, 1954.

Nos. 147-149 Overprinted

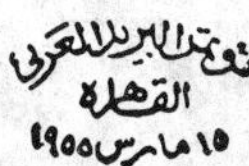

1955, Aug. 1

No.	Type	Value	Color	Unused	Used
150	A29	5m	yellow brn	22	20
151	A29	10m	green	32	32
152	A29	30m	violet	1.10	65

Arab Postal Congress, Cairo, Mar. 15.

Emblems of Tripolitania, Cyrenaica and Fezzan with Royal Crown — A30

1955 Engr. Wmk. 310 *Perf. 11½*

No.	Type	Value	Color	Unused	Used
153	A30	2m	lemon	65	35
154	A30	3m	slate blue	15	15
155	A30	4m	gray green	65	60
156	A30	5m	light blue grn	22	15
157	A30	10m	violet	40	15
158	A30	18m	crimson	15	15
159	A30	20m	orange	20	15
160	A30	30m	blue	45	15
161	A30	35m	brown	25	15
162	A30	40m	rose carmine	45	15
163	A30	50m	olive	42	16

Size: 27½x32½mm

No.	Type	Value	Color	Unused	Used
164	A30	100m	dk green & pur	65	25
165	A30	200m	ultra & rose car	6.50	2.50
166	A30	500m	grn & orange	8.00	6.00

Size: 26½x32mm

No.	Type	Value	Color	Unused	Used
167	A30	£1	ocher, brn & grn, *yel*	14.00	7.00
			Nos. 153-167 (15)	33.14	18.06

See Nos. 177-179, 192-206A.

No. 136 Surcharged 5 0

1955, Aug. 25 Unwmk.

No.	Type	Value	Color	Unused	Used
168	A27	5m	on 4m gray	80	80

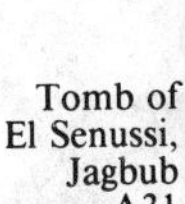

Tomb of El Senussi, Jagbub A31

Perf. 13x13½

1956, Sept. 14 Photo. Wmk. 195

No.	Type	Value	Color	Unused	Used
169	A31	5m	green	15	15
170	A31	10m	bright violet	16	15
171	A31	15m	rose carmine	25	25
172	A31	30m	sapphire	70	50

Death centenary of the Imam Seyyid Mohammed Aly El Senussi (in 1859).

Map, Flags and UN Headquarters A32

Globe and Postal Emblems A33

1956, Dec. 14 Litho. *Perf. 13½x13*

No.	Type	Value	Color	Unused	Used
173	A32	15m	bl, ocher & ol bis	25	15
174	A32	35m	bl, ocher & vio brn	40	28

Libya's admission to the UN, 1st anniv.

1957 Wmk. 195 *Perf. 13½x13*

No.	Type	Value	Color	Unused	Used
175	A33	15m	blue	90	30
176	A33	500m	yellow brown	4.50	3.50

Arab Postal Congress, Tripoli, Feb. 9.

Emblems Type of 1955

1957 Wmk. 310 Engr. *Perf. 11½*

No.	Type	Value	Color	Unused	Used
177	A30	1m	black, *yellow*	16	15
178	A30	2m	bister brown	16	15
179	A30	4m	brown carmine	16	15
			Set value		24

UN Emblem and Broken Chain — A34

Unwmk.

1958, Dec. 10 Photo. *Perf. 14*

No.	Type	Value	Color	Unused	Used
180	A34	10m	bluish violet	15	15
181	A34	15m	green	20	16
182	A34	30m	ultramarine	50	40

Universal Declaration of Human Rights, 10th anniv.

Date Palms and FAO Emblem A35

1959, Dec. 5 Unwmk. *Perf. 14*

No.	Type	Value	Color	Unused	Used
183	A35	10m	pale vio & black	15	15
184	A35	15m	bluish grn & blk	20	16
185	A35	45m	light blue & blk	50	45

1st Intl. Dates Conf., Tripoli, Dec. 5-11.

Arab League Center, Cairo, and Arms of Libya A36

Perf. 13x13½

1960, Mar. 22 Wmk. 328

No.	Type	Value	Color	Unused	Used
186	A36	10m	dull grn & blk	28	16

Opening of the Arab League Center and the Arab Postal Museum in Cairo.

Emblems of WRY and UN, Arms of Libya — A37

Palm Tree and Radio Mast — A38

1960, Apr. 7 Unwmk. *Perf. 14*

No.	Type	Value	Color	Unused	Used
187	A37	10m	violet & black	20	16
188	A37	45m	blue & black	70	62

World Refugee Year, July 1, 1959-June 30, 1960.

1960, Aug. 4 Engr. *Perf. 13x13½*

No.	Type	Value	Color	Unused	Used
189	A38	10m	violet	15	15
190	A38	15m	blue green	20	15
191	A38	45m	dk carmine rose	65	28
			Set value		45

3rd Arab Telecommunications Conf., Tripoli, Aug. 4.

Emblems Type of 1955

1960 Wmk. 310 Engr. *Perf. 11½*

Size: 18x21½mm

No.	Type	Value	Color	Unused	Used
192	A30	1m	black, *gray*	15	15
193	A30	2m	bis brn, *buff*	15	15
194	A30	3m	blue, *bluish*	15	15
195	A30	4m	brn car, *rose*	15	15
196	A30	5m	grn, *greenish*	15	15
197	A30	10m	vio, *pale vio*	15	15
198	A30	15m	brown, *buff*	15	15
199	A30	20m	orange, *buff*	15	15
200	A30	30m	red, *pink*	15	15
201	A30	40m	rose car, *rose*	15	15
202	A30	45m	blue, *bluish*	15	16
203	A30	50m	olive, *buff*	35	16

Size: 27½x32½mm

No.	Type	Value	Color	Unused	Used
204	A30	100m	dk grn & pur, *gray*	50	40
205	A30	200m	bl & rose car, *bluish*	1.50	60
206	A30	500m	green & org, *greenish*	8.25	2.50

Size: 26½x32mm

No.	Type	Value	Color	Unused	Used
206A	A30	£1	ocher, brn & grn, *brn*	16.00	14.00
			Nos. 192-206A (16)	28.25	19.32

Watchtower and Broken Chain — A39

1961, Aug. 9 Photo. Unwmk.

No.	Type	Value	Color	Unused	Used
207	A39	5m	lt yel grn & brn	35	15
208	A39	15m	light blue & brn	50	16

Issued for Army Day, Aug. 9, 1961.

Map of Zelten Oil Field and Tanker at Marsa Brega — A40

1961, Oct. 25 *Perf. 11½*

No.	Type	Value	Color	Unused	Used
209	A40	15m	ol grn & buff	15	15
210	A40	50m	red brn & pale vio	50	30
211	A40	100m	ultra & blue	1.00	65

Opening of first oil pipe line in Libya.

Hands Breaking Chain, Tractor and Cows — A41

Designs: 50m, Modern highways and buildings. 100m, Machinery.

1961, Dec. 24 *Perf. 11½*

Granite Paper

No.	Type	Value	Color	Unused	Used
212	A41	15m	pale grn, grn & brown	15	15
213	A41	50m	buff & brown	50	30
214	A41	100m	sal, vio & brn	1.00	65

10th anniversary of independence.

Camel Riders — A42

Designs: 15m, Well. 50m, Oil installations in desert.

1962, Feb. 20 Photo. *Perf. 12*

No.	Type	Value	Color	Unused	Used
215	A42	10m	choc & org brn	15	15
216	A42	15m	plum & yel grn	40	32
217	A42	50m	emer & ultra	1.10	80
a.			Souv. sheet of 3, #215-217, imperf.	20.00	13.00

Intl. Fair, Tripoli, Feb. 20-Mar. 20.

Nos. 215-217 exist imperf. Value about twice that of perf.

Malaria Eradication Emblem and Palm — A43

Ahmed Rafik El Mehdawi (1989-1961), Poet — A44

1962, Apr. 7 Unwmk. *Perf. 11½*

No.	Type	Value	Color	Unused	Used
218	A43	15m	multicolored	35	16
219	A43	50m	grn, yel & brn	45	45

WHO drive to eradicate malaria.

Exist imperf. Value about three times that of perf.

Two imperf. souvenir sheets exist, one containing the 15m, the other the 50m. Sold for 20m and 70m respectively. Value for both, $6.

1962, July 6 Engr. *Perf. 13x14*

No.	Type	Value	Color	Unused	Used
220	A44	15m	green	15	15
221	A44	20m	brown	28	22

El Mehdawi, 1st death anniv.

Clasped Hands and Scout Emblem — A45

Drop of Oil with New City, Desert, Oil Wells and Map of Coast Line — A46

Designs: 10m, 30m, Boy Scouts. 15m, 50m, Scout emblem and tents.

1962, July 13 Photo. *Perf. 12*

No.	Type	Value	Color	Unused	Used
222	A45	5m	yel, blk & red	15	15
223	A45	10m	bl, blk & yel	22	15
224	A45	15m	multicolored	28	20
			Set value		40

Souvenir Sheet

Imperf

No.	Type	Value	Color	Unused	Used
225			Sheet of 3	3.75	3.50
a.	A45	20m	yel, blk & red	65	65
b.	A45	30m	bl, blk & yel	65	65
c.	A45	50m	bl gray, yel, blk & grn	65	65

Third Libyan Scout meeting (Philia).

Nos. 222-224 exist imperf. Value for set, $1.50.

1962, Nov. 25 ***Perf. 11x11½***

226 A46 15m grn & vio blk 15 15
227 A46 50m brn org & ol 45 35

Opening of the Essider Terminal Sidrah pipeline system.

Centenary Emblem — A47

Litho. & Photo.

1963, Jan. 1 ***Perf. 11½***

228 A47 10m rose, blk, red & bl 15 15
229 A47 15m cit, blk, red & bl 20 15
230 A47 20m gray, blk, red & bl 45 35
Set value 55

Centenary of the International Red Cross.

Rainbow and Arches over Map of Africa and Libya — A48

1963, Feb. 28 **Litho.** ***Perf. 13½***

231 A48 15m multicolored 20 15
232 A48 30m multicolored 38 35
233 A48 50m multicolored 55 50

Tripoli Intl. Fair "Gateway of Africa," Feb. 28-Mar. 28. Every other horizontal row inverted in sheet of 50 (25 tete beche pairs).

Date Palm and Well — A49

Designs: 15m, Camel and flock of sheep. 45m, Sower and tractor.

1963, Mar. 21 **Photo.** ***Perf. 11½***

234 A49 10m green, lt bl & bis 15 15
235 A49 15m pur, lt grn & bis 15 15
236 A49 45m dk bl, sal & sep 55 28
Set value 48

FAO "Freedom from Hunger" campaign.

Man with Whip and Slave Reaching for UN Emblem A50

1963, Dec. 10 **Unwmk.** ***Perf. 11½***

237 A50 5m red brown & bl 15 15
238 A50 15m deep claret & bl 15 15
239 A50 50m green & blue 38 25
Set value 40

Universal Declaration of Human Rights, 15th anniv.

Values quoted in this catalogue are for stamps graded at Fine-Very Fine and with no faults. An illustrated guide to grade is provided in introductory material, beginning on Page 1A.

Exhibition Hall and Finger Pointing to Libya — A51

1964, Feb. 28 **Photo.** ***Perf. 11½***

240 A51 10m red brn, gray grn & brn 15 15
241 A51 15m pur, gray grn & brn 28 20
242 A51 30m dk bl, gray grn & brn 75 38

3rd Intl. Fair, Tripoli, Feb. 28-Mar. 20.

Child Playing with Blocks — A52

Design: 15m, Child in bird's nest.

1964, Mar. 22 ***Perf. 11½***

243 A52 5m multicolored 15 15
244 A52 15m multicolored 15 15
245 A52 45m multicolored 42 28
a. Souvenir sheet of 3, #243-245, imperf. 2.00 2.00
Set value 48

Children's Day. Exist imperf. Value about 1½ times that of perf.
No. 245a sold for 100m.

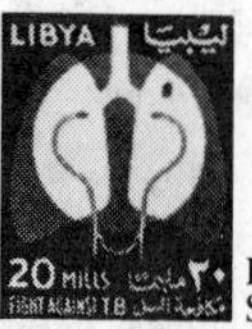
Lungs and Stethoscope — A53

1964, Apr. 7 **Photo.** ***Perf. 13½x14***

246 A53 20m deep purple 50 25

Campaign against tuberculosis.

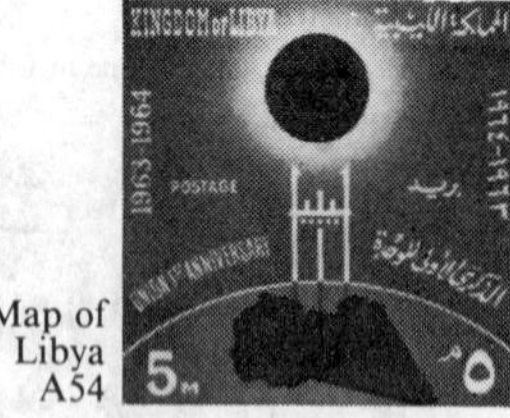
Map of Libya A54

1964, Apr. 27 **Unwmk.** ***Perf. 11½***

247 A54 5m emerald & org 15 15
248 A54 50m blue & yellow 38 28
Set value 32

First anniversary of Libyan union.

Moth Emerging from Cocoon, Veiled and Modern Women — A55

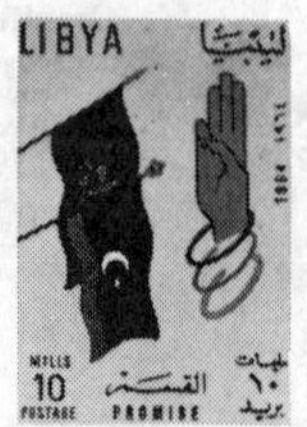
Hand Giving Scout Sign, Scout and Libyan Flags — A56

1964, June 15 **Litho. & Engraved**

249 A55 10m vio bl & lt grn 15 15
250 A55 20m vio blue & yel 15 15
251 A55 35m vio bl & pink 30 28
a. Souv. sheet of 3, #249-251 2.00 2.00
Set value 40

To honor Libyan women in a new epoch. No. 251a sold for 100m.

1964, July 24 **Photo.** ***Perf. 12x11½***

Design: 20m, Libyan Scout emblem and hands.

252 A56 10m lt bl & multi 65 25
253 A56 20m multicolored 1.10 40
a. Souvenir sheet of 2, #252-253, imperf. 2.75 2.75

Opening of new Boy Scout headquarters; installation of Crown Prince Hassan al-Rida el Senussi as Chief Scout. No. 253a sold for 50m.

Nos. 252-253 exist imperf. Value about 1½ times that of perf.

Bayonet, Wreath and Map A57

Ahmed Bahloul el-Sharef A58

1964, Aug. 9 **Litho.** ***Perf. 14x13½***

254 A57 10m yel grn & brn 15 15
255 A57 20m org & blk 25 15
Set value 32 16

Founding of the Senussi Army.

1964, Aug. 11 **Engr.** ***Perf. 11½***

256 A58 15m lilac 15 15
257 A58 20m greenish blue 35 16
Set value 20

Poet Ahmed Bahloul el-Sharef, died 1953.

Soccer A59

1964, Oct. 1 **Litho.** ***Perf. 14***

Black Inscriptions and Gold Olympic Rings

258 A59 5m shown 35 35
259 A59 10m Bicycling 35 35
260 A59 20m Boxing 35 35
261 A59 30m Sprinter 35 35
262 A59 35m Woman diver 35 35
263 A59 50m Hurdling 35 35
a. Block of 6, #258-263 2.25 2.25
Nos. 258-263 (6) 2.10 2.10

18th Olympic Games, Tokyo, Oct. 10-25. No. 263a printed in sheet of 48. The two blocks in each double row are inverted in relation to the two blocks in the next row, providing various tete beche and se-tenant arrangements.

#258-263 exist imperf. Value for set, $7.50.

Perf. and imperf. souvenir sheets exist containing six 15m stamps in the designs and colors of Nos. 258-263. Sheets sold for 100m. Value for both, $13.50.

Arab Postal Union Emblem — A59a

1964, Dec. 1 **Photo.** ***Perf. 11x11½***

264 A59a 10m yellow & blue 15 15
265 A59a 15m pale vio & org brn 16 15
266 A59a 30m lt yel grn & brn 55 40
Set value 56

Permanent Office of the APU, 10th anniv.

International Cooperation Year Emblem A60

1965, Jan. 1 **Litho.** ***Perf. 14½x14***

267 A60 5m vio bl & gold 15 15
268 A60 15m rose car & gold 50 50

Imperfs. exist. Value about twice that of perfs.

See Nos. C51-C51a.

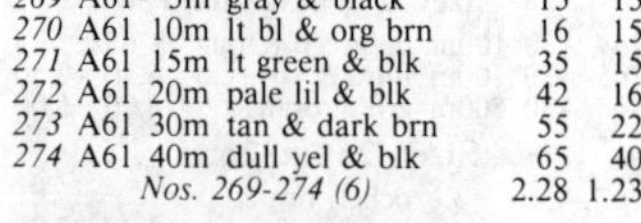
European Bee Eater — A61

Birds: 5m, Long-legged buzzard, vert. 15m, Chestnut-bellied sandgrouse. 20m, Houbara bustard. 30m, Spotted sandgrouse. 40m, Libyan Barbary partridge.

1965, Feb. 10 **Photo.** ***Perf. 11½***

Granite Paper

Birds in Natural Colors

269 A61 5m gray & black 15 15
270 A61 10m lt bl & org brn 16 15
271 A61 15m lt green & blk 35 15
272 A61 20m pale lil & blk 42 16
273 A61 30m tan & dark brn 55 22
274 A61 40m dull yel & blk 65 40
Nos. 269-274 (6) 2.28 1.23

Map of Africa with Libya A62

1965, Feb. 28 **Photo.** ***Perf. 11½***

Granite Paper

275 A62 50m multicolored 35 20

4th Intl. Tripoli Fair, Feb. 28-Mar. 20.

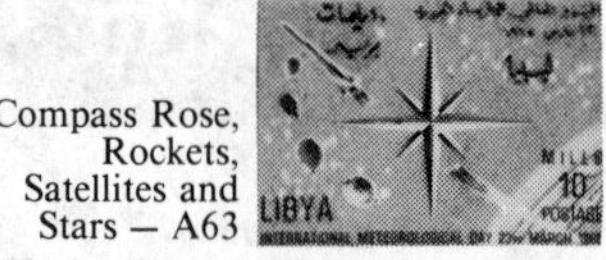
Compass Rose, Rockets, Satellites and Stars — A63

1965, Mar. 23 **Litho.**

276 A63 10m multicolored 15 15
277 A63 15m multicolored 15 15
278 A63 50m multicolored 40 28
Set value 56 30

Fifth World Meteorological Day.

ITU Emblem, Old and New Communication Equipment — A64

1965, May 17 **Unwmk.**

279 A64 10m sepia 15 15
280 A64 20m red lilac 15 15
281 A64 50m lilac rose 28 20
Set value 48 32

ITU, centenary.

Library Aflame and Lamp — A65

1965, June **Litho.** ***Perf. 11½***

282 A65 15m multicolored 15 15
283 A65 50m multicolored 40 20
Set value 28

Burning of the Library of Algiers, June 7, 1962.

Rose — A66

Jet Plane and Globe — A67

1965, Aug. **Litho.** ***Perf. 14***

284 A66 1m shown 16 15
285 A66 2m Iris 16 15
286 A66 3m Opuntia 35 15
287 A66 4m Sunflower 50 22
Set value 52

1965, Oct. **Photo.** ***Perf. 11½***

288 A67 5m multicolored 15 15
289 A67 10m multicolored 15 15
290 A67 15m multicolored 28 15
Set value 45 25

Issued to publicize Libyan Airlines.

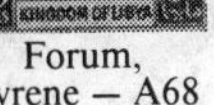

Forum, Cyrene — A68

Mausoleum at Germa — A69

Designs: 100m, Arch of Trajan. 200m, Temple of Apollo, Cyrene. 500m, Antonine Temple of Jupiter, Sabratha, horiz. £1, Theater, Sabratha.

Perf. 12x11½, 11½x12

1965, Dec. 24 **Engr.** **Wmk. 310**

291 A68 50m vio blue & ol 32 15
292 A68 100m Prus bl & dp org 65 22
293 A68 200m pur & Prus bl 1.60 32
294 A68 500m car rose & grn 2.50 1.40
295 A68 £1 grn & dp org 7.50 2.75
Nos. 291-295 (5) 12.57 4.84

Nos. 293-295 with "Kingdom of Libia" in both Arabic and English blocked out with a blue felt-tipped pen were issued June 21, 1970, by the Republic.

Perf. 11½

1966, Feb. 10 **Unwmk.** **Litho.**

296 A69 70m pur & salmon 35 25

"POLIGRAFICA & CARTEVALORI-NAPLES" and Libyan Coat of Arms printed on back in yellow green. See No. E13.

Booklet pane containing 4 No. 296 and 4 No. E13 exists.

Globe in Space, Satellites — A70

1966, Feb. 28 ***Perf. 12***

297 A70 15m multicolored 15 15
298 A70 45m multicolored 20 20
299 A70 55m multicolored 62 35
Set value 60

5th Intl. Fair at Tripoli, Feb. 28-Mar. 20.

Arab League Center, Cairo, and Emblem — A71

Litho. & Photo.

1966, Mar. 22 ***Perf. 11***

300 A71 20m car, emer & blk 15 15
301 A71 55m brt bl, ver & blk 30 25

Issued to publicize the Arab League.

Souvenir Sheet

WHO Headquarters, Geneva, and Emblem — A72

1966, May 3 **Litho.** ***Imperf.***

302 A72 50m multicolored 1.90 1.90

Inauguration of the WHO headquarters. See Nos. C55-C57.

Tuareg and Camel — A73

A74

Three Tuareg Riders — A75

Design: 20m, like 10m, facing left.

1966, June 20 **Unwmk.** ***Perf. 10***

303 A73 10m bright red 25 20
304 A73 20m ultramarine 55 40
305 A74 50m multicolored 90 80
a. Strip of 3, Nos. 303-305 1.90 1.90

Souvenir Sheet

Imperf

306 A75 100m multicolored 2.50 2.00

Gazelle A76

Emblem A77

Perf. 13x11, 11x13

1966, Aug. 12 **Litho.**

307 A76 5m lt grn, blk & red 16 15
308 A77 25m multicolored 35 20
309 A77 65m multicolored 65 35

1st Arab Girl Scout Camp (No. 307); 7th Arab Boy Scout Camp, Good Daim, Libya, Aug. 12 (Nos. 308-309).

UNESCO Emblem A78

1967, Jan. **Litho.** ***Perf. 10x10½***

310 A78 15m multicolored 15 15
311 A78 25m multicolored 20 16
Set value 24

UNESCO, 20th anniv. (in 1966).

Castle of Columns, Tolemaide A79

Fair Emblem A80

Design: 55m, Sebha Fort (horiz.).

Perf. 13x13½, 13½x13

1966, Dec. 24 **Engr.**

312 A79 25m lil, red brn & blk 16 15
313 A79 55m blk, lil & red brn 35 28

1967, Feb. 28 **Photo.** ***Perf. 11½***

314 A80 15m multicolored 16 15
315 A80 55m multicolored 35 20
Set value 25

6th Intl. Fair, Tripoli, Feb. 28-Mar. 20.

Oil Tanker, Marsa Al Hariga Terminal — A81

1967, Feb. 14 **Litho.** ***Perf. 10***

316 A81 60m multicolored 40 22

Opening of Marsa Al Hariga oil terminal.

Tourist Year Emblem — A82

1967, May 1 **Litho.** ***Perf. 10½x10***

317 A82 5m gray, blk & brt bl 15 15
318 A82 10m lt bl, blk & brt bl 15 15
319 A82 45m pink, blk & brt bl 28 16
Set value 40 25

International Tourist Year.

Map of Mediterranean and Runners — A83

1967, Sept. 8 **Litho.** ***Perf. 10½***

320 A83 5m shown 15 15
321 A83 10m Javelin 15 15
322 A83 15m Bicyling 15 15
323 A83 45m Soccer 20 16
324 A83 75m Boxing 50 25
Set value 90 55

5th Mediterranean Games, Tunis, Sept. 8-17.

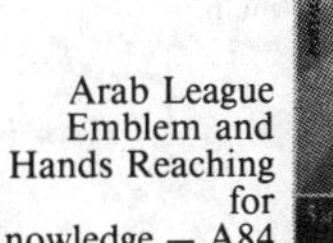

Arab League Emblem and Hands Reaching for Knowledge — A84

1967, Oct. 1 **Litho.** ***Perf. 12½x13***

325 A84 5m orange & dk pur 15 15
326 A84 10m brt grn & dk pur 15 15
327 A84 15m lilac & dk pur 15 15
328 A84 25m blue & dk pur 28 15
Set value 45 22

Literacy campaign.

Human Rights Flame — A85

1968, Jan. 15 Litho. *Perf. 13½x14*

329 A85 15m grn & vermilion	16	15
330 A85 60m org & vio bl	28	25
Set value		30

International Human Rights Year.

Map, Derrick, Plane and Camel Riders — A86

1968, Feb. 28 Photo. *Perf. 11½*

331 A86 55m car rose, brn & yel	45	35

7th Intl. Fair, Tripoli, Feb. 28-Mar. 20.

Arab League Emblem A87

1968, Mar. 22 Engr. *Perf. 13½*

332 A87 10m blue gray & car	15	15
333 A87 45m fawn & green	38	25

Issued for Arab League Week.

Children, Statuary Group — A88

Children's Day: 55m, Mother and children.

1968, Mar. 21 Litho. *Perf. 11*

334 A88 25m gray, blk & mag	16	15
335 A88 55m gray & multi	28	20
Set value		28

Hands Reaching for WHO Emblem — A89

1968, Apr. 7 Photo. *Perf. 13½x14½*

336 A89 25m rose cl, dk bl & gray bl	20	15
337 A89 55m bl, blk & gray	45	20
Set value		28

WHO, 20th anniversary.

The lack of a price for a listed item does not necessarily indicate rarity.

From Oil Field to Tanker — A90

1968, Apr. 23 Litho. *Perf. 11*

338 A90 10m multicolored	16	15
339 A90 60m multicolored	45	25

Opening of the Zueitina oil terminal.

Teacher and Crowd A91

1968, Sept. 8 Litho. *Perf. 13½*

340 A91 5m bright pink	15	15
341 A91 10m orange	15	15
342 A91 15m blue	15	15
343 A91 20m emerald	25	16
Set value	42	32

Literacy campaign.

Arab Labor Emblem A92

1968, Nov. 3 Photo. *Perf. 14x13½*

344 A92 10m multicolored	15	15
345 A92 15m multicolored	25	15
Set value		20

4th session of the Arab Labor Ministers' Conf., Tripoli, Nov. 3-10.

Wadi el Kuf Bridge and Road Sign — A93

1968, Dec. 25 Litho. *Perf. 11x11½*

346 A93 25m ultra & multi	16	15
347 A93 60m emer & multi	35	20

Opening of the Wadi el Kuf Bridge.

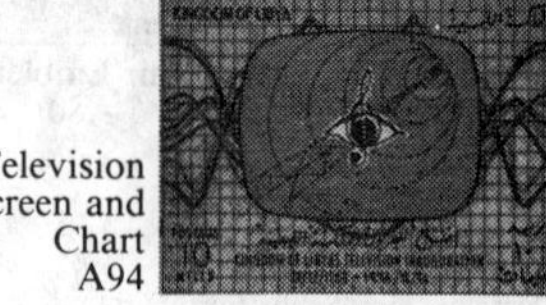

Television Screen and Chart A94

1968, Dec. 25 Photo. *Perf. 14x13½*

348 A94 10m yellow & multi	15	15
349 A94 30m lilac & multi	25	16
Set value		20

Inauguration of television service, Dec. 24.

Melons — A95

Designs: 10m, Peanuts. 15m, Lemons. 20m, Oranges. 25m, Peaches. 35m, Pears.

1969, Jan. Photo. *Perf. 11½*

Granite Paper

350 A95 5m shown	15	15
351 A95 10m Peanuts	15	15
352 A95 15m Lemons	15	15
353 A95 20m Oranges	30	15
354 A95 25m Peaches	38	15
355 A95 35m Pears	50	30
Set value	1.40	70

Nos. 350-355 with "Kingdom of Libya" in both English and Arabic blocked out with a blue felt-tipped pen were issued in December, 1971, by the Republic.

Tripoli Fair Emblem A96

1969, Apr. 8

Granite Paper

356 A96 25m silver & multi	15	15
357 A96 35m bronze & multi	15	15
358 A96 40m gold & multi	28	16
Set value	48	32

8th Intl. Fair, Tripoli, Mar. 6-26.

Weather Balloon and Observer A97

1969, Mar. 21 Photo. *Perf. 14x13*

359 A97 60m gray & multi	40	35

World Meteorological Day, Mar. 23.

Cogwheel and Workers A98

1969, Mar. 29 Litho. *Perf. 13½*

360 A98 15m blue & multi	15	15
361 A98 55m salmon & multi	35	20
Set value		28

10th anniversary of Social Insurance.

ILO Emblem — A99

1969, June 1 Photo. *Perf. 14*

362 A99 10m bl grn, blk & lt ol	15	15
363 A99 60m car rose, blk & lt ol	38	20
Set value		28

ILO, 50th anniversary.

African Tourist Year Emblem — A100

1969, July *Perf. 11½*

Emblem in Emerald, Light Blue & Red

364 A100 15m emer & silver	20	15
365 A100 30m blk & gold	40	20
Set value		28

Issued to publicize African Tourist Year.

Libyan Arab Republic

Soldiers, Tanks and Planes — A101

Radar, Flags and Carrier Pigeon — A102

1969, Dec. 7 Photo. *Perf. 12x12½*

366 A101 5m org & multi	15	15
367 A101 10m ultra & multi	15	15
368 A101 15m multicolored	20	15
369 A101 25m multicolored	30	15
370 A101 45m brt bl & multi	45	25
371 A101 60m multicolored	80	40
Nos. 366-371 (6)	2.05	
Set value		1.00

Establishment of the Libyan Arab Republic, Sept. 1, 1969. See Nos. 379-384.

1970, Mar. 1 Photo. *Perf. 11½*

Granite Paper

372 A102 15m multicolored	22	15
373 A102 20m multicolored	38	18
374 A102 25m multicolored	45	22
375 A102 40m multicolored	60	38

Map of Arab League Countries, Flag and Emblem A102a

1970, Mar. 22

376 A102a 10m lt bl, brn & grn	15	15
377 A102a 15m org, brn & grn	15	15
378 A102a 20m ol, brn & grn	22	20
Set value	42	35

25th anniversary of the Arab League.

Type A101 Redrawn — A103

1970, May 2 Photo. *Perf. 12x12½*

379 A103 5m org & multi	15	15
380 A103 10m ultra & multi	15	15
381 A103 15m multicolored	16	15
382 A103 25m multicolored	25	15

383 A103 45m brt bl & multi 50 20
384 A103 60m multicolored 60 25
Nos. 379-384 (6) 1.81
Set value 70

On Nos. 379-384 the numerals are in black, the bottom inscription is in 2 lines and several other changes.

Inauguration of UPU Headquarters, Bern — A104

1970, May 20 Photo. *Perf. 11½x11*
385 A104 10m multicolored 15 15
386 A104 25m multicolored 20 15
387 A104 60m multicolored 45 22
Set value 38

Arms of Libyan Arab Republic A105

Flags, Soldiers and Tank A106

1970, June 20 Photo. *Perf. 11*
388 A105 15m black & brt rose 15 15
389 A105 25m vio bl, yel & brt rose 22 15
390 A105 45m emer, yel & brt rose 55 20
Set value 35

Evacuation of US military base in Libya.

1970, Sept. 1 Photo. *Perf. 11x11½*
391 A106 20m multicolored 45 16
392 A106 25m multicolored 55 22
393 A106 30m blue & multi 90 45

Libyan Arab Republic, 1st anniv.

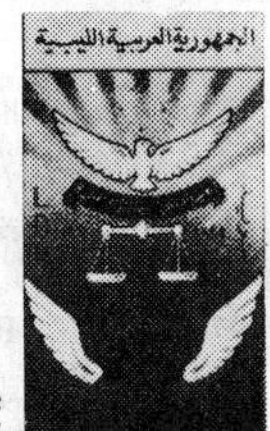

UN Emblem, Dove and Scales — A107

1970, Oct. 24 Photo. *Perf. 11x11½*
394 A107 5m org & multi 38 15
395 A107 10m olive & multi 45 22
396 A107 60m multicolored 90 40

25th anniversary of the United Nations.

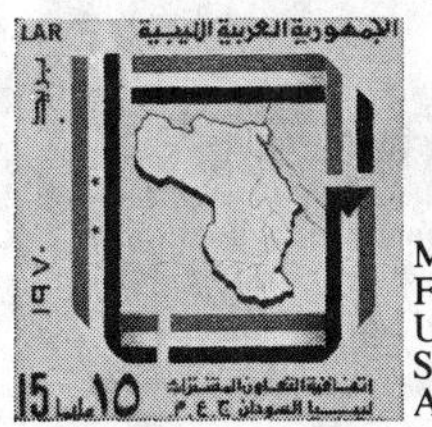

Map and Flags of UAR, Libya, Sudan A107a

1970, Dec. 27 Photo. *Perf. 11½*
397 A107a 15m lt grn, car & blk 1.50 60

Signing of the Charter of Tripoli affirming the unity of UAR, Libya and the Sudan, Dec. 27, 1970.

UN Emblem, Dove and Globe — A108

1971, Jan. 10 Litho. *Perf. 12x11½*
398 A108 15m multicolored 38 15
399 A108 20m multicolored 45 16
400 A108 60m lt vio & multi 90 30

UN declaration on granting of independence to colonial countries and peoples, 10th anniv.

Education Year Emblem A109

Al Fatah Fighter A110

1971, Jan. 16
401 A109 5m red, blk & ocher 16 15
402 A109 10m red, blk & emer 30 15
403 A109 20m red, blk & vio bl 60 15
Set value 28

International Education Year.

1971, Mar. 14 Photo. *Perf. 11*
404 A110 5m ol & multi 50 15
405 A110 10m yel & multi 80 15
406 A110 100m multicolored 1.90 20

Fight for the liberation of Palestine.

Tripoli Fair Emblem A111

10th Anniv. of OPEC A112

1971, Mar. 18 Litho. *Perf. 14*
407 A111 15m multicolored 20 15
408 A111 30m org & multi 30 15
Set value 22

9th International Fair at Tripoli.

1971, May 29 Litho. *Perf. 12*
409 A112 10m yellow & brown 15 15
410 A112 70m pink & vio bl 55 25
Set value 30

Globe and Waves A113

1971, June 10 *Perf. 14½x13½*
411 A113 25m brt grn, blk & vio bl 20 15
412 A113 35m gray & multi 22 15
Set value 24

3rd World Telecommunications Day, May 17, 1971.

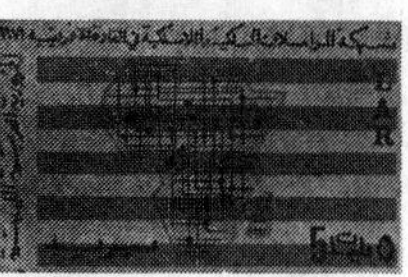

Map of Africa and Telecommunications Network — A114

1971, June 10
413 A114 5m yel, blk & grn 15 15
414 A114 15m dl bl, blk & grn 40 22
Set value 28

Pan-African telecommunications system.

Torchbearer and Banner A115

Ramadan Suehli A116

1971, June 15 Photo. *Perf. 11½x12*
415 A115 5m yel & multi 20 15
416 A115 10m org & multi 35 15
417 A115 15m multicolored 50 15
Set value 16

Evacuation of US military base, 1st anniv.

1971, Aug. 24 *Perf. 14x14½*
418 A116 15m multicolored 15 15
419 A116 55m bl & multi 22 15
Set value 20

Ramadan Suehli (1879-1920), freedom fighter.

See Nos. 422-423, 426-427, 439-440, 479-480.

Date Palm — A117

Gamal Abdel Nasser (1918-1970), President of Egypt — A118

1971, Sept. 1
420 A117 5m multicolored 20 15
421 A117 15m multicolored 40 15
Set value 16

Sept. 1, 1969 Revolution, 2nd anniv.

Portrait Type of 1971

Portrait: Omar el Mukhtar (1858-1931), leader of the Martyrs.

1971, Sept. 16 *Perf. 14x14½*
422 A116 5m lt grn & multi 15 15
423 A116 100m multicolored 70 25
Set value 30

1971, Sept. 28 Photo. *Perf. 11x11½*
424 A118 5m lil, grn & blk 15 15
425 A118 15m grn, lil & blk 22 15
Set value 22

Portrait Type of 1971

Portrait: Ibrahim Usta Omar (1908-1950), patriotic poet.

1971, Oct. 8 Litho. *Perf. 14x14½*
426 A116 25m vio bl & multi 20 15
427 A116 30m multicolored 25 15

Racial Equality Emblem A119

Arab Postal Union Emblem A120

1971, Oct. 24 *Perf. 13½x14½*
428 A119 25m multicolored 22 15
429 A119 35m multicolored 30 15
Set value 22

Intl. Year Against Racial Discrimination.

1971, Nov. 6 Litho. *Perf. 14½*
Emblem in Black, Yellow and Blue
430 A120 5m red 15 15
431 A120 10m violet 15 15
432 A120 15m bright rose lil 20 15
Set value 36 20

Conference of Sofar, Lebanon, establishing Arab Postal Union, 25th anniv.

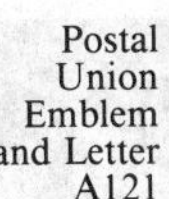

Postal Union Emblem and Letter A121

Design: 25m, 55m, APU emblem, letter and dove.

1971, Dec. Photo. *Perf. 11½x11*
433 A121 10m org brn, bl & blk 15 15
434 A121 15m org, lt bl & blk 15 15
435 A121 25m lt grn, org & blk 22 15
436 A121 55m lt brn, yel & blk 42 22
Set value 40

10th anniversary of African Postal Union.
Issue dates: 25m, 55m, Dec. 2; 10m, 15m, Dec. 12.

Book Year Emblem A122

Coat of Arms A123

1972, Jan. 1 Litho. *Perf. 12½x13*
437 A122 15d ultra, brn, gold & blk 20 15
438 A122 20d gold, brn, ultra & blk 22 15

International Book Year.

Portrait Type of 1971

Portrait: Ahmed Gnaba (1898-1968), poet of unity.

1972, Jan. 12 *Perf. 14x14½*
439 A116 20m red & multi 20 15
440 A116 35m olive & multi 22 15
Set value 20

1972, Feb. 10 Photo. *Perf. 14½*
Size: 19x23mm
441 A123 5m gray & multi 15 15
442 A123 10m lt ol & multi 16 15
443 A123 15d lilac & multi 15 15
445 A123 25m lt bl & multi 15 15
446 A123 30m rose & multi 22 15
447 A123 35m lt ol & multi 35 15
448 A123 40m dl yel & multi 25 15
449 A123 45m lt grn & multi 30 15
451 A123 55m multicolored 35 20
452 A123 60m bis & multi 50 20
453 A123 65d multicolored 40 22
454 A123 70d lt vio & multi 55 22
455 A123 80d ocher & multi 70 25
456 A123 90m bl & multi 1.10 35

Size: 27x32mm
Perf. 14x14½

457 A123 100d multicolored 1.50 38
458 A123 200d multicolored 2.25 45
459 A123 500d multicolored 4.50 2.50
460 A123 £1 multicolored 9.00 5.00
Nos. 441-460 (18) 22.58 10.97

A124

20m
50m

Coil Stamps

1972, July 27 Photo. *Perf. 14½x14*
461 A124 5m sl bl, ocher & black 70 15
462 A124 20m bl, lil & blk 2.75 30
463 A124 50m bl, ol & blk 6.00 1.10

See Nos. 496-498, 575-577.

Tombs at Ghirza A125

Fair Emblem A126

Designs: 10m, Kufic inscription, Agedabia, horiz. 15m, Marcus Aurelius Arch, Tripoli. 25m, Exchange of weapons, mural from Wan Amil Cave. 55m, Garamanthian (Berber) chariot, petroglyph, Wadi Zigza. 70m, Nymph Cyrene strangling a lion, bas-relief, Cyrene.

1972, Feb. 15 Litho. *Perf. 14*
464 A125 5m lilac & multi 15 15
465 A125 10m multicolored 15 15
466 A125 15m dp org & multi 16 15
467 A125 25m emer & multi 25 15
468 A125 55m scar & multi 70 22
469 A125 70m ultra & multi 1.00 38
Nos. 464-469 (6) 2.41
Set value 92

1972, Mar. 1
470 A126 25d gray & multi 22 15
471 A126 35d multicolored 30 18
472 A126 50d multicolored 55 25
473 A126 70d multicolored 70 38

10th International Fair at Tripoli.

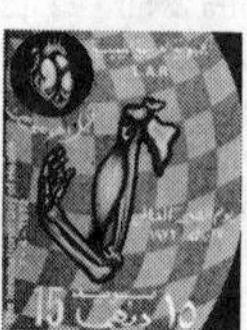
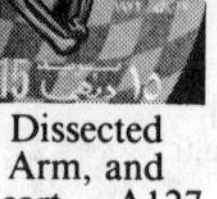
Dissected Arm, and Heart — A127

"Arab Unity" — A128

1972, Apr. 7 *Perf. 14½*
474 A127 15d multicolored 80 30
475 A127 25d multicolored 1.50 60

"Your heart is your health," World Health Day.

Litho. & Engr.
1972, Apr. 17 *Perf. 13½x13*
476 A128 15d bl, yel & blk 15 15
477 A128 20d lt grn, yel & blk 20 15
478 A128 25d lt ver, yel & blk 55 20
Set value 40

Federation of Arab Republics Foundation, 1st anniv.

Portrait Type of 1971

Portrait: Suleiman el Baruni (1870-1940), patriotic writer.

1972, May 1 Litho. *Perf. 14x14½*
479 A116 10m yellow & multi 70 22
480 A116 70m dp org & multi 1.10 60

Environment Emblem A129

Olympic Emblems A130

1972, Aug. 15 Litho. *Perf. 14½*
481 A129 15m red & multi 38 15
482 A129 55m green & multi 80 22

UN Conference on Human Environment, Stockholm, June 5-16.

1972, Aug. 26
483 A130 25d brt bl & multi 70 30
484 A130 35d red & multi 1.10 60

20th Olympic Games, Munich, Aug. 26-Sept. 11.

Emblem and Broken Chain A131

Dome of the Rock, Jerusalem A132

1972, Oct. 1 Litho. *Perf. 14x13½*
485 A131 15d blue & multi 15 15
486 A131 25d yellow & multi 30 15
Set value 18

Libyan Arab Republic, 3rd anniv.

1972 *Perf. 12½x13*
487 A132 10d multicolored 35 15
488 A132 25d multicolored 50 15
Set value 16

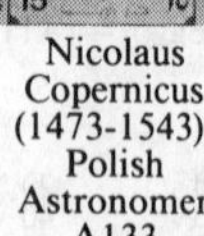
Nicolaus Copernicus (1473-1543), Polish Astronomer A133

Blind Person, Books, Loom and Basket A135

Eagle and Fair Buildings A134

Design: 25d, Copernicus in Observatory, by Jan Matejko, horiz.

Perf. 14½x13½, 13½x14½
1973, Feb. 26
489 A133 15d yellow & multi 18 15
490 A133 25d blue & multi 22 15
Set value 22

1973, Mar. 1 *Perf. 13½x14½*
491 A134 5d dull red & multi 20 15
492 A134 10d blue grn & multi 22 15
493 A134 15d vio blue & multi 45 15
Set value 28

11th International Fair at Tripoli.

1973, Apr. 18 Photo. *Perf. 12x11½*
494 A135 20d gray & multi 2.25 45
495 A135 25d dull yel & multi 4.50 1.40

Role of the blind in society.

Coil Stamps
Numeral Type of 1972
Denominations in Dirhams

5d 20d 50d

1973, Apr. 26 Photo. *Perf. 14½x14*
496 A124 5d sl bl, ocher & blk 50 15
497 A124 20d blue, lilac & blk 65 16
498 A124 50d blue, olive & blk 1.50 22
Set value 42

Map of Africa — A136

1973, May 25 Photo. *Perf. 11x11½*
499 A136 15d yel, green & brown 22 15
500 A136 25d lt yel grn, grn & blk 38 15
Set value 22

"Freedom in Unity" (Org. for African Unity).

INTERPOL Emblem and General Secretariat, Paris — A138

Perf. 13½x14½
1973, June 30 Litho.
501 A138 10d lilac & multi 15 15
502 A138 15d ocher & multi 22 15
503 A138 25d lt grn & multi 38 15
Set value 24

50th anniv. of Intl. Criminal Police Org.

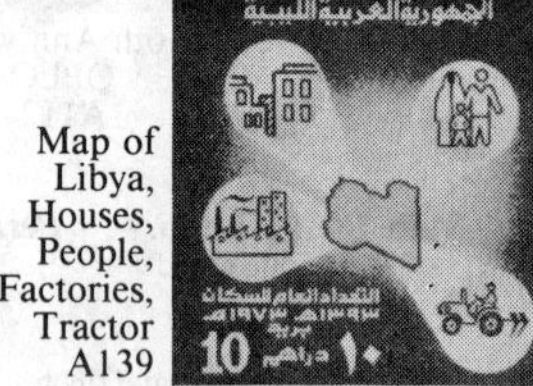
Map of Libya, Houses, People, Factories, Tractor A139

1973, July 15 Photo. *Perf. 11½*
504 A139 10d rose red, black & ultra 90 25
505 A139 25d ultra, blk & grn 1.50 50
506 A139 35d grn, blk & org 2.50 75

General census.

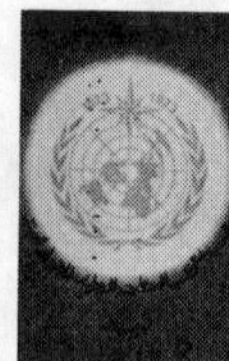
UN Emblem — A140

1973, Aug. 1 *Perf. 12½x11*
507 A140 5d ver, blk & bl 15 15
508 A140 10d yel grn, blk & bl 22 15
Set value 15

Intl. meteorological cooperation, cent.

Soccer — A141

1973, Aug. 10 Photo. *Perf. 11½*
509 A141 5d yel grn & dk brn 42 16
510 A141 25d orange & dk brn 80 15

2nd Palestinian Cup Soccer Tournament.

Torch and Grain A142

Writing Hand, Lamp and Globe A143

1973, Sept. 1 Litho. *Perf. 14*
511 A142 15d brown & multi 18 15
512 A142 25d emer & multi 45 15
Set value 16

4th anniv. of Sept. 1 Revolution.

1973, Sept. 8
513 A143 25d multicolored 30 15

Literacy campaign.

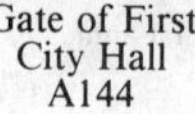
Gate of First City Hall A144

Militia, Flag and Factories A145

1973, Sept. 18 *Perf. 13*
514 A144 10d shown 20 15
515 A144 25d Khondok fountain 22 15
516 A144 35d Clock tower 38 15
Set value 24

Centenary of Tripoli as a municipality.

1973, Oct. 7 Photo. *Perf. 11½x11*
517 A145 15d yel, blk & red 20 15
518 A145 25d green & multi 22 15
Set value 16

Libyan Militia.

Revolutionary Proclamation by Khadafy — A146

Design: 70d, as 25d, with English inscription.

1973, Oct. 15 Litho. *Perf. 12½*
519 A146 25d orange & multi 20 15
520 A146 70d green & multi 45 22
Set value 28

Proclamation of People's Revolution by Pres. Muammar Khadafy.

FAO Emblem, Camel Pulling Plow A147

1973, Nov. 1 Photo. *Perf. 11*
521 A147 10d ocher & multi 15 15
522 A147 25d dk brn & multi 20 15
523 A147 35d black & multi 22 15
Set value 22

World Food Org., 10th anniv.

Human Rights Flame — A148

1973, Dec. 20 Photo. *Perf. 11x11½*
524 A148 25d pur, car & dk bl 20 15
525 A148 70d lt grn, car & dk bl 45 22
Set value 28

Universal Declaration of Human Rights, 25th anniv.

Fish A149

Designs: Various fish from Libyan waters.

1973, Dec. 31 Photo. *Perf. 14x13½*
526 A149 5d lt blue & multi 15 15
527 A149 10d lt blue & multi 20 15
528 A149 15d lt blue & multi 25 15
529 A149 20d lt blue & multi 42 15
530 A149 25d lt blue & multi 70 16
Nos. 526-530 (5) 1.72
Set value 45

1975, Jan. 5
526a A149 5d grnsh bl & multi 15 15
527a A149 10d grnsh bl & multi 15 15
528a A149 15d grnsh bl & multi 16 15
529a A149 20d grnsh bl & multi 35 15
530a A149 25d grnsh bl & multi 38 15
Nos. 526a-530a (5) 1.19
Set value 30

Scout, Sun and Scout Signs A150

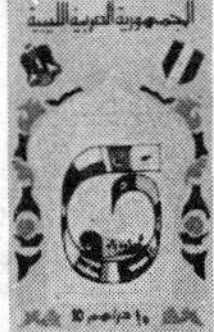
Fair Emblem, Flags of Participants A151

1974, Feb. 1 Litho. *Perf. 11½*
531 A150 5d blue & multi 28 15
532 A150 20d lt lil & multi 70 18
533 A150 25d lt grn & multi 1.50 30

Libyan Boy Scouts.

1974, Mar. 1 Litho. *Perf. 12x11½*
534 A151 10d lt ultra & multi 22 15
535 A151 25d tan & multi 38 15
536 A151 35d lt green & multi 50 15
Set value 25

12th Tripoli International Fair.

Protected Family, WHO Emblem — A152

Minaret and Star — A153

1974, Apr. 7 Litho. *Perf. 12½*
537 A152 5d lt green & multi 15 15
538 A152 25d red & multi 22 15
Set value 20

World Health Day.

1974, Apr. 16 *Perf. 11½x11*
539 A153 10d pink & multi 16 15
540 A153 25d yellow & multi 30 15
541 A153 35d orange & multi 60 22
Set value 38

City University of Bengazi, inauguration.

UPU Emblem and Star — A154

Traffic Signs — A156

Perf. 13½x14½
1974, May 22 Litho.
542 A154 25d multicolored 2.25 38
543 A154 70d multicolored 5.00 80

Centenary of Universal Postal Union.

1974, June 8 Photo. *Perf. 11*
547 A156 5d gold & multi 15 15
548 A156 10d gold & multi 15 15
549 A156 25d gold & multi 20 15
Set value 24

Automobile and Touring Club of Libya.

Tank, Oil Refinery, Book — A157

Symbolic "5" — A158

1974, Sept. 1 Litho. *Perf. 14*
550 A157 5d red & multi 15 15
551 A157 20d violet & multi 15 15
552 A157 25d vio bl & multi 15 15
553 A157 35d green & multi 15 15
Set value 34 22

Souvenir Sheet
Perf. 13
554 A158 55d yel & maroon 2.00 1.75

Revolution of Sept. 1, 5th anniv. English inscription on No. 553.

WPY Emblem and Crowd A159

Libyan Woman A160

1974, Oct. 19 *Perf. 14*
555 A159 25d multicolored 20 15
556 A159 35d lt brn & multi 22 15
Set value 22

World Population Year.

1975, Mar. 1 Litho. *Perf. 13x12½*

Libyan Costumes: 10d, 15d, Women. 20d, Old man. 25d, Man riding camel. 50d, Man on horseback.

557 A160 5d org yel & multi 15 15
558 A160 10d org yel & multi 15 15
559 A160 15d org yel & multi 15 15
560 A160 20d org yel & multi 15 15
561 A160 25d org yel & multi 20 15
562 A160 50d org yel & multi 42 20
Set value 95 45

Congress Emblem — A161

1975, Mar. 4 Litho. *Perf. 12x12½*
563 A161 10d brown & multi 15 15
564 A161 25d vio & multi 15 15
565 A161 35d gray & multi 22 15
Set value 38 25

Arab Labor Congress.

Teacher Pointing to Blackboard A162

1975, Mar. 10 *Perf. 11½*
566 A162 10d gold & multi 15 15
567 A162 25d gold & multi 15 15
Set value 22 15

Teacher's Day.

Bodies, Globe, Proclamation A163

Woman and Man in Library A164

1975, Apr. 7 Litho. *Perf. 12½*
568 A163 20d lilac & multi 15 15
569 A163 25d emer & multi 18 15
Set value 15

World Health Day.

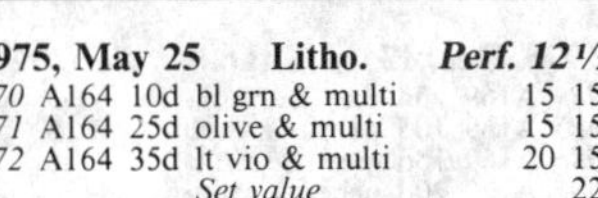

1975, May 25 Litho. *Perf. 12½*
570 A164 10d bl grn & multi 15 15
571 A164 25d olive & multi 15 15
572 A164 35d lt vio & multi 20 15
Set value 22

Libyan Arab Book Exhibition.

Festival Emblem — A165

Games Emblem and Arms — A166

1975, July 5 Litho. *Perf. 13x12½*
573 A165 20d lt bl & multi 15 15
574 A165 25d orange & multi 20 15
Set value 15

2nd Arab Youth Festival.

Coil Stamps
Redrawn Type of 1973 Without "LAR"

1975, Aug. 15 Photo. *Perf. 14½x14*
575 A124 5d blue, org & blk 25 15
576 A124 20d blue, yel & blk 50 15
577 A124 50d blue, grn & blk 65 15
Set value 22

1975, Aug. 23 *Perf. 13x12½*
578 A166 10d salmon & multi 15 15
579 A166 25d lilac & multi 15 15
580 A166 50d yellow & multi 30 16
Set value 28

7th Mediterranean Games, Algiers, Aug. 23-Sept. 6.

Peace Dove, Symbols of Agriculture and Industry — A167

Khadafy's Head Over Desert — A168

Design: 70d, Peace dove (different design).

1975, Sept. Litho. *Perf. 13x12½*
581 A167 25d multicolored 20 15
582 A167 70d multicolored 45 15

Souvenir Sheet
Imperf
Litho. & Embossed
583 A168 100d multicolored 1.90 1.90

6th anniversary of Sept. 1 revolution. No. 583 contains one stamp with simulated perforations.

Khalil Basha Mosque A169

Al Kharruba Mosque A170

Mosques: 10d, Sidi Abdulla El Shaab. 15d, Sidi Ali El Fergani. 25d, Katikhtha. 30d, Murad Agha. 35d, Maulai Mohammed.

1975, Dec. 13 Litho. *Perf. 12½*

584	A169	5d gray & multi	15	15
585	A169	10d purple & multi	15	15
586	A169	15d green & multi	16	15
587	A170	20d ocher & multi	20	15
588	A170	25d multicolored	22	15
589	A170	30d multicolored	25	15
590	A170	35d lilac & multi	35	15
		Nos. 584-590 (7)	1.48	
		Set value		40

Mohammed's 1405th birthday.

Arms of Libya and People — A171

Islamic-Christian Dialogue Emblem — A172

1976, Jan. 15 Photo. *Perf. 13*

591	A171	35d blue & multi	20	15
592	A171	40d multicolored	22	15
		Set value		18

General National (People's) Congress.

1976, Feb. 5 Litho. *Perf. 13x12½*

593	A172	40d gold & multi	20	15
594	A172	115d gold & multi	55	15
		Set value		20

Seminar of Islamic-Christian Dialogue, Tripoli, Feb. 1-5.

Woman Blowing Horn — A173

National Costumes: 20d, Lancer. 30d, Drummer. 40d, Bagpiper. 100d, Woman carrying jug on head.

1976, Mar. 1 Litho. *Perf. 13x12½*

595	A173	10d multicolored	15	15
596	A173	20d multicolored	15	15
597	A173	30d pink & multi	20	15
598	A173	40d multicolored	22	15
599	A173	100d yel & multi	70	28
		Nos. 595-599 (5)	1.42	
		Set value		64

14th Tripoli International Fair.

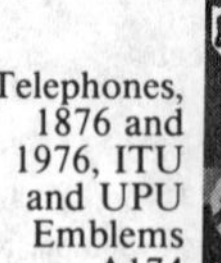

Telephones, 1876 and 1976, ITU and UPU Emblems A174

Design: 70d, Alexander Graham Bell, telephone, satellites, radar, ITU and UPU emblems.

1976, Mar. 10 Photo. *Perf. 13*

600	A174	40d multicolored	60	15
	a.	Souvenir sheet of 4	5.00	5.00
601	A174	70d multicolored	1.20	20
	a.	Souvenir sheet of 4	6.50	6.50

Centenary of first telephone call by Alexander Graham Bell, Mar. 10, 1876.

Mother and Child A175

Hands, Eye and Head A176

1976, Mar. 21 *Perf. 12*

602	A175	85d gray & multi	40	25
603	A175	110d pink & multi	60	30

International Children's Day.

1976, Apr. 7 Photo. *Perf. 13½x13*

604	A176	30d multicolored	15	15
605	A176	35d multicolored	16	15
606	A176	40d multicolored	20	15
		Set value		30

"Foresight prevents blindness;" World Health Day.

Little Bittern A177

Birds of Libya: 10d, Great gray shrike. 15d, Songbird. 20d, European bee-eater, vert. 25d, Hoopoe.

Perf. 13x13½, 13½x13

1976, May 1 Litho.

607	A177	5d orange & multi	*22*	15
608	A177	10d ultra & multi	*42*	16
609	A177	15d rose & multi	*80*	22
610	A177	20d yellow & multi	*1.20*	30
611	A177	25d blue & multi	*1.50*	45
		Nos. 607-611 (5)	*4.14*	1.28

Al Barambekh A178

Bicycling A179

Designs: 15d, Whale, horiz. 30d, Lizard (alwaral), horiz. 40d, Mastodon skull, horiz. 70d, Hawk. 115d, Wild mountain sheep.

1976, June 20 Litho. *Perf. 12½*

612	A178	10d multicolored	15	15
613	A178	15d multicolored	22	15
614	A178	30d multicolored	32	15
615	A178	40d multicolored	38	18
616	A178	70d multicolored	75	32
617	A178	115d multicolored	1.40	55
		Nos. 612-617 (6)	3.22	
		Set value		1.25

Museum of Natural History.

1976, July 17 Litho. *Perf. 12x11½*

Granite Paper

618	A179	15d shown	15	15
619	A179	25d Boxing	15	15
620	A179	70d Soccer	35	20
		Set value		32

Souvenir Sheet

621	A179	150d Symbolic of various sports	*9.00*	*9.00*

21st Olympic Games, Montreal, Canada, July 17-Aug. 1.

Tree Growing from Globe A180

Symbols of Agriculture and Industry A181

Drummer and Pipeline — A182

1976, Aug. 9 *Perf. 13*

622	A180	115d multicolored	45	30

5th Conference of Non-Aligned Countries, Colombo, Sri Lanka, Aug. 9-19.

Beginning with No. 622 numerous issues are printed with multiple coats of arms in pale green on back of stamps.

1976, Sept. 1 *Perf. 14½x14*

623	A181	30d yel & multi	15	15
624	A181	40d multicolored	15	15
625	A181	100d multicolored	40	25
		Set value		42

Souvenir Sheet

Perf. 13

626	A182	200d multicolored	1.90	1.90

Sept. 1 Revolution, 7th anniv.

Sports, Torch and Emblems A183

Chess Board, Rook, Knight, Emblem A184

Design: 145d, Symbolic wrestlers and various emblems, horiz.

1976, Oct. 6 Litho. *Perf. 13*

627	A183	15d multicolored	15	15
628	A183	30d multicolored	22	15
629	A183	100d multicolored	60	25
		Set value		38

Souvenir Sheet

630	A183	145d multicolored	1.50	1.50

5th Arab Games, Damascus, Syria.

1976, Oct. 24 Photo. *Perf. 11½*

631	A184	15d pink & multi	55	15
632	A184	30d buff & multi	1.10	20
633	A184	100d multicolored	1.40	30

The "Against" (protest) Chess Olympiad, Tripoli, Oct. 24-Nov. 15.

A185

Designs: Various local flowers.

1976, Nov. 1 Photo. *Perf. 11½*

Granite Paper

634	A185	15d lilac & multi	15	15
635	A185	20d multicolored	15	15
636	A185	35d yellow & multi	20	15
637	A185	40d salmon & multi	25	15
638	A185	70d multicolored	60	22
		Nos. 634-638 (5)	1.35	
		Set value		58

International Archives Council Emblem and Document — A186

1976, Nov. 10 Litho. *Perf. 13x13½*

639	A186	15d brown, org & buff	15	15
640	A186	35d brn, brt grn & buff	15	15
641	A186	70d brown, blue & buff	30	20
		Set value		32

Arab Regional Branch of International Council on Archives, Baghdad.

Holy Ka'aba and Pilgrims A187

Numeral A188

1976, Dec. 12 Litho. *Perf. 14*

642	A187	15d multicolored	15	15
643	A187	30d multicolored	15	15
644	A187	70d multicolored	25	20
645	A187	100d multicolored	40	25
		Set value	82	58

Pilgrimage to Mecca.

Coil Stamps

1977, Jan. 15 Photo. *Perf. 14½x14*

646	A188	5d multicolored	15	15
647	A188	20d multicolored	15	15
648	A188	50d multicolored	22	15
		Set value	36	25

Covered Basket — A189

Designs: 20d, Leather bag. 30d, Vase. 40d, Embroidered slippers. 50d, Ornate saddle. 100d, Horse with saddle and harness.

1977, Mar. 1 Litho. *Perf. 12½x12*

649 A189 10d multicolored 15 15
650 A189 20d multicolored 15 15
651 A189 30d multicolored 16 15
652 A189 40d multicolored 20 15
653 A189 50d multicolored 25 15
Set value 75 45

Souvenir Sheet

Imperf

654 A189 100d multicolored 60 60

15th Tripoli International Fair. No. 654 contains one stamp 49x53mm with simulated perforations.

Girl and Flowers, UNICEF Emblem A190

Children's drawings, UNICEF Emblem and: 30d, Clothing store. 40d, Farm yard.

1977, Mar. 28 Litho. *Perf. 13x13½*

655 A190 10d multicolored 15 15
656 A190 30d multicolored 16 15
657 A190 40d multicolored 20 15
Set value 40 28

Children's Day.

Gun, Fighters, UN Headquarters A191

1977, Mar. 13 *Perf. 13½*

658 A191 15d multicolored *50* 15
659 A191 25d multicolored *65* 15
660 A191 70d multicolored *1.40* 22
Set value 35

Battle of Al-Karamah, 9th anniversary.

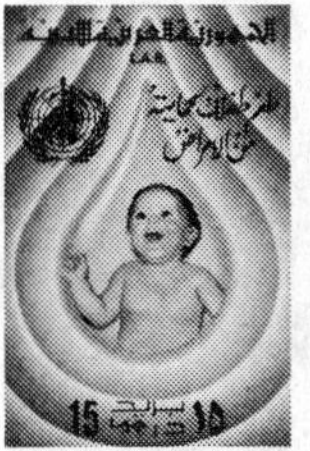

Child, Raindrop, WHO Emblem – A192

Arab Postal Union, 25th Anniv. – A193

1977, Apr. 7 Litho. *Perf. 13x12½*

661 A192 15d multicolored 15 15
662 A192 30d multicolored 25 15
Set value 15

World Health Day.

1977, Apr. 12 *Perf. 13½*

663 A193 15d multicolored 15 15
664 A193 30d multicolored 25 15
665 A193 40d multicolored 40 16
Set value 28

Maps of Africa and Libya A194

1977, May 8 Litho. *Perf. 14x13½*

666 A194 40d multicolored 50 20
667 A194 70d multicolored 65 30

African Labor Day.

Map of Libya and Heart – A195

1977, May 10 *Perf. 14½x14*

668 A195 5d multicolored 15 15
669 A195 10d multicolored 22 15
670 A195 30d multicolored 42 15
Set value 24

Libyan Red Crescent Society.

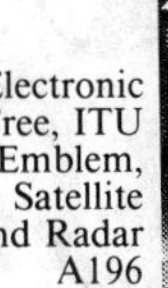

Electronic Tree, ITU Emblem, Satellite and Radar A196

Electronic Tree, ITU Emblem and: 115d, Communications satellite, Montreal Olympics emblem, boxer on TV screen. 200d, Spacecraft over earth. 300d, Solar system.

1977, May 17 Litho. *Perf. 13½x13*

671 A196 60d multicolored 30 20
672 A196 115d multicolored 62 38
673 A196 200d multicolored 1.20 62

Souvenir Sheet

674 A196 300d multicolored *3.00 3.00*

9th World Telecommunications Day. No. 674 contains one stamp 52x35mm.

Plane over Tripoli, Messenger A197

UPU Emblem and: 25d, Concorde, messenger on horseback. 150d, Loading transport plane and messenger riding camel. 300d, Graf Zeppelin LZ127 over Tripoli.

1977, May 17 Litho. *Perf. 13½*

675 A197 20d multicolored 15 15
676 A197 25d multicolored 15 15
677 A197 150d multicolored 90 45
Set value 58

Souvenir Sheet

678 A197 300d multicolored *3.00 3.00*

UPU centenary (in 1974). No. 678 contains one stamp 52x35mm.

Mosque – A198

Various Mosques. 50d, 100d, vertical.

1977, June 1 Photo. *Perf. 14*

679 A198 40d multicolored 20 15
680 A198 50d multicolored 25 15
681 A198 70d multicolored 35 20
682 A198 90d multicolored 45 30
683 A198 100d multicolored 55 38
684 A198 115d multicolored 62 40
Nos. 679-684 (6) 2.42 1.58

Palestinian Archbishop Hilarion Capucci, Jailed by Israel in 1974, Map of Palestine – A199

1977, Aug. 18 Litho. *Perf. 13½*

687 A199 30d multicolored 35 15
688 A199 40d multicolored 50 15
689 A199 115d multicolored 70 38
Set value 58

Raised Hands, Pylons, Wheel, Buildings A200

Star and Ornament A201

1977, Sept. 1 Litho. *Perf. 13½x12½*

690 A200 15d multicolored 16 15
691 A200 30d multicolored 35 15
692 A200 85d multicolored 50 22
Set value 35

Souvenir Sheet

Perf. 12½

693 A201 100d gold & multi 70 70

8th anniversary of Sept. 1 Revolution.

Soccer A202

1977, Oct. 8 *Perf. 13½*

694 A202 5d Swimmers, vert. 15 15
695 A202 10d shown 15 15
696 A202 15d Soccer, vert. 15 15
697 A202 25d Table tennis 22 20
698 A202 40d Basketball, vert. 38 22
Set value 85 60

7th Arab School Games.

Steeplechase – A203

Show Emblem and: 10d, Bedouin on horseback. 15d, Show emblem (Horse and "7"; vert.). 45d, Steeplechase. 100d, Hurdles. 115d, Bedouins on horseback.

1977, Oct. 10 *Perf. 14½*

699 A203 5d multicolored 15 15
700 A203 10d multicolored 15 15
701 A203 15d multicolored 15 15
702 A203 45d multicolored 30 15
703 A203 115d multicolored 70 40
Set value 1.25 70

Souvenir Sheet

704 A203 100d multicolored 70 70

7th Intl. Turf Championships, Tripoli, Oct. 1977.

Dome of the Rock, Jerusalem – A204

1977, Oct. 14 *Perf. 14½x14*

705 A204 5d multicolored 38 15
706 A204 10d multicolored 50 15
Set value 15

Palestinian fighters and their families.

"The Green Book" – A205

Designs: 35d, Hands with broken chain holding hook over citadel. 40d, Hands above chaos. 115d, Dove and Green Book rising from Africa, world map.

1977 Litho. *Perf. 14*

707 A205 Strip of 3 1.65 1.65
a. 35d multicolored 35 35
b. 40d multicolored 50 50
c. 115d multicolored 65 65

The Greek Book, by Khadafy outlines Libyan democracy. Green descriptive inscription on back beneath gum, in English on 35d, French on 40d, Arabic on 115d.

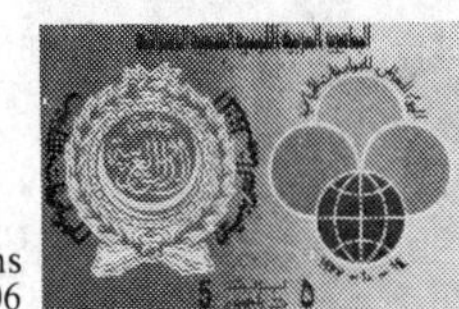

Emblems A206

1977 *Perf. 12½x13*

708 A206 5d multicolored 15 15
709 A206 15d multicolored 15 15
710 A206 30d multicolored 16 15
Set value 28 20

Standardization Day.

Crocodile and Young A207

Rock Carvings, Wadi Mathendous, c. 8000 B.C.: 15d, Elephant hunt. 20d, Giraffe, vert. 30d, Antelope. 40d, Trumpeting elephant.

1978, Jan. 1 *Perf. 12½x13, 13x12½*

711 A207 10d multicolored 15 15
712 A207 15d multicolored 15 15
713 A207 20d multicolored 15 15
714 A207 30d multicolored 20 15
715 A207 40d multicolored 22 20
Set value 70 50

Silver Pendant – A208

Emblem, Compass and Lightning – A209

Silver Jewelry: 10d, Ornamental plate. 20d, Necklace with pendants. 25d, Crescent-shaped brooch. 115d, Armband.

1978, Mar. 1 Litho. *Perf. 13x12½*

716 A208 5d multicolored 15 15

717 A208 10d multicolored 15 15

718 A208 20d multicolored 15 15

719 A208 25d multicolored 15 15

720 A208 115d multicolored 60 38

Set value 90 55

Tripoli International Fair.

1978, Mar. 10 *Perf. 13½*

721 A209 30d multicolored 20 15

722 A209 115d multicolored 70 38

Arab Cultural Education Organization.

Bride and Attendants A210

Children's drawings and UNESCO emblem.

1978, Mar. 21

723 A210 40d Dancing 20 15

724 A210 40d Children with posters 20 15

725 A210 40d Shopping street 20 15

726 A210 40d Playground 20 15

727 A210 40d shown 20 15

Nos. 723-727 (5) 1.00

Set value 60

Children's Day. Nos. 723-727 printed se-tenant.

Clenched Fist, Made of Bricks A211

1978, Mar. 22

728 A211 30d multicolored 65 15

729 A211 115d multicolored 1.20 38

Determination of Arab people.

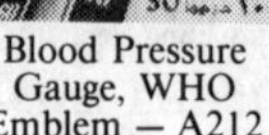

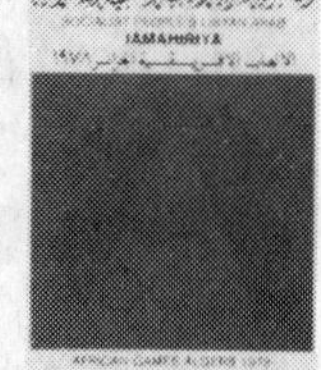

Blood Pressure Gauge, WHO Emblem — A212

Games Emblem — A214

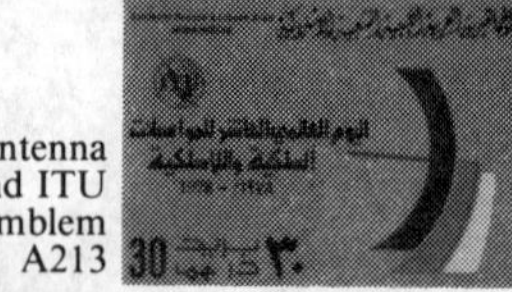

Antenna and ITU Emblem A213

1978, Apr. 7 *Perf. 13x12½*

730 A212 30d multicolored 16 15

731 A212 115d multicolored 55 38

World Health Day, drive against hypertension.

1978, May 17 Photo. *Perf. 13½*

732 A213 30d silver & multi 16 15

733 A213 115d gold & multi 55 38

10th World Telecommunications Day.

1978, July 13 Litho. *Perf. 12½*

734 A214 15d multicolored 15 15

735 A214 30d multicolored 15 15

736 A214 115d multicolored 60 38

Set value 50

3rd African Games, Algiers, 1978.

Inauguration of Tripoli International Airport — A215

1978, Aug. 10 Litho. *Perf. 13½*

737 A215 40d shown *50* 15

738 A215 115d Terminal *1.50* 38

View of Ankara — A216

Soldiers, Jet, Ship — A217

1978, Aug. 17

739 A216 30d multicolored *42* 15

740 A216 35d multicolored *45* 15

741 A216 115d multicolored *1.50* 38

Set value 55

Turkish-Libyan friendship.

1978, Sept. 1 *Perf. 14½*

Designs: 35d, Tower, Green Book, oil derrick. 100d, View of Tripoli with mosque and modern buildings. 115d, View of Tripoli within cogwheel.

742 A217 30d multicolored *42* 15

743 A217 35d org & multi *45* 15

744 A217 115d blue & multi *1.50* 38

Set value 55

Souvenir Sheet

745 A217 100d multicolored *2.50* 50

9th anniversary of Sept. 1 Revolution. No. 745 contains one stamp 50x41mm.

Quarry and Symposium Emblem — A218

Designs: 40d, Oasis lake. 115d, Crater.

1978, Sept. 16 *Perf. 13½*

746 A218 30d multicolored *20* 15

747 A218 40d multicolored *38* 15

748 A218 115d multicolored *60* 38

Set value 56

2nd Symposium on Libyan Geology.

Green Book and Three Races A219

1978, Oct. 18 *Perf. 12½*

749 A219 30d multicolored 15 15

750 A219 40d multicolored 20 15

751 A219 115d multicolored 45 38

Set value 56

International Anti-Apartheid Year.

Pilgrims, Minarets, Holy Kaaba A220

1978, Nov. 9 Photo. *Perf. 12*

752 A220 5d multicolored 15 15

753 A220 10d multicolored 15 15

754 A220 15d multicolored 15 15

755 A220 20d multicolored 15 15

Set value 30 22

Pilgrimage to Mecca.

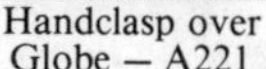

Handclasp over Globe — A221

Fists, Guns, Map of Israel — A222

1978, Nov. 10 Litho. *Perf. 13½*

756 A221 30d multicolored *42* 15

757 A221 40d multicolored *50* 15

758 A221 115d multicolored *1.50* 38

Set value 56

Technical Cooperation Among Developing Countries Conference, Buenos Aires, Argentina, Sept. 1978.

1978, Dec. 5 Litho. *Perf. 13½*

Designs: 40d, 115d, Map of Arab countries and Israel, eagle and crowd, horiz. 145d, like 30d.

759 A222 30d multicolored 22 15

760 A222 40d multicolored 40 15

761 A222 115d multicolored 70 38

762 A222 145d multicolored 1.40 40

Anti-Israel Summit Conference, Baghdad, Dec. 2-8.

Scales, Globe and Human Rights Flame — A223

Libyan Fort and Horse Racing — A224

1978, Dec. 10

763 A223 15d multicolored *20* 15

764 A223 30d multicolored *30* 15

765 A223 115d multicolored *60* 38

Universal Declaration of Human Rights, 30th anniv.

1978, Dec. 11

766 A224 20d multicolored *38* 15

767 A224 40d multicolored *50* 15

768 A224 115d multicolored *1.50* 38

Set value 55

Libyan Study Center.

Lilienthal's Glider, 1896 A225

Mounted Stag's Head A226

Designs: 25d, Spirit of St. Louis, 1927. 30d, Adm. Byrd's Polar flight, 1929. 50d, Graf Zeppelin, 1934, hydroplane and storks. 115d, Wilbur and Orville Wright and Flyer A. No. 774, Icarus falling. No. 775, Eagle and Boeing 727.

1978, Dec. 26 Litho. *Perf. 14*

769 A225 20d multicolored 15 15

770 A225 25d multicolored 15 15

771 A225 30d multicolored 16 15

772 A225 50d multicolored 20 15

773 A225 115d multicolored 50 38

Nos. 769-773 (5) 1.16

Set value 72

Souvenir Sheets

774 A225 100d multicolored 55 55

775 A225 100d multicolored 55 55

75th anniversary of 1st powered flight. Nos. 769-773 issued also in sheets of 4.

Coil Stamps

1979, Jan. 15 Photo. *Perf. 14½x14*

776 A226 5d multicolored *35* 15

777 A226 20d multicolored *50* 15

778 A226 50d multicolored *65* 15

Set value 22

Carpobrotus Acinaciformis A227

Flora of Libya: 15d, Caralluma europaea. 20d, Arum cirenaicum. 35d, Lavatera arborea. 40d, Capparis spinosa. 50d, Ranunculus asiaticus.

1979, May 15 Litho. *Perf. 14*

779 A227 10d multicolored 15 15

780 A227 15d multicolored 15 15

781 A227 20d multicolored 15 15

782 A227 35d multicolored 28 18

783 A227 40d multicolored 28 18

784 A227 50d multicolored 35 22

Set value 1.12 75

People, Torch, Olive Branches — A228

1979 Litho. *Perf. 13x12½*

Size: 18x23mm

785 A228 5d multi *15* 15

786 A228 10d multi *15* 15

787 A228 15d multi *15* 15

788 A228 30d multi *30* 15

789 A228 50d multi *38* 15

790 A228 60d multi *42* 15

791 A228 70d multi *48* 15

792 A228 100d multi *75* 18

793 A228 115d multi *1.10* 20

Perf. 13½

Size: 26½x32mm

794	A228	200d multi	*1.20*	35
795	A228	500d multi	*2.25*	70
796	A228	1000d multi	*5.00*	1.75
		Nos. 785-796 (12)	*12.33*	
		Set value		3.60

See Nos. 1053-1055.

Tortoise A229

Animals: 10d, Antelope. 15d, Hedgehog. 20d, Porcupine. 30d, Arabian camel. 35d, African wildcat. 45d, Gazelle. 115d, Cheetah. 10d, 30d, 35d, 45d, vert.

1979, Feb. 1 Litho. *Perf. 14½*

797	A229	5d multicolored	15	15
798	A229	10d multicolored	15	15
799	A229	15d multicolored	15	15
800	A229	20d multicolored	15	15
801	A229	30d multicolored	15	15
802	A229	35d multicolored	20	15
803	A229	45d multicolored	25	20
804	A229	115d multicolored	55	35
		Set value	1.40	90

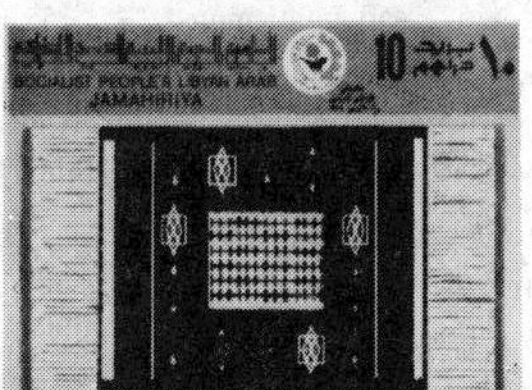

Rug and Tripoli Fair Emblem — A230

Tripoli Fair emblem and various rugs.

1979, Mar. 1 Litho. *Perf. 11*

805	A230	10d multicolored	15	15
806	A230	15d multicolored	15	15
807	A230	30d multicolored	15	15
808	A230	45d multicolored	15	15
809	A230	115d multicolored	50	38
		Set value	90	60

17th Tripoli Fair.

Shepherd, Sheep and Dog A231

Children's drawings and IYC emblem.

1979, Mar. 20 *Perf. 13½*

810	A231	20d Families and planes	50	15
811	A231	20d shown	50	15
812	A231	20d Beach umbrellas	50	15
813	A231	20d Boat in storm	50	15
814	A231	20d Traffic policeman	50	15
		Nos. 810-814 (5)	2.50	
		Set value		25

Intl. Year of the Child. Nos. 810-814 printed se-tenant.

Book, World Map, Arab Achievements A232

1979, Mar. 22 *Perf. 13*

815	A232	45d multicolored	20	15
816	A232	70d multicolored	30	20

WMO Emblem, Weather Map and Tower — A233

1979, Mar. 23

817	A233	15d multicolored	15	15
818	A233	30d multicolored	15	15
819	A233	50d multicolored	20	15
		Set value	38	25

World Meteorological Day.

Medical Services, WHO Emblem A234

1979, Apr. 7

820	A234	40d multicolored	18	15

Farmer Plowing and Sheep — A235

1979, Sept. 1 Litho. *Perf. 14½*

821	Block of 4	30	20
a.	A235 15d shown	15	15
b.	A235 15d Men holding Green Book	15	15
c.	A235 15d Oil field	15	15
d.	A235 15d Oil refinery	15	15
822	Block of 4	60	38
a.	A235 30d Dish antenna	15	15
b.	A235 30d Hospital	15	15
c.	A235 30d Doctor examining patient	15	15
d.	A235 30d Surgery	15	15
823	Block of 4	75	42
a.	A235 40d Street, Tripoli	18	15
b.	A235 40d Steel mill	18	15
c.	A235 40d Tanks	18	15
d.	A235 40d Tuareg horsemen	18	15
824	Block of 4	1.50	80
a.	A235 70d Revolutionaries, Green Book	35	20
b.	A235 70d Crowd, map of Libya	35	20
c.	A235 70d Mullah	35	20
d.	A235 70d Student	35	20

Souvenir Sheets

Imperf

825	A235	50d Revolution symbols, Green Book	80	65
826	A235	50d Monument	80	65

Sept. 1st revolution, 10th anniversary.

Volleyball A236

1979, Sept. 10

827	A236	45d shown	25	15
828	A236	115d Soccer	60	30

Universiade '79 World University Games, Mexico City, Sept.

Mediterranean Games, Split, Yugoslavia — A237

1979, Sept. 15 Litho. *Perf. 12x11½*

829	A237	15d multicolored	16	15
830	A237	30d multicolored	35	15
831	A237	70d multicolored	65	22
		Set value		36

Exhibition Emblem — A238

1979, Sept. 25 Photo. *Perf. 11½x11*

832	A238	45d multicolored	*28*	15
833	A238	115d multicolored	*75*	30

TELECOM '79, 3rd World Telecommunications Exhibition, Geneva, Sept. 20-26.

Seminar Emblem, Green Book, Crowd — A239

1979, Oct. 1

834	A239	10d shown	*15*	15

Size: 67x43½mm

835	A239	35d Meeting hall	*28*	15

Size: 32x43½mm

836	A239	100d Col. Khadafy	*65*	30
a.		Miniature sheet, imperf.	*90*	60
		Set value		46

Intl. Seminar of the Green Book, Benghazi, Oct. 1-3. Nos. 834-836 se-tenant in continuous design. No. 836a contains an imperf. design similar to type A239.

Evacuation of Foreign Forces — A240

1979, Oct. 7

837	A240	30d shown	26	15
838	A240	40d Tuareg horsemen	38	15
		Set value		22

Souvenir Sheet

Imperf

839	A240	100d Vignettes	40	40

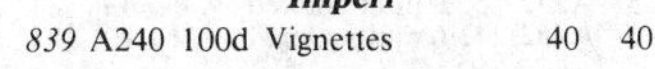

Cyclist, Championship Emblem — A241

1979, Nov. 21

840	A241	15d shown	15	15
841	A241	30d Cyclists, emblem, diff.	25	15
		Set value		15

Junior Cycling Championships, Tripoli, Nov. 21-23. Issued in sheetlets of 4.

Hurdles, Olympic Rings, Moscow '80 Emblem — A242

1979, Nov. 21

842	A242	45d Equestrian	*18*	*15*
843	A242	60d Javelin	*28*	*15*
844	A242	115d shown	*60*	*20*
845	A242	160d Soccer	*75*	*28*

Souvenir Sheets

846	A242	150d like #844	*1.25*	*65*
847	A242	150d like #845	*2.50*	*65*

Pre-Olympics (Moscow '80 Olympic Games). Nos. 842-845 issued in sheetlets of 4 and sheets of 20 (4x5) with silver Moscow '80 Emblem covering background of every 20 stamps.

Intl. Day of Cooperation with Palestinian People — A242a

1979, Nov. 29 Photo. *Perf. 12*

847A	A242a	30d multicolored	20	15
847B	A242a	115d multicolored	70	40

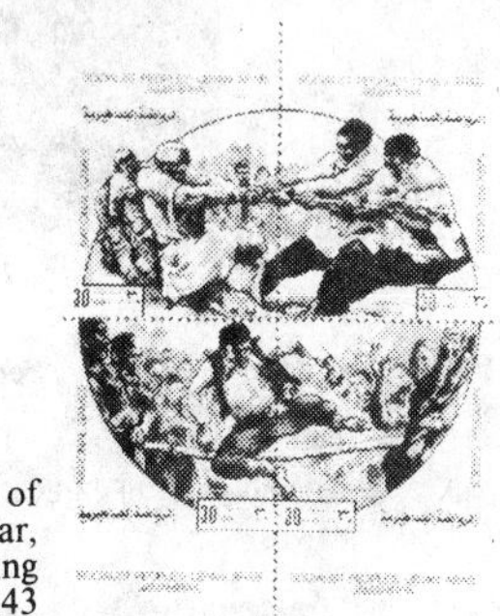

Tug of War, Jumping A243

National Games: No. 848, Polo, leap frog. No. 849, Racing, ball game. No. 850, Wrestling, log rolling. No. 852, Horsemen.

1980, Feb. 15

848	A243	Block of 4	40	40
a.-d.		10d, single stamp	15	15
849	A243	Block of 4	50	40
a.-d.		15d, single stamp	15	15
850	A243	Block of 4	70	40
a.-d.		20d, single stamp	16	15

851 A243 Block of 4 1.00 65
a.-d. 30d, single stamp 25 16
852 A243 Block of 4 1.65 1.00
a.-d. 45d, single stamp 40 25
Nos. 848-852 (5) 4.25 2.85

Battle of Gardabia, 1915 — A244

1980 Litho. *Perf. 14½*
853 A244 20d shown 24 15
854 A244 20d Shoghab, 1913 24 15
855 A244 20d Fundugh Al-Shibani, 1922 24 15
856 A244 20d Ghira 24 15
857 A244 35d Gardabia, diff. 45 15
858 A244 35d Shoghab, diff. 45 15
859 A244 35d Fundugh Al-Shibani, diff. 45 15
860 A244 35d Ghira, diff. 45 15
Nos. 853-860 (8) 2.76
Set value 88

Issue dates: Gardabia, Apr. 28. Shoghab, May 25. Fundugh Al-Shibani, June 1. Ghira, Aug. 15. Stamps of same battle se-tenant in continuous design.

See Nos. 893-900, 921-944, 980-1003, 1059-1082.

Girl Guides Examining Plant — A245

1980, Aug. 22 *Perf. 13½*
861 A245 15d shown 15 15
862 A245 30d Guides cooking 30 15
863 A245 50d Scouts at campfire 48 30
864 A245 115d Scouts reading map 1.25 60

Souvenir Sheets
865 A245 100d like #861 1.00 50
866 A245 100d like #863 1.00 50

8th Pan Arab Girl Guide and 14th Pan Arab Scout Jamborees, Aug.

Men Holding OPEC Emblem A246

1980, Sept. 15 *Perf. 14½*
867 A246 45d Emblem, globe 50 15
868 A246 115d shown 1.10 60

20th anniversary of OPEC.

Martyrdom of Omar Muktar, 1931 — A247

1980, Sept. 16
869 A247 20d multicolored 15 15
870 A247 35d multicolored 45 15
Set value 20

Souvenir Sheet
870A A247 100d multicolored 1.90 1.90

UNESCO Emblem and Avicenna A248

1980, Sept. 20
871 A248 45d Scientific symbols 70 15
872 A248 115d shown 1.65 60

School Scientific Exhibition, Sept. 20-24 and birth millenium of Arab physician Avicenna (115d).

18th Tripoli Fair A249

Various musical instruments. 15d vert.

1980 Litho. *Perf. 13½*
873 A249 5d multicolored 15 15
874 A249 10d multicolored 15 15
875 A249 15d multicolored 18 15
876 A249 20d multicolored 25 15
877 A249 25d multicolored 32 18
Set value 25

Souvenir Sheet
878 A249 100d Musicians 1.25 1.25

World Olive Oil Year A250

1980, Jan. 15 Litho. *Perf. 13½*
879 A250 15d multicolored 15 15
880 A250 30d multicolored 28 15
881 A250 45d multicolored 45 22
Set value 42

Intl. Year of the Child (1979) A251

Children's drawings: a, Riding horses. b, water sports. c, Fish. d, Gift sale. e, Preparing feast.

1980, Mar. 21
882 Strip of 5 1.25 60
a.-e. A251 20d any single 24 15

The Hegira, 1500th Anniv. A252

1980, Apr. 1
883 A252 50d multicolored 48 24
884 A252 115d multicolored 1.10 55

Operating Room, Hospital — A253

1980, Apr. 7 Litho. *Perf. 13½*
885 A253 20d multicolored 30 15
886 A253 50d multicolored 70 38

World Health Day.

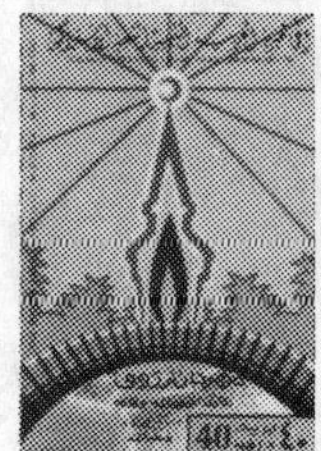

Sheik Zarruq Festival, Misurata, June 16-20 A254

Arabian Towns Organization A255

1980, June 16
887 A254 40d multicolored 52 24
888 A254 115d multicolored 1.25 65

Souvenir Sheet
889 A254 100d multicolored 1.25 1.25

1980, July 1 *Perf. 11½x12*
890 A255 15d Ghadames 15 15
891 A255 30d Derna 38 15
892 A255 50d Tripoli 60 30

Battles Type of 1980

1980 *Perf. 13½*
893 A244 20d Yefren, 1915 25 15
894 A244 20d El Hani, 1911 25 15
895 A244 20d Sebha, 1914 25 15
896 A244 20d Sirt, 1912 25 15
897 A244 35d Yefren, diff. 45 30
898 A244 35d El Hani, diff. 45 30
899 A244 35d Sebha, diff. 45 30
900 A244 35d Sirt, diff. 45 30
Nos. 893-900 (8) 2.80 1.80

Issue dates: Yefren, July 16. El Hani, Oct. 23. Sebha, Nov. 27. Sirt, Dec. 31. Stamps of same battle printed se-tenant in a continuous design.

Sept. 1 Revolution, 11th Anniv. — A256

Achievements of the Revolution.

1980, Sept. 1
901 A256 5d Oil industry 15 15
902 A256 10d Youth festival 15 15
903 A256 15d Agriculture 15 15
904 A256 25d Transportation 30 15
905 A256 40d Education 50 24
906 A256 115d Housing 1.40 65
Nos. 901-906 (6) 2.65
Set value 1.25

Souvenir Sheet
907 A256 100d Montage of achievements 1.25 1.25

No. 907 contains one stamp 30x50mm.

World Tourism Conference A257

1980, Sept. 10
908 A257 45d multicolored 50 30
909 A257 115d multicolored 1.40 65

Intl. Year of the Disabled — A258

1981, Jan. 1 *Perf. 15*
910 A258 20d multicolored 24 15
911 A258 45d multicolored 55 30
912 A258 115d multicolored 1.25 65

Redrawn

1981, Nov. 21 Litho. *Perf. 15*
913 A258 45d multicolored 55 30
914 A258 115d multicolored 1.25 65

UPA Disabled Persons Campaign. Design redrawn to include Arab League Emblem.

Mosaics — A259

1981, Jan. 15 *Perf. 13½*
915 A259 10d Horse 15 15
916 A259 20d Sailing ship 20 15
917 A259 30d Peacocks 30 15
918 A259 40d Panther 45 15
919 A259 50d Musician 55 25
920 A259 115d Fish 1.25 60
Nos. 915-920 (6) 2.90 1.45

Battles Type of 1980

Perf. 13½, 14½ (#926, 932, 938, 944)
1981
921 A244 20d Dernah, 1912 50 16
922 A244 20d Bir Tagreft, 1928 50 16
923 A244 20d Tawargha, 1923 50 16
924 A244 20d Zuara, 1912 50 16
925 A244 20d Funduk El-Jamel Misurata, 1915 50 16
926 A244 20d Sidi El-Khemri, 1915 35 16
927 A244 20d El-Khoms, 1913 50 16
928 A244 20d Roghdalin, 1912 50 16
929 A244 20d Rughbat El-Naga, 1925 50 16
930 A244 20d Tobruk, 1911 50 16
931 A244 20d Bir Ikshadia, 1924 35 16
932 A244 20d Ain Zara, 1924 50 16
933 A244 35d Dernah, diff. 80 30
934 A244 35d Bir Tagreft, diff. 80 30
935 A244 35d Tawargha, diff. 80 30
936 A244 35d Zuara, diff. 80 30
937 A244 35d Funduk El-Jamel Misurata, diff. 80 30
938 A244 35d Sidi El-Khemri, diff. 80 30
939 A244 35d El-Khoms, diff. 80 30
940 A244 35d Roghdalin, diff. 80 30
941 A244 35d Rughbat El-Naga, diff. 80 30
942 A244 35d Tobruk, diff. 80 30

943 A244 35d Bir Ikshadia, diff. 80 30
944 A244 35d Ain Zara, diff. 80 30
Nos. 921-944 (24) 15.30 5.52

Issue dates: Dernah, Jan. 17. Bir Tagreft, Feb. 25. Tawargha, Mar. 20. Zuara, Apr. 13. Funduk El-Jamel Misurata, May 26. Sidi El-Khemri, June 4. El-Khoms, July 27. Roghdalin, Aug. 15. Rughbat El-Naga, Sept. 16. Tobruk, Oct. 27. Bir Ikshadia, Nov. 19. Ain Zara, Dec. 4. Stamps of the same battle printed se-tenant in a continuous design.

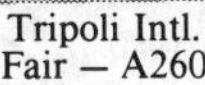

Tripoli Intl. Fair — A260

No. 707b, Crowd — A261

Ceramicware.

1981, Mar. 1 ***Perf. 13½***

945 A260 5d Bowls, horiz. 15 15
946 A260 10d Lamp 15 15
947 A260 15d Vase 20 15
948 A260 45d Water jar, horiz. 65 25
949 A260 115d Spouted water jar, horiz. 1.50 85
Nos. 945-949 (5) 2.65 1.55

1981, Mar. 2 ***Perf. 15***

950 A261 50d multicolored 50 15
951 A261 115d multicolored 1.10 55

People's Authority Declaration, The Green Book.

Children's Day, IYC — A262

Children's illustrations: a, Desert camp. b, Women doing chores. c, Village scene. d, Airplane over playground. e, Minaret, camel, man.

1981, Mar. 21 **Litho.** ***Perf. 13½***

952 Strip of 5 1.25 60
a.-e. A262 20d any single 24 15

Bank of Libya, 25th Anniv. — A263

1981, Apr. 1 **Litho.** ***Perf. 13½***

953 A263 45d multicolored 48 20
954 A263 115d multicolored 1.25 60

Souvenir Sheet

955 A263 50d multicolored 1.10 1.10

World Health Day A264

1981, Apr. 7 ***Perf. 14***

956 A264 45d multicolored 60 25
957 A264 115d multicolored 1.50 75

Intl. Year for Combating Racial Discrimination A265

1981, July 1 ***Perf. 15***

958 A265 45d multicolored 55 15
959 A265 50d multicolored 65 15

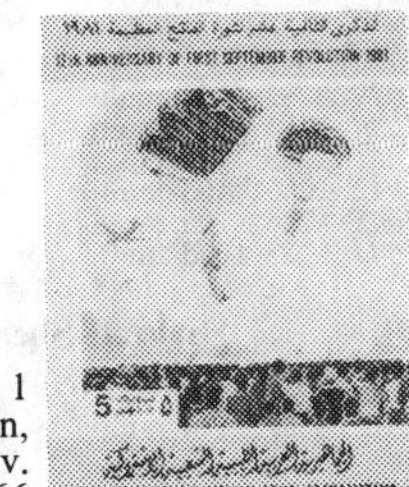

September 1 Revolution, 12th Anniv. A266

Designs: Nos. 960a-960b, Helicopter and jets. Nos. 960c-960d, Paratroopers. Nos. 961a-961b, Tanks. Nos. 961c-961d, Frogman parade. Nos. 962a-962b, Twelve-barrel rocket launchers. Nos. 962c-962d, Trucks with rockets. Nos. 963a-963b, Sailor parade. Nos. 963c-963d, Jeep and trucks with twelve-barrel rocket launchers. Nos. 964a-964b, Wheeled tanks and jeeps. Nos. 964c-964d, Tank parade.

1981, Sept. 1 ***Perf. 14½***

960 Block of 4 20 20
a.-d. A266 5d. any single 15 15
961 Block of 4 22 20
a.-d. A266 10d. any single 15 15
962 Block of 4 32 20
a.-d. A266 15d. any single 15 15
963 Block of 4 42 22
a.-d. A266 20d. any single 15 15
964 Block of 4 55 25
a.-d. A266 25d. any single 15 15
Nos. 961-964 (4) 1.51 87

Souvenir Sheet
Perf. 11

965 A266 50d Naval troop marching *1.25* 35

Horizontal pairs within 960-964 printed in continuous designs. Nos. 960-962 vert. No. 965 contains one stamp 63x38mm.

Miniature Sheet

Butterflies — A267

1981, Oct. 1 ***Perf. 14½***

966 Sheet of 16 *5.50*
a.-d. A267 5d. any single *15* 15
e.-h. A267 10d. any single *20* 15
i.-l. A267 15d. any single *30* 15
m.-p. A267 25d. any single *45* 15

Nos. 966a-966p printed se-tenant in a continuous design, stamps of same denomination in blocks of 4. Sheetlets exist containing blocks of 4 for each denomination.

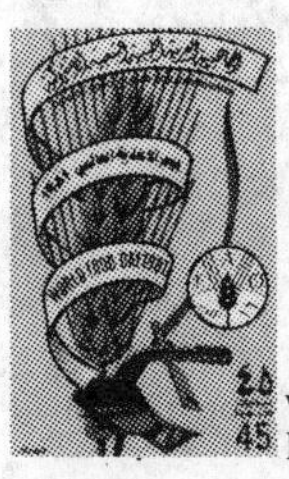

World Food Day — A268

1981, Oct. 16 ***Perf. 15***

967 A268 45d multicolored 45 15
968 A268 200d multicolored 2.25 1.10

Fruit — A269

1981, Nov. 17 ***Perf. 13½***

969 A269 5d Grapes 15 15
970 A269 10d Dates 15 15
971 A269 15d Lemons 22 15
972 A269 20d Oranges 30 15
973 A269 35d Cactus fruit 45 15
974 A269 55d Pomegranates 60 15
Nos. 969-974 (6) 1.87
Set value 50

Miniature Sheet

Orpheus Playing Music to the Animals — A270

Mosaics: d, Fish. e, Fishermen. f, Fish in basket. g, Farm yard. h, Birds eating fruit. i, Milking a goat. Illustration reduced.

1982, Jan. 1 ***Perf. 13½***

975 Sheet of 9 5.00
a.-i. A270 45d any single 50 22

Nos. 975a-975c, shown in illustration, printed in continuous design.

3rd Intl. Koran Reading Contest — A271

Designs: 10d, Stone tablets, Holy Ka'aba, Mecca. 35d, Open Koran, creation of the world. 115d, Scholar, students.

1982, Jan. 7

976 A271 10d multicolored 15 15
977 A271 35d multicolored 40 18
978 A271 115d multicolored 1.25 55

Souvenir Sheet

979 A271 100d like 115d 1.25 1.25

Battles Type of 1980

Perf. 13½, 14½ (#985-988, 997-1000)

1982

980 A244 20d Hun Gioffra, 1915 50 24
981 A244 20d Gedabia, 1914 50 24
982 A244 20d El-Asaba, 1913 50 24
983 A244 20d El-Habela, 1917 50 24
984 A244 20d Suk El-Ahad, 1915 50 24
985 A244 20d El-Tangi, 1913 50 24
986 A244 20d Sokna, 1913 50 24
987 A244 20d Wadi Smalus, 1925 50 24
988 A244 20d Sidi Abuagela, 1917 50 24
989 A244 20d Sidi Surur, 1914 50 24
990 A244 20d Kuefia, 1911 50 24
991 A244 20d Abunjeim, 1940 50 24
992 A244 35d Hun Gioffra, diff. 90 45
993 A244 35d Gedabia, diff. 90 45
994 A244 35d El-Asaba, diff. 90 45
995 A244 35d El-Habela, diff. 90 45
996 A244 35d Suk El-Ahad, diff. 90 45
997 A244 35d El-Tangi, diff. 90 45
998 A244 35d Sokna, diff. 90 45
999 A244 35d Wadi Smalus, diff. 90 45
1000 A244 35d Sidi Abuagela, diff. 90 45
1001 A244 35d Sidi Surur, diff. 90 45
1002 A244 35d Kuefia, diff. 90 45
1003 A244 35d Abunjeim, diff. 90 45
Nos. 980-1003 (24) 16.80 8.28

Issue dates: Nos. 980, 992, Jan. 26. Nos. 981, 993, Mar. 8. Nos. 982, 994, Mar. 23. Nos. 983, 995, Apr. 24. No. 984, 996, May 15. Nos. 985, 997, June 19. Nos. 986, 998, July 23. Nos. 987, 999, Aug. 11. Nos. 988, 1000, Sept. 4. Nos. 989, 1001, Oct. 14. Nos. 990, 1002, Nov. 28. Nos. 991, 1003, Dec. 13. Stamps of same battle printed se-tenant in a continuous design.

Tripoli Intl. Fair — A272

1982, Mar. 1 ***Perf. 13x12½***

1004 A272 5d Grinding stone 15 15
1005 A272 10d Ox-drawn plow 18 15
1006 A272 25d Pitching hay 30 15
1007 A272 35d Tapestry weaving 42 15
1008 A272 45d Traditional cooking 45 22
1009 A272 100d Grain harvest 1.10 55
Nos. 1004-1009 (6) 2.60
Set value 1.20

People's Authority Declaration, The Green Book A273

1982, Mar. 2 ***Perf. 13½***

1010 Strip of 3 7.50 3.50
a. A273 100d Harvester combine 1.10 48
b. A273 200d Khadafy, scholar, rifles 2.50 1.10
c. A273 300d Govt. building, citizens 3.75 1.50

Scouting Movement, 75th Anniv. A274

13th African Soccer Cup Championships A275

1982, Mar. 2

1011 Strip of 4 10.00 5.00
a. A274 100d Cub scout, blimp 1.00 50
b. A274 200d Scouts, dog 2.00 1.00
c. A274 300d Scholar, scout 3.00 1.40
d. A274 400d Boy scout, rocket 4.00 2.00

Souvenir Sheets

1012 A274 500d Green Book 5.00 5.00
1013 A274 500d Khadafy, scouts 5.00 5.00

Nos. 1012-1013 each contain one stamp 39x42mm.

1982, Mar. 5

1014 A275 100d multi 1.00 50
1015 A275 200d multi 2.00 1.00

1982 World Cup Soccer Championships, Spain — A276

World Cup trophy and various soccer plays.

1982, Mar. 15 *Perf. 14½*

1016 A276 45d multi 45 22
1017 A276 100d multi 1.00 50
1018 A276 200d multi 2.00 1.00
1019 A276 300d multi 3.00 1.65

Souvenir Sheets

1020 A276 500d like 45d 5.00 5.00
1021 A276 500d like 100d 5.00 5.00

Nos. 1016-1019 issued in sheets of 8 overprinted in silver with soccer ball in motion. Sheetlets of 4 in each denomination exist without overprint.

Nos. 1020 1021 have Arabic text in green on reverse.

Palestinian Children's Day — A277

Designs: a, Two children. b, Girl with bowl. c, Girl with kaffiyeh. d, Girl hiding. e, Boy.

1982, Mar. 7 *Perf. 13½*

1022 Strip of 5 2.00 85
a.-e. A277 20d. any single 35 16

Birds — A278

Arab Postal Union, 30th — A280

Teaching Hospitals Anniv. A279

Miniature Sheet

1982, Apr. 1 *Perf. 14½*

1023 Sheet of 16 9.00
a.-d. A278 15d. any single 15 15
e.-h. A278 25d. any single 35 15
i.-l. A278 45d. any single 60 22
m.-p. A278 95d. any single 95 45

No. 1023a-1023p printed se-tenant in a continuous design; stamps of same denomination in blocks of 4.

1982, Apr. 7 *Perf. 13x12½*

1024 A279 95d multi 90 45
1025 A279 100d multi 1.00 50
1026 A279 205d multi 2.00 1.00

1982, Apr. 12 *Perf. 13½*

1027 A280 100d multi 1.00 50
1028 A280 200d multi 2.00 1.00

1982 World Chess Championships — A281

Board positions and chessmen: a, Chinese piece. b, African piece. c, Modern piece. d, European piece.

1982, May 1

1029 Block of 4 4.00 1.75
a.-d. A281 100d. any single 1.00 40

Souvenir Sheet

1030 A281 500d Overhead view of chessboard 5.00 5.00

No. 1030 contains one stamp 39x42mm.

World Telecommunications Day — A282

1982, May 17

1031 A282 100d multi 1.00 50
1032 A282 200d multi 2.00 1.00

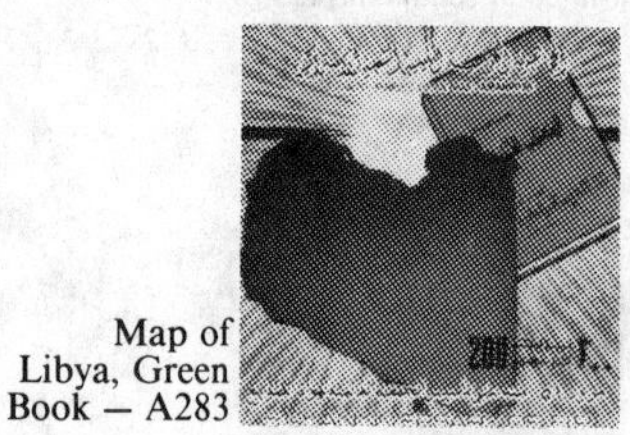

Map of Libya, Green Book — A283

1982, June 11

1033 A283 200d multi 2.00 75

Souvenir Sheet

1034 A283 300d multi 3.75 3.75

Post Day, FIP 51st anniv.

Organization of African Unity, 19th Summit — A284

1982, Aug. 5 *Perf. 14*

1035 A284 50d OAU flag, Arab family 50 25
1036 A284 100d Map of Africa, emblem 1.00 50

Size: 69x40mm

1037 A284 200d Khadafy, Green Book 2.00 1.00

Souvenir Sheet

Perf. 13x13½

1038 A284 300d Fist, map 3.75 3.75

No. 1038 contains one stamp 29x42mm.

September 1 Revolution, 13th Anniv. — A285

Khadafy in uniforms and various armed forces' exercises.

1982, Sept. 1 *Perf. 11½*

1039 A285 15d multi *24* 15
1040 A285 20d multi *30* 15
1041 A285 30d multi *32* 15
1042 A285 45d multi *50* 16
1043 A285 70d multi *65* 24
1044 A285 100d multi *90* 38
Nos. 1039-1044 (6) *2.91* 1.23

Souvenir Sheet

Imperf

1045 A285 200d multi *2.50 2.50*

Libyan Red Crescent, 25th Anniv. — A286

Intl. Day of Cooperation with Palestinian People — A287

1982, Oct. 5 *Perf. 13½*

1046 A286 100d Palm tree 1.00 50
1047 A286 200d "25," crescents 2.00 1.00

1982, Nov. 29

1048 A287 100d gray grn & blk 1.25 48
1049 A287 200d brt bl, gray grn & blk 2.75 90

Al-Fateh University Symposium on Khadafy's Green Book — A288

1982, Dec. 1 *Perf. 12*

1050 A288 100d Khadafy in uniform *1.00* 25
1051 A288 200d Khadafy, map, Green Book *2.00* 50

Flowers — A289

Customs Cooperation Council, 30th Anniv. — A290

Miniature Sheet

Designs: a, Philadelphus. b, Hypericum. c, Antinhinum. d, Lily. e, Capparis. f, Tropaeolum. g, Rose. h, Chrysanthemum. i, Nigella damascena. j, Guillardia lanceolata. k, Dahlia. l, Dianthus carophyllus. m, Notobasis syriaca. n, Nerium oleander. o, Iris histriodes. p, Scolymus hispanicus.

1983, Jan. 1 *Perf. 14½*

1052 Sheet of 16 5.00
a.-p. A289 25d. any single 30 20

Torch Type of 1979

1983, Jan. 2 *Perf. 13½*

Size: 26½x32mm

1053 A228 250d multi 3.50 1.10
1054 A228 1500d multi 15.00 6.50
1055 A228 2500d multi 27.50 10.00

1983, Jan. 15 *Perf. 14½x14*

1056 A290 25d Arab riding horse 25 15
1057 A290 50d Riding camel 50 25
1058 A290 100d Drawing sword 1.00 50

Battles Type of 1980

1983 *Perf. 13½*

1059 A244 50d Ghaser Ahmed, 1922 1.25 70
1060 A244 50d Same, right 1.25 70
1061 A244 50d Sidi Abuarghub, 1923 1.25 70
1062 A244 50d Same, right 1.25 70
1063 A244 50d Ghar Yunes, 1913 1.25 70
1064 A244 50d Same, right 1.25 70
1065 A244 50d Bir Otman, 1926 1.25 70
1066 A244 50d Same, right 1.25 70
1067 A244 50d Sidi Sajeh, 1922 1.25 70
1068 A244 50d Same, right 1.25 70
1069 A244 50d Ras El-Hamam, 1915 1.25 70
1070 A244 50d Same, right 1.25 70
1071 A244 50d Zawiet Ishghefa, 1913 1.25 70
1072 A244 50d Same, right 1.25 70
1073 A244 50d Wadi Essania, 1930 1.25 70
1074 A244 50d Same, right 1.25 70
1075 A244 50d El-Meshiashta, 1917 1.25 70
1076 A244 50d Same, right 1.25 70
1077 A244 50d Gharara, 1925 1.25 70
1078 A244 50d Same, right 1.25 70
1079 A244 50d Abughelan, 1922 1.25 70
1080 A244 50d Same, right 1.25 70
1081 A244 50d Mahruka, 1913 1.25 70
1082 A244 50d Same, right 1.25 70
Nos. 1059-1082 (24) 30.00 16.80

Issue dates: #1059-1060, Jan. 26. #1061-1062, Feb. 2. #1063-1064, Mar. 26. #1065-1066, Apr. 9. #1067-1068, May 2. #1069-1070, June 24. #1071-1072, July 13. #1073-1074, Aug. 8. #1075-1076, Sept. 9. #1077-1078, Oct. 22. #1079-1080, Nov. 17. #1081-1082, Dec. 24.

Miniature Sheet

Farm Animals — A291

Designs: a, Camel. b, Cow. c, Horse. d, Bull. e, Goat. f, Dog. g, Sheep. h, Ram. i, Goose. j, Turkey hen. k, Rabbit. l, Pigeon. m, Turkey. n, Rooster. o, Hen. p, Duck.

1983, Feb. 15 *Perf. 14½*

1083 Sheet of 16 5.00
a.-p. A291 25d any single 30 20

Tripoli Intl. Fair — A292

Libyans playing traditional instruments.

1983, Mar. 5 *Perf. 14½x14, 14x14½*

1084	A292	40d multi, vert.	40	15
1085	A292	45d multicolored	45	18
1086	A292	50d multi, vert.	50	22
1087	A292	55d multicolored	55	25
1088	A292	75d multi, vert.	75	40
1089	A292	100d multi, vert.	1.00	50
		Nos. 1084-1089 (6)	3.65	1.70

Intl. Maritime Organization, 25th Anniv. — A293

Early sailing ships.

1983, Mar. 17 *Perf. 14½*

1090	A293	100d Phoenician	1.10	60
1091	A293	100d Viking	1.10	60
1092	A293	100d Greek	1.10	60
1093	A293	100d Roman	1.10	60
1094	A293	100d Libyan	1.10	60
1095	A293	100d Pharoah's ship	1.10	60
		Nos. 1090-1095 (6)	6.60	3.60

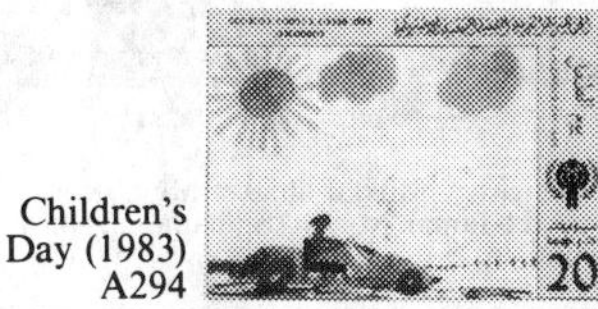

Children's Day (1983) A294

Children's illustrations: a, Car. b, Tractor towing trailer. c, Children, dove. d, Boy Scouts. e, Dinosaur.

1983, Mar. 21 *Perf. 14x14½*

1096	Strip of 5	*3.00*	35
a.-e.	A294 20d, any single	*55*	15

1st Intl. Symposium on Khadafy's Green Book — A295

1983, Apr. 1 *Perf. 13½*

1097	A295	50d Khadafy, Green Book, map	42	15
1098	A295	70d Lecture hall, emblem	60	20
1099	A295	80d Khadafy, Green Book, emblem	90	25

Souvenir Sheet

Perf. 12½

1100	A295	100d Khadafy, Green Books	*3.00*	1.25

No. 1100 contains one stamp 57x48mm.

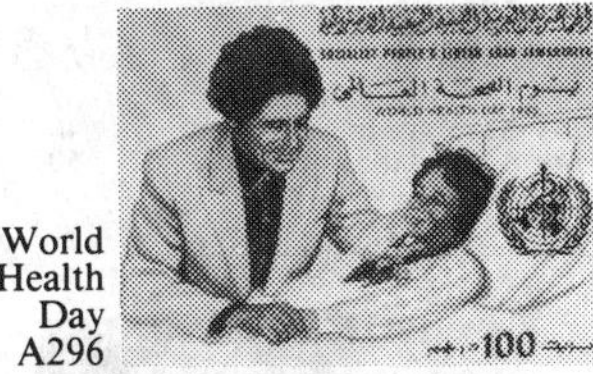

World Health Day A296

1983, Apr. 7 *Perf. 12½*

1101	A296	25d Healthy children, vert.	*25*	15
1102	A296	50d Man in wheelchair, vert.	*52*	16
1103	A296	100d Girl in hospital bed	*85*	32

Pan-African Economic Committee, 25th Anniv. — A297

1983, Apr. 20 *Perf. 13½*

1104	A297	50d multi	48	15
1105	A297	100d multi	90	45
1106	A297	250d multi	2.75	1.25

Miniature Sheet

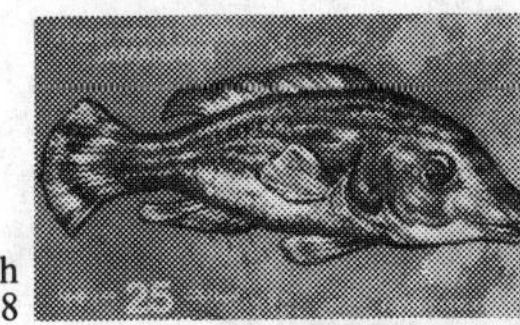

Fish A298

Designs: a, Labrus bimaculatus. b, Trigloporus lastoviza. c, Thalassoma pavo. d, Apogon imberbis. e, Scomber scombrus. f, Spondyliosoma cantharus. g, Trachinus draco. h, Blennius pavo. i, Scorpaena notata. j, Serranus scriba. k, Lophius piscatorius. l, Uranoscopus scaber. m, Auxis thazard. n, Zeus faber. o, Dactylopterus volitans. p, Umbrina cirrosa.

1983, May 15 *Perf. 14½*

1107	Sheet of 16	5.00	
a.-p.	A298 25d any single	30	20

Still-life by Gauguin (1848-1903) — A299

Paintings: No. 1108b, Abstract, unattributed. c, The Conquest of Tunis by Charles V, by Rubens. d, Arab Musicians in a Carriage, unattributed.

No. 1109a, Khadafy Glorified on Horseback, unattributed, vert. b, Triumph of David over the Syrians, by Raphael, vert. c, Laborers, unattributed, vert. d, Flower Vase, by van Gogh, vert.

1983, June 1 *Perf. 11*

1108	Strip of 4	2.00	90
a.-d.	A299 50d, any single	50	20
1109	Strip of 4	2.00	90
a.-d.	A299 50d, any single	50	20

Souvenir Sheet

Ali Siala — A300

Scientists: No. 1110b, Ali El-Najar.

1983, June 1

1110	Sheet of 2	*2.50*	1.50
a.-b.	A300 100d, any single	*1.10*	65

1984 Summer Olympic Games, Los Angeles — A301

1983, June 15 *Perf. 13½*

1111	A301	10d Basketball	15	15
1112	A301	15d High jump	15	15
1113	A301	25d Running	20	15
1114	A301	50d Gymnastics	40	20
1115	A301	100d Wind surfing	90	40
1116	A301	200d Shot put	1.90	90
		Nos. 1111-1116 (6)	3.70	1.95

Souvenir Sheets

1117	A301	100d Equestrian	*1.00*	*1.00*
1118	A301	100d Soccer	*1.00*	*1.00*

Nos. 1111-1116 also exist in miniature sheets of 4.

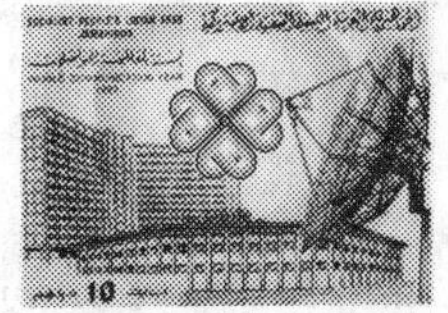

World Communications Year — A302

1983, July 1 *Perf. 13*

1119	A302	10d multicolored	15	15
1120	A302	50d multicolored	40	20
1121	A302	100d multicolored	90	40

The Green Book, by Khadafy A303

Ideologies: 10d, The House is to be served by its residents. 15d, Power, wealth and arms are in the hands of the people. 20d, Masters in their own castles, vert. 35d, No democracy without popular congress. 100d, The authority of the people, vert. 140d, The Green Book is the guide of humanity for final release.

1983, Aug. 1 *Perf. 13½*

1122	A303	10d multi	15	15
1123	A303	15d multi	20	15
1124	A303	20d multi	25	15
1125	A303	35d multi	38	15
1126	A303	100d multi	90	40
1127	A303	140d multi	1.40	75
		Nos. 1122-1127 (6)	3.28	1.75

Souvenir Sheet

Litho. & Embossed

1128	A303	200d Khadafy in uniform	1.65	1.65

No. 1128 contains one gold embossed stamp 36x51mm.

2nd African Youth Sports Festival — A304

Designs: a, Team Handball. b, Basketball. c, Javelin. d, Running. e, Soccer.

1983, Aug. 22 **Litho.**

1129	Strip of 5	5.00	2.75
a.-e.	A304 100d, any single	1.00	50

September 1 Revolution, 14th Anniv. — A305

Women in the Armed Forces.

1983, Sept. 1 *Perf. 11½*

1130	A305	65d multi	55	30
1131	A305	75d multi	75	40
1132	A305	90d multi	85	42
1133	A305	100d multi	90	45
1134	A305	150d multi	1.40	75
1135	A305	250d multi	2.75	1.25
		Nos. 1130-1135 (6)	7.20	3.57

Souvenir Sheet

Perf. 11

1136	A305	200d multi	2.00	2.00

No. 1136 contains one stamp 63x38mm.

2nd Islamic Scout Jamboree — A306

1983, Sept. 2 *Perf. 12½*

1137	A306	50d Saluting	60	18
1138	A306	100d Camping	90	35

Souvenir Sheet

1139	Sheet of 2	1.25	90
a.	A306 100d like 50d	60	40

No. 1139 contains Nos. 1138 and 1139a.

Traffic Day A307

Saadun (1893-1923) A308

1983, Oct. 1 *Perf. 14½x14*

1140	A307	30d Youth traffic monitors	30	15
1141	A307	70d Traffic officer	65	30
1142	A307	200d Motorcycle police	1.90	90

1983, Oct. 11 *Perf. 13½*

1143	A308	100d multicolored	1.00	50

1st Manned Flight, Bicent. — A309

Early aircraft and historic flights: a, Americana, 1910. b, Nulli Secundus, 1907. c, J. B. Meusnier, 1785. d, Blanchard and Jeffries, 1785, vert. e, Pilatre de Rozier, 1784, vert. f, Montgolfiere, Oct. 19, 1783, vert.

1983, Nov. 1

1144	Strip of 6	7.50	3.50
a.-f.	A309 100d. any single	1.25	55

Intl. Day of Cooperation with Palestinian People — A310

1983, Nov. 29 **Perf. 14½x14**

1145	A310	30d pale vio & lt bl grn	30	15
1146	A310	70d lil & lt yel grn	90	30
1147	A310	200d lt ultra & grn	2.75	90

Miniature Sheet

Roman Mosaic — A311

Designs: Nos. 1148a-1148c, Gladiators. Nos. 1148d-1148f, Musicians, Nos. 1148g-1148i, Hunters. Illustration reduced.

1983, Dec. 1 **Perf. 12**

1148	Sheet of 9	5.50	
a.-i.	A311 50d. any single	60	25

Nos. 1148a-1148c, 1148d-1148f and 1148g-1148i se-tenant in a continuous design.

Achievements of the Sept. 1 Revolution — A312

1983, Dec. 15 **Perf. 13½**

1149	A312	10d Mosque	15	15
1150	A312	15d Agriculture	15	15
1151	A312	20d Industry	22	15
1152	A312	35d Office building	35	15
1153	A312	100d Health care	90	40
1154	A312	140d Airport	1.25	65
		Nos. 1149-1154 (6)	3.02	1.65

Souvenir Sheet

Litho. & Embossed

1155	A312	200d Khadafy	2.50	2.50

No. 1155 contains one gold embossed stamp 36x51mm.

Khadafy, Irrigation Project Survey Map A313

1983, Dec. 15

1156	A313	150d multicolored	1.50	75

15-Cent Minimum Value
The minimum catalogue value is 15 cents. Separating se-tenant pieces into individual stamps does not increase the "value" of the stamps... since demand for the separated stamps may be small.

A314

A315

Famous men: No. 1157a, Mahmud Burkis. No. 1157b, Ahmed El-Bakbak. No. 1157c, Mohamed El-Misurati. No. 1157d, Mahmud Ben Musa. No. 1157e, Abdulhamid Ben Ashiur. No. 1158a, Hosni Fauzi El-Amir. No. 1158b, Ali Haidar El-Saati. No. 1159, Mahmud Mustafa Dreza. No. 1160, Mehdi El-Sherif. No. 1161a, Ali El-Gariani. No. 1161b, Muktar Shakshuki. No. 1161c, Abdurrahman El-Busayri. No. 1161d, Ibbrahim Bakir. No. 1161e, Mahmud El-Janzuri. No. 1162a, Ahmed El-Feghi Hasan. No. 1162b, Bashir El Jawab.

1984 **Litho.** **Perf. 13½**

1157	Strip of 5	5.00	2.75
a.-e.	A314 100d any single	1.00	55
1158	Pair	2.25	1.00
a.-b.	A314 100d any single	1.10	50
1159	A314 100d multi	1.10	50
1160	A315 100d multi	1.10	50
1161	Strip of 5	10.00	5.00
a.-e.	A314 200d any single	2.00	1.00
1162	Pair	4.00	2.25
a.-b.	A315 200d any single	2.00	1.00
	Nos. 1157-1162 (6)	23.45	12.00

Issue dates: Nos. 1158, 1161-1162, Jan. 1. Others, Feb. 20.

Miniature Sheet

Water Sports — A316

Designs: a, Two windsurfers. b, Two-man craft. c, Two-man craft, birds. d, Wind sailing, skis. e, Water skier facing front. f, Fisherman in boat. g, Power boating. h, Water skier facing right. i, Fisherman in surf. j, Kayaking. k, Surfing. l, Water skier wearing life jacket. m, Scuba diver sketching underwater. n, Diver. o, Snorkel diver removing fish from harpoon. p, Scuba diver surfacing.

1984, Jan. 10 **Perf. 14½**

1164	Sheet of 16	5.00	2.50
a.-p.	A316 25d any single	30	15

African Children's Day — A317

Designs: a, Khadafy, girl scouts. b, Khadafy, children. c, Map, Khadafy, children (size: 63x44mm).

1984, Jan. 15 **Litho.** **Perf. 14½**

1165	Strip of 3	1.90	50
a.-b.	A317 50d. any single	42	15
c.	A317 100d multi	80	20

Women's Emancipation — A318

Designs: 70d, Women, diff., vert. 100d, Soldiers, Khadafy.

1984, Jan. 20 **Perf. 12**

1166	A318	55d multicolored	55	25
1167	A318	70d multicolored	75	38
1168	A318	100d multicolored	1.00	45

Irrigation A319

Designs: No. 1169a, Desert, water. No. 1169b, Produce, sheep grazing. No. 1169c, Khadafy, irrigation of desert (size: 63x44mm). Nos. 1170-1171, Khadafy, map.

1984, Feb. 1 **Perf. 14½**

1169	Strip of 3	2.00	1.00
a.-b.	A319 50d any single	45	22
c.	A319 100d multicolored	1.00	50

Size: 72x36mm

Perf. 13½

1170	A319	100d multicolored	1.00	50

Souvenir Sheet

1171	A319	300d multicolored	*3.75*	*3.75*

World Heritage — A320

Architectural ruins. No. 1174 vert.

1984, Feb. 10 **Perf. 12**

1172	A320	50d Theater, Sabratha	48	15
1173	A320	60d Temple, Cyrene	60	30
1174	A320	70d Monument, Sabratha	75	35
1175	A320	100d Arena, Leptis Magna	1.00	45
1176	A320	150d Temple, Cyrene, diff.	1.50	75
1177	A320	200d Basilica, Leptis Magna	2.25	1.10
		Nos. 1172-1177 (6)	6.58	3.10

Silver Dirhams Minted A.D. 671-757 — A321

Designs: a, Hegira 115. b, Hegira 93. c, Hegira 121. d, Hegira 49. e, Hegira 135.

Litho. & Embossed

1984, Feb. 15 **Perf. 13½**

1178	Strip of 5	10.00	5.00
a.-e.	A321 200d. any single	2.00	1.00

Tripoli Intl. Fair A322

Tea served in various settings.

1984, Mar. 5 **Litho.** **Perf. 12½**

1179	A322	25d multicolored	20	15
1180	A322	35d multicolored	35	15
1181	A322	45d multicolored	45	16
1182	A322	55d multicolored	55	20
1183	A322	75d multicolored	75	35
1184	A322	100d multicolored	1.00	45
		Nos. 1179-1184 (6)	3.30	1.46

Musicians — A323

Designs: a, Muktar Shiaker Murabet. b, El-Aref El-Jamal. c, Ali Shiaalia. d, Bashir Fehmi.

1984, Mar. 15 **Perf. 14½**

1185	Strip of 4 + label	4.00	2.00
a.-d.	A323 100d. any single	95	45

No. 1185 has center label picturing musical instruments.

Children's Day, IYC A324

Children's drawings: a, Recreation. b, Rainy day. c, Military strength. d, Playground. e, Porch swing, children, motorcycle.

1984, Mar. 21 **Perf. 14**

1186	Strip of 5	2.00	90
a.-e.	A324 20d. any single	40	18

Arab League Constitution, 39th Anniv. A325

1984, Mar. 22 **Perf. 13½**

1187	A325	30d multicolored	32	15
1188	A325	40d multicolored	40	20
1189	A325	50d multicolored	50	25

Miniature Sheet

Automobiles, Locomotives — A326

1984, Apr. 1

1190 Sheet of 16 20.00 9.00
a.-h. A326 100d. Car, any single 1.25 55
i.-p. A326 100d. Locomotive, any single 1.25 55

No. 1190 pictures outline of two camels in gold. Size: 214x135mm.

World Health Day A327

1984, Apr. 7 ***Perf. 14½***

1191 A327 20d Stop Polio 20 15
1192 A327 30d No. 910 32 15
1193 A327 40d Arabic text 40 20

Crafts — A328

Designs: a, Shoemaker. b, Saddler. c, Women, wool. d, Spinner. e, Weaver. f, Tapestry weavers.

1984, May 1 ***Perf. 12½***

1194 Strip of 6 9.00 4.50
a.-f. A328 150d. any single 1.50 75

Postal and Telecommunications Union Congress — A329

Designs: a, Telephones, mail. b, Computer operators. c, Emblem.

1984, May 15 ***Perf. 14½***

1195 Strip of 3 2.00 1.00
a.-b. A329 50d. any single 50 25
c. A329 100d multicolored 1.00 50

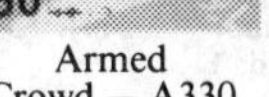

Armed Crowd — A330 Map, Fire, Military — A331

Designs: No. 1197b, Soldiers. No. 1197c, Khadafy. No. 1198, Khadafy giving speech.

1984, May 17 ***Perf. 12, 14½ (#1197)***

1196 A330 50d multi 55 25
1197 Strip of 3 2.25 1.25
a.-b. A331 50d. any single 55 28
c. A331 100d multi 1.10 55
1198 A330 100d multi 1.25 55
Nos. 1196-1198 (3) 4.05 2.05

Abrogation of the May 17 Treaty. Size of No. 1197c: 63x45mm.

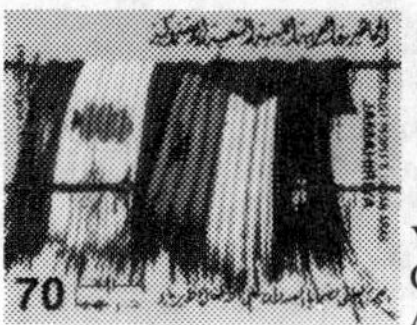

Youth War Casualties A332

1984, June 4 ***Perf. 10***

1199 A332 70d Damaged flag 75 35
1200 A332 100d Children imprisoned 1.00 45

Miniature Sheet

Green Book Quotations A333

Designs: a, The Party System Aborts Democracy. b, Khadafy. c, Partners Not Wage-Workers. d, No Representation in Lieu of the People . . . e, Green Book. f, Committees Everywhere. g, Forming Parties Splits Societies. h, Party building, text on track. i, No Democracy without Popular Congresses.

1984, June 20 ***Perf. 14***

1201 Sheet of 9 9.00 4.50
a.-i. A333 100d. any single 1.00 45

See No. 1270.

Folk Costumes — A334

1984, July 1 ***Perf. 14½x14***

**Background colors:
a, Green. b, Beige. c, Violet.
d, Pale greenish blue.
e, Salmon rose. f, Blue.**

1202 Strip of 6 6.00 3.00
a.-f. A334 100d. any single 1.00 50

Miniature Sheet

Natl. Soccer Championships — A335

Stadium, star, world cup and various action scenes.

1984, July 15 ***Perf. 13½***

1203 Sheet of 16 11.00 5.00
a.-p. A335 70d. any single 65 30

1984 Los Angeles Olympics — A336 World Food Day — A337

1984, July 28

1204 A336 100d Soccer 1.00 45
1205 A336 100d Basketball 1.00 45
1206 A336 100d Swimming 1.00 45
1207 A336 100d Sprinting 1.00 45
1208 A336 100d Windsurfing 1.00 45
1209 A336 100d Discus 1.00 45
Nos. 1204-1209 (6) 6.00 2.70

Souvenir Sheets

1210 A336 250d Equestrian 1.90 90
1211 A336 250d Arab equestrian 1.90 90

1984, Aug. 1 ***Perf. 12***

1212 A337 100d Forest scenes 1.00 45
1213 A337 200d Men riding camels, oasis 2.00 1.00

Miniature Sheet

Sept. 1 Revolution, 15th Anniv. — A338

Designs: a, Green books, building at right angle. b, Green book, building, minaret. c, Minaret, party building and grounds. d, Revolution leader. e, Eight-story building. f, Construction, dome. g, Highway, bridge. h, Green book, building at left angle. i, Shepherd, sheep. j, Harvester. k, Tractors. l, Industry. m, Khadafy. n, Irrigation pipe, man drinking. o, Silos, factory. p, Shipping.

1984, Sept. 15 ***Perf. 14½***

1214 Sheet of 16 5.00 5.00
a.-p. A338 25d any single 30 20

A339

Evacuation Day — A340

Designs: No. 1215b, Warrior facing left. No. 1215c, Khadafy leading battle (size: 63x45mm). No. 1216, Female rider. No. 1217, Battle scene. No. 1218, Italian whipping Libyan.

1984, Oct. 7

1215 Strip of 3 2.00 1.00
a.-b. A339 50d. any single 50 22
c. A339 100d multi 1.00 45

Perf. 11½

1216 A340 100d multicolored 1.00 45
1217 A340 100d multicolored 1.00 45
1218 A340 100d multicolored 1.00 45
Nos. 1215-1218 (4) 5.00 2.35

Miniature Sheet

Equestrians — A341

Various jumping, racing and dressage exercises printed in a continuous design.

1984, Oct. 15 ***Perf. 13½***

1219 Sheet of 16 5.00 5.00
a.-p. A341 25d any single 30 20

PHILAKOREA '84.

Agricultural Traditions — A342

Designs: a, Farmer. b, Well, man, ox. c, Basket weaver. d, Shepherd, ram. e, Tanning hide. f, Coconut picker.

1984, Nov. 1 ***Perf. 13½***

1220 Strip of 6 6.00 3.00
a.-f. A342 100d. any single 1.00 50

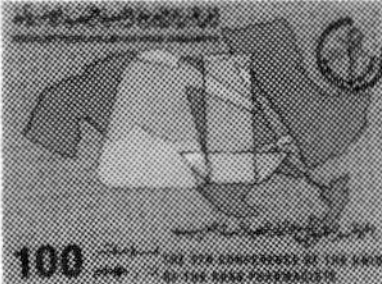

Union of Arab Pharmacists, 9th Congress A343

1984, Nov. 6 ***Perf. 12***

1221 A343 100d multicolored 1.00 45
1222 A343 200d multicolored 2.00 1.00

Arab-African Union A344

1984, Nov. 15 ***Perf. 12***

1223 A344 100d Map, banner, crowd 1.00 45
1224 A344 100d Men, flags 1.00 45

Nos. 1046, 1147 A345

1984, Nov. 29 ***Perf. 12½***

1225 A345 100d pink & multi 1.25 60
1226 A345 150d brt yel grn & multi 1.75 90

Intl. Day of Cooperation with the Palestinian People.

Miniature Sheet

Intl. Civil Aviation Organization, 40th Anniv. — A346

Aircraft: a, Boeing 747 SP, 1975. b, Concorde, 1969. c, Lockheed L1011-500 Tristar, 1978. d, Airbus A310, 1982. e, Tupolev TU-134A, 1962. f, Shorts 360, 1981. g, Boeing 727, 1963. h, Caravelle 10, 1965. i, Fokker F27, 1955. j, Lockheed 749A Constellation, 1946. k, Martin 130, 1955. l, Douglas DC-3, 1936. m, Junkers JU-52, 1932. n, Lindbergh's Spirit of St. Louis, 1927 Ryan. o, De Havilland Moth, 1925. p, Wright Flyer, 1903.

1984, Dec. 7 ***Perf. 13½***

1227 Sheet of 16 14.00 7.50
a.-p. A346 70d any single 85 45

African Development Bank, 20th Anniv. — A347

UN Child Survival Campaign — A348

"20" in different configurations and: 70d, Map, symbols of industry, education and agriculture. 100d, Symbols of research and development.

1984, Dec. 15

1228 A347 50d multicolored 50 25
1229 A347 70d multicolored 75 40
1230 A347 100d multicolored 1.10 50

1985, Jan. 1 ***Perf. 12***

1231 A348 70d Mother, child 70 30
1232 A348 70d Children 70 30
1233 A348 70d Boys at military school 70 30
1234 A348 70d Khadafy, children 70 30

Irrigation — A349

Drop of Water, Map A350

1985, Jan. 15 ***Perf. 14½x14***

1235 A349 100d shown 1.00 45
1236 A349 100d Flowers 1.00 45
1237 A349 100d Map, water 1.00 45

Souvenir Sheet

Perf. 14x14½

1238 A350 200d shown 2.50 2.50

Musicians — A351

Designs: No. 1239a, Kamel El-Ghadi. No. 1239b, Lute. No. 1240a, Ahmed El-Khogia. No. 1240b, Violin. No. 1241a, Mustafa El-Fallah. No. 1241b, Zither. No. 1242a, Mohamed Hamdi. No. 1242b, Mask.

1985, Feb. 1 ***Perf. 14½***

1239 Pair 3.00 1.50
a.-b. A351 100d, any single 1.50 75
1240 Pair 3.00 1.50
a.-b. A351 100d, any single 1.50 75
1241 Pair 3.00 1.50
a.-b. A351 100d, any single 1.50 75
1242 Pair 3.00 1.50
a.-b. A351 100d, any single 1.50 75
Nos. 1239-1242 (4) 12.00 6.00

Nos. 1239-1242 printed in sheets of 20, four strips of 5 consisting of two pairs each musician flanking center stamps picturing instruments.

Gold Dinars Minted A.D. 699-727 — A352

Designs: No. 1243a, Hegira 105. No. 1243b, Hegira 91. No. 1243c, Hegira 77. No. 1244, Dinar from Zuela.

Litho. and Embossed

1985, Feb. 15 ***Perf. 13½***

1243 Strip of 3 6.00 3.00
a.-c. A352 200d. any single 2.00 1.00

Souvenir Sheet

1244 A352 300d multi 3.75 1.75

Fossils A353

1985, Mar. 1 **Litho.** ***Perf. 13½***

1245 A353 150d Frog 1.40 65
1246 A353 150d Fish 1.40 65
1247 A353 150d Mammal 1.40 65

People's Authority Declaration A354

Khadafy wearing: a, Folk costume. b, Academic robe. c, Khaki uniform. d, Black uniform. e, White uniform.

1985, Mar. 2 **Litho.** ***Perf. 14½***

1248 Strip of 5 6.50 3.25
a.-e. A354 100d. any single 1.25 65

Tripoli Intl. Fair — A355

Musicians playing: a, Cymbals. b, Double flute, bongo. c, Wind instrument, drum. d, Drum. e, Tambourine.

1985, Mar. 5 ***Perf. 14***

1249 Strip of 5 5.00 2.50
a.-e. A355 100d. any single 1.00 50

Children's Day, IYC — A356

Children's drawings, various soccer plays: a, Goalie and player. b, Four players. c, Players as letters of the alphabet. d, Goalie save. e, Player heading the ball.

1985, Mar. 21 ***Perf. 12***

1250 Strip of 5 2.00 75
a.-e. A356 20d. any single 40 15

Intl. Program for Development of Telecommunications A357

World Health Day A358

1985, Apr. 1

1251 A357 30d multicolored 35 16
1252 A357 70d multicolored 75 35
1253 A357 100d multicolored 1.10 50

1985, Apr. 7

1254 A358 40d Invalid, nurses 38 18
1255 A358 60d Nurse, surgery 60 30
1256 A358 100d Nurse, child 1.10 50

Miniature Sheet

Sea Shells — A359

Designs: a, Mytilidae. b, Muricidae (white). c, Cardiidae. d, Corallophilidae. e, Muricidae. f, Muricacea. g, Turridae. h, Argonautidae. i, Tonnidae. j, Aporrhaidae. k, Trochidae. l, Cancellariidae. m, Epitoniidae. n, Turbnidae. o, Mitridae. p, Pectinidae.

1985, Apr. 20

1257 Sheet of 16 5.00 2.75
a.-p. A359 25d. any single 30 15

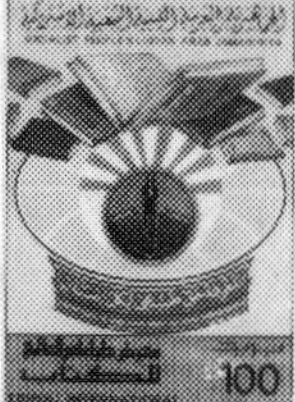

Tripoli Intl. Book Fair — A360

Intl. Youth Year — A361

1985, Apr. 28 ***Perf. 13½***

1258 A360 100d multi 1.00 50
1259 A360 200d multi 2.00 1.00

1985, May 1

Games: No. 1260a, Jump rope. No. 1260b, Board game. No. 1260c, Hopscotch. No. 1260d, Stickgame. No. 1260e, Tops. No. 1261a, Soccer. No. 1261b, Basketball.

1260 Strip of 5 1.90 90
a.-e. A361 20d. any single 55 18

Souvenir Sheet

1261 Sheet of 2 2.50 1.10
a.-b. A361 100d. any single 1.25 50

No. 1261 contains 2 stamps 30x42mm.

Miniature Sheet

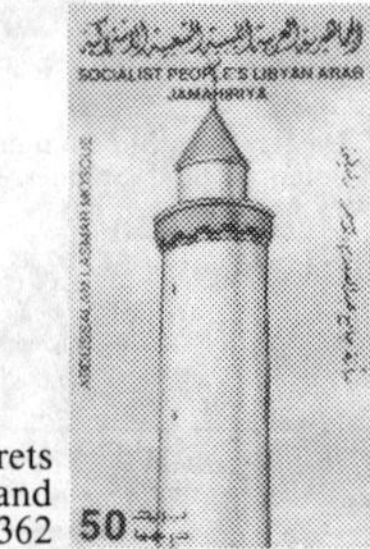

Mosque Minarets and Towers — A362

Mosques: a, Abdussalam Lasmar. b, Zaoviat Kadria. c, Zaoviat Amura. d, Gurgi. e, Mizran. f, Salem. g, Ghat. h, Ahmed Karamanli. i, Atya. j, El Kettani. k, Benghazi. l, Derna. m, El Derug. n, Ben Moussa. o, Ghadames. p, Abdulwahab.

1985, May 15 ***Perf. 12***

1262 Sheet of 16 11.00 5.00
a.-p. A362 50d. any single 60 30

Teachers' Day — A363

1985, June 1 **Litho.** ***Perf. 13½***

1263 A363 100d Hamida El-Anezi 1.00 40
1264 A363 100d Jamila Zemerli 1.00 40

Battle of the Philadelphia A364

Designs: a, Ship sinking. b, Militia. c, Hand-to-hand combat.

1985 June 12

1265 Strip of 3 2.00 1.00
a.-b. A364 50d. any single 50 25
c. A364 100d multicolored 1.00 50

Size of No. 1265c: 60x48mm. Continuous design with No. 1265c in middle.

A365

Khadafy's Islamic Pilgrimage A366

"The Holy Koran is the Law of Society" and Khadafy: a, Writing. b, Kneeling. c, With Holy Kaaba. d, Looking in window. e, Praying at pilgrimage ceremony.

1985, June 16

1266 Strip of 5 10.00 4.50
a.-e. A365 200d. any single 2.00 90

Souvenir Sheet

1267 A366 300d multicolored 5.50 5.50

Miniature Sheet

Mushrooms — A367

Designs: a, Leucopaxillus lepistoides. b, Amanita caesarea. c, Coriolus hirsutus. d, Cortinarius subfulgens. e, Dermocybe pratensis. f, Macrolepiota excoriata. g, Amanita curtipes. h, Trametes ljubarskyi. i, Pholiota aurivella. j, Boletus edulis. k, Geastrum sessile. l, Russula sanguinea. m, Cortinarius herculeus. n, Pholiota lenta. o, Amanita rubenscens. p, Scleroderma polyrhizum.

1985, July 15

1268 Sheet of 16 10.00 4.50
a.-p. A367 50d. any single 60 25

Women's Folk Costumes — A368

Designs: a, Woman in violet. b, In white. c, In brown and blue. d, In blue. e, In red.

1985, Aug. 1 ***Perf. 14½x14***

1269 Strip of 5 5.00 2.25
a.-e. A368 100d. any single 1.00 45

Green Book Quotations Type of 1984
Miniature Sheet

Designs: a, In Need Freedom Is Latent. b, Khadafy reading. c, To Make A Party You Split Society. d, Public Sport Is for All the Masses. e, Green Books, doves. f, Wage-Workers Are a Type of Slave . . . g, People Are Only Harmonious with Their Own Arts and Heritages. h, Khadafy orating. i, Democracy Means Popular Rule Not Popular Expression.

1985, Aug. 15 ***Perf. 14***

1270 Sheet of 9 9.00 4.50
a.-i. A333 100d. any single 1.00 50

A369

September 1 Revolution, 16th Anniv. — A370

Designs: a, Food. b, Oil pipeline, refinery. c, Capital, olive branch. d, Mosque, modern buildings. e, Flag, mountains. f, Telecommunications apparatus.

1985, Sept. 1 ***Perf. 12½***

1271 Strip of 6 6.00 3.00
a.-f. A369 100d. any single 1.00 50
1272 A370 200d multi 2.50 1.25

Mosque Entrances A371

Designs: a, Zauiet Amoura, Janzour. b, Shiaieb El-ain, Tripoli. c, Zauiet Abdussalam El-asmar, Zliten. d, Karamanli, Tripoli. e, Gurgi, Tripoli.

1985, Sept. 15 ***Perf. 14***

1273 Strip of 5 5.00 2.25
a.-e. A371 100d. any single 1.00 45

Miniature Sheet

Basketball A372

Various players in action.

1985, Oct. 1 Litho. ***Perf. 13x12½***

1274 Sheet of 16 5.00 2.50
a. A372 25d any single 30 15

Evacuation — A373

Designs: a, Man on crutches, web, tree. b, Man caught in web held by disembodied hands. c, Three men basking in light.

1985, Oct. 7 ***Perf. 15***

1275 Strip of 3 3.00 1.50
a.-c. A373 100d. any single 1.00 50

Stamp Day — A374

Italia 85: a, Man sitting at desk, Type A228, Earth. b, Magnifying glass, open stock book, Type A228. c, Stamps escaping envelope.

1985, Oct. 25 ***Perf. 12***

1276 Strip of 3 1.50 75
a.-c. A374 50d. any single 50 25

1986 World Cup Soccer Championships — A375

1985, Nov. 1 ***Perf. 13½***

1277 A375 100d Block, heading the ball 1.00 50
1278 A375 100d Kick, goalie catching ball 1.00 50
1279 A375 100d Goalie, block, dribble 1.00 50
1280 A375 100d Goalie, dribble, sliding block 1.00 50
1281 A375 100d Goalie catching the ball 1.00 50
1282 A375 100d Block 1.00 50
Nos. 1277-1282 (6) 6.00 3.00

Souvenir Sheet

1283 A375 200d Four players 2.50 1.25

Intl. Day of Cooperation with the Palestinian People A376

1985, Nov. 29 Litho. ***Perf. 12½***

1284 A376 100d multi 1.25 60
1285 A376 150d multi 1.90 90

Importation Prohibited
Importation of the stamps of Libya was prohibited as of Jan. 7, 1986.

General Post and Telecommunications Co. — A378

1986, Jan. 15 ***Perf. 12***

1298 A378 100d yel & multi
1299 A378 150d yel grn & multi

Peoples Authority Declaration A379

Designs: b, Hand holding globe and paper. c, Dove, Khadafy's Green Book (size: 53x37mm).

1986, Mar. 2 ***Perf. 12½x13***

1300 Strip of 3
a.-b. A379 50d, any single
c. A379 100d multicolored

Musical Instruments — A380

Designs: a, Flute. b, Drums. c, Horn. d, Cymbals. e, Hand drum.

1986, Mar. 5

1301 Strip of 5
a.-e. A380 100d any single

Tripoli International Fair.

Intl. Children's Day — A381

Designs: a, Boy Scout fishing. b, Riding camel. c, Chasing butterflies. d, Beating drum. e, Soccer game.

1986, Mar. 21 ***Perf. 13½***

1302 Strip of 5
a.-e. A381 50d any single

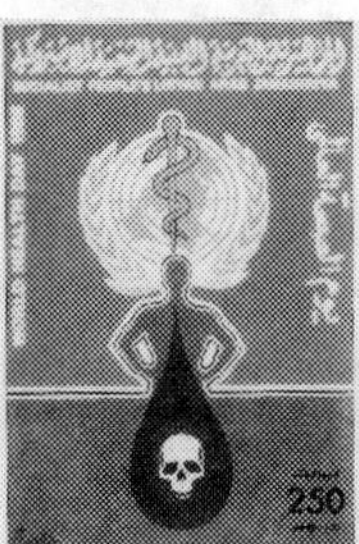

World Health Day — A382

1986, Apr. 7
1303 A382 250d sil & multi
1304 A382 250d gold & multi

Government Programs — A383

Designs: a, Medical examinations. b, Education. c, Farming (size: 63x42mm).

1986, May 1 *Perf. 14½*
1305 Strip of 3
a.-b. A383 50d any single
c. A383 100d multicolored

Miniature Sheet

World Cup Soccer Championships, Mexico — A384

Designs: No. 1306a, 2 players. No. 1306b, 3 players in red and white shirts, one in green. No. 1306c, 2 players, referee. No. 1306d, Shot at goal. No. 1306e, 2 players with striped shirts. No. 1306f, 2 players with blue shirts, one with red. No. 1307, 7 players. No. 1308, 1st Libyan team, 1931.

1986, May 31 *Perf. 13½*
1306 Sheet of 6
a.-f. A384 50d any single

Souvenir Sheets

1307 A384 200d multicolored
1308 A384 200d multicolored

Nos. 1307-1308 each contain one 52x37mm stamp.

Miniature Sheet

Vegetables A385

Designs: a, Peas. b, Zucchini. c, Beans. d, Eggplant. e, Corn. f, Tomato. g, Red pepper. h, Cucumbers. i, Garlic. j, Cabbage. k, Cauliflower. l, Celery. m, Onions. n, Carrots. o, Potato. p, Radishes.

1986, June 1 *Perf. 13x12½*
1309 Sheet of 16
a.-p. A385 50d any single

No. 1309 has a continuous design.

Miniature Sheet

Khadafy and Irrigation Project — A386

Khadafy and: a, Engineer reviewing plans, drill rig. b, Map. c, Well. d, Drought conditions. e, Water pipe. f, Pipes, pulleys, equipment. g, Lowering water pipe. h, Construction workers, trailer. i, Hands holding water. j, Opening water valve. k, Laying pipeline. l, Trucks hauling pipes. m, Khadafy holding green book, city. n, Giving vegetables to people. o, Boy drinking, man cultivating field. p, Men in prayer, irrigation. (Khadafy not shown on Nos. 1310h, 1310i, 1310k, 1310 l, 1310o.)

1986, July 1 *Perf. 13½*
1310 Sheet of 16
a.-p. A386 100d any single

A387

A388

American Attack on Libya, Apr. 15 — A389

Designs: Nos. 1311a-1311p, Various scenes in Tripoli during and after air raid. No. 1312a. F14 aircraft. No. 1312b, Aircraft carrier, people. No. 1312c, Sinking of USS *Philadelphia,* 1801.
Illustration A389 is reduced.

1986, July 13
1311 A387 Sheet of 16, #a.-p.
1312 Strip of 3
a.-b. A388 50d multicolored
c. A388 100d multicolored
1313 A389 100d multicolored

No. 1312 has a continuous design. Size of No. 1312b: 60x38mm.

Khadafy's Peace Methods A390

Khadafy: b, Reading Green Book. c, With old woman. d, Praying with children. e, Visiting sick. f, Driving tractor.

1986, July 13
1314 Sheet of 6
a.-f. A390 100d any single

Miniature Sheet

Green Book Quotations A391

Designs: a, The House Must be Served by its Own Tenant. b, Khadafy. c, The Child is Raised by His Mother. d, Democracy is the Supervision of the People by the People. e, Green Books. f, Representation is a Falsification of Democracy. g, The Recognition of Profit is an Acknowledgement of Exploitation. h, Flowers. i, Knowledge is a Natural Right of Every Human Being...

1986, Aug. 1 *Perf. 14*
1315 Sheet of 9
a.-i. A391 100d any single

Sept. 1st Revolution, 17th Anniv. A392

Designs: a, Public health. b, Agriculture. c, Sunflowers by Vincent Van Gogh. d, Defense. e. Oil industry.

1986, Sept. 1
1316 Strip of 5
a.-e. A392 200d any single

A393

Arab-African Union, 1st Anniv. — A394

1986, Sept. 15 *Perf. 12*
1317 A393 250d Libyan, Arab horsemen
1318 A394 250d Women in native dress

Evacuation Day A395

Designs: a, Mounted warrior. b, Two horsemen, infantry. c, Cavalry charge.

1986, Oct. 7 *Perf. 13½*
1319 Strip of 3
a. A395 50d multicolored
b. A395 100d multicolored
c. A395 150d multicolored

Intl. Peace Year A396

1986, Oct. 24 *Perf. 14½*
1320 A396 200d bl & multi
1321 A396 200d grn & multi

Solidarity with the Palestinians — A397

1986, Nov. 29 *Perf. 12½*
1322 A397 250d pink & multi
1323 A397 250d blue & multi

Music and Dance — A398

Designs: a, Man beating drum. b, Masked dancer. c, Woman dancing with jugs on her head. d, Man playing bagpipe. e, Man beating hand drum.

1986, Dec. 1 *Perf. 12*
1324 Strip of 5
a.-e. A398 70d any single

Gazella Leptoceros A399

1987, Mar. 2 **Litho.** *Perf. 13½*
1325 A399 100d Two adults
1326 A399 100d Fawn nursing
1327 A399 100d Adult sleeping
1328 A399 100d Adult drinking

World Wildlife Fund.

People's Authority Declaration — A400

Crowd of People and: a, Oilfields. b, Buildings. c, Khadafy, buildings, globe.

1987, Mar. 2 *Perf. 13½*
1329 Strip of 3
a.-b. A400 500d multicolored
c. A400 1000d multicolored

No. 1329 has a continuous design. Size of No. 1329c: 42x37mm.

Miniature Sheet

Sept. 1st Revolution, 18th Anniv. — A401

Designs: a, Shepherd, sheep. b, Khadafy. c, Mosque. d, Irrigation pipeline. e, Combine in field. f, Khadafy at microphones. g, Harvesting grain. h, Irrigation. i, Soldier. j, Militiaman. k, Fountain. l, Skyscrapers. m, House, women. n, Children. o, Assembly hall. p, Two girls.

1987, Sept. 1 ***Perf. 13 1/2***

1330 Sheet of 16
a.-p. A401 150d any single

No. 1330 has a continuous design.

Libyan Freedom Fighters — A402

No. 1331: a, Omer Abed Anabi Al Mansuri. b, Ahmed Ali Al Emrayd. c, Khalifa Said Ben Asker. d, Mohamed Ben Farhat Azawi. e, Mohamed Souf Al Lafi Al Marmori.

1988, Feb. 15

1331 Strip of 5
a. A402 100d multicolored
b. A402 200d multicolored
c. A402 300d multicolored
d. A402 400d multicolored
e. A402 500d multicolored

Freedom Festival Day — A403

1988, June 1

1332 A403 100d yel & multi
1333 A403 150d grn & multi
1334 A403 250d brn org & multi

Miniature Sheet

American Attack on Libya, 2nd Anniv. A404

Khadafy: a, With woman and children. b, Playing chess. c, Fleeing from bombing with children. d, Praying in desert. e, Praying with children. f, Visiting wounded child. g, With infants and children, horiz. h, Delivering speech, horiz. i, With family, horiz.

1988, July 13

1335 Sheet of 9
a.-i. A404 150d any single

No. 1335 exists imperf.

September 1st Revolution, 19th Anniv. — A405

1988, Sept. 19

1338 A405 100d brt bl & multi
1339 A405 250d gray & multi
1340 A405 300d cit & multi
1341 A405 500d bl grn & multi

1988 Summer Olympics, Seoul — A406

1988, Sept. 17

1342 A406 150d Tennis
1343 A406 150d Equestrian
1344 A406 150d Relay race
1345 A406 150d Soccer
1346 A406 150d Distance race
1347 A406 150d Cycling

Souvenir Sheet

1348 A406 750d Soccer, diff.

No. 1348 contains one 30x42mm stamp. Exists imperf. Nos. 1342-1347 exist in miniature sheets of 1.

Miniature Sheet

1988 Summer Olympics, Seoul — A407

1988, Sept 17

1350 Sheet of 3
a. A407 100d Bedouin rider
b. A407 200d shown
c. A407 200d Show jumping, diff.

Olymphilex '88, Seoul.

Libyan Palm Tree — A408

1988, Nov. 1

1351 A408 500d Fruit
1352 A408 1000d Palm tree

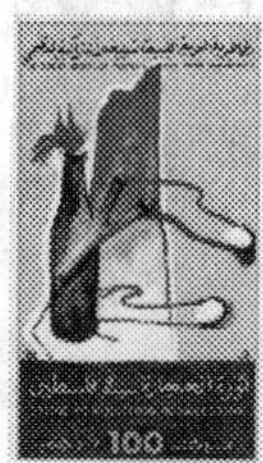
Palestinian Uprising — A409

1988

1353 Strip of 3
a. A409 100d shown
b. A409 200d Boy with rocks
c. A409 300d Flag, map

Size of No. 1353b: 45x39mm.

People's Authority Declaration — A410

1989

1354 A410 260d dk grn & multi
1355 A410 500d gold & multi

Miniature Sheet

September 1 Revolution, 20th Anniv. — A411

Designs: a, Crowd, Green Books, emblem. b, Soldiers, Khadafy, irrigation pipeline. c, Military equipment, Khadafy, communication and transportation. d, Mounted warriors. e, Battle scenes.

1989 ***Perf. 13 1/2***

1356 Sheet of 5
a.-e. A411 150d any single
f. Bklt. pane of 5, perf. 13 1/2 horiz.

Souvenir Sheet

1357 A411 250d Khadafy

No. 1357 contains one 36x51mm stamp. Stamps from No. 1356f have gold border at right.

Libyans Deported to Italy — A412

Designs: No. 1359, Libyans in boats. No. 1360, Khadafy, crescent moon. No. 1361, Khadafy at left, in desert. No. 1362, Khadafy at right, soldiers. No. 1363, Khadafy in center, Libyans.

1989

1358 A412 100d shown
1359 A412 100d multicolored
1360 A412 100d multicolored
1361 A412 100d multicolored
1362 A412 100d multicolored

Souvenir Sheet

1363 A412 150d multicolored

No. 1363 contains one 72x38mm stamp.

Demolition of Libyan-Tunisian Border Fortifications A413

1989 ***Perf. 12***

1364 A413 150d multicolored
1365 A413 200d multicolored

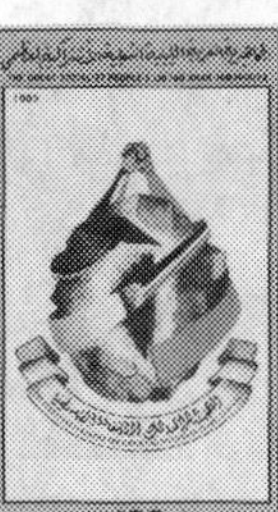
Solidarity With the Palestinians A414

1989 ***Perf. 12x11 1/2***

1366 A414 100d shown
1367 A414 300d Man, flag, crowd
1368 A414 500d Emblem

Ibn Annafis, Physician A415

1989 ***Perf. 12***

1369 A415 100d multicolored
1370 A415 150d multicolored

Intl. Literacy Year — A416

1990 **Litho.** ***Perf. 14***

Granite Paper

1371 A416 100d multicolored
1372 A416 300d multicolored

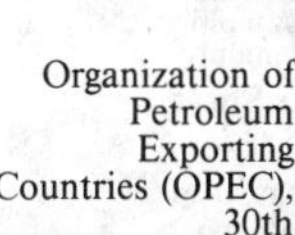

Organization of Petroleum Exporting Countries (OPEC), 30th Anniv. — A417

1990

Granite Paper

1373 A417 100d multicolored
1374 A417 400d multicolored

Evacuation of US Military Base, 20th Anniv. — A418

1990 ***Perf. 11 1/2x12***

1375 A418 100d brt org & multi
1376 A418 400d grn & multi

People's Authority Declaration A419

1990

1377	A419	300d bl & multi	
1378	A419	500d vio & multi	

Plowing Season in Libya — A420

Design: 2000d, Man on tractor plowing field.

1990 *Perf. 14*

Granite Paper

1379	A420	500d multicolored	
1380	A420	2000d multicolored	

World Cup Soccer Championships, Italy — A421

1990 *Perf. 14*

Granite Paper

1381	A421	100d grn & multi	
1382	A421	400d vio & multi	
1383	A421	500d bl & multi	

Souvenir Sheet

Perf. 11½

1384	A421	500d Trophy, map, horiz.	

No. 1384 contains one 38x33mm stamp.

Sept. 1st Revolution, 21st Anniv. A422

1990 *Perf. 14*

Granite Paper

1385	A422	100d multicolored	
1386	A422	400d multicolored	
1387	A422	1000d multicolored	

Imperf

Size: 120x90mm

1388	A422	200d multi, diff.	

SEMI-POSTAL STAMPS

Many issues of Italy and Italian Colonies include one or more semipostal denominations. To avoid splitting sets, these issues are generally listed as regular postage, semipostals or airmails, etc.

Semi-Postal Stamps of Italy Overprinted **LIBIA**

1915-16 **Wmk. 140** *Perf. 14*

B1	SP1	10c + 5c rose	1.25	*2.25*
B2	SP2	15c + 5c slate	3.00	*6.00*
B3	SP2	20c + 5c org ('16)	1.75	*3.25*

No. B2 with Additional Surcharge **20**

1916, Mar.

B4	SP2	20c on 15c + 5c sl	3.00	*6.00*

View of Port, Tripoli SP1

Designs: B5, B6, View of port, Tripoli. B7, B8, Arch of Marcus Aurelius. B9, B10, View of Tripoli.

1927, Feb. 15 **Litho.**

B5	SP1	20c + 5c brn vio & black	1.50	1.50
B6	SP1	25c + 5c bl grn & black	1.50	1.50
B7	SP1	40c + 10c blk brn & black	1.50	1.50
B8	SP1	60c + 10c org brn & black	1.50	1.50
B9	SP1	75c + 20c red & black	1.50	1.50
B10	SP1	1.25 l + 20c bl & blk	7.00	7.00
		Nos. B5-B10 (6)	14.50	14.50

First Sample Fair, Tripoli. Surtax aided fair. See Nos. EB1-EB2.

View of Tripoli — SP2

Knights of Malta Castle SP3

Designs: 50c+20c, Date palm. 1.25 l+20c, Camel riders. 2.55 l+50c, View of Tripoli. 5 l+1 l, Traction well.

1928, Feb. 20 **Wmk. 140** *Perf. 14*

B11	SP2	30c + 20c mar & blk	1.00	*2.50*
B12	SP2	50c + 20c bl grn & blk	1.00	*2.50*
B13	SP2	1.25 l + 20c red & blk	1.00	*2.50*
B14	SP3	1.75 l + 20c bl & blk	1.00	*2.50*
B15	SP3	2.55 l + 50c brn & blk	1.50	*4.00*
B16	SP3	5 l + 1 l pur & blk	2.00	*6.00*
		Nos. B11-B16 (6)	7.50	*20.00*

2nd Sample Fair, Tripoli, 1928. The surtax was for the aid of the Fair.

Olive Tree — SP4

Herding SP5

Designs: 50c+20c, Dorcas gazelle. 1.25 l+20c, Peach blossoms. 2.55 l+50c, Camel caravan. 5 l+1 l, Oasis with date palms.

1929, Apr. 7

B17	SP4	30c + 20c mar & blk	3.75	*7.00*
B18	SP4	50c + 20c bl grn & blk	3.75	*7.00*
B19	SP4	1.25 l + 20c scar & blk	3.75	*7.00*
B20	SP5	1.75 l + 20c bl & blk	3.75	*7.00*
B21	SP5	2.55 l + 50c yel brn & blk	3.75	*7.00*
B22	SP5	5 l + 1 l pur & blk	55.00	*100.00*
		Nos. B17-B22 (6)	73.75	*135.00*

3rd Sample Fair, Tripoli, 1929. The surtax was for the aid of the Fair.

Harvesting Bananas SP6

Water Carriers SP7

Designs: 50c, Tobacco plant. 1.25 l, Venus of Cyrene. 2.55 l+45c, Black bucks. 5 l+1 l, Motor and camel transportation. 10 l+2 l, Rome pavilion.

1930, Feb. 20 **Photo.**

B23	SP6	30c dark brown	85	*2.50*
B24	SP6	50c violet	85	*2.50*
B25	SP6	1.25 l deep blue	85	*2.50*
B26	SP7	1.75 l + 20c scar	1.25	*4.00*
B27	SP7	2.55 l + 45c dp grn	4.75	*7.00*
B28	SP7	5 l + 1 l dp org	3.50	*7.00*
B29	SP7	10 l + 2 l dk vio	6.00	*15.00*
		Nos. B23-B29 (7)	18.05	*40.50*

4th Sample Fair at Tripoli, 1930. The surtax was for the aid of the Fair.

Statue of Ephebus — SP8

Exhibition Pavilion SP9

Designs: 25c, Arab musician. 50c, View of Zeughet. 1.25 l, Snake charmer. 1.75 l+25c, Windmill. 2.75 l+45c, "Zaptie." 5 l+1 l, Mounted Arab.

1931, Mar. 8

B30	SP8	10c black brown	1.90	*3.00*
B31	SP8	25c green	1.90	*3.00*
B32	SP8	50c purple	1.90	*3.00*
B33	SP8	1.25 l blue	1.90	*3.00*
B34	SP8	1.75 l + 25c car rose	2.25	*5.00*
B35	SP8	2.75 l + 45c org	2.25	*5.00*
B36	SP8	5 l + 1 l dl vio	6.00	*9.00*
B37	SP9	10 l + 2 l brn	12.50	*37.50*
		Nos. B30-B37 (8)	30.60	*68.50*

Fifth Sample Fair, Tripoli, 1931. Surtax aided fair. See Nos. C3, EB3.

Papaya Tree SP10

Dorcas Gazelle SP12

Ar Tower, Mogadiscio SP11

Designs: 10c, 50c, Papaya tree. 20c, 30c, Euphorbia abyssinica. 25c, Fig cactus. 75c, Mausoleum, Ghirza. 1.75 l+25c, Lioness. 5 l+1 l, Bedouin with camel.

1932, Mar. 8

B38	SP10	10c ol brn	2.50	*5.00*
B39	SP10	20c brn red	2.50	*5.00*
B40	SP10	25c green	2.75	*5.00*
B41	SP10	30c ol black	2.50	*5.00*
B42	SP10	50c dk vio	2.50	*5.00*
B43	SP10	75c carmine	3.75	*7.00*
B44	SP11	1.25 l dk blue	3.00	*7.00*
B45	SP11	1.75 l + 25c ol brown	10.00	*22.50*
B46	SP11	5 l + 1 l dp bl	10.00	*22.50*
B47	SP12	10 l + 2 l brn violet	35.00	*65.00*
		Nos. B38-B47 (10)	74.50	*149.00*

Sixth Sample Fair, Tripoli, 1932. Surtax aided fair. See Nos. C4-C7.

Ostrich SP13

Arab Musician SP14

Designs: 25c, Incense plant. 30c, Arab musician. 50c, Arch of Marcus Aurelius. 1.25 l, African eagle. 5 l+1 l, Leopard. 10 l+2.50 l, Tripoli skyline and fasces.

1933, Mar. 2 **Photo.** **Wmk. 140**

B48	SP13	10c dp vio	15.00	7.00
B49	SP13	25c dp grn	4.50	*5.00*
B50	SP14	30c org brn	4.50	*7.00*
B51	SP13	50c purple	3.75	*5.00*
B52	SP13	1.25 l dk bl	20.00	*32.50*
B53	SP14	5 l + 1 l ol brn	22.50	*55.00*
B54	SP13	10 l + 2.50 l car	20.00	*62.50*
		Nos. B48-B54 (7)	90.25	*174.00*

Seventh Sample Fair, Tripoli, 1932. Surtax aided fair. See Nos. C8-C13.

Pomegranate Tree — SP15

Designs: 10c+10c, 20c+10c, Pomegranate tree. 50c+10c, 2 l+50c, Musician. 75c+15c, 1.25 l+25c, Tribesman.

1935, Feb. 16

B55	SP15	10c + 10c brown	62	*2.25*
B56	SP15	20c + 10c rose red	62	*2.25*
B57	SP15	50c + 10c purple	62	*2.25*
B58	SP15	75c + 15c car	62	*2.25*
B59	SP15	1.25 l + 25c dl blue	62	*2.25*
B60	SP15	2 l + 50c ol grn	62	*2.25*
		Nos. B55-B60 (6)	3.72	*13.50*

Ninth Sample Fair, Tripoli, 1935. Surtax aided fair. See Nos. C19-C24.

AIR POST STAMPS

Italy Nos. C3 and C5 Overprinted **Libia**

1928-29 Wmk. 140 *Perf. 14*

C1 AP2 50c rose red 2.00 1.50
C2 AP2 80c brn vio & brn ('29) 3.75 *11.00*

Airplane AP1

1931, Mar. 8 Photo. Wmk. 140

C3 AP1 50c blue 1.00 *5.00*

See note after No. B37.

Seaplane over Bedouin Camp AP2

Designs: 50c, 1 l, Seaplane over Bedouin camp. 2 l+1 l, 5 l+2 l, Seaplane over Tripoli.

1932, Mar. 1 *Perf. 14*

C4 AP2 50c dark blue 3.75 *7.00*
C5 AP2 1 l org brown 3.75 *7.00*
C6 AP2 2 l + 1 l dk gray 10.00 *30.00*
C7 AP2 5 l + 2 l car 37.50 *80.00*

See note after No. B47.

Seaplane Arriving at Tripoli AP3

Designs: 50c, 2 l+50c, Seaplane arriving at Tripoli. 75c, 10 l+2.50 l, Plane over Tagiura. 1 l, 4 l+1 l, Seaplane leaving Tripoli.

1933, Mar. 1

C8 AP3 50c deep grn 3.00 *7.00*
C9 AP3 75c carmine 3.00 *7.00*
C10 AP3 1 l dk bl 3.00 *7.00*
C11 AP3 2 l + 50c pur 6.00 *10.00*
C12 AP3 5 l + 1 l org brn 13.00 *25.00*
C13 AP3 10 l + 2.50 l gray blk 13.00 *25.00*
Nos. C8-C13 (6) 41.00 *81.00*

See note after No. B54.

Seaplane over Tripoli Harbor AP4

Airplane and Camel — AP5

Designs: 50c, 5 l+1 l, Seaplane over Tripoli harbor. 75c, 10 l+2 l, Plane and minaret.

1934, Feb. 17 Photo. Wmk. 140

C14 AP4 50c slate bl 3.00 *7.00*
C15 AP4 75c red org 3.00 *7.00*
C16 AP4 5 l + 1 l dp grn 30.00 *62.50*
C17 AP4 10 l + 2 l dl vio 30.00 *62.50*
C18 AP5 25 l + 3 l org brn 42.50 *80.00*
Nos. C14-C18 (5) 108.50 *219.00*

Eighth Sample Fair, Tripoli. Surtax aided fair. See Nos. CE1-CE2.

Plane and Ancient Tower AP6

Camel Train AP7

Designs: 25c+10c, 3 l+1.50 l, Plane and ancient tower. 50c+10c, 2 l+30c, Camel train. 1 l+25c, 10 l+5 l, Arab watching plane.

1935, Apr. 12

C19 AP6 25c + 10c green 60 *2.50*
C20 AP7 50c + 10c slate bl 60 *2.50*
C21 AP7 1 l + 25c blue 60 *2.50*
C22 AP7 2 l + 30c rose red 60 *2.50*
C23 AP6 3 l + 1.50 l brn 60 *2.50*
C24 AP7 10 l + 5 l dl vio 4.50 *12.50*
Nos. C19-C24 (6) 7.50 *25.00*

See note after No. B60.

Cyrenaica No. C6 Overprinted in Black **LIBIA**

1936, Oct.

C25 AP2 50c purple 38 15

Same on Tripolitania Nos. C8 and C12

1937

C26 AP1 50c rose carmine 20 15
C27 AP2 1 l deep blue 55 35
Set value 40

See Nos. C45-C50.

Ruins of Odeon Theater, Sabrata AP8

1937, Mar. 15 Photo.

C28 AP8 50c dark violet 1.00 *3.25*
C29 AP8 1 l vio black 1.00 *4.25*

Opening of a coastal road to the Egyptian frontier.

Nos. C28-C29 Overprinted "XI FIERA DI TRIPOLI"

1937, Mar. 15

C30 AP8 50c dark violet 3.25 *7.00*
C31 AP8 1 l violet blk 3.25 *7.00*

11th Sample Fair, Tripoli.

View of Tripoli AP9

Eagle Attacking Serpent AP10

1938, Mar. 12 *Perf. 14*

C32 AP9 50c dk olive grn 38 *62*
C33 AP9 1 l slate blue 50 *1.90*

12th Sample Fair, Tripoli.

1938, Apr. 25 Wmk. 140

C34 AP10 50c olive brown 30 *60*
C35 AP10 1 l brn violet 50 *1.40*

Birth bimillenary Augustus Caesar (Octavianus), first Roman emperor.

Arab and Camel AP11

Design: 50c, Fair entrance.

1939, Apr. 12 Photo.

C36 AP11 25c green 20 *65*
C37 AP11 50c olive brown 25 *65*
C38 AP11 1 l rose violet 30 *65*

13th Sample Fair, Tripoli.

Plane Over Modern City AP12

Design: 1 l, 5 l+2.50 l, Plane over oasis.

1940, June 3

C39 AP12 50c brn blk 25 *1.25*
C40 AP12 1 l brn vio 25 *1.25*
C41 AP12 2 l + 75c indigo 38 *1.60*
C42 AP12 5 l + 2.50 l cop brn 38 *1.60*

Triennial Overseas Exposition, Naples.

Hitler, Mussolini and Inscription "Two Peoples, One War" AP13

1941, Apr. 24

C43 AP13 50c slate green 25 *10.00*

Rome-Berlin Axis.

Cyrenaica No. C9 Overprinted in Black Like No. C25

1941

C44 AP3 1 l black 1.60 *10.00*

Same Overprint on Tripolitania Nos. C9-C11, C13-C15

C45 AP1 60c red orange 25
C46 AP1 75c deep blue 25
C47 AP1 80c dull violet 25
C48 AP2 1.20 l dark brown 25
C49 AP2 1.50 l orange red 25
C50 AP2 5 l green 25
Nos. C44-C50 (7) 3.10

Catalogue values for unused stamps in this section, from this point to the end of the section, are for Never Hinged items.

United Kingdom of Libya

ICY Type of Regular Issue

Perf. 14½x14

1965, Jan. 1 Litho. Unwmk.

C51 A60 50m dp lil & gold 80 80
a. Souvenir sheet 2.00 2.00

No. C51a exists imperf.; same value.

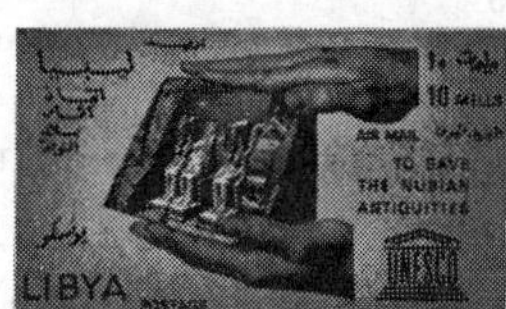

Hands Holding Facade of Abu Simbel — AP14

1966, Jan. 1 Photo. *Perf. 11½*

Granite Paper

C52 AP14 10m bis & dk brn 15 15
a. Souvenir sheet of 4 75 75
C53 AP14 15m gray grn & dk grn 15 15
a. Souvenir sheet of 4 75 75
C54 AP14 40m dl sal & dk brn 28 28
a. Souvenir sheet of 4 1.50 90
Set value 46 42

UNESCO world campaign to save historic monuments in Nubia.

Inauguration of WHO Headquarters, Geneva — AP15

Perf. 10x10½

1966, May 3 Litho. Unwmk.

C55 AP15 20m blk, yel & bl 15 15
C56 AP15 50m blk, yel grn & red 20 16
C57 AP15 65m blk, sal & brn red 35 25

Flag and Globe — AP16

1966, Oct. 1 Photo. *Perf. 11½*

Granite Paper

C58 AP16 25m multicolored 15 15
C59 AP16 60m multicolored 28 20
C60 AP16 85m gray & multi 40 35

Inauguration of Kingdom of Libya Airlines, 1st anniv.

AIR POST SPECIAL DELIVERY STAMPS

APSD1

Wmk. 140

1934, Feb. 17 Photo. *Perf. 14*

CE1 APSD1 2.25 l olive blk 12.50 *30.00*
CE2 APSD1 4.50 l + 1 l gray blk 12.50 *30.00*

8th Sample Fair at Tripoli. The surtax was for the aid of the Fair.

SPECIAL DELIVERY STAMPS

Special Delivery Stamps of Italy Overprinted **Libia**

1915, Nov. Wmk. 140 *Perf. 14*

E1 SD1 25c rose red 6.00 3.00
E2 SD2 30c blue & rose 2.00 *7.00*

"Italia" SD3

1921-23 Engr. *Perf. 13½*

E3 SD3 30c blue & rose 70 *1.50*
E4 SD3 50c rose red & brn 1.00 *2.00*
E5 SD3 60c dk red & brn ('23) 2.00 *4.00*
E6 SD3 2 l dk bl & red ('23) 4.00 *8.00*

30c, 2 l inscribed "EXPRES".

Special Delivery Stamps of 1915 Surcharged

Cent. 60   1,60 LIRE 1,60

1922, June 1

E7 SD1	60c on 25c rose red	2.00	*4.00*
E8 SD2	1.60 l on 30c bl & rose	5.00	*8.00*

Nos. E5-E6 Surcharged in Dark Blue or Red:

70   ٧٠

No. E9

2,50   ٢،٥٠

No. E10

1926, July

E9 SD3	70c on 60c	2.00	*4.00*
E10 SD3	2.50 l on 2 l (R)	4.00	*8.00*

Nos. E5-E6 Surcharged in Blue or Red:

LIRE 1,25

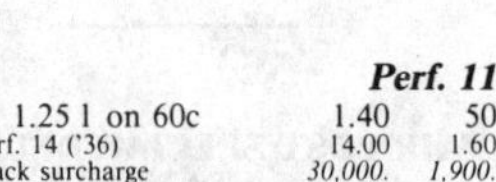

1927-36 ***Perf. 11***

E11 SD3	1.25 l on 60c	1.40	50
a.	Perf. 14 ('36)	14.00	1.60
b.	Black surcharge	*30,000.*	*1,900.*
E12 SD3	2.50 l on 2 l (R)	40.00	*100.00*

Catalogue values for unused stamps in this section, from this point to the end of the section, are for Never Hinged items.

United Kingdom of Libya

Zuela Saracen Castle SD4

Perf. 11½

1966, Feb. 10 Unwmk. Litho.

E13 SD4	90m car rose & lt grn	65	50

Coat of Arms of Libya and "POLIGRAFICA & CARTEVALORI - NAPLES" printed on back in yellow green.

SEMI-POSTAL SPECIAL DELIVERY STAMPS

Camel Caravan SPSD1

Wmk. 140

1927, Feb. 15 Litho. ***Perf. 14***

EB1 SPSD1	1.25 l + 30c pur & blk	5.00	5.00
EB2 SPSD1	2.50 l + 1 l yel & blk	5.00	5.00

See note after No. B10.

No. EB2 is inscribed "EXPRES."

War Memorial SPSD2

1931, Mar. 8 Photo.

EB3 SPSD2	1.25 l + 20c car rose	2.25	*7.00*

See note after No. B37.

AUTHORIZED DELIVERY STAMPS

Italy No. EY1 Overprinted in Black **LIBIA**

1929, May 11 Wmk. 140 ***Perf. 14***

EY1 AD1	10c dull blue	10.00	8.00
a.	Perf. 11	50.00	40.00

Italy No. EY2 Overprinted in Black **LIBIA**

1941, May ***Perf. 14***

EY2 AD2	10c dark brown	4.00	3.25

A variety of No. EY2, with larger "LIBIA" and yellow gum, was prepared in 1942, but not issued. Value 35 cents.

AD1

1942 Litho. Wmk. 140

EY3 AD1	10c sepia	35

No. EY3 was not issued.

POSTAGE DUE STAMPS

Italian Postage Due Stamps, 1870-1903 Overprinted in Black **Libia**

1915, Nov. Wmk. 140 ***Perf. 14***

J1 D3	5c buff & magenta	65	*1.25*
J2 D3	10c buff & magenta	85	*1.25*
J3 D3	20c buff & magenta	1.00	*2.50*
a.	Double overprint	50.00	50.00
b.	Inverted overprint	50.00	50.00
J4 D3	30c buff & magenta	1.00	*2.50*
J5 D3	40c buff & magenta	1.00	*2.50*
a.	"40" in black	*1,500.*	
J6 D3	50c buff & magenta	1.00	*2.50*
J7 D3	60c buff & magenta	2.00	*3.75*
J8 D3	1 l blue & magenta	1.00	60
a.	Double overprint	*2,000.*	*1,500.*
J9 D3	2 l blue & magenta	13.00	*12.50*
J10 D3	5 l blue & magenta	19.00	*16.00*
	Nos. J1-J10 (10)	40.50	*45.35*

1926

J11 D3	60c buff & brn	18.00	*37.50*

Postage Due Stamps of Italy, 1934, Overprinted in Black **LIBIA**

1934

J12 D6	5c brown	25	*60*
J13 D6	10c blue	25	*60*
J14 D6	20c rose red	62	50
J15 D6	25c green	70	50
J16 D6	30c red org	62	*80*
J17 D6	40c blk brn	70	*1.25*
J18 D6	50c violet	80	25
J19 D6	60c black	1.25	*3.00*
J20 D7	1 l red org	80	25
J21 D7	2 l green	15.00	3.75
J22 D7	5 l violet	35.00	9.00
J23 D7	10 l blue	7.50	*9.00*
J24 D7	20 l carmine	7.50	*11.00*
	Nos. J12-J24 (13)	70.99	*40.50*

In 1942 a set of 11 "Segnatasse" stamps, picturing a camel and rider and inscribed "LIBIA," was prepared but not issued. Value, $4.

Catalogue values for unused stamps in this section, from this point to the end of the section, are for Never Hinged items.

United Kingdom of Libya

Postage Due Stamps of Cyrenaica, 1950 Surcharged in Black

-- ليبيا --
٢ ليرة ع.
2 MAL.
LIBYA

For Use in Tripolitania

1951 Unwmk. ***Perf. 12½***

J25 D1	1mal on 2m dk brown	4.00	5.00
J26 D1	2mal on 4m dp grn	1.50	*5.00*
J27 D1	4mal on 8m scar	4.50	*10.00*
J28 D1	10mal on 20m org yel	10.00	*20.00*
a.	Arabic "20" for "10"	*200.00*	
J29 D1	20mal on 40m dp bl	14.00	*25.00*
	Nos. J25-J29 (5)	34.00	*65.00*

Cyrenaica Nos. J1-J7 Overprinted in Black

ليبيا
LIBYA

For Use in Cyrenaica

Overprint 13mm High

1952 Unwmk. ***Perf. 12½***

J30 D1	2m dk brn	2.00	*3.75*
J31 D1	4m dp grn	2.00	*3.75*
J32 D1	8m scarlet	2.00	*3.75*
J33 D1	10m vermilion	4.50	*7.00*
J34 D1	20m org yel	6.00	*10.00*
J35 D1	40m dp bl	11.00	*20.00*
J36 D1	100m dk gray	15.00	*25.00*
	Nos. J30-J36 (7)	42.50	*73.25*

D1

Castle at Tripoli — D2

1952 Litho. ***Perf. 11½***

J37 D1	2m chocolate	15	15
J38 D1	5m bl grn	60	30
J39 D1	10m carmine	1.10	65
J40 D1	50m vio blue	3.50	1.90

1964, Feb. 1 Photo. ***Perf. 14***

J41 D2	2m red brn	16	20
J42 D2	6m Prus grn	16	20
J43 D2	10m rose red	16	20
J44 D2	50m brt bl	50	60

Men in Boat, Birds, Mosaic — D3

Ancient Mosaics: 10d, Head of Medusa. 20d, Peacock. 50d, Fish.

1976, Nov. 15 Litho. ***Perf. 14***

J45 D3	5d bis & multi	15	15
J46 D3	10d org & multi	16	15
J47 D3	20d bl & multi	35	15
J48 D3	50d emer & multi	65	15
	Set value		26

Nos. J45-J48 have multiple coat of arms printed on back in pale green beneath gum.

OFFICIAL STAMPS

Catalogue values for unused stamps in this section are for Never Hinged items.

United Kingdom of Libya

Nos. 135-142 Overprinted in Black

رسمى
Official

1952 Unwmk. ***Perf. 11½***

O1 A27	2m yel brn	1.10	1.10
O2 A27	4m gray	25	38
O3 A27	5m bl grn	2.50	3.75
O4 A27	8m vermilion	1.00	1.10
O5 A27	10m purple	2.25	2.25
O6 A27	12m lil rose	4.75	3.75
O7 A27	20m dp bl	5.75	7.50
O8 A27	25m chocolate	7.50	11.00
	Nos. O1-O8 (8)	25.10	30.83

PARCEL POST STAMPS

These stamps were used by affixing them to the way bill so that one half remained on it following the parcel, the other half staying on the receipt given the sender. Most used halves are right halves. Complete stamps were obtainable canceled, probably to order. Both unused and used values are for complete stamps.

Italian Parcel Post Stamps, 1914-22, Overprinted **LIBIA**

1915-24 Wmk. 140 ***Perf. 13½***

Q1 PP2	5c brown	60	*2.00*
a.	Double overprint	50.00	
Q2 PP2	10c deep blue	60	*2.00*
Q3 PP2	20c blk ('18)	70	*2.00*
Q4 PP2	25c red	70	*2.00*
Q5 PP2	50c orange	1.00	*2.50*
Q6 PP2	1 l violet	1.00	*2.00*
Q7 PP2	2 l green	1.60	*3.00*
Q8 PP2	3 l bister	1.40	*3.00*
Q9 PP2	4 l slate	1.60	*3.00*
Q10 PP2	10 l rose lil ('24)	25.00	*30.00*
Q11 PP2	12 l red brn ('24)	37.50	*65.00*
Q12 PP2	15 l ol grn ('24)	37.50	*65.00*
Q13 PP2	20 l brn vio ('24)	37.50	*65.00*
	Nos. Q1-Q13 (13)	146.70	*246.50*

Same Overprint on Parcel Post Stamps of Italy, 1927-36

1927-38

Q14 PP3	10c dp bl ('36)	1.10	*3.00*
Q15 PP3	25c red ('36)	1.00	*3.00*
Q16 PP3	30c ultra ('29)	15	*1.00*
Q17 PP3	50c orange	120.00	150.00
a.	Overprint 8¾x2mm ('31)	70.00	*200.00*
Q18 PP3	60c red ('29)	15	*1.00*
Q19 PP3	1 l lilac ('36)	18.00	*30.00*
Q20 PP3	2 l grn ('38)	18.00	*30.00*
Q21 PP3	3 l bister	38	*1.50*
Q22 PP3	4 l gray	38	*1.50*
Q23 PP3	10 l rose lil ('36)	100.00	*125.00*
Q24 PP3	20 l brn vio ('36)	100.00	*150.00*
	Nos. Q14-Q24 (11)	359.16	*496.00*

The overprint measures 10x1½mm on No. Q17.

Same Overprint on Italy No. Q24

1939

Q25 PP3	5c brown	*5,000.*

The overprint was applied to the 5c in error. Few copies exist.

OCCUPATION STAMPS

Catalogue values for unused stamps in this section are for Never Hinged items.

Issued under French Occupation

Stamps of Italy and Libya were overprinted in 1943: "FEZZAN Occupation Française" and "R. F. FEZZAN" for use in this region when General Leclerc's forces 1st occupied it.

Fezzan-Ghadames

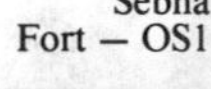

Sebha Fort — OS1

Mosque and Fort Turc Murzuch OS2

Map of Fezzan-Ghadames, Soldier and Camel — OS3

1946	Unwmk.	Engr.	*Perf. 13*	
N1	OS1	10c black	15	15
N2	OS1	50c rose	15	15
N3	OS1	1fr brown	15	15
N4	OS1	1.50fr green	15	15
N5	OS1	2fr ultramarine	15	15
N6	OS2	2.50fr violet	20	18
N7	OS2	3fr rose carmine	30	30
N8	OS2	5fr chocolate	35	38
N9	OS2	6fr dark green	22	25
N10	OS2	10fr blue	35	38
N11	OS3	15fr violet	35	38
N12	OS3	20fr red	50	65
N13	OS3	25fr sepia	50	65
N14	OS3	40fr dark green	70	80
N15	OS3	50fr deep blue	70	80
		Nos. N1-N15 (15)	4.92	5.52

FEZZAN

Catalogue values for unused stamps in this section are for Never Hinged items.

Monument, Djerma Oasis — OS1

Tombs of the Beni-Khettab — OS2

Well at Gorda OS3

Col. Colonna d'Ornano and Fort at Murzuch OS4

Philippe F. M. de Hautecloque (Gen. Jacques Leclerc) OS5

1949	Unwmk.	Engr.	*Perf. 13*	
2N1	OS1	1fr black	20	20
2N2	OS1	2fr lil pink	20	20
2N3	OS2	4fr red brn	70	70
2N4	OS2	5fr emerald	70	70
2N5	OS3	8fr blue	42	42
2N6	OS3	10fr brown	1.40	1.40
2N7	OS3	12fr dk grn	2.50	2.50
2N8	OS4	15fr sal red	3.50	3.50
2N9	OS4	20fr brn blk	1.10	1.10
2N10	OS5	25fr dk bl	1.60	1.60
2N11	OS5	50fr cop red	2.25	2.25
		Nos. 2N1-2N11 (11)	14.57	14.57

Camel Raising OS6

Agriculture OS7

Well Drilling OS8

Ahmed Bey OS9

1951				
2N12	OS6	30c brown	40	40
2N13	OS6	1fr dp bl	40	40
2N14	OS6	2fr rose car	40	40
2N15	OS7	4fr red	40	40
2N16	OS7	5fr green	42	42
2N17	OS7	8fr dp bl	42	42
2N18	OS8	10fr sepia	1.60	1.60
2N19	OS8	12fr dp grn	1.75	1.75
2N20	OS8	15fr brt red	2.00	2.00
2N21	OS9	20fr blk brn & vio brn	2.00	2.00
2N22	OS9	25fr dk bl & bl	2.50	2.50
2N23	OS9	50fr ind & brn org	2.50	2.50
		Nos. 2N12-2N23 (12)	14.79	14.79

OCCUPATION SEMI-POSTAL STAMPS

Catalogue values for unused stamps in this section are for Never Hinged items.

"The Unhappy Ones"
OSP1 OSP2

1950	Unwmk.	Engr.	*Perf. 13*	
2NB1	OSP1	15fr + 5fr red brn	1.00	1.00
2NB2	OSP2	25fr + 5fr blue	1.00	1.00

The surtax was for charitable works.

OCCUPATION AIR POST STAMPS

Catalogue values for unused stamps in this section are for Never Hinged items.

Airport in Fezzan OAP1

Plane over Fezzan — OAP2

1948	Unwmk.	Engr.	*Perf. 13*	
2NC1	OAP1	100fr red	2.50	2.50
2NC2	OAP2	200fr indigo	4.00	4.00

Oasis OAP3

Murzuch OAP4

1951				
2NC3	OAP3	100fr dk bl	4.00	4.50
2NC4	OAP4	200fr vermilion	5.00	5.50

OCCUPATION POSTAGE DUE STAMPS

Catalogue values for unused stamps in this section are for Never Hinged items.

Oasis of Brak — D1

1950	Unwmk.	Engr.	*Perf. 13*	
2NJ1	D1	1fr brown black	30	30
2NJ2	D1	2fr deep green	40	40
2NJ3	D1	3fr red brown	50	50
2NJ4	D1	5fr purple	60	60
2NJ5	D1	10fr red	1.10	1.10
2NJ6	D1	20fr deep blue	1.75	1.75
		Nos. 2NJ1-2NJ6 (6)	4.65	4.65

GHADAMES

Catalogue values for unused stamps in this section are for Never Hinged items.

Cross of Agadem — OS1

1949	Unwmk.	Engr.	*Perf. 13*	
3N1	OS1	4fr sep & red brn	60	60
3N2	OS1	5fr pck bl & dk grn	60	60
3N3	OS1	8fr sep & org brn	1.50	1.50
3N4	OS1	10fr blk & dk ultra	1.50	1.50
3N5	OS1	12fr vio & red vio	4.50	4.50
3N6	OS1	15fr brn & red brn	2.50	2.50
3N7	OS1	20fr sep & emer	3.50	3.50
3N8	OS1	25fr sep & bl	3.50	3.50
		Nos. 3N1-3N8 (8)	18.20	18.20

OCCUPATION AIR POST STAMPS

Catalogue values for unused stamps in this section are for Never Hinged items.

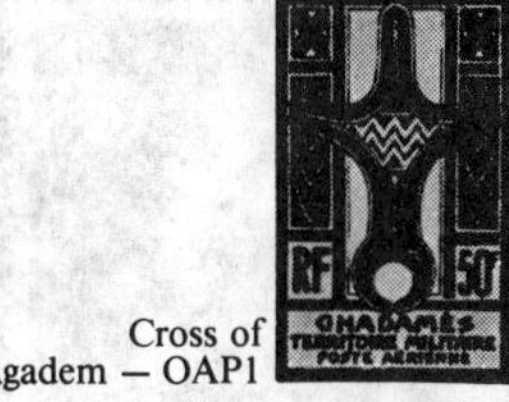

Cross of Agadem — OAP1

1949	Unwmk.	Engr.	*Perf. 13*	
3NC1	OAP1	50fr pur & rose	4.50	4.50
3NC2	OAP1	100fr sep & pur brn	5.50	5.50

LIECHTENSTEIN

LOCATION — Central Europe southeast of Lake Constance, between Austria and Switzerland
GOVT. — Principality
AREA — 61.8 sq. mi.
POP. — 4,896 (est. 1984)
CAPITAL — Vaduz

The Principality of Liechtenstein is a sovereign state consisting of the two counties of Schellenberg and Vaduz. Since 1921 the post office has been administered by Switzerland.

100 Heller = 1 Krone
100 Rappen = 1 Franc (1921)

Catalogue values for unused stamps in this country are for Never Hinged items, beginning with Scott 368 in the regular postage section, Scott B22 in the semi-postal section, and Scott O47 in the offical section.

Watermarks

Wmk. 183- Greek Cross

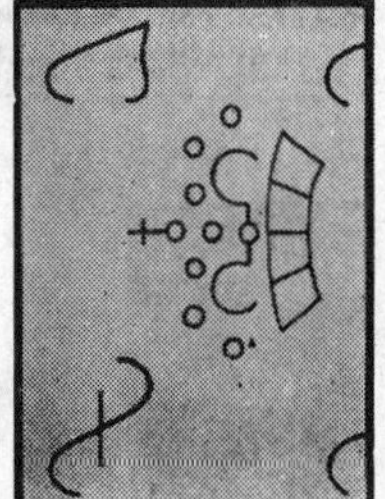

Wmk. 296- Crown and Initials

Austrian Administration of the Post Office

Prince Johann II – A1

1912 Unwmk. Typo. *Perf. 12½x13*

Thick Chalky Paper

No.	Design	Description	Unused	Used
1	A1	5h yellow green	10.50	4.50
2	A1	10h rose	32.50	4.50
3	A1	25h dark blue	40.00	22.50

1915

Thin Unsurfaced Paper

No.	Design	Description	Unused	Used
1a	A1	5h yellow green	3.50	6.75
2a	A1	10h rose	35.00	13.00
3a	A1	25h dark blue	375.00	90.00
b.		25h ultramarine	225.00	200.00

Coat of Arms – A2

Prince Johann II – A3

1917-18

No.	Design	Description	Unused	Used
4	A2	3h violet	75	60
5	A2	5h yellow green	75	60
6	A3	10h claret	75	60
7	A3	15h dull red	75	60
8	A3	20h dark green	75	60
9	A3	25h deep blue	75	60
		Nos. 4-9 (6)	4.50	3.60

Exist imperf.

Prince Johann II – A4

1918

Dates in Upper Corners

No.	Design	Description	Unused	Used
10	A4	20h dark green	42	65

Accession of Prince Johann II, 60th anniv. Exists imperf.

National Administration of the Post Office

Stamps of 1917-18 Overprinted or Surcharged

a

b

c

1920

No.	Design	Description	Unused	Used
11	A2(a)	5h yel grn	1.40	4.00
a.		Inverted overprint	70.00	
b.		Double overprint	22.50	*45.00*
12	A3(a)	10h claret	1.40	4.00
a.		Inverted overprint	70.00	
b.		Double overprint	22.50	*45.00*
c.		Overprint type "c"	15.00	70.00
13	A3(a)	25h deep blue	1.40	4.00
a.		Inverted overprint	70.00	
14	A2(b)	40h on 3h violet	1.40	4.00
a.		Inverted surcharge	70.00	
15	A3(c)	1k on 15h dl red	1.40	4.00
a.		Inverted surcharge	70.00	
b.		Overprint type "a"	62.50	*150.00*
16	A3(c)	2½k on 20h dk grn	1.40	4.00
a.		Inverted surcharge	70.00	
		Nos. 11-16 (6)	8.40	24.00

Coat of Arms A5

Chapel of St. Mamertus A6

Coat of Arms with Supporters A15

Designs: 40h, Gutenberg Castle. 50h, Courtyard, Vaduz Castle. 60h, Red Tower, Vaduz. 80h, Old Roman Tower, Schaan. 1k, Castle at Vaduz. 2k, View of Bendern. 5k, Prince Johann I. 7½k, Prince Johann II.

1920 Engr. *Imperf.*

No.	Design	Description	Unused	Used
18	A5	5h olive bister	15	15
19	A5	10h deep orange	15	15
20	A5	15h dark blue	15	15
21	A5	20h deep brown	15	15
22	A5	25h dark green	15	15
23	A5	30h gray black	15	15
24	A5	40h dark red	15	15
25	A6	1k blue	15	15

Perf. 12½

No.	Design	Description	Unused	Used
32	A5	5h olive bister	15	18
33	A5	10h deep orange	15	18
34	A5	15h deep blue	15	18
35	A5	20h red brown	15	18
36	A6	25h olive green	15	18
37	A5	30h dark gray	15	18
38	A6	40h claret	15	18
39	A6	50h yellow green	15	18
40	A6	60h red brown	15	18
41	A6	80h rose	15	18
42	A6	1k dull violet	15	18
43	A6	2k light blue	20	35
44	A6	5k black	28	35
45	A6	7½k slate	28	35
46	A15	10k ocher	28	35
		Nos. 18-46 (23)	3.89	4.58

Used values for Nos. 18-46 are for canceled to order stamps.

Many denominations of Nos. 32-46 are found imperforate, imperforate vertically and imperforate horizontally.

Madonna and Child – A16

1920, Oct. 5

No.	Design	Description	Unused	Used
47	A16	50h olive green	20	65
48	A16	80h brown red	20	65
49	A16	2k dark blue	20	65

80th birthday of Prince Johann II.

Imperf., Pairs

No.	Design	Description	Unused	Used
47a	A16	50h	4.25	
48a	A16	80h	4.25	
49a	A16	2k	4.25	

Swiss Administration of the Post Office

Coat of Arms
A17 A18

1921 Unwmk. Engr. *Imperf.*

No.	Design	Description	Unused	Used
51	A17	2rp on 10h dp org	30	*13.00*
a.		Double surcharge	30.00	*65.00*
b.		Inverted surcharge	30.00	*80.00*
c.		Double surch., one inverted	30.00	*65.00*
52	A18	2rp on 10h dp org	30	*13.00*
a.		Double surcharge	57.50	*150.00*
b.		Inverted surcharge	57.50	*150.00*
c.		Double surch., one inverted	57.50	*150.00*

Arms with Supporters A19

Chapel of St. Mamertus A20

View of Vaduz – A21

Designs: 25rp, Castle at Vaduz. 30rp, View of Bendern. 35rp, Prince Johann II. 40rp, Old Roman Tower at Schaan. 50rp, Gutenberg Castle. 80rp, Red Tower at Vaduz.

1921 *Perf. 12½*

Surface Tinted Paper (#54-61)

No.	Design	Description	Unused	Used
54	A19	2rp lemon, perf. 9½	60	*6.75*
55	A19	2½rp black	75	*8.00*
a.		Perf. 9½	75	*40.00*
56	A19	3rp orange	75	*7.25*
a.		Perf. 9½	90.00	*3,000.*
57	A19	5rp ol grn	4.75	45
a.		Perf. 9½	32.50	*6.50*
58	A19	7½rp dk bl	3.50	*18.00*
a.		Perf. 9½	150.00	*825.00*
59	A19	10rp yel grn, perf. 9½	27.50	1.65
a.		Perf. 12½	30.00	4.00
60	A19	13rp brown	5.50	*47.50*
a.		Perf. 9½	67.50	*2,000.*
61	A19	15rp dk vio, perf. 9½	8.50	5.75
a.		Perf. 12½	12.00	12.00
62	A20	20rp dl vio & blk	30.00	75
63	A20	25rp rose red & blk	95	1.50
64	A20	30rp dp grn & blk	42.50	6.50
65	A20	35rp brn & blk, *straw*	1.65	4.75
66	A20	40rp dk bl & blk	1.65	1.40
67	A20	50rp dk grn & blk	1.90	1.50

68 A20 80rp gray & blk 11.00 *42.50*
69 A21 1fr dp cl & blk 21.00 20.00
Nos. 54-69 (16) 162.50 *174.25*

Nos. 54-69 exist imperforate; Nos. 54-61, partly perforated. See Nos. 73, 81.

Nos. 58, 60a Surcharged in Red **10**

1924 ***Perf. 12½, 9½***
70 A19 5rp on 7½rp 70 1.50
a. Perf. 9½ 5.50 5.00
71 A19 10rp on 13rp 45 1.10
a. Perf. 12½ 10.50 25.00

Type of 1921

1924 **Wmk. 183** ***Perf. 11½***

Granite Paper

73 A19 10rp green 11.00 65

Peasant A28

Government Palace and Church at Vaduz A30

Design: 10rp, 20rp, Courtyard, Vaduz Castle.

1924-28 **Typo.** ***Perf. 11½***
74 A28 2½rp ol grn & red vio ('28) 1.40 *4.00*
75 A28 5rp brn & blue 2.25 65
76 A28 7½rp bl grn & brn ('28) 1.40 *4.00*
77 A28 15rp red brn & bl grn ('28) 4.25 *21.00*

Engr.

78 A28 10rp yel grn 7.50 65
79 A28 20rp dp red 17.00 65
80 A30 1½fr blue 52.50 65.00
Nos. 74-80 (7) 86.30 95.95

Bendern Type of 1921

1925
81 A20 30rp bl & blk 10.50 65

Prince Johann II — A31

Prince Johann II as Boy and Man — A32

1928, Nov. 12 **Typo.** **Wmk. 183**
82 A31 10rp lt brn & ol grn 1.40 3.00
83 A31 20rp org red & ol grn 3.50 5.75
84 A31 30rp sl bl & ol grn 17.00 18.00
85 A31 60rp red vio & ol grn 45.00 *62.50*

Engr.

Unwmk.

86 A32 1.20fr ultra 40.00 *100.00*
87 A32 1.50fr blk brn 60.00 *145.00*
88 A32 2fr dp car 60.00 *145.00*
89 A32 5fr dk grn 60.00 *200.00*
Nos. 82-89 (8) 286.90 *679.25*

70th year of the reign of Prince Johann II.

Prince Francis I, as a Child — A33

Prince Francis I as a Man — A34

Princess Elsa — A35

Prince Francis and Princess Elsa — A36

1929, Dec. 2 **Photo.**
90 A33 10rp ol grn 65 *2.00*
91 A34 20rp carmine 65 *3.25*
92 A35 30rp ultra 1.90 *13.00*
93 A36 70rp brown 14.00 *72.50*

Accession of Prince Francis I, Feb. 11, 1929.

Grape Girl — A37

Chamois Hunter — A38

Mountain Cattle — A39

Courtyard, Vaduz Castle — A40

Mt. Naafkopf A41

Chapel at Steg A42

Rofenberg Chapel A43

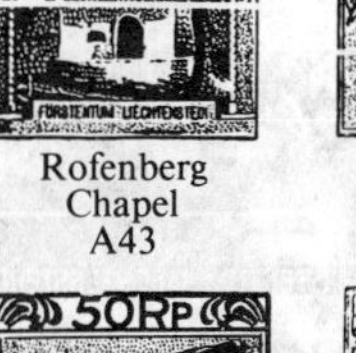

Chapel of St. Mamertus A44

Alpine Hotel, Malbun — A45

Gutenberg Castle — A46

Schellenberg Monastery A47

Castle at Vaduz A48

Mountain Cottage — A49

Prince Francis and Princess Elsa — A50

1930 ***Perf. 10½, 11½, 11½x10½***
94 A37 3rp brn lake 30 65
95 A38 5rp dp grn 60 45
96 A39 10rp dk vio 75 35
a. Perf. 11½x10½ 7.25 *19.00*
97 A40 20rp dp rose red 11.00 50
98 A41 25rp black 3.75 *21.00*
a. Perf. 11½ 92.50 *165.00*
99 A42 30rp dp ultra 2.50 90
a. Perf. 11½x10½ 1,200. 1,200.
100 A43 35rp dk grn 3.50 *9.25*
a. Perf. 11½ *4,250.* *4,250.*
101 A44 40rp lt brn 3.50 3.25
102 A45 50rp blk brn 42.50 11.50
a. Perf. 11½ 160.00 105.00
103 A46 60rp ol blk 42.50 12.50
104 A47 90rp vio brn 42.50 80.00
105 A48 1.20fr ol brn 42.50 *125.00*
a. Perf. 11½x10½ *2,400.* *3,250.*
106 A49 1.50fr blk vio 25.00 40.00
107 A50 2fr gray grn & red brn 32.50 65.00
a. Perf. 11½x10½ 2,500. *3,000.*
Nos. 94-107 (14) 253.40 *370.35*

Mt. Naafkopf A51

Gutenberg Castle A52

Vaduz Castle — A53

1933, Jan. 23 ***Perf. 14½***
108 A51 25rp red org 135.00 40.00
109 A52 90rp dk grn 8.50 *50.00*
110 A53 1.20fr red brn 75.00 *200.00*

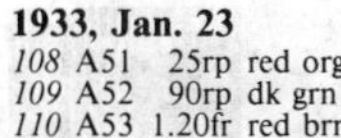

Prince Francis I A54 A55

1933, Aug. 28 ***Perf. 11***
111 A54 10rp purple 16.00 27.50
112 A54 20rp brn car 16.00 27.50
113 A54 30rp dk bl 16.00 27.50

80th birthday of Prince Francis I.

1933, Dec. 15 **Engr.** ***Perf. 12½***
114 A55 3fr vio bl 100.00 150.00

See No. 152.

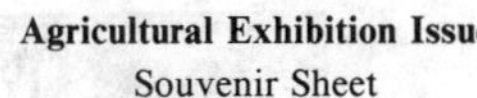

Agricultural Exhibition Issue

Souvenir Sheet

Arms of Liechtenstein — A56

1934, Sept. 29 ***Perf. 12***

Granite Paper

115 A56 5fr brown *1,100.* *2,000.*

See No. 131.

Coat of Arms A57

"Three Sisters" (Landmark) A58

Church of Schaan A59

Bendern A60

Rathaus, Vaduz A61

Samina Valley A62

Samina Valley in Winter A63

Ruin at Schellenberg A64

Government Palace — A65

Vaduz Castle — A66

Gutenberg Castle — A68

Alpine Hut – A69

Princess Elsa – A70

Coat of Arms – A71

Designs: 60rp, Vaduz castle, diff. 1.50fr, Valuna.

Perf. 11½, 11x11½, 12½

1934-35			**Photo.**	
116 A57	3rp cop red		20	52
117 A58	5rp emerald		2.75	45
118 A59	10rp dp vio		85	32
119 A60	15rp red org ('35)		40	1.00
120 A61	20rp red ('35)		70	45
121 A62	25rp brn ('35)		22.50	27.50
122 A63	30rp dk bl ('35)		3.75	1.25
123 A64	35rp gray grn ('35)		75	*4.00*
124 A65	40rp brn ('35)		85	2.50
125 A66	50rp lt brn		22.50	18.00
126 A66	60rp claret		1.25	*4.50*
127 A68	90rp dp grn		6.00	*18.00*
128 A69	1.20fr dp bl		1.65	*15.00*
129 A69	1.50fr brn car ('35)		2.50	*22.50*
	Nos. 116-129 (14)		66.65	*115.99*
	Engr.			
130 A70	2fr hn brn ('35)		57.50	*135.00*
131 A71	5fr dk vio ('35)		375.00	*725.00*

No. 131 has the same design as the 5fr in the souvenir sheet, No. 115. See #226, B14.

Bridge at Malbun A72

Labor: 20rp, Constructing Road to Triesenberg. 30rp, Binnen Canal. 50rp, Bridge near Planken.

1937, June 30		**Photo.**	
132 A72	10rp brt vio	95	65
133 A72	20rp red	95	65
134 A72	30rp brt bl	95	1.00
135 A72	50rp yel brn	95	1.65

Ruin at Schalun – A76

Peasant in Rhine Valley A77

Ruin at Schellenberg A78

Knight and Gutenberg Castle A79

Baron von Brandis and Vaduz Castle A80

Designs: 5rp, Chapel at Masescha. 10rp, Knight and Vaduz Castle. 15rp, Upper Valüna Valley. 20rp, Wooden Bridge over Rhine, Bendern. 25rp, Chapel at Steg. 90rp, "The Three Sisters". 1fr, Frontier stone. 1.20fr, Gutenberg Castle and Harpist. 1.50fr, Alpine View of Lawena and Schwartzhorn.

1937-38			
136 A76	3rp yel brn	18	35
	Pale Buff Shading		
137 A76	5rp emerald	18	22
138 A76	10rp violet	18	15
139 A76	15rp dk sl grn	30	45
140 A76	20rp brn org	30	22
141 A76	25rp chestnut	55	1.50
142 A77	30rp bl & gray	3.50	52
144 A78	40rp dk grn	2.75	1.00
145 A79	50rp dk brn	1.00	2.00
146 A80	60rp dp cl ('38)	2.25	1.50
147 A80	90rp gray vio ('38)	10.50	8.00
148 A80	1fr red brn	1.75	*6.25*
149 A80	1.20fr dp brn ('38)	8.25	*16.00*
150 A80	1.50fr sl bl ('38)	7.50	*16.00*
	Nos. 136-150 (14)	39.19	*54.16*

Souvenir Sheet

Josef Rheinberger A91

1938, July 30	**Engr.**	***Perf. 12***	
151	Sheet of 4	19.00	19.00
a.	A91 50rp slate gray	2.50	3.25

Issued in connection with the Third Philatelic Exhibition of Liechtenstein. Sheet size: 99¾x135mm.
See No. 153.

Francis Type of 1933
Thick Wove Paper

1938, Aug. 15	***Perf. 12½***		
152 A55	3fr blk, *buff*	11.00	*60.00*

Issued in memory of Prince Francis I, who died July 25, 1938. Sheets of 20.

Josef Rheinberger – A92

1939, Mar. 31			
153 A92	50rp slate green	70	*3.50*

Josef Gabriel Rheinberger (1839-1901), German composer and organist. Issued in sheets of 20.

Scene of Homage, 1718 – A93

1939, May 29			
154 A93	20rp grn lake	80	1.25
155 A93	30rp slate blue	80	1.25
156 A93	50rp gray grn	80	1.25

Issued to honor Prince Franz Joseph II. Sheets of 20.

Cantonal Coats of Arms – A94

Prince Franz Joseph II – A95

Design: 3fr, Arms of Principality.

1939			
157 A94	2fr dk grn, *buff*	5.25	*27.50*
158 A94	3fr indigo, *buff*	4.50	*30.00*
159 A96	5fr brn, *buff*	10.50	*32.50*
a.	Sheet of 4	85.00	*130.00*

Nos. 157-158 issued in sheets of 12; No. 159 in sheets of 4.

Prince Johann as a Child A100

Memorial Tablet A101

Prince Johann II – A102

Designs: 30rp, Prince Johann and Tower at Vaduz. 50rp, Prince Johann and Gutenberg Castle. 1fr, Prince Johann in 1920 and Vaduz Castle.

1940	**Photo.**	***Perf. 11½.***	
160 A100	20rp hn brn	45	*1.95*
161 A100	30rp indigo	60	*2.50*
162 A100	50rp dk sl grn	1.25	*5.75*
163 A100	1fr brn vio	6.50	*45.00*
164 A101	1.50fr vio blk	6.00	*45.00*
165 A102	3fr brown	1.75	*13.00*
	Nos. 160-165 (6)	17.80	*113.20*

Birth centenary of Prince Johann II. Nos. 160-164 issued in sheets of 25; No. 165 in sheets of 12.
Issue dates: 3fr, Oct. 5; others Aug. 10.

Gathering Corn A103

Wine Press A104

Sharpening Scythe A105

Milkmaid and Cow A106

Native Costume A107

1941, Apr. 7			
166 A103	10rp dl red brn	20	40
167 A104	20rp lake	35	85
168 A105	30rp royal bl	42	*1.50*
169 A106	50rp myrtle grn	1.65	*10.00*
170 A107	90rp dp claret	1.65	*13.00*
	Nos. 166-170 (5)	4.27	*25.75*

Madonna and Child – A108

1941, July 7		**Engr.**	
171 A108	10fr brn car	55.00	100.00

Issued in sheets of 4.

Johann Adam Andreas – A109

Designs: 30rp, Wenzel. 100rp, Anton Florian. 150rp, Joseph Adam.

1941, Dec. 18		**Photo.**	
172 A109	20rp brn car	40	55
173 A109	30rp ryl bl	45	*1.40*
174 A109	100rp vio blk	1.50	*10.50*
175 A109	150rp sl grn	1.50	*10.50*

Saint Lucius A113

Designs: 30rp, Reconstruction of Vaduz Castle. 50rp, Signing the Treaty of May 3, 1342. 1fr, Battle of Gutenberg. 2fr, Scene of Homage, 1718.

1942, Apr. 22	**Engr.**	***Perf. 11½***	
176 A113	20rp brn org, *buff*	1.00	52
177 A113	30rp steel bl, *buff*	80	1.50
178 A113	50rp dk ol grn, *buff*	2.00	*5.25*
179 A113	1fr dl brn, *buff*	2.00	*10.50*
180 A113	2fr vio blk, *buff*	1.75	*12.00*
	Nos. 176-180 (5)	7.55	*29.77*

600th anniversary of the separation of Liechtenstein from the House of Monfort.

Johann Karl – A118

Designs: 30rp, Franz Joseph I. 1fr, Alois I. 1.50fr, Johann I.

1942, Oct. 5 **Photo.**

181	A118	20rp rose	30	70
182	A118	30rp brt blue	45	*1.25*
183	A118	1fr rose lilac	1.25	*9.75*
184	A118	1.50fr deep brn	1.40	*9.75*

Prince Franz Joseph II A122

Countess Georgina von Wilczek A123

Prince and Princess — A124

1943, Mar. 5

185	A122	10rp dp rose vio	45	70
186	A123	20rp henna brn	45	70
187	A124	30rp slate blue	45	70

Marriage of Prince Franz Joseph II and Countess Georgina von Wilczek.

Prince Johann II — A126

Princes: 20rp, Alois II. 100rp, Franz Joseph I. 150rp, Franz Joseph II.

Perf. 11½

1943, July 5 **Unwmk.** **Photo.**

188	A126	20rp copper brn	20	40
189	A126	30rp deep blue	40	80
190	A126	100rp olive gray	1.10	*5.75*
191	A126	150rp slate grn	1.10	*5.75*

Sheets of 20.

Terrain before Reclaiming A129

Designs: 30rp, Draining the Canal. 50rp, Plowing Reclaimed Land. 2fr, Harvesting Crops.

1943, Sept. 6

192	A129	10rp violet blk	16	40
193	A129	30rp deep blue	35	*2.25*
194	A129	50rp slate grn	75	*6.00*
195	A129	2fr olive brn	1.65	*9.25*

Vaduz A133

Gutenberg A134

1943, Dec. 27

196	A133	10rp dk gray	50	35
197	A134	20rp chnt brn	65	90

Planken — A135

Bendern — A136

Designs: 10rp, Triesen. 15rp, Ruggell. 20rp, Vaduz. 25rp, Triesenberg. 30rp, Schaan. 40rp, Balzers. 50rp, Mauren. 60rp, Schellenberg. 90rp, Eschen. 1fr, Vaduz Castle. 120rp, Valuna Valley. 150rp, Lawena.

1944-45

198	A135	3rp dk brn & buff	15	22
199	A136	5rp sl grn & buff	15	15
200	A136	10rp gray & buff	18	15
201	A136	15rp bl gray & buff	28	*75*
202	A136	20rp org red & buff	24	18
203	A136	25rp dk rose vio & buff	28	*80*
204	A136	30rp bl & buff	35	45
205	A136	40rp brn & buff	55	95
206	A136	50rp bluish blk & pale gray	65	1.10
207	A136	60rp grn & buff	3.25	2.75
208	A136	90rp ol grn & buff	3.25	3.75
209	A136	1fr dp cl & buff	1.75	*3.50*
210	A136	120rp red brn	1.90	*3.75*
211	A136	150rp royal blue	1.90	*4.50*
		Nos. 198-211 (14)	14.88	*23.00*

Issue years: 10rp, 15rp, 40rp-1fr, 1945; others, 1944. See No. 239.

Crown and Rose — A149

1945, Apr. 9

212	A149	20rp multi	85	*52*
213	A149	30rp multi	85	*1.10*
214	A149	1fr multi	1.00	*3.75*

Birth of Prince Johann Adam Pius, Feb. 14, 1945. Sheets of 20.

Prince Franz Joseph II — A150

Arms of Liechtenstein and Vaduz Castle — A152

Design: 3fr, Princess Georgina.

1944-45 **Photo.**

215	A150	2fr brn, *buff*	5.75	*5.00*
216	A150	3fr dk grn	3.75	*4.75*

Engr.

217	A152	5fr bl gray, *cr* ('45)	10.50	*12.50*

Nos. 215-217 were issued in sheets of 8. See Nos. 222, 259-260.

Saint Lucius — A153

1946, Mar. 14 **Unwmk.** ***Perf. 11½***

218	A153	10fr gray blk, *cr*	26.00	*26.00*
		Sheet of four	115.00	*115.00*

Issued in sheets measuring 105x130mm.

Red Deer — A154

Varying Hare — A155

Capercaillie A156

1946, Dec. 10 **Photo.**

219	A154	20rp henna brn	1.25	1.25
220	A155	30rp grnsh bl	1.65	1.50
221	A156	150rp olive brn	2.75	*9.50*

Arms Type of 1945

1947, Mar. 20 **Engr.**

222	A152	5fr henna brn, *cr*	11.00	*27.50*

Issued in sheets of 8.

Chamois — A157

Alpine Marmot — A158

Golden Eagle — A159

1947, Oct. 15 **Photo.** **Unwmk.**

223	A157	20rp henna brn	1.65	2.75
224	A158	30rp grnsh bl	2.00	3.50
225	A159	150rp dark brn	3.00	*11.00*

Elsa Type of 1935

1947, Dec. 10 **Engr.** ***Perf. 14½***

226	A70	2fr black, *yelsh*	2.25	*10.00*

Issued in memory of Princess Elsa, who died Sept. 28, 1947. Sheets of 20.

Portrait of Ginevra dei Benci by Leonardo da Vinci — A160

Designs: 20rp, Girl, Rubens. 30rp, Self-portrait, Rembrandt. 40rp, Canon, Massys. 50rp, Madonna, Memling. 60rp, French Painter, 1456, Fouquet. 80rp, Lute Player, Gentileschi. 90rp, Man, Strigel. 120rp, Man, Raphael.

1949, Mar. 15 **Photo.** ***Perf. 11½***

227	A160	10rp dk grn	75	60
228	A160	20rp henna brn	1.00	60
229	A160	30rp sepia	1.90	2.50
230	A160	40rp blue	5.00	90
231	A160	50rp violet	4.25	6.25
232	A160	60rp grnsh gray	8.00	7.25
233	A160	80rp brn org	2.00	6.25
234	A160	90rp olive bis	8.00	6.25
235	A160	120rp claret	2.00	5.50
		Nos. 227-235 (9)	32.90	36.10

Issued in sheets of 12.

See No. 238.

No. 198 Surcharged with New Value and Bars in Dark Brown

1949, Apr. 14

236	A135	5rp on 3rp dk brn & buff	25	30

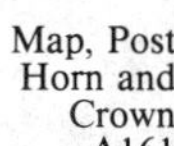

Map, Post Horn and Crown A161

1949, May 23

237	A161	40rp bl & ind	2.75	4.75

75th anniversary of the UPU.

Portrait Type of 1949
Souvenir Sheet

Unwmk.

1949, Aug. 6 **Photo.** ***Imperf.***

238		Sheet of 3	60.00	*110.00*
a.	A160	10rp dull green	10.50	14.00
b.	A160	20rp lilac rose	10.50	14.00
c.	A160	40rp blue	10.50	14.00

5th Philatelic Exhibition.
Sheet size: 121½x69½mm. Sold for 3fr.

Scenic Type of 1944

1949, Dec. 1 ***Perf. 11½***

239	A136	5rp dk brn & buff	16.00	45

Rossauer Castle, Vienna A163

Church at Bendern A164

Prince Johann Adam Andreas — A165

1949, Nov. 15 **Engr.** ***Perf. 14½***

240	A163	20rp dk vio	75	1.65
241	A164	40rp blue	4.00	8.00
242	A165	150rp brn red	5.50	8.50

250th anniv. of the purchase of the former dukedom of Schellenberg. Sheets of 20.

Roe Deer — A166

Black Grouse — A167

Badger — A168

1950, Mar. 7 **Photo.** ***Perf. 11½***

243	A166	20rp red brn	3.75	1.65
244	A167	30rp Prus grn	5.75	3.75
245	A168	80rp dk brn	21.00	40.00

Issued in sheets of 20.

No. 237 Surcharged with New Value and Bars Obliterating Commemorative Inscriptions

1950, Nov. 7

246	A161	1fr on 40rp bl & ind	16.00	*40.00*

Boy Cutting Bread — A169

Designs: 10rp, Laborer. 15rp, Cutting hay. 20rp, Harvesting corn. 25rp, Load of hay. 30rp, Wine grower. 40rp, Farmer and scythe. 50rp, Cattle raising. 60rp, Plowing. 80rp, Woman with potatoes. 90rp, Potato cultivation. 1fr, Tractor with potatoes.

Perf. 11½

1951, May 3 Unwmk. Photo.

247 A169	5rp	claret	28	15
248 A169	10rp	green	40	15
249 A169	15rp	yel brn	2.75	4.50
250 A169	20rp	ol brn	90	32
251 A169	25rp	rose brn	2.75	4.50
252 A169	30rp	grnsh gray	1.75	70
253 A169	40rp	dp bl	5.25	5.50
254 A169	50rp	vio brn	4.25	2.70
255 A169	60rp	brown	4.00	2.75
256 A169	80rp	hn brn	5.50	9.00
257 A169	90rp	ol grn	9.00	4.25
258 A169	1fr	indigo	32.50	6.00
		Nos. 247-258 (12)	69.33	40.52

Types of 1944, Redrawn

Perf. 12½x12

1951, Nov. 20 Engr. Wmk. 296

259 A150 2fr dk bl	7.75	*35.00*
a. Perf. 14½	575.00	165.00
260 A150 3fr dk red brn	100.00	80.00
a. Perf. 14½	90.00	*225.00*

Issued in sheets of 20.

Portrait, Savolodo A170

Madonna, Botticelli A171

Design: 40rp St. John, Del Sarto.

Perf. 11½

1952, May 27 Unwmk. Photo.

261 A170 20rp vio brn	24.00	3.75
262 A171 30rp brn olive	15.00	6.50
263 A170 40rp vio blue	9.00	5.25

Issued in sheets of 12.

Vaduz Castle — A172

Wmk. 296

1952, Sept. 25 Engr. *Perf. 14½*

264 A172 5fr dp grn 115.00 140.00

Issued in sheets of 9.

No. 241 Surcharged with New Value and Wavy Lines in Red

1952, Sept. 25 Unwmk.

265 A164 1.20fr on 40rp blue 20.00 *40.00*

Liechtenstein stamps can be mounted in Scott's annual Liechtenstein Supplement.

Portrait of a Young Man A173

St. Nicholas by Zeitblom A174

Designs: 30rp, St. Christopher by Cranach. 40rp, Leonhard, Duke of Hag, by Kulmbach.

Perf. 11½

1953, Feb. 5 Unwmk. Photo.

266 A173 10rp dk ol grn	42	1.00
267 A174 20rp olive brn	7.75	1.90
268 A174 30rp vio brn	17.00	7.50
269 A173 40rp slate bl	17.00	*45.00*

Issued in sheets of 12.

Lord Baden-Powell A175

1953, Aug. 4 Engr. *Perf. 13x13½*

270 A175 10rp dp grn	1.25	1.25
271 A175 20rp dk brn	8.50	2.75
272 A175 25rp red	8.50	16.00
273 A175 40rp dp bl	7.75	7.50

Intl. Scout Conf. Sheets of 20.

Alemannic Disc, 600 A. D. — A176

Prehistoric Settlement of Borscht — A177

Design: 1.20fr, Rössen jug.

1953, Nov. 26 *Perf. 11½*

274 A176 10rp org brn	5.00	*11.00*
275 A177 20rp dp gray grn	5.00	*8.25*
276 A176 1.20fr dk bl gray	27.50	*26.00*

Opening of National Museum, Vaduz.

Soccer Players — A178

Designs: 20rp, Player kicking ball. 25rp, Goalkeeper. 40rp, Two opposing players.

1954, May 18 Photo.

277 A178 10rp dl rose & brn	1.65	65
278 A178 20rp olive grn	2.50	65
279 A178 25rp org brn	9.25	*19.00*
280 A178 40rp lilac gray	6.25	5.00

See #289-292, 297-300, 308-311, 320-323.

Nos. B19-B21 Surcharged with New Value and Bars in Color of Stamp

1954, Sept. 28 Unwmk. *Perf. 11½*

281 SP15 35rp on 10rp+10rp	1.25	3.25
282 SP16 60rp on 20rp+10rp	13.00	10.00
283 SP15 65rp on 40rp+10rp	3.75	6.50

Madonna in Wood, 14th Century — A179

1954, Dec. 16 Engr.

284 A179 20rp henna brn	1.50	2.75
285 A179 40rp gray	8.50	18.00
286 A179 1fr dk brn	8.50	18.00

Prince Franz Joseph II A180

Princess Georgina A181

1955, Apr. 5 *Perf. 14½*

Cream Paper

287 A180 2fr dk brn	50.00	32.50
288 A181 3fr dk grn	50.00	32.50

Issued in sheets of 9.

Sports Type of 1954

Designs: 10rp, Slalom. 20rp, Mountain climbing. 25rp, Skiing. 40rp, Resting on summit.

1955, June 14 Photo. *Perf. 11½*

289 A178 10rp aqua & brn vio	1.00	85
290 A178 20rp grn & ol bis	2.50	85
291 A178 25rp lt ultra & sep	9.50	14.00
292 A178 40rp ol & pink	7.00	3.50

Prince Johann Adam A183

Eagle, Crown and Oak Leaves A184

Portraits: 20rp, Prince Philipp. 40rp, Prince Nikolaus. 60rp, Princess Nora.

1955, Dec. 14

Granite Paper

Cross in Red

293 A183 10rp dull vio	65	42
294 A183 20rp slate grn	3.50	1.40
295 A183 40rp olive brn	5.00	7.00
296 A183 60rp rose brown	3.50	5.25

Liechtenstein Red Cross, 10th anniversary.

Sports Type of 1954

Designs: 10rp, Javelin thrower. 20rp, Hurdling. 40rp, Pole vaulting. 1fr, Sprinters.

Perf. 11½

1956, June 21 Unwmk. Photo.

Granite Paper

297 A178 10rp lt red brn & ol grn	65	30
298 A178 20rp lt ol grn & pur	1.65	55
299 A178 40rp bl & vio brn	2.50	3.25
300 A178 1fr org ver & ol brn	7.00	7.75

1956, Aug. 21

Granite Paper

301 A184 10rp dk brn & gold	1.10	1.00
302 A184 120rp sl blk & gold	5.75	3.50

150th anniversary of independence.

Prince Franz Joseph II — A185

Prince Johann Adam — A186

1956, Aug. 21

303 A185 10rp dk grn	1.00	52
304 A185 15rp brt ultra	2.25	3.25
305 A185 25rp purple	2.50	3.25
306 A185 60rp dk brn	4.50	3.50

50th birthday of Prince Franz Joseph II.

1956, Aug. 21

Granite Paper

307 A186 20rp olive green 1.75 48

Issued to publicize the 6th Philatelic Exhibition, Vaduz, Aug. 25-Sept. 2. Sheets of 9.

Sports Type of 1954

Designs: 10rp, Somersault on bar. 15rp, Jumping over vaulting horse. 25rp, Exercise on rings. 1.50fr, Somersault on parallel bars.

1957, May 14 Photo. *Perf. 11½*

308 A178 10rp pale rose & ol grn	70	48
309 A178 15rp pale grn & dl pur	2.50	4.00
310 A178 25rp ol bis & Prus grn	2.50	5.75
311 A178 1.50fr lem & sepia	6.50	13.00

Pine A187

Lord Baden-Powell A188

Designs: 20rp, Wild roses. 1fr, Birches.

1957, Sept. 10 *Perf. 11½*

Granite Paper

312 A187 10rp dk vio	2.50	2.50
313 A187 20rp brn car	2.50	80
314 A187 1fr green	4.00	5.50

See Nos. 326-328, 332-334, 353-355.

1957, Sept. 10 Unwmk.

Design: 10rp, Symbolical torchlight parade.

315 A188 10rp bl blk	1.00	1.65
316 A188 20rp dk brn	1.00	1.65
a. Sheet of 12, 6 each #315-316	12.00	17.50

Cent. of the birth of Lord Baden-Powell and the 60th anniv. of the Boy Scout movement.

Chapel of St. Mamertus — A189

Designs: 40rp, Madonna and saints. 1.50fr, Pieta.

1957, Dec. 16 *Perf. 11½*

317	A189	10rp dk brn	40	32
318	A189	40rp dark blue	1.25	*5.00*
319	A189	1.50fr brn lake	7.00	8.75

Issued in sheets of 20. Sheet inscribed: "Furstentum Liechtenstein" and "Weihnacht 1957" (Christmas 1957).

Sports Type of 1954

Designs: 15rp, Girl swimmer. 30rp, Fencers. 40rp, Tennis. 90rp, Bicyclists.

1958, Mar. 18 **Photo.**

Granite Paper

320	A178	15rp lt bl & pur	70	95
321	A178	30rp pale rose lil & ol gray	3.50	5.75
322	A178	40rp sal pink & sl bl	3.50	5.75
323	A178	90rp lt ol grn & vio brn	1.75	3.75

Relief Map of Liechtenstein A190

1958, Mar. 18

324	A190	25rp bis, vio & red	35	90
325	A190	40rp bl, vio & red	35	90

World's Fair, Brussels, Apr. 17-Oct. 19. Sheets of 25.

Tree-Bush Design of 1957

Designs: 20rp, Maples at Lawena. 50rp, Holly at Schellenberg. 90rp, Yew at Maurerberg.

1958, Aug. 12 *Perf. 11½*

Granite Paper

326	A187	20rp chocolate	1.75	75
327	A187	50rp olive green	7.00	4.50
328	A187	90rp vio blue	1.75	2.75

Sts. Moritz and Agatha A191

"The Good Shepherd" A192

Christmas: 35rp, St. Peter. 80rp, Chapel of St. Peter, Mals-Balzers.

1958, Dec. 4 **Photo.** **Unwmk.**

Granite Paper

329	A191	20rp dk slate grn	2.50	2.50
330	A191	35rp dk blue vio	2.50	2.50
331	A191	80rp dark brown	2.50	2.50

Issued in sheets of 20.

Tree-Bush Type of 1957

Designs: 20rp, Larch in Lawena. 50rp, Holly on Alpila. 90rp, Linden in Schaan.

1959, Apr. 15 *Perf. 11½*

332	A187	20rp dark vio	2.75	2.00
333	A187	50rp henna brn	2.75	2.00
334	A187	90rp dark green	2.75	2.00

1959, Apr. 15 **Unwmk.**

335	A192	30rp rose vio & gold	50	85

Issued in memory of Pope Pius XII.

Flags and Rhine Valley — A193

Man Carrying Hay — A194

Apple Harvest A195

Designs: 5rp, Church at Bendern and sheaves. 20rp, Rhine embankment. 30rp, Gutenberg Castle. 40rp, View from Schellenberg. 50rp, Vaduz Castle. 60rp, Naafkopf, Falknis Range. 75rp, Woman gathering sheaves. 90rp, Woman in vineyard. 1fr, Woman in kitchen. 1.30fr, Return from the field. 1.50fr, Family saying grace.

1959-64

Granite Paper

336	A193	5rp gray ol ('61)	15	15
337	A193	10rp dl vio	15	15
338	A193	20rp lil rose	15	15
339	A193	30rp dk red	15	15
340	A193	40rp ol grn ('61)	1.25	55
341	A193	50rp deep blue	30	35
342	A193	60rp brt grnsh bl	45	55
343	A194	75rp dp ocher ('60)	1.25	1.00
344	A194	80rp ol grn ('61)	1.00	90
345	A194	90rp red lil ('61)	1.00	90
346	A194	1fr chnt ('61)	1.00	90
347	A195	1.20fr org ver ('60)	1.50	1.10
348	A195	1.30fr brt grn ('64)	1.25	90
349	A195	1.50fr brt bl ('60)	1.50	1.40
		Nos. 336-349 (14)	11.10	9.15

Belfry, Bendern Church — A196

Christmas: 60rp, Sculpture, bell, St. Theodul's church. 1fr, Sculpture, tower of St. Lucius' church.

1959, Dec. 2 **Unwmk.** *Perf. 11½*

350	A196	5rp dk slate grn	60	25
351	A196	60rp olive	4.00	4.50
352	A196	1fr dp claret	3.00	2.75

Issued in sheets of 20.

Tree-Bush Type of 1957

Designs: 20rp, Beech tree on Gafadura. 30rp, Juniper on Alpila. 50rp, Pine on Sass.

1960, Sept. 19

353	A187	20rp brown	5.00	5.00
354	A187	30rp deep plum	5.00	5.00
355	A187	50rp Prus grn	17.00	5.00

Europa Issue, 1960

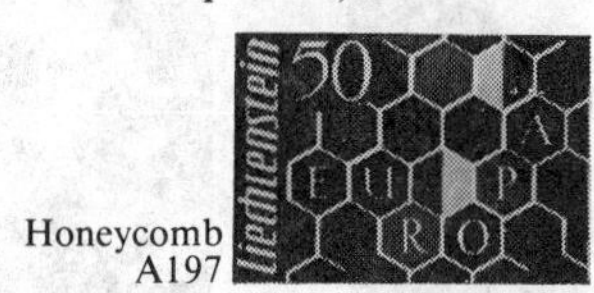

Honeycomb A197

1960, Sept. 19 *Perf. 14*

356	A197	50rp multi	100.00	60.00

Issued to promote the idea of a united Europe. Sheets of 20.

Princess Gina A198

Heinrich von Frauenberg A199

Portraits: 1.70fr, Prince Johann Adam Pius. 3fr, Prince Franz Joseph II.

1960-64 **Engr.** *Perf. 14*

356A	A198	1.70fr vio ('64)	1.00	1.50
b.		Imperf., pair	*1,750.*	*1,750.*
357	A198	2fr dk bl	2.50	2.25
a.		Imperf., pair	*1,750.*	*1,750.*
358	A198	3fr dp brn	2.50	2.25

Issued in sheets of 16.

1961-62 **Photo.** *Perf. 11½*

Minnesingers: 20rp, King Konradin. 25rp, Ulrich von Liechtenstein. 30rp, Kraft von Toggenburg. 35rp, Ulrich von Gutenberg. 40rp, Heinrich von Veldig. 1fr, Konrad von Alstetten. 1.50r, Walther von der Vogelweide. 2fr, Tannhäuser. (Designs from 14th century Manesse manuscript.)

359	A199	15rp multi	60	75
360	A199	20rp multi ('62)	30	30
361	A199	25rp multi	1.25	1.65
362	A199	30rp multi ('62)	40	40
363	A199	35rp multi	1.50	2.00
364	A199	40rp multi ('62)	65	65
365	A199	1fr multi	2.50	2.00
366	A199	1.50fr multi	9.25	15.00
367	A199	2fr multi ('62)	1.65	1.65
		Nos. 359-367 (9)	18.10	24.40

Issued in sheets of 20. See #381-384, 471.

Catalogue values for unused stamps in this section, from this point to the end of the section, are for Never Hinged items.

Europa Issue, 1961

Cogwheels A200

1961, Oct. 3 **Unwmk.** *Perf. 13½*

368	A200	50rp multi	25	25

Printed in sheets of 20.

Souvenir Sheet

Prince Johann II — A201

Portraits: 10rp, Francis I. 25rp, Franz Joseph II.

1962, Aug. 2 **Photo.** *Perf. 11½*

369		Sheet of 3	9.50	6.00
a.	A201	5rp gray green	1.10	85
b.	A201	10rp deep rose	3.50	2.75
c.	A201	25rp blue	1.10	85

50th anniv. of Liechtenstein's postage stamps and in connection with the Anniv. Stamp Exhib., Vaduz, Aug. 4-12. No. 369 sold for 3fr.

Hands A202

1962, Aug. 2

370	A202	50rp indigo & red	80	75

Europa. Issued in sheets of 20.

Malaria Eradication Emblem — A203

Pietà — A204

1962, Aug. 2 **Engr.**

371	A203	50rp turq blue	38	38

Issued for the World Health Organization drive to eradicate malaria. Sheets of 20.

1962, Dec. 6 **Photo.**

Designs: 50rp, Angel with harp, fresco. 1.20fr, View of Mauren.

372	A204	30rp magenta	60	60
373	A204	50rp dp org	85	85
374	A204	1.20fr deep blue	1.25	1.25

Issued in sheets of 20.

Prince Franz Joseph II A205

1963, Apr. 3 **Engr.** *Perf. 13½x14*

375	A205	5fr dull green	4.75	3.00

25th anniversary of the accession of Prince Franz Joseph II. Sheets of 8.
Exists imperf. Value $1,500.

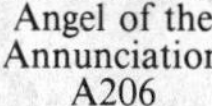

Angel of the Annunciation A206

Greek Architectural Elements A207

Designs: 80rp, Three Kings. 1fr, Family.

Perf. 11½

1963, Aug. 26 **Unwmk.** **Photo.**

376	A206	20rp multi	40	40
377	A206	80rp gray, pur & red	80	80
378	A206	1fr multi	80	80

Centenary of the International Red Cross.

Europa Issue, 1963

1963, Aug. 26

379	A207	50rp multi	2.00	1.50

Bread and Milk — A208

1963, Aug. 26
380 A208 50rp dk red pur & brn 40 40

FAO "Freedom from Hunger" campaign.

Minnesinger Type of 1961-62

Minnesingers: 25rp, Heinrich von Sax. 30rp, Kristan von Hamle. 75rp, Werner von Teufen. 1.70fr, Hartmann von Aue.

Perf. 11½
1963, Dec. 5 Unwmk. Photo.
381 A199 25rp multi 30 30
382 A199 30rp multi 30 30
383 A199 75rp multi 75 75
384 A199 1.70fr multi 1.25 1.25

Issued in sheets of 20.

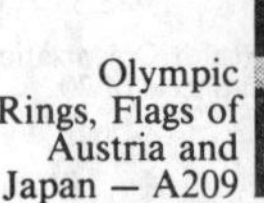

Olympic Rings, Flags of Austria and Japan — A209

1964, Apr. 15 *Perf. 11½*
385 A209 50rp Prus bl, red & blk 40 40

Olympic Games 1964. Sheets of 20.

Arms of Counts of Werdenberg-Vaduz A210

Coats of Arms: 30rp, Barons of Brandis. 80rp, Counts of Sulz. 1.50fr, Counts of Hohenems.

1964, Sept. 1 Photo.
386 A210 20rp multi 16 16
387 A210 30rp multi 25 25
388 A210 80rp multi 55 55
389 A210 1.50fr multi 80 80

See Nos. 396-399.

Europa Issue, 1964

Roman Castle, Schaan A211

1964, Sept. 1 *Perf. 13x14*
390 A211 50rp multi 3.75 95

Masescha Chapel — A212

Peter Kaiser — A213

Designs: 40rp, Mary Magdalene, altarpiece. 1.30fr, Madonna with Sts. Sebastian and Roch, altarpiece.

1964, Dec. 9 Photo. *Perf. 11½*
391 A212 10rp vio blk 15 15
392 A212 40rp dk bl 40 40
393 A212 1.30fr dp cl 1.10 1.10

Issued in sheets of 20.

1964, Dec. 9 Engr.
394 A213 1fr dk grn, *buff* 60 60

Kaiser (1793-1864), historian. Sheets of 20.

Madonna, Wood Sculpture, 18th Century — A214

Perf. 11½
1965, Apr. 22 Unwmk. Engr.
395 A214 10fr org red 8.25 6.00

Issued in sheets of 4.

Arms Type of 1965

Coats of Arms (Lords of): 20rp, Schellenberg. 30rp, Gutenberg. 80rp, Frauenberg. 1fr, Ramschwag.

Perf. 11½
1965, Aug. 31 Unwmk. Photo.
396 A210 20rp multi 15 15
397 A210 30rp multi 15 15
398 A210 80rp multi 50 50
399 A210 1fr multi 55 55

Alemannic Ornament A215

Europa: The design is from a belt buckle, about 600 A.D., found in a man's tomb near Eschen.

1965, Aug. 31
400 A215 50rp vio bl, gray & brn 70 45

The Annunciation by Ferdinand Nigg — A216

Princess Gina and Prince Franz Josef Wenzel — A217

Paintings by Nigg: 30rp, The Three Kings. 1.20fr, Jesus in the Temple (horiz.).

1965, Dec. 7 Photo. *Perf. 11½*
401 A216 10rp yel grn & dk grn 15 15
402 A216 30rp org & red brn 28 28
403 A216 1.20fr ultra & grnsh bl 55 55

Ferdinand Nigg (1865-1949), painter.

1965, Dec. 7
404 A217 75rp gray, buff & gold 45 45

Communication Symbols — A218

1965, Dec. 7
405 A218 25rp multi 22 22

Centenary of the ITU.

Soil Conservation, Tree — A219

Designs: 20rp, Clean air, bird. 30rp, Unpolluted water, fish. 1.50fr, Nature preservation, sun.

1966, Apr. 26 Photo. *Perf. 11½*
406 A219 10rp brt yel & grn 15 15
407 A219 20rp bl & dk bl 15 15
408 A219 30rp brt grn & ultra 25 25
409 A219 1.50fr yel & red 70 70

Issued to publicize nature conservation.

Prince Franz Joseph II A220

Arms of Barons of Richenstein A221

1966, Apr. 26
410 A220 1fr gray, gold, buff & dk brn 60 60

60th birthday of Prince Franz Joseph II.

1966, Sept. 6 Photo. *Perf. 11½*

Coats of Arms: 30rp, Vaistli knights. 60rp, Lords of Trisun. 1.20fr, von Schiel.

Light Gray Background
411 A221 20rp multi 15 15
412 A221 30rp multi 15 15
413 A221 60rp multi 25 25
414 A221 1.20fr multi 55 55

Europa Issue, 1966
Common Design Type
1966, Sept. 6 Photo. *Perf. 14x13*
Size: 25x32mm
415 CD9 50rp ultra, dp org & lt grn 45 40

Vaduz Parish Church A222

St. Florin A223

Designs: 30rp, Madonna. 1.70fr, God the Father.

1966, Dec. 6 Photo. *Perf. 11½*
416 A222 5rp org red & cit 15 15
417 A223 20rp lem & mag 15 15
418 A223 30rp dl rose & dp bl 20 20
419 A223 1.70fr gray & red brn 75 75

Restoration of the Vaduz Parish Church.

Europa Issue, 1967
Common Design Type
1967, Apr. 20 Photo. *Perf. 11½*
420 CD10 50rp multi 42 42

The Man from Malans and his White Horse — A225

Fairy Tales of Liechtenstein: 30rp, The Treasure of Gutenberg. 1.20fr, The Giant of Guflina slaying the Dragon.

1967, Apr. 20
421 A225 20rp multi 15 15
422 A225 30rp multi 18 15
423 A225 1.20fr grn & multi 70 65

See Nos. 443-445, 458-460.

Souvenir Sheet

Prince Hans Adam and Countess Kinsky — A226

1967, June 26 Engr. *Perf. 14x13½*
424 A226 Sheet of 2 2.25 2.25
a. 1.50fr slate blue (Prince) 1.10 1.10
b. 1.50fr red brown (Countess) 1.10 1.10

Wedding of Prince Hans Adam of Liechtenstein and Marie Aglae Countess Kinsky of Wichnitz and Tettau, July 30, 1967.

Common Design Types pictured in section at front of book.

EFTA Emblem A227

1967, Sept. 28 Photo. *Perf. 11½*
425 A227 50rp multi 55 55

European Free Trade Association. See note after Norway No. 501.

Trophaeum (The Victorious Cross) — A228

Christian Symbols: 20rp, Alpha and Omega. 70rp, Chrismon.

1967, Sept. 28
426 A228 20rp rose cl, blk, & gold 18 15
427 A228 30rp multi 25 18
428 A228 70rp dp ultra, blk & gold 60 48

Johann Baptist Büchel — A229

1967, Sept. 28 **Engr. & Litho.**

429 A229 1fr rose cl & pale grn 70 55

Issued in memory of Johann Baptist Büchel (1853-1927), priest, educator, historian and poet. Printed on fluorescent paper.

Peter and Paul, Patron Saints of Mauren — A230

Patron Saints: 5rp, St. Joseph, Planken. 10rp, St. Laurentius, Schaan. 30rp, St. Nicholas, Balzers. 40rp, St. Sebastian, Nendeln. 50rp, St. George, Schellenberg Chapel. 60rp, St. Martin, Eschen. 70rp, St. Fridolin, Ruggell. 80rp, St. Gallus, Triesen. 1fr, St. Theodul, Triesenberg. 1.20fr, St. Ann, Vaduz Castle. 1.50fr, St. Mary, Bendern-Gamprin. 2fr, St. Lucius, patron saint of the Principality.

1967-71 **Photo.** ***Perf. 11½***

430 A230 5rp multi ('68) 15 15
431 A230 10rp multi ('68) 15 15
432 A230 20rp bl & multi 15 15
433 A230 30rp dk red & multi 22 15
433A A230 40rp multi ('71) 45 35
434 A230 50rp multi ('68) 38 30
435 A230 60rp multi ('68) 45 35
436 A230 70rp multi 48 40
437 A230 80rp multi ('68) 55 50
438 A230 1fr multi ('68) 75 55
439 A230 1.20fr vio bl & multi 80 90
440 A230 1.50fr multi ('68) 1.10 95
441 A230 2fr multi ('68) 1.25 1.25
Nos. 430-441 (13) 6.88 6.15

Issue dates: 20rp, 30rp, 70rp, 1.20fr, Dec. 7, 1967; 5rp, 1.50fr, Aug. 29, 1968; 40rp, June 11, 1971. 2fr, Dec. 5, 1968. Others Apr. 25, 1968.

Europa Issue, 1968
Common Design Type

1968, Apr. 25
Size: 32½x23mm

442 CD11 50rp crim, gold & ultra 45 45

Fairy Tale Type of 1967

Fairy Tales of Liechtenstein: 30rp, The Treasure of St. Mamerten. 50rp, The Goblin from the Bergerwald. 80rp, The Three Sisters. (Denominations at right.)

1968, Aug. 29

443 A225 30rp Prus bl, yel & red 18 15
444 A225 50rp grn, yel & bl 32 32
445 A225 80rp brt bl, yel & lt bl 55 55

Arms of Liechtenstein and Wilczek A231

1968, Aug. 29

446 A231 75rp multi 75 70

Silver wedding anniversary of Prince Franz Joseph II and Princess Gina.

Sir Rowland Hill — A232

Coat of Arms — A233

Portraits: 30rp, Count Philippe de Ferrari. 80rp, Carl Lindenberg. 1fr, Maurice Burrus. 1.20fr, Theodore Champion.

1968-69 **Engr.** ***Perf. 14x13½***

447 A232 20rp green 15 15
448 A232 30rp red brown 22 22
449 A232 80rp dark brown 55 45
450 A232 1fr black 70 65
451 A232 1.20fr dark blue 90 70
Nos. 447-451 (5) 2.52 2.17

Issued to honor "Pioneers of Philately."
Issue dates: 80rp, 1.20fr, Aug. 28, 1969. Others, Dec. 5, 1968.
See Nos. 509-511.

1969, Apr. 24 **Engr.** ***Perf. 14x13½***

452 A233 3.50fr dk brn 2.50 1.65

Sheets of 16.

Europa Issue, 1969
Common Design Type

1969, Apr. 24 **Photo.** ***Perf. 14***
Size: 33x23mm

453 CD12 50rp brn red, yel & grn 60 60

"Biology" (Man and DNA Molecule) A234

Designs: 30rp, "Physics" (man and magnetic field). 50rp, "Astronomy" (man and planets). 80rp, "Art" (artist and Prince Franz Joseph II and Princess Gina).

1969, Aug. 28 **Photo.** ***Perf. 11½***

454 A234 10rp grn, dk bl & dp cl 15 15
455 A234 30rp brn & multi 24 16
456 A234 50rp ultra & grn 42 30
457 A234 80rp brn, dk brn & yel 70 50

250th anniv. of the Duchy of Liechtenstein.

Fairy Tale Type of 1967

Fairy Tales of Liechtenstein: 20rp, The Cheated Devil. 50rp, The Fiery Red Goat. 60rp, The Grafenberg Treasure (toad). (Denominations at right.)

1969, Dec. 4 **Photo.** ***Perf. 11½***

458 A225 20rp multi 15 15
459 A225 50rp yel & multi 38 35
460 A225 60rp red & multi 52 45

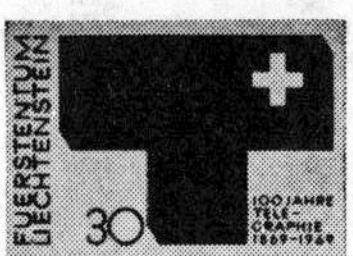

"T" and Arms of Austria-Hungary, Liechtenstein and Switzerland — A235

1969, Dec. 4 ***Perf. 13½***

461 A235 30rp gold & multi 28 28

Cent. of the Liechtenstein telegraph system.

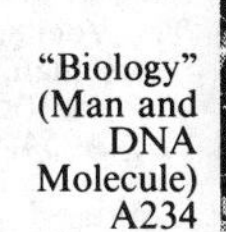

Arms of St. Lucius Monastery, Chur A236

Prince Wenzel A237

Arms of Ecclesiastic Patrons: 50rp, Pfäfers Abbey (dove). 1.50fr, Chur Bishopric (stag).

1969, Dec. 4 ***Perf. 11½***

462 A236 30rp multi 22 20
463 A236 50rp multi 38 35
464 A236 1.50fr multi 1.00 1.00

See Nos. 475-477, 486-488.

1970, Apr. 30 **Photo.** ***Perf. 11½***

465 A237 1fr sep & multi 90 90

25th anniv. of the Liechtenstein Red Cross.

Orange Lily — A238

Native Flowers: 30rp, Bumblebee orchid. 50rp, Glacier crowfoot. 1.20fr, Buck bean.

1970, Apr. 30

466 A238 20rp multi 18 18
467 A238 30rp grn & multi 30 30
468 A238 50rp ol & multi 60 60
469 A238 1.20fr multi 1.25 1.25

Issued to publicize the European Conservation Year 1970. See Nos. 481-484, 500-503.

Europa Issue, 1970
Common Design Type

1970, Apr. 30 **Litho.** ***Perf. 14***
Size: 31½x20½mm

470 CD13 50rp emer, dk bl & yel 60 60

Minnesinger Type of 1961-62
Souvenir Sheet

Minnesingers: 30rp, Wolfram von Eschenbach. 50rp, Reinmar der Fiedler. 80rp, Hartmann von Starkenberg. 1.20fr, Friedrich von Hausen.

1970, Aug. 27 **Photo.** ***Perf. 11½***

471 Sheet of 4 2.25 2.25
a. A199 30rp multi 15 15
b. A199 50rp multi 28 28
c. A199 80rp multi 48 48
d. A199 1.20fr multi 65 65

Wolfram von Eschenbach (1170-1220), German minnesinger (poet). Sold for 3fr.

Prince Franz Joseph II — A239

Mother & Child, Sculpture by Rudolf Schädler — A240

Portrait: 2.50fr, Princess Gina.

1970-71 **Engr.** ***Perf. 14x13½***

472 A239 2.50fr violet blue 1.90 1.10
473 A239 3fr black 2.00 1.25

Issue dates: 2.50fr, June 11, 1971. 3fr, Dec. 3, 1970. Sheets of 16.

1970, Dec. 3 **Photo.** ***Perf. 11½***

474 A240 30rp dk red & multi 28 28

Christmas.

Ecclesiastic Arms Type of 1969

Arms of Ecclesiastic Patrons: 20rp, Abbey of St. John in Thur Valley (Lamb of God). 30rp, Ladies' Abbey, Schänis (crown). 75rp, Abbey of St. Gallen (bear rampant).

1970, Dec. 3

475 A236 20rp lt bl & multi 16 16
476 A236 30rp gray, red & gold 25 25
477 A236 75rp multi 60 60

Bronze Boar, La Tene Period — A241

Designs: 30rp, Peacock, Roman, 2nd century. 75rp, Decorated copper bowl, 13th century.

1971, Mar. 11 **Photo.** ***Perf. 11½***

478 A241 25rp dp ultra & bluish blk 22 22
479 A241 30rp dk brn & grn 25 25
480 A241 75rp grn, yel & brn 60 60

Opening of the National Museum, Vaduz.

Flower Type of 1970

Flowers: 10rp, Cyclamen. 20rp, Moonwort. 50rp, Superb pink. 1.50fr, Alpine columbine.

1971, Mar. 11

481 A238 10rp multi 15 15
482 A238 20rp multi 15 15
483 A238 50rp multi 45 45
484 A238 1.50fr multi 1.40 1.25

Europa Issue, 1971
Common Design Type

1971, June 11 **Photo.** ***Perf. 13½***
Size: 31x21mm

485 CD14 50rp grnsh bl, yel & blk 55 55

Ecclesiastic Arms Type of 1969

Arms of Ecclesiastic Patrons: 30rp, Knights of St. John, Feldkirch (Latin and moline crosses). 50rp, Weingarten Abbey (grapes). 1.20fr, Ottobeuren Abbey (eagle and cross).

1971, Sept. 2 **Photo.** ***Perf. 11½***

486 A236 30rp bis & multi 22 22
487 A236 50rp multi 35 35
488 A236 1.20fr gray & multi 90 90

Princely Crown — A242

Design: 70rp, Page from constitution.

1971, Sept. 2

489 A242 70rp grn, gold, blk & cop 52 52
490 A242 80rp dk bl, gold, red & plum 65 65

50th anniversary of the constitution.

Madonna, by Andrea della Robbia A243

Long-distance Skiing A244

1971, Dec. 9
491 A243 30rp multi 30 28

Christmas 1971.

1971, Dec. 9

Designs (Olympic Rings and): 40rp, Ice hockey. 65rp, Downhill skiing, women's. 1.50fr, Figure skating, women's.

492 A244 15rp lem & dk brn 15 15
493 A244 40rp multi 32 28
494 A244 65rp multi 52 52
495 A244 1.50fr multi 1.25 1.10

11th Winter Olympic Games, Sapporo, Japan, Feb. 3-13, 1972.

1972, Mar. 16 Photo. *Perf. 11*

Designs (Olympic Rings and): 10rp, Gymnast. 20rp, High jump. 40rp, Running, women's. 60rp, Discus. (All horiz.).

496 A244 10rp cl, brn & gray 15 15
497 A244 20rp ol, brn & yel 20 20
498 A244 40rp red, brn & gray 35 35
499 A244 60rp brn, dk brn & bl 70 55

20th Olympic Games, Munich, Aug. 26-Sept. 10.

Flower Type of 1970

Flowers: 20rp, Anemone. 30rp, Turk's cap. 60rp, Alpine centaury. 1.20fr, Reed mace.

1972, Mar. 16
500 A238 20rp dk bl & multi 16 15
501 A238 30rp ol & multi 24 16
502 A238 60rp multi 52 52
503 A238 1.20fr multi 1.00 1.00

Europa Issue, 1972

Common Design Type

1972, Mar. 16
504 CD15 40rp dk ol, bl grn & rose red 60 50

Souvenir Sheet

Bendern and Vaduz Castle — A246

1972, June 8 Engr. *Perf. 13½*
505 A246 Sheet of 2 2.75 2.75
a. 1fr violet blue 90 90
b. 2fr carmine 1.75 1.75

8th Liechtenstein Philatelic Exhibition, LIBA 1972, Vaduz, Aug. 18-27.

Faun, by Rudolf Schädler A247

Madonna with Angels, by Ferdinand Nigg A248

1972, Sept. 7 Photo. *Perf. 11½*
506 A247 20rp shown 16 15
507 A247 30rp Dancer 25 22
508 A247 1.10fr Owl 95 80

Sculptures made of roots and branches by Rudolf Schädler.

Portrait Type of 1968-69

Portraits: 30rp, Emilio Diena. 40rp, André de Cock. 1.30fr, Theodore E. Steinway.

1972, Sept. 7 Engr. *Perf. 14x13½*
509 A232 30rp Prus grn 22 20
510 A232 40rp dk vio brn 35 30
511 A232 1.30fr vio bl 1.10 1.00

Pioneers of Philately.

1972, Dec. 7 Photo. *Perf. 11½*
512 A248 30rp blk & multi 30 28

Christmas 1972.

Lawena Springs — A249

Nautilus Cup — A250

Landscapes: 5rp, Silum. 15rp, Ruggell Marsh. 25rp, Steg, Kirchlispitz. 30rp, Fields, Schellenberg. 40rp, Rennhof, Mauren. 50rp, Tidrüfe Vaduz. 60rp, Eschner Riet. 70rp, Mittagspitz. 80rp, Three Sisters, Schaan Forest. 1fr, St. Peter's and Tower House, Mäls. 1.30fr, Road, Frommenhaus. 1.50fr, Ox Head Mountain. 1.80fr, Hehlawangspitz. 2fr, Saminaschlucht.

1972-73 Engr. & Litho. *Perf. 11½*
513 A249 5rp brn, yel & mag 15 15
514 A249 10rp sl grn & cit 15 15
515 A249 15rp red brn & cit 15 15
516 A249 25rp dk vio & pale grn 24 18
517 A249 30rp pur & buff 28 22
518 A249 40rp vio & pale sal 35 28
519 A249 50rp vio bl & rose 45 35
520 A249 60rp grn & yel 55 45
521 A249 70rp dk & lt bl 65 52
522 A249 80rp Prus grn & cit 70 55
523 A249 1fr red brn & lt grn 95 65
524 A249 1.30fr ultra & lt grn 1.25 1.00
525 A249 1.50fr brn & lt bl 1.40 1.00
526 A249 1.80fr brn & buff 1.65 1.25
527 A249 2fr sep & pale grn 1.75 1.40
Nos. 513-527 (15) 10.67 8.30

Issue dates: 10rp, 15rp, 80rp, 1fr, 1.50fr, Dec. 7. 30rp, 1.30fr, 1.80fr, Mar. 8, 1973. 50rp, 60rp, 70rp, June 7, 1973. 5rp, 25rp, 40rp, 2fr, Dec. 6, 1973.

Europa Issue, 1973

Common Design Type

1973, Mar. 8 Photo. *Perf. 11½*
Size: 33x23mm
528 CD16 30rp pur & multi 30 30
529 CD16 40rp bl & multi 45 45

1973, June 7 Photo. *Perf. 11½*

Designs: 70rp, Ivory tankard. 1.10fr, Silver goblet.

530 A250 30rp gray & multi 24 24
531 A250 70rp multi 55 55
532 A250 1.10fr dk bl & multi 95 95

Drinking vessels from the Princely Treasury.

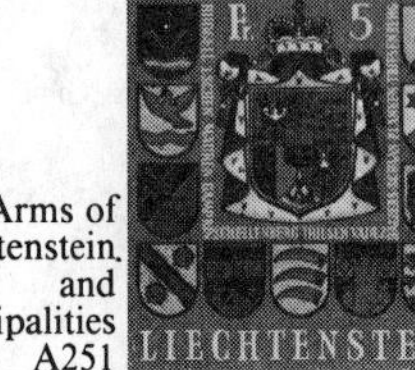

Arms of Liechtenstein and Municipalities A251

Engraved & Photogravure
1973, Sept. 6 *Perf. 14x13½*
533 A251 5fr blk & multi 4.00 3.00

Coenonympha Oedippus A252

Designs: 15rp, Alpine newt. 25rp, European viper (adder). 40rp, Common curlew. 60rp, Edible frog. 70rp, Dappled butterfly. 80rp, Grass snake. 1.10fr, Three-toed woodpecker.

1973-74 Photo. *Perf. 11½*
534 A252 15rp multi 15 15
535 A252 25rp multi 28 28
536 A252 30rp org & multi 25 25
537 A252 40rp brn & multi 35 35
538 A252 60rp multi 60 60
539 A252 70rp multi 65 60
540 A252 80rp multi 70 70
541 A252 1.10fr multi 1.00 1.00
Nos. 534-541 (8) 3.98 3.93

Issue dates: 30rp, 40rp, 60rp, 80rp, Dec. 6. Others, June 6, 1974.

Virgin and Child, by Bartolomeo di Tommaso A253

The Vociferant Horseman, by Andrea Riccio A254

Engraved & Lithographed
1973, Dec. 6 *Perf. 13½*
542 A253 30rp gold & multi 38 30

Christmas 1973.

1974, Mar. 21 Photo. *Perf. 11½*

Europa: 40rp, Kneeling Venus, by Antonio Susini.

543 A254 30rp tan & multi 42 35
544 A254 40rp ultra & multi 60 50

Chinese Vase, 19th Century A255

Soccer A256

Designs: Chinese vases from Princely Treasury.

1974, Mar. 21
545 A255 30rp shown 32 32
546 A255 50rp from 1740 50 50
547 A255 60rp from 1830 65 65
548 A255 1fr circa 1700 1.10 1.10

1974, Mar. 21
549 A256 80rp lem & multi 80 75

World Soccer Championships, Munich June 13-July 7.

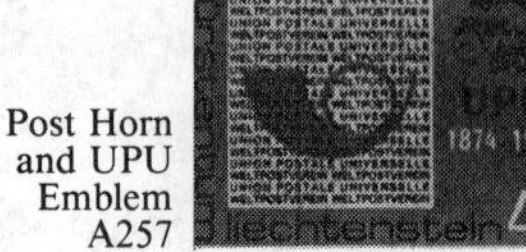

Post Horn and UPU Emblem A257

1974, June 6 *Perf. 13½*
550 A257 40rp gold, grn & blk 35 28
551 A257 60rp gold, red & blk 52 42

Centenary of Universal Postal Union.

Bishop F. A. Marxer — A258

Photogravure and Engraved
1974, June 6 *Perf. 14x13½*
552 A258 1fr multi 85 85

Bicentenary of the death of Bishop Franz Anton Marxer (1703-1775).

Prince Constantin A259

Prince Hans Adam — A260

Princess Gina and Prince Franz Joseph II — A261

Designs: 80rp, Prince Maximilian. 1.20fr, Prince Alois.

1974-75 Photo. *Perf. 11½*
553 A259 70rp dk grn & gold 70 55
554 A259 80rp dp cl & gold 75 65
555 A259 1.20fr bluish blk & gold 1.10 1.00

Engr.
Perf. 14x13½
556 A260 1.70fr slate grn 1.40 1.25

Photogravure and Engraved
Perf. 13½x14
557 A261 10fr gold & choc 8.00 8.00

No. 557 printed in sheets of 4.

Issue dates: 1.70fr, Dec. 5, 1974; 10fr, Sept. 5, 1974; others, Mar. 13, 1975.

St. Florian — A262

Designs: 50rp, St. Wendelin. 60rp, Virgin Mary with Sts. Anna and Joachim. 70rp, Nativity.

1974, Dec. 5 Photo. *Perf. 12*

560	A262	30rp multi	28	22
561	A262	50rp multi	40	35
562	A262	60rp multi	55	50
563	A262	70rp multi	70	65

Designs are from 19th century devotional glass paintings. Christmas 1974.

"Cold Sun," by Martin Frommelt A263

Europa: 60rp, "Village," by Louis Jaeger.

1975, Mar. 13 *Perf. 11½*

564	A263	30rp multi	28	28
565	A263	60rp multi	60	60

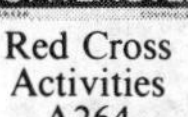

Red Cross Activities A264

Imperial Crown A266

Coronation Robe — A265

1975, June 5 Photo. *Perf. 11½*

566	A264	60rp dk bl & multi	55	55

30th anniversary of the Liechtenstein Red Cross.

1975 Engr. & Photo. *Perf. 14*

567	A266	30rp Imperial cross	55	45
568	A266	60rp Imperial sword	85	75
569	A266	1fr Orb	1.75	1.40
570	A265	1.30fr shown	21.00	18.00
571	A266	2fr shown	4.25	3.00
		Nos. 567-571 (5)	28.40	23.60

Treasures of the Holy Roman Empire from the Treasury of the Hofburg in Vienna, Austria.

Issue dates: 1.30fr, Sept. 4; others, June 5.

See Nos. 617-620.

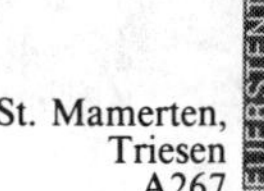

St. Mamerten, Triesen A267

Designs: 50rp, Red House, Vaduz, 14th century. 70rp, Prebendary House, Eschen, 14th century. 1fr, Gutenberg Castle.

1975, Sept. 4 Photo. *Perf. 11½*

572	A267	40rp multi	45	38
573	A267	50rp multi	48	40
574	A267	70rp plum & multi	95	95
575	A267	1fr dk bl & multi	1.25	1.25

European Architectural Heritage Year 1975.

Speed Skating A268

Designs (Olympic Rings and): 25rp, Ice hockey. 70rp, Downhill skiing. 1.20fr, Slalom.

1975, Dec. 4 Photo. *Perf. 11½*

576	A268	20rp multi	18	15
577	A268	25rp multi	22	18
578	A268	70rp multi	60	50
579	A268	1.20fr yel & multi	1.10	95

12th Winter Olympic Games, Innsbruck, Austria, Feb. 4-15, 1976.

Daniel in the Lions' Den A269

River Crayfish A270

Designs: 60rp, Virgin and Child. 90rp, St. Peter. All designs are after Romanesque sculptured capitals in Chur Cathedral, c. 1208.

Photogravure and Engraved

1975, Dec. 4 *Perf. 14*

580	A269	30rp gold & pur	22	22
581	A269	60rp gold & grn	40	40
582	A269	90rp gold & claret	75	75

Christmas and Holy Year 1975.

1976, Mar. 11 Photo. *Perf. 11½*

World Wildlife Fund: 40rp, European pond turtle. 70rp, Old-world otter. 80rp, Lapwing.

583	A270	25rp multi	32	32
584	A270	40rp multi	50	50
585	A270	70rp multi	85	85
586	A270	80rp multi	1.25	1.25

Mouflon — A271

Europa: 80rp, Pheasant family. Ceramics by Prince Hans von Liechtenstein.

1976, Mar. 11

587	A271	40rp multi	48	42
588	A271	80rp vio & multi	1.00	85

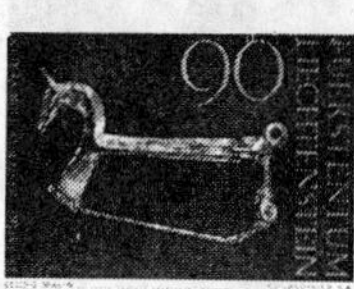

Roman Fibula, 3rd Century A272

1976, Mar. 11

589	A272	90rp vio bl, grn & gold	1.00	80

Historical Association of Liechtenstein, 75th anniversary.

Souvenir Sheet

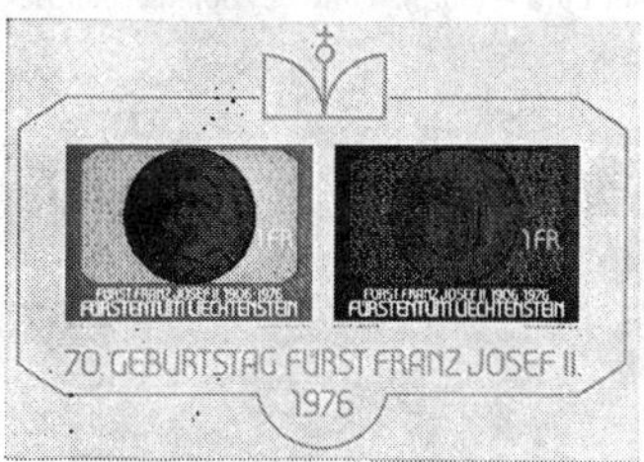

Franz Josef II 50fr-Memorial Coin — A273

1976, June 10 Photo. *Imperf.*

590	A273	Sheet of 2	1.75	1.75
a.		1fr blue & multi	85	85
b.		1fr red & multi	85	85

70th birthday of Prince Franz Joseph II of Liechtenstein.

Judo and Olympic Rings — A274

Rubens' Sons, Albrecht and Nikolas — A275

Designs (Olympic Rings and): 50rp, volleyball. 80rp, Relay race. 1.10fr, Long jump, women's.

1976, June 10 *Perf. 11½*

591	A274	35rp multi	30	30
592	A274	50rp multi	48	48
593	A274	80rp multi	70	70
594	A274	1.10fr multi	95	95

21st Olympic Games, Montreal, Canada, July 17-Aug. 1.

1976, Sept. 9 Engr. *Perf. 13½x14*

Rubens Paintings: 50rp, Singing Angels. 1fr, The Daughters of Cecrops (horiz.). (from Collection of Prince of Liechtenstein).

Size: 24x38mm

595	A275	50rp gold & multi	1.40	1.40
596	A275	70rp gold & multi	2.00	2.00

Size: 48x38mm

597	A275	1fr gold & multi	5.25	5.25

400th anniversary of the birth of Peter Paul Rubens (1577-1640), Flemish painter. Sheets of 8 (2x4).

Zodiac Signs — A276

1976-78 Photo. *Perf. 11½*

598	A276	20rp Pisces	22	22
599	A276	40rp Aries	38	38
600	A276	40rp Cancer ('77)	45	42
601	A276	40rp Scorpio ('78)	50	45
602	A276	50rp Sagittarius ('78)	55	50
603	A276	70rp Leo ('77)	75	75
604	A276	80rp Taurus	85	80
605	A276	80rp Virgo ('77)	85	85
606	A276	80rp Capricorn ('78)	85	80
607	A276	90rp Gemini	1.10	85
608	A276	1.10fr Libra ('77)	1.25	1.25
609	A276	1.50fr Aquarius	1.50	1.50
		Nos. 598-609 (12)	9.25	8.77

Flight into Egypt A277

Ortlieb von Brandis, Sarcophagus A278

Monastic Wax Works: 20rp, Holy Infant of Prague (horiz.). 80rp, Holy Family and Trinity. 1.50fr, Holy Family (horiz.).

1976, Dec. 9 Photo. *Perf. 11½*

610	A277	20rp multi	20	20
611	A277	50rp multi	40	40
612	A277	80rp multi	55	55
613	A277	1.50fr multi	1.25	1.25

Christmas 1976.

Photogravure and Engraved

1976, Dec. 9 *Perf. 13½x14*

614	A278	1.10fr gold & dk brn	90	70

Ortlieb von Brandis, Bishop of Chur (1458-1491).

Map of Liechtenstein, by J. J. Heber, 1721 — A279

Europa: 80rp, View of Vaduz, by Ferdinand Bachmann, 1815.

1977, Mar. 10 Photo. *Perf. 12½*

615	A279	40rp multi	45	45
616	A279	80rp multi	90	90

Treasure Type of 1975

Designs: 40rp, Holy Lance and Particle of the Cross. 50rp, Imperial Evangel of St. Matthew. 80rp, St. Stephen's Purse. 90rp, Tabard of Imperial Herald.

Engraved and Photogravure

1977, June 8 *Perf. 14*

617	A266	40rp gold & multi	40	32
618	A266	50rp gold & multi	48	45
619	A266	80rp gold & multi	75	65
620	A266	90rp gold & multi	1.10	1.00

Treasures of the Holy Roman Empire from the Treasury of the Hofburg in Vienna.

Emperor Constantius II Coin — A280

Coins: 70rp, Lindau bracteate, c. 1300. 80rp, Ortlieb von Brandis, 1458-1491.

1977, June 8 Photo. *Perf. 11½*

Granite Paper

621	A280	35rp gold & multi	35	28
622	A280	70rp sil & multi	60	52
623	A280	80rp sil & multi	80	65

Frauenthal Castle — A281

Castles: 50rp, Gross Ullersdorf. 80rp, Liechtenstein Castle near Mödling, Austria. 90rp, Liechtenstein Palace, Vienna.

Engraved and Photogravure

1977, Sept. 8 *Perf. 13½x14*

624	A281	20rp sl grn & gold	20	20
625	A281	50rp mag & gold	55	55
626	A281	80rp dk vio & gold	90	90
627	A281	90rp dk bl & gold	1.00	1.00

Children — A282

Traditional Costumes: 70rp, Two girls. 1fr, Woman in festival dress.

1977, Sept. 8 Photo. *Perf. 11½*
Granite Paper

628	A282	40rp multi	50	42
629	A282	70rp multi	75	70
630	A282	1fr multi	1.25	1.10

Princess Tatjana A283

1977, Dec. 7 Photo. *Perf. 11½*

631	A283	1.10fr brown & gold	90	85

Angel — A284

Liechtenstein Palace, Vienna — A285

Sculptures by Erasmus Kern: 50rp, St. Rochus. 80rp, Virgin and Child. 1.50fr, God the Father.

1977, Dec. 7

632	A284	20rp multi	18	18
633	A284	50rp multi	50	50
634	A284	80rp multi	80	80
635	A284	1.50fr multi	1.65	1.65

Christmas 1977.

Photogravure and Engraved
1978, Mar. 2 *Perf. 14*

Europa: 80rp, Feldsberg Castle.

636	A285	40rp gold & slate bl	42	42
637	A285	80rp gold & claret	85	85

Residential Tower, Balzers-Mäls — A286

Designs: 10rp, Farmhouse, Triesen. 20rp, Houses, Upper Village, Triesen. 35rp, Barns, Balzers. 40rp, Monastery, Bendern. 70rp, Parish house. 80rp, Farmhouse, Schellenberg. 90rp, Parish house, Balzers. 1fr, Rheinberger House, Music School, Vaduz. 1.10fr, Street, Mitteldorf, Vaduz. 1.50fr, Town Hall, Triesenberg. 2fr, National Museum and Administrator's Residence, Vaduz.

1978 Photo. *Perf. 11½*

638	A286	10rp multi	15	15
639	A286	20rp multi	16	16
640	A286	35rp multi	28	28
641	A286	40rp multi	30	30
642	A286	50rp multi	40	40
643	A286	70rp multi	55	55
644	A286	80rp multi	60	60
645	A286	90rp multi	70	70
646	A286	1fr multi	75	75
647	A286	1.10fr multi	90	90
648	A286	1.50fr multi	1.10	1.10
649	A286	2fr multi	1.50	1.50
		Nos. 638-649 (12)	7.39	7.39

Vaduz Castle — A287

Vaduz Castle: 50rp, Courtyard. 70rp, Staircase. 80rp, Triptych from High Altar, Castle Chapel.

Engraved and Photogravure
1978, June 1 *Perf. 13½x14*

650	A287	40rp gold & multi	52	52
651	A287	50rp gold & multi	70	70
652	A287	70rp gold & multi	1.00	1.00
653	A287	80rp gold & multi	1.25	1.25

40th anniversary of reign of Prince Franz Joseph II. Sheet of 8.

Prince Karl I, Coin, 1614 A288

Adoration of the Shepherds A289

Designs: 50rp, Prince Johann Adam, medal, 1694. 80rp, Prince Josef Wenzel, medal, 1773.

1978, Sept. 7 Photo. *Perf. 11½*

654	A288	40rp multi	42	42
655	A288	50rp multi	60	60
656	A288	80rp multi	1.10	1.10

1978, Dec. 7 Photo. *Perf. 11½*

Stained-glass Windows, Triesenberg: 50rp, Holy Family. 80rp, Adoration of the Kings.

657	A289	20rp multi	22	22
658	A289	50rp multi	55	55
659	A289	80rp multi	85	85

Christmas 1978.

Piebald, by Hamilton and Faistenberger A290

Golden Carriage of Prince Joseph Wenzel, by Martin von Meytens — A291

Design: 80rp, Black stallion, by Johann Georg von Hamilton.

Photo. & Engr.
1978, Dec. 7 *Perf. 13½x14*

660	A290	70rp multi	60	60
661	A290	80rp multi	70	70

Perf. 12

662	A291	1.10fr multi	95	95

Sheets of 8.

Mail Plane over Schaan A292

Europa: 80rp, Zeppelin over Vaduz Castle.

1979, Mar. 8 Photo. *Perf. 11½*

663	A292	40rp multi	80	80
664	A292	80rp multi	95	95

First airmail service, St. Gallen to Schaan, Aug. 31, 1930, and first Zeppelin flight to Liechtenstein, June 10, 1931.

Child Drinking — A293

Designs: 90rp, Child eating. 1.10fr, Child reading.

1979, Mar. 8

665	A293	80rp sil & multi	75	70
666	A293	90rp sil & multi	85	85
667	A293	1.10fr sil & multi	95	95

International Year of the Child.

Ordered Wave Fields A294

Sun over Continents A296

Council of Europe A295

1979, June 7 Litho. *Perf. 11½*

668	A294	50rp multi	38	38

Photo.

669	A295	80rp multi	75	75
670	A296	100rp multi	75	75

Intl. Radio Consultative Committee (CCIR) of the Intl. Telecommunications Union, 50th anniv. (50rp); Entry into Council of Europe (80rp); aid to developing countries (100rp).

Heraldic Panel of Carl Ludwig von Sulz — A297

Heraldic Panels of: 70rp, Barbara von Sulz, nee zu Staufen. 1.10fr, Ulrich von Ramschwag and Barbara von Hallwil.

Photogravure and Engraved
1979, June 1 *Perf. 13½*

671	A297	40rp multi	30	30
672	A297	70rp multi	52	52
673	A297	1.10fr multi	95	95

Sts. Lucius and Florin, Fresco in Waltensburg-Vuorz Church — A298

Photogravure and Engraved
1979, Sept. 6 *Perf. 13½*

674	A298	20fr multi	14.00	14.00

Patron saints of Liechtenstein. Printed in sheets of 4.

Annunciation, Embroidery — A299

Christmas 1979 (Ferdnand Nigg Embroideries): 50rp, Christmas. 80rp, Blessed Are the Peacemakers.

1979, Dec. 6 Engr. *Perf. 13½*

675	A299	20rp multi	20	20
676	A299	50rp multi	45	45
677	A299	80rp multi	70	70

Cross-Country Skiing — A300

Olympic Rings and: 70rp, Oxhead Mountain. 1.50fr, Ski lift.

1979, Dec. 6 Photo. *Perf. 12*

678	A300	40rp multi	30	28
679	A300	70rp multi	55	52
680	A300	1.50fr multi	1.25	1.10

13th Winter Olympic Games, Lake Placid, NY, Feb. 12-24, 1980.

Arms of Bailiff Andreas Buchel, 1690 — A301

Designs: Various arms.

1980, Mar. 10 Photo. *Perf. 11½*
Granite Paper

681 A301 40rp shown 30 30
682 A301 70rp Georg Marxer, 1745 50 50
683 A301 80rp Luzius Frick, 1503 60 60
684 A301 1.10fr Adam Oehri, 1634 95 95

See Nos. 704-707, 729-732.

Princess Maria Leopoldine Esterhazy, by Antonio Canova — A302

Europa: 80rp, Maria Theresa, Duchess of Savoy, by Martin van Meytens.

1980, Mar. 10

685 A302 40rp multi 1.00 1.00
686 A302 80rp multi 1.00 1.00

Milking Pail A303

Liechtenstein A304

Old Alpine Farm Tools: 50rp, Wooden heart, ceremonial cattle decoration. 80rp, Butter churn.

1980, Sept. 8

687 A303 20rp multi 18 18
688 A303 50rp multi 42 42
689 A303 80rp multi 75 75

1980, Sept 8

690 A304 80rp multi 75 75

Postal Museum, 50th anniversary.

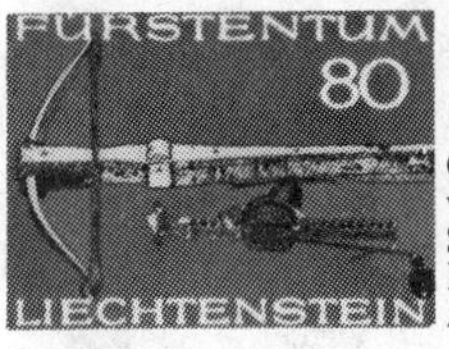

Crossbow with Spanning Device A305

1980, Sept. 8 Engr. *Perf. 13½x14*

691 A305 80rp shown 70 70
692 A305 90rp Spear, knife 75 75
693 A305 1.10fr Rifle, powderhorn 1.00 1.00

Triesenberg Family In Traditional Costumes A306

1980, Sept. 8 Photo. *Perf. 12*
Granite Paper

694 A306 40rp shown 35 35
695 A306 70rp Folk dancers, Schellenberg 55 55
696 A306 80rp Brass band, Mauren 65 65

Green Beeches, Matrula Forest — A307

Glad Tidings — A308

Photogravure and Engraved
1980, Dec. 9 *Perf. 14*

697 A307 40rp shown 35 35
698 A307 50rp White firs, Valorsch Valley 45 45
699 A307 80rp Beech forest, Schaan 65 65
700 A307 1.50fr Forest, Oberplanken 1.25 1.25

1980, Dec. 9 Photo. *Perf. 11½*
Granite Paper

701 A308 20rp shown 18 18
702 A308 50rp Creche 45 45
703 A308 80rp Epiphany 70 70

Christmas 1980.

Bailiff Arms Type of 1980

1981, Mar. 9 Photo. *Perf. 11½*
Granite Paper

704 A301 40rp Anton Meier, 1748 32 32
705 A301 70rp Kaspar Kindle, 1534 55 55
706 A301 80rp Hans Adam Negele, 1600 65 65
707 A301 1.10fr Peter Matt, 1693 1.00 1.00

Fireworks at Vaduz Castle — A309

Europa: 80rp, National Day procession.

1981, Mar. 9 *Perf. 12½*
Granite Paper

708 A309 40rp multi 52 52
709 A309 80rp multi 1.00 1.00

Souvenir Sheet

Prince Alois, Princess Elisabeth and Prince Franz Joseph II — A310

1981, June 9 Photo. *Perf. 13*
Granite Paper

710 Sheet of 3 2.50 2.50
a. A310 70rp shown 50 50
b. A310 80rp Princes Alois and Franz Joseph II 55 55
c. A310 150rp Prince Franz Joseph II 1.00 1.00

75th birthday of Prince Franz Joseph II.

Scout Emblems A311

Man in Wheelchair A312

1981, June 9

711 A311 20rp multi 18 18

50th anniversary of Boy Scouts and Girl Guides.

1981, June 9

712 A312 40rp multi 28 28

International Year of the Disabled.

St. Theodul, 1600th Birth Anniv. — A313

Mosses and Lichens — A314

1981, June 9

713 A313 80rp multi 55 55

Photogravure and Engraved
1981, Sept. 7 *Perf. 13½*

714 A314 40rp Xanthoria parietina 30 30
715 A314 50rp Parmelia physodes 38 38
716 A314 70rp Sphagnum palustre 52 52
717 A314 80rp Amblystegium 60 60

Gutenberg Castle — A315

1981, Sept. 7

718 A315 20rp shown 15 15
719 A315 40rp Castle yard 30 30
720 A315 50rp Parlor 38 38
721 A315 1.10fr Great Hall 90 90

St. Charles Borromeo (1538-1584) A316

St. Nicholas A317

Famous Visitors to Liechtenstein (Paintings): 70rp, Goethe (1749-1832), by Angelica Kauffmann. 80rp, Alexander Dumas (1824-1895). 1fr, Hermann Hesse (1877-1962), by Cuno Amiet.

Lithographed and Engraved
1981, Dec. 7 *Perf. 14*

722 A316 40rp multi 35 35
723 A316 70rp multi 60 60
724 A316 80rp multi 70 70
725 A316 1fr multi 80 80

See Nos. 747-750.

1981, Dec. 7 Photo. *Perf. 11½*
Granite Paper

726 A317 20rp shown 18 18
727 A317 50rp Adoration of the Kings 45 45
728 A317 80rp Holy Family 70 70

Christmas 1981.

Bailiff Arms Type of 1980

1982, Mar. 8 Photo.
Granite Paper

729 A301 40rp Johann Kaiser, 1664 35 35
730 A301 70rp Joseph Anton Kaufmann, 1748 55 55
731 A301 80rp Christoph Walser, 1690 70 70
732 A301 1.10fr Stephan Banzer, 1658 1.00 1.00

Europa 1982 — A318

1982, Mar. 8
Granite Paper

733 A318 40rp Peasants' Uprising, 1525 35 35
734 A318 80rp Imperial Direct Rule, 1396 70 70

Hereditary Prince Hans Adam — A319

1982, June 7 Granite Paper

735 A319 1fr shown 75 75
736 A319 1fr Princess Marie Aglae 75 75

LIBA '82, 10th Liechtenstein Philatelic Exhibition, Vaduz, July 31-Aug. 8.

1982 World Cup — A320

Designs: Sports arenas.

1982, June 7 Granite Paper

737 A320 15rp Triesenberg 15 15
738 A320 25rp Mauren 18 18
739 A320 1.80fr Balzers 1.40 1.40

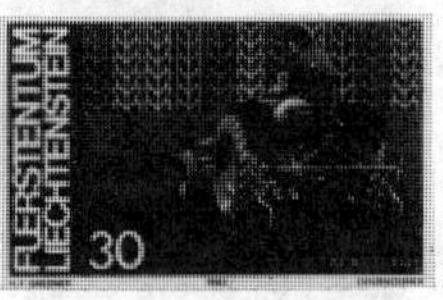

Farming A321

1982, Sept. 20 Photo. *Perf. 11½*
Granite Paper

740 A321 30rp shown 22 22
741 A321 50rp Horticulture 38 38
742 A321 70rp Forestry 52 52
743 A321 150rp Dairy farming 1.10 1.10

The Catalogue editors cannot undertake to appraise, identify or judge the genuineness or condition of stamps.

View of Neu-Schellenberg, 1861, by Moriz Menzinger (1832-1914) — A322

Photogravure and Engraved

1982, Sept. 20 *Perf. 13½x14*

744 A322 40rp shown 30 30
745 A322 50rp Vaduz, 1860 35 35
746 A322 100rp Bendern, 1868 85 85

Visitor Type of 1981

Paintings: 40rp, Emperor Maximilian I (1459-1519), by Bernhard Strigel. 70rp, Georg Jenatsch (1596-1639). 80rp, Angelika Kaufmann (1741-1807), self portrait. 1fr, Fidelis von Sigmaringen (1577-1622).

1982, Dec. 6 *Perf. 14*

747 A316 40rp multi 30 30
748 A316 70rp multi 52 52
749 A316 80rp multi 60 60
750 A316 1fr multi 75 75

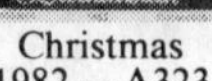

Christmas 1982 — A323

Europa 1983 — A324

Designs: Chur Cathedral sculptures.

1982, Dec. 6 Photo. *Perf. 11½*
Granite Paper

751 A323 20rp Angel playing lute 16 16
752 A323 50rp Virgin and Child 40 40
753 A323 80rp Angel playing organ 65 65

1983, Mar. 7 **Photo.**

Designs: 40rp, Notker Balbulus of St. Gall (840-912), Benedictine monk, poet and liturgical composer. 80rp, St. Hildegard of Bingen (1098-1179).

754 A324 40rp multi 32 32
755 A324 80rp multi 60 60

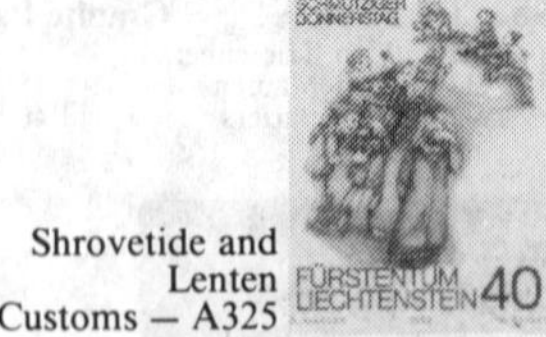

Shrovetide and Lenten Customs — A325

Designs: 40rp, Last Thursday before Lent. 70rp, Begging for eggs on Shrove Tuesday. 180fr, Bonfire, first Sunday in Lent.

Photogravure and Engraved

1983, Mar. 7 *Perf. 14*

756 A325 40rp multi 35 35
757 A325 70rp multi 60 60
758 A325 1.80fr multi 1.50 1.50

See Nos. 844-846, 915-917.

Landscapes by Anton Ender (b. 1898) — A326

1983, June 6 Photo. *Perf. 12*

759 A326 40rp Schaan, on the Zollstrasse 35 35
760 A326 50rp Balzers with Gutenberg Castle 42 42
761 A326 2fr Stag by the Reservoir 1.75 1.75

Protection of Shores and Coasts — A327

1983, June 6

762 A327 20rp shown 80 80
763 A327 40rp Manned flight bicentenary 30 30
764 A327 50rp World communications year 38 38
765 A327 80rp Humanitarian aid 60 60

Pope John Paul II — A328

1983, Sept. 5 **Photo.**

766 A328 80rp multi 1.00 1.00

Princess Gina — A329

1983, Sept. 5 *Perf. 12x11½*

767 A329 2.50fr shown 2.25 2.25
768 A329 3fr Prince Franz Joseph II 2.75 2.75

Christmas 1983 — A330

1983, Dec. 5 Photo. *Perf. 12*
Granite Paper

769 A330 20rp Seeking shelter 16 16
770 A330 50rp Child Jesus 42 42
771 A330 80rp The Three Magi 70 70

1984 Winter Olympics, Sarajevo — A331

Snowflakes.

1983, Dec. 5 Photo. *Perf. 11½x12*
Granite Paper

772 A331 40rp multi 40 40
773 A331 80rp multi 80 80
774 A331 1.80fr multi 1.65 1.65

Famous Visitors to Liechtenstein A332

Paintings: 40rp, Count Alexander Wassiljewitsch Suworow-Rimnikski (1730-1800), Austro-Russian Army general. 70rp, Karl Rudolf Count von Buol-Schauenstein (1760-1833). 80rp, Carl Zuckmayer (1896-1977), playwright. 1fr, Curt Goetz (1888-1960), actor and playwright.

Photogravure and Engraved

1984, Mar. 12 *Perf. 14*

775 A332 40rp multi 40 40
776 A332 70rp multi 70 70
777 A332 80rp multi 80 80
778 A332 1fr multi 1.00 1.00

Europa (1959-1984) A333

1984, Mar. 12 Photo. *Perf. 12*
Granite Paper

779 A333 50rp multi 45 45
780 A333 80rp multi 70 70

The Destruction of Trisona Fairy Tale Illustrations A334

Root Carvings by Beni Gassner.

Photogravure and Engraved

1984, June 12 *Perf. 14*

781 A334 35rp Warning messenger 35 35
782 A334 50rp Buried town 50 50
783 A334 80rp Spared family 80 80

1984 Summer Olympics A335

1984, June 12 Photo. *Perf. 11½*
Granite Paper

784 A335 70rp Pole vault 75 75
785 A335 80rp Discus 85 85
786 A335 1fr Shot put 1.10 1.10

Industries and Occupations — A336

1984, Sept. 10 Photo. *Perf. 11½*

787 A336 5rp Banking & trading 15 15
788 A336 10rp Construction, plumbing 15 15
789 A336 20rp Production, factory worker 22 22
790 A336 35rp Contracting, draftswoman 35 35
791 A336 45rp Manufacturing, sales rep 45 45
792 A336 50rp Catering 50 50
793 A336 60rp Carpentry 60 60
794 A336 70rp Public health 70 70
795 A336 80rp Industrial research 80 80
796 A336 1fr Masonry 1.00 1.00
797 A336 1.20fr Industrial management 1.25 1.25
798 A336 1.50fr Posta & communications 1.50 1.50
Nos. 787-798 (12) 7.67 7.67

Princess Marie Aglae — A337

Christmas 1984 — A338

Photogravure and Engraved

1984, Dec. 10 *Perf. 14x13½*

799 A337 1.70fr shown 1.65 1.65
800 A337 2fr Prince Hans Adam 2.00 2.00

1984, Dec. 10 Photo. *Perf. 11*

801 A338 35rp Annunciation 35 35
802 A338 50rp Holy Family 52 52
803 A338 80rp Three Kings 80 75

Europa 1985 — A339

1985, Mar. 11 Photo. *Perf. 11½*

804 A339 50rp Three Muses 48 48
805 A339 80rp Pan and Muses 75 75

Orders and Monestaries A340

Photogravure and Engraved

1985, Mar. 11 *Perf. 13½x14*

806 A340 50rp St. Elisabeth 60 60
807 A340 1fr Schellenberg Convent 1.25 1.25
808 A340 1.70fr Gutenberg Mission 2.00 2.00

Cardinal Virtues — A341

1985, June 10 Photo. *Perf. 11½x12*

809 A341 35rp Justice 40 40
810 A341 50rp Temperance 55 55
811 A341 70rp Prudence 75 75
812 A341 1fr Fortitude 1.10 1.10

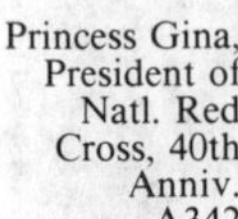

Princess Gina, President of Natl. Red Cross, 40th Anniv. A342

Portrait and: 20rp, Helping refugees, 1945. 50rp, Rescue service. 1.20fr, Child refugees, 1979.

1985, June 10 *Perf. 12x11½*

813 A342 20rp multi 22 22
814 A342 50rp multi 55 55
815 A342 1.20fr multi 1.40 1.40

Souvenir Sheet

State Visit of Pope John Paul II — A343

Designs: 50rp, Papal coat of arms. 80rp, Chapel of St. Maria zum Trost, Dux, Schaan. 1.70fr, Our Lady of Liechtenstein, St. Mary the Comforter.

1985, Feb. 2 ***Perf. 11½***

816 Sheet of 3 4.25 4.25
a. A343 50rp multi 1.40 1.40
b. A343 80rp multi 1.40 1.40
c. A343 1.70fr multi 1.40 1.40

Paintings from the Princely Collections A344

Christmas 1985 A345

Designs: 50rp, Portrait of a Canon, by Quintin Massys (1466-1530). 1fr, Portrait of Clara Serena Rubens, by Peter Paul Rubens (1577-1640). 1.20fr, Portrait of the Duke of Urbino, by Raphael (1483-1520).

Photogravure and Engraved

1985, Sept. 2 ***Perf. 14***

817 A344 50rp multi 55 55
818 A344 1fr multi 1.10 1.10
819 A344 1.20fr multi 1.40 1.40

1985, Dec. 9 **Photo.** ***Perf. 11½x12***

820 A345 35rp Frankincense 40 40
821 A345 50rp Gold 55 55
822 A345 80rp Myrrh 90 90

Kirchplatz Theater, 15th Anniv. — A346

Photogravure and Engraved

1985, Dec. 9 ***Perf. 14***

823 A346 50rp Tragedy 40 40
824 A346 80rp Commedia dell'arte 55 55
825 A346 1.50rp Opera buffa 1.75 1.75

Weapons from the Prince's Armory A347

Designs: 35rp, Halberd, bodyguard of Prince Charles I. 50rp, German morion, 16th cent. 80rp, Halberd, bodyguard of Prince Carl Eusebius.

1985, Dec. 9 ***Perf. 13½x14½***

826 A347 35rp multi 40 40
827 A347 50rp multi 55 55
828 A347 80rp multi 90 90

Europa 1986 — A348

1986, Mar. 10 **Photo.** ***Perf. 12***

829 A348 50rp Swallows 52 52
830 A348 90rp Robin 1.00 1.00

Views of Vaduz Castle A349

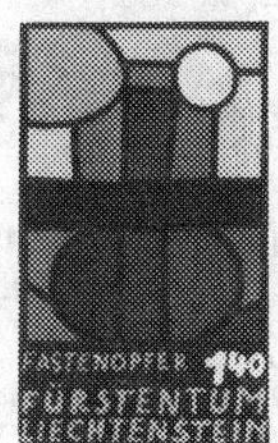

Fasting Sacrifice A350

1986-89 **Photo.** ***Perf. 11½x12***

Granite Paper

832 A349 20rp Outer courtyard 16 16
833 A349 25rp View from the south ('89) 35 35
835 A349 50rp Castle, mountains 40 40
838 A349 90rp Inner gate ('87) 1.20 1.20
840 A349 1.10fr Back view 90 90
841 A349 1.40fr Inner courtyard ('87) 1.85 1.85
Nos. 832-841 (6) 4.86 4.86

This is an expanding set. Numbers will change if necessary.

1986, Mar. 10 **Photo.** ***Perf. 12***

843 A350 1.40fr multi 1.40 1.40

Type of 1983

Photogravure and Engraved

1986, June 9 ***Perf. 13½***

844 A325 35rp shown 45 45
845 A325 50rp Wedding 65 65
846 A325 70rp Rogation Day procession 90 90

Karl Freiherr Haus von Hausen (1823-1889), Founder — A352

1986, June 9 **Photo.** ***Perf. 11½***

847 A352 50rp multi 58 58

Natl. Savings Bank, Vaduz, 125th anniv.

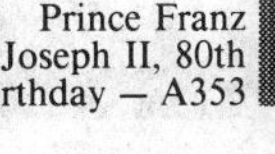

Prince Franz Joseph II, 80th Birthday — A353

Photogravure and Engraved

1986, June 9 ***Perf. 13½***

848 A353 3.50fr multi 4.50 4.50

Hunting — A354

1986, Sept. 9 ***Perf. 13x13½***

849 A354 35rp Roebuck, Ruggeller Riet 42 42
850 A354 50rp Chamois in winter, Rappenstein 60 60
851 A354 1.70fr Rutting stag, Lawena 2.05 2.05

Crops A355

1986, Sept. 9 **Photo.** ***Perf. 12x11½***

852 A355 50rp White cabbage, beets 65 65
853 A355 80rp Red cabbage 1.10 1.10
854 A355 90rp Potatoes, onions, garlic 1.25 1.25

Christmas A356

Trees A357

Archangels.

1986, Dec. 9 ***Perf. 11½***

855 A356 35rp Michael 45 40
856 A356 50rp Gabriel 65 65
857 A356 90rp Raphael 1.20 1.20

1986, Dec. 9

858 A357 25rp Silver fir 32 32
859 A357 90rp Spruce 1.20 1.20
860 A357 1.40fr Oak 1.75 1.75

Europa 1987 — A358

Nicholas Among the Thorns — A359

Modern architecture: 50rp, Primary school, 1980, Gamprin. 90rp, Parish church, c. 1960, Schellenburg.

1987, Mar. 9 **Photo.** ***Perf. 11½x12***

Granite Paper

861 A358 50rp multi 68 68
862 A358 90rp multi 1.20 1.20

1987, Mar. 9 ***Perf. 11½***

Granite Paper

863 A359 1.10fr multi 1.50 1.50

Nicholas von der Fiue (1417-1487), canonized in 1947.

Hereditary Prince Alois — A360

Fish — A361

Photo. & Engr.

1987, June 9 ***Perf. 14***

864 A360 2fr multi 2.40 2.40

No. 864 printed in sheets of 8.

1987, June 9 **Photo.** ***Perf. 11½***

865 A361 50rp Cottus gobio 60 60
866 A361 90rp Salmo trutta fario 1.10 1.10
867 A361 1.10fr Thymallus thymallus 1.40 1.40

Liechtenstein City Palace, Vienna — A362

1987, Sept. 7 **Photo.** ***Perf. 11½***

Granite Paper

868 A362 35rp Arch 48 48
869 A362 50rp Entrance 68 68
870 A362 90rp Staircase 1.20 1.20

Purchase of County of Vaduz, 275th Anniv. — A363

1987, Sept. 7 ***Perf. 11½***

871 A363 1.40fr House of Liechtenstein coat of arms 1.90 1.90

Diet, 125th Anniv. A364

1987, Sept. 7 ***Perf. 11½***

872 A364 1.70fr Constitution of 1862 2.25 2.25

Christmas — A365

The Evangelists, illuminated codices from the Golden Book, c. 1100, Abbey of Pfafers, purportedly made under the direction of monks from Reichenau Is.

Photo. & Engr.

1987, Dec. 7 **Perf. 14**

873 A365 35rp St. Matthew 30 30
874 A365 50rp St. Mark 42 42
875 A365 60rp St. Luke 50 50
876 A365 90rp St. John 75 75

1988 Winter Olympics, Calgary A366

Humorous drawings by illustrator Paul Flora of Austria: 25rp, The Toil of the Cross-country Skier. 90rp, Courageous Pioneer of Skiing. 1.10fr, As Grandfather Used to Ride on a Bobsled.

1987, Dec. 7 **Perf. 14x13½**

877 A366 25rp multi 35 35
878 A366 90rp multi 1.25 1.25
879 A366 1.10fr multi 1.50 1.50

See Nos. 888-891.

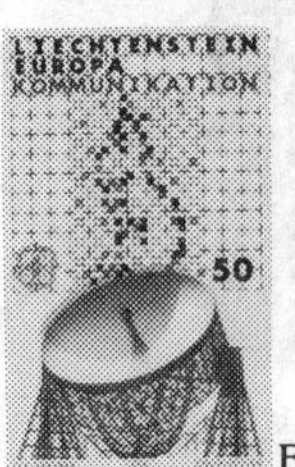

Europa 1988 — A367

Modern communication and transportation.

1988, Mar. 7 Photo. **Perf. 11½x12**

Granite Paper

880 A367 50rp Satellite dish 70 70
881 A367 90rp High-speed monorail 1.25 1.25

European Campaign to Protect Undeveloped and Developing Lands — A368

1988, Mar. 7 **Perf. 12**

Granite Paper

882 A368 80rp Forest preservation 1.10 1.10
883 A368 90rp Layout for village development 1.25 1.25
884 A368 1.70rp Traffic planning 2.25 2.25

Balancing nature conservation with natl. development.

Souvenir Sheet

Succession to the Throne — A369

Portraits: a, Crown Prince Hans-Adam. b, Prince Alois, successor to the crown prince. c, Prince Franz Josef II, ruler.

Perf. 14½x13½

1988, June 6 **Photo. & Engr.**

885 A369 Sheet of 3 4.25 4.25
a. 50rp blk, gold & brt blue 72 72
b. 50rp blk, gold & sage grn 72 72
c. 2fr blk, gold & deep rose 2.80 2.80

North and South Campaign A370

1988, June 6 Photo. **Perf. 12x11½**

Granite Paper

886 A370 50rp Public radio 72 72
887 A370 1.40fr Adult education 2.00 2.00

Cultural cooperation with Costa Rica. See Costa Rica Nos. 401-402.

Olympics Type of 1988

Humorous drawings by illustrator Paul Flora of Austria: 50rp, Cycling. 80rp, Gymnastics. 90rp, Running. 1.40fr, Equestrian.

Photo. & Engr.

1988, Sept. 5 **Perf. 14x13½**

888 A366 50rp multi 68 68
889 A366 80rp multi 1.05 1.05
890 A366 90rp multi 1.20 1.20
891 A366 1.40fr multi 1.85 1.85

Roadside Shrines A371

Christmas A372

1988, Sept. 5 Photo. **Perf. 11½x12**

Granite Paper

892 A371 25rp Kaltweh Chapel, Balzers 35 35
893 A371 35rp Oberdorf, Vaduz, c. 1870 48 48
894 A371 50rp Bangstrasse, Ruggell 68 68

1988, Dec. 5 Photo. **Perf. 11½x12**

Granite Paper

895 A372 35rp Joseph, Mary 48 48
896 A372 50rp Christ child 68 68
897 A372 90rp Adoration of the Magi 1.20 1.20

The Letter — A373

Europa 1989 — A374

Details of Portrait of Marie-Therese de Lamballe (The Letter), by Anton Hickel (1745-1798): 90rp, Handkerchief and writing materials in open desk. 2fr, Entire painting.

Photo. & Engr.

1988, Dec. 5 **Perf. 13x13½**

898 A373 50rp shown 68 68
899 A373 90rp multi 1.20 1.20
900 A373 2fr multi 2.70 2.70

1989, Mar. 6 Photo. **Perf. 11½x12**

Traditional children's games.

Granite Paper

901 A374 50rp Cat and Mouse 68 68
902 A374 90rp Stockleverband 1.20 1.20

Josef Gabriel Rheinberger (1839-1901), Composer, and Score — A375

Photo. & Engr.

1989, Mar. 6 **Perf. 14x13½**

903 A375 2.90fr multi 3.85 3.85

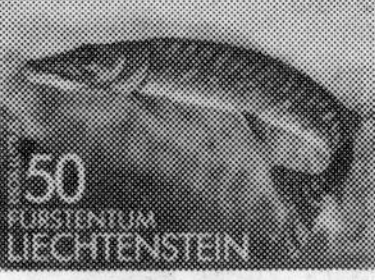

Fish — A376

1989, June 5 Photo. **Perf. 12x11½**

Granite Paper

904 A376 50rp *Esox lucius* 65 65
905 A376 1.10fr *Salmo trutta lacustris* 1.45 1.45
906 A376 1.40fr *Noemacheilus barbatulus* 1.85 1.85

World Wildlife Fund — A377

1989, June 5 **Perf. 12**

Granite Paper

907 A377 25rp *Charadrius dubuis* 32 32
908 A377 35rp *Hyla arborea* 45 45
909 A377 50rp *Libelloides coccajus* 65 65
910 A377 90rp *Putorius putorius* 1.15 1.15

Mountains A378

1989, Sept. 4 Photo. **Perf. 11½**

Granite Paper

911 A378 50rp Falknis 60 60
912 A378 75rp Plassteikopf 90 90
913 A378 80rp Naafkopf 95 95
914 A378 1.50fr Garselliturm 1.75 1.75

See Nos. 930-939.

Folklore Type of 1983

Autumn activities: 35rp, Alpine herdsman and flock return from pasture. 50rp, Shucking corn. 80rp, Cattle market.

Photo. & Engr.

1989, Sept. 4 **Perf. 14**

915 A325 35rp multi 42 42
916 A325 50rp multi 60 60
917 A325 80rp multi 95 95

Christmas — A379

Details of the triptych *Adoration of the Magi*, by Hugo van der Goes (50rp) and student (35rp, 90rp), late 15th cent.: 35rp, Melchior and Balthazar. 50rp, Caspar and holy family. 90rp, Donor with St. Stephen.

1989, Dec. 4 **Perf. 13½**

Size of 35rp and 90rp: 23x41mm

918 A379 35rp multi 45 45
919 A379 50rp shown 62 62
920 A379 90rp multi 1.10 1.10

Minerals A380

1989, Dec. 4 **Perf. 13½x13**

921 A380 50rp Scepter quartz 62 62
922 A380 1.10fr Pyrite ball 1.35 1.35
923 A380 1.50fr Calcite 1.85 1.85

Europa 1990 — A381

Postage Stamps, 150th Anniv. — A382

Post offices.

1990, Mar. 5 Photo. **Perf. 11½x12**

Granite Paper

924 A381 50rp shown 62 62
925 A381 90rp Modern p.o. 1.10 1.10

1990, Mar. 5 **Perf. 11½**

Granite Paper

926 A382 1.50fr Penny Black 1.85 1.85

1990 World Cup Soccer Championships, Italy — A383

1990, Mar. 5 Granite Paper **Perf. 12**

927 A383 2fr multicolored 2.50 2.50

Princess Gina A384

1990, June 5 Litho. **Perf. 11½**

Granite Paper

928 A384 2fr shown 2.70 2.70
929 A384 3fr Prince Franz Joseph II 4.10 4.10

1st anniv. of death.

Mountains Type of 1989

1990-91

Granite Paper

930 A378 5rp Augstenberg 15 15
931 A378 10rp Hahnenspiel 15 15
933 A378 35rp Nospitz 52 52
933A A378 40rp Ochsenkopf 52 52
934 A378 45rp Drei Schwestern 60 60
935 A378 60rp Kuhgrat 90 90
936 A378 70rp Galinakopf 95 95
938 A378 1fr Schonberg 1.35 1.35
939 A378 1.20fr Bleikaturm 1.80 1.80
Nos. 930-939 (9) 6.94 6.94

Issue dates: 5, 45, 70rp, 1fr, June 5. 10, 35, 60rp, 1.20fr, Sept. 3. 40rp, June 3, 1991.

This is an expanding set. Numbers will change if neccessary.

Paintings by Benjamin Steck (1902-1981) A385

Photo. & Engr.

1990, June 5 **Perf. 14**

942	A385	50rp shown	70	70
943	A385	80rp Fruit, dish	1.10	1.10
944	A385	1.50fr Basket, fruit, stein	2.10	2.10

Game Birds — A386

Photo. & Engr.

1990, Sept. 3 **Perf. 13x13½**

945	A386	25rp Pheasant	35	35
946	A386	50rp Blackcock	70	70
947	A386	2fr Mallard duck	2.75	2.75

European Postal Communications, 500th Anniv. — A387

1990, Dec. 3 **Perf. 13½x14**

948	A387	90rp multicolored	1.25	1.25

Lenten Cloth of Bendern — A388

Christmas: 35rp, The Annunciation. 50rp, Birth of Christ. 90rp, Adoration of the Magi.

1990, Dec. 3 **Photo.** **Perf. 12**

Granite Paper

949	A388	35rp multicolored	50	50
950	A388	50rp multicolored	72	72
951	A388	90rp multicolored	1.25	1.25

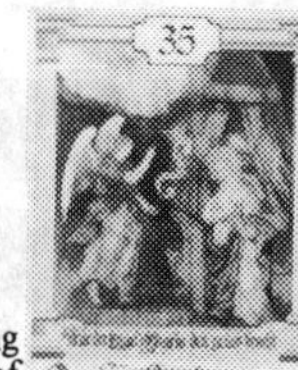

St. Nicholas Visiting Children on Feast of St. Nicholas — A389

Holiday Customs: 50rp, Waking "sleepy-heads" on New Year's Day. 1.50fr, Good wishes on New Year's Day.

Photo. & Engr.

1990, Dec. 3 **Perf. 14**

952	A389	35rp multicolored	50	50
953	A389	50rp multicolored	72	72
954	A389	1.50fr multicolored	2.15	2.15

Europa — A390

Designs: 50rp, Telecommunications satellite, Olympus I. 90rp, Weather satellite, Meteosat.

1991, Mar. 4 **Photo.** **Perf. 11½**

Granite Paper

955	A390	50rp multicolored	72	72
956	A390	90rp multicolored	1.25	1.25

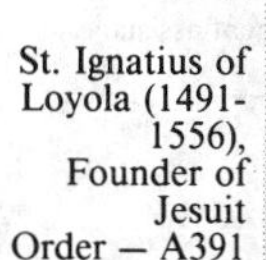

St. Ignatius of Loyola (1491-1556), Founder of Jesuit Order — A391

Designs: 90rp, Wolfgang Amadeus Mozart (1756-1791), composer.

1991, Mar. 4 **Perf. 11½**

Granite Paper

957	A391	80rp multicolored	1.15	1.15
958	A391	90rp multicolored	1.25	1.25

UN Membership, 1990 — A392

1991, Mar. 4 **Perf. 11½**

Granite Paper

959	A392	2.50fr multicolored	3.50	3.50

Swiss Confederation, 700th Anniv. — A393

Paintings: 50rp, Maloja, by Giovanni Giacometti. 80rp, Rheintal, by Ferdinand Gehr. 90rp, Bergell, by Augusto Giacometti. 1.10fr, Hoher Kasten, by Hedwig Scherrer.

1991, June 3 **Photo.** **Perf. 11½**

Granite Paper

960	A393	50rp multicolored	65	65
961	A393	80rp multicolored	1.05	1.05
962	A393	90rp multicolored	1.15	1.15
963	A393	1.10fr multicolored	1.45	1.45

Military Uniforms A394

Designs: 50rp, Non-commissioned officer, private. 70rp, Uniform tunic, trunk. 1fr, Sharpshooters, officer and private.

Photo. & Engr.

1991, June 3 **Perf. 13½x14**

964	A394	50rp multicolored	65	65
965	A394	70rp multicolored	90	90
966	A394	1fr multicolored	1.00	1.00

Last action of Liechtenstein's military, 1866 (70rp).

Princess Marie — A395

Photo. & Engr.

1991, Sept. 2 **Perf. 13x13½**

967	A395	3fr shown	3.90	3.90
968	A395	3.40fr Prince Hans-Adam II	4.50	4.50

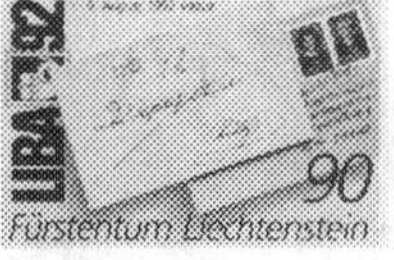

LIBA 92, Natl. Philatelic Exhibition A396

1991, Sept. 2 **Photo.** **Perf. 11½**

Granite Paper

969	A396	90rp multicolored	1.15	1.15

Christmas — A397

Altar of St. Mamertus Chapel, Triesen: 50rp, Mary. 80rp, Madonna and Child. 90rp, Angel Gabriel.

Photo. & Engr.

1991, Dec. 2 **Perf. 13½x14**

970	A397	50rp multicolored	70	70
971	A397	80rp multicolored	1.10	1.10
972	A397	90rp multicolored	1.25	1.25

1992 Winter Olympics, Albertville — A398

70rp, Cross-country skiers, doping check. 80rp, Hockey players, good sportsmanship. 1.60rp, Downhill skier, safety precautions.

1991, Dec. 2 **Photo.** **Perf. 11½x12**

Granite Paper

973	A398	70rp multicolored	95	95
974	A398	80rp multicolored	1.10	1.10
975	A398	1.60fr multicolored	2.25	2.25

SEMI-POSTAL STAMPS

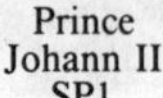
Prince Johann II SP1

Coat of Arms SP2

Wmk. 183

1925, Oct. 5 Engr. *Perf. 11½*

B1	SP1	10rp yel green	26.00	10.00
B2	SP1	20rp deep red	19.00	10.00
B3	SP1	30rp deep blue	5.50	3.50

85th birthday of the Prince Regent. Sold at a premium of 5rp each, the excess being devoted to charities.

1927, Oct. 5 Typo.

B4	SP2	10rp multi	7.50	*13.00*
B5	SP2	20rp multi	7.50	*13.00*
B6	SP2	30rp multi	7.50	*13.00*

87th birthday of Prince Johann II.
These stamps were sold at premiums of 5, 10 and 20rp respectively. The money thus obtained was devoted to charity.

Railroad Bridge Demolished by Flood — SP3

Designs: 10rp+10rp, Inundated Village of Ruggel. 20rp+10rp, Austrian soldiers rescuing refugees. 30rp+10rp, Swiss soldiers salvaging personal effects.

1928, Feb. 6 Litho. Unwmk.

B7	SP3	5rp + 5rp brn vio & brn	11.00	19.00
B8	SP3	10rp + 10rp bl grn & brn	14.00	19.00
B9	SP3	20rp + 10rp dl red & brn	14.00	19.00
B10	SP3	30rp + 10rp dp bl & brn	11.00	19.00

The surtax on these stamps was used to aid the sufferers from the Rhine floods.

Coat of Arms — SP7

Princess Elsa — SP8

Design: 30rp, Prince Francis I.

1932, Dec. 21 Photo.

B11	SP7	10rp (+ 5rp) ol grn	18.00	*24.00*
B12	SP8	20rp (+ 5rp) rose red	18.00	*24.00*
B13	SP8	30rp (+ 10rp) ultra	18.00	*24.00*

The surtax was for the Child Welfare Fund.

Postal Museum Issue
Souvenir Sheet

SP10

1936, Oct. 24 Litho. *Imperf.*

B14	SP10	Sheet of 4	15.00	*37.50*

Sheet contains 2 each, #120, 122. Sold for 2fr.

"Protect the Child" — SP11

Designs: No. B16, "Take Care of the Sick". No. B17, "Help the Aged".

Perf. 11½

1945, Nov. 27 Photo. Unwmk.

Cross in Red

B15	SP11	10rp + 10rp brn vio & buff	60	*1.75*
B16	SP11	20rp + 20rp hn brn & buff	70	*2.00*
B17	SP11	1fr + 1.40fr slate & buff	5.25	*16.00*

Souvenir Sheet

Post Coach SP14

1946, Aug. 10

B18	SP14	Sheet of 2	21.00	*30.00*
a.		10rp dark vio brn & buff	9.00	*13.00*

25th anniv. of the Swiss-Liechtenstein Postal Agreement. Sheet, size: 82x60½mm, sold for 3fr.

Canal by Albert Cuyp — SP15

Willem van Huythuysen by Frans Hals — SP16

Design: 40rp+10rp, Landscape by Jacob van Ruysdael.

1951, July 24 *Perf. 11½*

B19	SP15	10rp + 10rp ol grn	5.75	6.50
B20	SP16	20rp + 10rp dk vio brn	5.75	13.00
B21	SP15	40rp + 10rp bl	5.75	6.50

Issued in sheets of 12.

Catalogue values for unused stamps in this section, from this point to the end of the section, are for Never Hinged items.

Nos. 324-325 Surcharged with New Value and Uprooted Oak Emblem

1960, Apr. 7

B22	A190	30rp + 10rp on 40rp bl, vio & red	90	90
B23	A190	50rp + 10rp on 25rp bis, vio & red	1.50	1.50

World Refugee Year, July 1, 1959-June 30, 1960. The surtax was for aid to refugees.

Growth Symbol SP17

1967, Dec. 7 Photo. *Perf. 11½*

B24	SP17	50rp + 20rp multi	85	60

Surtax was for development assistance.

AIR POST STAMPS

Airplane over Snow-capped Mountain Peaks — AP1

Airplane above Vaduz Castle — AP2

Airplane over Rhine Valley — AP3

Perf. 10½, 10½x11½

1930, Aug. 12 Photo. Unwmk.

Gray Wavy Lines in Background

C1	AP1	15rp dk brn	6.00	6.25
C2	AP1	20rp slate	12.50	11.00
C3	AP2	25rp ol brn	9.00	9.50
C4	AP2	35rp sl bl	12.50	9.50
C5	AP3	45rp ol grn	22.50	37.50
C6	AP3	1fr lake	42.50	27.50
		Nos. C1-C6 (6)	105.00	101.25

For surcharge see No. C14.

Zeppelin over Naafkopf, Falknis Range AP4

Design: 2fr, Zeppelin over Valüna Valley.

1931, June 1 *Perf. 11½*

C7	AP4	1fr olive blk	52.50	95.00
C8	AP4	2fr blue blk	110.00	265.00

Golden Eagle — AP6

Designs: 15rp, Golden Eagle in flight, diff. 20rp, Golden Eagle in flight, diff. 30rp, Osprey. 50rp, Eagle.

1934-35

C9	AP6	10rp brt vio ('35)	4.50	13.00
C10	AP6	15rp red org ('35)	11.00	30.00
C11	AP6	20rp red ('35)	14.00	30.00
C12	AP6	30rp brt bl ('35)	12.50	30.00
C13	AP6	50rp emerald	8.00	21.00
		Nos. C9-C13 (5)	50.00	124.00

No. C6 Surcharged with New Value

1935, June 24 *Perf. 10½x11½*

C14	AP3	60rp on 1fr lake	27.50	35.00

Airship "Hindenburg" — AP11

Design: 2fr, Airship "Graf Zeppelin."

1936, May 1 *Perf. 11½*

C15	AP11	1fr rose car	30.00	67.50
C16	AP11	2fr violet	27.50	55.00

Barn Swallows — AP13

Designs: 15rp, Black-headed Gulls. 20rp, Gulls. 30rp, Eagle. 50rp, Northern Goshawk. 1fr, Lammergeier. 2fr, Lammergeier.

1939, Apr. 3 Photo.

C17	AP13	10rp violet	28	20
C18	AP13	15rp red org	80	1.50
C19	AP13	20rp dark red	1.00	42
C20	AP13	30rp dull blue	1.00	70
C21	AP13	50rp brt grn	2.75	1.50
C22	AP13	1fr rose car	2.75	*10.50*
C23	AP13	2fr violet	2.00	*10.50*
		Nos. C17-C23 (7)	10.58	*25.32*

Leonardo da Vinci — AP20

Designs: 15rp, Joseph Montgolfier. 20rp, Jacob Degen. 25rp, Wilhelm Kress. 40rp, E. G. Robertson. 50rp, W. S. Henson. 1fr, Otto Lilienthal. 2fr, S. A. Andree. 5fr, Wilbur Wright. 10fr, Icarus.

1948

C24	AP20	10rp dk grn	1.40	50
C25	AP20	15rp dk vio	1.10	1.10
C26	AP20	20rp brown	1.10	50
a.		20rp reddish brown	42.50	2.00
C27	AP20	25rp dark red	1.40	2.50
C28	AP20	40rp vio blue	2.00	1.25
C29	AP20	50rp Prus blue	2.75	2.25
C30	AP20	1fr chocolate	2.75	3.00
C31	AP20	2fr rose lake	4.00	4.00
C32	AP20	5fr olive grn	4.00	8.00
C33	AP20	10fr slate blk	25.00	13.00
		Nos. C24-C33 (10)	45.50	36.10

Issued in sheets of 9.
Exist imperf. Value, set $6,500.

Helicopter, Bell 47-J AP21

Planes: 40rp, Boeing 707 jet. 50rp, Convair 600 jet. 75rp, Douglas DC-8.

1960, Apr. 7 Unwmk. *Perf. 11½*

C34	AP21	30rp red orange	1.25	1.75
C35	AP21	40rp blue black	2.50	1.75
C36	AP21	50rp dp claret	4.75	3.75
C37	AP21	75rp olive grn	2.50	1.75

30th anniv. of Liechtenstein's air post stamps.

POSTAGE DUE STAMPS

National Administration of the Post Office

D1

1920 Unwmk. Engr. *Perf. 12 ½*

No.	Type	Denomination	Unused	Used
J1	D1	5h rose red	15	20
J2	D1	10h rose red	15	20
J3	D1	15h rose red	15	20
J4	D1	20h rose red	15	20
J5	D1	25h rose red	15	20
J6	D1	30h rose red	15	20
J7	D1	40h rose red	15	20
J8	D1	50h rose red	15	20
J9	D1	80h rose red	15	20
J10	D1	1k dull blue	15	20
J11	D1	2k dull blue	15	28
J12	D1	5k dull blue	15	28
		Set value		1.00

Nos. J1-J12 exist imperf. and part perf.

Swiss Administration of the Post Office

D2

Post Horn — D3

1928 Litho. Wmk. 183 *Perf. 11 ½*
Granite Paper

No.	Type	Denomination	Unused	Used
J13	D2	5rp pur & org	80	1.75
J14	D2	10rp pur & org	90	1.75
J15	D2	15rp pur & org	2.25	*8.50*
J16	D2	20rp pur & org	1.40	2.50
J17	D2	25rp pur & org	2.25	*7.00*
J18	D2	30rp pur & org	5.00	*8.75*
J19	D2	40rp pur & org	5.25	*9.75*
J20	D2	50rp pur & org	5.25	*12.00*
		Nos. J13-J20 (8)	23.10	*52.00*

Engraved; Value Typographed in Dark Red

1940 Unwmk. *Perf. 11 ½*

No.	Type	Denomination	Unused	Used
J21	D3	5rp gray blue	1.50	*5.50*
J22	D3	10rp gray blue	65	90
J23	D3	15rp gray blue	60	*3.50*
J24	D3	20rp gray blue	60	1.25
J25	D3	25rp gray blue	1.25	*3.25*
J26	D3	30rp gray blue	2.50	4.50
J27	D3	40rp gray blue	2.50	4.00
J28	D3	50rp gray blue	2.50	5.00
		Nos. J21-J28 (8)	12.10	*27.90*

OFFICIAL STAMPS

Regular Issue of 1930 Overprinted in Various Colors with Crown and:

REGIERUNGS DIENSTSACHE

Perf. 10 ½, 11 ½, 11 ½x10 ½

1932 Unwmk.

No.	Type	Denomination	Unused	Used
O1	A38	5rp dk grn (Bk)	5.50	9.00
O2	A39	10rp dk vio (R)	37.50	7.50
a.		Perf. 11½x10½	*650.00*	*1,050.*
O3	A40	20rp dp rose red (Bl)	50.00	7.50
a.		Perf. 10½	175.00	40.00
O4	A42	30rp ultra (R)	7.75	9.00
a.		Perf. 10½	22.50	13.00
O5	A43	35rp dp grn (Bk)	5.50	14.00
a.		Perf. 11½	*3,500.*	*5,500.*
O6	A45	50rp blk brn (Bl)	37.50	11.00
a.		Perf. 11½	130.00	130.00
O7	A46	60rp ol blk (R)	5.50	30.00
O8	A48	1.20fr ol brn (G)	77.50	265.00
		Nos. O1-O8 (8)	226.75	353.00

Nos. 108, 110 Overprinted in Black

1933 *Perf. 14 ½*

No.	Type	Denomination	Unused	Used
O9	A51	25rp red org	37.50	40.00
O10	A53	1.20fr red brn	60.00	*175.00*

Same Overprint in Various Colors on Regular Issue of 1934-35

1934-36 *Perf. 11 ½*

No.	Type	Denomination	Unused	Used
O11	A58	5rp emer (R)	45	1.25
O12	A59	10rp dp vio (Bk)	22	1.10
O13	A60	15rp red org (V)	22	40
O14	A61	20rp red (Bk)	35	1.10
O15	A62	25rp brn (R)	27.50	*80.00*
O16	A62	25rp brn (Bk)	1.50	*8.75*
O17	A63	30rp dk bl (R)	1.90	3.50
O18	A66	50rp lt brn (V)	85	2.00
O19	A68	90rp dp grn (Bk)	5.00	*24.00*
O20	A70	1.50fr brn car (Bl)	35.00	*105.00*
		Nos. O11-O20 (10)	72.99	*227.10*

Regular Issue of 1937-38 Overprinted in Black, Red or Blue

1937-41

No.	Type	Denomination	Unused	Used
O21	A77	5rp emer (Bk)	15	15
O22	A78	10rp vio & buff (R)	15	22
O23	A80	20rp brn org (Bl)	90	95
O24	A80	20rp brn org (Bk) ('41)	90	95
O25	A81	25rp chnt (Bk)	48	1.10
O26	A82	30rp bl & gray (Bk)	70	48
O27	A85	50rp dk brn & buff (R)	40	95
O28	A88	1fr red brn (Bk)	80	*4.00*
O29	A90	1.50fr sl bl (Bk) ('38)	2.75	*6.50*
		Nos. O21-O29 (9)	7.23	15.30

Stamps of 1944-45 Overprinted in Black DIENSTMARKE

1947

No.	Type	Denomination	Unused	Used
O30	A136	5rp sl grn & buff	55	75
O31	A136	10rp gray & buff	75	75
O32	A136	20rp org red & buff	75	75
O33	A136	30rp bl & buff	1.50	1.40
O34	A136	50rp bluish blk & pale gray	1.50	*3.00*
O35	A136	1fr dp cl & buff	3.75	*9.00*
O36	A136	150rp royal blue	4.75	*9.00*
		Nos. O30-O36 (7)	13.55	24.65

Crown — O1

Government Building, Vaduz — O2

Engr.; Value Typo.
1950-68 Unwmk. *Perf. 11 ½*
Buff Granite Paper
Narrow Gothic Numerals

No.	Type	Denomination	Unused	Used
O37	O1	5rp red vio & gray	15	15
O38	O1	10rp ol grn & mag	15	15
O39	O1	20rp org brn & bl	15	20
O40	O1	30rp dk red brn & org red	20	30
O41	O1	40rp bl & hn brn	25	42
O42	O1	55rp dk gray grn & red	1.10	1.50
a.		White paper ('68)	30.00	*125.00*
O43	O1	60rp sl & mag	1.10	1.50
a.		White paper ('68)	4.75	*32.50*
O44	O1	80rp red org & gray	52	75
O45	O1	90rp choc & bl	70	1.10
O46	O1	1.20fr grnsh bl & org	80	1.40
		Nos. O37-O46 (10)	5.12	7.47

Catalogue values for unused stamps in this section, from this point to the end of the section, are for Never Hinged items.

1968-69 *Perf. 11 ½*
White Granite Paper
Broad Numerals, Varying Thickness

No.	Type	Denomination	Unused	Used
O47	O1	5rp ol brn & org	15	15
O48	O1	10rp vio & car	15	15
O49	O1	20rp ver & emer	15	15
O50	O1	30rp grn & red	16	16
O51	O1	50rp ultra & red	20	20
O52	O1	60rp org & ultra	24	24
O53	O1	70rp mar & emer	30	30
O54	O1	80rp bl grn & car	35	35
O55	O1	95rp sl & red ('69)	60	60
O56	O1	1fr rose cl & grn	42	42
O57	O1	1.20fr lt red brn & grn	52	52
O58	O1	2fr brn & org ('69)	1.00	1.00
		Nos. O47-O58 (12)	4.24	4.24

Engr., Value Typo.

1976-89 *Perf. 14*

No.	Type	Denomination	Unused	Used
O59	O2	10rp yel brn & vio	15	15
O60	O2	20rp car lake & bl	15	16
O61	O2	35rp bl & red	18	24
O62	O2	40rp dl pur & grn	20	25
O63	O2	50rp slate & mag	25	35
O64	O2	70rp vio brn & bl grn	32	42
O65	O2	80rp grn & mag	40	50
O66	O2	90rp vio & bl grn	45	60
O67	O2	1fr olive & mag	52	70
O68	O2	1.10fr brn & ultra	60	75
O69	O2	1.50fr dl grn & red	85	1.10
O70	O2	2fr org & bl	1.00	1.25
O75	O2	5fr rose vio & brn org	6.00	6.00
		Nos. O59-O75 (13)	11.07	12.47

Issue dates: 5fr, Sept. 4, 1989. Others, Dec. 9, 1976.

This is an expanding set. Numbers will change if necessary.

LITHUANIA

(Lietuva)

LOCATION — Northern Europe bordering on the Baltic Sea
GOVT. — Independent republic
AREA — 22,959 sq. mi.
POP. — 2,879,070 (1940)
CAPITAL — Vilnius

Lithuania was under Russian rule when it declared its independence in 1918. The League of Nations recognized it in 1922. In 1940 it became a republic in the Union of Soviet Socialist Republics. Lithuanian independence was recognized by the Soviet Union on Sept. 6, 1991.

100 Skatiku = 1 Auksinas
100 Centai = 1 Litas (1922)
100 Kopecks = 1 Ruble (1991)

Catalogue values for unused stamps in this country are for Never Hinged items, beginning with Scott 400.

Nos. 1-26 were printed in sheets of 20 (5x4) which were imperf. at the outer sides, so that only 6 stamps in each sheet were fully perforated. Values are for the stamps partly imperf. The stamps fully perforated sell for at least double these values. There was also a printing of Nos. 19-26 in a sheet of 160, composed of blocks of 20 of each stamp. Pairs or blocks with different values se-tenant sell for considerably more than the values for the stamps singly.

Nos. 1-26 are without gum.

Watermarks

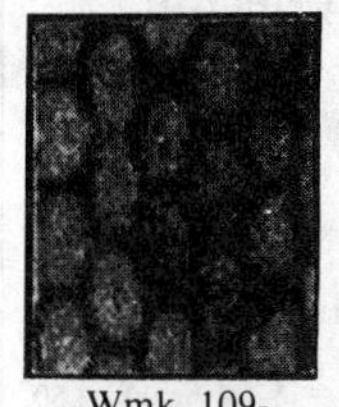
Wmk. 109- Webbing

Wmk. 144- Network

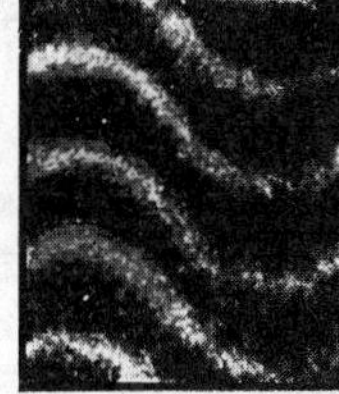
Wmk. 145- Wavy Lines

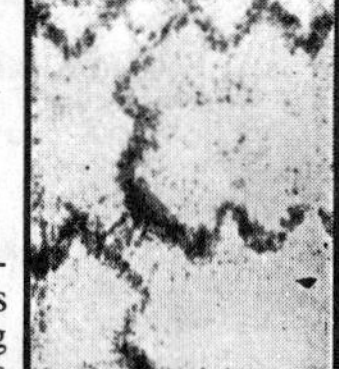
Wmk. 146- Zigzag Lines Forming Rectangles

Wmk. 147- Parquetry

Wmk. 198- Intersecting Diamonds

Wmk. 209- Multiple Ovals

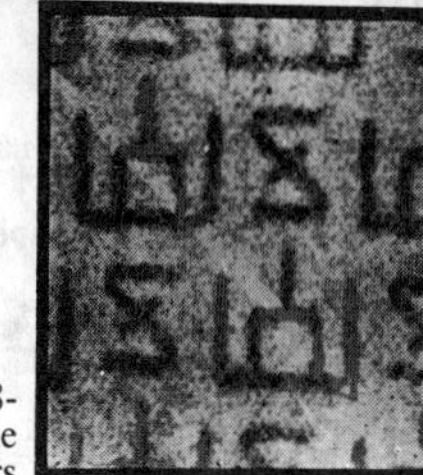
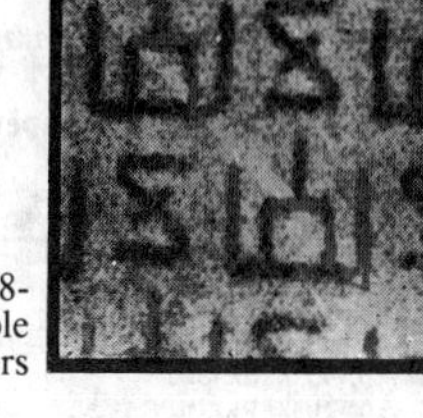
Wmk. 238- Multiple Letters

Lietuvos 30 skatiku pašta
A1

Lietuvos 10 skatiku paštas
A2

Perf. 11 ½
1918, Dec. 27 Unwmk. Typeset
First Vilnius Printing
Thin Figures

No.	Type	Denomination	Unused	Used
1	A1	10sk black	75.00	45.00
2	A1	15sk black	75.00	45.00

1918, Dec. 31

Second Vilnius Printing

Thick Figures

No.	Type	Description	Unused	Used
3	A1	10sk black	37.50	27.50
4	A1	15sk black	37.50	25.00
5	A1	20sk black	4.50	4.00
6	A1	30sk black	4.50	4.00
7	A1	40sk black	4.50	4.00
8	A1	50sk black	4.50	4.00
		Nos. 3-8 (6)	93.00	

First Kaunas Issue

1919

No.	Type	Description	Unused	Used
9	A2	10sk black	6.00	3.50
10	A2	15sk black	6.00	3.50
a.		"5" for "15"	37.50	37.50
11	A2	20sk black	6.00	3.50
12	A2	30sk black	6.00	3.50

A3 A4

Second Kaunas Issue

No.	Type	Description	Unused	Used
13	A3	10sk black	2.50	1.25
14	A3	15sk black	2.50	1.25
15	A3	20sk black	2.50	1.25
a.		"astas" for "pastas"	47.50	45.00
16	A3	30sk black	2.50	1.25
17	A3	40sk black	2.50	1.50
18	A3	50sk black	2.50	1.50
19	A3	60sk black	2.50	1.50
		Nos. 13-19 (7)	17.50	9.50

Third Kaunas Issue

No.	Type	Description	Unused	Used
20	A4	10sk black	1.50	1.25
21	A4	15sk black	1.50	1.25
22	A4	20sk black	1.50	1.25
23	A4	30sk black	1.50	1.25
24	A4	40sk black	1.50	1.25
25	A4	50sk black	1.50	1.25
26	A4	60sk black	1.50	1.50
		Nos. 20-26 (7)	10.50	9.00

The White Knight "Vytis"
A5 A6

A7 A8

Perf. 10½ to 14 & Compound

1919 Litho. Wmk. 144

Gray Granite Paper

No.	Type	Description	Unused	Used
30	A5	10sk dp rose	22	22
a.		Wmk. vert.	12.50	6.75
31	A5	15sk violet	22	20
a.		Wmk. vert.	12.50	6.75
32	A5	20sk dk bl	22	20
33	A5	30sk dp org	22	20
a.		Wmk. vert.	12.50	6.75
34	A5	40sk dk brn	22	20
35	A6	50sk bl grn	38	28
36	A6	75sk org & dp rose	38	20
37	A7	1auk gray & rose	38	28
38	A7	3auk bis brn & rose	38	30
39	A7	5auk bl grn & rose	38	38
		Nos. 30-39 (10)	3.00	2.46

Nos. 30a, 31a and 33a are from the first printing with watermark vertical showing points to left; various perforations.

Nos. 30-39 exist imperf. Value in pairs, $40.

1919 Wmk. 145

Thick White Paper

No.	Type	Description	Unused	Used
40	A5	10sk dl rose	15	15
41	A5	15sk violet	15	15
42	A5	20sk dk bl	15	15
43	A5	30sk orange	15	15
44	A5	40sk red brn	15	15
45	A6	50sk green	15	15
46	A6	75sk yel & dp rose	15	15
47	A7	1auk gray & rose	30	20
48	A7	3auk yel brn & rose, perf. 12½	30	20
49	A7	5auk bl grn & rose	42	28
		Nos. 40-49 (10)	2.07	1.73

Nos. 40-49 exist imperf. Value in pairs, $40.

1919 *Perf. 10½ to 14 & Compound*

Thin White Paper

No.	Type	Description	Unused	Used
50	A5	10sk red	15	15
51	A5	15sk lilac	15	15
52	A5	20sk dl bl	15	15
53	A5	30sk buff	15	15
54	A5	40sk gray brn	15	15
55	A6	50sk lt grn	15	15
56	A6	60sk vio & red	15	15
57	A6	75sk bis & red	15	15
58	A8	1auk gray & red	15	15
59	A8	3auk lt brn & red	15	15
60	A8	5auk bl grn & red	18	15
		Set value	1.00	95

Nos. 50-60 exist imperf. Value, pairs $50.
See Nos. 93-96.

"Lithuania" Receiving Benediction
A9

The Spirit of Lithuania Rises
A10

"Lithuania" with Chains Broken — A11

White Knight — A12

1920, Feb. 16 Wmk. 146 *Perf. 11½*

No.	Type	Description	Unused	Used
70	A9	10sk dp rose	1.50	1.25
71	A9	15sk lt vio	1.50	1.25
72	A9	20sk gray bl	1.50	1.25
73	A10	30sk yel brn	1.50	1.25
74	A11	40sk brn & grn	1.50	1.25
75	A10	50sk dp rose	1.50	1.25
76	A10	60sk lt vio	1.50	1.25
77	A11	80sk pur & red	1.50	1.25
78	A11	1auk grn & red	1.50	1.25
79	A12	3auk brn & red	1.50	1.25
80	A12	5auk grn & red	1.50	1.25
a.		Right "5" dbl., grn and red	50.00	62.50
		Nos. 70-80 (11)	16.50	13.75

Anniv. of natl. independence. The stamps were on sale only 3 days. Only a limited number of stamps was sold at post offices but 40,000 sets were delivered to the bank of Kaunas.

All values exist imperforate.

White Knight
A13

Grand Duke Vytautas
A14

Grand Duke Gediminas
A15

Sacred Oak and Altar
A16

1920, Aug. 25

No.	Type	Description	Unused	Used
81	A13	10sk rose	38	38
a.		Imperf., pair	6.00	
82	A13	15sk dk vio	38	38
83	A14	20sk grn & lt grn	38	38
84	A13	30sk brown	38	38
85	A15	40sk gray grn & vio	38	50
86	A14	50sk brn & brn org	1.00	1.00
87	A14	60sk red & org	1.00	1.00
88	A15	80sk blk, grn & red	1.00	1.00
89	A16	1auk org & blk	1.00	1.00
90	A16	3auk grn & blk	1.00	1.00
91	A16	5auk gray vio & blk	1.00	1.00
		Nos. 81-91 (11)	7.90	8.02

Opening of Lithuanian National Assembly. On sale for three days.

Nos. 82 and 84 were printed on the same sheet and are found in pairs, se-tenant. Value for pair, $6.

1920

No.	Type	Description	Unused	Used
92	A14	20sk grn & lil	40.00	
92A	A15	40sk gray grn, buff & vio	40.00	
92B	A14	50sk brn & gray lil	40.00	
92C	A14	60sk red & grn	40.00	
92D	A15	80sk blk, grn & red	40.00	
		Nos. 92-92D (5)	200.00	

Nos. 92 to 92D were trial printings. By order of the Ministry of Posts, 2,000 copies of each were placed on sale at post offices.

Type of 1919 Issue

1920 Unwmk. *Perf. 11½*

No.	Type	Description	Unused	Used
93	A5	15sk lilac	2.50	1.50
94	A5	20sk dp bl	2.00	1.50

Wmk. 109

No.	Type	Description	Unused	Used
95	A5	20sk dp bl	1.25	75
96	A5	40sk gray brn	1.75	1.00

Watermark horizontal on Nos. 95-96. No. 96 exists perf. 10½x11½.

Imperf., Pairs

No.	Type	Description	Unused	Used
93a	A5	15sk	3.00	2.00
94a	A5	20sk	3.00	2.00
95a	A5	20sk	3.25	2.50
96a	A5	40sk	3.25	3.75

Sower
A17

Peasant Sharpening Scythe
A18

Prince Kestutis
A19

Black Horseman
A20

Perf. 11, 11½ and Compound

1921-22

No.	Type	Description	Unused	Used
97	A17	10sk brt rose	15	55
98	A17	15sk violet	15	70
99	A17	20sk ultra	15	15
100	A18	30sk brown	38	1.10
101	A19	40sk red	15	15
102	A18	50sk olive	15	15
103	A18	60sk grn & vio	25	1.65
104	A19	80sk brn org & car	18	15
105	A19	1auk brn & grn	15	15
106	A19	2auk gray bl & red	15	15
107	A20	3auk yel brn & dk bl	30	42
108	A17	4auk yel & dk bl ('22)	25	15
109	A20	5auk gray blk & rose	38	1.00
110	A17	8auk grn & blk ('22)	38	15
111	A20	10auk rose & vio	75	55
112	A20	25auk bis brn & grn	90	85
113	A20	100auk dl red & gray blk	4.50	6.50
		Nos. 97-113 (17)	9.32	14.52

Imperf., Pairs

No.	Type	Description	Unused
97a	A17	10sk	12.50
98a	A17	15sk	10.00
99a	A17	20sk	12.50
100a	A18	30sk	17.50
102a	A18	50sk	1.25
103a	A18	60sk	12.50
104a	A19	80sk	12.50
105a	A19	1auk	12.50
106a	A19	2auk	12.50
107a	A20	3auk	12.50
109a	A20	5auk	15.00
110a	A17	8auk	10.00

No. 57 Surcharged **4 AUKSINAI**

Perf. 12½x11½

1922, May Wmk. 145

No.	Type	Description	Unused	Used
114	A6	4auk on 75sk bis & red	25	15
a.		Inverted surcharge	5.00	4.00

Same with Bars over Original Value

No.	Type	Description	Unused	Used
115	A6	4auk on 75sk bis & red	50	38
a.		Double surcharge	5.00	5.00

Povilas Luksis — A20a

Justinas Staugaitis, Antanas Smetona, Stasys Silingas
A20b

Portraits: 40s, Lt. Juozapavicius. 50s, Dr. Basanavicius. 60s, Mrs. Petkeviciute. 1auk, Prof. Voldemaras. 2auk, Pranas Dovidaitis. 3auk, Dr. Slezevicius. 4auk, Dr. Galvanauskas. 5auk, Kazys Grinius. 6auk, Dr. Stulginskis. 8auk, Pres. Smetona.

1922 Litho. Unwmk.

No.	Type	Description	Unused	Used
116	A20a	20s blk & car rose	42	42
116A	A20a	40s bl grn & vio	42	42
116B	A20a	50s plum & grnsh bl	42	42
117	A20a	60s pur & org	42	42
117A	A20a	1auk car & lt bl	42	42
117B	A20a	2auk dp bl & yel brn	42	42
c.		Center inverted	45.00	45.00
118	A20a	3auk mar & ultra	42	42
118A	A20a	4auk dk grn & red vio	42	42
118B	A20a	5auk blk brn & dp rose	42	42
119	A20a	6auk dk bl & grnsh bl	42	42
a.		Cliche of 8auk in sheet of 6auk	22.50	22.50
119B	A20a	8auk ultra & bis	55	55
119C	A20b	10auk dk vio & bl grn	1.10	1.10
		Nos. 116-119C (12)	5.85	5.85

League of Nations' recognition of Lithuania. Sold only on Oct. 1, 1922.

Forty sheets of the 6auk each included eight copies of the 8auk.

Stamps of 1919-22 Surcharged in Black, Carmine or Green

1 CENT **10 CENTU**

On Nos. 37-39

1922 Wmk. 144 *Perf. 11½x12*

Gray Granite Paper

No.	Type	Description	Unused	Used
120	A7	3c on 1auk	72.50	72.50
121	A7	3c on 3auk	57.50	57.50
122	A7	3c on 5auk	27.50	27.50

Excellent counterfeits exist.

White Paper

Wmk. 145

Perf. 14, 11½, 12½x11½

No.	Type	Description	Unused	Used
123	A5	1c on 10sk red	52	70
124	A5	1c on 15sk lil	52	70
125	A5	1c on 20sk dl bl	52	70
126	A5	1c on 30sk org	60.00	42.50
127	A5	1c on 30sk buff	25	22
128	A5	1c on 40sk gray brn	52	70
129	A6	2c on 50sk grn	52	70
130	A6	2c on 60sk vio & red	15	15
131	A6	2c on 75sk bis & red	35	70
132	A8	3c on 1auk gray & red	35	25
133	A8	3c on 3auk brn & red	18	18

134 A8 3c on 5auk bl grn & red 18 18
Nos. 123-125,127-134 (11) 4.06 5.18

On Stamps of 1920

1922 Unwmk. *Perf. 11*
136 A5 1c on 20sk dp bl (C) 50 75

Wmk. Webbing. (109)
Perf. 11, 11½
138 A5 1c on 20sk dp bl (C) 50 65
139 A5 1c on 40sk gray brn (C) 1.25 1.25

On Stamps of 1921-22
140 A18 1c on 50sk ol (C) 15 15
a. Imperf., pair 17.50
b. Inverted surcharge 7.50
c. Double surch., one invtd.
141 A17 3c on 10sk rose 1.25 1.25
142 A17 3c on 15sk vio 15 15
143 A17 3c on 20sk ultra 18 25
144 A18 3c on 30sk brn 90 1.00
145 A19 3c on 40sk red 15 15
a. Imperf., pair
146 A18 5c on 50sk ol 15 15
147 A18 5c on 60sk grn & vio 45 65
148 A19 5c on 80sk brn org & car 15 15
a. Imperf., pair 15.00 15.00

Wmk. Wavy Lines (145)
Perf. 12½x11½
149 A6 5c on 4auk on 75sk (No. 114) (G) 38 65
150 A6 5c on 4auk on 75sk (No. 115) (G) 1.25 1.50

Wmk. Webbing (109)
Perf. 11, 11½
151 A19 10c on 1auk brn & grn 30 15
a. Inverted surcharge 12.50
152 A19 10c on 2auk bl & red 15 15
a. Inverted surcharge 7.50
b. Imperf., pair 15.00
153 A17 15c on 4auk yel & dk bl 15 15
a. Inverted surcharge 5.00
154 A20 25c on 3auk yel brn & dk bl 2.25 2.50
155 A20 25c on 5auk gray blk & rose 1.90 1.50
156 A20 25c on 10auk rose & vio 1.50 1.00
a. Imperf., pair 15.00
157 A17 30c on 8auk grn & blk (C) 30 24
a. Inverted surcharge 7.50 7.50
158 A20 50c on 25auk bis brn & grn 1.75 1.75
160 A20 1 l on 100auk red & gray 2.50 2.00
Nos. 136-160 (23) 18.21 18.14

A21

Ruin — A22

Seminary Church, Kaunas — A23

1923 Litho. Wmk. 109 *Perf. 11*
165 A21 10c violet 3.00 15
166 A21 15c scarlet 1.25 15
167 A21 20c ol brn 1.25 15
168 A21 25c dp bl 1.25 15
169 A22 50c yel grn 1.25 15
170 A22 60c red 1.25 15
171 A23 1 l org & grn 7.50 15
172 A23 3 l red & gray 4.75 25
173 A23 5 l brn & bl 8.75 1.00
Nos. 165-173 (9) 30.25
Set value 1.85

See Nos. 189-209, 281-282.

Memel Coat of Arms — A24

Lithuanian Coat of Arms — A25

Biruta Chapel — A26

Kaunas, War Memorial — A27

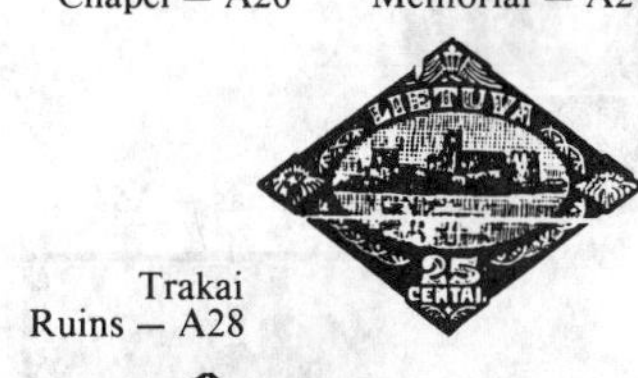
Trakai Ruins — A28

Memel Lighthouse A29

Memel Harbor A30

Perf. 11, 11½, 12
1923, Aug. Unwmk.
176 A24 1c rose, grn & blk 1.40 1.65
177 A25 2c dl vio & blk 1.40 1.65
178 A26 3c yel & blk 1.40 1.65
179 A24 5c bl, buff & blk 1.65 1.90
180 A27 10c org & blk 1.65 1.90
181 A27 15c grn & blk 1.90 2.50
182 A28 25c brt vio & blk 1.90 2.50
183 A25 30c red vio & blk 2.25 2.75
184 A29 60c ol grn & blk 2.25 2.75
185 A30 1 l bl grn & blk 2.25 2.75
186 A26 2 l red & blk 2.75 3.50
187 A28 3 l bl & blk 4.25 5.00
188 A29 5 l ultra & blk 5.50 6.75
Nos. 176-188 (13) 30.55 37.25

This series was issued ostensibly to commemorate the incorporation of Memel with Lithuania.

Type of 1923 Issue

1923 Unwmk. *Perf. 11*
189 A21 5c pale grn 1.75 15
190 A21 10c violet 2.50 15
a. Imperf., pair 22.50
191 A21 15c scarlet 3.00 15
a. Imperf., pair 22.50
193 A21 25c blue 4.75 15
Set value 20

1923 Wmk. 147
196 A21 2c pale brn 90 25
197 A21 3c olive bis 1.00 18
198 A21 5c pale grn 1.00 15
199 A21 10c violet 2.25 15
202 A21 25c deep blue 5.00 15
a. Imperf., pair 24.00
204 A21 36c org brn 7.50 50
Nos. 196-204 (6) 17.65 1.38

Perf. 11½, 14½, 11½x14½
1923-25 Wmk. 198
207 A21 25c deep blue 180.00 180.00
208 A22 50c dp grn ('25) 2.75 15
209 A22 60c car ('25) 3.25 15

Double- barred Cross A31

Dr. Jonas Basanavicius A32

1927, Jan. *Perf. 11½, 14½*
210 A31 2c orange 75 15
211 A31 3c dp brn 75 15
212 A31 5c green 1.25 15
a. Imperf., pair 10.00
213 A31 10c violet 2.00 15
214 A31 15c red 1.75 15
a. Imperf., pair 10.00
215 A31 25c blue 1.75 15
Nos. 210-215 (6) 8.25
Set value 48

1927-29 Wmk. 147 *Perf. 14½*
216 A31 5c green 20.00 10.00
217 A31 30c blue ('29) 12.50 2.50

See Nos. 233-240, 278-280.

Perf. 11½, 14½x11½
1927 Unwmk.
219 A32 15c claret & blk 70 38
220 A32 25c dl bl & blk 70 38
221 A32 50c dk grn & blk 1.25 75
222 A32 60c dk vio & blk 1.75 1.00

Dr. Jonas Basanavicius (1851-1927), patriot and folklorist.

National Arms — A33

1927, Dec. 23 Wmk. 109 *Perf. 14½*
223 A33 1 l bl grn & gray 1.40 15
224 A33 3 l vio & pale grn 2.25 45
225 A33 5 l brn & gray 4.00 80

Pres. Antanas Smetona A34

Decade of Independence A35

Dawn of Peace — A36

1928, Feb. Wmk. 109
226 A34 5c org brn & grn 42 28
227 A34 10c vio & blk 55 28
228 A34 15c org & brn 55 28
229 A34 25c bl & indigo 55 28
230 A35 50c ultra & dl vio 55 28
231 A35 60c car & blk 85 55
232 A36 1 l blk brn & db 85 70
Nos. 226-232 (7) 4.32 2.65

10th anniv. of Lithuanian independence.

Type of 1926 Issue

1929-31
233 A31 2c org ('31) 1.25 15
234 A31 5c green 1.25 15
235 A31 10c vio ('31) 6.00 15
237 A31 15c red 1.75 15
a. Tete beche pair 4.50 4.50
239 A31 30c dk bl 3.00 15

Unwmk.
240 A31 15c red 6.25 15
Nos. 233-240 (6) 19.50
Set value 52

Grand Duke Vytautas A37

Grand Duke, Mounted A38

1930, Feb. 16 *Perf. 14*
242 A37 2c yel brn & dk brn 25 15
243 A37 3c dk brn & vio 25 15
244 A37 5c yel grn & dp org 25 15
245 A37 10c vio & emer 25 15
246 A37 15c dp rose & vio 25 15
247 A37 30c dk bl & brn vio 38 15
248 A37 36c brn vio & ol blk 38 15
249 A37 50c dl grn & ultra 38 15
250 A37 60c dk bl & rose 38 15
251 A38 1 l bl grn, db & red brn 1.00 20
252 A38 3 l dk brn, sal & dk vio 1.25 1.00
253 A38 5 l ol brn, gray & red 2.50 1.00
254 A38 10 l multi 14.00 9.00
255 A38 25 l multi 27.50 20.00
Nos. 242-255 (14) 49.02 32.55

5th cent. of the death of the Grand Duke Vytautas.

Kaunas, Railroad Station A39

Cathedral at Vilnius — A39a

Designs: 15c, 25c, Landscape on the Neman River. 50c, Main Post Office, Kaunas.

Perf. 14, Imperf.
1932, July 21 Wmk. 238
256 A39 10c dk red brn & ocher 25 25
257 A39 15c dk brn & ol 38 38
258 A39 25c dk bl & ol 50 50
259 A39 50c gray blk & ol 75 90
260 A39a 1 l dk bl & ol 1.50 2.25
261 A39a 3 l red brn & gray grn 3.25 3.75

Wmk. 198
262 A39 5c vio bl & ocher 25 25
263 A39a 60c grnsh blk & lil 1.50 1.65
Nos. 256-263 (8) 8.38 9.93

Issued for the benefit of Lithuanian orphans.

In September, 1935, a red overprint was applied to No. 259: "ORO PASTAS / LITUANICA II / 1935 / NEW YORK-KAUNAS". Value $250.

Vytautas Fleeing from Prison, 1382 A40

Designs: 15c, 25c, Conversion of Ladislas II Jagello and Vytautas (1386). 50c, 60c, Battle at Tannenberg (1410). 1 l, 3 l, Meeting of the Nobles (1429).

1932 Wmk. 209 *Perf. 14, Imperf.*
264 A40 5c red & rose lake 28 28
265 A40 10c ol bis & org brn 28 28
266 A40 15c rose lil & ol grn 35 35
267 A40 25c dk vio brn & ocher 85 1.10
268 A40 50c dp grn & bis brn 1.10 1.25
269 A40 60c ol grn & brn car 1.40 1.50

270	A40	1 l ultra & ol grn	1.65	1.90
271	A40	3 l dk brn & dk grn	2.50	2.75
		Nos. 264-271 (8)	8.41	9.41

15th anniversary of independence.

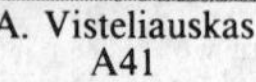

A. Visteliauskas
A41

Mother and Child
A42

Designs: 15c, 25c, Petras Vileisis. 50c, 60c, Dr. John Sliupas. 1 l, 3 l, Jonas Basanavicius.

1933 ***Perf. 14, Imperf.***

272	A41	5c yel grn & car	15	15
273	A41	10c ultra & car	15	15
274	A41	15c org & red	18	22
275	A41	25c dk bl & blk brn	30	35
276	A41	50c ol gray & dk bl	75	1.10
277	A41	60c org brn & chnt	1.50	2.00
277A	A41	1 l red & vio brn	1.75	2.25
277B	A41	3 l turq grn & vio brn	3.00	4.50
		Nos. 272-277B (8)	7.78	10.72

50th anniv. of the 1st newspaper "Ausra" in Lithuanian language.

1933, Sept. ***Perf. 14, Imperf.***

Designs: 15c, 25c, Boy reading. 50c, 60c, Boy playing with blocks. 1 l, 3 l, Woman and boy at the Spinning Wheel.

277C	A42	5c dp yel grn & org brn	15	15
277D	A42	10c rose brn & ultra	15	15
277E	A42	15c ol grn & plum	20	22
277F	A42	25c org & gray blk	30	32
277G	A42	50c ol grn & car	75	1.00
277H	A42	60c blk & yel org	1.50	1.90
277I	A42	1 l dk brn & ultra	1.75	2.00
277K	A42	3 l rose lil & ol grn	3.00	4.25
		Nos. 277C-277K (8)	7.80	9.99

Issued for the benefit of Lithuanian orphans.

Types of 1923-26 Issues

1933-34 **Wmk. 238** ***Perf. 14***

278	A31	2c orange	13.00	1.65
279	A31	10c dk vio	11.00	1.65
280	A31	15c red	17.50	80
281	A22	50c green	8.75	1.65
282	A22	60c red	11.00	80
		Nos. 278-282 (5)	61.25	6.55

Pres. Antanas Smetona, 60th Birthday — A43

1934 **Unwmk.** **Engr.** ***Perf. 11½***

283	A43	15c red	2.75	15
284	A43	30c green	4.50	15
285	A43	60c blue	6.75	20
		Set value		36

A44 A47

Arms — A45 Knight — A48

Girl with Wheat — A46

Wmk. 198; Wmk. 209 (35c, 10 l)

1934-35 **Litho.** ***Perf. 14***

286	A44	2c rose & dl org	60	15
287	A44	5c bl grn & grn	60	15
288	A45	10c chocolate	1.25	15
289	A46	25c dk brn & emer	2.25	15
290	A45	35c carmine	2.25	15
291	A46	50c dk bl & bl	2.75	15
292	A47	1 l sl & mar	12.00	15
293	A47	3 l grn & gray grn	18	15
294	A48	5 l mar & gray bl	24	45
295	A48	10 l choc & yel	1.50	1.50
		Nos. 286-295 (10)	23.62	
		Set value		2.05

No. 290 exists imperf. Value $25.

1936-37 **Wmk. 238** ***Perf. 14***

Size: 17½x23mm

296	A44	2c orange ('37)	15	15
297	A44	5c green	18	15
		Set value		18

Pres. Smetona
A49

Arms
A50

1936-37 **Unwmk.**

298	A49	15c carmine	4.00	15
299	A49	30c green ('37)	6.00	15
300	A49	60c ultra ('37)	6.00	15
		Set value		30

1937-39 **Wmk. 238** ***Perf. 14***

Paper with Gray Network

301	A50	10c green	1.00	15
302	A50	25c magenta	15	15
303	A50	35c red	50	15
304	A50	50c brown	15	15
305	A50	1 l dp vio bl ('39)	15	15
		Nos. 301-305 (5)	1.95	
		Set value		45

No. 304 exists in two types: I- "50" is fat and broad, with "0" leaning to right. II- "50" is thinner and narrower, with "0" straight.

Jonas Basanavicius Reading Act of Independence
A51

President Antanas Smetona
A52

Perf. 13x13½

1939, Jan. 15 **Engr.** **Unwmk.**

306	A51	15c dk red	32	30
307	A52	30c dp grn	32	30
308	A51	35c red lilac	70	45
309	A52	60c dark blue	70	45
a.		Souvenir sheet of 2, #308-309	5.50	11.00
b.		As "a," imperf.	15.00	19.00

20th anniv. of Independence.
Nos. 309a, 309b sold for 2 l.

Same Overprinted in Blue

1939

310	A51	15c dk red	50	80
311	A52	30c dp grn	65	80
312	A51	35c red lilac	75	90
313	A52	60c dark blue	1.00	90

Recovery of Vilnius.

View of Vilnius
A53

Gediminas — A54

Trakai Ruins — A55

Unwmk.

1940, May 6 **Photo.** ***Perf. 14***

314	A53	15c brn & pale brn	30	20
315	A54	30c dk grn & lt grn	40	20
316	A55	60c dk bl & lt bl	80	40
a.		Souvenir sheet of 3, #314-316, imperf.	3.00	6.00

Return of Vilnius to Lithuania, Oct. 10, 1939. Exist imperf.

No. 316a has simulated perforations in gold. Sold for 2 l.

White Knight — A56

Angel — A57

Woman Releasing Dove — A58

Mother and Children — A59

Liberty Bell — A60

Mythical Animal — A61

1940

317	A56	5c brown carmine	15	15
318	A57	10c green	15	15
319	A58	15c dull orange	15	15
320	A59	25c light brn	15	15
321	A60	30c Prussian grn	15	15
322	A61	35c red orange	15	25
		Set value	42	

Nos. 317-322 exist imperf.

Catalogue values for unused stamps in this section, from this point to the end of the section, are for Never Hinged items.

Grand Duke Gediminas, 650th Death Anniv. — A75

1991, Sept. 28 **Litho.** ***Perf. 13x13½***

400	A75	30k Castle	1.40	70
401	A75	50k Grand Duke	2.40	1.20
402	A75	70k Early view of Vilnius	3.30	1.65

Ciconia Nigra — A76

Design: 50k, Grus grus.

1991, Nov. 21 **Litho.** ***Perf. 14***

403	A76	30k +15k multi	2.35	1.15
404	A76	50k multicolored	2.60	1.30

SEMI-POSTAL STAMPS

Regular Issue of 1923-24 Surcharged in Blue, Violet or Black:

On A21 On A22

On A23

1924, Feb. **Wmk. 147** ***Perf. 11***

B1	A21	2c + 2c pale brn (Bl)	55	55
B2	A21	3c + 3c ol bis (Bl)	55	55
B3	A21	5c + 5c pale grn (V)	55	55
B4	A21	10c + 10c vio (Bk)	1.40	1.40
B5	A21	36c + 34c org brn (V)	4.75	4.75

Wmk. Webbing (109)

B6	A21	10c + 10c vio (Bk)	6.00	6.00
B7	A21	15c + 15c scar (V)	1.40	1.40
B8	A21	20c + 20c ol brn (Bl)	1.90	1.90
B9	A21	25c + 25c bl (Bk)	15.00	15.00
B10	A22	50c + 50c yel grn (V)	4.75	4.75
B11	A22	60c + 60c red (V)	6.00	6.00
B12	A23	1 l + 1 l org & grn (V)	6.00	6.00
B13	A23	3 l + 2 l red & gray (V)	7.75	7.75
B14	A23	5 l + 3 l brn & bl (V)	13.00	13.00

Unwmk.

B15	A21	25c + 25c dp bl (Bk)	3.75	3.75
		Nos. B1-B15 (15)	73.35	73.35

For War Invalids

Semi-Postal Stamps of 1924 Surcharged

Surcharged in Gold or Copper

1926, Dec. 3 **Wmk. 147**

B16	A21	1 + 1c on #B1	42	42
a.		Inverted surcharge	5.50	

B17 A21 2 + 2c on #B2 (C) 55 55
B19 A21 2 + 2c on #B3 55 55
a. Double surch.. one inverted 5.50
B20 A21 5 + 5c on #B4 1.10 1.10
B21 A21 14 + 14c on #B5 3.50 3.50

Wmk. Webbing (109)

B22 A21 5 + 5c on #B6 10.00 10.00
B23 A21 5 + 5c on #B7 1.10 1.10
B24 A21 10 + 10c on #B8 1.10 1.10
B25 A21 10 + 10c on #B9 55.00 55.00

Unwmk.

B26 A21 10 + 10c on #B15 2.75 2.75

Surcharged in Copper or Silver:

On A22

On A23

Wmk. Webbing (109)

B27 A22 20 + 20c on #B10 2.75 2.75
B28 A22 25 + 25c on #B11 4.25 4.25
B29 A23 30 + 30c on #B12 (S) 5.50 5.50
Nos. B16-B29 (13) 88.57 88.57

For War Orphans

Surcharged in Gold

1926, Dec. 3 Wmk. 147

B30 A21 1 + 1c on #B1 55 55
B31 A21 2 + 2c on #B2 55 55
a. Inverted surcharge 6.00
B32 A21 2 + 2c on #B3 55 55
a. Inverted surcharge
B33 A21 5 + 5c on #B4 1.10 1.10
B34 A21 19 + 19c on #B5 2.75 2.75

Wmk. Webbing (109)

B35 A21 5 + 5c on #B6 9.50 9.50
B36 A21 10 + 10c on #B7 1.10 1.10
B37 A21 15 + 15c on #B8 1.10 1.10
B38 A21 15 + 15c on #B9 55.00 55.00

Unwmk.

B39 A21 15 + 15c on #B15 2.75 2.75

Surcharged in Gold:

On A22

On A23

Wmk. 109

B40 A22 25c on #B10 3.25 3.25
B41 A22 30c on #B11 5.50 5.50
B42 A23 50c on #B12 5.50 5.50
Nos. B30-B42 (13) 89.20 89.20

Archery — SP1

Natl. Olympiad, July 15-20: 15c+5c, Javelin throwing. 30c+10c, Diving. 60c+15c, Running.

Unwmk.

1938, July 13 Photo. *Perf. 14*

B43 SP1 5c + 5c grn & dk grn 1.00 1.00
B44 SP1 15c + 5c org & red org 1.75 1.75
B45 SP1 30c + 10c bl & dk bl 3.00 3.00
B46 SP1 60c + 15c tan & brn 6.00 5.00

Same Overprinted in Red, Blue or Black:

k

l

1938, July 13

B47 SP1(k) 5c + 5c (R) 4.75 4.75
B48 SP2(l) 15c + 5c (Bl) 4.75 4.75
B49 SP3(l) 30c + 10c (R) 6.00 6.00
B50 SP4(k) 60c + 15c (Bk) 10.00 10.00

National Scout Jamboree, July 12-14.

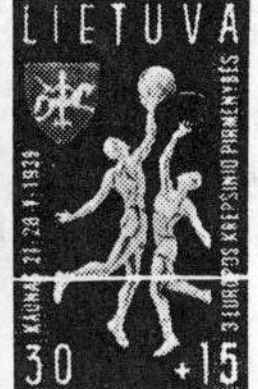

Basketball Players
SP6 SP7

Flags of Competing Nations and Basketball — SP8

1939 Photo. *Perf. 14*

B52 SP6 15c + 10c copper brn & brn 2.25 2.25
B53 SP7 30c + 15c myrtle grn & grn 3.50 2.25
B54 SP8 60c + 40c blue vio & gray vio 5.50 5.50

Issued to commemorate the 3rd European Basketball Championships held at Kaunas. The surtax was used for athletic equipment. Nos. B52-B54 exist imperf. Value, pair, $150.

AIR POST STAMPS

Winged Posthorn — AP1

Airplane over Neman River — AP2

Air Squadron AP3

Plane over Gediminas Castle — AP4

1921 Litho. Wmk. 109 *Perf. 11½*

C1 AP1 20sk ultra 90 75
C2 AP1 40sk red org 75 75
C3 AP1 60sk green 75 75
a. Imperf., pair 22.50
C4 AP1 80sk lt rose 75 75
a. Horiz. pair, imperf. vert. 25.00 22.50
C5 AP2 1auk grn & red 90 50
a. Imperf., pair 12.50 12.50
C6 AP3 2auk brn & blue 1.00 75
C7 AP4 5auk slate & yel 1.50 1.25
Nos. C1-C7 (7) 6.55 5.50

Allegory of Flight — AP5

1921, Nov. 6

C8 AP5 20sk org & gray bl 70 1.10
C9 AP5 40sk dl bl & lake 70 1.10
C10 AP5 60sk vio bl & ol grn 70 1.10
C11 AP5 80sk ocher & dp grn 70 1.10
a. Vertical pair, imperf. between 15.00 15.00
C12 AP5 1auk bl grn & bl 70 1.10
C13 AP5 2auk gray & brn org 85 1.10
C14 AP5 5auk dl lil & Prus bl 85 1.10
Nos. C8-C14 (7) 5.20 7.70

Opening of airmail service.

Plane over Kaunas — AP6

Black Overprint

1922, July 16 *Perf. 11, 11½*

C15 AP6 1auk ol brn & red 85 1.10
a. Imperf., pair 40.00
C16 AP6 3auk vio & grn 85 1.10
C17 AP6 5auk dp bl & yel 1.40 1.40

It was the intention to issue Nos. C15 to C17, without overprint, in commemoration of the founding of the Air Post service but they were not put in use at that time. Subsequently the word "ZENKLAS" (stamp) was overprinted over "ISTEIGIMAS" (founding) and the date "1921, VI, 25" was obliterated by short vertical lines.

Plane over Gediminas Castle — AP7

1922, July 22

C18 AP7 2auk bl & rose 85 85
C19 AP7 4auk brn & rose 85 85
C20 AP7 10auk blk & gray bl 1.40 1.40

Nos. C1-C7, C17-C20 Surcharged like Regular Issues in Black or Carmine

1922

C21 AP1 10c on 20sk 1.00 1.25
C22 AP1 10c on 40sk 1.00 1.25
C23 AP1 10c on 60sk 75 90
a. Inverted surcharge 17.50
C24 AP1 10c on 80sk 1.00 1.25
C25 AP2 20c on 1auk 2.50 3.00
C26 AP3 20c on 2auk 4.00 4.50
a. Without "CENT" 125.00 125.00
C27 AP7 25c on 2auk 75 50
a. Inverted surcharge 17.50 17.50
C28 AP7 30c on 4auk (C) 75 65
a. Double surcharge 20.00 20.00
C29 AP4 50c on 5auk 1.00 75
C30 AP7 50c on 10auk 65 65
a. Inverted surcharge 20.00 20.00
C31 AP6 1 l on 5auk 7.50 8.75
a. Double surcharge 27.50
Nos. C21-C31 (11) 20.90 23.45

Airplane and Carrier Pigeons AP8

"Flight" AP9

1924, Jan. 28 Wmk. 147 *Perf. 11*

C32 AP8 20c yellow 1.00 50
C33 AP8 40c emerald 1.00 50
a. Horiz. or vert. pair, imperf. between 30.00
C34 AP8 60c rose 1.25 50
a. Imperf., pair 55.00
C35 AP9 1 l dk brn 1.75 50

Most copies, if not all, of the "unwatermarked" varieties show faint traces of watermark, according to experts. Counterfeits show no trace of watermark.

Swallow — AP10

1926, June 17 Wmk. 198 *Perf. 14½*

C37 AP10 20c car rose 85 70
a. Horiz. or vert. pair, imperf. between 15.00
C38 AP10 40c vio & red org 85 70
a. Horiz. or vert. pair, imperf. between 15.00
C39 AP10 60c bl & blk 1.10 70
a. Horiz. or vert. pair, imperf. between 15.00
c. Center inverted 110.00 110.00

Juozas Tubelis AP11

Vytautas and Airplane over Kaunas AP12

Vytautas and Antanas Smetona AP13

1930, Feb. 16 Wmk. 109 *Perf. 14*

C40 AP11 5c blk, bis & brn 42 28
C41 AP11 10c dk bl, db & blk 42 28
C42 AP11 15c mar, gray & bl 42 28
C43 AP12 20c dk brn, org & dl red 42 35
C44 AP12 40c dk bl, lt bl & vio 70 42
C45 AP13 60c bl grn, lil & blk 85 55
C46 AP13 1 l dl red, lil & blk 1.10 70
Nos. C40-C46 (7) 4.33 2.86

5th cent. of the death of the Grand Duke Vytautas.

Map of Lithuania, Klaipeda and Vilnius — AP14

Designs: 15c, 20c, Airplane over Neman. 40c, 60c, City Hall, Kaunas. 1 l, 2 l, Church of Vytautas, Kaunas.

Wmk. Multiple Letters (238)

1932, July 21 *Perf. 14, Imperf.*

C47 AP14 5c ver & ol grn 25 38
C48 AP14 10c dk red brn & ocher 25 38
C49 AP14 15c dk bl & org yel 25 38
C50 AP14 20c sl blk & org 38 50

C51	AP14	60c ultra & ocher	1.50	1.65
C52	AP14	2 l dk bl & yel	2.25	2.50

Wmk. 198

C53	AP14	40c vio brn & yel	1.10	1.40
C54	AP14	1 l vio brn & grn	1.75	2.00
		Nos. C47-C54 (8)	7.73	9.19

Issued for the benefit of Lithuanian orphans.

Mindaugas in the Battle of Shauyai, 1236 — AP15

Designs: 15c, 20c, Coronation of Mindaugas (1253). 40c, Grand Duke Gediminas and his followers. 60c, Founding of Vilnius by Gediminas (1332). 1 l, Gediminas capturing the Russian Fortifications. 2 l, Grand Duke Algirdas before Moscow (1368).

Perf. 14, Imperf.

1932, Nov. 28 **Wmk. 209**

C55	AP15	5c grn & red lil	45	60
C56	AP15	10c emer & rose	45	60
C57	AP15	15c rose vio & bis brn	45	60
C58	AP15	20c rose red & blk brn	45	40
C59	AP15	40c choc & dk gray	75	90
C60	AP15	60c org & gray blk	1.25	1.50
C61	AP15	1 l rose vio & grn	1.50	1.75
C62	AP15	2 l dp bl & brn	2.25	2.75
		Nos. C55-C62 (8)	7.55	9.10

Anniv. of independence.

Nos. C58-C62 exist with overprint "DARIUS-GIRENAS / NEW YORK-1933-KAUNAS" below small plane. The overprint was applied in New York with the approval of the Lithuanian consul general. Lithuanian postal authorities seem not to have been involved in the creation or release of these overprints.

Trakai Castle, Home of the Grand Duke Kestutis — AP16

Designs: 15c, 20c, Meeting of Kestutis and the Hermit Birute. 40c, 60c, Hermit Birute. 1 l, 2 l, Kestutis and his Brother Algirdas.

1933, May 6 ***Perf. 14, Imperf.***

C63	AP16	5c ol gray & dp bl	25	38
C64	AP16	10c gray vio & org brn	25	38
C65	AP16	15c dp bl & lil	25	38
C66	AP16	20c org brn & lil	50	55
C67	AP16	40c lt ultra & lil	75	1.10
C68	AP16	60c brn & lt ultra	1.40	1.65
C69	AP16	1 l ol gray & dp bl	1.65	2.00
C70	AP16	2 l vio gray & yel grn	2.25	2.75
		Nos. C63-C70 (8)	7.30	9.19

Issued to commemorate the reopening of air service to Berlin-Kaunas-Moscow, and the 550th anniversary of the death of Kestutis.

Joseph Maironis — AP17

Lithuania German Occupation stamps can be mounted in Scott's Germany Part II Album.

Joseph Tumas-Vaizgantas — AP17a

Designs: 40c, 60c, Vincas Kudirka. 1 l, 2 l, Julia A. Zemaite.

1933, Sept. 15 ***Perf. 14, Imperf.***

C71	AP17	5c crim & dp bl	42	55
C72	AP17	10c bl vio & grn	42	55
C73	AP17a	15c dk grn & choc	42	55
C74	AP17a	20c brn car & ultra	55	60
C75	AP17	40c red brn & ol grn	85	1.10
C76	AP17	60c dk bl & choc	1.10	1.40
C77	AP17	1 l cit & ind	1.25	1.50
C78	AP17	2 l dp grn & red brn	1.90	2.25
		Nos. C71-C78 (8)	6.91	8.50

Issued for the benefit of Lithuanian orphans.

Capts. Steponas Darius and Stas. Girenas AP18

Ill-Fated Plane "Lituanica" AP19

The Dark Angel of Death — AP20

"Lituanica" over Globe — AP21

"Lituanica" and White Knight — AP22

Perf. 11½

1934, May 18 **Unwmk.** **Engr.**

C79	AP18	20c scar & blk	15	15
C80	AP19	40c dp rose & bl	15	15
C81	AP18	60c dk vio & blk	15	15
C82	AP20	1 l blk & rose	28	15
C83	AP21	3 l gray grn & org	70	45
C84	AP22	5 l dk brn & bl	1.40	1.10
		Nos. C79-C84 (6)	2.83	
		Set value		1.75

Issued to commemorate the death of Capts. Steponas Darius and Stas. Girenas on their New York-Kaunas flight of 1933.

No. C80 exists with diagonal overprint: "F. VAITKUS / nugalejo Atlanta / 21-22-IX-1935". Value $275.

Felix Waitkus and Map of Transatlantic Flight — AP23

Wmk. 238

1936, Mar. 24 **Litho.** ***Perf. 14***

C85	AP23	15c brown lake	65	55
C86	AP23	30c dark green	85	55
C87	AP23	60c blue	1.50	90

Transatlantic Flight of the Lituanica II, Sept. 21-22, 1935.

AIR POST SEMI-POSTAL STAMPS

Nos. C32-C35 Surcharged like Nos. B1-B9 (No. CB1), Nos. B10-B11 (Nos. CB2-CB3), and Nos. B12-B14 (No. CB4) in Red, Violet or Black

1924 **Wmk. 147** ***Perf. 11***

CB1	AP8	20c + 20c yel (R)	5.00	6.75
CB2	AP8	40c + 40c emer (V)	5.00	6.75
CB3	AP8	60c + 60c rose (V)	5.00	6.75
CB4	AP9	1 l + 1 l dk brn	5.00	6.75

Surtax for the Red Cross. See note following No. C35.

SOUTH LITHUANIA

GRODNO DISTRICT

Russian Stamps of 1909-12 Surcharged in Black or Red

Lietuva
Aітва.
50
skatikų
грашэй.

1919 **Unwmk.** ***Perf. 14, 14½x15***

L1	A14	50sk on 3k red	42.50	24.00
a.		Double surcharge		
L2	A14	50sk on 5k cl	24.00	24.00
a.		Imperf., pair	200.00	200.00
L3	A15	50sk on 10k dk bl (R)	24.00	24.00
L4	A11	50sk on 15k red brn & bl	24.00	24.00
a.		Imperf., pair	225.00	225.00
L5	A11	50sk on 25k grn & gray vio (R)	24.00	24.00
L6	A11	50sk on 35k red brn & grn	24.00	24.00
L7	A8	50sk on 50k vio & grn	24.00	24.00
L8	A11	50sk on 70k brn & org	24.00	24.00
		Nos. L1-L8 (8)	210.50	192.00

Excellent counterfeits are plentiful.

This surcharge exists on Russia No. 119, the imperf. 1k orange of 1917. Value, unused $90, used $60.

OCCUPATION STAMPS

ISSUED UNDER GERMAN OCCUPATION

German Stamps Overprinted in Black

Postgebiet
Ob. Ost

On Stamps of 1905-17

1916-17 **Wmk. 125** ***Perf. 14, 14½***

1N1	A22	2½pf gray	15	15
1N2	A16	3pf brown	15	15
1N3	A16	5pf green	20	15
1N4	A22	7½pf orange	15	15
1N5	A16	10pf carmine	18	18
1N6	A22	15pf yel brn	3.50	3.00
1N7	A22	15pf dk vio ('17)	20	18
1N8	A16	20pf ultra	52	52
1N9	A16	25pf org & blk, *yel*	20	35
1N10	A16	40pf lake & blk	75	1.00
1N11	A16	50pf vio & blk, *buff*	75	65
1N12	A17	1m car rose	10.50	3.75
		Nos. 1N1-1N12 (12)	17.25	10.23

These stamps were used in the former Russian provinces of Suvalki, Vilnius, Kaunas, Kurland.

ISSUED UNDER RUSSIAN OCCUPATION

Lithuanian Stamps of 1937-40 Overprinted in Red or Blue

LTSR
1940 VII 21

1940 **Wmk. 238** ***Perf. 14***

2N9	A44	2c orange (Bl)	25	38
2N10	A50	50c brown (Bl)	50	50

Unwmk.

2N11	A56	5c brn car (Bl)	25	38
2N12	A57	10c grn (R)	1.75	1.75
2N13	A58	15c dl org (Bl)	25	38
2N14	A59	25c lt brn (R)	25	38
2N15	A60	30c Prus grn (R)	50	50
2N16	A61	35c red org (Bl)	75	1.00
		Nos. 2N9-2N16 (8)	4.50	5.27

Values for used stamps are for CTOs. Postally used examples are considerably more.

The Lithuanian Soviet Socialist Republic was proclaimed July 21, 1940.

LOURENCO MARQUES

LOCATION — In the southern part of Mozambique in Southeast Africa
GOVT. — Part of Portuguese East Africa Colony
AREA — 28,800 sq. mi. (approx.)
POP. — 474,000 (approx.)
CAPITAL — Lourenço Marques

Stamps of Mozambique replaced those of Lourenço Marques in 1920. See Mozambique.

1000 Reis = 1 Milreis
100 Centavos = 1 Escudo (1913)

King Carlos — A1

Perf. 11½, 12½, 13½

1895 **Typo.** **Unwmk.**

1	A1	5r yellow	38	20
2	A1	10r redsh vio	38	28
3	A1	15r chocolate	60	45
4	A1	20r lavender	60	45
5	A1	25r bl grn	60	24
a.		Perf. 11½	2.50	70
6	A1	50r lt bl	75	60
a.		Perf. 13½	7.25	3.75
b.		Perf. 11½		
7	A1	75r rose	1.40	1.25
8	A1	80r yel grn	4.50	2.75
9	A1	100r brn, *yel*	1.50	85
a.		Perf. 12½	3.75	2.50
10	A1	150r car, *rose*	3.00	2.50
11	A1	200r dk bl, *bl*	3.75	2.10
12	A1	300r dk bl, *sal*	3.75	2.10
		Nos. 1-12 (12)	21.21	13.77

Saint Anthony of Padua Issue

Regular Issues of Mozambique, 1886 and 1894, Overprinted in Black

L. MARQUES
CENTENARIO
DE
S. ANTONIO
MDCCCXCV

1895 **Without Gum** ***Perf. 12½***

On 1886 Issue

13	A2	5r black	10.00	8.00
14	A2	10r green	14.00	8.00
15	A2	20r rose	17.00	8.75
16	A2	25r lilac	20.00	14.00
17	A2	40r chocolate	17.50	11.00
18	A2	50r bl, perf. 13½	15.00	8.75
a.		Perf. 12½	32.50	22.50
19	A2	100r yel brn	30.00	22.50
20	A2	200r gray vio	25.00	19.00
21	A2	300r orange	32.50	30.00

On 1894 Issue

Perf. 11½

22 A3 5r yellow 12.50 7.50
23 A3 10r redsh vio 20.00 11.00
24 A3 50r lt bl 25.00 14.00
a. Perf. 12½ 37.50 30.00
25 A3 75r rose, perf. 12½ 30.00 22.50
26 A3 80r yel grn 45.00 25.00
27 A3 100r brn, *buff* 125.00 35.00
28 A3 150r car, *rose*, perf. 12½ 40.00 25.00
Nos. 13-28 (16) 478.50 270.00

No. 12 Surcharged in Black

50 réis

1897, Jan. 2
29 A1 50r on 300r 140.00 75.00

No. 29 issued mostly without gum.

King Carlos — A2

1898-1903 ***Perf. 11½***

Name, Value in Black except 500r

30 A2 2½r gray 20 20
31 A2 5r orange 20 20
32 A2 10r lt grn 20 20
33 A2 15r brown 1.00 85
34 A2 15r gray grn ('03) 40 35
a. Imperf.
35 A2 20r gray vio 40 20
a. Imperf.
36 A2 25r sea grn 55 28
a. Perf. 13½ 25.00 6.75
b. 25r light green (error) *25.00 25.00*
c. Perf. 12½ *60.00* 55.00
37 A2 25r car ('03) 28 20
a. Imperf.
38 A2 50r blue 95 35
39 A2 50r brn ('03) 80 70
40 A2 65r dl bl ('03) 4.75 4.00
41 A2 75r rose 1.50 1.40
42 A2 75r lilac ('03) 1.10 95
a. Imperf.
43 A2 80r violet 1.50 1.25
44 A2 100r dk bl, *bl* 1.40 55
a. Perf. 13½ 14.00 4.75
45 A2 115r org brn, *pink* ('03) 4.50 4.00
46 A2 130r brn, *straw* ('03) 4.50 4.00
47 A2 150r brn, *straw* 1.75 1.40
48 A2 200r red lil, *pnksh* 2.50 1.25
49 A2 300r dk bl, *rose* 1.75 1.25
50 A2 400r dl bl, *straw* ('03) 5.75 4.00
51 A2 500r blk & red, *bl* ('01) 3.50 2.25
52 A2 700r vio, *yelsh* ('01) 6.75 5.75
Nos. 30-52 (23) 46.23 35.58

Coat of Arms — A3

Surcharged On Upper and Lower Halves of Stamp

1899 ***Imperf.***
53 A3 5r on 10r grn & brn 10.00 10.00
54 A3 25r on 10r grn & brn 10.00 10.00
55 A3 50r on 30r grn & brn 12.00 12.00
a. Inverted surcharge
56 A3 50r on 800r grn & brn 18.00 18.00

The lower half of No. 55 can be distinguished from that of No. 56 by the background of the label containing the word "REIS." The former is plain, while the latter is formed of white intersecting curved horizontal lines over vertical shading of violet brown.

Values are for undivided stamps. Halves sell for ¼ as much.

Nos. 53-56 issued mostly without gum.

No. 41 Surcharged in Black

50 Réis

1899 ***Perf. 11½***
57 A2 50r on 75r rose 3.25 2.50

No. 57 issued mostly without gum.

Surcharged in Black

On Issue of 1895

1902 ***Perf. 11½, 12½***
58 A1 65r on 5r yel 2.25 1.90
59 A1 65r on 15r choc 2.25 1.90
60 A1 65r on 20r lav 2.25 1.90
a. Perf. 12½ 22.50 12.00
61 A1 115r on 10r red vio 2.25 1.90
62 A1 115r on 200r bl, *bl* 2.25 1.90
63 A1 115r on 300r bl, *sal* 2.25 1.90
64 A1 130r on 25r grn, perf. 12½ 1.90 1.50
a. Perf. 11½ 24.00 19.00
65 A1 130r on 80r yel grn 2.00 1.90
66 A1 130r on 150r car, *rose* 2.00 1.90
67 A1 400r on 50r lt bl 6.00 4.00
68 A1 400r on 75r rose 6.00 4.00
69 A1 400r on 100r brn, *buff* 4.00 3.50

On Newspaper Stamp of 1893
70 N1 65r on 2½ brn 2.25 1.90
Nos. 58-70 (13) 37.65 30.10

Surcharge exists inverted on Nos. 61, 70.

Nos. 64, 67 and 68 have been reprinted on thin white paper with shiny white gum and clean-cut perforation 13½. Value $2 each.

Issue of 1898-1903 Overprinted in Black

PROVISORIO

1903 ***Perf. 11½***
71 A2 15r brown 1.25 85
72 A2 25r sea green 1.00 85
73 A2 50r blue 1.40 85
74 A2 75r rose 2.00 1.40
a. Inverted overprint 10.00 10.00

Surcharged in Black

50 RÉIS

1905
76 A2 50r on 65r dull blue 1.75 1.50

Regular Issues Overprinted in Carmine or Green

1911
77 A2 2½r gray 18 18
78 A2 5r orange 18 18
a. Double overprint 4.00 4.00
b. Inverted overprint 4.00 4.00
79 A2 10r lt grn 28 22
80 A2 15r gray grn 28 24
a. Inverted overprint 4.00 4.00
81 A2 20r dl vio 60 38
82 A2 25r car (G) 22 18
83 A2 50r brown 60 38
84 A2 75r lilac 60 38
85 A2 100r dk bl, *bl* 60 38
86 A2 115r org brn, *pink* 5.50 1.90
87 A2 130r brn, *straw* 60 40
88 A2 200r red lil, *pnksh* 60 40
89 A2 400r dl bl, *straw* 65 60
90 A2 500r blk & red, *bl* 90 75
91 A2 700r vio, *yelsh* 1.25 90
Nos. 77-91 (15) 13.04 7.47

Vasco da Gama Issue of Various Portuguese Colonies Common Design Types Surcharged

REPUBLICA
LOURENCO MARQUES
¼ C.

1913 ***Perf. 12½-16***

On Stamps of Macao
92 CD20 ¼c on ½a bl grn 1.75 1.75
93 CD21 ½c on 1a red 1.75 1.75
94 CD22 1c on 2a red vio 1.75 1.75
95 CD23 2½c on 4a yel grn 1.75 1.75
96 CD24 5c on 8a dk bl 1.75 1.75
97 CD25 7½c on 12a vio brn 3.50 3.50
98 CD26 10c on 16a bis brn 3.00 3.00
a. Inverted surcharge
99 CD27 15c on 24a bis 3.25 3.25
Nos. 92-99 (8) 18.50 18.50

On Stamps of Portuguese Africa
100 CD20 ¼c on 2½r bl grn 1.00 1.00
101 CD21 ½c on 5r red 1.00 1.00
102 CD22 1c on 10r red vio 1.00 1.00
103 CD23 2½c on 25r yel grn 1.00 1.00
104 CD24 5c on 50r dk bl 1.00 1.00
105 CD25 7½c on 75r vio brn 3.00 3.00
106 CD26 10c on 100r bis brn 2.00 2.00
107 CD27 15c on 150r bis 2.00 2.00
Nos. 100-107 (8) 12.00 12.00

On Stamps of Timor
108 CD20 ¼c on ½a bl grn 1.50 1.50
109 CD21 ½c on 1a red 1.50 1.50
110 CD22 1c on 2a red vio 1.50 1.50
111 CD23 2½c on 4a yel grn 1.50 1.50
112 CD24 5c on 8a dk bl 1.50 1.50
113 CD25 7½c on 12a vio brn 3.00 3.00
114 CD26 10c on 16a bis brn 2.50 2.50
115 CD27 15c on 24a bis 2.50 2.50
Nos. 108-115 (8) 15.50 15.50
Nos. 92-115 (24) 46.00 46.00

Ceres — A4

1914 **Typo.** ***Perf. 15x14***

Name and Value in Black
116 A4 ¼c ol brn 15 15
117 A4 ½c black 15 15
a. Value omitted
118 A4 1c bl grn 15 15
119 A4 1½c lil brn 15 15
a. Imperf.
120 A4 2c carmine 15 15
121 A4 2½c lt vio 15 15
122 A4 5c dp bl 15 15
123 A4 7½c yel brn 15 15
124 A4 8c slate 15 15
125 A4 10c org brn 1.50 70
126 A4 15c plum 40 35
127 A4 20c yel grn 1.75 50
128 A4 30c brn, *grn* 1.90 1.00
129 A4 40c brn, *pink* 4.50 4.00
130 A4 50c org, *sal* 2.25 2.25
131 A4 1e grn, *bl* 2.50 1.75
Nos. 116-131 (16) 16.15 11.90

Values of Nos. 116-124 are for stamps on ordinary paper. Those on chalky paper sell for 8 to 12 times as much. Nos. 127-131 issued only on chalky paper.

In 1921 Nos. 117 and 119 were surcharged 10c and 30c respectively, for use in Mozambique as Nos. 230 and 231. These same values, surcharged 5c and 10c respectively, with the addition of the word "PORTEADO," were used in Mozambique as postage dues, Nos. J44 and J45.

Provisional Issue of 1902 Overprinted Locally in Carmine

1914 ***Perf. 11½, 12½***
132 A1 115r on 10r red vio 70 45
a. "Republica" inverted
133 A1 115r on 200r bl, *bl* 70 45
134 A1 115r on 300r bl, *sal* 70 45
a. Double overprint 12.50 12.50
135 A1 130r on 25r grn 1.10 70
a. Perf. 12½ 3.25 1.65
136 A1 130r on 80r yel grn 70 35
137 A1 130r on 150r car, *rose* 70 35
Nos. 132-137 (6) 4.60 2.75

No. 135a was issued without gum.

Nos. 78 and 117 Perforated Diagonally and Surcharged in Carmine

¼

1915 ***Perf. 11½***
138 A2 ¼c on half of 5r org, pair 4.00 4.00
a. Pair without dividing perfs. 8.00 8.00

Perf. 15x14
139 A4 ¼c on half of ½c blk, pair 6.00 6.00

The added perforation on Nos. 138-139 runs from lower left to upper right corners, dividing the stamp in two. Values are for pairs, both halves of the stamp.

Provisional Issue of 1902 Overprinted in Carmine

1915 ***Perf. 11½, 12½***
140 A1 115r on 10r red vio 55 40
141 A1 115r on 200r bl, *bl* 55 40
142 A1 115r on 300r bl, *sal* 55 40
143 A1 130r on 150r car, *rose* 55 40

Nos. 34 and 80 Surcharged

Dois centavos

1915

On Issue of 1903
144 A2 2c on 15r gray grn 75 70

On Issue of 1911
145 A2 2c on 15r gray grn 75 70
a. New value inverted 15.00

Regular Issues of 1898-1903 Overprinted Locally in Carmine

REPUBLICA

1916
146 A2 15r gray grn 1.00 42
147 A2 50r brown 2.00 1.25
a. Inverted overprint
148 A2 75r lilac 2.25 1.40
149 A2 100r bl, *bl* 1.25 70
150 A2 115r org brn, *pink* 1.25 70
151 A2 130r brn, *straw* 8.00 4.25
152 A2 200r red lil, *pnksh* 2.00 1.10
153 A2 400r dl bl, *straw* 4.00 1.90
154 A2 500r blk & red, *bl* 3.00 1.40
155 A2 700r vio, *yelsh* 6.00 1.75
Nos. 146-155 (10) 30.75 14.87

Same Overprint on Nos. 67-68

1917
156 A1 400r on 50r lt bl 1.25 65
a. Perf. 13½ 11.50 9.00
157 A1 400r on 75r rose 2.50 1.00

No. 69 exists with this overprint. It was not officially issued.

Type of 1914 Surcharged in Red

Quatro centavos

1920 *Perf. 15x14*

159 A4 4c on 2½c violet	1.00	28

Stamps of 1914 Surcharged in Green or Black

Um quarto de centavo
a

1 Centavo
b

1921

160 A1(a) ¼c on 115r on 10r red vio (G)	80	80
161 A4(b) 1c on 2½c vio (Bk)	52	40
a. Inverted surcharge	20.00	
162 A4(b) 1½c on 2½c vio (Bk)	80	60

Nos. 159-162 were postally valid throughout Mozambique.

SEMI-POSTAL STAMPS

Regular Issue of 1914 Overprinted or Surcharged:

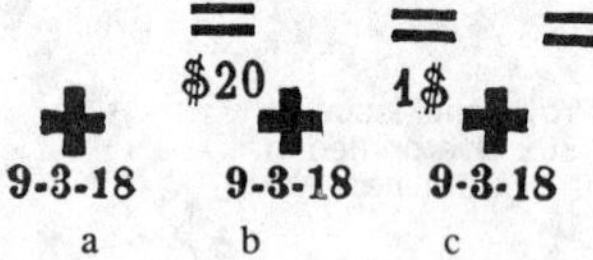

a b c

1918 *Perf. 15x14½*

B1	A4(a)	¼c ol brn	2.00	2.00
B2	A4(a)	½c black	2.00	2.00
B3	A4(a)	1c bl grn	2.00	2.00
B4	A4(a)	2½c violet	4.00	4.00
B5	A4(a)	5c blue	4.00	4.00
B6	A4(a)	10c org brn	5.00	5.00
B7	A4(b)	20c on 1½c lil brn	5.00	5.00
B8	A4(a)	30c brn, *grn*	5.00	5.00
B9	A4(b)	40c on 2c car	5.00	5.00
B10	A4(b)	50c on 7½c bis	8.00	8.00
B11	A4(b)	70c on 8c slate	10.00	10.00
B12	A4(c)	$1 on 15c mag	10.00	10.00
		Nos. B1-B12 (12)	62.00	62.00

Nos. B1-B12 were used in place of ordinary postage stamps on Mar. 9, 1918.

NEWSPAPER STAMPS

Numeral of Value — N1

Perf. 11½

1893, July 28 **Typo.** **Unwmk.**

P1 N1 2½r brown	25	65
a. Perf. 12½	20.00	17.50

Saint Anthony of Padua Issue

Mozambique No. P6 Overprinted

L. MARQUES
—
CENTENARIO
DE
S. ANTONIO
—
MDCCCXCV

1895, July 1 *Perf. 11½, 13½*

P2 N3 2½r brown	20.00	17.50
a. Inverted overprint	30.00	30.00

LUXEMBOURG

LOCATION — Western Europe between southern Belgium, Germany and France
GOVT. — Grand Duchy
AREA — 998 sq. mi.
POP. — 365,800 (est. 1984)
CAPITAL — Luxembourg

12½ Centimes = 1 Silbergroschen
100 Centimes = 1 Franc

Catalogue values for unused stamps in this country are for Never Hinged items, beginning with Scott 357 in the regular postage section, Scott B216 in the semi-postal section.

Values of early Luxembourg stamps vary according to condition. Quotations for Nos. 1-12 are for fine copies. Very fine to superb specimens sell at much higher prices, and inferior or poor copies sell at reduced prices, depending on the condition of the individual specimen.

Watermarks

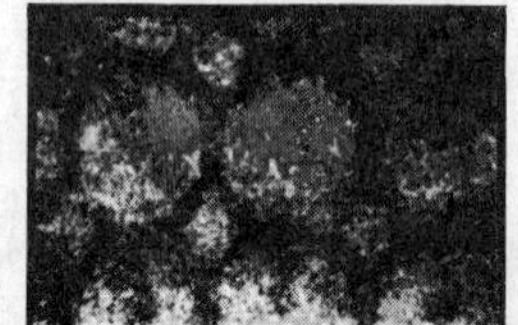

Wmk. 110- Octagons

Wmk. 149- W

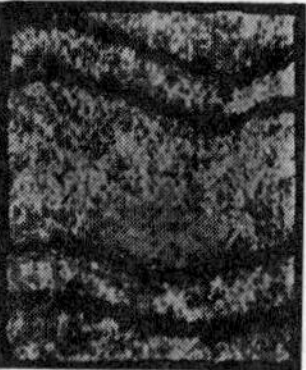

Wmk. 213 - Double Wavy Lines

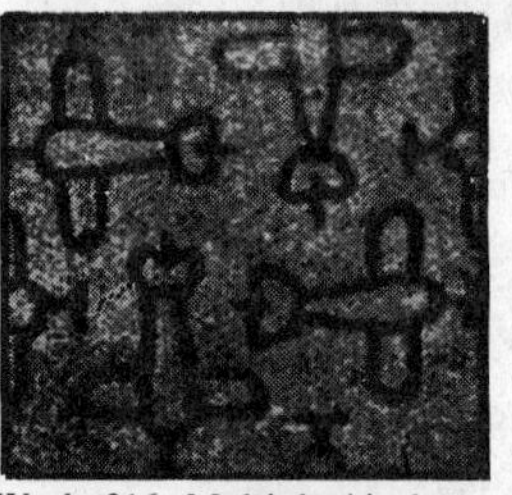

Wmk. 216- Multiple Airplanes

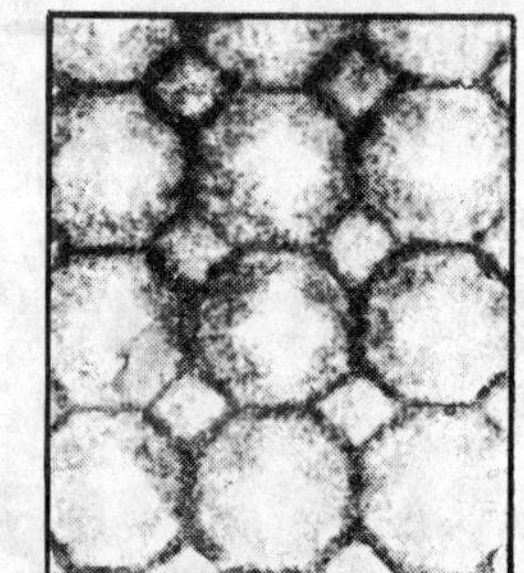

Wmk. 246- Multiple Cross Enclosed in Octagons

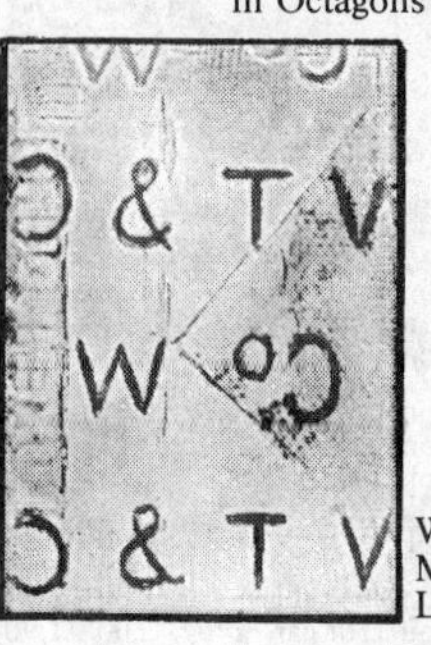

Wmk. 247- Multiple Letters

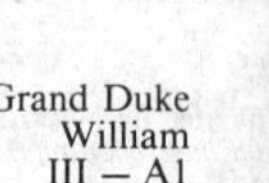

Grand Duke William III — A1

Luxembourg Print

Wmk. 149

1852, Sept. 15 **Engr.** ***Imperf.***

1	A1	10c gray blk	*925.00*	18.00
a.		10c black	*1,400.*	25.00
2	A1	1sg brick red	625.00	25.00
a.		1sg brown red	625.00	45.00
b.		1sg orange red	625.00	45.00
c.		1sg copper red	625.00	30.00
3	A1	1sg rose	625.00	60.00

Reprints of both values exist on watermarked paper. Some of the reprints show traces of lines cancelling the plates, but others can be distinguished only by an expert.

Coat of Arms
A2 A3

Frankfort Print

1859-63 **Typo.** **Unwmk.**

4	A2	1c	buff ('63)	75.00	*125.00*
5	A2	2c	blk ('60)	60.00	*180.00*
6	A2	4c	yel ('60)	100.00	75.00
a.		4c orange		125.00	100.00
7	A3	10c	blue	125.00	7.00
8	A3	12½c	rose	150.00	70.00
9	A3	25c	brown	175.00	100.00
10	A3	30c	rose lil	190.00	85.00
11	A3	37½c	green	190.00	80.00
12	A3	40c	red org	500.00	110.00

Counterfeits of Nos. 1-12 exist.

1865-71 ***Rouletted***

13	A2	1c	red brn	110.00	125.00
14	A2	2c	blk ('67)	12.00	8.50
15	A2	4c	yel ('67)	500.00	125.00
16	A2	4c	grn ('71)	25.00	15.00

A4

A5

1865-74 ***Rouletted in Color***

17	A2	1c	red brn ('72)	12.50	4.00
18	A2	1c	org ('69)	18.00	3.50
a.		1c brn org ('67)		75.00	22.50
19	A3	10c	lilac	75.00	1.00
a.		10c rose lil		75.00	1.00
b.		10c gray lil		77.50	1.00
20	A3	12½c	carmine	200.00	4.50
a.		12½c rose		250.00	6.00
21	A3	20c	gray brn ('72)	80.00	2.50
a.		20c yel brn ('69)		90.00	4.00
22	A3	25c	bl ('72)	650.00	9.00
22A	A3	25c	ultra ('65)	600.00	12.50
23	A3	30c	lil rose	650.00	40.00
24	A3	37½c	bis ('66)	600.00	150.00
25	A3	40c	pale org ('74)	30.00	55.00
a.		40c org red ('66)		800.00	40.00
26	A4	1fr	on 37½c bis ('73)	750.00	45.00
a.		Surcharge inverted			*3,250.*

Luxembourg Print

1874 **Typo.** ***Imperf.***

27	A2	4c	green	75.00	75.00

1875-79 ***Perf. 13***

Narrow Margins

29	A2	1c	red brn ('78)	30.00	3.00
30	A2	2c	black	125.00	15.00
31	A2	4c	green	1.50	*5.00*
32	A2	5c	yel ('76)	150.00	10.00
a.		5c orange yellow		600.00	100.00
b.		Imperf.		450.00	400.00
33	A3	10c	gray lil	400.00	1.00
b.		10c lilac		1,300.	15.00
c.		Imperf.		1,300.	*2,200.*
34	A3	12½c	lil rose ('76)	500.00	15.00
35	A3	12½c	car rose ('77)	300.00	12.50
36	A3	25c	bl ('77)	700.00	10.00
37	A3	30c	dl rose ('78)	650.00	400.00
38	A3	40c	org ('79)	1.00	*8.00*
39	A5	1fr	on 37½c bis ('79)	8.00	*15.00*
a.		"Pranc"		*5,000.*	*6,250.*
b.		Without surcharge		400.00	
c.		As "b." imperf.		400.00	

In the Luxembourg print the perforation is close to the border of the stamp. Excellent forgeries of No. 39a are plentiful, as well as faked cancellations on Nos. 31, 38 and 39.

Nos. 32b and 33c are said to be essays; Nos. 39b and 39c printer's waste.

Haarlem Print

Perf. 11½x12, 12½x12, 13½

1880-81

Wide Margins

40	A2	1c	yel brn ('81)	8.00	5.00
41	A2	2c	black	7.50	1.00
42	A2	5c	yel ('81)	175.00	75.00
43	A3	10c	gray lil	150.00	65
44	A3	12½c	rose ('81)	175.00	160.00
45	A3	20c	gray brn ('81)	40.00	11.00
46	A3	25c	blue	250.00	3.50
47	A3	30c	dl rose ('81)	3.00	13.00

Stamps on gray yellowish paper were not regularly issued.

Gray Yellowish Paper

Perf. 12½

42a	A2	5c	5.00
43a	A3	10c	1.50
44a	A3	12½c	7.50
46a	A3	25c	3.00

"Industry" and "Commerce" A6

Grand Duke Adolphe A7

Perf. 11½x12, 12½x12, 12½, 13½
1882, Dec. 1 **Typo.**
48 A6 1c gray lil 20 25
49 A6 2c olive gray 20 20
a. 2c olive brown 25 40
50 A6 4c olive bis 40 60
51 A6 5c lt grn 60 20
52 A6 10c rose 4.75 20
53 A6 12½c slate 3.00 6.00
54 A6 20c orange 4.50 1.40
55 A6 25c ultra 165.00 1.00
56 A6 30c gray grn 25.00 13.00
57 A6 50c bis brn 1.10 2.00
58 A6 1fr pale vio 1.10 6.00
59 A6 5fr brn org 30.00 70.00

Perf. 11, 11½, 11½x11 and 12½
1891-93 **Engr.**
60 A7 10c carmine 15 20
a. Sheet of 25 60.00
61 A7 12½c sl grn ('93) 28 30
62 A7 20c org ('93) 5.00 40
a. 20c brown (error) 90.00 165.00
63 A7 25c blue 38 25
a. Sheet of 25 725.00
64 A7 30c ol grn ('93) 90 80
65 A7 37½c grn ('93) 1.90 2.00
66 A7 50c brn ('93) 3.75 2.00
67 A7 1fr dp vio ('93) 7.75 3.75
68 A7 2½fr blk ('93) 75 6.00
69 A7 5fr lake ('93) 32.50 45.00

No. 62a was never on sale at any post office, but exists postally used.
Perf. 11½ stamps are from the sheets of 25.

Grand Duke Adolphe — A8

1895, May 4 **Typo.** *Perf. 12½*
70 A8 1c pearl gray 3.00 20
71 A8 2c gray brown 25 18
72 A8 4c olive bister 25 45
73 A8 5c green 3.00 18
74 A8 10c carmine 13.00 18

Coat of Arms — A9

Grand Duke William IV — A10

1906-26 **Typo.** *Perf. 12½*
75 A9 1c gray ('07) 15 15
76 A9 2c ol brn ('07) 15 15
77 A9 4c bis ('07) 15 15
78 A9 5c grn ('07) 15 15
79 A9 5c lil ('26) 15 15
80 A9 6c vio ('07) 15 32
81 A9 7½c org ('19) 15 65

Engr.
Perf. 11, 11½x11
82 A10 10c scarlet 1.40 15
a. Souvenir sheet of 10 375.00 725.00
83 A10 12½c sl grn ('07) 1.65 15
84 A10 15c org brn ('07) 1.65 50
85 A10 20c org ('07) 2.00 40
86 A10 25c ultra ('07) 42.50 20
87 A10 30c ol grn ('08) 90 40
88 A10 37½c grn ('07) 90 40
a. Perf. 12½ 25.00 4.50
89 A10 50c brn ('07) 2.75 60
90 A10 87½c dk bl ('08) 1.65 5.75
91 A10 1fr vio ('08) 3.25 1.25
92 A10 2½fr ver ('08) 60.00 65.00
93 A10 5fr claret ('08) 8.00 24.00
Nos. 75-93 (19) 127.70 100.52

No. 82a for accession of Grand Duke William IV to the throne.

Nos. 90, 92-93 Surcharged in Red or Black **62½ cts.**

1912-15
94 A10 62½c on 87½c (R) 1.10 2.00
95 A10 62½c on 2½fr (Bk) ('15) 1.10 2.50
96 A10 62½c on 5fr (Bk) ('15) 38 1.50

Grand Duchess Marie Adelaide A11

Grand Duchess Charlotte A12

1914-17 **Engr.** *Perf. 11½, 11½x11*
97 A11 10c lake 15 15
98 A11 12½c dl grn 15 15
99 A11 15c sepia 15 20
100 A11 17½c dp brn ('17) 15 25
101 A11 25c ultra 15 15
102 A11 30c bister 15 25
103 A11 35c dk bl 15 20
104 A11 37½c blk brn 15 20
105 A11 40c orange 15 20
106 A11 50c dk gray 20 33
107 A11 62½c bl grn 32 1.40
108 A11 87½c org ('17) 32 1.65
109 A11 1fr org brn 2.00 60
110 A11 2½fr red 1.00 1.65
111 A11 5fr dk vio 5.25 13.00
Nos. 97-111 (15) 10.44 20.38

Stamps of 1906-19 Surcharged with New Value and Bars in Black or Red

1916-24
112 A9 2½c on 5c grn ('18) 15 15
113 A9 3c on 2c ol brn ('21) 15 18
114 A9 5c on 1c gray ('23) 15 18
115 A9 5c on 4c bis ('23) 15 28
116 A9 5c on 7½c org ('24) 15 18
117 A9 6c on 2c ol brn (R) ('22) 15 20
118 A11 7½c on 10c lake ('18) 15 15
119 A11 17½c on 30c bis 15 38
120 A11 20c on 17½c brn ('21) 15 20
121 A11 25c on 37½c blk brn ('23) 15 18
a. Double surcharge 75.00
122 A11 75c on 62½c bl grn (R) ('22) 15 20
123 A11 80c on 87½c org ('22) 15 20
124 A11 87½c on 1fr org brn 60 1.50
Nos. 112-124 (13) 2.40 3.98

1921, Jan. 6 **Engr.** *Perf. 11½*
125 A12 15c rose 15 15
a. Sheet of 5, perf 11 125.00 125.00
b. Sheet of 25, perf. 11½, 11x11½, 12x11½ 4.50 14.00

Birth of Prince Jean, first son of Grand Duchess Charlotte, Jan. 5 (No. 125a). No. 125 was printed in sheets of 100.
See Nos. 131-148.

Vianden Castle — A13

Foundries at Esch — A14

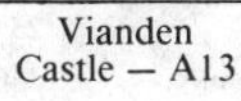

Adolphe Bridge — A15

1921-34 *Perf. 11, 11x11½, 11½*
126 A13 1fr carmine 15 30
127 A13 1fr dk bl ('26) 18 28
Perf. 11½x11; 11½ (#129)
128 A14 2fr indigo 15 50
129 A14 2fr dk brn ('26) 1.25 90
130 A15 5fr dk vio 7.50 4.50
a. Perf. 12½ ('34) 16.00 9.50
Nos. 126-130 (5) 9.23 6.48

Charlotte Type of 1921
1921-26 *Perf. 11½*
131 A12 2c brown 15 15
132 A12 3c ol grn 15 15
a. Sheet of 25 8.50 17.50
133 A12 6c violet 15 15
a. Sheet of 25 8.50 17.50
134 A12 10c yel grn 18 15
135 A12 10c ol brn ('24) 15 15
136 A12 15c brn ol 18 15
137 A12 15c pale grn ('24) 15 15
138 A12 15c dp org ('26) 15 15
139 A12 20c dp org 18 15
a. Sheet of 25 50.00 80.00
140 A12 20c yel grn ('26) 15 15
141 A12 25c dk grn 18 15
142 A12 30c car rose 18 15
143 A12 40c brn org 20 15
144 A12 50c dp bl 38 23
145 A12 50c red ('24) 25 35
146 A12 75c red 25 38
a. Sheet of 25 350.00
147 A12 75c dp bl ('24) 20 15
148 A12 80c black 38 30
a. Sheet of 25 350.00
Nos. 131-148 (18) 3.61 3.36

Philatelic Exhibition Issue
1922, Aug. 27 ***Imperf.***
Laid Paper
149 A12 25c dk grn 1.65 2.75
150 A12 30c car rose 1.65 2.75

Nos. 149 and 150 were sold exclusively at the Luxembourg Phil. Exhib., Aug. 1922.

Souvenir Sheet

View of Luxembourg — A16

1923, Jan. 3 ***Perf. 11***
151 A16 10fr dp grn, sheet 750.00 2,200.
Birth of Princess Elisabeth.

1923, Mar. ***Perf. 11½***
152 A16 10fr black 5.00 14.00
a. Perf. 12½ ('34) 4.00 8.50

The Wolfsschlucht near Echternach — A17

1923-34 ***Perf. 11½***
153 A17 3fr dk bl & bl 1.00 1.00
a. Perf. 12½ ('34) 80 60

Stamps of 1921-26 Surcharged with New Values and Bars

1925-28
154 A12 5c on 10c yel grn 20 20
155 A12 15c on 20c yel grn ('28) 15 20
a. Bars omitted
156 A12 35c on 40c brn org ('27) 15 20
157 A12 60c on 75c dp bl ('27) 15 20
158 A12 60c on 80c blk ('28) 35 32
Nos. 154-158 (5) 1.00 1.12

Grand Duchess Charlotte — A18

1926-35 **Engr.** ***Perf. 12***
159 A18 5c dk vio 15 15
160 A18 10c ol grn 15 15
161 A18 15c blk ('30) 15 25
162 A18 20c orange 15 18
163 A18 25c yel grn 15 18
164 A18 25c vio brn ('27) 15 20
165 A18 30c yel grn ('27) 20 38
166 A18 30c gray vio ('30) 16 30
167 A18 35c gray vio ('28) 1.00 22
168 A18 35c yel grn ('30) 15 15
169 A18 40c ol gray 15 18
170 A18 50c red brn 15 15
171 A18 60c bl grn ('28) 1.00 15
172 A18 65c blk brn 15 50
173 A18 70c bl vio ('35) 15 15
174 A18 75c rose 15 25
175 A18 75c bis brn ('27) 15 15
176 A18 80c bis brn 18 50
177 A18 90c rose ('27) 45 75
178 A18 1fr black 35 50
179 A18 1fr rose ('30) 16 40
180 A18 1¼fr dk bl 15 35
181 A18 1¼fr yel ('30) 4.75 1.00
182 A18 1¼fr bl grn ('31) 28 18
183 A18 1¼fr rose car ('34) 20.00 1.40
184 A18 1½fr dp bl ('27) 80 1.00
185 A18 1¾fr dk bl ('30) 32 38
Nos. 159-185 (27) 31.75 10.15

Stamps of 1926-35, Surcharged with New Values and Bars

1928-39
186 A18 10(c) on 30c yel grn ('29) 20 20
187 A18 15c on 25c yel grn 30 32
187A A18 30c on 60c bl grn ('39) 15 32
188 A18 60c on 65c blk brn 30 32
189 A18 60c on 75c rose 30 28
190 A18 60c on 80c bis brn 35 40
191 A18 70(c) on 75c bis brn ('35) 8.00 20
192 A18 75(c) on 90c rose ('29) 1.00 20
193 A18 1¾(fr) on 1½fr dp bl ('29) 2.00 1.40
Nos. 186-193 (9) 12.60 3.64

The surcharge on No. 187A has no bars.

View of Clervaux A19

1928-34 ***Perf. 12½***
194 A19 2fr blk ('34) 1.00 50
a. Perf. 11½ ('28) 1.25 50

See No. B66.

Coat of Arms — A20

1930, Dec. 20 **Typo.** ***Perf. 12½***
195 A20 5c claret 32 25
196 A20 10c ol grn 55 15
Set value 32

View of the Lower City of Luxembourg A21

Gate of "Three Towers" A22

1931, June 20 **Engr.**
197 A21 20fr dp grn 3.00 7.25

1934, Aug. 30 ***Perf. 14x13½***
198 A22 5fr bl grn 1.25 2.75

Castle From Our Valley A23

1935, Nov. 15 *Perf. 12½x12*

No.	Type	Description	Unused	Used
199	A23	10fr green	2.00	4.75

Municipal Palace — A24

1936, Aug. 26 Photo. *Perf. 11½*

Granite Paper

No.	Type	Description	Unused	Used
200	A24	10c brown	15	20
201	A24	35c green	15	40
202	A24	70c red org	18	60
203	A24	1fr car rose	1.00	4.00
204	A24	1.25fr violet	1.75	7.25
205	A24	1.75fr brt ultra	1.00	4.00
		Nos. 200-205 (6)	4.23	16.45

11th Cong. of Intl. Federation of Philately.

Arms of Luxembourg A25

William I A26

Designs: 70c, William II. 75c, William III. 1fr, Prince Henry. 1.25fr, Grand Duke Adolphe. 1.75fr, William IV. 3fr, Regent Marie Anne. 5fr, Grand Duchess Marie Adelaide. 10fr, Grand Duchess Charlotte.

1939, May 27 Engr. *Perf. 12½x12*

No.	Type	Description	Unused	Used
206	A25	35c brt grn	25	20
207	A26	50c orange	25	25
208	A26	70c slate grn	15	15
209	A26	75c sepia	55	1.00
210	A26	1fr red	1.40	2.75
211	A26	1.25fr brn vio	15	20
212	A26	1.75fr dark blue	15	20
213	A26	3fr lt brn	25	40
214	A26	5fr gray blk	40	80
215	A26	10fr copper red	65	2.25
		Nos. 206-215 (10)	4.20	8.20

Centenary of Independence.

Allegory of Medicinal Baths — A35

1939, Sept. 18 Photo. *Perf. 11½*

No.	Type	Description	Unused	Used
216	A35	2fr brn rose	40	1.10

Elevation of Mondorf-les-Bains to town status.

Souvenir Sheet

A36

1939, Dec. 20 Engr. *Perf. 14x13*

No.	Type	Description	Unused	Used
217	A36	Sheet of 3	27.50	65.00
a.		2fr vermilion, buff	7.50	12.50
b.		3fr dark green, buff	7.50	12.50
c.		5fr blue, buff	7.50	12.50

20th anniv. of the reign of Grand Duchess Charlotte (Jan. 15, 1919) and her marriage to Prince Felix (Nov. 6, 1919).

See Nos. B98-B103.

Grand Duchess Charlotte A37

Lion from Duchy Arms A38

1944-46 Unwmk. *Perf. 12*

No.	Type	Description	Unused	Used
218	A37	5c brn red	15	15
219	A37	10c black	15	15
219A	A37	20c org ('46)	15	15
220	A37	25c sepia	15	15
220A	A37	30c car ('46)	15	15
221	A37	35c green	15	15
221A	A37	40c dk bl ('46)	15	15
222	A37	50c dk vio	15	15
222A	A37	60c org ('46)	1.00	15
223	A37	70c rose pink	15	15
223A	A37	70c dp grn ('46)	30	55
223B	A37	75c sep ('46)	18	18
224	A37	1fr olive	15	15
225	A37	1¼fr red org	15	15
226	A37	1½fr red org ('46)	15	15
227	A37	1¾fr blue	15	25
228	A37	2fr rose car ('46)	1.50	25
229	A37	2½fr dp vio ('46)	2.25	4.00
230	A37	3fr dp yel grn ('46)	30	45
231	A37	3½fr brt bl ('46)	38	70
232	A37	5fr dk bl grn	15	18
233	A37	10fr carmine	18	55
234	A37	20fr dp bl	30	4.50
		Nos. 218-234 (23)	8.49	13.56

1945 Engr. *Perf. 14x13*

No.	Type	Description	Unused	Used
235	A38	20c black	15	15
236	A38	30c brt grn	15	15
237	A38	60c dp vio	15	15
238	A38	75c brn red	15	15
239	A38	1.20fr red	15	15
240	A38	1.50fr rose lil	15	15
241	A38	2.50fr lt bl	15	15
		Set value	62	85

Patton's Grave, US Military Cemetery, Hamm A39

Gen. Patton, Broken Chain and Advancing Tanks A40

1947, Oct. 24 Photo. *Perf. 11½*

No.	Type	Description	Unused	Used
242	A39	1.50fr dk car	15	20
243	A40	3.50fr dl bl	65	3.00
244	A39	5fr dk sl grn	65	2.00
245	A40	10fr chocolate	3.00	12.00

George S. Patton, Jr. (1885-1945), American general.

Oesling Mountain Forts A41

Luxembourg A44

Moselle River A42

Steel Mills — A43

Perf. 11½x11, 11x11½

1948, Aug. 5 Engr. Unwmk.

No.	Type	Description	Unused	Used
246	A41	7fr dk brn	5.00	60
247	A42	10fr dk grn	38	20
248	A43	15fr carmine	38	60
249	A44	20fr dk bl	50	20

Grand Duchess Charlotte — A45

1948-49 *Perf. 11½*

No.	Type	Description	Unused	Used
250	A45	15c ol brn ('49)	15	15
251	A45	25c slate	15	15
252	A45	60c brn ('49)	25	15
253	A45	80c grn ('49)	25	15
254	A45	1fr red lil	65	15
255	A45	1.50fr grnsh bl	65	15
256	A45	1.60fr sl gray ('49)	65	80
257	A45	2fr dk vio brn	65	15
258	A45	4fr vio bl	1.25	28
259	A45	6fr brt red vio ('49)	2.00	28
260	A45	8fr dl grn ('49)	2.00	60
		Nos. 250-260 (11)	8.65	
		Set value		2.50

See Nos. 265-271, 292, 337-340, B151.

Self-Inking Canceller A46

1949, Oct. 6 Photo.

No.	Type	Description	Unused	Used
261	A46	80c blk, Prus grn & pale grn	20	55
262	A46	2.50fr dk brn, brn red & sal rose	1.00	2.75
263	A46	4fr blk, bl & pale bl	2.75	7.25
264	A46	8fr dk brn, brn & buff	8.75	25.00

UPU, 75th anniv.

Charlotte Type of 1948-49

1951, Mar. 15 Engr. Unwmk.

No.	Type	Description	Unused	Used
265	A45	5c red org	15	15
266	A45	10c ultra	15	15
267	A45	40c crimson	15	20
268	A45	1.25fr dk brn	65	28
269	A45	2.50fr red	65	15
270	A45	3fr blue	2.50	28
271	A45	3.50fr rose lake	1.75	40
		Nos. 265-271 (7)	6.00	1.61

Agriculture and Industry A47

Globe and Scales A48

Design: 1fr, 3fr, People of Europe and Charter of Freedom.

1951, Oct. 25 Photo. *Perf. 11½*

No.	Type	Description	Unused	Used
272	A47	80c dp grn	6.00	5.00
273	A47	1fr purple	3.00	42
274	A48	2fr blk brn	15.00	42
275	A47	2.50fr dk car	19.00	13.00
276	A47	3fr org brn	35.00	21.00
277	A48	4fr blue	42.50	30.00
		Nos. 272-277 (6)	120.50	69.84

Issued to promote a united Europe.

Grand Duke William III — A49

Perf. 13½x13

1952, May 24 Engr. Unwmk.

Dates, Ornaments in Olive Green

No.	Type	Description	Unused	Used
278	A49	2fr black	25.00	50.00
279	A49	4fr red brn	25.00	50.00

Printed in sheets containing two panes of eight stamps each, alternating the two denominations. Centenary of Luxembourg's postage stamps. Price per set, 26fr, which included admission to the CENTILUX exhibition.

See Nos. C16-C20.

Hurdle Race — A50

Designs: 2fr, Football. 2.50fr, Boxing. 3fr, Water polo. 4fr, Bicycle racing. 8fr, Fencing.

1952, Aug. 20 Photo. *Perf. 11½*

Designs in Black

No.	Type	Description	Unused	Used
280	A50	1fr pale grn	20	30
281	A50	2fr brn buff	60	30
282	A50	2.50fr sal pink	1.40	1.00
283	A50	3fr buff	1.70	1.65
284	A50	4fr lt bl	8.50	8.25
285	A50	8fr lilac	5.00	5.50
		Nos. 280-285 (6)	17.40	17.00

15th Olympic Games, Helsinki; World Bicycling Championships of 1952.

Wedding of Princess Josephine-Charlotte of Belgium and Hereditary Grand Duke Jean — A51

1953, Apr. 1

No.	Type	Description	Unused	Used
286	A51	80c dl vio	22	20
287	A51	1.20fr lt brn	22	20
288	A51	2fr green	50	20
289	A51	3fr red lil	80	60

290 A51 4fr brt bl 3.00 1.10
291 A51 9fr brn red 3.00 1.10
Nos. 286-291 (6) 7.74 3.40

Charlotte Type of 1948-49

1953, May 18 **Engr.**
292 A45 1.20fr gray 45 28

Radio Luxembourg — A52

Victor Hugo's Home, Vianden A53

1953, May 18 ***Perf. 11½x11***
293 A52 3fr purple 2.50 1.40
294 A53 4fr Prussian bl 1.65 1.40

150th birth anniv. of Victor Hugo (No. 294).

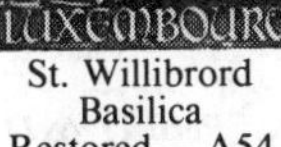

St. Willibrord Basilica Restored — A54

Pierre d'Aspelt — A55

Design: 2.50fr, Interior view.

1953, Sept. 18 ***Perf. 13x13½***
295 A54 2fr red 1.50 40
296 A54 2.50fr dk gray grn 2.50 6.50

Consecration of St. Willibrord Basilica at Echternach.

1953, Sept.
297 A55 4fr black 4.75 5.00

Pierre d'Aspelt (1250-1320), chancellor of the Holy Roman Empire and Archbishop of Mainz.

Fencing Swords, Mask and Glove — A56

Winged "L" Over Map — A57

1954, May 6 ***Perf. 13½x13***
298 A56 2fr red brn & blk brn, *gray* 4.50 50

World Fencing Championship Matches, Luxembourg, June 10-22.

1954, May 6 **Photo.** ***Perf. 11½***
299 A57 4fr dp bl, yel & red 6.00 3.50

6th Intl. Fair, Luxembourg, July 10-25.

Tulips — A58

Artisan, Wheel and Tools — A59

Flowers: 2fr, Daffodils. 3fr, Hyacinths. 4fr, Parrot tulips.

1955, Apr. 1
300 A58 80c dk brn, rose red & bl grn 15 15
301 A58 2fr cer, yel & grn 15 15
302 A58 3fr bl grn & lil rose 1.40 3.00
303 A58 4fr multi 1.65 3.50

Flower festival at Mondorf-les-Bains. See Nos. 351-353.

1955, Sept. 1 **Engr.** ***Perf. 13***
304 A59 2fr dk gray & blk brn 60 32

Natl. Handicraft Exposition at Luxembourg - Limpertsburg, Sept. 3-12.

Dudelange Television Station A60

1955, Sept. 1 **Unwmk.**
305 A60 2.50fr dk brn & redsh brn 60 32

Installation of the Tele-Luxembourg station at Dudelange.

United Nations Emblem and Children Playing A61

UN, 10th anniv.: 80c, "Charter". 4fr, "Justice" (Sword and Scales). 9fr, "Assistance" (Workers).

1955, Oct. 24 ***Perf. 11x11½***
306 A61 80c blk & dk bl 22 42
307 A61 2fr red & brn 1.75 15
308 A61 4fr dk bl & red 1.40 3.75
309 A61 9fr dk brn & sl grn 55 1.40

Anemones — A62

Design: 2.50fr, 4fr, Roses. 3fr, Crocuses.

1956 **Photo.** ***Perf. 11½***

Flowers in Natural Colors

310 A62 2fr gray vio 25 18
311 A62 2.50fr brt bl 2.25 4.50
312 A62 3fr red brn 95 1.50
313 A62 4fr purple 1.10 1.50

Flower Festival at Mondorf-Bains (Nos. 310, 312). Nos. 311 and 313 are inscribed: "Luxembourg-Ville des Roses."

Issue dates: Nos. 310, 312, Apr. 27; Nos. 311, 313, May 30.

Steel Beam and City Emblem — A63

1956, May 30
314 A63 2fr brt grnsh bl, red & blk 75 40

50th anniversary of Esch-sur-Alzette.

Bessemer Converter and Blast Furnaces A64

Steel Beam and Model of City of Luxembourg A65

"Rebuilding Europe" A66

Design: 4fr, 6-link chain, miner's lamp.

Perf. 11x11½, 11½x11

1956, Aug. 10 **Engr.**
315 A64 2fr dl red 9.50 2.25
316 A65 3fr dk bl 9.50 19.00
317 A64 4fr green 1.90 3.25

4th anniv. of the establishment in Luxembourg of the headquarters of the European Coal and Steel Community.

1956, Sept. 15 ***Perf. 13***
318 A66 2fr brn & blk 75.00 28
319 A66 3fr brick red & car 24.00 37.50
320 A66 4fr brt bl & dp bl 2.75 4.00

Cooperation among the six countries comprising the Coal and Steel Community.

Central Station from Train Window A67

1956, Sept. 29 ***Perf. 13x12½***
321 A67 2fr blk & sepia 75 45

Electrification of Luxembourg railways.

Ignace de la Fontaine A68

Design: 7fr, Grand Duchess Charlotte.

1956, Nov. 7 ***Perf. 11½***
322 A68 2fr gray brn 1.00 30
323 A68 7fr dl pur 2.00 65

Centenary of the Council of State.

Lord Baden-Powell and Luxembourg Scout Emblems — A69

Designs: 2.50fr, Lord Baden-Powell and Luxembourg Girl Scout emblems.

1957, June 17 ***Perf. 11½x11***
324 A69 2fr ol grn & red brn 52 28
325 A69 2.50fr dk vio & claret 2.50 *4.25*

Birth centenary of Robert Baden-Powell and the 50th anniversary of the founding of the Scout movement.

Prince Henry — A70

Children's Clinic — A71

Design: 4fr, Princess Marie-Astrid.

1957, June 17 **Photo.** ***Perf. 11½***
326 A70 2fr brown 45 16
327 A71 3fr bluish grn 1.75 *3.50*
328 A70 4fr ultra 2.00 *3.75*

Children's Clinic of the Prince Jean-Princess Josephine-Charlotte Foundation.

"United Europe" A72

Fair Building and Flags A73

1957, Sept. 16 **Engr.** ***Perf. 12½x12***
329 A72 2fr redsh brn 60 32
330 A72 3fr red 9.75 *18.00*
331 A72 4fr rose lil 9.75 11.00

A united Europe for peace and prosperity.

1958, Apr. 16 ***Perf. 12x11½***
332 A73 2fr ultra & multi 15 18

10th International Luxembourg Fair.

Luxembourg Pavilion, Brussels A74

1958, Apr. 16 **Unwmk.**
333 A74 2.50fr car & ultra 15 25

International Exposition at Brussels.

St. Willibrord — A75

Designs: 1fr, Sts. Willibrord and Irmina from "Liber Aureus." 5fr, St. Willibrord, young man and wine cask.

1958, May 23 Engr. *Perf. 13x13½*

334	A75	1fr red	15	32
335	A75	2.50fr ol brn	18	28
336	A75	5fr blue	48	*1.00*

1300th birth anniv. of St. Willibrord, apostle of the Low Countries and founder of Echternach Abbey.

Charlotte Type of 1948-49

1958 Unwmk. *Perf. 11½*

337	A45	20c dull claret	15	15
338	A45	30c olive	15	15
339	A45	50c dp org	18	15
340	A45	5fr violet	4.75	55
		Set value		78

Europa Issue, 1958

Common Design Type

1958, Sept. 13 Litho. *Perf. 12½x13*

Size: 21x34mm

341	CD1	2.50fr car & bl	15	15
342	CD1	3.50fr grn & org	15	22
343	CD1	5fr bl & red	35	55

Wiltz Open-Air Theater A76

Vintage, Moselle A77

1958, Sept. 13 Engr. *Perf. 11x11½*

344	A76	2.50fr slate & sepia	20	15
345	A77	2.50fr lt grn & sep	20	15
		Set value		24

No. 345 issued to publicize 2,000 years of grape growing in Luxembourg region.

Grand Duchess Charlotte A78

NATO Emblem A79

1959, Jan. 15 Photo. *Perf. 11½*

346	A78	1.50fr pale grn & dk grn	15	25
347	A78	2.50fr pink & dk brn	15	15
348	A78	5fr lt bl & dk bl	24	90

40th anniv. of the accession to the throne of the Grand Duchess Charlotte.

1959, Apr. 3 *Perf. 12½x12*

349	A79	2.50fr brt ol & bl	15	15
350	A79	8.50fr red brn & bl	24	45

NATO, 10th anniversary.

Flower Type of 1955, Inscribed "1959"

Flowers: 1fr, Iris. 2.50fr, Peonies. 3fr, Hydrangea.

1959, Apr. 3 *Perf. 11½*

Flowers in Natural Colors

351	A58	1fr dk bl grn	18	40
352	A58	2.50fr deep blue	24	50
353	A58	3fr dp red lil	24	50

Flower festival, Mondorf-les-Bains.

Europa Issue, 1959

Common Design Type

Perf. 12½x13½

1959, Sept. 19 Litho.

Size: 22x33mm

354	CD2	2.50fr olive	16	40
355	CD2	5fr dk bl	35	80

Locomotive of 1859 and Hymn — A80

1959, Sept. 19 Engr. *Perf. 13½*

356	A80	2.50fr red & ultra	42	18

Centenary of Luxembourg's railroads.

Catalogue values for unused stamps in this section, from this point to the end of the section, are for Never Hinged items.

Man and Child Knocking at Door — A81

Holy Family, Flight into Egypt A82

Perf. 11½x11, 11x11½

1960, Apr. 7 Unwmk.

357	A81	2.50fr org & slate	15	15
358	A82	5fr pur & slate	30	30

World Refugee Year, July 1, 1959-June 30, 1960.

Steel Worker Drawing CECA Initials and Map of Member Countries A83

1960, May 9 *Perf. 11x11½*

359	A83	2.50fr dk car rose	60	20

10th anniv. of the Schumann Plan for a European Steel and Coal Community.

European School and Children A84

1960, May 9

360	A84	5fr bl & gray blk	90	90

Establishment of the first European school in Luxembourg.

Heraldic Lion and Tools A85

1960, June 14 Photo. *Perf. 11½*

361	A85	2.50fr gray, red, bl & blk	1.40	32

Natl. Exhibition of Craftsmanship, Luxembourg-Limpertsberg, July 9-18.

Grand Duchess Charlotte — A86

1960-64 Engr. Unwmk.

362	A86	10c claret ('61)	15	15
363	A86	20c rose red ('61)	20	15
363A	A86	25c org ('64)	15	15
364	A86	30c gray olive	20	15
365	A86	50c dl grn	60	15
366	A86	1fr vio bl	75	15
367	A86	1.50fr rose lilac	75	20
368	A86	2fr blue ('61)	80	15
369	A86	2.50fr rose vio	1.40	20
370	A86	3fr vio brn ('61)	1.60	15
371	A86	3.50fr aqua ('64)	2.25	1.90
372	A86	5fr lt red brn	2.25	25
373	A86	6fr slate ('64)	2.75	20
		Nos. 362-373 (13)	13.85	3.95

The 50c, 1fr and 3fr were issued in sheets and in coils. Every fifth coil stamp has control number on back.

Europa Issue, 1960

Common Design Type

1960, Sept. 19 *Perf. 11x11½*

Size: 37x27mm

374	CD3	2.50fr indigo & emer	25	20
375	CD3	5fr mar & blk	40	35

Great Spotted Woodpecker A87

Clervaux and Abbey of St. Maurice and St. Maur A88

Designs: 1.50fr, Cat, horiz. 3fr, Filly, horiz. 8.50fr, Dachshund.

1961, May 15 Photo. *Perf. 11½*

376	A87	1fr multi	15	15
377	A87	1.50fr multi	15	15
378	A87	3fr gray, buff & red brn	40	40
379	A87	8.50fr lt grn, blk & ocher	80	60

Issued to publicize animal protection.

1961, June 8 Engr. *Perf. 11½x11*

380	A88	2.50fr green	25	15

General Patton Monument, Ettelbruck — A89

1961, June 8 *Perf. 11x11½*

381	A89	2.50fr dk bl & gray	25	15

The monument commemorates the American victory of the 3rd Army under Gen. George S. Patton, Jr., Battle of the Ardennes Bulge, 1944-45.

Europa Issue, 1961

Common Design Type

1961, Sept. 18 *Perf. 13x12½*

Size: 29½x27mm

382	CD4	2.50fr red	15	15
383	CD4	5fr blue	16	16
		Set value	24	24

Cyclist Carrying Bicycle A90

St. Laurent's Church, Diekirch A91

Design: 5fr, Emblem of 1962 championship

1962, Jan. 22 Photo. *Perf. 11½*

384	A90	2.50fr lt ultra, crim & blk	18	17
385	A90	5fr multi	42	40

Intl. Cross-country Bicycle Race, Esch-sur-Alzette, Feb. 18.

Europa Issue, 1962

Common Design Type

1962, Sept. 17 Unwmk. *Perf. 11½*

Size: 32½x23mm

386	CD5	2.50fr ol bis, yel grn & brn blk	15	15
387	CD5	5fr rose lil, lt grn & brn blk	30	25

1962, Sept. 17 Engr. *Perf. 11½x11*

388	A91	2.50fr brn & blk	28	18

Bock Rock Castle, 10th Century A92

Gate of Three Towers, 11th Century A93

Designs (each stamp represents a different century): No. 391, Benedictine Abbey, Munster. No. 392, Great Seal of Luxembourg, 1237. No. 393, Rham Towers. No. 394, Black Virgin, Grund. No. 395, Grand Ducal Palace. No. 396, The Citadel of the Holy Ghost. No. 397, Castle Bridge. No. 398, Town Hall. No. 399, Municipal theater, bridge and European Community Center.

Perf. 14x13 (A92), 11½ (A93)

Engr. (A92), Photo. (A93)

1963, Apr. 13

389	A92	1fr slate blue	42	42
390	A93	1fr multi	15	15
391	A92	1.50fr dl red brn	42	42
392	A93	1.50fr multi	15	15
393	A92	2.50fr gray grn	42	42
394	A93	2.50fr multi	18	18
395	A92	3fr brown	42	42
396	A93	3fr multi	15	15
397	A92	5fr brt vio	60	60
398	A93	5fr multi	60	60
399	A92	11fr multi	90	90
		Nos. 389-399 (11)	4.41	4.41

Millennium of the city of Luxembourg; MELUSINA Intl. Phil. Exhib., Luxembourg, Apr. 13-21. Set sold only at exhibition. Value of 62fr included entrance ticket. Nos. 390, 392, 394 and 396 however were sold without restriction.

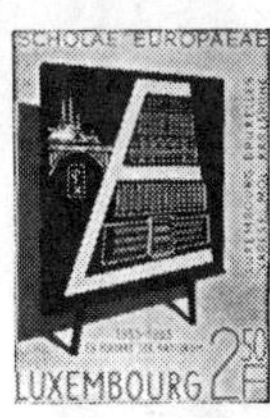

Blackboard Showing European School Buildings — A94

1963, Apr. 13 Photo. *Perf. 11½*

400 A94 2.50fr gray, grn & mag	20	20

10th anniv. of the European Schools in Luxembourg, Brussels, Varese, Mol and Karlsruhe.

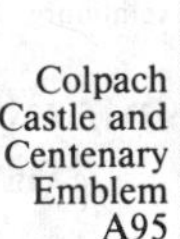

Colpach Castle and Centenary Emblem A95

1963, May 8 Engr. *Perf. 13*

401 A95 2.50fr hn brn, gray & red	20	20

Centenary of the Intl. Red Cross. Colpach Castle, home of Emile Mayrisch, was donated to the Luxembourg League of the Red Cross for a rest home.

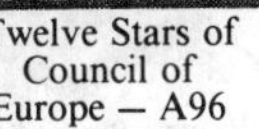

Twelve Stars of Council of Europe — A96

Brown Trout Taking Bait — A97

1963, June 25 *Perf. 13x14*

402 A96 2.50fr dp ultra, *gold*	20	20

10th anniv. of the European Convention of Human Rights.

Europa Issue, 1963

Common Design Type

1963, Sept. 16 Photo. *Perf. 11½*

Size: 32½x23mm

403 CD6 3fr bl grn, lt grn & org	25	15
404 CD6 6fr red brn, org red & org	30	30

1963, Sept. 16 Engr. *Perf. 13*

405 A97 3fr indigo	25	15

World Fly-Fishing Championship, Wormeldange, Sept. 22.

Map of Luxembourg, Telephone Dial and Stars — A98

Power House — A99

1963, Sept. 16 Photo. *Perf. 11½*

406 A98 3fr ultra, brt grn & blk	25	15

Completion of telephone automation.

1964, Apr. 17 Engr. *Perf. 13*

Designs: 3fr, Upper reservoir, horiz. 6fr, Lohmuhle dam.

407 A99 2fr red brn & sl	15	15
408 A99 3fr red, sl grn & lt bl	20	15
409 A99 6fr choc, grn & bl	22	22

Inauguration of the Vianden hydroelectric station.

Barge Entering Lock at Grevenmacher Dam — A100

1964, May 26 Unwmk.

410 A100 3fr ind & brt bl	35	18

Opening of Moselle River canal system.

Europa Issue, 1964

Common Design Type

1964, Sept. 14 Photo. *Perf. 11½*

Size: 22x38mm

411 CD7 3fr org brn, yel & dk bl	20	20
412 CD7 6fr yel grn, yel & dk brn	35	32

New Atheneum Educational Center and Students A101

1964, Sept. 14 Unwmk.

413 A101 3fr dk bl grn & blk	20	15

Benelux Issue

King Baudouin, Queen Juliana and Grand Duchess Charlotte — A101a

1964, Oct. 12

Size: 45x26mm

414 A101a 3fr dl bl, yel & brn	22	20

20th anniv. of the customs union of Belgium, Netherlands and Luxembourg.

Grand Duke Jean and Grand Duchess Josephine Charlotte A102

1964, Nov. 11 Photo. *Perf. 11½*

415 A102 3fr indigo	35	16
416 A102 6fr dk brn	35	28

Grand Duke Jean's accession to throne.

Rotary Emblem and Cogwheels A103

Grand Duke Jean A104

1965, Apr. 5 Photo. *Perf. 11½*

417 A103 3fr gold, car, gray & ultra	40	20

Rotary International, 60th anniversary.

1965-71 Engr. Unwmk.

418 A104 25c ol bis ('66)	15	15
419 A104 50c rose red	24	15
420 A104 1fr ultra	24	15
421 A104 1.50fr dk vio brn ('66)	15	15
422 A104 2fr mag ('66)	18	15
423 A104 2.50fr org ('71)	35	15
424 A104 3fr gray	48	15
425 A104 3.50fr brn org ('66)	35	20
426 A104 4fr vio brn ('71)	30	15
427 A104 5fr grn ('71)	35	15
428 A104 6fr purple	95	15
429 A104 8fr bl grn ('71)	80	15
Nos. 418-429 (12)	4.54	
Set value		1.05

The 50c, 1fr, 2fr, 3fr and 6fr were issued in sheets and in coils. Every fifth coil stamp has control number on back.

See Nos. 570-576.

ITU Emblem, Old and New Communication Equipment — A105

1965, May 17 Litho. *Perf. 13½*

431 A105 3fr dk pur, cl & blk	22	20

ITU, centenary.

Europa Issue, 1965

Common Design Type

Perf. 13x12½

1965, Sept. 27 Photo. Unwmk.

Size: 30x23½mm

432 CD8 3fr grn, mar & blk	25	18
433 CD8 6fr tan, dk bl & grn	40	40

Inauguration of WHO Headquarters, Geneva — A106

1966, Mar. 7 Engr. *Perf. 11x11½*

434 A106 3fr green	20	15

Torch and Banner — A107

Key and Arms of City of Luxembourg, and Arms of Prince of Chimay — A108

1966, Mar. 7 Photo. *Perf. 11½*

435 A107 3fr gray & brt red	20	15

50th anniversary of the Workers' Federation in Luxembourg.

1966, Apr. 28 Engr. *Perf. 13x14*

Designs: 2fr, Interior of Cathedral of Luxembourg, painting by Juan Martin. 3fr, Our Lady of Luxembourg, engraving by Richard Collin. 6fr, Column and spandrel with sculptured angels from Cathedral.

436 A108 1.50fr green	15	15
437 A108 2fr dl red	15	15
438 A108 3fr dk bl	15	15
439 A108 6fr red brn	25	25
Set value	55	55

300th anniv. of the Votum Solemne (Solemn Promise) which made the Virgin Mary Patron Saint of the City of Luxembourg.

Europa Issue, 1966

Common Design Type

Perf. 13½x12½

1966, Sept. 26 Litho.

Size: 25x37mm

440 CD9 3fr gray & vio bl	20	15
441 CD9 6fr ol & dk grn	30	30

Diesel Locomotive A109

Design: 3fr, Electric locomotive.

1966, Sept. 26 Photo. *Perf. 11½*

442 A109 1.50fr multi	20	20
443 A109 3fr multi	25	20

5th Intl. Philatelic Exhibition of Luxembourg Railroad Men, Sept. 30-Oct. 3.

Grand Duchess Charlotte Bridge A110

1966, Sept. 26 Engr. *Perf. 13*

444 A110 3fr dk car rose	20	15

Tower Building, Kirchberg, Seat of European Community — A111

Design: 13fr, Design for Robert Schuman monument, Luxembourg.

1966, Sept. 26

445 A111 1.50fr dk grn	16	16
446 A111 13fr dp bl	55	25

"Luxembourg, Center of Europe."

View of Luxembourg, 1850, by Nicolas Liez — A112

Map of Luxembourg Fortress, 1850, by Theodore de Cederstolpe — A113

1967, Mar. 6 Engr. *Perf. 13*

447 A112 3fr bl, vio brn & grn 20 15
448 A113 6fr bl, brn & red 25 20

Centenary of the Treaty of London, which guaranteed the country's neutrality after the dismantling of the Fortress of Luxembourg.

Europa Issue, 1967

Common Design Type

1967, May 2 Photo. *Perf. 11½*

Size: 33x22mm

449 CD10 3fr cl brn, gray & buff 30 20
450 CD10 6fr dk brn, vio gray & lt bl 35 35

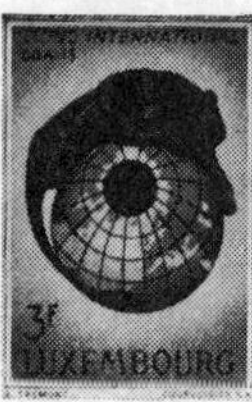

Lion, Globe and Lions Emblem A115

NATO Emblem and European Community Administration Building A116

1967, May 2 Photo. *Perf. 11½*

451 A115 3fr multi 18 15

Lions International, 50th anniversary.

> Canceled to Order
> Luxembourg's Office des Timbres, Direction des Postes, was offering, at least as early as 1967, to sell commemorative issues canceled to order.

1967, June 13 Litho. *Perf. 13x12½*

452 A116 3fr lt grn & dk grn 25 15
453 A116 6fr dp rose & dk car 40 40

NATO Council meeting, Luxembourg, June 13-14.

Youth Hostel, Ettelbruck A117

Home Gardener A118

1967, Sept. 14 Photo. *Perf. 11½*

454 A117 1.50fr multi 20 15

Luxembourg youth hostels.

1967, Sept. 14

455 A118 1.50fr brt grn & org 18 15

16th Congress of the Intl. Assoc. of Home Gardeners.

Shaving Basin with Wedding Scene, 1819 — A119

Design: 3fr, Ornamental vase, 1820.

1967, Sept. 14

456 A119 1.50fr ol grn & multi 15 15
457 A119 3fr ultra & lt gray 25 20

Faience industry in Luxembourg, 200th anniv.

Wormeldingen on Mosel River — A120

Mertert, Mosel River Port — A121

1967, Sept. 14 Engr. *Perf. 13*

458 A120 3fr dp bl, cl & ol 25 15
459 A121 3fr vio bl & sl 25 15

Swimming — A122

Sport: 1.50fr, Soccer. 2fr, Bicycling. 3fr, Running. 6fr, Walking. 13fr, Fencing.

1968, Feb. 22 Photo. *Perf. 11½*

460 A122 50c bl & grnsh bl 15 15
461 A122 1.50fr brt grn & emer 15 15
462 A122 2fr yel grn & lt yel grn 15 15
463 A122 3fr dp org & dl org 15 15
464 A122 6fr grnsh bl & pale grn 30 20
465 A122 13fr rose cl & rose 50 50
Nos. 460-465 (6) 1.40 1.30

Issued to publicize the 19th Olympic Games, Mexico City, Oct. 12-27.

Europa Issue, 1968

Common Design Type

1968, Apr. 29 Photo. *Perf. 11½*

Size: 32½x23mm

466 CD11 3fr ap grn, blk & org brn 20 15
467 CD11 6fr brn org, blk & ap grn 40 30

Kind Spring Pavilion A123

1968, Apr. 29 Photo. *Perf. 11½*

468 A123 3fr multi 20 15

Issued to publicize Mondorf-les-Bains.

Fair Emblem A124

1968, Apr. 29

469 A124 3fr dp vio, dl bl gold & red 20 15

20th Intl. Fair, Luxembourg City, May 23-June 2.

Children's Village of Mersch A125

Orphan and Foster Mother — A126

1968, Sept. 18 Engr. *Perf. 13*

470 A125 3fr sl grn & dk red brn 15 15
471 A126 6fr sl bl, blk & brn 28 20

Mersch children's village. (Modeled after Austrian SOS villages for homeless children.)

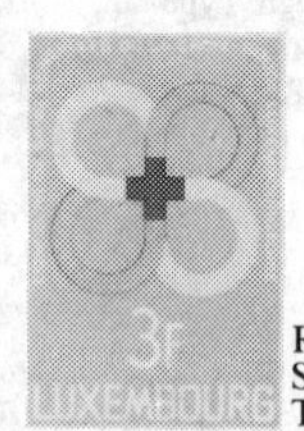

Red Cross and Symbolic Blood Transfusion — A127

1968, Sept. 18 Photo. *Perf. 11½*

472 A127 3fr lt bl & car 20 15

Voluntary Red Cross blood donors.

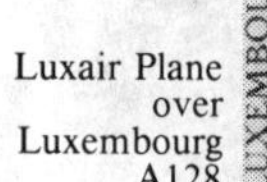

Luxair Plane over Luxembourg A128

1968, Sept. 18 Engr. *Perf. 13*

473 A128 50fr ol, bl & dk bl 1.65 70

Issued for tourist publicity.

Souvenir Sheet

"Youth and Leisure" — A129

Designs, 3fr, Doll. 6fr, Ballplayers. 13fr, Book, compass rose and ball.

1969, Apr. 3 Photo. *Perf. 11½*

Granite Paper

474 A129 Sheet of 3 3.25 3.25
a. 3fr ultra, blk & org 1.00 1.00
b. 6fr ultra, red & blk 1.00 1.00
c. 13fr dl grn, red & yel 1.00 1.00

1st Intl. Youth Phil. Exhib., JUVENTUS 1969, Luxembourg, Apr. 3-8.

No. 474 was on sale only at the exhibition. Sold only with entrance ticket for 40fr.

Europa Issue, 1969

Common Design Type

1969, May 19 Photo. *Perf. 11½*

Size: 32½x23mm

475 CD12 3fr gray, brn & org 25 15
476 CD12 6fr vio gray, blk & yel 38 35

Boy on Hobbyhorse, by Joseph Kutter (1894-1941) — A130

Design: 6fr, View of Luxembourg, by Kutter.

1969, May 19 Engr. *Perf. 12x13*

477 A130 3fr multi 25 15
a. Green omitted *150.00 150.00*
478 A130 6fr multi 35 35

ILO, 50th Anniv. A131

Photo.; Gold Impressed (Emblem)

1969, May 19 *Perf. 14x14½*

479 A131 3fr brt grn, vio & gold 20 15

Mobius Strip in Benelux Colors — A131a

1969, Sept. 8 Litho. *Perf. 12½x13½*

480 A131a 3fr multi 28 20

25th anniv. of the signing of the customs union of Belgium, Netherlands and Luxembourg.

NATO, 20th Anniv. A132

Grain and Mersch Agricultural Center A133

1969, Sept. 8 *Perf. 13½x12½*

481 A132 3fr org brn & dk brn 32 20

1969, Sept. 8 Photo. *Perf. 11½*

482 A133 3fr bl grn, gray & blk 20 15

Issued to publicize agricultural progress.

St. Willibrord's Basilica and Abbey, Echternach A134

Design: No. 484, Castle and open-air theater, Wiltz.

1969, Sept. 8 Engr. *Perf. 13*
483 A134 3fr dk bl & ind 22 15
484 A134 3fr sl grn & ind 22 15
Set value 24

Pasqueflower — A135

Design: 6fr, Hedgehog and 3 young.

1970, Mar. 9 Photo. *Perf. 11½*
485 A135 3fr multi 24 20
486 A135 6fr grn & multi 45 40

European Conservation Year.

Goldcrest A136

1970, Mar. 9 Engr. *Perf. 13*
487 A136 1.50fr org, grn & blk brn 20 15

Luxembourg Society for the protection and study of birds, 50th anniv.

Traffic Sign and Street Scene — A137

1970, May 4 Photo. *Perf. 11½*
488 A137 3fr rose mag, red & blk 22 15

The importance of traffic safety.

Europa Issue, 1970
Common Design Type

1970, May 4
Size: 32½x23mm
489 CD13 3fr brn & multi 24 15
490 CD13 6fr grn & multi 48 40

Empress Kunigunde and Emperor Henry II, Window, Luxembourg Cathedral — A138

1970, Sept. 14 Photo. *Perf. 12*
491 A138 3fr multi 20 20

Centenary of the Diocese of Luxembourg.

Census Symbol A139

1970, Sept. 14 *Perf. 11½*
492 A139 3fr dk grn, grnsh bl & red 20 15

Census of Dec. 31, 1970.

Lion, Luxembourg City Hall — A140

1970, Sept. 14
493 A140 3fr bis, lt bl & dk brn 18 15

50th anniversary of the City of Luxembourg through the union of 5 municipalities.

UN Emblem A141

Perf. 12½x13½
1970, Sept. 14 Litho.
494 A141 1.50fr bl & vio bl 18 15

25th anniversary of the United Nations.

Monks in Abbey Workshop A142

Olympic Rings, Arms of Luxembourg A143

Miniatures Painted at Echternach, about 1040: 3fr, Laborers going to the vineyard (Matthew 20:1-6). 6fr, Laborers toiling in vineyard. 13fr, Workers searching for graves of the saints.

1971, Mar. 15 Photo. *Perf. 12*
495 A142 1.50fr gold & multi 15 15
496 A142 3fr gold & multi 15 15
497 A142 6fr gold & multi 25 20
498 A142 13fr gold & multi 52 45
Set value 82

1971, May 3 Photo. *Perf. 12½*
499 A143 3fr ultra & multi 25 15

Intl. Olympic Committee, 71st session.

Europa Issue, 1971
Common Design Type

1971, May 3 *Perf. 12½x13*
Size: 34x25mm
500 CD14 3fr ver, brn & blk 32 15
501 CD14 6fr brt grn, brn & blk 45 35

A145

1971, May 3 Litho. *Perf. 13x13½*
502 A145 3fr org, dk brn & yel 20 20

Christian Workers Union, 50th anniv.

Artificial Lake, Upper Sure — A146

Designs: No. 504, Water treatment plant, Esch-sur-Sure. 15fr, ARBED Steel Corporation Headquarters, Luxembourg.

1971, Sept. 13 Engr. *Perf. 13*
503 A146 3fr ol, grnsh bl & ind 18 15
504 A146 3fr brn, sl grn & grnsh bl 24 15
505 A146 15fr ind & blk brn 70 40
Set value 60

School Girl with Coin — A147

1971, Sept. 13 Photo. *Perf. 11½*
506 A147 3fr vio & multi 22 15

School children's savings campaign.

Coins of Luxembourg and Belgium A148

Bronze Mask A149

1972, Mar. 6
507 A148 1.50fr lt grn, sil & blk 18 15

Economic Union of Luxembourg and Belgium, 50th anniversary.

1972, Mar. 6

Archaeological Objects, 4th to 1st centuries, B.C.: 1fr, Bronze bowl (horiz.). 8fr, Limestone head. 15fr, Glass jug in shape of head.

508 A149 1fr lem & multi 15 15
509 A149 3fr multi 15 15
510 A149 8fr multi 60 60
511 A149 15fr multi 80 80

Europa Issue 1972
Common Design Type

1972, May 2 Photo. *Perf. 11½*
Size: 22x33mm
512 CD15 3fr rose vio & multi 25 15
513 CD15 8fr gray bl & multi 80 80

Archer — A150

1972, May 2
514 A150 3fr crim, blk & ol 38 22

3rd European Archery Championships.

Robert Schuman Medal — A151

The Fox Wearing Tails — A152

1972, May 2 Engr. *Perf. 13*
515 A151 3fr gray & sl grn 50 18

Establishment in Luxembourg of the European Coal and Steel Community, 20th anniv.

1972, Sept. 11 Photo. *Perf. 11½*
516 A152 3fr scar & multi 35 20

Centenary of the publication of "Renert," satirical poem by Michel Rodange.

National Monument A153

Court of Justice of European Communities, Kirchberg — A154

1972, Sept. 11 Engr. *Perf. 13*
517 A153 3fr sl grn, ol & vio 22 15
518 A154 3fr brn, bl & sl grn 28 22

Epona on Horseback — A155

Archaeological Objects: 4fr, Panther killing swan (horiz.). 8fr, Celtic gold stater inscribed Pottina. 15fr, Bronze boar (horiz.).

1973, Mar. 14 Photo. *Perf. 11½*
519 A155 1fr sal & multi 15 15
520 A155 4fr beige & multi 20 15
521 A155 8fr multi 65 65
522 A155 15fr multi 65 65

Europa Issue 1973
Common Design Type

1973, Apr. 30 Photo. *Perf. 11½*
Size: 32x22mm
523 CD16 4fr org, dk vio & lt bl 38 15
524 CD16 8fr ol, vio blk & yel 1.10 75

An enhanced introduction to the Scott Catalogue begins on Page 1A. A thorough understanding of the material presented there will greatly aid your use of the catalogue itself.

Bee on Honeycomb A156

Nurse Holding Child A157

1973, Apr. 30 Photo. *Perf. 11½*
525 A156 4fr ocher & multi 35 15

Publicizing importance of beekeeping.

1973, Apr. 30
526 A157 4fr multi 28 20

Publicizing importance of day nurseries.

Laurel Branch A158

1973, Sept. 10 Photo. *Perf. 11½*
527 A158 3fr vio bl & multi 22 18

50th anniv. of Luxembourg Board of Labor.

Jerome de Busleyden A159

National Strike Memorial, Wiltz A160

1973, Sept. 10 Engr. *Perf. 13*
528 A159 4fr blk, brn & pur 28 20

Council of Mechelen, 500th anniv.

1973, Sept. 10
529 A160 4fr ol bis, sl & sl grn 22 20

In memory of the Luxembourg resistance heroes who died during the great strike of 1942.

Capital, Byzantine Hall, Vianden — A161

St. Gregory the Great — A161a

Designs: No. 534, Sts. Cecilia and Valerian crowned by angel, Hollenfels Church. No. 535, Interior, Septfontaines Church. 8fr, Madonna and Child, St. Irmina's Chapel, Rosport. 12fr, St. Augustine Sculptures by Jean-Georges Scholtus from pulpit in Feulen parish church, c. 1734.

1973-77 *Perf. 13x12½, 14 (6fr, 12fr)*
533 A161 4fr grn & rose vio 22 15
534 A161 4fr red brn, grn & lil 35 20
535 A161 4fr gray, brn & dk vio 35 20
536 A161a 6fr maroon 28 28
537 A161 8fr sep & vio bl 60 60
538 A161a 12fr slate bl 65 65
Nos. 533-538 (6) 2.45 2.08

Architecture of Luxembourg: Romanesque, Gothic, Baroque.
Issue dates: No. 533, 8fr, Sept. 10, 1973; Nos. 534-535, Sept. 9, 1974; 6fr, 12fr, Sept. 16, 1977.

Princess Marie Astrid — A162

Torch — A163

1974, Mar. 14 Photo. *Perf. 11½*
540 A162 4fr bl & multi 65 18

Princess Marie-Astrid, president of the Luxembourg Red Cross Youth Section.

1974, Mar. 14
541 A163 4fr ultra & multi 20 15

50th anniversary of Luxembourg Mutual Insurance Federation.

Royal Seal of Henri VII — A164

Seals from 13th-14th Centuries: 3fr, Equestrian, seal of Jean, King of Bohemia. 4fr, Seal of Town of Diekirch. 19fr, Virgin and Child, seal of Convent of Marienthal.

1974, Mar. 14
542 A164 1fr pur & multi 15 15
543 A164 3fr grn & multi 32 25
544 A164 4fr multi 45 15
545 A164 19fr multi 1.50 1.25

Hind, by Auguste Tremont A165

Winston Churchill, by Oscar Nemon A166

Europa: 8fr, "Growth," abstract sculpture, by Lucien Wercollier.

1974, Apr. 29 Photo. *Perf. 11½*
546 A165 4fr ocher & multi 38 24
547 A165 8fr brt bl & multi 1.25 1.00

1974, Apr. 29
548 A166 4fr lilac & multi 28 15

Sir Winston Churchill (1874-1965), statesman.

Fairground, Aerial View — A167

Theis, the Blind — A168

1974, Apr. 29
549 A167 4fr silver & multi 28 15

Publicity for New International Fairground, Luxembourg-Kirchberg.

1974, Apr. 29
550 A168 3fr multi 32 20

Mathias Schou, Theis the Blind (1747-1824), wandering minstrel.

UPU Emblem and "100" — A169

1974, Sept. 9 Photo. *Perf. 11½*
551 A169 4fr multi 32 32
552 A169 8fr multi 80 80

Centenary of Universal Postal Union.

"BENELUX" A170

1974, Sept. 9
553 A170 4fr bl grn, dk grn & lt bl 80 20

30th anniversary of the signing of the customs union of Belgium, Netherlands and Luxembourg.

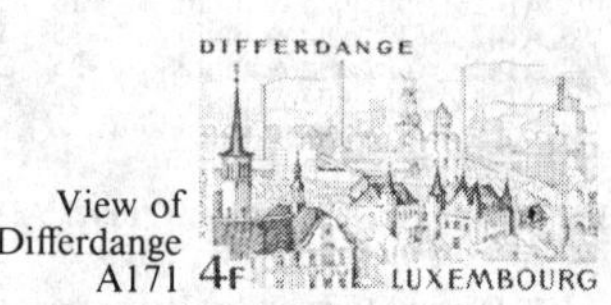

View of Differdange A171

1974, Sept. 9 Engr. *Perf. 13*
554 A171 4fr rose claret 22 15

Bourglinster A172

Designs: 1fr, Fish Market, Old Luxembourg, vert. 4fr, Market Square, Echternach. 19fr, St. Michael's Square, Mersch, vert.

Perf. 14x13½, 13½x14
1975, Mar. 10 Engr.
555 A172 1fr olive green 75 20
556 A172 3fr deep brown 1.40 40
557 A172 4fr dark purple 1.50 60
558 A172 19fr copper red 1.25 1.00

European Architectural Heritage Year.

Joseph Kutter, Self-portrait A173

Moselle Bridge, Remich, by Nico Klopp A174

Paintings: 8fr, Still Life, by Joseph Kutter. 20fr, The Dam, by Dominique Lang.

1975, Apr. 28 Photo. *Perf. 11½*
559 A173 1fr multi 28 18
560 A174 4fr multi 45 25
561 A174 8fr multi 2.20 75
562 A173 20fr multi 1.65 85

Cultural series. Nos. 560-561 are 1975 Europa Issue.

Robert Schuman, Gaetano Martino, Paul-Henri Spaak Medals A175

1975, Apr. 28
563 A175 4fr yel grn, gold & brn 1.10 25

25th anniversary of Robert Schuman's declaration establishing European Coal and Steel Community.

Albert Schweitzer (1875-1965), Medical Missionary — A176

1975, Apr. 28 Engr. *Perf. 13*
564 A176 4fr brt bl 90 20

Civil Defense Emblem A177

Figure Skating A178

1975, Sept. 8 Photo. *Perf. 11½*
565 A177 4fr multi 65 25

Civil Defense Org. for protection and rescue.

1975, Sept. 8 Engr. *Perf. 13*

Designs: 4fr, Water skiing (horiz.). 15fr, Mountain climbing.

566 A178 3fr grn, bl & lil 25 15
567 A178 4fr dk brn, grn & lt brn 40 30
568 A178 15fr brn, ind & grn 1.25 70

Grand Duke Type of 1965-71

1975-91 Engr. *Perf. 11½*
Granite Paper (14fr, 22fr)
570 A104 7fr org ('83) 35 20
571 A104 9fr yel grn 55 35
572 A104 10fr black 45 15
573 A104 12fr brick red 50 45
573A A104 14fr dark blue 85 85
574 A104 16fr green ('82) 70 60
574A A104 18fr brn ol ('86) 65 58

575	A104	20fr blue	90	40
576	A104	22fr orange brown	1.35	1.35
		Nos. 570-576 (9)	6.30	4.93

Issue dates: 10fr, Jan. 9; 9fr, 12fr, 20fr, Dec. 23; 16fr, Feb. 25, 1982; 7fr, July 1, 1983; 18fr, Mar. 3, 1986; 14fr, Jan. 2, 1990. 22fr, Sept. 23, 1991.

This is an expanding set. Numbers will change if necessary.

Grand Duchess Charlotte — A179

Design: No. 580, Prince Henri.

1976, Mar. 8 Litho. *Perf. 14x13 ½*

579	A179	6fr grn & multi	38	22
580	A179	6fr dl bl & multi	90	25

80th birthday of Grand Duchess Charlotte and 21st birthday of Prince Henri, heir to the throne.

Gold Brooch — A180

Designs: 5fr, Footless beaker (horiz.). 6fr, Decorated vessel (horiz.). 12fr, Gold coin. All designs show excavated items of Franco-Merovingian period.

Perf. 13 ½x12 ½, 12 ½x13 ½

1976, Mar. 8

581	A180	2fr bl & multi	15	15
582	A180	5fr blk & multi	28	28
583	A180	6fr lil & multi	45	28
584	A180	12fr multi	1.00	1.10

Soup Tureen A181

Europa: 12fr, Deep bowl. Tureen and bowl after pottery from Nospelt, 19th century.

1976, May 3 Photo. *Perf. 11 ½*

585	A181	6fr lt vio & multi	52	15
586	A181	12fr yel grn & multi	1.50	1.00

The indexes in each volume of the Scott Catalogue contain many listings which help to identify stamps.

Independence Hall, Philadelphia A182

Boomerang A183

1976, May 3

587	A182	6fr lt bl & multi	32	25

American Bicentennial.

1976, May 3

588	A183	6fr brt rose lil & gold	35	20

21st Olympic Games, Montreal, Canada, July 17-Aug. 1.

"Vibrations of Sound" A184

1976, May 3

589	A184	6fr red & multi	35	20

Jeunesses Musicales (Young Music Friends), association to foster interest in music and art.

Alexander Graham Bell — A185

Virgin and Child with St. Anne — A186

1976, Sept. 9 Engr. *Perf. 13*

590	A185	6fr slate green	35	25

Centenary of first telephone call by Alexander Graham Bell, Mar. 10, 1876.

1976, Sept. 9 Photo. *Perf. 11 ½*

Renaissance sculptures: 12fr, Grave of Bernard de Velbruck, Lord of Beaufort.

591	A186	6fr gold & multi	35	20
592	A186	12fr gold, gray & blk	70	70

Johann Wolfgang von Goethe A187

Old Luxembourg A188

Portraits: 5fr, J. M. William Turner. 6fr, Victor Hugo. 12fr, Franz Liszt.

1977, Mar. 14 Engr. *Perf. 13*

593	A187	2fr lake	15	15
594	A187	5fr purple	28	24
595	A187	6fr slate green	35	28
596	A187	12fr violet blue	70	65

Famous visitors to Luxembourg.

1977, May 3 Photo. *Perf. 11 ½*

Europa: 12fr, Adolphe Bridge and European Investment Bank headquarters.

597	A188	6fr multi	45	15
598	A188	12fr multi	1.25	65

Esch-sur-Sure A189

Marguerite de Busbach A190

Design: 6fr, View of Ehnen.

1977, May 3 Engr. *Perf. 13*

599	A189	5fr Prus bl	38	25
600	A189	6fr dp brn	32	25

1977, May 3 Photo. *Perf. 11 ½*

Design: No. 602, Louis Braille, by Lucienne Filippi.

601	A190	6fr multi	35	20
602	A190	6fr multi	35	20

Notre Dame Congregation, founded by Marguerite de Busbach, 350th anniversary; Louis Braille (1809-1852), inventor of the Braille system of writing for the blind.

Souvenir Sheet

Luxembourg Nos. 1-2 — A191

Engr. & Photo.

1977, Sept. 15 *Perf. 13 ½*

603	A191	40fr gray & red brn	4.50	4.50

125th anniv. of Luxembourg's stamps.

Head of Medusa, Roman Mosaic, Diekirch, 3rd Century A.D. — A192

1977, Sept. 15 Photo. *Perf. 11 ½*

604	A192	6fr multi	50	32

Orpheus and Eurydice, by C. W. Gluck A193

1977, Sept. 15 *Perf. 11 ½x12*

605	A193	6fr multi	60	25

Intl. Wiltz Festival, 25th anniv.

Europa Tamed, by R. Zilli, and Map of Europe A194

1977, Dec. 5 Photo. *Perf. 11 ½*

606	A194	6fr multi	60	30

20th anniversary of the Treaties of Rome, setting up the European Economic Community and the European Atomic Energy Commission.

Souvenir Sheet

Grand Duke and Grand Duchess of Luxembourg — A195

Photogravure and Engraved

1978, Apr. 3 *Perf. 13 ½x14*

607	A195	Sheet of 2	2.00	2.00
a.		6fr dk bl & multi	90	90
b.		12fr dk red & multi	90	90

Silver wedding anniversary of Grand Duke Jean and Grand Duchess Josephine Charlotte.

Souvenir Sheet

Youth Fountain, Streamer and Dancers — A196

1978, Apr. 3 Photo. *Perf. 11 ½*

608	A196	Sheet of 3	3.50	3.50
a.		5fr ultra & multi	1.10	1.10
b.		6fr org & multi	1.10	1.10
c.		20fr yel grn & multi	1.10	1.10

Juphilux 78, 5th International Young Philatelists' Exhibition, Luxembourg, Apr. 6-10.

Charles IV, Statue, Charles Bridge, Prague A197

Emile Mayrish, by Theo Van Rysselberghe A198

Europa: 12fr, Pierre d'Aspelt, tomb, Mainz Cathedral.

1978, May 18 Engr. *Perf. 13 ½*

609	A197	6fr dk vio bl	30	20
610	A197	12fr dl rose lil	85	70

Charles IV (1316-1378), Count of Luxembourg, Holy Roman Emperor, 600th death anniversary. Pierre d'Aspelt (c. 1250-1320), Archbishop of Mainz and Prince-Elector.

1978, May 18 **Perf. 11½**
611 A198 6fr multi 85 30

Emile Mayrish (1862-1928), president of International Steel Cartel and promoter of United Europe, 50th death anniversary.

Our Lady of Luxembourg A199

Trumpeters and Old Luxembourg A200

1978, May 18 **Photo.** **Perf. 11½**
612 A199 6fr multi 25 25
613 A200 6fr multi 25 25

Our Lady of Luxembourg, patroness, 300th anniversary; 135th anniversary of Grand Ducal Military Band.

Starving Child, Helping Hand, Millet A201

League Emblem, Lungs, Open Window A202

Open Prison Door — A203

1978, Sept. 11 **Photo.** **Perf. 11½**
614 A201 2fr multi 15 15
615 A202 5fr multi 25 25
616 A203 6fr multi 40 30

"Terre des Hommes," an association to help underprivileged children; Luxembourg Anti-Tuberculosis League, 70th anniversary; Amnesty International and 30th anniversary of Universal Declaration of Human Rights.

Squared Stone Emerging from Rock, City of Luxembourg — A204

1978, Sept. 11 **Engr.** **Perf. 13½x13**
617 A204 6fr vio bl 45 25

Masonic Grand Lodge of Luxembourg, 175th anniversary.

Julius Caesar on Denarius, c. 44 B.C. A205

St. Michael's Church, Mondorf-les-Bains A206

Roman Coins, Found in Luxembourg: 6fr, Empress Faustina I on Sestertius, 141 A.D. 9fr, Empress Helena on Follis, c. 324-330. 26fr, Emperor Valens on Solidus, c. 367-375.

1979, Mar. 5 **Photo.** **Perf. 11½**
618 A205 5fr multi 22 22
619 A205 6fr multi 22 22
620 A205 9fr multi 65 55
621 A205 26fr multi 1.25 1.00

1979, Mar. 5 **Engr.** **Perf. 13**

Design: 6fr, Luxembourg Central Station.

622 A206 5fr multi 30 20
623 A206 6fr rose claret 60 30

Troisvierges Stagecoach A207

Europa: 12fr, Early wall telephone (vert.).

1979, Apr. 30 **Photo.** **Perf. 11½**
624 A207 6fr multi 1.10 40
625 A207 12fr multi 2.50 90

Michel Pintz Facing Jury — A208

1979, Apr. 30 **Engr.** **Perf. 13**
626 A208 2fr rose lil 30 15

180th anniversary of peasant uprising against French occupation.

Antoine Meyer — A209

Abundance Crowning Work and Thrift, by Auguste Vinet — A210

Design: 6fr, Sidney Gilchrist Thomas.

1979, Apr. 30
627 A209 5fr carmine 32 20
628 A209 6fr lt bl 32 25
629 A210 9fr black 50 35

Antoine Meyer (1801-1857), mathematician and first national poet; centenary of acquisition of Thomas process for production of high-quality steel; 50th anniversary of Luxembourg Stock Exchange.

European Parliament A211

1979, June 7 **Photo.** **Perf. 11½**
630 A211 6fr multi 5.00 90

European Parliament, first direct elections, June 7-10.

Angel with Chalice, by Barthelemy Namur — A212

Rococo Art: 12fr, Angel with anchor, by Namur, from High Altar, St. Michael's Church, Luxembourg.

Engraved and Photogravure
1979, Sept. 10 **Perf. 13½**
631 A212 6fr multi 35 25
632 A212 12fr multi 65 50

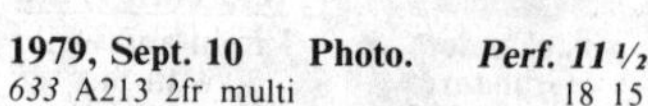

Road Safety for Children A213

1979, Sept. 10 **Photo.** **Perf. 11½**
633 A213 2fr multi 18 15

International Year of the Child.

Radio Tele-Luxembourg Emblem — A214

1979, Sept. 10
634 A214 6fr ultra, bl & red 45 25

50 years of broadcasting in Luxembourg.

John the Blind, Silver Coin, 1331 — A215

Ettelbruck Town Hall — A216

14th Century Coins: 2fr, Sts. Gervase and Protais, silver grosso. 6fr, Easter lamb, gold coin. 20fr, Crown and arms, silver grosso.

1980, Mar. 5 **Photo.** **Perf. 11½**
635 A215 2fr multi 15 15
636 A215 5fr multi 25 25
637 A215 6fr multi 35 35
638 A215 20fr multi 1.20 1.20

See Nos. 651-654.

1980, Mar. 5 **Engr.** **Perf. 13**

Design: No. 640, State Archives Building, horiz.

639 A216 6fr brn & dk red 35 25
640 A216 6fr multi 35 25

Jean Monnet — A217

Sports for All — A218

Europa: 12fr, St. Benedict of Nursia.

1980, Apr. 28 **Perf. 13½**
641 A217 6fr dk bl 52 25
642 A217 12fr ol grn 1.00 60

1980, Apr. 28 **Photo.** **Perf. 11½**
Granite Paper
643 A218 6fr multi 95 22

Worker Pouring Molten Iron — A219

Mercury by Jean Mich — A220

Design: 6fr, Man, hand, gears (horiz.).

1980, Apr. 28
644 A219 2fr multi 15 15
645 A219 6fr multi 42 22
Set value 30

9th World Congress on Prevention of Occupational Accidents and Diseases, Amsterdam, May 6-9.

1980, Sept. 10 **Engr.** **Perf. 14**

Art Nouveau Sculpture by Jean Mich.

646 A220 8fr shown 48 40
647 A220 12fr Ceres 70 55

Introduction of Postal Code A221

1980, Sept. 10 **Photo.** **Perf. 11½**
648 A221 4fr multi 42 15

Police Car and Officers A222

1980, Sept. 10
649 A222 8fr multi 48 32

State control of police force, 50th anniv.

Grand Duke Jean — A223

Arms of Grand Duke Jean — A224

Photo. & Engr.

1981, Jan. 5 *Perf. 13½*

650 Sheet of 3 2.50 2.50
a. A223 8fr multi 65 65
b. A224 12fr multi 75 75
c. A223 30fr multi 1.00 1.00

Grand Duke Jean, 60th birthday.

Coin Type of 1980

Silver Coins: 4fr, Philip IV patagon, 1635. 6fr, Empress Maria Theresa 12 sol, 1775. 8fr, Emperor Joseph II 12 sol, 1789. 30fr, Emperor Francois II 72 sol, 1795.

1981, Mar. 5 Photo. *Perf. 11½*

651 A215 4fr multi 18 16
652 A215 6fr multi 25 20
653 A215 8fr multi 32 32
654 A215 30fr multi 1.25 1.10

National Library A225

1981, Mar. 5 Engr. *Perf. 13*

655 A225 8fr shown 35 20
656 A225 8fr European Hemicycle, Kirchberg 35 20

Hammelsmarsch (Sheep Procession) A226

Europa: 12fr, Bird-shaped whistle, Eimaischen market.

1981, May 4 Photo. *Perf. 13½*

657 A226 8fr multi 38 30
658 A226 12fr multi 60 50

Knight on Chessboard A227

Savings Account Book, State Bank A228

First Bank Note, 1856 — A229

1981, May 4 *Perf. 11½*

Granite Paper

659 A227 4fr multi 25 22
660 A228 8fr multi 35 35
661 A229 8fr multi 35 35

Luxembourg Chess Federation, 50th anniversary; State Savings Bank, 125th anniversary; International Bank of Luxembourg, 125th anniversary of issuing rights.

Wedding of Prince Henri and Maria Teresa Mestre, Feb. 14 — A230

Photo. & Engr.

1981, June 22 *Perf. 13½*

662 A230 8fr multi 50 40

Sheets of 12.

Single-seater Gliders A231

Energy Conservation A232

1981, Sept. 28 Photo. *Perf. 11½*

Granite Paper

663 A231 8fr shown 30 30
664 A231 16fr Propeller planes, horiz. 60 60
665 A231 35fr Jet, Luxembourg Airport, horiz. 1.50 1.40

1981, Sept. 28

Granite Paper

666 A232 8fr multi 35 35

Apple Trees in Blossom, by Frantz Seimetz (1858-1914) A233

World War II Resistance A234

Landscape Paintings: 6fr, Summer Landscape, by Pierre Blanc (1872-1946). 8fr, The Larger Hallerbach, by Guido Oppenheim (1862-1942). 16fr, Winter Evening, by Eugene Mousset (1877-1941).

1982, Feb. 25 Engr. *Perf. 11½*

667 A233 4fr multi 18 18
668 A233 6fr multi 28 28
669 A233 8fr multi 40 40
670 A233 16fr multi 80 80

1982, Feb. 25

Design: Cross of Hinzert (Natl. Monument of the Resistance and Deportation) and Political Prisoner, by Lucien Wercollier.

671 A234 8fr multi 38 35

Europa 1982 A235

St. Theresa of Avila (1515-1582) A236

1982, May 4 Photo.

Granite Paper

672 A235 8fr Treaty of London, 1867 50 35
673 A235 16fr Treaty of Paris, 1951 90 65

1982, May 4

Design: 8fr, Raoul Follereau (1903-1977), "Apostle of the Lepers."

Granite Paper

674 A236 4fr multi 20 18
675 A236 8fr multi 40 38

State Museums A237

1982, May 4 Photo. & Engr.

676 A237 8fr shown 45 35
677 A237 8fr Synagogue of Luxembourg 45 35

Bourscheid Castle — A238

Intl. Youth Hostel Federation, 50th Anniv. — A239

Designs: Restored castles.

1982, Sept. 9 Engr. *Perf. 11½*

Granite Paper

678 A238 6fr shown 32 25
679 A238 8fr Vianden, horiz. 45 35

1982, Sept. 9 Photo.

680 A239 4fr shown 30 15
681 A239 8fr Scouting year, vert. 60 35

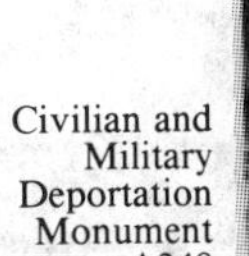
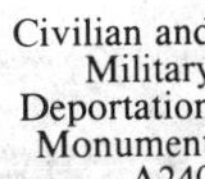
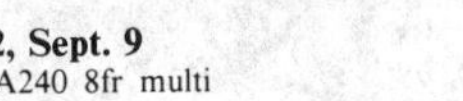

Civilian and Military Deportation Monument A240

1982, Sept. 9

682 A240 8fr multi 50 35

Mercury, Sculpture by Auguste Tremond A241

NATO Emblem, Flags A242

1983, Mar. 7 Photo. *Perf. 11½*

Granite Paper

683 A241 4fr multi 20 15

FOREX '83, 25th Intl. Assoc. of Foreign Exchange Dealers' Congress, June 2-5.

1983, Mar. 7

Granite Paper

684 A242 6fr multi 25 25

25th anniv. of NAMSA (NATO Maintenance and Supply Agency).

Echternach Cross of Justice, 1236 A243

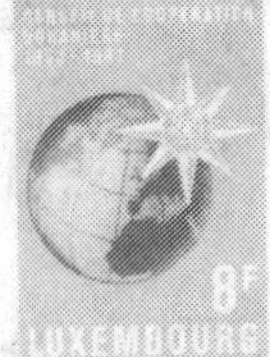

Globe, CCC Emblem A244

1983, Mar. 7

Granite Paper

685 A243 8fr multi 45 35

30th Congress of Intl. Union of Barristers, July 3-9.

1983, Mar. 7

Granite Paper

686 A244 8fr multi 45 35

30th anniv. of Council of Customs Cooperation.

Natl. Federation of Fire Brigades Centenary A245

1983, Mar. 7

Granite Paper

687 A245 8fr Fire engine, 1983 45 35
688 A245 16fr Hand pump, 1740 85 65

Europa 1983 — A246

The Good Samaritan, Codex Aureus Escorialensis Miniatures, 11th Cent., Echternach.

1983, May 3 Photo.

689 A246 8fr Highway robbers 52 35
690 A246 16fr Good Samaritan 1.00 65

Giant Bible, 11th Cent. — A247

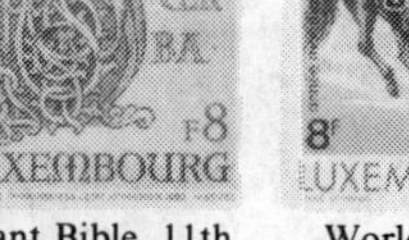

World Communications Year — A248

Illuminated Letters.

Photo. & Engr.

1983, May 3 *Perf. 14*

691 A247 8fr "h," Book of Baruch 45 35
692 A247 35fr "B," letter of St. Jerome 2.00 1.50

1983, May 3 Photo. *Perf. 11½*

693 A248 8fr Post code 42 35
694 A248 8fr Satellite relay, horiz. 42 35

Town Hall, Dudelange A249

Designs: 7fr, St. Lawrence Church, Diekirch (vert.).

1983, Sept. 7 Photo. & Engr.

695 A249 7fr multi 38 25
696 A249 10fr multi 55 35

Basketball Fed., 50th Anniv. A250

European Working Dog Championship A251

Tourism — A252

1983, Sept. 7 Photo.
Granite Paper

697 A250 7fr multi 38 25
698 A251 10fr Alsatian sheepdog 55 35
699 A252 10fr View of Luxembourg 55 35

Environment Protection A253

1984, Mar. 6 Photo. *Perf. 11½*
Granite Paper

700 A253 7fr Pedestrian zoning 35 16
701 A253 10fr Water purification 50 24

2nd European Parliament Election — A254

1984, Mar. 6
Granite Paper

702 A254 10fr Hands holding emblem 60 40

Anniversaries — A255

1984, Mar. 6 Engr. *Perf. 12½x13*

703 A255 10fr No. 1 50 35
704 A255 10fr Union meeting 50 35
705 A255 10fr Mail bag 50 35
706 A255 10fr Train 50 35

Philatelic Federation (1934); Civil Service Trade Union (1909); Postal Workers' Union (1909); Railroad (1859).

1984 Summer Olympics — A256

1984, May 7 Photo. *Perf. 11½x12*

707 A256 10fr The Race, by Jean Jacoby (1891-1936) 55 35

Europa (1959-84) A257

1984, May 7 *Perf. 11½*
Granite Paper

708 A257 10fr green 55 30
709 A257 16fr orange 80 60

Young Turk Caressing His Horse, by Delacroix A258

Paintings: 4fr, The Smoker, by David Teniers the Younger (1610-90). 10fr, Epiphany, by Han Steen (1626-79). 50fr, The Lacemaker, by Pieter van Slingelandt (1640-91). 4fr, 50fr vert.

Photo. & Engr.

1984, May 7 *Perf. 14*

710 A258 4fr multi 25 22
711 A258 7fr multi 40 24
712 A258 10fr multi 60 35
713 A258 50fr multi 2.75 2.00

Marine Life Fossils A259

Restored Castles A260

1984, Sept. 10 Photo. *Perf. 11½*

714 A259 4fr Pecten sp. 22 15
715 A259 7fr Gryphaea arcuata 38 25
716 A259 10fr Coeloceras raqyinianum 55 35
717 A259 16fr Daildius 90 60

1984, Sept. 10 Engr.

718 A260 7fr Hollenfels 38 25
719 A260 10fr Larochette 55 40

40th Anniv. of D Day (June 6) — A261

1984, Sept. 10 *Perf. 12x12½*

720 A261 10fr Soldier, US flag 75 35

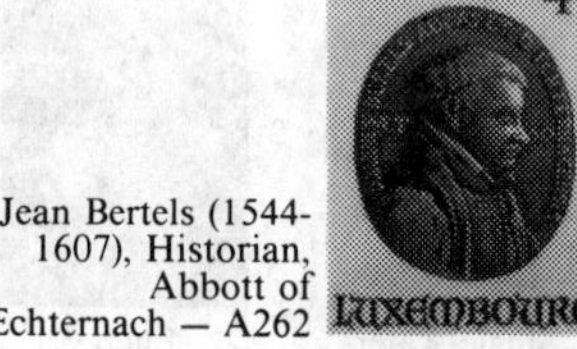

Jean Bertels (1544-1607), Historian, Abbott of Echternach — A262

Portrait medals in the state museum: 7fr, Emperor Charles V (1500-1558). 10fr, King Philip II of Spain (1527-1598). 30fr, Prince Maurice of Orange-Nassau, Count of Vianden (1567-1625).

1985, Mar. 4 Photo. *Perf. 11½*
Granite Paper

721 A262 4fr multi 24 22
722 A262 7fr multi 40 22
723 A262 10fr multi 60 32
724 A262 30fr multi 1.75 90

See Nos. 739-742.

Anniversaries A263

Designs: No. 725, Benz Velo, First automobile in Luxembourg, 1895. No. 726, Push-button telephone, sound waves. No. 727, Fencers.

1985, Mar. 4 *Perf. 12x11½*
Granite Paper

725 A263 10fr multi 65 40
726 A263 10fr multi 65 40
727 A263 10fr multi 65 40

Centenary of the first automobile; Luxembourg Telephone Service, cent.; Luxembourg Fencing Federation, 50th anniv.

Visit of Pope John Paul II — A264

Europa 1985 — A265

1985, Mar. 4 *Perf. 11½x12*
Granite Paper

728 A264 10fr Papal arms 75 40

1985, May 8 *Perf. 11½*

Designs: 10fr, Grand-Duke Adolphe Music Federation. 16fr, Luxembourg Music School.

729 A265 10fr multi 80 40
730 A265 16fr multi 1.25 60

Souvenir Sheet

End of World War II, 40th Anniv. — A266

Designs: a, Luxembourg resistance fighters, Wounded Fighters medal. b, Luxembourg War Cross. c, Badge of the Union of Luxembourg Resistance Movements. d, Liberation of the concentration camps.

1985, May 8 *Perf. 11½x12*
Granite Paper

731 Sheet of 4 2.75 2.75
a.-d. A266 10fr. any single 60 38

Endangered Wildlife — A267

1985, Sept. 23 Photo. *Perf. 12x11½*

732 A267 4fr Athene nocturna 20 15
733 A267 7fr Felis silvestris 38 22
734 A267 10fr Vanessa atalanti-ca, vert. 55 35
735 A267 50fr Hyla arborea, vert. 2.75 1.65

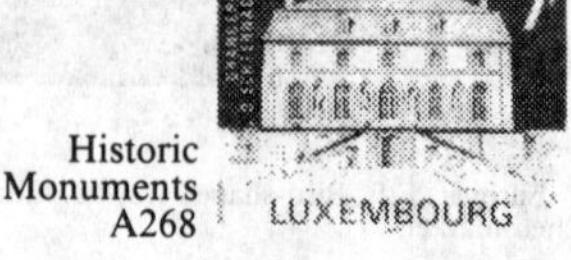

Historic Monuments A268

1985, Sept. 23 Engr. *Perf. 11½*

736 A268 7fr Echternach Orangery, 1750 45 22
737 A268 10fr Mohr de Waldt House, 17th cent. 65 45

Natl. Art Collection A269

Photo. & Engr.

1985, Sept. 23 *Perf. 14*

738 A269 10fr 18th cent. book cover, Natl. Library 40 22

Portrait Medals Type of 1985

1986, Mar. 3 Photo. *Perf. 11½*

Granite Paper

739 A262 10fr Count of Monterey, 1675 65 40
740 A262 12fr Louis XIV, 1684 70 45
741 A262 18fr Pierre de Weyms, c. 1700 1.10 70
742 A262 20fr Duke of Marlborough, 1706 1.25 80

Federation of Luxembourg Beekeepers' Associations, Cent. — A270

Mondorf State Spa, Cent. — A271

Natl. Table Tennis Federation, 50th Anniv. — A272

1986, Mar. 3 *Perf. 11½*

743 A270 12fr Bee collecting pollen 75 50
744 A271 12fr Mosaic 75 50
745 A272 12fr Boy playing table tennis 75 50

Europa 1986 A273

Fortifications A274

1986, May 5 Photo. *Perf. 12*

Granite Paper

751 A273 12fr Polluted forest, city 75 50
752 A273 20fr Man, pollution sources 1.25 80

1986, May 5

Granite Paper

753 A274 15fr Ft. Thungen, horiz. 90 60
754 A274 18fr Invalid's Gate 1.10 72
755 A274 50fr Malakoff Tower 3.00 2.00

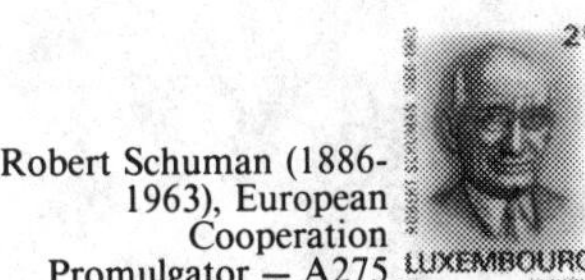

Robert Schuman (1886-1963), European Cooperation Promulgator — A275

1986, June 26 *Perf. 12 on 3 Sides*

Granite Paper

756 A275 2fr pink & blk 15 15
a. Bklt. pane of 4 32
757 A275 10fr lt bl & blk 65 40
a. Bklt. pane of 4 2.75
b. Bklt. pane of 2, #756-757, + 2 labels 1.40

Nos. 756-757 issued in booklets only.

European Road Safety Year A276

Countess Ermesinde (1186-1247), Ruler of Luxembourg A278

Bas-relief, Town Hall, Esch-Sur-Alzette — A277

1986, Sept. 15 Photo. *Perf. 11½*

758 A276 10fr multi 55 40

Photogravure & Engraved

1986, Sept. 15 *Perf. 14x13½*

Design: No. 760, Stairs to the Chapel of the Cross, Grevenmacher.

759 A277 12fr shown 75 50
760 A277 12fr multi 75 50

1986, Sept. 15 *Perf. 13½x14*

Designs: No. 761, Presentation of the letter of freedom to Echternach inhabitants, 1236, engraving (detail) by P.H. Witkamp, c. 1873. 30fr, Charter seal, Marienthal Convent, 1238.

761 A278 12fr multi 70 50
762 A278 30fr multi 1.65 1.20

Wildlife Conservation A279

Natl. Home Amateur Radio Operators Network, 50th Anniv. A280

Luxembourg Intl. Fair, 50th Anniv. A281

1987, Mar. 9 Photo. *Perf. 11½*

763 A279 6fr Eliomys quercinus 30 24
764 A279 10fr Calopteryx splendens, vert. 52 40
765 A279 12fr Cinclus cinclus, vert. 60 48
766 A279 25fr Salamandra salamandra terrestris 1.40 1.00

1987, Mar. 9

767 A280 12fr multi 62 48
768 A281 12fr multi 62 48

Europa 1987 — A282

Designs: 12fr, Aquatic Sports Center. 20fr, European Communities Court of Justice and abstract sculpture by Henry Moore (1898-1986).

1987, May 4 Photo. *Perf. 11½*

769 A282 12fr multi 75 48
770 A282 20fr multi 1.25 80

St. Michael's Church Millenary A283

Designs: 12fr, Consecration of the church by Archbishop Egbert of Trier, 987, stained glass window by Gustav Zanter. 20fr, Baroque organ-chest, 17th century.

Photogravure & Engraved

1987, May 4 *Perf. 14*

771 A283 12fr multi 75 48
772 A283 20fr multi 1.25 80

15th Century Paintings by Giovanni Ambrogio Bevilacqua — A284

Polyptych panels in the State Museum: 10fr, St. Bernard of Sienna and St. John the Baptist. 18fr, St. Jerome and St. Francis of Assisi.

1987, May 4 *Perf. 11½*

773 A284 10fr multi 55 40
774 A284 18fr multi 1.00 72

Rural Architecture A285

Photo. & Engr.

1987, Sept. 14 *Perf. 13½*

775 A285 10fr Hennesbau Bark Mill, 1826, Niederfeulen 50 40
776 A285 12fr Health Center, 18th cent., Mersch 60 48
777 A285 100fr Post Office, 18th cent., Bertrange 5.00 4.00

Chamber of Deputies (Parliament) 139th Anniv. — A286

Designs: 6fr, Charles Metz (1799-1853), first President. 12fr, Parliament, 1860, designed by Antoine Hartmann (1817-1891).

1987, Sept. 14 Engr. *Perf. 14*

778 A286 6fr violet brn 24 24
779 A286 12fr blue black 48 48

Flowers by Botanical Illustrator Pierre-Joseph Redoute (1759-1840) A287

1988, Feb. 8 Photo. *Perf. 11½x12*

780 A287 6fr Orange lily, water lily 35 35
781 A287 10fr Primula, double narcissus 60 60
782 A287 12fr Tulip 72 72
783 A287 50fr Iris, gorteria 3.00 3.00

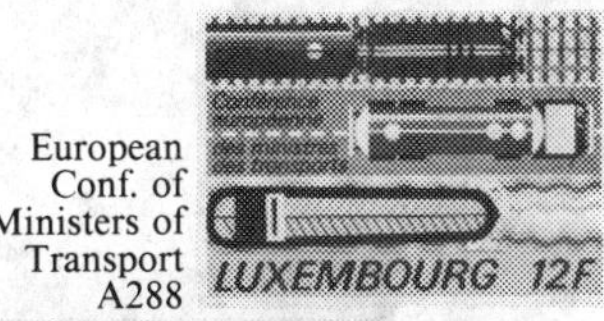

European Conf. of Ministers of Transport A288

Eurocontrol, 25th Anniv. A289

1988, Feb. 8 *Perf. 12*

784 A288 12fr multi 72 72
785 A289 20fr multi 1.20 1.20

Souvenir Sheet

Family of Prince Henri — A290

1988, Mar. 29 Photo. *Perf. 12*

786 A290 Sheet of 3 4.75 4.75
a. 12fr Maria Theresa 68 68
b. 18fr Guillaume, Felix and Louis 1.00 1.00
c. 50fr Prince Henri 2.75 2.75

JUVALUX '88, 9th intl. youth philatelic exhibition, Mar. 29-Apr. 4.

Europa 1988 — A291

Communication.

1988, June 6 Photo. *Perf. 11½*

787 A291 12fr Automatic mail handling 72 72
788 A291 20fr Electronic mail 1.20 1.20

Tourism A292

Designs: 10fr, Wiltz town hall and Cross of Justice Monument, c. 1502. 12fr, Castle, Differdange, 16th cent., vert.

Photo. & Engr.

1988, June 6 ***Perf. 13½***

789 A292 10fr multi 60 60
790 A292 12fr multi 72 72

See Nos. 824-825, 841-842.

League of Luxembourg Student Sports Associations (LASEL), 50th Anniv. A293

1988, June 6 **Photo.** ***Perf. 11½***

791 A293 12fr multi 72 72

Doorways A294

Architectural drawings by Joseph Wegener (1895-1980) and his students, 1949-1951: 12fr, Septfontaines Castle main entrance, 1785. 25fr, National Library regency north-wing entrance, c. 1720. 50fr, Holy Trinity Church baroque entrance, c. 1740.

Litho. & Engr.

1988, Sept. 12 ***Perf. 14***

792 A294 12fr black & buff 65 65
793 A294 25fr blk & citron 1.30 1.30
794 A294 50fr blk & yel bis 2.60 2.60

Jean Monnet (1888-1979), French Economist — A295

1988, Sept. 12 **Engr.**

795 A295 12fr multi 65 65

European Investment Bank, 30th Anniv. — A296

1988, Sept. 12 **Litho. & Engr.**

796 A296 12fr yel grn & blk 65 65

1988 Summer Olympics, Seoul — A297

1988, Sept. 12 **Photo.** ***Perf. 11½***

797 A297 12fr multi 65 65

C.M. Spoo (1837-1914), Advocate of Luxembourgish as the Natl. Language — A298

Design: 12fr, Portrait and excerpt from his speech to the Chamber of Deputies, 1896.

1989, Mar. 6 **Photo.** ***Perf. 11½x12***

798 A298 12fr multi 62 62

Book Workers' Fed., 125th Anniv. — A299

Natl. Red Cross, 75th Anniv. — A300

1989, Mar. 6

799 A299 18fr multi 95 95

1989, Mar. 6

800 A300 20fr Henri Dunant 1.05 1.05

Independence of the Grand Duchy, 150th Anniv. A301

Design: 12fr, Lion, bronze sculpture by Auguste Tremont (1892-1980) guarding the grand ducal family vault, Cathedral of Luxembourg.

Photo. & Engr.

1989, Mar. 6 ***Perf. 14***

801 A301 12fr multi 62 62

Astra Telecommunications Satellite — A302

1989, Mar. 6 **Photo.** ***Perf. 11½***

802 A302 12fr multi 62 62

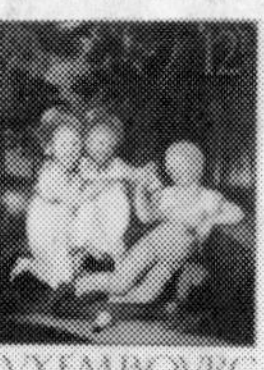
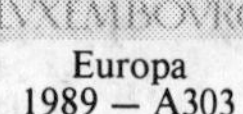

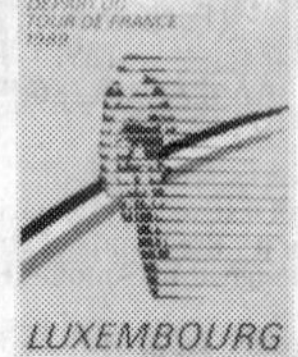

Europa 1989 — A303

Tour de France — A304

Paintings (children at play): 12fr, *Three Children in a Park,* 19th cent., anonymous. 20fr, *Child with Drum,* 17th cent., anonymous.

1989, May 8 **Photo.** ***Perf. 11½x12***

803 A303 12fr multi 62 62
804 A303 20fr multi 1.05 1.05

1989, May 8 ***Perf. 11½***

805 A304 9fr multi 48 48

Start of the bicycle race in Luxembourg City.

Interparliamentary Union, Cent. — A305

1989, May 8 ***Perf. 11½x12***

806 A305 12fr multi 62 62

European Parliament 3rd Elections — A306

1989, May 8

807 A306 12fr multi 62 62

Council of Europe, 40th Anniv. A307

1989, May 8 ***Perf. 12x11½***

808 A307 12fr multi 62 62

Reign of Grand Duke Jean, 25th Anniv. A308

Charles IV (1316-1378) A309

1989, Sept. 18 **Photo.** ***Perf. 12x11½***

Booklet Stamps

810 A308 3fr 15 15
816 A308 9fr 42 42
a. Bklt. pane, 5 each #810, 816 2.85

This is an expanding set. Numbers will change if necessary.

Photo. & Engr.

1989, Sept. 18 ***Perf. 13½x14***

Stained-glass windows by Joseph Oberberger in the Grand Ducal Loggia, Cathedral of Luxembourg: 20fr, John the Blind (1296-1346). 25fr, Wenceslas II (1361-1419).

821 A309 12fr shown 58 58
822 A309 20fr multi 95 95
823 A309 25fr multi 1.20 1.20

Independence of the Grand Duchy, 150th anniv.

Tourism Type of 1988

Designs: 12fr, Clervaux Castle interior courtyard, circa 12th cent. 18fr, Bronzed wild boar of Titelberg, 1st cent., vert.

Litho. & Engr.

1989, Sept. 18 ***Perf. 13½***

824 A292 12fr multi 58 58
825 A292 18fr multi 88 88

Views of the Former Fortress of Luxembourg, 1814-1815, Engravings by Christoph Wilhelm Selig (1791-1837) — A310

1990, Mar. 5 **Photo.** ***Perf. 12x11½***

826 A310 9fr shown 52 52
827 A310 12fr multi, diff. 70 70
828 A310 20fr multi, diff. 1.15 1.15
829 A310 25fr multi, diff. 1.40 1.40

Congress of Vienna, 1815, during which the Duchy of Luxembourg was elevated to the Grand Duchy of Luxembourg.

Schueberfouer Carnival, 650th Anniv. — A311

1990, Mar. 15 ***Perf. 11½x12***

830 A311 9fr Carnival ride 52 52

Batty Weber (1860-1940), Writer — A312

ITU, 125th Anniv. — A313

1990, Mar. 15

831 A312 12fr multi 70 70

1990, Mar. 15

832 A313 18fr multicolored 1.05 1.05

Europa — A314

Post offices: 12fr, Luxembourg City. 20fr, Esch-Sur-Alzette, vert.

Litho. & Engr.

1990, May 28 ***Perf. 13½***

833 A314 12fr buff & blk 72 72
834 A314 20fr lt bl & blk 1.20 1.20

Paul Eyschen (1841-1915) A315

Prime Ministers: 12fr, Emmanuel Servais (1811-1890).

Photo. & Engr.

1990, May 28 *Perf. 14x13½*

835 A315 9fr multicolored 55 55
836 A315 12fr multicolored 72 72

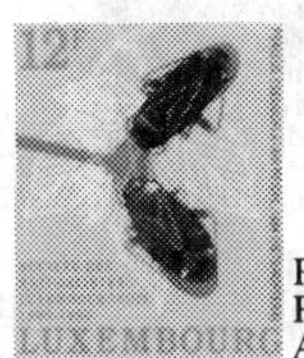

Psallus Pseudoplatani A316

1990, May 28 Photo. *Perf. 11½*

837 A316 12fr multicolored 72 72

Luxembourg Naturalists' Society, cent.

Fountains — A317

Designs: 12fr, Sheep's march by Will Lofy. 25fr, Fountain of Doves. 50fr, "Maus Ketty" by Lofy.

Litho. & Engr.

1990, Sept. 24 *Perf. 14*

838 A317 12fr 72 72
839 A317 25fr 1.50 1.50
840 A317 50fr 3.00 3.00

Tourism Type of 1988

1990, Sept. 24 *Perf. 13½*

841 A292 12fr Mondercange 72 72
842 A292 12fr Schifflange 72 72

Souvenir Sheet

Nassau-Weilbourg Dynasty, Cent. — A318

Designs: a, Grand Duke Adolphe. b, Grand Duchess Marie-Adelaide. c, Grand Ducal House arms. d, Grand Duchess Charlotte. e, Grand Duke Guillaume. f, Grand Duke Jean. Illustration reduced.

Photo. & Engr.

1990, Nov. 26 *Perf. 14x13½*

843 A318 Sheet of 6 6.00 6.00
a.-b. 12fr mulitcolored 72 72
c.-d. 18fr mulitcolored 1.10 1.10
e.-f. 20fr multicolored 1.20 1.20

View From the Trier Road by Sosthene Weis (1872-1941) — A319

Paintings: 18fr, Vauban Street and the Viaduct. 25fr, St. Ulric Street.

Perf. 12x11½, 11½x12

1991, Mar. 4 **Photo.**

844 A319 14fr multicolored 85 85
845 A319 18fr multicolored 1.10 1.10
846 A319 25fr multi, vert. 1.50 1.50

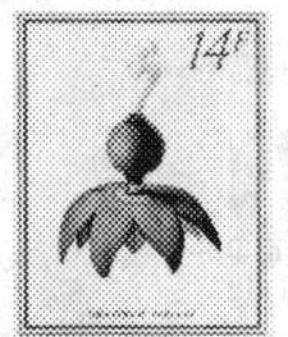

Fungi — A320

1991, Mar. 4 *Perf. 11½*

847 A320 14fr Geastrum varians 85 85
848 A320 14fr Agaricus (Gymnopus) thiebautii 85 85
849 A320 18fr Agaricus (lepiota) lepidocephalus 1.10 1.10
850 A320 25fr Morchella favosa 1.50 1.50

Europa A321

1991, May 13 Photo. *Perf. 12x11½*

851 A321 14fr Astra 1A, 1B satellites 85 85
852 A321 18fr Betzdorf ground station 1.10 1.10

Natl. Miners' Monument, Kayl — A322

Art by Emile Kirscht — A323

Designs: No. 854, Magistrates' Court, Redange-Sur-Attert, horiz.

Perf. 11½x12, 12x11½

1991, May 23

853 A322 14fr multicolored 85 85
854 A322 14fr multicolored 85 85

1991, May 23 *Perf. 11½*

Design: No. 856, Edmund de la Fontaine (1823-1891), Poet.

855 A323 14fr multicolored 85 85
856 A323 14fr multicolored 85 85

Labor Unions, 75th anniv. (No. 855).

Post and Telecommunications Museum — A324

Perf. 11½ on 3 sides

1991, Sept. 23 **Photo.**

Booklet Stamps

857 A324 4fr Old telephone 24 24
a. Bklt. pane of 1 + 3 labels 24
858 A324 14fr Old postbox 85 85
a. Bklt. pane of 4 3.40

Stamp Day, 50th Anniv. — A325

1991, Sept. 23 *Perf. 11½*

859 A325 14fr Stamp of Type A24 85 85

Gargoyles — A326

Photo. & Engr.

1991, Sept. 23 *Perf. 14*

860 A326 14fr Young girl's head 85 85
861 A326 25fr Woman's head 1.50 1.50
862 A326 50fr Man's head 3.00 3.00

SEMI-POSTAL STAMPS

Clervaux Monastery SP1

Designs: 15c+10c, View of Pfaffenthal. 25c+10c, View of Luxembourg.

Engr.; Surcharge Typo. in Red

1921, Aug. 2 Unwmk. *Perf. 11½*

B1 SP1 10c + 5c grn 15 *90*
B2 SP1 15c + 10c org red 15 *1.10*
B3 SP1 25c + 10c dp grn 15 *90*

The amount received from the surtax on these stamps was added to a fund for the erection of a monument to the soldiers from Luxembourg who died in World War I.

Nos. B1-B3 with Additional Surcharge in Red or Black

+ 25

x 27 mai 1923 x

1923, May 27

B4 SP1 25c on #B1 (R) 1.00 *5.75*
B5 SP1 25c on #B2 1.25 *7.25*
B6 SP1 25c on #B3 1.00 *5.75*

Unveiling of the monument to the soldiers who died in World War I.

CARITAS

Regular Issue of 1914-15 Surcharged in Black or Red

+10c

1924, Apr. 17 *Perf. 11½x11*

B7 A11 12½c + 7½c grn 15 18
B8 A11 35c + 10c dk bl (R) 15 18
B9 A11 2½fr + 1fr red 60 *4.50*
B10 A11 5fr + 2fr dk vio 35 *2.50*

Nurse and Patient SP4

Prince Jean SP5

1925, Dec. 21 Litho. *Perf. 13*

B11 SP4 5c (+ 5c) dl vio 15 20
B12 SP4 30c (+ 5c) org 15 28
B13 SP4 50c (+ 5c) red brn 24 *80*
B14 SP4 1fr (+ 10c) dp bl 35 *2.00*

1926, Dec. 15 Photo. *Perf. 12½x12*

B15 SP5 5c (+ 5c) vio & blk 15 15
B16 SP5 40c (+ 10) grn & blk 15 20
B17 SP5 50c (+ 15c) lem & blk 15 20
B18 SP5 75c (+ 20c) lt red & blk 25 *1.50*
B19 SP5 1.50fr (+ 30c) gray bl & blk 30 *2.50*
Nos. B15-B19 (5) 1.00 *4.55*

Grand Duchess Charlotte and Prince Felix — SP6

1927, Sept. 4 Engr. *Perf. 11½*

B20 SP6 25c dp vio 70 *4.50*
B21 SP6 50c green 1.10 *7.50*
B22 SP6 75c rose lake 70 *4.50*
B23 SP6 1fr gray blk 70 *4.50*
B24 SP6 1½fr dp bl 70 *4.50*
Nos. B20-B24 (5) 3.90 *25.50*

Introduction of postage stamps in Luxembourg, 75th anniv. These stamps were sold exclusively at the Luxembourg Philatelic Exhibition, September 4-8, 1927, at a premium of 3 francs per set, which was donated to the exhibition funds.

Princess Elisabeth SP7

Princess Marie Adelaide SP8

1927, Dec. 1 Photo. *Perf. 12½*

B25 SP7 10c (+ 5c) turq bl & blk 15 28
B26 SP7 50c (+ 10c) dk brn & blk 15 *45*
B27 SP7 75c (+ 20c) org & blk 15 *75*
B28 SP7 1fr (+ 30c) brn lake & blk 24 *3.00*
B29 SP7 1½fr (+ 50c) ultra & blk 18 *3.00*
Set value 66

The surtax was for Child Welfare societies.

1928, Dec. 12 *Perf. 12½x12*

B30 SP8 10c (+ 5c) ol grn & brn vio 15 *80*
B31 SP8 60c (+ 10c) brn & ol grn 25 *1.65*
B32 SP8 75c (+ 15c) vio rose & bl grn 40 *3.00*
B33 SP8 1fr (+ 25c) dk grn & brn 80 *4.75*
B34 SP8 1½fr (+ 50c) cit & bl 80 *4.75*
Nos. B30-B34 (5) 2.40 *14.95*

Princess Marie Gabrielle SP9

Prince Charles SP10

1929, Dec. 14 *Perf. 13*

B35 SP9 10c (+ 10c) mar & dp grn 15 *90*
B36 SP9 35c (+ 15c) dk grn & red brn 60 *4.25*
B37 SP9 75c (+ 30c) ver & blk 60 *4.25*
B38 SP9 1¼fr (+ 50c) mag & bl grn 1.10 *7.75*
B39 SP9 1¾fr (+ 75c) Prus bl & sl 1.10 *7.75*
Nos. B35-B39 (5) 3.55 *24.90*

The surtax was for Child Welfare societies.

1930, Dec. 10 *Perf. 12½*

B40 SP10 10c (+ 5c) bl grn & ol brn 15 35
B41 SP10 75c (+ 10c) vio brn & bl grn 60 *2.25*
B42 SP10 1fr (+ 25c) car rose & vio 1.75 *6.75*
B43 SP10 1¼fr (+ 75c) ol bis & dk brn 2.50 *9.00*
B44 SP10 1¾fr (+ 1.50fr) ultra & red brn 4.00 *12.00*
Nos. B40-B44 (5) 9.00 *30.35*

The surtax was for Child Welfare societies.

Princess Alix SP11

Countess Ermesinde SP12

1931, Dec. 10

B45 SP11 10c (+ 5c) brn org & gray 18 38
B46 SP11 75c (+ 10c) claret & bl grn 1.65 *8.25*
B47 SP11 1fr (+ 25c) dp grn & gray 3.50 *16.00*
B48 SP11 1¼fr (+ 75c) dk vio & bl grn 3.50 *12.50*
B49 SP11 1¾fr (+ 1.50fr) bl & gray 6.75 *32.50*
Nos. B45-B49 (5) 15.58 *69.63*

The surtax was for Child Welfare societies.

1932, Dec. 8

B50 SP12 10c (+ 5c) ol bis 28 48
B51 SP12 75c (+ 10c) dp vio 1.25 *5.75*
B52 SP12 1fr (+ 25c) scar 5.00 *22.50*
B53 SP12 1¼fr (+ 75c) red brn 6.00 *24.00*
B54 SP12 1¾fr (+ 1.50fr) dp bl 6.00 *24.00*
Nos. B50-B54 (5) 18.53 *76.73*

The surtax was for Child Welfare societies.

Count Henry VII — SP13

John the Blind — SP14

1933, Dec. 12

B55 SP13 10c (+ 5c) yel brn 35 35
B56 SP13 75c (+ 10c) dp vio 2.00 *7.25*
B57 SP13 1fr (+ 25c) car rose 7.50 *22.50*
B58 SP13 1¼fr (+ 75c) org brn 9.50 *32.50*
B59 SP13 1¾fr (+ 1.50fr) brt bl 9.50 *32.50*
Nos. B55-B59 (5) 28.85 *95.10*

1934, Dec. 5

B60 SP14 10c (+ 5c) dk vio 18 28
B61 SP14 35c (+ 10c) dp grn 1.00 *4.75*
B62 SP14 75c (+ 15c) rose lake 1.00 *4.75*
B63 SP14 1fr (+ 25c) dp rose 7.50 *30.00*
B64 SP14 1¼fr (+ 75c) org 9.50 *32.50*
B65 SP14 1¾fr (+ 1.50fr) brt bl 9.50 *32.50*
Nos. B60-B65 (6) 28.68 *104.78*

Teacher SP15

Sculptor and Painter — SP16

Journalist SP17

Engineer SP18

Scientist SP19

Lawyer SP20

University SP21

Surgeon SP22

1935, May 1 Unwmk. *Perf. 12½*

B65A SP15 5c vio 15 *28*
B65B SP16 10c brn red 20 *32*
B65C SP17 15c ol 25 *55*
B65D SP18 20c org 40 *1.00*
B65E SP19 35c yel grn 52 *1.50*
B65F SP20 50c gray blk 55 *1.50*
B65G SP21 70c dk grn 85 *2.00*
B65H SP22 1fr car red 1.10 *3.00*
B65J SP19 1.25fr turq 4.50 *12.00*
B65K SP18 1.75fr bl 5.75 *22.50*
B65L SP16 2fr lt brn 22.50 *57.50*
B65M SP17 3fr dk brn 27.50 *67.50*
B65N SP20 5fr lt bl 45.00 *110.00*
B65P SP15 10fr red vio 130.00 *300.00*
B65Q SP22 20fr dk grn 165.00 *350.00*
Nos. B65A-B65Q (15) 404.27 *929.65*

Sold at double face, surtax going to intl. fund to aid professional people.

Philatelic Exhibition Issue

Type of Regular Issue of 1928

Wmk. 246

1935, Aug. 15 Engr. *Imperf.*

B66 A19 2fr (+ 50c) blk 4.00 *12.00*

Philatelic exhibition held at Esch-sur-Alzette.

Charles I — SP23

Perf. 11½

1935, Dec. 2 Photo. Unwmk.

B67 SP23 10c (+ 5c) vio 15 16
B68 SP23 35c (+ 10c) grn 18 *70*
B69 SP23 70c (+ 20c) dk brn 42 *1.40*
B70 SP23 1fr (+ 25c) rose lake 8.00 *22.50*
B71 SP23 1.25fr (+ 75c) org brn 8.00 *22.50*
B72 SP23 1.75fr (+ 1.50fr) bl 8.00 *22.50*
Nos. B67-B72 (6) 24.75 *69.76*

Wenceslas I, Duke of Luxembourg — SP24

1936, Dec. 1 *Perf. 11½x13*

B73 SP24 10c + 5(c) blk brn 15 20
B74 SP24 35c + 10(c) bl grn 15 *40*
B75 SP24 70c + 20(c) blk 25 *80*
B76 SP24 1fr + 25(c) rose car 1.00 *4.00*
B77 SP24 1.25fr + 75(c) vio 2.00 *8.75*
B78 SP24 1.75fr + 1.50(fr) saph 1.55 *6.00*
Nos. B73-B78 (6) 5.10 *20.15*

Wenceslas II — SP25

1937, Dec. 1 *Perf. 11½x12½*

B79 SP25 10c + 5c car & blk 15 18
B80 SP25 35c + 10c red vio & grn 15 20
B81 SP25 70c + 20c ultra & red brn 18 40
B82 SP25 1fr + 25c dk grn & scar 1.10 *3.25*
B83 SP25 1.25fr + 75c dk brn & vio 1.25 *3.75*
B84 SP25 1.75fr + 1.50fr blk & ultra 1.40 *4.50*
Nos. B79-B84 (6) 4.23 *12.28*

Souvenir Sheet

SP26

Wmk. 110

1937, July 25 Engr. *Perf. 13*

B85 SP26 Sheet of 2 2.25 *7.00*
a. 2fr red brown, single stamp 85 *2.75*

National Philatelic Exposition at Dudelange on July 25-26.

Sold for 5fr per sheet, of which 1fr was for the aid of the exposition.

Portrait of St. Willibrord SP28

St. Willibrord, after a Miniature SP29

Abbey at Echternach — SP30

Designs: No. B87, The Rathaus at Echternach. No. B88, Pavilion in Abbey Park, Echternach. No. B91, Dancing Procession in Honor of St. Willibrord.

Perf. 14x13, 13x14

1938, June 5 Engr. Unwmk.

B86 SP28 35c + 10c dk bl grn 15 *40*
B87 SP28 70c + 10c ol gray 40 *42*
B88 SP28 1.25fr + 25c brn car 85 *1.25*

B89	SP29	1.75fr + 50c sl bl	1.40	1.75
B90	SP30	3fr + 2fr vio brn	4.75	5.25
B91	SP30	5fr + 5fr dk vio	4.75	5.25
		Nos. B86-B91 (6)	12.30	14.32

12th centenary of the death of St. Willibrord. The surtax was used for the restoration of the ancient Abbey at Echternach.

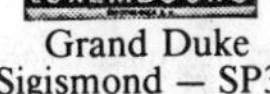

Grand Duke Sigismond — SP32

Prince Jean — SP33

1938, Dec. 1 Photo. *Perf. 11½*

B92	SP32	10c + 5c lil & blk	15	15
B93	SP32	35c + 10c grn & blk	15	15
B94	SP32	70c + 20c buff & blk	18	*42*
B95	SP32	1fr + 25c red org & blk	1.50	*4.00*
B96	SP32	1.25fr + 75c gray bl & blk	1.50	*4.00*
B97	SP32	1.75fr + 1.50fr bl & blk	1.75	*5.75*
		Nos. B92-B97 (6)	5.23	*14.47*

1939, Dec. 1 Litho. *Perf. 14x13*

Designs: Nos. B99, B102, Prince Felix. Nos. B100, B103, Grand Duchess Charlotte.

B98	SP33	10c + 5c red brn, *buff*	15	20
B99	SP33	35c + 10c sl grn, *buff*	15	45
B100	SP33	70c + 20c blk, *buff*	18	*90*
B101	SP33	1fr + 25c red org, *buff*	1.75	*8.00*
B102	SP33	1.25fr + 75c vio brn, *buff*	2.25	*8.75*
B103	SP33	1.75fr + 1.50fr lt bl, *buff*	5.00	*20.00*
		Nos. B98-B103 (6)	9.48	*38.30*

See No. 217 (souvenir sheet).

Allegory of Medicinal Baths — SP36

1940, Mar. 1 Photo. *Perf. 11½*

B104	SP36	2fr + 50c gray, blk & slate grn	1.00	*6.00*

Stamps of 1944, type A37, surcharged "+50C," "+5F" or "+15F" in black, were sold only in canceled condition, affixed to numbered folders. The surtax was for the benefit of Luxembourg evacuees. Value for folder, $15.

Homage to France SP37

Thanks to: No. B118, Russia. No. B119, Britannia. No. B120, America.

1945, Mar. 1 Engr. *Perf. 13*

B117	SP37	60c + 1.40fr dp grn	15	15
B118	SP37	1.20fr + 1.80fr red	15	15
B119	SP37	2.50fr + 3.50fr dp bl	15	20
B120	SP37	4.20fr + 4.80fr dp vio	15	20
		Set value	38	60

Issued to honor the Allied Nations. Exist imperf. Value, set $60.

Statue Carried in Procession SP41

Statue of Our Lady "Patrona Civitatis" SP42

"Our Lady of Luxembourg" SP43

Cathedral Façade SP44

Altar with Statue of Madonna — SP45

1945, June 4

B121	SP41	60c + 40c grn	15	25
B122	SP42	1.20fr + 80c red	15	25
B123	SP43	2.50fr + 2.50fr dp bl	15	*1.10*
B124	SP44	5.50fr + 6.50fr dk vio	60	*9.25*
B125	SP45	20fr + 20fr choc	60	*9.25*
		Nos. B121-B125 (5)	1.65	*20.10*

Exist imperf. Value, set $52.50.

Souvenir Sheet

"Our Lady of Luxembourg" — SP46

1945, Sept. 30 Engr. *Imperf.*

B126	SP46	50fr + 50fr blk	1.10	*50.00*

Young Fighters SP47

Refugee Mother and Children SP48

Political Prisoner SP49

Executed Civilian SP50

1945, Dec. 20 Photo. *Perf. 11½*

B127	SP47	20c + 30c sl grn & buff	15	*80*
B128	SP48	1.50fr + 1fr brn red & buff	15	*80*
B129	SP49	3.50fr + 3.50fr bl, dp bl & buff	18	*5.75*
B130	SP50	5fr + 10fr brn, dk brn & buff	16	*5.75*
		Set value	48	

Souvenir Sheet

1946, Jan. 30 Unwmk. *Perf. 11½*

B131		Sheet of 4	8.00	*225.00*
	a.	SP47 2.50fr + 2.50fr sl grn & buff	2.00	*45.00*
	b.	SP48 3.50fr + 6.50fr brn red & buff	2.00	*45.00*
	c.	SP49 5fr + 15fr bl, dp bl & buff	2.00	*45.00*
	d.	SP50 20fr + 20fr brn, dk brn & buff	2.00	*45.00*

Tribute to Luxembourg's heroes and martyrs.

The surtax was for the National Welfare Fund.

Souvenir Sheet

Old Rolling Mill, Dudelange — SP52

1946, July 28 Engr. & Typo.

B132	SP52	50fr brn & dk bl, *buff*	5.00	*15.00*

National Postage Stamp Exhibition, Dudelange, July 28-29, 1946. The sheets sold for 55fr.

Jean l'Aveugle — SP53

1946, Dec. 5 Photo.

B133	SP53	60c + 40c dk grn	15	*40*
B134	SP53	1.50fr + 50c brn red	15	*55*
B135	SP53	3.50fr + 3.50fr dp bl	55	*4.50*
B136	SP53	5fr + 10fr sepia	28	*3.75*

600th anniv. of the death of Jean l'Aveugle (John the Blind), Count of Luxembourg.

Ruins of St. Willibrord Basilica — SP54

Twelfth Century Miniature of St. Willibrord SP59

Designs: #B138, Statue of Abbot Jean Bertels. #B139, Emblem of Echternach Abbey. #B140, Ruins of the Basilica's Interior. #B141, St. Irmine and Pepin of Hersta Holding Model of the Abbey.

Perf. 13x14, 14x13

1947, May 25 Engr.

B137	SP54	20c + 10c blk	20	25
B138	SP54	60c + 10c dk grn	35	45
B139	SP54	75c + 25c dk car	50	70
B140	SP54	1.50fr + 50c dk brn	65	70
B141	SP54	3.50fr + 2.50fr dk bl	1.25	*3.00*
B142	SP59	25fr + 25fr dk pur	14.00	*22.50*
		Nos. B137-B142 (6)	16.95	*27.60*

The surtax was to aid in restoring the Basilica of Saint Willibrord at Echternach.

Michel Lentz SP60

Edmond de La Fontaine (Dicks) SP61

1947, Dec. 4 Photo. *Perf. 11½*

B143	SP60	60c + 40c sep & buff	25	80
B144	SP60	1.50fr + 50c dp plum & buff	25	80
B145	SP60	3.50fr + 3.50fr dp bl & gray	2.25	*7.25*
B146	SP60	10fr + 5fr dk grn & gray	2.25	*7.25*

1948, Nov. 18

B147	SP61	60c + 40c brn & pale bis	20	55
B148	SP61	1.50fr + 50c brn car & buff	30	60
B149	SP61	3.50fr + 3.50fr dp bl & gray	3.75	*9.25*
B150	SP61	10fr + 5fr dk grn & gray	3.75	*9.25*

125th anniversary of the birth of Edmond de La Fontaine, poet and composer.

Type of Regular Issue of 1948
Souvenir Sheet

1949, Jan. 8 Unwmk. *Perf. 11½*

B151		Sheet of three	55.00	70.00
	a.	A45 8fr + 3fr bl gray	15.00	24.00
	b.	A45 12fr + 5fr grn	15.00	24.00
	c.	A45 15fr + 7fr brn	15.00	24.00

30th anniversary of Grand Duchess Charlotte's ascension to the throne. Border and dates "1919-1949" in gray.

Michel Rodange — SP62

1949, Dec. 5

No.	Type	Description	Unused	Used
B152	SP62	60c + 40c ol grn & gray	22	45
B153	SP62	2fr + 1fr dk vio & rose	2.00	*5.50*
B154	SP62	4fr + 2fr sl blk & gray	2.50	*6.75*
B155	SP62	10fr + 5fr brn & buff	3.25	*8.50*

Wards of the Nation
SP63 SP64

1950, June 24 Engr. *Perf. 12½x12*

No.	Type	Description	Unused	Used
B156	SP63	60c + 15c dk sl bl	30	40
B157	SP64	1fr + 20c dk car rose	70	90
B158	SP63	2fr + 30c red brn	70	90
B159	SP64	4fr + 75c dk bl	6.00	*12.00*
B160	SP63	8fr + 3fr blk	20.00	*40.00*
B161	SP64	10fr + 5fr lil rose	20.00	*40.00*
		Nos. B156-B161 (6)	47.70	*94.20*

The surtax was for child welfare.

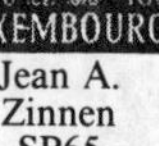

Jean A. Zinnen
SP65

Laurent Menager
SP66

1950, Dec. 5 Photo. *Perf. 11½*

No.	Type	Description	Unused	Used
B162	SP65	60c + 10c ind & gray	18	40
B163	SP65	2fr + 15c cer & buff	24	55
B164	SP65	4fr + 15c vio bl & bl gray	1.25	*5.00*
B165	SP65	8fr + 5fr dk brn & buff	8.00	*15.00*

1951, Dec. 5

Gray Background

No.	Type	Description	Unused	Used
B166	SP66	60c + 10c sepia	15	35
B167	SP66	2fr + 15c dl ol grn	24	55
B168	SP66	4fr + 15c blue	1.00	*3.00*
B169	SP66	8fr + 5fr vio brn	8.50	*24.00*

50th anniversary of the death of Laurent Menager, composer.

J. B. Fresez
SP67

Candlemas Singing
SP68

1952, Dec. 3

No.	Type	Description	Unused	Used
B170	SP67	60c + 15c dk bl grn & pale bl	15	35
B171	SP67	2fr + 25c chnt brn & buff	20	55
B172	SP67	4fr + 25c dk vio bl & gray	1.10	*3.50*
B173	SP67	8fr + 4.75fr dp plum & lil gray	8.25	*24.00*

1953, Dec. 3

Designs: 80c+20c, 4fr+50c, Procession with ratchets. 1.20fr+30c, 7fr+3.35fr, Breaking Easter eggs.

No.	Type	Description	Unused	Used
B174	SP68	25c + 15c red org & dp car	15	18
B175	SP68	80c + 20c vio brn & bl gray	15	18
B176	SP68	1.20fr + 30c bl grn & ol grn	25	70
B177	SP68	2fr + 25c brn car & brn	15	35
B178	SP68	4fr + 50c grnsh bl & vio bl	1.90	*4.25*
B179	SP68	7fr + 3.35fr vio & pur	4.75	*12.00*
		Nos. B174-B179 (6)	7.35	*17.66*

The surtax was for the National Welfare Fund of Grand Duchess Charlotte.

Clay Censer and Whistle — SP69

Toys for St. Nicholas Day — SP70

Designs: 80c+20c, 4fr+50c, Sheep and bass drum. 1.20fr+30c, 7fr+3.45fr, Merry-go-round horses. 2fr+25c, As No. B180.

1954, Dec. 3

No.	Type	Description	Unused	Used
B180	SP69	25c + 5c car lake & cop brn	15	16
B181	SP69	80c + 20c dk gray	15	16
B182	SP69	1.20fr + 30c dk bl grn & cr	32	65
B183	SP69	2fr + 25c brn & ocher	15	32
B184	SP69	4fr + 50c brt bl	2.00	*3.25*
B185	SP69	7fr + 3.45fr pur	5.75	*12.00*
		Nos. B180-B185 (6)	8.52	*16.54*

1955, Dec. 5 Unwmk. *Perf. 11½*

Designs: 80c+20c, 4fr+50c, Christ child and lamb (Christmas). 1.20fr+30c, 7fr+3.45fr, Star, crown and cake (Epiphany).

No.	Type	Description	Unused	Used
B186	SP70	25c + 5c sal & dk car	15	15
B187	SP70	80c + 20c gray & gray blk	15	15
B188	SP70	1.20fr + 30c ol grn & sl grn	35	60
B189	SP70	2fr + 25c buff & dk brn	25	20
B190	SP70	4fr + 50c lt bl & brt bl	1.40	*2.75*
B191	SP70	7fr + 3.45fr rose vio & cl	6.00	*12.00*
		Nos. B186-B191 (6)	8.30	*15.85*

Arms of Echternach — SP71

Arms: 80c+20c, 4fr+50c, Esch-sur-Alzette. 1.20fr+30c, 7fr+3.45fr, Grevenmacher.

1956, Dec. 5 Photo.

Arms in Original Colors

No.	Type	Description	Unused	Used
B192	SP71	25c + 5c blk & sal pink	15	25
B193	SP71	80c + 20c ultra & yel	15	25
B194	SP71	1.20fr + 30c ultra & gray	22	40
B195	SP71	2fr + 25c blk & buff	15	25
B196	SP71	4fr + 50c ultra & lt bl	1.10	*3.25*
B197	SP71	7fr + 3.45fr ultra & pale vio	3.00	*8.75*
		Nos. B192-B197 (6)	4.77	*13.15*

1957, Dec. 4 Unwmk. *Perf. 11½*

Arms: 25c+5c, 2fr+25c, Luxembourg. 80c+20c, 4fr+50c, Mersch. 1.20fr+30c, 7fr+3.45fr, Vianden.

Arms in Original Colors

No.	Type	Description	Unused	Used
B198	SP71	25c + 5c ultra & org	15	22
B199	SP71	80c + 20c blk & lem	15	22
B200	SP71	1.20fr + 30c ultra & lt bl grn	22	32
B201	SP71	2fr + 25c ultra & pale brn	15	22
B202	SP71	4fr + 50c blk & pale vio bl	45	70
B203	SP71	7fr + 3.45fr ultra & rose lil	3.00	4.50
		Nos. B198-B203 (6)	4.12	6.18

1958, Dec. 3 *Perf. 11½*

Arms: 30c+10c, 2.50fr+50c, Capellen. 1fr+25c, 5fr+50c, Diekirch. 1.50fr+25c, 8.50fr+4.60fr, Redange.

Arms in Original Colors

No.	Type	Description	Unused	Used
B204	SP71	30c + 10c blk & pink	15	15
B205	SP71	1fr + 25c ultra & buff	15	15
B206	SP71	1.50fr + 25c ultra & pale grn	15	24
B207	SP71	2.50fr + 50c blk & gray	15	15
B208	SP71	5fr + 50c ultra	40	60
B209	SP71	8.50fr + 4.60fr ultra & lil	2.25	*4.75*
		Nos. B204-B209 (6)	3.25	*6.04*

1959, Dec. 2

Arms: 30c+10c, 2.50fr+50c, Clervaux. 1fr+25c, 5fr+50c, Remich. 1.50fr+25c, 8.50fr+4.60fr, Wiltz.

Arms in Original Colors

No.	Type	Description	Unused	Used
B210	SP71	30c + 10c ultra & pink	15	15
B211	SP71	1fr + 25c ultra & pale lem	15	15
B212	SP71	1.50fr + 25c blk & pale grn	15	20
B213	SP71	2.50fr + 50c ultra & pale fawn	15	15
B214	SP71	5fr + 50c ultra & lt bl	40	75
B215	SP71	8.50fr + 4.60fr blk & pale vio	1.90	*3.75*
		Nos. B210-B215 (6)	2.90	*5.15*

Catalogue values for unused stamps in this section, from this point to the end of the section, are for Never Hinged items.

Princess Marie-Astrid
SP72

Prince Jean
SP73

Designs: 1fr+25c, 5fr+50c, Princess in party dress. 1.50fr+25c, 8.50fr+4.60fr, Princess with book.

1960, Dec. 5 Photo. *Perf. 11½*

No.	Type	Description	Unused	Used
B216	SP72	30c + 10c brn & lt bl	15	15
B217	SP72	1fr + 25c brn & pink	15	15
B218	SP72	1.50fr + 25c brn & lt bl	20	20
B219	SP72	2.50fr + 50c brn & yel	15	15
B220	SP72	5fr + 50c brn & pale lil	1.25	1.25
B221	SP72	8.50fr + 4.60fr brn & pale ol	4.50	4.25
		Nos. B216-B221 (6)	6.40	6.15

Type of 1960

Prince Henri: 30c+10c, 2.50fr+50c, Infant in long dress. 1fr+25c, 5fr+50c, Informal portrait. 1.50fr+25c, 8.50fr+ 4.60fr, In dress suit.

1961, Dec. 4 Unwmk. *Perf. 11½*

No.	Type	Description	Unused	Used
B222	SP72	30c + 10c brn & brt pink	15	15
B223	SP72	1fr + 25c brn & lt vio	15	15
B224	SP72	1.50fr + 25c brn & sal	15	15
B225	SP72	2.50fr + 50c brn & pale grn	15	15
B226	SP72	5fr + 50c brn & cit	32	32
B227	SP72	8.50fr + 4.60fr brn & gray	1.75	1.75
		Nos. B222-B227 (6)	2.67	2.67

1962, Dec. 3 Photo. *Perf. 11½*

Designs: Different portraits of the twins Prince Jean and Princess Margaretha. Nos. B228 and B233 are horizontal.

Inscriptions and Portraits in Dark Brown

No.	Type	Description	Unused	Used
B228	SP73	30c + 10c org yel	15	15
B229	SP73	1fr + 25c lt bl	15	15
B230	SP73	1.50fr + 25c pale ol	15	15
B231	SP73	2.50fr + 50c rose	15	15
B232	SP73	5fr + 50c lt yel grn	24	24
B233	SP73	8.50fr + 4.60fr lil gray	2.00	2.00
		Nos. B228-B233 (6)	2.84	2.84

St. Roch, Patron of Bakers — SP74

Three Towers — SP75

Patron Saints: 1fr+25c, St. Anne, tailors. 2fr+25c, St. Eloi, smiths. 3fr+50c, St. Michael, shopkeepers. 6fr+50c, St. Bartholomew, butchers. St. Theobald, seven crafts.

1963, Dec. 2 Unwmk. *Perf. 11½*

Multicolored Design

No.	Type	Description	Unused	Used
B234	SP74	50c + 10c pale lil	15	15
B235	SP74	1fr + 25c tan	15	15
B236	SP74	2fr + 25c lt grnsh bl	15	15
B237	SP74	3fr + 50c lt bl	15	22
B238	SP74	6fr + 50c buff	70	80
B239	SP74	10fr + 5.90fr pale yel grn	80	95
		Nos. B234-B239 (6)	2.10	2.42

1964, Dec. 7 Photo. *Perf. 11½*

Children's paintings: 1fr+25c, 6fr+50c, Grand Duke Adolphe Bridge, horiz. 2fr+25c, 10fr+5.90fr, The Lower City.

No.	Type	Description	Unused	Used
B240	SP75	50c + 10c multi	15	15
B241	SP75	1fr + 25c multi	15	15
B242	SP75	2fr + 25c multi	15	30
a.		Value omitted	*300.00*	
B243	SP75	3fr + 50c multi	15	30
B244	SP75	6fr + 50c multi	70	1.50
B245	SP75	10fr + 5.90fr multi	80	1.50
		Nos. B240-B245 (6)	2.10	3.90

The Roman Lady of Titelberg — SP76

Fairy Tales of Luxembourg: 1fr+25c, Schäppchen, the Huntsman. 2fr+25c, The Witch of Koerich. 3fr+50c, The Gnomes of Schoenfels. 6fr+50c, Tollchen, Watchman of Hesperange. 10fr+5.90fr, The Old Spinster of Heispelt.

1965, Dec. 6 Photo. *Perf. 11½*

No.	Type	Description	Unused	Used
B246	SP76	50c + 10c multi	15	15
B247	SP76	1fr + 25c multi	15	15
B248	SP76	2fr + 25c multi	15	15
B249	SP76	3fr + 50c multi	15	20
B250	SP76	6fr + 50c multi	48	90
B251	SP76	10fr + 5.90fr multi	85	1.40
		Nos. B246-B251 (6)	1.93	2.95

Fairy Tale Type of 1965

Fairy Tales of Luxembourg: 50c+10c, The Veiled Matron of Wormeldange. 1.50fr+25c, Jekel, Warden of the Wark. 2fr+25c, The Black Man of Vianden. 3fr+50c, The Gracious Fairy of Rosport. 6fr+1fr, The Friendly Shepherd of Donkolz. 13fr+6.90fr, The Little Sisters of Trois-Vierges.

1966, Dec. 6 Photo. *Perf. 11½*

No.	Type	Description	Unused	Used
B252	SP76	50c + 10c multi	15	15
B253	SP76	1.50fr + 25c multi	15	15
B254	SP76	2fr + 25c multi	15	15
B255	SP76	3fr + 50c multi	15	30
B256	SP76	6fr + 1fr multi	28	60
B257	SP76	13fr + 6.90fr multi	85	1.90
		Nos. B252-B257 (6)	1.73	3.25

Prince Guillaume
SP77

Castle of Berg
SP78

Portraits: 1.50fr+25c, Princess Margaretha. 2fr+25c, Prince Jean. 3fr+50c, Prince Henri as Boy Scout. 6fr+1fr, Princess Marie-Astrid.

1967, Dec. 6 Photo. *Perf. 11½*

B258 SP77 50c + 10c yel & brn 15 15
B259 SP77 1.50fr + 25c gray bl & brn 15 15
B260 SP77 2fr + 25c pale rose & brn 15 15
B261 SP77 3fr + 50c lt ol & brn 32 60
B262 SP77 6fr + 1fr lt vio & brn 45 60
B263 SP78 13fr + 6.90fr multi 60 1.40
Nos. B258-B263 (6) 1.82 3.05

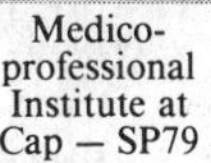

Medico-professional Institute at Cap — SP79

Deaf-mute Child Imitating Bird — SP80

Handicapped Children: 2fr+25c, Blind child holding candle. 3fr+50c, Nurse supporting physically handicapped child. 6fr+1fr, Cerebral palsy victim. 13fr+6.90fr, Mentally disturbed child.

1968, Dec. 5 Photo. *Perf. 11½*

Designs and Inscriptions in Dark Brown

B264 SP79 50c + 10c lt bl 15 15
B265 SP80 1.50fr + 25c lt grn 15 15
B266 SP80 2fr + 25c yel 15 15
B267 SP80 3fr + 50c bl 16 24
B268 SP80 6fr + 1fr buff 50 1.10
B269 SP80 13fr + 6.90fr pink 75 1.50
Nos. B264-B269 (6) 1.86 3.29

Vianden Castle SP81

Children of Bethlehem SP82

Castles in Luxembourg: 1.50fr+25c, Lucilinburhuc. 2fr+25c, Bourglinster. 3fr+50c, Hollenfels. 6fr+1fr, Ansembourg. 13fr+6.90fr, Beaufort.

1969, Dec. 8 Photo. *Perf. 11½*

B270 SP81 50c + 10c multi 15 15
B271 SP81 1.50fr + 25c multi 15 15
B272 SP81 2fr + 25c multi 15 15
B273 SP81 3fr + 50c multi 15 30
B274 SP81 6fr + 1fr multi 60 1.00
B275 SP81 13fr + 6.90fr multi 85 1.50
Nos. B270-B275 (6) 2.05 3.25

1970, Dec. 7 Photo. *Perf. 11½*

Castles in Luxembourg: 50c+10c, Clervaux. 1.50fr+25c, Septfontaines. 2fr+25c, Bourscheid. 3fr+50c, Esch-sur-Sure. 6fr+1fr, Larochette. 13fr+6.90fr, Brandenbourg.

B276 SP81 50c + 10c multi 15 15
B277 SP81 1.50fr + 25c multi 15 15
B278 SP81 2fr + 25c multi 15 15
B279 SP81 3fr + 50c multi 15 30
B280 SP81 6fr + 1fr multi 60 1.00
B281 SP81 13fr + 6.90fr multi 85 1.75
Nos. B276-B281 (6) 2.05 3.50

The surtax on Nos. B180-B281 was for charitable purposes.

1971, Dec. 6 Photo. *Perf. 11½*

Wooden Statues from Creche of Beaufort Church: 1.50fr+25c, Shepherds. 3fr+50c, Nativity. 8fr+1fr, Herdsmen. 18fr+6.50fr, King offering gift.

Sculptures in Shades of Brown

B282 SP82 1fr + 25c lilac 15 15
B283 SP82 1.50fr + 25c olive 15 15
B284 SP82 3fr + 50c gray 16 35
B285 SP82 8fr + 1fr lt ultra 1.10 1.50
B286 SP82 18fr + 6.50fr grn 1.90 4.00
Nos. B282-B286 (5) 3.46 6.15

The surtax was for various charitable organizations.

Angel — SP83

Sts. Anne and Joachim — SP84

Stained Glass Windows, Luxembourg Cathedral: 1.50fr+25c, St. Joseph. 3fr+50c, Virgin and Child. 8fr+1fr, People of Bethlehem. 18fr+6.50fr, Angel facing left.

1972, Dec. 4

B287 SP83 1fr + 25c multi 15 15
B288 SP83 1.50fr + 25c multi 15 15
B289 SP83 3fr + 50c multi 15 15
B290 SP83 8fr + 1fr multi 95 1.00
B291 SP83 18fr + 6.50fr multi 2.25 3.75
Nos. B287-B291 (5) 3.65 5.20

Surtax was for charitable purposes.

1973, Dec. 5 Photo. *Perf. 11½*

Sculptures: 3fr+25c, Mary meeting Elizabeth. 4fr+50c, Virgin and Child and a King. 8fr+1fr, Shepherds. 15fr+7fr, St. Joseph holding candle. Designs from 16th century reredos, Hermitage of Hachiville.

B292 SP84 1fr + 25c multi 15 15
B293 SP84 3fr + 25c multi 15 16
B294 SP84 4fr + 50c multi 24 70
B295 SP84 8fr + 1fr multi 1.10 2.00
B296 SP84 15fr + 7fr multi 1.90 3.75
Nos. B292-B296 (5) 3.54 6.76

Annunciation SP85

Crucifixion SP86

Designs: 3fr+25c, Visitation. 4fr+50c, Nativity. 8fr+1fr, Adoration of the King. 15fr+7fr, Presentation at the Temple. Designs of Nos. B297-B301 are from miniatures in the "Codex Aureus Epternacensis" (Gospel from Echternach Abbey). The Crucifixion is from the carved ivory cover of the Codex, by the Master of Echternach, c. 983-991.

1974, Dec. 5 Photo. *Perf. 11½*

B297 SP85 1fr + 25c multi 15 15
B298 SP85 3fr + 25c multi 15 18
B299 SP85 4fr + 50c multi 20 35
B300 SP85 8fr + 1fr multi 1.10 1.75
B301 SP85 15fr + 7fr multi 1.75 2.75
Nos. B297-B301 (5) 3.35 5.18

Souvenir Sheet

Photogravure & Engraved

Perf. 13½

B302 SP86 20fr + 10fr multi 3.50 5.00

50th anniversary of Caritas issues. No. B302 contains one 34x42mm stamp.

Fly Orchid SP87

Lilies of the Valley SP88

Flowers: 3fr+25c, Pyramidal orchid. 4fr+50c, Marsh hellebore. 8fr+1fr, Pasqueflower. 15fr+7fr, Bee orchid.

1975, Dec. 4 Photo. *Perf. 11½*

B303 SP87 1fr + 25c multi 15 15
B304 SP87 3fr + 25c multi 16 18
B305 SP87 4fr + 50c multi 24 35
B306 SP87 8fr + 1fr multi 1.00 1.40
B307 SP87 15fr + 7fr multi 2.25 3.00
Nos. B303-B307 (5) 3.80 5.08

The surtax on Nos. B303-B317 was for various charitable organizations.

1976, Dec. 6

Flowers: 2fr+25c, Gentian. 5fr+25c, Narcissus. 6fr+50c, Red hellebore. 12fr+1fr, Late spider orchid. 20fr+8fr, Two-leafed squill.

B308 SP87 2fr + 25c multi 15 15
B309 SP87 5fr + 25c multi 22 30
B310 SP87 6fr + 50c multi 30 60
B311 SP87 12fr + 1fr multi 65 1.10
B312 SP87 20fr + 8fr multi 2.00 2.75
Nos. B308-B312 (5) 3.32 4.90

1977, Dec. 5 Photo. *Perf. 11½*

Flowers: 5fr+25c, Columbine. 6fr+50c, Mezereon. 12fr+1fr, Early spider orchid. 20fr+8fr, Spotted orchid.

B313 SP88 2fr + 25c multi 15 15
B314 SP88 5fr + 25c multi 15 20
B315 SP88 6fr + 50c multi 22 40
B316 SP88 12fr + 1fr multi 95 1.75
B317 SP88 20fr + 8fr multi 1.90 2.75
Nos. B313-B317 (5) 3.37 5.25

St. Matthew — SP89

Spring — SP90

Behind-glass Paintings, 19th Century: 5fr+25c, St. Mark. 6fr+50c, Nativity. 12fr+1fr, St. Luke. 20fr+8fr, St. John.

1978, Dec. 5 Photo. *Perf. 11½*

B318 SP89 2fr + 25c multi 15 15
B319 SP89 5fr + 25c multi 24 32
B320 SP89 6fr + 50c multi 25 35
B321 SP89 12fr + 1fr multi 65 90
B322 SP89 20fr + 8fr multi 1.90 2.50
Nos. B318-B322 (5) 3.19 4.22

Surtax was for charitable organizations.

1979, Dec. 5 Photo. *Perf. 12*

Behind-glass Paintings, 19th Century: 5fr+25c, Summer. 6fr+50c, Charity. 12fr+1fr, Autumn. 20fr+8fr, Winter.

B323 SP90 2fr + 25c multi 15 15
B324 SP90 5fr + 25c multi 25 25
B325 SP90 6fr + 50c multi 30 30
B326 SP90 12fr + 1fr multi 85 85
B327 SP90 20fr + 8fr multi 1.75 1.75
Nos. B323-B327 (5) 3.30 3.30

St. Martin — SP91

Behind-glass Paintings, 19th Century: 6fr+50c, St. Nicholas. 8fr+1fr, Madonna and Child. 30fr+1fr, St. George the Martyr.

1980, Dec. 5 Photo. *Perf. 11½*

B328 SP91 4fr + 50c multi 20 20
B329 SP91 6fr + 50c multi 25 25
B330 SP91 8fr + 1fr multi 45 45
B331 SP91 30fr + 10fr multi 1.75 1.75

Surtax was for charitable organizations.

Arms of Petange SP92

Nativity, by Otto van Veen (1556-1629) SP93

1981, Dec. 4 Photo.

Granite Paper

B332 SP92 4fr + 50c shown 22 28
B333 SP92 6fr + 50c Larochette 30 35
B334 SP93 8fr + 1fr shown 50 60
B335 SP92 16fr + 2fr Stadtbredimus 90 1.10
B336 SP92 35fr + 12fr Weiswampach 2.25 2.75
Nos. B332-B336 (5) 4.17 5.08

Surtax was for charitable organizations.

1982, Dec. 6 Photo. *Perf. 11½*

Design: 8fr+1fr, Adoration of the Shepherds, stained-glass window, by Gust Zanter, Hoscheid Parish Church.

Granite Paper

B337 SP92 4fr + 50c Bettembourg 18 16
B338 SP92 6fr + 50c Frisange 35 30
B339 SP93 8fr + 1fr multi 45 40
B340 SP92 16fr + 2fr Mamer 90 80
B341 SP92 35fr + 12fr Heinerscheid 2.25 2.00
Nos. B337-B341 (5) 4.13 3.66

Surtax was for charitable organizations.

1983, Dec. 5 Photo.

B342 SP92 4fr + 1fr Winseler 20 20
B343 SP92 7fr + 1fr Beckerich 40 40
B344 SP93 10fr + 1fr Nativity 50 50
B345 SP92 16fr + 2fr Feulen 85 85
B346 SP92 40fr + 13fr Mertert 3.00 3.00
Nos. B342-B346 (5) 4.95 4.95

Surtax was for charitable organizations.

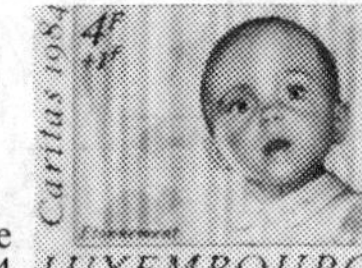

Inquisitive Child — SP94

Children Exhibiting Various Moods.

1984, Dec. 5 Photo.

B347 SP94 4fr + 1fr shown 20 18
B348 SP94 7fr + 1fr Daydreaming 45 40
B349 SP94 10fr + 1fr Nativity 55 50
B350 SP94 16fr + 2fr Sulking 95 85
B351 SP94 40fr + 13fr Admiring 3.25 3.00
Nos. B347-B351 (5) 5.40 4.93

Surtax was for charitable organizations.

1985, Dec. 5 Photo.

B352 SP94 4fr + 1fr Girl drawing 20 16
B353 SP94 7fr + 1fr Two boys 30 25
B354 SP94 10fr + 1fr Adoration of the Magi 40 32
B355 SP94 16fr + 2fr Fairy tale characters 1.00 85
B356 SP94 40fr + 13fr Embarrassed girl 2.75 2.25
Nos. B352-B356 (5) 4.65 3.83

Surtax was for charitable organizations.

SP95

SP96

Book of Hours, France, c. 1550, Natl. Library — SP97

Christmas: illuminated text.

1986, Dec. 8 Photo. *Perf. 11½*
B357 SP95 6fr + 1fr Annunciation 38 30
B358 SP95 10fr + 1fr Angel appears to the Shepherds 55 45
B359 SP95 12fr + 2fr Nativity 70 58
B360 SP95 18fr + 2fr Adoration of the Magi 1.00 82
B361 SP95 20fr + 8fr Flight into Egypt 1.40 1.15
Nos. B357-B361 (5) 4.03 3.30

Surtax for social work organizations.

1987, Dec. 1 Photo. *Perf. 12*

Christmas: illuminated text.

B362 SP96 6fr + 1fr Annunciation 40 40
B363 SP96 10fr + 1fr Visitation 62 62
B364 SP96 12fr + 2fr Adoration of the Magi 78 78
B365 SP96 18fr + 2fr Presentation in the Temple 1.15 1.15
B366 SP96 20fr + 8fr Flight into Egypt 1.60 1.60
Nos. B362-B366 (5) 4.55 4.55

Surtax for charitable organizations.

1988, Dec. 5 Photo. *Perf. 11½*

Christmas: illuminated text.

B367 SP97 9fr +1fr Annunciation to the Shepherds 55 55
B368 SP97 12fr +2fr Adoration of the Magi 75 75
B369 SP97 18fr +2fr Virgin and Child 1.10 1.10
B370 SP97 20fr +8fr Pentecost 1.50 1.50

Surtax for charitable organizations.

Christmas SP98

Chapels: No. B371, St. Lambert and St. Blase, Fennange, vert. No. B372, St. Quirinus, Luxembourg. No. B373, St. Anthony the Hermit, Reisdorf, vert. No. B374, The Hermitage, Hachiville.

1989, Dec. 11 Photo. *Perf. 12x11½*
B371 SP98 9fr +1fr multi 50 50
B372 SP98 12fr +2fr multi 70 70
B373 SP98 18fr +3fr multi 1.10 1.10
B374 SP98 25fr +8fr multi 1.65 1.65

Surtax for social work.

1990, Nov. 26 Photo. *Perf. 11½*

Chapels: No. B375, Congregation of the Blessed Virgin Mary, Vianden, vert. No. B376, Our Lady, Echternach. No. B377, Our Lady, Consoler of the Afflicted, Grentzingen. B378, St. Pirmin, Kaundorf, vert.

B375 SP98 9fr +1fr multi 60 60
B376 SP98 12fr +2fr multi 85 85
B377 SP98 18fr +3fr multi 1.25 1.25
B378 SP98 25fr +8fr multi 2.00 2.00

Surtax for charitable organizations.

Chapels: No. B379, St. Donatus, Arsdorf, vert. No. B380, Our Lady of Sorrows, Brandenbourg. No. B381, Our Lady, Luxembourg. No. B382, The Hermitage, Wolwelange, vert.

1991, Dec. 9 Photo. *Perf. 11½*
B379 SP98 14fr +2fr multi 95 95
B380 SP98 14fr +2fr multi 95 95
B381 SP98 18fr +3fr multi 1.25 1.25
B382 SP98 22fr +7fr multi 1.75 1.75

Surtax used for philanthropic work.

AIR POST STAMPS

Airplane over Luxembourg — AP1

1931-33 Unwmk. Engr. *Perf. 12½*
C1 AP1 50c grn ('33) 50 *1.10*
C2 AP1 75c dk brn 35 80
C3 AP1 1fr red 35 80
C4 AP1 1¼fr dk vio 35 80
C5 AP1 1¾fr dk bl 35 80
C6 AP1 3fr gray blk ('33) 50 *1.65*
Nos. C1-C6 (6) 2.40 *5.95*

Air View of Mosel River AP2

Wing and View of Luxembourg AP3

Vianden Castle — AP4

1946, June 7 Photo. *Perf. 11½*
C7 AP2 1fr dk ol grn & gray 15 15
C8 AP3 2fr chnt brn & buff 15 15
C9 AP4 3fr sep & brn 15 15
C10 AP2 4fr dp vio & gray vio 15 25
C11 AP3 5fr dp mag & buff 15 25
C12 AP4 6fr dk brn & gray 15 32
C13 AP2 10fr hn brn & buff 90 32
C14 AP3 20fr dk bl & cr 90 1.50
C15 AP4 50fr dk grn & gray 1.75 1.50
Nos. C7-C15 (9) 4.45 4.59

1852 and 1952 AP5

1952, May 24

Stamps in Gray and Dark Violet Brown

C16 AP5 80c ol grn 32 48
C17 AP5 2.50fr brt car 75 1.25
C18 AP5 4fr brt bl 1.50 2.75
C19 AP5 8fr brn red 27.50 *50.00*
C20 AP5 10fr dl brn 20.00 *42.50*
Nos. C16-C20 (5) 50.07 *96.98*

Centenary of Luxembourg's postage stamps. Nos. C16-C18 were available at face, but complete sets sold for 45.30fr, which included admission to the CENTILUX exhibition.

POSTAGE DUE STAMPS

Coat of Arms — D1

1907 Unwmk. Typo. *Perf. 12½*
J1 D1 5c grn & blk 15 15
J2 D1 10c grn & blk 2.50 18
J3 D1 12½c grn & blk 60 70
J4 D1 20c grn & blk 60 45
J5 D1 25c grn & blk 24.00 1.40
J6 D1 50c grn & blk 60 1.40
J7 D1 1fr grn & blk 30 *1.10*
Nos. J1-J7 (7) 28.75 5.38

See Nos. J10-J22.

Nos. J3, J5 Surcharged **15**

1920
J8 D1 15c on 12½c 2.75 2.25
J9 D1 30c on 25c 2.75 3.00

Arms Type of 1907

1921-35
J10 D1 5c grn & red 30 30
J11 D1 10c grn & red 30 30
J12 D1 20c grn & red 45 30
J13 D1 25c grn & red 45 30
J14 D1 30c grn & red 50 55
J15 D1 35c grn & red ('35) 1.10 30
J16 D1 50c grn & red 50 55
J17 D1 60c grn & red ('28) 85 30
J18 D1 70c grn & red ('35) 1.10 30
J19 D1 75c grn & red ('30) 85 25
J20 D1 1fr grn & red 65 70
J21 D1 2fr grn & red ('30) 1.50 2.00
J22 D1 3fr grn & red ('30) 3.50 5.50
Nos. J10-J22 (13) 12.05 11.65

D2

D3

1946-48 Photo. *Perf. 11½*
J23 D2 5c brt grn 15 25
J24 D2 10c brt grn 15 25
J25 D2 20c brt grn 15 25
J26 D2 30c brt grn 15 25
J27 D2 50c brt grn 15 25
J28 D2 70c brt grn 15 50
J29 D2 75c brt grn ('48) 65 25
J30 D3 1fr carmine 15 25
J31 D3 1.50fr carmine 15 25
J32 D3 2fr carmine 15 25
J33 D3 3fr carmine 18 25
J34 D3 5fr carmine 50 40
J35 D3 10fr carmine 85 1.00
J36 D3 20fr carmine 2.50 5.00
Nos. J23-J36 (14) 6.03 9.40

OFFICIAL STAMPS

Forged overprints on Nos. O1-O64 abound.

Regular Issues Overprinted Reading Diagonally Up or Down

Frankfort Print

Rouletted in Color except 2c

1875 Unwmk.
O1 A2 1c red brown 13.00 30.00
O2 A2 2c black 15.00 30.00
O3 A3 10c lilac 1,300. 1,000.
O4 A3 12½c rose 350.00 450.00
O5 A3 20c gray brn 25.00 30.00
O6 A3 25c blue 150.00 100.00
O7 A3 25c ultra 1,400. 1,000.
O8 A3 30c lilac rose 26.00 *60.00*
O9 A3 40c pale org 135.00 160.00
a. 40c org red, thick paper 140.00 150.00
c. As "a," thin paper 1,000. 825.00
O10 A4 1fr on 37½c bis 85.00 15.00

Double overprints exist on Nos. O1-O6, O8-O10.

Overprints reading diagonally down sell for more.

Inverted Overprint

O1a A2 1c 100.00 160.00
O2a A2 2c 110.00 175.00
O3a A3 10c 1,600. 1,600.
O4a A3 12½c 500.00 550.00
O5a A3 20c 25.00 32.50
O6a A3 25c 725.00 725.00
O7a A3 25c 1,600. 1,350.
O8a A3 30c 360.00 450.00
O9b A3 40c pale orange 175.00 225.00
O10a A4 1fr on 37½ 140.00 35.00

Luxembourg Print

1875-76 *Perf. 13*
O11 A2 1c red brn 10.00 20.00
O12 A2 2c black 12.50 20.00
O13 A2 4c green 110.00 175.00
O14 A2 5c yellow 50.00 90.00
a. 5c orange yellow 55.00 90.00
O15 A3 10c gray lil 75.00 90.00
O16 A3 12½c rose 65.00 37.50
O17 A3 12½c lil rose 140.00 125.00
O18 A3 25c blue 6.75 *35.00*
O19 A5 1fr on 37½c bis 37.50 60.00

Double overprints exist on Nos. O11-O15.

Inverted Overprint

O11a A2 1c 40.00 *85.00*
O12a A2 2c 135.00 175.00
O13a A2 4c 150.00 200.00
O14b A2 5c 450.00 600.00
O15a A3 10c 140.00 175.00
O16a A3 12½c 350.00 475.00
O17a A3 12½c 350.00 475.00
O18a A3 25c 110.00 150.00
O19a A5 1fr on 37½ 175.00 250.00

Haarlem Print

1880 *Perf. 11½x12, 12½x12, 13½*
O22 A3 25c blue 3.00 4.00

Overprinted

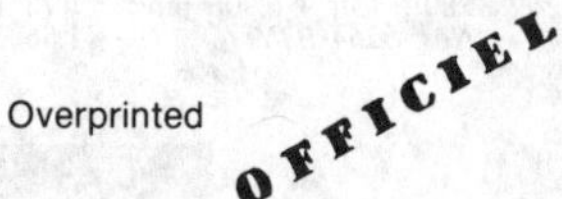

Frankfort Print

1878 *Rouletted in Color*
O23 A2 1c red brn 80.00 95.00
O25 A3 20c gray brn 125.00 125.00
O26 A3 30c lilac rose 525.00 500.00
O27 A3 40c orange 225.00 300.00
O28 A4 1fr on 37½c bis 400.00 90.00

Inverted Overprint

O23a A2 1c 275.00 350.00
O25a A3 20c 275.00 350.00
O26a A3 30c 800.00 650.00
O27a A3 40c 800.00 800.00
O28a A4 1fr on 37½c 625.00 135.00

Luxembourg Print

1878-80 *Perf. 13*
O29 A2 1c red brn 575.00 675.00
O30 A2 2c black 150.00 200.00
O31 A2 4c green 165.00 165.00
O32 A2 5c yellow 375.00 350.00
O33 A3 10c gray lil 350.00 375.00
O34 A3 12½c rose 65.00 75.00
O35 A3 25c blue 475.00 575.00

Inverted Overprint

O29a A2 1c 90.00 140.00
O30a A2 2c 13.00 20.00
O31a A2 4c 100.00 125.00
O32a A2 5c
O33a A3 10c 75.00 85.00
O34a A3 12½c 425.00 500.00
O35a A3 25c 650.00 750.00

Overprinted **S. P.**

Frankfort Print

1881 *Rouletted in Color*
O39 A3 40c orange 30.00 57.50
a. Inverted overprint 185.00 250.00

"S.P." are initials of "Service Public."

Luxembourg Print

Perf. 13
O40 A2 1c red brn 125.00 150.00
O41 A2 4c green 190.00 185.00
a. Inverted overprint 225.00
O42 A2 5c yellow 500.00 450.00
O43 A5 1fr on 37½c bis 24.00 35.00

Haarlem Print
Perf. 11½x12, 12½x12, 13½

O44 A2 1c yel brn 6.75 8.00
O45 A2 2c black 8.00 8.00
O46 A2 5c yellow 110.00 140.00
a. Inverted overprint 200.00
O47 A3 10c gray lil 110.00 140.00
O48 A3 12½c rose 200.00 225.00
O49 A3 20c gray brn 60.00 85.00
O50 A3 25c blue 65.00 85.00
O51 A3 30c dl rose 67.50 90.00

Stamps of the 1881 issue with overprint of type "d" were never issued.

Overprinted **S. P.** d

Perf. 11½x12, 12½x12, 12½, 13½

1882
O52 A6 1c gray lil 40 45
a. "S" omitted
O53 A6 2c ol gray 40 45
O54 A6 4c ol bis 60 60
O55 A6 5c lt grn 1.00 75
O56 A6 10c rose 20.00 18.00
O57 A6 12½c slate 3.50 2.75
O58 A6 20c orange 3.50 2.75
O59 A6 25c ultra 25.00 25.00
O60 A6 30c gray grn 7.50 9.00
O61 A6 50c bis brn 1.25 2.00
O62 A6 1fr pale vio 1.25 2.00
O63 A6 5fr brn org 19.00 22.50

Nos. O52-O63 exist without one or both periods, also with varying space between "S" and "P". Nine denominations exist with double overprint, six with inverted overprint.

Overprinted **S. P.**

1883 *Perf. 13½*
O64 A6 5fr brn org *2,250. 1,700.*

Overprinted **S. P.**

Perf. 11, 11½, 11½x11, 12½

1891-93
O65 A7 10c carmine 32 30
a. Sheet of 25 60.00
O66 A7 12½c sl grn 8.00 5.50
O67 A7 20c orange 12.00 6.50
O68 A7 25c blue 40 35
a. Sheet of 25 75.00
O69 A7 30c ol grn 9.00 7.50
O70 A7 37½c green 9.00 9.00
O71 A7 50c brown 11.00 9.00
O72 A7 1fr dp vio 11.00 10.00
O73 A7 2½fr black 35.00 62.50
O74 A7 5fr lake 25.00 37.50

1895 *Perf. 12½*
O75 A8 1c pearl gray 1.50 1.75
O76 A8 2c gray brn 1.50 1.75
O77 A8 4c ol bis 1.50 1.75
O78 A8 5c green 3.50 4.00
O79 A8 10c carmine 42.50 32.50

Nos. O66-O79 exist without overprint and perforated "OFFICIEL" through the stamp. Value for set, $25.

Nos. O65a and O68a were issued to commemorate the coronation of Duke Adolphe.

Regular Issue of 1906-26 Overprinted

1908-26 *Perf. 11x11½, 12½*
O80 A9 1c gray 15 18
a. Inverted overprint 110.00
O81 A9 2c ol brn 15 16
O82 A9 4c bister 15 16
a. Double overprint 125.00
O83 A9 5c green 15 16
O84 A9 5c lilac ('26) 15 20
O85 A9 6c violet 15 16
O86 A9 7½c org ('19) 15 16
O87 A10 10c scarlet 24 32
O88 A10 12½c sl grn 24 32
O89 A10 15c org brn 35 42
O90 A10 20c orange 35 60
O91 A10 25c ultra 35 32
O92 A10 30c ol grn 3.50 3.75
O93 A10 37½c green 60 60
O94 A10 50c brown 1.00 1.10
O95 A10 87½c dk bl 2.50 2.50
O96 A10 1fr violet 3.50 3.25
O97 A10 2½fr vermilion 42.50 42.50
O98 A10 5fr claret 42.50 42.50
Nos. O80-O98 (19) 98.68 99.36

On Regular Issue of 1914-17

1915-17
O99 A11 10c lake 28 40
O100 A11 12½c dl grn 28 40
O101 A11 15c ol blk 28 40
O102 A11 17½c dp brn ('17) 28 40
O103 A11 25c ultra 28 40
O104 A11 30c bister 85 1.25
O105 A11 35c dk bl 28 40
O106 A11 37½c blk brn 28 40
O107 A11 40c orange 40 80
O108 A11 50c dk gray 40 80
O109 A11 62½c bl grn 40 80
O110 A11 87½c org ('17) 40 80
O111 A11 1fr org brn 40 80
O112 A11 2½fr red 40 80
O113 A11 5fr dk vio 40 80
Nos. O99-O113 (15) 5.61 9.65

On Regular Issues of 1921-26 in Black

1922-26 *Perf. 11½, 11½x11, 12½*
O114 A12 2c brown 15 15
O115 A12 3c ol grn 15 15
O116 A12 6c violet 15 15
O117 A12 10c yel grn 15 30
O118 A12 10c ol grn ('24) 15 28
O119 A12 15c brn ol 15 30
O120 A12 15c pale grn ('24) 15 28
O121 A12 15c dp org ('26) 15 25
O122 A12 20c dp org 15 30
O123 A12 20c yel grn ('26) 15 25
O124 A12 25c dk grn 15 30
O125 A12 30c car rose 15 30
O126 A12 40c brn org 15 30
O127 A12 50c dp bl 16 40
O128 A12 50c red ('24) 15 28
O129 A12 75c red 16 40
O130 A12 75c dp bl ('24) 16 40
O131 A12 80c black 4.25 10.00
O132 A13 1fr carmine 32 80
O133 A14 2fr indigo 2.75 6.00
O134 A14 2fr dk brn ('26) 1.65 4.50
O135 A15 5fr dk vio 16.00 37.50
Nos. O114-O135 (22) 27.55 63.59

On Regular Issues of 1921-26 in Red
Perf. 11, 11½, 11½x11, 12½

1922-34
O136 A12 80c blk, perf. 11½ 15 32
O137 A13 1fr dk bl, perf. 11½ ('26) 22 50
O138 A14 2fr ind, perf. 11½x11 40 1.10
O139 A17 3fr dk bl & bl, perf. 11 2.50 2.50
a. Perf. 11½ 80 1.25
b. Perf. 12½ 1.50 2.00
O140 A15 5fr dk vio, perf. 11½x11 3.50 6.75
a. Perf. 12½ ('34) 25.00 25.00
O141 A16 10fr blk, perf. 11½ 9.25 19.00
a. Perf. 12½ 25.00 25.00
Nos. O136-O141 (6) 16.02 30.17

On Regular Issue of 1926-35

1926-27 *Perf. 12*
O142 A18 5c dk vio 15 22
O143 A18 10c ol grn 15 22
O144 A18 20c org 15 22
O145 A18 25c yel grn 15 22
O146 A18 25c blk brn ('27) 30 48
O147 A18 30c yel grn ('27) 60 1.00
O148 A18 40c ol gray 15 22
O149 A18 50c red brn 15 22
O150 A18 65c blk brn 15 22
O151 A18 75c rose 15 22
O152 A18 75c bis brn ('27) 38 65
O153 A18 80c bis brn 18 32
O154 A18 90c rose ('27) 30 48
O155 A18 1fr black 18 32
O156 A18 1¼fr dk bl 15 22
O157 A18 1¾fr dp bl ('27) 48 80
Nos. O142-O157 (16) 3.77 6.03

Type of Regular Issue, 1926-35, Overprinted *Officiel*

1928-35 **Wmk. 213**
O158 A18 5c dk vio 15 20
O159 A18 10c ol grn 15 20
O160 A18 15c blk ('30) 20 60
O161 A18 20c orange 40 60
O162 A18 25c vio brn 40 60
O163 A18 30c yel grn 42 65
O164 A18 30c gray vio ('30) 20 60
O165 A18 35c yel grn ('30) 20 60
O166 A18 35c gray vio 42 65
O167 A18 40c ol gray 42 65
O168 A18 50c red brn 40 60
O169 A18 60c bl grn 40 60
O170 A18 70c bl vio ('35) 3.25 6.50
O171 A18 75c bis brn 40 60
O172 A18 90c rose 42 65
O173 A18 1fr black 42 65
O174 A18 1fr rose ('30) 20 60
O175 A18 1¼fr yel ('30) 1.65 4.00
O176 A18 1¼fr bl grn ('31) 1.65 4.00
O177 A18 1½fr dp bl 42 65
O178 A18 1¾fr dk bl ('30) 20 60
Nos. O158-O178 (21) 12.37 24.80

Type of Regular Issues of 1928-31 Overprinted Like Nos. O80-O98

1928-31 **Wmk. 216** *Perf. 11½*
O179 A19 2fr black 42 95

Wmk. 110 *Perf. 12½*
O180 A21 20fr dp grn ('31) 2.00 4.50

No. 198 Overprinted Like Nos. O80-O98

1934 **Unwmk.** *Perf. 14x13½*
O181 A22 5fr bl grn 1.50 3.00

Type of Regular Issue of 1935 Overprinted Like Nos. O158-O178 in Red

1935 **Wmk. 247** *Perf. 12½x12*
O182 A23 10fr green 1.50 3.50

OCCUPATION STAMPS

Issued under German Occupation
Stamps of Germany, 1933-36, Overprinted in Black

Luxemburg

1940 **Wmk. 237** *Perf. 14*
N1 A64 3pf olive bis 18 *48*
N2 A64 4pf dull blue 18 *52*
N3 A64 5pf bright grn 18 *48*
N4 A64 6pf dark green 18 *48*
N5 A64 8pf vermilion 18 *48*
N6 A64 10pf chocolate 18 *48*
N7 A64 12pf deep car 18 *48*
N8 A64 15pf maroon 25 *70*
a. Inverted overprint *450.00 1,300.*
N9 A64 20pf bright bl 25 *1.25*
N10 A64 25pf ultra 32 *1.75*
N11 A64 30pf olive grn 32 *1.75*
N12 A64 40pf red vio 48 *1.90*
N13 A64 50pf dk grn & blk 48 *2.00*
N14 A64 60pf claret & blk 48 *2.75*
N15 A64 80pf dk bl & blk 1.00 *3.75*
N16 A64 100pf org & blk 1.25 *5.75*
Nos. N1-N16 (16) 6.09 *25.00*

Nos. 159-162, 164, 168-171, 173, 175, 179, 182, 216, 198-199 Surcharged in Black

— 60 Rpf
b

80 Rpf

4 Rpf
a
c

100 Rpf
d

Perf. 12, 14x13½, 12½x12, 11½

1940 **Unwmk.**
N17 A18(a) 3rpf on 15c 15 *32*
N18 A18(a) 4rpf on 20c 15 *40*
N19 A18(a) 5rpf on 35c 15 *40*
N20 A18(a) 6rpf on 10c 15 *40*
N21 A18(a) 8rpf on 25c 15 *40*
N22 A18(a) 10rpf on 40c 15 *40*
N23 A18(a) 12rpf on 60c 15 *40*
N24 A18(a) 15rpf on 1fr rose 15 *40*
N25 A18(a) 20rpf on 50c 15 *75*
N26 A18(a) 25rpf on 5c 15 *1.25*
N27 A18(a) 30rpf on 70c 15 *60*
N28 A18(a) 40rpf on 75c 15 *1.00*
N29 A18(a) 50rpf on 1¼fr 15 *60*
N30 A35(b) 60rpf on 2fr 1.40 *12.50*
N31 A22(c) 80rpf on 5fr 40 *2.25*
N32 A23(d) 100rpf on 10fr 50 *3.00*
Set value 3.00

OCCUPATION SEMI-POSTAL STAMPS

Semi-Postal Stamps of Germany, 1940 Overprinted in Black — Luxemburg

1941 **Unwmk.** *Perf. 14*
NB1 SP153 3pf + 2pf dk brn 20 *85*
NB2 SP153 4pf + 3pf bluish blk 20 *85*
NB3 SP153 5pf + 3pf yel grn 20 *85*
NB4 SP153 6pf + 4pf dk grn 20 *85*
NB5 SP153 8pf + 4pf dp org 20 *85*
NB6 SP153 12pf + 6pf car 20 *85*
NB7 SP153 15pf + 10pf dk vio brn 28 *1.90*
NB8 SP153 25pf + 15pf dp ultra 85 *3.75*
NB9 SP153 40pf + 35pf red lil 1.50 *6.25*
Nos. NB1-NB9 (9) 3.83

MACAO

LOCATION — Off the Chinese coast at the mouth of the Canton River
GOVT. — Portuguese Overseas Territory
AREA — 6 sq. mi.
POP. — 261,680 (1981)
CAPITAL — Macao

The territory includes the two small adjacent islands of Coloane and Taipa.

1000 Reis = 1 Milreis
78 Avos = 1 Rupee (1894)
100 Avos = 1 Pataca (1913)

Catalogue values for unused stamps in this country are for Never Hinged items, beginning with Scott 339 in the regular postage section, Scott C16 in the air post section, Scott J50 in the semi-postal section, and Scott RA11 in the postal tax section.

Watermark

Wmk. 232- Maltese Cross

Portuguese Crown — A1

Perf. 12½, 13½

1884-85 **Typo.** **Unwmk.**
1 A1 5r black 4.00 1.90
2 A1 10r orange 5.50 2.50
3 A1 10r grn ('85) 6.00 3.50
a. Perf. 13½ 19.00 12.00
4 A1 20r bister 6.00 4.50
5 A1 20r rose ('85) 5.50 3.50
6 A1 25r rose 2.00 3.50
7 A1 25r vio ('85) 2.00 1.90
a. Perf. 13½ 27.50 19.00
8 A1 40r blue 17.50 7.50
a. Perf. 12½ 27.50 10.00
9 A1 40r yel ('85) 5.75 4.50
a. Perf. 13½ 17.00 10.00

10 A1 50r green	19.00	8.00
a. Perf. 12½	60.00	25.00
11 A1 50r bl ('85)	2.25	1.90
a. Perf. 13½	20.00	14.00
12 A1 80r gray ('85)	21.50	8.00
13 A1 100r red lil	3.00	2.25
a. 100r lil	4.00	2.25
14 A1 200r orange	6.75	4.00
a. Perf. 12½	20.00	14.00
15 A1 300r chocolate	5.75	4.50
a. Perf. 13½	30.00	22.50

The reprints of the 1885 issue are printed on smooth, white chalky paper, ungummed and on thin white paper with shiny white gum and clean-cut perforation 13½.

No. 13a Surcharged in Black

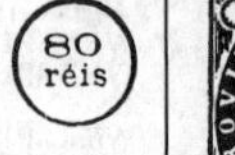

1884

16 A1 80r on 100r lil	6.75	5.50
a. Inverted surcharge	9.00	7.50
b. Without accent on "e" of "reis"	6.75	5.50
c. Perf. 13½	6.75	5.50

Nos. 16-23, 25 and 27 were issued without gum.

Nos. 6 and 10 Surcharged in Black, Blue or Red:

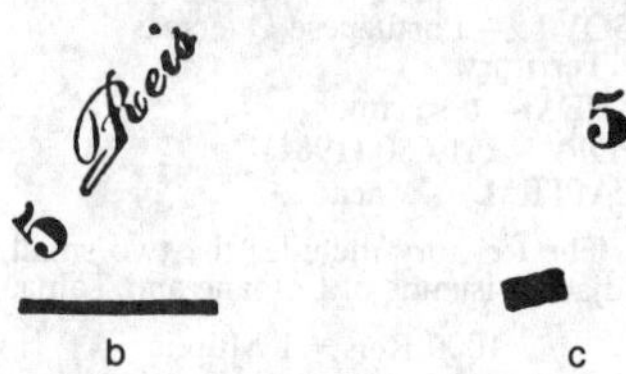

1885

17 A1(b) 5r on 25r rose, perf. 12½ (Bk)	2.00	1.40
a. With accent on "e" of "Reis"	3.00	2.50
b. Double surcharge		
c. Inverted surcharge	47.50	27.50
d. Perf. 13½	27.50	15.00
18 A1(b) 10r on 25r rose (Bl)	4.00	2.75
a. Accent on "e" of "Reis"		
b. Pair, one without surcharge	55.00	
19 A1(b) 10r on 50r grn, perf. 13½ (Bl)	37.50	22.50
a. Perf. 12½	42.50	22.50
20 A1(b) 20r on 50r grn (Bk)	2.75	1.40
a. Double surcharge		35.00
b. Accent on "e" of "Reis"		
21 A1(b) 40r on 50r grn, perf. 13½ (R)	35.00	17.00
a. Perf. 12½	24.00	19.00

1885

22 A1(c) 5r on 25r rose (Bk)	3.00	2.00
a. Original value not obliterated		
23 A1(c) 10r on 50r grn (Bk)	3.00	2.00
a. Inverted surcharge		
b. Perf. 12½	4.00	2.75

Nos. 12, 13a and 14 Surcharged in Black

5
Reis

1887

24 A1 5r on 80r gray	3.50	2.00
a. "R" of "Reis" 4mm high	19.00	17.50
b. Perf. 12½	10.50	8.75
25 A1 5r on 100r lilac	12.50	7.00
a. Perf. 12½	11.50	8.50
26 A1 10r on 80r gray	4.50	3.50
a. "R" 4mm high	17.50	17.00
27 A1 10r on 200r org	16.00	11.50
a. "R" 4mm high	25.00	19.00
b. Perf. 13½	14.00	7.75
28 A1 20r on 80r gray	7.00	4.25
a. "R" 4mm high	22.50	21.00
b. Perf. 12½		

The surcharges with larger "R" (4mm) have accent on "e." Smaller "R" is 3mm high.

Coat of Arms — A6

Red Surcharge

1887, Oct. 20 ***Perf. 12½***

Without Gum

32 A6 5r grn & buff	2.50	1.90
a. With labels, 5r on 10r	30.00	20.00
b. With labels, 5r on 20r	30.00	20.00
c. With labels, 5r on 60r	30.00	20.00
33 A6 10r grn & buff	2.50	1.90
a. With labels, 10r on 10r	27.50	20.00
b. With labels, 10r on 60r	50.00	24.00
34 A6 40r grn & buff	2.75	2.75
a. With labels, 40r on 20r	22.50	25.00

The 10r also exists with 20r labels, and 40r with 10r labels.

King Luiz — A7

King Carlos — A9

Typographed and Embossed

1888, Jan. ***Perf. 12½, 13½***

Chalk-surfaced Paper

35 A7 5r black	1.90	1.25
36 A7 10r green	1.90	1.25
a. Perf. 13½	8.25	6.50
37 A7 20r carmine	2.75	1.50
38 A7 25r violet	2.75	1.90
39 A7 40r chocolate	3.00	1.90
a. Perf. 13½	5.50	3.50
40 A7 50r blue	3.00	2.25
41 A7 80r gray	3.75	2.75
a. Imperf., pair	50.00	
42 A7 100r brown	3.75	2.75
43 A7 200r gray lil	7.50	4.25
44 A7 300r orange	10.00	5.00

No. 43 Surcharged in Red **30 30**

1892

Without Gum

45 A7 30r on 200r gray lil	6.00	4.75
a. Inverted surcharge	30.00	20.00

1894, Nov. 15 Typo. ***Perf. 11½***

46 A9 5r yellow	1.25	90
47 A9 10r redsh vio	1.25	90
48 A9 15r chocolate	1.50	1.10
49 A9 20r lavender	1.65	1.25
50 A9 25r green	3.75	1.90
51 A9 50r lt bl	4.00	1.90
a. Perf. 13½	30.00	27.50
52 A9 75r carmine	4.00	1.90
53 A9 80r yel grn	4.50	3.75
54 A9 100r brn, *buff*	3.75	3.50
55 A9 150r car, *rose*	6.75	4.25
56 A9 200r dk bl, *bl*	7.50	4.75
57 A9 300r dk bl, *sal*	8.50	6.00
Nos. 46-57 (12)	48.40	32.10

Stamps of 1888 Surcharged in Red, Green or Black

1894 Without Gum ***Perf. 12½***

58 A7 1a on 5r blk (R)	75	60
a. Short "1"	90	75
b. Inverted surcharge	6.00	6.00
c. Double surcharge		
d. Surch. on back instead of face	18.00	15.00
59 A7 3a on 20r car (G)	1.90	1.25
a. Inverted surcharge		
60 A7 4a on 25r vio (Bk)	2.25	1.25
a. Inverted surcharge	12.50	12.50
61 A7 6a on 40r choc (Bk)	2.10	1.25
a. Perf. 13½	5.25	4.50
62 A7 8a on 50r bl (R)	4.50	3.25
a. Double surch., one inverted		
b. Inverted surcharge	20.00	19.00
c. Perf. 13½	15.00	10.50
63 A7 13a on 80r gray (Bk)	2.50	1.90
a. Double surcharge		
64 A7 16a on 100r brn (Bk)	3.50	2.75
a. Inverted surcharge		
b. Perf. 13½	35.00	21.00
65 A7 31a on 200r gray lil	7.25	5.00
a. Inverted surcharge	25.00	18.00
b. Perf. 13½	8.00	5.50
66 A7 47a on 300r org (G)	6.50	5.00
a. Double surcharge		

The style of type used for the word "PROVISORIO" on Nos. 58 to 66 differs for each value.

A 2a on 10r green was unofficially surcharged and denounced by the authorities.

On No. 45

66B A7 5a on 30r on 200r gray lil	12.00	5.00

Vasco da Gama Issue

Common Design Types

1898, Apr. 1 Engr. ***Perf. 12½ to 16***

67 CD20 ½a bl grn	70	60
68 CD21 1a red	70	60
69 CD22 2a red vio	75	70
70 CD23 4a yel grn	75	70
71 CD24 8a dk bl	1.65	1.10
72 CD25 12a vio brn	3.00	1.90
73 CD26 16a bis brn	1.90	1.25
74 CD27 24a bister	3.75	2.75
Nos. 67-74 (8)	13.20	9.60

King Carlos — A11

1898-1910 Typo. ***Perf. 11½***

Name and Value in Black except #103

75 A11 ½a gray	30	20
a. Perf. 12½	1.40	1.10
76 A11 1a orange	30	20
a. Perf. 12½	1.40	1.10
77 A11 2a yel grn	45	22
78 A11 2a gray grn ('03)	75	52
79 A11 2½a red brn	1.25	70
80 A11 3a gray vio	1.25	70
81 A11 3a slate ('03)	75	52
82 A11 4a sea grn	1.25	95
83 A11 4a car ('03)	75	60
84 A11 5a gray brn ('00)	1.50	1.25
85 A11 5a pale yel brn ('03)	95	75
86 A11 6a red brn ('03)	1.40	1.40
87 A11 8a blue	1.75	95
88 A11 8a gray brn ('03)	2.10	1.25
89 A11 10a slate bl ('00)	1.90	1.25
90 A11 12a rose	2.10	1.90
91 A11 12a red lil ('03)	6.50	5.00
92 A11 13a violet	2.10	1.90
93 A11 13a gray lil ('03)	2.75	1.90
94 A11 15a pale ol grn ('00)	6.75	5.75
95 A11 16a dk bl, *bl*	2.75	1.90
96 A11 18a org brn, *pink* ('03)	4.25	3.50
97 A11 20a brn, *yelsh* ('00)	2.75	1.90
98 A11 24a brn, *buff*	2.75	1.90
99 A11 31a red lil	3.50	2.25
100 A11 31a red lil, *pink* ('03)	4.25	3.75
101 A11 47a dk bl, *rose*	4.25	3.50
102 A11 47a dl bl, *straw* ('03)	5.75	5.00
103 A11 78a blk & red, *bl* ('00)	5.75	4.25
Nos. 75-103 (29)	72.85	55.86

Issued without gum: Nos. 76a, 77, 79-80, 82, 84, 89, 94, 97 and 103.

Nos. 92, 95, 98-99 Surcharged in Black

5 ≡
PROVISORIO

1900

104 A11 5a on 13a vio	1.25	90
105 A11 10a on 16a dk bl, *bl*	1.40	90
106 A11 15a on 24a brn, *buff*	1.40	1.00
107 A11 20a on 31a red lil	1.75	1.40

Regular Issues Surcharged

On Stamps of 1884-85

1902 ***Perf. 11½***

Black Surcharge

108 A1 6a on 10r org	3.00	2.25
a. Double surcharge	30.00	25.00
109 A1 6a on 10r grn	1.50	1.25

On Stamps of 1888

Perf. 12½, 13½

Red Surcharge

110 A7 6a on 5r blk	95	75
a. Inverted surcharge	25.00	20.00

Black Surcharge

111 A7 6a on 10r grn	95	75
112 A7 6a on 40r choc	1.10	75
a. Double surcharge	25.00	19.00
b. Perf. 13½	3.50	2.75
113 A7 18a on 20r rose	1.50	1.40
a. Double surcharge	30.00	25.00
114 A7 18a on 25r vio	15.00	9.00
115 A7 18a on 80r gray	17.00	13.00
a. Double surcharge	40.00	37.50
116 A7 18a on 100r brn	3.50	2.25
a. Perf. 13½	12.00	10.50
117 A7 18a on 200r gray lil	13.00	12.00
a. Perf. 12½	17.00	12.00
118 A7 18a on 300r org	4.25	2.75
a. Perf. 13½	8.25	8.25

Issued without gum: Nos. 110-118.

Nos. 109 to 118 inclusive, except No. 111, have been reprinted. The reprints have white gum and clean-cut perforation 13½ and the colors are usually paler than those of the originals. Value $1 each.

On Stamps of 1894

1902-10 ***Perf. 11½, 13½***

119 A9 6a on 5r yel	70	60
a. Inverted surcharge	5.25	5.00
120 A9 6a on 10r red vio	70	60
121 A9 6a on 15r choc	70	60
122 A9 6a on 25r grn	70	60
123 A9 6a on 80r yel grn	70	60
124 A9 6a on 100r brn, *buff*	70	60
a. Perf. 11½	4.25	3.25
125 A9 6a on 200r bl, *bl*	90	70
a. Vert. half used as 3a on cover ('10)		
126 A9 18a on 20r lav	2.25	1.75
127 A9 18a on 50r lt bl	2.25	1.75
a. Perf. 13½	7.75	6.50
128 A9 18a on 75r car	2.25	1.75
129 A9 18a on 150r car, *rose*	2.25	1.75
130 A9 18a on 300r bl, *salmon*	2.25	1.75

On Newspaper Stamp of 1893

Perf. 12½

131 N3 18a on 2½r brn	2.10	1.40
a. Perf. 13½	4.00	2.10
b. Perf. 11½	7.75	5.25
Nos. 108-131 (24)	80.20	60.60

Issued without gum: Nos. 122-130, 131b.

Stamps of 1898-1900 Overprinted in Black **PROVISORIO**

1902 ***Perf. 11½***

132 A11 2a yel grn	3.25	1.75
133 A11 4a sea grn	2.50	1.40
134 A11 8a blue	2.50	1.40
135 A11 10a sl bl	2.50	1.40
136 A11 12a rose	4.00	2.75
Nos. 132-136 (5)	14.75	8.70

Issued without gum: Nos. 133, 135.

Reprints of No. 133 have shiny white gum and clean-cut perforation 13½. Value $1.

No. 91 Surcharged **10 AVOS**

1905

141 A11 10a on 12a red lil	3.00	2.50

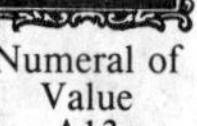

Numeral of Value A13

Coat of Arms A14

Postage Due Stamps of 1904 Overprinted with Bars

1910, Oct. ***Perf. 11½x12***

144 A13 ½a gray grn	1.75	1.25
a. Inverted overprint	3.50	3.50
145 A13 1a yel grn	1.75	1.25
a. Inverted overprint	3.50	3.50
146 A13 2a slate	1.75	1.50
a. Inverted overprint	8.50	8.50

Stamps of 1898-1903 Overprinted in Carmine or Green

Lisbon Overprint

1911, Apr. 2 *Perf. 11½*

147 A11 ½a gray 18 15
- *a.* Inverted overprint

147B A11 1a orange 18 15
- *c.* Inverted overprint

148 A11 2a gray grn 18 15
149 A11 3a slate 18 15
150 A11 4a car (G) 75 60
- *a.* 4a pale yel brn (error) 25.00 20.00

151 A11 5a pale yel brn 75 60
152 A11 6a red brn 75 60
153 A11 8a gray brn 75 60
154 A11 10a sl bl 75 60
155 A11 13a gray lil 90 75
156 A11 16a dk bl, *bl* 90 75
157 A11 18a org brn, *pink* 1.90 1.25
157A A11 20a brn, *straw* 1.90 1.25
157B A11 31a red lil, *pink* 1.90 1.25
157C A11 47a dl bl, *straw* 3.00 2.50
157D A11 78a blk & red, *bl* 4.00 3.00
Nos. 147-157D (16) 18.97 14.35

Issued without gum: Nos. 153-157D.

1911 *Perf. 11½x12*

Red Surcharge

158 A14 1a on 5r brn & buff 1.50 1.10
- *a.* "1" omitted 11.50 9.50
- *b.* Inverted surcharge 5.75 5.75

Stamps of 1900-03 Surcharged

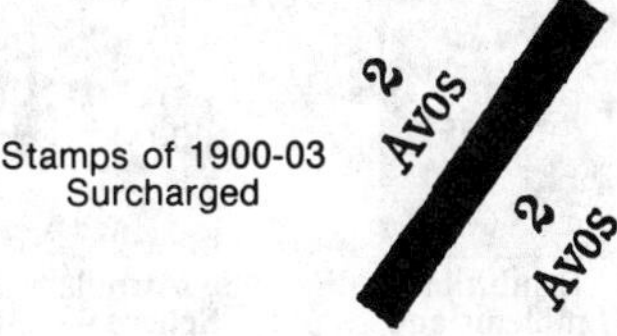

Diagonal Halves

1911 **Without Gum** *Perf. 11½*

Black Surcharge

159 A11 2a on half of 4a car 2.00 2.00
- *a.* "2" omitted 15.00 15.00
- *b.* Inverted surcharge 12.50 12.50
- *d.* Entire stamp 15.00 15.00

159C A11 5a on half of 10a sl bl (#89) *400.00 400.00*
- *e.* Entire stamp

Red Surcharge

160 A11 5a on half of 10a sl bl (#89) *250.00 200.00*
- *a.* Inverted surcharge
- *b.* Entire stamp

161 A11 5a on half of 10a sl bl (#135) 8.00 6.50
- *a.* Inverted surcharge 20.00 18.00
- *b.* Entire stamp 27.50 24.00

A15

1911 *Perf. 12x11½*

Laid or Wove Paper

162 A15 1a black 175.00 100.00
- *a.* "Corrieo" 350.00 350.00

163 A15 2a black 200.00 115.00
- *a.* "Corrieo" 350.00 350.00

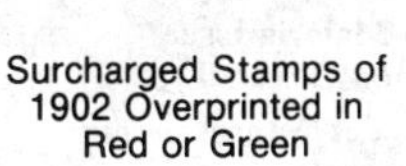

Surcharged Stamps of 1902 Overprinted in Red or Green

Local Overprint

1913 **Without Gum** *Perf. 11½*

164 A1 6a on 10r grn (R) 7.25 3.00

Perf. 12½, 13½

165 A7 6a on 5r blk (G) 2.75 1.25
166 A7 6a on 10r grn (R) 7.25 3.00
167 A7 6a on 40r choc (R) 2.75 1.25
- *a.* Perf. 13½ 6.00 4.75

168 A7 18a on 20r car (G) 5.00 1.90
169 A7 18a on 100r brn (R) 15.00 6.00
- *a.* Perf. 13½ 14.00 10.00

170 A7 18a on 300r org (R) 9.00 4.00
- *a.* Perf. 12½ 6.00 4.75

Nos. 164-170 (7) 49.00 20.40

"Republica" overprint exists inverted on Nos. 164-170.

"Republica" overprint exists double on No. 164.

1913 **Without Gum** *Perf. 11½, 13½*

171 A9 6a on 10r red vio (G) 1.40 85
172 A9 6a on 10r red vio (R) 30.00 3.50
173 A9 6a on 15r choc (R) 1.40 1.00
174 A9 6a on 25r grn (R) 1.75 1.40
175 A9 6a on 80r yel grn (R) 1.40 1.25
176 A9 6a on 100r brn, *buff*(R) 1.40 1.25
- *a.* Perf. 11½ 3.50 1.75

177 A9 18a on 20r lav (R) 2.00 1.75
178 A9 18a on 50r lt bl (R) 2.00 1.75
- *a.* Perf. 13½ 3.00 1.75

179 A9 18a on 75r car (G) 2.00 1.75
180 A9 18a on 150r car, *rose* (G) 3.00 2.00
181 A9 18a on 300r dk bl, *buff* (R) 2.50 2.00

On No. 141

182 A11 10a on 12a red lil (R) 1.75 1.75
Nos. 171-182 (12) 50.60 20.25

"Republica" overprint exists inverted on Nos. 171-181.

Stamps of Preceding Issue Surcharged 2

1913 **Without Gum** *Perf. 11½*

183 A9 2a on 18a on 20r lav (R) 1.00 85
184 A9 2a on 18a on 50r lt bl (R) 1.00 85
- *a.* Perf. 13½ 1.75 1.40

185 A9 2a on 18a on 75r car (G) 1.00 85
186 A9 2a on 18a on 150r car, *rose* (G) 1.00 85

"Republica" overprint exists inverted on Nos. 183-186. Value, each $3.50.

The 2a surcharge exists inverted or double on Nos. 183-186. Value, each $5.

Vasco da Gama Issue Overprinted or Surcharged:

REPUBLICA

REPUBLICA 10 A.

j k

187 CD20 (j) ½a bl grn 70 60
188 CD21 (j) 1a red 70 60
189 CD22 (j) 2a red vio 70 80
- *a.* Dbl. ovpt., one inverted 20.00

190 CD23 (j) 4a yel grn 70 60
- *a.* Half used as 2a on cover

191 CD24 (j) 8a dk bl 1.10 70
192 CD25 (k) 10a on 12a vio brn 2.00 1.65
193 CD26 (j) 16a bis brn 1.10 90
194 CD27 (j) 24a bister 1.75 1.40
Nos. 187-194 (8) 8.75 7.25

Stamps of 1898-1903 Overprinted in Red or Green

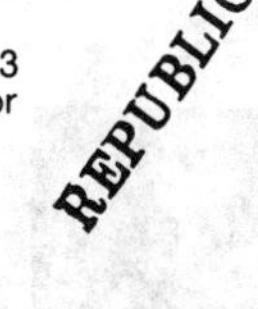

1913 **Without Gum** *Perf. 11½*

195 A11 4a car (G) 25.00 11.50
196 A11 5a yel brn 7.50 2.75
- *a.* Inverted overprint

197 A11 6a red brn 7.50 2.75
198 A11 8a gray brn 65.00 19.00
199 A11 13a violet 15.00 6.00
- *a.* Inverted overprint 30.00

200 A11 13a gray lil 7.50 2.75
201 A11 16a bl, *bl* 7.50 2.75
202 A11 18a org brn, *pink* 7.50 2.75
203 A11 20a brn, *yelsh* 7.50 2.75
204 A11 31a red lil, *pink* 7.50 2.75
205 A11 47a dl bl, *straw* 7.50 2.75
Nos. 195-205 (11) 165.00 58.50

Stamps of 1911-13 Surcharged ½ Avo

On Stamps of 1911 With Lisbon "Republica"

1913

206 A11 ½a on 5a yel brn (R) 1.10 90
- *a.* "½ Avo" inverted 15.00

207 A11 4a on 8a gray brn (R) 1.40 1.10
- *a.* "4 Avos" inverted 15.00

On Stamps of 1913 With Local "Republica"

208 A11 1a on 13a vio (R) 20.00 17.50
209 A11 1a on 13a gray lil (R) 1.10 70
- *a.* "REPUBLICA" omitted

Issued without gum: Nos. 207-209.

"Ceres" — A16

1913-24 *Perf. 12x11½, 15x14*

Name and Value in Black

210 A16 ½a ol brn 20 15
- *a.* Inscriptions inverted 10.00

211 A16 1a black 24 15
- *a.* Inscriptions inverted 10.00
- *b.* Inscriptions double 10.00

212 A16 1½a yel grn ('24) 20 15
213 A16 2a bl grn 20 15
- *a.* Inscriptions inverted 5.00

214 A16 3a org ('23) 1.10 95
215 A16 4a carmine 75 28
216 A16 4a lem ('24) 1.50 95
217 A16 5a lil brn 1.40 95
218 A16 6a lt vio 1.10 70
219 A16 6a gray ('23) 4.50 2.25
220 A16 8a lil brn 95 60
221 A16 10a dp bl 95 60
222 A16 10a pale bl ('23) 3.00 1.75
223 A16 12a yel brn 1.40 75
224 A16 14a lil ('24) 6.00 3.50
225 A16 16a slate 1.90 1.40
226 A16 20a org brn 3.50 1.50
227 A16 24a sl grn ('23) 2.75 1.90
228 A16 32a org brn ('24) 3.00 2.75
229 A16 40a plum 2.50 1.50
230 A16 56a dl rose ('24) 6.50 3.75
231 A16 58a brn, *grn* 4.50 3.00
232 A16 72a brn ('23) 7.50 5.25
233 A16 76a brn, *pink* 6.50 3.75
234 A16 1p org, *sal* 7.50 4.50
235 A16 1p org ('24) 24.00 7.50
236 A16 3p grn, *bl* 30.00 14.00
237 A16 3p pale turq ('24) 55.00 22.50
238 A16 5p car rose ('24) 40.00 22.50
Nos. 210-238 (29) 218.64 109.68

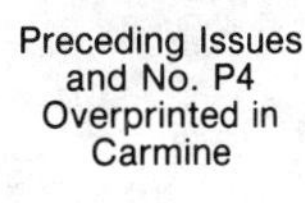

Preceding Issues and No. P4 Overprinted in Carmine

REPUBLICA

On Stamps of 1902

Perf. 11½, 12, 12½, 13½, 11½x12

1915

239 A7 6a on 10r grn 90 60
240 A9 6a on 5r yel 90 65
241 A9 6a on 10r red vio 90 65
242 A9 6a on 15r choc 65 42
243 A9 6a on 25r grn 65 42
244 A9 6a on 80r yel grn 65 42
245 A9 6a on 100r brn, *buff* 1.25 70
246 A9 6a on 200r bl, *bl* 60 42
247 A9 18a on 20r lav 1.25 1.10
248 A9 18a on 50r lt bl 1.65 1.10
249 A9 18a on 75r car 1.40 1.25
250 A9 18a on 150r car, *rose* 1.65 1.25
251 A9 18a on 300r bl, *sal* 1.40 1.25
252 N3 18a on 2½r brn 1.10 60

With Additional Overprint PROVISORIO

253 A11 8a blue 65 52
254 A11 10a slate blue 65 52
- *a.* "Provisorio" double 5.25

On Stamp of 1905

255 A11 10a on 12a red lil 65 52
Nos. 239-255 (17) 16.90 12.39

Issued without gum: Nos. 243-251 and 255.

No. 217 Surcharged ½ AVO

1919-20

Without Gum

256 A16 ½a on 5a lil brn 7.50 3.25

Nos. 243 and 244 Surcharged 2

257 A9 2a on 6a on 25r grn 12.50 7.00
258 A9 2a on 6a on 80r yel grn 12.50 4.50

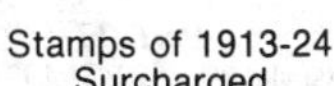

No. 152 Surcharged 2 avos

258A A11 2a on 6a red brn 14.00 6.00

Issued without gum: Nos. 256-258A.

Stamps of 1913-24 Surcharged 7 avos

1931-33

259 A16 1a on 24a sl grn 70 55
260 A16 2a on 32a org brn 70 55
261 A16 4a on 12a bis brn 70 55
262 A16 5a on 6a lt gray 2.75 1.40
263 A16 5a on 6a lt vio 1.90 1.40
264 A16 7a on 8a lil brn ('31) 1.40 80
265 A16 12a on 14a lil ('31) 1.25 80
266 A16 15a on 16a dk gray 1.25 80
267 A16 20a on 56a dl rose 1.75 1.10
Nos. 259-267 (9) 12.40 7.95

"Portugal" and Vasco da Gama's Flagship "San Gabriel" — A17

Wmk. 232

1934, Feb. 1 **Typo.** *Perf. 11½*

268 A17 ½a bister 15 15
269 A17 1a ol brn 15 15
270 A17 2a bl grn 15 15
271 A17 3a violet 15 15
272 A17 4a black 24 15
273 A17 5a gray 24 15
274 A17 6a brown 24 15
275 A17 7a brt rose 32 22
276 A17 8a brt bl 32 25
277 A17 10a red org 65 42
278 A17 12a dk bl 65 42
279 A17 14a ol grn 65 42
280 A17 15a maroon 65 42
281 A17 20a orange 65 42
282 A17 30a ap grn 1.40 70
283 A17 40a violet 1.40 70
284 A17 50a ol bis 3.00 90
285 A17 1p lt bl 12.50 1.75
286 A17 2p brn org 15.00 4.00
287 A17 3p emerald 30.00 5.25
288 A17 5p dk vio 65.00 10.50
Nos. 268-288 (21) 133.51 27.42

See Nos. 316-323.

Common Design Types

Perf. 13½x13

1938, Aug. 1 **Engr.** **Unwmk.**

Name and Value in Black

289 CD34 1a gray grn 15 15
290 CD34 2a org brn 15 15
291 CD34 3a dk vio brn 15 15
292 CD34 4a brt grn 15 15

293 CD35 5a dk car 15 15
294 CD35 6a slate 15 15
295 CD35 8a rose vio 24 20
296 CD36 10a brt red vio 28 20
297 CD36 12a red 35 20
298 CD36 15a orange 35 20
299 CD37 20a blue 60 40
300 CD37 40a gray blk 1.40 55
301 CD37 50a brown 1.40 55
302 CD38 1p brn car 4.25 1.40
303 CD38 2p ol grn 10.00 2.00
304 CD38 3p bl vio 14.00 4.00
305 CD38 5p red brn 30.00 6.75
Nos. 289-305 (17) 63.77 17.35

Stamps of 1934 Surcharged in Black:

5 avos a — **5 avos** b

1941 Wmk. 232 *Perf. 11½x12*

306 A17(a) 1a on 6a brn 1.75 85
307 A17(b) 2a on 6a brn 70 55
308 A17(b) 3a on 6a brn 70 55
309 A17(a) 5a on 7a brt rose 67.50 24.00
310 A17(b) 5a on 7a brt rose 70 55
311 A17(a) 5a on 8a brt bl 2.50 1.75
312 A17(b) 5a on 8a brt bl 70 55
313 A17(b) 8a on 30a ap grn 1.50 1.25
314 A17(b) 8a on 40a vio 1.50 1.25
315 A17(b) 8a on 50a ol bis 1.50 1.25
Nos. 306-315 (10) 79.05 32.55

No. 294 Surcharged in Black:

3 avos

1941 Unwmk. *Perf. 13½x13*

315A CD35 3a on 6a slate 22.50 13.00

Counterfeits exist.

"Portugal" Type of 1934

1942 Litho. *Rough Perf. 12*

Thin Paper Without Gum

316 A17 1a ol brn 40 35
317 A17 2a bl grn 40 35
318 A17 3a vio, perf. 11 2.00 1.40
a. Perf. 12 3.75 1.50
319 A17 6a brown 3.00 1.25
a. Perf. 10 6.75 4.00
b. Perf. 11 5.75 3.00
320 A17 10a red org 1.90 1.25
321 A17 20a orange 1.90 1.25
a. Perf. 11 5.75 3.00
322 A17 30a ap grn 3.00 1.40
323 A17 40a violet 4.00 1.75
Nos. 316-323 (8) 16.60 9.00

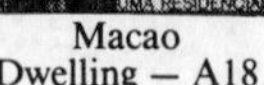

Macao Dwelling — A18

Gate of Cerco — A19

Designs: 2a, Mountain fort. 3a, View of Macao. 8a, Praia Grande Bay. 10a, Leal Senado Square. 20a, Sao Jeronimo Hill. 30a, Marginal Ave. 50a, Relief of Goddess Ma. 2p, Pagoda of Barra. 3p, Post Office. 5p, Solidao Walk.

1948, Dec. 20 Litho. *Perf. 10½*

324 A18 1a dk brn & org 24 15
325 A19 2a rose brn & rose 18 15
326 A18 3a brn vio & lil 38 15
327 A18 8a rose car & rose 24 15
328 A18 10a lil rose & rose 38 22
329 A18 20a dk bl & gray 45 22
330 A18 30a blk & gray 90 30
331 A18 50a brn & pale bis 1.40 38
332 A19 1p emer & pale grn 10.50 3.75
333 A19 2p scar & rose 9.00 3.75
334 A19 3p dl grn & gray grn 15.00 4.25
335 A18 5p vio bl & gray 21.00 6.75
Nos. 324-335 (12) 59.67 20.22

See Nos. 341-347A.

Lady of Fatima Issue
Common Design Type

1949, Feb. 1 Unwmk. *Perf. 14½*

336 CD40 8a scarlet 2.50 2.00

Symbols of the UPU A20

Dragon A21

1949, Dec. 24 Litho. Unwmk.

337 A20 32a cl & rose 18.00 6.00

75th anniv. of the formation of the UPU.

Catalogue values for unused stamps in this section, from this point to the end of the section, are for Never Hinged items.

Holy Year Issue
Common Design Types

1950, July 26 *Perf. 13x13½*

339 CD41 32a dk sl gray 1.90 90
340 CD42 50a carmine 1.90 90

Scenic Types of 1948

Designs as before.

1950-51 *Perf. 14*

341 A18 1a vio & rose 24 18
342 A19 2a ol bis & yel 24 18
343 A18 3a org red & buff 32 18
344 A18 8a sl & gray 32 18
345 A18 10a red brn & org 40 24
346 A18 30a vio bl & bl 1.40 42
347 A18 50a ol grn & yel grn 1.65 42
347A A19 1p dk org brn & org brn 1.65 60
Nos. 341-347A (8) 6.22 2.40

A 1p ultra & vio, perf. 11, was not sold in Macao. Value $6.

The 1p was issued in 1950, Nos. 341-347 in 1951.

1951 *Perf. 11½x12*

348 A21 1a org yel, *lem* 32 45
349 A21 2a dk grn, *bl* 32 45
350 A21 10a vio brn, *bl* 32 45
351 A21 10a brt pink, *bl* 32 45

Holy Year Extension Issue
Common Design Type

1951, Dec. 3 Litho. *Perf. 14*

352 CD43 60a mag & pink 2.50 1.25

Fernao Mendes Pinto — A22

Portraits: 2a and 10a, St. Francis Xavier. 3a and 50a, Jorge Alvares. 6a and 30a, Luis de Camoens.

1951, Aug. 27 *Perf. 11½*

353 A22 1a stl bl & gray bl 15 15
354 A22 2a dk brn & ol grn 16 15
355 A22 3a dp grn & grn 15 15
356 A22 6a purple 40 18
357 A22 10a red brn & org 80 22
358 A22 20a brn car 1.25 42
359 A22 30a dk brn & ol grn 1.25 42
360 A22 50a red & org 2.75 75
Nos. 353-360 (8) 6.91 2.44

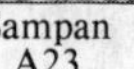

Sampan A23

Junk A24

Design: 5p, Junk.

1951, Nov. 1 Unwmk.

361 A23 1p vio bl & bl 2.50 60
362 A24 3p blk & vio 16.00 1.75
363 A23 5p henna brn 32.50 5.50

Medical Congress Issue
Common Design Type

Design: Sao Rafael Hospital.

1952, June 16 Unwmk. *Perf. 13½*

364 CD44 6a blk & pur 40 24

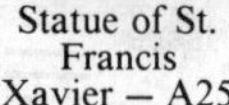

Statue of St. Francis Xavier — A25

Statue of Virgin Mary — A26

St. Francis Xavier Issue

Designs: 16a, Arm of St. Francis. 40a, Tomb of St. Francis.

1952, Nov. 28 Litho. *Perf. 14*

365 A25 3a blk, *grnsh gray* 25 15
366 A25 16a choc, *buff* 1.25 42
367 A25 40a blk, *blue* 2.75 1.10

Issued to commemorate the 400th anniversary of the death of St. Francis Xavier.

1953, Apr. 28 Unwmk. *Perf. 13½*

368 A26 8a choc & dl ol 24 18
369 A26 10a bl blk & buff 1.00 42
370 A26 50a sl grn & ol grn 2.75 1.25

Issued to commemorate the Exhibition of Sacred Missionary Art, held at Lisbon in 1951.

Stamp of Portugal and Arms of Colonies — A27

1954, Mar. 9 Photo. *Perf. 13*

371 A27 10a multi 90 60

Cent. of Portugal's first postage stamps.

Firecracker Flower — A28

Map of Colony — A29

Flowers: 3a, Forget-me-not. 5a, Dragon claw. 10a, Nunflower. 16a, Narcissus. 30a, Peach flower. 39a, Lotus flower. 1p, Chrysanthemum. 3p, Cherry blossoms. 5p, Tangerine blossoms.

1953, Sept. 22 *Perf. 11½*

Flowers in Natural Colors

372 A28 1a dk red 15 15
373 A28 3a dk grn 15 15
374 A28 5a dk brn 15 15
375 A28 10a dp grnsh bl 20 15
376 A28 16a yel brn 16 15
377 A28 30a dk ol grn 16 15
378 A28 39a vio bl 24 15
379 A28 1p dp plum 2.00 75
380 A28 3p dk gray 4.00 1.25
381 A28 5p dp car 6.00 2.50
Nos. 372-381 (10) 13.21 5.55

Sao Paulo Issue
Common Design Type

1954, Aug. 4 Litho. *Perf. 13½*

382 CD46 39a org, cr & blk 60 38

Sao Paulo founding, 400th anniversary.

Perf. 12½x13½

1956, May 10 Photo.

Inscriptions and design in brown, red, green, ultra & yellow (buff on 10a, 40a, 90a)

383 A29 1a gray 15 15
384 A29 3a pale gray 15 15
385 A29 5a pale pink 15 15
386 A29 10a buff 15 15
387 A29 30a lt bl 24 15
388 A29 40a pale grn 32 18
389 A29 90a pale gray 1.00 30
390 A29 1.50p pink 1.25 40
Nos. 383-390 (8) 3.41
Set value 1.25

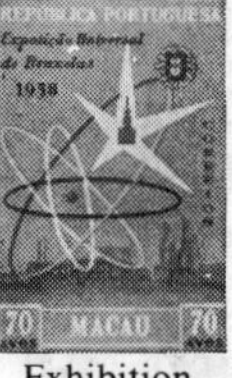

Exhibition Emblems and View — A30

Armillary Sphere — A31

1958, Nov. 8 Litho. *Perf. 14½*

391 A30 70a multi 48 24

World's Fair, Brussels, Apr. 17-Oct. 19.

Tropical Medicine Congress Issue
Common Design Type

Design: Cinnamomum camphora.

1958, Nov. 15 *Perf. 13½*

392 CD47 20a multi 2.00 1.25

1960, June 25 Litho. *Perf. 13½*

393 A31 2p multi 1.25 60

Issued to commemorate the 500th anniversary of the death of Prince Henry the Navigator.

Sports Issue
Common Design Type

Sports: 10a, Field hockey. 16a, Wrestling. 20a, Table tennis. 50a, Motorcycling. 1.20p, Relay race. 2.50p, Badminton.

1962, Feb. 9 *Perf. 13½*

Multicolored Design

394 CD48 10a bl & yel grn 20 15
395 CD48 16a brt pink 90 40
396 CD48 20a orange 70 48
397 CD48 50a rose 70 48
398 CD48 1.20p bl & beige 2.00 1.00
399 CD48 2.50p gray & brn 4.25 2.00
Nos. 394-399 (6) 8.75 4.51

Anti-Malaria Issue
Common Design Type

Design: Anopheles hyrcanus sinensis.

1962, Apr. 7 Litho. *Perf. 13½*

400 CD49 40a multi 1.25 55

Bank Building — A32

1964, May 16 Unwmk. *Perf. 13½*
401 A32 20a multi 1.00 48

Issued to commemorate the centenary of the National Overseas Bank of Portugal.

ITU Issue
Common Design Type

1965, May 17 Litho. *Perf. 14½*
402 CD52 10a pale grn & multi 1.25 60

National Revolution Issue
Common Design Type

Design: 10a, Infante D. Henrique School and Count de S. Januario Hospital.

1966, May 28 Litho. *Perf. 11½*
403 CD53 10a multi 80 35

Drummer, 1548 — A32a

Designs: 15a, Soldier with sword, 1548. 20a, Harquebusier, 1649. 40a, Infantry officer, 1783. 50a, Infantry soldier, 1783. 60a, Colonial infantry soldier (Indian), 1902. 1p, Colonial infantry soldier (Chinese), 1903. 3p, Colonial infantry soldier (Chinese) 1904.

1966, Aug. 8 Litho. *Perf. 13*
404 A32a 10a multi 40 28
405 A32a 15a multi 50 28
406 A32a 20a multi 50 28
407 A32a 40a multi 70 35
408 A32a 50a multi 70 35
409 A32a 60a multi 1.00 48
410 A32a 1p multi 1.75 55
411 A32a 3p multi 4.50 1.75
Nos. 404-411 (8) 10.05 4.32

Navy Club Issue, 1967
Common Design Type

Designs: 10a, Capt. Oliveira E. Carmo and armed launch Vega. 20a, Capt. Silva Junior and frigate Dom Fernando.

1967, Jan. 31 Litho. *Perf. 13*
412 CD54 10a multi 40 20
413 CD54 20a multi 1.00 48

Arms of Pope Paul VI and Golden Rose — A33

Cabral Monument, Lisbon — A34

1967, May 13 *Perf. 12½x13*
414 A33 50a multi 80 35

Issued to commemorate the 50th anniversary of the apparition of the Virgin Mary to three shepherd children at Fatima.

Cabral Issue

Design: 70a, Cabral monument, Belmonte.

1968, Apr. 22 Litho. *Perf. 14*
415 A34 20a multi 80 40
416 A34 70a multi 1.50 48

500th anniversary of the birth of Pedro Alvares Cabral, navigator who took possession of Brazil for Portugal.

Admiral Coutinho Issue
Common Design Type

Design: 20a, Adm. Coutinho with sextant (vert.).

1969, Feb. 17 Litho. *Perf. 14*
417 CD55 20a multi 40 28

Church of Our Lady of the Relics, Vidigueira A35

Bishop D. Belchior Carneiro A36

Vasco da Gama Issue

1969, Aug. 29 Litho. *Perf. 14*
418 A35 1p multi 70 28

Issued to commemorate the 500th anniversary of the birth of Vasco da Gama (1469-1524), navigator.

Administration Reform Issue
Common Design Type

1969, Sept. 25 Litho. *Perf. 14*
419 CD56 90a multi 70 35

1969, Oct. 16 Litho. *Perf. 13*
420 A36 50a multi 60 28

Issued to commemorate the 4th centenary of the founding of the Santa Casa da Misericordia in Macao.

King Manuel I Issue

Portal of Mother Church, Golega — A37

1969, Dec. 1 Litho. *Perf. 14*
421 A37 30a multi 50 28

Issued to commemorate the 500th anniversary of the birth of King Manuel I.

Marshal Carmona Issue
Common Design Type

Design: 5a, Antonio Oscar Carmona in general's uniform.

1970, Nov. 15 Litho. *Perf. 14*
422 CD57 5a multi 50 28

Dragon Mask — A38

1971, Sept. 30 *Perf. 13½*
423 A38 5a lt bl & multi 20 15
424 A38 10a Lion mask 40 20

Lusiads Issue

Portuguese Delegation at Chinese Court — A39

1972, May 25 Litho. *Perf. 13*
425 A39 20a cit & multi 50 28

4th centenary of publication of The Lusiads by Luiz Camoens.

Olympic Games Issue
Common Design Type

Design: Hockey and Olympic emblem.

1972, June 20 *Perf. 14x13½*
426 CD59 50a multi 50 28

Lisbon-Rio de Janeiro Flight Issue
Common Design Type

Design: "Santa Cruz" landing in Rio de Janeiro.

1972, Sept. 20 Litho. *Perf. 13½*
427 CD60 5p multi 4.50 1.75

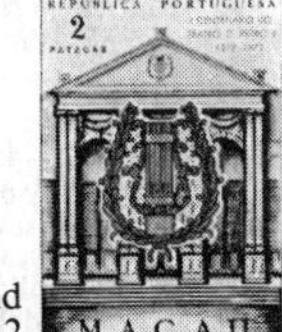

Pedro V Theater and Lyre — A42

1972, Dec. 25 Litho. *Perf. 13½*
428 A42 2p multi 1.50 55

Centenary of Pedro V Theater, Macao.

WMO Centenary Issue
Common Design Type

1973, Dec. 15 Litho. *Perf. 13*
429 CD61 20a bl grn & multi 60 28

Viscount St. Januario — A44

Design: 60a, Hospital, 1874 and 1974.

1974, Jan. 25 Litho. *Perf. 13½*
430 A44 15a multi 20 15
431 A44 60a multi 60 20
Set value 26

Centenary of Viscount St. Januario Hospital, Macao.

Macao stamps can be mounted in Scott's annual Portugal Supplement.

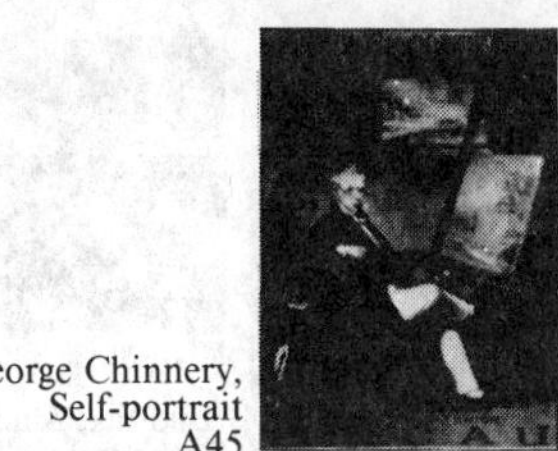
George Chinnery, Self-portrait A45

1974, Sept. 23 Litho. *Perf. 14*
432 A45 30a multi 60 28

George Chinnery (1774-1852), English painter who lived in Macao.

Macao-Taipa Bridge — A46

Design: 2.20p, Different view of bridge.

1974, Oct. 7 Litho. *Perf. 14x13½*
433 A46 20a multi 30 15
434 A46 2.20p multi 1.70 55

Inauguration of the Macao-Taipa Bridge.

Man Raising Banner A47

1975, Apr. 25 *Perf. 12*
435 A47 10a ocher & multi 30 20
436 A47 1p multi 1.25 70

Revolution of Apr. 25, 1974, 1st anniv.

Pou Chai Pagoda — A48

Design: 20p, Tin Hau Pagoda.

1976, Jan. 30 Litho. *Perf. 13½x13*
437 A48 10p multi 6.00 2.00
438 A48 20p multi 14.00 2.75

A 1p stamp for the 400th anniv. of the Macao Diocese was prepared but not issued. Some copies were sold in Lisbon.

"The Law" — A50

1978 Litho. *Perf. 13½*
440 A50 5a blk, dk & lt bl 30 15
441 A50 2p blk, org brn & buff 2.00 1.00
442 A50 5p blk, ol & yel grn 3.75 1.75

Legislative Assembly, Aug. 9, 1976.

Nos. 376, 378, 382, 434 Surcharged

1979, Nov.
443 A28 10a on 16a 1.50 70
444 A28 30a on 39a (#378) 1.50 70
445 CD46 30a on 39a (#382) 10.00 2.75
446 A46 2p on 2.20p 4.00 1.00

Luis de Camoens (1524-80), Poet — A51

Buddha, Macao Cathedral — A52

1981, June **Litho.** ***Perf. 13½***

447 A51 10a multi 15 15
448 A51 30a multi 20 15
449 A51 1p multi 60 28
450 A51 3p multi 1.75 55

1981, Sept.

451 A52 15a multi 15 15
452 A52 40a multi 20 15
453 A52 50a multi 30 15
454 A52 60a multi 40 15
455 A52 1p multi 60 28
456 A52 2.20p multi 1.50 48
Nos. 451-456 (6) 3.15 1.36

Transcultural Psychiatry Symposium.

No. 431 Surcharged

1981 **Litho.** ***Perf. 13½***

457 A44 30a on 60a multi 40 20

Health Services Building A53

Designs: Public Buildings and Monuments.

1982, June 10 **Litho.** ***Perf. 12x12½***

458 A53 30a shown 20 15
459 A53 40a Guia Lighthouse 25 15
460 A53 1p Portas do Cerco 70 24
461 A53 2p Luis de Camoes Museum 1.40 48
462 A53 10p School Welfare Service Building 7.00 2.50
Nos. 458-462 (5) 9.55 3.52

See Nos. 472-476, 489-493.

Autumn Festivals A54

Designs: Painted paper lanterns.

1982, Oct. 1 ***Perf. 12x11½***

463 A54 40a multi 25 15
464 A54 1p multi 70 24
465 A54 2p multi 1.40 48
466 A54 5p multi 3.50 1.25

Geographical Position — A55

1982, Dec. 1 **Litho.** ***Perf. 13***

467 A55 50a Aerial view 35 15
468 A55 3p Map 2.10 70

World Communications Year — A56

1983, Feb. 16 ***Perf. 13½***

469 A56 60a Telephone operators 40 15
470 A56 3p Mailman, mailbox 2.10 70
471 A56 6p Globe, satellites 4.25 1.40

Architecture Type of 1982

1983, May 12 **Litho.** ***Perf. 13***

472 A53 10a Social Welfare Institute 15 15
473 A53 80a St. Joseph's Seminary 50 18
474 A53 1.50p St. Dominic's Church 1.05 38
475 A53 2.50p St. Paul's Church ruins 1.75 60
476 A53 7.50p Senate House 5.25 1.75
Nos. 472-476 (5) 8.70 3.06

Medicinal Plants A57

1983, July 14 **Litho.** ***Perf. 13½x14***

477 A57 20a Asclepias curassavica 20 15
478 A57 40a Acanthus ilicifolius 30 20
479 A57 60a Melastoma sanguineum 50 20
480 A57 70a Nelumbo nucifera 60 20
481 A57 1.50p Bombax malabaricum 1.40 55
482 A57 2.50p Hibiscus mutabilis 2.00 70
a. Souv. sheet of 6, #477-482 7.00 85
Nos. 477-482 (6) 5.00 2.00

No. 482a sold for 6.50p.

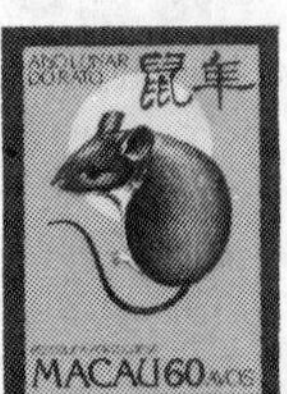

16th Century Discoveries A58 A59

1983, Nov. 15 **Litho.** ***Perf. 13½x14***

483 A58 4p multi 2.00 70
484 A59 4p multi 2.00 70

Nos. 483-484 printed se-tenant.

New Year 1984 (Year of the Rat) — A60

1984, Jan. 25 **Litho.** ***Perf. 13½***

485 A60 60a multi 25 15
a. Bklt. pane of 5 1.50

See Nos. 504, 522, 540, 560, 583, 611.

Centenary of Macao Postage Stamps — A61

Design of First Stamp Issue, 1884.

1984, Mar. 1 **Litho.** ***Perf. 12½***

486 A61 40a org & blk 15 15
487 A61 3p gray & blk 90 35
488 A61 5p sep & blk 1.50 55
a. Souv. sheet of 3, #486-488 2.50 1.00

Architecture Type of 1982

1984, May 18 **Litho.** ***Perf. 13½***

489 A53 20a Holy House of Mercy 15 15
490 A53 60a St. Lawrence Church 15 15
491 A53 90a King Peter V Theater 22 15
492 A53 3p Palace of St. Sancha 72 24
493 A53 15p Moorish barracks 3.50 1.25
Nos. 489-493 (5) 4.74
Set value 1.70

Birds, Ausipex '84 Emblem A62

1984, Sept. 21 **Litho.** ***Perf. 13***

494 A62 30a Kingfishers 15 15
495 A62 40a European jay 15 15
496 A62 50a White eyes 20 15
497 A62 70a Hoopoe 25 15
498 A62 2.50p Peking nightingale 90 28
499 A62 6p Wild duck 1.75 55
Nos. 494-499 (6) 3.40
Set value 1.08

Philakorea '84 Emblem, Fishing Boats A63

1984, Oct. 22 **Litho.**

500 A63 20a Hok lou t'eng 15 15
501 A63 60a Tai t'ong 18 15
502 A63 2p Tai mei chai 60 24
503 A63 5p Ch'at pong t'o 1.50 60
Set value 95

New Year Type of 1984

1985, Feb. 13 **Litho.** ***Perf. 13½***

504 A60 1p Buffalo 40 15
a. Bklt. pane of 5 2.00

Intl. Youth Year — A65

1985, Apr. 19 **Litho.** ***Perf. 13½***

505 A65 2.50p shown 60 60
506 A65 3p Clasped hands 72 72

Visit of President Eanes of Portugal A66

1985, May 27 **Litho.**

507 A66 1.50p multi 50 50

Luis de Camoens Museum, 25th Anniv. — A67

Silk paintings by Chen Chi Yun.

1985, June 27 **Litho.**

508 A67 2.50p Two travelers, hermit 85 85
509 A67 2.50p Traveling merchant 85 85
510 A67 2.50p Conversation in a garden 85 85
511 A67 2.50p Veranda of a house 85 85
a. Strip of 4, #508-511 3.50 3.50

Butterflies, World Tourism Assoc. Emblem — A68

1985, Sept. 27 **Litho.**

512 A68 30a Euploea midamus 15 15
513 A68 50a Hebomoia glaucippe 15 15
514 A68 70a Lethe confusa 18 18
515 A68 2p Heliophorus epicles 50 50
516 A68 4p Euthalia phemius seitzi 1.25 1.25
517 A68 7.50p Troides helena 2.00 2.00
a. Sheet of 6, Nos. 512-517 4.00 4.00
Nos. 512-517 (6) 4.23 4.23

World Tourism Day.

Cargo Boats — A69

Designs: 50a, Tou. 70a, Veng Seng Lei motor junk. 1p, Tong Heng Long No. 2 motor junk. 6p, Fong Vong San cargo ship.

1985, Oct. 25 ***Perf. 14***

518 A69 50a multi 15 15
519 A69 70a multi 18 18
520 A69 1p multi 25 25
521 A69 6p multi 1.50 1.50

New Year Type of 1984

1986, Feb. 3 ***Perf. 13½***

522 A60 1.50p Tiger 38 38
a. Bklt. pane of 5 2.00

City of Macau, 400th Anniv. A71

1986, Apr. 10 **Litho.** ***Perf. 13½***

523 A71 2.20p multi 55 55

Musical Instruments A72

1986, May 22

524 A72 20a Suo-na 15 15
525 A72 50a Sheng 15 15
526 A72 60a Er-hu 15 15
527 A72 70a Ruan 18 18
528 A72 5p Cheng 1.25 1.25
529 A72 8p Pi-pa 2.00 2.00
a. Souvenir sheet of 6, #524-529 3.75 3.75
Nos. 524-529 (6) 3.88 3.88

AMERIPEX '86.

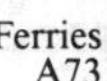

Ferries
A73

1986, Aug. 28 Litho. *Perf. 13*

530 A73 10a Hydrofoil 15 15
531 A73 40a Hovermarine 15 15
532 A73 3p Jetfoil 85 85
533 A73 7.5p High-speed ferry 2.00 2.00

Fortresses
A74

1986, Oct. 3 Litho. *Perf. 12½*

534 A74 2p Taipa 50 50
535 A74 2p Sao Paulo do Monte 50 50
536 A74 2p Our Lady of Guia 50 50
537 A74 2p Sao Francisco 50 50
a. Strip of 4, #534-537 3.50 3.50

Macao Security Forces, 10th anniv. No. 537a has continuous design.

Dr. Sun Yat-sen
A75 A76

1986, Nov. 12 Litho. *Perf. 12½*

538 A75 70a multi *1.00 1.00*

Souvenir Sheet

539 A76 1.30p shown *5.00 5.00*

New Year Type of 1984

1987, Jan. 21 *Perf. 13½*

540 A60 1.50p Hare 38 38
a. Bklt. pane of 5 2.00

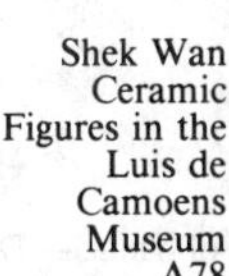

Shek Wan Ceramic Figures in the Luis de Camoens Museum
A78

1987, Apr. 10 Litho. *Perf. 13½*

541 A78 2.20p Medicine man 55 55
542 A78 2.20p Choi San, god of good fortune 55 55
543 A78 2.20p Yi, sun god 55 55
544 A78 2.20p Chung Kuei, conqueror of demons 55 55

Printed se-tenant in blocks of four.

Dragon Boat Festival
A79

1987, May 29 Litho. *Perf. 13½*

545 A79 50a Dragon boat race 15 15
546 A79 5p Figurehead 1.25 1.25

Decorated Fans — A80
Casino Gambling — A81

1987, July 29 Litho. *Perf. 12½*

547 A80 30a multi 15 15
548 A80 70a multi, diff. 20 20
549 A80 1p multi, diff. 28 28
550 A80 6p multi, diff. 1.75 1.75
a. Souv. sheet of 4, Nos. 547-550 2.50 2.50

1987, Sept. 30 *Perf. 13½*

551 A81 20a Fan-tan 15 15
552 A81 40a Cussec 15 15
553 A81 4p Baccarat 1.15 1.15
554 A81 7p Roulette 2.00 2.00

Traditional Transportation — A82

1987, Nov. 18 Litho. *Perf. 13½*

555 A82 10a Market wagon 15 15
556 A82 70a Sedan chair 20 20
557 A82 90a Rickshaw 28 28
558 A82 10p Tricycle rickshaw 2.85 2.85

Souvenir Sheet

559 A82 7.50p Sedan chair, diff. 2.25 2.25

New Year Type of 1984

1988, Feb. 10 Litho. *Perf. 13½*

560 A60 2.50p Dragon 75 75
a. Bklt. pane of 5 3.75

Wildlife Protection
A84

1988, Apr. 14 Litho. *Perf. 12½x12*

561 A84 3p Erinacens europaeus 80 80
562 A84 3p Meles meles 80 80
563 A84 3p Lutra lutra 80 80
564 A84 3p Manis pentadactyla 80 80
a. Strip of 4, Nos. 561-564 3.20 3.20

World Health Organization, 40th Anniv. — A85

1988, June 1 Litho. *Perf. 13½*

565 A85 60a Breast-feeding 15 15
566 A85 80a Immunization 20 20
567 A85 2.40p Blood donation 60 60

Modes of Transportation — A86

1988, July 15 Litho.

568 A86 20a Bicycles 15 15
569 A86 50a Vespa, Lambretta 15 15
570 A86 3.30p 1907 Rover 20hp 82 82
571 A86 5p 1912 Renault delivery truck 1.25 1.25

Souvenir Sheet

572 A86 7.50p 1930s Sedan 1.90 1.90

1988 Summer Olympics, Seoul
A87

1988, Sept. 19 Litho.

573 A87 40a Hurdles 15 15
574 A87 60a Basketball 15 15
575 A87 1p Soccer 25 25
576 A87 8p Table tennis 2.00 2.00
577 Sheet of 5, Nos. 573-576, 577a 3.75 3.75
a. A87 5p Tae kwon do 1.25 1.25

World Post Day — A88
35th Macao Grand Prix — A89

1988, Oct. 10 Litho. *Perf. 14*

578 A88 13.40p Electronic mail 3.35 3.35
579 A88 40p Express mail 10.00 10.00

1988, Nov. 24 Litho. *Perf. 12½*

580 A89 80a Sedan 20 20
581 A89 2.80p Motorcycle 70 70
582 A89 7p Formula 3 1.75 1.75
a. Souv. sheet of 3, Nos. 580-582 2.25 2.25

New Year Type of 1984

1989, Jan. 20 Litho. *Perf. 13½*

583 A60 3p Snake 75 75
a. Bklt. pane of 5 3.75

Occupations
A91

1989, Mar. 1 Litho. *Perf. 12x12½*

584 A91 50a Water carrier 15 15
585 A91 1p Tan-kya woman 25 25
586 A91 4p Tin-tin (junk) man 1.00 1.00
587 A91 5p Tofu peddler 1.25 1.25

See Nos. 612-615, 640-643.

Watercolors by George Smirnoff in the Luis de Camoens Museum
A92

1989, Apr. 10 Litho. *Perf. 12½x12*

588 A92 2p multi (4-1) 50 50
589 A92 2p multi (4-2) 50 50
590 A92 2p multi (4-3) 50 50
591 A92 2p multi (4-4) 50 50
a. Strip of 4, Nos. 588-591 2.00 2.00

Snakes
A93

1989, July 7 Litho.

592 A93 2.50p *Naja naja* 62 62
593 A93 2.50p *Bungarus fasciatus* 62 62
594 A93 2.50p *Trimeresurus albolabris* 62 62
595 A93 2.50p *Elaphe radiata* 62 62
a. Strip of 4, Nos. 592-595 2.50 2.50

Traditional Games — A94

1989, July 31 Litho. *Perf. 13½*

596 A94 10a Talu 15 15
597 A94 60a Triol 15 15
598 A94 3.30p Chiquia 82 82
599 A94 5p Xadrez Chines 1.25 1.25

Seaplanes — A95

1989, Oct. 9 Litho.

600 A95 50a Over church 15 15
601 A95 70a American over lighthouse 18 18
602 A95 2.80p shown 70 70
603 A95 4p Over junk 1.00 1.00

Souvenir Sheet

604 A95 7.50p Over harbor 1.90 1.90

No. 604 contains one 40x30mm stamp.

World Stamp Expo '89, Washington, DC — A96

1989, Nov. 17 Litho. *Perf. 12½*

605 A96 40a Malaca 15 15
606 A96 70a Thailand 18 18
607 A96 90a India 22 22
608 A96 2.50p Japan 62 62
609 A96 7.50p China 1.85 1.85
Nos. 605-609 (5) 3.02 3.02

Souvenir Sheet

610	Sheet of 6, #605-609, 610a	3.75	3.75
a.	A96 3p Macao	75	75

Influence of the Portuguese in the Far East.

New Year Type of 1984

1990, Jan. 19 Litho. *Perf. 13½*

611	A60 4p Horse		1.00	1.00
a.	Bklt. pane of 5		5.00	

Occupations Type of 1989

1990, Mar. 1 Litho. *Perf. 12x12½*

612	A91	30a Long chau singer	15	15
613	A91	70a Cobbler	18	18
614	A91	1.50p Scribe	38	38
615	A91	7.50p Net fisherman	1.85	1.85

Souvenir Sheet

Penny Black, 150th Anniv. — A99

1990, May 3 Litho. *Perf. 12*

616	A99 10p multicolored	2.50	2.50

Stamp World London 90.

Lutianus Malabaricus A100

1990, June 8 *Perf. 12x12½*

617	A100 2.40p shown	62	62
618	A100 2.40p Epinephelus megachir	62	62
619	A100 2.40p Macropodus opercularis	62	62
620	A100 2.40p Ophiocephalus maculatus	62	62
a.	Strip of 4, #617-620	2.50	2.50

Decorative Porcelain A101

1990, Aug. 24 Litho. *Perf. 12½*

621	A101 3p shown	75	75
622	A101 3p Furniture	75	75
623	A101 3p Toys	75	75
624	A101 3p Artificial flowers	75	75
a.	Souvenir sheet of 4, #621-624	3.00	3.00

Asian Games, Beijing — A102

1990, Sept. 22 Litho. *Perf. 13½*

625	A102	80a Cycling	20	20
626	A102	1p Swimming	25	25
627	A102	3p Judo	75	75
628	A102	4.20p Shooting	1.05	1.05

Souvenir Sheet

629	Sheet of 5, #625-628, 629a	3.95	3.95
a.	A102 6p Martial arts	1.50	1.50

Compass Roses from Portuguese Charts — A103

Charts by 16th century cartographers: Lazaro Luis, Diogo Homem, Fernao Vaz Dourado, and Luiz Teixeira.

1990, Oct. 9 Litho. *Perf. 13½*

630	A103	50a shown	15	15
631	A103	1p multi, diff.	25	25
632	A103	3.50p multi, diff.	90	90
633	A103	6.50p multi, diff.	1.60	1.60

Souvenir Sheet

634	A103	5p multi, diff.	1.30	1.30

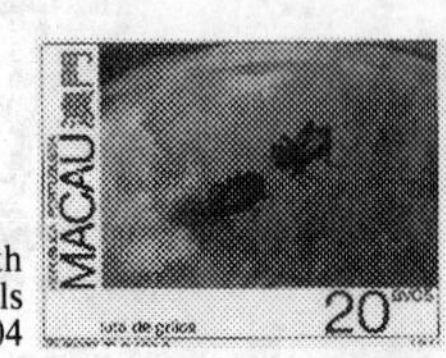

Games with Animals A104

1990, Nov. 15 Litho. *Perf. 14*

635	A104 20a Cricket fight	15	15
636	A104 80a Bird fight	20	20
637	A104 1p Greyhound race	25	25
638	A104 10p Horse race	2.50	2.50

Year of the Sheep — A105

1991, Feb. 8 Litho. *Perf. 13½*

639	A105 4.50p multicolored	1.15	1.15
a.	Perf. 13½ vert.	1.15	1.15
b.	Booklet pane of 5, #639a	5.85	5.85

Occupations Type of 1987

1991, Mar. 1 *Perf. 14*

640	A91	80a Knife grinder	20	20
641	A91	1.70p Flour puppet vender	45	45
642	A91	3.50p Street barber	90	90
643	A91	4.20p Fortune teller	1.05	1.05

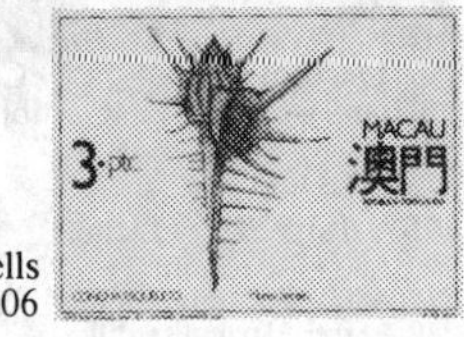

Shells A106

1991, Apr. 18 Litho. *Perf. 14*

644	A106 3p Murex pecten	75	75
645	A106 3p Harpa harpa	75	75
646	A106 3p Chicoreus rosarius	75	75
647	A106 3p Tonna zonata	75	75
a.	Strip of 4, #644-647	3.00	3.00

Chinese Opera — A107

Various performers in costume.

1991, June 5 Litho. *Perf. 13½*

648	A107 60a multicolored	15	15
649	A107 80a multicolored	20	20
650	A107 1p multicolored	26	26
651	A107 10p multicolored	2.60	2.60

Flowers A108

Designs: 1.70p, Delonix regia. 3p, Ipomoea cairica. 3.50p, Jasminum mesnyi. 4.20p, Bauhinia variegata.

1991, Oct. 9 Litho. *Perf. 13½*

652	A108 1.70p multicolored	45	45
653	A108 3p multicolored	78	78
654	A108 3.50p multicolored	90	90
655	A108 4.20p multicolored	1.10	1.10
a.	Souvenir sheet of 4, #652-655	3.25	3.25

Cultural Exchange A109

Namban screen: No. 656, Unloading boat.

1991, Nov. 16 Litho. *Perf. 12*

656	A109 4.20p multicolored	1.10	1.10
657	A109 4.20p shown	1.10	1.10
a.	Souvenir sheet of 2, #656-657	2.20	2.20

AIR POST STAMPS

Stamps of 1934 Overprinted or Surcharged in Black

Avião — a

Avião 5 avos — b

1936 Wmk. 232 *Perf. 11½*

C1	A17 (a)	2a bl grn	1.65	70
C2	A17 (a)	3a violet	1.65	70
C3	A17 (b)	5a on 6a brn	1.65	70
C4	A17 (a)	7a brt rose	1.65	70
C5	A17 (a)	8a brt bl	3.00	90
C6	A17 (a)	15a maroon	9.75	4.00
		Nos. C1-C6 (6)	19.35	7.70

Common Design Type
Name and Value in Black

Perf. 13½x13

1938, Aug. 1 Engr. Unwmk.

C7	CD39	1a scarlet	18	15
C8	CD39	2a purple	18	15
C9	CD39	3a orange	28	28
C10	CD39	5a ultra	60	38
C11	CD39	10a lil brn	75	38
C12	CD39	20a dk grn	1.25	90
C13	CD39	50a red brn	1.90	1.10
C14	CD39	70a rose car	3.00	1.40
C15	CD39	1p magenta	5.25	5.00
		Nos. C7-C15 (9)	13.39	9.74

No. C13 exists with overprint "Exposicao Internacional de Nova York, 1939-1940" and Trylon and Perisphere.

Catalogue values for unused stamps in this section, from this point to the end of the section, are for never hinged items.

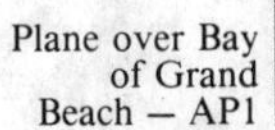

Plane over Bay of Grand Beach — AP1

1960, Dec. 11 Litho. *Perf. 14*

C16	AP1	50a shown	48	18
C17	AP1	76a Penha Chapel	80	28
C18	AP1	3p Macao	1.40	60
C19	AP1	5p Bairro de Mong Ha	2.50	90
C20	AP1	10p Penha and Bay	5.00	1.25
		Nos. C16-C20 (5)	10.18	3.21

No. C17 Surcharged

1979, Aug. 3 Litho. *Perf. 14*

C21	AP1 70a on 76a multi	5.75	1.50

POSTAGE DUE STAMPS

Numeral of Value — D1

Perf. 11½x12

1904, July Typo. Unwmk.

Name and Value in Black

J1	D1	½a gray grn	24	24
a.		Name & value inverted	10.00	10.00
J2	D1	1a yel grn	28	28
J3	D1	2a slate	28	28
J4	D1	4a pale brn	28	28
J5	D1	5a red org	85	70
J6	D1	8a gray brn	85	70

J7 D1 12a red brn 1.00 70
J8 D1 20a dl bl 2.00 1.40
J9 D1 40a carmine 2.75 2.50
J10 D1 50a orange 4.75 4.00
J11 D1 1p gray vio 10.00 6.75
Nos. J1-J11 (11) 23.28 17.83

Issued without gum: Nos. J7-J11.

Issue of 1904 Overprinted in Carmine or Green

1911
J12 D1 ½a gray grn 15 15
J13 D1 1a yel grn 15 15
J14 D1 2a slate 15 15
J15 D1 4a pale brn 18 18
J16 D1 5a orange 18 18
J17 D1 8a gray brn 18 18
J18 D1 12a red brn 48 40
J19 D1 20a dl bl 1.00 85
J20 D1 40a car (G) 1.75 1.25
J21 D1 50a orange 3.50 2.50
J22 D1 1p gray vio 4.50 3.50
Nos. J12-J22 (11) 12.22 9.49

Issued without gum: Nos. J19-J22.

Issue of 1904 Overprinted in Red or Green

1914
J22A D1 ½a gray grn *475.00 425.00*
J23 D1 1a yel grn 35 35
J24 D1 2a slate 35 35
J25 D1 4a pale brn 35 35
J26 D1 5a orange 40 35
J27 D1 8a gray brn 40 35
J28 D1 12a red brn 40 35
J29 D1 20a dl bl 1.50 1.40
J30 D1 40a car (G) 4.00 2.50
a. Double ovpt., red and grn 15.00 8.00
J31 D1 50a orange 4.00 2.50
J32 D1 1p gray vio 10.00 5.00
Nos. J23-J32 (10) *21.75 13.50*

Issued without gum: Nos. J28, J30-J32.

D2

Name and Value in Black

1947 Typo. *Perf. 11½x12*
J33 D2 1a red vio 1.00 85
J34 D2 2a purple 1.00 85
J35 D2 4a dk bl 1.00 85
J36 D2 5a chocolate 1.00 85
J37 D2 8a red vio 1.00 85
J38 D2 12a org brn 3.00 85
J39 D2 20a yel grn 1.75 2.00
J40 D2 40a brt car 3.00 2.25
J41 D2 50a org yel 7.50 5.00
J42 D2 1p blue 7.50 3.50
Nos. J33-J42 (10) 27.75 17.85

Stamps of 1934 Surcharged "PORTEADO" and New Values in Carmine

1949, May 1 Wmk. 232
J43 A17 1a on 4a blk 1.00 85
J44 A17 2a on 6a brn 1.00 85
J45 A17 4a on 8a brt bl 1.25 85
J46 A17 5a on 10a red org 1.50 85
J47 A17 8a on 12a dk bl 1.50 1.40
J48 A17 12a on 30a ap grn 2.00 1.50
J49 A17 20a on 40a vio 2.00 1.50
Nos. J43-J49 (7) 10.25 7.80

Catalogue values for unused stamps in this section, from this point to the end of the section, are for Never Hinged items.

Nos. 348, 349 and 351 Overprinted or Surcharged in Black or Carmine

PORTEADO

1951, June 6 Unwmk.
J50 A21 1a org yel, *lem* 28 18
J51 A21 2a dk grn, *bl* (C) 28 18
J52 A21 7a on 10a brt pink, *bl* 28 18

Common Design Type

1952 Photo. & Typo. *Perf. 14*
Numeral in Red; Frame Multicolored
J53 CD45 1a vio bl 15 15
J54 CD45 3a chocolate 15 15
J55 CD45 5a indigo 15 15
J56 CD45 10a dk red 32 24
J57 CD45 30a indigo 40 30
J58 CD45 1p chocolate 1.25 90
Nos. J53-J58 (6) 2.42
Set value 1.60

WAR TAX STAMPS

Victory
WT1

1919, Aug. 11 Unwmk. *Perf. 15x14*
Overprinted in Black or Carmine
MR1 WT1 2a green 1.40 1.00
MR2 WT1 11a grn (C) 2.00 1.40

Nos. MR1-MR2 were also for use in Timor. A 9a value was issued for revenue use.

NEWSPAPER STAMPS

King Luiz
N1 N2

Typographed and Embossed
1892-93 Unwmk. *Perf. 12½, 13½*
Black Surcharge
P1 N1 2½r on 40r choc 75 70
a. Inverted surcharge 15.00 15.00
P2 N1 2½r on 80r gray 75 70
a. Inverted surcharge 15.00 15.00
b. Double surcharge
c. Perf. 13½ 15.00 11.00
P3 N2 2½r on 10r grn ('93) 75 70
a. Double surcharge

N3 N4

Perf. 11½, 12½, 13½
1893-94 Typo.
P4 N3 2½r brown 35 28
P5 N4 ½a on 2½r brn (Bk) ('94) 75 55
a. Double surcharge

POSTAL TAX STAMPS

Pombal Commemorative Issue
Common Design Types
Perf. 12½
1925, Nov. 3 Engr. Unwmk.
RA1 CD28 2a red org & blk 50 70
RA2 CD29 2a red org & blk 50 70
RA3 CD30 2a red org & blk 50 70

Symbolical of Charity
PT1 PT2

1930, Dec. 25 Litho. *Perf. 11*
RA4 PT1 5a dk brn, *yel* 14.00 9.00

1945-47 *Perf. 11½, 12, 10*
RA5 PT2 5a blk brn, *yel* 10.50 7.50
RA6 PT2 5a bl, *bluish* ('47) 8.50 6.75
RA7 PT2 10a grn, *citron* 4.50 3.75
RA8 PT2 15a org, *buff* 4.50 3.75
RA9 PT2 20a rose red, *sal* 9.75 6.75
RA10 PT2 50a red vio, *pnksh* 5.00 3.00

Catalogue values for unused stamps in this section, from this point to the end of the section, are for Never Hinged items.

1953-56 *Perf. 10½x11½*
RA11 PT2 10a bl, *pale grn* ('56) 40 18
RA12 PT2 20a chocolate, *yel* 5.75 2.50
RA13 PT2 50a car, *pale rose* 5.25 2.75

1958 *Perf. 12x11½*
RA14 PT2 1a gray grn, *grnsh* 16 15
RA15 PT2 2a rose lilac, *grysh* 16 15
Set value 18

Type of 1945-47 Redrawn
Imprint: "Lito. Imp. Nac.-Macau"

1961-66 *Perf. 11*
RA16 PT2 1a gray grn, *grnsh* 16 15
RA17 PT2 2a rose lil, *grysh* 16 15
RA18 PT2 10a bl, *pale grn* ('62) 24 18
RA19 PT2 20a brn, *yel* ('66) 32 18
Set value 54

Nos. RA16-RA19 have accent added to "E" in "Assistencia."
Nos. RA4-RA19 were issued without gum.

POSTAL TAX DUE STAMPS

Pombal Commemorative Issue
Common Design Types

1925 Unwmk. *Perf. 12½*
RAJ1 CD31 4a red org & blk 70 70
RAJ2 CD32 4a red org & blk 70 70
RAJ3 CD33 4a red org & blk 70 70

MADAGASCAR

Malagasy Republic

LOCATION — Large island off the coast of southeastern Africa
GOVT. — Republic
AREA — 226,658 sq. mi.
POP. — 9,735,000 (est. 1984)
CAPITAL — Antananarivo

Madagascar became a French protectorate in 1885 and a French colony in 1896 following several years of dispute among France, Great Britain, and the native government. The colony administered the former protectorates of Anjouan, Grand Comoro, Mayotte, Diego-Suarez, Nossi-Be and Sainte-Marie de Madagascar. Previous issues of postage stamps are found under these individual headings. The Malagasy Republic succeeded the colony in 1958 and became the Democratic Republic of Madagascar in 1975.

For Madagascar's British Consular Mail stamps of 1884-1886, see Vol. 1.

100 Centimes = 1 Franc
100 Centimes = 1 Ariary (1976)

Catalogue values for unused stamps in this country are for Never Hinged items, beginning with Scott 241 in the regular postage section, Scott B15 in the semi-postal section, Scott C37 in the airpost section, and Scott J31 in the postage due section.

French Offices in Madagascar

The general issues of French Colonies were used in these offices in addition to the stamps listed here.

Stamps of French Colonies Surcharged in Black:

25 05 5
a b c

1889 Unwmk. *Perf. 14x13½*
Overprint Type "a"
1 A9 05c on 10c blk, *lav* 200.00 80.00
a. Inverted surcharge 900.00 650.00
2 A9 05c on 25c blk, *rose* 200.00 80.00
a. Inverted surcharge 900.00 650.00
b. 25c on 10c lav (error) *4,500. 3,500.*
3 A9 25c on 40c red, *straw* 190.00 65.00
a. Inverted surcharge 825.00 575.00

1891
Overprint Type "b"
4 A9 05c on 40c red, *straw* 100.00 42.50
5 A9 15c on 25c blk, *rose* 100.00 42.50
a. Surcharge vertical 100.00 62.50
Overprint Type "c"
6 A9 5c on 10c blk, *lav* 140.00 65.00
a. Double surcharge 400.00
7 A9 5c on 25c blk, *rose* 140.00 65.00

Forgeries of Nos. 1-7 exist.

A4

1891 Type-set *Imperf.*
Without Gum
8 A4 5c blk, *green* 65.00 14.00
9 A4 10c blk, *lt bl* 60.00 15.00
10 A4 15c ultra, *pale bl* 60.00 15.00
11 A4 25c brn, *buff* 10.00 6.00
12 A4 1fr blk, *yellow* 650.00 190.00
13 A4 5fr vio & blk, *lil* 1,200. 600.00

Ten varieties of each. Nos. 12-13 have been extensively forged.

Stamps of France 1876-90, Overprinted in Red or Black

POSTE FRANÇAISE
Madagascar

1895 *Perf. 14x13½*
14 A15 5c grn, *grnsh* (R) 6.00 3.50
15 A15 10c blk, *lav* (R) 22.50 14.00
16 A15 15c bl (R) 30.00 8.25
17 A15 25c blk, *rose* (R) 49.00 10.00
18 A15 40c red, *straw* (Bk) 40.00 15.00
19 A15 50c rose, *rose* (Bk) 49.00 22.00
20 A15 75c dp vio, *org* (R) 49.00 22.00
21 A15 1fr brnz grn, *straw* (Bk) 50.00 27.50
22 A15 5fr vio, *lav* (Bk) 82.50 45.00

Majunga Issue
Stamps of France, 1876-86, Surcharged with New Value

1895

Manuscript Surcharge in Red

22A A15 0,15c on 25c blk, *rose* 4,500.
22B A15 0,15c on 1fr brnz grn, *straw* 3,750.

Handstamped in Black

22C A15 15c on 25c blk, *rose* 4,000.
22D A15 15c on 1fr brnz grn, *straw* 9,000. 4,250.

Three types of "15" were used for No. 22C.

Stamps of France, 1876-84, Surcharged with New Value

1896

23 A15 5c on 1c blk, *bl* 4,000. 1,500.
24 A15 15c on 2c brn, *buff* 1,500. 750.00
25 A15 25c on 3c gray, *grysh* 1,750. 750.00
26 A15 25c on 4c cl, *lav* 4,000. 750.00
27 A15 25c on 40c red, *straw* 850.00 575.00

The oval of the 5c and 15c surcharges is smaller than that of the 25c, and it does not extend beyond the edges of the stamp as the 25c surcharge does.

Excellent counterfeits of the surcharges on Nos. 22A to 27 exist.

Issues of the Colony

Navigation and Commerce — A7

1896-1906 Typo. *Perf. 14x13½*

Colony Name in Blue or Carmine

28 A7 1c blk, *lil bl* 72 55
29 A7 2c brn, *buff* 72 55
a. Name in blue black 2.50 2.50
30 A7 4c claret, *lav* 80 55
31 A7 5c grn, *grnsh* 3.25 72
32 A7 5c yel grn ('01) 75 48
33 A7 10c blk, *lav* 3.50 80
34 A7 10c red ('00) 75 48
35 A7 15c blue, quadrille paper 4.75 55
36 A7 15c gray ('00) 80 70
37 A7 20c red, *grn* 2.50 70
38 A7 25c blk, *rose* 3.25 2.50
39 A7 25c blue ('00) 10.00 10.00
40 A7 30c brn, *bis* 4.00 2.00
41 A7 35c blk, *yel* ('06) 20.00 3.50
42 A7 40c red, *straw* 3.50 2.50
43 A7 50c car, *rose* 5.25 75
44 A7 50c brn, *az* ('00) 14.00 13.00
45 A7 75c dp vio, *org* 1.40 80
46 A7 1fr brnz grn, *straw* 5.25 1.75
a. Name in blue ('99) 14.00 7.00
47 A7 5fr red lil, *lav* ('99) 16.00 12.00
Nos. 28-47 (20) 101.19 54.88

Perf. 13½x14 stamps are counterfeits.

Surcharged in Black **05**

1902

48 A7 05c on 50c car, *rose* 3.00 3.00
a. Inverted surcharge 52.50 52.50
49 A7 10c on 5fr red lil, *lav* 11.00 9.00
a. Inverted surcharge 57.50 57.50
50 A7 15c on 1fr ol grn, *straw* 3.00 3.00
a. Inverted surcharge 57.50 57.50
b. Double surcharge 175.00 175.00

Surcharged in Black **0,01**

51 A7 0,01 on 2c brn, *buff* 3.75 3.75
a. Inverted surcharge 32.50 32.50
b. "00.1" instead of "0.01" 45.00 45.00
c. As "b" inverted
d. Comma omitted 75.00 75.00
e. Name in blue black 4.25 4.25
52 A7 0,05 on 30c brn, *bis* 4.50 4.50
a. Inverted surcharge 32.50 32.50
b. "00,5" instead of "0,05" 45.00 45.00
c. As "b" inverted 175.00 175.00
d. Comma omitted 75.00 75.00
53 A7 0,10 on 50c car, *rose* 4.50 4.50
a. Inverted surcharge 32.50 32.50
b. Comma omitted 75.00 75.00
54 A7 0,15 on 75c vio, *org* 3.75 3.75
a. Inverted surcharge 40.00 40.00
b. Comma omitted 90.00 90.00
55 A7 0,15 on 1fr ol grn, *straw* 6.75 6.75
a. Inverted surcharge 50.00 50.00
b. Comma omitted 100.00 100.00

Surcharged On Stamps of Diego-Suarez

56 A11 0,05 on 30c brn, *bis* 62.50 62.50
a. "00,5" instead of "0,05" 425.00 425.00
b. Inverted surcharge 600.00 600.00
57 A11 0,10 on 50c car, *rose* 3,250. 3,250.

Counterfeits of Nos. 56-57 exist with surcharge both normal and inverted.

Surcharged in Black **0,01**

58 A7 0,01 on 2c brn, *buff* 3.25 3.25
a. Inverted surcharge 32.50 32.50
b. Comma omitted 75.00 75.00
59 A7 0,05 on 30c brn, *bis* 3.75 3.75
a. Inverted surcharge 32.50 32.50
b. Comma omitted 75.00 75.00
60 A7 0,10 on 50c car, *rose* 3.25 3.25
a. Inverted surcharge 32.50 32.50
b. Comma omitted 90.00 90.00

Surcharged On Stamps of Diego-Suarez

61 A11 0,05 on 30c brn, *bister* 85.00 85.00
a. Inverted surcharge 600.00 600.00
62 A11 0,10 on 50c car, *rose* 3,250. 3,250.

BISECTS

During alleged stamp shortages at several Madagascar towns in 1904, it is claimed that bisects were used. After being affixed to letters, these bisects were handstamped "Affranchissement - exceptionnel - (faute de timbres)" and other inscriptions of similar import. The stamps bisected were 10c, 20c, 30c and 50c denominations of Madagascar type A7 and Diego-Suarez type A11. The editors believe these provisionals were unnecessary and speculative.

Zebu, Traveler's Tree and Lemur — A8

Transportation by Sedan Chair — A9

1903 Engr. *Perf. 11½*

63 A8 1c dk vio 70 68
a. On bluish paper 4.00 3.25
64 A8 2c ol brn 70 68
65 A8 4c brown 70 68
66 A8 5c yel grn 4.00 68
67 A8 10c red 4.00 70
68 A8 15c carmine 7.75 70
a. On bluish paper 75.00
69 A8 20c orange 3.00 90
70 A8 25c dl bl 16.00 2.50
71 A8 30c pale red 18.00 5.75
72 A8 40c gray vio 16.00 2.50
73 A8 50c brn org 32.50 10.50
74 A8 75c org yel 32.50 10.50
75 A8 1fr dp grn 32.50 15.00
76 A8 2fr slate 40.00 18.00
77 A8 5fr gray blk 52.50 20.00
Nos. 63-77 (15) 260.85 89.77

Nos. 63-77 exist imperf. Value of set, $700.

1908-28 Typo. *Perf. 13½x14*

79 A9 1c vio & ol 15 15
80 A9 2c red & ol 15 15
81 A9 4c ol brn & brn 15 15
82 A9 5c bl grn & ol 15 15
83 A9 5c blk & rose ('22) 15 15
84 A9 10c rose & brn 15 15
85 A9 10c bl grn & ol grn ('22) 15 15
86 A9 10c org brn & vio ('25) 15 15
87 A9 15c dl vio & rose ('16) 15 15
88 A9 15c dl grn & lt grn ('27) 15 15
89 A9 15c dk bl & rose red ('28) 65 50
90 A9 20c org & brn 15 15
91 A9 25c bl & blk 80 20
92 A9 25c vio & blk ('22) 15 15
93 A9 30c brn & blk 1.00 62
94 A9 30c rose red & brn ('22) 15 15
95 A9 30c grn & red vio ('25) 15 15
96 A9 30c dp grn & yel grn ('27) 60 55
97 A9 35c red & blk 60 25
98 A9 40c vio brn & blk 60 22
99 A9 45c bl grn & blk 42 22
100 A9 45c red & ver ('25) 15 15
101 A9 45c gray lil & mag ('27) 60 42
102 A9 50c vio & blk 42 20
103 A9 50c bl & blk ('22) 15 15
104 A9 50c blk & org ('25) 28 15
105 A9 60c vio, *pnksh* ('25) 28 25
106 A9 65c blk & bl ('25) 55 45
107 A9 75c rose red & blk 42 15
108 A9 85c grn & ver ('25) 55 50
109 A9 1fr brn & ol 35 15
110 A9 1fr dl bl ('25) 55 40
111 A9 1fr rose & grn ('28) 3.50 2.75
112 A9 1.10fr bis & bl grn ('28) 60 50
113 A9 2fr bl & ol 2.25 60
114 A9 5fr vio & vio brn 4.75 3.50
Nos. 79-114 (36) 22.17 14.98

75c violet on pinkish stamps of type A9 are No. 138 without surcharge.

Preceding Issues Surcharged in Black or Carmine

05 **10**

1912, Nov. *Perf. 14x13½*

115 A7 5c on 15c gray (C) 35 35
116 A7 5c on 20c red, *grn* 42 42
a. Inverted surcharge 60.00 60.00
117 A7 5c on 30c brn, *bis* (C) 50 50
118 A7 10c on 75c vio, *org* 5.00 5.00
a. Double surcharge 100.00 100.00
119 A8 5c on 2c ol brn (C) 35 35
120 A8 5c on 20c org 40 40
121 A8 5c on 30c pale red 60 60
122 A8 10c on 40c gray vio (C) 65 65
123 A8 10c on 50c brn org 1.60 1.60
124 A8 10c on 75c org yel 3.50 3.50
a. Inverted surcharge 110.00 110.00
Nos. 115-124 (10) 13.37 13.37

Two spacings between the surcharged numerals are found on Nos. 115 to 118.

Stamps of Anjouan, Grand Comoro Island, Mayotte and Moheli with similar surcharges were also available for use in Madagascar and the entire Comoro archipelago.

Preceding Issues Surcharged in Red or Black

0,30 (g) **1 FR.** (h)

1921

On Nos. 98 & 107

125 A9 (g) 30c on 40c (R) 1.00 1.00
126 A9 (g) 60c on 75c 1.40 1.40

On Nos. 45 & 47

127 A7 (g) 60c on 75c (R) 3.25 3.25
a. Inverted surcharge 120.00 120.00
128 A7 (h) 1fr on 5fr 48 48

On No. 77

129 A8 (h) 1fr on 5fr (R) 40.00 40.00

Stamps and Type of 1908-16 Surcharged in Black or Red

0,25

1 cent.

130 A9 1c on 15c dl vio & rose 48 48
131 A9 25c on 35c red & blk 2.25 2.25
132 A9 25c on 35c red & blk (R) 7.25 7.25
133 A9 25c on 40c brn & blk 2.25 2.25
134 A9 25c on 45c grn & blk 1.60 1.60
Nos. 125-134 (10) 59.96 59.96

Stamps and Type of 1908-28 Surcharged with New Value and Bars

1922-27

135 A9 25c on 15c dl vio & rose ('25) 15 15
a. Double surcharge 25.00
136 A9 25c on 2fr bl & ol ('24) 15 15
137 A9 25c on 5fr vio & vio brn ('24) 15 15
138 A9 60c on 75c vio, *pnksh* ('22) 18 16
139 A9 65c on 75c rose red & blk ('25) 30 22
140 A9 85c on 45c bl grn & blk ('25) 30 22
141 A9 90c on 75c dl red & rose red ('27) 24 20
142 A9 1.25fr on 1fr lt bl (R) ('26) 18 15
143 A9 1.50fr on 1fr dp bl & dl bl ('27) 18 15
144 A9 3fr on 5fr grn & vio ('27) 50 40
145 A9 10fr on 5fr org & rose lil ('27) 3.00 2.00
146 A9 20fr on 5fr rose & sl bl ('27) 5.00 3.75
Nos. 135-146 (12) 10.33 7.70

See Nos. 178-179.

Sakalava Chief A10

Hova Woman A12

Hova with Oxen — A11

Betsileo Woman A13

Perf. 13½x14, 14x13½

1930-44 Typo.

147 A11 1c dk bl & bl grn ('33) 15 15
148 A10 2c brn red & dk brn 15 15
149 A10 4c dk brn & vio 15 15
150 A11 5c lt grn & red 15 15
151 A12 10c ver & dp grn 15 15
152 A13 15c dp red 15 15
153 A11 20c yel brn & dk bl 15 15
154 A12 25c vio & dk brn 15 15
155 A13 30c Prus bl 25 15
156 A10 40c grn & red 30 30
157 A13 45c dl vio 55 40
158 A11 65c ol grn & vio 55 32
159 A13 75c dk brn 45 32

160 A11 90c brn red & dk red 58 45
161 A12 1fr yel brn & dk bl 75 60
162 A12 1fr dk red & car rose ('38) 40 32
163 A12 1.25fr dp bl & dk brn ('33) 60 45
164 A10 1.50fr dk & dp bl 3.25 85
165 A10 1.50fr brn & dk red ('38) 15 15
165A A10 1.50fr dk red & brn ('44) 16 16
166 A10 1.75fr dk brn & dk red ('33) 1.75 65
167 A10 5fr vio & dk brn 68 32
168 A10 20fr yel brn & dk bl 1.10 90
Nos. 147-168 (23) 12.72
Set value 6.60

Colonial Exposition Issue
Common Design Types

1931 Engr. *Perf. 12½*
Name of Country in Black

169 CD70 40c dp grn 42 35
170 CD71 50c violet 85 40
171 CD72 90c red org 70 50
172 CD73 1.50fr dl bl 1.00 60

General Joseph Simon Galliéni — A14

1931 Engr. *Perf. 14*
Size: 21½x34½mm

173 A14 1c ultra 28 15
174 A14 50c org brn 60 15
175 A14 2fr dp red 3.50 2.25
176 A14 3fr emerald 3.00 1.10
177 A14 10fr dp org 1.75 1.10
Nos. 173-177 (5) 9.13 4.75

See Nos. 180-190.

25c

Nos. 113 and 109 Surcharged

1932 *Perf. 13½x14*

178 A9 25c on 2fr bl & ol 35 25
179 A9 50c on 1fr brn & ol 35 25

No. 178 has numerals in thick block letters. No. 136 has thin shaded numerals.

Galliéni Type of 1931

1936-40 Photo. *Perf. 13½, 13x13½*
Size: 21x34mm

180 A14 3c saph ('40) 15 15
181 A14 45c brt grn ('40) 15 15
182 A14 50c yel brn 15 15
183 A14 60c brt red lil ('40) 15 15
184 A14 70c brt rose ('40) 20 20
185 A14 90c cop brn ('39) 15 15
186 A14 1.40fr org yel ('40) 35 22
187 A14 1.60fr pur ('40) 35 28
188 A14 2fr dk car 15 15
189 A14 3fr green 2.00 1.00
190 A14 3fr ol blk ('39) 60 32
Nos. 180-190 (11) 4.40
Set value 2.50

Paris International Exposition Issue
Common Design Types

1937, Apr. 15 Engr. *Perf. 13*

191 CD74 20c dp vio 60 60
192 CD75 30c dk grn 60 60
193 CD76 40c car rose 60 60
194 CD77 50c dk brn & blk 50 50
195 CD78 90c red 75 75
196 CD79 1.50fr ultra 75 75
Nos. 191-196 (6) 3.80 3.80

Common Design Types pictured in section at front of book.

Colonial Arts Exhibition Issue
Common Design Type
Souvenir Sheet

1937 *Imperf.*

197 CD74 3fr org red 2.50 2.50

Jean Laborde A15

1938-40 *Perf. 13*

198 A15 35c green 35 20
199 A15 55c dp pur 35 20
200 A15 65c org red 53 20
201 A15 80c vio brn 35 20
202 A15 1fr rose car 35 20
203 A15 1.25fr rose car ('39) 15 15
204 A15 1.75fr dk ultra 65 20
205 A15 2.15fr yel brn 1.20 80
206 A15 2.25fr dk ultra ('39) 28 15
207 A15 2.50fr blk brn ('40) 20 20
208 A15 10fr dk grn ('40) 60 35
Nos. 198-208 (11) 5.01 2.85

Nos. 198 to 202, 204 and 205 were issued in commemoration of the 60th anniversary of the death of Jean Laborde, explorer.

New York World's Fair Issue
Common Design Type

1939, May 10 Engr. *Perf. 12½x12*

209 CD82 1.25fr car lake 65 65
210 CD82 2.25fr ultra 65 65

Porters Carrying Man in Chair, and Marshal Petain — A15a

1941 Engr. *Perf. 12x12½*

210A A15a 1fr bister brn 35
210B A15a 2.50fr blue 35

Nos. 210A-210B were issued by the Vichy government and were not placed on sale in the colony.

Type of 1930-44 Surcharged in Black with New Value

1942 *Perf. 14x13½*

211 A11 50c on 65c dk brn & mag 65 15

V2

Stamps of the design shown above and types A10, A11, A12 and A14, without "RF," were issued in 1942-44 by the Vichy government, but were not placed on sale in the colony.

Nos. 143, 145-146 with Additional Overprint in Red or Black **FRANCE LIBRE**

1942 Unwmk. *Perf. 14x13½*

212 A9 1.50fr on 1fr (R) 55 55
213 A9 10fr on 5fr (Bk) 3.50 3.50
214 A9 20fr on 5fr (R) 5.00 5.00

Stamps of 1930-40 Overprinted Like Nos. 212-214 in Black or Red or:

FRANCE LIBRE

215 A10 2c brn red & dk brn 55 55
216 A14 3c saph (R) 65.00 65.00
217 A13 15c dp red 4.50 4.50
218 A11 65c dk brn & mag 45 45
219 A14 70c brt rose 40 40
220 A15 80c vio brn 1.10 1.10
221 A14 1.40fr org yel 40 40
222 A10 1.50fr dk bl & dp bl (R) 65 65
223 A10 1.50fr brn & dk red 65 65
224 A14 1.60fr purple 45 45
225 A15 2.25fr dk ultra (R) 35 35
226 A15 2.50fr blk brn (R) 1.60 1.60
227 A15 10fr dk grn 2.25 2.25
228 A10 20fr yel brn & dk bl (R) *450.00 450.00*

Stamps of 1930-40 Surcharged in Black or Red **FRANCE LIBRE 0,10 x**

229 A11 5c on 1c dk bl & bl grn 28 28
230 A15 10c on 55c dp pur 65 65
231 A15 30c on 65c org red 40 40
232 A14 50c on 90c cop brn 20 20
233 A12 1fr on 1.25fr dp bl & dk brn 1.00 1.00
234 A15 1fr on 1.25fr rose car 4.00 4.00
235 A10 1.50fr on 1.75fr dk brn & dk red 35 35
236 A15 1.50fr on 1.75fr ultra (R) 35 35
237 A15 2fr on 2.15fr yel brn 80 80

No. 211 with additional Overprint Like Nos. 217-218 in Black

239 A11 50c on 65c dk brn & mag 28 28

New York World's Fair Stamp Overprinted Like #217-218 in Red
Perf. 12½x12

240 CD82 2.25fr ultra 28 28
Nos. 212-227,229-240 (27) 95.99 95.99

Catalogue values for unused stamps in this section, from this point to the end of the section, are for Never Hinged items.

Traveler's Tree — A16

1943 Unwmk. Photo. *Perf. 14x14½*

241 A16 5c ol gray 15 15
242 A16 10c pale rose vio 15 15
243 A16 25c emerald 15 15
244 A16 30c dp org 15 15
245 A16 40c sl bl 15 15
246 A16 80c dk red brn 15 15
247 A16 1fr dl bl 15 15
248 A16 1.50fr crim rose 28 28
249 A16 2fr dl yel 15 15
250 A16 2.50fr brt ultra 15 15
251 A16 4fr aqua & red 20 20
252 A16 5fr grn & blk 35 22
253 A16 10fr sal pink & dk bl 45 38
254 A16 20fr dl vio & brn 60 60
Set value 2.50 2.30

Nos. 241 and 242 Surcharged with New Values and Bars in Red or Blue

1944

255 A16 1.50fr on 5c (R) 32 32
256 A16 1.50fr on 10c (Bl) 42 42

Nos. 229 and 224 Surcharged with New Values and Bars in Red or Black
Perf. 14x13½, 14

257 A11 50c on 5c on 1c (R) 28 28
258 A14 1.50fr on 1.60fr (Bk) 35 35

Eboue Issue
Common Design Type

1945 Engr. *Perf. 13*

259 CD91 2fr black 28 28
260 CD91 25fr Prus grn 62 62

Nos. 241, 243 and 250 Surcharged with New Values and Bars in Carmine or Black

1945 *Perf. 14x14½*

261 A16 50c on 5c ol gray (C) 20 20
262 A16 60c on 5c ol gray (C) 35 35
263 A16 70c on 5c ol gray (C) 15 15
264 A16 1.20fr on 5c ol gray (C) 25 25
265 A16 2.40fr on 25c emer 20 20
266 A16 3fr on 25c emer 15 15
267 A16 4.50fr on 25c emer 38 38
268 A16 15fr on 2.50fr brt ultra (C) 28 28
Nos. 261-268 (8) 1.96 1.96

Southern Dancer A17

Gen. J. S. Gallieni A20

Herd of Zebus A18

Sakalava Man and Woman A19

Betsimisaraka Mother and Child — A21

General Jacques C. R. A. Duchesne A22

Marshal Joseph J. C. Joffre A23

Perf. 13x13½, 13½x13

1946 Photo. Unwmk.

269 A17 10c green 15 15
270 A17 30c orange 15 15
271 A17 40c brn ol 15 15
272 A17 50c vio brn 15 15
273 A18 60c dp ultra 15 15
274 A18 80c bl grn 15 15
275 A19 1fr brown 15 15
276 A19 1.20fr green 15 15
276A A20 1.50fr dk red 15 15
277 A20 2fr slate blk 15 15
278 A20 3fr dp claret 15 15
278A A21 3.60fr dk car rose 55 50
279 A21 4fr dp ultra 15 15
280 A21 5fr red org 28 15
281 A22 6fr dk grnsh bl 15 15
282 A22 10fr red brn 28 15
283 A23 15fr vio brn 55 15

284	A23	20fr dk vio bl	62	38
285	A23	25fr brown	70	45
		Set value	3.60	2.00

Military Medal Issue
Common Design Type
Engraved and Typographed

1952, Dec. 1 Unwmk. *Perf. 13*
286 CD101 15fr multi 1.00 75

Centenary of the creation of the French Military Medal.

Tropical Flowers A24

Long-tailed Ground Roller A25

1954 Engr.

287	A24	7.50fr ind & gray grn	80	15
288	A25	8fr brn car	60	20
289	A25	15fr dk grn & dp ultra	1.60	15
		Set value		35

Colonel Lyautey and Royal Palace, Tananarive A26

1954-55

290	A26	10fr vio bl, ind & bl ('55)	65	15
291	A26	40fr dk sl bl & red brn	1.10	15
		Set value		20

FIDES Issue
Common Design Type

Designs: 3fr, Tractor and modern settlement. 5fr, Gallieni school. 10fr, Pangalanes Canal. 15fr, Irrigation project.

1956, Oct. 22 Engr. *Perf. 13x12½*

292	CD103	3fr gray vio & vio brn	20	15
293	CD103	5fr org brn & dk vio brn	15	15
294	CD103	10fr ind & lil	35	15
295	CD103	15fr grn & bl grn	40	15
		Set value		26

Coffee A26a

1956, Oct. 22 *Perf. 13*
296 A26a 20r red brn & dk brn 40 15

Manioc — A27

Vanilla — A28

Design: 4fr, Cloves.

1957, Mar. 12 Unwmk. *Perf. 13*

297	A27	2fr bl, grn & sep	15	15
298	A28	4fr dp grn & red	22	15
299	A28	12fr dk vio, dl grn & sep	40	22
		Set value		36

Malagasy Republic
Human Rights Issue
Common Design Type

1958, Dec. 10 Engr. *Perf. 13*
300 CD105 10fr brn & dk bl 22 15

Universal Declaration of Human Rights, 10th anniversary.
"CF" stands for "Communauté française."

> Imperforates
> Most Malagasy stamps from 1958 onward exist imperforate in issued and trial colors, and also in small presentation sheets in issued colors.

Flower Issue
Common Design Type
Perf. 12½x12, 12x12½

1959, Jan. 31 Photo.

301	CD104	6fr Datura, horiz.	15	15
302	CD104	25fr Poinsettia	22	15
		Set value	28	15

Flag and Assembly Building A29

Flag and Map — A30

French and Malagasy Flags and Map — A31

1959, Feb. 28 Engr. *Perf. 13*

303	A29	20fr brn vio, car & emer	22	15
304	A30	25fr gray, red & emer	30	16

Proclamation of the Malagasy Republic.

1959, Feb. 28
305 A31 60fr multi 60 30

Issued to honor the French Community.

Chionaema Pauliani A32

Ylang-ylang — A33

Designs: 30c, 40c, 50c, 3fr, Various butterflies. 5fr, Sisal. 8fr, Pepper. 10fr, Rice. 15fr, Cotton.

1960 Unwmk. *Perf. 13*

306	A32	30c multi	15	15
307	A32	40c emer, sep & red brn	15	15
308	A32	50c vio brn, blk & stl bl	15	15
309	A32	1fr ind, red & dl pur	15	15
310	A32	3fr ol, vio blk & org	15	15
311	A32	5fr red, brn & emer	15	15
312	A33	6fr dk grn & brt yel	15	15
313	A32	8fr crim rose, emer & blk	15	15
314	A33	10fr dk grn, yel grn & lt brn	15	15
315	A32	15fr brn & grn	18	15
		Set value	75	60

Family Planting Trees — A34

1960, Feb. 1 Engr. *Perf. 13*
316 A34 20fr red brn, buff & grn 22 15

Issued for the "Week of the Tree," Feb. 1-7.

C.C.T.A. Issue
Common Design Type

1960, Feb. 22
317 CD106 25fr lt bl grn & plum 40 30

Pres. Philibert Tsiranana and Map — A36

1960, Mar. 25 Unwmk. *Perf. 13*
318 A36 20fr grn & brn 20 15

Athletes of Two Races — A37

Pres. Philibert Tsiranana — A38

1960 Engr. *Perf. 13*
319 A37 25fr choc, org brn & ultra 35 22

First Games of the French Community, Apr. 13-18, at Tananarive.

1960, July 29 Unwmk. *Perf. 13*
320 A38 20fr red, blk & brt grn 20 15

Issued to honor Pres. Tsiranana, "Father of Independence." See No. B18.

Gray Lemur — A39

Designs: 4fr, Ruffed lemur (horiz.). 12fr, Mongoose lemur.

1961, Dec. 9 *Perf. 13*

321	A39	2fr brn & grnsh bl	15	15
322	A39	4fr brn, grn & blk	15	15
323	A39	12fr grn & red brn	20	15
		Nos. 321-323,C67-C69 (6)	4.45	2.25

Pres. Tsiranana Bridge, Sofia River — A40

1962, Jan. 4 Unwmk. *Perf. 13*
324 A40 25fr brt bl 22 15

First Train Built at Tananarive A41

1962, Feb. 1
325 A41 20fr dk grn 20 15

UN and Malagasy Flags over Government Building, Tananarive — A42

1962, Mar. 14 *Perf. 13*

326	A42	25fr multi	22	16
327	A42	85fr multi	80	55

Issued to commemorate the Malagasy Republic's admission to the United Nations.

Ranomafana Village A43

Designs: 30fr, Tritriva crater lake. 50fr, Foulpointe shore. 60fr, Fort Dauphin.

1962, May 7 Engr. *Perf. 13*

328	A43	10fr sl grn, grnsh bl & cl	15	15
329	A43	30fr sl grn, cl & grnsh bl	22	15
330	A43	50fr ultra, cl & sl grn	40	25
331	A43	60fr cl, ultra & sl grn	50	35

See No. C70 and souvenir sheet No. C70a.

African and Malgache Union Issue
Common Design Type

1962, Sept. 8 Photo. *Perf. 12½x12*
332 CD110 30fr grn, bluish grn, red & gold 42 35

First anniversary of the African and Malgache Union.

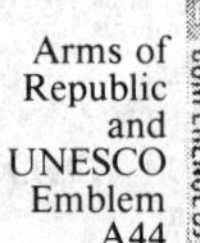

Arms of Republic and UNESCO Emblem A44

1962, Sept. 3 Unwmk.
333 A44 20fr rose, emer & blk 25 20

First Conference on Higher Education in Africa, Tananarive, Sept. 3-12.

Power Station — A45

Designs: 8fr, Atomic reactor and atom symbol (horiz.). 10fr, Oil derrick. 15fr, Tanker (horiz.).

Perf. 12x12½, 12½x12

1962, Oct. 18 **Litho.**

334	A45	5fr bl, yel & red	15	15
335	A45	8fr bl, red & yel	15	15
336	A45	10fr multi	15	15
337	A45	15fr bl, red brn & blk	15	15
		Set value	38	26

Industrialization of Madagascar.

Factory and Globe A46

1963, Jan. 7 **Typo.** ***Perf. 14x13½***

338	A46	25fr dp org & blk	22	15

International Fair at Tamatave.

Hertzian Cable, Tananarive-Fianarantsoa — A47

1963, Mar. 7 **Photo.** ***Perf. 12½x12***

339	A47	20fr multi	20	15

Madagascar Blue Pigeon A48

Gastrorchis Humblotii A49

Birds: 2fr, Blue coua. 3fr, Red fody. 6fr, Madagascar pigmy kingfisher. Orchids: 10fr, Eulophiella Roempleriana. 12fr, Angraecum sesquipedale.

1963 **Unwmk.** ***Perf. 13***

340	A48	1fr multi	20	20
341	A48	2fr multi	20	20
342	A48	3fr multi	20	20
343	A48	6fr multi	20	20
344	A49	8fr multi	16	15
345	A49	10fr multi	25	22
346	A49	12fr multi	25	22
		Nos. 340-346,C72-C74 (10)	4.81	2.86

Arms of Fianarantsoa — A50

Arms of: 1.50fr, Antsirabe. 5fr, Antalaha. 10fr, Tulear. 15fr, Majunga. 25fr, Tananarive. 50fr, Diego-Suarez.

Imprint: "R. Louis del. So. Ge. Im."

1963-65 **Litho.** ***Perf. 13***

Size: 23½x35½mm

347	A50	1.50fr multi ('64)	15	15
348	A50	5fr multi ('65)	15	15
349	A50	10fr multi ('64)	15	15
350	A50	15fr multi ('64)	15	15
351	A50	20fr multi	20	15
352	A50	25fr multi	22	15
353	A50	50fr multi ('65)	40	30
		Set value	1.10	70

See Nos. 388-390, 434-439.

Map and Centenary Emblem A51

Globe and Hands Holding Torch A52

1963, Sept. 2 ***Perf. 12x12½***

354	A51	30fr multi	55	50

Centenary of the International Red Cross.

1963, Dec. 10 **Engr.** ***Perf. 12½***

355	A52	60fr ol, ocher & car	50	35

15th anniversary of the Universal Declaration of Human Rights.

Scouts and Campfire A53

1964, June 6 **Engr.** ***Perf. 13***

356	A53	20fr dk red, org & car	22	15

Issued to commemorate the 40th anniversary of the Boy Scouts of Madagascar.

Europafrica Issue, 1964

Dove and Globe A54

1964, July 20 **Engr.**

357	A54	45fr ol grn, brn red & blk	40	25

First anniversary of economic agreement between the European Economic Community and the African and Malgache Union.

Carved Statue of Woman A55

University Emblem A56

Malagasy Art: 30fr, Statue of sitting man.

1964, Oct. 20 **Unwmk.** ***Perf. 13***

358	A55	6fr dk bl, brt bl & sep	15	15
359	A55	30fr dp grn, ol bis & dk brn	30	20

See No. C79.

Cooperation Issue

Common Design Type

1964, Nov. 7 **Engr.** ***Perf. 13***

360	CD119	25fr blk, dk brn & org brn	25	16

1964, Dec. 5 **Litho.** ***Perf. 13x12½***

361	A56	65fr red, blk & grn	50	35

Issued to commemorate the founding of the University of Madagascar, Tannanarive. The inscription reads: "Foolish is he who does not do better than his father."

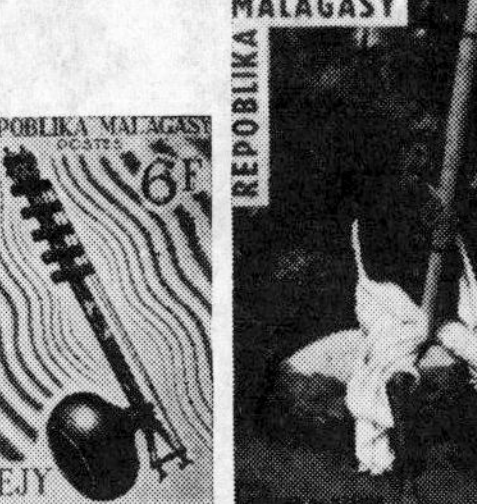

Jejy — A57 Valiha Player — A58

Musical instruments: 3fr, Kabosa (lute). 8fr, Hazolahy (sacred drum).

1965 **Engr.** ***Perf. 13***

Size: 22x36mm

362	A57	3fr mag, vio bl & dk brn	15	15
363	A57	6fr emer, rose lil & dk brn	15	15
364	A57	8fr brn, grn & blk	15	15

Photo. ***Perf. 12½x13***

365	A58	25fr multi	25	16
		Nos. 362-365,C80 (5)	2.60	
		Set value		1.35

PTT Receiving Station, Foulpointe A59

1965, May 8 **Engr.** ***Perf. 13***

366	A59	20fr red org, dk grn & ocher	16	15

Issued for Stamp Day, 1965.

ITU Emblem, Old and New Telecommunication Equipment — A60

1965, May 17

367	A60	50fr ultra, red & grn	65	40

ITU, centenary.

Jean Joseph Rabearivelo A61

Pres. Philibert Tsiranana A62

1965, June 22 **Photo.** ***Perf. 13x12½***

368	A61	40fr dk brn & org	38	22

Issued to honor the poet Jean Joseph Rabearivelo, pen name of Joseph Casimir, (1901-37).

1965, Oct. 18 ***Perf. 13x12½***

369	A62	20fr multi	15	15
a.		Souv. sheet of 4	55	55
370	A62	25fr multi	15	15
a.		Souv. sheet of 4	65	65
		Set value		18

Issued to commemorate the 55th birthday of President Philibert Tsiranana.

Mail Coach A63

History of the Post: 3fr, Early automobile. 4fr, Litter. 10fr, Mail runner (vert.). 12fr, Mail boat. 25fr, Oxcart. 30fr, Old railroad mail car. 65fr, Hydrofoil.

1965-66 **Engr.** ***Perf. 13***

371	A63	3fr vio, dp bis & sky bl ('66)	15	15
372	A63	4fr ultra, grn & dk brn ('66)	15	15
373	A63	10fr multi	15	15
374	A63	12fr multi	15	15
375	A63	20fr bis, grn & red brn	25	15
376	A63	25fr sl grn, dk brn & org	30	15
377	A63	30fr pck bl, red & sep ('66)	35	20
378	A63	65fr vio, brn & Prus bl ('66)	55	35
		Nos. 371-378 (8)	2.05	1.45

Leper's Crippled Hands A64

1966, Jan. 30

379	A64	20fr dk grn, dk brn & red	25	20

Issued for the 13th World Leprosy Day.

Couple Planting Trees — A65

1966, Feb. 21

380	A65	20fr dk brn, pur & bl grn	20	15

Reforestation as a national duty.

Tiger Beetle — A66

Insects: 6fr, Mantis. 12fr, Long-horned beetle. 45fr, Weevil.

1966 **Photo.** ***Perf. 12½x12***

Insects in Natural Colors

381	A66	1fr brick red	15	15
382	A66	6fr rose claret	15	15
383	A66	12fr Prus blue	15	15
384	A66	45fr lt yel grn	38	20
		Set value	60	40

Stamp of 1903 — A67

1966, May 8 **Engr.** ***Perf. 13***

385	A67	25fr red & sepia	25	20

Issued for Stamp Day 1966.

Betsileo Dancers A68

1966, June 13 Photo. ***Perf.*** ***12½x13***
Size: 36x23mm

386 A68 5fr multi 15 15

See No. C83.

Symbolic Tree and Emblems — A69

1966, June 26

387 A69 25fr multi 22 15

Issued to commemorate the conference of the Organisation Commune Africaine et Malgache (OCAM), Tananarive.

No. 387 dated "JUIN 1966," original date "Janvier 1966" obliterated with bar. Exists without overprint "JUIN 1966" and bar. Value $45.

Arms Type of 1963-65
Imprint: "S. Gauthier So. Ge. Im."

Arms: 20fr, Mananjary. 30fr, Nossi-Be. 90fr, Antsohihy.

1966-68 Litho. ***Perf. 13***
Size: 23½x35½mm

388 A50 20fr multi ('67) 15 15
389 A50 30fr multi 20 15
390 A50 90fr multi ('68) 55 35
Set value 50

Singers and Map of Madagascar — A70

1966, Oct. 14 Engr. ***Perf. 13***

392 A70 20fr red brn, grn & dk car rose 15 15

Issued in honor of the National Anthem.

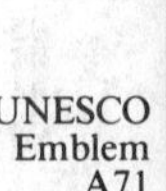

UNESCO Emblem A71

1966, Nov. 4

393 A71 30fr red, yel & slate 25 20

UNESCO, 20th anniv.

Lions Emblem — A72

1967, Jan. 14 Photo. ***Perf. 13x12½***

394 A72 30fr multi 25 16

50th anniversary of Lions International.

Rice Harvest A73

1967, Jan. 27 ***Perf. 12½x13***

395 A73 20fr multi 16 15

FAO International Rice Year.

Adventist Temple, Tanambao-Tamatave — A74

Designs: 5fr, Catholic Cathedral, Tananarive (vert.). 10fr, Mosque, Tamatave.

1967, Feb. 20 Engr. ***Perf. 13***

396 A74 3fr lt ultra, grn & bis 15 15
397 A74 5fr brt rose lil, grn & vio 15 15
398 A74 10fr dp bl, brn & grn 15 15
Set value 20 15

Norbert Raharisoa at Piano — A75

1967, Mar. 23 Photo. ***Perf. 12½x12***

399 A75 40fr cit & multi 35 15

Issued in memory of Norbert Raharisoa (1914-1963), composer.

Jean Raoult Flying Bleriot Plane, 1911 — A76

Design: 45fr, Barnard-Bougault and hydroplane, 1926.

1967, Apr. 28 Engr. ***Perf. 13***
Size: 35½x22mm

400 A76 5fr gray bl, brn & grn 15 15
401 A76 45fr brn, stl bl & blk 40 22
Set value 26

History of aviation in Madagascar. See No. C84.

Ministry of Equipment and Communications — A77

1967, May 8 Engr. ***Perf. 13***

402 A77 20fr ocher, ultra & grn 16 15

Issued for Stamp Day, 1967.

Lutheran Church, Tananarive, Madagascar Map A78

Map of Madagascar and Emblems A79

1967, Sept. 24 Photo. ***Perf. 12x12½***

403 A78 20fr multi 16 15

Issued to commemorate the centenary of the Lutheran Church in Madagascar.

1967, Oct. 16 Engr. ***Perf. 13***

404 A79 90fr red brn, bl & dk red 65 40

Hydrological Decade (UNESCO), 1965-74.

Dance of the Bilo Sakalavas — A80

Design: 30fr, Atandroy dancers.

1967, Nov. 25 Photo. ***Perf. 13x12½***
Size: 22x36mm

405 A80 2fr lt grn & multi 15 15
406 A80 30fr multi 25 15
Set value 30 18

See Nos. C86-C87.

Woman's Face, Scales and UN Emblem A81

1967, Dec. 16 ***Perf. 12½x13***

407 A81 50fr emer, dk bl & brn 38 25

Issued to publicize the United Nations Commission on the Status of Women.

Human Rights Flame — A82

1968, Mar. 16 Litho. ***Perf. 13x12½***

408 A82 50fr blk, ver & grn 38 22

International Human Rights Year.

No. 327 Surcharged with New Value and 3 Bars

1968, June 4 Engr. ***Perf. 13***

409 A42 20fr on 85fr multi 16 15

"Industry" A83

Designs: 20fr, "Agriculture" (mother and child carrying fruit and grain, and cattle) (vert.). 40fr, "Communications and Investments," (train, highway, factory and buildings).

1968, July 15

410 A83 10fr rose car, grn & dk pur 15 15
411 A83 20fr dp car, grn & blk 16 15
412 A83 40fr brn, vio & sl bl 35 16
Set value 32

Completion of Five-year Plan, 1964-68.

Church, Translated Bible, Cross and Map of Madagascar A84

1968, Aug. 18 Photo. ***Perf. 12½x12***

413 A84 20fr multi 16 15

Issued to commemorate the sesquicentennial of Christianity in Madagascar.

Isotry-Fitiavana Protestant Church — A85

Designs: 12fr, Catholic Cathedral, Fianarantsoa. 50fr, Aga Khan Mosque, Tananarive.

1968, Sept. 10 Engr. ***Perf. 13***

414 A85 4fr red brn, brt grn & dk brn 15 15
415 A85 12fr plum, bl & hn brn 15 15
416 A85 50fr brt grn, bl & ind 35 20
Set value 52 32

President and Mrs. Tsiranana A86

1968, Oct. 14 Photo. ***Perf. 12½x12***

417 A86 20fr car, org & blk 15 15
418 A86 30fr car, grnsh bl & blk 20 15
a. Souv. sheet of 4, 2 each #417-418 1.10 1.10
Set value 17

10th anniv. of the Republic.

For unused stamps, more recent issues are valued as never hinged, with the beginning point determined on a country-by-country basis. Notes to show the beginning points are prominently placed in the text.

Madagascar Map and Cornucopia with Coins
A87

Striving Mankind
A88

1968, Nov. 3 Photo. *Perf. 12x12½*
419 A87 20fr multi 16 15

Issued to commemorate the 50th anniversary of the Malagasy Savings Bank.

1968, Dec. 3 Photo. *Perf. 12½x12*

Design: 15fr, Mother, child and physician (horiz.).

420 A88 15fr ultra, yel & crim 15 15
421 A88 45fr vio bl & multi 35 22
Set value 30

Completion of Five-Year Plan, 1964-68.

Queen Adelaide Receiving Malagasy Delegation, London, 1836 — A89

1969, Mar. 29 Photo. *Perf. 12x12½*
422 A89 250fr multi 2.25 1.40

Issued to commemorate the Malagasy delegation visiting London, 1836-1837.

Cogwheels, Wrench and ILO Emblem
A90

1969, Apr. 11 *Perf. 12½x12*
423 A90 20fr grn & multi 16 15

ILO, 50th anniv.

Telecommunications and Postal Building, Tananarive — A91

1969, May 8 Engr. *Perf. 13*
424 A91 30fr bl, brt grn & car lake 22 15

Issued for Stamp Day 1969.

Steering Wheel, Map, Automobiles — A92

1969, June 1 Photo. *Perf. 12*
425 A92 65fr multi 50 25

Issued to commemorate the 20th anniversary of the Automobile Club of Madagascar.

Pres. Philibert Tsiranana
A93

Banana Plants
A94

1969, June 26 Photo. *Perf. 12x12½*
426 A93 20fr multi 15 15

10th anniversary of the inauguration of Pres. Philibert Tsiranana.

1969, July 7 Engr. *Perf. 13*
427 A94 5fr shown 15 15
428 A94 15fr Lichi tree 15 15
Set value 18 15

Runners
A95

1969, Sept. 9 Engr. *Perf. 13*
429 A95 15fr yel grn, brn & red 16 15

Issued to commemorate the 19th Olympic Games, Mexico City, Oct. 12-27, 1968.

Malagasy House, Highlands
A96

Carnelian
A97

Designs (Malagasy Houses): No. 430, Betsileo house, Highlands. No. 431, Tsimihety house, West Coast (horiz.). 60fr, Malagasy house, Highlands.

1969-70 Engr. *Perf. 13*
430 A96 20fr bl, ol & ver 15 15
431 A96 20fr sl, brt grn & red 15 15
432 A96 40fr blk, bl & dk red 30 15
433 A96 60fr vio bl, dp grn & brn 45 20
Set value 48

Issues dates: 40fr, 60fr, Nov. 25, 1969. Others, Nov. 25, 1970.

Arms Type of 1963-65

Arms: 1fr, Maintirano. 10fr, Ambalavao. No. 436, Morondava. No. 437, Ambatondrazaka. No. 438, Fenerive-Est. 80fr, Tamatave.

1970-72 Photo. *Perf. 13*
434 A50 1fr multi ('72) 15 15
435 A50 10fr multi ('72) 15 15
436 A50 25fr multi ('71) 22 15
437 A50 25fr multi ('71) 22 15
438 A50 25fr multi ('72) 20 15
439 A50 80fr pink & multi 55 30
Nos. 434-439 (6) 1.49
Set value 80

The 10fr and 80fr are dated "1970." No. 437 is dated "1971." Nos. 434, 438 are dated "1972."

Sizes: 22x37mm (Nos. 434, 438); 25½x36mm (others).

Imprints: "S. Gauthier" on Nos. 434, 438. "S. Gauthier Delrieu" on others.

Perf. 12x12½ (5, 20fr), 13 (12, 15fr)
1970-71 Photo.

Semi-precious Stones: 12fr, Yellow calcite. 15fr, Quartz. 20fr, Ammonite.

440 A97 5fr brn, dl rose & yel 15 15
441 A97 12fr multi ('71) 15 15
442 A97 15fr multi ('71) 16 15
443 A97 20fr grn & multi 20 15
Set value 42

UPU Headquarters Issue
Common Design Type

1970, May 20 Engr. *Perf. 13*
444 CD133 20fr lil rose, brn & ultra 20 15

UN Emblem and Symbols of Justice
A98

1970, June 26 Engr. *Perf. 13*
445 A98 50fr blk, ultra & org 38 20

25th anniversary of the United Nations.

Fruits of Madagascar — A99

1970, Aug. 18 Photo. *Perf. 13*
446 A99 20fr multi 15 15

Volute Delessertiana
A100

Shells: 10fr, Murex tribulus. 20fr, Spondylus.

1970, Sept. 9 Photo. *Perf. 13*
447 A100 5fr Prus bl & multi 15 15
448 A100 10fr vio & multi 15 15
449 A100 20fr multi 20 15
Set value 36 18

Aye-aye — A101

1970, Oct. 7 Photo. *Perf. 12½*
450 A101 20fr multi 35 25

Intl. Conference for Nature Conservation, Tananarive, Oct. 7-10.

Pres. Tsiranana — A102

1970, Dec. 30 Photo. *Perf. 12½*
451 A102 30fr grn & lt brn 20 15

60th birthday of Pres. Philibert Tsiranana.

Tropical Soap Factory, Tananarive
A103

Designs: 15fr, Comina chromium smelting plant, Andriamena. 50fr, Textile mill, Majunga.

1971, Apr. 14 Photo. *Perf. 12½x12*
452 A103 5fr multi 15 15

Engr. *Perf. 13*
453 A103 15fr vio bl, blk & ocher 15 15

Photo. *Perf. 13*
454 A103 50fr multi 38 20
Set value 55 32

Economic development.

Globe, Agriculture, Industry, Science
A104

1971, Apr. 22 Photo. *Perf. 12½x12*
455 A104 5fr multi 15 15

Extraordinary meeting of the Council of the C.E.E.-E.A.M.A. (Communaute Economique Europeen-Etats Africains et Malgache Associes).

Mobile Rural Post Office
A105

1971, May 8 *Perf. 13*
456 A105 25fr multi 20 15

Stamp Day.

Gen. Charles de Gaulle A106

Madagascar Hilton, Tananarive A107

1971, June 26 Engr. *Perf. 13*
457 A106 30fr ultra, blk & rose 40 20

In memory of Charles de Gaulle (1890-1970), President of France.

1971, July 23 Photo.

Design: 25fr, Hotel Palm Beach, Nossi-Bé.

458 A107 25fr multi 20 15

Engr.

459 A107 65fr vio bl, brn & lt grn 45 25

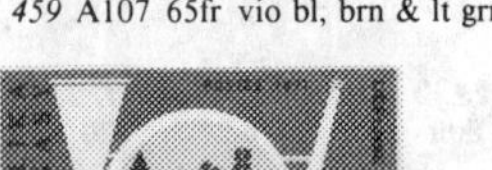

Trees and Post Horn A108

1971, Aug. 6 Photo. *Perf. 12½x12*
460 A108 3fr red, yel & grn 15 15

Forest preservation campaign.

House, South West Madagascar A109

Design: 10fr, House from Southern Madagascar.

1971, Nov. 25 *Perf. 13x12½*
461 A109 5fr lt bl & multi 15 15
462 A109 10fr lt bl & multi 15 15
Set value 15 15

Children Playing, and Cattle A110

1971, Dec. 11 Litho. *Perf. 13*
463 A110 50fr grn & multi 40 22

UNICEF, 25th anniv.

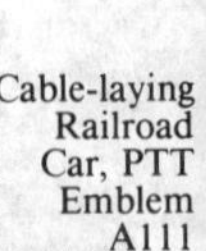

Cable-laying Railroad Car, PTT Emblem A111

1972, Apr. 8 Engr. *Perf. 13*
464 A111 45fr sl grn, red & choc 35 22

Coaxial cable connection between Tananarive and Tamatave.

Philibert Tsiranana Radar Station — A112

1972, Apr. 8 Photo. *Perf. 13½*
465 A112 85fr bl & multi 65 38

Voters and Pres. Tsiranana — A113

1972, May 1 *Perf. 12½x13*
466 A113 25fr yel & multi 40 35

Commemorating the Presidential election, Jan. 30, 1972.

Mail Delivery — A114

1972, May 30 Photo. *Perf. 12x12½*
467 A114 10fr multi 15 15

Stamp Day 1972.

Emblem and Stamps of Madagascar A115

Design: Stamps shown are Madagascar Nos. 352, 410, 429, 449.

1972, June 26 *Perf. 13*
468 A115 25fr org & multi 15 15
469 A115 40fr org & multi 25 16
470 A115 100fr org & multi 65 35
a. Souv. sheet of 3, #468-470 1.40 1.40

2nd Malgache Philatelic Exhibition, Tananarive, June 26-July 9.

Andapa-Sambava Road and Monument — A116

1972, July 6 *Perf. 12½x12*
471 A116 50fr multi 30 20

Opening of the Andapa-Sambava road.

Diesel Locomotive A117

1972, July 6 Engr. *Perf. 13*
472 A117 100fr multi 65 40

Razafindrahety College — A118

1972, Aug. 6
473 A118 10fr choc, bl & red brn 15 15

Sesquicentennial of Razafindrahety College, Tananarive.

Volleyball A119

1972, Aug. 6 Typo. *Perf. 12½x13*
474 A119 12fr org, blk & brn 15 15

African volleyball championship.

Oil Refinery, Tamatave A120

1972, Sept. 18 Engr. *Perf. 13*
475 A120 2fr bl, bis & sl grn 15 15

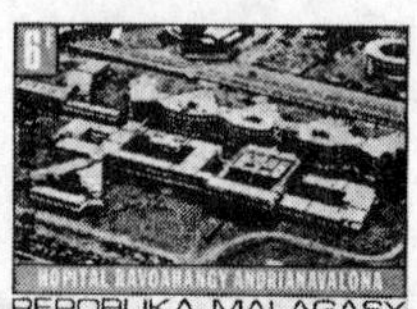

Ravoahangy Andrianavalona Hospital — A121

1972, Oct. 14 Photo. *Perf. 13x12½*
476 A121 6fr multi 15 15

Plowing A122

1972, Nov. 15 Photo. *Perf. 13½x14*
477 A122 25fr gold & multi 15 15

Betsimisaraka Costume — A123

Design: 15fr, Merina costume.

1972, Dec. 30 Photo. *Perf. 13x12½*
478 A123 10fr bl & multi 15 15
479 A123 15fr brn & multi 15 15
Set value 16 15

Farmer and Produce — A124

1973, Feb. 6 Photo. *Perf. 13*
480 A124 25fr lt bl & multi 16 15

10th anniversary of the Malagasy Committee of "Freedom from Hunger Campaign."

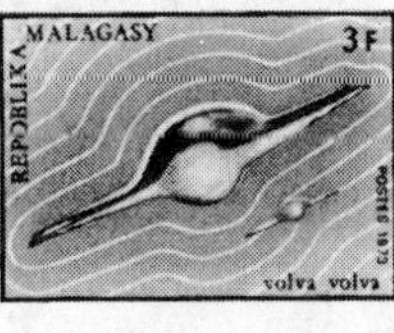

Volva Volva A125

Shells: 10fr, 50fr, Lambis chiragra. 15fr, 40fr, Harpa major. 25fr, Like 3fr.

1973, Apr. 5 Litho. *Perf. 13*
481 A125 3fr ol & multi 15 15
482 A125 10fr bl grn & multi 15 15
483 A125 15fr brt bl & multi 15 15
484 A125 25fr lt bl & multi 16 15
485 A125 40fr multi 25 16
486 A125 50fr red lil & multi 40 22
Nos. 481-486 (6) 1.26 98

Tsimandoa Mail Carrier — A126

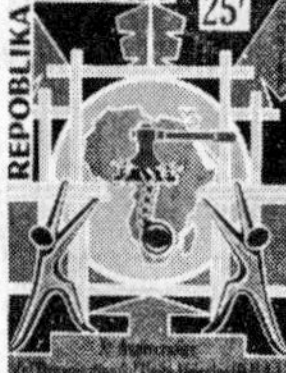

Builders and Map of Africa — A127

1973, May 13 Engr. *Perf. 13*
487 A126 50fr ind, ocher & sl grn 35 16

Stamp Day 1973.

1973, May 25 Photo. *Perf. 13*
488 A127 25fr multi 15 15

Organization for African Unity, 10th anniversary.

Campani Chameleon A128

Various Chameleons: 5fr, 40fr, Male nasutus. 10fr, 85fr, Female nasutus. 60fr, Like 1fr.

1973, June 15 Photo. *Perf. 13x12½*
489 A128 1fr dp car & multi 15 15
490 A128 5fr brn & multi 15 15
491 A128 10fr grn & multi 15 15
492 A128 40fr red lil & multi 25 15
493 A128 60fr dk bl & multi 42 22
494 A128 85fr brn & multi 65 35
Set value 1.50 85

Lady's Slipper
A129

Orchids: 25fr, 40fr, Pitcher plant. 100fr, Like 10fr.

1973, Aug. 6 Photo. *Perf. 12½*

495 A129 10fr multi 15 15
496 A129 25fr rose & multi 16 15
497 A129 40fr lt bl & multi 22 15
498 A129 100fr multi 52 40
Set value 70

No. 480 Surcharged with New Value, 2 Bars, and Overprinted in Ultramarine: "SECHERESSE / SOLIDARITE AFRICAINE"

1973, Aug. 16 *Perf. 13*

499 A124 100fr on 25fr multi 52 35

African solidarity in drought emergency.

African Postal Union Issue
Common Design Type

1973, Sept. 12 Engr. *Perf. 13*

500 CD137 100fr vio, red & sl grn 55 35

Greater Dwarf Lemur
A131

Design: 25fr, Weasel lemur (vert.).

1973, Oct. 9 Engr. *Perf. 13*

501 A131 5fr brt grn & multi 15 15
502 A131 25fr ocher & multi 15 15
Set value 18 15

Lemurs of Madagascar. See Nos. C117-C118.

25Fmg

No. 389 Surcharged

1974, Feb. 9 Litho. *Perf. 13*

503 A50 25fr on 30fr multi 15 15

Scouts Helping to Raise Cattle – A132

Mother with Children and Clinic – A133

Design: 15fr, Scouts building house; African Scout emblem.

1974, Feb. 14 Engr. *Perf. 13*

504 A132 4fr bl, sl & emer 15 15
505 A132 15fr choc & multi 15 15
Set value 15 15

Malagasy Boy Scouts. See Nos. C122-C123.

1974, May 24 Photo. *Perf. 13*

506 A133 25fr multi 15 15

World Population Year.

Rainibetsimisaraka
A134

1974, July 26 Photo. *Perf. 13*

507 A134 25fr multi 15 15

In memory of Rainibetsimisaraka, independence leader.

Marble Blocks
A135

Design: 25fr, Marble quarry.

1974, Sept. 27 Photo. *Perf. 13*

508 A135 4fr multi 15 15
509 A135 25fr multi 15 15
Set value 18 15

Malagasy marble.

Europafrica Issue, 1974

Links, White and Black Faces, Map of Europe and Africa – A136

1974, Oct. 17 Engr. *Perf. 13*

510 A136 150fr dk brn & org 80 35

Grain and Hand
A137

1974, Oct. 29

511 A137 80fr lt bl & ocher 42 25

World Committee against Hunger.

Tuléar Dog – A138

Design: 100fr, Hunting dog.

1974, Nov. 26 Photo. *Perf. 13x13½*

512 A138 50fr multi 25 20
513 A138 100fr multi 55 42

Malagasy Citizens – A139

1974, Dec. 9 *Perf. 13½x13*

514 A139 5fr bl grn & multi 15 15
515 A139 10fr multi 15 15
516 A139 20fr yel grn & multi 15 15
517 A139 60fr org & multi 35 20
Set value 56 36

Introduction of "Fokonolona" community organization.

Symbols of Development
A140

1974, Dec. 16 Photo. *Perf. 13x13½*

518 A140 25fr ultra & multi 16 15
519 A140 35fr bl grn & multi 20 15
Set value 24

National Council for Development.

Woman, Rose, Dove and Emblem – A141

1975, Jan. 21 Engr. *Perf. 13*

520 A141 100fr brn, emer & org 55 22

International Women's Year 1975.

Col. Richard Ratsimandrava – A142

1975, Apr. 25 Photo. *Perf. 13*

521 A142 15fr brn & sal 15 15
522 A142 25fr blk, bl & brn 15 15
523 A142 100fr blk, lt grn & brn 52 25
Set value 75 36

Col. Richard Ratsimandrava (1933-1975), head of state.

Sofia Bridge
A143

1975, May 29 Litho. *Perf. 12½*

524 A143 45fr multi 22 15

Count de Grasse and "Randolph" – A144

Design: 50fr, Marquis de Lafayette, "Lexington" and HMS "Edward."

1975, June 30 Litho. *Perf. 11*

525 A144 40fr multi 30 15
526 A144 50fr multi 38 16
Nos. 525-526,C137-C139 (5) 4.38 1.91

American Bicentennial.

Euphorbia Viguieri
A145

Tropical Plants: 25fr, Hibiscus. 30fr, Plumieria rubra acutitolia. 40fr, Pachypodium rosulatum.

1975, Aug. 4 Photo. *Perf. 12½*

527 A145 15fr lem & multi 15 15
528 A145 25fr blk & multi 15 15
529 A145 30fr org & multi 16 15
530 A145 40fr dk red & multi 22 20
Nos. 527-530,C141 (5) 1.13 1.00

Brown, White, Yellow and Black Hands Holding Globe – A146

1975, Aug. 26 Litho. *Perf. 12*

531 A146 50fr multi 25 16

Namibia Day (independence for South-West Africa.)

Woodpecker – A147

Designs: 40fr, Rabbit. 50fr, Frog. 75fr, Tortoise.

1975, Sept. 16 Litho. *Perf. 14x13½*

532 A147 25fr multi 20 15
533 A147 40fr multi 25 15
534 A147 50fr multi 35 20
535 A147 75fr multi 45 25
Nos. 532-535,C145 (5) 2.05 1.20

International Exposition, Okinawa.

Lily Waterfall A148

Design: 40fr, Lily Waterfall, different view.

1975, Sept. 17 Litho. *Perf. 12½*

536 A148 25fr multi	15	15
537 A148 40fr multi	22	15
Set value		20

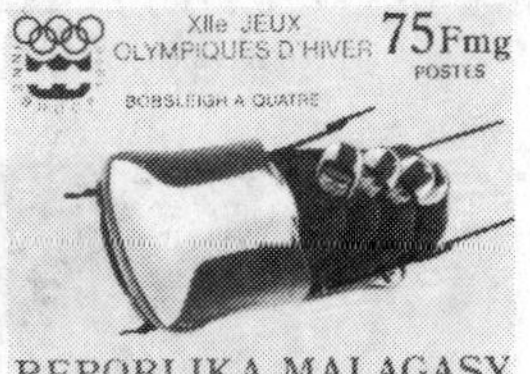

4-man Bob Sled — A149

Designs: 100fr, Ski jump. 140fr, Speed skating.

1975, Nov. 19 Litho. *Perf. 14*

538 A149 75fr multi	45	20
539 A149 100fr multi	60	22
540 A149 140fr multi	90	30
Nos. 538-540,C149-C150 (5)	4.70	1.92

12th Winter Olympic games, Innsbruck, 1976.

Pirogue A150

Designs: 45fr, Boutre (Arabian coastal vessel).

1975, Nov. 20 Photo. *Perf. 12½*

541 A150 8fr multi	15	15
542 A150 45fr ultra & multi	22	15
Set value	36	18

Canadian Canoe and Kayak — A151

Design: 50fr, Sprint and Hurdles.

1976, Jan. 21 Litho. *Perf. 14x13½*

543 A151 40fr multi	25	15
544 A151 50fr multi	35	16
Nos. 543-544,C153-C155 (5)	4.35	2.01

21st Summer Olympic games, Montreal.

A particular stamp may be scarce, but if few collectors want it, its market value may remain relatively low.

Count Zeppelin and LZ-127 over Fujiyama, Japan — A152

Designs (Count Zeppelin and LZ-127 over): 50fr, Rio de Janeiro, Brazil. 75fr, New York City. 100fr, Sphinx, Egypt.

1976, Mar. 3 *Perf. 11*

545 A152 40fr multi	28	15
546 A152 50fr multi	38	15
547 A152 75fr multi	55	20
548 A152 100fr multi	60	25
Nos. 545-548,C158-C159 (6)	4.81	2.25

75th anniversary of the Zeppelin.

Worker, Globe, Eye Chart and Eye — A153

1976, Apr. 7 Photo. *Perf. 12½*

549 A153 100fr multi	55	35

World Health Day: "Foresight prevents blindness."

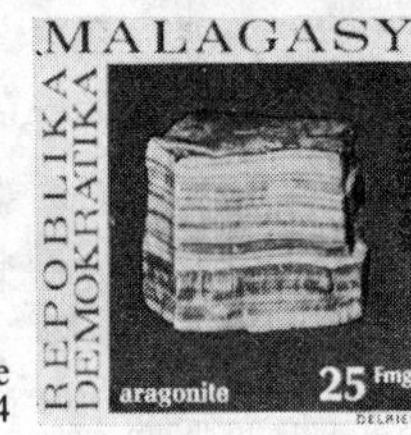

Aragonite A154

Designs: 50fr, Petrified wood. 150fr, Celestite.

1976, May 7 Photo. *Perf. 12½*

550 A154 25fr bl & multi	15	15
551 A154 50fr bl grn & multi	25	15
552 A154 150fr org & multi	80	42

Alexander Graham Bell and First Telephone — A155

Designs: 50fr, Telephone lines, 1911. 100fr, Central office, 1895. 200fr, Cable ship, 1925. 300fr, Radio telephone. 500fr, Telstar satellite and globe.

1976, May 13 Litho. *Perf. 14*

553 A155 25fr multi	16	15
554 A155 50fr multi	35	15
555 A155 100fr multi	62	30
556 A155 200fr multi	1.20	55
557 A155 300fr multi	1.90	75
Nos. 553-557 (5)	4.23	1.90

Souvenir Sheet

558 A155 500fr multi	3.25	1.40

Cent. of 1st telephone call by Alexander Graham Bell, Mar. 10, 1876.

Children with Books A156

Design: 25fr, Children with books (vert.).

1976, May 25 Litho.

559 A156 10fr multi	15	15
560 A156 25fr multi	15	15
Set value	18	15

Books for children.

Nos. 538-540 Overprinted

a. VAINQUEUR ALLEMAGNE FEDERALE
b. VAINQUEUR KARL SCHNABL AUTRICHE
c. VAINQUEUR SHEILA YOUNG ETATS-UNIS

1976, June 17

561 A149 (a) 75fr multi	40	20
562 A149 (b) 100fr multi	55	30
563 A149 (c) 140fr multi	70	42
Nos. 561-563,C161-C162 (5)	3.50	1.87

12th Winter Olympic games winners.

Nos. 525-526 Overprinted "4 Juillet / 1776-1976"

1976, July 4

564 A144 40fr multi	30	15
565 A144 50fr multi	35	16
Nos. 564-565,C164-C166 (5)	4.45	1.91

American Bicentennial.

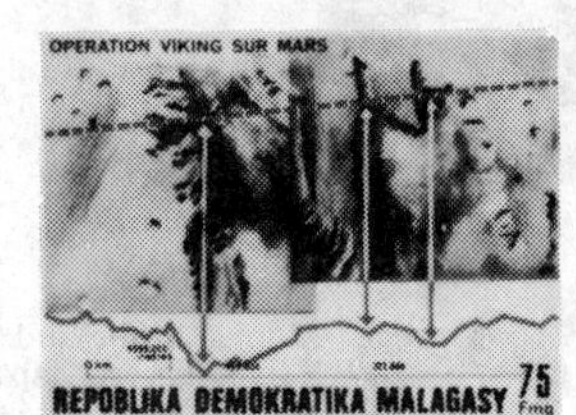

Graph of Projected Landing Spots on Mars — A157

Viking project to Mars: 100fr, Viking probe in flight. 200fr, Viking probe on Mars. 300fr, Viking probe over projected landing spot. 500fr, Viking probe approaching Mars.

1976, July 17 Litho. *Perf. 14*

566 A157 75fr multi	35	20
567 A157 100fr multi	50	20
568 A157 200fr multi	1.00	40
569 A157 300fr multi	1.50	60

Souvenir Sheet

570 A157 500fr multi	2.50	1.00

Nos. 543-544 Overprinted

a. A. ROGOV / V. DIBA
b. H. CRAWFORD / J. SCHALLER

1977, Jan.

571 A151 (a) 40fr multi	30	15
572 A151 (b) 50fr multi	38	16
Nos. 571-572,C168-C170 (5)	4.25	1.91

21st Summer Olympic games winners.

Rainandriamampandry — A158

Portrait: No. 574, Rabezavana.

1976-77 Litho. *Perf. 12x12½*

573 A158 25fr multi	15	15
574 A158 25fr multi	15	15
Set value		20

Rainandriamampandry was Malagasy Foreign Minister who signed treaties in 1896.

Issue dates: No. 573, Oct. 15, 1976. No. 574, Mar. 29, 1977.

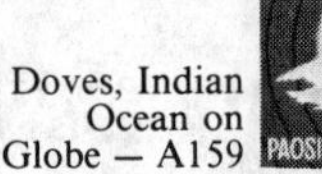

Doves, Indian Ocean on Globe — A159

Design: 12a, Globe with Africa and Indian Ocean, doves (vert.).

Perf. 12½x12, 12x12½

1976, Nov. 18

575 A159 60fr multi	35	20
576 A159 160fr multi	90	50

"Indian Ocean - Zone of Peace."

Coat of Arms — A160

1976, Dec. 30 Litho. *Perf. 12*

577 A160 25fr multi	15	15

Democratic Republic of Malagasy, first anniversary.

Lt. Albert Randriamaromanana — A161

Portrait: #578, Avana Ramanantoanina.

1977, Mar. 29

578 A161 25fr multi	15	15
579 A161 25fr multi	15	15
Set value		20

National Mausoleum — A162

1977, Mar. 29 *Perf. 12½x12*

580 A162 100fr multi	50	35

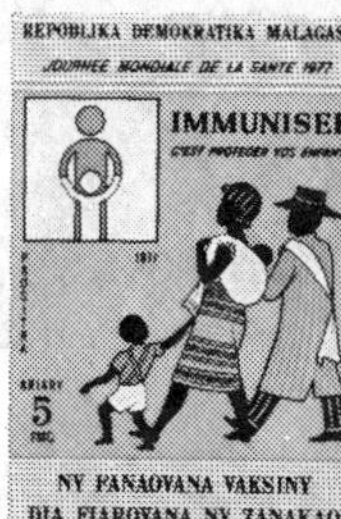

Family
A163

1977, Apr. 7 ***Perf. 12x12½***
581 A163 5fr yel & multi 15 15

World Health Day: Immunization protects the children.

Tananarive Medical School — A164

1977, June 30 Litho. ***Perf. 12½x12***
582 A164 250fr multi 1.40 65

80th anniversary of Tananarive Medical School.

Mail
Bus
A165

1977, Aug. 18 Litho. ***Perf. 12½x12***
583 A165 35fr multi 20 15

Rural mail delivery.

Telegraph Operator — A166

1977, Sept. 13 Litho. ***Perf. 12½x12***
584 A166 15fr multi 15 15

90th anniversary of telegraph service Tananarive-Tamatave.

Malagasy
Art — A167

1977, Sept. 29 ***Perf. 12x12½***
585 A167 10fr multi 15 15

Malagasy Academy, 75th anniversary.

Lenin and Russian Flag — A168

1977, Nov. 7 Litho. ***Perf. 12½x12***
586 A168 25fr multi 15 15

60th anniversary of Russian October Revolution.

Raoul
Follereau, Map
of Malagasy
A169

1978, Jan. 28 Litho. ***Perf. 12x12½***
587 A169 5fr multi 15 15

25th anniversary of Leprosy Day.

Antenna,
ITU Emblem
A170

1978, May 17 Litho. ***Perf. 12x12½***
588 A170 20fr multi 41 15

10th World Telecommunications Day.

Black and White Men
Breaking Chains of
Africa — A171

1978, June 22 Photo. ***Perf. 12½x12***
589 A171 60fr multi 40 16

Anti-Apartheid Year.

Boy and Girl,
Arch: Pen,
Gun and Hoe
A172

Farm Workers,
Factory,
Tractor
A173

1978, July 28 Litho. ***Perf. 12½x12***
590 A172 125fr multi 80 35

Youth, the pillar of revolution.

1978, Aug. 24
591 A173 25fr multi 16 15

Socialist cooperation.

Women
A174

Children Bringing
Gifts
A175

1979, Mar. 8 Litho. ***Perf. 12½x12***
592 A174 40fr multi 25 15

Women, supporters of the revolution.

1979, June 1 Litho. ***Perf. 12x12½***
593 A175 10fr multi 15 15

International Year of the Child.

Lemur
Macaco
A176

Fauna: 25fr, Lemur catta (vert.). 1000fr, Foussa.

Perf. 12½x12, 12x12½

1979, July 6 **Litho.**

594 A176	25fr multi	16	15
595 A176	125fr multi	80	35
596 A176	1000fr multi	6.50	2.50
Nos. 594-596,C172-C173 (5)		8.23	3.37

Jean Verdi
Salomon
A177

1979, July 25 ***Perf. 12x12½***
597 A177 25fr multi 16 15

Jean Verdi Salomon (1913-1978), poet.

Talapetraka (Medicinal Plant) — A178

1979, Sept. 27 Litho. ***Perf. 12½***
598 A178 25fr multi 16 15

Map of Magagascar, Dish
Antenna — A179

1979, Oct. 12
599 A179 25fr multi 16 15

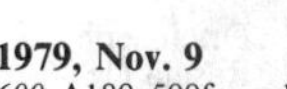

Stamp
Day 1979
A180

1979, Nov. 9
600 A180 500fr multi 3.50 1.40

Jet, Map
of Africa
A181

1979, Dec. 12 ***Perf. 12½***
601 A181 50fr multi 35 15

ASECNA (Air Safety Board), 20th anniversary.

Lenin
Addressing
Workers in the
Winter
Palace — A182

1980, Apr. 22 Litho. ***Perf. 12x12½***
602 A182 25fr multi 16 15

Lenin's 110th birth anniversary.

Bus and Road in
Madagascar
Colors — A183

Flag and Map
under
Sun — A184

1980, June 15 Litho. ***Perf. 12x12½***
603 A183 30fr multi 20 15

Socialist Revolution, 5th anniversary.

1980, June 26 ***Perf. 12½x12***
604 A184 75fr multi 50 22

Independence, 20th anniversary.

Armed Forces Day — A185

1980, Aug. Litho. ***Perf. 12½x12***
605 A185 50fr multi 35 15

Dr. Joseph Raseta (1886-1979)
A186

1980, Oct. 15 Litho. ***Perf. 12x12½***
606 A186 30fr multi 20 15

Anatirova Temple Centenary — A187

1980, Nov. 27 Litho. ***Perf. 12½x12***
607 A187 30fr multi 20 15

Hurdles, Olympic Torch, Moscow '80 Emblem — A188

1980, Dec. 29
608 A188 30fr shown 20 15
609 A188 75fr Boxing 50 22
Set value 30

22nd Summer Olympic Games, Moscow, July 19-Aug. 3. See Nos. C175-C176.

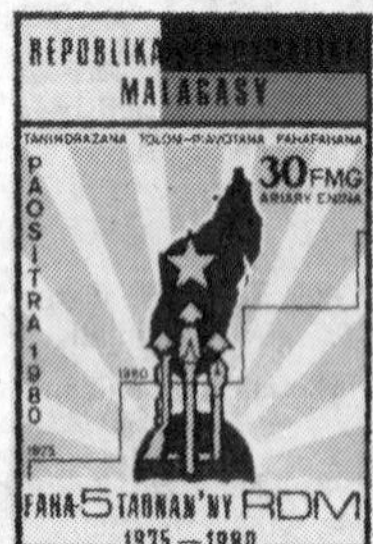

Democratic Republic of Madagascar, 5th Anniversary
A189

1980, Dec. 30 ***Perf. 12x12½***
610 A189 30fr multi 20 15

Downhill Skiing — A190

1981, Jan. 26 Litho. ***Perf. 12½x12***
611 A190 175fr multi 1.20 50

13th Winter Olympic Games, Lake Placid, Feb. 12-24, 1980.

Angraecum Leonis — A191

1981, Mar. 23 Litho. ***Perf. 11½***
612 A191 5fr shown 15 15
613 A191 80fr Angraecum ramosum 55 22
614 A191 170fr Angraecum sesquipedale 1.10 45

Carpenter — A192

1981, June 12 Litho. ***Perf. 12***
615 A192 25fr Student at desk 16 15
616 A192 80fr shown 55 22
Set value 28

Intl. Year of the Disabled.

13th World Telecommunications Day — A193

1981, July 10 Litho. ***Perf. 12½x12***
617 A193 15fr multi 15 15
618 A193 45fr multi 30 15
Set value 15

Neil Armstrong on Moon (Apollo 11) — A194

Space Anniversaries.

1981, July 23 ***Perf. 11½***
619 A194 30fr Valentina Tereshkova 20 15
620 A194 80fr shown 55 22
621 A194 90fr Yuri Gagarin 60 25

Brother Raphael Louis Rafiringa (1854-1919)
A195

1981, Aug. 10 Litho. ***Perf. 12***
622 A195 30fr multi 20 15

World Literacy Day — A196

1981, Sept. 8
623 A196 30fr multi 20 15

World Food Day — A197

1981, Oct. 16 Litho. ***Perf. 12x12½***
624 A197 200fr multi 1.40 55

See No. 635.

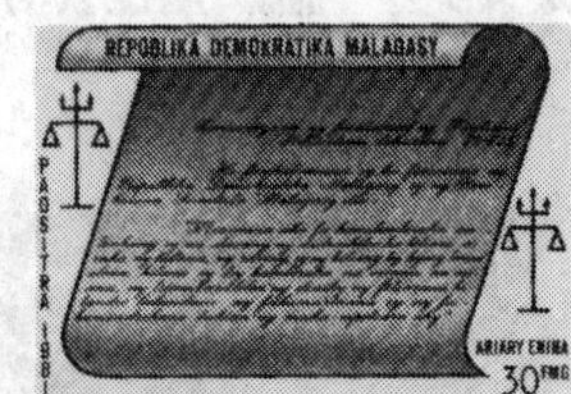

Oaths of Magistracy Renewal — A198

1981, Oct. 30 ***Perf. 12½x12***
625 A198 30fr blk & lil rose 20 15

Dove, by Pablo Picasso (1881-1973) — A199

1981, Nov. 18 Photo. ***Perf. 11½x12***
626 A199 80fr multi 55 20

20th Anniv. of UPU Membership — A200

Design; Nos. C76, C77, emblem.

1981, Nov. 19 Litho. ***Perf. 12***
627 A200 5fr multi 15 15
628 A200 30fr multi 20 15
Set value 25 15

TB Bacillus Centenary
A201

1982, June 21 Litho. ***Perf. 12***
629 A201 30fr multi 20 15

Jeannette Mpihira (1903-1981), Actress and Singer
A202

Haliaeetus Vociferoides
A203

1982, June 24 ***Perf. 12½***
630 A202 30fr multi 20 15

1982, July
631 A203 25fr Vanga curvirostris, horiz. 16 15
632 A203 30fr Leptostomus discolor, horiz. 20 15
633 A203 200fr shown 1.40 55
Set value 70

Pierre Louis Boiteau (1911-1980), Educator
A204

1982, Sept. 13
634 A204 30fr multi 20 15

World Food Day Type of 1981

1982, Oct. 16 ***Perf. 12x12½***
635 A197 80fr multi 55 22

25th Anniv. of Launching of Sputnik I — A205

1982, Oct. 4 Litho. *Perf. 12*

636	A205	10fr	Sputnik I	15	15
637	A205	80fr	Yuri Gagarin, Vostok I	55	22
638	A205	100fr	Soyuz-Salyut	65	25
			Set value		50

1982 World Cup — A206

Designs: Various soccer players.

1982, Oct. 14 *Perf. 12x12½*

639	A206	30fr	multi	15	15
640	A206	40fr	multi	20	15
641	A206	80fr	multi	40	18
			Set value		32

Souvenir Sheet

Perf. 11½x12½

642	A206	450fr	multi	2.25	90

Scene at a Bar, by Edouard Manet (1832-1883) — A207

1982, Nov. 25 *Perf. 12½x12*

643	A207	5fr	shown	15	15
644	A207	30fr	Lady in a White Dress	20	15
645	A207	170fr	Portrait of Mallarme	1.10	50
			Set value		62

Souvenir Sheet

Perf. 11½x12½

646	A207	400fr	The Fifer, vert.	2.50	1.00

Local Fish — A208

1982, Dec. 14 *Perf. 11½*

647	A208	5fr	Lutianus sebae	15	15
648	A208	20fr	Istiophorus platypterus	15	15
649	A208	30fr	Pterois volitans	20	15
650	A208	50fr	Thunnus albacares	35	15
651	A208	200fr	Epinephelus fasciatus	1.40	50
			Nos. 647-651 (5)	2.25	
			Set value		80

Souvenir Sheet

Perf. 12½x12

652	A208	450fr	Latimeria chalumnae	3.00	1.20

No. 652 contains one stamp 38x26mm.

Fort Mahavelona Ruins — A209

1982, Dec. 22 *Perf. 12½x12*

653	A209	10fr	shown	15	15
654	A209	30fr	Ramena Beach	20	15
655	A209	400fr	Flowering jacaranda trees	2.50	1.00

60th Anniv. of USSR — A210

1982, Dec. 29

656	A210	10fr	Tractors	15	15
657	A210	15fr	Pylon	15	15
658	A210	30fr	Kremlin, Lenin	20	15
659	A210	150fr	Arms	1.00	40
			Set value		55

World Communications Year — A211

Design: 80fr, Stylized figures holding wheel.

1983, May 17 Litho. *Perf. 12*

660	A211	30fr	multi	20	15
661	A211	80fr	multi	55	20

United African Organization, 20th Anniv. A212

1983, May 25 Litho. *Perf. 12*

662	A212	30fr	multi	20	15

Henri Douzon, Lawyer and Patriot — A213

1983, June 27 Litho. *Perf. 12*

663	A213	30fr	multi	20	15

Souvenir Sheet

Manned Flight Bicentenary A214

1983, July 20 Litho. *Perf. 12*

664	A214	500fr	Montgolfiere balloon	1.60	80

Souvenir Sheet

Raphael, 500th Birth Anniv. A215

1983, Aug. 10 Litho. *Perf. 12*

665	A215	500fr	The Madonna Connestable	1.60	80

Lemur — A216

Various lemurs. Nos. 668-669, 671 vert.

Perf. 12½x12, 12x12½

1983, Dec. 6 Litho.

666	A216	30fr	Daubentonia madagascariensis	15	15
667	A216	30fr	Microcebus murinus	15	15
668	A216	30fr	Lemur variegatus	15	15
669	A216	30fr	Propithecus verreauxi	15	15
670	A216	200fr	Indri indri	65	35
			Set value	1.00	50

Souvenir Sheet

671	A216	500fr	Perodicticus potto	1.60	80

1984 Winter Olympics A217

1984, Jan. 20 Litho. *Perf. 11½*

672	A217	20fr	Ski jumping	15	15
673	A217	30fr	Speed skating	15	15
674	A217	30fr	Downhill skiing	15	15
675	A217	30fr	Hockey	15	15
676	A217	200fr	Figure skating	50	25
			Set value	78	40

Souvenir Sheet

677	A217	500fr	Cross-country skiing	1.25	65

No. 677 contains one stamp 48x32mm.

Vintage Cars — A218

1984, Jan. 27 *Perf. 12½x12*

678	A218	15fr	Renault, 1907	15	15
679	A218	30fr	Benz, 1896	15	15
680	A218	30fr	Baker, 1901	15	15
681	A218	30fr	Blake, 1901	15	15
682	A218	200fr	FIAL, 1908	65	35
			Set value	1.00	50

Souvenir Sheet

Perf. 12½x11½

683	A218	450fr	Russo-Baltique, 1909	1.50	80

Pastor Ravelojaona (1879-1956), Encyclopedist A219

1984, Feb. 14 *Perf. 12x12½*

684	A219	30fr	multi	15	15

Madonna and Child, by Correggio (1489-1534) A220

Various Correggio paintings.

1984, May 5 Litho. *Perf. 12x12½*

685	A220	5fr	multi	15	15
686	A220	20fr	multi	15	15
687	A220	30fr	multi	15	15
688	A220	80fr	multi	25	15
689	A220	200fr	multi	65	35
			Set value	1.10	60

Souvenir Sheet

690	A220	400fr	multi	1.40	65

World Chess Federation, 60th Anniv. — A221

1984, July 27

691	A221	5fr	Paris landmarks	15	15
692	A221	20fr	Wilhelm Steinitz	15	15
693	A221	30fr	Champion, cup	15	15
694	A221	30fr	Vera Menchik	15	15
695	A221	215fr	Champion, cup, diff.	70	38
			Set value	1.00	55

Souvenir Sheet

696 A221 400fr Children playing chess 1.40 65

1984 Summer Olympics — A222

1984, Aug. 10

697 A222 100fr Soccer 35 16

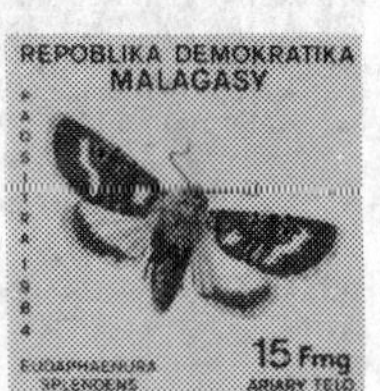

Butterflies A223

1984, Aug. 30 Litho. *Perf. 11½*

698 A223 15fr Eudaphaenura splendens 15 15
699 A223 50fr Othreis boseae 15 15
700 A223 50fr Pharmacophagus antenor 15 15
701 A223 50fr Acraea hova 15 15
702 A223 200fr Epicausis smithii 55 25
Nos. 698-702 (5) 1.15
Set value 50

Miniature Sheet

Perf. 11½x12½

703 A223 400fr Papilio delandii 1.10 55

No. 703 contains one stamp 37x52mm.

Jean Ralaimongo (1884-1944), Birth Centenary — A224

1984, Oct. 4 *Perf. 12x12½*

704 A224 50fr Portrait 15 15

Children's Rights A225

1984, Nov. 20 Litho. *Perf. 12½x12*

705 A225 50fr Youths in school bag 15 15

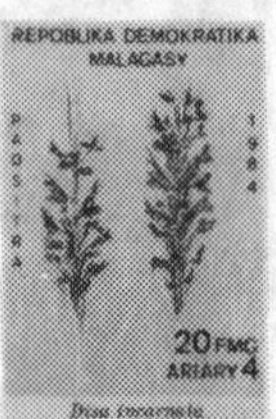

Malagasy Orchids A226

Cotton Seminar, UN Trade and Development Conference A227

1984, Nov. 20 Litho. *Perf. 12*

706 A226 20fr Disa incarnata 15 15
707 A226 235fr Eulophiella roempleriana 62 32
Nos. 706-707,C180-C182 (5) 1.22
Set value 56

Miniature Sheet

Perf. 12x12½

708 A226 400fr Gastrorchis tuberculosa 1.10 55

No. 708 contains one stamp 30x42mm.

1984, Dec. 15 Litho. *Perf. 13x12½*

709 A227 100fr UN emblem, cotton bolls 25 15

Malagasy Language Bible, 150th Anniv. A228

1985, Feb. 11 Litho. *Perf. 12½x12*

710 A228 50fr multi 16 15

1985 Agricultural Census — A229

1985, Feb. 21 Litho. *Perf. 12x12½*

711 A229 50fr Census taker, farmer 15 15

Allied Defeat of Nazi Germany, 40th Anniv. — A230

Designs: 20fr, Russian flag-raising, Berlin, 1945. 50fr, Normandy-Niemen squadron shooting down German fighter planes. No. 714, Soviet Victory Parade, Red Square, Moscow. No. 715, Victorious French troops marching through Arc de Triomphe, vert.

1985 *Perf. 12½x12, 12x12½*

712 A230 20fr multi 15 15
713 A230 50fr multi 15 15
714 A230 100fr multi 30 15
715 A230 100fr multi 30 15
Set value 42

Issue dates: #712-714, May 9. #715, Oct.

Cats and Dogs A231

Perf. 12x12½, 12½x12

1985, Apr. 25

716 A231 20fr Siamese 15 15
717 A231 20fr Bichon 15 15
718 A231 50fr Abyssinian, vert. 15 15
719 A231 100fr Cocker spaniel, vert. 30 15
720 A231 235fr Poodle 65 35
Nos. 716-720 (5) 1.40
Set value 65

Souvenir Sheet

721 A231 400fr Kitten 1.20 1.20

No. 721 contains one stamp 42x30mm, perf. 12½x12.

Gymnastic Event, Natl. Stadium, Atananarivo — A232

1985, July 9 *Perf. 12½x12*

722 A232 50fr multi 15 15

Natl. Socialist Revolution, 10th anniv.

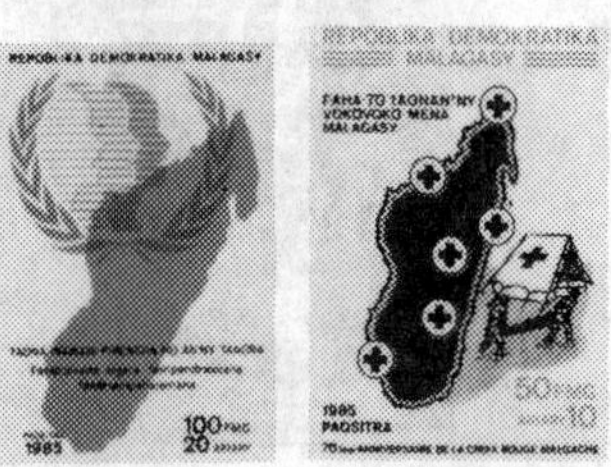
Commemorative Medal, Memorial Stele — A233

1985, July 9

723 A233 50fr multi 15 15

Independence, 25th anniv.

Intl. Youth Year — A234

Natl. Red Cross, 70th Anniv. — A235

1985, Sept. 18 *Perf. 12*

724 A234 100fr Emblem, map 30 15

1985, Oct. 3 *Perf. 12x12½*

725 A235 50fr multi 15 15

Indira Gandhi — A236

22nd World Youth and Student's Festival, Moscow — A237

1985, Oct. 31 *Perf. 13½*

726 A236 100fr multi 30 15

1985, Nov. *Perf. 12*

727 A237 50fr multi 15 15

Rouen Cathedral at Night, by Monet — A238

UN, 40th Aniv. — A239

Impressionist paintings: No. 729, View of Sea at Sainte-Marie, by van Gogh, horiz. 45fr, Young Women in Black, by Renoir. 50fr, The Red Vineyard at Arles, by van Gogh, horiz. 100fr, Boulevard des Capucines in Paris, by Monet, horiz. 400fr, In the Garden, by Renoir.

1985, Oct. 25 Litho. *Perf. 12*

728 A238 20fr multi 15 15
729 A238 20fr multi 15 15
730 A238 45fr multi 15 15
731 A238 50fr multi 15 15
732 A238 100fr multi 30 15
Set value 65 38

Souvenir Sheet

733 A238 400fr multi 1.20 1.20

No. 733 contains one stamp 30x42mm, perf. 12x12½.

1985, Oct. 31

734 A239 100fr multi 30 15

Orchids A240

1985, Nov. 8

735 A240 20fr Aeranthes grandiflora 15 15
736 A240 45fr Angraecum magdalanae 15 15
737 A240 50fr Aerangis stylosa 15 15
738 A240 100fr Angraecum eburneum longicalcar 30 15
739 A240 100fr Angraecum sesquipedale 30 15
Nos. 735-739 (5) 1.05
Set value 50

Souvenir Sheet

740 A240 400fr Angraecum aburneum superbum 1.20 1.20

Nos. 735, 737-740 vert. No. 740 contains one stamp 30x42mm, perf. 12x12½.

INTERCOSMOS — A241

Cosmonauts, natl. flags, rockets, satellites and probes.

1985, Nov. *Perf. 12x12½*

741 A241 20fr USSR, Czechoslovakia 15 15
742 A241 20fr Soyuz-Apollo emblem 15 15
743 A241 50fr USSR, India 15 15
744 A241 100fr USSR, Cuba 30 15
745 A241 200fr USSR, France 60 30
Nos. 741-745 (5) 1.35 90

Souvenir Sheet

746 A241 400fr Halley's Comet, probe 1.20 1.20

No. 746 contains one stamp 42x30mm.

Independence, 10th Anniv. — A242

1985, Dec. 30 Litho. *Perf. 12½x12*
747 A242 50fr Industrial symbols 16 15

Natl. Insurance and Securities Co. (ARO), 10th Anniv. — A243

1986, Jan. 20 *Perf. 12x12½*
748 A243 50fr dk brn, yel org & gray brn 16 15

Paintings in the Tretyakov Gallery, Moscow — A244

Designs: 20fr, Still-life with Flowers and Fruit, 1839, by I. Chroutzky. No. 750, Portrait of Alexander Pushkin, 1827, by O. Kiprenski, vert. No. 751, Portrait of an Unknown Woman, 1883, by I. Kramskoi. No. 752, The Crows Have Returned, 1872, by A. Sakrassov, vert. 100fr, March, 1895, by I. Levitan. 450fr, Portrait of Pavel Tretyakov, 1883, by I. Repin, vert.

Perf. 12½x12, 12x12½
1986, Apr. 26 Litho.
749 A244 20fr multi 15 15
750 A244 50fr multi 16 15
751 A244 50fr multi 16 15
752 A244 50fr multi 16 15
753 A244 100fr multi 35 16
Nos. 749-753 (5) 98
Set value 45

Souvenir Sheet
754 A244 450fr multi 1.50 70

1986 World Cup Soccer Championships, Mexico — A245

1986, May 31 *Perf. 13½*
755 A245 150fr multi 50 25

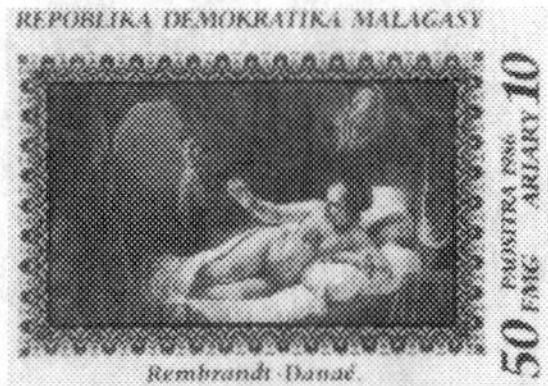

Paintings in Russian Museums — A246

Designs: No. 756, David and Urie, by Rembrandt, vert. No. 757, Danae, by Rembrandt. No. 758, Portrait of the Nurse of the Infant Isabella, by Rubens, vert. No. 759, The Alliance of Earth and Water, by Rubens, vert. No. 760, Portrait of an Old Man in Red, by Rembrandt. No. 761, The Holy Family, by Raphael.

Perf. 12x12½, 12½x12
1986, Mar. 24 Litho.
756 A246 20fr multi 15 15
757 A246 50fr multi 16 15
758 A246 50fr multi 16 15
759 A246 50fr multi 16 15
760 A246 50fr multi 16 15
Nos. 756-760 (5) 79
Set value 35

Souvenir Sheet
Perf. 11½x12½
761 A246 450fr multi 1.50 70

UN Child Survival Campaign — A247

A248

Wildcats A249

1986, June 1 Litho. *Perf. 12x12½*
762 A247 60fr multi 20 15

1986, July 17
763 A248 10fr Sable 15 15
764 A248 10fr Chaus 15 15
765 A248 60fr Serval 20 15
766 A248 60fr Caracal 20 15
767 A248 60fr Bengal 20 15
Set value 70 38

Souvenir Sheet
Perf. 12½x12
768 A249 450fr Golden 1.40 65

Intl. Peace Year A249a

1986, Sept. 12 *Perf. 12*
769 A249a 60fr shown 20 15
770 A249a 150fr Hemispheres, emblem, vert. 42 22

World Post Day — A250

1986, Oct. 9 Litho. *Perf. 13x12½*
771 A250 60fr multi 20 15
772 A250 150fr multi 42 22

No. 772 is airmail.

A251

Birds A252

Perf. 12x12½, 12½x12
1986, Dec. 23 Litho.
773 A251 60fr Xenopirostris daimi, vert. 20 15
774 A251 60fr Falculea palliata 20 15
775 A251 60fr Coua gigas 20 15
776 A251 60fr Coua cristata 20 15
777 A251 60fr Cianolanius madagascariensis, vert. 20 15
Nos. 773-777 (5) 1.00
Set value 50

Souvenir Sheet
778 A252 450fr Bubulcus ibis ibis 1.50 70

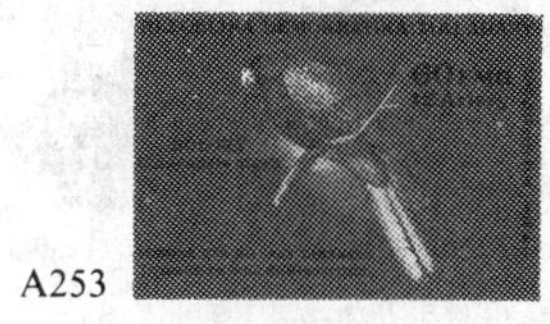
A253

Endangered Species — A254

Perf. 12x12½, 12½x12
1987, Mar. 13 Litho.
779 A253 60fr Lophotibis cristata, vert. 20 15
780 A253 60fr Coracopsis nigra 20 15
781 A254 60fr Crocodylus niloticus 20 15
782 A254 60fr Geochelone yniphora 20 15
Set value 40

Souvenir Sheet
783 A253 450fr Centropus toulou, vert. 1.50 70

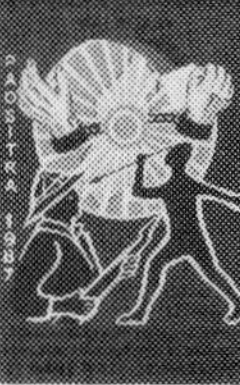

Anti-Colonial Revolt, 40th Anniv.
A255 A256

1987, Mar. 29 *Perf. 12*
784 A255 60fr multi 20 15
785 A256 60fr multi 20 15
Set value 20

1st Games of Indian Ocean Towns — A257

1987, Apr. 15 *Perf. 13½*
786 A257 60fr multi 22 15
787 A257 150fr multi 60 30

Le Sarimanok A258

1987, Apr. 15
788 A258 60fr Port side 22 15
789 A258 150fr Starboard side 60 30

African and Madagascar Coffee Organization, 25th Anniv. — A259

1987, Apr. 24 Litho. *Perf. 12*
790 A259 60fr Coffee plant 22 15
791 A259 150fr Map 60 30

Halley's Comet — A260

Space probes.

1987, May 13 *Perf. 13½*
792 A260 60fr Giotto, ESA 20 15
793 A260 150fr Vega 1, Russia 50 25
794 A260 250fr Vega 2, Russia 85 40
795 A260 350fr Planet-A1, Japan 1.10 60
796 A260 400fr Planet-A2, Japan 1.40 65
797 A260 450fr ICE, US 1.50 70
Nos. 792-797 (6) 5.55 2.75

Souvenir Sheet
798 A260 600fr Halley, Giotto 2.00 1.00

Litho. & Embossed 'Gold Foil' Stamps

These stamps generally are of a different design format than the rest of the issue. Since there is a commemorative inscription tying them to the issue a separate illustration is not being shown.

1988 Calgary Winter Olympics — A261

Jean-Joseph Rabearivelo (d. 1937), Poet — A263

Men's Downhill A262

1987, May 13

799 A261 60fr Biathlon 20 15
800 A261 150fr shown 50 25
801 A261 250fr Luge 85 40
802 A261 350fr Speed skating 1.10 60
803 A261 400fr Hockey 1.40 65
804 A261 450fr Pairs figure skating 1.50 70
Nos. 799-804 (6) 5.55 2.75

Litho. & Embossed

804A A261 1500fr Speed skating

Souvenir Sheets

Litho.

805 A262 600fr shown 2.00 1.00

Litho. & Embossed

805A A262 1500fr Slalom skiing

1987, June 22 ***Perf. 13½***

806 A263 60fr multi 20 15

1992 Summer Olympics, Barcelona — A264

Athletes, emblem and art or architecture: 60fr, Equestrian, and the Harlequin, by Picasso. 150fr, Weight lifting, church. 250fr, Hurdles, Canaletas Fountain. 350fr, High jump, amusement park. 400fr, Men's gymnastics, abbey. 450fr, Rhythmic gymnastics, Arc de Triomphe. 600fr, Equestrian, Columbus monument.

1987, Oct. 7 **Litho.** ***Perf. 13½***

807 A264 60fr multi 20 15
808 A264 150fr multi 50 25
809 A264 250fr multi 85 42
810 A264 350fr multi 1.10 60
811 A264 400fr multi 1.40 65
812 A264 450fr multi 1.50 70
Nos. 807-812 (6) 5.55 2.77

Souvenir Sheet

813 A264 600fr multi 2.00 1.00

Nos. 811-813 are airmail.

A265

Discovery of America, 500th Anniv. (in 1992) — A266

Anniv. emblem and: 60fr, Bartolomeu Dias (c. 1450-1500), Portuguese navigator, departure from De Palos, 1492. 150fr, Henry the Navigator (1394-1460), prince of Portugal, Samana Cay. 250fr, A. De Marchena landing, 1492. 350fr, Paolo Toscanelli dal Pozzo (1397-1482), Italian physician and cosmographer, La Navidad Fort. 400fr, Queen Isabella I, Barcelona, 1493. 450fr, Christopher Columbus, the Nina. 600fr, Landing in New World, 1492.

1987, Sept. 24 **Litho.** ***Perf. 13½***

814 A265 60fr multi 28 15
815 A265 150fr multi 70 35
816 A265 250fr multi 1.10 55
817 A265 350fr multi 1.65 85
818 A265 400fr multi 1.90 1.00
819 A265 450fr multi 2.25 1.10
Nos. 814-819 (6) 7.88 4.00

Souvenir Sheet

820 A266 600fr multi 3.00 1.50

Natl. Telecommunications Research Laboratory — A267

1987, July 27 ***Perf. 12½x12***

821 A267 60fr multi 22 15

Rafaravavy Rasalama (d. 1837), Christian Martyr — A268

1987, Aug. 14

822 A268 60fr lt blue, blk & brt ultra 22 15

Antananarivo-Tamatave Telegraph Link, Cent. — A269

1987, Sept. 15 ***Perf. 12x12½***

823 A269 60fr multi 22 15

Pasteur Institute, Paris, Cent. A270

1987, Oct. 26 ***Perf. 13½***

824 A270 250fr multi 1.00 45

City of Berlin, 750th Anniv. — A271

Design: Anniv. emblem, television tower and the Interhotel in East Berlin.

1987, Oct. 18 **Litho.** ***Perf. 12½x12***

825 A271 150fr multi 22 15

Schools Festival A272

1987, Oct. 23 ***Perf. 12x12½***

826 A272 60fr multi 15 15

Paintings in the Pushkin Museum, Moscow — A273

Designs: 10fr, After the Shipwreck (1847), by Eugene Delacroix (1798-1863). No. 828, Still-life with Swan (c. 1620), by Frans Snyders (1579-1647). No. 829, Jupiter and Callisto (1744), by Francois Boucher (1703-1770), vert. No. 830, Chalet in the Mountains (1874), by Jean Desire Gustav Courbet (1819-1877). 150fr, At the Market (1564), by Joachim Bueckelaer. 1000fr, Minerva (1560), by Paolo Veronese (1528-1588), vert.

Perf. 12½x12, 12x12½

1987, Nov. 10

827 A273 10fr multi 15 15
828 A273 60fr multi 15 15
829 A273 60fr multi 15 15
830 A273 60fr multi 15 15
831 A273 150fr multi 22 15
Set value 55 35

Souvenir Sheet

832 A273 1000fr multi 1.50 1.50

Pan-African Telecommunications Union, 10th Anniv. — A274

1987, Dec. 28 ***Perf. 13x12½***

833 A274 250fr multi 1.00 45

Intl. Year of Shelter for the Homeless A275

1988, Feb. 15 **Litho.** ***Perf. 12***

834 A275 80fr shown 16 15
835 A275 250fr Family in shelter, rain, vert. 52 25

Fauna A276

1988, Apr. 18 **Litho.** ***Perf. 13½***

836 A276 60fr Hapalemur simus 15 15
837 A276 150fr Propithecus diadema diadema 32 16
838 A276 250fr Indri indri 55 28
839 A276 350fr Varecia variegata variegata 75 38
840 A276 550fr Madagascar young heron 1.20 60
841 A276 1500fr Nosy-be chameleon 3.15 1.60
Nos. 836-841 (6) 6.12 3.17

Souvenir Sheet

842 A276 1500fr Uratelornis (bird) 3.25 3.25

Conservation and service organization emblems: World Wildlife Fund (60fr, 150fr, 250fr and 350fr); Rotary Intl. (550fr and No. 842); and Scouting trefoil (No. 841).

October Revolution, Russia, 70th Anniv. A277

1988, Mar. 7 **Litho.** ***Perf. 12x12½***

843 A277 60fr Lenin 15 15
844 A277 60fr Revolutionaries 15 15
845 A277 150fr Lenin, revolutionaries 32 16
Set value 32

1988 Winter Olympics, Calgary A278

1988, May 11 ***Perf. 11½***

846 A278 20fr Pairs figure skating 15 15
847 A278 60fr Slalom 15 15
848 A278 60fr Speed skating 15 15
849 A278 100fr Cross-country skiing 22 15
850 A278 250fr Ice hockey 55 28
Nos. 846-850 (5) 1.22
Set value 58

Souvenir Sheet

851 A278 800fr Ski jumping 1.75 1.75

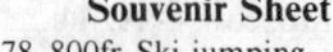

Discovery of Radium by Pierre and Marie Curie, 90th Anniv. A279

1988, July 14 **Litho.** ***Perf. 12***

852 A279 150fr blk & rose lil 35 18

OAU, 25th Anniv. A280

1988, May 25 **Litho.** ***Perf. 13***

853 A280 80fr multi 20 15

Natl. Telecommunications and Posts Institute, 20th Anniv. — A281

1988, June 22 ***Perf. 13½***

854 A281 80fr multi 20 15

Saint-Michel College, Cent.
A282

1988, July 9

855	A282	250fr multi	55	28

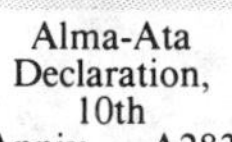

Alma-Ata Declaration, 10th Anniv. — A283

WHO, 40th Anniv. — A284

1988, Aug. 11 Litho. *Perf. 12*

856	A283	60fr multi	15	15

1988, Aug. 11

857	A284	150fr multi	32	16

Tsimbazaza Botanical and Zoological Park, 150th Anniv. — A285

Perf. 12x12½, 12½x12

1988, Aug. 22

858	A285	20fr Lemur habitat	15	15
859	A285	80fr Lemur and young	20	15
860	A285	250fr shown	55	28
		Set value		42

Souvenir Sheet

861	A285	1000fr Lemur and mate	2.25	2.25

Size of No. 859: 25x37mm.

Boy Scouts Studying Birds and Butterflies — A286

Designs: 80fr, Upupa epops maginata, Coua caerulea and scout photographing bird. 250fr, Chrysiridia croesus and comparing butterfly to a sketch. 270fr, Nelicurvius nelicourvi, Foudia omissa and constructing bird feeder. 350fr, Papilio dardanus and studying butterflies with magnifying glass. 550fr, Coua critata and tagging bird. No. 867, Argema mittrei and writing observations. No. 868, Merops superciliosus and recording bird calls.

1988, Sept. 29

862	A286	80fr multi	20	15
863	A286	250fr multi	55	28
864	A286	270fr multi	60	30
865	A286	350fr multi	78	40
866	A286	550fr multi	1.20	60
867	A286	1500fr multi	3.25	1.65
		Nos. 862-867 (6)	6.58	3.38

Souvenir Sheet

868	A286	1500fr multi	3.25	3.25

No. 868 contains one stamp 36x51mm.

Composers and Entertainers
A287

Designs: 80fr, German-made clavier and Carl Philipp Emanuel Bach (1714-1788), organist and composer. 250fr, Piano and Franz Peter Schubert (1797-1828), Austrian composer. 270fr, Scene from opera Carmen, 1875, and Georges Bizet (1838-1875), French composer. 350fr, Scene from opera Pelleas et Melisande, 1902, and Claude Debussy (1862-1918), French composer. 550fr, George Gershwin (1898-1937), American composer. No. 874, Elvis Presley (1935-1977), American entertainer. No. 875, Rimsky-Korsakov (1844-1908), Russian composer, and Le Coq d'Or from the opera of the same name.

1988, Oct. 28

869	A287	80fr multi	20	15
870	A287	250fr multi	55	28
871	A287	270fr multi	60	30
872	A287	350fr multi	78	40
873	A287	550fr multi	1.20	60
874	A287	1500fr multi	3.25	1.65
		Nos. 869-874 (6)	6.58	3.38

Souvenir Sheet

875	A287	1500fr multi	3.25	3.25

Intl. Fund for Agricultural Development (IFAD), 10th Anniv. — A288

1988, Sept. 4 Litho. *Perf. 12*

876	A288	250fr multi	48	25

School Feast — A289

1988, Nov. 22

877	A289	80fr multi	16	15

A290

Ships — A291

Paintings: 20fr, The Squadron of the Sea, Black Feodossia, by Ivan Aivazovski, vert. No. 879, Seascape with Sailing Ships, by Simon de Vlieger, vert. No. 880, The Ship Lesnoie, by N. Semenov, vert. 100fr, The Merchantman, Orel, by N. Golitsine. 250fr, Naval Exercises, by Adam Silo, vert. 550fr, On the River, by Abraham Beerstraten.

1988, Dec. 5 *Perf. 12x12½, 12½x12*

878	A290	20fr multi	15	15
879	A290	80fr multi	16	15
880	A290	80fr multi	16	15
881	A290	100fr shown	20	15
882	A290	250fr multi	48	25
		Nos. 878-882 (5)	1.15	
		Set value		55

Souvenir Sheet

Perf. 11½x12½

883	A291	550fr shown	1.05	1.05

World Wildlife Fund — A292

Insect species in danger of extinction: 20fr, Tragocephala crassicornis. 80fr, Polybothris symptuosa-gema. 250fr, Euchroea auripigmenta. 350fr, Stellognata maculata.

1988, Dec. 13 *Perf. 12*

884	A292	20fr multi	15	15
885	A292	80fr multi	16	15
886	A292	250fr multi	48	25
887	A292	350fr multi	68	35
		Set value		72

Intl. Red Cross and Red Crescent Organizations, 125th Annivs. — A293

1988, Dec. 27 Litho. *Perf. 12*

888	A293	80fr Globe, stretcher-bearers, vert.	16	15
889	A293	250fr Emblems, Dunant	48	24
		Set value		32

UN Declaration of Human Rights, 40th Anniv. (in 1988) — A294

1989, Jan. 10

890	A294	80fr shown	16	15
891	A294	250fr Hands, "4" and "0"	48	24
		Set value		32

Dated 1988.

Transportation — A295

Designs: 80fr, 1909 Mercedes-Benz Blitzen Benz. 250fr, Micheline ZM 517 Tsikirity, Tananarive-Moramanga line. 270fr, Bugatti Coupe Binder 41. 350fr, Electric locomotive 1020-DES OBB, Germany. 1500fr, Souleze Autorail 701 DU CFN, Madagascar. No. 897. 1913 Opel race car. No. 898, Bugatti Presidential Autorail locomotive and Bugatti Type 57 Atalante automobile.

1989, Jan. 24 *Perf. 13½*

892	A295	80fr multi	16	15
893	A295	250fr multi	48	24
894	A295	270fr multi	52	25
895	A295	350fr multi	70	35
896	A295	1500fr multi	2.85	1.45
897	A295	2500fr multi	4.75	2.40
		Nos. 892-897 (6)	9.46	4.84

Souvenir Sheet

898	A295	2500fr multi	4.75	4.75

Dinosaurs — A296

1989, Feb. 1 Litho. *Perf. 12½x12*

899	A296	20fr Tyrannosaurus	15	15
900	A296	80fr Stegosaurus	16	15
901	A296	250fr Arsinoitherium	48	24
902	A296	450fr Triceratops	90	45
		Set value		80

Souvenir Sheet

Perf. 11½x12½

903	A296	600fr Sauralophus, vert.	1.20	1.20

Women as the Subject of Paintings — A297

Designs: 20fr, *Tahitian Pastorales,* by Gauguin. No 905, *Portrait of a Young Woman,* by Titian, vert. No. 906, *Portrait of a Little Girl,* by Jean-Baptiste Greuze (1725-1805), vert. 100fr, *Woman in Black,* by Renoir, vert. 250fr, *Lacemaker,* by Vassili Tropinine, vert. 550fr, *The Annunciation,* by Cima Da Conegliano (c. 1459-1517), vert.

Perf. 12½x12, 12x12½

1989, Feb. 10

904	A297	20fr multi	15	15
905	A297	80fr multi	16	15
906	A297	80fr multi	16	15
907	A297	100fr multi	20	15
908	A297	250fr multi	48	24
		Nos. 904-908 (5)	1.15	
		Set value		55

Souvenir Sheet

Perf. 11½x12½

909	A297	550fr multi	1.05	1.05

Orchids
A298

1989, Feb. 28 Litho. *Perf. 12*

910 A298 5fr *Sobennikoffia robusta,* vert. 15 15
911 A298 10fr *Grammangis fallax* 15 15
912 A298 80fr *Cymbidiella humblotii,* vert. 15 15
913 A298 80fr *Angraecum sororium,* vert. 15 15
914 A298 250fr *Oenia oncidiiflora,* vert. 38 18
Set value 70 40

Souvenir Sheet

915 A298 1000fr *Aerangis curnowiana* 1.40 1.40

Jawaharlal Nehru (1889-1964), 1st Prime Minister of Independent India — A299

1989, Mar. 7 Litho. *Perf. 13*

916 A299 250fr multi 48 24

Ornamental Mineral Industry — A300

1989, Apr. 12 Litho. *Perf. 13½*

917 A300 80fr Rose quartz 16 15
918 A300 250fr Petrified wood 48 24
Set value 32

Views of Antananarivo A301

Designs: 5fr, Mahamasina Sports Complex, Ampefiloha Quarter. 20fr, Andravoahangy and Anjanahary Quarters. No. 921, Zoma Market and Faravohitra Quarter. No. 922, Andohan'Analakely Quarter and March 29th monument. 250fr, Independence Avenue and Jean Ralaimongo monument. 550fr, Queen's Palace and Andohalo School on Lake Anosy.

1989, Mar. 31 Litho. *Perf. 13½*

919 A301 5fr multi 15 15
920 A301 20fr multi 15 15
921 A301 80fr multi 48 24
922 A301 80fr multi 48 24
923 A301 250fr multi 1.50 75
924 A301 550fr multi 3.25 1.65
Nos. 919-924 (6) 6.01 3.18

Visit of Pope John Paul II — A302

1989, Apr. 28 *Perf. 12x12½*

925 A302 80fr shown 48 24
926 A302 250fr Pope, map 1.50 75

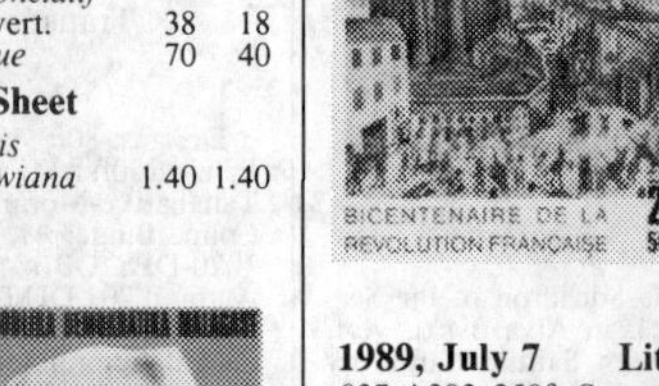

French Revolution, Bicent. A303

1989, July 7 Litho. *Perf. 12½*

927 A303 250fr Storming of the Bastille 48 24

Phobos Space Program for the Exploration of Mars — A304

1989, Aug. 29 Litho. *Perf. 12½x12*

928 A304 20fr Mars 1 15 15
929 A304 80fr Mars 3 15 15
930 A304 80fr Sond 2 15 15
931 A304 250fr Mariner 9 32 16
932 A304 270fr Viking 2 35 18
Set value 90 45

Souvenir Sheet

933 A304 550fr Phobos 70 70

PHILEXFRANCE '89 and French Revolution Bicent. — A305

Exhibition emblems, key people and scenes from the revolution: 250fr, Honore-Gabriel Riqueti (1749-1791), Count of Mirabeau, at the meeting of Estates-General, June 23, 1789. 350fr, Camille Desmoulins (1760-1794), call to arms, July 12, 1789. 1000fr, Lafayette (1757-1834), women's march on Versailles, Oct. 5, 1789. 1500fr, King tried by the National Convention, Dec. 26, 1792. 2500fr, Charlotte Corday (1768-1793), assassination of Marat, July 13, 1793. 3000fr, Bertrand Barere de Vieuzac, Robespierre, Jean-Marie Collot D'Herbois, Lazare Nicolas Carnot, George Jacques Danton, Georges Auguste Couthon, Pierre-Louis Prieur, Antoine Saint-Just and Marc Guillaume Vadiez, Committee of Public Safety, July, 1793.

1989, July 14 Litho. *Perf. 13½*

934 A305 250fr multicolored 32 16
935 A305 350fr multicolored 45 22
936 A305 1000fr multicolored 1.30 65
937 A305 1500fr multicolored 1.95 98
938 A305 2500fr multicolored 3.25 1.65
Nos. 934-938 (5) 7.27 3.66

Souvenir Sheet

939 A305 3000fr multicolored 4.00 4.00

French Revolution, Bicent. — A306

Paintings and sculpture: 5fr, *Liberty Guiding the People,* by Eugene Delacroix. 80fr, "La Marseillaise" from *Departure of the Volunteers in 1792,* high relief on the Arc de Triomphe, 1833-35, by Francois Rude. 250fr, *The Tennis Court Oath,* by David.

1989, Oct. 25 *Perf. 12½x12*

940 A306 5fr multicolored 15 15
941 A306 80fr multicolored 15 15
942 A306 250fr multicolored 32 16
Set value 46 20

No. 942 is airmail.

Rene Cassin (1887-1976), Nobel Peace Prize Winner and Institute Founder — A307

1989, Nov. 21 *Perf. 12*

943 A307 250fr multicolored 35 18

Intl. Law Institute of the French-Speaking Nations, 25th anniv.

Hapalemur aureus A308

1989, Dec. 5 Litho. *Perf. 12*

944 A308 250fr multicolored 38 20

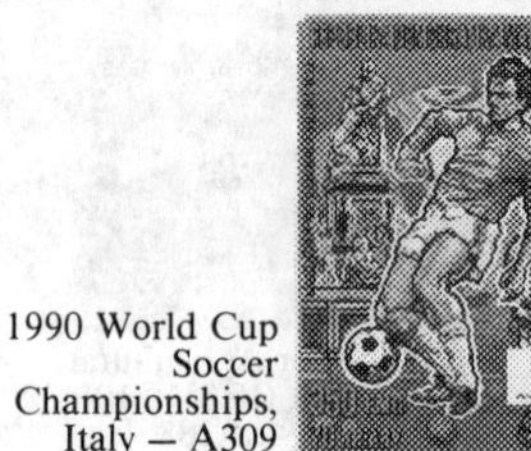

1990 World Cup Soccer Championships, Italy — A309

Various athletes, cup and: 350fr, Cavour Monument, Turin. 1000fr, Christopher Columbus Monument, Genoa, 1903. 1500fr, Michelangelo's *David.* 2500fr, *Abduction of Prosperina,* by Bernini, Rome. 3000fr, Statue of Leonardo da Vinci, 1903.

1989, Dec. 12 Litho. *Perf. 13½*

945 A309 350fr multicolored 45 22
946 A309 1000fr multicolored 1.30 65
947 A309 1500fr multicolored 2.00 1.00
948 A309 2500fr multicolored 3.25 1.65

Souvenir Sheet

949 A309 3000fr multicolored 4.00 2.00

1992 Summer Olympics, Barcelona — A310

1989, Oct. 7 Litho. *Perf. 13½*

950 A310 80fr Long jump 15 15
951 A310 250fr Pole vault 35 18
952 A310 550fr Hurdles 78 40
953 A310 1500fr Cycling 2.15 1.10
954 A310 2000fr Baseball 2.85 1.45
955 A310 2500fr Tennis 3.50 1.75
Nos. 950-955 (6) 9.78 5.03

Souvenir Sheet

956 A310 3000fr Soccer 4.25 2.15

Scenic Views and Artifacts A311

1990, May 29

Size: 47x33mm (#958, 960)

957 A311 70fr Queen Isalo Rock 15 15
958 A311 70fr Sakalava pipe 15 15
959 A311 150fr Sakalava combs 22 15
960 A311 150fr Lonjy Is., Diego Suarez Bay 22 15
Set value 64 32

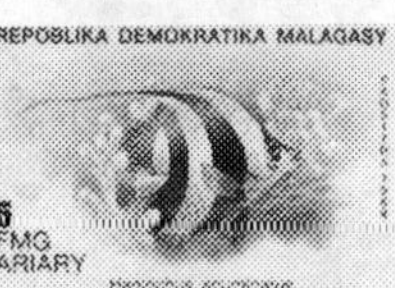

Fish A312

1990, Apr. 26 Litho. *Perf. 12*

961 A312 5fr Heniochus acuminatus 15 15
962 A312 20fr Simenhelys dofleinl 15 15
963 A312 80fr Phinobatos perceli 15 15
964 A312 250fr Epinephelus fasciatus 40 20
965 A312 320fr Sphurna zygaena 50 25
Set value 1.10 60

Souvenir Sheet

966 A312 550fr Latimeria chalumnae 90 90

Nos. 962-963 vert. Nos. 961-966 inscribed 1989.

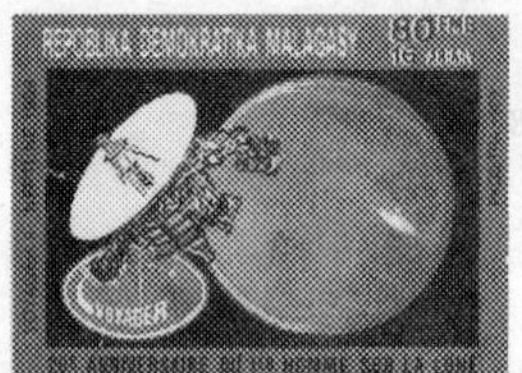

Moon Landing, 20th Anniv. — A314

Designs: 80fr, Voyager 2, Neptune. 250fr, Hydro 2000 flying boat. 550fr, NOAA satellite. 1500fr, Magellan probe, Venus. 2000fr, Concorde. 2500fr, Armstrong, Aldrin, Collins, lunar module. 3000fr, Apollo 11 astronauts, first step on moon.

1990, June 19 Litho. *Perf. 13½*

967 A314 80fr multicolored 15 15
968 A314 250fr multicolored 35 18
969 A314 550fr multicolored 82 40
970 A314 1500fr multicolored 2.25 1.10
971 A314 2000fr multicolored 3.00 1.50
972 A314 2500fr multicolored 3.75 1.90
Nos. 967-972 (6) 10.32 5.23

Souvenir Sheet

973 A314 3000fr multicolored 4.50 2.25

1992 Winter Olympics, Albertville — A315

1990, July 17

974 A315 350fr Bobsled 52 25
975 A315 1000fr Speed skating 1.50 75
976 A315 1500fr Nordic skiing 2.25 1.10

977 A315 2500fr Super giant slalom 3.75 1.90

Souvenir Sheet

978 A315 3000fr Giant slalom 4.50 2.25

Intl. Maritime Organization, 30th Anniv. — A316

1990, June 19 Litho. *Perf. 12*

979 A316 250fr blk, ultra & bl 40 20

African Development Bank, 25th Anniv. A317

1990, June 19

980 A317 80fr multicolored 15 15

Campaign Against Polio — A318

1990, June 28

981 A318 150fr multicolored 22 15

Independence, 30th Anniv. — A319

1990, Aug. 22

982 A319 100fr multicolored 16 15

3rd Indian Ocean Games — A320

1990, Aug. 24 *Perf. 12½x12*

983 A320 100fr yellow & multi 16 15
984 A320 350fr lil rose & multi 52 25
Set value 32

Stamp Day — A321

1990, Oct. 9 Litho. *Perf. 13x12½*

985 A321 350fr multicolored 60 30

Ho Chi Minh (1890-1969), Vietnamese Leader — A322

1990, Oct. 19 Litho. *Perf. 12*

986 A322 350fr multicolored 60 30

Lemurs A323

1990, Nov. 23 Litho. *Perf. 11½*

987 A323 10fr Avahi laniger 15 15
988 A323 20fr Lemur fulvus sanfordi 15 15
989 A323 20fr Lemur fulvus albifrons 15 15
990 A323 100fr Lemur fulvus collaris 18 15
991 A323 100fr Lepulemur ruficaudatus 18 15
Set value 46 23

Souvenir Sheet

992 A323 350fr Lemur fulvus fulvus 60 30

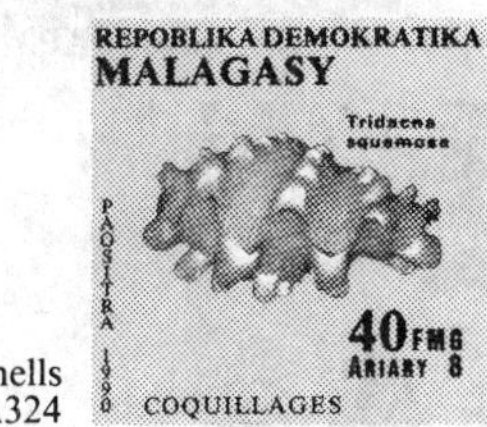

Shells A324

1990, Dec. 21 *Perf. 12½*

993 A324 40fr Tridacna squamosa 15 15
994 A324 50fr Terebra demidiata, Terebra subulata 15 15
Set value 18 15

Anniversaries and Events — A325

Designs: 100fr, Charles de Gaulle, liberation of Paris, 1944. 350fr, Galileo probe orbiting Jupiter. 800fr, Apollo 11 crew and Columbia command module, first Moon landing, 1969. 900fr, De Gaulle, 1942. 1250fr, Concorde jet, TGV high-speed train. 2500fr, De Gaulle as head of provisional government, 1944. 300fr, Apollo 11 crew, Eagle lunar module.

1990, Dec. 28 Litho. *Perf. 13½*

995 A325 100fr multi 18 15
996 A325 350fr multi 60 30
997 A325 800fr multi 1.40 70
998 A325 900fr multi 1.60 80
999 A325 1250fr multi 2.20 1.10
1000 A325 2500fr multi 4.40 2.20
Nos. 995-1000 (6) 10.38 5.25

Souvenir Sheet

1001 A325 3000fr multi 5.30 2.65

Nos. 995-1000 exist in souvenir sheets of 1.

Intl. Literacy Year A326

1990, Dec. 30 *Perf. 12*

1002 A326 20fr Book, guiding hands, vert. 15 15
1003 A326 100fr shown 18 15
Set value 22 15

Democratic Republic of Madagascar, 15th Anniv. (in 1990) A327

1991, Apr. 8 Litho. *Perf. 12*

1004 A327 100fr multicolored 18 15

Dated 1990.

Trees — A328

1991 Litho. *Perf. 13½*

1005 A328 140fr Adansonia fony 22 15
1006 A328 500fr Didierea madagascariensis 75 40

SEMI-POSTAL STAMPS

No. 84 Surcharged in Red **+5c**

1915, Feb. Unwmk. *Perf. 13½x14*

B1 A9 10c + 5c rose & brn 45 45

Curie Issue
Common Design Type

1938, Oct. 24 *Perf. 13*

B2 CD80 1.75fr + 50c brt ultra 5.75 5.75

French Revolution Issue
Common Design Type
Name and Value Typographed in Black

1939, July 5 Photo.

B3 CD83 45c + 25c grn 3.75 3.75
B4 CD83 70c + 30c brn 3.75 3.75
B5 CD83 90c + 35c red org 3.75 3.75
B6 CD83 1.25fr + 1fr rose pink 3.75 3.75
B7 CD83 2.25fr + 2fr blue 3.75 3.75
Nos. B3-B7 (5) 18.75 18.75

Common Design Type and

Malgache Sharpshooter — SP1

Tank Corpsman SP2

1941 Photo. *Perf. 13½*

B8 SP1 1fr + 1fr red 80
B9 CD86 1.50fr + 3fr maroon 80
B10 SP2 2.50fr + 1fr blue 1.00

Nos. B8-B10 were issued by the Vichy government, and were not placed on sale in the colony.

Nos. 162 and 190 surcharged "SECOURS +50c NATIONAL," and Nos. 210A-210B surcharged "OEUVRES COLONIALES" and surtax (including change of denomination of the 2.50fr to 50c) were issued in 1942-44 by the Vichy government, and not placed on sale in the colony.

Catalogue values for unused stamps in this section, from this point to the end of the section, are for Never Hinged items.

Red Cross Issue
Common Design Type

1944 Unwmk. *Perf. 14½x14*

B15 CD90 5fr + 20fr dk grn 38 38

The surtax was for the French Red Cross and national relief.

Gen. J. S. Galliéni and Malagasy Plowing — SP3

1946, Nov. Engr. *Perf. 13*

B16 SP3 10fr + 5fr dk vio brn 28 28

Issued to commemorate the 50th anniversary of Madagascar's existence as a French Colony.

Tropical Medicine Issue
Common Design Type

1950, May 15

B17 CD100 10fr + 2fr dk Prus grn & brn vio 2.75 2.75

The surtax was for charitable work.

Malagasy Republic
No. 320 Surcharged in Ultramarine with New Value and: "FETES DE L'INDEPENDANCE"

1960, July 29 Engr. *Perf. 13*

B18 A38 20fr + 10fr red, blk & brt grn 40 35

Anti-Malaria Issue
Common Design Type

1962, Apr. 7 *Perf. 12½x12*

B19 CD108 25fr + 5fr yel grn 50 50

Post Office, Tamatave SP4

1962, May 8 **Engr.** ***Perf. 13***
B20 SP4 25fr + 5fr sl grn, bl & lt red brn 25 25

Issued for Stamp Day, 1962.

Freedom from Hunger Issue
Common Design Type

1963, Mar. 21 ***Perf. 13***
B21 CD112 25fr + 5fr red org, plum & brn 45 45

FAO "Freedom from Hunger" campaign.

Type of 1962

Design: 20fr+5fr, Central Parcel Post Office, Tananarive.

1963, May 8 **Engr.**
B22 SP4 20fr + 5fr bl grn & red brn 30 30

Issued for Stamp Day, 1963.

Postal Savings and Checking Accounts Building, Tananarive — SP5

1964, May 8 **Unwmk.** ***Perf. 13***
B23 SP5 25fr + 5fr bl, bis & dk grn 40 40

Issued for Stamp Day, 1964.

No. 457 Surcharged in Violet Blue

+ 20F
MEMORIAL

1972, June 26 **Engr.** ***Perf. 13***
B24 A106 30fr + 20fr multi 40 40

Charles de Gaulle memorial.

Village Games — SP6

1989, June 15 **Litho.**
B25 SP6 80fr +20fr Torch bearer 20 15

3rd Indian Ocean Games — SP7

1990, Aug. 7 **Litho.** ***Perf. 12***
B26 SP7 100fr+20fr on 80fr+20fr 20 15
B27 SP7 350fr+20fr on 250fr+20fr 60 30

Nos. B26-B27 were not issued without surcharge.

AIR POST STAMPS

Airplane and Map of Madagascar — AP1

Perf. 13x13½

1935-41		**Photo.**	**Unwmk.**	
C1	AP1	50c yel grn & red	48	32
C2	AP1	90c yel grn & red ('41)	28	
C3	AP1	1.25fr cl & red	35	32
C4	AP1	1.50fr brt bl & red	35	32
C5	AP1	1.60fr brt bl & red ('41)	15	15
C6	AP1	1.75fr org & red	4.50	2.75
C7	AP1	2fr Prus bl & red	48	32
C8	AP1	3fr dp org & red ('41)	15	15
C9	AP1	3.65fr ol blk & red ('38)	35	32
C10	AP1	3.90fr pck grn & red ('41)	15	15
C11	AP1	4fr rose & red	30.00	2.00
C12	AP1	4.50fr blk & red	15.00	1.25
C13	AP1	5.50fr ol blk & red ('41)	18	15
C14	AP1	6fr rose lil & red ('41)	18	18
C15	AP1	6.90fr dl vio & red ('41)	15	15
C16	AP1	8fr rose lil & red	60	52
C17	AP1	8.50fr grn & red	70	70
C18	AP1	9fr ol grn & red ('41)	32	35
C19	AP1	12fr vio brn & red	52	40
C20	AP1	12.50fr dl vio & red	1.00	60
C21	AP1	15fr org yel & red ('41)	68	48
C22	AP1	16fr ol grn & red	90	70
C23	AP1	20fr dk brn & red	1.40	70
C24	AP1	50fr brt ultra & red ('38)	2.50	2.00
		Nos. C1,C3-C24 (23)	61.09	14.98

According to some authorities the 90c was not placed on sale in Madagascar.

V5

Stamps of type AP1, without "RF" monogram, and stamp of design shown above were issued in 1942 to 1944 by the Vichy Government, but were not placed on sale in the colony.

Air Post Stamps of 1935-38 Overprinted in Black

FRANCE LIBRE

1942		***Perf. 13x13½***		
C27	AP1	1.50fr brt bl & red	2.75	2.75
C28	AP1	1.75fr org & red	42.50	42.50
C29	AP1	8fr rose lil & red	75	75
C30	AP1	12fr vio brn & red	1.10	1.10
C31	AP1	12.50fr dl vio & red	80	80
C32	AP1	16fr ol grn & red	2.75	2.75
C33	AP1	50fr brt ultra & red	1.75	1.75

FRANCE LIBRE

Nos. C3, C9, C17 Surcharged in Black

1,00 ×

C34	AP1	1fr on 1.25fr	2.00	2.00
C35	AP1	3fr on 3.65fr	65	65
C36	AP1	8fr on 8.50fr	65	65
		Nos. C27-C36 (10)	55.70	55.70

Catalogue values for unused stamps in this section, from this point to the end of the section, are for Never Hinged items.

Common Design Type

1943		**Photo.**	***Perf. 14½x14***	
C37	CD87	1fr dk org	15	15
C38	CD87	1.50fr brt red	15	15
C39	CD87	5fr brn red	15	15
C40	CD87	10fr black	20	20
C41	CD87	25fr ultra	35	25
C42	CD87	50fr dk grn	50	38
C43	CD87	100fr plum	80	50
		Nos. C37-C43 (7)	2.30	
		Set value		1.50

Victory Issue
Common Design Type
Perf. 12½

1946, May 8 **Unwmk.** **Engr.**
C44 CD92 8fr brn red 30 20

Issued to commemorate the European victory of the Allied Nations in World War II.

Chad to Rhine Issue
Common Design Types

1946, June 6				
C45	CD93	5fr brt bl	50	50
C46	CD94	10fr dk car rose	50	50
C47	CD95	15fr gray grn	50	50
C48	CD96	20fr brn ol	60	60
C49	CD97	25fr dk vio	65	65
C50	CD98	50fr brn org	65	65
		Nos. C45-C50 (6)	3.40	3.40

Tamatave — AP2

Allegory of Air Mail — AP3

Plane over Map of Madagascar — AP4

Perf. 13½x12½, 12½x13½

1946		**Photo.**	**Unwmk.**	
C51	AP2	50fr bl vio & car	65	25
C52	AP3	100fr brn & car	1.65	40
C53	AP4	200fr bl grn & brn	3.25	1.00

No. C52 Overprinted in Carmine

TERRE ADÉLIE
DUMONT D'URVILLE
1840

1948, Oct. 26 ***Perf. 12½x13½***
C54 AP3 100fr brn & car 22.50 24.00

Issued to publicize the French claim to Antarctic Adelie Land, discovered by Jules S. C. Dumont d'Urville in 1840.

UPU Issue
Common Design Type

1949, July 4 **Engr.** ***Perf. 13***
C55 CD99 25fr multi 1.90 1.50

Scene Near Bemananga — AP5

1952, June 30 **Unwmk.** ***Perf. 13***
C56 AP5 500fr brn, blk brn & dk grn 10.50 3.25

Liberation Issue
Common Design Type

1954, June 6
C57 CD102 15fr vio & vio brn 80 65

Pachypodes — AP6

Designs: 100fr, Antsirabé viaduct. 200fr, Ring-tailed lemurs.

1954, Sept. 20				
C58	AP6	50fr dk bl grn & dk grn	1.00	15
C59	AP6	100fr dp ultra, blk & choc	1.60	65
C60	AP6	200fr dk grn & sep	4.00	1.20

Malagasy Republic

Sugar Cane Harvest — AP7

Charaxes Antamboulou — AP8

Designs: 40fr, Tobacco field. 100fr, Chrysiridia Madagascariensis. 200fr, Argema mittrel (vert.). 500fr, Mandrare bridge.

1960	**Unwmk.**	**Engr.**	***Perf. 13***	
C61	AP7	30fr grn, vio brn & pale brn	42	15
C62	AP7	40fr Prus grn & ol gray	65	20
C63	AP8	50fr multi	70	16
C64	AP8	100fr sl grn, emer & org	1.50	22
C65	AP8	200fr pur & yel	2.25	60
C66	AP7	500fr Prus grn, bis & ultra	5.50	1.50
		Nos. C61-C66 (6)	11.02	2.83

Diademed Sifakas — AP9

Lemurs: 85fr, Indri. 250fr, Verreaux's sifaka.

1961, Dec. 9 Unwmk. Perf. 13
C67 AP9 65fr sl grn & red brn 65 25
C68 AP9 85fr ol, blk & brn 80 35
C69 AP9 250fr Prus grn, blk & mar 2.50 1.20

Plane over Nossi-Be — AP10

1962, May 7 Engr. Perf. 13
C70 AP10 100fr red brn, bl & dk grn 70 40
a. Souv. sheet of 5, #328-331, C70 1.50 1.50

1st Malagasy Philatelic Exhibition, Tananarive, May 5-13.

Turbojet Airliner, Emblem — AP11

1963, Apr. 18 Unwmk. Perf. 13
C71 AP11 500fr dk bl, red & grn 3.50 1.25

Madagascar commercial aviation.

Helmet Bird — AP12

Birds: 100fr, Pitta-like ground roller. 200fr, Crested wood ibis.

1963, Aug. 12 Photo. Perf. 13x12½
C72 AP12 40fr multi 35 25
C73 AP12 100fr multi 1.00 42
C74 AP12 200fr multi 2.00 80

African Postal Union Issue
Common Design Type

1963, Sept. 8 Perf. 12½
C75 CD114 85fr grn, ocher & red 1.00 70

Map of Madagascar, Jet Plane and UPU Emblem — AP13

1963, Nov. 2 Engr. Perf. 13
C76 AP13 45fr dk car, grnsh bl & ultra 40 20
C77 AP13 85fr dk car, vio & bl 70 40

Malagasy Republic's admission to the UPU, Nov. 2, 1961.

Meteorological Center, Tananarive and Tiros Satellite — AP14

1964, Mar. 23 Unwmk.
C78 AP14 90fr org brn, ultra & grn 1.20 50

UN 4th World Meteorological Day, Mar. 23.

Zebu, Wood Sculpture — AP15

1964, Oct. 20 Engr. Perf. 13
C79 AP15 100fr lil rose, dk vio & brn 90 62

Musical Instrument Type of Regular Issue

Design: 200fr, Lokanga bara (stringed instrument).

1965, Feb. 16 Unwmk. Perf. 13
Size: 26x47mm
C80 A57 200fr grn, org & choc 1.90 1.00

Nurse Weighing Infant, and ICY Emblem — AP16

Design: 100fr, Small boy and girl, child care scenes and ICY emblem.

1965, Sept. 20 Engr. Perf. 13
C81 AP16 50fr multi 42 25
C82 AP16 100fr multi 80 50

International Cooperation Year.

Dance Type of Regular Issue

Design: 250fr, Dance of a young girl, Sakalava (vert.).

1966, June 13 Photo. Perf. 13
Size: 27x49mm
C83 A68 250fr multi 2.00 80

Aviation Type of Regular Issue

Design: 500fr, Dagnaux-Dufert and his Breguet biplane, 1927.

1967, Apr. 28 Engr. Perf. 13
Size: 48x27mm
C84 A76 500fr Prus bl, blk & brn 4.00 1.40

No. C84 for the 40th anniv. of the 1st Majunga-Tananarive flight.

African Postal Union Issue, 1967
Common Design Type

1967, Sept. 9 Engr. Perf. 13
C85 CD124 100fr ol bis, red brn & brt pink 80 35

Dancer Type of Regular Issue

Designs: 100fr, Tourbillon dance (horiz.). 200fr, Male dancer from the South.

1967-68 Photo. Perf. 11½
Size: 38x23mm
C86 A80 100fr multi ('68) 65 38
Perf. 13
Size: 27x48mm
C87 A80 200fr multi 1.60 70

Issue dates: 100fr, Nov. 25. 200fr, Nov. 25.

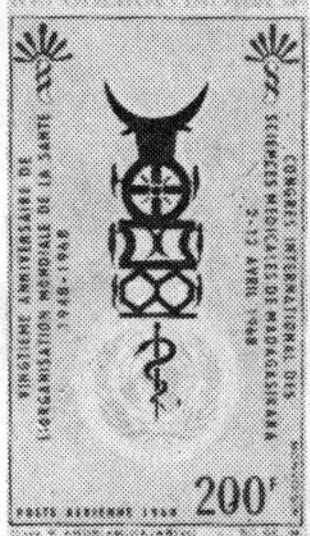
WHO Emblem, Bull's Head Totem and Palm Fan — AP17

1968, Apr. 7 Photo. Perf. 12½x13
C88 AP17 200fr bl, yel brn & red 1.50 80

WHO, 20th anniv.; Intl. Congress of Medical Science, Apr. 2-12.

Tananarive-Ivato International Airport — AP18

1968, May 8 Engr. Perf. 13
C89 AP18 500fr lt red brn, dl bl & dl grn 3.75 2.00

Issued for Stamp Day.

No. C68 Surcharged in Vermilion with New Value and 2 Bars

1968, June 24 Engr. Perf. 13
C90 AP9 20fr on 85fr multi 16 15

PHILEXAFRIQUE Issue

Lady Sealing Letter, by Jean Baptiste Santerre AP19

1968, Dec. 30 Photo. Perf. 12½x12
C91 AP19 100fr lil & multi 1.10 60

Issued to publicize PHILEXAFRIQUE Philatelic Exhibition in Abidjan, Feb. 14-23. Printed with alternating lilac label.

2nd PHILEXAFRIQUE Issue
Common Design Type

Design: 50fr, Madagascar No. 274, map of Madagascar and Malagasy emblem.

1969, Feb. 14 Engr. Perf. 13
C92 CD128 50fr gray, brn red & sl grn 60 35

Sunset over Madagascar Highlands, by Henri Ratovo — AP20

Painting: 100fr, On the Seashore of the East Coast of Madagascar, by Alfred Razafinjohany.

1969, Nov. 5 Photo. Perf. 12x12½
C93 AP20 100fr brn & multi 80 50
C94 AP20 150fr multi 1.20 80

Lunar Landing Module and Man on the Moon — AP21

1970, July 20 Engr. Perf. 13
C95 AP21 75fr ultra, dk gray & sl grn 45 38

Issued to commemorate the first anniversary of man's first landing on the moon.

Boeing 737 — AP22

1970, Dec. 18 Engr. Perf. 13
C96 AP22 200fr bl, red brn & grn 1.20 65

Jean Ralaimongo (1884-1944) AP23

Portraits: 40fr, René Rakotobe (1918-1971). 65fr, Albert Sylla (1909-1967). 100fr, Joseph Ravoahangy Andrianavalona (1893-1970).

1971-72 Photo. *Perf. 12½; 13 (40fr)*

C97 AP23 25fr red brn, org & blk 16 15
C98 AP23 40fr dp cl, ocher & blk 22 16
C99 AP23 65fr grn, lt grn & blk 35 25
C100 AP23 100fr vio bl, lt bl & blk 60 35

Famous Malagasy men.

Issue dates: No. C98, July 25, 1972; others, Oct. 14, 1971.

African Postal Union Issue, 1971

"Mpisikidy" by G. Rakotovao and UAMPT Building, Brazzaville, Congo — AP24

1971, Nov. 13 Photo. *Perf. 13x13½*

C105 AP24 100fr bl & multi 65 42

10th anniv. of African and Malagasy Posts and Telecommunications Union (UAMPT).

Running, Olympic Village AP25

Design: 200fr, Judo, Olympic Stadium.

1972, Sept. 11 Photo. *Perf. 13½*

C106 AP25 100fr multi 65 35
C107 AP25 200fr multi 1.10 55

20th Olympic Games, Munich, Aug. 26-Sept. 11.

Mohair Goat AP26

1972, Nov. 15

C108 AP26 250fr multi 1.90 1.00

Adoration of the Kings, by Andrea Mantegna — AP27

Christmas: 85fr, Virgin and Child, Florentine School, 15th century (vert.).

1972, Dec. 15 Photo. *Perf. 13*

C109 AP27 85fr gold & multi 50 25
C110 AP27 150fr gold & multi 90 42

Landing Module, Astronauts and Lunar Rover AP28

1973, Jan. 25 Engr. *Perf. 13*

C111 AP28 300fr dp cl, gray & brn 1.50 1.25

Apollo 17 moon mission, Dec. 7-19, 1972.

The Burial of Christ, by Grunewald — AP29

Easter: 200fr, Resurrection, by Mattias Grunewald (horiz.). Both paintings from panels of Issenheim altar.

1973, Mar. 22 Photo. *Perf. 13*

C112 AP29 100fr gold & multi 45 25
C113 AP29 200fr gold & multi 1.00 50

Early Excursion Car — AP30

Design: 150fr, Early steam locomotive.

1973, July 25 Photo. *Perf. 13x12½*

C114 AP30 100fr multi 45 25
C115 AP30 150fr multi 70 40

Set Values

A 15-cent minimum now applies to individual stamps and sets. Where the 15-cent minimum per stamp would increase the "value" of a set beyond retail, there is a "Set Value" notation giving the retail value of the set.

WMO Emblem, Radar, Map of Madagascar, Hurricane AP31

Pres. John F. Kennedy, US Flag AP32

1973, Sept. 3 Engr. *Perf. 13*

C116 AP31 100fr blk, ultra & org 60 30

Cent. of intl. meteorological cooperation.

Lemur Type of Regular Issue

Designs: 150fr, Lepilemur mustelinus (vert.). 200fr, Cheirogaleus major.

1973, Oct. 9 Engr. *Perf. 13*

C117 A131 150fr multi 90 55
C118 A131 200fr multi 1.20 80

1973, Nov. 22 Photo. *Perf. 13*

C119 AP32 300fr multi 1.60 1.00

10th anniv. of the death of John F. Kennedy.

Soccer — AP33

1973, Dec. 20 Engr. *Perf. 13*

C120 AP33 500fr lil rose, dk brn & org brn 3.00 2.00

World Soccer Cup, Munich, 1974.

Copernicus, Skylab and Heliocentric System — AP34

1974, Jan. 22

C121 AP34 250fr multi 1.20 45

500th anniversary of the birth of Nicolaus Copernicus (1473-1543), Polish astronomer.

Scout Type of Regular Issue

Designs (African Scout Emblem and): 100fr, Scouts bringing sick people to Red Cross tent (horiz.). 300fr, Scouts fishing and fish (horiz.).

1974, Feb. 14 Engr. *Perf. 13*

C122 A132 100fr multi 55 22
C123 A132 300fr multi 1.60 70

Camellia, Hummingbird, Table Tennis Player — AP35

Design: 100fr, Girl player, flower and bird design.

1974, Mar. 19 Engr. *Perf. 13*

C124 AP35 50fr bl & multi 25 15
C125 AP35 100fr multi 55 25

Table Tennis Tournament, Peking.

Autorail Micheline — AP36

Designs (Malagasy Locomotives): 85fr, Track inspection trolley. 200fr, Garratt (steam).

1974, June 7 Engr. *Perf. 13*

C126 AP36 50fr multi 25 16
C127 AP36 85fr multi 42 22
C128 AP36 200fr multi 1.10 80

Letters and UPU Emblem — AP37

1974, July 9 Engr. *Perf. 13*

C129 AP37 250fr multi 1.40 65

Centenary of Universal Postal Union.

No. C120 Overprinted: "R.F.A. 2 / HOLLANDE 1"

1974, Aug. 20 Engr. *Perf. 13*

C130 AP33 500fr multi 2.50 1.50

World Cup Soccer Championship, 1974, victory of German Federal Republic.

Link-up in Space, Globe, Emblem — AP38

Design: 250fr, Link-up, globe and emblem (different).

1974, Sept. 12

C131 AP38 150fr org, bl & sl grn 80 65
C132 AP38 250fr bl, brn & sl grn 1.40 90

Russo-American space cooperation.

No. C129 Overprinted

**100 ANS
DE
COLLABORATION
INTERNATIONALE**

1974, Oct. 9 Engr. *Perf. 13*

C133 AP37 250fr multi 1.40 65

100 years of international collaboration.

Adoration of the Kings, by J. L. David
AP39

Christmas: 300fr, Virgin of the Cherries and Child, by Quentin Massys.

1974, Dec. 20 Photo. *Perf. 13*
C134 AP39 200fr gold & multi 90 40
C135 AP39 300fr gold & multi 1.40 60

UN Emblem and Globe — AP40

1975, June 24 Litho. *Perf. 12½*
C136 AP40 300fr grn, bl & blk 1.60 80

United Nations Charter, 30th anniversary.

American Bicentennial Type, 1975

Designs: 100fr, Count d'Estaing and "Languedoc." 200fr, John Paul Jones, "Bonhomme Richard" and "Serapis." 300fr, Benjamin Franklin, "Millern" and "Montgomery." 500fr, George Washington and "Hanna."

1975, June 30 Litho. *Perf. 11*
C137 A144 100fr multi 60 25
C138 A144 200fr multi 1.20 55
C139 A144 300fr multi 1.90 80

Souvenir Sheet

C140 A144 500fr multi 3.25 1.50

Flower Type of 1975

Design: 85fr, Turraea sericea.

1975, Aug. 4 Photo. *Perf. 12½*
C141 A145 85fr dp grn, yel & org 45 35

Nos. C131-C132 Overprinted **JONCTION 17 JUILLET 1975**

1975, Aug. 5 Engr. *Perf. 13*
C142 AP38 150fr multi 80 40
C143 AP38 250fr multi 1.40 65

Apollo Soyuz link-up in space, July 17, 1975.

Bas-relief and Stupas — AP41

1975, Aug. 10 Engr. *Perf. 13*
C144 AP41 50fr bl, car & bis 25 16

UNESCO campaign to save Borobudur Temple, Java.

Exposition Type, 1975

Designs: 125fr, Deer. 300fr, Jay.

1975, Sept. 16 Litho. *Perf. 14x13½*
C145 A147 125fr multi 80 45

Souvenir Sheet

C146 A147 300fr multi 2.00 1.00

Hurdling and Olympic Rings — AP42

Design: 200fr, Weight lifting and Olympic rings (vert.).

1975, Oct. 9 Litho. *Perf. 12½*
C147 AP42 75fr multi 40 20
C148 AP42 200fr multi 1.10 55

Pre-Olympic Year 1975.

12th Winter Olympics Type, 1975

Designs: 200fr, Cross-country skiing. 245fr, Down-hill skiing. 450fr, Figure skating, pairs.

1975, Nov. 19 *Perf. 14*
C149 A149 200fr multi 1.25 55
C150 A149 245fr multi 1.50 65

Souvenir Sheet

C151 A149 450fr multi 3.00 1.50

Landing Module, Apollo 14 Emblem — AP43

1976, Jan. 18 Engr. *Perf. 13*
C152 AP43 150fr red, grn & ind 80 40

Apollo 14 moon landing, 5th anniversary.

21st Summer Olympics Type, 1976

Designs: 100fr, Shot-put and long jump. 200fr, Gymnastics, horse and balance bar. 300fr, Diving, 3-meter and platform. 500fr, Swimming, free-style and breast stroke.

1976, Jan. 21 Litho. *Perf. 13½*
C153 A151 100fr multi 60 28
C154 A151 200fr multi 1.25 62
C155 A151 300fr multi 1.90 80

Souvenir Sheet

C156 A151 500fr multi 3.25 1.50

No. C152 Overprinted: "5e Anniversaire / de la mission / APOLLO XIV"

1976, Feb. 5 Engr. *Perf. 13*
C157 AP43 150fr red, grn & ind 80 40

Apollo 14 moon landing, 5th anniversary.

Zeppelin Type of 1976

Designs (Count Zeppelin and LZ-127 over): 200fr, Brandenburg Gate, Berlin 300fr, Parliament, London. 450fr, St. Peter's Cathedral, Rome.

1976, Mar. 3 Litho. *Perf. 11*
C158 A152 200fr multi 1.40 60
C159 A152 300fr multi 1.60 90

Souvenir Sheet

C160 A152 450fr multi 3.00 1.40

Nos. C149-C151 Overprinted

a. VAINQUEUR IVAR FORMO NORVEGE
b. VAINQUEUR ROSI MITTERMAIER ALLEMAGNE DE L'OUEST
c. VAINQUEUR IRINA RODNINA ALEXANDER ZAITSEV URSS

1976, June 17
C161 A149 (a) 200fr multi 85 45
C162 A149 (b) 245fr multi 1.00 50

Souvenir Sheet

C163 A149 (c) 450fr multi 1.75 1.20

12th Winter Olympic games winners.

Nos. C137-C140 Overprinted "4 Juillet / 1776-1976"

1976, July 4
C164 A144 100fr multi 65 25
C165 A144 200fr multi 1.25 55
C166 A144 300fr multi 1.90 80

Souvenir Sheet

C167 A144 500fr multi 3.25 1.60

American Bicentennial.

Nos. C153-C156 Overprinted

a. U. BEYER / A. ROBINSON
b. N. ANDRIANOV / N. COMANECI
c. K. DIBIASI / E. VAYTSEKHOVSKAIA,
d. J. MONTGOMERY / H. ANKE

1977, Jan.
C168 A151 (a) 100fr multi 62 25
C169 A151 (b) 200fr multi 1.20 55
C170 A151 (c) 300fr multi 1.75 80

Souvenir Sheet

C171 A151 (d) 500fr multi 3.25 1.60

21st Summer Olympic Games winners.

Fauna Type of 1979

Designs: 20fr, Tortoises. 95fr, Macaco lemurs.

1979, July 6
C172 A176 20fr multi 15 15
C173 A176 95fr multi 62 22
Set value 36

International Palestinian Solidarity Day — AP44

1979, Nov. 29 Litho. *Perf. 12x12½*
C174 AP44 60fr multi 40 16

Olympic Type of 1980

1980, Dec. 29 Litho. *Perf. 12½x12*
C175 A188 250fr Judo 1.60 70
C176 A188 500fr Swimming 3.50 1.50

Stamp Day — AP45

1981, Dec. 17 Litho. *Perf. 12x12½*
C177 AP45 90fr multi 60 22

20th Anniv. of Pan-African Women's Org. — AP46

1982, Aug. 6 Litho. *Perf. 12*
C178 AP46 80fr dk brn & lt brn 55 22

Hydroelectric Plant, Andekaleka — AP47

1982, Sept. 13 *Perf. 12½x12*
C179 AP47 80fr multi 55 22

Orchid Type of 1984

1984, Nov. 20 Litho. *Perf. 12*
C180 A226 50fr Eulophiella elisabethae, horiz. 15 15
C181 A226 50fr Grammangis ellisii, horiz. 15 15
C182 A226 50fr Grammangis spectabilis 15 15
Set value 20

Solar Princess, by Sadiou Diouf
AP48

1984, Dec. 22 Litho. *Perf. 12*
C183 AP48 100fr multi 30 15

Intl. Civil Aviation Org., 40th anniv.

Halley's Comet
AP49

1986, Apr. 5 Litho. *Perf. 12½x13*
C184 AP49 150fr multi 50 25

Admission of Madagascar into the UPU, 25th Anniv. — AP50

1986, Dec. 23 Litho. *Perf. 11½*
C185 AP50 150fr multi 50 25

Air Madagascar, 25th Anniv.
AP51

1987, June 17 Litho. *Perf. 12x12½*
C186 AP51 60fr Piper Aztec 22 15
C187 AP51 60fr Twin Otter 22 15
C188 AP51 150fr Boeing 747 60 28
Set value 48

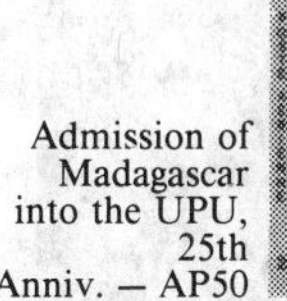

Socialist Revolution, 15th Anniv. — AP52

1990, June 16 Litho. *Perf. 13½*
C189 AP52 100fr Map 16 15
C190 AP52 350fr Architecture 58 30
Set value 38

Madagascan Bible Society, 25th Anniv. AP53

1990, Sept. 17 *Perf. 12½*
C191 AP53 25fr lt bl & multi 15 15
C192 AP53 100fr bl, blk & grn, vert. 16 15
Set value 20 15

AIR POST SEMI-POSTAL STAMPS

French Revolution Issue
Common Design Type
Unwmk.
1939, July 5 Photo. *Perf. 13*
Name and Value in Orange
CB1 CD83 4.50fr + 4fr brn blk 8.00 8.00

V6

V7

V8

Stamps of the designs shown above, and type of Cameroun V10 inscribed "Madagascar", were issued in 1942 by the Vichy Government, but were not placed on sale in the colony.

POSTAGE DUE STAMPS

D1

Governor's Palace — D2

Postage Due Stamps of French Colonies Overprinted in Red or Blue

1896 Unwmk. *Imperf.*
J1 D1 5c blue (R) 4.00 3.75
J2 D1 10c brn (R) 4.00 3.25
J3 D1 20c yel (Bl) 4.50 4.00
J4 D1 30c rose red (Bl) 4.50 4.00
J5 D1 40c lilac (R) 35.00 22.50
J6 D1 50c gray vio (Bl) 6.00 4.75
J7 D1 1fr dk grn (R) 37.50 35.00
Nos. J1-J7 (7) 95.50 77.25

1908-24 Typo. *Perf. 13½x14*
J8 D2 2c vio brn 15 15
J9 D2 4c violet 15 15
J10 D2 5c green 15 15
J11 D2 10c dp rose 15 15
J12 D2 20c olive grn 15 15
J13 D2 40c brn, *straw* 15 15
J14 D2 50c brn, *bl* 15 15
J15 D2 60c org ('24) 35 35
J16 D2 1fr dark blue 42 42
Set value 1.25 1.25

Type of 1908 Issue Surcharged **60c**

1924-27
J17 D2 60c on 1fr org 1.00 1.00

Surcharged **2f**

J18 D2 2fr on 1fr lil rose ('27) 42 42
J19 D2 3fr on 1fr ultra ('27) 42 42

Postage Due Stamps of 1908-27 Overprinted or Surcharged in Black

FRANCE LIBRE

1943 *Perf. 13½x14*
J20 D2 10c dp rose 52 52
J21 D2 20c olive grn 52 52
J22 D2 30c on 5c green 52 52
J23 D2 40c brn, *straw* 52 52
J24 D2 50c brn, *blue* 52 52
J25 D2 60c orange 52 52
J26 D2 1fr dark blue 52 52
J27 D2 1fr on 2c vio brn 2.25 2.25
J28 D2 2fr on 1fr lil rose 52 52
J29 D2 2fr on 4c vio 90 90
J30 D2 3fr on 1fr ultra 52 52
Nos. J20-J30 (11) 7.83 7.83

Catalogue values for unused stamps in this section, from this point to the end of the section, are for Never Hinged items.

D3

Independence Monument — D4

1947 Photo. *Perf. 13*
J31 D3 10c dk vio 15 15
J32 D3 30c brown 15 15
J33 D3 50c dk bl grn 15 15
J34 D3 1fr dp org 15 15
J35 D3 2fr red vio 15 15
J36 D3 3fr red brn 15 15
J37 D3 4fr blue 25 25
J38 D3 5fr henna brown 30 30
J39 D3 10fr slate green 42 42
J40 D3 20fr vio blue 80 80
Set value 2.30 2.30

Malagasy Republic
Engraved; Denomination Typographed
1962, May 7 Unwmk. *Perf. 13*
J41 D4 1fr brt grn 15 15
J42 D4 2fr copper brn 15 15
J43 D4 3fr brt vio 15 15
J44 D4 4fr slate 15 15
J45 D4 5fr red 15 15
J46 D4 10fr yel grn 15 15
J47 D4 20fr dull claret 20 15
J48 D4 40fr blue 45 38
J49 D4 50fr rose red 70 65
J50 D4 100fr black 1.40 1.20
Set value 3.00 2.65

MADEIRA

LOCATION — A group of islands in the Atlantic Ocean northwest of Africa
GOVT. — Part of the Republic of Portugal
AREA — 314 sq. mi.
POP. — 150,574 (1900)
CAPITAL — Funchal

These islands are considered an integral part of Portugal and since 1898 postage stamps of Portugal have been in use. See Portugal for issues also inscribed Madeira, starting in 1980.

1000 Reis = 1 Milreis
100 Centavos = 1 Escudo (1925)

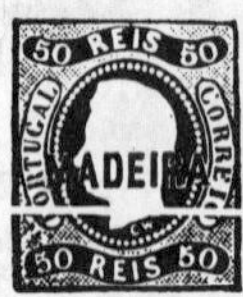

King Luiz
A1 A2

Stamps of Portugal Overprinted

1868, Jan. 1 Unwmk. *Imperf.*
Black Overprint
2 A1 20r bister 150.00 65.00
a. Inverted overprint
b. Rouletted
3 A1 50r green 150.00 60.00
4 A1 80r orange 165.00 75.00
a. Double overprint
5 A1 100r lilac 165.00 60.00

The 5r black does not exist as a genuinely imperforate original.

Reprints of 1885 are on stout white paper, ungummed. (Also, 5r, 10r and 25r values were overprinted.) Reprints of 1905 are on ordinary white paper with shiny gum and have a wide "D" and "R." Value, $12 each.

Lozenge Perf.

2c A1 20r
3a A1 50r
4b A1 80r
5a A1 100r

Overprinted in Red or Black

1868-70 *Perf. 12½*
6 A1 5r black (R) 30.00 17.50
8 A1 10r yellow 70.00 30.00
9 A1 20r bister 70.00 30.00
10 A1 25r rose 42.50 6.25
a. Inverted overprint
11 A1 50r green 125.00 40.00
a. Inverted overprint
12 A1 80r orange 175.00 70.00
13 A1 100r lilac 150.00 50.00
a. Inverted overprint
14 A1 120r blue 85.00 45.00
15 A1 240r violet ('70) 315.00 110.00

Two types of 5r differ in the position of the "5" at upper right.

The reprints are on stout white paper, ungummed, with rough perforation 13½, and on thin white paper with shiny white gum and clean-cut perforation 13½. The overprint has the wide "D" and "R" and the first reprints included the 5r with both black and red overprint. Value $10 each.

Common Design Types pictured in section at front of book.

Overprinted in Red or Black

1871-80 *Perf. 12½, 13½*
16 A2 5r black (R) 4.25 3.50
a. Inverted overprint
b. Double overprint
c. Perf. 14 65.00 30.00
18 A2 10r yellow 17.50 9.75
19 A2 10r bl grn ('79) 62.50 30.00
a. Perf. 13½ 75.50 62.50
20 A2 10r yel grn ('80) 27.50 25.00
21 A2 15r brn ('75) 8.50 7.00
22 A2 20r bister 14.00 10.50
23 A2 25r rose 8.50 2.00
a. Inverted overprint
24 A2 50r green ('72) 35.00 14.00
a. Double overprint
b. Inverted overprint
25 A2 50r blue ('80) 62.50 25.00
26 A2 80r orange ('72) 60.00 30.00
27 A2 100r pale lil ('73) 37.50 21.00
a. Perf. 14 225.00 175.00
b. Perf. 13½ 42.50 27.50
28 A2 120r blue 67.50 30.00
29 A2 150r blue ('76) 140.00 60.00
a. Perf. 13½ 150.00 100.00
30 A2 150r yel ('79) 195.00 175.00
31 A2 240r vio ('74) 500.00 200.00
32 A2 300r vio ('76) 62.50 25.00

There are two types of the overprint, the second one having a broad "D."

The reprints have the same characteristics as those of the 1868-70 issues.

King Luiz
A4 A5

1880-81
33 A4 5r black 13.00 9.00
34 A5 25r pearl gray 13.00 9.25
a. Inverted overprint
35 A4 25r lilac 15.00 4.50

No. 35 is overprinted on Portugal type A18.

Nos. 33, 34 and 35 have been reprinted on stout white paper, ungummed, and the last three on thin white paper with shiny white gum. The perforations are as previously described.

Vasco da Gama Issue
Common Design Types
1898, Apr. 1 Engr. *Perf. 14-15*
37 CD20 2½r blue grn 1.50 55
38 CD21 5r red 1.50 55
39 CD22 10r red violet 2.75 1.25
40 CD23 25r yel green 1.50 60
41 CD24 50r dk blue 4.50 2.25
42 CD25 75r vio brown 6.50 4.50
43 CD26 100r bister brn 4.50 3.75
44 CD27 150r bister 9.25 5.75
Nos. 37-44 (8) 32.00 19.20

Nos. 37-44 with "REPUBLICA" overprint and surcharges are listed as Portugal Nos. 199-206.

Ceres — A6

1928, May 1 Engr. *Perf. 13½*
Value Typographed in Black
45 A6 3c deep violet 18 *50*
46 A6 4c orange 18 *50*
47 A6 5c light blue 18 *50*
48 A6 6c brown 18 *50*
49 A6 10c red 18 *50*
50 A6 15c yel green 18 *50*
51 A6 16c red brown 22 *50*
52 A6 25c violet rose 22 *50*
53 A6 32c blue grn 22 *50*
54 A6 40c yel brown 52 *1.50*
55 A6 50c slate 52 *1.50*
56 A6 64c Prussian bl 75 *2.50*
57 A6 80c dk brown 75 *2.50*
58 A6 96c carmine rose 75 *2.50*
59 A6 1e black 75 *2.50*
a. Value omitted
60 A6 1.20e light rose 75 *2.50*
61 A6 1.60e ultra 75 *2.50*
62 A6 2.40e yellow 80 *3.00*
63 A6 3.36e dull green 1.50 *5.00*
64 A6 4.50e brown red 1.65 *8.00*
65 A6 7e dk bl 2.75 *15.00*
Nos. 45-65 (21) 13.98 *53.50*

It was obligatory to use these stamps in place of those in regular use on May 1, June 5, July 1 and Dec. 31, 1928, Jan. 1 and 31, May 1 and June 5, 1929. The amount obtained from this sale was donated to a fund for building a museum.

NEWSPAPER STAMP

Numeral of Value — N1

Newspaper Stamp of Portugal Overprinted in Black

Perf. 12½, 13½

1876, July 1 **Unwmk.**

P1	N1 2½r olive	4.50	1.90
a.	Inverted overprint	20.00	

The reprints have the same papers, gum, perforations and overprint as the reprints of the regular issues.

POSTAL TAX STAMPS

Pombal Commemorative Issue

Common Design Types

1925 Unwmk. Engr. ***Perf. 12½***

RA1	CD28 15c gray & black	55	60
RA2	CD29 15c gray & black	55	60
RA3	CD30 15c gray & black	55	60

POSTAL TAX DUE STAMPS

Pombal Commemorative Issue

Common Design Types

1925 Unwmk. ***Perf. 12½***

RAJ1	CD31 30c gray & black	75	1.10
RAJ2	CD32 30c gray & black	75	1.10
RAJ3	CD33 30c gray & black	75	1.10

MALI

Federation of Mali

LOCATION — West Africa
GOVT. — Republic within French Community
AREA — 531,000 sq. mi.
POP. — 5,862,000 (est.)
CAPITAL — Dakar and Bamako

The Federation of Mali, founded Jan. 17, 1959, consisted of the Republic of Senegal and the Sudanese Republic. It broke up in June, 1960. See Senegal.

100 Centimes = 1 Franc

Catalogue values for all unused stamps in this country are for Never Hinged items.

Flag and Map of Mali A1

Unwmk.

1959, Nov. 7 Engr. ***Perf. 13***

1	A1 25fr grn, car & dp claret	35	35

Founding of the Federation of Mali.

Imperforates

Most Mali stamps exist imperforate in issued and trial colors, and also in small presentation sheets in issued colors.

Parrotfish A2

Fish: 10fr, Triggerfish. 15fr, Psetta. 20fr, Blepharis crinitus. 25fr, Butterflyfish. 30fr, Surgeonfish. 85fr, Dentex.

1960, Mar. 5

Fish in Natural Colors

2	A2 5fr olive	18	15
3	A2 10fr brt grnsh bl	20	15
4	A2 15fr dk bl	25	16
5	A2 20fr gray grn	38	20
6	A2 25fr sl grn	42	25
7	A2 30fr dk bl	60	40
8	A2 85fr dk grn	1.40	1.00
	Nos. 2-8 (7)	3.43	2.31

C.C.T.A. Issue

Common Design Type

1960, May 21 ***Perf. 13***

9	CD106 25fr lt vio & mag	70	55

REPUBLIC OF MALI

GOVT. — Republic
AREA — 463,500 sq. mi.
POP. — 5,990,000 (est. 1977)
CAPITAL — Bamako

The Republic of Mali, formerly the Sudanese Republic, proclaimed its independence on June 20, 1960, when the Federation of Mali ceased to exist. See French Sudan.

Nos. 5, 6 and 8 Overprinted "REPUBLIQUE DU MALI" and Bar

Unwmk.

1961, Jan. 15 Engr. ***Perf. 13***

Fish in Natural Colors

10	A2 20fr gray grn	32	25
11	A2 25fr sl grn	40	25
12	A2 85fr dk grn	90	55

Pres. Mamadou Konate — A3

Design: 25fr, Pres. Modibo Keita.

1961, Mar. 18

13	A3 20fr grn & blk	15	15
14	A3 25fr mar & blk	18	15
	Set value		15

For miniature sheet see No. C11a.

Reading Class, Bullock Team and Factory — A4

1961, Sept. 22 Unwmk. ***Perf. 13***

15	A4 25fr multi	35	20

First anniversary of Independence.

Common Design Types pictured in section at front of book.

Shepherd and Sheep — A5

Designs: 1fr, 10fr, 40fr, Cattle. 2fr, 15fr, 50fr, Mali Arts Museum. 3fr, 20fr, 60fr, Plowing. 4fr, 25fr, 85fr, Harvester.

Unwmk.

1961, Dec. 24 Engr. ***Perf. 13***

16	A5 50c car rose, blk & dk grn	15	15
17	A5 1fr grn, bl & bis	15	15
18	A5 2fr ultra, grn & org red	15	15
19	A5 3fr bl, grn & brn	15	15
20	A5 4fr bl grn, ind & bis	15	15
21	A5 5fr bl, ol & mar	15	15
22	A5 10fr ol blk, bl & sep	15	15
23	A5 15fr ultra, grn & bis brn	15	15
24	A5 20fr bl, grn & org red	16	15
25	A5 25fr dk bl & yel grn	20	15
26	A5 30fr vio, grn & dk brn	24	16
27	A5 40fr sl grn, bl & org red	32	15
28	A5 50fr ultra, grn & rose car	30	15
29	A5 60fr bl, grn & brn	40	16
30	A5 85fr bl, bis & dk red brn	60	20
	Set value	2.65	1.20

King Mohammed V of Morocco and Map of Africa — A6

1962, Jan. 4 Photo. ***Perf. 12***

31	A6 25fr multi	20	15
32	A6 50fr multi	38	15
	Set value		24

Issued to commemorate the first anniversary of the conference of African heads of state at Casablanca.

Patrice Lumumba A7

1962, Feb. 12 Unwmk. ***Perf. 12***

33	A7 25fr choc & brn org	16	15
34	A7 100fr choc & emer	65	38

Issued in memory of Patrice Lumumba, Premier of the Congo (Democratic) Republic.

Pegasus and UPU Monument, Bern — A8

1962, Apr. 21 ***Perf. 12½x12***

35	A8 85fr red brn, yel & brt grn	65	50

1st anniv. of Mali's admission to the UPU.

Map of Africa and Post Horn — A8a

1962, Apr. 23 ***Perf. 13½x13***

36	A8a 25fr dk red brn & dp grn	18	15
37	A8a 85fr dp grn & org	60	35

Establishment of African Postal Union.

Sansanding Dam — A9

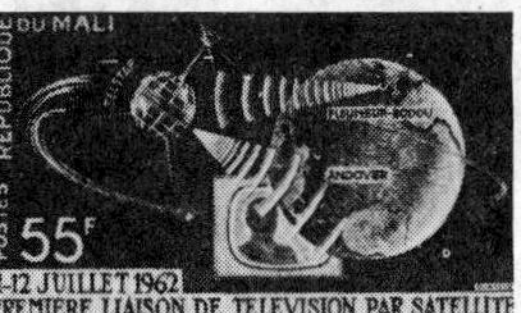

Cotton Plant A10

1962, Oct. 27 Photo. ***Perf. 12***

38	A9 25fr dk gray, ultra & grn	18	15
39	A10 45fr multi	42	20

Telstar, Earth and Television Set — A10a

1962, Nov. 24 Engr. ***Perf. 13***

40	A10a 45fr dk car, vio & brn	50	40
41	A10a 55fr grn, vio & ol	70	50

Issued to commemorate the first television connection of the United States and Europe through the Telstar satellite, July 11-12.

Bull, Chemical Equipment, Chicks — A11

1963, Feb. 23 Unwmk. ***Perf. 13***

42	A11 25fr red brn & grnsh bl	22	15

Issued to publicize the Sotuba Zootechnical Institute. See No. C15.

Tractor A12

1963, Mar. 21 **Engr.**

43	A12 25fr vio bl, dk brn & blk	18	15
44	A12 45fr bl grn, red brn & grn	40	25

FAO "Freedom from Hunger" campaign.

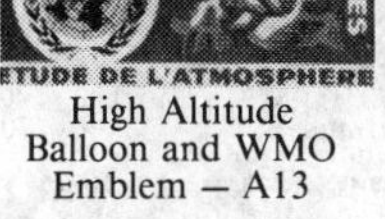

High Altitude Balloon and WMO Emblem — A13

Winners, 800-meter Race — A14

1963, June 12 Photo. *Perf. 12½*

Green Emblem; Yellow and Black Balloon.

45	A13 25fr ultra	20	15
46	A13 45fr car rose	38	25
47	A13 60fr red brn	50	40

Studies of the atmosphere.

1963, Aug. 10 Unwmk. *Perf. 12*

Designs: 20fr, Acrobatic dancers (horiz.). 85fr, Soccer (horiz.).

48	A14 5fr multi	15	15
49	A14 10fr multi	15	15
50	A14 20fr multi	18	15
51	A14 85fr multi	60	35
	Set value	92	62

Issued to publicize Youth Week.

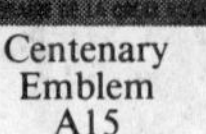

Centenary Emblem A15

Kaempferia Aethiopica A16

1963, Sept. 1 *Perf. 13½x13*

Emblem in Gray, Yellow and Red

52	A15 5fr lt ol grn & blk	15	15
53	A15 10fr yel & blk	15	15
54	A15 85fr red & blk	60	40
	Set value		58

Centenary of the International Red Cross.

1963, Dec. 23 Unwmk. *Perf. 13*

Tropical plants: 70fr, Bombax costatum. 100fr, Adenium Honghel.

55	A16 30fr multi	22	15
56	A16 70fr multi	55	22
57	A16 100fr multi	70	25

Plane Spraying, Locust and Village A17

Designs (each inscribed "O.I.C.M.A."): 5fr, Head of locust and map of Africa (vert.). 10fr, Locust in flight over map of Mali (vert.).

1964, June 15 Engr. *Perf. 13*

58	A17 5fr org brn, dl cl & grn	15	15
59	A17 10fr org brn, ol & bl grn	15	15
60	A17 20fr bis, org brn & yel grn	20	15
	Set value		26

Anti-locust campaign.

Soccer Player and Tokyo Stadium — A18

Designs (stadium in background): 10fr, Boxer (vert.). 15fr, Runner (vert.). 85fr, Hurdler.

1964, June 27 Unwmk.

61	A18 5fr red, brt grn & dk pur	15	15
62	A18 10fr blk, dl bl & org brn	15	15
63	A18 15fr vio & dk red	16	15
64	A18 85fr vio, dk brn & sl grn	65	45
a.	Min. sheet of 4, #61-64	1.40	1.40
	Set value		70

18th Olympic Games, Tokyo, Oct. 10-25.

IQSY Emblem and Eclipse of Sun — A19

1964, July 27 Engr. *Perf. 13*

65	A19 45fr multi	45	20

International Quiet Sun Year, 1964-65.

Map of Viet Nam A20

Defassa Waterbuck A21

1964, Nov. 2 Photo. *Perf. 12x12½*

66	A20 30fr multi	22	15

Issued to publicize the solidarity of the workers of Mali and those of South Viet Nam.

1965, Apr. 5 Engr.

Designs: 5fr, Cape buffalo (horiz.). 10fr, Scimitar-horned oryx. 30fr, Leopard (horiz.). 90fr, Giraffe.

67	A21 1fr choc, brt bl & grn	15	15
68	A21 5fr grn, ocher & choc	15	15
69	A21 10fr grn, brt pink & bis brn	15	15
70	A21 30fr dk red, grn & choc	22	15
71	A21 90fr bis brn, sl & yel grn	60	42
	Set value	1.00	72

Abraham Lincoln A22

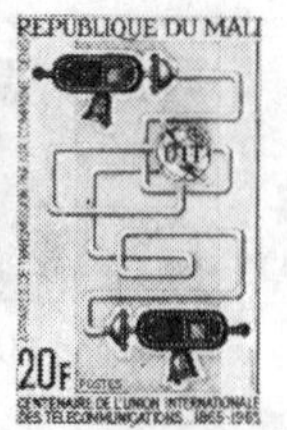

Denis Compressed Air Transmitter A23

1965, Apr. 15 Photo. *Perf. 13x12½*

72	A22 45fr blk & multi	40	30
73	A22 55fr dp grn & multi	45	40

Centenary of the death of Lincoln.

1965, May 17 Engr. *Perf. 13*

Designs: 30fr, Hughes telegraph system (horiz.). 50fr, Lescurre heliograph.

74	A23 20fr org, blk & bl	18	15
75	A23 30fr org, ocher & sl grn	22	16
76	A23 50fr org, dk brn & sl grn	38	25

Issued to commemorate the centenary of the International Telecommunication Union.

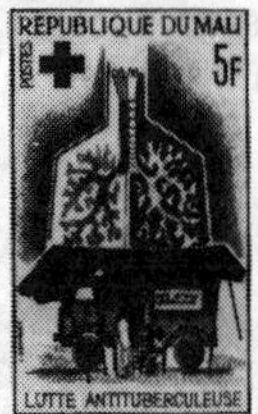

Mobile X-ray Unit and Lungs — A24

Designs: 10fr, Mother and infants. 25fr, Examination of patient at Marchoux Institute and slide. 45fr, Biology laboratory.

1965, July 5 Unwmk. *Perf. 13*

77	A24 5fr lake, red & vio	15	15
78	A24 10fr brn ol, red & sl grn	15	15
79	A24 25fr dk brn, red & grn	18	15
80	A24 45fr dk brn, red & sl grn	35	22
	Set value	68	48

Issued to publicize the Health Service.

Swimmer A25

1965, July 19 Engr.

81	A25 5fr shown	15	15
82	A25 15fr Judo	16	15
	Set value	24	16

1st African Games, Brazzaville, July 18-25.

Globe, Vase, Quill, Trumpet A26

Designs: 55fr, Mask, palette and microphones. 90fr, Dancers, mask and printed cloth.

1966, Apr. 4 Engr. *Perf. 13*

83	A26 30fr blk, red & ocher	22	15
84	A26 55fr car rose, emer & blk	38	25
85	A26 90fr ultra, org & dk brn	60	38

Issued to commemorate the International Negro Arts Festival, Dakar, Senegal, Apr. 1-24.

WHO Headquarters, Geneva — A27

1966, May 3 Photo. *Perf. 12½x13*

86	A27 30fr org yel, bl & ol grn	22	15
87	A27 45fr org yel, bl & dl red	30	20

Inauguration of the WHO Headquarters.

Fishermen with Nets — A28

River Fishing: 4fr, 60fr, Group fishing with large net. 20fr, 85fr, Commercial fishing boats.

1966, May 30 Engr. *Perf. 13*

88	A28 3fr ultra & brn	15	15
89	A28 4fr Prus bl & org brn	15	15
90	A28 20fr dk brn, ultra & grn	15	15
91	A28 25fr dk brn, bl & brt grn	18	15
92	A28 60fr mag, brn & brt grn	38	16
93	A28 85fr dk pur, dl bl & grn	50	25
	Set value	1.30	65

Initiation of Pioneers A29

Design: 25fr, Dance and Pioneer emblem.

1966, July 25 Engr. *Perf. 13*

94	A29 5fr multi	15	15
95	A29 25fr multi	18	15
	Set value	22	15

Issued to honor the pioneers of Mali.

Inoculation of Zebu — A30

1967, Jan. 16 Photo. *Perf. 12½x13*

96	A30 10fr dp grn, yel grn & brn	15	15
97	A30 30fr Prus bl, bl & brn	20	15
	Set value	26	20

Campaign against cattle plague.

View of Timbuktu and Tourist Year Emblem A31

1967, May 15 Engr. *Perf. 13*

98	A31 25fr Prus bl, red lil & org	18	15

International Tourist Year, 1967.

Ugada Grandicollis A32

Insects: 5fr, Chelorrhina polyphemus (vert.). 50fr, Phymateus cinctus.

1967, Aug. 14 Engr. *Perf. 13*

99	A32 5fr brt bl, sl grn & brn	15	15
100	A32 15fr sl grn, dk brn & red	16	15
101	A32 50fr sl grn, dk brn & dp org	35	20
	Set value		32

Teacher and Adult Class — A33

1967, Sept. 8 Photo. *Perf. 12½x13*

102	A33 50fr blk, grn & car	35	15

International Literacy Day, Sept. 8.

Europafrica Issue

Birds, New Buildings and Map — A34

1967, Sept. 18 *Perf. 12½x12*

103	A34 45fr multi	38	16

Lions Emblem and Crocodile — A35

1967, Oct. 16 Photo. *Perf. 13x12½*

104 A35 90fr yel & multi 45 25

50th anniversary of Lions International.

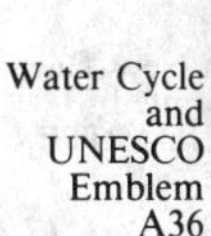

Water Cycle and UNESCO Emblem A36

1967, Nov. 15 Photo. *Perf. 13*

105 A36 25fr multi 16 15

Hydrological Decade (UNESCO), 1965-74.

WHO Emblem A37

1968, Apr. 8 Engr. *Perf. 13*

106 A37 90fr sl grn, dk car rose & bl 38 15

20th anniv. of the World Health Organization.

Linked Hearts and People A38

1968, Apr. 28 Engr. *Perf. 13*

107 A38 50fr sl grn, red & vio bl 22 18

International Day of Sister Communities.

Books, Student, Chart, and Map of Africa A39

1968, Aug. 12 Engr. *Perf. 13*

108 A39 100fr car, ol & blk 40 20

10th anniv. of the Intl. Assoc. for the Development of Libraries and Archives in Africa.

Draisienne, 1809 — A40

Designs: 5fr, De Dion-Bouton automobile, 1894 (horiz.). 10fr, Michaux bicycle, 1861. 45fr, Panhard & Levassor automobile, 1914 (horiz.).

1968, Aug. 12

109 A40 2fr grn, ol & mag 15 15
110 A40 5fr lem, ind & red 15 15
111 A40 10fr brt grn, ind & brn 15 15
112 A40 45fr ocher, gray grn & blk 18 15
Set value 38 25

See Nos. C60-C61.

Tourist Emblem with Map of Africa and Dove A41

1969, May 12 Photo. *Perf. 12½x13*

113 A41 50fr lt ultra, grn & red 18 15

Year of African Tourism.

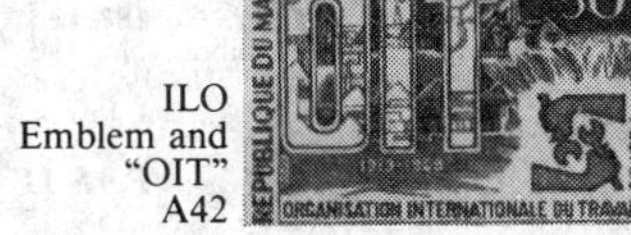

ILO Emblem and "OIT" A42

1969, May 12 Engr. *Perf. 13*

114 A42 50fr vio, sl grn & brt bl 22 15
115 A42 60fr sl, red & ol brn 25 15
Set value 20

Issued to commemorate the 50th anniversary of the International Labor Organization.

Panhard, 1897, and Citroen 24, 1969 — A43

Design: 30fr, Citroen, 1923, and Citroen DS 21, 1969.

1969, May 30 Engr. *Perf. 13*

116 A43 25fr blk, mar & lem 15 15
117 A43 30fr blk, brt grn & dk grn 16 15
Set value 16

See Nos. C71-C72.

Play Blocks A44

Toys: 10fr, Mule on wheels. 15fr, Ducks. 20fr, Racing car and track.

1969 Photo. *Perf. 12½x13*

118 A44 5fr red, gray & yel 15 15
119 A44 10fr red, yel & ol 15 15
120 A44 15fr red, sal & yel grn 15 15
121 A44 20fr red, ind & org 15 15
Set value 38 22

Issued to publicize the International Toy Fair in Nuremberg, Germany.

Ram — A45

1969, Aug. 18 Engr. *Perf. 13*

122 A45 1fr shown 15 15
123 A45 2fr Goat 15 15
124 A45 10fr Donkey 15 15
125 A45 35fr Horse 22 16
126 A45 90fr Dromedaries 55 35
Set value 90 68

Development Bank Issue
Common Design Type

1969, Sept. 10

127 CD130 50fr brt lil, grn & ocher 20 15
128 CD130 90fr ol brn, grn & ocher 38 15

Boy Being Vaccinated A46

1969, Nov. 10 Engr. *Perf. 13*

129 A46 50fr brn, ind & brt grn 22 15

Campaign against smallbox and measles.

ASECNA Issue
Common Design Type

1969, Dec. 12 Engr. *Perf. 13*

130 CD132 100fr dk sl grn 40 20

African and Japanese Women A47

Design: 150fr, Flags and maps of Mali and Japan.

1970, Apr. 13 Engr. *Perf. 13*

131 A47 100fr brn, bl & ocher 42 16
132 A47 150fr dk red, yel grn & org 60 20

Issued to publicize EXPO '70 International Exhibition, Osaka, Japan, Mar. 15-Sept. 13.

Satellite Telecommunications, Map of Africa and ITU Emblem — A48

1970, May 17 Engr. *Perf. 13*

133 A48 90fr car rose & brn 40 20

World Telecommunications Day.

UPU Headquarters Issue
Common Design Type

1970, May 20 Engr. *Perf. 13*

134 CD133 50fr dk red, bl grn & ol 20 15
135 CD133 60fr red lil, ultra & red brn 25 16

Post Office, Bamako A49

Public Buildings: 40fr, Chamber of Commerce, Bamako. 60fr, Public Works Ministry, Bamako. 80fr, City Hall, Segou.

1970, Nov. 23 Engr. *Perf. 13*

136 A49 30fr brn, brt grn & ol 15 15
137 A49 40fr brn, sl grn & dp cl 15 15
138 A49 60fr brn red, sl grn & gray 20 15
139 A49 80fr brn, brt grn & emer 25 16
Set value 45

Gallet 030T, 1882 — A50

Old Steam Locomotives: 40fr, Felou 030T, 1882. 50fr, Bechevel 230T, 1882. 80fr, Type 231, 1930. 100fr, Type 141, 1930.

1970, Dec. 14 Engr. *Perf. 13*

140 A50 20fr brt grn, dk car & blk 15 15
141 A50 40fr blk, dk grn & ocher 18 15
142 A50 50fr bis brn, bl grn & blk 20 15
143 A50 80fr car rose, blk & bl grn 25 20
144 A50 100fr ocher, bl grn & blk 40 22
Nos. 140-144 (5) 1.18 87

Scout Sounding Retreat — A51

Bambara Mask, San — A52

Designs (Boy Scouts): 5fr, Crossing river (horiz.). 100fr, Canoeing (horiz.).

Perf. 13x12½, 12½x13

1970, Dec. 28 Litho.

145 A51 5fr multi 15 15
146 A51 30fr multi 15 15
147 A51 100fr multi 38 18
Set value 56 30

1971, Jan. 25 Photo. *Perf. 12x12½*

Designs: 25fr, Dogon mask, Bandiagara. 50fr, Kanaga ideogram. 80fr, Bambara ideogram.

148 A52 20fr org & multi 15 15
149 A52 25fr brt grn & multi 15 15
150 A52 50fr dk pur & multi 20 15
151 A52 80fr bl & multi 30 15
Set value 68 36

Boy, Medical and Scientific Symbols A53

1971, Mar. 22 Engr. *Perf. 13*

152 A53 100fr dp car, ocher & grn 42 22

B.C.G. inoculation (Bacillus-Calmette-Guerin) against tuberculosis, 50th anniv.

Boy Scouts, Mt. Fuji, Japanese Print — A54

1971, Apr. 19

153 A54 80fr lt ultra, dp plum & brt grn 22 15

13th Boy Scout World Jamboree, Asagiri Plain, Japan, Aug. 2-10.

UNICEF Emblem, Hands and Rose — A55

Design: 60fr, UNICEF emblem, women and children (vert.).

1971, May 24 Engr. *Perf. 13*

154 A55 50fr brn org, car & dk brn 16 15
155 A55 60fr vio bl, grn & red brn 18 15
Set value 22

25th anniv. of UNICEF.

Mali Farmer — A56

Map of Africa with Communications Network — A57

Costumes of Mali: 10fr, Mali farm woman. 15fr, Tuareg. 60fr, Embroidered robe, Grand Boubou. 80fr, Ceremonial robe, woman.

1971, June 14 Photo. *Perf. 13*

156 A56 5fr gray & multi 15 15
157 A56 10fr vio bl & multi 15 15
158 A56 15fr yel & multi 15 15
159 A56 60fr gray & multi 18 15
160 A56 80fr tan & multi 22 16
Set value 60 40

1971, Aug. 16 Photo. *Perf. 13*

161 A57 50fr bl, vio bl & org 20 15

Pan-African telecommunications system.

Hibiscus A58

Flowers: 50fr, Poinsettia. 60fr, Adenium obesum. 80fr, Dogbane. 100fr, Satanocrater berhautii.

1971, Oct. 4 Litho. *Perf. 14x13½*

162 A58 20fr multi 15 15
163 A58 50fr multi 16 15
164 A58 60fr multi 22 15
165 A58 80fr multi 25 15
166 A58 100fr multi 35 15
Nos. 162-166 (5) 1.13
Set value 42

Mother, Child and Bird (Sculpture) A59

1971, Dec. 27 Engr. *Perf. 13x12½*

167 A59 70fr mag, sep & bl grn 22 15

National Institute of Social Security, 15th anniversary.

ITU Emblem A60

1972, May 17 Photo. *Perf. 13x13½*

168 A60 70fr bl, mar & blk 22 15

4th World Telecommunications Day.

Clay Funerary Statuette — A61

Mali Art: 40fr, Female torso, wood. 50fr, Masked figure, painted stone. 100fr, Animals and men, wrought iron.

1972, May 29 *Perf. 12½x13*

169 A61 30fr org red & multi 15 15
170 A61 40fr yel & multi 15 15
171 A61 50fr red & multi 16 15
172 A61 100fr lt grn & multi 30 15
Set value 42

Morse and Telegraph A62

1972, June 5 Engr. *Perf. 13*

173 A62 80fr red, emer & choc 22 15

Centenary of the death of Samuel F. B. Morse (1791-1872), inventor of the telegraph.

Weather Balloon over Africa — A63

1972, July 10 Photo. *Perf. 12½x13*

174 A63 130fr multi 40 22

12th World Meteorology Day.

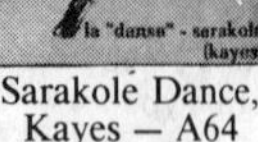

Sarakole Dance, Kayes — A64

People, Book, Pencil — A65

Designs: Folk dances.

1972, Aug. 21 Photo. *Perf. 13*

175 A64 10fr shown 15 15
176 A64 20fr LaGomba, Bamako 15 15
177 A64 50fr Hunters' dance, Bougouni 15 15
178 A64 70fr Kore Duga, Segou 18 15
179 A64 80fr Kanaga, Sanga 20 15
180 A64 120fr Targui, Timbuktu 25 16
Set value 90 65

1972, Sept. 8 Typo. *Perf. 12½x13*

181 A65 80fr blk & yel grn 20 15

World Literacy Day, Sept. 8.

"Edison Classique," Mali Instruments — A66

1972, Sept. 18 Engr. *Perf. 13*

182 A66 100fr multi 30 15

First Anthology of Music of Mali.

Aries A67

Signs of the Zodiac: No. 184, Taurus. No. 185, Gemini. No. 186, Cancer. No. 187, Leo. No. 188, Virgo. No. 189, Libra. No. 190, Scorpio. No. 191, Sagittarius. No. 192, Capricorn. No. 193, Aquarius. No. 194, Pisces.

1972, Oct. 23 Engr. *Perf. 11*

183 A67 15fr lil & bis brn 15 15
184 A67 15fr bis brn & blk 15 15
185 A67 35fr mar & ind 15 15
186 A67 35fr emer & mar 15 15
187 A67 40fr bl & red brn 15 15
188 A67 40fr dk pur & red brn 15 15
189 A67 45fr dk bl & mar 16 15
190 A67 45fr mar & brt grn 16 15
191 A67 65fr dk vio & ind 20 15
192 A67 65fr dk vio & gray ol 20 15
193 A67 90fr brt pink & ind 22 16
194 A67 90fr brt pink & grn 22 16
Set value 1.75 1.20

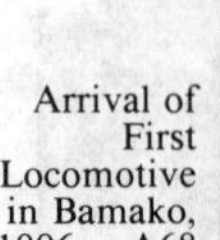

Arrival of First Locomotive in Bamako, 1906 — A68

Designs (Locomotives): 30fr, Thies-Bamako, 1920. 60fr, Thies-Bamako, 1927. 120fr, Two Alsthom BB, 1947.

1972, Dec. 11 Engr. *Perf. 13*

195 A68 10fr ind, brn & sl grn 15 15
196 A68 30fr sl grn, ind & brn 15 15
197 A68 60fr sl grn, ind & brn 20 15
198 A68 120fr sl grn & choc 35 20
Set value 72 45

2nd African Games, Lagos, Nigeria, Jan. 7-18 — A69

1973, Jan. 15 Photo. *Perf. 12½*

199 A69 70fr High jump 22 15
200 A69 270fr Discus 80 40
201 A69 280fr Soccer 85 40

INTERPOL Emblem and Headquarters A70

1973, Feb. 28 Photo. *Perf. 13*

202 A70 80fr multi 22 15

50th anniversary of International Criminal Police Organization (INTERPOL).

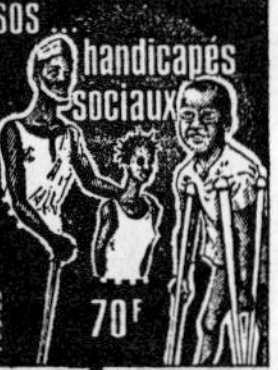

Blind Man and Disabled Boy — A71

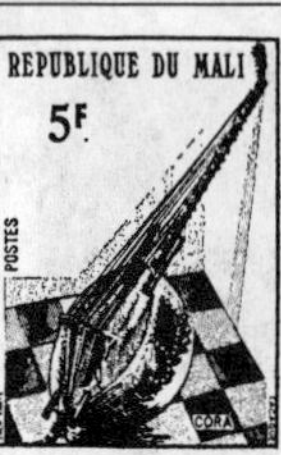

Cora — A72

1973, Apr. 24 Engr. *Perf. 12½x13*

203 A71 70fr dk car, brick red & blk 22 15

Help for the handicapped.

No. 166 Surcharged with New Value, 2 Bars, and Overprinted: "SECHERESSE / SOLIDARITE AFRICAINE"

1973, Aug. 16 Litho. *Perf. 13½*

204 A58 200fr on 100fr multi 55 35

African solidarity in drought emergency.

Perf. 12½x13, 13x12½

1973, Dec. 10 Engr.

Musical Instruments: 10fr, Balafon (horiz.). 15fr, Djembe. 20fr, Guitar. 25fr, N'Djarka. 30fr, M'Bolon. 35fr, Dozo N'Goni. 40fr, N'Tamani.

205 A72 5fr mar, dk grn & brn 15 15
206 A72 10fr bl & choc 15 15
207 A72 15fr brn, dk red & yel 15 15
208 A72 20fr mar & brn ol 15 15
209 A72 25fr org, yel & blk 15 15
210 A72 30fr vio bl & blk 15 15
211 A72 35fr dk red & brn 15 15
212 A72 40fr dk red & choc 15 15
Set value 65 45

Farmer with Newspaper, Corn — A73

Soccer, Goalkeeper, Symbolic Globe and Net — A74

1974, Mar. 11 Engr. *Perf. 12½x13*

213 A73 70fr multi 20 15

2nd anniversary of "Kibaru," rural newspaper.

1974, May 6 Engr. *Perf. 13*

Design: 280fr, Games' emblem, soccer and ball.

214 A74 270fr multi 80 42
215 A74 280fr multi 85 42

World Cup Soccer Championships, Munich, June 13-July 7.

Old and New Ships, UPU Emblem — A75

Artisans of Mali — A76

Designs: 90fr, Old and new planes, UPU emblem. 270fr, Old and new trains, UPU emblem.

1974, June 2 Engr. *Perf. 12½x13*

216	A75	80fr brn & multir	22	16
217	A75	90fr ultra & multi	30	20
218	A75	270fr lt grn & multi	80	42

Centenary of Universal Postal Union.

Nos. 214-215 Surcharged and Overprinted in Black or Red: "R.F.A. 2 / HOLLANDE 1"

1974, Aug. 28 Engr. *Perf. 13*

219	A74	300fr on 270fr multi	90	45
220	A74	330fr on 280fr multi (R)	90	45

World Cup Soccer Championship, 1974, victory of German Federal Republic.

1974, Sept. 16 Photo. *Perf. 12½x13*

221	A76	50fr Weaver	15	15
222	A76	60fr Potter	16	15
223	A76	70fr Smiths	20	15
224	A76	80fr Sculptor	22	15
		Set value		44

Niger River near Gao — A77

Landscapes: 20fr, The Hand of Fatma (rock formation; vert.). 40fr, Gouina Waterfall. 70fr, Dogon houses (vert.).

Perf. 13x12½, 12½x13

1974, Sept. 23

225	A77	10fr multi	15	15
226	A77	20fr multi	15	15
227	A77	40fr multi	15	15
228	A77	70fr multi	20	15
		Set value	40	40

Nos. 216 and 218 Surcharged and Overprinted in Black or Red: "9 OCTOBRE 1974"

1974, Oct. 9 Engr. *Perf. 13*

229	A75	250fr on 80fr multi	90	45
230	A75	300fr on 270fr multi (R)	90	45

UPU Day.

Mao Tse-tung, Flags, Great Wall — A78

1974, Oct. 21 Engr. *Perf. 13*

231	A78	100fr multi	25	16

People's Republic of China, 25th anniversary.

Artisans and Lions Emblem — A79

Design: 100fr, View of Samanko and Lions emblem.

1975, Feb. 3 Photo. *Perf. 13*

232	A79	90fr red & multi	25	16
233	A79	100fr bl & multi	30	20

5th anniversary of lepers' rehabilitation village, Samanko, sponsored by Lions International.

Tetrodon Fahaka A80

Designs: Fish.

1975, May 12 Engr. *Perf. 13*

234	A80	60fr *shown*	16	15
235	A80	70fr *Malopterurus electricus*	20	15
236	A80	80fr *Citharinus latus*	20	15
237	A80	90fr *Hydrocyon forskali*	22	15
238	A80	110fr *Lates niloticus*	25	15
		Nos. 234-238 (5)	1.03	
		Set value		62

See Nos. 256-260.

Woman and IWY Emblem — A81

1975, June 9 Engr. *Perf. 13*

239	A81	150fr red & grn	40	20

International Women's Year 1975.

Morris "Oxford," 1913 — A82

Automobiles: 130fr, Franklin "E," 1907. 190fr, Daimler, 1900. 230fr, Panhard & Levassor, 1895.

1975, June 16

240	A82	90fr blk, ol & lil	22	15
241	A82	130fr vio bl, gray & red	35	20
242	A82	190fr bl, grn & ind	50	30
243	A82	230fr red, ultra & brn ol	60	38

Carthaginian Tristater, 500 B.C. — A83

Ancient Coins: 170fr, Decadrachma, Syracuse, 413 B.C. 190fr, Acanthe tetradrachma, 400 B.C. 260fr, Didrachma, Eritrea, 480-445 B.C.

1975, Oct. 13 Engr. *Perf. 13*

244	A83	130fr bl, cl & blk	35	18
245	A83	170fr emer, brn & blk	42	22
246	A83	190fr grn, red & blk	50	30
247	A83	260fr dp bl, org & blk	65	42

UN Emblem and "ONU" — A84

1975, Nov. 10 Engr. *Perf. 13*

248	A84	200fr emer & brt bl	55	35

30th anniversary of UN.

A. G. Bell, Waves, Satellite, Telephone — A85

1976, Mar. 8 Litho. *Perf. 12x12½*

249	A85	180fr brn, ultra & ocher	50	25

Centenary of first telephone call by Alexander Graham Bell, Mar. 10, 1876.

Chameleon A86

1976, Mar. 31 Litho. *Perf. 12½*

250	A86	20fr shown	15	15
251	A86	30fr Lizard	15	15
252	A86	40fr Tortoise	15	15
253	A86	90fr Python	22	15
254	A86	120fr Crocodile	35	20
		Set value	80	45

Konrad Adenauer and Cologne Cathedral — A87

1976, Apr. 26 Engr. *Perf. 13*

255	A87	180fr mag & dk brn	45	25

Konrad Adenauer (1876-1967), German Chancellor, birth centenary.

Fish Type of 1975

1976, June 28 Engr. *Perf. 13*

256	A80	100fr *Heterotis niloticus*	25	16
257	A80	120fr *Synodontis budgetti*	35	18
258	A80	130fr *Heterobranchus bidorsalis*	38	18
259	A80	150fr *Tilapia monodi*	40	20
260	A80	220fr *Alestes macrolepidotus*	55	35
		Nos. 256-260 (5)	1.93	1.07

Buying Sets
Frequently it is less expensive to purchase complete sets rather than the individual stamps that make up the set. "Set Values" are provided for many such sets.

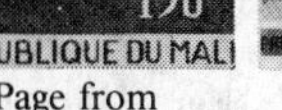

Page from Children's Book — A88

"Le Roi de l'Air" — A89

1976, July 19

261	A88	130fr red & multi	35	20

Books for children.

1976, July 26 Litho. *Perf. 12½x13*

262	A89	120fr multi	30	16

First lottery, sponsored by L'Essor newspaper.

"Do not overload scaffold" — A90

1976, Aug. 16 Litho. *Perf. 13*

263	A90	120fr multi	30	16

National Insurance Institute, 20th anniv.

Letters, UPU and UN Emblems — A91

1976, Oct. 4 Engr. *Perf. 13*

264	A91	120fr lil, org & grn	30	16

UN Postal Administration, 25th anniv.

Moto-Guzzi 254, Italy — A92

Motorcycles: 120fr, BMW 900, Germany. 130fr, Honda-Egli, Japan. 140fr, Motobecane LT-3, France.

1976, Oct. 18 Engr. *Perf. 13*

265	A92	90fr multi	22	15
266	A92	120fr multi	32	20
267	A92	130fr multi	35	20
268	A92	140fr multi	38	22

Fishing Boat, Masgat — A93

Designs: 180fr, Coaster, Cochin China. 190fr, Fireboat, Dunkirk, 1878. 200fr, Nile river boat.

1976, Dec. 6 **Engr.** ***Perf. 13***

269	A93	160fr multi	42	18
270	A93	180fr multi	45	22
271	A93	190fr multi	50	25
272	A93	200fr multi	55	25

Indigo Finch — A94

Birds: 25fr, Yellow-breasted barbet. 30fr, Vitelline masked weaver. 40fr, Bee-eater. 50fr, Senegal parrot.

1977, Apr. 18 **Photo.** ***Perf. 13***

273	A94	15fr multi	15	15
274	A94	25fr multi	15	15
275	A94	30fr multi	15	15
276	A94	40fr multi	16	15
277	A94	50fr multi	20	15
		Set value	62	40

See Nos. 298-302.

Braille Statue, Script and Reading Hands — A95

1977, Apr. 25 **Engr.** ***Perf. 13***

278	A95	200fr multi	55	30

Louis Braille (1809-1852), inventor of the reading and writing system for the blind.

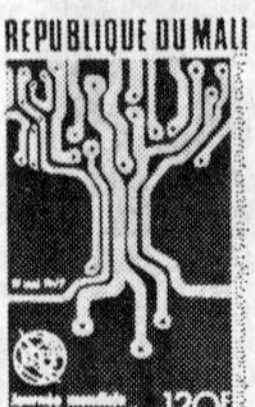

Electronic Tree, ITU Emblem — A96

1977, May 17 **Photo.**

279	A96	120fr dk brn & org	32	18

World Telecommunications Day.

Dragonfly A97

Insects: 10fr, Praying mantis. 20fr, Tropical wasp. 35fr, Cockchafer. 60fr, Flying stag beetle.

1977, June 15 **Photo.** ***Perf. 13x12½***

280	A97	5fr multi	15	15
281	A97	10fr multi	15	15
282	A97	20fr multi	15	15
283	A97	35fr multi	15	15
284	A97	60fr multi	22	16
		Set value	52	40

Knight and Rook — A98

Chess Pieces: 130fr, Bishop and pawn (vert.). 300fr, Queen and King.

1977, June 27 **Engr.** ***Perf. 13***

285	A98	120fr multi	50	25
286	A98	130fr multi	50	25
287	A98	300fr multi	1.20	65

Europafrica Issue

Symbolic Ship, White and Brown Persons — A99

1977, July 18 **Litho.** ***Perf. 13***

288	A99	400fr multi	1.10	65

Horse, by Leonardo da Vinci A100

Drawings by Leonardo da Vinci: 300fr, Head of Young Woman. 500fr, Self-portrait.

1977, Sept. 5 **Engr.** ***Perf. 13***

289	A100	200fr dk brn & blk	55	35
290	A100	300fr dk brn & ol	80	42
291	A100	500fr dk brn & red	1.40	62

Hotel de l'Amitié, Bamako — A101

1977, Oct. 15 **Litho.** ***Perf. 13x12½***

292	A101	120fr multi	35	18

Opening of the Hotel de l'Amitié, Oct. 15.

Dome of the Rock Jerusalem — A102

1977, Oct. 17 ***Perf. 12½***

293	A102	120fr multi	35	18
294	A102	180fr multi	45	25

Palestinian fighters and their families.

Black Man, Chains and UN Emblem A103

Design: 130fr, Statue of Liberty, people and UN emblem. 180fr, Black children and horse behind fence.

1978, Mar. 13 **Engr.** ***Perf. 13***

295	A103	120fr multi	35	18
296	A103	130fr multi	35	18
297	A103	180fr multi	45	25

International Year against Apartheid.

Bird Type of 1977

Birds: 20fr, Granatine bengala. 30fr, Lagonosticta vinacea. 50fr, Lagonosticta. 70fr, Turtle dove. 80fr, Buffalo weaver.

1978, Apr. 10 **Litho.** ***Perf. 13***

298	A94	20fr multi	15	15
299	A94	30fr multi	15	15
300	A94	50fr multi	15	15
301	A94	70fr multi	18	15
302	A94	80fr multi	20	15
		Set value	65	40

Nos. 232-233 Surcharged with New Value, Bar and: "XXe ANNIVERSAIRE DU LIONS CLUB DE BAMAKO 1958-1978"

1978, May 8 **Photo.**

303	A79	120fr on 90fr multi	32	16
304	A79	130fr on 100fr multi	35	18

20th anniversary of Bamako Lions Club.

Wall and Desert — A105

1978, May 18 **Litho.** ***Perf. 13***

306	A105	200fr multi	55	25

Hammamet Conference for reclamation of the desert.

Demand, as well as supply, determines a stamp's market value. One is as important as the other.

Mahatma Gandhi and Roses — A106

1978, May 29 **Engr.**

307	A106	140fr blk, brn & red	38	18

Mohandas K. Gandhi (1869-1948), Hindu spiritual leader, 30th death anniversary.

Dermestes — A107

Insects: 25fr, Ground beetle. 90fr, Cricket. 120fr, Ladybird. 140fr, Goliath beetle.

1978, June 12 **Photo.** ***Perf. 13***

308	A107	15fr multi	15	15
309	A107	25fr multi	15	15
310	A107	90fr multi	22	15
311	A107	120fr multi	35	18
312	A107	140fr multi	38	20
		Set value	1.05	60

Bridge — A108

Design: 100fr, Dominoes (vert.).

1978, June 26 **Engr.**

313	A108	100fr multi	25	15
314	A108	130fr multi	35	18

Aristotle — A109

1978, Oct. 16 **Engr.** ***Perf. 13***

315	A109	200fr multi	55	25

Aristotle (384-322 B.C.), Greek philosopher.

Human Rights and UN Emblems — A110

1978, Dec. 11 **Engr.** ***Perf. 13***
316 A110 180fr red, bl & brn 48 22

Universal Declaration of Human Rights, 30th anniversary.

Manatee — A111

Endangered Wildlife: 120fr, Chimpanzee. 130fr, Damaliscus antelope. 180fr, Oryx. 200fr, Derby's eland.

1979, Apr. 23 **Litho.** ***Perf. 12½***
317 A111 100fr multi 25 15
318 A111 120fr multi 32 16
319 A111 130fr multi 35 18
320 A111 180fr multi 48 25
321 A111 200fr multi 55 30
Nos. 317-321 (5) 1.95 1.04

Boy Praying and IYC Emblem — A112

Designs (IYC emblem and): 200fr, Girl and Boy Scout holding bird. 300fr, IYC emblem, boys with calf.

1979, May 7 **Engr.** ***Perf. 13***
322 A112 120fr multi 32 20
323 A112 200fr multi 55 30
324 A112 300fr multi 80 40

International Year of the Child.

Judo and Notre Dame, Paris — A113

1979, May 14 **Engr.** ***Perf. 13***
325 A113 200fr multi 55 30

World Judo Championship, Paris.

Telecommunica-tions A114

Wood Carving A115

1979, May 17 **Litho.**
326 A114 120fr multi 32 16

11th Telecommunications Day.

1979, May 18 ***Perf. 13x12½***

Sculptures from National Museum: 120fr, Ancestral figures. 130fr, Animal heads, and kneeling woman.

327 A115 90fr multi 25 16
328 A115 120fr multi 32 16
329 A115 130fr multi 35 18

International Museums Day.

Rowland Hill and Mali No. 15 — A116

Designs: 130fr, Zeppelin and Saxony No. 1. 180fr, Concorde and France No. 3. 200fr, Stagecoach and US No. 2. 300fr, UPU emblem and Penny Black.

1979, May 21 **Engr.** ***Perf. 13***
330 A116 120fr multi 32 16
331 A116 130fr multi 35 18
332 A116 180fr multi 50 25
333 A116 200fr multi 55 30
334 A116 300fr multi 80 45
Nos. 330-334 (5) 2.52 1.34

Sir Rowland Hill (1795-1879), originator of penny postage.

Cora Players — A117

1979, June 4 **Litho.** ***Perf. 13***
335 A117 200fr multi 55 30

Adenium Obesum and Sankore Mosque — A118

Design: 300fr, Satellite, mounted messenger, globe and letter (vert.).

1979, June 8 **Photo.**
336 A118 120fr multi 32 16

Engr.
337 A118 300fr multi 80 45

Philexafrique II, Libreville, Gabon, June 8-17. Nos. 336, 337 printed in sheets of 10 and 5 labels showing exhibition emblem.

Map of Mali — A119

Design: 300fr, Men planting trees.

1979, June 18 **Litho.** ***Perf. 13x12½***
338 A119 200fr multi 55 30
339 A119 300fr multi 80 45

Operation Green Sahel.

Lemons — A120

Sigmund Freud — A121

1979, June 25 ***Perf. 12½x13***
340 A120 10fr shown 15 15
341 A120 60fr Pineapple 16 15
342 A120 100fr Papayas 25 15
343 A120 120fr Soursops 32 16
344 A120 130fr Mangoes 35 18
Nos. 340-344 (5) 1.23
Set value 60

1979, Sept. 17 **Engr.** ***Perf. 13***
345 A121 300fr vio bl & sep 80 45

Sigmund Freud (1856-1939), founder of psychoanalysis.

Timbuktu, Man and Camel A122

Design: 130fr, Caillié, Map of Sahara.

1979, Sept. 27 ***Perf. 13x12½***
346 A122 120fr multi 32 16
347 A122 130fr multi 35 18

René Caillié (1799-1838), French explorer, 180th birth anniversary.

Eurema Brigitta A123

1979, Oct. 15 **Litho.** ***Perf. 13***
348 A123 100fr *shown* 25 15
349 A123 120fr *Papilio pylades* 32 16
350 A123 130fr *Melanitis leda satyridae* 35 18
351 A123 180fr *Gonimbrasia belina occidentalis* 48 25
352 A123 200fr *Bunaea alcinoe* 55 30
Nos. 348-352 (5) 1.95 1.04

Greyhound A124

Designs: Dogs.

1979, Nov. 12 **Litho.** ***Perf. 12½***
353 A124 20fr multi 15 15
354 A124 50fr multi 15 15
355 A124 70fr multi 18 15
356 A124 80fr multi 20 15
357 A124 90fr multi 25 15
Nos. 353-357 (5) 93
Set value 35

Wild Donkey — A125

1980, Feb. 4 **Litho.** ***Perf. 13x13½***
358 A125 90fr shown 25 15
359 A125 120fr Addax 32 15
360 A125 130fr Leopards 35 15
361 A125 140fr Mouflon 35 15
362 A125 180fr Buffalo 50 20
Nos. 358-362 (5) 1.77 80

Photovoltaic Cell Pumping Station, Koni — A126

Solar Energy Utilization: 100fr, Sun shields, Dire. 120fr, Solar stove, Bamako. 130fr, Heliodynamic solar energy generating station, Dire.

1980, Mar. 10 **Litho.** ***Perf. 13***
363 A126 90fr multi 25 15
364 A126 100fr multi 25 15
365 A126 120fr multi 32 15
366 A126 130fr multi 35 15
Set value 45

Horse Breeding, Mopti — A127

1980, Mar. 17
367 A127 100fr shown 25 15
368 A127 120fr Nioro 32 15
369 A127 130fr Koro 35 15
370 A127 180fr Coastal zone 50 20
371 A127 200fr Banamba 55 22
Nos. 367-371 (5) 1.97 87

Alexander Fleming (Discoverer of Penicillin) A128

1980, May 5 **Engr.** ***Perf. 13***
372 A128 200fr multi 55 20

Avicenna and Medical Instruments A129

Design: 180fr, Avicenna as teacher (12th century manuscript illustration)

1980, May 12 ***Perf. 13x12½***
373 A129 120fr multi 32 15
374 A129 180fr multi 50 20

Avicenna (980-1037), Arab physician and philosopher, 1000th birth anniversary.

Pilgrim at Mecca — A130

Guavas — A131

1980, May 26 **Litho.** ***Perf. 13***
375 A130 120fr shown 32 15
376 A130 130fr Praying hands, stars, Mecca 35 15
377 A130 180fr Pilgrims, camels, horiz. 50 20

Hegira, 1500th Anniversary.

1980, June 9
378 A131 90fr shown 22 15
379 A131 120fr Cashews 32 15
380 A131 130fr Oranges 35 15
381 A131 140fr Bananas 38 15
382 A131 180fr Grapefruit 50 20
Nos. 378-382 (5) 1.77 80

League of Nations, 60th Anniversary A132

1980, June 23 **Engr.** ***Perf. 13***
383 A132 200fr multi 55 20

Festival Emblem, Mask, Xylophone A133

1980, July 5 **Litho.** ***Perf. 12½***
384 A133 120fr multi 32 15

6th Biennial Arts and Cultural Festival, Bamako, July 5-15.

Sun Rising over Map of Africa — A134

1980, July 7 **Engr.** ***Perf. 13***
385 A134 300fr multi 80 38

Afro-Asian Bandung Conference, 25th anniversary.

Market Place, Conference Emblem A135

1980, Sept. 15 **Litho.** ***Perf. 13***
386 A135 120fr View of Mali, vert. 32 15
387 A135 180fr shown 50 20

World Tourism Conf., Manila, Sept. 27.

Hydro-electric Dam and Power Station — A136

20th Anniversary of Independence: 120fr, Pres. Traore, flag of Mali, National Assembly building. 130fr, Independence monument, Bamako, Political Party badge (vert.).

1980, Sept. 15 ***Perf. 13x12½***
388 A136 100fr multi 25 15
389 A136 120fr multi 32 15
390 A136 130fr multi 35 15
Set value 35

Utetheisa Pulchella A137

1980, Oct. 6 ***Perf. 13½***
391 A137 50fr *shown* 15 15
392 A137 60fr *Mylothis chloris pieridae* 16 15
393 A137 70fr *Hypolimnas misippus* 18 15
394 A137 80fr *Papilio demodocus* 20 15
Nos. 391-394,C402 (5) 1.89
Set value 75

Fight Against Cigarette Smoking — A138

1980, Oct. 13 **Litho.** ***Perf. 12½x12***
395 A138 200fr multi 55 20

European-African Economic Convention — A139

1980, Oct. 20 ***Perf. 12½***
396 A139 300fr multi 80 38

Agricultural Map of West Africa A140

West African Economic Council, 5th anniversary (Economic Maps): 120fr, Transportation. 130fr, Industry. 140fr, Communications.

1980, Nov. 5 ***Perf. 13½x13***
397 A140 100fr multi 25 15
398 A140 120fr multi 32 15
399 A140 130fr multi 35 15
400 A140 140fr multi 38 16
Set value 52

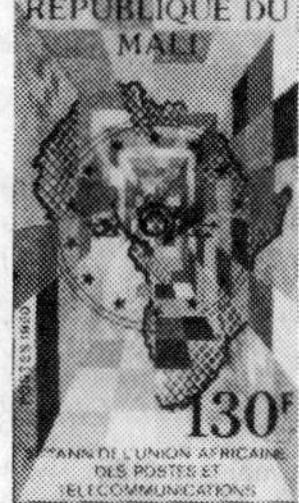

African Postal Union, 5th Anniv. — A141

Senuofo Fertility Statue — A142

1980, Dec. 24 **Photo.** ***Perf. 13½***
401 A141 130fr multi 35 15

1981, Jan. 12 **Litho.** ***Perf. 13***

Designs: Fertility statues.

402 A142 60fr Nomo dogon 16 15
403 A142 70fr shown 18 15
404 A142 90fr Bamanan 25 15
405 A142 100fr Spirit 25 15
406 A142 120fr Dogon 32 15
Nos. 402-406 (5) 1.16
Set value 46

Mambi Sidibe — A143

Hegira (Pilgrimage Year) — A144

Designs: Philosophers.

1981, Feb. 16 ***Perf. 12½x13***
407 A143 120fr shown 32 15
408 A143 130fr Amadou Hampate 35 15

1981, Feb. 23 ***Perf. 13***
409 A144 120fr multi 32 15
410 A144 180fr multi 50 20

Maure Zebu A145

Designs: Cattle breeds.

1981, Mar. 9 ***Perf. 12½***
411 A145 20fr Kaarta zebu 15 15
412 A145 30fr Peul du Macina zebu 15 15
413 A145 40fr Maure zebu 15 15
414 A145 80fr Touareg zebu 20 15
415 A145 100fr N'Dama cow 25 15
Set value 65 35

See Nos. 433-437.

Hibiscus Double Rose — A146

Designs: Flowers.

1981, Mar. 16
416 A146 50fr Crinum de Moore 15 15
417 A146 100fr Double Rose Hibiscus 25 15
418 A146 120fr Pervenche 32 15
419 A146 130fr Frangipani 35 15
420 A146 180fr Orgueil de Chine 50 20
Nos. 416-420 (5) 1.57
Set value 60

See Nos. 442-446.

Wrench Operated by Artificial Hand A147

Perf. 13x12½, 12x13

1981, May 4 **Engr.**
421 A147 100fr Heads, vert. 25 15
422 A147 120fr shown 32 15
Set value 22

Intl. Year of the Disabled.

13th World Telecommunications Day — A148

1981, May 17 **Litho.** ***Perf. 13x12½***
423 A148 130fr multi 35 15

Pierre Curie, Lab Equipment A149

1981, May 25 **Engr.**
424 A149 180fr multi 50 20

Curie (1859-1906), discoverer of radium.

Scouts at Water Hole — A150

1981, June 8 **Litho.** ***Perf. 13***
425 A150 110fr shown 30 15
426 A150 160fr Sending signals 42 20
427 A150 300fr Salute, vert. 80 35

Souvenir Sheet

428 A150 500fr Lord Baden-Powell 1.40 65

4th African Scouting Conf., Abidjan, June.

Nos. 425-428 Overprinted in Red in 2 or 3 Lines: "DAKAR 8 AOUT 1981/28e CONFERENCE MONDIALE DU SCOUTISME"

1981, June 29

429 A150 110fr multi 30 15
430 A150 160fr multi 42 20
431 A150 300fr multi 80 35

Souvenir Sheet

432 A150 500fr multi 1.40 65

28th World Scouting Conf., Dakar, Aug. 8.

Cattle Type of 1981

Various goats.

1981, Sept. 14 Litho. *Perf. 13x13½*

433 A145 10fr Maure 15 15
434 A145 25fr Peul 15 15
435 A145 140fr Sahel 40 16
436 A145 180fr Tuareg 50 20
437 A145 200fr Djallonke 55 20
Nos. 433-437 (5) 1.75
Set value 65

World UPU Day — A151

1981, Oct. 9 Engr. *Perf. 13*

438 A151 400fr multi 1.10 42

World Food Day — A152

1981, Oct. 16

439 A152 200fr multi 55 20

Europafrica Economic Convention — A153

1981, Nov. 23 Engr. *Perf. 13*

440 A153 700fr multi 1.90 1.20

60th Anniv. of Tuberculosis Inoculation A154

1981, Dec. 7 *Perf. 13x12½*

441 A154 200fr multi 55 20

Flower Type of 1981

1982, Jan. 18 Litho. *Perf. 13*

442 A146 170fr White water lilies 45 20
443 A146 180fr Red kapok bush 50 20
444 A146 200fr Purple mimosa 55 22
445 A146 220fr Pobego lilies 60 22
446 A146 270fr Satan's chalices 70 30
Nos. 442-446 (5) 2.80 1.14

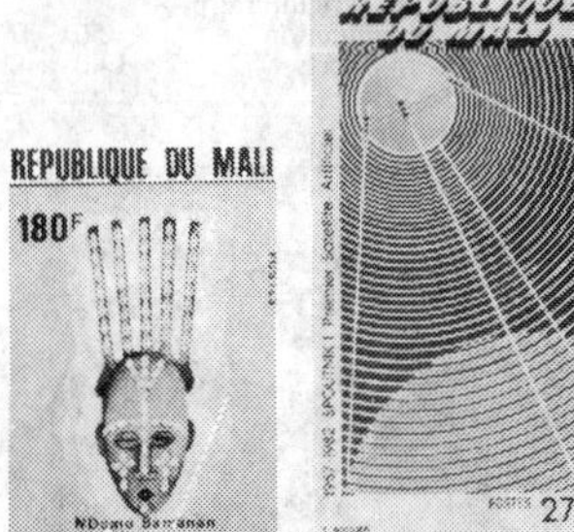

Ceremonial Mask — A155

25th Anniv. of Sputnik I Flight — A156

Designs: Various masks.

1982, Feb. 22 Litho. *Perf. 12½*

447 A155 5fr multi 15 15
448 A155 35fr multi 15 15
449 A155 180fr multi 50 20
450 A155 200fr multi 55 22
451 A155 250fr multi 65 25
Nos. 447-451 (5) 2.00
Set value 75

1982, Mar. 29 Litho. *Perf. 13*

452 A156 270fr multi 70 28

Fight Against Polio — A157

1982, May 3

453 A157 180fr multi 50 20

Lions Intl. and Day of the Blind A158

1982, May 10 Engr.

454 A158 260fr multi 65 25

"Good Friends" Hairstyle — A159

Designs: Various hairstyles.

1982, May 24 Litho.

455 A159 140fr multi 40 16
456 A159 150fr multi 42 18
457 A159 160fr multi 45 20
458 A159 180fr multi 50 20
459 A159 270fr multi 70 30
Nos. 455-459 (5) 2.47 1.04

Zebu A160

Designs: Various breeds of zebu.

1982, July 5 *Perf. 12½*

460 A160 10fr multi 15 15
461 A160 60fr multi 16 15
462 A160 110fr multi 30 15
463 A160 180fr multi 50 20
464 A160 200fr multi 55 22
Nos. 460-464 (5) 1.66
Set value 62

Wind Surfing (New Olympic Class) — A161

Pres. John F. Kennedy — A162

Designs: Various wind surfers.

1982, Nov. 22 Litho. *Perf. 12½x13*

465 A161 200fr multi 55 20
466 A161 270fr multi 70 30
467 A161 300fr multi 90 38

1983, Apr. 4 Engr. *Perf. 13*

468 A162 800fr shown 2.25 90
469 A162 800fr Martin Luther King 2.50 90

Oua Traditional Hairstyle — A163

1983, Apr. 25 Litho.

470 A163 180fr shown 50 20
471 A163 200fr Nation 60 22
472 A163 270fr Rond point 70 28
473 A163 300fr Naamu-Naamu 80 35
474 A163 500fr Bamba-Bamba 1.40 55
Nos. 470-474 (5) 4.00 1.60

World Communications Year — A164

1983, May 17 Litho. *Perf. 13*

475 A164 180fr multi 50 20

Bicent. of Lavoisier's Water Analysis A165

Musicians A166

1983, May 27 Engr. *Perf. 13*

476 A165 300fr multi 90 38

1983, June 13 Litho. *Perf. 13x13½*

477 A166 200fr Banzoumana Sissoko 60 22
478 A166 300fr Batourou Sekou Kouyate 90 38

Nicephore Niepce, Photography Pioneer, (1765-1833) A167

1983, July 4 Engr. *Perf. 13*

479 A167 400fr Portrait, early camera 1.20 45

2nd Pan African Youth Festival — A168

Palestinian Solidarity — A169

14th World UPU Day — A170

1983, Aug. 22 Litho. *Perf. 12½*

480 A168 240fr multi 70 30
481 A169 270fr multi 80 32

1983, Oct. 10 Engr. *Perf. 12½*

482 A170 240fr multi 70 30

Sahel Goat — A171

1984, Jan. 30 Litho. *Perf. 13*

483 A171 20fr shown 15 15
484 A171 30fr Billy goat 15 15
485 A171 50fr Billy goat, diff. 15 15
486 A171 240fr Kaarta goat 70 18
487 A171 350fr Southern goats 1.10 32
Nos. 483-487 (5) 2.25
Set value 68

Rural Development A172

Fragrant Trees A173

1984, June 1 Litho. *Perf. 13*

488 A172 5fr Crop disease prevention 15 15
489 A172 90fr Carpenters, horiz. 28 15
490 A172 100fr Tapestry weaving, horiz. 32 16
491 A172 135fr Metal workers, horiz. 42 20
Set value 55

1984, June 1

492 A173 515fr Borassus flabelifer 1.60 80
493 A173 1225fr Vitelaria paradoxa 4.00 1.90

UN Infant Survival Campaign — A174

1984, June 12 Engr.

494 A174 120fr Child, hearts 40 20
495 A174 135fr Children 42 20

1984 UPU Congress — A175

1984, June 18

496 A175 135fr Anchor, UPU emblem, view of Hamburg 42 20

Nos. 482-487 Overprinted and Surcharged

1984

497 A171 10fr on 20fr #483 15 15
498 A171 15fr on 30fr #484 15 15
499 A171 25fr on 50fr #485 15 15
500 A170 120fr on 240fr #482 35 16
501 A171 120fr on 240fr #486 35 16
502 A171 175fr on 350fr #487 45 22
Set value 1.35 65

West African Economic Community, CEAO, 10th Anniv. A176

1984, Oct. 22 Litho. *Perf. 13½*

503 A176 350fr multi 1.00 35

Prehistoric Animals A177

1984, Nov. 5 Litho. *Perf. 12½*

504 A177 10fr Dimetrodon 15 15
505 A177 25fr Iguanodon, vert. 15 15
506 A177 30fr Archaeopteryx, vert. 15 15
507 A177 120fr Like 10fr 35 15
508 A177 175fr Like 25fr 50 15
509 A177 350fr Like 30fr 1.00 30
510 A177 470fr Triceratops 1.40 40
Nos. 504-510 (7) 3.70
Set value 1.00

No. 366 Overprinted "Aide au Sahel 84" and Surcharged

1984 Litho. *Perf. 13*

511 A126 470fr on 130fr 1.40 40

Issued to publicize drought relief efforts.

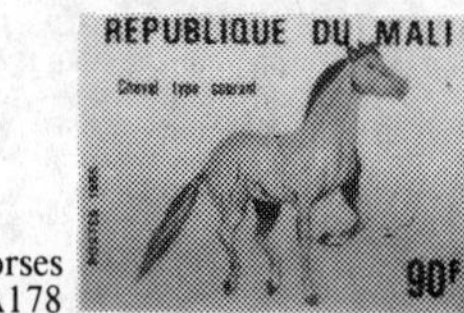

Mali Horses A178

1985, Jan. 21 Litho. *Perf. 13½*

512 A178 90fr Modern horse 25 15
513 A178 135fr Horse from Beledougou 38 15
514 A178 190fr Horse from Nara 50 16
515 A178 530fr Horse from Trait 1.50 45

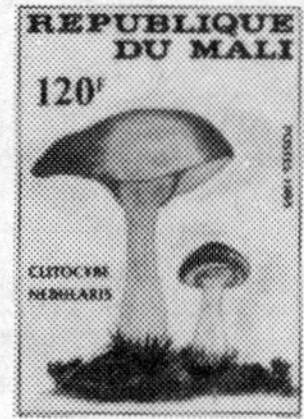

Fungi — A179

1985, Jan. 28 Litho. *Perf. 12½*

516 A179 120fr Clitocybe nebularis 35 15
517 A179 200fr Lepiota cortinarius 55 18
518 A179 485fr Agavicus semotus 1.40 42
519 A179 525fr Lepiota procera 1.50 45

Health — A180

Designs: 120fr, 32nd World Leprosy Day, Emile Marchoux (1862-1943), Marchoux Institute, 150th anniv. 135fr, Lions Intl., Samanko Convalescence Village, 15th anniv. 470fr, Anti-polio campaign, research facility, victim.

1985, Feb. 18 Litho. *Perf. 13*

520 A180 120fr multi 35 15
521 A180 135fr multi 38 15
522 A180 470fr multi 1.40 40

No. 522 is airmail.

Cultural and Technical Cooperation Agency, 15th Anniv. — A181

1985, Mar. 20

523 A181 540fr brn & brt bl grn 1.50 45

Intl. Youth Year A182

Youth activities.

1985, May 13 *Perf. 12½x13*

524 A182 120fr Natl. Pioneers Movement emblem 35 15
525 A182 190fr Agricultural production 50 16
526 A182 500fr Sports 1.40 42

PHILEXAFRICA '85, Lome, Togo — A183

1985, June 24 *Perf. 13*

527 A183 250fr Education, telecommunications 65 20
528 A183 250fr Road, dam, computers 65 20

Nos. 527-528 show the UPU emblem and are printed se-tenant with center label picturing map of Africa or UAPT emblem. See Nos. C517-C518.

Cats A184

1986, Feb. 15 Litho. *Perf. 13½*

529 A184 150fr Gray 60 20
530 A184 200fr White 70 25
531 A184 300fr Tabby 1.25 40

Fight Against Apartheid — A185

1986, Feb. 24 *Perf. 13*

532 A185 100fr shown 38 15
533 A185 120fr Map, broken chain 42 15

Telecommunications and Agriculture — A186

1986, May 17 Litho. *Perf. 13*

534 A186 200fr multi 75 25

1986 World Cup Soccer Championships, Mexico — A187

Various soccer plays.

1986, May 24 Litho. *Perf. 12½*

535 A187 160fr multi 60 20
536 A187 225fr multi 80 25

Souvenir Sheet

537 A187 500fr multi 2.00 60

James Watt (1736-1819), Inventor, and Steam Engine — A188

1986, May 26 *Perf. 12½x12*

538 A188 110fr multi 40 15

Nos. 535-537 Ovptd. "ARGENTINE 3 / R.F.A. 2" in Red

1986, July 30 Litho. *Perf. 12½*

539 A187 160fr multi 60 20
540 A187 225fr multi 80 28

Souvenir Sheet

541 A187 500fr multi 2.00 60

World Wildlife Fund — A189

Derby's Eland, Taurotragus derbianus.

1986, Aug. 11 Litho. *Perf. 13*

542 A189 5fr Adult head 15 15
543 A189 20fr Adult in brush 15 15
544 A189 25fr Adult walking 15 15
545 A189 200fr Calf suckling 75 25
Set value 98 40

Henry Ford (1863-1947), Auto Manufacturer, Inventor of Mass Production — A190

1987, Feb. 16 Litho. *Perf. 13*

546 A190 150fr Model A, 1903 60 20
547 A190 200fr Model T, 1923 70 25
548 A190 225fr Thunderbird, 1968 80 28
549 A190 300fr Lincoln Continental, 1963 1.10 38

Bees A191

1987, May 11 Litho. *Perf. 13½*

550 A191 100fr Apis florea, Asia 38 20
551 A191 150fr Apis dorsata, Asia 55 25
552 A191 175fr Apis adansonii, Africa 65 35
553 A191 200fr Apis mellifica, worldwide 70 38

Lions Club Activities — A192

1988, Jan. 13 Litho. *Perf. 12½*
554 A192 200fr multi 1.00 50

World Health Organization, 40th Anniv. — A193

1988, Feb. 22 Litho. *Perf. 12½x12*
555 A193 150fr multi 70 38

John F. Kennedy (1917-1963), 35th US President — A194

1988, June 6 Litho. *Perf. 13*
556 A194 640fr multi 4.25 2.15

No. 555 Surcharged in Dark Red

MISSION MALI
HOPITAL de MOPTI
300F

1988, June 13 *Perf. 12½x12*
557 A193 300fr on 150fr multi 2.00 1.00

Mali Mission Hospital in Mopti and World Medicine organization.

Organization of African Unity, 25th Anniv. — A194a

1988, June 27 Litho. *Perf. 12½*
558 A194a 400fr multi 2.65 1.35

Universal Immunization Campaign — A195

1989, May 2 Litho. *Perf. 13½*
559 A195 20fr shown 15 15
560 A195 30fr Inoculating woman 18 15
561 A195 50fr Emblem, needles, diff. 30 15
562 A195 175fr Inoculating boy 1.05 52
Set value 82

Intl. Law Institute of the French-Speaking Nations — A196

1989, May 15 *Perf. 12½*
563 A196 150fr multi 90 45
564 A196 200fr multi 1.20 60

World Post Day — A197

1989, Oct. 9 Litho. *Perf. 13*
565 A197 625fr multicolored 4.00 2.00

Visit of Pope John Paul II — A198

1990, Jan. 28 Litho. *Perf. 13x12½*
566 A198 200fr multicolored 1.45 72

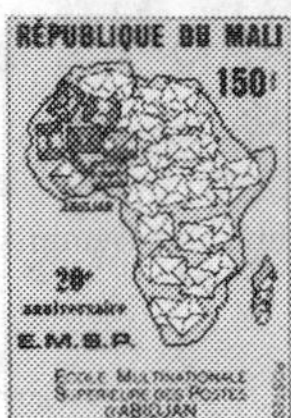
Multinational Postal School, 20th Anniv. — A199

1990, May 31 Litho. *Perf. 12½*
567 A199 150fr multicolored 1.10 55

Independence, 30th Anniv. — A200

1990, Sept. 20 Litho. *Perf. 13x12½*
568 A200 400fr multicolored 3.00 1.50

Intl. Literacy Year A201

1990, Sept. 24 Litho. *Perf. 13½*
569 A201 150fr grn & multi 1.30 65
570 A201 200fr org & multi 1.75 90

Lions Intl. Water Project, 6th Anniv. — A202

Design: No. 572, Rotary Club fight against polio, 30th anniv.

1991, Feb. 25 Litho. *Perf. 13x12½*
571 A202 200fr multicolored 1.75 90
572 A202 200fr multicolored 1.75 90

Tribal Dances of Mali — A203

1991, Apr. 29 Litho. *Perf. 12½*
573 A203 50fr Takamba 45 22
574 A203 100fr Mandiani 90 45
575 A203 150fr Kono 1.40 70
576 A203 200fr Songho 1.75 90

SEMI-POSTAL STAMPS

Anti-Malaria Issue
Common Design Type
Perf. 12½x12

1962, Apr. 7 Engr. Unwmk.
B1 CD108 25fr + 5fr pale vio bl 50 50

Algerian Family — SP1

1962, Dec. 24 Photo. *Perf. 12x12½*
B2 SP1 25fr + 5fr multi 22 22

Issued for the national campaign to show the solidarity of the peoples of Mali and Algeria.

AIR POST STAMPS

Federation

Composite View of St. Louis, Senegal — AP1

Unwmk.

1959, Dec. 11 Engr. *Perf. 13*
C1 AP1 85fr multi 1.00 80

Issued to commemorate the tercentenary of the founding of St. Louis, Senegal, and to honor the opening of the 6th meeting of the executive council of the French Community.

Amethyst Starling — AP2

Birds: 200fr, Bateleur eagle (horiz.). 500fr, Barbary shrike.

Perf. 12½x13, 13x12½

1960, Feb. 13 Photo.

Birds in Natural Colors

C2 AP2 100fr multi 1.00 55
C3 AP2 200fr multi 1.65 1.00
C4 AP2 500fr blk & bl 6.50 4.50

Republic

Nos. C2-C4 Overprinted or Surcharged "REPUBLIQUE DU MALI" and Bars

1960, Dec. 18

Birds in Natural Colors

C5 AP2 100fr multi 1.40 90
C6 AP2 200fr multi 2.25 1.50
C7 AP2 300fr on 500fr blk & bl 3.50 3.00
C8 AP2 500fr blk & bl 6.25 4.75

Pres. Modibo Keita — AP3

Designs: 200fr, Mamadou Konate.

1961, Mar. 18 Engr. *Perf. 13*
C9 AP3 200fr cl & gray brn 1.60 65
C10 AP3 300fr grn & blk 2.25 90

Flag, Map, UN Emblem — AP4

1961, Mar. 18

C11 AP4 100fr multi	75	60
a. Min. sheet of 3, #13, 14, C11	1.40	1.40

Proclamation of independence and admission to UN.

Sankore Mosque, Timbuktu — AP5

Designs: 200fr, View of Timbuktu. 500fr, Bamako and arms.

1961, Apr. 15 **Unwmk.** ***Perf. 13***

C12 AP5 100fr Prus bl, red brn & gray	65	20
C13 AP5 200fr grn, brn & red	1.25	65
C14 AP5 500fr red brn, Prus bl & dk grn	3.50	1.25

Issued for the inauguration of Timbuktu airport and Air Mali.

Bull, Chemical Equipment and Chicks — AP6

1963, Feb. 23 **Engr.**

C15 AP6 200fr bis, mar & grnsh bl	1.50	70

Sotuba Zootechnical Institute.

Air Ambulance — AP7

Designs: 55fr, National Line plane loading. 100fr, Intl. Line Vickers Viscount in flight.

1963, Nov. 2 **Unwmk.** ***Perf. 13***

C16 AP7 25fr dk bl, emer & red brn	22	15
C17 AP7 55fr bis, bl & red brn	50	25
C18 AP7 100fr dk bl, red brn & yel grn	80	42

Issued to publicize Air Mali.

Crowned Crane and Giant Tortoise — AP8

1963, Nov. 23 **Unwmk.** ***Perf. 13***

C19 AP8 25fr sep, org & ver	40	25
C20 AP8 200fr multi	1.90	1.25

Animal protection.

UN Emblem, Flag, Doves — AP9

1963, Dec. 10 **Engr.**

C21 AP9 50fr lt grn, yel & red	40	20

15th anniversary of the Universal Declaration of Human Rights.

Cleopatra and Ptolemy at Kom Ombo — AP10

1964, Mar. 9 **Unwmk.** ***Perf. 12***

C22 AP10 25fr dp cl & bis	35	15
C23 AP10 55fr dp cl & lt ol grn	60	30

UNESCO world campaign to save historic monuments in Nubia.

Pres. John F. Kennedy — AP11

1964, Oct. 26 **Photo.** ***Perf. 12½***

C24 AP11 100fr sl, red brn & blk	65	65
a. Souv. sheet of 4	3.00	3.00

Touracos — AP12

Birds: 200fr, Abyssinian ground hornbills (vert.). 300fr, Egyptian vultures (vert.). 500fr, Goliath herons.

1965, Feb. 15 **Engr.** ***Perf. 13***

C25 AP12 100fr grn, dk bl & red	65	38
C26 AP12 200fr blk, red & brt bl	1.10	55
C27 AP12 300fr blk, sl grn & yel	1.65	1.00
C28 AP12 500fr sl grn, dk brn & claret	3.50	1.50

UN Headquarters, New York, and ICY Emblem — AP13

1965, Mar. 15 **Unwmk.** ***Perf. 13***

C29 AP13 55fr bis, dk bl & vio brn	45	30

International Cooperation Year.

Pope John XXIII AP14

Perf. 12½x13

1965, Sept. 14 **Photo.** **Unwmk.**

C30 AP14 100fr multi	90	60

Winston Churchill — AP15

1965, Oct. 11 **Engr.** ***Perf. 13***

C31 AP15 100fr brn & ind	90	60

Dr. Albert Schweitzer and Sick Child — AP16

1965, Dec. 20 **Photo.** ***Perf. 12½***

C32 AP16 100fr multi	1.00	60
a. Souv. sheet of 4	4.00	3.25

Major Edward H. White and Gemini 4 — AP17

Designs: No. C34, Lt. Col. Alexei A. Leonov. 300fr, Gordon Cooper, Charles Conrad, Alexei Leonov and Pavel Belyayev, Parthenon, Athens, and vase (vert.).

1966, Jan. 10

C33 AP17 100fr vio, yel, lt bl & blk	90	40
C34 AP17 100fr bl, red, yel & blk	90	40
C35 AP17 300fr multi	2.75	1.75

Achievements in space research and 16th Intl. Astronautical Congress, Athens, Sept. 12-18, 1965.

Papal Arms and UN Emblem — AP18

1966, July 11 **Engr.** ***Perf. 13***

C36 AP18 200fr brt bl, grnsh bl & grn	1.60	55

Visit of Pope Paul VI to the UN, NYC, Oct. 4, 1965.

People and UNESCO Emblem — AP19

1966, Sept. 5 **Engr.** ***Perf. 13***

C37 AP19 100fr dk car rose, sl grn & ultra	70	42

20th anniv. of UNESCO.

Soccer Players, Ball, Globe, and Jules Rimet Cup — AP20

1966, Oct. 31 **Photo.** ***Perf. 13***

C38 AP20 100fr multi	70	42

8th International Soccer Championship Games, Wembley, England, July 11-30.

Crab and Mt. Fuji — AP21

UNICEF Emblem and Children — AP22

1966, Nov. 30 **Photo.** ***Perf. 13***

C39 AP21 100fr multi	70	35

9th International Anticancer Congress, Tokyo, Oct. 23-29.

1966, Dec. 10 **Engr.**

C40 AP22 45fr dp bl, bis brn & red lil	38	16

20th anniv. of UNICEF.

Land Cruisers in Hoggar Mountain Pass — AP23

1967, Mar. 20 **Engr.** ***Perf. 13***
C41 AP23 200fr multi 1.25 65

"Black Cruise 1924," which crossed Africa from Beni-Abbes, Algeria to the Indian Ocean and on to Tananarive, Madagascar, Oct. 28, 1924-June 26, 1925.

Diamant Rocket and Francesco de Lana's 1650 Flying Boat — AP24

Designs: 100fr, A-1 satellite and rocket launching adapted from Jules Verne. 200fr, D-1 satellite and Leonardo da Vinci's bird-borne flying machine.

1967, Apr. 17 **Engr.** ***Perf. 13***
C42 AP24 50fr brt bl, pur & grn 60 35
C43 AP24 100fr dk Prus bl, dk car & lil 1.40 65
C44 AP24 200fr sl bl, ol & pur 2.25 1.00

Honoring French achievements in space.

Amelia Earhart and Map of Mali — AP25

1967, May 29 **Photo.** ***Perf. 13***
C45 AP25 500fr bl & multi 2.75 1.25

30th anniversary of Amelia Earhart's stop at Gao, West Africa.

Paul as Harlequin, by Picasso AP26

Picasso Paintings: 50fr, Bird Cage. 250fr, The Flutes of Pan.

1967, June 16 ***Perf. 12½***
C46 AP26 50fr multi 30 16
C47 AP26 100fr multi 60 32
C48 AP26 250fr multi 1.40 75

See No. C82.

Jamboree Emblem, Scout Knots and Badges — AP27

Design: 100fr, Scout with portable radio transmitter, tents and Jamboree badge.

1967, July 10 **Engr.** ***Perf. 13***
C49 AP27 70fr dk car, emer & bl grn 42 22
C50 AP27 100fr dk car lake, sl grn & blk 65 30
a. Strip of 2, #C49-C50 + label 1.40 1.20

12th Boy Scout World Jamboree, Farragut State Park, Idaho, Aug. 1-9.

Head of Horse, by Toulouse-Lautrec — AP28

Design: 300fr, Cob-drawn gig, by Toulouse-Lautrec (vert.).

Perf. 12x12½, 12½x12
1967, Dec. 11 **Photo.**
C51 AP28 100fr multi 60 40
C52 AP28 300fr multi 1.75 75

See Nos. C66-C67.

Grenoble — AP29

Design: 150fr, Bobsled course on Huez Alp.

1968, Jan. 8 **Engr.** ***Perf. 13***
C53 AP29 50fr bl, yel brn & grn 25 15
C54 AP29 150fr brn, vio bl & stl bl 65 30

10th Winter Olympic Games, Grenoble, France, Feb. 6-18.

Roses and Anemones, by Van Gogh — AP30

Paintings: 150fr, Peonies in Vase, by Edouard Manet (vert., 36x49mm). 300fr, Bouquet, by Delarcroix (41x42mm). 500fr, Daisies in Vase, by Jean François Millet (horiz., 49x37mm).

Perf. 13, 12½x12, 12x12½
1968, June 24 **Photo.**
C55 AP30 50fr multi 25 15
C56 AP30 150fr grn & multi 65 30
C57 AP30 300fr grn & multi 1.20 65
C58 AP30 500fr car & multi 2.25 90

Martin Luther King, Jr. — AP31

Long Jumper and Satellite — AP32

1968, July 22 ***Perf. 12½***
C59 AP31 100fr rose lil, sal pink & blk 38 16

Bicycle Type of Regular Issue

Designs: 50fr, Bicyclette, 1918. 100fr, Mercedes Benz, 1927 (horiz.).

1968, Aug. 12 **Engr.** ***Perf. 13***
C60 A40 50fr gray, dk grn & brick red 22 20
C61 A40 100fr lem, ind & car 45 22

1968, Nov. 25 **Photo.** ***Perf. 12½***

Design: 100fr, Soccer goalkeeper and satellite (horiz.).

C62 AP32 100fr multi 42 25
C63 AP32 150fr multi 65 35

Issued to commemorate the 19th Olympic Games, Mexico City, Oct. 12-27.

PHILEXAFRIQUE Issue

Editorial Department, by François Marius Granet AP33

1968, Dec. 23 **Photo.** ***Perf. 12½x12***
C64 AP33 200fr multi 90 65

Issued to publicize PHILEXAFRIQUE Philatelic Exhibition in Abidjan, Feb. 14-23. Printed with alternating light green label.

See Nos. C85-C87, C110-C112, C205-C207, C216-C217.

2nd PHILEXAFRIQUE Issue
Common Design Type

Design: 100fr, French Sudan No. 64 and sculpture.

1969, Feb. 14 **Engr.** ***Perf. 13***
C65 CD128 100fr pur & multi 50 50

Painting Type of 1967

Paintings: 150fr, Napoleon as First Consul, by Antoine Jean Gros (vert.). 250fr, Bivouac at Austerlitz, by Louis François Lejeune.

Perf. 12½x12, 12x12½
1969, Feb. 25 **Photo.**
C66 AP28 150fr multi 1.20 70
C67 AP28 250fr multi 1.60 1.20

Napoleon Bonaparte (1769-1821).

Concorde — AP34

Designs: 50fr, Montgolfier's balloon. 150fr, Ferber 5, experimental biplane.

1969, Mar. 10 **Photo.** ***Perf. 13***
C68 AP34 50fr multi 25 15
C69 AP34 150fr multi 65 25
C70 AP34 300fr multi 1.40 70

1st flight of the prototype Concorde plane at Toulouse, France, Mar. 1, 1969. Nos. C68-C70 are printed se-tenant.

Auto Type of Regular Issue

Designs: 55fr, Renault, 1898, and Renault 16, 1969. 90fr, Peugeot, 1893, and Peugeot 404, 1969.

1969, May 30 **Engr.** ***Perf. 13***
C71 A43 55fr rose car, blk & brt pink 25 20
C72 A43 90fr blk, dp car & ind 40 20

Ronald Clark, Australia, 10,000-meter Run, 1965 — AP35

World Records: 90fr, Yanis Lusis, USSR, Javelin, 1968. 120fr, Yoshinobu Miyake, Japan, weight lifting, 1967. 140fr, Randy Matson, USA, shot put, 1968. 150fr, Kipchoge Keino, Kenya, 3,000-meter run, 1965.

1969, June 23 **Engr.** ***Perf. 13***
C73 AP35 60fr bl & ol brn 18 15
C74 AP35 90fr car rose & red brn 28 16
C75 AP35 120fr emer & gray ol 35 16
C76 AP35 140fr gray & brn 45 20
C77 AP35 150fr red org & blk 50 25
Nos. C73-C77 (5) 1.76 92

Issued to honor sports world records.

Nos. C68-C70 Overprinted in Red with Lunar Landing Module and: "L'HOMME SUR LA LUNE / JUILLET 1969 / APOLLO 11"

1969, July 25 **Photo.** ***Perf. 13***
C78 AP34 50fr multi 42 30
C79 AP34 150fr multi 1.10 80
C80 AP34 300fr multi 2.25 1.60

Man's 1st landing on moon, July 20, 1969. US astronauts Neil A. Armstrong and Col. Edwin E. Aldrin, Jr., with Lieut. Col. Michael Collins piloting Apollo 11.
Printed se-tenant.

Apollo 8, Moon and Earth AP35a

Embossed on Gold Foil
1969, July 24 ***Die-cut perf 10½***
C81 AP35a 2000fr gold 9.00 9.00

US Apollo 8 mission, the 1st men in orbit around the moon, Dec. 21-27, 1968.

Painting Type of 1967

Design: 500fr, Mona Lisa, by Leonardo da Vinci.

1969, Oct. 20 Photo. *Perf. 12½*
C82 AP26 500fr multi 2.25 1.65

Mahatma Gandhi — AP36

1969, Nov. 24 Engr. *Perf. 13*
C83 AP36 150fr brt bl, ol brn & red brn 65 35

Map of West Africa, Post Horns and Lightning Bolts — AP37

1970, Feb. 23 Photo. *Perf. 12½*
C84 AP37 100fr multi 42 25

11th anniversary of the West African Postal Union (CAPTEAO).

Painting Type of 1968

Paintings: 100fr, Madonna and Child, from Rogier van der Weyden school. 150fr, Nativity, by the master of Flemalle. 250fr, Madonna and Child with St. John, from the Dutch School.

1970, Mar. 2
C85 AP33 100fr multi 38 22
C86 AP33 150fr multi 55 35
C87 AP33 250fr multi 90 55

Roosevelt AP38

Lenin AP39

1970, Mar. 30 Photo. *Perf. 12½*
C88 AP38 500fr red, lt ultra & blk 2.75 1.35

Pres. Franklin D. Roosevelt (1882-1945).

1970, Apr. 22
C89 AP39 300fr pink, grn & blk 1.25 55

Jules Verne and Firing of Moon Rockets — AP40

Designs: 150fr, Jules Verne, rockets, landing modules and moon. 300fr, Jules Verne and splashdown.

1970, May 4
C90 AP40 50fr multi 35 16
C91 AP40 150fr multi 1.20 42
C92 AP40 300fr multi 2.00 80

Nos. C90-C92 Overprinted in Red or Blue: "APOLLO XIII / EPOPEE SPATIALE / 11-17 AVRIL 1970"

1970, June Photo. *Perf. 12½*
C93 AP40 50fr multi (Bl) 40 25
C94 AP40 150fr multi (R) 1.00 42
C95 AP40 300fr multi (Bl) 2.25 1.40

Flight and safe return of Apollo 13, Apr. 11-13, 1970.

Intelsat III — AP41

Telecommunications Through Space: 200fr, Molniya I satellite. 300fr, Radar. 500fr, "Project Symphony" (various satellites).

1970, July 13 Engr. *Perf. 13*
C96 AP41 100fr gray, brt bl & org 65 35
C97 AP41 200fr bl, gray & red lil 1.40 60
C98 AP41 300fr org, dk brn & gray 1.90 80
C99 AP41 500fr dk brn, sl & grnsh bl 3.00 1.40

Auguste and Louis Lumiere, Jean Harlow and Marilyn Monroe AP42

1970, July 27 Photo. *Perf. 12½x12*
C100 AP42 250fr multi 90 55

Issued to honor Auguste Lumière (1862-1954), and his brother Louis Jean Lumière (1864-1948), inventors of the Lumière process of color photography and of a motion picture camera.

Soccer — AP43

1970, Sept. 7 Engr. *Perf. 13*
C101 AP43 80fr bl, dp car & brn ol 35 16
C102 AP43 200fr dp car, bl grn & ol brn 70 42

Issued to commemorate the 9th World Soccer Championships for the Jules Rimet Cup, Mexico City, May 30-June 21, 1970.

Rotary Emblem, Map of Mali and Ceremonial Antelope Heads — AP44

Men Holding UN Emblem, and Doves — AP45

1970, Sept. 21 Photo. *Perf. 12½*
C103 AP44 200fr multi 70 42

Issued to honor Rotary International.

1970, Oct. 5 Engr. *Perf. 13*
C104 AP45 100fr dk pur, red brn & dk bl 38 22

25th anniversary of the United Nations.

Koran Page, Baghdad, 11th Century AP46

Moslem Art: 200fr, Tree, and lion killing deer, mosaic, Jordan, c. 730 (horiz.). 250fr, Scribe, miniature, Baghdad, 1287.

1970, Oct. 26 Photo. *Perf. 12½x12*
C105 AP46 50fr multi 22 15
C106 AP46 200fr multi 60 30
C107 AP46 250fr multi 70 38

Nos. C97-C98 Surcharged and Overprinted: "LUNA 16 / PREMIERS PRELEVEMENTS AUTOMATIQUES / SUR LA LUNE / SEPTEMBRE 1970"

1970, Nov. 9 Engr. *Perf. 13*
C108 AP41 150fr on 200fr multi 1.10 55
C109 AP41 250fr on 300fr multi 2.00 85

Unmanned moon probe of the Russian space ship Luna 16, Sept. 12-24.

Painting Type of 1968

Paintings: 100fr, Nativity, Antwerp School, c. 1530. 250fr, St. John the Baptist, by Hans Memling. 300fr, Adoration of the Kings, Flemish School, 17th century.

1970, Dec. 1 Photo. *Perf. 12½x12*
C110 AP33 100fr brn & multi 32 16
C111 AP33 250fr brn & multi 65 32
C112 AP33 300fr brn & multi 90 40

Christmas 1970.

Gamal Abdel Nasser — AP47

Embossed on Gold Foil

1970, Nov. 25 *Perf. 12½*
C113 AP47 1000fr gold 5.00 5.00

In memory of Gamal Abdel Nasser (1918-1970), President of Egypt.

Charles de Gaulle AP48

Embossed on Gold Foil

1971, Feb. 8 *Die-cut Perf. 10*
C114 AP48 2000fr gold, red & dp ultra 12.00 12.00

In memory of Gen. Charles de Gaulle (1890-1970), President of France.

Alfred Nobel — AP49

Tennis, Davis Cup — AP50

1971, Feb. 22 Engr. *Perf. 13*
C115 AP49 300fr cl, brt grn & dk brn 90 60

75th anniversary of the death of Alfred Nobel (1833-1896), inventor of dynamite, sponsor of Nobel Prize.

1971, Mar. 8

Designs: 150fr, Derby at Epsom (horiz.). 200fr, Racing yacht, America's Cup.

C116 AP50 100fr bl, lil & sl 25 15
C117 AP50 150fr brn, brt grn & ol 38 16
C118 AP50 200fr brt bl, ol & brn 65 22

The Arabian Nights — AP51

Designs: 180fr, Ali Baba and the 40 Thieves. 200fr, Aladdin's Lamp.

1971, Apr. 5 Photo. *Perf. 13*
C119 AP51 120fr gold & multi 35 22
C120 AP51 180fr gold & multi 42 25
C121 AP51 200fr gold & multi 65 38

Olympic Rings and Sports — AP52

1971, June 28 Photo. *Perf. 12½*
C122 AP52 80fr ultra, yel grn & brt mag 22 15

Pre-Olympic Year.

Mariner 4 — AP53

Design: 300fr, Venera 5 in space.

1971, Sept. 13 Engr. *Perf. 13*
C123 AP53 200fr multi 55 30
C124 AP53 300fr multi 80 42

Space explorations of US Mariner 4 (200fr); and USSR Venera 5 (300fr).

Santa Maria, 1492 — AP54

Famous Ships: 150fr, Mayflower, 1620. 200fr, Potemkin, 1905. 250fr, Normandie, 1935.

1971, Sept. 27
C125 AP54 100fr brn, bluish grn & pur 22 15
C126 AP54 150fr sl grn, brn & pur 38 20
C127 AP54 200fr car, bl & dk ol 60 35
C128 AP54 250fr blk, bl & red 70 42

Symbols of Justice and Maps — AP55

1971, Oct. 18
C129 AP55 160fr mar, ocher & dk brn 50 22

25th anniversary of the International Court of Justice in The Hague, Netherlands.

Statue of Zeus, by Phidias — AP56

Nat "King" Cole — AP57

The Seven Wonders of the Ancient World: 80fr, Cheops Pyramid and Sphinx. 100fr, Temple of Artemis, Ephesus (horiz.). 130fr, Lighthouse at Alexandria. 150fr, Hanging Gardens of Babylon (horiz.). 270fr, Mausoleum of Halicarnassus. 280fr, Colossus of Rhodes.

1971, Dec. 13
C130 AP56 70fr ind, dk red & pink 22 15
C131 AP56 80fr brn, bl & blk 22 15
C132 AP56 100fr org, ind & pur 30 16
C133 AP56 130fr rose lil, blk & grnsh bl 40 16
C134 AP56 150fr brn, brt grn & bl 42 16
C135 AP56 270fr sl, brn & plum 80 20
C136 AP56 280fr sl lil & ol 80 20
Nos. C130-C136 (7) 3.16 1.18

1971, Dec. 6 Photo. *Perf. 13x12½*

Famous American Black Musicians: 150fr, Erroll Garner. 270fr, Louis Armstrong.

C137 AP57 130fr blk, brn & yel 40 16
C138 AP57 150fr blk, bl & yel 42 18
C139 AP57 270fr blk, rose car & yel 80 35

Slalom and Japanese Child AP58

Design: 200fr, Ice hockey and character from Noh play.

1972, Jan. 10 Engr. *Perf. 13*
C140 AP58 150fr sl grn, dk brn & red 42 20
C141 AP58 200fr red, sl grn & dk brn 60 35
a. Souv. sheet of 2, #C140-C141 1.40 1.40

11th Winter Olympic Games, Sapporo, Japan, Feb. 3-13.

Santa Maria della Salute, by Ippolito Caffi — AP59

Paintings of Venice, by Ippolito Caffi: 270fr, Rialto Bridge. 280fr, St. Mark's Square (vert.).

1972, Feb. 21 Photo. *Perf. 13*
C142 AP59 130fr gold & multi 45 22
C143 AP59 270fr gold & multi 80 42
C144 AP59 280fr gold & multi 90 55

UNESCO campaign to save Venice.

Hands of 4 Races Holding Scout Flag — AP60

1972, Mar. 27 Engr. *Perf. 13*
C145 AP60 200fr dk red, ocher & ol gray 55 28

World Boy Scout Seminar, Cotonou, Dahomey, March, 1972.

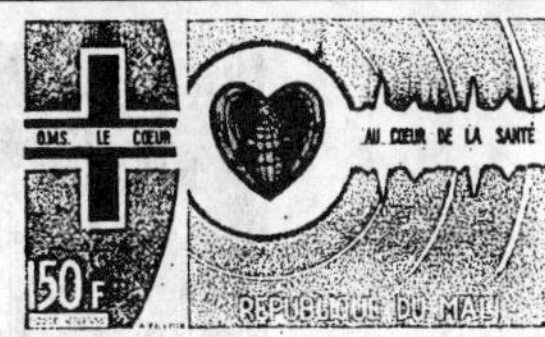
"Your Heart is your Health" — AP61

1972, Apr. 7 Engr. *Perf. 13*
C146 AP61 150fr brt bl & red 42 25

World Health Day.

Soccer Player and Frauenkirche, Munich — AP62

Designs (Sport and Munich Landmarks): 150fr, Wrestling and TV Tower (vert.). 200fr, Steeplechase and Propylaeum (vert.). 300fr, Runner and Church of the Theatines.

1972, Apr. 17
C147 AP62 50fr ocher, dk bl & grn 20 15
C148 AP62 150fr dk bl, ocher & grn 45 20
C149 AP62 200fr grn, dk bl & ocher 60 28
C150 AP62 300fr dk bl, grn & ocher 90 40
a. Min. sheet of 4, #C147-C150 3.00 3.00

20th Olympic Games, Munich, Aug. 26-Sept. 10.

Apollo 15, Lunar Rover, Landing Module — AP63

Design: 250fr, Cugnot's steam wagon and Montgolfier's Balloon.

1972, Apr. 27
C151 AP63 150fr ver, sl grn & rose mag 55 25
C152 AP63 250fr ultra, grn & rose red 80 38

Development of transportation.

Cinderella AP64

Fairy Tales: 80fr, Puss in Boots. 150fr, Sleeping Beauty.

1972, June 19 Engr. *Perf. 13x12½*
C153 AP64 70fr car rose, sl grn & ol 25 15
C154 AP64 80fr choc, brt grn & dp org 35 18
C155 AP64 150fr vio, bl & lil 55 25

Charles Perrault (1628-1703), French writer.

Astronauts and Lunar Rover on Moon — AP65

1972, July 24 Engr. *Perf. 13*
C156 AP65 500fr ol bis, vio & brt grn 1.60 75

US Apollo 16 moon mission, Apr. 15-27.

Book Year Emblem — AP66

1972, Aug. 7 Litho. *Perf. 12½*
C157 AP66 80fr bl, gold & grn 25 16

International Book Year 1972.

Bamako Rotary Emblem with Crocodiles — AP67

1972, Oct. 9 Engr. *Perf. 13*
C158 AP67 170fr dk brn, red & ultra 55 20

10th anniv. of the Bamako Rotary Club.

Hurdler, Olympic Rings, Melbourne Cathedral, Kangaroo — AP68

Designs (Olympic Rings and): 70fr, Boxing, Helsinki Railroad Station, arms of Finland (vert.). 140fr, Running, Colosseum, Roman wolf. 150fr, Weight lifting, Tokyo stadium, phoenix (vert.). 170fr, Swimming, University Library, Mexico City; Aztec sculpture. 210fr, Javelin, Munich Stadium, Arms of Munich. Stamps inscribed with name of gold medal winner of event shown.

1972, Nov. 13 Engr. *Perf. 13*
C159 AP68 70fr red, ocher & ind 20 15
C160 AP68 90fr red brn, bl & sl 25 16
C161 AP68 140fr brn, brt grn & ol gray 40 16
C162 AP68 150fr dk car, emer & gray ol 42 18
C163 AP68 170fr red lil, brn & Prus bl 45 20
C164 AP68 210fr ultra, emer & brick red 65 35
Nos. C159-C164 (6) 2.37 1.20

Retrospective of Olympic Games 1952-1972.

Nos. C148-C150 and C164 Overprinted:

a. JUDO / RUSKA / 2 MEDAILLES D'OR
b. STEEPLE / KEINO / MEDAILLE D'OR
c. MEDAILLE D'OR / 90m. 48
d. 100m.-200m. / BORZOV / 2 MEDAILLES D'OR

1972, Nov. 27 Engr. *Perf. 13*

C165 AP62 150fr multi (a) 42 22
C166 AP62 200fr multi (b) 55 25
C167 AP68 210fr multi (c) 60 30
C168 AP62 300fr multi (d) 90 42

Gold medal winners in 20th Olympic Games: Wim Ruska, Netherlands, heavyweight judo (#C165); Kipchoge Keino, Kenya, 3000m. steeplechase (#C166); Klaus Wolfermann, Germany, javelin (#C167); Valery Borzov, USSR, 100m., 200m. race (#C168).

Emperor Haile Selassie AP69

1972, Dec. 26 Photo. *Perf. 12½*

C169 AP69 70fr grn & multi 22 15

80th birthday of Emperor Haile Selassie of Ethiopia.

Plane, Balloon, Route Timbuktu to Bamako — AP70

Design: 300fr, Balloon, jet and route Timbuktu to Bamako.

1972, Dec. 29 *Perf. 13½*

C170 AP70 200fr multi 65 30
C171 AP70 300fr bl & multi 90 42

First postal balloon flight in Mali.

Bishop of 14th Century European Chess Set — AP71

Design: 200fr, Knight (elephant), from 18th century Indian set.

1973, Feb. 19 Engr. *Perf. 13*

C172 AP71 100fr dk car, bl & ind 40 20
C173 AP71 200fr blk, red & brn 65 30

World Chess Championship, Reykjavik, Iceland, July-Sept., 1972.

Postal Union Emblem, Letter and Dove AP72

1973, Mar. 9 Photo. *Perf. 11½x11*

C174 AP72 70fr bl, blk & org 22 16

10th anniv. (in 1971) of African Postal Union.

No. C20, Collector's Hand and Philatelic Background AP73

1973, Mar. 12 Engr. *Perf. 13*

C175 AP73 70fr multi 30 16

Stamp Day, 1973.

Astronauts and Lunar Rover on Moon AP74

1973, Mar. 26

C176 AP74 250fr bl, ind & bis 70 42

Souvenir Sheet

C177 AP74 350fr choc, vio bl & ultra 1.10 1.10

Apollo 17 US moon mission, Dec. 7-19, 1972.

Nicolaus Copernicus — AP75

1973, Apr. 9 Engr. *Perf. 13*

C178 AP75 300fr brt bl & mag 1.00 50

500th anniversary of the birth of Nicolaus Copernicus (1473-1543), Polish astronomer.

Dr. Armauer G. Hansen and Leprosy Bacillus — AP76

1973, May 7 Engr. *Perf. 13*

C179 AP76 200fr blk, yel grn & red 65 40

Centenary of the discovery of the Hansen bacillus, the cause of leprosy.

Bentley and Alfa Romeo, 1930 — AP77

Designs: 100fr, Jaguar and Talbot, 1953. 200fr, Matra and Porsche, 1972.

1973, May 21 Engr. *Perf. 13*

C180 AP77 50fr bl, org & grn 16 15
C181 AP77 100fr grn, ultra & car 35 15
C182 AP77 200fr ind, grn & car 65 25
Set value 46

50th anniversary of the 24-hour automobile race at Le Mans, France.

Camp Fire, Fleur-de-Lis AP78

Designs (Fleur-de-Lis and): 70fr, Scouts saluting flag (vert.). 80fr, Scouts with flags. 130fr, Lord Baden-Powell (vert.). 270fr, Round dance and map of Africa.

1973, June 4

C183 AP78 50fr dk red, ultra & choc 16 15
C184 AP78 70fr sl grn, dk brn & red 22 15
C185 AP78 80fr mag, sl grn & ol 25 15
C186 AP78 130fr brn, ultra & sl grn 45 20
C187 AP78 270fr mag, gray & vio bl 90 45
Nos. C183-C187 (5) 1.98 1.10

Mali Boy and Girl Scouts and International Scouts Congress.

Swimming, US and "Africa" Flags — AP79

Designs (US, Africa Flags and): 80fr, Discus and javelin (vert.). 330fr, Runners.

1973, July 30 Engr. *Perf. 13*

C188 AP79 70fr red, sl grn & bl 22 15
C189 AP79 80fr vio bl, dk ol & red 30 16
C190 AP79 330fr red & vio bl 1.00 42

First African-United States Sports Meet.

Head and City Hall, Brussels — AP80

Perseus, by Benvenuto Cellini — AP81

1973, Sept. 17 Engr. *Perf. 13*

C191 AP80 70fr brt ultra, ol & vio 22 15

Africa Weeks, Brussels, Sept. 15-30, 1973.

1973, Sept. 24

Famous Sculptures: 150fr, Pieta, by Michelangelo. 250fr, Victory of Samothrace, Greek 1st century B.C.

C192 AP81 100fr dk car & sl grn 35 20
C193 AP81 150fr dk car & dp cl 45 25
C194 AP81 250fr dk car & dk ol 80 42

Stephenson's Rocket and Buddicom Engine — AP82

Locomotives: 150fr, Union Pacific, 1890, and Santa Fe, 1940. 200fr, Mistral and Tokaido, 1970.

1973, Oct. 8 Engr. *Perf. 13*

C195 AP82 100fr brn, bl & blk 30 15
C196 AP82 150fr red, brt ultra & dk car 45 20
C197 AP82 200fr ocher, bl & ind 65 30

Apollo XI on Moon AP83

Designs: 75fr, Landing capsule, Apollo XIII. 100fr, Astronauts and equipment on moon, Apollo XIV. 280fr, Rover, landing module and astronauts on moon, Apollo XV. 300fr, Lift-off from moon, Apollo XVII.

1973, Oct. 25

C198 AP83 50fr vio, org & sl grn 16 15
C199 AP83 75fr sl, red & bl 22 15
C200 AP83 100fr sl, bl & ol brn 35 16
C201 AP83 280fr vio bl, red & sl grn 80 38
C202 AP83 300fr sl, red & sl grn 1.00 45
Nos. C198-C202 (5) 2.53 1.29

Apollo U.S. moon missions.

Pablo Picasso AP84

John F. Kennedy AP85

1973, Nov. 7 Litho. *Perf. 12½*

C203 AP84 500fr multi 1.60 80

Pablo Picasso (1881-1973), painter.

1973, Nov. 12

C204 AP85 500fr gold, brt rose lil & blk 1.60 80

10th anniversary of the death of President John F. Kennedy (1917-1963).

Painting Type of 1968

Paintings: 100fr, Annunciation, by Vittore Carpaccio (horiz.). 200fr, Virgin of St. Simon, by Federigo Baroccio. 250fr, Flight into Egypt, by Andrea Solario.

Perf. 13x12½, 12½x12, 12½x13

1973, Nov. 30 Litho.

C205 AP33 100fr blk & multi 30 20
C206 AP33 200fr blk & multi 65 30
C207 AP33 250fr blk & multi 80 40

Christmas 1973.

Soccer Player and Ball — AP86

Designs: 250fr, Goalkeeper and ball. 500fr, Frauenkirche, Munich, Arms of Munich and soccer ball (horiz.).

1973, Dec. 3 Engr. *Perf. 13*

C208 AP86 150fr emer, ol brn & red 50 25
C209 AP86 250fr emer, vio bl & ol brn 80 38

Souvenir Sheet

C210 AP86 500fr bl & multi 1.60 1.60

World Soccer Cup, Munich.

Musicians, Mosaic from Pompeii — AP87

Designs (Mosaics from Pompeii): 250fr, Alexander the Great in battle (vert.). 350fr, Bacchants (vert.).

1974, Jan. 21 Engr. *Perf. 13*

C211 AP87 150fr sl bl, ol & rose 45 25
C212 AP87 250fr mag, ol & ocher 80 42
C213 AP87 350fr ol, dp brn & ocher 1.25 60

Winston Churchill — AP88

1974, Mar. 18 Engr. *Perf. 13*

C214 AP88 500fr black 1.25 85

Centenary of the birth of Sir Winston Churchill (1874-1965), statesman.

Chess Game — AP89

1974, Mar. 25 Engr. *Perf. 13*

C215 AP89 250fr multi 90 42

21st Chess Olympic Games, Nice 1974.

Painting Type of 1968

Paintings: 400fr, Crucifixion, Alsatian School, c. 1380 (vert.). 500fr, Burial of Christ, by Titian.

Perf. 12½x13, 13x12½

1974, Apr. 12 Photo.

C216 AP33 400fr multi 90 50
C217 AP33 500fr multi 1.10 55

Easter 1974.

Lenin — AP90

1974, Apr. 22 Engr. *Perf. 13*

C218 AP90 150fr vio bl & lake 40 20

50th anniversary of the death of Lenin.

Women's Steeplechase — AP91

1974, May 20 Engr. *Perf. 13*

C219 AP91 130fr bl, lil & brn 40 22

World Horsewomen's Championship, La Baule, France, June 30-July 7.

Skylab Docking in Space — AP92

Design: 250fr, Skylab over globe with Africa.

1974, July 1 Engr. *Perf. 13*

C220 AP92 200fr bl, sl & org 55 30
C221 AP92 250fr lil, sl & org 65 38

Skylab's flight over Africa, 1974.

Nos. C184-C185 Surcharged in Violet Blue with New Value, Two Bars and:

a. 11e JAMBOREE ARABE / AOUT 1974 LIBAN
b. CONGRES PANARABE LIBAN / AOUT 1974

1974, July 8 Engr. *Perf. 13*

C222 AP78 130fr on 70fr (a) 40 25
C223 AP78 170fr on 80fr (b) 55 40

11th Pan-Arab Jamboree and Pan-Arab Congress, Batrun, Lebanon, Aug. 1974.

Nos. C200-C201 Surcharged in Red with New Value, Two Bars and:

c. ler DEBARQUEMENT / SUR LA LUNE / 20-VII-69
d. ler PAS SUR LA / LUNE 21-VII-69

1974, July 15

C224 AP83 130fr on 100fr (c) 38 25
C225 AP83 300fr on 280fr (d) 80 42

First manned moon landing, July 20, 1969, and first step on moon, July 21, 1969.

1906 and 1939 Locomotives — AP93

Locomotives: 120fr, Baldwin, 1870, and Pacific, 1920. 210fr, Al., 1925, and Buddicom, 1847. 330fr, Hudson, 1938, and La Gironde, 1839.

1974, Oct. 7 Engr. *Perf. 13*

C226 AP93 90fr dk car & multi 25 16
C227 AP93 120fr ocher & multi 35 20
C228 AP93 210fr org & multi 55 30
C229 AP93 330fr grn & multi 90 42

Skier, Winter Sports and Olympic Rings AP94

1974, Oct. 7

C230 AP94 300fr multi 80 42

Holy Family, by Hans Memling AP95

Designs: 310fr, Virgin and Child, Bourgogne School. 400fr, Adoration of the Kings, by Martin Schongauer.

1974, Nov. 4 Photo. *Perf. 12½*

C231 AP95 290fr multi 80 38
C232 AP95 310fr multi 80 42
C233 AP95 400fr multi 1.10 55

Christmas 1974.

See Nos. C238-C240, C267-C269.

Raoul Follereau — AP96

1974, Nov. 18 Engr. *Perf. 13*

C234 AP96 200fr brt bl 55 35

Raoul Follereau (1903-1977), apostle to the lepers and educator of the blind. See No. C468.

Europafrica Issue

Train, Jet, Cogwheel, Grain, Maps of Africa and Europe — AP97

1974, Dec. 27 Engr. *Perf. 13*

C235 AP97 100fr brn, grn & ind 25 16
C236 AP97 110fr ocher, vio bl & pur 30 20

Painting Type of 1974

Designs: 200fr, Christ at Emmaus, by Philipe de Champaigne (horiz.). 300fr, Christ at Emmaus, by Paolo Veronese (horiz.). 500fr, Christ in Majesty, Limoges, 13th century.

Perf. 13x12½, 12½x13

1975, Mar. 24 Litho.

C238 AP95 200fr multi 55 35
C239 AP95 300fr multi 80 42
C240 AP95 500fr multi 1.40 70

Easter 1975.

"Voyage to the Center of the Earth" — AP99

Jules Verne's Stories: 170fr, "From Earth to Moon" and Verne's portrait. 190fr, "20,000 Leagues under the Sea." 220fr, "A Floating City."

1975, Apr. 7 Engr. *Perf. 13*

C241 AP99 100fr multi 25 18
C242 AP99 170fr multi 45 25
C243 AP99 190fr multi 55 30
C244 AP99 220fr multi 60 38

Dawn, by Michelangelo AP100

Design: 500fr, Moses, by Michelangelo.

1975, Apr. 28 Photo. *Perf. 13*

C245 AP100 400fr multi 1.10 65
C246 AP100 500fr multi 1.40 80

500th birth anniversary of Michelangelo Buonarroti (1475-1564), Italian sculptor, painter and architect.

Astronaut on Moon — AP101

Designs: 300fr, Constellations Virgo and Capricorn. 370fr, Statue of Liberty, Kremlin, Soyuz and Apollo spacecraft.

1975, May 19 Engr. *Perf. 13*

C247 AP101 290fr multi 1.20 50
C248 AP101 300fr multi 1.20 65
C249 AP101 370fr multi 1.50 80

Russo-American space cooperation.

Boy Scout, Globe, Nordjamb 75 Emblem AP103

Designs (Globe, Nordjamb 75 Emblem and): 150fr, Boy Scout giving Scout sign. 290fr, Scouts around campfire.

1975, June 23 Engr. *Perf. 13*

C251 AP103 100fr cl, brn & bl 25 16
C252 AP103 150fr red, brn & grn 40 20
C253 AP103 290fr bl, grn & cl 80 42

Nordjamb 75, 14th Boy Scout Jamboree, Lillehammer, Norway, July 29-Aug. 7.

Battle Scene and Marquis de Lafayette — AP104

Designs: 300fr, Battle scene and George Washington. 370fr, Battle of Chesapeake Bay and Count de Grasse.

1975, July 7 Engr. *Perf. 13*

C254 AP104 290fr lt bl & ind 80 42
C255 AP104 300fr lt bl & ind 80 42
C256 AP104 370fr lt bl & ind 90 55
a. Strip of 3. #C254-C256 2.50 1.90

Bicentenary of the American Revolution. No. C256a has continuous design.

Schweitzer, Bach and Score AP105

Designs: No. C257, Albert Einstein (1879-1955), theoretical physicist. No. No. C258, Andre-Marie Ampere (1775-1836), French physicist. 100fr, Clement Ader (1841-1925), French aviation pioneer. No. C260, Dr. Albert Schweitzer (1875-1965), Medical missionary and musician. No. C261, Sir Alexander Fleming (1881-1955), British bacteriologist, discoverer of penicillin.

1975 Engr. *Perf. 13*

C257 AP105 90fr multi 22 16
C258 AP105 90fr pur, org & bis 22 15
C259 AP105 100fr bl, red & lil 25 16
C260 AP105 150fr grn, bl & dk grn 40 20
C261 AP105 150fr lil, bl & brick red 40 20
Nos. C257-C261 (5) 1.49 87

Issue dates: No. C257, May 26. No. C258, Sept. 23. 100fr, Dec. 8. No. C260, Jan. 14. No. C261, July 21.

Olympic Rings and Globe — AP106

Design: 400fr, Montreal Olympic Games' emblem.

1975, Oct.

C262 AP106 350fr pur & bl 70 40
C263 AP106 400fr blue 80 45

Pre-Olympic Year 1975.

Nos. C247-C249 Overprinted: "ARRIMAGE / 17 Juil. 1975"

1975, Oct. 20 Engr. *Perf. 13*

C264 AP101 290fr multi 80 38
C265 AP101 300fr multi 80 38
C266 AP101 370fr multi 1.00 55

Apollo-Soyuz link-up in space, July 17, 1975.

Painting Type of 1974

Designs: 290fr, Visitation, by Ghirlandaio. 300fr, Nativity, Fra Filippo Lippi school. 370fr, Adoration of the Kings, by Velazquez.

1975, Nov. 24 Litho. *Perf. 12½x13*

C267 AP95 290fr multi 80 38
C268 AP95 300fr multi 80 42
C269 AP95 370fr multi 1.00 55

Christmas 1975.

Concorde — AP107

1976, Jan. 12 Litho. *Perf. 13*

C270 AP107 500fr multi 1.40 90

Concorde supersonic jet, first commercial flight, Jan. 21, 1976.

Figure Skating — AP108

Designs (Games Emblem and): 420fr, Ski jump. 430fr, Slalom.

1976, Feb. 16 Litho. *Perf. 13*

C271 AP108 120fr grn, lt grn & blk 35 16
C272 AP108 420fr brn, rose & blk 1.10 60
C273 AP108 430fr ultra, lt bl & blk 1.20 60

12th Winter Olympic Games, Innsbruck, Austria, Feb. 4-15.

Eye Examination, WHO Emblem — AP109

1976, Apr. 5 Litho. *Perf. 12½*

C274 AP109 130fr multi 35 18

World Health Day: "Foresight prevents blindness."

Space Ship with Solar Batteries — AP110

Design: 300fr, Astronaut working on orbital space station (vert.).

1976, May 10 Engr. *Perf. 13*

C275 AP110 300fr org, dk & lt bl 65 32
C276 AP110 400fr mag, dk bl & org 80 45

Futuristic space achievements.

American Eagle, Flag and Liberty Bell — AP111

Designs: 400fr, Revolutionary War naval battle and American eagle. 440fr, Indians on horseback and American eagle (vert.).

1976, May 24 Litho. *Perf. 12½*

C277 AP111 100fr multi 25 16
C278 AP111 400fr multi 1.10 65
C279 AP111 440fr multi 1.25 70

American Bicentennial. Nos. C278-C279 also commemorate Interphil 76, International Philatelic Exhibition, Philadelphia, Pa, May 29-June 6.

Running AP112

Designs (Olympic Rings and): 250fr, Swimming. 300fr, Field ball. 440fr, Soccer.

1976, June 7 Engr. *Perf. 13*

C280 AP112 200fr red brn & blk 55 25
C281 AP112 250fr multi 65 38
C282 AP112 300fr multi 80 42
C283 AP112 440fr multi 1.25 60

21st Olympic Games, Montreal, Canada, July 17-Aug. 1.

Cub Scout and Leader — AP113

Designs: 180fr, Scouts tending sick animal (horiz.). 200fr, Night hike.

1976, June 14 Engr. *Perf. 13*

C284 AP113 140fr ultra & red brn 38 30
C285 AP113 180fr dk brn & multi 45 35
C286 AP113 200fr brn org & vio bl 55 38

First African Boy Scout Jamboree, Nigeria.

Mohenjo-Daro, Bull from Wall Relief — AP114

Design: 500fr, Man's head, animals, wall and UNESCO emblem.

1976, Sept. 6 Engr. *Perf. 13*

C287 AP114 400fr blk, bl & pur 1.10 55
C288 AP114 500fr dk red, bl & grn 1.40 80

UNESCO campaign to save Mohenjo-Daro excavations.

Europafrica Issue

Freighter, Plane, Map of Europe and Africa — AP115

1976, Sept. 20

C289 AP115 200fr vio brn & bl 55 35

Nativity, by Taddeo Gaddi — AP116

Paintings: 300fr, Adoration of the Kings, by Hans Memling. 320fr, Nativity, by Carlo Crivelli.

1976, Nov. 8 Litho. *Perf. 13x12½*

C290 AP116 280fr multi 70 38
C291 AP116 300fr multi 80 42
C292 AP116 320fr multi 90 45

Christmas 1976.

Viking Flying to Mars — AP117

Design: 1000fr, Viking landing craft on Mars.

1976, Dec. 8 Engr. *Perf. 13*

C293 AP117 500fr red, brn & bl 1.25 55
C294 AP117 1000fr multi 2.50 1.25
a. Miniature sheet of 2 4.50 2.50

Operation Viking, US Mars mission, No. C294a contains 2 stamps similar to Nos. C293-C294 in changed colors.

The only foreign revenue stamps listed in this Catalogue are those authorized for prepayment of postage.

Pres. Giscard d'Estaing, Village and Bambara Antelope — AP118

1977, Feb. 13 Photo. *Perf. 13*
C295 AP118 430fr multi 1.00 42

Visit of Pres. Valéry Giscard d'Estaing of France, Feb. 13-15.

Elizabeth II and Prince Philip — AP119

Designs: 200fr, Charles de Gaulle (vert.). 250fr, Queen Wilhelmina (vert.). 300fr, King Baudouin and Queen Fabiola. 480fr, Coronation of Queen Elizabeth II (vert.).

1977, Mar. 21 Litho. *Perf. 12*
C296 AP119 180fr multi 45 25
C297 AP119 200fr multi 55 35
C298 AP119 250fr multi 65 38
C299 AP119 300fr multi 80 45
C300 AP119 480fr multi 1.40 65
Nos. C296-C300 (5) 3.85 2.08

Personalities involved in de-colonization.

Newton, Rocket and Apple — AP120

1977, May 7 Engr. *Perf. 13*
C301 AP120 400fr grn, brn & red 1.20 55

Isaac Newton (1643-1727), natural philosopher and mathematician, 250th death anniversary.

Charles Lindbergh and Spirit of St. Louis — AP121

Design: 430fr, Spirit of St. Louis flying over clouds.

1977, Apr. 4 Litho. *Perf. 12*
C302 AP121 420fr org & pur 80 40
C303 AP121 430fr multi 85 40

Charles A. Lindbergh's solo transatlantic flight from New York to Paris, 50th anniversary.

Sassenage Castle, Grenoble — AP122

1977, May 21 Litho. *Perf. 12½*
C304 AP122 300fr multi 80 42

10th anniversary of International French Language Council.

Zeppelin No. 1, 1900 — AP123

Designs: 130fr, Graf Zeppelin, 1924. 350fr, Hindenburg aflame at Lakehurst, N.J., 1937. 500fr, Ferdinand von Zeppelin and Graf Zeppelin.

1977, May 30 Engr. *Perf. 13*
C305 AP123 120fr multi 35 18
C306 AP123 130fr multi 35 18
C307 AP123 350fr multi 90 55
C308 AP123 500fr multi 1.40 65

History of the Zeppelin.

Martin Luther King, American and Swedish Flags — AP124

Design: 600fr, Henri Dunant, Red Cross, Swiss and Swedish flags.

1977, July 4 Engr. *Perf. 13*
C309 AP124 600fr multi 1.20 65
C310 AP124 700fr multi 1.40 70

Nobel Peace Prize recipients.

Soccer — AP125

Designs: 200fr, 3 soccer players (vert.). 420fr, 3 soccer players.

1977, Oct. 3 Engr. *Perf. 13*
C311 AP125 180fr multi 35 20
C312 AP125 200fr multi 40 25
C313 AP125 420fr multi 90 45

World Soccer Cup Elimination Games.

Mao Tse-tung and COMATEX Hall, Bamako — AP126

1977, Nov. 7 Engr. *Perf. 13*
C314 AP126 300fr dl red 80 42

Chairman Mao Tse-tung (1893-1976), first death anniversary.

No. C270 Overprinted in Violet Blue: "PARIS NEW-YORK 22.11.77"

1977, Nov. 22 Litho. *Perf. 13*
C315 AP107 500fr multi 3.50 1.90

Concorde, first commerical transatlantic flight, Paris to New York.

Virgin and Child, by Rubens AP127

Rubens Paintings: 400fr, Adoration of the Kings. 600fr, Detail from Adoration of the Kings (horiz.).

1977, Dec. 5 *Perf. 12½x12, 12x12½*
C316 AP127 400fr gold & multi 1.10 60
C317 AP127 500fr gold & multi 1.40 80
C318 AP127 600fr gold & multi 1.60 90

Christmas 1977, and 400th birth anniversary of Peter Paul Rubens (1577-1640).

Battle of the Amazons, by Rubens — AP128

Rubens Paintings: 300fr, Return from the fields. 500fr, Hercules fighting the Nemean Lion (vert.).

Perf. 12x12½, 12½x12
1978, Jan. 16 Litho.
C319 AP128 200fr multi 55 35
C320 AP128 300fr multi 80 50
C321 AP128 500fr multi 1.40 80

Peter Paul Rubens, 400th birth anniversary.

Schubert Composing "Winterreise" — AP129

Design: 300fr, Schubert and score (vert.).

1978, Feb. 13
C322 AP129 300fr multi 80 50
C323 AP129 420fr multi 1.20 60

Franz Schubert (1797-1828), Austrian composer, death sesquicentennial.

Capt. Cook Receiving Hawaiian Delegation — AP130

Design: 300fr, Cook landing on Hawaii. Designs after sketches by John Weber.

1978, Feb. 27 Engr. *Perf. 13*
C324 AP130 200fr multi 55 35
C325 AP130 300fr multi 80 42

Capt. James Cook (1728-1779), bicentenary of his arrival in Hawaii.

Soccer — AP131

Designs: 250fr, One player. 300fr, Two players (horiz.).

1978, Mar. 20
C326 AP131 150fr multi 40 22
C327 AP131 250fr multi 65 40
a. "REPUPLIQUE" 65 40
C328 AP131 300fr multi 80 42
a. Min. sheet of 3, #C326-C328 + label 1.90 1.50
b. As "a," #C326, C327a, C328

World Soccer Cup Championships, Argentina, 1978, June 1-25.

Nos. C327 and C328a were issued in July to correct the spelling error.

Jesus with Crown of Thorns, by Dürer AP132

Design: 430fr, Resurrection, by Albrecht Dürer.

1978, Mar. 28
C329 AP132 420fr multi 1.10 65
C330 AP132 430fr multi 1.20 65

Easter 1978. See Nos. C359-C361.

Citroen, C3-Trefle, 1922 — AP133

Citroen Cars: 130fr, Croisiere Noire, 1924, tractor. 180fr, B14G, 1927. 200fr, "11" Tractor Avant, 1934.

1978, Apr. 24 Engr. *Perf. 13*

C331 AP133 120fr multi 30 20
C332 AP133 130fr multi 35 20
C333 AP133 180fr multi 50 25
C334 AP133 200fr multi 55 30

Andre Citroen (1878-1935), automobile designer and manufacturer.

UPU Emblem, World Map, Country Names — AP133a

Design: 130fr, UPU emblem, globe and names of member countries.

1978, May 15

C334A AP133a 120fr multi 32 16
C335 AP133a 130fr red, grn & emer 35 20

Centenary of Congress of Paris where General Postal Union became the Universal Postal Union.

Europafrica Issue

Ostrich Incubating Eggs, Syrian Manuscript, 14th Century — AP134

Design: 110fr, Zebra, Miniature by Mansur, Jehangir School, 1620.

1978, July 24 Litho. *Perf. 13x12½*

C336 AP134 100fr multi 25 16
C337 AP134 110fr multi 30 18

Nos. C326-C328a Overprinted in Black:

a. CHAMPION / 1978 / ARGENTINE
b. 2e HOLLANDE
c. 3e BRESIL / 4e ITALIE

1978, Aug. 7 Engr. *Perf. 13*

C338 AP131 150fr multi (a) 40 22
C339 AP131 250fr multi (b) 65 40
C340 AP131 300fr multi (c) 80 42
a. Souvenir sheet of 3 1.50 1.50

Winners, World Soccer Cup Championship, Argentina. Overprints on No. C340a are green including label overprint: FINALE / ARGENTINA 3 HOLLANDE 1.

Elizabeth II in Coronation Robes AP135

Design: 500fr, Coronation coach.

1978, Sept. 18 Litho. *Perf. 12½x12*

C341 AP135 500fr multi 1.00 65
C342 AP135 1000fr multi 2.00 1.50

25th anniversary of coronation of Queen Elizabeth II.

US No. C3a and Douglas DC-3 AP136

History of Aviation: 100fr, Belgium No. 252 and Stampe SV-4. 120fr, France No. C48 and Ader's plane No. 3. 130fr, Germany No. C2 and Junker Ju-52. 320fr, Japan No. C25 and Mitsubishi A-6M "Zero".

1978, Oct. 16 Engr. *Perf. 13*

C343 AP136 80fr multi 20 15
C344 AP136 100fr multi 25 18
C345 AP136 120fr multi 32 20
C346 AP136 130fr multi 35 22
C347 AP136 320fr multi 90 55
Nos. C343-C347 (5) 2.02 1.30

Annunciation, by Dürer — AP137

Etchings by Dürer: 430fr, Virgin and Child. 500fr, Adoration of the Kings.

1978, Nov. 6

C348 AP137 420fr blk & rose car 85 45
C349 AP137 430fr ol grn & brn 90 50
C350 AP137 500fr blk & red 1.00 65

Christmas 1978 and 450th death anniversary of Albrecht Dürer (1471-1528), German painter.

Rocket and Trajectory Around Moon — AP138

Design: 300fr, Spaceship circling moon.

1978, Nov. 20 Engr. *Perf. 13*

C351 AP138 200fr multi 80 55
C352 AP138 300fr multi 1.20 70

10th anniversary of 1st flight around moon. Nos. C351-C352 printed se-tenant with label between showing earth, moon and US astronauts' names.

Ader's Plane and Concorde — AP139

Designs: 130fr, Wright Flyer A and Concorde. 200fr, Spirit of St. Louis and Concorde.

1979, Jan. 25 Litho. *Perf. 13*

C353 AP139 120fr multi 35 20
C354 AP139 130fr multi 35 22
C355 AP139 200fr multi 55 38

Third anniversary of 1st supersonic commercial flight.

Philexafrique II-Essen Issue
Common Design Types

Designs: No. C356, Dromedary and Mali No. C26. No. C357, Bird and Lubeck No. 1.

1979, Jan. 29 Litho. *Perf. 13x12½*

C356 CD138 200fr multi 55 38
C357 CD139 200fr multi 55 38

Nos. C356-C357 printed se-tenant.

No. C257 Surcharged

"1879-1979"
130 F

1979, Mar. 26 Engr. *Perf. 13*

C358 AP105 130fr on 90fr multi 35 22

Centenary of the birth of Albert Einstein (1879-1955).

Easter Type of 1978

Dürer Etchings: 400fr, Jesus Carrying Cross. 430fr, Crucified Christ. 480fr, Pieta.

1979, Apr. 9

C359 AP132 400fr bl & blk 1.10 70
C360 AP132 430fr red & blk 1.20 80
C361 AP132 480fr ultra & blk 1.25 90

Easter 1979.

Basketball and St. Basil's Cathedral, Moscow — AP140

Design: 430fr, Soccer and Kremlin.

1979, Apr. 17 Litho. *Perf. 13*

C362 AP140 420fr multi 1.10 75
C363 AP140 430fr multi 1.20 80

Pre-Olympic Year.

Mali No. C92, Apollo Spacecraft AP141

Design: 500fr, Mali No. C176, lift-off.

1979, Oct. 22 Litho. *Perf. 12½x13*

C364 AP141 430fr multi 1.20 60
C365 AP141 500fr multi 1.40 70

Apollo 11 moon landing, 10th anniversary.

Capt. Cook, Ship, Kerguelen Island — AP142

Design: 480fr, Capt. Cook, Ship, Hawaii.

1979, Oct. 29 *Perf. 13x12½*

C366 AP142 300fr multi 1.20 65
C367 AP142 480fr multi 1.40 1.00

Capt. James Cook (1728-1779), explorer, death bicentenary.

David Janowski (1868-1927), Chess Pieces — AP143

Chess Pieces and Grand Masters: 140fr, Alexander Alekhine (1892-1946). 200fr, W. Schlage. 300fr, Effim D. Bogoljubow (1889-1952).

1979, Nov. 30 Engr. *Perf. 13*

C368 AP143 100fr red & brn 35 16
C369 AP143 140fr multi 42 20
C370 AP143 200fr multi 65 35
C371 AP143 300fr multi 1.00 50

Adoration of the Kings, by Dürer AP144

Christmas 1979: 400fr, 500fr, Adoration of the Kings by Dürer (diff.).

1979, Dec. 10 *Perf. 13x13½*

C372 AP144 300fr brn org & brn 80 35
C373 AP144 400fr bl & brn 1.10 42
C374 AP144 500fr dk grn & brn 1.40 55

Jet, Map of Africa AP145

1979, Dec. 27 Litho. *Perf. 12½*

C375 AP145 120fr multi 32 15

ASECNA (Air Safety Board), 20th anniv.

Train, Globe, Rotary Emblem AP146

Rotary International, 75th Anniversary: 250fr, Jet. 430fr, Bamako Club emblem, meeting hall.

1980, Jan. 28 Litho. *Perf. 12½*

C376	AP146	220fr multi	70	35
C377	AP146	250fr multi	90	40
C378	AP146	430fr multi	1.50	60

Speed Skating, Lake Placid '80 Emblem, Snowflake AP147

1980, Feb. 11 *Perf. 13*

C379	AP147	200fr shown	55	22
C380	AP147	300fr Ski jump	80	35
a.		Souvenir sheet of 2	1.40	65

13th Winter Olympic Games, Lake Placid, NY, Feb. 12-24. No. C380a contains Nos. C379-C380 in changed colors.

Stephenson's Rocket, Mali No. 196 — AP148

Liverpool-Manchester Railroad, 150th Anniversary: 300fr, Stephenson's Rocket, Mali No. 142.

1980, Feb. 25 Engr.

C381	AP148	200fr multi	55	22
C382	AP148	300fr multi	80	35

Equestrian, Moscow '80 Emblem — AP149

1980, Mar. 10 Engr. *Perf. 13*

C383	AP149	200fr shown	55	20
C384	AP149	300fr Yachting	80	35
C385	AP149	400fr Soccer	1.10	42
a.		Souv. sheet of 3, #C383-C385	3.00	3.00

22nd Summer Olympic Games, Moscow, July 19-Aug. 3.

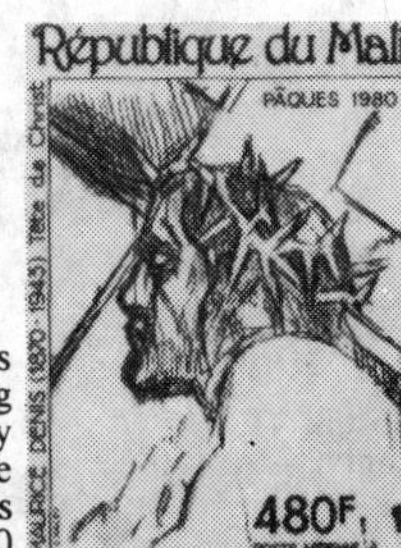

Jesus Carrying Cross, by Maurice Denis AP150

Easter 1980: 500fr, Jesus before Pilate, by Dürer.

1980, Mar. 31

C386	AP150	480fr brn & org red	1.25	50
C387	AP150	500fr org red & brn	1.40	55

Kepler, Copernicus and Solar System Diagram — AP151

Design: 200fr, Kepler and diagram of earth's orbit (vert.).

1980, Apr. 7 Engr. *Perf. 13*

C388	AP151	200fr multi	55	20
C389	AP151	300fr multi	80	35

Discovery of Pluto, 50th Anniversary — AP152

1980, Apr. 21

C390	AP152	420fr multi	1.10	70

Lunokhod I, Russian Flag — AP153

Design: 500fr, Apollo and Soyuz spacecraft, flags of US and Russia.

1980, Apr. 28

C391	AP153	480fr multi	1.25	50
C392	AP153	500fr multi	1.40	55

Lunokhod I, 10th anniversary; Apollo-Soyuz space test program, 5th anniversary.

Rochambeau, French Fleet Landing at Newport, R.I. — AP154

French Cooperation in American Revolution: 430fr, Rochambeau and George Washington, eagle.

1980, June 16 Engr. *Perf. 13*

C393	AP154	420fr multi	1.10	70
C394	AP154	430fr multi	1.20	70

Jet Flying Around Earth — AP155

Designs: No. C396, Ship, people, attack. No. C397, Astronaut on moon. No. C398, Space craft, scientists, moon. Nos. C395-C396 from "Around the World in 80 Days;" Nos. C397-C398 from "From Earth to Moon."

1980, June 30 Engr. *Perf. 11*

C395	AP155	100fr multi	25	15
C396	AP155	100fr multi	25	15
C397	AP155	150fr multi	40	15
C398	AP155	150fr multi	40	15
		Set value		50

Jules Verne (1828-1905), French science fiction writer. Nos. C395-C398 each printed se-tenant with label showing various space scenes.

Nos. C383-C385a Overprinted:
200fr- CONCOURS COMPLET/ INDIVIDUEL/ROMAN (It.)/ BLINOV (Urss)/SALNIKOV (Urss)
300fr- FINN/RECHARDT (Fin.)/ MAYRHOFER (Autr.)/ BALACHOV (Urss)
400fr- TCHECOSLOVAQUIE/ ALLEMAGNE DE L'EST/URSS

1980, Sept. 8 Engr. *Perf. 13*

C399	AP149	200fr multi	55	20
C400	AP149	300fr multi	80	35
C401	AP149	400fr multi	1.10	42
a.		Souvenir sheet of 3	2.50	2.50

Butterfly Type of 1980

1980, Oct. 6 Litho. *Perf. 13x12½*
Size: 48x36mm

C402	A137	420fr *Denaus chrysippus*	1.20	45

Charles De Gaulle, Map and Colors of France — AP156

1980, Nov. 9 Litho. *Perf. 13½x13*

C403	AP156	420fr shown	1.40	65
C404	AP156	430fr De Gaulle, cross	1.40	70

Charles De Gaulle, 10th anniv. of death.

Mali No. 140, Amtrak Train — AP157

Mali Stamps and Trains: 120fr, No. 195, Tokaido, Japan (vert.). 200fr, No. 144, Rembrandt, Germany. 480fr, No. 143, TGV-001 France (vert.).

1980, Nov. 17 Engr. *Perf. 13*

C405	AP157	120fr multi	32	15
C406	AP157	130fr multi	35	15
C407	AP157	200fr multi	55	20
C408	AP157	480fr multi	1.25	50

Holy Family, by Lorenzo Lotto — AP158

Christmas 1980 (Paintings): 400fr, Flight to Egypt, by Rembrandt (vert.). 500fr, Christmas Night, by Gauguin.

1980, Dec. 1 Litho. *Perf. 13x12½*

C409	AP158	300fr multi	80	38
C410	AP158	400fr multi	1.10	42
C411	AP158	500fr multi	1.40	60

Self-portrait, by Picasso AP159

1981, Jan. 26 Litho. *Perf. 12½x13*

C412	AP159	1000fr multi	2.50	1.10

Pablo Picasso (1881-1973), birth centenary.

Soccer Players — AP160

Designs: Soccer players.

1981, Feb. 28 *Perf. 13*

C413	AP160	100fr multi	25	15
C414	AP160	200fr multi	55	20
C415	AP160	300fr multi	80	35

Souvenir Sheet

C416	AP160	600fr multi	1.60	65

World Cup Soccer preliminary games.

Mozart and Instruments — AP161

225th Birth Anniversary of Wolfgang Amadeus Mozart: 430fr, Mozart and instruments (diff.).

1981, Mar. 30 Litho. *Perf. 13*

C417	AP161	420fr multi	1.10	45
C418	AP161	430fr multi	1.20	50

Jesus Falls on the Way to Calvary, by Raphael AP162

Easter 1981: 600fr, Ecce Homo, by Rembrandt.

1981, Apr. 6 *Perf. 12½x13*

C419	AP162	500fr multi	1.40	60
C420	AP162	600fr multi	1.60	65

Alan B. Shepard — AP163 Exploration of Saturn — AP164

Space Anniversaries: No. C422, Yuri Gagarin's flight, 1961. 430fr, Uranus discovery bicentennial (horiz.).

1981, Apr. 21 Litho. *Perf. 13*

C421 AP163 200fr multi 55 20
C422 AP163 200fr multi 55 20
C423 AP164 380fr multi 1.00 40
C424 AP163 430fr multi 1.20 50

No. C408 Overprinted: "26 fevrier 1981/Record du monde de/vitesse-380 km/h."

1981, June 15 Engr.

C425 AP157 480fr multi 1.25 50

New railroad speed record.

US No. 233, Columbus and His Fleet — AP165

475th Death Anniversary of Christopher Columbus (Santa Maria and): 200fr, Spain No. 418 (vert.). 260fr, Spain No. 421 (vert.). 300fr, US No. 232.

1981, June 22

C426 AP165 180fr multi 50 20
C427 AP165 200fr multi 55 20
C428 AP165 260fr multi 70 30
C429 AP165 300fr multi 80 35

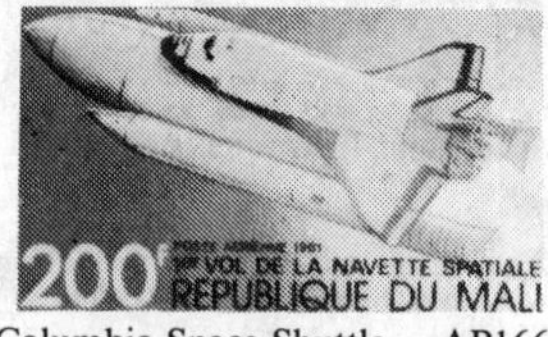

Columbia Space Shuttle — AP166

Designs: Space shuttle.

1981, July 6 Litho. *Perf. 13*

C430 AP166 200fr multi 55 20
C431 AP166 500fr multi 1.40 50
C432 AP166 600fr multi 1.60 65

Souvenir Sheet

Perf. 12

C433 AP166 700fr multi 2.00 80

Harlequin on Horseback AP167

Picasso Birth Centenary: 750fr, Child Holding a Dove.

1981, July 15 *Perf. 12½x13*

C434 AP167 600fr multi 1.60 65
C435 AP167 750fr multi 2.25 1.00

Prince Charles and Lady Diana, St. Paul's Cathedral AP168

1981, July 20 *Perf. 12½*

C436 AP168 500fr shown 1.40 50
C437 AP168 700fr Couple, coach 2.00 80

Royal wedding.

Christmas 1981 AP169

Designs: Virgin and Child paintings.

1981, Nov. 9 Litho. *Perf. 12½x13*

C438 AP169 500fr Grunewald 1.40 50
C439 AP169 700fr Correggio 2.00 80

See Nos. C451-C452, C464-C466, C475-C477, C488-C489, C511.

No. C433 Overprinted In Blue: "JOE ENGLE / RICHARD TRULY / 2 eme VOL SPATIAL"

1981, Nov. 12 Litho. *Perf. 12*

C440 AP166 700fr multi 2.00 80

Nos. C369, C371 Overprinted with Winners' Names and Dates

1981, Dec. Engr. *Perf. 13*

C441 AP143 140fr multi 38 15
C442 AP143 300fr multi 80 35

Lewis Carroll (1832-1908) — AP170

Designs: Scenes from Alice in Wonderland.

1982, Jan. 30 Litho. *Perf. 12½*

C443 AP170 110fr multi 30 15
C444 AP170 130fr multi 35 15
C445 AP170 140fr multi 38 15

George Washington's Birth, 250th Anniv. — AP171

1982, Feb. 8 *Perf. 13*

C446 AP171 700fr Portrait, by Gilbert Stuart 2.00 80

Incorrectly inscribed "Stuart Gilbert."

1982 World Cup — AP172

Designs: Various soccer players.

1982, Mar. 15 Litho. *Perf. 13*

C447 AP172 220fr multi 60 22
C448 AP172 420fr multi 1.20 45
C449 AP172 500fr multi 1.40 50

Souvenir Sheet

Perf. 12½

C450 AP172 680fr multi 1.90 65

Art Type of 1981

Paintings: 680fr, Transfiguration, by Fra Angelico. 1000fr, Pieta, by Bellini (horiz.).

Perf. 12½x13, 13x12½

1982, Apr. 19 Litho.

C451 AP169 680fr multi 1.90 65
C452 AP169 1000fr multi 2.50 1.00

Mali No. O30, France No. 1985 — AP174

1982, June 1 *Perf. 13*

C453 AP174 180fr shown 50 20
C454 AP174 200fr No. C356 55 20

PHILEXFRANCE '82 Intl. Stamp Exhibition, Paris, June 11-21. Nos. C453-C454 se-tenant with label showing show emblem and dates.

Fire Engine, France, 1850 — AP175

Designs: French fire engines.

1982, June 14

C455 AP175 180fr shown 50 20
C456 AP175 200fr 1921 55 22
C457 AP175 270fr 1982 70 28

Nos. C447-C450 Overprinted with Finalists' and Scores in Brown, Black, Blue or Red

1982, Aug. 16 Litho. *Perf. 13*

C458 AP172 220fr multi (Brn) 60 22
C459 AP172 420fr multi 1.20 45
C460 AP172 500fr multi (Bl) 1.40 50

Souvenir Sheet

Perf. 12½

C461 AP172 680fr multi (R) 1.90 65

Italy's victory in 1982 World Cup.

Scouting Year — AP176

1982 *Perf. 12½*

C462 AP176 300fr Tent, Baden-Powell 80 35
C463 AP176 500fr Salute, emblem 1.40 50

Art Type of 1981

Design: Boy with Cherries, by Edouard Manet (1832-83).

1982, Oct. 28 Litho. *Perf. 12½x13*

C464 AP169 680fr multi 1.90 65

Art Type of 1981

Madonna and Child Paintings.

1982, Nov. 10

C465 AP169 500fr Titian 1.40 50
C466 AP169 1000fr Bellini 2.50 1.00

Johann von Goethe (1749-1832), Poet — AP179

1982, Dec. 13 Engr. *Perf. 13*

C467 AP179 500fr multi 1.40 50

Follereau Type of 1974

1983, Jan. 24

C468 AP96 200fr dk brn 55 16

Vostok VI, 20th Anniv. — AP180 Manned Flight, 200th Anniv. — AP181

1983, Feb. 14 Litho. *Perf. 12½*

C469 AP180 400fr Valentina Tereshkova 1.10 35

1983, Feb. 28 *Perf. 13*

C470 AP181 500fr Eagle transatlantic balloon 1.40 50
C471 AP181 700fr Montgolfiere 2.00 90

Pre-Olympic Year — AP182

1983, Mar. 14 **Litho.** *Perf. 13*

C472 AP182 180fr Soccer 50 20
C473 AP182 270fr Hurdles 70 28
C474 AP182 300fr Wind surfing 80 35

Art Type of 1981

Raphael paintings.

1983, Mar. 28 *Perf. 12½x13*

C475 AP169 400fr Deposition 1.20 40
C476 AP169 600fr Transfiguration 1.60 55

Art Type of 1981

Design: Family of Acrobats with Monkey, by Picasso (1881-1973).

1983, Apr. 30 **Litho.** *Perf. 12½x13*

C477 AP169 680fr multi 1.60 80

Lions Intl. — AP185

1983, May 9 *Perf. 12½*

C478 Pair 4.00 1.90
a. AP185 700fr shown 2.00 90
b. AP185 700fr Rotary Intl. 2.00 90

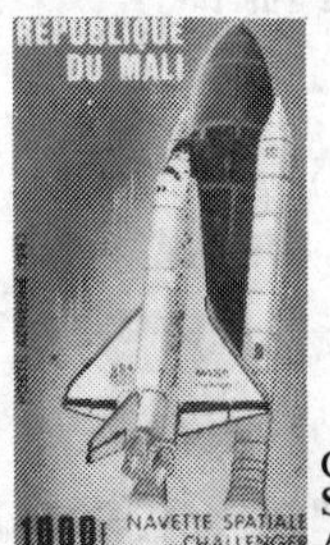

Challenger Spacecraft AP186

1983, July 29 **Litho.** *Perf. 13*

C479 AP186 1000fr multi 2.50 90

Printed se-tenant with orange red label showing astronaut Sally Ride.

Paris-Dakar Auto Race — AP187

1983, Sept. 5 **Litho.** *Perf. 12½*

C480 AP187 240fr Mercedes, 1914 55 20
C481 AP187 270fr SSK, 1929 60 22
C482 AP187 500fr W196, 1954 1.20 42

Souvenir Sheet

C483 AP187 1000fr Mercedes van 2.50 1.00

Chess Game — AP188

1983, Oct. 24 **Engr.** *Perf. 13*

C484 AP188 300fr Pawn, bishop 90 35
C485 AP188 420fr Knight, castle 1.40 60
C486 AP188 500fr King, Queen 1.60 60

Souvenir Sheet

C487 AP188 700fr Various chess pieces 2.00 80

Art Type of 1981

Raphael Paintings.

1983, Nov. 7 **Litho.** *Perf. 12½x13*

C488 AP169 700fr Canigiani Madonna 2.00 80
C489 AP169 800fr Madonna with Lamb 2.50 90

Portrait of Leopold Zborowski, by Amedeo Modigliani (1884-1920) AP190

1984, Feb. 13 **Litho.** *Perf. 12½x13*

C490 AP190 700fr multi 2.00 60

Abraham Lincoln AP191

Duke Ellington AP192

1984, Feb. 27 *Perf. 12½*

C491 AP191 400fr Henri Dunant 1.20 35
C492 AP191 540fr shown 1.60 50

1984, Mar. 12 *Perf. 13½x13*

C493 AP192 470fr Sidney Bechet 1.50 40
C494 AP192 500fr shown 1.50 40

Glider — AP193

1984, Mar. 26

C495 AP193 270fr shown 80 25
C496 AP193 350fr Hang glider 1.10 40

1984 Summer Olympics — AP194

1984, Apr. 9 *Perf. 13*

C497 AP194 265fr Weight lifting 80 22
C498 AP194 440fr Equestrian 1.40 40
C499 AP194 500fr Hurdles 1.60 45

Souvenir Sheet

Perf. 12½

C500 AP194 700fr Wind surfing 2.00 90

Easter 1984 — AP195

Paintings: 940fr, Crucifixion, by Rubens (vert.). 970fr, Resurrection, by Mantegna.

1984, Apr. 24 **Engr.**

C501 AP195 940fr multi 3.00 80
C502 AP195 970fr multi 3.25 90

Gottlieb Daimler Birth Sesquicentenary — AP196

1984, June 1 **Engr.** *Perf. 13*

C503 AP196 350fr Mercedes Simplex 1.10 55
C504 AP196 470fr Mercedes-Benz 370-S 1.50 70
C505 AP196 485fr 500-SEC 1.60 80

No. C480 Overprinted and Surcharged

1984 **Litho.** *Perf. 12½*

C506 AP187 120fr on 240fr #C480 32 16

Nos. C497-C500 Overprinted and Surcharged

1984, Oct. **Litho.** *Perf. 13*

C507 AP194 135fr on 265fr 40 15
C508 AP194 220fr on 440fr 60 20
C509 AP194 250fr on 500fr 70 20

Souvenir Sheet

C510 AP194 350fr on 700fr 90 40

Overprints refer to the winners of the events depicted.

Art Type of 1981

Painting: Virgin and Child, by Lorenzo Lotto.

1984, Nov. 20 **Litho.** *Perf. 12½x13*

C511 AP169 500fr multi 1.40 42

Audubon Birth Bicentenary — AP198

1985, Apr. 15 **Litho.** *Perf. 13*

C512 AP198 180fr Kingfisher 45 16
C513 AP198 300fr Bustard, vert. 70 25
C514 AP198 470fr Ostrich, vert. 1.20 40
C515 AP198 540fr Buzzard 1.40 45

ASECNA Airlines, 25th Anniv. — AP199

1985, June 10 *Perf. 12½*

C516 AP199 700fr multi 1.90 60

PHILEXAFRICA Type of 1985

1985, June 24 *Perf. 13*

C517 A183 200fr Boy Scouts, lion 50 16
C518 A183 200fr Satellite communications 50 16

Nos. C517-C518 are printed se-tenant with center label picturing map of Africa or UAPT emblem.

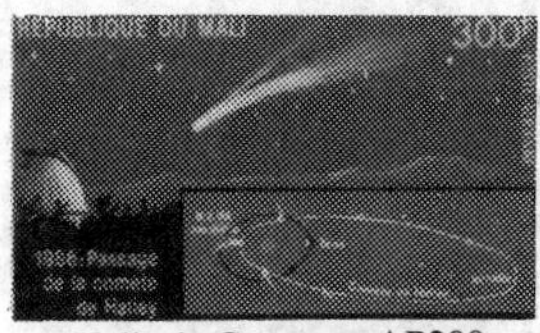

Halley's Comet — AP200

1986, Mar. 24 **Litho.** *Perf. 12½*

C519 AP200 300fr multi 1.10 38

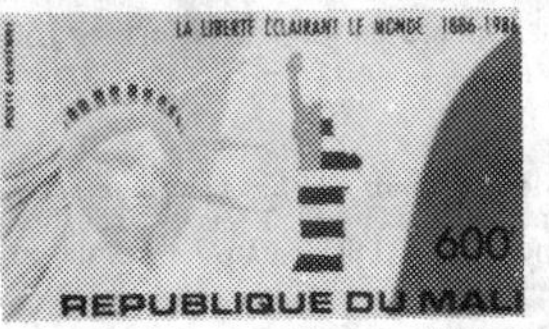

Statue of Liberty, Cent. — AP201

1986, Apr. 7 *Perf. 13*

C520 AP201 600fr multi 2.25 70

Gottlieb Daimler Motorcycle — AP202

1986, Apr. 14

C521 AP202 400fr multi 1.50 50

1st Internal combustion automotive engine, cent.

Paul Robeson (1898-1976), American Actor, Singer — AP203

1986, May 10

C522 AP203 500fr Portrait, Show Boat 2.00 65

Karl Eberth (1835-1926), Bacteriologist, and Typhoid Bacilli AP204

World Chess Championships AP205

1986, June 7 Litho. *Perf. 12x12½*

C523 AP204 550fr multi 2.00 65

1986, June 16 *Perf. 12½*

C524 AP205 400fr Chessmen 1.50 50
C525 AP205 500fr Knight 2.00 60

Disappearance of Jean Mermoz, 50th Anniv. — AP206

Mermoz and: 150fr, Latecoere-300 seaplane. 600fr, Cams 53 Oiseau Tango, seaplane. 625fr, Flight map, Le Comte de La Vaulx aircraft.

1986, Aug. 18 Litho. *Perf. 13*

C526 AP206 150fr multi 60 22
C527 AP206 600fr multi 2.50 85
C528 AP206 625fr multi 2.50 85

Nos. C353-C355 Surcharged "1986-10e Anniversaire du ler Vol/Commercial Supersonique" and New Value

1986, Sept. 29

C529 AP139 175fr on 120fr 70 38
C530 AP139 225fr on 130fr 1.00 50
C531 AP139 300fr on 200fr 1.10 60

Hansen, Leprosy Bacillus, Follereau and Lepers — AP207

1987, Jan. 26 Litho. *Perf. 13*

C532 AP207 500fr multi 2.00 1.00

Gerhard Hansen (1841-1912), Norwegian physician who discovered the leprosy bacillus (1869); Raoul Follereau (1903-1977), philanthropist.

Konrad Adenauer (1876-1967), West German Chancellor AP208

1987, Mar. 9 Litho. *Perf. 13*

C533 AP208 625fr org, buff & blk 2.25 1.10

Pre-Olympics Year — AP209

Buddha and: 400fr, Runners. 500fr, Soccer players.

1987, Apr. 6 Engr.

C534 AP209 400fr blk & red brn 1.50 70
C535 AP209 500fr lil rose, ol grn & ol 2.00 1.00

25th Summer Olympics, Seoul, 1988.

Al Jolson in The Jazz Singer — AP210

1987, Apr. 20

C536 AP210 550fr dk red brn & car rose 2.00 1.00

Sound films, 60th anniv.

Albert John Luthuli (1899-1967), 1960 Nobel Peace Prize Winner — AP211

1987, May 26 Engr. *Perf. 13*

C537 AP211 400fr multi 1.50 75

Service Organizations AP212

1987, June 8 Litho. *Perf. 13*

C538 AP212 500fr Rotary Int'l. 2.00 1.00
C539 AP212 500fr Lions Int'l. 2.00 1.00

Coubertin, Ancient Greek Runners, Contemporary Athletes — AP213

1988, Feb. 14 Litho. *Perf. 13*

C540 AP213 240fr shown 1.10 60
C541 AP213 400fr 5-ring emblem, stadium 2.00 1.00

125th birth anniv. of Baron Pierre de Coubertin (1863-1937), French educator and sportsman who promulgated revival of the Olympic Games; 1988 Summer Olympics, Seoul.

Harlequin, by Pablo Picasso (1881-1973), Spanish Painter and Sculptor AP214

1988, Apr. 4 Litho. *Perf. 13*

C542 AP214 600fr multi 4.25 1.15

1st Scheduled Transatlantic Flight of the Concorde (London-New York), 15th Anniv. — AP215

1988, May 2 *Perf. 13*

C543 AP215 500fr multi 3.50 1.75

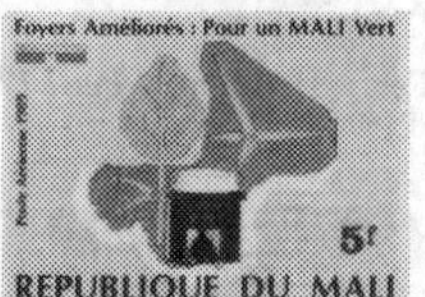

Home Improvement for a Verdant Mali — AP216

1989, Feb. 6 Litho. *Perf. 12½*

C544 AP216 5fr shown 15 15
C545 AP216 10fr Furnace, tree, field 15 15
C546 AP216 25fr like 5fr 18 15
C547 AP216 100fr like 10fr 70 35
Set value 1.00 50

1st Man on the Moon, 20th Anniv. — AP217

1989, Mar. 13 Engr. *Perf. 13*

C548 AP217 300fr multi. 2.10 1.05
C549 AP217 500fr multi, vert. 3.50 1.75

French Revolution, Bicent. AP218

1989, July 3 Engr. *Perf. 13*

C550 AP218 400fr Women's march on Versailles 2.35 1.20
C551 AP218 600fr Storming of the Bastille 3.50 1.75

World Cup Soccer Championships, Italy — AP219

1990, June 4 Litho. *Perf. 13*

C552 AP219 200fr multi 1.20 60
C553 AP219 225fr multi, diff. 1.35 68

Souvenir Sheet

C554 AP219 500fr like #C552 3.00 1.50

No. C552 overprinted in red "ITALIE : 2 / ANGLETERRE : 1"
No. C553 overprinted in red "R.F.A. : 1 / ARGENTINE : 0"
No. C554 overprinted in red in margin "1er : R.F.A. 2eme : ARGENTINE 3eme : ITALIE"

1990

C555 AP219 200fr on #C552 1.20 60
C556 AP219 225fr on #C553 1.35 68

Souvenir Sheet

C557 AP219 500fr on #C554 3.00 1.50

POSTAGE DUE STAMPS

Bambara Headpiece — D1

Perf. 14x13½

1961, Mar. 18 Engr. Unwmk.

J1 D1 1fr black 15 15
J2 D1 2fr brt ultra 15 15
J3 D1 5fr red lilac 15 15
J4 D1 10fr orange 16 15
J5 D1 20fr bright grn 20 15
J6 D1 25fr red brown 22 18
Set value 80 65

Polyptychus Roseus — D2

Designs: No. J8, Deilephila Nerii. No. J9, Gynanisa maja. No. J10, Bunaea alcinoe. No. J11, Teracolus eris. No. J12, Colotis antevippe. No. J13, Charaxes epijasius. No. J14, Manatha microcera. No. J15, Hypokopelates otraeda. No. J16, Lipaphnaeus leonina. No. J17, Gonimbrasia hecate. No. J18, Lobounaea christyi. No. J19, Hypolimnas misippus. No. J20, Catopsilia florella.

1964, June 1 Photo. *Perf. 11*

Butterflies and Moths in Natural Colors

J7	D2	1fr ol grn	15	15
J8	D2	1fr org & brn	15	15
J9	D2	2fr emer & brn	15	15
J10	D2	2fr emer & brn	15	15
J11	D2	3fr rose lil & brn	15	15
J12	D2	3fr rose lil & brn	15	15
J13	D2	5fr blk & rose	15	15
J14	D2	5fr green	15	15
J15	D2	10fr yel, org & blk	15	15
J16	D2	10fr blue	15	15
J17	D2	20fr lt bl & brn	22	22
J18	D2	20fr lt bl & brn	22	22
J19	D2	25fr grn & yel	30	30
J20	D2	25fr dp grn & blk	30	30
		Set value	1.80	1.80

The two stamps of the same denomination are printed together in the sheet, se-tenant at the base.

Nos. J7-J20 Surcharged

1984 Photo. *Perf. 11*

J21	D2	5fr on 1fr #J7	15	15
J22	D2	5fr on 1fr #J8	15	15
J23	D2	10fr on 2fr #J9	15	15
J24	D2	10fr on 2fr #J10	15	15
J25	D2	15fr on 3fr #J11	15	15
J26	D2	15fr on 3fr #J12	15	15
J27	D2	25fr on 5fr #J13	15	15
J28	D2	25fr on 5fr #J14	15	15
J29	D2	50fr on 10fr #J15	15	15
J30	D2	50fr on 10fr #J16	15	15
J31	D2	100fr on 20fr #J17	25	25
J32	D2	100fr on 20fr #J18	25	25
J33	D2	125fr on 25fr #J19	35	35
J34	D2	125fr on 25fr #J20	35	35
		Set value	1.85	1.85

OFFICIAL STAMPS

Dogon Mask
O1

Mali Coat of Arms
O2

Perf. 14x13½

1961, Mar. 18 Engr. Unwmk.

O1	O1	1fr gray	15	15
O2	O1	2fr red org	15	15
O3	O1	3fr black	15	15
O4	O1	5fr lt bl	15	15
O5	O1	10fr bis brn	15	15
O6	O1	25fr brt ultra	15	15
O7	O1	30fr car rose	20	15
O8	O1	50fr Prus grn	35	15
O9	O1	85fr red brn	50	30
O10	O1	100fr emerald	65	35
O11	O1	200fr red lil	1.20	75
		Set value	3.25	1.85

1964, June 1 Photo. *Perf. 12½*

National Colors and Arms in Multicolor, Background in Light Green

O12	O2	1fr green	15	15
O13	O2	2fr lt vio	15	15
O14	O2	3fr gray	15	15
O15	O2	5fr lil rose	15	15
O16	O2	10fr brt bl	15	15
O17	O2	25fr ocher	16	16
O18	O2	30fr dk grn	18	18
O19	O2	50fr orange	25	25
O20	O2	85fr dk brn	40	40
O21	O2	100fr red	50	40
O22	O2	200fr dk vio bl	1.10	40
		Set value	2.80	2.00

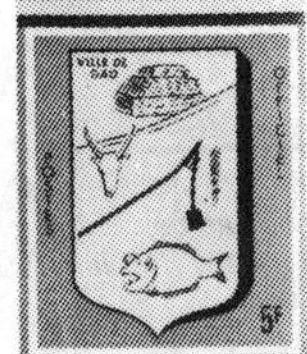

City Coats of Arms — O3

1981, Sept. Photo. *Perf. 12½x13*

O23	O3	5fr Gao	15	15
O24	O3	15fr Timbuktu	15	15
O25	O3	50fr Mopti	15	15
O26	O3	180fr Segou	30	16
O27	O3	200fr Sikasso	40	20
O28	O3	680fr Koulikoro	1.20	60
O29	O3	700fr Kayes	1.40	65
O30	O3	1000fr Bamako	2.00	1.00
		Nos. O23-O30 (8)	5.75	3.06

Nos. O23-O30 Surcharged

1984 Photo. *Perf. 12½x13*

O31	O3	15fr on 5fr	15	15
O32	O3	50fr on 15fr	15	15
O33	O3	120fr on 50fr	35	15
O34	O3	295fr on 180fr	80	40
O35	O3	470fr on 200fr	1.25	60
O36	O3	515fr on 680fr	1.40	65
O37	O3	845fr on 700fr	2.25	1.10
O38	O3	1225fr on 1000fr	3.50	1.40
		Nos. O31-O38 (8)	9.85	4.60

MANCHUKUO

LOCATION — Covering Manchuria, or China's three northeastern provinces--Fengtien, Kirin and Heilungkiang--plus Jehol province.

GOVT. — A former independent state under Japanese influence.

AREA — 503,013 sq. mi. (estimated).

POP. — 43,233,954 (estimated 1940).

CAPITAL — Hsinking (Changchun).

Manchukuo was formed in 1932 with the assistance of Japan. In 1934 Henry Pu-yi, Chief Executive, was enthroned as Emperor Kang Teh. In 1945, when Japan surrendered to the Allies, the terms included the return of Manchukuo to China. The puppet state was dissolved.

100 Fen = 1 Yuan

Watermarks

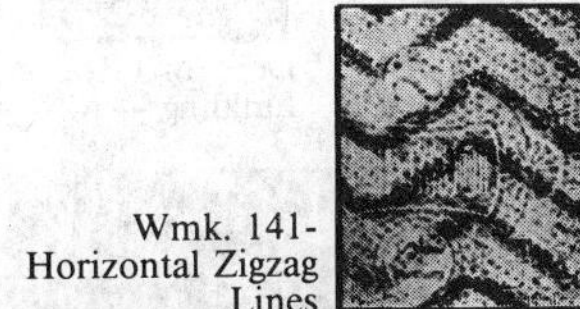

Wmk. 141-Horizontal Zigzag Lines

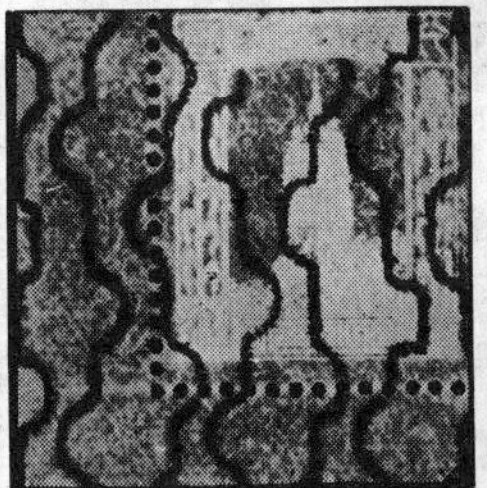

Wmk. 239-Curved Wavy Lines

Wmk. 242-Characters

Pagoda at Liaoyang
A1

Chief Executive Henry Pu-yi
A2

Five characters in top label.

Inscription reads "Manchu State Postal Administration."

Perf. 13x13½

Lithographed

1932, July 26 Unwmk.

White Paper

1	A1	½f gray brown	1.00	65
2	A1	1f dull red	1.40	30
3	A1	1½f lilac	3.50	2.00
4	A1	2f slate	2.75	80
5	A1	3f dull brown	6.25	3.00
6	A1	4f olive green	2.00	40
7	A1	5f green	2.50	50
8	A1	6f rose	7.25	1.50
9	A1	7f gray	2.50	80
10	A1	8f ocher	11.00	6.00
11	A1	10f orange	3.25	40
12	A2	13f dull brown	8.75	4.50
13	A2	15f rose	8.75	2.00
14	A2	16f turquoise grn	19.00	7.50
15	A2	20f gray brown	6.25	1.50
16	A2	30f orange	6.25	1.75
17	A2	50f olive green	14.00	3.00
18	A2	1y violet	30.00	7.50
		Nos. 1-18 (18)	136.40	44.10

A local provisional overprint of a horizontal line of four characters in red or black, reading "Chinese Postal Administration," was applied to Nos. 1-18 by followers of Gen. Su Ping-wen, who rebelled against the Manchukuo government in September, 1932. Many counterfeits exist.

See Nos. 23-31. For surcharges see Nos. 36, 59-61.

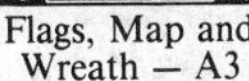

Flags, Map and Wreath — A3

Old State Council Building — A4

1933, Mar. 1 *Perf. 12½*

19	A3	1f orange	4.00	3.00
20	A4	2f dull green	10.50	7.00
21	A3	4f light red	4.00	3.00
22	A4	10f deep blue	27.50	18.00

1st anniv. of the establishing of the State. Nos. 19-22 were printed in sheets of 100 with a special printing in sheets of 20.

Type of 1932

Perf. 13x13½

1934, Feb. Engr. Wmk. 239

Granite Paper

23	A1	½f dk brn	1.50	1.00
24	A1	1f red brn	1.50	75
25	A1	1½f dk vio	2.50	1.25
26	A1	2f slate	3.50	1.00
27	A1	3f brown	2.25	40
28	A1	4f ol brn	20.00	2.50
29	A1	10f dp org	6.00	70
30	A2	15f rose	340.00	150.00
31	A2	1y violet	17.00	7.50
		Nos. 23-31 (9)	394.25	165.10

For surcharge see No. 60.

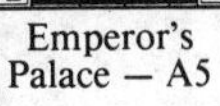

Emperor's Palace — A5

Phoenix — A6

1934, Mar. 1 *Perf. 12½*

32	A5	1½f org brn	3.50	1.75
33	A6	3f carmine	3.50	1.50
34	A5	6f green	6.50	6.00
35	A6	10f dk bl	17.50	7.00

Enthronement of Emperor Kang Teh. Nos. 32-35 were printed in sheets of 100, with a special printing in sheets of 20.

No. 6 Surcharged in Black

壹 暫
分 作

Perf. 13x13½

1934 Unwmk. White Paper

36	A1	1f on 4f ol grn	3.50	2.00
a.		Brown surcharge	24.00	15.00
b.		Upper left character of surcharge omitted		
c.		Inverted surcharge	80.00	80.00

Pagoda at Liaoyang
A7

Emperor Kang Teh
A8

Six characters in top label instead of five as in 1932-34 issues.

Inscription reads "Manchu Empire Postal Administration."

Perf. 13x13½

1934-36 Wmk. 239 Engr.

Granite Paper

37	A7	½f brown	40	25
38	A7	1f red brn	50	25
39	A7	1½f dk vio	85	40
a.		Booklet pane of 6	40.00	
41	A7	3f brn ('35)	50	30
a.		Booklet pane of 6	45.00	
42	A7	5f dk bl ('35)	5.00	90
43	A7	5f gray ('36)	2.25	75
44	A7	6f rose ('35)	2.25	40
45	A7	7f dk gray ('36)	2.00	1.50
47	A7	9f red org ('35)	2.25	50
50	A8	15f ver ('35)	1.75	60
51	A8	18f Prus grn ('35)	20.00	3.00
52	A8	20f dk brn ('35)	2.75	60
53	A8	30f org brn ('35)	3.50	60
54	A8	50f ol grn ('35)	4.50	1.25
55	A8	1y dk vio ('35)	14.00	4.50
a.		1y violet	14.00	6.75
		Nos. 37-55 (15)	62.50	15.80

4f and 8f, type A7, were prepared but not issued.

1935 Wmk. 242 *Perf. 13x13½*

57	A7	10f deep blue	7.00	85
58	A8	13f light brown	7.50	3.25

Nos. 6 and 28 Surcharged in Black

三 暫
分 作

1935 White Paper Unwmk.

59	A1	3f on 4f ol grn	47.50	40.00

1935 Granite Paper Wmk. 239

60	A1	3f on 4f ol brn	4.75	2.75

Similar Surcharge on No. 14

1935 White Paper Unwmk.

61	A2	3f on 16f turq grn	11.00	7.25

Orchid Crest of Manchukuo
A9

Sacred White Mountains and Black Waters
A10

1935, Jan. 1 Litho. Wmk. 141

Granite Paper

62	A9	2f green	3.00	1.25
63	A10	4f dl ol grn	1.10	90
64	A9	8f ocher	2.50	1.00
65	A10	12f brn red	8.50	2.50

Nos. 62-65 exist imperforate.

1935 Wmk. 242

66	A9	2f yel grn	3.00	45
68	A9	8f ocher	5.25	1.40
70	A10	12f brown red	9.00	3.25

Nos. 62-70 issued primarily to pay postage to China, but valid for any postal use.

See Nos. 75-78, 113, 115, 158. For surcharges see Nos. 101, 103-104, 106-109, People's Republic of China No. 2L19.

Mt. Fuji — A11

Phoenix — A12

Perf. 11, 12½ and Compound

1935, Apr. 1 Engr. Wmk. 242

No.	Type	Description	Unused	Used
71	A11	1½f dl grn	1.90	1.10
72	A12	3f orange	2.00	1.75
a.		3f red orange	5.00	4.00
73	A11	6f dk car	4.50	3.75
a.		Horiz. pair, imperf. btwn.	175.00	
b.		Perf. 11x12½	25.00	25.00
74	A12	10f dk bl	5.00	5.25
a.		Perf. 12½x11	20.00	17.50
b.		Perf. 12½	20.00	

Visit of the Emperor of Manchukuo to Tokyo.

Orchid Crest — A13

Types of A9 & A10

Redrawn and Engraved

1936 Wmk. 242 *Perf. 13x13½*

No.	Type	Description	Unused	Used
75	A13	2f lt grn	50	22
76	A10	4f ol grn	2.25	50
77	A13	8f ocher	1.25	50
78	A10	12f org brn	30.00	17.50

Unbroken lines of shading in the background of Nos. 76 and 78. Shading has been removed from right and left of the mountains. Nearly all lines have been removed from the lake. There are numerous other alterations in the design.

Issued primarily to pay postage to China, but valid for any postal use.

See #112. For surcharges see #102-106.

Wild Goose over Sea of Japan — A14

Communications Building at Hsinking — A15

Perf. 12x12½, 12½x12

1936, Jan. 26 Wmk. 242

No.	Type	Description	Unused	Used
79	A14	1½f blk brn	1.90	1.75
80	A15	3f rose lilac	1.90	50
81	A14	6f car rose	5.00	4.00
82	A15	10f blue	6.25	5.00

Postal convention with Japan.

New State Council Building A16

Carting Soybeans A17

North Mausoleum at Mukden A18

Summer Palace at Chengteh A19

1936-37 Wmk. 242 *Perf. 13x13½*

No.	Type	Description	Unused	Used
83	A16	½f brown	35	15
84	A16	1f red brn	35	15
85	A16	1½f violet	3.00	2.25
a.		Booklet pane of 6	55.00	
86	A17	2f lt grn ('37)	35	15
a.		Booklet pane of 6	12.00	
87	A16	3f chocolate	35	15
a.		Booklet pane of 6	100.00	
88	A18	4f lt ol grn ('37)	35	15
a.		Booklet pane of 6	12.00	
89	A16	5f gray blk	15.00	6.00
90	A17	6f carmine	40	15
91	A18	7f brn blk	50	15
92	A18	9f red org	60	20
93	A19	10f blue	60	15
94	A18	12f dp org ('37)	50	15
95	A18	13f brown	27.50	19.00
96	A18	15f carmine	1.00	30
97	A17	20f dk brn	1.00	30
98	A19	30f chnt brn	1.00	30
99	A17	50f olive grn	1.25	40
100	A19	1y violet	2.50	50
		Nos. 83-100 (18)	56.60	30.60

Nos. 83, 84, 86, 88 and 93 are known imperforate but were not regularly issued.

See Nos. 159-163. For overprints see Nos. 140-141, 148-151. For surcharges see People's Republic of China Nos. 2L1-2L2, 2L11-2L18, 2L20-2L37, 2L40-2L52.

暫作 貳分五厘

a

暫作 五分

b

暫作 壹角參分

c

暫作 二分五厘

d

1937

Surcharged on No. 66

No.	Type	Description	Unused	Used
101	A9 (a)	2½f on 2f	1.50	1.25

Surcharged on Nos. 75, 76 and 78

No.	Type	Description	Unused	Used
102	A13 (a)	2½f on 2f	1.50	1.25
103	A10 (b)	5f on 4f	2.00	1.75
104	A10 (c)	13f on 12f	8.00	7.50

Surcharged in Black on Nos. 75, 76 and 70

Space between bottom characters of surcharge 4½mm

No.	Type	Description	Unused	Used
105	A13 (d)	2½f on 2f	1.50	1.25
a.		Inverted surcharge	100.00	75.00
b.		Vert. pair, one without surch.	85.00	
106	A10 (b)	5f on 4f ol grn	2.25	1.50
107	A10 (c)	13f on 12f brn red	7.00	4.50

Surcharged on No. 70

Space between characters 6½mm

No.	Type	Description	Unused	Used
108	A10 (c)	13f on 12f	150.00	105.00

Same Surcharge on No. 63

Space between characters 4½mm

Wmk. 141

No.	Type	Description	Unused	Used
109	A10 (b)	5f on 4f	4.75	3.00
		Nos. 101-109 (9)	178.50	127.00

Nos. 101-109 were issued primarily to pay postage to China, but were valid for any postal use.

Rising Sun over Manchurian Plain — A20

Composite Picture of Manchurian City — A21

Perf. 12½

1937, Mar. 1 Litho. Unwmk.

No.	Type	Description	Unused	Used
110	A20	1½f car rose	2.25	1.65
111	A21	3f bl grn	2.00	1.65

5th anniv. of the founding of the State of Manchukuo.

Types of 1936

Perf. 13x13½

1937 Wmk. 242 Engr.

No.	Type	Description	Unused	Used
112	A13	2½f dk vio	60	25
113	A10	5f black	20	15
115	A10	13f dk red brn	40	25

Issued primarily to pay postage to China, but were valid for any postal use.

Pouter Pigeon A22

National Flag and Buildings A23

Perf. 12x12½

1937, Sept. 16 Unwmk.

No.	Type	Description	Unused	Used
116	A22	2f dk vio	1.25	1.25
117	A23	4f rose car	1.25	85
118	A22	10f dk grn	2.75	1.65
119	A23	20f dk bl	3.75	3.50

Issued in commemoration of the completion of the national capital, Hsinking, under the first Five-Year Construction Plan.

Map — A24

Dept. of Justice Building — A27

Japanese Residents' Association Building — A25

Postal Administration Building — A26

Perf. 12x12½, 13

1937, Dec. 1 Litho. Unwmk.

No.	Type	Description	Unused	Used
121	A24	2f dk car	80	65
122	A25	4f green	1.40	90
123	A25	8f orange	3.25	2.50
124	A26	10f blue	3.25	3.00
125	A27	12f lt vio	4.00	3.75
126	A26	20f lil brn	4.50	4.00
		Nos. 121-126 (6)	17.20	14.80

Issued in commemoration of the abolition of extraterritorial rights within Manchukuo.

New Year Greetings A28

Map and Cross A29

1937, Dec. 15 Engr. *Perf. 12x12½*

No.	Type	Description	Unused	Used
127	A28	2f dk bl & red	1.65	50
a.		Double impression of border		

Issued to pay postage on New Year's greeting cards.

Wmk. 242

1938, Oct. 15 Litho. *Perf. 13*

No.	Type	Description	Unused	Used
128	A29	2f lake & scar	55	50
129	A29	4f slate grn & scar	55	50

Issued in commemoration of the founding of the Red Cross Society in Manchukuo.

Network of State Railroads in Manchukuo A30

Express Train "Asia" A31

1939, Oct. 21

No.	Type	Description	Unused	Used
130	A30	2f dk org, blk & dp bl	75	65
131	A31	4f dp bl & indigo	75	65

Attainment of 10,000 kilometers in the railway mileage in Manchuria.

Stork Flying above Mast of Imperial Flagship — A32

1940 Photo. Unwmk.

No.	Type	Description	Unused	Used
132	A32	2f brt red vio	16	16
133	A32	4f brt grn	20	20

Second visit of Emperor Kang Teh to Emperor Hirohito of Japan.

Census Taker and Map of Manchukuo A33

Census Form A34

1940, Sept. 10 Litho. Wmk. 242

No.	Type	Description	Unused	Used
134	A33	2f vio brn & org	16	16
135	A34	4f blk & grn	25	20
a.		Double impression of green	27.50	

National census starting Oct. 1.

Message of Congratulation from Premier Chang Ching-hui — A35

Dragon Dance A36

1940, Sept. 18 Engr.

No.	Type	Description	Unused	Used
136	A35	2f carmine	16	20
137	A36	4f indigo	25	30
a.		Imperf., pair	80.00	

2600th anniversary of the birth of the Japanese Empire.

Soldier — A37

1941, May 25 **Photo.** **Unwmk.**

138	A37	2f dp car	18	18
139	A37	4f brt ultra	25	25

Conscription Law, effective June 1, 1941.

Nos. 86 and 88 Overprinted in Red or Blue

紀念新嘉坡 復歸我東亞
年九德康

Perf. 13x13½

1942, Feb. 16 **Wmk. 242**

140	A17	2f lt grn (R)	16	16
141	A18	4f lt ol grn (Bl)	20	20

"Return of Singapore to East Asia, 9th year of Kang Teh."

Kengoku Shrine A38

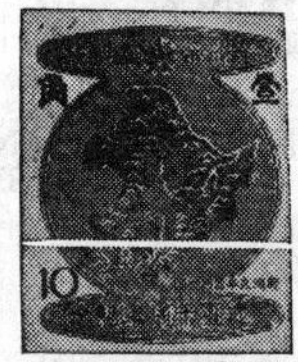
Map of Manchukuo A39

Flag of Manchukuo A40

Perf. 12x12½, 12½x12

1942, Mar. 1 **Engr.**

142	A38	2f carmine	25	25
143	A38	4f lilac	25	25
144	A39	10f red, *yel*	70	70
145	A40	20f indigo, *yel*	90	90

"10th anniv. of Manchukuo, Mar. 1, 1942".

Allegory of National Harmony A41

Women of Five Races, Dancing A42

1942, Sept. 15

146	A41	3f orange	25	25
147	A42	6f light green	35	35

"10th anniv. of the founding of Manchukuo, Sept. 15, 1942."

Nos. 87 and 90 Overprinted in Green or Blue

1942, Dec. 8 ***Perf. 13x13½***

148	A16	3f chocolate (G)	20	20
149	A17	6f carmine (Bl)	20	20

1st anniv. of the "Greater East Asia War."
The overprint reads "Asiatic Prosperity Began This Day December 8, 1941."

Nos. 87 and 90 Overprinted in Red or Blue

1943, May 1

150	A16	3f chocolate (R)	20	20
151	A17	6f carmine (Bl)	20	20

Proclamation of the labor service law.

Red Cross Nurse Carrying Stretcher A43

Smelting Furnace A44

1943, Oct. 1 **Photo.**

152	A43	6f green	20	20

5th anniv. of the founding of the Red Cross Society of Manchukuo, Oct. 1, 1938.

1943, Dec. 8 **Unwmk.** ***Perf. 13***

153	A44	6f red brown	20	20

2nd anniv. of the "Greater East Asia War."

"Japan's Progress Is Manchukuo's Progress"

Chinese Characters A45

Japanese Characters A46

Perf. 13x13½

1944 **Wmk. 242** **Litho.**

154	A45	10f rose	60	60
a.		Imperf., vert. pair #154 + 155	4.00	4.00
155	A46	10f rose	60	60
156	A45	40f gray green	1.50	1.50
a.		Imperf., vert. pair #156 + 157	7.50	7.50
b.		40f with 10f vignette, perf.	45.00	40.00
c.		40f with 10f vignette, imperf.	90.00	
157	A46	40f gray green	1.50	1.50

Issued as propaganda for the close relationship of Japan and Manchukuo. Sheets contain alternate horizontal rows of stamps with Chinese and Japanese inscriptions.

Frames of the 10f vignettes have rounded corners, those of the 40f vignettes have indented corners.

Types of 1935 and 1936-37

1944-45 **Litho.**

158	A10	5f gray black	50	60
a.		Imperf., pair	3.50	
159	A17	6f crimson rose	1.25	1.25
160	A19	10f light blue	90	1.50
161	A17	20f brown	1.00	1.50
162	A19	30f buff ('45)	1.25	1.50
163	A19	1y dull lilac	1.50	2.25
		Nos. 158-163 (6)	6.40	8.60

For surcharges see People's Republic of China Nos. 2L1, 2L14, 2L19, 2L24, 2L27, 2L30-2L31, 2L35, 2L37, 2L49, 2L52.

"One Heart, One Soul" — A47

1945, May 2

164	A47	10f red	25	25
a.		Imperf., pair	2.00	2.00

10th anniv. of the emperor's edict issued May 2, 1935.

AIR POST STAMPS

Sheep Grazing AP1

Railroad Bridge AP2

Wmk. Characters (242)

1936-37 **Engr.** ***Perf. 13x13½***

Granite Paper

C1	AP1	18f green	10.00	5.50
C2	AP1	19f bl grn ('37)	2.50	1.75
C3	AP2	38f blue	10.00	10.00
C4	AP2	39f dp bl ('37)	1.10	1.00

MARIANA ISLANDS

LOCATION — A group of 14 islands in the West Pacific Ocean, about 1500 miles east of the Philippines.
GOVT. — Former possession of Spain, then of Germany.
AREA — 246 sq. mi.
POP. — 44,025 (1935).
CAPITAL — Saipan.

Until 1899 this group belonged to Spain but in that year all except Guam were ceded to Germany.

100 Centavos = 1 Peso
100 Pfennig = 1 Mark (1899)

Issued under Spanish Dominion

King Alfonso XIII — A1

Stamps of the Philippines Handstamped Vertically in Blackish Violet Reading Up or Down

1899, Sept. **Unwmk.** ***Perf. 14***

1	A1	2c dk bl grn	350.00	70.00
2	A1	3c dk brn	250.00	67.50
3	A1	5c car rose	350.00	70.00
4	A1	6c dark blue	1,500.	425.00
5	A1	8c gray brn	225.00	70.00
6	A1	15c slate grn	850.00	425.00

Overprint forgeries of Nos. 1-6 exist.

Issued under German Dominion

Stamps of Germany, 1889-90, Overprinted in Black at 56 degree Angle

Perf. 13½x14½

1900, May **Unwmk.**

11	A9	3pf dk brn	15.00	*30.00*
12	A9	5pf green	18.00	*30.00*
13	A10	10pf carmine	22.50	*30.00*
14	A10	20pf ultra	27.50	*115.00*
15	A10	25pf orange	60.00	*125.00*
b.		Inverted overprint	*2,500.*	
16	A10	50pf red brn	60.00	*125.00*
		Nos. 11-16 (6)	203.00	*455.00*

Forged cancellations exist on Nos. 11-16, 17-29.

Overprinted at 48 degree Angle

1899, Nov. 18

11a	A9	3pf light brown	*1,500.*	*1,100.*
12a	A9	5pf green	*2,000.*	*1,050.*
13a	A10	10pf carmine	225.00	225.00
14a	A10	20pf ultra	250.00	275.00
15a	A10	25pf orange	*2,500.*	*1,750.*
16a	A10	50pf red brown	*2,500.*	*1,750.*

Kaiser's Yacht "Hohenzollern" A4

A5

1901, Jan. **Typo.** ***Perf. 14***

17	A4	3pf brown	90	90
18	A4	5pf green	90	90
19	A4	10pf carmine	90	*2.75*
20	A4	20pf ultra	1.00	*6.25*
21	A4	25pf org & blk, *yel*	1.75	*12.00*
22	A4	30pf org & blk, *sal*	1.75	*12.00*
23	A4	40pf lake & blk	1.90	*12.00*
24	A4	50pf pur & blk, *sal*	1.90	*14.00*
25	A4	80pf lake & blk, *rose*	3.00	*27.50*

Engr.

Perf. 14½x14

26	A5	1m carmine	3.50	*70.00*
27	A5	2m blue	6.25	*85.00*
28	A5	3m blk vio	9.00	*130.00*
29	A5	5m slate & car	150.00	*450.00*
		Nos. 17-29 (13)	182.75	

Wmk. Lozenges (125)

1916-19 **Typo.** ***Perf. 14***

30	A4	3pf brown ('19)	1.00	

Engr.

Perf. 14½x14

31	A5	5m slate & car	22.50	

Nos. 30 and 31 were never placed in use.

MARIENWERDER

LOCATION — In northeastern Germany, bordering on Poland.
GOVT. — A former district of West Prussia.

By the Versailles Treaty the greater portion of West Prussia was ceded to Poland but the district of Marienwerder was allowed a plebiscite which was held in 1920 and resulted in favor of Germany.

100 Pfennig = 1 Mark

Plebiscite Issues

Symbolical of Allied Supervision of the Plebiscite — A1

1920 **Unwmk.** **Litho.** ***Perf. 11½***

1	A1	5pf green	42	35
2	A1	10pf rose red	32	28
3	A1	15pf gray	45	40
4	A1	20pf brn org	28	22
5	A1	25pf deep blue	65	55
6	A1	30pf orange	1.00	85
7	A1	40pf brown	65	55
8	A1	50pf violet	65	45
9	A1	60pf red brn	4.00	2.75
10	A1	75pf chocolate	1.00	90
11	A1	1m brn & grn	80	70
12	A1	2m dk vio	4.00	3.25
13	A1	3m red	4.75	3.75
14	A1	5m blue & rose	20.00	16.00
		Nos. 1-14 (14)	38.97	31.00

These stamps occasionally show parts of two papermakers' watermarks, consisting of the letters "O. B. M." with two stars before and after, or "P. & C. M."

Nos. 1-14 exist imperf.; value for set, $700. Nearly all exist part perf.

Stamps of Germany, 1905-19, Overprinted

Commission
Interalliée
Marienwerder

1920 **Wmk. 125** ***Perf. 14, 14½***

24	A16	5pf green	15.00	25.00
a.		Inverted overprint	130.00	210.00
26	A16	20pf bl vio	6.00	*10.00*
a.		Inverted overprint	80.00	130.00
b.		Double overprint	165.00	150.00

28 A16 50pf vio & blk, *buff* 225.00 600.00
29 A16 75pf grn & blk 4.25 6.00
a. Inverted overprint 80.00 100.00
30 A16 80pf lake & blk, *rose* 85.00 150.00
31 A17 1m car rose 90.00 *175.00*
a. Inverted overprint 250.00 *425.00*
Nos. 24-31 (6) 425.25 966.00

Trial impressions were made in red, green and lilac, and with 2½mm instead of 3mm space between the lines of the overprint. These were printed on the 75pf and 80pf. The 1 mark was overprinted with the same words in 3 lines of large sans-serif capitals. All these are essays. Some were passed through the post, apparently with speculative intent.

Stamps of Germany, 1905-18, Surcharged

1 Mark 1
Commission
Interalliée
Marienwerder

32 A22 1m on 2pf gray 18.00 30.00
33 A22 2m on 2½pf gray 9.00 17.50
a. Inverted surcharge 55.00 110.00
34 A16 3m on 3pf brn 9.00 15.00
a. Double surcharge 55.00 110.00
b. Inverted surcharge 55.00 110.00
35 A22 5m on 7½pf org 9.00 12.00
a. Inverted surcharge 55.00 110.00
b. Double surcharge 55.00 110.00

There are two types of the letters "M", "C", "i" and "e" and of the numerals "2" and "5" in these surcharges.

Counterfeits exist of Nos. 24-35.

Stamps of Germany, 1920, Overprinted

Commission
Interalliée
Marienwerder

1920, July *Perf. 15x14½*
36 A17 1m red 2.50 4.25
37 A17 1.25m green 2.75 5.25
38 A17 1.50m yel brn 2.75 6.75
39 A21 2.50m lil rose 2.50 4.25

A2

1920 **Unwmk.** *Perf. 11½*
40 A2 5pf green 2.25 1.90
41 A2 10pf rose red 2.25 1.90
42 A2 15pf gray 11.00 10.50
43 A2 20pf brn org 1.50 1.50
44 A2 25pf dp bl 13.00 12.00
45 A2 30pf orange 1.25 95
46 A2 40pf brown 90 55
47 A2 50pf violet 1.50 1.10
48 A2 60pf red brn 4.50 3.50
49 A2 75pf chocolate 5.50 5.00
50 A2 1m brn & grn 90 75
51 A2 2m dk vio 1.25 1.00
52 A2 3m lt red 1.75 1.10
53 A2 5m bl & rose 2.25 1.40
Nos. 40-53 (14) 49.80 43.15

MARSHALL ISLANDS

LOCATION — Two chains of islands in the West Pacific Ocean, northwest of the Gilbert and Ellice group
GOVT. — Former German possession
AREA — 176 sq. mi.
POP. — 15,179 (1913)
CAPITAL — Jaluit

100 Pfennig = 1 Mark

Issued under German Dominion

A1

A2

Stamps of Germany Overprinted "Marschall-Inseln" in Black

1897 **Unwmk.** *Perf. 13½x14½*
1 A1 3pf dk brn 140.00 *550.00*
a. 3pf light brown *3,500.* *1,500.*
2 A1 5pf green 100.00 *500.00*
3 A2 10pf carmine 37.50 *80.00*
4 A2 20pf ultra 37.50 *95.00*
5 A2 25pf orange 110.00
6 A2 50pf red brown 110.00

Nos. 5 and 6 were not placed in use, but canceled copies exist.

A small quantity of the 3pf, 5pf, 10pf and 20pf were issued at Jaluit. These have yellowish, dull gum. Later overprintings of Nos. 1-6 were sold only at Berlin, and have white, smooth, shiny gum. No. 1a belongs to the Jaluit issue.

Forged cancellations are found on almost all Marshall Islands stamps.

Overprinted "Marshall-Inseln"

1899-1900
7 A1 3pf dk brn ('00) 4.00 4.75
a. 3pf light brown 130.00 *310.00*
8 A1 5pf green 9.00 6.75
9 A2 10pf car ('00) 11.00 17.00
10 A2 20pf ultra ('00) 18.00 *25.00*
11 A2 25pf orange 20.00 *40.00*
12 A2 50pf red brown 30.00 *55.00*
Nos. 7-12 (6) 92.00 *148.50*

Kaiser's Yacht "Hohenzollern"
A3 A4

1901 **Unwmk.** **Typo.** *Perf. 14*
13 A3 3pf brown 70 1.00
14 A3 5pf green 70 1.00
15 A3 10pf carmine 70 *4.25*
16 A3 20pf ultra 85 *8.25*
17 A3 25pf org & blk, *yel* 95 *14.00*
18 A3 30pf org & blk, *sal* 95 *14.00*
19 A3 40pf lake & blk 95 *14.00*
20 A3 50pf pur & blk, *sal* 1.90 *20.00*
21 A3 80pf lake & blk, *rose* 2.75 *45.00*

Engr.
Perf. 14½x14
22 A4 1m carmine 3.75 *65.00*
23 A4 2m blue 5.75 *110.00*
24 A4 3m blk vio 8.75 *165.00*
25 A4 5m slate & car 125.00 *375.00*
Nos. 13-25 (13) 153.70

Wmk. Lozenges (125)
1916 **Typo.** *Perf. 14*
26 A3 3pf brown 65

Engr.
Perf. 14½x14
27 A4 5m slate & car 22.50

Nos. 26 and 27 were never placed in use.

The stamps of Marshall Islands overprinted "G. R. I." and new values in British currency were all used in New Britain and are, therefore, listed among the issues for that country, in Volume I of the Standard Postage Stamp Catalogue.

See Vol. 1 for issues beginning in 1984 for the Marshall Islands as a US Trust Territory.

MARTINIQUE

LOCATION — Island in the West Indies, southeast of Puerto Rico
GOVT. — Former French Colony
AREA — 385 sq. mi.
POP. — 261,595 (1946)
CAPITAL — Fort-de-France

Formerly a French colony, Martinique became an integral part of the Republic, acquiring the same status as the departments in metropolitan France, under a law effective Jan. 1, 1947.

100 Centimes = 1 Franc

Marshall Islands under German Dominion stamps can be mounted in Scott's Germany Part II Album.

Catalogue values for unused stamps in this country are for Never Hinged items, beginning with Scott 196 in the regular postage section, Scott C1 in the airpost section, and Scott J37 in the postage due section.

See France Nos. 780, 1278, 1508 for French stamps inscribed "Martinique."

Stamps of French Colonies 1881-86 Surcharged in Black

MARTINIQUE 5 (a) — MARTINIQUE 5c (b) — MQE 15 c. (c) — MQE 15 c. (d) — MARTINIQUE 01 (e) — MARTINIQUE 01c. (f)

1886-91 **Unwmk.** *Perf. 14x13½*
1 A9 (a) 5 on 20c red, *grn* 24.00 19.00
a. Double surcharge *325.00* *325.00*
2 A9 (b) 5c on 20c red, *grn* *9,000.* *9,000.*
3 A9 (c) 15c on 20c red, *grn* ('87) 110.00 100.00
a. Inverted surcharge *1,200.* *1,200.*
4 A9 (d) 15c on 20c red, *grn* ('87) 42.50 37.50
a. Inverted surcharge *575.00* *575.00*
5 A9 (e) 01 on 20c red, *grn* ('88) 5.50 4.00
a. Inverted surcharge *150.00* *125.00*
6 A9 (e) 05 on 20c red, *grn* 5.00 3.00
7 A9 (a) 15 on 20c red, *grn* ('88) 90.00 60.00
c. Inverted surcharge *325.00* *325.00*
8 A9 (e) 015 on 20c red, *grn* ('87) 24.00 22.50
a. Inverted surcharge *400.00* *400.00*
9 A9 (f) 01c on 2c brn, *buff* ('88) 1.25 90
a. Double surcharge *175.00* *140.00*
10 A9 (f) 01c on 4c cl, *lav* ('88) 5.00 1.25
11 A9 (f) 05c on 4c cl, *lav* ('88) 825.00 600.00
12 A9 (f) 05c on 10c blk, *lav* ('90) 42.50 17.50
a. Slanting "5" *125.00* *75.00*
13 A9 (f) 05c on 20c red, *grn* ('88) 9.00 6.00
a. Slanting "5" *50.00* *35.00*
b. Inverted surcharge *175.00* *140.00*
14 A9 (f) 05c on 30c brn, *bis* ('91) 12.50 9.00
a. Slanting "5" *60.00* *37.50*
15 A9 (f) 05c on 35c dp vio, *org* ('91) 7.50 5.00
a. Slanting "5" *45.00* *37.50*
b. Inverted surcharge *150.00* *90.00*
16 A9 (f) 05c on 40c red, *straw* ('91) 25.00 16.00
a. Slanting "5" *90.00* *60.00*
17 A9 (f) 15c on 4c cl, *lav* ('88) *7,000.* *5,500.*
18 A9 (f) 15c on 20c red, *grn* ('87) 62.50 37.50
a. Slanting "5" *225.00* *140.00*
b. Double surcharge *275.00* *225.00*
19 A9 (f) 15c on 25c blk, *rose* ('90) 7.00 5.25
a. Slanting "5" *45.00* *35.00*
b. Inverted surcharge *175.00* *125.00*
20 A9 (f) 15c on 75c car, *rose* ('91) 80.00 50.00
a. Slanting "5" *250.00* *190.00*

French Colonies No. 47 Surcharged

TIMBRE-POSTE 01c. MARTINIQUE

1891
21 A9 01c on 2c brn, *buff* 4.25 3.25

French Colonies Nos. J5-J9 Surcharged

TIMBRE-POSTE 05c. MARTINIQUE

1891-92 **Black Surcharge** *Imperf.*
22 D1 05c on 5c blk ('92) 5.50 4.50
a. Slanting "5" *32.50* *22.50*
23 D1 05c on 15c blk 4.00 2.75
b. Slanting "5" *32.50* *22.50*
24 D1 15c on 20c blk 5.50 5.00
a. Inverted surcharge *125.00* *125.00*
b. Double surcharge *125.00* *125.00*
25 D1 15c on 30c blk 5.50 5.00
a. Inverted surcharge *125.00* *125.00*
b. Slanting "5" *32.50* *27.50*

Red Surcharge
26 D1 05c on 10c blk 4.00 4.00
a. Inverted surcharge *125.00* *110.00*
27 D1 05c on 15c blk 5.25 4.50
28 D1 15c on 20c blk 19.00 12.50
a. Inverted surcharge *180.00* *140.00*

French Colonies No. 54 Surcharged in Black

1892 MARTINIQUE 05c. (j) — 1892 05c. MARTINIQUE (k)

1892 *Perf. 14x13½*
29 A9 (j) 05c on 25c blk, *rose* 25.00 19.00
a. Slanting "5" *125.00* *100.00*
30 A9 (j) 15c on 25c blk, *rose* 10.00 8.00
a. Slanting "5" *125.00* *100.00*
31 A9 (k) 05c on 25c blk, *rose* 25.00 19.00
a. "1882" instead of "1892" *250.00* *190.00*
b. "95" instead of "05" *325.00* *225.00*
c. Slanting "5" *125.00* *100.00*
32 A9 (k) 15c on 25c blk, *rose* 10.00 8.00
a. "1882" instead of "1892" *225.00* *175.00*
b. Slanting "5" *75.00* *60.00*

Navigation and Commerce — A15

1892-1906 **Typo.** *Perf. 14x13½*
Name of Colony in Carmine or Blue
33 A15 1c blk, *lil bl* 65 62
a. Name in blue 325.00 325.00
34 A15 2c brn, *buff* 65 62
35 A15 4c cl, *lav* 65 62
36 A15 5c grn, *grnsh* 90 40
37 A15 5c yel grn ('99) 90 40
38 A15 10c blk, *lav* 4.00 62
39 A15 10c red ('99) 1.10 40
40 A15 15c blue, quadrille paper 15.00 3.50
41 A15 15c gray ('99) 4.00 60
42 A15 20c red, *grn* 6.50 2.75
43 A15 25c blk, *rose* 8.00 80
44 A15 25c bl ('99) 5.50 5.00
45 A15 30c brn, *bis* 15.00 5.00
46 A15 35c blk, *yel* ('06) 5.75 3.75
47 A15 40c red, *straw* 15.00 5.00
48 A15 50c car, *rose* 12.50 6.50
49 A15 50c brn, *az* ('99) 13.50 10.00
50 A15 75c dp vio, *org* 12.50 7.00
51 A15 1fr brnz grn, *straw* 10.00 5.50
52 A15 2fr vio, *rose* ('04) 42.50 37.50
53 A15 5fr lil, *lav* ('03) 50.00 42.50
Nos. 33-53 (21) 224.60 139.08

Perf. 13½x14 stamps are counterfeits.

Stamps of 1892-1903 Surcharged in Black

10c

1904

54 A15 10c on 30c brn, *bis* 3.50 3.50
a. Double surcharge
55 A15 10c on 5fr lil, *lav* 4.25 4.25

Surcharged **1904 0f10**

56 A15 10c on 30c brn, *bis* 7.00 7.00
57 A15 10c on 40c red, *straw* 7.00 7.00
a. Double surcharge 225.00 225.00
58 A15 10c on 50c car, *rose* 7.00 7.00
59 A15 10c on 75c dp vio, *org* 5.75 5.75
60 A15 10c on 1fr brnz grn, *straw* 7.00 7.00
a. Double surcharge 125.00 125.00
61 A15 10c on 5fr lil, *lav* 100.00 100.00
Nos. 54-61 (8) 141.50 141.50

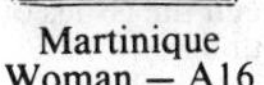

Martinique Woman — A16

Girl Bearing Pineapple in Cane Field — A18

View of Fort-de-France — A17

1908-30 **Typo.**

62 A16 1c red brn & brn 15 15
63 A16 2c ol grn & brn 15 15
64 A16 4c vio brn & brn 15 15
65 A16 5c grn & brn 15 15
66 A16 5c org & brn ('22) 15 15
67 A16 10c car & brn 28 15
68 A16 10c bl grn & grn ('22) 15 15
69 A16 10c brn vio & rose ('25) 15 15
70 A16 15c brn vio & rose ('17) 15 15
71 A16 15c bl grn & gray grn ('25) 15 15
72 A16 15c dp bl & red org ('27) 60 60
73 A16 20c vio & brn 60 38
74 A17 25c bl & brn 60 15
75 A17 25c org & brn ('22) 15 15
76 A17 30c brn org & brn 60 32
77 A17 30c dl red & brn ('22) 15 15
78 A17 30c rose & ver ('24) 15 15
79 A17 30c ol grn & brn ('25) 15 15
80 A17 30c sl bl & bl grn ('27) 60 60
81 A17 35c vio & brn 28 20
82 A17 40c gray grn & brn 28 15
83 A17 45c dk brn & brn 28 20
84 A17 50c rose & brn 60 28
85 A17 50c bl & brn ('22) 60 55
86 A17 50c org & grn ('25) 15 15
87 A17 60c dk bl & lil rose ('25) 15 15
88 A17 65c vio & ol brn ('27) 65 65
89 A17 75c sl & brn 60 28
90 A17 75c ind & dk bl ('25) 15 15
91 A17 75c org brn & lt bl ('27) 1.10 1.10
92 A17 90c brn red & brt red ('30) 2.25 2.25
93 A18 1fr dl bl & brn 28 15
94 A18 1fr dk bl ('25) 28 15
95 A18 1fr ver & ol grn ('27) 80 80
96 A18 1.10fr vio & dk brn ('28) 1.50 1.50
97 A18 1.50fr ind & ultra ('30) 2.50 2.50
98 A18 2fr gray & brn 1.40 50
99 A18 3fr red vio ('30) 3.50 3.50
100 A18 5fr org red & brn 4.00 3.50
Nos. 62-100 (39) 26.58 22.86

Nos. 41, 43, 47 and 53 Surcharged in Carmine or Black

05 **10**

1912, Aug.

101 A15 5c on 15c gray (C) 42 42
102 A15 5c on 25c blk, *rose* (C) 65 65
103 A15 10c on 40c red, *straw* 65 65
104 A15 10c on 5fr lil, *lav* 1.00 1.00

Two spacings between the surcharged numerals are found on Nos. 101 to 104.

Nos. 62, 63, 70 Surcharged **05**

1920, June 15

105 A16 5c on 1c 70 70
a. Double surcharge 12.50 12.50
b. Inverted surcharge 12.50 12.50
106 A16 10c on 2c 65 65
a. Inverted surcharge 12.50 12.50
107 A16 25c on 15c 50 50
a. Double surcharge 21.00 21.00
b. Inverted surcharge 21.00 21.00

No. 70 Surcharged in Various Colors **0,01**

1922, Dec.

108 A16 1c on 15c (Bk) 15 15
109 A16 2c on 15c (Bl) 15 15
110 A16 5c on 15c (R) 15 15
a. Imperf., pair 40.00
Set value 34 34

Types of 1908-30 Surcharged **60**

1923-25

111 A17 60c on 75c bl & rose 22 22
112 A17 65c on 45c ol brn & brn ('25) 50 50
113 A17 85c on 75c blk & brn (R) ('25) 60 60

Nos. 63, 73, 76-77, 84-85 Surcharged in Brown **0,01**

Surcharge is horiz. on Nos. 114-115, vert. reading up on Nos. 116, 119 and down on Nos. 117-118.

1924, Feb. 14

114 A16 1c on 2c ol grn & brn 70 70
a. Double surcharge 150.00 150.00
b. Inverted surcharge 27.50 27.50
115 A16 5c on 20c vio & brn 80 80
a. Inverted surcharge 27.50 27.50
116 A17 15c on 30c brn org & brn 4.50 4.50
a. Surch. reading down 15.00 15.00
117 A17 15c on 30c dl red & brn 6.25 6.25
a. Surch. reading up 20.00 20.00
118 A17 25c on 50c rose & brn 140.00 140.00
119 A17 25c on 50c bl & brn 1.90 1.90
a. Surch. reading down 15.00 15.00
Nos. 114-119 (6) 154.15 154.15

Stamps and Types of 1908-30 Surcharged with New Value and Bars

1924-27

120 A16 25c on 15c brn vio & rose ('25) 20 20
121 A18 25c on 2fr gray & brn 15 15
122 A18 25c on 5fr org red & brn (Bl) 40 35
123 A17 90c on 75c brn red & red ('27) 1.40 1.10
124 A18 1.25fr on 1fr dk bl ('26) 15 15
125 A18 1.50fr on 1fr dk bl & ultra ('27) 52 40
126 A18 3fr on 5fr dl red & grn ('27) 90 70
127 A18 10fr on 5fr dl grn & dp red ('27) 4.25 4.25
128 A18 20fr on 5fr org brn & red vio ('27) 6.50 6.00
Nos. 120-128 (9) 14.47 13.30

Colonial Exposition Issue
Common Design Types

1931, Apr. 13 **Engr.** ***Perf. 12½***
Name of Country in Black

129 CD70 40c dp grn 1.60 1.60
130 CD71 50c violet 1.60 1.60
131 CD72 90c red org 1.60 1.60
132 CD73 1.50fr dull blue 1.60 1.60

Village of Basse-Pointe A19

Government Palace, Fort-de-France — A20

Martinique Women A21

1933-40 **Photo.** ***Perf. 13½***

133 A19 1c red, *pink* 15 15
134 A20 2c dull blue 15 15
135 A20 3c sepia ('40) 15 15
136 A19 4c olive grn 15 15
137 A20 5c dp rose 15 15
138 A19 10c blk, *pink* 15 15
139 A20 15c blk, *org* 15 15
140 A21 20c org brn 15 15
141 A19 25c brn vio 15 15
142 A20 30c green 15 15
143 A20 30c lt ultra ('40) 15 15
144 A21 35c dl grn ('38) 15 15
145 A21 40c olive brn 15 15
146 A20 45c dk brn 65 65
147 A20 45c grn ('40) 15 15
148 A20 50c red 15 15
149 A19 55c brn red ('38) 28 28
150 A19 60c lt bl ('40) 15 15
151 A21 65c red, *grn* 20 20
152 A21 70c brt red vio ('40) 15 15
153 A19 75c dk brn 40 40
154 A20 80c vio ('38) 15 15
155 A19 90c carmine 65 65
156 A19 90c brt red vio ('39) 28 28
157 A20 1fr blk, *grn* 65 55
158 A20 1fr rose red ('38) 28 15
159 A21 1.25fr dk vio 28 15
160 A21 1.25fr dp rose ('39) 28 28
161 A19 1.40fr lt ultra ('40) 28 28
162 A20 1.50fr dp bl 28 15
163 A20 1.60fr chnt ('40) 28 28
164 A21 1.75fr ol grn 3.75 2.00
165 A21 1.75fr dp bl ('38) 15 15
166 A19 2fr dk bl, *grn* 15 15
167 A21 2.25fr blue ('39) 35 35
168 A19 2.50fr sepia ('40) 40 40
169 A21 3fr brn vio 15 15
170 A21 5fr red, *pink* 58 28
171 A19 10fr dk bl, *bl* 28 20
172 A20 20fr red, *yel* 60 40
Nos. 133-172 (40) 13.90
Set value 9.50

Landing of Bélain d'Esnambuc — A22

Freed Slaves Paying Homage to Victor Schoelcher A23

1935, Oct. 22 **Engr.** ***Perf. 13***

173 A22 40c blk brn 1.50 90
174 A22 50c dl red 1.50 90
175 A22 1.50fr ultra 12.00 7.50
176 A23 1.75fr lil rose 10.00 7.00
177 A23 5fr brown 10.00 7.00
178 A23 10fr bl grn 8.25 5.25
Nos. 173-178 (6) 43.25 28.55

Tercentenary of French possessions in the West Indies.

Colonial Arts Exhibition Issue
Common Design Type
Souvenir Sheet

1937 ***Imperf.***

179 CD74 3fr brt grn 2.25 2.25

Paris International Exposition Issue
Common Design Types

1937, Apr. 15 ***Perf. 13***

180 CD74 20c dp vio 60 60
181 CD75 30c dk grn 60 60
182 CD76 40c car rose 60 60
183 CD77 50c dk brn & blk 80 80
184 CD78 90c red 80 80
185 CD79 1.50fr ultra 80 80
Nos. 180-185 (6) 4.20 4.20

New York World's Fair Issue
Common Design Type

1939, May 10 ***Perf. 12½x12***

186 CD82 1.25fr car lake 60 60
187 CD82 2.25fr ultra 60 60

View of Fort-de-France and Marshal Petain — A23a

1941 **Engr.** ***Perf. 12½x12***

188 A23a 1fr dull lilac 22
189 A23a 2.50fr blue 22

Nos. 188-189 were issued by the Vichy government, and were not placed on sale in Martinique.

Nos. 134, 135, 136 and 151 Surcharged with New Values and Bars or Wavy Lines in Red, Black or Blue

1945 ***Perf. 13½, 13x13½***

190 A20 1fr on 2c dl bl (R) 15 15
191 A19 2fr on 4c ol grn 20 20
192 A20 3fr on 2c dl bl (R) 22 22
193 A21 5fr on 65c red, *grn* 42 42
194 A21 10fr on 65c red, *grn* 42 42
195 A20 20fr on 3c sepia (Bl) 55 55
Nos. 190-195 (6) 1.96 1.96

Catalogue values for unused stamps in this section, from this point to the end of the section, are for Never Hinged items.

Eboue Issue
Common Design Type

1945 **Engr.** ***Perf. 13***

196 CD91 2fr black 15 15
197 CD91 25fr Prussian green 42 42

Victor Schoelcher and View of Town of Schoelcher A24

1945 **Unwmk.** **Litho.** ***Perf. 11½***

198 A24 10c dp bl vio & ultra 15 15
199 A24 30c dk org brn & lt org brn 15 15
200 A24 40c grnsh bl & pale bl 15 15
201 A24 50c car brn & rose lil 15 15
202 A24 60c org yel & yel 15 15
203 A24 70c brn & pale brn 15 15
204 A24 80c lt bl grn & pale grn 15 15
205 A24 1fr bl & lt bl 15 15
206 A24 1.20fr rose vio & rose lil 15 15
207 A24 1.50fr red org & org 15 15
208 A24 2fr blk & gray 15 15
209 A24 2.40fr red & pink 65 60
210 A24 3fr pink & pale pink 15 15
211 A24 4fr ultra & lt ultra 20 15
212 A24 4.50fr yel grn & lt grn 38 15

213	A24	5fr org brn & lt org brn	15	15
214	A24	10fr dk vio & lil	38	22
215	A24	15fr rose car & lil rose	45	22
216	A24	20fr ol grn & lt ol grn	65	60
		Set value	3.75	2.85

Martinique Girl A25

Mountains A30

Cliffs — A26

Gathering Sugar Cane — A27

Mount Pelee — A28

Tropical Fruit — A29

1947, June 2 Engr. *Perf. 13*

217	A25	10c red brown	15	15
218	A25	30c deep blue	15	15
219	A25	50c olive brown	15	15
220	A26	60c dark green	15	15
221	A26	1fr red brown	15	15
222	A26	1.50fr purple	20	20
223	A27	2fr blue green	50	35
224	A27	2.50fr blk brn	40	30
225	A27	3fr deep blue	38	22
226	A28	4fr dk brown	38	28
227	A28	5fr dark green	35	30
228	A28	6fr lilac rose	38	28
229	A29	10fr indigo	62	38
230	A29	15fr red brown	70	62
231	A29	20fr blk brown	1.00	62
232	A30	25fr violet	1.00	70
233	A30	40fr blue grren	1.25	80
		Nos. 217-233 (17)	7.91	5.80

SEMI-POSTAL STAMPS

Regular Issue of 1908 Surcharged in Red

Perf. 13½x14

1915, May 15 Unwmk.

B1	A16	10c + 5c car & brn	80	62

Curie Issue
Common Design Type

1938, Oct. 24 *Perf. 13*

B2	CD80	1.75fr + 50c brt ultra	5.00	5.00

French Revolution Issue
Common Design Type

Photo.; Name & Value Typo. in Black

1939, July 5

B3	CD83	45c + 25c grn	3.50	3.50
B4	CD83	70c + 30c brn	3.50	3.50
B5	CD83	90c + 35c red org	3.50	3.50
B6	CD83	1.25fr + 1fr rose pink	3.50	3.50
B7	CD83	2.25fr + 2fr blue	3.50	3.50
		Nos. B3-B7 (5)	17.50	17.50

Common Design Type and

Colonial Infantry with Machine Gun — SP1

Naval Rifleman SP2

1941 Photo. *Perf. 13½*

B8	SP1	1fr + 1fr red	40
B9	CD86	1.50fr + 3fr maroon	40
B10	SP2	2.50fr + 1fr blue	40

Nos. B8-B10 were issued by the Vichy government, and were not placed on sale in Martinique.

Nos. 188-189 were surcharged "OEUVRES COLONIALES" and surtax (including change of denomination of the 2.50fr to 50c). These were issued in 1944 by the Vichy government, and were not placed on sale in Martinique.

Red Cross Issue
Common Design Type

1944 *Perf. 14½x14*

B11	CD90	5fr + 20fr dk pur	40	40

The surtax was for the French Red Cross and national relief.

AIR POST STAMPS

Catalogue values for unused stamps in this section are for Never Hinged items.

Common Design Type

1945 Unwmk. Photo. *Perf. 14½x14*

C1	CD87	50fr dark green	40	22
C2	CD87	100fr plum	45	35

Two other values, 8.50fr orange and 18fr red brown, were prepared but not issued. Value, $50 each.

Victory Issue
Common Design Type

1946, May 8 Engr. *Perf. 12½*

C3	CD92	8fr indigo	60	60

Issued to commemorate the European victory of the Allied Nations in World War II.

Chad to Rhine Issue
Common Design Types

1946, June 6

C4	CD93	5fr orange	35	35
C5	CD94	10fr slate grn	35	35
C6	CD95	15fr carmine	40	40
C7	CD96	20fr chocolate	40	40
C8	CD97	25fr deep blue	55	55
C9	CD98	50fr gray blk	70	70
		Nos. C4-C9 (6)	2.75	2.75

Seaplane and Beach Scene — AP1

Plane over Tropic Shore — AP2

Albatross — AP3

1947, June 2 *Perf. 13*

C10	AP1	50fr dk brn vio	1.50	1.25
C11	AP2	100fr dk bl grn	2.25	1.75
C12	AP3	200fr violet	14.00	10.00

AIR POST SEMI-POSTAL STAMPS

Stamps similar to French Guiana type V6 inscribed "Martinique" and stamp of Cameroun type V10 inscribed "Martinique" were issued in 1942 by the Vichy Government, but were not placed on sale in Martinique.

POSTAGE DUE STAMPS

The set of 14 French Colonies postage due stamps (Nos. J1-14) overprinted "MARTINIQUE" diagonally in red in 1887 was not an official issue.

Postage Due Stamps of France, 1893-1926 Overprinted

MARTINIQUE

1927, Oct. 10 *Perf. 14x13½*

J15	D2	5c light blue	62	62
J16	D2	10c brown	70	70
J17	D2	20c olive green	70	70
J18	D2	25c rose	1.10	1.10
J19	D2	30c red	1.20	1.20
J20	D2	45c green	1.20	1.20
J21	D2	50c brn violet	2.50	2.50
J22	D2	60c blue green	2.75	2.75
J23	D2	1fr red brown	3.75	3.75
J24	D2	2fr bright vio	4.50	4.50
J25	D2	3fr magenta	5.75	5.75
		Nos. J15-J25 (11)	24.77	24.77

Tropical Fruit — D3

Map — D4

1933, Feb. 15 Photo. *Perf. 13½*

J26	D3	5c dk bl, *green*	22	22
J27	D3	10c orange brown	22	22
J28	D3	20c dk blue	55	55
J29	D3	25c red, *pink*	55	55
J30	D3	30c dk vio	35	35
J31	D3	45c red, *yel*	22	22
J32	D3	50c dk brn	55	55
J33	D3	60c dl grn	55	55
J34	D3	1fr blk, *org*	65	65
J35	D3	2fr dp rose	55	55
J36	D3	3fr dk blue, *bl*	55	55
		Nos. J26-J36 (11)	4.96	4.96

Stamps of type D3 without the "RF" monogram were issued in 1943 by the Vichy Government, but were not placed on sale in Martinique.

1947, June 2 Engr. *Perf. 14x13*

J37	D4	10c ultra	15	15
J38	D4	30c brt bl grn	15	15
J39	D4	50c sl gray	15	15
J40	D4	1fr org red	15	15
J41	D4	2fr dk vio brn	30	30
J42	D4	3fr lil rose	30	30
J43	D4	4fr dk brn	42	42
J44	D4	5fr red	45	45
J45	D4	10fr black	70	70
J46	D4	20fr ol grn	70	70
		Nos. J37-J46 (10)	3.47	3.47

PARCEL POST STAMP

Postage Due Stamp of French Colonies Surcharged in Black

TIMBRE POSTE
5 F.
MARTINIQUE
COLIS POSTAUX

1903, Oct. Unwmk. *Imperf.*

Q1	D1	5fr on 60c brn, *buff*	375.00	400.00
a.		Inverted surcharge	*425.00*	*500.00*

MAURITANIA

LOCATION — Northwestern Africa, bordering on the Atlantic Ocean
GOVT. — Republic
AREA — 398,000 sq. mi.
POP. — 1,834,500 (est. 1984)
CAPITAL — Nouakchott

The Islamic Republic of Mauritania was proclaimed Nov. 28, 1958.

Stamps of French West Africa were used in the period between the issues of the colony and the republic.

100 Centimes = 1 Franc
Ouguiya ("um") (1973)

Catalogue values for unused stamps in this country are for Never Hinged items, beginning with Scott 116 in the regular postage section, Scott B16 in the semi-postal section, Scott C14 in the airpost section, Scott J19 in the postage due section, and Scott O1 in the official section.

General Louis Faidherbe — A1

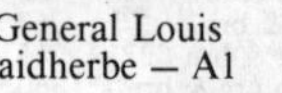

Oil Palms — A2

Dr. Noel Eugene Ballay — A3

Perf. 14x13½

1906-07 Typo. Unwmk.

"Mauritanie" in Red or Blue

1	A1	1c slate	20	20
2	A1	2c chocolate	38	32
3	A1	4c choc, *gray bl*	50	40
4	A1	5c green	38	25
5	A1	10c car (B)	3.25	2.00
7	A2	20c blk, *azure*	10.00	6.25
8	A2	25c bl, *pnksh*	3.25	2.25
9	A2	30c choc, *pnksh*	45.00	32.50
10	A2	35c blk, *yellow*	3.25	2.25
11	A2	40c car, *az* (B)	3.50	2.25
12	A2	45c choc, *grnsh* ('07)	3.25	2.50
13	A2	50c dp vio	3.25	2.50
14	A2	75c bl, *org*	3.25	2.50
15	A3	1fr blk, *azure*	6.50	5.50
16	A3	2fr bl, *pink*	22.50	21.50
17	A3	5fr car, *straw* (B)	70.00	60.00
		Nos. 1-17 (16)	178.46	143.17

Crossing Desert — A4

1913-38

18 A4 1c brn vio & brn 15 15
19 A4 2c blk & bl 15 15
20 A4 4c vio & blk 15 15
21 A4 5c yel grn & bl grn 20 20
22 A4 5c brn vio & rose ('22) 15 15
23 A4 10c rose & red org 40 40
24 A4 10c yel grn & bl grn ('22) 15 15
25 A4 10c lil rose, *bluish* ('25) 20 20
26 A4 15c dk brn & blk ('17) 20 20
27 A4 20c bis brn & org 15 15
28 A4 25c bl & vio 42 42
29 A4 25c grn & rose ('22) 15 15
30 A4 30c bl grn & rose 35 35
31 A4 30c rose & red org ('22) 40 40
32 A4 30c blk & yel ('26) 15 15
33 A4 30c bl grn & yel grn ('28) 58 58
34 A4 35c brn & vio 28 28
35 A4 35c dp grn & lt grn ('38) 40 40
36 A4 40c gray & bl grn 90 90
37 A4 45c org & bis brn 38 38
38 A4 50c brn vio & rose 28 28
39 A4 50c dk bl & ultra ('22) 15 15
40 A4 50c gray grn & dp bl ('26) 35 35
41 A4 60c vio, *pnksh* ('26) 15 15
42 A4 65c yel brn & lt bl ('26) 42 42
43 A4 75c ultra & brn 35 35
44 A4 85c myr grn & lt brn ('26) 55 55
45 A4 90c brn red & rose ('30) 65 65
46 A4 1fr rose & blk 35 35

47 A4 1.10fr vio & ver ('28) 5.50 5.50
48 A4 1.25fr dk bl & blk brn ('33) 90 90
49 A4 1.50fr lt bl & dp bl ('30) 35 35
50 A4 1.75fr bl grn & brn red ('33) 40 40
51 A4 1.75fr dk bl & ultra ('38) 40 40
52 A4 2fr red org & vio 80 62
53 A4 3fr red vio ('30) 80 80
54 A4 5fr vio & bl 1.20 1.00
Nos. 18-54 (37) 19.51 19.13

Stamp and Type of 1913-38 Surcharged

= 60   = 60

1922-25

55 A4 60c on 75c vio, *pnksh* 40 40
56 A4 65c on 15c dk brn & blk ('25) 70 70
57 A4 85c on 75c ultra & brn ('25) 70 70

Stamp and Type of 1913-38 Surcharged with New Value and Bars

1924-27

58 A4 25c on 2fr red org & vio 50 50
59 A4 90c on 75c brn red & cer ('27) 1.00 1.00
60 A4 1.25fr on 1fr dk bl & ultra ('26) 20 20
61 A4 1.50fr on 1fr bl & dp bl ('27) 60 60
62 A4 3fr on 5fr ol brn & red vio ('27) 4.00 4.00
63 A4 10fr on 5fr mag & bl grn ('27) 3.25 3.25
64 A4 20fr on 5fr bl vio & dp org ('27) 3.25 3.25
Nos. 58-64 (7) 12.80 12.80

Colonial Exposition Issue
Common Design Types

Engr.; Name of Country Typo. in Black

1931, Apr. 13 ***Perf. 12½***

65 CD70 40c dp grn 2.25 2.25
66 CD71 50c violet 1.60 1.60
67 CD72 90c red org 1.60 1.60
68 CD73 1.50fr dull blue 1.60 1.60

Paris International Exposition Issue
Common Design Types

1937, Apr. 15 ***Perf. 13***

69 CD74 20c dp vio 55 55
70 CD75 30c dk grn 55 55
71 CD76 40c car rose 50 50
72 CD77 50c dk brn & blk 50 50
73 CD78 90c red 58 58
74 CD79 1.50fr ultra 58 58
Nos. 69-74 (6) 3.26 3.26

Colonial Arts Exhibition Issue
Common Design Type
Souvenir Sheet

1937 ***Imperf.***

75 CD76 3fr dark blue 2.25 2.25

Camel Rider — A5

Mauri Couple — A8

Mauris on Camels A6

Family before Tent — A7

1938-40 ***Perf. 13***

76 A5 2c vio blk 15 15
77 A5 3c dp ultra 15 15
78 A5 4c rose vio 15 15
79 A5 5c org red 15 15
80 A5 10c brn car 15 15
81 A5 15c dk vio 15 15
82 A6 20c red 15 15
83 A6 25c dp ultra 15 15
84 A6 30c dp brn 15 15
85 A6 35c Prus grn 20 20
86 A6 40c rose car ('40) 15 15
87 A6 45c Prus grn ('40) 15 15
88 A6 50c purple 15 15
89 A7 55c rose vio 28 28
90 A7 60c vio ('40) 20 20
91 A7 65c dp grn 38 38
92 A7 70c red ('40) 40 40
93 A7 80c dp bl 70 70
94 A7 90c rose vio ('39) 30 30
95 A7 1fr red 70 70
96 A7 1fr dp grn ('40) 30 30
97 A7 1.25fr rose car ('39) 65 65
98 A7 1.40fr dp bl ('40) 30 30
99 A7 1.50fr violet 30 30
99A A7 1.50fr red brn ('40) 50.00 50.00
100 A7 1.60fr blk brn ('40) 65 65
101 A8 1.75fr dp ultra 42 42
102 A8 2fr rose vio 42 42
103 A8 2.25fr dl ultra ('39) 38 38
104 A8 2.50fr blk brn ('40) 50 50
105 A8 3fr dp grn 30 30
106 A8 5fr scarlet 60 60
107 A8 10fr dp brn 80 80
108 A8 20fr brn car 80 80
Nos. 76-108 (34) 61.38 61.38

Nos. 91 and 109 surcharged with new values are listed under French West Africa.

Caillie Issue
Common Design Type

1939, Apr. 5 **Engr.** ***Perf. 12½x12***

109 CD81 90c org brn & org 50 50
110 CD81 2fr brt vio 50 50
111 CD81 2.25fr ultra & dk bl 50 50

New York World's Fair Issue
Common Design Type

1939, May 10

112 CD82 1.25fr car lake 35 35
113 CD82 2.25fr ultra 35 35

Caravan and Marshal Petain — A9

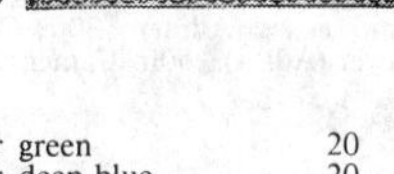

1941

114 A9 1fr green 20
115 A9 2.50fr deep blue 20

Nos. 114-115 were issued by the Vichy government, and were not placed on sale in the colony. This also holds true for six stamps of types A5-A7 without "RF," issued in 1943-44.

Catalogue values for unused stamps in this section, from this point to the end of the section, are for Never Hinged items.

Islamic Republic

Camel and Hands Raising Flag — A10

Unwmk.

1960, Jan. 20 **Engr.** ***Perf. 13***

116 A10 25fr multi, *pink* 35 20

Issued to commemorate the proclamation of the Islamic Republic of Mauritania.

Imperforates
Most Mauritania stamps from 1960 onward exist imperforate in issued and trial colors, and also in small presentation sheets in issued colors.

C.C.T.A. Issue
Common Design Type

1960, May 16

117 CD106 25fr bluish grn & ultra 38 22

Flag and Map — A11

1960, Dec. 15 **Engr.** ***Perf. 13***

118 A11 25fr org brn, emer & sep 22 16

Proclamation of independence, Nov. 28, 1960.

Pastoral Well — A12

Scimitar-horned Oryx — A15

Spotted Hyena A13

Ore Train and Camel Riders A14

Designs: 50c, 1fr, Well. 2fr, Date harvesting. 3fr, Aoudad. 4fr, Fennecs. 5fr, Millet harvesting. 10fr, Shoemaker. 15fr, Fishing boats. 20fr, Nomad school. 25fr, 30fr, Seated dance. No. 130, Religious student. 60fr, Metalworker.

1960-62 **Unwmk.** ***Perf. 13***

119 A12 50c mag, yel & brn ('61) 15 15
120 A12 1fr brn, yel brn & grn 15 15
121 A12 2fr dk brn, bl & grn 15 15
122 A13 3fr bl grn, red brn & gray ('61) 15 15
123 A13 4fr yel grn & ocher ('61) 15 15
124 A12 5fr red, dk brn & yel brn 15 15
125 A14 10fr dk bl & org 15 15
126 A14 15fr ver, dk brn, grn & bl 15 15
127 A14 20fr grn, sl grn & red brn 22 15
128 A12 25fr ultra & gray grn ('61) 25 15
129 A12 30fr lil, bis & ind 30 15
130 A12 50fr org brn & grn 60 20
131 A14 50fr red brn, bl & ol ('62) 55 38
132 A12 60fr grn, cl & pur 65 20
133 A15 85fr bl, brn & blk ('61) 1.00 50
Set value 4.00 1.75

An overprint, "Jeux Olympiques / Rome 1960 / Tokyo 1964," the 5-ring Olympic emblem and a 75fr surcharge were applied to Nos. 126-127 in 1962.

An overprint, "Aide aux Refugies" with uprooted oak emblem, was applied in 1962 to No. 132 and to pink-paper printings of Nos. 129-130.

Other overprints, applied to airmail stamps, are noted after No. C16.

1963, July 6

Designs: 50c, Striped hyena. 1.50fr, Cheetah. 2fr, Guinea baboons. 5fr, Dromedaries. 10fr, Leopard. 15fr, Bongo antelopes. 20fr, Aardvark. 25fr, Patas monkeys. 30fr, Crested porcupine. 50fr, Dorcas gazelle. 60fr, Common chameleon.

134 A15 50c sl grn, blk & org brn 15 15
135 A13 1fr ultra, blk & yel 15 15
136 A15 1.50fr ol grn, brn & bis 15 15
137 A13 2fr dk brn, grn & dp org 15 15
138 A15 5fr brn, ultra & bis 15 15
139 A13 10fr blk & bis 15 15
140 A13 15fr vio bl & red brn 16 15
141 A13 20fr dk red brn, dk bl & bis 18 15
142 A15 25fr brt grn, red brn & ol bis 30 15
143 A13 30fr dk brn, dk bl & ol bis 40 15
144 A15 50fr grn, ocher & brn 55 25
145 A13 60fr dk bl, emer & ocher 80 45
Set value 2.80 1.30

UN Headquarters, New York, and View of Nouakchott — A15a

1962, June 1 **Engr.** ***Perf. 13***

167 A15a 15fr blk, ultra & cop red 16 15
168 A15a 25fr cop red, sl grn & ultra 25 22
169 A15a 85fr dk bl, dl pur & cop red 80 65

Mauritania's admission to the UN.

African-Malagasy Union Issue
Common Design Type

1962, Sept. 8 **Photo.** ***Perf. 12½x12***

170 CD110 30fr multi 35 30

Organization Emblem and View of Nouakchott — A16

1962, Oct. 15 ***Perf. 12½***

171 A16 30fr dk red brn, ultra & brt grn	25	22

8th Conf. of the Organization to Fight Endemic Diseases, Nouakchott, Oct. 15-18.

Map, Mechanized and Manual Farm Work — A17

1962, Nov. 28 **Engr.** ***Perf. 13***

172 A17 30fr blk, grn & vio brn	30	22

2nd anniversary of independence.

People in European and Mauritanian Clothes A18

1962, Dec. 24 **Unwmk.**

173 A18 25fr multi	22	16

First anniversary of Congress for Unity.

Weather and WMO Symbols — A20

1964, Mar. 23 **Unwmk.** ***Perf. 13***

175 A20 85fr dk brn, dk bl & org	1.25	80

UN 4th World Meteorological Day, Mar. 23.

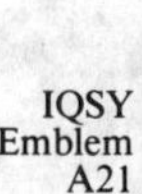

IQSY Emblem A21

1964, July 3 **Engr.**

176 A21 25fr dk bl, red & grn	22	16

International Quiet Sun Year, 1964-65.

Striped Mullet A22

Designs: 5fr, Mauritanian lobster (vert.). 10fr, Royal lobster (vert.). 60fr, Maigre fish.

1964, Oct. 5 **Engr.** ***Perf. 13***

177 A22 1fr org brn, dk bl & grn	15	15
178 A22 5fr org brn, sl grn & choc	15	15
179 A22 10fr dk bl, bis & sl grn	20	15
180 A22 60fr dk brn, dp grn & dl bl	60	45
Set value	94	70

Cooperation Issue

Common Design Type

1964, Nov. 7 **Unwmk.** ***Perf. 13***

181 CD119 25fr mag, sl grn & dk brn	25	20

Water Lilies A23

Tropical Plants: 10fr, Acacia (vert.). 20fr, Adenium obesum. 45fr, Caralluma retrospiciens (vert.).

1965, Jan. 11 **Engr.** ***Perf. 13***

182 A23 5fr grn, dk bl & pink	15	15
183 A23 10fr grn, dl pur & bis	15	15
184 A23 20fr dk car, dk brn & pale brn	15	15
185 A23 45fr plum, dk sl grn & Prus bl	35	25
Set value	68	54

Hardine A24

Musical Instruments: 8fr, Tobol (drums). 25fr, Tidinit (stringed instruments). 40fr, Musicians.

1965, Mar. 8 ***Perf. 13***

186 A24 2fr red brn, brt bl & sep	15	15
187 A24 8fr red brn, red & brn	15	15
188 A24 25fr red brn, emer & blk	20	15
189 A24 40fr vio bl, plum & blk	30	18
Set value	65	40

Abraham Lincoln (1809-1865) — A25

1965, Apr. 23 **Photo.** ***Perf. 13x12½***

190 A25 50fr lt ultra & multi	50	25

Palms at Adrar A26

Designs: 4fr, Chinguetti mosque (vert.). 15fr, Clay pit and donkeys. 60fr, Decorated door, Oualata.

1965, June 14 **Engr.** ***Perf. 13***

191 A26 1fr brn, bl & grn	15	15
192 A26 4fr dk red, bl & brn	15	15
193 A26 15fr multi	15	15
194 A26 60fr grn, dk brn & red brn	55	35
Set value	75	50

Issued for tourist publicity.

Tea Service in Inlaid Box — A27

Designs: 7fr, Tobacco pouch and pipe (vert.). 25fr, Dagger (vert.). 50fr, Mederdra ornamental chest.

1965, Sept. 13 **Unwmk.** ***Perf. 13***

195 A27 3fr gray, choc & ocher	15	15
196 A27 7fr red lil, Prus bl & org	15	15
197 A27 25fr blk, org red & brn	16	15
198 A27 50fr brt grn, brn org & mar	35	20
Set value	60	40

Choum Railroad Tunnel — A28

Designs: 10fr, Nouakchott wharf, ships and anchor (horiz.). 85fr, Nouakchott hospital and caduceus (horiz.).

1965, Oct. 18 **Engr.** ***Perf. 13***

199 A28 5fr dk brn & brt grn	15	15
200 A28 10fr dk vio bl, brn red & Prus bl	15	15
201 A28 30fr brn red, red & red brn	25	15
202 A28 85fr dp bl, rose cl & lil	65	40
Set value	1.00	55

Sculptured Heads A29

Designs: 30fr, "Music and Dance." 60fr, Movie camera and huts.

1966, Apr. **Engr.** ***Perf. 13***

203 A29 10fr brt grn, blk & brn	15	15
204 A29 30fr brt bl, red lil & blk	25	16
205 A29 60fr red, org & dk brn	55	35

Intl. Negro Arts Festival, Dakar, Senegal, Apr. 1-24.

Mimosa — A30

Myrina Silenus — A31

Flowers: 15fr, Schouwia purpurea. 20fr, Ipomea asarifolia. 25fr, Grewia bicolor. 30fr, Pancratium trianthum. 60fr, Blepharis linariifolia.

1966, Aug. 8 **Photo.** ***Perf. 13x12½***

Flowers in Natural Colors

206 A30 10fr dl bl & dk bl	15	15
207 A30 15fr dk brn & buff	15	15
208 A30 20fr grnsh bl & lt bl	20	15
209 A30 25fr brn & buff	22	15
210 A30 30fr lil & vio	30	15
211 A30 60fr grn & pale grn	50	25
Nos. 206-211 (6)	1.52	
Set value		65

1966, Oct. 3 **Photo.** ***Perf. 12x12½***

Various Butterflies

212 A31 5fr buff & multi	15	15
213 A31 30fr bl grn & multi	35	15
214 A31 45fr yel grn & multi	50	16
215 A31 60fr dl bl & multi	65	30
Set value		62

Hunter, Petroglyph from Adrar A32

Designs: 3fr, Two men fighting, petroglyph from Tenses (Adrar). 30fr, Copper jug, Le Mreyer (Adrar). 50fr, Camel caravan.

1966, Oct. 24 **Engr.** ***Perf. 13***

216 A32 2fr dk brn & brn org	15	15
217 A32 3fr bl & brn org	15	15
218 A32 30fr sl grn & dk red	30	15
219 A32 50fr mag, sl grn & brn	50	35
Set value	90	55

Issued for tourist publicity.

UNESCO, 20th Anniv. A33

1966, Dec. 5 **Litho.** ***Perf. 12½x13***

220 A33 30fr multi	30	15

Plaza of Three Cultures, Mexico City — A34

Olympic Village, Grenoble A35

Designs: 40fr, Olympic torch and skating rink. 100fr, Olympic Stadium, Mexico City.

1967, Mar. 11 **Engr.** ***Perf. 13***

221 A34 20fr dl bl, brn & sl grn	20	15
222 A35 30fr dl bl, brn & grn	30	15
223 A34 40fr brt bl, dk brn & sep	38	16
224 A35 100fr brn, emer & blk	70	42

Nos. 221 and 223 publicize the 19th Olympic Games, Mexico City; Nos. 222 and 224 the 10th Winter Olympic Games, Grenoble.

Prosopis Tree A36

1967 Jamboree Emblem and Campsite A37

Trees: 15fr, Jujube. 20fr, Date palm. 25fr, Peltophorum. 30fr, Baobab.

1967, May 15 **Engr.** ***Perf. 13***

225 A36 10fr brn, bl & sl grn	15	15
226 A36 15fr dk brn, vio bl & sl grn	15	15
227 A36 20fr sl grn, bl & dk brn	16	15
228 A36 25fr brn & sl grn	22	15
229 A36 30fr ver, sl grn & yel brn	25	15
Nos. 225-229 (5)	93	
Set value		45

1967, June 5

Design: 90fr, 1967 Jamboree emblem and Mauritanian Boy Scouts (horiz.).

230 A37 60fr brn, ultra & sl grn	55	25
231 A37 90fr dl red, bl & sl grn	80	38

12th Boy Scout World Jamboree, Farragut State Park, Idaho, Aug. 1-9.

Weavers A38

Design: 10fr, Embroiderer (vert.). 20fr, Nurse, mother and infant. 30fr, Laundress (vert.). 50fr, Seamstresses.

1967, July 3 Engr. *Perf. 13*

232 A38 5fr plum, blk & cl 15 15
233 A38 10fr plum, brt grn & blk 15 15
234 A38 20fr brt bl, plum & blk 15 15
235 A38 30fr dk bl, brn & blk 20 15
236 A38 50fr plum, sl & blk 35 16
Set value 80 45

Progress made by working women.

Cattle and Hypodermic Syringe A39

1967, Aug. 21 Engr. *Perf. 13*

237 A39 30fr sl grn, brt bl & rose cl 20 15

Campaign against cattle plague.

Monetary Union Issue
Common Design Type

1967, Nov. 4 Engr. *Perf. 13*

238 CD125 30fr gray & org 30 15

Fruit of Doom Palm — A40

Human Rights Flame — A41

Fruit: 2fr, Bito (horiz.). 3fr, Baobab. 4fr, Jujube (horiz.). 5fr, Date.

1967, Dec. 4 Engr. *Perf. 13*

239 A40 1fr brt grn, bis & red brn 15 15
240 A40 2fr brn, red, yel & brt grn 15 15
241 A40 3fr pur, brt grn & ol 15 15
242 A40 4fr dk brn, brt grn & dk car rose 15 15
243 A40 5fr emer, org & brn 15 15
Set value 26 24

1968, Jan. 8 Photo. *Perf. 13x12½*

244 A41 30fr brt grn, blk & yel 25 15
245 A41 50fr brn org, blk & yel 40 18

International Human Rights Year.

Nouakchott Mosque A42

Designs: 45fr, Amogjar Pass. 90fr, Cavaliers' Towers.

1968, Apr. 1 Photo. *Perf. 12½x13*

246 A42 30fr multi 20 15
247 A42 45fr multi 25 15
248 A42 90fr multi 55 25

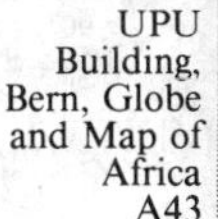

UPU Building, Bern, Globe and Map of Africa A43

1968, June 3 Engr. *Perf. 13*

249 A43 30fr ver, ultra & ol 20 15

Mauritania's admission to the UPU.

Symbolic Water Cycle — A44

1968, June 24

250 A44 90fr car, lake, grn & sl grn 55 30

Hydrological Decade (UNESCO), 1965-74.

Land Yacht Racing — A45

Donkey and Foal — A46

Designs: 40fr, Three land yachts racing (horiz.). 60fr, Crew changing wheel of land yacht.

1968, Oct. 7 Engr. *Perf. 13*

251 A45 30fr ultra, org & ocher 20 15
252 A45 40fr ultra, dp org & plum 25 15
253 A45 60fr brt grn, dp org & ocher 40 18

1968, Dec. 16 Photo. *Perf. 13*

Domestic Animals: 10fr, Ewe and lamb. 15fr, Camel and calf. 30fr, Mare and foal. 50fr, Cow and calf. 90fr, Goat and kid.

254 A46 5fr ocher & multi 15 15
255 A46 10fr multi 15 15
256 A46 15fr multi 15 15
257 A46 30fr multi 20 15
258 A46 50fr pur & multi 30 15
259 A46 90fr multi 55 30
Set value 1.25 70

ILO Emblem and Map A47

Desert Monitor A48

1969, Apr. 14 Photo. *Perf. 13x12½*

260 A47 50fr dk & lt bl, pur & org 42 16

ILO, 50th anniversary.

1969, May 5 Photo. *Perf. 13x12½*

Reptiles: 10fr, Horned viper. 30fr, Common spitting cobra. 60fr, Rock python. 85fr, African crocodile.

261 A48 5fr brn, pink & yel 15 15
262 A48 10fr brn, lt grn & yel 16 15
263 A48 30fr dk brn, pink & yel 25 15
264 A48 60fr dk brn, lt bl & yel 45 25
265 A48 85fr dk brn, yel & red 65 45
Nos. 261-265 (5) 1.66 1.15

Lady Beetle Eating Noxious Insects A49

1969, May 26 Engr. *Perf. 13*

266 A49 30fr ind, grn & mar 25 15

Natural protection of date palms.

Development Bank Issue
Common Design Type

1969, Sept. 10 Engr. *Perf. 13*

267 CD130 30fr Prus bl, grn & ocher 22 15

Pendant — A50

Design: 20fr, Rahla headdress (horiz.).

1969, Oct. 13 Engr. *Perf. 13*

268 A50 10fr dk brn, lil & brn 15 15
269 A50 20fr blk, Prus bl & mag 16 15
Set value 24 15

Desalination Plant — A51

Designs: 15fr, Fishing harbor, Nouadhibou. 30fr, Meat refrigeration plant, Kaedi.

1969, Dec. 1 Engr. *Perf. 13*

270 A51 10fr brt rose lil, dk bl & red brn 15 15
271 A51 15fr dk car, blk & dp bl 15 15
272 A51 30fr blk, dk bl & rose brn 20 15
Set value 36 25

Issued to publicize economic progress.

Lenin (1870-1924) A52

Sternocera Interrupta A53

1970, Feb. 16 Photo. *Perf. 12x12½*

273 A52 30fr car, lt bl & blk 22 15

1970, Mar. 16 Engr. *Perf. 13*

Insects: 10fr, Anoplocnemis curvipes. 20fr, Julodis aequinoctialis. 30fr, Thermophilum sexmaculatum marginatum. 40fr, Plocaederus denticornis.

274 A53 5fr red brn, buff & blk 15 15
275 A53 10fr red brn, yel & brn 15 15
276 A53 20fr red brn, lil & dk ol 15 15
277 A53 30fr red brn, grn & vio 20 15
278 A53 40fr red brn, lt bl & brn 25 16
Set value 70 42

Soccer Players and Hemispheres A54

Designs: Hemispheres and various views of soccer play.

1970, May 11 Engr. *Perf. 13*

279 A54 25fr bl, vio bl & dk brn 16 15
280 A54 30fr vio bl, brn & ol brn 20 15
281 A54 70fr brt pink, mar & dk brn 40 22
282 A54 150fr brn red, grn & dk brn 90 50

Issued to publicize the 9th World Soccer Championships for the Jules Rimet Cup, Mexico City, May 29-June 21.

UPU Headquarters Issue
Common Design Type

1970, May 20 Engr. *Perf. 13*

283 CD133 30fr grn, dk brn & red brn 20 15

Woman Wearing "Boubou" — A55

Various Traditional Costumes: 30fr, 70fr, Men. 40fr, 50fr, Women.

1970, Sept. 21 Engr. *Perf. 12½x13*

284 A55 10fr red brn & org 15 15
285 A55 30fr ol, red brn & ind 16 15
286 A55 40fr red brn, plum & dk brn 25 15
287 A55 50fr dk brn & brt bl 30 16
288 A55 70fr bl, brn & dk brn 40 20
Nos. 284-288 (5) 1.26
Set value 65

People of Various Races — A55a

Design: 40fr, Outstretched hands (vert.).

1971, Mar. 22 Engr. *Perf. 13*

288A A55a 30fr brn vio, ol & brt bl 20 15
288B A55a 40fr brn red, bl & blk 22 15
Set value 24

Intl. year against racial discrimination.

Gen. Charles de Gaulle (1890-1970), President of France A56

Design: 100fr, De Gaulle as President.

1971, June 18 Photo. *Perf. 13*

289 A56 40fr gold, blk & grnsh bl 40 40
290 A56 100fr lt bl, gold & blk 1.10 1.10
a. Souvenir sheet of 2, #289-290 1.90 1.90

Iron Ore Freight Train of Miferma Mines
A57 A58

1971, Nov. 8 Photo. *Perf. 12½x12*
291 A57 35fr bl & multi 25 15
292 A58 100fr bl & multi 70 40

Nos. 291-292 printed se-tenant.

UNICEF Emblem and Child A59

1971, Dec. 11 Litho. *Perf. 13½*
293 A59 35fr lt ultra, blk & brn 22 15

UNICEF, 25th anniv.

Samuel F. B. Morse and Telegraph — A60

Designs: 40fr, Relay satellite over globes. 75fr, Alexander Graham Bell.

1972, May 17 Engr. *Perf. 13*
294 A60 35fr lil, ind & vio 25 15
295 A60 40fr bl, ocher & choc 28 16
296 A60 75fr grn, ol grn & Prus bl 45 25

4th World Telecommunications Day.

Fossil Spirifer Shell — A61

1972, July 31 Litho. *Perf. 12½*
297 A61 25fr shown 16 15
298 A61 75fr Phacops rana 42 30

Fossil shells.

West African Monetary Union Issue
Common Design Type

1972, Nov. 2 Engr. *Perf. 13*
299 CD136 35fr brn, yel grn & gray 22 15

Mediterranean Monk Seal and Pup — A63

1973, Feb. 28 Litho. *Perf. 13*
300 A63 40fr multi 30 16

See No. C130.

Food Program Symbols and Emblem A64

1973, Apr. 30 Photo. *Perf. 12x12½*
301 A64 35fr gray bl & multi 22 15

World Food Program, 10th anniversary.

UPU Monument and Globe A65

1973, May 28 Engr. *Perf. 13*
302 A65 100fr grn, ocher & bl 65 50

Universal Postal Union Day.

Currency Change to Ouguiya ("um")

No. 258 Surcharged with New Value, 2 Bars, and Overprinted: "SECHERESSE / SOLIDARITE / AFRICAINE"

1973, Aug. 16 Photo. *Perf. 13*
303 A46 20um on 50fr multi 60 38

African solidarity in drought emergency.

African Postal Union Issue
Common Design Type

1973, Sept. 12 Engr. *Perf. 13*
304 CD137 20um org, brn & ocher 60 38

INTERPOL Emblem, Detective, Criminal, Fingerprint A66

1973, Sept. 24
305 A66 15um brn, ver & vio 50 30

50th anniv. of Intl. Criminal Police Org.

Nos. 297-298, 300 and 268-269 Surcharged with New Value and Two Bars in Ultramarine, Red or Black

1973-74 Litho. *Perf. 12½*
306 A61 5um on 25fr (U) ('74) 16 15
307 A63 8um on 40fr (R) 25 15
308 A61 15um on 75fr (U) ('74) 45 25

Engr.
Perf. 13
309 A50 27um on 10fr (B) ('74) 70 38
310 A50 28um on 20fr (R) ('74) 80 42
Nos. 306-310 (5) 2.36 1.35

Nos. 274-278 Surcharged with New Value and Two bars in Violet Blue or Red

1974, July 29 Engr. *Perf. 13*
311 A53 5um on 5fr 16 15
312 A53 7um on 10fr 22 15
313 A53 8um on 20fr 22 16
314 A53 10um on 30fr (R) 35 20
315 A53 20um on 40fr 65 40
Nos. 311-315 (5) 1.60 1.06

UPU Emblem and Globes — A67

1974, Aug. 5 Photo. *Perf. 13*
316 A67 30um multi 90 65
317 A67 50um multi 1.50 90

Centenary of Universal Postal Union.

5-Ouguiya Coin and Bank Note — A68

Designs: 8um, 10-ouguiya coin. 20um, 20-ouguiya coin. Each design includes picture of different bank note.

1974, Aug. 12 Engr.
318 A68 7um blk, ultra & grn 20 15
319 A68 8um blk, sl grn & mag 22 15
320 A68 20um blk, red & bl 60 35
Set value 52

First anniversary of currency reform.

Nos. 316-317 Overprinted in Red: "9 OCTOBRE / 100 ANS D'UNION POSTALE / INTERNATIONALE"

1974, Oct. 9 Photo. *Perf. 13*
321 A67 30um multi 90 50
322 A67 50um multi 1.50 65

Centenary of Universal Postal Union.

Nos. 239-243 Surcharged with New Value and Two Bars in Black or Violet Blue

1975, Feb. 14 Engr. *Perf. 13*
323 A40 1um on 5fr multi (B) 15 15
324 A40 2um on 4fr multi (VB) 15 15
325 A40 3um on 2fr multi (B) 15 15
326 A40 10um on 1fr multi (B) 30 15
327 A40 12um on 3fr multi (VB) 35 15
Set value 85 40

Hunters, Rock Carvings — A69

White and Black Men, Map of Europe and Africa — A70

Rock Carvings from Zemmour Cave: 5um, Ostrich. 10um, Elephant (horiz.).

1975, May 26 Engr. *Perf. 13*
328 A69 4um lt brn & car 15 15
329 A69 5um red lil 16 15
330 A69 10um blue 30 16
Set value 28

Europafrica Issue

1975, July 7 Engr. *Perf. 13*
331 A70 40um dk brn & red 1.20 70

Nos. 247-248 Surcharged in Red or Black

15UM

SECHERESSE SOLIDARITE
AFRICAINE

1975, Aug. 25 Photo. *Perf. 12½x13*
332 A42 15um on 45fr (R) 42 30
333 A42 25um on 90fr 70 50

African solidarity in drought emergency.

Map of Africa with Mauritania, Akjoujt Blast Furnace, Camel — A71

Fair Emblem — A72

Design: 12um, Snim emblem, furnace, dump truck, excavator.

1975, Sept. 22 Engr. *Perf. 13*
334 A71 10um brt bl, choc & org 30 16
335 A71 12um brt bl & multi 38 20

Mining and industry: Somima (Société Minière de Mauritanie) and Snim (Société Nationale Industrielle et Minière).

1975, Oct. 5 Litho. *Perf. 12*
336 A72 10um multi 30 15

National Nouakchott Fair, Nov. 28-Dec. 7.

Commemorative Medal — A73

Design: 12um, Map of Mauritania (vert.).

1975, Nov. 28 Litho. *Perf. 12*
337 A73 10um sil & multi 30 15
338 A73 12um grn, yel & grn 38 20

15th anniversary of independence.

Docked Space Ships and Astronauts — A74

Docked Space Ships and: 10um, Soyuz rocket launch.

1975, Dec. 29 Litho. *Perf. 14*
339 A74 8um multi 30 16
340 A74 10um multi 38 20
Nos. 339-340,C156-C158 (5) 3.68 1.88

Apollo Soyuz space test project, Russo-American cooperation, launched July 15, link-up July 17, 1975.

French Legion Infantryman A75

Uniform: 10um, Green Mountain Boy.

1976, Jan. 26 *Perf. 13½x14*

341 A75 8um multi 25 15
342 A75 10um multi 30 15
Nos. 341-342,C160-C162 (5) 3.80 1.60

American Bicentennial.

10e ANNIVERSAIRE DE LA
CHARTE ARABE DU TRAVAIL

No. 296
Surcharged

12UM

1976, Mar. 1 **Engr.** *Perf. 13*

343 A60 12um on 75fr multi 35 16

Arab Labor Charter, 10th anniversary.

Map of Mauritania with Spanish Sahara Incorporated — A76

1976, Mar. 15 **Litho.** *Perf. 13x12½*

344 A76 10um grn & multi 30 16

Reunified Mauritania, Feb. 29, 1976.

LZ-4 over Hangar — A77

75th anniv. of the Zeppelin: 10um, Dr. Hugo Eckener and "Schwaben" (LZ-10). 12um, "Hansa" (LZ-13) over Heligoland. 20um, "Bodensee" (LZ-120) and Dr. Ludwig Dürr.

1976, June 28 **Litho.** *Perf. 11*

345 A77 5um multi 18 15
346 A77 10um multi 38 18
347 A77 12um multi 42 22
348 A77 20um multi 70 30
Nos. 345-348,C167-C168 (6) 5.08 2.30

Mohenjo-Daro — A78

1976, Sept. 6 **Litho.** *Perf. 12*

349 A78 15um multi 42 20

UNESCO campaign to save Mohenjo-Daro excavations, Pakistan.

A. G. Bell, Telephone and Satellite — A79

1976, Oct. 11 **Engr.** *Perf. 13*

350 A79 10um bl, car & red 30 16

Centenary of first telephone call by Alexander Graham Bell, Mar. 10, 1876.

Mohammed Ali Jinnah (1876-1948), Governor General of Pakistan — A80

1976, Dec. 25 **Litho.** *Perf. 13*

351 A80 10um multi 30 16

NASA Control Room, Houston — A81

Design: 12um, Viking components (vert.).

1977, Feb. 28 *Perf. 14*

352 A81 10um multi 35 15
353 A81 12um multi 42 20
Nos. 352-353,C173-C175 (5) 3.97 1.77

Viking Mars project.

Jackals — A82

Designs: 5um, Wild rabbits. 12um, Wart-hogs. 14um, Lions. 15um, Elephants.

1977, Mar. 14 **Litho.** *Perf. 12½*

354 A82 5um multi 15 15
355 A82 10um multi 30 16
356 A82 12um multi 38 20
357 A82 14um multi 40 20
358 A82 15um multi 45 20
Nos. 354-358 (5) 1.68 91

Irene and Frederic Joliot-Curie, Chemistry — A83

Nobel prize winners: 15um, Emil A. von Bering, medicine.

1977, Apr. 29 **Litho.** *Perf. 14*

359 A83 12um multi 40 20
360 A83 15um multi 45 25
Nos. 359-360,C177-C179 (5) 3.92 1.90

APU Emblem, Member's Flags — A84

1977, May 30 **Photo.** *Perf. 13*

361 A84 12um multi 38 20

Arab Postal Union, 25th anniversary.

Oil Lamp — A85

Tegdaoust Pottery: 2um, 4-handled pot. 5um, Large jar. 12um, Jug with filter.

1977, June 13 **Engr.** *Perf. 13*

362 A85 1um multi 15 15
363 A85 2um multi 15 15
364 A85 5um multi 15 15
365 A85 12um multi 38 18
Set value 64 32

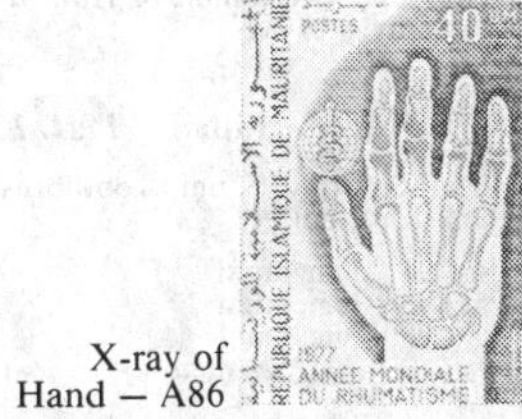

X-ray of Hand — A86

1977, June 27 **Engr.** *Perf. 12½x13*

366 A86 40um multi 1.20 65

World Rheumatism Year.

Charles Lindbergh and "Spirit of St. Louis" — A87

History of aviation: 14um, Clement Ader and "Eole!" 15um, Louis Bleriot over channel. 55um, Italo Balbo and seaplanes. 60um, Concorde. 100um, Charles Lindbergh and "Spirit of St. Louis."

1977, Sept. 19

367 A87 12um multi 40 20
368 A87 14um multi 42 20
369 A87 15um multi 45 25
370 A87 55um multi 1.75 80
371 A87 60um multi 1.90 90
Nos. 367-371 (5) 4.92 2.35

Souvenir Sheet

372 A87 100um multi 3.00 1.75

Dome of the Rock, Jerusalem — A88

1977, Oct. 31 **Litho.** *Perf. 12½*

373 A88 12um multi 38 20
374 A88 14um multi 40 22

Palestinian fighters and their families.

Soccer and Emblems — A89

Emblems and: 14um, Alf Ramsey and stadium. 15um, Players and goalkeeper.

1977, Dec. 19 **Litho.** *Perf. 13½*

375 A89 12um multi 40 18
376 A89 14um multi 45 22
377 A89 15um multi 50 22
Nos. 375-377,C182-C183 (5) 4.05 1.77

Elimination Games for World Cup Soccer Championship, Argentina, 1978.

Helen Fourment and her Children, by Rubens A90

Paintings by Peter Paul Rubens (1577-1640): 14um, Knight in armor. 67um, Three Burghers. 69um, Landscape (horiz.). 100um, Rubens with wife and son.

1977, Dec. 26

378 A90 12um multi 40 18
379 A90 14um multi 45 25
380 A90 67um multi 2.25 80
381 A90 69um multi 2.25 80

Souvenir Sheet

382 A90 100um gold & multi 3.75 1.60

Sable Antelope and Wildlife Fund Emblem — A91

Endangered Animals: 12um, Gazelles (vert.). 14um, Manatee. 55um, Aoudad (vert.). 60um, Elephant. 100um, Ostrich (vert.).

1978, Feb. 28 Litho. *Perf. 13½x14*

383 A91	5um multi	18	15
384 A91	12um multi	40	16
385 A91	14um multi	42	20
386 A91	55um multi	1.75	62
387 A91	60um multi	1.90	65
388 A91	100um multi	3.25	1.10
	Nos. 383-388 (6)	7.90	2.88

Soccer and Games' Emblem — A92

Designs: 14um, Rimet Cup. 20um, Soccer ball and F.I.F.A. flag. 50um, Soccer ball and Rimet Cup (horiz.).

1978, June 26 Photo. *Perf. 13*

389 A92	12um multi	40	16
390 A92	14um multi	45	20
391 A92	20um multi	65	25

Souvenir Sheet

392 A92	50um multi	1.75	1.00

11th World Cup Soccer Championship, Argentina, June 1-25.

Raoul Follereau and St. George Slaying Dragon — A93

1978, Sept. 4 Engr. *Perf. 13*

393 A93	12um brn & dp grn	40	16

25th anniversary of the Raoul Follereau Anti-Leprosy Foundation.

Anti-Apartheid Emblem, Fenced-in People — A94

Design: 30um, Anti-Apartheid emblem and free people (vert.).

1978, Oct. 9

394 A94	25um bl, red & brn	80	38
395 A94	30um grn, bl & brn	1.00	42

Anti-Apartheid Year.

Charles de Gaulle A95

Portraits: 14um, King Baudouin. 55um, Queen Elizabeth II.

1978, Oct. 16 Litho. *Perf. 12½x12*

396 A95	12um multi	40	16
397 A95	14um multi	45	20
398 A95	55um multi	1.90	80

Rulers who helped in de-colonization. No. 398 also commemorates 25th anniversary of coronation of Queen Elizabeth II.

Nos. 375-377 Overprinted in Arabic and French in Silver: "ARGENTINE- / PAYS BAS 3-1"

1978, Dec. 11 Litho. *Perf. 13½*

399 A89	12um multi	40	16
400 A89	14um multi	45	20
401 A89	15um multi	50	20
	Nos. 399-401,C187-C188 (5)	4.10	1.71

Argentina's victory in World Cup Soccer Championship 1978.

View of Nouakchott — A96

1978, Dec. 18 Litho. *Perf. 12*

402 A96	12um multi	40	16

20th anniversary of Nouakchott.

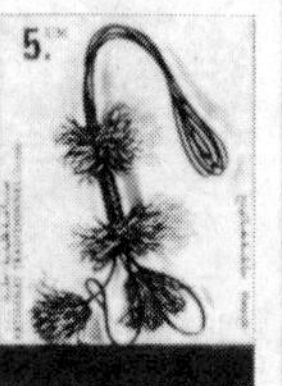

Flame Emblem — A97 Leather Key Holder — A98

1978, Dec. 26 *Perf. 12½*

403 A97	55um ultra & red	1.90	80

Universal Declaration of Human Rights, 30th anniv.

1979, Feb. 5 Litho. *Perf. 13½x14*

Leather Craft: 7um, Toothbrush case. 10um, Knife holder.

404 A98	5um multi	16	15
405 A98	7um multi	22	15
406 A98	10um multi	35	16
	Set value		35

Farmers at Market, by Dürer A99

Engravings by Albrecht Durer (1471-1528): 14um, Young Peasant and Wife. 55um, Mercenary with flag. 60um, St. George Slaying Dragon. 100um, Mercenaries (horiz.).

Litho.; Red Foil Embossed

1979, May 3 *Perf. 13½x14*

407 A99	12um blk, *buff*	40	20
408 A99	14um blk, *buff*	45	22
409 A99	55um blk, *buff*	1.90	90
410 A99	60um blk, *buff*	2.00	1.10

Souvenir Sheet

Perf. 14x13½

411 A99	100um blk, *buff*	3.50	1.60

Buddha, Borobudur Temple and UNESCO Emblem — A100

UNESCO Emblem and: 14um, Hunter on horseback, Carthage. 55um, Caryatid, Acropolis.

1979, May 14 Photo. *Perf. 12½*

412 A100	12um multi	40	20
413 A100	14um multi	45	22
414 A100	55um multi	1.90	90

Preservation of art treasures with help from UNESCO.

Paddle Steamer Sirius, Rowland Hill — A101

Sir Rowland Hill (1795-1879), originator of penny postage, and: 14um, Paddle steamer Great Republic. 55um, S.S. Mauritania. 60um, M.S. Stirling Castle. 100um, Mauritania No. 8.

1979, June 4 Litho. *Perf. 13½x14*

415 A101	12um multi	50	22
416 A101	14um multi	65	30
417 A101	55um multi	2.25	1.20
418 A101	60um multi	2.50	1.40

Souvenir Sheet

419 A101	100um multi	3.50	2.00

Embossed Leather Cushion — A102

Design: 30um, Satellite, jet, ship, globe and UPU emblem (vert.).

1979, June 8 Litho. *Perf. 12½*

420 A102	12um multi	40	22

Engr.

Perf. 13

421 A102	30um multi	1.00	55

Philexafrique II, Libreville, Gabon, June 8-17. Nos. 420, 421 each printed in sheets of 10 and 5 labels showing exhibition emblem.

Mother and Children, IYC Emblem — A103

1979, Oct. 2 Litho. *Perf. 12½*

422 A103	12um multi	40	20
423 A103	14um multi	45	22
424 A103	40um multi	1.40	65

International Year of the Child

Nos. 352-353 Overprinted in Silver: "ALUNISSAGE / APOLLO XI / JUILLET 1969" and Emblem

1979, Oct. 24 Litho. *Perf. 14*

425 A81	10um multi	35	16
426 A81	12um multi	40	20
	Nos. 425-426,C192-C194 (5)	3.85	1.94

Apollo 11 moon landing, 10th anniversary.

Runner, Moscow '80 Emblem A104

Moscow '80 Emblem and: 14um, 55um, 100um, Running (diff.). 60um, Hurdles.

1979, Oct. 26 Litho. *Perf. 13½*

427 A104	12um multi	40	20
428 A104	14um multi	45	22
429 A104	55um multi	1.90	90
430 A104	60um multi	2.00	1.00

Souvenir Sheet

431 A104	100um multi	3.50	3.50

Pre-Olympic Year.

Scomberesox Saurus Walbaum — A104a

1979, Nov. 12 Photo. *Perf. 14*

431A A104a	1um shown	15	15
431B A104a	5um Trigla lucerna	16	15
	Set value	20	15

Ice Hockey, Lake Placid '80 Emblem A105

Lake Placid '80 Emblem and various ice hockey plays.

1979, Dec. 6 Litho. *Perf. 14½*

432 A105	10um multi	35	15
433 A105	12um multi	40	20
434 A105	14um multi	45	25
435 A105	55um multi	1.90	90
436 A105	60um multi	2.00	1.10
437 A105	100um multi	3.50	1.60
	Nos. 432-437 (6)	8.60	4.20

13th Winter Olympic Games. Lake Placid, NY, Feb. 12-24, 1980.

Arab Achievements — A106

1980, Mar. 22 Litho. *Perf. 13*

438	A106	12um multi	40	20
439	A106	15um multi	50	25

Nos. 432-437 Overprinted:
a. Medaille / de bronze / SUÈDE
b. MÉDAILLE / DE BRONZE / SUÈDE
c. Medaille / d'argent / U.R.S.S.
d. MÉDAILLE / D'ARGENT/ U.R.S.S.
e. MÉDAILLE / D'OR / ÉTATS-UNIS
f. Medaille / d'or / ÉTATS-UNIS

1980, June 14 Litho. *Perf. 14½*

440	A105(a)	10um multi	35	15
441	A105(b)	12um multi	40	20
442	A105(c)	14um multi	45	25
443	A105(d)	55um multi	1.90	90
444	A105(e)	60um multi	2.00	1.10
445	A105(f)	100um multi	3.50	1.75
		Nos. 440-445 (6)	8.60	4.35

Equestrian, Olympic Rings — A107

Designs: Equestrian scenes. 10um, 20um, 70um, 100um, vert.

1980, June Litho. *Perf. 14*

446	A107	10um multi	35	15
447	A107	20um multi	65	30
448	A107	50um multi	1.60	70
449	A107	70um multi	2.25	1.00

Souvenir Sheet

450	A107	100um multi	3.50	1.50

22nd Summer Olympic Games, Moscow, July 19-Aug. 3.

Armed Forces Day — A108

1980, July 9 *Perf. 13x12½*

451	A108	12um multi	40	20
452	A108	14um multi	45	25

World Red Cross Day — A109

1980, June 14 *Perf. 13*

453	A109	20um multi	65	30

Pilgrimage to Mecca — A110

Design: 50um, Mosque, outside view.

1980

454	A110	10um multi	35	15
455	A110	50um multi	1.60	70

Man with Turban, by Rembrandt A111

Rembrandt Paintings: 10um, Self-portrait. 20um, His mother. 70um, His son Titus reading. 100um, Polish knight (horiz.).

1980, July Litho. *Perf. 12½*

456	A111	10um multi	35	15
457	A111	20um multi	65	30
458	A111	50um multi	1.60	70
459	A111	70um multi	2.25	1.00

Souvenir Sheet

460	A111	100um multi	3.50	3.50

Tea Time A112

1980, Mar. 11 Litho. *Perf. 12½*

460A	A112	1um multi	15	15
461	A112	5um multi	16	15
462	A112	12um multi	40	20
		Set value	60	32

Arbor Day — A113

1980, Aug. 29

463	A113	12um multi	40	20

Nos. 446-450 Overprinted with Winner and Country

1980, Oct. Litho. *Perf. 14*

464	A107	10um multi	35	15
465	A107	20um multi	65	30
466	A107	50um multi	1.60	70
467	A107	70um multi	2.25	1.00

Souvenir Sheet

468	A107	100um multi	3.50	1.50

Mastodont Locomotive, 1850 — A114

Designs: Various locomotives.

1980, Nov. *Perf. 12½*

469	A114	10um shown	35	15
470	A114	12um Iron ore train	40	20
471	A114	14um Chicago-Milwaukee line, 1900	45	25
472	A114	20um Bury, 1837	65	30
473	A114	67um Reseau North line, 1870	2.25	1.00
474	A114	100um Potsdam, 1840	3.50	1.40
		Nos. 469-474 (6)	7.60	3.30

20th Anniversary of Independence — A115

1980, Nov. 27 *Perf. 13*

475	A115	12um multi	40	20
476	A115	15um multi	50	22

El Haram Mosque — A116

1981, Apr. 13 Litho. *Perf. 12½*

477	A116	2um shown	15	15
478	A116	12um Medina Mosque	40	20
479	A116	14um Chinguetti Mosque	45	25
		Set value		50

Hegira, 1500th anniversary.

Prince Charles and Lady Diana, Coach A117

Designs: Coaches.

1981, July 8 Litho. *Perf. 14½*

480	A117	14um multi	35	35
481	A117	18um multi	45	45
482	A117	77um multi	1.90	1.10

Souvenir Sheet

483	A117	100um multi	5.00	2.50

Royal wedding.

Intl. Year of the Disabled A119

1981, June 29 Litho. *Perf. 13x13½*

486	A119	12um multi	40	20

Battle of Yorktown Bicentenary (American Revolution) — A120

1981, Oct. 5 *Perf. 12½*

487	A120	14um George Washington, vert.	45	22
488	A120	18um Admiral de Grasse, vert.	60	30
489	A120	63um Surrender of Cornwallis	2.00	1.10
490	A120	81um Battle of Chesapeake Bay	2.50	1.40

450th Death Anniv. of Christopher Columbus (1451-1506) — A121

1981, Oct. 5

491	A121	19um Pinta	62	32
492	A121	55um Santa Maria	1.90	90

World Food Day — A122

Kemal Ataturk Birth Cent. — A123

1981, Oct. 16 *Perf. 13*

493	A122	19um multi	62	32

1981, Oct. 29 *Perf. 12½*

494	A123	63um multi	2.00	1.10

Scouting Year — A124

Designs: Boating scenes. 92um vert.

1982, Jan. 20 Litho. *Perf. 12½*

495	A124	14um multi	45	22
496	A124	19um multi	62	32
497	A124	22um multi	70	40
498	A124	92um multi	3.00	1.25

Souvenir Sheet

Perf. 13

499	A124	100um Baden-Powell, scout	3.50	1.60

75th Anniv. of Grand Prix — A125

Designs: Winners and their Cars.

1982, Jan. 23 *Perf. 13½*

500	A125	7um Deusenberg, 1921	22	15
501	A125	12um Alfa Romeo, 1932	40	20
502	A125	14um Juan Fangio, 1949	45	22
503	A125	18um Renault, 1979	60	30

504 A125 19um Niki Lauda, 1974 62 32
Nos. 500-504 (5) 2.29 1.19

Souvenir Sheet

505 A125 100um Race 3.50 1.60

Birds of the Arguin Bank
A126

1981, Dec. 17 Photo. *Perf. 13*
506 A126 2um White pelicans 15 15
507 A126 18um Pink flamingoes 60 30
Set value 35

Battle of Karameh
A127

1982, Dec. 19 Litho.
508 A127 14um Hand holding tattered flag 45 22

Deluth Turtle — A128

APU, 30th Anniv. — A129

Designs: Sea turtles.

1981, Dec. 21 Photo. *Perf. 14x13½*
509 A128 1um shown 15 15
510 A128 3um Green turtle 15 15
511 A128 4um Shell turtle 15 15
Set value 28 16

1982, May 14 Litho. *Perf. 13*
512 A129 14um org & brn 45 22

14th World Telecommunications Day — A130

1982, May 17 Photo. *Perf. 13½x13*
513 A130 21um multi 70 35

15-Cent Minimum Value
The minimum value for a single stamp is 15 cents. This value reflects the costs of the handlling of inexpensive stamps.

UN Conference on Human Environment, 10th Anniv. — A131

1982, June 7 Litho. *Perf. 12½*
514 A131 14um grnsh bl 45 22

21st Birthday of Princess Diana of Wales — A132

Portraits.

1982, July *Perf. 14x13½*
515 A132 21um multi 70 35
516 A132 77um multi 2.50 1.10

Souvenir Sheet

517 A132 100um multi 3.50 1.60

Nos. 480-483 Overprinted in Blue: "NAISSANCE ROYALE 1982"

1982, Aug. 2 *Perf. 14½*
518 A117 14um multi 45 22
519 A117 18um multi 60 30
520 A117 77um multi 2.50 1.20

Souvenir Sheet

521 A117 100um multi 3.50 1.60

Birth of Prince William of Wales, June 21.

Manned Flight Bicentenary
A133

1982, Dec. 29 Litho. *Perf. 14*
522 A133 14um Montgolfiere balloon, 1783, vert. 45 22
523 A133 18um Hydrogen balloon, 1783 60 30
524 A133 19um Zeppelin, vert. 62 32
525 A133 55um Nieuport plane 1.90 90
526 A133 63um Concorde 2.25 1.10
527 A133 77um Apollo II, vert. 2.50 1.10
Nos. 522-527 (6) 8.32 3.94

Preservation of Ancient Cities — A134

1983, Feb. 16 Litho. *Perf. 14x14½*
528 A134 14um City Wall, Ouadane 45 22
529 A134 18um Chinguetti 60 30
530 A134 24um Staircase, panels, Qualata 80 42
531 A134 30um Ruins, Tichitt 1.00 50

World Communications Year — A135

1983, June 21 Litho. *Perf. 13*
532 A135 14um multi 45 22

30th Anniv. of Customs Cooperation Council — A136

1983, June 25
533 A136 14um multi 45 22

Traditional Houses — A137

Ancient Manuscript Page — A138

1983, June 14 Photo. *Perf. 13½*
534 A137 14um Peule 38 18
535 A137 18um Toucouleur 50 25
536 A137 19um Tent 52 28

1983, June 15 Photo. *Perf. 12½x13*
537 A138 2um shown 15 15
538 A138 5um Ornamental scroll-work 15 15
539 A138 7um Sheath 18 15
Set value 36 22

Manned Flight Bicentenary — A139

Early Fliers and their Balloons or Dirigibles. 10um, 14um vert.

1983, Oct. 17 Litho. *Perf. 13½*
540 A139 10um F. Pilatre de Rozier 25 15
541 A139 14um John Wise 38 18
542 A139 25um Charles Renard 65 35
543 A139 100um Henri Julliot 2.50 1.40

Souvenir Sheet

544 A139 100um Joseph Montgolfier 2.50 1.40

No. 544 contains one stamp 47x37mm. Nos. 543-544 airmail.

Mortar — A140

Various prehistoric grinding implements.

1983, Dec. 28 Litho. *Perf. 13*
545 A140 10um multi 25 15
546 A140 14um multi 38 18
547 A140 18um multi 50 25

Pre-Olympics — A141

1983, Dec. 31 Litho. *Perf. 13½*
548 A141 1um Basketball 15 15
549 A141 20um Wrestling 25 15
550 A141 50um Equestrian 65 35
551 A141 77um Running 1.00 50

Souvenir Sheet

552 A141 100um Soccer 1.40 65

No. 552 contains one stamp 41x36mm. Nos. 551-552 airmail.

Scouting Year — A142

Artemis, by Rembrandt — A142a

Designs: 14um, Johann Wolfgang von Goethe. 25um, Virgin and Child, by Peter Paul Rubens.
No. 553C illustration reduced.

1984, Jan. 24
553 A142 5um Flag, Baden-Powell 15 15
553A A142 14um multicolored 22 15
553B A142 25um multicolored 35 16

Souvenir Sheet

553C A142a 100um multicolored 1.40 65

No. 553C is airmail and contains one 42x51mm stamp.

Sand Rose — A143

1984, Mar. Litho. *Perf. 14*
554 A143 21um multi 28 15

Inscribed 1982.

Anniversaries and Events — A145

1984, Apr. 26

555 A145 10um Albrecht Durer (1471-1528) 15 15
556 A145 12um Apollo XI, 15th anniv. 16 15
557 A145 50um Chess 65 35
Set value 50

1984, Apr. 16 Litho. *Perf. 13 1/2*

Designs: 77um, Prince Charles, Princess Diana. 100um, Prince Charles, Princess Diana (vert.).

557A A145 77um multi 1.50 70

Miniature Sheet

557B A145 100um multi 2.00 1.00

Nos. 557A-557B airmail.

Fishing Industry A146

1984

558 A146 1um Tuna 15 15
559 A146 2um Mackerel 15 15
560 A146 5um Haddock 15 15
561 A146 14um Black chinchard 18 15
562 A146 18um Boat building 25 15
Set value 55 35

Nouakchott Olympic Complex A148

1984, Sept. 26 Litho. *Perf. 13 1/2*

569 A148 14um multi 28 15

Infant Survival Campaign — A149

1984, Sept. 26 Litho. *Perf. 12 1/2*

570 A149 1um Feeding by glass 15 15
571 A149 4um Breastfeeding 15 15
572 A149 10um Vaccinating 20 15
573 A149 14um Weighing 28 15
Set value 60 35

Pilgrimage to Mecca — A150

1984, Oct. 3 Litho. *Perf. 13*

574 A150 14um Tents, mosque 28 15
575 A150 18um Tents, courtyard 38 18

10th Anniv., West African Union — A151

1984, Nov. Litho. *Perf. 13*

576 A151 14um Map of member nations 28 15

No. 355 Overprinted "Aide au Sahel 84" and Surcharged

1984 Litho. *Perf. 12 1/2*

577 A82 18um on 10um 38 18

Issued to publicize drought relief efforts.

Technical & Cultural Cooperation Agency, 15th Anniv. — A152

1985, Mar. 20 Litho. *Perf. 12 1/2*

578 A152 18um Profiles, emblem 35 16

League of Arab States, 40th Anniv. — A153

1985, May 7 *Perf. 13*

579 A153 14um brt yel grn & blk 28 15

German Railways 150th Anniv. — A154

Anniversaries and events: 12um, Adler, 1st German locomotive, 1835. 18um, Series 10, 1956, last Fed. German Railways locomotive. 44um, European Music Year, Johann Sebastian Bach, composer, and Angels Making Music, unattributed painting. 77um, George Frideric Handel. 90um, Statue of Liberty, cent., vert. 100um, Queen Mother, 85th birthday, vert.

1985, Sept.

580 A154 12um multi 22 15
581 A154 18um multi 35 16
582 A154 44um multi 80 40
583 A154 77um multi 1.50 80
584 A154 90um multi 1.60 80
Nos. 580-584 (5) 4.47 2.31

Souvenir Sheet

585 A154 100um multi 2.00 1.00

World Food Day — A155

1985, Oct. 16 *Perf. 13x12 1/2*

586 A155 18um multi 35 16

UN Food and Agriculture Org., 40th anniv.

Fight Against Drought A156

1985 Litho. *Perf. 13*

587 A156 14um Antelope 28 15
588 A156 18um Oasis 35 16

Fight Against Desert Encroachment — A157

1985

589 A157 10um Grain harvest, vert. 20 15
590 A157 14um Brush fire 28 15
591 A157 18um Planting brush 35 16
Set value 40

Natl. Independence, 25th Anniv. — A158

1985 *Perf. 15x14 1/2*

592 A158 18um multi 35 16

Intl. Youth Year A159

1986, Feb. 13 Litho. *Perf. 13*

593 A159 18um Development 15 15
594 A159 22um Participation 15 15
595 A159 25um Peace, vert. 15 15
Set value 35 18

Toujounine Satellite Station — A160

1986, May 22 Litho. *Perf. 12 1/2*

596 A160 25um multi 15 15

World Wildlife Fund — A161

Monk seal (Monachus monachus).

1986, June 12 *Perf. 13*

597 A161 2um multi 15 15
598 A161 5um multi 15 15
599 A161 10um multi 15 15
600 A161 18um multi 15 15
Set value 25 25

Souvenir Sheet

601 A161 50um multi 28 15

Weaving — A162

1986, July 20 Litho. *Perf. 12 1/2*

602 A162 18um multi 35 18

Sabra and Chatila Massacre, 4th Anniv. — A163

1986, Oct. 18

603 A163 22um multi 45 22

A164

Christopher Columbus — A165

Indians, maps on globe and: 2um, Santa Maria. 22um, Nina. 35um, Pinta. 150um, Columbus.

1986, Oct. 14 Litho. *Perf. 13½*

604 A164 2um multi 15 15
605 A164 22um multi 65 32
606 A164 35um multi 1.05 52
607 A164 150um multi 4.50 2.25

Souvenir Sheet

608 A165 100um Columbus, Earth 3.00 1.50

Nos. 607-608 are airmail.

US Space Shuttle Challenger Explosion, Jan. 28, 1986 — A166

Crew members and: 7um, Space shuttle. 22um, Canadarm. 32um, Sky, moon. 43um, Memorial emblem.

1986, Oct. 14

609 A166 7um multi 22 15
610 A166 22um multi 65 32
611 A166 32um multi 95 48
612 A166 43um multi 1.30 65

Souvenir Sheet

613 A166 100um Crew, lift-off 3.00 1.50

Nos. 612-613 are airmail.

Fish A167

1986, Oct. 16 *Perf. 13*

614 A167 4um Dorade 15 15
615 A167 98um Truite de mer 3.00 1.50

See Nos. 631-633.

Birds A168

1986, Oct. 16

616 A168 22um Spatule blanche 65 32
617 A168 32um Sterne bridee 95 48

See Nos. 634-635.

World Food Day — A169

1986, Nov. 6 *Perf. 12½*

618 A169 22um multi 65 32

A170

Halley's Comet — A171

Space probes and portraits: 5um, J.H. Dort, Giotto probe. 18um, Sir William Huggins (1824-1910), English astronomer, and launch of Giotto on Ariane rocket. 26um, E.J. Opik, Giotto and Vega. 80um, F.L. Whipple, Planet-A. 100um, Edmond Halley, Giotto.

1986, Oct. 14 Litho. *Perf. 13½*

619 A170 5um multi 15 15
620 A170 18um multi 30 15
621 A170 26um multi 40 20
622 A170 80um multi 1.25 60

Souvenir Sheet

623 A171 100um multi 2.00 1.00

Nos. 622-623 are airmail.

Jerusalem Day — A172

1987, May 21 Litho. *Perf. 13½*

624 A172 22um Dome of the Rock 65 32

Cordoue Mosque, 1200th Anniv. A173

1987, Sept. 5 Litho. *Perf. 13½*

625 A173 30um multi 1.10 55

Literacy Campaign A174

1987, Sept. 12

626 A174 18um Classroom 65 32
627 A174 22um Family reading, vert. 80 40

World Health Day — A175

1987, Oct. 1 *Perf. 13*

628 A175 18um multi 65 32

Natl. Population Census A176

1988, Aug. 21 Litho. *Perf. 13½*

629 A176 20um multi 60 30

WHO, 40th Anniv. — A177

Arab Scouting Movement, 75th Anniv. — A178

1988, Sept. 19 *Perf. 13*

630 A177 30um multi 90 45

Fish Type of 1986

1988, Sept. 10 Litho. *Perf. 13*

631 A167 1um Rascasse blanche 15 15
632 A167 7um Baliste 48 25
633 A167 15um Bonite a ventre raye 1.00 50

Bird Type of 1986

1988, Sept. 15

634 A168 18um Grand cormorant 1.20 60
635 A168 80um Royal tern 5.40 2.70

1988, Sept. 29 Litho. *Perf. 13*

636 A178 35um multi 1.15 58

1st Municipal Elections — A179

1988, Nov. 22 *Perf. 13½*

637 A179 20um Men casting ballots 65 32
638 A179 24um Woman casting ballot 78 40

Organization of African Unity, 25th Anniv. (in 1988) — A180

Intl. Fund for Agricultural Development, 10th Anniv. (in 1988) — A181

1988, Dec. 7 Litho. *Perf. 13*

639 A180 40um multi 1.30 65

1988, Dec. 15

640 A181 35um multi 1.15 58

Autonomy of Nouakchott (Amitie) Port, 1st Anniv. — A182

1988, Dec. 20 Litho. *Perf. 13*

641 A182 24um multi 78 40

French Revolution Bicent., PHILEXFRANCE '89 — A183

1989, July 7 Litho. *Perf. 13*

642 A183 35um multi 1.10 55

1990 World Cup Soccer Championships, Italy — A184

1989, July 17

643 A184 20um multi 60 30

Pilgrimage to Mecca A185

1989, Aug. 26 Litho. *Perf. 13½*

644 A185 20um Mosque 65 32

African Development Bank, 25th Anniv. — A186

1989, Sept. 2

645 A186 37um lt vio & blk 1.20 60

Tapestry — A187

1989, Oct. 1 ***Perf. 13***

646 A187 50um multicolored 1.60 80

Locusts, Moths and Ladybugs A188

1989, Dec. 29

647	A188	2um	*Heliothis armigera*	15	15
648	A188	5um	Locust	16	15
649	A188	6um	*Aphis gossypii*	20	15
650	A188	10um	*Agrotis ypsilon*	35	17
651	A188	20um	*Chilo*	68	35
652	A188	20um	Two locusts, egg case	68	35
653	A188	24um	Locusts emerging	80	40
654	A188	24um	*Plitella xylostella*	80	40
655	A188	30um	*Henosepilachna elaterii*	1.00	50
656	A188	40um	Locust flying	1.35	68
657	A188	42um	*Trichoplusia ni*	1.40	70
658	A188	88um	Locust, diff.	2.85	1.45
			Nos. 647-658 (12)	10.42	5.45

Revolt — A189

1989, Dec. 8 Litho. ***Perf. 13***

659 A189 35um multicolored 1.10 55

2nd Anniv. of the Palestinian Uprising and 1st anniv. of the declaration of a Palestinian State.

Maghreb Arab Union, 1st Anniv. — A190

Illustration reduced.

1990, Feb. 17 Litho. ***Perf. 13½***

660 A190 50um multicolored 1.35 65

Mineral Resources A191

1990, July 27 ***Perf. 11½***

661 A191 60um multicolored 1.65 85

Intl. Literacy Year — A192

1990, July 27

662 A192 60um multicolored 1.65 85

1992 Summer Olympics, Barcelona A193

1990 Litho. & Typo. ***Perf. 13½***

663	A193	5um	Equestrian	15	15
664	A193	50um	Archery	1.35	65
665	A193	60um	Hammer throw	1.65	85
666	A193	75um	Field hockey	2.00	1.00
667	A193	90um	Handball	2.50	1.25
668	A193	220um	Table tennis	6.00	3.00
			Nos. 663-668 (6)	13.65	6.90

Souvenir Sheet

669 A193 150um Runner 4.00 2.00

Nos. 668-669 airmail.

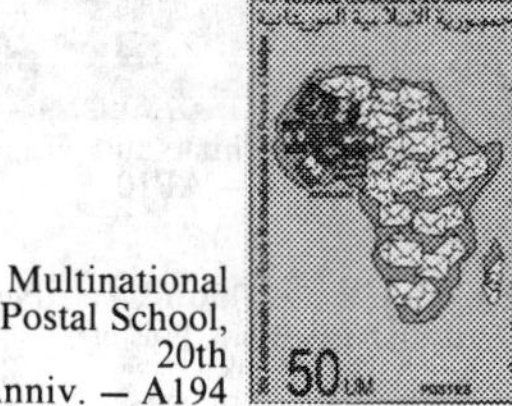

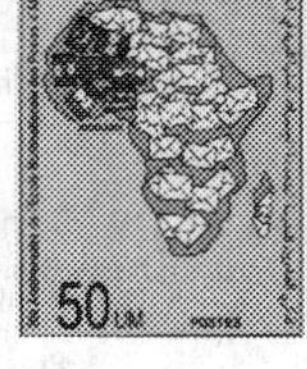

Multinational Postal School, 20th Anniv. — A194

1990 ***Perf. 11½***

670 A194 50um multicolored 1.35 65

Declaration of the Palestinian State, 2nd Anniv. — A195

1990, Nov. 21 Litho. ***Perf. 11½***

671 A195 85um multicolored 3.20 1.60

Release of Nelson Mandela A197

1990, Dec. 10

677 A197 85um multicolored 3.20 1.60

Return of Senegalese Refugees A198

1990, Dec. 10

678	A198	50um	Cooking at encampment	1.90	95
679	A198	75um	Women sewing	2.80	1.40
680	A198	85um	Drawing water	3.40	1.70

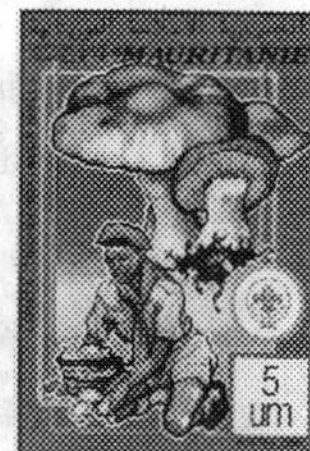

Boy Scouts Observing Nature — A199

Scout: 5um, Picking mushrooms. 50um, Holding mushroom. 60um, Drawing butterfly. 75um, Feeding butterfly. 90um, Photographing butterfly. 220um, Drying mushrooms. No. 687, Using microscope.

1991, Jan. 16 Litho. ***Perf. 13½***

681	A199	5um	multicolored	20	15
682	A199	50um	multicolored	1.90	95
683	A199	60um	multicolored	2.25	1.15
684	A199	75um	multicolored	2.80	1.40
685	A199	90um	multicolored	3.40	1.70
686	A199	220um	multicolored	8.25	4.15
			Nos. 681-686 (6)	18.80	9.50

Souvenir Sheet

687 A199 150um multicolored 5.85 2.95

Nos. 684 and 687 are airmail. Nos. 683-685 exist in souvenir sheets of 1.

Independence, 30th Anniv. — A200

1991, Mar. 5

688	A200	50um	Satellite dish antennae	1.90	95
689	A200	60um	Container ship	2.25	1.15
690	A200	100um	Harvesting rice	3.80	1.90

World Meteorology Day — A201

1991, Mar. 23 ***Perf. 14x15***

691 A201 100um multicolored 3.80 1.90

SEMI-POSTAL STAMPS

Nos. 23 and 26 Surcharged in Red

1915-18 Unwmk. ***Perf. 14x13½***

B1	A4	10c + 5c rose & red org	38	38
B2	A4	15c + 5c dk brn & blk ('18)	25	25

Curie Issue

Common Design Type

1938, Oct. 24 ***Perf. 13***

B3 CD80 1.75fr + 50c brt ultra 3.75 3.75

French Revolution Issue

Common Design Type

Photo.; Name and Value Typographed in Black

1939, July 5 Unwmk.

B4	CD83	45c + 25c grn	3.75	3.75
B5	CD83	70c + 30c brn	3.75	3.75
B6	CD83	90c + 35c red org	3.75	3.75
B7	CD83	1.25fr + 1fr rose pink	3.75	3.75
B8	CD83	2.25fr + 2fr bl	3.75	3.75
		Nos. B4-B8 (5)	18.75	18.75

Stamps of 1938 Surcharge in Red or Black

SECOURS + 1 fr. NATIONAL

1941

B9	A6	50c + 1fr pur (R)	80	80
B10	A7	80c + 2fr dp bl (R)	3.50	3.50
B11	A7	1.50fr + 2fr vio (R)	3.50	3.50
B12	A8	2fr + 3fr rose vio (Bk)	3.50	3.50

Common Design Type and

Moorish Goumier SP1

White Goumier SP2

1941 Photo. ***Perf. 13½***

B13	SP1	1fr + 1fr red	40
B14	CD86	1.50fr + 3fr claret	40
B15	SP2	2.50fr + 1fr blue	40

Nos. B13-B15 were issued by the Vichy government, and were not placed on sale in the colony.

Nos. 114-115 were surcharged "OEUVRES COLONIALES" and surtax (including change of denomination of the 2.50fr to 50c). These were issued in 1944 by the Vichy government and were not placed on sale in the colony.

Catalogue values for unused stamps in this section, from this point to the end of the section, are for Never Hinged items.

Islamic Republic
Anti-Malaria Issue
Common Design Type

1962, Apr. 7 Engr. *Perf. 12½x12*
B16 CD108 25fr + 5f lt ol grn 40 40

Freedom from Hunger Issue
Common Design Type

1963, Mar. 21 Unwmk. *Perf. 13*
B17 CD112 25fr + 5fr dp cl, dp bl & ocher 35 35

Nurse Tending Infant — SP3

1972, May 8 Photo. *Perf. 12½x13*
B18 SP3 35fr + 5fr grn, red & brn 25 25

Surtax was for Mauritania Red Crescent Society.

AIR POST STAMPS

Common Design Type
Perf. 12½x12

1940, Feb. 8 Engr. Unwmk.
C1 CD85 1.90fr ultra 20 20
C2 CD85 2.90fr dk red 20 20
C3 CD85 4.50fr dk gray grn 28 28
C4 CD85 4.90fr yel bis 60 60
C5 CD85 6.90fr dp org 60 60
Nos. C1-C5 (5) 1.88 1.88

Common Design Types

1942
C6 CD88 50c car & bl 15
C7 CD88 1fr brn & blk 16
C8 CD88 2fr dk grn & red brn 20
C9 CD88 3fr dk bl & scar 22
C10 CD88 5fr vio & brn red 30

Frame Engraved, Center Typo.
C11 CD89 10fr ultra, ind & hn 32
a. Center inverted *600.00*
C12 CD89 20fr rose car, mag & buff 35
C13 CD89 50fr yel grn, dl grn & org 45 1.00
Nos. C6-C13 (8) 2.15

There is doubt whether Nos. C6-C12 were officially placed in use.

Catalogue values for unused stamps in this section, from this point to the end of the section, are for Never Hinged items.

Islamic Republic

Flamingoes — AP1

Designs: 200fr, African spoonbills. 500fr, Slender-billed gull (horiz.).

A little time given to the study of the arrangement of the Scott Catalogue can make it easier to use effectively.

Unwmk.

1961, June 30 Engr. *Perf. 13*
C14 AP1 100fr red org, brn & ultra 1.40 90
C15 AP1 200fr red org, sep & sl grn 2.75 1.90
C16 AP1 500fr red org, gray & bl 6.50 3.75

An overprint, "Europa / CECA / MIFERMA," was applied in carmine to No. C16 in 1962.

The anti-malaria emblem, including slogan "Le Monde contre le Paludisme," was overprinted on Nos. C14-C15 in 1962.

Air Afrique Issue
Common Design Type

1962, Feb. 17
C17 CD107 100fr sl grn, choc & bis 1.00 65

UN Headquarters, New York; View of Nouakchott — AP2

1962, Oct. 27 Engr. *Perf. 13*
C18 AP2 100fr bluish grn, dk bl & org brn 1.00 70

Mauritania's admission to the UN.

Plane, Nouakchott Airport — AP3

1963, May 3 Unwmk. *Perf. 13*
C19 AP3 500fr dp bl, gldn brn & slate grn 3.75 2.25

Miferma Open-pit Mine at Zouerate — AP4

Design: 200fr, Ore transport at Port Etienne.

1963, June Photo. *Perf. 13x12*
C20 AP4 100fr multi 65 35
C21 AP4 200fr multi 1.50 75

African Postal Union Issue
Common Design Type

1963, Sept. 8 Unwmk. *Perf. 12½*
C22 CD114 85fr blk brn, ocher & red 70 40

Globe and Telstar — AP5

Design: 150fr, Relay satellite and stars.

1963, Oct. 7 Engr. *Perf. 13*
C23 AP5 50fr yel grn, pur & red brn 50 32
C24 AP5 150fr red brn & sl grn 1.40 1.00

Communication through space.

Tiros Satellite and Emblem of WMO — AP6

UN Emblem, Doves and Sun — AP7

1963, Nov. 4
C25 AP6 200fr ultra, brn & grn 1.50 90

Space research for meteorology and navigation.

1963 Air Afrique Issue
Common Design Type

1963, Nov. 19 Photo. *Perf. 13x12*
C26 CD115 25fr multi 30 18

1963, Dec. 10 Engr. *Perf. 13*
C27 AP7 100fr vio, brn, & dk bl 1.00 55

Universal Declaration of Human Rights, 15th anniv.

Symbols of Agriculture and Industry — AP8

Lichtenstein's Sand Grouse — AP9

Europafrica Issue

1964, Jan. 6 Photo.
C28 AP8 50fr multi 80 50

Signing of economic agreement between the European Economic Community and the African and Malgache Union at Yaounde, Cameroun, July 20, 1963.

1964, Feb. 3 Engr. *Perf. 13*

Birds: 200fr, Long-tailed cormorant. 500fr, Chanting goshawk.

C29 AP9 100fr ocher, ol & dk brn 1.00 40
C30 AP9 200fr blk, dk bl & brn 1.90 80
C31 AP9 500fr rose red, grn & sl 4.50 2.00

Isis, Temple at Philae and Trajan's Kiosk — AP10

1964, Mar. 8 Unwmk. *Perf. 13*
C32 AP10 10fr red brn, Prus bl & blk 25 18
C33 AP10 25fr red brn, ind & Prus bl 40 30
C34 AP10 60fr blk brn, Prus bl & red brn 80 60

UNESCO world campaign to save historic monuments in Nubia.

Syncom Satellite, Globe — AP11

1964, May 4 Engr.
C35 AP11 100fr red, red brn & ultra 1.00 60

Issued to publicize space communications.

Horse Race on Bowl — AP12

Sport Designs from Ancient Pottery: 50fr, Runner (vert.). 85fr, Wrestlers (vert.). 100fr, Charioteer.

1964, Sept. 27 Unwmk. *Perf. 13*
C36 AP12 15fr ol bis & choc 15 15
C37 AP12 50fr bl & org brn 38 22
C38 AP12 85fr crim & brn 65 38
C39 AP12 100fr emer & dk red brn 75 45
a. Min. sheet of 4, #C36-C39 2.25 2.25

18th Olympic Games, Tokyo, Oct. 10-25.

Pres. John F. Kennedy (1917-1963) AP13

1964, Dec. 7 Photo. *Perf. 12½*
C40 AP13 100fr red brn, bl grn & dk brn 75 65
a. Souv. sheet of 4 3.25 3.25

ITU Emblem, Induction Telegraph and Relay Satellite — AP14

1965, May 17 Engr. *Perf. 13*
C41 AP14 250fr multi 1.90 1.25

ITU, centenary.

Fight Against Cancer AP15

Winston Churchill AP16

1965, July 19 Unwmk. *Perf. 13*
C42 AP15 100fr bis, Prus bl & red 1.00 42

Issued to publicize the fight against cancer.

1965, Dec. 6 Photo. *Perf. 13*
C43 AP16 200fr multi 1.50 60

Sir Winston Spencer Churchill (1874-1965), statesman and WWII leader.

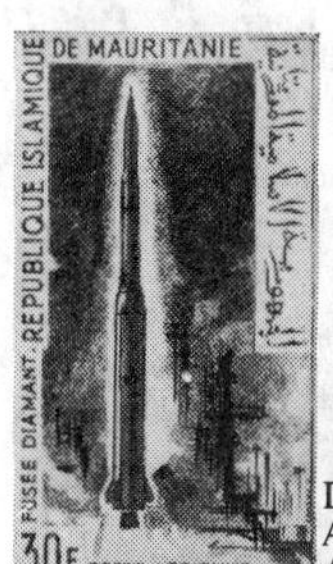

Diamant Rocket Ascending AP17

French achievements in space: 60fr, Satellite A-1 and earth (horiz.). 90fr, Scout rocket and satellite FR-1 (horiz.).

1966, Feb. 7 Engr. *Perf. 13*
C44 AP17 30fr dp bl, red & grn 60 22
C45 AP17 60fr mar, Prus grn & bl 1.10 40
C46 AP17 90fr dp bl, rose cl & vio 1.40 65

Dr. Albert Schweitzer and Clinic — AP18

1966, Feb. 21 Photo. *Perf. 12½*
C47 AP18 50fr multi 50 22

Schweitzer (1875-1965), medical missionary to Gabon, theologian and musician.

Thomas P. Stafford, Walter M. Schirra and Gemini 6 — AP19

Designs: 100fr, Frank A. Borman, James A. Lovell, Jr., and Gemini 7. 200fr, Pavel Belyayev, Alexei Leonov, Voskhod 2.

1966, Mar. 7 Photo. *Perf. 12½*
C48 AP19 50fr multi 40 18
C49 AP19 100fr multi 70 35
C50 AP19 200fr multi 1.50 60

Issued to honor achievements in space.

Map of Africa and Dove — AP20

D-1 Satellite over Earth — AP21

1966, May 9 Photo. *Perf. 13*
C51 AP20 100fr red brn, sl & yel grn 90 38

Organization for African Unity.

1966, June 6 Engr.
C52 AP21 100fr bl, dk pur & ocher 1.90 42

Launching of the D-1 satellite at Hammaguir, Algeria, Feb. 17, 1966.

Breguet 14 — AP22

Planes: 100fr, Goliath Farman, and camel caravan. 150fr, Couzinet "Arc-en-Ciel." 200fr, Latecoere 28 hydroplane.

1966, July 4 Engr. *Perf. 13*
C53 AP22 50fr sl bl, dl grn & ol bis 50 18
C54 AP22 100fr brt bl, dk grn & dk red brn 90 30
C55 AP22 150fr dl brn, Prus bl & saph 1.40 45
C56 AP22 200fr dk red brn, bl & ind 2.00 70

Air Afrique Issue, 1966
Common Design Type

1966, Aug. 31 Photo. *Perf. 13*
C57 CD123 30fr red, blk & gray 30 15

"The Raft of the Medusa," by Theodore Gericault — AP23

1966, Sept. 5 Photo. *Perf. 12½*
C58 AP23 500fr multi 3.75 2.00

Sinking of the frigate "Medusa" off Mauritania, July 2, 1816.

Symbols of Agriculture and Industry — AP24

1966, Nov. 7 Photo. *Perf. 13x12*
C59 AP24 50fr multi 42 16

Third anniversary, economic agreement between the European Economic Community and the African and Malgache Union.

Crowned Crane — AP25

Eye, Globe and Rockets — AP26

Birds: 200fr, Common egret. 500fr, Ostrich.

1967, Apr. 3 *Perf. 12½x13*
C60 AP25 100fr multi 65 40
C61 AP25 200fr multi 1.40 60
C62 AP25 500fr multi 3.50 1.60

1967, May 2 Engr. *Perf. 13*
C63 AP26 250fr brn, Prus bl & blk 1.90 1.00

EXPO '67 Intl. Exhibition, Montreal, Apr. 28-Oct. 27.

Emblem of Atomic Energy Commission AP27

1967, Aug. 7 Engr. *Perf. 13*
C64 AP27 200fr dk red, brt grn & ultra 2.25 1.00

International Atomic Energy Commission.

African Postal Union Issue, 1967
Common Design Type

1967, Sept. 9 Engr. *Perf. 13*
C65 CD124 100fr brn org, vio brn & brt grn 90 40

Francesca da Rimini, by Ingres AP28

Paintings by and of Ingres: 100fr, Young man's torso. 150fr, "The Iliad" (seated woman). 200fr, Ingres in his Studio, by Alaux. 250fr, "The Odyssey" (seated woman).

1967-68 Photo. *Perf. 12½*
C66 AP28 90fr multi 90 42
C67 AP28 100fr multi ('68) 80 45
C68 AP28 150fr multi ('68) 1.40 65
C69 AP28 200fr multi 2.00 90
C70 AP28 250fr multi ('68) 2.25 1.20
Nos. C66-C70 (5) 7.35 3.62

Jean Dominique Ingres (1780-1867), French painter.

Issue dates: Oct. 2, 1967, 90fr, 200fr. Sept. 2, 1968, others.

See No. C79.

Konrad Adenauer — AP29

Gymnast — AP30

1968, Feb. 5 Photo. *Perf. 12½*
C71 AP29 100fr org brn, lt bl & blk 75 35
a. Souv. sheet of 4 3.00 2.50

Adenauer (1876-1967), chancellor of West Germany (1949-63).

1968, Mar. 4 Engr. *Perf. 13*

Sports: 20fr, Slalom (horiz.). 50fr, Ski jump. 100fr, Hurdling (horiz.).

C72 AP30 20fr plum, blk & bl 16 15
C73 AP30 30fr dl pur, brt grn & brn 22 15
C74 AP30 50fr Prus bl, bis & bl grn 40 18
C75 AP30 100fr brn, grn & ver 80 35
Set value 70

1968 Olympic Games.

WHO Emblem, Man and Insects — AP31

1968, May 2 Engr. *Perf. 13*
C76 AP31 150fr red lil, dp bl & org red 1.20 60

WHO, 20th anniversary.

Martin Luther King — AP32

Design: No. C78, Mahatma Gandhi.

1968, Nov. 4 Photo. *Perf. 12½*

C77	AP32	50fr sl bl, cit & blk	35	18
C78	AP32	50fr sl bl, lt bl & blk	35	18
a.		Souv. sheet of 4, 2 each #C77-C78	1.60	1.60

Issued to honor two apostles of peace.

PHILEXAFRIQUE Issue
Painting Type of 1967

Design: 100fr, The Surprise Letter, by Charles Antoine Coypel.

1968, Dec. 9 Photo. *Perf. 12½*

C79	AP28	100fr multi	1.00	1.00

PHILEXAFRIQUE, Phil. Exhib., Abidjan, Feb. 14-23. Printed with alternating brown red label.

2nd PHILEXAFRIQUE Issue
Common Design Type

Design: 50fr, Mauritania No. 89 and family on jungle trail.

1969, Feb. 14 Engr. *Perf. 13*

C80	CD128	50fr sl grn, vio brn & red brn	55	55

Napoleon Installed in Council of State, by Louis Charles Couder AP33

Paintings: 50fr, Napoleon at Council of the 500, by F. Bouchot. 250fr, Farewell at Fontainebleau, by Horace Vernet.

1969, Feb. 24 Photo. *Perf. 12½*

C81	AP33	50fr pur & multi	80	65
C82	AP33	90fr multi	1.20	1.00
C83	AP33	250fr multi	3.50	2.25

Napoleon Bonaparte (1769-1821).

Camel, Gazelles, and Tourist Year Emblem — AP34

1969, June 9 Engr. *Perf. 13*

C84	AP34	50fr org, dk brn & lt bl	42	22

Year of African Tourism.

Dancers and Temple Ruins, Baalbek — AP35

1969, June 16

C85	AP35	100fr Prus bl, ol brn & rose car	65	35

International Baalbek Festival, Lebanon.

Apollo 8 and Moon Surface — AP36

Embossed on Gold Foil

1969 *Die-cut Perf. 10*

C86	AP36	1000fr gold	9.00	9.00

Man's first flight around the moon, Dec. 21-28, 1968 (US astronauts Col. Frank Borman, Capt. James Lovell and Maj. William Anders).

Mamo Wolde, Ethiopia, Marathon AP37

Designs: 70fr, Bob Beamon, USA, broad jump. 150fr, Vera Caslavska, Czechoslovakia, gymnastics.

1969, July 7 Engr. *Perf. 13*

C87	AP37	30fr multi	20	15
C88	AP37	70fr multi	42	20
C89	AP37	150fr multi	90	55

Issued to honor gold medal winners in the 19th Olympic Games, Mexico City.

Map of London-Istanbul Route — AP38

London to Sydney automobile rally: 20fr, Map showing Ankara to Teheran route, and compass rose. 50fr, Map showing Kandahar to Bombay route, arms of Afghanistan and elephant. 70fr, Map of Australia with Perth to Sydney route, and kangaroo.

1969, Aug. 14 Engr. *Perf. 13*

C90	AP38	10fr multicolored	15	15
C91	AP38	20fr multicolored	15	15
C92	AP38	50fr multicolored	35	15
C93	AP38	70fr multicolored	40	18
a.		Min. sheet of 4, #C90-C93	1.40	1.40
		Set value		45

Palette with World Map, Geisha and EXPO '70 Emblem — AP39

Designs (EXPO '70 Emblem and): 75fr, Fan and fireworks. 150fr, Stylized bird, map of Japan and boat.

1970, June 15 Photo. *Perf. 12½*

C94	AP39	50fr multi	38	16
C95	AP39	75fr multi	50	25
C96	AP39	150fr multi	1.10	45

Issued to publicize EXPO '70 International Exhibition, Osaka, Japan, Mar. 15-Sept. 13.

UN Emblem, Balloon, Rocket, Farm Woman, Tractor, Old and New Record Players — AP40

1970, June 22 Engr. *Perf. 13*

C97	AP40	100fr ultra, dk brn & grn	70	42

25th anniversary of the United Nations.

Elliott See (1927-1966), American Astronaut AP41

Apollo 13 Capsule with Parachutes AP42

Portraits: No. C99, Vladimir Komarov (1927-1967). C100, Yuri Gagarin (1934-1968). No. C101, Virgil Grissom (1926-1967). No. C102, Edward White (1930-1967). No. C103, Roger Chaffee (1935-1967).

1970 Engr. *Perf. 13*

Portrait in Brown

C98	AP41	150fr gray & brt bl	1.00	42
C99	AP41	150fr gray & org	1.00	42
C100	AP41	150fr gray & org	1.00	42
a.		Souv. sheet of 3, #C98-C100	4.00	4.00
C101	AP41	150fr ultra & grnsh bl	1.00	42
C102	AP41	150fr ultra & org	1.00	42
C103	AP41	150fr ultra & grnsh bl	1.00	42
a.		Souv. sheet of 3, #C101-C103	6.00	6.00
		Nos. C98-C103 (6)	6.00	2.52

American and Russian astronauts who died in space explorations.

Gold Embossed

1970, Aug. 17 *Perf. 12½*

C104	AP42	500fr gold, crim & bl	4.00	4.00

Safe return of Apollo 13 crew.

Parliament, Nouakchott, and Coat of Arms — AP43

1970, Nov. 28 Photo. *Perf. 12½*

C105	AP43	100fr multi	65	35

10th anniversary of Independence.

Hercules Wrestling Antaeus — AP44

1971, Mar. 8 Engr. *Perf. 13*

C106	AP44	100fr red lil, brn & ultra	80	50

Pre-Olympic Year. Design from a vase decoration by Euphronius.

Gamal Abdel Nasser (1918-1970), President of U.A.R. — AP46

1971, May 10 Photo. *Perf. 12½*

C109	AP46	100fr gold & multi	60	30

Boy Scout, Emblem and Map of Mauritania AP47

1971, Aug. 16 Photo. *Perf. 12½*

C110	AP47	35fr yel & multi	20	15
C111	AP47	40fr pink & multi	22	16
C112	AP47	100fr multi	60	35

13th Boy Scout World Jamboree, Asagiri Plain, Japan, Aug. 2-10.

African Postal Union Issue, 1971
Common Design Type

Design: 100fr, Women musicians and UAMPT building, Brazzaville, Congo.

1971, Nov. 13 Photo. *Perf. 13x13½*

C113	CD135	100fr bl & multi	65	42

Letter and Postal Emblem AP48

1971, Dec. 2 *Perf. 13*

C114	AP48	35fr bis & multi	22	15

10th anniversary of African Postal Union.

Mosul Monarch, from Book of Songs, c. 1218 AP49

Designs from Mohammedan Miniatures: 40fr, Prince holding audience, Egypt, 1334. 100fr, Pilgrim caravan, from "Maquamat," Baghdad, 1237.

1972, Jan. 10 Photo. *Perf. 13*

C115 AP49 35fr gold & multi 22 16
C116 AP49 40fr gray & multi 25 20
C117 AP49 100fr buff & multi 65 42

Grand Canal, by Canaletto — AP50

Designs: 45fr, Venice Harbor, by Carlevaris (vert.). 250fr, Santa Maria della Salute, by Canaletto.

1972, Feb. 14

C118 AP50 45fr gold & multi 20 15
C119 AP50 100fr gold & multi 45 25
C120 AP50 250fr gold & multi 1.25 60

UNESCO campaign to save Venice.

Hurdles and Olympic Rings — AP51

1972, Apr. 27 Engr. *Perf. 13*

C121 AP51 75fr org, vio brn & blk 35 16
C122 AP51 100fr Prus bl, vio brn & brn 50 25
C123 AP51 200fr lake, vio brn & blk 1.00 40
a. Min. sheet of 3, #C121-C123 1.90 1.90

20th Olympic Games, Munich, Aug. 26-Sept. 11.

Luna 17 on Moon — AP52

Design: 75fr, Luna 16 take-off from moon (vert.).

1972, Oct. 9

C124 AP52 75fr vio bl, bis & grn 45 20
C125 AP52 100fr dl pur, sl & ol bis 65 35

Russian moon missions, Luna 16, Sept. 12-14, 1970; and Luna 17, Nov. 10-17, 1970.

Nos. C121-C123 Overprinted in Violet Blue or Red:

a. 110m HAIES / MILBURN MEDAILLE D'OR
b. 400m HAIES / AKII-BUA MEDAILLE D'OR
c. 3.000m STEEPLE / KEINO MEDAILLE D'OR

1972, Oct. 16

C126 AP51(a) 75fr multi (VB) 45 20
C127 AP51(b) 100fr multi (R) 65 35
C128 AP51(c) 200fr multi (VB) 1.40 55

Gold medal winners in 20th Olympic Games: Rod Milburn, US, John Akii-Bua, Uganda, and Kipchoge Keino, Kenya.

No. C62 Surcharged with New Value, Two Bars and: "Apollo XVII / December 1972"

1973, Jan. 29 Photo. *Perf. 12½x13*

C129 AP25 250fr on 500fr multi 1.50 65

Apollo 17 moon mission, Dec. 7-19, 1972.

Seal Type of Regular Issue

1973, Feb. 28 Litho. *Perf. 13*

C130 A63 135fr Seal's head 1.20 70

Lion Eating Caiman, by Delacroix — AP53

Painting: 250fr, Lion Eating Boar, by Delacroix.

1973, Mar. 26 Photo. *Perf. 13x12½*

C131 AP53 100fr blk & multi 80 42
C132 AP53 250fr blk & multi 2.00 1.10

Villagers Observing Solar Eclipse — AP54

Designs: 40fr, Rocket take-off and Concord (vert.). 140fr, Scientists with telescopes observing eclipse.

1973, June 20 Engr. *Perf. 13*

C133 AP54 35fr grn & pur 22 15
C134 AP54 40fr ultra, pur & scar 25 15
C135 AP54 140fr scar & pur 90 55
a. Souvenir sheet of 3 2.00 2.00

Solar eclipse, June 30, 1973. No. C135a contains 3 stamps similar to Nos. C133-C135 in changed colors (35fr, 140fr in magenta and violet blue; 40fr in magenta, violet blue and orange).

Soccer AP55

1973, Dec. 24 Photo. *Perf. 13*

C136 AP55 7um multi 22 15
C137 AP55 8um multi 22 15
C138 AP55 20um multi 65 42

Souvenir Sheet

C139 AP55 30um multi 1.10 1.10

World Soccer Cup, Munich, 1974.

Nos. C115-C117, C130 and C133-C135 Surcharged with New Value and Two Bars in Red, Black or Ultramarine

1973-74 Photo., Litho. or Engr.

C140 AP49 7um on 35fr (R) ('74) 22 15
C141 AP54 7um on 35fr (B) 25 15
C142 AP54 8um on 40fr (B) 25 16
C143 AP49 8um on 40fr (U) ('74) 25 16
C144 AP49 20um on 100fr (R) ('74) 70 42
C145 A63 27um on 135fr (R) 80 50
C146 AP54 28um on 140fr (B) 95 55
Nos. C140-C146 (7) 3.42 2.09

Winston Churchill (1874-1965) AP56

Lenin (1870-1924) AP57

1974, June 3 Engr. *Perf. 13*

C147 AP56 40um blk, brn & hn brn 1.00 60

Nos. C131-C132 Surcharged with New Value and Two Bars in Red

1974, July 15 Photo. *Perf. 13x12½*

C148 AP53 20um on 100fr multi 45 28
C149 AP53 50um on 250fr multi 1.20 70

1974, Sept. 16 Engr. *Perf. 13*

C150 AP57 40um sl grn & red 1.00 60

Women, IWY Emblem AP58

Design: 40um, Woman's head and IWY emblems.

1975, June 16 Engr. *Perf. 13*

C151 AP58 12um multi 38 20
C152 AP58 40um dk brn, lt brn & bl 1.25 65

International Women's Year.

Albert Schweitzer and Patients Arriving — AP59

1975, Aug. 4 Engr. *Perf. 13*

C153 AP59 60um multi 1.60 1.00

Schweitzer (1875-1965), medical missionary.

Javelin and Olympic Emblem — AP60

Design: 52um, Running and Olympic emblem.

1975, Nov. 17 Engr. *Perf. 13*

C154 AP60 50um sl grn, red & ol 1.50 80
C155 AP60 52um car, ocher & ultra 1.40 80

Pre-Olympic Year 1975.

Apollo Soyuz Type, 1975

Docked Space Ships and: 20um, Apollo rocket launch. 50um, Handshake in linked-up cabin. 60um, Apollo splash-down. 100um, Astronauts and Cosmonauts.

1975, Dec. 29 Litho. *Perf. 14*

C156 A74 20um multi 50 22
C157 A74 50um multi 1.10 60
C158 A74 60um multi 1.40 70

Souvenir Sheet

C159 A74 100um multi 2.40 1.25

American Bicentennial Type, 1976

Uniforms: 20um, French Hussar officer. 50um, 3rd Continental Artillery officer. 60um, French infantry regiment grenadier. 100um, American infantryman.

1976, Jan. 26

C160 A75 20um multi 50 20
C161 A75 50um multi 1.25 50
C162 A75 60um multi 1.50 60

Souvenir Sheet

C163 A75 100um multi 2.50 1.25

Running and Olympic Rings AP61

Olympic Rings and: 12um, High jump. 52um, Fencing.

1976, June 14 Engr. *Perf. 13*

C164 AP61 10um pur, grn & brn 30 16
C165 AP61 12um pur, grn & brn 38 20
C166 AP61 52um pur, grn & brn 1.50 80

21st Olympic Games, Montreal, Canada, July 17-Aug. 1.

Zeppelin Type, 1976

Designs: 50um, "Graf Zeppelin" (LZ-127) over U.S. Capitol. 60um, "Hindenburg" (LZ-130) over Swiss Alps. 100um, "Führersland" (LZ-129) over 1936 Olympic stadium.

1976, June 28 Litho. *Perf. 11*

C167 A77 50um multi 1.50 65
C168 A77 60um multi 1.90 80

Souvenir Sheet

C169 A77 100um multi 3.25 1.40

Marabou Storks — AP62

African Birds: 50um, Sacred ibis (vert.). 200um, Long-crested eagles (vert.).

1976, Sept. 20 Litho. *Perf. 13½*

C170 AP62 50um multi 1.50 62
C171 AP62 100um multi 3.00 1.40
C172 AP62 200um multi 5.75 2.25

Viking Type, 1977

Designs: 20um, Viking orbiter in flight to Mars. 50um, Viking "B" in descent to Mars. 60um, Various phases of descent. 100um, Viking lander using probe.

1977, Feb. 28 *Perf. 14*

C173 A81 20um multi 50 22
C174 A81 50um multi 1.20 55
C175 A81 60um multi 1.50 65

Souvenir Sheet

C176 A81 100um multi 2.50 1.00

Nobel Prize Type, 1977

Designs: 14um, George Bernard Shaw, literature. 55um, Thomas Mann, literature. 60um, International Red Cross Society, peace. 100um, George C. Marshall, peace.

1977, Apr. 29 Litho. *Perf. 14*

C177	A83	14um multi	32	20
C178	A83	55um multi	1.25	60
C179	A83	60um multi	1.50	65

Souvenir Sheet

C180	A83	100um multi	2.50	1.00

Holy Kaaba — AP63

1977, July 25 Litho. *Perf. 12½*

C181	AP63	12um multi	38	20

Pilgrimage to Mecca.

Soccer Type of 1977

Designs (Emblems and): 50um, Soccer ball. 60um, Eusebio Ferreira. 100um, Players holding pennants.

1977, Dec. 19 Litho. *Perf. 13½*

C182	A89	50um multi	1.20	50
C183	A89	60um multi	1.50	65

Souvenir Sheet

C184	A89	100um multi	2.40	1.00

Franco-African Co-operation — AP63a

1978, June 7 Embossed *Perf. 10½*

C184A	AP63a	250um silver
C184B	AP63a	500um gold

Philexafrique II - Essen Issue
Common Design Types

Designs: No. C185, Hyena and Mauritania No. C60. No. C186, Wading bird and Hamburg No. 1.

1978, Nov. 1 Litho. *Perf. 12½*

C185	CD138	20um multi	65	35
C186	CD139	20um multi	65	35

Nos. C185-C186 printed se-tenant.

Nos. C182-C184 Overprinted in Arabic and French in Silver: "ARGENTINE- / PAYS BAS 3-1"

1978, Dec. 11 Litho. *Perf. 13½*

C187	A89	50um multi	1.25	50
C188	A89	60um multi	1.50	65

Souvenir Sheet

C189	A89	100um multi	2.75	1.25

Argentina's victory in World Cup Soccer Championship 1978.

Flyer A and Prototype Plane — AP64

Design: 40um, Flyer A and supersonic jet.

1979, Jan. 29 Engr. *Perf. 13*

C190	AP64	15um multi	42	20
C191	AP64	40um multi	1.10	55

75th anniversary of first powered flight.

Nos. C173-C176 Overprinted and Surcharged in Silver: "ALUNISSAGE / APOLLO XI / JUILLET 1969" and Emblem

1979, Oct. 24 Litho. *Perf. 14*

C192	A81	14um on 20um multi	35	18
C193	A81	50um multi	1.25	65
C194	A81	60um multi	1.50	75

Souvenir Sheet

C195	A81	100um multi	2.75	2.75

Apollo 11 moon landing, 10th anniversary.

Soccer Players — AP65

Designs: Various soccer scenes.

1980, Sept. 29 Litho. *Perf. 12½*

C196	AP65	10um multi	35	15
C197	AP65	12um multi	40	18
C198	AP65	14um multi	45	20
C199	AP65	20um multi	65	30
C200	AP65	67um multi	2.25	1.10
		Nos. C196-C200 (5)	4.10	1.93

Souvenir Sheet

C201	AP65	100um multi	3.50	1.50

World Soccer Cup 1982.

Flight of Columbia Space Shuttle — AP66

Designs: Views of Columbia space shuttle.

1981, Apr. 27 Litho. *Perf. 12½*

C202	AP66	12um multi	40	20
C203	AP66	20um multi	65	30
C204	AP66	50um multi	1.60	80
C205	AP66	70um multi	2.25	1.20

Souvenir Sheet

C206	AP66	100um multi	3.50	1.60

Dinard Landscape, by Pablo Picasso — AP67

Picasso Birth Centenary: 12um, Harlequin (vert.). 20um, Vase of Flowers (vert.). 50um, Three Women at the Well. 100um, Picnic.

1981, June 29 Litho. *Perf. 12½*

C207	AP67	12um multi	40	20
C208	AP67	20um multi	65	35
C209	AP67	50um multi	1.60	80
C210	AP67	70um multi	2.25	1.10
C211	AP67	100um multi	3.50	1.60
		Nos. C207-C211 (5)	8.40	4.05

Nos. C196-C201 Overprinted in Red with Finalists' and Score on 1 or 2 Lines

1982, Sept. 18 Litho. *Perf. 12½*

C212	AP65	10um multi	35	15
C213	AP65	12um multi	40	18
C214	AP65	14um multi	45	20
C215	AP65	20um multi	65	30
C216	AP65	67um multi	2.25	1.10
		Nos. C212-C216 (5)	4.10	1.93

Souvenir Sheet

C217	AP65	100um multi	3.50	1.50

Italy's victory in 1982 World Cup.

25th Anniv. of Intl. Maritime Org. — AP68

1983, June 18 Litho. *Perf. 12½x13*

C218	AP68	18um multi	60	28

Paul Harris, Rotary Founder AP69

1984, Jan. 20 Litho. *Perf. 13½*

C219	AP69	100um multi	1.40	65

1984 Summer Olympics — AP70

1984, July 15 Litho. *Perf. 14*

C223	AP70	14um Running, horiz.	18	15
C224	AP70	18um Shot put	25	15
C225	AP70	19um Hurdles	25	15
C226	AP70	44um Javelin	60	30
C227	AP70	77um High jump	1.00	50
		Nos. C223-C227 (5)	2.28	1.25

Souvenir Sheet

C228	AP70	100um Hurdles, diff.	1.40	65

Olympics Winners — AP71

1984, Dec. 20 Litho. *Perf. 13*

C229	AP71	14um Van den Berg, sailboard, Netherlands	28	15
C230	AP71	18um Coutts, Finn sailing, N.Z.	38	18
C231	AP71	19um 470 class, Spain	40	20
C232	AP71	44um Soling, US	90	45

Souvenir Sheet

C233	AP71	100um Sailing, US	2.00	1.00

PHILEXAFRICA '85, Lome, Togo — AP72

1985, May 23 Litho. *Perf. 13*

C234	AP72	40um Youths, map, IYY emblem	70	40
C235	AP72	40um Oil refinery, Nouadhibou	70	40

1985, Nov. 12 *Perf. 13x12½*

C236	AP72	50um Iron mine, train	1.00	50
C237	AP72	50um Boy reading, herding sheep	1.00	50

Nos. C234-C237 printed se-tenant with center labels picturing map of Africa or UAPT emblem.

Audubon Birth Bicentenary AP73

1985, Aug. 14

C238	AP73	14um Passeriformes thraupidae	28	15
C239	AP73	18um Larus philadelphia	35	16
C240	AP73	19um Cyanocitta cristata	38	18
C241	AP73	44um Rhyncops nigra	80	40

Souvenir Sheet

C242	AP73	100um Anhinga anhinga	2.00	1.00

1st South Atlantic Crossing, 55th Anniv. — AP74

1986, May 19 Litho. *Perf. 13*

C243	AP74	18um	Comte de Vaux, 1930	55	28
C244	AP74	50um	Flight reenactment, 1985	1.50	75

Nos. C243-C244 printed se-tenant with center label.

1986 World Cup Soccer Championships, Mexico — AP75

Various soccer plays.

1986, June 19 Litho. *Perf. 13*

C245	AP75	8um	No. 279	24	15
C246	AP75	18um	No. 280	55	28
C247	AP75	22um	No. 281	65	32
C248	AP75	25um	No. 282	75	38
C249	AP75	40um	Soccer cup	1.20	60
			Nos. C245-C249 (5)	3.39	1.73

Souvenir Sheet

C250	AP75	100um	multi	3.00	1.50

Air Africa, 25th Anniv. — AP76

1986, Oct. 6 Litho. *Perf. 13*

C251	AP76	26um	multi	80	40

1988 Summer Olympics, Seoul — AP77

1987, Aug. 13 Litho. *Perf. 13*

C252	AP77	30um	Boxing	90	45
C253	AP77	40um	Judo	1.20	60
C254	AP77	50um	Fencing	1.50	75
C255	AP77	75um	Wrestling	2.25	1.10

Souvenir Sheet

C256	AP77	150um	Judo, diff.	4.50	2.25

1988 Winter Olympics, Calgary — AP78

1987, Sept.

C257	AP78	30um	Women's slalom	90	45
C258	AP78	40um	Speed skating	1.20	60
C259	AP78	50um	Ice hockey	1.50	75
C260	AP78	75um	Women's downhill skiing	2.25	1.10

Souvenir Sheet

C261	AP78	150um	Men's cross-country skiing	4.50	2.25

1988 Summer Olympics, Seoul AP79

1988, Sept. 17 Litho. *Perf. 13*

C262	AP79	20um	Hammer throw	60	30
C263	AP79	24um	Discus	72	35
C264	AP79	30um	Shot put	90	45
C265	AP79	150um	Javelin	4.50	4.50

Souvenir Sheet

C266	AP79	170um	Javelin, diff.	5.00	2.50

Nos. C257-C261 Overprinted "Medaille d'or" in Red or Bright Blue and:

a. "Vreni Schneider (Suisse)"
b. "1500 m / Andre Hoffman (R.D.A.)"
c. "U.R.S.S."
d. "Marina Kiehl (R.F.A.)"
e. "15 km / Mikhail Deviatiarov (U.R.S.S.)"

1988, Sept. 18

C267	AP78(a)	30um	multi	90	45
C268	AP78(b)	40um	multi (BB)	1.20	60
C269	AP78(c)	50um	multi	1.50	75
C270	AP78(d)	75um	multi	2.25	1.10

Souvenir Sheet

C271	AP78(e)	150um	multi	4.50	2.25

World Cup Soccer Championships, Italy — AP80

Map of Italy and various soccer plays.

1990 Litho. *Perf. 13*

C272	AP80	50um	multicolored	1.35	65
C273	AP80	60um	multicolored	1.65	85
C274	AP80	70um	multicolored	1.90	95
C275	AP80	90um	multicolored	2.50	1.25
C276	AP80	150um	multicolored	4.00	2.00
			Nos. C272-C276 (5)	11.40	5.70

POSTAGE DUE STAMPS

D1

D2

Perf. 14x13½

1906-07 Unwmk. Typo.

J1	D1	5c	grn, *grnsh*	1.40	1.40
J2	D1	10c	red brn	2.25	2.25
J3	D1	15c	dk bl	5.00	3.75
J4	D1	20c	blk, *yellow*	5.25	4.75
J5	D1	30c	red, *straw*	5.25	5.25
J6	D1	50c	violet	7.25	7.25
J7	D1	60c	blk, *buff*	5.50	5.00
J8	D1	1fr	blk, *pinkish*	9.25	8.00
			Nos. J1-J8 (8)	41.15	37.65

Issue dates: 20c, 1906; others 1907.

Regular postage stamps canceled "T" in a triangle were used for postage due.

1914

J9	D2	5c	green	15	15
J10	D2	10c	rose	15	15
J11	D2	15c	gray	15	15
J12	D2	20c	brown	15	15
J13	D2	30c	blue	15	15
J14	D2	50c	black	80	80
J15	D2	60c	orange	38	38
J16	D2	1fr	violet	60	60
			Nos. J9-J16 (8)	2.53	2.53

Type of 1914 Issue Surcharged **2F.**

1927, Oct. 10

J17	D2	2fr	on 1fr lil rose	1.25	1.25
J18	D2	3fr	on 1fr org brn	1.60	1.60

Catalogue values for unused stamps in this section, from this point to the end of the section, are for Never Hinged items.

Islamic Republic

Oualata Motif — D3

Perf. 14x13½

1961, July 1 Typo. Unwmk.

Denominations in Black

J19	D3	1fr	plum & org yel	15	15
J20	D3	2fr	red & gray	15	15
J21	D3	5fr	mar & pink	15	15
J22	D3	10fr	dk grn & grn	25	15
J23	D3	15fr	ol & brn org	30	16
J24	D3	20fr	red brn & lt bl	40	20
J25	D3	25fr	grn & ver	60	38
			Nos. J19-J25 (7)	2.00	
			Set value		1.10

Vulture (Ruppell's Griffon) — D4

Birds: No. J27, Eurasian crane. No. J28, Pink-backed pelican. No. J29, Garganey teal. No. J30, European golden oriole. No. J31, Variable sunbird. No. J32, Shoveler ducks. No. J33, Great snipe. No. J34, Vulturine guinea fowl. No. J35, Black stork. No. J36, Gray heron. No. J37, White stork. No. J38, Red-legged partridge. No. J39, Paradise whydah. No. J40, Sandpiper (little stint). No. J41, Sudan bustard.

1963, Sept. 7 Engr. *Perf. 11*

J26	D4	50c	blk, yel org & red	15	15
J27	D4	50c	blk, yel org & red	15	15
J28	D4	1fr	blk, red & yel	15	15
J29	D4	1fr	blk, red & yel	15	15
J30	D4	2fr	blk, bl grn & yel	15	15
J31	D4	2fr	blk, bl grn & yel	15	15
J32	D4	5fr	blk, grn & red brn	15	15
J33	D4	5fr	blk, grn & red brn	15	15
J34	D4	10fr	blk, red & tan	38	38
J35	D4	10fr	blk, red & tan	38	38
J36	D4	15fr	blk, emer & red	45	45
J37	D4	15fr	blk, emer & red	45	45
J38	D4	20fr	blk, yel grn & red	70	70
J39	D4	20fr	blk, yel grn & red	70	70
J40	D4	25fr	blk, yel grn & brn	1.00	1.00
J41	D4	25fr	blk, yel grn & brn	1.00	1.00
			Nos. J26-J41 (16)	6.26	6.26

Ornament D5

1976, May 10 Litho. *Perf. 12½x13*

J42	D5	1um	buff & multi	15	15
J43	D5	3um	buff & multi	15	15
J44	D5	10um	buff & multi	38	38
J45	D5	12um	buff & multi	42	42
J46	D5	20um	buff & multi	70	70
			Nos. J42-J46 (5)	1.80	1.80

OFFICIAL STAMPS

Catalogue values for unused stamps in this section are for Never Hinged items.

Islamic Republic

Cross of Trarza — O1

Perf. 14x13½

1961, July 1 Typo. Unwmk.

O1	O1	1fr	vio & lilac	15	15
O2	O1	3fr	red & slate	15	15
O3	O1	5fr	grn & brown	15	15
O4	O1	10fr	grn & vio bl	18	15
O5	O1	15fr	blue & org	26	15
O6	O1	20fr	sl grn & emer	30	15
O7	O1	25fr	red org & mar	35	26
O8	O1	30fr	maroon & grn	42	30
O9	O1	50fr	dk red & dk brn	85	42
O10	O1	100fr	org & blue	1.50	80
O11	O1	200fr	grn & red org	3.00	1.50
			Nos. O1-O11 (11)	7.31	4.18

Ornament O2

1976, May 3 Litho. *Perf. 12½x13*

O12	O2	1um	blk & multi	15	15
O13	O2	2um	blk & multi	15	15
O14	O2	5um	blk & multi	20	15
O15	O2	10um	blk & multi	40	16
O16	O2	12um	blk & multi	55	22
O17	O2	40um	blk & multi	1.50	70
O18	O2	50um	blk & multi	2.00	1.00
			Nos. O12-O18 (7)	4.95	
			Set value		2.20

AIR POST SEMI-POSTAL STAMPS

Stamps of Dahomey types V1, V2, V3 and V4 inscribed "Mauritanie" were issued in 1942 by the Vichy Government, but were not placed on sale in the colony.

MAYOTTE

LOCATION — One of the Comoro Islands situated in the Mozambique Channel midway between Madagascar and Mozambique (Africa)
GOVT. — Former French Colony
AREA — 140 sq. mi.
POP. — 13,783 (1914).
CAPITAL — Dzaoudzi
See Comoro Islands

100 Centimes = 1 Franc

See France No. 2271 for French stamp inscribed "Mayotte."

Navigation and Commerce — A1

Perf. 14x13½

1892-1907 Typo. Unwmk.

Name of Colony in Blue or Carmine

1 A1 1c blk, *lil bl* 35 35
2 A1 2c brn, *buff* 40 40
a. Name double 200.00 200.00
3 A1 4c claret, *lav* 62 55
4 A1 5c grn, *grnsh* 1.25 1.00
5 A1 10c blk, *lavender* 1.50 1.25
6 A1 10c red ('00) 20.00 14.00
7 A1 15c blue, quadrille paper 5.00 3.25
8 A1 15c gray ('00) 40.00 32.50
9 A1 20c red, *grn* 4.00 3.25
10 A1 25c blk, *rose* 3.00 2.25
11 A1 25c blue ('00) 3.50 2.25
12 A1 30c brn, *bis* 5.75 4.25
13 A1 35c blk, *yel* 2.50 2.25
14 A1 40c red, *straw* 5.00 4.25
15 A1 45c blk, *gray grn* ('07) 5.75 4.50
16 A1 50c carmine, *rose* 8.00 6.00
17 A1 50c brn, *az* ('00) 6.00 6.00
18 A1 75c dp vio, *org* 9.00 6.00
19 A1 1fr brnz grn, *straw* 7.00 6.00
20 A1 5fr red lil, *lav* ('99) 45.00 40.00
Nos. 1-20 (20) 173.62 140.30

Perf. 13½x14 stamps are counterfeits.

Issues of 1892-1907 Surcharged in Black or Carmine

05 **10**

1912

22 A1 5c on 2c brn, *buff* 65 65
23 A1 5c on 4c cl, *lav* (C) 60 60
24 A1 5c on 15c bl (C) 45 45
25 A1 5c on 20c red, *grn* 60 60
26 A1 5c on 25c blk, *rose* (C) 60 60
a. Double surcharge 150.00
27 A1 5c on 30c brn, *bis* (C) 60 60
28 A1 10c on 40c red, *straw* 60 60
a. Double surcharge 100.00
29 A1 10c on 45c blk, *gray grn* (C) 60 60
a. Double surcharge 100.00
30 A1 10c on 50c car, *rose* 1.10 1.10
31 A1 10c on 75c dp vio, *org* 75 75
32 A1 10c on 1fr brnz grn, *straw* 75 75
Nos. 22-32 (11) 7.30 7.30

Two spacings between the surcharged numerals are found on Nos. 22 to 32.

Nos. 22 to 32 were available for use in Madagascar and the entire Comoro archipelago.

Stamps of Mayotte were replaced successively by those of Madagascar, Comoro Islands and France.

MEMEL

LOCATION — In northern Europe, bordering on the Baltic Sea
GOVT. — Special commission (see below)
AREA — 1099 sq. mi.
POP. — 151,960

Following World War I this territory was detached from Germany and by Treaty of Versailles assigned to the government of a commission of the Allied and Associated Powers (not the League of Nations), which administered it until January, 1923, when it was forcibly occupied by Lithuania. In 1924 Memel became incorporated as a semi-autonomous district of Lithuania with the approval of the Allied Powers and the League of Nations.

100 Pfennig = 1 Mark
100 Centu = 1 Litas (1923)

Stamps of Germany, 1905-20, Overprinted **Memel-gebiet**

Wmk. Lozenges (125)

1920, Aug. 1 *Perf. 14, 14½*

1 A16 5pf green 22 35
2 A16 10pf car rose 2.00 4.50
3 A16 10pf orange 15 32
4 A22 15pf vio brn 2.00 5.00
5 A16 20pf bl vio 20 15
6 A16 30pf org & blk, *buff* 1.00 1.25
7 A16 30pf dl bl 15 32
8 A16 40pf lake & blk 15 15
9 A16 50pf pur & blk, *buff* 15 15
10 A16 60pf ol grn 45 1.45
11 A16 75pf grn & blk 1.75 4.00
12 A16 80pf bl vio 85 1.75

Overprinted **Memelgebiet**

13 A17 1m car rose 24 45
14 A17 1.25m green 8.25 18.00
15 A17 1.50m yel brn 3.00 6.00
16 A21 2m blue 1.25 2.50
17 A21 2.50m red lil 8.25 14.00
Nos. 1-17 (17) 30.06 60.34

Stamps of France, Surcharged in Black

On A22: MEMEL 5 pfennig

On A18: MEMEL 60 pfennig

1920 Unwmk. *Perf. 14x13½*

18 A22 5pf on 5c grn 15 15
19 A22 10pf on 10c red 15 15
20 A22 20pf on 25c bl 15 15
21 A22 30pf on 30c org 15 15
22 A22 40pf on 20c red brn 15 15
23 A22 50pf on 35c vio 15 30
24 A18 60pf on 40c red & pale bl 18 40
25 A18 80pf on 45c grn & bl 15 18
26 A18 1m on 50c brn & lav 15 16
27 A18 1m 25pf on 60c vio & ultra 75 1.65
28 A18 2m on 1fr cl & ol grn 15 20
29 A18 3m on 5fr bl & buff 9.00 12.00
Nos. 18-29 (12) 11.28 15.64

French Stamps of 1900-20 Surcharged like Nos. 24 to 29 in Red or Black

4 4
Four Marks
Type I Type II

1920-21 Unwmk. *Perf. 14x13½*

30 A18 3m on 2fr org & pale bl 8.50 14.00
31 A18 4m on 2fr org & pale bl (I) (Bk) 15 28
a. Type II 50.00 *125.00*
32 A18 10m on 5fr bl & buff 1.50 2.75
33 A18 20m on 5fr bl & buff 27.50 40.00

New Value with Initial Capital

1921

39 A18 60Pf on 40c red & pale bl 2.00 3.75
40 A18 3M on 60c vio & ultra 50 70
41 A18 10M on 5fr bl & buff 60 95
42 A18 20M on 45c grn & bl 2.25 5.00

The surcharged value on No. 40 is in italics.

Stamps of 1920 Surcharged with Large Numerals in Dark Blue or Red

1921-22

43 A22 15pf on 10pf on 10c 15 25
a. Inverted surcharge 52.50 67.50
44 A22 15pf on 20pf on 25c 18 32
a. Inverted surcharge 60.00 67.50
45 A22 15pf on 50pf on 35c (R) 15 28
a. Inverted surcharge 60.00 67.50
46 A22 60pf on 40pf on 20c 15 18
a. Inverted surcharge 52.50 67.50
47 A18 75pf on 60pf on 40c 40 55
48 A18 1.25m on 1m on 50c 15 20
49 A18 5.00m on 2m on 1fr 55 60
a. Inverted surcharge 240.00 280.00
Nos. 43-49 (7) 1.73 2.38

Stamps of France Surcharged in Black or Red

On A22: MEMEL 5 Pfennig

On A18: MEMEL 40 Pfennig

1922

50 A22 5pf on 5c org 15 15
51 A22 10pf on 10c red 50 1.10
52 A22 10pf on 10c grn 15 15
53 A22 15pf on 10c grn 20 35
54 A22 20pf on 20c red brn 2.25 5.50
55 A22 20pf on 25c bl 2.25 5.50
56 A22 25pf on 5c org 15 15
57 A22 30pf on 30c red 35 1.40
58 A22 35pf on 35c vio 15 15
59 A22 50pf on 50c dl bl 15 18
60 A22 75pf on 15c grn 15 15
61 A22 75pf on 35c vio 15 18
62 A22 1m on 25c bl 15 15
63 A22 1¼m on 30c red 15 15
64 A22 3m on 5c org 15 40
65 A22 6m on 15c grn (R) 22 40
66 A22 8m on 30c red 20 80

Type A18

67 40pf on 40c red & pale bl 15 18
68 80pf on 45c grn & bl 15 18
69 1m on 40c red & pale bl 15 18
70 1.25m on 60c vio & ultra (R) 15 18
71 1.50m on 45c grn & bl (R) 15 18
72 2m on 45c grn & bl 15 15
73 2m on 1fr cl & ol grn 15 18
74 2¼m on 40c red & pale bl 15 15
75 2½m on 60c vio & ultra (R) 20 32
76 3m on 60c vio & ultra (R) 40 60
77 4m on 45c grn & bl 15 15
78 5m on 1fr cl & ol grn 18 30
79 6m on 60c vio & ultra 15 15
80 6m on 2fr org & pale bl 18 30
81 9m on 1fr cl & ol grn 22 22
82 9m on 5fr bl & buff (R) 24 40
83 10m on 45c grn & bl (R) 18 35
84 12m on 40c red & pale bl 22 22
85 20m on 40c red & pale bl 18 35
86 20m on 2fr org & pale bl 22 22
87 30m on 60c vio & ultra 18 35
88 30m on 5fr dk bl & buff 1.90 4.75
89 40m on 1fr cl & ol grn 18 35
90 50m on 2fr org & pale bl 5.50 12.50
91 80m on 2fr org & pale bl (R) 18 40
92 100m on 5fr bl & buff 25 48
Nos. 50-92 (43) 19.38 40.65

Nos. 59, 60 and 65 are on France type A20.

A 500m on 5fr dark blue and buff was prepared, but not officially issued. Value, $750.

Nos. 52, 54, 67, 59 Surcharged "Mark"

1922-23

93 A22 10m on 10pf on 10c 55 1.50
a. Double surcharge 125.00 140.00
94 A22 20m on 20pf on 20c 40 40
95 A18 40m on 40pf on 40c ('23) 40 70
96 A20 50m on 50pf on 50c 1.10 1.90

Nos. 72, 61, 70 Surcharged with New Values in Red or Black

1922-23

97 A18 10m on 2m on 45c75 95
98 A22 25m on 1m on 25c 75 95
99 A18 80m on 1.25m on 60c (Bk) ('23) 40 70

AIR POST STAMPS

Nos. 24-26, 28, 31, 39-40 Overprinted in Dark Blue

1921, July 6 Unwmk. *Perf. 14x13½*

C1 A18 60pf on 40c 27.50 45.00
C2 A18 80pf on 45c 1.40 3.50
C3 A18 1m on 50c 1.25 2.75
C4 A18 2m on 1fr 1.40 4.00
a. "Flugpost" inverted 200.00 240.00
C5 A18 4m on 2fr (I) 1.90 6.25
a. Type II 200.00 240.00

New Value with Initial Capital

C6 A18 60Pf on 40c 1.75 4.25
a. "Flugpost" inverted 200.00 240.00
C7 A18 3M on 60c 1.75 4.25
a. "Flugpost" inverted 200.00 225.00
Nos. C1-C7 (7) 36.95 70.00

The surcharged value on No. C7 is in italics.

Nos. 67-71, 73, 76, 78, 80, 82 Overprinted in Dark Blue

1922, May 12

C8 A18 40pf on 40c 30 75
C9 A18 80pf on 45c 30 75
C10 A18 1m on 40c 30 75
C11 A18 1.25m on 60c 45 1.25
C12 A18 1.50m on 45c 45 1.25
C13 A18 2m on 1fr 45 1.25
C14 A18 3m on 60c 45 1.25
C15 A18 5m on 1fr 55 1.40
C16 A18 6m on 2fr 55 1.40
C17 A18 9m on 5fr 55 1.40

Same Overprint On Nos. 40, 31

C18 A18 3m on 60c 80.00 *400.00*
C19 A18 4m on 2fr 45 1.25
Nos. C8-C17,C19 (11) 4.80 12.70

Nos. 67, 69-71, 73, 76, 78, 80, 82 Overprinted in Black or Red **FLUGPOST**

1922, Oct. 17

C20 A18 40pf on 40c 55 *2.50*
C21 A18 1m on 40c 55 *2.50*
C22 A18 1.25m on 60c (R) 55 *2.50*
C23 A18 1.50m on 45c (R) 55 *2.50*
C24 A18 2m on 1fr 55 *2.50*
C25 A18 3m on 60c (R) 55 *2.50*
C26 A18 4m on 2fr 55 *2.50*
C27 A18 5m on 1fr 55 *2.50*
C28 A18 6m on 2fr 55 *2.50*
C29 A18 9m on 5fr (R) 55 *2.50*
Nos. C20-C29 (10) 5.50 *25.00*

No. C26 is not known without the "FLUGPOST" overprint.

OCCUPATION STAMPS

Issued under Lithuanian Occupation

Surcharged in Various Colors on Unissued Official Stamps of Lithuania Similar to Type O4

Klaipėda (Memel) 10 Markių — On Nos. N1-N6

KLAIPĖDA (MEMEL) 25 MARKĖS — On Nos. N7-N11

Memel Printing

1923 Unwmk. Litho. *Perf. 11*

N1	O4	10m on 5c bl (Bk)	65	1.25
a.		"Memel" and bars omitted	5.00	12.50
N2	O4	25m on 5c bl (R)	65	1.25
N3	O4	50m on 25c red (Bk)	65	1.25
N4	O4	100m on 25c red (G)	65	1.25
N5	O4	400m on 1 l brn (R)	75	1.50
N6	O4	500m on 1 l brn (Bl)	75	1.50
		Nos. N1-N6 (6)	4.10	8.00

Nos. N1 and N3-N6 exist with double surcharge. Value $50 each.

Kaunas Printing

Black Surcharge

N7	O4	10m on 5c bl	30	55
N8	O4	25m on 5c bl	30	55
N9	O4	50m on 25c red	30	55
N10	O4	100m on 25c red	45	80
N11	O4	400m on 1 l brn	75	1.40
		Nos. N7-N11 (5)	2.10	3.85

No. N8 has the value in "Markes," others of the group have it in "Markiu."

Surcharged in Various Colors on Unissued Official Stamps of Lithuania Similar to Type O4

KLAIPĖDA (Memel) 25 *MARKĖS*

1923

N12	O4	10m on 5c bl (R)	50	1.10
a.		"Markes" instead of "Markiu"	22.50	50.00
N13	O4	20m on 5c bl (R)	50	1.10
N14	O4	25m on 25c red (Bl)	50	1.10
N15	O4	50m on 25c red (Bl)	55	1.40
a.		Inverted surcharge	40.00	
N16	O4	100m on 1 l brn (Bk)	70	1.65
a.		Inverted surcharge	40.00	
N17	O4	200m on 1 l brn (Bk)	70	1.65
		Nos. N12-N17 (6)	3.45	8.00

No. N14 has the value in "Markes," others of the group have it in "Markiu."

"Vytis"

O4 O5

1923, Mar.

N18	O4	10m lt brn	22	28
N19	O4	20m yellow	22	28
N20	O4	25m orange	22	28
N21	O4	40m violet	22	28
N22	O4	50m yel grn	50	55
N23	O5	100m carmine	28	32
N24	O5	300m olive grn	2.50	22.50
N25	O5	400m olive brn	35	40
N26	O5	500m lilac	2.50	22.50
N27	O5	1000m blue	50	55
		Nos. N18-N27 (10)	7.51	47.94

No. N20 has the value in "Markes."

Memel stamps can be mounted in Scott's Germany Part II Album.

No. 99 Surcharged in Green

Klaipėda 400 M

1923, Apr. 13

N28	A18	100m on No. 99	3.00	5.00
N29	A18	400m on No. 99	3.00	5.00
N30	A18	500m on No. 99	3.00	5.00

The normal position of the green surcharge is sideways, with the top at the left. It exists reversed on the three stamps.

Ship — O7

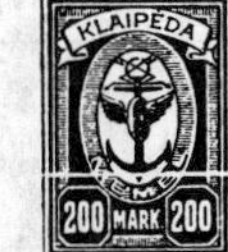

Seal — O8

Lighthouse — O9

1923, Apr. 12 Litho.

N31	O7	40m olive grn	2.00	6.00
N32	O7	50m brown	2.00	6.00
N33	O7	80m green	2.00	6.00
N34	O7	100m red	2.00	6.00
N35	O8	200m deep blue	2.00	6.00
N36	O8	300m brown	2.00	6.00
N37	O8	400m lilac	2.00	6.00
N38	O8	500m orange	2.00	6.00
N39	O8	600m olive grn	2.00	6.00
N40	O9	800m deep blue	2.00	6.00
N41	O9	1000m lilac	2.00	6.00
N42	O9	2000m red	2.00	6.00
N43	O9	3000m green	2.00	6.00
		Nos. N31-N43 (13)	26.00	78.00

Union of Memel with Lithuania. Forgeries exist.

Nos. N20, N24, N26 Surcharged in Various Colors

3 CENTŲ

1923

Thin Figures

N44	O5	2c on 300m (R)	2.50	3.75
N45	O5	3c on 300m (R)	2.50	3.75
N46	O4	10c on 25m (Bk)	2.50	3.75
a.		Double surcharge	65.00	
N47	O4	15c on 25m (Bk)	2.50	3.75
N48	O5	20c on 500m (Bl)	3.00	6.25
N49	O5	30c on 500m (Bk)	2.50	3.75
N50	O5	50c on 500m (G)	5.00	9.50
a.		Inverted surcharge	125.00	
		Nos. N44-N50 (7)	20.50	34.50

Nos. N19, N21-N27 Surcharged:

2 CENT. — 1 LITAS

N51	O4	2c on 20m yel	1.65	2.50
N52	O4	2c on 50c yel grn	1.65	2.75
N53	O4	3c on 40m vio	2.00	2.50
a.		Double surcharge	65.00	
N54	O5	3c on 300m ol grn	1.65	2.00
a.		Double surcharge	65.00	
N55	O5	5c on 100m car	2.00	2.00
N56	O5	5c on 300m ol grn (R)	2.75	3.75
N57	O5	10c on 400m ol brn	4.00	4.00
N58	O5	30c on 500m lil	2.25	6.25
N59	O5	1 l on 1000m bl	8.00	12.50
		Nos. N51-N59 (9)	25.95	38.25

There are several types of the numerals in these surcharges. Nos. N56 and N58 have "CENT" in short, thick letters, as on Nos. N44 to N50.

Nos. N18-N23, N25, N27 Surcharged

2 CENT.

Thick Figures

N60	O4	2c on 10m lt brn	75	3.75
N61	O4	2c on 20m yel	6.25	37.50
N62	O4	2c on 50m yel grn	1.50	4.50
N63	O4	3c on 10m lt brn	1.50	4.50
a.		Double surcharge	60.00	
N64	O4	3c on 40m vio	10.00	50.00
N65	O5	5c on 100m car	1.50	4.50
a.		Double surcharge	60.00	
N66	O5	10c on 400m ol brn	50.00	250.00
N67	O4	15c on 25m org	50.00	250.00
N68	O5	50c on 1000m bl	1.50	4.50
a.		Double surcharge	60.00	
N69	O5	1 l on 1000m bl	3.00	7.50
a.		Double surcharge	90.00	
		Nos. N60-N69 (10)	126.00	616.75

No. N69 is surcharged like type "b" in the following group.

Nos. N31-N43 Surcharged:

30 CENT. — a

1 LITAS — b

N70	O7(a)	15c on 40m ol grn	3.25	6.25
N71	O7(a)	30c on 50m brn	2.75	5.00
N72	O7(a)	30c on 80m grn	3.25	6.25
N73	O7(a)	30c on 100m red	2.75	5.00
N74	O8(a)	50c on 200m dp bl	3.25	6.25
N75	O8(a)	50c on 300m brn	2.75	5.00
N76	O8(a)	50c on 400m lil	3.25	6.25
N77	O8(a)	50c on 500m org	2.75	5.00
N78	O8(b)	1 l on 600m ol grn	3.25	6.25
N79	O9(b)	1 l on 800m dp bl	3.25	6.25
N80	O9(b)	1 l on 1000m lil	3.25	6.25
N81	O9(b)	1 l on 2000m red	3.25	6.25
N82	O9(b)	1 l on 3000m grn	3.25	6.25
		Nos. N70-N82 (13)	40.25	76.25

These stamps are said to have been issued to commemorate the institution of autonomous government.

Double or inverted surcharges exist on Nos. N71, N75-N77. Value, each $60.

Nos. N32, N34, N36, N38 Surcharged in Green

25 CENT.

1923

N83	O7	15c on 50m brn	87.50	1,200.
N84	O7	25c on 100m red	57.50	800.00
N85	O8	30c on 300m brn	87.50	1,000.
N86	O8	60c on 500m org	52.50	800.00

Surcharges on Nos. N83-N86 are of two types, differing in width of numerals. Values are for stamps with narrow numerals, as illustrated. Stamps with wide numerals sell for two to four times as much.

Nos. N8, N10-N11, N3 Surcharged in Red or Green

15 Centų

N87	O4	10c on 25m on 5c bl (R)	12.50	22.50
N88	O4	15c on 100m on 25c red (G)	15.00	50.00
a.		Inverted surcharge	125.00	75.00
N89	O4	30c on 400m on 1 l brn (R)	3.75	7.50
N90	O4	60c on 50m on 25c red (G)	16.00	50.00

Nos. N18-N22 Surcharged in Green or Red

15 Centų

N91	O4	15c on 10m	3.75	15.00
N92	O4	15c on 20m	2.00	8.75
N93	O4	15c on 25m	2.50	9.00
N94	O4	15c on 40m	2.00	8.75
N95	O4	15c on 50m (R)	1.50	6.50
N96	O4	25c on 10m	2.75	12.50
N97	O4	25c on 20m	2.00	8.75
N98	O4	25c on 25m	2.50	9.00
N99	O4	25c on 40m	2.00	8.75
N100	O4	25c on 50m (R)	1.50	6.50
N101	O4	30c on 10m	3.75	15.00
N102	O4	30c on 20m	2.00	8.75
N103	O4	30c on 25m	2.50	9.00
N104	O4	30c on 40m	2.00	8.75
N105	O4	30c on 50m (R)	1.50	6.50
		Nos. N91-N105 (15)	34.25	141.50

Nine stamps between Nos. N95 and N114 exist with inverted surcharge. No. 102 exists with double surcharge.

Nos. N23, N25, N27 Surcharged in Green or Red

15 Centų

N106	O5	15c on 100m	1.40	6.50
N107	O5	15c on 400m	1.25	6.00
N108	O5	15c on 1000m (R)	27.50	200.00
N109	O5	25c on 100m	1.40	6.50
N110	O5	25c on 400m	1.25	6.00
N111	O5	25c on 1000m (R)	30.00	225.00
N112	O5	30c on 100m	1.40	6.50
N113	O5	30c on 400m	1.25	6.00
N114	O5	30c on 1000m (R)	27.50	200.00
		Nos. N106-N114 (9)	92.95	662.50

Nos. N96 to N100 and N109 to N111 are surcharged "Centai", the others "Centu."

Excellent counterfeits of all Memel issues exist.

MEXICO

LOCATION — Extreme southern part of the North American continent, south of the United States

GOVT. — Republic

AREA — 756,198 sq. mi.

POP. — 76,791,819 (est. 1984)

CAPITAL — Mexico, D.F

8 Reales = 1 Peso

100 Centavos = 1 Peso

Catalogue values for unused stamps in this country are for Never Hinged items, beginning with Scott 960 in the regular postage section, Scott C302 in the airpost section, Scott E22 in the special delivery section, and Scott G21 in the insured letter section.

Values of early Mexico stamps vary according to condition. Quotations for Nos. 1-104 are for fine copies. Very fine to superb specimens sell at much higher prices, and inferior or poor copies sell at reduced prices, depending on the condition of the individual specimen.

District Overprints

Nos. 1-149 are overprinted with names of various districts, and sometimes also with district numbers and year dates. Some of the district overprints are rare and command high prices. Values given for Nos. 1-149 are for the more common district overprints.

Watermarks

Wmk. 150- PAPEL SELLADO in Sheet

Wmk. 151- R. P. S. in the Sheet (R.P.S. stands for "Renta Papel Sellado")

Wmk. 152- "CORREOS E U M" on Every Horizontal Line of Ten Stamps

Wmk. 153- "R M" Interlaced

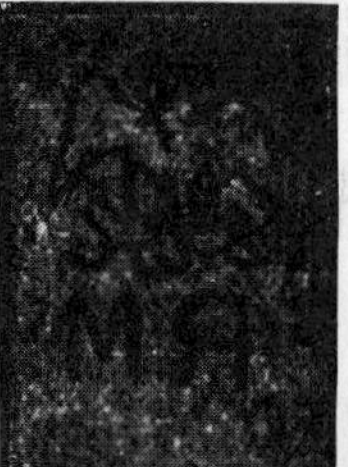

Wmk. 154- Eagle and R M

Wmk. 155- SERVICIO POSTAL DE LOS ESTADOS UNIDOS MEXICANOS

Wmk. 156- CORREOS MEXICO

Wmk. 248- SECRETARIA DE HACIENDA MEXICO

Wmk. 260- Lines and SECRETARIA DE HACIENDA MEXICO

Wmk. 272- "S. H. C. P. MEXICO" and Eagle in Circle

The first price column gives the catalogue value of an unused stamp, the second that of a used stamp.

Wmk. 279- GOBIERNO MEXICANO and Eagle in Circle

Wmk. 300- MEX-MEX and Eagle in Circle, Multiple (Letters 6mm)

Wmk. 350- MEX and Eagle in Circle, Multiple. Letters 8-9mm

Miguel Hidalgo y Costilla — A1

Handstamped with District Name

1856 Unwmk. Engr. *Imperf.*

No.	Description	Unused	Used
1	A1 ½r blue	35.00	17.50
a.	½r dark blue	35.00	17.50
b.	Without overprint	20.00	22.00
c.	Double impression		150.00
2	A1 1r yellow	17.50	2.50
a.	1r deep yellow	17.50	2.50
b.	Half used as ½r on cover		*5,000*
c.	Without overprint	10.00	12.00
d.	1r green (error)		
3	A1 2r yel grn	17.50	2.50
a.	2r blue green	140.00	25.00
b.	2r emerald	175.00	40.00
c.	Half used as 1r on cover		400.00
d.	Without overprint	25.00	15.00
e.	Printed on both sides (yel green)	150.00	175.00
4	A1 4r red	110.00	60.00
a.	Half used as 2r on cover		140.00
b.	Quarter used as 1r on cover		250.00
c.	Without overprint	90.00	120.00
d.	Three quarters used as 3r on cover		*7,000.*
5	A1 8r red lilac	225.00	140.00
a.	8r violet	200.00	130.00
b.	Without overprint	120.00	150.00
c.	Eighth used as 1r on cover		*2,500.*
d.	Quarter used as 2r on cover		160.00
e.	Half used as 4r on cover		250.00

The 1r and 2r were printed in sheets of 60 with wide spacing between stamps, and in sheets of 190 or 200 with narrow spacing.

All values have been reprinted, some of them several times. The reprints usually show signs of wear and the impressions are often smudgy. The paper is usually thicker than that of the originals. Reprints are usually on very white paper. Reprints are found with and without overprints and with cancellations made both from the original handstamps and from forged ones.

Counterfeits exist.

See Nos. 6-12. For overprints see Nos. 35-45.

1861

No.	Description	Unused	Used
6	A1 ½r blk, *buff*	35.00	20.00
a.	Without overprint	20.00	27.50
7	A1 1r blk, *green*	13.00	3.50
a.	Impression of 2r on back		400.00
b.	Without overprint	4.00	4.50
c.	Printed on both sides		300.00
d.	As "b," blk, *pink* (error)		
f.	Double impression		150.00
8	A1 2r blk, *pink*	10.00	2.00
a.	Impression of 1r on back	450.00	
b.	Half used as 1r on cover		325.00
c.	Without overprint	2.25	5.00
d.	Printed on both sides		2,250.
e.	Double impression		100.00
9	A1 4r blk, *yellow*	125.00	40.00
a.	Half used as 2r on cover		175.00
b.	Without overprint	35.00	55.00
c.	Quarter used as 1r on cover		275.00
d.	Three-quarters used as 3r on cover		*3,000.*
10	A1 4r dl rose, *yel*	140.00	50.00
a.	Half used as 2r on cover		450.00
b.	Without overprint	80.00	100.00
c.	Printed on both sides		*1,500.*
d.	Quarter used as 1r on cover		500.00
11	A1 8r blk, *red brn*	250.00	150.00
b.	Quarter used as 2r on cover		150.00
c.	Half used as 4r on cover		275.00
d.	Without overprint	75.00	150.00
e.	Three quarters used as 6r on cover		*3,500.*
12	A1 8r grn, *red brn*	350.00	140.00
a.	Half used as 4r on cover		
b.	Without overprint	100.00	125.00
c.	Quarter used as 2r on cover		
d.	Printed on both sides	*1,250.*	*1,250.*

Nos. 6, 9, 10, 11 and 12 have been reprinted. Most reprints of the ½r, 4r and 8r are on vertically grained paper. Originals are on horizontally grained paper. The original ½r stamps are much worn but the reprints are unworn. The paper of the 4r is too deep and rich in color and No. 10 is printed in too bright red.

Reprints of the 8r can only be told by experts. All these reprints are found in fancy colors and with overprints and cancellations as in the 1856 issue.

Counterfeits exist.

Hidalgo A3

Coat of Arms A4

With District Name

1864 *Perf. 12*

No.	Description	Unused	Used
14	A3 1r red	*500.00*	*1,000.*
a.	Without District Name	50	
15	A3 2r blue	*450.00*	*800.00*
a.	Without District Name	50	
16	A3 4r brown	*1,000.*	*2,000.*
a.	Without District Name	75	
b.	Vert. pair, imperf. between		
17	A3 1p black	*2,500.*	*22,500.*
a.	Without District Name	1.50	

Nos. 14 to 17 were issued with district overprints of Saltillo or Monterrey on the toned paper of 1864. Overprints on the 1867 white paper are fraudulant. Counterfeit cancellations are plentiful. The 1r red with "½" surcharge is bogus.

Overprint of District Name, etc.

1864-66 *Imperf.*

Five types of overprints:
I- District name only.
II- District name, consignment number and "1864" in large figures.
III- District name, number and "1864" in small figures.
IV- District name, number and "1865."
V- District name, number and "1866."

No.	Description	Unused	Used
18	A4 3c brn (IV, V)	1,000.	*1,900.*
a.	Without overprint	550.00	
b.	Laid paper	*3,500.*	*5,500.*
19	A4 ½r brown (I)	300.00	210.00
a.	Type II	1,500.	1,000.
b.	Without overprint	140.00	350.00
20	A4 ½r lilac (IV)	55.00	45.00
a.	Type III	60.00	55.00
b.	Type II	110.00	100.00
c.	Type V		*3,000.*
d.	½r gray (V)	65.00	65.00
e.	Without overprint	4.00	
21	A4 1r blue (IV, V)	13.00	8.00
a.	Type III	20.00	12.00
b.	Without overprint	2.00	
c.	Half used as ½r on cover		3,000.
22	A4 1r ultra (I, II)	100.00	27.50
a.	Type III	75.00	35.00
b.	Without overprint	130.00	120.00
c.	Half used as ½r on cover		*3,000.*
23	A4 2r org (III, IV, V)	4.00	2.50
a.	Type II	15.00	3.00
b.	Type I	40.00	4.50
c.	2r dp org, without ovpt., early plate	150.00	50.00
d.	Without ovpt., late plate	1.25	
e.	Half used as 1r on cover		1,000.
24	A4 4r grn (III, IV, V)	85.00	50.00
a.	Types I, II	120.00	60.00
b.	4r dk grn, without ovpt.	3.50	*125.00*
d.	Half used as 2r on cover		675.00

25 A4 8r red (IV, V) 125.00 75.00
a. Types II, III 150.00 70.00
b. Type I 300.00 115.00
c. 8r dk red, without ovpt. 5.25 *250.00*
f. Quarter used as 2r on cover 3,000.
g. Three-quarters used as 6r on cover

The 2r printings from the early plates are 25½mm high; those from the late plate, 24½mm.

Varieties listed as "Without overprint" in unused condition are remainders.

Besides the overprints of district name, number and date, Nos. 18-34 often received, in the district offices, additional overprints of numbers and sometimes year dates. Copies with these "sub-consignment numbers" sell for more than stamps without them.

Faked quarterlings and bisects of 1856-64 are plentiful.

The 3c has been reprinted from a die on which the words "TRES CENTAVOS," the outlines of the serpent and some of the background lines have been retouched.

Emperor Maximilian — A5

Overprinted with District Name, Number and Date 1866 or 866; also with Number and Date only, or with Name only

1866 **Litho.**

26 A5 7c lilac gray 50.00 95.00
a. 7c deep gray 70.00 95.00
27 A5 13c blue 18.00 18.00
a. Half used as 7c on cover *5,000.*
b. 13c cobalt blue 22.50 22.50
c. Without overprint
28 A5 25c buff 8.00 5.00
29 A5 25c orange 8.00 7.00
a. 25c red orange 15.00 11.00
b. 25c red brown 35.00 25.00
c. 25c brown 50.00 30.00
30 A5 50c green 18.00 18.00

Litho. printings have round period after value numerals.

Overprinted with District Name, Number and Date 866 or 867; also with Number and Date only

Engr.

31 A5 7c lilac 350.00 *4,000.*
a. Without overprint 2.75
32 A5 13c blue 6.00 9.00
a. Without overprint 1.00
33 A5 25c org brn 5.00 8.00
a. Without overprint 1.00
34 A5 50c green 550.00 55.00
a. Without overprint 2.00

See "sub-consignment" note after No. 25.

Engraved printings have square period after value numerals.

Varieties listed as "Without overprint" in unused condition are remainders.

Stamps of 1856-61 Overprinted Mexico

1867

35 A1 ½r blk, *buff* 1,400. 1,750.
36 A1 1r blk, *green* 40.00 6.00
37 A1 2r blk, *pink* 17.50 3.00
a. Printed on both sides 125.00
38 A1 4r red, *yel* 250.00 14.00
a. Printed on both sides 175.00
39 A1 4r red 4,000. 1,200.
40 A1 8r blk, *red brn* 1,100. 250.00
41 A1 8r grn, *red brn* 2,000.

Dangerous counterfeits exist of the "Mexico" overprint.

Same Overprint

Thin Gray Blue Paper

Wmk. 151

42 A1 ½r gray 225.00 175.00
a. Without overprint 175.00 175.00
43 A1 1r blue 375.00 60.00
b. Without overprint 300.00 75.00
44 A1 2r green 70.00 7.00
a. Printed on both sides 900.00
b. Without overprint 75.00 20.00
45 A1 4r rose 1,400. 55.00
a. Without overprint 60.00

Reprints of the ½r and 4r exist on watermarked paper. Reprints of ½r and 8r also exist in gray on thick grayish wove paper, unwatermarked.

Hidalgo — A6

Thin Figures of Value, without Period

6 CENT. 12 CENT.
25 CENT. 50 CENT.
100 CENT.

Overprinted with District Name, Number and Abbreviated Date

1868 **Unwmk.** **Litho.** ***Imperf.***

46 A6 6c blk, *buff* 27.50 14.00
47 A6 12c blk, *green* 25.00 12.00
a. Period after "12" 40.00
48 A6 25c bl, *pink* 45.00 10.00
a. Without overprint 100.00
49 A6 50c blk, *yellow* 400.00 40.00
50 A6 100c blk, *brown* 500.00 90.00
51 A6 100c brn, *brn* 1,200. 400.00

Perf.

52 A6 6c blk, *buff* 16.00 12.00
a. Without overprint 100.00
53 A6 12c blk, *green* 16.00 6.00
a. Period after "12" 60.00 20.00
b. Very thick paper 22.50 15.00
c. Without overprint 85.00
54 A6 25c bl, *pink* 35.00 4.00
b. Without overprint 125.00
55 A6 50c blk, *yellow* 200.00 20.00
56 A6 100c blk, *brown* 275.00 65.00
c. Without overprint 250.00
57 A6 100c brn, *brn* 650.00 200.00
a. Printed on both sides 850.00 700.00

Four kinds of perforation are found in the 1868 issue: serrate, square, pin and regular.

Thick Figures of Value with Period

6.CENT. 12.CENT
25.CENT. 50.CENT.
100.CENT

Overprinted with District Name, Number and Abbreviated Date

Imperf

58 A6 6c blk, *buff* 7.00 4.00
59 A6 12c blk, *green* 3.00 1.00
a. Very thick paper 7.50
c. 12c black, *buff* (error) 425.00 425.00
61 A6 25c blue, *pink* 5.50 75
a. No period after "25" 85.00
c. Very thick paper 20.00 5.00
d. "85" for "25" 50.00 25.00
e. "35" for "25" 40.00
62 A6 50c blk, *yellow* 100.00 12.00
a. No period after "50" 150.00 20.00
b. 50c blue, *lt pink* (error) *2,500.* *1,750.*
c. Half used as 25c on cover 600.00
d. Very thick paper 40.00
64 A6 100c blk, *brown* 100.00 35.00
a. No period after "100" 110.00 40.00
b. Very thick paper 50.00
c. Quarter used as 25c on cover *1,000.*

Perf.

65 A6 6c blk, *buff* 30.00 15.00
a. Very thick paper 40.00 25.00
66 A6 12c blk, *green* 4.00 4.00
a. Very thick paper 14.00 10.00
b. 12c black, *buff* (error) 450.00 450.00
68 A6 25c blue, *pink* 15.00 1.50
a. No period after "25" 60.00
c. Thick paper 10.00
d. "85" for "25" 50.00 30.00
69 A6 50c blk, *yellow* 150.00 20.00
a. No period after "50" 170.00 24.00
b. 50c blue, *lt pink* (error) *2,000.* *1,500.*
c. Thick paper 40.00
70 A6 100c blk, *brown* 150.00 45.00
a. No period after "100" 160.00 50.00
b. Very thick paper 60.00

Postal forgeries of Nos. 58-70 were printed from original plates with district name overprints forged. These include the pelure paper varieties and some thick paper varieties. The "Anotado" handstamp was applied to some of the confiscated forgeries and they were issued, including Nos. 73a and 78a.

Stamps of 1868 Handstamped

Overprinted with District Name, Number and Abbreviated Date
Thick Figures with Period

1872				***Imperf.***
71	A6	6c blk, *buff*	500.00	550.00
72	A6	12c blk, *green*	50.00	55.00
73	A6	25c bl, *pink*	30.00	35.00
a.		Pelure paper	40.00	50.00
b.		"85" for "25"		100.00
74	A6	50c blk, *yellow*	650.00	350.00
a.		No period after "50"	700.00	375.00
75	A6	100c blk, *brown*	1,200.	1,000.
a.		No period after "100"		1,050.

Perf.

76	A6	6c blk, *buff*		
77	A6	12c blk, *green*	70.00	70.00
78	A6	25c blue, *pink*	25.00	30.00
a.		Pelure paper	65.00	70.00
79	A6	50c blk, *yellow*	700.00	400.00
a.		No period after "50"		425.00
80	A6	100c blk, *brown*		1,200.

Counterfeit "Anotado" overprints abound. Genuine cancellations other than Mexico City are unknown.

The stamps of the 1872 issue are found perforated with square holes, pin-perf. 13, 14 or 15, and with serrate perforation.

Counterfeits of the 1868 6c, 12c buff, 50c and 100c (both colors) from new plates have clear, sharp impressions and more facial shading lines than the originals. These counterfeits are found perf. and imperf., with thick and thin numerals, and with the "Anotado" overprint.

Hidalgo — A8

Moiré on White Back
Overprinted with District Name, Number and Abbreviated Date
White Wove Paper

1872	**Litho.**	**Wmk. 150**		***Imperf.***
81	A8	6c green	60.00	45.00
82	A8	12c blue	35.00	25.00
a.		Laid paper		
83	A8	25c red	90.00	20.00
a.		Laid paper		
84	A8	50c yellow	400.00	200.00
a.		50c blue (error)		800.00
b.		Laid paper		
c.		As "a," without ovpt.	55.00	
86	A8	100c gray lilac	265.00	150.00

Wmk. "LA + F"

81a	A8	6c green	175.00	100.00
82b	A8	12c blue	125.00	45.00
83b	A8	25c red	160.00	35.00
c.		Without overprint	200.00	
84d	A8	50c yellow	1,000.	750.00
86a	A8	100c gray lilac	700.00	500.00

1872		**Wmk. 150**		***Pin-perf.***
87	A8	6c green	250.00	250.00
88	A8	12c blue	40.00	35.00
89	A8	25c red	95.00	30.00
b.		Laid paper		
90	A8	50c yellow	450.00	225.00
a.		50c blue (error)	*500.00*	*625.00*
b.		As "a," without overprint	75.00	
92	A8	100c gray lilac	250.00	200.00

Wmk. "LA + F"

87a	A8	6c green	325.00	265.00
88a	A8	12c blue	100.00	100.00
89a	A8	25c red	300.00	60.00
90c	A8	50c yellow	900.00	650.00
92a	A8	100c gray lilac	650.00	425.00

The watermark "LA+F" stands for La Croix Freres, the paper manufacturers, and is in double-lined block capitals 13mm high. A single stamp will show only part of this watermark.

1872		**Unwmk.**		***Imperf.***
93	A8	6c green	10.00	10.00
a.		Without moire on back	50.00	55.00
b.		Vertically laid paper		1,300.
c.		Bottom label retouched	80.00	75.00
d.		Very thick paper		20.00
94	A8	12c blue	1.60	1.40
a.		Without moire on back	20.00	30.00
b.		Vertically laid paper	300.00	175.00
c.		Thin gray bl paper of 1867 (Wmk 151)		
95	A8	25c red	5.50	1.50
a.		Without moire on back	20.00	30.00
b.		Vertically laid paper	400.00	175.00
c.		Thin gray bl paper of 1867 (Wmk 151)		
96	A8	50c yellow	110.00	25.00
a.		50c orange	110.00	25.00
b.		Without moire on back	40.00	55.00
c.		Vertically laid paper		1,500.
d.		50c blue (error)		550.00
e.		As "d," without overprint	35.00	
f.		As "e," without moire on back	55.00	
98	A8	100c gray lilac	75.00	40.00
a.		100c lilac	80.00	35.00
b.		Without moire on back	40.00	90.00
c.		Vertically laid paper		800.00

Counterfeits of these stamps are 24½mm high instead of 24mm. The printing is sharper and more uniform than the genuine. Forged district names and consignment numbers exist.

Pin-perf. and Serrate Perf.

99	A8	6c green	60.00	50.00
100	A8	12c blue	2.25	1.90
a.		Vertically laid paper		225.00
b.		Horiz. pair, imperf. vert.	75.00	75.00
c.		Vert. pair, imperf. between		
101	A8	25c red	2.50	1.00
a.		Vertically laid paper		300.00
b.		Horiz. pair, imperf. vert.	75.00	75.00
102	A8	50c yellow	110.00	40.00
a.		50c orange	110.00	40.00
b.		50c blue (error)	325.00	
c.		As "b," without overprint	30.00	
104	A8	100c lilac	100.00	55.00
a.		100c gray lilac	85.00	55.00

Hidalgo
A9 A10

A11

A12

A13

A14

Overprinted with District Name and Number and Date; also with Number and Date only
Thick Wove Paper, Some Showing Vertical Ribbing

1874-80	**Unwmk.**	**Engr.**		***Perf. 12***
105	A9	4c org ('80)	10.00	9.00
a.		Vert. pair, imperf. btwn.	50.00	
b.		Without overprint	5.50	10.00
c.		Half used as 2c on cover		1,000.
106	A10	5c brown	3.50	2.25
a.		Horizontally laid paper	75.00	45.00
b.		Imperf., pair	50.00	
c.		Horiz. pair, imperf. btwn.	40.00	
d.		Vert. pair, imperf. btwn.	90.00	90.00
e.		Without overprint	30.00	
f.		As "a," wmkd. "LACROIX"	250.00	175.00
107	A11	10c black	1.75	1.00
a.		Horizontally laid paper	2.00	2.00
b.		Horiz. pair, imperf. btwn.	50.00	50.00
c.		Without overprint	22.50	22.50
d.		Half used as 5c on cover		600.00
e.		Imperf., pair		
f.		As "a," wmkd. "LACROIX"	50.00	37.50
108	A11	10c org ('78)	1.75	1.00
a.		10c yellow bister	5.00	3.50
b.		Imperf., pair		
c.		Without overprint	45.00	45.00
d.		Half used as 5c on cover		100.00
109	A12	25c blue	70	60
b.		Horizontally laid paper	1.80	
c.		Imperf., pair	35.00	25.00
d.		Without overprint	30.00	17.50
e.		Horiz. pair, imperf. btwn.	100.00	
f.		As "b," horiz. pair, imperf. vert.	100.00	
g.		As "b," wmkd. "LACROIX"	40.00	30.00
h.		Printed on both sides		
110	A13	50c green	11.00	10.00
a.		Without overprint	40.00	
b.		Half used as 25c on cover		
111	A14	100c carmine	15.00	13.00
a.		Imperf., pair	150.00	
b.		Without overprint	40.00	
		Nos. 105-111 (7)	43.70	36.85

The "LACROIX" watermark is spelled out "LACROIX FRERES" in 2 lines of block capitals without serifs once to a sheet of horiz. laid paper. 6-12 stamps may have a portion of the wmk.

1875-77				**Wmk. 150**
112	A10	5c brown	30.00	30.00
113	A11	10c black	30.00	30.00
114	A12	25c blue	27.50	27.50
115	A13	50c green	175.00	175.00
116	A14	100c carmine	140.00	140.00

1881	**Unwmk.**	**Thin Wove Paper**		
117	A9	4c orange	37.50	37.50
a.		Without overprint	11.00	11.00
118	A10	5c brown	6.00	4.00
a.		Without overprint	32	11.00
b.		As "a," vert. pair, imperf. horiz.	87.50	
119	A11	10c orange	3.25	1.90
a.		Imperf., pair		
b.		Vert. pair, imperf. horiz.	37.50	37.50
c.		Without overprint	45	2.25
d.		Vert. pair, imperf. btwn.	37.50	37.50
120	A12	25c blue	2.25	1.40
a.		Imperf., pair		
b.		Without overprint	32	
c.		Double impression		37.50
121	A13	50c green	26.00	21.00
a.		Without overprint	2.25	16.00
122	A14	100c carmine	35.00	27.50
a.		Without overprint	3.25	
		Nos. 117-122 (6)	110.00	93.30

The stamps of 1874-81 are found with number and date wide apart, close together or omitted, and in various colors.

The thin paper is fragile and easily damaged. Values for Nos. 117-122 are for undamaged, 4 margined copies.

Benito Juárez — A15

Overprinted with District Name and Number and Date;
also with Number and Date only

1879				***Perf. 12***

Thick Wove Paper, Some Showing Vertical Ribbing

123	A15	1c brown	3.00	2.75
a.		Without overprint	60.00	110.00
b.		1c gray	14.00	12.00
124	A15	2c dk vio	2.75	2.40
a.		Without overprint	60.00	75.00
b.		Printed on both sides		
c.		2c dark gray	15.00	12.00
125	A15	5c orange	2.10	1.25
a.		Without overprint	40.00	60.00
126	A15	10c blue	2.50	1.90
a.		Without overprint	45.00	70.00
b.		10c ultra	150.00	150.00
127	A15	25c rose	6.50	7.50
a.		Without overprint	1.50	
128	A15	50c green	10.00	9.50
a.		Without overprint	1.00	
b.		Printed on both sides		150.00
129	A15	85c violet	17.50	15.00
a.		Without overprint	2.00	
130	A15	100c black	20.00	17.50
a.		Without overprint	2.25	
		Nos. 123-130 (8)	64.35	57.80

1882

Thin Wove Paper

131	A15	1c brown	24.00	20.00
a.		Without overprint	82.50	
132	A15	2c dk vio	18.00	14.00
a.		2c slate	25.00	20.00
b.		Without overprint	65.00	
c.		Half used as 1c on cover		
133	A15	5c orange	6.00	3.00
a.		Without overprint	80	
b.		Half used as 2c on cover		
134	A15	10c blue	6.00	3.00
a.		Without overprint	80	
b.		Half used as 5c on cover		
135	A15	10c brown	6.00	
a.		Imperf., pair	2.00	
136	A15	12c brown	5.00	5.00
a.		Without overprint	1.65	
b.		Imperf. pair	5.00	5.00
c.		Half used as 6c on cover		
137	A15	18c org brn	6.00	5.00
a.		Horiz. pair, imperf. btwn.	60.00	60.00
b.		Without overprint	1.40	8.25
138	A15	24c violet	6.00	5.00
a.		Without overprint	1.40	11.00
139	A15	25c rose	30.00	30.00
a.		Without overprint	2.75	
140	A15	25c org brn	3.50	
141	A15	50c green	27.50	30.00
a.		Without overprint	4.25	
142	A15	50c yellow	55.00	60.00
a.		Without overprint	90.00	
143	A15	85c red vio	35.00	
144	A15	100c black	40.00	*60.00*
a.		Without overprint	3.25	
b.		Vert. pair, imperf. btwn.	110.00	110.00
145	A15	100c orange	65.00	75.00
a.		Without overprint	100.00	
		Nos. 131-145 (15)	333.00	

No. 135, 140 and 143 exist only without overprint. They were never placed in use.

Used values for 50c, 85c and 100c of type A15 (Juarez) are for privately canceled copies.

Postally used examples sell for several times as much.

See note on thin paper after No. 122.

A16

Hidalgo — A17

Overprinted with District Name, Number and Abbreviated Date

1882-83

146 A16 2c green 5.00 4.00
a. Without overprint 12.00 9.00
147 A16 3c car lake 5.00 4.00
a. Without overprint 2.50 3.00
148 A16 6c blue ('83) 18.00 15.00
a. Without overprint 12.50 17.00
149 A16 6c ultra 4.00 3.00
a. Without overprint 1.50 3.00
b. Imperf., pair 40.00

See note on thin paper after No. 122.

1884 ***Perf. 11, 12***

Wove or Laid Paper

150 A17 1c green 2.00 50
a. Imperf., pair 17.50
b. 1c blue (error) 325.00 325.00
151 A17 2c green 3.00 75
a. Imperf., pair 30.00 30.00
b. Half used as 1c on cover
152 A17 3c green 6.00 1.25
a. Imperf., pair 60.00 60.00
b. Horiz. pair, imperf. vert. 50.00
153 A17 4c green 8.00 1.25
a. Imperf., pair 45.00 45.00
b. Half used as 2c on cover 100.00
154 A17 5c green 8.00 1.00
a. Imperf., pair 60.00 60.00
155 A17 6c green 7.25 90
a. Imperf., pair 45.00 45.00
156 A17 10c green 7.50 50
a. Imperf., pair 20.00 20.00
157 A17 12c green 14.00 2.00
a. Vert. pair, imperf. between 45.00 45.00
b. Half used as 6c on cover 90.00
158 A17 20c green 40.00 1.50
a. Diagonal half used as 10c on cover 100.00
b. Imperf., pair 85.00 85.00
159 A17 25c green 70.00 3.00
a. Imperf., pair 150.00 150.00
160 A17 50c green 50 *2.00*
a. Imperf., pair 14.00 14.00
161 A17 1p blue 50 *7.50*
a. Imperf., pair 30.00 30.00
b. Vert. pair, imperf. between
162 A17 2p blue 50 *14.00*
a. Imperf., pair 40.00 40.00
163 A17 5p blue 190.00 125.00
164 A17 10p blue 275.00 150.00
Nos. 150-162 (13) 167.25 *36.15*

Imperforate varieties should be purchased in pairs or larger. Single imperforates are usually trimmed perforated stamps.

See Nos. 165-173, 230-231.

1885

165 A17 1c pale grn 15.00 5.00
166 A17 2c carmine 10.00 2.25
a. Diagonal half used as 1c on cover 75.00
167 A17 3c org brn 14.00 4.00
a. Imperf., pair 60.00 60.00
168 A17 4c red org 20.00 12.00
169 A17 5c ultra 14.00 2.50
170 A17 6c dk brn 16.00 4.00
a. Half used as 3c on cover 75.00
171 A17 10c orange 12.00 90
a. 10c yellow 12.00 90
b. Horiz. pair, imperf. btwn. 60.00 60.00
172 A17 12c olive brn 25.00 6.00
173 A17 25c grnsh blue 90.00 14.00
Nos. 165-173 (9) 216.00 50.65

Numeral of Value — A18

1886 ***Perf. 12***

174 A18 1c blue grn 75 25
a. 1c yellow green 75 25
b. Horiz. pair, imperf. btwn. 20.00 15.00
c. Perf. 11 10.00 10.00
175 A18 2c carmine 1.00 35
a. Horiz. pair, imperf. btwn. 20.00
b. Vert. pair, imperf. between 20.00 20.00
c. Perf. 11 10.00 10.00
d. Half used as 1c on cover 75.00
176 A18 3c lilac 4.00 2.00
177 A18 4c lilac 7.00 1.50
a. Perf. 11 12.00 12.00
178 A18 5c ultra 75 25
a. 5c blue 80 30
179 A18 6c lilac 8.00 1.00
180 A18 10c lilac 8.00 30
a. Perf. 11 10.00 10.00
181 A18 12c lilac 8.00 5.00
182 A18 20c lilac 65.00 35.00
183 A18 25c lilac 25.00 6.00
Nos. 174-183 (10) 127.50 51.65

Nos. 175, 191, 194B, 196, 202 with blue or black surcharge "Vale 1 Cvo." These were made by the Colima postmaster.

1887

184 A18 3c scarlet 60 20
a. Imperf., pair
185 A18 4c scarlet 2.50 60
186 A18 6c scarlet 4.00 75
a. Horiz. pair, imperf. btwn. 20.00
187 A18 10c scarlet 1.10 20
a. Imperf., pair
b. Horiz. pair, imperf. btwn. 15.00
188 A18 20c scarlet 6.00 50
a. Horiz. pair, imperf. btwn. 25.00
189 A18 25c scarlet 5.00 1.25
Nos. 184-189 (6) 19.20 3.50

Perf. 6

190 A18 1c blue grn 6.00 4.00
191 A18 2c brn car 8.00 4.00
191A A18 3c scarlet *150.00* 60.00
192 A18 5c ultra 4.50 1.50
a. 5c blue 4.50 1.50
193 A18 10c lilac 5.00 1.50
193A A18 10c brn lil 4.00 1.00
194 A18 10c scarlet 10.00 5.00

Perf. 6x12

194A A18 1c blue grn 20.00 15.00
194B A18 2c brn car 25.00 20.00
194C A18 3c scarlet 100.00
194D A18 5c ultra 20.00 15.00
194E A18 10c lilac 20.00 18.00
194F A18 10c scarlet 25.00 20.00
194G A18 10c brn lil 25.00 15.00

Paper ruled with blue lines on face or reverse of stamp

1887 ***Perf. 12***

195 A18 1c green 25.00 14.00
196 A18 2c brn car 40.00 15.00
196A A18 3c scarlet
198 A18 5c ultra 40.00 8.00
199 A18 10c scarlet 40.00 7.00

Perf. 6

201 A18 1c green 20.00 6.00
202 A18 2c brn car 20.00 7.50
204 A18 5c ultra 16.00 4.00
205 A18 10c brn lil 14.00 3.00
206 A18 10c scarlet 85.00 12.00

Perf. 6x12

207 A18 1c green 80.00 50.00
208 A18 2c brn car 80.00 50.00
209 A18 5c ultra 80.00 50.00
210 A18 10c brn lil 100.00 40.00
211 A18 10c scarlet 110.00 70.00

1890-95 Wmk. 152 ***Perf. 11 & 12***

Wove or Laid Paper

212 A18 1c yel grn 20 15
a. 1c blue green 20 15
b. Horiz. pair, imperf. btwn. 14.00 14.00
c. Laid paper 1.00 1.00
d. Horiz. pair, imperf. vert. 14.00 14.00
213 A18 2c brn car 50 30
a. 2c carmine 50 25
b. Vert. pair, imperf. btwn. 60.00
c. Imperf., pair 80.00
214 A18 3c vermilion 30 20
b. Horiz. pair, imperf. between 12.00
215 A18 4c vermilion 1.25 80
a. Horiz. pair, imperf. between 30.00
216 A18 5c ultra 20 15
a. 5c dull blue 30 20
217 A18 6c vermilion 1.25 1.00
a. Horiz. pair, imperf. btwn. 15.00
218 A18 10c vermilion 15 15
b. Horiz. or vert. pair, imperf. btwn. 15.00
c. Vert. pair, imperf. horiz. 15.00 15.00
d. Imperf., pair 20.00
219 A18 12c ver ('95) 5.00 6.00
220 A18 20c vermilion 1.00 40
220A A18 20c dk violet 50.00 60.00
221 A18 25c vermilion 1.50 75
Nos. 212-220,221 (10) 11.35 9.90

No. 219 has been reprinted in slightly darker shade than the original.

1892

Change of Colors

222 A18 3c orange 1.50 75
223 A18 4c orange 1.75 1.00
224 A18 6c orange 2.25 75
225 A18 10c orange 12.00 75
226 A18 20c orange 20.00 2.50
227 A18 25c orange 6.50 1.75
Nos. 222-227 (6) 44.00 7.50

1892

228 A18 5p carmine 550.00 375.00
229 A18 10p carmine 900.00 550.00
230 A17 5p bl grn 1,600. 600.00
231 A17 10p bl grn *4,000. 1,250.*

1894 ***Perf. 5½, 6***

232 A18 1c yel grn 85 85
233 A18 3c vermilion 2.75 2.75
234 A18 4c vermilion 14.00 10.00
235 A18 5c ultra 4.00 1.50
236 A18 10c vermilion 2.50 1.00
236A A18 20c vermilion 40.00 40.00
237 A18 25c vermilion 20.00 20.00

Perf. 5½x11, 11x5½, Compound and Irregular

238 A18 1c yel grn 1.75 1.75
238A A18 2c brn car 5.00 5.00
238B A18 3c vermilion 10.00 10.00
238C A18 4c vermilion 15.00 15.00
239 A18 5c ultra 4.00 4.00
a. 5c blue 4.00 4.00
239C A18 6c vermilion 20.00 20.00
240 A18 10c vermilion 7.00 2.00
240A A18 20c vermilion 75.00 50.00
241 A18 25c vermilion 20.00 15.00

The stamps of the 1890 to 1895 issues are also to be found unwatermarked, as part of the sheet frequently escaped the watermark.

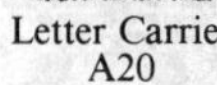

Letter Carrier A20

Mounted Courier with Pack Mule A21

Statue of Cuauhtémoc A22

Mail Coach A23

Mail Train — A24

Regular or Pin Perf. 12

1895 Wmk. 152

Wove or Laid Paper

242 A20 1c green 45 20
a. Vert. pair, imperf. horiz. 50.00
243 A20 2c carmine 65 25
a. Half used as 1c on cover 30.00
244 A20 3c org brn 65 25
a. Vert. pair, imperf. horiz. 50.00
246 A21 4c orange 2.40 55
a. 4c org red 2.40 55
247 A22 5c ultra 1.20 15
a. Imperf., pair 25.00 25.00
b. Horiz. or vert. pair, imperf. between 25.00 25.00
e. Half used as 2c on cover 60.00
248 A23 10c lil rose 1.00 25
a. Horiz. or vert. pair, imperf. between 40.00
b. Half used as 5c on cover 40.00
249 A21 12c olive brn 13.00 6.00
251 A23 15c brt blue 6.50 1.25
252 A23 20c brn rose 6.50 1.00
b. Half used as 10c on cover 50.00
253 A23 50c purple 19.00 7.50
a. Half used as 25c on cover 75.00
254 A24 1p brown 37.50 18.00
255 A24 5p scarlet 125.00 75.00
256 A24 10p deep blue 200.00 140.00
Nos. 242-256 (13) 413.85 250.40

No. 248 exists in perf. 11.

Perf. 6

242b A20 1c green
243b A20 2c carmine
244b A20 3c org brn
247c A22 5c ultra
248c A23 10c lil rose
249a A21 12c olive brn

Perf. 6x12, 12x6 & Compound or Irregular

242c A20 1c green
244c A20 3c org brn
246b A21 4c orange
247d A22 5c ultra

248d A23 10c lil rose
249b A21 12c olive brn
251a A23 15c brt blue
252a A23 20c brn rose
253b A23 50c purple

See Nos. 257-291. For overprints see Nos. O10-O48A.

"Irregular" Perfs.
Some copies perf. 6x12, 12x6, 5½x11 and 11x5½ have both perf. 6 and 12 or perf. 5½ and 11 on one or more sides of the stamp. These are known as irregular perfs.

1896-97 Wmk. 153 *Perf. 12*

257 A20 1c green 2.00 35
c. Imperf., pair
258 A20 2c carmine 2.50 40
a. Horiz. pair, imperf. vert.
259 A20 3c org brn 2.75 45
260 A21 4c orange 5.00 55
c. 4c deep orange 8.00 2.00
261 A22 5c ultra 2.00 20
a. Imperf., pair 24.00
b. Vert. pair, imperf. btwn. 40.00
262 A21 12c ol brn 35.00 24.00
263 A23 15c brt bl 35.00 4.00
264 A23 20c brn rose 250.00 125.00
265 A23 50c purple 40.00 35.00
266 A24 1p brown 110.00 50.00
267 A24 5p scarlet 325.00 200.00
268 A24 10p dp bl 500.00 240.00
Nos. 257-268 (12) 1,309. 679.95

Perf. 6

257a A20 1c green
259a A20 3c org brn
260a A21 4c orange
261c A22 5c ultra
263a A23 15c brt bl

Perf. 6x12, 12x6 and Compound or Irregular

257b A20 1c green
258b A20 2c carmine
259b A20 3c org brn
260b A21 4c orange
261d A22 5c ultra
262a A21 12c ol brn
263b A23 15c brt bl
264a A23 20c brn rose
265a A23 50c purple

1897-98 Wmk. 154 *Perf. 12*

269 A20 1c green 3.00 70
270 A20 2c scarlet 5.00 1.00
271 A21 4c orange 12.00 80
a. Horizontal pair, imperf. vertical
272 A22 5c ultra 7.00 45
a. Imperf., pair 40.00
273 A21 12c ol brn 36.00 10.00
275 A23 15c brt bl 55.00 30.00
276 A23 20c brn rose 40.00 4.00
277 A23 50c purple 60.00 20.00
278 A24 1p brown 110.00 45.00
278A A24 5p scarlet *10,000.* *10,000.*
Nos. 269-278 (9) 328.00 111.95

Perf. 6

269a A20 1c green
270a A20 2c scarlet
272b A22 5c ultra
273a A21 12c ol brn
276a A23 20c brn rose

Perf. 6x12, 12x6 and Compound or Irregular

269b A20 1c green
270b A20 2c scarlet
271b A21 4c orange
272c A22 5c ultra
273b A21 12c ol brn
275a A23 15c brt bl
276b A23 20c brn rose
277a A23 50c purple

1898 Unwmk. *Perf. 12*

279 A20 1c green 45 15
a. Horiz. pair, imperf. vert
b. Imperf., pair 45.00
280 A20 2c scarlet 1.10 25
a. 2c green (error) *210.00*
281 A20 3c org brn 1.00 25
a. Imperf., pair 55.00
b. Pair, imperf. between 30.00
282 A21 4c orange 6.00 1.20
b. 4c deep orange 15.00 5.00
283 A22 5c ultra 60 15
a. Imperf., pair 25.00 25.00
b. Pair, imperf. between 45.00
284 A23 10c lil rose 165.00 85.00
285 A21 12c ol brn 17.50 7.00
a. Imperf., pair 110.00
286 A23 15c brt bl 47.50 3.00
287 A23 20c brn rose 15.00 2.00
a. Imperf., pair 110.00
288 A23 50c purple 37.50 16.00
289 A24 1p brown 55.00 24.00

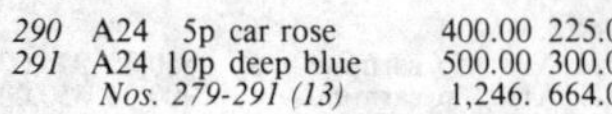

290 A24 5p car rose 400.00 225.00
291 A24 10p deep blue 500.00 300.00
Nos. 279-291 (13) 1,246. 664.00

Perf. 6

279c A20 1c green
280b A20 2c scarlet
281c A20 3c org brn
283c A22 5c ultra
287b A23 20c brn rose
291a A24 10p deep blue

Perf. 6x12, 12x6 and Compound or Irregular

279d A20 1c green
280c A20 2c scarlet
281d A20 3c org brn
282a A21 4c orange
283d A22 5c ultra
284a A23 10c lil rose
286a A23 15c brt bl
287c A23 20c brn rose
288a A23 50c purple

Forgeries of the 6 and 6x12 perforations of 1895-98 are plentiful.

Coat of Arms
A25 A26

A27

A28

A29

A30

A31

Juanacatlan Falls — A32

View of Mt. Popocatepetl A33

Cathedral, Mexico, D. F. — A34

1899 Wmk. 155 *Perf. 14, 15*

294 A25 1c green 1.65 15
295 A26 2c vermilion 3.75 20
296 A27 3c org brn 2.50 15
297 A28 5c dark blue 4.00 15
298 A29 10c vio & org 5.25 30
299 A30 15c lav & claret 6.75 25
300 A31 20c rose & dk bl 7.75 35
301 A32 50c red lil & blk 30.00 2.00
a. 50c lilac & black 35.00 2.00
302 A33 1p bl & blk 67.50 3.00
303 A34 5p car & blk 200.00 10.00
Nos. 294-303 (10) 329.15 16.55

See Nos. 304-305, 307-309. For overprints see Nos. 420-422, 439-450, 452-454, 482-483, 515-516, 539, 550, O49-O60, O62-O66, O68-O74, O101.

A35

1903

304 A25 1c violet 1.25 15
a. Booklet pane of 6 50.00
305 A26 2c green 1.65 15
a. Booklet pane of 6 75.00
306 A35 4c carmine 4.00 40
307 A28 5c orange 95 15
a. Booklet pane of 6 75.00
308 A29 10c blue & org 4.00 30
309 A32 50c car & blk 65.00 5.50
Nos. 304-309 (6) 76.85 6.65

For overprints see Nos. 451, O61, O67.

Independence Issue

Josefa Ortiz — A36

Leona Vicario — A37

López Rayon — A38

Juan Aldama — A39

Miguel Hidalgo — A40

Ignacio Allende — A41

Epigmenio Gonzalez — A42

Mariano Abasolo — A43

Declaration of Independence A44

Mass on the Mount of Crosses A45

Capture of Granaditas A46

1910 *Perf. 14*

310 A36 1c dull vio 15 20
a. Booklet pane of 4 35.00
311 A37 2c green 15 15
a. Booklet pane of 8 35.00
312 A38 3c org brn 55 25
313 A39 4c carmine 2.00 40
314 A40 5c orange 15 15
a. Booklet pane of 8 25.00
315 A41 10c blue & org 1.25 20
316 A42 15c gray bl & cl 7.00 45
317 A43 20c red & bl 4.00 35
318 A44 50c red brn & blk 10.00 1.50
319 A45 1p blue & blk 12.00 1.75
320 A46 5p car & blk 45.00 4.50
Nos. 310-320 (11) 82.25 9.90

Centenary of the independence of Mexico from Spain.

For overprints and surcharges see Nos. 370-380, 423-433, 455-465, 484-494, 517-538, 540-549, 551-558, 577-590, O75-O85, O102-O112, O191-O192, O195, RA13, Merida 1.

CIVIL WAR ISSUES

During the 1913-16 Civil War, provisional issues with various handstamped overprints were circulated in limited areas.

Sonora

A47

Seal

Typeset in a row of five varieties. Two impressions placed tete beche (foot to foot) constitute a sheet. The settings show various wrong font and defective letters, "!" for "1" in "1913," etc. The paper occasionally has a manufacturer's watermark.

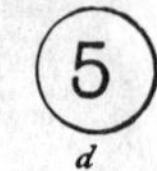

a *b* *c* *d*

Four Types of the Numerals.
a- Wide, heavy-faced numerals.
b- Narrow Roman numerals.
c- Wide Roman numerals.
d- Gothic or sans-serif numerals.

Embossed "CONSTITUCIONAL"

1913 Typeset Unwmk. *Perf. 12*

321 A47 (a) 5c blk & red 2,500. 650.00
a. "CENTAVOB" *2,750.* *700.00*

Colorless Roulette

322 A47(b) 1c blk & red 10.00 12.00
a. With green seal *750.00* *650.00*
323 A47(a) 2c blk & red 7.00 7.00
a. With green seal *1,000.* *1,000.*
324 A47(c) 2c blk & red 35.00 35.00
a. With green seal *2,000.* *2,000.*
325 A47(a) 3c blk & red 45.00 37.50
a. With green seal *400.00* *400.00*
326 A47(a) 5c blk & red 150.00 37.50
a. "CENTAVOB" 175.00 42.50
327 A47(d) 5c blk & red 400.00 200.00
a. With green seal 650.00
328 A47(b) 10c blk & red 12.50 15.00

Black Roulette

329 A47(d) 5c blk & red 75.00 45.00
a. "MARO" 85.00 50.00

Stamps are known with the embossing double or omitted.

The varieties with green seal are from a few sheets embossed "Constitucional" which were in stock at the time the green seal control was adopted.

Without Embossing
With Green Seal
Colorless Roulette

336 A47(b) 1c blk & red 5.00 5.00
337 A47(a) 3c blk & red 4.50 4.50
a. Imperf. 250.00
338 A47(a) 5c blk & red 700.00 200.00
a. "CENTAVOB" *750.00* 225.00
339 A47(b) 10c blk & red 3.00 3.00

Colored Roulette

340 A47(d) 5c brnsh blk & red 6.00 3.00
a. 5c lilac brown & red 45.00 11.00
b. Double seal *1,000.* *750.00*
c. Red printing omitted *1,000.*

1913-14 ***Black Roulette***

With Green Seal

341 A47(a) 1c blk & red 1.20 1.00
b. "erano" ('14) 60.00 60.00
342 A47(d) 2c blk & red 1.20 90
a. "erano" ('14) 30.00 35.00
343 A47(a) 3c blk & red 1.75 1.50
a. "CENTAVO" 25.00 25.00
b. "erano" ('14) 35.00 35.00
344 A47(d) 5c blk & red 1.75 1.00
b. Heavy black penetrating roulette 2.75 1.75
c. As "b." "MARO" 7.50 5.00

Stamps without seal are unfinished remainders.

On Nos. 341-344 the rouletting cuts the paper slightly or not at all. On Nos. 344b-344c the rouletting is heavy, cutting deeply into the paper.

1914

345 A47(a) 5c blk & red 2.00 1.75
346 A47(b) 10c blk & red 1.20 1.20

Coat of Arms — A49

Revenue Stamps Used for Postage

1913 **Litho.** ***Rouletted 14, 14x7***

347 A49 1c yel grn 1.50 1.50
a. With coupon 5.00 5.00
348 A49 2c violet 3.00 3.00
a. With coupon 12.00 12.00
349 A49 5c brown 45 45
a. With coupon 1.25 1.25
350 A49 10c claret 2.00 2.00
a. With coupon 10.00 10.00
351 A49 20c gray grn 2.25 2.75
a. With coupon 15.00 15.00
352 A49 50c ultra 8.00 10.00
a. With coupon 50.00 40.00
353 A49 1p orange 35.00 40.00
a. With coupon 125.00 100.00
Nos. 347-353 (7) 52.20 59.70

For a short time these stamps (called "Ejercitos") were used for postage with coupon attached. Later this was required to be removed unless they were to be used for revenue. Values above 1p were used for revenue. Imperfs exist of all values, but were not issued.

Use of typeset Sonora revenue stamps for postage was not authorized or allowed.

Coat of Arms
A50 A51

5c (A50): "CINCO CENTAVOS" 14x2mm

1914 ***Rouletted 9½x14***

354 A50 1c dp bl 45 45
355 A50 2c yel grn 60 35
a. 2c green 3.00 1.75
356 A50 4c bl vio 11.00 2.50
a. Horiz. pair, imperf. btwn. 225.00
357 A50 5c gray grn 11.00 3.00
a. Horiz. pair imperf. btwn. 65.00
358 A50 10c red 45 45
359 A50 20c yel brn 60 60
a. 20c deep brown 2.25 2.25
b. Horiz. pair, imperf. btwn. 225.00
360 A50 50c claret 2.50 3.50
a. Horiz. pair, imperf. btwn. 225.00
361 A50 1p brt vio 14.00 16.00
a. Horiz. pair, imperf. btwn. 200.00
Nos. 354-361 (8) 40.60 26.85

Nos. 354-361 (called "Transitorios") exist imperf. but were not regularly issued.

See No. 369. For overprints see Nos. 362-368, 559-565.

Overprinted in Black

Victoria de
TORREON
ABRIL 2-1914

1914

362 A50 1c dp bl 150.00 125.00
363 A50 2c yel grn 175.00 150.00
364 A50 4c bl vio 200.00 250.00
365 A50 5c gray grn 18.00 20.00
a. Horiz. pair, imperf. btwn. 425.00
366 A50 10c red 100.00 100.00
367 A50 20c yel brn *1,750.* *1,750.*
368 A50 50c claret *2,000.* *2,000.*

Excellent counterfeits of this overprint exist.

Redrawn

"CINCO CENTAVOS" 16x2½mm

1914 ***Perf. 12***

369 A51 5c gray green 15 15

Imperfs are printers' waste.

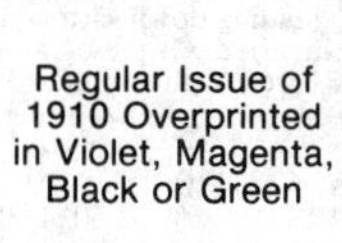

Regular Issue of 1910 Overprinted in Violet, Magenta, Black or Green

1914 **Wmk. 155** ***Perf. 14***

370 A36 1c dl vio 70 60
a. Booklet pane of 4 75.00
371 A37 2c green 1.50 1.25
a. Booklet pane of 8 75.00
372 A38 3c org brn 1.50 1.25
373 A39 4c carmine 2.50 2.00
374 A40 5c orange 50 30
a. Booklet pane of 8 60.00
375 A41 10c bl & org 3.00 2.00
376 A42 15c gray bl & cl 5.00 3.00
377 A43 20c red & blue 10.00 6.00
378 A44 50c red brn & blk 12.00 8.00
379 A45 1p bl & blk 25.00 10.00
380 A46 5p car & blk 165.00 150.00
Nos. 370-380 (11) 226.70 184.40

Overprinted On Postage Due Stamps of 1908

381 D1 1c blue 14.00 16.00
382 D1 2c blue 14.00 16.00
383 D1 4c blue 14.00 16.00
384 D1 5c blue 14.00 16.00
385 D1 10c blue 14.00 16.00
Nos. 381-385 (5) 70.00 80.00

This overprint is found double, inverted, sideways and in pairs with and without the overprint.

There are two or more types of this overprint.

The Postage Due Stamps and similar groups of them which follow were issued and used as regular postage stamps.

Values are for copies where the overprint is clear enough to be expertised.

Counterfeits abound.

A52 A53

1914 **Unwmk.** **Litho.** ***Perf. 12***

386 A52 1c pale blue 35 50
387 A52 2c light green 30 45
388 A52 3c orange 50 50
389 A52 5c deep rose 50 30
390 A52 10c rose 70 85
391 A52 15c rose lilac 1.20 1.75
392 A52 50c yellow 2.00 2.50
a. 50c ocher 1.75
393 A52 1p violet 8.50 12.00
Nos. 386-393 (8) 14.05 18.85

Nos. 386-393, are known imperforate.

This set is usually called the Denver Issue because it was printed there.

For overprints and surcharges see Nos. 566-573, 591-592.

Revenue Stamps Used for Postage

1914, July ***Perf. 12***

393A A53 1c rose 1.25 20.00
393B A53 2c lt grn 1.25 18.00
393C A53 3c lt org 1.25 20.00
393D A53 5c red 1.00 8.00
393E A53 10c gray grn 1.00 35.00

Nos. 393A-393E were used in the northeast. Values are for examples with postal cancellations.

Background as A55 — A54

A55

1914 ***Imperf.***

Values and Inscriptions in Black

Inscribed "SONORA"

394 A54 1c bl & red 25 25
a. Double seal
b. Without seal 20.00
395 A54 2c grn & org 30 30
a. Without seal 100.00
396 A54 5c yel & grn 30 30
a. 5c orange & green 1.50 1.25
b. Without seal 200.00
397 A54 10c lt bl & red 3.50 1.75
a. 10c blue & red 40.00 15.00
398 A54 20c yel & grn 1.75 2.00
399 A54 20c org & bl 15.00 17.50
400 A54 50c grn & org 1.25 1.25
Nos. 394-400 (7) 22.35 23.35

Stamps of type A54 are usually termed the "Coach Seal Issue".

Inscribed "DISTRITO SUR DE LA BAJA CAL"

401 A54 1c yel & bl 2.00 *30.00*
a. Without seal 50.00
402 A54 2c gray & ol grn 2.50 *25.00*
403 A54 5c olive & rose 2.00 *20.00*
a. Without seal 50.00
404 A54 10c pale red & dl vio 2.00 *20.00*
a. Without seal 50.00

Counterfeit cancellations exist.

Inscribed "SONORA"

405 A55 1c blue & red 6.00
a. Without seal 50.00
406 A55 2c grn & org 50
407 A55 5c yel & grn 50 *2.50*
a. Without seal 75.00
408 A55 10c blue & red 50 *2.50*
409 A55 20c yel & grn 30.00 *15.00*
a. Without seal 50.00
b. Double seal *80.00*
Nos. 405-409 (5) 37.50

With "PLATA" added to the inscription

410 A55 1c bl & red 1.00
a. "PLATA" inverted 60.00
b. Pair, one without "PLATA" 15.00
411 A55 10c blue & red 1.00
412 A55 20c yel & grn 2.50
a. "PLATA" double 50.00
413 A55 50c gray grn & org 1.75
a. Without seal 1.00
b. As "a," "P" of "PLATA" missing 150.00

Stamps of type A55 are termed the "Anvil Seal Issue".

Nos. 394-413 were issued without gum.

Nos. 410-413 were not placed in use.

Oaxaca

Coat of Arms — A56

5c:

Type I- Thick numerals, 2mm wide.

Type II- Thin numerals, 1½mm wide.

1915 **Typo.** **Unwmk.** ***Perf. 8½ to 14***

414 A56 1c dull vio 85 1.25
415 A56 2c emerald 1.50 2.25
a. Inverted numeral 30.00
e. Numeral omitted 35.00
416 A56 3c red brn 2.25 3.50
b. Inverted numeral 24.00
417 A56 5c org (type I) 20.00 25.00
a. Tete beche pair 60.00 60.00
418 A56 5c org (type II) 50 75
a. Types I and II in pair 70.00
419 A56 10c bl & car 1.75
Nos. 414-419 (6) 26.85

Many printing errors, imperfs and part perfs exist. Mostly these are printers' waste, private reprints or counterfeits.

Nos. 414-419 printed on backs of post office receipt forms.

Regular Issues of 1899-1910 Overprinted in Black

1914 **Wmk. 155** ***Perf. 14***

On Issues of 1899-1903

420 A28 5c orange
421 A30 15c lav & claret 150.00 150.00
422 A31 20c rose & dk bl 500.00 400.00

Counterfeits exist.

On Issue of 1910

423 A36 1c dl vio 20 20
424 A37 2c green 25 25
425 A38 3c org brn 40 40
426 A39 4c carmine 50 50
427 A40 5c orange 15 15
428 A41 10c bl & org 25 25
429 A42 15c gray bl & claret 70 60
430 A43 20c red & bl 75 70

Overprinted

GOBIERNO
Y
CONSTITUCIONALISTA

431 A44 50c red brn & blk 1.75 1.50
432 A45 1p bl & blk 7.50 5.00
433 A46 5p car & blk 40.00 30.00
Nos. 423-433 (11) 52.45 39.55

In the first setting of the overprint on 1c to 20c, the variety "GONSTITUCIONALISTA" occurs 4 times in each sheet of 100. In the second setting it occurs on the last stamp in each row of 10.

The overprint exists reading downward on Nos. 423-430; inverted on Nos. 431-433; double on Nos. 423-425, 427.

Postage Due Stamps of 1908 Overprinted

GOBIERNO
$
CONSTITUCIONALISTA

434 D1 1c blue 1.75 1.75
435 D1 2c blue 2.00 2.00
436 D1 4c blue 15.00 15.00
437 D1 5c blue 15.00 15.00
438 D1 10c blue 2.50 2.50
a. Double overprint
Nos. 434-438 (5) 36.25 36.25

Preceding Issues Overprinted

This is usually called the "Villa" monogram. Counterfeits abound.

1915

On Issue of 1899

439 A25 1c green *100.00*
440 A26 2c vermilion *100.00*
441 A27 3c org brn *50.00*
442 A28 5c dark blue *100.00*
443 A29 10c vio & org *100.00*
444 A30 15c lav & claret *100.00*
445 A31 20c rose & bl *100.00*
446 A32 50c red lil & blk *250.00*
447 A33 1p blue & blk *250.00*
448 A34 5p car & blk *500.00*

On Issue of 1903

449 A25 1c violet *100.00*
450 A26 2c green *100.00*
451 A35 4c carmine *100.00*
452 A28 5c orange 12.50
a. Inverted overprint *20.00*
453 A29 10c blue & org *75.00*
454 A32 50c car & blk *200.00*

In Sept. 1915 Postmaster Hinojosa ordered a special printing of Nos. 439-454 (as valued) for sale to collectors. Earlier a small quantity of Nos. 444-445, 448 and 452-454 was regularly issued. They are hard to distinguish and sell for much more. Counterfeits abound.

On Issue of 1910

455 A36 1c dl vio 85 1.00
456 A37 2c green 40 60
457 A38 3c org brn 60 75
458 A39 4c carmine 4.00 4.50
459 A40 5c orange 18 18
460 A41 10c bl & org 7.00 7.50
461 A42 15c gray bl & cl 3.00 4.00
462 A43 20c red & bl 5.50 7.00
463 A44 50c red brn & blk 13.00 14.00
464 A45 1p bl & blk 17.00 20.00
465 A46 5p car & blk *150.00*
Nos. 455-464 (10) 51.53 59.53

Nos. 455-465 are known with overprint inverted, double and other variations. Most were ordered by Postmaster General Hinojosa for philtelic purposes. They were sold at a premium. This applies to Nos. 354-361, 386-393, 431-433 with this monogram as well.

Overprinted On Postage Due Stamps of 1908

466 D1 1c blue 9.50 10.00
467 D1 2c blue 9.50 10.00
468 D1 4c blue 9.50 10.00
469 D1 5c blue 9.50 10.00
470 D1 10c blue 9.50 10.00
Nos. 466-470 (5) 47.50 50.00

Nos. 466 to 470 are known with inverted overprint. All other values of the 1899 and 1903 issues exist with this overprint. See note after No. 465.

Issues of 1899-1910 Overprinted

This is called the "Carranza" or small monogram. Counterfeits abound.

On Issues of 1899-1903

482 A28 5c orange 20.00 20.00
483 A30 15c lav & claret 80.00 80.00

On Issue of 1910

484 A36 1c dl vio 70 70
485 A37 2c green 70 60
486 A38 3c org brn 75 75
487 A39 4c carmine 2.00 2.00
488 A40 5c orange 25 25
489 A41 10c bl & org 1.50 1.50
a. Double ovpt., one invtd. 25.00
490 A42 15c gray bl & cl 1.50 1.50
491 A43 20c red & blue 1.50 1.50
492 A44 50c red brn & blk 10.00 10.00
493 A45 1p bl & blk 15.00 15.00
494 A46 5p car & blk 150.00 *150.00*
Nos. 484-494 (11) 183.90 *183.80*

All values exist with inverted overprint; all but 5p with double overprint.

Overprinted On Postage Due Stamps of 1908

495 D1 1c blue 11.00 12.00
496 D1 2c blue 11.00 12.00
497 D1 4c blue 11.00 12.00
498 D1 5c blue 11.00 12.00
499 D1 10c blue 11.00 12.00
Nos. 495-499 (5) 55.00 60.00

Nos. 495-499 exist with inverted overprint.

It is stated that, in parts of Mexico occupied by the revolutionary forces, instructions were given to apply a distinguishing overprint to all stamps found in the post offices. This overprint was usually some arrangement or abbreviation of "Gobierno Constitucionalista". Such overprints as were specially authorized or were in general use in large sections of the country are listed. Numerous other handstamped overprints were used in one town or locality. They were essentially military faction control marks necessitated in most instances by the chaotic situation following the split between Villa and Carranza. The fact that some were often struck in a variety of colors and positions suggests the influence of philatelists.

Coat of Arms
A57

Statue of Cuauhtemoc
A58

Ignacio Zaragoza
A59

José María Morelos
A60

Francisco Madero
A61

Benito Juárez
A62

1915 Unwmk. Litho. *Rouletted 14*

500 A57 1c violet 15 15
501 A58 2c green 25 20
502 A59 3c brown 25 25
503 A60 4c carmine 30 25
504 A61 5c orange 30 25
505 A62 10c ultra 25 20
Nos. 500-505 (6) 1.50 1.30

Nos. 500-505 exists imperf.; some exist imperf. vertically or horizontally; some with rouletting and perforation combined. These probably were not regularly issued in these forms.

See Nos. 506-511. For overprints see Nos. O86-O97.

Map of Mexico — A63

Veracruz Lighthouse
A64

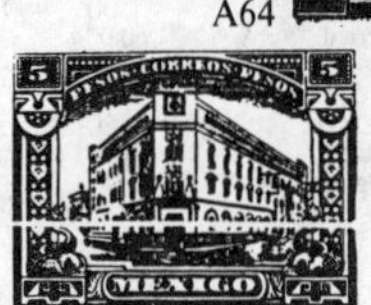

Post Office, Mexico, D.F. — A65

TEN CENTAVOS:
Type I- Size 19½x24mm. Crossed lines on coat.
Type II- Size 19x23½mm. Diagonal lines only on coat.

1915-16 *Perf. 12*

506 A57 1c violet 20 30
507 A58 2c green 20 30
508 A59 3c brown 30 30
509 A60 4c carmine 30 35
a. "CEATRO" 5.00 7.00
510 A61 5c orange 35 35
511 A62 10c ultra, type I 35 35
a. 10c ultra, II 20 25

Engr.

512 A63 40c slate 50 45
513 A64 1p brn & blk 70 1.00
a. Inverted center 200.00
514 A65 5p cl & ultra ('16) 8.00 9.00
a. Inverted center 400.00
Nos. 506-514 (9) 10.90 12.40

Nos. 507-508, 510-514, exist imperf; Nos. 513-514 imperf with inverted center. These varieties were not regularly issued.

See Nos. 626-628, 647. For overprints see Nos. O92-O100, O121-O123, O132-O133, O142-O144, O153-O154, O162-O164, O174, O188, O193, O207, O222.

Issues of 1899-1910 Overprinted in Blue, Red or Black

1916 Wmk. 155 *Perf. 14*

On Issues of 1899-1903

515 A28 5c org (Bl) 85.00
516 A30 15c lav & cl (Bl) 425.00 425.00

On Issue of 1910

517 A36 1c dl vio (R) 3.50 *5.00*
518 A37 2c grn (R) 50 35
519 A38 3c org brn (Bl) 55 35
a. Double overprint 500.00
520 A39 4c car (Bl) 6.00 *8.00*
521 A40 5c org (Bl) 25 25
a. Double overprint 75.00
522 A41 10c bl & org (R) 1.25 1.50
523 A42 15c gray bl & cl (Bk) 1.75 3.00
524 A43 20c red & bl (Bk) 1.75 3.00
525 A44 50c red brn & blk (R) 8.50 5.00
526 A45 1p bl & blk (R) 15.00 6.50
527 A46 5p car & blk (R) 150.00 125.00
Nos. 517-527 (11) 189.05 157.95

Nos. 519-524 exist with this overprint (called the "Corbata") reading downward and Nos. 525-527 with it inverted. Of these varieties only Nos. 519-521 were regularly issued.

On Nos. 423-430

528 A36 1c dl vio (R) 2.50 4.00
529 A37 2c grn (R) 75 60
530 A38 3c org brn (Bl) 60 60
531 A39 4c car (Bl) 60 60
532 A40 5c org (Bl) 1.00 30
533 A41 10c bl & org (R) 75 60
534 A42 15c gray bl & cl (Bk) 80 80
535 A43 20c red & bl (Bk) 80 80

On Nos. 431-433 in Red

536 A44 50c red brn & blk 7.50 6.00
537 A45 1p bl & blk 16.00 16.00
538 A46 5p car & blk 150.00 140.00
a. Tablet inverted 200.00
Nos. 528-538 (11) 181.30 170.30

Nos. 529 to 535 are known with the overprint reading downward and Nos. 536 to 538 with it inverted.

On No. 482

539 A28 5c org (Bl) 60.00 *60.00*

On Nos. 484-494

540 A36 1c dl vio (R) 2.50 *3.50*
541 A37 2c grn (R) 60 60
a. Monogram inverted 40.00
542 A38 3c org brn (Bl) 50 60
543 A39 4c car (Bl) 5.00 6.00
544 A40 5c org (Bl) 85 25
545 A41 10c bl & org (R) 1.50 2.00
546 A42 15c gray bl & cl (Bk) 1.25 60
a. Tablet double *500.00* *500.00*
b. Monogram double *500.00*
547 A43 20c red & bl (Bk) 1.20 1.10
548 A44 50c red brn & blk (R) 7.50 9.00
a. Monogram inverted 65.00
b. Tablet inverted 75.00
549 A45 1p bl & blk (R) 11.00 12.00
a. Tablet double 175.00
b. Monogram inverted 60.00
Nos. 539-549 (11) 91.90 *95.65*

Nos. 541-547 exist with overprint reading downward. A few 5p were overprinted for the Post Office collection.

On No. 453

550 A28 5c org (Bl) 90.00 *90.00*

On Nos. 455-462

551 A36 1c dl vio (R) 11.00 *15.00*
552 A37 2c grn (R) 1.50 90
553 A38 3c org brn (Bl) 3.25 *4.50*
554 A39 4c car (Bl) 13.00 *15.00*
555 A40 5c org (Bl) 4.50 *6.00*
556 A41 10c bl & org (R) 12.00 *14.00*
a. Monogram inverted 125.00
557 A42 15c gray bl & cl (Bk) 12.00 *14.00*
a. Monogram inverted 90.00
558 A43 20c red & bl (Bk) 12.00 *14.00*
a. Monogram inverted 82.50
Nos. 550-558 (9) 159.25 *173.40*

Stamps of 50c, 1p and 5p were overprinted for the Post Office collection but were not regularly issued.

Issues of 1914 Overprinted

On "Transitorio" Issue

Rouletted 9½x14

Unwmk.

559 A50 1c dp bl (R) 24.00 24.00
560 A50 2c yel grn (R) 12.00 18.00
561 A50 4c bl vio (R) 250.00 200.00
562 A50 10c red (Bl) 2.00 6.00
a. Vertical overprint 125.00
563 A50 20c yel brn (Bl) 3.00 6.00
564 A50 50c cl (Bl) 15.00 20.00
565 A50 1p vio (Bl) 24.00 24.00
a. Horiz. pair, imperf. btwn.

Overprinted in Blue

On "Denver" Issue

Perf. 12

566 A52 1c pale bl 3.75
567 A52 2c lt grn 3.75
568 A52 3c orange 45
569 A52 5c dp rose 45
570 A52 10c rose 45
571 A52 15c rose lil 45
572 A52 50c yellow 1.10
573 A52 1p violet 9.50
Nos. 566-573 (8) 19.90

Many of the foregoing stamps exist with the "G. P. DE M." overprint printed in other colors than those listed. These "trial color" stamps were not regularly on sale at post offices but were available for postage and used copies are known.

There appears to have been speculation in Nos. 516, 517, 520, 528, 539, 540, 543, 566, and 567. A small quantity of each of these stamps was sold at post offices but subsequently they could be obtained only from officials or their agents at advanced prices.

Venustiano Carranza
A66

Coat of Arms
A67

1916, June 1 Engr. *Perf. 12*

574 A66 10c blue 1.25 65
a. Imperf., pair 22.50
575 A66 10c lil brn 12.00 13.00
a. Imperf., pair 45.00

Entry of Carranza into Mexico, D.F.

Stamps of type A66 with only horizontal lines in the background of the oval are essays.

1916

576 A67 1c lilac 20 20

Issue of 1910 Surcharged in Various Colors

This overprint is called the "Barril."

1916 Wmk. 155 *Perf. 14*

577 A36 5c on 1c dl vio (Br) 25 30
a. Vertical surcharge 1.25 1.25
b. Double surcharge 150.00
578 A36 10c on 1c dl vio (Bl) 35 40
a. Double surcharge 100.00
579 A40 20c on 5c org (Br) 20 30
a. Double surcharge 90.00
580 A40 25c on 5c org (G) 40 50
581 A37 60c on 2c grn (R) 17.00 20.00
Nos. 577-581 (5) 18.20 21.50

On Nos. 423-424, 427

582 A36 5c on 1c dl vio (Br) 25 35
a. Double tablet, one vertical 100.00
b. Inverted tablet 250.00 250.00
583 A36 10c on 1c dl vio (Bl) 90 90
584 A40 25c on 5c org (G) 35 45
a. Inverted tablet 225.00 225.00
585 A37 60c on 2c grn (R) 200.00 *275.00*

No. 585 was not regularly issued.

The variety "GONSTITUCIONALISTA" is found on Nos. 582 to 585.

On No. 459

586 A40 25c on 5c org (G) 20 15

On Nos. 484-485, 488

587 A36 5c on 1c dl vio (Br) 15.00 20.00
a. Vertical tablet 100.00 125.00
588 A36 10c on 1c dl vio (Bl) 5.00 7.50
589 A40 25c on 5c org (G) 1.00 1.50
a. Inverted tablet 225.00
590 A37 60c on 2c grn (R) 225.00

No. 590 was not regularly issued.

Surcharged on "Denver" Issue of 1914

1916 **Unwmk.** ***Perf. 12***

591	A52	60c on 1c pale bl (Br)	3.00	6.00
592	A52	60c on 2c lt grn (Br)	3.00	6.00
a.		Inverted surcharge	500.00	

Postage Due Stamps Surcharged Like Nos. 577-581

1916 **Wmk. 155** ***Perf. 14***

593	D1	5c on 1c bl (Br)	2.50	
594	D1	10c on 2c bl (V)	2.50	
595	D1	20c on 4c bl (Br)	2.50	
596	D1	25c on 5c bl (G)	2.50	
597	D1	60c on 10c bl (R)	1.50	
598	D1	1p on 1c bl (C)	1.50	
599	D1	1p on 2c bl (C)	1.50	
600	D1	1p on 4c bl (C)	80	80
601	D1	1p on 5c bl (C)	2.50	
602	D1	1p on 10c bl (C)	2.50	
		Nos. 593-602 (10)	20.30	

There are numerous "trial colors" and "essays" of the overprints and surcharges on Nos. 577 to 602. They were available for postage though not regularly issued.

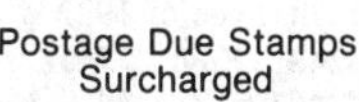
Postage Due Stamps Surcharged

1916

603	D1	2.50p on 1c bl	1.25	1.25
604	D1	2.50p on 2c bl	10.00	
605	D1	2.50p on 4c bl	10.00	
606	D1	2.50p on 5c bl	10.00	
607	D1	2.50p on 10c bl	10.00	
		Nos. 603-607 (5)	41.25	

Regular Issue

Ignacio Zaragoza A68

Ildefonso Vázquez A69

M. J. Pino Suarez A70

Jesús Carranza A71

Maclovio Herrera A72

F. I. Madero A73

Belisario Dominguez A74

Aquiles Serdán A75

Rouletted 14½

1917-20 **Engr.** **Unwmk.**

Thick Paper

608	A68	1c dl vio	40	20
609	A68	1c gray ('20)	2.00	1.50
a.		1c lilac gray ('20)	1.00	25
610	A69	2c gray grn	50	15
611	A70	3c bis brn	50	15
612	A71	4c carmine	1.00	40
613	A72	5c ultra	1.50	25
a.		Horiz. pair, imperf. btwn.	50.00	
b.		Imperf., pair		50.00
614	A73	10c blue	2.00	15
a.		Without imprint	3.00	25
615	A74	20c rose	22.50	60
a.		20c brown rose	25.00	60
616	A75	30c gray brn	60.00	1.00
617	A75	30c gray blk ('20)	70.00	1.00
		Nos. 608-617 (10)	160.40	5.40

Perf. 12

Thick or Medium Paper

618	A68	1c dl vio	20.00	20.00
619	A69	2c gray grn	5.00	5.00
620	A70	3c bis brn ('17)	100.00	100.00
621	A71	4c carmine	*300.00*	*300.00*
622	A72	5c ultra	2.00	20
623	A73	10c bl ('17)	4.50	20
a.		Without imprint ('17)	12.00	12.00
624	A74	20c rose ('20)	95.00	2.00
625	A75	30c gray blk ('20)	80.00	1.65

Thin or Medium Paper

626	A63	40c violet	40.00	50
627	A64	1p bl & blk	35.00	1.00
a.		With center of 5p	450.00	
b.		1p bl & dk bl (error)	500.00	20.00
c.		Vert. pair, imperf. btwn.		250.00
628	A65	5p grn & blk	1.00	1.00
a.		With violet or red control number		7.50
b.		With center of 1p	425.00	

The 1, 2, 3, 5 and 10c are known on thin paper perforated. It is stated they were printed for Postal Union and "specimen" purposes.

All values exist imperf; these are not known to have been regularly issued. Nos. 627a and 628b were not regularly issued.

All values except 3c have an imprint.

For overprints and surcharges see Nos. B1-B2, O113-O165.

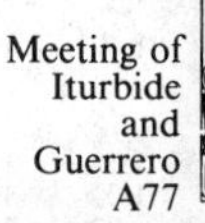
Meeting of Iturbide and Guerrero A77

Entering City of Mexico — A78

1921

632	A77	10c bl & brn	15.00	3.00
a.		Center inverted		*6,000.*
633	A78	10p blk brn & blk	15.00	35.00

Commemorating the meeting of Augustin de Iturbide and Vincente Guerrero and the entry into City of Mexico in 1821.

For overprint see No. O194.

"El Salto de Agua," Public Fountain A79

Pyramid of the Sun at Teotihuacán A80

Chapultepec Castle A81

Columbus Monument A82

Juárez Colonnade, Mexico, D. F. — A83

Monument to Josefa Ortiz de Dominguez A84

Cuauhtémoc Monument A85

1923 **Unwmk.** ***Rouletted 14½***

634	A79	2c scarlet	1.75	20
635	A80	3c bis brn	1.75	25
636	A81	4c green	2.50	75
637	A82	5c orange	4.25	20
638	A83	10c brown	3.75	15
639	A85	10c claret	3.00	15
640	A84	20c dk bl	40.00	1.75
641	A85	30c dk grn	27.50	2.00
		Nos. 634-641 (8)	84.50	5.45

See Nos. 642-646, 650-657, 688-692, 727A, 735A-736. For overprints see Nos. O166-O173, O178-O181, O183-O187, O196-O197, O199-O206, O210, O212-O214, O217-O222.

Communications Building — A87

Palace of Fine Arts (National Theater) — A88

Two types of 1p:
I- Eagle on palace dome.
II- Without eagle.

1923 **Wmk. 156** ***Perf. 12***

642	A79	2c scarlet	9.00	9.00
643	A81	4c green	1.40	35
644	A82	5c orange	8.00	7.00
645	A85	10c brn lake	11.00	6.00
646	A83	30c dk grn	95	20
647	A63	40c violet	1.00	25
648	A87	50c ol brn	60	25
649	A88	1p red brn & bl (I)	1.00	55
a.		Type II	3.00	*10.00*
		Nos. 642-649 (8)	32.95	23.60

Most of Nos. 642-649 are known imperforate or part perforate but probably were not regularly issued.

For overprints see Nos. O175-O176, O189-O190, O208-O209, O223.

1923-34 ***Rouletted 14½***

650	A79	2c scarlet	25	15
651	A80	3c bis brn ('27)	25	15
652	A81	4c green	20.00	8.00
653	A82	4c grn ('27)	25	15
654	A82	5c orange	25	15
655	A85	10c lake	25	15
656	A84	20c dp bl	75	30
657	A83	30c dk grn ('34)	75	30
		Nos. 650-657 (8)	22.75	9.35

Nos. 650 to 657 inclusive exist imperforate.

Medallion A90

Map of Americas A91

Francisco García y Santos A92

Post Office, Mexico, D. F. A93

1926 ***Perf. 12***

658	A90	2c red	2.00	75
659	A91	4c green	2.00	85
660	A90	5c orange	2.00	60
661	A91	10c brn red	3.00	60
662	A92	20c dk bl	3.00	1.00
663	A92	30c dk grn	5.00	3.00
664	A92	40c violet	10.00	2.50
665	A93	1p brn & blue	20.00	6.00
a.		1p red & blue	30.00	12.00
		Nos. 658-665 (8)	47.00	15.30

Pan-American Postal Congress.

Nos. 658-665 were also printed in black, on unwatermarked paper, for presentation to delegates to the Universal Postal Congress at London in 1929. Remainders were overprinted in 1929 for use as airmail official stamps, and are listed as Nos. CO3-CO10.

For overprints see Nos. 667-674, 675A-682, CO3-CO10.

Benito Juárez — A94

1926 ***Rouletted 14½***

666	A94	8c orange	30	15

For overprint see No. O182.

Nos. 658-665 Overprinted

HABILITADO 1930

1930 ***Perf. 12***

667	A90	2c red	3.50	2.25
a.		Reading down	12.50	14.00
668	A91	4c green	3.50	2.00
a.		Reading down	12.50	14.00
669	A90	5c orange	3.50	1.75
a.		Reading down	12.50	
b.		Double overprint	60.00	*60.00*
670	A91	10c brn red	6.00	2.00
671	A92	20c dk bl	8.00	3.00
672	A92	30c dk grn	7.00	3.50
a.		Reading down	8.50	12.00
673	A92	40c violet	10.00	7.00
a.		Reading down	40.00	
674	A93	1p red brn & bl	9.00	6.00
a.		Double overprint	125.00	
b.		Triple overprint	175.00	
		Nos. 667-674 (8)	50.50	27.50

Overprint horizontal on 1p.

Arms of Puebla — A95

1931, May 1 **Engr.**

675	A95	10c dk bl & dk brn	2.50	50

400th anniversary of Puebla.

Nos. 658-665a Overprinted

HABILITADO
1931

1931

No.	Type	Description	Unused	Used
675A	A90	2c red	750.00	
676	A91	4c green	55.00	60.00
677	A90	5c orange	10.00	14.00
678	A91	10c brn red	10.00	12.00
679	A92	20c dk bl	10.00	15.00
680	A92	30c dk grn	17.50	20.50
681	A92	40c violet	25.00	30.00
682	A93	1p brn & bl	22.50	30.00
a.		1p red & blue	35.00	40.00
		Nos. 676-682 (7)	150.00	181.50

Overprint horizontal on 1p.

Nos. 676 and 682 are not known to have been sold to the public through post offices.

Forgeries of overprint exist.

Bartolomé de las Casas — A96

Emblem of Mexican Society of Geography and Statistics — A97

1933, Mar. 3 Engr. *Rouletted 14½*

No.	Type	Description	Unused	Used
683	A96	15c dark blue	20	15

For overprint see No. O215.

1933, Oct. *Rouletted 14½*

No.	Type	Description	Unused	Used
684	A97	2c dp grn	1.50	60
685	A97	5c dk brn	1.75	50
686	A97	10c dk bl	75	15
687	A97	1p dk vio	50.00	60.00

XXI International Congress of Statistics and the first centenary of the Mexican Society of Geography and Statistics.

Types of 1923 and PT1

1934 *Perf. 10½, 11 (4c)*

No.	Type	Description	Unused	Used
687A	PT1	1c brown	1.00	30
688	A79	2c scarlet	35	15
689	A82	4c green	35	15
690	A85	10c brn lake	35	15
691	A84	20c dk bl	75	75
692	A83	30c dk bl grn	1.00	1.25
		Nos. 687A-692 (6)	3.80	2.75

See 2nd note after Postal Tax stamp No. RA3.

Indian Archer A99

Indian A100

Woman Decorating Pottery A101

Peon A102

Potter A103

Sculptor A104

Craftsman A105

Offering to the Gods A106

Worshiper — A107

1934, Sept. 1 Wmk. 156 *Perf. 10½*

No.	Type	Description	Unused	Used
698	A99	5c dk grn	1.65	35
699	A100	10c brn lake	2.00	60
700	A101	20c ultra	8.00	5.00
701	A102	30c black	14.00	12.00
702	A103	40c blk brn	24.00	16.00
703	A104	50c dl bl	45.00	50.00
704	A105	1p brn lake & blk	50.00	47.50
705	A106	5p brn blk & red brn	190.00	250.00
706	A107	10p brn & vio	800.00	1,050.
a.		Unwatermarked	*3,250.*	
		Nos. 698-706 (9)	1,134.	1,431.

National University.
See Nos. C54-C61, RA13B.

Yalalteca Indian — A108

Tehuana Indian — A109

Arch of the Revolution A110

Tower of Los Remedios A111

Cross of Palenque A112

Independence Monument A113

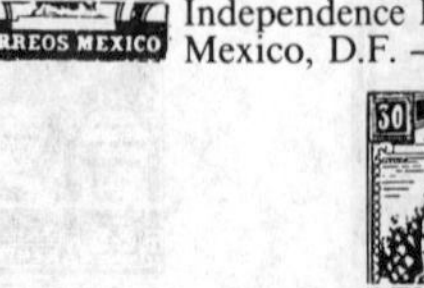
Monument, Puebla Independence Building, Mexico, D.F. — A114

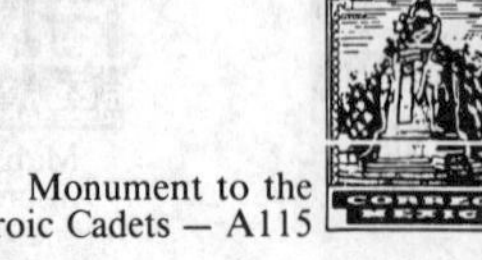
Monument to the Heroic Cadets — A115

Stone of Tizoc — A116

Ruins of Mitla — A117

Coat of Arms — A118

Cowboy — A119

Imprint: "Oficina Impresora de Hacienda-Mexico"

1934-40 Wmk. 156 *Perf. 10½*
Size: 20x26mm

No.	Type	Description	Unused	Used
707	A108	1c orange	65	15
a.		Unwmkd.		350.00
708	A109	2c green	65	15
a.		Unwmkd.	3.75	3.75
709	A110	4c carmine	90	20
710	A111	5c ol brn	65	15
a.		Unwmkd.	400.00	350.00
711	A112	10c dk bl	80	15
712	A112	10c vio ('35)	1.25	15
a.		Unwmkd.	200.00	40.00
713	A113	15c lt bl	4.00	30
714	A114	20c gray grn	1.90	20
a.		20c olive green	2.00	20
715	A114	20c ultra ('35)	1.40	15
a.		Unwmkd.		150.00
716	A115	30c lake	90	15
a.		Unwmkd.	350.00	
716B	A115	30c lt ultra ('40)	1.00	15
717	A116	40c red brn	1.00	15
718	A117	50c grnsh blk	90	15
a.		Imperf., pair	110.00	
b.		Unwmkd.		375.00
719	A118	1p dk brn & org	2.50	15
a.		Imperf., pair	350.00	
720	A119	5p org & vio	7.75	75
		Nos. 707-720 (15)	26.25	
		Set value		2.60

No. 718a was not regularly issued.
See Nos. 729-733, 733B, 735, 784-788, 795A-800A, 837-838, 840-841, 844, 846-851. For overprints see Nos. 728, O224-O232.

Tractor — A120

1935, Apr. 1 Wmk. 156 *Perf. 10½*

No.	Type	Description	Unused	Used
721	A120	10c violet	4.00	50

Industrial census of Apr. 10, 1935.

Arms of Chiapas A121

Emiliano Zapata A122

1935, Sept. 14

No.	Type	Description	Unused	Used
722	A121	10c dark blue	50	20
a.		Unwmkd.	125.00	100.00

The 111th anniversary of the joining of the state of Chiapas with the federal republic of Mexico. See No. 734.

1935, Nov. 20 Wmk. 156

No.	Type	Description	Unused	Used
723	A122	10c violet	75	20

25th anniversary of the Plan of Ayala.

US and Mexico Joined by Highways A123

Matalote Bridge A124

View of Nuevo Laredo Highway — A125

1936 Wmk. 248 *Perf. 14*

No.	Type	Description	Unused	Used
725	A123	5c bl grn & rose	30	15
726	A124	10c sl bl & blk	50	15
727	A125	20c brn & dk grn	1.50	1.00

Issued to commemorate the opening of the Nuevo Laredo Highway. See Nos. C77-C79.

Monument Type of 1923

1936 Wmk. 248 Engr. *Perf. 10½*

No.	Type	Description	Unused	Used
727A	A85	10c brn lake	*1,150.*	650.00

No. 712 Overprinted in Green

PRIMER CONGRESO
NAL. DE HIGIENE Y
MED. DEL TRABAJO

1936, Dec. 15 Wmk. 156

No.	Type	Description	Unused	Used
728	A112	10c violet	60	50

1st National Congress of Industrial Hygiene and Medicine.

Type of 1934
Redrawn size: 17½x21mm
Imprint: "Talleres de Imp. de Est. y Valores-Mexico"

1937 Photo. Wmk. 156 *Perf. 14*

No.	Type	Description	Unused	Used
729	A108	1c orange	60	15
a.		Imperf., pair	12.50	
730	A109	2c dl grn	60	15
a.		Imperf., pair	12.50	
731	A110	4c carmine	90	15
a.		Imperf., pair	12.50	
732	A111	5c ol brn	80	15
a.		Unwmkd.		*150.00*
733	A112	10c violet	70	15
a.		Imperf., pair	10.00	
		Nos. 729-733 (5)	3.60	75

The imperfs were not regularly issued.

Types of 1934-35

1937 Wmk. 260
Size: 17½x21mm

No.	Type	Description	Unused	Used
733B	A111	5c ol brn	650.00	185.00

1937 Engr. *Perf. 10½*

No.	Type	Description	Unused	Used
734	A121	10c dark blue	15.00	12.00

1937
Size: 20x26mm

No.	Type	Description	Unused	Used
735	A112	10c violet	275.00	35.00

Types of 1923

1934-37 Wmk. 260 *Perf. 10½*

No.	Type	Description	Unused	Used
735A	A79	2c scarlet		*4,000.*
735B	A85	10c brn lake		

Forged perforations exist.

Rouletted 14½

No.	Type	Description	Unused	Used
736	A85	10c claret	*1,800.*	*125.00*

Blacksmith
A126

Revolutionary Soldier
A127

Revolutionary Envoy — A128

Wmk. 156

1938, Mar. 26 Photo. *Perf. 14*

737	A126	5c blk & brn	80	20
738	A127	10c red brn	35	15
739	A128	20c maroon & org	5.00	1.00

25th anniv. of the Plan of Guadalupe. See Nos. C82-C84.

Arch of the Revolution
A129

National Theater
A130

Liberty Monument — A131

1938, July 1

740	A129	5c bis brn	1.25	60
741	A129	5c red brn	2.50	2.25
742	A130	10c orange	14.00	11.00
743	A130	10c chocolate	60	18
744	A131	20c brn lake	3.50	4.00
745	A131	20c black	18.00	15.00
		Nos. 740-745 (6)	39.85	33.03

16th International Congress of Planning and Housing. See Nos. C85-C90.

Arch of the Revolution
A132

1939, May 1

746	A132	10c Prus blue	65	20

New York World's Fair. See Nos. C91-C93.

Indian — A133

1939, May 17

747	A133	10c red orange	45	15

Tulsa World Philatelic Convention. See Nos. C94-C96.

Juan Zumárraga
A134

First Printing Shop in Mexico, 1539
A135

Design: 10c, Antonio de Mendoza.

1939, Sept. 1 Engr. *Perf. 10½*

748	A134	2c brn blk	75	25
749	A135	5c green	75	20
750	A134	10c red brn	25	15

400th anniversary of printing in Mexico. See Nos. C97-C99.

View of Taxco
A137

Allegory of Agriculture
A138

Design: 10c, Two hands holding symbols of commerce.

1939, Oct. 1 Photo. *Perf. 12x13*

751	A137	2c dk car	1.25	20
752	A138	5c sl grn & gray grn	15	15
753	A138	10c org brn & buff	15	15
		Set value		40

Census Taking. See Nos. C100-C102.

"Penny Black" of 1840
A140

Roadside Monument
A141

1940, May *Perf. 14*

754	A140	5c blk & lem	90	50
755	A140	10c dk vio	25	15
756	A140	20c lt bl & car	32	15
757	A140	1p gray & red org	7.00	4.00
758	A140	5p blk & Prus bl	37.50	30.00
		Nos. 754-758 (5)	45.97	34.80

Issued to commemorate the centenary of the postage stamp. See Nos. C103-C107.

1940 Wmk. 156

759	A141	6c dp grn	50	15

Opening of the highway between Mexico, D. F., and Guadalajara. See Nos. 789, 842.

Vasco de Quiroga
A142

Melchor Ocampo
A143

College Seal — A144

1940, July 15 Engr. *Perf. 10½*

760	A142	2c violet	1.30	50
761	A143	5c copper red	80	20
762	A144	10c olive bister	80	30
a.		Imperf., pair	150.00	

400th anniv. of the founding of the National College of San Nicolas de Hidalgo. See Nos. C108-C110.

Coat of Arms of Campeche
A145

1940, Aug. 7 Photo. *Perf. 12x13*

763	A145	10c bis brn & dk car	3.00	1.25

400th anniversary of the founding of Campeche. See Nos. C111-C113.

Man at Helm
A146

1940, Dec. 1

764	A146	2c red org & blk	1.65	60
765	A146	5c pck bl & red brn	6.25	3.50
766	A146	10c sl grn & dk brn	2.25	85

Inauguration of Pres. Manuel Avila Camacho. See Nos. C114-C116.

Javelin Thrower — A147

1941, Nov. 4 *Perf. 14*

767	A147	10c dl yel grn	3.50	50

National Athletic Games of the Revolution, Nov. 4-20, 1941.

Serpent Columns, Chichen Itza
A148

Mayan Sculpture
A149

Coat of Arms of Merida — A150

1942, June 30

768	A148	2c dk ol bis	1.40	75
769	A149	5c dp org	2.25	60
770	A150	10c dk vio	1.65	25

400th anniversary of the founding of Merida. See Nos. C117-C119.

Independence Monument to Hidalgo
A151

Government Palace
A152

View of Guadalajara — A153

1942, Feb. 11 Engr. *Perf. 10x10½*

771	A151	2c bl vio & vio brn	35	30
772	A152	5c blk & cop red	1.25	50
773	A153	10c red org & ultra	1.25	40

Founding of Guadalajara, 400th anniv. See Nos. C120-C122.

No. 773 exists imperf. on unwatermarked paper.

Black Cloud in Orion
A154

Designs: 5c, Total solar eclipse. 10c, Spiral galaxy in the "Hunting Dogs."

1942, Feb. 17 Photo. *Perf. 12x13*

774	A154	2c lt vio & ind	1.65	1.00
775	A154	5c bl & ind	8.75	2.00
776	A154	10c red org & ind	8.75	75

Astrophysics Congress and the inauguration of an observatory at Tonanzintla, Feb. 17, 1942. See Nos. C123-C125.

"Mother Earth"
A157

Sowing Wheat
A158

Western Hemisphere Carrying Torch
A159

1942, July 1

777	A157	2c chestnut	85	40
778	A158	5c turq bl	3.00	1.10
779	A159	10c red org	1.25	55

2nd Inter-American Agricultural Conference. See Nos. C126-C128.

Fuente Academy
A160

1942, Nov. 16 *Perf. 14*

780	A160	10c grnsh blk	1.75	75

75th anniversary of Fuente Academy.

Las Monjas Church
A161

Generalissimo Ignacio José de Allende
A163

Design: 5c, San Miguel Church.

1943, May 11

781	A161	2c int bl	1.00	35
782	A161	5c dp brn	1.10	30
783	A163	10c dl blk	3.50	1.00

400th anniv. of the founding of San Miguel de Allende. See Nos. C129-C131.

Types of 1937

1944 Photo. Wmk. 272

784	A108	1c orange	1.10	15
785	A109	2c dl grn	1.10	15
786	A110	4c carmine	2.00	20
787	A111	5c ol brn	1.75	15
788	A112	10c violet	90	15

Type of 1940

789	A141	6c green	90	15
		Nos. 784-789 (6)	7.75	95

"Liberty"
A164

Juan M. de Castorena
A165

1944 Photo.

790	A164	12c vio brn	35	15

See No. 845.

1944, Oct. 12 Engr. *Perf. 10*

791	A165	12c dk brn	60	15

Third Book Fair. See No. C142.

Hands Holding Globe Showing Western Hemisphere
A166

1945, Feb. 27 Photo. *Perf. 12x13*

792	A166	12c dk car	60	15
793	A166	1p slate grn	1.00	25
794	A166	5p olive brn	5.75	4.50
795	A166	10p black	10.00	8.00

Inter-American Conf. held at Chapultepec, Feb. 1945. See Nos. C143-C147.

Types of 1934-40

Wmk. 272

1945-46 Engr. *Perf. 10½*

795A	A113	15c lt grnsh bl ('46)	190.00	40.00
796	A114	20c gray grn	2.50	15
797	A115	30c lt ultra	3.25	15
798	A116	40c brown	2.50	20
799	A117	50c grnsh blk	1.65	20
800	A118	1p dk brn & org	2.50	20
b.		Imperf., pair		
800A	A119	5p org & vio ('46)	9.00	6.00
		Nos. 795A-800A (7)	211.40	46.90

Theater of Peace, San Luis Potosi
A167

Fountain of Diana, the Huntress
A168

1945, July 27 Photo. *Perf. 12x13*

801	A167	12c blk & vio brn	45	15
802	A167	1p blk & bl gray	60	40
803	A167	5p blk & brn lake	5.50	5.00
804	A167	10p blk & grnsh bl	12.50	12.00

Reconstruction of the Peace Theater (Teatro de la Paz), San Luis Potosi. See Nos. C148-C152.

1945 *Perf. 14*

805	A168	3c vio blue	55	15

See No. 839.

Removing Blindfold
A169

1945, Nov. 2 *Perf. 12x13*

806	A169	2c bluish grn	40	20
807	A169	6c orange	40	20
808	A169	12c ultra	40	20
809	A169	1p olive	60	25
810	A169	5p gray & pale rose	3.50	3.00
811	A169	10p bl & yel grn	20.00	20.00
		Nos. 806-811 (6)	25.30	23.85

Issued to publicize the national literacy campaign. See Nos. C153-C157.

M. E. de Almanza — A170

1946 *Perf. 14*

812	A170	8c black	1.25	25

Martines Enriquez de Almanza, founder of the Mexican posts. See No. 843.

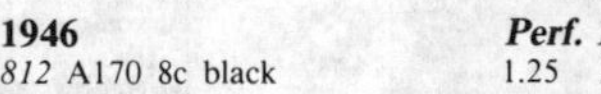

Allegory of World Peace
A171

1946, Apr. 10 *Perf. 12x13*

813	A171	2c dk ol bis	35	20
814	A171	6c red brn	30	20
815	A171	12c Prus grn	25	15
816	A171	1p lt grn	60	40
817	A171	5p dl red vio	5.00	5.00
818	A171	10p lt ultra	22.50	20.00
		Nos. 813-818 (6)	29.00	25.95

United Nations. See Nos. C158-C162.

Arms of Zacatecas
A173

Monument to Gen. Gonzalez Ortega
A174

Ramon Lopez Velarde
A175

Francisco Garcia Salinas
A176

Wmk. 279

1946, Sept. 1 Photo. *Perf. 14*

820	A173	2c org brn	55	15
821	A173	12c Prus blue	25	15

Engr.

Perf. 10x10½

822	A174	1p lilac rose	70	20
823	A175	5p red	5.50	3.00
824	A176	10p dk bl & blk	30.00	10.00
		Nos. 820-824 (5)	37.00	13.50

400th anniversary of the founding of the city of Zacatecas. See Nos. C163-C166.

Postman — A177

1947 Photo. *Perf. 14*

825	A177	15c grnsh bl	25	15
a.		Imperf., pair	110.00	

Franklin D. Roosevelt and Stamp of 1st Mexican Issue — A178

Design: 15c, Arms of Mexico and Stamp of 1st US Issue.

1947, May 16

826	A178	10c yel brn	1.65	1.00
827	A178	15c green	25	15

Cent. Intl. Phil. Exhib., NYC, May 17-25, 1947.

See Nos. C167-C169.

Justo Sierra — A180

Communications Building — A181

Perf. 10x10½, 10½x10

1947, Engr. Wmk. 279

828	A180	10p brn & dl grn	85.00	15.00
829	A181	20p dk grn & lil	1.65	2.00

Cadet Francisco Marquez A182

Gen. Manuel Rincon A186

Flag of San Blas Battalion — A188

Designs: 5c, Cadet Fernando Montes de Oca. 10c, Cadet Juan Escutia. 15c, Cadet Agustin Melgar. 1p, Gen. Lucas Balderas.

1947, Sept. 8 Photo. *Perf. 14*

830 A182 2c brn blk 42 15
831 A182 5c red org 30 15
832 A182 10c dk brn 25 15
833 A182 15c dk Prus grn 25 15
834 A182 30c dl ol grn 35 15

Engr.

Perf. 10x10½

835 A186 1p aqua 45 45
836 A188 5p dk bl & claret 1.90 1.90
Nos. 830-836 (7) 3.92 3.10

Centenary of the battles of Chapultepec, Churubusco and Molino del Rey. See Nos. C180-C184.

Types of 1934-46

1947-50 Wmk. 279 Photo. *Perf. 14*

837 A108 1c orange 1.00 30
a. Imperf., pair 90.00
838 A109 2c dk grn 60 15
839 A168 3c vio bl 60 15
840 A110 4c dl red 1.90 15
841 A111 5c ol brn 2.50 15
842 A141 6c dp grn 45 15
a. Imperf., pair 90.00
843 A170 8c black 35 15
844 A112 10c violet 1.90 25
845 A164 12c vio brn 9.00 75

Types A108 to A112 are in the redrawn size of 1937.

Size: 19x25mm

Engr. *Perf. 10½*

846 A114 20c ol grn 1.25 20
a. 20c green 3.00 30
847 A115 30c lt ultra 8.75 40
848 A116 40c red brn 1.40 25
849 A117 50c green 1.90 20
a. Imperf., pair 110.00
850 A118 1p dk brn & org 25.00 9.00
851 A119 5p org & vio ('50) 16.00 11.00
Nos. 837-851 (15) 72.60 23.25

Puebla Cathedral — A189

Designs: 3c, Modernistic church, Nuevo Leon. 5c, Modern building, Mexico City. 10c, Convent, Morelos. 15c, Benito Juarez. 30c, Indian dancer, Michoacan. 40c, Stone head, Tabasco. 50c, Carved head, Veracruz. 1p, Convent and carved head, Hidalgo. 5p, Galleon, arms of Campeche. 10p, Francisco I. Madero. 20p, Modern building, Mexico City.

1950-52 Wmk. 279 Photo. *Perf. 14*

856 A189 3c bl vio ('51) 50 15
857 A189 5c dk red brn 75 15
858 A189 10c dk grn 3.50 15
859 A189 15c dk grn ('51) 1.75 15
860 A189 20c bl vio 14.00 15
861 A189 30c red 50 15
862 A189 40c red org ('51) 1.00 15
863 A189 50c blue 1.25 15

Engr.

864 A189 1p dl brn 4.50 15
865 A189 5p ultra & bl grn 7.00 4.00
866 A189 10p blk & dp ultra ('52) 7.00 7.00
867 A189 20p pur & grn ('52) 10.00 10.00
Nos. 856-867 (12) 51.75 22.35

See Nos. 875-885, 909, 928-931, 943-952, 1003-1004, 1054-1055, 1072, 1076, 1081, 1090-1091, 1094-1102.

Highway Bridge A190

Symbolical of Construction in 1950 A191

Railroad Laborer A192

Perf. 10½x10, 10x10½

1950, May 5 Photo.

868 A190 15c purple 60 15
869 A191 20c deep blue 40 20

Completion of the International Highway between Ciudad Juarez and the Guatemala border. See Nos. C199-C200.

Inscribed: "Ferrocarril del Sureste 1950"

Design: 20c, Map and locomotive.

1950, May 24 *Perf. 10x10½*

870 A192 15c chocolate 1.25 15
871 A192 20c dp car 45 15
Set value 20

Opening of the Southeastern Railroad between Veracruz, Coatzocoalcos and Yucatan, 1950. See Nos. C201-C202.

Postal Service A193

Miguel Hidalgo y Costilla A194

1950, June 25 *Perf. 10x10½*

872 A193 50c purple 40 15

75th anniv. (in 1949) of the UPU. See Nos. C203-C204.

1953, May 8 Wmk. 300 *Perf. 14*

873 A194 20c grnsh bl & dk brn 1.75 25

Bicentenary of birth of Miguel Hidalgo y Costilla. See Nos. C206-C207.

Type of 1950-52
Designs as before.

Two types of 5p:
I- Imprint ½mm high and blurred.
II- Imprint ¾mm high and clear.

1954-67 Photo. *Perf. 14*

875 A189 5c red brn 50 15
876 A189 10c dk grn 2.50 15
a. 10c green, redrawn 65 15
877 A189 15c dk grn 40 15
878 A189 20c dk bl 3.50 15
a. 20c bluish blk, white paper, colorless gum ('67) 60 15
879 A189 30c brn red 75 15
a. 30c redsh brn 75 15
880 A189 40c red org 1.50 15
881 A189 50c lt bl 1.00 15

Engr.

882 A189 1p ol brn 12.00 20
a. 1p olive green 7.00 20
b. As "a.", perf. 11, vert. wmk. ('58) 4.00 25
883 A189 5p ultra & bl grn, I 7.00 1.00
a. Type II 500.00 8.00
884 A189 10p sl & dp ultra ('56) 9.00 5.00
a. 10p slate green & ultra 35.00 5.00
885 A189 20p pur & grn 11.00 9.00
a. 20p brn vio & yel grn 75.00 20.00
Nos. 875-885 (11) 49.15 16.25

Nos. 875-881 comes only with watermark vertical, and in various shades. Watermark inverted on Nos. 884, 885.

On No. 876a, imprint extends full width of stamp.

Vert. pairs, imperf. horiz. of Nos. 878, 880 are noted after No. 1004.

Aztec Messenger of the Sun A195

Symbolizing Adoption of National Anthem A196

1954, Mar. 6

886 A195 20c rose & bl gray 1.10 15

7th Central American and Caribbean Games. See Nos. C222-C223.

1954, Sept. 16 Photo.

887 A196 5c rose lil & dk bl 75 20
888 A196 20c yel brn & brn vio 90 20
889 A196 1p gray grn & cer 65 40

Centenary of the adoption of Mexico's National Anthem. See Nos. C224-C226.

Torch-Bearer and Stadium A197

"Motion" A198

1955, Mar. 12 Wmk. 300 *Perf. 14*

890 A197 20c dk grn & red brn 85 20

Issued to publicize the second Pan American Games, 1955. See Nos. C227-C228.

1956, Aug. 1

Aztec Designs: 10c, Bird. 30c, Flowers. 50c, Corn. 1p, Deer. 5p, Man.

891 A198 5c org brn & brt grn 50 15
892 A198 10c lil gray & dp bl 50 15
893 A198 30c red & dk pur 40 15
894 A198 50c aqua & hn brn 50 15
895 A198 1p emer & blk 60 20
896 A198 5p dl yel & dk brn 2.25 2.25
a. Souv. sheet, #891-896, imperf. 30.00 30.00
Nos. 891-896 (6) 4.75 3.05

Centenary of Mexico's 1st postage stamps. No. 896a sold for 15p. See Nos. C229-C234.

Stamp of 1856 A199

Francisco Zarco A200

1956, Aug. 1

897 A199 30c brn & intense bl 75 25

Centenary International Philatelic Exhibition, Mexico City, Aug. 16, 1956.

1956-63

Portraits: 25c, 45c, Guillermo Prieto. 60c, Ponciano Arriaga.

897A A200 25c dk brn ('63) 75 50
898 A200 45c dk bl grn 35 25
899 A200 60c red lil 35 35
900 A200 70c vio bl 40 20

Centenary of the constitution (in 1957). See Nos. C236-C237A, C289, 1075, 1092-1093.

"Mexico" A201

Mexican Eagle and Oil Derrick A202

Design: 1p, National Assembly.

1957, Aug. 31 Photo. *Perf. 14*

901 A201 30c mar & gold 50 15
902 A201 1p pale brn & metallic grn 35 25

Centenary of the constitution. See Nos. C239-C240.

1958, Aug. 30 Wmk. 300 *Perf. 14*

Design: 5p, Map of Mexico and refinery.

903 A202 30c lt bl & blk 50 15
904 A202 5p hn brn & Prus grn 4.00 4.00

20th anniv. of the nationalization of Mexico's oil industry. See Nos. C243-C244.

UNESCO Building and Eiffel Tower — A203

UN Headquarters, New York — A204

1959, Jan. 20

905 A203 30c dl lil & blk 50 15

Opening of UNESCO Headquarters in Paris, Nov. 9.

1959, Sept. 7 Litho. *Perf. 14*

906 A204 30c org yel & bl 50 15

Meeting of UNESCO.

Pres. Venustiano Carranza A205

Alexander von Humboldt Statue A206

1960, Jan. 15 Photo. Wmk. 300
907 A205 30c pale grn & plum 35 15

Issued to commemorate the birth centenary of Pres. Venustiano Carranza. See No. C246.

1960, Mar. 16 Wmk. 300 *Perf. 14*
908 A206 40c bis brn & grn 35 15

Issued to commemorate the centenary of the death (in 1859) of Alexander von Humboldt, German naturalist and geographer.

Type of 1950-52 Inscribed: "HOMENAJE AL COLECCIONISTA DEL TIMBRE DE MEXICO-JUNIO 1960"

1960, June 8 Engr. Wmk. 300
909 A189 10p lil, brn & grn 35.00 42.50

25th anniversary visit of the Elmhurst (Ill.) Philatelic Society of Mexico Specialists to Mexico. See No. C249.

Independence Bell & Monument
A207 A208

Designs: 5p, Bell of Dolores and Miguel Hidalgo.

Wmk. 300

1960, Sept. 15 Photo. *Perf. 14*
910 A207 30c grn & rose red 1.00 15
911 A208 1p dl grn & dk brn 50 20
912 A208 5p mar & dk bl 5.00 5.00

150th anniv. of Mexican independence. See US No. 1157, Mexico Nos. C250-C252.

Agricultural Reform A209

Symbols of Health Education — A210

Designs: 20c, Sailor and Soldier, 1960, and Fighter of 1910. 30c, Electrification. 1p, Political development (schools). 5p, Currency stability (Bank and money).

1960-61 Photo. *Perf. 14*
913 A209 10c sl grn, blk & red org 75 20
914 A210 15c grn & org brn 2.75 50
915 A210 20c brt bl & lt brn ('61) 1.00 15
916 A210 30c vio brn & sep 40 15
917 A210 1p redsh brn & sl 50 15
918 A210 5p mar & gray 3.50 3.50
Nos. 913-918 (6) 8.90 4.65

50th anniversary (in 1960) of the Mexican Revolution. See Nos. C253-C256.

Tunnel A211

Microscope, Mosquito and Globe A212

1961, Dec. Wmk. 300 *Perf. 14*
919 A211 40c blk & brt grn 40 15

Opening of the railroad from Chihuahua to the Pacific Ocean. See Nos. C258-C259.

1962, Apr. 6
920 A212 40c dl bl & maroon 40 15

WHO drive to eradicate malaria.

President Joao Goulart of Brazil — A213

Mexican Indian at Marker for Battle of Puebla — A214

Wmk. 300

1962, Apr. 11 Photo. *Perf. 14*
921 A213 40c brn olive 1.00 25

Issued to commemorate the visit of Joao Goulart, president of Brazil, to Mexico.

1962, May 5
922 A214 40c sepiaz & dk grn 35 15

Centenary of the Battle of May 5 at Puebla and the defeat of French forces by Gen. Ignacio Zaragoza. See No. C260.

Canceled-to-order stamps are often from remainders. Most collectors of canceled stamps prefer postally used specimens.

Draftsman and Surveyor A215

Plumbline A216

1962, June 11
923 A215 40c sl grn & dk bl 90 20

25th anniversary of the National Polytechnic Institute. See No. C261.

1962, June 21
924 A216 20c dp bl & blk 1.40 20

Issued to publicize the importance of mental health.

"Space Needle" and Gear Wheels A217

Globe A218

1962, July 6
925 A217 40c dk grn & gray 35 15

"Century 21" International Exposition, Seattle, Wash., Apr. 21-Oct. 12.

1962, Oct. 1 *Perf. 14*
926 A218 40c gray & brn 35 15

1962 meeting of the Inter-American Economic and Social Council. See No. C263.

Pres. Alessandri of Chile A219

Pres. Betancourt of Venezuela A220

1962, Dec. 20 Wmk. 300 *Perf. 14*
927 A219 20c olive black 75 20

Visit of President Jorge Alessandri Rodriguez of Chile to Mexico, Dec. 17-20.

Type of 1950-52

Designs as before.

Wmk. 300, Vertical

1962-74 Photo. *Perf. 14*
928 A189 1p ol gray ('67) 1.25 15
a. 1p green 4.00 20
929 A189 5p dl bl & dk grn 3.50 75
a. 5p bluish gray & dk grn, white paper ('67) 3.50 50
930 A189 10p gray & bl ('63) 8.50 5.00
a. 10p grn & dp bl ('74) 7.50 5.50
931 A189 20p lil & blk ('63) 9.00 7.50

No. 928 is on thick, luminescent paper. No. 929 is 20½mm high; No. 929a, 20¾mm. See No. 1102 for unwmkd. 20p with more shading in sky, spots on first floor windows and 1mm space between vignette and "Correos."

1963, Feb. 28 Wmk. 300
932 A220 20c slate 70 20

Visit of President Romulo Betancourt of Venezuela to Mexico.

Congress Emblem A221

Wheat Emblem A222

1963, Apr. 22 Wmk. 300 *Perf. 14*
933 A221 49c fawn & blk 60 20

19th International Chamber of Commerce Congress. See No. C271.

1963, June 17 Wmk. 300 *Perf. 14*
934 A222 40c crim & dk bl 60 20

FAO "Freedom from Hunger" campaign.

Mercado Mountains and Arms of Durango A223

Belisario Dominguez A224

1963, July 13 Photo.
935 A223 20c dk bl & choc 60 20

400th anniv. of the founding of Durango.

1963, July 13 Photo.
936 A224 20c dk grn & ol gray 60 20

Centenary of the birth of Belisario Dominguez, revolutionary leader.

Stamp of 1956 — A225

1963, Oct. 9 Wmk. 350 *Perf. 14*
937 A225 1p int bl & brn 1.25 75

77th Annual Convention of the American Philatelic Society, Mexico City, Oct. 7-13. See No. C274.

Tree of Life
A226

José Morelos
A227

1963, Oct. 26 Wmk. 350 *Perf. 14*
938 A226 20c dl bl grn & car 40 20

Centenary of the International Red Cross. See No. C277.

1963, Nov. 9
939 A227 40c grn & dk sl grn 55 20

150th anniv. of the 1st congress of Anahuac.

Pres. Victor Paz Estenssoro
A228

Arms of Sinaloa University
A229

1963, Nov. 9 Wmk. 350 *Perf. 14*
940 A228 40c dk brn & dk red brn 60 20

Issued to commemorate the visit of President Victor Paz Estenssoro of Bolivia.

1963 Photo.
941 A229 40c sl grn & ol bis 60 20

90th anniversary of the founding of the University of Sinaloa.

Diesel Train, Rail Cross Section and Globe
A230

1963, Nov. 29 Photo.
942 A230 20c blk & dk brn 90 50

Issued to commemorate the 11th Pan-American Railroad Congress. See No. C279.

Type of 1950-52

Designs as before.

1963-66 Wmk. 350 Photo. *Perf. 14*

943	A189	5c red brn ('65)	60	15
944	A189	10c dk grn ('64)	65	15
945	A189	15c dk grn ('66)	60	15
946	A189	20c dark blue	60	15
948	A189	40c red org	70	15
949	A189	50c bl ('64)	1.25	15
950	A189	1p ol grn ('64)	3.00	15
951	A189	5p dl bl & dk grn ('66)	100.00	30.00
952	A189	10p gray & Prus bl ('65)	35.00	25.00
		Nos. 943-952 (9)	142.40	56.05

The 20c is redrawn; clouds almost eliminated and other slight variations.

"F.S.T.S.E." Emblem
A231

Academy of Medicine Emblem
A232

1964, Feb. 15
954 A231 20c red org & dk brn 40 15

25th anniv. (in 1963) of the Civil Service Statute affecting federal employees.

1964, May 18 Wmk. 350 *Perf. 14*
955 A232 20c gold & blk 40 15

National Academy of Medicine, cent.

José Rizal
A233

View of Zacatecas
A234

Design: 40c, Miguel Lopez de Legaspi, Spanish navigator.

1964, Nov. 10 Photo. *Perf. 14*
956 A233 20c dk bl & dp grn 50 20
957 A233 40c dk bl & brt vio 60 20

Issued to honor 400 years of Mexican-Philippine friendship. See Nos. C300-C301.

1964, Nov. 10 Wmk. 350
958 A234 40c slate grn & red 55 20

50th anniv. of the capture of Zacatecas.

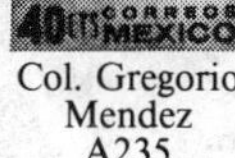

Col. Gregorio Mendez
A235

Morelos Theater, Aguascalientes
A236

1964, Nov. 10
959 A235 40c grysh blk & dk brn 50 20

Cent. of the Battle of Jahuactal, Tabasco.

Catalogue values for unused stamps in this section, from this point to the end of the section, are for Never Hinged items.

1965, Jan. 9 Photo. *Perf. 14*
960 A236 20c dl cl & dk gray 35 15

50th anniversary of the Aguascalientes Convention, Oct. 1-Nov. 9, 1914.

Andrés Manuel del Rio — A237

1965, Feb. 19 Wmk. 350 *Perf. 14*
961 A237 30c gray 40 20

Bicentenary of the birth of Andrés Manuel del Rio, founder of the National School of Mining and discoverer of vanadium.

José Morelos and Constitution
A238

Trees
A239

1965, Apr. 24 Photo. *Perf. 14*
962 A238 40c brt grn & dk red brn 45 20

Sesquicentennial (in 1964) of the 1st Mexican constitution.

1965, July 14 Wmk. 350 *Perf. 14*
963 A239 20c bl & grn 30 15

Issued to commemorate Tree Day, July 8.

ICY Emblem
A240

1965, Sept. 13 Photo.
964 A240 40c ol gray & sl grn 30 15

International Cooperation Year, 1965.

Athlete with Sling, Clay Figure
A241

Design: 40c, Batter. Clay figures on 20c and 40c found in Colima, period 300-650 A.D.

1965, Dec. 17 Wmk. 350 *Perf. 14*
965 A241 20c ol & vio bl 90 20
966 A241 40c pink & blk 30 15

Issued to publicize the 19th Olympic Games, Mexico, 1968. For souvenir sheet see No. C310a. See Nos. C309-C311.

José Morelos by Diego Rivera
A242

Emiliano Zapata
A243

1965, Dec. 22
967 A242 20c lt vio bl & blk 40 20

José Maria Morelos y Pavon (1765-1815), priest and patriot in 1810 revolution against Spain.

1966, Jan. 10 Photo.

Design: 20c, Corn, cotton, bamboo, wheat and cow.

968 A243 20c car rose 35 15
969 A243 40c black 45 20

50th anniv. of the Agrarian Reform Law.

Mexican Postal Service Emblem
A244

Bartolomé de Las Casas
A245

1966, June 24 Wmk. 300 *Perf. 14*
970 A244 40c brt grn & blk 40 15

Congress of the Postal Union of the Americas and Spain, UPAE, Mexico City, June 24-July 23. See Nos. C314-C315.

1966, Aug. 1 Photo. Wmk. 300
971 A245 20c blk & buff 40 15

400th anniv. of the death of Bartolomé de Las Casas (1474-1566), "Apostle of the Indies."

Mechanical Drawings and Cogwheels — A246

1966, Aug. 15 Photo. *Perf. 14*
972 A246 20c gray & grn 30 15

50th anniversary of the founding of the School of Mechanical and Electrical Engineering (ESIME).

FAO Emblem — A247

1966, Sept. 30 Wmk. 300 *Perf. 14*
973 A247 40c green 30 15

FAO International Rice Year.

Running and Jumping, by Diego Rivera
A248

1966, Oct. 15

Size: 35x21mm

974	A248	20c shown	70	20
975	A248	40c Wrestling	35	15
a.		Souvenir sheet	1.40	1.40

Issued to publicize the 19th Olympic Games, Mexico City, D.F., 1968. No. 975a contains 2 imperf. stamps similar to Nos. 974-975 with simulated perforations. Sold for 90c.

See Nos. C318-C320.

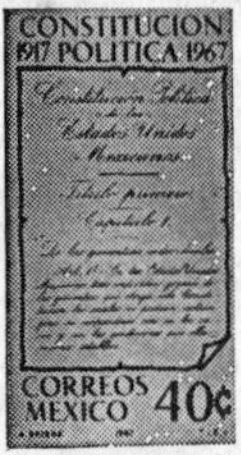

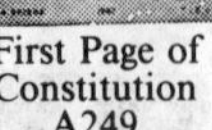

First Page of Constitution
A249

Oil Refinery and Pyramid of the Sun
A250

Wmk. 300

1967, Feb. 5 Photo. *Perf. 14*

976	A249	40c black	50	20

50th anniversary of the Constitution. See No. C322.

1967, Apr. 2 Wmk. 300 *Perf. 14*

977	A250	40c lt bl & blk	35	15

Issued to publicize the 7th International Oil Congress, Mexico City, September, 1967.

Nayarit Indian — A251

Wmk. 300

1967, May 1 Photo. *Perf. 14*

978	A251	20c pale grn & blk	30	15

50th anniversary of Nayarit State.

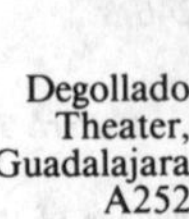

Degollado Theater, Guadalajara
A252

Wmk. 300

1967, June 12 Photo. *Perf. 14*

979	A252	40c pink & blk	20	20

Centenary of the founding of the Degollado Theater, Guadalajara.

Mexican Eagle over Imperial Crown — A253

Perf. 10x10½

1967, June 19 Litho. Wmk. 350

980	A253	20c blk & ocher	30	15

Centenary of the victory of the Mexican republican forces and of the execution of Emperor Maximilian I.

Canoeing
A254

Designs: 40c, Basketball. 50c, Hockey. 80c, Bicycling. 2p, Fencing.

Wmk. 300

1967, Oct. 12 Photo. *Perf. 14*

981	A254	20c bl & blk	35	15
982	A254	40c brick red & blk	30	15
983	A254	50c brt yel grn & blk	30	15
a.		Souvenir sheet of 3, #981-983, imperf.	1.10	1.10
984	A254	80c brt pur & blk	42	15
985	A254	2p org & blk	70	30
a.		Souvenir sheet of 2, #984-985, imperf.	2.00	2.00
		Nos. 981-985 (5)	2.07	90

Issued to publicize the 19th Olympic Games, Mexico City, Oct. 12-27, 1968.

No. 983a sold for 1.50p; No. 985a sold for 3.50p. Both sheets are watermark 350.

See Nos. 990-995, C328-C331, C335-C338.

Artemio de Valle-Arizpe
A255

Pedro Moreno
A256

1967, Nov. 1 Photo.

986	A255	20c brn & slate	35	30

Centenary of the Ateneo Fuente, a college at Saltillo, Coahuila.

1967, Nov. 18 Wmk. 300 *Perf. 14*

987	A256	40c blk & lt bl	35	15

Moreno (1775-1817), revolutionary leader.

Gabino Barreda
A257

Staircase, Palace of Mining
A258

1968, Jan. 27 Photo. *Perf. 14*

988	A257	40c dk bl & rose cl	40	15
989	A258	40c blk & bl gray	40	15

Centenary of the founding of the National Preparatory and Engineering Schools.

Type of Olympic Issue, 1967

Designs: 20c, Wrestling. 40c, Pentathlon. 50c, Water polo. 80c, Gymnastics. 1p, Boxing. 2p, Pistol shoot.

1968, Mar. 21 Wmk. 300 *Perf. 14*

990	A254	20c ol & blk	40	15
991	A254	40c red lil & blk	40	20
992	A254	50c brt grn & blk	40	20
a.		Souvenir sheet of 3, #990-992, imperf.	1.25	1.25
993	A254	80c brt pink & blk	45	25
994	A254	1p org brn & blk	2.25	50
995	A254	2p gray & blk	2.50	1.50
a.		Souvenir sheet of 3, #993-995, imperf.	3.00	3.00
		Nos. 990-995 (6)	6.40	2.80

19th Olympic Games, Mexico City, Oct. 12-27. No. 992a sold for 1.50p; No. 995a sold for 5p. Both sheets are watermark 350.

See Nos. C335-C338.

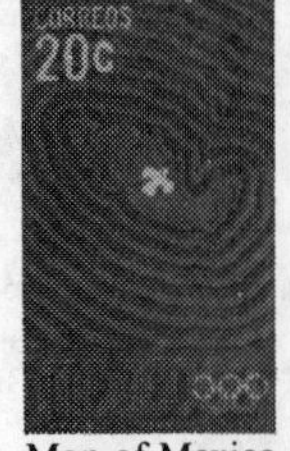

Map of Mexico, Peace Dove — A259

Arms of Veracruz — A261

Symbols of Cultural Events
A260

Designs: 40c, University City Olympic stadium. 50c, Telecommunications tower. 2p, Sports Palace. 10p, Pyramid of the Sun, Teotihuacan, and Olympic torch.

Wmk. 350

1968, Oct. Photo. *Perf. 14*

996	A259	20c bl, yel & grn	25	15
997	A259	40c multi	35	20
998	A259	50c multi	35	20
a.		Souv. sheet of 3, #996-998, imperf.	6.50	7.00
999	A260	2p multi	55	50
1000	A260	5p sil & blk	2.25	1.25
a.		Souv. sheet of 2, #999-1000, imperf.	6.00	6.50
1001	A259	10p multi	3.00	2.00
		Nos. 996-1001 (6)	6.75	4.30

19th Olympic Games, Mexico City, Oct. 12-27 (Nos. 996-1000). Arrival of the Olympic torch in Veracruz (No. 1001).

No. 998a sold for 1.50p. No. 1000a sold for 9p.

See Nos. C340-C344a.

1969, May 20 Wmk. 350 *Perf. 14*

1002	A261	40c multi	35	15

450th anniv. of the founding of Veracruz.

Type of 1950-52
Coil Stamps
Perf. 11 Vert.

1969 Wmk. 300 Photo.

1003	A189	20c dk bl	1.00	75
1004	A189	40c red org	1.50	1.60

Vert. pairs, imperf. horiz. may be from uncut rolls of coils.

Subway Train — A262

1969, Sept. 4 Wmk. 350 *Perf. 14*

1005	A262	40c multi	35	15

Inauguration of Mexico City subway.

Honeycomb, Bee and ILO Emblem
A263

Gen. Allende, by Diego Rivera
A264

1969, Oct. 18 Photo. *Perf. 14*

1006	A263	40c multi	25	15

50th anniversary of the ILO.

1969, Nov. 15 Wmk. 350 *Perf. 14*

1007	A264	40c multi	25	15

Issued to commemorate the bicentenary of the birth of Gen. Ignacio Allende Unzaga (1769-1811), father of Mexican independence.

Tourist Issue

Pyramid of Niches at El Tajin, Veracruz, and Dancers Swinging from Pole
A265

Anthropology Museum, Mexico City — A266

Deer Dance, Sonora — A267

Designs: No. 1010, View of Puerto Vallarta. No. 1011, Puebla Cathedral. No. 1012, Calle Belaunzaran. No. 1014, Ocotlan Cathedral (horiz.).

1969-73 Photo. Wmk. 350

1008	A265	40c shown	45	15
1009	A266	40c shown ('70)	45	15
1010	A266	40c Jalisco ('70)	45	15
1011	A266	40c Puebla ('70)	45	15
1012	A266	40c Guanajuato ('70)	45	15

Wmk. 300

1013	A267	40c shown ('73)	25	15
1014	A267	40c Tlaxcala ('73)	25	15
		Nos. 1008-1014 (7)	2.75	1.05

No. 1010 is inscribed "1970" below the design. Copies inscribed "1969" are from an earlier, unissued printing.

See Nos. C357-C358.

Luminescence

Fluorescent stamps include Nos. 1013-1014, 1035, 1038, 1041, 1043-1045, 1047-1050, 1054-1059. (See Luminescence note over No. C527.)

"How Many, Who and What are We?" — A268

Design: 40c, "What, How and How Much do we produce?" (horse's head and symbols of agriculture).

1970, Jan. 26 Wmk. 350 *Perf. 14*

1024	A268	20c multi	30	15
1025	A268	40c bl & multi	25	15

Issued to publicize the 1970 census.

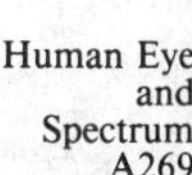

Human Eye and Spectrum A269

1970, Mar. 8 Photo. Wmk. 350

1026	A269	40c multi	25	15

21st International Congress of Ophthalmology, Mexico City, Mar. 8-14.

Helmets of 1920 and 1970 A270

1970, Apr. 11 Wmk. 350 *Perf. 14*

1027	A270	40c dk car rose, blk & lt brn	20	15

50th anniversary of the Military College.

José Maria Pino Suarez A271

Coat of Arms of Celaya A272

1970, Apr. 25 Photo.

1028	A271	40c blk & multi	20	15

Centenary of the birth of José Maria Pino Suarez (1869-1913), lawyer, poet and Vice President of Mexico.

1970, Oct. 12 Photo. *Perf. 14*

1029	A272	40c blk & multi	20	15

City of Celaya, 400th anniversary.

Eclipse of Sun — A273

1970, Nov. 11 Wmk. 350 *Perf. 14*

1030	A273	40c black & gray	25	15

Total eclipse of the sun, Mar. 7, 1970.

Spheres with Dates 1970-1770 A274

1971, June 26 Photo. *Perf. 14*

1031	A274	40c emer & blk	25	15

Bicentenary of National Lottery.

Vasco de Quiroga, Mural by O'Gorman A275

1971, July 10 Photo.

1032	A275	40c multi	20	15

500th anniversary of the birth of Vasco de Quiroga (1470-1565), Archbishop of Michoacan, founder of hospitals and schools.

Amado Nervo (1870-1919), Poet — A276

1971, Aug. 7 Wmk. 350 *Perf. 14*

1033	A276	40c multi	20	15

Waves and Transformer — A277

1971, Oct. 9

1034	A277	40c blk, lt bl & lt grn	30	15

50th anniversary of Mexican radio.

Pres. Lazaro Cardenas (1895-1970) — A278

1971, Oct. 19 Wmk. 300

1035	A278	40c blk & pale lil	30	15

Keyboard and Lara's Signature A279

1971, Nov. 6 Wmk. 350

1036	A279	40c blk, buff & pale bl	30	15

Agustin Lara (1900-70), composer.

Arms of Monterrey A280

Cardiology Institute and WHO Emblems A281

1971, Dec. 18

1037	A280	40c blk & multi	30	15

375th anniv. of the founding of Monterrey.

1972, Apr. 8 Wmk. 300

1038	A281	40c multi	25	15

"Your heart is your health," World Health Day 1972. See No. C395.

Gaceta de Mexico, Jan. 1, 1722 A282

1972, June 24 Wmk. 350

1039	A282	40c multi	25	15

250th anniv. of 1st Mexican newspaper.

Lions International Emblem A283

Sailing Ship Zaragoza A284

1972, June 28

1040	A283	40c blk & multi	25	15

55th Lions International Convention.

1972, July 1

1041	A284	40c bl & multi	25	15

75th anniv. of the Naval School of Veracruz.

Olive Tree and Branch — A285

1972, July 18 Wmk. 350 *Perf. 14*

1042	A285	40c lt grn, ocher & blk	25	15
a.		40c light green, yellow & black	50	35

Centenary of Chilpancingo as capital of Guerrero State.

Margarita Maza de Juarez A286

Design: 40c, Benito Juárez, by Diego Rivera.

1972, Sept. 15 Photo. Wmk. 300

1043	A286	20c pink & multi	40	15
1044	A286	40c dp yel & multi	40	15
		Nos. 1043-1044,C403-C405 (5)	1.57	
		Set value		66

Benito Juárez (1806-1872), revolutionary leader and president of Mexico.

Emperor Justinian I, Mosaic A287

1972, Sept. 30 Wmk. 300

1045	A287	40c multi	65	15

Mexican Bar Association, 50th anniv.

Caravel — A288

Library, Book Year Emblem — A290

Olympic Emblems A289

1972, Oct. 12 Wmk. 350

1046	A288	80c buff, pur & ocher	40	15

Stamp Day of The Americas.

1972, Dec. 9 Wmk. 300

1047	A289	40c multi	35	15

20th Olympic Games, Munich, Aug. 26-Sept. 11. See Nos. C410-C411.

1972, Dec. 16

1048	A290	40c blk & multi	25	15

International Book Year 1972.

Fish in Clean Water A291

1972, Dec. 16

1049	A291	40c blk & lt bl	40	15

Anti-pollution campaign. See No. C412.

Metlac Railroad Bridge — A292

1973, Feb. 2 ***Perf. 14***
1050 A292 40c multi 85 15

Centenary of Mexican railroads.

Cadet — A293

1973, Oct. 11 **Photo.** **Wmk. 300**
1051 A293 40c blk & multi 45 15

Sesquicentennial of Military College.

Madero, by Diego Rivera A294

Antonio Narro A295

1973, Nov. 9 **Wmk. 350** ***Perf. 14***
1052 A294 40c multi 20 15

Pres. Francisco I. Madero (1873-1913).

1973, Nov. 9 **Photo.**
1053 A295 40c stl gray 35 15

50th anniversary of the Antonio Narro Agriculture School in Saltillo.

Type of 1950-52

Designs as before

1973 **Unwmk.** ***Perf. 14***
1054 A189 20c bl vio 2.00 1.50
1055 A189 40c red org 2.00 1.50

Fluorescent printing on back (or on front of 40c) consisting of beehive pattern and diagonal inscription.

Hydrocarbon Molecule — A296

Wmk. 300
1973, Dec. 7 **Photo.** ***Perf. 14***
1056 A296 40c blk, dk car & yel 20 15

Footnotes often refer to other stamps of the same design.

Pointing Hand Emblem of Foreign Trade Institute — A297

1974, Jan. 11 **Photo.** **Wmk. 300**
1057 A297 40c dk grn & blk 20 15

Export promotion.

A298

1974, Jan. 18 **Litho.** **Wmk. 300**
1058 A298 40c black 20 15

EXMEX 73 Philatelic Exhibition, Cuernavaca, Apr. 7-15. See No. C424.

Manuel M. Ponce at Keyboard A299

1974, Jan. 18 **Photo.** **Wmk. 300**
1059 A299 40c gold & multi 20 15

Manuel M. Ponce (1882-1948), composer.

Silver Statuette of Mexican Woman — A300

1974, Mar. 23 **Photo.** ***Perf. 14***
1060 A300 40c red & multi 20 15

First World Silver Fair.

Mariano Azuela A301

1974, Apr. 10 **Wmk. 300** ***Perf. 14***
1061 A301 40c multi 20 15

Mariano Azuela (1873-1952), writer.

Dancing Dogs, Pre-Columbian A302

1974, Apr. 10
1062 A302 40c multi 20 15

6th Traveling Dog Exhibition, Mexico City, Nov. 23-Dec. 1.

Aqueduct, Tepotzotlan — A303

1974, July 10 **Photo.** **Wmk. 300**
1063 A303 40c brt bl & blk 45 15

National Engineers' Day, July 1.

Dr. Rodolfo Robles A304

1974, July 19 ***Perf. 14***
1064 A304 40c bis & grn 20 15

25th anniv. of WHO (in 1973).

EXFILMEX 74 Emblem — A305

1974, July 26 ***Perf. 13x12***
1065 A305 40c buff, grn & blk 20 15

EXFILMEX 74, Fifth Inter-American Philatelic Exhibition honoring centenary of Universal Postal Union, Mexico City, Oct. 26-Nov. 3. See No. C429.

Demosthenes — A306

1974, Aug. 2 **Photo.** ***Perf. 14***
1066 A306 20c grn & brn 35 15

2nd Spanish-American Cong. for Reading and Writing Studies, Mexico City, May 7-14.

Map of Chiapas and Head A307

1974, Sept. 14 **Wmk. 300** ***Perf. 14***
1067 A307 20c blk & grn 20 15

Centenary of Chiapas statehood.

Law of 1824 A308

Sebastian Lerdo de Tejada A309

1974, Oct. 11 **Wmk. 300**
1068 A308 40c gray & grn 20 15

Sesquicentennial of the establishment of the Federal Republic of Mexico.

1974, Oct. 11 **Photo.**
1069 A309 40c blk & lt bl 20 15

Centenary of restoration of the Senate.

UPU Monument, Bern — A310

1974, Dec. 13 **Wmk. 300** ***Perf. 14***
1070 A310 40c ultra & org brn 20 15

Cent. of UPU. See Nos. C437-C438.

Types of 1950-56

Designs (as 1951-56 issues): 2.30p, Guillermo Prieto. 3p, Modernistic church, Nuevo Leon. 50p, Benito Juarez.

1975 **Photo.** **Wmk. 300** ***Perf. 14***
1072 A189 80c green 55 25
1075 A200 2.30p dp vio bl 85 35
1076 A189 3p brick red 85 35
1081 A189 50p org & grn 10.00 7.50

See No. 1097 for unwmkd. 3p with no shading under "Leon."

Gov. José Maria Mora — A312

1975, Feb. 21 **Photo.** **Wmk. 300**
1084 A312 20c yel & multi 20 15

Sesquicentennial (in 1974) of establishment of the State of Mexico.

Merchants with Pre-Columbian Goods — A313

1975, Apr. 18 Photo. Unwmk.
1085 A313 80c multi 20 15

Centenary (in 1974) of the National Chamber of Commerce in Mexico City. Design from Florentine Codex.

Juan Aldama, by Diego Rivera A314

1975, June 6 *Perf. 14*
1086 A314 80c multi 20 15

Juan Aldama (1774-1811), officer and patriot, birth bicentenary.

Indians and Eagle on Cactus Destroying Serpent, from Duran Codex A315

1975, Aug. 1 Photo. Unwmk.
1087 A315 80c multi 20 15

650th anniv. of Tenochtitlan (Mexico City).

Julián Carrillo A316

Academy Emblem A317

1975, Sept. 12 Photo. Unwmk.
1088 A316 80c brt grn & red brn 20 15

Julián Carrillo (1875-1965), violinist and composer, birth centenary.

1975, Sept. 13 *Perf. 14*
1089 A317 80c brn & ocher 20 15

Cent. of Mexican Academy of Languages.

Types of 1950-56

Designs (as 1950-56 issues): 80c, Indian dancer, Michoacan. 2p, Convent, Morelos.

1975-76 Photo. Unwmk.
1090 A189 40c orange 30 15
1091 A189 50c blue 35 15
1092 A200 60c red lil 45 15
1093 A200 70c vio bl 40 15
1094 A189 80c green 40 15
1095 A189 1p ol grn 40 15
1096 A189 2p scarlet 80 50
1097 A189 3p brick red 80 50
1099 A189 5p gray bl & grn 1.75 1.00
1101 A189 10p grn & dp ultra ('76) 4.00 2.00
1102 A189 20p lil & blk ('76) 8.25 4.00
Nos. 1090-1102 (11) 17.90 8.90

University of Guadalajara — A318

1975, Oct. 1 Photo. *Perf. 14*
1107 A318 80c multi 20 15

University of Guadalajara, 50th anniversary.

Road Workers — A319

1975, Oct. 17 Photo. Unwmk.
1108 A319 80c gray grn, grn & blk 20 15

50 years of road building for progress.

Pistons A320

Designs: Export Emblem and 5c, 6p, Steel pipes. 20c, Chemistry flasks. 40c, Cup of coffee. 80c, Meat cuts marked on steer. 1p, Electrical conductor. 2p, Abalone. 3p, Men's shoes. 4p, Tiles. 5p, Minerals. 7p, 8p, 9p, Overalls. 10p, Tequila. 15p, Honey. 20p, Wrought iron. 25p, Copper vase. 35p, 40p, No. 1132, 80p, Jewelry. No. 1133, Books. 100p, Strawberry. 200p, Citrus fruit. 300p, Motor vehicles. 400p, Circuit board. 500p, Cotton.

Some stamps have a gray burelage;

Type I- Burelage lines run lower left to upper right with arch towards lower right.

Type II- Burelage lines run lower left to upper right with arch towards upper left.

1975-87 Photo. Unwmk. *Perf. 14*
1109 A320 5c sl bl ('77) 15 15
1110 A320 20c blk ('76) 15 15
1111 A320 40c dk brn ('76) 50 20
 a. 40c claret brn ('81) 1.00 25
1112 A320 50c dl bl 60 15
 a. 50c slate blue ('76) 20 15
 b. 50c black ('83) 15 15
 c. 50c sl, thin paper ('81) 30 15
1113 A320 80c brt car ('76) 20 15
 a. Perf. 11 40 15
 b. Perf. 11½x11 20 15
 c. As "a," thin paper ('81) 30 25
 d. As "b," thin paper ('81) 15 15
1114 A320 1p vio bl & org ('78) 15 15
1115 A320 1p lt vio & org ('83) 15 15
1116 A320 1p blk & org ('84) 15 15
1117 A320 2p bl grn & dk bl ('76) 75 15
 a. 2p grn & brt bl ('81) 15 15
1118 A320 3p red brn 15 15
 a. 3p brn, perf 11½x11 ('82) 30 15
 b. Gldn brn, thin paper ('81) 30 15
1119 A320 4p tan & dk brn ('80) 20 15
1120 A320 5p gray ol ('78) 20 15
 a. Perf 11½x11 ('84) 15 15
1121 A320 6p brt org ('83) 30 15
 a. Perf 11½x11 ('83) 30 15
 b. Perf 11 ('84) 1.00 15
1121C A320 6p gray, perf. 11½x11 ('84) 15 15
1122 A320 7p Prus bl ('84) 15 15
 a. 7p bl gray ('84) 5.00 15
1123 A320 8p bis brn, perf 11 ('84) 1.25 15
 a. Perf 11½x11 ('84) 15 15
1124 A320 9p dk bl ('84) 15 15
1125 A320 10p dk & lt grn ('78) 15 15
 a. Thin paper ('81) 30 30
 b. Dk ol grn & yel grn ('86) 15 15
 c. Dark olive grn & brt olive grn ('87) 15 15
1126 A320 15p yel org & red brn ('84) 15 15
1127 A320 20p blk ('78) 60 15
1128 A320 20p dk gray ('84) 15 15
1129 A320 25p org brn ('84) 15 15
1130 A320 35p brt cer & yel ('84) 20 20
1131 A320 40p org brn & lt yel ('84) 20 20
1132 A320 50p gray, sil, brt vio & pur ('80) 2.00 75
1133 A320 50p brt bl & lt yel ('83) 35 15
1133A A320 80p pink & gold ('85) 35 35
1134 A320 100p scar & brt grn, I ('83) 1.00 25
1135 A320 200p emer & yel grn, II ('83) 3.00 50
 a. Emer & lem, I ('87) 2.00 1.00
 b. Emer & yel grn, I ('83) 1.00 25
1136 A320 300p brt bl & red, I ('83) 1.00 1.00
 a. Type II ('87) 80 60
1137 A320 400p lem & red brn, I ('84) 1.50 60
1138 A320 500p lt ol grn & yel org, I ('84) 3.00 50
Nos. 1109-1138 (32) 19.15
Set value 6.40

No. 1125b is 2mm wider than No. 1125. Size of No. 1125b: 37x21mm.

Nos. 1117, 1119, 1126, 1135 exist with one or more colors missing. These were not regularly issued.

See Nos. 1166-1176, 1465-1470A, 1491-1505, 1579-1603, C486-C508, C594-C603.

Aguascalientes Cathedral A323

Jaime Torres Bodet A324

1975, Nov. 28
1140 A323 50c bl grn & blk 75 20

400th anniversary of Aguascalientes.

1975, Nov. 28
1141 A324 80c blue & brn 20 15

Jaime Torres Bodet (1920-1974), writer, director general of UNESCO (1958-1962).

Allegory, by José Clemente Orozco — A325

1975, Dec. 9 *Perf. 14*
1142 A325 80c multi 20 15

Sesquicentennial of Supreme Court.

The Death of Cuauhtemoc, by Chavez Morado — A326

1975, Dec. 12 **Photo.**
1143 A326 80c multi 20 15

450th anniv. of the death of Cuauhtemoc (1495?-1525), last Aztec emperor.

Netzahualcoyotl (Water God) — A327

1976, Jan. 9 Unwmk. *Perf. 14*
1144 A327 80c bl & vio bl 20 15

50th anniv. of Mexican irrigation projects.

Arch, León A328

1976, Jan. 20
1145 A328 80c dk brn & ocher 20 15

400th anniversary of León, Guanajuato.

Forest Fire A329

1976, July 8 Photo. *Perf. 14*
1146 A329 80c blk, grn & red 20 15

Prevent fires!

Hat and Scout Emblem A330

Exhibition Emblem A331

1976, Aug. 24 Photo. Unwmk.
1147 A330 80c ol & red brn 20 15

Mexican Boy Scout Assoc., 50th anniv.

1976, Sept. 2
1148 A331 80c blk, red & grn 20 15

Mexico Today and Tomorrow Exhibition.

New Building, Military College A332

1976, Sept. 13 *Perf. 14*
1149 A332 50c red brn & ocher 20 15

Military College, new installations.

Dr. Ricardo Vertiz — A333

1976, Sept. 24 **Photo.** *Perf. 14*
1150 A333 80c blk & redsh brn 20 15

Our Lady of Light Ophthalmological Hospital, centenary.

National Basilica of Guadeloupe — A334

1976, Oct. 12
1151 A334 50c blk & ocher 20 15

Inauguration of the new National Basilica of Our Lady of Guadeloupe.

"40" and Emblem A335

1976, Oct. 28 **Photo.** *Perf. 14*
1152 A335 80c blk, lt grn & car 20 15

Natl. Polytechnic Institute, 40th anniv.

Blast Furnace A336

1976, Nov. 4
1153 A336 50c multi 20 15

Inauguration of the Lazaro Cardenas Steel Mill, Las Truchas.

Saltillo Cathedral A337

Electrification A338

1977, July 25 **Photo.** *Perf. 14*
1154 A337 80c yel & dk brn 20 15

400th anniversary of the founding of Saltillo.

1977, Aug. 14 **Photo.** *Perf. 14*
1155 A338 80c multi 20 15

40 years of Mexican development program.

Flags of Spain and Mexico A339

1977, Oct. 8 **Photo.** **Wmk. 300**
1156 A339 50c multi 20 15
1157 A339 80c multi 20 15
Nos. 1156-1157,C537-C539 (5) 1.02
Set value 58

Resumption of diplomatic relations with Spain.

Aquiles Serdan (1877-1910), Martyr of the Revolution — A340

1977, Nov. 18 **Photo.** *Perf. 14*
1158 A340 80c lt & dk grn & blk 20 15

Poinsettia A341

1977, Dec. 2 **Wmk. 300** *Perf. 14*
1159 A341 50c multi 15 15

Christmas 1977.

Old and New Telephones — A342

1978, Mar. 15 **Photo.** *Perf. 14*
1160 A342 80c sal & mar 20 15

Centenary of first telephone in Mexico.

Oil Derrick A343

1978, Mar. 18
1161 A343 80c dp org & mar 20 15

40th anniversary of nationalization of oil industry. See Nos. C556-C557.

Institute Emblem A344

1978, July 21 **Photo.** *Perf. 14*
1162 A344 80c bl & blk 20 15

Pan-American Institute for Geography and History, 50th anniv. See Nos. C574-C575.

Dahlias A345

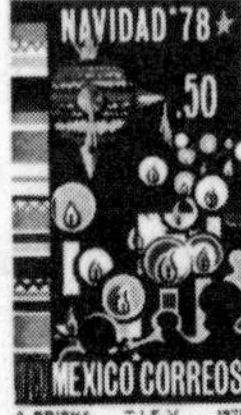

Decorations and Candles A346

1978, Sept. 29 **Photo.** **Wmk. 300**
1163 A345 50c shown 20 15
1164 A345 80c Frangipani 20 15

1978, Nov. 22 **Photo.** *Perf. 14*
1165 A346 50c multi 15 15

Christmas 1978.

Export Type of 1975

Designs as before. 50p, Jewelry.

1979-81 **Photo.** **Wmk. 300** *Perf. 14*
1166 A320 20c blk ('81) 40 20
1167 A320 50c slate bl 20 20
a. 50c bluish black 30 20
1168 A320 80c brt car 75 20
a. Perf. 11 30 20
1169 A320 1p ultra & org 30 15
1170 A320 2p brt grn & bl 30 20
1171 A320 3p dk brn 30 15
1172 A320 4p tan & dk brn ('80) 30 20
1173 A320 5p gray olive 40 35
1174 A320 10p dk & lt grn 1.50 75
1175 A320 20p black 2.00 75
1176 A320 50p gray, sil, brt vio & pur 4.00 2.50
Nos. 1166-1176 (11) 10.45 5.65

A347

Soccer Ball — A348

1979, Apr. 26 **Wmk. 300** *Perf. 14*
1177 A347 80c multi 15 15

Centenary of Hermosillo, Sonora.

1979, June 15 **Photo.** **Wmk. 300**

Designs: 80c, Aztec ball player. 1p, Wall painting showing athletes. 5p, Runners (horiz.).

1178 A348 50c bl & blk 15 15
1179 A348 80c multi 15 15
1180 A348 1p multi 15 15
Nos. 1178-1180,C606-C607 (5) 91
Set value 56

Souvenir Sheet

Imperf

1181 A348 5p multi 80 80

Universiada '79, World Games, Mexico City, Sept. 1979. No. 1181 has simulated perforations.

Josefa Ortiz de Dominguez, Mayor of Queretaro, 150th Death Anniv. — A349

1979, July 6 *Perf. 14*
1182 A349 80c multi 15 15

Allegory of National Culture, by Alfaro Siqueiros — A350

Design: 3p, Conquest of Energy, by Chavez Morado.

1979, July 10
1183 A350 80c multi 16 15
1184 A350 3p multi 24 15

National University, 50th anniversary of autonomy. See Nos. C609-C610.

Emiliano Zapata, by Diego Rivera — A351

1979, Aug. 8 **Photo.** *Perf. 14*
1185 A351 80c multi 20 15

Emiliano Zapata (1879-1919), revolutionist.

Soccer A352

Designs: 80c, Women's volleyball. 1p, Basketball. 5p, Fencing.

1979, Sept. 2
1186 A352 50c multi 15 15
1187 A352 80c multi 15 15
1188 A352 1p multi 15 15
Nos. 1186-1188,C612-C613 (5) 88
Set value 56

Souvenir Sheet

Imperf

1189 A352 5p multi 80 80

Universiada '79 World University Games, Mexico City. No. 1189 has simulated perforations.

Tepoztlan, Morelos — A353

Tourism: No. 1191, Mexcaltitan, Nayarit.

1979, Sept. 28 Photo. *Perf. 14*

1190 A353 80c multi 15 15
1191 A353 80c multi 15 15
Set value 15

See Nos. C615-C616, 1274-1277, 1318-1321, 1513-1516.

Postmaster Martin de Olivares — A354

Shepherd and Sheep — A355

1979 Wmk. 300 *Perf. 14*

1192 A354 80c multi 15 15

Royal proclamation of mail service in the New World (New Spain), 400th anniversary. See Nos. C618-C620.

1979, Nov. 15

1193 A355 50c multi 15 15

Christmas 1979. See No. C623.

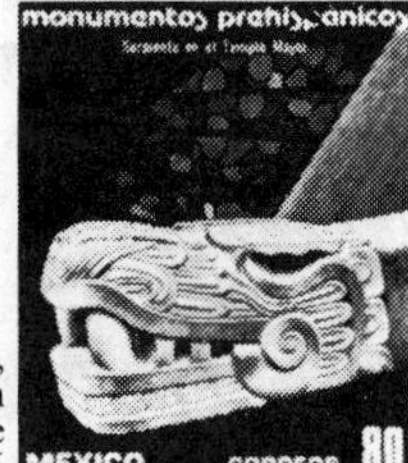
Serpent, Mayan Temple A356

1980, Feb. 16 Photo. *Perf. 14x14½*

1194 A356 80c multi 15 15

Pre-Hispanic monuments. See Nos. C625-C626.

North American Turkey A357

Tajetes Erecta A358

Wmk. 300

1980, Mar. 8 Photo. *Perf. 14*

1195 A357 80c multi 15 15
1196 A358 80c multi 15 15
Set value 15

See Nos. C632-C633, 1234-1237.

China Poblana (Woman's Costume), Puebla — A359

Wmk. 300

1980, Apr. 26 Photo. *Perf. 14*

1197 A359 50c shown 15 15
1198 A359 80c Jarocha, Veracruz 15 15
Set value 15

See No. C636, 1231-1233.

10th National Census — A360

1980, June 4 Unwmk.

1200 A360 3p silver & blk 20 15

Cuauhtemoc (Last Aztec Emperor), 1520, Matritense Codex A361

Pre-Hispanic Art (Leaders): 1.60p, Nezahualcoyotl (1402-1472), governor of Tetzcoco, poet, Azcatitlan Codex. 5.50p, Eight Deer Tiger's Claw (1011-1063), 11th king of Mixtec, Nuttall Codex.

1980, June 21

1201 A361 80c multi 15 15
1202 A361 1.60p multi 16 15
1203 A361 5.50p multi 42 20
Set value 40

See Nos. 1285-1287, 1510-1512.

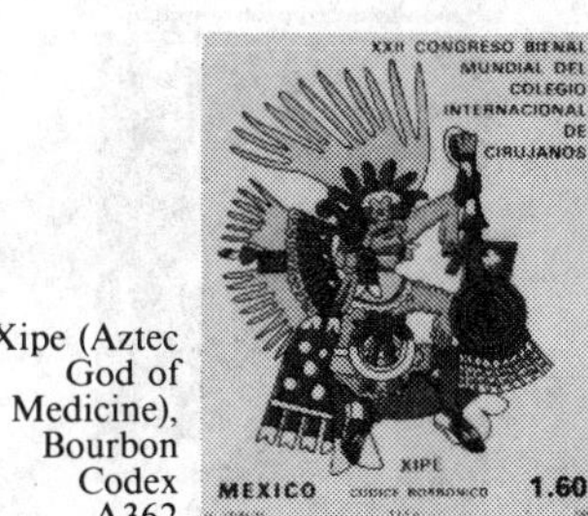
Xipe (Aztec God of Medicine), Bourbon Codex A362

1980, June 29

1204 A362 1.60p multi 15 15

22nd International Biennial Congress of the International College of Surgeons, Mexico City, June 29-July 4.

Moscow '80 Bronze Medal, Emblem, Misha, Olympic Rings — A363

1980, July 19 Photo. *Perf. 14*

1205 A363 1.60p shown 15 15
1206 A363 3p Silver medal 26 15
1207 A363 5.50p Gold medal 38 25

22nd Summer Olympic Games, Moscow, July 19-Aug. 3.

Ceremonial Vessel, Tenochtitlan Temple A364

Wmk. 300

1980, Aug. 23 Photo. *Perf. 14*

1208 A364 80c shown 15 15
1209 A364 1.60p Caracol 15 15
1210 A364 5.50p Chacmool 28 15
Set value 30

Pre-Columbian Art.

Sacromonte Sanctuary, Amecameca — A365

Colonial Monuments: No. 1212, St. Catherine's Convent, Patzcuaro. No. 1213, Basilica, Cuilapan (vert.). No. 1214, Calvary Hermitage, Cuernavaca.

1980, Sept. 26 Photo. *Perf. 14*

1211 A365 2.50p black 20 15
1212 A365 2.50p black 20 15
1213 A365 3p black 25 15
1214 A365 3p black 25 15
Set value 40

See Nos. 1260-1263, 1303-1306, 1338-1341.

Quetzalcoatl (God) A366

Sinaloa Coat of Arms A367

1980, Sept. 27

1215 A366 2.50p multi 20 15

World Tourism Conf., Manila, Sept. 27.

1980, Oct. 13

1216 A367 1.60p multi 20 15

Sinaloa state sesquicentennial.

Straw Angel — A368

Christmas 1980: 1.60p, Poinsettias.

1980, Nov. 17 Photo. *Perf. 14*

1217 A368 50c multi 15 15
1218 A368 1.60p multi 15 15
Set value 20

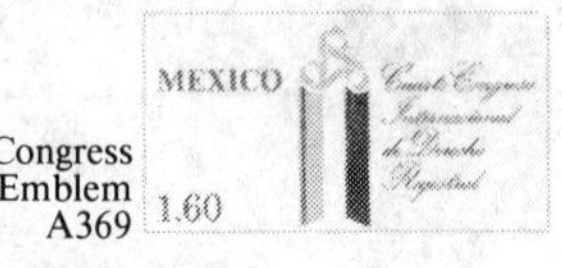
Congress Emblem A369

1980, Dec. 10

1219 A369 1.60p multi 15 15

4th International Civil Justice Congress.

Glass Vase and Animals A370

1980, Dec. 13 Wmk. 300

1220 A370 50c shown 15 15
1221 A370 1p Poncho 15 15
1222 A370 3p Wooden mask, 17th century 30 15
Set value 35

See Nos. 1267-1269.

Simon Bolivar, by Paulin Guerin A371

Vicente Guerrero A372

1980, Dec. 17

1223 A371 4p multi 40 25

Simon Bolivar death sesquicentennial.

1981, Feb. 14

1224 A372 80c multi 15 15

Vicente Guerrero (1783-1831), statesman.

Valentin Gomez Farias — A373

1981, Feb. 14
1225 A373 80c brt grn & gray 15 15

First Latin-American Table Tennis Cup — A374

Wmk. 300

1981, Feb. 27 Photo. *Perf. 14*
1226 A374 4p multi 40 25

Jesus Gonzalez Ortega, Politician, Birth Cent. A375

Gabino Barreda (1818-1881), Physician A376

Wmk. 300

1981, Mar. 10 Photo. *Perf. 14*
1227 A375 80c brn & yel org 15 15

1981, Feb. 28
1228 A376 80c multi 15 15

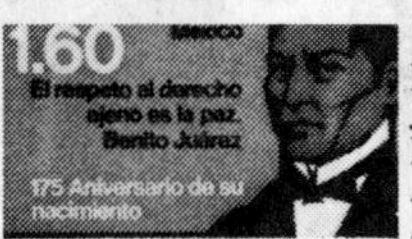

Benito Juarez, 175th Death Anniv. A377

1981, Mar. 21
1229 A377 1.60p multi 15 15

450th Anniv. of Puebla City — A378

1981, Apr. 16 Unwmk.
1230 A378 80c multi 15 15
a. Wmk. 300 40 20

Costume Type of 1980

1981, Apr. 25 Unwmk.
1231 A359 50c Purepecha, Michoacan 15 15
1232 A359 80c Charra, Jalisco 15 15
1233 A359 1.60p Mestiza, Yucatan 15 15
Set value 30 15

Flora and Fauna Types of 1980

Wmk. 300 (#1235), Unwmkd.

1981, May 30
1234 A357 80c Mimus polyglottos 15 15
1235 A358 80c Persea americana 15 15
1236 A357 1.60p Trogon mexicanus 15 15
1237 A358 1.60p Theobromo cacao 15 15
Set value 40 20

Workers' Strike, by David Altaro Siqueiros — A379

1981, June 10 Photo. *Perf. 14*
1238 A379 1.60p multi 15 15

Labor strike martyrs of Cananea, 75th anniversary.

Intl. Year of the Disabled A380

1981, July 4 Unwmk. *Perf. 14*
1239 A380 4p multi 40 25

450th Anniv. of Queretaro City — A381

1981, July 25 Unwmk.
1240 A381 80c multi 15 15
a. Wmk. 300 40 15

Alexander Fleming (1881-1955), Discoverer of Penicillin — A382

1981, Aug. 1 Unwmk.
1241 A382 5p bl & org 40 15

No. 1 A383

1981, Aug. 6
1242 A383 4p multi 32 15
a. Wmk. 300 40 15

125th anniv. of Mexican stamps.

St. Francis Xavier Clavijero, 250th Birth Anniv. — A384

1981, Sept. 9 Unwmk. *Perf. 14*
1243 A384 80c multi 15 15

Union Congress Building Opening — A385

1981, Sept. 10
1244 A385 1.60p red & brt grn 15 15

1300th Anniv. of Bulgarian State A386

1981, Sept. 19 Photo. *Perf. 14*
1245 A386 1.60p Desislava, mural, 1259 15 15
1246 A386 4p Thracian gold cup 30 15
1247 A386 7p Horseman 45 15
Set value 35

Pre-Hispanic Art — A387

1981, Sept. 26
1248 A387 80c Squatting diety 20 15
1249 A387 1.60p Animal head 30 15
1250 A387 4p Fish 40 25
Set value 45

Pablo Picasso (1881-1973) — A388

1981, Oct. 5
1251 A388 5p lt ol grn & grn 40 24

Christmas 1981 — A389

1981, Oct. 15
1252 A389 50c Shepherd 15 15
1253 A389 1.60p Girl 20 15
Set value 20

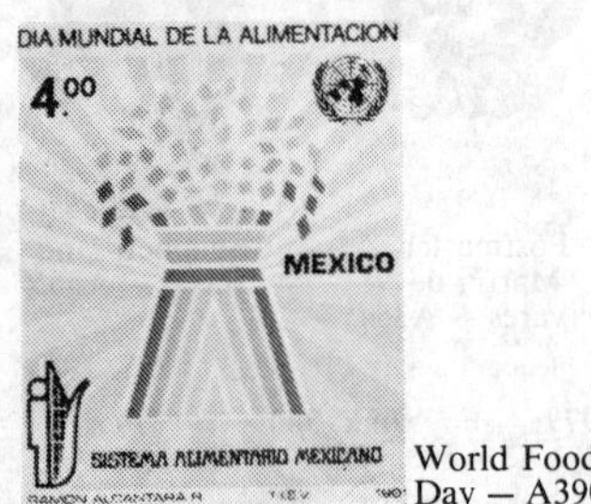

World Food Day — A390

1981, Oct. 16
1254 A390 4p multi 30 18

50th Death Anniv. of Thomas Edison A391

1981, Oct. 18
1255 A391 4p multi 30 18

Intl. Meeting on Cooperation and Development — A392

1981, Oct. 22
1256 A392 4p multi 30 15

Pan-American Railway Congress — A393

1981, Oct. 25 **Unwmk.**
1257 A393 1.60p multi 15 15

50th Anniv. of Mexican Sound Movies A394

1981, Nov. 3 **Photo.** ***Perf. 14***
1258 A394 4p multi 30 15

Inauguration of Zip Codes A395

1981, Nov. 12
1259 A395 80c multi 15 15

Colonial Monument Type of 1980

Design: No. 1260, Mascarones House. No. 1261, La Merced Order Convent. No. 1262, Third Order Chapel, Texoco. No. 1263, Friar Tembleque Aqueduct, Otumba.

1981, Nov. 28
1260 A365 4p black 18 15
1261 A365 4p black 18 15
1262 A365 5p black 20 15
1263 A365 5p black 20 15
Set value 40

Martyrs of Rio Blanco, 75th Anniv. A396

1982, Jan. 7 **Photo.** ***Perf. 14***
1264 A396 80c multi 15 15

Death Sesquicentennial of Ignacio Lopez Rayon — A397

1982, Feb. 2
1265 A397 1.60p multi 15 15

75th Anniv. of Postal Headquarters — A398

1982, Feb. 17
1266 A398 4p grn & ocher 20 15

Crafts Type of 1980

1982, Mar. 6 **Photo.** ***Perf. 14***
1267 A370 50c Huichole art 15 15
1268 A370 1p Ceramic snail 20 15
1269 A370 3p Tiger mask, Madera 20 15
Set value 15

"Use Zip Codes" A399

1982, Mar. 20
1270 A399 80c multi 15 15

TB Bacillus Centenary and World Health Day A400

1982, Apr. 7 **Photo.** ***Perf. 14***
1271 A400 4p multi 20 15

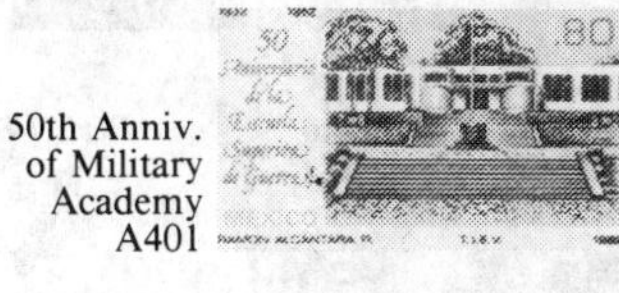

50th Anniv. of Military Academy A401

1982, Apr. 15
1272 A401 80c multi 15 15

City Oaxaca, 450th Anniv. — A402

1982, Apr. 25
1273 A402 1.60p multi 15 15

Tourism Type of 1979

Designs: No. 1274, Basaseachic Cascade, Chihuahua. No. 1275, Silence Zone, Durango. No. 1276, Ruins, Maya city of Edzna, Campeche. No. 1277, Olmec sculpture, Tabasco.

1982, May 29 **Photo.** ***Perf. 14***
1274 A353 80c multi 15 15
1275 A353 80c multi 15 15
1276 A353 1.60p multi 15 15
1277 A353 1.60p multi 15 15
Set value 20

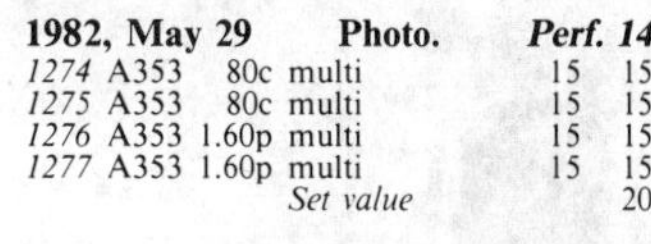

1982 World Cup A403

Designs: Various soccer players.

1982, June 13
1278 A403 1.60p multi 16 15
1279 A403 4p multi 20 15
1280 A403 7p multi 24 15
Set value 15

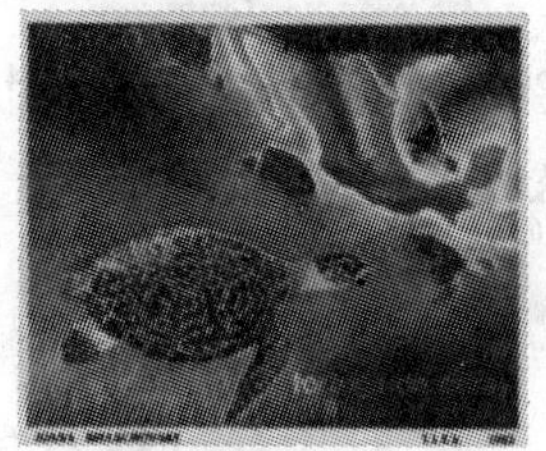

Turtles and Map — A404

1982, July 3
1281 A404 1.60p shown 20 15
1282 A404 4p Gray whales 25 15
Set value 15

Gen. Vicente Guerrero (1782-1831) — A405

1982, Aug. 10 **Photo.** ***Perf. 14***
1283 A405 80c multi 15 15

2nd UN Conference on Peaceful Uses of Outer Space, Vienna, Aug. 9-21 — A406

1982, Aug. 14
1284 A406 4p multi 20 15

Pre-Hispanic Art Type of 1980

Designs: 80c, Tariacuri, founder of Tarasco Kingdom, Chronicle of Michoacan, 16th cent. 1.60p, Acamapichtli, Aztec emperor, 1376-1396, Azcatitlan Codex. 4p, 10-Deer Tiger's Breastplate, wife of Lord 13-Eagle Tlaloc Copal Ball, 12th cent., Nuttal Mixtec Codex.

1982, Sept. 4
1285 A361 80c multi 15 15
1286 A361 1.60p multi 20 15
1287 A361 4p multi 25 15
Set value 15

Papaya A407

Perf. 14x14½

1982, Sept. 18 **Unwmk.**
1288 A407 80c shown 15 15
1289 A407 1.60p Corn 20 15
Set value 15

Florentine Codex Illustrations — A408

1982, Oct. 2
1290 A408 80c Astrologer 15 15
1291 A408 1.60p School 15 15
1292 A408 4p Musicians 18 15
Set value 15

See Nos. 1520-1522.

Manuel Gamio (1883-1960) Anthropologist — A409

Scientists: No. 1294, Isaac Ochoterena (1855-1950), biologist. No. 1295, Angel Maria Garibay K. (1892-1976), philologist. No. 1296, Manuel Sandoval Vallarta (1899-), nuclear physicist. No. 1297, Guillermo Gonzalez Camarena (b. 1917), electronic engineer.

1982, Oct. 16 **Photo.** ***Perf. 14x14½***
1293 A409 1.60p multi 20 15
1294 A409 1.60p multi 20 15
1295 A409 1.60p multi 20 15
1296 A409 1.60p multi 20 15
1297 A409 1.60p multi 20 15
a. Strip of 5, #1293-1297 1.25 75
Nos. 1293-1297 (5) 1.00
Set value 25

Natl. Archives Opening, Aug. 27 — A410

1982, Oct. 23 ***Perf. 14½x14***
1298 A410 1.60p brt grn & blk 20 15

Christmas 1982
A411

1982, Oct. 30 *Perf. 14*
1299 A411 50c Dove 15 15
1300 A411 1.60p Dove, diff. 20 15
Set value 15

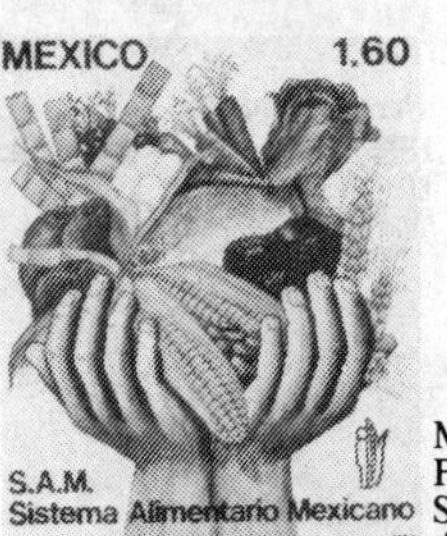

Mexican Food System
A412

1982, Nov. 13 Photo. *Perf. 14x14½*
1301 A412 1.60p multi 20 15

Opening of Revolutionary Museum, Chihuahua — A413

1982, Nov. 17 *Perf. 14½x14*
1302 A413 1.60p No. C232 20 15

Colonial Monument Type of 1980

Designs: 1.60p, College of Sts. Peter and Paul, Mexico City, 1576. 8p, Convent of Jesus Maria, Mexico City, 1603. 10p, Open Chapel, Tlalmanalco, 1585. 14p, Convent at Actopan, Hidalgo State, 1548.

1982, Nov. 27
1303 A365 1.60p blk & gray 20 15
1304 A365 8p blk & gray 30 15
1305 A365 10p blk & gray 30 15
1306 A365 14p blk & gray 40 15
Set value 34

Alfonso Garcia Robles, 1982 Nobel Peace Prize Winner
A414

Perf. 14x14½

1982, Nov. 30 **Unwmk.**
1307 A414 1.60p multi 15 15
1308 A414 14p multi 30 15
Set value 18

15-Cent Minimum Value
The minimum catalogue value is 15 cents. Separating se-tenant pieces into individual stamps does not increase the "value" of the stamps... since demand for the separated stamps may be small.

Jose Vasconcelos, Philosopher — A415

1982, Dec. 11 *Perf. 14*
1309 A415 1.60p bl & blk 20 15

World Communications Year — A416

1983, Feb. 12 Photo. *Perf. 14*
1310 A416 16p multi 30 16

First Philatelic Exposition of the Mexican Revolution
A417

1983, Mar. 13 Photo. *Perf. 14*
1311 A417 6p No. 326 20 15

25th Anniv. of Intl. Maritime Org. — A418

1983, Mar. 17
1312 A418 16p multi 32 18

Year of Constitutional Right to Health Protection — A419

1983, Apr. 7
1313 A419 6p red & ol 20 15

Society of Geography and Statistics Sesquicentennial — A420

1983, Apr. 18
1314 A420 6p Founder Gomez Farias 20 15

2nd World Youth Soccer Championships
A421

1983, June 2 Photo. *Perf. 14*
1315 A421 6p grn & blk 20 15
1316 A421 13p red & blk 32 15
1317 A421 14p bl & blk 32 15
Set value 32

Tourism Type of 1979

Designs: No. 1318, Federal Palace Building, Queretaro. No. 1319, Fountain, San Luis Potosi. 13p, Cable car, Zacatecas. 14p, Mayan stone head, Quintana Roo.

1983, June 24 Photo. *Perf. 14*
1318 A353 6p multi 20 15
1319 A353 6p multi 20 15
1320 A353 13p multi 32 15
1321 A353 14p multi 32 15
a. Vert. strip of 4, #1318-1321 + label 1.25 1.00
Set value 38

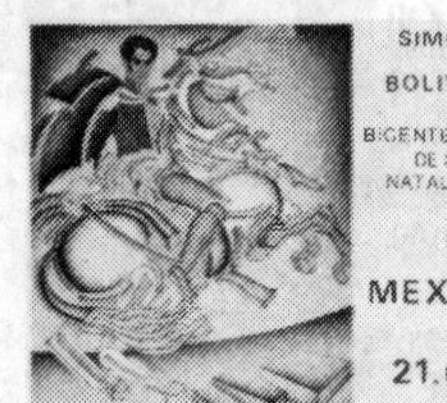

Simon Bolivar (1783-1830) — A422

1983, July 14
1322 A422 21p multi 38 20

Angela Peralta, Opera Singer (1845-1883) — A423

1983, Photo. *Perf. 14*
1323 A423 9p multi 25 15

Mexican Flora
A424

1983, Sept. 23 Photo. *Perf. 14*
1324 A424 9p Achras zapota 25 15
1325 A424 9p Agave atrovirens 25 15
Set value 20

Mexican Fauna
A425

1983, Sept. 23 Photo. *Perf. 14*
1326 A425 9p Boa constrictor imperator 25 15
1327 A425 9p Papilio machaon 25 15
Set value 20

Christmas 1983 — A426

1983, Oct. 15 Photo. *Perf. 14*
1328 A426 9p multi 20 15
1329 A426 20p multi 30 18

Integral Communications and Transportation Systems — A427

1983, Oct. 17 Photo. *Perf. 14*
1330 A427 13p brt bl & blk 30 15

Carlos Chavez (1899-1978), Musician, Composer — A428

Contemporary Artists: No. 1332, Francisco Goitia (1882-1960), Painter. No. 1333, Salvador Diaz Miron (1853-1927), Lyrical Poet. No. 1334, Carlos Bracho (1899-1966), Sculptor. No. 1335, Fanny Anitua (1887-1968), Singer.

1983, Nov. 7 Photo. *Perf. 14*
1331 A428 9p brn & multi 24 15
1332 A428 9p brn & multi 24 15
1333 A428 9p brn & multi 24 15
1334 A428 9p brn & multi 24 15
1335 A428 9p brn & multi 24 15
a. Horiz. strip of 5, #1331-1335 1.40 1.00
Nos. 1331-1335 (5) 1.20
Set value 50

Jose Clemente Orozco (1883-1949), Painter — A429

1983, Nov. 23 Photo. *Perf. 14*
1336 A429 9p multi 25 15

35th Anniv. of Human Rights Declaration A430

1983, Dec. 10 *Perf. 14*
1337 A430 20p multi 30 18

Colonial Monument Type of 1980

Designs: 9p, Convent Garden, Malinalco, 16th cent. 20p, Open Chapel, Cuernavaca Cathedral, Morelos. 21p, Tepeji del Rio Convent, Hidalgo. 24p, Atlatlahuacan Convent, Morelos.

1983, Dec. 16 Photo. *Perf. 14½x14*
1338 A365 9p blk & gray 28 15
1339 A365 20p blk & gray 40 18
1340 A365 21p blk & gray 40 20
1341 A365 24p blk & gray 40 22

Antonio Caso (1883-1946), Philosopher — A431

1983, Dec. 19
Granite Paper
1342 A431 9p multi 25 15

Royal Mining Decree Bicentenary A432

1983, Dec. 21
1343 A432 9p Joaquin Velazquez Leon, reform author 25 15

Postal Code Centenary A433

1984, Jan. 2 Photo. *Perf. 14*
1344 A433 12p Envelopes 32 15

Fight Against Polio A434

1984, Apr. 7 Photo. *Perf. 14*
1345 A434 12p Children dancing 32 15

Aquatic Birds — A435

1984, May 4 Photo. *Perf. 14*
1346 A435 12p Muscovy duck 40 15
1347 A435 20p Black-bellied whistling tree duck 45 15
Set value 20

World Dog Exposition, Mexico City A436

1984, May 27
1348 A436 12p multi 32 15

Natl. Bank of Mexico Centenary — A437

1984, June 2
1349 A437 12p multi 32 15

Forest Protection and Conservation — A438

1984, July 12 Photo. *Perf. 14*
1350 A438 20p Hands holding trees 38 15

1984 Summer Olympics A439

1984, July 28
1351 A439 14p Shot put 25 15
1352 A439 20p Equestrian 28 15
1353 A439 23p Gymnastics 28 16
1354 A439 24p Diving 28 16
1355 A439 25p Boxing 30 16
1356 A439 26p Fencing 30 16

Size: 56x62mm

Imperf

1357 A439 40p Rings 52 30
Nos. 1351-1357 (7) 2.21 1.24

Mexico-Russian Diplomatic Relations, 60th Anniv. — A440

1984, Aug. 4
1358 A440 23p Flags 38 16

Intl. Population Conference, Aug. 5-14 — A441

1984, Aug. 6
1359 A441 20p UN emblem, hand 38 15

Economic Culture Fund, 50th Anniv. — A442

1984, Sept. 3
1360 A442 14p multi 30 15

Gen Francisco J. Mugica A443

1984,
1361 A443 14p blk & brn 18 15

Red Cactus, by Sebastian A444

Airline Emblem A445

1984, Sept. 14 Photo. *Perf. 14x14½*
1362 A444 14p multi 15 15
1363 A445 20p blk & org 20 15

Aeromexico (airline), 50th anniv.

Palace of Fine Arts, 50th Anniv. A446

1984, Sept. 29
1364 A446 14p multi 15 15

275th Anniv. of Chihuahua City A447

1984, Oct. 12
1365 A447 14p Cathedral exterior detail 15 15

Scott's editorial staff cannot undertake to identify, authenticate or appraise stamps and postal markings.

Coatzacoalcos Bridge Inauguration — A448

1984, Oct. 17 ***Perf. 14½x14***

1366 A448 14p Aerial view 15 15

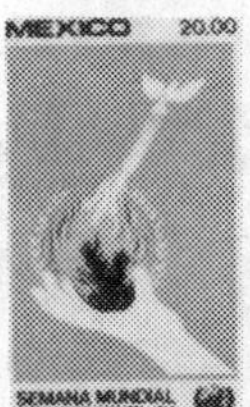

UN Disarmament Week — A449

1984, Oct. 14 **Photo.** ***Perf. 14***

1367 A449 20p multi 20 15

Christmas 1984 A450

1984, Oct. 31 **Photo.** ***Perf. 14***

1368 A450 14p Toy train & tree 15 15
1369 A450 20p Pinata breaking 20 15

Politician-Journalist Ignacio M. Altamirano (1834-1893) — A451

1984, Nov. 13 **Photo.** ***Perf. 14***

1370 A451 14p blk & lt red brn 15 15

State Audit Office, 160th Anniv. A452

1984, Nov. 16

1371 A452 14p multi 15 15

1986 World Cup Soccer Championships, Mexico — A453

1984, Nov. 19

1372 A453 20p multi *16* *15*
1373 A453 24p multi *20* *15*

Printed se-tenant and has label in center vertical row of sheet.

Romulo Gallegos (1884-1969), Author and Former Pres. of Venezuela — A454

1984, Dec. 6

1374 A454 20p bl & gray 20 15

State Registry Office, 125th Anniv. A455

1984, Dec. 13

1375 A455 24p slate blue 24 18

Natl. Flag, 50th Anniv. A456

1985, Feb. 24

1376 A456 22p multi 22 16

Johann Sebastian Bach — A457

Intl. Youth Year — A458

1985, Mar. 21 **Photo.** ***Perf. 14***

1377 A457 35p dl red brn, gold & blk 24 18

1985, Mar. 28 **Photo.** ***Perf. 14***

1378 A458 35p rose vio, gold & blk 24 18

Child Survival Campaign A459

1985, Mar. 28 **Photo.** ***Perf. 14***

1379 A459 36p multi 24 18

Mexican Mint, 450th Anniv. A460

1985, May 11 **Photo.** ***Perf. 14***

1380 A460 35p 1st gold & copper coins 24 18

Victor Hugo A461

1985, May 22 **Photo.** ***Perf. 14***

1381 A461 35p slate 24 18

MEXFIL '85 — A462

1985, June 9 **Photo.** ***Perf. 14***

1382 A462 22p No. 5 15 15
1383 A462 35p No. 574 22 18
1384 A462 36p No. 1081 24 18

Souvenir Sheet

1985, June 27 ***Imperf.***

1385 A462 90p No. 111 on cover 50 35

Morelos Telecommunications Satellite Launch — A463

1985, June 17 ***Perf. 14x14½***

1386 A463 22p Shuttle launch 15 15
1387 A463 36p Ground receiver 20 18
1388 A463 90p Modes of communication 50 38
a. Strip of 3, #1386-1388 + 2 labels 1.25 1.00

Souvenir Sheet

Imperf

1389 A463 100p multi 60 45

Nos. 1386-1388 has continuous design. No. 1389 pictures uninscribed continuous design of Nos. 1386-1388.

9th World Forestry Congress, Mexico City, July 1-9 A464

1985, July 1 ***Perf. 14x14½***

1390 A464 22p Conifer 15 15
1391 A464 35p Silk-cotton tree 18 15
1392 A464 36p Mahogany 20 16
a. Strip of 3, #1390-1392 + 2 labels 1.25 1.00
Set value 38

Martin Luis Guzman (1887-1977), Journalist, Politician — A465

Contemporary writers: No. 1394, Agustin Yanez (1904-1980), politician. No. 1395, Alfonso Reyes (1889-1959), diplomat. No. 1396, Jose Ruben Romero (1890-1952), diplomat. No. 1397, Artemio de Valle Arizpe (1888-1961), historian.

1985, July 19 ***Perf. 14***

1393 A465 22p multi 15 15
1394 A465 22p multi 15 15
1395 A465 22p multi 15 15
1396 A465 22p multi 15 15
1397 A465 22p multi 15 15
a. Strip of 5, #1393-1397 75 75
Set value 50 50

Heroes of the Mexican Revolution, 1810 A466

1985, Sept. 15

1398 A466 22p Miguel Hidalgo 15 15
1399 A466 35p Jose Morelos 15 15
1400 A466 35p Ignacio Allende 15 15
1401 A466 36p Leona Vicario 18 18
1402 A466 110p Vicente Guerrero 50 50
Nos. 1398-1402 (5) 1.13 1.13

Souvenir Sheet

Imperf

1403 A466 90p Bell, church 40 30

175th anniv. of independence from Spanish rule. #1403 contains one 56x49mm stamp.

University of Mexico, 75th Anniv. A467

1985, Sept. 22 Photo. *Perf. 14x14½*

1404 A467 26p San Ildefonso, 1910 15 15
1405 A467 26p University emblem 15 15
1406 A467 40p Rectory, 1985 22 18
1407 A467 45p 1st Rector Justo Sierra, crest, 1910 25 20
1408 A467 90p Crest, 1985 50 38
a. Strip of 5, #1404-1407 1.50 1.00
Nos. 1404-1408 (5) 1.27 1.06

Interamerican Development Bank, 25th Anniv. — A468

1985, Oct. 23 Photo. *Perf. 14½x14*

1409 A468 26p multi 15 15

UN Disarmament Week — A469

1985, Oct. 24 *Perf. 14x14½*

1410 A469 36p Guns, doves 20 15

UN, 40th Anniv. — A470

1985, Oct. 25 *Perf. 14½x14*

1411 A470 26p Hand, dove 15 15

Christmas 1985 A471

Children's drawings.

1985, Nov. 15 Photo. *Perf. 14x14½*

1412 A471 26p multi 15 15
1413 A471 35p multi 15 15
Set value 22

1910 Revolution, 75th Anniv. A472

1985, Nov. 18 *Perf. 14*

1414 A472 26p Soldadera 15 15
1415 A472 35p Francisco Villa 15 15
1416 A472 40p Emiliano Zapata 16 15
1417 A472 45p Venustiano Carranza 18 15
1418 A472 110p Francisco Madero 32 25
Nos. 1414-1418 (5) 96 85

Souvenir Sheet

Imperf

1419 A472 90p Liberty bell 35 28

No. 1419 contains one 48x40mm stamp.

Astronaut, by Sebastian A473

The Watchman, by Federico Silva A474

Mexican Astronaut, Rodolfo Neri, by Cauduro — A475

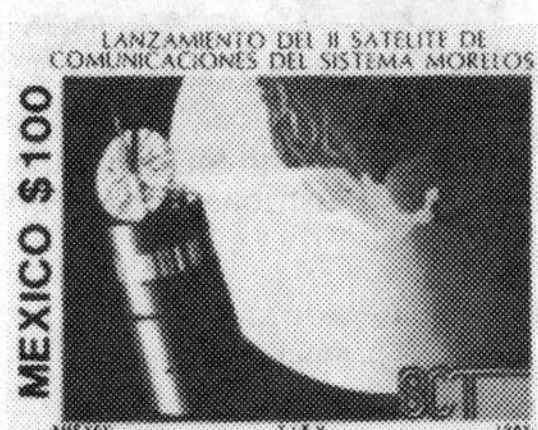

Morelos and Telecommunications Satellite Launch — A476

1985, Nov. 26 *Perf. 14x14½*

1420 A473 26p multi 15 15
1421 A474 35p multi 15 15
1422 A475 45p multi 18 15
Set value 36

Miniature Sheet

Imperf

1423 A476 100p multi 35 28

1986 World Cup Soccer Championships, Mexico — A477

1985, Dec. 15 Photo. *Perf. 14½x14*

1424 A477 26p Olympic Stadium 15 15
1425 A477 45p Aztec Stadium 20 15

1st Free Textbook for Primary Education, 25th Anniv. — A478

1985, Dec. 16

1426 A478 26p Book cover 15 15

Colonial Monuments — A479

Landmarks in Mexico City: 26p, College of the Vizcainas, c. 1735. 35p, Palace of the Counts of Heras and Soto. 40p, Palace of the Counts of Calimaya, 16th cent. 45p, San Carlos Academy, 16th cent.

1985, Dec. 27 *Perf. 14x14½*

1427 A479 26p grnsh blk & fawn 15 15
1428 A479 35p grnsh blk & fawn 16 15
1429 A479 40p grnsh blk & fawn 18 15
1430 A479 45p grnsh blk & fawn 20 15
a. Strip of 4, #1427-1430 + label 1.00 75
Set value 50

Natl. Polytechnic Institute, 50th Anniv. A480

1986, Feb. 7 *Perf. 14*

1431 A480 40p Luis Enrique Erro Planetarium 15 15
1432 A480 65p School of Arts & Communications 24 20
1433 A480 75p Emblem, founders 28 24
a. Strip of 3, #1431-1433 + 2 labels 90 75

Fruit — A481

1986, Feb. 21 *Perf. 14½x14*

1434 A481 40p Cucurbita pepo 18 15
1435 A481 65p Nopalea coccinellifera 30 24

World Health Day — A482

1986, Apr. 7 Photo. *Perf. 14*

1436 A482 65p Doll 20 16

Halley's Comet A483

1986, Apr. 25

1437 A483 90p multi 25 20

Natl. Geology Institute, Cent. A484

1986, May 26

1438 A484 40p multi 16 15

1986 World Cup Soccer Championships — A485

Paintings by Angel Zarraga (1886-1946) and Sergio Guerrero Morales: 30p, Three Soccer Players with Cap. 40p, Portrait of Ramon Novaro. 65p, Dimanche. 70p, Portrait of Ernest Charles Gimpel. 90p, Three Soccer Players. 110p, Poster for 1986 championships, by Morales.

1986, May 31

1439 A485 30p multi 15 15
1440 A485 40p multi 16 15
1441 A485 65p multi 25 18
1442 A485 70p multi 28 22
1443 A485 90p multi 35 28

Size: 120x91mm

Imperf

1444 A485 110p multi 35 25
Nos. 1439-1444 (6) 1.54 1.23

Independence War Heroes — A486

175th Death anniv. of: 40p, Ignacio Allende (1769-1811). 65p, Juan Aldama (1774-1811). 75p, Mariano Jimenez (1781-1811).

1986, June 26 Photo. *Perf. 14*

1445	A486	40p multi	15	15
1446	A486	65p multi	22	16
1447	A486	75p multi	25	18

Miguel Hidalgo y Costilla (1753-1811), Mural by Jose Clemente Orozco — A487

1986, July 30 Photo. *Perf. 14*

1448	A487	40p multi	15	15

Federal Tax Court, 50th Anniv. A488

Gen. Nicolas Bravo (1786-1854) A489

1986, Aug. 27 *Perf. 14½x14*

1449	A488	40p gray, bl & blk	15	15

1986, Sept. 10 *Perf. 14*

1450	A489	40p multi	15	15

Paintings by Diego Rivera — A490

Designs: 50p, Paisaje Zapatista, 1915, vert. 80p, Desnudo con Alcatraces, 1944, vert. 110p, Sueno de una Tarde Dominical en la Alameda Central, 1947-48.

Perf. 14x14½, 14½x14
1986, Sept. 26

1451	A490	50p multi	15	15
1452	A490	80p multi	22	18
1453	A490	110p multi	32	25

See Nos. 1571-1573.

Guadalupe Victoria (1786-1843), 1st President — A491

1986, Sept. 29 *Perf. 14½x14*

1454	A491	50p multi	15	15

Natl. Storage Warehouse, 50th Anniv. — A492

1986, Oct. 3

1455	A492	40p multi	15	15

Intl. Post Day A493

1986, Oct. 9 *Perf. 14x14½*

1456	A493	120p multi	25	20

Natl. Committee Commemorating the 500th Anniv. (1992) of the Meeting of Two Worlds — A494

1986, Oct. 12 *Perf. 14½x14*

1457	A494	50p blk & lake	15	15

15th Pan American Highways Congress, Mexico City A495

1986, Oct. 17 Photo. *Perf. 14x14½*

1458	A495	80p Palacio de Mineria	18	16

Franz Liszt, Composer, 175th Birth Anniv. — A496

1986, Oct. 22 *Perf. 14½x14*

1459	A496	100p blk & brn	22	18

Intl. Peace Year A497

1986, Oct. 24

1460	A497	80p blk, bl & dk red	18	16

Interment of Pino Suarez in the Rotunda of Illustrious Men — A498

1986, Nov. 6

1461	A498	50p multi	15	15

Jose Maria Pino Suarez, vice-president of 1st revolutionary government, 1911.

See Nos. 1472, 1475, 1487, 1563.

Christmas — A499

Clay figurines from Tonala, Jalisco.

1986, Nov. 28

1462	A499	50p King	15	15
1463	A499	80p Angel	15	15

Diego Rivera (1886-1957), Painter A500

1986, Dec. 4 Photo. *Perf. 14x14½*

1464	A500	80p Self-portrait	18	15

Export Type of 1975

Designs as before and: 60p, Men's shoes. 70p, Copperware. 80p, Denim overalls. 90p, Abalone. 100p, Cup of coffee.

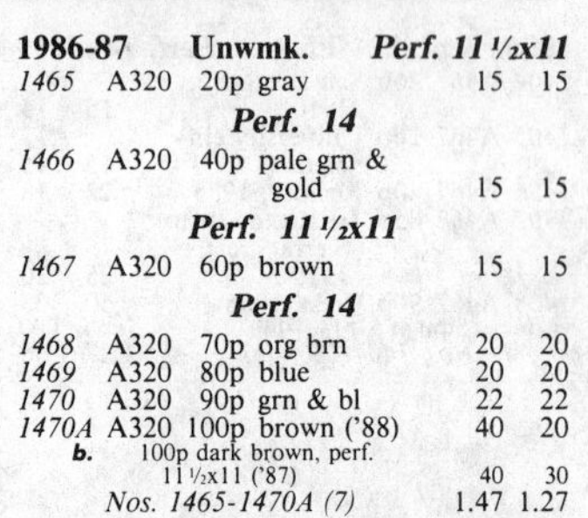

1986-87 Unwmk. *Perf. 11½x11*

1465	A320	20p gray	15	15
		Perf. 14		
1466	A320	40p pale grn & gold	15	15
		Perf. 11½x11		
1467	A320	60p brown	15	15
		Perf. 14		
1468	A320	70p org brn	20	20
1469	A320	80p blue	20	20
1470	A320	90p grn & bl	22	22
1470A	A320	100p brown ('88)	40	20
b.		100p dark brown, perf. 11½x11 ('87)	40	30
		Nos. 1465-1470A (7)	1.47	1.27

Natl. Polio Vaccination Program, Jan. 24-Mar. 28 — A501

1987, Jan. 20 Photo. *Perf. 14½x14*

1471	A501	50p Oral vaccine	15	15

Rotunda of Illustrious Men Type of 1986

1987, Feb. 4

1472	A498	100p multi	28	22

Jose Maria Iglesias (1823-1891), president in 1876.

Natl. Teachers' College, 100th Anniv. A503

1987, Feb. 24 *Perf. 14x14½*

1473	A503	100p multi	28	22

Exploration of Pima Indian Territory by Eusebio Francisco Kino, 300th Anniv. — A504

1987, Feb. 27 *Perf. 14½x14*

1474	A504	100p multi	28	22

Rotunda of Illustrious Men Type of 1986

1987, Mar. 20 Photo. *Perf. 14*

1475	A498	100p Pedro Sainz de Baranda	28	22

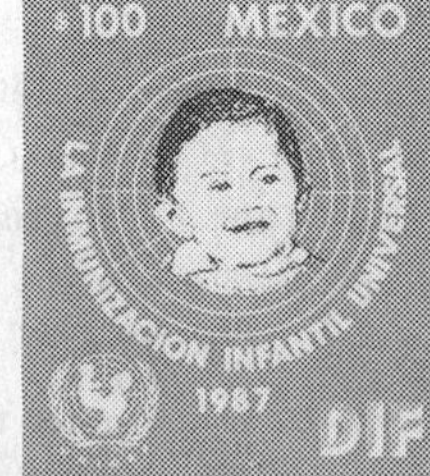

World Health Day, UN Child Survival Program A505

1987, Apr. 7

1476 A505 100p blue & slate blue 28 22

Autonomous University of Puebla, 50th Anniv. — A506

1987, Apr. 23

1477 A506 200p multi 48 35

Battle of Puebla, 125th Anniv. — A507

1987, May 5 Photo. *Perf. 14½x14*

1478 A507 100p multi 24 18

METROPOLIS '87 — A508

1987, May 19

1479 A508 310p gray blk, grn & red 65 45

Cong. of metropolitan areas, Mexico City.

Handicrafts — A509

Designs: 100p, Lacquerware tray, Uruapan, Michoacan. 200p, Blanket, Santa Ana Chiautempan, Tlaxcala. 230p, Lidded jar, Puebla, Pue.

1987, May 29 Photo. *Perf. 14*

1480 A509 100p multi 22 15
1481 A509 200p multi 45 32
1482 A509 230p multi 50 38

Genaro Estrada, (1887-1937) Political Reformer — A510

1987, June 2

1483 A510 100p pale pink, blk & pale rose 22 16

See Nos. 1509, 1568-1569.

Native Traders, 1961, Mural by P. O'Higgins — A511

1987, June 8

1484 A511 100p multi 22 16

Nat'l. Bank of Int'l. Commerce, 50th anniv.

Publication of the 1st Shipbuilding Manual in the Americas, by Diego Garcia Palacio, 400th Anniv. — A512

1987, June 15

1485 A512 100p multi 22 16

Nat'l. Food Program, 50th Anniv. A513

1987, June 22

1486 A513 100p multi 22 16

Rotunda of Illustrious Men Type of 1986

1987, June 22

1487 A498 100p multi 22 16

Leandro Valle (1833-1861), revolution leader.

Paintings by Saturnino Herran (1887-1918) A514

1917 paintings: No. 1488, Self-portrait with Skull. No. 1489, The Offering. No. 1490, Creole Woman with Mantilla.

1987, July 9

1488 A514 100p blk & red brn 24 18
1489 A514 100p multi 24 18
1490 A514 400p multi 95 75

Export Type of 1975

Designs: 10p, Meat cuts marked on steer. 20p, Bicycle. 50p, Tomatoes. 300p, Motor vehicle. 500p, Petroleum valves. 600p, Jewelry. 700p, Film. 800p, Construction materials. 900p, Pistons. 1,000p, Agricultural machinery. 2,000p, Wrought iron. 3,000p, Electric wiring. 4,000p, Honey. 5,000p, Cotton.

1987-88 Photo. *Perf. 14*

1491 A320 10p brt car 15 15
1492 A320 20p blk & org 15 15
1493 A320 50p verm & yel grn 15 15
1494 A320 300p chalky blue & scar, type I ('88) 30 15
1495 A320 300p Prus blue & brt rose ('88) 30 15
1496 A320 500p dark gray & Prus blue ('88) 48 25
1497 A320 600p multi ('88) 58 30
1498 A320 700p brt yel grn, dark red & blk ('88) 68 35
a. Brt yel grn, lil rose & blk ('88) 68 35
1499 A320 800p dark red brn & golden brn ('88) 78 40
1500 A320 900p blk ('88) 88 45

Wmk. 300
Granite Paper
Type I Burelage in Gray

1501 A320 1000p dark red & blk ('88) 98 50
1502 A320 2000p blk ('88) 1.95 1.00
1503 A320 3000p gray blk & org ('88) 2.90 1.45
1504 A320 4000p yel org & red brn ('88) 3.85 1.90
1505 A320 5000p apple grn & org ('88) 4.75 2.40
Nos. 1491-1505 (15) 18.88 9.75

See No. 1590 for No. 1501 without burelage.

A515

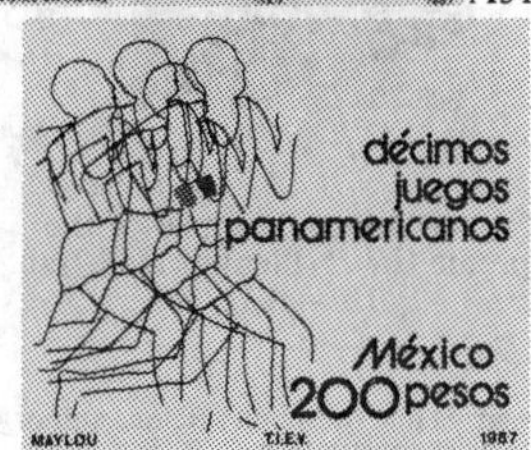

10th Pan American Games, Indianapolis — A516

Perf. 14½x14

1987, Aug. 7 Photo. Unwmk.

1506 A515 100p multi 15 15
1507 A516 200p blk, brt grn & dark red 24 20

Federal Power Commission, 50th Anniv. — A517

1987, Aug. 14 Photo. *Perf. 14x14½*

1508 A517 200p multi 28 22

Art and Science Type of 1987

Design: J.E. Hernandez y Davalos (1827-1893), historian.

1987, Aug. 25 *Perf. 14½x14*

1509 A510 100p buff, blk & dull red brn 15 15

Pre-Hispanic Art Type of 1980

Designs: 100p, Xolotl (d. 1232), king of Amaquemecan. 200p, Nezahualpilli (1460-1516), king of Texcoco, conqueror. 400p, Motecuhzoma Ilhuicamina (Montezuma I d. 1469), emperor of Tenochtitlan (1440-1469).

1987, Aug. 31 *Perf. 14x14½*

1510 A361 100p multi 18 15
1511 A361 200p multi 35 28
1512 A361 400p multi 72 35

Tourism Type of 1979

Designs: 100p, Central Public Library, Mexico State. No. 1514, Patzcuaro Harbor, Michoacan. No. 1515, Garcia Caverns, Nuevo Leon. No. 1516, Beach resort, Mazatlan, Sinaloa.

1987 *Perf. 14½x14*

1513 A353 100p multi 15 15
1514 A353 150p multi 18 15
1515 A353 150p multi 18 15
1516 A353 150p multi 18 15
Set value 52

Issue dates: 100p, Sept. 11. Others, Oct. 19.

Formula 1 Grand Prix Race, Oct. 18 — A518

1987, Sept. 11

1517 A518 100p multi 15 15

13th Intl. Cartography Conference — A519

1987, Oct. 12

1518 A519 150p Map, 16th cent. 18 15

Discovery of America, 500th Anniv. (in 1992) A520

Design: Santa Maria, emblem of the Discovery of America Festival to be held in 1992.

1987, Oct. 12 ***Perf. 14x14½***
1519 A520 150p multi 18 15

Illuminated Codices Type of 1982

Mendocino Codex (c. 1541): No. 1520, Founding of Tenochtitlan by the Aztecs, 1324. No. 1521, Pre-Hispanic wedding. No. 1522, Montezuma's Council.

1987, Nov. 3
1520 A408 150p multi 18 15
1521 A408 150p multi 18 15
1522 A408 150p multi 18 15

Christmas 1987 A521

1987, Nov. 6
1523 A521 150p brt pink 18 15
1524 A521 150p dull blue 18 15

World Post Day — A522

Documents: 150p, Ordinance for expediting mail by sea, 1777. 600p, Roster of correspondence transported by coach, 1857.

1987, Nov. 12
1525 A522 150p pale gray & slate gray 18 15

Size: 129x102mm

Imperf

1526 A522 600p rose lake & yel bis 75 55

Meeting of Eight Latin American Presidents, 1st Anniv. — A523

1987, Nov. 26 ***Perf. 14½x14***
1527 A523 250p shown 25 18
1528 A523 500p Flags, peace doves 50 38

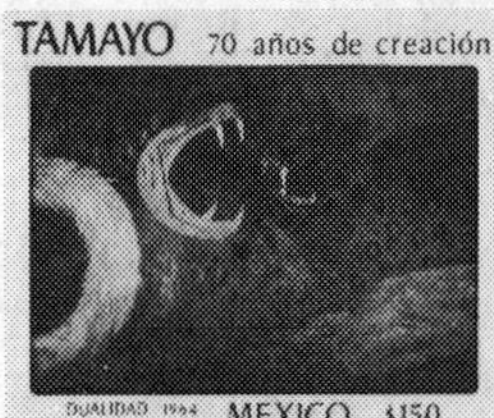

Dualidad 1964, by Rufino Tamayo (b. 1899) — A524

1987, Dec. 9
1529 A524 150p multi 18 15

Nationalization of Mexican Railroads, 50th Anniv. — A525

1987, Dec. 15
1530 A525 150p Metlac Bridge 18 15

Antonio Stradivarius (c. 1644-1737), Italian Violin Maker — A526

1987, Dec. 18 ***Perf. 14x14½***
1531 A526 150p bluish lil 18 15

Constitutional Tribunal of the Supreme Court, Plenum Hall, Jan. 15 — A527

Design: Statue of Manuel Rejon, author of the Mexican constitution.

1988, Jan. 15 **Photo.** ***Perf. 14x14½***
1532 A527 300p multi 35 28

Fauna A528

1988, Feb. 29 **Photo.** ***Perf. 14***
1533 A528 300p *Ambystoma mexicanum* 30 22
1534 A528 300p *Trichechus manatus* 30 22

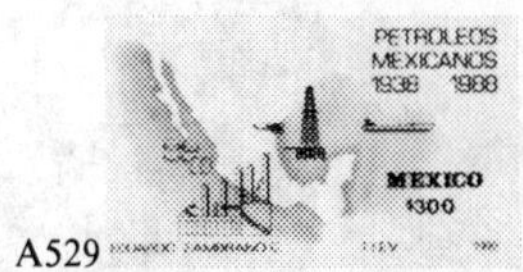

A529

Nationalization of the Petroleum Industry, 50th Anniv. — A530

1988, Mar. 18
1535 A529 300p blue & blk 30 22
1536 A530 300p PEMEX emblem, vert. 30 22
1537 A530 500p shown 45 35

Vaccination, Detroit, 1932, Mural (detail) by Diego Rivera — A531

1988, Apr. 7
1538 A531 300p olive grn & henna brn 35 25

World Health Day: child immunization.

The People in Pursuit of Health, 1953, by Diego Rivera A532

1988, Apr. 7
1539 A532 300p multi 35 25

World Health Organization, 40th anniv.

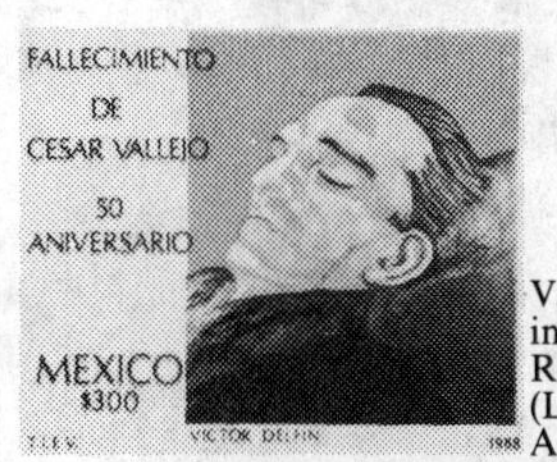

Vallejo in Repose (Large) A533

Vallejo in Repose (Small) A534

1988, Apr. 15
1540 A533 300p shown 32 22
1541 A533 300p Portrait, diff. (large) 32 22
b. Bklt. pane of 4 (2 each #1540-1541) + label
1542 A534 300p shown 32 22
1543 A534 300p As #1541 (small) 32 22

Cesar Vallejo (1892-1938), Peruvian poet. Stamps of the same type printed se-tenant in sheets of 20 stamps containing 10 pairs plus 5 labels between inscribed with various Vallejo quotes or commemorative text.

Issue date: No. 1541b, Nov. 9, 1990. Label in No. 1541b is overprinted in red with Mexican Chicagopex '90 souvenir cancel.

Sketch of Carlos Pellicer Camara (1897-1977), Poet, by Fontanelly — A535

1988, Apr. 23
1544 A535 300p pale vio, blk & sal 35 25

MEPSIRREY '88 Philatelic Exhibition, Monterrey, May 27-29 — A536

1988, May 27
1545 A536 300p Youth collectors 35 25
1546 A536 300p Handstamped cover 35 25
1547 A536 500p Emblem 55 42

Mexico-Elmhurst Philatelic Society Intl. (MEPSI).

1988 Formula I Championships, Mexico — A537

Design: Layout of Hermanos Rodriguez race track, Mexico City, and car.

1988, May 28 **Photo.** ***Perf. 14***
1548 A537 500p multi 48 35

A538

Ramon Lopez Velarde (1888-1921), Poet — A539

1988, June 15
1549 A538 300p multi 30 22
1550 A539 300p multi 30 22
a. Bklt. pane of 4 + label

Issue date: No. 1550a, Nov. 9, 1990. Label in No. 1550a is overprinted in red with Mexican Chicagopex '90 souvenir cancel.

University Military Pentathlon, 50th Anniv. — A540

1988, July 9 Photo. *Perf. 14*
1551 A540 300p multi 30 22

1st Mexico-Japan Friendship, Commerce and Navigation Treaty, Cent. — A541

1988, Aug. 16
1552 A541 500p multi 48 35

Joint Oceanographic Assembly, Acapulco, Aug. 23-31 — A542

1988, Aug. 23
1553 A542 500p multi 48 35

1988 Summer Olympics, Seoul — A543

1988, Aug. 31 Photo. *Perf. 14½x14*
1554 A543 500p multi 48 35

Size: 71x55mm

Imperf

1555 A543 700p Emblems, torch 68 52

World Boxing Council, 25th Anniv. A544

1988, Sept. 9
1556 A544 500p multi 48 35

Intl. Red Cross and Red Crescent Organizations, 125th Annivs. — A545

1988, Sept. 23 Photo. *Perf. 14x14½*
1557 A545 300p blk, gray & scar 30 22

Jose Guadalupe Posada (1852-1913), Painter, Illustrator — A546

1988, Sept. 29
1558 A546 300p sil & blk 30 22

World Wildlife Fund — A547

Various monarch butterflies, *Danaus plexippus.*

1988, Sept. 30 *Perf. 14½x14*
1559 A547 300p shown 30 22
1560 A547 300p Three adults 30 22
1561 A547 300p Larva, adult, pupa 30 22
1562 A547 300p Five adults 30 22

Rotunda of Illustrious Men Type of 1986

Portrait and eternal flame: Manuel Sandoval Vallarta (1899-1977), physicist.

1988, Oct. 5
1563 A498 300p multi 30 22

World Post Day A548

1988, Oct. 9 *Perf. 14x14½*
1564 A548 500p World map 48 35

Size: 75x44mm

Imperf

1565 A548 700p Envelope, doves, Earth 68 52

Discovery of America, 500th Anniv. (in 1992) — A549

Illuminations: Aztec painter Tlacuilo from the Mendocine Codex, 1541, and Dominican scribe from the Yanhuitlan Codex, 1541-50.

1988, Oct. 12 *Perf. 14½x14*
1566 A549 500p multi 48 35

World Food Day — A550

1988, Oct. 15 *Perf. 14x14½*
1567 A550 500p multi 48 35

Art and Science Type of 1987

Designs: No. 1568, Alfonso Caso (1896-1970), educator, founder of the Natl. Museum of Anthropology. No. 1569, Vito Alessio Robles (1879-1957), historian.

1988, Oct. 24 *Perf. 14½x14*
1568 A510 300p gray & blk 30 22
1569 A510 300p pale yel, blk & red brn 30 22

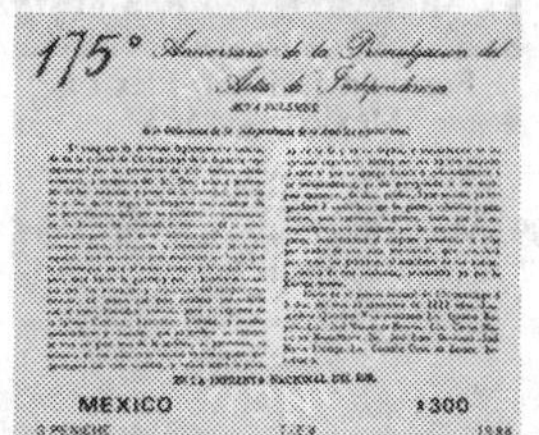

Act of Independence, 175th Anniv. — A551

1988, Nov. 9
1570 A551 300p claret brn & fawn 30 22

Art Type of 1986

Paintings by Antonio M. Ruiz (1895-1964): No. 1571, *Parade,* 1936. No. 1572, *La Malinche,* 1939. No. 1573, *Self-portrait,* 1925, vert.

Perf. 14½x14, 14x14½
1988, Nov. 21
1571 A490 300p multi 30 22
1572 A490 300p multi 30 22
1573 A490 300p multi 30 22

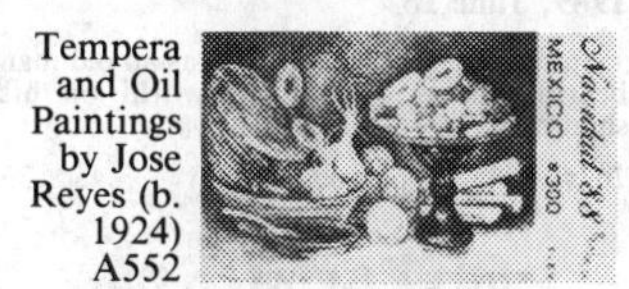

Tempera and Oil Paintings by Jose Reyes (b. 1924) A552

Perf. 14x14½, 14½x14
1988, Nov. 25
1574 A552 300p Feast 30 22
1575 A552 300p Pinata, vert. 30 22

Christmas.

Municipal Workers' Trade Union, 50th Anniv. A553

1988, Dec. 5 *Perf. 14x14½*
1576 A553 300p pale bister & blk 30 22

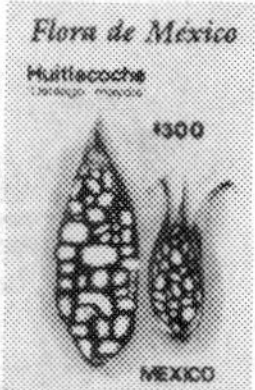

Flora — A554

1988, Dec. 20 *Perf. 14½x14*
1577 A554 300p *Ustilago maydis* 30 22
1578 A554 300p *Mimosa tenuiflora* 30 22

Exporta Type of 1975

Designs: 40p, Chemistry flasks. 200p, Citrus fruit. 450p, Circuit board. 750p, Film. 950p, Pistons. 1000p, Agricultural machinery. 1100p, Minerals. 2100p, Bicycles. 2500p, Overalls.

Nos. 1601-1602 have gray burelage Type I.

1988-91 Photo. Unwmk. *Perf. 14*
1579 A320 40p black 15 15
1581 A320 200p emer & brt yel 20 15
a. Thin paper 20 15
1583 A320 450p yel bister & lil rose 45 22
a. Thin paper 45 22
1587 A320 750p brt yel grn, dark red & dark gray 75 38
1589 A320 950p indigo 95 42
a. Thin paper 95 42
1590 A320 1000p dark red & blk 70 40
1592 A320 1100p dark gray, type I 1.10 55
1592A A320 1100p dark gray, type II 1.10 55
1593 A320 1300p red & grn, type II 90 62
1594 A320 1300p red & grn, type I 90 62
1595 A320 1400p black 95 66
1596 A320 1500p tan 1.00 70
a. 1500p orange brown 1.00 70
1597 A320 1600p red orange 1.05 72
1598 A320 1700p dk grn & yel grn 1.15 80
1600 A320 1900p bl grn & bl 1.30 90
1601 A320 2100p black & orange 1.65 82
1602 A320 2500p dark blue 2.00 1.40
Nos. 1579-1602 (17) 16.30 10.06

Issue dates: 40p, Jan. 5. 200p, Feb. 27, 1989. 450p, Feb. 10, 1989. No. 1583a, 950p, Nos. 1589a, 1592, Mar. 30, 1989. 1,000p, 1989. No. 1592A, 2100p, 2500p, 1991. Others, 1990.

This is an expanding set. Numbers will change if necessary.

Graphic Arts Workshop, 50th Anniv. A555

1989, Feb. 9 Photo. *Perf. 14*
1604 A555 450p yel bis, red & blk 45 35

Coat of Arms and *E Santo Domingo,* the Natl. Hymn — A556

1989, Feb. 27
1605 A556 450p multi 45 35

Dominican Republic independence, 145th anniv.

Intl. Border and Territorial Waters Commission of Mexico and the U.S., Cent. — A557

1989, Mar. 1
1606 A557 1100p multi 1.10 80

10th Intl. Book Fair — A558

1989, Mar. 4
1607 A558 450p UNAM School of Engineering 45 35

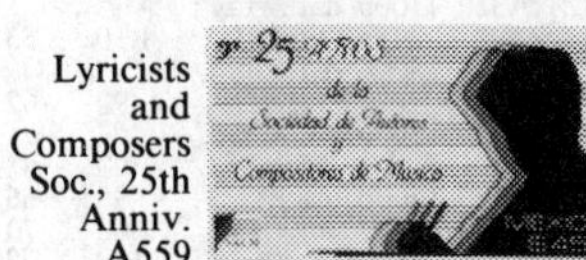

Lyricists and Composers Soc., 25th Anniv. A559

1989, Mar. 17
1608 A559 450p multi 45 35

World Day for the Fight Against AIDS A560

1989, Apr. 7
1609 A560 450p multi 45 35

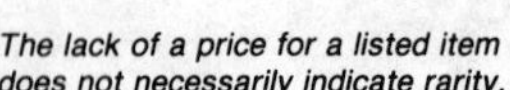
The lack of a price for a listed item does not necessarily indicate rarity.

Leona Vicario (1779-1842), Heroine of the Independence Movement A561

Alfonso Reyes (1879-1959), Author, Educator A562

1989, Apr. 20 Photo. *Perf. 14*
1610 A561 450p blk, sepia & golden brn 45 35

1989, May 17
1611 A562 450p multi 45 35

Formula 1 Grand Prix of Mexico — A563

1989, May 28 *Perf. 14*
1612 A563 450p multi 45 35

14th Tourism Congress, Acapulco A564

14th Intl. Gerontology Congress, Mexico A565

1989, June 11 *Perf. 14*
1613 A564 1100p multi 1.10 80

1989, June 18

Statue: The god Huehueteotl as an old man bearing the weight of the world on his shoulders.

1614 A565 450p multi 45 35

Baseball Hall of Fame of Mexico — A567

1989, June 25
1616 A567 550p Umpire, catcher 55 42
1617 A567 550p Batter 55 42

Printed se-tenant in continuous design in sheet of 20 + 5 labels.

35th World Archery Championships, Lausanne, Switzerland, July 4-8 — A568

1989, July 2
1618 A568 650p Bows and arrows 65 50
1619 A568 650p Arrows, target 65 50

Printed se-tenant in a continuous design in sheets of 20 + 5 labels.

Tijuana, Cent. A569

1989, July 11 Photo. *Perf. 14x14½*
1620 A569 1100p Municipal arms 90 68

Gen. Francisco Xavier Mina (1789-1817), Revolution Martyr — A571

French Revolution, Bicent. A570

1989, July 14
1621 A570 1300p blue, blk & dark red 1.10 80

1989, Sept. 7
1622 A571 450p green, blk & dark red 38 28

Natl. Museum of Anthropology, Chapultepec, 25th Anniv. — A572

1989, Sept. 17 *Perf. 14½x14*
1623 A572 450p multicolored 38 28

7th Mexico City Marathon — A573

1989, Sept. 24
1624 A573 450p multicolored 38 28

Printing in America, 450th Anniv. — A574

1989, Sept. 28
1625 A574 450p multicolored 38 28

World Post Day A575

1989, Oct. 9 Photo. *Perf. 14*
1626 A575 1100p multicolored 82 62

Sovereign Revolutionary Convention of Aguascalientes, 75th Anniv. — A576

1989, Oct. 10
1627 A576 450p multicolored 35 25

Battle of Zacatecas, 75th Anniv. — A566

1989, June 23
1615 A566 450p black 45 35

Exploration and Colonization of the Americas by Europeans A577

1989, Oct. 12
1628 A577 1300p multicolored 98 72

America Issue — A578

UPAE emblem and symbols like those produced on art by pre-Columbian peoples.

1989, Oct. 12
1629 A578 450p shown 35 25
1630 A578 450p multi, diff., vert. 35 25

Natl. Tuberculosis Foundation, 50th Anniv. — A579

1989, Nov. 10
1631 A579 450p multicolored 35 25

Mask of the Bat God, Zapoteca Culture, c. 200-300 A580

1989, Nov. 28
1632 A580 450p multicolored 35 25

Serfin Commercial Bank of Mexico, 125th Anniv. — A581

1989, Nov. 29
1633 A581 450p deep blue, gold & blk 35 25

Pres. Adolfo Ruiz Cortines (1889-1973) — A582

1989, Dec. 3
1634 A582 450p multicolored 35 25

Christmas A583

1989, Dec. 11
1635 A583 450p Candlelight vigil 35 25
1636 A583 450p Man sees star, vert. 35 25

Natl. Institute of Anthropology and Natural History, 50th Anniv. — A584

1989, Dec. 13
1637 A584 450p dark red, gold & black 35 25

Nationalization of the Railway System in Mexico, 80th Anniv. — A585

1989
1638 A585 450p multicolored 35 25

Issue dates for some 1990-1991 issues are based on First Day cancels. Original printings were small. Later printings, made in 1991, were distributed to the stamp trade and seem to be the ones used for "First Day Covers."

Tampico Bridge — A586

1990, Jan. 11 **Photo.** ***Perf. 14***
1639 A586 600p gold, blk & red 42 30

Eradication of Polio — A587

1990, Feb. 1
1640 A587 700p multicolored 50 35

Natl. Census A588

1990, Mar. 12
1641 A588 700p lt grn & yel 50 35

Mexican Philatelic Assoc., 10th Anniv. — A589

1990, Apr. 19
1642 A589 700p multicolored 50 35

Natl. Archives, Bicentennial — A590

1990, Apr. 24
1643 A590 700p pale violet 50 35

Intl. Conf. of Advertising Agencies — A591

1990, Apr. 27
1644 A591 700p multicolored 50 35

Stamp World London '90 — A592

1990, May 3
1645 A592 700p multicolored 50 35

First Postage Stamps, 150th Anniv. — A593

1990, May 6
1646 A593 700p lake, gold & blk 50 35

15th Tourism Exposition — A594

1990, May 6
1647 A594 700p multicolored 50 35

Visit of Pope John Paul II A595

1990, May 6
1648 A595 700p multicolored 50 35

Health of Young Mothers A596

1990, May 10
1649 A596 700p multicolored 50 35

Fight Against Smoking — A597

1990, May 31
1650 A597 700p multicolored 50 35

World Environment Day — A598

1990, June 5
1651 A598 700p multicolored 50 35

Formula 1 Grand Prix of Mexico — A599

1990, June 24
1652 A599 700p grn, red & blk 50 35

Airport & Auxiliary Services, 25th Anniv. — A600

1990, June 25 Photo. *Perf. 14*
1653 A600 700p multicolored 50 35

Fight Against Drugs — A601

1990, June 26
1654 A601 700p multicolored 50 35

Protection of Rain Forests — A602

1990, July 6
1655 A602 700p multicolored 50 35

Solidarity with Poor People — A603

1990, Aug. 8
1656 A603 700p multicolored 50 35

Oaxaca Cultural Heritage — A604

1990, Aug. 10
1657 A604 700p multicolored 50 35

Nature Conservation A605

1990, Aug. 21
1658 A605 700p blk, gray & org 50 35

Mexican Institute of Petroleum, 25th Anniv. A606

1990, Aug. 23
1659 A606 700p black & blue 50 35

8th Mexico City Marathon — A607

1990, Aug. 24
1660 A607 700p blk, red & grn 50 35

University of Colima, 50th Anniv. A608

1990, Sept. 16
1661 A608 700p gray, bister, red & grn 50 35

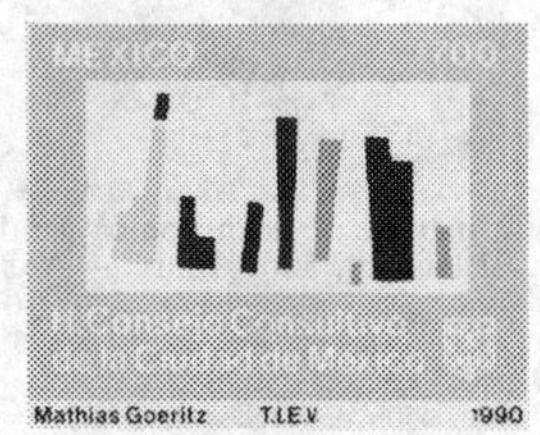

Mexico City Advisory Council, 61st Anniv. — A609

1990, Sept. 17
1662 A609 700p sil, yel, blk & org 50 35

Nationalization of Electric Industry, 30th Anniv. — A610

1990, Sept. 27
1663 A610 700p gray, grn, red & blk 50 35

City of Campeche, 450th Anniv. — A611

1990, Oct. 4
1664 A611 700p multicolored 50 35

Silvestre Revueltas (1899-1940), Musician — A612

1990, Oct. 4
1665 A612 700p multicolored 50 35

Plan of San Luis, 80th Anniv. A613

1990, Oct. 5
1666 A613 700p multicolored 50 35

14th World Conference of Supreme Counselors — A614

1990, Oct. 8
1667 A614 1500p vio, sil, gold & grn 1.10 78

Discovery of America, 498th Anniv. — A615

1990, Oct. 12
1668 A615 700p multicolored 50 35

Mexican Archaeology, Bicentennial — A616

1990, Nov. 18
1669 A616 1500p multicolored 1.10 78

16th Central American and Caribbean Games — A617

1990, Nov. 20

1670 A617 750p shown 55 40
1671 A617 750p Mayan ball player 55 40
1672 A617 750p Mayan ball player, vert. 55 40
1673 A617 750p Ball court, stone ring, vert. 55 40
a. Strip of 4, #1670-1673 2.20 1.60

Christmas
A618 A619

1990, Dec. 3

1674 A618 700p Poinsettias 50 35
1675 A619 700p Candles 50 35

Mexican Canine Federation, 50th Anniv. A620

1990, Dec. 9

1676 A620 700p multicolored 50 35

World Post Day A621

1990, Oct. 9 Photo. *Perf. 14x14½*

1677 A621 1500p multicolored 1.10 78

America Issue A622

Designs: No. 622, Flowers, galleon. No. 623, Galleon, parrot.

1990, Oct. 12

1678 A622 700p multicolored 50 35
1679 A622 700p multicolored 50 35
a. Pair, #1678-1679 1.00 70

No. 1679a has continuous design. Printed in sheets of 20+5 blank labels.

Mexican Brewing Industry, Cent. — A623

1990, Nov. 8 ***Perf. 14½x14***

1680 A623 700p multicolored 50 35

National Chamber of Industrial Development, 50th Anniv. — A624

1990, Dec. 5 ***Perf. 14½x14***

1681 A624 1500p multicolored 1.10 78

Naval Secretariat, 50th Anniv. — A625

1991 Photo. *Perf. 14*

1682 A625 1000p bl, blk & gold 70 50

Prevent Transportation Accidents — A626

1991, Jan. 11 Photo. *Perf. 14½x14*

1683 A626 700p multicolored 55 38

Natl. Consumers Institute, 15th Anniv. — A627

1991, Feb. 11

1684 A627 1000p multicolored 78 55

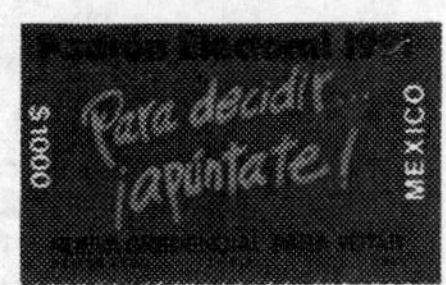
Voter Registration — A628

1991, Feb. 13 ***Perf. 14x14½***

1685 A628 1000p org, blk & grn 78 55

Olympic Basketball — A629

1991, Feb. 25 ***Perf. 14½x14***

1686 A629 1000p black & yellow 78 55

Campaign Against Polio — A630

1991, Mar. 8

1687 A630 1000p multicolored 78 55

Childrens' Walk for Peace and Development — A631

Health and Family Life A632

1991, Apr. 16 ***Perf. 14½x14***

1688 A631 1000p multicolored 78 55

Perf. 14x14½

1689 A632 1000p multicolored 78 55

Mining in Mexico, 500th Anniv. — A633

1991, Apr. 25 ***Perf. 14½x14***

1690 A633 1000p multicolored 78 55

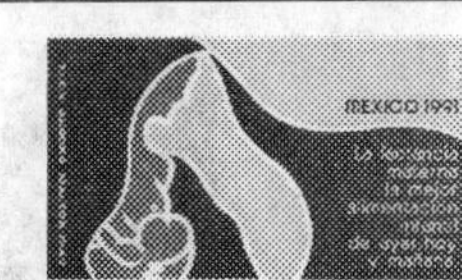
Promotion of Breastfeeding — A634

1991, May 10 ***Perf. 14x14½***

1691 A634 1000p multicolored 78 55

16th Tourism Exposition — A635

1991, May 12 ***Perf. 14½x14***

1692 A635 1000p brt grn & dk grn 85 60

Rotary Intl. Convention — A636

1991, June 2 ***Rouletted 6½***

1693 A636 1000p blue & gold 85 60

Integrated Communications and Transportation Systems (SCT), Cent. — A637

Designs: No. 1695a, 1000p, Jet landing. b, 1500p, Airport control tower. c, 1000p, FAX machine. d, 1500p, Upper floors, SCT headquarters. e, 1000p, Communications van. f, 1500p, Satellite. g, 1000p, Satellite in orbit, earth. h, 1000p, Boxcars. i, 1500p, Locomotives. j, 1000p, People using telephones. k, 1500p, Lower floors, SCT headquarters. l, 1000p, Hillside road, left section, highway bridge. m, 1500p, Center section, highway bridge. n, 1000p, Right section of bridge. o, 1000p, Cranes loading cargo ship. p, 1500p, Bow of cargo ship. q, 1000p, Television camera. r, 1500p, Bus. s, 1000p, Truck. t, 1500p, Trailers passing through toll plaza. u, 1000p, Bridge construction. Continuous design.

1991, June 11 ***Rouletted 6½***

1694 A637 1000p gray & multi 85 60
1695 A637 Block of 21, #a.-u. 22.00 15.00

Jaguar A638

1991, June 12 ***Perf. 14½x14***

1696 A638 1000p black & orange 85 60

Conservation of the rain forests.

Total Solar Eclipse — A640

Designs: No. 1699a, 1000p, Denomination at lower right. b, Globe showing Mexico. c, 1000p, Denomination at lower left. Continuous design.

1991, July 5 ***Rouletted 6½***
1699 A640 Strip of 3, #a.-c. 3.50 2.50

First Latin American Presidential Summit, Guadalajara A641

1991, July 18
1700 A641 1500p blk, org & yel 1.10 78

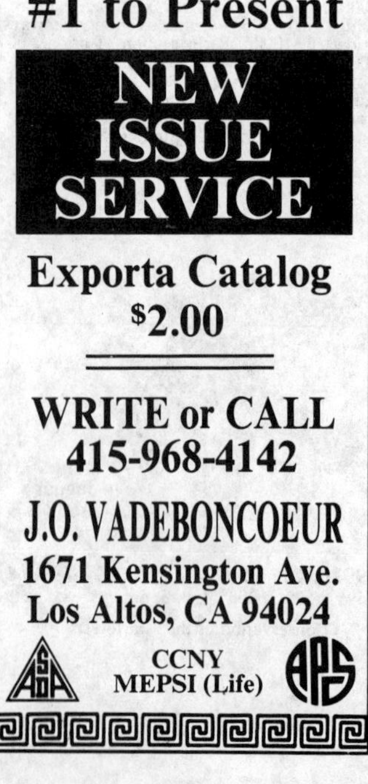

A642

1991, July 31
1701 A642 2000p multicolored 1.70 1.20

Ninth Mexico City Marathon — A643

1991, Aug. 22
1702 A643 1000p multicolored 85 60

Federal Tax Court, 55th Anniv. — A644

1991, Aug. 27
1703 A644 1000p blue & silver 85 60

Solidarity Type of 1990 and

A645

1991 ***Perf. 14½x14***
1704 A603 1000p multicolored 85 60

Rouletted 6½
1705 A645 1000p multicolored 85 60

Issue dates: No. 1704, Dec. 17; No. 1705, Sept. 9.

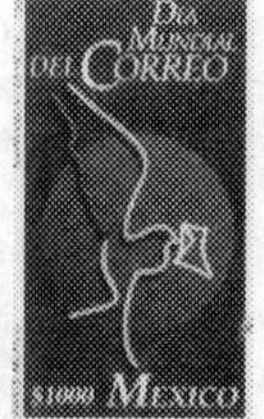

World Post Day — A646

1991, Oct. 9 ***Rouletted 6½***
1706 A646 1000p multicolored 85 60

Voyages of Discovery A647

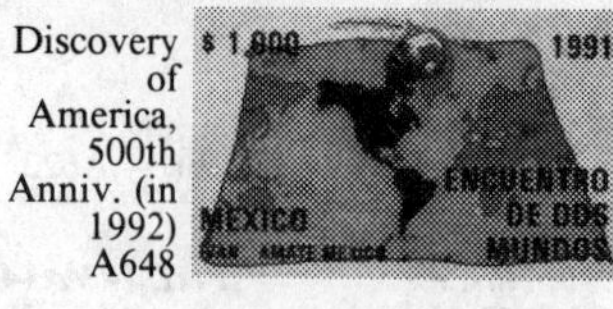

Discovery of America, 500th Anniv. (in 1992) A648

Designs: No. 1708, Sailing ship, storm.

1991, Oct. 12
1707 A647 1000p multicolored 85 60
1708 A647 1000p multicolored 85 60
a. Pair, #1707-1708 1.70 1.20
1709 A648 1000p multicolored 85 60

No. 1708a has continuous design. Printed in sheets of 20+5 labels.

A649

Christmas A650

1991, Nov. 26
1710 A649 1000p multicolored 85 60
1711 A650 1000p multicolored 85 60

Carlos Merida, Birth Cent. A651

1991, Dec. 2 **Photo.** ***Rouletted 6½***
1712 A651 1000p multicolored 85 60

Wolfgang Amadeus Mozart, Death Bicent. A652

1991, Dec. 5
1713 A652 1000p multicolored 85 60

Merida, 450th Anniv. A655

1992, Jan. 6 **Photo.** ***Rouletted 6½***
1716 A655 1300p multicolored 1.00 70

Engineering Education in Mexico, Bicent. — A656

1992, Jan. 15
1717 A656 1300p blue & red 1.00 70

SEMI-POSTAL STAMPS

Regular Issue of 1916 Surcharged in Red **+ 3 ¢**

1918, Dec. 25 **Unwmk.** ***Perf. 12***
B1 A72 5c + 3c ultra 14.00 15.00

Rouletted
B2 A73 10c + 5c blue 17.50 15.00

AIR POST STAMPS

Eagle — AP1

Unwmk.

1922, Apr. 2 **Engr.** ***Perf. 12***
C1 AP1 50c bl & red brn 60.00 40.00
a. 50c dk bl & claret ('29) 90.00 90.00

See Nos. C2-C3. For overprints and surcharges see Nos. C47-C48, CO1-CO2B, CO18-CO19, CO29.

1927, Oct. 13 **Wmk. 156**
C2 AP1 50c dk bl & red brn 75 25
a. 50c dark blue & claret ('29) 75 25
b. Vert. strip of 3, imperf. btwn. *10,000.*

The vignettes of Nos. C1a and C2a fluoresce a bright rose red under UV light.

1928
C3 AP1 25c brn car & gray brn 45 15
C4 AP1 25c dk grn & gray brn 45 20

On May 3, 1929, certain proofs or essays were sold at the post office in Mexico, D. F. They were printed in different colors from those of the regularly issued stamps. There were 7 varieties perf. and 2 imperf. and a total of 225 copies. They were sold with the understanding that they were for collections but the majority of them were used on air mail sent out that day.

Capt. Emilio Carranza and his Airplane "Mexico Excelsior" AP2

1929, June 19
C5 AP2 5c ol grn & sep 1.15 65
C6 AP2 10c sep & brn red 1.30 70
C7 AP2 15c vio & dk grn 3.00 1.25
C8 AP2 20c brn & blk 1.20 75
C9 AP2 50c brn red & blk 6.00 2.00
C10 AP2 1p blk & brn 12.50 2.75
Nos. C5-C10 (6) 25.15 8.10

1st anniv. of death of Carranza (1905-28).
For overprints see Nos. C29-C36, C40-C44.

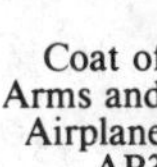

Coat of Arms and Airplane AP3

1929-34 *Perf. 11½, 12*

C11 AP3 10c violet	35	15
C12 AP3 15c carmine	1.35	20
C13 AP3 20c brn ol	27.50	1.25
C14 AP3 30c gray blk	20	20
C15 AP3 35c blue grn	35	25
a. Imperf., pair	1,200.	
C16 AP3 50c red brn ('34)	1.25	65
C17 AP3 1p blk & dk bl	1.25	65
C18 AP3 5p cl & dp bl	4.00	3.50
C19 AP3 10p vio & ol brn	6.00	7.00
Nos. C11-C19 (9)	42.25	13.85

1930-32 *Rouletted 13, 13½*

C20 AP3 5c lt bl ('32)	25	15
C21 AP3 10c violet	25	15
C22 AP3 15c carmine	35	15
a. 15c rose carmine	40	15
C23 AP3 20c brown olive	1.50	15
a. 20c brown	50	15
b. 20c yellow brown	50	15
c. Horiz. pair, imperf. btwn.		
C24 AP3 25c violet	95	80
C25 AP3 50c red brown	90	75
Nos. C20-C25 (6)	4.20	2.15

Trial impressions of No. C20 were printed in orange but were never sold at post offices.

See Nos. C62-C64, C75. For overprints and surcharges see Nos. C28, C38-C39, C46, C49-C50, CO17, CO20-CO28, CO30.

Plane over Plaza, Mexico City — AP4

1929, Dec. 10 **Wmk. 156** *Perf. 12*

C26 AP4 20c blk vio	1.25	1.00
C27 AP4 40c slate grn	85.00	75.00

Aviation Week, Dec. 10-16.
For overprint see No. CO11.

No. C21 Overprinted in Red

Primer Congreso Nacional de Turismo. México. Abril 20-27 de 1930.

1930, Apr. 20 *Rouletted 13, 13½*

C28 AP3 10c violet	2.00	1.25

National Tourism Congress at Mexico, D. F., Apr. 20-27, 1930.

Nos. C5 and C7 Overprinted **HABILITADO 1930**

1930, Sept. 1 *Perf. 12*

C29 AP2 5c ol grn & sep	5.50	4.50
a. Double overprint	220.00	
C30 AP2 15c vio & dk grn	9.00	7.75

Nos. C5-C10 Overprinted **HABILITADO Aéreo 1930-1931**

1930, Dec. 18

C31 AP2 5c ol grn & sep	6.00	6.50
C32 AP2 10c sep & brn red	3.50	4.00
a. Double overprint	50.00	50.00
C33 AP2 15c vio & dk grn	6.50	7.00
C34 AP2 20c brn & blk	7.00	5.50
C35 AP2 50c brn red & blk	14.00	10.00
C36 AP2 1p blk & brn	2.00	2.75
Nos. C31-C36 (6)	41.00	35.75

Plane over Flying Field AP5

1931, May 15 **Engr.** *Perf. 12*

C37 AP5 25c lake	4.00	4.50
a. Imperf., pair	80.00	72.50

Aeronautic Exhibition of the Aero Club of Mexico. Of the 25c, 15c paid air mail postage and 10c went to a fund to improve the Mexico City airport.

For surcharge see No. C45.

Nos. C13 and C23 Surcharged in Red

HABILITADO Quince centavos

1931

C38 AP3 15c on 20c brn ol	32.50	35.00

Rouletted 13, 13½

C39 AP3 15c on 20c brn ol	30	15
a. Inverted surcharge	150.00	
b. Double surcharge	150.00	
c. Pair, one without surcharge	350.00	

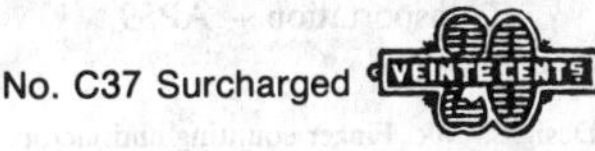
Nos. C5 to C9 Overprinted **HABILITADO AEREO-1932**

1932, July 13 *Perf. 12*

C40 AP2 5c ol grn & sep	6.00	5.00
a. Imperf., pair	60.00	60.00
C41 AP2 10c sep & brn red	5.00	3.00
a. Imperf., pair	60.00	60.00
C42 AP2 15c vio & bk grn	6.00	4.00
a. Imperf., pair	60.00	60.00
C43 AP2 20c brn & blk	5.00	2.75
a. Imperf., pair	60.00	60.00
C44 AP2 50c brn red & blk	35.00	35.00
a. Imperf., pair	60.00	60.00
Nos. C40-C44 (5)	57.00	49.75

Issued to commemorate the fourth anniversary of the death of Capt. Emilio Carranza.

No. C37 Surcharged

1932

C45 AP5 20c on 25c lake	70	30
a. Imperf., pair	72.50	72.50

No. C13 Surcharged HABILITADO TREINTA 30

C46 AP3 30c on 20c brn ol	30.00	30.00

Similar Surcharge on Nos. C3 and C4

C47 AP1 40c on 25c (#C3)	90	90
a. Inverted surcharge	1,000.	
C48 AP1 40c on 25c (#C4)	40.00	40.00

Surcharged on Nos. C23 and C24
Rouletted 13, 13½

C49 AP3 30c on 20c brn ol	35	18
a. Inverted surcharge	2,750.	
C50 AP3 80c on 25c dl vio	1.80	1.20

Palace of Fine Arts — AP6

1933, Oct. 1 **Engr.** *Perf. 12*

C51 AP6 20c dk red & dl vio	3.50	1.40
C52 AP6 30c dk brn & dl vio	6.75	6.00
C53 AP6 1p grnsh blk & dl vio	67.50	70.00

21st Intl. Cong. of Statistics and the cent. of the Mexican Soc. of Geography and Statistics.

National University Issue

Nevado de Toluca AP7

Pyramids of the Sun and Moon AP8

View of Ajusco AP9

Volcanoes Popocatepetl and Iztaccihuatl — AP10

Bridge over Tepecayo AP11

Chapultepec Fortress AP12

Orizaba Volcano (Citlaltepetl) — AP13

Mexican Girl and Aztec Calendar Stone AP14

1934, Sept. 1 **Wmk. 156** *Perf. 10½*

C54 AP7 20c orange	2.75	2.50
C55 AP8 30c red lil & vio	5.75	6.75
C56 AP9 50c ol grn & bis brn	6.50	10.00
C57 AP10 75c blk & yel grn	7.50	14.00
C58 AP11 1p blk & pck bl	8.00	10.00
C59 AP12 5p bis brn & dk bl	42.50	95.00
C60 AP13 10p ind & mar	125.00	200.00
C61 AP14 20p brn & brn lake	750.00	1,200.
Nos. C54-C61 (8)	948.00	1,538.

Type of 1929-34

1934-35 *Perf. 10½, 10½x10*

C62 AP3 20c ol grn	35	15
a. 20c slate	500.00	500.00
C63 AP3 30c slate	40	40
C64 AP3 50c red brn ('35)	2.00	2.00

Symbols of Air Service AP15

Tláloc, God of Water (Quetzalcóatl Temple) — AP16

Orizaba Volcano (Citlaltepetl) — AP17

"Eagle Man" AP18

Symbolical of Flight AP19

Aztec Bird-Man — AP20

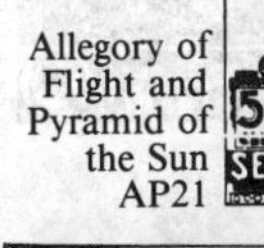

Allegory of Flight and Pyramid of the Sun AP21

"Eagle Man" and Airplanes AP22

Natives Looking at Airplane and Orizaba Volcano — AP23

Imprint: "Oficina Impresora de Hacienda-Mexico"

Perf. 10½x10, 10x10½

1934-35 **Wmk. 156**

C65 AP15 5c black	42	15
a. Imperf., pair		
C66 AP16 10c red brn	90	15
C67 AP17 15c gray grn	1.25	15
a. Imperf., pair	300.00	
C68 AP18 20c brn car	3.00	15
a. 20c lake	4.00	15
b. Imperf. pair		
C69 AP19 30c brn ol	70	15
C70 AP20 40c bl ('35)	1.25	15
C71 AP21 50c green	2.50	15
a. Imperf., pair	275.00	
C72 AP22 1p gray grn & red brn	3.50	15
C73 AP23 5p dk car & blk	7.25	70
Nos. C65-C73 (9)	20.77	
Set value		1.55

See Nos. C76A, C80, C81, C132-C140, C170-C177A. For overprint see No. C74.

No. C68 Overprinted in Violet

AMELIA EARHART
VUELO DE BUENA VOLUNTAD
MEXICO
1935

1935, Apr. 16
C74 AP18 20c lake *3,000. 4,000.*

Amelia Earhart's goodwill flight to Mexico.

Arms-Plane Type of 1929-34

1935 Wmk. 248 *Perf. 10½x10*
C75 AP3 30c slate 3.00 5.00

Francisco I. Madero AP24

1935, Nov. 20 Wmk. 156
C76 AP24 20c scarlet 30 15

25th anniversary of the Plan of San Luis. See No. C76B.

Eagle Man Type of 1934-35

1936 Wmk. 260
C76A AP18 20c lake *5,500.* 52.50

Madero Type of 1935
C76B AP24 20c scarlet *15,000.*

Tasquillo Bridge AP25

Corona River Bridge AP26

Bridge on Nuevo Laredo Highway AP27

Wmk. 248
1936, July 1 Photo. *Perf. 14*
C77 AP25 10c sl bl & lt bl 20 15
C78 AP26 20c dl vio & org 28 15
C79 AP27 40c dk bl & dk grn 55 50

Opening of Nuevo Laredo Highway.

Eagle Man Type of 1934-35
Perf. 10½x10
1936, June 18 Engr. Unwmk.
C80 AP18 20c brn car 6.50 7.00

Imprint: "Talleres de Imp. de Est. y Valores-Mexico"

1937 Wmk. 156 Photo. *Perf. 14*
C81 AP18 20c rose red 1.25 15
a. 20c brown carmine 1.50 15
b. 20c dark carmine 2.00 15
c. Imperf., pair 37.50 42.50

There are two sizes of watermark 156. No. C81c was not regularly issued.

Cavalryman AP28

Early Biplane over Mountains AP29

Venustiano Carranza on Horseback — AP30

1938, Mar. 26
C82 AP28 20c org red & bl 50 20
C83 AP29 40c bl & org red 75 30
C84 AP30 1p bl & bis brn 4.75 2.25

Plan of Guadalupe, 25th anniversary.

The Zocalo and Cathedral, Mexico City AP31

Designs: Nos. C87, C88, Reconstructed edifices of Chichen Itza. Nos. C89, C90, View of Acapulco.

1938, July 1
C85 AP31 20c car rose 35 25
C86 AP31 20c purple 14.00 10.00
C87 AP31 40c brt grn 7.75 5.00
C88 AP31 40c dk grn 7.00 5.00
C89 AP31 1p lt bl 7.00 5.00
C90 AP31 1p sl bl 7.00 5.00
Nos. C85-C90 (6) 43.10 30.25

16th Intl. Cong. of Planning & Housing.

Statue of José María Morelos AP34

Statue of Pioneer Woman, Ponca City, OK AP35

1939 Engr. *Perf. 10½*
C91 AP34 20c green 70 50
C92 AP34 40c red vio 2.00 1.25
C93 AP34 1p vio brn & car 1.40 1.00

New York World's Fair. Released in New York May 2, in Mexico May 24.

SARABIA
Vuelo MEXICO-NUEVA YORK

Type of 1939 Overprinted in Cerise

1939, May 23
C93A AP34 20c bl & red 250.00 500.00

Issued for the flight of Francisco Sarabia from Mexico City to New York on May 25.

1939, May 17
C94 AP35 20c gray brown 1.00 40
C95 AP35 40c slate grn 2.50 1.25
C96 AP35 1p violet 1.65 90

Tulsa World Philatelic Convention.

First Engraving Made in Mexico, 1544 — AP36

First Work of Legislation Printed in America, 1563 — AP37

Designs: 1p, Reproduction of oldest preserved Mexican printing.

1939, Sept. 7 Wmk. 156
C97 AP36 20c slate blue 25 15
a. Unwmkd.
C98 AP37 40c slate green 65 15
a. Imperf., pair *700.00*
C99 AP37 1p dk brn & car 1.10 70

400th anniversary of printing in Mexico.

Transportation — AP39

Designs: 40c, Finger counting and factory. 1p, "Seven Censuses."

Perf. 12x13, 13x12
1939, Oct. 2 Photo.
C100 AP39 20c dk bl & bl 1.00 20
C101 AP39 40c red org & org 75 25
C102 AP39 1p ind & vio bl 2.75 75

National Census of 1939-40.

Penny Black Type of Regular Issue, 1940

1940, May *Perf. 14*
C103 A140 5c blk & dk grn 65 60
C104 A140 10c bis brn & dp bl 52 25
C105 A140 20c car & bl vio 38 20
C106 A140 1p car & choc 3.50 5.00
C107 A140 5p gray grn & red brn 40.00 55.00
Nos. C103-C107 (5) 45.05 61.05

Issue dates: 5c-1p, May 2; 5p, May 15.

Part of Original College at Patzcuaro AP43

College at Morelia (18th Century) — AP44

College at Morelia (1940) AP45

1940, July 15 Engr. *Perf. 10½*
C108 AP43 20c brt grn 45 20
C109 AP44 40c orange 50 30
C110 AP45 1p dp pur, red brn & org 1.25 1.00

400th anniv. of the founding of the National College of San Nicolas de Hidalgo.

Pirate Ship AP46

Designs: 40c, Castle of San Miguel. 1p, Temple of San Francisco.

Perf. 12x13, 13x12
1940, Aug. 7 Photo.
C111 AP46 20c red brn & bis brn 1.15 70
C112 AP46 40c blk & sl grn 1.50 75
C113 AP46 1p vio bl & blk 5.00 3.00

400th anniversary of Campeche.

Inauguration Type of Regular Issue, 1940

1940, Dec. 1 *Perf. 12x13*
C114 A146 20c gray blk & red org 1.90 1.00
C115 A146 40c chnt brn & dk sl 2.00 1.50
C116 A146 1p brt vio bl & rose 3.50 2.00

Tower of the Convent of the Nuns AP50

Casa de Montejo — AP51

Campanile of Cathedral at Merida AP52

1942, Jan. 2 *Perf. 14*
C117 AP50 20c Prus bl 1.50 75
C118 AP51 40c grnsh blk (C) 2.25 2.00
a. Without overprint 7.50 7.50
C119 AP52 1p carmine 2.50 2.00

400th anniversary of Merida.
No. C118 bears the overprint "Servicio Aereo" in carmine.

Church of Zapopan
AP53

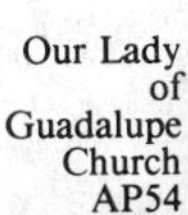

Our Lady of Guadalupe Church
AP54

Guadalajara Arms
AP55

1942, Feb. 11 Engr. *Perf. 10½x10*

C120	AP53	20c grn & blk	1.65	75
C121	AP54	40c ol & yel grn	1.75	1.00
C122	AP55	1p pur & sep	1.65	1.25

400th anniversary of Guadalajara.

Astrophysics Type of Regular Issue, 1942

Designs: 20c, Spiral Galaxy NGC 4594. 40c, Planetary Nebula in Lyra. 1p, Russell Diagrams.

1942, Feb. 17 Photo. *Perf. 12x13*

C123	A154	20c dk grn & ind	12.50	3.00
C124	A154	40c car lake & ind	11.00	4.00
C125	A154	1p org & blk	11.00	4.50

Corn
AP59

1942, July 1

C126	AP59	20c shown	1.90	70
C127	AP59	40c Coffee	1.50	75
C128	AP59	1p Bananas	2.50	2.00

2nd Inter-American Agricultural Conf.

View of San Miguel de Allende
AP62

Designs: 40c, Birthplace of Allende. 1p, Church of Our Lady of Health.

1943, May 18 *Perf. 14*

C129	AP62	20c dk sl grn	95	60
C130	AP62	40c purple	1.25	60
C131	AP62	1p dp car	2.75	2.50

400th anniversary of the founding of San Miguel de Allende.

Types of 1934-35

1944 Photo. Wmk. 272

C132	AP18	20c brn car	75	15

Perf. 10½x10

1944-46 Engr. Wmk. 272

C133	AP15	5c black	50	15
C134	AP16	10c red brn ('45)	1.25	15
C135	AP17	15c gray grn ('45)	85	15
C136	AP19	30c brn ol ('45)	12.50	75
C137	AP20	40c gray bl ('45)	1.10	20
C138	AP21	50c green	85	15
C139	AP22	1p gray grn & red brn ('45)	6.00	1.50
C140	AP23	5p dk car & blk ('46)	4.75	2.00
		Nos. C133-C140 (8)	27.80	5.05

Symbol of Flight
AP65

Microphone, Book and Camera
AP66

1944 Photo. *Perf. 14*

C141	AP65	25c chestnut brn	35	15

See No. C185.

1944, Nov. 8 Wmk. 272

C142	AP66	25c dl slate grn	65	15

Issued to commemorate the third Book Fair.

Globe-in-Hands Type of Regular Issue, 1945

1945, Feb. 27 *Perf. 12x13*

C143	A166	25c red org	28	15
C144	A166	1p brt grn	35	25
C145	A166	5p indigo	2.00	1.75
C146	A166	10p brt rose	5.50	4.50
C147	A166	20p brt vio bl	11.50	11.00
		Nos. C143-C147 (5)	19.63	17.65

Theater Type of Regular Issue, 1945

1945, July 27

C148	A167	30c sl & ol	20	15
C149	A167	1p sl & lil	30	30
C150	A167	5p sl & blk	2.25	2.00
C151	A167	10p sl & lt ultra	4.25	3.50
C152	A167	20p blk & gray grn	9.75	8.50
		Nos. C148-C152 (5)	16.75	14.45

Blindfold Type of Regular Issue, 1945

1945, Nov. 21

C153	A169	30c sl grn	16	16
C154	A169	1p brn red	30	20
C155	A169	5p red brn & pale bl	2.50	2.25
C156	A169	10p sl blk & pale lil	4.25	4.25
C157	A169	20p grn & lt brn	21.00	20.00
		Nos. C153-C157 (5)	28.21	26.86

Torch, Laurel and Flag-decorated ONU — AP70

1946, Apr. 10

C158	AP70	30c chocolate	16	15
C159	AP70	1p sl grn	28	24
C160	AP70	5p chnt & dk grn	1.40	1.00
C161	AP70	10p dk brn & chnt	4.25	3.25
C162	AP70	20p sl grn & org red	9.75	7.75
		Nos. C158-C162 (5)	15.84	12.39

Issued to honor the United Nations.

Father Margil de Jesus and Plane over Zacatecas
AP71

Designs (Zacatecas scene and): 1p, Genaro Codina. 5p, Gen. Enrique Estrada. 10p, Fernando Villalpando.

Perf. 10½x10

1946, Sept. 13 Engr. Wmk. 279

C163	AP71	30c gray	16	15
C164	AP71	1p brn & Prus grn	35	30
C165	AP71	5p red & ol	2.50	2.50
C166	AP71	10p Prus grn & dk brn	8.75	4.25

400th anniversary of Zacatecas.

Franklin D. Roosevelt and Stamp of 1st Mexican Issue
AP72

Design: 30c, Arms of Mexico and Stamp of 1st US Issue.

1947, May 16 Photo. *Perf. 14*

C167	AP72	25c lt vio bl	75	40
C168	AP72	30c gray blk	50	20
a.		Imperf., pair	450.00	
C169	AP72	1p blue & car	1.00	35

Centenary International Philatelic Exhibition, New York, May 17-25, 1947.

Type of 1934-35

Perf. 10½x10, 10x10½

1947 Engr. Wmk. 279

C170	AP15	5c black	90	15
C171	AP16	10c red brn	1.50	25
C172	AP17	15c ol grn	1.50	25
C173	AP19	30c brn ol	1.00	15
C174	AP20	40c bl gray	1.00	15
C175	AP21	50c green	9.00	25
a.		Imperf., pair	450.00	
C176	AP22	1p gray grn & red brn	2.25	20
a.		Imperf., pair	500.00	
C177	AP23	5p red & blk	6.00	1.00
c.		5p dk car & blk	200.00	3.00

Perf. 14

C177A	AP18	20c brn car	2.00	40
b.		Imperf., pair	250.00	
		Nos. C170-C177A (9)	25.15	2.80

Emilio Carranza
AP74

Douglas DC-4
AP75

1947, June 25 Engr. *Perf. 10½x10*

C178	AP74	10p red & dk brn	1.40	1.25
a.		10p dk car & brn		6.50
C179	AP75	20p bl & red brn	2.00	2.00

Cadet Vincente Suarez
AP76

Chapultepec Castle
AP78

Designs: 30c, Lieut. Juan de la Barrera. 1p, Gen. Pedro M. Anaya. 5p, Gen. Antonio de Leon.

1947, Sept. 8 Photo. *Perf. 14*

C180	AP76	25c dl vio	20	15
C181	AP76	30c blue	20	15

Engr.

Perf. 10x10½

C182	AP78	50c dp grn	30	15
C183	AP78	1p violet	40	15
C184	AP78	5p aqua & brn	1.65	1.65
a.		Imperf. pair	600.00	
		Nos. C180-C184 (5)	2.75	2.25

Centenary of the battles of Chapultepec, Churubusco and Molino del Rey.

Flight Symbol Type of 1944

1947 Wmk. 279 Photo. *Perf. 14*

C185	AP65	25c chnt brn	35	15
a.		Imperf., pair	250.00	

Puebla, Dance of the Half Moon
AP81

Designs: 5c, Guerrero, Acapulco waterfront. 10c, Oaxaca, dance. 20c, Chiapas, musicians (Mayan). 25c, Michoacan, masks. 30c, Cuauhtemoc. 35c, Guerrero, view of Taxco. 40c, San Luis Potosi, head. 50c, Chiapas, bas-relief profile, Mayan culture. 80c, Mexico City University Stadium. 5p, Queretaro, architecture. 10p, Miguel Hidalgo. 20p, Modern building.

Two types of 20p:

I- Blue gray part 21¼mm wide. Child's figure touching left edge.

II- Blue gray part 21¾mm wide; "LQ" at lower left corner. Child's figure 1mm from left edge.

Imprint: "Talleres de Impresion de Estampillas y Valores-Mexico"

Perf. 10½x10

1950-52 Wmk. 279 Engr.

C186	AP81	5c aqua ('51)	40	15
C187	AP81	10c brn org ('51)	2.00	40
C188	AP81	20c carmine	90	15
C189	AP81	25c redsh brn	90	15
C190	AP81	30c ol bis	40	15
C191	AP81	35c violet	2.00	15
a.		Retouched die	16.00	25
b.		As "a," imperf., pair	400.00	
C192	AP81	40c dk gray bl ('51)	1.75	15
a.		Imperf., pair	400.00	
C193	AP81	50c green	3.00	15
C194	AP81	80c cl ('52)	1.75	40
a.		Imperf., pair	400.00	
C195	AP81	1p bl gray	1.00	15
C196	AP81	5p dk brn & org ('51)	4.25	75
a.		Imperf., pair		*1,800.*
C197	AP81	10p blk & aqua ('52)	55.00	17.50
C198	AP81	20p car & bl gray, I ('52)	7.00	7.75
a.		Type II	600.00	75.00
		Nos. C186-C198 (13)	80.35	28.00

No. C191a: A patch of heavy shading has been added at right of "MEXICO;" lines in sky increased and strengthened.

Many shades exist of Nos. C186-C198.

See Nos. C208-C221, C249, C265-C268, C285-C288, C290-C298, C347-C349, C422, C444, C446-C450, C471-C480.

Pres. Aleman and Highway Bridging Map of Mexico
AP82

Design: 35c, Pres. Juarez and map.

1950, May 21 Engr.

C199	AP82	25c lil rose	2.50	20
C200	AP82	35c dp grn	20	15

Completion of the Intl. Highway between Ciudad Juarez and the Guatemala border.

Trains Crossing Isthmus of Tehuantepec
AP83

Design: 35c, Pres. Aleman and bridge.

1950, May 24

C201 AP83 25c green	40	20
C202 AP83 35c ultra	30	20

Issued to commemorate the opening of the Southeastern Railroad between Veracruz, Coatzocoalcos and Yucatan, 1950.

Aztec Courier, Plane, Train AP84

Design: 80c, Symbols of universal postal service.

1950, June 15

C203 AP84 25c red org	30	15
C204 AP84 80c blue	40	25

75th anniv. (in 1949) of the UPU.

Miguel Hidalgo AP86

Design: 35c, Hidalgo and Mexican Flag.

Wmk. 300

1953, May 8 Photo. *Perf. 14*

C206 AP86 25c gray bl & dk red brn	70	15
C207 AP86 35c slate grn	70	20

Bicentenary of birth of Miguel Hidalgo y Costilla (1753-1811), priest and revolutionist.

Type of 1950-52

Designs as before.

Imprint: "Talleres de Impresion de Estampillas y Valores-Mexico"

Wmk. 300, Horizontal

1953-56 Engr. *Perf. 10½x10*

C208 AP81 5c aqua	38	15
C209 AP81 10c org brn	4.50	70
a. 10c orange	9.00	2.00
C210 AP81 30c gray ol	15.00	1.00
C211 AP81 40c gray bl ('56)	15.00	1.50
C212 AP81 50c green	225.00	115.00
C213 AP81 80c claret	85.00	6.00
C214 AP81 1p bl gray	2.50	25
C215 AP81 5p dk brn & org	2.25	50
C216 AP81 10p blk & aqua	4.75	1.00
C217 AP81 20p car & bl gray (II) ('56)	45.00	8.00
Nos. C208-C211,C213-C217 (9)	174.38	19.10

Printed in sheets of 30.

Type of 1950-52

Designs as in 1950-52. 2p, Guerrero, view of Taxco. 2.25p, Michoacan, masks.

Two types of 2p:

I- No dots after "Colonial". Frame line at right broken near top.

II- Three dots in a line after "Colonial". Right frame line unbroken.

Wmk. 300, Vertical

1955-65 *Perf. 11½x11*

C218 AP81 5c bluish grn ('56)	15	15

Perf. 11

C219 AP81 10c org brn ('60)	28	15
a. Perf. 11½x11	90	35
C220 AP81 20c car ('60)	28	15
k. Perf. 11½x11 ('57)	1.40	15
C220A AP81 25c vio brn, perf. 11½x11	1.50	15
C220B AP81 30c ol gray ('60)	15	15
l. Perf. 11½x11	70	15
C220C AP81 35c dk vio, perf. 11½x11	70	15
C220D AP81 40c sl bl ('60)	28	15
m. Perf. 11½x11	8.50	15
C220E AP81 50c green, perf. 11½x11	70	15
n. Perf. 11 ('60)	90	15
q. 50c yellow green	90	18
C220F AP81 80c cl ('60)	4.25	50
o. Perf. 11½x11	4.25	50
C220G AP81 1p grn gray ('60)	90	25
p. Perf. 11½x11	10.50	25
C220H AP81 2p dk org brn, II ('63)	90	50
i. 2p lt org brn, perf. 11½x11 ('65)	110.00	35.00
j. 2p org brn, I, perf. 11	7.00	1.00
C221 AP81 2.25p mar ('63)	55	60
Nos. C218-C221 (12)	10.64	3.05

Printed in sheets of 50. Nos. C218-C221 have been re-engraved.

No. C218 has been redrawn and there are many differences. "CTS" measures 7mm; it is 5½mm on No. C208.

Nos. C208-C221 exist in various shades.

No. C220n was privately overprinted in red: "25vo Aniversario / Primer Cohete Internacional / Reynosa, Mexico-McAllen, U.S.A. / 1936-1961".

Mayan Ball Court and Player AP87

Design: 35c, Modern Stadium, Mexico.

1954, Mar. 6 Photo. *Perf. 14*

C222 AP87 25c brn & dk bl grn	75	30
C223 AP87 35c dl sl grn & lil rose	60	20

7th Central American & Caribbean Games.

Allegory AP88

1954, Sept. 15

C224 AP88 25c red brn & dp bl	42	20
C225 AP88 35c dk bl & vio brn	18	15
C226 AP88 80c blk & bl grn	20	20

Centenary of national anthem.

Aztec God Tezcatlipoca and Map — AP89

Design: 35c, Stadium and map.

1955, Mar. 12

C227 AP89 25c dk Prus grn & red brn	60	25
C228 AP89 35c car & brn	60	25

2nd Pan American Games, 1955.

Ornaments and Mask, Archeological Era — AP90

Designs: 10c, Virrey Enriquez de Almanza, bell tower and coach, colonial era. 50c, Jose Maria Morelos and cannon, heroic Mexico. 1p, Woman and child and horse back rider, revolutionary Mexico. 1.20p, Sombrero and Spurs, popular Mexico. 5p, Pointing hand and school, modern Mexico.

Perf. 11½x11

1956, Aug. 1 Engr. Wmk. 300

C229 AP90 5c black	35	15
C230 AP90 10c lt bl	35	15
C231 AP90 50c vio brn	25	15
C232 AP90 1p bl gray	35	15
C233 AP90 1.20p magenta	35	20
C234 AP90 5p bl grn	1.00	1.00
a. Souv. sheet of 6, #C229-C234, perf. 10½x10	30.00	30.00
Nos. C229-C234 (6)	2.65	1.80

Centenary of Mexico's 1st postage stamps. No. C234a sold for 15 pesos.

Paricutin Volcano AP91

1956, Sept. 5 Photo. *Perf. 14*

C235 AP91 50c dk vio bl	40	15

20th Intl. Geological Cong., Mexico City.

Valentin Gomez Farias and Melchor Ocampo AP92

Design: 1.20p, Leon Guzman and Ignacio Ramirez.

1956-63 Wmk. 300 *Perf. 14*

C236 AP92 15c intense bl	40	15
C237 AP92 1.20p dk grn & pur	70	30
b. Dark green omitted	90.00	
c. Purple omitted	100.00	
C237A AP92 2.75p pur ('63)	1.00	65

Centenary of the constitution (in 1957). See Nos. C289, C445, C451, C471A.

Map — AP93

1956, Dec. 1

C238 AP93 25c gray & dk bl	30	15

Issued to publicize the 4th Inter-American Regional Tourism Congress of the Gulf of Mexico and the Caribbean (in 1955).

Eagle Holding Scales AP94

Design: 1p, Allegorical figure writing the law.

1957, Aug. 31 Photo. *Perf. 14*

C239 AP94 50c metallic red brn & green	30	15
C240 AP94 1p metallic lilac & ultra	40	20

Centenary of 1857 Constitution.

Globe, Weights and Measure AP95

1957, Sept. 21

C241 AP95 50c metallic bl & blk	40	15

Issued to commemorate the centenary of the adoption of the metric system in Mexico.

Death of Jesus Garcia AP96

1957, Nov. 7 Wmk. 300 *Perf. 14*

C242 AP96 50c car rose & dk vio	35	15

50th anniversary of the death of Jesus Garcia, hero of Nacozari.

Oil Industry Symbols AP97

Design: 1p, Derricks at night.

1958, Aug. 30

C243 AP97 50c emer & blk	25	15
C244 AP97 1p car & bluish blk	40	15
Set value		20

20th anniversary of the nationalization of Mexico's oil industry.

Independence Monument Figure — AP98

1958, Dec. 15 Engr. *Perf. 11*

C245 AP98 50c gray blue	25	15

10th anniversary of the signing of the Universal Declaration of Human Rights.

Pres. Venustiano Carranza AP99

1960, Jan. 15 Photo. *Perf. 14*

C246 AP99 50c salmon & dk bl	25	15

Centenary of the birth of President Venustiano Carranza.

Alberto Braniff's 1910 Plane, Douglas DC-7 and Mexican Airlines Map AP100

1960, May 15 Wmk. 300 *Perf. 14*

C247 AP100 50c lt brn & vio	50	15
C248 AP100 1p lt brn & bl grn	40	20

50th anniversary of Mexican aviation.

Type of 1950-52 inscribed: "HOMENAJE AL COLECCIONISTA DEL TIMBRE DEL MEXICO-JUNIO 1960"

1960, June 8 Engr. *Perf. 10½x10*

C249 AP81 20p lil, brn & lt grn	42.50	80.00

See note below No. 909.

Flag AP101

Designs: 1.20p, Bell of Dolores and eagle. 5p, Dolores Church.

Wmk. 300

1960, Sept. 16 Photo. *Perf. 14*

C250	AP101	50c dp grn & brt red	35	15
C251	AP101	1.20p grnsh bl & dk brn	45	20
C252	AP101	5p sep & grn	4.50	1.75

150th anniversary of independence.

Aviation (Douglas DC-8 Airliner) AP102

Designs: 1p, Oil industry. 1.20p, Road development. 5p, Water power (dam).

1960, Nov. 20 Photo. *Perf. 14*

C253	AP102	50c gray bl & blk	35	15
C254	AP102	1p dk grn & rose car	40	20
C255	AP102	1.20p dk grn & sep	40	25
C256	AP102	5p bl & lil	2.00	90

50th anniversary of Mexican Revolution.

Count de Revilla Gigedo — AP103

1960, Dec. 23

C257	AP103	60c dk car & blk	50	15

80th census and to honor Juan Vicente Güemez Pacheco de Padilla Horcasitas, Count de Revilla Gigedo, was conducted the 1st census in America, 1793.

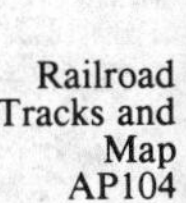

Railroad Tracks and Map AP104

Design: 70c, Railroad bridge.

1961, Nov. Wmk. 300 *Perf. 14*

C258	AP104	60c chlky bl & dk grn	35	15
C259	AP104	70c dk bl & gray	35	15

Opening of the railroad from Chihuahua to the Pacific Ocean.

Gen. Ignacio Zaragoza and View of Puebla AP105

1962, May 5

C260	AP105	1p gray grn & sl grn	50	15

Centenary of the Battle of May 5 at Puebla and the defeat of French forces by Gen. Ignacio Zaragoza.

Laboratory AP106

1962, June 11

C261	AP106	1p ol & vio bl	50	15

25th anniversary of the National Polytechnic Institute.

Pres. John F. Kennedy AP107

1962, June 29

C262	AP107	80c brt bl & car	1.50	35

Issued to commemorate the visit of President John F. Kennedy to Mexico, June 29-30.

Globe AP108

1962, Oct. 20

C263	AP108	1.20p vio & dk brn	50	20

Inter-American Economic and Social Council meeting.

Balloon over Mexico City, 1862 — AP109

1962, Dec. 21 Wmk. 300 *Perf. 14*

C264	AP109	80c lt bl & blk	1.40	50

Cent. of the 1st Mexican balloon ascension by Joaquin de la Cantolla y Rico.

Type of 1950-52
Imprint: "Talleres de Imp. de Est. y Valores-Mexico"

Designs as before.

Wmk. 300, Vertical

1962-72 Photo. *Perf. 14*

Two sizes of 80c:
I- 35½x20mm.
II- 37x20½mm.

C265	AP81	80c cl, I ('63)	1.25	25
a.		Perf. 11½x11, size II ('63)	3.50	30
b.		Perf. 11, size II ('63)	3.00	25
c.		Perf. 11, size I ('72)	2.00	15
C266	AP81	5p dk brn & yel org	3.50	85
C267	AP81	10p blk & lt grn ('63)	6.00	3.00
C268	AP81	20p car & bl gray	14.00	3.00

Vert. pairs, imperf. horiz. of No. C265, perf. 11, may be from uncut rolls of No. C348.

ALALC Emblem AP110

1963, Feb. 15 Wmk. 300

C269	AP110	80c org & dl pur	90	25

2nd general session of the Latin American Free Trade Assoc. (ALALC), held in 1962.

Mexican Eagle and Refinery AP111

1963, Mar. 23

C270	AP111	80c red org & slate	50	15

25th anniversary of the nationalization of the oil industry.

Polyconic Map AP112

1963, Apr. 22 Photo. *Perf. 14*

C271	AP112	80c bl & blk	75	25

Issued to commemorate the 19th International Chamber of Commerce Congress.

EXMEX Emblem and Postmark AP113

1963, Oct. 9 Wmk. 350 *Perf. 14*

C274	AP113	5p rose red	2.25	1.50

77th Annual Convention of the American Philatelic Society, Mexico City, Oct. 7-13.

Marshal Tito AP114

1963, Oct. 15 Wmk. 350 *Perf. 14*

C275	AP114	2p dk grn & vio	1.75	60

Visit of Marshal Tito of Yugoslavia.

Modern Architecture — AP115

1963, Oct. 19

C276	AP115	80c dk bl & gray	60	20

Issued to publicize the International Architects' Convention, Mexico City.

Dove AP116

1963, Oct. 26

C277	AP116	80c dl bl grn & car	1.00	30

Centenary of the International Red Cross.

Don Quixote by Jose Guadalupe Posada AP117

1963, Nov. 9 Engr. *Perf. 10½x10*

C278	AP117	1.20p black	1.50	40

50th anniversary of the death of José Guadalupe Posada, satirical artist and Mexican independence hero.

Horse-drawn Rail Coach, Old and New Trains AP118

Wmk. 350

1963, Nov. 29 Photo. *Perf. 14*

C279	AP118	1.20p vio bl & bl	80	30

11th Pan-American Railroad Congress.

Eleanor Roosevelt, Flame and UN Emblem AP119

1964, Feb. 22 Wmk. 350 *Perf. 14*

C280	AP119	80c lt ultra & red	70	20

15th anniversary (in 1963) of the Universal Declaration of Human Rights and to honor Eleanor Roosevelt.

Gen. Charles de Gaulle AP120

1964, Mar. 16 Photo.

C281	AP120	2p dl vio bl & brn	2.00	70

Visit of President Charles de Gaulle of France to Mexico, Mar. 16-18.

Pres. John F. Kennedy and Pres. Adolfo Lopez Mateos and Map AP121

1964, Apr. 11 Photo.

C282	AP121	80c vio bl & gray	75	20

Ratification of the Chamizal Treaty, returning the Chamizal area of El Paso, Texas, to Mexico, July 18, 1963.

Queen Juliana AP122

1964, May 8 Wmk. 350 *Perf. 14*

C283	AP122	80c bis & vio bl	1.00	20

Visit of Queen Juliana of the Netherlands.

Lt. José Azueta and Cadet Virgilio Uribe
AP123

1964, June 18 Wmk. 350 *Perf. 14*

C284 AP123 40c dk brn & blk 45 15

50th anniversary of the defense of Veracruz (against US Navy).

Types of 1950-62

Designs as before.

Engraved; Photogravure (C296-C298)
Perf. 11 (20c, 40c, 50c, 80c, 2p); 14

1964-73 Wmk. 350

C285	AP81	20c car ('71)	70	1.00
C286	AP81	40c gray bl ('71)	125.00	*125.00*
C287	AP81	50c grn ('71)	45	45
C288	AP81	80c cl, I ('73)	45	45
C289	AP92	1.20p dk grn & pur	5.50	2.00
C290	AP81	2p red brn, II ('71)	1.40	1.25
C296	AP81	5p brn & org ('66)	9.00	7.50
C297	AP81	10p blk & aqua	20.00	15.00
C298	AP81	20p car & bl gray	32.50	22.50
	Nos. C285-C290,C296-C298 (9)		195.00	*175.15*

National Emblem, Cahill's Butterfly World Map, Sword and Scales of Justice
AP124

1964, July 29 Photo.

C299 AP124 40c sep & dp bl 60 15

10th conference of the International Bar Association, Mexico City, July 27-31.

Galleon
AP125

Map Showing 16th Century Voyages Between Mexico and Philippines — AP126

1964, Nov. 10 Wmk. 350 *Perf. 14*

C300	AP125	80c ultra & ind	2.25	35
C301	AP126	2.75p brt yel & blk	2.75	1.00

400 years of Mexican-Philippine friendship.

Catalogue values for unused stamps in this section, from this point to the end of the section, are for Never Hinged items.

Netzahualcoyotl Dam, Grijalva River — AP127

1965, Feb. 19 Photo. *Perf. 14*

C302 AP127 80c vio gray & dk brn 50 15

Radio-electric Unit of San Benito, Chiapas — AP128

Design: 80c, Microwave tower, Villahermosa, Tabasco.

1965, June 19 Wmk. 350 *Perf. 14*

C303	AP128	80c lt bl & dk bl	65	30
C304	AP128	1.20p dk grn & blk	70	30

Centenary of the ITU.

Campfire, Tent and Scout Emblem
AP129

1965, Sept. 27 Photo. *Perf. 14*

C305 AP129 80c lt ultra & vio bl 65 30

Issued to publicize the 20th World Scout Conference, Mexico City, Sept. 27-Oct. 3.

King Baudouin, Queen Fabiola and Arms of Belgium
AP130

1965, Oct. 18 Wmk. 350 *Perf. 14*

C306 AP130 2p sl grn & dl bl 1.00 40

Visit of the King and Queen of Belgium.

Mayan Antiquities and Unisphere
AP131

1965, Nov. 9 Photo.

C307 AP131 80c lem & emer 50 20

Issued for the NY World's Fair, 1964-65.

Dante by Raphael — AP132

Perf. 10x10½

1965, Nov. 23 Wmk. 350 Engr.

C308 AP132 2p hn brn 1.25 65

700th anniv. of the birth of Dante Alighieri.

Runner in Starting Position, Terra Cotta Found in Colima, 300-650 A.D.
AP133

Designs: 1.20p, Chin cultic disk, ball game scoring stone with ball player in center, Mayan culture, c. 500 A.D., found in Chiapas. 2p, Clay sculpture of ball court, players, spectators and temple. Pieces on 80c and 2p from 300-650 A.D.

1965, Dec. 17 Photo. *Perf. 14*
Size: 35x21mm

C309	AP133	80c org & sl	65	25
C310	AP133	1.20p bl & vio bl	80	30
a.		Souv. sheet of 4, #965-966, C309-C310, imperf.	1.50	1.50

Size: 43x36mm

C311	AP133	2p brt bl & dk brn	65	25
a.		Souv. sheet, imperf.	1.50	1.50

19th Olympic Games, Mexico, 1968. No. C310a sold for 3.90p. No. C311a sold for 3p. Nos. C310a and C311a have large watermark of national arms (diameter 54mm) and "SECRETARIA DE HACIENDA Y CREDITO PUBLICO." Issued without gum.

Ruben Dario — AP134

1966, Mar. 17 Wmk. 350 *Perf. 14*

C312 AP134 1.20p sepia 60 32

Ruben Dario (pen name of Felix Ruben Garcia Sarmiento, 1867-1916), Nicaraguan poet, newspaper correspondent and diplomat.

Father Andres de Urdaneta and Compass Rose
AP135

Perf. 10½x10

1966, June 4 Engr. Wmk. 350

C313 AP135 2.75p bluish blk 1.25 60

4th centenary of Father Urdaneta's return trip from the Philippines.

UPAE Type of Regular Issue

Designs: 80c, Pennant and post horn. 1.20p, Pennant and UPAE emblem (horiz.).

Wmk. 300

1966, June 24 Photo. *Perf. 14*

C314	A244	80c mag & blk	25	15
C315	A244	1.20p lt ultra & blk	32	15
		Set value		24

U Thant and UN Emblem
AP136

1966, Aug. 24 Photo. Wmk. 300

C316 AP136 80c blk & ultra 50 20

Visit of U Thant, Secretary General of the UN.

AP137

1966, Aug. 26 *Perf. 14*

C317 AP137 80c grn & red 22 15

Issued to publicize the year of friendship between Mexico and Central America.

Olympic Type of Regular Issue, 1966

Designs by Diego Rivera: 80c, Obstacle race. 2.25p, Football. 2.75p, Lighting Olympic torch.

1966, Oct. 15 Wmk. 300 *Perf. 14*
Size: 57x21mm

C318	A248	80c org brn & blk	40	15
C319	A248	2.25p grn & blk	60	35
C320	A248	2.75p dp pur & blk	1.00	50
a.		Souv. sheet of 3	3.00	3.00

Issued to publicize the 19th Olympic Games, Mexico City, D.F., 1968. No. C320a contains 3 imperf. stamps similar to Nos. C318-C320 with simulated perforations. Sold for 8.70p.

UNESCO Emblem
AP138

Litho. & Engr.

1966, Nov. 4 *Perf. 11*

C321	AP138	80c blk, car, brt grn & org	50	15
a.		Perf. 10½	5.00	2.00
b.		Perf. 10½x11	25.00	
c.		Perf. 11x10½	12.50	5.00

UNESCO 20th anniv.

Venustiano Carranza
AP139

Tiros Satellite over Earth
AP140

1967, Feb. 5 Photo. *Perf. 14*

C322 AP139 80c dk red brn & ocher 35 15

50th anniversary of the constitution. Venustiano Carranza (1859-1920), was president of Mexico 1917-20.

1967, Mar. 23 Photo. Wmk. 300

C323 AP140 80c blk & dk bl 50 20

World Meteorological Day, Mar. 23.

Medical School Emblem AP141

Captain Horacio Ruiz Gavino AP142

1967, July 10 Wmk. 300 *Perf. 14*

C324 AP141 80c blk & ocher	32	15

Issued to commemorate the 50th anniversary of the Mexican Military Medical School.

1967, July 17 Photo.

Design: 2p, Biplane (horiz.).

C325 AP142 80c blk & brn	24	15
C326 AP142 2p blk & brn	42	25

50th anniv. of the 1st Mexican airmail flight, from Pachuca to Mexico City, July 6, 1917.

Marco Polo and ITY Emblem — AP143

1967, Sept. 9 Wmk. 300 *Perf. 14*

C327 AP143 80c rose cl & blk	22	15

Issued for International Tourist Year, 1967.

Olympic Games Type of Regular Issue, 1967

Designs: 80c, Diving. 1.20p, Runners. 2p, Weight lifters. 5p, Soccer.

1967, Oct. 12 Photo. *Perf. 14*

C328 A254 80c dp lil rose & blk	24	15
C329 A254 1.20p brt grn & blk	28	20
a. Souv. sheet of 2, #C328-C329, imperf.	1.75	1.75
C330 A254 2p yel & blk	1.00	40
C331 A254 5p ol & blk	1.65	75
a. Souv. sheet of 2, #C330-C331, imperf.	4.25	3.75

No. C329a sold for 2.50p; No. C331a sold for 9p. Both sheets are watermark 350.

Heinrich Hertz and James Clerk Maxwell AP144

1967, Nov. 15 Photo. Wmk. 300

C332 AP144 80c brt grn & blk	28	15

2nd Intl. Telecommunications Plan Conf., Mexico City, Oct. 30-Nov. 15.

EFIMEX Emblem, Showing Official Stamp of 1884 — AP145

1968, Feb. 24 Wmk. 300 *Perf. 14*

C333 AP145 80c blk & grn	45	24
C334 AP145 2p blk & ver	45	24

EFIMEX '68, International Philatelic Exhibition, Mexico City, Nov. 1-9, 1968.

Olympic Games Type of Regular Issue, 1967

Designs: 80c, Sailing. 1p, Rowing. 2p, Volleyball. 5p, Equestrian.

1968, Mar. 21 Photo. *Perf. 14*

C335 A254 80c ultra & blk	22	15
C336 A254 1p brt bl grn & blk	28	20
a. Souv. sheet of 2, #C335-C336, imperf.	1.50	1.50
C337 A254 2p yel & blk	60	30
C338 A254 5p red brn & blk	1.25	1.10
a. Souv. sheet of 2, #C337-C338, imperf.	2.75	2.75

No. C336a sold for 2.40p; No. C338a sold for 9p. Both sheets are watermark 350.

Martin Luther King, Jr. — AP146

1968, June 8 Photo. Wmk. 300

C339 AP146 80c blk & gray	35	15

Rev. Dr. Martin Luther King, Jr. (1929-1968), American civil rights leader.

Olympic Types of Regular Issue, 1968

Designs: 80c, Peace dove and Olympic rings. 1p, Discobolus. 2p, Olympic medals. 5p, Symbols of Olympic sports events. 10p, Symbolic design for Mexican Olympic Games.

1968, Oct. 12 Wmk. 350 *Perf. 14*

C340 A259 80c grn, lil & org	24	15
C341 A259 1p grn, bl & blk	28	15
C342 A259 2p multi	75	50
a. Souvenir sheet of 3, #C340-C342, imperf.	4.50	4.50
C343 A260 5p multi	3.00	1.40
C344 A260 10p blk & multi	2.50	1.50
a. Souvenir sheet of 2, #C343-C344, imperf.	7.50	7.50
Nos. C340-C344 (5)	6.77	3.70

19th Olympic Games, Mexico City, Oct. 12-27. No. C342a sold for 5p. No. C344a sold for 20p.

Souvenir Sheet

EFIMEX Emblem — AP147

1968, Nov. 1 Photo. *Imperf.*

C345 AP147 5p blk & ultra	2.10	2.10

EFIMEX '68 International philatelic exhibition, Mexico City, Nov. 1-9. No. C345 contains one stamp with simulated perforations.

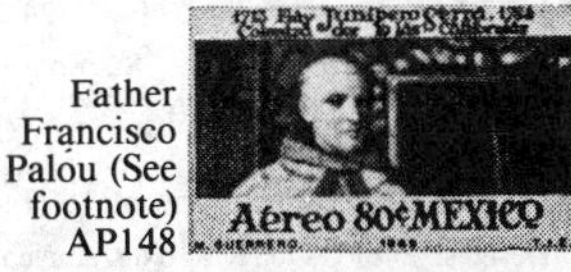

Father Francisco Palou (See footnote) AP148

1969, July 16 Wmk. 350 *Perf. 14*

C346 AP148 80c multi	38	15

Issued to honor Father Junipero Serra (1713-1784), Franciscan missionary, founder of San Diego, Calif. The portrait was intended to be that of Father Serra. By error the head of Father Palou, his coworker, was taken from a painting (c. 1785) by Mariano Guerrero which also contains a Serra portrait.

Type of 1950-52 Redrawn Coil Stamps

Wmk. 300 Vert.

1969 Photo. *Perf. 11 Vert.*

Imprint: "T.I.E.V."

C347 AP81 20c carmine	90	90

Imprint: "Talleres de Est. y Valores-Mexico"

C348 AP81 80c claret	1.10	1.10

Imprint: "T.I.E.V."

C349 AP81 1p gray grn	1.25	1.25

Soccer Ball AP149

Design: 2p, Foot and soccer ball.

1969, Aug. 16 Wmk. 350 *Perf. 14*

C350 AP149 80c red & multi	32	15
C351 AP149 2p grn & multi	50	15

Issued to publicize the 9th World Soccer Championships for the Jules Rimet Cup, Mexico City, May 30-June 21, 1970.

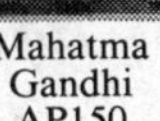

Mahatma Gandhi AP150

Astronaut's Footprint AP151

1969, Sept. 27 Photo. *Perf. 14*

C352 AP150 80c multi	28	15

of Mohandas K. Gandhi (1869-1948), leader in India's fight for independence.

1969, Oct. 29 Photo.

C353 AP151 2p black	50	22

Man's 1st landing on the moon, July 20, 1969. See note after US No. C76.

Tourist Issue

Type of Regular Issue, 1969-73 and

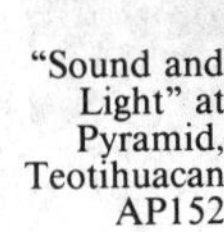

"Sound and Light" at Pyramid, Teotihuacan AP152

Designs: No. C355, Acapulco Bay. No. C356, El Caracol Observatory, Yucatan. No. C357, Dancer with fruit basket, Oaxaca. No. C358, Sports fishing, Lower California (horiz.).

1969-73 Wmk. 350 *Perf. 14*

C354 AP152 80c shown	90	30
C355 AP152 80c multi	90	30
C356 AP152 80c multi	90	30

Wmk. 300

C357 A267 80c multi	35	25
C358 A267 80c multi	35	20
Nos. C354-C358 (5)	3.40	1.35

Issue dates: Nos. C354-C356, Nov. 1, 1969. Nos. C357-C358, Mar. 16, 1973.

Red Crosses AP154

1969, Nov. 8 Photo. Wmk. 350

C370 AP154 80c blk & multi	28	15
a. Red omitted	150.00	

Issued to commemorate the 50th anniversary of the League of Red Cross Societies.

Radar Satellite Ground Station — AP155

1969, Dec. 6 Wmk. 350 *Perf. 14*

C371 AP155 80c multi	32	15

Issued to publicize the installation of the ground station for communications by satellite at Tulancingo, Hidalgo.

Soccer Ball, and Mexican Masks — AP156

Design: 2p, Pre-Columbian sculptured heads and soccer ball.

1970, May 31 Wmk. 350 *Perf. 14*

C372 AP156 80c bl & multi	24	15
C373 AP156 2p multi	42	18

Issued to publicize the World Soccer Championships for the Jules Rimet Cup, Mexico City, May 30-June 21, 1970. The design of Nos. C372-C373 is continuous.

SPORTMEX '70 Emblem — AP157

1970, June 19 *Rouletted 13*

C374 AP157 2p gray & car	3.75	3.00

SPORTMEX '70 philatelic exposition devoted to sports, especially soccer, on stamps. Mexico City, June 19-28. The 2p stamp of No. C374 is imperf.

The Catalogue editors cannot undertake to appraise, identify or judge the genuineness or condition of stamps.

Ode to Joy and Beethoven's Signature AP158

1970, Sept. 26 Wmk. 350 *Perf. 14*

C375 AP158 2p multi 48 22

200th anniversary of the birth of Ludwig van Beethoven (1770-1827), composer.

UN General Assembly Floor Plan AP159

1970, Oct. 24 Photo. *Perf. 14*

C376 AP159 80c multi 30 15

25th anniversary of United Nations.

Isaac Newton AP160

1971, Feb. 27 Wmk. 350 *Perf. 14*

C377 AP160 2p shown 45 20
C378 AP160 2p Galileo 45 20
C379 AP160 2p Johannes Kepler 45 20

Mayan Warriors, Dresden Codex AP161

Designs: No. C381, Sister Juana, by Miguel Cabrera (1695-1768). No. C382, Jose Maria Velasco (1840-1912), self-portrait. No. C383, El Paricutin (volcano), by Gerardo Murillo ("Dr. Atl," 1875-1964). No. C384, Detail of mural, Man in Flames, by Jose Clemente Orozco (1883-1949).

Imprint includes "1971"

1971, Apr. 24 Photo. Wmk. 350

C380 AP161 80c multi 30 18
C381 AP161 80c multi 30 18
C382 AP161 80c multi 30 18
C383 AP161 80c multi 30 18
C384 AP161 80c multi 30 18
Nos. C380-C384 (5) 1.50 90

Mexican art and science through the centuries. See Nos. C396-C400, C417-C421, C439-C443, C513-C517, C527-C531.

The Scott Catalogue value is a retail price, what you could expect to pay for the stamp in a grade of Fine-Very Fine. The value listed is a reference which reflects recent actual dealer selling price.

Stamps of Venezuela, Mexico and Colombia AP162

1971, May 22 Photo. Wmk. 350

C385 AP162 80c multi 35 20

EXFILCA 70, 2nd Interamerican Philatelic Exhibition, Caracas, Venezuela, Nov. 27-Dec. 6, 1970.

Francisco Javier Clavijero AP163

1971, July 10 Wmk. 350 *Perf. 14*

C386 AP163 2p lt ol bis & dk brn 50 22

Francisco Javier Clavijero (1731-1786), Jesuit and historian, whose remains were returned from Italy to Mexico in 1970.

Waves AP164

Mariano Matamoros, by Diego Rivera AP165

1971, Aug. 7 Wmk. 350 *Perf. 14*

C387 AP164 80c multi 22 15

3rd World Telecommunications Day, May 17.

1971, Aug. 28 Photo.

C388 AP165 2p multi 42 20

Bicentenary of the birth of Mariano Matamoros (1770-1814), priest and patriot.

Vicente Guerrero AP166

Circles AP167

1971, Sept. 27

C389 AP166 2p multi 38 18

Vicente Guerrero (1783-1831), independence leader, president of Mexico. Painting by Juan O'Gorman.

1971, Nov. 4 Wmk. 300

C390 AP167 80c grnsh bl, dk bl & blk 30 15

25th anniv. of UNESCO.

Stamps of Venezuela, Mexico, Colombia and Peru AP168

1971, Nov. 4

C391 AP168 80c multi 42 15

EXFILIMA '71, 3rd Interamerican Philatelic Exhibition, Lima, Peru, Nov. 6-14.

Faces and Hand AP169

1971, Nov. 29

C392 AP169 2p blk, dk bl & pink 45 18

5th Congress of Psychiatry, Mexico City, Nov. 28-Dec. 4.

Ex Libris by Albrecht Dürer AP170

1971, Dec. 18

C393 AP170 2p blk & buff 65 18

Albrecht Dürer (1471-1528), German painter and engraver.

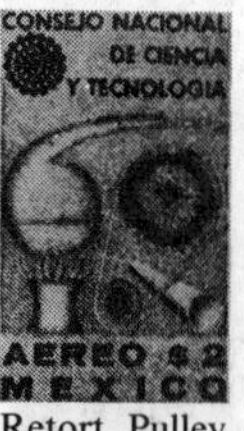
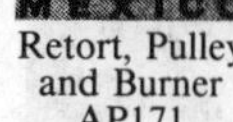

Retort, Pulley and Burner AP171

Scientists and WHO Emblem AP172

1972, Feb. 26 Wmk. 300 *Perf. 14*

C394 AP171 2p lil, blk & yel 35 15

Anniversary of the National Council on Science and Technology.

1972, Apr. 8

C395 AP172 80c multi 24 15

World Health Day 1972. Stamp shows Willem Einthoven and Frank Wilson.

Art and Science Type of 1971

Designs: No. C396, King Netzahuacoyotl (1402-1472) of Texcoco, art patron. No. C397, Juan Ruiz de Alarcon (c. 1580-1639), lawyer. No. C398, Jose Joaquin Fernandez de Lizardi (1776-1827), author. No. C399, Ramon Lopez Velarde (1888-1921), writer. No. C400, Enrique Gonzalez Martinez (1871-1952), poet.

Imprint includes "1972"

1972, Apr. 15 Wmk. 350

Black Inscriptions

C396 AP161 80c ocher 1.25 25
C397 AP161 80c green 1.25 25
C398 AP161 80c brown 1.25 25
C399 AP161 80c carmine 1.25 25
C400 AP161 80c gray bl 1.25 25
Nos. C396-C400 (5) 6.25 1.25

Mexican art and science through the centuries.

Rotary Emblem AP173

1972, Apr. 5

C401 AP173 80c multi 28 15

Rotary Intl. in Mexico, 50th anniv.

Tire Treads AP174

1972, May 11 Wmk. 300

C402 AP174 80c gray & blk 28 15

74th Assembly of the International Tourism Alliance, Mexico City, May 8-11.

Benito Juarez AP175

Design: 80c, Page of Civil Register. 1.20p, Juarez, by Pelegrin Clave.

1972 Photo. *Perf. 14*

C403 AP175 80c gray bl & blk 20 15
C404 AP175 1.20p multi 25 15
C405 AP175 2p yel & multi 32 20

Centenary of the death of Benito Juarez (1806-1872), revolutionary leader and president of Mexico.

Issue dates: 80c, 2p, July 18; 1.20p, Sept. 15.

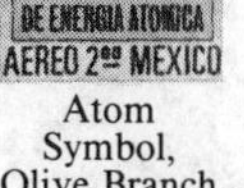

Atom Symbol, Olive Branch AP176

"Over the Waves," by Juventina Rosas AP177

1972, Oct. 3 Photo. Wmk. 300

C406 AP176 2p gray, bl & blk 40 15

16th Conference of the Atomic Energy Commission, Mexico City, Sept. 26.

1972, Oct. 16 *Perf. 14*

C407 AP177 80c olive bister 25 15

28th Intl. Cong. of the Societies of Authors and Composers, Mexico City, Oct. 16-21.

Child with Doll, by Guerrero Galvan, UNICEF Emblem — AP178

1972, Nov. 4
C408 AP178 80c multi 75 20

25th anniv. (in 1971) of UNICEF.

Pedro de Gante, by Rodriguez y Arangorti AP179

Map of Americas with Tourists' Footprints AP180

1972, Nov. 22 ***Perf. 14***
C409 AP179 2p multi 28 15

400th anniversary of the death of Brother Pedro de Gante (Pedro Moor or van der Moere; 1480 ?-1572), Franciscan brother who founded first school in Mexico, and writer.

Olympic Games Type of Regular Issue, 1972

Designs: 80c, Olympic emblems and stylized soccer game. 2p, Olympic emblems (vert.).

1972, Dec. 9 **Photo.** **Wmk. 300**
C410 A289 80c grn & multi 20 15
C411 A289 2p yel grn, blk & bl 32 15
Set value 24

20th Olympic Games, Munich, Aug. 26-Sept. 11.

Anti-pollution Type of Regular Issue

Design: 80c, Bird sitting on ornamental capital (vert.).

1972, Dec. 16
C412 A291 80c lt bl & blk 24 16

Anti-pollution campaign.

1972, Dec. 23
C413 AP180 80c blk, yel & grn 24 15

Tourism Year of the Americas.

Mexico #O1, Brazil #992, Colombia #130, Venezuela #22, Peru #C320 AP181

1973, Jan. 19 ***Perf. 14***
C414 AP181 80c multi 24 15

4th Interamerican Philatelic Exhibition, EXFILBRA 72, Rio de Janeiro, Brazil, Aug. 26-Sept. 2, 1972.

Aeolus, God of Winds AP182

1973, Sept. 14 **Photo.** **Wmk. 300**
C415 AP182 80c brt pink, blk & bl 60 20

Cent. of intl. meteorological cooperation.

Nicolaus Copernicus AP183

San Martin Monument AP184

Wmk. 300
1973, Oct. 10 **Photo.** ***Perf. 14***
C416 AP183 80c sl grn 30 15

500th anniversary of the birth of Nicolaus Copernicus (1473-1543), Polish astronomer.

Art and Science Type of 1971

Designs: No. C417, Aztec calendar stone. No. C418, Carlos de Sigüenza y Gongora (1645-1700), mathematician, astronomer. No. C419, Francisco Diaz Covarrubias (1833-1889), topographer. No. C420, Joaquin Gallo (1882-1965), geographer, astronomer. No. C421, Luis Enrique Erro (1897-1955), founder of Tonanzintla Observatory.

Imprint includes "1973"

1973, Nov. 21 **Wmk. 350**
C417 AP161 80c car & sl grn 15 15
C418 AP161 80c multi 15 15
C419 AP161 80c multi 15 15
C420 AP161 80c multi 15 15
C421 AP161 80c multi 15 15
Nos. C417-C421 (5) 75
Set value 60

Type of 1950-52

Design: Mexico City University Stadium.

Imprint: "Talleres de. Imp. de Est. y Vallores-Mexico"

1973 **Unwmk.** ***Perf. 11***
C422 AP81 80c claret, I 1.25 95

Fluorescent printing on front or back of stamps consisting of beehive pattern and diagonal inscription.

Wmk. 350
1973, Nov. 9 **Photo.** ***Perf. 14***
C423 AP184 80c org, ind & yel 18 15

Erection of a monument to San Martin in Mexico City, a gift of Argentina.

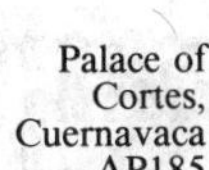

Palace of Cortes, Cuernavaca AP185

Wmk. 300
1974, Jan. 18 **Litho.** ***Perf. 14***
C424 AP185 80c blk & multi 18 15

EXMEX 73 Philatelic Exhibition, Cuernavaca, Apr. 7-15.

Gold Brooch, Mochica Culture AP186

1974, Mar. 6 **Photo.** **Wmk. 300**
C425 AP186 80c gold & multi 18 15

Exhibition of Peruvian gold treasures, Mexico City, 1973-74.

Luggage — AP187

1974, Mar. 22 ***Perf. 14***
C426 AP187 80c multi 20 15

16th Convention of the Federation of Latin American Tourist Organizations (COTAL), Acapulco, May 1974.

CEPAL Emblem AP188

1974, Mar. 22
C427 AP188 80c blk & multi 18 15
a. Red omitted 100.00

25th anniversary (in 1973) of the Economic Commission for Latin America (CEPAL).

"The Enameled Casserole," by Picasso — AP189

1974, Mar. 29 **Wmk. 300**
C428 AP189 80c multi 30 15

Pablo Ruiz Picasso (1881-1973), painter and sculptor.

EXFILMEX Type of 1974

1974, July 26 ***Perf. 13x12***
C429 A305 80c buff, red brn & blk 18 15

See note after No. 1065.

Biplane — AP190

Perf. 13x12
1974, Aug. 20 **Photo.** **Wmk. 300**
C430 AP190 80c shown 15 15
C431 AP190 2p Jet plane 22 15
Set value 20

50th anniversary of Mexican Airlines (MEXICANA).

Transmitter and Waves Circling Globe — AP191

1974, Oct. 4 **Wmk. 300** ***Perf. 14***
C432 AP191 2p multi 20 15

First International Congress of Electric and Electronic Communications, Sept. 17-21.

Volleyball AP192

1974, Oct. 12 ***Perf. 13x12***
C433 AP192 2p org, bis & blk 20 15

8th World Volleyball Championship. Perforation holes are of two sizes.

Souvenir Sheet

FILATELIA PARA LA PAZ

M E X I C O $10 A E R E O

Mexico #O1, Colombia #130, Venezuela #22, Peru #C320, Brazil #992, Mexico #123 — AP193

Wmk. 300
1974, Oct. 28 **Photo.** ***Imperf.***
C434 AP193 10p multi 1.50 1.50

EXFILMEX 74, 5th Inter-American Philatelic Exhibition, Mexico City, Oct. 26-Nov. 3. Exists with red omitted.

Felipe Carrillo Puerto AP194

1974, Nov. 8 ***Perf. 14***
C435 AP194 80c grn & gldn brn 20 15

Birth centenary of Felipe Carrillo Puerto (1874-1924), politician and journalist.

Mask, Bat and Catcher's Mitt — AP195

1974, Nov. 29 **Wmk. 350** ***Perf. 14***
C436 AP195 80c multi 20 15

Mexican Baseball League, 50th anniversary.

Man's Face, Mailbox, Colonial Period AP196

Design: 2p, Heinrich von Stephan, contemporary engraving.

1974, Dec. 13 **Photo.** **Wmk. 300**
C437 AP196 80c multi 18 15
C438 AP196 2p grn & ocher 18 15
Set value 24

Centenary of Universal Postal Union.

Art and Science Type of 1971

Designs: No. C439, Mayan mural (8th century), Bonampak, Chiapas. No. C440, First musical score printed in Mexico, 1556. No. C441, Miguel Lerdo de Tejada (1869-1941), composer. No. C442, Silvestre Revueltas (1899-1940), composer (bronze bust). No. C443, Angela Peralta (1845-1883), singer.

Imprint includes "1974"

1974, Dec. 20 **Wmk. 300**
C439 AP161 80c multi 15 15
C440 AP161 80c multi 15 15
C441 AP161 80c multi 15 15
C442 AP161 80c multi 15 15
C443 AP161 80c multi 15 15
Nos. C439-C443 (5) 75
Set value 60

Types of 1950-56

Designs (as 1950-56 issues): 40c, San Luis Potosi, head. 60c, Leon Guzman and Ignacio Ramirez. 1.60p, Chiapas, Mayan bas-relief. 1.90p, Guerrero, Acapulco waterfront. 4.30p, Oaxaca, dance. 5.20p, Guerrero, view of Taxco. 5.60p, Michoacan, masks. 50p, Valentin Gomez Farias and Melchor Ocampo.

Engraved (40c), Photogravure
Perf. 11 (40c, 1.60p), 14

1975 **Wmk. 300**
C444 AP81 40c bluish gray 22 15
C445 AP92 60c yel grn 22 15
C446 AP81 1.60p red 90 15
C447 AP81 1.90p rose red 60 15
C448 AP81 4.30p ultra 75 15
C449 AP81 5.20p purple 1.10 40
C450 AP81 5.60p bl grn 2.25 50
C451 AP92 50p dk bl & brick red 13.00 2.50
Nos. C444-C451 (8) 19.04 4.15

Women's Year Emblem — AP199

1975, Jan. 3 **Wmk. 300** ***Perf. 14***
C456 AP199 1.60p brt pink & blk 20 15

International Women's Year 1975.

Declaration, UN Emblem, Mexican Flag AP200

1975, Feb. 7 **Photo.** **Wmk. 300**
C457 AP200 1.60p multi 15 15

Declaration of Economic Rights and Duties of Nations.

Balsa Raft "Acali" — AP201

1975, Mar. 7 **Wmk. 300** ***Perf. 14***
C458 AP201 80c multi 20 15

Trans-Atlantic voyage of the "Acali" from Canary Islands to Yucatan, May-Aug. 1973.

Dr. Miguel Jimenez, by I. Ramirez AP202

Miguel de Cervantes AP203

1975, Mar. 24 **Unwmk.** ***Perf. 14***
C459 AP202 2p multi 20 15

Fifth World Gastroenterology Congress.

1975, Apr. 26 **Photo.** **Unwmk.**
C460 AP203 1.60p bl blk & dk car 20 15

Third International Cervantes Festival, Guanajuato, Apr. 26-May 11.

Four-reales Coin, 1675 — AP204

1975, May 2
C461 AP204 1.60p bl, gold & blk 20 15

Intl. Numismatic Convention, Mexico City, Mar. 28-30, 1974, and 300th anniv. of 1st coin struck by Mexico City Mint.

Salvador Novo, by Roberto Montenegro AP205

1975, May 9
C462 AP205 1.60p multi 20 15

Salvador Novo (1904-1974), author.

Mural, Siqueiros — AP206

1975, May 16
C463 AP206 1.60p multi 20 15

David Alfaro Siqueiros (1896-1974), painter.

UN and IWY Emblems AP207

1975, June 19
C464 AP207 1.60p ultra & pink 20 15

International Women's Year World Conference, Mexico City, June 19-July 2.

Mexico City Coat of Arms AP208

Unwmk.

1975, Aug. 1 **Photo.** ***Perf. 14***
C465 AP208 1.60p multi 20 15

650th anniv. of Tenochtitlan (Mexico City).

Domingo F. Sarmiento AP209

Teachers' Monument AP210

Unwmk.

1975, Aug. 9 **Photo.** ***Perf. 14***
C466 AP209 1.60p brn & sl grn 20 15

1st International Congress of Third World Educators, Acapulco, Aug. 5-9. Domingo Faustino Sarmiento (1811-1888), Argentinian statesman, writer and educator.

1975, Aug. 9
C467 AP210 4.30p grn & ocher 30 15

Mexican-Lebanese friendship. The monument in Mexico City, by I Naffa al Rozzi, shows Cadmus, a mythical Phoenician, teaching the alphabet.

7th Pan American Games' Emblem AP211

1975, Aug. 29
C468 AP211 1.60p multi 20 15

Pan American Games, Mexico City, Oct. 13-26.

Dr. Atl, Self-portrait AP212

Unwmk.

1975, Oct. 3 **Photo.** ***Perf. 14***
C469 AP212 4.30p multi 30 15

Geraldo Murillo ("Dr. Atl," 1875-1924), painter and writer, birth centenary.

Globe and Traffic Circle — AP213

1975, Oct. 12
C470 AP213 1.60p bl, blk & gray 20 15

15th World Road Congress, Mexico City, Oct. 12-26.

Type of 1950-52

Designs: 40c, San Luis Potosi, head. 80c, Mexico City University stadium. 1p, Puebla, Half Moon dance. 1.60p, Chiapas, Mayan bas-relief. 5p, Queretaro, architecture. 5.60p, Michoacan, masks. 10p, Miguel Hidalgo. 20p, Modern building.

Engraved (40c, 1p), Photogravure
Perf. 11 (40c, 80c, 1p, 1.60p), 14

1975-76				**Unwmk.**	
C471	AP81	40c	bluish gray	32	32
C471A	AP92	60c	yel grn		
C472	AP81	80c	claret, II	60	48
C473	AP81	1p	grysh grn	1.00	80
C474	AP81	1.60p	red	1.40	1.00
C476	AP81	5p	dk brn & org ('76)	1.25	1.00
C477	AP81	5.60p	bluish grn ('76)	4.75	3.25
C479	AP81	10p	blk & grn	3.50	2.50
C480	AP81	20p	red & dl grn ('76)	6.25	4.00
	Nos. C471,C472-C480 (8)			19.07	13.35

Bicycle and Export Emblem AP214

Designs: Export Emblem and 30c, Copper vase. 80c, Overalls. 1.90p, Oil valves. 2p, Books. 4p, Honey. 4.30p, Strawberry. 5p, Motor vehicles. 5.20p, Farm machinery. 5.60p, Cotton. 20p, Film. 50p, Cotton thread.

1975-82	**Unwmk.**		**Photo.**	***Perf. 14***	
C486	AP214	30c	cop ('76)	15	15
C489	AP214	80c	dl bl ('76)	20	15
C491	AP214	1.60p	blk & org	15	15
a.			Thin paper ('81)	40	15
C492	AP214	1.90p	ver & dk grn	35	15
C493	AP214	2p	ultra & gold ('76)	40	15
C495	AP214	4p	yel bis & brn ('82)	1.00	20
C496	AP214	4.30p	brt pink & ol	15	15
C497	AP214	5p	dk bl & ocher ('76)	20	20
C498	AP214	5.20p	red & blk ('76)	40	40
C499	AP214	5.60p	yel grn & org ('76)	20	20
C503	AP214	20p	multi, thin paper ('81)	60	20
C508	AP214	50p	multi ('82)	2.00	2.00
	Nos. C486-C508 (12)			5.80	4.10

See Nos. C594-C603.

Art and Science Type of 1971

Designs: No. C513, Title page of "Medical History of New Spain," by Francisco Hernandez, 1628. No. C514, Alfonso L. Herrera (1868-1942), biologist. No. C515, Title page, Aztec Herbal, 1552. No. C516, Arturo S. Rosenblueth (1900-1970). No. C517, Alfredo Augusto Duges (1826-1910) French-born naturalist.

Imprint includes "1975"

1975, Nov. 21	**Unwmk.**			***Perf. 14***	
C513	AP161	1.60p	buff, red & blk	15	15
C514	AP161	1.60p	vio bl & multi	15	15
C515	AP161	1.60p	blk & multi	15	15
C516	AP161	1.60p	gray & multi	15	15
C517	AP161	1.60p	grn & multi	15	15
	Nos. C513-C517 (5)			75	
	Set value				25

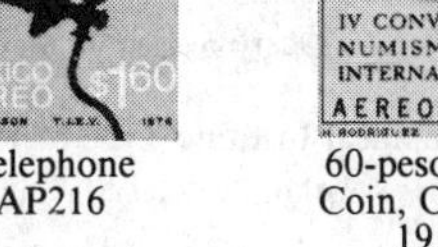

Telephone AP216

60-peso Gold Coin, Oaxaca, 1917 AP217

1976, Mar. 10				**Photo.**	
C518	AP216	1.60p	gray & blk	20	15

Centenary of first telephone call by Alexander Graham Bell, Mar. 10, 1876.

1976, Mar. 25	**Photo.**			**Unwmk.**	
C519	AP217	1.60p	blk, ocher & yel	20	15

4th International Numismatic Convention, Mexico City, March 1976.

Rain God Tlaloc and Calles Dam AP218

1976, Mar. 29				***Perf. 14***	
C520	AP218	1.60p	vio brn & dk grn	20	15

12th International Great Dams Congress, Mar. 29-Apr. 2.

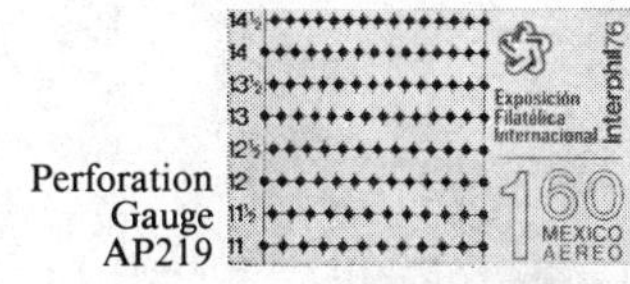

Perforation Gauge AP219

1976, May 7	**Photo.**			**Unwmk.**	
C521	AP219	1.60p	blk, red & bl	20	15

Interphil 76 International Philatelic Exhibition, Philadelphia, Pa., May 29-June 6.

Rainbow over City — AP220

1976, May 31	**Unwmk.**			***Perf. 14***	
C522	AP220	1.60p	blk & multi	20	15

Habitat, UN Conf. on Human Settlements, Vancouver, Canada, May 31-June 11.

Liberty Bell AP221

"Peace" AP222

1976, July 4	**Photo.**			***Perf. 14***	
C523	AP221	1.60p	ultra & red	20	15

American Bicentennial.

1976, Aug. 3 Photo. *Perf. 14*

Design: "Peace" written in Chinese, Japanese, Hebrew, Hindi and Arabic.

C524	AP222	1.60p	multi	20	15

30th Intl. Cong. of Science and Humanities of Asia and North Africa, Mexico, Aug. 3-8.

Television Screen AP223

1976, Aug. 24	**Photo.**			**Unwmk.**	
C525	AP223	1.60p	multi	20	15

1st Latin-American Forum on Children's Television.

Luminescence

Fluorescent airmail stamps include Nos. C265, C265c, C288, C357-C358, C390-C415, C422-C423.

Airmail stamps issued on both ordinary and fluorescent paper include Nos. C220, C220D-C220E, C220G-C220H, C265b, C266-C268, C286.

Sky, Sun, Water and Earth AP224

1976, Nov. 8	**Photo.**			***Perf. 14***	
C526	AP224	1.60p	multi	20	15

World Conservation Day.

Art and Science Type of 1971

Designs: No. C527, Coatlicue, Mother of Earth, Aztec sculpture. No. C528, El Caballito, statue of Charles IV of Spain, by Manuel Tolsa. No. C529, Chief Tlahuicole, bronze statue by Manuel Vilar. No. C530, Today's God, Money, seated ceramic figure, by L. Ortiz Monasterio. No. C531, Signal, abstract sculpture by Angela Gurria.

Imprint includes "1976"

1976, Dec. 10	**Photo.**			***Perf. 14***	
C527	AP161	1.60p	blk & yel	15	15
C528	AP161	1.60p	blk & red brn	15	15
C529	AP161	1.60p	blk & multi	15	15
C530	AP161	1.60p	car & multi	15	15
C531	AP161	1.60p	car & blk	15	15
	Nos. C527-C531 (5)			75	
	Set value				25

Score for El Pesebre by Casals AP225

1976, Dec. 29					
C532	AP225	4.30p	lt bl, blk & brn	35	15

Pablo Casals (1876-1973), cellist and composer, birth centenary.

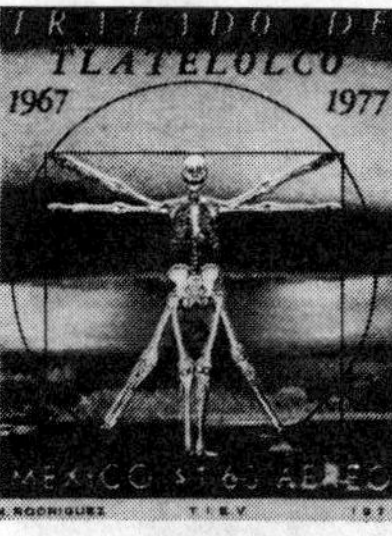

Mankind Destroyed by Nuclear Power AP226

1977, Feb. 14	**Photo.**			***Perf. 14***	
C533	AP226	1.60p	multi	20	15
a.			Wmk. 300	40.00	40.00

10th anniv. of the Agreement of Tlatelolco, banning nuclear arms in Latin America.

Soccer AP227

Anniversary Emblem — AP228

1977, Aug. 23	**Wmk. 300**			***Perf. 14***	
C534	AP227	1.60p	multi	18	15
C535	AP228	4.30p	blk, bl & yel	28	15

Mexican Soccer Fed., 50th anniv.

Hands and Scales AP229

1977, Sept. 28	**Photo.**			***Perf. 14***	
C536	AP229	1.60p	org, brn & blk	18	15

Federal Council of Reconciliation and Arbitration, 50th anniversary.

Arms of Mexico and Spain AP230

Designs: 1.90p, Maps of Mexico and Spain. 4.30p, Pres. Jose Lopez Portillo and King Juan Carlos.

1977, Oct. 8				***Perf. 14***	
C537	AP230	1.60p	dl bl & blk	18	15
C538	AP230	1.90p	lt grn & mar	22	15
C539	AP230	4.30p	tan, grn & brn	22	15

Resumption of diplomatic relations with Spain.

Tlaloc, the Rain God AP231

Ludwig van Beethoven AP232

Wmk. 300

1977, Nov. 4	**Photo.**			***Perf. 14***	
C540	AP231	1.60p	multi	18	15

National Central Observatory, centenary.

1977, Nov. 12				**Photo.**	
C541	AP232	1.60p	brt grn & brn	15	15
C542	AP232	4.30p	lil rose & bl	25	15

The indexes in each volume of the Scott Catalogue contain many listings which help to identify stamps.

Tractor and Dam AP233

1977, Nov. 25 Photo. *Perf. 14*

C543 AP233 1.60p multi 18 15

United Nations Desertification Conference.

Mexico City-Cuernavaca Highway — AP234

1977, Nov. 30

C544 AP234 1.60p multi 18 15

25th anniversary of first national highway.

Arms of Campeche — AP235

1977, Dec. 3

C545 AP235 1.60p multi 18 15

200th anniv. of the naming of Campeche.

Congress Emblem AP236

1977, Dec. 9

C546 AP236 1.60p multi 18 15

20th World Congress for Education, Hygiene and Recreation, July 18-24, 1977.

Freighter Navimex AP237

1977, Dec. 16

C547 AP237 1.60p multi 18 15

60th anniv. of National Merchant Marine.

Mayan Dancer, Jaina — AP238

Pre-Columbian Sculptures: No. C549, Aztec dance god. No. C550, Snake dancer, bas-relief. No. C551, Monte Alban, bas-relief. No. C552, Totonaca figurine.

1977, Dec. 26 *Perf. 14*

C548 AP238 1.60p sal, blk & car 15 15
C549 AP238 1.60p lt & dk bl & blk 15 15
C550 AP238 1.60p yel, blk & gray 15 15
C551 AP238 1.60p bl grn, blk & grn 15 15
C552 AP238 1.60p gray, blk & red brn 15 15
Nos. C548-C552 (5) 75
Set value 25

Mexican art.

Tumor Clinic, by David A. Siqueiros — AP239

Design: 4.30p, La Raza Medical Center, by Diego Rivera.

1978, Jan. 19 Photo. Wmk. 300

C553 AP239 1.60p multi 18 15
C554 AP239 4.30p multi 28 15

35th anniversary of Mexican Social Security Institute.

Moorish Fountain — AP240

1978, Mar. 1 Photo. *Perf. 14*

C555 AP240 1.60p multi 18 15

450th anniversary of the founding of Chiapa de Corzo, Chiapas.

Oil Industry Type of 1978

Designs: 1.60p, Gen. Lazaro Cardenas. 4.30p, Offshore oil rig.

Wmk. 300

1978, Mar. 18 Photo. *Perf. 14*

C556 A343 1.60p brt bl & lil rose 18 15
C557 A343 4.30p bl, brt bl & blk 28 15

Oil industry nationalization, 40th anniv.

Arms of Diego de Mazariegos AP241

Wmk. 300

1978, Apr. 3 Photo. *Perf. 14*

C558 AP241 1.60p pink, blk & pur 18 15

400th anniversary of the founding of San Cristobal de las Casas, Chiapas, by Diego de Mazariegos.

Blood Pressure Gauge, Map of Mexico AP242

Globe, Snake, Hand Holding Stethoscope AP243

1978, Apr. 30

C559 AP242 1.60p dk bl & car 18 15
C560 AP243 4.30p org & dk bl 28 15

Drive against hypertension and World Health Day.

X-ABC1 Plane AP244

1978, Mar. 15

C561 AP244 1.60p ultra & multi 18 15
C562 AP244 4.30p ultra & multi 28 15

1st Mexican airmail route, 50th anniv.

Globe, Cogwheel, UN Emblem — AP245

Design: 4.30p, Globe, flags, cogwheel, UN emblem.

1978, Apr. 21

C563 AP245 1.60p multi 18 15
C564 AP245 4.30p multi 28 15

World Conference on Technical Cooperation of Underdeveloped Countries.

Soccer — AP246

Designs: 1.90p, Goalkeeper catching ball. 4.30p, Soccer player.

Wmk. 300

1978, June 1 Photo. *Perf. 14*

C565 AP246 1.60p multi 15 15
C566 AP246 1.90p multi 15 15
C567 AP246 4.30p multi 28 15

11th World Cup Soccer Championship, Argentina, June 1-25.

Francisco (Pancho) Villa AP247

1978, June 5

C568 AP247 1.60p multi 18 15

Pancho Villa (1878-1923), revolutionary leader, birth centenary.

Mexico No. C6, Independence Monument, Washington Monument — A248

1978, June 11

C569 AP248 1.60p ol gray & red 18 15

50th anniversary of flight Mexico to Washington by Emilio Carranza (1905-1928).

Woman and Calendar Stone — AP249

Wmk. 300

1978, July 15 Photo. *Perf. 14*

C570 AP249 1.60p rose, blk & brn 18 15
C571 AP249 1.90p brt grn, blk & brn 18 15
C572 AP249 4.30p org, blk & brn 28 15

Miss Universe contest, Acapulco, July 1978.

Alvaro Obregon AP250

1978, July 17

C573 AP250 1.60p multi 18 15

Obregón (1880-1928), president of Mexico.

Geographical Institute Type of 1978

Designs: Institute emblem in different arrangements.

1978, July 21 Photo. Wmk. 300

C574 A344 1.60p emer & blk 18 15
C575 A344 4.30p ocher & blk 28 15

Pan-American Institute for Geography and History, 50th anniversary.

Sun Rising over Obregon AP251

1978, Aug. 4 ***Perf. 14***
C576 AP251 1.60p multi 18 15

50th anniv. of the founding of Obregon.

Mayan Figure, Castle and Pawn AP252

Aristotle (384-322 B.C.), Philosopher AP253

1978, Aug. 19 **Photo.** ***Perf. 14***
C577 AP252 1.60p multi 18 15
C578 AP252 4.30p multi 28 15

World Youth Team Chess Championship, Ajedrez, Aug. 19-Sept. 7.

1978, Aug. 25

Design: 4.30p, Statue of Aristotle.

C579 AP253 1.60p multi 18 15
C580 AP253 4.30p multi 28 15

Mule Deer AP254

Man's Head, Dove, UN Emblem AP255

1978, Sept. 8 **Photo.** **Wmk. 300**
C581 AP254 1.60p shown 18 15
C582 AP254 1.60p Ocelot 18 15
Set value 24

Protected animals.

1978, Sept. 22 ***Perf. 14***

Design: 4.30p, Woman's head, dove, UN emblem.

C583 AP255 1.60p ver, gray & blk 18 15
C584 AP255 4.30p lil, gray & blk 28 15

Anti-Apartheid Year.

Emblem — AP256

Wmk. 300
1978, Oct. 23 **Photo.** ***Perf. 14***
C585 AP256 1.60p multi 18 15

13th Congress of International Union of Architects, Mexico City, Oct. 23-27.

Dr. Rafael Lucio (1819-1886) AP257

Franz Schubert, "Death and the Maiden" AP258

1978, Nov. 13 **Wmk. 350**
C586 AP257 1.60p yel grn 18 15

11th International Anti-Leprosy Congress.

1978, Nov. 19 **Photo.** ***Perf. 14***
C587 AP258 4.30p brn, grn & blk 28 15

Schubert (1797-1828), Austrian composer.

Children, Christmas Decorations AP259

Antonio Vivaldi AP260

Wmk. 350
1978, Nov. 22 **Photo.** ***Perf. 14***
C588 AP259 1.60p multi 18 15

Christmas 1978.

1978, Dec. 1
C589 AP260 4.30p multi 28 15

Antonio Vivaldi (1675-1741), Italian violinist and composer.

Wright Brothers' Flyer AP261

Design: 4.30p, Flyer, different view.

1978, Dec. 17
C590 AP261 1.60p multi 18 15
C591 AP261 4.30p multi 28 15

75th anniversary of 1st powered flight.

Einstein and his Equation AP262

Wmk. 300
1979, Apr. 20 **Photo.** ***Perf. 14***
C592 AP262 1.60p multi 18 15

Albert Einstein (1879-1955), theoretical physicist.

Rowland Hill — AP263

1979, Apr. 27
C593 AP263 1.60p multi 18 15

Sir Rowland Hill (1795-1879), originator of penny postage.

Export Type of 1975

Designs: Export Emblem and 50c, Circuit board. 1.60p, Bicycle. 1.90p, Oil valves. 2.50p, Tomato. 4p, Honey. 5p, Motor vehicles. 10p, Citrus fruit. 50p, Cotton thread.

1979-81 **Photo.** **Wmk. 300**
C594 AP214 50c ocher & red brn 15 15
C596 AP214 1.60p blk & org 20 15
C597 AP214 1.90p ver & dk grn ('81) 45 40
C599 AP214 2.50p ver & grn 15 15
C600 AP214 4p yel bis & brn ('81) 35 25
C601 AP214 5p dk bl & dl org 1.50 50
C602 AP214 10p grn & yel grn ('81) 90 75
C603 AP214 50p multi 2.50 1.50
Nos. C594-C603 (8) 6.20 3.85

No. C600 exists with brown omitted.

Children, Child's Drawing — AP264

1979, May 16
C604 AP264 1.60p multi 15 15

International Year of the Child.

Registered Letter from Mexico to Rome, 1860 — AP265

Wmk. 300
1979, June 7 **Photo.** ***Perf. 14***
C605 AP265 1.60p multi 15 15

MEPSIPEX '79, 3rd International Exhibition of Elmhurst Philatelic Society, Mexico City, June 7-10.

Sports Type of 1979

Designs: 1.60p, Games emblem. 4.30p, Symbolic flame and birds. 10p, Women gymnasts (horiz.).

1979, June 15
C606 A348 1.60p multi 18 15
C607 A348 4.30p multi 28 15

Souvenir Sheet
Imperf

C608 A348 10p multi 1.00

No. C608 has simulated perforations.

University Type of 1979

Paintings: 1.60p, The Return of Quetzalcoatl, by Chavez Morado. 4.30p, Students Reaching for Culture, by Alfaro Siqueiros.

1979, July 10 ***Perf. 14***
C609 A350 1.60p multi 15 15
C610 A350 4.30p multi 28 15

Messenger and UPU Emblem AP266

1979, July 27 **Photo.** **Wmk. 300**
C611 AP266 1.60p multi 18 15

Cent. of Mexico's membership in UPU.

Sports Type of 1979

Designs: 1.60p, Tennis. 5.50p, Swimming. 10p, Various sports.

1979, Sept. 2 **Wmk. 300** ***Perf. 14***
C612 A352 1.60p multi 15 15
C613 A352 5.50p multi 28 15

Souvenir Sheet
Imperf

C614 A352 10p multi 1.10

Tourism Type of 1979

Designs: No. C615, Agua Azul Waterfall, Chiapas. No. C616, King Coliman statue, Colima.

Wmk. 300
1979, Sept. 28 **Photo.** ***Perf. 14***
C615 A353 1.60p multi 18 15
C616 A353 1.60p multi 18 15
Set value 24

Graphic Design AP267

1979, Oct. 14 **Photo.** **Wmk. 300**
C617 AP267 1.60p multi 18 15

ICSID, 11th Congress and Assembly of the Intl. Industrial Design Council, Oct. 1979.

Mail Service Type of 1979

Designs: 1.60p, Martin Enriquez de Almanza, Viceroy of New Spain. 5.50p, King Philip II of Spain. 10p, Sailing ship (horiz.).

1979
C618 A354 1.60p multi 15 15
C619 A354 5.50p multi 30 20

Souvenir Sheet
Imperf

C620 A354 10p multi 90 90

No. C620 contains stamp with simulated perforations.

Early Lamp — AP268

1979, Oct. 21 **Wmk. 300**
C621 AP268 1.60p multi 18 15

Centenary of invention of electric light.

Union Emblem AP269

Wmk. 300

1979, Nov. 12 Photo. ***Perf. 14***
C622 AP269 1.60p multi 18 15

Latin American Universities Union, 8th general assembly.

Christmas Type of 1979

Design: 1.60p, Girl and Christmas tree.

1979, Nov. 15
C623 A355 1.60p multi 18 15

Moon Symbol from Mexican Codex AP270

1979, Nov. 30
C624 AP270 2.50p multi 18 15

Apollo 11 moon landing, 10th anniversary.

Monument Type of 1980

Stone Sculptures: 1.60p, Tlaloc, water god. 5.50p, Coyolxauqui, goddess.

1980, Feb. 16 Photo. ***Perf. 14x14½***
C625 A356 1.60p multi 18 15
C626 A356 5.50p multi 28 20

16th Century Church, Acolman AP271

16th Century Churches in: No. C628, Actopan Convent. No. C629, Tlayacapan. No. C630, Yanhuitlan. No. C631, Yuriria. No. C628 actually shows Tlayacapan; No. C629, Actopan convent (inscriptions reversed).

1980
C627 AP271 1.60p multi 15 15
C628 AP271 1.60p multi 15 15
C629 AP271 1.60p multi 15 15
C630 AP271 1.60p multi 15 15
C631 AP271 1.60p multi 15 15
Nos. C627-C631 (5) 75
Set value 60

Flora and Fauna Types of 1980

Designs: No. C632, Flamingo. No. C633, Vanilla plant.

1980, Mar. 8 ***Perf. 14***
C632 A357 1.60p multi 15 15
C633 A358 1.60p multi 15 15
Set value 24

Jules Verne AP272

Perf. 14x14½
1980, Mar. 24 Photo. Wmk. 300
C634 AP272 5.50p blk & red brn 30 15

Jules Verne (1828-1905) French science fiction writer.

Skeleton Smoking Cigar, UN Emblem AP273

1980, Apr. 7 ***Perf. 14x14½***
C635 AP273 1.60p multi 18 15

World Health Day/Fight against cigarette smoking.

Costume Type

1980, Apr. 26 ***Perf. 14***
C636 A359 1.60p Chiapaneca, Chiapas 18 15

AIR POST OFFICIAL STAMPS

Nos. C4 and C3 Overprinted in Black or Red **OFICIAL.**

1929 Wmk. 156 ***Perf. 12***
CO1 AP1 25c dk grn & gray brn 2.50 3.00
a. Without period 10.00 10.00
CO2 AP1 25c dk grn & gray brn (R) 2.50 3.50
a. Without period 12.00 14.00
CO2B AP1 25c brn car & gray brn 7.00 8.50
c. Without period 15.00 17.50

Types of Regular Issue of 1926 Overprinted in Red **HABILITADO Servicio Oficial Aereo**

1929, Oct. 15 Unwmk.
CO3 A90 2c black 42.50 42.50
CO4 A91 4c black 42.50 42.50
CO5 A90 5c black 42.50 42.50
CO6 A91 10c black 42.50 42.50
CO7 A92 20c black 42.50 42.50
CO8 A92 30c black 42.50 42.50
CO9 A92 40c black 42.50 42.50
Nos. CO3-CO9 (7) 297.50 297.50

Horizontal Overprint
CO10 A93 1p black *1,500. 1,500.*

Nos. CO3-CO9 also exist with overprint reading up.

No. C26 Overprinted in Black **OFICIAL.**

1930 Wmk. 156
CO11 AP4 20c blk vio 75 *1.25*
a. Without period 12.00 *14.00*
b. Inverted overprint 10.00 *14.00*
c. As "a," inverted overprint 125.00

No. CO11 with red overprint is believed not to have been issued for postal purposes.

Plane over Mexico City OA1

1930 Engr.
CO12 OA1 20c gray blk 4.50 4.50
CO13 OA1 35c lt vio 85 *1.50*
CO14 OA1 40c ol brn & dp bl 1.00 *1.40*
CO15 OA1 70c vio & ol gray 1.00 *1.50*

No. CO12 Surcharged in Red

HABILITADO Quince centavos

1931
CO16 OA1 15c on 20c gray blk 65 *1.00*
a. Inverted surcharge 125.00
b. Double surcharge 125.00

No. C20 Overprinted **OFICIAL.**

1932 ***Rouletted 13, 13½***
CO17 AP3 5c lt bl 65 75

Air Post Stamps of 1927-32 Overprinted

SERVICIO OFICIAL

On No. C1a

1932 Unwmk. ***Perf. 12***
CO18 AP1 50c dk bl & cl 650.00 650.00

On Nos. C2, C2a
Wmk. 156
CO19 AP1 50c dk bl & red brn 1.00 *1.25*
a. 50c dark blue & claret 1.25 *1.50*

See note after No. C2.

On Nos. C11 and C12

1932 ***Perf. 12***
CO20 AP3 10c violet 15.00 18.00
CO21 AP3 15c carmine 225.00 250.00

On Nos. C21 to C23
Rouletted 13, 13½
CO22 AP3 10c violet 25 *40*
CO23 AP3 15c carmine 1.00 *1.40*
CO24 AP3 20c brn olive 1.00 *1.40*

Nos. C20, C21 C23 and C25 Overprinted **SERVICIO OFICIAL**

1933-34 ***Rouletted 13½***
CO25 AP3 5c light blue 25 *40*
CO26 AP3 10c vio ('34) 25 *60*
CO27 AP3 20c brn olive 50 *75*
CO28 AP3 50c red brn ('34) 65 *1.50*

On No. C2
Perf. 12
CO29 AP1 50c dk bl & red brn 1.00 *1.40*
a. 50c dark blue & claret 1.50 *2.00*

On No. C11
Perf. 12
CO30 AP3 10c vio ('34) 100.00 *125.00*
a. Double overprint *300.00*

SPECIAL DELIVERY STAMPS

Motorcycle Postman SD1

1919 Unwmk. Engr. ***Perf. 12***
E1 SD1 20c red & black 50.00 2.25

1923 Wmk. 156
E2 SD1 20c blk car & blk 25 20

For overprint see No. E7

Toltec Messenger with Quipu SD2

1934
E3 SD2 10c brn red & blue 25 40

Indian Archer — SD3

Imprint: "Oficina Impresora de Hacienda Mexico."

1934 ***Perf. 10x10½***
E4 SD3 10c blk vio 1.25 40

See Nos. E5-E6, E8-E9.

Redrawn
Imprint: "Talleres de Imp. de Est. y Valores-Mexico."

1938-41 Photo. ***Perf. 14***
E5 SD3 10c slate violet 60 20
E6 SD3 20c orange red ('41) 40 15

Imperforate copies of No. E6 were not regularly issued.

No. E2 Overprinted "1940" in Violet

1940 Engr. ***Perf. 12***
E7 SD1 20c red & black 32 16

Redrawn Archer Type of 1941

1944-47 Wmk. 272 Photo. ***Perf. 14***
E8 SD3 20c org red 1.10 20

Wmk. 279
E9 SD3 20c org red ('47) 1.40 20

Special Delivery Messenger SD4

Messengers' Hands Transferring Letter — SD5

1950-51 Photo. Wmk. 279
E10 SD4 25c bright red 30 15
E11 SD5 60c dk bl grn ('51) 1.75 75

Redrawn

1951

E12 SD4 25c bright red 24.00 3.00

Sharper Impression, heavier shading; motorcycle sidecar ½mm from "s" of "centavos;" imprint wider, beginning under "n" of "inmediata."

Second Redrawing

1952

E13 SD4 25c bright red 7.00 1.00

Design 35½mm wide (33mm on Nos. E10 and E12); finer lettering at left, and height of letters in imprint reduced 50 per cent; three distinct lines in tires.

Redrawn Type of 1951

1954 **Wmk. 300**

E14 SD4 25c red orange 40 15

Type of 1951

1954

E15 SD5 60c dk bl grn 50 *1.00*

Hands and Pigeon SD6

Plane Circling Globe SD7

1956 **Wmk. 300** **Photo.** ***Perf. 14***

E16 SD6 35c red lilac 20 15
E17 SD7 80c henna brown 30 *1.25*

1962

E18 SD6 50c green 70 15
E19 SD7 1.20p dark purple 1.10 *1.25*

1964 **Wmk. 350**

E20 SD6 50c green 60 15
E21 SD7 1.20p dk pur 1.25 90

Catalogue values for unused stamps in this section, from this point to the end of the section, are for Never Hinged items.

1973 **Unwmk.**

E22 SD6 50c green 3.50 3.25

Fluorescent printing on front or back consists of beehive pattern and diagonal inscription.

1975 **Wmk. 300**

E23 SD6 2p orange 20 *1.00*
E24 SP7 5p vio bl 1.25 90

1976 **Unwmk.**

E25 SD6 2p red org 25 40
E26 SD7 5p dk vio bl 35 1.00

Watch — SD8

1976 **Unwmk.** **Photo.** ***Perf. 14***

E27 SD8 2p org & blk 15 *1.00*

INSURED LETTER STAMPS

Insured Letters — IL1

Registered Mailbag — IL2

Safe — IL3

1935 **Engr.** **Wmk. 156** ***Perf. 10½***

G1 IL1 10c vermilion 1.75 75
a. Perf. 10x10½
G2 IL2 50c dk bl 1.25 60
G3 IL3 1p turq grn 1.25 85

Nos. G1 and G4 were issued both with and without imprint.

1944-45 **Wmk. 272** ***Perf. 10x10½***

G4 IL1 10c ver ('45) 9.50 1.50
G5 IL2 50c dk bl 1.40 50
G6 IL3 1p turq grn 2.50 65

1947 **Wmk. 279** ***Perf. 10x10½***

G7 IL1 10c vermilion 8.00 85
G8 IL2 50c dark blue 10.00 1.50
G9 IL3 1p turq grn 3.50 1.00

Vault — IL4

1950-51 **Photo.** ***Perf. 14***

G10 IL4 20c blue 2.00 45
G11 IL4 40c purple 30 20
G12 IL4 1p yel grn ('51) 65 50
G13 IL4 5p dk bl & gray grn ('51) 1.00 1.00
G14 IL4 10p car & ultra ('51) 4.00 4.00
Nos. G10-G14 (5) 7.95 6.15

1954-71 **Wmk. 300**

G15 IL4 20c bl ('56) 20 15
G16 IL4 40c lt pur ('56) 20 15
G17 IL4 1p yel grn 30 20
a. Size: 37x20¼mm ('71) 1.10 1.10
G18 IL4 5p bl grn ('59) 1.00 1.00
G19 IL4 10p car & ultra ('63) 4.75 2.50
Nos. G15-G19 (5) 6.45 4.00

No. G17 measures 35x19½mm. Vertical measurement excludes imprint.

Catalogue values for unused stamps in this section, from this point to the end of the section, are for Never Hinged items.

1967 **Wmk. 350** ***Perf. 14***

G21 IL4 40c light purple 1.25 1.50
G22 IL4 1p yellow green 1.25 1.50

1975 **Photo.** **Wmk. 300**

G23 IL4 2p lilac rose 30 30
G24 IL4 20p orange & gray 1.80 3.00

Padlock — IL5

1976-81 **Unwmk.** **Photo.** ***Perf. 14***

G25 IL5 40c black & blue 15 15
G26 IL5 1p black & blue 15 15
G26A IL5 2p blk & bl ('81) 15 15
G27 IL5 5p black & blue 15 15
G28 IL5 10p black & blue 15 15
G28A IL5 20p black & blue 30 30
Set value 65 65

1979 **Photo.** **Wmk. 300**

G29 IL5 40c black & blue 15 40
G30 IL5 1p black & blue 15 20
G31 IL5 5p black & blue 15 40
G32 IL5 10p black & blue 15 20
G33 IL5 20p black & blue 50 65
Nos. G29-G33 (5) 1.10 1.85

Perf. 14½x14

1983-86 **Photo.** **Unwmk.**

Size of Lock: 20x31mm

G36 IL5 5p black & blue 45 40
G37 IL5 10p black & blue 45 40
G38 IL5 20p black & blue 80 80
G39 IL5 50p black & blue 1.50 1.50
G40 IL5 100p blk & bl ('86) 1.00 1.00
Nos. G36-G40 (5) 4.20 4.10

This is an expanding set. Numbers will change if necessary.

POSTAGE DUE STAMPS

D1

1908 **Engr.** **Wmk. 155** ***Perf. 14***

J1 D1 1c blue 1.00 1.00
J2 D1 2c blue 1.00 1.00
J3 D1 4c blue 1.00 1.00
J4 D1 5c blue 1.00 1.00
J5 D1 10c blue 1.00 1.00
Nos. J1-J5 (5) 5.00 5.00

For overprints and surcharges see Nos. 381-385, 434-438, 466-470, 495-499, 593-607.

PORTE DE MAR STAMPS

These stamps were used to indicate the amount of cash to be paid to the captains of the mail steamers taking outgoing foreign mail.

PM2

PM3

1875 **Unwmk.** **Litho.** ***Imperf.***

JX9 PM2 2c black 60 *50.00*
a. "5" added to make 25c 12.00 *100.00*
JX10 PM2 10c black 80 *30.00*
JX11 PM2 12c black 80 *50.00*
JX12 PM2 20c black 1.00 *50.00*
JX13 PM2 25c black 3.25 *50.00*
JX14 PM2 35c black 3.25 *60.00*
JX15 PM2 50c black 3.00 *60.00*
JX16 PM2 60c black 3.00 *75.00*
JX17 PM2 75c black 3.50 *75.00*
JX18 PM2 85c black 3.25 *100.00*
JX19 PM2 100c black 4.00 *100.00*
Nos. JX9-JX19 (11) 26.45

Same, Numerals Larger

JX20 PM2 5c black 1.00 *50.00*
JX21 PM2 25c black 1.65 *50.00*
JX22 PM2 35c black 175.00
JX23 PM2 50c black 1.00 *50.00*
JX24 PM2 60c black 65.00
JX25 PM2 100c black 60 *100.00*
Nos. JX20-JX25 (6) 244.25

In Nos. JX9-JX19 the figures of value are 7mm high and "CENTAVOS" is 7½mm long. On Nos. JX20-JX25 the figures of value are 8mm high and "CENTAVOS" is 9½mm long.

Nos. JX9-JX25 exist with overprints of district names.

Counterfeits exist of Nos. JX9-JX31.

1879

JX26 PM3 2c brown 50
JX27 PM3 5c yellow 50
JX28 PM3 10c red 50
JX29 PM3 25c blue 50
JX30 PM3 50c green 50
JX31 PM3 100c violet 50
Nos. JX26-JX31 (6) 3.00

Nos. JX26 to JX31 were never put in use.

Stamps of this design were never issued. Copies appeared on the market in 1884. Value, set, $22.

All were printed in same sheet of 49 (7x7). Sheet consists of 14 of 10c; 7 each of 25c, 35c, 50c; 4 each of 60c, 85c; 3 each of 75c, 100c. There are four varieties of 10c, two of 25c, 35c and 50c.

OFFICIAL STAMPS

Hidalgo — O1

Wove or Laid Paper

1884-93 **Unwmk.** **Engr.** ***Perf. 11, 12***

O1 O1 red 70 50
a. Vert. pair, imperf. betwn. 90.00
O2 O1 olive brn ('87) 45 30
a. Blue ruled lines on paper
O3 O1 orange 1.25 45
a. Vert. pair, imperf. betwn. 80.00
O4 O1 blue grn ('93) 70 40
a. Imperf., pair 10.00 8.00

Pin-perf. 6

O5 O1 olive brown 40.00 16.00

Wmk. "Correos E U M" on every Vertical Line of Ten Stamps (152)

1894 ***Perf. 5½***

O6 O1 ultra 1.50 1.40
a. Vert. pair, imperf. horiz. 30.00
b. Imperf., pair 40.00

Perf. 11 and 12

O7 O1 ultra 90 80

Perf. 5½x11, 11x5½

O9 O1 ultra 6.00 4.00

Regular Issues with Handstamped Overprint in Black **OFICIAL**

1895 ***Perf. 12***

O10 A20 1c green 6.00 2.00
O11 A20 2c carmine 7.00 2.00
O12 A20 3c org brn 6.00 2.00
O13 A21 4c red org 9.00 4.00
a. 4c orange 14.00 5.00

O14 A22 5c ultra 12.00 4.00
O15 A23 10c lil rose 11.00 1.00
O16 A21 12c ol brn 24.00 10.00
O17 A23 15c brt bl 14.00 6.00
O18 A23 20c brn rose 14.00 6.00
O19 A23 50c purple 30.00 15.00
O20 A24 1p brown 75.00 30.00
O21 A24 5p scarlet 175.00 90.00
O22 A24 10p deep blue 300.00 165.00

Similar stamps with red overprint were not officially placed in use.

Black Overprint

1896-97 Wmk. 153

O23 A20 1c green 20.00 3.50
O24 A20 2c carmine 20.00 4.00
O25 A20 3c org brn 20.00 4.00
O26 A21 4c red org 20.00 4.00
a. 4c orange 25.00 7.50
O27 A22 5c ultra 20.00 4.00
O28 A21 12c ol brn 30.00 10.00
O29 A23 15c brt bl 35.00 15.00
O29A A23 50c purple 275.00 275.00
Nos. O23-O29A (8) 440.00 319.50

Black Overprint

1897 Wmk. 154

O30 A20 1c green 35.00 10.00
O31 A20 2c scarlet 30.00 12.00
O33 A21 4c orange 45.00 20.00
O34 A22 5c ultra 35.00 12.00
O35 A21 12c ol brn 45.00 15.00
O36 A23 15c brt bl 60.00 15.00
O37 A23 20c brn rose 40.00 6.00
O38 A23 50c purple 50.00 10.00
O39 A24 1p brown 125.00 40.00
Nos. O30-O39 (9) 465.00 140.00

Black Overprint

1898 Unwmk.

O40 A20 1c green 12.00 3.00
O41 A20 2c scarlet 12.00 3.00
O42 A20 3c org brn 12.00 3.00
O43 A21 4c orange 20.00 4.00
O44 A22 5c ultra 20.00 7.00
O45 A23 10c lil rose 260.00 175.00
O46 A21 12c ol brn 45.00 10.00
O47 A23 15c brt bl 45.00 10.00
O48 A23 20c brn rose 75.00 25.00
O48A A23 50c purple 125.00 50.00
Nos. O40-O48A (10) 626.00 290.00

The 10p unwatermarked exists.

Black Overprint

1900 Wmk. 155 *Perf. 14, 15*

O49 A25 1c green 15.00 1.00
O50 A26 2c vermilion 20.00 1.50
O51 A27 3c yel brn 20.00 1.00
O52 A28 5c dk bl 20.00 1.75
O53 A29 10c vio & org 25.00 2.25
O54 A30 15c lav & cl 25.00 2.25
O55 A31 20c rose & dk bl 30.00 1.00
O56 A32 50c red lil & blk 60.00 10.00
O57 A33 1p bl & blk 125.00 10.00
O58 A34 5p car & blk 250.00 30.00
Nos. O49-O58 (10) 590.00 60.75

Black Overprint

1903

O59 A25 1c violet 14.00 1.50
O60 A26 2c green 14.00 1.50
O61 A35 4c carmine 25.00 1.00
O62 A28 5c orange 25.00 5.00
O63 A29 10c bl & org 30.00 1.50
O64 A32 50c car & blk 75.00 10.00
Nos. O59-O64 (6) 183.00 20.50

Regular Issues Overprinted OFICIAL

On Issues of 1899-1903

1910

O65 A26 2c green 70.00 2.50
O66 A27 3c org brn 70.00 1.75
O67 A35 4c carmine 85.00 4.00
O68 A28 5c orange 90.00 20.00
O69 A29 10c bl & org 80.00 1.50
O70 A30 15c lav & cl 90.00 2.50
O71 A31 20c rose & dk bl 110.00 1.20
O72 A32 50c car & blk 150.00 14.00
O73 A33 1p bl & blk 275.00 50.00
O74 A34 5p car & blk 80.00 50.00
Nos. O65-O74 (10) 1,100. 147.45

On Issue of 1910

1911

O75 A36 1c violet 2.00 2.00
O76 A37 2c green 1.50 90
O77 A38 3c org brn 2.00 1.00
O78 A39 4c carmine 3.00 90
O79 A40 5c orange 5.00 2.75
O80 A41 10c bl & org 3.00 1.00
O81 A42 15c gray bl & cl 5.00 3.25
O82 A43 20c red & blue 4.00 1.00
O83 A44 50c red brn & blk 14.00 6.00
O84 A45 1p blue & blk 24.00 10.00
O85 A46 5p car & blk 90.00 50.00
Nos. O75-O85 (11) 153.50 78.80

Nos. 500 to 505 Overprinted OFICIAL

1915 Unwmk. *Rouletted 14½*

O86 A57 1c violet 50 1.00
O87 A58 2c green 50 1.00
O88 A59 3c brown 60 1.00
O89 A60 4c carmine 50 1.00
O90 A61 5c orange 50 1.00
O91 A62 10c ultra 60 1.00
Nos. O86-O91 (6) 3.20 6.00

All values are known with inverted overprint. All values exist imperforate and part perforate but were not regularly issued in these forms.

On Nos. 506 to 514

1915-16 *Perf. 12*

O92 A57 1c violet 50 1.00
O93 A58 2c green 50 1.00
O94 A59 3c brown 50 1.00
O95 A60 4c carmine 50 1.00
a. "CEATRO" 7.00 15.00
O96 A61 5c orange 50 1.00
O97 A62 10c ultra, type II 50 1.00
a. Double overprint 12.00
O98 A63 40c slate 4.00 6.00
a. Inverted overprint 12.00 10.00
b. Double overprint 20.00
O99 A64 1p brn & blk 5.00 6.00
a. Inverted overprint 14.00 14.00
O100 A65 5p cl & ultra 30.00 25.00
a. Inverted overprint 40.00
Nos. O92-O100 (9) 42.00 43.00

Nos. O98 and O99 exist imperforate but probably were not issued in that form.

Preceding Issues Overprinted in Red, Blue or Black G.P.DE M.

On No. O74

1916 Wmk. 155

O101 A34 5p car & blk 650.00

On Nos. O75 to O85

O102 A36 1c violet 3.00
O103 A37 2c green 60
O104 A38 3c org brn (Bl) 75
O105 A39 4c car (Bl) 3.25
O106 A40 5c org (Bl) 75
O107 A41 10c bl & org 75
O108 A42 15c gray bl & cl (Bk) 75
O109 A43 20c red & bl (Bk) 85
O110 A44 50c red brn & blk 90.00
O111 A45 1p bl & blk 5.00
O112 A46 5p car & blk *2,500.*
Nos. O102-O111 (10) 105.70

No. O102 with blue overprint is a trial color. Counterfeits exist of Nos. O110, O112.

Nos. 608, 610 to 612, 615 and 616 Overprinted Vertically in Red or Black OFICIAL

Thick Paper

1918 Unwmk. *Rouletted 14½*

O113 A68 1c vio (R) 25.00 14.00
O114 A69 2c gray grn (R) 27.50 15.00
O115 A70 3c bis brn (R) 25.00 14.00
O116 A71 4c car (Bk) 25.00 15.00
O117 A74 20c rose (Bk) 50.00 40.00
O118 A75 30c gray brn (R) 80.00 70.00

On Nos. 622-623

Medium Paper

Perf. 12

O119 A72 5c ultra (R) 17.50 17.50
O120 A73 10c bl (R) 15.00 10.00
a. Double overprint 200.00
Nos. O113-O120 (8) 265.00 195.50

Overprinted Horizontally in Red OFICIAL

On Nos. 626-628

Thin Paper

O121 A63 40c vio (R) 14.00 12.00
O122 A64 1p bl & blk (R) 35.00 30.00
O123 A65 5p grn & blk (R) *225.00 250.00*

Nos. 608 and 610 to 615 Overprinted Vertically Up in Red or Black OFICIAL

Thick Paper

1919 *Rouletted 14½*

O124 A68 1c dl vio (R) 2.50 2.50
a. "OFICIAN" 30.00 30.00
O125 A69 2c gray grn (R) 4.00 1.50
a. "OFICIAN" 30.00 30.00
O126 A70 3c bis brn (R) 6.00 2.50
a. "OFICIAN" 40.00 40.00
O127 A71 4c car (Bk) 12.00 5.50
O127A A72 5c ultra 70.00 50.00
b. "OFICIAN"
O128 A73 10c bl (R) 4.00 1.00
a. "OFICIAN" 35.00 20.00
O129 A74 20c rose (Bk) 25.00 20.00
a. "OFICIAN" 60.00

On Nos. 618, 622

Perf. 12

O130 A68 1c dl vio (R) 20.00 20.00
a. "OFICIAN" 60.00 40.00
O131 A72 5c ultra (R) 20.00 9.00
a. "OFICIAN" 60.00 40.00

Overprinted Horizontally On Nos. 626-627

Thin Paper

O132 A63 40c vio (R) 20.00 14.00
O133 A64 1p bl & blk (R) 12.00 10.00
Nos. O124-O133 (11) 195.50 136.00

Nos. 608 to 615 and 617 Overprinted Vertically down in Black, Red or Blue OFICIAL

Size: 17½x3mm

1921 *Rouletted 14½*

O134 A68 1c gray (Bk) 12.00 5.00
a. 1c dull violet (Bk) 7.00 3.00
O135 A69 2c gray grn (R) 2.00 1.20
O136 A70 3c bis brn (R) 3.50 1.25
O137 A71 4c car (Bk) 8.00 6.00
O138 A72 5c ultra (R) 10.00 5.00
O139 A73 10c bl, reading down (R) 12.50 5.00
a. Overprint reading up 25.00 25.00
O140 A74 20c rose (Bl) 20.00 12.00
O141 A75 30c gray blk (R) 10.00 10.00

Overprinted Horizontally On Nos. 626-628

Perf. 12

O142 A63 40c vio (R) 12.50 12.50
O143 A64 1p bl & blk (R) 10.00 10.00
O144 A65 5p grn & blk (Bk) *200.00 200.00*
Nos. O134-O144 (11) *300.50* 267.95

Nos. 609 to 615 Overprinted Vertically in Black OFICIAL.

1921-30 *Rouletted 14½*

O145 A68 1c gray 2.00 1.00
a. 1c lilac gray 40 30
O146 A69 2c gray grn 75 25
O147 A70 3c bis brn 35 25
a. "OFICAL" 20.00 10.00
b. "OIFCIAL" 20.00 10.00
c. Double overprint 60.00
O148 A71 4c carmine 6.00 1.00
O149 A72 5c ultra 40 25
O150 A73 10c blue 40 20
a. "OIFCIAL" 20.00
O151 A74 20c brn rose 4.00 4.00
a. 20c rose 2.00 1.00

On No. 625

Perf. 12

O152 A75 30c gray blk 6.00 2.00

Overprinted Horizontally On Nos. 626, 628

O153 A63 40c violet 3.00 2.00
a. "OFICAL" 25.00 25.00
b. "OICIFAL" 25.00 25.00
c. Inverted overprint 35.00
O154 A65 5p grn & blk ('30) 100.00 *125.00*
Nos. O145-O154 (10) 122.90 *135.95*

Overprinted Vertically in Red On Nos. 609, 610, 611, 613 and 614

1921-24 *Rouletted 14½*

O155 A68 1c lilac 65 40
O156 A69 2c gray grn 60 35
O157 A70 3c bis brn 1.65 40
O158 A72 5c ultra 65 35
O159 A73 10c blue 15.00 1.50
a. Double overprint

On Nos. 624-625

Perf. 12

O160 A74 20c rose 3.00 65
O161 A75 30c gray blk 8.00 2.00

Overprinted Horizontally On Nos. 626-628

O162 A63 40c violet 6.00 3.00
O163 A64 1p bl & blk 15.00 10.00
O164 A65 5p grn & blk 90.00 *150.00*

Overprinted Vertically in Blue on No. 612

Rouletted 14½

O165 A71 4c carmine 3.00 1.50
Nos. O155-O165 (11) 143.55 *170.15*

Same Overprint Vertically in Red or Blue On Nos. 635 and 637

1926-27 *Rouletted 14½*

O166 A80 3c bis brn, ovpt. horiz. (R) 6.00 6.00
a. Period omitted 15.00 15.00
O167 A82 5c org (R) 14.00 15.00

Same Overprint Vertically Down On Nos. 650, 651, 655 and 656

Wmk. 156

O168 A79 2c scar (Bl) 10.00 10.00
a. Overprint reading up 15.00 15.00
O169 A80 3c bis brn, ovpt. horiz. (R) 2.50 2.50
a. Inverted overprint 30.00
O170 A85 10c claret (Bl) 17.50 8.00
O171 A84 20c dp bl (R) 7.00 6.00
a. Overprint reading up 7.00 6.00

Overprinted Horizontally On Nos. 643, 646 to 649

Perf. 12

O172 A81 4c grn (R) 3.00 3.00
O173 A83 30c dk grn (R) 3.00 3.00
O174 A63 40c vio (R) 8.00 8.00
a. Inverted overprint 40.00
O175 A87 50c ol brn (R) 75 75
a. 50c yellow brown (R) 9.00 9.00
O176 A88 1p red brn & bl (R) 7.50 7.50
Nos. O168-O176 (9) 59.25 48.75

Same Overprint Horizontally on No. RA3, Vertically Up on Nos. 650-651, 653-656, 666

1927-31 *Rouletted 14½*

O177 PT1 1c brn ('31) 30 50
O178 A79 2c scarlet 30 50
a. "OFICAIL" 15.00 15.00
b. Overprint reading down 75 1.00
O179 A80 3c bis brn, ovpt. horiz. 1.00 75
a. "OFICAIL" 20.00 15.00
O180 A82 4c green 75 55
a. "OFICAIL" 20.00 20.00
b. Overprint reading down 5.00 1.00
O181 A82 5c orange 2.00 1.50
a. Overprint reading down 2.00 1.25
O182 A94 8c orange 6.00 4.00
a. Overprint reading down 3.50 3.00
O183 A85 10c lake 1.00 1.00
a. Overprint reading down 1.00 1.00
O184 A84 20c dk bl 5.00 4.00
a. "OFICAIL" 20.00 20.00
b. Overprint reading down 10.00 10.00
Nos. O177-O184 (8) 16.35 12.80

Overprinted Horizontally On Nos. 643 and 645 to 649

1927-33 *Perf. 12*

O185 A81 4c green 3.00 2.50
a. Inverted overprint 15.00 15.00
O186 A85 10c brn lake 27.50 27.50
O187 A83 30c dk grn 70 50
a. Inverted overprint 15.00 15.00
b. Pair, tete beche overprints 17.50 17.50
c. "OFICAIL" 17.50 17.50
O188 A63 40c violet 6.00 4.00
O189 A87 50c ol brn ('33) 1.75 2.00
O190 A88 1p red brn & bl 12.00 10.00
Nos. O185-O190 (6) 50.95 46.50

The overprint on No. O186 is vertical.

Nos. 320, 628, 633 Overprinted Horizontally OFICIAL

On Stamp No. 320

1927-28 Wmk. 155 *Perf. 14, 15*

O191 A46 5p car & blk (R) 90.00 *125.00*
O192 A46 5p car & blk (Bl) 90.00 *125.00*

Unwmk. ***Perf. 12***

O193 A65 5p grn & blk (Bk) 85.00 *125.00*
a. Inverted overprint 120.00 *120.00*
O194 A78 10p blk brn & blk (Bl) 100.00 *150.00*

No. 320 Overprinted Horizontally **OFICIAL.**

Wmk. 155 ***Perf. 14***

O195 A46 5p car & blk 150.00

Nos. 650 and 655 Overprinted Horizontally **OFICIAL**

1928-29 Wmk. 156 ***Rouletted 14½***
Size: 16x2½mm

O196 A79 2c dull red 9.00 6.00
O197 A85 10c rose lake 14.00 6.00

Nos. RA1, 650-651, 653-656 Overprinted **SERVICIO OFICIAL**

1932-33

O198 PT1 1c brown 30 50
O199 A79 2c dl red 40 40
O200 A80 3c bis brn 1.50 1.50
O201 A82 4c green 5.00 4.00
O202 A82 5c orange 6.00 4.00
O203 A85 10c rose lake 1.75 1.50
O204 A84 20c dark blue 7.50 5.00
a. Double overprint 75.00 *45.00*
Nos. O198-O204 (7) 22.45 16.90

Nos. 651, 646-649 Overprinted Horizontally **SERVICIO OFICIAL**

1933 ***Rouletted 14½***

O205 A80 3c bis brn 1.50 1.50

Perf. 12

O206 A83 30c dk grn 4.00 1.50
O207 A63 40c violet 7.50 3.00
O208 A87 50c ol brn 1.25 1.50
a. "OFICIAL OFICIAL" 25.00 25.00
O209 A88 1p red brn & bl, type I 1.50 1.50
a. Type II 1.40 1.75

Overprinted Vertically On No. 656
Rouletted 14½

O210 A84 20c dk bl 9.00 5.00
Nos. O205-O210 (6) 24.75 14.00

Nos. RA1, 651, 653, 654, 683 Overprinted Horizontally **OFICIAL**

1934-37 ***Rouletted 14½***
Size: 13x2mm

O211 PT1 1c brown 2.50 3.00
O212 A80 3c bis brn 30 30
O213 A82 4c green 6.00 5.00
O214 A82 5c orange 30 30
O215 A96 15c dk bl ('37) 50 50
Nos. O211-O215 (5) 9.60 9.10

See No. O217a.

Same Overprint on Nos. 687A-692

1934-37 ***Perf. 10½***

O216 PT1 1c brn ('37) 50 60
O217 A79 2c scarlet 50 75
a. On No. 650 (error) 175.00
b. Double overprint 75.00
O218 A82 4c grn ('35) 70 80
O219 A85 10c brn lake 50 50
O220 A84 20c dk bl ('37) 60 60
O221 A83 30c dk bl grn ('37) 1.00 1.00

On Nos. 647 and 649
Perf. 12, 11½x12

O222 A63 40c violet 1.50 1.75
O223 A88 1p red brn & bl (I) 2.50 3.00
a. Type II 2.00 2.00
Nos. O216-O223 (8) 7.80 9.00

On Nos. 707 to 709, 712, 715, 716, 717, 718 and 719

O224 A108 1c orange 1.00 *2.00*
O225 A109 2c green 60 *1.00*
O226 A110 4c carmine 60 *70*
O227 A112 10c violet 60 *1.25*
O228 A114 20c ultra 80 *1.25*
O229 A115 30c lake 1.00 *2.00*
O230 A116 40c red brn 1.25 *2.00*
O231 A117 50c black 1.40 *1.40*
O232 A118 1p dk brn & org 4.00 *6.00*
Nos. O224-O232 (9) 11.25 *17.60*

PARCEL POST STAMPS

Railroad Train — PP1

1941 Photo. Wmk. 156 ***Perf. 14***

Q1 PP1 10c brt rose 2.75 35
Q2 PP1 20c dk vio bl 1.75 35

1944-46 Wmk. 272

Q3 PP1 10c brt rose 1.75 1.00
Q4 PP1 20c dk vio bl ('46) 5.00 2.50

1947-49 Wmk. 279

Q5 PP1 10c brt rose 1.25 60
Q6 PP1 20c dk vio bl ('49) 1.60 60

Streamlined Locomotive — PP2

1951

Q7 PP2 10c rose pink 2.00 40
Q8 PP2 20c bl vio 1.75 70

1954 Wmk. 300

Q9 PP2 10c rose pink 1.25 60
Q10 PP2 20c bl vio 1.25 1.50

POSTAL TAX STAMPS

Morelos Monument — PT1

Rouletted 14½

1925 Engr. Wmk. 156

RA1 PT1 1c brown 35 15
a. Imperf. 30.00

1926 ***Perf. 12***

RA2 PT1 1c brown 75 5.00
a. Booklet pane of 2 12.00

1925 Unwmk. ***Rouletted 14½***

RA3 PT1 1c brown 25.00 9.00

It was obligatory to add a stamp of type PT1 to the regular postage on every article of domestic mail matter. The money obtained from this source formed a fund to combat a plague of locusts.

In 1931, 1c stamps of type PT1 were discontinued as Postal Tax stamps. It was subsequently used for the payment of postage on drop letters (announcement cards and unsealed circulars) to be delivered in the city of cancellation. See No. 687A.

For overprints see Nos. O177, O198, O211, O216, RA4.

Protección a la Infancia

Mother and Child — PT3

Red Overprint

1929 Wmk. 156

RA4 PT1 1c brown 35 15
a. Overprint reading down 40.00 40.00

There were two settings of this overprint. They may be distinguished by the two lines being spaced 4mm or 6mm apart.

The money from sales of this stamp was devoted to child welfare work.

1929 Litho. ***Rouletted 13, 13½***

RA5 PT3 1c violet 25 15

PT4

PT5

1929 Unwmk.
Size: 18x24½mm

RA6 PT4 2c dp grn 40 15
RA7 PT4 5c brown 40 15
a. Imperf., pair 40.00 40.00
Set value 20

For surcharges see Nos. RA10-RA11.

1929 Size: 19x25¼mm

Two types of 1c:

Type I- Background lines continue through lettering of top inscription. Denomination circle hangs below second background line. Paper and gum white.

Type II- Background lines cut away behind some letters. Circle rests on second background line. Paper and gum yellowish.

RA8 PT5 1c vio, type I 15 15
a. Booklet pane of 4 10.00
b. Booklet pane of 2 18.00
c. Type II 40 15
d. Imperf., pair 35.00 35.00
RA9 PT5 2c deep green 40 15
a. Imperf., pair 12.00

The use of these stamps, in addition to the regular postage, was compulsory. The money obtained from their sale was used for child welfare work.

For surcharge see No. RA12.

Nos. RA6, RA7, RA9 Surcharged **HABILITADO $0.01**

1930

RA10 PT4 1c on 2c dp grn 75 40
RA11 PT4 1c on 5c brn 1.00 60
RA12 PT5 1c on 2c dp grn 2.00 1.00

No. 423 Overprinted **PRO INFANCIA**

1931, Jan. 30 Wmk. 155 ***Perf. 14***

RA13 A36 1c dull vio 30 40
a. "PRO INFANCIA" double 50.00

Indian Mother and Child — PT6

Mosquito Attacking Man — PT7

1934, Sept. 1 Wmk. 156 ***Perf. 10½***

RA13B PT6 1c dull orange 20 15

1939 Photo. Wmk. 156

RA14 PT7 1c Prus blue 1.50 15
a. Imperf. 3.00 3.00

This stamp was obligatory on all mail, the money being used to aid in a drive against malaria.

See Nos. RA16, RA19.

Miguel Hidalgo y Costilla — PT8

Learning Vowels — PT9

1941

RA15 PT8 1c brt car 45 15

Type of 1939

1944 Wmk. 272 ***Perf. 14***

RA16 PT7 1c Prus blue 1.00 15

1946 Photo. Wmk. 279

RA17 PT9 1c blk brn 45 15
a. 1c green black 1.00 1.00

1947 Wmk. 272

RA18 PT9 1c blk brn 40.00 4.00

Type of 1939
Wmk. 279

RA19 PT7 1c Prus blue 3.50 30

PROVISIONAL ISSUES

During the struggle led by Juarez to expel the Emperor Maximilian, installed June, 1864 by Napoleon III and French troops, a number of towns when free of Imperial forces issued provisional postage stamps. Maximilian was captured and executed June 19, 1867, but provisional issues continued current for a time pending re-establishment of Republican Government.

Campeche

A southern state in Mexico, comprising the western part of the Yucatan peninsula.

A1

White Paper
Numerals in Black

1876 Handstamped ***Imperf.***

1 A1 5c gray bl & bl *2,000.*
2 A1 25c gray bl & bl *1,100.*
3 A1 50c gray bl & bl *4,500.*

The stamps printed in blue-black and blue on yellowish paper, formerly listed as issued in 1867, are now known to be an unofficial production of later years. They are reprints, but produced without official sanction.

Chiapas

A southern state in Mexico, bordering on Guatemala and the Pacific Ocean.

A1

1866 **Typeset**

No.	Type	Description	Unused	Used
1	A1	½r blk, *gray bl*	2,000.	1,300.
2	A1	1r blk, *lt grn*		850.00
3	A1	2r blk, *rose*		900.00
4	A1	4r blk, *lt buff*		2,000.
a.		Vertical half used as 2r on cover		3,000.
5	A1	8r blk, *rose*		15,000.
a.		Quarter used as 2r on cover		4,000.
b.		Half used as 4r on cover		5,000.

Chihuahua

A city of northern Mexico and capital of the State of Chihuahua.

A1

1872 **Handstamped**

No.	Type	Description	Unused	Used
1	A1	12(c) black		1,200.
2	A1	25(c) black		900.00

Cuautla

A town in the state of Morelos.

A1

1867 **Handstamped**

No.	Type	Description	Unused	Used
1	A1	(2r) black	7,000.	

Cuernavaca

A city of Mexico, just south of the capital, and the capital of the State of Morelos.

A1

1867 **Handstamped**

No.	Type	Description	Unused	Used
1	A1	(2r) black	1,500.	1,750.

The CUERNAVACA district name handstamp was used to cancel the stamp.
Counterfeits exist.

Guadalajara

A city of Mexico and capital of the State of Jalisco.

A1

Dated "1867"
1st Printing
Medium Wove Paper

1867 **Handstamped** ***Imperf.***

No.	Type	Description	Unused	Used
1	A1	Medio r blk, *white*	125.00	90.00
2	A1	un r blk, *gray bl*		90.00
3	A1	un r blk, *dk bl*		80.00
4	A1	un r blk, *white*		70.00
5	A1	2r blk, *dk grn*	40.00	18.00
6	A1	2r blk, *white*		70.00
7	A1	4r blk, *rose*	110.00	70.00
a.		Half used as 2r on cover		250.00
8	A1	4r blk, *white*		100.00
9	A1	un p blk, *lilac*	120.00	125.00

Serrate Perf.

No.	Type	Description	Unused	Used
10	A1	un r blk, *gray bl*		125.00
11	A1	2r blk, *dk grn*		70.00
12	A1	4r blk, *rose*		80.00

2nd Printing
No Period after "2" or "4"
Thin Quadrille Paper
Imperf

No.	Type	Description	Unused	Used
13	A1	2r blk, *green*	25.00	17.50
a.		Half used as 1r on cover		250.00

Serrate Perf.

No.	Type	Description	Unused	Used
14	A1	2r blk, *green*		50.00

Thin Laid Batonné Paper
Imperf

No.	Type	Description	Unused	Used
15	A1	2r blk, *green*	37.50	20.00

Serrate Perf.

No.	Type	Description	Unused	Used
16	A1	2r blk, *green*		42.50

3rd Printing
Capital "U" in "Un" on 1r, 1p
Period after "2" and "4"
Thin Wove Paper
Imperf

No.	Type	Description	Unused	Used
16A	A1	Un r blk, *white*		75.00
17	A1	Un r blk, *blue*		50.00
17A	A1	Un r blk, *lilac*	70.00	
18	A1	2r blk, *rose*		42.50
18A	A1	4r blk, *blue*		

Serrate Perf.

No.	Type	Description	Unused	Used
19	A1	Un r blk, *blue*		85.00

Thin Quadrille Paper
Imperf

No.	Type	Description	Unused	Used
20	A1	2r blk, *rose*	35.00	35.00
21	A1	4r blk, *blue*	12.50	25.00
22	A1	4r blk, *white*	55.00	
23	A1	Un p blk, *lilac*	12.50	50.00
24	A1	Un p blk, *rose*	55.00	

Serrate Perf.

No.	Type	Description	Unused	Used
25	A1	Un p blk, *lilac*		125.00
25A	A1	Un p blk, *rose*		125.00

Thin Laid Batonné Paper
Imperf

No.	Type	Description	Unused	Used
26	A1	Un r blk, *green*	18.00	14.00
27	A1	2r blk, *rose*	22.50	19.00
27A	A1	2r blk, *green*		40.00
28	A1	4r blk, *blue*	14.00	35.00
29	A1	4r blk, *white*	55.00	
30	A1	Un p blk, *lilac*	25.00	45.00
31	A1	Un p blk, *rose*	55.00	

Serrate Perf.

No.	Type	Description	Unused	Used
32	A1	Un r blk, *green*	55.00	
33	A1	2r blk, *rose*	60.00	*70.00*
34	A1	4r blk, *blue*		85.00

Thin Oblong Quadrille Paper
Imperf

No.	Type	Description	Unused	Used
35	A1	Un r blk, *blue*		19.00
36	A1	4r blk, *blue*		150.00

Serrate Perf.

No.	Type	Description	Unused	Used
37	A1	Un r blk, *blue*		65.00

4th Printing
Dated "1868"
Wove Paper

1868 ***Imperf.***

No.	Type	Description	Unused	Used
38	A1	2r blk, *lilac*	25.00	12.00
a.		Half used as 1r on cover		275.00
39	A1	2r blk, *rose*	45.00	55.00

Serrate Perf.

No.	Type	Description	Unused	Used
40	A1	2r blk, *lilac*		45.00
41	A1	2r blk, *rose*		80.00

Laid Batonné Paper
Imperf

No.	Type	Description	Unused	Used
42	A1	un r blk, *green*	10.00	10.00
a.		"nu" instead of "un"		70.00
43	A1	2r blk, *lilac*	10.00	10.00

Serrate Perf.

No.	Type	Description	Unused	Used
44	A1	un r blk, *green*	60.00	45.00

Quadrille Paper.
Imperf

No.	Type	Description	Unused	Used
45	A1	2r blk, *lilac*	20.00	12.00

Serrate Perf.

No.	Type	Description	Unused	Used
46	A1	2r blk, *lilac*	55.00	55.00

Laid Paper
Imperf

No.	Type	Description	Unused	Used
47	A1	un r blk, *green*	11.00	14.00
a.		"nu" instead of "un"		60.00
48	A1	2r blk, *lilac*	27.50	27.50
49	A1	2r blk, *rose*	32.50	32.50

Serrate Perf.

No.	Type	Description	Unused	Used
50	A1	un r blk, *green*		47.50
51	A1	2r blk, *rose*	90.00	

Counterfeits of Nos. 1-51 abound.

Merida

A city of southeastern Mexico, capital of the State of Yucatan.

Mexico No. 521 Surcharged **25**

1916 **Wmk. 155** ***Perf. 14***

No.	Type	Description	Unused	Used
1	A40	25(c) on 5c org, on cover		*500.00*

The G.P.DE.M. overprint reads down.

Authorities consider the Monterrey, Morelia and Patzcuaro stamps to be bogus.

Tlacotalpan

A village in the state of Veracruz.

A1

1856, Oct. **Handstamped**

No.	Type	Description	Unused	Used
1	A1	½(r) black		10,000.

REVOLUTIONARY ISSUES

SINALOA

A northern state in Mexico, bordering on the Pacific Ocean. Stamps were issued by a provisional government.

Coat of Arms — A1

1929 **Unwmk.** **Litho.** ***Perf. 12***

No.	Type	Description	Unused	Used
1	A1	10c blk, red & bl	2.50	
a.		Tete beche pair	30.00	
2	A1	20c blk, red & gray	2.50	

Just as Nos. 1 and 2 were ready to be placed on sale the state was occupied by the Federal forces and the stamps could not be used. At a later date a few copies were canceled by favor.

YUCATAN

A southeastern state of Mexico.

Mayan Altar Support
A1

"Casa de Monjas"
A2

Temple of the Tigers — A3

1924 **Unwmk.** **Litho.** ***Imperf.***

No.	Type	Description	Unused	Used
1	A1	5c violet	10.00	10.00
2	A2	10c carmine	35.00	35.00
3	A3	50c olive green	175.00	

Perf. 12

No.	Type	Description	Unused	Used
4	A1	5c violet	20.00	20.00
5	A2	10c carmine	60.00	60.00
6	A3	50c olive green	250.00	

Nos. 3 and 6 were not regularly issued.

MIDDLE CONGO

LOCATION — Western Africa at the Equator, bordering on the Atlantic Ocean
GOVT. — Former French Colony
AREA — 166,069
POP. — 746,805 (1936)
CAPITAL — Brazzaville

In 1910 Middle Congo, formerly a part of French Congo, was declared a separate colony. It was grouped with Gabon and the Ubangi-Shari and Chad Territories and officially designated French Equatorial Africa. This group became a single administrative unit in 1934. See Gabon.

See Congo Republic (ex-French) for issues of 1959 onward.

100 Centimes = 1 Franc

Leopard
A1

Bakalois Woman
A2

Coconut Grove
A3

Perf. 14x13½

1907-22 **Typo.** **Unwmk.**

No.	Type	Description	Unused	Used
1	A1	1c ol gray & brn	15	15
2	A1	2c vio & brn	15	15
3	A1	4c bl & brn	15	15
4	A1	5c dk grn & bl	20	15
5	A1	5c yel & bl ('22)	38	38
6	A1	10c car & bl	22	15
7	A1	10c dp grn & bl grn ('22)	90	90
8	A1	15c brn vio & rose	65	42
9	A1	20c brn & bl	1.00	70
10	A2	25c bl & grn	30	28
11	A2	25c bl grn & gray ('22)	38	38
12	A2	30c scar & grn	60	40
13	A2	30c dp rose & rose ('22)	60	60
14	A2	35c vio brn & bl	45	45
15	A2	40c dl grn & brn	45	45
16	A2	45c vio & red	2.25	1.50
17	A2	50c bl grn & red	60	50
18	A2	50c bl & grn ('22)	60	60
19	A2	75c brn & bl	2.50	2.25
20	A3	1fr dp grn & vio	4.50	3.50
21	A3	2fr vio & gray grn	4.00	2.50
22	A3	5fr bl & rose	12.00	10.00
		Nos. 1-22 (22)	33.03	26.56

For stamps of types A1-A3 in changed colors, see Chad, French Congo and Ubangi-Shari.

For overprints and surcharges see Nos. 23-60, B1-B2.

Stamps and Types of 1907-22 Overprinted in Black, Blue or Red

AFRIQUE EQUATORIALE FRANÇAISE

1924-30

23 A1 1c ol gray & brn 15 15
24 A1 2c vio & brn 15 15
25 A1 4c bl & brn 15 15
26 A1 5c yel & bl 15 15
27 A1 10c grn & bl grn (R) 15 15
28 A1 10c car & gray ('25) 15 15
29 A1 15c brn vio & rose (Bl) 15 15
a. Double surcharge 50.00
30 A1 20c brn & bl 15 15
31 A1 20c bl grn & yel grn ('26) 15 15
32 A1 20c dp brn & rose lil ('27) 35 15

Overprinted **AFRIQUE EQUATORIALE FRANÇAISE**

33 A2 25c bl grn & gray 20 20
34 A2 30c rose & pale rose (Bl) 30 20
35 A2 30c gray & bl vio (R) ('25) 28 20
36 A2 30c dk grn & grn ('27) 55 42
37 A2 35c choc & bl 25 20
38 A2 40c ol grn & brn 30 20
39 A2 45c vio & pale red (Bl) 58 35
a. Inverted overprint 50.00 50.00
40 A2 50c bl & grn (R) 30 22
41 A2 50c org & blk ('25) 28 20
a. Without overprint 82.50
42 A2 65c org brn & bl ('27) 1.20 80
43 A2 75c brn & bl 32 22
44 A2 90c brn red & pink ('30) 1.60 1.40
45 A3 1fr grn & vio 58 45
a. Double overprint 90.00 85.00
46 A3 1.10fr vio & brn ('28) 1.60 1.00
47 A3 1.50fr ultra & bl ('30) 2.50 2.25
48 A3 2fr vio & gray grn 62 55
49 A3 3fr red vio ('30) 3.25 2.50
50 A3 5fr bl & rose 2.00 1.10
Nos. 23-50 (28) 18.41 13.96

Nos. 48 and 50 Surcharged with New Values

1924

51 A3 25c on 2fr vio & gray grn 28 28
52 A3 25c on 5fr bl & rose (Bl) 28 28

Types of 1924-27 Surcharged with New Values in Black or Red

1925-27

53 A3 65c on 1fr red org & ol brn 40 40
54 A3 85c on 1fr red org & ol brn 40 40
55 A2 90c on 75c brn red & rose red ('27) 55 55
56 A3 1.25fr on 1fr dl bl & ultra (R) 20 16
57 A3 1.50fr on 1fr ultra & bl ('27) 70 55
a. New value omitted 60.00
58 A3 3fr on 5fr org brn & dl red ('27) 80 65
a. New value omitted 110.00
59 A3 10fr on 5fr ver & bl grn ('27) 4.00 3.50
60 A3 20fr on 5fr org brn & vio ('27) 6.00 4.50
Nos. 53-60 (8) 13.05 10.71

Bars cover old values on Nos. 56-60.

Colonial Exposition Issue
Common Design Types

1931 **Engr.** ***Perf. 12½***
Name of Country in Black

61 CD70 40c dp grn 1.60 1.50
62 CD71 50c violet 90 80
63 CD72 90c red org 1.20 1.00
64 CD73 1.50fr dl bl 1.60 1.00

Viaduct at Mindouli A4

Pasteur Institute at Brazzaville A5

Government Building, Brazzaville A6

1933 **Photo.** ***Perf. 13½***

65 A4 1c lt brn 15 15
66 A4 2c dl bl 15 15
67 A4 4c ol grn 15 15
68 A4 5c red vio 15 15
69 A4 10c slate 15 15
70 A4 15c dk vio 20 20
71 A4 20c red, *pink* 2.75 2.00
72 A4 25c orange 28 20
73 A4 30c yel grn 80 65
74 A5 40c org brn 65 45
75 A5 45c blk, *green* 80 60
76 A5 50c blk vio 50 30
77 A5 65c brn red, *grn* 50 40
78 A5 75c blk, *pink* 4.00 2.50
79 A5 90c carmine 50 45
80 A5 1fr dk red 50 40
81 A5 1.25fr Prus bl 80 60
82 A5 1.50fr dk bl 2.50 1.10
83 A6 1.75fr dk vio 80 62
84 A6 2fr grnsh blk 65 62
85 A6 3fr orange 1.25 1.25
86 A6 5fr slate bl 5.75 4.50
87 A6 10fr black 25.00 12.00
88 A6 20fr dk brn 16.00 10.00
Nos. 65-88 (24) 64.98 39.59

SEMI-POSTAL STAMPS

No. 6 Surcharged in Black

1916 **Unwmk.** ***Perf. 14x13½***

B1 A1 10c + 5c car & bl 60 40
a. Double surcharge 45.00 45.00
b. Inverted surcharge 40.00 40.00

A printing with the surcharge placed lower and more to the left was made and used in Ubangi.

No. 6 Surcharged in Red

B2 A1 10c + 5c car & bl 40 40

POSTAGE DUE STAMPS

Postage Due Stamps of France Overprinted

MOYEN-CONGO

A. E. F.

1928 **Unwmk.** ***Perf. 14x13½***

J1 D2 5c lt bl 28 28
J2 D2 10c gray brn 28 28
J3 D2 20c ol grn 42 42
J4 D2 25c brt rose 42 42
J5 D2 30c lt red 42 42
J6 D2 45c bl grn 50 50
J7 D2 50c brn vio 60 60
J8 D2 60c yel brn 70 70
J9 D2 1fr red brn 70 70
J10 D2 2fr org red 1.25 1.25
J11 D2 3fr brt vio 2.25 2.25
Nos. J1-J11 (11) 7.82 7.82

Village on Ubangi, Dance Mask — D3

Steamer on Ubangi River — D4

1930 **Typo.**

J12 D3 5c dp bl & ol 35 35
J13 D3 10c dp red & brn 45 45
J14 D3 20c grn & brn 1.20 1.20
J15 D3 25c lt bl & brn 1.40 1.40
J16 D3 30c bis brn & Prus bl 2.25 2.25
J17 D3 45c Prus bl & ol 2.25 2.25
J18 D3 50c red vio & brn 2.25 2.25
J19 D3 60c gray lil & bl blk 2.50 2.50
J20 D4 1fr bis brn & bl blk 4.25 4.25
J21 D4 2fr vio & brn 5.25 5.25
J22 D4 3fr dk red & brn 5.25 5.25
Nos. J12-J22 (11) 27.40 27.40

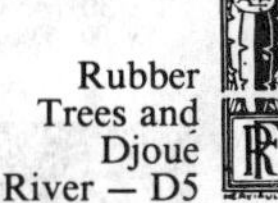

Rubber Trees and Djoue River — D5

1933 **Photo.** ***Perf. 13½***

J23 D5 5c ap grn 32 32
J24 D5 10c dk bl, *bl* 32 32
J25 D5 20c red, *yel* 45 45
J26 D5 25c chocolate 45 45
J27 D5 30c org red 52 52
J28 D5 45c dk vio 52 52
J29 D5 50c gray blk 90 90
J30 D5 60c blk, *orange* 1.25 1.25
J31 D5 1fr brn rose 2.00 2.00
J32 D5 2fr org yel 2.75 2.75
J33 D5 3fr Prus bl 4.50 4.50
Nos. J23-J33 (11) 13.98 13.98

MOHELI

LOCATION — One of the Comoro Islands, situated in the Mozambique Channel midway between Madagascar and Mozambique (Africa)
GOVT. — Former French Colony
AREA — 89 sq. mi.
POP. — 4,000
CAPITAL — Fomboni

See Comoro Islands

100 Centimes = 1 Franc

Navigation and Commerce — A1

Perf. 14x13½

1906-07 **Typo.** **Unwmk.**
Name of Colony in Blue or Carmine

1 A1 1c blk, *lil bl* 65 65
2 A1 2c brn, *buff* 65 60
3 A1 4c claret, *lav* 1.00 90
4 A1 5c yel grn 1.00 90
5 A1 10c carmine 1.25 1.00
6 A1 20c red, *grn* 4.50 2.25
7 A1 25c blue 4.50 2.50
8 A1 30c brn, *bis* 7.00 5.00
9 A1 35c blk, *yellow* 3.50 1.75
10 A1 40c red, *straw* 6.00 3.75
11 A1 45c blk, *gray grn* ('07) 35.00 22.50
12 A1 50c brn, *az* 10.00 6.50
13 A1 75c dp vio, *org* 10.00 9.00
14 A1 1fr brnz grn, *straw* 10.00 6.50
15 A1 2fr vio, *rose* 16.00 14.00
16 A1 5fr lil, *lav* 65.00 55.00
Nos. 1-16 (16) 176.05 132.80

Perf. 13½x14 stamps are counterfeits.

Issue of 1906-07 Surcharged in Carmine or Black

05 **10**

1912

17 A1 5c on 4c cl, *lav* (C) 60 60
18 A1 5c on 20c red, *grn* 1.50 1.50
19 A1 5c on 30c brn, *bis* (C) 65 65
20 A1 10c on 40c red, *straw* 65 65
21 A1 10c on 45c blk, *gray grn* (C) 65 65
a. "Moheli" double 150.00
b. "Moheli" triple 150.00
22 A1 10c on 50c brn, *az* (C) 1.00 1.00
Nos. 17-22 (6) 5.05 5.05

Two spacings between the surcharged numerals are found on Nos. 17 to 22.

The stamps of Moheli were supposed to have been superseded by those of Madagascar, January, 1908. However, Nos. 17-22 were surcharged in 1912 to use up remainders. These were available for use in Madagascar and the entire Comoro archipelago. In 1950 stamps of Comoro Islands came into use.

MONACO

LOCATION — Southern coast of France, bordering on the Mediterranean Sea
GOVT. — Principality
AREA — 481 acres
POP. — 27,063 (1982)
CAPITAL — Monaco

100 Centimes = 1 Franc

Catalogue values for unused stamps in this country are for Never Hinged items, beginning with Scott 182 in the regular postage section, Scott B51 in the semi-postal section, Scott C2 in the airpost section, Scott CB1 in the airpost semi-postal section, and Scott J28 in the postage due section.

Prince Charles III — A1

Prince Albert I — A2

1885 **Unwmk.** **Typo.** ***Perf. 14x13½***

1 A1 1c olive grn 6.50 3.75
2 A1 2c dull lilac 20.00 8.50
3 A1 5c blue 27.50 10.00
4 A1 10c brn, *straw* 35.00 11.00
5 A1 15c rose 110.00 4.00
6 A1 25c green 275.00 17.00
7 A1 40c slate, *rose* 32.50 13.00
8 A1 75c blk, *rose* 85.00 25.00
9 A1 1fr blk, *yellow* 700.00 130.00
10 A1 5fr rose, *grn* 1,500. 875.00

1891-1921

11 A2 1c ol grn 40 38
12 A2 2c dl vio 40 38
13 A2 5c blue 20.00 85
14 A2 5c yel grn ('01) 38 25
15 A2 10c brn, *straw* 52.50 4.25
16 A2 10c car ('01) 1.50 35
17 A2 15c rose 70.00 85
18 A2 15c vio brn, *straw* ('01) 1.40 60
19 A2 15c gray grn ('21) 1.50 1.25
20 A2 25c green 190.00 9.00
21 A2 25c dp bl ('01) 5.00 90
22 A2 40c sl, *rose* ('94) 1.75 70
23 A2 50c vio, *org* 3.00 1.65
24 A2 75c vio brn, *buff* ('94) 7.50 4.25
a. 75c lilac brown, *buff* 14.00 6.00
25 A2 75c ol brn, *buff* ('21) 9.50 8.00
26 A2 1fr blk, *yellow* 6.25 3.25
27 A2 5fr rose, *grn* 52.50 18.00
28 A2 5fr dl vio ('21) 140.00 80.00
29 A2 5fr dk grn ('21) 16.00 15.00
Nos. 11-29 (19) 579.58 149.91

The handstamp "OL" in a circle of dots is a cancellation, not an overprint.

See No. 1782. For overprints and surcharges see Nos. 30-35, 57-59, B1.

Stamps of 1901-21 Overprinted or Surcharged:

28 DÉCEMBRE 1920

28 DÉCEMBRE 1920 2f

1921, Mar. 5

No.	Type	Description	Unused	Used
30	A2	5c lt grn	70	60
31	A2	75c brn, *buff*	4.50	4.50
32	A2	2fr on 5fr dl vio	35.00	35.00

Issued to commemorate the birth of Princess Antoinette, daughter of Princess Charlotte and Prince Pierre, Comte de Polignac.

Stamps and Type of 1891-1921 Surcharged 25c.

1922

No.	Type	Description	Unused	Used
33	A2	20c on 15c gray grn	1.00	90
34	A2	25c on 10c rose	60	60
35	A2	50c on 1fr blk, *yel*	5.50	4.50

Prince Albert I A5

Oceanographic Museum A6

"The Rock" of Monaco — A7

Royal Palace — A8

1922-24 **Engr.** ***Perf. 11***

No.	Type	Description	Unused	Used
40	A5	25c olive brn	5.00	4.00
41	A6	30c dk grn	80	80
42	A6	30c scar ('23)	32	32
43	A6	50c ultra	3.25	3.25
44	A7	60c blk brn	25	25
45	A7	1fr blk, *yellow*	16	16
46	A7	2fr scarlet	32	32
47	A8	5fr red brn	32.50	25.00
48	A8	5fr dk grn, *lil* ('24)	6.00	6.00
49	A8	10fr carmine	11.00	11.00
		Nos. 40-49 (10)	59.60	51.10

Nos. 40-49 exist imperf.

Prince Louis II A9 A10

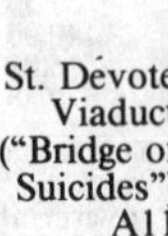

St. Devote Viaduct ("Bridge of Suicides") A11

1923-24 **Engr.**

No.	Type	Description	Unused	Used
50	A9	10c deep green	28	28
51	A9	15c car rose ('24)	42	42
52	A9	20c red brn	26	26
53	A9	25c violet	26	26
a.		Without engraver's name	4.00	4.00
54	A11	40c org brn ('24)	38	38
55	A10	50c ultra	26	26
		Nos. 50-55 (6)	1.86	1.86

The 25c comes in 2 types, one with larger "5" and "c" touching frame of numeral tablet.

Stamps of the 1922-24 issues sometimes show parts of the letters of a papermaker's watermark.

The engraved stamps of type A11 measure 31x21½mm. The typographed stamps of that design measure 36x21½mm.

See #86-88. For surcharges see #95-96.

Stamps and Type of 1891-1921 Surcharged 45

1924, Aug. 5 ***Perf. 14x13½***

No.	Type	Description	Unused	Used
57	A2	45c on 50c brn ol, *buff*	52	52
a.		Double surcharge	600.00	600.00
58	A2	75c on 1fr blk, *yel*	30	30
a.		Double surcharge	475.00	475.00
59	A2	85c on 5fr dk grn	30	30
a.		Double surcharge	530.00	530.00

Grimaldi Family Coat of Arms — A12

Prince Louis II — A13

Louis II — A14

View of Monaco — A15

1924-33 **Typo.**

No.	Type	Description	Unused	Used
60	A12	1c gray black	15	15
61	A12	2c red brown	15	15
62	A12	3c brt vio ('33)	1.25	28
63	A12	5c org ('26)	22	22
64	A12	10c blue	15	15
65	A13	15c apple grn	15	15
66	A13	15c dl vio ('29)	1.25	60
67	A13	20c violet	16	15
68	A13	20c rose	22	15
69	A13	25c rose	15	15
70	A13	25c red, *yel*	16	16
71	A13	30c orange	15	15
72	A13	40c blk brn	16	15
73	A13	40c lt bl, *bluish*	22	22
74	A13	45c gray blk ('26)	52	32
75	A14	50c myr grn ('25)	16	16
76	A13	50c brn, *org*	15	15
77	A14	60c yel brn ('25)	16	16
78	A13	60c ol grn, *grnsh*	16	15
79	A13	75c ol grn, *grnsh* ('26)	32	22
80	A13	75c car, *straw* ('26)	16	15
81	A13	75c slate	42	22
82	A13	80c red, *yel* ('26)	26	22
83	A13	90c rose, *straw* ('27)	80	80
84	A13	1.25fr bl, *bluish* ('26)	15	15
85	A13	1.50fr bl, *bluish* ('27)	1.40	90

Size: 36x21½mm

No.	Type	Description	Unused	Used
86	A11	1fr blk, *orange*	16	16
87	A11	1.05fr red vio ('26)	16	16
88	A11	1.10fr bl grn ('27)	5.75	3.25
89	A15	2fr vio & ol brn ('25)	65	50
90	A15	3fr rose & ultra, *yel* ('27)	10.00	6.00
91	A15	5fr grn & rose ('25)	4.50	3.00
92	A15	10fr yel brn & bl ('25)	11.00	8.75
		Nos. 60-92 (33)	41.42	28.25

Nos. 60 to 74 and 76 exist imperforate. For surcharges see Nos. 93-94, 97-99, C1.

Type of 1924-33 Surcharged with New Value and Bars

1926-31

No.	Type	Description	Unused	Used
93	A13	30c on 25c rose	22	20
94	A13	50c on 60c ol grn, *grnsh* ('28)	75	22
95	A11	50c on 1.05fr red vio ('28)	45	30
a.		Double surcharge		
96	A11	50c on 1.10fr bl grn ('31)	5.25	3.25
97	A13	50c on 1.25fr bl, *bluish* (R) ('28)	66	32
98	A13	1.25fr on 1fr bl, *bluish*	38	22
99	A15	1.50fr on 2fr vio & ol brn ('28)	2.75	2.25
		Nos. 93-99 (7)	10.46	6.76

Princes Charles III, Louis II and Albert I — A17

1928, Feb. 18 **Engr.** ***Perf. 11***

No.	Type	Description	Unused	Used
100	A17	50c dl car	75	75
101	A17	1.50fr dk bl	75	75
102	A17	3fr dk vio	75	75

Nos. 100-102 were sold exclusively at the Intl. Phil. Exhib. at Monte Carlo, Feb., 1928. One set was sold to each purchaser of a ticket of admission to the exhibition which cost 5fr.

Exist imperf. Value, set $20.

Old Watchtower A20

Royal Palace — A21

Church of St. Devote A22

Prince Louis II A23

"The Rock" of Monaco A24

Gardens of Monaco A25

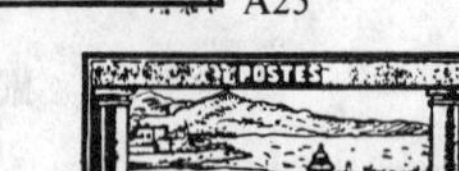

Fortifications and Harbor A26

1932-37 ***Perf. 13, 14x13½***

No.	Type	Description	Unused	Used
110	A20	15c lil rose	52	15
111	A20	20c org brn	52	15
112	A21	25c ol blk	60	30
113	A22	30c yel grn	48	30
114	A23	40c dk brn	1.25	75
115	A24	45c brn red	1.40	52
a.		45c red	300.00	300.00
116	A23	50c purple	1.25	55
117	A25	65c bl grn	1.40	40
118	A26	75c dp bl	1.75	85
119	A23	90c red	3.25	1.75
120	A22	1fr red brn ('33)	7.50	4.00
121	A26	1.25fr rose lil	2.50	1.90
122	A23	1.50fr ultra	12.00	6.00
123	A21	1.75fr rose lil	16.00	4.00
124	A21	1.75fr car rose ('37)	14.00	5.00
125	A24	2fr dk bl	3.00	1.90
126	A20	3fr purple	4.25	2.75
127	A21	3.50fr org ('35)	27.50	20.00
128	A22	5fr violet	9.00	8.50
129	A21	10fr dp bl	65.00	30.00
130	A25	20fr black	85.00	50.00
		Nos. 110-130 (21)	258.17	139.77

Postage Due Stamps of 1925-32 Surcharged or Overprinted in Black:

POSTES =5

POSTES

1937-38 ***Perf. 14x13***

No.	Type	Description	Unused	Used
131	D3	5c on 10c vio	52	52
132	D3	10c violet	52	52
133	D3	15c on 30c bis	52	52
134	D3	20c on 30c bis	52	52
135	D3	25c on 60c red	85	85
136	D3	30c bister	1.50	1.40
137	D3	40c on 60c red	1.40	1.40
138	D3	50c on 60c red	1.90	1.75
139	D3	65c on 1fr lt bl	1.50	1.40
140	D3	85c on 1fr lt bl	3.25	3.00
141	D3	1fr light blue	3.75	3.50
142	D3	2.15fr on 2fr dl red	3.75	3.75
143	D3	2.25fr on 2fr dl red ('38)	9.25	9.25
144	D3	2.50fr on 2fr dl red ('38)	12.00	11.00
		Nos. 131-144 (14)	41.23	39.38

Grimaldi Arms A27

Prince Louis II A28

1937-43 **Engr.**

No.	Type	Description	Unused	Used
145	A27	1c dk vio brn ('38)	15	15
146	A27	2c emerald	15	15
147	A27	3c brt red vio	15	15
148	A27	5c red	15	15
149	A27	10c ultra	15	15
149A	A27	10c blk ('43)	15	15
150	A27	15c vio ('39)	85	75
150A	A27	30c dl grn ('43)	15	15
150B	A27	40c rose car ('43)	15	15
150C	A27	50c brt vio ('43)	15	15
151	A28	55c red brn ('38)	1.90	75
151A	A27	60c Prus bl ('43)	15	15
152	A28	65c vio ('38)	17.00	6.00
153	A28	70c red brn ('39)	15	15
153A	A27	70c red brn ('43)	15	15
154	A28	90c vio ('39)	16	16
155	A28	1fr rose red ('38)	3.00	1.75
156	A28	1.25fr rose red ('39)	16	15
157	A28	1.75fr ultra ('38)	7.25	3.25
158	A28	2.25fr ultra ('39)	16	15
		Nos. 145-158 (20)	32.28	14.76

Nos. 151, 152, 155 and 157 exist imperforate.

Souvenir Sheet

Prince Louis II — A29

1938, Jan. 17 **Unwmk.** ***Imperf.***

No.	Type	Description	Unused	Used
159	A29	10fr magenta	25.00	25.00

"Fête Nationale" Jan. 17, 1938. Size: 99x120mm.

Cathedral of Monaco — A30

St. Nicholas Square — A31

Palace Gate — A32

Palace of Monaco — A34

Panorama of Monaco A33

Harbor of Monte Carlo — A35

1939-46			Perf. 13	
160	A30	20c rose lil	20	20
161	A31	25c gldn brn	40	22
162	A32	30c dk bl grn	28	22
162A	A32	30c brn red ('40)	26	20
163	A31	40c hn brn	60	35
164	A33	45c brt red vio	26	22
165	A34	50c dk bl grn	28	20
166	A32	60c rose car	35	22
166A	A32	60c dk grn ('40)	28	22
166B	A35	70c brt red vio ('41)	26	16
167	A35	75c dk grn	26	16
167A	A30	80c dl grn ('43)	20	20
168	A34	1fr brn blk	26	16
168A	A33	1fr cl ('43)	15	15
168B	A35	1.20fr ultra ('46)	16	16
168C	A34	1.30fr brn blk ('41)	26	16
168D	A31	1.50fr ultra ('46)	26	26
169	A31	2fr rose vio	35	22
169A	A35	2fr lt ultra ('43)	15	15
169B	A34	2fr grn ('46)	15	15
170	A33	2.50fr red	20.00	11.00
171	A33	2.50fr dp bl ('40)	1.00	40
172	A35	3fr brn red	40	20
172A	A31	3fr blk ('43)	15	15
172B	A30	4fr rose lil ('46)	28	28
172C	A34	4.50fr brt vio ('43)	15	15
173	A30	5fr Prus bl	2.00	40
173A	A32	5fr dp grn ('43)	15	15
173B	A34	6fr lt vio ('46)	45	45
174	A33	10fr green	1.40	35
174A	A30	10fr dp bl ('43)	20	20
174B	A35	15fr rose pink ('43)	26	20
175	A32	20fr brt ultra	1.40	35
175A	A33	20fr sep ('43)	26	20
175B	A35	25fr bl grn ('46)	1.25	85
		Nos. 160-175B (35)	34.72	19.31

See Nos. 214-221, 228-232, 274-275, 319-320, 407-408, 423, 426, 428-429, B36-B50.

Louis II Stadium A36

1939, Apr. 23			Engr.	
176	A36	10fr dk grn	85.00	85.00

Inauguration of Louis II Stadium.

Louis II Stadium A37

1939, Aug. 15				
177	A37	40c dl grn	80	80
178	A37	70c brn blk	90	90
179	A37	90c dk vio	1.25	1.25
180	A37	1.25fr cop red	1.50	1.50
181	A37	2.25fr dk bl	2.25	2.25
		Nos. 177-181 (5)	6.70	6.70

8th International University Games.

Imperforates

Nearly all Monaco stamps from 1940 onward exist imperforate. Officially 20 sheets, ranging from 25 to 100 subjects, were left imperforate.

Catalogue values for unused stamps in this section, from this point to the end of the section, are for Never Hinged items.

Prince Louis II
A38 A39

1941-46			Perf. 14x13	
182	A38	40c brn car	30	30
183	A38	80c dp grn	30	30
184	A38	1fr rose vio	15	15
185	A38	1.20fr grn ('42)	15	15
186	A38	1.50fr rose	15	15
187	A38	1.50fr vio ('42)	15	15
187A	A38	2fr lt grn ('46)	22	18
188	A38	2.40fr red ('42)	15	15
189	A38	2.50fr dp ultra	55	55
190	A38	4fr bl ('42)	15	15
		Set value	1.70	1.65

1943			Perf. 13	
191	A39	50fr purple	70	70

Prince Louis II
A40 A41

1946	Unwmk.	Engr.	Perf. 14x13	
192	A40	2.50fr dk bl grn	25	20
193	A40	3fr brt red vio	25	20
194	A40	6fr brt red	30	30
195	A40	10fr brt ultra	38	40
		Perf. 13		
196	A41	50fr dp Prus grn	1.65	1.50
197	A41	100fr red	2.50	2.25
		Nos. 192-197 (6)	5.33	4.85

Nos. 196-197 exist imperforate.

See Nos. 222-227, 233-236. For overprints see Nos. C8-C9.

Franklin D. Roosevelt — A42

Harbor of Monte Carlo — A43

Palace of Monaco A44

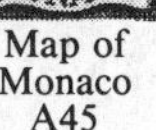

Map of Monaco A45

Prince Louis II A46

1946, Dec. 13		Unwmk.	Perf. 13	
198	A42	10c red vio	15	15
199	A43	30c dp bl	15	15
200	A44	60c bl blk	15	15
201	A45	1fr sepia	35	35
202	A45	3fr lt vio	65	65
		Nos. 198-202,B93,C14-C15,CB6 (9)	3.43	3.33

Issued in tribute to the memory of Franklin D. Roosevelt.

1947, May 15				
203	A46	10fr dk bl grn	1.40	1.40

See No. C20a.

Hurdler A47

Runner — A48

Designs: 2fr, Discus thrower. 2.50fr, Basketball. 4fr, Swimmer.

1948, July 1			Perf. 13	
204	A47	50c bl grn	22	22
205	A48	1fr rose brn	25	25
206	A48	2fr grnsh bl	50	50
207	A48	2.50fr vermilion	80	80
208	A48	4fr sl gray	1.00	1.00
		Nos. 204-208,CB7-CB10 (9)	62.27	62.27

Issued to publicize Monaco's participation in the 1948 Olympic Games held at Wembley, England, during July and August.

Nymph Salmacis A49

Hercules A50

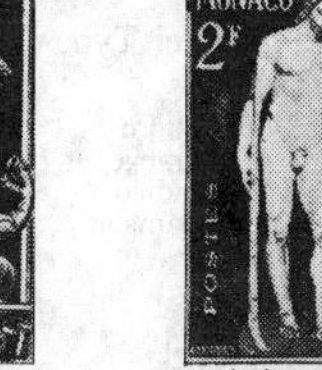

Aristaeus A51

Hyacinthus A52

François J. Bosio and Louis XIV Statue — A53

1948, July 12				
209	A49	50c dk grn	15	15
210	A50	1fr red	18	18
211	A51	2fr dp ultra	20	20
212	A52	2.50fr dp vio	35	35
213	A53	4fr purple	60	60
		Nos. 209-213,CB11-CB14 (9)	39.98	39.98

Issued to honor François J. Bosio (1768-1845), sculptor. No. 213 inscribed "J F Bosio."

Scenic Types of 1939

1948			Engr.	
214	A30	50c sepia	30	22
215	A31	60c rose pink	30	22
216	A32	3fr vio rose	50	30
217	A31	4fr emerald	50	30
218	A34	8fr red brn	1.75	75
219	A34	10fr brn red	3.00	60
220	A33	20fr car rose	1.25	45
221	A35	25fr gray blk	25.00	11.00
		Nos. 214-221 (8)	32.60	13.84

Louis II Type of 1946

1948, July			Perf. 14x13	
222	A40	30c black	28	15
223	A40	5fr org brn	42	28
224	A40	6fr purple	1.50	45
225	A40	10fr orange	42	28
226	A40	12fr dp car	2.25	70
227	A40	18fr dk bl	4.75	4.25
		Nos. 222-227 (6)	9.62	6.11

Scenic Types of 1939

1949			Perf. 13	
228	A33	5fr bl grn	45	15
229	A35	10fr orange	72	26
230	A32	25fr blue	14.00	5.50
231	A30	40fr brn red	5.25	2.50
232	A30	50fr purple	3.50	65
		Nos. 228-232 (5)	23.92	9.06

Louis II Type of 1946

1949, Mar. 10			Perf. 14x13	
233	A40	50c olive	28	15
234	A40	1fr dk vio bl	20	20
235	A40	12fr dk sl grn	4.50	2.50
236	A40	15fr brn car	4.50	3.00

Hirondelle I A54

Cactus Plants A55

Designs: 4fr, Oceanographic Museum. 5fr, Princess Alice II at Spitzbergen. 6fr, Albert I Monument. 10fr, Hirondelle II. 12fr, Albert I whaling. 18fr, Bison.

1949, Mar. 5			Perf. 13	
237	A54	2fr brt bl	15	15
238	A55	3fr dk grn	18	18
239	A54	4fr blk brn & bl	28	28
240	A54	5fr crimson	32	32
241	A55	6fr dk vio	55	55
242	A54	10fr blk brn	65	65
243	A54	12fr brt red vio	85	85
244	A54	18fr dk brn & org brn	2.25	2.25
		Nos. 237-244 (8)	5.23	5.23

See Nos. C21-C26.

Palace, Globe and Pigeon A56

1949-50 **Engr.** **Unwmk.**

245	A56	5fr bl grn	26	26
245A	A56	10fr org ('50)	2.25	2.25
246	A56	15fr carmine	32	32
		Nos. 245-246,C30-C33 (7)	8.23	8.23

75th anniversary of the UPU.
Nos. 245, 245A and 246 exist imperf.

Prince Rainier III
A57 A58

1950, Apr. 11

247	A57	10c red & blk brn	15	15
248	A57	50c dp yel & dk brn	15	15
249	A57	1fr purple	18	18
250	A57	5fr dk grn	65	65
251	A57	15fr carmine	1.25	1.25
252	A57	25fr ultra, ol grn & ind	1.90	1.90
		Nos. 247-252,C34-C35 (8)	11.53	11.53

Enthronement of Prince Rainier III.

1950, Apr. **Engr.** ***Perf. 14x13***

253	A58	50c purple	15	15
254	A58	1fr org brn	24	20
255	A58	8fr bl grn	3.25	1.25
256	A58	12fr blue	1.10	45
257	A58	15fr crimson	1.50	48
		Nos. 253-257 (5)	6.24	2.53

1951, Apr. 31 **Typo.**

258	A58	5fr emerald	4.75	3.00
259	A58	10fr orange	8.25	4.25

See Nos. 276-279.

Statue of Prince Albert I — A59

1951, Apr. 11 **Engr.** ***Perf. 13***

260	A59	15fr deep blue	6.25	5.25

Edmond and Jules de Goncourt A60

1951, Apr. 11

261	A60	15fr vio brn	7.00	5.75

Issued to commemorate the 50th anniversary of the foundation of Goncourt Academy.

St. Vincent de Paul A61

Judgment of St. Devote — A62

Symbolizing Monaco's Adoption of Catholicism — A63

Mosaic of the Immaculate Conception A64

Blessed Rainier of Westphalia A65

Designs: 50c, Pope Pius XII. 12fr, Prince Rainier III at Prayer. 15fr, St. Nicholas de Patare. 20fr, St. Roman. 25fr, St. Charles Borromée. 40fr, Cross, arms and Roman Coliseum. 50fr, Chapel of St. Devote.

Inscribed: "Anno Santo"

1951, June 4 **Unwmk.** ***Perf. 13***

262	A61	10c ultra & red	18	18
263	A61	50c dk rose lake & pur	18	18
264	A62	1fr brn & dk grn	24	24
265	A63	2fr vio brn & ver	30	30
266	A64	5fr bl grn	35	35
267	A63	12fr rose vio	48	48
268	A63	15fr vermilion	2.50	2.50
269	A63	20fr red brn	3.75	3.75
270	A63	25fr ultra	4.00	4.00
271	A63	40fr dk car rose & pur	5.00	5.00
272	A63	50fr ol grn & dk vio brn	6.25	6.25
273	A65	100fr dk vio brn	17.00	17.00
		Nos. 262-273 (12)	40.23	40.23

Issued to commemorate the Holy Year, 1951.

Scenic Types of 1939-46

1951, Dec. 22 ***Perf. 13***

274	A31	3fr dp turq grn	85	40
275	A32	30fr slate blk	4.75	2.75

Rainier Type of 1950

1951, Dec. 22 ***Perf. 14x13***

276	A58	6fr bl grn	65	45
277	A58	8fr orange	70	45
278	A58	15fr indigo	85	28
279	A58	18fr crimson	2.50	1.25

Radio Monte Carlo — A66

Knight in Armor — A67

1951, Dec. 22 ***Perf. 13***

280	A66	1fr bl, car & org	20	16
281	A66	15fr pur, car & rose vio	80	28
282	A66	30fr ind & red brn	1.65	85

1951, Dec. 22

283	A67	1fr purple	1.00	48
284	A67	5fr gray blk	2.50	1.00
285	A67	8fr dp car	4.75	2.75
286	A67	15fr emerald	6.50	5.50
287	A67	30fr sl blk	9.25	5.50
		Nos. 283-287 (5)	24.00	15.23

See Nos. 328-332.

Nos. B96-B99a Surcharged with New Values and Bars in Black

1951, Dec. ***Perf. 13½x13, Imperf.***

288	SP51	1fr on 10fr + 5fr	5.50	5.50
289	SP52	3fr on 15fr + 5fr	5.50	5.50
290	SP52	5fr on 25fr + 5fr	5.50	5.50
291	SP51	6fr on 40fr + 5fr	5.50	5.50
b.		Block of 4, #288-291	27.50	27.50

Gallery of Hercules, Royal Palace A68

1952, Apr. 26 **Engr.** ***Perf. 13***

292	A68	5fr red brn & brn	38	35
293	A68	15fr pur & lil rose	55	35
294	A68	30fr ind & ultra	70	55

Issued on the occasion of the opening of a philatelic museum at the royal palace, April 26, 1952.

Basketball — A69

Designs: 2fr, Soccer. 3fr, Sailing. 5fr, Cyclist. 8fr, Gymnastics. 15fr, Louis II Stadium.

1953, Feb. 23 **Unwmk.** ***Perf. 11***

295	A69	1fr dk pur & mag	22	20
296	A69	2fr dk grn & sl bl	28	22
297	A69	3fr bl & lt bl	30	28
298	A69	5fr dk brn & grnsh blk	70	35
299	A69	8fr brn lake & red	1.40	85
300	A69	15fr bl, brn blk & dk grn	85	60
		Nos. 295-300,C36-C39 (10)	43.25	37.50

Issued to publicize Monaco's participation in the Helsinki Olympic Games.

Books, Pens and Proof Pages — A70

1953, June 29 ***Perf. 13***

301	A70	5fr dk grn	42	38
302	A70	15fr red brn	80	62

Issued to publicize the publication of a first edition of the unexpurgated diary of Edmond and Jules Goncourt.

Physalia and Laboratory Ship Hirondelle II — A71

1953, June 29

303	A71	2fr Prus grn, pur & choc	20	15
304	A71	5fr dp mag, red & Prus grn	32	32
305	A71	15fr ultra, vio brn & Prus grn	1.40	1.40

Issued to commemorate the 50th anniversary of the discovery of anaphylaxis by Charles Richet and Paul Portier.

Frederic Ozanam A72 Nun A73

1954, Apr. 12 **Engr.** ***Perf. 13***

306	A72	1fr brt red	15	15
307	A73	5fr dk bl	35	35
308	A72	15fr black	80	80

Issued to commemorate the centenary of the death of Frederic Ozanam, founder of the Society of Saint Vincent de Paul.

Jean Baptiste de la Salle
A74 A75

1954, Apr. 12

309	A74	1fr dk car	15	15
310	A75	5fr blk brn	35	35
311	A74	15fr brt ultra	80	80

Issued to honor Jean Baptiste de la Salle, founder of the Christian Brothers Institute and saint.

A76

A77

Grimaldi Arms — A78

Knight in Armor — A79

Perf. 13½x14, 14x13½

1954, Apr. 12 **Typo.**

Various Forms of Grimaldi Arms in Black and Red or Black, Red and Deep Plum (5fr)

312 A76 50c blk & mag 15 15
313 A77 70c blk & aqua 15 15
314 A76 80c blk, red & dk grn 15 15
315 A77 1fr vio bl 15 15
316 A77 2fr blk & dp org 15 15
317 A77 3fr blk & grn 15 15
318 A78 5fr blk & lt grn 20 20
Set value 72 72

Scenic Types of 1939-46

1954, Apr. 12 **Engr.** ***Perf. 13***
319 A34 25fr brt red 1.50 85
320 A31 75fr dk grn 12.50 7.25

1954, Apr. 12 **Unwmk.** ***Perf. 13***
321 A79 4fr dk red 85 38
322 A79 8fr dk grn 70 70
323 A79 12fr dk pur 3.00 1.25
324 A79 24fr dk mar 6.50 3.50

Nos. 321-324 were issued precanceled only. Values for precanceled stamps in first column are for those which have not been through the post and have original gum. Values in the second column are for postally used, gumless stamps.

See Nos. 400-404, 430-433, 466-469.

Lambarene Landing, Gabon — A80

Dr. Albert Schweitzer — A81

Design: 15fr, Lambarene hospital.

1955, Jan. 14 ***Perf. 11x11½***
325 A80 2fr ol grn, bl grn & ind 15 15
326 A81 5fr dk grnsh bl & grn 80 80
327 A81 15fr dk bl grn, dp cl & brn blk 1.50 1.50

Issued to honor Dr. Albert Schweitzer, medical missionary. See No. C40.

Knight Type of 1951

1955, Jan. 14 ***Perf. 13***
328 A67 5fr purple 1.90 85
329 A67 6fr red 2.25 1.25
330 A67 8fr red brn 2.50 1.65
331 A67 15fr ultra 6.60 3.75
332 A67 30fr dk grn 7.50 4.75
Nos. 328-332 (5) 20.75 12.25

Automobile and Representation of Eight European Cities — A82

Prince Rainier III — A83

1955, Jan. 14 **Unwmk.**
333 A82 100fr dk brn & red 50.00 50.00

25th Monte Carlo Automobile Rally.

1955, June 7 **Engr.** ***Perf. 13***
334 A83 6fr grn & vio brn 24 38
335 A83 8fr red & vio 24 38
336 A83 12fr car & grn 24 38
337 A83 15fr pur & bl 60 22
338 A83 18fr org & bl 60 40
339 A83 30fr ultra & gray 8.25 5.50
Nos. 334-339 (6) 10.17 7.26

See Nos. 405-406, 424-425, 427, 462-465, 586, 603-604A, 725-728, 730, 789, 791.

"Five Weeks in a Balloon" — A84

"A Floating City" and Jules Verne — A85

"Michael Strogoff" — A86

"Around the World in 80 Days" — A87

USS Nautilus and Verne — A88

Designs (Scenes from Jules Verne's Books): 3fr, The House of Vapors. 6fr, The 500 Millions of the Begum. 8fr, The Magnificent Orinoco. 10fr, A Journey to the Center of the Earth. 25fr, Twenty Thousand Leagues under the Sea.

1955, June 7
340 A84 1fr red brn & bl gray 15 15
341 A85 2fr bl, ind & brn 15 15
342 A85 3fr red brn, gray & sl 15 15
343 A86 5fr car & blk brn 26 26
344 A84 6fr blk brn & bluish gray 30 30
345 A86 8fr ol grn & aqua 38 38
346 A85 10fr ind, turq & brn 1.00 90
347 A87 15fr rose brn & ver 75 70
348 A85 25fr bl grn, grn & gray 1.50 1.25
349 A88 30fr vio, turq & blk 3.75 3.75
Nos. 340-349,C45 (11) 28.39 27.99

50th anniv. of the death of Jules Verne.

Virgin by Francois Brea — A89

Blessed Rainier — A90

Design: 10fr, Pieta by Louis Brea.

1955, June 7
350 A89 5fr vio brn, gray & dk grn 25 25
351 A89 10fr vio brn, gray & dk grn 35 35
352 A90 15fr blk brn & org brn 50 50

Issued to commemorate the Marian Year.

Rotary Emblem, World Map — A91

1955, June 7
353 A91 30fr bl & org 75 75

Issued to commemorate the 50th anniversary of the founding of Rotary International.

George Washington A92

Franklin D. Roosevelt — A93

Dwight D. Eisenhower — A94

Palace of Monaco, c. 1790 — A95

Palace of Monaco, c. 1750 — A96

Designs: 3fr, Abraham Lincoln. 30fr, Columbus landing in America. 40fr, Prince Rainier III. 100fr, Early Louisiana scene.

1956, Apr. 3 **Engr.** ***Perf. 13***
354 A92 1fr dk pur 15 15
355 A93 2fr cl & dk pur 15 15
356 A93 3fr vio & dp ultra 18 18
357 A94 5fr brn lake 30 30
358 A95 15fr brn blk & vio brn 55 55
359 A95 30fr ind, blk & ultra 1.00 1.00
360 A94 40fr dk brn & vio brn 1.10 80
361 A96 50fr vermilion 1.25 1.10
362 A96 100fr Prus grn 1.50 1.50
a. Strip of 3, #360-362 4.25 4.00
Nos. 354-362 (9) 6.18 5.73

5th Intl. Phil. Exhib. (FIPEX), NYC, Apr. 28-May 6, 1956.

Ski Jump, Cortina d'Ampezzo — A97

Design: 30fr, Olympic Scenes.

1956, Apr. 3
363 A97 15fr brn vio, brn & dk grn 85 52
364 A97 30fr red org 1.40 1.25

Issued to publicize Monaco's participation in the 1956 Olympic Games.

"Glasgow to Monte Carlo" A98

1956, Apr. 3 **Unwmk.**
365 A98 100fr red brn & red 19.00 19.00

The 26th Monte Carlo Automobile Rally.

See Nos. 411, 437, 460, 483, 500, 539, 549, 600, 629.

Princess Grace and Prince Rainier III – A99

1956, Apr. 19 Engr. *Perf. 13*

Portraits in Black

366 A99 1fr dk grn 15 15
367 A99 2fr dk car 15 15
368 A99 3fr ultra 28 20
369 A99 5fr brt yel grn 35 22
370 A99 15fr redsh brn 35 28
Nos. 366-370,C46-C48 (8) 4.98 4.70

Wedding of Prince Rainier III to Grace Kelly, Apr. 19, 1956.

Nos. J41-J47, J50-J56 Overprinted with Bars and Surcharged in Indigo, Red or Black

Unwmk.

1956, Apr. 3 Engr. *Perf. 11*

Designs: Early Transportation.

371 D6 2fr on 4fr (I) 38 38
372 D6 3fr (R) 38 38
373 D6 5fr on 4fr 60 60
374 D6 10fr on 4fr (R) 75 75
375 D6 15fr on 5fr (I) 1.50 1.50
376 D6 20fr (R) 2.50 2.50
377 D6 25fr on 20fr 3.25 3.25
378 D6 30fr on 10fr (I) 5.25 5.25
379 D6 40fr on 50fr (R) 6.00 6.00
380 D6 50fr on 100fr 8.50 8.50

Designs: Modern Transportation.

381 D7 2fr on 4fr (I) 38 38
382 D7 3fr (R) 38 38
383 D7 5fr on 4fr 60 60
384 D7 10fr on 4fr (R) 75 75
385 D7 15fr on 5fr (I) 1.50 1.50
386 D7 20fr (R) 2.50 2.50
387 D7 25fr on 20fr 3.25 3.25
388 D7 30fr on 10fr (I) 5.25 5.25
389 D7 40fr on 50fr (R) 6.00 6.00
390 D7 50fr on 100fr 8.50 8.50
Nos. 371-390,C49-C50 (22) 76.72 76.72

The two types of each value in Nos. 371-390 were printed tete beche, se-tenant at the base.

Princess Grace – A100

1957, May 11 Engr. *Perf. 13*

391 A100 1fr bl vio 15 15
392 A100 2fr lt ol grn 15 15
393 A100 3fr yel brn 15 15
394 A100 5fr magenta 18 18
395 A100 15fr pink 18 18
396 A100 25fr Prus bl 35 22
397 A100 30fr purple 35 26
398 A100 50fr scarlet 52 26
399 A100 75fr orange 70 60
Nos. 391-399 (9) 2.73 2.15

Birth of Princess Caroline of Monaco.

Knight Type of 1954

1957 Unwmk. *Perf. 13*

400 A79 5fr dk bl 24 18
401 A79 10fr yel grn 24 15
402 A79 15fr brt org 80 60
403 A79 30fr brt bl 1.00 70
404 A79 45fr crimson 1.50 1.00
Nos. 400-404 (5) 3.78 2.63

Nos. 400-404 were issued precanceled only. See note after No. 324.

Types of 1955 and 1939-46

1957

405 A83 20fr grnsh bl 70 45
406 A83 35fr red brn 2.25 1.25
407 A33 65fr brt vio 7.00 5.50
408 A30 70fr org yel 8.00 7.25

Princesses Grace and Caroline A101

1958, May 15 Engr. *Perf. 13*

409 A101 100fr bluish blk 3.75 3.75

Issued to commemorate the birth of Prince Albert Alexander Louis, Mar. 14.

Order of St. Charles – A102

1958, May 15

410 A102 100fr car, grn & bis 1.65 1.65

Issued to commemorate the centenary of the National Order of St. Charles.

Rally Type of 1956

Design: 100fr, "Munich to Monte Carlo."

1958, May 15

411 A98 100fr red, grn & sep 6.50 6.00

27th Monte Carlo Automobile Rally.

Virgin Mary, Popes Pius IX and XII – A103

Bernadette Soubirous – A104

Tomb of Bernadette, Nevers A105

Designs: 3fr, Shepherdess Bernadette at Bartres. 5fr, Bouriette kneeling (first miracle). 8fr, Stained glass window showing apparition. 10fr, Empty grotto at Lourdes. 12fr, Grotto with statue and altar. 20fr, Bernadette praying. 35fr, High Altar at St. Peter's during canonization of Bernadette. 50fr, Bernadette, Pope Pius XI, Mgr. Laurence and Abbe Peyramale.

1958, May 15 Unwmk.

412 A103 1fr lil gray & vio brn 15 15
413 A104 2fr bl & vio 15 15
414 A104 3fr grn & sep 15 15
415 A104 5fr gray brn & vio bl 15 15
416 A104 8fr blk, ol bis & ind 30 25
417 A105 10fr multi 28 25
418 A105 12fr ind, ol bis & ol grn 30 25
a. Strip of 3, #416-418 1.00 90
419 A104 20fr dk sl grn & rose 35 30
420 A104 35fr ol, gray ol & dk sl grn 45 35
421 A103 50fr lake, ol grn & ind 60 50
422 A105 65fr ind & grnsh bl 1.00 65
Nos. 412-422,C51-C52 (13) 7.38 6.15

Centenary of the apparition of the Virgin Mary at Lourdes.

Sizes: Nos. 413-415, 419-420 26x36mm. No. 416 22x36mm. Nos. 417-418 48x36mm. No. 422 36x26mm.

Types of 1939-46 and 1955

1959 Engr. *Perf. 13*

423 A32 5fr cop red 90 80
424 A83 25fr org & blk 1.10 80
425 A83 30fr dk vio 1.75 1.50
426 A34 35fr dk bl 5.50 2.00
427 A83 50fr bl grn & rose cl 2.50 1.50
428 A31 85fr dk car rose 9.00 4.50
429 A33 100fr brt grnsh bl 8.00 6.25
Nos. 423-429 (7) 28.75 17.35

Knight Type of 1954

1959

430 A79 8fr dp mag 52 22
431 A79 20fr brt grn 70 65
432 A79 40fr chocolate 1.40 70
433 A79 55fr ultra 3.25 1.40

Nos. 430-433 were issued precanceled only. See note after No. 324.

Princess Grace Polyclinic – A106

1959, May 16

434 A106 100fr gray, brn & grn 1.25 1.25

Opening of Princess Grace Hospital.

UNESCO Building, Paris, and Cultural Emblems – A107

Design: 50fr, UNESCO Building and children of various races.

1959, May 16

435 A107 25fr multi 28 20
436 A107 50fr ol, bl grn & blk brn 55 48

Opening of UNESCO Headquarters in Paris, Nov. 3, 1958.

Rally Type of 1956

Design: 100fr, "Athens to Monaco."

1959, May 16

437 A98 100fr vio bl, red & sl grn, *bl* 4.75 4.75

28th Monte Carlo Automobile Rally.

Carnations – A108

Bougainvillea – A109

Flowers: 10fr on 3fr, Princess Grace Carnations. 15fr on 1fr, Mimosa (vert.). 25fr on 6fr, Geranium (vert.). 35fr, Oleander. 50fr, Jasmine. 85fr on 65fr, Lavender. 100fr, Grace de Monaco Rose.

1959, May 16

438 A108 5fr brn, Prus grn & rose car 22 15
439 A108 10fr on 3fr brn, grn & rose 22 15
440 A109 15fr on 1fr dk grn & cit 30 15
441 A109 20fr ol grn & mag 40 32
442 A109 25fr on 6fr yel grn & red 55 38
443 A109 35fr dk grn & pink 75 70
444 A109 50fr dk brn & dk grn 1.10 90
445 A109 85fr on 65fr ol grn & gray vio 1.50 1.50
446 A108 100fr grn & pink 1.90 1.75
Nos. 438-446 (9) 6.94 6.00

Nos. 439-440, 442 and 445 were not issued without surcharge.

View of Monaco and Uprooted Oak Emblem – A110

1960, June 1 Unwmk. *Perf. 13*

447 A110 25c bl, ol grn & sep 20 20

Issued to publicize World Refugee Year, July 1, 1959-June 30, 1960.

Entrance to Oceanographic Museum – A111

Museum and Aquarium – A112

Designs: 15c, Museum conference room. 20c, Arrival of equipment, designed by Prince Albert I. 25c, Research on electrical qualities of cephalopodes. 50c, Albert I and vessels Hirondelle I and Princesse Alice.

1960, June 1 Engr. *Perf. 13*

448 A111 5c bl, sep & cl 22 15
449 A112 10c multi 40 28
450 A112 15c sep, ultra & bis 25 15
451 A112 20c rose lil, blk & bl 48 22
452 A112 25c grnsh bl 1.00 75
453 A112 50c lt ultra & brn 1.10 90
Nos. 448-453 (6) 3.45 2.45

Issued to commemorate the 50th anniversary of the inauguration of the Oceanographic Museum of Monaco. See No. 475.

Horse Jumping — A113

Sports: 10c, Women swimmers. 15c, Broad jumper. 20c, Javelin thrower. 25c, Girl figure skater. 50c, Skier.

1960, June 1

454 A113 5c dk brn, car & emer 15 15
455 A113 10c red brn, bl & grn 18 18
456 A113 15c dl red brn, ol & mag 18 18
457 A113 20c blk, bl & grn 2.25 2.25
458 A113 25c dk grn & dl pur 60 60
459 A113 50c dk bl, grnsh bl & dl pur 90 90
Nos. 454-459 (6) 4.26 4.26

Nos. 454-457 issued to commemorate the 17th Olympic Games, Rome, Aug. 25-Sept. 11; Nos. 458-459 commemorate the 8th Winter Olympic Games, Squaw Valley, Feb. 18-29.

Rally Type of 1956

Design: 25c, "Lisbon to Monte Carlo."

1960, June 1

460 A98 25c bl, brn & car, *bluish* 1.90 1.90

29th Monte Carlo Automobile Rally.

Stamps of Sardinia and France, 1860, and Stamp of Monaco, 1885
A114

1960, June 1 Engr. & Embossed

461 A114 25c vio, bl & ol 80 70

Issued to commemorate the 75th anniversary of postage stamps of Monaco.

Prince Rainier Type of 1955

1960 Engr. *Perf. 13*

462 A83 25c org & blk 15 15
463 A83 30c dk vio 22 15
464 A83 50c bl grn & rose lil 42 15
465 A83 65c yel brn & slate 3.25 60
Set value 85

Knight Type of 1954

1960

466 A79 8c dp mag 1.40 42
467 A79 20c brt grn 1.90 42
468 A79 40c chocolate 2.25 80
469 A79 55c ultra 40 1.25

Nos. 466-469 were issued precanceled only. See note after No. 324.

Sea Horse — A115

Designs: Nos. 471 Cactus (Cereanee). No. 472, Cactus (Nopalea dejecta). No. 473, Scorpion fish (horiz.).

1960, June 1

470 A115 15c org brn & sl grn 50 20
471 A115 15c ol grn, yel & brn 60 15
472 A115 20c mar & ol grn 40 15
473 A115 20c brn, red brn, red & ol 60 15
Set value 54

See Nos. 581-584.

Type of 1960 and

Palace of Monaco
A116

Designs: 10c, Type A111 without inscription. 45c, Aerial view of Palace. 85c, Honor court. 1fr, Palace at night.

1960, June 1 Engr.

474 A116 5c grn & sepia 15 15
475 A111 10c dk bl & vio brn 48 24
476 A116 45c dk bl, sep & grn 75 24
477 A116 85c sl, gray & bis 3.50 24
478 A116 1fr dk bl, red brn & sl grn 1.40 35
Nos. 474-478 (5) 6.28 1.22

See Nos. 585, 602, 729, 731, 731A, 790, 792.

Sphinx of Wadi-es-Sebua — A117

1961, June 3 Unwmk. *Perf. 13*

479 A117 50c choc, dk bl & ocher 80 80

Issued as publicity to save historic monuments in Nubia.

Murena, Starfish, Sea Urchin, Sea Cucumber and Coral — A118

Medieval Town and Leper — A119

1961, June 3

480 A118 25c vio buff & dk red 22 20

Issued to commemorate the World Congress of Aquariology, Monaco, Nov. 1960.

1961, June 3

481 A119 25c ol gray, ocher & car 22 18

Issued to honor the Sovereign Order of the Knights of Malta.

Hand and Ant — A120

1961, June 3

482 A120 25c mag & dp car 22 16

Issued to publicize "Respect for Life."

Rally Type of 1956

Design: 1fr, "Stockholm to Monte Carlo."

1961, June 3

483 A98 1fr multi 1.50 1.50

30th Monte Carlo Automobile Rally.

Turcat-Mery, 1911 Winner, and 1961 Car — A121

1961, June 3

484 A121 1fr org brn, vio & rose red 1.50 1.25

Issued to commemorate the 50th anniversary of the founding of the Monte Carlo Automobile Rally.

Chevrolet, 1912
A122

Automobiles (pre-1912): 2c, Peugeot. 3c, Fiat. 4c, Mercedes. 5c, Rolls Royce. 10c, Panhard-Levassor. 15c, Renault. 20c, Ford. 25c, Rochet-Schneider. 30c, FN-Herstal. 45c, De Dion Bouton. 50c, Buick. 65c, Delahaye. 1fr, Cadillac.

1961, June 13 Engr.

485 A122 1c org brn, dk brn & grn 15 15
486 A122 2c org red, dk bl & brn 15 15
487 A122 3c multi 15 15
488 A122 4c multi 15 15
489 A122 5c ol bis, sl grn & car 15 15
490 A122 10c brn, sl & red 18 18
491 A122 15c grnsh bl & dk sl grn 20 20
492 A122 20c pur, blk & red 24 24
493 A122 25c dk brn lil & red 32 32
494 A122 30c ol grn & dl pur 60 60
495 A122 45c multi 1.25 1.25
496 A122 50c brn blk, red & ultra 1.25 1.25
497 A122 65c multi 1.25 1.25
498 A122 1fr brt pur, ind & red 2.50 2.50
Nos. 485-498 (14) 8.54 8.54

See Nos. 648-661.

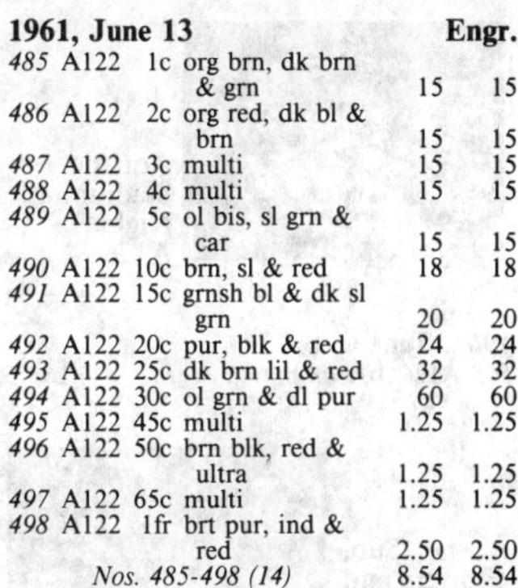

Bugatti, First Winner, and Course — A123

1962, June 6 Unwmk. *Perf. 13*

499 A123 1fr lil rose 1.50 1.25

20th Automobile Grand Prix of Monaco.

Rally Type of 1956

Design: 1fr, "Oslo to Monte Carlo."

1962, June 6

500 A98 1fr multi 1.40 1.25

31st Monte Carlo Automobile Rally.

Louis XII and Lucien Grimaldi
A124

Designs: 50c, Document granting sovereignty. 1fr, Seals of Louis XII and Lucien Grimaldi.

1962, June 6 Engr.

501 A124 25c ver, blk & vio bl 26 20
502 A124 50c dk bl, brn & mag 26 20
503 A124 1fr dk brn, grn & car 70 60

450th anniversary of Monaco's reception of sovereignty from Louis XII.

Mosquito and Swamp
A125

1962, June 6

504 A125 1fr brn ol & lt grn 60 55

WHO drive to eradicate malaria.

Aquatic Stadium at Night A126

1962, June 6
505 A126 10c dk bl, ind & grn 16 15

Sun, Flowers and Hope Chest A127

1962, June 6
506 A127 20c multi 20 16

Issued to publicize the National Multiple Sclerosis Society of New York.

Wheat Harvest A128

1962, June 6
507 A128 25c dk bl, red brn & brn 15 15
508 A128 50c ind, ol bis & dk bl grn 25 25
509 A128 1fr red lil & ol bis 60 60

Europa. See No. C61.

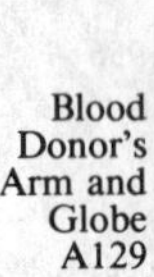

Blood Donor's Arm and Globe A129

1962, Nov. 15 Engr. *Perf. 13*
510 A129 1fr dk red, blk & org 50 45

3rd International Blood Donors' Congress, Nov. 15-18 at Monaco.

Yellow Wagtails — A130

Birds: 10c, European robins. 15c, European goldfinches. 20c, Blackcaps. 25c, Great spotted woodpeckers. 30c, Nightingale. 45c, Barn owls. 50c, Common starlings. 85c, Red crossbills. 1fr, White storks.

1962, Dec. 12 Unwmk.
511 A130 5c grn, sep & yel 15 15
512 A130 10c bis, dk pur & red 18 18
513 A130 15c multi 24 24
514 A130 20c mag, grn & blk 28 24
515 A130 25c multi 35 22
516 A130 30c brn, sl grn & bl 42 30
517 A130 45c vio & gldn brn 60 48
518 A130 50c bl grn, blk & yel 85 65
519 A130 85c multi 1.10 85
520 A130 1fr blk, grn & red 1.25 1.10
Nos. 511-520 (10) 5.42 4.41

Protection of useful birds.

Divers A131

Designs: 10c, Galeazzi's turret (vert.). 25c, Williamson's photosphere, 1914 and bathyscape "Trieste," 1962. 45c, Diving suits. 50c, Diving chamber. 85c, Fulton's "Nautilus," 1800 and modern submarine. 1fr, Alexander the Great's underwater chamber and bathysphere of the New York Zoological Society.

1962, Dec. 12
521 A131 5c bluish grn, vio & blk 15 15
522 A131 10c multi 15 15
523 A131 25c bis, bluish grn & sl grn 20 20
524 A131 45c grn, ind & blk 30 30
525 A131 50c cit & dk bl 45 45
526 A131 85c Prus grn & dk vio bl 60 60
527 A131 1fr dk bl, dk brn & dk grn 1.00 1.00
Nos. 521-527 (7) 2.85 2.85

Issued in connection with an exhibition at the Oceanographic Museum "Man Under Water," showing ancient and modern methods of under-water exploration.

Dancing Children and UN Emblem — A132

Children on Scales A133

Designs: 10c, Bird feeding nestlings (vert.). 20c, Sun shining on children of different races (vert.). 25c, Mother and child (vert.). 50c, House and child. 95c, African mother and child (vert.). 1fr, Prince Albert and Princess Caroline.

1963, May 3 Unwmk. *Perf. 13*
528 A132 5c ocher, dk red & ultra 15 15
529 A133 10c vio bl, emer & ol gray 16 15
530 A133 15c ultra, red & grn 20 15
531 A133 20c multi 20 15
532 A133 25c bl, brn & pink 20 20
533 A133 50c multi 45 40
534 A133 95c multi 60 55
535 A132 1fr grnsh bl, dl pur & rose red 1.10 1.00
Nos. 528-535 (8) 3.06 2.75

Publicizing the UN Children's Charter.

Figurehead with Red Cross, Red Crescent and Red Lion and Sun — A134

Design: 1fr, Centenary emblem, Gustave Moynier, Henri Dunant and Gen. Henri Dufour (horiz.).

1963, May 3 Engr.
536 A134 50c bluish grn, red & red brn 38 38
537 A134 1fr bl, sl grn & red 60 60

Centenary of International Red Cross.

Racing Cars on Monte Carlo Course and Map of Europe A135

1963, May 3
538 A135 50c multi 45 38

European Automobile Grand Prix.

Rally Type of 1956

Design: 1fr, "Warsaw to Monte Carlo."

1963, May 3
539 A98 1fr multi 1.40 1.25

32nd Monte Carlo Auto Race.

Lions International Emblem A136

1963, May 3
540 A136 50c bis, lt vio & bl 75 75

Issued to commemorate the founding of the Lions Club of Monaco, Mar. 24, 1962.

Hôtel des Postes, Paris, and UPU Allegory — A137

1963, May 3
541 A137 50c multi 60 60

Centenary of the first International Postal Conference, Paris, 1863.

Globe and Telstar A138

1963, May 3
542 A138 50c grn, dk pur & mar 75 75

1st television connection of the US and Europe through the Telstar satellite, July 11-12, 1962.

Holy Spirit over St. Peter's and World A139

1963, May 3
543 A139 1fr grn, red brn & bl 75 75

Issued to commemorate Vatican II, the 21st Ecumenical Council of the Roman Catholic Church.

Wheat Emblem and Dove Feeding Nestlings A140

1963, May 3 Engr.
544 A140 1fr multi 85 85

FAO "Freedom from Hunger" campaign.

Henry Ford and 1903 Model A — A141

1963, Dec. 12 Unwmk. *Perf. 13*
545 A141 20c sl grn & lil rose 38 32

Issued to commemorate the centenary of the birth of Henry Ford, American automobile manufacturer.

Bicyle Racer in Town A142

Design: 50c, Bicyclist on country road.

1963, Dec. 12
546 A142 25c bl, sl grn & red brn 30 25
547 A142 50c bl, gray grn, & blk brn 38 38

Issued to commemorate the 50th anniversary of the Bicycle Tour de France.

Pierre de Coubertin and Myron's Discobolus A143

1963, Dec. 12
548 A143 1fr dp cl, car & ocher 1.00 90

Issued to commemorate the centenary of the birth of Baron Pierre de Coubertin, organizer of the modern Olympic Games.

Rally Type of 1956

Design: 1fr, "Paris to Monte Carlo."

1963, Dec. 12
549 A98 1fr multi 1.40 1.40

33rd Monte Carlo Automobile Rally.

Children with Stamp Album and UNESCO Emblem A144

1963, Dec. 12
550 A144 50c dp ultra, red & vio 45 42

Issued to publicize the International Philatelic and Educational Exposition, Monaco, Nov.-Dec., 1963.

Europa Issue, 1963

Woman, Dove and Lyre — A145

1963, Dec. 12
551 A145 25c brn, grn & car 30 25
552 A145 50c dk brn, bl & car 60 48

Wembley Stadium and British Football Association Emblem — A146

Overhead Kick A147

Soccer Game, Florence, 16th Century A148

Tackle A149

Designs: 3c, Goalkeeper. 4c, Louis II Stadium and emblem of Sports Association of Monaco, with black overprint: "Championnat /1962-1963/Coupe de France." 15c, Soule Game, Brittany, 19th century. 20c, Soccer, England, 1827. 25c, Soccer, England, 1890. 50c, Clearing goal area. 95c, Heading the ball. 1fr, Kicking the ball.

1963, Dec. 12
553 A146 1c grn, vio & dk red 15 15
554 A147 2c blk, red & grn 15 15
555 A147 3c gray ol, org & red 15 15
556 A146 4c bl, red, grn, pur & blk 15 15
557 A148 10c dk bl, car & sep 15 15
558 A148 15c sepia & car 15 15
559 A148 20c sepia & dk bl 22 22
560 A148 25c sepia & lilac 22 22
a. Block of 4 70 70
561 A149 30c grn, sep & red 45 45
562 A149 50c sep, grn & red 52 52
563 A149 95c sep, grn & red 1.00 1.00
564 A149 1fr sep, grn & red 1.25 1.25
a. Block of 4 3.50 3.50
Nos. 553-564 (12) 4.56 4.56

Cent. of British Football Assoc. (organized soccer). No. 556 also for the successes of the soccer team of Monaco, 1962-63 (overprint typographed). No. 556 was not regularly issued without overprint. Value $525.

The 4 stamps of No. 560a are connected by an 1863 soccer ball in red brown; the stamps of No. 564a by a modern soccer ball.

Design from 1914 Rally Post Card — A150

Farman Biplane over Monaco — A151

Designs: 3c, Nieuport monoplane. 4c, Breguet biplane. 5c, Morane-Saulnier monoplane. 10c, Albatros biplane. 15c, Deperdussin monoplane. 20c, Vickers-Vimy biplane and map (Ross Smith's flight London-Port Darwin, 1919). 25c, Douglas Liberty biplane (first American around-the-world flight. 4 planes, 1924). 30c, Savoia S-16 hydroplane (De Pinedo's Rome-Australia-Japan-Rome flight, 1925). 45c, Trimotor Fokker F-7 monoplane (first aerial survey of North Pole, Richard E. Byrd and James Gordon Bennett, 1925). 50c, Spirit of St. Louis (first crossing of Atlantic, New York-Paris, Charles Lindbergh, 1927). 65c, Breguet 19 (Paris-New York, Coste and Bellonte, 1930). 95c, Laté 28 hydroplane (first South Atlantic airmail route, Dakar-Natal, 1930). 1fr, Dornier DO-X, (Germany-Rio de Janeiro, 1930).

1964, May 22 Engr. *Perf. 13*
565 A150 1c grn, bl & ol 15 15
566 A151 2c bl, bis & red brn 15 15
567 A151 3c ol, grn & bl 15 15
568 A151 4c red brn, bl & Prus grn 15 15
569 A151 5c gray ol, vio & mag 15 15
570 A151 10c vio, bl & ol 15 15
571 A151 15c bl, org & brn 15 15
572 A151 20c brt grn, blk & bl 16 15
573 A151 25c red, bl & ol 20 15
574 A151 30c bl, sl grn & dp cl 28 20
575 A151 45c red brn, grnsh bl & blk 48 32
576 A151 50c pur, ol & bis 60 45
577 A151 65c stl bl, blk & red 70 48
578 A151 95c ocher, sl grn & red 96 65
579 A151 1fr sl grn, bl & vio brn 1.10 80
Nos. 565-579,C64 (16) 9.03 7.25

Issued to commemorate the 50th anniversary of the first airplane rally of Monte Carlo. Nos. 565-571 show planes which took part in the 1914 rally, Nos. 572-579 and C64 show important flights from 1919 to 1961.

Ancient Egyptian Message Transmitters and Rocket — A152

1964, May 22 Unwmk.
580 A152 1fr dk bl, ind & org brn 80 80

Issued to publicize "PHILATEC", International Philatelic and Postal Techniques Exhibition, Paris, June 5-21, 1964.

Types of 1955-60

Designs: 1c, Crab (Macrocheira Kampferi) (horiz.). 2c, Flowering cactus (Selenicereus Gr.). 12c, Shell (Fasciolaria trapezium). 18c, Aloe ciliaris. 70c, Honor court of palace (like No. 477). 95c, Prince Rainier III.

1964, May 19 *Perf. 13*
581 A115 1c bl grn & dk red 15 15
582 A115 2c dk grn & multi 15 15
583 A115 12c vio & brn red 42 18
584 A115 18c grn, yel & car 55 15
585 A116 70c lt grn, choc & red org 55 32
586 A83 95c ultra 1.50 38
Nos. 581-586 (6) 3.32
Set value 1.05

Rainier III Aquatic Stadium A153

1964-67 Engr. *Perf. 13*
587 A153 10c dk car, rose, bl & blk 1.50 18
587A A153 15c dk car, rose, brt bl & blk ('67) 65 18
588 A153 25c dl grn, dk bl & blk 65 18
589 A153 50c lil, bl grn & blk 1.50 65

Nos. 587-589 were issued precanceled only. See note after No. 324. The "1962" date has been obliterated with 2 bars. See Nos. 732-734, 793-796, 976-979.

Europa Issue, 1964
Common Design Type

1964, Sept. 12
Size: 22x34½mm
590 CD7 25c brt red, brt grn & dk grn 18 18
591 CD7 50c ultra, ol bis & dk red brn 45 45

Weight Lifter — A154

1964, Dec. 3 Unwmk. *Perf. 13*
592 A154 1c shown 15 15
593 A154 2c Judo 15 15
594 A154 3c Pole vault 15 15
595 A154 4c Archery 15 15
Set value 20 20

Issued to commemorate the 18th Olympic Games, Tokyo, Oct. 10-25. See No. C65.

Pres. John F. Kennedy and Mercury Capsule — A155

1964, Dec. 3
596 A155 50c brt bl & indigo 65 65

Issued in memory of Pres. John F. Kennedy (1917-63).

Television Set and View of Monte Carlo A156

1964, Dec. 3
597 A156 50c dk car rose, dk bl & brn 38 38

Fifth International Television Festival.

Fréderic Mistral A157

1964, Dec. 3 Engr.
598 A157 1fr gray ol & brn red 45 45

Issued to commemorate the 50th anniversary of the death of Frederic Mistral, (1830-1914), Provençal poet.

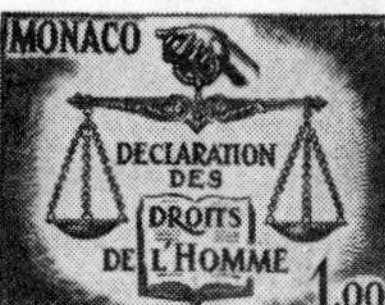

Scales of Justice and Code A158

1964, Dec. 3
599 A158 1fr gldn brn & sl grn 60 60

Universal Declaration of Human Rights.

Rally Type of 1956

Design: 1fr, "Minsk to Monte Carlo."

1964, Dec. 3
600 A98 1fr bl grn, ocher & brn 65 60

34th Monte Carlo Automobile Rally.

International Football Association Emblem — A159

1964, Dec. 3
601 A159 1fr red, bl & ol bis 70 70

Issued to commemorate the 60th anniversary of FIFA, the Federation Internationale de Football (soccer).

Types of 1955 and 1960

Designs: 40c, Aerial view of palace. 60c, 1.30fr, 2.30fr, Prince Rainier III.

1965-66 Engr. *Perf. 13*

602	A116	40c sl grn, dl cl & brt grn	30	15
603	A83	60c sl grn & blk	38	20
604	A83	1.30fr dk red & blk	2.75	65
604A	A83	2.30fr org & rose lil ('66)	90	40

Telstar and Pleumeur-Bodou Relay Station — A160

Alexander Graham Bell and Telephone A161

Designs (ITU Emblem and): 5c, Syncom II and Earth. 10c, Echo II and Earth. 12c, Relay satellite and Earth (vert.). 18c, Lunik III and Moon. 50c, Samuel Morse and telegraph. 60c, Edouard Belin, belinograph and newspaper. 70c, Roman signal towers and Chappe telegraph. 95c, Cable laying ships; "The Great Eastern" (British, 1858) and "Alsace" (French, modern). 1fr, Edouard Branly, Guglielmo Marconi and map of English Channel.

1965, May 17

605	A161	5c vio bl & sl grn	15	15
606	A161	10c dk bl & sep	15	15
607	A161	12c gray, brn & dk car	15	15
608	A161	18c ind, dk car & plum	15	15
609	A160	25c vio, ol & rose brn	15	15
610	A161	30c dk brn, ol & bis brn	18	18
611	A161	50c grn & ind	24	24
612	A161	60c dl red brn & brt bl	26	26
613	A160	70c brn blk, org & dk bl	45	45
614	A160	95c ind, blk & bl	55	55
615	A160	1fr brn, blk & ultra	80	80
		Nos. 605-615,C66 (12)	7.48	7.48

Issued to commemorate the centenary of the International Telecommunication Union.

Europa Issue, 1965
Common Design Type

1965, Sept. 25 Engr. *Perf. 13*
Size: 36x22mm

616	CD8	30c red brn & grn	18	18
617	CD8	60c vio & dk car	40	40

Palace of Monaco, 18th Century A162

Views of Palace: 12c, From the Bay, 17th century. 18c, Bay with sailboats, 18th century. 30c, From distance, 19th century. 60c, Close-up, 19th century. 1.30fr, Aerial view, 20th century.

1966, Feb. 1 Engr. *Perf. 13*

618	A162	10c vio, dl grn & ind	15	15
619	A162	12c bl, bis brn & dk brn	15	15
620	A162	18c blk, grn & bl	15	15
621	A162	30c vio bl, sep & red brn	24	24
622	A162	60c bl, grn & brn	38	38
623	A162	1.30fr dk grn & red brn	75	75
		Nos. 618-623 (6)	1.82	1.82

750th anniversary of Palace of Monaco.

Dante Alighieri — A163

Designs: 60c, Dante facing Panther of Envy. 70c, Dante and Virgil boating across muddy swamp of 5th Circle. 95c, Dante watching the arrogant and Cross of Salvation. 1fr, Invocation of St. Bernard; Dante and Beatrice.

1966, Feb. 1

624	A163	30c crim & dp grn	38	38
625	A163	60c dl grn, Prus bl & ind	65	65
626	A163	70c blk, sep & car	85	85
627	A163	95c red lil & bl	1.25	1.25
628	A163	1fr ultra & bluish grn	1.40	1.40
		Nos. 624-628 (5)	4.53	4.53

Issued to commemorate the 700th anniversary (in 1965) of the birth of Dante (1265-1321), poet.

Rally Type of 1956

Design: 1fr, "London to Monte Carlo."

1966, Feb. 1

629	A98	1fr pur, red & ind	95	95

The 35th Monte Carlo Automobile Rally.

Nativity by Gerard van Honthorst A164

1966, Feb. 1

630	A164	30c brown	22	22

Issued to honor the World Association for the Protection of Children.

Casino, Monte Carlo A165

View of La Condamine, 1860, and Francois Blanc — A166

Designs: 12c, Prince Charles III (vert.). 40c, Charles III monument, Bowling Green Gardens. 60c, Seaside Promenade and Rainier III. 70c, René Blum, Sergei Diaghilev and "Petroushka." 95c, Jules Massenet and Camille Saint-Saens. 1.30fr, Gabriel Faure and Maurice Ravel.

1966, June 1 Engr. *Perf. 13*

631	A165	12c dp bl, blk & mag	15	15
632	A165	25c multi	15	15
633	A166	30c bl, plum, grn & org	15	15
634	A165	40c multi	16	16
635	A166	60c multi	40	40
636	A166	70c rose cl & ind	40	40
637	A165	95c pur & blk	60	60
638	A165	1.30fr brn org, ol bis & brn	1.00	1.00
		Nos. 631-638,C68 (9)	5.51	5.51

Centenary of founding of Monte Carlo.

Europa Issue, 1966
Common Design Type

1966, Sept. 26 Engr. *Perf. 13*
Size: 21½x35½mm

639	CD9	30c orange	16	16
640	CD9	60c lt grn	32	32

Prince Albert I, Yachts Hirondelle I and Princesse Alice — A167

1966, Dec. 12 Engr. *Perf. 13*

641	A167	1fr ultra & dk vio brn	70	60

Issued to commemorate the first International Congress of the History of Oceanography, Monaco, Dec. 12-17. Issued in sheets of 10.

Red Chalk Drawing by Domenico Zampieri A168

Television Screen and Cross over Monaco A169

1966, Dec. 12

642	A168	30c brt rose & dk brn	16	16
643	A168	60c brt bl & yel brn	26	26

20th anniv. of UNESCO.

1966, Dec. 12

644	A169	60c dk car rose, lil & red	28	18

Issued to commemorate the 10th meeting of "UNDA" the International Catholic Association for Radio and Television.

Precontinent III and Divers on Ocean Floor — A170

1966, Dec. 12

645	A170	1fr Prus bl, yel & dk brn	45	38

Issued to commemorate the first anniversary of the submarine research station Precontinent III.

WHO Headquarters, Geneva — A171

1966, Dec. 12

646	A171	30c dp bl, ol brn & dp bl grn	15	15
647	A171	60c dk grn, crim & dk brn	22	20

Opening of WHO Headquarters, Geneva.

Automobile Type of 1961

Automobiles (Previous Winners): 1c, Bugatti, 1931. 2c, Alfa Romeo, 1932. 5c, Mercedes, 1936. 10c, Maserati, 1948. 18c, Ferrari, 1955. 20c, Alfa Romeo, 1950. 25c, Maserati, 1957. 30c, Cooper-Climax, 1958. 40c, Lotus-Climax, 1960. 50c, Lotus-Climax, 1961. 60c, Cooper-Climax, 1962. 70c, B.R.M., 1963-66. 1fr, Walter Christie, 1907. 2.30fr, Peugeot, 1910.

1967, Apr. 28 Engr. *Perf. 13x12½*

648	A122	1c ind, red & brt bl	15	15
649	A122	2c grn, red & blk	15	15
650	A122	5c red, ind & gray	15	15
651	A122	10c vio, red & ind	15	15
652	A122	18c ind & red	15	15
653	A122	20c dk grn, red & ind	15	15
654	A122	25c ultra, red & ind	15	15
655	A122	30c brn, ind & grn	20	15
656	A122	40c car rose, ind & grn	28	20
657	A122	50c lil, ind & grn	40	25
658	A122	60c car, ind & grn	55	35
659	A122	70c dl yel, bl grn & ind	65	45
660	A122	1fr brn red, blk & gray	80	60
661	A122	2.30fr multi	1.75	1.25
		Nos. 648-661,C73 (15)	7.93	6.30

25th Grand Prix of Monaco, May 7.

Dog, Egyptian Statue — A172

1967, Apr. 28 *Perf. 12½x13*

662	A172	30c dk grn, brn & blk	45	38

Issued to commemorate the congress of the International Dog Fanciers Federation, Monaco, Apr. 5-9.

View of Monte Carlo — A173

1967, Apr. 28 *Perf. 13*

663	A173	30c sl grn, brt bl & brn	25	18

International Tourist Year, 1967.

Chessboard and Monte Carlo Harbor — A174

1967, Apr. 28

664	A174	60c brt bl, dk pur & blk	65	60

International Chess Championships, Monaco, Mar. 19-Apr. 1.

Melvin Jones, View of Monte Carlo and Lions Emblem — A175

1967, Apr. 28
665 A175 60c ultra, sl bl & choc 42 32

50th anniversary of Lions International.

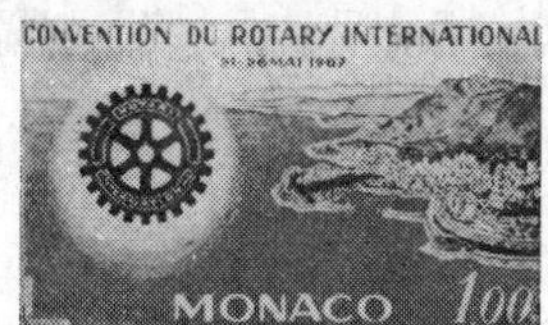

Rotary Emblem and View of Monte Carlo — A176

1967, Apr. 28
666 A176 1fr brt bl & lt ol grn 50 40

Issued to publicize the Rotary International Convention, Monaco, May 21-26.

EXPO '67 Monaco Pavilion — A177

1967, Apr. 28
667 A177 1fr multi 38 32

Issued to commemorate EXPO '67, International Exhibition, Montreal, Apr. 28-Oct. 27, 1967.

Map of Europe A178

1967, Apr. 28
668 A178 1fr choc, lem & Prus bl 38 30

Issued to publicize the International Committee for European Migration, CIME.

Europa Issue, 1967
Common Design Type

1967, Apr. 28 ***Perf. 12½x13***
669 CD10 30c brt car, rose lil & brt vio 18 18
670 CD10 60c grn ol & bl grn 35 32

Skier and Olympic Emblem — A179

1967, Dec. 7 **Engr.** ***Perf. 13***
671 A179 2.30fr red brn, gray & brt bl 1.10 95

Issued to commemorate the 10th Winter Olympic Games, Grenoble, France, Feb. 6-18, 1968.

Sounding Line and Map — A180

1967, Dec. 7
672 A180 1fr dk bl, grn & ol 50 40

Issued to commemorate the 9th International Hydrographic Conference, Monte Carlo, April-May, 1967.

Marie Curie, Chemical Apparatus and Atom Symbol — A181

1967, Dec. 7
673 A181 1fr brn, ultra & ol 52 40

Issued to commemorate the centenary of the birth of Marie Curie (1867-1934), discoverer of radium and polonium.

Princes of Monaco Issue

Rainier I, by Eugene Charpentier A182

Design: No. 675, Lucien Grimaldi, by Ambrogio di Predis.

1967, Dec. 7 ***Perf. 12x13***
674 A182 1fr multi 95 70
675 A182 1fr multi 95 70

See Nos. 710-711, 735-736, 774-775, 813-814, 860-861, 892-893, 991-992, 1035-1036, 1093, 1135-1136, 1187-1188, 1246-1247, 1302-1303.

Shot Put — A183

Sport: 30c, High jump. 60c, Gymnast on rings. 70c, Water polo. 1fr, Wrestling. 2.30fr, Gymnast.

1968, Apr. 29 **Engr.** ***Perf. 13***
676 A183 20c brt bl, grn & brn 15 15
677 A183 30c vio bl, sep & brn vio 15 15
678 A183 60c car, brt rose lil & dp bl 24 24
679 A183 70c ocher, brn org & Prus bl 30 30
680 A183 1fr brn org, brn & ind 48 48
681 A183 2.30fr dk car, vio bl & ol 1.00 1.00
Nos. 676-681,C74 (7) 4.32 4.07

Issued to publicize the 19th Olympic Games, Mexico City, Oct. 12-27.

St. Martin and the Beggar A184

1968, Apr. 29
682 A184 2.30fr brn red, Prus bl & blk brn 1.00 90

Red Cross of Monaco, 20th anniversary.

Anemones, by Raoul Dufy A185

1968, Apr. 29 **Photo.** ***Perf. 12x13***
683 A185 1fr lt bl & multi 60 48

Issued to publicize the International Flower Show in Monte Carlo. See Nos. 766, 776, 815-816, 829, 865.

Arms of Pope Pius IX and Prince Charles III — A186

St. Nicholas — A187

Designs: 30c, St. Benedict. 60c, Benedictine Monastery, Subiaco (Italy). 1fr, Church of St. Nicholas, Monaco, 13th century (horiz.).

Perf. 12½x13, 13x12½

1968, Apr. 29 **Engr.**
684 A186 10c red & brn 15 15
685 A187 20c sl grn, ocher & car 15 15
686 A187 30c ultra & ol grn 22 16
687 A187 60c lt bl, brn & dk grn 30 30
688 A187 1fr ind, bl & ol bis 55 45
Nos. 684-688 (5) 1.37 1.21

Centenary of the elevation of St. Nicholas Church to an Abbey *Nullius,* directly subject to the Holy See.

Europa Issue, 1968
Common Design Type

1968, Apr. 29 ***Perf. 13***
Size: 36x22mm
689 CD11 30c dp org & car 20 15
690 CD11 60c car & ultra 30 18
691 CD11 1fr grn & red brn 65 42

Locomotive 030, 1868 — A188

Locomotives and Views: 30c, Type "C"-220, 1898. 60c, Type 230-"C", 1910. 70c, Type 231-"F," 1925. 1fr, Type 241-"A," 1932. 2.30fr, Type "BB," 1968.

1968, Dec. 12 **Engr.** ***Perf. 13***
692 A188 20c vio bl, brn & blk 22 16
693 A188 30c dk ol grn, bl & blk 32 18
694 A188 60c bl, bis & blk 50 24
695 A188 70c vio, red brn & blk 60 38
696 A188 1fr bl, brn red & blk 1.10 65
697 A188 2.30fr sal pink, brt bl & blk 2.25 1.65
Nos. 692-697 (6) 4.99 3.26

Centenary of the Nice-Monaco Railroad.

Chateaubriand and Combourg Castle — A189

Scenes from Chateaubriand Novels: 20c, The Genius of Christianity. 25c, René. 30c, The Last Abencerage. 60c, The Martyrs. 2.30fr, Atala.

1968, Dec. 12
698 A189 10c dk grn, grn & pur 15 15
699 A189 20c brt bl, vio & mag 15 15
700 A189 25c sl, pur & brn 16 15
701 A189 30c dp brn, brn & pur 25 16
702 A189 60c brn red, bl grn & dk brn 32 30
703 A189 2.30fr dk bl, ol & mag 1.10 95
Nos. 698-703 (6) 2.13 1.86

Issued to commemorate the 200th anniversary of the birth of Vicomte François René de Chateaubriand (1768-1848), novelist and statesman.

"France" and "Fidelity" by Bosio — A190

François Joseph Bosio (1768-1845), Sculptor — A191

Designs: 25c, Henri IV as a boy. 60c, Louis XIV on horseback, Place des Victoires. 2.30fr, Busts of Louis XVIII, Napoleon I and Charles X.

1968, Dec. 12
704 A190 20c brown 15 15
705 A191 25c sal pink & dk brn 15 15
706 A191 30c sl & vio bl 16 15

707 A191 60c dk ol grn & gray grn 28 20
708 A190 2.30fr blk & sl 90 70
Nos. 704-708 (5) 1.64 1.35

WHO Emblem — A192

1968, Dec. 12 **Photo.**
709 A192 60c multi 30 25

Issued to commemorate the 20th anniversary of the World Health Organization.

Princes of Monaco Type of 1967

Designs: 1fr, Charles II (1581-89). 2.30fr, Jeanne Grimaldi (1596-1620).

1968, Dec. 12 **Engr.** ***Perf. 12x13***
710 A182 1fr multi 42 42
711 A182 2.30fr multi 1.10 1.10

Faust and Mephistopheles — A193

Scenes from "Damnation of Faust" by Berlioz: 10c, Rakoczy March. 25c, Auerbach's Cellar. 30c, Dance of the Sylphs. 40c, Dance of the Sprites. 50c, Faust and Marguerite. 70c, Woods and Meadows. 1fr, The Ride to the Abyss. 1.15fr, Heaven.

1969, Apr. 26 **Engr.** ***Perf. 13***
712 A193 10c bl grn, pur & org brn 15 15
713 A193 20c mag, dk ol & lt brn 15 15
714 A193 25c ind, brn & mag 15 15
715 A193 30c yel grn, sl & blk 15 15
716 A193 40c org red, sl & blk 18 15
717 A193 50c ol, plum & sl 22 20
718 A193 70c dp grn, sl & lt brn 35 28
719 A193 1fr mag, blk & ol bis 48 40
720 A193 1.15fr Prus bl, blk & ultra 60 60
Nos. 712-720,C75 (10) 3.68 3.33

Issued to commemorate the centenary of the death of Hector Berlioz (1803-1869), French composer.

St. Elizabeth and Husband, Louis IV, Landgrave of Thuringia A194

1969, Apr. 26
721 A194 3fr dk red, sl & gray 1.65 1.40

Issued for the Red Cross.

See Nos. 767, 812, 830, 905, 963, 1037, 1094, 1189.

Europa Issue, 1969
Common Design Type

1969, Apr. 26
Size: 36x26mm
722 CD12 40c scar & pur 18 15
723 CD12 70c brt bl & blk 42 26
724 CD12 1fr yel bis, brn & bl 55 38

Prince Rainier Type of 1955 and Palace Type of 1960

Designs: 80c, Aerial view of Palace. 1.15fr, 1.30fr, Honor Court.

1969-70 **Engr.** ***Perf. 13***
725 A83 40c ol & rose red 20 15
726 A83 45c sl & ocher 25 15
727 A83 50c ocher & mar 40 15
728 A83 70c dk pur & brt vio bl 55 30
729 A116 80c bl, red brn & grn 60 30
730 A83 85c dk vio & brt grn 65 45
731 A116 1.15fr blk, bl & mar 1.00 60
731A A116 1.30fr ol brn, lt bl & dl grn ('70) 75 40
Nos. 725-731A (8) 4.40 2.50

Aquatic Stadium Type of 1964-67, "1962" Omitted

1969 **Engr.** ***Perf. 13***
732 A153 22c choc, brt bl & blk 35 15
733 A153 35c Prus bl, brt bl & blk 35 28
734 A153 70c blk & vio bl 60 24

Nos. 732-734 were issued precanceled only. See note after No. 324.

Princes of Monaco Type of 1967

Designs: 1fr, Honoré II (1604-1662), by Philippe de Champaigne. 3fr, Louise-Hippolyte (1697-1731), by Pierre Gobert.

1969, Nov. 25 **Engr.** ***Perf. 12x13***
735 A182 1fr multi 38 38
736 A182 3fr multi 1.10 1.10

Woman's Head, by Leonardo da Vinci — A195

Drawings by Leonardo da Vinci: 40c, Self-portrait. 70c, Head of old man. 80c, Study for head of St. Magdalene. 1.15fr, Man's head. 3fr, Professional soldier.

1969, Nov. 25 ***Perf. 13***
737 A195 30c dl brn 20 15
738 A195 40c brn & rose red 22 16
739 A195 70c gray grn 30 22
740 A195 80c dk brn 35 30
741 A195 1.15fr org brn 60 55
742 A195 3fr ol brn 1.50 1.10
Nos. 737-742 (6) 3.17 2.48

Issued to commemorate the 450th anniversary of the death of Leonardo da Vinci (1452-1519), Florentine painter, sculptor and scientist.

Alphonse Daudet and Scenes from "Letters from My Windmill" — A196

Various Scenes from "Letters from My Windmill" (Lettres de Mon Moulin).

1969, Nov. 25
743 A196 30c bl grn & multi 16 15
744 A196 40c brn, vio bl & ol 28 24
745 A196 70c pur, brn & ol gray 32 30
746 A196 80c sl grn, vio bl & mar 38 35
747 A196 1.15fr ocher, sep & blk 50 48
Nos. 743-747 (5) 1.64 1.52

Centenary of publication of "Letters from My Windmill," by Alphonse Daudet (1840-1897).

ILO Emblem A197

1969, Nov. 25 ***Perf. 13x12½***
748 A197 40c dk bl & dk pur 35 28

50th anniv. of the ILO.

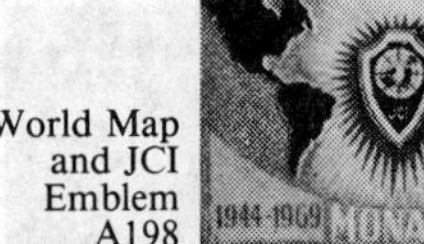

World Map and JCI Emblem A198

1969, Nov. 25
749 A198 40c ol, dk bl & bl 24 20

Issued to commemorate the 25th anniversary of the Junior Chamber of Commerce in Monaco.

Television Camera and View of Monte Carlo A199

1969, Nov. 25
750 A199 40c red brn, lil & bl 24 20

Issued to publicize the 10th International Television Festival in 1970.

King Alfonso XIII, Prince Albert I and Underwater Scene — A200

1969, Nov. 25 ***Perf. 12½x13***
751 A200 40c dk brn, blk & grnsh bl 28 28

Issued to commemorate the 50th anniversary of the International Commission for the Scientific Exploration of the Mediterranean.

Congress Building, Princes Albert I and Rainier III — A201

1970, Feb. 21 **Engr.** ***Perf. 13***
752 A201 40c gray & car 22 16

Issued to commemorate the meeting of the Interparliamentary Union, Monaco, Mar. 30-Apr. 5.

EXPO '70 Emblem, Japanese Scroll — A202

Designs (EXPO '70 Emblem and): 30c, Ibis. 40c, Torii. 70c, Cherry blossoms (horiz.) 1.15fr, Palace and arms of Monaco, Osaka Castle and arms (horiz.).

1970, Mar. 16
753 A202 20c brn, yel grn & car 15 15
754 A202 30c brn, yel grn & buff 15 20
755 A202 40c ol bis & pur 22 22
756 A202 70c lt gray & red 55 55
757 A202 1.15fr red & multi 60 60
Nos. 753-757 (5) 1.67 1.72

Issued to publicize EXPO '70 International Exposition, Osaka, Japan, Mar. 15-Sept. 13.

Harbor Seal Pup — A203

1970, Mar. 16
758 A203 40c red lil, bl & gray 50 42

Protection of seal pups.

Doberman Pinscher A204

1970, Apr. 25
759 A204 40c ocher & blk 1.65 60

International Dog Show, Monte Carlo, Apr. 25. See No. 996.

Basque Ponies A205

Designs: 30c, Parnassius Apollo butterfly. 50c, Harbor seal in Somme Bay. 80c, Pyrenean chamois (vert.). 1fr, Whitetailed sea eagles (vert.). 1.15fr, European otter (vert.).

1970, May 4
760 A205 30c Prus bl & multi 22 15
761 A205 40c bl & multi 28 16
762 A205 50c grnsh bl, bis & brn 40 16
763 A205 80c gray grn, sl bl & brn 58 28
764 A205 1fr gray, brn & bis 95 38
765 A205 1.15fr dk brn, lt bl & yel grn 1.10 45
Nos. 760-765 (6) 3.53 1.58

Issued to commemorate the 20th anniversary of the International Federation of Animal Protection.

Flower Type of 1968

Design: 3fr, Roses and Anemones, by Vincent van Gogh.

1970, May 4 Photo. *Perf. 12x13*
766 A185 3fr blk & multi 1.50 1.50

International Flower Show, Monte Carlo.

Red Cross Type of 1969

Design: 3fr, St. Louis giving alms to the poor.

1970, May 4 Engr. *Perf. 13*
767 A194 3fr dk gray, ol gray & slate grn 1.50 1.50

Issued for the Red Cross.

Europa Issue, 1970
Common Design Type

1970, May 4
Size: 26x36mm
768 CD13 40c deep rose lilac 22 15
769 CD13 80c bright green 45 28
770 CD13 1fr deep blue 55 35

UPU Headquarters and Monument, Bern — A206

1970, May 4
771 A206 40c brn ol, gray & bl grn 22 16

New UPU Headquarters in Bern opening.

Plaque and Flag on the Moon, Presidents Kennedy and Nixon — A207

Design: 80c, Astronauts and landing module on moon, and Apollo 11 emblem.

1970, May 4 Photo.
772 A207 40c multi 28 24
773 A207 80c multi 55 42

Man's first landing on moon, July 20, 1969. US astronauts Neil A. Armstrong and Col. Edwin E. Aldrin, Jr., with Lt. Col. Michael Collins piloting Apollo 11.

Princes of Monaco Type of 1967

Designs: 1fr, Louis I (1662-1701), by Jean Francois de Troy. 3fr, Charlotte de Gramont (1639-1678), by Sebastian Bourdon.

1970, Dec. 15 Engr. *Perf. 12x13*
774 A182 1fr multi 45 45
775 A182 3fr multi 1.25 1.40

Painting Type of 1968

Design: 3fr, Portrait of Dédie, by Amedeo Modigliani (1884-1920).

1970, Dec. 15
776 A185 3fr multi 1.00 70

Beethoven and "Ode to Joy" A208

1970, Dec. 15
777 A208 1.30fr brn & mar 1.00 70

Bicentenary of the birth of Ludwig van Beethoven (1770-1827), composer.

Dumas and Scene from "Three Musketeers" — A209

Designs: 40c, Henri Rougier and biplane over Monaco. 80c, Alphonse de Lamartine and scenes from his works.

1970, Dec. 15
778 A209 30c bl, brn & gray 15 15
779 A209 40c bl, sep & gray 26 18
780 A209 80c multi 35 22

Nos. 778-780 commemorate: Centenary of the death of Alexandre Dumas, pere (1802-1870), novelist; 60th anniversary of first flight over the Mediterranean by Henri Rougier; 150th anniversary of the publication of **"Meditations Poetiques" by Alphonse de** Lamartine (1790-1869), poet.

Camargue Horse A210

Horses: 20c, Anglo-Arabian thoroughbred. 30c, French saddle horse. 40c, Lippizaner. 50c, Trotter. 70c, English thoroughbred. 85c, Arabian. 1.15fr, Barbary.

1970, Dec. 15 Engr. *Perf. 13*
781 A210 10c bl, ol bis & dk bl 15 15
782 A210 20c vio bl, brn & ol 15 15
783 A210 30c bl, brn & grn 22 15
784 A210 40c gray, ind & ol bis 32 18
785 A210 50c bl, dk brn & ol 45 22
786 A210 70c dk grn, ol brn & red brn 55 28
787 A210 85c dk grn, ol & sl 70 45
788 A210 1.15fr bl, emer & blk 95 55
Nos. 781-788,C77 (9) 5.74 4.13

Prince Rainier Type of 1955 and Palace Type of 1960

Designs: 90c, Honor Court. 1.40fr, Aerial view of Palace.

1971 Engr. *Perf. 13*
789 A83 60c plum & blk 65 32
790 A116 90c dk car, ultra & blk 90 42
791 A83 1.10fr gray & ultra 1.10 65
792 A116 1.40fr pur, org & grn 1.25 1.00

Aquatic Stadium Type of 1964-67, "1962" Omitted

1971
793 A153 26c pur, ultra & blk 35 18
794 A153 30c cop red, bl, lil & blk 45 18
795 A153 45c sl grn, vio bl & blk 70 24
796 A153 90c ol, Prus bl & blk 1.25 40

Nos. 793-796 were issued precanceled only. See note after No. 324.

Europa Issue, 1971
Common Design Type

1971, Sept. 6
797 CD14 50c car rose 25 15
798 CD14 80c brt bl 38 22
799 CD14 1.30fr sl grn 90 32

Old Bridge at Sospel — A211

Designs: 80c, Roquebrune Castle. 1.30fr, Grimaldi Castle. 3fr, Roman Monument, La Turbie (vert.). All views in Alpes-Maritimes Department, France.

1971, Sept. 6
800 A211 50c sl grn, bl & ol brn 20 15
801 A211 80c sl grn, sl & brn 35 16
802 A211 1.30fr brn, sl grn & red 50 35
803 A211 3fr brt bl, sl & ol 1.25 85

Protection of historic monuments.

Theodolite, Underwater Scene and Coast Line — A212

1971, Sept. 6
804 A212 80c bl grn & multi 42 35

50th anniversary of International Hydrographical Bureau.

Sea Bird Covered with Oil — A213

1971, Sept. 6
805 A213 50c dp bl & ind 45 35

Against pollution of the seas.

"Arts" (Organ Pipes and Michelangelo's Creation of Adam) — A214

"Science" (Alchemist, Radar and Rocket) — A215

Prince Pierre of Monaco — A216

Design: 80c, "Culture" (medieval scholar, book, film and television).

1971, Sept. 6 Engr. *Perf. 13*
806 A214 30c brt bl, pur & brn 15 15
807 A215 50c sl & brn org 18 15
808 A214 80c emer & brn 28 18

Photo. *Perf. 12½x13*
809 A216 1.30fr gray grn 42 32
Set value 66

25th anniv. of UNESCO.

Cocker Spaniel A217

1971, Sept. 6 *Perf. 13x12½*
810 A217 50c multi 1.25 1.00

Intl. Dog Show. See Nos. 826, 879, 910.

Hand Holding Blood Donor Emblem A218

1971, Sept. 6 Engr. *Perf. 13*
811 A218 80c red, vio & gray 45 32

7th International Blood Donors Congress, Monaco, Oct. 21-24.

Red Cross Type of 1969

Design: 3fr, St. Vincent de Paul appearing to prisoners.

1971, Sept. 6
812 A194 3fr bl grn, ol grn & dp grn 1.40 1.10

For the Red Cross

Princes of Monaco Type of 1967

Designs: 1fr, Antoine I (1701-1731), by Hyacinthe Rigaud. 3fr, Marie de Lorraine (1674-1724), French School.

1972, Jan. 18 *Perf. 12x13*
813 A182 1fr multi 45 45
814 A182 3fr multi 1.40 1.25

Painting Type of 1968

Designs: 2fr, The Cradle, by Berthe Morisot. 3fr, Clown, by Jean Antoine Watteau.

1972, Jan. 18
815 A185 2fr grn & multi 1.10 95
816 A185 3fr multi 1.50 1.25

No. 815 issued for 25th anniv. (in 1971) of UNICEF.

Christ Before Pilate, by Dürer A219

1972, Jan. 18 *Perf. 13*
817 A219 2fr lt brn & blk 1.25 1.00

500th anniversary of the birth of Albrecht Dürer (1471-1528), German painter and engraver.

La Fontaine and Animals — A220

Saint-Saens and "Samson et Dalila" — A221

Design: 1.30fr, Charles Baudelaire, nudes and cats.

1972, Jan. 18

818 A220 50c brn, grn & sl grn 35 24
819 A221 90c dk brn & yel brn 52 38
820 A220 1.30fr blk, red & vio brn 65 52

350th anniversary of the birth of Jean de La Fontaine (1621-1695), fabulist (50c); 50th anniversary of the death of Camille Saint-Saens (1835-1921), composer (90c); 150th anniversary of the birth of Charles Baudelaire (1821-1867), poet (1.30fr).

Father Christmas — A222

1972, Jan. 18

821 A222 30c bis, sl bl & red 15 15
822 A222 50c vio brn, grn & red 24 15
823 A222 90c ocher, ind & red 40 22

Christmas 1971.

Battle of Lepanto — A223

1972, Jan. 18

824 A223 1fr dl bl, red & brn 50 40

400th anniversary of the Battle of Lepanto against the Turks.

Steam and Diesel Locomotives, UIC Emblem — A224

1972, Apr. 27 Engr. *Perf. 13*

825 A224 50c dk car, lil & choc 42 32

50th anniversary of the founding of the International Railroad Union (UIC).

Dog Type of 1971

1972, Apr. 27 Photo. *Perf. 13x12½*

826 A217 60c Great Dane 80 70

International Dog Show.

Serene Landscape, Pollution, Destruction — A225

1972, Apr. 27 Engr. *Perf. 13*

827 A225 90c grn, brn & blk 48 30

Anti-pollution fight.

Ski Jump, Sapporo '72 Emblem — A226

1972, Apr. 27

828 A226 90c bl grn, dk red & blk 50 40

11th Winter Olympic Games, Sapporo, Japan, Feb. 3-13.

Flower Type of 1968

Design: 3fr, Flowers in Vase, by Paul Cezanne.

1972, Apr. 27 Photo. *Perf. 12x13*

829 A185 3fr multi 1.65 1.10

International Flower Show, Monte Carlo.

Red Cross Type of 1969

Design: 3fr, St. Francis of Assisi comforting poor man.

1972, Apr. 27 Engr. *Perf. 13*

830 A194 3fr dk pur & brn 1.65 1.40

For the Red Cross.

Europa Issue 1972

Common Design Type

1972, Apr. 27 *Perf. 12½x13*

Size: 26x36mm

831 CD15 50c vio bl & org 68 35
832 CD15 90c vio bl & emer 1.25 80

Church of Sts. John and Paul (detail), by Canaletto A227

Designs: 60c, Church of St. Peter of Castello, by Francesco Guardi. 2fr, St. Mark's Square, by Bernardo Bellotto.

1972, Apr. 27 *Perf. 13*

Sizes: 36x48mm (30c, 2fr); 26½x48mm (60c)

833 A227 30c rose red 24 20
834 A227 60c brt pur 32 24
835 A227 2fr Prus bl 1.75 1.25

UNESCO campaign to save Venice.

Dressage A228

Designs (Equestrian Events): 90c, Jump over fences. 1.10fr, Jump over wall. 1.40fr, Jump over gates.

1972, Apr. 27

836 A228 60c rose car, vio bl & brn 70 70
837 A228 90c vio bl, rose car & brn 1.10 1.10
838 A228 1.10fr brn, rose car & vio bl 1.75 1.75
839 A228 1.40fr vio bl, rose car & brn 2.50 2.50
a. Block of 4 + 2 labels 8.00 8.00

20th Olympic Games, Munich, Aug. 26-Sept. 10. Nos. 836-839 printed se-tenant in sheets of 24 stamps and 6 labels.

Auguste Escoffier and his Birthplace A229

1972, May 6 Engr. *Perf. 13*

840 A229 45c blk & olive 32 24

125th anniversary of the birth of Georges Auguste Escoffier (1846-1935), French chef.

Young Drug Addict — A230

Congress Emblem, Birds and Animals — A231

1972, July 3

841 A230 50c car, sep & org 40 22
842 A230 90c sl grn, sep & ind 60 38

Fight against drug abuse.

1972, Sept. 25

Designs: 50c, Congress emblem, Neptune, sea, earth and land creatures (horiz.). 90c, Globe, land, sea and air creatures.

843 A231 30c ol, brt grn & car 15 15
844 A231 50c ocher, brn & org brn 25 15
845 A231 90c org brn, bl & ol 38 24

17th International Zoology Congress, Monaco, Sept. 24-30.

Arrangement of Lilies and Palm — A232

Designs: Floral arrangements.

1972, Nov. 13 Photo. *Perf. 13*

846 A232 30c org red & multi 24 15
847 A232 50c multi 35 24
848 A232 90c blk & multi 60 32

International Flower Show, Monte Carlo, May, 1973. See Nos. 894-896.

Child and Adoration of the Kings A233

1972, Nov. 13 Engr.

849 A233 30c gray, vio bl & brt pink 15 15
850 A233 50c dp car, lil & brn 22 15
851 A233 90c vio bl & pur 45 24

Christmas 1972.

Louis Bleriot and his Monoplane — A234

Designs: 50c, Roald Amundsen and Antarctic landscape. 90c, Louis Pasteur and laboratory.

1972, Dec. 4

852 A234 30c choc & brt bl 22 15
853 A234 50c Prus bl & ind 35 28
854 A234 90c choc & ocher 60 50

Anniversaries of the births of: Louis Bleriot (1872-1936), French aviation pioneer (30c); Roald Amundsen (1872-1928), Norwegian polar explorer (50c); Louis Pasteur (1822-1895), French chemist and bacteriologist (90c).

Gethsemane, by Giovanni Canavesio — A235

Frescoes by Canavesio, 15th century, Chapel of Our Lady of Fountains at La Brique: 50c, Christ Stripped of His Garments. 90c, Christ Carrying the Cross. 1.40fr, Resurrection. 2fr, Crucifixion.

1972, Dec. 4

855 A235 30c brt rose 16 15
856 A235 50c indigo 28 22
857 A235 90c sl grn 50 32
858 A235 1.40fr brt red 60 45
859 A235 2fr purple 1.10 70
Nos. 855-859 (5) 2.64 1.84

Protection of historic monuments.

Princes of Monaco Type of 1967

Designs: 1fr, Jacques I, by Nicolas de Largilliere. 3fr, Louise Hippolyte (1697-1731), by Jean Baptiste Vanloo.

1972, Dec. 4 *Perf. 12x13*
860 A182 1fr multi 60 35
861 A182 3fr multi 1.50 1.25

Girl, Syringe, Addicts A236

1973, Jan. 5 **Engr.** *Perf. 13*
862 A236 50c brt bl, cl & sl grn 24 15
863 A236 90c org, lil & emer 52 38

Fight against drug abuse.

Souvenir Sheet

Sts. Barbara, Devote and Agatha, by Louis Brea A237

1973, Apr. 30
864 A237 5fr dull red 10.50 10.50

Red Cross of Monaco, 25th anniv.

Flower Type of 1968

Design: 3.50fr, Flowers in Vase, by Ambrosius Bosschaert.

1973, Apr. 30 **Photo.** *Perf. 12x13*
865 A185 3.50fr multi 1.90 1.50

International Flower Show, Monte Carlo.

Europa Issue 1973
Common Design Type

1973, Apr. 30 **Engr.** *Perf. 13*
Size: 36x26mm
866 CD16 50c orange 65 52
867 CD16 90c bl grn 1.20 75

Molière, Scene from "Le Malade Imaginaire" A238

Costumed Players and Mask A239

1973, Apr. 30
868 A238 20c red, vio bl & brn 38 18

Tricentenary of the death of Molière (1622-1673), French actor and writer.

1973, Apr. 30
869 A239 60c red, lil & bl 48 28

5th International Amateur Theater Festival.

Virgin Mary, St. Teresa, Lisieux Basilica — A240

1973, Apr. 30
870 A240 1.40fr ind, ultra & brn 65 45

Centenary of the birth of St. Teresa of Lisieux (Therese Martin, 1873-1897), Carmelite nun.

Charles Peguy and Cathedral of Chartres — A241

1973, Apr. 30
871 A241 50c dp cl, ol brn & sl 38 24

Centenary of the birth of Charles Pierre Peguy (1873-1914), French writer.

Colette, Books and Cat — A242

Designs: No. 873, Eugene Ducretet and transmission from Eiffel Tower to Pantheon. 45c, Jean Henri Fabre and insects. 50c, Blaise Pascal (vert.). 60c, Radar installation and telegraph wire insulators. No. 877, William Webb Ellis and rugby. No. 878, Sir George Cayley and early model plane.

1973, Apr. 30
872 A242 30c dp org, bl & dk bl 48 24
873 A242 30c brn & multi 30 24
874 A242 45c dp bl & multi 48 30
875 A242 50c vio bl, lil & dk pur 30 24
876 A242 60c brn, bl blk & brt bl 38 30
877 A242 90c brn & car rose 60 40
878 A242 90c red & multi 60 48
Nos. 872-878 (7) 3.14 2.20

Anniversaries: Colette (1873-1954), French writer (#872); 75th anniv. of 1st Hertzian wave transmission (#873); Fabre (1823-1915), entomologist (45c); Pascal (1623-1662), scientist and philosopher (50c); 5th Intl. Telecommunications Day (60c); Sesquicentennial of the invention of rugby (#877); Cayley (1821-95), aviation pioneer (#878).

Dog Type of 1971

Design: German shepherd.

1973, Apr. 30 **Photo.** *Perf. 13x12½*
879 A217 45c multi 3.75 1.90

International Dog Show.

The First Crèche, by Giotto — A243

Paintings of the Nativity by: 45c, School of Filippo Lippi. 50c, Giotto. 1fr, 15th century miniature (vert.). 2fr, Fra Angelico (vert.).

Perf. 13x12, 12x13

1973, Nov. 12 **Engr.**
880 A243 30c purple 38 25
881 A243 45c rose mag 60 45
882 A243 50c brn org 75 50
883 A243 1fr sl grn 1.25 85
884 A243 2fr ol grn 2.00 1.65
Nos. 880-884,C78 (6) 7.73 5.70

750th anniversary of the first crèche assembled by St. Francis of Assisi.

Picnic and View of Monte Carlo — A244

Designs: 20c, Dance around maypole (vert.). 30c, "U Brandi" folk dance. 45c, Dance around St. John's fire. 50c, Blessing of the Christmas bread. 60c, Blessing of the sea. 1fr, Good Friday procession.

1973, Nov. 12 *Perf. 13*
885 A244 10c sl grn, dk bl & sep 15 15
886 A244 20c bl, ol & lil 15 15
887 A244 30c lt grn, bl & brn 22 22
888 A244 45c dk brn, vio & red brn 28 28
889 A244 50c blk, brn & ver 28 28
890 A244 60c bl, mag & vio bl 42 42
891 A244 1fr ind, vio & ol bis 70 70
Nos. 885-891 (7) 2.20 2.20

Monegasque customs.

Princes of Monaco Type of 1967

Paintings of Charlotte Grimaldi, by Pierre Gobert, 1733: No. 892, in court dress, No. 893, in nun's habit.

1973, Nov. 12 *Perf. 12x13*
892 A182 2fr multi 1.25 1.10
893 A182 2fr multi 1.25 1.10

Flower Type of 1972

Designs: Floral arrangements.

1973, Nov. 12 **Photo.** *Perf. 13*
894 A232 45c vio bl & multi 42 28
895 A232 60c dk brn & multi 55 42
896 A232 1fr brn org & multi 90 70

International Flower Show, Monte Carlo, May 1974.

Children, Syringes, Drug Addicts A245

1973, Nov. 12 **Engr.**
897 A245 50c bl, grn & brn 28 22
898 A245 90c red, brn & ind 70 42

Fight against drug abuse.

Souvenir Sheet

RAINIER III
PRINCE DE MONACO

Prince Rainier III — A246

1974, May 8 **Engr.** *Imperf.*
899 A246 10fr black 6.00 6.00

25th anniv. of the accession of Prince Rainier III.

Art from Around the World — A247

King of Rome (Napoleon's Son), by Bosio — A248

Designs (UPU Emblem and): 70c, Hands holding letters. 1.10fr, Famous buildings, Statue of Liberty and Sphinx.

1974, May 8 *Perf. 13*
900 A247 50c choc & org brn 22 18
901 A247 70c aqua & multi 35 30
902 A247 1.10fr ind & multi 90 65

Centenary of the Universal Postal Union.

1974, May 8

Europa: 1.10fr, Madame Elisabeth (sister of Louis XVI), by Francois Josef Bosio.

903 A248 45c sl grn & sep 85 65
904 A248 1.10fr brn & ol brn 1.50 1.00
a. Souv. sheet, 5 #903, 5 #904 20.00 20.00

Red Cross Type of 1969

Design: St. Bernard of Menthon rescuing mountain traveler.

1974, May 8
905 A194 3fr Prus bl & vio brn 1.65 1.25

For the Red Cross.

Henri Farman and Farman Planes A249

Designs: 40c, Guglielmo Marconi, circuit diagram and ships which conducted first tests. 45c, Ernest Duchesne and penicillin. 50c, Fernand Forest and 4-cylinder motor.

1974, May 8
906 A249 30c multi 18 15
907 A249 40c multi 20 15
908 A249 45c multi 25 18
909 A249 50c multi 24 18

Centenary of the birth of Henri Farman (1874-1934), French aviation pioneer (30c); centenary of the birth of Guglielmo Marconi (1874-1937), Italian inventor (40c); centenary of the birth of Ernest Duchesne (1874-1912), French biologist (45c); 60th anniversary of the death of Fernand Forest (1851-1914), inventor (50c).

Dog Type of 1971

1974, May 8 **Photo.** *Perf. 13x12½*
910 A217 60c Schnauzer 1.25 85

Intl. Dog Show, Monte Carlo, Apr. 6-7.

Ronsard and Scenes from his Sonnet à Hélène — A250

1974, May 8 **Engr.** *Perf. 13*
911 A250 70c choc & dk car 42 32

450th anniversary of the birth of Pierre de Ronsard (1524-1585), French poet.

Winston Churchill — A251

1974, May 8

912	A251	1fr gray & brn	52	32

Centenary of the birth of Sir Winston Churchill (1874-1965), statesman.

Palaces of Monaco and Vienna — A252

1974, May 8

913	A252	2fr multi	1.00	85

60th anniversary of the first International Police Congress, Monaco, Apr. 1914.

The Box, by Auguste Renoir A253

Rising Sun, by Claude Monet — A254

Impressionist Paintings: No. 915, Dancing Class, by Edgar Degas. No. 917, Entrance to Voisins Village, by Camille Pissarro. No. 918, House of the Hanged Man, by Paul Cezanne. No. 919, The Flooding of Port Marly, by Alfred Sisley.

Perf. 12x13, 13x12

1974, Nov. 12 Engr.

914	A253	1fr multi	1.25	95
915	A253	1fr multi	1.25	95
916	A254	2fr multi	1.90	1.25
917	A254	2fr multi	1.90	1.25
918	A254	2fr multi	1.90	1.25
919	A254	2fr multi	1.90	1.25
		Nos. 914-919 (6)	10.10	6.90

Trainer and Tigers A255

Prancing Horses — A256

Perf. 13x12½, 12½x13

1974, Nov. 12

920	A255	2c shown	15	15
921	A256	3c shown	15	15
922	A255	5c Elephants	15	15
923	A256	45c Equestrian act	40	18
924	A255	70c Clowns	52	32
925	A256	1.10fr Jugglers	90	65
926	A256	5fr Trapeze act	3.75	2.50
		Nos. 920-926 (7)	6.02	4.10

International Circus Festival.

Honoré II Coin A257

1974, Nov. 12 ***Perf. 13***

927	A257	60c rose red & blk	45	32

350th anniversary of coins of Monaco.

Underwater Fauna and Flora — A258

Designs: 45c, Fish, and marine life. 1.10fr, Coral.

1974, Nov. 12 Photo. ***Perf. 13x12½***

Size: 35x25mm

928	A258	45c multi	48	35

Size: 48x27mm

Perf. 13

929	A258	70c multi	60	35
930	A258	1.10fr multi	80	60

Congress of the International Commission for the Scientific Exploration of the Mediterranean, Monaco, Dec. 6-14.

Floral Arrangements
A259 A260

1974, Nov. 12 ***Perf. 13x12½***

931	A259	70c multi	60	35
932	A260	1.10fr multi	85	48

International Flower Show, Monte Carlo, May 1975. See Nos. 1003-1004, 1084-1085.

Prince Rainier III — A261

1974-78 Engr. ***Perf. 13***

933	A261	60c slate grn	42	15
934	A261	80c red	70	15
935	A261	80c brt grn	48	15
936	A261	1fr brown	85	42
937	A261	1fr scarlet	75	15
938	A261	1fr slate grn	60	15
939	A261	1.20fr vio bl	1.25	80
940	A261	1.20fr red	70	15
941	A261	1.25fr blue	1.00	48
942	A261	1.50fr black	80	24
943	A261	1.70fr dp bl	80	30
944	A261	2fr dk pur	2.25	80
945	A261	2.10fr olive bis	1.00	65
946	A261	2.50fr indigo	1.75	70
947	A261	9fr brt vio	4.25	2.00
		Nos. 933-947 (15)	17.60	7.29

Issue dates: 60c, Nos. 934, 936, 939, 2fr, Dec. 23. Nos. 935, 937, 1.25fr, 2.50fr, Jan. 10, 1977. Nos. 938, 940, 1.50fr, 1.70fr, 2.10fr, 9fr, Aug. 18, 1978.

See Nos. 1200-1204, 1255-1256.

Monte Carlo Beach A262

Clock Tower — A263

Prince Albert I Statue and Museum — A264

1974-77

948	A262	25c shown	30	20
949	A263	50c shown	42	26
950	A262	1.10fr shown ('77)	95	40
951	A264	1.40fr shown	1.25	52
952	A262	1.70fr All Saints' Tower	1.65	1.10
953	A263	3fr Fort Antoine	3.50	1.50
954	A262	5.50fr La Condamine (view)	5.00	2.25
		Nos. 948-954 (7)	13.07	6.23

Issue dates: 1.10fr, Jan. 10. Others, Dec. 23.

See Nos. 1005-1008, 1030-1033, 1069-1072, 1138-1152.

Haageocereus A265

1974, Dec. 23 Photo. ***Perf. 12½x13***

955	A265	10c *shown*	15	15
956	A265	20c *Matucana*	15	15
957	A265	30c *Parodia*	26	20
958	A265	85c *Mediolobivia*	55	40
959	A265	1.90fr *Matucana*	1.50	1.10
960	A265	4fr *Echinocereus*	3.00	1.65
		Nos. 955-960 (6)	5.61	3.65

Plants from Monaco Botanical Gardens.

Europa Issue 1975

Sailor, by Philibert Florence — A266

St. Dévote, by Ludovic Brea — A267

1975, May 13 Engr. ***Perf. 13***

961	A266	80c brt red lil	95	80
962	A267	1.20fr brt bl	1.25	90
a.		Souv. sheet, 5 each #961-962	18.00	18.00

Red Cross Type of 1969

Design: St. Bernardino of Siena (1380-1444) burying the dead.

1975, May 13

963	A194	4fr pur & Prus bl	2.75	1.75

For the Red Cross.

Carmen, at the Tavern A268

Scenes from Carmen: 30c, Prologue (vert.). 80c, The smugglers' hide-out. 1.40fr, Entrance to bull ring.

1975, May 13

964	A268	30c multi	16	15
965	A268	60c multi	28	16
966	A268	80c multi	55	35
967	A268	1.40fr multi	1.00	75

Centenary of first performance of opera Carmen by George Bizet (1838-1875).

Louis de Saint-Simon A269

Albert Schweitzer A270

1975, May 13

968	A269	40c bluish blk	40	32
969	A270	60c blk & dl red	48	40

300th birth anniversary of Louis de Saint-Simon (1675-1755), statesman and writer, and birth centenary of Albert Schweitzer (1875-1965), medical missionary.

ARPHILA 75 Emblem, G Clef — A271

1975, May 13

970	A271	80c sep & org brn	65	45

ARPHILA 75 International Philatelic Exhibition, Paris, June 6-16.

Seagull and Rising Sun — A272

1975, May 13 **Photo.**

971	A272	85c multi	55	45

Oceanexpo 75, International Exhibition, Okinawa, July 20, 1975-Jan. 1976.

Charity Label and "1f" Destroying Cancer A273

1975, May 13 **Engr.**
972 A273 1fr multi 80 60

Fight against cancer.

Jesus with Crown of Thorns, Holy Year Emblem — A274

1975, May 13
973 A274 1.15fr lil, bis & ind 85 60

Holy Year 1975.

Villa Sauber, by Charles Garnier A275

1975, May 13
974 A275 1.20fr multi 90 65

European Architectural Heritage Year 1975.

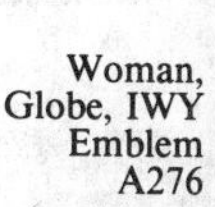

Woman, Globe, IWY Emblem A276

1975, May 13
975 A276 1.20fr multi 85 65

International Women's Year.

Nos. 793-796 Surcharged

1975, Apr. 1 **Engr.** ***Perf. 13***

976	A153	42c on 26c multi	1.10	65
977	A153	48c on 30c multi	1.75	80
978	A153	70c on 45c multi	3.75	1.10
979	A153	1.35fr on 90c multi	4.75	1.40

Nos. 976-979 were issued precanceled only. See note after No. 324.

Rolls Royce "Silver Ghost" 1907 — A277

1975, Nov. **Engr.** ***Perf. 13***

980	A277	5c	shown	15	15
981	A277	10c	Hispano Suiza, 1926	15	15
982	A277	20c	Isotta Fraschini, 1928	15	15
983	A277	30c	Cord L. 29	26	16
984	A277	50c	Voisin, 1930	45	26
985	A277	60c	Duesenberg, 1933	52	32
986	A277	80c	Bugatti, 1938	80	45
987	A277	85c	Delahaye, 1940	1.25	65
988	A277	1.20fr	Cisitalia, 1946	2.00	85
989	A277	1.40fr	Mercedes Benz, 1955	2.25	1.25
990	A277	5.50fr	Lamborghini, 1974	5.25	2.75
			Nos. 980-990 (11)	13.23	7.14

Development of the automobile.

Princes of Monaco Type of 1967

Paintings (Unknown Artists): 2fr, Prince Honore III (1733-1795). 4fr, Princess Catherine de Brignole (1759-1813).

1975, Nov.
991 A182 2fr multi 1.25 90
992 A182 4fr multi 2.50 1.50

Caged Dog A278

Designs: 80c, Cat chased up a tree (vert.). 1.20fr, Horses pulling heavy load.

1975, Nov.
993 A278 60c blk & brn 60 42
994 A278 80c blk, gray & brn 75 48
995 A278 1.20fr mag & sl grn 1.00 60

125th anniversary of the Grammont (J. P. Delmas Grammont) Law against cruelty to animals.

Dog Type of 1970

1975, Nov.
996 A204 60c Poodle 1.40 1.00

International Dog Show, Monte Carlo.

Maurice Ravel — A279

Clown — A280

Design: 1.20fr, Johann Strauss and dancers.

1975, Nov.
997 A279 60c mar & sep 48 35
998 A279 1.20fr mar & ind 90 70

Maurice Ravel (1875-1937), birth centenary, and Johann Strauss (1804-1849), sesquicentennial of birth, composers.

1975, Nov. **Photo.** ***Perf. 12½x13***
999 A280 80c multi 55 38

2nd International Circus Festival, Monte Carlo, Dec. 1975.

Honoré II Florin, 1640 — A281

1975, Nov. **Engr.** ***Perf. 13***
1000 A281 80c slate & gray 55 38

See Nos. 1040, 1088, 1234.

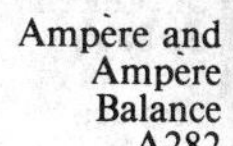

Ampère and Ampère Balance A282

1975, Nov.
1001 A282 85c ultra & ind 52 38

André Marie Ampère (1775-1836), physicist, birth bicentennial.

Lamentation for the Dead Christ, by Michelangelo — A283

1975, Nov.
1002 A283 1.40fr blk & ol gray 95 65

Michelangelo Buonarroti (1475-1564), Italian sculptor, painter and architect, 500th anniversary of birth.

Flower Types of 1974

Designs: Floral arrangements.

1975, Nov. **Photo.** ***Perf. 13x12½***
1003 A259 60c multi 48 25
1004 A260 80c multi 60 35

International Flower Show, Monte Carlo, May 1976.

Clock Tower Type, 1974

1976, Jan. 26 **Engr.** ***Perf. 13***
1005 A263 50c brn lake 55 38
1006 A263 60c ol grn 65 52
1007 A263 90c purple 1.00 75
1008 A263 1.60fr brt bl 1.50 1.40

Nos. 1005-1008 were issued precanceled only. See note after No. 324.

Prince Pierre — A284

André Maurois and Colette — A285

Portraits: 25c, Jean and Jerome Tharaud. 30c, Emile Henriot, Marcel Pagnol, Georges Duhamel. 50c, Philippe Heriat, Jules Supervielle, L. Pierard. 60c, Roland Dorgeles, M. Achard, G. Bauer. 80c, Franz Hellens, A. Billy, Msgr. Grente. 1.20fr, Jean Giono, L. Pasteur-Vallery-Radot, M. Garcon.

1976, May 3 **Engr.** ***Perf. 13***

1009	A284	10c	black	15	15
1010	A285	20c	red & sl	15	15
1011	A285	25c	red, dk bl & blk	20	15
1012	A285	30c	brown	30	20
1013	A285	50c	brn, red & vio bl	38	24
1014	A285	60c	grn, brn & lt brn	52	30
1015	A285	80c	blk & mag	70	35
1016	A285	1.20fr	blk, vio & cl	1.25	70
			Nos. 1009-1016 (8)	3.65	2.24

Literary Council of Monaco, 25th anniv.

Dachshunds — A286

1976, May 3 **Photo.**
1017 A286 60c multi 1.00 65

International Dog Show, Monte Carlo.

Bridge Table, Coast A287

1976, May 3 **Engr.**
1018 A287 60c multi 52 35

Fifth Bridge Olympiade, Monte Carlo.

A. G. Bell, Telephone, 1876, Satellite Dish A288

1976, May 3
1019 A288 80c multi 50 35

Centenary of first telephone call by Alexander Graham Bell, Mar. 10, 1876.

Federation Emblem — A289

1976, May 3
1020 A289 1.20fr multi 80 55

International Federation of Philately (F.I.P.), 50th anniversary.

U.S. Liberty Bell Type of 1926 — A290

1976, May 3
1021 A290 1.70fr car & blk 1.25 95

American Bicentennial.

A particular stamp may be scarce, but if few collectors want it, its market value may remain relatively low.

Fritillaria, by Vincent van Gogh
A291

1976, May 3 Photo. *Perf. 12x13*

1022 A291 3fr multi 3.50 2.75

International Flower Show, Monte Carlo, May 1976.

Plate with Lemon Branch — A292

Diving — A293

Europs: 1.20fr, The Peddler, 19th century figurine, and CEPT emblem.

1976, May 3 *Perf. 12½x13*

1023 A292 80c sal & multi 85 55
1024 A292 1.20fr ultra & multi 1.25 70
a. Souv. sheet of 10, 5 each #1023-1024 16.00 16.00

1976, May 3 Engr. *Perf. 13*

Designs (Olympic Rings and): 80c, Athlete on parallel bars. 85c, Hammer throw. 1.20fr, Rowing (horiz.). 1.70fr, Boxing (horiz.).

1025 A293 60c multi 32 26
1026 A293 80c multi 42 32
1027 A293 85c multi 52 42
1028 A293 1.20fr multi 70 60
1029 A293 1.70fr multi 1.10 1.00
a. Souv. sheet of 5, #1025-1029, perf. 14 3.50 3.50
Nos. 1025-1029 (5) 3.06 2.60

21st Olympic Games, Montreal, Canada, July 17-Aug. 1.

Clock Tower Type, 1974

1976, Sept. 1 Engr. *Perf. 13*

1030 A263 52c bister 35 24
1031 A263 62c red lil 48 30
1032 A263 95c scarlet 70 50
1033 A263 1.70fr bl grn 1.25 85

Nos. 1030-1033 were issued precanceled only. See note after No. 324.

Princes of Monaco Type of 1967

Paintings: 2fr, Honore IV (1815-1819), by Francois Lemoyne. 4fr, Louise d'Aumont-Mazarin (1750-1826), by Marie Verroust.

1976, Nov. 9 *Perf. 12½x13*

1035 A182 2fr vio brn 1.25 1.00
1036 A182 4fr multi 2.50 1.65

Red Cross Type of 1969

Design: St. Louise de Marillac and children.

1976, Nov. 9 *Perf. 13*

1037 A194 4fr grn, gray & plum 2.25 1.40

Values quoted in this catalogue are for stamps graded at Fine-Very Fine and with no faults. An illustrated guide to grade is provided in introductory material, beginning on Page 1A.

St. Vincent de Paul, View of Monaco
A294

1976, Nov. 9

1038 A294 60c multi 55 45

St. Vincent de Paul Conference, Monaco, July 31, 1876, centenary.

Marquise de Sevigne — A295

1976, Nov. 9

1039 A295 80c multi 42 28

Marie de Rabutin-Chantal, Marquise de Sevigne (1626-1696), writer.

Coin Type of 1975

Design: 80c, Honore II 2-gros coin.

1976, Nov. 9

1040 A281 80c grn & stl bl 60 38

Richard E. Byrd, Roald Amundsen, North Pole — A296

1976, Nov. 9

1041 A296 85c ol, blk & bl 75 55

First flights over the North Pole, 50th anniversary.

Gulliver Holding King, Queen and Enemy Fleet — A297

1976, Nov. 9

1042 A297 1.20fr ind, bl & brn 70 55

250th anniversary of the publication of Gulliver's Travels, by Jonathan Swift.

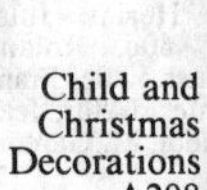

Child and Christmas Decorations
A298

1976, Nov. 9 *Perf. 13x12½*

1043 A298 60c multi 38 24
1044 A298 1.20fr multi 75 42

Christmas 1976.

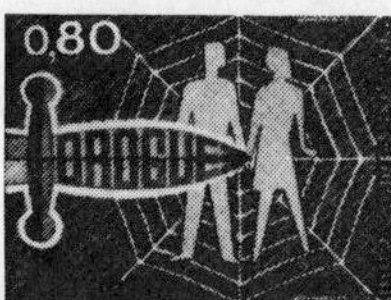

"Trapped by Drugs"
A299

1976, Nov. 9

1045 A299 80c grn, ultra & org 60 35
1046 A299 1.20fr red brn, vio & car 85 48

Fight against drug abuse.

Floral Arrangement
A300

Clown and Circus Acts
A301

Design: 1fr, Floral arrangement. Designs by Princess Grace.

1976, Nov. 9 Photo. *Perf. 13½x13*

1047 A300 80c yel grn & multi 60 30
1048 A300 1fr lt bl & multi 85 40

International Flower Show, Monte Carlo, May 1977. See Nos. 1124-1125, 1191.

1976, Nov. 9

1049 A301 1fr multi 85 70

3rd Intl. Circus Festival, Dec. 26-30.

L'Hirondelle I — A302

Prince Albert I — A303

Designs (Gouaches by Louis Tinayre): 30c, Crew of L'Hirondelle. 80c, L'Hirondelle in Storm. 1fr, The Helmsman (vert.). 1.25fr, L'Hirondelle in Storm. 1.40fr, Shrimp Fishermen in Boat. 1.90fr, Hauling in the Net (vert.). 2.50fr, Catching Opah Fish.

1977, May 3 Engr. *Perf. 13*

1050 A302 10c multi 15 15
1051 A303 20c multi 18 15
1052 A302 30c multi 25 18
1053 A302 80c multi 42 30
1054 A302 1fr multi 65 35
1055 A302 1.25fr multi 75 50
1056 A302 1.40fr multi 1.10 75
1057 A302 1.90fr multi 1.50 1.00
1058 A302 2.50fr multi 2.00 1.50
Nos. 1050-1058 (9) 7.00 4.88

75th anniversary of publication of "The Career of a Sailor," by Prince Albert I. See Nos. 1073-1081.

Pyreneean Mountain Dogs — A304

1977, May 3 Photo.

1059 A304 80c multi 1.40 1.00

International Dog Show, Monte Carlo. See No. 1199.

Motherhood, by Mary Cassatt — A305

1977, May 3 Engr.

1060 A305 80c multi 55 40

World Association of the Friends of Children.

Archers, Target and Monte Carlo — A306

1977, May 3

1061 A306 1.10fr multi 65 48

10th International Rainier III Archery Championships.

Spirit of St. Louis and Lindbergh — A307

1977, May 3

1062 A307 1.90fr multi 1.10 85

50th anniversary of first transatlantic flight by Charles Lindbergh.

The Dock at Deauville, by Dufy — A308

1977, May 3 Photo.

1063 A308 2fr multi 1.90 1.40

Raoul Dufy (1877-1953), painter, birth centenary.

Young Girl, by Rubens — A309

Helmet Tower, Monaco — A310

Rubens Paintings: 1fr, Duke of Buckingham. 1.40fr, Rubens' son Nicolas, 2 years old.

1977, May 3 **Engr.**
1064 A309 80c multi 40 35
1065 A309 1fr multi 55 35
1066 A309 1.40fr multi 95 70

Peter Paul Rubens (1577-1640), 400th birth anniversary.

1977, May 3

Europa: 1.40fr, St. Michael's Church, Menton.

1067 A310 1fr multi 60 48
1068 A310 1.40fr multi 1.25 70
a. Souv. sheet of 10, 5 each #1067-1068 15.00 15.00

Clock Tower Type of 1974

1977, Apr. 1 **Engr.** ***Perf. 13***
1069 A263 54c brt grn 38 32
1070 A263 68c orange 52 45
1071 A263 1.05fr olive 75 52
1072 A263 1.85fr brown 1.40 1.00

Nos. 1069-1072 were issued precanceled only. See note after No. 324.

Career of a Sailor Types of 1977

Designs (Gouaches by Louis Tinayre): 10c, Yacht Princess Alice II, Kiel harbor. 20c, Laboratory on board ship. 30c, Yacht amidst ice floes. 80c, Crew in arctic outfits. 1fr, Yacht in polar region. 1.25fr, Yacht in snow storm. 1.40fr, Building camp on ice. 1.90fr, Yacht under steam amidst ice floes. 3fr, Yacht passing iceberg.

1977, Nov. **Engr.** ***Perf. 13***
1073 A302 10c blk & brt bl 15 15
1074 A302 20c Prus bl 18 15
1075 A302 30c blk & brt bl 25 18
1076 A303 80c multi 42 30
1077 A302 1fr brt grn & blk 62 35
1078 A302 1.25fr vio, sep & blk 70 48
1079 A302 1.40fr ol, bl & pur 1.10 70
1080 A302 1.90fr blk & brt bl 1.50 1.00
1081 A302 3fr dk grn, ol & brt bl 2.00 1.50
Nos. 1073-1081 (9) 6.92 4.81

75th anniversary of publication of "The Career of a Sailor," by Prince Albert I.

Santa Claus A311

1977, Nov.
1082 A311 80c multi 40 24
1083 A311 1.40fr multi 65 40

Christmas 1977.

Flowers Types of 1974

Designs: 80c, Snapdragons and bellflowers. 1fr, Ikebana arrangement.

1977, Nov. **Photo.** ***Perf. 13½x13***
1084 A259 80c multi 60 32
1085 A260 1fr multi 75 45

International Flower Show, Monte Carlo, May 1978.

Face (Van Gogh), Syringe, Hallucination Pattern A312

Clown, Flags of Participants A313

1977, Nov. **Engr.** ***Perf. 13***
1086 A312 1fr multi 75 45

Fight against drug abuse.

1977, Nov. **Photo.** ***Perf. 13½x13***
1087 A313 1fr multi 75 55

Fourth International Circus Festival. Monte Carlo, December 1977.

Coin Type of 1975

Design: 80c, Doubloon of Honoré II, 1648.

1977, Nov. **Engr.** ***Perf. 13***
1088 A281 80c lil & brn 60 45

Mediterranean Landscape and Industrial Pollution — A314

1977, Nov.
1089 A314 1fr multi 85 52

Protection of the Mediterranean. Meeting of the UN Mediterranean Environmental Protection Group, Monte Carlo, Nov. 28-Dec. 6.

Men Spreading Tar, Dr. Guglielminetti, 1903 Car — A315

1977, Nov.
1090 A315 1.10fr multi 60 42

75th anniversary of first tarred roads, invented by Swiss Dr. Guglielminetti.

View of Monaco and Tennis Emblem — A316

First Match at Wimbledon and Stadium — A317

1977, Nov.
1091 A316 1fr multi 65 48
1092 A317 1.40fr multi 90 70

50th anniversary of the Lawn Tennis Federation of Monaco and centenary of first international tennis match at Wimbledon.

Prince of Monaco Type of 1967

Painting: 6fr, Honoré V (1819-1841), by Marie Verroust.

1977, Nov. ***Perf. 12½x13***
1093 A182 6fr multi 3.00 2.00

Red Cross Type of 1969

Design: 4fr, St. John Bosco and boys.

1977, Nov. ***Perf. 13***
1094 A194 4fr multi 2.00 1.40

Nos. 1069-1072 Surcharged

1978, Jan. 17
1095 A263 58c on 54c brt grn 45 35
1096 A263 73c on 68c org 65 45
1097 A263 1.15fr on 1.05fr ol 85 55
1098 A263 2fr on 1.85fr brn 1.50 1.10

See note after No. 324.

The Abandoned Ship, from "Mysterious Island" — A318

Illustrations, Novels by Jules Verne: 5c, Shipwreck. 30c, Secret of the Island. 80c, Robur, the Conqueror. 1fr, Master Zacharius. 1.40fr, The Castle in the Carpathians. 1.70fr, The Children of Capt. Grant. 5.50fr, Jules Verne and allegories.

1978, May 2 **Engr.** ***Perf. 13***
1099 A318 5c multi 15 15
1100 A318 25c multi 15 15
1101 A318 30c multi 18 15
1102 A318 80c multi 40 28
1103 A318 1fr multi 60 35
1104 A318 1.40fr multi 80 52
1105 A318 1.70fr multi 1.10 70
1106 A318 5.50fr multi 3.25 1.65
Nos. 1099-1106 (8) 6.63 3.95

Jules Verne (1828-1905), science fiction writer, birth sesquicentennial.

Congress Center and Monte Carlo — A319

Design: 1.40fr, Congress Center, view from the sea.

1978, May 2
1107 A319 1fr multi 52 42
1108 A319 1.40fr multi 65 52

Inauguration of Monaco Congress Center.

Soccer Players and Globe — A320

1978, May 2
1109 A320 1fr multi 52 42

11th World Soccer Cup Championship, Argentina, June 1-25.

Vivaldi and St. Mark's Place, Venice — A321

Control Ship and Grimaldi Palace — A322

1978, May 2
1110 A321 1fr dk brn & red 60 52

Antonio Vivaldi (1675?-1741), Italian violinist and composer.

1978, May 2

Design: 1fr, Map of coastal area and city emblems (horiz.).

Size: 26x36mm

1111 A322 80c multi 48 30

Size: 48x27mm

1112 A322 1fr multi 60 40

Protection of the environment, signing of "Ra Mo Ge" agreement for the protection of the Mediterranean Coast between Saint-Raphael, France, and Genoa, Italy (including Monaco).

Monaco Cathedral — A323

Europa: 1.40fr, View of Principality from East.

1978, May 2 ***Perf. 12½x13***
1113 A323 1fr multi 70 42
1114 A323 1.40fr multi 1.00 55
a. Souv. sheet, 5 each #1113-1114 12.00 12.00

Cinderella — A324

Mother Goose Tales: 25c, Puss in Boots. 30c, Sleeping Beauty. 80c, Fairy tale princess. 1fr, Little Red Riding Hood. 1.40fr, Bluebeard. 1.70fr, Tom Thumb. 1.90fr, Riquet with the Tuft of Hair. 2.50fr, The Fairies.

1978, Nov. 8 **Engr.** ***Perf. 13***
1115 A324 5c multi 15 15
1116 A324 25c multi 15 15
1117 A324 30c multi 15 15
1118 A324 80c multi 35 22
1119 A324 1fr multi 45 32
1120 A324 1.40fr multi 90 42
1121 A324 1.70fr multi 1.10 52
1122 A324 1.90fr multi 1.10 65
1123 A324 2.50fr multi 1.25 75
Nos. 1115-1123 (9) 5.60 3.33

Charles Perrault (1628-1703), compiler of Mother Goose Tales.

Flower Type of 1976

Van Gogh Paintings: 1fr, Sunflowers. 1.70fr, Iris.

1978, Nov. 8 **Photo.** ***Perf. 12½x13***
1124 A300 1fr multi 75 55
1125 A300 1.70fr multi 1.00 80

Intl. Flower show, Monte Carlo, May 1979, and 125th birth anniv. of Vincent van Gogh (1853-1890), Dutch painter.

Afghan Hound A325

Design: 1.20fr, Russian wolfhound.

1978, Nov. 8 *Perf. 13x12½*

1126	A325	1fr multi	1.25	90
1127	A325	1.20fr multi	1.65	1.10

International Dog Show, Monte Carlo.

Child Holding Gift of Shoes — A326

1978, Nov. 8 **Engr.** *Perf. 12½x13*

1128	A326	1fr multi	52	40

Christmas 1978.

Catherine and William Booth, Salvation Army Band — A327

1978, Nov. 8 **Engr.** *Perf. 13*

1129	A327	1.70fr multi	80	70

Centenary of founding of Salvation Army.

Trained Seals A328

Designs: 1fr, Lions (vert.). 1.40fr, Equestrian act. 1.90fr, Monkey music band. 2.40fr, Trapeze act.

1978, Nov. 8 *Perf. 13x12½*

1130	A328	80c multi	40	30
1131	A328	1fr multi	55	40
1132	A328	1.40fr multi	95	60
1133	A328	1.90fr multi	1.10	85
1134	A328	2.40fr multi	1.50	1.10
		Nos. 1130-1134 (5)	4.50	3.25

5th Intl. Circus Festival, Monte Carlo.

Princes of Monaco Type of 1967

Paintings: 2fr, Florestan I (1841-1856), by G. Dauphin. 4fr, Caroline Gilbert de Lametz (1793-1879), by Marie Verroust.

1978, Nov. 8 **Engr.** *Perf. 12½x13*

1135	A182	2fr multi	95	65
1136	A182	4fr multi	2.00	1.25

Demand, as well as supply, determines a stamp's market value. One is as important as the other.

Souvenir Sheet

Henri Dunant and Battle Scene — A329

1978, Nov. 8 **Engr.** *Perf. 13*

1137	A329	5fr multi	3.25	3.25

Henri Dunant (1828-1910), founder of Red Cross.

View Types of 1974

1978-80

1138	A262	25c All Saints' Tower	15	15
1139	A262	65c Monte Carlo Beach	32	32
1140	A263	70c Exotic Garden, cacti ('80)	35	20
1142	A262	1.10fr Palais de Justice ('80)	48	20
1144	A263	1.30fr Cathedral	65	26
1145	A264	1.50fr Prince Albert Statue and Museum ('80)	80	42
1146	A262	1.80fr La Condamine	1.00	60
1148	A262	2.30fr Palace ('80)	1.10	60
1152	A262	6.50fr Monte Carlo Auditorium	3.00	1.65
		Nos. 1138-1152 (9)	7.85	4.40

Convention Center, Monte Carlo A330

1978-79

1154	A330	61c vermilion	42	20
1155	A330	64c green	38	24
1156	A330	68c brt bl	30	20
1157	A330	78c dp rose lil	55	26
1158	A330	83c vio bl	42	26
1159	A330	88c orange	38	26
1160	A330	1.25fr brown	90	42
1161	A330	1.30fr purple	75	45
1162	A330	1.40fr brt yel grn	70	42
1163	A330	2.10fr vio bl	1.40	80
1164	A330	2.25fr brn org	1.25	75
1165	A330	2.35fr lil rose	1.10	60
		Nos. 1154-1165 (12)	8.55	4.86

Issued precanceled only. See note after No. 324.

Issue dates: 61c, 78c, 1.25fr, 2.10fr, July 10, 1978. Others, 1979.

Souvenir Sheet

Prince Albert — A331

1979, Apr. 30 **Engr.** *Perf. 12½x13*

1166	A331	10fr multi	6.25	6.25

21st birthday of Hereditary Prince Albert.

The Juggler of Notre Dame, by Jules Massenet A332

Designs: 1.20fr, Hans, the Flute Player, by Gaston L. Ganne. 1.50fr, Don Quichotte, by Massenet. 1.70fr, L'Aiglon, by Jacques Ibert and Arthur Honegger (vert.). 2.10fr, The Child and the Sorcerer, by Maurice Ravel. 3fr, Monte Carlo Opera and Charles Garnier, architect.

1979, Apr. 30 *Perf. 13*

1167	A332	1fr multi	52	24
1168	A332	1.20fr multi	65	30
1169	A332	1.50fr multi	85	55
1170	A332	1.70fr multi	1.25	70
1171	A332	2.10fr multi	1.50	1.10
1172	A332	3fr multi	2.00	1.25
		Nos. 1167-1172 (6)	6.77	4.14

Centenary of the Salle Garnier, Monte Carlo Opera.

Flower, Bird, Butterfly, IYC Emblem A333

Children's Drawings (IYC Emblem and): 1fr, Horse and child. 1.20fr, Children shaking hands, and heart. 1.50fr, Children of the world for peace. 1.70fr, Children against pollution.

1979, Apr. 30

1173	A333	50c multi	24	15
1174	A333	1fr multi	45	32
1175	A333	1.20fr multi	65	42
1176	A333	1.50fr multi	75	52
1177	A333	1.70fr multi	1.10	65
		Nos. 1173-1177 (5)	3.19	2.06

International Year of the Child.

Armed Messenger, 15th-16th Centuries A334

Europa (designs similar to 1960 postage dues); 1.50fr, Felucca, 18th cent. 1.70fr, Arrival of 1st train, Dec. 12, 1868.

1979, Apr. 30

1178	A334	1.20fr multi	55	40
1179	A334	1.50fr multi	75	45
1180	A334	1.70fr multi	90	60
a.		Souv. sheet of 6, 2 each #1178-1180, perf. 13x12½	7.50	7.50

Les Biches, by Francis Poulenc A335

Ballets: 1.20fr, Les Matelots, by George Auric. 1.50fr, Le Spectre de la Rose, by Carl Maria Weber (vert.). 1.70fr, GaietePari-sienne, by Jacques Offenbach. 2.10fr, Dance of Salome, by Richard Strauss (vert.). 3fr, Instrumental Music, ceiling decoration of Salle Garnier.

1979, Nov. 12

Size: 26x36mm, 36x26mm

1181	A335	1fr multi	55	22
1182	A335	1.20fr multi	70	35
1183	A335	1.50fr multi	95	55
1184	A335	1.70fr multi	1.10	75
1185	A335	2.10fr multi	1.40	1.10

Size: 48x27mm

1186	A335	3fr multi	2.00	1.40
		Nos. 1181-1186 (6)	6.70	4.37

Centenary of the Salle Garnier, Monte Carlo Opera.

Princes of Monaco Type of 1967

Paintings: 3fr, Charles III (1856-1889). 4fr, Antoinette de Merode (1828-1864).

1979, Nov. 12 *Perf. 12½x13*

1187	A182	3fr multi	1.24	95
1188	A182	4fr multi	1.75	1.25

Red Cross Type of 1969

Design: 5fr, St. Peter Claver preaching to slaves.

1979, Nov. 12 *Perf. 13*

1189	A194	5fr multi	2.00	1.65

Princess Grace Orchid — A336

Clown Balancing on Globe — A337

1979, Nov. 12 **Photo.**

1190	A336	1fr multi	65	60

International Orchid Exhibition, Monte Carlo, April 1980.

Flower Type of 1976

Design: 1.20fr, Princess Grace rose.

1979, Nov. 12

1191	A300	1.20fr multi	65	55

International Flower Show, Monte Carlo, May 1980.

1979, Nov. 12

1192	A337	1.20fr multi	65	52

6th International Circus Festival, Monte Carlo, Dec. 6-10.

Rowland Hill, Penny Black — A338

1979, Nov. 12 **Engr.** *Perf. 13*

1193	A338	1.70fr multi	70	52

Sir Rowland Hill (1795-1879), originator of penny postage.

Albert Einstein, Equations A339

St. Patrick's Cathedral A340

1979, Nov. 12

1194	A339	1.70fr multi	75	55

Albert Einstein (1879-1955), theoretical physicist.

1979, Nov. 12

1195	A340	2.10fr multi	1.00	75

St. Patrick's Cathedral, New York City, centenary.

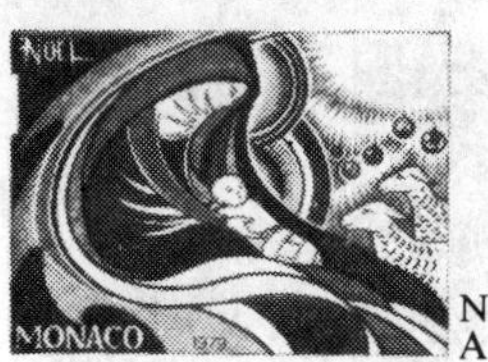

Nativity
A341

1979, Nov. 12
1196 A341 1.20fr multi 60 26

Christmas 1979.

Bugatti, Monte Carlo, 1929 Winner — A342

1979, Nov. 12
1197 A342 1fr multi 60 40

50th anniversary of Grand Prix auto race, Monte Carlo.

Arms of Charles V and Monaco, View of Monaco — A343

1979, Nov. 12
1198 A343 1.50fr multi 65 45

Emperor Charles V visit to Monaco, 450th anniversary.

Dog Type of 1977

Design: 1.20fr, Setter and pointer.

1979, Nov. 12 **Photo.**
1199 A304 1.20fr multi 1.40 80

International Dog Show, Monte Carlo.

Prince Rainier Type of 1974

1980, Jan. 17 **Engr.** ***Perf. 13***
1200 A261 1.10fr emerald 55 15
1201 A261 1.30fr rose red 60 15
1202 A261 1.60fr dk bl gray 75 18
1203 A261 1.80fr grnsh bl 90 26
1204 A261 2.30fr red lil 1.00 30
Nos. 1200-1204 (5) 3.80 1.04

Chestnut Branch in Spring
A344

Designs of 1980, 1981 stamps show chestnut branch. 1982 stamps show peach branch. 1983 stamps show apple branch.

1980-83 **Engr.** ***Perf. 13x12½***
1205 A344 76c shown 40 28
1206 A344 88c Spring ('81) 40 28
1207 A344 97c Spring ('82) 45 28
1208 A344 99c Summer 55 35
1209 A344 1.05fr Spring ('83) 40 25
1210 A344 1.14fr Summer ('81) 55 35
1211 A344 1.25fr Summer ('82) 60 35
1212 A344 1.35fr Summer ('83) 48 32
1213 A344 1.60fr Autumn 85 65
1214 A344 1.84fr Autumn ('81) 85 65
1215 A344 2.03fr Autumn ('82) 1.10 60
1216 A344 2.19fr Autumn ('83) 85 52
1217 A344 2.65fr Winter 1.50 1.10
1218 A344 3.05fr Winter ('81) 1.50 1.10
1219 A344 3.36fr Winter ('82) 1.65 1.10
1220 A344 3.63fr Winter ('83) 1.40 1.10
Nos. 1205-1220 (16) 13.53 9.28

Issued precanceled only. See note after No. 324. See Nos. 1406-1409, 1457-1460.

Gymnast — A345

1980, Apr. 28
1221 A345 1.10fr shown 32 22
1222 A345 1.30fr Handball 35 28
1223 A345 1.60fr Shooting 55 40
1224 A345 1.80fr Volleyball 70 52
1225 A345 2.30fr Ice hockey 95 60
1226 A345 4fr Slalom 1.40 1.00
Nos. 1221-1226 (6) 4.27 3.02

22nd Summer Olympic Games, Moscow, July 19-Aug. 3; 13th Winter Olympic Games, Lake Placid, NY, Feb. 12-24.

Colette, Novelist — A346

Europa: 1.80fr, Marcel Pagnol (1895-1974), French playwright.

1980, Apr. 28 ***Perf. 12½x13***
1227 A346 1.30fr multi 45 42
1228 A346 1.80fr multi 65 45
a. Souv. sheet, 5 each #1227-1228 5.00 5.00

The Source, by Ingres
A347

1980, Apr. 28
1229 A347 4fr multi 2.75 1.90

Jean Auguste Dominique Ingres (1780-1867).

Michel Eyquem de Montaigne
A348

Guillaume Apollinaire
A349

1980, Apr. 28 ***Perf. 13***
1230 A348 1.30fr multi 52 35

Essays of Montaigne (1533-1592), 400th anniversary of publication.

1980, Apr. 28
1231 A349 1.10fr multi 42 30

Guillaume Apollinaire (1880-1918), French writer.

Paul P. Harris, Chicago Skyline, Rotary Emblem — A350

1980, Apr. 28
1232 A350 1.80fr multi 75 42

Rotary International, 75th anniversary.

Convention Center, Map of Europe, Kiwanis Emblem — A351

1980, Apr. 28
1233 A351 1.30fr multi 55 48

Kiwanis International, European Convention, Monte Carlo, June.

Coin Type of 1975

Design: 1.50fr, Honoré II silver ecu, 1649.

1980, Apr. 28
1234 A281 1.50fr multi 65 52

Lhasa Apso and Shih-Tzu — A352

1980, Apr. 28 **Photo.**
1235 A352 1.30fr multi 1.25 75

International Dog Show, Monte Carlo.

The Princess and the Pea — A353

Hans Christian Andersen (1805-1875) Fairy Tales: 1.30fr, The Little Mermaid. 1.50fr, The Chimneysweep and the Shepherdess. 1.60fr, The Brave Little Tin Soldier. 1.80fr, The Little Match Girl. 2.30fr, The Nightingale.

1980, Nov. 6 **Engr.** ***Perf. 13***
1236 A353 70c multi 25 18
1237 A353 1.30fr multi 38 24
1238 A353 1.50fr multi 60 20
1239 A353 1.60fr multi 75 55
1240 A353 1.80fr multi 1.00 60
1241 A353 2.30fr multi 1.10 75
Nos. 1236-1241 (6) 4.08 2.52

Women on Balcony, by Van Dongen — A354

Paintings from 1905 Paris Fall Salon: 2fr, The Road, by de Vlaminck. 4fr, Woman Reading, by Matisse. 5fr, Three Women in a Meadow, by Andre Derain.

1980, Nov. 6 ***Perf. 13x12***
1242 A354 2fr multi 1.25 95
1243 A354 3fr multi 1.75 1.50
1244 A354 4fr multi 2.50 1.90
1245 A354 5fr multi 3.25 2.50

Princes of Monaco Type of 1967

Paintings: No. 1246, Prince Albert I (1848-1922), by Leon Bonnat. No. 1247, Princess Alice (1857-1925), by L. Maeterlinck.

1980, Nov. 6 ***Perf. 12½x13***
1246 A182 4fr multi 1.75 1.40
1247 A182 4fr multi 1.75 1.40

Sun and Birds, by Perrette Lambert — A355

1980, Nov. 6 ***Perf. 13***
1248 A355 6fr multi 2.50 2.25

Red Cross.

7th International Circus Festival
A356

1980, Nov. 6 ***Perf. 13x12½***
1249 A356 1.30fr multi 70 50

Christmas 1980
A357

1980, Nov. 6
1250 A357 1.10fr multi 38 26
1251 A357 2.30fr multi 85 65

Princess Stephanie of Monaco Rose — A358

1980, Nov. 6 Photo. Perf. 12½x13

1252	A358	1.30fr	shown	60	48
1253	A358	1.80fr	Ikebana	80	60

International Flower Show, Monte Carlo, May 1981.

Prince Rainier Type of 1974

1980 Engr. Perf. 13

1255	A261	1.20fr	brt grn	52	20
1256	A261	1.40fr	red	75	15

Issue dates: 1.20fr, Aug. 19; 1.40fr, Aug. 11.

Paramuricea Clavata A359

5c-20c, 40c, 50c, vert.

1980, Nov. 6 Perf. 13x12½

1259	A359	5c	Spirographis spallanzanii	15	15
1260	A359	10c	Anemonia sulcata	15	15
1261	A359	15c	Leptosammia pruvoti	15	15
1262	A359	20c	Pteroides	15	15
1263	A359	30c	shown	16	15
1264	A359	40c	Alcyonium	20	15
1265	A359	50c	Corallium rubrum	24	16
1266	A359	60c	Caliactis parisitica	45	16
1267	A359	70c	Cerianthus membranaceus	55	20
1268	A359	1fr	Actinia equina	60	20
1269	A359	2fr	Protula	1.10	35
			Nos. 1259-1269 (11)	3.90	
			Set value		1.50

See Nos. 1316-1321, 1380.

25th Wedding Anniversary of Prince Rainier and Princess Grace — A360

1981, May 4 Perf. 13

1270	A360	1.20fr	grn & blk	55	25
1271	A360	1.40fr	car & blk	70	25
1272	A360	1.70fr	ol grn & blk	85	38
1273	A360	1.80fr	brn & blk	90	42
1274	A360	2fr	brt bl & blk	1.10	60
			Nos. 1270-1274 (5)	4.10	1.90

Mozart with his Father and Sister, by Carmontelle — A361

Wolfgang Amadeus Mozart (1756-1791), 225th Birth Anniversary (Paintings): 2fr, Portrait, by Lorenz Vogel (26x36mm). 3.50fr, Conducting his Requiem Two Days Before his Death, by F.C. Baude. Nos. 1275-1277 se-tenant.

1981, May 4 Engr. Perf. 13½x13

1275	A361	2fr	multi	1.25	1.10
1276	A361	2.50fr	multi	1.75	1.50
1277	A361	3.50fr	multi	2.25	1.90

Cross of Palms — A362

Europa (Palm Sunday Traditions): 2fr, Children with palms at benediction.

1981, May 4 Perf. 12½x13

1278	A362	1.40fr	multi	40	25
1279	A362	2fr	multi	60	40
a.			Souv. sheet, 5 each #1278-1279	6.00	6.00

European Soccer Cup, 25th Anniversary — A363

1981, May 4 Perf. 13

1280	A363	2fr	black & blue	75	65

International Year of the Disabled A364

1981, May 4

1281	A364	1.40fr	brt grn & bl	52	38

Monegasque National Pavilion Centenary — A365

1981, May 4

1282	A365	2fr	multi	85	70

Oceanographic Institute, Monaco and Museum, Paris — A366

1981, May 4

1283	A366	1.20fr	multi	52	38

75th anniversary of the Oceanographic Institute (Monaco-France).

50th Anniversary of the International Hydrographic Bureau — A367

1981, May 4

1284	A367	2.50fr	multi	90	80

Rough Collies and Shetland Sheepdogs — A368

1981, May 4 Photo.

1285	A368	1.40fr	multi	1.65	1.40

International Dog Show, Monte Carlo.

Marine Life Preservation A369

Prince Rainier and Hereditary Prince Albert A370

1981, Mar. 21 Photo.

1286	A369	1.20fr	multi	85	52

1981-84 Engr. Perf. 13

1287	A370	1.40fr	dk grn	80	15
1288	A370	1.60fr	carmine	95	15
1289	A370	1.60fr	ol grn ('82)	70	15
1290	A370	1.70fr	bluish grn ('84)	70	15
1291	A370	1.80fr	mag ('82)	95	15
1292	A370	2fr	red ('83)	1.00	15
1293	A370	2.10fr	red ('84)	95	15
1294	A370	2.30fr	blue	1.65	70
1295	A370	2.60fr	vio bl ('82)	1.25	48
1296	A370	2.80fr	stl bl ('83)	1.25	60
1297	A370	3fr	sky bl ('84)	1.25	48
1298	A370	4fr	brown	1.50	40
1299	A370	5.50fr	black	1.90	1.10
			Nos. 1287-1299 (13)	14.85	4.81

See Nos. 1505-1515.

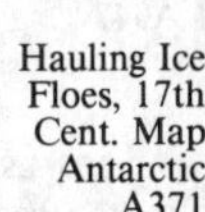

Hauling Ice Floes, 17th Cent. Map Antarctic A371

1981, Oct. 5

1301	A371	1.50fr	multi	75	38

First Intl. Arctic Committee Congress, Rome, Oct. 5-9.

Princes of Monaco Type of 1967

Paintings by P.A. de Laszlo, 1929: 3fr, Prince Louis II. 5fr, Princess Charlotte.

1981, Nov. 5 Engr. Perf. 12½x13

1302	A182	3fr	multi	1.25	85
1303	A182	5fr	multi	2.00	1.40

Ettore Bugatti, Auto Designer and Racer, Birth Centenary A372

George Bernard Shaw (1856-1950) A373

1981, Nov. 5 Perf. 13

1304	A372	1fr	multi	42	35

1981, Nov. 5

Design: 2.50fr, Fernand Leger, painter, birth centenary.

1305	A373	2fr	multi	90	65
1306	A373	2.50fr	multi	1.10	80

Self-portrait, by Pablo Picasso (1881-1973) — A374

Design: No. 1308, Self-portrait, by Rembrandt (1606-1669).

1981, Nov. 5 Perf. 12½x13

1307	A374	4fr	multi	2.00	1.65
1308	A374	4fr	multi	2.00	1.65

Ikebana, Painting by Ikenobo, 1673 — A375

Intl. Flower Show, Monte Carlo, 1982: 1.40fr, Elegantines, morning glories.

1981, Nov. 5 Photo. Perf. 12½

1309	A375	1.40fr	multi	50	38
1310	A375	2fr	multi	75	58

Catherine Deneuve Rose A376

1981, Nov. 5 Perf. 13x12½

1311	A376	1.80fr	multi	85	70

First Intl. Rose Competition, Monte Carlo, June 12-14.

8th Intl. Circus Festival, Monte Carlo, Dec. 10-14 — A377

1981, Nov. 5 Engr. *Perf. 13*
1312 A377 1.40fr multi 65 50

Christmas 1981 A378

1981, Nov. 5
1313 A378 1.20fr multi 50 42

50th Monte Carlo Auto Race — A379

1981, Nov. 5
1314 A379 1fr Lancia-Stratos 42 30

Souvenir Sheet

Persimmon Branch in Spring A380

1981, Nov. 5 *Perf. 13x12½*
1315 Sheet of 4 4.25 4.25
a. A380 1fr shown 42 42
b. A380 2fr Summer 80 80
c. A380 3fr Autumn 1.10 1.10
d. A380 4fr Winter 1.65 1.65

Coral Type of 1980

Exotic Plants. 1.40fr, 1.60fr, 2.30fr vert.

Perf. 12½x13, 13x12½

1981-82 Photo.

1316	A359	1.40fr Hoya bella	1.10	30
1317	A359	1.60fr Bolivicereus samaipatanus	75	30
1317A	A359	1.80fr Trichocereus grandiflorus	1.00	60
1318	A359	2.30fr Euphorbia milii	90	52
1319	A359	2.60fr Echinocereus fitchii	1.00	75
1320	A359	2.90fr Rebutia heliosa	1.25	1.00
1321	A359	4.10fr Echinopsis multiplex	1.65	1.25
		Nos. 1316-1321 (7)	7.65	4.72

Issue dates: 1.80fr, June 7, others Dec. 10.

Miniature Sheet

1982 World Cup A381

Designs: Various soccer players.

1982, May 3 *Perf. 13*
1322 Sheet of 4 4.50 4.50
a. A381 1fr multi 48 48
b. A381 2fr multi 80 80
c. A381 3fr multi 1.25 1.25
d. A381 4fr multi 1.75 1.75

Mercantour Natl. Park Birds — A382

Europa — A383

1982, May 3 *Perf. 12½x13, 13x12½*

1323	A382	60c Nutcracker	30	22
1324	A382	70c Black grouse	38	22
1325	A382	80c Rock partridge	38	30
1326	A382	90c Wall creeper, horiz.	52	30
1327	A382	1.40fr Ptarmigan, horiz.	95	38
1328	A382	1.60fr Golden eagle	1.25	38
		Nos. 1323-1328 (6)	3.78	1.80

1982, May 3 *Perf. 12½x13*

1329	A383	1.60fr Guelph attacking Fortress of Monaco, 1297	52	25
1330	A383	2.30fr Treaty of Peronne, 1641	80	38
a.		Souv. sheet, 5 each #1329-1330	6.25	6.25

Fontvielle Landfill Project A384

1982, May 3 *Perf. 13x12½*
1331 A384 1.40fr Old coastline 48 24
1332 A384 1.60fr Landfill site 55 24
1333 A384 2.30fr Completed site 90 55

Fontvielle Stadium — A385

1982, May 3 *Perf. 13*
1334 A385 2.30fr multi 85 70

PHILEXFRANCE '82 Stamp Exhibition, Paris, June 11-21 — A386

1982, May 3
1335 A386 1.40fr multi 52 42

Intl. Dog Show, Monte Carlo A387

1982, May 3 Photo. *Perf. 13x12½*
1336 A387 60c Old English sheepdog 52 35
1337 A387 1fr Briard terrier 70 45

See No. 1366, 1431, 1479, 1539, 1676, 1704, 1756.

Monaco Cathedral, Arms of Pope John Paul II and Monaco A388

1982, May 3 Engr.
1338 A388 1.60fr multi 55 40

Creation of archbishopric of Monaco, July 25, 1981.

800th Birth Anniv. of St. Francis of Assisi — A389

TB Bacillus Cent. — A390

1982, May 3 *Perf. 12½x13*
1339 A389 1.40fr multi 55 45

1982, May 3
1340 A390 1.40fr multi 45 35

Scouting Year — A391

Intl. Hunting Council, 29th Meeting — A392

1982, May 3
1341 A391 1.60fr dk brn & blk 60 42

1982, June 11 Photo. *Perf. 12½*
1342 A392 1.60fr St. Hubert 60 45

Intl. Bibliophile Assoc. General Assembly — A393

1982, Sept. 30 Engr. *Perf. 13*
1343 A393 1.60fr multi 50 35

Monte Carlo and Monaco During the Belle Epoch (1870-1925), by Hubert Clerissi — A394

Photogravure and Engraved

1982, Nov. 8 *Perf. 13x12½*
1344 A394 3fr Casino, 1870 1.25 80
1345 A394 5fr Palace, 1893 2.25 1.25

See Nos. 1385-1386, 1436-1437, 1488-1489, 1546-1547, 1605-1606, 1638-1639, 1695-1696.

Nicolo Paganini (1782-1840), Composer and Violinist — A395

Designs: 1.80fr, Anna Pavlova (1881-1931), ballerina. 2.60fr, Igor Stravinsky (1882-1971), composer.

1982, Nov. 8 Engr. *Perf. 12½x13*
1346 A395 1.60fr multi 70 45
1347 A395 1.80fr multi 1.00 45
1348 A395 2.60fr multi 1.25 60

In a Boat, by Manet (1832-1883) — A396

Design: No. 1348, Les Poissons Noir, by Georges Braque (1882-1963).

Photogravure and Engraved

1982, Nov. 8 *Perf. 13x12½*
1349 A396 4fr multi 1.65 90
1350 A396 4fr multi 1.65 90

Intl. Flower Show, Monte Carlo — A397

Designs: Various floral arrangements.

1982, Nov. 8 Photo. *Perf. 12½x13*
1351 A397 1.60fr multi 60 38
1352 A397 2.60fr multi 85 65

Bouquet — A398

Christmas 1982 — A399

1982 *Perf. 13*
1353 A398 1.60fr multi 70 45

1982, Nov. 8 Engr. *Perf. 12½x13*
1354 A399 1.60fr Three Kings 48 35
1355 A399 1.80fr Holy Family 70 35
1356 A399 2.60fr Shepherds 90 48
a. Souv. sheet of 3, #1354-1356 2.50 2.50

Intl. Polar Year Centenary — A400

1982, Nov. 8 Engr. *Perf. 13*
1358 A400 1.60fr Prince Louis, Discovery 75 55

Discovery of Greenland Millenium — A401

1982, Nov. 8
1359 A401 1.60fr Erik the Red's longship 70 52

Death Bimillenium of Virgil — A402

1982, Nov. 8
1360 A402 1.80fr Scene from Aeneid, Book 6 75 60

50th Anniv. of Botanical Garden A403

1983, Feb. 11 Photo. *Perf. 12½x13*
1361 A403 1.80fr Cacti, vert. 65 35
1362 A403 2fr Exotic plants, vert. 80 35
1363 A403 2.30fr Intl. exhibits, vert. 80 65
1364 A403 2.60fr Cave 90 70
1365 A403 3.30fr Prehistoric Anthropology Museum 1.40 1.00
Nos. 1361-1365 (5) 4.55 3.05

Monte Carlo Dog Show Type

1983, Apr. 13 *Perf. 13x12½*
1366 A387 1.80fr Alaskan malamute 1.25 85

Souvenir Sheet

Princess Grace (1929-1982) — A405

1983, Apr. 19 Engr. *Perf. 13*
1367 A405 10fr black 7.50 7.50

Europa 1983 — A406

1983, Apr. 27 *Perf. 12½x13*
1368 A406 1.80fr Montgolfiere balloon flight, 1783 60 42
1369 A406 2.60fr Columbia space shuttle 90 65
a. Souv. sheet, 5 each #1368-1369 7.25 7.25

Centenary of St. Charles' Church, Monte Carlo — A407

1983, Apr. 27 Engr.
1370 A407 2.60fr St. Charles Borromeo 80 48

Franciscan College Centenary A408

1983, Apr. 27 *Perf. 13x12½*
1371 A408 2fr Church, medallion 70 45

Fontvielle Stadium Interior — A409

1983, Apr. 28 *Perf. 13*
1372 A409 2fr multi 70 50

Automobile Centenary — A410

1983, Apr. 27
1373 A410 2.90fr Benz, 1883, Formula One racer 95 65

Save the Whales Campaign — A411

1983, Apr. 27
1374 A411 3.30fr Blue whale 1.65 95

World Communications Year — A412

1983, Apr. 27
1375 A412 4fr lil rose & brn vio 1.25 90

Souvenir Sheet

Fig Branch in Spring A413

1983, Nov. 9 Engr. *Perf. 13x12½*
1376 Sheet of 4 4.00 4.00
a. A413 1fr shown 38 38
b. A413 2fr Summer 75 75
c. A413 3fr Autumn 1.10 1.10
d. A413 4fr Winter 1.40 1.40

Exotic Plant Type of 1980

1983, Nov. 9 Photo. *Perf. 13*
1380 A359 2fr Argyroderma roseum 95 40

Belle Epoch Type of 1982

Paintings by Hubert Clerissi: 3fr, Thermes Valentia from the Beach, 1902. 5fr, Cafe de Paris and Place du Casino, 1905.

Photogravure and Engraved

1983, Nov. 9 *Perf. 13x12½*
1385 A394 3fr multi 1.10 70
1386 A394 5fr multi 1.50 1.10

Portrait of a Young Man, by Raphael (1483-1520) A414

Passage Cottin, by Maurice Utrillo (1883-1955) A415

Photogravure and Engraved

1983, Nov. 9 *Perf. 13*
1387 A414 4fr multi 1.25 75
1388 A415 4fr multi 1.25 75

Johannes Brahms (1833-1897), Composer — A416

Design: No. 1390, Giacomo Puccini (1858-1924), composer, scene from Madame Butterfly.

1983, Nov. 9 Engr. *Perf. 13½x13*
1389 A416 3fr multi 95 48
1390 A416 3fr multi 95 48

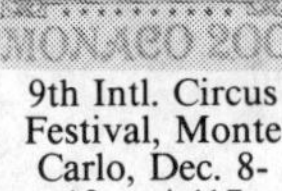

9th Intl. Circus Festival, Monte Carlo, Dec. 8-12 — A417

Intl. Flower Show, Monte Carlo — A418

1983, Nov. 9 *Perf. 13*
1391 A417 2fr multi 80 65

1983, Nov. 9 Photo.
1392 A418 1.60fr Pansies, convolvulus, carnations 60 35
1393 A418 2.60fr Oriental poppies 85 65

Christmas 1983 — A419

1983, Nov. 9 Photo.
1394 A419 2fr Provencal creche figures 65 42

Alfred Nobel (1833-1896), Literature Medal — A420

1983, Nov. 9 Engr.
1395 A420 2fr multi 65 42

Sesquicentenary of Society of St. Vincent de Paul — A421

1983, Nov. 9 **Engr.**
1396 A421 1.80fr F. Ozanam, founder, Paris headquarters 60 48

Offshore Petroleum Plant — A422

1983, Nov. 9
1397 A422 5fr multi 1.50 95

19th Cent. Figurines, Galea Toy Collection — A423

1983, Nov. 9 **Photo.** ***Perf. 12½x13***

1398 A423	50c	Water pipe smoker	16	15
1399 A423	60c	Clown with yo-yo	20	15
1400 A423	70c	Smoking monkey	20	16
1401 A423	80c	Farmer and pig	24	16
1402 A423	90c	Buffalo Bill	30	20
1403 A423	1fr	Snake charmer	35	15
1404 A423	1.50fr	Piano and harp player	45	30
1405 A423	2fr	Girl powdering her face	65	30
		Nos. 1398-1405 (8)	2.55	1.57

Quince Branch in Spring A424

1984, May 10 **Photo.** ***Perf. 13x12½***

1406 A424	1.14fr	shown	35	25
1407 A424	1.47fr	Summer	45	32
1408 A424	2.38fr	Autumn	70	42
1409 A424	3.95fr	Winter	1.40	85

Issued precanceled only. See note after No. 324.

Place de la Visitation, by Hubert Clerissi — A425

Drawings by Hubert Clerissi: 10c, Town Hall. 15c, Rue Basse. 20c, Place Saint-Nicolas. 30c, Quai du Commerce. 40c, Rue des Iris. 3fr, Bandstand. 6fr, Opera House.

1984, May 10 **Engr.** ***Perf. 12½x13***

1410 A425	5c	brown	15	15
1411 A425	10c	claret	15	15
1412 A425	15c	violet	15	15
1413 A425	20c	dark blue	15	15
1414 A425	30c	deep blue	15	15
1415 A425	40c	dark green	15	15
1416 A425	3fr	red brown	1.10	55
1417 A425	6fr	yellow green	2.00	1.25
		Set value	3.40	2.10

See Nos. 1516-1524, 1750-1755.

Souvenir Sheet

1984 Los Angeles Olympics A426

Rhythmic Gymnastics.

1984, May 10 ***Perf. 13***

1418	Sheet of 4	5.25	5.25
a.	A426 2fr Ball	70	70
b.	A426 3fr Clubs	1.10	1.10
c.	A426 4fr Ribbon	1.40	1.40
d.	A426 5fr Hoop	1.75	1.75

1984 Winter Olympics — A427

1984, May 10
1422 A427 2fr Rink, speed skater 65 48
1423 A427 4fr Skater, snowflake 1.25 95

Europa (1959-84) A428

1984, May 10 ***Perf. 13x12½***

1424 A428 2fr blue		70	38
1425 A428 3fr yel grn		95	70
a.	Souv. sheet, 4 each #1424-1425	8.00	8.00

Butterflies and Rare Flowers, Mercantour Natl. Park A429

1.60fr, Boloria graeca tendensis, ranunculus montanus. 2fr, Zygaena vesubiana, saxifraga aizoides. 2.80fr, Erebia aethiopella, myosotis alpestris. 3fr, Parnassius phoebus gazeli, rhododendron ferrugineum. 3.60fr, Papilio alexanor, myrrhis odorata. Nos. 1426-1428 vert.

Perf. 12½x13, 13x12½
1984, May 10 **Photo.**

1426 A429	1.60fr	multi	52	20
1427 A429	2fr	multi	70	20
1428 A429	2.80fr	multi	90	35
1429 A429	3fr	multi	1.00	48
1430 A429	3.60fr	multi	1.40	70
		Nos. 1426-1430 (5)	4.52	1.93

Monte Carlo Dog Show Type

1984, May 10 ***Perf. 13x12½***
1431 A387 1.60fr Auvergne pointer 75 52

Sanctuary of Our Lady of Laghet — A431

1984, May 10 **Engr.** ***Perf. 12½x13***
1432 A431 2fr Statue, rosary, pilgrimage sanctuary 65 40

Auguste Piccard Birth Centenary — A432

1984, May 10
1433 A432 2.80fr Stratosphere balloon 1.00 60
1434 A432 4fr Bathyscaphe 1.50 85

25th Anniv. of Princely Palace Concerts A433

1984, May 10 ***Perf. 13x12½***
1435 A433 3.60fr Orchestra 1.00 60

Belle Epoch Type of 1982

Paintings by Hubert Clerissi: 4fr, Rue Grimaldi, 1908. 5fr, Train Entering Monte Carlo Station, 1910.

Photo. & Engr.
1984, Nov. 8 ***Perf. 12½x13***
1436 A394 4fr multi 1.10 1.00
1437 A394 5fr multi 1.65 1.40

25th Intl. Television Festival, Monte Carlo, Feb. 1985 — A434

1984, Nov. 8 **Engr.** ***Perf. 13***
1438 A434 2.10fr Lights 60 35
1439 A434 3fr Golden nymph (prize) 75 55

Intl. Flower Show, Monte Carlo — A435

Pharmaceuticals, Cosmetics Industry — A436

1984, Nov. 8 **Photo.** ***Perf. 12½x13***
1440 A435 2.10fr Mixed bouquet 60 32
1441 A435 3fr Ikebana 80 60

See Nos. 1491-1492, 1552-1553.

1984, Nov. 8 **Engr.** ***Perf. 13***
1442 A436 2.40fr multi 1.10 85

Illustration from Gargantua, by Rabelais — A437

Francois Rabelais (1490-1553), 17th Cent. Drawing A438

1984, Nov. 8 ***Perf. 13x12½, 12½x13***
1443 A437 2fr With animals 70 52
1444 A437 2fr With sheep of Panurge 70 52
1445 A438 4fr multi 1.40 1.10

Souvenir Sheet

10th Intl. Circus Festival, Dec. 6-10 — A439

1984, Nov. 8 **Photo.** ***Perf. 13***
1446 A439 5fr Poster 1.65 1.65

La Femme a la Potiche, by Degas A440

1984, Nov. 8 **Engr.** ***Perf. 12x13***
1447 A440 6fr multi 2.00 1.75

Christmas 1984 — A441

Figurines from Provence.

1984, Nov. 8 ***Perf. 12½x13***

1448 A441	70c	Shepherd	26	20
1449 A441	1fr	Blind man	32	26
1450 A441	1.70fr	Happy man	52	45
1451 A441	2fr	Woman spinning	60	52
1452 A441	2.10fr	Angel	65	55
1453 A441	2.40fr	Garlic seller	80	60
1454 A441	3fr	Drummer	90	75
1455 A441	3.70fr	Knife grinder	1.25	85
1456 A441	4fr	Elderly couple	1.25	95
		Nos. 1448-1456 (9)	6.55	5.13

See Nos. 1737-1739, 1766-1768.

Cherry Tree A442

1985, Mar. 1 Engr. *Perf. 13*

1457 A442 1.22fr Spring 40 20
1458 A442 1.57fr Summer 48 28
1459 A442 2.55fr Fall 80 42
1460 A442 4.23fr Winter 1.40 85

Issued precanceled only. See note after No. 324.

No. 1 in Green A443

1985, Mar. 25

1461 A443 1.70fr shown 60 42
1462 A443 2.10fr No. 1 in scar 70 22
1463 A443 3fr No. 1 in lt pck bl 90 42

Stamp centenary, Natl. Stamp Exhibition, Dec. 5-8, Monte Carlo.

Europa 1985 — A444

Portraits: 2.10fr Prince Antoine I (1661-1731), Founder of Monaco Palace, music library. 3fr, Jean-Baptiste Lully (1632-1687), composer, violinist, superintendent of music to King Louis XIV.

1985, May 23 *Perf. 12½x13*

1464 A444 2.10fr brt bl 70 52
1465 A444 3fr dk car 1.00 85
a. Souv. sheet, 5 #1464, 5 #1465 10.50 10.50

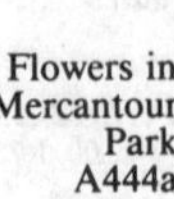

Flowers in Mercantour Park A444a

Perf. 13x12½, 12½x13

1985, May 23 Photo.

1466 A444a 1.70fr Berardia subacaulis 60 38
1467 A444a 2.10fr Saxifraga florulenta, vert. 70 38
1468 A444a 2.40fr Fritillaria moggridgei, vert. 75 70
1469 A444a 3fr Sempervivum allionii, vert. 1.00 90
1470 A444a 3.60fr Silene cordifolia, vert. 1.25 1.00
1471 A444a 4fr Primula allionii 1.40 1.10
Nos. 1466-1471 (6) 5.70 4.46

Japanese Medlar A445

1985, May 23 Engr. *Perf. 13x12½*

1472 Sheet of 4 3.25 3.25
a. A445 1fr Spring 32 32
b. A445 2fr Summer 65 65
c. A445 3fr Autumn 85 85
d. A445 4fr Winter 1.25 1.25

Nadia Boulanger (1887-1979), Musician, Composer, Conductor — A446

Portraits, manuscripts and music: 2.10fr, Georges Auric (1899-1983), composer of film, ballet music, Music Foundation council president.

1985, May 23 *Perf. 13*

1473 A446 1.70fr brown 55 48
1474 A446 2.10fr brt ultra 77 55

Prince Pierre de Monaco Music Foundation composition prize, 25th anniv.

Natl. Oceanographic Museum, 75th Anniv. — A447

1985, May 23

1475 A447 2.10fr brt bl, grn & blk 70 45

Graphs, Fish, Molecular Structures, Lab Apparatus — A448

1985, May 23

1476 A448 3fr dk bl grn, blk & dk rose lil 90 60

Prince Rainier III Scientific Research Center, 25th anniv.

Intl. Athletic Championships, May 25-26 — A449

1985, May 23

1477 A449 1.70fr Running 52 30
1478 A449 2.10fr Swimming 70 35

Opening of Louis II Stadium, May 25.

Monte Carlo Dog Show Type

1985, May 3 Photo. *Perf. 13x12½*

1479 A387 2.10fr Boxer 1.25 70

Intl. Youth Year A450

1985, May 23 Engr. *Perf. 13*

1480 A450 3fr fawn, sep & dp grn 95 55

Fish, Natl. Oceanographic Museum Aquarium A451

1985, Aug. 13 Photo. *Perf. 12½x13*

1481 A451 1.80fr Pygoplites diacanthus 60 35
1482 A451 2.20fr Acanthurus leucosternon 70 32
1483 A451 3.20fr Chaetodon collare 1.10 70
1484 A451 3.90fr Balistoides conspicillum 1.25 75

Size: 40x52mm

Perf. 13

1485 A451 7fr Aquarium 2.25 1.65
Nos. 1481-1485 (5) 5.90 3.77

See Nos. 1560-1561, 1610-1615.

Souvenir Sheet

Transatlantic Yachting Race, Oct. 13 — A452

Yacht classes: No. 1486a, Catamaran. No. 1486b, Monocoque. No. 1486c, Trimaran.

1985, Oct. Engr. *Perf. 13*

1486 Sheet of 3 4.25 4.25
a.-c. A452 4fr, any single 1.25 1.25

Monaco-New York competition.

ITALIA '85, Rome, Oct. 25-Nov. 3 — A453

Design: Exhibition emblem, St. Peter's Cathedral and Temple of Castor ruins.

1985, Oct. 25 *Perf. 13½x13*

1487 A453 4fr int blk, brt grn & red rose 1.40 80

Belle Epoch Type of 1982

Illustrations by Hubert Clerissi.

Photo. & Engr.

1985, Nov. 7 *Perf. 13x12½*

1488 A394 4fr Port of Monaco, 1912 1.40 1.40
1489 A394 6fr La Gare Vers Avenue, 1920 2.00 2.00

11th Intl. Circus Festival, Dec. 5-9 — A454

1985, Nov. 7 Photo. *Perf. 13*

1490 A454 1.80fr multi 55 22

Intl. Flower Show Type of 1984

1985, Nov. 7

1491 A435 2.20fr Roses, tulips, jonquils 75 26
1492 A435 3.20fr Ikebana of chrysanthemums, bryony 1.10 52

Dated 1986.

Factory, Ship, Fish, Crustaceans A455

Christmas 1985 A456

1985, Nov. 7 Engr. *Perf. 13x13½*

1493 A455 2.20fr brt bl, dp brn & dk grnsh bl 75 38

Monagasque fishing industry, Fontvieille District. See No. 1555.

1985, Nov. 7 Photo. *Perf. 12½x13*

1494 A456 2.20fr multi 75 25

EUTELSAT Orbiting Earth — A457

1985, Nov. 7 Engr. *Perf. 13*

1495 A457 3fr int blk, dp rose lil & dk bl 1.00 60

European Telecommunications Satellite Org.

Sacha Guitry (1885-1957), Actor, Dramatist — A458

Authors, composers: 4fr, Brothers Grimm. 5fr, Frederic Chopin and Robert Schumann, composers. 6fr, Johann Sebastian Bach and George Frideric Handel, composers.

1985, Nov. 7

1496 A458 3fr brn blk & gldn brn 1.10 75
1497 A458 4fr dp rose lil, sep & turq bl 1.50 95
1498 A458 5fr stl bl, dp bl & grnsh bl 1.65 1.25
1499 A458 6fr blk, brn & stl bl 1.90 1.50

Souvenir Sheet

Natl. Postage Stamp Cent. — A459

Altered designs: a, Type A1. b, Type A2. c, Type A13. d, Type A83.

1985, Dec. 5
1500 Sheet of 4 7.75 7.75
a.-d. A459 5fr, any single 1.90 1.90

Rainier and Albert Type of 1981-84

1985-88 **Engr.** ***Perf. 13***
1505 A370 1.80fr brt grn 55 15
1506 A370 1.90fr ol grn ('86) 58 30
1507 A370 2fr emer grn ('87) 68 35
1508 A370 2.20fr red rose 60 15
1509 A370 2.50fr dk brn 65 30
1510 A370 3.20fr brt bl 95 22
1511 A370 3.40fr ind ('86) 1.05 52
1512 A370 3.60fr dp ultra ('87) 1.20 60
1513 A370 10fr cl ('86) 2.50 1.50
1514 A370 15fr dk bl grn ('86) 4.75 2.40
1515 A370 20fr brt blue ('88) 7.20 3.60
Nos. 1505-1515 (11) 20.71 10.09

This is an expanding set. Numbers will change if necessary.

Views of Old Monaco Type of 1984

Illustrations by Hubert Clerissi: 50c, Port of Monaco. 60c, St. Charles Church. 70c, Promenade. 80c, Harbor, olive trees. 90c, Quay. 1fr, Palace Square. 2fr, Ships, harbor mouth. 4fr, Monaco Tram Station. 5fr, Mail coach.

1986, Jan. 23
1516 A425 50c red 15 15
1517 A425 60c Prus blue 15 15
1518 A425 70c orange 18 15
1519 A425 80c brt yel grn 20 18
1520 A425 90c rose violet 32 20
1521 A425 1fr brt blue 32 15
1522 A425 2fr black 65 28
1523 A425 4fr ultramarine 1.40 55
1524 A425 5fr olive green 1.50 70
Nos. 1516-1524 (9) 4.87 2.51

Hazel Nut Tree A460

1986, Feb. 24 **Engr.** ***Perf. 13x12½***
1525 A460 1.28fr Spring 42 25
1526 A460 1.65fr Summer 52 38
1527 A460 2.67fr Fall 85 50
1528 A460 4.44fr Winter 1.50 85

Nos. 1525-1528 known only precanceled. See note after No. 324.

See Nos. 1580-1583, 1616-1619, 1685-1688, 1719-1722.

Port of Monaco, 18th Cent. A461

1986, Feb. 24
1529 A461 2.20fr ultra, gray & brown 75 38

Publication of Annales Monegasques, 10th anniv.

Europa 1986 — A462

1986 World Cup Soccer Championships, Mexico — A463

1986, May 22 **Engr.** ***Perf. 12½x13***
1530 A462 2.20fr Ramoge Nature Protection Treaty 85 42
1531 A462 3.20fr Natl. marine reserve 95 65
a. Souv. sheet, 5 each #1530-1531 9.00 9.00

Souvenir Sheet

1986, May 22
1532 Sheet of 2 3.75 3.75
a. A463 5fr Player 1.50 1.50
b. A463 7fr Goalie 2.00 2.00

Ovis Musimon A464

1986, May 22 ***Perf. 13x12½***
1533 A464 2.20fr shown 65 24
1534 A464 2.50fr Capra ibex 70 35
1535 A464 3.20fr Rupicapra rupicapra 1.00 35
1536 A464 3.90fr Marmota marmota 1.10 48
1537 A464 5fr Lepus timidus varronis 1.40 80
1538 A464 7.20fr Mustela erminea 2.25 1.25
Nos. 1533-1538 (6) 7.10 3.47

Nos. 1536-1538 vert.

Monte Carlo Dog Show Type

1986, May 22 **Photo.** ***Perf. 13x12½***
1539 A387 1.80fr Terriers 75 38

Prince Albert I, Parliament — A465

1986, May 22 ***Perf. 13***
1540 A465 2.50fr brn & ol grn 70 52

First Constitution, 75th anniv.

Serge Diaghilev, Founder — A466

1986, May 22 ***Perf. 13***
1541 A466 3.20fr brn blk, carm rose & blk 90 75

Diaghilev's first permanent ballet company, 75th anniv., and creation of Monte Carlo Ballet Company, 1986.

1st Monte Carlo Auto Rally, 75 Anniv. — A467

Design: Winner Henri Rougier and Turcat-Mery, 1911.

1986, May 22
1542 A467 3.90fr rose mag & car 1.10 90

Statue of Liberty, Cent. — A468

1986, May 22
1543 A468 5fr multi 1.40 1.10

Halley's Comet — A469

1986, May 22
1544 A469 10fr Sightings, 1986, 1352 2.75 2.25

AMERIPEX '86, Chicago, May 22-June 1 — A470

1986, May 22
1545 A470 5fr US flag, skyline 1.40 1.10

Belle Epoch Type of 1982

Illustrations by Hubert Clerissi.

Photo. & Engr.

1986, Oct. 28 ***Perf. 12½x13***
1546 A394 6fr Pavilion, 1920, vert. 1.80 90
1547 A394 7fr Beau Rivage Avenue, 1925, vert. 2.10 1.05

Premiere of El Cid, by Pierre Corneille, 350th Anniv. — A471

1986, Oct. 28 **Engr.** ***Perf. 13***
1548 A471 4fr Scenes 1.20 60

Franz Liszt, Composer — A472

1986, Oct. 28
1549 A472 5fr dk red brn & brt ultra 1.50 75

The Olympic Swimmer, 1961, by Emma de Sigaldi A473

1986, Oct. 28 ***Perf. 12½x13***
1550 A473 6fr multi 1.80 90

Intl. Insurers Congress, Monte Carlo, Sept. 30 — A474

1986, Oct. 28 ***Perf. 13½x13***
1551 A474 3.20fr brn, dp grn & brt bl 95 48

Intl. Flower Show Type of 1984

Designs: 2.20fr, Bouquet of roses, acidenthera. 3.90fr, Ikebana of lilies, beech branches.

1986, Oct. 28 **Photo.** ***Perf. 12½x13***
1552 A435 2.20fr multi 65 32
1553 A435 3.90fr multi 1.15 58

Dated 1987.

12th Intl. Circus Festival, Dec. 4-8 — A475

1986, Oct. 28 ***Perf. 13***
1554 A475 2.20fr multi 65 32

Industries Type of 1985

Design: 3.90fr, Plastics industry.

1986, Oct. 28 **Engr.**
1555 A455 3.90fr dk red, dk gray & bl grn 1.15 58

Christmas — A476

1986, Oct. 28 Photo. *Perf. 12½x13*

1556 A476 1.80fr Holly 55 28
1557 A476 2.50fr Poinsettia 75 38

Ascent of Mt. Blanc by J. Balmat and M.G. Paccard, Bicent. — A477

1986, Oct. 28 Engr. *Perf. 13*

1558 A477 5.80fr red, brt bl & slate bl 1.75 90

Miniature Sheet

Arbutus Tree A478

1986, Oct. 28 *Perf. 13x12½*

1559 Sheet of 4 5.40 2.70
a. A478 3fr Spring .90 .45
b. A478 4fr Summer 1.20 .60
c. A478 5fr Fall 1.50 .75
d. A478 6fr Winter 1.80 .90

See Nos. 1645, 1680, 1736, 1775.

Aquarium Type of 1985

1986, Sept. 25 Photo. *Perf. 12½x13*

1560 A451 1.90fr like No. 1481 58 30
1561 A451 3.40fr like No. 1483 1.05 52

Prince Rainier III — A479

Villa Miraflores, Seat of the Philatelic Bureau — A480

Design: No. 1562b, Prince Louis II, founder of the bureau.

1987, Apr. 23 Engr. *Perf. 12½x13*

1562 Strip of 3 5.50 2.75
a. A479 4fr brt bl 1.35 .68
b. A479 4fr dk red 1.35 .68
c. A480 8fr multi 2.70 1.35

Philatelic Bureau, 50th anniv.
See No. 1607.

Louis II Stadium A481

1987, Apr. 23 *Perf. 13x12½*

1563 A481 2.20fr Exterior 75 38
1564 A481 3.40fr Interior 1.15 58
a. Min. sheet of 10, 5 each #1563-1564 9.50 4.80

Europa 1987.

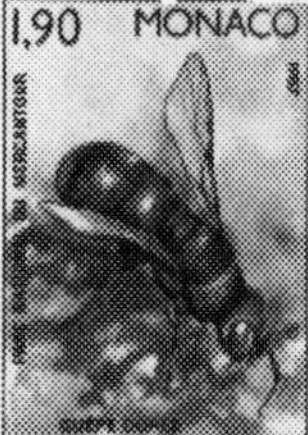

Insects — A482 St. Devote Parish, Cent. — A483

1987, Apr. 23 Photo.

1565 A482 1fr Carabe de solier 35 18
1566 A482 1.90fr Guepe dorec 65 32
1567 A482 2fr Cicindele 68 35
1568 A482 2.20fr Grande aeschne 75 38
1569 A482 3fr Chrysomele 1.00 50
1570 A482 3.40fr Grande sauterelle verte 1.15 58
Nos. 1565-1570 (6) 4.58 2.31

Nos. 1565, 1567 and 1569 horiz.

1987, Apr. 23 Engr. *Perf. 12½x13*

1571 A483 1.90fr black 65 32

Monaco Diocese, Cent. — A484

1987, Apr. 23

1572 A484 2.50fr dk yel grn 85 42

50th Intl. Dog Show, Monte Carlo A485

1987, Apr. 23 *Perf. 13x12½*

1573 A485 1.90fr Dog breeds 65 32
1574 A485 2.70fr Poodle 90 45

Stamp Day — A486

1987, Apr. 23 *Perf. 13*

1575 A486 2.20fr multi 75 38

Red Curley Tail, Mobile by Alexander Calder (1898-1976), Sculptor — A487

1987, Apr. 23 Photo.

1576 A487 3.70fr multi 1.25 62

Sculpture Exhibition, Monte Carlo.

2nd Small European Countries Games, May 14-17 — A488

1987, Apr. 23 Engr.

1577 A488 3fr Tennis 1.00 50
1578 A488 5fr Windsurfing 1.70 85

Miniature Sheet

Grape Vines A489

1987, Apr. 23 *Perf. 13x12½*

1579 Sheet of 4 6.00 3.00
a. A489 3fr Spring 1.00 .50
b. A489 4fr Summer 1.30 .65
c. A489 5fr Autumn 1.70 .85
d. A489 6fr Winter 2.00 1.00

Four Seasons Type of 1986

Life cycle of the chestnut tree.

1987, Mar. 17 Engr. *Perf. 13x12½*

1580 A460 1.31fr Spring 45 22
1581 A460 1.69fr Summer 55 28
1582 A460 2.74fr Fall 90 45
1583 A460 4.56fr Winter 1.50 75

Nos. 1580-1583 known only precanceled. See note after No. 324.

The Life of St. Devote, Patron Saint of Monaco A490

Text: 4fr, Born in 283, in Quercio, Devote was martyred in Mariana, Corsica. 5fr, Devote's nurse teaches the saint about Christianity.

1987, Nov. 13 Photo. *Perf. 13x12½*

1584 A490 4fr multi 1.30 65
1585 A490 5fr multi 1.65 82

Red Cross of Monaco.
See Nos. 1643-1644, 1692-1693, 1714-1715, 1776-1777.

Philately A491

Butterflies and butterflies on simulated stamps.

1987, July 28 Engr.

1586 A491 1.90fr brt grn & dk gray 62 30
1587 A491 2.20fr rose red & rose lake 72 35
1588 A491 2.50fr red lil & vio 82 40
1589 A491 3.40fr brt bl & bluish blk 1.15 58

13th Int'l. Circus Festival, Monte Carlo, Jan. 28-Feb. 1 — A492

1987, Nov. 13 Photo. *Perf. 12½x13*

1590 A492 2.20fr multi 72 35

Ikebanas — A493

1987, Nov. 13

1591 A493 2.20fr shown 72 35
1592 A493 3.40fr multi, horiz. 1.15 58

1988 Int'l Flower Show, Concours. Dated 1988. See Nos. 1651, 1749.

Christmas A494

1987, Nov. 13 Engr. *Perf. 13x12½*

1593 A494 2.20fr crimson 72 35

5-Franc Prince Honore V Coin A495

1987, Nov. 13 *Perf. 13*

1594 A495 2.50fr scar & dk gray 82 40

Recapture of the Mint, 150th anniv.

Electronics Industry — A496

1987, Nov. 13

1595 A496 2.50fr henna brn, vio bl & grn 82 40

Int'l. Marine Radioactivity Laboratory, 25th Anniv. — A497

Design: Monaco Oceanographic Museum and Int'l. Agency of Atomic Energy, Vienna.

1987, Nov. 13
1596 A497 5fr brt bl, red brn & blk 1.65 82

Louis Jouvet (b.1887), French Actor A498

1987, Nov. 16 ***Perf. 13x12½***
1597 A498 3fr black 1.00 50

Paul and Virginia, by Bernardin de Saint-Pierre, First Edition Bicent. (in 1988) A499

1987, Nov. 16
1598 A499 3fr The River Crossing 1.00 50

Marc Chagall (1887-1985), Painter — A500

1987, Nov. 16 ***Perf. 13***
1599 A500 4fr terra cotta & bl gray 1.30 65

Jean Jenneret (Le Corbusier, 1887-1965), French Architect — A501

1987, Nov. 16
1600 A501 4fr Architect, Ronchamp Chapel 1.30 65

Newton's Theory of Gravity, 300th Anniv. — A502

Invention of the Telegraph by Samuel Morse, 150th Anniv. — A503

1987, Nov. 16
1601 A502 4fr mag & dk bl 1.30 65
1602 A503 4fr brt vio, turq bl & brn 1.30 65

Don Juan, Opera by Mozart, Bicent. — A504

Mass of the Dead, by Berlioz — A505

1987, Nov. 16
1603 A504 5fr ind, vio brn & sage grn 1.65 82
1604 A505 5fr sl grn, vio brn & bl 1.65 82

Belle Epoch Type of 1982

Illustrations by Hubert Clerissi. Nos. 1605-1606 vert.

Photo. & Engr.

1987, Nov. 16 ***Perf. 12½x13***
1605 A394 6fr Rampe Major 2.00 1.00
1606 A394 7fr Old Monte Carlo Station 2.35 1.20

Philatelic Bureau Type of 1987

1987, Nov. 13 Engr. ***Perf. 12½x13***
1607 Sheet of 3 5.50 5.50
a. A479 4fr blk vio, like #1562a 1.35 1.35
b. A479 4fr blk vio, like #1562b 1.35 1.35
c. A480 8fr blk vio, like #1562c 2.70 2.70

Postage Due Arms Type of 1985
Booklet Stamps

1987-88 Photo. ***Perf. 13 on 3 Sides***
1608 D10 2fr multi ('88) 72 35
a. Bklt. pane of 10 7.25
1609 D10 2.20fr multi 72 35
a. Bklt. pane of 10 7.25

Dates of issue: No. 1608, Jan. 15. No. 1609, Nov. 13.

Aquarium Type of 1985
Perf. 13x12½, 12½x13

1988, Jan. 15 **Photo.**
1610 A451 2fr Bodianus rufus 72 35
1611 A451 2.20fr Chelmon rostratus 80 40
1612 A451 2.50fr Oxymonacanthus longirostris 90 45
1613 A451 3fr Ostracion lentiginosum 1.10 55
1614 A451 3.70fr Pterois volitans 1.30 65
1615 A451 7fr Thalassoma lunare, horiz. 2.50 1.25
Nos. 1610-1615 (6) 7.32 3.65

Life Cycle of the Pear Tree A505a

1988, Feb. 15 ***Perf. 13x12½***
1616 A505a 1.36fr Spring 50 25
1617 A505a 1.75fr Summer 65 32
1618 A505a 2.83fr Fall 1.00 50
1619 A505a 4.72fr Winter 1.70 85

Nos. 1616-1619 known only precanceled. See note after No. 324.

Souvenir Sheet

Biathlon, 1988 Winter Olympics, Calgary — A506

Litho. & Engr.

1988, Feb. 15 ***Perf. 13***
1620 Sheet of 2 3.60 3.60
a. A506 4fr Skiing 1.45 1.45
b. A506 6fr Shooting 2.15 2.15

51st Intl. Dog Show, Monte Carlo — A507

1988, Mar. 30 Photo. ***Perf. 12½x13***
1621 A507 3fr Dachshunds 1.10 55

World Assoc. of the Friends of Children (AMADE), 25th Anniv. A508

1988, Mar. 30 Engr. ***Perf. 13***
1622 A508 5fr dark vio blue, dark brn & brt olive grn 1.80 90

Europa 1988 — A509

Transport and communication: 2.20fr, Globe picturing hemispheres, man, brain, telecommunications satellite. 3.60fr, Plane propeller and high-speed locomotive.

1988, Apr. 21 ***Perf. 12½x13***
1623 A509 2.20fr multi 80 40
1624 A509 3.60fr multi 1.30 65
a. Souv. sheet, 5 each #1623-1624 10.50 10.50

Mushrooms of Mercantour Natl. Park A510

Perf. 13x12½, 12½x13

1988, May 26 **Photo.**
1625 A510 2fr Leccinum rotundifoliae 70 35
1626 A510 2.20fr Hygrocybe punicea 78 40
1627 A510 2.50fr Pholiota flammans 90 45
1628 A510 2.70fr Lactarius lignyotus 95 42
1629 A510 3fr Cortinarius traganus 1.05 52
1630 A510 7fr Russula olivacea 2.50 1.25
Nos. 1625-1630 (6) 6.88 3.39

Nos. 1629-1630 vert.

Nautical Soc., Cent. — A511

1988, May 26 Engr. ***Perf. 13***
1631 A511 2fr dark red, lt blue & dark grn 70 35

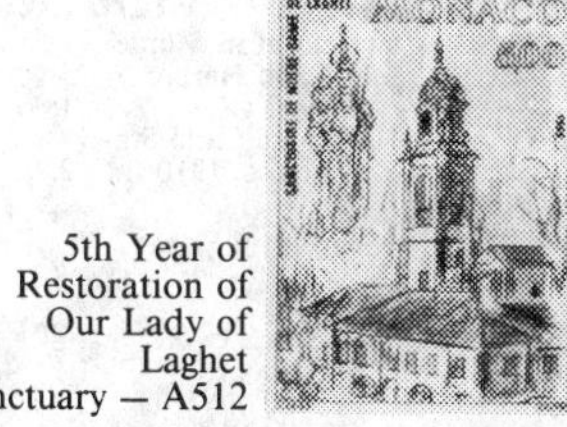
5th Year of Restoration of Our Lady of Laghet Sanctuary — A512

1988, May 26 ***Perf. 12½***
1632 A512 5fr multi 1.75 88

World Health Organization, 40th Anniv. — A513

1988, May 26 ***Perf. 13***
1633 A513 6fr brt blue & lake 2.15 1.10

Intl. Red Cross and Red Crescent Organizations, 125th Annivs. — A514

1988, May 26 Photo. ***Perf. 13x12½***
1634 A514 6fr dull red, blk & gray 2.15 1.10

Jean Monnet (1888-1979), Nobel Peace Prize Winner in 1922 — A515

Maurice Chevalier (1888-1972), Actor — A516

1988, May 26 Engr. ***Perf. 12½x13***
1635 A515 2fr brt blue, dark olive bister & blk 70 35
1636 A516 2fr blk & dark blue 70 35

1st Crossing of Greenland by Fridtjof Nansen (1861-1930), Cent. — A517

1988, May 26 *Perf. 13*
1637 A517 4fr brt vio 1.40 70

Belle Epoch Type of 1982

Illustrations by Hubert Clerissi.

Photo. & Engr.

1988, Sept. 8 *Perf. 13x12½*
1638 A394 6fr Packet in Monte Carlo Harbor, 1910 1.90 95
1639 A394 7fr Monte Carlo Station, c. 1910 2.25 1.15

Souvenir Sheet

1988 Summer Olympics, Seoul A518

Woman wearing Korean regional costume, Games emblem and event: 2fr, Women's tennis. 3fr, Women's table tennis. 5fr, Women's yachting. 7fr, Women's cycling.

1988, Sept. 8 **Engr.**
1640 Sheet of 4 5.50 5.50
a. A518 2fr blk, lt ultra & brn 65 65
b. A518 3fr blk, lt ultra & brn 95 95
c. A518 5fr blk, lt ultra & brn 1.60 1.60
d. A518 7fr blk, lt ultra & brn 2.25 2.25

A519

Monte Carlo Congress Center, 10th Anniv. A520

1988, Sept. 8 *Perf. 13*
1641 A519 2fr dark blue grn 68 35
1642 A520 3fr henna brn 1.00 50
a. Pair, #1641-1642 1.75 1.00

Monegasque Red Cross Type of 1987

The Life of St. Devote, patron saint of Monaco: 4fr, Devote witnessing the arrival of the governor of Rome. 5fr, Devote and the governor.

1988, Oct. 20 **Photo.** *Perf. 13x12½*
1643 A490 4fr multi 1.30 65
1644 A490 5fr multi 1.60 80

Tree Type of 1986

Life cycle of the olive tree.

1988, Oct. 20 **Engr.** *Perf. 13x12½*
1645 Sheet of 4 5.75 5.75
a. A478 3fr Spring 95 95
b. A478 4fr Summer 1.30 1.30
c. A478 5fr Fall 1.60 1.60
d. A478 6fr Winter 1.90 1.90

Le Nain and Brothers, Detail of a Painting in the Louvre, by Antoine Le Nain (c. 1588-1648) A521

1988, Oct. 20 *Perf. 12½x13*
1646 A521 5fr ol brn, dull brn & car rose 1.60 80

Les Grands Archeologues, Bronze Sculpture by Giorgio De Chirico (1888-1978), Italian Painter and Sculptor — A522

1988, Oct. 20 *Perf. 13*
1647 A522 5fr ol bis, blk brn & dark bl 1.60 80

Pierre Carlet de Chamblain de Marivaux (1688-1763), French Playwright and Novelist — A523

Lord Byron (1788-1824), English Poet — A524

1988, Oct. 20
1648 A523 3fr dull ol & ultra 95 48

1988, Oct. 20
1649 A524 3fr grnsh bl, brn & blk 95 48

14th Intl. Circus Festival, Monte Carlo, Feb. 2-6, 1989 — A525

1988, Oct. 20 **Photo.** *Perf. 12½x13*
1650 A525 2fr multi 65 32

Intl. Flower Show Type of 1987

1988, Oct. 20
1651 A493 3fr Ikebana 95 48

22nd Intl. Flower Show and Flower Arranging Contest, Monte Carlo.

Textile Industry (Ready-to-Wear Clothes by Bettina and Le Squadra) — A526

1988, Oct. 20 **Engr.** *Perf. 13*
1652 A526 3fr blk, yel org & dk ol grn 95 48

Christmas — A527

1988, Oct. 20 **Litho.** *Perf. 12½x13*
1653 A527 2fr blk & lem 65 32

Petroglyphs, Mercantour Natl. Park A528

Perf. 13x12½, 12½x13

1989, Feb. 8 **Litho.**
1654 A528 2fr multi 65 32
1655 A528 2.20fr multi, diff. 72 35
1656 A528 3fr multi, diff. 98 50
1657 A528 3.60fr multi, diff. 1.20 60
1658 A528 4fr multi, diff., vert. 1.30 65
1659 A528 5fr multi, diff., vert. 1.65 82
Nos. 1654-1659 (6) 6.50 3.24

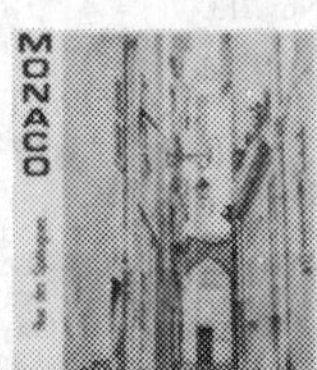

Rue des Spelugues A528a

1989, Feb. 8 **Litho.** *Perf. 13½x13*

Booklet Stamps
1660 A528a 2fr shown 65 32
b. Bklt. pane of 10 6.50
1660A A528a 2.20fr St. Nicolas Place 72 35
c. Bklt. pane of 10 7.25

See Nos. 1702-1703.

Prince Rainier III — A529

1989-91 **Photo. & Engr.** *Perf. 13*
1661 A529 2fr pale blue grn & Prus grn 65 16
1662 A529 2.10fr lt blue & Prus blue 75 18
1663 A529 2.20fr pink & rose brn 72 18
1664 A529 2.20fr pale greenish bl & greenish bl 80 40
1665 A529 2.30fr pale pink & car lake 82 20
1666 A529 2.50fr pale rose & rose lake 90 45
1667 A529 3.20fr pale blue & brt blue 1.15 28
1668 A529 3.40fr lt bl & dk bl 1.25 62
1669 A529 3.60fr lt blue & sapphire 1.20 30
1670 A529 3.80fr pale pink & dk lil rose 1.35 32
1671 A529 4fr pale vio & rose vio 1.40 70
1672 A529 5fr buff & dark vio brn 1.65 55
1673 A529 15fr pale vio & indigo 4.75 2.40
1673A A529 20fr pink & rose car 6.80 3.40
1674 A529 25fr pale gray & blk 9.00 4.50
Nos. 1661-1674 (15) 33.19 14.64

Issue dates: 2fr, No. 1663, 3.60fr, 5fr, 15fr, Mar. 14. 2.10fr, 2.30fr, 25fr, Jan. 11, 1990. 3.20fr, 3.80fr, Mar. 15, 1990. 20fr, Apr. 26, 1991. No. 1664, 2.50fr, 3.40fr, 4fr, Sept. 24, 1991.

See No. 1797.

5th Magic Grand Prix, Monte Carlo, Mar. 17-19 A530

1989, Mar. 14 **Engr.** *Perf. 13x12½*
1675 A530 2.20fr multi 72 35

Dog Show Type of 1982

1989, Mar. 14 **Photo.**
1676 A387 2.20fr Yorkshire terrier 72 35

Our Lady of Mercy Soc., 350th Anniv. A531

1989, Mar. 14 **Engr.** *Perf. 13*
1677 A531 3fr choc, dark red & blk 98 50

Theater & Film — A532

Designs: 3fr, Jean Cocteau (1889-1963), French writer, artist. 4fr, Charlie Chaplin (1889-1977), English actor, film producer.

1989, Mar. 14
1678 A532 3fr Prus grn, olive grn & deep rose lil 98 50
1679 A532 4fr dark grn, dark vio & dark red 1.30 65

Tree Type of 1986

Life cycle of the pomegranate tree.

1989, Mar. 14 *Perf. 13x12½*

Miniature Sheet
1680 Sheet of 4 5.90 5.90
a. A478 3fr Spring 98 98
b. A478 4fr Summer 1.30 1.30
c. A478 5fr Fall 1.65 1.65
d. A478 6fr Winter 1.95 1.95

Souvenir Sheet

Reign of Prince Rainier III, 40th Anniv. A533

1989, May 9 Engr. *Perf. 13*
1681 A533 20fr rose vio 6.00 6.00

Europa 1989 — A534

Children's games.

1989, May 9 *Perf. 12½x13*
1682 A534 2.20fr Marbles 68 35
1683 A534 3.60fr Jumping rope 1.10 55
a. Souv. sheet, 5 each #1682-1683 9.00 9.00

Souvenir Sheet

French Revolution, Bicent., PHILEXFRANCE '89 — A535

Designs: a, Liberty. b, Equality. c, Fraternity.

1989, July 7 Engr. *Perf. 12½x13*
1684 A535 Sheet of 3 4.35 4.35
a. 5fr sapphire 1.45 1.45
b. 5fr black 1.45 1.45
c. 5fr dark red 1.45 1.45

Four Seasons Type of 1986

Life cycle of the pear tree.

1989, July 27 Photo. *Perf. 13x12½*
1685 A460 1.39fr like No. 1616 45 22
1686 A460 1.79fr like No. 1617 58 30
1687 A460 2.90fr like No. 1618 92 45
1688 A460 4.84fr like No. 1619 1.55 78

Nos. 1685-1688 known only precanceled. See note after No. 324.

Portrait of the Artist's Mother, by Philibert Florence A536

Regatta at Molesey, by Alfred Sisley (1839-1899) — A537

Paintings: 8fr, *Enclosed Courtyard, Auvers,* by Paul Cezanne (1839-1906), vert.

Perf. 13, 13x12½ (6fr), 12½x13 (8fr)
1989, Sept. 7 Engr.
1689 A536 4fr olive black 1.20 60
1690 A537 6fr multi 1.80 90
1691 A537 8fr multi 2.40 1.20

Birth sesquicentennials of painters.

Monegasque Red Cross Type of 1987

The life of St. Devote, patron saint of Monaco: 4fr, Eutychius refuses to betray Devote to Barbarus and is poisoned. 5fr, Devote is condemned to torture by Barbarus when she refuses to make sacrifices to the Gods.

1989, Sept. 7 Photo. *Perf. 13x12½*
1692 A490 4fr multi 1.20 60
1693 A490 5fr multi 1.50 75

Interparliamentary Union, Cent. — A538

1989, Oct. 26 Engr. *Perf. 13*
1694 A538 4fr multi 1.20 60

Belle Epoch Type of 1982

Illustrations by Hubert Clerissi.

1989, Oct. 26 *Perf. 12½x13*
1695 A394 7fr Ship in Monaco Port 2.10 1.05
1696 A394 8fr Gaming hall, Monte Carlo Casino 2.40 1.20

Souvenir Sheet

Princess Grace Foundation, 25th Anniv. — A539

Designs: a, Princess Grace. b, Princess Caroline.

1989, Oct. 26
1697 Sheet of 2 3.00 3.00
a.-b. A539 5fr any single 1.50 1.50

20th UPU Congress — A540

Design: Views of the Prince of Monaco's palace and the White House.

1989, Oct. 26 *Perf. 13*
1698 A540 6fr multi 1.80 90

Christmas — A541

1989, Oct. 26 Litho. *Perf. 12½x13*
1699 A541 2fr Poinsettia 65 32

15th Intl. Circus Festival, Monte Carlo, Feb. 1-5, 1990 — A542

1989, Dec. 7 Photo. *Perf. 12½x13*
1700 A542 2.20fr multicolored 78 40

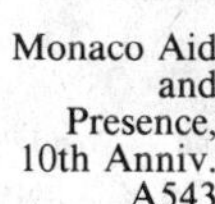

Monaco Aid and Presence, 10th Anniv. A543

1989, Dec. 7 Engr. *Perf. 13x12½*
1701 A543 2.20fr brown & red 78 40

Avenues Type of 1989

1990, Feb. 8 Litho. *Perf. 13½x13*
1702 A528a 2.10fr The Great Stairs 75 38
a. Bklt. pane of 10 + 2 labels 7.50
1703 A528a 2.30fr Mayoral Court of Honor 82 40
a. Bklt. pane of 10 + 2 labels 8.25

Dog Show Type of 1982

1990, Mar. 15 *Perf. 13x12½*
1704 A387 2.30fr Bearded collie 82 40

Sir Rowland Hill, Great Britain No. 1 — A544

1990, Mar. 15 Engr. *Perf. 13*
1705 A544 5fr royal blue & black 1.80 90

Penny Black, 150th anniv.

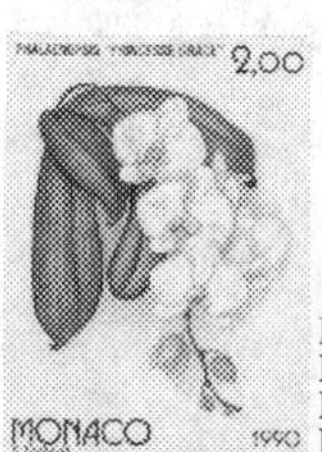

Flowers Named for Members of the Royal Family — A545

1990, Mar. 15 Litho. *Perf. 12½x13*
1706 A545 2fr Princess Grace 72 35
1707 A545 3fr Prince Rainier III 1.05 52
1708 A545 3fr Grace Patricia 1.05 52
1709 A545 4fr Principessa Grace 1.45 72
1710 A545 5fr Caroline of Monaco 1.75 90
Nos. 1706-1710 (5) 6.02 3.01

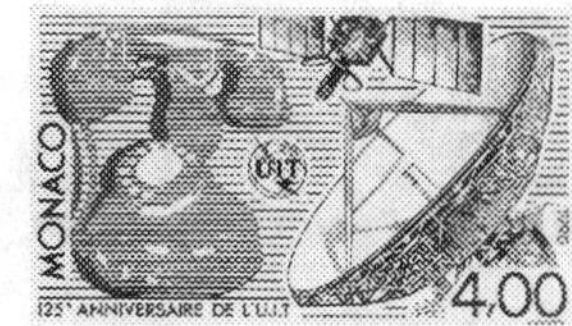

Intl. Telecommunications Union, 125th Anniv. — A546

1990, Mar. 15 Engr. *Perf. 13*
1711 A546 4fr pink, deep vio & dull blue grn 1.45 72

Antony Noghes (1890-1978), Creator of the Monaco Grand Prix and Monte Carlo Rally — A547

1990, Mar. 15
1712 A547 3fr deep vio, blk & dark red 1.10 55

Automobile Club, Cent. — A548

1990, Mar. 15
1713 A548 4fr brt pur, sepia & brt blue 1.45 72

Monegasque Red Cross Type of 1987

The life of St. Devote, patron saint of Monaco: 4fr, Devote tortured to death (whipped). 5fr, Body layed out in a small boat.

1990, Mar. 15 Litho. *Perf. 13x12½*
1714 A490 4fr multicolored 1.45 72
1715 A490 5fr multicolored 1.75 88

Europa — A549

1990, May 3 Engr. *Perf. 12½x12*
1716 A549 2.30fr multicolored 80 40
1717 A549 3.70fr multicolored 1.30 60
a. Souv. sheet of 8, 4 each #1716, 1717, perf. 12½x13 8.75 8.75

The only foreign revenue stamps listed in this Catalogue are those authorized for prepayment of postage.

Souvenir Sheet

World Cup Soccer Championships, Italy — A550

1990, May 3 ***Perf. 13x12½***
1718 A550 Sheet of 4 7.00 7.00
a. 5fr Players, trophy 1.75 1.75
b. 5fr Player dribbling ball 1.75 1.75
c. 5fr Ball 1.75 1.75
d. 5fr Players, stadium 1.75 1.75

Four Seasons Type of 1986

Life cycle of the plum tree.

1990, Sept. 17 ***Perf. 13***
1719 A460 1.46fr Spring 52 26
1720 A460 1.89fr Summer 65 32
1721 A460 3.06fr Fall 1.10 55
1722 A460 5.10fr Winter 1.80 90

Nos. 1719-1722 known only precanceled. See note after No. 324.

Minerals, Mercantour Natl. Park A551

Perf. 13x12½, 12½x13
1990, Sept. 4 **Litho.**
1723 A551 2.10fr Anatase 75 38
1724 A551 2.30fr Albite 80 40
1725 A551 3.20fr Rutile 1.15 58
1726 A551 3.80fr Chlorite 1.35 68
1727 A551 4fr Brookite 1.40 70
1728 A551 6fr Quartz 2.10 1.05
Nos. 1723-1728 (6) 7.55 3.79

Nos. 1727-1728 vert.

Pierrot Ecrivain — A552

1990, Sept. 4 **Engr.** ***Perf. 12½x13***
1729 A552 3fr dark blue 1.10 55

Helicopter, Monaco Heliport A553

Design: 5fr, Helicopters, Monte Carlo skyline.

1990, Sept. 4 ***Perf. 13***
1730 A553 3fr red, brn & blk 1.10 55
1731 A553 5fr blk, gray bl & brn 1.80 90

30th World Congress of Civilian Airports, Monte Carlo.

C. Samuel Hahnemann (1755-1843), Physician — A554

1990, Sept. 4
1732 A554 3fr multicolored 1.10 55

Homeopathic medicine, bicentennial.

Jean-Francois Champollion (1790-1832), Egyptologist — A555

1990, Sept. 4
1733 A555 5fr blue & brown 1.80 90

Offshore Power Boating World Championships A556

Design: 6fr, Petanque World Championships.

1990, Sept. 4
1734 A556 2.30fr brt ultra, brn & red 90 45
1735 A556 6fr brn org, brn & bl 2.25 1.10

Tree Type of 1986
Miniature Sheet

Life cycle of the lemon tree.

1990, Oct. 17 **Litho.** ***Perf. 13x12½***
1736 Sheet of 4 6.75 6.75
a. A478 3fr Spring 1.15 1.15
b. A478 4fr Summer 1.50 1.50
c. A478 5fr Fall 1.90 1.90
e. A478 6fr Winter 2.25 2.25

Type of 1984

1990, Oct. 17 **Litho.** ***Perf. 12½x13***
1737 A441 2.30fr Miller riding donkey 90 45
1738 A441 3.20fr Woman carrying firewood 1.25 65
1739 A441 3.80fr Baker 1.50 75

The Cathedral, by Auguste Rodin (1840-1917) A558

1990, Oct. 17 **Engr.** ***Perf. 12½***
1740 A558 5fr bl & cream 1.90 95

La Pie by Claude Monet (1840-1926) — A559

1990, Oct. 17 ***Perf. 13x12***
1741 A559 7fr multicolored 2.60 1.30

Peter Ilich Tchaikovsky, Composer (1840-1893) A560

1990, Oct. 17 ***Perf. 12½x13***
1742 A560 5fr dark grn & bl 1.90 95

16th Intl. Circus Festival, Monte Carlo — A561

1991, Jan. 2 **Photo.** ***Perf. 13***
1743 A561 2.30fr multicolored 90 45

See No. 1801.

Migratory Birds — A562

Birds and their continents: 2fr, Ciconia abdimii, Africa. 3fr, Selasphorus platycercus, America. 4fr, Anas querquedula, Asia. 5fr, Eurystomus orientalis, Australia. 6fr, Merops apiaster, Europe.

1991, Feb. 22 **Litho.** ***Perf. 12½x13***
1744 A562 2fr multicolored 80 40
1745 A562 3fr multicolored 1.20 60
1746 A562 4fr multicolored 1.60 80
1747 A562 5fr multicolored 2.00 1.00
1748 A562 6fr multicolored 2.40 1.20
Nos. 1744-1748 (5) 8.00 4.00

Intl. Symposium on Migratory Birds.

Intl. Flower Show Type of 1987

1991, Feb. 22
1749 A493 3fr Cyclamen 1.20 60

Views of Old Monaco Type of 1984

Designs: 20c, Cliffs of Monaco, Port de Fontvieille. 40c, Place du Casino. 50c, Place de la Cremaillere. 70c, Prince's Palace. 80c, Avenue du Beau Rivage. 1fr, Place d'Armes.

1991, Feb. 22 **Engr.**
1750 A425 20c rose violet 15 15
1751 A425 40c dk green 15 15
1752 A425 50c claret 20 15
1753 A425 70c ol green 25 15
1754 A425 80c ultramarine 30 15
1755 A425 1fr dk blue 40 20
Nos. 1750-1755 (6) 1.45
Set value 78

Dog Show Type of 1982

1991, Feb. 22 **Litho.** ***Perf. 12***
1756 A387 2.50fr Schnauzer 1.00 50

Phytoplankton A563

1991, Feb. 22
1757 A563 2.10fr multicolored 85 42

Oceanographic Museum.

1992 Olympics A564

Design: No. 1758b, Cross country skiiers, diff. No. 1759a, Relay runner receiving baton. No. 1759b, Runner passing baton.

1991, Apr. 26 **Engr.** ***Perf. 13x12½***
1758 Pair 2.80 1.40
a. A564 3fr dk grn, bl & olive 1.20 60
b. A564 4fr dk grn, bl & olive 1.60 80
1759 Pair 3.20 1.60
a. A564 3fr brn & Prus bl 1.20 60
b. A564 5fr brn & Prus bl 2.00 1.00

Nos. 1758 and 1759 have continuous designs.

Europa A565

1991, Apr. 26
1760 A565 2.30fr Eutelsat 90 45
1761 A565 3.20fr Inmarsat 1.25 65
a. Min. sheet, 5 ea. #1760-1761 10.75 5.35

25th Intl. Contemporary Art Competition A566

Prince Pierre Foundation, 25th Anniv. A567

1991, Apr. 26 **Engr.** ***Perf. 12½x13***
1762 A566 4fr multicolored 1.40 70

1991, Apr. 26
1763 A567 5fr multicolored 1.75 88

Coral — A568

1991, Apr. 26 **Photo.** ***Perf. 12***

1764 A568	2.20fr shown		75	38
1765 A568	2.40fr Coral necklace		85	42

Christmas Type of 1984

1991, Nov. 7 **Litho.** ***Perf. 12***

1766 A441	2.50fr Consul	90	45
1767 A441	3.50fr Woman from Arles	1.30	65
1768 A441	4fr Mayor	1.45	75

Conifers, Mercantour Natl. Park A569

1991, Nov. 7

1769 A569	2.50fr Epicea	90	45
1770 A569	3.50fr Sapin	1.30	65
1771 A569	4fr Pin a crochets	1.45	75
1772 A569	5fr Pin sylvestre, vert.	1.85	90
1773 A569	6fr Pin cembro	2.20	1.10
1774 A569	7fr Meleze, vert.	2.55	1.30
	Nos. 1769-1774 (6)	10.25	5.15

Tree Type of 1986
Miniature Sheet

Life cycle of an orange tree.

1991, Nov. 7 **Engr.** ***Perf. 13x12½***

1775	Sheet of 4	6.60	3.30
a.	A478 3fr Spring	1.10	55
b.	A478 4fr Summer	1.45	75
c.	A478 5fr Fall	1.85	90
d.	A478 6fr Winter	2.20	1.10

Monagasque Red Cross Type of 1987

Life of St. Devote, Monaco's Patron Saint: 4.50fr, The Storm is Rising. 5.50fr, Arrival of the Rock of Monaco.

1991, Nov. 7 **Photo.**

1776 A490	4.50fr multicolored	1.65	85
1777 A490	5.50fr multicolored	2.00	1.00

Testudo Hermanni A570

1991, Nov. 7 **Litho.** ***Perf. 12***

1778 A570	1.25fr Two crawling right	45	22
1779 A570	1.25fr Peering from shell	45	22
1780 A570	1.25fr Walking in grass	45	22
1781 A570	1.25fr Walking amid plants	45	22
a.	Block or strip of 4, #1778-1781	1.80	90

Prince Albert I Type of 1891
Miniature Sheet

1991, Nov. 7 **Engr.** ***Perf. 13***

Stamp size: 22½x28mm

1782	Sheet of 3	11.10	5.55
a.	A2 10fr dark red	3.70	1.85
b.	A2 10fr dark blue green	3.70	1.85
c.	A2 10fr deep violet	3.70	1.85

Portrait of Claude Monet by Auguste Renoir A571

1991, Nov. 7 **Engr.** ***Perf. 12½x13***

1783 A571	5fr multicolored	1.80	90

Treaty of Peronne, 350th Anniv. A572

Portraits by Philippe de Champaigne (1602-1674): 6fr, Honore II (1604-1662), Monaco. 7fr, Louis XIII (1610-1643), France.

1991, Nov. 7

1784 A572	6fr multicolored	2.20	1.10
1785 A572	7fr multicolored	2.55	1.30

Princess Grace Theatre, 10th Anniv. A573

1991, Nov. 7 **Litho.**

1786 A573	8fr Princess Grace	3.00	1.50

Prince Rainier III Type of 1989

Photo. & Engr.

1991, Nov. 7 ***Perf. 13***

1797 A529	10fr lt bl grn & deep bl grn	3.70	1.85

This is an expanding set. Numbers will change if necessary.

16th Intl. Circus Festival Type of 1991

1992, Jan. 6 **Photo.** ***Perf. 12½x13***

1801 A561	2.50fr multicolored	90	45

Inscribed "30 janvier au 5 fevrier 1992".

SEMI-POSTAL STAMPS

No. 16 Surcharged in Red ✚ 5c

1914, Oct. **Unwmk.** ***Perf. 14x13½***

B1 A2	10c + 5c car	4.25	3.25

View of Monaco — SP2

1919, Sept. 20 **Typo.**

B2 SP2	2c + 3c lilac	10.00	10.00
B3 SP2	5c + 5c green	7.25	7.25
B4 SP2	15c + 10c rose	7.25	7.25
B5 SP2	25c + 15c blue	17.00	17.00
B6 SP2	50c + 50c brn, *buff*	70.00	70.00
B7 SP2	1fr + 1fr blk, *yel*	235.00	235.00
B8 SP2	5fr + 5fr dl red	750.00	750.00
	Nos. B2-B8 (7)	1,096.	1,096.

Nos. B4-B8 Surcharged

20 mars
1920
2c + 3c

1920, Mar. 20

B9 SP2	2c + 3c on #B4	24.00	24.00
a.	"c" of "3c" inverted	*2,000.*	*2,000.*
B10 SP2	2c + 3c on #B5	24.00	24.00
a.	"c" of "3c" inverted	*2,000.*	*2,000.*
B11 SP2	2c + 3c on #B6	24.00	24.00
a.	"c" of "3c" inverted	*2,000.*	*2,000.*
B12 SP2	5c + 5c on #B7	24.00	24.00
B13 SP2	5c + 5c on #B8	24.00	24.00

Overprinted

20 mars
1920

B14 SP2	15c + 10c rose	16.00	16.00
B15 SP2	25c + 15c blue	6.50	6.50
B16 SP2	50c + 50c brn, *buff*	27.50	27.50
B17 SP2	1fr + 1fr blk, *yel*	37.50	37.50
B18 SP2	5fr + 5fr red	*6,000.*	*6,000.*
	Nos. B9-B17 (9)	207.50	207.50

Marriage of Princess Charlotte to Prince Pierre, Comte de Polignac.

Palace Gardens SP3

"The Rock" of Monaco SP4

Bay of Monaco SP5

Prince Louis II — SP6

1937, Apr. **Engr.** ***Perf. 13***

B19 SP3	50c + 50c grn	1.90	1.90
B20 SP4	90c + 90c car	1.90	1.90
B21 SP5	1.50fr + 1.50fr bl	4.00	4.00
B22 SP6	2fr + 2fr vio	5.25	5.25
B23 SP6	5fr + 5fr brn red	52.50	52.50
	Nos. B19-B23 (5)	65.55	65.55

The surtax was used for welfare work.

Pierre and Marie Curie — SP7

Monaco Hospital, Date Palms SP8

1938, Nov. 15 ***Perf. 13***

B24 SP7	65c + 25c dp bl grn	4.25	4.25
B25 SP8	1.75fr + 50c dp ultra	5.00	5.00

B24 and B25 exist imperforate.

The surtax was for the International Union for the Control of Cancer.

Lucien — SP9

Honore II — SP10

Louis I SP11

Charlotte de Gramont SP12

Antoine I SP13

Marie de Lorraine SP14

Jacques I SP15

Louise-Hippolyte SP16

Honore III — SP17

"The Rock," 18th Century SP18

1939, June 26

B26 SP9	5c + 5c brn blk	60	60
B27 SP10	10c + 10c rose vio	60	60
B28 SP11	45c + 15c brt grn	1.10	1.10
B29 SP12	70c + 30c brt red vio	2.75	2.75
B30 SP13	90c + 35c vio	2.75	2.75
B31 SP14	1fr + 1fr ultra	11.00	11.00
B32 SP15	2fr + 2fr brn org	12.00	12.00
B33 SP16	2.25fr + 1.25fr Prus bl	20.00	20.00
B34 SP17	3fr + 3fr dp rose	27.50	27.50
B35 SP18	5fr + 5fr red	55.00	55.00
	Nos. B26-B35 (10)	133.30	133.30

Types of Regular Issue, 1939 Surcharged in Red

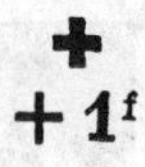

1940, Feb. 10 **Engr.** ***Perf. 13***

No.	Type	Description	Unused	Used
B36	A30	20c + 1fr vio	1.65	1.65
B37	A31	25c + 1fr dk grn	1.65	1.65
B38	A32	30c + 1fr brn red	1.65	1.65
B39	A31	40c + 1fr dk bl	1.65	1.65
B40	A33	45c + 1fr rose car	1.65	1.65
B41	A34	50c + 1fr brn	1.65	1.65
B42	A32	60c + 1fr dk grn	1.65	1.65
B43	A35	75c + 1fr brn blk	1.65	1.65
B44	A34	1fr + 1fr scar	1.90	1.90
B45	A31	2fr + 1fr ind	1.90	1.90
B46	A33	2.50fr + 1fr dk grn	5.50	5.50
B47	A35	3fr + 1fr dk bl	6.00	6.00
B48	A30	5fr + 1fr brn blk	7.00	7.00
B49	A33	10fr + 5fr lt bl	11.00	11.00
B50	A32	20fr + 5fr brn vio	12.00	12.00
		Nos. B36-B50 (15)	58.50	58.50

The surtax was used to purchase ambulances for the French government.

Catalogue values for unused stamps in this section, from this point to the end of the section, are for Never Hinged items.

Symbol of Charity and View of Monaco SP19

Symbol of Charity and View of Monaco — SP20

1941, May 15

No.	Type	Description	Unused	Used
B51	SP19	25c + 25c brt red vio	1.65	1.65
B52	SP20	50c + 25c dk brn	1.65	1.65
B53	SP20	75c + 50c rose vio	2.00	2.00
B54	SP19	1fr + 1fr dk bl	2.00	2.00
B55	SP20	1.50fr + 1.50fr rose red	3.00	3.00
B56	SP19	2fr + 2fr Prus grn	3.00	3.00
B57	SP20	2.50fr + 2fr brt ultra	3.50	3.50
B58	SP19	3fr + 3fr dl red brn	3.50	3.50
B59	SP20	5fr + 5fr dk bl grn	6.75	6.75
B60	SP19	10fr + 8fr brn blk	12.50	12.50
		Nos. B51-B60 (10)	39.55	39.55

The surtax was for various charities.

Rainier Grimaldi SP21

Charles II SP22

Jeanne Grimaldi SP23

Charles-August Goyon de Matignon SP24

Jacques I SP25

Louise-Hippolyte SP26

Charlotte Grimaldi SP27

Marie-Charles Grimaldi SP28

Honoré III — SP29

Honoré IV — SP30

Honoré V — SP31

Florestan I — SP32

Charles III — SP33

Albert I — SP34

Marie-Victoire SP35

1942, Dec. 10

No.	Type	Description	Unused	Used
B61	SP21	2c + 3c ultra	18	18
B62	SP22	5c + 5c org ver	18	18
B63	SP23	10c + 5c blk	18	18
B64	SP24	20c + 10c brt grn	18	18
B65	SP25	30c + 30c brn vio	18	18
B66	SP26	40c + 40c rose red	18	18
B67	SP27	50c + 50c vio	18	18
B68	SP28	75c + 75c brt red vio	18	18
B69	SP29	1fr + 1fr dk grn	18	18
B70	SP30	1.50fr + 1fr car brn	18	18
B71	SP31	2.50fr + 2.50fr pur	2.25	2.25
B72	SP32	3fr + 3fr turq bl	2.50	2.50
B73	SP33	5fr + 5fr sep	2.50	2.50
B74	SP34	10fr + 5fr rose lil	2.50	2.50
B75	SP35	20fr + 5fr ultra	2.50	2.50
		Nos. B61-B75 (15)	14.05	14.05

Saint Devote SP36

Procession SP37

Procession SP38

Church of St. Devote SP39

Burning of Symbolic Boat SP40

Blessing of the Sea — SP41

Church of St. Devote SP42

Trial of St. Barbara — SP43

Arrival of St. Devote at Monaco — SP44

1944, Jan. 27 **Unwmk.** ***Perf. 13***

No.	Type	Description	Unused	Used
B76	SP36	50c + 50c sep	22	22
B77	SP37	70c + 80c dp ultra	22	22
B78	SP38	80c + 70c grn	18	18
B79	SP39	1fr + 1fr rose vio	18	18
B80	SP40	1.50fr + 1.50fr red	35	35
B81	SP41	2fr + 2fr brn vio	40	40
B82	SP42	5fr + 2fr vio	45	45
B83	SP43	10fr + 40fr ryl bl	45	45
B84	SP44	20fr + 60fr chlky bl	4.25	4.25
		Nos. B76-B84 (9)	6.70	6.70

Issued in honor of St. Devote.

Type SP43 is inscribed "Jugement de Sainte Devote," but actually shows the trial of St. Barbara in 235 A.D.

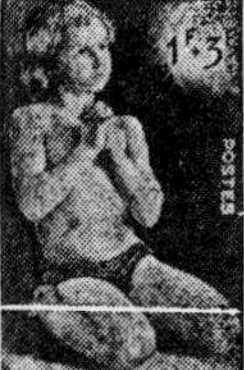

Needy Child — SP45

Nurse and Child — SP46

1946, Feb. 18 **Engr.**

No.	Type	Description	Unused	Used
B85	SP45	1fr + 3fr dp bl grn	18	18
B86	SP45	2fr + 4fr rose pink	18	18
B87	SP45	4fr + 6fr dk bl	18	18
B88	SP45	5fr + 40fr dk vio	40	40
B89	SP45	10fr + 60fr brn red	48	48
B90	SP45	15fr + 100fr indigo	65	65
		Nos. B85-B90 (6)	2.07	2.07

The surtax was for child welfare.

1946, Feb. 18

No.	Type	Description	Unused	Used
B91	SP46	2fr + 8fr brt bl	15	15

The surtax was used for prevention of tuberculosis.

19th Century Steamer and Map SP47

1946

No.	Type	Description	Unused	Used
B92	SP47	3fr + 2fr deep blue	16	16

Stamp Day, June 23, 1946.

Harbor of Monte Carlo SP48

1946, Dec. 13

No.	Type	Description	Unused	Used
B93	SP48	2fr + 3fr dk bluish grn	38	38

Issued in tribute to the memory of Franklin D. Roosevelt. The surtax was for a fund to erect a monument in his honor.

Souvenir Sheet

SP49

Unwmk.

1947, May 15 **Engr.** ***Imperf.***

No.	Type	Description	Unused	Used
B94	SP49	200fr + 300fr dk red & choc	8.75	8.75

25th anniv. of the reign of Prince Louis II.

Prince Charles III — SP50

1948, Mar. 6 ***Perf. 14x13***

No.	Type	Description	Unused	Used
B95	SP50	6fr + 4fr dk bl grn, *lt bl*	24	24

Issued for Stamp Day, Mar. 6.

Princess Charlotte SP51

Prince Rainier III SP52

Perf. 13½x13, Imperf.

1949, Dec. 27 **Engr.**

Cross Typo. in Red

B96	SP51 10fr + 5fr red brn	7.25	7.25
B97	SP52 15fr + 5fr brt red	7.25	7.25
B98	SP52 25fr + 5fr dk vio bl	7.25	7.25
B99	SP51 40fr + 5fr dl grn	7.25	7.25
a.	Block of 4, #B96-B99	30.00	30.00

Printed in sheets measuring 151x173mm, perf. and imperf., containing 4 of No. B99a.

The surtax was for the Red Cross.

For surcharges see Nos. 288-291.

Hercules Strangling the Lion of Nemea — SP53

Twelve Labors of Hercules: No. B101, Capturing the Erymanthean boar. No. B102, Killing the Hydra of Lerna. No. B103, Killing Stymphalian birds. No. B104, Hercules and the Ceryneian Hind. No. B105, The Augean Stables. No. B106, Hercules and the Cretan Bull. No. B107, Wild horses of Diomedes. No. B108, Hercules and the Oxen of Geryon. No. B109, Hercules and the Belt of Hippolytus. No. B110, Winning the golden apple of Hesperides. No. B111, Battling Cerberus.

1981-82 **Engr.** ***Perf. 13***

B100	SP53 2.50fr + 50c multi	1.25	1.25
B101	SP53 2.50fr + 50c multi	1.10	1.10
B102	SP53 3.50fr + 50c multi	1.40	1.40
B103	SP53 3.50fr + 50c multi	1.25	1.25

Issue dates: Nos. B100, B102 Nov. 5. Nos. B101, B103 Nov. 8, 1982.

1983, Nov. 9

B104	SP53 2.50fr + 50c multi	1.10	1.10
B105	SP53 3.50fr + 50c multi	1.25	1.25

1984, Nov. 8

B106	SP53 3fr + 50c multi	1.25	1.25
B107	SP53 4fr + 50c multi	1.65	1.65

1985, Nov. 7

B108	SP53 3fr + 70c dp red lil, red & gray ol	1.25	48
B109	SP53 4fr + 80c dk bl, red & brn	1.65	62

1986, Oct. 28

B110	SP53 3fr + 70c red, dp yel grn & yel	1.25	42
B111	SP53 4fr + 80c dp bis, red & int bl	1.50	55
	Nos. B100-B111 (12)	15.90	12.32

Surtax on #B100-B111 for the Red Cross.

AIR POST STAMPS

No. 91 Surcharged in Black

1f50

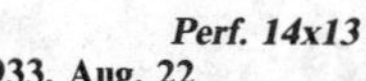

Perf. 14x13½

1933, Aug. 22 **Unwmk.**

C1	A15 1.50fr on 5fr	20.00	15.00
a.	Imperf., pair	275.00	

Catalogue values for unused stamps in this section, from this point to the end of the section, are for Never Hinged items.

Plane over Monaco AP1

Plane Propeller and Buildings AP2

Pegasus — AP3

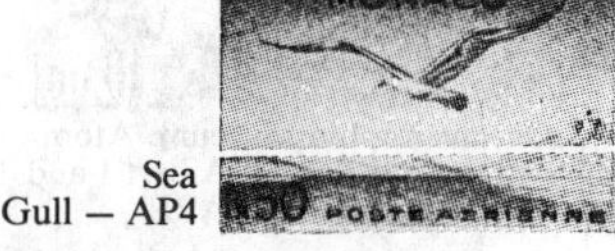
Sea Gull — AP4

Plane, Globe and Arms of Monaco AP5

1942, Apr. 15 **Engr.** ***Perf. 13***

C2	AP1 5fr bl grn	22	22
C3	AP1 10fr ultra	22	22
C4	AP2 15fr sepia	35	35
C5	AP3 20fr hn brn	55	55
C6	AP4 50fr red vio	2.50	1.40
C7	AP5 100fr red & vio brn	2.25	1.40
	Nos. C2-C7 (6)	6.09	4.14

For surcharges see Nos. CB1-CB5.

Nos. 196-197 Overprinted in Blue

1946, May 20

C8	A41 50fr dp Prus grn	1.65	1.65
C9	A41 100fr red	2.50	2.55
a.	Inverted overprint	17,000.	
b.	Double overprint	13,000.	

Douglas DC-3 and Arms — AP6

1946, May 20

C10	AP6 40fr red	80	50
C11	AP6 50fr red brn	90	70
C12	AP6 100fr dp bl grn	1.40	1.25
C13	AP6 200fr violet	2.25	2.00

Exist imperforate. See Nos. C27-C29.

Harbor of Monte Carlo AP7

Map of Monaco — AP8

1946, Dec. 13

C14	AP7 5fr car rose	38	38
C15	AP8 10fr vio blk	42	42

Issued in tribute to the memory of Franklin D. Roosevelt.

Franklin D. Roosevelt Examining his Stamp Collection AP9

Main Post Office, New York City — AP10

Oceanographic Museum, Monaco — AP11

Harbor of Monte Carlo — AP12

Statue of Liberty and New York City Skyline — AP13

1947, May 15 **Unwmk.**

C16	AP9 50c violet	32	32
C17	AP10 1.50fr rose vio	42	42
C18	AP11 3fr hn brn	50	50
C19	AP12 10fr dp bl	1.75	1.75
C20	AP13 15fr rose car	2.25	2.25
a.	Strip of 3, #C20, 203, C19	5.50	5.50
	Nos. C16-C20 (5)	5.24	5.24

Issued to commemorate the principality's participation in the Centenary International Philatelic Exhibition, New York, May, 1947.

Crowd Acclaiming Constitution of 1911 AP14

Anthropological Museum — AP15

Designs: 25fr, Institute of Human Paleontology, Paris. 50fr, Albert I. 100fr, Oceanographic Institute, Paris. 200fr, Albert I medal.

1949, Mar. 5 **Engr.** ***Perf. 13***

C21	AP14 20fr brn red	70	70
C22	AP14 25fr indigo	80	80
C23	AP15 40fr bl grn	1.25	1.25
C24	AP15 50fr blk, brn & grn	1.50	1.50
C25	AP15 100fr cerise	5.50	5.50
C26	AP14 200fr dp org	8.25	8.25
	Nos. C21-C26 (6)	18.00	18.00

Plane-Arms Type of 1946

1949, Mar. 10

C27	AP6 300fr dp ultra & ind	47.50	35.50
C28	AP6 500fr grnsh blk & bl grn	32.50	32.50
C29	AP6 1000fr blk & red vio	52.50	42.50

Palace, Globe and Pigeon AP16

1949-50

C30	AP16 25fr deep blue	55	55
C31	AP16 40fr red brn & sep ('50)	85	85
C32	AP16 50fr dk grn & ultra ('50)	1.25	1.25
C33	AP16 100fr dk car & dk grn ('50)	2.75	2.75

75th anniv. of the UPU.

Nos. C30 to C33 exist imperforate, also No. C30 in deep plum and violet, imperforate.

Rainier Type of Regular Issue

1950, Apr. 11 **Unwmk.**

C34	A57 50fr blk & red brn	2.75	2.75
C35	A57 100fr red brn, sep & ind	4.50	4.50

Enthronement of Prince Rainier III.

Runner — AP18

Designs: 50fr, Fencing. 100fr, Target Shooting. 200fr, Olympic Torch.

1953, Feb. 23 ***Perf. 11***

C36	AP18 40fr black	8.25	7.00
C37	AP18 50fr brt pur	8.25	7.00
C38	AP18 100fr dk sl grn	11.00	10.00
C39	AP18 200fr dp car	12.00	11.00

Issued to publicize Monaco's participation in the Helsinki Olympic Games.

Dr. Albert Schweitzer and Ogowe River Scene, Gabon — AP19

1955, Jan. 14 ***Perf. 13***

C40 AP19 200fr sl blk, dk bl grn & bl 19.00 19.00

Issued to honor Dr. Albert Schweitzer, medical missionary.

Mediterranean Sea Swallows — AP20

Birds: 200fr, Sea gulls. 500fr, Albatross. 1000fr, Great cormorants.

1955-57 ***Perf. 11***

C41 AP20 100fr dp bl & ind 21.00 8.00
 a. Perf. 13 ('57) 19.00 9.25
C42 AP20 200fr bl & blk 21.00 8.00
 a. Perf. 13 ('57) 275.00 27.50
C43 AP20 500fr gray & dk grn 30.00 14.00

Perf. 13

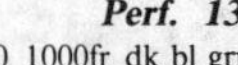

C44 AP20 1000fr dk bl grn & blk brn ('57) 80.00 32.50
 a. Perf. 11 200.00 87.50

Issue dates: Perf. 11, Jan. 14, 1955. Perf. 13, 1957.

"From the Earth to the Moon" and Jules Verne — AP21

1955, June 7 **Unwmk.**

C45 AP21 200fr dp bl & sl 20.00 20.00

50th anniv. of the death of Jules Verne.

Princess Grace and Prince Rainier III — AP22

1956, Apr. 19 **Engr.**

Portraits in Brown

C46 AP22 100fr purple 55 55
C47 AP22 200fr carmine 90 90
C48 AP22 500fr gray vio 2.25 2.25

Wedding of Prince Rainier III to Grace Kelly, Apr. 19, 1956.

Nos. J45 and J54 Surcharged and Overprinted "Poste Aerienne" and bars

1956, Apr. ***Perf. 11***

C49 D6 100fr on 20fr 9.25 9.25
 a. Double surcharge *425.00 425.00*
C50 D7 100fr on 20fr 9.25 9.25
 a. Double surcharge *425.00 425.00*

See footnote after No. 390.

Basilica of Lourdes — AP23

Design: 200fr, Pope Pius X and underground basilica.

1958, May 15 **Unwmk.** ***Perf. 13***

C51 AP23 100fr dk bl, grn & gray 1.50 1.10
C52 AP23 200fr red brn & sep 2.00 1.90

Issued to commemorate the centenary of the apparition of the Virgin Mary at Lourdes.

Prince Rainier III and Princess Grace — AP24

1959, May 16

C53 AP24 300fr dk pur 5.25 4.25
C54 AP24 500fr blue 9.50 6.25

St. Devote AP25

1960, June 1 **Engr.** ***Perf. 13***

C55 AP25 2fr grn, bl & vio 1.40 85
C56 AP24 3fr dk pur 32.50 12.00
C57 AP24 5fr blue 32.50 13.00
C58 AP25 10fr grn & brn 6.50 3.00

1961, June 3

C59 AP25 3fr ultra, grn & gray ol 1.75 1.00
C60 AP25 5fr rose car 3.50 50

Europa Issue, 1962

Mercury over Map of Europe AP26

1962, June 6 **Unwmk.** ***Perf. 13***

C61 AP26 2fr dk grn, sl grn & brn 1.25 1.00

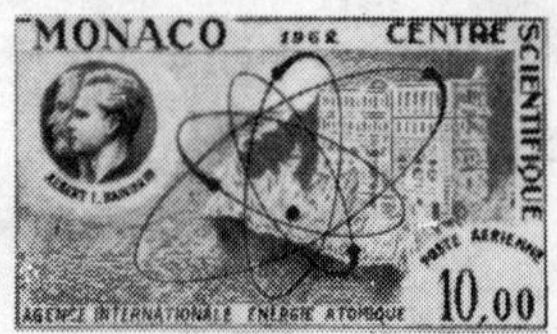

Oceanographic Museum, Atom Symbol and Princes Albert I and Rainier III — AP27

1962, June 6

C62 AP27 10fr vio, bl & bis 8.50 7.75

Issued to commemorate the establishment of a scientific research center by agreement with the International Atomic Energy Commission.

Roland Garros AP28

1963, Dec. 12 **Engr.** ***Perf. 13***

C63 AP28 2fr dk bl & dk brn 1.25 95

Issued to commemorate the 50th anniversary of the first airplane crossing of the Mediterranean by Roland Garros (1888-1918).

Type of Regular Issue, 1964

Design: 5fr, Convair B-58 Hustler (New York-Paris in 3 hours, 19 minutes, 41 seconds, Maj. William R. Payne, USAF, 1961).

1964, May 22 **Unwmk.** ***Perf. 13***

C64 A151 5fr brn, blk & bl 3.50 3.00

Issued to commemorate the 50th anniversary of the first airplane rally of Monte Carlo.

Bobsledding — AP29

1964, Dec. 3 **Engr.** ***Perf. 13***

C65 AP29 5fr multi 2.75 2.75

Issued to commemorate the 9th Winter Olympic Games, Innsbruck, Austria, Jan. 29-Feb. 9, 1964.

ITU Type of Regular Issue

Design: 10fr, ITU Emblem and Monte Carlo television station on Mount Agel (vert.).

1965, May 17 **Engr.** ***Perf. 13***

C66 A161 10fr bis brn, sl grn & bl 4.25 4.25

Princess Grace with Albert Alexander Louis, Caroline and Stephanie — AP30

1966, Feb. 1 **Engr.** ***Perf. 13***

C67 AP30 3fr pur, red brn & Prus bl 2.25 1.75

Issued to commemorate the birth of Princess Stephanie, Feb. 1, 1965.

Opera House Interior AP31

1966, June 1 **Engr.** ***Perf. 13***

C68 AP31 5fr Prus bl, bis & dk car rose 2.50 2.50

Centenary of founding of Monte Carlo.

Prince Rainier III and Princess Grace — AP32

1966-71 **Engr.** ***Perf. 13***

C69 AP32 2fr pink & sl 1.00 40
C70 AP32 3fr emer & sl 2.00 65
C71 AP32 5fr lt bl & sl 2.50 1.10
C72 AP32 10fr lem & sl ('67) 4.00 2.75

C72A AP32 20fr org & brn ('71) 30.00 15.00
Nos. C69-C72A (5) 39.50 19.90

Issue dates: 10fr, Dec. 7, 1967; 20fr, Sept. 6, 1971. Others, Dec. 12, 1966.

Panhard-Phenix, 1895 — AP33

1967, Apr. 28 **Engr.** ***Perf. 13***
C73 AP33 3fr Prus bl & blk 2.25 2.00

25th Grand Prix of Monaco.

Olympic Games Type of Regular Issue

1968, Apr. 29 **Engr.** ***Perf. 13***
C74 A183 3fr Field hockey 2.00 1.75

Berlioz Monument, Monte Carlo — AP34

1969, Apr. 26 **Engr.** ***Perf. 13***
C75 AP34 2fr grn, blk & ultra 1.25 1.10

Issued to commemorate the centenary of the death of Hector Berlioz (1803-1869), French composer.

Napoleon, by Paul Delaroche AP35

1969, Apr. 26 **Photo.** ***Perf. 12x13***
C76 AP35 3fr multi 1.50 1.25

Bicentenary of birth of Napoleon I.

Horses, Prehistoric Drawing from Lascaux Cave — AP36

1970, Dec. 15 **Engr.** ***Perf. 13***
C77 AP36 3fr multi 2.25 2.00

Nativity Type of Regular Issue

Design: 3fr, Nativity, Flemish School, 15th century (vert.).

1973, Nov. 12 **Engr.** ***Perf. 12x13***
C78 A243 3fr Prus grn 2.75 2.00

Prince Rainier III — AP37

1974, Dec. 23 **Engr.** ***Perf. 12½x13***
C81 AP37 10fr dk pur 3.00 2.25
C82 AP37 15fr hn brn 4.75 3.50
C83 AP37 20fr ultra 6.75 4.50

Prince Rainier and Hereditary Prince Albert — AP38

1982-84 **Engr.** ***Perf. 13x13½***
C84 AP38 5fr dp vio 1.40 75
C85 AP38 10fr red 2.75 1.50
C86 AP38 15fr dk bl grn 4.00 2.25
C87 AP38 20fr brt bl 5.00 3.00
C88 AP38 30fr brn ('84) 7.75 4.25
Nos. C84-C88 (5) 20.90 11.75

AIR POST SEMI-POSTAL STAMPS

Catalogue values for unused stamps in this section are for Never Hinged items.

Types of 1942 Air Post Stamps Surcharged with New Values and Bars

Unwmk.

1945, Mar. 27 **Engr.** ***Perf. 13***
CB1 AP1 1fr + 4fr on 10fr rose red 25 25
CB2 AP2 1fr + 4fr on 15fr red brown 25 25
CB3 AP3 1fr + 4fr on 20fr sep 25 25
CB4 AP4 1fr + 4fr on 50fr ultra 25 25
CB5 AP5 1fr + 4fr on 100fr brt red violet 25 25
Nos. CB1-CB5 (5) 1.25 1.25

Surtax for the benefit of prisoners of war.

Franklin D. Roosevelt — SPAP1

1946, Dec. 13
CB6 SPAP1 15fr + 10fr red 80 70

Issued in tribute to the memory of Franklin D. Roosevelt. The surtax was for a fund to erect a monument in his honor.

Rowing SPAP2 Sailboat Race SPAP3

1948, July
CB7 SPAP2 5fr +5fr shown 8.00 8.00
CB8 SPAP2 6fr +9fr Skiing 11.50 11.50
CB9 SPAP2 10fr +15fr Tennis 16.00 16.00
CB10 SPAP3 15fr +25fr shown 24.00 24.00

Issued to publicize Monaco's participation in the 1948 Olympic Games held at Wembley, England, during July and August.

Salmacis Nymph SPAP4

Designs similar to regular issue.

1948, July
CB11 A50 5fr + 5fr blk bl 8.00 8.00
CB12 A51 6fr + 9fr dk grn 9.50 9.50
CB13 A52 10fr + 15fr crim 10.00 10.00
CB14 SPAP4 15fr + 25fr red brn 11.00 11.00

François J. Bosio (1769-1845), sculptor.

POSTAGE DUE STAMPS

D1

Prince Albert I — D2

Perf. 14x13½

1905-43 **Unwmk.** **Typo.**
J1 D1 1c olive green 52 52
J2 D1 5c green 65 52
J3 D1 10c rose 52 52
J4 D1 10c brn ('09) 250.00 72.50
J5 D1 15c vio brn, *straw* 1.90 1.10
J6 D1 20c bis brn, *buff* ('26) 18 18
J7 D1 30c blue 52 52
J8 D1 40c red vio ('26) 18 18
J9 D1 50c brn, *org* 4.00 2.25
J10 D1 50c bl grn ('27) 18 18
J11 D1 60c gray blk ('26) 55 55
J12 D1 60c brt vio ('34) 8.50 8.50
J13 D1 1fr red brn, *straw* ('26) 15 15
J14 D1 2fr red org ('27) 38 38
J15 D1 3fr mag ('27) 38 38
J15A D1 5fr ultra ('43) 52 52
Nos. J1-J15A (16) 269.13 88.95

For surcharge see No. J27.

1910
J16 D2 1c olive grn 22 22
J17 D2 10c light vio 32 32
J18 D2 30c bister 140.00 110.00

In January, 1917, regular postage stamps overprinted "T" in a triangle were used as postage due stamps.

Nos. J17 and J18 Surcharged **20c.**

1918
J19 D2 20c on 10c lt vio 2.00 2.00
a. Double surcharge 725.00
J20 D2 40c on 30c bister 2.00 2.00

D3

1925-32
J21 D3 1c gray green 20 20
J22 D3 10c violet 20 20
J23 D3 30c bister 30 30
J24 D3 60c red 40 40
J25 D3 1fr lt bl ('32) 47.50 32.50
J26 D3 2fr dl red ('32) 72.50 47.50
Nos. J21-J26 (6) 121.10 81.10

Nos. J25 and J26 have the numerals of value double-lined.

"Recouvrements" stamps were used to recover charges due on undelivered or refused mail which was returned to the sender.

No. J9 Surcharged **1 franc à percevoir**

1925
J27 D1 1fr on 50c brn, *org* 50 40
a. Double surcharge 650.00

Catalogue values for unused stamps in this section, from this point to the end of the section, are for Never Hinged items.

D4

D5

1946-57 **Engr.** ***Perf. 14x13, 13***
J28 D4 10c sepia 18 18
J29 D4 30c dk vio 18 18
J30 D4 50c dp bl 18 18
J31 D4 1fr dk grn 18 18
J32 D4 2fr yel brn 18 18
J33 D4 3fr brt red vio 25 25
J34 D4 4fr carmine 38 38
J35 D5 5fr chocolate 30 30
J36 D5 10fr dp ultra 55 55
J37 D5 20fr grnsh bl 60 60
J38 D5 50fr red vio & red ('50) 50.00 50.00
J38A D5 100fr dk grn & red ('57) 8.75 8.75
Nos. J28-J38A (12) 61.73 61.73

Sailing Vessel — D6

Early Postal Transport: 1fr, Carrier pigeons. 3fr, Old railroad engine. 4fr, Old monoplane. 5fr, Steam automobile. 10fr, daVinci's flying machine. 20fr, Balloon. 50fr, Post rider. 100fr, Old mail coach.

1953-54 ***Perf. 11***

No.	Design	Description	Unused	Used
J39	D6	1fr dk grn & brt red ('54)	15	15
J40	D6	2fr dp ultra & bl grn	15	15
J41	D6	3fr Prus grn & brn lake	16	16
J42	D6	4fr dk brn & Prus grn	26	26
J43	D6	5fr ultra & pur	65	65
J44	D6	10fr dp ultra & dk bl	6.75	6.75
J45	D6	20fr ind & pur	2.25	2.25
J46	D6	50fr red & dk brn	6.00	6.00
J47	D6	100fr vio brn & dp grn	12.00	12.00

The two types of each value in Nos. J39-J56 (early and modern transportation) were printed tete beche, se-tenant at the base.

S. S. United States D7

Modern Postal Transport: 1fr, Sikorsky S-51 helicopter. 3fr, Modern locomotive. 4fr, Comet airliner. 5fr, Sabre sports car. 10fr, Rocket. 20fr, Graf Zeppelin. 50fr, Motorcyclist. 100fr, Railroad mail car.

No.	Design	Description	Unused	Used
J48	D7	1fr brt red & dk grn ('54)	15	15
J49	D7	2fr bl grn & dp ultra	15	15
J50	D7	3fr brn lake & Prus grn	16	16
J51	D7	4fr Prus grn & dk brn	26	26
J52	D7	5fr pur & ultra	65	65
J53	D7	10fr dk bl & dp ultra	6.75	6.75
J54	D7	20fr pur & ind	2.25	2.25
J55	D7	50fr dk brn & red	6.00	6.00
J56	D7	100fr dp grn & vio brn	12.00	12.00
		Nos. J39-J56 (18)	56.74	56.74

See note following No. J47.
For overprints see Nos. 371-390.

Felucca, 18th Century D8

Designs: 2c, Paddle steamer La Palmaria, 19th century. 5c, Arrival of first train. 10c, Armed messenger, 15th-16th century. 20c, Monaco-Nice courier, 18th century. 30c, "Charles III," 1866. 50c, Courier on horseback, 17th century. 1fr, Diligence, 19th century.

1960-69 **Engr.** ***Perf. 13***

No.	Design	Description	Unused	Used
J57	D8	1c bl grn, bis brn & bl	40	40
J58	D8	2c sl grn, sep & ultra	15	15
J59	D8	5c grnsh bl, gray & red brn	15	15
J60	D8	10c vio bl, blk & grn	25	25
J61	D8	20c bl, brn & grn	90	90
J62	D8	30c brn, brt grn & brt bl ('69)	50	50
J63	D8	50c dk bl, brn & sl grn	90	90
J64	D8	1fr sl grn, bl & brn	1.25	1.25
		Nos. J57-J64 (8)	4.50	4.50

Knight in Armor D9

1980-83 **Engr.** ***Perf. 13***

No.	Design	Description	Unused	Used
J65	D9	5c red & gray	15	15
J66	D9	10c sal & red	15	15
J67	D9	15c vio & red	15	15
J68	D9	20c lt grn & red	15	15
J69	D9	30c bl & red	15	15
J70	D9	40c lt brn & red	16	16
J71	D9	50c lil & red	16	16
J72	D9	1fr blk & bl	38	38
J73	D9	2fr dk brn & org ('82)	70	70
J74	D9	3fr sl bl & rose car ('83)	1.10	1.10
J75	D9	4fr red & dk grn ('82)	1.25	1.25
J76	D9	5fr mag & brn ('83)	2.00	2.00
		Nos. J65-J76 (12)	6.50	6.50

Nos. J65-J76 printed in horizontal rows with princely coat of arms between stamps. Sold in strips of 3 only.
Issue dates: Nos. J65-J72, Feb. 8; Nos. J73, J75, Feb. 15; Nos. J74, J76, Jan. 3.

Natl. Coat of Arms — D10

1985-86 **Photo.** ***Perf. 13x12½***

No.	Design	Description	Unused	Used
J77	D10	5c multi	15	15
J78	D10	10c multi	15	15
J79	D10	15c multi	15	15
J80	D10	20c multi	15	15
J81	D10	30c multi	15	15
J82	D10	40c multi	15	15
J83	D10	50c multi ('86)	15	15
J84	D10	1fr multi ('86)	30	15
J85	D10	2fr multi ('86)	60	30
J86	D10	3fr multi	70	35
J87	D10	4fr multi ('86)	1.25	60
J88	D10	5fr multi	1.25	60
		Set value	4.40	2.30

See Nos. 1608-1609.

MONGOLIA

Mongolian People's Republic (Outer Mongolia)

LOCATION — Central Asia, bounded on the north by Siberia, on the west by Sinkiang, on the south and east by China proper and Manchuria
GOVT. — Republic
AREA — 604,250 sq. mi.
POP. — 1,820,000 (est. 1984)
CAPITAL — Ulan Bator

Outer Mongolia, which had long been under Russian influence although nominally a dependency of China, voted at a plebescite on October 20, 1945, to sever all ties with China and become an independent nation. See Tannu Tuva.

100 Cents = 1 Dollar
100 Mung = 1 Tugrik (1926)

Catalogue values for unused stamps in this country are for Never Hinged items, beginning with Scott 149 in the regular postage section, Scott B1 in the semi-postal section, Scott C1 in the airpost section, and Scott CB1 in the airpost semi-postal section.

Watermark

Wmk. 170- Greek Border and Rosettes

Scepter of Indra — A1

A2

1924 **Litho.** **Unwmk.** ***Perf. 10, 13½***
Surface Tinted Paper

No.	Design	Description	Unused	Used
1	A1	1c multi, *bis*	2.75	2.50
2	A1	2c multi, *brnsh*	2.50	2.50
a.		Perf. 13½	15.00	13.00
3	A1	5c multi	19.00	13.00
a.		Perf. 10	19.00	17.00
4	A1	10c multi, *gray bl*	4.50	3.75
a.		Perf. 10	5.50	4.00
5	A1	20c multi, *gray*	6.50	5.50
6	A1	50c multi, *sal*	19.00	12.00
7	A1	$1 multi, *yel*	25.00	25.00
b.		Perf. 10	30.00	30.00
		Nos. 1-7 (7)	79.25	64.25

These stamps vary in size from 19x25mm (1c) to 30x39mm ($1). They also differ in details of the design.
Errors of perforating and printing exist.
Some quantities of Nos. 1-2, 4-7 were defaced with horizontal perforation across the center.
The 5c exists perf 11½.

Revenue Stamps Handstamp Overprinted "POSTAGE" in Violet

Sizes: 1c to 20c: 22x36mm
50c, $1: 26x43½mm
$5: 30x45½mm

1926 ***Perf. 11***

No.	Design	Description	Unused	Used
16	A2	1c blue	5.00	5.00
17	A2	2c orange	5.00	5.00
18	A2	5c plum	5.00	5.00
19	A2	10c green	5.00	5.00
20	A2	20c yel brn	5.00	5.00
21	A2	50c brn & ol grn	*85.00*	*85.00*
22	A2	$1 brn & sal	*275.00*	*275.00*
23	A2	$5 red, yel & gray	*175.00*	*175.00*

Black Overprint

No.	Design	Description	Unused	Used
16a	A2	1c blue	8.75	8.75
17a	A2	2c orange	8.75	8.75
18a	A2	5c plum	8.75	8.75
19a	A2	10c green	8.75	8.75
20a	A2	20c yel brn	8.75	8.75
21a	A2	50c brn & ol grn	*125.00*	*125.00*
22a	A2	$1 brn & sal	*300.00*	*300.00*
23a	A2	$5 red, yel & gray		
		Nos. 16a-22a (7)	*468.75*	*468.75*

Red Overprint

No.	Design	Description	Unused	Used
16b	A2	1c blue		
17b	A2	2c orange		
18b	A2	5c plum		
19b	A2	10c green		
20b	A2	20c yel brn		

The preceding handstamped overprints may be found inverted, double, etc. Counterfeits abound.
For overprints and surcharges see #48-61.

Yin Yang and other Symbols
A3 A4

TYPE I - The pearl above the crescent is solid. The devices in the middle of the stamp are not outlined.
TYPE II - The pearl is open. The devices and panels are all outlined in black.

1926-29 ***Perf. 11***

Type I

Size: 22x28mm

No.	Design	Description	Unused	Used
32	A3	5m lil & blk	2.50	2.50
33	A3	20m bl & blk	2.00	2.00

Type II

Size: 22x29mm

No.	Design	Description	Unused	Used
34	A3	1m yel & blk	60	60
35	A3	2m brn org & blk	75	75
36	A3	5m lil & blk	1.25	1.25
37	A3	10m lt bl & blk	75	60
a.		Imperf.		
38	A3	20m dp bl & blk ('29)	5.50	4.75
a.		Imperf.		
39	A3	25m yel grn & blk	2.50	2.50
a.		Imperf.		

Size: 26x34mm

No.	Design	Description	Unused	Used
40	A3	40m lem & blk	2.50	2.50
41	A3	50m buff & blk	3.00	2.75

Size: 28x37mm

No.	Design	Description	Unused	Used
42	A4	1t brn, grn & blk	11.00	11.00
43	A4	3t red, yel & blk	25.00	25.00
44	A4	5t brn vio, rose & blk	50.00	45.00
		Nos. 32-44 (13)	107.35	101.20

In 1929 a change was made in the perforating machine. Every fourth pin was removed, which left the perforation holes in groups of three with blank spaces between the groups. Nos. 38 and 44A have only this interrupted perforation. Nos. 37 and 39 are found with both perforations.
For overprints and surcharges see #45-47.

Yin Yang and other Symbols — A5

1929

No.	Design	Description	Unused	Used
44A	A5	5m lil & blk	6.00	6.00

See note after No. 44.

Nos. 34, 35, 40 Handstamped With New Values in Black

1930

No.	Design	Description	Unused	Used
45	A3	10m on 1m yel & blk	12.50	10.00
46	A3	20m on 2m brn org & blk	12.50	10.00
47	A3	25m on 40m lem & blk	17.50	14.00

Mongolia stamps through 1932 can be mounted in Scott's Soviet Republics Part I Album.

Symbols of Government
A6 A7

Violet Overprint, Handstamped

1931

48	A6	1c blue	5.50	5.50
a.		Blue overprint	8.00	5.50
49	A6	2c orange	8.00	5.50
50	A6	5c brn vio	8.00	6.50
a.		Blue overprint	8.50	6.00
51	A6	10c green	8.50	6.00
a.		Blue overprint	11.00	9.50
52	A6	20c bis brn	11.00	6.00
53	A6	50c brn & ol yel	65.00	50.00
54	A6	$1 brn & sal	85.00	67.50
		Nos. 48-54 (7)	191.00	147.00

Revenue Stamps Surcharged in Black, Red or Blue

1931

59	A7	5m on 5c brn vio (Bk)	12.50	6.00
a.		Inverted surcharge		17.50
b.		Imperf., pair	22.00	22.00
60	A7	10m on 10c grn (R)	25.00	12.50
a.		Inverted surcharge	15.00	12.50
b.		Imperf., pair	35.00	35.00
61	A7	20m on 20c bis brn (Bl)	32.50	19.00
a.		Inverted surcharge		18.00
b.		Imperf., pair	55.00	55.00

On Nos. 59-61, "Postage" is always diagonal, and may read up or down.

Weaver at Loom — A8

Telegrapher
A9

Sukhe Bator
A10

Lake and Mountains — A11

Designs: 5m, Mongol at lathe. 10m, Government building, Ulan Bator. 15m, Young Mongolian revolutionary. 20m, Studying Latin alphabet. 25m, Mongolian soldier. 50m, Monument to Sukhe Bator. 3t, Sheep shearing. 5t, Camel caravan. 10t, Chasing wild horses.

Perf. 12½x12

1932 **Photo.** **Wmk. 170**

62	A8	1m brown	40	35
63	A9	2m red vio	40	35
64	A8	5m indigo	35	28
65	A8	10m dl grn	35	28
66	A9	15m dp brn	35	28
67	A9	20m rose red	35	28
68	A9	25m dl vio	35	28
69	A10	40m gray blk	38	35
70	A10	50m dl bl	38	38

Perf. 11x12

71	A11	1t dl grn	40	40
72	A11	3t dl vio	1.25	1.25
73	A11	5t brown	3.50	3.50
74	A11	10t ultra	7.00	7.00
		Nos. 62-74 (13)	15.46	14.98

Marshal Kharloin Choibalsan — A21

1945 **Unwmk.** ***Perf. 12½***

83	A21	1t blk brn	2.75	2.75

Choibalsan
A22

Victory Medal
A24

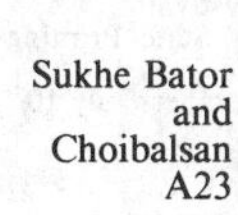

Sukhe Bator and Choibalsan
A23

Designs: #86, Choibalsan as young man. #87, Choibalsan University, Ulan Bator. 1t, Anniversary medal. 2t, Sukhe Bator.

1946, July **Photo.** ***Perf. 12½***

84	A22	30m ol bis	1.40	1.40
85	A23	50m dl pur	2.00	2.00
86	A24	60m black	2.00	2.00
87	A23	60m org brn	2.50	2.50
88	A24	80m dk org brn	2.75	2.75
89	A24	1t indigo	5.75	5.75
90	A24	2t dp brn	7.50	7.50
		Nos. 84-90 (7)	23.90	23.90

25th anniversary of independence.

New Housing
A25

School Children — A26

Mongolian Arms and Flag — A27

Sukhe Bator — A28

Flags of Communist Countries — A29

Lenin — A30

Designs: 15m, Altai Hotel. No. 94, State Store. No. 95, Like 30m. 25m, University. 40m, National Theater. 50m, Pedagogical Institute. 60m, Sukhe Bator monument. Sizes of type A25: Nos. 91, 93-94, 98-99, 32½x22mm. 25m, 55x26mm.

1951

91	A25	5m brn, *pink*	80	80
92	A26	10m dp bl, *pink*	1.00	1.00
93	A25	15m grn, *grnsh*	1.00	1.00
94	A25	20m red org	1.40	1.40
95	A27	20m dk bl & multi	1.40	1.40
96	A25	25m bl, *bluish*	1.50	1.50
97	A27	30m red & multi	1.50	1.50
98	A25	40m pur, *pink*	1.50	1.50
99	A25	50m brn, *grysh*	5.50	5.50
100	A28	60m brn blk	5.50	5.50
101	A29	1t multi	5.50	5.50
102	A28	2t dk brn & org brn	6.75	6.75
103	A30	3t multi	14.00	14.00
		Nos. 91-103 (13)	47.35	47.35

30th anniversary of independence.

Choibalsan
A31

Choibalsan and Farmer
A32

Choibalsan and Sukhe Bator — A33

Designs: No. 108, 30m, Choibalsan and factory worker (47x33mm). 50m, Choibalsan and Young Pioneer. No. 112, 2t, Choibalsan in uniform.

1953, Dec. **Photo.** ***Perf. 12½***

104	A31	15m dl bl	1.00	1.00
105	A32	15m dl grn	1.00	1.00
106	A31	20m dl grn	1.40	1.40
107	A32	20m sepia	1.50	1.50
108	A32	20m vio bl	1.50	1.50
109	A32	30m dk brn	1.75	1.75
110	A33	50m org brn	2.00	2.00
111	A33	1t car rose	2.00	2.00
112	A31	1t sepia	2.00	2.00
113	A31	2t red	2.00	2.00
114	A33	3t sepia	2.75	2.75
115	A33	5t red	4.00	4.00
		Nos. 104-115 (12)	22.90	22.90

First anniversary of death of Marshal Karloin Choibalsan (1895-1952).

Arms of Mongolia — A34

1954, Mar. **Litho.** ***Perf. 12½***

116	A34	10m carmine	2.00	1.75
117	A34	20m carmine	4.00	2.75
118	A34	30m carmine	2.50	1.90
119	A34	40m carmine	3.50	1.75
120	A34	60m carmine	3.00	1.75
		Nos. 116-120 (5)	15.00	9.90

Sukhe Bator and Choibalsan — A35

Lake Hubsugul — A36

Guard with Dog — A37

Designs: No. 122, Lenin Statue, Ulan Bator. 50m, Choibalsan University. 1t, Arms and flag of Mongolia.

1955, June **Photo.** ***Perf. 12½***

121	A35	30m green	20	15
122	A35	30m org ver	28	15
123	A36	30m brt bl	20	15
124	A37	40m dp red lil	35	15
125	A36	50m ocher	70	30
126	A37	1t red & multi	1.50	1.00
		Nos. 121-126 (6)	3.23	
		Set value		1.65

35th anniversary of independence.

1955

Design: 2t, Lenin.

127	A35	2t brt bl	2.50	1.25

85th anniversary of birth of Lenin.

Flags of Communist Countries
A38

Arms of Mongolia
A39

1955

128	A38	60m bl & multi	1.00	55

Fight for peace.

1956 **Photo.** ***Perf. 12½***

129	A39	20m dark brown	18	15
130	A39	30m dark olive	20	15
131	A39	40m bright blue	28	20
132	A39	60m blue green	40	28
133	A39	1t deep carmine	70	28
		Nos. 129-133 (5)	1.76	1.06

Kremlin, Moscow, Train and Sukhe Bator Monument
A40

Design: 2t, Flags of Mongolia and USSR.

1956

134	A40	1t dk bl & multi	1.40	70
135	A40	2t red & multi	2.75	1.00

Establishment of railroad connection between Moscow and Ulan Bator.

Mongolian Arms and Flag A41

Hunter with Golden Eagle A42

Wrestlers A43

Designs: No. 138, 3 children (33x26½mm).

1956, July **Typo.** ***Perf. 9***

136	A41	30m blue	2.00	2.00
137	A42	30m pale brn	8.00	8.00
138	A42	60m orange	9.00	8.00
139	A43	60m yel grn	9.00	8.00

35th anniversary of independence.

Types A41 and A43 without "XXXV"

1958

140	A41	20m red	50	50
141	A43	50m brn, *pink*	2.75	2.75

Nos. 140-143 were issued both with and without gum.

Poster — A44

Globe and Dove — A45

1958, Mar. **Litho.** ***Perf. 9***

142	A44	30m mar & sal	2.25	1.40

13th Congress of Mongolian People's Party.

1958, May

143	A45	60m deep blue	2.00	85

4th Congress of International Democratic Women's Federation, Vienna, June, 1958. Nos. 142-143 exist imperf.

Yak — A46

Designs: No. 144, Pelicans (vert.). No. 145, Siberian ibex (vert.). No. 147, Yak. No. 148, Camels.

1958, July **Typo.** ***Perf. 9***

144	A46	30m lt bl	70	35
145	A46	30m brt grn	70	35
146	A46	60m orange	1.00	50
147	A46	1t blue	2.50	1.00
148	A46	1t rose	2.50	1.00
		Nos. 144-148 (5)	7.40	3.20

Shades exist.

Canceled to Order

From Nos. 149-158 onward, almost all stamps were printed by the Hungarian State Printing Office, Budapest. A few issues (as noted) were printed by the State Printing Works, Ulan Bator.

Canceling to order was done at Budapest to some quantity of all issues printed there, except Nos. 296-303, the anti-malaria set.

Used values are for canceled to order stamps. Postally used specimens sell for considerably more.

Catalogue values for unused stamps in this section, from this point to the end of the section, are for Never Hinged items.

Stallion A47

Holy Flame (Tulaga) A48

Designs: 5m, 40m, Goat. 10m, 30m, Ram. 15m, 60m, Stallion. 20m, 50m, Bull. 25m, 1t, Bactrian camel.

Perf. 10½x11½

1958, Nov. 11 **Litho.**

149	A47	5m yel & brn	15	15
150	A47	10m lt grn & brn	15	15
151	A47	15m lil & brn	15	15
152	A47	20m lt bl & brn	15	15
153	A47	25m rose & brn	15	15
154	A47	30m lil & pur	15	15
155	A47	40m lt & dk grn	15	15
156	A47	50m sal & brn	18	15
157	A47	60m lt bl & ind	20	15
158	A47	1t yel & brn	50	20
		Set value	1.40	75

1959, May 1 **Litho.** ***Perf. 9***

159	A48	1t multi	1.75	70

See No. C36.

Archer — A49

Mongol Sports: 5m, Taming wild horse. 10m, Wrestlers. 15m, Horseback riding. 25m, Horse race. 30m, Archers. 70m, Hunting wild horse. 80m, Proclaiming a champion.

1959, June 6 **Photo.** ***Perf. 11***

160	A49	5m multi	15	15
161	A49	10m multi	15	15
162	A49	15m multi	15	15
163	A49	20m multi	15	15
164	A49	25m multi	18	15
165	A49	30m multi	18	15
166	A49	70m multi	35	15
167	A49	80m multi	55	24
		Set value	1.55	75

Young Wrestlers A50

Youth Festival Emblem A51

Designs: 5m, Young musician (horiz.). 20m, Boy on horseback. 25m, Two opera singers. 40m, Young Pioneers with flags (horiz.).

Photo.; Litho. (30m)

1959, July ***Perf. 12, 11 (30m)***

168	A50	5m vio bl & rose car	15	15
169	A50	10m bl grn & brn	15	15
170	A50	20m claret & grn	15	15
171	A50	25m grn & vio bl	18	15
172	A51	30m lil & lt bl	18	15
173	A50	40m grn & pur	35	20
		Set value	1.00	62

Mongolian Youth Festival.

The 30m was printed by State Printing Works, Ulan Bator.

Issue dates: 30m, July 11; others July 10.

"Mongol" in Stylized Uighur Script — A52

"Mongol" in Various Scripts: 40m, Soyombo. 50m, Kalmuck. 60m, Square (Pagspa). 1t, Cyrillic.

Printed by State Printing Works, Ulan Bator.

1959, Sept. 1 **Litho.** ***Perf. 11***

Size: 29x42½mm

174	A52	30m blk & multi	2.00	2.00
175	A52	40m blk & multi	2.00	2.00
176	A52	50m blk & multi	2.75	2.75
177	A52	60m blk & multi	4.00	4.00

Size: 21x31mm

Perf. 9

178	A52	1t blk & multi	8.50	8.50
		Nos. 174-178 (5)	19.25	19.25

1st Intl. Mongolian Language Congress.

Battle Emblem A53

Battle Monument A54

1959, Sept. 15 **Photo.** ***Perf. 12½x12***

179	A53	40m yel, brn & car	24	15
180	A54	50m multi	28	15
		Set value		20

Battle of Ha-lo-hsin (Khalka) River, 20th anniversary.

Congress Emblem A55

Printed by State Printing Works, Ulan Bator.

1959, Dec. **Litho.** ***Perf. 11***

181	A55	30m green	1.40	1.40

2nd meeting of rural economy cooperatives of Mongolia.

Sable — A56

Pheasants — A57

Perf. 15, 11x13

1959, Dec. 21 **Photo.**

182	A56	5m shown	15	15
183	A57	10m shown	15	15
184	A56	15m Muskrat	15	15
185	A57	20m Otter	15	15
186	A56	30m Argali	16	15
187	A57	50m Saigas	35	20
188	A57	1t Musk deer	70	38
		Set value	1.50	90

Lunik 3 — A58

Design: 50m, Lunik 3 with path around moon (horiz.).

1959, Dec. 30 **Photo.** ***Perf. 12***

189	A58	30m vio & yel grn	40	18
190	A58	50m red, dk bl & grn	60	20

Lunik 3 Russian moon mission, Oct. 7, 1959.

Motherhood Badge — A59

Flower Emblem — A60

1960, Mar. 8 *Perf. 11, 12½x11½*

191	A59	40m	bl & bis	40	15
192	A60	50m	bl, grn & yel	55	20

International Women's Day.

Lenin — A61

Jacob's-ladder — A62

1960, Apr. 22 Photo. *Perf. 11½x12*

193	A61	40m	dk rose car	35	15
194	A61	50m	rose vio	48	15
			Set value		24

90th anniversary, birth of Lenin.

1960, May 31 *Perf. 11½x12*

195	A62	5m	Larkspur	15	15
196	A62	10m	Tulips	15	15
197	A62	15m	shown	15	15
198	A62	20m	Globeflowers	15	15
199	A62	30m	Bellflowers	15	15
200	A62	40m	Parnassia	15	15
201	A62	50m	Geranium	20	18
202	A62	1t	Begonia	40	30
			Set value	1.05	85

For overprints see Nos. 296-303.

Equestrian — A63

Running — A64

1960, Aug. 1 *Perf. 15, 11*

203	A63	5m	shown	15	15
204	A64	10m	shown	15	15
205	A63	15m	Diving	15	15
206	A64	20m	Wrestling	15	15
207	A63	30m	Hurdling	18	15
208	A64	50m	Gymnastics, women's	28	15
209	A63	70m	High jump	35	15
210	A64	1t	Discus, women's	70	28
			Nos. 203-210 (8)	2.11	
			Set value		80

17th Olympic Games, Rome, Aug. 25-Sept. 11.

Red Cross A65

1960, Aug. 29 *Perf. 11*

211	A65	20m	bl, red & yel	24	15

Newspaper "Unen" (Truth) A66

1960, Dec. 19 *Perf. 12x11½*

212	A66	20m	red, yel & sl grn	15	82
213	A66	30m	grn, yel & red	20	15

40th anniversary of Mongolian press.

Golden Orioles — A67

Songbirds: 5m, Rose-colored starling. 10m, Hoopoe. 20m, Black-billed capercaillie. 50m, Oriental broad-billed roller. 70m, Tibetan sandgrouse. 1t, Mandarin duck. (Triangle points down on 5m, 50m, 70m, 1t.)

1961, Jan. 3 *Perf. 11*

214	A67	5m	multi	15	15
215	A67	10m	multi	15	15
216	A67	15m	multi	15	15
217	A67	20m	multi	15	15
218	A67	50m	multi	28	15
219	A67	70m	multi	40	18
220	A67	1t	multi	60	24
			Nos. 214-220 (7)	1.88	
			Set value		80

Federation Emblem A68

Design: 30m, Worker and emblem (vert.).

Perf. 11½x12, 12x11½

1961, Jan. 29 **Photo.**

221	A68	30m	dk gray & rose	15	15
222	A68	50m	ultra & red	20	15
			Set value		18

World Federation of Trade Unions, 15th anniv.

Patrice Lumumba (1925-1961), Premier of Congo — A69

1961, Apr. 8 *Perf. 11½x12*

223	A69	30m	brown	85	28
224	A69	50m	vio gray	1.75	40

Bridge — A70

Designs: 10m, Shoemaker. 15m, Department Store, Ulan Bator. 20m, Government building. 30m, State Theater, Ulan Bator. 50m, Machinist. 1t, Modern and old buildings.

1961, Apr. 30 *Perf. 11½x12, 15*

Sizes: 31½x21mm, 59x20mm (20m)

225	A70	5m	emerald	15	15
226	A70	10m	blue	15	15
227	A70	15m	rose red	15	15
228	A70	20m	brown	18	15
229	A70	30m	blue	28	18
230	A70	50m	ol grn	35	24
231	A70	1t	violet	50	35
			Nos. 225-231 (7)	1.76	
			Set value		1.05

40th anniversary of independence; modernization of Mongolia.

Yuri Gagarin and Globe — A71

Designs: 20m, Gagarin with rocket (vert.). 50m, Gagarin making parachute descent (vert.). 1t, Gagarin wearing helmet; globe.

1961, May 31 *Perf. 15*

232	A71	20m	multi	20	15
233	A71	30m	multi	28	15
234	A71	50m	multi	50	18
235	A71	1t	multi	70	45

Yuri A. Gagarin, first man in space, Apr. 12, 1961.

Postman on Reindeer A72

Designs: 15m, No. 241a, Postman on camel. 10m, 20m, Postman with yaks. 25m, No. 241c, Postman with ship. 30m, 50m, Diesel train.

1961, June 5 *Perf. 15*

236	A72	5m	multi	15	15
237	A72	15m	multi	15	15
238	A72	20m	multi	15	15
239	A72	25m	multi	18	15
240	A72	30m	multi	24	18
			Nos. 236-240,C1-C3 (8)	2.02	
			Set value		95

Souvenir Sheet

Perf. 11

241	Sheet of 4	1.25	1.25
a.	A72 5m lt bl & brn	28	28
b.	A72 10m grn, brn & bl	28	28
c.	A72 15m grn, vio & brn	28	28
d.	A72 50m vio, grn & blk	28	28

40th anniv. of independence; postal modernization. See No. C4b for 25m, perf. 11.

Souvenir Sheet

Ornamental Column — A73

1961, June 20 *Perf. 12*

242	A73		Sheet of 2 + label	2.00	1.75
a.			2t bl, red & gold	85	85

40th anniversary of the Mongolian People's Revolution. No. 242 contains two No. 242a and label, imperf. between.

Herdsman and Oxen — A74

Designs: Herdsmen and domestic animals (except 1t and No. 252a).

1961, July 10 *Perf. 13*

243	A74	5m	Rams	15	15
244	A74	10m	shown	15	15
245	A74	15m	Camels	15	15
246	A74	20m	Pigs and geese	15	15
247	A74	25m	Angora goats	15	15
248	A74	30m	Horses	18	15
249	A74	40m	Sheep	20	15
250	A74	50m	Cows	28	20
251	A74	1t	Combine harvester	48	35
			Set value	1.60	1.15

Souvenir Sheets

Perf. 12

252	Sheet of 3	1.00	1.00
a.	A74 5m Combine harvester	28	28
b.	A74 15m Angora goats	28	28
c.	A74 40m Oxen	28	28
253	Sheet of 3	1.00	1.00
a.	A74 10m Pigs and geese	28	28
b.	A74 20m Horses	28	28
c.	A74 30m Cows	28	28
254	Sheet of 3	1.00	1.00
a.	A74 25m Camels	28	28
b.	A74 50m Rams	28	28
c.	A74 1t Sheep	28	28

40th anniversary of independence. Nos. 252-254 each contain 3 stamps imperf. between.

Horseback Riders — A75

Designs: 5m, Young wrestlers and instructor. 15m, Camel and pony riders. 20m, Falconers. 30m, Skier. 50m, Archers. 1t, Male dancers.

1961, Aug. 10 *Perf. 11*

255	A75	5m	multi	15	15
256	A75	10m	multi	15	15
257	A75	15m	multi	15	15
258	A75	20m	multi	15	15
259	A75	30m	multi	18	15
260	A75	50m	multi	35	15
261	A75	1t	multi	50	24
			Set value	1.30	70

40th anniversary of independence; Mongolian youth sports.

Statue of Sukhe Bator A76

Arms of Mongolia A77

Designs: 5m, Mongol youth. 10m, Mongol chieftain. 20m, Singer. 30m, Dancer. 50m,

Dombra player. 70m, Musicians. 1t, Gymnast. (5m, 10m, 70m, 1t, horiz.).

Perf. 12x11½, 11½x12

1961, Sept. 16

262	A76	5m brt grn & red lil	15	15
263	A76	10m red & dk bl	15	15
264	A76	15m bl & lt brn	15	15
265	A76	20m pur & brt grn	15	15
266	A76	30m vio bl & car	15	15
267	A76	50m ol & vio	28	28
268	A76	70m brt lil rose & ol	38	38
269	A76	1t dk bl & ver	50	45
		Nos. 262-269 (8)	1.91	1.86

40th anniversary of independence; Mongolian culture.

1961, Nov. 17 *Perf. 11½x12*

270	A77	5m multi	15	15
271	A77	10m multi	15	15
272	A77	15m multi	15	15
273	A77	20m multi	15	15
274	A77	30m multi	18	15
275	A77	50m multi	20	15
276	A77	70m multi	28	18
277	A77	1t multi	50	28
		Set value	1.50	88

Congress Emblem A78

1961, Dec. 4 **Litho.** *Perf. 11½*

278	A78	30m vio bl, yel & red	18	15
279	A78	50m brn, yel & red	24	18
		Set value		28

5th World Congress of Trade Unions, Moscow, Dec. 4-16.

UN Emblem and Arms of Mongolia — A79

Designs: 10m, Globe, map of Mongolia and dove. 50m, Flags of UN and Mongolia. 60m, UN Headquarters, New York and Parliament, Ulan Bator. 70m, UN assembly, UN and Mongolian flags.

1962, Mar. 15 **Photo.** *Perf. 11*

280	A79	10m gold & multi	15	15
281	A79	30m gold & multi	15	15
282	A79	50m gold & multi	20	15
283	A79	60m gold & multi	40	18
284	A79	70m gold & multi	60	35
		Nos. 280-284 (5)	1.50	
		Set value		75

Mongolia's admission to UN.

Soccer — A80

Designs: 10m, Soccer ball, globe and flags. 50m, Soccer players, globe and ball. 60m, Goalkeeper. 70m, Stadium.

1962, May 15 **Litho.** *Perf. 10½*

285	A80	10m multi	15	15
286	A80	30m multi	15	15
287	A80	50m multi	18	15
288	A80	60m multi	35	18
289	A80	70m multi	50	20
		Nos. 285-289 (5)	1.33	
		Set value		55

World Soccer Championship, Chile, May 30-June 17.

D. Natsagdorji A81

Solidarity Emblem A82

1962, May 15 **Photo.** *Perf. 15x14½*

290	A81	30m brown	18	15
291	A81	50m bluish grn	24	15
		Set value		20

Mongolian writers' congress.
For overprints see Nos. 430-431.

Perf. 11½x10½

1962, May 22 **Litho.**

292	A82	20m yel grn & multi	18	15
293	A82	30m bl & multi	24	15
		Set value		20

Afro-Asian Peoples' solidarity.

Flags of USSR and Mongolia — A83

Perf. 11½x10½

1962, June 25 **Litho.**

294	A83	30m brn & multi	15	15
295	A83	50m vio bl & multi	20	15
		Set value		20

Mongol-Soviet friendship.

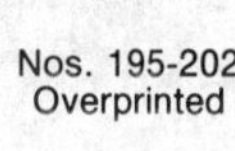

Nos. 195-202 Overprinted

1962, July 20 **Photo.** *Perf. 11½x12*

296	A62	5m multi	15	15
297	A62	10m multi	15	15
298	A62	15m multi	20	20
299	A62	20m multi	20	20
300	A62	30m multi	24	24
301	A62	40m multi	30	30
302	A62	50m multi	48	48
303	A62	1t multi	75	75
		Nos. 296-303 (8)	2.47	2.47

WHO drive to eradicate malaria.

Military Field Emblem — A84

Designs: 30m, Tablets with inscriptions. 50m, Stone column. 60m, Genghis Khan.

1962, July 20 *Perf. 11½x12*

304	A84	20m bl & multi	70	70
305	A84	30m red & multi	70	70
306	A84	50m pink, brn & blk	1.50	1.50
307	A84	60m bl & multi	2.25	2.25

Genghis Khan (1162-1227), Mongol conqueror.
For overprints see Nos. 1846-1849.

River Perch — A85

1962, Dec. 28 *Perf. 11*

308	A85	5m shown	15	15
309	A85	10m Burbot	15	15
310	A85	15m Arctic grayling	15	15
311	A85	20m Shorthorn sculpin	15	15
312	A85	30m Marine zander	18	15
313	A85	50m Siberian sturgeon	20	15
314	A85	70m Waleck's chub minnow	35	18
315	A85	1.50t Cottocomephorid	55	30
		Set value	1.60	85

Sukhe Bator (1893-1923), National Hero — A86

1963, Feb. 2 **Photo.** *Perf. 11½x12*

316	A86	30m blue	15	15
317	A86	60m rose car	20	15
		Set value		20

Laika and Rocket — A87

Designs: 15m, Rocket launching (vert.). 25m, Lunik 2 (vert.). 70m, Andrian G. Nikolayev and Pavel R. Popovich. 1t, Mars rocket.

1963, Apr. 1 **Litho.** *Perf. 12½x12*

Size: 46x32mm

318	A87	5m multi	15	15

Size: 20x68mm

319	A87	15m multi	15	15
320	A87	25m multi	24	15

Size: 46x32mm

321	A87	70m multi	38	20
322	A87	1t multi	60	35
		Nos. 318-322 (5)	1.52	
		Set value		78

Soviet space explorations.

Blood Transfusion — A88

1963, Aug. 15 *Perf. 10½*

323	A88	20m Packing Red Cross parcels	15	15
324	A88	30m shown	15	15
325	A88	50m Vaccination	18	15
326	A88	60m Ambulance service	24	18
327	A88	1.30t Centenary emblem	50	40
		Nos. 323-327 (5)	1.22	
		Set value		80

Red Cross centenary.

Karl Marx — A89

Mongolian Woman — A90

1963, Sept. 16 **Photo.** *Perf. 11½x12*

328	A89	30m blue	15	15
329	A89	60m dk car rose	20	15
		Set value		20

145th anniversary of birth of Karl Marx.

1963, Sept. 26

330	A90	30m bl & multi	18	15

5th International Women's Congress, Moscow, June 24-29.

Inachis A91

Designs: Mongolian butterflies.

1963, Nov. 7 **Litho.** *Perf. 11½*

331	A91	5m shown	15	15
332	A91	10m Gonepteryxrhamni	15	15
333	A91	15m Aglais urticae	15	15
334	A91	20m Parnassius apollo	15	15
335	A91	30m Papilio machaon	20	15
336	A91	60m Agrodiaetus damon	35	20
337	A91	1t Limenitis populi	48	28
		Set value	1.38	85

UNESCO Emblem, Globe and Scales — A92

1963, Dec. 10 Photo. *Perf. 12*
338 A92 30m multi 18 15
339 A92 60m multi 28 15
Set value 18

Universal Declaration of Human Rights, 15th anniversary.

Coprinus Comatus — A93

Designs: Mushrooms.

1964, Jan. 1 Litho. *Perf. 10½*
340 A93 5m shown 15 15
341 A93 10m Lactarius torminosus 15 15
342 A93 15m Psalliota campestris 15 15
343 A93 20m Russula delica 15 15
344 A93 30m Ixocomus granulatus 20 15
345 A93 50m Lactarius scrobiculatus 24 18
346 A93 70m Lactarius deliciosus 35 20
347 A93 1t Ixocomus variegatus 50 28
Set value 1.60 95

Souvenir Sheet

Skier A94

1964, Feb. 12 Photo. *Perf. 12x11½*
348 A94 4t gray 2.00 2.00

9th Winter Olympic Games, Innsbruck, Jan. 29-Feb. 9.

Lenin — A95

1964 Photo. *Perf. 11½x12*
349 A95 30m sal & multi 48 15
350 A95 50m bl & multi 55 15
Set value 20

60th anniversary of Communist Party. Nos. 349-350 printed with alternating label showing Lenin quotation.

Javelin — A96

1964, Apr. 30 Litho. *Perf. 10½*
351 A96 5m Gymnastics, women's 15 15
352 A96 10m shown 15 15
353 A96 15m Wrestling 15 15
354 A96 20m Running, women's 15 15
355 A96 30m Equestrian 20 15
356 A96 50m Diving, women's 28 15
357 A96 60m Bicycling 35 20
358 A96 1t Olympic Games emblem 60 28
Set value 1.70 95

Souvenir Sheet
Perf. 12x11½
359 A96 4t Wrestling 2.50 2.50

18th Olympic Games, Toyko, Oct. 10-25. No. 359 contains one horizontal stamp, 37x27½mm. Issued Sept. 1.

Congress Emblem — A97

1964, Sept. 30 Photo. *Perf. 11*
360 A97 30m multi 24 15

4th Mongolian Women's Congress.

Lunik 1 — A98

Russian Space Research: 10m, Vostok 1 and 2. 15m, Tiros weather satellite (vert.). 20m, Cosmos circling earth (vert.). 30m, Mars probe (vert.). 60m, Luna 4 (vert.). 80m, Echo 2. 1t, Radar and rockets.

1964, Oct. 30
361 A98 5m multi 15 15
362 A98 10m multi 15 15
363 A98 15m multi 15 15
364 A98 20m multi 15 15
365 A98 30m multi 20 15
366 A98 60m multi 24 15
367 A98 80m multi 24 15
368 A98 1t multi 45 24
Set value 1.50 70

Rider Carrying Flag — A99

1964, Nov. 26 Photo. *Perf. 11½x12*
369 A99 25m multi 20 15
370 A99 50m multi 30 15
Set value 20

40th anniversary of Mongolian constitution.

Weather Balloon A100

Designs: 5m, Oceanographic exploration. 60m, Northern lights and polar bears. 80m, Gemagnetism. 1t, I.Q.S.Y. emblem and Mercator map.

1965, May 15 Photo. *Perf. 13½*
371 A100 5m gray & multi 15 15
372 A100 10m grn & multi 15 15
373 A100 60m bl, blk & pink 20 15
374 A100 80m cit & multi 40 20
375 A100 1t brt grn & multi 70 38
Nos. 371-375,C6-C8 (8) 2.10
Set value 1.10

International Quiet Sun Year.

Horses — A101

Designs: Mongolian horses.

1965, Aug. 25 *Perf. 11*
376 A101 5m shown 15 15
377 A101 10m Falconers 15 15
378 A101 15m Taming wild horse 15 15
379 A101 20m Horse race 15 15
380 A101 30m Hurdles 18 15
381 A101 60m Wolf hunt 20 15
382 A101 80m Milking a mare 28 20
383 A101 1t Mare and foal 45 30
Set value 1.40 95

Girl Holding Lambs — A102

1965, Oct. 10 Photo. *Perf. 11*
384 A102 5m shown 15 15
385 A102 10m Boy and girl drummers 15 15
386 A102 20m Camp fire 15 15
387 A102 30m Wrestlers 24 15
388 A102 50m Emblem 35 28
Set value 82 58
Nos. 384-388 (5) 1.04 88

40th anniv. of Mongolian Youth Org.

Chinese Perch — A103

1965, Nov. 25
389 A103 5m shown 15 15
390 A103 10m Lenok trout 15 15
391 A103 15m Siberian sturgeon 15 15
392 A103 20m Amur salmon 15 15
393 A103 30m Bagrid catfish 18 15
394 A103 60m Siluri catfish 24 15
395 A103 80m Northern pike 35 18
396 A103 1t River perch 50 28
Nos. 389-396 (8) 1.87
Set value 90

Marx and Lenin — A104

1965, Dec. 15 *Perf. 11½x12*
397 A104 10m red & blk 15 15

6th Conference of Postal Ministers of Communist Countries, Peking, June 21-July 15.

Sable — A105

1966, Feb. 15 Photo. *Perf. 12½*
398 A105 5m shown 15 15
399 A105 10m Fox 15 15
400 A105 15m Otter, vert. 15 15
401 A105 20m Cheetah, vert. 15 15
402 A105 30m Pallas's cat 18 15
403 A105 60m Stone marten 24 15
404 A105 80m Ermine, vert. 30 20
405 A105 1t Woman in mink coat, vert. 50 28
Set value 1.50 90

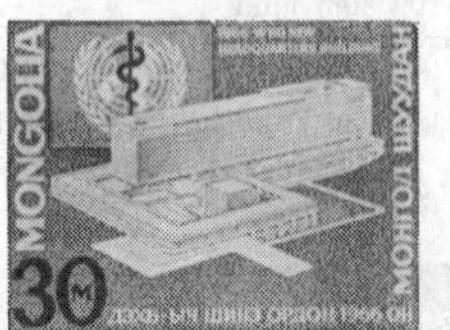

Opening of WHO Headquarters, Geneva — A106

1966, May 3 Photo. *Perf. 12x11½*
406 A106 30m bl grn, bl & gold 15 15
407 A106 50m red, bl & gold 28 15
Set value 16

For overprints see Nos. 483-484.

Soccer — A107

Designs: 30m, 60m, 80m, Various soccer plays. 1t, British flag and World Soccer Cup emblem. 4t, Wembley Stadium (horiz.).

1966, May 31 Photo. *Perf. 11*
408 A107 10m multi 15 15
409 A107 30m multi 15 15
410 A107 60m multi 18 15
411 A107 80m multi 30 18
412 A107 1t multi 50 30
Nos. 408-412 (5) 1.28
Set value 70

Souvenir Sheet

Perf. 12½, Imperf.

413 A107 4t gray & brn 2.00 2.00

World Soccer Championship for Jules Rimet Cup, Wembley, England, July 11-30. No. 413 contains one stamp 61x83mm.

Sukhe Bator, Parliament Building, Ulan Bator A108

1966, June 7 Litho. *Perf. 12x12½*

414 A108 30m red, bl & brn 20 15

15th Congress of Mongolian Communist Party.

Wrestling — A109

Designs: Various wrestling holds.

1966, June 15 Photo. *Perf. 11½x12*

415 A109 10m multi 15 15
416 A109 30m multi 15 15
417 A109 60m multi 24 15
418 A109 80m multi 28 18
419 A109 1t multi 35 28
Set value 1.00 68

World Wrestling Championship, Toledo, Spain.

Emblem and Map of Mongolia — A110

Sukhe Bator, Grain and Factories A111

Perf. 11½x12, 12x11½

1966, July 11 Litho.

420 A110 30m red & multi 20 15
421 A111 50m red & multi 30 18

45th anniversary of independence. For overprints see Nos. 552-553.

Lilium Tenuifolium — A112

1966, Oct. 15 Photo. *Perf. 12x11½*

422 A112 5m Physochlaena physaloides 15 15
423 A112 10m Allium polyrrchizum 15 15
424 A112 15m shown 15 15
425 A112 20m Thermopsis lanceolata 15 15
426 A112 30m Amygdalus mongolica 18 15
427 A112 60m Caryopteris mongolica 24 15
428 A112 80m Piptanthus mongolicus 30 20
429 A112 1t Iris bungei 45 30
Set value 1.55 90

Nos. 290-291 Overprinted: "1906/1966"

1966, Oct. 26 Photo. *Perf. 15x14½*

430 A81 30m brown 28 15
431 A81 50m bluish grn 35 15
Set value 22

60th anniv. of birth of D. Natsagdorji, writer.

50m exists double, one invtd.

Child with Dove — A113

1966, Dec. 2 *Perf. 11½x12, 12x11½*

432 A113 10m shown 15 15
433 A113 15m Children with reindeer 15 15
434 A113 20m Boys wrestling, vert. 15 15
435 A113 30m Horseback riding 20 15
436 A113 60m Children riding camel, vert. 24 15
437 A113 80m Child with sheep 35 15
438 A113 1t Boy archer, vert. 50 28
Nos. 432-438 (7) 1.74
Set value 80

Children's Day.

Proton 1 — A114

Perf. 11½x12½, 12½x11½

1966, Dec. 28 Photo.

439 A114 5m Vostok 2, vert. 15 15
440 A114 10m shown 15 15
441 A114 15m Telstar 1, vert. 15 15
442 A114 20m Molnija 1, vert. 15 15
443 A114 30m Syncom 3, vert. 18 15
444 A114 60m Luna 9 24 15
445 A114 80m Luna 12, vert. 30 18
446 A114 1t Mariner 4 45 20
Set value 1.55 90

Space exploration.

Tarbosaurus — A115

1967, Mar. 31 *Perf. 12x11½*

447 A115 5m shown 15 15
448 A115 10m Talarurus 15 15
449 A115 15m Proceratops 15 15
450 A115 20m Indricotherium 15 15
451 A115 30m Saurolophus 18 15
452 A115 60m Mastodon 20 15
453 A115 80m Mongolotherium 30 18
454 A115 1t Mammoth 45 20
Set value 1.50 90

Prehistoric animals.

Congress Emblem — A116

1967, June 9 Litho. *Perf. 12*

455 A116 30m lt bl & multi 18 15
456 A116 50m pink & multi 24 20

9th Youth Festival for Peace and Friendship, Sofia.

Sukhe Bator and Soldiers — A117

Design: 60m, Lenin and soldiers.

1967, Oct. 25 Litho. *Perf. 11½x12*

457 A117 40m red & multi 28 24
458 A117 60m red & multi 35 28

Russian October Revolution, 50th anniv.

Ice Hockey and Olympic Rings A118

1967, Dec. 29 *Perf. 12x12½*

459 A118 5m Figure skating 15 15
460 A118 10m Speed skating 15 15
461 A118 15m shown 15 15
462 A118 20m Ski jump 18 15
463 A118 30m Bobsledding 20 15
464 A118 60m Figure skating, pair 40 15
465 A118 80m Slalom 55 24
Nos. 459-465 (7) 1.78
Set value 72

Souvenir Sheet

Perf. 12

466 A118 4t Women's figure skating 2.00 2.00

10th Winter Olympic Games, Grenoble, France, Feb. 6-18.

Bactrian Camels A119

1968, Jan. 15 Photo. *Perf. 12*

467 A119 5m shown 15 15
468 A119 10m Yak 15 15
469 A119 15m Lamb 18 15
470 A119 20m Foal 20 15
471 A119 30m Calf 24 15
472 A119 60m Bison 30 15
473 A119 80m Roe deer 38 18
474 A119 1t Reindeer 55 28
Nos. 467-474 (8) 2.15
Set value 90

Young animals.

Black Currants A120

Berries: 5m, Rosa acicularis. 15m, Gooseberries. 20m, Malus. 30m, Strawberries. 60m, Ribes altissimum. 80m, Blueberries. 1t, Hippophae rhamnoides.

Lithographed & Engraved

1968, Feb. 15

475 A120 5m bl & ultra 15 15
476 A120 10m buff & brn 15 15
477 A120 15m lt grn & grn 15 15
478 A120 20m yel & red 18 15
479 A120 30m pink & car 28 15
480 A120 60m sal & org brn 35 15
481 A120 80m pale & dl bl 45 18
482 A120 1t lt yel & red 60 24
Nos. 475-482 (8) 2.31
Set value 85

Nos. 406-407 Overprinted ДЭХБ 20 ЖИЛ WHO

1968, Apr. 16 Photo. *Perf. 12x11½*

483 A106 30m bl grn, bl & gold 18 15
484 A106 50m red, bl & gold 24 15
Set value 22

WHO, 20th anniversary.

Human Rights Flame — A121

1968, June 20 Litho. *Perf. 12*

485 A121 30m turq & vio bl 15 15

International Human Rights Year.

"Das Kapital," by Karl Marx A122

Design: 50m, Karl Marx.

1968, July 1 Litho. *Perf. 12*

486 A122 30m bl & multi 18 15
487 A122 50m red & multi 24 15
Set value 20

Karl Marx (1818-1883).

Artist, by A. Sangatzohyo A123

Paintings: 10m, On Remote Roads, by Sangatzohyo. 15m, Camel calf, by B. Avarzad. 20m, Milk, by Avarzad. 30m, The Bowman, by B. Gombosuren. 80m, Girl Sitting on Yak, by Sangatzohyo. 1.40t, Cagan Dara Eke, by Janaivajara. 4t, Meeting, by Sangatzohyo (horiz.).

1968, July 11 Litho. *Perf. 12*

488 A123 5m brn & multi 15 15
489 A123 10m brn & multi 15 15
490 A123 15m brn & multi 15 15
491 A123 20m brn & multi 24 15
492 A123 30m brn & multi 35 15
493 A123 80m brn & multi 48 18
494 A123 1.40t brn & multi 70 35
Nos. 488-494 (7) 2.22
Set value 90

Miniature Sheets

Perf. 11½, Imperf.

495 A123 4t brn & multi 2.25 2.25

Paintings from national museum, Ulan Bator. #495 contains one 54x84mm stamp.

Volleyball — A124

Sports (Olympic Rings and): 10m, Wrestling. 15m, Bicycling. 20m, Javelin, women's. 30m, Soccer. 60m, Running. 80m, Gymnastics, women's. 1t, Weight lifting. 4t, Equestrian.

1968, Sept. 1 Litho. *Perf. 12*

496 A124 5m multi 15 15
497 A124 10m multi 15 15
498 A124 15m multi 15 15
499 A124 20m multi 15 15
500 A124 30m multi 20 15
501 A124 60m multi 28 15
502 A124 80m multi 30 18
503 A124 1t multi 60 20
Set value 1.75 78

Souvenir Sheets

Perf. 11½, Imperf.

504 A124 4t org & multi 2.75 2.75

19th Olympic Games, Mexico City, Oct. 12-27. #504 contains one 52x44mm stamp.

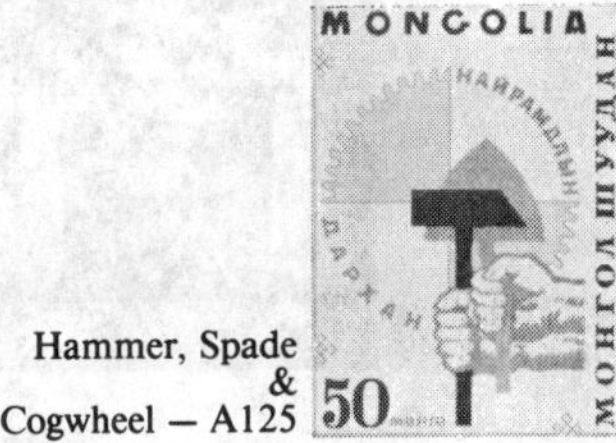

Hammer, Spade & Cogwheel — A125

1968, Sept. 17 Litho. *Perf. 11½*

505 A125 50m bl & ver 15 15

Industrial development in town of Darhan.

Maxim Gorki (1868-1936), Russian Writer — A126

1968, Nov. 6 Litho. *Perf. 12*

506 A126 60m turq & sep 18 15

Madonna and Child, by Boltraffio A127

Paintings: 10m, St. Roch Healed by an Angel, by Brescia. 15m, Madonna and Child with St. Anne, by Macchietti. 20m, St. John on Patmos, by Cano. 30m, Lady with Viola da Gamba, by Kupetzky. 80m, Boy, by Amerling. 1.40t, Death of Adonis, by Furini. 4t, Portrait of a Lady, by Renoir.

1968, Nov. 20 Litho. *Perf. 12*

507 A127 5m gray & multi 15 15
508 A127 10m gray & multi 15 15
509 A127 15m gray & multi 15 15
510 A127 20m gray & multi 20 15
511 A127 30m gray & multi 30 15
512 A127 80m gray & multi 45 20
513 A127 1.40t gray & multi 60 28
Nos. 507-513 (7) 2.00
Set value 94

Miniature Sheet

514 A127 4t gray & multi 2.25 2.25

UNESCO, 22nd anniv.

Jesse Owens, USA — A128

Olympic Gold Medal Winners: 5m, Paavo Nurmi, Finland. 15m, Fanny Blankers-Koen, Netherlands. 20m, Laszlo Papp, Hungary. 30m, Wilma Rudolph, US. 60m, Boris Sahlin, USSR. 80m, Donald Schollander, US. 1t Akinori Nakayama, Japan. 4t, Jigjidin Munhbat, Mongolia.

1969, Mar. 25 Litho. *Perf. 12*

515 A128 5m multi 15 15
516 A128 10m multi 15 15
517 A128 15m multi 15 15
518 A128 20m multi 15 15
519 A128 30m multi 15 15
520 A128 60m multi 15 15
521 A128 80m multi 28 24
522 A128 1t multi 60 28
Set value 1.30 85

Souvenir Sheet

523 A128 4t grn & multi 2.75 2.75

Bayit Woman A129

Regional Costumes: 10m, Torgut man. 15m, Dzakhachin woman. 20m, Khalkha woman. 30m, Dariganga woman. 60m, Mingat woman. 80m, Khalkha man. 1t, Bargut woman.

1969, Apr. 20 Litho. *Perf. 12*

524 A129 5m multi 15 15
525 A129 10m multi 15 15
526 A129 15m multi 15 15
527 A129 20m multi 15 15
528 A129 30m multi 18 15
529 A129 60m multi 24 15
530 A129 80m multi 30 15
531 A129 1t multi 48 20
Set value 1.55 75

Red Cross Emblem and Helicopter — A130

Design: 50m, Emblem, Red Cross car and shepherd.

1969, May 15 Litho. *Perf. 12*

532 A130 30m multi 15 15
533 A130 50m multi 20 15
Set value 22

30th anniversary of Mongolian Red Cross.

Landscape and Edelweiss — A131

Designs: Mongolian landscapes and flowers.

1969, May 20

534 A131 5m shown 15 15
535 A131 10m Pinks 15 15
536 A131 15m Dianthus superbus 15 15
537 A131 20m Geranium 15 15
538 A131 30m Dianthus ramosissimus 18 15
539 A131 60m Globeflowers 24 15
540 A131 80m Delphinium 28 20
541 A131 1t Haloxylon 45 28
Set value 1.50 90

See No. 1105.

Bull Fight, by Tsewegdjaw — A132

Paintings from National Museum: 10m, Fighting Colts, by O. Tsewegdjaw. 15m, Horseman and Herd, by A. Sangatzohyo. 20m, Camel Caravan, by D. Damdinsuren. 30m, On the Steppe, by N. Tsultem. 60m, Milking Mares, by Tsewegdjaw. 80m, Going to School, by B. Avarzad. 1t, After Work, by G. Odon. 4t, Horses, by Damdinsuren.

1969, July 11 Litho. *Perf. 12*

542 A132 5m multi 15 15
543 A132 10m multi 15 15
544 A132 15m multi 15 15
545 A132 20m multi 15 15
546 A132 30m multi 18 15
547 A132 60m multi 24 15
548 A132 80m multi 28 18
549 A132 1t multi 45 20
Set value 1.45 80

Souvenir Sheet

550 A132 4t multi 1.75 1.75

10th anniversary of cooperative movement. No. 550 contains one stamp 65x42mm.

Mongolian Flag and Emblem — A133

1969, Sept. 20 Litho. *Perf. 12*

551 A133 50m multi 18 15

Battle of Ha-lo-hsin (Khalka) River, 30th anniversary.

Nos. 420-421 Overprinted

ВНМАУ-ыг
түнхагласны
45
жилийн ой
1969—XI—26

Perf. 11½x12, 12x11½

1969, Nov. 26 Photo.

552 A110 30m red & multi 20 15
553 A111 50m red & multi 28 20

45th anniv. of Mongolian People's Republic.

Mercury 7 — A134

Designs: 5m, Sputnik 3. 10m, Vostok 1. 20m, Voskhod 2. 30m, Apollo 8. 60m, Soyuz 5. 80m, Apollo 12.

1969, Dec. 6 Photo. *Perf. 12x11½*

554 A134 5m multi 15 15
555 A134 10m multi 15 15
556 A134 15m multi 15 15
557 A134 20m multi 18 15
558 A134 30m multi 28 15
559 A134 60m multi 38 18
560 A134 80m multi 55 20
Nos. 554-560 (7) 1.84
Set value 65

Souvenir Sheet

561 A134 4t multi 2.25 2.25

Space achievements of US and USSR.

Wolf — A135

Designs: 10m, Brown bear. 15m, Lynx. 20m, Wild boar. 30m, Moose. 60m, Bobac marmot. 80m, Argali. 1t, Old wall carpet showing hunter and dog.

1970, Mar. 25 Photo. *Perf. 12*

562 A135 5m multi 15 15
563 A135 10m multi 15 15
564 A135 15m multi 15 15
565 A135 20m multi 15 15
566 A135 30m multi 15 15
567 A135 60m multi 24 15
568 A135 80m multi 35 18
569 A135 1t multi 45 28
Set value 1.55 90

Lenin and Mongolian Delegation, by Sangatzohyo — A136

Designs: 20m, Lenin, embroidered panel, by Cerenhuu (vert.). 1t, Lenin, by Mazhig (vert.).

1970, Apr. 22 **Photo. & Litho.**
570 A136 20m multi 15 15
571 A136 50m multi 18 15
572 A136 1t lt bl, blk & red 35 18
Set value 56 32

Centenary of the birth of Lenin.

Souvenir Sheet

EXPO '70 Pavilion of Matsushita Electric Co. and Time Capsule — A137

1970, May 26 **Photo.** ***Perf. 12½***
573 A137 4t gold & multi 2.25 2.25

EXPO '70 International Exposition, Osaka, Japan, Mar. 15-Sept. 13.

Sumitomo Fairy Tale Pavilion A138

1970, June 5 **Photo.** ***Perf. 12x11½***
574 A138 1.50t multi 50 40

EXPO '70 International Exposition, Osaka. No. 574 printed in sheets of 20 (5x4) with alternating horizontal rows of tabs showing various fairy tales and EXPO '70 emblem.

Soccer, Rimet Cup — A139

Designs: Soccer players of various teams in action.

1970, June 20 ***Perf. 12½x11½***
575 A139 10m multi 15 15
576 A139 20m multi 15 15
577 A139 30m multi 15 15
578 A139 50m multi 15 15
579 A139 60m multi 20 15
580 A139 1t multi 40 20
581 A139 1.30t multi 50 30
Nos. 575-581 (7) 1.70
Set value 85

Souvenir Sheet

Perf. 12½

582 A139 4t multi 2.00 2.00

World Soccer Championship for Jules Rimet Cup, Mexico City, May 30-June 21. No. 582 contains one stamp 51x37mm.

Old World Buzzard A140

Birds of Prey: 20m, Tawny owls. 30m, Northern goshawk. 50m, White-tailed sea eagle. 60m, Peregrine falcon. 1t, Old world kestrel. 1.30t, Black kite.

1970, June 30 **Litho.** ***Perf. 12***
583 A140 10m bl & multi 15 15
584 A140 20m pink & multi 15 15
585 A140 30m yel grn & multi 15 15
586 A140 50m bl & multi 18 15
587 A140 60m yel & multi 20 15
588 A140 1t grn & multi 35 24
589 A140 1.30t bl & multi 50 28
Nos. 583-589 (7) 1.68
Set value 90

Russian War Memorial, Berlin — A141

1970, July 11 **Litho.** ***Perf. 12***
590 A141 60m bl & multi 18 15

25th anniversary of end of World War II.

Bogdo-Gegen Palace A142

Designs: 10m, Archer. 30m, Horseman. 40m, "White Mother" Goddess. 50m, Girl in national costume. 60m, Lion statue. 70m, Dancer's mask. 80m, Detail from Bogdo-Gegen Palace, Ulan Bator.

1970, Sept. 20 **Litho.** ***Perf. 12***
591 A142 10m multi 15 15
592 A142 20m multi 15 15
593 A142 30m multi 18 15
594 A142 40m multi 20 15
595 A142 50m multi 28 20
596 A142 60m multi 35 28
597 A142 70m multi 40 35
598 A142 80m multi 50 40
Nos. 591-598 (8) 2.21 1.83

Nos. 595-598 printed se-tenant in blocks of 4, in sheets of 40.

Souvenir Sheet

Recovery of Apollo 13 Capsule A143

1970, Nov. 1 **Litho.** ***Perf. 12***
599 A143 4t bl & multi 2.00 2.00

Space missions of Apollo 13, Apr. 11-17, and Soyuz 9, June 1-10, 1970.

Mongolian Flag, UN and Education Year Emblems — A144

1970, Nov. 7
600 A144 60m multi 40 18

International Education Year.

Mounted Herald A145

1970, Nov. 7 **Litho.** ***Perf. 12***
601 A145 30m gold & multi 15 15

50th anniv. of newspaper Unen (Truth).

Apollo 11 Lunar Landing Module — A146

Designs: 10m, Vostok 2 and 3. 20m, Voskhod 2 and space walk. 30m, Gemini 6 and 7 capsules. 50m, Soyuz 4 and 5 docking in space. 60m, Soyuz 6, 7 and 8 group flight. 1t, Apollo 13 with damaged capsule. 1.30t, Luna 16 unmanned moon landing. 4t, Radar ground tracking station.

1971, Feb. 25 **Litho.** ***Perf. 12***
602 A146 10m multi 15 15
603 A146 20m multi 15 15
604 A146 30m multi 15 15
605 A146 50m multi 20 15
606 A146 60m multi 26 15
607 A146 80m multi 26 15
608 A146 1t multi 45 15
609 A146 1.30t multi 55 15
Nos. 602-609 (8) 2.17
Set value 65

Souvenir Sheet

610 A146 4t vio bl & multi 2.25 2.25

US and USSR space explorations.

Rider with Mongolian Flag — A147

Designs: 30m, Party meeting. 90m, Lenin with Mongolian leader. 1.20t, Marchers, pictures of Lenin and Marx.

1971, Mar. 1 **Photo.** ***Perf. 12½***
611 A147 30m gold & multi 15 15
612 A147 60m gold & multi 15 15
613 A147 90m gold & multi 18 15
614 A147 1.30t gold & multi 35 28
Set value 54

50th anniversary of Mongolian Revolutionary Party.

Souvenir Sheet

Lunokhod 1 on Moon — A148

Design: No. 615b, Apollo 14 on moon.

1971, Apr. 15 **Photo.** ***Perf. 14***
615 A148 Sheet of 2 2.00 2.00
a.-b. 2t any single 80 80

Luna 17 unmanned automated moon mission, Nov. 10-17, 1970, and Apollo 14 moon landing, Jan. 31-Feb. 9, 1971.

Dancer's Mask — A149

Designs: Various masks for dancers.

1971, Apr. 25 **Litho.** ***Perf. 12***
616 A149 10m gold & multi 15 15
617 A149 20m gold & multi 15 15
618 A149 30m gold & multi 20 15
619 A149 50m gold & multi 24 15
620 A149 60m gold & multi 28 15
621 A149 1t gold & multi 55 20
622 A149 1.30t gold & multi 75 24
Nos. 616-622 (7) 2.32
Set value 75

Red Flag and Emblems A150

1971, May 31 **Photo.** ***Perf. 12x11½***
623 A150 60m bl, red & gold 18 15

16th Congress of Mongolian Revolutionary Party.

Steam Locomotive — A151

1971, July 11 Litho. *Perf. 12*

624	A151	20m shown	15	15
625	A151	30m Diesel locomotive	15	15
626	A151	40m Truck	15	15
627	A151	50m Automobile	20	15
628	A151	60m Biplane PO-2	24	15
629	A151	80m AN-24 plane	32	18
630	A151	1t Fishing boat	40	20
		Nos. 624-630 (7)	1.61	
		Set value		72

50th anniversary of modern transportation. For overprints see Nos. 850A-850G.

Arms of Mongolia and Soldier — A152

Design: 1.50t, Arms, policeman and child.

1971, July 11 Litho. *Perf. 12*

631	A152	60m multi	15	15
632	A152	1.50t multi	40	18
		Set value		26

50th anniversary of the people's army and police.

Mongolian Flag and Emblem A153

1971, Aug. 25 Photo. *Perf. 12x11½*

633	A153	60m lt bl & multi	18	15

International Year Against Racial discrimination.

Flag of Youth Organization — A154

1971, Aug. 25 Litho. *Perf. 12*

634	A154	60m org & multi	20	15

50th anniversary of Mongolian revolutionary youth organization.

The Woodsman and the Tiger A155

Designs: Various Mongolian fairy tales.

1971, Sept. 15 Litho. *Perf. 12*

635	A155	10m gold & multi	15	15
636	A155	20m gold & multi	15	15
637	A155	30m gold & multi	15	15
638	A155	50m gold & multi	18	15
639	A155	60m gold & multi	25	15
640	A155	80m gold & multi	30	15
641	A155	1t gold & multi	38	18
642	A155	1.30t gold & multi	55	24
		Nos. 635-642 (8)	2.11	
		Set value		88

Bactrian Camel — A156

1971, Nov. 1 Litho. *Perf. 12½*

643	A156	20m Yaks	15	15
644	A156	30m shown	15	15
645	A156	40m Sheep	15	15
646	A156	50m Goats	18	15
647	A156	60m Cattle	28	18
648	A156	80m Horses	35	20
649	A156	1t White horse	45	24
		Nos. 643-649 (7)	1.71	
		Set value		90

Mongolian livestock breeding.

Cross-country Skiing — A157

Designs (Sapporo Olympic Emblem and): 20m, Bobsledding. 30m, Women's figure skating. 50m, Slalom. 60m, Speed skating. 80m, Downhill skiing. 1t, Ice hockey. 1.30t, Figure skating, pairs. 4t, Ski jump.

Perf. 12½x11½

1972, Jan. 20 Photo.

650	A157	10m multi	15	15
651	A157	20m ol & multi	15	15
652	A157	30m ultra & multi	15	15
653	A157	50m brt bl & multi	15	15
654	A157	60m multi	20	15
655	A157	80m grn & multi	24	15
656	A157	1t bl & multi	30	18
657	A157	1.30t vio & multi	38	24
		Set value	1.50	90

Souvenir Sheet

Perf. 12½

658	A157	4t lt bl & multi	2.00	2.00

11th Winter Olympic Games, Sapporo, Japan, Feb. 3-13.

Taming Wild Horse A158

Paintings: 20m, Mythological animal in winter. 30m, Lancer on horseback. 50m, Athletes. 60m, Waterfall and horses. 80m, The Wise Musician, by Sarav. 1t, Young musician. 1.30t, Old sage with animals.

1972, Apr. 15 Litho. *Perf. 12*

659	A158	10m multi	15	15
660	A158	20m multi	15	15
661	A158	30m multi	15	15
662	A158	50m multi	15	15
663	A158	60m multi	20	15
664	A158	80m multi	24	15
665	A158	1t multi	30	20
666	A158	1.30t multi	38	24
		Set value	1.50	90

Paintings by contemporary artists in Ulan Bator Museum.

Calosoma Fischeri A159

Designs: Various insects.

1972, Apr. 30 Litho. *Perf. 12*

667	A159	10m multi	15	15
668	A159	20m multi	15	15
669	A159	30m multi	15	15
670	A159	50m multi	15	15
671	A159	60m multi	24	15
672	A159	80m multi	28	15
673	A159	1t multi	35	20
674	A159	1.30t multi	40	24
		Nos. 667-674 (8)	1.87	
		Set value		90

UN Emblem — A160

1972, Aug. 30 Photo. *Perf. 12*

675	A160	60m multi	20	15

ECAFE (UN Economic Commission for Asia and the Far East), 25th anniv.

Slow Lizard — A161

Designs: 15m, Radd's toad. 20m, Pallas's viper. 25m, Toad-headed agamid. 30m, Siberian wood frog. 60m, Przewalski's lizard. 80m, Taphrometopon lineolatum (snake). 1t, Stoliczka's agamid.

1972, Sept. 5 Litho. *Perf. 12*

676	A161	10m multi	15	15
677	A161	15m multi	15	15
678	A161	20m multi	15	15
679	A161	25m multi	15	15
680	A161	30m multi	18	15
681	A161	60m multi	28	15
682	A161	80m multi	35	20
683	A161	1t multi	40	24
		Nos. 676-683 (8)	1.81	
		Set value		90

Symbols of Technical Knowledge — A162

Design: 60m, University of Mongolia.

1972, Sept. 25

684	A162	50m org & multi	18	15
685	A162	60m lil & multi	20	15
		Set value		15

30th anniversary of Mongolian State University.

Virgin and Child with St. John, by Bellini — A163

Paintings by Venetian Masters: 20m, Transfiguration, by Bellini (vert.). 30m, Virgin and Child, by Bellini (vert.). 50m, Presentation in the Temple, by Bellini. 60m, St. George, by Mantegna (vert.). 80m, Departure of St. Ursula, by Carpaccio (vert.). 1t, Departure of St. Ursula, by Carpaccio.

1972, Oct. 1

686	A163	10m multi	15	15
687	A163	20m multi	15	15
688	A163	30m multi	15	15
689	A163	50m multi	20	15
690	A163	60m multi	35	18
691	A163	80m multi	40	20
692	A163	1t multi	55	24
		Nos. 686-692 (7)	1.95	
		Set value		95

Save Venice campaign. See No. B3.

Manlay Bator Ramdinsuren A164

Designs: 20m, Ard Ayus (horiz.). 50m, Hatan Bator Magsarzhav. 60m, Has Bator (horiz.). 1t, Sukhe Bator.

1972, Oct. 20 Litho. *Perf. 12*

693	A164	10m gold & multi	15	15
694	A164	20m gold & multi	15	15
695	A164	50m gold & multi	20	15

696	A164	60m gold & multi	30	18
697	A164	1t gold & multi	40	28
		Nos. 693-697 (5)	1.20	
		Set value		68

Paintings of national heroes.

Spasski Tower, Moscow — A165

1972, Nov. 7 Photo. *Perf. 11*

698	A165	60m multi	20	15

50th anniversary of USSR. Printed with small label showing arms of USSR.

Mark Spitz, US, Gold Medal — A166

Designs (Medal and): 10m, Ulrike Meyfarth, Germany. 20m, Sawao Kato, Japan. 30m, Andras Balczo, Hungary. 60m, Lasse Viren, Finland. 80m, Shane Gould, Australia. 1t, Anatoli Bondarchuk, USSR. 4t, Khorloo Baianmunk, Mongolia.

1972, Dec. 15 Photo. *Perf. 12½*

699	A166	5m grn & multi	15	15
700	A166	10m ver & multi	15	15
701	A166	20m bl & multi	15	15
702	A166	30m multi	20	15
703	A166	60m lt vio & multi	28	15
704	A166	80m ol & multi	35	18
705	A166	1t lem & multi	50	28
		Nos. 699-705 (7)	1.78	
		Set value		85

Souvenir Sheet

706	A166	4t red & multi	2.00	2.00

Winners in 20th Olympic Games, Munich.

Chimpanzee on Bicycle A167

Circus Scenes: 10m, Seal playing ball. 15m, Bear riding wheel. 20m, Woman acrobat on camel. 30m, Woman equestrian. 50m, Clown playing flute. 60m, Woman gymnast. 1t, Circus building, Ulan Bator (horiz.).

1973, Jan. 29 Litho. *Perf. 12*

707	A167	5m multi	15	15
708	A167	10m multi	15	15
709	A167	15m multi	15	15
710	A167	20m multi	15	15
711	A167	30m multi	18	15
712	A167	50m multi	20	15
713	A167	60m multi	28	15
714	A167	1t multi	38	24
		Set value	1.40	80

Postrider — A168

Designs: 60m, Diesel locomotive. 1t, Truck.

1973, Jan. 31 Photo. *Perf. 12*

715	A168	50m brown	24	15
716	A168	60m green	30	15
717	A168	1t rose claret	50	20
		Set value		36

See No. C34.

Sukhe Bator and Merchants A169

Paintings of Sukhe Bator: 20m, With elders. 50m, Leading partisans. 60m, With revolutionary council. 1t, Receiving deputation (horiz.).

1973, Feb. 2 Photo. *Perf. 11½x12*

718	A169	10m gold & multi	15	15
719	A169	20m gold & multi	15	15
720	A169	50m gold & multi	18	15
721	A169	60m gold & multi	20	18
722	A169	1t gold & multi	35	28
		Nos. 718-722 (5)	1.03	
		Set value		66

80th anniversary of birth of Sukhe Bator (1893-1923).

Nicolaus Copernicus A170

Marx and Lenin A171

Designs: 60m, 2t, Copernicus in laboratory, by Jan Matejko (horiz.; 55x35mm.). 1t (No. 725, 726b), Portrait. 1t (No. 726a), like 50m.

1973, Mar. Litho. *Perf. 12*

723	A170	50m gold & multi	18	15
724	A170	60m gold & multi	24	15
725	A170	1t gold & multi	38	20

Souvenir Sheet

726		Sheet of 3	2.00	2.00
a.	A170	1t multi	35	35
b.	A170	1t multi	35	35
c.	A170	2t multi	70	70

500th anniversary of the birth of Nicolaus Copernicus (1473-1543), Polish astronomer.

1973, July 15 Photo. *Perf. 11½x12*

727	A171	60m gold, car & ultra	28	15

9th meeting of postal administrations of socialist countries, Ulan Bator.

Common Shelducks — A172

Designs: Aquatic birds.

1973, Aug. 10 Litho. *Perf. 12x11*

728	A172	5m shown	15	15
729	A172	10m Arctic loons	15	15
730	A172	15m Bar-headed geese	15	15
731	A172	30m Great crested grebe	18	15
732	A172	50m Mallards	24	15
733	A172	60m Mute swans	30	20
734	A172	1t Greater scaups	55	28
		Nos. 728-734 (7)	1.72	
		Set value		88

1973, Aug. 25 Litho. *Perf. 12x11*

Designs: Fur-bearing animals.

735	A172	5m Siberian weasel	15	15
736	A172	10m Siberian chipmunk	15	15
737	A172	15m Flying squirrel	15	15
738	A172	20m Eurasian badger	15	15
739	A172	30m Eurasian red squirrel	15	15
740	A172	60m Wolverine	20	15
741	A172	80m Mink	24	20
742	A172	1t White hare	30	24
		Set value	1.15	90

1973, Dec. 15 Litho. *Perf. 12x11*

Designs: Flowers.

743	A172	5m Alpine aster	15	15
744	A172	10m Mongolian silene	15	15
745	A172	15m Rosa davurica	15	15
746	A172	20m Mongolian dandelion	15	15
747	A172	30m Rhododendron dahuricum	15	15
748	A172	50m Clematis tanguti-ca	18	15
749	A172	60m Siberian primula	24	18
750	A172	1t Pasqueflower	35	24
		Set value	1.20	90

Globe and Red Flag Emblem — A173

1973, Dec. 10 Photo. *Perf. 12x12½*

751	A173	60m gold, red & bl	28	15

15th anniversary of the review "Problems of Peace and Socialism," published in Prague.

Limenitis Populi A174

Butterflies: 10m, Arctia hebe. 15m, Rhyparia purpurata. 20m, Catocala pacta. 30m, Isoceras kaszabi. 50m, Celerio costata. 60m, Arctia caja. 1t, Diacrisia sannio.

1974, Jan. 15 Litho. *Perf. 11*

752	A174	5m lil & multi	15	15
753	A174	10m brn & multi	15	15
754	A174	15m bl & multi	15	15
755	A174	20m brn org & multi	15	15
756	A174	30m lt vio & multi	15	15
757	A174	50m dl red & multi	20	16
758	A174	60m yel grn & multi	28	24
759	A174	1t ultra & multi	40	30
		Set value	1.35	1.00

"Hehe Namshil" by L. Merdorsh A175

Designs (Various Scenes from): 20m, "Sive Hiagt," by D. Luvsansharav. 25m, 80m, 1t, "Edre," by D. Namdag. 30m, "The 3 Khans of Sara-Gol" (legend). 60m, "Amarsana," by B. Damdinsuren. 20m and 30m horizontal.

1974, Feb. 20 Litho. *Perf. 12*

760	A175	15m sil & multi	15	15
761	A175	20m sil & multi	15	15
762	A175	25m sil & multi	15	15
763	A175	30m sil & multi	18	15
764	A175	60m sil & multi	24	15
765	A175	80m sil & multi	35	18
766	A175	1t sil & multi	38	20
		Nos. 760-766 (7)	1.60	
		Set value		80

Mongolian operas and dramas.

Government Building and Sukhe Bator — A176

1974, Mar. 1 Photo. *Perf. 11*

767	A176	60m gold & multi	20	15

50th anniv. of renaming capital Ulan Bator.

Juggler A177

Designs: 10m, Dressage (horiz.). 30m, Trained elephant. 40m, Yak pushing ball (horiz.). 60m, Acrobats with ring. 80m, Woman acrobat on unicycle.

1974, May 4 Litho. *Perf. 12*

768	A177	10m multi	15	15
769	A177	20m multi	15	15
770	A177	30m multi	15	15
771	A177	40m multi	16	15

772 A177 60m multi 28 20
773 A177 80m multi 35 24
Nos. 768-773,C65 (7) 1.72
Set value 1.00

Mongolian Circus. No. 773 has se-tenant label, with similar design.

Girl on Bronco A178

Children's Activities: 20m, Boy roping calf. 30m, 40m, Boy taming horse (different designs). 60m, Girl with doves. 80m, Wrestling. 1t, Dancing.

1974, June 2 **Litho.** ***Perf. 12***
774 A178 10m dl yel & multi 15 15
775 A178 20m lt bl & multi 15 15
776 A178 30m grn & multi 15 15
777 A178 40m yel & multi 18 15
778 A178 60m pink & multi 24 15
779 A178 80m lil & multi 35 18
780 A178 1t dl bl & multi 38 20
Set value 1.35 72

Children's Day.

Archer — A179

National Sports: 20m, Two horsemen fighting for goatskin. 30m, Archer on horseback. 40m, Horse race. 60m, Riding wild horse. 80m, Rider chasing riderless horse. 1t, Boys wrestling.

1974, July 11 **Photo.** ***Perf. 11***
781 A179 10m vio bl & multi 15 15
782 A179 20m yel & multi 15 15
783 A179 30m lil & multi 15 15
784 A179 40m multi 15 15
785 A179 60m multi 20 15
786 A179 80m multi 30 18
787 A179 1t multi 45 24
Set value 1.30 76

Nadam, Mongolian national festival.

Grizzly Bear — A180

1974, July **Litho.** ***Perf. 12***
788 A180 10m shown 15 15
789 A180 20m Common panda 15 15
790 A180 30m Giant panda 15 15
791 A180 40m Two brown bears 18 15
792 A180 60m Sloth bear 28 15
793 A180 80m Asiatic black bears 40 18
794 A180 1t Giant brown bear 55 20
Nos. 788-794 (7) 1.86
Set value 80

Stag in Zuun Araat Wildlife Preserve — A181

1974, Sept. **Litho.** ***Perf. 12***
795 A181 10m shown 15 15
796 A181 20m Beaver 15 15
797 A181 30m Leopard 15 15
798 A181 40m Great black-backed gull 15 15
799 A181 60m Deer 20 15
800 A181 80m Mouflon 30 20
801 A181 1t Deer and entrance to Bogd-uul Preserve 45 28
Set value 1.30 90

Protected fauna in Mongolian wildlife preserves.

Buddhist Temple, Bogdo Gegen Palace — A182

Mongolian Architecture: 15m, Buddhist Temple, now Museum. 30m, Entrance to Charity Temple, Ulan Bator. 50m, Mongolian yurta. 80m, Gazebo in convent yard.

1974, Oct. 15 **Litho.** ***Perf. 12***
802 A182 10m bl & multi 15 15
803 A182 15m multi 15 15
804 A182 30m grn & multi 15 15
805 A182 50m multi 24 15
806 A182 80m yel & multi 40 24
Set value 88 56

Spasski Tower, Sukhe Bator Statue — A183

1974, Nov. 26 **Photo.** ***Perf. 11½x12***
807 A183 60m multi 28 15

Visit of General Secretary Brezhnev and a delegation from the USSR to participate in celebration of 50th anniversary of People's Republic of Mongolia.

Sukhe Bator Proclaiming Republic — A184

Designs: No. 808, "First Constitution," symbolic embroidery. No. 809, Flag over landscape, lane and communications tower.

1974, Nov. 28 **Litho.**
808 A184 60m multi 28 15
809 A184 60m multi 28 15
810 A184 60m multi 28 15
Set value 30

50th anniversary of People's Republic of Mongolia.

Decanter A185

Designs: 20m, Silver jar. 30m, Night lamp. 40m, Tea jug. 60m, Candelabra. 80m, Teapot. 1t, Silver bowl on 3-legged stand.

1974, Dec. 1 **Photo.**
811 A185 10m bl & multi 15 15
812 A185 20m cl & multi 15 15
813 A185 30m multi 15 15
814 A185 40m dp bl & multi 15 15
815 A185 60m multi 20 15
816 A185 80m grn & multi 35 18
817 A185 1t lil & multi 45 24
Set value 1.35 75

Mongolian 19th century goldsmiths' work.

Lapwing (plover) — A186

1974, Dec. **Litho.** ***Perf. 11***
818 A186 10m shown 15 15
819 A186 20m Fish 15 15
820 A186 30m Marsh marigolds 16 15
821 A186 40m White pelican 25 15
822 A186 60m Perch 32 20
823 A186 80m Mink 50 28
Nos. 818-823,C66 (7) 2.08
Set value 1.10

Water and nature protection.

American Mail Coach, UPU Emblem — A187

Designs (UPU Emblem and): 20m, French two-wheeled coach. 30m, Changing horses, Russian coach. 40m, Swedish caterpillar mail truck. 50m, First Hungarian mail truck. 60m, German Daimler-Benz mail truck. 1t, Mongolian dispatch rider.

1974, Dec. **Litho.** ***Perf. 12***
824 A187 10m multi 15 15
825 A187 20m multi 15 15
826 A187 30m multi 15 15
827 A187 40m multi 18 15
828 A187 50m multi 20 15
829 A187 60m multi 28 15
830 A187 1t multi 45 24
Nos. 824-830 (7) 1.56
Set value 80

See note after No. C68.

Mongolian Flag, Broken Swastika — A188

1975, May 9 **Photo.** ***Perf. 11½x12***
832 A188 60m multi 28 15

30th anniversary of the end of World War II and victory over fascism.

Mongolian Woman A189

1975, May
833 A189 60m multi 28 15

International Women's Year 1975.

Zygophyllum Xanthoxylon — A190

Medicinal Plants: 20m, Ingarvillea potaninii. 30m, Lancea tibetica. 40m, Jurinea mongolica. 50m, Saussurea involucrata. 60m, Allium mongolicum. 1t, Adonis mongolica.

1975, May 24 **Photo.** ***Perf. 11x11½***
834 A190 10m dp org & multi 15 15
835 A190 20m grn & multi 15 15
836 A190 30m yel & multi 15 15
837 A190 40m vio & multi 15 15
838 A190 50m brn & multi 24 15
839 A190 60m bl & multi 28 18
840 A190 1t multi 48 28
Set value 1.35 88

12th International Botanists' Conference.

Shepherd — A191

Puppet Theater: 20m, Boy on horseback. 30m, Boy and disobedient bull calf. 40m, Little orphan camel's tale. 50m, Boy and obedient little yak. 60m, Boy riding swan. 1t, Children's choir.

1975, June 30 **Litho.** ***Perf. 12***
841 A191 10m multi 15 15
842 A191 20m multi 15 15
843 A191 30m multi 15 15
844 A191 40m multi 15 15
845 A191 50m multi 24 15

846 A191 60m multi 28 18
847 A191 1t multi 48 28
Set value 1.35 88

Pioneers Tending Fruit Tree — A192

Designs: 60m, Pioneers studying, and flying model plane. 1t, New emblem of Mongolian Pioneers.

1975, July 15 ***Perf. 12x11½***
848 A192 50m multi 20 15
849 A192 60m multi 24 15
850 A192 1t multi 35 24
Set value 44

Mongolian Pioneers, 50th anniversary.

Nos. 624-630 Overprinted — Тээвэр—50 1975—7—15

1975, July 15 **Litho.** ***Perf. 12***
850A A151 20m multi 85 85
850B A151 30m multi 85 85
850C A151 40m multi 1.25 1.25
850D A151 50m multi 1.25 1.25
850E A151 60m multi 1.40 1.40
850E A151 80m multi 2.00 2.00
850G A151 1t multi 2.50 2.50
Nos. 850A-850G (7) 10.10 10.10

Fifty years of communication.

Golden Eagle Hunting Fox — A193

Hunting Scenes: 20m, Dogs treeing lynx (vert.). 30m, Hunter stalking marmots. 40m, Hunter riding reindeer (vert.). 50m, Boar hunt. 60m, Trapped wolf (vert.). 1t, Bear hunt.

1975, Aug. 25 **Litho.** ***Perf. 12***
851 A193 10m multi 15 15
852 A193 20m multi 20 15
853 A193 30m multi 30 15
854 A193 40m multi 35 15
855 A193 50m multi 45 18
856 A193 60m multi 60 20
857 A193 1t multi 1.00 35
Nos. 851-857 (7) 3.05
Set value 1.00

Hunting in Mongolia.

Mesocottus Haitej — A194

Various Fish: 20m, Pseudaspius leptocephalus. 30m, Oreoleuciscus potanini. 40m, Tinca tinca. 50m, Coregonus lavaretus pidschian. 60m, Erythroculter mongolicus. 1t, Carassius auratus.

1975, Sept. 15 **Photo.** ***Perf. 11***
858 A194 10m multi 15 15
859 A194 20m multi 15 15
860 A194 30m multi 15 15
861 A194 40m bl & multi 18 15
862 A194 50m grn & multi 28 18
863 A194 60m lil & multi 35 20
864 A194 1t vio bl & multi 55 35
Nos. 858-864 (7) 1.81
Set value 1.00

Neck and Bow of Musical Instrument (Morin Hur) — A195

National Handicraft: 20m, Saddle. 30m, Silver headgear. 40m, Boots. 50m, Tasseled Woman's cap. 60m, Pipe and tobacco pouch. 1t, Sable cap.

Perf. 11½x12½
1975, Oct. 10 **Litho.**
865 A195 10m multi 15 15
866 A195 20m multi 15 15
867 A195 30m multi 15 15
868 A195 40m multi 18 15
869 A195 50m multi 28 18
870 A195 60m multi 35 20
871 A195 1t multi 55 35
Nos. 865-871 (7) 1.81
Set value 1.00

Revolutionists with Flags — A196

1975, Nov. 15 **Litho.** ***Perf. 11½x12***
872 A196 60m multi 28 15

70th anniversary of Russian Revolution.

Ski Jump, Olympic Games Emblem A197

Designs (Winter Olympic Games Emblem and): 20m, Ice hockey. 30m, Skiing. 40m, Bobsled. 50m, Biathlon. 60m, Speed skating. 1t, Figure skating, women's. 4t, Skier carrying torch.

Perf. 11½x12½
1975, Dec. 20 **Litho.**
873 A197 10m multi 15 15
874 A197 20m multi 15 15
875 A197 30m brn & multi 15 15
876 A197 40m grn & multi 18 15
877 A197 50m multi 28 18
878 A197 60m ol & multi 35 20
879 A197 1t multi 55 35
Nos. 873-879 (7) 1.81
Set value 1.00

Souvenir Sheet

880 A197 4t multi 3.00 3.00

12th Winter Olympic Games, Innsbruck, Austria, Feb. 4-15, 1976.

Taming Wild Horse A198

Mongolian Paintings: 20m, Camel caravan (horiz.). 30m, Man playing lute. 40m, Woman adjusting headdress (horiz.). 50m, Woman wearing ceremonial costume. 60m, Women fetching water. 1t, Woman musician. 4t, Warrior on horseback.

1975, Nov. 30 ***Perf. 12***
881 A198 10m brn & multi 15 15
882 A198 20m bl & multi 15 15
883 A198 30m ol & multi 15 15
884 A198 40m lil & multi 15 15
885 A198 50m bl & multi 24 18
886 A198 60m lil & multi 28 18
887 A198 1t sil & multi 48 30
Set value 1.40 95

Souvenir Sheet

888 A198 4t bl & multi 1.75 1.75

House of Young Technicians A199

Designs: 60m, Hotel Ulan Bator. 1t, Museum of the Revolution.

1975, Dec. 30 **Photo.** ***Perf. 12x11½***
893 A199 50m ultra 20 15
894 A199 60m bl grn 40 15
895 A199 1t brick red 60 20
Set value 40

Camels in Gobi Desert — A200

Designs: 20m, Horse taming. 30m, Horseback riding. 40m, Pioneers' camp. 60m, Young musician. 80m, Children's festival. 1t, Mongolian wrestling.

1976, June 1 **Litho.** ***Perf. 12***
896 A200 10m multi 15 15
897 A200 20m multi 15 15
898 A200 30m multi 15 15
899 A200 40m multi 20 15
900 A200 60m multi 35 15
901 A200 80m multi 48 24
902 A200 1t multi 60 28
Nos. 896-902 (7) 2.08
Set value 90

International Children's Day.

Red Star — A201

1976, May 1 **Photo.** ***Perf. 11x12½***
903 A201 60m red, mar & sil 30 15

17th Congress of the Mongolian People's Revolutionary Party, June 14.

Archery, Montreal Games' Emblem, Canadian Flag — A202

Designs (Montreal Olympic Games' Emblem, Canadian Flag and): 20m, Judo. 30m, Boxing. 40m, Vaulting. 60m, Weight lifting. 80m, High Jump. 1t, Target shooting.

Perf. 12½x11½
1976, May 20 **Litho.**
904 A202 10m yel & multi 15 15
905 A202 20m yel & multi 15 15
906 A202 30m yel & multi 15 15
907 A202 40m yel & multi 18 15
908 A202 60m yel & multi 28 15
909 A202 80m yel & multi 35 24
910 A202 1t yel & multi 45 28
Set value 1.45 90

21st Olympic Games, Montreal, Canada, July 17-Aug. 1. See No. C81.

Partisans A203

Fighter and Sojombo Independence Symbol A204

Perf. 12x11½, 11½x12
1976, June 15 **Litho.**
911 A203 60m multi 35 15
912 A204 60m multi 40 15

55th anniversary of Mongolia's independence. See No. C82.

Souvenir Sheet

Sukhe Bator Medal — A205

1976, July 11 *Perf. 11½*
913 A205 4t multi 1.75 1.75

Mongolian honors medals.

Osprey — A206

Protected Birds: 20m, Griffon vulture. 30m, Bearded lammergeier. 40m, Marsh harrier. 60m, Black vulture. 80m, Golden eagle. 1t, Tawny eagle.

1976, Aug. 16 **Litho.** *Perf. 12*
914 A206 10m multi 15 15
915 A206 20m multi 15 15
916 A206 30m multi 15 15
917 A206 40m multi 20 15
918 A206 60m multi 35 18
919 A206 80m multi 40 28
920 A206 1t multi 55 35
Nos. 914-920 (7) 1.95
Set value 1.05

"Nadom" Military Game — A207

Paintings by O. Cevegshava: 10m, Taming Wild Horse (vert.). 30m, Hubsugul Lake Harbor. 40m, The Steppe Awakening. 80m, Wrestlers. 1.60t, Yak Descending in Snow (vert.).

1976, Sept. **Litho.** *Perf. 12*
921 A207 10m multi 15 15
922 A207 20m multi 15 15
923 A207 30m multi 15 15
924 A207 40m multi 20 15
925 A207 80m multi 40 24
926 A207 1.60t multi 55 28
Nos. 921-926 (6) 1.60
Set value 78

Interlocking Circles, Industry and Transport — A208

1976, Oct. 15 **Photo.** *Perf. 12x11½*
927 A208 60m brn, bl & red 35 18

Soviet-Mongolian friendship.

John Naber, US Flag, Gold Medals — A209

Designs: 20m, Nadia Comaneci, Romanian flag. 30m, Kornelia Ender, East German flag. 40m, Mitsuo Tsukahara, Japanese flag. 60m, Gregor Braun, German flag. 80m, Lasse Viren, Finnish flag. 1t, Nikolai Andrianov, Russian flag.

1976, Nov. 30 **Litho.** *Perf. 12*
928 A209 10m multi 15 15
929 A209 20m multi 15 15
930 A209 30m multi 15 15
931 A209 40m multi 20 15
932 A209 60m multi 35 15
933 A209 80m multi 40 24
934 A209 1t multi 55 28
Nos. 928-934 (7) 1.95
Set value 90

Gold medal winners, 21st Olympic Games, Montreal. See No. C83.

Stone Tablet on Tortoise A210

Carved Tablet, 6th-8th Centuries A211

1976, Dec. 15 **Litho.** *Perf. 11½x12*
935 A210 50m brn & lt bl 85 15
936 A211 60m gray & brt grn 1.25 15
Set value 24

International Archaeological Conference, Ulan Bator.

R-1 Plane — A212

Designs: Various Mongolian planes.

1976, Dec. 22 *Perf. 12*
937 A212 10m multi 15 15
938 A212 20m multi 15 15
939 A212 30m multi 15 15
940 A212 40m multi 18 15
941 A212 60m multi 35 18
942 A212 80m multi 40 24
943 A212 1t multi 48 30
Nos. 937-943 (7) 1.86
Set value 95

Dancers — A213

Folk Dances: 20m, 13th century costumes. 30m, West Mongolian dance. 40m, "Ekachi," or horse-dance. 60m, "Bielge," West Mongolian trunk dance. 80m, "Hodak," or friendship dance. 1t, "Dojarka."

1977, Mar. 20 **Litho.** *Perf. 12½*
944 A213 10m multi 15 15
945 A213 20m multi 15 15
946 A213 30m multi 15 15
947 A213 40m multi 18 15
948 A213 60m multi 35 18
949 A213 80m multi 40 28
950 A213 1t multi 48 35
Nos. 944-950 (7) 1.86
Set value 1.10

Miniature Sheet

Path of Pioneer from Earth to Jupiter, deflected by Mars — A214

Isaac Newton — A215

1977, Mar. 31 **Litho.** *Perf. 11½x12*
951 Sheet of 9 2.00 85
a. A214 60m shown 20 15
b. A215 60m Apple tree 20 15
c. A214 60m Sextant and planets 20 15
d. A214 60m Astronauts in space 20 15
e. A215 60m shown 20 15
f. A214 60m Prism and spectrum 20 15
g. A214 60m Rain falling on earth 20 15
h. A215 60m Motion of celestial bodies 20 15
i. A214 60m Pioneer 10 over Jupiter 20 15

Sir Isaac Newton (1642-1727), English natural philosopher and mathematician.

Nos. 951a-951i arranged in 3 rows of 3. Nos. 951d and 951i inscribed AIR MAIL.

D. Natsagdorji, Writer, and Quotation — A216

Design: No. 953, Grazing horses, landscape, ornament and quotation.

1977 *Perf. 11½x12*
952 A216 60m multi 35 18
953 A216 60m multi 40 18

D. Natsagdorji, founder of modern Mongolian literature. Label and vignette separated by simulated perforations.

Primitive Tortoises — A217

Prehistoric Animals: 20m, Ungulate (titanothere). 30m, Flying lizard. 40m, Entelodon (swine). 60m, Antelope. 80m, Hipparion. 1t, Aurochs.

1977, May 7 **Photo.** *Perf. 12½*
954 A217 10m multi 15 15
955 A217 20m multi 15 15
956 A217 30m multi 15 15
957 A217 40m multi 18 15
958 A217 60m multi 35 18
959 A217 80m multi 40 28
960 A217 1t multi 48 35
Nos. 954-960 (7) 1.86
Set value 1.10

Souvenir Sheet

Mongolia, Type A2 and Netherlands No. 1 — A218

1977, May 20
961 A218 4t multi 2.00 2.00

AMPHILEX '77 International Philatelic Exhibition, Amsterdam, May 27-June 5. No. 961 contains one 37x52mm stamp.

Boys on Horseback — A219

Designs: 20m, Girl on horseback. 30m, Hunter on horseback. 40m, Grazing horses. 60m, Mare and foal. 80m, Grazing horse and student. 1t, White stallion.

1977, June 15 **Litho.** *Perf. 12*
962 A219 10m multi 15 15
963 A219 20m multi 18 15
964 A219 30m multi 24 15
965 A219 40m multi 38 15
966 A219 60m multi 65 15
967 A219 80m multi 75 24
968 A219 1t multi 1.00 28
Nos. 962-968 (7) 3.35
Set value 90

Copper and Molybdenum Plant, Vehicles — A220

1977, June 15 **Litho.** *Perf. 12*
969 A220 60m multi 35 18

Erdenet, a new industrial town.

Bucket Brigade Fighting Fire — A221

Fire Fighting: 20m, Horse-drawn fire pump. 30m, Horse-drawn steam pump. 40m, Men in protective suits fighting forest fire. 60m, Modern foam extinguisher. 80m, Truck and ladder. 1t, Helicopter fighting fire on steppe.

1977, Aug. **Litho.** *Perf. 12*
970 A221 10m multi 15 15
971 A221 20m multi 15 15
972 A221 30m multi 15 15

973 A221 40m multi 20 15
974 A221 60m multi 35 18
975 A221 80m multi 40 28
976 A221 1t multi 55 35
Nos. 970-976 (7) 1.95
Set value 1.05

Radar and Molnya Satellite on TV Screen — A222

1977, Sept. 12 Photo. *Perf. 12x11½*
977 A222 60m gray, bl & blk 35 18

40th anniversary of Technical Institute.

Lenin Museum, Ulan Bator A223

1977, Oct. 1 Litho. *Perf. 12*
978 A223 60m multi 40 18

Inauguration of Lenin Museum in connection with the 60th anniversary of the Russian October Revolution.

Dove, Globe, Decree of Peace A224

Designs: 50m, Cruiser Aurora and Russian flag (vert.). 1.50t, Globe and "Freedom."

Perf. 11½x12, 12x11½

1977, Oct. 1 Photo.
979 A224 50m gold & multi 28 15
980 A224 60m gold & multi 35 18
981 A224 1.50t gold & multi 80 48

60th anniversary of the Russian Revolution.

Aporia Crataegi — A225

Moths: 20m, Gastropacha quercifolia. 30m, Colias chrysoteme. 40m, Dasychira fascelina. 60m, Malocosoma neustria. 80m, Diacrisia sanno. 1t, Heodes virgaureae.

1977, Sept. 25 Photo. *Perf. 12½*
982 A225 10m multi 15 15
983 A225 20m multi 15 15
984 A225 30m multi 18 15
985 A225 40m multi 24 15
986 A225 60m multi 38 18
987 A225 80m multi 48 28
988 A225 1t multi 60 35
Nos. 982-988 (7) 2.18
Set value 1.05

An enhanced introduction to the Scott Catalogue begins on Page 1A. A thorough understanding of the material presented there will greatly aid your use of the catalogue itself.

Giant Pandas — A226

Pandas: 10m, Eating bamboo (vert.). 30m, Female and cub in washtub (vert.). 40m, Male and cub playing with bamboo. 60m, Female and cub (vert.). 80m, Family. 1t, Male (vert.).

1977, Nov. 25 Litho. *Perf. 12*
989 A226 10m multi 15 15
990 A226 20m multi 15 15
991 A226 30m multi 15 15
992 A226 40m multi 20 15
993 A226 60m multi 35 18
994 A226 80m multi 40 28
995 A226 1t multi 55 35
Nos. 989-995 (7) 1.95
Set value 1.05

Souvenir Sheet

Helen Fourment and her Children, by Rubens — A227

1977, Dec. 5 *Perf. 11½x10½*
996 A227 4t multi 2.25 2.25

Peter Paul Rubens (1577-1640).

Ferrari Racing Car — A228

Experimental Racing Cars: 30m, Ford McLaren. 40m, Madi, USSR. 50m, Mazda. 60m, Porsche. 80m, Russian model car. 1.20t, The Blue Flame, US speed car.

1978, Jan. 28 Litho. *Perf. 12*
997 A228 20m multi 15 15
998 A228 30m multi 15 15
999 A228 40m multi 18 15
1000 A228 50m multi 24 18
1001 A228 60m multi 28 20
1002 A228 80m multi 35 28
1003 A228 1.20t multi 55 38
Nos. 997-1003 (7) 1.90
Set value 1.25

Boletus Variegatus — A229

Mushrooms: 30m, Russula cyanoxantha. 40m, Boletus aurantiacus. 50m, Boletus scaber. 60m, Russula flava. 80m, Lactarius resimus. 1.20t, Flammula spumosa.

1978, Feb. 28 Photo. *Perf. 11x11½*
1004 A229 20m yel & multi 15 15
1005 A229 30m yel & multi 15 15
1006 A229 40m yel & multi 18 15
1007 A229 50m yel & multi 24 18
1008 A229 60m yel & multi 30 20
1009 A229 80m yel & multi 38 28
1010 A229 1.20t yel & multi 60 38
Nos. 1004-1010 (7) 2.00
Set value 1.25

Young Couple with Youth Flag — A230

1978, Apr. Litho. *Perf. 11½x12*
1011 A230 60m multi 35 18

17th Congress of Mongolian Youth Organization, Ulan Bator, Apr. 1978.

Soccer, Sugar Loaf Mountain, Rio de Janeiro, Brazil 1950 Emblem — A231

Designs (Various Soccer Scenes and): 30m, Old Town Tower, Bern, Switzerland, 1954. 40m, Town Hall, Stockholm, Sweden, 1958. 50m, University of Chile, Chile, 1962. 60m, Parliament and Big Ben, London, 1966. 80m, Degolladeo Theater, Guadalajara, Mexico, 1970. 1.20t, Town Hall and TV Tower, Munich, Germany.

1978, Apr. 15 *Perf. 12*
1012 A231 20m multi 15 15
1013 A231 30m multi 15 15
1014 A231 40m multi 20 15
1015 A231 50m multi 28 15
1016 A231 60m multi 35 18
1017 A231 80m multi 40 20
1018 A231 1.20t multi 70 28
Nos. 1012-1018 (7) 2.23
Set value 1.00

11th World Cup Soccer Championship, Argentina, June 1-25. See No. C109.

Capex Emblem, Eurasian Beaver and Canada No. 336 — A232

Designs: 30m, Tibetan sand grouse and Canada No. 478. 40m, Red-throated loon and Canada No. 369. 50m, Argali and Canada No. 324. 60m, Eurasian brown bear and Canada No. 322. 80m, Moose and Canada No. 323. 1.20t, Great black-backed gull and Canada No. 343.

1978, June Litho. *Perf. 12*
1019 A232 20m multi 15 15
1020 A232 30m multi 15 15
1021 A232 40m multi 18 15
1022 A232 50m multi 20 18
1023 A232 60m multi 28 20
1024 A232 80m multi 40 30
1025 A232 1.20t multi 60 40
Nos. 1019-1025 (7) 1.96
Set value 1.30

CAPEX '78 International Philatelic Exhibition, Toronto, June 9-18. See No. C110.

Marx, Engels and Lenin A233

1978, July 11 Photo. *Perf. 12x11½*
1026 A233 60m gold, blk & red 35 18

50th anniversary of publication in Prague of "Problems of Peace and Socialism."

Souvenir Sheet

Outdoor Rest, by Amgalan — A234

Paintings by D. Amgalan: No. 1027b, Winter Night (dromedary and people in snow). No. 1027c, Saddling up.

1978, Aug. 10 Litho. *Perf. 12*
1027 Sheet of 3 2.75 2.75
a.-c. A234 1.50t any single 80

Philatelic cooperation between Hungary and Mongolia, 20th anniversary. No. 1027 contains 3 stamps and 3 labels.

Papillon — A235

Dogs: 20m, Black Mongolian sheepdog. 30m, Puli. 40m, St. Bernard. 50m, German shepherd. 60m, Mongolian watchdog. 70m, Samoyed. 80m, Laika (1st dog in space) and rocket. 1.20t, Cocker spaniels and poodle.

1978, Sept. 25 Litho. *Perf. 12*
1028 A235 10m multi 15 15
1029 A235 20m multi 15 15
1030 A235 30m multi 15 15
1031 A235 40m multi 18 15
1032 A235 50m multi 20 15
1033 A235 60m multi 24 15
1034 A235 70m multi 28 18
1035 A235 80m multi 30 20
1036 A235 1.20t multi 50 24
Nos. 1028-1036 (9) 2.15
Set value 1.10

Open Book and Pen — A236

1978, Oct. 20 Photo. *Perf. 12x11½*
1037 A236 60m car & ultra 35 18

Mongolian Writers' Association, 50th anniversary.

Souvenir Sheets

Clothed Maya, by Goya — A237

Melancholy, by Dürer — A238

Paintings: No. 1038b, "Ta Matete," by Gauguin. No. 1038c, Bridge at Arles, by Van Gogh.

1978, Oct. 30 **Litho.** ***Perf. 12***

1038	Sheet of 3 + 3 labels	2.75	2.75
a.-c.	A237 1.50t any single	80	80

Perf. 11½

1039	A238 4t black	2.25	2.25

Anniversaries of European painters: Francisco Goya; Paul Gauguin; Vincent van Gogh; Albrecht Dürer.

Camel and Calf — A239

Bactrian Camels: 30m, Young camel. 40m, Two camels. 50m, Woman leading pack camel. 60m, Old camel. 80m, Camel pulling cart. 1.20t, Race.

1978, Nov. 30 **Litho.** ***Perf. 12***

1040	A239 20m multi	15	15
1041	A239 30m multi	15	15
1042	A239 40m multi	20	15
1043	A239 50m multi	24	15
1044	A239 60m multi	35	15
1045	A239 80m multi	40	15
1046	A239 1.20t multi	60	20
	Nos. 1040-1046 (7)	2.09	
	Set value		75

Flags of Comecon Members, Globe A240

1979, Jan. 2 **Litho.** ***Perf. 12***

1047	A240 60m multi	28	15

30th anniversary of the Council of Mutual Assistance (Comecon).

Silver Tabby — A241

Domestic Cats: 30m, White Persian. 50m, Red Persian. 60m, Cream Persian. 70m, Siamese. 80m, Smoky Persian. 1t, Burmese.

1979, Feb. 10

1048	A241 10m multi	15	15
1049	A241 30m multi	15	15
1050	A241 50m multi	20	15
1051	A241 60m multi	24	15
1052	A241 70m multi	28	15
1053	A241 80m multi	35	18
1054	A241 1t multi	40	28
	Nos. 1048-1054 (7)	1.77	
	Set value		98

Potaninia Mongolica — A242

Flowers: 30m, Sophora alopecuroides. 50m, Halimodendron halodendron. 60m, Forget-me-nots. 70m, Pincushion flower. 80m, Leucanthemum Sibiricum. 1t, Edelweiss.

1979, Mar. 10 **Litho.** ***Perf. 12***

1055	A242 10m multi	15	15
1056	A242 30m multi	15	15
1057	A242 50m multi	22	15
1058	A242 60m multi	28	15
1059	A242 70m multi	30	15
1060	A242 80m multi	38	15
1061	A242 1t multi	45	18
	Nos. 1055-1061 (7)	1.93	
	Set value		75

Finland-Czechoslovakia, Finnish Flag — A243

Ice Hockey Games and 1980 Olympic Emblems: 30m, German Fed. Rep.-Sweden, German flag. 50m, USA-Canada, US flag. 60m, USSR-Sweden, Russian flag. 70m, Canada-USSR, Canadian flag. 80m, Swedish goalie and flag. 1t, Czechoslovakia-USSR, Czechoslovak flag.

1979, Apr. 10 **Litho.** ***Perf. 12***

1062	A243 10m multi	15	15
1063	A243 30m multi	15	15
1064	A243 50m multi	22	15
1065	A243 60m multi	28	15
1066	A243 70m multi	35	15
1067	A243 80m multi	40	18
1068	A243 1t multi	50	20
	Nos. 1062-1068 (7)	2.05	
	Set value		82

Ice Hockey World Championship, Moscow, Apr. 14-27.

Lambs — A244

Paintings: 30m, Milking, camels. 50m, Plane bringing supplies in winter. 60m, Herdsmen and horses. 70m, Milkmaids (vert.). 80m, Summer Evening (camels). 1t, Landscape with herd. 4t, After the Storm.

Perf. 12x11½, 11½x12

1979, May 3 **Litho.**

1069	A244 10m multi	15	15
1070	A244 30m multi	15	15
1071	A244 50m multi	18	15
1072	A244 60m multi	24	15
1073	A244 70m multi	32	15
1074	A244 80m multi	40	18
1075	A244 1t multi	48	20
	Nos. 1069-1075 (7)	1.92	
	Set value		82

Souvenir Sheet

1076	A244 4t multi	2.25	2.25

20th anniv. of 1st agricultural cooperative.

Souvenir Sheet

Mongolia No. 4, Bulgaria No. 1, Philaserdica Emblem — A245

Designs (Rowland Hill and): No. 1077b, American mail coach. No. 1077c, Mail car, London-Birmingham railroad, 1838. 1077d, Packet leaving Southampton, Sept. 24, 1842, opening Indian mail service.

1979, May 15 **Litho.** ***Perf. 12***

1077	Sheet of 4, multi	1.75	1.75
a.-d.	A245 1t any single	38	38

Philaserdica '79, Sofia, May 18-27, and Rowland Hill (1795-1879), originator of penny postage.

Rocket, Manchester, 1829 — A246

Locomotives: 20m, "Adler" Nuremberg-Furth, 1835. 30m, American engine, 1860. 40m, Ulan Bator-Nalajh run, 1931. 50m, Moscow-Ulan Bator run, 1936. 60m, Moscow-Ulan Bator, 1970. 70m, Tokyo-Osaka run, 1963. 80m, Orleans Aerotrain, 1967. 1.20t, Soviet Rapidity, experimental train.

1979, June 8 **Litho.** ***Perf. 12***

1078	A246 10m multi	15	15
1079	A246 20m multi	15	15
1080	A246 30m multi	15	15
1081	A246 40m multi	18	15
1082	A246 50m multi	20	15
1083	A246 60m multi	28	15
1084	A246 70m multi	30	15
1085	A246 80m multi	35	15
1086	A246 1.20t multi	48	20
	Nos. 1078-1086 (9)	2.24	
	Set value		85

Intl. Transportation Exhibition, Hamburg.

Mongolian and Russian Flags — A247

Battle Scene and Emblem — A248

1979, Aug. 10 **Photo.** ***Perf. 11½x12***

1087	A247 60m multi	28	15
1088	A248 60m multi	28	15
	Set value		24

Battle of Ha-lo-hsin River, 40th anniversary.

Manuls A249

Wild Cats: 30m, Lynx. 50m, Tigers. 60m, Snow leopards. 70m, Black panthers. 80m, Leopards. 1t, Lions.

1979, Sept. 10 **Litho.** ***Perf. 12***

1089	A249 10m multi	15	15
1090	A249 30m multi	15	15
1091	A249 50m multi	20	15
1092	A249 60m multi	24	15
1093	A249 70m multi	28	15
1094	A249 80m multi	35	15
1095	A249 1t multi	40	18
	Nos. 1089-1095 (7)	1.77	
	Set value		72

Souvenir Sheet

Brazil No. 1582 A250

Designs: No. 1096b, Brazil No. 1144 (Pele). No. 1096c, Mongolia No. C1.

1979, Sept. 15 **Litho.** ***Perf. 11***

1096	Sheet of 3 + 3 labels	2.50	2.50
a.-c.	A250 1.50t any single	75	75

Brasiliana '79, 3rd World Thematic Stamp Exhibition, Rio de Janeiro, Sept. 15-23.

Cross-Country Skiing, Lake Placid '80 Emblem A251

Lake Placid '80 Emblem and: 30m, Biathlon. 40m, Ice hockey. 50m, Ski jump. 60m, Downhill skiing. 80m, Speed skating. 1.20t, Bobsledding. 4t, Figure skating.

Perf. 11½x12½

1980, Jan. 20 **Litho.**

1097	A251 20m multi	15	15
1098	A251 30m multi	16	15
1099	A251 40m multi	22	15
1100	A251 50m multi	25	15
1101	A251 60m multi	35	15
1102	A251 80m multi	42	15
1103	A251 1.20t multi	65	22
	Nos. 1097-1103 (7)	2.20	

Set value 75

Souvenir Sheet

1104 A251 4t multi 2.75 2.75

13th Winter Olympic Games, Lake Placid, N.Y., Feb. 12-24.

Flower Type of 1969
Souvenir Sheet

Design: Landscape and edelweiss.

1980, May 5 Litho. *Perf. 11*
1105 A131 4t multi 3.00 3.00

London 1980 Intl. Stamp Exhib., May 6-14. No. 1105 contains one stamp 43x26mm.

Weightlifting, Moscow '80 Emblem — A252

1980, June 2 Litho. *Perf. 12*
1106 A252 20m shown 15 15
1107 A252 30m Archery 15 15
1108 A252 40m Gymnast 18 15
1109 A252 50m Running 20 15
1110 A252 60m Boxing 24 15
1111 A252 80m Judo 35 15
1112 A252 1.20t Bicycling 50 18
Nos. 1106-1112 (7) 1.77
Set value 66

Souvenir Sheet

1113 A252 4t Wrestling 2.75 2.75

22nd Summer Olympic Games, Moscow, July 19-Aug. 3.

Gold Medal, Swimmer, Moscow '80 Emblem — A253

Gold Medal, Moscow '80 Emblem and Number of Medals won by Top Countries: 30m, Fencing. 50m, Judo. 60m, Track. 80m, Boxing. 1t, Weight lifting. 1.20t, Kayak.

1980, Sept. 15 Litho. *Perf. 12½*
1114 A253 20m multi 15 15
1115 A253 30m multi 16 15
1116 A253 50m multi 28 15
1117 A253 60m multi 32 15
1118 A253 80m multi 45 15
1119 A253 1t multi 55 15
1120 A253 1.20t multi 65 18
Nos. 1114-1120 (7) 2.56
Set value 75

See No. C144.

Jumdshaigiin Zedenbal A254

1980, Sept. 17 *Perf. 11½x12*
1121 A254 60m shown 32 15
1122 A254 60m Zedenbal, 1941, grn 32 15
1123 A254 60m Zedenbal, 1979, gray grn 32 15
1124 A254 60m with Brezhnev, horiz. 32 15
1125 A254 60m with children 32 15
1126 A254 60m Sukhe Bator, dk brn 32 15
1127 A254 60m Choibalsan, ultra 32 15
Nos. 1121-1127 (7) 2.24
Set value 84

Miniature Sheet

A. Gubarjev — A255

Cosmonauts from various Intercosmos flights: b, Czechoslovakia #2222. c, P. Klimuk. d, Poland #2270. e, V. Bykovsky. f, DDR #1947. g, N. Rukavishnikov. h, Bulgaria #2576. i, V. Kubasov. j, Hungary #C417.

1980, Oct. 10 Litho. *Perf. 12*
1128 Sheet of 12 2.50 2.50
a.-j. A255 40m any single 22 22

Intercosmos cooperative space program. See No. 1232.

Benz, Germany, 1885 — A256

Antique Cars: 30m, President, Austria-Hungary, 1897. 40m, Armstrong Siddley, 1904. 50m, Russo-Balt, 1909. 60m, Packard, United States, 1909. 80m, Lancia, Italy, 1911. 1.60t, Marne taxi, France, 1914. 4t, Nami-1, Russia, 1927.

1980, Nov. 20 Litho. *Perf. 12½*
1129 A256 20m multi 15 15
1130 A256 30m multi 16 15
1131 A256 40m multi 22 15
1132 A256 50m multi 28 15
1133 A256 60m multi 32 15
1134 A256 80m multi 45 15
1135 A256 1.60t multi 90 28
Nos. 1129-1135 (7) 2.48
Set value 82

Souvenir Sheet

1136 A256 4t multi 2.50 2.50

Penguins A257

1980, Dec. 1 *Perf. 12*
1137 A257 20m shown 15 15
1138 A257 30m Giant blue whale 16 15
1139 A257 40m Albatross 22 15
1140 A257 50m Weddell seals 28 15
1141 A257 60m Emperor penguins 32 15
1142 A257 70m Skua 38 15
1143 A257 80m Grampus 45 15
1144 A257 1.20t Penguins, Soviet plane 65 18
Nos. 1137-1144 (8) 2.61
Set value 78

Souvenir Sheet

1145 A257 4t World map showing continental drift 2.50 2.50

Antarctic animals and exploration. No. 1145 contains one 44mm circular stamp.

Souvenir Sheet

A258

1980, Dec. 20 Litho. *Perf. 11*
1146 Sheet of 2 2.50 85
a. A258 2t shown 1.25 40
b. A258 2t Old Marketplace 1.25 40

The Shepherd Speaking the Truth, IYC Emblem A259

IYC Emblem and Nursery Tales: 30m, Above Them the Sky is Always Clear. 40m, Winter's Joys. 50m, Little Musicians. 60m, Happy Birthday. 80m, The First Day of School. 1.20t, May Day. 4t, The Wonder-working Squirrels.

1980, Dec. 29 *Perf. 12*
1147 A259 20m multi 15 15
1148 A259 30m multi 16 15
1149 A259 40m multi 22 15
1150 A259 50m multi 35 15
1151 A259 60m multi 40 15
1152 A259 80m multi 55 16
1153 A259 1.20t multi 75 22
Nos. 1147-1153 (7) 2.58
Set value 75

Souvenir Sheet

1154 A259 4t multi 2.50 2.50

Intl. Year of the Child (1979).

60th Anniversary of People's Army — A260

1981, Jan. 31 Litho. *Perf. 12*
1155 A260 60m multi 32 15

60th Anniversary of People's Revolutionary Party — A261

1981, Feb. 2
1156 A261 60m multi 32 15

Ice Racing — A262

Designs: Various racing motorcycles.

1981, Feb. 28 *Perf. 12½*
1157 A262 10m multi 15 15
1158 A262 20m multi 15 15
1159 A262 30m multi 16 15
1160 A262 40m multi 22 15
1161 A262 50m multi 28 15
1162 A262 60m multi 32 15
1163 A262 70m multi 35 15
1164 A262 80m multi 45 15
1165 A262 1.20t multi 65 18
Nos. 1157-1165 (9) 2.73
Set value 82

Cosmonauts Boarding Soyuz 39 — A263

Designs: 30m, Rocket designer Koroljov. 40m, Vostok I, Yuri Gagarin. 50m, Salyut space station. 60m, Satellite photographing earth. 80m, Light crystallization from Salyut spacecraft. 1.20t, Salyut, Kremlin, Sukhe Bator statue. 4t, Soviet and Mongolian cosmonauts.

1981, Mar. 22 Litho. *Perf. 12*
1166 A263 20m multi 15 15
1167 A263 30m multi 16 15
1168 A263 40m multi 22 15
1169 A263 50m multi 28 15
1170 A263 60m multi 35 15
1171 A263 80m multi 45 15
1172 A263 1.20t multi 65 22
Nos. 1166-1172 (7) 2.26
Set value 75

Souvenir Sheet
Perf. 11½

1173 A263 4t multi 2.50 2.50

Intercosmos cooperative space program (Mongolia-USSR). No. 1173 contains one 29x39mm stamp.

No. 240, Ulan Bator A264

1981, Apr. 28 Litho. *Perf. 12*
1174 Sheet of 4 2.50 2.50
a. A264 1t shown 55 20
b. A264 1t Wurttemberg #8N4, 8N34 55 20
c. A264 1t Austria #B110 55 20
d. A264 1t Japan #827 55 20

1981 Stamp Exhibitions: Mongolian Natl., Ulan Bator; Naposta, Stuttgart; WIPA, Vienna; Japex, Tokyo. Nos. 1174a-1174d se-tenant with labels showing show emblems.

Star Shining on Factories and Sheep — A265

1981, May 5
1175 A265 60m multi 32 15

18th Congress of Revolutionary People's Party, May.

Souvenir Sheet

Statue of Sukhe Bator, Mongolian Flag — A266

1981, May 20 *Perf. 12½*
1176 A266 4t multi 2.50 2.50

Mongolian Revolutionary People's Party, 60th anniv.

Sheep Farming (Economic Development) — A267

1981, June 1 *Perf. 12½x11½*
1177 A267 20m shown 15 15
1178 A267 30m Transportation 16 15
1179 A267 40m Telecommunications 22 15
1180 A267 50m Public health service 28 15
1181 A267 60m Agriculture 35 15
1182 A267 80m Power plant 45 15
1183 A267 1.20t Public housing 65 22
Nos. 1177-1183 (7) 2.26
Set value 75

Souvenir Sheet

20th Anniv. of UN Membership A268

Perf. 12½x11½
1981, July 11 **Litho.**
1184 A268 4t multi 2.50 2.50

Hansa Cog, 12th Cent. — A269

Designs: Sailing ships. 10m, 20m, horiz.

1981, Aug. 1 *Perf. 12*
1185 A269 10m Egyptian, 15th cent. BC 15 15
1186 A269 20m Mediterranean, 9th cent. 15 15
1187 A269 40m shown 22 15
1188 A269 50m Venitian, 13th cent. 28 15
1189 A269 60m Santa Maria 35 15
1190 A269 80m Endeavor 45 15
1191 A269 1t Poltava, 18th cent. 55 20
1192 A269 1.20t US schooner, 19th cent. 65 22
Nos. 1185-1192 (8) 2.80
Set value 95

Mongolian-USSR Friendship Pact — A270

1981, Sept. 1 *Perf. 11½x12*
1193 A270 60m multi 35 15

Flora, by Rembrandt A271

1981, Sept. 1 *Perf. 11½x12½*
1194 A271 20m shown 15 15
1195 A271 30m Hendrickje in the Bed 16 15
1196 A271 40m Young Woman with Earrings 22 15
1197 A271 50m Young Girl in the Window 28 15
1198 A271 60m Hendrickje like Flora 35 15
1199 A271 80m Saskia with Red Flower 45 15
1200 A271 1.20t Holy Family with Drape 65 22
Nos. 1194-1200 (7) 2.26
Set value 75

Souvenir Sheet

1201 A271 4t Self-portrait with Saskia 2.50 2.50

375th birth anniv. of Rembrandt.

Goat (Pawn) A272

Designs: Wood chess pieces.

1981, Sept. 30 **Litho.** *Perf. 12½*
1202 A272 20m shown 15 15
1203 A272 40m Cart (castle) 22 15
1204 A272 50m Camel (bishop) 28 15
1205 A272 60m Horse (knight) 35 15
1206 A272 80m Lion (queen) 45 15
1207 A272 1.20t Man and dog (king) 65 15
Nos. 1202-1207 (6) 2.10
Set value 58

Souvenir Sheet

1208 A272 4t Men playing 2.50 2.50

Camel and Circus Tent A273

1981, Oct. 30 **Litho.** *Perf. 12*
1209 A273 10m shown 15 15
1210 A273 20m Horsemen 15 15
1211 A273 40m Wrestlers 22 15
1212 A273 50m Archers 28 15
1213 A273 60m Folksinger 35 15
1214 A273 80m Girl playing jatga 45 15
1215 A273 1t Ballet dancers 55 18
1216 A273 1.20t Statue 65 20
Nos. 1209-1216 (8) 2.80
Set value 85

Wolfgang Amadeus Mozart and Scene from his Magic Flute — A274

Designs: Composers and Scenes from their Works.

1981, Nov. 16
1217 A274 20m shown 15 15
1218 A274 30m Beethoven, Fidelio 16 15
1219 A274 40m Bartok, Miraculous Mandarin 22 15
1220 A274 50m Verdi, Aida 28 15
1221 A274 60m Tchaikovsky, Sleeping Beauty 35 15
1222 A274 80m Dvorak, New World Symphony score 45 15
1223 A274 1.20t Chopin, piano 65 20
Nos. 1217-1223 (7) 2.26
Set value 70

Ribbon Weaver A275

Designs: Mongolian women.

Perf. 11½x12½
1981, Dec. 10 **Litho.**
1224 A275 20m multi 15 15
1225 A275 30m multi 16 15
1226 A275 40m multi 22 15
1227 A275 50m multi 28 15
1228 A275 60m multi 35 15
1229 A275 80m multi 45 15
1230 A275 1.20t multi 65 22
Nos. 1224-1230 (7) 2.26
Set value 75

Souvenir Sheet

1231 A275 4t multi 2.75 2.75

Intercosmos Type of 1980

Designs: a, V. Gorbatko. b, Y. Romanenko. c, V. Dzhanibekov. d, L. Popov. e, Vietnamese stamp. f, Cuban stamp. g, No. 1173. h, Romania No. C241.

1981, Dec. 28 *Perf. 12*
1232 Sheet of 8, multi 2.50 2.50
a.-h. A255 50m, any single 30 30

Historic Bicycles A276

1982, Mar. 25 **Litho.** *Perf. 11*
1233 A276 10m Germany, 1816 15 15
1234 A276 20m Scotland, 1838 15 15
1235 A276 40m US, 1866 22 15
1236 A276 50m France, 1863 28 15
1237 A276 60m "Kangaroo", 1877 35 15
1238 A276 80m England, 1870 45 15
1239 A276 1t 1878 55 20
1240 A276 1.20t Modern bike 65 22
Nos. 1233-1240 (8) 2.80
Set value 95

Souvenir Sheet

Perf. 12½

1241 A276 4t Racing 2.75 2.75

No. 1241 contains one stamp 47x47mm.

1982 World Cup — A277

1982, Apr. 20 *Perf. 12*
1242 A277 10m Brazil, 1950 15 15
1243 A277 20m Switzerland, 1954 15 15
1244 A277 40m Sweden, 1958 22 15
1245 A277 50m Chile, 1962 28 15
1246 A277 60m England, 1966 35 15
1247 A277 80m Mexico, 1970 45 15
1248 A277 1t Germany, 1974 55 20
1249 A277 1.20t Argentina, 1978 65 22
Nos. 1242-1249 (8) 2.80
Set value 95

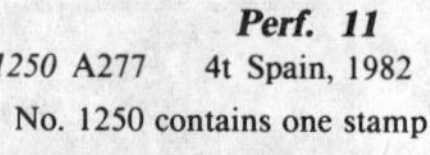

Souvenir Sheet

Perf. 11

1250 A277 4t Spain, 1982 2.50 2.50

No. 1250 contains one stamp 48x48mm.

12th Trade Union Congress, Ulan Bator A278

Perf. 11½x12½

1982, May 20 **Litho.**

1251 A278 60m multi 35 15

Souvenir Sheet

PHILEXFRANCE Intl. Stamp Exhibition, Paris, June 11-21 — A279

1982, June 11 ***Perf. 10½***

1252 A279 4t No. B13 design 2.50 2.50

George Dimitrov (1882-1949), First Prime Minister of Bulgaria — A280

1982, June 18 ***Perf. 12***

1253 A280 60m gold & blk 35 15

Chicks — A281

1982, June 25 ***Perf. 11***

1254 A281 10m shown 15 15
1255 A281 20m Colt 15 15
1256 A281 30m Lamb 16 15
1257 A281 40m Fawn 22 15
1258 A281 50m Camel calf 28 15
1259 A281 60m Kid 35 15
1260 A281 70m Calf 38 15
1261 A281 1.20t Young boar 65 22
Nos. 1254-1261 (8) 2.34
Set value 75

Coal Mining Industry — A282

1982, July 5 ***Perf. 12***

1262 A282 60m Mine, truck 35 15

18th Mongolian Youth Org. Congress A283

1982, Aug. 14 ***Perf. 11½x12***

1263 A283 60m multi 35 15

Siberian Pine A284

1982, Aug. 16

1264 A284 20m shown 15 15
1265 A284 30m Abies sibirica 15 15
1266 A284 40m Populus diversifolia 18 15
1267 A284 50m Larix sibirica 20 15
1268 A284 60m Pinus silvestris 28 15
1269 A284 80m Betula platyphylla 35 15
1270 A284 1.20t Picea obovata 50 22
Nos. 1264-1270 (7) 1.81
Set value 75

60th Anniv. of Mongolian Youth Org. — A285

1982, Aug. 30

1271 A285 60m multi 35 15

Iseki-6500 Tractor, Japan — A286

1982, Oct. 1 **Litho.** ***Perf. 12½***

1272 A286 10m shown 15 15
1273 A286 20m Deutz-DX-230, Germany 15 15
1274 A286 40m Bonser, Gt. Britain 18 15
1275 A286 50m Intl.-884, US 22 15
1276 A286 60m Renault TX-145-14, France 28 15
1277 A286 80m Belarus-611, USSR 35 15
1278 A286 1t K-7100, USSR 45 15
1279 A286 1.20t DT-75, USSR 55 18
Nos. 1272-1279 (8) 2.33
Set value 70

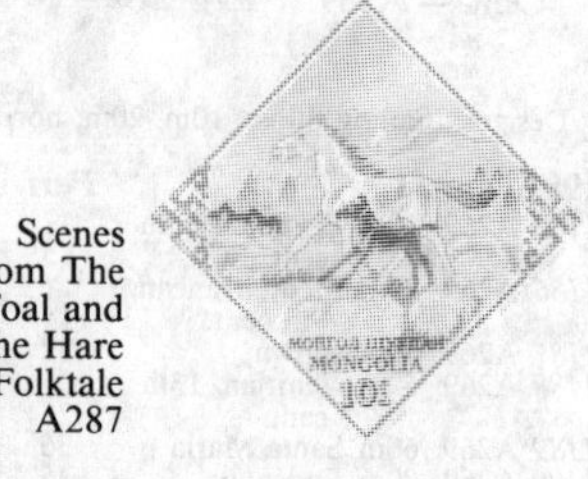

Scenes from The Foal and The Hare Folktale A287

1983, Jan. 1 **Litho.** ***Perf. 14***

1280 A287 10m multi 15
1281 A287 20m multi 15
1282 A287 30m multi 15
1283 A287 40m multi 22
1284 A287 50m multi 26
1285 A287 60m multi 35
1286 A287 70m multi 38
1287 A287 80m multi 42
1288 A287 1.20t multi 70
Nos. 1280-1288 (9) 2.78

Souvenir Sheet

Imperf

1289 A287 7t multi 4.00

No. 1289 contains one stamp 58x58mm.

Scenes from Walt Disney's The Sorcerer's Apprentice — A288

1983, Jan. 1

1290 A288 25m multi 15
1291 A288 35m multi 16
1292 A288 45m multi 24
1293 A288 55m multi 28
1294 A288 65m multi 32
1295 A288 75m multi 35
1296 A288 85m multi 42
1297 A288 1.40t multi 70
1298 A288 2t multi 95
Nos. 1290-1298 (9) 3.57

Souvenir Sheet

1299 A288 7t multi 4.00

Fish, Lake Hevsgel — A289

1982, Nov. 30 ***Perf. 12***

1300 A289 20m shown 15
1301 A289 30m Sheep, Zavhan Highlands 15
1302 A289 40m Beaver, Lake Hovd 18
1303 A289 50m Horses, Lake Uvs 22
1304 A289 60m Chamois, Bajanhongor Steppe 28
1305 A289 80m Mounted hunter, eagle, Bajan-Elgij Highlands 35
1306 A289 1.20t Camels, Gobi Desert 55
Nos. 1300-1306 (7) 1.88

Mongolian Skin Tent (Yurt) — A290

1983, Mar. 30 **Litho.** ***Perf. 14***

1307 A290 20m Antonov AN-24B plane 15
1308 A290 30m shown 15
1309 A290 40m Deer 18
1310 A290 50m Bighorn sheep 22
1311 A290 60m Eagle 28
1312 A290 80m Museum of the Khans, Ulan Bator 35
1313 A290 1.20t Sukhe Bator monument, Ulan Bator 55
Nos. 1307-1313 (7) 1.88

Souvenir Sheet

90th Birth Anniv. of Sukhe Bator — A291

1983 ***Perf. 13x14***

1314 A291 4t multi 2.50

Local Flowers — A292

1983, Feb. 4 **Photo.** ***Perf. 13***

1315 A292 20m Rose 15
1316 A292 30m Dahlias 16
1317 A292 40m Tagetes faula 22
1318 A292 50m Narcissus 28
1319 A292 60m Violets 35
1320 A292 80m Tulips 40
1321 A292 1.20t Heliopsis helianthoides 70
Nos. 1315-1321 (7) 2.26

50th Anniv. of Border Forces — A293

1983, Feb. 9 **Litho.** ***Perf. 14***

1322 A293 60m multi 35

For unused stamps, more recent issues are valued as never hinged, with the beginning point determined on a country-by-country basis. Notes to show the beginning points are prominently placed in the text.

Souvenir Sheet

BRASILIANA, Philatelic Exhibition — A294

1983, July 10 **Litho.** ***Perf. 14***

1323	A294	4t multi	2.50

Karl Marx — A295

1983, Oct. 1 **Litho.** ***Perf. 14***

1324	A295	60m gold, dp car & bl	40

18th Party Congress, Ulan Bator — A296

1983, Nov. 1 **Litho.** ***Perf. 14***

1325	A296	10m	Cattle	15
1326	A296	20m	Coal	15
1327	A296	30m	Garment	20
1328	A296	40m	Agricultural	28
1329	A296	60m	Communications	40
1330	A296	80m	Transportation	55
1331	A296	1t	Educational System	70
	Nos. 1325-1331 (7)			2.43

Souvenir Sheet

Sistine Madonna, by Raphael (1483-1520) A297

1983, Dec. 15 **Litho.** ***Perf. 14x13½***

1332	A297	4t multi	2.75

A298

Children in Various Activities.

1984, Jan. 1 **Photo.** ***Perf. 13***

1333	A298	10m	multi	15
1334	A298	20m	multi	15
1335	A298	30m	multi	20
1336	A298	40m	multi	28
1337	A298	50m	multi	35
1338	A298	70m	multi	48
1339	A298	1.20t	multi	80
	Nos. 1333-1339 (7)			2.41

Rodents — A299

Various rodents.

1984, Jan. 15 **Litho.** ***Perf. 13½x13***

1340	A299	20m	multi	15
1341	A299	30m	multi	20
1342	A299	40m	multi	28
1343	A299	50m	multi	35
1344	A299	60m	multi	40
1345	A299	80m	multi	55
1346	A299	1.20t	multi	80
	Nos. 1340-1346 (7)			2.73

1984 Winter Olympics — A300

1984, Feb. 15 **Litho.** ***Perf. 14***

1347	A300	20m	Bobsledding	15
1348	A300	30m	Cross-country skiing	20
1349	A300	40m	Hockey	28
1350	A300	50m	Speed skating	35
1351	A300	60m	Downhill skiing	40
1352	A300	80m	Figure skating	55
1353	A300	1.20t	Biathlon	80
	Nos. 1347-1353 (7)			2.73

Souvenir Sheet

1354	A300	4t	Ski jumping	2.75

Size of No. 1354: 134x106mm. Nos. 1347-1352 vert.

Children Feeding Lambs — A301

1984, Mar. 1 **Litho.** ***Perf. 12***

1355	A301	20m	Ice skating	15
1356	A301	30m	shown	20
1357	A301	40m	Planting tree	28
1358	A301	50m	Playing on beach	35
1359	A301	60m	Carrying pail	40
1360	A301	80m	Dancing	55
1361	A301	1.20t	Dancing, diff.	80
	Nos. 1355-1361 (7)			2.73

Souvenir Sheet

1362	A301	4t	Boy, girl	2.75

No. 1362 contains one stamp 48x46mm.

Mail Car, Communications Emblems — A302

1984, Apr. 15 ***Perf. 13½x14***

1363	A302	10m	shown	15
1364	A302	20m	Earth satellite receiving station	15
1365	A302	40m	Airplane	28
1366	A302	50m	Central PO	35
1367	A302	1t	Radar station	70
1368	A302	1.20t	Train	80
	Nos. 1363-1368 (6)			2.43

Souvenir Sheet

Imperf

1369	A302	4t	Dish antenna	2.75

1984 Summer Olympics — A303

1984, June 1 **Photo.** ***Perf. 14***

1370	A303	20m	Gymnastics	15
1371	A303	30m	Bicycling	20
1372	A303	40m	Weight lifting	28
1373	A303	50m	Judo	35
1374	A303	60m	Archery	40
1375	A303	80m	Boxing	55
1376	A303	1.20t	High jump	80
	Nos. 1370-1376 (7)			2.73

Souvenir Sheet

1377	A303	4t	Wrestling	2.75

Souvenir Sheet

AUSIPEX '84 and ESPANA '84 — A304

1984, May **Litho.** ***Perf. 14***

1378	A304	4t Jet	2.75

Cuban Revolution, 25th Anniv. — A304a

1984, June 2 **Litho.** ***Perf. 14***

1378A	A304a	60m multi	24

State Bank, 60th Anniv. A304b

1984, Sept. 25 ***Perf. 13½x13***

1378B	A304b	60m Commemorative coins, 1981	24

Scenes from Walt Disney's Mickey and the Beanstalk — A305

1984, Dec. 20 **Litho.** ***Perf. 11***

1379	A305	25m	multi	15
1380	A305	35m	multi	15
1381	A305	45m	multi	20
1382	A305	55m	multi	24
1383	A305	65m	multi	28
1384	A305	75m	multi	30
1385	A305	85m	multi	35
1386	A305	1.40t	multi	60
1387	A305	2t	multi	80
	Nos. 1379-1387 (9)			3.07

Miniature Sheet

Perf. 14

1388	A305	7t	multi	3.75

Fairy Tales — A306

1984, Dec. 20 **Litho.** ***Perf. 13½***

1389	A306	10m	multi	15
1390	A306	20m	multi	15
1391	A306	30m	multi	16
1392	A306	40m	multi	20
1393	A306	50m	multi	28
1394	A306	60m	multi	35
1395	A306	70m	multi	40
1396	A306	80m	multi	45
1397	A306	1.20t	multi	65
	Nos. 1389-1397 (9)			2.79

Miniature Sheet

1398	A306	4t	multi	3.00

Souvenir Sheet

60th Anniv. of Mongolian Stamps — A308

1984, Dec. 20 **Litho.** ***Perf. 14***

1400	A308	4t No. 1	2.75

Mongolian People's Party, 60th Anniv. — A311

1984, Nov. 26 **Litho.** ***Perf. 14***

1403	A311	60m	multi	35

Native Masks — A312

1984, Dec. 31 **Litho.** ***Perf. 14***

1404	A312	20m	multi	15
1405	A312	30m	multi	20
1406	A312	40m	multi	25
1407	A312	50m	multi	35
1408	A312	60m	multi	40
1409	A312	80m	multi	60
1410	A312	1.20t	multi	85
			Nos. 1404-1410 (7)	2.80

Souvenir Sheet

1411	A312	4t	multi	2.75

Dogs A313

1984, Dec. 31 **Litho.** ***Perf. 13***

1412	A313	20m	Collie	15
1413	A313	30m	German Sheep-dog	20
1414	A313	40m	Papillon	25
1415	A313	50m	Cocker Spaniel	35
1416	A313	60m	Puppy	40
1417	A313	80m	Dalmatians	60
1418	A313	1.20t	Mongolian Sheepdog	85
			Nos. 1412-1418 (7)	2.80

Cattle — A314

1985, Jan. ***Perf. 14***

1419	A314	20m	Shar tarlan	15
1420	A314	30m	Bor khaliun	18
1421	A314	40m	Sarlag	25
1422	A314	50m	Dornod taliin bukh	32
1423	A314	60m	Char tarlan	38
1424	A314	80m	Nutgiin uulderi-in unee	50
1425	A314	1.20t	Tsagaan tolgoit	75
			Nos. 1419-1425 (7)	2.53

1984 Olympic Winners — A315

Gold medalists: 20m, Gaetan Boucher, Canada, 1500-meter speed skating. 30m, Eirik Kvalfoss, Norway, 10-kilometer biathlon. 40m, Marja-Lissa Haemaelainen, Finland, 5-kilometer Nordic skiing. 50m, Max Julen, Switzerland, men's giant slalom. 60m, Jens Weissflag, German Democratic Republic, 70-meter ski jump. 80m, W. Hoppe and D. Schauerhammer, German Democratic Republic, 2-man bobsled. 1.20t, Elena Valova and Oleg Vassiliev, USSR, pairs figure skating. 4t, USSR, ice hockey. Nos. 1430-1432 vert.

1985, Apr. 25

1426	A315	20m	multi	15
1427	A315	30m	multi	15
1428	A315	40m	multi	20
1429	A315	50m	multi	25
1430	A315	60m	multi	30
1431	A315	80m	multi	40
1432	A315	1.20t	multi	60
			Nos. 1426-1432 (7)	2.05

Souvenir Sheet

1433	A315	4t	multi	2.00

Souvenir Sheet

Girl, Fawn — A316

1985, Apr. 25

1434	A316	4m	multi	2.00

Birds — A317

World Youth Festival, Moscow — A318

1985, May 1 ***Perf. 12½x13***

1435	A317	20m	Ciconia nigra	15
1436	A317	30m	Haliaetus albicilla	15
1437	A317	40m	Grus leucogeranus	20
1438	A317	50m	Paradoxornis heudei	25
1439	A317	60m	Grus monahas	30
1440	A317	80m	Grus vipio	40
1441	A317	1.20t	Buteo lagopus	60
			Nos. 1435-1441 (7)	2.05

National Wildlife Preservation Association.

1985, June ***Perf. 14***

1442	A318	60m	Girls in folk costumes	30

Camelus Bactrianus — A319

Panthera Unicias — A320

Cervus Elaphus — A321

Camels, leopards and deer.

1985

1443	A319	50m	Adults, young	25
1444	A319	50m	Facing right	25
1445	A319	50m	Facing left	25
1446	A319	50m	Trotting	25
1447	A320	50m	Hunting	25
1448	A320	50m	Standing in snow	25
1449	A320	50m	Female, young	25
1450	A320	50m	Adults	25
1451	A321	50m	Fawn	25
1452	A321	50m	Doe in woods	25
1453	A321	50m	Adult male	25
1454	A321	50m	Adults, fawn	25
			Nos. 1443-1454 (12)	3.00

#1443-1446 show the World Wildlife Fund emblem, #1447-1454 the Natl. Wildlife Preservation emblem. Issue dates: #1443-1446, July 1; #1447-1454, Aug. 1.

UN, 40th Anniv. A322

1985, Aug. 1 ***Perf. 13½x13***

1455	A322	60m	Flags, UN building	30

Indigenous Flowering Plants — A323

1985, Aug. 1 ***Perf. 14***

1456	A323	20m	Rosa dahurica	15
1457	A323	30m	Matricaria chamomilla	15
1458	A323	40m	Taraxacum officinale	20
1459	A323	50m	Saxzitraga nircu-lus	25
1460	A323	60m	Vaccinium vitis idaea	30
1461	A323	80m	Sanguisorba officinalis	40
1462	A323	1.20t	Plantago major	60
			Nos. 1456-1462 (7)	2.05

Souvenir Sheet

1463	A323	4t	Hyppopae thamnoides	2.00

Defeat of Nazi Germany, 40th Anniv. — A324

1985, Sept. 15 ***Perf. 13x13½***

1464	A324	60m	Monument	30

1985 Junior World Soccer Championships, Moscow — A325

Various soccer plays. No. 1472 horiz.

1985, Oct. 1 ***Perf. 14***

1465	A325	20m	multi	15
1466	A325	30m	multi	15
1467	A325	40m	multi	20
1468	A325	50m	multi	25
1469	A325	60m	multi	30
1470	A325	80m	multi	40
1471	A325	1.20t	multi	60
			Nos. 1465-1471 (7)	2.05

Souvenir Sheet

1472	A325	4t	multi	2.00

Souvenir Sheet

ITALIA '85 — A326

1985, Oct. 1

1473	A326	4t	Horseman	2.00

Conquest of Space — A327

Russian spacecraft.

1985, Nov. 1

1474	A327	20m	Soyuz	15
1475	A327	30m	Cosmos	15
1476	A327	40m	Venera 9	20
1477	A327	50m	Salyut	25
1478	A327	60m	Luna 9	30
1479	A327	80m	Train	40
1480	A327	1.20t	Dish receiver	60
			Nos. 1474-1480 (7)	2.05

Souvenir Sheet

1985, Dec. 15

1481	A327	4t	Cosmonaut on space walk	2.00

Mushrooms — A328

1985, Dec. 1 *Perf. 13½*

1482 A328 20m Tricholoma mongolica 15
1483 A328 30m Cantharellus cibarius 15
1484 A328 40m Armillariella mellea 20
1485 A328 50m Amanita caesarea 25
1486 A328 70m Xerocomus badius 35
1487 A328 80m Agaricus silvaticus 40
1488 A328 1.20t Boletus edulis 60
Nos. 1482-1488 (7) 2.10

Souvenir Sheet

Phalacrocorax Penicillatus — A329

1986, Jan. 15 *Perf. 12½x13*

1489 A329 4t multi 3.00

No. 1489 contains one stamp plus 2 labels picturing various bird species.

Young Pioneers A330

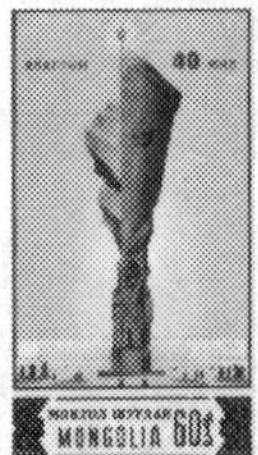

Victory Monument A331

1985, Dec. 31 Litho. *Perf. 13x13½*

1490 A330 60m multi 38

1985, Dec. 31 *Perf. 12½x13*

1491 A331 60m multi 38

Victory over Japan ending WWII, 40th anniv.

Natl. Costumes A332

1986, Mar. 1 Litho. *Perf. 14*

Background Color

1492 A332 60m yel grn, shown 20
1493 A332 60m red 20
1494 A332 60m pale yel grn 20
1495 A332 60m violet 20
1496 A332 60m ultra 20
1497 A332 60m bluish grn 20
1498 A332 60m pale org brn 20
Nos. 1492-1498 (7) 1.40

Ernst Thalmann (1886-1944) A333

1986, May 15 Litho. *Perf. 14*

1499 A333 60m gold, redsh brn & dk brn 28

Natl. Revolution, 65th Anniv. — A334

1986, May 15

1500 A334 60m Statue of Sukhe Bator 28

19th Socialist Party Congress A335

1986, May 15

1501 A335 60m multi 28

1986 World Cup Soccer Championships, Mexico — A336

FIFA emblem and various soccer plays. Nos. 1502-1503, 1505-1508 vert.

1986, May 31

1502 A336 20m multi 15
1503 A336 30m multi 15
1504 A336 40m multi 20
1505 A336 50m multi 24
1506 A336 60m multi 28
1507 A336 80m multi 38
1508 A336 1.20t multi 55
Nos. 1502-1508 (7) 1.95

Souvenir Sheet

1509 A336 4t multi 1.90

Mink, Wildlife Conservation — A337

1986, June 15

1510 A337 60m Spring 35
1511 A337 60m Summer 35
1512 A337 60m Autumn 35
1513 A337 60m Winter 35

Flowers A338

Butterflies A339

1986, June 1 Litho. *Perf. 14*

1514 A338 20m Valeriana officinalis 15
1515 A338 30m Hyoscymus niger 16
1516 A338 40m Ephedra sinica 20
1517 A338 50m Thymus gobica 25
1518 A338 60m Paeonia anomala 30
1519 A338 80m Achilea millefolium 40
1520 A338 1.20t Rhododendron adamsii 60
Nos. 1514-1520 (7) 2.06

1986, Aug. 1 *Perf. 13½*

1521 A339 20m Neptis coenobita 15
1522 A339 30m Colias tycha 20
1523 A339 40m Leptidea amurensis 28
1524 A339 50m Oeneis tarpenledevi 32
1525 A339 60m Mesoacidalia charlotta 40
1526 A339 80m Smerinthus ocellatus 50
1527 A339 1.20t Pericalia matronula 80
Nos. 1521-1527 (7) 2.65

Circus — A340

Animal trainers and acrobats. Nos. 1531-1534 vert.

1986, Aug. 1 *Perf. 14*

1528 A340 20m multi 15
1529 A340 30m multi 16
1530 A340 40m multi 20
1531 A340 50m multi 25
1532 A340 60m multi 30
1533 A340 80m multi 40
1534 A340 1.20t multi 60
Nos. 1528-1534 (7) 2.06

Przewalski's Horses — A341

1986, Aug. 1 Litho. *Perf. 14*

1535 A341 50m Two horses, foal 35
1536 A341 50m One facing left, two facing right 35
1537 A341 50m Three facing right 35
1538 A341 50m Four in storm 35

Pelicans *(Pelecanus)* — A341a

1986, Sept. 1 Litho. *Perf. 14*

1538A A341a 60m *crispus* feeding 58
1538B A341a 60m *crispus* wading 58
1538C A341a 60m *onocrotalus* flying 58
1538D A341a 60m *onocrotalus* on land 58

Saiga tatarica mongolica — A341b

1986, Sept. 15

1538E A341b 60m Spring (doe, fawn) 58
1538F A341b 60m Summer (buck, doe) 58
1538G A341b 60m Fall (buck) 58
1538H A341b 60m Winter (buck, doe) 58

Musical Instruments — A342

1986, Sept. 4

1539 A342 20m Morin khuur 15
1540 A342 30m Bishguur 20
1541 A342 40m Ever buree 28
1542 A342 50m Shudarga 35
1543 A342 60m Khiil 40
1544 A342 80m Janchir 55
1545 A342 1.20t Jatga 80
Nos. 1539-1545 (7) 2.73

Souvenir Sheet

1546 A342 4t like 20m, vert. 2.75

STOCKHOLMIA '86. Nos. 1539-1543 vert.

Set Values

A 15-cent minimum now applies to individual stamps and sets. Where the 15-cent minimum per stamp would increase the "value" of a set beyond retail, there is a "Set Value" notation giving the retail value of the set.

North American Bird Species — A343

1986, Oct. 1
1547 A343 60m Anthus spinoletta 35
1548 A343 60m Aythya americana 35
1549 A343 60m Bonasa umbellus 35
1550 A343 60m Olor columbianus 35

Eastern Architecture — A343a

Various two-story buildings.

1986, Oct. 1
Color of Border
1551 A343a 60m dark grn & blk 70
1552 A343a 60m beige & blk 70
1553 A343a 60m apple grn & blk 70
1554 A343a 60m red brn & blk 70

Classic Automobiles — A344

1986, Oct. 1 **Litho.** ***Perf. 14***
1554A A344 20m 1922 Alfa Romeo RL Sport, Italy 15
1554B A344 30m 1912 Stutz Bearcat, US 24
1554C A344 40m 1902 Mercedes Simplex, Germany 30
1554D A344 50m 1923 Tatra 11, Czechoslovakia 38
1554E A344 60m 1908 Ford Model T, US 45
1554F A344 80m 1905 Vauxhall, England 60
1554G A344 1.20t 1913 Russo-Baltik, Russia 90
Nos. 1554A-1554G (7) 3.02
Souvenir Sheet
1554H A344 4t like 1.20t 3.00

Woodpeckers A344a

1986, Nov. 1
1555 A344a 20m Picus canus 16
1556 A344a 30m Jynx torquilla 24
1557 A344a 40m Dryobates major 32
1558 A344a 50m Dryobates leucotos 40
1559 A344a 60m Dryobates minor 48
1560 A344a 80m Dryocopus martius 65
1561 A344a 1.20t Picoides tridactylus 90
Nos. 1555-1561 (7) 3.15
Souvenir Sheet
1562 A344a 4t Saphopipo noguchi 3.25

Chess Champions — A345

Portraits and chessmen on boards in match-winning configurations. No. 1562H, Chess champions Gary Kasparov, Jose R. Capablanca, Max Euwe, Vassily Smyslow, Mikhail Tal, Tigran Petrosian, Boris Spasski and Bobby Fischer; W. Menchik, L. Rudenko, E. Bykowa and O. Rubzowa.

1986, Nov. 1 ***Perf. 14***
1562A A345 20m Steinitz, Austria 15
1562B A345 30m Lasker, Germany 24
1562C A345 40m Alekhine, France 30
1562D A345 50m Botvinnik, USSR 38
1562E A345 60m Karpov, USSR 45
1562F A345 80m N. Gaprindashvili 60
1562G A345 1.20t M. Chiburdanidze 90
Size: 110x100mm
Imperf
1562H A345 4t multi 3.00
Nos. 1562A-1562H (8) 6.02

Ovis Ammon Ammon — A347

1987, Jan. 1
1564 A347 60m shown 42
1565 A347 60m In the mountains 42
1566 A347 60m Close-up of head 42
1567 A347 60m Male, female, lamb 42

Children's Activities A348

1987, Feb. 1
1568 A348 20m Backpacking, hunting butterflies 15
1569 A348 30m Playing with calves 24
1570 A348 40m Chalk-writing on cement 30
1571 A348 50m Playing soccer 38
1572 A348 60m Go-cart, model rocket, boat 45
1573 A348 80m Agriculture 60
1574 A348 1.20t Playing the morin khuur, dancing 90
Nos. 1568-1574 (7) 3.02

Int'l. Peace Year (40m); Child Survival Campaign (50m).

13th Trade Unions Congress — A349

1987, Feb. 15 ***Perf. 13½x13***
1575 A349 60m multi 45

Equestrian Sports — A350

1987, Mar. 1
1576 A350 20m Lassoer 15
1577 A350 30m Breaking horse 24
1578 A350 40m Shooting bow 30
1579 A350 50m Race 38
1580 A350 60m Retrieving flags 45
1581 A350 80m Tug-of-war 60
1582 A350 1.20t Racing wolf 90
Nos. 1576-1582 (7) 3.02

Admission into Comecon, 25th Anniv. — A351

1987, Apr. 15 ***Perf. 13x13½***
1583 A351 60m multi 45

Fruit — A352

A353

1987, June 1 ***Perf. 13½***
1584 A352 20m Hippophae rhamnoides 15
1585 A352 30m Ribes nigrum 24
1586 A352 40m Ribes rubrus 30
1587 A352 50m Ribes altissimum 38
1588 A352 60m Rubus sachalinensis 45
1589 A352 80m Padus asiatica 60
1590 A352 1.20t Fragaria orientalis 90
Nos. 1584-1590 (7) 3.02

Souvenir Sheet
Perf. 14
1591 A353 4t Malus domestica 3.00

Soviet-Mongolian Diplomatic Relations, 50th Anniv. — A354

Russian Revolution, 70th Anniv. — A355

1987, July 1 ***Perf. 13x13½***
1592 A354 60m multi 55

1987, July 1
1593 A355 60m multi 55

Folk Dances — A356

1987, Aug. 1 ***Perf. 14***
1594 A356 20m multi 15
1595 A356 30m multi, diff. 24
1596 A356 40m multi, diff. 30
1597 A356 50m multi, diff. 38
1598 A356 60m multi, diff. 45
1599 A356 80m multi, diff. 60
1600 A356 1.20t multi, diff. 90
Nos. 1594-1600 (7) 3.02

Antiques A357

Full costume and accessories.

1987, Aug. 10
1601 A357 20m Folk costumes 15
1602 A357 30m Gilded nunchaku 24
1603 A357 40m Brooches 30
1604 A357 50m Draw-string pouch, rice bowl 38
1605 A357 60m Headdress 45
1606 A357 80m Pouches, bottle, pipe 60
1607 A357 1.20t Sash, brooch 90
Nos. 1601-1607 (7) 3.02

Souvenir Sheet

HAFNIA '87 — A358

1987, Aug. 10

No.	Type	Value	Description	Price
1608	A358	4t	multi	3.00

Swans — A359

1987, Aug. 15

No.	Type	Value	Description	Price
1609	A359	60m	Cygnus olor on land	35
1610	A359	60m	Cygnus olor in water	35
1611	A359	60m	Cygnus beruickii	35
1612	A359	60m	Cygnus beruickii, gunus and olor	35

Domestic and Wild Cats — A360

1987, Oct. 1 **Litho.** ***Perf. 14***

No.	Type	Value	Description	Price
1613	A360	20m	multi, vert.	15
1614	A360	30m	multi, vert.	24
1615	A360	40m	multi, vert.	30
1616	A360	50m	shown	38
1617	A360	60m	multi	45
1618	A360	80m	multi	60
1619	A360	1.20t	multi	90
			Nos. 1613-1619 (7)	3.02

Miniature Sheet

No.	Type	Value	Description	Price
1620	A360	4t	multi, vert.	3.00

Helicopter — A361

1987, Oct. 3 ***Perf. 12½x11½***

No.	Type	Value	Description	Price
1621	A361	20m	B-12	15
1622	A361	30m	Westland-WG-30	24
1623	A361	40m	Bell-S-206L	30
1624	A361	50m	Kawasaki-369HS	38
1625	A361	60m	KA-32	45
1626	A361	80m	MI-17	60
1627	A361	1.20t	MI-10K	90
			Nos. 1621-1627 (7)	3.02

Disney Cartoons — A362

The Brave Little Tailor (25m-55m, 2t, No. 1637), and The Celebrated Jumping Frog of Calaveras County (65m-1.40t, No. 1638).

1987, Nov. 23 ***Perf. 14***

No.	Type	Value	Description	Price
1628	A362	25m	multi	15
1629	A362	35m	multi	18
1630	A362	45m	multi	22
1631	A362	55m	multi	28
1632	A362	65m	multi	32
1633	A362	75m	multi	38
1634	A362	85m	multi	40
1635	A362	1.40t	multi	70
1636	A362	2t	multi	1.00
			Nos. 1628-1636 (9)	3.63

Souvenir Sheets

No.	Type	Value	Description	Price
1637	A362	7t	multi	3.25
1638	A362	7t	multi	3.25

A363

Tropical Fish — A364

1987, Oct. ***Perf. 13x12½, 12½x13***

No.	Type	Value	Description	Price
1639	A363	20m	Betta splendens	15
1640	A363	30m	Carassius auratus	24
1641	A363	40m	Rasbora hengeli	30
1642	A363	50m	Aequidens	38
1643	A363	60m	Xiphophorus macalatus	45
1644	A363	80m	Xiphophorus helleri	60
1645	A363	1.20t	Pterophyllum scalare, vert.	90
			Nos. 1639-1645 (7)	3.02

Miniature Sheet

Perf. 14

No.	Type	Value	Description	Price
1646	A364	4t	Crenuchus spilurus	3.00

19th Communist Party Congress — A365

1987, Dec. ***Perf. 14***

No.	Type	Value	Description	Price
1647	A365	60m	Family	45
1648	A365	60m	Construction	45
1649	A365	60m	Jet, harvesting, produce	45
1650	A365	60m	Education	45
1651	A365	60m	Transportation	45
1652	A365	60m	Heavy industry	45
1653	A365	60m	Science and technology	45
			Nos. 1647-1653 (7)	3.15

Vulpes Vulpes (Fox) — A366

1987, Dec.

No.	Type	Value	Description	Price
1654	A366	60m	Adult in snow	45
1655	A366	60m	Adult, young	45
1656	A366	60m	Adult in field	45
1657	A366	60m	Close-up of head	45

Souvenir Sheet

INTERCOSMOS — A367

1987, Dec. 15 **Litho.** ***Perf. 14***

No.	Type	Value	Description	Price
1658	A367	4t	multi	3.00

Souvenir Sheet

PRAGA '88 — A368

1988, Jan. 30

No.	Type	Value	Description	Price
1659	A368	4t	1923 Tatra 11	3.00

Sukhe Bator — A369

1988, Feb. 2 ***Perf. 13x13½***

No.	Type	Value	Description	Price
1660	A369	60m	multi	60

Roses — A370

1988, Feb. 20 ***Perf. 14***

No.	Type	Value	Description	Price
1661	A370	20m	Invitation	15
1662	A370	30m	Meilland	24
1663	A370	40m	Pascali	30
1664	A370	50m	Tropicana	40
1665	A370	60m	Wendy cussons	45
1666	A370	80m	Blue moon	60
1667	A370	1.20t	Diorama	90
			Nos. 1661-1667 (7)	3.04

Souvenir Sheet

No.	Type	Value	Description	Price
1668	A370	4t	shown	3.00

19th Communist Youth Congress — A371

1988, Apr. 15 ***Perf. 12½x13***

No.	Type	Value	Description	Price
1669	A371	60m	multi	60

Puppets — A372

Folk tales.

1988, Apr. 1 **Litho.** ***Perf. 14***

No.	Type	Value	Description	Price
1670	A372	20m	Ukhaant Ekhner	20
1671	A372	30m	Altan Everte Mungun Turuut	30
1672	A372	40m	Aduuchyn Khuu	40
1673	A372	50m	Suulenkhuu	48
1674	A372	60m	Khonchyn Khuu	60
1675	A372	80m	Argat Byatskhan Baatar	80
1676	A372	1.20t	Botgochyn Khuu	1.25
			Nos. 1670-1676 (7)	4.03

1988 Summer Olympics, Seoul A373

Soviet Space Achievements A374

1988, Feb. 15

No.	Type	Value	Description	Price
1677	A373	20m	Judo	15
1678	A373	30m	Women's archery	24
1679	A373	40m	Weight lifting	30
1680	A373	50m	Women's gymnastics	40
1681	A373	60m	Cycling	45
1682	A373	80m	Running	60
1683	A373	1.20t	Wrestling	90
			Nos. 1677-1683 (7)	3.04

Souvenir Sheet

No.	Type	Value	Description	Price
1684	A373	4t	Boxing	3.00

1988, May 15

No.	Type	Value	Description	Price
1685	A374	20m	Cosmos	15
1686	A374	30m	Meteor	24
1687	A374	40m	Salyut-Soyuz	30
1688	A374	50m	Prognoz-6	40
1689	A374	60m	Molniya-1	45
1690	A374	80m	Soyuz	60
1691	A374	1.20t	Vostok	90
			Nos. 1685-1691 (7)	3.04

Effigies of Buddhist Deities — A375

Various statues.

1988, June 15 Litho. *Perf. 14*

1692 A375 20m multi 15
1693 A375 30m multi, diff. 20
1694 A375 40m multi, diff. 28
1695 A375 50m multi, diff. 35
1696 A375 60m multi, diff. 40
1697 A375 70m multi, diff. 48
1698 A375 80m multi, diff. 55
1699 A375 1.20t multi, diff. 80
Nos. 1692-1699 (8) 3.21

Wildlife Conservation — A376

Eagles, Haliaeetus albicilla. Nos. 1700-1702 vert.

1988, Aug. 1 Litho. *Perf. 14*

1700 A376 60m Eagle facing left, diff. 40
1701 A376 60m Landing on branch 40
1702 A376 60m Facing right 40
1703 A376 60m shown 40

Souvenir Sheet

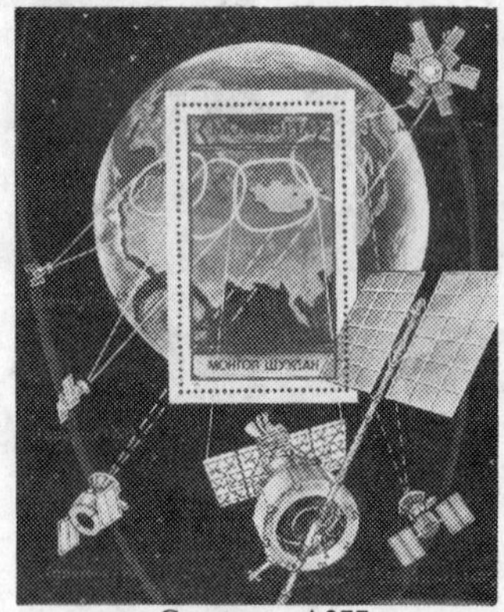

Cosmos — A377

1988, Sept. 15 Litho. *Perf. 14*

1704 A377 4t Satellite links 3.25

Opera A378

1988, Oct. 1 Litho. *Perf. 13x12½*

1705 A378 60m multi 90

No. 1705 printed se-tenant with label picturing composer.

Equus hemionus — A380

1988, May 3

1713 A380 60m Mare, foal 58
1714 A380 60m Horse's head 58
1715 A380 60m Horse galloping 58
1716 A380 60m Horses cantering 58

Winners of the 1988 Winter Olympics, Calgary — A381

1988, July 1

1717 A381 1.50t Matti Nykaenen, Finland 58
1718 A381 1.50t Bonnie Blair, US 58
1719 A381 1.50t Alberto Tomba, Italy 58
1720 A381 1.50t USSR hockey team 58

Souvenir Sheet

1721 A381 4t Katarina Witt, DDR 2.35

Nos. 1718-1720 vert.

Sports — A382

1988, Sept. 1

1722 A382 10m shown 15
1723 A382 20m Horsemanship 20
1724 A382 30m Archery 30
1725 A382 40m Wrestling 40
1726 A382 50m Archery, diff. 50
1727 A382 70m Horsemanship, diff. 70
1728 A382 1.20t Horsemanship, wrestling, archery 1.20
Nos. 1722-1728 (7) 3.45

Socialism and Peace — A383

1988, Dec. 1 *Perf. 13x13½*

1729 A383 60m multicolored 80

Goats — A384

Various species.

1989, Jan. 15 *Perf. 14*

1730 A384 20m multi 25
1731 A384 30m multi 38
1732 A384 40m multi 50
1733 A384 50m multi 62
1734 A384 60m multi 75
1735 A384 80m multi 1.00
1736 A384 1.20t multi 1.50
Nos. 1717-1723 (7) 5.02

Souvenir Sheet

1737 A384 4t multi, vert. 5.00

Souvenir Sheet

Child Survival — A385

1989, Jan. 28 Litho. *Perf. 14*

1738 A385 4t Drawing by H. Jargalsuren 5.00

Karl Marx — A386

1989, Feb. 25 Litho. *Perf. 13x13½*

1739 A386 60m multicolored 80

Miniature Sheet

Statue of Sukhe Bator — A387

Mongolian Airline Jet — A388

1989, July 1 *Perf. 14*

1740 Sheet of 3 2.60
a. A387 20m Concorde jet 25
b. A387 60m TGV high-speed train 78
c. A387 1.20t shown 1.55

Souvenir Sheet

1741 A388 4t shown 4.25

PHILEXFRANCE '89, BULGARIA '89.
For overprint see No. 1756.

World War II Memorial A389

1989, Sept. 2

1742 A389 60m multicolored 80

Cacti — A390

1989, Sept. 7

1743 A390 20m *O. microdasys* 22
1744 A390 30m *E. multipiex* 32
1745 A390 40m *R. tephracanthus* 42
1746 A390 50m *B. haselbergii* 55
1747 A390 60m *G. mihanovichii* 65
1748 A390 80m *C. strausii* 85
1749 A390 1.20t *Horridocactus tuberisvicatus* 1.25
Nos. 1743-1749 (7) 4.26

Souvenir Sheet

1750 A390 4t *Astrophytum ornatum* 4.25

Winners of the 1988 Summer Olympics, Seoul — A391

1989, Oct. 1

1751 A391 60m Kristin Otto, East Germany 58
1752 A391 60m Florence Griffith-Joyner, US 58
1753 A391 60m Gintaoutas Umaras, USSR 58
1754 A391 60m Stefano Cerioni, Italy 58

Souvenir Sheet

1755 A391 4t N. Enkhbat, Mongolia 4.25

No. 1740 Overprinted for WORLD STAMP EXPO '89

1989, Nov. 17 **Miniature Sheet**

1756 Sheet of 3 2.60
a. A387 20m multicolored 25
b. A387 60m multicolored 78
c. A387 1.20t multicolored 1.55

Books, Fountain Pen — A392

1989, Dec. 1

1757 A392 60m multicolored 58

Beavers *(Castor fiber birulai)* — A393

1989, Dec. 10

1758 A393 60m Cutting down saplings 58
1759 A393 60m Rolling wood across ground 58
1760 A393 60m Beaver on land, in water 58
1761 A393 60m Beaver and young 58

Medals and Military Decorations A394

1989, Dec. 31 ***Perf. 13x13½***

1762 A394 60m pink & multi 58
1763 A394 60m lt blue grn & multi 58
1764 A394 60m vio & multi 58
1765 A394 60m org & multi 58
1766 A394 60m brt blue & multi 58
1767 A394 60m ver & multi 58
1768 A394 60m vio blue & multi 58
Nos. 1762-1768 (7) 4.06

Bears and Giant Pandas — A395

1990, Jan. 1 ***Perf. 14***

1769 A395 20m *Ursus pruinosis* 22
1770 A395 30m *Ursus arctos syriacus* 32
1771 A395 40m *Ursus thibetanus* 42
1772 A395 50m *Ursus maritimus* 55
1773 A395 60m *Ursus arctos bruinosus* 65
1774 A395 80m *Ailuropus melanoleucus* 85
1775 A395 1.20t *Ursus arctos isabellinus* 1.25
Nos. 1771-1775 (5) 3.72

Souvenir Sheet

1776 A395 4t *Ailuropus melanoleucus*, diff. 4.25

Winter Sports — A396

1990, Jan. 6

1777 A396 20m 4-man bobsled 22
1778 A396 30m Luge 32
1779 A396 40m Women's figure skating 42
1780 A396 50m 1-man bobsled 55
1781 A396 60m Pairs figure skating 65
1782 A396 80m Speed skating 85
1783 A396 1.20t Ice speedway 1.25
Nos. 1777-1783 (7) 4.26

Souvenir Sheet

1784 A396 4t Ice hockey 4.25

Space Exploration — A397

Rockets and spacecraft: 20m, Soyuz, USSR. 30m, Apollo-Soyuz, US-USSR. 40m, *Columbia* space shuttle, US, vert. 50m, *Hermes,* France. 60m, *Nippon,* Japan, vert. 80m, *Energy,* USSR, vert. 1.20t, *Buran,* USSR, vert. 4t, *Sanger,* West Germany.

1990, Jan. 30

1785 A397 20m shown 22
1786 A397 30m multicolored 32
1787 A397 40m multicolored 42
1788 A397 50m multicolored 55
1789 A397 60m multicolored 65
1790 A397 80m multicolored 85
1791 A397 1.20t multicolored 1.25
Nos. 1785-1791 (7) 4.26

Souvenir Sheet

1792 A397 4t multicolored 4.25

Jawaharlal Nehru, 1st Prime Minister of Independent India — A398

1990, Feb. 10

1793 A398 10m gold, blk & dark red brn 80

Statue of Sukhe Bator — A399

1990, Feb. 27

1794 A399 10m multicolored 80

Mongolian Ballet — A400

Dancers in scenes from various ballets. 40m, 80m, 1.20t vert.

1990, Feb. 28

1795 A400 20m shown 22
1796 A400 30m multi 32
1797 A400 40m multi 42
1798 A400 50m multi 55
1799 A400 60m multi 65
1800 A400 80m multi 85
1801 A400 1.20t multi 1.20
Nos. 1795-1801 (7) 4.21

Automobiles — A401

1990, Mar. 26

1802 A401 20m Citroen, France 22
1803 A401 30m Volvo 760 GLF, Sweden 32
1804 A401 40m Honda, Japan 42
1805 A401 50m Volga, USSR 55
1806 A401 60m Ford Granada, US 65
1807 A401 80m BAZ 21099, USSR 85
1808 A401 1.20t Mercedes Class 190, West Germany 1.25
Nos. 1802-1808 (7) 4.26

Souvenir Sheet

1809 A401 4t like 50m 4.25

Lenin — A402

1990, Mar. 27 ***Perf. 13x13½***

1810 A402 60m gold, black & ver 80

Unen Newspaper, 70th Anniv. — A403

1990, Apr. 1 ***Perf. 14***

1811 A403 60m multicolored 80

End of World War II, 45th Anniv. — A404

1990, Apr. 1

1812 A404 60m multicolored 80

Buddhist Deities (18th-20th Cent. Paintings) A405

1990, Apr. 1

1813 A405 20m Damdin Sandub 22
1814 A405 30m Pagwa Lama 32
1815 A405 40m Chu Lha 42
1816 A405 50m Agwanglobsan 55
1817 A405 60m Dorje Dags Dan 65
1818 A405 80m Wangchikdorje 85
1819 A405 1.20t Buddha 1.25
Nos. 1813-1819 (7) 4.26

Souvenir Sheet

1820 A405 4t Migjed Jang-Rasek 4.25

A406

Aspects of a Cooperative Settlement — A407

Paintings: 20m, Animals on plain, rainbow. 30m, Workers, reindeer, dog, vert. 40m, Two men, mountains, Bactrian camels. 50m, Man, Bactrian camels. 60m, Huts, animal shelter, corral. 60m, Breaking horses, vert. 1.20t, Sheep, shepherd girl on horse. 4t, Wrestling match.

1990, Apr. 1

1821	A406	20m	shown	22
1822	A406	30m	multicolored	32
1823	A406	40m	multicolored	42
1824	A406	50m	multicolored	55
1825	A406	60m	multicolored	65
1826	A406	80m	multicolored	85
1827	A406	1.20t	multicolored	1.25
			Nos. 1821-1827 (7)	4.26

Souvenir Sheet

1828	A407	4t	shown	4.25

Scenes from Various Mongolian-made Films — A408

1990, Apr. 1

1829	A408	20m	shown	22
1830	A408	30m	multi, diff.	32
1831	A408	40m	multi, diff.	42
1832	A408	50m	multi, diff.	55
1833	A408	60m	multi, diff.	65
1834	A408	80m	multi, diff.	85
1835	A408	1.20t	multi, diff.	1.25
			Nos. 1829-1835 (7)	4.26

Souvenir Sheet

1836	A408	4t	multi, diff., vert.	4.25

Souvenir Sheet

Stamp World London '90 — A409

1990, Apr. 1

1837	A409	4t	multicolored	4.25

1990 World Cup Soccer Championships, Italy — A410

Trophy and various athletes.

1990, Apr. 30

1838	A410	20m	multicolored	22
1839	A410	30m	multicolored	32
1840	A410	40m	multicolored	42
1841	A410	50m	multicolored	55
1842	A410	60m	multicolored	65
1843	A410	80m	multicolored	85
1844	A410	1.20t	multicolored	1.25
			Nos. 1838-1844 (7)	4.26

Souvenir Sheet

1845	A410	4t	Trophy, vert.	4.25

Nos. 304-307 Ovptd. CHINGGIS KHAN CROWNATION 1189

1990, May 1 Photo. *Perf. 11½x12*

1846	A84	20m	multicolored	*2.50*
1847	A84	30m	multicolored	*3.75*
1848	A84	50m	multicolored	*6.25*
1849	A84	60m	multicolored	*7.50*

Coronation of Genghis Khan, 800th anniv. (in 1989).

Souvenir Sheet

Genghis Khan A411

1990, May 8 Litho. *Perf. 13½*

1850	A411	7t	multicolored	4.90

Stamp World London '90. Exists imperf. Exists without "Stamp World London '90" and Great Britain No. 1.

Cranes *(Grus vipio pallas)* — A412

1990, May 23 *Perf. 14*

1851	A412	60m	brt blue & multi	58
1852	A412	60m	brt rose lil & multi	58
1853	A412	60m	red lil & multi	58
1854	A412	60m	car rose & multi	58

Nos. 1853-1854 are vert.

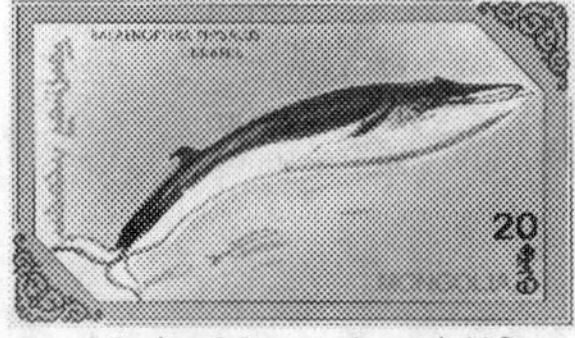
Marine Mammals — A413

1990 Litho. *Perf. 14*

1855	A413	20m	Balaenoptera physalus	24
1856	A413	30m	Megaptera novaeangliae	35
1857	A413	40m	Monodon monoceros	48
1858	A413	50m	Grampus griseus	60
1859	A413	60m	Tursiops truncatus	70
1860	A413	80m	Lagenorhynchus acutius	95
1861	A413	1.20t	Balaena mysticetus	1.40
			Nos. 1855-1861 (7)	4.72

Souvenir Sheet

1861A	A413	4t	Killer whale	4.65

Cultural Heritage
A414 A415

1990 *Perf. 13x12½*

1862	A414	10m	shown	15
1863	A414	10m	Like No. 1862, arrows at left	15
1864	A415	40m	Fire ring	48
1865	A415	60m	Genghis Khan	70
1866	A414	60m	Tent	70
1867	A414	60m	Horses	70
1868	A414	80m	Royal family (green panel)	95
1869	A414	80m	Royal court (dk bl panel)	95
a.			Souv. sheet, #1862-1869 + label	5.00
			Nos. 1862-1869 (8)	4.78

20th Party Congress A416

1990 Litho. *Perf. 14*

1870	A416	60m	multicolored	90

Dinosaurs — A417

1990

1871	A417	20m	shown	25
1872	A417	30m	multi, diff.	35
1873	A417	40m	multi, diff.	50
1874	A417	50m	multi, diff.	60
1875	A417	60m	multi, vert.	70
1876	A417	80m	multi, diff.	1.00

Size: 60x21mm

Perf. 13

1877	A417	1.20t	multi, diff.	1.40
			Nos. 1871-1877 (7)	4.80

Souvenir Sheet

1878	A417	4t	multi, diff.	4.75

Giant Pandas — A418

1990 Litho. *Perf. 14*

1879	A418	10m	Adult on rock, vert.	15
1880	A418	20m	Adult, eating, vert.	25
1881	A418	30m	Adult and cub, vert.	35
1882	A418	40m	shown	50
1883	A418	50m	Adult and cub, resting	60
1884	A418	60m	Adult, mountains	70
1885	A418	80m	Adult and cub, playing	1.00
1886	A418	1.20t	Adult, in winter	1.40
			Nos. 1879-1886 (8)	4.95

Souvenir Sheet

1887	A418	4t	Family	4.70

Pyramids of Egypt — A419

Seven wonders of the ancient world: 20m, Lighthouse of Alexander, vert. 40m, Statue of Zeus, vert. 50m, Colossus of Rhodes, vert. 60m, Mausoleum of Halicarnassus, vert. 80m, Temple of Artemis. 1.20t, Hanging gardens of Babylon, vert. 4t, Pyramids of Egypt, vert.

1990

1888	A419	20m	multicolored	25
1889	A419	30m	shown	35
1890	A419	40m	multicolored	50
1891	A419	50m	multicolored	62
1892	A419	60m	multicolored	70
1893	A419	80m	multicolored	1.00
1894	A419	1.20t	multicolored	1.40
			Nos. 1888-1894 (7)	4.82

Souvenir Sheet

1895	A419	4t	multicolored	4.65

Moschus Moschiferus — A419a

1990, Sept. 26 Litho. *Perf. 14*

1895A	A419a	60m	shown	70
1895B	A419a	60m	In snow	70
1895C	A419a	60m	Facing left	70
1895D	A419a	60m	Two, one on ground	70

Parrots — A420

1990 **Litho.** ***Perf. 14***

1896	A420	20m shown	25
1897	A420	30m multi, diff.	35
1898	A420	40m multi, diff.	50
1899	A420	50m multi, diff.	60
1900	A420	60m multi, diff.	70
1901	A420	80m multi, diff.	1.00
1902	A420	1.20t multi, diff.	1.50
		Nos. 1896-1902 (7)	4.90

Souvenir Sheet

1903	A420	4t multi, diff.	4.65

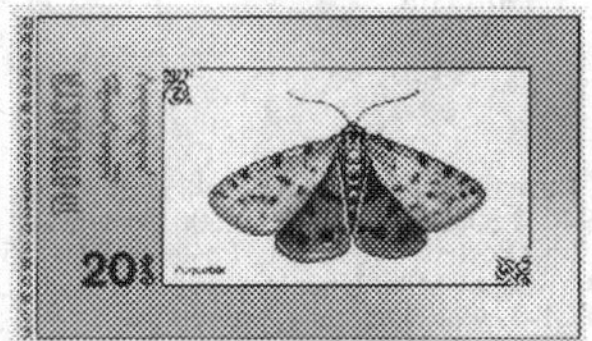

Butterflies — A421

Designs: 20m, Purpurbar. 30m, Grosses nachtpfauenauge. 40m, Grosser C-Falter. 50m, Stachelbeerspanner. 60m, Damenbrett. 80m, Schwalbenschwanz. 1.20t, Aurorafalter. 4t, Linienschwarmer, vert.

1990 **Litho.** ***Perf. 14***

1904	A421	20m multicolored	25
1905	A421	30m multicolored	35
1906	A421	40m multicolored	50
1907	A421	50m multicolored	60
1908	A421	60m multicolored	70
1909	A421	80m multicolored	1.00
1910	A421	1.20t multicolored	1.50
		Nos. 1904-1910 (7)	4.90

Souvenir Sheet

1911	A421	4t multicolored	4.65

Flintstones Visit Mongolia — A422

Designs: 25m, Dino, Bam-Bam. 35m, Dino, Bamm-Bamm, diff., vert. 45m, Betty, Wilma, Bamm-Bamm, Pebbles. 55m, Fred, Barney, Dino. 65m, Flintstones & Rubbles. 75m, Bamm-Bamm riding Dino. 85m, Fred, Barney, Bamm-Bamm. 1.40t, Flintstones, Rubbles in car. 2t, Fred, Barney. No. 1921, Wilma, Betty & Bamm-Bamm. No. 1922, Bamm-Bamm, Pebbles riding Dino.

1991, Feb. 10 **Litho.** ***Perf. 14***

1912	A422	25m multicolored	30
1913	A422	35m multicolored	42
1914	A422	45m multicolored	55
1915	A422	55m multicolored	65
1916	A422	65m multicolored	78
1917	A422	75m multicolored	90
1918	A422	85m multicolored	1.00
1919	A422	1.40t multicolored	1.70
1920	A422	2t multicolored	2.40
		Nos. 1912-1920 (9)	8.70

Souvenir Sheets

1921	A422	7t multicolored	3.50
1922	A422	7t multicolored	3.50

The Jetsons A423

Designs: 20m, Jetsons blasting off in spaceship. 25m, Jetsons on planet, horiz. 30m, George, Jane, Elroy & Astro. 40m, George, Judy, Elroy & Astro. 50m, Jetsons in spaceship, horiz. 60m, George, Jane, Elroy & Mr. Spacely, horiz. 70m, George, Elroy wearing jet packs. 80m, Elroy. 1.20t, Elroy, Judy & Astro. No. 1932, Elroy, red flowers. No. 1933, Elroy, blue flowers.

1991, Feb. 10

1923	A423	20m multicolored	25
1924	A423	25m multicolored	30
1925	A423	30m multicolored	35
1926	A423	40m multicolored	50
1927	A423	50m multicolored	60
1928	A423	60m multicolored	70
1929	A423	70m multicolored	85
1930	A423	80m multicolored	1.00
1931	A423	1.20t multicolored	1.50
		Nos. 1923-1931 (9)	6.05

Souvenir Sheets

1932	A423	7t multicolored	3.50
1933	A423	7t multicolored	3.50

Stamp World London '90 — A424

A425

Various birds.

1991, Mar. 3 **Litho.** ***Perf. 14½***

1934	A424	25m multicolored	30
1935	A424	35m multicolored	42
1936	A424	45m multicolored	55
1937	A424	55m multicolored	65
1938	A424	65m multicolored	78
1939	A424	75m multi, horiz.	90
1940	A424	85m multicolored	1.00
1941	A424	1.40t multicolored	1.70
1942	A424	2t multicolored	2.40
		Nos. 1934-1942 (9)	8.70

Souvenir Sheets

1943	A424	7t multicolored	3.50
1944	A425	7t multicolored	3.50

Butterflies and Flowers of Mongolia — A426

Designs: 20m, 30m-60m, various butterflies. Others, various flowers.

1991, Mar. 3 **Litho.** ***Perf. 14½***

1945	A426	20m multicolored	25
1946	A426	25m multicolored	30
1947	A426	30m multicolored	35
1948	A426	40m multicolored	48
1949	A426	50m multicolored	60
1950	A426	60m multicolored	70
1951	A426	70m multicolored	80

1952 A426 80m multicolored 95
1953 A426 1.20t multicolored 1.40
Nos. 1945-1953 (9) 5.83

Nos. 1945-1953 and Types Overprinted

EXPO'90

1991, Mar. 3
1954 A426 20m multicolored 25
1955 A426 25m multicolored 30
1956 A426 30m multicolored 35
1957 A426 40m multicolored 48
1958 A426 50m multicolored 60
1959 A426 60m multicolored 70
1960 A426 70m multicolored 80
1961 A426 80m multicolored 95
1962 A426 1.20t multicolored 1.40
Nos. 1954-1962 (9) 5.83

Souvenir Sheets

1963 A426 7t Butterfly 5.35
1964 A426 7t Flower 5.35

Nos. 1963-1964 were not issued without overprint which appears in sheet margin only.

Birds — A427

1991, Apr. 1 ***Perf. 14***
1965 A427 20m Lururus tetrix 25
1966 A427 30m Tadorna tadorna 35
1967 A427 40m Phasianus colchicus 48
1968 A427 50m Clangula byemalis 60
1969 A427 60m Tetrastes bonasia 70
1970 A427 80m Mergus serrator 95
1971 A427 1.20t Bucephaia clangula 1.40
Nos. 1965-1971 (7) 4.73

Souvenir Sheet

1972 A427 4t Anas crecca, vert. 4.65

Flowers — A428

1991, Apr. 15
1973 A428 20m Dianthus superbus 25
1974 A428 30m Gentiana puenmonanthe 35
1975 A428 40m Taraxacum officinale 48
1976 A428 50m Iris sibrica 60
1977 A428 60m Lilium martagon 70
1978 A428 80m Aster amellus 95
1979 A428 1.20t Cizsium rivulare 1.40
Nos. 1973-1979 (7) 4.73

Souvenir Sheet

1980 A428 4t Campanula persicifolia 4.65

A little time given to the study of the arrangement of the Scott Catalogue can make it easier to use effectively.

Buddhist Effigies — A429

1991, May 1
1981 A429 20m Defend 25
1982 A429 30m Badmasanhava 35
1983 A429 40m Avalokitecvara 48
1984 A429 50m Buddha 60
1985 A429 60m Mintugwa 70
1986 A429 80m Shyamatara 95
1987 A429 1.20t Samvara 1.40
Nos. 1981-1987 (7) 4.73

Souvenir Sheet

1988 A429 4t Lamidhatara 4.65

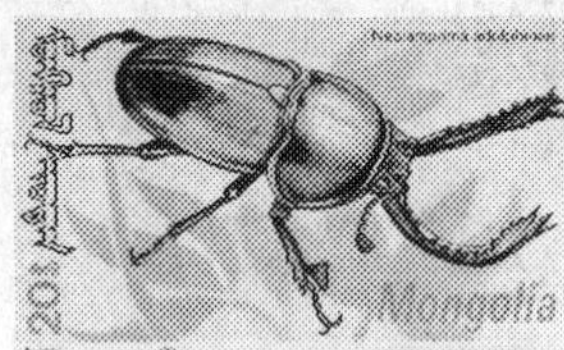
Insects — A430

1991, May 22
1989 A430 20m Neolamprima adolphinae 25
1990 A430 30m Chelorrhina polyphemus 35
1991 A430 40m Coptolabrus coelestis 48
1992 A430 50m Epepeotes togatus 60
1993 A430 60m Cicindela chinensis 70
1994 A430 80m Macrodontia cervicornis 95
1995 A430 1.20t Dynastes hercules 1.40
Nos. 1989-1995 (7) 4.73

African Animals — A431

1991, May 23
1996 A431 20m Zebras 25
1997 A431 30m Cheetah 35
1998 A431 40m Black rhinos 48
1999 A431 50m Giraffe, vert. 60
2000 A431 60m Gorilla 70
2001 A431 80m Elephants 95
2002 A431 1.20t Lion, vert. 1.40
Nos. 1996-2002 (7) 4.73

Souvenir Sheet

2003 A431 4t Gazelle 4.65

No. 1997 is incorrectly spelled "Cheetan."

Exhibition of Meiso Mizuhara's Mongolian Stamp Collection — A432

1991, June **Litho.** ***Perf. 13½***
2004 A432 1.20t multicolored 1.10

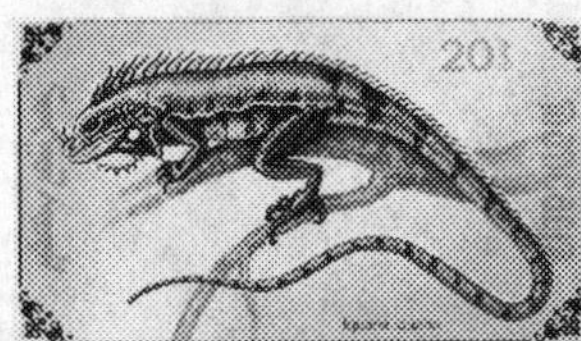
Lizards — A433

1991, Oct. 29 ***Perf. 14***
2005 A433 20m Iguana iguana 30
2006 A433 30m Ptychozoon kihli 45
2007 A433 40m Chlamydosaurus kingii 62
2008 A433 50m Cordylus cordylus 78
2009 A433 60m Basiliscus basilisus 90
2010 A433 80m Tupinambis teguixin 1.25
2011 A433 1.20t Amblyrhynchus cristatus 1.85
Nos. 2005-2011 (7) 6.15

Souvenir Sheet

2012 A433 4t Varanus bengalensis, vert. 4.75

Masks and Costumes A434

Various masks and costumes.

1991, Oct. 1
2013 A434 35m multicolored 40
2014 A434 45m multicolored 52
2015 A434 55m multicolored 65
2016 A434 65m multicolored 75
2017 A434 85m multicolored 1.00
2018 A434 1.40t multicolored 1.65
2019 A434 2t multicolored 2.35
Nos. 2013-2019 (7) 7.32

Souvenir Sheet

2020 A434 4t multicolored 4.75

Phila Nippon '91 — A435

1991, Oct. 29
2021 A435 1t Pagoda
2022 A435 2t Japanese beauty
2023 A435 3t Mongolian woman
2024 A435 4t Mongolian building

Fantasia, 50th Anniv. A436

Designs: 1.70t, Poster, 1985. 2t, Poster, 1940. 2.30t, Poster, 1982. 2.60t, Poster, 1981. 4.20t, Poster, 1969. 10t, Poster, 1941. 15t, Drawing of Mlle. Upanova, 1940. 16t, Sketch of Mickey as Sorcerer's Apprentice.

1991, Dec. 31 ***Perf. 13½x14***
2025 A436 1.70t multicolored 28
2026 A436 2t multicolored 32
2027 A436 2.30t multicolored 38
2028 A436 2.60t multicolored 42
2029 A436 4.20t multicolored 68
2030 A436 10t multicolored 1.60
2031 A436 15t multicolored 2.40
2032 A436 16t multicolored 2.60
Nos. 2025-2032 (8) 8.68

1992 Winter Olympics, Albertville — A437

1992, Feb. 1 ***Perf. 14***
2037 A437 60m Speed skating, vert. 90
2038 A437 80m Ski jumping, vert. 1.20
2039 A437 1t Hockey, vert. 1.50
2040 A437 1.20t Figure skating, vert. 1.80
2041 A437 1.50t Biathlon 2.25
2042 A437 2t Downhill skiing 3.00
2043 A437 2.40t Two-man bobsled 3.60
Nos. 2037-2043 (7) 14.25

Souvenir Sheet

2044 A437 8t Four-man bobsled, vert. 4.75

SEMI-POSTAL STAMPS

Catalogue values for unused stamps in this section are for Never Hinged items.

Vietnamese Mother and Child SP1

1967, Dec. 22 **Photo.** ***Perf. 12x11½***
B1 SP1 30m + 20m multi 20 15
B2 SP1 50m + 30m multi 30 20

Solidarity with Vietnam.

Save Venice Type of Regular Issue Souvenir Sheet

Design: 3t+1t, Departure of St. Ursula, by Carpaccio.

1972, Oct. 1 **Litho.** ***Perf. 12***
B3 A163 3t + 1t multi 3.25 3.25

Save Venice Campaign. No. B3 contains one horizontal stamp.

Girl Feeding Lambs SP2

Designs (UNICEF Emblem and): 20+5m, Boy playing flute and dancing girl. 30+5m, Girl chasing butterflies. 40+5m, Girl with ribbon. 60+5m, Girl with flowers. 80+5m, Girl carrying bucket. 1t+5m, Boy going to school.

1977, June 1 Litho. *Perf. 12*

B4	SP2 10m + 5m multi	15	15
B5	SP2 20m + 5m multi	18	15
B6	SP2 30m + 5m multi	30	18
B7	SP2 40m + 5m multi	40	25
B8	SP2 60m + 5m multi	60	30
B9	SP2 80m + 5m multi	70	40
B10	SP2 1t + 5m multi	90	55
	Nos. B4-B10 (7)	3.23	1.98

Surtax was for Mongolian Children's Village. See No. CB1.

Boys on Horseback — SP3

Mongolian Children and IYC Emblem: 30+5m, Raising chickens. 50+5m, With deer. 60+5m, With flowers. 70+5m, Planting tree. 80+5m, Studying space project. 1t+5m, Dancing. 4t+50m, Girl on horseback.

1979, Jan. 10

B11	SP3 10m + 5m multi	15	15
B12	SP3 30m + 5m multi	18	15
B13	SP3 50m + 5m multi	32	15
B14	SP3 60m + 5m multi	35	15
B15	SP3 70m + 5m multi	45	22
B16	SP3 80m + 5m multi	55	32
B17	SP3 1t + 5m multi	70	40
	Nos. B11-B17 (7)	2.70	
	Set value		1.25

Souvenir Sheet

B18	SP3 4t + 50m multi	3.00	3.00

International Year of the Child.

AIR POST STAMPS

Catalogue values for unused stamps in this section are for Never Hinged items.

Postal Modernization Type of Regular Issue

Designs: 10m, 20m, Postman with horses. 25m, Postman with reindeer. 30m, 50m, Plane over map of Mongolia. 1t, Post horn and flag of Mongolia.

1961, June 5 Photo. *Perf. 15*

C1	A72 10m multi	15	15
C2	A72 50m multi	30	15
C3	A72 1t multi	70	40
	Set value		58

Souvenir Sheet

Perf. 11

C4	Sheet of 4	1.00	1.00
a.	A72 20m lt bl grn & multi	24	24
b.	A72 25m lt bl & multi	24	24
c.	A72 30m lt grn & multi	24	24
d.	A72 1t rose car & multi	24	24

40th anniversary of independence; postal modernization. No. C4b is not inscribed Airmail.

Souvenir Sheet

Austria Type SP55, Austrian and Mongolian Stamps Circling Globe — AP1

1965, May 1 Engr. *Perf. 11½*

C5	AP1 4t brn car	2.50	2.50

Vienna Intl. Philatelic Exhibition, WIPA, June 4-13. #C5 contains one 61x38mm stamp.

Weather Satellite AP2

Designs: 20m, Antarctic exploration. 30m, Space exploration.

1965, May 15 Photo. *Perf. 13½*

C6	AP2 15m lil, gold & blk	15	15
C7	AP2 20m bl & multi	15	15
C8	AP2 30m rose & multi	20	15
	Set value		28

International Quiet Sun Year, 1964-65.

ITU Emblem — AP3

Design: 4t, Communications satellite.

1965, Dec. 20 *Perf. 11½x12*

C9	AP3 30m bl & bis	15	15
C10	AP3 50m red & bis	20	15
	Set value		16

Souvenir Sheet

Perf. 11, Imperf.

C11	AP3 4t gold, bl & blk	2.25	2.25

ITU, centenary. No. C11 contains one stamp, 38x51mm.

Souvenir Sheet

Luna 10, Moon and Earth — AP4

1966, July 10 Photo. *Imperf.*

C12	AP4 4t multi	2.50	2.50

Luna 10 Russian moon mission, Apr. 3, 1966.

Souvenir Sheet

Astronaut and Landing Module — AP5

1969, Aug. 20 Litho. *Perf. 11½*

C13	AP5 4t ultra & multi	2.50	2.50

Apollo 11 US moon mission, first man landing on moon.

Souvenir Sheet

Apollo 16 — AP6

Perf. 12½x11½

1972, Apr. 16 Photo.

C14	AP6 4t multi	2.50	2.50

Apollo 16 moon mission, Apr. 15-27.

Souvenir Sheet

Mongolian Horse — AP7

1972, May 10 Photo. *Perf. 12½*

C15	AP7 4t multi	2.50	2.50

Centenary of the discovery of the Przewalski wild horse, bred in captivity in Berlin Zoo.

Telecommunication — AP8

Designs: 30m, Horse breeding. 40m, Train and plane. 50m, Corn and farm machinery. 60m, Red Cross ambulance and hospital. 80m, Actors. 1t, Factories.

1972, July 11 Litho. *Perf. 12*

C16	AP8 20m ol & multi	15	15
C17	AP8 30m vio & multi	15	15
C18	AP8 40m rose & multi	15	15
C19	AP8 50m red & multi	20	15
C20	AP8 60m multi	35	15
C21	AP8 80m lt bl & multi	35	18
C22	AP8 1t grn & multi	40	28
	Nos. C16-C22 (7)	1.75	
	Set value		88

Mongolian Achievements.

Mongolian Flag, Globe and Radar — AP9

Perf. 12½x11½

1972, July 20 Photo.

C23	AP9 60m ol & multi	28	18

Intl. Telecommunications Day, May 17, 1972.

Running and Olympic Rings — AP10

Olympic Rings and: 15m, Boxing. 20m, Judo. 25m, High jump. 30m, Rifle shooting. 60m, Wrestling. 80m, Weight lifting. 1t, Mongolian flag and sport emblem. 4t, Woman archer (vert.).

Perf. 12½x11½

1972, July 30 Photo.

C24	AP10 10m multi	15	15
C25	AP10 15m multi	15	15
C26	AP10 20m multi	15	15
C27	AP10 25m multi	18	15
C28	AP10 30m multi	20	15
C29	AP10 60m multi	30	20
C30	AP10 80m multi	38	24
C31	AP10 1t multi	55	32
	Nos. C24-C31 (8)	2.06	
	Set value		1.10

Souvenir Sheet

Perf. 11½x12½

C32	AP10 4t org & multi	2.00	2.00

20th Olympic Games, Munich, Aug. 26-Sept. 11.

Dragon and Mariner 2 — AP11

Designs: a, Snake, Mars 1. c, Hare, Soyuz 5. d, Monkey, Explorer 6. e, Cock, Venus 1. f, Rat, Apollo 15. g, Horse, Apollo 8. h, Boar, Cosmos 110. i, Tiger, Gemini 7. j, Sheep, Electron 2. k, Dog, Ariel 2. l, Ram, Venus 4.

1972, Dec. 4 Photo. *Perf. 12*
C33 AP11 Sheet of 12 4.00 1.50

Size: 55x35mm

a.-f. 60m any single 30 15

Size: 35x35mm

g.-l. 60m any single 30 15

Space achievements of US and USSR, and signs of Eastern Calendar.

Airliner — AP12

1973, Jan. Photo. *Perf. 12*
C34 AP12 1.50t blue 70 20

Weather Satellite, Earth Station, WMO Emblem — AP13

1973, Feb. Photo. *Perf. 12x11½*
C35 AP13 60m multi 28 15

Intl. meteorological cooperation, cent.

Holy Flame Type of 1959
Souvenir Sheet

1973, Apr. 15 Photo. *Perf. 12½*
C36 A48 4t gold & multi 1.75 1.75

IBRA München 1973 Intl. Stamp Exhibition, Munich, May 11-20. No. C36 contains one 40x63mm stamp in redrawn design of A48 with simulated perforations and wide gold margin.

Russia No. 3100 — AP14

Designs: Stamps (with mail-connected designs) of participating countries.

1973, July 31 Litho. *Perf. 12½*
C37 AP14 30m shown 20 15
C38 AP14 30m Mongolia #236 20 15
C39 AP14 30m Bulgaria #1047 20 15
C40 AP14 30m Hungary #B202 20 15
C41 AP14 30m Czechoslavia #C72 20 15
C42 AP14 30m German Dem. Rep. #369 20 15
C43 AP14 30m Cuba #C31 20 15
C44 AP14 30m Romania #2280 20 15
C45 AP14 30m Poland #802 20 15
Nos. C37-C45 (9) 1.80 1.35

Conference of Permanent Committee for Posts and Telecommunications of Council for Economic Aid (COMECON), Ulan Bator, Aug. 1973.

Launching of Soyuz Spacecraft — AP15

1973, Oct. 26 Litho. *Perf. 12½*
C46 AP15 5m shown 15 15
C47 AP15 10m Apollo 8 15 15
C48 AP15 15m Soyuz 4 & 5 docking 15 15
C49 AP15 20m Apollo 11 lunar module 15 15
C50 AP15 30m Apollo 14 splashdown 28 15
C51 AP15 50m Soyuz 6, 7 & 8 35 16
C52 AP15 60m Apollo 16 moon rover 40 28
C53 AP15 1t Lunokhod 1 on moon 60 38
Nos. C46-C53 (8) 2.23
Set value 1.20

Souvenir Sheet

C54 AP15 4t Soyuz and Apollo 2.25 2.25

US and Russian achievements in space.

Comecon Building, Moscow — AP16

1974, Feb. 28 Photo. *Perf. 11½x12*
C55 AP16 60m bl & multi 28 15

25th anniversary of the Council of Mutual Economic Assistance.

Souvenir Sheet

Mongolia No. 4 — AP17

1974, Mar. 15 Photo. *Perf. 12½*
C56 AP17 4t multi 1.90 1.90

50th anniv. of 1st stamps of Mongolia.

Postrider and UPU Emblem — AP18

Designs: UPU emblem and means of transportation.

1974, Apr. Litho. *Perf. 12*
C57 AP18 50m shown 35 18
C58 AP18 50m Reindeer post 35 18
C59 AP18 50m Mail coach 35 18
C60 AP18 50m Balloon post 35 18
C61 AP18 50m Steamship and AN-2 plane 35 18
C62 AP18 50m Train, truck and city 35 18
C63 AP18 50m Rocket over North Pole 35 18
Nos. C57-C63 (7) 2.45 1.26

Souvenir Sheet

C64 AP18 4t Globe and post horn, vert. 2.50 2.50

Centenary of Universal Postal Union.

Circus Type of 1974

Design: 1t, Two women contortionists.

1974, May 4 Litho. *Perf. 12*
C65 A177 1t multi 48 30

No. C65 has se-tenant label, with similar design.

Nature Type of Regular Issue

Designs: 1t, Scientist checking water, globe. 4t, Wild rose.

1974, Dec. Litho. *Perf. 11*
C66 A186 1t multi 55 30

Souvenir Sheet
Perf. 12½

C67 A186 4t multi 2.25 2.25

UPU Type of 1974
Souvenir Sheet

Design: UPU Emblem (vert.).

1974, Dec. *Perf. 11½x12*
C68 A187 4t multi 4.00 4.00

Soyuz on Launching Pad, Project Emblem — AP19

Project Emblem and: 20m, Radar and Apollo. 30m, Apollo, Soyuz and earth. 40m, Spacecraft before docking. 50m, Spacecraft after docking. 60m, Soyuz circling earth. 1t, Spacecraft, space station and earth. 4t, Russian and American astronauts.

1975, June 14 Litho. *Perf. 12*
C69 AP19 10m bl & multi 15 15
C70 AP19 20m multi 15 15
C71 AP19 30m sep & multi 20 15
C72 AP19 40m sil & multi 24 15
C73 AP19 50m multi 35 15
C74 AP19 60m multi 48 20
C75 AP19 1t multi 60 30
Nos. C69-C75 (7) 2.17
Set value 90

Souvenir Sheet

C76 AP19 4t blk & multi 3.00 3.00

Apollo Soyuz space test project (Russo-American space cooperation), launching July 15; link-up July 17.

Mongolian Mountain Sheep — AP20

1975, Aug. 4 Litho. *Perf. 12*
C77 AP20 1.50t multi 80 30

South Asia Tourism Year. No. C77 printed se-tenant with label showing modern hotel, map and stone turtle.

Satellite over Weather Map of Mongolia AP21

1976, Mar. 20 *Perf. 12x11½*
C78 AP21 60m bl & yel 35 15

40th anniversary of meteorological service.

Souvenir Sheet

Girl with Books and Flowers — AP22

1976, Mar. 30 *Perf. 12*
C79 AP22 4t multi 2.25 2.25

30th anniversary of UNESCO.

Souvenir Sheet

The Wise Musician, by Sarav — AP23

1976, May 3 Litho. *Perf. 11½x12½*
C80 AP23 4t multi 2.25 2.25

Interphil 76 Phil. Exhib., Philadelphia, Pa., May 29-June 6.

Olympic Games Type of 1976
Souvenir Sheet

1976, May 20 *Perf. 12½x11½*
C81 A202 4t Wrestling 2.25 2.25

Independence Type of 1976

Design: 60m, Progress in agriculture and industry.

1976, June 20 Litho. *Perf. 12x11½*
C82 A203 60m multi 35 18

Olympic Medalists Type, 1976
Souvenir Sheet

Design: 4t, Oidov Zeveg, Mongolian flag.

1976, Nov. 30 Litho. *Perf. 11x11½*
C83 A209 4t multi 2.00 2.00

Mounting Carrier Rocket with Bell-shaped Gear — AP24

Designs: 20m, Launching of Intercosmos 3. 30m, Marine Observatory Gagarin (ship). 40m, Satellite observation of lunar eclipse. 60m, Observatory with multiple antenna system. 80m, Examination of Van Allen Zone, magnetosphere. 1t, Meteorological earth satellite. 4t, Intercosmos satellite with lines showing participating countries on globe.

1977, June 20 Litho. *Perf. 12*

C84 AP24 10m multi 15 15
C85 AP24 20m multi 15 15
C86 AP24 30m multi 18 15
C87 AP24 40m multi 28 15
C88 AP24 60m multi 48 20
C89 AP24 80m multi 60 28
C90 AP24 1t multi 75 38
Nos. C84-C90 (7) 2.59
Set value 1.15

Souvenir Sheet

Perf. 12½

C91 AP24 4t multi 2.50 2.50

11th anniv. of Intercosmos program, cooperation of 9 socialist countries for space research. No. C91 contains one stamp 58x37mm.

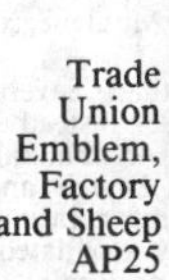

Trade Union Emblem, Factory and Sheep AP25

1977, June *Perf. 12x11½*

C92 AP25 60m multi 40 18

11th Congress of Mongolian Trade Unions, May 12.

Montgolfier's Balloon — AP26

Dirigibles: 30m, Zeppelin over North Pole, 1931. 40m, Osoaviahim, Russian Arctic cargo. 50m, North, Russian heavy duty cargo. 60m, Aeron-340, Russian planned. 80m, Machinery transport, Russian planned. 1.20t, Flying crane, French planned. 4t, Russia No. C26 (stamp) and Sukhe Bator statue.

1977, Dec. Litho. *Perf. 12*

C93 AP26 20m multi 15 15
C94 AP26 30m multi 15 15
C95 AP26 40m multi 20 15
C96 AP26 50m multi 28 15
C97 AP26 60m multi 35 18
C98 AP26 80m multi 40 24
C99 AP26 1.20t multi 60 38
Nos. C93-C99 (7) 2.13
Set value 1.20

Souvenir Sheet

Perf. 12½x11½

C100 AP26 4t multi 2.00 2.00

History of airships.

A. F. Mozhaiski and his Plane, 1884 — AP27

Designs: 30m, Henry Farman and his plane, 1909. 40m, Geoffrey de Havilland and D. H. 66 Hercules, 1920's. 50m, Charles A. Lindbergh, Spirit of St. Louis and route New York to Paris, 1927. 60m, Mongolian pilots Shagdarsuren and Demberel and plane over Altai Mountains, 1935. 80m, Soviet aviators Chkalov, Baidukov, Beliakov, plane and route Moscow to Vancouver, 1937. 1.20t, A. N. Tupolev, supersonic plane TU 154, route Moscow to Alma-Ata, 1968. 4t, Wilbur and Orville Wright and their plane.

1978, Mar. 25 Litho. *Perf. 12½x11*

C101 AP27 20m multi 15 15
C102 AP27 30m multi 15 15
C103 AP27 40m multi 20 15
C104 AP27 50m multi 28 15
C105 AP27 60m multi 35 18
C106 AP27 80m multi 40 24
C107 AP27 1.20t multi 70 38
Nos. C101-C107 (7) 2.23
Set value 1.20

Souvenir Sheet

C108 AP27 4t multi 3.00 3.00

75th anniversary of first powered flight, Wright brothers, 1903.

Soccer Type of 1978
Souvenir Sheet

Design: 4t, Two soccer players.

1978, Apr. 15 *Perf. 11½*

C109 A231 4t multi 2.50 2.50

World Soccer Championships, Argentina 78, June 1-25. No. C109 contains one stamp 45x38mm.

Souvenir Sheet

Canada No. 553 and Mongolia No. 549 — AP28

1978, June Litho. *Perf. 12½*

C110 AP28 4t multi 3.00 3.00

CAPEX '78, Intl. Phil. Exhibition, Toronto, June 9-18.

Map of Cuba, Ship, Plane and Festival Emblem — AP29

1978, July 28 Litho. *Perf. 12*

C111 AP29 1t multi 60 24

11th World Youth Festival, Havana, July 28-Aug. 5.

Souvenir Sheet

Aleksei Gubarev and Vladimir Remek, PRAGA '78 Emblem — AP30

1978, Sept. 5 Litho. *Perf. 12*

C112 AP30 4t multi 3.00 3.00

PRAGA '78 Intl. Phil. Exhib., Prague, Sept. 8-17, and Russian-Czechoslovak space cooperation, Intercosmos.

DDR Flag, TV Tower, Berlin, Satellite — AP31

1979, Oct. 9 Litho. *Perf. 11½x12*

C113 AP31 60m multi 35 15

German Democratic Republic, 30th anniv.

Demoiselle Crane AP32

Protected Birds: 30m, Hawk warbler. 50m, Ruddy shelduck. 60m, Blue magpie. 70m, Goldfinch. 80m, Titmouse. 1t, Golden oriole.

1979, Oct. 25

C114 AP32 10m multi 15 15
C115 AP32 30m multi 15 15
C116 AP32 50m multi 28 15
C117 AP32 60m multi 30 15
C118 AP32 70m multi 30 15
C119 AP32 80m multi 35 15
C120 AP32 1t multi 45 18
Nos. C114-C120 (7) 1.98
Set value 72

Venera 5 and 6 — AP33

American and Russian Space Missions: 30m, Mariner 5. 50m, Mars 3. 60m, Viking 1 and 2. 70m, Luna 1, 2 and 3. 80m, Lunokhod 2. 1t, Apollo 15. 4t, Apollo 11, astronauts on moon.

Perf. 12½x11½

1979, Nov. 24 Litho.

C121 AP33 10m multi 15 15
C122 AP33 30m multi 16 15
C123 AP33 50m multi 28 15
C124 AP33 60m multi 32 15
C125 AP33 70m multi 38 15
C126 AP33 80m multi 45 15
C127 AP33 1t multi 55 18
Nos. C121-C127 (7) 2.29
Set value 75

Souvenir Sheet

C128 AP33 4t multi 2.50 2.50

Apollo 11 moon landing, 10th anniversary.

Andrena Scita — AP34

Insects: 30m, Paravespula germanica. 40m, Perilampus ruficornis. 50m, Bumblebee. 60m, Honey bee. 80m, Stilbum cyanurum. 1.20t, Ruby tail.

1980, Feb. 25 Litho. *Perf. 11x12*

C129 AP34 20m multi 15 15
C130 AP34 30m multi 16 15
C131 AP34 40m multi 25 15
C132 AP34 50m multi 40 15
C133 AP34 60m multi 45 15
C134 AP34 80m multi 60 25
C135 AP34 1.20t multi 80 30
Nos. C129-C135 (7) 2.81
Set value 1.05

Z-526 AFS Stunt Planes, Czechoslovakia — AP35

1980, Aug. 4 Litho. *Perf. 12*

C136 AP35 20m shown 15 15
C137 AP35 30m RS-180 "Sportsman," Germany 20 15
C138 AP35 40m Yanki-Anu, US 28 15
C139 AP35 50m MJ-2 "Tempete," France 35 15
C140 AP35 60m "Pits," Canada 40 15
C141 AP35 80m "Acrostar," Switzerland 55 18
C142 AP35 1.20t JAK-50, USSR 85 20
Nos. C136-C142 (7) 2.78
Set value 78

Souvenir Sheet

C143 AP35 4t JAK-52, USSR 2.00 1.75

10th World Aerobatic Championship, Oshkosh, Wisconsin, Aug. 17-30. Nos. C143 contains one stamp 50x43mm.

Olympic Type of 1980
Souvenir Sheet

1980, Sept. 15 Litho. *Perf. 12½*

C144 A253 4t Wrestlers 2.00 1.75

J. Davaajav, Mongolian silver medalist, 22nd Summer Olympic Games, Moscow. Inscribed "Los Angeles '84".

Johannes Kepler — AP36

1980, Dec. 10 Litho. *Perf. 11½x11*

C145 AP36 4t multi 3.00 2.75

Johannes Kepler (1571-1630), German astronomer.

Germany No. C40, Graf Zeppelin, Sea Eagle — AP37

Graf Zeppelin and: 30m, Germany No. C41, polar fox, 40m, Germany No. C42, sea ox. 50m, Russia No. C26, polar bear. 60m, Russia No. C27, snowy owl. 80m, Russia No.

C28, puffin. 1.20t, Russia No. C29, seal. 4t, Icebreaker Maligin.

1981, Oct. 5 Litho. *Perf. 12x11½*
C146 AP37 20m multi 15 15
C147 AP37 30m multi 18 15
C148 AP37 40m multi 28 15
C149 AP37 50m multi 35 15
C150 AP37 60m multi 40 15
C151 AP37 80m multi 50 15
C152 AP37 1.20t multi 70 22
Nos. C146-C152 (7) 2.56
Set value 75

Souvenir Sheet

C153 AP37 4t multi 2.50 2.50

Graf Zeppelin polar flight, 50th anniv. No. C153 contains one stamp 36x51mm.

ITU Plenipotentiaries Conference, Nairobi, Sept. — AP38

1982, Sept. 27 Litho. *Perf. 12*
C154 AP38 60m Map 28 15

2nd UN Conference on Peaceful Uses of Outer Space, Vienna, Aug. 9-21 — AP39

1982, Dec. 15 Litho. *Perf. 12*
C155 AP39 60m Sputnik 1 28 15
C156 AP39 60m Sputnik 2 28 15
C157 AP39 60m Vostok 1 28 15
C158 AP39 60m Venera 8 28 15
C159 AP39 60m Vostok 6 28 15
C160 AP39 60m Voskhod 2 28 15
C161 AP39 60m Apollo II 28 15
C162 AP39 60m Soyuz 6 28 15
Nos. C155-C162 (8) 2.24
Set value 65

Souvenir Sheet
Perf. 12½x12

C163 AP39 4t Soyuz 39, Salyut 6 3.00 3.00

Balloon Flight Bicentenary AP40

1982, Dec. 31 *Perf. 11½x12½*
C164 AP40 20m Montgolfiere, 1783 15 15
C165 AP40 30m Blanchard, 1785 15 15
C166 AP40 40m Royal-Vauzhall, 1836 20 15
C167 AP40 50m Oernen, 1897 24 15
C168 AP40 60m Gordon Bennett Race, 1906 35 15
C169 AP40 80m Paris, 1931 40 15
C170 AP40 1.20t USSR-VR-62, 1933 70 18
Nos. C164-C170 (7) 2.19
Set value 60

Souvenir Sheet

C171 AP40 4t Mongolia, 1977 3.00 2.50

Souvenir Sheet

Revolutionary Mongolia Monument — AP41

1983 Litho. *Imperf.*
C172 AP41 4t multi 2.50

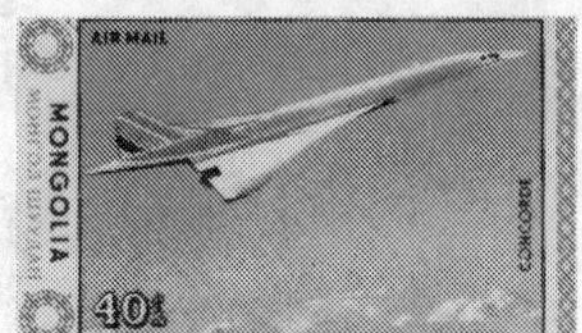

Concorde — AP42

1984, Aug. 15 Litho. *Perf. 14*
C173 AP42 20m DC-10, vert. 15
C174 AP42 30m Airbus A-300 B-2 20
C175 AP42 40m shown 28
C176 AP42 50m Boeing 747 35
C177 AP42 60m IL-62 40
C178 AP42 80m TU-154 55
C179 AP42 1.20t IL-86 80
Nos. C173-C179 (7) 2.73

Souvenir Sheet

C180 AP42 4t Yak-42 2.75

1988 Winter Olympics, Calgary — AP43

1988, Jan. 20 Litho. *Perf. 14*
C181 AP43 20m Bobsled 15
C182 AP43 30m Ski jumping 22
C183 AP43 40m Downhill skiing 30
C184 AP43 50m Biathlon 40
C185 AP43 60m Speed skating 45
C186 AP43 80m Women's figure skating 60
C187 AP43 1.20t Ice hockey 90
Nos. C181-C187 (7) 3.02

Souvenir sheet

C188 AP43 4t Cross-country skiing 3.00

AIR POST SEMI-POSTAL STAMP

Catalogue values for unused stamps in this section are for Never Hinged items.

UNICEF Type of 1977
Souvenir Sheet

Design: 4t+50m, Balloon with Mongolian flag, children and UNICEF emblem.

1977, June 1 Litho. *Perf. 12*
CB1 SP2 4t + 50m multi 2.50 2.50

First balloon flight in Mongolia. Surtax was for Children's Village.

MONTENEGRO

LOCATION — Southern Europe, bordering on the Adriatic Sea
GOVT. — A former Kingdom
AREA — 5,603 sq. mi.
POP. — 516,000 (estimated)
CAPITAL — Cetinje

This kingdom, formerly a Turkish Protectorate, later became independent. On December 1, 1918, Montenegro united with Serbia, Bosnia and Herzegovina, Croatia, Dalmatia and Slovenia to form the Kingdom of the Serbs, Croats and Slovenes which became Yugoslavia in 1929.

100 Novcic = 1 Florin
100 Helera = 1 Kruna (1902)
100 Para = 1 Kruna (1907)
100 Para = 1 Perper (1910)

Canceled to Order
Used values are for canceled to order stamps. Postally used specimens sell for considerably more.

Watermarks

Wmk. 91- "BRIEF-MARKEN" (#1-14) or "ZEITUNGS-MARKEN" (#15-21) in Double-lined Capitals once across sheet

Prince Nicholas I — A1

1874 Typo. Wmk. 91
Early Printings
Perf. 10½ Large Holes, pointed teeth
Narrow Spacing (2-2½mm)

1 A1 2n yellow 30.00 30.00
2 A1 3n green 45.00 40.00
3 A1 5n rose red 32.50 30.00
4 A1 7n lt lil 40.00 32.50
5 A1 10n blue 95.00 60.00
6 A1 15n yel bis 100.00 82.50
7 A1 25n lil gray 200.00 165.00

Middle Printings (1879)
Perf. 12, 12½, 13 and Compound
Narrow spacing

8 A1 2n yellow 8.00 5.50
a. Perf. 12-13x10½ 65.00 65.00
9 A1 3n green 6.50 4.00
10 A1 5n red 6.50 4.00
11 A1 7n rose lilac 6.50 3.75
a. 7n lilac 16.00 13.00
12 A1 10n blue 8.50 5.50
a. Perf. 12-13x10½ 65.50 52.50
13 A1 15n bis brn 17.00 10.00
14 A1 25n gray lilac 17.00 13.00

Late Printings (1891-93)
Perf. 10½, 11, 11½ Small holes, broad teeth
(Perf. 11½ also with pointed teeth)
Narrow and wide spacing
(2¾-3½mm)

15 A1 2n yellow 2.25 1.50
a. Perf. 11 ('91) 20.00 16.00
16 A1 3n green 1.50 1.00
17 A1 5n red 1.50 70
18 A1 7n rose 1.50 70
a. Perf. 11 ('91) 5.25 5.00
19 A1 10n blue 1.75 1.50
20 A1 15n brown 1.75 1.50
21 A1 25n brn vio 1.65 1.50
Nos. 15-21 (7) 11.90 8.40

Прослава
Types of 1874-93 Overprinted in Black or Red
1493 1893
Штампарије

1893 *Perf. 10½, 11, 11½*
22 A1 2n yellow 27.50 5.00
a. Perf. 11 *40.00* *35.00*
23 A1 3n green 1.75 1.50
24 A1 5n red 1.10 85
25 A1 7n rose 2.75 1.50
a. Perf. 12 50.00 42.50
c. 7n lilac, perf. 12 *125.00*
d. Perf. 11 *22.50* *20.00*
26 A1 10n blue 1.65 1.65
27 A1 10n blue (R) 2.25 2.25
28 A1 15n brown 1.10 1.10
a. Perf. 12 50.00 42.50
29 A1 15n brn (R) *1,500.* *1,500.*
30 A1 25n brn vio 2.00 2.00
31 A1 25n brn vio (R) 2.00 2.00
a. Perf. 12½ *225.00*

Introduction of printing to Montenegro, 400th anniversary.

This overprint had three settings. Several values exist with "1494" or "1495" instead of "1493", or with missing letters or numerals due to wearing of the cliches. Double and inverted overprints exist. Some printings were made after 1893 to supply a philatelic demand, but were available for postage.

The 7n with red overprint was not issued.

1894-98 Wmk. 91 *Perf. 10½, 11½*
32 A1 1n gray blue 15 15
33 A1 2n emer ('98) 20 15
34 A1 3n car rose ('98) 15 15
35 A1 5n orange ('98) 50 22
36 A1 7n gray lilac ('98) 20 15
37 A1 10n magenta ('98) 18 15
38 A1 15n red brn ('98) 22 20
39 A1 20n brn org 15 15
40 A1 25n dl bl ('98) 22 20
41 A1 30n maroon 15 15
42 A1 50n ultra 24 22
43 A1 1fl dp grn 40 35
44 A1 2fl red brown 70 70
Nos. 32-44 (13) 3.46 2.94

Monastery at Cetinje (Royal Mausoleum) A3

Perf. 10½, 11½
1896, Sept. 1 Litho. Unwmk.
45 A3 1n dk bl & bis 15 15
46 A3 2n mag & yel 22 22
47 A3 3n org brn & yel grn 22 22
48 A3 5n bl grn & bis 22 22
49 A3 10n yel & ultra 22 22
50 A3 15n dk bl & grn 22 22
a. Perf. 11½ 27.50 27.50
51 A3 20n bl grn & ultra 22 22
a. Perf. 11½ 27.50 27.50
52 A3 25n dk bl & yel 22 22
53 A3 30n mag & bis 22 22
54 A3 50n red brn & gray bl 22 22
55 A3 1fl rose & gray bl 42 42
56 A3 2fl brn & blk 42 42
Nos. 45-56 (12) 2.97 2.97

Bicentenary of the ruling dynasty, founded by the Vladika, Danilo Petrovich of Nyegosh.

Inverted centers and other errors exist, but experts believe these to be printer's waste.

Perf. 11½ counterfeits are common.

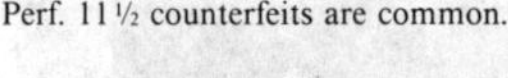

Prince Nicholas I
A4 A5

Perf. 13x13½, 13x12½ (2h, 5h, 50h, 2k, 5k), 12½ (1h, 25h)
1902, July 12
57 A4 1h ultra 15 15
58 A4 2h rose lilac 15 15
59 A4 5h green 15 15
60 A4 10h rose 25 25
61 A4 25h dull blue 15 15
62 A4 50h gray grn 25 25
63 A4 1k chocolate 25 25

64 A4 2k pale brn 40 40
65 A4 5k buff 65 65
Nos. 57-65 (9) 2.40 2.40

The 2h black brown and 25h indigo were not issued.

Constitution Issue

Same Overprinted in Red or Black "Constitution" 15mm

УСТАВ
Constitution
Николђан
1905

1905, Dec. 5
66 A4 1h ultra (R) 15 15
67 A4 2h rose lil 15 15
68 A4 5h green (R) 20 20
69 A4 10h rose 20 20
70 A4 25h dl bl (R) 20 20
71 A4 50h gray grn (R) 20 20
72 A4 1k choc (R) 22 22
73 A4 2k pale brn (R) 40 40
74 A4 5k buff 50 50
Nos. 66-74 (9) 2.22 2.22

Overprints in other colors are proofs.

1906

"Constitution" 16½mm
66a A4 1h ultra (R) 15 15
67a A4 2h rose lilac 15 15
68a A4 5h green (R) 15 15
69a A4 10h rose 15 15
70a A4 25h dull blue (R) 15 15
71a A4 50h gray green (R) 15 15
72a A4 1k chocolate (R) 15 15
73a A4 2k pale brown (R) 25 25
74a A4 5k buff 50 50
Nos. 66a-74a (9) 1.80 1.80

Three settings of Nos. 66a-74a containing four types of "УСТАВ": I, 9¾mm, II, 11¼mm, III, 10¼mm, IV, 8½mm. One setting contains two type IV. Nos. 67a, 69a-74a, H3a exist in type IV.

Two errors occur: "Constitutton" and "Coustitution." Many other varieties including reversed color overprints exist.

Values are for types I and II.

1907, June 1 **Engr.** ***Perf. 12½***
75 A5 1pa ocher 15 15
76 A5 2pa black 15 15
77 A5 5pa yel grn 15 15
78 A5 10pa rose red 15 15
79 A5 15pa ultra 15 15
80 A5 20pa red org 15 15
81 A5 25pa indigo 15 15
82 A5 35pa bis brn 15 15
83 A5 50pa dl vio 20 20
84 A5 1kr car rose 28 28
85 A5 2kr green 32 32
86 A5 5kr red brn 35 35
Nos. 75-86 (12) 2.35 2.35

Many Montenegro stamps exist imperforate or part perforate. Experts believe these to be printer's waste.

King Nicholas I as a Youth — A6

King Nicholas I and Queen Milena — A7

King Nicholas I — A11

Prince Nicholas — A12

Designs: 5pa, 10pa, 35pa, Nicholas in 1910. 15pa, Nicholas in 1878. 20pa, King and Queen, diff.

1910, Aug. 28 **Engr.**
87 A6 1pa black 15 15
88 A7 2pa pur brn 15 15
89 A6 5pa dk grn 15 15
90 A6 10pa carmine 15 15
91 A6 15pa sl bl 15 15
92 A7 20pa ol grn 15 15
93 A6 25pa dp bl 15 15
94 A6 35pa chestnut 22 22
95 A11 50pa violet 25 25
96 A11 1per lake 25 25
97 A11 2per yel grn 42 42
98 A12 5per pale bl 65 65
Nos. 87-98 (12) 2.84 2.84

Proclamation of Montenegro as a kingdom, the 50th anniv. of the reign of King Nicholas and the golden wedding celebration of the King and Queen.

King Nicholas I — A13

1913, Apr. 1 **Typo.**
99 A13 1pa orange 15 15
100 A13 2pa plum 15 15
101 A13 5pa dp grn 15 15
102 A13 10pa dp rose 15 15
103 A13 15pa bl gray 15 15
104 A13 20pa dk brn 15 15
105 A13 25pa dp bl 15 15
106 A13 35pa vermilion 25 25
107 A13 50pa pale bl 15 15
108 A13 1per yel brn 15 15
109 A13 2per gray vio 22 22
110 A13 5per yel grn 22 22
Nos. 99-110 (12) 2.04 2.04

ACKNOWLEDGMENT OF RECEIPT STAMPS

Prince Nicholas I
AR1 AR2

Perf. 10½, 11½
1895 **Litho.** **Wmk. 91**
H1 AR1 10n ultra & rose 40 40

1902 **Unwmk.** ***Perf. 12½***
H2 AR2 25h org & car 40 40

Constitution Issue

No. H2 Overprinted in Black Like Nos. 66-74

1905
H3 AR2 25h org & car 40 40
a. "Constitution" 16½mm ('06) 40 40

See note after 74a.

Nicholas I
AR3 AR4

1907 **Engr.**
H4 AR3 25pa olive 25 25

1913 **Typo.**
H5 AR4 25pa olive green 25 25

Montenegro under German Occupation stamps can be mounted in Scott's Germany Part II Album.

POSTAGE DUE STAMPS

D1

D2

Perf. 10½, 11, 11½
1894 **Litho.** **Wmk. 91**
J1 D1 1n red 1.75 1.75
J2 D1 2n yel grn 32 32
J3 D1 3n orange 32 32
J4 D1 5n ol grn 20 20
J5 D1 10n violet 20 20
J6 D1 20n ultra 20 20
J7 D1 30n emerald 20 20
J8 D1 50n pale gray grn 20 20
Nos. J1-J8 (8) 3.39 3.39

1902 **Unwmk.** ***Perf. 12½***
J9 D2 5h orange 15 15
J10 D2 10h ol grn 15 15
J11 D2 25h dl lil 15 15
J12 D2 50h emerald 15 15
J13 D2 1k pale gray grn 15 15
Set value 50 50

Constitution Issue

Postage Due Stamps of 1902 Overprinted in Black or Red Like Nos. 66-74

1905
J14 D2 5h orange 15 15
J15 D2 10h ol grn (R) 15 15
a. "Constitution" 16½mm ('06) 15 15
J16 D2 25h dl lil 15 15
J17 D2 50h emerald 15 15
J18 D2 1k pale gray grn 15 15
Set value 52 52

D3

D4

1907 **Typo.** ***Perf. 13x13½***
J19 D3 5pa red brn 15 15
J20 D3 10pa violet 15 15
J21 D3 25pa rose 15 15
J22 D3 50pa green 15 15
Set value 40 40

1913 ***Perf. 12½***
J23 D4 5pa gray 22 22
J24 D4 10pa violet 20 20
J25 D4 25pa bl gray 20 20
J26 D4 50pa lil rose 22 22

ISSUED UNDER AUSTRIAN OCCUPATION

Austrian Military Stamps of 1917 Overprinted

K.U.K. MILIT.-VERWALTUNG
MONTENEGRO

1917 **Unwmk.** ***Perf. 12½***
1N1 M1 10h blue 5.75 3.50
1N2 M1 15h car rose 5.75 3.50

Austrian Military Stamps of 1917 Overprinted

Montenegro

1918
1N3 M1 10h blue 25.00
1N4 M1 15h car rose 1.65

Nos. 1N3-1N4 were never placed in use.

ISSUED UNDER ITALIAN OCCUPATION

Yugoslavia Nos. 142, 144-154 Overprinted

Montenegro
Црна Гора
17-IV-41-XIX

1941 **Unwmk.** **Typo.** ***Perf. 12½***
2N1 A16 25p black 15 20
2N2 A16 1d yel grn 15 20
2N3 A16 1.50d red 15 20
2N4 A16 2d dp mag 15 20
2N5 A16 3d dl red brn 15 20
2N6 A16 4d ultra 15 20
2N7 A16 5d dk bl 1.00 1.50
2N8 A16 5.50d dk vio brn 1.00 1.50
2N9 A16 6d slate bl 1.00 1.50
2N10 A16 8d sepia 1.00 1.50
2N11 A16 12d brt vio 1.00 1.50
2N12 A16 16d dl vio 1.00 1.50
2N13 A16 20d blue 110.00 125.00
2N14 A16 30d brt pink 65.00 85.00
Nos. 2N1-2N14 (14) 181.90 220.20

The 25p, 1d, 3d, 6d and 8d exist with inverted overprint.

Stamps of Italy, 1929, Overprinted in Red or Black

ЦРНА ГОРА

1941 **Wmk. 140** ***Perf. 14***
2N15 A90 5c ol brn (R) 15 *35*
2N16 A92 10c dk brn 15 *35*
2N17 A93 15c sl grn (R) 15 *35*
2N18 A91 20c rose red 15 *35*
2N19 A94 25c dp grn 15 *35*
2N20 A95 30c ol brn (R) 15 *35*
2N21 A95 50c pur (R) 15 *35*
2N22 A94 75c rose red 15 *35*
2N23 A94 1.25 l dp bl (R) 15 *35*
Set value 90

Yugoslavia Nos. 144-145, 147-148, 148B, 149-152 Overprinted in Black

Governatorato del Montenegro
Valore
LIRE

1942 **Unwmk.** **Typo.** ***Perf. 12½***
2N24 A16 1d yel grn 65 85
2N25 A16 1.50d red 20.00 22.50
2N26 A16 3d dl red brn 65 85
2N27 A16 4d ultra 65 85
2N28 A16 5.50d dk vio brn 65 85
2N29 A16 6d slate bl 65 85
2N30 A16 8d sepia 65 85
2N31 A16 12d brt vio 65 85
2N32 A16 16d dl vio 65 85
Nos. 2N24-2N32 (9) 25.20 29.30

Yugoslavia Nos. 142 and 146 with this overprint in red were not officially issued.

Red overprint
2N24a A16 1d 65 *1.65*
2N25a A16 1.50d 20.00 *22.50*
2N26a A16 3d 65 *1.65*
2N27a A16 4d 65 *1.65*
2N28a A16 5.50d 65 *1.65*
2N29a A16 6d 65 *1.65*
2N30a A16 8d 65 *1.65*
2N31a A16 12d 65 *1.65*
2N32a A16 16d 65 *1.65*
Nos. 2N24a-2N32a (9) 25.20 *35.70*

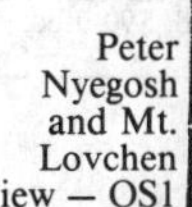

Peter Nyegosh and Mt. Lovchen View — OS1

Mt. Lovchen Scene OS2

Peter Petrovich Nyegosh — OS3

Designs: 15c, Mountain Church, Eve of Trinity Feast. 20c, Chiefs at Cetinje Monastery. 25c, Folk Dancing at Cetinje Monastery. 50c, Eagle dance. 1.25 l, Chiefs taking loyalty oath. 2 l, Moslem wedding procession. 5 l, Group sitting up with injured standard bearer.

Perf. 14.

1943, May 9		Unwmk.	Photo.	
2N33	OS1	5c dp vio	15	*60*
2N34	OS2	10c dl ol grn	15	*60*
2N35	OS1	15c brown	15	*60*
2N36	OS1	20c dl org	15	*60*
2N37	OS1	25c dl grn	15	*60*
2N38	OS1	50c rose pink	15	*60*
2N39	OS1	1.25 l sapphire	24	*1.00*
2N40	OS1	2 l bl grn	35	*1.50*
2N41	OS2	5 l dk red, *sal*	1.75	*5.00*
2N42	OS3	20 l dk vio, *gray*	5.25	*10.50*
		Nos. 2N33-2N42 (10)	8.49	*21.60*

Quotations from national poem on backs of stamps.

OCCUPATION AIR POST STAMPS

Yugoslavia Nos. C7-C14 Overprinted Like Nos. 2N1-2N14

Perf. 12½, 11½x12½, 12½x11½

1941		Photo.		Unwmk.
2NC1	AP6	50p brown	3.25	4.00
2NC2	AP7	1d yel grn	1.50	2.00
2NC3	AP8	2d bl gray	1.50	2.00
2NC4	AP9	2.50d rose red	3.25	4.00
2NC5	AP6	5d brn vio	30.00	30.00
2NC6	AP7	10d brn lake	30.00	30.00
2NC7	AP8	20d dk grn	45.00	45.00
2NC8	AP9	30d ultra	30.00	30.00
		Nos. 2NC1-2NC8 (8)	144.50	147.00

Italy No. C13 Overprinted in Red Like Nos. 2N15-2N23

1941		Wmk. 140		*Perf. 14*
2NC9	AP3	50c ol brn	15	50

Yugoslavia Nos. C7-C14 Overprinted in Black

Governatorato del Montenegro Valore in Lire
a

Governatorato del Montenegro Valore in Lire
b

Perf. 12½, 11½x12½, 12½x11½

1942, Jan. 9				Unwmk.
2NC10	AP6(a)	50p brown	1.10	*2.00*
2NC11	AP7(a)	1d yel grn	1.10	*2.00*
2NC12	AP8(b)	2d bl gray	1.10	*2.00*
2NC13	AP9(b)	2.50d rose red	1.10	*2.00*
2NC14	AP6(a)	5d brn vio	1.10	*2.00*
2NC15	AP7(a)	10d brn lake	1.10	*2.00*
2NC16	AP8(b)	20d dk grn	100.00	100.00
2NC17	AP9(b)	30d ultra	32.50	32.50
		Nos. 2NC10-2NC17 (8)	139.10	144.50

Nos. 2NC10-2NC17 exist with red overprints. Value, each $80 unused, $90 used.

Governatorato del Montenegro
c

Overprints *a*, *b* or *c* were applied in 1941-42 to the following Yugoslavia stamps under Italian occupation:

a. or *b.* Nos. B120-B123 (4 values) in black and in red.

c. Nos. B116-B119 (4 values) in black and in red.

Cetinje AP1

Mt. Durmitor — AP6

Designs: 1 l, Seacoast. 2 l, Budus. 5 l, Mt. Lovchen. 10 l, Rieka River.

1943		Unwmk. Photo.		*Perf. 14*
2NC18	AP1	50c brown	15	60
2NC19	AP1	1 l ultra	15	60
2NC20	AP1	2 l rose pink	24	*1.00*
2NC21	AP1	5 l green	35	*1.50*
2NC22	AP1	10 l lake, *rose buff*	2.00	*6.00*
2NC23	AP6	20 l ind, *rose*	7.25	*10.50*
		Nos. 2NC18-2NC23 (6)	10.14	*20.20*

OCCUPATION POSTAGE DUE STAMPS

Yugoslavia Nos. J28-J32 Overprinted Like Nos. 2N1-2N14

1941		Unwmk. Typo.		*Perf. 12½*
2NJ1	D4	50p violet	24	50
2NJ2	D4	1d dp mag	24	50
2NJ3	D4	2d dp bl	24	50
2NJ4	D4	5d orange	16.00	20.00
2NJ5	D4	10d chocolate	1.65	3.50
		Nos. 2NJ1-2NJ5 (5)	18.37	25.00

Postage Due Stamps of Italy, 1934, Overprinted in Black Like Nos. 2N15-2N23

1942		Wmk. 140		*Perf. 14*
2NJ6	D6	10c blue	15	*70*
2NJ7	D6	20c rose red	15	*70*
2NJ8	D6	30c red org	15	*70*
2NJ9	D6	50c violet	15	*70*
2NJ10	D7	1 l red org	15	*70*
		Set value	60	

ISSUED UNDER GERMAN OCCUPATION

Yugoslavia Nos. 147-148 Surcharged

Deutsche Militaer-Verwaltung Montenegro

0.50 LIRE

1943		Unwmk. Typo.		*Perf. 12½*
3N1	A16	50c on 3d	2.25	*10.00*
3N2	A16	1 l on 3d	2.25	*10.00*
3N3	A16	1.50 l on 3d	2.25	*10.00*
3N4	A16	2 l on 3d	4.50	*20.00*
3N5	A16	4 l on 3d	4.00	*20.00*
3N6	A16	5 l on 4d	4.50	*20.00*
3N7	A16	8 l on 4d	5.50	*50.00*
3N8	A16	10 l on 4d	11.50	*65.00*
3N9	A16	20 l on 4d	16.00	*130.00*
		Nos. 3N1-3N9 (9)	52.75	*335.00*

Montenegro Nos. 2N37-2N41 Ovptd.

Nationaler Verwaltungsausschuss 10.XI.1943

1943		Photo.		*Perf. 14*
3N10	OS1	25c dl grn	6.50	*65.00*
3N11	OS1	50c rose pink	6.50	*65.00*
3N12	OS1	1.25 l sapphire	6.50	*65.00*
3N13	OS1	2 l bl grn	6.50	*65.00*
3N14	OS2	5 l dk red, *sal*	230.00	*1,600.*
		Nos. 3N10-3N14 (5)	256.00	*1,860.*

Counterfeits exist.

SEMI-POSTAL STAMPS

Yugoslavia Nos. 147-148 Surcharged

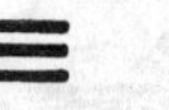

Flüchtlingshilfe Montenegro 0.15+0.85 RM.

1944		Unwmk. Typo.		*Perf. 12½*
3NB1	A16	15pf + 85pf on 3d	6.50	*55.00*
3NB2	A16	15pf + 85pf on 4d	6.50	*85.00*

Montenegro Nos. 2N37-2N40 Surcharged

Flüchtlingshilfe Montenegro 0,15 + 0,85 RM.
d

1944		Photo.		*Perf. 14*
3NB3	OS1	15pf +85pf on 25c	6.00	*85.00*
3NB4	OS1	15pf +1.35m on 50c	6.50	*85.00*
3NB5	OS1	25pf +1.75m on 1.25 l	6.50	*85.00*
3NB6	OS1	25pf +1.75m on 2 l	6.50	*85.00*
		Nos. 3NB1-3NB6 (6)	38.50	*480.00*

Surtax on Nos. 3NB1-3NB6 aided refugees.

Montenegro Nos. 2N37-2N38 Surcharged

+ Crveni krst Montenegro 0.25+1.75 RM.
e

1944				
3NB7	OS1	15pf + 85pf on 25c	6.00	*65.00*
3NB8	OS1	15pf + 1.35m on 50c	6.00	*65.00*

Yugoslavia Nos. 147-148 Surcharged

+ Crveni krst Montenegro 0.50+2.50 RM.

		Typo.		*Perf. 12½*
3NB9	A16	50pf + 2.50m on 3d	6.00	*65.00*
3NB10	A16	50pf + 2.50m on 4d	6.00	*65.00*

The surtax on Nos. 3NB7-3NB10 aided the Montenegro Red Cross.

AIR POST STAMPS

Montenegro Nos. 2NC18-2NC22 Overprinted Like Nos. 3N10-3N14

1943		Unwmk. Photo.		*Perf. 14*
3NC1	AP1	50c brown	8.00	*85.00*
3NC2	AP1	1 l ultra	8.00	*85.00*
3NC3	AP1	2 l rose pink	8.00	*85.00*
3NC4	AP1	5 l green	8.00	*85.00*
3NC5	AP1	10 l lake, *rose buff*	*1,500.*	*15,000.*

Counterfeits exist.

AIR POST SEMI-POSTAL STAMPS

Montenegro Nos. 2NC18-2NC20 Surcharged Type "d"

1944		Unwmk. Photo.		*Perf. 14*
3NCB1	AP1	15pf +85pf on 50c	6.50	*65.00*
3NCB2	AP1	25pf +1.25m on 1 l	6.50	*65.00*
3NCB3	AP1	50pf +1.50m on 2 l	6.50	*65.00*

The surtax aided refugees.

Same Surcharged Type "e"

1944				
3NCB4	AP1	25pf +1.75m on 50c	6.00	*65.00*
3NCB5	AP1	25pf +2.75m on 1 l	6.00	*65.00*
3NCB6	AP1	50pf +2m on 2 l	6.00	*65.00*

The surtax aided the Montenegro Red Cross.

MOROCCO

LOCATION — Northwest coast of Africa
GOVT. — Kingdom
AREA — 171,953 sq. mi.
POP. — 21,160,000 (est. 1984)
CAPITAL — Rabat

In 1956 the three zones of Morocco, French, Spanish and Tangier, were united to form an independent nation. Nos. 1-24 and C1-C3 were intended for use only in the southern (French currency) zone. Issues of the northern zone (Spanish currency) are listed after Postage Due stamps.

For earlier issues see French Morocco and Spanish Morocco.

100 Centimes = 1 Franc
100 Centimes = 1 Dirham (1962)

Catalogue values for all unused stamps in this country are for Never Hinged items.

Sultan Mohammed V — A1

Men Reading — A2

1956-57		Unwmk. Engr.		*Perf. 13*
1	A1	5fr brt bl & ind	15	15
2	A1	10fr bis brn & choc	15	15
3	A1	15fr dp grn & mag	16	15
4	A1	25fr purple ('57)	50	15
5	A1	30fr green ('57)	90	15
6	A1	50fr rose red ('57)	1.40	15
7	A1	70fr dk brn & brn red ('57)	2.00	40
		Nos. 1-7 (7)	5.26	
		Set value		78

For surcharges, see Nos. B1-B5, B8-B9.

1956, Nov. 5

Campaign against illiteracy: 15fr, Girls reading. 20fr, Instructor and pupils. 30fr, Old man and child reading. 50fr, Girl pointing out poster.

8 A2 10fr pur & vio 85 65
9 A2 15fr car & rose lake 1.10 70
10 A2 20fr bl grn & grn 1.25 1.25
11 A2 30fr rose lake & brt red 2.00 1.40
12 A2 50fr dp bl & bl 3.50 2.25
Nos. 8-12 (5) 8.70 6.25

Sultan Mohammed V – A3

Prince Moulay el Hassan – A4

1957, Mar. 2 Photo. ***Perf. 13½x13***

13 A3 15fr blue green 75 65
14 A3 25fr gray olive 1.00 65
15 A3 30fr deep rose 1.40 90

Anniversary of independence.

1957, July 9 ***Perf. 13***

16 A4 15fr blue 70 50
17 A4 25fr green 85 65
18 A4 30fr car rose 1.40 90

Designation of Prince Moulay el Hassan as heir to the throne.

King Mohammed V – A5

1957, Nov. ***Perf. 12½***

19 A5 15fr blk & brt grn 45 40
20 A5 25fr blk & rose red 70 50
21 A5 30fr blk & vio 75 65

Enthronement of Mohammed V, 30th anniv.

Morocco Pavilion, Brussels World's Fair – A6

1958, Apr. 20 Engr. ***Perf. 13***

22 A6 15fr brt grnsh bl 20 15
23 A6 25fr carmine 20 15
24 A6 30fr indigo 25 20

World's Fair, Brussels.

UNESCO Building, Paris, and Mohammed V – A7

1958, Nov. 23

25 A7 15fr green 20 15
26 A7 25fr lake 20 15
27 A7 30fr blue 25 20

Opening of UNESCO Headquarters in Paris, Nov. 3.

Ben Smin Sanatorium A8

1959, Jan. 18 Unwmk. ***Perf. 13***

28 A8 50fr dk brn, car & sl grn 38 25

Red Cross-Red Crescent Society.

Mohammed V – A9

Princess Lalla Amina – A10

1959, Aug. 18 Engr. ***Perf. 13***

29 A9 15fr dk car rose 30 20
30 A9 25fr brt bl 40 22
31 A9 45fr dk grn 45 30

50th birthday of King Mohammed V.

1959, Nov. 17

32 A10 15fr blue 20 15
33 A10 25fr green 22 15
34 A10 45fr rose lil 25 20

Issued for International Children's Week.

Map of Africa and Symbols of Agriculture, Industry and Commerce – A11

1960, Jan. 31 ***Perf. 13***

35 A11 45fr vio, ocher & emer 45 30

Issued to publicize the meeting of the Economic Commission for Africa, Tangier.

Refugees and Uprooted Oak Emblem A12

Design: 45fr, Refugee family and uprooted oak emblem.

1960, Apr. 7 Unwmk. ***Perf. 13***

36 A12 15fr ocher, blk & grn 16 15
37 A12 45fr blk & grn 28 20

World Refugee Year, July 1, 1959-June 30, 1960.

Marrakesh A13

1960, Apr. 25 Engr. ***Perf. 13***

38 A13 100fr grn, bl & red brn 55 40

900th anniversary of Marrakesh.

Lamp – A14

Wrestlers – A16

Arab League Center, Cairo and Mohammed V – A15

Designs: 25fr, Fountain and arched door. 30fr, Minaret. 35fr, Ornamented wall. 45fr, Moorish architecture.

1960, May 12 ***Perf. 13½***

39 A14 15fr rose lil 25 22
40 A14 25fr dk bl 30 25
41 A14 30fr org red 55 40
42 A14 35fr black 70 50
43 A14 45fr yel grn 1.00 70
Nos. 39-43 (5) 2.80 2.07

1,100th anniversary of Karaouiyne University, Fez.

1960, June 28 Photo. ***Perf. 12½***

44 A15 15fr grn & blk 15 15

Opening of the Arab League Center and the Arab Postal Museum, Cairo.

1960, Sept. 26 Engr. ***Perf. 13***

Sports: 10fr, Gymnast. 15fr, Bicyclist. 20fr, Weight lifter. 30fr, Runner. 40fr, Boxers. 45fr, Sailboat. 70fr, Fencers.

45 A16 5fr ol, vio bl & plum 15 15
46 A16 10fr org brn, bl & brn 15 15
47 A16 15fr emer, bl & org brn 15 15
48 A16 20fr ultra, ol & brn 20 16
49 A16 30fr vio bl, mar & sep 25 20
50 A16 40fr grnsh bl, dk pur & red brn 40 20
51 A16 45fr grn, plum & ultra 45 25
52 A16 70fr dk brn, bl & gray 70 30
Nos. 45-52 (8) 2.45 1.56

17th Olympic Games, Rome, Aug. 25-Sept. 11.

Runner A17

1961, Aug. 30 Unwmk. ***Perf. 13***

53 A17 20fr dk grn 15 15
54 A17 30fr dk car rose 25 15
55 A17 50fr brt bl 32 25

3rd Pan-Arabic Games, Casablanca.

Post Office, Tangier A18

View of Tangier and Gibraltar A19

Design: 30fr, Telephone operator.

1961, Dec. 8 Litho. ***Perf. 12½***

56 A18 20fr red vio 20 16
57 A18 30fr green 25 20
57A A19 90fr lt bl & vio bl 50 32

Conference of the African Postal and Telecommunications Union, Tangier.

Mohammed V and Map of Africa – A20

Patrice Lumumba and Map of Congo – A21

1962, Jan. 4 Unwmk. ***Perf. 11½***

58 A20 20c buff & vio brn 15 15
59 A20 30c lt & dk bl 20 15
Set value 22

1st anniv. of the conference of African heads of state at Casablanca.

1962, Feb. 12 ***Perf. 12½***

60 A21 20c bis & blk 15 15
61 A21 30c dl red brn & blk 20 16
Set value 25

1st death anniv. of Patrice Lumumba, Premier of Congo Democratic Republic.

Moroccan Students A22

Arab League Building, Cairo A23

1962, Mar. 5 **Engr.**

62 A22 20fr multi 20 15
63 A22 30fr multi 25 20
64 A22 90fr gray grn, ind & brn 45 32

Issued to honor the nation's students.

1962, Mar. 22 Photo. ***Perf. 13½x13***

65 A23 20c red brn 38 15

Arab Propaganda Week, Mar. 22-28. See No. 146.

Malaria Eradication Emblem and Swamp A24

Design: 50c, Dagger stabbing mosquito, vert.

1962, Sept. 3 Engr. ***Perf. 13***

66 A24 20c dk grn & grnsh blk 15 15
67 A24 50c dk grn & mag 25 15
Set value 22

WHO drive to eradicate malaria.

The first price column gives the catalogue value of an unused stamp, the second that of a used stamp.

Fish and Aquarium — A25

1962, Nov. 5 Unwmk. *Perf. 13*

68 A25 20c shown 25 16
69 A25 30c Moray eel 25 16

Casablanca Aquarium.

Courier and Sherifian Stamp of 1912 — A26

Designs: 30c, Courier on foot and round Sherifian cancellation. 50c, Sultan Hassan I and octagonal cancellation.

1962, Dec. 15 Unwmk.

70 A26 20c Prus grn & redsh brn 30 20
71 A26 30c dk car rose & blk 40 22
72 A26 50c bl & bister 65 30

Stamp Day; 1st National Stamp Exhibition, Dec. 15-23; 75th anniv. of the Sherifian Post and the 50th anniv. of its reorganization.

Boy Scout — A27

King Hassan II — A28

1962, Aug. 8 Litho. *Perf. 11½*

73 A27 20c vio brn & lt bl 15 15

5th Arab Boy Scout Jamboree, Rabat.

1962 Engr. *Perf. 13½x13*

75 A28 1c gray ol 15 15
76 A28 2c violet 15 15
77 A28 5c black 15 15
78 A28 10c brn org 15 15
79 A28 15c Prus grn 15 15
80 A28 20c purple 16 15
81 A28 30c dp yel grn 20 15
82 A28 50c vio brn 40 15
83 A28 70c deep blue 65 15
84 A28 80c magenta 1.00 16
Set value 2.70 60

See Nos. 110-114. "Mazelin" (designer-engraver) reads down on Nos. 75-84.

King Moulay Ismail A29

Al Idrissi, Geographer A30

1963, Mar. 3 *Perf. 12½*

85 A29 20c sepia 25 16

Tercentenary of Meknes as Ismaili capital.

1963-66 Engr.

Portraits: Nos. 87, 88A, Ibn Batota, explorer. No. 88, Ibn Khaldoun, historian and sociologist.

86 A30 20c dk sl grn 25 15
87 A30 20c dk car rose 25 15
88 A30 20c black 25 15
88A A30 40c dk vio bl ('66) 25 15

Famous medieval men of Morocco (Maghreb). No. 88A also marks the inauguration of the ferryboat "Ibn Batota" connecting Tangier and Malaga.

Issue dates: Nos. 86-88, May 7, 1963. No. 88A, July 15, 1966.

Sugar Beet and Sugar Refinery, Sidi Slimane A31

1963, June 10 Unwmk. *Perf. 13*

89 A31 20c shown 20 15
90 A31 50c Tuna fisherman, vert. 32 22

FAO "Freedom from Hunger" campaign.

Heads of Ramses II, Abu Simbel A32

Designs: 30c, Isis, Kalabsha Temple, vert. 50c, Temple of Philae.

1963, July 15 Engr. *Perf. 11½*

91 A32 20c black 15 15
92 A32 30c vio, *grysh* 20 16
93 A32 50c maroon, *buff* 30 22

Campaign to save historic monuments in Nubia.

Agadir Before Earthquake A33

Designs: 30c, Like 20c, with "29 Février 1960" and crossed bars added. 50c, Agadir rebuilt.

Engr.; Engr. & Photo. (No. 95)

1963, Oct. 10 *Perf. 13½x13*

94 A33 20c bl & brn red 22 20
95 A33 30c bl, brn red & red 30 22
96 A33 50c bl & brn red 80 32

Issued to publicize the rebuilding of Agadir.

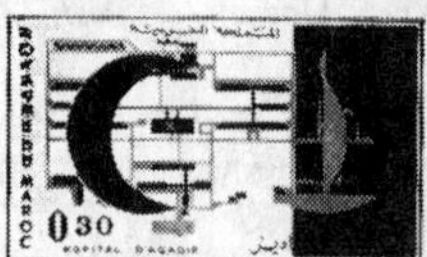
Centenary Emblem and Plan of Agadir Hospital A34

1963, Oct. 28 Photo. *Perf. 12½x13*

97 A34 30c blk, dp car & sil 20 16

Centenary of the International Red Cross.

Arms of Morocco and Rabat — A35

Flag — A37

Hands Breaking Chain A36

1963, Nov. 18 *Perf. 13x12½*

98 A35 20c gold, red, blk & emer 16 16

Installation of Parliament.

1963, Dec. 10 Engr. *Perf. 13*

99 A36 20c dk brn, grn & org 20 16

15th anniversary of the Universal Declaration of Human Rights.

1963, Dec. 25 Photo. *Perf. 13x12½*

100 A37 20c blk, dp car & grn 20 16

Evacuation of all foreign military forces from Moroccan territory.

Moulay Abd-er-Rahman, by Delacroix — A38

1964, Mar. 3 Engr. *Perf. 12x13*

101 A38 1d multi 1.50 1.00

Coronation of King Hassan II, 3rd anniv.

Weather Map of Africa and UN Emblem A39

Children on Vacation A40

Designs: 30c, World map and barometer trace (horiz.).

1964, Mar. 23 Photo. *Perf. 11½*

Granite Paper

102 A39 20c multi 20 16
103 A39 30c multi 25 20

UN 4th World Meteorological Day. See No. C10.

1964, July 6 Litho. *Perf. 12½*

Design: 30c, Heads of boy and girl, buildings.

104 A40 20c multi 20 16
105 A40 30c multi 25 22

Issued for vacation camps for children of P.T.T. employees.

Olympic Torch A41

Cape Spartel Lighthouse, Sultan Mohammed ben Abd-er-Rahman A42

1964, Sept. 22 Engr. *Perf. 13*

106 A41 20c car lake, dk pur & grn 25 16
107 A41 30c bl, dk grn & red brn 38 20
108 A41 50c grn, red & brn 50 25

18th Olympic Games, Tokyo, Oct. 10-25.

Perf. 12½x11½

1964, Oct. 15 Photo.

109 A42 25c multi 20 16

Centenary of the Cape Spartel lighthouse.

King Type of 1962

1964-65 Engr. *Perf. 12½x13*

Size: 17x23mm

110 A28 20c pur (redrawn) 38 25

Perf. 13½x13

Size: 18x22mm

111 A28 25c rose red ('65) 22 15
112 A28 35c slate ('65) 35 15
113 A28 40c ultra ('65) 38 15
114 A28 60c red lil ('65) 55 15
Nos. 110-114 (5) 1.88
Set value 45

The Arabic inscription touches the frame on No. 110. "Mazelin" (designer-engraver) reads up on No. 110, down on Nos. 111-114. No. 110 is a coil stamp with red control numbers on the back of some copies.

Iris — A43

Mohammed V Arriving by Plane — A44

1965 Photo. *Perf. 11½*

Granite Paper

115 A43 25c shown 45 30
116 A43 40c Gladiolus segetum 50 38
117 A43 60c Capparis spinosa, horiz. 85 65

Printed in sheets of 10. Five tête-bêche pairs in every sheet; vertical stamps arranged 5x2, horizontal stamps 2x5.

See Nos. 129-131.

1965, Mar. 15 Litho. *Perf. 12½*

118 A44 25c lt bl & dk grn 20 15

10th anniv. of the return of King Mohammed V from exile and the restoration of the monarchy.

ITU Emblem, Punched-Tape Writer and Telegraph Wires — A45

Design: 40c, ITU emblem, Syncom satellite, radio waves and "ITU" in Morse code.

Perf. 13x14

1965, May 17 Unwmk. Typo.

119 A45 25c multi 16 16
120 A45 40c lt bl, dp bl & bis 25 20

ITU, centenary.

ICY Emblem A46

1965, June 14 Engr. *Perf. 13*

121 A46 25c slate grn 16 15
122 A46 60c dk car rose 25 15
Set value 22

International Cooperation Year.

Triton Shell — A47

Designs: No. 124, Varnish shell (pitaria chione). No. 125, Great voluted shell (cymbium neptuni). No. 126, Helmet crab, vert. 40c, Mantis shrimp, vert. 1d, Royal prawn.

1965 Photo. *Perf. 11½*
Granite Paper

123 A47 25c vio & multi 38 15
124 A47 25c lt bl & multi 38 15
125 A47 25c org & multi 38 16
126 A47 25c lt grn & multi 38 25
127 A47 40c bl & multi 75 45
128 A47 1d yel & multi 1.00 65
Nos. 123-128 (6) 3.27 1.81

Printed in sheets of 10. Nos. 126-127 (5x2); others (2x5). Five tete beche pairs in every sheet.

Flower Type of 1965

Orchids: 25c, Ophrys speculum. 40c, Ophrys fusca. 60c, Ophrys tenthredinifera (front and side view; horiz.).

1965, Dec. 13 Photo. *Perf. 11½*
Granite Paper

129 A43 25c yel & multi 25 22
130 A43 40c dl rose & multi 38 22
131 A43 60c lt bl & multi 75 55

Note on tête bêche pairs after No. 117 also applies to Nos. 129-131.

Grain — A48

Designs: 40c, Various citrus fruit. 60c, Olives, horiz.

1966 Photo. *Perf. 11½*
Granite Paper

133 A48 25c blk & bis 15 15
136 A48 40c multi 20 16
137 A48 60c gray & multi 25 15
Set value 35

For surcharge, see No. 231.

Flag, Map and Dove — A49

1966, Mar. 2 Typo. *Perf. 14x13*

139 A49 25c brt grn & red 15 15

Tenth anniversary of Independence.

King Hassan II — A50

1966, Mar. 2 Engr. *Perf. 13*

140 A50 25c red, brt grn & ind 15 15

Coronation of King Hassan II, 5th anniv.

Cross-country Runner — A51

1966, Mar. 20 Engr. *Perf. 13*

141 A51 25c blue green 16 15

53rd International Cross-country Race.

WHO Headquarters from West — A52

Design: 40c, WHO Headquarters from the East.

1966, May 3 Engr. *Perf. 13*

142 A52 25c rose lil & blk 15 15
143 A52 40c dp bl & blk 20 15

Inauguration of the WHO Headquarters, Geneva.

Crown Prince Hassan Kissing Hand of King Mohammed V — A53

Design: 25c, King Hassan II and parachutist.

Perf. 12½x12

1966, May 14 Photo. Unwmk.

144 A53 25c gold & blk 30 22
145 A53 40c gold & blk 30 22
a. Strip of 2, #144-145 + label 65 50

10th anniv. of the Royal Armed Forces.

Type of 1962 Inscribed: "SEMAINE DE LA PALESTINE"

1966, May 16 *Perf. 11x11½*

146 A23 25c slate blue 15 15

Issued for Palestine Week.

Train A54

1966, Dec. 19 Photo. *Perf. 13½*

147 A54 25c shown 22 16
148 A54 40c Ship 30 20
149 A54 1d Autobus 38 25

Twaite Shad A55

Fish: 40c, Plain bonito. 1d, Bluefish, vert.

1967, Feb. 1 Photo. *Perf. 11½*
Granite Paper

150 A55 25c yel & multi 38 15
151 A55 40c yel & multi 50 22
152 A55 1d lt grn & multi 1.00 55

Printed tête bêche in sheets of 10. Nos. 150-151 (2x5); No. 152 (5x2).

Ait Aadel Dam A56

1967, Mar. 3 Engr. *Perf. 13*

153 A56 25c sl grn, Prus bl & gray 20 16
154 A56 40c Prus bl & lt brn 28 16

Inauguration of Ait Aadel Dam.

Rabat Hilton Hotel, Map of Morocco and Roman Arch — A57

1967, Mar. 3

155 A57 25c brt bl & blk 20 16
156 A57 1d brt bl & pur 38 16

Opening of the Rabat Hilton Hotel.

Torch, Globe, Town and Lions Emblem — A58

1967, Apr. 22 Photo. *Perf. 12½*

157 A58 40c gold & saph bl 22 16
158 A58 1d gold & slate grn 45 25

Lions International, 50th anniversary.

Three Hands Holding Pickax — A59

1967, July 9 Engr. *Perf. 13*

159 A59 25c slate green 15 15

Community Development Campaign.

Intl. Tourism Year Emblem A60

1967, Aug. 9 Photo. *Perf. 12½*

160 A60 1d lt ultra & dk bl 38 25

Arrow and Map of Mediterranean A61

1967, Sept. 8 *Perf. 13x12*

161 A61 25c dk bl, ultra, red & tan 16 15
162 A61 40c blk, bl grn, red & tan 20 15
Set value 24

Mediterranean Games, Tunis, Sept. 8-17.

Steeplechase A62

1967, Oct. 14 Photo. *Perf. 12½*

163 A62 40c yel grn, blk & brt rose lilac 22 15
164 A62 1d lt ultra, blk & brt rose lilac 32 22

International Horseshow.

Cotton — A63

Human Rights Flame — A64

1967, Nov. 15 Photo. *Perf. 12½*

165 A63 40c lt bl, grn & yel 22 15

1968, Jan. 10 Engr. *Perf. 13*

166 A64 25c gray 15 15
167 A64 1d rose claret 22 20

International Human Rights Year.

King Hassan II — A65

1968-74 Litho. *Perf. 13*

Portrait in Magenta, Brown and Black

Size: 23x30mm

169 A65 1c cream & blk 15 15
170 A65 2c lt grnsh bl & blk 15 15
171 A65 5c lt ol grn & blk 15 15
172 A65 10c pale rose & blk 15 15
173 A65 15c gray bl & blk 15 15
174 A65 20c pink & blk 15 15
175 A65 25c black 18 15
176 A65 30c pale rose & blk 20 15
177 A65 35c bl & blk 22 25
178 A65 40c gray & blk 22 15
179 A65 50c lt bl & blk 32 15
180 A65 60c sal & blk 85 15
181 A65 70c gray & blk 2.00 50
182 A65 75c pale yel ('74) 50 25
183 A65 80c ocher & blk 1.00 15

Perf. 13½x14

Size: 26x40mm

184 A65 90c lt bl grn & blk 65 35
185 A65 1d tan & blk 85 15
186 A65 2d lt ultra & blk 1.90 25
187 A65 3d bluish lil & blk 2.75 45
188 A65 5d apple grn & blk 3.75 1.50
Nos. 169-188 (20) 16.29
Set value 4.40

For overprints or surcharges, see Nos. 224, B17-B18.

Nurse and Child — A66

Pendant — A67

1968, Apr. 8 Engr. *Perf. 13*

189 A66 25c ultra, red & olive 15 15
190 A66 40c slate, red & ol 16 15
Set value 18

WHO, 20th anniv.

1968, May 15 Photo. *Perf. 11½*

Design: 40c, Bracelet.

191 A67 25c dk ol bis & multi 38 20
192 A67 40c ultra & multi 50 25

Moroccan Red Crescent Society.

Nos. 191-192 were printed se-tenant in sheets of 10 (5x2) arranged vertically tete beche.

See Nos. 373-374.

Map of Morocco and Rotary Emblem — A68

1968, May 23 *Perf. 13*

193 A68 40c multi 30 15
194 A68 1d ultra & multi 45 22

Rotary Intl. District Conference, Casablanca, May 24-25.

Ornamental Design — A69

Designs: Various patterns used for sashes.

1968, July 12 Photo. *Perf. 11½*

195 A69 25c multi 90 40
196 A69 40c multi 1.10 50
197 A69 60c multi 1.75 85
198 A69 1d multi 3.00 1.65

Berber (Riff), North Morocco — A70

Princess Lalla Meryem — A71

Regional Costumes: 10c, Man from Ait Moussa ou Ali. 15c, Woman from Ait Mouhad. No. 200, Bargeman from Rabat Sale. No. 201, Citadin man. 40c, Citadin woman. 60c, Royal Mokhazni. No. 204, Zemmours man. No. 204A, Man from Meknassa. No. 206, Msouffa woman, Sahara.

1968-74 Litho. *Perf. 13x12½*

198A A70 10c multi ('69) 45 32
199 A70 15c yel & multi ('69) 75 40
200 A70 25c bis & multi 75 45
201 A70 25c tan & multi ('69) 85 45
202 A70 40c lt bl & multi 90 65
203 A70 60c emer & multi 1.25 85
204 A70 1d lt bl & multi 1.65 1.10
204A A70 1d gray & multi ('69) 1.50 75

Perf. 15

205 A70 1d bis & multi 1.40 90
206 A70 1d grn & multi 1.40 90
a. Souvenir sheet of 10, #198A-206, perf. 13 13.75 12.50
b. As "a," with red overprint & surcharge 15.00 15.00
Nos. 198A-206 (10) 10.90 6.77

No. 206a issued June 30, 1970, for the opening of the National P.T.T. Museum, Rabat. Sold for 10d.

No. 206b issued Nov. 22, 1974, for the 8th Cong. of the Intl. Fed. of Blood Donors. Each stamp overprinted vertically "8eme Congres de la F.I.O.D.S." and blood container emblem. Black marginal inscription partially obliterated with lines, new Arabic inscription and price added. Sold for 20d.

1968, Oct. 7 Litho. *Perf. 13½*

Children's Week: 40c, Princess Lalla Asmaa. 1d, Crown Prince Sidi Mohammed.

207 A71 25c red & multi 30 15
208 A71 40c yel & multi 38 22
209 A71 1d lt bl & multi 50 38

Wrestling, Aztec Calendar Stone and Olympic Rings — A72

1968, Oct. 25 Photo. *Perf. 12x11½*

210 A72 15c shown 15 15
211 A72 20c Basketball 15 15
212 A72 25c Cycling 22 20
213 A72 40c Boxing 25 16
214 A72 60c Running 32 20
215 A72 1d Soccer 50 30
Nos. 210-215 (6) 1.59 1.16

19th Olympic Games, Mexico City, Oct. 12-27.

10 Dirham Coin of Tetuan, 1780 — A73

Women from Zagora — A74

Coins: 25c, Dirham, Agmat, c. 1138 A.D. 40c, Dirham, El Alya (Fes), c. 840 A.D. 60c, Dirham, Marrakesh, c. 1248 A.D.

1968, Dec. 17 Photo. *Perf. 11½*

Granite Paper

216 A73 20c dp plum, sil & blk 22 15
217 A73 25c dk rose brn, gold & blk 32 22
218 A73 40c dk grn, sil & blk 55 30
219 A73 60c dk red, gold & blk 75 45

See Nos. C16-C17.

1969, Jan. 21 Litho. *Perf. 12*

Design: 25c, Women from Ait Adidou.

220 A74 15c multi 55 30
221 A74 25c multi 75 45

See No. C15.

Painting by Belkahya A75

King Hassan II A76

1969, Mar. 27 Litho. *Perf. 11½x12*

222 A75 1d lt grnsh bl, blk & brn 32 16

International Day of the Theater.

1969, July 9 Photo. *Perf. 11½*

223 A76 1d gold & multi 55 22

40th birthday of King Hassan II. A souvenir sheet contains one of No. 223. Size: 75x105mm. Sold for 2.50d.

No. 185 Overprinted مؤتمر القمة الاسلامي الرباط ١٠ رجب 1389

1969, Sept. 22 Litho. *Perf. 13*

224 A65 1d tan & multi 2.25 1.90

First Arab Summit Conference, Rabat.

Mahatma Gandhi — A77

1969, Oct. 16 Photo. *Perf. 11½*

225 A77 40c pale vio, blk & gray 50 25

Mohandas K. Gandhi (1869-1948), leader in India's struggle for independence.

ILO Emblem A78

1969, Oct. 29

226 A78 50c multi 38 20

ILO, 50th anniv.

King Hassan II on Way to Prayer — A79

1969, Nov. 20 Photo. *Perf. 11½*

227 A79 1d multi 50 25

1st Arab Summit Conference, Rabat, Sept. 1969. For overprint, see No. 311.

Spahi Horsemen, by Haram al Glaoui A80

1970, Jan. 23 Engr. *Perf. 12x13*

228 A80 1d multi 50 25

Main Sewer, Fez — A81

Guedra Dance, by P. C. Beaubrun — A82

1970, Mar. 23 **Litho.** ***Perf. 12***
229 A81 60c multi 28 15

50th Congress of Municipal Engineers, Rabat, Mar. 1970.

1970, Apr. 15
230 A82 40c multi 38 20

Folklore Festival, Marrakesh, May 1970.

No. 137 Overprinted "1970", "Census" in Arabic in Red and Surcharged in Black

1970 حصاء 0,25

1970, July 9 **Photo.** ***Perf. 11½***
231 A48 25c on 60c multi 50 30

Issued to publicize the 1970 census.

Radar Station at Souk El Arba des Sehoul, and Satellite A83

Ruddy Shelduck A84

1970, Aug. 20
232 A83 1d lt ultra & multi 50 30

Revolution of King and People, 17th anniv.

1970, Sept. 25 **Photo.** ***Perf. 11½***
233 A84 25c shown 42 22
234 A84 40c Houbara bustard 55 30

Campaign to save Moroccan wildlife.

Man Reading Book, Intl. Education Year Emblem — A85

1970, Oct. 20 **Litho.** ***Perf. 12x11½***
235 A85 60c dl yel & multi 50 25

Symbols of Peace, Justice and Progress A86

1970, Oct. 27 ***Perf. 13½***
236 A86 50c multi 38 25

United Nations, 25th anniversary.

Arab League Countries and Emblem A87

1970, Nov. 13 **Photo.** ***Perf. 11½***
237 A87 50c multi 38 25

Arab League, 25th anniversary.

Olive Grove, Tree and Branch A88

1970, Dec. 3 **Litho.** ***Perf. 12***
238 A88 50c red brn & grn 45 28

International Olive Year.

Es Sounna Mosque, Rabat — A89

1971, Jan. 5 **Engr.** ***Perf. 13***
239 A89 60c ol bis, bl & sl grn 40 22

Restoration of Es Sounna Mosque, Rabat, built in 1785.

Heart and Horse — A90

1971, Feb. 23 **Photo.** ***Perf. 12x12½***
240 A90 50c blk & multi 35 18

European heart research week, Feb. 21-28.

Dam and Hassan II — A91

1971, Mar. 3 ***Perf. 11½***
241 A91 25c multi 35 15
a. Souv. sheet of 4 1.50 1.50

Accession of King Hassan II, 10th anniv. No. 241a issued Mar. 24. Sold for 2.50d.

Black and White Hands with Dove and Emblem A92

1971, June 16 **Photo.** ***Perf. 13***
242 A92 50c brn & multi 35 20

Intl. Year against Racial Discrimination.

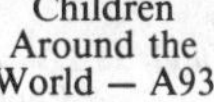

Children Around the World — A93

Shah Mohammed Riza Pahlavi of Iran — A94

1971, Oct. 4 **Litho.** ***Perf. 13x14***
243 A93 40c emer & multi 32 15

International Children's Day.

1971, Oct. 11 **Photo.** ***Perf. 11½***
244 A94 1d bl & multi 30 22

2500th anniv. of the founding of the Persian empire by Cyrus the Great.

Mausoleum of Mohammed V — A95

Designs: 50c, Mausoleum, close-up view, and Mohammed V. 1d, Decorated interior wall, vert.

1971, Nov. 10 **Litho.** ***Perf. 14***
245 A95 25c multi 15 15
246 A95 50c multi 20 15
247 A95 1d multi 40 25

Soccer Ball and Games Emblem A96

1971, Nov. 30 **Photo.** ***Perf. 13x13½***
248 A96 40c shown 22 20
249 A96 60c Runner 30 20

Mediterranean Games, Izmir, Turkey, Oct. 6-17.

Arab Postal Union Emblem A97

1971, Dec. 23 **Litho.** ***Perf. 13x12½***
250 A97 25c dk & lt bl & org 15 15

25th anniv. of the Conference of Sofar, Lebanon, establishing APU.

Sun over Cultivated Sand Dunes — A98

Torch and Book Year Emblem — A99

1971, Dec. 30 **Photo.** ***Perf. 12½***
251 A98 70c blk, bl & yel 22 15

Sherifian Phosphate Office (fertilizer production and export), 50th anniversary.

1972, Jan. 12 ***Perf. 11½***
252 A99 1d sil & multi 25 15

International Book Year.

National Lottery — A100

Bridge of Sighs — A101

1972, Feb. 7 **Photo.** ***Perf. 13***
253 A100 25c tan, blk & gold 15 15

Creation of a national lottery.

1972, Feb. 25

Designs: 50c, St. Mark's Basilica and waves, horiz. 1d, Lion of St. Mark.

254 A101 25c multi 15 15
255 A101 50c red, blk & buff 15 15
256 A101 1d lt bl & multi 30 15
Set value 35

UNESCO campaign to save Venice.

Bridge, Road, Map of Africa — A102

1972, Apr. 21 ***Perf. 13***
257 A102 75c blue & multi 22 15

2nd African Road Conf., Rabat, Apr. 17-22.

Morocco No. 223 — A103

1972, Apr. 27 ***Perf. 11½***
258 A103 1d lt ultra & multi 30 20

Stamp Day.

The Engagement of Imilchil, by Tayeb Lahlou A104

1972, May 26 Litho. *Perf. 13x13½*
259 A104 60c blk & multi 38 22

Folklore Festival, Marrakesh, May 26-June 4.

Map of Africa, Dove and OAU Emblem — A105

1972, June 12 Photo. *Perf. 11½*
260 A105 25c multi 15 15

9th Summit Conference of Organization for African Unity, Rabat, June 12-15.

Landscape, Environment Emblem — A106

1972, July 20 Photo. *Perf. 12½x12*
261 A106 50c bl & multi 20 15

UN Conference on Human Environment, Stockholm, June 5-16

Olympic Emblems, Running A107

1972, Aug. 29 Photo. *Perf. 13x13½*
262 A107 25c shown 15 15
263 A107 50c Wrestling 15 15
264 A107 75c Soccer 25 20
265 A107 1d Cycling 32 22
Set value 60

20th Olympic Games, Munich, Aug. 26-Sept. 11.

Sow Thistle A108

Mountain Gazelle A109

1972, Sept. 15 Litho. *Perf. 14*
266 A108 25c shown 20 15
267 A108 40c Amberboa crupinoides 25 20
Set value 28

See No. 305-306.

1972, Sept. 29 Photo. *Perf. 11½*
268 A109 25c shown 22 20
269 A109 40c Barbary sheep 32 25

Nos. 266-269 issued for nature protection.

Rabat Rug — A110

Child and UNICEF Emblem — A111

Designs: 25c, High Atlas rug. 70c, Tazenakht rug. 75c, Rabat rug, different pattern.

Perf. 13½ (25fr, 70fr), 11½
1972-73 Photo.
270 A110 25c multi 50 15
270A A110 50c multi 75 22
271 A110 70c multi 90 30
271A A110 75c multi 1.00 30

Issue dates: 50c, 75c, Oct. 27, 1972; 25c, 70c, Dec. 28, 1973.
See Nos. 326-327.

1972, Dec. 20 Photo. *Perf. 13½x13*
272 A111 75c brt grn & bl 22 15

International Children's Day.

Symbolic Letter Carrier and Stamp A112

1973, Jan. 30 Photo. *Perf. 13x13½*
273 A112 25c brn & multi 15 15

Stamp Day.

Weather Map, Northern Hemisphere A113

1973, Feb. 23 Photo. *Perf. 13*
274 A113 70c sil & multi 25 16

Intl. meteorological cooperation, cent.

King Hassan II, Coat of Arms — A114

1973-76 Photo. *Perf. 14*
275 A114 1c pale yel & multi 15 15
276 A114 2c pale bl & multi 15 15
277 A114 5c pale ol & multi 15 15
278 A114 10c brn org & multi 15 15
279 A114 15c vio gray & multi 15 15
280 A114 20c pink & multi 22 15
281 A114 25c pale bl & multi 15 15
282 A114 30c rose & multi 22 15
283 A114 35c org yel & multi 15 15
284 A114 40c lt gray & multi 1.50 25
285 A114 50c ultra & multi 22 15
286 A114 60c sal & multi 25 15
287 A114 70c yel grn & multi 20 15
288 A114 75c lem & multi 38 15
289 A114 80c multi 25 20
290 A114 90c brt grn & multi 50 15
291 A114 1d beige & multi 65 15
292 A114 2d gray & multi 2.00 38
293 A114 3d lt lil & multi 2.25 50
294 A114 5d lt brn & multi ('75) 2.00 55
294A A114 5d pink & multi ('76) 2.00 70
Nos. 275-294A (21) 13.69
Set value 3.50

مناظرة
السماحة
1973

Nos. B26-B27 Surcharged to Obliterate Surtax

1973, Mar. 13 *Perf. 11½*
295 SP1 25c multi 1.10 1.10
296 SP1 70c multi 1.10 1.10

Tourism Conference 1973. Arabic overprint and date on one line on No. 296.
See se-tenant note below No. B11.
See Nos. 351-352.

Holy Ka'aba, Mecca, Mosque and Minaret, Rabat A115

1973, May 3 Photo. *Perf. 13½x14*
297 A115 25c lt bl & multi 15 15

Mohammed's 1,403rd birthday.

Roses and M'Gouna A116

1973, May 14 *Perf. 13*
298 A116 25c bl & multi 15 15

Rose Festival of M'Gouna.

Hands, Torch, OAU Emblem — A117

1973, May 25 Photo. *Perf. 14x13*
299 A117 70c dp cl & multi 20 15

OAU, 10th anniversary.

Dancers with Tambourines — A118

Design: 1d, Dancer with handbells, Marrakesh Minaret, Atlas Mountain.

1973, May 30 *Perf. 12½x13*
300 A118 50c multi 20 15
301 A118 1d multi 25 20

Folklore Festival, Marrakesh.

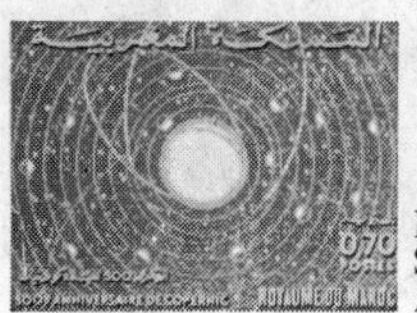

Heliocentric System A119

1973, June 29 *Perf. 13x13½*
302 A119 70c dk bl & multi 30 15

Nicolaus Copernicus (1473-1543), Polish astronomer.

Microscope, WHO Emblem, World Map — A120

1973, July 16 Photo. *Perf. 13x12½*
303 A120 70c multi 22 15

WHO, 25th anniversary.

INTERPOL Emblem, Fingerprint A121

1973, Sept. 12 Photo. *Perf. 13x13½*
304 A121 70c brn, sil & bl 20 15

50th anniv. of Intl. Criminal Police Org.

Flower Type of 1972

1973, Oct. 12 Litho. *Perf. 14*
305 A108 25c Daisies, horiz. 38 15
306 A108 1d Thistle 75 25

Nature protection.

Berber Hyena A122

Design: 50c, Eleonora's falcon, vert.

1973, Nov. 23 Photo. *Perf. 14*
307 A122 25c multi 38 15
308 A122 50c multi 50 20

Nature protection.

Map and Colors of Morocco, Algeria and Tunisia A123

1973, Dec. 7 *Perf. 13x13½*
309 A123 25c gold & multi 15 15

Maghreb Committee for Coordination of Posts and Telecommunications.

Fairway and Drive over Water Hazard — A124

Map of Africa, Scales, Human Rights Flame — A125

1974, Feb. 8 **Photo.** ***Perf. 14x13***
310 A124 70c multi 30 20

International Golf Grand Prix for the Hassan II Morocco trophy.

No. 227 Overprinted in Red

المؤتمر الاسلامي - لاهور
1394

1974, Feb. 25 ***Perf. 11½***
311 A79 1d multi 1.40 75

Islamic Conference, Lahore, India, 1974.

1974, Mar. 15 **Photo.** ***Perf. 14x13½***
312 A125 70c gold & multi 40 25

25th anniversary of the Universal Declaration of Human Rights.

Vanadinite A126

Minaret, Marrakesh Mosque, Rotary Emblem A127

1974-75 **Photo.** ***Perf. 13***

313	A126 25c shown	15	15
313A	A126 50c Aragonite	38	15
314	A126 70c Erythrine	38	22
314A	A126 1d Agate	75	16

Issue dates: 25c, 70c, Apr. 30, 1974; 50c, 1d, Feb. 14, 1975.

1974, May 11 **Photo.** ***Perf. 14***
315 A127 70c multi 25 15

District 173 Rotary International annual meeting, Marrakesh, May 10-12.

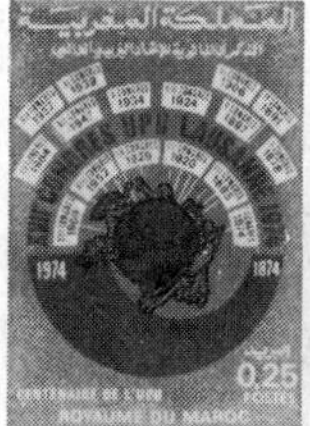

UPU Emblem, Congress Dates — A128

Drummer and Dancers — A129

Design: 1d, Scroll with UPU emblem, Lausanne coat of arms and 17th UPU Congress emblem, horiz.

1974, May 30 **Photo.**
316 A128 25c lt grn, org & blk 15 15
317 A128 1d dk grn & multi 32 20

Centenary of Universal Postal Union.

1974, June 7 **Photo.** ***Perf. 14***

Design: 70c, Knife juggler and women.

318 A129 25c multi 22 15
319 A129 70c multi 50 22

National folklore festival, Marrakesh.

Environment Emblem, Polution, Clean Water and Air — A130

1974, June 25 ***Perf. 13***
320 A130 25c multi 15 15

World Environment Day.

Simulated Stamps, Cancel and Magnifier A131

1974, Aug. 2 **Photo.** ***Perf. 13***
321 A131 70c sil & multi 22 15

Stamp Day.

No. J5 Surcharged الاحصاء الفلاحي

1,00

1974, Sept. 25 **Photo.** ***Perf. 14***
322 D2 1d on 5c multi 85 65

Agricultural census.

World Soccer Cup — A132

Double-spurred Francolin — A133

1974, Oct. 11
323 A132 1d brt bl & multi 50 30

World Cup Soccer Championship, Munich, June 13-July 7.

A stamp similar to No. 323, also issued Oct. 11, has gold inscription: "CHAMPION: R.F.A." in French and Arabic, honoring the German Federal Republic as championship winner. Value $32.50

Perf. 14x13½, 13½x14

1974, Dec. 5 **Photo.**
324 A133 25c shown 38 15
325 A133 70c Leopard, horiz. 70 22

Nature protection.

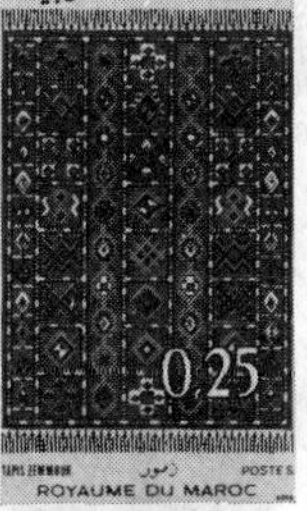

Zemmour Rug A134

Columbine A135

Design: 1d, Beni Mguilo rug.

1974, Dec 20 ***Perf. 13***
326 A134 25c multi 38 15
327 A134 1d multi 75 22

See Nos. 349-350, 398-400.

1975 **Photo.** ***Perf. 13½***

328	A135 10c Daisies	15	15
329	A135 25c Columbine	20	15
330	A135 35c Orange lilies	22	15
331	A135 50c Anemones	22	15
332	A135 60c White starflower	30	20
333	A135 70c Poppies	32	22
334	A135 90c Carnations	45	32
335	A135 1d Pansies	50	38
	Nos. 328-335 (8)	2.36	
	Set value		1.50

Issue dates: 25c, 35c, 70c, 90c, Jan. 10; others, Apr. 29.

Water Carrier, by Feu Tayeb Lahlou A136

1975, Apr. 3 ***Perf. 13***
338 A136 1d multi 65 30

Stamp Collector, Carrier Pigeon, Globe — A137

Musicians and Dancers — A138

1975, May 21 **Photo.** ***Perf. 13***
339 A137 40c gold & multi 15 15

Stamp Day.

1975, June 12 **Photo.** ***Perf. 14x13½***
340 A138 1d multi 40 22

16th Folklore Festival, Marrakesh, May 30-June 15.

Guitar and Association for the Blind Emblem A139

1975, July 8 ***Perf. 13x13½***
341 A139 1d pur & multi 38 15

Week of the Blind.

Animals in Forest — A140

1975, July 25 **Photo.** ***Perf. 13x13½***
342 A140 25c multi 15 15

Children's Week.

Games' Emblem, Runner, Weight Lifter — A141

1975, Sept. 4 **Photo.** ***Perf. 13***
343 A141 40c gold, mar & buff 15 15

7th Mediterranean Games, Algiers, Aug. 23-Sept. 6.

Bald Ibis A142

1975, Oct. 21 **Photo.** ***Perf. 13***
344 A142 40c shown 38 15
345 A142 1d Persian lynx, vert. 55 30

Nature protection.

King Mohammed V Greeting Crowd, Prince Moulay Hassan at Left — A143

Canceled-to-order stamps are often from remainders. Most collectors of canceled stamps prefer postally used specimens.

King Hassan II — A144

Design: No. 348, King Mohammed V wearing fez.

1975, Nov. 21 Photo. *Perf. 13½*

346 A143 40c blk, sil & dk bl 20 15
347 A144 1d blk, gold & dk bl 32 20
348 A144 1d blk, gold & dk bl 32 20
a. Sheet of 3, #346-348 9.00 9.00

20th anniversary of independence.

Rug Type of 1974

Designs: 25c, Ouled Besseba rug. 1d, Ait Ouaouzguid rug.

1975, Dec. 11

349 A134 25c red & multi 38 25
350 A134 1d org & multi 55 32

المسيرة الخضراء
1975

Nos. B29-B30 Surcharged in Green to Obliterate Surtax

1975 *Perf. 11½*

351 SP1 25c bl & multi 1.50 1.50
352 SP1 70c org & multi 1.50 1.50

March of Moroccan people into Spanish Sahara, Dec. 1975.
See se-tenant note after No. B11.

"Green March of the People" — A145

Copper Coin, Fez, 1883-84 — A146

1975, Dec. 30 Photo. *Perf. 13½x13*

353 A145 40c multi 15 15

March of Moroccan people into Spanish Sahara, Dec. 1975.

1976 Photo. *Perf. 14x13½*

Coins: 15c, 50c, silver coin, Rabat, 1774-75. 35c, 65c, Gold coin, Sabta, 13th-14th centuries. 1d, Square coin, Sabta, 12th-13th centuries. 40c, as 5c.

354 A146 5c dl rose & multi 15 15
355 A146 15c brn & multi 15 15
356 A146 35c gray & multi 38 15
357 A146 40c ocher & multi 16 15
358 A146 50c ultra & blk 25 15
359 A146 65c yel & multi 30 22
360 A146 1d multi 40 25
Nos. 354-360 (7) 1.79
Set value 98

Issue dates: Nos. 354-356, Apr. 26. Nos. 357-360, Jan. 20.

1976, Sept. 9

Designs: Various Moroccan coins.

361 A146 5c grn & multi 15 15
362 A146 15c dp rose & multi 15 15
363 A146 20c lt bl & multi 18 15
364 A146 30c lil rose & multi 20 15
365 A146 35c grn & multi 38 15
366 A146 70c org & multi 50 18
Nos. 361-366 (6) 1.56
Set value 64

See Nos. 403-406A, 524B-524C.

Family — A147

Arch, Ibn Zaidoun Mosque — A148

1976, Feb. 12 *Perf. 14x13½*

367 A147 40c multi 25 20

Family planning.

Perf. 13½x14, 14x13½

1976, Feb. 12 Photo.

Design: 40c, Hall, Ibn Zaidoun Mosque, horiz.

368 A148 40c multi 15 15
369 A148 65c multi 25 20
Set value 28

Ibn Zaidoun Mosque, millennium.

Medersa bou Anania, Fez A149

1976, Feb. 26 *Perf. 13x14½*

370 A149 1d multi 25 20

Borobudur Temple — A150

Design: 40c, Bas-relief, Borobudur.

1976, Mar. 11 Photo. *Perf. 13*

371 A150 40c multi 15 15
372 A150 1d multi 25 15
Set value 24

UNESCO campaign to save Borobudur Temple, Java.

Islamic Conference, 6th Anniv. — A151

1976 Litho. *Perf. 13½x13*

372A A151 1d Dome of the Rock 3.50 1.25

Jewelry Type of 1968

Designs: 40c, Pendant. 1d, Breastplate.

1976, June 29 Photo. *Perf. 14x13½*

373 A67 40c bl & multi 25 15
374 A67 1d ol & multi 38 20

Moroccan Red Crescent Society.

Nos. 373-374 were printed se-tenant in sheets of 10 (5x2) arranged vertically tete-beche.

Bicentennial Emblem, Flags and Map of US and Morocco — A152

Design: 1d, George Washington, King Hassan, Statue of Liberty and Royal Palace, Rabat, vert.

1976, July 27 Photo. *Perf. 14*

375 A152 40c multi 20 15
376 A152 1d multi 32 22

American Bicentennial.

Wrestling A153

1976, Aug. 11 *Perf. 13x13½*

377 A153 35c shown 15 15
378 A153 40c Cycling 22 15
379 A153 50c Boxing 35 22
380 A153 1d Running 50 38

21st Olympic Games, Montreal, Canada, July 17-Aug. 1.

Old and New Telephones, Radar — A154

1976, Sept. 29 Photo. *Perf. 14*

381 A154 1d gold & multi 30 15

Centenary of first telephone call by Alexander Graham Bell, Mar. 10, 1876.

Blind Person's Identification A155

1976, Oct. 12 Photo. *Perf. 13½x14*

382 A155 50c multi 16 15

Week of the Blind.

Chanting Goshawk A156

1976, Oct. 29 *Perf. 13x13½*

383 A156 40c shown 45 15
384 A156 1d Purple gallinule 75 30

Nature protection.

King Hassan, Star, Torch, Map of Morocco — A157

Africa Cup — A159

Globe and Dove A158

1976, Nov. 19 Photo. *Perf. 12½x13*

385 A157 40c multi 15 15

First anniversary of Green March into Spanish Sahara.

Nos. B34-B35 Overprinted with 2 Bars over Surcharge and 4-line Arabic Inscription

1976, Nov. 29 Photo. *Perf. 13½*

386 SP1 25c ultra, blk & org 75 75
387 SP1 70c red, blk & org 90 90

5th African Tuberculosis Conference, Rabat.

1976, Dec. 16 *Perf. 13*

388 A158 1d bl, blk & red 22 15

5th Summit Meeting of Non-aligned Countries, Colombo, Aug. 9-19, and 25th anniv. of Org. of Non-aligned Countries.

1976, Dec. 29 Photo. *Perf. 14*

389 A159 1d multi 25 16

African Soccer Cup.

Letters Circling Globe, Postmark A160

1977, Jan. 24 Photo. *Perf. 13½*

390 A160 40c multi 16 15

Stamp Day.

Aeonium Arboreum — A161

Malope Trifida — A162

Design: 1d, Hesperolaburnum platyclarpum.

Perf. 13x13½, 14 (A162)

1977, Feb. 22

391 A161 40c multi 32 15
392 A162 50c multi 45 22
393 A161 1d multi 55 22

Ornamental Lamps, View of Sale — A163

1977, Mar. 24 Photo. *Perf. 14*
394 A163 40c multi 20 15

Candle procession of Sale.

موسم حب الملوك
1977

No. J6 Surcharged in Orange

0,40

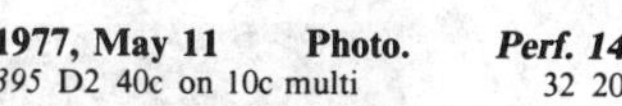

1977, May 11 Photo. *Perf. 14*
395 D2 40c on 10c multi 32 20

Cherry Festival.

Map of Arab Countries, Emblem A164

1977, June 2 Photo. *Perf. 14*
396 A164 50c multi 20 15

5th Congress of Organization of Arab Cities.

APU Emblem, Members' Flags A165

1977, June 20
397 A165 1d multi 35 20

Arab Postal Union, 25th anniversary.

Rug Type of 1974

Designs: 35c, No. 399A, Marmoucha rug (diff.). No. 399, Ait Haddou rug. 1d, Sale rug.

Perf. 11½x12, 13½ (#399A)
1977-79 Photo.

398	A134 35c multi	25	15
399	A134 40c multi	32	15
399A	A134 40c multi	32	15
400	A134 1d multi	45	22
	Set value		56

Issue dates: No. 399A, Mar. 8, 1979, others, July 21, 1977.

Cithara — A166

Ali Jinnah and Map of Pakistan — A167

1977, Aug. 18 Photo. *Perf. 14*
401 A166 1d multi 25 15

Week of the Blind.

1977, Oct. 10 Photo. *Perf. 13½x13*
402 A167 70c multi 20 15

Mohammed Ali Jinnah (1876-1948), first Governor General of Pakistan.

Coin Type of 1976

Designs: Various Moroccan coins.

1977-81 *Perf. 14x13½*

403	A146 10c gray & multi	15	15
403A	A146 25c ap grn & multi ('81)	15	15
404	A146 60c dk red & multi ('78)	22	15
405	A146 75c citron & multi	25	15
405A	A146 80c pale vio & mult ('81)	20	15
406	A146 2d yel grn & multi	75	25
406A	A146 3d beige & multi ('81)	75	40
	Nos. 403-406A (7)	2.47	
	Set value		1.00

Marcher with Flag, Map of Morocco and Spanish Sahara — A168

1977, Nov. 6 Photo. *Perf. 14*
407 A168 1d multi 28 15

Green March into Spanish Sahara, 2nd anniv.

Chamber of Representatives — A169

1977, Nov. 6 *Perf. 13½*
408 A169 1d multi 25 15
a. Souvenir sheet 1.40 1.40

Opening of Chamber of Representatives. No. 408a sold for 3d.

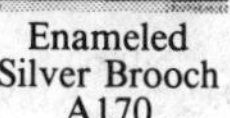

Enameled Silver Brooch A170

Copper Vessel A171

1977, Dec. 14 Photo. *Perf. 11½*
409 A170 1d multi 30 16

Moroccan Red Crescent Society.

1978, Jan. 5 Photo. *Perf. 13*

Design: 1d, Standing filigree copper bowl with cover.

410	A171 40c gold & multi	25	15
411	A171 1d gold & multi	45	20
	Set value		28

Printed se-tenant in sheets of 10 (5x2) arranged vertically tete beche.

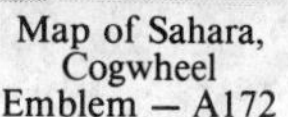

Map of Sahara, Cogwheel Emblem — A172

Covered Jar — A173

Design: 1d, Map of North Africa, fish in net, camels, horiz.

1978, Feb. 27 Photo. *Perf. 14*
412 A172 40c multi 15 15
413 A172 1d multi 30 15

Promotion of the Sahara. See Nos. 441-442 for similar stamps overprinted.

1978, Mar. 27 *Perf. 13½x13*
414 A173 1d shown 38 22
415 A173 1d Vase 38 22

Week of the Blind.

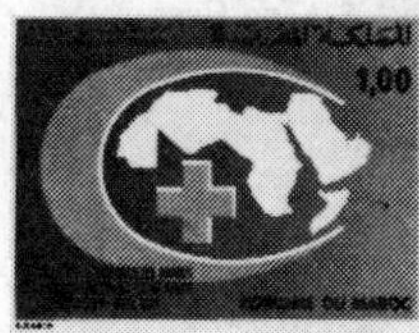

Red Crescent, Red Cross, Arab Countries A174

1978, Apr. 14 *Perf. 13x13½*
416 A174 1d multi 25 15

10th Conference of Arab Red Crescent and Red Cross Societies, Apr. 10-15.

View of Fez, Rotary Emblem — A175

1978, Apr. 22 Photo. *Perf. 14*
417 A175 1d multi 25 15

Rotary Intl. Meeting, Fez, District 173.

Dome of the Rock, Jerusalem A176

Folk Dancers and Flutist A177

1978, May 29 *Perf. 14½*

418	A176 5c multi	15	15
419	A176 10c multi	15	15
	Set value	24	18

Palestinian fighters and their families. For overprints, see Nos. 502-502A.

1978, June 15 *Perf. 13½x13*
420 A177 1d multi 50 25

National Folklore Festival, Marrakesh.

Sugar Cane Field, and Conveyor Belt A178

1978, July 24 Photo. *Perf. 13*
421 A178 40c multi 15 15

Sugar industry.

Games Emblem — A179

Bird, Tree, Tent, Scout Emblem — A180

1978, Aug. 25
422 A179 1d multi 30 20

World sailing championships.

1978, Sept. 26 Photo. *Perf. 13*
423 A180 40c multi 1.75 50

Pan-Arab Scout Jamboree, Rabat.

View of Fez A181

1978, Oct. 10
424 A181 40c multi 15 15

Moulay Idriss the Great, Festival, Fez.

Flame Emblem — A182

Houses, Agadir — A183

1978, Dec. 21 **Photo.** ***Perf. 14***
425 A182 1d multi 38 20

30th anniversary of Universal Declaration of Human Rights.

1979, Jan. 25 **Photo.** ***Perf. 12***
426 A183 40c shown 15 15
427 A183 1d Old Fort, Marrakesh 30 15

Soccer and Cup A184

1979, Mar. 2 ***Perf. 13***
428 A184 40c multi 15 15

Mohammed V Soccer Cup.

Vase — A185 Procession — A186

1979, Mar. 29 **Photo.** ***Perf. 14***
429 A185 1d multi 25 20

Week of the Blind.

Perf. 13x13½, 13½x13

1979, Apr. 18

Design: 1d, Festival, by Mohamed Ben Ali Rbati, horiz.

430 A186 40c multi 15 15
431 A186 1d multi 30 20

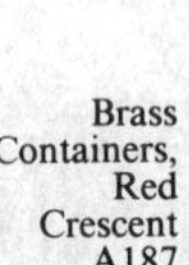

Brass Containers, Red Crescent A187

Perf. 13x13½, 13½x13

1979, May 16 **Photo.**
432 A187 40c shown 25 15
433 A187 1d Heated coffee urn, vert. 50 20

Red Crescent Society.

Dancers — A188

Silver Dagger — A189

1979, June 1 **Photo.** ***Perf. 13***
434 A188 40c multi 15 15

National Festival of Marrakech.

1979, June 20 ***Perf. 14***
435 A189 1d multi 30 15

King Hassan II, 50th Birthday — A190

1979, July 9 **Photo.** ***Perf. 14***
436 A190 1d multi 25 15

4th Arab Youth Festival, Rabat A191

1979, July 30 **Photo.** ***Perf. 13½x14***
437 A191 1d multi 25 15

King Hassan II and Crowd — A192

1979, Aug. 20 ***Perf. 14x13½***
438 A192 1d multi 22 15

Revolution of the King and the People, 25th anniv.

Intl. Bureau of Education, 50th Anniv. — A193

1979, Sept. 28 **Photo.** ***Perf. 13x13½***
439 A193 1d multi 38 20

Pilgrimage to Mecca, Mt. Arafat, Holy Ka'aba — A194

1979, Oct. 25 ***Perf. 13½***
440 A194 1d multi 25 15

No. 413 Redrawn in Smaller Size and Overprinted in Red

استرجاع اقليم وادى الذهب
١٩٧٩-٨-١٤

1979, Nov. 7 **Litho.** ***Perf. 14***
Size: 33x23mm

441 A172 40c multi 25 15
442 A172 1d multi 38 25

Return of Oued Eddahab province, Aug. 14.

Leucanthemum Catanance A195

Children, Globe, IYC Emblem A196

1979, Nov. 21 **Photo.** ***Perf. 14½***
443 A195 40c Centaurium 15 15
444 A195 1d shown 32 15
Set value 22

1979, Dec. 3 ***Perf. 14***
445 A196 40c multi 65 25

International Year of the Child.

Otter — A197

Traffic Signs and Road — A198

1979, Dec. 18 ***Perf. 13½x13***
446 A197 40c shown 25 15
447 A197 1d Redstart 40 22
Set value 30

1980, Jan. 3 **Photo.** ***Perf. 14***
448 A198 40c shown 15 15
449 A198 1d Children at curb 20 15
Set value 16

Fortress A199

1980, Jan. 29 ***Perf. 13x13½***
450 A199 1d multi 25 15

Copper Bowl and Lid, Red Crescent — A200

Week of the Blind — A201

Red Crescent Society: 70c, Copper kettle and brazier. Nos. 451-452 tete-beche.

1980, Feb. 28 **Photo.** ***Perf. 14***
451 A200 50c multi 20 15
452 A200 70c multi 28 15

1980, Mar. 19 **Photo.** ***Perf. 14***
453 A201 40c multi 15 15

Rabat Mechanical Sorting Office A202

1980, Apr. 17
454 A202 40c multi 15 15

Stamp Day.

Rotary Intl., 75th Anniv. — A203

Cloth and Leather Goods — A204

1980, May 14 **Photo.** ***Perf. 14***
455 A203 1d multi 22 15

1980, May 31 **Photo.** ***Perf. 13½x13***
456 A204 1d multi 22 15

4th Textile and Leather Exhibition, Casablanca, May 2-9.

Gypsum A205

Falcon A206

1980, June 19 **Photo.** ***Perf. 13½x13***
457 A205 40c multi 20 15

See Nos. 477-478.

1980, July 26 ***Perf. 11½***
458 A206 40c multi 20 15

Hunting with falcons.

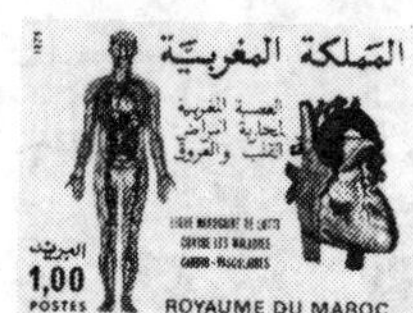
Fight against Heart Disease A207

1980, Aug. 7 Photo. *Perf. 13x13½*
459 A207 1d multi 30 15

Women's Decade and UN Emblems — A208

1980, Aug. 18 *Perf. 14*
460 A208 40c shown 15 15
461 A208 1d Emblems, diff. 25 15
Set value 16

United Nations Decade for Women.

Ornamental Saddle and Harness — A209

1980, Sept. 3 *Perf. 14½*
462 A209 40c Saddle, harness, diff. 15 15
463 A209 1d shown 30 15
Set value 22

World Meteorological Day — A210

1980, Sept. 18
464 A210 40c multi 15 15

Hand Holding Dry Gas Pump A211

1980, Oct. 6 Photo. *Perf. 14*
465 A211 40c Light bulb, gas can 15 15
466 A211 1d shown 25 15
Set value 18

Energy conservation.

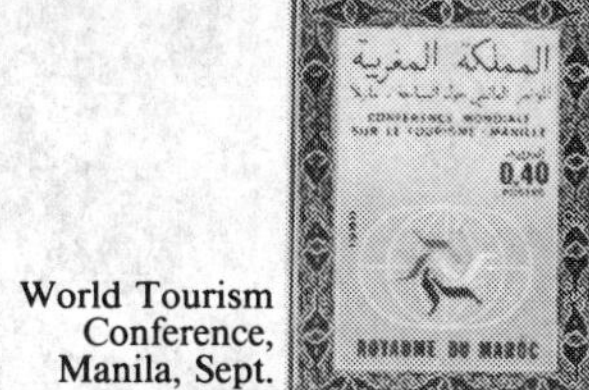
World Tourism Conference, Manila, Sept. 27 — A212

1980, Oct. 22 *Perf. 11½x12*
467 A212 40c multi 15 15

Symbolic Tree Rooted in Europe and Africa A213

1980, Oct. 30 *Perf. 14*
468 A213 1d multi 25 15

Straits of Gibraltar linking Europe and Africa.

5th Anniversary of the Green March — A214

1980, Nov. 6
469 A214 1d multi 22 15

Holy Ka'aba A215

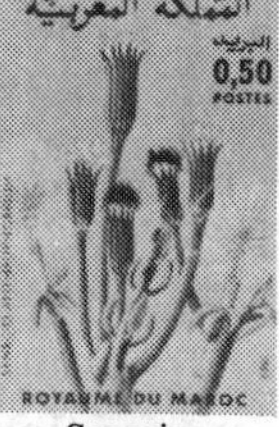
Senecio Antheuphorbium A216

1980, Nov. 9
470 A215 40c shown 15 15
471 A215 1d Mecca Mosque 25 15
a. Souv. sheet of 2, #480-471 1.25
Set value 22

No. 471a sold for 3d.

1980, Dec. 4 *Perf. 13*
472 A216 50c shown 15 15
473 A216 1d Periploca laevigata 30 16
Set value 25

Leaves, by Mahjoubi Aherdan A217

Nejjarine Fountain, Fes A218

Design: 40c. Untitled painting by Mahjoubi Aherdan (23x38mm).

1980, Dec. 18 *Perf. 12*
474 A217 40c multi 15 15
475 A217 1d multi 25 15
Set value 22

1981, Jan. 22 *Perf. 14x13½*
476 A218 40c multi 15 15

Mineral Type of 1980

1981, Feb. 19 Photo. *Perf. 13½x13*
477 A205 40c Onyx 16 15
478 A205 1d Malachite-azurite 35 20
Set value 28

Inscribed 1980.

King Hassan II — A219

1981, Mar. 2 *Perf. 14*
479 A219 60c shown 15 15
480 A219 60c Map of Morocco 15 15
481 A219 60c King Mohammed V 15 15
Set value 26

25th anniv. of independence. Nos. 479-481 se-tenant.

25th Anniv. of King Hassan II Coronation A220

1981, Mar. 3
482 A220 1.30d multi 30 20

The Source, by Jillali Gharbaoui — A221

1981, Apr. 8 *Perf. 13x12½*
483 A221 1.30d multi 30 20

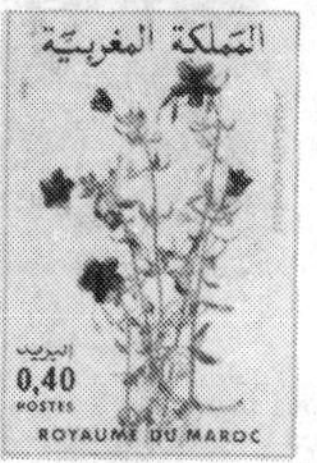
Anagalis Monelli — A222

Army Badge — A223

1981, Apr. 23 *Perf. 13*
484 A222 40c shown 15 15
485 A222 70c Bubonium intricatum 22 15
Set value 20

1981, May 14 Photo. *Perf. 14x13½*

Moroccan Armed Forces, 25th Anniv: Nos. 486, 488, King Hassan as army major general. Nos. 486-488 se-tenant.

486 A223 60c multi 15 15
487 A223 60c multi 15 15
488 A223 60c multi 15 15
Set value 26

13th World Telecommunications Day — A224

1981, May 18 *Perf. 14x13*
489 A224 1.30d multi 25 16

Hand-painted Plate — A225

22nd Marrakesh Arts Festival — A226

1981, June 5 *Perf. 14*
490 A225 50c shown 15 15
491 A225 1.30d Plate, diff. 25 15
Set value 22

Week of the Blind.

1981, June 18 *Perf. 13½x13*
492 A226 1.30d multi 30 20

For overprint, see No. 579.

Seboula Dagger, Oujda — A227

Copper Mortar and Pestle, Red Crescent — A228

1981, Sept. 7 Photo. *Perf. 13½*
493 A227 1.30d multi 25 16

1981, Sept. 24 *Perf. 14*
494 A228 60c shown 25 15
495 A228 1.30d Tripod 40 16
Set value 25

Footnotes often refer to other stamps of the same design.

Intl. Year of the Disabled A229

Iphiclides Feisthamelii A230

1981, Oct. 15 *Perf. 13½*
496 A229 60c multi 22 15

1981, Oct. 29 *Perf. 13½x13*
497 A230 60c shown 20 15
498 A230 1.30d Zerynthia rumina 40 22

See Nos. 528-529.

6th Anniv. of Green March — A231

Intl. Palestinian Solidarity Day — A232

1981, Nov. 6 *Perf. 13x13½*
499 A231 1.30d multi 50 25

1981, Nov. 22 *Perf. 13½x13*
500 A232 60c multi 38 25

Congress Emblem — A233

1981, Nov. 22 *Perf. 13½*
501 A233 1.30d multi 38 25

World Federation of Twin Cities, 10th Congress, Casablanca, Nov. 15-18.

Nos. 418-419 Overprinted

مؤتمر القمة العربي
الثاني عشر
فاس 1981

0,40

ROYAUME DU MAROC

1981, Nov. 25 **Photo.** *Perf. 14½*
502 A176 40c on 5c multi 3.00 3.00
502A A176 40c on 10c multi 2.25 2.25

First Anniv. of Mohammed V Airport — A234

King Hassan II — A236

Al Massirah Dam Opening A235

1981, Dec. 8 **Photo.** *Perf. 14x13*
503 A234 1.30d multi 25 20

1981, Dec. 17 *Perf. 11½*
504 A235 60c multi 15 15

1981, Dec. 28 *Perf. 13x12½*

505	A236	5c multi	15	15
506	A236	10c multi	15	15
507	A236	15c multi	15	15
508	A236	20c multi	15	15
509	A236	25c multi	15	15
510	A236	30c multi	15	15
511	A236	35c multi	15	15
512	A236	40c multi	38	15
513	A236	50c multi	15	15
514	A236	60c multi	18	15
515	A236	65c multi	18	15
516	A236	70c multi	20	15
517	A236	75c multi	20	15
518	A236	80c multi	22	15
519	A236	90c multi	28	15

1983, Mar. 1 **Photo.** *Perf. 14½*
Size: 25x32mm

520	A236	1d multi	32	15
521	A236	1.40d multi	38	15
522	A236	2d multi	45	15
523	A236	3d multi	65	20
524	A236	5d multi	85	40
524A	A236	10d multi	1.65	70
		Nos. 505-524A (21)	7.14	
		Set value		2.40

See Nos. 566-575, 715.

Type of 1976

1979-81 **Photo.** *Perf. 12½*
Size: 18x23mm
524B A146 40c ocher & multi 15 15
524C A146 50c brt bl, blk & dk brn ('81) 15 15
d. Bklt. pane of 10 1.25
Set value 20 15

Equestrian Sports A237

1981, Dec. 29 *Perf. 13x13½*
525 A237 1.30d multi 30 20

Traditional Carpet Design — A238

1982, Jan. 21
526 A238 50c Glaoua pattern 15 15
527 A238 1.30d Ouled Besseba pattern 30 20
Set value 28

Butterfly Type of 1981

1982, Feb. 25 *Perf. 13½x13*
528 A230 60c Celerio oken lineata 15 15
529 A230 1.30d Mesoacidalia aglaja lyauteyi 32 22

World Forest Day — A240

Blind Week — A241

1982, Apr. 8 *Perf. 14*
531 A240 40c multi 15 15

1982, May 10
532 A241 1d Jug 20 15

Folk Dancers, Rabat A242

Copper Candlestick, Red Crescent A243

1982, June 3
533 A242 1.40d multi 25 16

1982, July 1
534 A243 1.40d multi 25 16

Women in Traditional Clothing, by M. Mezian — A244

ITU Conf., Nairobi, Sept. — A246

Natl. Census A245

1982, Aug. 16 **Photo.** *Perf. 14*
535 A244 1.40d multi 25 16

1982, Sept. 6 **Photo.** *Perf. 11½*
536 A245 60c multi 15 15

1982 *Perf. 13½x13*
537 A246 1.40d multi 25 15

TB Bacillus Centenary A247

World Food Day A248

1982, Sept. 30
538 A247 1.40d multi 25 15

1982, Oct. 16 *Perf. 14*
539 A248 60c multi 15 15

Unity Railroad A249

1982, Nov. 6 *Perf. 13x13½*
540 A249 1.40d multi 25 16

30th Anniv. of Arab Postal Union A250

1982, Nov. 17 *Perf. 14*
541 A250 1.40d multi 25 15

Intl. Palestinian Solidarity Day A251

Red Coral, Al-Hoceima A252

1982, Nov. 29 *Perf. 14*
542 A251 1.40d sil & multi 38 18

1982, Dec. 20 *Perf. 13½*
543 A252 1.40d multi 25 15

Stamp Day — A253

Week of the Blind — A254

1983, Jan. 26 *Perf. 13½x13*
544 A253 1.40d Nos. 3, 178 25 15

1983, Apr. 20 **Photo.** *Perf. 14*
545 A254 1.40d multi 25 15

Popular Arts A255

1983, June 27 Photo. Perf. 14
546 A255 1.40d multi 25 15

Wrought-Iron Lectern — A256

Moroccan Flora — A258

Economic Commission for Africa, 25th Anniv. — A257

1983, July 7 Litho. Perf. 13½
547 A256 1.40d multi 25 16

1983, July 18 Photo. Perf. 14
548 A257 1.40d multi 25 15

1983, Aug. 1 Litho. Perf. 14
549 A258 60c Tecoma 15 15
550 A258 1.40d Strelitzia 25 15
Set value 34 22

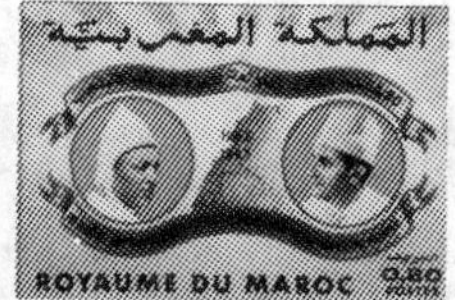
Kings Mohammed V and Hassan II — A259

1983, Aug. 20 Litho. Perf. 14
551 A259 80c multi 15 15
a. Souvenir sheet of 1 90 90

King and People's Revolution, 30th Anniv. No. 551a sold for 5 dinars.

Mediterranean Games A260

Palestinian Solidarity A262

Touiza A261

1983, Sept. 3 Photo. Perf. 14
552 A260 80c Stylized sportsmen 15 15
553 A260 1d Emblem 16 15
554 A260 2d Stylized runner, horiz. 32 22
a. Souv. sheet of 3, #552-554, imperf. 90 90

No. 554a sold for 5d.

1983, Sept. 30 Photo. Perf. 13
555 A261 80c Tractors 15 15

1983, Nov. 10 Photo. Perf. 13½x13
556 A262 80c multi 25 15

8th Anniv. of the Green March into Spanish Sahara A263

1983, Nov. 17 Perf. 13x13½
557 A263 80c multi 15 15

Ouzoud Waterfall — A264

1983, Nov. 28 Perf. 14
558 A264 80c multi 15 15

Children's Day — A265

Zemmouri Carpet — A266

1983, Dec. 5 Photo. Perf. 13½x13
559 A265 2d multi 32 15

1983, Dec. 15 Perf. 13½

Various carpets.

560 A266 60c multi 15 15
561 A266 1.40d multi 25 15
Set value 34 22

World Communications Year — A267

1983, Dec. 20 Perf. 14
562 A267 2d multi 32 15

Union of Cities Al-Qods and Fez — A268

1984, Jan. 16 Photo. Perf. 13x13½
563 A268 2d multi 32 15

Desert Fox — A269

Perf. 11½x12, 12x11½

1984, Feb. 13
564 A269 80c shown 15 15
565 A269 2d Jumping mouse, vert. 32 20
Set value 28

King Hassan II Type of 1981

1984-88 Photo. Perf. 14½

Size: 25x32mm

566	A236	1.20d multi ('88)	32	15
567	A236	1.25d multi	20	15
568	A236	1.60d multi ('87)	18	15
569	A236	2.50d multi ('87)	28	15
570	A236	3.60d multi ('88)	1.00	40
571	A236	4d multi	65	25
572	A236	5.20d multi ('88)	1.45	58
573	A236	6.50d multi ('87)	70	28
574	A236	7d multi ('87)	75	30
575	A236	8.50d multi ('87)	90	35
		Nos. 566-575 (10)	6.43	2.76

Dated 1986: 1.60d, 2.50d, 6.50d, 7d and 8.50d. Issue date: 1.20d, 3.60d, 5.20d, Dec. 26, 1988.

39th Anniv. of Arab League A270

1984, May 24 Perf. 14½x14
578 A270 2d Emblem 32 15

No. 492 Overprinted with Arabic and 25

1984, June 12 Perf. 13½x13
579 A226 1.30d multi 30 20

25th Anniv. of Marrakesh Arts Festival.

Local Plants — A271

Red Crescent — A273

Week of the Blind A272

1984, June 13 Perf. 14
580 A271 80c Mentha viridis 15 15
581 A271 2d Aloe 32 20
Set value 28

See Nos. 602-603.

1984, July 10 Perf. 13x13½
582 A272 80c Painted bowl 15 15

1984, July 16 Perf. 14
583 A273 2d Octagonal brass container 32 20

1984 Summer Olympics — A274

Intl. Child Victims' Day — A275

1984, Aug. 8 Perf. 13½x13
584 A274 2d Sports 32 20

1984, Aug. 22 Perf. 14
585 A275 2d Children held by dove 32 15

UPU Day — A276

World Food Day — A277

1984, Oct. 9 Photo. Perf. 13½
586 A276 2d multi 50 25

1984, Oct. 16 Perf. 14
587 A277 80c multi 20 15

Intl. Civil Aviation Org., 40th Anniv. — A278

Green March, 9th Anniv. — A279

1984, Oct. 20 Perf. 13½
588 A278 2d multi 1.00 50

1984, Nov. 6 Perf. 14
589 A279 80c Scroll, text 40 20

Palestinian Solidarity — A281

UN Human Rights Declaration, 36th Anniv. — A282

1984, Nov. 29 *Perf. 13½*
591 A281 2d Arab Revolt flag, 1918-19 1.00 50

1984, Dec. 10 *Perf. 14*
592 A282 2d multi 65 35

Native Dogs A283

UN Child Survival Campaign A284

1984, Dec. 21 **Photo.** *Perf. 14*
593 A283 80c Aidi 15 15
594 A283 2d Sloughi 32 15
Set value 22

1985, Mar. 5 **Photo.** *Perf. 14*
595 A284 80c Growth monitoring 20 15

1st SOS Children's Village in Morocco A285

1985, Mar. 11 *Perf. 13x13½*
596 A285 2d multi 50 25

Sherifian Hand Stamp, 1892 — A287

World Environment Day — A288

1985, Mar. 25 **Photo.** *Perf. 14*
597 A287 2d dl pink, blk & gray 50 25

Souvenir Sheet
Perf. 13½

598 Sheet of 6 1.25 1.25
a. A287 80c grn, blk & gray 20 15
b. A287 80c yel, blk & gray 20 15
c. A287 80c blue, blk & gray 20 15
d. A287 80c red, blk & gray 20 15
e. A287 80c pur, blk & gray 20 15
f. A287 80c brn, blk & gray 20 15

Stamp Day. No. 598 sold for 5d. See Nos. 615-616, 633-634, 668-669, 684-685, 701-702.

1985, June 5 *Perf. 13*
599 A288 80c Emblem, ecosystem 20 15

Susi Dancers from Marrakesh and Kutabia, Minaret — A289

1985, June 7 *Perf. 13x13½*
600 A289 2d multi 50 25

Folk Arts Festival.

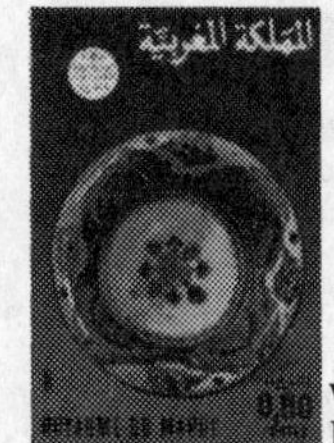
Week of the Blind — A290

1985, June 24 *Perf. 14*
601 A290 80c Ceramic bowl 20 15

Flower Type of 1984

1985, July 1
602 A271 80c Bougainvillea 20 15
603 A271 2d Red hibiscus 50 25

Berber Woman — A291

6th Pan-Arab Games — A292

1985, July 15 *Perf. 14*
604 A291 2d multi 50 25

Red Crescent Society.

1985 *Perf. 14½x13½*
605 A292 2d Torch, emblem, map 50 25

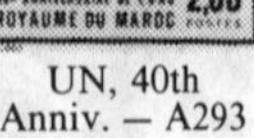
UN, 40th Anniv. — A293

Intl. Youth Year — A294

1985, Oct. 7 *Perf. 13*
606 A293 2d multi 50 25

1985, Oct. 21
607 A294 2d multi 50 25

Green March, 10th Anniv. — A295

Palestinian Solidarity — A296

1985, Nov. 6 *Perf. 14½x13½*
608 A295 2d Commemorative medal 50 25

1985, Nov. 29 *Perf. 13½*
609 A296 2d multi 50 25

Butterflies A297

1985, Dec. 16 **Photo.** *Perf. 14*
610 A297 80c Euphydryas desfontainii 15 15
611 A297 2d Colotis evagore 20 15
Set value 18

Accession of King Hassan II, 25th Anniv. — A298

Perf. 13x13½, 13½x13

1986, Mar. 3 **Litho.**
612 A298 80c Natl. arms, vert. 25 16
613 A298 2d shown 65 40
a. Souvenir sheet of 2, #612-613, imperf. 1.00 1.00

26th Intl. Military Medicine and Pharmaceutical Congress — A299

1986, Mar. 24 **Photo.** *Perf. 14*
614 A299 2d multi 42 25

Hand Stamp Type of 1985

Sherifian postal seals of Maghzen-Safi, 1892.

1986, Apr. 7
615 A287 80c orange & blk 18 15
616 A287 2d green & blk 42 25

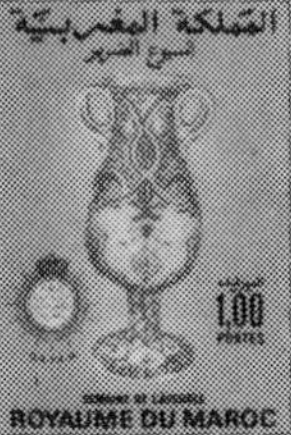
Week of the Blind — A300

1986 World Cup Soccer Championships, Mexico — A301

1986, Apr. 21
617 A300 1d multi 22 15

1986, May 31 *Perf. 13½*
618 A301 1d Emblems, horiz. 22 15
619 A301 2d Soccer cup, emblems 42 25

Red Crescent Soc. — A302

Flowers — A304

Popular Arts A303

1986, June *Perf. 14*
620 A302 2d multi 42 25

1986, June
621 A303 2d Folk band, dancers 42 25

1986, July 21 **Photo.** *Perf. 14*
622 A304 1d Warionia saharae 22 15
623 A304 2d Mandragora autumnalis 42 25

Intl. Peace Year A305

18th Skydiving Championships A306

1986, Aug. 4 *Perf. 13*
624 A305 2d multi 42 25

1986, Aug. 18 *Perf. 13½x13*
625 A306 2d multi 42 25

Horse Week A307

1986, Oct. 10 *Perf. 13*
626 A307 1d multicolored 22 15

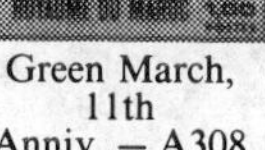

Green March, 11th Anniv. — A308

World Food Day — A309

1986, Nov. 6 **Photo.** ***Perf. 14***
627 A308 1d multicolored 22 15

1986, Nov. 12
628 A309 2d multicolored 42 25

Aga Khan Architecture Prize A310

1986, Nov. 24 **Litho.** ***Perf. 13***
629 A310 2d multicolored 42 25

Operation Grain: One Million Hectares — A311

Butterflies — A312

1986, Dec. 8
630 A311 1d multicolored 22 15

1986, Dec. 22 ***Perf. 14***
631 A312 1d Elphinstonia charlonia 22 15
632 A312 2d Anthocharis belia 42 25

Hand Stamp Type of 1985

Stamp Day: Sherifian postal seals of Maghzen-Tetouan, 1892.

1987, Jan. 26 **Photo.**
633 A287 1d blue & blk 22 15
634 A287 2d red & black 42 25

King Mohammed V, Flag, 1947 — A313

1987, Apr. 9 **Photo.** ***Perf. 13½x13***
635 A313 1d shown 22 15
636 A313 1d King Hassan II, 1987 22 15
a. Souvenir sheet of 2, Nos. 635-636 75 75

Tangiers Conf., 40th anniv. #636a sold for 3d.

Red Crescent Society A314

UN Child Survival Campaign A315

1987, May 1 **Photo.** ***Perf. 14***
637 A314 2d Brass lamp 50 35

1987, May 25 ***Perf. 12½x13***
638 A315 1d Oral rehydration 25 18

See Nos. 647, 687.

Week of the Blind — A316

1987, June 8 ***Perf. 14***
639 A316 1d Porcelain cup 25 18

Flowering Plants — A317

US-Morocco Diplomatic Relations, 200th Anniv. — A318

1987, July 6 **Photo.**
640 A317 1d Zygophyllum fontanesii 25 18
641 A317 2d Otanthus maritimus 50 35

See Nos. 661-662.

1987, July 22 **Litho & Engr.**
642 A318 1d lt bl, blk & scar 25 18

See United States No. 2349.

Give Blood — A319

1987, Aug. 20 **Photo.** ***Perf. 13x13½***
643 A319 2d King Hassan II, map 60 45

Desert Costumes, the Sahara — A320

13th Intl. Cong. on Irrigation and Drainage — A321

1987, Sept. 14 ***Perf. 13***
644 A320 1d Woman from Melhfa 32 24
645 A320 2d Man from Derraa 65 48

See Nos. 711-712.

1987, Sept. 21
646 A321 1d multi 35 28

UN Child Survival Type of 1987

1987, Sept. 28
647 A315 1d Universal immunization 35 28

Congress on Mineral Industries, Marrakesh A322

Green March, 12th Anniv. A323

1987, Oct.
648 A322 1d Azurite 32 24
649 A322 2d Wulfenite 65 48

1987, Nov. 6 **Photo.** ***Perf. 14***
650 A323 1d multi 30 22

See Nos. 667, 683, 695, 727.

Royal Armed Forces Social Services Month A324

1987, Nov. 13 ***Perf. 13x12½***
651 A324 1d multicolored 30 22

Birds — A325

1987, Dec. 1 **Litho.** ***Perf. 14***
652 A325 1d Passer simplex saharae 30 22
653 A325 2d Alectoris barbara 60 45

Natl. Postage Stamp 75th Anniv. — A326

Design: Postmark and Sherifian postage stamp (French Morocco) of 1912.

1987, Dec. 31 **Photo.** ***Perf. 14x13½***
654 A326 3d pale lil rose, blk & blue grn 92 70

Cetiosaurus Mogrebiensis — A327

1988, Jan. 18 **Photo.** ***Perf. 13½***
655 A327 2d multicolored 62 48

Intl. Symposium on Mohammed V, Aug. 16-Nov. 20, 1987 — A328

1988, Feb. 16 **Litho.** ***Perf. 14***
656 A328 2d multicolored 62 45

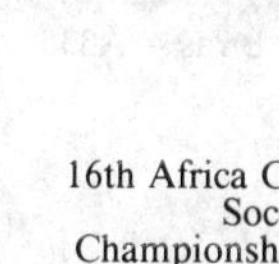

16th Africa Cup Soccer Championships A329

Perf. 14½x13½

1988, Mar. 13 **Photo.**
657 A329 3d multi 85 75

Horse Week A330

1988, Mar. 20 **Litho.** ***Perf. 14***
658 A330 3d multi 85 75

Intl. Red Cross and Red Crescent Orgs., 125th Annivs. — A331

1988, Apr. 30 Photo. ***Perf. 12½x13***
659 A331 3d pink, blk & dark red 85 65

Week of the Blind A332

UN Child Survival Campaign A333

1988, May 25 Litho. ***Perf. 14***
660 A332 3d Pottery bottle 85 65

Flower Type of 1987

1988, June 27 Litho. ***Perf. 14***
661 A317 3.60d Citrullus colocynthis 95 75
662 A317 3.60d Calotropis procera 95 75

1988, July 18 Litho. ***Perf. 12½x13***
663 A333 3d multi 82 62

1988 Summer Olympics, Seoul — A334

Birds — A335

Perf. 14½x13½

1988, Sept. 19 **Litho.**
664 A334 2d multi 62 48

1988, Oct. 26 Litho. ***Perf. 14***
665 A335 3.60d Grande outarde 1.00 75
666 A335 3.60d Flamant rose 1.00 75

Green March Anniv. Type of 1987

1988, Nov. 6
667 A323 2d multi 55 42

Green March, 13th anniv.

Hand Stamp Type of 1985

Sherifian postal seals of Maghzen-El Jadida, 1892: No. 668, Octagonal. No. 669, Circular.

1988, Nov. 22 Photo. ***Perf. 14***
668 A287 3d olive bister & blk 82 62
669 A287 3d violet & blk 82 62

Stamp Day.

Scott's editorial staff cannot undertake to identify, authenticate or appraise stamps and postal markings.

Housing of the Ksours and Casbahs A336

1989, Jan. 23 ***Perf. 13x13½***
670 A336 2d multi 55 42

Royal Chess Federation, 25th Anniv. — A337

1989, Apr. 17 Litho. ***Perf. 14***
671 A337 2d multi 52 38

Red Crescent Society — A338

Week of the Blind — A339

1989, May 29 Litho. ***Perf. 14x13½***
672 A338 2d multi 55 42

1989, June 12 ***Perf. 14***
673 A339 2d multi 55 42

King Hassan II, 60th Birthday A340

1989, July 9 Litho. ***Perf. 13x13½***
674 A340 2d multi 52 40
675 A340 2d King Hassan II, diff. 52 40
a. Souvenir sheet of 2, #674-675, imperf. & embossed 1.30 1.30

No. 675a sold for 5d.

Flowering Plants — A341

1989, Sept. 11 Litho. ***Perf. 14***
676 A341 2d *Narcissus papyraceus* 60 45
677 A341 2d *Cerinthe major* 60 45

See Nos. 709-710.

World Telecommunications Day — A342

1989, Sept. 25 ***Perf. 13x12½***
678 A342 2d multicolored 60 45

13th World Congress on Fertility and Sterility — A343

1989, Oct. 6 ***Perf. 14***
679 A343 2d multicolored 60 45

Birds A344

1989, Oct. 16 ***Perf. 14***
680 A344 2d Desert beater 60 45
681 A344 3d Gorget lark 90 68

Interparliamentary Union, Cent. — A345

1989, Oct. 27
682 A345 2d multicolored 60 45

Green March Anniv. Type of 1987

1989, Nov. 6
683 A323 3d multicolored 90 68

Green March, 14th anniv.

Hand Stamp Type of 1985

Sherifian postal seals of Maghzen-Casablanca, 1892: 2d, Circular. 3d, Octagonal.

1990, Jan. 15 Photo. ***Perf. 14***
684 A287 2d orange & blk 62 45
685 A287 3d green & blk 95 72

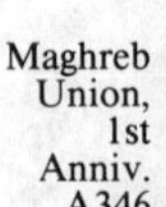

Maghreb Union, 1st Anniv. A346

1990, Feb. 17 ***Perf. 13½x14***
686 A346 2d multicolored 62 45
a. Souv. sheet of one, perf. 13½ 95 95

No. 686a sold for 3d.

Child Survival Type of 1987

1990 ***Perf. 12½x13***
687 A315 3d Breast feeding 95 72

3rd World Olive Day A347

1990, May 14 Litho. ***Perf. 14***
688 A347 2d Olive press 50 36
689 A347 3d King Hassan II 75 55

Week of the Blind A348

1990, May 28 Litho. ***Perf. 14***
690 A348 2d multicolored 70 52

Red Crescent Society A349

1990, June 11
691 A349 2d multicolored 50 36

Intl. Literacy Year — A350

1990, Sept. 17 Litho. ***Perf. 14***
692 A350 3d blk, yel grn & grn 1.10 82

Birds A351

1990, Oct. 26
693 A351 2d Tourterelle, vert. 70 52
694 A351 3d Huppe fasciee 1.10 82

Green March Type of 1987

1990, Nov. 5
695 A323 3d multicolored 1.10 82

Green March, 15th anniv.

Independence, 35th Anniv. — A353

1990, Nov. 18
696 A353 3d multicolored 1.10 82

Dam A354

1990, Nov. 26
697 A354 3d multicolored 1.10 82

Royal Academy of Morocco, 10th Anniv. — A355

1990, Dec. 28 Litho. *Perf. 14*
698 A355 3d multicolored 1.00 75

Opening of Postal Museum, 20th Anniv. — A356

Designs: No. 699, Telegraph machine. No. 700, Horse-drawn mail carriage fording river.

1990, Dec. 31 Litho. *Perf. 13½x13*
699 A356 2d multicolored 65 50
700 A356 3d multicolored 1.00 75
a. Souvenir sheet of 2, #699-700, imperf. 2.15 2.15

No. 700a sold for 6d, has simulated perforations.

Hand Stamp Type of 1985

Sherifian postal seals of Maghzen-Rabat, 1892: 2d, Circular. 3d, Octagonal.

1991, Jan. 25 *Perf. 14*
701 A287 2d ver & blk 65 50
702 A287 3d blue & blk 1.00 75

UN Development Program, 40th Anniv. — A357

1991, Feb. 18
703 A357 3d multicolored 1.00 75

Coronation of King Hassan II, 30th Anniv. — A358

1991, Mar. 3 Litho. *Perf. 14½x13*
704 A358 3d shown 1.00 75
705 A358 3d Wearing business suit 1.00 75
a. Souvenir sheet of 2, #704-705, imperf. 3.00 2.35

Nos. 704-705 exist tete beche. No. 705a has simulated perforations and sold for 10d.

Phosphate Mining, 70th Anniv. — A359

1991, Mar. 28 Litho. *Perf. 14*
706 A359 3d multicolored 1.00 75

Week of the Blind — A360 Red Crescent Society — A361

1991, May 15 Photo. *Perf. 14*
707 A360 3d multicolored 1.00 75

1991, May 27 Litho. *Perf. 14*
708 A361 3d multicolored 95 70

Flowering Plants Type of 1989

1991, June 27 Litho. *Perf. 14*
709 A341 3d Pyrus mamorensis 95 70
710 A341 3d Cynara humilis 95 70

Desert Costumes Type of 1987

Costumes of Ouarzazate.

1991, July 31 Photo.
711 A320 3d Woman 95 70
712 A320 3d Man 95 70

King Hassan II Type of 1981

1991 Photo. *Perf. 14½*
Size: 25x32mm
715 A236 1.35d multicolored 42 16

Issue date: 1.35d, Sept. 2.
This is an expanding set. Numbers will change if necessary.

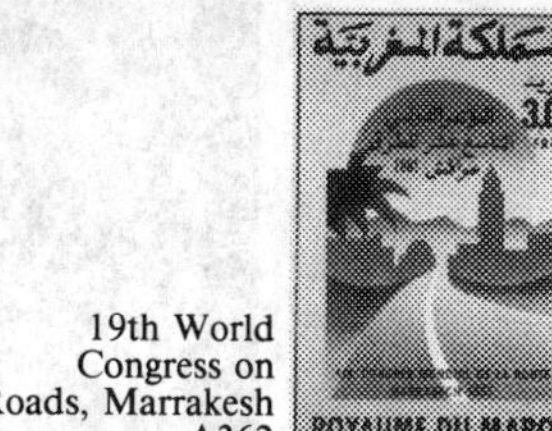

19th World Congress on Roads, Marrakesh A362

1991, Sept. 23 Litho. *Perf. 14*
725 A362 3d multicolored 95 70

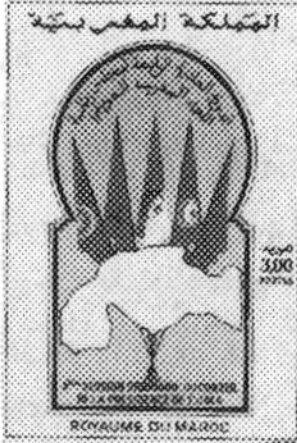

4th Session of the Council of Presidents of the Maghreb Arab Union — A363

1991, Oct. 30 Litho.
726 A363 3d multicolored 95 70

Green March Anniv. Type of 1987

1991, Nov. 6 Photo. *Perf. 14*
727 A323 3d multicolored 95 70

Green March, 16th anniv.

Birds — A364 Fight Against AIDS — A365

1991, Nov. 20 Litho. *Perf. 14*
728 A364 3d Merops apiaster 1.00 80
729 A364 3d Ciconia ciconia 1.00 80

1991, Dec. 16
730 A365 3d multicolored 1.00 80

Organization of the Islamic Conference, 20th Anniv. — A366

1991, Dec. 16
731 A366 3d multicolored 1.00 80

SEMI-POSTAL STAMPS

+10f

Nos. 1-5 Surcharged

اعانة ضحايا
الزيوت المسممة
اكتوبر 1959

1960, Mar. Unwmk. Engr. *Perf. 13*
B1 A1 5fr + 10fr brt bl & ind 22 20
B2 A1 10fr + 10fr bis brn & choc 30 28
B3 A1 15fr + 10fr dp grn & mag 55 45
B4 A1 25fr + 15fr purple 65 55
B5 A1 30fr + 20fr green 1.00 1.00
Nos. B1-B5 (5) 2.72 2.48

The surtax aided families whose members consumed adulterated cooking oil with crippling or fatal results.

French Morocco Nos. 321 and 322 Surcharged

اسبوعا
التضامن
1380
1960
15+3

1960, Sept. 12
B6 A71 15fr + 3fr on 18fr dk grn 32 32
B7 A71 20fr + 5fr brown lake 50 50

فيضانات
1
9
6
3
20+5

Nos. 1 and 6 Surcharged in Red or Black

1963, Jan. 28 Engr. *Perf. 13*
B8 A1 20c + 5c on 5fr brt bl & ind (R) 38 38
B9 A1 30c + 10c on 50fr rose red 45 38

The surtax was for flood victims.

Moroccan Brooch — SP1

Design: 40c+10c, Brooch with pendants.

1966, May 23 Photo. *Perf. 11½*
Granite Paper
B10 SP1 25c + 5c ultra, sil, blk & red 38 30
B11 SP1 40c + 10c mag, sil, blk, ultra & bl 55 38

Meeting in Morocco of the Middle East and North African Red Cross-Red Crescent Seminar. The surtax was for the Moroccan Red Crescent Society.

Nos. B10-B11 were printed se-tenant in sheets of 10 (5x2) arranged vertically tete beche.

See Nos. B12-B13, B15-B16, B19-B22, B26-B27, B29-B30, B34-B35.

1967, May 15 Granite Paper

Designs: 60c+5c, Two brooches linked by silver drapery. 1d+10c, Two bracelets.

B12 SP1 60c + 5c yel bis & multi 40 40
B13 SP1 1d + 10c emer & multi 85 85

The surtax was for the Moroccan Red Crescent Society. Each value printed tete beche in sheets of 10 (5x2).

Hands Reading Braille and Map of Morocco — SP2

1969, Mar. 21 Photo. *Perf. 12½*
B14 SP2 25c + 10c multi 15 15

Week of the Blind, Mar. 21-29.

Jewelry Type of 1966

Designs: 25c+5c, Silver earrings. 40c+10c, Gold ear pendant.

1969, May 9 Photo. *Perf. 11½*
Granite Paper
B15 SP1 25c + 5c gray grn & multi 38 30
B16 SP1 40c + 10c tan & multi 55 38

50th anniversary of the League of Red Cross Societies. Surtax was for Moroccan Red Crescent Society.

See se-tenant note after No. B11.

Nos. 173-174 Surcharged + 0.25 فيضانات 1970

1970, Feb. 26 Litho. *Perf. 13*
B17 A65 10c + 25c multi 1.50 1.50
B18 A65 15c + 25c multi 1.50 1.50

The surtax was for flood victims.

Jewelry Type of 1966

Designs: 25c+5c, Necklace with pendants. 50c+10c, Earring with 5 pendants.

1970, May 25 Photo. *Perf. 11½*
Granite Paper
B19 SP1 25c + 5c gray & multi 40 38
B20 SP1 50c + 10c brt vio & multi 65 65

Surtax for Moroccan Red Crescent Society.

See se-tenant note after No. B11.

1971, May 10

Designs: 25c+5c, Brooch. 40c+10c, Stomacher.

Granite Paper
B21 SP1 25c + 5c gray & multi 30 30
B22 SP1 40c + 10c yel & multi 45 38

See se-tenant note after No. B11.

Globe and Map of Palestine SP3

1971, Apr. 30 *Perf. 13*
B23 SP3 25c + 10c multi 50 25

Palestine Week, May 3-8.

String Instrument and Bow — SP4

1971, June 28 Photo. *Perf. 12*
B24 SP4 40c + 10c multi 20 15

Week of the Blind.

Mizmar (Double Flute) — SP5

1972, Mar. 31 Photo. *Perf. 13x13½*
B25 SP5 25c + 10c multi 22 22

Week of the Blind.

Jewelry Type of 1966

Designs: 25c+5c, Jeweled bracelets. 70c+10c, Rectangular pendant with ball drop.

1972, May 8 Photo. *Perf. 11½*
Granite Paper
B26 SP1 25c + 5c brn & multi 30 30
B27 SP1 70c + 10c dp grn & multi 45 38

See se-tenant note after No. B11. For overprints, see Nos. 295-296.

Drums SP6

1973, Mar. 30 Photo. *Perf. 13x14*
B28 SP6 70c + 10c multi 30 25

Week of the Blind.

Jewelry Type of 1966

Designs: 25c+5c, Silver box pendant. 70c+10c, Bracelet.

1973, June 15 Photo. *Perf. 11½*
B29 SP1 25c + 5c bl & multi 40 30
B30 SP1 70c + 10c org & multi 50 38

Moroccan Red Crescent Society. See 2nd note after No. B11. For overprints, see Nos. 351-352.

Pistol — SP7 Erbab (Fiddle) — SP8

Design: 70c+10c, Decorated antique powder box.

1974, July 8 Photo. *Perf. 14x13½*
B31 SP7 25c + 5c multi 30 30
B32 SP7 70c + 10c multi 45 38

Moroccan Red Crescent Society. See se-tenant note after B11.

1975, Jan. 10 Photo. *Perf. 13*
B33 SP8 70c + 10c multi 38 22

Week of the Blind.

Jewelry Type of 1966

Designs: 25c+5c, Silver pendant. 70c+10c, Earring.

1975, Mar. 13 Photo. *Perf. 13½*
B34 SP1 25c + 5c multi 30 30
B35 SP1 70c + 10c multi 45 38

Moroccan Red Crescent Society. See se-tenant note after No. B11. For overprints, see Nos. 386-387.

AIR POST STAMPS

Sultan's Star over Casablanca AP1

King Hassan II AP2

Unwmk.
1957, May 4 Engr. *Perf. 13*
C1 AP1 15fr car & brt grn 55 50
C2 AP1 25fr brt grnsh bl 1.00 70
C3 AP1 30fr red brn 1.40 90

Intl. Fair, Casablanca, May 4-19.

1962
C5 AP2 90c black 32 15
C6 AP2 1d rose red 50 15
C7 AP2 2d deep blue 65 32
C8 AP2 3d dl bl grn 1.10 65
C9 AP2 5d purple 2.25 90
Nos. C5-C9 (5) 4.82 2.17

Meteorological Day Type of Regular Issue

Design: 90c, Anemometer and globe.

1964, Mar. 23 Photo. *Perf. 11½*
Granite Paper
C10 A39 90c multi 40 30

Intl. Fair, Casablanca, 20th Anniv. AP3

1964, Apr. 30 Photo. *Perf. 12½*
C11 AP3 1d bl, bis & org 50 38

Moroccan Pavilion and Unisphere AP4

1964, May 25 Unwmk. *Perf. 12½*
C12 AP4 1d dk grn, red & bl 55 40

New York World's Fair, 1964-65.

Ramses II and UNESCO Emblem — AP5

Litho. & Engr.
1966, Oct. 3 *Perf. 12x11½*
C13 AP5 1d magenta, *yel* 55 38

UNESCO, 20th anniv.

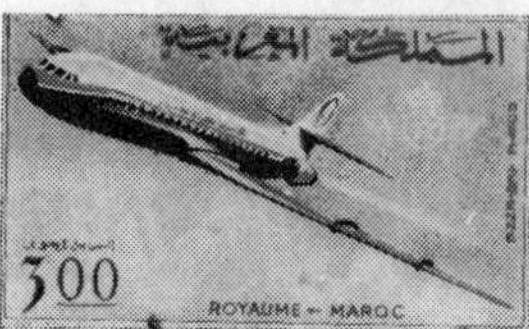

Jet Plane — AP6

Perf. 12½x13½
1966, Dec. 19 Photo.
C14 AP6 3d multi 2.25 1.25

Costume Type of Regular Issue

Design: 1d, Women from Ait Ouaouzguit.

1969, Jan. 21 Litho. *Perf. 12*
C15 A74 1d multi 1.20 55

Coin Type of Regular Issue, 1968

Coins: 1d, King Mohammed V, 1960. 5d, King Hassan II, 1965.

1969, Mar. 3 Photo. *Perf. 11½*
Granite Paper
C16 A73 1d brt bl, sil & blk 2.25 1.50
C17 A73 5d vio blk, sil & blk 6.00 3.75

King Hassan II — AP7

1983, Mar. 1 Photo. *Perf. 12*
Granite Paper
C18 AP7 1.40d multi 38 15
C19 AP7 2d multi 45 15
C20 AP7 3d multi 65 20
C21 AP7 5d multi 1.00 30
C22 AP7 10d multi 2.00 65
Nos. C18-C22 (5) 4.48 1.45

No. C19 Overprinted الملتقى العالمى الاول لخطباء الجمعة

1987, Mar. 23 Photo. *Perf. 12*
Granite Paper
C23 AP7 2d multi 42 25

1st World Congress of Friday Preachers, Al Joumouaa.

No. C18 Overprinted اتحاد المغرب العربى مراكش ـ فبراير 89

1989, Mar. 27 Photo. *Perf. 12*
Granite Paper
C24 AP7 1.40d multi 38 20

Maghreb Union, agreement between Morocco, Algeria and Tunisia.

POSTAGE DUE STAMPS

D1

Oranges — D2

1965 Unwmk. Typo. *Perf. 14x13½*

J1	D1	5c green	75	20
J2	D1	10c bister brown	30	15
J3	D1	20c red	45	15
J4	D1	30c brown black	75	20

1974-86 Photo. *Perf. 14*

J5	D2	5c shown	15	15
J6	D2	10c Cherries	15	15
J7	D2	20c Grapes	18	15
J8	D2	30c Peaches, horiz.	22	15
J9	D2	40c Grapes ('78)	15	15
J10	D2	60c Peaches, horiz. ('78)	20	15
J11	D2	80c Oranges ('78)	28	15
J12	D2	1d Apples ('86)	22	15
J13	D2	1.20d Cherries ('84)	25	15
J14	D2	1.60d Peaches ('85)	48	25
J15	D2	2d Strawberries ('86)	42	25
		Nos. J5-J15 (11)	2.70	
		Set value		1.45

For surcharges, see Nos. 322, 395.
Type D2 is an expanding set. Numbers will change again if more stamps are added.

NORTHERN ZONE

100 Centimos = 1 Peseta

Sultan Mohammed V — A1

Villa Sanjurjo Harbor A2

Designs: 25c, Polytechnic school. 50c, 10p, Institute of Culture, Tetuan.

Perf. 13x12½, 12½x13

1956, Aug. 23 Photo. Unwmk.

1	A1	10c deep rose	15	15
2	A2	15c yellow brn	15	15
3	A2	25c dk bl gray	15	15
4	A1	50c dark olive	15	15
5	A1	80c bright grn	15	15
6	A2	2p brt red lil	1.40	1.00
7	A2	3p brt blue	3.00	1.65
8	A1	10p green	10.50	7.00
		Nos. 1-8 (8)	15.65	10.40

Sultan Mohammed V
A3 A4

1957, Mar. 2 *Perf. 13½x13*

9	A3	80c blue green	22	15
10	A3	1.50p gray olive	85	55
11	A3	3p deep rose	2.75	1.75

1st anniversary of independence. See Morocco Nos. 13-15.

1957 Engr. *Perf. 13*

12	A4	30c brt bl & ind	15	15
13	A4	70c bis, brn & choc	15	15
14	A4	80c brt vio	50	15
15	A4	1.50p dp grn & mag	15	15
16	A4	3p green	20	15
17	A4	7p rose red	1.00	25
		Nos. 12-17 (6)	2.15	
		Set value		55

Prince Moulay el Hassan — A5

King Mohammed V — A6

1957, July 15 Photo. *Perf. 13*

18	A5	80c blue	18	15
19	A5	1.50p green	75	50
20	A5	3p carmine rose	2.25	1.65

Nos. 13 and 15 Surcharged in Carmine or Black

بسيطة 1'20 PESETAS

1957 Engr.

21	A4	15c on 70c (C)	18	15
22	A4	1.20p on 1.50p (Bk)	42	18

The surcharge is in two lines on No. 21.

1957, Nov. Photo. *Perf. 12½*

23	A6	1.20p blk & brt grn	20	20
24	A6	1.80p blk & rose red	22	22
25	A6	3p black & vio	65	42

Enthronement of Mohammed V, 30th anniv.

AIR POST STAMPS

Plane over Lau Dam AP1

Design: 1.40p, 4.80p, Plane over Nekor bridge.

Perf. 12½x13

1956, Dec. 17 Photo. Unwmk.

C1	AP1	25c rose violet	15	15
C2	AP1	1.40p lilac rose	15	15
C3	AP1	3.40p org vermilion	75	65
C4	AP1	4.80p dull violet	1.25	1.00

MOZAMBIQUE

LOCATION — Southeastern Africa, bordering on the Mozambique Channel
GOVT. — Republic
AREA — 308,642 sq. mi.
POP. — 14,140,000 (est. 1983)
CAPITAL — Maputo

Formerly a Portuguese colony, Mozambique, or Portuguese East Africa, was divided into eight districts: Lourenco Marques, Inhambane, Quelimane, Tete, Mozambique, Zambezia, Nyassa and the Manica and Sofala region formerly administered by the Mozambique Company. At various times the districts issued their own stamps which were eventually replaced by those inscribed "Mocambique."

Mozambique achieved independence June 25, 1975, taking the name People's Republic of Mozambique.

1000 Reis = 1 Milreis
100 Centavos = 1 Escudo (1913)
100 Centavos = 1 Metical (1980)

Catalogue values for unused stamps in this country are for Never Hinged items, beginning with Scott 330 in the regular postage section, Scott C29 in the airpost section, Scott J51 in the postage due section, and Scott RA55 in the postal tax section.

Portuguese Crown — A1

King Luiz — A2

Perf. 12½, 13½

1877-85 Typo. Unwmk.

1	A1	5r black	70	50
a.		Perf. 13½	1.50	1.40
2	A1	10r yellow	5.00	4.00
3	A1	10r green ('81)	85	60
4	A1	20r bister	1.00	60
a.		Perf. 13½	2.00	1.25
5	A1	20r rose ('85)	250.00	135.00
6	A1	25r rose	50	35
a.		Perf. 13½	5.50	1.35
7	A1	25r vio ('85)	2.50	1.35
8	A1	40r blue	14.00	8.00
9	A1	40r yel buff ('81)	1.75	1.35
a.		Perf. 12½	2.50	2.00
10	A1	50r green	60.00	20.00
a.		Perf. 13½	100.00	67.50
11	A1	50r blue ('81)	50	40
12	A1	100r lilac	70	48
13	A1	200r orange	1.90	1.40
a.		Perf. 12½	3.75	3.00
14	A1	300r chocolate	1.90	1.50

The reprints of the 1877-85 issues are printed on a smooth white chalky paper, ungummed, with rough perforation 13½, also on thin white paper, with shiny white gum and clean-cut perforation 13½.

Typographed and Embossed

1886 *Perf. 12½, 13½*

15	A2	5r black	1.00	60
a.		Perf. 13½	3.00	2.25
16	A2	10r green	1.00	60
a.		Perf. 13½	3.75	2.50
17	A2	20r rose	1.10	85
a.		Perf. 13½	10.00	4.50
18	A2	25r dull lilac	12.50	1.75
a.		Perf. 13½	13.00	4.00
19	A2	40r chocolate	1.40	85
a.		Perf. 13½	10.00	7.00
20	A2	50r blue	1.50	50
a.		Perf. 13½	12.50	3.00
21	A2	100r yel brn	1.75	50
22	A2	200r gray violet	2.50	1.75
a.		Perf. 13½	12.50	10.00
23	A2	300r orange	2.75	2.00

Nos. 15, 18, 19, 20, 21 and 23 have been reprinted. The reprints have shiny white gum and clean-cut perforation 13½. Many of the colors are paler than those of the originals.

No. 19 Surcharged in Black

PROVISORIO
5 5

1893, Jan. *Perf. 12½*

Without Gum

23A	A2	5r on 40r choc	95.00	45.00

There are three varieties of No. 23A:
I- "PROVISORIO" 19mm long, numerals 4½mm high.
II- "PROVISORIO" 19½mm long, numerals 5mm high.
III- "PROVISORIO" 19½mm long, numerals of both sizes.

King Carlos I — A3

1894 Typo. *Perf. 11½, 12½*

24	A3	5r yellow	50	35
25	A3	10r red lil	50	35
26	A3	15r red brn	70	50
27	A3	20r gray lil	85	50
28	A3	25r bl grn	70	20
29	A3	50r lt bl	5.00	1.00
a.		Perf. 12½	7.50	2.00
30	A3	75r rose	1.40	1.25
31	A3	80r yel grn	2.75	1.40
32	A3	100r brn, *buff*	1.75	1.50
33	A3	150r car, *rose*	13.00	6.75
a.		Perf. 11½		
34	A3	200r dk bl, *bl*	2.75	2.00
35	A3	300r dk bl, *sal*	3.50	2.50

Nos. 28 and 31-33 have been reprinted with shiny white gum and clean-cut perf. 13½.

Stamps of 1886 Overprinted in Red or Black

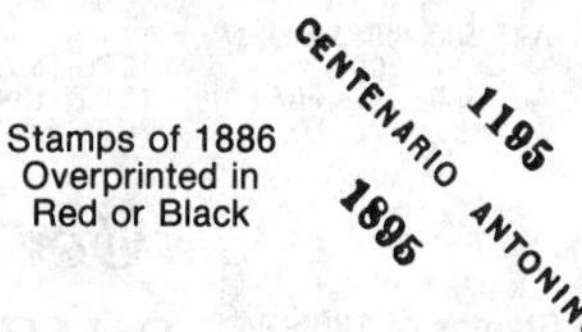

1895, July 1 *Perf. 12½*

Without Gum

36	A2	5r blk (R)	6.00	5.50
37	A2	10r green	6.75	6.00
38	A2	20r rose	8.00	6.00
39	A2	25r violet	8.00	6.00
a.		Double overprint		
40	A2	40r chocolate	9.00	7.50
41	A2	50r blue	9.00	7.50
a.		Perf. 13½	67.50	55.00
42	A2	100r yel brn	9.00	7.50
43	A2	200r gray vio	19.00	11.00
a.		Perf. 13½	67.50	55.00
44	A2	300r orange	20.00	14.00

Commemorating the seventh centenary of the birth of Saint Anthony of Padua.

No. 35 Surcharged in Black

50
réis

1897, Jan. 2 *Perf. 12½*

Without Gum

45	A3	50r on 300r dk bl, *sal*	150.00	50.00

Nos. 17, 19 Surcharged

a: MOCAMBIQUE 2½ REIS

b: MOCAMBIQUE 2½ RÉIS

c: MOÇAMBIQUE 5 RÉIS

1898

Without Gum

46	A2 (a)	2½r on 20r rose	35.00	14.00
47	A2 (b)	2½r on 20r rose	26.00	12.00
a.		Inverted surcharge	50.00	30.00
48	A2 (c)	5r on 40r choc	30.00	12.00
a.		Inverted surcharge	80.00	45.00

King Carlos I — A4

1898-1903 Typo. *Perf. 11½*

Name and Value in Black except 500r

No.	Type	Description	Unused	Used
49	A4	2½r gray	18	15
50	A4	5r orange	18	15
51	A4	10r lt grn	20	18
52	A4	15r brown	3.50	1.50
53	A4	15r gray grn ('03)	70	55
54	A4	20r gray vio	85	40
55	A4	25r sea grn	85	40
56	A4	25r car ('03)	70	28
57	A4	50r dk bl	1.00	48
58	A4	50r brn ('03)	1.90	1.50
59	A4	65r dl bl ('03)	7.50	6.00
60	A4	75r rose	4.75	2.75
61	A4	75r red lil ('03)	1.90	1.75
62	A4	80r violet	4.75	2.75
63	A4	100r dk bl, *bl*	1.90	1.00
64	A4	115r org brn, *pink* ('03)	5.50	4.00
65	A4	130r brn, *straw* ('03)	5.50	4.00
66	A4	150r brn, *straw*	4.75	2.75
67	A4	200r red lil, *pnksh*	1.90	1.40
68	A4	300r dk bl, *rose*	4.75	2.75
69	A4	400r dl bl, *straw* ('03)	9.00	6.00
70	A4	500r blk & red, *bl* ('01)	12.00	6.75
71	A4	700r vio, *yelsh* ('01)	12.00	8.00
		Nos. 49-71 (23)	86.26	55.49

Stamps of 1886-94 Surcharged

65
RÉIS

1902 *Perf. 12½, 13½*

On Stamps of 1886

Red Surcharge

No.	Type	Description	Unused	Used
72	A2	115r on 5r blk	1.75	1.25

Black Surcharge

No.	Type	Description	Unused	Used
73	A2	65r on 20r rose	3.00	2.00
a.		Double surcharge	20.00	20.00
74	A2	65r on 40r choc	4.00	3.75
75	A2	65r on 200r vio	3.00	1.50
76	A2	115r on 50r bl	1.25	1.00
77	A2	130r on 25r red vio	1.65	85
78	A2	130r on 300r org	1.40	85
79	A2	400r on 10r grn	4.50	3.00
80	A2	400r on 100r yel brn	27.50	20.00

The reprints of Nos. 74, 75, 76, 77, 79 and 80 have shiny white gum and clean-cut perforation 13½.

On Stamps of 1894

Perf. 11½

No.	Type	Description	Unused	Used
81	A3	65r on 10r red lil	2.00	1.90
82	A3	65r on 15r red brn	2.25	1.90
a.		Pair, one without surcharge		
83	A3	65r on 20r gray lil	2.25	1.90
84	A3	115r on 5r yel	2.25	1.90
a.		Inverted surcharge		
85	A3	115r on 25r bl grn	2.25	1.90
86	A3	130r on 75r rose	2.25	1.90
87	A3	130r on 100r brn, *buff*	4.00	4.00
88	A3	130r on 150r car, *rose*	2.25	1.90
89	A3	130r on 200r bl, *bl*	3.75	3.50
90	A3	400r on 50r lt bl	1.00	85
91	A3	400r on 80r yel grn	1.00	85
92	A3	400r on 300r bl, *sal*	1.00	85

On Newspaper Stamp of 1893

Perf. 13½

No.	Type	Description	Unused	Used
93	N3	115r on 2½r brn	2.00	1.90

Reprints of No. 87 have shiny white gum and clean-cut perforation 13½.

Overprinted in Black PROVISORIO

On Stamps of 1898

Perf. 11½

No.	Type	Description	Unused	Used
94	A4	15r brown	1.40	85
95	A4	25r sea green	1.40	85
96	A4	50r blue	2.00	1.75
97	A4	75r rose	3.75	2.00

No. 59 Surcharged in Black

50
RÉIS

1905

No.	Type	Description	Unused	Used
98	A4	50r on 65r dull blue	1.90	1.75

Stamps of 1898-1903 Overprinted in Carmine or Green

1911

No.	Type	Description	Unused	Used
99	A4	2½r gray	20	18
a.		Inverted overprint	5.00	5.00
100	A4	5r orange	20	18
101	A4	10r lt grn	1.00	50
102	A4	15r gray grn	20	18
103	A4	20r gray vio	85	40
104	A4	25r car (G)	18	15
a.		25r gray violet (error)		
105	A4	50r brown	28	20
106	A4	75r red lilac	60	48
107	A4	100r dk bl, *bl*	60	48
108	A4	115r org brn, *pink*	85	75
109	A4	130r brn, *straw*	85	75
a.		Double overprint		
110	A4	200r red lil, *pnksh*	1.25	70
111	A4	400r dl bl, *straw*	1.25	85
112	A4	500r blk & red, *bl*	1.25	85
113	A4	700r vio, *straw*	1.25	85
		Nos. 99-113 (15)	10.81	7.50

King Manoel — A5

Overprinted in Carmine or Green

1912 *Perf. 11½x12*

No.	Type	Description	Unused	Used
114	A5	2½r violet	15	15
115	A5	5r black	15	15
116	A5	10r gray grn	20	18
117	A5	20r car (G)	55	40
118	A5	25r vio brn	15	15
119	A5	50r dp bl	40	35
120	A5	75r bis brn	40	35
121	A5	100r brn, *lt grn*	40	35
122	A5	200r dk grn, *sal*	85	70
123	A5	300r blk, *azure*	85	70

Perf. 14x15

No.	Type	Description	Unused	Used
124	A5	500r ol grn & vio brn	1.25	1.00
		Nos. 114-124 (11)	5.35	4.48

Vasco da Gama Issue of Various Portuguese Colonies Common Design Types Surcharged

REPUBLICA
MOCAMBIQUE
¼ C.

1913

On Stamps of Macao

No.	Type	Description	Unused	Used
125	CD20	¼c on ½a bl grn	1.50	1.50
126	CD21	½c on 1a red	1.50	1.50
127	CD22	1c on 2a red vio	1.50	1.50
128	CD23	2½c on 4a yel grn	1.50	1.50
a.		Double surcharge	22.50	22.50
129	CD24	5c on 8a dk bl	3.50	3.50
130	CD25	7½c on 12a vio brn	2.50	2.50
131	CD26	10c on 16a bis brn	2.00	2.00
132	CD27	15c on 24a bis	2.00	2.00
		Nos. 125-132 (8)	16.00	16.00

On Stamps of Portuguese Africa

No.	Type	Description	Unused	Used
133	CD20	¼c on 2½r bl grn	1.00	1.00
134	CD21	½c on 5r red	1.00	1.00
135	CD22	1c on 10r red vio	1.00	1.00
a.		Inverted surcharge	15.00	15.00
136	CD23	2½c on 25r yel grn	1.00	1.00
137	CD24	5c on 50r dk bl	1.00	1.00
138	CD25	7½c on 75r vio brn	1.50	1.50
139	CD26	10c on 100r bis brn	1.25	1.25
140	CD27	15c on 150r bis	1.25	1.25
		Nos. 133-140 (8)	9.00	9.00

On Stamps of Timor

No.	Type	Description	Unused	Used
141	CD20	¼c on ½a bl grn	1.50	1.50
142	CD21	½c on 1a red	1.50	1.50
143	CD22	1c on 2a red vio	1.50	1.50
144	CD23	2½c on 4a yel grn	1.50	1.50
145	CD24	5c on 8a dk bl	1.50	1.50
146	CD25	7½c on 12a vio brn	3.00	3.00
147	CD26	10c on 16a bis brn	1.50	1.50
148	CD27	15c on 24a bis	2.00	2.00
		Nos. 141-148 (8)	14.00	14.00
		Nos. 125-148 (24)	39.00	39.00

Ceres — A6

1914-26 Typo. *Perf. 15x14, 12x11½*

Name and Value in Black

No.	Type	Description	Unused	Used
149	A6	¼c olive brown	15	15
150	A6	½c black	15	15
151	A6	1c blue green	15	15
152	A6	1½c lilac brown	15	15
153	A6	2c carmine	15	15
154	A6	2c gray ('26)	18	18
155	A6	2½c lt vio	15	15
156	A6	3c org ('21)	15	15
157	A6	4c pale rose ('21)	15	15
158	A6	4½c gray ('21)	15	15
159	A6	5c deep blue	15	15
160	A6	6c lilac ('21)	15	15
a.		Name and value printed twice		
161	A6	7c ultra ('21)	15	15
162	A6	7½c yel brn	15	15
163	A6	8c slate	15	15
164	A6	10c org brn	15	15
165	A6	12c gray brn ('21)	18	15
166	A6	12c bl grn ('22)	18	15
167	A6	15c plum	1.40	1.00
a.		Perf. 12x11½ ('30)	35	18
168	A6	15c brn rose ('22)	15	15
169	A6	20c yel grn	15	15
170	A6	24c ultra ('26)	4.50	95
171	A6	25c choc ('26)	70	50
172	A6	30c brn, *grn*	1.00	70
173	A6	30c dp grn ('21)	28	15
174	A6	30c gray bl, *pink* ('21)	1.00	85
175	A6	40c brn, *pink*	1.25	85
176	A6	40c turq bl ('22)	60	20
177	A6	50c org, *sal*	2.50	2.00
178	A6	50c lt vio ('26)	28	15
179	A6	60c red brn, *pink* ('21)	1.00	70
180	A6	60c dk bl ('22)	70	30
181	A6	60c rose ('26)	70	24
182	A6	80c dk brn, *bl* ('21)	1.00	70
183	A6	80c brt rose ('22)	70	24
184	A6	1e grn, *bl*, perf. 12x11½ ('21)	1.40	60
a.		Perf. 15x14	17.00	4.75
185	A6	1e rose ('21)	1.10	48
186	A6	1e blue ('26)	1.00	50
187	A6	2e brt vio, *pink* ('21)	1.40	60
188	A6	2e dk vio ('22)	70	35
189	A6	5e buff ('26)	6.75	2.50
190	A6	10e pink ('26)	12.00	4.75
191	A6	20e pale turq ('26)	35.00	15.00
		Nos. 149-191 (43)	80.05	37.34

Stamps of 1902 Overprinted Locally in Carmine

REPUBLICA

1915

On Provisional Stamps of 1902

No.	Type	Description	Unused	Used
192	A2	115r on 5r blk	20.00	15.00
193	A3	115r on 5r yel	85	75
194	A3	115r on 25r bl grn	85	75
195	A3	130r on 75r rose	85	75
196	A3	130r on 100r brn, *buff*	85	75
197	A3	130r on 150r car, *rose*	85	75
198	A3	130r on 200r bl, *bl*	85	75
199	A3	115r on 2½r brn	60	40

On No. 97

No.	Type	Description	Unused	Used
200	A4	75r rose	1.25	70
		Nos. 192-200 (9)	26.95	20.60

Stamps of 1902-05 Overprinted in Carmine

1915

On Provisional Stamps of 1902

No.	Type	Description	Unused	Used
201	A3	115r on 5r yel	55	48
202	A3	115r on 25r bl grn	55	48
203	A3	130r on 75r rose	55	48
204	A3	130r on 150r car, *rose*	70	50
205	A3	130r on 200r bl, *bl*	70	50
206	A3	115r on 2½r brn	55	48

On No. 96

No.	Type	Description	Unused	Used
207	A4	50r blue	70	50

On No. 98

No.	Type	Description	Unused	Used
208	A4	50r on 65r dull blue	70	50
		Nos. 201-208 (8)	5.00	3.92

Stamps of 1898-1903 Overprinted Locally in Carmine Like Nos. 192-200

1917

No.	Type	Description	Unused	Used
209	A4	2½r gray	14.00	10.00
210	A4	15r gray grn	10.00	6.00
211	A4	20r gray vio	11.00	7.50
212	A4	50r brown	10.00	6.75
213	A4	75r red lil	20.00	17.00
214	A4	100r bl, *bl*	3.50	1.90
215	A4	115r org brn, *pink*	3.50	1.90
216	A4	130r brn, *straw*	3.50	1.90
217	A4	200r red lil, *pnksh*	3.50	1.90
218	A4	400r dl bl, *straw*	3.50	1.90
219	A4	500r blk & red, *bl*	3.50	1.90
220	A4	700r vio, *yelsh*	4.75	3.00
		Nos. 209-220 (12)	90.75	61.65

War Tax Stamps of 1916-18 Surcharged

2 ½
CENTAVOS

1918 *Rouletted 7*

No.	Type	Description	Unused	Used
221	WT2	2½c on 5c rose	95	70

Perf. 11, 12

No.	Type	Description	Unused	Used
222	WT2	2½c on 5c red	95	70
a.		"PETRIA"	2.00	1.75
b.		"PEPUBLICA"	2.00	1.75
c.		"1910" for "1916"	5.00	2.50

War Tax Stamps of 1916-18 Surcharged

"CORREIOS" 1 C.

1919 *Perf. 11*

No.	Type	Description	Unused	Used
224	WT1	1c on 1c gray grn	55	40
a.		"PEPUBLICA"	3.50	2.75
b.		Rouletted 7	*125.00*	*45.00*

Perf. 12

No.	Type	Description	Unused	Used
225	WT2	1½c on 5c red	40	35
a.		"PETRIA"	2.50	2.00
b.		"PEPUBLICA"	2.50	2.00
c.		"1910" for "1916"	3.50	2.75

Stamps of 1902 Overprinted Locally in Carmine Like Nos. 192-200

1920

No.	Type	Description	Unused	Used
226	A3	400r on 50r lt bl	1.00	85
227	A3	400r on 80r yel grn	1.00	85
228	A3	400r on 300r bl, *sal*	1.00	85

War Tax Stamp of 1918 Surcharged in Green

SEIS
CENTAVOS

No.	Type	Description	Unused	Used
229	WT2	6c on 5c red	60	48
a.		"1910" for "1916"	6.00	3.50
b.		"PETRIA"	2.00	1.40
c.		"PEPUBLICA"	2.00	1.40

Lourenco Marques Nos. 117, 119 Surcharged in Red or Bue

10 c.

1921 *Perf. 15x14*

No.	Type	Description	Unused	Used
230	A4	10c on ½c blk (R)	55	40
231	A4	30c on 1½c brn (Bl)	55	40

Same Surcharge on Mozambique Nos. 150, 152, 155 in Red, Blue or Green

No.	Type	Description	Unused	Used
232	A6	10c on ½c blk (R)	1.25	85
233	A6	30c on 1½c brn (Bl)	1.25	85
234	A6	60c on 2½c vio (G)	1.75	1.00
		Nos. 230-234 (5)	5.35	3.50

War Tax Stamp of 1918 Surcharged in Green

2$00

1921 *Perf. 12*

235 WT2 2e on 5c red	1.00	50
a. "PETRIA"	1.75	1.40
b. "PEPUBLICA"	3.50	2.00
c. "1910" for "1916"	6.00	5.00

No. 157 Surcharged

50 c.

1923 *Perf. 12x11½*

236 A6 50c on 4c pale rose	85	55

No. 183 Overprinted in Green

Vasco da Gama 1924

1924

237 A6 80c brt rose	85	60

To commemorate the fourth centenary of the death of Vasco da Gama.

Nos. 90 and 91 Surcharged

República

40 C.

1925 *Perf. 11½*

238 A3 40c on 400r on 50r	70	48
239 A3 40c on 400r on 80r	60	48
a. "a" omitted	25.00	25.00

Postage Due Stamp of 1917 Overprinted in Black and Bars in Red

CORREIOS

1929, Jan. *Perf. 12*

247 D1 50c gray	85	55

No. 188 Surcharged

70 C.

1931 *Perf. 11½*

249 A6 70c on 2e dk vio	70	50
250 A6 1.40e on 2e dk vio	1.00	50

"Portugal" Holding Volume of the "Lusiads" — A7

Wmk. Maltese Cross (232)

1933, July 13 Typo. *Perf. 14*

Value in Red or Black

251	A7	1c bis brn (R)	15	15
252	A7	5c blk brn	15	15
253	A7	10c dp vio	15	15
254	A7	15c blk (R)	15	15
255	A7	20c lt gray	15	15
256	A7	30c blue green	15	15
257	A7	40c org red	15	15
258	A7	45c brt bl	20	15
259	A7	50c dk brn	15	15
260	A7	60c ol grn	20	15
261	A7	70c org brn	20	15
262	A7	80c emerald	20	15
263	A7	85c dp rose	85	50
264	A7	1e red brn	50	15
265	A7	1.40e dk bl (R)	8.00	1.40
266	A7	2e dk vio	1.25	35
267	A7	5e apple grn	2.00	50
268	A7	10e ol bis	4.75	1.00
269	A7	20e orange	25.00	1.75
		Nos. 251-269 (19)	44.35	
		Set value		6.40

See Nos. 298 and 299.

Common Design Types

Perf. 13½x13

1938, Aug. Engr. Unwmk.

Name and Value in Black

270	CD34	1c gray grn	15	15
271	CD34	5c org brn	15	15
272	CD34	10c dk car	15	15
273	CD34	15c dk vio brn	15	15
274	CD34	20c slate	15	15
275	CD35	30c rose vio	15	15
276	CD35	35c brt grn	18	15
277	CD35	40c brown	28	15
278	CD35	50c brt red vio	28	15
279	CD36	60c gray blk	28	15
280	CD36	70c brn vio	28	15
281	CD36	80c orange	50	15
282	CD36	1e red	40	20
283	CD37	1.75e blue	1.50	30
284	CD37	2e brn car	1.50	30
285	CD37	5e olive green	3.50	50
286	CD38	10e bl vio	9.00	1.00
287	CD38	20e red brn	25.00	1.40
		Nos. 270-287 (18)	43.60	
		Set value		4.80

Common Design Types pictured in section at front of Catalogue.

No. 258 Surcharged in Black

40 centavos

1938, Jan. 16 Wmk. 232 *Perf. 14*

288 A7 40c on 45c brt bl	2.50	1.00

Map of Africa — A7a

Perf. 11½x12

1939, July 17 Litho. Unwmk.

289	A7a	80c vio, *pale rose*	2.00	1.75
290	A7a	1.75e bl, *pale bl*	5.50	2.75
291	A7a	3e grn, *yel grn*	10.00	5.75
292	A7a	20e brn, *buff*	47.50	27.50

Presidential visit.

New Cathedral, Lourenço Marques — A8

Railroad Station A9

Municipal Hall — A10

1944, Dec. Litho. *Perf. 11½*

293	A8	50c dk brn	70	40
294	A8	50c dk grn	70	40
295	A9	1.75e ultra	3.75	85
296	A10	20e dk gray	8.50	85

Issued to commemorate the 4th centenary of the founding of Lourenço Marques. See No. 302.

No. 283 Surcharged in Carmine

60

1946 Engr. *Perf. 13½x13*

297 CD37 60c on 1.75e blue	85	40

Lusiads Type of 1933

1947 Wmk. 232 Typo. *Perf. 14*

Value in Black

298 A7 35c yel grn	4.00	1.40
299 A7 1.75e deep blue	4.00	1.40

No. 296 Surcharged in Pink

2$00

1946 Unwmk. *Perf. 11½*

300 A10 2e on 20e dk gray	1.40	40

No. 273 Surcharged with New Value and Wavy Lines

Perf. 13½x13

301 CD34 10c on 15c dk vio brn	70	40
a. Inverted surcharge	6.00	

Cathedral Type of 1944

Commemorative Inscription Omitted

1948 Litho. *Perf. 11½*

302 A8 4.50e brt ver	1.40	38

Antonio Enes — A11

1948, Oct. 4 *Perf. 14*

303 A11 50c blk & cream	1.40	35
304 A11 5e vio brn & cream	5.75	85

Birth centenary of Antonio Enes.

Gogogo Peak — A12

Zambezi River Bridge — A13

Zumbo River A14

Waterfall at Nhanhangare A15

Lourenço Marques — A16

Plantation, Baixa — A17

Pungwe River at Beira — A18

Polana Beach — A19

Lourenço Marques — A20

Malema River — A21

Perf. 13½x13, 13x13½

1948-49 Typo. Unwmk.

305	A12	5c org brn	18	15
306	A13	10c vio brn	18	15
307	A14	20c dk brn	18	15
308	A12	30c plum	18	15
309	A14	40c dl grn	18	15
310	A16	50c slate	18	15
311	A15	60c brn car	18	15
312	A16	80c vio blk	18	15
313	A17	1e carmine	35	18
314	A13	1.20e sl gray	35	18
315	A18	1.50e dk pur	35	18
316	A19	1.75e dk bl ('49)	1.00	24
317	A18	2e brown	50	18
318	A20	2.50e dk sl ('49)	2.25	20
319	A19	3e gray ol ('49)	1.25	20
320	A15	3.50e ol gray	1.75	20
321	A17	5e bl grn	1.75	20
322	A20	10e choc ('49)	4.00	35
323	A21	15e dp car ('49)	8.00	1.75
324	A21	20e org ('49)	17.00	1.75
		Nos. 305-324 (20)	39.99	6.81

On No. 320 the "$" is reversed.

Lady of Fatima Issue

Common Design Type

1948, Oct. Litho. *Perf. 14½*

325	CD40	50c blue	1.40	70
326	CD40	1.20e red vio	3.75	1.40
327	CD40	4.50e emerald	12.00	4.00
328	CD40	20e chocolate	24.00	5.00

Symbols of the UPU — A21a

1949, Apr. 11 *Perf. 14*

329 A21a 4.50e ultra & pale gray	1.00	50

75th anniversary of UPU.

Catalogue values for unused stamps in this section, from this point to the end of the section, are for Never Hinged items.

Holy Year Issue
Common Design Types

1950, May *Perf. 13x13½*
330 CD41 1.50e red org 70 24
331 CD42 3e brt bl 1.00 28

Spotted Triggerfish — A22

Pennant Coral Fish — A22a

Fish: 10c, Golden butterflyfish. 15c, Orange butterflyfish. 20c, Lionfish. 30c, Sharpnose puffer. 40c, Porky filefish. 50c, Dark brown surgeonfish. 1.50e Rainbow wrasse. 2e, Orange-spotted gray-skin. 2.50e, Kasmir snapper. 3e, Convict fish. 3.50e, Stellar triggerfish. 4e, Cornetfish. 4.50e, Vagabond butterflyfish. 5e, Mail-cheeked fish. 6e, Pinnate batfish. 8e, Moorish idol. 9e, Triangulate boxfish. 10e, Flying gurnard. 15e, Redtooth triggerfish. 20e, Striped triggerfish. 30e, Horned cowfish. 50e, Spotted cowfish.

Photogravure and Lithographed

1951 **Unwmk.** *Perf. 14x14½*

Fish in Natural Colors

332 A22 5c dp yel 24 *50*
333 A22 10c lt bl 15 *50*
334 A22 15c yellow 60 *1.00*
335 A22 20c pale olvn 28 18
336 A22 30c gray 24 18
337 A22 40c pale grn 18 15
338 A22 50c pale buff 18 15
339 A22a 1e aqua 18 15
340 A22 1.50e olive 15 15
341 A22 2e blue 20 18
342 A22 2.50e brnsh lil 50 18
343 A22 3e aqua 50 18
344 A22 350e ol grn 40 18
345 A22 4e bl gray 85 70
346 A22 4.50e green 85 70
347 A22 5e buff 85 18
348 A22a 6e sal pink 85 20
349 A22a 8e gray bl 85 24
350 A22 9e lil rose 1.50 30
351 A22 10e gray lil 12.50 2.00
352 A22 15e gray 35.00 6.50
353 A22 20e lemon 17.50 3.50
354 A22 30e yel grn 13.00 4.00
355 A22 50e gray vio 32.50 6.50
Nos. 332-355 (24) 120.05 28.50

Holy Year Extension Issue
Common Design Type

1951, Oct. **Litho.** *Perf. 14*
356 CD43 5e car & rose 1.75 1.00

Victor Cordon
A23

Plane and Ship
A24

1951, Oct. *Perf. 11½*
357 A23 1e dk brn 1.25 35
358 A23 5e blk & sl 7.50 1.00

Issued to commemorate the centenary of the birth of Victor Cordon, explorer.

Medical Congress Issue
Common Design Type

Design: Miguel Bombarda Hospital.

1952, June 19 **Litho.** *Perf. 13½*
359 CD44 3e dk bl & brn buff 85 35

1952, Sept. 15 **Unwmk.**
360 A24 1.50e multi 48 35

4th African Tourism Congress.

Missionary
A25

Papilio Demodocus
A26

1953
361 A25 10c red brn & pale vio 15 15
362 A25 1e red brn & pale yel grn 50 20
363 A25 5e blk & lt bl 1.40 35
Set value 60

Exhibition of Sacred Missionary Art, held at Lisbon in 1951.

Canceled to Order
Certain issues, including Nos. 364-383, were canceled to order under Republican administration.

Photogravure and Lithographed

1953, May 28 *Perf. 13x14*

Various Butterflies and Moths in Natural Colors

364 A26 10c lt bl 15 15
365 A26 15c cream 15 15
366 A26 20c yel grn 15 15
367 A26 30c lt vio 15 15
368 A26 40c brown 15 15
369 A26 50c bluish gray 15 15
370 A26 80c brt bl 15 15
371 A26 1e gray bl 15 15
372 A26 1.50e ocher 18 15
373 A26 2e org brn 4.50 50
374 A26 2.30e blue 3.50 35
375 A26 2.50e citron 6.00 35
376 A26 3e lil rose 1.75 15
377 A26 4e lt bl 24 15
378 A26 4.50e orange 28 15
379 A26 5e green 28 15
380 A26 6e pale vio 35 15
381 A26 7.50e buff 3.25 30
382 A26 10e pink 6.25 75
383 A26 20e grnsh gray 8.00 70
Nos. 364-383 (20) 35.78
Set value 4.00
Set value, CTO 50

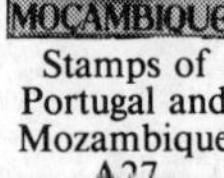

Stamps of Portugal and Mozambique
A27

Stamp of Portugal and Arms of Colonies
A27a

1953, July 23 **Litho.** *Perf. 14*
384 A27 1e multi 85 40
385 A27 3e multi 2.50 70

Issued in connection with the Lourenço Marques philatelic exhibition, July 1953.

Stamp Centenary Issue

1953 **Photo.** *Perf. 13*
386 A27a 50c multi 55 40

Map — A28

1954, Oct. 15 **Litho.**

Colors (except Colony) on map: Gray, Light Blue, Blue, Carmine and Black

387 A28 10c pale rose lil 15 15
388 A28 20c pale yel 15 15
389 A28 50c lilac 15 15
390 A28 1e org yel 18 15
391 A28 2.30e white 45 18
392 A28 4e pale salmon 60 20
393 A28 10e lt grn 1.90 20
394 A28 20e brn buff 2.50 35
Nos. 387-394 (8) 6.08
Set value 1.10

Sao Paulo Issue
Common Design Type

1954, July 2
395 CD46 3.50e dk gray, cr & ol 35 28

Arms of Beira
A29

Mousinho de Albuquerque
A30

Paper with network as in parenthesis

1954, Dec. 1 *Perf. 13x13½*

Arms in Silver, Gold, Red and Pale Green

396 A29 1.50e dk bl *(bl)* 35 28
397 A29 3.50e brn *(buff)* 75 35

Issued to publicize the first philatelic exhibition of Manica and Sofala.

1955, Feb. 1 **Litho.** *Perf. 11½x12*

Design: 2.50e, Statue of Mousinho de Albuquerque.

398 A30 1e gray, blk & buff 60 35
399 A30 2.50e ol bis, blk & bl 1.00 60

Issued to commemorate the 100th anniversary of the birth of Mousinho de Albuquerque, statesman.

Eight Races Holding Arms of Portugal
A31

View of Beira
A32

1956, Aug. 4 **Unwmk.** *Perf. 14½*

Central Design in Multicolor

400 A31 1e pale yel 28 20
401 A31 2.50e lt bl 70 28

Issued to commemorate the visit of President Antonio Oscar de Fragoso Carmona.

1957, Aug. 15 **Litho.**
402 A32 2.50e multi 48 28

50th anniversary of the city of Beira.

Brussels Fair Issue

Exhibition Emblems and View — A32a

1958, Oct. 8 **Unwmk.** *Perf. 14½*
403 A32a 3.50c blk, grn, yel, red & bl 20 15

Tropical Medicine Congress Issue
Common Design Type

Design: Strophanthus grandiflorus.

1958, Sept. 14 *Perf. 13½*
404 CD47 1.50e sal brn, grn & red 1.25 70

Caravel
A33

Technical Instruction
A34

1960, June 25 **Litho.** *Perf. 13½*
405 A33 5e multi 28 15

Issued to commemorate the 500th anniversary of the death of Prince Henry the Navigator.

1960, Nov. 21 **Unwmk.** *Perf. 14½*
406 A34 3e multi 40 28

Issued to commemorate the 10th anniversary of the Commission for Technical Co-operation in Africa South of the Sahara (C.C.T.A.).

Arms of Lourenço Marques — A35

Arms of various cities of Mozambique.

1961, Jan. 30 **Litho.** *Perf. 13½*

Arms in Original Colors; Black, Ultramarine and Red Inscriptions

407 A35 5c salmon 15 15
408 A35 15c pale grn 15 15
409 A35 20c lt vio gray 15 15
410 A35 30c buff 15 15
411 A35 50c bluish gray 15 15
412 A35 1e pale ol 30 15
413 A35 1.50e lt bl 30 15
414 A35 2e pale pink 45 15
415 A35 2.50e lt bl grn 1.00 15
416 A35 3e beige 60 20
417 A35 4e yellow 38 15
418 A35 4.50e pale gray 38 15
419 A35 5e pale bluish grn 85 15
420 A35 7.50e rose 1.00 24
a. "CORREIOS 7$50" omitted
421 A35 10e lt yel grn 1.50 24
422 A35 20e beige 4.00 50
423 A35 50e gray 4.75 1.00
Nos. 407-423 (17) 16.26
Set value 3.00

Sports Issue
Common Design Type

Sports: 50c, Water skiing. 1e, Wrestling. 1.50e, Woman gymnast. 2.50e, Field hockey. 4.50e, Women's basketball. 15e, Speedboat racing.

1962, Feb. 10 **Unwmk.** *Perf. 13½*

Multicolored Designs

424 CD48 50c gray grn 15 15
425 CD48 1e dk gray 70 35
426 CD48 1.50e pink 28 15
427 CD48 2.50e buff 35 15
428 CD48 4.50e gray 70 40
429 CD48 15e gray grn 1.75 1.00
Nos. 424-429 (6) 3.93 2.20

Anti-Malaria Issue
Common Design Type

Design: Anopheles funestus.

1962, Apr. 5 *Perf. 13½*
430 CD49 2.50e multi 60 35

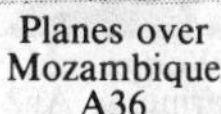

Planes over Mozambique A36

Lourenço Marques 1887 and 1962 A37

1962, Oct. 15 Litho. *Perf. 14½*
431 A36 3e multi 35 20

25th anniversary of DETA airlines.

1962, Nov. 1 *Perf. 13*
432 A37 1e multi 28 15

75th anniversary of Lourenço Marques.

Vasco da Gama Statue and Arms — A38

1963, Apr. 25 Unwmk. *Perf. 14½*
433 A38 3e multi 28 15

Issued to commemorate the 200th anniversary of the founding of Mozambique City.

Airline Anniversary Issue
Common Design Type

1963, Oct. 21 Litho. *Perf. 14½*
434 CD50 2.50e brt pink & multi 28 15

Barque, 1430 — A39

Caravel, 1436 — A40

Development of Sailing Ships: 30c, Lateen-rigged caravel, 1460. 50c, "Sao Gabriel," 1497. 1e, Dom Manuel's ship, 1498. 1.50e, Warship, 1500. 2e, "Flor de la Mar," 1511. 2.50e, Redonda caravel, 1519. 3.50e, 800-ton ship, 1520. 4e, Portuguese India galley, 1521. 4.50e, "Santa Tereza," 1639. 5e, "Nostra Senhora da Conceiçao," 1716. 6e, "Nostra Senhora do Bom Sucesso," 1764. 7.50e, Launch with mortar, 1788. 8e, Brigantine, 1793. 10e, Corvette, 1799. 12.50e, Schooner "Maria Teresa," 1820. 15e, "Vasco da Gama," 1841. 20e, Frigate "Dom Fernando II," 1843. 30e, Training Ship "Sagres," 1924.

1963, Dec. 1 Litho. *Perf. 14½*

435 A39	10c	multi	15	15
436 A40	20c	multi	15	15
437 A40	30c	multi	15	15
438 A40	50c	multi	15	15
439 A40	1e	multi	35	15
440 A40	1.50e	multi	18	15
441 A40	2e	multi	24	15
442 A39	2.50e	multi	50	15
443 A40	3.50e	multi	38	28
444 A39	4e	multi	45	15
445 A40	4.50e	multi	70	18
446 A40	5e	multi	7.50	18
447 A39	6e	multi	70	20
448 A39	7.50e	multi	90	24
449 A39	8e	multi	90	28
450 A39	10e	multi	1.25	40
451 A39	12.50e	multi	1.40	50
452 A39	15e	multi	1.40	50
453 A40	20e	multi	2.00	70
454 A40	30e	multi	2.75	1.25
Nos. 435-454 (20)			22.20	
Set value				5.35

National Overseas Bank Issue

Modern Bank Building, Luanda — A40a

1964, May 16 *Perf. 13½*
455 A40a 1.50e bl, yel gray & grn 35 20

Issued to commemorate the centenary of the National Overseas Bank of Portugal.

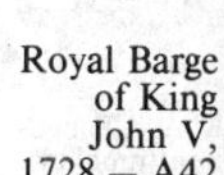

Pres. Americo Rodrigues Thomaz — A41

Perf. 13½x12½
1964, July 23 Litho.
456 A41 2.50e multi 20 15

Issued to commemorate the visit of Pres. Americo Rodrigues Thomaz of Portugal to Mozambique, in July.

Royal Barge of King John V, 1728 — A42

Designs: 35c, Barge of Dom Jose I, 1753. 1e, Customs barge, 1768. 1.50e, Sailor, 1780 (vert.). 2.50e, Royal barge, 1780. 5e, Barge of Dona Carlota Joaquina, 1790. 9e, Barge of Dom Miguel, 1831.

1964, Dec. 18 Litho. *Perf. 14½*

457 A42	15c	multi	15	15
458 A42	35c	lt bl & multi	15	15
459 A42	1e	gray & multi	40	15
460 A42	1.50e	gray & multi	28	15
461 A42	2.50e	multi	20	15
462 A42	5e	multi	28	15
463 A42	9e	multi	48	40
Nos. 457-463 (7)			1.94	
Set value				90

ITU Issue
Common Design Type

1965, May 17 Unwmk. *Perf. 14½*
464 CD52 1e yel & multi 40 28

National Revolution Issue
Common Design Type

Design: 1e, Beira Railroad Station, and Antonio Enes School.

1966, May 28 Litho. *Perf. 11½*
465 CD53 1e multi 20 20

Harquebusier, 1560 — A42a

Designs: 30c, Harquebusier, 1640. 40c, Infantry soldier, 1777. 50c, Infantry officer, 1777. 80c, Drummer, 1777. 1e, Infantry sergeant, 1777. 2e, Infantry major, 1784. 2.50e, Colonial officer, 1788. 3e, Infantry soldier, 1789. 5e, Colonial bugler, 1801. 10e, Colonial officer, 1807. 15e, Colonial infantry soldier, 1817.

1967, Jan. 12 Photo. *Perf. 14*

466 A42a	20c	multi	15	15
467 A42a	30c	multi	15	15
468 A42a	40c	multi	15	15
469 A42a	50c	multi	15	15
470 A42a	80c	multi	40	28
471 A42a	1e	multi	28	15
472 A42a	2e	multi	28	20
473 A42a	2.50e	multi	48	28
474 A42a	3e	multi	35	20
475 A42a	5e	multi	48	28
476 A42a	10e	multi	60	35
477 A42a	15e	multi	75	55
Nos. 466-477 (12)			4.22	2.89

Navy Club Issue
Common Design Type

Designs: 3e, Capt. Azevedo Coutinho and gunboat (stern-wheeler) Tete. 10e, Capt. Joao Roby and gunboat (paddle steamer) Granada.

1967, Jan. 31 Litho. *Perf. 13*
478 CD54 3e multi 35 15
479 CD54 10e multi 85 40

Virgin's Crown, Presented by Portuguese Women — A43

1967, May 13 Litho. *Perf. 12½x13*
480 A43 50c multi 15 15

Issued to commemorate the 50th anniversary of the appearance of the Virgin Mary to 3 shepherd children at Fatima.

Cabral Issue

Raising the Cross at Porto Seguro — A44

Designs: 1.50e, First mission to Brazil. 3e, Grace Church, Santarem (vert.).

1968, Apr. 22 Litho. *Perf. 14*
481 A44 1e multi 15 15
482 A44 1.50e multi 20 15
483 A44 3e multi 40 20
Set value 30

500th anniversary of the birth of Pedro Alvares Cabral, navigator who took possession of Brazil for Portugal.

Admiral Coutinho Issue
Common Design Type

Design: 70c, Adm. Coutinho and Adm. Gago Coutinho Airport.

1969, Feb. 17 Litho. *Perf. 14*
484 CD55 70c multi 15 15

Luiz Vaz de Camoens A45

Sailing Ship, 1553 A46

Designs: 1.50e, Map of Mozambique, 1554. 2.50e, Chapel of Our Lady of Baluarte, 1552. 5e, Excerpt from Lusiads about Mozambique (1st Song, 14th Stanza).

Perf. 12½x13, 13x12½
1969, June 10 Litho.

485 A45	15c	multi	15	15
486 A46	50c	multi	15	15
487 A45	1.50e	multi	15	15
488 A46	2.50e	multi	15	15
489 A45	5e	multi	28	15
Set value			75	40

Issued to commemorate the 400th anniversary of the visit to Mozambique of Luiz Vaz de Camoens (1524-1580), poet.

Vasco da Gama Issue

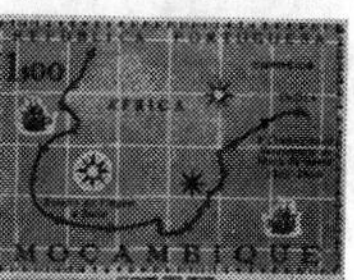

Map Showing Voyage to Mozambique and India — A47

1969, Aug. 29 Litho. *Perf. 14*
490 A47 1e multi 15 15

Issued to commemorate the 500th anniversary of the birth of Vasco da Gama (1469-1524), navigator.

Administration Reform Issue
Common Design Type

1969, Sept. 25 Litho. *Perf. 14*
491 CD56 1.50e multi 15 15

King Manuel I Issue

Illuminated Miniature of King's Arms — A48

1969, Dec. 1 Litho. *Perf. 14*
492 A48 80c multi 15 15

Issued to commemorate the 500th anniversary of the birth of King Manuel I.

Marshal Carmona Issue
Common Design Type

Design: 5e, Antonio Oscar Carmona in marshal's uniform.

1970, Nov. 15 Litho. *Perf. 14*
493 CD57 5e multi 20 15

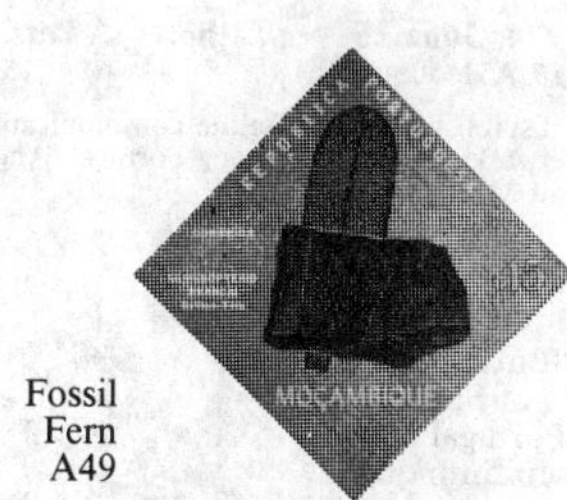

Fossil Fern A49

Fossils and Minerals: 50c, Fossil snail. 1e, Stibnite. 1.50e, Pink beryl. 2e, Dinosaur. 3e, Tantalocolumbite. 3.50e, Verdelite. 4e, Zircon. 10e, Petrified wood.

1971, Jan. 15 Litho. *Perf. 13*

494 A49	15c	gray & multi	15	15
495 A49	50c	lt ultra & multi	15	15
496 A49	1e	grn & multi	15	15
497 A49	1.50e	multi	15	15
498 A49	2e	multi	20	15
499 A49	3e	lt bl & multi	20	15
500 A49	3.50e	lil & multi	40	20
501 A49	4e	multi	40	20
502 A49	10e	dl red & multi	1.10	48
Set value			2.05	1.25

Mozambique Island — A49a

1972, May 25 Litho. *Perf. 13*
503 A49a 4e ultra & multi 28 15

4th centenary of publication of The Lusiads by Luiz Camoens.

Olympic Games Issue
Common Design Type

Design: 3e, Hurdles and swimming, Olympic emblem.

1972, June 20 ***Perf. 14x13½***
504 CD59 3e multi 20 15

Lisbon-Rio de Janeiro Flight Issue
Common Design Type

Design: 1e, "Santa Cruz" over Recife harbor.

1972, Sept. 20 Litho. ***Perf. 13½***
505 CD60 1e multi 15 15

Sailboats
A50

Designs: Various sailboats.

1973, Aug. 21 Litho. ***Perf. 12x11½***
506 A50 1e multi 15 15
507 A50 1.50e multi 15 15
508 A50 3e multi 28 15
Set value 25

World Sailing Championships, Vauriens Class, Lourenço Marques, Aug. 21-30.

WMO Centenary Issue
Common Design Type

1973, Dec. 15 Litho. ***Perf. 13***
509 CD61 2e rose red & multi 20 15

Radar Station
A51

1974, June 25 Litho. ***Perf. 13***
510 A51 50c multi 15 15

Establishment of satellite communications network via Intelsat among Portugal, Angola and Mozambique.

"Bird" Made of Flags of Portugal and Mozambique
A52

1975, Jan. Litho. ***Perf. 14½***
511 A52 1e pink & multi 15 15
512 A52 1.50e yel & multi 15 15
513 A52 2e gray & multi 20 15
514 A52 3.50e lem & multi 28 15
515 A52 6e lt bl & multi 75 28
a. Souv. sheet of 5, #511-515 + label 3.50
Nos. 511-515 (5) 1.53
Set value 70

Lusaka Agreement, Sept. 7, 1974, which gave Mozambique independence from Portugal, effective June 25, 1975.
No. 515a sold for 25e.

Republic
Issues of 1953-74 Overprinted in Red or Black:

a

INDEPENDÊNCIA
25 JUN 75

b

1975, June 25
516 A28 (a) 10c (R; #387) 15 15
517 A26 (a) 40c (R; #368) 15 15
518 A51 (b) 50c (B; #510) 15 15
519 A50 (b) 1e (B; #506) 15 15
520 A50 (b) 1.50e (B; #507) 20 15
521 CD61 (a) 2e (B; #509) 20 15
522 CD48 (b) 2.50e (B; #427) 40 20
523 CD59 (a) 3e (R; #504) 40 20
524 A50 (b) 3e (B; #508) 40 40
525 A49 (b) 3.50e (B; #500) 40 40
526 CD48 (b) 4.50e (B; #428) 2.50 1.75
527 A26 (a) 7.50e (R; #381) 85 40
528 A49 (b) 10e (B; #502) 1.75 60
529 CD48 (b) 15e (B; #429) 1.75 85
530 A28 (a) 20e (R; #394) 1.00 60
Nos. 516-530,C35-C38 (19) 13.60 7.26

Workers, Farmers and Children
A53

Designs: 30c, 50c, 2.50e, like 20c. 4.50e, 5e, 10e, 50e, Dancers, workers, armed family.

1975 Litho. ***Perf. 12x11½***
531 A53 20c pink & multi 15 15
532 A53 30c bis & multi 15 15
533 A53 50c bl & multi 15 15
534 A53 2.50e grn & multi 15 15
535 A53 4.50e brn & multi 18 15
536 A53 5e bis & multi 18 15
537 A53 10e bl & multi 35 20
538 A53 50e yel & multi 1.65 80
a. Souvenir sheet of 8 3.25 3.25
Set value 2.60 1.35

No. 538a contains 8 stamps similar to Nos. 531-538 with simulated perforation. Sold for 75e.

Farm Woman — A54

Designs: 1.50e, Teacher. 2.50e, Nurse. 10e, Mother.

1976, Apr. 7 Litho. ***Perf. 14½***
539 A54 1e yel grn & blk 15 15
540 A54 1.50e tan & multi 16 16
541 A54 2.50e lt ultra & multi 25 25
542 A54 10e red & multi 50 35

Day of the Mozambique Woman, Apr. 7.

Nos. 513-515 Overprinted in Red:
"PRESIDENTE KENNETH KAUNDA / PRIMEIRA VISITA 20/4/1976"

1976, Apr. 20 Litho. ***Perf. 14½***
543 A52 2e gray & multi 18 18
544 A52 3.50e lem & multi 30 30
545 A52 6e lt bl & multi 50 50

Visit of President Kaunda of Zambia.

Pres. Machel's Arrival at Maputo — A55

Mozambique No. 1 — A56

Designs: 1e, Independence proclamation ceremony. 2.50e, Pres. Samora Moises Machel taking office. 7.50e, Military parade. 20e, Flame of Unity and festival.

1976, June 25
546 A55 50c multi 15 15
547 A55 1e multi 15 15
548 A55 2.50e multi 24 20
549 A55 7.50e multi 40 24
550 A55 20e multi 1.00 50
Nos. 546-550 (5) 1.94 1.24

First anniversary of independence.

1976, July ***Perf. 11½x12***
551 A56 1.50e ocher & multi 18 18
552 A56 6e red & multi 35 28

Centenary of Mozambique postage stamps.

Flag and Weapons
A57

1976, Sept. 25 Litho. ***Perf. 14½***
553 A57 3e multi 24 15

Army Day 1976.

No. 534 Overprinted in Silver: "FACIM"

1976 Litho. ***Perf. 12x11½***
554 A53 2.50e multi 28 15

FACIM, Industrial Fair.

Bush Baby — A58

Animals: 1e, Honey badger. 1.50e, Pangolin. 2e, Steinbok. 2.50e, Guenon (monkey). 3e, Cape hunting dog. 4e, Cheetah. 5e, Spotted hyena. 7.50e, Wart hog. 8e, Hippopotamus. 10e, Rhinoceros. 15e, Sable antelope. 1e, 2e, 3e, 4e, 7.50e, 8e, 10e horiz.

1977, Jan. Litho. ***Perf. 14½***
555 A58 50c multi 15 15
556 A58 1e multi 15 15
557 A58 1.50e multi 15 15
558 A58 2e multi 15 15
559 A58 2.50e multi 18 15
560 A58 3e multi 20 15
561 A58 4e multi 28 15
562 A58 5e multi 35 15
563 A58 7.50e multi 50 20
564 A58 8e multi 55 28
565 A58 10e multi 70 28
566 A58 15e multi 1.00 40
Nos. 555-566 (12) 4.36
Set value 2.00

Congress Emblem — A59

Monument in Maputo — A60

Design: 3.50e, Monument in Macheje, site of 2nd Frelimo Congress (horiz.).

1977, Feb. 7 ***Perf. 14½***
567 A59 3e multi 20 20

Perf. 12x11½, 11½x12
568 A60 3.50e multi 28 28
569 A60 20e multi 1.00 35

3rd FRELIMO Party Congress, Maputo, Feb. 3-7.

Women, Child's Design — A61

Worker and Farmer — A62

1977, Apr. 7 Litho. ***Perf. 14½***
570 A61 5e dp org & multi 28 18
571 A61 15e lt grn & multi 70 20

Mozambique Women's Day 1977.

1977, May 1 Litho. ***Perf. 14½***
572 A62 5e red, blk & yel 38 28

Labor Day.

People, Flags and Rising Sun — A63

1977, June 25 Litho. ***Perf. 11½x12***
573 A63 50c multi 15 15
574 A63 1.50e multi 15 15
575 A63 3e multi 20 15
576 A63 15e multi 70 20
Set value 48

2nd anniversary of independence.

Bread Palm — A64

1977, Dec. 21 Litho. ***Perf. 12x11½***
577 A64 1e shown 15 15
578 A64 10e Nyala 50 24
Set value 30

Nature protection and Stamp Day.

Chariesthes Bella Rufoplagiata
A65

Violet-crested Touraco
A66

Beetles: 1e, Tragocephalus variegata. 1.50e, Monochamus leuconotus. 3e, Prospocera lactator meridionalis. 5e, Dinocephalus ornatus. 10e, Tragiscoschema nigroscriptum maculata.

1978, Jan. 20 Litho. ***Perf. 11½x12***
579 A65 50c multi 15 15
580 A65 1e multi 15 15
581 A65 1.50e multi 15 15
582 A65 3e multi 20 20
583 A65 5e multi 35 35
584 A65 10e multi 50 35
Set value 1.25 1.10

1978, Mar. 20 Litho. ***Perf. 11½***

Birds of Mozambique: 1e, Lilac-breasted roller. 1.50e, Weaver. 2.50e, Violet-backed starling. 3e, Peter's twinspot. 15e, European bee-eater.

585 A66 50c multi 15 15
586 A66 1e multi 15 15
587 A66 1.50e multi 15 15
588 A66 2.50e multi 18 18
589 A66 3e multi 20 20
590 A66 15e multi 70 35
Set value 1.30 92

Mother and Child, WHO Emblem A67

1978, Apr. 17 ***Perf. 12***
591 A67 15e multi 50 28

Smallpox eradication campaign.

Crinum Delagoense A68

No. 1, Canada No. 1 A69

Flowers of Mozambique: 1e, Gloriosa superba. 1.50e, Eulophia speciosa. 3e, Erithrina humeana. 5e, Astripomoea malvacea. 10e, Kigelia africana.

1978, May 16 ***Perf. 11½x12***
592 A68 50c multi 15 15
593 A68 1e multi 15 15
594 A68 1.50e multi 15 15
595 A68 3e multi 20 20
596 A68 5e multi 24 24
597 A68 10e multi 48 28
Set value 1.12 92

1978, June 9
598 A69 15e multi 50 28

CAPEX Canadian International Philatelic Exhibition, Toronto, Ont., June 9-18.

National Flag — A70

Soldiers, Festival Emblem — A71

Designs: 1.50e, Coat of arms. 7.50e, Page of Constitution and people. 10e, Music band and national anthem.

1978, June 25 ***Perf. 11½x12***
599 A70 1e multi 15 15
600 A70 1.50e multi 15 15
601 A70 7.50e multi 28 18
602 A70 10e multi 50 24
a. Souvenir sheet of 4 1.75 1.75
Set value 58

3rd anniversary of proclamation of independence. No. 602a contains 4 stamps similar to Nos. 599-602 with simulated perforations. Sold for 30e.

1978, July 28

Designs (Festival Emblem and): 2.50e, Students. 7.50e, Farmworkers.

603 A71 2.50e multi 18 15
604 A71 3e multi 20 15
605 A71 7.50e multi 25 18

11th World Youth Festival, Havana, July 28-Aug. 5.

Czechoslovakia No. B126 and PRAGA '78 Emblem — A72

1978, Sept. 8 Litho. ***Perf. 12x11½***
606 A72 15e multi 50 24
a. Souvenir sheet 2.50 2.50

PRAGA '78 International Philatelic Exhibition, Prague, Sept. 8-17.

No. 606a contains one stamp with simulated perforations. Sold for 30e.

Soccer A73

Stamp Day: 1.50e, Shotput. 3e, Hurdling. 7.50e, Fieldball. 12.50e, Swimming. 25e, Roller skate hockey.

1978, Dec. 21 Litho. ***Perf. 12x11½***
607 A73 50c multi 15 15
608 A73 1.50e multi 15 15
609 A73 3e multi 15 15
610 A73 7.50e multi 28 15
611 A73 12.50e multi 35 20
612 A73 25e multi 70 35
Nos. 607-612 (6) 1.78
Set value 92

Carrier Pigeon, UPU Emblem A74

1979, Jan. 1 Litho. ***Perf. 11x11½***
613 A74 20e multi 55 40

Membership in Universal Postal Union.

Soldier Giving Gourd to Woman — A75

Edward Chivambo Mondlane A76

Designs: 3e, Frelimo soldiers. 7.50e, Mozambique children in school.

1979, Feb. 3 ***Perf. 11½x11, 11x11½***
614 A75 1e multi 15 15
615 A75 3e multi 20 15
616 A75 7.50e multi 28 15
617 A76 12.50e multi 55 20
Set value 55

10th anniversary of death of Dr. Edward Chivambo Mondlane (1920-1969), educator, founder of Frelimo Party.

Shaded Silver Cat — A77

Cats: 1.50e, Manx. 2.50e, English blue. 3e, Turkish. 12.50e, Long-haired Mid-East tabby. 20e, African wild cat.

1979, Mar. 27 Litho. ***Perf. 11***
618 A77 50c multi 15 15
619 A77 1.50e multi 15 15
620 A77 2.50e multi 15 15
621 A77 3e multi 18 15
622 A77 12.50e multi 50 20
623 A77 20e multi 70 28
Nos. 618-623 (6) 1.83
Set value 85

Wrestling and Moscow '80 Emblem — A78

Sport and Moscow '80 Emblem: 2e, Running. 3e, Equestrian. 5e, Canoeing. 10e, High jump. 15e, Archery.

1979, Apr. 24 Litho. ***Perf. 11***
624 A78 1e gray grn & blk 15 15
625 A78 2e brt bl & blk 15 15
626 A78 3e lt brn & blk 15 15
627 A78 5e multi 18 15
628 A78 10e grn & blk 30 15
629 A78 15e lil rose & blk 50 18
Nos. 624-629 (6) 1.43
Set value 58

Souvenir Sheet

Imperf

630 A78 30e rose & dk brn 1.75 1.75

22nd Olympic Games, Moscow, July 10-Aug. 3, 1980. No. 630 contains one 47x37mm stamp.

Garden and IYC Emblem A79

Children's Drawings and IYC Emblem: 1.50e, Dancers. 3e, City. 5e, Farmers. 7.50e, Village. 12.50e, Automobiles, train and flowers.

1979, June 1 Litho. ***Perf. 11***
631 A79 50c multi 15 15
632 A79 1.50e multi 15 15
633 A79 3e multi 15 15
634 A79 5e multi 15 15
635 A79 7.50e multi 20 15
636 A79 12.50e multi 40 15
Set value 1.00 55

International Year of the Child.

Flight from Colonialism — A80

Designs: 2e, Founding of FRELIMO and Pres. Eduardo Chivambo Mondlane. 3e, Advance of armed strruggle and death of Mondlane. 7.50e, Final fight for liberation. 15e, Proclamation of victory, Pres. Samora Moises Machel, flag and torch. Designs after mural in Heroes' Square, Maputo. 30e, Building up the country. Nos. 637-641 printed se-tenant.

1979, June 25
637 A80 50c multi 15 15
638 A80 2e multi 15 15
639 A80 3e multi 15 15
640 A80 7.50e multi 20 15
641 A80 15e multi 50 20
Nos. 637-641 (5) 1.15
Set value 48

Souvenir Sheet

1979 ***Imperf.***
641A A80 30e multi 3.25 3.25

4th anniversary of independence. No. 641A contains one stamp with simulated perforations.

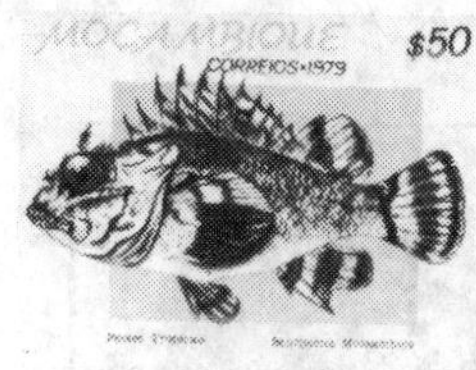

Scorpion Fish A81

Tropical Fish: 1.50e, King fish. 2.50e, Gobius inhaca. 3e, Acanthurus lineatus. 10e, Gobuchthys lemayi. 12.50e, Variola louti.

1979, Aug. 7 Litho. ***Perf. 11***
642 A81 50c multi 15 15
643 A81 1.50e multi 15 15
644 A81 2.50e multi 18 15
645 A81 3e multi 20 15
646 A81 10e multi 50 15
647 A81 12.50e multi 60 20
Nos. 642-647 (6) 1.78
Set value 65

Quartz A82

Mozambique Minerals: 1.50e, Beryl. 2.50e, Magnetite. 5e, Tourmaline. 10e, Euxenite. 20e, Fluorite.

1979, Sept. 10
648 A82 1e multi 15 15
649 A82 1.50e multi 15 15
650 A82 2.50e multi 18 15
651 A82 5e multi 20 15
652 A82 10e multi 35 15
653 A82 20e multi 70 35
Nos. 648-653 (6) 1.73
Set value 82

Mozambique stamps can be mounted in Scott's annual Portugal Supplement.

Citizens Gathering Arms A83

1979, Sept. 25

654 A83	5e multi		28	15

15th anniversary of independence.

Locomotive — A85

Designs: Historic Locomotives.

1979, Nov. 11 Litho. *Perf. 11*

656 A85	50c multi		15	15
657 A85	1.50e multi		15	15
658 A85	3e multi		15	15
659 A85	7.50e multi		24	15
660 A85	12.50e multi		35	18
661 A85	15e multi		50	20
	Nos. 656-661 (6)		1.54	
	Set value			72

Dalmatian — A86

Perf. 11½x11, 11x11½

1979, Dec. 17 Litho.

662 A86	50c	Basenji, vert.	15	15
663 A86	1.50e	shown	15	15
664 A86	3e	Boxer	15	15
665 A86	7.50e	Blue gasconha braco	25	15
666 A86	12.50e	Cocker spaniel	35	15
667 A86	15e	Pointer	50	18
	Nos. 662-667 (6)		1.55	
	Set value			60

Nireus Lyaeus — A87

Butterflies: 1.50e, Amauris ochlea. 2.50e, Pinacopterix eriphia. 5e, Junonia hierta cebrene. 10e, Nephronia argia. 20e, Catacroptera cloanthe.

1979, Dec. 21

668 A87	1e multi		15	15
669 A87	1.50e multi		15	15
670 A87	2.50e multi		15	15
671 A87	5e multi		20	15
672 A87	10e multi		45	24
673 A87	20e multi		1.00	50
	Nos. 668-673 (6)		2.10	
	Set value			1.00

Dermacentor Rhinocerinus, Rhinoceros — A88

Ticks and Animals: 50c, Dermacentor circumguttatus cunhasilvai, elephant. 2.50e, Green tick, giraffe. 3e, Red tick, antelope. 5e, Amblyomma theilerae, cattle. 7.50e, Buffalo tick, buffalo.

1980, Jan. 29 Litho. *Perf. 11½x11*

674 A88	50c multi		15	15
675 A88	1.50e multi		15	15
676 A88	2.50e multi		15	15
677 A88	3e multi		15	15
678 A88	5e multi		18	15
679 A88	7.50e multi		24	15
	Set value		85	58

Ford Hercules, 1950 A89

Public Transportation: 1.50e, Scania Marcopolo, 1978. 3e, Bussing Nag, 1936. 5e, Articulated Ikarus, 1978. 7.50e, Ford taxi, 1929. 12.50e, Fiat 131 taxi, 1978.

1980, Feb. 29 Litho. *Perf. 11*

680 A89	50c multi		15	15
681 A89	1.50e multi		15	15
682 A89	3e multi		15	15
683 A89	5e multi		20	15
684 A89	7.50e multi		35	15
685 A89	12.50e multi		50	15
	Nos. 680-685 (6)		1.50	
	Set value			58

Marx, Engels, and Lenin A90

1980, May 1 Litho. *Perf. 11*

686 A90	10e multi		28	15

Workers' Day.

"Heads," by Malangatana, London 1980 Emblem — A91

Paintings by Mozambique Artists: 1.50e, Crowded Market, by Moises Simbine. 3e, Heads with Helmets, by Malangatana. 5e, Women with Goods, by Machiana. 7.50e, Crowd with Masks, by Malangatana. 12.50e, Man and Woman with Spear, by Mankeu.

1980, May 6

687 A91	50c multi		15	15
688 A91	1.50e multi		15	15
689 A91	3e multi		15	15
690 A91	5e multi		18	15
691 A91	7.50e multi		28	15
692 A91	12.50e multi		50	15
	Nos. 687-692 (6)		1.41	
	Set value			58

London 1980 International Stamp Exhibition, May 6-14.

World Telecommunications Day — A92

1980, May 17 Litho. *Perf. 12*

693 A92	15e multi		50	28

Mueda Massacre, 20th Anniv. — A93

People with Weapons and Flag — A94

1980, June 16 Litho. *Perf. 11*

694 A93	15e multi		50	28

1980, June 25

695 A94	1e	Development projects, 1975	15	15
696 A94	2e	shown	15	15
697 A94	3e	Arms, flags, 1977	15	15
698 A94	4e	Raised fists, 1978	20	15
699 A94	5e	Hand holding grain, flags, 1979	24	15
700 A94	10e	Year banners, 1980	38	15
	Nos. 695-700 (6)		1.27	
	Set value			60

Souvenir Sheet

Litho. *Imperf.*

700A A94	30e Soldiers		3.00	

5th anniv. of independence. No. 700A contains one stamp with simulated perforations.

Gymnast, Moscow '80 Emblem A95

1980, July 19

701 A95	50c	shown	15	15
702 A95	1.50e	Soccer	15	15
703 A95	2.50e	Running	15	15
704 A95	3e	Volleyball	15	15
705 A95	10e	Bicycling	40	18
706 A95	12.50e	Boxing	50	28
	Set value		1.25	80

22nd Summer Olympic Games, Moscow, July 19-Aug. 3.

Soldier, Map of Southern Africa Showing Zimbabwe — A96

1980, Apr. 18

707 A96	10e multi		28	15

Establishment of independent Zimbabwe, Apr. 18.

Narina Trogon — A97

1980, July 30 Litho. *Perf. 11*

708 A97	1m	shown	15	15
709 A97	1.50m	Crowned crane	15	15
710 A97	2.50m	Red-necked francolin	15	15
711 A97	5m	Ostrich	18	15
712 A97	7.50m	Spur-winged goose	30	15
713 A97	12.50m	Fish eagle	50	24
	Set value		1.20	75

First Census, Aug. 1-15 A98

1980, Aug. 12 *Perf. 11*

714 A98	3.5m multi		15	15

Brush Fire Control Campaign — A99

1980, Sept. 7

715 A99	3.5m multi		15	15

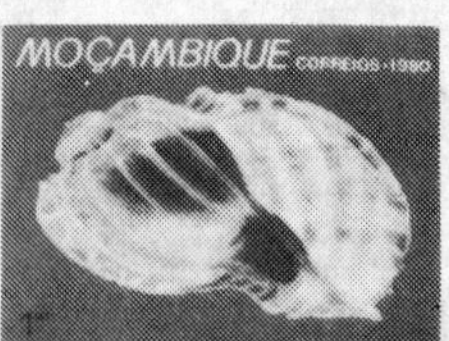

Harpa Major A100

1980, Dec. 12 Litho. *Perf. 11*

716 A100	1m	*shown*	15	15
717 A100	1.50m	*Lambis chiragra*	15	15
718 A100	2.50m	*Murex pecten*	15	15
719 A100	5m	*Architectonia perspectiva*	15	15
720 A100	7.50m	*Murex ramosus*	28	15
721 A100	12.50m	*Strombus aurisdinae*	50	24
	Set value		1.12	68

Pres. Machel and Symbols of Industry and Transportation — A101

Decade of Development, 1981-1990 (Pres. Machel and): 7.50m, Soldiers. 12.50m, Symbols of education.

1981, Jan. 1 Litho. *Perf. 11x11½*

722 A101 3.50m red & bl 15 15
723 A101 7.50m grn & red brn 30 15
724 A101 12.50m dk bl & lil rose 48 15

Bilbao Soccer Stadium, Soccer Player — A102

Designs: Soccer players and various stadiums.

1981, Jan. 30 Litho. *Perf. 11*

725 A102 1m multi 15 15
726 A102 1.50m multi 15 15
727 A102 2.50m multi 15 15
728 A102 5m multi 15 15
729 A102 7.50m multi 28 15
730 A102 12.50m multi 50 20
c. Souvenir sheet of 6 1.25 1.25
Set value 1.12 65

Souvenir Sheets

Imperf

730A A102 20m multi 85 85
730B A102 20m multi 85 85

ESPANA '82 World Cup Soccer Championship. No. 730c contains Nos. 725-730 with simulated perforations. Sizes: No. 730A, 105x85mm; 730B, 141x111mm.

Giraffe — A103

1981, Mar. 3 *Perf. 11*

731 A103 50c shown 15 15
732 A103 1.50m Tsessebe 15 15
733 A103 2.50m Aardvark 15 15
734 A103 3m African python 15 15
735 A103 5m Loggerhead turtle 18 15
736 A103 10m Marabou 40 15
737 A103 12.50m Saddlebill stork 50 20
738 A103 15m Kori bustard 60 28
Nos. 731-738 (8) 2.28
Set value 1.12

Pankwe A104

1981, Apr. 8 Litho. *Perf. 11*

739 A104 50c Chitende, vert. 15 15
740 A104 2m shown 15 15
741 A104 2.50m Kanyembe, vert. 15 15
742 A104 7m Nyanga 28 28
743 A104 10m Likuti and m'petheni 40 40
Set value 90 90

International Year of the Disabled — A105

1981, Apr. 18

744 A105 5m multi 20 15

African Buffalo and Helicopter, Exhibition Emblem — A106

1981, June 14 *Perf. 11*

745 A106 2m shown 15 15
746 A106 5m Hunters, blue kids 15 15
747 A106 6m Hunter, impala 18 15
748 A106 7.5m Hunters shooting 30 15
749 A106 12.5m Elephants 50 15
750 A106 20m Trap 80 30
a. Souv. sheet of 6, #745-750, imperf. 2.50 2.50
Nos. 745-750 (6) 2.08
Set value 80

World Hunting Exhibition, Plovdiv, Bulgaria.

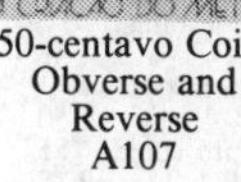

50-centavo Coin, Obverse and Reverse A107

Sunflower A108

First Anniversary of New Currency (Coins on stamps of matching denomination).

1981, June 16

751 A107 50c multi 15 15
752 A107 1m multi 15 15
753 A107 2.50m multi 15 15
754 A107 5m multi 20 15
755 A107 10m multi 40 20
756 A107 20m multi 80 28
a. Souvenir sheet of 6, #751-756, imperf. 1.75 1.75
Set value 1.55 75

1981, July 24 Litho. *Perf. 14½*

757 A108 50c shown 15 15
758 A108 1m Cotton 15 15
759 A108 1.50m Sisal 15 15
760 A108 2.50m Cashews 15 15
761 A108 3.50m Tea leaves 15 15
762 A108 4.50m Sugar cane 20 15
763 A108 10m Castor-oil plant 40 15
764 A108 12.50m Coconut 50 18
765 A108 15m Tobacco leaves 60 20
766 A108 25m Rice 1.00 40
767 A108 40m Corn 1.65 60
768 A108 60m Peanut 2.50 85
Nos. 757-768 (12) 7.60
Set value 2.75

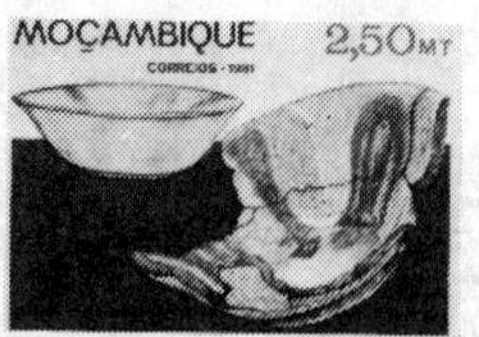

9th Cent. Persian Bowl, Chibuene Excavation Site — A109

1981, Aug. 30 *Perf. 11*

769 A109 1m Manyikeni Museum 15 15
770 A109 1.50m Hand ax, Massingir Dam 15 15
771 A109 2.50m shown 15 15
772 A109 7.50m Pot, Chibuene, 9th cent. 30 15
773 A109 12.50m Gold beads, Manyikeni 50 20
774 A109 20m Iron, Manyikeni, 15th cent. 80 30
Nos. 769-774 (6) 2.05
Set value 80

Sculptures A110

1981, Sept. 25 Litho. *Perf. 11*

775 A110 50c Mapiko mask 15 15
776 A110 1m Suffering woman 15 15
777 A110 2.50m Mother and child 15 15
778 A110 3.50m Man making fire 20 15
779 A110 5m Chietane 50 28
780 A110 12.50m Chietane, diff. 50 50
Set value 1.40 1.00

World Food Day A111

1981, Oct. 16 Litho. *Perf. 11*

781 A111 10m multi 40 15

Ocean Tanker Matchedje — A112

1981, Nov. 22 Litho. *Perf. 11*

782 A112 50c shown 15 15
783 A112 1.50m Tugboat Macuti 15 15
784 A112 3m Prawn trawler Vega 7 15 15
785 A112 5m Freighter Linde 20 15
786 A112 7.50m Ocean freighter Pemba 30 20
787 A112 12.50m Dredger Rovuma 50 25
Set value 1.22 75

Chinaman Crab A113

1981, Dec. 6

788 A113 50c shown 15 15
789 A113 1.50m Scylla serrata 15 15
790 A113 3m White prawn 15 15
791 A113 7.50m Palinurus delagoae 30 15
792 A113 12.50m Mantis shrimp 50 18
793 A113 15m Panulirus ornatus 60 28
Nos. 788-793 (6) 1.85
Set value 80

Hypoxis Multiceps A114

1981, Dec. 21 Litho. *Perf. 11*

794 A114 1m shown 15 15
795 A114 1.50m Pelargonium luridum 15 15
796 A114 2.50m Caralluma melananthera 15 15
797 A114 7.50m Ansellia gigantea 30 15
798 A114 12.50m Stapelia leendertsiae 50 18
799 A114 25m Adenium multiflorium 1.00 28
Nos. 794-799 (6) 2.25
Set value 75

First Anniv. of Posts and Telecommunications Dept. — A115

1982, Jan. 1 Litho. *Perf. 11*

800 A115 6m Phone, globe 25 15
801 A115 15m Envelope 60 20

Gasoline Conservation — A116

1982, Jan. 25

802 A116 5m Piston 20 15
803 A116 7.50m Car 30 15
804 A116 10m Truck 40 15
Set value 30

Sea Snake A117

1982, Feb. 27 Litho. *Perf. 11*

805 A117 50c shown 15 15
806 A117 1.50m Mozambique spitting cobra 15 15
807 A117 3m Savanna vine snake 15 15
808 A117 6m Black mamba 25 15
809 A117 15m Boomslang 60 20
810 A117 20m Bitis arietans 80 28
Nos. 805-810 (6) 2.10
Set value 78

TB Bacillus Centenary A118

1982, Mar. 15 Litho. *Perf. 11*

811 A118 20m multi 80 28

ITU Plenipotentiary Conference, Nairobi, Sept. 28-Nov. 5 — A119

1982, Mar. 31 *Perf. 13½*

812 A119 20m multi 80 35

1982 World Cup — A120

Designs: Various soccer players.

1982, Apr. 19 Litho. *Perf. 13½*

813 A120 1.5m multi 15 15
814 A120 3.5m multi 15 15
815 A120 7m multi 30 15
816 A120 10m multi 40 15
817 A120 20m multi 80 28
Nos. 813-817 (5) 1.80
Set value 65

Souvenir Sheet

Imperf

818 A120 50m multi 2.00 2.00

Souvenir Sheet

Two Tahitian Women, by Gauguin — A121

1982, June 11 Litho. *Imperf.*

819 A121 35m multi 1.75 1.75

PHILEXFRANCE '82 Intl. Stamp Exhibition, Paris, June 11-21.

Natl. Liberation Front, 20th Anniv. — A122

Vangueria Infausta — A123

1982, June 25 *Perf. 13*

820 A122 4m Pres. Mondland addressing crowd 16 15
821 A122 8m Guarded fields 35 15
822 A122 12m Procession 50 18
Set value 38

1982, Sept. 13 *Perf. 11*

Designs: Fruits.

823 A123 1m shown 15 15
824 A123 2m Mimusops caffra 15 15
825 A123 4m Sclerocarya caffra 16 15
826 A123 8m Strychnos spinosa 35 15
827 A123 12m Salacia kraussi 50 18
828 A123 32m Trichilia emetica 1.40 40
Nos. 823-828 (6) 2.71
Set value 90

25th Anniv. of Sputnik 1 Flight A124

1982, Oct. 4 Litho. *Perf. 11*

829 A124 1m Sputnik, 1957 15 15
830 A124 2m Yuri Gagarin's flight, 1961 15 15
831 A124 4m A. Leonov's spacewalk, 1965 18 15
832 A124 8m Apollo 11, 1969 35 15
833 A124 16m Apollo-Soyuz, 1975 70 24
834 A124 20m Salyut-6, 1978 85 30
a. Min. sheet of 6, #829-834 2.50 2.50
Nos. 829-834 (6) 2.38
Set value 85

People's Vigilance Day — A125

Caique — A126

1982, Oct. 11 *Perf. 13½*

835 A125 4m multi 18 15

1982, Nov. 29

Traditional boats. 4m, 8m, 12m, 16m horiz.

836 A126 1m shown 15 15
837 A126 2m Machua 15 15
838 A126 4m Calaua 18 15
839 A126 8m Chitatarro 35 15
840 A126 12m Cangaia 50 18
841 A126 16m Chata (flatboat) 70 24
Nos. 836-841 (6) 2.03
Set value 72

Marine Life — A127

1982, Dec. 21 Litho. *Perf. 11*

842 A127 1m Ophiomastix venosa 15 15
843 A127 2m Protoreaster lincki 15 15
844 A127 4m Tropiometra carinata 18 15
845 A127 8m Holothuria scabra 35 18
846 A127 12m Prionocidaris baculosa 50 18
847 A127 16m Colobocentrotus atnatus 70 24
Nos. 842-847 (6) 2.03
Set value 80

Frelimo Party 4th Congress — A128

1983, Jan. 17

848 A128 4m Map, soldier 18 15
849 A128 8m Voters 35 15
850 A128 16m Farm workers 70 18
Set value 38

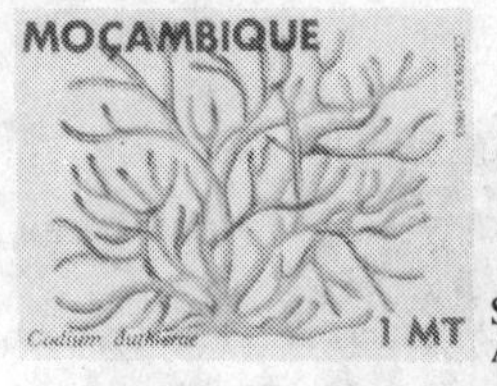

Seaweed A129

1983, Feb. 28 Litho. *Perf. 11*

851 A129 1m Codium duthierae 15 15
852 A129 2m Halimeda cuncata 15 15
853 A129 4m Dictyota liturata 18 15
854 A129 8m Encorachne bing hamiae 35 15
855 A129 12m Laurencia flexuosa 50 18
856 A129 20m Acrosorium sp. 85 35
Nos. 851-856 (6) 2.18
Set value 85

1984 Olympic Games, Los Angeles — A130

1983, Mar. 31 Litho. *Perf. 11*

857 A130 1m Diving 15 15
858 A130 2m Boxing 15 15
859 A130 4m Basketball 18 15
860 A130 8m Handball 35 15
861 A130 12m Volleyball 50 18
862 A130 16m Running 70 24
863 A130 20m Sailing 85 35
Nos. 857-863 (7) 2.88
Set value 1.12

Souvenir Sheet

Imperf

864 A130 50m Discus 2.00 2.00

Steam Locomotives — A131

1983, Apr. 29 Litho. *Perf. 11*

865 A131 1m 1912 15 15
866 A131 2m 1947 15 15
867 A131 4m 1923 18 15
868 A131 8m 1924 35 18
869 A131 16m 1924, diff. 70 28
870 A131 32m 1950 1.40 40
Nos. 865-870 (6) 2.93
Set value 1.05

20th Anniv. of Org. of African Unity A132

1983, May 25 Litho. *Perf. 11*

871 A132 4m multi 18 15

Mammals A133

1983, May 30

872 A133 1m Petrodromus tetradactylus 15 15
873 A133 2m Rhabdomys pumilio 15 15
874 A133 4m Paraxerus vincenti 18 15
875 A133 8m Cryptomys hottentotus 35 15
876 A133 12m Pronolagus crassicaudatus 50 18
877 A133 16m Eidolon helvum 70 28
Nos. 872-877 (6) 2.03
Set value 78

Souvenir Sheet

Marimba Players — A134

1983, July 29 Litho. *Perf. 11*

878 A134 30m multi 1.50 1.50

BRASILIANA '83 Intl. Stamp Show, Rio de Janeiro, July 29-Aug. 7.

World Communications Year — A135

1983, Aug. 26 **Litho.** ***Perf. 11***

879 A135 8m multi 35 15

Fishing Techniques — A136

1983, Oct. 29 **Litho.** ***Perf. 11***

880 A136 50c Line fishing 15 15
881 A136 2m Chifonho 15 15
882 A136 4m Momba 15 15
883 A136 8m Gamboa 28 15
884 A136 16m Mono 55 18
885 A136 20m Lema 70 28
Nos. 880-885 (6) 1.98
Set value 75

World Communications Year, Stamp Day — A137

1983, Dec. 21 **Litho.**

886 A137 50c Horn 15 15
887 A137 1m Drum 15 15
888 A137 4m Native mail carriers 15 15
889 A137 8m Boat 28 15
890 A137 16m Truck 55 20
891 A137 20m Train 70 28
Nos. 886-891 (6) 1.98
Set value 75

2nd Anniv. of Mozambique Red Cross (July 10) — A138

1983, Oct. 29 **Litho.** ***Perf. 11***

892 A138 4m Flood relief 15 15
893 A138 8m Rescue truck 28 15
894 A138 16m First aid 55 20
895 A138 32m Field first aid 1.10 40
Set value 75

Olympic Games 1984, Los Angeles — A139

1984, Jan. 2 **Litho.** ***Perf. 11***

896 A139 50c Swimming 15 15
897 A139 4m Soccer 15 15
898 A139 8m Hurdles 28 20
899 A139 16m Basketball 55 25
900 A139 32m Handball 1.10 30
901 A139 60m Boxing 2.00 50
Nos. 896-901 (6) 4.23 1.55

Indigenous Trees — A140

1984, Mar. 30 **Litho.** ***Perf. 11***

902 A140 50c Trichilia emetica 15 15
903 A140 2m Brachystegia spiciformis 15 15
904 A140 4m Androstachys johnsonii 15 15
905 A140 8m Pterocarpus angolensis 16 15
906 A140 16m Milletia stuhlmannii 32 20
907 A140 50m Dalbergia melanoxylon 1.00 40
Set value 1.65 85

Nkomati Accord, Mar. 16 — A141

1984, Mar. 16

908 A141 4m Dove 15 15

Natl. Arms A142

1984, May 1

909 A142 4m shown 15 15
910 A142 8m Natl. flag 16 15
Set value 24 15

Traditional Dances — A143

1984, May 9

911 A143 4m Makway 15 15
912 A143 8m Mapiko 16 15
913 A143 16m Wadjaba 32 15
Set value 30

LUBRAPEX '84, May 9-17.

Museums and Artifacts — A144

Designs: 50c, Nampula Museum, African carrying water jar, wooden statue. 4m, Museum of Natural History, preserved bird. 8m, Revolution Museum, guerrilla fighter statue. 16m, Colonial Occupation Museum, fort and cannon. 20m, Numismatic Museum, coins. 30m, Palace of St. Paul, char, 19th cent.

1984, June 25

914 A144 50c multi 15 15
915 A144 4m multi 15 15
916 A144 8m multi 16 15
917 A144 16m multi 32 20
918 A144 20m multi 40 25
919 A144 30m multi 60 30
Nos. 914-919 (6) 1.78
Set value 1.00

Freshwater Fish — A145

1984, Aug. 24

920 A145 50c Alestes imberi 15 15
921 A145 4m Labeo congoro 15 15
922 A145 12m Syndontis zambezensis 40 20
923 A145 16m Noto branchius zachovii 55 30
924 A145 40m Barbus paludinosus 1.40 40
925 A145 60m Barilius zambezensis 2.00 60
Nos. 920-925 (6) 4.65 1.80

Traditional Weapons A146

1984, Sept. 25

926 A146 50c Knife, cudgel *18* *15*
927 A146 4m Axes *25* *15*
928 A146 8m Shield, assagai *45* *20*
929 A146 16m Bow and arrow *75* *30*
930 A146 32m Muzzleloader *2.00* *40*
931 A146 50m Assagai, arrow *3.00* *50*
Nos. 926-931 (6) *6.63* *1.70*

Natl. Revolution, 20th anniv.

Natl. Trade Unions, 1st Anniv. A147

1984, Oct. 13 ***Perf. 13½***

932 A147 4m Workers, emblem 15 15

Stamp Day — A149

Cancellations on altered stamps and stationery: 4m, Barue cancel on 1885 20r postal card. 8m, Zumbo cancel on design similar to No. 52. 12m, Mozambique Co. cancel on design similar to Mozambique Company Type API. 16m, Macequece cancel on design similar to Mozambique Company No. 190.

1984, Dec. 21 ***Perf. 11½x11***

936 A149 4m multi 15 15
937 A149 8m multi 28 15
938 A149 12m multi 40 20
939 A149 16m multi 55 25

African Development Bank, 20th Anniv. — A150

1984, Sept. 16 **Photo.** ***Perf. 11½x11***

940 A150 4m multi 15 15

Apiculture A151

1985, Feb. 3

941 A151 4m Beekeeper 15 15
942 A151 8m Bee gathering pollen 15 15
943 A151 16m Entering nest 22 15
944 A151 20m Building honeycomb 28 20
Set value 50

OLYMPHILEX '85, Lausanne A152

1985, Mar. 18 ***Perf. 11***

945 A152 16m Shot putter 22 15

15-Cent Minimum Value
The minimum value for a single stamp is 15 cents. This value reflects the costs of the handling of inexpensive stamps.

World Meteorology Day — A153

1985, Mar. 23 Litho. *Perf. 11*

946	A153	4m	multi	15	15

Southern African Development Coordination Conference, 5th Anniv. — A154

1985, Apr. 1

947	A154	4m	Map	15	15
948	A154	8m	Map, transmission tower	15	15
949	A154	16m	Industry	22	15
950	A154	32m	Flags	45	20
			Set value		50

Independence, 10th Anniv. — A155

Colonial resistance battles: 1m, Mujenga, 1896. 4m, Mungari, 1917. 8m, Massangano, 1868. 16m, Marracuene, 1895, and Gungunhana (c. 1840-1906), resistance leader.

1985, June 25 Litho. *Perf. 11*

951	A155	1m	multi	15	15
952	A155	4m	multi	15	15
953	A155	8m	multi	15	15
954	A155	16m	multi	22	15
			Set value	45	35

UN, 40th Anniv. — A156

1985, June 26

955	A156	16m	multi	*1.10*	*15*

Traditional Games — A157

1985, Aug. 28 Litho. *Perf. 11*

956	A157	50c	Mathacuzana	15	15
957	A157	4m	Mudzobo	18	18
958	A157	8m	Muravarava	35	35
959	A157	16m	N'Tshuwa	70	70

Frogs and Toads A158

1985, Oct. 25 Litho. *Perf. 11*

960	A158	50c	Rana angolensis	15	15
961	A158	1m	Hyperolius pictus	15	15
962	A158	4m	Ptychadena porosissima	15	15
963	A158	8m	Afrixalus formasinii	15	15
964	A158	16m	Bufo regularis	22	15
965	A158	32m	Hyperolius marmoratus	45	25
			Set value	90	62

Medicinal Plants — A159

1985, Nov. 28 Litho. *Perf. 11*

966	A159	50c	Aloe ferox	15	15
967	A159	1m	Boophone disticha	15	15
968	A159	3.50m	Gloriosa superba	15	15
969	A159	4m	Cotyledon orbiculata	15	15
970	A159	8m	Homeria breyniana	15	15
970A	A159	50m	Haemanthus coccineus	70	25
			Set value	1.00	54

Stamp Day A160

Stamps: 1m, Mozambique Company No. 126. 4m, Nyassa Type A6. 8m, Mozambique Company No. 110. 16m, Nyassa No. J2.

1985, Dec. 21

971	A160	1m	multi	15	15
972	A160	4m	multi	15	15
973	A160	8m	multi	15	15
974	A160	16m	multi	22	15
			Set value	45	35

Halley's Comet — A161

Comet and: 4m, Space probe. 8m, Trajectory diagram. 16m, Newton's telescope, observatory, probe. 30m, Earth.

1986, Jan. 2

975	A161	4m	multi	15	15
976	A161	8m	multi	15	15
977	A161	16m	multi	22	15
978	A161	30m	multi	45	25
			Set value		55

1986 World Cup Soccer Championships, Mexico — A162

Players.

1986, Feb. 28 Litho. *Perf. 11½x11*

979	A162	3m	Vicente	15	15
980	A162	4m	Coluna	15	15
981	A162	8m	Costa Pereira	15	15
982	A162	12m	Hilario	16	15
983	A162	16m	Matateu	22	20
984	A162	50m	Eusebio	70	40
			Set value	1.30	95

Intl. Peace Year — A163

1986, Mar. 18 *Perf. 11*

985	A163	16m	multi	22	15

Mushrooms A164

1986, Apr. 8

986	A164	4m	Amanita muscaria	15	15
987	A164	8m	Lactarius deliciosus	15	15
988	A164	16m	Amanita phaloides	22	15
989	A164	30m	Tricholoma nudum	40	20
			Set value	78	50

Souvenir Sheet

Statue of Liberty, Cent. — A165

1986, May 22 *Imperf.*

990	A165	100m	multi	1.40	1.40

AMERIPEX '86. No. 990 has simulated perforations.

Traditional Women's Hair Styles — A166

1986, June Litho. *Perf. 11½x11*

991	A166	1m	Tanzanian	15	15
992	A166	4m	Miriam	15	15
993	A166	8m	Estrelinhas	15	15
994	A166	16m	Toto	22	20
			Set value	45	42

Marine Mammals A167

1986, Aug. *Perf. 11*

995	A167	1m	Dugongo dugon	15	15
996	A167	8m	Delphinus delphis	15	15
997	A167	16m	Neobalena marginata	22	15
998	A167	50m	Balaenoptera physalus	70	25
			Set value		50

Continuing Youth Education Organization, 1st Anniv. — A168

1986, Sept. 16 Litho. *Perf. 11½x11*

999	A168	4m	multi	15	15

Natl. Savings Campaign — A169

Bank notes, front and back.

1986, Oct. 22 Litho. *Perf. 11½x11*

1000	A169	4m	50m note	15	15
1001	A169	8m	100m note	15	15
1002	A169	16m	500m note	22	15
1003	A169	30m	1000m note	40	20
			Set value	80	50

Stamp Day A170

Post offices.

1986, Dec. 21 Litho. *Perf. 11*

1004	A170	3m	Quelimane	15	15
1005	A170	4m	Maputo	15	15
1006	A170	8m	Beira	15	15
1007	A170	16m	Nampula	22	20
			Set value	45	50

Minerals
A171

1987, Jan. 2 *Perf. 11x11½*

1008 A171 4m Pyrite 15 15
1009 A171 8m Emerald 15 15
1010 A171 12m Agate 16 15
1011 A171 16m Malachite 22 20
1012 A171 30m Garnet 40 25
1013 A171 50m Amethyst 70 40
Nos. 1008-1013 (6) 1.78 1.30

Frelimo Party, 10th Anniv. — A172

1987, Feb. 3 *Perf. 11*

1014 A172 4m multi 15 15

Pequenos Libombos Dam — A173

1987, Feb. 17 *Perf. 11½x11*

1015 A173 16m multi 22 15

World Health Day
A174

1987, Apr. 7 **Litho.** *Perf. 11x11½*

1016 A174 50m multi 70 25

Birds — A175

1987, Apr. 27 **Litho.** *Perf. 11½x11*

1017 A175 3m Granatina granatina 15 15
1018 A175 4m Halcyon senegalensis 15 15
1019 A175 8m Mellittophagus bullockoides 15 15
1020 A175 12m Perinestes minor 16 20
1021 A175 16m Coracias naevia mosambica 22 25
1022 A175 30m Cimmyris neergardi 40 30
Set value 1.00 1.00

Souvenir Sheet

CAPEX '87, Toronto, June 13-21 — A176

1987, June *Imperf.*

1023 A176 200m multi 2.00 2.00

No. 1023 contains one stamp having simulated perforations.

1988 Summer Olympics, Seoul — A177

1987, May **Litho.** *Perf. 11½x11*

1024 A177 12.50m Soccer players and ball 15 15
1025 A177 25m Runner's legs 25 20
1026 A177 50m Volleyball 50 30
1027 A177 75m Chess 75 40
1028 A177 100m Basketball 1.00 50
1029 A177 200m Swimming 2.00 75
Nos. 1024-1029 (6) 4.65 2.30

Tapestries — A178

1987, Aug. *Perf. 11*

1030 A178 20m Incomplete pattern on loom 15 15
1031 A178 40m Diamond-shaped pattern 16 15
1032 A178 80m Landscape pattern 32 25
1033 A178 200m Oriental pattern 80 40

Maputo City
A179

Early Portuguese map of Lourenco Marques.

1987, Nov. 10 **Litho.** *Perf. 11*

1034 A179 20m multi 15 15

No. 762 Surcharged in Silver and Dark Red **4,00 MT**

1987 **Litho.** *Perf. 14½*

1034A A108 4m on 4.50m multi 25 25

1988 Summer Olympics, Seoul — A180

Flowering Plants — A181

1988, Feb. 10 **Litho.** *Perf. 11*

1035 A180 10m Javelin 15 15
1036 A180 20m Baseball 28 15
1037 A180 40m Boxing 58 25
1038 A180 80m Field hockey 1.15 40
1039 A180 100m Gymnastic rings 1.40 50
1040 A180 400m Cycling 5.65 1.90
Nos. 1035-1040 (6) 9.21 3.35

Nos. 1036-1040 horiz.

1988, Mar. 18 *Perf. 11½x11*

1041 A181 10m Heamanthus nelsonii 15 15
1042 A181 20m Crinum polyphyllum 28 15
1043 A181 40m Boophane disticha 58 25
1044 A181 80m Cyrtanthus contractus 1.15 40
1045 A181 100m Nerine angustifolia 1.40 50
1046 A181 400m Cyrtanthus galpinnii 5.65 1.90
Nos. 1041-1046 (6) 9.21 3.35

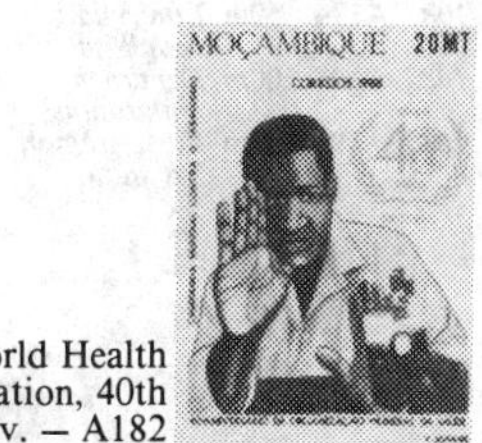

World Health Organization, 40th Anniv. — A182

1988, Apr. 7

1047 A182 20m multi 28 28

Anti-smoking campaign.

Wickerwork — A183

1988, June 16 **Litho.** *Perf. 11*

1048 A183 20m Mat 16 15
1049 A183 25m Lidded container 20 15
1050 A183 80m Market basket 62 20
1051 A183 100m Fan 78 25
1052 A183 400m Flat basket 3.15 1.00
1053 A183 500m Funnel basket 3.90 1.25
Nos. 1048-1053 (6) 8.81 3.00

Souvenir Sheet

FINLANDIA '88 — A184

1988, June 12 **Litho.** *Imperf.*

1054 A184 500m multi 2.50 1.00

Stamp in No. 1054 has simulated perfs.

Souvenir Sheet

State Visit of Pope John Paul II, Sept. 16-19 — A185

1988 **Litho.** *Perf. 13½*

1055 A185 500m multi 1.50 1.50

Horses
A186

1988, Sept. 20 **Litho.** *Perf. 11*

1056 A186 20m Percheron 20 15
1057 A186 40m Arab 38 15
1058 A186 80m Purebred 75 25
1059 A186 100m Pony 92 30

Pres. Samora Machel (1933-1986)
A187

1988, Oct. 19 **Litho.** *Perf. 11*

1060 A187 20m multi 15 15

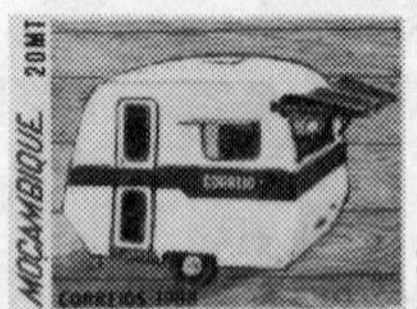

Stamp Day A188

Perf. 11x11½, 11½x11

1988, Dec. 21

1061 A188 20m P.O. trailer 15 15
1062 A188 40m Mailbox, vert. 20 15

Ports A189

1988, Nov. 30 ***Perf. 11***

1063 A189 25m Inhambane 15 15
1064 A189 50m Quelimane, vert. 20 15
1065 A189 75m Pemba 30 15
1066 A189 100m Beira 42 15
1067 A189 250m Nacala, vert. 1.05 25
1068 A189 500m Maputo 2.05 50
Nos. 1063-1068 (6) 4.17
Set value 1.00

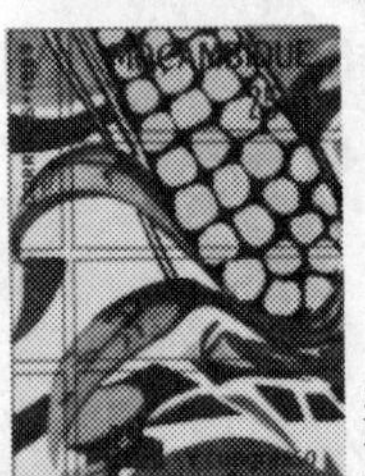
5th Frelimo Party Congress A190

1989, Jan. 19

1069 Strip of 5 2.40 1.25
a. A190 25m Corn 15 15
b. A190 50m Axe 24 15
c. A190 75m Abstract shapes 35 18
d. A190 100m 2½ Gearwheels 48 24
e. A190 250m ½ Gearwheel 1.20 60

Printed se-tenant in a continuous design.

French Revolution Bicent. — A191

Designs: 100m, *Storming of the Bastille,* by Thevenin. 250m, *Liberty Guiding the People,* by Delacroix. 500m, *Declaration of Human Rights and Citizenship,* a print by Blanchard.

1989, Feb. 16 ***Perf. 11***

1070 A191 100m multi 30 15
1071 A191 250m multi 75 25

Souvenir Sheet

1072 A191 500m multi 1.50 75

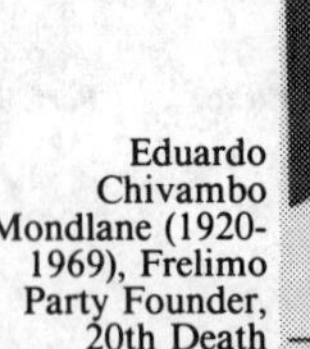

Eduardo Chivambo Mondlane (1920-1969), Frelimo Party Founder, 20th Death Anniv. — 192

1989, Feb. 3 **Litho.** ***Perf. 11***

1073 A192 25m blk, gold & dark red 15 15

Venomous Species — A193

1989, Mar. 23

1074 A193 25m *Pandinus* 15 15
1075 A193 50m *Naja haje* 20 15
1076 A193 75m *Bombus* 30 15
1077 A193 100m *Paraphysa* 42 15
1078 A193 250m *Conus marmoreus* 1.05 25
1079 A193 500m *Pterois volitans* 2.05 50
Nos. 1074-1079 (6) 4.17
Set value 1.00

Coral A194

1989, May 2 **Litho.** ***Perf. 11***

1080 A194 25m *Acropora pulchra* 15 15
1081 A194 50m *Eunicella papilosa* 15 15
1082 A194 100m *Dendrophyla migrantus* 28 15
1083 A194 250m *Favia fragum* 68 25
Set value 40

1990 World Cup Soccer Championships, Italy — A195

Athletes executing various plays.

1989, June 22 **Litho.** ***Perf. 11½x11***

1084 A195 30m multi 15 15
1085 A195 60m multi 16 15
1086 A195 125m multi 32 15
1087 A195 200m multi 55 18
1088 A195 250m multi 68 22
1089 A195 500m multi 1.35 45
Nos. 1084-1089 (6) 3.21
Set value 1.00

Lighthouses A196

1989, July 24 **Litho.** ***Perf. 11***

1090 A196 30m Macuti 15 15
1091 A196 60m Pinda 16 15
1092 A196 125m Cape Delgado 35 15
1093 A196 200m Isle of Goa 55 18
1094 A196 250m Caldeira Point 68 22
1095 A196 500m Vilhena 1.35 45
Nos. 1090-1095 (6) 3.24
Set value 1.00

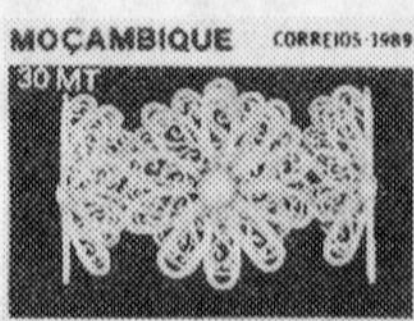

Filigree Workmanship in Silver — A197

1989, Aug. 30 **Litho.** ***Perf. 11x11½***

1096 A197 30m shown 15 15
1097 A197 60m Flower on band 15 15
1098 A197 125m Necklace 32 15
1099 A197 200m Decorative box 50 15
1100 A197 250m Utensils 62 22
1101 A197 500m Butterfly 1.25 45
Nos. 1096-1101 (6) 2.99
Set value 1.00

Natl. Liberation War, 25th Anniv. A198

1989, Sept. 25

1102 A198 30m multicolored 15 15

Meteorological Instruments A199

Designs: 30m, Rain gauge. 60m, Weather system on radar. 125m, Instrument shelter. 200m, Computer monitor and keyboard.

1989, Oct. 12 ***Perf. 11½x11***

1103 A199 30m multicolored 15 15
1104 A199 60m multicolored 15 15
1105 A199 125m multicolored 32 16
1106 A199 200m multicolored 50 25

Souvenir Sheet

World Stamp Expo '89, Washington, DC — A200

1989, Nov. 17 ***Perf. 13½***

1107 A200 500m Washington Monument 1.25 75

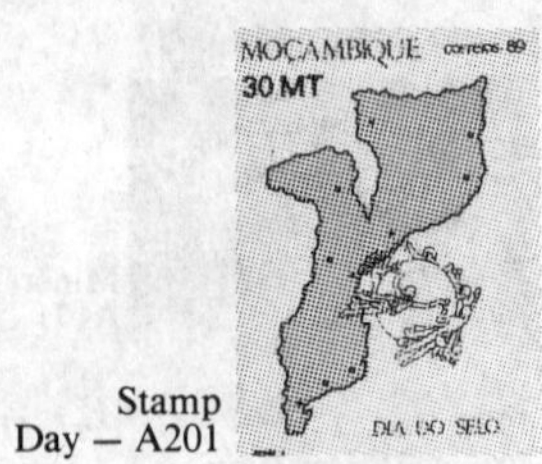

Stamp Day — A201

Maps and emblems.

1989, Dec. 21 **Litho.** ***Perf. 11½x11***

1108 A201 30m UPU emblem 15 15
1109 A201 60m P.O. emblem 16 16
Set value 24 24

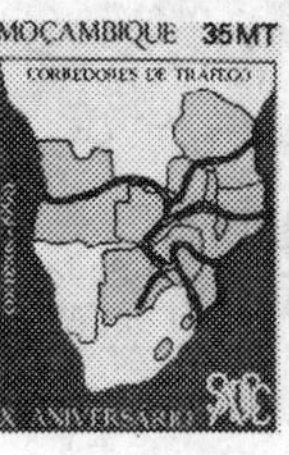

Southern African Development Coordination Conf. (SADCC), 10th Anniv. — A201a

1990, Jan. 31 ***Perf. 11½x11***

1109A A201a 35m multicolored 15 15

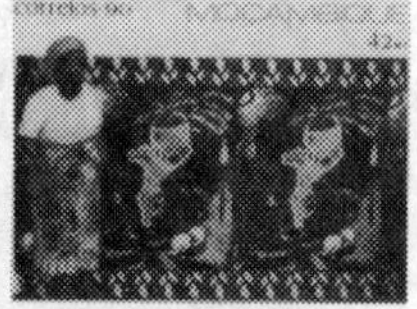
Textile Designs A202

1990, Feb. 28 **Litho.** ***Perf. 11x11½***

1110 A202 42m multi, diff. 15 15
1111 A202 90m multi, diff. 28 16
1112 A202 150m multi, diff. 45 22
1113 A202 200m multi, diff. 60 30
1114 A202 400m multi, diff. 1.20 60
1115 A202 500m multi, diff. 1.50 75
Nos. 1110-1115 (6) 4.18 2.18

Forts A203

1990, Mar. 20 ***Perf. 11x11½***

1116 A203 45m Sena 15 15
1117 A203 90m Santo Antonio 28 16
1118 A203 150m Santo Sebastiao 45 22
1119 A203 200m Santo Caetano 60 30
1120 A203 400m Our Lady of Conceicao 1.20 60
1121 A203 500m Santo Luis 1.50 75
Nos. 1116-1121 (6) 4.18 2.18

The lack of a price for a listed item does not necessarily indicate rarity.

Souvenir Sheet

Penny Black, Mozambique No. 1 — A204

1990, May 3 Litho. *Perf. 11½x11*
1122 A204 1000m red, blk & bl 2.85 1.50

Penny Black, 150th anniversary. Stamp World London '90.

Bank of Mozambique, 15th Anniv. — A205

1990, May 17 Litho. *Perf. 11x11½*
1123 A205 100m multicolored 30 16

Natl. Independence, 15th Anniv. — A206

1990, June 25 *Perf. 11*
1124 A206 42.50m Eduardo Mondlane 15 15
1125 A206 150m Samora Machel 45 22

Endangered Species A207

1990, Aug. 20 Litho. *Perf. 11x11½*
1126 A207 42.50m Ceratotherium simum 15 15
1127 A207 100m Dugong dugon 30 16
1128 A207 150m Loxodonta africana 45 22
1129 A207 200m Acinonix jubatus 60 30
1130 A207 400m Lutra maculicollis 1.20 60
1131 A207 500m Eretmochelys imbricata 1.45 70
Nos. 1126-1131 (6) 4.15 2.13

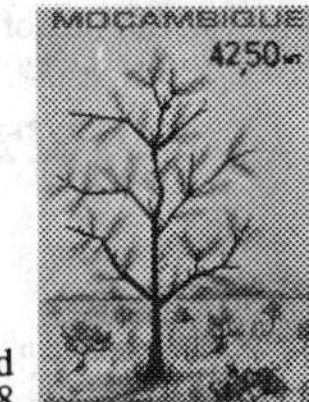

Trees and Plants — A208

1990, Oct. 15 Litho. *Perf. 11½x11*
1132 A208 42.50m Dichrostachys cinerea 15 15
1133 A208 100m Queimadas 30 16
1134 A208 150m Casuariana equisetifolia 45 22
1135 A208 200m Rhizophora muronata 60 30
1136 A208 400m Estrato herbaceo 1.20 60
1137 A208 500m Atzelia cuanzensis 1.45 70
Nos. 1132-1137 (6) 4.15 2.13

Stamp Day — A209

Designs: a, Pick-up at letter box. b, Canceling letters. c, Letter carrier. d, Delivery to recipient.

1990 Litho. *Perf. 11½x11*
1138 Strip of 4 60 40
a.-d. A209 42.50m any single 15 15

Post Office Dept., 10th Anniv. — A210

Design: #1140, Telecommunications Dept.

1991, Jan. 2
1139 A210 50m dk bl, red & blk 20 15
1140 A210 50m grn, blk & brn 20 15
Set value 20

Flowers A211

Alcelaphus Lichtensteini A212

1991, Feb. 25 Litho. *Perf. 11½x11*
1141 A211 50m Strilitzia reginae 20 15
1142 A211 125m Anthurium andraeanum 50 25
1143 A211 250m Zantedeschia pentlandii 1.00 50
1144 A211 300m Canna indica 1.20 60

1991, Mar. 27 *Perf. 14*
1145 Strip of 4 3.60 1.85
a. A212 50m Two adults 20 15
b. A212 100m Adult 40 20
c. A212 250m Adult grazing 1.00 50
d. A212 500m Nursing calf 2.00 1.00

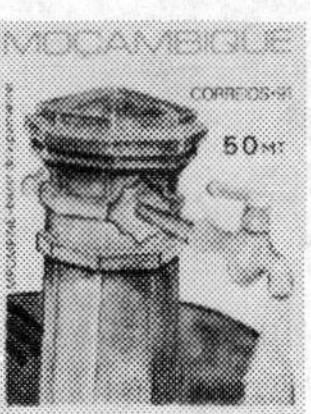

Fountains of Maputo — A213

Fountains: 50m, Mpompine. 125m, Chinhambanine. 250m, Sao Pedro-Zaza. 300m, Xipamanine.

1991 Litho. *Perf. 11½x11*
1146 A213 50m multicolored 15 15
1147 A213 125m multicolored 28 15
1148 A213 250m multicolored 55 28
1149 A213 300m multicolored 65 32
Set value 80

Paintings by Mozambican Artists — A214

1991, May 18 Litho. *Perf. 11½x11*
1150 A214 180m Samale 40 20
1151 A214 250m Malangatana 55 30
1152 A214 560m Malangatana, diff. 1.25 60

1992 Summer Olympics, Barcelona — A215

1991, June 25 Litho. *Perf. 11½x11*
1153 A215 10m Swimming 15 15
1154 A215 50m Roller hockey 15 15
1155 A215 100m Tennis 22 15
1156 A215 200m Table tennis 45 22
1157 A215 500m Running 1.10 55
1158 A215 1000m Badminton 2.20 1.10
Nos. 1153-1158 (6) 4.27 2.32

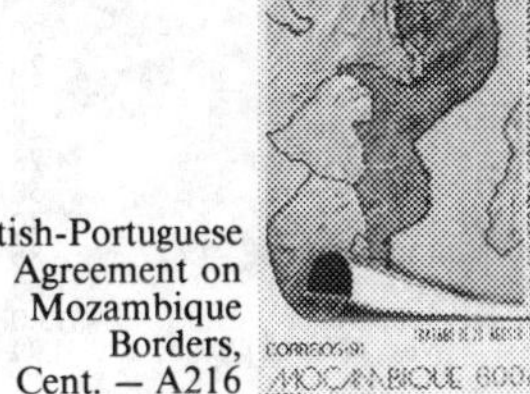

British-Portuguese Agreement on Mozambique Borders, Cent. — A216

1991, Oct. 9 Litho. *Perf. 11½x11*
1159 A216 600m Map of 1890 85 42
1160 A216 800m Map of 1891 1.15 58

SEMI-POSTAL STAMPS

"History" Pointing out to "the Republic" Need for Charity SP1

Nurse Leading Wounded Soldiers SP2

Veteran Relating Experiences SP3

Perf. 11½

1920, Dec. 1 Litho. Unwmk.
B1 SP1 ¼c olive 1.90 1.50
B2 SP1 ½c ol blk 1.90 1.50
B3 SP1 1c dp bis 1.90 1.50
B4 SP1 2c lil brn 1.90 1.50
B5 SP1 3c lilac 1.90 1.50
B6 SP1 4c green 1.90 1.50
B7 SP2 5c grnsh bl 1.90 1.50
B8 SP2 6c lt bl 1.90 1.50
B9 SP2 7½c red brn 1.90 1.50
B10 SP2 8c lemon 1.90 1.50
B11 SP2 10c gray lil 1.90 1.50
B12 SP2 12c pink 1.90 1.50
B13 SP3 18c rose 1.90 1.50
B14 SP3 24c vio brn 1.90 1.50
B15 SP3 30c pale ol grn 1.90 1.50
B16 SP3 40c dl red 1.90 1.50
B17 SP3 50c yellow 1.90 1.50
B18 SP3 1e ultra 1.90 1.50
Nos. B1-B18 (18) 34.20 27.00

Nos. B1-B18 were used Dec. 1, 1920, in place of ordinary stamps. The proceeds were for war victims.

AIR POST STAMPS

Common Design Type
Perf. 13½x13

1938, Aug. Engr. Unwmk.
Name and Value in Black
C1 CD39 10c scarlet 28 22
C2 CD39 20c purple 28 22
C3 CD39 50c orange 28 20
C4 CD39 1e ultra 38 28
C5 CD39 2e lil brn 85 30
C6 CD39 3e dk grn 1.25 38
C7 CD39 5e red brn 2.00 70
C8 CD39 9e rose car 3.75 75
C9 CD39 10e magenta 4.75 1.10
Nos. C1-C9 (9) 13.82 4.15

No. C7 exists with overprint "Exposicao Internacional de Nova York, 1939-1940" and Trylon and Perisphere.

3$00

No. C7 Surcharged in Black

1946, Nov. 2 *Perf. 13½x13*
C10 CD39 3e on 5e red brn 4.50 1.75
a. Inverted surcharge

Plane AP1

1946, Nov. 2 Typo. *Perf. 11½*
Denomination in Black
C11 AP1 1.20e carmine 1.10 85
C12 AP1 1.60e blue 1.40 90
C13 AP1 1.70e plum 3.50 1.40
C14 AP1 2.90e brown 3.50 1.90
C15 AP1 3e green 3.00 1.75
Nos. C11-C15 (5) 12.50 6.80

Inscribed "Taxe perçue" and Denomination in Brown Carmine or Black

1947, May 20

C16 AP1	50c blk (BrC)		60	40
C17 AP1	1e pink		60	40
C18 AP1	3e green		1.50	70
C19 AP1	4.50e yel grn		3.00	1.00
C20 AP1	5e red brn		2.50	1.10
C21 AP1	10e ultra		10.00	3.00
C22 AP1	20e violet		17.00	6.75
C23 AP1	50e orange		35.00	14.00
	Nos. C16-C23 (8)		70.20	27.35

Dangerous counterfeits exist.

Planes Circling Globe — AP2

Oil Refinery, Sonarep — AP3

1949, Mar.

C24 AP2	50c sepia	28	15
C25 AP2	1.20e violet	50	28
C26 AP2	4.50e dl bl	1.25	50
C27 AP2	5e bl grn	1.75	50
C28 AP2	20e chocolate	4.00	85
	Nos. C24-C28 (5)	7.78	2.28

Catalogue values for unused stamps in this section, from this point to the end of the section, are for Never Hinged items.

1963, Mar. 5 **Litho.** ***Perf. 13***

Designs: 2e, Salazar High School, Lourenço Marques. 3.50e, Lourenço Marques harbor. 4.50e, Salazar dam. 5e, Trigo de Morais bridge. 20e, Marcelo Caetano bridge.

C29 AP3	1.50e multi	60	15
C30 AP3	2e multi	30	15
C31 AP3	3.50e multi	60	15
C32 AP3	4.50e multi	38	20
C33 AP3	5e multi	38	20
C34 AP3	20e multi	1.10	50
	Nos. C29-C34 (6)	3.36	1.35

Republic

Nos. C31-C34 Overprinted in Red

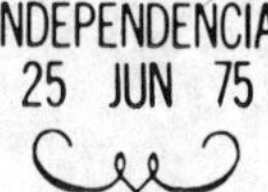

1975, June 25 **Litho.** ***Perf. 13***

C35 AP3	3.50e multi	20	18
C36 AP3	4.50e multi	35	18
C37 AP3	5e multi	85	20
C38 AP3	20e multi	1.75	40

DeHavilland Dragonfly, 1937 — AP4

1981, May 14 **Litho.** ***Perf. 11***

C39 AP4	50c shown	15	15
C40 AP4	1.50m Junker JU-52-3M, 1938	15	15
C41 AP4	3m Lockheed Lodestar L-18-08, 1940	14	15
C42 AP4	7.50m DeHavilland Dove DH-104, 1948	30	15
C43 AP4	10m Douglas Dakota DC-3, 1956	40	18
C44 AP4	12.5m Fokker Friendship F-27, 1962	50	35
	Nos. C39-C44 (6)	1.64	
	Set value		92

Piper Navajo Over Hydroelectric Dam — AP5

1987, Oct. 28 **Litho.** ***Perf. 11***

C45 AP5	20m shown	15	15
C46 AP5	40m De Havilland Hornet trainer, 1936	16	15
C47 AP5	80m Boeing 737, Maputo Airport, 1973	30	20
C48 AP5	120m Beechcraft King-Air	48	25
C49 AP5	160m Piper Aztec	60	30
C50 AP5	320m Douglas DC-10, 1982	1.25	40
	Nos. C45-C50 (6)	2.94	1.45

POSTAGE DUE STAMPS

D1

1904 **Unwmk.** **Typo.** ***Perf. 11½x12***
Name and Value in Black

J1 D1	5r yel grn	28	20
J2 D1	10r slate	28	20
J3 D1	20r yel brn	28	20
J4 D1	30r orange	50	40
J5 D1	50r gray brn	70	40
J6 D1	60r red brn	2.50	1.25
J7 D1	100r red lil	2.50	1.25
J8 D1	130r dl bl	1.00	85
J9 D1	200r carmine	1.75	1.00
J10 D1	500r violet	1.75	1.00
	Nos. J1-J10 (10)	11.54	6.75

Same Overprinted in Carmine or Green

1911

J11 D1	5r yel grn	20	20
J12 D1	10r slate	20	20
J13 D1	20r yel brn	28	20
J14 D1	30r orange	28	20
J15 D1	50r gray brn	28	20
J16 D1	60r red brn	50	35
J17 D1	100r red lil	40	35
J18 D1	130r dl bl	85	60
J19 D1	200r car (G)	1.00	85
J20 D1	500r violet	1.00	85
	Nos. J11-J20 (10)	4.99	4.00

Nos. J1-J10 Overprinted Locally in Carmine

1916

J21 D1	5r yel grn	2.50	2.00
J22 D1	10r slate	3.50	1.25
J23 D1	20r yel brn	57.50	35.00
J24 D1	30r orange	10.00	7.50
J25 D1	50r gray brn	45.00	35.00
J26 D1	60r red brn	40.00	27.50
J27 D1	100r red lil	57.50	40.00
J28 D1	130r dl bl	1.75	1.40
J29 D1	200r carmine	1.75	1.90
J30 D1	500r violet	3.50	3.00
	Nos. J21-J30 (10)	223.00	154.55

War Tax Stamps of 1916 Overprinted Diagonally

PORTEADO

1918 ***Rouletted 7***

J31 WT1	1c gray grn	85	70
J32 WT2	5c rose	85	70
a.	Inverted overprint	6.50	5.00

Perf. 11

J33 WT1	1c gray grn	85	70
a.	"PEPUBLICA"	3.75	2.75

Type of 1904 Issue With Value in Centavos

1917 ***Perf. 12***

J34 D1	½c yel grn	15	15
J35 D1	1c slate	15	15
J36 D1	2c org brn	15	15
J37 D1	3c orange	15	15
J38 D1	5c gray brn	15	15
J39 D1	6c pale brn	15	15
J40 D1	10c red vio	15	15
J41 D1	13c dp bl	15	15
J42 D1	20c rose	15	15
J43 D1	50c gray	18	18
	Set value	90	90

Lourenco Marques Nos. 117, 119 Surcharged in Red

10 C.
PORTEADO

1921

J44 A4	5c on ½c blk	1.00	70
J45 A4	10c on 1½c brn	1.00	70

Same Surcharge on Mozambique Nos. 151, 155, 157 in Red or Green

J46 A6	6c on 1c bl grn (R)	85	70
J47 A6	20c on 2½c vio (R)	85	70
J48 A6	50c on 4c rose (G)	85	70
	Nos. J44-J48 (5)	4.55	3.50

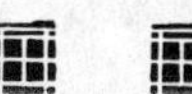

Regular Issues of 1921-22 Surcharged in Black or Red

Porteado
50 C.

1924 ***Perf. 12x11½***

J49 A6	20c on 30c ol grn (Bk)	55	40
a.	Perf. 15x14	17.50	4.00
J50 A6	50c on 60c dk bl (R)	85	55

Catalogue values for unused stamps in this section, from this point to the end of the section, are for Never Hinged items.

Common Design Type
Photo. and Typo.
1952 **Unwmk.** ***Perf. 14***
Numeral in Red Orange or Red; Frame Multicolored

J51 CD45	10c car (RO)	15	15
J52 CD45	30c blk brn	15	15
J53 CD45	50c black	15	15
J54 CD45	1e vio bl	15	15
J55 CD45	2e ol grn	20	15
J56 CD45	5e org brn	50	28
	Set value	1.00	72

WAR TAX STAMPS

Coats of Arms of Portugal and Mozambique on Columns, Allegorical Figures of History of Portugal and the Republic Holding Scroll with Date of Declaration of War — WT1

Prow of Galley of Discoveries. Left, "Republic" Teaching History of Portugal; Right "History" with Laurels (Victory) and Sword (Symbolical of Declaration of War) WT2

1916 **Unwmk.** **Litho.** ***Rouletted 7***

MR1 WT1	1c gray grn	2.00	48
a.	Imperf., pair		
MR2 WT2	5c rose	2.00	48
a.	Imperf., pair		

1918 ***Perf. 11, 12***

MR3 WT1	1c gray grn	50	48
a.	"PEPUBLICA"	3.75	3.50
MR4 WT2	5c red	70	60
a.	"PETRIA"	1.75	1.75
b.	"PEPUBLICA"	2.00	1.75
c.	"1910" for "1916"	3.75	2.75
d.	Imperf., pair		

See Nos. 221-225, 229, 235, J31-J33.

NEWSPAPER STAMPS

No. 19 Surcharged in Black, Red or Blue:

JORNAES JORNAES

2 ½ REIS 2½ 2½
a b

Perf. 11½, 12½, 13½
1893 **Unwmk.**

P1	A2 (a)	2½r on 40r	165.00	60.00
P2	A2 (a)	5r on 40r	110.00	60.00
P3	A2 (a)	5r on 40r (R)	100.00	47.50
P4	A2 (a)	5r on 40r (Bl)	140.00	57.50
P5	A2 (b)	2½r on 40r	24.00	17.50

Nos. P1-P5 exist with double surcharge, Nos. P2-P4 with inverted surcharge.

N3

1893 **Typo.** ***Perf. 11½, 13½***

P6 N3	2½r brown	35	28

No. P6 has been reprinted on chalk-surfaced paper with clean-cut perforation 13½. Value, 50 cents.

POSTAL TAX STAMPS

Pombal Commemorative Issue
Common Design Types

1925 **Engr.** ***Perf. 12½***

RA1 CD28	15c brn & blk	30	24
RA2 CD29	15c brn & blk	30	24
RA3 CD30	15c brn & blk	30	24

Seal of Local Red Cross Society
PT7 PT8

Surcharged in Various Colors

1925 Typo. *Perf. 11½*
RA4 PT7 50c sl & yel (Bk) 1.40 1.40

1926
RA5 PT8 40c sl & yel (Bk) 1.90 1.90
RA6 PT8 50c sl & yel (R) 1.90 1.90
RA7 PT8 60c sl & yel (V) 1.90 1.90
RA8 PT8 80c sl & yel (Br) 1.90 1.90
RA9 PT8 1e sl & yel (Bl) 1.90 1.90
RA10 PT8 2e sl & yel (G) 1.90 1.90
Nos. RA5-RA10 (6) 11.40 11.40

Obligatory on mail certain days of the year. The tax benefited the Cross of the Orient Society.

Type of 1926 Issue

1927
Black Surcharge
RA11 PT8 5c red & yel 1.75 1.75
RA12 PT8 10c grn & yel 1.75 1.75
RA13 PT8 20c gray & yel 1.75 1.75
RA14 PT8 30c lt bl & yel 1.75 1.75
RA15 PT8 40c vio & yel 1.75 1.75
RA16 PT8 50c car & yel 1.75 1.75
RA17 PT8 60c brn & yel 1.75 1.75
RA18 PT8 80c bl & yel 1.75 1.75
RA19 PT8 1e ol & yel 1.75 1.75
RA20 PT8 2e yel brn & yel 1.75 1.75
Nos. RA11-RA20 (10) 17.50 17.50

See note after No. RA10.

PT9

1928 Litho.
RA21 PT9 5c grn, yel & blk 2.50 2.50
RA22 PT9 10c sl bl, yel & blk 2.50 2.50
RA23 PT9 20c gray blk, yel & blk 2.50 2.50
RA24 PT9 30c brn rose, yel & blk 2.50 2.50
RA25 PT9 40c cl brn, yel & blk 2.50 2.50
RA26 PT9 50c red org, yel & blk 2.50 2.50
RA27 PT9 60c brn, yel & blk 2.50 2.50
RA28 PT9 80c dk brn, yel & blk 2.50 2.50
RA29 PT9 1e gray, yel & blk 2.50 2.50
RA30 PT9 2e red, yel & blk 2.50 2.50
Nos. RA21-RA30 (10) 25.00 25.00

See note after RA10.

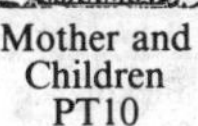

Mother and Children
PT10

Mousinho de Albuquerque
PT11

1929 Photo. *Perf. 14*
RA31 PT10 40c ultra, cl & blk 1.75 1.75

The use of this stamp was compulsory on all correspondence to Portugal and Portuguese Colonies for eight days beginning July 24th, 1929.

1930-31 *Perf. 14½x14*
Inscribed: "MACONTENE"
RA32 PT11 50c lake, red & gray 6.00 6.00
Inscribed: "COOLELA"
RA33 PT11 50c red vio, red brn & gray 6.00 6.00
Inscribed: "MUJENGA"
RA34 PT11 50c org red, red & gray 6.00 6.00
Inscribed: "CHAIMITE"
RA35 PT11 50c dp grn, bl grn & gray 6.00 6.00
Inscribed: "IBRAHIMO"
RA36 PT11 50c dk bl, blk & gray 6.00 6.00
Inscribed: "MUCUTO-MUNO"
RA37 PT11 50c ultra, blk & gray 6.00 6.00
Inscribed: "NAGUEMA"
RA38 PT11 50c dk vio, lt vio & gray 6.00 6.00
Nos. RA32-RA38 (7) 42.00 42.00

The portrait is that of Mousinho de Albuquerque, the celebrated Portuguese warrior, and the names of seven battles in which he took part appear at the foot of the stamps. The stamps were issued for the memorial fund bearing his name and their use was obligatory on all correspondence posted on eight specific days in the year.

Type of 1929 Issue
Denominations in Black

1931 *Perf. 14*
RA39 PT10 40c rose & vio 2.75 2.75

1932
RA40 PT10 40c ol grn & vio 2.75 2.75

1933
RA41 PT10 40c bis brn & rose 2.75 2.75

Without Denomination

1934
RA42 PT10 bl grn & rose 2.75 2.75

Denominations in Black

1936-40
RA43 PT10 40c org & ultra 2.75 2.75
RA44 PT10 40c choc & ultra ('37) 2.75 2.75
RA45 PT10 40c grn & brn car ('38) 4.00 4.00
RA46 PT10 40c yel & blk ('39) 4.00 4.00
RA47 PT10 40c gray brn ('40) 4.00 4.00

Allegory of Charity
PT12

White Pelican
PT13

1942 Unwmk. Litho. *Perf. 11½*
Denomination in Black
RA48 PT12 50c rose car 6.75 1.40

1943-51 *Perf. 11½, 14*
Denomination in Black
RA49 PT13 50c rose car 10.00 30
RA50 PT13 50c emerald 6.75 30
RA51 PT13 50c purple 8.00 30
RA52 PT13 50c blue 6.75 30
RA53 PT13 50c red brn 10.00 30
RA54 PT13 50c ol bis 6.75 30
Nos. RA49-RA54 (6) 48.25 1.80

There are two sizes of the numeral on No. RA49.

Catalogue values for unused stamps in this section, from this point to the end of the section, are for Never Hinged items.

Inscribed: "Provincia de Mocambique"

1954-56 *Perf. 14½x14*
RA55 PT13 50c orange 1.40 28
RA56 PT13 50c ol grn ('56) 1.40 28
RA57 PT13 50c brn ('56) 1.40 28

No. RA57 Surcharged with New Value and Wavy Lines

1956
RA58 PT13 30c on 50c brown 70 35

Pelican Type of 1954-56

1958 Litho. *Perf. 14*
Denomination in Black
RA59 PT13 30c yellow 70 35
RA60 PT13 50c salmon 70 35

Imprint: "Imprensa Nacional de Mocambique"

1963-64
Denomination Typographed in Black
RA61 PT13 30c yellow ('64) 48 20
RA62 PT13 50c salmon 35 20

Women and Children
PT14

Lineman on Pole and Map of Mozambique
PT15

1963-65 Litho. *Perf. 14*
RA63 PT14 50c blk, bis & red 28 15
RA64 PT14 50c blk, pink & red ('65) 28 15

See Nos. RA68-RA76.

1965, Apr. 1 Unwmk. *Perf. 14*

Design: 30c, Telegraph poles and map of Mozambique.

Size: 23x30mm
RA65 PT15 30c blk, sal & lil 15 15
Size: 19x36mm
RA66 PT15 50c blk, bl & sep 18 15
RA67 PT15 1e blk, yel & org 18 15
Set value 42 24

The tax was for improvement of the telecommunications system. Obligatory on inland mail. A 2.50e in the design of the 30c was issued for use on telegrams.

Type of 1963

1967, June 29 Litho. *Perf. 14*
RA68 PT14 50c blk, lt yel grn & red 28 18

1969
RA69 PT14 50c blk, lt bl & red 40 18

1970
RA70 PT14 50c blk, buff & brt red 40 18

1972-73
RA71 PT14 30c blk, lt grn & red 15 15
RA72 PT14 50c blk, gray & red ('73) 1.00 18
RA73 PT14 1e blk, bis & red ('73) 18 15
Set value 30

1974-75
RA74 PT14 50c bl, yel & red 15 15
RA75 PT14 1e blk, gray & ver 70 15
RA76 PT14 1e blk, lil rose & red ('75) 28 15
Set value 35

POSTAL TAX DUE STAMPS

Pombal Commemorative Issue
Common Design Types

1925 Unwmk. *Perf. 12½*
RAJ1 CD31 30c brn & blk 50 60
RAJ2 CD32 30c brn & blk 50 60
RAJ3 CD33 30c brn & blk 50 60

MOZAMBIQUE COMPANY

LOCATION — Comprises the territory of Manica and Sofala of the Mozambique Colony in southeastern Africa
GOVT. — A part of the Portuguese Colony of Mozambique
AREA — 51,881 sq. mi.
POP. — 368,447 (1939)
CAPITAL — Beira

The Mozambique Company was chartered by Portugal in 1891 for 50 years. The territory was under direct administration of the Company until July 18, 1941

1000 Reis = 1 Milreis
100 Centavos = 1 Escudo (1916)

Mozambique Nos. 15-23 Overprinted in Carmine or Black

COMP.ª DE
MOÇAMBIQUE

1892 Unwmk. *Perf. 12½, 13½*
1 A2 5r blk (C) 70 24
a. Pair, one without overprint 12.50 12.50
2 A2 10r green 70 24
3 A2 20r rose 70 24
a. Perf. 13½ 25.00 19.00
4 A2 25r violet 85 35
a. Double overprint 12.50
5 A2 40r chocolate 70 30
a. Double overprint 7.50
6 A2 50r blue 75 24
7 A2 100r yel brown 75 35
8 A2 200r gray violet 1.00 45
9 A2 300r orange 1.00 70
Nos. 1-9 (9) 7.15 3.11

Nos. 1 to 6, 8-9 were reprinted in 1905. These reprints have white gum and clean-cut perf. 13½ and the colors are usually paler than those of the originals.

Company Coat of Arms — A2

Perf. 11½, 12½, 13½
1895-1907 Typo.
Black or Red Numerals
10 A2 2½r olive yel 18 18
11 A2 2½r gray ('07) 60 35
12 A2 5r orange 18 18
a. Value omitted 3.00
b. Perf. 13½ 1.40 70
13 A2 10r red lilac 30 30
14 A2 10r yel grn ('07) 85 40
a. Value inverted at top of stamp 7.50 4.00
15 A2 15r red brn 50 28
16 A2 15r dk grn ('07) 75 40
17 A2 20r gray lilac 70 28
18 A2 25r green 50 28
a. Perf. 13½ 1.75 1.00
19 A2 25r car ('07) 1.00 60
a. Value omitted 6.00 6.00
20 A2 50r blue 70 28
21 A2 50r brown ('07) 1.00 60
a. Value omitted 6.00
22 A2 65r slate bl ('02) 40 35
23 A2 75r rose 38 28
24 A2 75r red lilac ('07) 1.40 1.00
25 A2 80r yel grn 35 28
26 A2 100r brown, *buff* 40 30
27 A2 100r dk bl, *bl* ('07) 1.40 1.00
28 A2 115r car, *pink* ('04) 1.00 70
29 A2 115r org brn, *pink* ('07) 2.00 1.40
30 A2 130r grn, *pink* ('04) 1.00 70
31 A2 130r brn, *yel* ('07) 2.00 1.40
32 A2 150r org brn, *pink* 35 35
33 A2 200r dk bl, *bl* 35 35
a. Perf. 13½ 1.75 1.25
34 A2 200r red lil, *pink* ('07) 2.00 1.40
35 A2 300r dk bl, *salmon* 48 30
a. Perf. 13½ 2.50 1.40
36 A2 400r brn, *bl* ('04) 1.00 70
37 A2 400r dl bl, *yel* ('07) 2.50 1.90
38 A2 500r blk & red 55 40
39 A2 500r blk & red, *bl* ('07) 2.50 1.90
a. 500r pur & red, *yel* (error)

No.	Type	Description	Unused	Used
40	A2	700r sl, *buff* ('04)	3.50	2.00
41	A2	700r pur, *yel* ('07)	2.50	2.00
42	A2	1000r vio & red	85	40
		Nos. 10-42 (33)	34.17	23.24

Nos. 12b, 18a, 33a and 35a were issued without gum.

Nos. 25 and 6 Surcharged or Overprinted in Red:

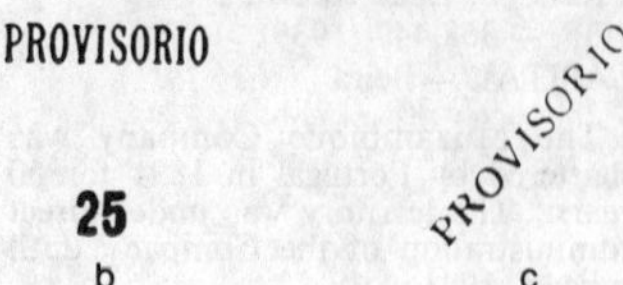
PROVISORIO
25
b
PROVISORIO
c

1895 *Perf. 12½, 13½*

No.	Type	Description	Unused	Used
43	A2(b)	25r on 80r yel grn	12.00	10.00
44	A2(c)	50r blue	2.75	2.00

Overprint "c" on No. 44 also exists reading from upper left to lower right.

Stamps of 1895 Overprinted in Bister, Orange, Violet, Green, Black or Brown

1498
Centenario da India
1898

1898 *Perf. 12½, 13½*

Without Gum

No.	Type	Description	Unused	Used
45	A2	2½r ol yel (Bi)	95	70
a.		Double overprint	7.00	7.00
b.		Red overprint	8.00	8.00
46	A2	5r orange (O)	1.10	85
47	A2	10r red lil (V)	1.10	85
48	A2	15r red brn (V)	2.25	1.25
a.		Red overprint		
49	A2	20r gray lil (V)	1.65	1.25
50	A2	25r green (G)	2.75	1.40
a.		Inverted overprint	15.00	8.00
51	A2	50r blue (Bk)	1.90	1.40
a.		Inverted overprint	15.00	15.00
52	A2	75r rose (V)	2.75	2.25
a.		Inverted overprint	17.50	17.50
b.		Red overprint		
53	A2	80r yel grn (G)	3.00	1.90
a.		Inverted overprint		
54	A2	100r brn, *buff* (Br)	3.25	2.50
55	A2	150r org brn, *pink* (O)	3.25	2.50
a.		Inverted overprint	8.50	8.50
b.		Double overprint		
56	A2	200r dk bl, *bl* (Bk)	4.50	3.00
57	A2	300r dk bl, *sal* (Bk)	5.25	4.00
a.		Inverted overprint	15.00	15.00
b.		Green overprint		
		Nos. 45-57 (13)	33.70	23.85

Vasco da Gama's discovery of route to India, 400th anniversary.

No. 57b was prepared but not issued.

Nos. 45 and 49 were also issued with gum.

The "Centenario" overprint on stamps perf. 11½ is forged.

Surcharged in Black, Carmine or Violet

25

PROVISORIO

e

25
Réis
f

50
RÉIS
g

1899 *Perf. 12½*

No.	Type	Description	Unused	Used
59	A2(e)	25r on 75r rose (Bk)	2.00	1.40

1900 *Perf. 12½, 12½x11½*

No.	Type	Description	Unused	Used
60	A2(f)	25r on 5r org (C)	1.40	1.00
61	A2(g)	50r on half of 20r gray lil (V)	85	70
b.		Entire stamp	4.00	4.00

No. 61b is perf. 11½ vertically through center.

Stamps of 1895-1907 Overprinted Locally in Carmine or Green

REPUBLICA

1911 *Perf. 11½, 13½*

No.	Type	Description	Unused	Used
61A	A2	2½r gray (C)	60	40
62	A2	5r orange (G)	90	60
63	A2	10r yel grn (C)	70	50
64	A2	15r dk grn (C)	70	50
a.		Double overprint	6.00	4.00
65	A2	20r gray lil (G)	85	50
a.		Perf. 13½	85	60
66	A2	25r carmine (G)	85	60
67	A2	50r brown (G)	70	45
68	A2	75r red lil (G)	85	45
69	A2	100r dk bl, *bl* (C)	90	50
70	A2	115r org brn, *pink* (G)	1.00	60
71	A2	130r brn, *yel* (G)	1.40	60
72	A2	200r red lil, *pink* (G)	1.40	60
73	A2	400r dl bl, *yel* (C)	1.40	60
74	A2	500r blk & red, *bl* (C)	1.50	95
75	A2	700r pur, *yel* (G)	1.50	95
		Nos. 61A-75 (15)	15.25	8.80

Nos. 63, 67 and 71 exist with inverted overprint; Nos. 63, 72 and 75 with double overprint.

Overprinted in Lisbon in Carmine or Green

1911 *Perf. 11½, 12½*

No.	Type	Description	Unused	Used
75B	A2	2½r gray	28	18
76	A2	5r orange	28	15
77	A2	10r yel grn	24	15
78	A2	15r dk grn	35	15
79	A2	20r gray lilac	28	15
80	A2	25r car (G)	35	15
a.		Value inverted at top of stamp	7.50	
81	A2	50r brown	35	15
82	A2	75r red lil	35	15
a.		Value omitted	6.00	
83	A2	100r dk bl, *bl*	60	20
84	A2	115r org brn, *pink*	85	30
85	A2	130r brn, *yel*	90	35
a.		Double overprint	7.50	
86	A2	200r red lil, *pink*	50	24
87	A2	400r dl bl, *yel*	70	28
88	A2	500r blk & red, *bl*	70	28
89	A2	700r pur, *yel*	85	48
		Nos. 75B-89 (15)	7.58	3.36

Nos. 75B-89 Surcharged ¼ C

1916 *Perf. 11½*

No.	Type	Description	Unused	Used
90	A2	¼c on 2½r gray	18	18
91	A2	½c on 5r org	18	18
a.		"½c" double	6.00	
92	A2	1c on 10r yel grn	40	18
93	A2	1½c on 15r dk grn	40	18
a.		Imperf., pair	4.00	
94	A2	2c on 20r gray lil	50	18
95	A2	2½c on 25r car	70	18
96	A2	5c on 50r brn	40	20
a.		Imperf., pair	4.00	
97	A2	7½c on 75r red lil	50	20
98	A2	10c on 100r dk bl, *bl*	65	30
a.		Inverted surcharge	6.75	6.75
99	A2	11½c on 115r org brn, *pink*	1.50	35
a.		Inverted surcharge	15.00	15.00
100	A2	13c on 130r brn, *yel*	2.00	30
101	A2	20c on 200r red lil, *pink*	1.50	30
102	A2	40c on 400r dl bl, *yel*	2.00	35
103	A2	50c on 500r blk & red, *bl* (R)	2.25	70
104	A2	70c on 700r pur, *yel*	2.50	75
		Nos. 90-104 (15)	15.66	4.53

Nos. 87 to 89 Surcharged

½
Cent.

1918 *Perf. 11½*

No.	Type	Description	Unused	Used
105	A2	½c on 700r pur, *yel*	1.00	95
106	A2	2½c on 500r blk & red, *bl* (Bl)	1.00	95
107	A2	5c on 400r dl bl, *yel*	1.00	95

Native and Village — A9

Man and Ivory Tusks — A10

Corn — A11

Tapping Rubber Tree — A12

Sugar Refinery — A13

Buzi River Scene — A14

Tobacco Field — A15

View of Beira — A16

Coffee Plantation A17

Orange Tree A18

Cotton Field A19

Sisal Plantation A20

Scene on Beira R. R. — A21

Court House at Beira — A22

Coconut Palm A23

Mangroves A24

Cattle — A25

Company Arms — A26

1918-31 **Engr.** *Perf. 14, 15, 12½*

No.	Type	Description	Unused	Used
108	A9	¼c brn & yel grn	15	15
109	A9	¼c ol grn & blk ('25)	15	15
110	A10	½c black	15	15
111	A11	1c grn & blk	15	15
112	A12	1½c blk & grn	15	15
113	A13	2c car & blk	15	15
114	A13	2c ol blk & blk ('25)	15	15
115	A14	2½c lil & blk	15	15
116	A11	3c ocher & blk ('23)	20	15
117	A15	4c grn & brn ('21)	20	15
118	A15	4c red & blk ('25)	18	15
119	A9	4½c gray & blk ('23)	20	18
120	A16	5c bl & blk	18	18
121	A17	6c cl & bl ('21)	45	28
122	A17	6c lil & blk ('25)	18	15
123	A21	7c ultra & blk ('23)	70	45
124	A18	7½c org & grn	40	24
125	A19	8c vio & blk	20	18
126	A20	10c red org & blk	20	15
128	A19	12c brn & blk ('23)	70	35
129	A19	12c bl grn & blk ('25)	40	24
130	A21	15c car & blk	40	28
131	A22	20c dp grn & blk	35	20
132	A23	30c red brn & blk	1.75	70
133	A23	30c gray grn & blk ('25)	85	20
134	A23	30c bl grn & blk ('31)	1.75	28
135	A24	40c yel grn & blk	85	45
136	A24	40c grnsh bl & blk ('25)	70	28
137	A25	50c org & blk	1.25	75
138	A25	50c lt vio & blk ('25)	1.25	35
139	A25	60c rose & brn ('23)	85	48
140	A20	80c ultra & brn ('23)	1.25	70
141	A20	80c car & blk ('25)	70	35
142	A26	1e dk grn & blk	1.25	45
143	A26	1e bl & blk ('25)	1.00	35
144	A16	2e rose & vio ('23)	1.90	70
145	A16	2e lil & blk ('25)	1.40	35
		Nos. 108-145 (37)	22.89	10.92

Shades exist of several denominations.

Nos. 132, 142, 115, 120, 131, 135, 125, 137 Surcharged with New Values in Red, Blue, Violet or Black:

Um e·meio
Centavo
h

4 Cent.
i

Seis
Centavos
j

1920 *Perf. 14, 15*

No.	Type	Description	Unused	Used
146	A23(h)	½c on 30c (Bk)	3.50	3.00
147	A26(h)	½c on 1e (R)	3.50	3.00
148	A14(h)	1½c on 2½c (Bl)	1.50	1.25
149	A16(h)	1½c on 5c (V)	2.50	2.00
150	A14(h)	2c on 2½c (R)	1.50	1.10
151	A22(i)	4c on 20c (V)	3.50	3.00
152	A24(i)	4c on 40c (V)	3.50	3.00
153	A19(j)	6c on 8c (R)	3.50	3.00
154	A25(j)	6c on 50c (Bk)	3.50	3.00
		Nos. 146-154 (9)	26.50	22.35

The surcharge on No. 148 is placed vertically between two bars. On No. 154 the two words of the surcharge are 13mm apart.

Native — A27

View of Beira — A28

Tapping Rubber Tree — A29

Picking Tea — A30

Zambezi River — A31

1925-31 Engr. *Perf. 12*

No.	Type	Description	Unused	Used
155	A27	24c ultra & blk	1.25	75
156	A28	25c choc & ultra	1.25	75
157	A27	85c brn red & blk ('31)	85	45
158	A28	1.40e dl bl & blk ('31)	85	45
159	A29	5e yel brn & ultra	1.25	30
160	A30	10e rose & blk	1.75	75
161	A31	20e grn & blk	2.00	75
		Nos. 155-161 (7)	9.20	4.20

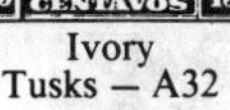
Ivory Tusks — A32

Panning Gold — A33

1931 Litho. *Perf. 14*

No.	Type	Description	Unused	Used
162	A32	45c lt bl	2.00	85
163	A33	70c yel brn	1.40	35

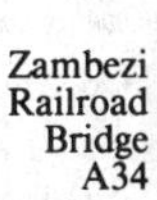

Zambezi Railroad Bridge A34

1935 Engr. *Perf. 12½*

No.	Type	Description	Unused	Used
164	A34	1e dk bl & blk	2.00	1.40

Issued to commemorate the opening of a new bridge over the Zambezi River.

Airplane over Beira — A35

1935

No.	Type	Description	Unused	Used
165	A35	5c bl & blk	45	35
166	A35	10c red org & blk	45	35
a.		Square pair, imperf. between	22.50	
167	A35	15c red & blk	45	35
a.		Square pair imperf. between	22.50	
168	A35	20c yel grn & blk	45	35
169	A35	30c grn & blk	45	35
170	A35	40c gray bl & blk	45	35
171	A35	45c bl & blk	45	35
172	A35	50c vio & blk	45	35
a.		Square pair imperf. between	30.00	
173	A35	60c car & brn	60	35
174	A35	80c car & blk	60	35
		Nos. 165-174 (10)	4.80	3.50

Issued to commemorate the opening of the Blantyre-Beira Salisbury air service.

Giraffe — A36

Thatched Huts — A37

Rock Python A41

Coconut Palms A50

Zambezi Railroad Bridge A52

Sena Gate — A53

Company Arms — A54

Designs: 10c, Dhow. 15c, St. Caetano Fortress, Sofala. 20c, Zebra. 40c, Black rhinoceros. 45c, Lion. 50c, Crocodile. 60c, Leopard. 70c, Mozambique woman. 80c, Hippopotami. 85c, Vasco da Gama's flagship. 1e, Man in canoe. 2e, Greater kudu.

1937, May 16 *Perf. 12½*

No.	Type	Description	Unused	Used
175	A36	1c yel grn & vio	15	*20*
176	A37	5c bl & yel grn	15	*15*
177	A36	10c ver & ultra	15	*15*
178	A37	15c car & blk	15	*15*
179	A36	20c grn & ultra	15	*15*
180	A41	30c dk grn & ind	15	*28*
181	A41	40c gray bl & blk	15	*28*
182	A41	45c bl & brn	15	*28*
183	A41	50c dk vio & emer	15	*28*
184	A37	60c car & bl	15	*15*
185	A36	70c yel brn & pale grn	15	*15*
186	A37	80c car & pale grn	24	*30*
187	A41	85c org red & blk	24	40
188	A41	1e dp bl & blk	20	15
189	A50	1.40e dk bl & pale grn	18	15
190	A41	2e pale lil & brn	40	15
191	A52	5e yel brn & bl	50	*70*
192	A53	10e car & blk	1.25	*1.40*
193	A54	20e grn & brn vio	1.75	*2.75*
		Set value	5.65	

Stamps of 1937 Overprinted in Red or Black

28-VII-1939
Visita Presidencial

1939, Aug. 28

No.	Type	Description	Unused	Used
194	A41	30c dk grn & ind (R)	85	70
195	A41	40c gray bl & blk (R)	85	70
196	A41	45c bl & brn (Bk)	85	70
197	A41	50c dk vio & emer (R)	85	70
198	A41	85c org red & blk (Bk)	85	70
199	A41	1e dp bl & blk (R)	1.25	1.00
200	A41	2e pale lil & brn (Bk)	1.25	1.40
		Nos. 194-200 (7)	6.75	5.90

Visit of the President of Portugal to Beira in 1939.

King Alfonso Henriques A55

King John IV A56

1940, Feb. 16 Typo. *Perf. 11½x12*

No.	Type	Description	Unused	Used
201	A55	1.75e bl & lt bl	70	55

800th anniv. of Portuguese independence.

1941 Engr. *Perf. 12½*

No.	Type	Description	Unused	Used
202	A56	40c gray grn & blk	30	20
203	A56	50c dk vio & brt grn	30	20
204	A56	60c brt car & dp bl	30	20
205	A56	70c brn org & dk grn	30	20
206	A56	80c car & dp grn	30	20
207	A56	1e dk bl & blk	30	20
		Nos. 202-207 (6)	1.80	1.20

300th anniv. of the restoration of the Portuguese Monarchy.

Mozambique Company's charter terminated July 18th, 1941 after which date its stamps were superseded by those of the territory of Mozambique.

SEMI-POSTAL STAMPS

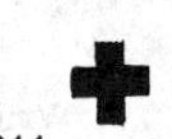

Lisbon Issue of 1911 Overprinted in Red

31.7.17.

1917 Unwmk. *Perf. 11½*

No.	Type	Description	Unused	Used
B1	A2	2½r gray	7.50	*9.00*
a.		Double overprint	30.00	*35.00*
B2	A2	10r yel grn	7.50	*12.50*
B3	A2	20r gray lil	9.00	*15.00*
B4	A2	50r brown	20.00	*20.00*
B5	A2	75r red lil	55.00	*65.00*
B6	A2	100r dk bl, *bl*	55.00	*65.00*
B7	A2	700r pur, *yel*	165.00	*200.00*
		Nos. B1-B7 (7)	319.00	386.50

Nos. B1-B7 were used on July 31, 1917, in place of ordinary stamps. The proceeds were given to the Red Cross.

AIR POST STAMPS

Airplane over Beira — AP1

1935 Unwmk. Engr. *Perf. 12½*

No.	Type	Description	Unused	Used
C1	AP1	5c bl & blk	15	15
C2	AP1	10c org red & blk	15	15
C3	AP1	15c red & blk	15	15
C4	AP1	20c yel grn & blk	15	15
C5	AP1	30c grn & blk	15	15
C6	AP1	40c gray bl & blk	15	15
C7	AP1	45c bl & blk	15	15
C8	AP1	50c dk vio & blk	15	15
C9	AP1	60c car & brn	15	15
C10	AP1	80c car & blk	15	15
C11	AP1	1e bl & blk	15	15
C12	AP1	2e mauve & blk	70	24
C13	AP1	5e bis brn & bl	70	40
C14	AP1	10e car & blk	1.00	60
C15	AP1	20e bl grn & blk	1.90	85
		Set value	5.00	2.75

POSTAGE DUE STAMPS

D1

1906 Unwmk. Typo. *Perf. 11½x12*
Denominations in Black

No.	Type	Description	Unused	Used
J1	D1	5r yel grn	40	18
J2	D1	10r slate	40	18
J3	D1	20r yel brn	40	18
J4	D1	30r orange	50	24
J5	D1	50r gray brn	50	24
J6	D1	60r red brn	12.50	3.50
J7	D1	100r red lil	1.25	70
J8	D1	130r dl bl	15.00	4.00
J9	D1	200r carmine	6.00	1.75
J10	D1	500r violet	7.50	2.00
		Nos. J1-J10 (10)	44.45	12.97

Nos. J1-J10 Overprinted in Carmine or Green

1911

No.	Type	Description	Unused	Used
J11	D1	5r yel grn	15	15
J12	D1	10r slate	15	15
J13	D1	20r yel brn	15	15
J14	D1	30r orange	20	15
J15	D1	50r gray brn	30	20
J16	D1	60r red brn	40	28
J17	D1	100r red lil	40	28
J18	D1	130r dl bl	1.50	1.00
J19	D1	200r car (G)	95	85
J20	D1	500r violet	2.00	1.00
		Nos. J11-J20 (10)	6.20	4.21

D2

Company Arms — D3

1916 Typo.
With Value in Centavos in Black

No.	Type	Description	Unused	Used
J21	D2	½c yel grn	15	15
J22	D2	1c slate	15	15
J23	D2	2c org brn	15	15
J24	D2	3c orange	18	15
J25	D2	5c gray brn	20	15
J26	D2	6c pale brn	18	15
J27	D2	10c red lil	20	18
J28	D2	13c gray bl	40	35
J29	D2	20c rose	50	35
J30	D2	50c gray	70	50
		Nos. J21-J30 (10)	2.81	2.28

Perf. 11½, 13½, 14 to 15½
1919 Engr.

No.	Type	Description	Unused	Used
J31	D3	½c green	15	15
J32	D3	1c slate	15	15
J33	D3	2c red brn	15	15
J34	D3	3c orange	15	15
J35	D3	5c gray brn	20	20
J36	D3	6c lt brn	45	45
J37	D3	10c lil rose	45	45
J38	D3	13c dl bl	45	45
J39	D3	20c rose	45	45
J40	D3	50c gray	45	45
		Nos. J31-J40 (10)	3.05	3.05

NEWSPAPER STAMP

Newspaper Stamp of Mozambique Overprinted Like Nos. 1-9

1894 Unwmk. *Perf. 11½*

No.	Type	Description	Unused	Used
P1	N3	2½r brown	48	40
a.		Inverted overprint	6.00	6.00
b.		Perf. 12½	85	50

Reprints are on stout white paper with clean-cut perf. 13½. Value $1.

POSTAL TAX STAMPS

No. 116 Surcharged in Black

Assistencia
Publica

2 Ctvos. 2

1932 *Perf. 12½*

No.	Type	Description	Unused	Used
RA1	A11	2c on 3c org & blk	1.40	*2.00*

Charity — PT2

1933 **Litho.** ***Perf. 11***

RA2	PT2	2c mag & blk	1.00	*2.00*

PT3 PT4

1940 **Unwmk.** ***Perf. 10½***

RA3	PT3	2c blk & ultra	12.00	*15.00*

1941

RA4	PT4	2c blk & brt red	12.00	*15.00*

NETHERLANDS

(Holland)

LOCATION — Northwestern Europe, bordering on the North Sea
GOVT. — Kingdom
AREA — 13,203 sq. mi.
POP. — 14,394,589 (1984)
CAPITAL — Amsterdam

100 Cents = 1 Gulden
(Guilder or Florin)

Catalogue values for unused stamps in this country are for Never Hinged items, beginning with Scott 216 in the regular postage section, Scott B123 in the semi-postal section, Scott C15 in the airpost section, and Scott J80 in the postage due section.

Values of early Netherlands stamps vary according to condition. Quotations for Nos. 4-12 are for copies with perforations cutting into the design (with original gum if unused).

Watermarks

Wmk. 158

Wmk. 202

King William III
A1 A2

Wmk. 158

1852, Jan. 1 **Engr.** ***Imperf.***

1	A1	5c blue	350.00	17.50
a.		5c light blue	350.00	14.00
b.		5c steel blue	1,500.	47.50
c.		5c dark blue	350.00	20.00
2	A1	10c lake	400.00	12.00
3	A1	15c orange	575.00	65.00

In 1895 the 10c was privately reprinted in several colors on unwatermarked paper by Joh. A. Moesman, whose name appears on the back.

1864 **Unwmk.** ***Perf. 12½x12***

4	A2	5c blue	225.00	10.00
5	A2	10c lake	350.00	4.00
6	A2	15c orange	800.00	65.00
a.		15c yellow	975.00	70.00

The paper varies considerably in thickness. It is sometimes slightly bluish, also vertically ribbed.

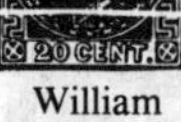

William III — A3 Coat of Arms — A4

Perf. 12½x12, 13, 13½, 14 and Compound

1867

7	A3	5c ultra	57.50	90
8	A3	10c lake	90.00	1.75
9	A3	15c org brn	425.00	22.50
10	A3	20c dk grn	350.00	15.00
11	A3	25c dk vio	1,000.	60.00
12	A3	50c gold	1,500.	110.00

The paper of Nos. 7-22 sometimes has an accidental bluish tinge of varying strength. During its manufacture a chemical whitener (bluing agent) was added in varying quantities. No particular printing was made on bluish paper.

Two varieties of numerals in each value, differing chiefly in the thickness.

Oxidized copies of the 50c are worth much less.

Imperforate varieties of Nos. 7-12 are proofs.

1869 ***Perf. 10½x10***

7c	A3	5c ultra	110.00	6.50
8c	A3	10c lake	160.00	3.25
9c	A3	15c org brn	*2,000.*	375.00
10c	A3	20c dk grn	*850.00*	100.00

1869-71 **Typo.** ***Perf. 13½, 14***

17	A4	½c red brn ('71)	20.00	1.75
c.		Perf. 14	*2,000.*	550.00
18	A4	1c black	160.00	57.50
19	A4	1c green	8.00	90
c.		Perf. 14	20.00	4.50
20	A4	1½c rose	90.00	65.00
b.		Perf. 14	100.00	60.00
21	A4	2c buff	37.50	8.00
c.		Perf. 14	40.00	8.00
22	A4	2½c vio ('71)	375.00	37.50
c.		Perf. 14	575.00	300.00

Imperforate varieties are proofs.

A5 A6

Perf. 12½, 13, 13½, 14, 12½x12 and 11½x12

1872-88

23	A5	5c ultra	9.00	24
a.		5c blue	9.00	24
24	A5	7½c red brn ('88)	24.00	15.00
25	A5	10c rose	42.50	70
26	A5	12½c gray ('75)	35.00	1.10
27	A5	15c brn org	260.00	3.50
28	A5	20c green	300.00	3.50
29	A5	22½c dk grn ('88)	50.00	35.00
30	A5	25c dl vio	375.00	2.75
31	A5	50c bister	425.00	8.00
32	A5	1g gray vio ('88)	375.00	20.00
33	A6	2g50c rose & ultra	550.00	75.00

Imperforate varieties are proofs.

Numeral of Value — A7

HALF CENT:
Type I- Fraction bar 8 to 8½mm long.
Type II- Fraction bar 9mm long and thinner.

1876-94 ***Perf. 12½***

34	A7	½c rose, II	2.75	15
a.		½c rose, I	9.25	16
c.		Laid paper		40.00
d.		Perf. 14, I	1,100.	500.00
35	A7	1c emer grn ('94)	1.65	15
b.		Laid paper	35.00	4.00
c.		1c green	6.50	16
36	A7	2c ol yel ('94)	24.00	1.75
a.		2c yellow	50.00	2.25
37	A7	2½c vio ('94)	11.00	16
b.		2½c dark violet ('94)	14.00	32
c.		2½c lilac	72.50	40

Imperforate varieties are proofs.

Queen Wilhelmina
A8 A9

1891-94 ***Perf. 12½***

40	A8	3c org ('94)	5.25	70
a.		3c org yel ('92)	8.50	70
41	A8	5c lt ultra ('94)	2.75	15
a.		5c dull blue	3.00	15
42	A8	7½c brn ('94)	10.50	3.00
a.		7½c red brn	21.00	3.25
43	A8	10c brt rose ('94)	16.00	50
a.		10c brick red	45.00	2.00
44	A8	12½c bluish gray ('94)	13.00	50
a.		12½c gray	21.00	65
45	A8	15c yel brn ('94)	30.00	2.75
a.		15c org brn	85.00	3.00
46	A8	20c grn ('94)	35.00	1.25
a.		20c yel grn	100.00	2.50
47	A8	22½c dk grn ('94)	27.50	8.00
a.		22½c dp bl grn	35.00	8.00
48	A8	25c dl vio ('94)	55.00	2.00
a.		25c dk vio	60.00	2.50
49	A8	50c yel brn ('94)	300.00	12.00
a.		50c bister	325.00	25.00
50	A8	1g gray vio	375.00	35.00

The paper used in 1891-93 was white, rough and somewhat opaque. In 1894, a thinner, smooth and sometimes transparent paper was introduced.

The 5c orange was privately produced.

1891-96 ***Perf. 11½x11***

51	A9	50c emer & yel brn ('96)	72.50	8.00
a.		Perf. 11	*2,750.*	225.00
52	A9	1g brn & ol grn ('96)	180.00	20.00
a.		Perf. 11	240.00	20.00
53	A9	2g 50c brt rose & ultra	525.00	125.00
a.		2g 50c lil rose & ultra, perf. 11	525.00	130.00
b.		Perf. 11½	575.00	150.00

Perf. 11

54	A9	5g brnz grn & red brn ('96)	400.00	200.00

A10 Wilhelmina — A11

1898-1924 ***Perf. 12½, 11½, 11½x11***

55	A10	½c violet	40	15
56	A10	1c red	85	15
b.		Imperf., pair	*4,000.*	*5,000.*
57	A10	1½c ultra ('08)	2.25	50
58	A10	1½c dp bl ('13)	3.25	15
59	A10	2c yel brn	3.25	15
60	A10	2½c dp grn	3.25	15
b.		Imperf., pair	*8,000.*	
61	A11	3c orange	9.00	3.00
62	A11	3c pale ol grn ('01)	90	15
63	A11	4c cl ('21)	1.10	80
64	A11	4½c vio ('19)	3.25	3.00
65	A11	5c car rose	1.25	15
66	A11	7½c brown	50	15
a.		Tete beche pair ('24)	60.00	70.00
67	A11	10c gray lil	5.50	15
68	A11	12½c blue	3.25	15
69	A11	15c yel brn	70.00	2.25
70	A11	15c bl & car ('08)	3.75	15
71	A11	17½c vio ('06)	40.00	9.00
73	A11	17½c ultra & brn ('10)	14.00	45
74	A11	20c yel grn	75.00	65
75	A11	20c ol grn & gray ('08)	8.00	22
76	A11	22½c brn & ol grn	6.00	18
77	A11	25c car & bl	6.00	15
78	A11	30c lil & vio brn ('17)	18.00	15
79	A11	40c grn & org ('20)	35.00	50
80	A11	50c brnz grn & red brn	37.50	70
81	A11	50c gray & vio ('14)	40.00	50
a.		Perf. 11½x11	80.00	7.50
82	A11	60c ol grn & grn ('20)	30.00	80
a.		Perf. 11½	175.00	20.00
		Nos. 55-82 (27)	421.25	24.50

See Nos. 107-112. For overprints and surcharges see Nos. 102-102, 106, 117-123, 135-136, O1-O8.

A12 Type I Type II

Type I- The figure "1" is 3¾mm high and 2¾mm wide.

Type II- The figure "1" is 3½mm high and 2½mm wide, it is also thinner than in type I.

Perf. 11, 11x11½, 11½, 11½x11

1898-1905 **Engr.**

83	A12	1g dk grn (type II) ('99)	45.00	30
a.		1g dk grn (type I) ('98)	95.00	47.50
84	A12	2½g brn lil ('99)	65.00	3.25
85	A12	5g claret ('99)	150.00	5.25
86	A12	10g org ('05)	500.00	550.00

For surcharge see No. 104.

Admiral M. A. de Ruyter and Fleet — A13

King William I — A14

1907, Mar. 23 Typo. *Perf. 12x12½*

87	A13	½c blue	80	75
88	A13	1c claret	3.25	2.85
89	A13	2½c vermilion	10.00	2.25

De Ruyter (1607-1676), naval hero.
For surcharges see Nos. J29-J41.

Perf. 11½, 11½x11

1913, Nov. 29 Engr.

Designs: 2½c, 12½c, 1g, King William I. 3c, 20c, 2½g, King William II. 5c, 25c, 5g, King William III. 10c, 50c, 10g, Queen Wilhelmina.

90	A14	2½c grn, *grn*	65	60
91	A14	3c buff, *straw*	90	75
92	A14	5c rose red, *sal*	80	40
93	A14	10c gray blk	2.25	1.00
94	A14	12½c dp bl, *bl*	1.50	1.00
95	A14	20c org brn	8.00	4.00
96	A14	25c pale bl	8.25	4.00
97	A14	50c yel grn	20.00	14.00
98	A14	1g claret	30.00	8.25
a.		Perf. 11½	40.00	10.50
99	A14	2½g dl vio	85.00	32.50
100	A14	5g yel, *straw*	175.00	30.00
101	A14	10g red, *straw*	525.00	500.00
		Nos. 90-101 (12)	857.35	596.50

Centenary of Dutch independence.
For surcharge see No. 105.

No. 78 Surcharged in Red or Black

Veertig Cent
a

Zestig Cent
b

1919, Dec. 1 *Perf. 12½*

102	A11	(a) 40c on 30c (R)	20.00	3.25
103	A11	(b) 60c on 30c (Bk)	18.00	3.00

Nos. 86 and 101 Surcharged in Black

2.50

1920, Aug. 17 *Perf. 11, 11½*

104	A12	2.50g on 10g	85.00	95.00
105	A14	2.50g on 10g	95.00	60.00

No. 64 Surcharged in Red

—4C—

1921, Mar. 1 *Perf. 12½*

106	A11	4c on 4½c vio	3.75	1.40

A17

1921, Aug. 5 Typo. *Perf. 12½*

107	A17	5c green	8.00	15
108	A17	12½c vermilion	10.50	1.50
109	A17	20c blue	17.00	15

Queen Type of 1898-99, 10c Redrawn

1922 *Perf. 12½*

110	A11	10c gray	20.00	15

Imperf

111	A11	5c car rose	5.25	5.25
112	A11	10c gray	6.25	5.75

In redrawn 10c the horizontal lines behind the Queen's head are wider apart.

Orange Tree and Lion of Brabant A18

Post Horn and Lion A19

Numeral of Value — A20

1923, Mar. *Perf. 12½*

113	A18	1c dk vio	50	55
114	A18	2c orange	6.75	15
115	A19	2½c bluish grn	1.75	75
116	A20	4c dp bl	1.40	55

Nos. 56, 58, 62, 65, 68, 73, 76 Surcharged in Various Colors

c

d

1923, Aug. *Perf. 12½, 11½x11, 11½*

117	A10(c)	2c on 1c (Bl)	45	15
118	A10(c)	2c on 1½c (Bk)	45	15
119	A11(d)	10c on 3c ol (Br)	4.75	15
120	A11(d)	10c on 5c (Bk)	9.00	35
121	A11(d)	10c on 12½c (R)	8.00	60
122	A11(d)	10c on 17½c (R)	2.75	3.75
a.		Perf. 11½	*1,600.*	*900.00*
b.		Perf. 11½x11	2.75	3.75
123	A11(d)	10c on 22½c (R)	2.75	3.75
a.		Perf. 11½	2.75	3.75
b.		Perf. 11½x11	2.75	3.75
		Nos. 117-123 (7)	28.15	8.90

Queen Wilhelmina A21 A22

Perf. 11, 11½, 12, 12½ and Compound

1923, Aug. 31 Engr.

124	A22	2c myr grn	15	15
a.		Vert. pair, imperf. between	*2,250.*	
125	A21	5c green	15	15
a.		Vert. pair, imperf. between	*2,400.*	
126	A22	7½ carmine	15	15
127	A22	10c vermilion	15	15
a.		Vert. pair, imperf. between	*750.00*	*800.00*
128	A22	20c ultra	1.00	32
129	A22	25c yellow	1.65	52
130	A22	35c orange	2.00	1.25
131	A22	50c black	8.50	20
132	A21	1g red	13.00	3.00
133	A21	2½g black	115.00	125.00
134	A21	5g dk bl	100.00	100.00
		Nos. 124-134 (11)	241.75	230.89

25th anniv. of the assumption of the Government of the Netherlands by Queen Wilhelmina at the age of 18.

Nos. 119, 73 Overprinted in Red "DIENSTZEGEL PORTEN AANTEEKENRECHT; No. 73 with New Value in Blue

1923 *Perf. 12½*

135	A11	10c on 3c	85	52
136	A11	1g on 17½c	50.00	12.00
a.		Perf. 11½	60.00	22.50
b.		Perf. 11½x11	52.50	18.00

Stamps with red surcharge were prepared for use as Officials but were not issued.

Queen Wilhelmina — A23

1924, Sept. 6 Photo. *Perf. 12½*

137	A23	10c slate green	27.50	27.50
138	A23	15c gray black	32.50	35.00
139	A23	35c brown org	27.50	27.50

These stamps were available solely to visitors to the International Philatelic Exhibition at The Hague and were not obtainable at regular post offices.

See Nos. 147-160, 172-193. For overprints and surcharge see Nos. 194, O11, O13-O15.

Ship in Distress A23a

Lifeboat A23b

1924, Sept. 15 Litho. *Perf. 11½*

140	A23a	2c blk brn	90	1.10
141	A23b	10c org brn	4.75	1.00

Centenary of Royal Dutch Lifeboat Society

Type A23 and

Gull — A24

1924-26 *Perf. 12½*

142	A24	1c dp red	40	42
143	A24	2c red org	1.65	15
144	A24	2½c dp grn	1.75	45
145	A24	3c yel grn ('25)	8.00	65
146	A24	4c dp ultra	1.65	35

Photo.

147	A23	5c dl grn	3.00	60
148	A23	6c org brn ('25)	50	40
149	A23	7½c org ('25)	25	15
150	A23	9c org red & blk ('26)	1.00	90
151	A23	10c red	85	15
152	A23	12½c dp rose	1.25	32
153	A23	15c ultra	3.50	25
154	A23	20c dp bl ('25)	8.00	45
155	A23	25c ol bis ('25)	14.00	40
156	A23	30c violet	8.25	40
157	A23	35c ol brn ('25)	18.00	5.00
158	A23	40c dp brn	18.00	45
159	A23	50c bl grn ('25)	27.50	45
160	A23	60c dk vio ('25)	18.00	52
		Nos. 142-160 (19)	135.55	12.46

See Nos. 164-171. For overprints and surcharges see Nos. 226-243, O9-O10.

Syncopated Perforations

Type A

Type C

Type B

These special "syncopated" or "interrupted" perforations, devised for coil stamps, are found on Nos. 142-156, 158-160, 164-166, 168-185, 187-193 and certain semipostals of 1925-33, between Nos. B9 and B69. There are four types:

A. On two shorter sides, groups of four holes separated by blank spaces equal in width to two or three holes.

B. As "A," but on all four sides.

C. On two shorter sides, end holes are omitted.

D. Four-hole sequence on horiz. sides, three-hole on vert. sides.

Syncopated, Type A (2 Sides)

1925-26

142a	A24	1c dp red	45	45
143a	A24	2c red org	2.75	1.50
144a	A24	2½c dp grn	1.90	60
145a	A24	3c yel grn	20.00	20.00
146a	A24	4c dp ultra	1.50	1.25
147a	A23	5c dl grn	3.75	1.25
148a	A23	6c org brn	100.00	95.00
149a	A23	7½c orange	80	75
150a	A23	9c org red & blk	1.25	75
151a	A23	10c red	18.00	2.75
152a	A23	12½c dp rose	1.25	75
153a	A23	15c ultra	67.50	7.50
154a	A23	20c dp bl	11.00	3.25
155a	A23	25c ol bis	47.50	45.00
156a	A23	30c violet	17.00	6.75
158a	A23	40c dp brn	50.00	30.00
159a	A23	50c bl grn	57.50	12.00
160a	A23	60c dk vio	27.50	7.50
		Nos. 142a-160a (18)	429.65	237.05

A25

1925-27 Engr. *Perf. 11½, 12½*
161 A25 1g ultra 4.75 25
162 A25 2½g car ('27) 60.00 1.50
163 A25 5g gray blk 110.00 2.00

Types of 1924-26 Issue

Perf. 12½, 13½x12½, 12½x13½

1926-39 Wmk. 202 Litho.
164 A24 ½c gray ('28) 1.00 80
165 A24 1c dp red ('27) 15 15
166 A24 1½c red vio ('28) 1.40 15
c. "CEN" for "CENT" 300.00 300.00
167 A24 1½c gray ('35) 15 15
a. 1½c dk gray 15 15
168 A24 2c dp org 15 15
a. 2c red org 15 15
169 A24 2½c grn ('27) 2.75 18
170 A24 3c yel grn ('27) 20 15
171 A24 4c dp ultra ('27) 15 15

Photo.

172 A23 5c dp grn 25 15
173 A23 6c org brn ('27) 25 15
174 A23 7½c dk vio ('27) 3.75 15
175 A23 7½c red ('28) 20 15
176 A23 9c org red & blk ('28) 12.00 10.00
b. Value omitted *12,500.*
177 A23 10c red 1.25 15
178 A23 10c dl vio ('29) 2.75 15
179 A23 12½c dp rose ('27) 40.00 3.75
180 A23 12½c ultra ('28) 45 15
181 A23 15c ultra 6.25 28
182 A23 15c org ('29) 1.10 20
183 A23 20c dp bl ('28) 6.25 20
184 A23 21c ol brn ('31) 22.50 80
185 A23 22½c ol brn ('27) 6.25 2.00
186 A23 22½c dp org ('39) 12.50 21.00
187 A23 25c ol bis ('27) 4.00 15
188 A23 27½c gray ('28) 4.00 80
189 A23 30c violet 4.75 15
190 A23 35c ol brn 60.00 14.00
191 A23 40c dp brn 9.75 30
192 A23 50c bl grn 5.50 30
193 A23 60c blk ('29) 27.50 95
Nos. 164-193 (30) 237.20 57.81

See Nos. 243A-243Q.

Syncopated, Type A (2 Sides), 12½

1926-27
168b A24 2c dp org 50 40
170a A24 3c yel grn 85 50
171a A24 4c dp ultra 85 1.00
172a A23 5c dp grn 1.00 1.65
173a A23 6c org brn 60 80
174a A23 7½c dk vio 4.75 2.00
177a A23 10c red 1.25 1.10
181a A23 15c ultra 8.75 3.25
185a A23 22½c ol brn 9.50 3.25
187a A23 25c ol bis 25.00 17.00
189a A23 30c violet 16.00 8.50
190a A23 35c ol brn 65.00 17.00
191a A23 40c dp brn 57.50 52.50
Nos. 168b-191a (13) 191.55 108.95

1928 *Syncopated, Type B (4 Sides)*
164a A24 ½c gray 1.10 80
165a A24 1c dp red 35 30
166a A24 1½c red vio 1.10 20
168c A24 2c dp org 1.25 1.25
169a A24 2½c green 2.75 30
170b A24 3c yel grn 85 1.10
171b A24 4c dp ultra 85 80
172b A23 5c dp grn 1.10 85
173b A23 6c org brn 85 60
174b A23 7½c dk vio 4.50 1.90
175a A23 7½c red 25 20
176a A23 9c org red & blk 11.00 15.00
178a A23 10c dl vio 6.25 5.50
179a A23 12½c dp rose 72.50 80.00
180a A23 12½c ultra 1.65 50
181b A23 15c ultra 9.25 2.25
182a A23 15c orange 85 50
183a A23 20c dp bl 7.25 3.25
187b A23 25c ol bis 13.00 9.75
188a A23 27½c gray 4.00 2.25
189b A23 30c violet 13.00 8.50
191b A23 40c dp brn 42.50 21.00
192a A23 50c bl grn 62.50 47.50
193a A23 60c black 50.00 30.00
Nos. 164a-193a (24) 308.70 234.30

Syncopated, Type C (2 Sides, Corners Only)

1930
164b A24 ½c gray 1.10 80
165b A24 1c dp red 1.10 60
166b A24 1½c red vio 1.10 15
168d A24 2c dp org 85 80
169b A24 2½c green 2.75 30
170c A24 3c yel grn 1.25 80
171c A24 4c dp ultra 60 30
172c A23 5c dp grn 85 80
173c A23 6c org brn 85 85
178b A23 10c dl vio 10.50 10.50
183b A23 20c dp bl 8.00 4.25
184a A23 21c ol brn 22.50 10.50
189c A23 30c violet 14.00 9.00
192b A23 50c bl grn 50.00 47.50
Nos. 164b-192b (14) 115.45 87.15

Syncopated, Type D (3 Holes Vert., 4 Holes Horiz.)

1927
174c A23 7½c dk vio *2,750. 2,750.*

No. 185 Surcharged in Red

21

1929, Nov. 11 *Perf. 12½*
194 A23 21c on 22½c ol brn 18.00 1.25

Queen Wilhelmina — A26

1931, Oct. Photo. *Perf. 12½*
195 A26 70c dk bl & red 20.00 50
a. Perf. 14½x13½ ('39) 27.50 4.50

Arms of the House of Orange A27

William I, Portrait by Goltzius A28

Designs: 6c, Portrait of William I by Van Key. 12½c, Portrait attributed to Moro.

Perf. 12½

1933, Apr. 1 Unwmk. Engr.
196 A27 1½c black 60 15
197 A28 5c dk grn 1.65 28
198 A28 6c dl vio 4.00 15
199 A28 12½c dp bl 17.50 3.25

400th anniv. of the birth of William I, Count of Nassau and Prince of Orange, frequently referred to as William the Silent.

Star, Dove and Sword A31

Queen Wilhelmina and Ships A32

1933, May 18 Photo. Wmk. 202
200 A31 12½c dp ultra 10.50 35

For overprint see No. O12.

Perf. 14½x13½

1933, July 26 Unwmk.
201 A32 80c Prus bl & red 110.00 3.25

Willemstad Harbor A33

Van Walbeeck's Ship — A34

1934, July 2 Engr. *Perf. 14x12½*
202 A33 6c vio blk 3.25 15
203 A34 12½c dull blue 19.00 3.25

Tercentenary of Curacao.

Minerva — A35

Design: 12½c, Gisbertius Voetius.

Wmk. 202

1936, May 15 Photo. *Perf. 12½*
204 A35 6c brn lake 1.90 22
205 A35 12½c indigo 3.25 3.25

300th anniversary of the founding of the University at Utrecht.

Boy Scout Emblem A37

"Assembly" A38

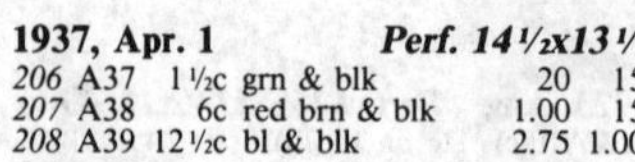
Mercury — A39

1937, Apr. 1 *Perf. 14½x13½*
206 A37 1½c grn & blk 20 15
207 A38 6c red brn & blk 1.00 15
208 A39 12½c bl & blk 2.75 1.00

Fifth Boy Scout World Jamboree, Vogelenzang, Netherlands, July 31-Aug. 13, 1937.

Wilhelmina A40

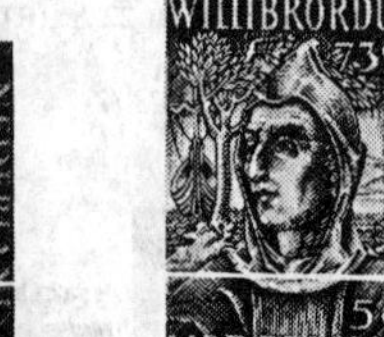
St. Willibrord A41

1938, Aug. 27 *Perf. 12½x12*
209 A40 1½c black 20 15
210 A40 5c red orange 30 15
211 A40 12½c royal blue 4.25 1.25

40th anniversary of the reign of Queen Wilhelmina.

Perf. 12½x13½

1939, June 15 Engr. Unwmk.

Design: 12½c, St. Willibrord as older man.

212 A41 5c dk sl grn 75 15
213 A41 12½c slate blue 4.00 2.50

12th centenary of the death of St. Willibrord.

Wood- burning Engine A43

Queen Wilhelmina A45

Design: 12½c, Streamlined electric car.

Perf. 14½x13½

1939, Sept. 1 Photo. Wmk. 202
214 A43 5c dk sl grn 1.00 15
215 A43 12½c dark blue 8.00 3.50

Centenary of Dutch Railroads.

Catalogue values for unused stamps in this section, from this point to the end of the section, are for Never Hinged items.

1940-47 *Perf. 13½x12½*
216 A45 5c dk grn 15 15
216B A45 6c hn brn ('47) 25 18
217 A45 7½c brt red 15 15
218 A45 10c brt red vio 15 15
219 A45 12½c sapphire 15 15
220 A45 15c lt bl 15 15
220B A45 17½c sl bl ('46) 1.00 80
221 A45 20c purple 15 15
222 A45 22½c ol grn 45 60
223 A45 25c rose brn 15 15
224 A45 30c bister 32 40
225 A45 40c brt grn 60 60
225A A45 50c org ('46) 6.75 75
225B A45 60c pur brn ('46) 5.75 2.75
Nos. 216-225B (14) 16.17 7.13

Imperf. copies of Nos. 216, 218-220 were released through philatelic channels during the German occupation, but were never issued at any post office. Value, set, $1.

For overprints see Nos. O16-O24.

Type of 1924-26 Surcharged in Black or Blue

Perf. 12½x13½

1940, Oct. Photo. Wmk. 202
226 A24 2½c on 3c ver 60 15
227 A24 5c on 3c lt grn 15 15
228 A24 7½c on 3c ver 15 15
a. Pair, #226, 228
229 A24 10c on 3c lt grn 15 15
230 A24 12½c on 3c lt bl (Bl) 15 30
231 A24 17½c on 3c lt grn 30 60
232 A24 20c on 3c lt grn 18 15
233 A24 22½c on 3c lt grn 45 85
234 A24 25c on 3c lt grn 25 20
235 A24 30c on 3c lt grn 30 40
236 A24 40c on 3c lt grn 38 70
237 A24 50c on 3c lt grn 50 40
238 A24 60c on 3c lt grn 85 1.00
239 A24 70c on 3c lt grn 1.40 1.75
240 A24 80c on 3c lt grn 2.25 4.50
241 A24 1g on 3c lt grn 25.00 45.00
242 A24 2.50g on 3c lt grn 25.00 45.00
243 A24 5g on 3c lt grn 25.00 45.00
Nos. 226-243 (18) 83.06 146.45

No. 228a is from coils.

Gull Type of 1924-26

1941
243A A24 2½c dk grn 1.25 35
b. Booklet pane of 6 10.00
243C A24 5c brt grn 15 15
243E A24 7½c henna 15 15
r. Pair, #243A, 243E 1.00
243G A24 10c brt vio 15 15
243H A24 12½c ultra 15 15
243J A24 15c lt bl 15 15
243K A24 17½c red org 15 15
243L A24 20c lt vio 18 20
243M A24 22½c dk ol grn 15 15
243N A24 25c lake 15 20
243O A24 30c olive 3.50 20
243P A24 40c emerald 15 20
243Q A24 50c org brn 15 20
Nos. 243A-243Q (13) 6.43 2.40

No. 243r is from coils.

Post Horn and Lion — A46

Gold Surcharge

1943, Jan. 15 Photo. *Perf. 12½x12*

244	A46	10c on 2½c yel	15	25
a.		Surcharge omitted	6,000.	6,500.

Founding of the European Union of Posts and Telegraphs at Vienna, Oct. 19, 1942. Surcharge reads: "Europeesche P T T Vereeniging 19 October 1942 10 Cent."

Sea Horse — A47

Triple-crown Tree — A48

Admiral M. A. de Ruyter — A54

Designs: 2c, Swans. 2½c, Tree of Life. 3c, Tree with snake roots. 4c, Man on horseback. 5c, Prancing white horses. 10c, Johan Evertsen. 12½c, Martin Tromp. 15c, Piet Hein. 17½c, Willem van Ghent. 20c, Witte de With. 22½c, Cornelis Evertsen. 25c, Tjerk de Vries. 30c, Cornelis Tromp. 40c, Cornelis Evertsen De Jongste.

Perf. 12x12½, 12½x12

1943-44 Photo. Wmk. 202

245	A47	1c black	15	15
246	A48	1½c rose lake	15	15
247	A47	2c dk bl	15	15
248	A48	2½c dk bl grn	15	15
249	A47	3c cop red	15	15
250	A48	4c blk brn	15	15
251	A47	5c dl yel grn	15	15

Unwmk.

252	A54	7½c henna brn	15	15
a.		Thinner numerals and letters ('44)	15	15
253	A54	10c dk grn	15	15
254	A54	12½c blue	15	18
255	A54	15c dl lil	15	15
256	A54	17½c sl ('44)	15	15
257	A54	20c dl brn	15	15
258	A54	22½c org red	15	25
259	A54	25c vio rose ('44)	35	55
260	A54	30c cob bl ('44)	15	18

Engr.

261	A54	40c bluish blk	15	20
		Nos. 245-261 (17)	2.75	3.16

In 1944, 200,000 copies of No. 247 were privately punched with a cross and printed on the back with a number and the words "Prijs 15 Cent toeslag ten bate Ned. Roode Kruis." These were sold at an exhibition, the surtax going to the Red Cross. The Dutch post office tolerated these stamps.

Soldier A64

S. S. "Nieuw Amsterdam" A65

Pilot — A66

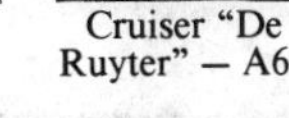
Cruiser "De Ruyter" — A67

Queen Wilhelmina — A68

Perf. 12, 12½

1944-46 Unwmk. Engr.

262	A64	1½c black	15	15
263	A65	2½c yel grn	15	15
264	A66	3c dl red brn	15	15
265	A67	5c dk bl	15	15
266	A68	7½c vermilion	15	15
267	A68	10c yel org	15	20
268	A68	12½c ultra	15	18
269	A68	15c dl red brn ('46)	1.40	4.50
270	A68	17½c gray grn ('46)	1.00	2.50
271	A68	20c violet	15	28
272	A68	22½c rose red ('46)	55	1.00
273	A68	25c brn org ('46)	2.00	2.75
274	A68	30c bl grn	15	20
275	A68	40c dk vio brn ('46)	2.00	4.50
276	A68	50c red vio ('46)	1.10	2.00
		Nos. 262-276 (15)	9.40	18.86

These stamps were used on board Dutch war and merchant ships until Netherlands' liberation.

Lion and Dragon A69

Queen Wilhelmina A70

1945, July 15 *Perf. 12½x14*

277	A69	7½c red org	15	15

Issued to commemorate Netherlands' liberationor "rising again."

1946 Engr. *Perf. 13½x14*

278	A70	1g dk bl	45	28
279	A70	2½g brick red	100.00	3.25
280	A70	5g dk ol grn	100.00	12.50
281	A70	10g dk pur	100.00	11.00

A71

Perf. 12½x13½

1946-47 Wmk. 202 Photo.

282	A71	1c dk red	15	15
283	A71	2c ultra	15	15
284	A71	2½c dp org ('47)	7.75	1.65
285	A71	4c ol grn	25	15

The 1c was reissued in 1969 on phosphorescent paper in booklet pane No. 345b. The 4c was reissued on fluorescent paper in 1962.

The 2c was issued in coils in 1972. Every fifth stamp has black control number on back. See Nos. 340-343A, 404-406.

Queen Wilhelmina
A72 A73

1947-48 *Perf. 13½x12½*

286	A72	5c ol grn ('48)	50	15
287	A72	6c brn blk	15	15
288	A72	7½c dp red brn ('48)	15	15
289	A72	10c brt red vio	38	15
290	A72	12½c scar ('48)	38	65
291	A72	15c purple	1.65	15
292	A72	20c dp bl	3.25	15
293	A72	22½c ol brn ('48)	75	90
294	A72	25c ultra	10.50	15
295	A72	30c dp org	4.25	35
296	A72	35c dk bl grn	4.25	50
297	A72	40c henna brn	14.00	50

Engr.

298	A73	45c dp bl ('48)	17.00	16.00
299	A73	50c brn ('48)	14.00	40
300	A73	60c red ('48)	15.00	3.75
		Nos. 286-300 (15)	86.21	24.10

For surcharge see No. 330.

Type of 1947

1948 Photo.

301	A72	6c gray blue	25	15

Queen Wilhelmina A74

Queen Juliana A75

Perf. 12½x14

1948, Aug. 30 Engr. Unwmk.

302	A74	10c vermilion	15	15
303	A74	20c dp bl	1.25	1.50

Issued to commemorate the 50th anniversary of the reign of Queen Wilhelmina.

Perf. 14x13

1948, Sept. 7 Photo. Wmk. 202

304	A75	10c dk brn	90	15
305	A75	20c ultra	1.75	60

Investiture of Queen Juliana, Sept. 6, 1948.

Queen Juliana
A76 A77

1949 *Perf. 13½x12½*

306	A76	5c olive grn	80	15
307	A76	6c gray blue	42	15
308	A76	10c dp org	42	15
309	A76	12c org red	1.10	1.00
310	A76	15c olive brn	4.00	15
311	A76	20c brt bl	4.00	15
312	A76	25c org brn	8.25	15
313	A76	30c violet	4.00	15
314	A76	35c gray	8.25	20
315	A76	40c red vio	19.00	20
316	A76	45c red org	1.65	1.00
317	A76	50c blue grn	7.00	20
318	A76	60c red brown	11.00	20
		Nos. 306-318 (13)	69.89	3.85

See No. 325-327. For surcharge see No. B248.

1949 Unwmk. Engr. *Perf. 12½x12*

319	A77	1g rose red	2.75	15
320	A77	2½g blk brn	120.00	1.00
321	A77	5g org brn	300.00	2.50
322	A77	10g dk vio brn	300.00	12.00

Two types exist of No. 321.

Post Horns Entwined — A78

Janus Dousa — A79

Perf. 11½x12½

1949, Oct. 1 Photo. Wmk. 202

323	A78	10c brn red	15	15
324	A78	20c dl bl	5.00	2.75

75th anniversary of the UPU.

Juliana Type of 1949

1950-51 *Perf. 13½x12½*

325	A76	12c scar ('51)	4.00	60
326	A76	45c vio brn	25.00	30
327	A76	75c car rose ('51)	60.00	1.25

1950, Oct. 3 *Perf. 11½x13*

Design: 20c, Jan van Hout.

328	A79	10c olive brn	3.00	20
329	A79	20c deep blue	3.25	1.65

375th anniversary of the founding of the University of Leyden.

No. 288 Surcharged with New Value

1950 *Perf. 13½x12½*

330	A72	6c on 7½c dp red brn	2.00	15

Miner — A80

Perf. 12x12½

1952, Apr. 16 Engr. Unwmk.

331	A80	10c dk bl	2.50	15

50th anniversary of the founding of Netherlands' mining and chemical industry.

Telegraph Poles and Train of 1852 — A81

Designs: 6c, Radio towers. 10c, Mail Delivery 1852. 20c, Modern postman.

1952, June 28 *Perf. 13x14*

332	A81	2c gray vio	30	20
333	A81	6c vermilion	35	35
334	A81	10c green	50	20
335	A81	20c gray bl	4.25	2.75

Issued to commemorate the centenary of Dutch postage stamps and of the telegraph service.

1952, June 28

336	A81	2c chocolate	10.50	17.00
337	A81	6c dk bluish grn	10.50	17.00
338	A81	10c brn car	10.50	17.00
339	A81	20c vio bl	10.50	17.00

Nos. 336 to 339 sold for 1.38g, which included the price of admission to the International Postage Stamp Centenary Exhibition, Utrecht.

Numeral Type of 1946-47

Perf. 12½x13½

1953-57 Wmk. 202 Photo.

340	A71	3c dp org brn	15	15
341	A71	5c orange	15	15
342	A71	6c gray ('54)	25	15
343	A71	7c red org	15	15
343A	A71	8c brt lil ('57)	15	15
		Set value	65	40

The 5c and 7c perf. on 3 sides, and with watermark vertical, are from booklet panes Nos. 346a-346b. The 5c perf. on 3 sides, with wmk. horiz., is from No. 349a.

In 1972 the 5c was printed on phosphorescent paper.

Queen Juliana
A82 A83

1953-71 Wmk. 202 *Perf. 13½x12½*

344	A82 10c dk red brn	18	15
a.	Bklt. pane of 6 (1 #344 + 5 #346C)('65)	8.00	
345	A82 12c dk Prus grn ('54)	15	15
a.	Bklt. pane of 7 + label (5 #345 + 2 #347)('67)	7.50	
b.	Bklt. pane, 4 #282 + 8 #345 ('69)	13.00	
346	A82 15c dp car	15	15
a.	Bklt. pane of 8 (2 #341 in vert. pair + 6 #346)('64)	18.00	
b.	Bklt. pane of 12 (10 #343 + 2 #346)('64)	13.00	
e.	Bklt. pane of 8 (2 #341 in horiz. pair + 6 #346)('70)	13.00	
346C	A82 18c dl bl ('65)	40	15
d.	Bklt. pane of 10 (8 #343A + 2 #346C)('65)	12.50	
347	A82 20c dk gray	25	15
b.	Bklt. pane of 5 + label ('66)	6.00	
347A	A82 24c ol ('63)	45	15
348	A82 25c dp bl	28	15
349	A82 30c dp org	60	15
a.	Bklt. pane of 5 + label (2 #341 + 3 #349)('71)	22.50	
350	A82 35c dk ol brn ('54)	1.00	15
351	A82 37c aqua ('58)	50	15
352	A82 40c dk sl	35	15
353	A82 45c scarlet	50	15
354	A82 50c dk bl grn	45	15
355	A82 60c brn bis	45	15
356	A82 62c dl red lil ('58)	3.75	4.75
357	A82 70c bl ('57)	50	15
358	A82 75c dp plum	50	15
359	A82 80c brt vio ('58)	50	15
360	A82 85c brt bl grn ('56)	1.00	15
360A	A82 95c org brn ('67)	3.25	32
	Nos. 344-360A (20)	15.21	
	Set value		6.65

Coils of the 12, 15, 20, 25, 30, 40, 45, 50, 60, 70, 75 and 80c were issued in 1972. Black control number on back of every fifth stamp.

Watermark is vertical on some stamps from booklet panes.

Some booklet panes, Nos. 344a, 347b, 349a, etc., have a large selvage the size of four or six stamps, with printed inscription and sometimes illustration.

Phosphorescent paper was introduced in 1967 for the 12, 15, 20 and 45c; in 1969 for the 25c, and in 1971 for the 30, 40, 50, 60, 70, 75 and 80c.

Of the booklet panes, Nos. 345a, 345b, 346d, 346e and 347b were issued on both ordinary and phosphorescent paper, and No. 349a only on phosphorescent paper.

See No. 407. For surcharge see No. 374.

Perf. 12½x12

1954-57 Unwmk. Engr.

361	A83 1g vermilion	2.50	15
362	A83 2½g dk grn ('55)	8.00	15
363	A83 5g blk ('55)	1.90	30
364	A83 10g vio bl ('57)	14.00	1.25

St. Boniface
A84

Flaming
Sword
A85

1954, June 16

365	A84 10c blue	1.65	15

1200th anniversary of the death of St. Boniface.

> *Netherlands stamps can be mounted in Scott's annual Netherlands Supplement.*

Charter of the Kingdom Issue

Type of Netherlands Antilles, 1954, with "Nederland" above portrait

Wmk. 202

1954, Dec. 15 Photo. *Perf. 13½*

366	A48 10c scarlet	65	15

Issued to publicize the Charter of the Kingdom, adopted December 15, 1954.

1955, May 4 *Perf. 12½x12*

367	A85 10c crimson	90	15

10th anniv. of Netherlands' liberation.

"Rebuilding
Europe"
A86

Admiral M.
A. de Ruyter
A87

1956, Sept. 15 Unwmk. *Perf. 13x14*

368	A86 10c rose brn & blk	65	15
369	A86 25c brt bl & blk	32.50	2.50

Europa. Issued to symbolize the cooperation among the six countries comprising the Coal and Steel Community.

1957, July 2 Engr. *Perf. 12½x12*

Design: 30c, Flagship "De Zeven Provincien."

370	A87 10c orange	30	15
371	A87 30c dk bl	3.00	2.50

350th anniversary of the birth of Adm. M. A. de Ruyter (1607-1676).

"United
Europe" — A88

1957, Sept. 16 Photo. *Perf. 13x14*

372	A88 10c blk, gray & ultra	50	15
373	A88 30c dl grn & ultra	5.00	2.50

United Europe for peace and prosperity.

No. 344 Surcharged in Silver with New Value and Bars

Perf. 13½x12½

1958, May 16 Photo. Wmk. 202

374	A82 12c on 10c	1.10	15
a.	Double surcharge	550.00	550.00
b.	Inverted surcharge	550.00	550.00

Europa Issue, 1958

Common Design Type

Perf. 13x14

1958, Sept. 13 Litho. Unwmk.

Size: 22x33mm

375	CD1 12c org ver & blue	25	15
376	CD1 30c blue & red	1.00	1.10

NATO Emblem — A89

1959, Apr. 3 *Perf. 12½x12*

377	A89 12c yel org & bl	15	15
378	A89 30c red & blue	65	80

10th anniversary of NATO.

Europa Issue, 1959.

Common Design Type

1959, Sept. 19 *Perf. 13x14*

Size: 22x33mm

379	CD2 12c crimson	38	15
380	CD2 30c yel grn	2.00	1.75

Douglas DC-8 and
World Map — A90

J. C.
Schroeder van
der
Kolk — A91

Design: 30c, Douglas DC-8 in flight.

1959, Oct. 5 Engr. *Perf. 14x13*

381	A90 12c car & ultra	22	15
382	A90 30c dp bl & dp grn	1.00	1.40

Issued to commemorate the 40th anniversary of the founding of KLM, Royal Dutch Airlines.

Perf. 12½x12

1960, July 18 Unwmk.

Design: 30c, Johannes Wier.

383	A91 12c red	16	15
384	A91 30c dk bl	3.75	2.25

Issued to publicize Mental Health Year and to honor Schroeder van der Kolk and Johannes Wier, pioneers of mental health.

Europa Issue, 1960

Common Design Type

1960, Sept. 19 Photo. *Perf. 12x12½*

Size: 27x21mm

385	CD3 12c car rose & org	24	20
386	CD3 30c dk bl & yel	2.50	1.90

1st anniv. of CEPT. Spokes symbolize 19 founding members of Conference.

Europa Issue, 1961

Common Design Type

1961, Sept. 18 *Perf. 14x13*

Size: 32½x21½mm

387	CD4 12c golden brn	15	15
388	CD4 30c Prus bl	24	20
	Set value		28

Queen Juliana and
Prince
Bernhard — A92

Telephone
Dial — A93

Perf. 14x13

1962, Jan. 5 Unwmk. Photo.

389	A92 12c dk red	20	15
390	A92 30c dk grn	1.75	1.00

Issued to commemorate the silver wedding anniversary of Queen Juliana and Prince Bernhard.

1962, May 22 *Perf. 13x14, 14x13*

Designs: 12c, Map showing telephone network. 30c, Arch and dial (horiz.).

391	A93 4c brn red & blk	20	15
392	A93 12c brn ol & blk	32	15
393	A93 30c blk, bis & Prus bl	2.00	1.50

Issued to commemorate the completion of the automation of the Netherlands telephone network.

Europa Issue, 1962

Common Design Type

1962, Sept. 17 *Perf. 14x13*

Size: 33x22mm

394	CD5 12c lem, yel & blk	20	15
395	CD5 30c bl, yel & blk	95	75

Polder with Canals
and Windmills — A94

Design: 4c, Cooling towers, Limburg State Coal Mines. 10c, Dredging in Delta.

Perf. 12½x13½

1962-66 Wmk. 202 Photo.

399	A94 4c dk bl ('63)	20	15
401	A94 6c grn & dk grn	70	15
403	A94 10c dp cl ('63)	20	15
a.	Bklt. pane of 10 ('66)	6.00	
	Set value		24

The 10c was issued in coils in 1972. Every fifth stamp has black control number on back. See No. 461b.

Types of 1946 and 1953

1962-73 Unwmk.

Phosphorescent Paper

404	A71 4c olive green	40	20
405	A71 5c orange ('73)	40	15
406	A71 8c bright lilac	18.00	12.00
407	A82 12c dark Prus grn	60	40

The 5c is from booklets and has the phosphor on the front only.

Issue dates: 5c, Jan. 12; others Aug. 27.

See Nos. 460d, 461c, 461d and 463a.

Wheat Emblem and
Globe — A95

Inscription in
Circle — A96

1963, Mar. 21 Photo. *Perf. 14x13*

413	A95 12c dl bl, dk bl & yel	15	15
414	A95 30c dl car, rose & yel	1.10	95

FAO "Freedom from Hunger" campaign.

Perf. 13x14

1963, May 7 Unwmk. Litho.

415	A96 30c brt bl, blk & grn	1.40	1.00

1st Intl. Postal Conf., Paris, cent.

Europa Issue, 1963

Common Design Type

1963, Sept. 16 Photo. *Perf. 14x13*

Size: 33x22mm

416	CD6 12c red brn & yel	15	15
417	CD6 30c Prus grn & yel	1.65	1.40

Prince William of
Orange Landing at
Scheveningen
A97

Designs: 12c, G. K. van Hogendorp, A. F. J. A. Graaf van der Duyn van Maasdam and L. Graaf van Limburg Stirum, Dutch leaders, 1813. 30c, Prince William taking oath of allegiance.

1963, Nov. 18 Photo. *Perf. 12x12½*
Size: 27½x27½mm

418 A97 4c dl bl, blk & brn 15 15
419 A97 5c dk grn, blk & red 15 15
420 A97 12c ol & blk 15 15
421 A97 30c mar & blk 60 55
Set value 84 78

Issued to commemorate the 150th anniversary of the founding of the Kingdom of the Netherlands.

Knights' Hall, The Hague A98

Arms of Groningen University A99

1964, Jan. 9 *Perf. 14x13*

422 A98 12c olive & blk 15 15

Issued to commemorate the 500th anniversary of the meeting of the States-General (Parliament).

1964, June 16 Engr. *Perf. 12½x12*

Design: 30c, Initials "AG" and crown.

423 A99 12c slate 15 15
424 A99 30c yel brn 20 20

Issued to commemorate the 350th anniversary of the University of Groningen.

Railroad Light Signal — A100

Design: 40c, Electric locomotive.

1964, July 28 Photo. *Perf. 14x13*

425 A100 15c blk & brt grn 15 15
426 A100 40c blk & yel 90 55

Issued to commemorate the 125th anniversary of the Netherlands railroads.

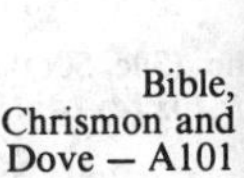

Bible, Chrismon and Dove — A101

1964, Aug. 25 Unwmk.

427 A101 15c brn red 15 15

150th anniversary of the founding of the Netherlands Bible Society.

Europa Issue, 1964
Common Design Type

1964, Sept. 14 Photo. *Perf. 13x14*
Size: 22x33mm

428 CD7 15c dp ol grn 15 15
429 CD7 20c yel brn 32 32

Benelux Issue

King Baudouin, Queen Juliana and Grand Duchess Charlotte A101a

1964, Oct. 12 *Perf. 14x13*
Size: 33x22mm

430 A101a 15c pur & buff 15 15

Issued to commemorate the 20th anniversary of the signing of the customs union of Belgium, Netherlands and Luxembourg.

Queen Juliana A102

"Killed in Action" and "Destroyed Town" A103

1964, Dec. 15 Photo. *Perf. 13x14*

431 A102 15c green 15 15

Issued to commemorate the 10th anniversary of the Charter of the Kingdom of the Netherlands.

1965, Apr. 6 Photo. *Perf. 12x12½*

Statues: 15c, "Docker" Amsterdam, and "Killed in Action" Waalwijk. 40c, "Destroyed Town" Rotterdam, and "Docker" Amsterdam.

432 A103 7c blk & dk red 15 15
433 A103 15c blk & dk ol 15 15
434 A103 40c blk & dk red 85 60
Set value 1.00 75

Resistance movement of World War II.

Knight Class IV, Order of William A104

ITU Emblem A105

1965, Apr. 29 *Perf. 13x14*

435 A104 1g gray 90 75

Issued to commemorate the 150th anniversary of the establishment of the Military Order of William.

1965, May 17 Litho. *Perf. 14x13*

436 A105 20c dl bl & tan 18 15
437 A105 40c tan & dl bl 40 32

Issued to commemorate the centenary of the International Telecommunication Union.

Europa Issue, 1965
Common Design Type

1965, Sept. 27 Photo.
Size: 33x22mm

438 CD8 18c org brn, dk red & blk 15 15
439 CD8 20c saph, brn & blk 28 16
Set value 24

Marines of 1665 and 1965 — A106

1965, Dec. 10 Engr. *Perf. 13x14*

440 A106 18c dk vio bl & car 15 15

Issued to commemorate the 300th anniversary of the Netherlands Marine Corps.

Europa Issue, 1966
Common Design Type

1966, Sept. 26 Photo. *Perf. 13x14*
Size: 22x33mm

441 CD9 20c citron 15 15
442 CD9 40c dull blue 25 16
Set value 24

Assembly Hall, Delft University A107

1967, Jan. 5 Litho. *Perf. 14x13*

443 A107 20c lemon & sepia 15 15

125th anniversary of the founding of the Delft University of Technology.

Europa Issue, 1967
Common Design Type
Perf. 13x14

1967, May 2 Unwmk. Photo.
Ordinary Paper
Size: 22x32½mm

444 CD10 20c dull blue 50 20
445 CD10 45c dl vio brn 1.50 80

Wmk. 202

446 CD10 20c dull blue 1.00 25
447 CD10 45c dl vio brn 1.50 95

Nos. 446-447 are on phosphorescent paper.

Stamp of 1852, #1 — A108

1967, May 8 Engr. Unwmk.

448 A108 20c shown 2.00 2.00
449 A108 25c No. 5 2.00 2.00
450 A108 75c No. 10 2.00 2.00

Issued to publicize AMPHILEX 67, Amsterdam, May 11-21. Sold only in complete sets together with a 2.50g admission ticket to Amsterdam Philatelic Exhibition. Issued in sheets of 10 (5x2).

Coins and Punched Card — A109

1968, Jan. 16 Photo. *Perf. 14x13*

451 A109 20c ver, blk & dl yel 20 15

Issued to commemorate the 50th anniversary of the postal checking service.

Luminescence
All commemorative issues from No. 451 to No. 511 are printed on phosphorescent paper except No. 478 which is printed with phosphorescent ink, and Nos. 490-492. Some later issues are tagged.

Europa Issue, 1968
Common Design Type

1968, Apr. 29 Photo. *Perf. 14x13*
Size: 32½x22mm

452 CD11 20c dp bl 35 15
453 CD11 45c crimson 1.10 85

National Anthem A110

Fokker F.2, 1919, and Friendship F.29 A111

1968, Aug. 27 Litho. *Perf. 13x14*

454 A110 20c gray, org, car & dk bl 25 15

400th anniversary of the national anthem "Wilhelmus van Nassouwe."

1968, Oct. 1 Photo. *Perf. 14x13*

Planes: 12c, Wright A, 1909, and Cessna sports plane. 45c, De Havilland DH-9, 1919, and Douglas DC-9.

455 A111 12c crim, pink & blk 15 15
456 A111 20c brt grn, bl grn & blk 15 15
457 A111 45c brt bl, lt grn & blk 1.40 1.10

50th anniversaries of the founding in 1919 of Royal Dutch Airlines and the Royal Netherlands Aircraft Factories Fokker, and the 60th anniversary in 1967 of the Royal Netherlands Aeronautical Association.

"iao" — A112

Design is made up of 28 minute lines, each reading "1919 internationale arbeidsorganisatie 1969".

1969, Feb. 25 Engr. *Perf. 14x13*

458 A112 25c brick red & blk 45 15
459 A112 45c ultra & bl 1.00 65

International Labor Organization, 50th anniversary.

Queen Juliana
A113 A114

Perf. 13½ horiz. x 12½ on one vert. side

1969-75 Photo.

460 A113 25c org ver 3.50 32
a. Bklt. pane of 4 + 2 labels 15.00
460B A113 25c dl red ('73) 2.25 15
c. Booklet pane of 6 (#460B + 5 #461A) 27.50
d. Booklet pane of 12 (5 #405 + 7 #460B) 16.00

Perf. 13x12½

461 A113 30c choc ('72) 1.00 15
d. Bklt. pane of 10 (4 #405 + 6 #461 + 2 labels)('74) 7.50
461A A113 35c grnsh bl ('72) 1.00 15
b. Bklt. pane of 5 (3 #403, 2 #461A + label)('72) 18.00
c. Bklt. pane of 10 (5 #405 + 5 #461A + 2 labels)('75) 4.50
462 A113 40c car rose ('72) 1.00 15
a. Bklt. pane of 5 + label ('73) 7.50
463 A113 45c ultra ('72) 1.75 15
a. Bklt. pane of 8 (4 #405 + 4 #463) ('74) 6.00
464 A113 50c lil ('72) 38 15
a. Bklt. pane of 4 + 2 labels ('75) 4.00
465 A113 60c sl bl ('72) 32 15
a. Bklt. pane of 5 + label ('80) 1.65
466 A113 70c bis ('72) 38 15
467 A113 75c grn ('72) 38 15
468 A113 80c red org ('72) 45 15
468A A113 90c gray ('75) 50 18

Perf. 13x14

469 A114 1g yel grn 75 15
470 A114 1.25g maroon 70 15
471 A114 1.50g yel bis ('71) 85 15

471A	A114	2g dp rose lil ('72)	1.10	70
472	A114	2.50g grnsh bl	1.40	15
473	A114	5g gray ('70)	2.50	20
474	A114	10g vio bl ('70)	5.00	1.75
		Nos. 460-474 (19)	25.21	
		Set value		4.50

Both 25c stamps issued only in booklets.

Printings were both ordinary and phosphorescent paper for Nos. 460, 460a, 469, 471-474.

Coil printings were issued later for Nos. 461, 462-471. Black control number on back of every fifth stamp.

Booklet panes have a large selvage the size of 4 or 6 stamps, with printed inscription.

See No. 542.

Europa Issue, 1969

Common Design Type

1969, Apr. 28 Photo. *Perf. 14x13*

Size: 33½x22mm

475	CD12	25c dk bl	1.40	15
476	CD12	45c red	2.50	2.25

Möbius Strip in Benelux Colors — A114a

1969, Sept. 8 Photo. *Perf. 13x14*

477 A114a 25c multi 40 15

25th anniversary of the signing of the customs union of Belgium, Netherlands and Luxembourg.

Desiderius Erasmus (1469-1536), Scholar — A115

Photo. & Engr.

1969, Sept. 30 *Perf. 13x14*

478 A115 25c yel grn & mar 40 15

Queen Juliana and Rising Sun — A116

1969, Dec. 15 Photo. *Perf. 14x13*

479 A116 25c bl & multi 32 15

15th anniversary of the Charter of the Kingdom of the Netherlands.

Prof. E. M. Meijers A117

1970, Jan. 13 Photo. *Perf. 14x13*

480 A117 25c bl, vio bl & grn 38 15

Issued to publicize the new Civil Code and to honor Prof. Meijers, who prepared it.

Dutch Pavilion, EXPO '70 — A118

1970, Mar. 16 Photo. *Perf. 14x13*

481 A118 25c multi 32 15

EXPO '70 International Exposition, Osaka, Japan, Mar. 15-Sept. 13.

"V" for Victory — A119

1970, Apr. 21 Photo. *Perf. 13x14*

482 A119 12c red, ultra, brn ol & lt bl 1.10 15

25th anniv. of liberation from the Germans.

Europa Issue, 1970

Common Design Type

1970, May 4 Photo. *Perf. 14x13*

Size: 32½x21½mm

483	CD13	25c carmine	45	15
484	CD13	45c dk bl	2.00	2.00

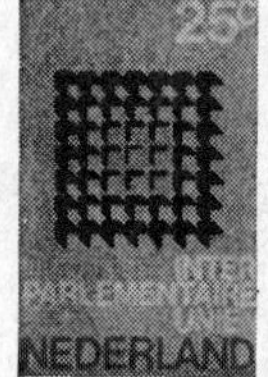

Panels — A120

Globe — A121

1970, June 23 Photo. *Perf. 13x14*

485	A120	25c gray, blk & brt yel grn	45	15
486	A121	45c ultra, blk & pur	1.00	85

No. 485 publicizes the meeting of the interparliamentary Union; No. 486 for the 25th anniv. of the UN.

Punch Cards — A122

1971, Feb. 16 Photo. *Perf. 14x13*

487 A122 15c dp rose lil 22 15

14th national census, 1971.

Europa Issue, 1971

Common Design Type

1971, May 3 Photo. *Perf. 14x13*

Size: 33x22mm

488	CD14	25c lil rose, yel & blk	55	15
489	CD14	45c ultra, yel & blk	2.50	1.50

No. 488 was issued in coils and sheets. In the coils every fifth stamp has a black control number on the back.

Prince Bernhard, Fokker F27, Boeing 747 B — A123

Designs: 15c, Stylized carnation (Prince Bernhard Fund). 20c, Giant Panda (World Wildlife Fund). 15c, 20c horiz.

Photo., Litho. (20c)

1971, June 29 *Perf. 13x14*

490	A123	15c blk & yel	30	15
491	A123	20c multi	50	20
492	A123	25c multi	65	15
		Set value		40

60th birthday of Prince Bernhard. See No. B475.

Map of Delta — A124

1972, Feb. 15 Photo. *Perf. 14x13*

493 A124 20c bl, grn, blk & red 42 15

Publicity for the Delta plan, a project to shorten the coastline and to build roads.

Europa Issue 1972

Common Design Type

1972, May 52 Photo. *Perf. 13x14*

Size: 22x33mm

494	CD15	30c bl & bis	1.10	15
495	CD15	45c org & bis	2.00	1.50

No. 494 was issued in coils and sheets. In the coils every fifth stamp has a black control number on the back.

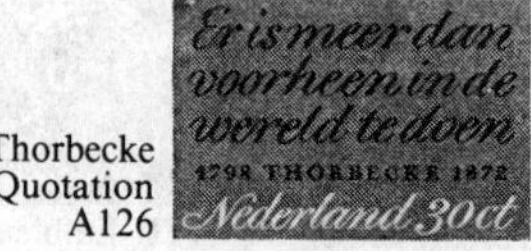

Thorbecke Quotation A126

1972, June 2 Photo. *Perf. 14x13*

496 A126 30c lt ultra & blk 45 15

Centenary of the death of Jan Rudolf Thorbecke (1798-1872), statesman, who said: "There is more to be done in the world than ever before."

Dutch Flag — A127

1972 *Perf. 13x14*

497	A127	20c blue & multi	75	15
498	A127	25c blue & multi	2.50	15

400th anniversary of the Dutch flag.

Issue dates: 20c, July 4; 25c, Nov. 1.

Woman Hurdler A128

Designs: 30c, Woman swimmer. 45c, Bicycling.

1972, July 11 *Perf. 14x13*

499	A128	20c multi	30	15
500	A128	30c crim & multi	35	15
501	A128	45c vio & multi	1.40	1.10

20th Olympic Games, Munich, Aug. 26-Sept. 11.

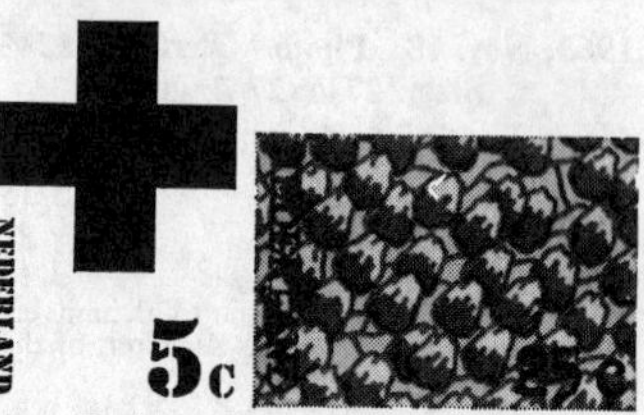

Red Cross — A129 Tulips — A130

1972, Aug. 15 Photo. *Perf. 13x14*

502	A129	5c red	15	15
		Nos. 502,B485-B488 (5)	3.95	2.95

Netherlands Red Cross.

1973, Mar. 20 Photo. *Perf. 14x13*

503 A130 25c rose, brt grn & blk 1.50 15

Dutch flower and bulb exports.

Europa Issue 1973

Common Design Type

1973, May 1 Photo. *Perf. 14x13*

Size: 32½x22mm

504	CD16	35c brt bl	70	15
505	CD16	50c purple	1.65	1.10

Hockey A132

Woman Gymnast A133

Antenna, Burum A134

Rainbow, Measures A135

Photo. (25c, 35c); Litho. (30c, 50c)

1973, July 31 *Perf. 13x14, 14x13*

506	A132	25c blk & grn	25	15
507	A133	30c gray & multi	2.50	55
508	A134	35c bl & multi	30	15
509	A135	50c bl & multi	70	65

Netherlands Hockey Assoc., 75th anniv. (25c); Rhythmical Gymnastics World Championship, Rotterdam (30c); inauguration of satellite ground station at Burum (35c); cent. of intl. meteorological cooperation (50c).

Queen Juliana, Dutch and House of Orange Colors A136

Engr. & Photo.

1973, Sept. 4 *Perf. 13x12*

510 A136 40c silver & multi 60 15

25th anniversary of reign of Queen Juliana.

Chain with Open Link — A137

1973, Oct. 16 Photo. *Perf. 13x14*
511 A137 40c grn, blk, gold & sil 3.00 15

Development Corporation.

Nature and Environment — A138

1974, Feb. 19 Photo. *Perf. 13x14*
512 A138 Strip of 3 8.00 5.25
a. 25c Bird of prey 2.25 52
b. 25c Tree 2.25 52
c. 25c Fisherman in boat and frog 2.25 52

75th anniversary of the Netherlands Association for the Protection of Birds and of the State Forestry Service. No. 512 printed se-tenant in sheets of 90.

Soccer Ball — A139

Tennis Ball — A140

Perf. 14x13, 13x14
1974, June 5 Photo.
513 A139 25c multi 35 15
514 A140 40c multi 40 15

World Cup Soccer Championship, Munich, June 13-July 7 (25c) and 75th anniversary of the Royal Dutch Lawn Tennis Association (40c).

Cattle — A141

Pierced Crab under Lens — A142

Shipwreck Seen Through Binoculars — A143

1974, July 30 *Perf. 13x14*
515 A141 25c multi 10.00 1.75
516 A142 25c sal pink & multi 16 16
517 A143 40c dk vio & multi 24 15

Centenary of the Netherlands Cattle Herdbook Society (No. 515); 25th anniversary of Queen Wilhelmina Fund (for cancer research) (No. 516); sesquicentennial of Royal Dutch Lifeboat Society (No. 517).

BENELUX Issue

"BENELUX" A143a

1974, Sept. 10 Photo. *Perf. 14x13*
518 A143a 30c bl grn, dk grn & lt bl 45 15

30th anniversary of the signing of the customs union of Belgium, Netherlands and Luxembourg.

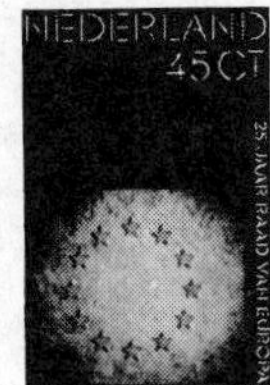

Council of Europe Emblem A144

NATO Emblem and Sea Gull A145

1974, Sept. 10 *Perf. 13x14*
519 A144 45c blk, bl & yel 45 15
520 A145 45c dk bl & sil 70 15

25th anniversaries of Council of Europe (No. 519) and of North Atlantic Treaty Organization (No. 520).

Letters and Hands, Papier-mache Sculpture — A146

1974, Oct. 9
521 A146 60c pur & multi 80 50

Centenary of Universal Postal Union.

People and Map of Dam Square A147

Brain with Window Symbolizing Free Thought A148

Design: No. 523, Portuguese Synagogue and map of Mr. Visser Square. 35c, No. 526, like No. 522.

1975 Photo. *Perf. 13x14*
522 A147 30c multi 35 15
523 A147 30c multi 30 20
524 A147 35c multi 45 15
525 A148 45c dp bl & multi 38 20

Coil Stamps
Perf. 13 Horiz.
526 A147 30c multi 42 20
527 A147 35c multi 60 20

700th anniversary of Amsterdam (No. 522); 300th anniversary of the Portuguese Synagogue in Amsterdam (No. 523) and 400th anniversary of the founding of the University of Leyden and the beginning of higher education in the Netherlands (No. 525).

Issue dates: Nos. 522-523, 525-526, Feb. 26; Nos. 524, 527, Apr. 1.

Eye Looking over Barbed Wire — A149

1975, Apr. 29 Photo. *Perf. 13x14*
528 A149 35c blk & car 45 15

Liberation of the Netherlands from Nazi occupation, 30th anniversary.

Company Emblem and "Stad Middelburg" A150

1975, May 21 Photo. *Perf. 14x13*
529 A150 35c multi 30 15

Zeeland Steamship Company, centenary.

Albert Schweitzer in Boat — A151

1975, May 21
530 A151 50c multi 40 15

Albert Schweitzer (1875-1965), medical missionary.

Symbolic Metric Scale — A152

1975, July 29 Litho. *Perf. 14x13*
531 A152 50c multi 40 15

Centenary of International Meter Convention, Paris, 1875.

Playing Card with Woman, Man, Pigeons, Pens — A153

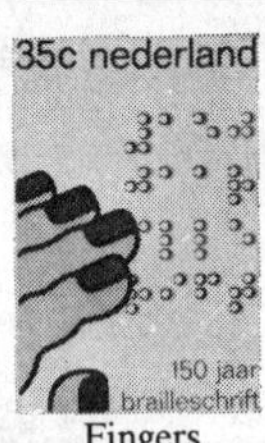

Fingers Reading Braille — A154

1975, July 29 *Perf. 13x14*
532 A153 35c multi 30 15

International Women's Year 1975.

1975, Oct. 7 Photo. *Perf. 13x14*
533 A154 35c multi 30 15

Sesquicentennial of the invention of Braille system of writing for the blind by Louis Braille (1809-1852).

Rubbings of 25¢ Coins — A155

1975, Oct. 7 *Perf. 14x13*
534 A155 50c grn, blk & bl 40 15

To publicize the importance of saving.

Lottery Ticket, 18th Century A156

1976, Feb. 3 Photo. *Perf. 14x13*
535 A156 35c multi 25 15

250th anniversary of National Lottery.

Queen Type of 1969 and

A157

1976-86 Photo. *Perf. 12½x13½*
536 A157 5c gray 15 15
Booklet Panes
a. (3 #536, 2 #537, 3 #542) 3.00
b. (4 #536, 2 #537, 4 #539 + 2 labels) 3.25
c. (#536, 2 #537, 5 #542) 3.00
d. (4 #536, 7 #539 + label) 3.00
e. (2 #536, 2 #540, 4 #541) 3.00
f. (5 #536, 2 #537, 2 #540, 3 #542) + 2 labels 4.00
g. (1 #536, 2 #537, 5 #543) ('86) 3.00
537 A157 10c ultra 15 15
538 A157 25c violet 18 15
539 A157 40c sepia 28 15
540 A157 45c brt bl 35 15
541 A157 50c lil rose ('80) 42 15
542 A113 55c carmine 50 15
543 A157 55c brt grn ('81) 45 20
544 A157 60c apple grn ('81) 45 20
545 A157 65c dk red brn ('86) 60 60
a. Bklt. pane of 10+2 labels (5 each Nos. 537, 545) 2.50
Nos. 536-545 (10) 3.53
Set value 1.50

Compare No. 544 with No. 790.

Coil Stamps

1976-86 *Perf. 13½ Vert.*
546 A157 5c slate gray 15 15
547 A157 10c ultra 15 15
548 A157 25c violet 18 15
549 A157 40c sepia ('77) 38 15
550 A157 45c brt bl 40 15
551 A157 50c brt rose ('79) 50 20
552 A157 55c brt grn ('81) 50 20

553 A157 60c apple grn ('81) 50 20
554 A157 65c dk red brn ('86) 60 60
Nos. 546-554 (9) 3.36
Set value 1.60

See Nos. 773, 776, 785, 787, 790.

De Ruyter Statue, Flushing
A158

1976, Apr. 22 **Photo.** ***Perf. 14x13***
555 A158 55c multi 55 15

Adm. Michiel Adriaenszon de Ruyter (1607-1676), Dutch naval hero, 300th death anniversary.

Van Prinsterer and Page — A159

1976, May 19 **Photo.** ***Perf. 14x13***
556 A159 55c multi 55 15

Guillaume Groen van Prinsterer (1801-1876), statesman and historian.

Women Waving American Flags
A160

Design is from a 220-year old permanent wooden calendar from Ameland Island.

1976, May 25 **Litho.**
557 A160 75c multi 70 55

American Bicentennial.

Marchers
A161

1976, June 15 **Photo.** ***Perf. 14x13***
558 A161 40c multi 35 15

Nijmegen 4-day march, 60th anniversary.

Runners
A162

1976, June 15 **Litho.**
Tagged
559 A162 55c multi 1.25 15

Royal Dutch Athletic Soc., 75th anniv.

Printing: One Communicating with Many — A163

1976, Sept. 2 **Photo.** ***Perf. 13x14***
560 A163 45c blue & red 35 15

Netherlands Printers Organization, 75th anniversary.

Sailing Ship and City — A164

Design: 75c, Sea gull over coast.

1976, Sept. 2 **Litho.** ***Perf. 14x13***
Tagged
561 A164 40c bis, red & bl 35 15
562 A164 75c ultra, yel & red 65 40

Zuider Zee Project, the conversion of water areas into land.

Radiation of Heat and Light — A165

Ballot and Pencil — A166

Perf. 13x14, 14x13
1977, Jan. 25 **Photo.**
563 A165 40c multi 28 15
564 A166 45c blk, red & ocher 48 15
Set value 24

Coil Stamps
Perf. 13 Horiz.
565 A165 40c multi 28 15
Perf. 13 Vert.
566 A166 45c multi 35 15

Publicity for wise use of energy (40c) and forthcoming elections (45c). Nos. 565-566 have black control number on back of every 5th stamp.

For overprint see No. 569.

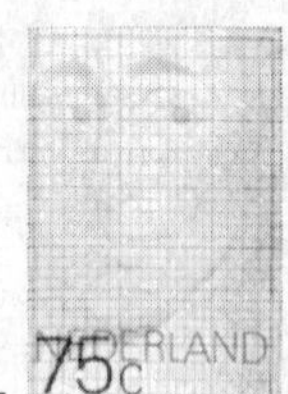

Spinoza — A167

1977, Feb. 21 **Photo.** ***Perf. 13x14***
567 A167 75c multi 60 40

Baruch Spinoza (1632-1677), philosopher, 300th death anniversary.

Delft Bible Text, Old Type, Electronic "a" — A168

1977, Mar. 8 ***Perf. 14x13***
568 A168 55c ocher & blk 45 20

Delft Bible (Old Testament), oldest book printed in Dutch, 500th anniversary. Printed in sheets of 50 se-tenant with label inscribed with description of stamp design and purpose.

No. 564 Overprinted in Blue **25 MEI'77**

1977, Apr. 15 **Photo.** ***Perf. 14x13***
569 A166 45c multi 50 15

Elections of May 25.

Kaleidoscope of Activities — A169

1977, June 9 **Litho.** ***Perf. 13x14***
570 A169 55c multi 40 15

Netherlands Society for Industry and Commerce, bicentenary.

Man in Wheelchair Looking at Obstacles
A170

Engineer's Diagram of Water Currents
A171

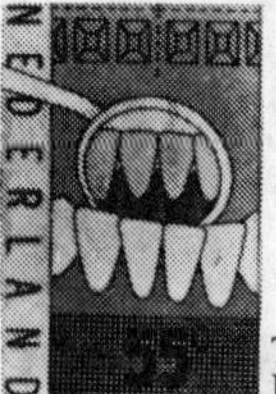

Teeth, Dentist's Mirror — A172

1977, Sept. 6 **Photo.** ***Perf. 14x13***
571 A170 40c multi 30 15
Litho.
572 A171 45c multi 30 15
Perf. 13x14
573 A172 55c multi 40 15

50th anniversaries of AVO (Actio vincit omnia), an organization to help the handicapped (40c), and of Delft Hydraulic Laboratory (45c); centenary of Dentists' Training in the Netherlands (55c).

"Postcode"
A173

1978, Mar. 14 **Photo.** ***Perf. 14x13***
574 A173 40c dk bl & red 30 15
575 A173 45c red, dk & lt bl 30 15
Set value 24

Introduction of new postal code.

European Human Rights Treaty — A174

Haarlem City Hall — A175

1978, May 2 **Photo.** ***Perf. 13x14***
576 A174 45c gray, bl & blk 32 15

European Treaty of Human Rights, 25th anniversary.

Europa Issue

1978, May 2
577 A175 55c multi 60 15

Chess Board and Move Diagram
A176

Korfball
A177

1978, June 1 **Photo.** ***Perf. 13x14***
578 A176 40c multi 30 15
Litho.
579 A177 45c red & vio bl 30 15

18th IBM Chess Tournament, Amsterdam, July 12, and 75th anniversary of korfball in the Netherlands.

Man Pointing to his Kidney
A178

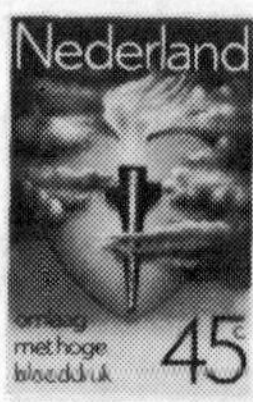

Heart, Torch, Gauge and Clouds
A179

1978, Aug. 22 **Photo.** ***Perf. 13x13½***
580 A178 40c multi 30 15
Perf. 13x14
581 A179 45c multi 30 15

Importance of kidney transplants and drive against hypertension.

Epaulettes, Military Academy — A180

1978, Sept. 12 Photo. *Perf. 13x14*
582 A180 55c multi 40 15

Royal Military Academy, sesquicentennial. Printed in continuous design in sheets of 100 (10x10).

Verkade as Hamlet A181

1978, Oct. 17 Photo. *Perf. 14x13*
583 A181 45c multi 30 15

Eduard Rutger Verkade (1878-1961), actor and producer.

Unie van Utrecht
Nederland 55 ct
Clasped Hands and Arrows — A182

1979, Jan. 23 Engr. *Perf. 13x14*
584 A182 55c blue 40 15

Union of Utrecht, 400th anniversary.

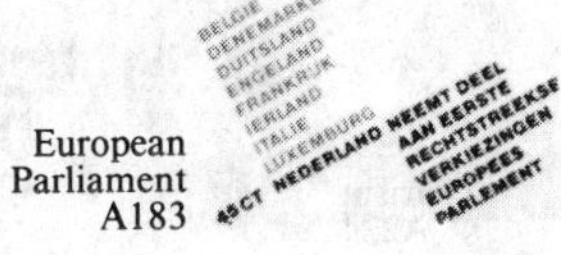

European Parliament A183

1979, Feb. 20 Litho. *Perf. 13½x13*
585 A183 45c bl, blk & red 35 15

European Parliament, first direct elections, June 7-10.

Queen Juliana A184

1979, Mar. 13 Photo. *Perf. 13½x14*
586 A184 55c multi 48 20

70th birthday of Queen Juliana.

Dutch Stamps and Magnifying Glass — A185

Europa: 75c, Hand on Morse key, and ship at sea.

1979, May 2 Litho. *Perf. 13x13½*
587 A185 55c multi 45 20
588 A185 75c multi 60 40

Map of Netherlands with Chamber Locations — A186

1979, June 5 Litho. *Perf. 13x14*
589 A186 45c multi 35 15

Netherlands Chambers of Commerce and 175th anniversary of Maastricht Chamber.

Soccer A187

1979, Aug. 28 Litho. *Perf. 14x13*
590 A187 45c multi 30 15

Centenary of soccer in the Netherlands.

Suffragettes — A188

1979, Aug. 28 Photo. *Perf. 13x14*
591 A188 55c multi 40 15

Voting right for women, 60th anniversary.

Inscribed Tympanum and Architrave A189

1979, Oct. 2 Photo. *Perf. 14x13*
592 A189 40c multi 30 15

Joost van den Vondel (1587-1679), Dutch poet and dramatist.

"Gay Company," Tile Floor — A190

1979, Oct. 2
593 A190 45c multi 30 15

Jan Steen (1626-1679), Dutch painter.

Alexander de Savorin Lohman (1837-1924) — A191

Politicians: 50c, Pieter Jelles Troelstra (1860-1930), Social Democratic Workmen's Party leader. 60c, Pieter Jacobus Oud (1886-1968), mayor of Rotterdam.

1980, Mar. 4 Photo. *Perf. 13x13½*
594 A191 45c multi 24 15
595 A191 50c multi 32 15
596 A191 60c multi 50 15
Set value 36

British Bomber Dropping Food, Dutch Flag — A192

Anne Frank — A193

Perf. 13x14, 14x13
1980, Apr. 25 Photo.
597 A192 45c multi 30 15
598 A193 60c multi 40 15
Set value 22

35th anniv. of liberation from the Germans.

Queen Beatrix, Palace — A194

1980, Apr. 30 *Perf. 13x14, 13x13½*
599 A194 60c multi 42 20

Installation of Queen Beatrix.
See No. 608.

Boy and Girl Inspecting Stamp A195

1980, May 1 *Perf. 14x13*
600 A195 50c multi 32 25

Youth philately; NVPH Stamp Show, s'Gravenhagen, May 1-3 and JUPOSTEX Stamp Exhibition, Eindhoven, May 23-27. No. 600 printed se-tenant with label.

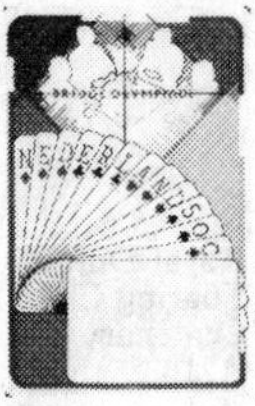

Bridge Players, "Netherlands" Hand — A196

1980, June 3 Litho. *Perf. 13x14*
601 A196 50c multi 32 15

6th Bridge Olympiad, Valkenburg, Sept. 27-Oct. 11.

Truck Transport A197

1980, Aug. 26 Photo. *Perf. 13½x13*
602 A197 50c shown 32 15
603 A197 60c Two-axle railway hopper truck 42 15
604 A197 80c Inland navigation barge 60 32

Queen Wilhelmina, Excerpt from Speech, Netherlands Flag — A198

1980, Sept. 23 Litho. *Perf. 13½x13*
605 A198 60c shown 42 15
606 A198 80c Winston Churchill, British flag 60 32

Europa.

Abraham Kupyer, University Emblem, "100" — A199

1980, Oct. 14 Litho. *Perf. 13½x13*
607 A199 50c multi 35 15

Free University centennial (founded by Kupyer).

Queen Beatrix Type of 1980
Perf. 13x13½, 13x14
1981, Jan. 6 Photo.
608 A194 65c multi 50 15

Parcel — A200

Designs: 55c, Dish antenna and telephone. 65c, Bank books.

1981, May 19 Litho. *Perf. 13½x13*
609 A200 45c multi 30 18
610 A200 55c multi 38 18
611 A200 65c multi 50 18
a. Souv. sheet of 3, #609-611 1.25 1.25

Centenaries: Parcel Post Service (45c); Public telephone service (55c); National Savings Bank (65c).

Huis ten Bosch (Royal Palace), The Hague — A201

1981, June 16 Litho. *Perf. 13½x13*
612 A201 55c multi 38 15

Europa Issue 1981

Carillon A202

1981, Sept. 1 Litho. *Perf. 13½x13*
613 A202 45c shown 30 18
614 A202 65c Barrel organ 50 18

450th Anniv. of Council of State — A203

1981, Oct. 1 Photo. *Perf. 13½x13*

615 A203 65c multi	50	15

Excavator and Ship's Screw (Exports) A204

1981, Oct. 20 Photo. *Perf. 13½x13*

616 A204 45c shown	30	15
617 A204 55c Cast iron component, scale	35	15
618 A204 60c Tomato, lettuce	42	15
619 A204 65c Egg, cheese	45	15
Set value		48

Queen Beatrix — A205

1981-86 Photo. *Perf. 13½x12½*

620	65c tan & blk	52	15
621	70c lt vio & blk ('82)	55	15
a.	Bklt. pane (4 #536, 4 #621) ('85)	2.50	
622	75c pale pink & blk ('82)	60	15
a.	Bklt. pane of 4 ('86)	2.20	
623	90c lt grn & blk ('82)	70	15
624	1g lt vio & blk ('82)	75	15
625	1.40g pale grn & blk ('82)	1.10	15
626	2g lem & blk ('82)	1.50	15
627	3g pale vio & blk ('82)	2.25	70
628	4g brt yel grn & blk ('82)	3.00	1.00
629	5g lt grnsh bl & blk ('82)	4.00	1.50
630	6.50g lt lil rose & blk ('82)	5.00	2.50
631	7g pale bl & blk ('86)	5.75	5.25
	Nos. 620-631 (12)	25.72	12.00

Coil Stamps

Perf. 13½ Horiz.

632	70c lt vio & blk ('82)	55	50
633	75c pale pink & blk ('86)	60	58
634	1g lt vio & blk ('82)	75	70
635	2g lem & blk ('82)	1.50	1.40
636	6.50g lt lil rose & blk ('82)	5.00	2.50
637	7g pale bl & blk ('86)	5.75	5.25
	Nos. 632-637 (6)	14.15	10.93

See Nos. 685-699.

University of Amsterdam, 350th Anniv. A206

1982, Jan. 14 Litho. *Perf. 13½x13*

638 A206 65c multi	45	15

Royal Dutch Skating Assoc. Centenary — A207

1982, Feb. 26 Litho. *Perf. 13x13½*

639 A207 45c multi	32	22

Bicentenary of US-Netherlands Diplomatic Relations — A208

1982, Apr. 20 Photo. *Perf. 13½x13*

640 A208 50c multi	32	22
641 A208 65c multi	45	22

See US No. 2003.

Sandwich Tern and Eider Duck, Waddenzee A209

1982, June 8 Litho. *Perf. 13½x13*

642 A209 50c shown	32	22
643 A209 70c Barnacle geese	45	22

Dutch Road Safety Assoc, 50th Anniv. — A210

Europa 1982 — A211

1982, Aug. 24 Photo. *Perf. 13x14*

644 A210 60c multi	45	25

1982, Sept. 16 Litho. *Perf. 13x13½*

Fortification Layouts.

645 A211 50c Enkhuizen, 1590	38	15
646 A211 70c Coevorden, 1680	50	15
Set value		24

Royal Palace, Dam Square, Amsterdam — A212

1982, Oct. 5 Litho. *Perf. 13x13½*

647 A212 50c Facade, cross-section	38	20
648 A212 60c Aerial view	45	25

Royal Dutch Touring Club Centenary A213

1983, Mar. 1 Litho. *Perf. 13½x13*

649 A213 70c multi	50	25

Europa 1983 — A214

Designs: 50c, Netherlands Newspaper Publishers Assoc., 75th anniv. 70c, Launching of European Telecommunication Satellite Org. ECS F-1 rocket, June 3.

1983, May 17 Litho. *Perf. 13x13½*

650 A214 50c multi	38	18
651 A214 70c multi	50	20

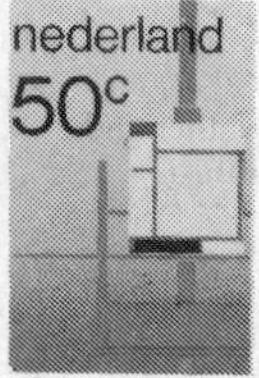

De Stijl ("The Style") Modern Art Movement, 1917-31 — A215

Designs: 50c, Composition 1922, by P. Mondriaan. 65c, Maison Particuliere contra Construction, by C. van Eesteren and T. van Doesburg.

1983, June 21 Litho. *Perf. 13x13½*

652 A215 50c multi	38	20
653 A215 65c multi	45	25

Symbolic Separation of Church — A216

1983, Oct. 11 Litho. *Perf. 13x13½*

654 A216 70c multi	50	25

Martin Luther (1483-1546).

2nd European Parliament Election, June 14 — A217

1984, Mar. 13 Litho. *Perf. 13½x13*

655 A217 70c multi	45	18

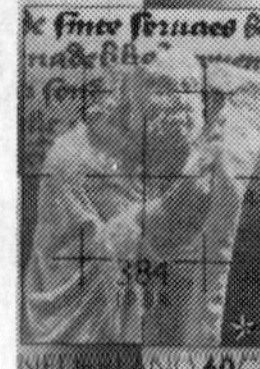

St. Servatius (d. 384) — A218

1984, May 8 Photo. *Perf. 13x14*

656 A218 60c Statue, 1732	60	15

Europa (1959-84) A219

1984, May 22 *Perf. 13½x13*

657	A219 50c blue	45	15
a.	Perf. 14x13	*10.00*	*1.00*
658	A219 70c yel grn	70	18
a.	Perf. 14x13	*10.00*	*1.00*

Perf. 14x13 stamps are coils. Every fifth stamp has a control number on the back.

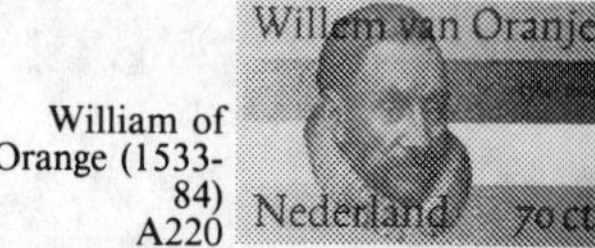

William of Orange (1533-84) A220

1984, July 10 Photo. *Perf. 14x13*

659 A220 70c multi	70	18

World Wildlife Fund — A221

1984, Sept. 18 Litho. *Perf. 14x13*

660 A221 70c Pandas, globe	65	18

11th Intl. Small Business Congress, Amsterdam, Oct. 24-26 — A222

1984, Oct. 23 Litho. *Perf. 13x13½*

661 A222 60c Graph, leaf	60	15

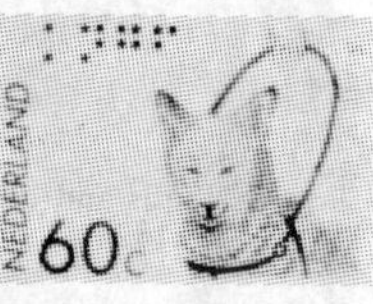

Guide Dog Fund — A223

Photogravure and Engraved

1985, Jan. 21 *Perf. 14x13*

662 A223 60c Sunny, first guide dog	60	15

Tourism A224

1985, Feb. 26 Photo.

663 A224 50c Dinner place setting	50	15
664 A224 70c Spiral, antlers	75	15

Liberation from German Forces, 40th Anniv. A225

Designs: 50c, Jewish star, mastheads of underground newspapers, resistance fighter. 60c, Allied supply air drop, masthead of The Flying Dutchman, Polish soldier at Arnhem. 65c, Liberation Day in Amsterdam, masthead, first edition of Het Parool (underground newspaper), American cemetary at Margraten. 70c, Dutch women in Japanese prison camp, Japanese occupation currency, building of the Burma Railway.

1985, May 5 Photo. *Perf. 14x13*

665 A225 50c blk, buff & red	50	15
666 A225 60c blk, buff & brt bl	60	15
667 A225 65c blk, buff & org	60	15
668 A225 70c blk, buff & brt grn	70	18

WWII resistance effort (1940-1945) and liberation of Europe, 1945.

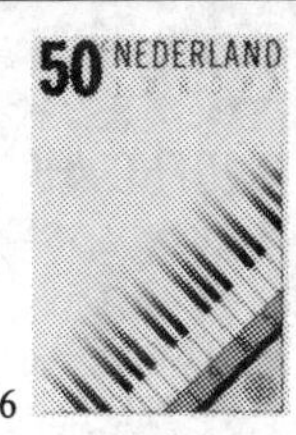

Europa '85 — A226

1984, June 4 Litho. *Perf. 13x13½*
669 A226 50c Piano keyboard 75 15
670 A226 70c Stylized organ pipes 1.00 18

Natl. Museum of Fine Arts, Amsterdam, Cent. — A227

Anniversaries and events: 60c, Nautical College, Amsterdam, bicent. 70c, SAIL-85, Amsterdam.

1985, July 2 Photo. *Perf. 13½x13*
671 A227 50c Museum in 1885, 1985 50 15
672 A227 60c Students training 60 15

Perf. 14x13
673 A227 70c Sailboat rigging 70 18

Wildlife Conservation A228

Designs: 50c, Porpoise, statistical graph. 70c, Seal, molecular structure models.

1985, Sept. 10 Litho. *Perf. 13½x13*
674 A228 50c multi 50 15
675 A228 70c multi 70 18

Penal Code, Cent. — A229

Amsterdam Datum Ordinance, 300th Anniv. A230

Lithographed, Photogravure (60c)
1986, Jan. 21 *Perf. 14x13*
676 A229 50c Text 52 15
677 A230 60c Elevation gauge 60 15

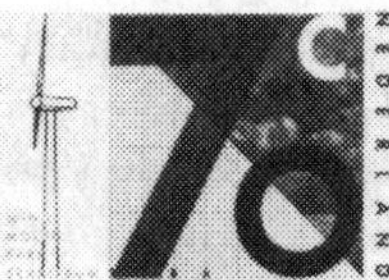

Sexbierum Windmill Test Station Inauguration A231

1986, Mar. 4 Litho. *Perf. 14x13*
678 A231 70c multi 70 18

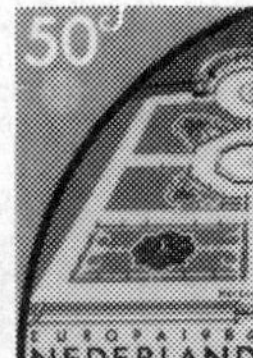

Het Loo Palace Gardens, Apeldorn — A232

1986, May 13 Litho. *Perf. 13x14*
679 A232 50c shown 55 15

Photo.
680 A232 70c Air and soil pollution 70 18

Europa 1986.

Utrecht Cathedral A233

Willem Drees (1886-), Statesman A234

1986, June 10 Photo. *Perf. 13x14*
681 A233 50c shown 48 15
682 A233 60c German House, c.1350 55 15

Perf. 14x13
683 A233 70c Utrecht University charter, horiz. 65 18

Cathedral restoration, 1986. Heemschut Conservation. Soc., 75th anniv. Utrecht University, 350th anniv.

1986, July 1 Litho. *Perf. 13x13½*
684 A234 55c multi 52 15

Queen Type of 1981

1986-90 Photo. *Perf. 13½x12½*
685 A205 1.20g citron & blk 1.10 15
686 A205 1.50g lt rose vio & blk 1.40 15
688 A205 2.50g tan & blk 2.25 15
694 A205 7.50g lt grn & blk 8.00 8.00

Coil Stamps
Perf. 13½ Horiz.
697 A205 1.50g lt rose vio & blk 1.40 15
699 A205 2.50g tan & blk 2.25 15

Issue dates: Nos. 685, 688, 699, Sept. 23. Nos. 686, 697, Aug. 19. 7.50g, May 29, 1990.
This is an expanding set. Numbers will change if necessary.

Billiards A235

Perf. 14x13, 13x14
1986, Sept. 9 Photo.
705 A235 75c shown 70 58
706 A235 75c Checkers, vert. 70 58

Royal Dutch Billiards Assoc., Checkers Association, 75th annivs.

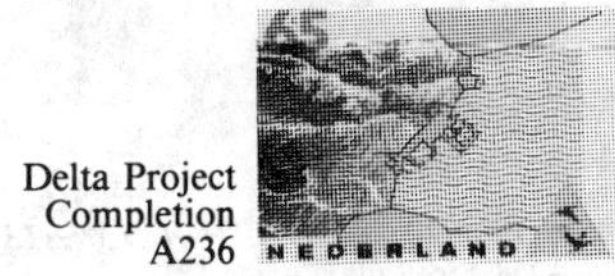

Delta Project Completion A236

1986, Oct. 7 Photo. *Perf. 14x13*
708 A236 65c Storm-surge barrier 70 15
709 A236 75c Barrier withstanding flood 75 15

Princess Juliana and Prince Bernhard, 50th Wedding Anniv. — A237

1987, Jan. 6 Photo. *Perf. 13x14*
710 A237 75c multi 75 15

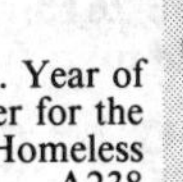

Intl. Year of Shelter for the Homeless A238

Designs: 75c, Salvation Army, cent.

1987, Feb. 10 Photo. *Perf. 14x13*
711 A238 65c multi 60 15
712 A238 75c multi 70 15

Dutch Literature A239

Authors: 55c, Eduard Douwes Dekker (1820-1887) and De Harmonie Club, Batavia. 75c, Constantijn Huygens (1596-1687) and Scheveningseweg, The Hague.

1987, Mar. 10 Litho. *Perf. 13½x13*
713 A239 55c multi 52 15
714 A239 75c multi 70 15
Set value 24

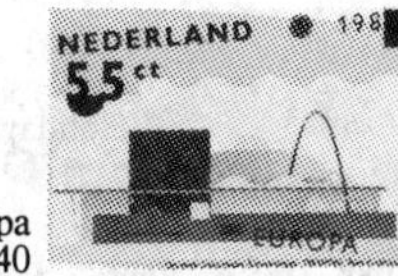

Europa 1987 — A240

Modern architecture: 55c, Scheveningen Dance Theater, designed by Rem Koolhaas. 75c, Montessori School, Amsterdam, designed by Herman Hertzberger.

1987, May 12 Litho. *Perf. 14x13*
715 A240 55c multi 55 15
716 A240 75c multi 80 15

Produce Auction at Broeck op Langedijk, 1887 A241

Designs: 65c, Field in Groningen Province, signatures of society founders. 75c, Auction, bidding, clock, 1987.

1987, June 16 Photo. *Perf. 14x13*
717 A241 55c shown 55 15
718 A241 65c multi 65 15
719 A241 75c multi 80 15
Set value 36

Sale of produce by auction in the Netherlands, cent., and Groningen Agricultural Society, 150th anniv. (No. 718).

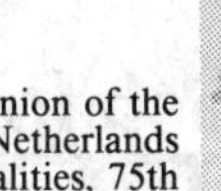

Union of the Netherlands Municipalities, 75th Anniv. — A242

1987, Oct. 6 Litho. *Perf. 13x14*
720 A242 75c multi 80 15

Noordeinde Palace, The Hague A243

1987, Oct. 27 Photo. *Perf. 14x13*
721 A243 65c multicolored 65 15

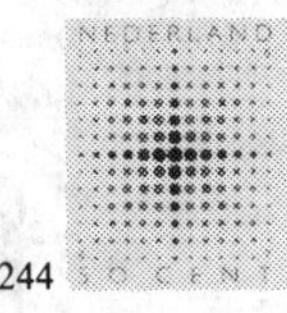

A244

Booklet Stamps
Perf. 13½x13 on 3 Sides
1987, Dec. 1 Photo.
722 A244 50c dark ultra, emer & dark red 50 15
723 A244 50c dark red, dark ultra & yel 50 15
724 A244 50c dark ultra, yel & dark red 50 15
725 A244 50c dark red, emer & yel 50 15
726 A244 50c emer, dark red & dark ultra 50 15
a. Bklt. pane of 20, 4 each #722-726 10.50
Nos. 722-726 (5) 2.50 75

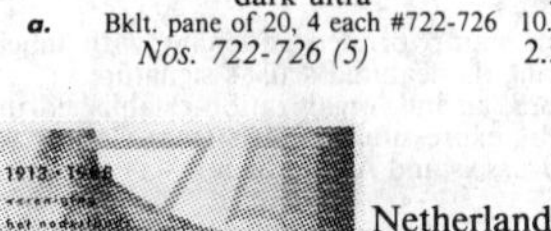

Netherlands Cancer Institute, 75th Anniv. A246

1988, Apr. 19 Litho. *Perf. 13½x13*
728 A246 75c multi 80 16

Europa 1988 — A247

Modern transportation meeting ecological requirements: 55c, Cyclist, rural scenery, chemical formulas, vert. 75c, Cyclists seen through car-door mirror.

1988, May 17 Litho. *Perf. 13x13½*
729 A247 55c multi 60 15

Perf. 13½x13
730 A247 75c multi 80 20

Coronation of William III and Mary Stuart, King and Queen of England, 300th Anniv. (in 1989) — A248

Designs: 65c, Prism splitting light as discovered by Sir Isaac Newton, planet Saturn as observed by Christian Huygens, and pendulum clock, c. 1688. 75c, William of Orange (1650-1702) and Mary II (1662-1694).

1988, June 14 *Perf. 14x13*
731 A248 65c multi 70 18
732 A248 75c multi 80 20

Arrival of Dutch William in England, 300th anniv.

Modern Art — A249

Paintings by artists belonging to Cobra: 55c, *Cobra Cat*, 1950, by Appel. 65c, *Stag Beetle*, 1948, by Corneille. 75c, *Fallen Horse*, 1950, by Constant.

1988, July 5 Litho. *Perf. 13½x13*
733 A249 55c multi 55 15
734 A249 65c multi 65 16
735 A249 75c multi 75 18

Each stamp printed se-tenant with label picturing the featured artist's signature.
Cobra, an intl. organization established in 1948 by expressionist artists from Copenhagen, Brussels and Amsterdam.

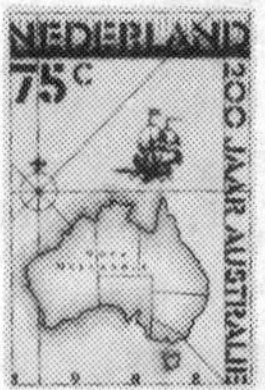
Australia Bicentennial — A250

1988, Aug. 30 Photo. *Perf. 13x14*
736 A250 75c multi 72 18

Erasmus University, Rotterdam, 75th Anniv. — A251

Amsterdam Concertgebouw and Orchestra, Cent. — A252

1988, Sept. 27 Litho. *Perf. 13x13½*
737 A251 75c dark grn & grn 72 18
738 A252 75c brt vio 72 18

Holiday Greetings — A253

1988, Dec. 1 Photo. *Perf. 13½x12½*
739 A253 50c multi 52 15

"Holland," etc.
Stamps inscribed "Holland," "Stadspost," etc., are private issues. In some cases overprints or surcharges on Netherlands stamps may be created.

Privatization of the Netherlands Postal Service — A254

Design: Mailbox, sorting machine, mailbag, mailman, telephone key pad, fiber optics cable, microwave transmitter and telephone handset.

Litho. & Engr.
1989, Jan. 3 *Perf. 13x13½*
740 A254 75c multi 78 20

Dutch Trade Unions — A255

1989, Feb. 7 Litho. *Perf. 13x13½*
741 A255 55c shown 55 15

Photo.
Perf. 13x14
742 A255 75c Hands, mouths 72 15

NATO, 40th Anniv. A256

1989, Mar. 14 Litho. *Perf. 14x13*
743 A256 75c multi 75 20

Europa 1989 — A257

Children's games (string telephone): 55c, Boy. 75c Girl.

1989, May 9 Litho. *Perf. 13½x13*
744 A257 55c multi 55 15
745 A257 75c multi 75 20

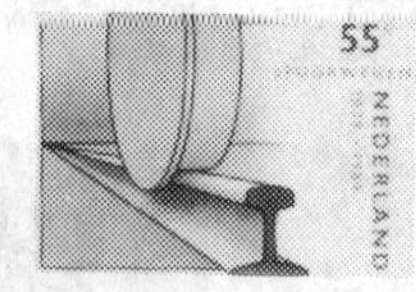
Dutch Railways, 150th Anniv. A258

1989, June 20 Litho. *Perf. 13½x13*
746 A258 55c Rails 55 15
747 A258 65c Trains 65 16

Perf. 14x13
748 A258 75c Passengers 75 20

Royal Dutch Soccer Assoc., Cent. — A259

Treaty of London, 150th Anniv. — A260

1989, Sept. 5 Photo. *Perf. 13x14*
749 A259 75c multi 72 18

1989, Oct. 2 Litho. *Perf. 13x14*
750 A260 75c Map of Limburg Provinces 72 18

See Belgium No. 1327.

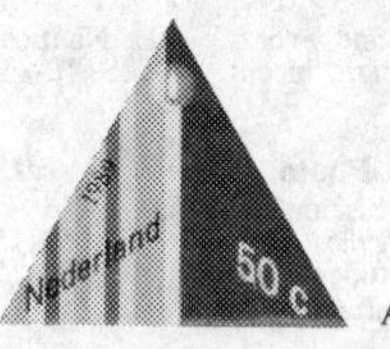
A261

Perf. 13x13x13½
1989, Nov. 30 **Photo.**
751 A261 50c multicolored 48 15

Sold only in sheets of 20.

Anniversaries A262

Vincent van Gogh (1853-1890) A263

Designs: 65c, Leiden coat of arms (tulip), and layout of the Hortus Botanicus in 1601. 75c, Assessing work conditions (clock, sky, wooden floor), horiz.

Perf. 13x13½,13½x13
1990, Feb. 6 **Litho.**
752 A262 65c multicolored 70 18
753 A262 75c multicolored 80 22

Hortus Botanicus, Leiden, 400th anniv. (65c); Labor Inspectorate, cent. (75c).

1990, Mar. 6 *Perf. 13x13½*

Details of works by van Gogh: 55c, *Self-portrait*, pencil sketch, 1886-87. 75c, *The Green Vineyard*, painting, 1888.

754 A263 55c multicolored 58 16
755 A263 75c multicolored 80 22

Rotterdam Reconstruction — A264

1990, May 8 Litho. *Perf. 13½x13*
756 A264 55c shown 58 16
757 A264 65c Diagram 70 18
758 A264 75c Modern bldgs. 80 22

Europa A264a

Post offices.

1990, June 12

759	A264a	55c Veere	58	16
760	A264a	75c Groningen	80	22

Dutch East India Co. Ships — A265

Sail '90 — A266

1990, July 3 *Perf. 13x13½*

761	A265	65c multi	70	18
762	A266	75c multi	80	22

Queens of the House of Orange A267

1990, Sept. 5 **Litho.** *Perf. 13½*

763	A267	150c multi	1.60	60

Century of rule by Queens Emma, Wilhelmina, Juliana and Beatrix.

Natl. Emergency Phone Number — A268

1990, Oct. 9 **Photo.** *Perf. 13x14*

764	A268	65c multicolored	70	18

A269

1990, Nov. 29 **Photo.** *Perf. 14*

765	A269	50c multicolored	55	15

Threats to the Environment A270

1991, Jan. 30 **Litho.** *Perf. 13½x13*

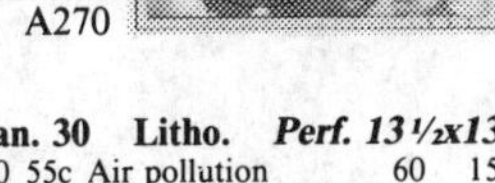

766	A270	55c Air pollution	60	15
767	A270	65c Water pollution	70	15
768	A270	75c Soil pollution	80	16

General Strike, 50th Anniv. A271

1991, Feb. 25 **Photo.** *Perf. 14x13*

769	A271	75c multicolored	80	16

Queen Beatrix and Prince Claus, 25th Wedding Anniv. A272

1991, Mar. 11 **Litho.** *Perf. 13½x13*

770	A272	75c shown	82	20
771	A272	75c Riding horses	82	20
a.		Pair, #770-771	1.64	40

Numeral Type of 1976 and

Queen Beatrix — A273

Perf. 12½x13½, 13½x12½

1991 **Photo.**

773	A157	70c gray violet	75	18
774	A273	75c green	78	15
a.		Bklt. pane of 4 + 2 labels	3.25	
776	A157	80c red lilac	85	20
781	A273	1.60g magenta	1.70	40

Coil Stamp

Perf. 13½ Vert. (A157), Horiz. (A273)

785	A157	70c gray violet	75	18
786	A273	75c green	80	15
787	A157	80c red lilac	85	20
788	A273	1.60g magenta	1.70	40

Booklet Stamp

790	A157	60c lemon	62	15
a.		Bklt. pane of 2 #790, 4 #773	4.25	
791	A273	80c red brown	85	20
a.		Booklet pane of 5 + label	4.25	

Issue dates: 75c, Mar. 14; 60c, 70c, 80c, 1.60g, June 25.

This is an expanding set. Numbers will change if neccesary.

Gerard Philips, Carbon Filament Experiments, 1890 — A274

Electrical Wiring A275

Europa — A276

Designs: 75c, Laser video disk experiment.

Perf. 13x14, 14x13

1991, May 15 **Photo.**

792	A274	55c multicolored	60	15
793	A275	65c multicolored	72	18
794	A274	75c multicolored	82	20

Philips Electronics, cent. (Nos. 792, 794). Netherlands Normalization Institute, 75th anniv. (No. 793).

1991, June 11 **Litho.** *Perf. 13x13½*

Design: 75c, Ladders to another world.

795	A276	55c multicolored	60	15
796	A276	75c multicolored	82	20

Nijmegen Four Days Marches, 75th Anniv. A277

1991, July 9 **Photo.** *Perf. 14x13*

797	A277	80c multicolored	85	20

Dutch Nobel Prize Winners A278

Designs: 60c, Jacobus H. Van't Hoff, chemistry, 1901. 70c, Pieter Zeeman, physics, 1902. 80c, Tobias M. C. Asser, peace, 1911.

1991, Sept. 3 *Perf. 14x13*

798	A278	60c multicolored	62	15
799	A278	70c multicolored	75	18
800	A278	80c multicolored	85	20

A280

1991, Nov. 28 **Photo.** *Perf. 14*

803	A280	55c multicolored	65	16

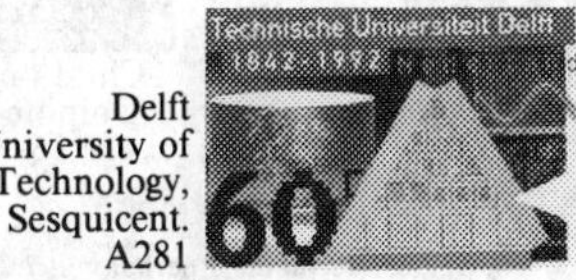

Delft University of Technology, Sesquicent. A281

New Civil Code A282

1992, Jan. 7 **Litho.** *Perf. 13½x13*

804	A281	60c multicolored	70	18
805	A282	80c multicolored	95	25

SEMI-POSTAL STAMPS

Design Symbolical of the Four Chief Means for Combating Tuberculosis: Light, Water, Air and Food — SP1

Perf. 12½

1906, Dec. 21 **Typo.** **Unwmk.**

B1	SP1	1c (+1c) rose red	2.25	1.10
B2	SP1	3c (+3c) pale ol grn	22.50	11.00
B3	SP1	5c (+5c) gray	22.50	3.75

Surtax aided the Society for the Prevention of Tuberculosis.

Nos. B1-B3 canceled-to-order "AMSTERDAM 31.07 10-12 N," sell at $2.75 a set.

Symbolical of Charity SP2

SP3

1923, Dec. 15 *Perf. 11½*

B4	SP2	2c (+5c) vio bl	10.50	8.00
B5	SP3	10c (+5c) org red	11.00	8.00

The surtax was for the benefit of charity.

Allegory, Charity Protecting Child — SP6

1924, Dec. 15 **Photo.** *Perf. 12½*

B6	SP6	2c (+2c) emer	55	95
B7	SP6	7½c (+3½c) dk brn	3.25	3.50
B8	SP6	10c (+2½c) ver	3.00	60

These stamps were sold at a premium over face value for the benefit of Child Welfare Societies.

Arms of North Brabant SP7

Arms of Gelderland SP8

Arms of South Holland — SP9

1925, Dec. 17 *Perf. 12½ Syncopated*

B9	SP7	2c (+2c) grn & org	75	65
B10	SP8	7½c (+3½c) vio & bl	2.50	2.25
B11	SP9	10c (+2½c) red & org	2.00	30

Surtax went to Child Welfare Societies. See note after No. 141.

Syncopated Perfs., Type A

B9a	SP7	2c (+2c)	6.75	6.75
B10a	SP8	7½c (+3½c)	20.00	22.50
B11a	SP9	10c (+2½c)	55.00	47.50

Arms of Utrecht SP10

Arms of Zeeland SP11

Arms of North Holland SP12

Arms of Friesland SP13

1926, Dec. 1 Wmk. 202 *Perf. 12½*

B12	SP10	2c (+2c) sil & red	40	25
B13	SP11	5c (+3c) grn & gray bl	95	50
B14	SP12	10c (+3c) red & gold	1.90	18
B15	SP13	15c (+3c) ultra & yel	4.75	2.50

The surtax on these stamps was devoted to Child Welfare Societies.

Syncopated Perfs., Type A

B12a	SP10	2c (+2c)	3.00	3.00
B13a	SP11	5c (+3c)	6.00	6.50
B14a	SP12	10c (+3c)	11.50	6.50
B15a	SP13	15c (+3c)	14.00	16.00

King William III SP14

Red Cross and Doves SP18

Designs: 3c, Queen Emma. 5c, Prince Consort Henry. 7½c, Queen Wilhelmina.

Perf. 11½, 11½x12

1927, June Photo. Unwmk.

B16	SP14	2c (+2c) scar	1.00	1.25
		Engr.		
B17	SP14	3c (+2c) dp grn	3.50	4.50
B18	SP14	5c (+3c) slate bl	40	35
		Photo.		
B19	SP14	7½c (+3½c) ultra	2.50	1.00
B20	SP18	15c (+5c) ultra & red	7.25	7.25
		Nos. B16-B20 (5)	14.65	14.35

60th anniversary of the Netherlands Red Cross Society. The surtaxes in parentheses were for the benefit of the Society.

Arms of Drenthe SP19

Arms of Groningen SP20

Arms of Limburg SP21

Arms of Overijssel SP22

1927, Dec. 15 Wmk. 202 *Perf. 12½*

B21	SP19	2c (+2c) dp rose & vio	32	22
B22	SP20	5c (+3c) ol grn & yel	1.00	90
B23	SP21	7½c (+3½c) red & blk	2.50	15
B24	SP22	15c (+3c) ultra & org brn	3.50	2.50

The surtax on these stamps was for the benefit of Child Welfare Societies.

Syncopated Perfs., Type A

B21a	SP19	2c (+2c)	1.65	1.65
B22a	SP20	5c (+3c)	3.00	2.75
B23a	SP21	7½c (+3½c)	4.75	1.75
B24a	SP22	15c (+3c)	8.50	6.50

Rowing — SP23

Fencing — SP24

Soccer SP25

Yachting SP26

Putting the Shot SP27

Running SP28

Riding SP29

Boxing SP30

Perf. 11½, 12, 11½x12, 12x11½

1928, Mar. 27 Litho.

B25	SP23	1½c (+1c) dk grn	65	50
B26	SP24	2c (+1c) red vio	95	70
B27	SP25	3c (+1c) green	95	70
B28	SP26	5c (+1c) lt bl	1.10	70
B29	SP27	7½c (+2½c) org	1.50	70
B30	SP28	10c (+2c) scarlet	3.00	2.75
B31	SP29	15c (+2c) dk bl	3.00	1.65
B32	SP30	30c (+3c) dk brn	15.00	15.00
		Nos. B25-B32 (8)	26.15	22.70

The surtax on these stamps was used to help defray the expenses of the Olympic Games of 1928.

Jean Pierre Minckelers SP31

Child on Dolphin SP35

Designs: 5c, Hermann Boerhaave. 7½c, Hendrik Antoon Lorentz. 12½c, Christian Huygens.

1928, Dec. 10 Photo. *Perf. 12x12½*

B33	SP31	1½c (+1½c) vio	30	20
B34	SP31	5c (+3c) grn	50	65
		Perf. 12		
B35	SP31	7½c (+3½c) ver	1.50	45
a.		Perf. 12x12½	4.00	70
B36	SP31	12½c (+3½c) ultra	5.75	3.75
a.		Perf. 12x12½	60.00	5.25

The surtax on these stamps was for the benefit of Child Welfare Societies.

1929, Dec. 10 Litho. *Perf. 12½*

B37	SP35	1½c (+1½c) gray	95	25
B38	SP35	5c (+3c) bl grn	1.50	85
B39	SP35	6c (+4c) scar	1.25	30
B40	SP35	12½c (+3½c) dk bl	8.25	6.50

Surtax for child welfare.

Syncopated Perfs., Type B

B37a	SP35	1½c (+1½c)	1.65	70
B38a	SP35	5c (+3c)	3.50	1.10
B39a	SP35	6c (+4c)	3.00	70
B40a	SP35	12½c (+3½c)	13.00	6.75

Rembrandt and His "Cloth Merchants of Amsterdam" SP36

"Spring" SP37

Perf. 11½

1930, Feb. 15 Engr. Unwmk.

B41	SP36	5c (+5c) bl grn	4.75	4.75
B42	SP36	6c (+5c) gray blk	2.50	1.75
B43	SP36	12½c (+5c) dp bl	5.75	5.75

The surtax on these stamps was for the benefit of the Rembrandt Society.

1930, Dec. 10 *Perf. 12½*

Designs: 5c, Summer. 6c, Autumn. 12½c, Winter.

B44	SP37	1½c (+1½c) lt red	70	45
B45	SP37	5c (+3c) gray grn	1.10	70
B46	SP37	6c (+4c) claret	1.10	25
B47	SP37	12½c (+3½c) lt ultra	10.00	8.00

Surtax was for Child Welfare work.

Syncopated Perfs., Type C

B44a	SP37	1½c (+1½c)	2.25	1.10
B45a	SP37	5c (+3c)	2.25	1.10
B46a	SP37	6c (+4c)	2.25	1.10
B47a	SP37	12½c (+3½c)	14.00	12.00

Stained Glass Window and Detail of Repair Method SP41

Deaf Mute Learning Lip Reading SP43

Design: 6c, Gouda Church and repair of window frame.

Wmk. 202

1931, Oct. 1 Photo. *Perf. 12½*

B48	SP41	1½c (+1½c) bl grn	7.25	7.50
B49	SP41	6c (+4c) car rose	15.00	16.00

1931, Dec. 10 *Perf. 12½*

Designs: 5c, Imbecile child. 6c, Blind girl learning to read Braille. 12½c, Child victim of malnutrition.

B50	SP43	1½c (+1½c) ver & ultra	90	25
B51	SP43	5c (+3c) Prus bl & vio	1.25	85
B52	SP43	6c (+4c) vio & grn	1.10	15
B53	SP43	12½c (+3½c) ultra & dp org	17.00	16.00

The surtax was for Child Welfare work.

Syncopated Perfs., Type C

B50a	SP43	1½c (+1½c)	1.25	1.10
B51a	SP43	5c (+3c)	3.50	1.40
B52a	SP43	6c (+4c)	3.50	1.40
B53a	SP43	12½c (+3½c)	21.00	17.50

Windmill and Dikes SP47

Furze and Boy SP51

Designs: 6c, Council House, Zierikzee. 7½c, Drawbridge. 12½c, Flower fields.

1932, May 23 *Perf. 12½*

B54	SP47	2½c (+1½c) turq grn & blk	2.25	2.00
B55	SP47	6c (+4c) gray blk & blk	4.50	2.00
B56	SP47	7½c (+3½c) brt red & blk	26.00	15.00
B57	SP47	12½c (+2½c) ultra & blk	30.00	17.00

The surtax was for the benefit of the National Tourist Association.

1932, Dec. 10 *Perf. 12½*

Designs (Heads of children and flowers typifying the seasons): 5c, Cornflower. 6c, Sunflower. 12½c, Christmas rose.

B58	SP51	1½c (+1½c) brn & yel	1.25	30
B59	SP51	5c (+3c) red org & ultra	1.25	1.00
B60	SP51	6c (+4c) dk grn & ocher	1.25	25
B61	SP51	12½c (+3½c) ocher & ultra	19.00	14.00

The surtax aided Child Welfare Societies.

Syncopated Perfs., Type C

B58a	SP51	1½c (+1½c)	2.50	1.25
B59a	SP51	5c (+3c)	3.00	1.25
B60a	SP51	6c (+4c)	3.00	1.25
B61a	SP51	12½c (+3½c)	25.00	21.00

Monument at Den Helder SP55

The "Hope," A Church and Hospital Ship SP56

Lifeboat in a Storm SP57

Dutch Sailor and Sailors' Home SP58

1933, June 10 *Perf. 14½x13½*

B62	SP55	1½c (+1½c) dp red	3.00	1.50
B63	SP56	5c (+5c) bl grn & red org	6.50	2.75
B64	SP57	6c (+4c) dp grn	10.00	2.75
B65	SP58	12½c (+3½c) ultra	12.00	13.00

The surtax was for the aid of Sailors' Homes.

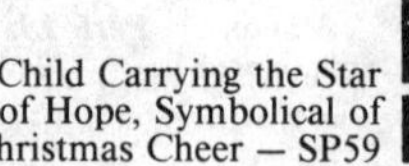
Child Carrying the Star of Hope, Symbolical of Christmas Cheer — SP59

1933, Dec. 11 *Perf. 12½*

B66	SP59	1½c (+1½c) sl & org brn	75	28
B67	SP59	5c (+3c) dk brn & ocher	90	48
B68	SP59	6c (+4c) bl grn & gold	1.00	18
B69	SP59	12½c (+3½c) dk bl & sil	13.00	12.50

The surtax aided Child Welfare Societies.

Syncopated Perfs., Type C

B66a	SP59	1½c (+1½c)	1.40	55
B67a	SP59	5c (+3c)	1.75	65
B68a	SP59	6c (+4c)	2.25	65
B69a	SP59	12½c (+3½c)	16.00	9.50

Queen Wilhelmina
SP60

Princess Juliana
SP61

Perf. 12½

1934, Apr. 28 Engr. Unwmk.

B70	SP60	5c (+4c) dk vio	6.00	1.50
B71	SP61	6c (+5c) blue	7.00	2.50

The surtax was for the benefit of the Anti-Depression Committee.

Dowager Queen Emma
SP62

Poor Child
SP63

1934, Oct. 1 ***Perf. 13x14***

B72	SP62	6c (+2c) blue	6.50	80

Surtax for the Fight Tuberculosis Society.

Perf. 13½x13

1934, Dec. 10 Photo. Wmk. 202

B73	SP63	1½c (+1½c) olive	80	35
B74	SP63	5c (+3c) rose red	1.25	90
B75	SP63	6c (+4c) bl grn	1.25	20
B76	SP63	12½c (+3½c) ultra	14.00	13.00

The surtax aided child welfare.

Henri D. Guyot
SP64

A. J. M. Diepenbrock
SP65

F. C. Donders
SP66

J. P. Sweelinck
SP67

Perf. 12½ x 12, 12

1935, June Engr. Unwmk.

B77	SP64	1½c (+1½c) dk car	90	1.50
B78	SP65	5c (+3c) blk brn	2.50	2.25
B79	SP66	6c (+4c) myr grn	2.75	20
B80	SP67	12½c (+3½c) dp bl	17.50	2.75

Surtax for social and cultural projects.

Netherlands Map, DC-3 Planes' Shadows
SP68

Girl Picking Apple
SP69

Perf. 14x13

1935, Oct. 16 Photo. Wmk. 202

B81	SP68	6c (+4c) brn	14.00	2.25

Surtax for Natl. Aviation.

1935, Dec. 4 ***Perf. 14½x13½***

B82	SP69	1½c (+1½c) crim	30	18
B83	SP69	5c (+3c) dk yel grn	80	75
B84	SP69	6c (+4c) blk brn	75	18
B85	SP69	12½c (+3½c) ultra	12.50	4.50

The surtax aided child welfare.

H. Kamerlingh Onnes
SP70

Dr. A. S. Talma
SP71

Msgr. Hjam Schaepman
SP72

Desiderius Erasmus
SP73

Perf. 12½x12

1936, May 1 Engr. Unwmk.

B86	SP70	1½c (+1½c) brn blk	80	75
B87	SP71	5c (+3c) dl grn	3.25	3.25
B88	SP72	6c (+4c) dk red	1.10	35
B89	SP73	12½c (+3½c) dl bl	10.00	2.50

Surtax for social and cultural projects.

Cherub — SP74

Perf. 14½x13½

1936, Dec. 1 Photo. Wmk. 202

B90	SP74	1½c (+1½c) lil gray	42	22
B91	SP74	5c (+3c) turq grn	1.25	70
B92	SP74	6c (+4c) dp red brn	1.25	22
B93	SP74	12½c (+3½c) ind	8.50	2.75

The surtax aided child welfare.

Jacob Maris
SP75

Franciscus de la Boe Sylvius
SP76

Joost van den Vondel
SP77

Anthony van Leeuwenhoek
SP78

Perf. 12½x12

1937, June 1 Engr. Unwmk.

B94	SP75	1½c (+1½c) blk brn	32	30
B95	SP76	5c (+3c) dl grn	2.50	2.50
B96	SP77	6c (+4c) brn vio	55	15
B97	SP78	12½c (+3½c) dl bl	5.00	1.00

Surtax for social and cultural projects.

"The Laughing Child" after Frans Hals — SP79

Perf. 14½x13½

1937, Dec. 1 Photo. Wmk. 202

B98	SP79	1½c (+1½c) blk	15	15
B99	SP79	3c (+2c) grn	70	85
B100	SP79	4c (+2c) hn brn	32	25
B101	SP79	5c (+3c) bl grn	28	15
B102	SP79	12½c (+3½c) dk bl	3.50	1.10
		Nos. B98-B102 (5)	4.95	2.50

The surtax aided child welfare.

Marnix de Sint Aldegonde
SP80

Otto Gerhard Heldring
SP81

Maria Tesselschade
SP82

Hermann Boerhaave
SP84

Harmenszoon Rembrandt van Rijn — SP83

Perf. 12½x12

1938, May 16 Engr. Unwmk.

B103	SP80	1½c (+1½c) sep	22	40
B104	SP81	3c (+2c) dk grn	25	22
B105	SP82	4c (+2c) rose lake	80	1.10
B106	SP83	5c (+3c) dk sl grn	1.00	16
B107	SP84	12½c (+3½c) dl bl	4.25	60
		Nos. B103-B107 (5)	6.52	2.48

The surtax was for the benefit of cultural and social relief.

Child with Flowers, Bird and Fish — SP85

Perf. 14½x13½

1938, Dec. 1 Photo. Wmk. 202

B108	SP85	1½c (+1½c) blk	15	15
B109	SP85	3c (+2c) mar	22	15
B110	SP85	4c (+2c) dk bl grn	45	65
B111	SP85	5c (+3c) hn brn	20	15
B112	SP85	12½c (+3½c) dp bl	4.00	1.40
		Nos. B108-B112 (5)	5.02	2.50

The surtax aided child welfare.

Mathijs Maris
SP86

Anton Mauve
SP87

Gerard van Swieten
SP88

Nikolaas Beets
SP89

Peter Stuyvesant — SP90

Perf. 12½x12

1939, May 1 Engr. Unwmk.

B113	SP86	1½c (+1½c) sep	26	32
B114	SP87	2½c (+2½c) gray grn	1.90	2.00
B115	SP88	3c (+3c) ver	48	60
B116	SP89	5c (+3c) dk sl grn	95	18
B117	SP90	12½c (+3½c) ind	3.50	60
		Nos. B113-B117 (5)	7.09	3.70

The surtax was for the benefit of cultural and social relief.

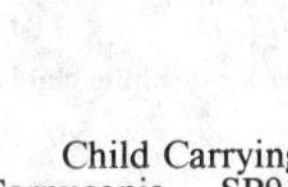

Child Carrying Cornucopia — SP91

Perf. 14½x13½

1939, Dec. 1 Photo. Wmk. 202

B118	SP91	1½c (+1½c) blk	15	15
B119	SP91	2½c (+2½c) dk ol grn	2.00	1.50
B120	SP91	3c (+3c) hn brn	30	15
B121	SP91	5c (+3c) dk grn	50	15
B122	SP91	12½c (+3½c) dk bl	2.25	85
		Nos. B118-B122 (5)	5.20	2.80

The surtax was used for destitute children.

Catalogue values for unused stamps in this section, from this point to the end of the section, are for Never Hinged items.

Vincent van Gogh SP92

E. J. Potgieter SP93

Petrus Camper SP94

Jan Steen SP95

Joseph Scaliger — SP96

Perf. 12½x12

1940, May 11 Engr. Unwmk.

B123	SP92	1½c +1½c brn blk	1.50	16
B124	SP93	2½c +2½c dk grn	5.00	70
B125	SP94	3c +3c car	3.00	65
B126	SP95	5c +3c dp grn	6.25	15
a.		Bklt. pane of 4	250.00	
B127	SP96	12½c +3½c dp bl	5.50	40

Surtax for social and cultural projects.

Type of 1940 Surcharged in Black 7½+2½

1940, Sept. 7

B128	SP95	7½c +2½c on 5c +3c dk red	45	20
		Nos. B123-B128 (6)	21.70	2.26

Child with Flowers and Doll — SP97

Perf. 14½x13½

1940, Dec. 2 Photo. Wmk. 202

B129	SP97	1½c +1½c dl bl gray	52	15
B130	SP97	2½c +2½c dp ol	2.00	50
B131	SP97	4c +3c royal bl	2.00	65
B132	SP97	5c +3c dk bl grn	2.00	15
B133	SP97	7½c +3½c hn	52	15
		Nos. B129-B133 (5)	7.04	1.60

The surtax was used for destitute children.

Dr. Antonius Mathijsen SP98

Dr. Jan Ingenhousz SP99

Aagje Deken SP100

Johannes Bosboom SP101

A. C. W. Staring — SP102

Perf. 12½x12

1941, May 29 Engr. Unwmk.

B134	SP98	1½c +1½c blk brn	60	15
B135	SP99	2½c +2½c dk sl grn	60	15
B136	SP100	4c +3c red	60	15
B137	SP101	5c +3c sl grn	60	15
B138	SP102	7½c +3½c rose vio	60	15
		Nos. B134-B138 (5)	3.00	
		Set value		60

The surtax was for cultural and social relief.

Rembrandt's Painting of Titus, His Son — SP103

Perf. 14½x13½

1941, Dec. 1 Photo. Wmk. 202

B139	SP103	1½c +1½c vio blk	20	15
B140	SP103	2½c +2½c dk ol	20	15
B141	SP103	4c +3c ryl bl	20	15
B142	SP103	5c +3c dp grn	20	15
B143	SP103	7½c +3½c dp hn brn	20	15
		Nos. B139-B143 (5)	1.00	
		Set value		50

The surtax aided child welfare.

Legionary SP104 SP105

1942, Nov. 1 *Perf. 12½x12, 12x12½*

B144	SP104	7½c +2½c dk red	35	15
a.		Sheet of 10	65.00	80.00
B145	SP106	12½c +87½c ultra	4.50	3.50
a.		Sheet of 4	60.00	90.00

The surtax aided the Netherlands Legion. #B144a, B145a measure 155x111mm and 94x94mm respectively.

19th Century Mail Cart — SP108

1943, Oct. 9 Unwmk. *Perf. 12x12½*

B148	SP108	7½c +7½c hn brn	15	15

Issued to commemorate Stamp Day.

Child and House — SP109

Designs: No. B150, Mother and Child. No. B151, Mother and Children. No. B152, Child Carrying Sheaf of Wheat. No. B153, Mother and Children, diff.

Perf. 12½x12

1944, Mar. 6 Wmk. 202

B149	SP109	1½c +3½c dl blk	15	15
B150	SP109	4c +3½ rose lake	15	15
B151	SP109	5c +5c dk bl grn	15	15
B152	SP109	7½c +7½c dp hn brn	15	15
B153	SP109	10c +40c ryl bl	15	15
		Set value		50

The surtax aided National Social Service and winter relief.

Child SP114

Fortuna SP115

1945, Dec. 1 Photo. *Perf. 14½x13½*

B154	SP114	1½c +2½c gray	18	15
B155	SP114	2½c +3½c dk bl grn	18	15
B156	SP114	5c +5c brn red	18	15
B157	SP114	7½c +4½c red	18	15
B158	SP114	12½c +5½c brt bl	18	15
		Nos. B154-B158 (5)	90	
		Set value		60

The surtax was for Child Welfare.

Perf. 12½x12

1946, May 1 Engr. Unwmk.

B159	SP115	1½c +3½c brn blk	45	15
B160	SP115	2½c +5c dl grn	60	32
B161	SP115	5c +10c dk vio	65	40
B162	SP115	7½c +15c car lake	45	15
B163	SP115	12½c +37½c dk bl	75	30
		Nos. B159-B163 (5)	2.90	1.32

The surtax was for victims of World War II.

Princess Irene SP116

Child on Merry-go-round SP119

Designs: Nos. B165, B167, Princess Margriet. Nos. B168-B169, Princess Beatrix.

1946, Sept. 16

B164	SP116	1½c +1½c blk brn	50	42
B165	SP116	2½c +1½c bl grn	50	42
B166	SP116	4c +2c mag	52	42
B167	SP116	5c +2c brn	52	42
B168	SP116	7½c +2½c red	50	15
B169	SP116	12½c +7½c dk bl	50	42
		Nos. B164-B169 (6)	3.04	2.25

The surtax was for child welfare and anti-tuberculosis work.

1946, Dec. 2 Photo. Wmk. 202

B170	SP119	2c +2c lil gray	42	20
B171	SP119	4c +2c dk grn	42	20
B172	SP119	7½c +2½c brt red	42	20
B173	SP119	10c +5c dp plum	42	15
B174	SP119	20c +5c dp bl	42	28
		Nos. B170-B174 (5)	2.10	1.03

The surtax was for child welfare.

Dr. Hendrik van Deventer SP120

Peter Cornelisz Hooft SP121

Johan de Witt SP122

Jean F. van Royen SP123

Hugo de Groot — SP124

1947, Aug. 1 Engr. Unwmk.

B175	SP120	2c +2c dk red	60	25
B176	SP121	4c +2c dk grn	1.25	42
B177	SP122	7½c +2½c dk pur brn	1.90	42
B178	SP123	10c +5c brn	1.40	15
B179	SP124	20c +5c dk bl	1.10	42
		Nos. B175-B179 (5)	6.25	1.66

The surtax was for social and cultural purposes.

Children SP125

Infant SP126

1947, Dec. 1 Photo. *Perf. 13x14*

B180	SP125	2c +2c red brn	15	15
B181	SP126	4c +2c bl grn	1.25	40
B182	SP126	7½c +2½c sepia	1.25	55
B183	SP126	10c +5c dk red	75	15
B184	SP125	20c +5c blue	1.25	65
		Nos. B180-B184 (5)	4.65	1.90

The surtax was for child welfare.

Hall of Knights, The Hague SP127

Boy in Kayak SP128

Designs: 6c+4c, Royal Palace, Amsterdam. 10c+5c, Kneuterdyk Palace, The Hague. 20c+5c, New Church, Amsterdam.

1948, June 17 Engr. *Perf. 13½x14*

B185	SP127	2c +2c dk brn	1.50	25
B186	SP127	6c +4c grn	1.50	25
B187	SP127	10c +5c brt red	1.25	15
B188	SP127	20c +5c dp bl	1.50	65

The surtax was for cultural and social purposes.

1948, Nov. 15 Photo. *Perf. 13x14*

Designs: 5c+3c, Swimming. 6c+4c, Sledding. 10c+5c, Swinging. 20c+8c, Figure skating.

B189 SP128 2c +2c yel grn 15 15
B190 SP128 5c +3c dk bl grn 2.00 65
B191 SP128 6c +4c gray 85 15
B192 SP128 10c +5c red 15 15
B193 SP128 20c +8c bl 2.25 65
Nos. B189-B193 (5) 5.40 1.75

The surtax was for child welfare.

Beach Terrace SP129

Boy and Girl Hikers SP130

Campers SP131

Reaping SP132

Sailboats SP133

1949, May 2 Wmk. 202 *Perf. 14x13*

B194 SP129 2c +2c bl & org yel 75 15
B195 SP130 5c +3c bl & yel 1.25 1.00
B196 SP131 6c +4c dk bl grn 1.25 30
B197 SP132 10c +5c bl & org yel 2.00 15
B198 SP133 20c +5c bl 1.50 1.25
Nos. B194-B198 (5) 6.75 2.85

The surtax was for cultural and social purposes.

Hands Reaching for Sunflower SP134

"Autumn" SP135

Perf. 14½x13½

1949, Aug. 1 Photo. Unwmk.

Flower in Yellow

B199 SP134 2c +3c gray 1.10 20
B200 SP134 6c +4c red brn 70 32
B201 SP134 10c +5c brt bl 2.25 20
B202 SP134 30c +10c dk brn 6.25 2.00

The surtax was for the Red Cross and for Indonesia Relief work.

1949, Nov. 14 Engr. *Perf. 13x14*

Designs: 5c+3c, "Summer." 6c+4c, "Spring." 10c+5c, "Winter." 20c+7c, "New Year."

B203 SP135 2c +3c brn 15 15
B204 SP135 5c +3c red 3.25 95
B205 SP135 6c +4c dl grn 1.10 20
B206 SP135 10c +5c gray 22 15
B207 SP135 20c +7c bl 3.50 85
Nos. B203-B207 (5) 8.22 2.30

The surtax was for child welfare.

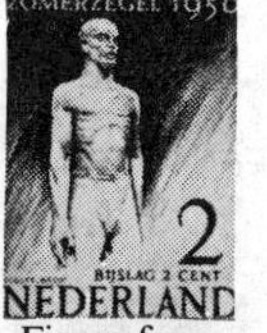

Figure from PTT Monument, The Hague SP136

Grain Binder SP137

Designs: 4c+2c, Dike repairs. 5c+3c, Apartment House, Rotterdam. 10c+5c, Bridge section being towed. 20c+5c, Canal freighter.

1950, May 2 *Perf. 12½x12, 12x12½*

B208 SP136 2c +2c dk brn 80 65
B209 SP136 4c +2c dk grn 7.50 6.00
B210 SP136 5c +3c sepia 3.75 2.00
B211 SP137 6c +4c purple 1.65 60
B212 SP137 10c +5c bl gray 1.65 20
B213 SP137 20c +5c dp bl 7.50 7.00
Nos. B208-B213 (6) 22.85 16.45

The surtax was for social and cultural works.

Church Ruins and Good Samaritan SP138

Baby and Bees SP139

1950, July 17 Photo. *Perf. 12½x12*

B214 SP138 2c +2c ol brn 1.50 85
B215 SP138 5c +3c brn red 8.25 *9.00*
B216 SP138 6c +4c dp grn 4.75 1.00
B217 SP138 10c +5c brt lil rose 5.00 20
B218 SP138 20c +5c ultra 12.00 *16.00*
Nos. B214-B218 (5) 31.50 *27.05*

The surtax was for the restoration of ruined churches.

1950, Nov. 13 *Perf. 13x12*

Designs: 5c+3c, Boy and rooster. 6c+4c, Girl feeding birds. 10c+5c, Boy and fish. 20c+7c, Girl, butterfly and toad.

B219 SP139 2c +3c car 15 15
B220 SP139 5c +3c ol grn 5.00 1.90
B221 SP139 6c +4c dk bl grn 1.50 40
B222 SP139 10c +5c lil 15 15
B223 SP139 20c +7c bl 9.00 5.00
Nos. B219-B223 (5) 15.80 7.60

The surtax was to aid needy children.

Hillenraad Castle SP140

Bergh Castle SP141

Castles: 6c+4c, Hernen. 10c+5c, Rechteren. 20c+5c, Moermond.

Perf. 12x12½, 12½x12

1951, May 15 Engr. Unwmk.

B224 SP140 2c +2c pur 2.00 1.00
B225 SP141 5c +3c dk red 6.00 5.00
B226 SP140 6c +4c dk brn 1.00 80
B227 SP141 10c +5c dk grn 2.00 35
B228 SP141 20c +5c dp bl 5.00 *5.00*
Nos. B224-B228 (5) 16.00 *12.15*

The surtax was for cultural, medical and social purposes.

Girl and Windmill SP142

Jan van Riebeeck SP143

Designs: 5c+3c, Boy and building construction. 6c+4c, Fisherboy and net. 10c+5c, Boy, chimneys and steelwork. 20c+7c, Girl and apartment house.

1951, Nov. 12 Photo. *Perf. 13x14*

B229 SP142 2c +3c dp grn 25 15
B230 SP142 5c +3c sl vio 4.75 2.75
B231 SP142 6c +4c dk brn 4.75 15
B232 SP142 10c +5c red brn 18 15
B233 SP142 20c +7c dp bl 6.25 *4.50*
Nos. B229-B233 (5) 16.18 *7.70*

The surtax was for child welfare.

1952, Mar. *Perf. 12½x12*

B234 SP143 2c +3c dk gray 2.50 1.65
B235 SP143 6c +4c dk bl grn 5.75 4.00
B236 SP143 10c +5c brt red 6.00 3.00
B237 SP143 20c +5c brt bl 2.50 1.65

Tercentenary of Van Riebeeck's landing in South Africa. Surtax was for Van Riebeeck monument fund.

Scotch Rose — SP144

Girl and Dog — SP145

Designs: 5c+3c, Marsh marigold. 6c+4c, Tulip. 10c+5c, Ox-eye daisy. 20c+5c, Cornflower.

1952, May 1

B238 SP144 2c +2c cer & dl grn 60 40
B239 SP144 5c +3c dp grn & yel 85 65
B240 SP144 6c +4c red & dl grn 1.10 30
B241 SP144 10c +5c org yel & dl grn 1.25 15
B242 SP144 20c +5c bl & dl grn 11.00 7.50
Nos. B238-B242 (5) 14.80 9.00

The surtax was for social, cultural and medical purposes.

Perf. 12x12½

1952, Nov. 17 Unwmk.

Designs: 2c+3c, Boy and goat. 5c+3c, Girl on donkey. 10c+5c, Boy and kitten. 20c+7c, Boy and rabbit.

Design in Black

B243 SP145 2c +3c ol 15 15
B244 SP145 5c +3c dp rose 90 45
B245 SP145 6c +4c aqua 1.90 28
B246 SP145 10c +5c org yel 15 15
B247 SP145 20c +7c bl 6.75 4.75
Nos. B243-B247 (5) 9.85 5.78

The surtax was for child welfare.

No. 308 Surcharged in Black

19 53

10c +10

WATERSNOOD

Perf. 13½x13

1953, Feb. 10 Wmk. 202

B248 A76 10c +10c org yel 38 15

The surtax was for flood relief.

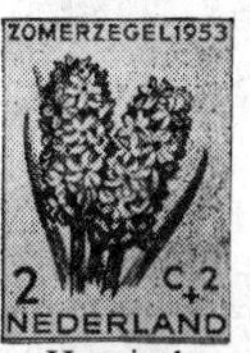

Hyacinth SP146

Red Cross on Shield SP147

Designs: 5c+3c, African Marigold. 6c+4c, Daffodil. 10c+5c, Anemone. 20c+5c, Iris.

1953, May 1 Unwmk. *Perf. 12½x12*

B249 SP146 2c +2c vio & grn 50 20
B250 SP146 5c +3c dp org & grn 75 65
B251 SP146 6c +4c grn & yel 1.00 30
B252 SP146 10c +5c dk red & grn 1.90 15
B253 SP146 20c +5c dp ultra & grn 10.50 *9.00*
Nos. B249-B253 (5) 14.65 *10.30*

The surtax was for social, cultural and medical purposes.

1953, Aug. 24 Engr.

Designs: 6c+4c, Man holding lantern. 7c+5c, Worker and ambulance at flood. 10c+5c, Nurse giving blood transfusion. 25c+8c, Red Cross flags.

Cross in Red

B254 SP147 2c +3c dk ol 50 20
B255 SP147 6c +4c dk vio brn 2.00 1.65
B256 SP147 7c +5c dk gray grn 1.00 25
B257 SP147 10c +5c red 75 15
B258 SP147 25c +8c dp bl 5.25 3.50
Nos. B254-B258 (5) 9.50 5.75

The surtax was for the Red Cross.

Spade, Flag, Bucket and Girl's Head — SP148

Designs: Head of child and: 5c+3c, Apple. 7c+5c, Pigeon. 10c+5c, Sailboat. 25c+8c, Tulip.

1953, Nov. 16 Litho. *Perf. 12x12½*

B259 SP148 2c +3c yel & bl gray 20 15
B260 SP148 5c +3c ap grn & brn car 1.50 60
B261 SP148 7c +5c lt bl & sep 3.25 70
B262 SP148 10c +5c ol bis & lil 20 15
B263 SP148 25c +8c pink & bl grn 12.00 7.75
Nos. B259-B263 (5) 17.15 9.35

The surtax was for child welfare.

Martinus Nijhoff, Poet SP149

Boy Flying Model Plane SP150

Portraits: 5c+3c, Willem Pijper, composer. 7c+5c, H. P. Berlage, architect. 10c+5c, Johan Huizinga, historian. 25c+ 8c, Vincent van Gogh, painter.

1954, May 1 Photo. *Perf. 12½x12*

B264 SP149 2c +3c dp bl 1.40 1.00
B265 SP149 5c +3c ol brn 70 40
B266 SP149 7c +5c dk red 2.25 85
B267 SP149 10c +5c dl grn 5.00 15
B268 SP149 25c +8c plum 9.00 *8.75*
Nos. B264-B268 (5) 18.35 *11.15*

The surtax was for social and cultural purposes.

1954, Aug. 23 *Perf. 12½x12*

Portrait: 10c+4c, Albert E. Plesman.

B269 SP150 2c +2c ol grn 55 48
B270 SP150 10c +4c dk gray bl 1.90 48

The surtax was for the Netherlands Aviation Foundation.

Children Making Paper Chains
SP151

Girl Brushing Teeth
SP152

Designs: 7c+5c, Boy sailing toy boat. 10c+5c, Nurse drying child. 25c+8c, Young convalescent, drawing.

Perf. 12x12½, 12½x12

1954, Nov. 15

B271 SP151 2c +3c brn 15 15
B272 SP152 5c +3c ol grn 70 35
B273 SP152 7c +5c gray bl 1.00 30
B274 SP152 10c +5c brn red 15 15
B275 SP151 25c +8c dp bl 7.50 5.00
Nos. B271-B275 (5) 9.50 5.95

The surtax was for child welfare.

Factory, Rotterdam
SP153

Amsterdam Stock Exchange
SP154

Designs: 5c+3c, Post office, The Hague. 10c+5c, Town hall, Hilversum. 25c+8c, Office building, The Hague.

1955, Apr. 25 Engr.

B276 SP153 2c +3c brnsh bis 85 95
B277 SP153 5c +3c bl grn 28 20
B278 SP154 7c +5c rose brn 85 95
B279 SP153 10c +5c stl bl 1.25 15
B280 SP153 25c +8c choc 10.00 *7.00*
Nos. B276-B280 (5) 13.23 *9.25*

The surtax was for social and cultural purposes.

Microscope and Crab
SP155

Willem van Loon by Dirck Santvoort
SP156

1955, Aug. 15 Photo. *Perf. 12½x12*
Crab in Red

B281 SP155 2c +3c dk gray 70 40
B282 SP155 5c +3c dk grn 42 25
B283 SP155 7c +5c dk vio 90 50
B284 SP155 10c +5c dk bl 90 15
B285 SP155 25c +8c ol 6.00 4.75
Nos. B281-B285 (5) 8.92 6.05

The surtax was for cancer research.

1955, Nov. 14 Unwmk.

Portraits: 5+3c, Boy by Jacob Adriaanszoon Backer. 7+5c, Girl by unknown artist. 10+5c, Philips Huygens by Adriaan Hanneman. 25+8c, Constantijn Huygens by Adriaan Hanneman.

B286 SP156 2c +3c dk grn 15 15
B287 SP156 5c +3c dp car 38 38
B288 SP156 7c +5c dl red brn 1.75 45
B289 SP156 10c +5c dp bl 15 15
B290 SP156 25c +8c pur 8.00 5.75
Nos. B286-B290 (5) 10.43 6.88

The surtax was for child welfare.

Farmer Wearing High Cap
SP157

Sailboat
SP158

Rembrandt Etchings: 5c+3c, Young Tobias with Angel. 7c+5c, Persian Wearing Fur Cap. 10c+5c, Old Blind Tobias. 25c+ 8c, Self-portrait of 1639.

1956, Apr. 23 Engr. *Perf. 13½x14*

B291 SP157 2c +3c bluish blk 1.90 *3.25*
B292 SP157 5c +3c ol grn 1.00 1.10
B293 SP157 7c +5c brn 3.25 *3.25*
B294 SP157 10c +5c dk grn 12.00 20
B295 SP157 25c +8c redsh brn 14.00 *14.00*
Nos. B291-B295 (5) 32.15 *21.80*

Issued to commemorate the 350th anniversary of the birth of Rembrandt van Rijn.
Surtax for social and cultural purposes.

1956, Aug. 27 Litho. *Perf. 12½x12*

Designs: 5c+3c, Woman runner. 7c+5c, Amphora depicting runners. 10c+5c, Field hockey. 25c+8c, Waterpolo player.

B296 SP158 2c +3c brt bl & blk 22 20
B297 SP158 5c +3c dl yel & blk 22 20
B298 SP158 7c +5c red brn & blk 85 65
B299 SP158 10c +5c gray & blk 1.10 65
B300 SP158 25c +8c brt grn & blk 4.75 *4.75*
Nos. B296-B300 (5) 7.14 *6.45*

Issued to publicize the forthcoming 16th Olympic Games at Melbourne, Nov. 22-Dec. 8, 1956.
The surtax was for the benefit of the Netherlands Olympic Committee.

Boy by Jan van Scorel
SP159

Motor Freighter
SP160

Children's Portraits: 5c+3c, Boy, 1563. 7c+5c, Girl, 1563. 10c+5c, Girl, 1590. 25c+8c, Eechie Pieters, 1592.

Perf. 12½x12

1956, Nov. 12 Photo. Unwmk.

B301 SP159 2c +3c blk vio 15 15
B302 SP159 5c +3c ol grn 42 30
B303 SP159 7c +5c brn vio 1.65 50
B304 SP159 10c +5c dp red 15 15
B305 SP159 25c +8c dk bl 4.75 2.75
Nos. B301-B305 (5) 7.12 3.85

The surtax was for child welfare.

1957, May 13 Photo. *Perf. 14x13*

Ships: 6+4c, Coaster. 7+5c, "Willem Barendsz." 10+8c, Trawler. 30+8c, S. S. "Nieuw Amsterdam."

B306 SP160 4c +3c brt bl 90 95
B307 SP160 6c +4c brt vio 55 40
B308 SP160 7c +5c dk car rose 1.10 85
B309 SP160 10c +8c grn 1.50 15
B310 SP160 30c +8c choc 5.00 *4.00*
Nos. B306-B310 (5) 9.05 *6.35*

The surtax was for social and cultural purposes.

White Pelican Feeding Young
SP161

Girl by B. J. Blommers
SP162

Designs: 6c+4c, Vacation ship, "Castle of Staverden." 7c+5c, Cross and dates: 1867-1957. 10c+8c, Cross and laurel wreath. 30c+8c, Globe and Cross.

1957, Aug. 19 Litho. *Perf. 12x12½*
Cross in Red

B311 SP161 4c +3c bl & red 55 65
B312 SP161 6c +4c dk grn 45 30
B313 SP161 7c +5c dk grn & pink 60 40
B314 SP161 10c +8c yel org 60 15
B315 SP161 30c +8c vio bl 2.50 *2.75*
Nos. B311-B315 (5) 4.70 *4.25*

Issued for the 90th anniversary of the founding of the Netherlands Red Cross.

1957, Nov. 18 Photo. *Perf. 12½x12*

Girls' Portraits by: 6c+4c, William B. Tholen. 8c+4c, Jan Sluyters. 12c+9c, Matthijs Maris. 30c+9c, Cornelis Kruseman.

B316 SP162 4c +4c dp car 15 15
B317 SP162 6c +4c ol grn 1.45 50
B318 SP162 8c +4c gray 1.75 1.00
B319 SP162 12c +9c dp cl 15 15
B320 SP162 30c +9c dk bl 5.25 5.00
Nos. B316-B320 (5) 8.75 6.80

The surtax was for child welfare.

Woman from Walcheren, Zeeland
SP163

Girl on Stilts and Boy on Tricycle
SP164

Regional Costumes: 6c+4c, Marken. 8c+4c, Scheveningen. 12c+9c, Friesland. 30c+9c, Volendam.

Perf. 12½x12

1958, Apr. 28 Photo. Unwmk.

B321 SP163 4c +4c bl 50 40
B322 SP163 6c +4c bis 75 60
B323 SP163 8c +4c dk car rose 2.25 1.25
B324 SP163 12c +9c org brn 80 20
B325 SP163 30c +9c vio 4.75 *5.00*
Nos. B321-B325 (5) 9.05 *7.45*

The surtax was for social and cultural purposes.

1958, Nov. 17 Litho.

Children's Games: 6c+4c, Boy and girl on scooters. 8c+4c, Leapfrog. 12c+9c, Roller skating. 30c+9c, Boy in toy car and girl jumping rope.

B326 SP164 4c +4c lt bl 15 15
B327 SP164 6c +4c dp red 1.10 65
B328 SP164 8c +4c brt bl grn 1.10 65
B329 SP164 12c +9c red org 15 15
B330 SP164 30c +9c dk bl 3.50 3.25
Nos. B326-B330 (5) 6.00 4.85

The surtax was for child welfare.

Tugs and Caisson
SP165

Designs: 6c+4c, Dredger. 8c +4c, Laborers making fascine mattresses. 12c+9c, Grab cranes. 30c+9c, Sand spouter.

1959, May 11 *Perf. 14x13*

B331 SP165 4c +4c dk bl, *bl grn* 70 80
B332 SP165 6c +4c red org, *gray* 80 60
B333 SP165 8c +4c bl vio, *lt bl* 1.25 90
B334 SP165 12c +9c bl grn, *brt yel* 2.50 15
B335 SP165 30c +9c dk brn, *brick red* 4.50 *5.00*
Nos. B331-B335 (5) 9.75 *7.45*

Issued to publicize the endless struggle to keep the sea out and the land dry.
The surtax was for social and cultural purposes.

Child in Playpen
SP166

Refugee Woman
SP167

Designs: 6c+4c, Playing Indian. 8c+4c, Child feeding geese. 12c+9c, Children crossing street. 30c+9c, Doing homework.

Perf. 12½x12

1959, Nov. 16 Unwmk.

B336 SP166 4c +4c dp rose & dk bl 15 15
B337 SP166 6c +4c red brn & emer 1.25 85
B338 SP166 8c +4c red & bl 1.25 1.00
B339 SP166 12c +9c grnsh bl, org & gray 15 15
B340 SP166 30c +9c yel & bl 2.50 2.50
Nos. B336-B340 (5) 5.30 4.65

The surtax was for child welfare.

1960, Apr. 7 Photo. *Perf. 13x14*

B341 SP167 12c +8c dp claret 48 15
B342 SP167 30c +10c dk ol grn 2.50 1.25

Issued to publicize World Refugee Year, July 1, 1959-June 30, 1960. The surtax was for aid to refugees.

Tulip
SP168

Girl from Marken
SP169

Flowers: 6c+4c, Gorse. 8c+4c, White waterlily (horiz.). 12c+8c, Red poppy. 30c+10c, Blue sea holly.

Perf. 12½x12, 12x12½

1960, May 23 Unwmk.

B343 SP168 4c +4c gray, grn & red 80 40
B344 SP168 6c +4c sal, grn & yel 60 30
B345 SP168 8c +4c multi 1.75 85
B346 SP168 12c +8c dl org, red & grn 1.75 30

B347 SP168 30c +10c yel, grn & ultra	6.25	4.50
Nos. B343-B347 (5)	11.15	6.35

The surtax was for social and cultural purposes.

1960, Nov. 14 ***Perf. 12½x12***

Regional Costumes: 6c+4c, Volendam. 8c+4c, Bunschoten. 12c+9c, Hindeloopen. 30c+9c, Huizen.

B348 SP169 4c +4c multi	16	15
B349 SP169 6c +4c multi	1.10	80
B350 SP169 8c +4c multi	3.50	1.10
B351 SP169 12c +9c multi	16	15
B352 SP169 30c +9c multi	6.00	3.50
Nos. B348-B352 (5)	10.92	5.70

The surtax was for child welfare.

Herring Gull SP170

St. Nicholas on his Horse SP171

Birds: 6c+4c, Oystercatcher (horiz.). 8c+4c, Curlew. 12c+8c, Avocet (horiz.). 30c+10c, Lapwing.

Perf. 12½x12, 12x12½

1961, Apr. 24 **Litho.** **Unwmk.**

B353 SP170 4c +4c yel & grnsh gray	85	85
B354 SP170 6c +4c fawn & blk	40	20
B355 SP170 8c +4c ol & red brn	85	70
B356 SP170 12c +8c lt bl & gray	1.75	20
B357 SP170 30c +10c grn & blk	3.50	2.75
Nos. B353-B357 (5)	7.35	4.70

The surtax was for social and cultural purposes.

1961, Nov. 13 ***Perf. 12½x12***

Holiday folklore: 6c+4c, Epiphany. 8c+4c, Palm Sunday. 12c+9c, Whitsun bride, Pentecost. 30c+9c, Martinmas.

B358 SP171 4c +4c brt red	15	15
B359 SP171 6c +4c brt bl	1.10	85
B360 SP171 8c +4c ol	1.10	85
B361 SP171 12c +9c dp grn	15	15
B362 SP171 30c +9c dp org	3.00	2.00
Nos. B358-B362 (5)	5.50	4.00

The surtax was for child welfare.

Christian Huygens' Pendulum Clock by van Ceulen SP172

Children Cooking SP173

Designs: 4c+4c, Cat, Roman sculpture (horiz.). 6c+4c, Fossil Ammonite. 12c+ 8c, Figurehead from admiralty ship model. 30c+10c, Guardsmen Hendrick van Berckenrode and Jacob van Lourensz, by Frans Hals (horiz.).

Perf. 14x13, 13x14

1962, Apr. 27 **Photo.**

B363 SP172 4c +4c ol grn	1.00	85
B364 SP172 6c +4c gray	50	40
B365 SP172 8c +4c dp cl	1.10	85
B366 SP172 12c +8c ol bis	1.10	20
B367 SP172 30c +10c bl blk	1.25	1.25
Nos. B363-B367 (5)	4.95	3.55

The surtax was for social and cultural purposes. Issued to publicize the International Congress of Museum Experts, July 4-11.

1962, Nov. 12 ***Perf. 12½x12***

Children's Activities: 6c+4c, Bicycling. 8c+4c, Watering flowers. 12c+9c, Feeding chickens. 30c+9c, Music making.

B368 SP173 4c +4c red	15	15
B369 SP173 6c +4c yel bis	1.25	30
B370 SP173 8c +4c ultra	1.50	85
B371 SP173 12c +9c dp grn	15	15
B372 SP173 30c +9c dk car rose	2.50	1.90
Nos. B368-B372 (5)	5.55	3.35

The surtax was for child welfare.

Gallery Windmill SP174

Roadside First Aid Station SP175

Windmills: 6c+4c, North Holland polder mill. 8c+4c, South Holland polder mill (horiz.). 12c+8c, Post mill. 30c+10c, Wip mill.

Perf. 13x14, 14x13

1963, Apr. 24 **Litho.** **Unwmk.**

B373 SP174 4c +4c dk bl	1.00	75
B374 SP174 6c +4c dk pur	1.00	75
B375 SP174 8c +4c dk grn	1.25	90
B376 SP174 12c +8c blk	2.00	25
B377 SP174 30c +10c dk car	2.00	1.75
Nos. B373-B377 (5)	7.25	4.40

The surtax was for social and cultural purposes.

1963, Aug. 20 ***Perf. 14x13***

Designs: 6c+4c, Book collection box. 8c+4c, Crosses. 12c+9c, International aid to Africans. 30c+9c, First aid team.

B378 SP175 4c +4c dk bl & red	35	20
B379 SP175 6c +4c dl pur & red	24	20
B380 SP175 8c +4c blk & red	85	50
B381 SP175 12c +9c red brn & red	50	15
B382 SP175 30c +9c yel grn & red	1.50	1.00
Nos. B378-B382 (5)	3.44	2.05

Issued to commemorate the centenary of the International Red Cross. The surtax went to the Netherlands Red Cross.

"Aunt Lucy Sat on a Goosey" SP176

Seeing-Eye Dog SP177

Nursery Rhymes: 6c+4c, "In the Hague there lives a count." 8c+4c, "One day I passed a puppet's fair." 12c+9c, "Storky, storky, Billy Spoon." 30c+9c, "Ride on in a little buggy."

1963, Nov. 12 **Litho.** ***Perf. 13x14***

B383 SP176 4c +4c grnsh bl & dk bl	15	15
B384 SP176 6c +4c org red & sl grn	60	40
B385 SP176 8c +4c dl grn & dk brn	85	40
B386 SP176 12c +9c yel & dk pur	15	15
B387 SP176 30c +9c rose & dk bl	1.50	1.00
Nos. B383-B387 (5)	3.25	2.10

The surtax was for mentally and physically handicapped children.

1964, Apr. 21 ***Perf. 12x12½***

Designs: 8c+5c, Three red deer. 12c+9c, Three kittens. 30c+9c, European bison and young.

B388 SP177 5c +5c gray ol, red & blk	35	20
B389 SP177 8c +5c dk red, pale brn & blk	35	15
B390 SP177 12c +9c dl yel, blk & gray	35	15
B391 SP177 30c +9c bl, gray & blk	55	38

The surtax was for social and cultural purposes.

Child Painting SP178

View of Veere SP179

"Artistic and Creative Activities of Children": 10c+5c, Ballet dancing. 15c+10c, Girl playing the flute. 20c+10c, Little Red Riding Hood (masquerading children). 40c+15c, Boy with hammer at work bench.

Perf. 13x14

1964, Nov. 17 **Photo.** **Unwmk.**

B392 SP178 7c +3c lt ol grn & bl	45	32
B393 SP178 10c +5c red, brt pink & grn	35	25
B394 SP178 15c +10c yel bis, blk & yel	15	15
B395 SP178 20c +10c brt pink, brn & red	45	25
B396 SP178 40c +15c bl & yel grn	75	48
Nos. B392-B396 (5)	2.15	1.45

The surtax was for child welfare.

1965, June 1 **Litho.** ***Perf. 14x13***

Views: 10c+6c, Thorn. 18c+12c, Dordrecht. 20c+10c, Staveren. 40c+10c, Medemblik.

B397 SP179 8c +6c yel & blk	24	15
B398 SP179 10c +6c grnsh bl & blk	25	20
B399 SP179 18c +12c sal & blk	24	15
B400 SP179 20c +10c bl & blk	25	20
B401 SP179 40c +10c ap grn & blk	50	30
Nos. B397-B401 (5)	1.48	1.00

The surtax was for social and cultural purposes.

Child — SP180

Designs by Children: 10c+6c, Ship. 18c+12c, Woman (vert.). 20c+10c, Child, lake and swan. 40c+10c, Tractor.

Perf. 14x13, 13x14

1965, Nov. 16 **Photo.**

B402 SP180 8c +6c multi	15	15
B403 SP180 10c +6c multi	45	38
B404 SP180 18c +12c multi	15	15
a. Min. sheet of 11, 5 #B402, 5 #B404 + label	18.00	8.00
B405 SP180 20c +10c multi	48	38
B406 SP180 40c +10c multi	80	45
Nos. B402-B406 (5)	2.03	1.51

The surtax was for child welfare.

"Help them to a safe haven" SP181

1966, Jan. 31 **Photo.** ***Perf. 14x13***

B407 SP181 18c +7c blk & org yel	40	18
B408 SP181 40c +20c blk & red	40	15
a. Min. sheet of 3, #B407, 2 #B408	4.00	3.00

The surtax was for the Intergovernmental Committee for European Migration (ICEM). The message on the stamps was given and signed by Queen Juliana.

Inkwell, Goose Quill and Book — SP182

Designs: 12c+8c, Fragment of Gysbert Japicx manuscript. 20c+10c, Knight on horseback, miniature from "Roman van Walewein" manuscript, 1350. 25c+10c, Initial "D" from "Ferguut" manuscript, 1350. 40c+20c, Print shop, 16th century woodcut.

1966, May 3 ***Perf. 13x14***

B409 SP182 10c +5c multi	32	30
B410 SP182 12c +8c multi	35	32
B411 SP182 20c +10c multi	45	40
B412 SP182 25c +10c multi	48	42
B413 SP182 40c +20c multi	55	50
Nos. B409-B413 (5)	2.15	1.94

Issued to commemorate the 300th anniversary of the death of Gysbert Japicx (1603-1666), Friesian poet, and the 200th anniversary of the founding of the Netherlands Literary Society.

The surtax was for social and cultural purposes.

Infant — SP183

Designs: 12c+8c, Daughter of the painter S. C. Lixenberg. 20c+10c, Boy swimming. 25c+10c, Dominga Blazer, daughter of Carel Blazer, photographer of this set. 40c+20c, Boy and horse.

1966, Nov. 15 **Photo.** ***Perf. 14x13***

B414 SP183 10c +5c dp org & bl	15	15
B415 SP183 12c +8c ap grn & red	15	15
B416 SP183 20c +10c brt bl & red	15	15
a. Min. sheet of 12, 4 #B414, 5 #B415, 3 #B416	3.00	3.00
B417 SP183 25c +10c brt rose lil & dk bl	80	75
B418 SP183 40c +20c dp car & dk grn	70	65
Nos. B414-B418 (5)	1.95	1.85

The surtax was for child welfare.

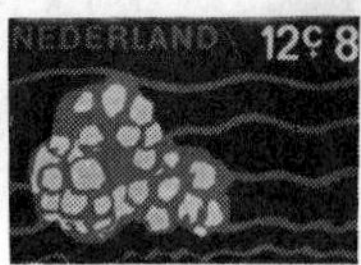

Whelk Eggs — SP184

Designs: 15c+10c, Whelk. 20c+10c, Mussel with acorn shells. 25c+10c, Jellyfish. 45c+20c, Crab.

1967, Apr. 11 **Unwmk.** **Litho.**

B419 SP184 12c +8c ol grn & tan	28	25
B420 SP184 15c +10c lt bl, ultra & blk	28	25
B421 SP184 20c +10c gray, blk & red	28	15
B422 SP184 25c +10c brn car, plum & ol brn	55	52
B423 SP184 45c +20c multi	70	65
Nos. B419-B423 (5)	2.09	1.82

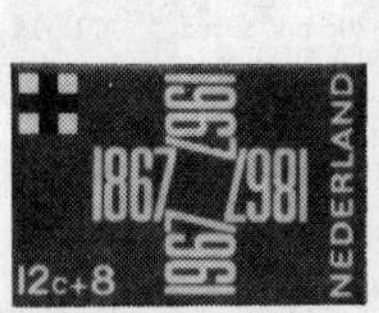

Red Cross and Dates Forming Cross
SP185

"Lullaby for the Little Porcupine"
SP186

Designs (Red Cross and): 15c+10c, Crosses. 20c+10c, Initials "NRK" forming cross. 25c+10c, Maltese cross and crosses. 45c+20c, "100" forming cross.

1967, Aug. 8 ***Perf. 14x13***

B424 SP185 12c +8c dl bl & red 30 24
B425 SP185 15c +10c red 38 35
B426 SP185 20c +10c ol & red 28 15
B427 SP185 25c +10c ol grn & red 38 35
B428 SP185 45c +20c gray & red 70 48
Nos. B424-B428 (5) 2.04 1.57

Centenary of the Dutch Red Cross.

1967, Nov. 7 **Litho.** ***Perf. 13x14***

Nursery Rhymes: 15c+10c, "Little Whistling Kettle." 20c+10c, "Dikkertje Dap and the Giraffe." 25c+10c, "The Nicest Flowers." 45c+20c, "Pippeljoentje, the Little Bear."

B429 SP186 12c +8c multi 15 15
B430 SP186 15c +10c multi 15 15
B431 SP186 20c +10c multi 15 15
a. Min. sheet of 10, 3 #B429, 4 #B430, 3 #B431 4.25 4.25
B432 SP186 25c +10c multi 85 75
B433 SP186 45c +20c multi 1.00 75
Nos. B429-B433 (5) 2.30 1.95

The surtax was for child welfare.

St. Servatius Bridge, Maastricht
SP187

Bridges: 15c+10c, Narrow Bridge, Amsterdam. 20c+10c, Railroad Bridge, Culenborg. 25c+10c, Van Brienenoord Bridge, Rotterdam. 45c+20c, Zeeland Bridge, Schelde Estuary.

1968, Apr. 9 **Photo.** ***Perf. 14x13***

B434 SP187 12c +8c grn 65 85
B435 SP187 15c +10c ol brn 75 90
B436 SP187 20c +10c rose red 65 25
B437 SP187 25c +10c gray 65 85
B438 SP187 45c +20c ultra 1.00 1.25
Nos. B434-B438 (5) 3.70 4.10

Goblin
SP188

Fairy Tale Characters: 15c+10c, Giant. 20c+10c, Witch. 25c+10c, Dragon. 45c+ 20c, Magician.

1968, Nov. 12 **Photo.** ***Perf. 14x13***

B439 SP188 12c +8c grn, pink & blk 15 15
B440 SP188 15c +10c bl, pink & blk 15 15
B441 SP188 20c +10c bl, emer & blk 15 15
a. Min. sheet of 10, 3 #B439, 4 #B440, 3 #B441 8.00 6.25
B442 SP188 25c +10c org red, org & blk 2.00 1.90
B443 SP188 45c +20c yel, org & blk 1.90 1.90
Nos. B439-B443 (5) 4.35 4.25

The surtax was for child welfare.

Villa Huis ter Heide, 1915 — SP189

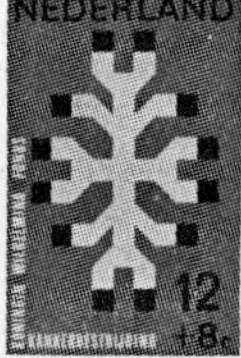

Stylized Crab — SP190

Contemporary Architecture: 15c+10c, House, Utrecht, 1924. 20c+10c, First open-air school, Amsterdam, 1960. 25c+ 10c, Burgweeshuis (orphanage), Amsterdam, 1960. 45c+20c, Netherlands Congress Building, The Hague, 1969.

1969, Apr. 15 **Photo.** ***Perf. 14x13***

B444 SP189 12c +8c lt brn & sl 85 85
B445 SP189 15c +10c bl, gray & red 85 1.10
B446 SP189 20c +10c vio & blk 85 1.10
B447 SP189 25c +10c grn & gray 1.00 52
B448 SP189 45c +20c gray, bl & yel 1.10 1.25
Nos. B444-B448 (5) 4.65 4.82

Surtax for social and cultural purposes.

1969, Aug. 12 **Photo.** ***Perf. 13x14***

B449 SP190 12c +8c vio 1.00 1.10
B450 SP190 25c +10c org 1.40 55
B451 SP190 45c +20c bl grn 1.75 2.50

20th anniv. of the Queen Wilhelmina Fund. The surtax was for cancer research.

Child with Violin
SP191

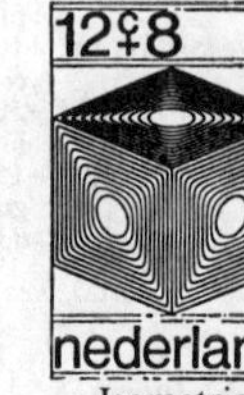

Isometric Projection from Circle to Square
SP192

Designs: 12c+8c, Child with flute. 20c+10c, Child with drum. 25c+10c, Three children singing (horiz.). 45c+20c, Two girls dancing (horiz.).

1969, Nov. 11 ***Perf. 13x14, 14x13***

B452 SP191 12c +8c ultra, blk & yel 25 15
B453 SP191 15c +10c blk & red 25 15
B454 SP191 20c +10c red, blk & yel 2.00 1.75
B455 SP191 25c +10c yel, blk & red 32 15
a. Min. sheet of 10, 4 #B452, 4 #B453, 2 #B455 8.75 7.25
B456 SP191 45c +20c grn, blk & red 2.75 2.75
Nos. B452-B456 (5) 5.57 4.95

The surtax was for child welfare.

Lithographed and Engraved

1970, Apr. 7 ***Perf. 13x14***

Designs made by Computer: 15c+10c, Parallel planes in a cube. 20c+10c, Two overlapping scales. 25c+10c, Transition phases of concentric circles with increasing diameters. 45c+20c, Four spirals.

B457 SP192 12c +8c yel & blk 1.25 1.75
B458 SP192 15c +10c sil & blk 1.25 1.50
B459 SP192 20c +10c blk 1.25 1.40
B460 SP192 25c +10c brt bl & blk 1.25 70
B461 SP192 45c +20c sil & white 1.25 1.75
Nos. B457-B461 (5) 6.25 7.10

Surtax for social and cultural purposes.

Bleeding Heart — SP193

Toy Block — SP194

1970, July 28 **Photo.** ***Perf. 13x14***

B462 SP193 12c +8c org yel, red & blk 90 1.10
B463 SP193 25c +10c pink, red & blk 90 55
B464 SP193 45c +20c brt grn, red & blk 90 1.10

The surtax was for the Netherlands Heart Foundation.

1970, Nov. 10 **Photo.** ***Perf. 13x14***

B465 SP194 12c +8c bl, vio bl & grn 15 15
B466 SP194 15c +10c grn, bl & yel 1.75 2.00
B467 SP194 20c +10c lil rose, red & vio bl 1.75 2.00
B468 SP194 25c +10c red, yel & lil rose 25 15
a. Min. sheet of 11, 9 #B465, 2 #B468 + label 13.00 13.00
B469 SP194 45c +20c gray & blk 2.25 2.50
Nos. B465-B469 (5) 6.15 6.80

The surtax was for child welfare.

St. Paul
SP195

Detail from Borobudur
SP196

Designs: 15c+10c, "50" and people. 25c+10c, Joachim and Ann. 30c+15c, John the Baptist and the Scribes. 45c+ 20c, St. Anne. The sculptures are wood, 15th century, and in Dutch museums.

1971, Apr. 20 **Litho.** ***Perf. 13x14***

B470 SP195 15c +10c multi 1.75 1.40

Lithographed and Photogravure

B471 SP195 20c +10c gray, grn & blk 1.40 1.40
B472 SP195 25c +10c buff, org & blk 1.40 55
B473 SP195 30c +15c gray, bl & blk 1.75 1.50
B474 SP195 45c +20c pink, ver & blk 1.75 1.50
Nos. B470-B474 (5) 8.05 6.35

50th anniversary of the Federation of Netherlands Universities for Adult Education.

1971, June 29 **Litho.** ***Perf. 13x14***

B475 SP196 45c +20c pur, yel & blk 2.50 2.50

60th birthday of Prince Bernhard. Surtax for Save Borobudur Temple Fund.

"Earth"
SP197

Stylized Fruits
SP198

Designs: 20c+10c, "Air" (butterfly). 25c+10c, "Sun" (horiz.). 30c+15c, "Moon" (horiz.). 45c+20c, "Water" (child looking at reflection).

Perf. 13x14, 14x13

1971, Nov. 9 **Photo.**

B476 SP197 15c +10c blk, lil & org 15 15
B477 SP197 20c +10c yel, blk & rose lil 55 42
B478 SP197 25c +10c multi 42 15
a. Min. sheet of 9, 6 #B476, #B477, 2 #B478 10.00 7.25
B479 SP197 30c +15c bl, blk & pur 1.50 55
B480 SP197 45c +20c grn, blk & bl 2.50 2.50
Nos. B476-B480 (5) 5.12 3.77

The surtax was for child welfare.

Luminescence

Some semipostal issues from Nos. B481-B484 onward are on phosphorescent paper.

1972, Apr. 11 **Litho.** ***Perf. 13x14***

B481 SP198 20c +10c shown 1.25 1.50
B482 SP198 25c +10c Flower 1.25 1.50
B483 SP198 30c +15c "Sunlit Landscape" 1.25 75
B484 SP198 45c +25c "Music" 1.25 1.50

Summer festivals: Nos. B481-B482 publicize the Floriade, flower festival; Nos. B483-B484 the Holland Festival of Arts.

Red Cross, First Aid
SP199

Prince Willem-Alexander
SP200

Designs (Red Cross and): 25c+10c, Blood bank. 30c+15c, Disaster relief. 45c+25c, Child care.

1972, Aug. 15 ***Perf. 13x14***

B485 SP199 20c +10c brt pink & red 80 45
B486 SP199 25c +10c org & red 95 80
B487 SP199 30c +15c blk & red 95 30
B488 SP199 45c +25c ultra & red 1.10 1.25

Surtax for the Netherlands Red Cross.

Perf. 13x14, 14x13

1972, Nov. 7 **Photo.**

Photographs of Dutch Princes: 30c+10c, Johan Friso. 35c+15c, Constantijn. 50c+20c, Johan Friso, Constantijn and Willem-Alexander. All are horizontal.

B489 SP200 25c +15c multi 28 15
B490 SP200 30c +10c multi 1.10 90
B491 SP200 35c +15c multi 1.10 15
a. Min. sheet of 7, 4 #B489, #B490, 2 #B491 + label 7.75 6.50
B492 SP200 50c +20c multi 2.50 2.50

Surtax was for child welfare.

"W. A. Scholten," 1874 — SP201

Ships: 25c+15c, Flagship "De Seven Provincien," 1673 (vert.). 35c+15c, "Veendam," 1923. 50c+20c, Zuider Zee fish well boat, 17th century (vert.).

1973, Apr. 10 **Litho.**

B493 SP201 25c +15c multi 1.50 1.40
B494 SP201 30c +10c multi 1.50 1.40
B495 SP201 35c +15c multi 1.50 90
B496 SP201 50c +20c multi 1.50 1.40

Tercentenary of the Battle of Kijkduin and centenary of the Holland-America Line.
Surtax for social and cultural purposes.

Chessboard — SP202

Games: 30c+10c, Tick-tack-toe. 40c+ 20c, Labyrinth. 50c+20c, Dominoes.

1973, Nov. 13 Photo. *Perf. 13x14*

B497 SP202 25c +15c multi 60 28
B498 SP202 30c +10c multi 1.10 70
B499 SP202 40c +20c multi 1.10 15
a. Min. sheet of 6, 2 #B497, #B498, 3 #B499 8.75 6.75
B500 SP202 50c +20c multi 2.00 2.00

Surtax was for child welfare.

Music Bands SP203

Herman Heijermans SP204

Designs: 30c+10c, Ballet dancers and traffic lights. 50c+20c, Kniertje, the fisher woman, from play by Heijermans.

1974, Apr. 23 Litho. *Perf. 13x14*

B501 SP203 25c +15c multi 95 95
B502 SP203 30c +10c multi 95 95

Photo.

B503 SP204 40c +20c multi 95 45
B504 SP204 50c +20c multi 95 95

Surtax was for various social and cultural institutions.

Boy with Hoop — SP205

Designs: 35c+20c, Girl and infant. 45c+20c, Two girls. 60c+20c, Girl sitting on balustrade. Designs are from turn-of-the-century photographs.

1974, Nov. 12 Photo. *Perf. 13x14*

B505 SP205 30c +15c blk & grn 38 30
B506 SP205 35c +20c mar 50 45
B507 SP205 45c +20c blk brn 60 18
a. Min. sheet of 6, 4 #B505, #B506, #B507 4.25 3.75
B508 SP205 60c +20c ind 1.25 1.40

Surtax was for child welfare.

Beguinage, Amsterdam SP206

Cooper's Gate, Middelburg SP207

Designs: 35c+20c, St. Hubertus Hunting Lodge (horiz.). 60c+20c, Orvelte Village (horiz.).

Perf. 14x13, 13x14

1975, Apr. 4 Litho.

B509 SP206 35c +20c multi 65 55
B510 SP206 40c +15c multi 65 70
B511 SP207 50c +20c multi 80 55
B512 SP207 60c +20c multi 1.10 70

European Architectural Heritage Year 1975. Surtax was for various social and cultural institutions.

Orphans, Sculpture, 1785 — SP208

Designs: 40c+15c, Milkmaid, 17th century. 50c+25c, Aymon's 4 sons on steed Bayard, 17th century. 60c+25c, Life at orphanage, 1557. All designs are after ornamental stones from various buildings.

1975, Nov. 11 Photo. *Perf. 14x13*

B513 SP208 35c +15c multi 28 15
B514 SP208 40c +15c multi 55 55
B515 SP208 50c +25c multi 42 15
a. Min. sheet of 5, 3 #B513, 2 #B515 + label 2.75 2.75
B516 SP208 60c +25c multi 90 90

Surtax was for child welfare.

Hedgehog SP209

Book with "ABC" and Grain; Open Field — SP210

Green Frog and Spawn — SP212

People and Initials of Social Security Acts — SP211

Perf. 14x13, 13x14

1976, Apr. 6 Litho.

B517 SP209 40c +20c multi 50 50
B518 SP210 45c +20c multi 50 38

Photo.

B519 SP211 55c +20c multi 80 38
B520 SP212 75c +25c multi 80 65

Surtax for various social and cultural institutions. #B517, B520 for wildlife protection; #B518 cent. of agricultural education and 175th anniv. of elementary education legislation; #B519 75th anniv. of social legislation and the Social Insurance Bank.

Patient Surrounded by Caring Hands — SP213

Netherlands No. 41 — SP214

1976, Sept. 2 Litho. *Perf. 13x14*

B521 SP213 55c +25c multi 60 60

Dutch Anti-Rheumatism Association, 50th anniversary.

1976, Oct. 8 Litho. *Perf. 13x14*

Designs: No. B523, #64. No. B524, #155. No. B525, #294. No. B526, #220.

B522 SP214 55c +55c multi 85 1.00
B523 SP214 55c +55c multi 85 1.00
B524 SP214 55c +55c multi 85 1.00

Photo.

B525 SP214 75c +75c multi 85 1.00
B526 SP214 75c +75c multi 85 1.00
Nos. B522-B526 (5) 4.25 5.00

Amphilex 77 Philatelic Exhibition, Amsterdam, May 26-June 5, 1977. Nos. B522-B524 printed se-tenant in sheets of 90; Nos. B525-B526 printed checkerwise in sheets of 100.

See Nos. B535-B538.

Soccer SP215

Designs (Children's Drawings): 45c+20c, Sailboat. 55c+20c, Elephant. 75c+25c, Mobile home.

1976, Nov. 16 Photo. *Perf. 14x13*

B527 SP215 40c +20c multi 32 15
B528 SP215 45c +20c multi 32 18
B529 SP215 55c +20c multi 32 15
a. Min. sheet of 6, 2 each #B527-B529 2.75 2.75
B530 SP215 75c +25c multi 85 85

Surtax was for child welfare.

Hot Room, Thermal Bath, Heerlen SP216

Designs: 45c+20c, Altar of Goddess Nehalennia, 200 A.D., Eastern Scheldt. 55c+20c, Part of oaken ship, Zwammerdam. 75c+25c, Helmet with face, Waal River at Nijmegen.

1977, Apr. 19 Photo. *Perf. 14x13*

B531 SP216 40c +20c multi 32 32
B532 SP216 45c +20c multi 32 32
B533 SP216 55c +20c multi 32 32
B534 SP216 75c +25c multi 48 48

Archaeological finds of Roman period.

Type of 1976

Designs: No. B535, Netherlands No. 83. No. B536, Netherlands No. 128. No. B537, Netherlands No. 211. No. B538, Netherlands No. 302.

1977, May 26 Litho. *Perf. 13x14*

B535 SP214 55c +45c multi 55 52
B536 SP214 55c +45c multi 55 52
B537 SP214 55c +45c multi 55 52
B538 SP214 55c +45c multi 55 52
a. Souv. sheet of 2, #B535, B538 1.25 1.25

Amphilex 77 International Philatelic Exhibition, Amsterdam May 26-June 5. Nos. B535-B536 and B537-B538 each printed se-tenant in sheets of 100. No. B538a sold at Exhibition only.

Risk of Drowning — SP217

Childhood Dangers: 45c+20c, Poisoning. 55c+20c, Following ball into street. 75c+ 25c, Playing with matches.

1977, Nov. 15 Photo. *Perf. 13x14*

B539 SP217 40c +20c multi 24 16
B540 SP217 45c +20c multi 24 16
B541 SP217 55c +20c multi 30 16
a. Min. sheet of 6, 2 each #B539-B541 2.50 2.50
B542 SP217 75c +25c multi 75 75

Surtax was for child welfare.

Anna Maria van Schuurman SP218

Delft Plate SP219

Designs: 45c+20c, Part of letter written by author Belle van Zuylen (1740-1805). 75c+25c, Makkum dish with dog.

1978, Apr. 11 Litho. *Perf. 13x14*

B543 SP218 40c +20c multi 32 32
B544 SP218 45c +20c multi 32 32

Photo.

B545 SP219 55c +20c multi 35 24
B546 SP219 75c +25c multi 48 48

Dutch authors and pottery products.

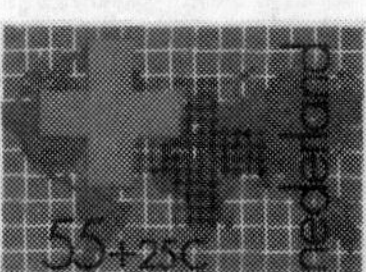

Red Cross and World Map — SP220

1978, Aug. 22 Photo. *Perf. 14x13*

B547 SP220 55c +25c multi 45 32
a. Souvenir sheet of 3 1.75 1.50

Surtax was for Dutch Red Cross.

Boy Ringing Doorbell SP221

Designs: 45c+20c, Child reading book. 55c+20c, Boy writing "30x Children for Children" (vert.). 75c+25c, Girl at blackboard, arithmetic lesson.

Perf. 14x13, 13x14

1978, Nov. 14 Photo.

B548 SP221 40c +20c multi 28 15
B549 SP221 45c +20c multi 30 15
B550 SP221 55c +20c multi 32 15
a. Min. sheet of 6, 2 each #B548-B550 2.25 2.25
B551 SP221 75c +25c multi 60 60

Surtax was for child welfare.

Psalm Trilogy, by Jurriaan Andriessen SP222

Birth of Christ (detail) Stained-glass Window SP223

Designs: 45c+20c, Amsterdam Toonkunst Choir. 75c+25c, William of Orange, stained-glass window, 1603. Windows from St. John's Church, Gouda.

1979, Apr. 5 Photo. *Perf. 13x14*
B552 SP222 40c +20c multi 30 25
B553 SP222 45c +20c multi 30 25
B554 SP223 55c +20c multi 35 25
B555 SP223 75c +25c multi 50 48

Surtax for social and cultural purposes.

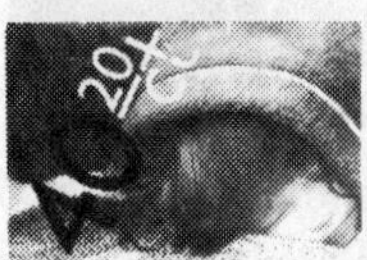

Child Sleeping Under Blanket SP224

Designs: 45c+20c, Infant. 55c+20c, African boy (vert.). 75c+25c, Children (vert.).

1979, Nov. 13 *Perf. 14x13, 13x14*
B556 SP224 40c +20c blk, red & yel 30 15
B557 SP224 45c +20c blk & red 30 15
B558 SP224 55c +20c blk & yel 38 15
a. Min. sheet, 2 each #B556-B558 2.00 2.00
B559 SP224 75c +25c blk, ultra & red 60 60

Surtax was for child welfare (in conjuction with International Year of the Child).

Roads Through Sand Dunes SP225

Designs: 50c+20c, Park mansion (vert.). 60c+25c, Sailing. 80c+35c, Bicycling, moorlands.

Perf. 14x13, 13x14
1980, Apr. 15 Litho.
B560 SP225 45c +20c multi 28 28
B561 SP225 50c +20c multi 35 28
B562 SP225 60c +25c multi 42 22
B563 SP225 80c +35c multi 52 52

Socicty for the Promotion of Nature Preserves, 75th anniv. Surtax for social and cultural purposes.

Wheelchair Basketball — SP226

1980, June 3 Litho. *Perf. 13x14*
B564 SP226 60c +25c multi 48 20

Olympics for the Disabled, Arnhem and Veenendaal, June 21-July 5. Surtax was for National Sports for the Handicapped Fund.

Harlequin and Girl Standing in Open Book — SP227

Designs: 50c+20c, Boy on flying book (vert.). 60c+30c, Boy reading King of Frogs (vert.). 80c+30c, Boy "engrossed" in book.

Perf. 14x13, 13x14
1980, Nov. 11 Photo.
B565 SP227 45c +20c multi 30 22
B566 SP227 50c +20c multi 35 35
B567 SP227 60c +30c multi 42 22
a. Min. sheet of 5, 2 #B565, 3 #B567 + label 2.00 2.00
B568 SP227 80c +30c multi 52 52

Surtax was for child welfare.

Salt Marsh with Outlet Ditch at Low Tide — SP228

Designs: 55c+25c, Dike. 60c+25c, Land drainage. 65c+30c, Cultivated land.

1981, Apr. 7 Photo. *Perf. 13x14*
B569 SP228 45c +20c multi 30 30
B570 SP228 55c +25c multi 38 38
B571 SP228 60c +25c multi 42 42
B572 SP228 65c +30c multi 55 55

Intl. Year of the Disabled SP229

Perf. 14x13, 13x14
1981, Nov. 10 Photo.
B573 SP229 45c +25c multi 32 25
B574 SP229 55c +20c multi, vert 35 32
B575 SP229 60c +25c multi, vert. 38 38
B576 SP229 65c +30c multi 45 38
a. Min. sheet of 5, 3 #B573, 2 #B576 + label 2.00 1.50

Surtax was for child welfare.

Floriade '82, Amsterdam, Apr. — SP230

1982, Apr. 7 Litho. *Perf. 13½x13*
B577 SP230 50c +20c shown 40 40
B578 SP230 60c +25c Anemones 45 45
B579 SP230 65c +25c Roses 52 52
B580 SP230 70c +30c African violets 55 55

Surtax was for culture and social welfare institutions.

Birds on Child's Head — SP231

Children and Animals: 60c+20c, Boy and cat. 65c+20c, Boy and rabbit. 70c+30c, Boy and bird.

1982, Nov. 16 Photo. *Perf. 13x14*
B581 SP231 50c +30c multi 45 45
B582 SP231 60c +20c multi 45 45
a. Min. sheet of 5, 4 #B581, #B582 2.75 2.75
B583 SP231 65c +20c multi 50 50
B584 SP231 70c +30c multi 55 55

Surtax was for child welfare.

Johan van Oldenbarneveldt (1547-1619), Statesman, by J. Houbraken — SP232

Paintings: 60c+25c, Willem Jansz Blaeu (1571-1638), cartographer, by Thomas de Keijser. 65c+25c, Hugo de Groot (1583-1645), statesman, by J. van Ravesteyn. 70c+30c, Portrait of Saskia van Uylenburch, by Rembrandt (1606-1669).

1983, Apr. 19 Photo. *Perf. 14x13*
B585 SP232 50c +20c multi 42 42
B586 SP232 60c +25c multi 48 48
B587 SP232 65c +25c multi 55 55
B588 SP232 70c +30c multi 60 60

Surtax was for cultural and social welfare institutions.

Red Cross Workers — SP233

Designs: 60c+20c, Principles. 65c+25c, Sociomedical work. 70c+30c, Peace.

1983, Aug. 30 Photo. *Perf. 13x14*
B589 SP233 50c +25c multi 42 42
B590 SP233 60c +20c multi 48 48
B591 SP233 65c +25c multi 55 55
B592 SP233 70c +30c multi 60 60
a. Bklt. pane, 4 #B589, 2 #B592 6.00

Surtax was for Red Cross.

Children's Christmas SP235

1983, Nov. 16 Photo. *Perf. 14x13*
B596 SP235 50c +10c Ox and donkey 42 42
B597 SP235 50c +25c Snowman 50 50
B598 SP235 60c +30c Stars 60 60
B599 SP235 70c +30c Epiphany 70 70
a. Min. sheet, 4 #B597, 2 #B599 3.25 3.25

Surtax was for Child Welfare.

Eurasian Lapwings SP236

Birds: 60c+25c, Ruffs. 65c+25c, Redshanks (vert.). 70c+30c, Black-tailed godwits (vert.).

1984, Apr. 3 *Perf. 14x13, 13x14*
B600 SP236 50c +20c multi 55 55
B601 SP236 60c +25c multi 70 70
B602 SP236 65c +25c multi 75 75
B603 SP236 70c +30c multi 85 85
a. Bklt. pane, 2 #B600, 2 #B603 3.25

Surtax for cultural and social welfare institutions.

FILACENTO '84 — SP237

Centenary of Organized Philately: 50c+20c, Eye, magnifying glass (36x25mm). 60c+25c, Cover, 1909 (34½x25mm). 70c+30c, Stamp club meeting, 1949 (34½x24mm).

1984, June 13 Litho. *Perf. 14x13*
B604 SP237 50c +20c multi 60 60
B605 SP237 60c +25c multi 70 70
B606 SP237 70c +30c multi 90 90
a. Souv. sheet of 3, #B604-B606 2.00 2.00

No. B606a issued Sept. 5, 1984.

Comic Strips — SP238

1984, Nov. 14 Litho. *Perf. 13x13½*
B607 SP238 50c +25c Music lesson 60 60
B608 SP238 60c +20c Dentist 65 65
B609 SP238 65c +25c Plumber 70 70
B610 SP238 70c +30c King 80 80
a. Min. sheet, 4 #B607, 2 #B610 4.00 4.00

Surtax was for child welfare.

Winterswijk Synagogue, Holy Arc — SP239

Religious architecture: 50+20c, St. Martin's Church, Zaltbommel (vert.). 65+25c, Village Congregational Church, Bolsward (vert.). 70+30c, St. John's Cathedral, 'S-Hertogenbosch, detail of buttress.

Perf. 13x14, 14x13
1985, Mar. 26 Photo.
B611 SP239 50c +20c gray & brt bl 65 65
B612 SP239 60c +25c dk red brn, Prus bl & pck bl 75 75
B613 SP239 65c +25c sl bl, red brn & gray ol 80 80
B614 SP239 70c +30c gray, brt bl & bis 90 90
a. Bklt. pane, 2 #B611, 2 #B614 3.75

Surtax for social and cultural purposes.

Traffic Safety — SP240

1985, Nov. 13 Photo. *Perf. 13x14*
B615 SP240 50c +25c Photograph, lock, key 75 75
B616 SP240 60c +20c Boy, target 80 80
B617 SP240 65c +20c Girl, hazard triangle 90 90
B618 SP240 70c +30c Boy, traffic sign 1.00 1.00
a. Souv. sheet, 4 #B615, 2 #B618 5.00 5.00

Surtax was for child welfare organizations.

Antique Measuring Instruments SP241

Perf. 13½x13, 13x13½

1986, Apr. 8 **Litho.**

B619	SP241	50c +20c Balance	65	65
B620	SP241	60c +25c Clock mechanism	85	85
B621	SP241	65c +25c Barometer	90	90
B622	SP241	70c +30c Jacob's staff	95	95
a.		Bklt. pane, 2 each #B619, B622	4.75	

Nos. B620-B621 vert.

Youth and Culture SP242

1986, Nov. 12 **Litho.** ***Perf. 14x13***

B623	SP242	55c +25c Music	80	80

Perf. 13½x13

B624	SP242	65c +35c Visual arts	95	95
B625	SP242	75c +35c Theater	1.00	1.00
a.		Min. sheet of 5, #B623, 2 each #B624-B625, perf. 14x13	4.75	

Surtax for child welfare organizations.

Traditional Industries SP243

Designs: 55c+30c, Steam pumping station, Nijkerk. 65c+35c, Water tower, Deventer. 75c+35c, Brass foundry, Joure.

1987, Apr. 7 **Photo.** ***Perf. 14x13***

B626	SP243	55c +30c multi	70	70
B627	SP243	65c +35c multi	80	80
B628	SP243	75c +35c multi	90	90
a.		Bklt. pane, 2 #B626, 2 #B628	3.50	

Surtax for social and cultural welfare organizations.

Red Cross SP244

1987, Sept. 1 **Photo.** ***Perf. 14x13***

B629	SP244	55c +30c multi	70	70
B630	SP244	65c +35c multi, diff.	80	80
B631	SP244	75c +35c multi, diff.	90	90
a.		Bklt. pane, 2 #B629, 2 #B631)	3.75	

Surtax for nat'l. Red Cross.

Youth and Professions SP245

Perf. 13x14, 14x13

1987, Nov. 11 **Photo.**

B632	SP245	55c +25c Woodcutter, vert.	80	80
B633	SP245	65c +35c Sailor	95	95
B634	SP245	75c +35c Pilot	1.00	1.00
a.		Miniature sheet of 5, #B632, 2 #B633, 2 #B634	4.75	4.75

Surtax for child welfare organizations.

FILACEPT '88, October 18, The Hague SP246

Designs: 55c +55c, Narcissus cyclamineus and poem "I call you flowers," by Jan Hanlo. No. B636, Rosa gallica versicolor. No. B637, Eryngium maritimum and map of The Hague from 1270.

1988, Feb. 23 **Litho.** ***Perf. 13½x13***

B635	SP246	55c +55c multi	1.10	1.10
B636	SP246	75c +70c multi	1.40	1.40
B637	SP246	75c +70c multi	1.40	1.40
a.		Souv. sheet of 3 + 3 labels, #B635-B637	4.00	4.00

Surtax helped finance exhibition. No. B637a issued Oct. 18, 1988.

Man and the Zoo — SP247

Perf. 14x13, 13x14

1988, Mar. 22 **Photo.**

B638	SP247	55c +30c Equus quagga quagga	80	80
B639	SP247	65c +35c Carribean sea cow	95	95
B640	SP247	75c +35c Sam the orangutan, vert.	1.10	1.10
a.		Bklt. pane, 2 #B638, 2 #B640	3.75	

Natural Artis Magistra zoological soc., 150th anniv. Surtax for social and cultural welfare organizations.

Royal Dutch Swimming Federation, Cent. SP248

Children's drawings on the theme "Children and Water."

1988, Nov. 16 **Photo.** ***Perf. 14x13***

B641	SP248	55c +25c Rain	82	82
B642	SP248	65c +35c Getting Ready for the Race	1.00	1.00
B643	SP248	75c +35c Swimming Test	1.15	1.15
a.		Souv. sheet of 5, #B641, 2 each #B642-B643	5.15	5.15

Surtax to benefit child welfare organizations.

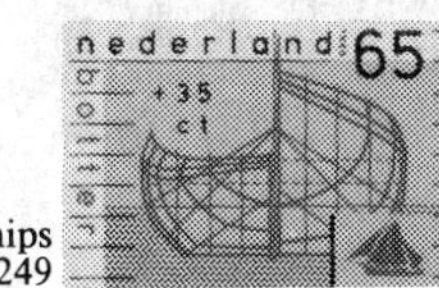

Ships SP249

Designs: No. B644, Pleasure yacht (boyer), vert. No. B645, Zuiderzee fishing boat (smack). No. B646, Clipper.

Perf. 13x14, 14x13

1989, Apr. 11 **Photo.**

B644	SP249	55c +30c multi	85	85
B645	SP249	65c +35c multi	98	98
B646	SP249	75c +35c multi	1.05	1.05
a.		Bklt. pane of 4 (Nos. B644-B645, 2 No. B646)	4.00	

Surtax for social and cultural organizations.

Children's Rights SP250

1989, Nov. 8 **Litho.** ***Perf. 13½x13***

B647	SP250	55c +25c Housing	75	75
B648	SP250	65c +35c Food	95	95
B649	SP250	75c +35c Education	1.05	1.05
a.		Min. sheet of 5, #B647, 2 each #B648-B649	4.75	4.75

UN Declaration of Children's Rights, 30th anniv. Surtax for child welfare.

Summer Weather SP251

Perf. 14x13, 13x14

1990, Apr. 3 **Photo.**

B650	SP251	55c +30c Girl, flowers	90	90
B651	SP251	65c +35c Clouds, isobars, vert.	1.05	1.05
B652	SP251	75c +35c Weather map, vert.	1.15	1.15
a.		Bklt. pane of 4, #B650-B651, 2 #B652	4.25	

Surtax for social and culture welfare organizations.

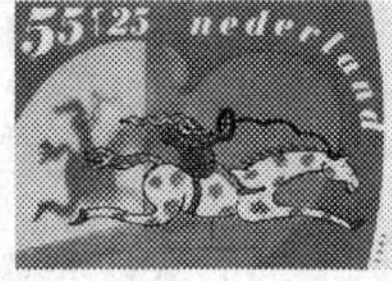

Children's Hobbies SP252

1990, Nov. 7 **Litho.** ***Perf. 13½x13***

B653	SP252	55c +25c Riding	85	85
B654	SP252	65c +35c Computers	1.05	1.05
B655	SP252	75c +35c Philately	1.20	1.20
a.		Souv. sheet of 5, #B653, 2 each #B654-B655	5.35	

Surtax for child welfare.

Dutch Farms SP253

Designs: 55c+30c, Frisian farm, Wartena. 65c+35c, Guelders T-style farm, Kesteren. 75c+35c, Closed construction farm, Nuth (Limburg).

1991, Apr. 16 **Litho.** ***Perf. 13½x13***

B656	SP253	55c +30c multi	95	25
a.		Photo.	95	25
B657	SP253	65c +35c multi	1.10	28
B658	SP253	75c +35c multi	1.20	30
a.		Photo.	1.20	30
b.		Bklt. pane, 2 #B656a, 3 #B658a	5.50	

Surtax for social and cultural welfare organizations.

AIR POST STAMPS

Stylized Seagull — AP1

Perf. 12½

1921, May 1 **Unwmk.** **Typo.**

C1	AP1	10c red	1.10	75
C2	AP1	15c yel grn	5.75	1.50
C3	AP1	60c dp bl	17.00	15

Nos. C1-C3 were used to pay airmail fee charged by the carrier, KLM.

Lt. G. A. Koppen AP2

Capt. Jan van der Hoop AP3

Wmk. Circles (202)

1928, Aug. 20 **Litho.** ***Perf. 12***

C4	AP2	40c org red	25	25
C5	AP3	75c bl grn	25	25

Mercury AP4

Queen Wilhelmina AP5

Perf. 11½

1929, July 16 **Unwmk.** **Engr.**

C6	AP4	1½g gray	2.25	1.40
C7	AP4	4½g carmine	1.75	2.50
C8	AP4	7½g bl grn	21.00	3.75

Perf. 12½, 14x13

1931, Sept. 24 **Photo.** **Wmk. 202**

C9	AP5	36c org red & dk bl	7.25	30

Fokker Pander AP6

1933, Oct. 9 ***Perf. 12½***

C10	AP6	30c dark green	35	35

Nos. C10-C12 were issued for use on special flights.

Crow in Flight AP7

1938-53 ***Perf. 13x14***

C11	AP7	12½c dk bl & gray	15	18
C12	AP7	25c dk bl & gray ('53)	90	1.10

Seagull AP8

Airplane AP9

15-Cent Minimum Value
The minimum catalogue value is 15 cents. Separating se-tenant pieces into individual stamps does not increase the "value" of the stamps... since demand for the separated stamps may be small.

Perf. 13x14

1951, Nov. 12 **Engr.** **Unwmk.**
C13 AP8 15g gray 130.00 65.00
C14 AP8 25g blue gray 130.00 65.00

Catalogue values for unused stamps in this section, from this point to the end of the section, are for Never Hinged items.

1966, Sept. 2 **Litho.** ***Perf. 14x13***
C15 AP9 25c gray, blk & bl 32 32

Issued for use on special flights.

AP10

1980, May 13 **Photo.** ***Perf. 13x14***
C16 AP10 1g multi 70 70

MARINE INSURANCE STAMPS

Floating Safe Attracting Gulls — MI1

Floating Safe with Night Flare — MI2

Fantasy of Floating Safe — MI3

Perf. 11½

1921, Feb. 2 **Unwmk.** **Engr.**
GY1 MI1 15c slate grn 3.50 *27.50*
GY2 MI1 60c car rose 3.50 *32.50*
GY3 MI1 75c gray brn 5.50 *37.50*
GY4 MI2 1.50g dk bl 60.00 *310.00*
GY5 MI2 2.25g org brn 150.00 *400.00*
GY6 MI3 4½g black 150.00 *500.00*
GY7 MI3 7½g red 180.00 *700.00*
Nos. GY1-GY7 (7) 552.50 *2,007.*

POSTAGE DUE STAMPS

Postage due types of Netherlands were also used for Curacao, Netherlands Indies and Surinam in different colors.

D1

D2

Perf. 12½x12, 13

1870, May 15 **Typo.** **Unwmk.**
J1 D1 5c brn, *org* 35.00 7.00
  a. Imperf., pair 450.00
J2 D1 10c vio, *bl* 100.00 8.75
  a. Imperf., pair 300.00

Type I- 34 loops. "T" of "BETALEN" over center of loop; top branch of "E" of "TE" shorter than lower branch.

Type II- 33 loops. "T" of "BETALEN" between two loops.

Type III- 32 loops. "T" of "BETALEN" slightly to the left of loop; top branch of first "E" of "BETALEN" shorter than lower branch.

Type IV- 37 loops. Letters of "PORT" larger than in the other three types.

Perf. 11½x12, 12½x12, 12½, 13½
1881-87

Value in Black

J3 D2 1c lt bl (III) 8.75 8.75
  a. Type I 10.50 12.50
  b. Type II 14.00 14.00
  c. Type IV 32.50 35.00
J4 D2 1½c lt bl (III) 12.50 10.00
  a. Type I 14.00 14.00
  b. Type II 19.00 17.00
  c. Type IV 50.00 50.00
J5 D2 2½c lt bl (III) 22.50 2.75
  a. Type I 27.50 3.50
  b. Type II 35.00 4.00
  c. Type IV 140.00 85.00
J6 D2 5c lt bl (III) ('87) 87.50 2.75
  a. Type I 110.00 3.50
  b. Type II 120.00 4.00
  c. Type IV 1,500. 225.00
J7 D2 10c lt bl (III) ('87) 100.00 2.75
  a. Type I 125.00 3.50
  b. Type II 130.00 4.00
  c. Type IV 2,100. 240.00
J8 D2 12½c lt bl (III) 87.50 22.50
  a. Type I 100.00 27.50
  b. Type II 120.00 30.00
  c. Type IV 325.00 87.50
J9 D2 15c lt bl (III) 80.00 2.75
  a. Type I 90.00 3.50
  b. Type II 100.00 4.00
  c. Type IV 120.00 18.00
J10 D2 20c lt bl (III) 22.50 2.75
  a. Type I 30.00 3.50
  b. Type II 32.50 4.00
  c. Type IV 125.00 18.50
J11 D2 25c lt bl (III) 230.00 2.50
  a. Type I 240.00 2.75
  b. Type II 260.00 3.50
  c. Type IV 450.00 125.00

Value in Red

J12 D2 1g lt bl (III) 80.00 20.00
  a. Type I 85.00 27.50
  b. Type II 100.00 27.50
  c. Type IV 150.00 50.00

See Nos. J13-J26, J44-J60. For surcharges see Nos. J27-J28, J42-J43, J72-J75.

1896-1910 ***Perf. 12½***

Value in Black

J13 D2 ½c dk bl (I) ('01) 15 15
J14 D2 1c dk bl (I) 1.10 20
  a. Type III 1.90 2.25
J15 D2 1½c dk bl (I) 55 15
  a. Type III 1.90 1.90
J16 D2 2½c dk bl (I) 1.20 15
  a. Type III 2.25 24
J17 D2 3c dk bl (I) ('10) 1.10 1.00
J18 D2 4c dk bl (I) ('09) 1.25 1.50
J19 D2 5c dk bl (I) 8.50 15
  a. Type III 11.00 16
J20 D2 6½c dk bl (I) ('07) 30.00 27.50
J21 D2 7½c dk bl (I) ('04) 1.00 38
J22 D2 10c dk bl (I) 22.50 30
  a. Type III 35.00 1.00
J23 D2 12½c dk bl (I) 20.00 75
  a. Type III 27.50 2.25
J24 D2 15c dk bl (I) 22.50 60
  a. Type III 35.00 60
J25 D2 20c dk bl (I) 12.50 5.00
  a. Type III 12.50 5.25
J26 D2 25c dk bl (I) 27.50 60
  a. Type III 30.00 60
Nos. J13-J26 (14) 149.85 38.43

Surcharged in Black **50 CENT**

1906, Jan. 10 ***Perf. 12½***
J27 D2 50c on 1g lt bl (III) 110.00 100.00
  a. 50c on 1g light blue (I) 110.00 110.00
  b. 50c on 1g light blue (II) 125.00 110.00

Surcharged in Red **6½**

1906, Oct. 6
J28 D2 6½c on 20c dk bl (I) 3.75 3.75

Nos. 87-89 Surcharged

PORTZEGEL

CENT

1907, Nov. 1
J29 A13 ½c on 1c cl 1.10 90
J30 A13 1c on 1c cl 30 30
J31 A13 1½c on 1c cl 35 35
J32 A13 2½c on 1c cl 1.10 1.10
J33 A13 5c on 2½c ver 1.10 30
J34 A13 6½c on 2½c ver 2.75 2.75
J35 A13 7½c on ½c bl 1.50 90
J36 A13 10c on ½c bl 1.50 42
J37 A13 12½c on ½c bl 3.00 3.00
J38 A13 15c on 2½c ver 4.50 3.00
J39 A13 25c on ½c bl 6.00 5.25
J40 A13 50c on ½c bl 30.00 25.00
J41 A13 1g on ½c bl 45.00 40.00
Nos. J29-J41 (13) 98.20 83.27

Two printings of the above surcharges were made. Some values show differences in the setting of the fractions; others are practically impossible to distinguish.

No. J20 Surcharged in Red

1909, June
J42 D2 4c on 6½c dk bl 4.50 4.50

No. J12 Surcharged in Black **3 CENT**

1910, July 11
J43 D2 3c on 1g lt bl, type III 22.50 22.50
  a. Type I 27.50 27.50
  b. Type II 25.00 25.00

Type I

1912-21 ***Perf. 12½, 13½x13***

Value in Color of Stamp

J44 D2 ½c pale ultra 15 15
J45 D2 1c pale ultra ('13) 15 15
J46 D2 1½c pale ultra ('15) 90 90
J47 D2 2½c pale ultra 15 15
J48 D2 3c pale ultra 32 20
J49 D2 4c pale ultra ('13) 15 15
J50 D2 4½c pale ultra ('16) 3.50 3.50
J51 D2 5c pale ultra 15 15
J52 D2 5½c pale ultra ('16) 3.50 3.50
J53 D2 7c pale ultra ('21) 1.75 1.50
J54 D2 7½c pale ultra ('13) 1.75 60
J55 D2 10c pale ultra ('13) 15 15
J56 D2 12½c pale ultra ('13) 15 15
J57 D2 15c pale ultra ('13) 15 15
J58 D2 20c pale ultra ('20) 15 15
J59 D2 25c pale ultra ('17) 60.00 50
J60 D2 50c pale ultra ('20) 25 15
Nos. J44-J60 (17) 73.32 12.20

D3

Perf. 12½, 13½x12½

1921-38 **Typo.**
J61 D3 3c pale ultra ('28) 15 15
J62 D3 6c pale ultra ('27) 15 15
J63 D3 7c pale ultra ('28) 15 15
J64 D3 7½c pale ultra ('26) 18 15
J65 D3 8c pale ultra ('38) 15 15
J66 D3 9c pale ultra ('30) 15 15
J67 D3 11c ultra ('21) 8.00 2.50
J68 D3 12c pale ultra ('28) 15 15
J69 D3 25c pale ultra ('25) 15 15
J70 D3 30c pale ultra ('35) 18 15
J71 D3 1g ver ('21) 52 15
Nos. J61-J71 (11) 9.93
Set value 3.45

Stamps of 1912-21 Surcharged

1923, Dec. ***Perf. 12½***
J72 D2 1c on 3c ultra 25 30
J73 D2 2½c on 7c ultra 25 20
J74 D2 25c on 1½c ultra 6.75 30
J75 D2 25c on 7½c ultra 6.75 15

D4

D5

1924, Aug.
J76 D4 4c on 3c ol grn 90 90
J77 D4 5c on 1c red 30 15
  a. Surcharge reading down 450.00 450.00
J78 D4 10c on ½c bl 60 15
  a. Tete beche pair 8.50 8.50
J79 D4 12½c on 5c car 65 15
  a. Tete beche pair 12.00 12.00
Set value 1.15

The basic stamps of Nos. J76 and J79 are type A11; those of J77-J78 are type A10.

Stamps of type D4 of denominations of 11c on 22½c and 15c on 17½c exist. These were used by the postal service for accounting of parcel post fees.

Catalogue values for unused stamps in this section, from this point to the end of the section, are for Never Hinged items.

Perf. 13½x12½

1947-58 **Wmk. 202** **Photo.**
J80 D5 1c lt bl ('48) 15 15
J81 D5 3c lt bl ('48) 15 15
J82 D5 4c lt bl 11.50 80
J83 D5 5c lt bl ('48) 15 15
J84 D5 6c lt bl ('50) 18 28
J85 D5 7c lt bl 15 15
J86 D5 8c lt bl ('48) 15 15
J87 D5 10c lt bl 15 15
J88 D5 11c lt bl 20 32
J89 D5 12c lt bl ('48) 25 35
J90 D5 14c lt bl ('53) 40 65
J91 D5 15c lt bl 20 15
J92 D5 16c lt bl 55 85
J93 D5 20c lt bl 20 15
J94 D5 24c lt bl ('57) 65 1.00
J95 D5 25c lt bl ('48) 18 15
J96 D5 26c lt bl ('58) 90 1.40
J97 D5 30c lt bl ('48) 38 15
J98 D5 35c lt bl 45 15
J99 D5 40c lt bl 50 15
J100 D5 50c lt bl ('48) 50 15
J101 D5 60c lt bl ('58) 70 40
J102 D5 85c lt bl ('50) 15.00 40
J103 D5 90c lt bl ('56) 1.75 40
J104 D5 95c lt bl ('57) 1.75 45
J105 D5 1g car ('48) 1.50 15
J106 D5 1.75g car ('57) 3.75 28
Nos. J80-J106 (27) 42.39 9.68

OFFICIAL STAMPS

Regular Issues of 1898-1908 Overprinted **ARMENWET**

1913 **Typo.** **Unwmk.** ***Perf. 12½***
O1 A10 1c red 2.00 1.00
O2 A10 1½c ultra 65 85
O3 A10 2c yel brn 3.25 3.25
O4 A10 2½c dp grn 8.00 6.00
O5 A11 3c ol grn 2.00 40
O6 A11 5c car rose 2.00 2.00
O7 A11 10c gray lil 22.50 20.00
Nos. O1-O7 (7) 40.40 33.50

Same Overprint in Red on No. 58

1919
O8 A10 1½c dp bl (R) 75.00 75.00

Nos. O1 to O8 were used to defray the postage on matter relating to the Poor Laws.

Counterfeit overprints exist.

For the International Court of Justice

Regular Issue of 1926-33 Overprinted in Gold

COUR PERMANENTE DE JUSTICE INTERNATIONALE

1934 **Wmk. 202** ***Perf. 12½***
O9 A24 1½c red vio 40
O10 A24 2½c dp grn 40
O11 A23 7½c red 65
O12 A31 12½c dp ultra 25.00
O13 A23 15c orange 90
O14 A23 30c violet 1.50
  a. Perf. 13½x12½ 1.50
Nos. O9-O14 (6) 28.85

Same Overprint on No. 180 in Gold

1937 ***Perf. 13½x12½***
O15 A23 12½c ultra 12.00

"Mint" Officials
Nos. O9-O15, O20-O43 were sold to the public only canceled. Uncanceled, they were obtainable only by favor of an official or from UPU specimen copies.

Same on Regular Issue of 1940 Overprinted in Gold

1940 *Perf. 13½x12½*
O16 A45 7½c brt red 12.00 6.50
O17 A45 12½c sapphire 12.00 6.50
O18 A45 15c lt bl 12.00 6.50
O19 A45 30c bister 12.00 6.50

Nos. 217 to 219, 221 and 223 Overprinted in Gold

COUR INTERNATIONALE DE JUSTICE

1947
O20 A45 7½c brt red 80
O21 A45 10c brt red vio 80
O22 A45 12½c sapphire 80
O23 A45 20c purple 80
O24 A45 25c rose brn 80
Nos. O20-O24 (5) 4.00

O1

Perf. 14½x13½
1950 Unwmk. Photo.
O25 O1 2c ultra 5.50
O26 O1 4c olive green 5.50

Palace of Peace, The Hague — O2

Queen Juliana — O3

1951-58 *Perf. 12½x12*
O27 O2 2c red brn 35
O28 O2 3c ultra ('53) 35
O29 O2 4c dp grn 35
O30 O2 5c ol brn ('53) 35
O31 O2 6c ol grn ('53) 70
O32 O2 7c red ('53) 55

Engr.
O33 O3 6c brn vio 5.50
O34 O3 10c dull grn 15
O35 O3 12c rose red 65
O36 O3 15c rose brn ('53) 15
O37 O3 20c dull blue 15
O38 O3 25c vio brn 15
O39 O3 30c rose lil ('58) 28
O40 O3 1g slate gray 70
Nos. O27-O40 (14) 10.38

1977, May Photo. *Perf. 12½x12*
O41 O2 40c brt grnsh bl 32
O42 O2 45c brick red 32
O43 O2 50c brt rose lil 32

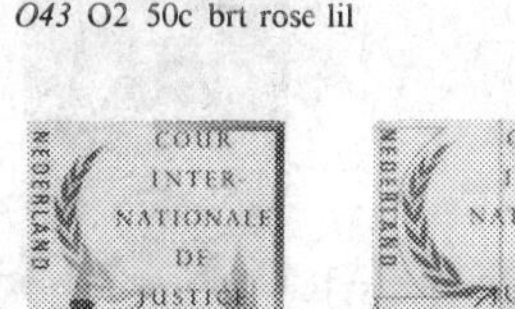
Peace Palace, The Hague — O4

Palm, Sun, Column — O5

1989, Oct. 24 Litho. *Perf. 13x14*
O44 O4 55c blk & pink 52 55
O45 O4 75c blk & yellow 70 70

Litho. & Engr.
O46 O5 7g multi 6.50 6.50

1990, Oct. 23 Litho.
O47 O4 65c blk & bl grn 75 75
O48 O4 1g blk & org 1.10 1.10
O49 O4 1.50g blk & bl 1.60 1.60

Litho. & Engr.
O50 O5 5g multi 5.50 5.50
Nos. O44-O50 (7) 16.67 16.70

This is an expanding set. Numbers will change when complete.

NETHERLANDS ANTILLES

(Curacao)

LOCATION — Two groups of islands about 500 miles apart in the West Indies, north of Venezuela
AREA — 383 sq. mi.
POP. — 260,000 (est. 1983)
CAPITAL — Willemstad

Formerly a colony, Curacao, Netherlands Antilles became an integral part of the Kingdom of the Netherlands under the Constitution of 1954. On Jan. 1, 1986, the island of Aruba achieved a separate status within the Kingdom and began issuing its own stamps.

100 Cents = 1 Gulden

Catalogue values for unused stamps in this country are for Never Hinged items, beginning with Scott 164 in the regular postage section, Scott B1 in the semi-postal section, Scott C18 in the airpost section, Scott CB9 in the airpost semi-postal section, and Scott J41 in the postage due section.

Watermark

Wmk. 202- Circles

King William III A1

Numeral A2

Regular Perf. 11½, 12½, 11½x12, 12½x12, 13½x13, 14
1873 Typo. Unwmk.
1 A1 2½c green 3.00 6.50
2 A1 3c bister 45.00 *110.00*
3 A1 5c rose 6.00 6.00
4 A1 10c ultra 42.50 12.00
5 A1 25c brn org 35.00 6.00
6 A1 50c violet 1.40 2.50
7 A1 2.50g bis & pur 25.00 21.00

See bluish paper note with Netherlands Nos. 7-22.
The gulden denominations, Nos. 7 and 12, are of larger size.
See 8-12. For surcharges see #18, 25-26.

Perf. 14, Small Holes
1b A1 2½c 9.00 13.00
2b A1 3c 50.00 *100.00*
3b A1 5c 9.00 15.00
4b A1 10c 50.00 60.00
5b A1 25c 50.00 40.00
6b A1 50c 24.00 26.00

"Small hole" varieties have the spaces between the holes wider than the diameter of the holes.

Perf. 11½, 12½, 12½x12, 13½
1886-89
8 A1 12½c yellow 70.00 32.50
9 A1 15c olive 19.00 11.00
10 A1 30c pearl gray 25.00 35.00
11 A1 60c ol bis 30.00 12.50
12 A1 1.50g lt & dk bl 80.00 65.00

Nos. 1-12 were issued without gum until 1890. Imperfs. are proofs.

1889 *Perf. 12½*
13 A2 1c gray 65 85
14 A2 2c violet 48 1.00
15 A2 2½c green 3.25 2.00
16 A2 3c bister 3.75 4.50
17 A2 5c rose 16.00 1.10
Nos. 13-17 (5) 24.13 9.45

King William III A3

Queen Wilhelmina A4

Black Surcharge, Handstamped
1891 *Perf. 12½x12*
Without Gum
18 A3 25c on 30c pearl gray 13.00 13.00

No. 18 exists with dbl. surch., value $225, and with invtd. surch., value $275.

1892-95 *Perf. 12½*
19 A4 10c ultra 70 95
20 A4 12½c green 26.00 7.00
21 A4 15c rose 2.25 2.50
22 A4 25c brn org 82.50 6.50
23 A4 30c gray 2.25 *6.50*
Nos. 19-23 (5) 113.70 23.45

King William III
A5 A6

Magenta Surcharge, Handstamped
1895 *Perf. 12½, 13½*
25 A5 2½c on 10c ultra 10.00 6.75
Perf. 12½x12
Black Surcharge, Handstamped
26 A6 2½c on 30c gray 125.00 5.00

Nos. 25-26 exist with surcharge double or inverted. Values: No. 25, double $275 and $200; inverted $350 and $250. No. 26, double $275, inverted $550.
No. 26 and No. 25, perf. 13½, were issued without gum.

Queen Wilhelmina
A7 A8

1902, Jan. 1 *Perf. 12½*
Black Surcharge
27 A7 25c on 25c car & bl 90 90

1901, May 1 Engr. *Perf. 11½x11*
28 A8 1.50g on 2.50g brn lil 14.00 19.00

1902, Mar. 1 Typo. *Perf. 12½*
29 A7 12½c on 12½c blue 25.00 6.75

A9

A10

1904-08
30 A9 1c ol grn 1.10 60
31 A9 2c yel brn 11.00 3.50
32 A9 2½c bl grn 3.50 28
33 A9 3c orange 6.50 3.50
34 A9 5c rose red 5.75 28
35 A9 7½c gray ('08) 27.50 5.75
36 A10 10c slate 9.75 3.50
37 A10 12½c dp bl 1.10 18
38 A10 15c brown 14.00 9.25
39 A10 22½c brn & ol ('08) 14.00 7.50
40 A10 25c violet 14.00 1.90
41 A10 30c brn org 32.50 13.00
42 A10 50c red brn 27.50 8.25
Nos. 30-42 (13) 168.20 57.49

Queen Wilhelmina — A11

1906, Nov. 1 Engr. *Perf. 11½*
Without Gum
43 A11 1½g red brown 35.00 24.00
44 A11 2½g slate blue 35.00 24.00

A12

Queen Wilhelmina
A13 A14

Perf. 12½, 11½, 11x11½

1915-33 **Typo.**

No.	Type	Description	Unused	Used
45	A12	½c lilac ('20)	40	85
46	A12	1c olive grn	18	15
47	A12	1½c blue ('20)	15	15
48	A12	2c yel brn	1.25	1.40
a.		Diag. half used as 1c on cover		4.50
49	A12	2½c green	1.10	16
a.		Diag. half used as 1c on cover		9.00
50	A12	3c yellow	1.25	1.50
51	A12	3c grn ('26)	2.25	2.50
52	A12	5c rose	1.40	15
53	A12	5c grn ('22)	2.50	2.75
54	A12	5c lilac ('26)	1.10	15
55	A12	7½c drab	1.50	32
56	A12	7½c bis ('20)	1.10	15
57	A12	10c lilac ('22)	4.25	4.50
58	A12	10c rose ('26)	4.25	1.25
59	A13	10c car rose	13.00	3.00
60	A13	12½c blue	1.50	50
61	A13	12½c red ('22)	1.40	1.65
62	A13	15c ol grn	45	65
63	A13	15c lt bl ('26)	3.00	2.50
64	A13	20c blue ('22)	6.00	3.00
65	A13	20c ol grn ('26)	1.65	2.25
66	A13	22½c orange	1.40	2.25
67	A13	25c red vio	3.00	90
68	A13	30c slate	3.00	65
69	A13	35c sl & red ('22)	3.00	4.25

Perf. 11½x11, 11½, 12½, 11

Engr.

No.	Type	Description	Unused	Used
70	A14	50c green	2.50	16
71	A14	1½g violet	12.00	10.00
72	A14	2½g carmine	20.00	19.00
a.		Perf. 12½ ('33)	140.00	300.00
		Nos. 45-72 (28)	94.58	66.74

Some stamps of 1915 were issued without gum.

For surcharges see #74, 107-108, C1-C3.

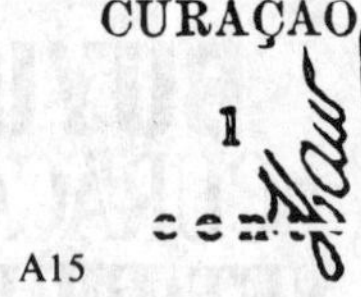

A15

Laid Paper, without Gum

1918, July 16 **Typo.** ***Perf. 12***

No.	Type	Description	Unused	Used
73	A15	1c black, *buff*	6.75	3.75

"HAW" are the initials of Postmaster H. A. Willemsen.

No. 60 Surcharged in Black **5 CENT**

1918, Sept. 1 ***Perf. 12½***

No.	Type	Description	Unused	Used
74	A13	5c on 12½c blue	3.75	2.00
a.		"5" 2½mm wide	55.00	30.00
b.		Double surcharge		450.00

The "5" of No. 74 is 3mm wide. Illustration shows No. 74a surcharge.

Queen Wilhelmina
A16 A17

1923 **Engr.** ***Perf. 11½, 11x11½***

No.	Type	Description	Unused	Used
75	A16	5c green	60	2.00
76	A16	7½c ol grn	1.10	1.65
77	A16	10c car rose	1.10	2.00
78	A16	20c indigo	1.90	3.50
a.		Perf. 11x11½	2.50	4.00
79	A16	1g brn vio	25.00	19.00
80	A16	2½g gray blk	60.00	*45.00*
81	A16	5g brown	80.00	*55.00*
a.		Perf. 11x11½	750.00	
		Nos. 75-81 (7)	169.70	*128.15*

25th anniv. of the assumption of the government of the Netherlands by Queen Wilhelmina, at the age of 18.

Nos. 80-81 with clear cancel between Aug. 1923 and Apr. 1924 sell for considerably more.

Types of Netherlands Marine Insurance Stamps, Inscribed "CURACAO" Surcharged in Black

FRANKEER = ZEGEL = 10 CENT

1927, Oct. 3

No.	Type	Description	Unused	Used
87	MI1	3c on 15c dk grn	18	24
88	MI1	10c on 60c car rose	22	30
89	MI1	12½c on 75c gray brn	24	30
90	MI2	15c on 1.50g dk bl	3.00	2.50
a.		Double surcharge	*475.00*	
91	MI2	25c on 2.25g org brn	6.50	6.25
92	MI3	30c on 4½g blk	14.00	11.00
93	MI3	50c on 7½g red	7.50	7.25
		Nos. 87-93 (7)	31.64	27.84

Nos. 90, 91 and 92 have "FRANKEER-ZEGEL" in one line of small capitals. Nos. 90 and 91 have a heavy bar across the top of the stamp.

1928-30 **Engr.** ***Perf. 11½, 12½***

No.	Type	Description	Unused	Used
95	A17	6c org red ('30)	1.50	18
a.		Booklet pane of 6		
96	A17	7½c org red	60	42
97	A17	10c carmine	1.50	35
98	A17	12½c red brn	1.50	1.00
a.		Booklet pane of 6		
99	A17	15c dk bl	1.50	28
a.		Booklet pane of 6		
100	A17	20c bl blk	5.75	55
101	A17	21c yel grn ('30)	9.25	14.00
102	A17	25c brn vio	3.50	1.40
103	A17	27½c blk ('30)	12.00	14.00
104	A17	30c dp grn	5.75	55
105	A17	35c brnsh blk	2.00	1.75
		Nos. 95-105 (11)	44.85	34.48

No. 96 Surcharged in Black with Bars over Original Value **6 ct.**

1929, Nov. 1

No.	Type	Description	Unused	Used
106	A17	6c on 7½c org red	1.40	1.00
a.		Inverted surcharge	300.00	260.00

No. 51 Surcharged in Red **2½**

1931, Mar. 1 **Typo.** ***Perf. 12½***

No.	Type	Description	Unused	Used
107	A12	2½c on 3c grn	1.10	1.10

No. 49 Surcharged in Red **1½**

1932, Oct. 29

No.	Type	Description	Unused	Used
108	A12	1½c on 2½c grn	3.50	3.50

Prince William I, Portrait by Van Key — A18

1933 **Photo.** ***Perf. 12½***

No.	Type	Description	Unused	Used
109	A18	6c deep orange	1.75	1.40

400th birth anniv. of Prince William I, Count of Nassau and Prince of Orange, frequently referred to as William the Silent.

Willem Usselinx
A19

Van Walbeeck's Ship
A22

Designs: 2½c, 5c, 6c, Frederik Hendrik. 10c, 12½c, 15c, Jacob Binckes. 27½c, 30c, 50c, Cornelis Evertsen the Younger. 1.50g, 2.50g, Louis Brion.

1934, Jan. 1 **Engr.** ***Perf. 12½***

No.	Type	Description	Unused	Used
110	A19	1c black	1.00	1.25
111	A19	1½c dl vio	75	30
112	A19	2c orange	1.00	1.25
113	A19	2½c dl grn	85	1.25
114	A19	5c blk brn	85	85
115	A19	6c vio bl	75	25
116	A19	10c lake	2.00	1.00
117	A19	12½c bis brn	6.50	7.00
118	A19	15c blue	1.65	1.00
119	A22	20c black	3.00	2.00
120	A22	21c brown	10.00	13.00
121	A22	25c dl grn	10.00	10.50
122	A19	27½c brn vio	13.00	16.00
123	A19	30c scarlet	10.00	4.50
124	A19	50c orange	10.00	7.50
125	A19	1.50g indigo	45.00	47.50
126	A19	2.50g yel grn	52.50	47.50
		Nos. 110-126 (17)	168.85	162.65

3rd centenary of the founding of the colony.

Numeral
A25

Queen Wilhelmina
A26

1936, Aug. 1 **Litho.** ***Perf. 13½x13***

Size: 18x22mm

No.	Type	Description	Unused	Used
127	A25	1c brn blk	15	15
128	A25	1½c dp ultra	18	15
129	A25	2c orange	22	22
130	A25	2½c green	20	20
131	A25	5c scarlet	18	15

Engr.

Perf. 12½

Size: 20¼x30½mm

No.	Type	Description	Unused	Used
132	A26	6c brn vio	45	15
133	A26	10c org red	85	15
134	A26	12½c dk bl grn	1.25	95
135	A26	15c dk bl	1.00	38
136	A26	20c org yel	1.00	45
137	A26	21c dk gray	1.90	2.25
138	A26	25c brn lake	1.25	75
139	A26	27½c vio brn	2.25	2.75
140	A26	30c ol brn	50	15

Perf. 13x14

Size: 22x33mm

No.	Type	Description	Unused	Used
141	A26	50c dl yel grn	2.50	15
a.		Perf. 14	30.00	25
142	A26	1.50g blk brn	18.00	15.00
a.		Perf. 14	30.00	22.50
143	A26	2.50g rose lake	10.50	8.50
a.		Perf. 14	10.00	8.50
		Nos. 127-143 (17)	42.38	32.50

See Nos. 147-151. For surcharges see Nos. B1-B3.

Queen Wilhelmina
A27

Perf. 12½x12

1938, Aug. 27 **Photo.** **Wmk. 202**

No.	Type	Description	Unused	Used
144	A27	1½c dl pur	15	22
145	A27	6c red org	80	75
146	A27	15c royal blue	1.50	1.25

Reign of Queen Wilhelmina, 40th anniv.

Numeral Type of 1936 and

Queen Wilhelmina — A28

1941-42 **Unwmk.** **Litho.** ***Perf. 12½***

Thick Paper

Size: 17¾x22mm

No.	Type	Description	Unused	Used
147	A25	1c gray brn ('42)	55	75
148	A25	1½c dl bl ('42)	6.50	15
149	A25	2c lt org ('42)	3.75	3.50
150	A25	2½c grn ('42)	32	15
151	A25	5c crim ('42)	32	15

Photo.

Perf. 12½, 13

Size: 18½x23mm

No.	Type	Description	Unused	Used
152	A28	6c rose vio	1.75	4.25
153	A28	10c red org	1.10	75
154	A28	12½c lt grn	1.50	50
155	A28	15c brt ultra	3.00	1.75
156	A28	20c orange	22	35
157	A28	21c gray	1.40	1.10
158	A28	25c brn lake	1.65	1.40
159	A28	27½c dp brn	1.90	2.50
160	A28	30c ol bis	8.25	2.50

Size: 21x26½mm

No.	Type	Description	Unused	Used
161	A28	50c ol grn ('42)	9.00	15
162	A28	1½g gray ol ('42)	11.00	75
163	A28	2½g rose lake ('42)	10.00	90
		Nos. 147-163 (17)	62.21	21.60

Imperfs. are printers waste.

See Nos. 174-187.

Catalogue values for unused stamps in this section, from this point to the end of the section, are for Never Hinged items.

Bonaire
A29

St. Eustatius
A30

Designs: 2c, View of Saba. 2½c, St. Maarten. 5c, Aruba. 6c, Curacao.

Perf. 13x13½, 13½x13

1943, Feb. 1 **Engr.** **Unwmk.**

No.	Type	Description	Unused	Used
164	A29	1c rose vio & org brn	15	15
165	A30	1½c dp bl & yel grn	15	15
166	A29	2c sl blk & org brn	42	25
167	A29	2½c grn & org	18	18
168	A29	5c red & sl blk	80	15
169	A29	6c rose lil & lt bl	50	45
		Nos. 164-169 (6)	2.20	1.33

Royal Family — A35

1943, Nov. 8 ***Perf. 13½x13***

No.	Type	Description	Unused	Used
170	A35	1½c deep org	15	15
171	A35	2½c red	15	15
172	A35	6c black	75	45
173	A35	10c deep blue	75	60

Issued in honor of Princess Margriet Francisca of the Netherlands.

Wilhelmina Type of 1941

1947 **Photo.** ***Perf. 13½x12½***

Size: 18x22mm

174 A28 6c brn vio 1.25 1.65
175 A28 10c org red 1.25 1.65
176 A28 12½c dk bl grn 1.25 1.65
177 A28 15c dk bl 1.25 1.65
178 A28 20c org yel 1.25 2.50
179 A28 21c dk gray 1.50 1.65
180 A28 25c brn lake 15 15
181 A28 27½c chocolate 1.25 1.10
182 A28 30c ol bis 1.40 65
183 A28 50c dl yel grn 1.65 15

Perf. 13x14

Engr.

Size: 25x31¼mm

184 A28 1½g dk brn 80 45
185 A28 2½g rose lake 15.00 3.75
186 A28 5g ol grn 80.00 105.00
187 A28 10g red org 110.00 175.00
Nos. 174-187 (14) 218.00 297.00

Used values for Nos. 186-187 are for genuinely canceled copies clearly dated before the end of 1949.

Queen Wilhelmina
A36 A37

Perf. 13½x12½

1948 **Unwmk.** **Photo.**

188 A36 6c dk vio brn 95 90
189 A36 10c scarlet 95 1.25
190 A36 12½c dk bl grn 95 75
191 A36 15c dp bl 95 90
192 A36 20c red org 95 1.50
193 A36 21c black 95 1.50
194 A36 25c brt red vio 30 15
195 A36 27½c hn brn 16.00 13.00
196 A36 30c ol brn 13.00 75
197 A36 50c ol grn 13.00 18

Perf. 12½x12

Engr.

198 A37 1.50g chocolate 21.00 3.50
Nos. 188-198 (11) 69.00 24.38

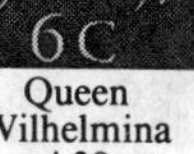

Queen Wilhelmina A38 Queen Juliana A39

1948, Aug. 30 ***Perf. 13x14***

199 A38 6c vermilion 45 45
200 A38 12½c dp bl 45 45

Reign of Queen Wilhelmina, 50th anniv.

Perf. 14x13

1948, Oct. 18 **Photo.** **Wmk. 202**

201 A39 6c red brn 35 35
202 A39 12½c dk grn 35 35

Investiture of Queen Juliana, Sept. 6, 1948. Nos. 201-202 were issued in Netherlands Sept. 6.

Ship of Ojeda — A40 Alonso de Ojeda — A41

Perf. 14x13, 13x14

1949, July 26 **Photo.** **Unwmk.**

203 A40 6c ol grn 2.50 1.75
204 A41 12½c brn red 3.25 3.00
205 A40 15c ultra 3.25 2.00

450th anniversary of the discovery of Curacao by Alonso de Ojeda, 1499.

Post Horns Entwined — A42

1949, Oct. 3 ***Perf. 12x12½***

206 A42 6c brown red 3.00 2.00
207 A42 25c dull blue 3.00 95

UPU, 75th anniversary.

A43

Queen Juliana
A44 A45

1950-79 **Photo.** ***Perf. 13x13½***

208 A43 1c red brn 15 15
209 A43 1½c blue 15 15
210 A43 2c orange 15 15
211 A43 2½c green 60 15
212 A43 3c purple 15 15
212A A43 4c yel grn ('59) 32 30
213 A43 5c dk red 15 15

Perf. 13½x13

214 A44 6c dp plum 65 15
215 A44 7½c red brn ('54) 3.50 15
216 A44 10c red 1.10 15
a. Redrawn ('79) 15 15
217 A44 12½c dk grn 1.40 15
218 A44 15c dp bl 1.40 15
a. Redrawn ('79) 15 15
219 A44 20c orange 1.65 15
a. Redrawn ('79) 18 15
220 A44 21c black 1.65 1.25
221 A44 22½c bl grn ('54) 4.50 15
222 A44 25c violet 2.00 15
a. Redrawn ('79) 22 15
223 A44 27½c henna brn 3.75 1.50
224 A44 30c ol brn 4.50 15
225 A44 50c ol grn 4.50 15

Perf. 12½x12

Engr.

226 A45 1½g slate grn 7.50 20
227 A45 2½g blk brn 12.00 75
228 A45 5g rose red 35.00 7.75
229 A45 10g dk vio brn 135.00 40.00
Nos. 208-229 (23) 221.77 54.15

Nos. 216a, 218a, 219a and 222a are from booklets Nos. 427a and 428a. Background design is sharper and stamps have one or two straight edges.

See Nos. 427-429. For surcharge see No. B20.

Fort Beekenburg A46

1953, June 16 **Photo.** ***Perf. 13x12½***

230 A46 22½c olive brown 3.00 32

250th anniversary of the founding of Fort Beekenburg.

Beach at Aruba A47

1954, May 1 ***Perf. 11x11½***

231 A47 15c dk bl, sal & dp bl 3.25 2.00

3rd congress of the Caribbean Tourist Assoc., Aruba, May 3-6.

Queen Juliana — A48

1954, Dec. 15 ***Perf. 13½***

232 A48 7½c ol grn 70 60

Charter of the Kingdom, adopted Dec. 15, 1954. See Netherlands #366 & Surinam #264.

Beach A49

Petroleum Refinery, Aruba — A50

1955, Dec. 5 **Litho.** ***Perf. 12***

233 A49 15c chnt, bl & emer 2.25 1.75
234 A50 25c chnt, bl & emer 2.50 2.00

Caribbean Commission, 21st meeting, Aruba.

St. Annabaai Harbor and Flags — A51

1956, Dec. 6 **Unwmk.** ***Perf. 14x13***

235 A51 15c lt bl, blk & red 28 28

Caribbean Commission, 10th anniversary.

Man Watching Rising Sun — A52

1957, Mar. 14 **Photo.** ***Perf. 11x11½***

236 A52 15c brn, blk & yel 28 28

1st Caribbean Mental Health Conference, Aruba, Mar. 14-19.

Saba — A53

Views: 15c, St. Maarten. 25c, St. Eustatius.

1957, July 1 **Litho.** ***Perf. 14x13***

237 A53 7½c multi 32 32
238 A53 15c multi 32 32
239 A53 25c multi 32 32

Issued to publicize these islands as tourist attractions.

Curacao Intercontinental Hotel — A54

1957, Oct. 12 ***Perf. 14x13***

240 A54 15c lt ultra 28 28

Opening of the Intercontinental Hotel, Willemstad.

Map of Curacao A55

1957, Dec. 10 ***Perf. 14x13***

241 A55 15c ind & lt bl 60 55

International Geophysical Year.

Flamingoes, Bonaire — A56

Designs: 7½c, 8c, 25c, 1½g, Old buildings, Curacao. 10c, 5g, Extinct volcano and palms, Saba. 15c, 30c, 1g, Fort Willem III, Aruba. 20c, 35c, De Ruyter obelisk, St. Eustatius. 12c, 40c, 2½g, Town Hall, St. Maarten.

1958-59 **Litho.** ***Perf. 14x13***

Size: 33x22mm

242 A56 6c lt ol grn & pink 2.00 15
243 A56 7½c red brn & org 15 15
244 A56 8c dk bl & org ('59) 15 15
245 A56 10c gray & org yel 15 15
246 A56 12c bluish grn & gray ('59) 15 15
247 A56 15c grn & lt ultra 15 15
a. 15c green & lilac 15 15
248 A56 20c crim & gray 16 15
249 A56 25c Prus bl & yel grn 20 15
250 A56 30c brn & bl grn 22 15
251 A56 35c gray & rose ('59) 28 15
252 A56 40c mag & grn 30 15
253 A56 50c grysh brn & pink 35 15
254 A56 1g brt red & gray 75 15
255 A56 1½g rose vio & pale brn 1.10 18
256 A56 2½g bl & cit 1.25 38
257 A56 5g lt red brn & rose lil 3.75 75
Nos. 242-257 (16) 11.11
Set value 2.50

See Nos. 340-348, 400-403. For surcharge see No. B58.

Globe — A57

1958, Oct. 16 ***Perf. 11x11½***

258 A57 7½c bl & lake 15 15
259 A57 15c red & ultra 28 28

50th anniv. of the Netherlands Antilles Radio and Telegraph Administration.

Hotel Aruba Caribbean A58

1959, July 18 *Perf. 14x13*

260 A58 15c multi 28 28

Opening of the Hotel Aruba Caribbean, Aruba.

Sea Water Distillation Plant — A59

1959, Oct. 16 Photo. *Perf. 14x13*

261 A59 20c bright blue 32 32

Opening of sea water distillation plant at Balashi, Aruba.

Netherlands Antilles Flag — A60

1959, Dec. 14 Litho. *Perf. 13½*

262 A60 10c ultra & red 28 28
263 A60 20c ultra, yel & red 28 28
264 A60 25c ultra, grn & red 28 28

5th anniv. of the new constitution (Charter of the Kingdom).

Fokker "Snip" and Map of Caribbean A61

Designs: 20c, Globe showing route flown, and plane. 25c, Map of Atlantic ocean and view of Willemstad. 35c, Map of Atlantic ocean and plane on Aruba airfield.

1959, Dec. 22 Unwmk. *Perf. 14x13*

265 A61 10c yel, lt & dk bl 32 28
266 A61 20c yel, lt & dk bl 32 28
267 A61 25c yel, lt & dk bl 32 15
268 A61 35c yel, lt & dk bl 32 40

25th anniv. of Netherlands-Curacao air service.

Msgr. Martinus J. Niewindt — A62

1960, Jan. 12 Photo. *Perf. 13½*

269 A62 10c dp cl 32 32
270 A62 20c dp vio 48 48
271 A62 25c ol grn 32 32

Death centenary of Monsignor Niewindt, first apostolic vicar for Curacao.

Worker, Flag and Factories — A63

1960, Apr. 29 *Perf. 12½x13*

272 A63 20c multi 32 32

Issued for Labor Day, May 1, 1960.

US Brig "Andrea Doria" and Gun at Fort Orange, St. Eustatius A64

1961, Nov. 16 Litho. *Perf. 14x13*

273 A64 20c bl, red, grn & blk 50 50

185th anniversary of first salute by a foreign power to the US flag flown by an American ship.

Silver Wedding Issue

Type of Netherlands, 1962

1962, Jan. 31 Photo. *Perf. 14x13*

274 A92 10c dp org 15 15
275 A92 25c dp bl 20 20

Silver wedding anniversary of Queen Juliana and Prince Bernhard.

Benta Player — A65

Designs: 6c, Corn masher. 20c, Petji kerchief. 25c, "Jaja" (nurse) with child, sculpture.

1962, Mar. 14 Photo. *Perf. 12½x13*

276 A65 6c red brn & yel 15 15
277 A65 10c multi 18 15
278 A65 20c crim, ind & brt grn 30 28
279 A65 25c brt grn, brn & gray 32 28
a. Souv. sheet of 4, #276-279 1.25 1.25

Emblem of Family Relationship A66

Design: 25c, Emblem of mental health (cross).

1963, Apr. 17 Litho. *Perf. 14x13*

280 A66 20c dk bl & ocher 28 28
281 A66 25c bl & red 28 28

Fourth Caribbean Conference for Mental Health, Curacao, Apr. 17-23.

Dove with Olive Branch — A67

1963, July 1 Unwmk. *Perf. 14x13*

282 A67 25c org yel & dk brn 22 22

Centenary of emancipation of the slaves.

Hotel Bonaire — A68

1963, Aug. 31 *Perf. 14x13*

283 A68 20c dk red brn 22 22

Opening of Hotel Bonaire on Bonaire.

Prince William of Orange Taking Oath of Allegiance — A69

1963, Nov. 21 Photo. *Perf. 13x13½*

284 A69 25c grn, blk & rose 22 22

150th anniversary of the founding of the Kingdom of the Netherlands.

Chemical Equipment A70

1963, Dec. 10 Litho. *Perf. 14x13*

285 A70 20c bl grn, brt yel grn & red 32 32

Opening of chemical factories on Aruba.

Airmail Letter and Wings A71

Design: 25c, Map of Caribbean, Miami-Curacao route and planes of 1929 and 1964.

1964, June 22 Photo. *Perf. 11x11½*

286 A71 20c lt bl, red & ultra 28 28
287 A71 25c lt grn, bl, red & blk 28 28

35th anniversary of the first regular Curacao airmail service.

Map of the Caribbean A72

1964, Nov. 30 Litho. Unwmk.

288 A72 20c ultra, org & dk red 22 22

5th meeting of the Caribbean Council, Curacao, Nov. 30-Dec. 4.

Netherlands Antilles Flags, Map of Curacao and Crest — A73

1964, Dec. 14 Litho. *Perf. 11½x11*

289 A73 25c lt bl & multi 22 22

10th anniversary of the Charter of the Kingdom of the Netherlands. The flags, shaped like seagulls, represent the six islands comprising the Netherlands Antilles.

Princess Beatrix — A74

1965, Feb. 22 Photo. *Perf. 13x14*

290 A74 25c brick red 28 28

Visit of Princess Beatrix of Netherlands.

ITU Emblem, Old and New Communication Equipment — A75

1965, May 17 Litho. *Perf. 13½*

291 A75 10c brt bl & dk bl 15 15

ITU, centenary.

Shell Refinery, Curacao A76

Designs: 10c, Catalytic cracking installation (vert.). 25c, Workers operating manifold, primary distillation plant (vert.).

Perf. 13x14, 14x13

1965, June 22 Photo.

292 A76 10c blk, red & yel 15 15
293 A76 20c multi 15 15
294 A76 25c multi 22 22

50th anniv. of the oil industry in Curacao.

Floating Market, Curacao A77

Designs (flag and): 2c, Divi-divi tree and Haystack Mountain, Aruba. 3c, Lace, Saba. 4c, Flamingoes, Bonaire. 5c, Church ruins, St. Eustatius. 6c, Lobster, St. Maarten.

1965, Aug. 25 Litho. *Perf. 14x13*

295 A77 1c lt grn, ultra & red 15 15
296 A77 2c yel, ultra & red 15 15
297 A77 3c chlky bl, ultra & red 15 15
298 A77 4c org, ultra & red 15 15
299 A77 5c lt bl, ultra & red 15 15
300 A77 6c pink, ultra & red 15 15
Set value 36 36

Marine Guarding Beach — A78

1965, Dec. 10 Photo. *Perf. 13x10½*
301 A78 25c multi 15 15

Issued to commemorate the 300th anniversary of the Netherlands Marine Corps.

Budgerigars, Wedding Rings and Initials — A79

1966, Mar. 10 Photo. *Perf. 13x14*
302 A79 25c gray & multi 15 15

Issued to commemorate the marriage of Princess Beatrix and Claus van Amsberg.

M. A. de Ruyter and Map of St. Eustatius — A80

1966, June 19 Photo. *Perf. 13½*
303 A80 25c vio, ocher & lt bl 15 15

Visit of Adm. Michiel Adriaanszoon de Ruyter (1607-1676) to St. Eustatius, 1666.

Liberal Arts and Grammar — A81

Designs: 10c, Rhetoric and dialectic. 20c, Arithmetic and geometry. 25c, Astronomy and music.

Perf. 13x12½
1966, Sept. 19 Litho. Unwmk.
304 A81 6c yel, bl & blk 15 15
305 A81 10c yel grn, red & blk 15 15
306 A81 20c bl, yel & blk 15 15
307 A81 25c red, yel grn & blk 15 15
Set value 38 38

25th anniversary of secondary education.

Cruiser — A82

Ships: 10c, Sailing ship. 20c, Tanker. 25c, Passenger ship.

Perf. 13x14
1967, Mar. 29 Litho. Unwmk.
308 A82 6c lt & dk grn 15 15
309 A82 10c org & brn 15 15
310 A82 20c sep & brn 15 15
311 A82 25c chlky bl & dk bl 16 15
Set value 44 44

60th anniv. of *Onze Vloot* (Our Fleet), an organization which publicizes the Dutch navy and merchant marine and helps seamen.

Manuel Carlos Piar (1777-1817), Independence Hero — A83

Discobolus after Myron — A84

1967, Apr. 26 Photo. *Perf. 14x13*
312 A83 20c red & blk 15 15

1968, Feb. 19 Litho. *Perf. 13x14*

Designs: 10c, Hand holding torch, and Olympic rings. 25c, Stadium, doves and Olympic rings.

313 A84 10c multi 20 20
314 A84 20c dk brn, ol & yel 20 20
315 A84 25c bl, dk bl & brt yel grn 20 20

19th Olympic Games, Mexico City, Oct. 12-27.

Friendship 500 — A84a

Designs: 20c, Beechcraft Queen Air. 25c, Friendship and DC-9.

1968, Dec. 3 Litho. *Perf. 14x13*
315A A84a 10c dl yel, blk & brt bl 22 22
315B A84a 20c tan, blk & brt bl 22 22
315C A84a 25c sal pink, blk & brt bl 22 22

Issued to publicize Dutch Antillean Airlines (ALM).

Map of Bonaire, Radio Mast and Waves — A85

Code of Law — A86

1969, Mar. 6 Litho. *Perf. 14x13*
316 A85 25c bl, emer & blk 22 22

Opening of the relay station of the Dutch World Broadcasting System on Bonaire.

1969, May 19 Photo. *Perf. 12½x13*

Designs: 25c, Scales of Justice.

317 A86 20c dk grn, yel grn & gold 22 22
318 A86 25c vio bl, bl & gold 22 22

Court of Justice, centenary.

ILO Emblem, Cactus and House — A87

1969, Aug. 25 Litho. *Perf. 14x13*
319 A87 10c bl & blk 15 15
320 A87 25c dk red & blk 15 16

ILO, 50th anniversary.

Queen Juliana and Rising Sun — A87a

1969, Dec. 15 Photo. *Perf. 14x13*
321 A87a 25c bl & multi 22 22

15th anniv. of the Charter of the Kingdom of the Netherlands. Phosphorescent paper.

Radio Bonaire Studio and Transmitter — A88

Design: 15c, Radio waves and cross set against land, sea and air.

1970, Feb. 5 Photo. *Perf. 12½x13*
322 A88 10c multi 15 15
323 A88 15c multi 15 16

5th anniv. of the opening of the Trans World Missionary Radio Station, Bonaire.

Altar, St. Anna's Church, Otrabanda 1752 — A89

Designs: 20c, Interior, Synagogue at Punda, 1732, horiz. 25c, Pulpit, Fort Church, Fort Amsterdam, 1769.

Perf. 13x14, 14x13
1970, May 12 Photo.
324 A89 10c gold & multi 20 20
325 A89 20c gold & multi 20 20
326 A89 25c gold & multi 20 20

St. Theresia Church, St. Nicolaas — A90

1971, Feb. 9 Litho. *Perf. 14x13*
327 A90 20c dl bl, gray & rose 22 22

40th anniversary of the Parish of St. Theresia at St. Nicolaas, Aruba.

Lions Emblem — A91

1971, Feb. 24 *Perf. 13x13½*
328 A91 25c dk bl & multi 28 28

Lions Club in the Netherlands Antilles, 25th anniversary.

Prince Bernhard Type of Netherlands

1971, June 29 Photo. *Perf. 13x14*
329 A123 45c multi 40 40

60th birthday of Prince Bernhard.

Pedro Luis Brion (1782-1821), Naval Commander in Fight for South American Independence — A92

1971, Sept. 27 Photo. *Perf. 13x12½*
330 A92 40c multi 28 28

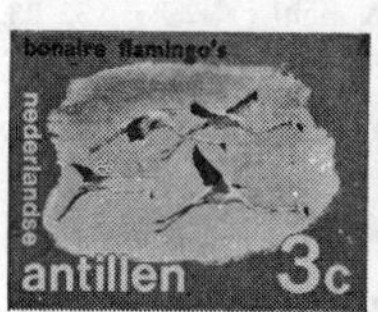

Flamingoes, Bonaire — A93

Ship in Dry Dock — A94

Designs: 1c, Queen Emma Bridge, Curaçao. 2c, The Bottom, Saba. 4c, Water tower, Aruba. 5c, Fort Amsterdam, St. Maarten. 6c, Fort Orange, St. Eustatius.

1972, Jan. 17 Litho. *Perf. 13x13½*
331 A93 1c yel & multi 15 15
332 A93 2c yel grn & multi 15 15
333 A93 3c dp org & multi 15 15
334 A93 4c brt bl & multi 15 15
335 A93 5c red org & multi 15 15
336 A93 6c lil rose & multi 15 15
Set value 36 36

1972, Apr. 7 *Perf. 13½x13*
337 A94 30c bl gray & multi 28 28

Inauguration of large dry dock facilities in Willemstad.

Juan Enrique Irausquin — A95

Costa Gomez — A96

1972, June 20 Photo. *Perf. 13x14*
338 A95 30c dp org 28 28

Irausquin (1904-1962), financier and patriot.

1972, Oct. 27 Litho.
339 A96 30c yel grn & blk 28 28

Moises Frumencio da Costa Gomez (1907-1966), lawyer, legislator, patriot.

Island Series Type of 1958-59

Designs: 45c, 85c, Extinct volcano and palms, Saba. 55c, 90c, De Ruyter obelisk, St. Eustatius. 65c, 75c, 10g, Flamingoes, Bonaire. 70c, Fort Willem III, Aruba. 95c, Town Hall, St. Maarten.

1973, Feb. 12 Litho. *Perf. 14x13*
Size: 33x22mm
340 A56 45c vio bl & lt bl 32 15
341 A56 55c dk car rose & emer 42 18
342 A56 65c grn & pink 48 22
343 A56 70c gray vio & org 50 25
344 A56 75c brt lil & sal 55 28
345 A56 85c brn ol & ap grn 60 30
346 A56 90c bl & ocher 70 35
347 A56 95c org & yel 70 38
348 A56 10g brt ultra & sal 7.00 3.75
Nos. 340-348 (9) 11.27 5.86

Mailman — A97

Designs: 15c, King William III from 1873 issue. 30c, Emblem of Netherlands Antilles postal service.

1973, May 23 Photo. *Perf. 13x14*
349 A97 15c lil, gold & vio 28 22
350 A97 20c dk grn & multi 32 28
351 A97 30c org & multi 32 28

Centenary of first stamps of Netherlands Antilles.

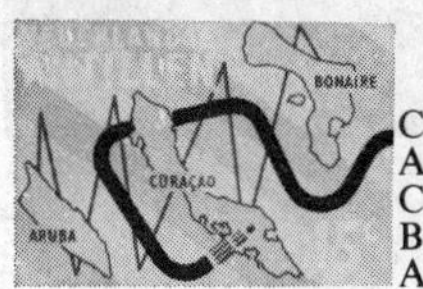
Cable Linking Aruba, Curacao and Bonaire A98

Designs: 30c, 6 stars symbolizing the islands, and cable. 45c, Saba, St. Maarten and St. Eustatius linked by cable.

1973, June 20 Litho. *Perf. 14x13*
352 A98 15c multi 32 32
353 A98 30c multi 32 32
354 A98 45c multi 32 23
a. Souvenir sheet of 3, #352-354 2.00 1.50

Inauguration of the inter-island submarine cable.

Queen Juliana, Netherlands Antilles and House of Orange Colors A99a

Engr. & Litho.
1973, Sept. 4 *Perf. 12½x12*
355 A99a 15c silver & multi 40 40

25th anniversary of reign of Queen Juliana.

Jan Hendrik Albert Eman — A99

Lionel Bernard Scott — A100

1973, Oct. 17 Litho. *Perf. 13x14*
356 A99 30c lt yel grn & blk 28 28

Eman (1888-1957), founder of the People's Party in Aruba, member of Antillean Parliament.

1974, Jan. 28
357 A100 30c lt bl & multi 28 28

Scott (1897-1966), architect and statesman.

Netherlands Antilles stamps can be mounted in Scott's annual Netherlands Supplement.

Family at Supper — A101

Designs: 12c, Parents watching children at play. 15c, Mother and daughter sewing, father and son gardening.

1974, Feb. 18 Litho. *Perf. 13x14*
358 A101 6c bl & multi 15 15
359 A101 12c bis & multi 22 20
360 A101 15c grn & multi 28 22
Set value 56 48

Planned parenthood and World Population Year.

Desulphurization Plant, Lago — A102

Designs: 30c, Distillation plant. 45c, Lago refinery at night.

1974, Aug. 12 Litho. *Perf. 14x13*
361 A102 15c lt bl, blk & yel 28 28
362 A102 30c lt bl, blk & yel 28 28
363 A102 45c dk brn & multi 28 28

Oil industry in Aruba, 50th anniversary.

UPU Emblem — A103

1974, Oct. 9 Litho. *Perf. 13x14*
364 A103 15c yel grn, blk & gold 32 32
365 A103 30c bl, blk & gold 32 32

Centenary of Universal Postal Union.

Queen Emma Bridge — A104

Willemstad Bridges: 30c, Queen Juliana Bridge. 40c, Queen Wilhelmina Bridge.

1975, Feb. 5 Litho. *Perf. 14x13*
366 A104 20c ultra & multi 32 32
367 A104 30c ultra & multi 32 32
368 A104 40c ultra & multi 40 40

Dedication of new Queen Juliana Bridge spanning Caracao Harbor.

Salt Crystals A105

Designs: 20c, Solar salt pond. 40c, Map of Bonaire and location of solar salt pond, vert.

Perf. 14x13, 13x14
1975, Apr. 24 Litho.
369 A105 15c multi 32 32
370 A105 20c multi 32 32
371 A105 40c multi 40 32

Bonaire's salt industry.

Aruba Airport, 1935 and Fokker F-18 — A106

Designs: 30c, Aruba Airport, 1950, and Douglas DC-9. 40c, New Princess Beatrix Airport and Boeing 727.

1975, June 19 Litho. *Perf. 14x13*
372 A106 15c vio & multi 28 22
373 A106 30c blk & multi 32 28
374 A106 40c yel & multi 32 32

40th anniversary of Aruba Airport.

International Women's Year Emblem A107

Designs: 12c, "Women's role in social development." 20c, Embryos within female and male symbols.

1975, Aug. 1 Photo. *Perf. 14x13*
375 A107 6c multi 15 15
376 A107 12c multi 28 22
377 A107 20c multi 32 28

International Women's Year 1975.

Beach, Aruba — A108

Tourist Publicity: No. 379, Beach pavilion and boat, Bonaire. No. 380, Table Mountain and Spanish Water, Curacao.

1976, June 21 Litho. *Perf. 14x13*
378 A108 40c blue & multi 40 40
379 A108 40c blue & multi 40 40
380 A108 40c blue & multi 40 40

Julio Antonio Abraham A109

Dike and Produce A110

1976, Aug. 10 Photo. *Perf. 13x14*
381 A109 30c tan & claret 32 32

Julio Antonio Abraham (1909-1960), founder of Democratic Party of Bonaire.

1976, Sept. 21 Litho.
382 A110 15c shown 28 22
383 A110 35c Cattle 40 32
384 A110 45c Fish 40 40

Agriculture, husbandry and fishing in Netherlands Antilles.

Plaque, Fort Oranje Memorial A111

Designs: 40c, Andrea Doria in St. Eustatius harbor receiving salute. 55c, Johannes de Graaff, Governor of St. Eustatius, holding Declaration of Independence.

1976, Nov. 16 Litho. *Perf. 14x13*
385 A111 25c multi 55 32
386 A111 40c multi 90 32
387 A111 55c multi 60 55

First gun salute to US flag, St. Eustatius, Nov. 16, 1776.

Dancer with Cactus Headdress A112

Bird Petroglyph, Aruba A113

Carnival: 35c, Woman in feather costume. 40c, Woman in pompadour costume.

1977, Jan. 20 Litho. *Perf. 13x14*
388 A112 25c multi 40 32
389 A112 35c multi 40 32
390 A112 40c multi 40 32

1977, Mar. 29

Indian Petroglyphs: 35c, Loops and spiral, Savonet Plantation, Curacao. 40c, Tortoise, Onima, Bonaire.

391 A113 25c red & multi 32 28
392 A113 35c brn & multi 32 32
393 A113 40c yel & multi 40 32

Cordia Sebestena A114

Chimes, Spritzer & Fuhrmann Building A115

Tropical Trees: 40c, East Indian walnut, vert. 55c, Tamarind.

1977, July 20 *Perf. 14x13, 13x14*
394 A114 25c blk & multi 32 28
395 A114 40c blk & multi 40 32
396 A114 55c blk & multi 48 48

1977, Sept. 27 Litho. *Perf. 13x14*

Designs: 40c, Globe with Western Hemisphere and sun over Curacao. 55c, Diamond ring and flag of Netherlands Antilles.

397 A115 20c brt grn & multi 32 28
398 A115 40c yel & multi 40 40
399 A115 55c bl & multi 48 48

Spritzer & Fuhrmann, jewelers of Netherlands Antilles, 50th anniversary.

Type of 1958-59

Designs: 20c, 35c, 55c, De Ruyter obelisk, St. Eustatius. 40c, Town Hall, St. Maarten.

Perf. 13½ Horiz.
1977, Nov. 30 Photo.
Size: 39x22mm
400 A56 20c crim & gray 70 50
a. Bklt. pane of 6 (2 #400, 4 #402) 5.25

401 A56 35c gray & rose 1.10 80
a. Bklt. pane of 4 (1 #401, 3 #403) 6.00
402 A56 40c magenta & grn 70 50
403 A56 55c dk car rose & emer 1.10 1.10

Nos. 400-403 issued in booklets only. No. 400a has label with red inscription in size of 3 stamps; No. 401a has label with dark carmine rose inscription in size of 2 stamps.

Winding Road, Map of Saba — A116

Tourist Publicity: 35c, Ruins of Synagogue, map of St. Eustatius. 40c, Greatbay, Map of St. Maarten.

1977, Nov. 30 Litho. *Perf. 14x13*
404 A116 25c multi 15 15
405 A116 35c multi 15 15
406 A116 40c multi 22 22
Set value 42 42

Treasure Chest — A117

Designs: 20c, Logo of Netherlands Antilles Bank. 40c, Safe deposit door.

1978, Feb. 7 Litho. *Perf. 14x13*
407 A117 15c brt & dk bl 15 15
408 A117 20c org & gold 15 15
409 A117 40c brt & dk grn 15 15
Set value 28 28

Bank of Netherlands Antilles, 150th anniv.

Flamboyant A118 — Polythysana Rubrescens A119

Flowers: 25c, Erythrina velutina. 40c, Guaiacum officinale, horiz. 55c, Gliricidia sepium, horiz.

Perf. 13x14, 14x13
1978, May 31 Litho.
410 A118 15c multi 15 15
411 A118 25c multi 22 20
412 A118 40c multi 28 25
413 A118 55c multi 32 32

1978, June 20 *Perf. 13x14*

Butterflies: 25c, Caligo eurilochus. 35c, Prepona omphale amesis. 40c, Morpho aega.

414 A119 15c multi 15 15
415 A119 25c multi 22 20
416 A119 35c multi 28 25
417 A119 40c multi 32 32

"Conserve Energy" — A120

1978, Aug. 31 Litho. *Perf. 13x14*
418 A120 15c org & blk 15 15
419 A120 20c dp grn & blk 18 15
420 A120 40c dk red & blk 30 30

Morse Ship-to-Shore Service A121

Designs: 40c, Ship-to-shore telex service. 55c, Future radar-satellite service, vert.

Perf. 14x13, 13x14
1978, Oct. 16 Litho.
421 A121 20c multi 22 22
422 A121 40c multi 28 28
423 A121 55c multi 40 40

70th anniversary of ship-to-shore communications.

Villa Maria Waterworks A122

Designs: 35c, Leonard B. Smith, vert. 40c, Opening of Queen Emma Bridge, Willemstadt, 1888.

1978, Dec. 13
424 A122 25c multi 18 16
425 A122 35c multi 22 20
426 A122 40c multi 30 25

Leonard B. Smith, engineer, 80th death anniversary.

Queen Juliana Type of 1950

1979, Jan. 11 Photo. *Perf. 13½x12*
427 A44 5c dp yel 15 15
a. Bklt. pane of 10 (4 #427, 1 #216a, 2 #222a, 3 #429) 3.00
428 A44 30c brown 25 15
a. Bklt. pane of 10 (1 #428, 4 #218a, 3 #219a, 2 #222a) 3.00
429 A44 40c brt bl 32 15
Set value 20

Nos. 427-429 issued in booklets only. Nos. 427a-428a have 2 labels and selvages the size of 6 stamps. Background design of booklet stamps sharper than 1950 issue. All stamps have 1 or 2 straight edges.

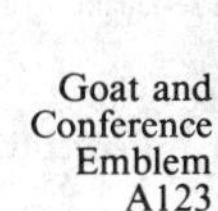

Goat and Conference Emblem A123

Designs: 75c, Horse and map of Curacao. 150c, Cattle, Netherlands Antilles flag, UN and Conference emblems.

1979, Apr. 18 Litho. *Perf. 14x13*
437 A123 50c multi 28 28
438 A123 75c multi 40 40
439 A123 150c multi 75 75
a. Souv. sheet of 3, perf. 13½x13 1.50 1.50

12th Inter-American Meeting at Ministerial Level on Foot and Mouth Disease and Zoonosis Control, Curacao, Apr. 17-20. No. 439a contains Nos. 437-439 in changed colors.

Dutch Colonial Soldier, Emblem — A124

1979, July 4 Litho. *Perf. 13x14*
440 A124 1g multi 55 52

50th anniversary of Netherlands Antilles Volunteer Corps. See Nos. B166-B167.

Casearia Tremula — A125

Flowering Trees: 40c, Cordia cylindrostachya. 1.50g, Melochia tomentosa.

1979, Sept. 3 Litho. *Perf. 13x14*
441 A125 25c multi 18 18
442 A125 40c multi 28 28
443 A125 1.50g multi 75 75

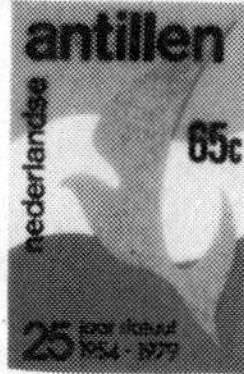

Dove and Netherlands Flag — A126

Design: 1.50g, Dove and Netherlands Antilles flag.

1979, Dec. 6 Litho. *Perf. 13x14*
444 A126 65c multi 48 40
445 A126 1.50g multi 80 80

Constitution, 25th anniversary.

Map of Aruba, Foundation Emblem A127

Design: 1g, Foundation headquarters, Aruba.

1979, Dec. 18 *Perf. 14x13*
446 A127 95c multi 60 60
447 A127 1g multi 70 70

Cultural Foundation Center, Aruba, 30th anniv.

Cupola, 1910, Fort Church — A128

1980, Jan. 9 *Perf. 13x14*
448 A128 100c multi 60 60

Fort Church, Curacao, 210th anniversary (1979). See Nos. B172-B173.

Rotary Emblem A129

Designs: 50c, Globe and cogwheels. 85c, Cogwheel and Rotary emblem.

1980, Feb. 22 Litho. *Perf. 14x13*
449 A129 45c multi 25 25
450 A129 50c multi 30 30
451 A129 85c multi 48 48
a. Souvenir sheet of 3, #449-451, perf. 13½x13 1.10 1.10

, Rotary Intl., 75th anniv. No. 449-451 se-tenant in continuous design.

Coin Box, 1905 — A130

Post Office Savings Bank of Netherlands Antilles, 75th Anniversary: 150c, Coin box, 1980.

1980, Apr. 2 Litho. *Perf. 14x13*
452 A130 25c multi 18 18
453 A130 150c multi 90 90

Netherlands Antilles No. 200, Arms — A131

1980, Apr. 29 Photo.
454 A131 25c shown 15 15
455 A131 60c No. 290, royal crown 32 32
a. Bklt. pane of 5 + 3 labels (#428, 2 #454, 2 #455) 3.00

Abdication of Queen Juliana of the Netherlands.

Sir Rowland Hill (1795-1879), Originator of Penny Postage A132

1980, May 6 Litho.
456 A132 45c shown 28 28
457 A132 60c London 1980 emblem 32 32
458 A132 1g Airmail label 70 70
a. Souv. sheet of 3, perf. 13½x14 1.40 1.40

London 1980 Intl. Stamp Exhibition, May 6-14. No. 458a contains Nos. 456-458 in changed colors.

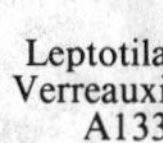

Leptotila Verreauxi A133

1980, Sept. 3 Litho. *Perf. 14x13*
459 A133 45c shown 28 25
460 A133 60c Mockingbird 55 55
461 A133 85c Coereba flaveola 75 75

Rudolf Theodorus Palm — A134 — Alliance Mission Emblem, Map of Aruba — A135

1981, Jan. 27 Litho. *Perf. 13x14*
462 A134 60c shown 40 38
463 A134 1g Score, hand playing piano 75 70

Palm, composer, birth centenary.

1981, Mar. 24 *Perf. 14x13*
464 A135 30c shown 22 22
465 A135 50c Curacao map 40 32
466 A135 1g Bonaire map 75 70

Evangelical Alliance Mission anniversaries: 35th in Aruba, 50th in Curacao, 30th in Bonaire.

St. Elisabeth's Hospital, 125th Anniv.
A136

1981, June 24 Litho. *Perf. 14x13*

467 A136 60c Gateway 40 40
468 A136 1.50g shown 1.00 1.00

Oregano Blossom
A137

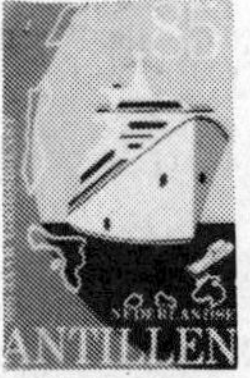

Ship Pilot Service Cent.
A138

1981, Nov. 24 Litho. *Perf. 13x14*

469 A137 45c shown 30 30
470 A137 70c Flaira 52 52
471 A137 100c Welisali 70 70

1982, Jan. 13 Litho. *Perf. 13x14*

Designs: Various ships.

472 A138 70c multi 55 55
473 A138 85c multi 60 60
474 A138 1g multi 70 70

250th Anniv. of Community Mikve Israel-Emanuel Synagogue — A139

1982, Mar. 15 Litho. *Perf. 13x14*

475 A139 75c Altar 60 60
476 A139 85c Building 60 60
477 A139 150c Pulpit 1.00 1.00

US-Netherlands Diplomatic Relations Bicentenary
A140

Intl. Air Traffic Controllers' Year
A141

1982, Apr. 21 Litho. *Perf. 13x14*

478 A140 75c Flags, Peter Stuyvesant 70 70
a. Souvenir sheet 75 75

1982, May 5

479 A141 35c Radar screen 28 28
480 A141 75c Control tower 60 60
481 A141 150c Antenna 1.00 1.00

PHILEXFRANCE '82 Stamp Exhibition, Paris, June 11-21 — A142

1982, June 9 Litho. *Perf. 13x14*

482 A142 45c Emblem 32 32
483 A142 85c Mail bag 60 60
484 A142 150c Flags of France, Neth. Ant. 1.10 1.00
a. Souvenir sheet of 3, #482-484 2.25 2.25

Brown Chromis
A143

1982, Sept. 15 Litho. *Perf. 14x13*

485 A143 35c shown 48 48
486 A143 75c Spotted trunkfish 1.00 1.00
487 A143 85c Blue tang 1.10 1.10
488 A143 100c French angelfish 1.40 1.40

Natural Bridge, Aruba
A144

1983, Apr. 12 Litho. *Perf. 14x13*

489 A144 35c shown 32 32
490 A144 45c Lac-Bay, Bonaire 40 40
491 A144 100c Willemstad, Curacao 90 90

World Communications Year — A145

1983, May 17 Litho. *Perf. 13x14*

492 A145 1g multi 90 90
a. Souvenir sheet 95 95

BRASILIANA '83 — A146

Fruit Tree — A147

1983, June 19 Litho. *Perf. 13x14*

493 A146 45c Ship, postal building, Waaigat 48 48
494 A146 55c Flags, emblem 55 55
495 A146 100c Governor's Palace, Sugar Loaf Mt. 95 95
a. Souvenir sheet of 3, #493-495 2.25 2.25

1983, Sept. 13 Litho. *Perf. 13x14*

496 A147 45c Mangifera indica 70 70
497 A147 55c Malpighia punicifolia 80 80
498 A147 100c Citrus aurantifolia 1.40 1.40

Local Government Buildings
A148

1983, Dec. 20 Litho. *Perf. 14x13*

499 A148 20c Saba 20 20
500 A148 25c St. Eustatius 22 22
501 A148 30c St. Maarten 28 28
502 A148 35c Aruba 30 30
503 A148 45c Bonaire 38 38
a. Perf. 13½ horiz. ('86) 20 20
504 A148 55c Curacao 48 48
a. Perf. 13½ horiz. ('86) 25 25
b. Bklt. pane of 4 + label (2 #503a, 504a) ('86) 1.75
Nos. 499-504 (6) 1.86 1.86

See Nos. 515-520, 543A-555.

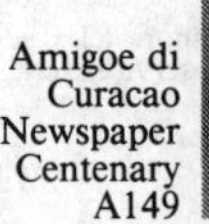

Amigoe di Curacao Newspaper Centenary
A149

1984, Jan. 5 Litho.

505 A149 45c Copy programming 40 40
506 A149 55c Printing press 48 48
507 A149 85c Man reading newspaper 90 90

40th Anniv. of Intl. Civil Aviation Org. — A150

Various emblems.

1984, Feb. 28 Litho. *Perf. 14x13*

508 A150 25c Winair 20 20
509 A150 45c ICAO 40 40
510 A150 55c ALM 50 50
511 A150 100c Plane 90 90

Chamber of Commerce and Industry Centenary — A151

1984, May 29 Litho. *Perf. 13½*

512 A151 45c Bonnet maker 60 60
513 A151 55c Emblem 60 60
514 A151 100c River, bridge, boat 95 95

Nos. 512-514 printed se-tenant.

Govt. Building Type of 1983

1984, June 26 Litho. *Perf. 14x13*

515 A148 60c like 20c 55 55
516 A148 65c like 25c 60 60
517 A148 75c like 30c 75 75
518 A148 85c like 35c 85 85
519 A148 90c like 45c 90 90
520 A148 95c like 55c 1.00 1.00
Nos. 515-520 (6) 4.65 4.65

Local Birds — A152

1984, Sept. 18 Litho. *Perf. 14x13*

521 A152 45c Tiaris bicolor 85 85
522 A152 55c Zonotrichia capensis 1.10 1.10
523 A152 150c Chlorostilbon mellisugus 2.25 2.25

Eleanor Roosevelt (1884-1962) — A153

1984, Oct. 11 Litho. *Perf. 13x14*

524 A153 45c At Hyde Park 48 48
525 A153 85c Portrait 80 80
526 A153 100c Reading to children 90 90

Flamingos
A154

Curacao Masonic Lodge Bicent.
A155

1985, Jan. 9 Litho. *Perf. 14x13*

527 A154 25c Adult pullets 55 55
528 A154 45c Juveniles 90 90
529 A154 55c Adults wading 1.10 1.10
530 A154 100c Adults flying 1.65 1.65

1985, Feb. 21 Litho. *Perf. 13x14*

531 A155 45c Compass, sun, moon and stars 50 50
532 A155 55c Doorway, columns and 5 steps 70 70
533 A155 100c Star, 7 steps 1.10 1.10

UN, 40th Anniv. — A156

1985, June 5 Litho. *Perf. 14x13*

534 A156 55c multi 60 60
535 A156 1g multi 1.00 1.00

Papiamentu, Language of the Antilles
A157

Designs: 45c, Pierre Lauffer (1920-1981), author and poem Patria. 55c, Waves of Papiamentu.

1985, Sept. 4 Litho. *Perf. 14x13*

536 A157 45c multi 45 45
537 A157 55c multi 60 60

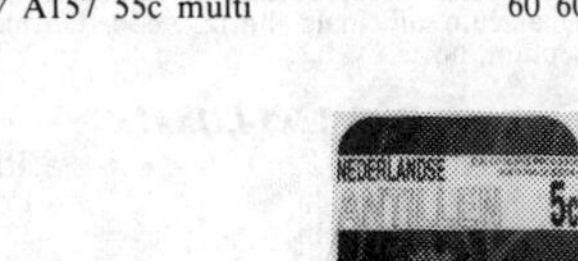

Flora — A158

1985, Nov. 6 *Perf. 13x14*

538 A158 5c Calotropis procera 15 15
539 A158 10c Capparis flexuosa 22 22
540 A158 20c Mimosa distachya 28 28
541 A158 45c Ipomoea nil 60 60
542 A158 55c Heliotropium ternatum 70 70
543 A158 1.50g Ipomoea incarnata 2.00 2.00
Set value 1.35 1.35

Govt. Building Type of 1983

1985-89 *Perf. 14x13*

543A A148 70c like 20c ('88) 52 52
543B A148 85c like 45c ('88) 60 60
544 A148 1g like 20c 85 85
545 A148 1.50g like 25c 1.10 1.10
546 A148 2.50g like 30c ('86) 2.00 2.00
551 A148 5g like 45c ('86) 3.50 3.50

554	A148	10g like 55c ('87)	7.25	7.25
555	A148	15g like 20c ('89)	14.50	14.50
		Nos. 543A-555 (8)	30.32	30.32

Issue dates: 70c, 85c, Mar. 16. 1g, 1.50g, Dec. 4. 2.50g, Jan. 8. 5g, Dec. 3. 10g, May 20. 15g, Feb. 8.

This is an expanding set. Numbers will change if necessary.

Curacao Town Hall, 125th Anniv. — A159

1986, Jan. 8 ***Perf. 14x13, 13x14***

561	A159 5c Town Hall		15	15
562	A159 15c State room, vert.		18	18
563	A159 25c Court room		25	25
564	A159 55c Entrance, vert.		52	52
	Set value		50	50

Amnesty Intl., 25th Anniv. A160

1986, May 28 **Litho.** ***Perf. 14x13***

565 A160	45c Prisoner chained	40	40
566 A160	55c Peace bird imprisoned	50	50
567 A160	100c Prisoner behind bars	90	90

Mailboxes A161

Perf. 14x13, 13x14

1986, Sept. 3 **Litho.**

568 A161	10c PO mailbox	15	15
569 A161	25c Steel mailbox	22	22
570 A161	45c Mailbox on brick wall	35	35
571 A161	55c Pillar box	42	42

Nos. 569-571 vert.

Friars of Tilburg in the Antilles, Cent. — A162

Designs: 10c, Brother Mauritius Vliegendehond, residence, 1886. 45c, Monsignor Ferdinand Kieckens, St. Thomas College, Roodeweg. 55c, Father F.S. de Beer, 1st general-superior, and college courtyard.

1986, Nov. 13 **Litho.** ***Perf. 13x14***

572 A162	10c multi	15	15
573 A162	45c multi	35	35
574 A162	55c multi	42	42

Princess Juliana & Prince Bernhard, 50th Wedding Anniv. A163

Maduro Holding, Inc., Sesquicent. A164

1987, Jan. 7 **Litho.** ***Perf. 13x14***

575 A163	1.35g multi	1.10	1.10
a.	Souvenir sheet	1.25	1.25

1987, Jan. 26

576 A164	70c Expansion map	48	48
577 A164	85c Corporate divisions	60	60
578 A164	1.55g S.E.L. Maduro, founder	1.10	1.10

Curacao Rotary Club, 50th Anniv. A165

1987, Apr. 2 **Litho.** ***Perf. 14x13***

579 A165	15c Map of the Antilles	20	20
580 A165	50c Rotary headquarters	42	42
581 A165	65c Map of Curacao	52	52

Bolivar-Curacao Friendship, 175th Anniv. — A166

Designs: 60c, Octagon, residence of Simon Bolivar in Curacao. 70c, Bolivarian Society Headquarters, 1949, Willemstad. 80c, Octagon interior (bedroom). 90c, Manual Carlos Piar, Simon Bolivar (1783-1830) and Pedro Luis Brion.

1987, July 24 **Litho.** ***Perf. 14x13***

582 A166	60c multi	42	42
583 A166	70c multi	52	52
584 A166	80c multi	55	55
585 A166	90c multi	65	65

Bolivarian Society, 50th anniv. (70c, 90c).

Antilles Natl. Parks Foundation, 25th Anniv. A167

1987, Dec. 1 **Litho.** ***Perf. 14x13***

586 A167	70c Phaethon lepturus	65	65
587 A167	85c Odocoileus virginianus curassavicus	80	80
588 A167	1.55g Iguana iguana	1.50	1.50

The Curacao Courant, 175th Anniv. A168

Designs: 55c, 19th Cent. printing press, lead type. 70c, Keyboard, modern press.

1987, Dec. 11

589 A168	55c multi	48	48
590 A168	70c multi	60	60

Mijnmaatschappij Phosphate Mining Co., Curacao, 75th Anniv. — A169

1988, Jan. 21

591 A169	40c William Godden, founder	30	30
592 A169	105c Processing plant	80	80
593 A169	155c Tafelberg	1.25	1.25

States of the Netherlands Antilles, 50th Anniv. A170

Designs: 65c, John Horris Sprockel, 1st president, and natl. colors, crest. 70c, Development of state elections, women's suffrage. 155c, Natl. colors, crest, constellation representing the 5 islands and separation of Aruba.

1988, Apr. 5 **Litho.**

594 A170	65c multi	50	50
595 A170	70c multi	52	52
596 A170	155c multi	1.10	1.10

Abolition of Slavery, 125th Anniv. A171

1988, July 1 **Litho.** ***Perf. 14x13***

597 A171	155c shown	1.25	1.25
598 A171	190c Slave Wall, Curacao	1.40	1.40

3rd Conference for Great Cities of the Americas, Curacao, Aug. 24-27 — A172

1988, Aug. 24 **Litho.**

599 A172	80c shown	60	60
600 A172	155c Bridge, globe	1.25	1.25

Interamerican Foundation of Cities conference on building bridges between peoples.

Charles Ernst Barend Hellmund (1896-1952) A173

Cacti A174

Men and women who initiated community development: 65c, Atthelo Maud Edwards Jackson (1901-1970). 90c, Nicolaas Debrot (1902-1981). 120c, William Charles De La Try Ellis (1881-1977).

1988, Sept. 20 ***Perf. 13x14***

601 A173	55c multi	42	42
602 A173	65c multi	50	50
603 A173	90c multi	65	65
604 A173	120c multi	85	85

1988, Dec. 13 **Litho.** ***Perf. 13x14***

605 A174	55c Cereus hexagonus	58	58
606 A174	115c Melocactus	1.20	1.20
607 A174	125c Opuntia wentiana	1.30	1.30

Wildlife Protection and Curacao Foundation for the Prevention of Cruelty to Animals A175

1989, Mar. 9 **Litho.** ***Perf. 14x13***

608 A175	65c Crested quail	65	65
609 A175	115c Dogs, cats	1.15	1.15

Cruise Ships at St. Maarten and Curacao A176

1989, May 8 **Litho.**

610 A176	70c Great Bay Harbor	55	55
611 A176	155c St. Annabay	1.25	1.25

Tourism.

Social and Political Figures — A177

Designs: 40c, Paula Clementina Dorner (1901-1969), teacher. 55c, John Aniceto de Jongh (1885-1951), pharmacist, Parliament member. 90c, Jacobo Palm (1887-1982), composer. 120c, Abraham Mendes Chumaceiro (1841-1902), political reformer.

1989, Sept. 20 **Litho.** ***Perf. 13x14***

612 A177	40c multi	35	35
613 A177	55c multi	45	45
614 A177	90c multi	80	80
615 A177	120c multi	1.10	1.10

Queen Wilhelmina Fund, 40th Anniv. — A178

1989, Nov. 7 **Litho.**

616 A178	30c 7 Symptoms of cancer	30	30
617 A178	60c Radiation treatment	58	58
618 A178	80c Fund emblem, healthy person	75	75

Nos. 616-618 printed se-tenant with inscribed labels.

Souvenir Sheet

World Stamp Expo '89 and 20th UPU Congress, Washington, DC — A179

Designs: 70c, Monument, St. Eustatius, where the sovereignty of the US was 1st recognized by a foreign officer, Nov. 16, 1776.

155c, Peter Stuyvesant, flags representing bicent. of US-Antilles diplomatic relations, vert. 250c, 9-Gun salute of the *Andrea Doria.*

1989, Nov. 17 Litho. *Perf. 13*

619 Sheet of 3 3.75 3.75
- ***a.*** A179 70c multicolored 55 55
- ***b.*** A179 155c multicolored 1.25 1.25
- ***c.*** A179 250c multicolored 1.75 1.75

Christmas 1989 and New Year 1990 — A180

1989, Dec. 1 *Perf. 13x14*

620 A180 30c Fireworks 22 22
621 A180 100c Ornaments on tree 75 75

Nos. 620-621 printed se-tenant with labels inscribed "Merry X-mas and Happy New Year" in four languages.

Flowering Plants — A181

1990, Jan. 31 Litho. *Perf. 13x14*

622 A181 30c *Tephrosia cinerea* 22 22
623 A181 55c *Erithalis fruticosa* 40 40
624 A181 65c *Evolvulus antillanus* 50 50
625 A181 70c *Jacquinia arborea* 55 55
626 A181 125c *Tournefortia gnaphalodes* 1.00 1.00
627 A181 155c *Sesuvium portulacastrum* 1.10 1.10
Nos. 622-627 (6) 3.77 3.77

Dominican Nuns in the Netherlands Antilles, Cent. — A182

Designs: 10c, Nurse, flag, map. 55c, St. Rose Hospital and St. Martin's Home. 60c, St. Joseph School.

1990, May 7 Litho. *Perf. 14x13*

628 A182 10c multicolored 16 16
629 A182 55c multicolored 62 62
630 A182 60c multicolored 70 70

Carlos Alberto Nicolaas-Perez (1915-1989) — A183

Poets: 60c, Evert Stephanus Jordanus Kruythoff (1893-1967). 80c, John De Pool (1873-1947). 150c, Joseph Sickman Corsen (1853-1911).

1990, Aug. 8 Litho. *Perf. 13x14*

631 A183 40c multicolored 46 46
632 A183 60c multicolored 70 70
633 A183 80c multicolored 95 95
634 A183 150c multicolored 1.75 1.75

Queens of the House of Orange — A184

1990, Sept. 5 *Perf. 13x14*

635 A184 100c Emma 1.15 1.15
636 A184 100c Wilhelmina 1.15 1.15
637 A184 100c Juliana 1.15 1.15
638 A184 100c Beatrix 1.15 1.15

Souvenir Sheet

Perf. 14x13

639 A184 250c Four Queens, horiz. 2.85 2.85

Oil Refining in Curacao, 75th Anniv. A185

1990, Oct. 1 Litho. *Perf. 14x13*

640 A185 100c multicolored 1.15 1.15

Christmas — A186

1990, Dec. 5 Litho. *Perf. 13x14*

641 A186 30c Gifts 35 35
642 A186 100c shown 1.15 1.15

Nos. 641-642 printed with setenant label showing holiday greetings. 25th anniv. of Bon Bisina Project (No. 641).

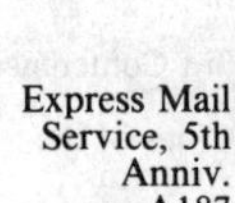

Express Mail Service, 5th Anniv. A187

1991, Jan. 16 Litho. *Perf. 14x13*

643 A187 20g multicolored 24.00 24.00

Fish — A188

Designs: 10c, Scuba diver, French grunt. 40c, Spotted trunkfish. 55c, Coppersweeper. 75c, Skindiver, yellow goatfish. 100c, Blackbar soldierfish.

1991, Mar. 13 *Perf. 13x14*

644 A188 10c multicolored 15 15
645 A188 40c multicolored 50 50
646 A188 55c multicolored 65 65
647 A188 75c multicolored 90 90
648 A188 100c multicolored 1.20 1.20
Nos. 644-648 (5) 3.40 3.40

Greetings A189

1991, May 8 *Perf. 14x13*

649 A189 30c Good luck 35 35
650 A189 30c Thank you 35 35
651 A189 30c Love you 35 35
652 A189 30c Happy day 35 35
653 A189 30c Get well soon 35 35
654 A189 30c Happy birthday 35 35
Nos. 649-654 (6) 2.10 2.10

Lighthouses — A190

1991, June 19 Litho. *Perf. 13x14*

655 A190 30c Westpoint, Curacao 35 35
656 A190 70c Willem's Tower, Bonaire 85 85
657 A190 115c Little Curacao, Curacao 1.40 1.40

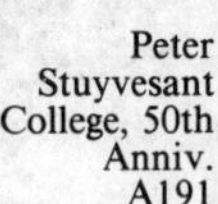

Peter Stuyvesant College, 50th Anniv. A191

Espamer '91 — A192

1991, July 5 *Perf. 14x13, 13x14*

658 A191 65c multicolored 78 78
659 A192 125c multicolored 1.50 1.50

Christmas — A193

1991, Dec. 2 Litho. *Perf. 13½x14*

660 A193 30c shown 35 35
661 A193 100c Angel, shepherds 1.10 1.10

Nos. 660-661 printed with se-tenant labels.

Maduro and Curiel's Bank NV, 75th Anniv. — A194

Litho. & Typo.

1991, Dec. 16 *Perf. 13x14*

662 A194 30c J. A. Correa 35 35
663 A194 70c "75," coat of arms 85 85
664 A194 155c I. H. Capriles 1.85 1.85
- ***a.*** Strip of 3, #662-664 3.05 3.05

Odocoileus Virginianus A195

1992, Jan. 29 Litho. *Perf. 14x13*

666 A195 5c Fawn 15 15
667 A195 10c Two does 15 15
668 A195 30c Buck 35 35
669 A195 40c Buck & doe in water 45 45
670 A195 200c Buck drinking 2.20 2.20
671 A195 355c Buck, diff. 4.00 4.00
Nos. 666-671 (6) 7.30 7.30

World Wildlife Fund. Nos. 670-671 are airmail and do not have the WWF emblem.

SEMI-POSTAL STAMPS

Catalogue values for unused stamps in this section are for Never Hinged items.

NIWIN

Nos. 132, 133 and 135 Surcharged in Black

1½ ct.
+ 2½ ct.

1947, Dec. 1 Unwmk. *Perf. 12½*

B1 A26 1½c + 2½c on 6c 85 75
B2 A26 2½c + 5c on 10c 85 75
B3 A26 5c + 7½c on 15c 85 75

The surtax was for the National Inspanning Welzijnszorg in Nederlandsch Indie, relief organization for Netherlands Indies.

Curaçao Children SP1 SP2

Design: Nos. B6, B9, Girl.

1948, Nov. 3 Photo. *Perf. 12½x12*

B4 SP1 6c + 10c ol brn 2.25 1.75
B5 SP2 10c + 15c brt red 2.25 1.75
B6 SP2 12½c + 20c Prus grn 2.25 1.75
B7 SP1 15c + 25c brt bl 2.25 1.75
B8 SP2 20c + 30c red brn 2.25 1.75
B9 SP2 25c + 35c pur 2.25 1.75
Nos. B4-B9 (6) 13.50 10.50

The surtax was for crippled children.

Leapfrog — SP4

Ship and Gull — SP5

Designs: 5c+2½c, Flying kite. 6c+2½c, Girls swinging, 12½c+5c, "London Bridge." 25c+10c, Rolling hoops.

1951, Aug. 16 Unwmk. *Perf. 14x13*

B10 SP4 1½c + 1c pur 1.65 2.00
B11 SP4 5c + 2½c brn 8.50 4.00
B12 SP4 6c + 2½c blue 8.50 4.00
B13 SP4 12½c + 5c red 8.50 4.00
B14 SP4 25c + 10c dl grn 8.50 3.50
Nos. B10-B14 (5) 35.65 17.50

The surtax was for child welfare.

1952, July 16 *Perf. 13x14*

Designs: 6c+4c, Sailor and lighthouse. 12½c+7c, Prow of sailboat. 15c+10c, Ships. 25c+15c, Ship, compass and anchor.

B15	SP5	1½c + 1c dk grn	90	1.00
B16	SP5	6c + 4c choc	6.25	3.00
B17	SP5	12½c + 7c red vio	6.25	3.25
B18	SP5	15c + 10c dp bl	8.00	4.00
B19	SP5	25c + 15c red	8.00	3.00
		Nos. B15-B19 (5)	29.40	14.25

The surtax was for the seamen's welfare fund.

No. 226 Surcharged in Black

22½ Ct. +7½ Ct.
WATERSNOOD NEDERLAND 1953

1953, Feb. 21

B20	A45	22½c + 7½c on 1½g	90	1.00

The surtax was for flood relief in the Netherlands.

Tribulus Cistoides SP6

Flowers: 7½c+5c, Yellow hibiscus. 15c+5c, Oleander. 22½c+7½c, Cactus. 25c+10c, Red hibiscus.

1955, May 17 Photo. *Perf. 14x13*

Flowers in Natural Colors

B21	SP6	1½c + 1c bl grn & dk bl	30	35
B22	SP6	7½c + 5c dp ultra	2.50	1.75
B23	SP6	15c + 5c ol grn	2.50	1.90
B24	SP6	22½c + 7½c dk bl	2.50	1.75
B25	SP6	25c + 10c ind & gray	2.50	1.90
		Nos. B21-B25 (5)	10.30	7.65

The surtax was for child welfare.

Prince Bernhard and Queen Juliana SP7

1955 *Perf. 11x11½*

B26	SP7	7½c + 2½c rose brn	15	15
B27	SP7	22½c + 7½c dp bl	80	80

Royal visit to the Netherlands Antilles, Oct. 1955.
Surtax paid for a gift.

Lord Baden-Powell SP8

1957, Feb. 22 *Perf. 14x13*

B28	SP8	6c + 1½c org yel	40	40
B29	SP8	7½c + 2½c dp grn	40	40
B30	SP8	15c + 5c red	40	40

Issued to commemorate the 50th anniversary of the Boy Scout movement.

Soccer Player — SP9

Map of Central America and the Caribbean SP10

Designs: 15c+5c, Goalkeeper catching ball. 22½c+7½c, Men playing soccer.

Perf. 11½x11, 11x11½

1957, Aug. 16

B31	SP9	6c + 2½c org	40	55
B32	SP10	7½c + 5c dk red	80	90
B33	SP9	15c + 5c brt bl grn	90	90
B34	SP9	22½c + 7½c brt bl	90	70

8th Central American and Caribbean Soccer Championships, Aug. 11-25.
Surtax was for organizing costs.

American Kestrel — SP11 Flag and Map — SP12

Birds: 7½+1½c, Yellow oriole. 15+2½c, Common ground doves. 22½+2½c, Brown-throated parakeet.

1958, Apr. 15 Photo. *Perf. 13x14*

B35	SP11	2½c + 1c multi	22	22
B36	SP11	7½c + 1½c multi	70	60
B37	SP11	15c + 2½c multi	80	80
B38	SP11	22½c + 2½c multi	90	70

The surtax was for child welfare.

1958, Dec. 1 Litho. *Perf. 13½*

Cross in Red

B39	SP12	6c + 2c red brn	28	28
B40	SP12	7½c + 2½c bl grn	40	40
B41	SP12	15c + 5c org yel	40	40
B42	SP12	22½c + 7½c blue	40	40

The surtax was for the Red Cross.

Community House, Zeeland SP13

Designs (historic buildings): 7½c+2½c, Molenplein. 15c+5c, Saba (vert.). 22½c+7½c, Scharlooburg. 25c+7½c, Community House, Brievengat.

Perf. 13½x13, 13x13½

1959, Sept. 16 **Litho.**

B43	SP13	6c + 1½c multi	80	70
B44	SP13	7½c + 2½c multi	80	80
B45	SP13	15c + 5c multi	80	80
B46	SP13	22½c + 7½c multi	80	80
B47	SP13	25c + 7½c multi	80	80
		Nos. B43-B47 (5)	4.00	3.90

The surtax went to the Foundation for the Preservation of Historical Monuments.

Fish — SP14

Designs. 10c+2c, SCUBA diver with spear gun, vert. 25c+5c, Two fish.

1960, Aug. 24 **Photo.**

B48	SP14	10c + 2c saph	80	80
B49	SP14	20c + 3c multi	1.10	1.10
B50	SP14	25c + 5c blk, brt pink & dk bl	1.10	1.10

The surtax was for the fight against cancer.

Infant — SP15

Designs: 10c+3c, Girl and doll. 20c+6c, Boy on beach. 25c+8c, Children in school.

1961, July 24 Litho. *Perf. 13x14*

Designs in Black

B51	SP15	6c + 2c lt yel grn	20	20
B52	SP15	10c + 3c rose red	20	20
B53	SP15	20c + 6c yel	20	20
B54	SP15	25c + 8c org	20	20

The surtax was for child welfare.

Globe and Knight — SP16

1962, May 2 *Perf. 13x14*

B55	SP16	10c + 5c grn	60	55
B56	SP16	20c + 10c car	60	55
B57	SP16	25c + 10c dk bl	60	55

Intl. Candidates Chess Tournament, Willemstad, May-June.

No. 248 Surcharged

TEGEN DE HONGER
+10c

1963, Mar. 21

B58	A56	20c + 10c crim & gray	40	40

FAO "Freedom from Hunger" campaign.

Child and Flowers SP17

Bougainvillea SP18

Designs: 6c+3c, Three girls and flowers, horiz. 10c+5c, Girl with ball and trees, horiz. 20c+10c, Three boys with flags, horiz. 25c+12c, Singing boy.

Perf. 14x13, 13x14

1963, Oct. 23 Photo. Unwmk.

B59	SP17	5c + 2c multi	22	22
B60	SP17	6c + 3c multi	22	22
B61	SP17	10c + 5c multi	22	22
B62	SP17	20c + 10c multi	22	22
B63	SP17	25c + 12c multi	22	22
		Nos. B59-B63 (5)	1.10	1.10

The surtax was for the Antillean Youth Federation.

1964, Oct. 21 *Perf. 14x13*

Designs: 10c+5c, Wild rose. 20c+10c, Chalice flower. 25c+11c, Bellisima.

Flowers in Natural Colors

B64	SP18	6c + 3c bl vio & blk	15	15
B65	SP18	10c + 5c yel brn, yel & blk	15	15
B66	SP18	20c + 10c dl red & blk	15	15
B67	SP18	25c + 11c cit & brn	15	15

The surtax was for child welfare.

Sea Anemones and Star Coral — SP19

Corals: 6c+3c, Blue cup sponges. 10c+5c, Green cup sponges. 25c+11c, Basket sponge, knobbed brain coral and reef fish.

1965, Nov. 10 Photo. *Perf. 14x13*

B68	SP19	6c + 3c multi	15	15
B69	SP19	10c + 5c multi	15	15
B70	SP19	20c + 10c multi	15	15
B71	SP19	25c + 11c multi	20	20
		Set value	55	55

The surtax was for child welfare.

ICEM Type of Netherlands

1966, Jan. 31 Photo. *Perf. 14x13*

B72	SP181	35c + 15c brn & dl yel	20	20

The surtax was for the Intergovernmental Committee for European Migration (ICEM). The message on the stamps was given and signed by Queen Juliana.

Girl Cooking SP20

Helping Hands Supporting Women SP21

Youth at Work: 10c+5c, Nurse's aide with infant. 20c+10c, Young metalworker. 25c+11c, Girl ironing.

1966, Nov. 15 *Perf. 13½*

B73	SP20	6c + 3c multi	15	15
B74	SP20	10c + 5c multi	15	15
B75	SP20	20c + 10c multi	15	15
B76	SP20	25c + 11c multi	20	20
		Set value	46	46

The surtax was for child welfare.

1967, July 4 Litho. *Perf. 13x14*

B77	SP21	6c + 3c bl & blk	15	15
B78	SP21	10c + 5c brt pink & blk	15	15
B79	SP21	20c + 19c lil	15	15
B80	SP21	25c + 11c dk bl	15	15
		Set value	44	44

The surtax was for various social and cultural institutions.

Nanzi the Spider and the Tiger — SP22

Nanzi Stories (Folklore): 6c+3c, Princess Longnose, vert. 10c+5c, The Turtle and the Monkey. 25c+11c, Adventure of Shon Arey.

Perf. 14x13, 13x14

1967, Nov. 15 **Photo.**

B81	SP22 6c + 3c dk red, pink & org	15	15
B82	SP22 10c + 5c vio bl & org	15	15
B83	SP22 20c + 10c grn & org	18	18
B84	SP22 25c + 11c brt bl & org	18	18

The surtax was for child welfare.

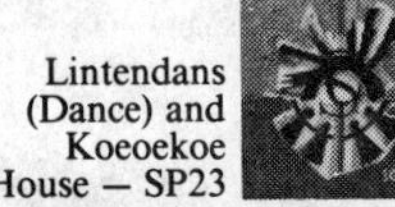

Lintendans (Dance) and Koeoekoe House — SP23

1968, May 29 **Litho.** ***Perf. 14x13***

B85	SP23 10c + 5c multi	15	15
B86	SP23 15c + 5c multi	15	15
B87	SP23 20c + 10c multi	15	15
B88	SP23 25c + 10c multi	15	15

The surtax was for various social and cultural institutions.

Boy and Pet Cat — SP24

Designs: 6c+3c, Boy and goat. 10c+5c, Girl and poodle. 25c+11c, Girl and duckling.

1968, Nov. 13 **Photo.** ***Perf. 13½***

B89	SP24 6c + 3c multi	15	15
B90	SP24 10c + 5c multi	15	15
B91	SP24 20c + 10c multi	18	18
B92	SP24 25c + 11c multi	18	18

The surtax was for child welfare.

Carnival Headpiece — SP25

Designs (Folklore): 15c+5c, Harvest-home festival. 20c+10c, Feast of St. John (dancers and cock). 25c+10c, "Dande" New Year's celebration.

1969, July 23 **Litho.** ***Perf. 13½***

B93	SP25 10c + 5c multi	22	22
B94	SP25 15c + 5c multi	22	22
B95	SP25 20c + 10c multi	32	32
B96	SP25 25c + 10c multi	32	32

The surtax was for various social and cultural institutions.

Boy Playing Guitar — SP26

Designs: 10c+5c, Girl with English flute. 20c+10c, Boy playing the marimula. 25c+11c, Girl playing the piano.

1969, Nov. 3 **Litho.** ***Perf. 14x13***

B97	SP26 6c + 3c org & vio	20	20
B98	SP26 10c + 5c yel & brt grn	28	28
B99	SP26 20c + 10c bl & car	28	28
B100	SP26 25c + 11c pink & brn	32	32

The surtax was for child welfare.

Printing Press and Quill — SP27

Mother and Child — SP28

Mass Media: 15c+5c, Filmstrip and reels. 20c+10c, Horn and radio mast. 25c+10c, Television antenna and eye focused on globe.

1970, July 14 **Litho.** ***Perf. 13½***

B101	SP27 10c + 5c multi	32	32
B102	SP27 15c + 5c multi	32	32
B103	SP27 20c + 10c multi	32	32
B104	SP27 25c + 10c multi	32	32

The surtax was for various social and cultural institutions.

1970, Nov. 16 **Litho.** ***Perf. 13x14***

Designs: 10c+5c, Girl holding piggy bank. 20c+10c, Boys wrestling (Judokas). 25c+11c, Youth carrying small boy on his shoulders.

B105	SP28 6c + 3c multi	50	50
B106	SP28 10c + 5c multi	50	50
B107	SP28 20c + 10c multi	50	50
B108	SP28 25c + 11c multi	50	50

The surtax was for child welfare.

Charcoal Burner — SP29

Kitchen Utensils: 15c+5c, Earthenware vessel for water. 20c+10c, Baking oven. 25c+10c, Soup plate, stirrer and kneading stick.

1971, May 12 **Litho.** ***Perf. 13½***

B109	SP29 10c + 5c multi	40	40
B110	SP29 15c + 5c multi	40	40
B111	SP29 20c + 10c multi	40	40
B112	SP29 25c + 10c multi	40	40

Surtax was for various social and cultural institutions.

Homemade Dolls and Comb — SP30

Homemade Toys: 20c+10c, Cars. 30c+15c, Musical top made from calabash.

1971, Nov. 16 **Litho.** ***Perf. 13x14***

B113	SP30 15c + 5c multi	48	48
B114	SP30 20c + 10c multi	48	48
B115	SP30 30c + 15c multi	48	48

Surtax was for child welfare.

Steel Band SP31

Designs: 20c+10c, Harvest festival (Seu). 30c+15c, Tambu dancers.

1972, May 16 **Litho.** ***Perf. 13½***

B116	SP31 15c + 5c multi	60	60
B117	SP31 20c + 10c multi	60	60
B118	SP31 30c + 15c multi	60	60

Surtax was for various social and cultural institutions.

Child at Play on Ground SP32

Designs: 20c+10c, Child playing in water. 30c+15c, Child throwing ball into air.

1972, Nov. 14 **Litho.** ***Perf. 14x13***

B119	SP32 15c + 5c multi	70	70
B120	SP32 20c + 10c multi	70	70
B121	SP32 30c + 15c multi	70	70

Surtax was for child welfare.

Pedestrian Crossing, Traffic Sign — SP33

Designs: 15c+7c, School crossing. 40c+20c, Traffic light, road and car.

1973, Apr. 9 **Litho.** ***Perf. 13x14***

B122	SP33 12c + 6c multi	60	60
B123	SP33 15c + 7c multi	60	60
B124	SP33 40c + 20c multi	60	60

Surtax was for various social and cultural institutions.

"1948-73" SP34

Designs: 20c+10c, Children. 30c+15c, Mother and child.

1973, Nov. 19 **Litho.** ***Perf. 14x13***

B125	SP34 15c + 5c multi	70	70
B126	SP34 20c + 10c multi	70	70
a.	Min. sheet, 2 each #B125-B126	2.00	2.50
B127	SP34 30c + 15c multi	1.10	1.10

25th anniversary of first Child Welfare semi-postal stamps.

Girl Combing her Hair — SP35

Designs: 15c+7c, Young people listening to rock music. 40c+20c, Drummer, symbolizing rock music.

1974, Apr. 9 **Litho.** ***Perf. 14x13***

B128	SP35 12c + 6c multi	80	80
B129	SP35 15c + 7c multi	80	80
B130	SP35 40c + 20c multi	80	80

Surtax was for various social and cultural institutions.

Child, Saw and Score — SP36

Designs: 20c+10c, Footprints in circle. 30c+15c, Moon and sun. Each design includes score of a children's song.

1974, Nov. 12 **Litho.** ***Perf. 13x14***

B131	SP36 15c + 5c multi	60	60
B132	SP36 20c + 10c multi	60	60
B133	SP36 30c + 15c multi	60	60

Surtax was for child welfare.

Carved Stone Grid, Flower Pot SP37

Jewish Tombstone, Mordecai's Procession SP38

Design: 40c+20c, Ornamental stone from facade of Jewish House, 1728.

1975, Mar. 21 **Litho.** ***Perf. 13x14***

B134	SP37 12c + 6c multi	60	60
B135	SP38 15c + 7c multi	60	60
B136	SP37 40c + 20c multi	60	60

Surtax was for various social and cultural institutions.

Children Building Curacao Windmill SP39

Designs: 20c+10c, Girl molding clay animal. 30c+15c, Children drawing picture.

1975, Nov. 12 **Litho.** ***Perf. 14x13***

B137	SP39 15c + 5c multi	55	55
B138	SP39 20c + 10c multi	55	55
B139	SP39 30c + 15c multi	55	55

Surtax was for child welfare.

Carrying a Child — SP40

Designs: Different ways of carrying a child. 40c+18c is vertical.

Perf. 14x13, 13x14

1976, Oct. 4 **Litho.**

B140	SP40 20c + 10c multi	45	45
B141	SP40 25c + 12c multi	45	45
B142	SP40 40c + 18c multi	45	45

Surtax was for child welfare.

The Catalogue editors cannot undertake to appraise, identify or judge the genuineness or condition of stamps.

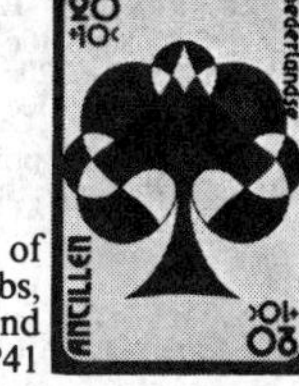

Composite: Aces of Hearts, Clubs, Diamonds and Spades — SP41

Designs: 25c+12c, "King" and inscription. 40c+18c, Hand holding cards; map of Aruba as ace of hearts, horiz.

Perf. 13x14, 14x13

1977, May 6 **Litho.**

B143 SP41 20c + 10c red & blk 32 28
B144 SP41 25c + 12c multi 32 32
a. Min. sheet, 2 each #B143-B144 1.40 1.10
B145 SP41 40c + 18c multi 48 48

Central American and Caribbean Bridge Championships, Aruba.

Souvenir Sheet

1977, May 26 ***Perf. 13x14***

B146 SP41 Sheet of 3 2.75 2.50

Amphilex 77 International Philatelic Exhibition, Amsterdam, May 26-June 5. No. B146 contains 3 stamps similar to Nos. B143-B145 with bright green background.

Children and Toys — SP42

Designs: Children playing with fantasy animals.

1977, Oct. 25 **Litho.** ***Perf. 14x13***

B147 SP42 15c + 5c multi 28 22
B148 SP42 20c + 10c multi 32 32
B149 SP42 25c + 12c multi 38 38
B150 SP42 40c + 18c multi 48 42
a. Min. sheet, 2 each #B148, B150 1.75 1.65

Surtax was for child welfare.

Water Skiing SP43

Roller Skating SP45

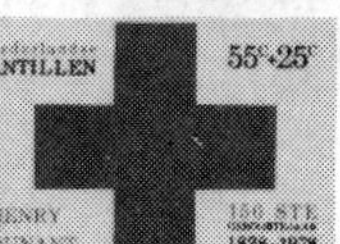

Red Cross — SP44

Designs: 20c+10c, Sailing. 25c+12c, Soccer. 40c+18c, Baseball.

1978, Mar. 31 **Litho.** ***Perf. 13x14***

B151 SP43 15c + 5c multi 15 15
B152 SP43 20c + 10c multi 15 15
B153 SP43 25c + 12c multi 15 15
B154 SP43 40c + 18c multi 22 22
Set value 56 56

Surtax was for sports.

1978, Sept. 19 **Litho.** ***Perf. 14x13***

B155 SP44 55c + 25c red & blk 22 22
a. Souv. sheet of 3, perf. 13½x13 1.65 1.65

Henri Dunant (1828-1910), founder of Red Cross. Surtax for the Red Cross.

1978, Nov. 7 **Litho.** ***Perf. 13x14***

Children's Activities: 20c+10c, Kite flying. 25c+12c, Playing marbles. 40c+18c, Bicycling.

B156 SP45 15c + 5c multi 32 28
B157 SP45 20c + 10c multi 40 32
a. Min. sheet, 2 each #B156-B157 1.75 1.50
B158 SP45 25c + 12c multi 40 38
B159 SP45 40c + 18c multi 48 45

Surtax was for child welfare.

Carnival King SP46

Regatta Emblem SP47

25th Aruba Carnival: 75c+20c, Carnival Queen and coat of arms.

1979, Feb. 20 **Litho.** ***Perf. 13x14***

B160 SP46 40c + 10c multi 38 30
B161 SP46 75c + 20c multi 55 52

Perf. 13x14, 14x13

1979, May 16 **Litho.**

Designs: 35c+10c, Race. 40c+15c, Globe and yacht, horiz. 55c+25c, Yacht, birds and sun.

B162 SP47 15c + 5c multi 15 15
B163 SP47 35c + 10c multi 25 25
B164 SP47 40c + 15c multi 32 32
B165 SP47 55c + 25c multi 40 40
a. Souv. sheet of 4, #B162-B165 1.10 1.10

12th International Sailing Regatta, Bonaire.

Volunteer Corps Type, 1979

Designs: 15c+10c, Soldiers, 1929 and 1979. 40c+20c, Soldier guarding oil refinery, Guard emblem.

1979, July 4 **Litho.** ***Perf. 13x14***

B166 A124 15c + 10c multi 18 16
B167 A124 40c + 20c multi 38 35

Girls Reading Book, IYC Emblem SP48

Volleyball, Olympic Rings SP49

IYC Emblem and Children's Drawings: 25c+12c, Infant and cat. 35c+15c, Girls walking under palm trees. 50c+20c, Children wearing adult clothing.

1979, Oct. 24 **Litho.** ***Perf. 13x14***

B168 SP48 20c + 10c multi 20 20
B169 SP48 25c + 12c multi 30 28
B170 SP48 35c + 15c multi 38 32
a. Souv. sheet, 2 #B168, 2 #B170 1.25 1.20
B171 SP48 50c + 20c multi 48 48

International Year of the Child.

Fort Church Type of 1980

Designs: 20c+10c, Brass chandelier, 1909, horiz. 50c+25c, Pipe organ.

Perf. 14x13, 13x14

1980, Jan. 9 **Litho.**

B172 A128 20c + 10c multi 18 18
B173 A128 50c + 15c multi 45 45

1980, June 25 **Litho.** ***Perf. 13x14***

Designs: 25c+10c, Woman gymnast. 30c+15c, Male gymnast. 60c+25c, Basketball.

B174 SP49 25c + 10c multi 18 18
B175 SP49 30c + 15c multi 30 30
B176 SP49 45c + 20c multi 38 35
B177 SP49 60c + 25c multi 50 45
a. Souvenir sheet of 6, 3 each #B174, B177, perf. 14x13½ 2.25 1.90

22nd Summer Olympic Games, Moscow, July 19-Aug. 3.

St. Maarten Landscape SP50

Children's Drawings: 30c+15c, House in Bonaire. 40c+20c, Child at blackboard. 60c+25c, Cancers, vert.

Perf. 14x13, 13x14

1980, Oct. 22 **Litho.**

B178 SP50 25c + 10c multi 28 24
B179 SP50 30c + 15c multi 35 32
B180 SP50 40c + 20c multi 40 38
B181 SP50 60c + 25c multi 50 48
a. Souvenir sheet of 6+ 4 labels, 3 each #B178, B181 2.50 2.25

Surtax was for Federation of Antillean Youth Care.

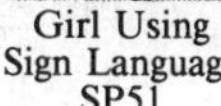

Girl Using Sign Language SP51

Tennis Player SP52

Designs: 25c+10c, Blind woman. 30c+15c, Man in wheelchair. 45c+20c, Infant in walker.

1981, Apr. 7 **Litho.** ***Perf. 13x14***

B182 SP51 25c + 10c multi 25 25
B183 SP51 30c + 15c multi 32 32
B184 SP51 45c + 20c multi 55 55
B185 SP51 60c + 25c multi 60 60

International Year of the Disabled. Surtax was for handicapped children.

1981, May 27 **Litho.** ***Perf. 13x14***

B186 SP52 30c + 15c shown 35 35
B187 SP52 50c + 20c Diving 55 55
B188 SP52 70c + 25c Boxing 75 75
a. Min. sheet of 3, #B186-B188 1.75 1.75

Surtax was for sporting events.

Den Mother and Cub Scout — SP53

Scouting in Netherlands Antilles, 50th Anniv.: 70c+25c, van der Maarel, national founder. 1g+50c, Ronde Klip (headquarters).

1981, Sept. 16 **Litho.** ***Perf. 14x13***

B189 SP53 45c + 20c multi 60 60
B190 SP53 70c + 25c multi 80 80
B191 SP53 1g + 50c multi 1.25 1.25
a. Min. sheet of 3, #B189-B191, perf. 13½x13 2.75 2.50

Surtax was for various social and cultural institutions.

Girl and Teddy Bear — SP54

Designs: 35c+15c, Mother and child. 45c+20c, Two children. 55c+25c, Boy and cat.

1981, Oct. 21 **Litho.** ***Perf. 13x14***

B192 SP54 35c + 15c multi 32 32
B193 SP54 45c + 20c multi 48 48
B194 SP54 55c + 25c multi 60 60
B195 SP54 85c + 40c multi 90 90
a. Min. sheet of 4, #B192-B195 2.50 2.50

Surtax was for Federation of Antillean Youth Care.

Fencing SP55

1982, Feb. 17 **Litho.** ***Perf. 14x13***

B196 SP55 35c + 15c shown 32 32
B197 SP55 45c + 20c Judo 50 50
B198 SP55 70c + 35c Soccer 80 80
a. Miniature sheet of 2 + label 1.75 1.75
B199 SP55 85c + 40c Bicycling 90 90

Surtax was for sporting events.

Girl Playing Accordion SP56

1982, Oct. 20 **Litho.**

B200 SP56 35c + 15c shown 40 40
B201 SP56 75c + 35c Guitar 90 90
B202 SP56 85c + 40c Violin 1.00 1.00
a. Min. sheet of 3, #B200-B202 2.50 2.50

Traditional House, Saba — SP57

1982, Nov. 17 **Litho.**

B203 SP57 35c + 15c shown 40 40
B204 SP57 75c + 35c Aruba 90 90
B205 SP57 85c + 40c Curacao 1.00 1.00
a. Souv. sheet of 3, #B203-B205 2.50 2.50

Surtax was for various social and cultural institutions.

High Jump SP58

1983, Feb. 22 **Litho.**

B206 SP58 35c + 15c shown 32 32
B207 SP58 45c + 20c Weight lifting 60 60
B208 SP58 85c + 40c Wind surfing 1.00 1.00

Surtax was for sporting events.

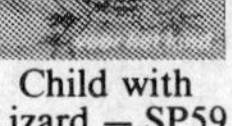
Child with Lizard — SP59

Pre-Columbian Artifacts — SP60

1983, Oct. 18 Litho. *Perf. 13x14*
B209 SP59 45c + 20c shown 60 60
B210 SP59 55c + 25c Child with insects 75 75
B211 SP59 100c + 50c Child with animal 1.40 1.40
a. Souv. sheet of 3, #B209-B211 2.75 2.75

Surtax was for Childrens' Charity.

1983, Nov. 22 Litho. *Perf. 13x14*
B212 SP60 45c + 20c multi 70 70
B213 SP60 55c + 25c multi 80 80
B214 SP60 85c + 40c multi 1.00 1.00
B215 SP60 100c + 50c multi 1.40 1.40

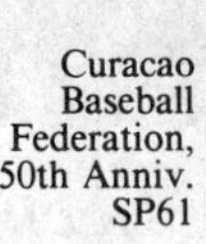

Curacao Baseball Federation, 50th Anniv. SP61

1984, Mar. 27 Litho. *Perf. 14x13*
B216 SP61 25c + 10c Catching 40 40
B217 SP61 45c + 20c Batting 75 75
B218 SP61 55c + 25c Pitching 95 95
B219 SP61 85c + 40c Running 1.10 1.10
a. Min. sheet of 3, #B217-B219 3.25 3.25

Surtax was for baseball fed., 1984 Olympics.

Microphones, Radio — SP62

Designs: 55c+25c, Radio, record player. 100c+50c, Record players.

1984, Apr. 24 Litho. *Perf. 14x13*
B220 SP62 45c + 20c multi 75 75
B221 SP62 55c + 25c multi 1.00 1.00
B222 SP62 100c + 50c multi 1.25 1.25

Surtax was for social and cultural institutions.

Boy Reading — SP63

Designs: 55c+25c, Parents reading to children. 100c+50c, Family worship.

1984, Nov. 7 Litho. *Perf. 13x14*
B223 SP63 45c + 20c multi 70 70
B224 SP63 55c + 25c multi 1.00 1.00
B225 SP63 100c + 50c multi 1.25 1.25
a. Souv. sheet of 3, #B223-B225 3.25 3.25

Surtax was for children's charity.

Soccer Players SP64

1985, Mar. 27 Litho. *Perf. 14x13*
B226 SP64 10c + 5c multi 22 22
B227 SP64 15c + 5c multi 25 25
B228 SP64 45c + 20c multi 70 70
B229 SP64 55c + 25c multi 90 90
B230 SP64 85c + 40c multi 1.25 1.25
Nos. B226-B230 (5) 3.32 3.32

The surtax was for sporting events.

Intl. Youth Year — SP65

1985, Apr. 29 Litho.
B231 SP65 45c + 20c Youth, computer keyboard 75 75
B232 SP65 55c + 25c Girl listening to music 1.00 1.00
B233 SP65 100c + 50c Youth breakdancing 1.50 1.50

Surtax for youth, social and cultural organizations.

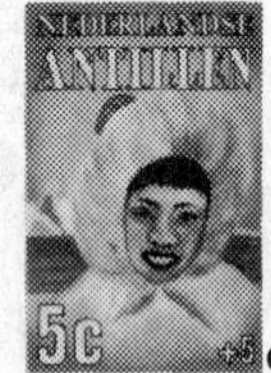
Children — SP66

1985, Oct. 16 Litho. *Perf. 13x14*
B234 SP66 5c + 5c Eskimo 18 18
B235 SP66 10c + 5c African 20 20
B236 SP66 25c + 10c Asian 42 42
B237 SP66 45c + 20c Dutch 70 70
B238 SP66 55c + 25c American Indian 80 80
a. Souv. sheet of 3, #B236-B238 2.00 2.00
Nos. B234-B238 (5) 2.30 2.30

Surtax for Youth Care Federation.

Sports SP67

Handicrafts SP68

1986, Feb. 19 Litho. *Perf. 13x14*
B239 SP67 15c + 5c Running 18 18
B240 SP67 25c + 10c Horse racing 38 38
B241 SP67 45c + 20c Car racing 65 65
B242 SP67 55c + 25c Soccer 75 75

Surtax for the natl. Sports Federation.

1986, Apr. 29
B243 SP68 30c + 15c Painting 40 40
B244 SP68 45c + 20c Sculpting 55 55
B245 SP68 55c + 25c Ceramics 70 70

Surtax for Curacao Youth Care Federation.

Sports SP69

Social and Cultural Programs SP70

1986, Oct. 15 Litho. *Perf. 13x14*
B246 SP69 20c + 10c Soccer 26 26
B247 SP69 25c + 15c Tennis 35 35
B248 SP69 45c + 20c Judo 52 52
B249 SP69 55c + 25c Baseball 65 65
a. Min. sheet of 2, #B248-B249 1.25 1.25

Surtax for the natl. Sports Foundation.

1987, Mar. 11 Litho.
B250 SP70 35c + 15c Musicians 38 38
B251 SP70 45c + 25c Handicapped 50 50
B252 SP70 85c + 40c Pavilion 95 95

Surtax for the Jong Wacht (Youth Guard) and the natl. Red Cross.

Boy in Various Stages of Growth SP71

1987, Oct. 21 Litho. *Perf. 14x13*
B253 SP71 40c +15c Infant 45 45
B254 SP71 55c +25c Toddler 60 60
B255 SP71 115c +50c Boy 1.25 1.25
a. Souv. sheet of 3, #B253-B255 2.50 2.50

Surtax benefited Youth Care programs.

Queen Emma Bridge, Cent. SP72

Designs: 55c+25c, Bridge, vert. 115c+55c, View of Willemstad Harbor and quay. 190c+60c, Flags of the Netherlands, Antilles and United States, Leonard B. Smith, engineer.

Perf. 13x14, 14x13

1988, May 9 Litho.
B256 SP72 55c +25c multi 60 60
B257 SP72 115c +55c multi 1.25 1.25
B258 SP72 190c +60c multi 1.75 1.75

Surtax for social and cultural purposes.

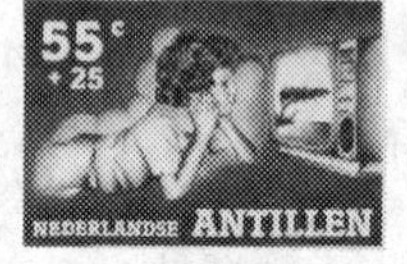
Youth Care Campaign SP73

1988, Oct. 26 Litho. *Perf. 14x13*
B259 SP73 55c +25c Girl, television 60 60
B260 SP73 65c +30c Boy, portable stereo 70 70
B261 SP73 115c +55c Girl, computer 1.25 1.25
a. Souv. sheet of 3, #B259-B261 2.50 2.50

Surtax for the Antillean Youth Care Federation.

Curacao Stamp Assoc., 50th Anniv. — SP75

Designs: 30c+10c, Type A25 and No. 461 under magnifying glass. 55c+20c, Simulated stamp (learning to use tongs). 80c+30c, Barn owl, album, magnifying glass, tongs.

1989, Jan. 18 Litho. *Perf. 13x14*
B264 SP75 30c +10c multi 30 30
B265 SP75 55c +20c multi 55 55
B266 SP75 80c +30c multi 75 75

Nos. B264-B266 printed se-tenant in a continuous design. Surtaxed for welfare organizations.

SP76

1989, Oct. 25 Litho. *Perf. 14x13*
B267 SP76 40c +15c Girl, boy, tree 35 35
B268 SP76 65c +30c Playing on beach 70 70
B269 SP76 115c +55c Father and child 1.25 1.25

Souvenir Sheet

B270 SP76 155c +75c At the beach, diff. 1.65 1.65

Surtax for child welfare.

Natl. Girl Scout Movement, 60th Anniv. SP77

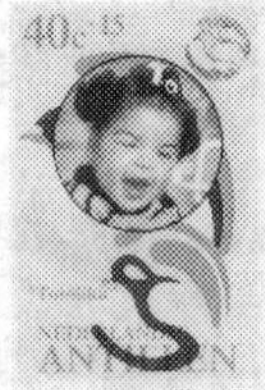
Totolika, 60th Anniv. SP78

Natl. Boy Scout Movement, 60th Anniv. — SP79

1990, Mar. 7 Litho. *Perf. 13x14*
B271 SP77 30c +10c multi 35 35
B272 SP78 40c +15c multi 45 45
B273 SP79 155c +65c multi 1.75 1.75

Parents' and Friends Association of Persons with a Mental Handicap (Totolika).

Sport Unie Brion Trappers Soccer Club — SP80

1990, June 13 Litho. *Perf. 13x14*
B274 SP80 65c +30c multi 90 90

Anti-drug Campaign — SP81

1990, June 13
B275 SP81 115c +55c multi 1.60 1.60

Youth Care Campaign SP82

1990, Oct. 31 Litho. *Perf. 14x13*

B276	SP82	30c +5c Bees, flowers	40	40
B277	SP82	55c +10c Dolphins	72	72
B278	SP82	65c +15c Donkey, bicycle	90	90
B279	SP82	100c +20c Goat, house	1.35	1.35
B280	SP82	115c +25c Rabbit	1.60	1.60
B281	SP82	155c +55c Lizard, moon	2.35	2.35
		Nos. B276-B281 (6)	7.32	7.32

Surtax for the benefit of the Antillean Youth Care Federation.
See Nos. B285-B288.

Social and Cultural Care — SP83

Designs: 30c+10c, Youth philately. 65c+25c, St. Vincentius Brass Band, 50th anniv. 155c+55c, Curacao Community Center Federation.

1991, Apr. 3 Litho. *Perf. 14x13*

B282	SP83	30c +10c multi	50	50
B283	SP83	65c +25c multi	1.10	1.10
B284	SP83	155c +55c multi	2.55	2.55

Youth Care Campaign Type of 1990

Fight illiteracy: 40c+15c, Octopus holding numbers and letters. 65c+30c, Birds, blackboard. 155c+65c, Turtle telling time. No. B288a, Owl, flag. b, Books, bookworms. c, Seahorse.

1991, Oct. 31 Litho. *Perf. 14x13*

B285	SP82	40c +15c multi	60	60
B286	SP82	65c +30c multi	1.00	1.00
B287	SP82	155c +65c multi	2.35	2.35

Souvenir Sheet

Imperf

B288		Sheet of 3	4.25	4.25
a.	SP82	55c +25c multi	90	90
b.	SP82	100c +35c multi	1.50	1.50
c.	SP82	115c +50c multi	1.85	1.85

Surtax for the benefit of the Antillean Yorth Care Federation.

AIR POST STAMPS

Regular Issues of 1915-22 Surcharged in Black

LUCHTPOST
1
gld.

Perf. 12½

1929, July 6 Typo. Unwmk.

C1	A13	50c on 12½c red	9.75	12.00
C2	A13	1g on 20c blue	9.75	12.00
C3	A13	2g on 15c ol grn	40.00	50.00

Excellent forgeries exist.

Allegory, "Flight" — AP1

1931-39 Engr.

C4	AP1	10c Prus grn ('34)	15	15
C5	AP1	15c dl bl ('38)	15	15
C6	AP1	20c red	60	15
C7	AP1	25c gray ('38)	32	28
C8	AP1	30c yel ('39)	22	15
C9	AP1	35c dl bl	65	55
C10	AP1	40c green	48	15
C11	AP1	45c orange	1.90	2.25
C12	AP1	50c lake ('38)	32	42
C13	AP1	60c brn vio	50	28
C14	AP1	70c black	5.75	2.25
C15	AP1	1.40g brown	3.75	4.75
C16	AP1	2.80g bister	4.50	5.00
		Nos. C4-C16 (13)	19.29	16.53

No. C6 Surcharged in Black

10 CT

1934, Aug. 25

C17	AP1	10c on 20c red	18.00	17.00

Catalogue values for unused stamps in this section, from this point to the end of the section, are for Never Hinged items.

Map of the Atlantic AP2

Plane over Islands — AP3

Map of Curaçao, Aruba and Bonaire — AP4

Planes — AP5

Plane — AP6

1942, Oct. 20 *Perf. 13x13½*

C18	AP2	10c grn & bl	15	15
C19	AP3	15c rose car & yel grn	20	15
C20	AP4	20c red brn & grn	24	35
C21	AP5	25c dp ultra & org brn	15	15
C22	AP6	30c red & lt vio	30	18
C23	AP2	35c dk vio & ol grn	45	18
C24	AP3	40c gray ol & chnt	50	28
C25	AP4	45c dk red & blk	35	42
C26	AP5	50c vio & blk	85	15
C27	AP6	60c lt yel brn & dl bl	85	45
C28	AP2	70c red brn & Prus bl	1.10	45
C29	AP3	1.40g bl vio & sl grn	4.50	1.10
C30	AP4	2.80g int bl & lt bl	5.50	2.25
C31	AP5	5g rose lake & sl grn	12.00	9.50
C32	AP6	10g grn & red brn	18.00	14.00
		Nos. C18-C32 (15)	45.14	29.76

For surcharges see Nos. CB9-CB12.

Plane and Post Horn — AP7

DC-4 above Waves — AP8

1947 Photo. *Perf. 12½x12*

C32A	AP7	6c gray blk	15	15
C33	AP7	10c dp red	15	15
C33A	AP7	12½c plum	18	15
C34	AP7	15c dp bl	18	16
C35	AP7	20c dl yel grn	25	20
C36	AP7	25c org yel	25	15
C37	AP7	30c lil gray	25	22
C38	AP7	35c org red	32	45
C39	AP7	40c bl grn	38	45
C40	AP7	45c brt vio	45	60
C41	AP7	50c carmine	38	15
C42	AP7	60c brt bl	60	45
C43	AP7	70c brown	1.25	90

Engr.

Perf. 12x12½

C44	AP8	1.50g black	90	45
C45	AP8	2.50g dk car	7.75	2.50
C46	AP8	5g green	16.00	5.50
C47	AP8	7.50g dk bl	47.50	42.50
C48	AP8	10g dk red vio	35.00	10.50
C49	AP8	15g red org	55.00	50.00
C50	AP8	25g chocolate	55.00	42.50
		Nos. C32A-C50 (20)	221.94	158.13

AIR POST SEMI-POSTAL STAMPS

Flags of the Netherlands and the House of Orange with Inscription "Netherlands Shall Rise Again" — SPAP1

Engr. & Photo.

1941, Dec. 11 Unwmk. *Perf. 12*

CB1	SPAP1	10c + 10c multi	2.50	1.90
CB2	SPAP1	15c + 25c multi	12.50	8.00
CB3	SPAP1	20c + 25c multi	12.50	10.00
CB4	SPAP1	25c + 25c multi	12.50	10.00
CB5	SPAP1	30c + 50c multi	12.50	10.00
CB6	SPAP1	35c + 50c multi	12.50	10.00
CB7	SPAP1	40c + 50c multi	12.50	10.00
CB8	SPAP1	50c +100c multi	12.50	10.00
		Nos. CB1-CB8 (8)	90.00	69.90

The surtax was used by the Prince Bernhard Committee to purchase war material for the Netherlands' fighting forces in Great Britain.

Catalogue values for unused stamps in this section, from this point to the end of the section, are for Never Hinged items.

Nos. C29-C32 Surcharged in Black

Voor Krijgs-
gevangenen

50 ct. + 75 ct

1943, Dec. 1 *Perf. 13x13½*

CB9	AP3	40c + 50c on 1.40g	4.50	3.50
CB10	AP4	45c + 50c on 2.80g	4.50	3.25
CB11	AP5	50c + 75c on 5g	4.50	3.25
CB12	AP6	60c + 100c on 10g	4.50	3.25

The surtax was for the benefit of prisoners of war. These stamps were not sold to the public in the normal manner. All were sold in sets by advance subscription, the majority to philatelic speculators.
On No. CB9 overprint reads: "Voor / Krijgsgevangenen".

Princess Juliana — SPAP2

Engr. & Photo.

1944, Aug. 16 *Perf. 12*

Frame in carmine & deep blue, cross in carmine

CB13	SPAP2	10c + 10c lt brn	1.50	1.25
CB14	SPAP2	15c + 25c turq grn	1.40	1.25
CB15	SPAP2	20c + 25c dk ol gray	1.40	1.25
CB16	SPAP2	25c + 25c slate	1.40	1.25
CB17	SPAP2	30c + 50c sepia	1.40	1.25
CB18	SPAP2	35c + 50c chnt	1.40	1.25
CB19	SPAP2	40c + 50c grn	1.40	1.25
CB20	SPAP2	50c + 100c dk vio	1.50	1.40
		Nos. CB13-CB20 (8)	11.40	10.15

The surtax was for the Red Cross.

Map of Netherlands Indies SPAP3

Map of Netherlands SPAP4

Photo. & Typo.

1946, July 1 *Perf. 11x11½*

CB21	SPAP3	10c + 10c	75	75
CB22	SPAP3	15c + 25c	85	75
CB23	SPAP3	20c + 25c	85	75
CB24	SPAP3	25c + 25c	85	75
CB25	SPAP3	30c + 50c	85	1.00
a.		Double impression of denomination	325.00	325.00
CB26	SPAP3	35c + 50c	85	1.00
CB27	SPAP3	40c + 75c	85	1.10
CB28	SPAP3	50c + 100c	85	1.10
CB29	SPAP4	10c + 10c	75	75
CB30	SPAP4	15c + 25c	85	75
CB31	SPAP4	20c + 25c	85	75
CB32	SPAP4	25c + 25c	85	75
CB33	SPAP4	30c + 50c	85	1.00
CB34	SPAP4	35c + 50c	85	1.00
CB35	SPAP4	40c + 75c	85	1.10
CB36	SPAP4	50c + 100c	85	1.10
		Nos. CB21-CB36 (16)	13.40	14.40

The surtax on Nos. CB21 to CB36 was for the National Relief Fund.

POSTAGE DUE STAMPS

D1

D2

Type I - 34 loops. "T" of *"BETALEN"* over center of loop, top branch of "E" of *"TE"* shorter than lower branch.
Type II - 33 loops. "T" of *"BETALEN"* over center of two loops.
Type III - 32 loops. "T" of *"BETALEN"* slightly to the left of loop, top of first "E" of *"BETALEN"* shorter than lower branch.

Value in Black

1889 Unwmk. Typo. *Perf. 12½*

Type III

J1	D1	2½c green	2.00	3.25
J2	D1	5c green	1.50	1.75
J3	D1	10c green	30.00	27.50
J4	D1	12½c green	275.00	140.00
J5	D1	15c green	20.00	18.00
J6	D1	20c green	9.00	9.00
J7	D1	25c green	140.00	90.00
J8	D1	30c green	9.00	9.00
J9	D1	40c green	9.00	9.00
J10	D1	50c green	40.00	37.50

Nos. J1 to J10 were issued without gum.

Type I

J1a	D1	2½c	3.00	4.00
J2a	D1	5c	40.00	35.00
J3a	D1	10c	35.00	35.00
J4a	D1	12½c	300.00	150.00
J5a	D1	15c	21.00	19.00
J6a	D1	20c	55.00	55.00
J7a	D1	25c	375.00	250.00
J8a	D1	30c	60.00	60.00
J9a	D1	40c	60.00	60.00

J10a D1 50c 45.00 40.00

Type II

J1b D1 2½c 5.00 4.75
J2b D1 5c 175.00 125.00
J3b D1 10c 40.00 37.50
J4b D1 12½c 300.00 175.00
J5b D1 15c 22.50 20.00
J6b D1 20c 300.00 300.00
J7b D1 25c *1,000.* *1,000.*
J8b D1 30c 300.00 300.00
J9b D1 40c 300.00 27.50
J10b D1 50c 47.50 47.50

Value in Black

1892-98 ***Perf. 12½***
J11 D2 2½c grn (III) 22 18
J12 D2 5c grn (III) 55 42
J13 D2 10c grn (III) 90 40
J14 D2 12½c grn (III) 1.00 45
J15 D2 15c grn (III) ('95) 1.40 95
J17 D2 25c grn (III) 1.10 95

Type I

J11a D2 2½c 45 45
J12a D2 5c 1.40 1.40
J13a D2 10c 1.90 1.90
J14a D2 12½c 1.40 1.40
J16 D2 20c grn ('95) 1.75 1.10
J17a D2 25c 1.50 1.50
J18 D2 30c grn ('95) 14.00 9.25
J19 D2 40c grn ('95) 14.00 12.50
J20 D2 50c grn ('95) 17.00 12.50

Type II

J11b D2 2½c 16.00 16.00
J12b D2 5c 90 90
J13b D2 10c 1.10 1.10
J14b D2 12½c 6.75 6.75
J17b D2 25c *9.50* *9.50*

Type I
On Yellowish or White Paper
Value in Color of Stamp

1915 ***Perf. 12½, 13½x12½***
J21 D2 2½c green 1.00 95
J22 D2 5c green 1.00 95
J23 D2 10c green 90 80
J24 D2 12½c green 1.25 1.10
J25 D2 15c green 1.90 2.00
J26 D2 20c green 1.00 1.75
J27 D2 25c green 35 16
J28 D2 30c green 4.25 4.00
J29 D2 40c green 4.25 4.00
J30 D2 50c green 3.50 3.50
Nos. J21-J30 (10) 19.40 19.21

1944 ***Perf. 11½***

Yellow Green

J23a D2 10c yellow green 15.00 16.00
J24a D2 12½c yellow green 13.00 9.00
J27a D2 25c yellow green 32.50 1.10

Type of 1915
Type I
Value in Color of Stamp
Perf. 13½x12½

1948-49 Unwmk. Photo.
J31 D2 2½c bl grn ('48) 38 1.00
J32 D2 5c bl grn ('48) 38 1.00
J33 D2 10c bl grn 9.25 8.50
J34 D2 12½c bl grn 9.25 1.50
J35 D2 15c bl grn 15.00 15.00
J36 D2 20c bl grn 13.00 15.00
J37 D2 25c bl grn 1.10 26
J38 D2 30c bl grn 15.00 19.00
J39 D2 40c bl grn 15.00 19.00
J40 D2 50c bl grn 15.00 15.00
Nos. J31-J40 (10) 93.36 95.26

Catalogue values for unused stamps in this section, from this point to the end of the section, are for Never Hinged items.

D3

1953-59 Photo.
J41 D3 1c dk bl grn ('59) 15 15
J42 D3 2½c dk bl grn 50 45
J43 D3 5c dk bl grn 15 15
J44 D3 6c dk bl grn ('59) 45 30
J45 D3 7c dk bl grn ('59) 45 30
J46 D3 8c dk bl grn ('59) 45 30
J47 D3 9c dk bl grn ('59) 45 30
J48 D3 10c dk bl grn 22 15
J49 D3 12½c dk bl grn 22 15
J50 D3 15c dk bl grn 30 18
J51 D3 20c dk bl grn 30 30
J52 D3 25c dk bl grn 45 15
J53 D3 30c dk bl grn 1.10 90
J54 D3 35c dk bl grn ('59) 1.25 90
J55 D3 40c dk bl grn 1.10 90
J56 D3 45c dk bl grn ('59) 1.25 90
J57 D3 50c dk bl grn 1.10 65
Nos. J41-J57 (17) 9.89 7.13

NETHERLANDS INDIES

(Dutch Indies, Indonesia)

LOCATION — East Indies
GOVT. — Former Dutch colony
AREA — 735,268 sq. mi.
POP. — 76,000,000 (estimated 1949)
CAPITAL — Jakarta (formerly Batavia)

Netherlands Indies consisted of the islands of Sumatra, Java, the Lesser Sundas, Madura, two thirds of Borneo, Celebes, the Moluccas, western New Guinea and many small islands.

Netherlands Indies changed its name to Indonesia in 1948. Holland transferred sovereignty on Dec. 28, 1949, to the Republic of the United States of Indonesia (see "Indonesia"), except for the western part of New Guinea (see "Netherlands New Guinea"). The Republic of Indonesia was proclaimed Aug. 15, 1950.

100 Cents = 1 Gulden
100 Sen = 1 Rupiah (1949)

Catalogue values for unused stamps in this country are for Never Hinged items, beginning with Scott 250 in the regular postage section, Scott B57 in the semi-postal section, and Scott J43 in the postage due section.

Watermarks

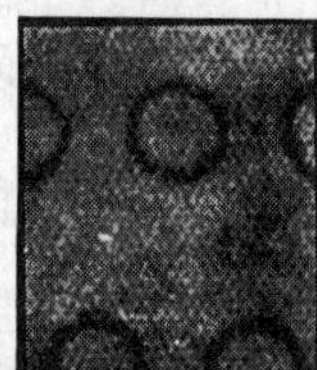

Wmk. 202- Circles

Wmk. 228- Small Crown and C of A Multiple

King William III
A1 A2

1864, Apr. 1 Unwmk. Engr. *Imperf.*
1 A1 10c lake 165.00 75.00

1868 ***Perf. 12½x12***
2 A1 10c lake 600.00 115.00

Privately perforated examples of No. 1 sometimes are mistaken for No. 2.

Perf. 11½x12, 12½, 12½x12, 13x14, 13½, 14, 13½x14

1870-88 Typo.

ONE CENT:
Type I - "CENT" 6mm long.
Type II - "CENT" 7½mm long.

3 A2 1c sl grn, type I 5.25 4.25
4 A2 1c sl grn, type II 2.00 1.25
5 A2 2c red brn 4.75 2.75
a. 2c fawn 4.75 3.25
6 A2 2c vio brn 90.00 75.00
7 A2 2½c orange 27.50 19.00
8 A2 5c pale grn 47.50 3.00
a. Perf. 14, small holes 45.00 3.25
b. Perf. 13x14, small holes 40.00 4.25
9 A2 10c org brn 11.00 15
a. Perf. 14, small holes 20.00 55
b. Perf. 13x14, small holes 27.50 75
10 A2 12½c gray 2.25 95
a. Perf. 12½x12 725.00
11 A2 15c bister 15.00 70
a. Perf. 13x14, small holes 22.50 1.50
12 A2 20c ultra 85.00 1.70
a. Perf. 14, small holes 85.00 1.75
b. Perf. 13x14, small holes 85.00 1.90
13 A2 25c dk vio 14.00 55
b. Perf. 13x14, small holes 20.00 1.50
c. Perf. 14, large holes 325.00 72.50
14 A2 30c green 24.00 2.25
15 A2 50c carmine 13.00 65
a. Perf. 14, small holes 16.00 65
b. Perf. 13x14, small holes 13.00 85
c. Perf. 14, large holes 18.00 1.25
16 A2 2.50g grn & vio 72.50 11.00
b. Perf. 14, small holes 72.50 11.00
c. Perf. 14, large holes 72.50 11.00

Imperforate examples of Nos. 3-16 are proofs. The 1c red brown and 2c yellow are believed to be bogus.

"Small hole" varieties have the spaces between the holes wider than the diameter of the holes.

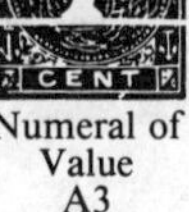

Numeral of Value
A3

Queen Wilhelmina
A4

1883-90 ***Perf. 12½***
17 A3 1c sl grn ('88) 55 15
a. Perf. 12½x12 1.10 65
18 A3 2c brn ('84) 55 15
a. Perf. 12½x12 75 30
b. Perf. 11½x12 65.00 22.50
19 A3 2½c yellow 65 65
a. Perf. 12½x12 1.25 75
b. Perf. 11½x12 12.00 4.75
20 A3 3c lil ('90) 75 15
21 A3 5c grn ('87) 24.00 15.00
22 A3 5c ultra ('90) 8.00 15

1892-97 ***Perf. 12½***
23 A4 10c org brn 3.75 15
24 A4 12½c gray 6.75 12.50
25 A4 15c bister 11.00 70
26 A4 20c ultra 27.50 80
27 A4 25c violet 27.50 1.10
28 A4 30c green 35.00 1.50
29 A4 50c carmine 25.00 60
30 A4 2.50g org brn & ultra 110.00 27.50

Queen Wilhelmina — A5

Stamps of Netherlands, 1898-99 Surcharged in Black

1900, July 1
31 A5 10c on 10c gray lil 1.25 15
32 A5 12½c on 12½c blue 1.90 55
33 A5 15c on 15c yel brn 2.25 18
34 A5 20c on 20c yel grn 13.00 45
35 A5 25c on 25c car & bl 13.00 55
36 A5 50c on 50c brnz grn & red brn 22.50 75

2.50 2.50

Netherlands No. 84, Surcharged in Black

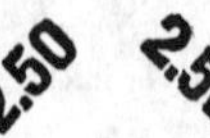

Perf. 11½x11
37 A12 2.50g on 2½g brn lil 42.50 7.50
a. Perf. 11 47.50 8.25
Nos. 31-37 (7) 96.40 10.13

A6

1902-09 ***Perf. 12½***
38 A6 ½c violet 30 15
39 A6 1c ol grn 30 15
a. Booklet pane of 6
40 A6 2c yel brn 2.25 18
41 A6 2½c green 1.50 15
a. Booklet pane of 6
42 A6 3c orange 1.50 1.10
43 A6 4c ultra ('09) 9.25 8.75
44 A6 5c rose red 4.00 15
a. Booklet pane of 6
45 A6 7½c gray ('09) 2.00 28
Nos. 38-45 (8) 21.10 10.91

A7

A8

1902
46 A7 ½c on 2c yel brn 20 20
a. Double surcharge 175.00 150.00
47 A8 2½c on 3c vio 25 25

Queen Wilhelmina
A9 A10

1902-08
48 A9 10c slate 85 15
a. Booklet pane of 6
49 A9 12½c dp bl 1.40 15
a. Booklet pane of 6
50 A9 15c chocolate 7.25 2.00
a. Ovptd. with 2 horiz. bars 1.50 75
51 A9 17½c bister ('08) 2.50 15
52 A9 20c grnsh slate 1.50 1.75
53 A9 20c ol grn 20.00 15
54 A9 22½c brn & ol grn ('08) 3.75 15
55 A9 25c violet 7.75 15
56 A9 30c org brn 25.00 15
57 A9 50c red brn 17.50 15
Nos. 48-57 (10) 87.50 4.95

No. 52 Surcharged in Black

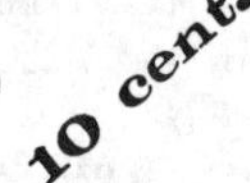

1905, July 6
58 A9 10c on 20c grnsh slate 1.90 1.25

1905-12 Engr. *Perf. 11x11½*
59 A10 1g dl lil ('05) 42.50 20
a. Perf. 11½x11 42.50 35
b. Perf. 11 52.50 3.50
60 A10 1g dl lil, *bl* ('12) 45.00 6.50
a. Perf. 11 55.00 57.50
61 A10 2½g sl bl ('05) 52.50 1.50
a. Perf. 11½ 52.50 1.65
b. Perf. 11½x11 60.00 1.65
c. Perf. 11 675.00
62 A10 2½g sl bl, *bl* ('12) 65.00 32.50
a. Perf. 11 75.00 75.00

Sheets of Nos. 60 & 62 were soaked in an indigo solution.

Previous Issues Overprinted

BUITEN BEZIT.

1908, July 1
63 A6 ½c violet 18 18
64 A6 1c ol grn 28 18
65 A6 2c yel brn 1.25 2.00
66 A6 2½c green 55 18
67 A6 3c orange 45 95
68 A6 5c rose red 1.90 38

69 A6 7½c gray 2.00 2.25
70 A9 10c slate 45 15
71 A9 12½c dp blue 7.50 2.00
72 A9 15c choc (#50a) 3.50 1.90
73 A9 17½c bister 1.25 95
74 A9 20c ol grn 6.25 1.25
75 A9 22½c brn & ol grn 5.25 3.50
76 A9 25c violet 4.00 28
77 A9 30c org brn 14.00 1.90
78 A9 50c red brn 6.25 60
79 A10 1g dl lil 47.50 3.50
80 A10 2½g slate blue 72.50 57.50
Nos. 63-80 (18) 175.06 79.65

The above stamps were overprinted for use in the territory outside of Java and Madura, stamps overprinted "Java" being used in these latter places.

The 15c is overprinted, in addition, with two horizontal lines, 2½mm apart.

Overprint Reading Down

63a A6 ½c 50 3.25
64a A6 1c 42 2.25
65a A6 2c 2.00 4.25
66a A6 2½c 85 2.75
67a A6 3c 14.00 37.50
68a A6 5c 1.00 2.50
70a A9 10c 50 1.90
71a A9 12½c 4.50 8.00
72a A9 15c 22.50 57.50
74a A9 20c 4.25 8.00
75a A9 22½c 1,300 1,300.
76a A9 25c 4.25 6.50
77a A9 30c 11.00 15.00
78a A9 50c 7.50 9.00
79a A10 1g 175.00 200.00
80a A10 2½g 1,900. 2,400.

Overprinted **JAVA.**

1908, July 1

81 A6 ½c violet 15 18
a. Inverted overprint 48 2.25
b. Double overprint 350.00
82 A6 1c ol grn 16 16
a. Inverted overprint 38 2.75
83 A6 2c yel brn 1.50 1.50
a. Inverted overprint 1.40 6.00
84 A6 2½c green 75 15
a. Inverted overprint 1.90 3.25
85 A6 3c orange 55 75
a. Inverted overprint 16.00 22.50
86 A6 5c rose red 2.00 15
a. Inverted overprint 1.40 2.50
87 A6 7½c gray 1.90 1.65
88 A9 10c slate 45 15
a. Inverted overprint 45 2.00
89 A9 12½c dp bl 2.75 55
a. Inverted overprint 2.75 5.00
b. Dbl. ovpt., one inverted 95.00 95.00
90 A9 15c choc (on No. 50a) 3.00 2.25
a. Inverted overprint 2.75 9.00
91 A9 17½c bister 1.50 60
92 A9 20c ol grn 8.50 55
a. Inverted overprint 8.25 10.00
93 A9 22½c brn & ol grn 4.00 2.00
94 A9 25c violet 3.50 18
a. Inverted overprint 4.50 9.00
95 A9 30c org brn 24.00 2.00
a. Inverted overprint 18.00 26.00
96 A9 50c red brn 15.00 55
a. Inverted overprint 12.00 19.00
97 A10 1g dl lil 37.50 2.25
a. Inverted overprint 150.00 150.00
b. Perf. 11 47.50 4.00
98 A10 2½g slate blue 57.50 40.00
a. Inverted overprint 1,900. 2,400.
Nos. 81-98 (18) 164.71 55.62

A11

Queen Wilhelmina
A12 A13

Typo., Litho. (#114A)

1912-40 *Perf. 12½*

101 A11 ½c lt vio 15 15
102 A11 1c ol grn 15 15
103 A11 2c yel brn 30 15
104 A11 2c gray blk ('30) 32 15
105 A11 2½c green 1.25 15
106 A11 2½c lt red ('22) 22 15
107 A11 3c yellow 32 15
108 A11 3c grn ('29) 60 15
109 A11 4c ultra 55 25
110 A11 4c dp grn ('28) 1.25 20
111 A11 4c yel ('30) 8.50 4.00
112 A11 5c rose 75 15
113 A11 5c grn ('22) 90 15
114 A11 5c chlky bl ('28) 38 15
114A A11 5c ultra ('40) 80 15
115 A11 7½c bister 35 15
116 A11 10c lil ('22) 95 15
117 A12 10c car rose ('14) 55 15
118 A12 12½c dl bl ('14) 85 15
119 A12 12½c red ('22) 85 15
120 A12 15c bl ('29) 7.50 15
121 A12 17½c red brn ('15) 85 15
122 A12 20c grn ('15) 1.40 15
123 A12 20c blue ('22) 1.40 15
124 A12 20c org ('32) 13.00 15
125 A12 22½c org ('15) 1.40 45
126 A12 25c red vio ('15) 1.40 15
127 A12 30c slate ('15) 1.65 15
128 A12 32½c vio & red ('22) 1.65 15
129 A12 35c org brn ('29) 8.50 52
130 A12 40c grn ('22) 1.65 15

Perf. 11½

Engr.

131 A13 50c grn ('13) 2.75 15
a. Perf. 11x11½ 3.50 15
b. Perf. 12½ 4.25 22
132 A13 60c dp bl ('22) 3.50 15
133 A13 80c org ('22) 3.75 15
134 A13 1g brn ('13) 2.75 15
a. Perf. 11x11½ 3.50 15
135 A13 1.75g dk vio, p. 12½ ('31) 14.00 1.90
136 A13 2½g car ('13) 11.00 38
a. Perf. 11x11½ 13.00 60
b. Perf. 12½ 14.00 48
Nos. 101-136 (37) 98.14 12.20

Water Soluble Ink

Some values of types A11 and A12 and late printings of types A6 and A9 are in soluble ink and the design disappears when immersed in water.

Nos. 105, 109, 54, 59 Surcharged

½ 1 17½

30 CENT

1917-18 **Typo.** *Perf. 12½*

137 A11 ½c on 2½c 22 18
138 A11 1c on 4c ('18) 55 45
139 A9 17½c on 22½c ('18) 90 38
a. Inverted surcharge 350.00 425.00

Perf. 11x11½

140 A10 30c on 1g ('18) 7.00 1.40
a. Perf. 11½x11 110.00 42.50

Nos. 121, 125, 131, 134 Surcharged in Red or Blue

12½ CENT — On A14

40 CENT — On A13

Two types of 32½c on 50c:
I- Surcharge bars spaced as in illustration.
II- Bars more closely spaced.

1922, Jan. *Perf. 12½*

144 A14 12½c on 17½c (R) 28 15
145 A14 12½c on 22½c (R) 38 15
146 A14 20c on 22½c (Bl) 38 15

Perf. 11½, 11x11½

147 A13 32½c on 50c (Bl) (I, perf. 11½) 1.25 15
a. Type II, perf. 11½ 10.00 15
b. Type I, perf. 11x11½ 275.00 7.00
c. Type II, perf. 11x11½ 22.50 1.25
148 A13 40c on 50c (R) 3.75 45
149 A13 60c on 1g (Bl) 6.00 38
150 A13 80c on 1g (R) 6.75 80
Nos. 144-150 (7) 18.79 2.23

Stamps of 1912-22 Overprinted in Red, Blue, Green or Black

a: 3de N.I. JAARBEURS BANDOENG 1922

b: 3de N. I. JAARBEURS BANDOENG 1922

1922, Sept. 18 **Typo.** *Perf. 12½*

102a A11(a) 1c ol grn (R) 5.75 4.75
103a A11(a) 2c yel brn (Bl) 5.75 4.75
106a A11(a) 2½c lt red (G) 47.50 52.50
107a A11(a) 3c yel (R) 5.75 5.75
109a A11(a) 4c ultra (R) 32.50 30.00
113a A11(a) 5c grn (R) 11.00 8.25
115a A11(a) 7½c db (Bl) 7.50 4.75
116a A11(a) 10c lil (Bk) 57.50 67.50
145a A14(b) 12½c on 22½c org (Bl) 5.75 5.75
121a A12(b) 17½c red brn (Bk) 3.75 4.75
123a A12(b) 20c bl (Bk) 5.75 4.75
Nos. 102a-123a (11) 188.50 193.50

Issued to publicize the 3rd Netherlands Indies Industrial Fair at Bandoeng, Java. On No. 145a the overprint is vertical.

Nos. 102a-123a were sold at a premium for 3, 4, 5, 6, 8, 9, 10, 12½, 15, 20 and 22½ cents respectively.

Queen Wilhelmina
A15

Prince William I, Portrait by Van Key
A16

1923, Aug. 31 **Engr.** *Perf. 11½*

151 A15 5c myr grn 15 15
a. Perf. 11½x11 350.00 110.00
b. Perf. 11x11½ 4.50 55
152 A15 12½c rose 18 15
a. Perf. 11x11½ 1.25 18
b. Perf. 11½x11 1.75 25
153 A15 20c dk bl 35 15
a. Perf. 11½x11 3.25 40
154 A15 50c red org 1.40 60
a. Perf. 11x11½ 6.50 1.25
b. Perf. 11½x11 2.00 90
c. Perf. 11 4.50 85
155 A15 1g brn vio 2.75 38
a. Perf. 11½x11 7.50 80
156 A15 2½g gray blk 22.50 8.75
157 A15 5g org brn 90.00 87.50
Nos. 151-157 (7) 117.33 97.68

25th anniversary of the assumption of the government of the Netherlands by Queen Wilhelmina, at the age of 18.

No. 123 Surcharged

12½

1930, Dec. 13 **Typo.** *Perf. 12½*

158 A12 12½c on 20c bl (R) 32 15
a. Inverted surcharge 375.00 475.00

1933, Apr. 18 **Photo.**

163 A16 12½c dp org 1.25 18

400th anniv. of the birth of Prince William I, Count of Nassau and Prince of Orange, frequently referred to as William the Silent.

Rice Field Scene
A17

Queen Wilhelmina
A18

Queen Wilhelmina
A19

1933-37 **Unwmk.** *Perf. 12x12½*

164 A17 1c lil gray ('34) 20 15
165 A17 2c plum ('34) 20 15
166 A17 2½c bis ('34) 20 15
167 A17 3c yel grn ('34) 20 15
168 A17 3½c dk gray ('37) 15 15
169 A17 4c dk ol ('34) 85 15
170 A17 5c ultra ('34) 15 15
171 A17 7½c vio ('34) 1.25 15
172 A17 10c ver ('34) 1.75 15
173 A18 10c ver ('37) 25 15
174 A18 12½c dp org ('34) 25 15
a. 12½c lt org, perf. 12½ 6.25 35
175 A18 15c ultra ('34) 25 15
176 A18 20c plum ('34) 38 15
177 A18 25c bl grn ('34) 1.75 15
178 A18 30c lil gray ('34) 2.75 15
179 A18 32½c bis ('34) 7.50 6.50
180 A18 35c vio ('34) 4.25 95
181 A18 40c yel grn ('34) 2.50 15
182 A18 42½c yel ('34) 2.50 18

1934, Jan 16 *Perf. 12½*

183 A19 50c lilac gray 3.25 18
184 A19 60c ultra 4.00 45
185 A19 80c vermilion 4.00 55
186 A19 1g violet 6.25 38
187 A19 1.75g yel grn 16.00 11.00
188 A19 2.50g plum 19.00 1.25
Nos. 164-188 (25) 79.83 23.84

See Nos. 200-225, 272-275.

Water Soluble Ink

Nos. 164-188 and the first printing of No. 163 have soluble ink and the design disappears when immersed in water.

Nos. C6-C7, C14, C9-C10 Surcharged in Black:

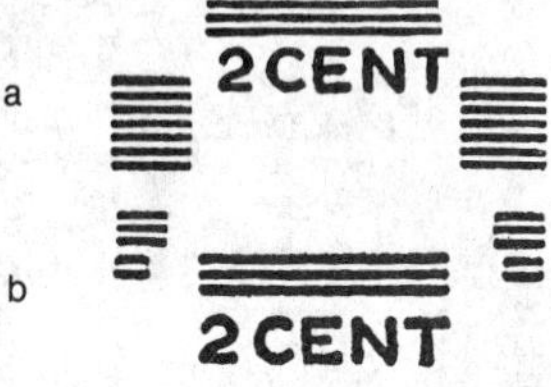

1934 **Typo.** *Perf. 12½x11½, 12½*

189 AP1(a) 2c on 10c 28 45
190 AP1(a) 2c on 20c 18 18
191 AP3(b) 2c on 30c 38 60
192 AP1(a) 42½c on 75c 4.25 28
193 AP1(a) 42½c on 1.50g 4.25 38
Nos. 189-193 (5) 9.34 1.89

Nos. 127-128 Surcharged with New Value in Red or Black

1937, Sept. *Perf. 12½*

194 A12 10c on 30c (R) 2.50 25
a. Double surcharge 675.00
195 A12 10c on 32½c (Bk) 2.75 28

Wilhelmina — A20

Perf. 12½x12

1938, Aug. 30 **Photo.** **Wmk. 202**

196 A20 2c dull pur 15 15
197 A20 10c car lake 15 15
198 A20 15c royal blue 1.25 75
199 A20 20c red orange 48 28

Issued in commemoration of the 40th anniversary of the reign of Queen Wilhelmina.

Types of 1933-37

1938-40 **Photo.** *Perf. 12½x12*

200 A17 1c lil gray ('39) 28 80
201 A17 2c plum ('39) 15 15
202 A17 2½c bis ('39) 48 48
203 A17 3c yel grn ('39) 1.50 1.25
205 A17 4c gray ol ('39) 1.50 1.25
206 A17 5c ultra ('39) 15 15
a. Perf. 12x12½ 1.25 15
207 A17 7½c vio ('39) 2.50 1.00
208 A18 10c ver ('39) 15 15
210 A18 15c ultra ('39) 15 15
211 A18 20c plum ('39) 18 15
a. Perf. 12x12½ 1.25 18
212 A18 25c bl grn ('39) 25.00 24.00
213 A18 30c lil gray ('39) 6.50 80
215 A18 35c vio ('39) 2.75 65
216 A18 40c dp yel grn ('40) 5.00 20

Perf. 12½

218 A19 50c lil gray ('40) 275.00
219 A19 60c ultra ('39) 10.50 1.25
220 A19 80c ver ('39) 62.50 26.00

221	A19	1g vio ('39)	27.50	85
223	A19	2g Prus grn	27.50	14.00
225	A19	5g yel brn	25.00	6.00
		Nos. 200-216,219-225 (19)	199.29	79.28

The note following No. 188 applies also to this issue.

The 50c was sold only at the philatelic window in Amsterdam.

War Dance of Nias Island — A23

Legong Dancer of Bali — A24

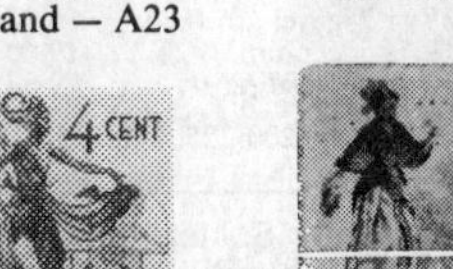
Wayang Wong Dancer of Java — A25

Padjoge Dancer, Southern Celebes — A26

Dyak Dancer of Borneo — A27

1941 Unwmk. *Perf. 12½*

228	A23	2½c rose vio	15	20
229	A24	3c green	16	48
230	A25	4c ol grn	15	45
231	A26	5c blue	15	15
232	A27	7½c dk vio	50	15
		Nos. 228-232 (5)	1.11	1.43

See Nos. 279-280, 293, N38.
Imperfs. are printers waste.

Queen Wilhelmina
A28 A28a

1941 *Perf. 12½*

Size: 18x22¾mm

234	A28	10c red org	15	15
235	A28	15c ultra	1.50	1.25
236	A28	17½c orange	40	60
237	A28	20c plum	21.00	35.00
238	A28	25c Prus grn	30.00	47.50
239	A28	30c ol bis	1.90	1.10
240	A28	35c pur	95.00	*325.00*
241	A28	40c yel grn	8.00	2.50

Perf. 13½

Size: 20½x26mm

242	A28	50c car lake	2.00	68
243	A28	60c ultra	1.65	58
244	A28	80c red org	1.90	95
245	A28	1g purple	2.00	28
246	A28	2g Prus grn	10.00	1.10
247	A28	5g bis, perf. 12½	250.00	*675.00*
248	A28	10g green	30.00	15.00

Size: 26x32mm

249	A28a	25g orange	175.00	125.00
		Nos. 234-249 (16)	630.50	*1,231.*

Nos. 242-246 come with pin-perf. 13½.

Catalogue values for unused stamps in this section, from this point to the end of the section, are for Never Hinged items.

Rice Fields — A29

Barge on Java Lake — A30

University of Medicine, Batavia — A31

Palms on Shore — A32

Plane over Bromo Volcano — A33

Queen Wilhelmina
A34 A35

1945, Oct. 1 Engr. *Perf. 12*

250	A29	1c green	22	18
251	A30	2c rose lilac	22	30
252	A31	2½c dull lilac	22	15
253	A32	5c blue	15	15
254	A33	7½c olive gray	48	15
255	A34	10c red brown	15	15
256	A34	15c dark blue	15	15
257	A34	17½c rose lake	15	20
258	A34	20c sepia	15	15
259	A34	30c slate gray	28	15
260	A35	60c gray black	65	15
261	A35	1g blue green	1.10	18
262	A35	2½g red orange	3.75	52
		Nos. 250-262 (13)	7.67	2.58

Railway Viaduct Near Soekaboemi A36

Dam and Power Station A37

Palm Tree and Menangkabau House — A38

Huts on Piles — A39

Buddhist Stupas — A40

Perf. 14½x14

1946 Typo. Wmk. 228

263	A36	1c dk grn	15	15
264	A37	2c blk brn	15	15
265	A38	2½c scarlet	18	15
266	A39	5c indigo	15	15
267	A40	7½c ultra	18	15
		Set value	65	52

Nos. 265, 267, 263 Surcharged

1947, Sept. 25

268	A38	3c on 2½c scar	15	15
269	A40	3c on 7½c ultra	15	15
a.		Double surcharge	150.00	150.00
270	A36	4c on 1c dk grn	15	18
		Set value		32

No. 219 Surcharged with New Value and Bars in Red

1947, Sept. 25 Wmk. 202 *Perf. 12½*

271	A19	45c on 60c ultra	1.25	1.25

Nos. 212, 218 and 220 Overprinted "1947" in Red or Black

1947, Sept. 25 *Perf. 12½x12, 12½*

272	A18	25c bl grn (R)	18	15
a.		Unwmkd.		125.00
273	A19	50c lil gray (R)	75	25
274	A19	80c vermilion	1.10	75
a.		Unwmkd.	500.00	140.00

Bar above "1947" on No. 274.

Nos. 174, 241, 247 and Type of 1941 Overprinted "1947" in Black

Perf. 12½, 12½x12 (2g)

1947, Sept. 25 Unwmk.

275	A18	12½c dp org	15	15
276	A28	40c yel grn	38	15
277	A28	2g Prus grn	3.75	50
278	A28	5g bister	11.00	7.50

The overprint is vertical on #276-278.

Dancer Types of 1941, 1945

1948, May 13 Litho. *Perf. 12½*

279	OS21	3c rose red	15	15
280	A24	4c dl ol grn	15	15
		Set value	24	24

Queen Wilhelmina — A41

1948 Photo. *Perf. 12½*

Size: 18x22mm

281	A41	15c red org	60	80
282	A41	20c brt bl	15	15
283	A41	25c dk grn	18	15
284	A41	40c dp yel grn	18	15
285	A41	45c plum	38	60
286	A41	50c red brn	22	15
287	A41	80c brt red	30	15

Perf. 13

Size: 20½x26mm

288	A41	1g dp vio	22	15
a.		Perf. 12½ x 12	75	38
289	A41	10g green	30.00	8.25
290	A41	25g orange	62.50	45.00
		Nos. 281-290 (10)	94.73	55.55

Wilhelmina Type of 1948
Inscribed: "1898 1948"

1948, Aug. 31 *Perf. 12½x12*

Size: 21x26½mm

291	A41	15c orange	28	20
292	A41	20c ultra	28	16

Reign of Queen Wilhelmina, 50th anniv.

Dancer Type of 1941

1948, Sept. Photo. *Perf. 12½*

293	A27	7½c olive bister	70	80

Juliana Type of Netherlands 1948

Perf. 14½x13½

1948, Sept. 25 Wmk. 202

293A	A75	15c red org	30	20
293B	A75	20c dp ultra	30	16

Investiture of Queen Juliana, Sept. 6, 1948.

Indonesia

Nos. 281 to 287 Overprinted in Black

INDONESIA

Two types of overprint:
I- Shiny ink, bar 1.8mm wide. By G. C. T. van Dorp & Co.
II- Dull ink, bar 2.2mm. By G. Kolff & Co.

1948 *Perf. 12½*

294	A41	15c red orange (I)	60	15
a.		Type II	55	15
295	A41	20c bright bl (I)	16	15
a.		Type II	16	15
296	A41	25c dark grn (I)	22	15
a.		Type II	15	15
297	A41	40c dp yel grn (I)	22	15
298	A41	45c plum ('49) (II)	80	70
299	A41	50c red brn ('49) (II)	18	15
300	A41	80c bright red (I)	65	15
a.		Type II	65	15

Nos. 288 to 290 Overprinted in Black

INDONESIA

Two or Three Bars

Perf. 12½x12

301	A41	1g dp vio	55	15
a.		Perf. 13	95	15

Perf. 13

302	A41	10g green	50.00	6.25
303	A41	25g orange	60.00	47.50
		Nos. 294-303 (10)	113.38	55.50

Same Overprint in Black on No. 262

1949 Engr. *Perf. 12*

Bars 28½mm long

304	A35	2½g red orange	14.00	5.50

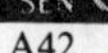
A42

Tjandi Puntadewa Temple Entrance, East Java — A43

Detail, Temple of the Dead, Bedjuning, Bali A44

Menangkabau House, Sumatra A45

Toradja House, Celebes — A46

Globe and Arms of Bern — A48

Designs: 5r, 10r, 25r, Temple entrance.

Perf. 12½, 11½

1949 Unwmk. Photo.

307	A42	1s gray	20	15
308	A42	2s claret	25	15
a.		Perf. 11½	5.00	*14.00*
309	A42	2½s ol brn	20	15
310	A42	3s rose pink	25	15
a.		Perf. 11½	1.10	75
311	A42	4s green	32	50
312	A42	5s blue	15	15
a.		Perf. 11½	1.00	20
313	A42	7½s dk grn	38	15
a.		Perf. 11½	1.00	75

314 A42 10s violet 16 15
a. Perf. 11½ 375.00
315 A42 12½s brt red 32 15
a. Perf. 11½ 4.00 4.00
316 A43 15s rose red 30 15
317 A43 20s gray blk 30 15
318 A43 25s ultra 30 15
319 A44 30s brt red 30 15
320 A44 40s gray grn 32 15
321 A44 45s claret 32 25
a. Perf. 12½ 2.75 50
322 A45 50s org brn 32 15
323 A45 60s brown 38 15
324 A45 80s scarlet 32 15
a. Perf. 12½ 4.00 25

Perf. 12½

325 A46 1r purple 22 15
326 A46 2r gray grn 2.00 15
327 A46 3r red vio 21.00 15
328 A46 5r dk brn 21.00 15
329 A46 10r gray 42.50 22
330 A46 25r org brn 22 25
Nos. 307-330 (24) 92.03
Set value 3.25

The 4s, 1r-25r are perf. 12½. Others come both 12½ and 11½.

1949 ***Perf. 12½***
331 A48 15s brt red 70 35
332 A48 25s ultra 70 25

75th anniv. of UPU.

See Indonesia (republic) for subsequent listings.

SEMI-POSTAL STAMPS

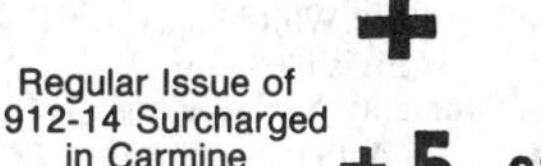

Regular Issue of 1912-14 Surcharged in Carmine

1915, June 10 Unwmk. ***Perf. 12½***
B1 A11 1c + 5c ol grn 3.25 3.25
B2 A11 5c + 5c rose 4.00 4.00
B3 A12 10c + 5c rose 6.25 6.25

Surtax for the Red Cross.

Bali Temple SP1

Watchtower SP2

Menangkabau Compound — SP3

Borobudur Temple, Java — SP4

Perf. 11½x11, 11x11½

1930, Dec. 1 **Photo.**
B4 SP1 2c (+ 1c) vio & brn 80 75
B5 SP2 5c (+ 2½c) dk grn & brn 3.25 2.25
B6 SP3 12½c (+ 2½c) dp red & brn 2.25 45
B7 SP4 15c (+ 5c) ultra & brn 4.25 5.00

Surtax for youth care.

Farmer and Carabao SP5

Designs: 5c, Fishermen. 12½c, Dancers. 15c, Musicians.

1931, Dec. 1 Engr. ***Perf. 12½***
B8 SP5 2c (+ 1c) olive bis 2.00 1.65
B9 SP5 5c (+ 2½c) bl grn 3.25 3.00
B10 SP5 12½c (+ 2½c) dp red 2.00 45
B11 SP5 15c (+ 5c) dl bl 8.00 6.75

The surtax was for the aid of the Leper Colony at Salatiga.

Weaving — SP9

Designs: 5c, Plaiting rattan. 12½c, Woman batik dyer. 15c, Coppersmith.

1932, Dec. 1 Photo. ***Perf. 12½***
B12 SP9 2c (+ 1c) dp vio & bis 40 38
B13 SP9 5c (+ 2½c) dp grn & bis 2.50 2.00
B14 SP9 12½c (+ 2½c) brt rose & bis 80 28
B15 SP9 15c (+ 5c) bl & bis 3.25 3.00

The surtax was donated to the Salvation Army.

Woman and Lotus — SP13

Designs: 5c, "The Light that Shows the Way." 12½c, YMCA emblem. 15c, Jobless man.

1933, Dec. 1 ***Perf. 12½***
B16 SP13 2c (+ 1c) red vio & ol bis 65 28
B17 SP13 5c (+ 2½c) grn & ol bis 2.25 1.90
B18 SP13 12½c (+ 2½c) ver & ol bis 2.50 28
B19 SP13 15c (+ 5c) bl & ol bis 2.75 2.00

The surtax was for the Amsterdam Young Men's Society for Relief of the Poor in Netherlands Indies.

Dowager Queen Emma SP17

A Pioneer at Work SP18

1934, Sept. 20 ***Perf. 13x14***
B20 SP17 12½c (+ 2½c) blk brn 1.25 45

Issued in memory of the late Dowager Queen Emma of Netherlands. The surtax was for the Anti-Tuberculosis Society.

1935 ***Perf. 12½***

Designs: 5c, Cavalryman rescuing wounded native. 12½c, Artilleryman under fire. 15c, Bugler.

B21 SP18 2c (+ 1c) plum & ol bis 1.25 1.00
B22 SP18 5c (+ 2½c) grn & ol bis 3.25 2.25
B23 SP18 12½c (+ 2½c) red org & ol bis 3.25 22
B24 SP18 15c (+ 5c) brt bl & ol bis 4.50 4.50

The surtax was for the Indian Committee of the Christian Military Association for the East and West Indies.

Child Welfare Work — SP22 Boy Scouts — SP23

1936, Dec. 1 **Size: 23x20mm**
B25 SP22 2c (+ 1c) plum 1.00 60

Size: 30x26½mm

B26 SP22 5c (+ 2½c) gray vio 1.25 1.10
B27 SP22 7½c (+ 2½c) dk vio 1.25 1.25
B28 SP22 12½c (+ 2½c) red org 1.25 28
B29 SP22 15c (+5c) brt bl 2.00 1.75
Nos. B25-B29 (5) 6.75 4.98

Surtax for Salvation Army.

1937, May 1
B30 SP23 7½c + 2½c dk ol brn 1.25 1.00
B31 SP23 12½c + 2½c rose car 1.25 50

Fifth Boy Scout World Jamboree, Vogelenzang, Netherlands, July 31-Aug. 13, 1937. Surtax for Netherlands Indies Scout association.

Sifting Rice — SP24

Designs: 3½c, Mother and children. 7½c, Plowing with carabao team. 10c, Carabao team and cart. 20c, Native couple.

1937, Dec. 1
B32 SP24 2c (+ 1c) dk brn & org 1.10 80
B33 SP24 3½c (+ 1½c) gray 1.10 80
B34 SP24 7½c (+ 2½c) Prus grn & org 1.25 95
B35 SP24 10c (+ 2½c) car & org 1.25 18
B36 SP24 20c (+ 5c) brt bl 1.25 1.10
Nos. B32-B36 (5) 5.95 3.83

Surtax for the Public Relief Fund for indigenous poor.

Modern Plane — SP28

Design: 20c, Plane nose facing left.

Wmk. 202

1938, Oct. 15 Photo. ***Perf. 12½***
B36A SP28 17½c (+5c) ol brn 85 85
B36B SP28 20c (+5c) slate 85 55

10th anniversary of the Dutch East Indies Royal Air Lines. (K. N. I. L. M.)

Surtax for the Aviation Fund in the Netherlands Indies.

Nun and Child SP29 SP30

Designs: 7½c, Nurse examining child's arm. 10c, Nurse bathing baby. 20c, Nun bandaging child's head.

1938, Dec. 1 Wmk. 202 ***Perf. 12½***
B37 SP29 2c (+ 1c) vio 60 45

Perf. 11½x12

B38 SP30 3½c (+ 1½c) brt grn 1.00 90

Perf. 12x11½

B39 SP30 7½c (+ 2½c) cop red 80 85
B40 SP30 10c (+ 2½c) ver 90 18
B41 SP30 20c (+ 5c) brt ultra 1.00 95
Nos. B37-B41 (5) 4.30 3.33

The surtax was for the Central Mission Bureau in Batavia.

Social Workers SP34

Indonesian Nurse Tending Patient SP35

European Nurse Tending Patient — SP36

Perf. 13x11½, 11½x13

1939, Dec. 1 **Photo.**
B42 SP34 2c (+ 1c) purple 22 16
B43 SP35 3½c (+ 1½c) bl grn & pale bl grn 32 22
B44 SP34 7½c (+ 2½c) cop brn 22 18
B45 SP35 10c (+ 2½c) scar & pink 1.40 80
B46 SP36 10c (+ 2½c) scar 1.40 80
B47 SP36 20c (+ 5c) dk bl 40 35
Nos. B42-B47 (6) 3.96 2.51

No. B44 shows native social workers.

Nos. B45 and B46 were issued se-tenant vertically and horizontally. The surtax was used for the Bureau of Social Service.

No. 174 Surcharged in Brown

10+5 ct

1940, Dec. 2 Unwmk. ***Perf. 12x12½***
B48 A18 10c + 5c on 12½c dp org 1.10 40

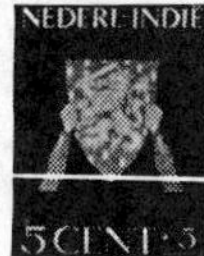

Netherlands Coat of Arms and Inscription "Netherlands Shall Rise Again" — SP37

1941, May 10 Typo. ***Perf. 12½***
B49 SP37 5c + 5c multi 15 15
B50 SP37 10c + 10c multi 22 15
B51 SP37 1g + 1g multi 9.00 6.75

The surtax was used to purchase fighter planes for Dutch pilots fighting with the Royal Air Force in Great Britain.

Doctor and Child — SP38

Designs: 3½c, Rice eater. 7½c, Nurse and patient. 10c, Nurse and children. 15c, Basket weaver.

1941, Sept. 22 **Photo.**
B52 SP38 2c (+ 1c) yel grn 60 55
B53 SP38 3½c (+ 1½c) vio brn 4.00 3.50
B54 SP38 7½c (+ 2½c) vio 3.25 2.75

B55	SP38	10c (+ 2½c) dk red	90	18
B56	SP38	15c (+ 5c) saph	9.50	6.00
		Nos. B52-B56 (5)	18.25	12.98

The surtax was used for various charities.

Catalogue values for unused stamps in this section, from this point to the end of the section, are for Never Hinged items.

Indonesia

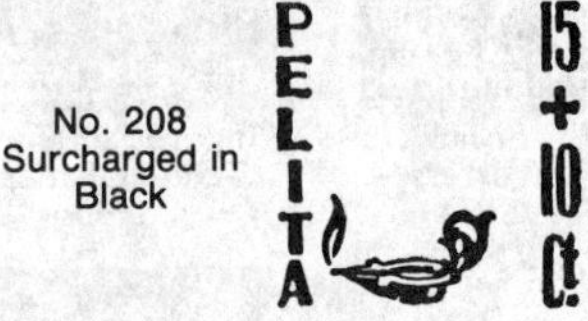

No. 208 Surcharged in Black

Perf. 12½x12

1948, Feb. 2 **Wmk. 202**

B57	A18	15c + 10c on 10c	15	15
a.		Inverted surcharge	210.00	210.00

The surtax was for war victims and other charitable purposes.

AIR POST STAMPS

Regular Issues of 1913-1923 Surcharged and New Values in Black or Blue

Perf. 12½, 11½

1928, Sept. 20 **Unwmk.**

C1	A12	10c on 12½c red	90	85
C2	A12	20c on 25c red vio	1.90	1.90
C3	A13	40c on 80c org	1.50	1.10
C4	A13	75c on 1g brn (Bl)	80	35
C5	A13	1½g on 2½g car	5.25	4.25
		Nos. C1-C5 (5)	10.35	8.45

On Nos. C4 and C5 there are stars over the original values and the airplane is of different shape. On No. C3 there are no bars under "OST".

Planes over Temple — AP1

1928, Dec. 1 **Litho.** ***Perf. 12½x11½***

C6	AP1	10c red vio	22	15
C7	AP1	20c brown	65	55
C8	AP1	40c rose	90	55
C9	AP1	75c green	1.65	14
C10	AP1	1.50g orange	3.25	45
		Nos. C6-C10 (5)	6.67	1.84

No. C8 Surcharged in Black or Green

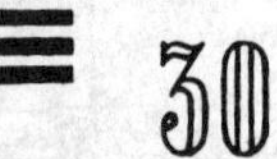

1930-32

C11	AP1	30c on 40c rose	75	15
C12	AP1	30c on 40c rose (G) ('32)	90	15

Pilot at Controls of Plane — AP2

1931, Apr. 1 **Photo.** ***Perf. 12½***

C13	AP2	1g bl & brn	10.00	12.00

Issued for the first air mail flight from Java to Australia.

Landscape and Garudas AP3

1931, May

C14	AP3	30c red vio	1.75	15
C15	AP3	4½g brt bl	7.25	2.75
C16	AP3	7½g yel grn	8.00	3.00

No. C10 Surcharged in Blue

1932, July 21 ***Perf. 12½x11½***

C17	AP1	50c on 1.50g org	2.50	38
a.		Inverted surcharge	*1,400.*	*1,600.*

Airplane AP4

1933, Oct. 18 **Photo.** ***Perf. 12½***

C18	AP4	30c deep blue	1.10	1.50

MARINE INSURANCE STAMPS

Floating Safe Attracting Gulls — MI1

Floating Safe with Night Flare — MI2

Artistic Fantasy of Floating Safe — MI3

Perf. 11½

1921, Nov. 1 **Unwmk.** **Engr.**

GY1	MI1	15c slate grn	1.90	*30.00*
GY2	MI1	60c rose	3.75	*45.00*
GY3	MI1	75c gray brn	3.75	*50.00*
GY4	MI2	1.50g dk bl	22.50	*225.00*
GY5	MI2	2.25g org brn	30.00	*300.00*
GY6	MI3	4½g black	57.50	*500.00*
GY7	MI3	7½g red	67.50	*575.00*
		Nos. GY1-GY7 (7)	186.90	*1,725.*

The indexes in each volume of the Scott Catalogue contain many listings which help to identify stamps.

POSTAGE DUE STAMPS

Aangebragt per Land-Mail.
Te betalen port duiten.
BATAVIA,

D1

Aangebragt per Land-Mail.
Te betalen port *f* koper.
BATAVIA, .

D2

1845-46 **Unwmk.** **Typeset** ***Imperf.***

Bluish Paper

J1	D1	black ('46)	*1,400.*	
J2	D2	black ('46)	*1,400.*	
a.		"Maill" instead of "Mail"	*3,200.*	

D3

Perf. 12½x12, 13x14, 10½x12

1874 **Typo.**

J3	D3	5c ocher	210.00	225.00
J4	D3	10c grn, *yel*	95.00	75.00
J5	D3	15c ocher, *org*	18.00	12.00
a.		Perf. 11½x12	35.00	30.00
J6	D3	20c grn, *bl*	30.00	7.50
a.		Perf. 11½x12	60.00	15.00

D4

D5

Type I - 34 loops. "T" of "Betalen" over center of loop, top branch of "E" of "Te" shorter than lower branch.

Type II - 33 loops. "T" of "Betalen" over center of two loops.

Type III - 32 loops. "T" of "Betalen" slightly to the left of loop, top branch of first "E" of "Betalen" shorter than lower branch.

Type IV - 37 loops and letters of "PORT" larger than in the other three types.

Value in Black

Perf. 11½x12, 12½, 12½x12, 13½

1882-88

Type III

J7	D4	2½c carmine	40	1.10
J8	D4	5c carmine	22	40
J9	D4	10c carmine	2.50	3.00
J10	D4	15c carmine	3.00	3.00
J11	D4	20c carmine	82.50	50
J12	D4	30c carmine	1.75	2.50
J13	D4	40c carmine	1.25	2.00
J14	D4	50c deep salmon	55	60
J15	D4	75c carmine	45	50

Type I

J7a	D4	2½c carmine	42	1.10
J8a	D4	5c carmine	25	45
J9a	D4	10c carmine	3.25	4.00
J10a	D4	15c carmine	3.25	3.50
J11a	D4	20c carmine	95.00	50
J12a	D4	30c carmine	3.25	4.00
J13a	D4	40c carmine	1.40	2.00
J14a	D4	50c deep salmon	65	60
J15a	D4	75c carmine	45	60

Type II

J7b	D4	2½c carmine	50	1.40
J8b	D4	5c carmine	28	50
J9b	D4	10c carmine	3.50	4.50
J10b	D4	15c carmine	3.75	4.00
J11b	D4	20c carmine	110.00	65
J12b	D4	30c carmine	7.00	7.50
J13b	D4	40c carmine	1.50	2.50
J14b	D4	50c deep salmon	75	75
J15b	D4	75c carmine	65	85

Type IV

J7c	D4	2½c carmine	2.25	3.00
J8c	D4	5c carmine	1.00	1.50
J9c	D4	10c carmine	20.00	24.00
J10c	D4	15c carmine	13.00	14.00
J11c	D4	20c carmine	200.00	5.00
J13c	D4	40c carmine	2.50	3.50
J14c	D4	50c deep salmon	9.00	14.00
J15c	D4	75c carmine	1.25	2.50

1892-95 ***Perf. 12½***

Type I

J16	D5	10c carmine	1.65	30
J17	D5	15c carmine ('95)	9.50	1.75
J18	D5	20c carmine	2.00	20

Type III

J16a	D5	10c dull red	2.75	1.75
J18a	D5	20c dull red	3.75	1.40

Type II

J16b	D5	10c dull red	13.00	13.00
J18b	D5	20c dull red	18.00	6.50

1906-09

Type I

J19	D5	2½c carmine ('08)	48	30
J20	D5	5c carmine ('09)	2.00	15
J21	D5	30c carmine	17.50	5.75
J22	D5	40c carmine ('09)	12.50	1.50
J23	D5	50c carmine ('09)	8.50	90
J24	D5	75c carmine ('09)	16.00	4.00

Value in Color of Stamp

1913-39 ***Perf. 12½***

J25	D5	1c salmon ('39)	15	*1.25*
J26	D5	2½c salmon	15	15
J27	D5	3½c salmon ('39)	15	*1.25*
J28	D5	5c salmon	15	15
J29	D5	7½c salmon ('22)	15	15
J30	D5	10c salmon	15	15
J31	D5	12½c salmon ('22)	2.75	15
J32	D5	15c salmon	2.75	15
J33	D5	20c salmon	16	15
J34	D5	25c salmon ('22)	18	15
J35	D5	30c salmon	20	20
J36	D5	37½c salmon ('30)	18.00	19.00
J37	D5	40c salmon	20	15
J38	D5	50c salmon	1.40	15
J39	D5	75c salmon	2.50	18
		Nos. J25-J39 (15)	29.04	23.38

Thick White Paper
Invisible Gum
Numerals Slightly Larger

1941 **Litho.** ***Perf. 12½***

J25a	D5	1c light red	60	*2.00*
J28a	D5	5c light red	65	1.00
J30a	D5	10c light red	10.50	10.00
J32a	D5	15c light red	1.00	1.00
J33a	D5	20c light red	80	80
J35a	D5	30c light red	1.25	1.00
J37a	D5	40c light red	1.00	80
		Nos. J25a-J37a (7)	15.80	16.60

No. J36 Surcharged with New Value

1937, Oct. 1 **Unwmk.** ***Perf. 12½***

J40	D5	20c on 37½c salmon	24	30

D6

D7

1939-40

J41	D6	1g salmon	4.50	6.50
J42	D6	1g blue ('40)	20	*3.00*
a.		1g light blue, thick paper, invisible gum	65	80

Catalogue values for unused stamps in this section, from this point to the end of the section, are for Never Hinged items.

TE BETALEN

PORT

Nos. 233, 237 and 241 Surcharged or Overprinted in Black

1946, Mar. 11 **Unwmk.** ***Perf. 12½***

J43	A28	2½c on 10c red org	60	55
J44	A28	10c red org	1.25	1.10
J45	A28	20c plum	6.25	3.50
J46	A28	40c yel grn	60.00	45.00

Perf. 14½x14

1946, Aug. 14 **Wmk. 228** **Typo.**

J47	D7	1c purple	1.00	1.40
J48	D7	2½c brn org	3.50	2.00
J49	D7	3½c ultra	1.00	1.40
J50	D7	5c red org	1.00	1.40
J51	D7	7½c Prus grn	1.00	1.40
J52	D7	10c dp mag	1.00	1.40
J53	D7	20c lt ultra	1.00	1.40
J54	D7	25c olive	1.50	2.00
J55	D7	30c red brn	1.50	2.00
J56	D7	40c yel grn	2.25	1.50

J57	D7	50c yellow	2.25	1.50
J58	D7	75c aqua	2.25	1.50
J59	D7	100c apple green	2.25	1.50
		Nos. J47-J59 (13)	21.50	20.40

1948 Unwmk. *Perf. 12½*

J59A	D7	2½c brn org	75	1.50

OFFICIAL STAMPS

Regular Issues of 1883-1909 Overprinted

1911, Oct. 1 Unwmk. *Perf. 12½*

O1	A6	½c violet	15	30
O2	A6	1c ol grn	15	15
O3	A6	2c yel brn	15	15
O4	A3	2½c yellow	55	55
O5	A6	2½c bl grn	1.00	1.10
O6	A6	3c orange	28	28
O7	A6	4c ultra	16	15
O8	A6	5c rose red	55	55
b.		Double overprint		*300.00*
O9	A6	7½c gray	2.50	2.75
O10	A9	10c slate	15	15
O11	A9	12½c dp bl	2.00	2.25
O12	A9	15c chocolate	48	48
a.		Overprinted with two bars	27.50	
b.		As "a," "Dienst," inverted	52.50	
O13	A9	17½c bister	2.50	2.25
O14	A9	20c ol grn	48	48
O15	A9	22½c brn & ol grn	3.25	2.75
O16	A9	25c violet	2.00	1.75
O17	A9	30c org brn	65	48
O18	A9	50c red brn	11.00	7.00
O19	A10	1g dl lil	2.00	1.25
O20	A10	2½g slate bl	27.50	32.50
		Nos. O1-O20 (20)	57.50	

The overprint reads diagonally downward on Nos. O1-O3 and O5-O9.

Overprint Inverted

O1a	A6	½c	42.50	*130.00*
O2a	A6	1c	3.00	*19.00*
O3a	A6	2c	3.00	*20.00*
O5a	A6	2½c	7.75	*30.00*
O6a	A6	3c	115.00	*40.00*
O8a	A6	5c	3.00	*20.00*
O10a	A9	10c	3.00	*7.00*
O11a	A9	12½c	32.50	*55.00*
O14a	A9	20c	175.00	70.00
O16a	A9	25c	*1,250.*	*850.00*
O17a	A9	30c	225.00	140.00
O18a	A9	50c	32.50	32.50
O19a	A10	1g	*525.00*	*850.00*
O20a	A10	2½g	225.00	*625.00*

Regular Issue of 1892-1894 Overprinted

1911, Oct. 1

O21	A4	10c org brn	1.00	60
O22	A4	12½c gray	2.25	4.50
O23	A4	15c bister	2.25	2.25
O24	A4	20c blue	1.50	80
O25	A4	25c lilac	8.00	8.00
O26	A4	50c carmine	1.00	80
O27	A4	2.50g org brn & bl	45.00	45.00
		Nos. O21-O27 (7)	61.00	61.95

Inverted Overprints

O21a	A4	10c	9.25	*32.50*
O22a	A4	12½c	275.00	275.00
O23a	A4	15c	300.00	300.00
O24a	A4	20c	80.00	90.00
O25a	A4	25c	425.00	425.00
O26a	A4	50c	9.25	*85.00*
O27a	A4	2.50g	500.00	800.00

OCCUPATION STAMPS

Issued under Japanese Occupation

During the Japanese occupation of the Netherlands Indies, 1942-45, the occupation forces applied a great variety of overprints to supplies of Netherlands Indies stamps of 1933-42. A few typical examples are shown above.

Most of these overprinted stamps were for use in limited areas, such as Java, Sumatra, Bangka and Billiton, etc. The anchor overprints were applied by the Japanese naval authorities for areas under their control.

For a time, stamps of Straits Settlements and some of the Malayan states, with Japanese overprints, were used in Sumatra and the Riouw archipelago. Stamps of Japan without overprint were also used in the Netherlands Indies during the occupation.

For Use in Java and Sumatra

100 Sen (Cents) = 1 Rupee (Gulden)

Globe Showing Japanese Empire — OS1

Farmer Plowing Rice Field — OS2

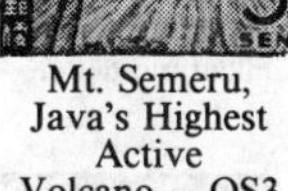

Mt. Semeru, Java's Highest Active Volcano — OS3

Bantam Bay, Northwest Java — OS4

Values in Sen

1943 Unwmk. Litho. *Perf. 12½*

N1	OS1	2s red brn	1.25	4.25
N2	OS2	3½s carmine	1.25	1.25
N3	OS3	5s green	1.25	1.25
N4	OS4	10s lt bl	14.00	2.50

Issued to mark the anniversary of Japan's "Victory" in Java.

For Use in Java (also Sumatra, Borneo and Malaya)

Javanese Dancer — OS5

Javanese Puppet — OS6

Buddha Statue, Borobudur — OS7

Map of Java — OS8

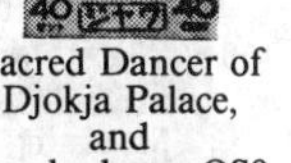

Sacred Dancer of Djokja Palace, and Borobudur — OS9

Bird of Vishnu, Map of Java and Mt. Semeru — OS10

Plowing with Carabao — OS11

Terraced Rice Fields — OS12

Values in Cents, Sen or Rupees

1943-44 Unwmk. *Perf. 12½*

N5	OS5	3½c rose red	50	55
N6	OS6	5s yel grn	50	55
N7	OS7	10c dk bl	50	38
N8	OS8	20c gray ol	65	90
N9	OS9	40c rose lil	1.65	2.25
N10	OS10	60c red org	2.25	1.10
N11	OS11	80s fawn ('44)	5.00	3.75
N12	OS12	1r vio ('44)	19.00	7.75
		Nos. N5-N12 (8)	30.05	17.23

Indies Soldier — OS13

1943

N13	OS13	3½c rose	9.00	9.25
N14	OS13	10c blue	45.00	5.75

Issued to commemorate reaching the postal savings goal of 5,000,000 gulden.

For Use in Sumatra

Batta Tribal House — OS14

Menangkabau House — OS15

Plowing with Carabao — OS16

Nias Island Scene — OS17

Carabao Canyon — OS18

1943 Unwmk. *Perf. 12½*

N15	OS14	1c ol grn	38	28
N16	OS14	2c brt yel brn	38	28
N17	OS14	3c bluish grn	38	28
N18	OS15	3½c rose red	1.65	28
N19	OS15	4c ultra	1.90	55
N20	OS15	5c red org	52	28
N21	OS16	10c bl gray	52	28
N22	OS16	20c org brn	75	40
N23	OS17	30c red vio	75	80
N24	OS17	40c dl brn	6.75	2.50
N25	OS18	50c bis brn	6.75	2.50
N26	OS18	1r lt bl vio	35.00	10.50
		Nos. N15-N26 (12)	55.73	18.93

For Use in the Lesser Sunda Islands, Molucca Archipelago and Districts of Celebes and South Borneo Controlled by the Japanese Navy

Japanese Flag, Island Scene — OS19

Mt. Fuji, Kite, Flag, Map of East Indies — OS20

Values in Cents and Gulden

1943 Wmk. 257 Typo. *Perf. 13*

N27	OS19	2c brown	35	*15.00*
N28	OS19	3c yel grn	35	*15.00*
N29	OS19	3½c brn org	3.00	*15.00*
N30	OS19	5c blue	35	*15.00*
N31	OS19	10c carmine	35	*15.00*
N32	OS19	15c ultra	52	*15.00*
N33	OS19	20c dl vio	70	*15.00*

Engr.

N34	OS20	25c orange	5.00	*15.00*
N35	OS20	30c blue	7.00	*10.00*
N36	OS20	50c sl grn	8.50	*25.00*
N37	OS20	1g brn lil	42.50	*45.00*
		Nos. N27-N37 (11)	68.62	*200.00*

Issued under Nationalist Occupation

Menari Dancer of Amboina — OS21

Perf. 12½

1945, Aug. Photo. Unwmk.

N38	OS21	2c carmine	15	35

This stamp was prepared in 1941 or 1942 by Netherlands Indies authorities as an addition to the 1941 "dancers set," but was issued in 1945 by the Nationalists (Indonesian Republic). It was not recognized by the Dutch. Exists imperforate.

NETHERLANDS NEW GUINEA

(Dutch New Guinea)

LOCATION — Western half of New Guinea, southwest Pacific Ocean
GOVT. — Former Overseas Territory of the Netherlands
AREA — 151,789 sq. mi.
POP. — 730,000 (est. 1958)
CAPITAL — Hollandia

Netherlands New Guinea came under temporary United Nations administration Oct. 1, 1962, when stamps of this territory overprinted "UNTEA" were introduced to replace issues of Netherlands New Guinea. See West New Guinea (West Irian) in Vol. IV.

100 Cents = 1 Gulden

Catalogue values for all unused stamps in this country are for Never Hinged items.

A1

Queen Juliana
A2 A3

Perf. 12½x13½

1950-52 Unwmk. Photo.

No.	Type	Description	Unused	Used
1	A1	1c slate bl	15	15
2	A1	2c deep org	15	15
3	A1	2½c olive brn	15	15
4	A1	3c deep plum	1.50	1.10
5	A1	4c blue grn	1.50	1.00
6	A1	5c ultra	3.00	15
7	A1	7½c org brown	32	15
8	A1	10c purple	1.65	15
9	A1	12½c crimson	1.65	1.25

Perf. 13½x12½

No.	Type	Description	Unused	Used
10	A2	15c brown org	1.10	50
11	A2	20c blue	32	15
12	A2	25c org red	32	15
13	A2	30c deep bl ('52)	3.25	24
14	A2	40c blue grn	65	15
15	A2	45c brown ('52)	3.00	50
16	A2	50c deep org	65	15
17	A2	55c brn blk ('52)	4.50	50
18	A2	80c purple	5.75	2.75

Engr. *Perf. 12½x12*

No.	Type	Description	Unused	Used
19	A3	1g red	10.00	15
20	A3	2g yel brn ('52)	8.25	1.10
21	A3	5g dk ol grn	8.25	90
		Nos. 1-21 (21)	56.11	11.49

For surcharges see Nos. B1-B3.

Bird of Paradise
A4

Queen Victoria Crowned Pigeon
A5

Queen Juliana — A6

Designs: 10c, 15c and 20c, Bird of Paradise with raised wings.

Photo.; Litho. (Nos. 24, 26, 28)

1954-60 *Perf. 12½x12*

No.	Type	Description	Unused	Used
22	A4	1c ver & yel ('58)	15	15
23	A4	5c choc & yel	15	15
24	A5	7c org red, bl & brn vio ('59)	15	18
25	A4	10c aqua & red brn	15	15
26	A5	12c grn, bl & brn vio ('59)	15	18
27	A4	15c dp yel & red brn	15	15
28	A5	17c brn vio & bl ('59)	15	15
29	A4	20c lt bl grn & red brn ('56)	50	30
30	A6	25c red	15	15
31	A6	30c deep blue	15	15
32	A6	40c dp org ('60)	1.25	1.40
33	A6	45c dk olive ('58)	42	65
34	A6	55c dk blue grn	30	15
35	A6	80c dl gray vio	55	20
36	A6	85c dk vio brn ('56)	65	30
37	A6	1g plum ('59)	3.25	1.50
		Nos. 22-37 (16)	8.27	5.91

Stamps overprinted "UNTEA" are listed under West New Guinea in Vol. IV.
For surcharges see Nos. B4-B6.

The Scott Catalogue value is a retail price, what you could expect to pay for the stamp in a grade of Fine-Very Fine. The value listed is a reference which reflects recent actual dealer selling price.

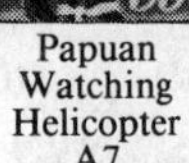

Papuan Watching Helicopter
A7

Mourning Woman
A8

1959, Apr. 10 Photo. *Perf. 11½x11*

No.	Type	Description	Unused	Used
38	A7	55c red brown & blue	85	65

1959 expedition to the Star Mountains of New Guinea.

1960, Apr. 7 Unwmk. *Perf. 13x14*

No.	Type	Description	Unused	Used
39	A8	25c blue	38	38
40	A8	30c yellow bister	38	50

World Refugee Year, July 1, 1959-June 30, 1960.

Council Building
A9

1961 Litho. *Perf. 11x11½*

No.	Type	Description	Unused	Used
41	A9	25c bluish green	18	25
42	A9	30c rose	18	25

Inauguration of the New Council.

School Children Crossing Street — A10

Design: 30c, Men looking at traffic sign.

1962, Mar. 16 Photo. *Perf. 14x13*

No.	Type	Description	Unused	Used
43	A10	25c dp bl & red	18	25
44	A10	30c brt grn & red	18	25

Need for road safety.

Silver Wedding Issue

Type of Netherlands, 1962

1962, Apr. 28 Unwmk. *Perf. 14x13*

No.	Type	Description	Unused	Used
45	A92	55c olive brown	25	30

Tropical Beach
A11

Design: 30c, Palm trees on beach.

1962, July 18 *Perf. 14x13*

No.	Type	Description	Unused	Used
46	A11	25c multi	18	28
47	A11	30c multi	18	28

5th So. Pacific Conf., Pago Pago, July 1962.

SEMI-POSTAL STAMPS

Regular Issue of 1950-52 Surcharged in Black

hulp
nederland
1953
+ 5 ct

Perf. 13½x12½, 12½x13½

1953, Feb. 9 Unwmk.

No.	Type	Description	Unused	Used
B1	A1	5c + 5c ultra	6.50	6.50
B2	A2	15c + 10c brn org	6.50	6.50
B3	A2	25c + 10c org red	6.50	6.50

The tax was for flood relief work in the Netherlands.

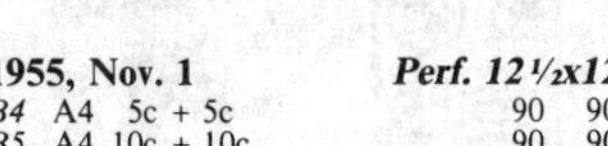

Nos. 23, 25, 27 Surcharged in Red

+ 5

1955, Nov. 1 *Perf. 12½x12*

No.	Type	Description	Unused	Used
B4	A4	5c + 5c	90	90
B5	A4	10c + 10c	90	90
B6	A4	15c + 10c	90	90

The surtax was for the Red Cross.

Leprosarium
SP1

Papuan Girl and Beach Scene
SP2

Design: 10c+5c, 30c+10c, Young Papuan and huts.

Perf. 12x12½

1956, Dec. 15 Unwmk. Photo.

No.	Type	Description	Unused	Used
B7	SP1	5c + 5c dk slate grn	75	75
B8	SP1	10c + 5c brn violet	75	75
B9	SP1	25c + 10c brt blue	75	75
B10	SP1	30c + 10c ocher	75	75

The surtax was for the fight against leprosy.

1957, Oct. 1 *Perf. 12½x12*

Design: 10c+5c, 30c+10c, Papuan boy and pile dwelling.

No.	Type	Description	Unused	Used
B11	SP2	5c + 5c maroon	65	65
B12	SP2	10c + 5c slate grn	65	65
B13	SP2	25c + 10c brown	65	65
B14	SP2	30c + 10c dark blue	65	65

The surtax was to fight infant mortality.

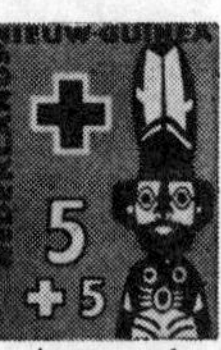

Ancestral Image, North Coast New Guinea
SP3

Bignonia
SP4

Design: 10c+5c, 30c+10c, Bowl in form of human figure, Asmat-Papua.

1958, Oct. 1 Litho. *Perf. 12½x12*

No.	Type	Description	Unused	Used
B15	SP3	5c + 5c bl, blk & red	75	75
B16	SP3	10c + 5c rose lake, blk, red & yel	75	75
B17	SP3	25c + 10c bl grn, blk & red	75	75
B18	SP3	30c + 10c ol gray, blk, red & yel	75	75

The surtax was for the Red Cross.

1959, Nov. 16 Photo. *Perf. 12½x13*

Flowers: 10c+5c, Orchid. 25c+10c, Rhododendron. 30c+10c, Gesneriaceа.

No.	Type	Description	Unused	Used
B19	SP4	5c + 5c car rose & grn	48	35
B20	SP4	10c + 5c ol, yel & lil	48	35
B21	SP4	25c + 10c red, org & grn	48	45
B22	SP4	30c + 10c vio & grn	48	45

Birdwing — SP5

Various Butterflies.

Perf. 13x12½

1960, Sept. 1 Unwmk. Litho.

No.	Type	Description	Unused	Used
B23	SP5	5c + 5c lt bl, blk, emer & yel	65	65
B24	SP5	10c + 5c sal, blk & bl	65	65
B25	SP5	25c + 10c yel, blk & org red	75	70
B26	SP5	30c + 10c lt grn, brn & yel	75	70

Surtax for social care.

Rhinoceros Beetle and Coconut Palm Leaf — SP6

Beetles and leaves of host plants: 10c+5c, Ectocemus 10-maculatus Montri, a primitive weevil. 25c+10c, Stag beetle. 30c+10c, Tortoise beetle.

1961, Sept. 15 *Perf. 13x12½*

Beetles in Natural Colors

No.	Type	Description	Unused	Used
B27	SP6	5c + 5c deep org	20	22
B28	SP6	10c + 5c lt ultra	20	22
B29	SP6	25c + 10c citron	25	28
B30	SP6	30c + 10c green	32	35

Surtax for social care.

Crab — SP7

Designs: 10c+5c, Lobster, vert. 25c+10c, Spiny lobster, vert. 30c+10c, Shrimp.

Perf. 14x13, 13x14

1962, Sept. 17 Unwmk.

No.	Type	Description	Unused	Used
B31	SP7	5c + 5c red, grn, brn & yel	15	15
B32	SP7	10c + 5c Prus bl & yel	15	15
B33	SP7	25c + 10c multicolored	18	18
B34	SP7	30c + 10c bl, org red & yel	18	22

The surtax on Nos. B19-B34 went to various social works organizations.

POSTAGE DUE STAMPS

Type of Netherlands Antilles, 1953

Perf. 13½x12½

1957 Photo. Unwmk.

No.	Type	Description	Unused	Used
J1	D3	1c vermilion	15	15
J2	D3	5c vermilion	38	75
J3	D3	10c vermilion	1.10	1.50
J4	D3	25c vermilion	1.65	55
J5	D3	40c vermilion	1.65	65
J6	D3	1g blue	2.00	2.25
		Nos. J1-J6 (6)	6.93	5.85

NEW CALEDONIA

LOCATION — Island in the South Pacific Ocean, east of Queensland, Australia
GOVT. — French Overseas Territory
AREA — 7,375 sq. mi.
POP. — 147,200 (est. 1984)
CAPITAL — Noumea

Dependencies of New Caledonia are the Loyalty Islands, Isle of Pines, Huon Islands and Chesterfield Islands.

100 Centimes = 1 Franc

Catalogue values for unused stamps in this country are for Never Hinged items, beginning with Scott 252 in the regular postage section, Scott B13 in the semi-postal section, Scott C14 in the airpost section, Scott J32 in the postage due section, and Scott O1 in the official section.

Napoleon III — A1

1859 Unwmk. Litho. *Imperf.*
Without Gum

1 A1 10c black 140.00

Fifty varieties. Counterfeits abound. See No. 315.

Type of French Colonies, 1877 Surcharged in Black:

NCE 5 — Nos. 2-5

N C E 5 — Nos. 6-7

1881-83

2 A8 5c on 40c red, *straw* ('82) 225.00 200.00
a. Inverted surcharge 550.00 550.00
3 A8 05c on 40c red, *straw* ('83) 14.00 14.00
4 A8 25c on 35c dp vio, *yel* 85.00 90.00
a. Inverted surcharge 400.00 400.00
5 A8 25c on 75c rose car, *rose* ('82) 165.00 165.00
a. Inverted surcharge 400.00 400.00

1883-84

6 A8 5c on 40c red, *straw* ('84) 9.50 9.50
a. Inverted surcharge 10.00 10.00
7 A8 5c on 75c rose car, *rose* ('83) 19.00 19.00
a. Inverted surcharge 22.50 22.50

In type "a" surcharge, the narrower-spaced letters measure 14½mm, and an early printing of No. 4 measures 13½mm. Type "b" letters measure 18mm.

French Colonies No. 59 Surcharged in Black:

N.C.E. 5c. — No. 8

N·C·E· 5c. — Nos. 9-10

1886 *Perf. 14x13½*

8 A9 5c on 1fr brnz grn, *straw* 8.75 8.75
a. Inverted surcharge 12.00 12.00
9 A9 5c on 1fr brnz grn, *straw* 6.75 6.75
b. Inverted surcharge 20.00 20.00

French Colonies No. 29 Surcharged
Imperf

10 A8 5c on 1fr brnz grn, *straw* 7,000. 7,000.

Types of French Colonies, 1877-86, Surcharged in Black:

N.-C. E. 10 c. — Nos. 11, 13

N.-C. E. 10 centimes — No. 12

1891-92 *Imperf.*

11 A8 10c on 40c red, *straw* ('92) 13.00 12.00
a. Inverted surcharge 16.00 16.00
b. Double surcharge 30.00 30.00
c. No period after "10c" 13.00 12.00

Perf. 14x13½

12 A9 10c on 30c brn, *bis* 6.50 6.50
a. Inverted surcharge 7.50 7.50
b. Double surcharge 19.00 19.00
c. Double surcharge, inverted 19.00 19.00
13 A9 10c on 40c red, *straw* ('92) 6.50 6.50
a. Inverted surcharge 7.50 7.50
b. No period after "10c" 6.50 6.50
c. Double surcharge 19.00 19.00

Variety "double surcharge, one inverted" exists on Nos. 11-13. Value same as for "double surcharge."

Types of French Colonies, 1877-86, Handstamped in Black

g

1892 *Imperf.*

16 A8 20c red, *grn* 175.00 175.00
17 A8 35c vio, *org* 30.00 30.00
18 A8 40c red, *straw*
19 A8 1fr brnz grn, *straw* 130.00 130.00

The 1c, 2c, 4c and 75c of type A8 are believed not to have been officially made or actually used.

1892 *Perf. 14x13½*

23 A9 5c grn, *grnsh* 5.75 5.25
24 A9 10c blk, *lavender* 50.00 30.00
25 A9 15c blue 37.50 19.00
26 A9 20c red, *grn* 37.50 24.00
27 A9 25c yel, *straw* 7.50 6.50
28 A9 25c blk, *rose* 37.50 6.50
29 A9 30c brn, *bis* 30.00 25.00
30 A9 35c vio, *org* 100.00 82.50
32 A9 75c car, *rose* 82.50 60.00
33 A9 1fr brnz grn, *straw* 67.50 57.50

The note following No. 19 also applies to the 1c, 2c, 4c and 40c of type A9.

Surcharged in Blue or Black

h

1892-93 *Imperf.*

34 A8 10c on 1fr brnz grn, *straw* (Bl) 2,400. 2,000.

Perf. 14x13½

35 A9 5c on 20c red, *grn* (Bk) 7.50 5.75
a. Inverted surcharge 50.00 47.50
b. Double surcharge inverted
36 A9 5c on 75c car, *rose* (Bk) 5.75 3.75
a. Inverted surcharge 50.00 47.50
37 A9 5c on 75c car, *rose* (Bl) 5.25 3.50
a. Inverted surcharge 50.00 47.50
38 A9 10c on 1fr brnz grn, *straw* (Bk) 5.25 3.75
a. Inverted surcharge 250.00 225.00
39 A9 10c on 1fr brnz grn, *straw* (Bl) 6.50 5.75
a. Inverted surcharge 50.00 47.50

Navigation and Commerce — A12

1892-1904 Typo. *Perf. 14x13½*
Name of Colony in Blue or Carmine

40 A12 1c blk, *blue* 35 28
41 A12 2c brn, *buff* 48 40
42 A12 4c claret, *lav* 85 70
43 A12 5c grn, *grnsh* 1.00 60
44 A12 5c yel grn ('00) 70 65
45 A12 10c blk, *lavender* 3.00 1.75
46 A12 10c rose red ('00) 3.50 70
47 A12 15c bl, quadrille paper 9.25 70
48 A12 15c gray ('00) 5.25 65
49 A12 20c red, *grn* 7.50 5.00
50 A12 25c blk, *rose* 8.50 3.00
51 A12 25c blue ('00) 7.00 4.00
52 A12 30c brn, *bis* 8.50 4.75
53 A12 40c red, *straw* 8.50 6.50
54 A12 50c car, *rose* 30.00 13.00
55 A12 50c brn, *az* (name in car) ('00) 47.50 40.00
56 A12 50c brn, *az* (name in bl) ('04) 30.00 25.00
57 A12 75c vio, *org* 14.00 10.00
58 A12 1fr brnz grn, *straw* 15.00 11.00
Nos. 40-58 (19) 200.88 128.68

Perf. 13½x14 stamps are counterfeits.

For overprints and surcharges see Nos. 59-87, 117-121.

Nos. 41-42, 52, 57-58, 53 Surcharged in Black:

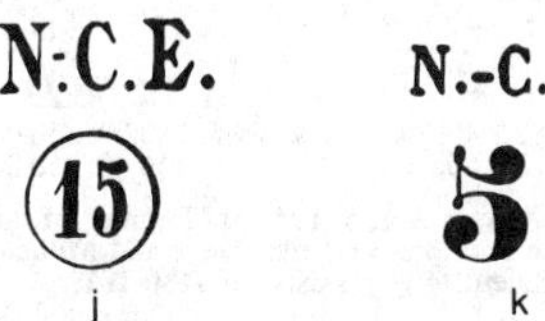

j k

1900-01

59 A12 (h) 5c on 2c ('01) 3.50 3.00
a. Double surcharge 52.50 52.50
b. Inverted surcharge 52.50 52.50
60 A12 (h) 5c on 4c 75 75
a. Inverted surcharge 30.00 30.00
b. Double surcharge 30.00 30.00
61 A12 (j) 15c on 30c 75 75
a. Inverted surcharge 25.00 25.00
b. Double surcharge 25.00 25.00
62 A12 (j) 15c on 75c ('01) 3.00 2.00
a. Pair, one without surcharge
b. Inverted surcharge 52.50 52.50
c. Double surcharge 52.50 52.50
63 A12 (j) 15c on 1fr ('01) 4.50 4.25
a. Double surcharge 65.00 65.00
b. Inverted surcharge 65.00 65.00
Nos. 59-63 (5) 12.50 10.75

1902

64 A12 (k) 5c on 30c 4.00 3.50
a. Inverted surcharge 16.00 16.00
65 A12 (k) 15c on 40c 3.25 3.25
a. Inverted surcharge 16.00 16.00

Jubilee Issue

Samps of 1892-1900 Overprinted in Blue, Red, Black or Gold

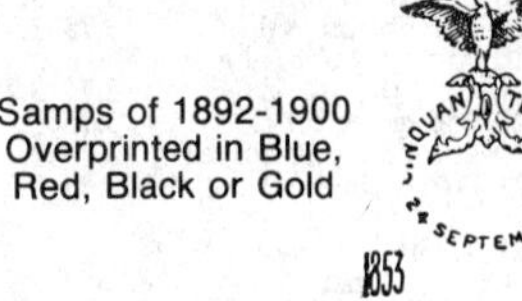

1903

66 A12 1c blk, *lil bl* (Bl) 75 70
a. Inverted overprint 90.00 90.00
67 A12 2c brn, *buff* (Bl) 2.25 1.40
68 A12 4c cl, *lav* (Bl) 2.75 1.40
a. Double overprint 150.00 150.00
69 A12 5c dk grn, *grnsh* (R) 2.75 1.50
70 A12 5c yel grn (R) 3.75 3.00
71 A12 10c blk, *lav* (R) 7.25 5.00
72 A12 10c blk, *lav* (double G & Bk) 4.50 4.50
73 A12 15c gray (R) 4.75 2.75
74 A12 20c red, *grn* (Bl) 8.50 5.75
75 A12 25c blk, *rose* (Bl) 8.50 6.25
a. Double overprint
76 A12 30c brn, *bis* (R) 11.00 7.25
77 A12 40c red, *straw* (Bl) 15.00 9.50
78 A12 50c car, *rose* (Bl) 25.00 11.00
a. Pair, one without overprint
79 A12 75c vio, *org* (Bk) 37.50 27.50
a. Dbl. ovpt. in blk and red 250.00 250.00
80 A12 1fr brnz grn, *straw* (Bl) 45.00 37.50
a. Dbl. ovpt., one in red 250.00 250.00
Nos. 66-80 (15) 179.25 125.00

With Additional Surcharge of New Value in Blue

81 A12 1c on 2c #67 42 42
a. Numeral double 40.00 40.00
b. Numeral only
82 A12 2c on 4c #68 90 90
83 A12 4c on 5c #69 90 90
a. Small "4" 375.00 375.00
84 A12 4c on 5c #70 1.40 1.40
a. Pair, one without numeral
85 A12 10c on 15c #73 1.40 1.40
86 A12 15c on 20c #74 1.40 1.40
87 A12 20c on 25c #75 2.50 2.50
Nos. 81-87 (7) 8.92 8.92

50 years of French occupation.

Surcharge on Nos. 81-83, 85-86 is horizontal, reading down.

There are three types of numeral on No. 83. The numeral on No. 84 is identical with that of No. 83a except that its position is upright.

Nos. 66-87 are known with "I" of "TENAIRE" missing.

Kagu A16

Landscape A17

Ship — A18

1905-28 Typo. *Perf. 14x13½*

88 A16 1c blk, *green* 15 15
89 A16 2c red brn 15 15
90 A16 4c bl, *org* 15 15
91 A16 5c pale grn 15 15
92 A16 5c dl bl ('21) 15 15
93 A16 10c carmine 48 40
94 A16 10c grn ('21) 30 30
95 A16 10c red, *pink* ('25) 15 15
96 A16 15c violet 24 15
97 A17 20c brown 15 15
98 A17 25c bl, *grn* 15 15
99 A17 25c red, *yel* ('21) 15 15
100 A17 30c brn, *org* 15 15
101 A17 30c dp rose ('21) 60 60
102 A17 30c org ('25) 15 15
103 A17 35c blk, *yellow* 15 15
104 A17 40c car, *grn* 48 35
105 A17 45c vio brn, *lav* 30 30
106 A17 50c car, *org* 95 60
107 A17 50c dk bl ('21) 55 55
108 A17 50c gray ('25) 28 28
109 A17 65c dp bl ('28) 15 15
110 A17 75c ol grn, *straw* 15 15
111 A17 75c bl, *bluish* ('25) 15 15
112 A17 75c vio ('27) 30 30
113 A18 1fr bl, *yel grn* 38 15
114 A18 1fr dp bl ('25) 60 60
115 A18 2fr car, *bl* 85 70
116 A18 5fr blk, *straw* 2.50 2.50
Nos. 88-116 (29) 11.06 10.03

See Nos. 311, 317a. For surcharges see Nos. 122-135, B1-B3, Q1-Q3.

Stamps of 1892-1904 Surcharged in Carmine or Black

05 10

1912

117 A12 5c on 15c gray (C) 35 35
a. Inverted surcharge 60.00 60.00
118 A12 5c on 20c red, *grn* 45 45
119 A12 5c on 30c brn, *bis* (C) 45 45
120 A12 10c on 40c red, *straw* 85 85
121 A12 10c on 50c brn, *az* (C) 85 85
Nos. 117-121 (5) 2.95 2.95

Two spacings between the surcharged numerals are found on Nos. 117 to 121.

No. 96 Surcharged in Brown

5 CENTIMES

1918

122 A16 5c on 15c vio 60 60
a. Double surcharge 32.50 32.50
b. Inverted surcharge 17.50 17.50

The color of the surcharge on No. 122 varies from red to dark brown.

No. 96 Surcharged 0,05 =

1922

123 A16 5c on 15c vio (R) 28 28
a. Double surcharge 27.50 27.50

Stamps and Types of 1905-28 Surcharged New Value and Bars in Red or Black 60=

1924-27

124 A16 25c on 15c vio 20 20
a. Double surcharge 27.50
125 A18 25c on 2fr car, *bl* 20 20
126 A18 25c on 5fr blk, *straw* 28 28
a. Double surcharge 45.00 45.00
127 A17 60c on 75c bl grn (R) 15 15
128 A17 65c on 45c red brn 55 55
129 A17 85c on 45c red brn 55 55
130 A17 90c on 75c dp rose 28 28
131 A18 1.25fr on 1fr dp bl (R) 20 20
132 A18 1.50fr on 1fr dp bl, *bl* 45 45
133 A18 3fr on 5fr red vio 48 48
134 A18 10fr on 5fr ol, *lav* (R) 3.00 3.00
135 A18 20fr on 5fr vio rose, *org* 6.25 6.25
Nos. 124-135 (12) 12.59 12.59

Issue years: Nos. 125-127, 1924. Nos. 124, 128-129, 1925. Nos. 131, 134, 1926. Nos. 130, 132-133, 135, 1927.

Bay of Paletuviers Point — A19

Landscape with Chief's House A20

Admiral de Bougainville and Count de La Perouse A21

1928-40 **Typo.**

136 A19 1c brn vio & ind 15 15
137 A19 2c dk brn & yel grn 15 15
137B A19 3c brn vio & ind 15 15
138 A19 4c org & Prus grn 15 15
139 A19 5c Prus bl & dp ol 15 15
140 A19 10c gray lil & dk brn 15 15
141 A19 15c yel brn & dp bl 15 15
142 A19 20c brn red & dk brn 15 15
143 A19 25c dk grn & dk brn 15 15
144 A20 30c gray grn & bl grn 15 15
145 A20 35c blk & brt vio 15 15
146 A20 40c brt red & olvn 15 15
147 A20 45c dp bl & red org 35 28
147A A20 45c bl grn & dl grn 28 28
148 A20 50c vio & brn 15 15
149 A20 55c vio bl & car 1.25 60
150 A20 60c vio bl & car 20 20
151 A20 65c org brn & bl 30 28
152 A20 70c dp rose & brn 15 15
153 A20 75c Prus bl & ol gray 60 28
154 A20 80c red brn & grn 30 15
155 A20 85c grn & brn 60 35
156 A20 90c dp red & brt red 30 28
157 A20 90c ol grn & rose red 28 28
158 A21 1fr dp ol & sal red 2.25 1.25
159 A21 1fr rose red & dk car 60 60
160 A21 1fr brn red & grn 15 15

161 A21 1.10fr dp grn & brn 5.50 5.00
162 A21 1.25fr brn red & grn 38 28
163 A21 1.25fr rose red & dk car 28 28
164 A21 1.40fr dk bl & red org 28 28
165 A21 1.50fr dp bl & bl 15 15
166 A21 1.60fr dp grn & brn 55 55
167 A21 1.75fr dk bl & red org 30 28
168 A21 1.75fr vio bl 28 28
169 A21 2fr red org & brn 22 15
170 A21 2.25fr vio bl 30 30
171 A21 2.50fr brn & lt brn 55 55
172 A21 3fr mag & brn 30 28
173 A21 5fr dk bl & brn 30 28
174 A21 10fr vio & brn, *pnksh* 60 48
175 A21 20fr red & brn, *yel* 1.00 70
Nos. 136-175 (42) 20.55 16.92

The 35c in Prussian green and dark green without overprint is listed as Wallis and Futuna No. 53a.

Issue years: 35c, 70c, 85c, Nos. 162, 167, 1933. 55c, 80c, Nos. 159, 168, 1938. No. 157, 163, 2.25fr, 1939. 3c, 55c, 1.40fr, 1.60fr, 2.50fr, Nos. 147A, 160, 1940. Others, 1928.

For overprints see Nos. 180-207, 217-251, Q4-Q6.

Colonial Exposition Issue
Common Design Types

1931 **Engr.** ***Perf. 12½***
Country Name Typo. in Black

176 CD70 40c dp grn 1.75 1.75
177 CD71 50c violet 1.75 1.75
178 CD72 90c red org 1.75 1.75
179 CD73 1.50fr dl bl 1.75 1.75

Paris-Noumea Flight Issue
Regular Issue of 1928 Overprinted:

PARIS-NOUMEA
Verneilh-Dévé-Munch
5 Avril 1932

1932 ***Perf. 14x13½***

180 A20 40c brt red & olvn 250.00 250.00
181 A20 50c vio & brn 250.00 250.00

Arrival on Apr. 5, 1932 at Noumea, of the French aviators, Verneilh, Deve and Munch. Excellent forgeries exist of #180-181.

Types of 1928-33 Overprinted in Black or Red:

PARIS-NOUMÉA
Première liaison aérienne
5 Avril 1932

1933

182 A19 1c red vio & dl bl 3.75 3.75
183 A19 2c dk brn & yel grn 3.75 3.75
184 A19 4c dl org & Prus bl 3.75 3.75
185 A19 5c Prus grn & ol (R) 3.75 3.75
186 A19 10c gray lil & dk brn (R) 3.75 3.75
187 A19 15c yel brn & dp bl (R) 3.75 3.75
188 A19 20c brn red & dk brn 3.75 3.75
189 A19 25c dk grn & dk brn (R) 3.75 3.75
190 A20 30c gray grn & bl grn (R) 3.75 3.75
191 A20 35c blk & lt vio 3.75 3.75
192 A20 40c brt red & olvn 3.75 3.75
193 A20 45c dp bl & red org 3.75 3.75
194 A20 50c vio & brn 3.75 3.75
195 A20 70c dp rose & brn 3.75 3.75
196 A20 75c Prus bl & ol gray (R) 3.75 3.75
197 A20 85c grn & brn 3.75 3.75
198 A20 90c dp red & brt red 3.75 3.75
199 A21 1fr dp ol & sal red 3.75 3.75
200 A21 1.25fr brn red & grn 3.75 3.75
201 A21 1.50fr dp bl & bl (R) 4.00 4.00
202 A21 1.75fr dk bl & red org 4.00 4.00
203 A21 2fr red org & brn 4.25 4.25
204 A21 3fr mag & brn 4.25 4.25
205 A21 5fr dk bl & brn (R) 4.25 4.25
206 A21 10fr vio & brn, *pnksh* 4.25 4.25
207 A21 20fr red & brn, *yel* 4.25 4.25
Nos. 182-207 (26) 100.50 100.50

1st anniv., Paris-Noumea flight. Plane centered on Nos. 190-207.

Paris International Exposition Issue
Common Design Types

1937 **Engr.** ***Perf. 13***

208 CD74 20c dp vio 60 60
209 CD75 30c dk grn 60 60
210 CD76 40c car rose 65 65
211 CD77 50c dk brn & bl 65 65
212 CD78 90c red 65 65
213 CD79 1.50fr ultra 65 65
Nos. 208-213 (6) 3.80 3.80

Colonial Arts Exhibition Issue
Souvenir Sheet
Common Design Type

1937 ***Imperf.***

214 CD78 3fr sepia 2.50 2.50

New York World's Fair Issue
Common Design Type

1939 ***Perf. 12½x12***

215 CD82 1.25fr car lake 45 45
216 CD82 2.25fr ultra 45 45

Noumea Roadstead and Marshal Petain A21a

1941 **Engr.** ***Perf. 12½x12***

216A A21a 1fr bluish grn 30
216B A21a 2.50fr dk bl 30

Nos. 216A-216B were issued by the Vichy government and were not placed on sale in the colony.

A 10c, type A19, without "RF," and a 60c, type A20, without "REPUBLIQUE FRANCAISE," were also issued by the Vichy government and not placed on sale in New Caledonia.

Types of 1928-40 Overprinted in Black **France Libre**

1941 ***Perf. 14x13½***

217 A19 1c red vio & dl bl 8.00 8.00
218 A19 2c dk brn & yel grn 8.00 8.00
219 A19 3c brn vio & ind 8.00 8.00
220 A19 4c dl org & Prus bl 8.00 8.00
221 A19 5c Prus bl & dp ol 8.00 8.00
222 A19 10c gray lil & dk brn 8.00 8.00
223 A19 15c yel brn & dp bl 8.00 8.00
224 A19 20c brn red & dk brn 8.00 8.00
225 A19 25c dk grn & dk brn 8.00 8.00
226 A20 30c gray grn & bl grn 8.00 8.00
227 A20 35c blk & brt vio 8.00 8.00
228 A20 40c brt red & olvn 8.00 8.00
229 A20 45c bl grn & dl grn 8.00 8.00
230 A20 50c vio & brn 8.00 8.00
231 A20 55c vio bl & car 8.00 8.00
232 A20 60c vio bl & car 8.00 8.00
233 A20 65c org brn & bl 8.00 8.00
234 A20 70c dp rose & brn 8.00 8.00
235 A20 75c Prus bl & ol gray 8.00 8.00
236 A20 80c red brn & grn 8.00 8.00
237 A20 85c grn & brn 9.00 9.00
238 A20 90c dp red & brt red 9.00 9.00
239 A21 1fr rose red & dk car 9.00 9.00
240 A21 1.25fr brn red & grn 9.00 9.00
241 A21 1.40fr dk bl & red org 9.00 9.00
242 A21 1.50fr dp bl & bl 9.00 9.00
243 A21 1.60fr dp grn & brn 9.00 9.00
244 A21 1.75fr dk bl & red org 9.00 9.00
245 A21 2fr red org & brn 9.00 9.00
246 A21 2.25fr vio bl 9.00 9.00
247 A21 2.50fr brn & lt brn 10.00 10.00
248 A21 3fr mag & brn 10.00 10.00
249 A21 5fr dk bl & brn 10.00 10.00
250 A21 10fr vio & brn, *pnksh* 10.00 10.00
251 A21 20fr red & brn, *yel* 10.00 10.00
Nos. 217-251 (35) 300.00 300.00

Issued to note this colony's affiliation with the "Free France" movement.

Catalogue values for unused stamps in this section, from this point to the end of the section, are for Never Hinged items.

Kagu A22

1942 **Photo.** ***Perf. 14½x14***

252 A22 5c brown 15 15
253 A22 10c dk gray bl 15 15
254 A22 25c emerald 15 15
255 A22 30c red org 15 15
256 A22 40c dk sl grn 15 15
257 A22 80c dl red brn 15 15
258 A22 1fr rose vio 15 15
259 A22 1.50fr red 15 15
260 A22 2fr gray blk 35 35
261 A22 2.50fr brt ultra 35 35
262 A22 4fr dl vio 28 28
263 A22 5fr bister 35 35
264 A22 10fr dp brn 50 50
265 A22 20fr dp grn 70 70
Nos. 252-265 (14) 3.73 3.73

Stamps of 1942 Surcharged in Carmine or Black 60 c. =

1945-46 **Unwmk.** ***Perf. 14½x14***

266 A22 50c on 5c brn (C) ('46) 45 45
267 A22 60c on 5c brn (C) 45 45
268 A22 70c on 5c brn (C) 45 45
269 A22 1.20fr on 5c brn (C) 20 20
270 A22 2.40fr on 25c emer 20 20
271 A22 3fr on 25c emer ('46) 20 20
272 A22 4.50fr on 25c emer 45 45
273 A22 15fr on 2.50fr brt ultra (C) 85 85
Nos. 266-273 (8) 3.25 3.25

Eboue Issue
Common Design Type

1945 **Engr.** ***Perf. 13***

274 CD91 2fr black 28 28
275 CD91 25fr Prus grn 85 85

Kagus A23

Ducos Sanatorium A24

Porcupine Isle — A25

Nickel Foundry A26

"Towers of Notre Dame" A27

Chieftain's House A28

1948 **Unwmk.** **Photo.** ***Perf. 13½x13***

276 A23 10c yel & brn 15 15
277 A23 30c grn & brn 15 15
278 A23 40c org & brn 15 15
279 A24 50c pink & brn 15 15
280 A24 60c yel & brn 15 15
281 A24 80c lt grn & bl grn 15 15
282 A25 1fr brn, pur & org 15 15
283 A25 1.20fr pale gray, brn & bl 20 15

284 A25 1.50fr cr, dk bl & yel 20 15
285 A26 2fr pck grn & brn 30 20
286 A26 2.40fr ver & dp rose 22 20
287 A26 3fr org & pur 2.50 60
288 A26 4fr bl & dk bl 48 28
289 A27 5fr ver & pur 60 35
290 A27 6fr yel & brn 75 45
291 A27 10fr org & dk bl 75 28
292 A28 15fr brn & gray 75 65
293 A28 20fr pur & yel 85 65
294 A28 25fr dk bl & org 1.25 95
Nos. 276-294 (19) 9.90 5.96

Military Medal Issue
Common Design Type

1952 Engr. & Typo. *Perf. 13*
295 CD101 2fr multi 2.00 2.00

Admiral Bruni d'Entrecasteaux and his Two Frigates — A29

Designs: 2fr, Msgr. Douarre and Cathedral of Nouméa. 6fr, Admiral Dumont d'Urville and map. 13fr, Admiral Auguste Febvrier-Despointes and Nouméa roadstead.

1953, Sept. 24 Engr.
296 A29 1.50fr org brn & dp cl 3.50 2.50
297 A29 2fr ind & aqua 2.50 1.75
298 A29 6fr dk brn, bl & car 5.25 2.75
299 A29 13fr bl grn & dk grnsh bl 5.50 4.00

Centenary of the presence of the French in New Caledonia.

"Towers of Notre Dame" A30

Coffee A31

1955, Nov. 21 Unwmk. *Perf. 13*
300 A30 2.50fr dk brn, ultra & grn 35 30
301 A30 3fr grn, ultra & red brn 2.75 1.50
302 A31 9fr vio bl & ind 55 30

FIDES Issue
Common Design Type

1956, Oct. 22 Engr. *Perf. 13x12½*
303 CD103 3fr Dumbea Dam 60 45

Flower Issue
Common Design Type

Designs: 4fr, Xanthostemon. 15fr, Hibiscus.

1958, July 7 Photo. *Perf. 12x12½*
304 CD104 4fr multi 1.10 45
305 CD104 15fr grn, red & yel 2.50 75

Imperforates
Most stamps of New Caledonia from 1958 onward exist imperforate, in trial colors, or in small presentation sheets in which the stamps are printed in changed colors.

Human Rights Issue
Common Design Type

1958, Dec. 10 Engr. *Perf. 13*
306 CD105 7fr car & dk bl 60 45

Brachyrus Zebra — A32

Lienardella Fasciata A33

Designs: 10fr, Claucus and Spirographe. 26fr, Fluorescent corals.

1959, Mar. 21 Engr. *Perf. 13*
307 A32 1fr lil gray & red brn 38 28
308 A33 3fr bl, grn & red 45 24
309 A32 10fr dk brn, Prus bl & org brn 1.10 60
310 A33 26fr multi 2.50 1.75

Types of 1859, 1905 and

Girl Operating Check Writer A34

Telephone Receiver and Exchange A35

Port-de-France (Nouméa) in 1859 — A36

Designs: 9fr, Wayside mailbox and mail bus (vert.). 33fr, Like 19fr without stamps.

Perf. 13½x13, 13

1960, May 20 Unwmk.
311 A16 4fr red 45 30
312 A34 5fr cl & org brn 45 30
313 A36 9fr dk grn & brn 45 38
314 A35 12fr bl & blk 55 45
315 A1 13fr sl bl 1.75 90
316 A36 19fr bl grn, dl grn & red 1.75 65
317 A36 33fr Prus bl & dl red 1.90 1.25
a. Souv. sheet of 3, #315, 311, 317 + label 4.50 4.50
Nos. 311-317 (7) 7.30 4.23

Cent. of postal service and stamps in New Caledonia.
No. 317a has label between 4fr and 33fr stamps.

Melanesian Sailing Canoes A37

Designs: 4fr, Spear fisherman (vert.). 5fr, Sail Rock and sailboats, Nouméa.

1962, July 2 Engr. *Perf. 13*
318 A37 2fr sl grn, ultra & brn 40 28
319 A37 4fr brn, car & grn 40 30
320 A37 5fr sep, grn & bl 75 45

See Nos. C29-C32.

Map of Australia and South Pacific — A37a

1962, July 18 Photo. *Perf. 13x12*
321 A37a 15fr multi 1.10 55

Fifth South Pacific Conf., Pago Pago, 1962.

Air Currents over Map of New Caledonia and South Pacific, Barograph and Compass Rose — A38

1962, Nov. 5 *Perf. 12x12½*
322 A38 50fr multi 4.50 3.00

3rd regional assembly of the World Meteorological Association, Nouméa, November 1962.

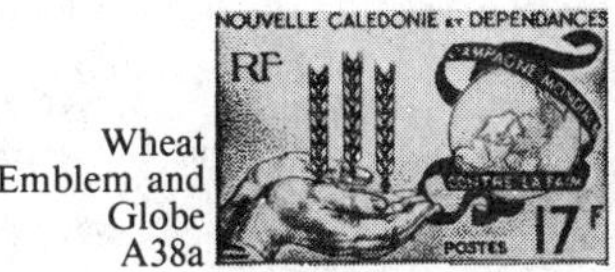

Wheat Emblem and Globe A38a

1963, Mar. 21 Engr. *Perf. 13*
323 A38a 17fr choc & dk bl 1.00 70

FAO "Freedom from Hunger" campaign.

Relay Race — A39

Designs: 7fr, Tennis. 10fr, Soccer. 27fr, Throwing the javelin.

Perf. 12½

1963, Aug. 29 Unwmk. Photo.
324 A39 1fr dk gray & dl red 42 30
325 A39 7fr dl bl & org brn 75 42
326 A39 10fr grn & brn 1.10 75
327 A39 27fr dk plum & ultra 2.25 1.75

Issued to publicize the South Pacific Games, Suva, Aug. 29-Sept. 7.

Red Cross Centenary Issue
Common Design Type

1963 Sept. 2 Engr. *Perf. 13*
328 CD113 37fr bl, gray & car 2.75 2.25

Human Rights Issue
Common Design Type

1963, Dec. 10 Unwmk. *Perf. 13*
329 CD117 50fr sl grn & dp cl 3.00 2.50

Bikkia Fritillarioides A40

Sea Squirts A41

Flowers: 1fr, Freycinettia Sp. 3fr, Xanthostemon Francii. 4fr, Psidiomyrtus locellatus. 5fr, Callistemon suberosum. 7fr, Montrouziera sphaeroidea (horiz.). 10fr, Ixora collina (horiz.). 17fr, Deplanchea speciosa.

Photogravure; Lithographed (2fr, 3fr)

1964-65 *Perf. 13x12½*
330 A40 1fr multi 25 20
331 A40 2fr multi 32 20
332 A40 3fr multi 48 25
333 A40 4fr multi ('65) 80 40
334 A40 5fr multi ('65) 90 45
335 A40 7fr multi 2.00 70
336 A40 10fr multi 2.00 70
337 A40 17fr multi 3.25 1.90
Nos. 330-337 (8) 10.00 4.80

1964-65 Engr. *Perf. 13*

Design: 10fr, Alcyonium catalai. 17fr, Shrimp (hymenocera elegans).

338 A41 7fr dk bl, org & brn 75 60
339 A41 10fr dk red & dk vio bl ('65) 1.10 50
340 A41 17fr dk bl, mag & grn 1.90 1.40

Nouméa Aquarium. See Nos. C41-C43.

Philatec Issue
Common Design Type

1964, Apr. 9 Unwmk. *Perf. 13*
341 CD118 40fr dk vio, grn & choc 3.50 3.50

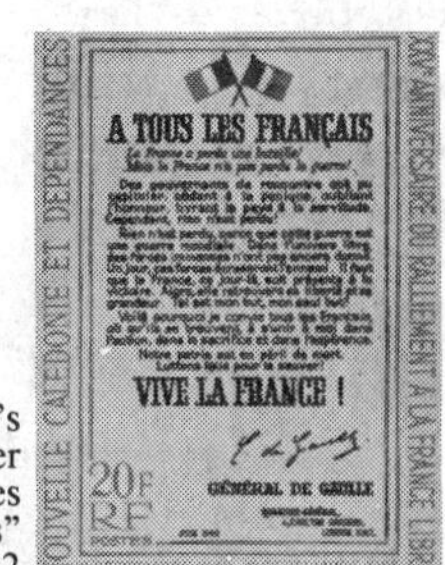

De Gaulle's 1940 Poster "A Tous les Francais" A42

1965, Sept. 20 Engr. *Perf. 13*
342 A42 20fr red, bl & blk 4.00 2.75

25th anniversary of the rallying of the Free French.

Amedee Lighthouse A43

Games' Emblem A44

1965, Nov. 25
343 A43 8fr dk vio bl, bis & grn 65 35

Centenary of the Amedee lighthouse.

1966, Feb. 28 Engr. *Perf. 13*
344 A44 8fr dk red, brt bl & blk 40 25

Issued to publicize the Second South Pacific Games, Nouméa, December, 1966.

Red-throated Parrot Finch — A45

Design: 3fr, Giant imperial pigeon.

1966, Oct. 10 Litho. *Perf. 13x12½*
Size: 22x37mm

345 A45 1fr grn & multi 70 55
346 A45 3fr cit & multi 1.40 85

See #361-366, 380-381, C48-C49A, C70-C71.

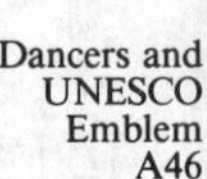

Dancers and UNESCO Emblem A46

1966, Nov. 4 Engr. *Perf. 13*
347 A46 16fr pur, ocher & grn 55 40

20th anniv. of UNESCO.

High Jump and Games' Emblem A47

Designs: 20fr, Hurdling. 40fr, Running. 100fr, Swimming.

1966, Dec. 8 Engr. *Perf. 13*
348 A47 17fr mar, vio & grn 1.00 50
349 A47 20fr mar, lil & bl grn 1.65 85
350 A47 40fr mar, sl grn & vio 2.00 1.65
351 A47 100fr mar, bl grn & lil 4.00 2.75
a. Souv. sheet of 4, #348-351 + label 12.00 12.00

2nd So. Pacific Games, Nouméa, Dec. 8-18.

Lekine Cliffs — A48

1967, Jan. 14 Engr. *Perf. 13*
352 A48 17fr brt grn, ultra & sl grn 75 40

Magenta Stadium, Nouméa A49

Design: 20fr, Fish hatchery, Nouméa.

1967, June 5 Photo. *Perf. 12x13*
353 A49 10fr multi 65 40
354 A49 20fr multi 1.40 60

> *A particular stamp may be scarce, but if few collectors want it, its market value may remain relatively low.*

ITY Emblem, Beach at Nouméa A50

1967, June 19 Engr. *Perf. 13*
355 A50 30fr multi 2.25 1.40

Issued for International Tourist Year, 1967.

19th Century Mailman A51

1967, July 12
356 A51 7fr dk car, bl grn & brn 50 40

Issued for Stamp Day.

Papilio Montrouzieri — A52

Butterflies: 9fr, Polyura clitarchus. 13fr, 15fr, Hypolimnas bolina, male and female respectively.

1967-68 Engr. *Perf. 13*
Size: 36x22mm

357 A52 7fr lt grn, blk & ultra 95 60
358 A52 9fr brn, lil & ind ('68) 1.40 85
359 A52 13fr vio bl, brn org & dk brn 2.00 1.25
360 A52 15fr dk brn, bl & yel 3.00 2.00
Nos. 357-360,C51-C53 (7) 23.35 13.70

Issue dates: 9fr, Mar. 26, 1968. Others, Aug. 10, 1967.

Bird Type of 1966

Birds: 1fr, New Caledonian grass warbler. 2fr, New Caledonia whistler. 3fr, New Caledonia white-throated pigeon. 4fr, Kagus. 5fr, Crested parakeet. 10fr, Crow honey-eater.

1967-68 Photo. *Perf. 13x12½*
Size: 22x37mm

361 A45 1fr multi ('68) 40 25
362 A45 2fr multi ('68) 55 32
363 A45 3fr multi ('68) 55 45
364 A45 4fr grn & multi 90 60
365 A45 5fr lt yel & multi 1.50 70
366 A45 10fr pink & multi 3.75 1.75
Nos. 361-366 (6) 7.65 4.07

Issue dates: Nos. 364-366, Dec. 16, 1967. Others May 14, 1968.

WHO Anniversary Issue
Common Design Type

1968, May 4 Engr. *Perf. 13*
367 CD126 20fr mar, vio & dk bl grn 1.25 90

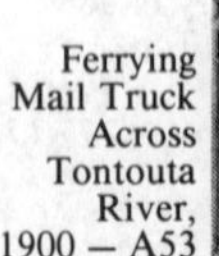

Ferrying Mail Truck Across Tontouta River, 1900 — A53

1968, July 1 Engr. *Perf. 13*
368 A53 9fr dk red brn, grn & ultra 1.00 50

Issued for Stamp Day, 1968.

Human Rights Year Issue
Common Design Type

1968, Aug. 10 Engr. *Perf. 13*
369 CD127 12fr sl grn, dp car & org yel 75 55

Conus Geographus A54

1968, Nov. 9 Engr. *Perf. 13*
Size: 36x22mm

370 A54 10fr dk brn, brt bl & gray 1.10 65

See Nos. C58-C60.

Car on Road — A55

1968, Dec. 26 Engr. *Perf. 13*
371 A55 25fr dp bl, sl grn & hn brn 2.50 1.10

2nd Automobile Safari of New Caledonia.

Cattle Dip — A56

Design: 25fr, Cattle branding.

1969, May 10 Engr. *Perf. 13*
Size: 36x22mm

372 A56 9fr sl grn, ultra & brn 70 55
373 A56 25fr grn, brn & lil 2.25 85

Issued to publicize cattle breeding in New Caledonia. See No. C64.

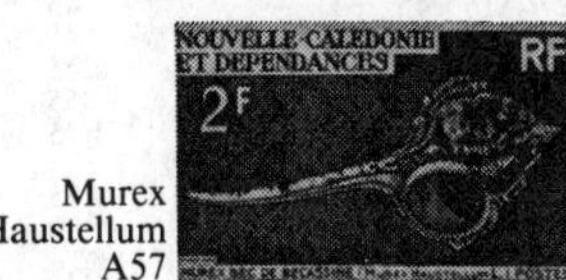

Murex Haustellum A57

Sea Shells: 5fr, Venus comb. 15fr, Murex ramosus.

1969, June 21 Engr. *Perf. 13*
Size: 35½x22mm

374 A57 2fr ver, bl & brn 55 35
375 A57 5fr dl red, pur & beige 70 48
376 A57 15fr ver, dl grn & gray 2.50 1.00

See No. C65.

Judo — A58

1969, Aug. 7 Engr. *Perf. 13*
Size: 36x22mm

377 A58 19fr shown 2.00 1.00
378 A58 20fr Boxers 2.00 1.00

3rd South Pacific Games. Port Moresby, Papua and New Guinea, Aug. 13-23. See Nos. C66-C67.

ILO Issue
Common Design Type

1969, Nov. 24 Engr. *Perf. 13*
379 CD131 12fr org, brn vio & brn 60 40

Bird Type of 1966

Birds: 15fr, Friarbird. 30fr, Sacred kingfisher.

1970, Feb. 19 Photo. *Perf. 13*
Size: 22x37mm

380 A45 15fr yel grn & multi 2.50 1.10
381 A45 30fr pale sal & multi 3.75 1.90

See Nos. C70-C71.

UPU Headquarters Issue
Common Design Type

1970, May 20 Engr. *Perf. 13*
382 CD133 12fr brn, gray & dk car 70 55

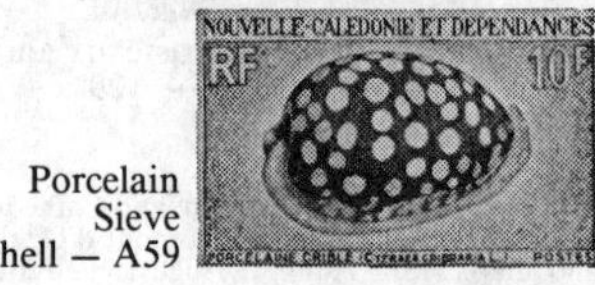

Porcelain Sieve Shell — A59

Designs: 1fr, Strombus epidromis linne (vert.). No. 385, Strombus variabilis swainson (vert.). 21fr, Mole porcelain shell.

1970
Size: 22x36mm, 36x22mm

383 A59 1fr brt grn & multi 55 28
384 A59 10fr rose & multi 1.40 55
385 A59 10fr blk & multi 1.40 55
386 A59 21fr bl grn, brn & dk brn 2.75 1.00
Nos. 383-386,C73-C76 (8) 20.10 10.28

See Nos. 395-396, C89-C90.

Packet Ship "Natal," 1883 — A60

1970, July 23 Engr. *Perf. 13*
387 A60 9fr Prus bl, blk & brt grn 80 45

Issued for Stamp Day.

Dumbea Railroad Post Office A61

1971, Mar. 13 Engr. *Perf. 13*
388 A61 10fr red, sl grn & blk 1.25 75

Stamp Day, 1971.

Racing Yachts — A62

1971, Apr. 17 Engr. *Perf. 13*
389 A62 16fr bl, Prus bl & sl grn 3.25 1.75

Third sailing cruise from Whangarei, New Zealand, to Nouméa.

Morse Recorder, Communications Satellite — A63

1971, May 17 Engr. *Perf. 13*
390 A63 19fr red, lake & org 85 40

3rd World Telecommunications Day.

Weight Lifting — A64

1971, June 24 Engr. *Perf. 13*
391 A64 11fr shown 75 50
392 A64 23fr Basketball 1.50 75

4th South Pacific Games, Papeete, French Polynesia, Sept. 8-19. See Nos. C82-C83.

De Gaulle Issue
Common Design Type

Designs: 34fr, Gen. de Gaulle, 1940. 100fr, Pres. de Gaulle, 1970.

1971, Nov. 9
393 CD134 34fr dk pur & blk 3.00 1.25
394 CD134 100fr dk pur & blk 7.00 3.50

Sea Shell Type of 1970

Designs: 1fr, Scorpion conch (vert.). 3fr, Common spider conch. (vert.).

1972, Mar. 4 Engr. *Perf. 13*
Size: 22x36mm
395 A59 1fr vio & dk brn 28 20
396 A59 3fr grn & ocher 40 28

See Nos. C89-C90.

Carved Wooden Pillow — A66

Chamber of Commerce Emblem — A67

1972-73 Photo. *Perf. 12½x13*
397 A66 1fr Doorpost, Goa ('73) 35 22
398 A66 2fr shown 35 28
399 A66 5fr Monstrance 60 40
400 A66 12fr Tchamba mask 1.75 75
Nos. 397-400,C102-C103 (6) 5.05 3.15

Objects from Nouméa Museum.

1972, Dec. 16
401 A67 12fr blk, yel & brt bl 80 50

10th anniversary of the Junior Chamber of Commerce.

Tchamba Mask A68

Black-back Butterflyfish (Day) A69

1973, Mar. 15 Engr. *Perf. 13*
402 A68 12fr lilac 1.25 85
a. Booklet pane of 5 10.00

No. 402 issued in booklets only. See No. C99.

1973, June 23 Photo. *Perf. 13x12½*
403 A69 8fr shown 95 60
404 A69 14fr same fish (night) 1.40 85

Nouméa Aquarium. See No. C105.

Emblem A70

1973, July 21 *Perf. 13*
405 A70 20fr grn, yel & vio bl 80 45

School Coordinating Office, 10th anniv.

"Nature Protection" — A72

1974, June 22 Photo. *Perf. 13x12½*
406 A72 7fr multi 45 30

Scorched Landscape A73

Calanthe Veratrifolia A74

1975, Feb. 3 Photo. *Perf. 13*
407 A73 20fr multi 60 50

"Prevent brush fires."

1975, May 30 Photo. *Perf. 13*

Design: 11fr, Liperanthus gigas.

408 A74 8fr pur & multi 70 40
409 A74 11fr dk bl & multi 85 48

Orchids. See Nos. 425-426, C125.

Festival Emblem — A75

1975, Sept. 6 Photo. *Perf. 12½x13*
410 A75 12fr ultra, org & yel 40 28

Melanesia 2000 Festival.

Birds in Flight A76

Georges Pompidou A77

1975, Oct. 18 Photo. *Perf. 13½x13*
411 A76 5fr ocher, yel & blk 32 18

Nouméa Ornithological Society, 10th anniversary.

1975, Dec. 6 Engr. *Perf. 13*
412 A77 26fr dk grn, blk & sl 90 45

Georges Pompidou (1911-1974), president of France.

Brown Booby A78

Sea Birds: 2fr, Blue-faced booby. 8fr, Red-footed booby (vert.).

Perf. 13x12½, 12½x13
1976, Feb. 21 Photo.
413 A78 1fr multi 18 15
414 A78 2fr multi 30 18
415 A78 8fr multi 75 40

Festival Emblem A79

1976, Mar. 13 Litho. *Perf. 12½*
416 A79 27fr bl, org & blk 80 45

Rotorua 1976, South Pacific Arts Festival, New Zealand.

Lion and Lions Emblem — A80

1976, Mar. 13 Photo. *Perf. 12½x13*
417 A80 49fr multi 1.40 1.10

Lions Club of Nouméa, 15th anniversary.

Music Pavilion — A81

Design: 30fr, Fountain (vert.).

1976, July 3 Litho. *Perf. 12½*
418 A81 25fr multi 55 40
419 A81 30fr bl & multi 75 50

Old Nouméa.

Polluted Shore — A82

1976, Aug. 21 Photo. *Perf. 13*
420 A82 20fr dp bl & multi 60 45

Nature protection.

South Pacific People A83

1976, Oct. 23 Photo. *Perf. 13*
421 A83 20fr bl & multi 75 45

16th South Pacific Commission Conference, Nouméa, Oct. 1976.

Giant Grasshopper A84

Design: 31fr, Beetle and larvae.

1977, Feb. 21 Engr. *Perf. 13*
422 A84 26fr multi 95 85
423 A84 31fr multi 95 85

Ground Satellite Station, Nouméa — A85

1977, Apr. 16 Litho. *Perf. 13*
424 A85 29fr multi 80 48

Orchid Type of 1975

Designs: 22fr, Phajus daenikeri. 44fr, Dendrobium finetianum.

1977, May 23 Photo. *Perf. 13*
425 A74 22fr brn & multi 75 60
426 A74 44fr bl & multi 1.50 85

Mask, Palms, "Stamps" — A86

1977, June 25 Photo. *Perf. 13*
427 A86 35fr multi 80 70

Philately in school, Philatelic Exhibition, La Perouse Lyceum, Noumea.

Trees — A87

1977, July 16 Photo. *Perf. 13*
428 A87 20fr multi 85 55

Nature protection.

Congress Emblem — A88

1977, Aug. 6 Photo. *Perf. 13*
429 A88 200fr multi 5.25 3.50

French Junior Economic Chambers Congress, Noumea.

Young Frigate Bird — A89

Designs: 22fr, Terns (horiz.). 40fr, Sooty terns (horiz.).

1977, Sept. 17 Photo. *Perf. 13*
430 A89 16fr multi 65 45
431 A89 22fr multi 85 60
432 A89 40fr multi 1.75 85

Issue dates: 16fr, Sept. 17, 1977. 22fr, 40fr, Feb. 11, 1978.
See No. C138.

Mare and Foal — A90

1977, Nov. 19 Engr. *Perf. 13*
433 A90 5fr multi 40 24

10th anniversary of the Society for Promotion of Caledonian Horses.

Araucaria Montana A91

Halityle Regularis A92

1978, Mar. 17 Photo. *Perf. 12½x13*
434 A91 16fr multi 55 35

See No. C149.

1978, May 20 Photo. *Perf. 13*
436 A92 10fr vio bl & multi 35 22

Nouméa Aquarium.

Stylized Turtle and Globe — A93

1978, May 20
437 A93 30fr multi 85 70

Protection of the turtle.

Flying Fox — A94

1978, June 10
438 A94 20fr multi 85 60

Nature protection.

Maurice Leenhardt A95

Soccer Player, League Emblem A96

1978, Aug. 16 Engr. *Perf. 13*
439 A95 37fr multi 1.00 80

Pastor Maurice Leenhardt (1878-1954).

1978, Nov. 4 Photo. *Perf. 13*
440 A96 26fr multi 70 42

New Caledonia Soccer League, 50th anniversary.

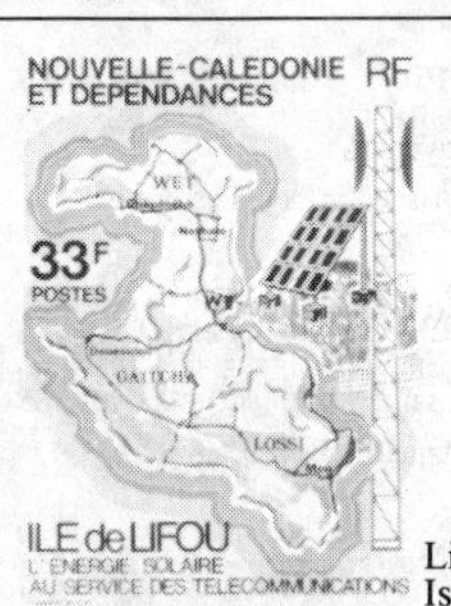

Lifu Island — A97

1978, Dec. 9 Litho. *Perf. 13*
441 A97 33fr multi 1.00 65

Petroglyph, Mere — A98

Map of Ouvea — A99

1979, Jan. 27 Engr. *Perf. 13*
442 A98 10fr brick red 40 30

Perf. 12½x13, 13x12½
1979, Feb. 17 Photo.

Design: 31fr, Map of Mare Island (horiz.).

443 A99 11fr multi 35 28
444 A99 31fr multi 60 45

House at Artillery Point — A100

1979, Apr. 28 Photo. *Perf. 13*
445 A100 20fr multi 65 48

Auguste Escoffier — A101

1979, July 21 Engr. *Perf. 12½x13*
446 A101 24fr multi 65 48

Auguste Escoffier Hotel School.

Regatta and Games Emblem A102

1979, Aug. 11 Photo. *Perf. 13*
447 A102 16fr multi 65 35

6th South Pacific Games, Suva, Fiji, Aug. 27-Sept. 8.

Agathis Ovata A103

1979, Oct. 6 Photo. *Perf. 13x12½*
448 A103 5fr *shown* 24 15
449 A103 34fr *Cyathea intermedia* 70 48

Pouembout Rodeo A104

1979, Oct. 27 Engr. *Perf. 13x12½*
450 A104 12fr multi 45 28

Bantamia Merleti A105

1979, Dec. 1 Photo. *Perf. 13x11½*
451 A105 23fr multi 60 40

Fluorescent corals from Nouméa Aquarium.

Map of Pine Tree Island, Fishermen with Nets — A106

1980, Jan. 12 Photo. *Perf. 13x12½*
452 A106 23fr multi 45 28

Hibbertia Virotii A107

1980, Apr. 19 Photo. *Perf. 13x12½*
453 A107 11fr shown 35 20
454 A107 12fr Grevillea meisneri 35 20

Philately at School — A108

1980, May 10 Litho. *Perf. 12½*
455 A108 30fr multi 60 40

Prevention of Traffic Accidents A109

1980, July 5 Photo. *Perf. 13x12½*
456 A109 15fr multi 35 20

Parribacus Caledonicus A110

Noumea Aquarium Crustacea: 8fr, Panulirus versicolor.

1980, Aug. 23 Litho. *Perf. 13x13½*
457 A110 5fr multi 15 15
458 A110 8fr multi 22 15

Solar Energy A111

1980, Oct. 11 Photo. *Perf. 13x12½*
459 A111 23fr multi 45 24

Manta Birostris A112

1981, Feb. 18 Photo. *Perf. 13x12½*
460 A112 23fr shown 45 20
461 A112 25fr Carcharhinus amblyrhnchos 50 24

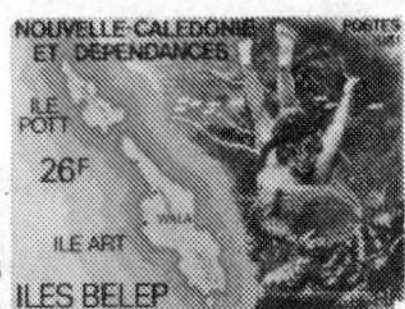

Belep Islands A113

1981, May 4
462 A113 26fr multi 55 28

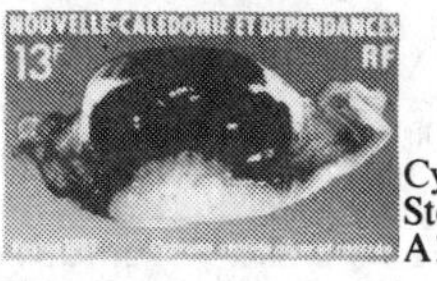

Cypraea Stolida A114

1981, June 17 Photo. *Perf. 13*
463 A114 1fr Cymbiola rossiniana, vert. 15 15
464 A114 2fr Connus floccatus, vert. 15 15
465 A114 13fr shown 22 15
Set value 32 22

See Nos. 470-471.

Corvette Constantine, 1854 — A115

1981, July 22 Engr. *Perf. 13*
466 A115 10fr shown 22 15
467 A115 25fr Aviso le Phoque, 1853 45 18

See Nos. 476-477.

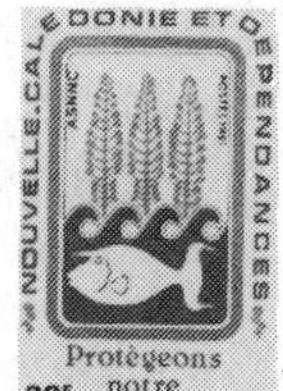

Intl. Year of the Disabled A116

1981, Sept. 2 Litho. *Perf. 12½*
468 A116 45fr multi 85 48

Nature Preservation — A117

1981, Nov. 7 Photo. *Perf. 13*
469 A117 28fr multi 50 24

Marine Life Type of 1981

1982, Jan. 20 Photo. *Perf. 13x13½*
470 A114 13fr Calappa calappa 22 15
471 A114 25fr Etisus splendidus 45 18

Chalcantite A118

1982, Mar. 17 Photo. *Perf. 13x13½*
472 A118 15fr shown 28 15
473 A118 30fr Anortnosite 55 20

Melaleuca Quinquenervia — A119

1982, June 23 Photo. *Perf. 13*
474 A119 20fr Savannah trees, vert. 38 18
475 A119 29fr shown 55 18

Ship Type of 1981

1982, July 7 Engr.
476 A115 44fr Barque Le Cher 75 35
477 A115 59fr Naval dispatch vessel Kersaint 1.00 55

Ateou Tribe Traditional House — A120

Grey's Ptilope — A121

1982, Oct. 13 Photo. *Perf. 13½x13*
478 A120 52fr multi 85 35

1982, Nov. 6
479 A121 32fr shown 60 24
480 A121 35fr Caledonian loriquet 65 24

Central Education Coordination Office — A122

1982, Nov. 27 Litho. *Perf. 13½x13*
481 A122 48fr Boat 75 28

Bernheim Library, Noumea — A123

1982, Dec. 15 Engr. *Perf. 13*
482 A123 36fr multi 60 28

Caledonian Orchids A123a

1983, Feb. 2 Photo. *Perf. 13x13½*
482A A123a 10fr Dendrobium oppositifolium 15 15
482B A123a 15fr Dendrobium munificum 20 15
482C A123a 29fr Dendrobium fractiflexum 40 20

Xanthostemon Aurantiacum — A124

1983, Mar. 23 Litho. *Perf. 13*
483 A124 1fr Crinum asiaticum 15 15
484 A124 2fr Xanthostemon aurantiacum 15 15
485 A124 4fr Metrosideros demonstrans, vert. 15 15
Set value 15 15

25th Anniv. of Posts and Telecommunications Dept. — A125

Telephones and post offices.

1983, Apr. 30 Litho. *Perf. 13*
486 A125 30fr multicolored 50 24
487 A125 40fr multicolored 60 28
488 A125 50fr multicolored 85 35
a. Souvenir sheet of 3 2.50 2.50

Nos. 486-488 se-tenant. No. 488a contains Nos. 486-488 with changed background colors.

Local Snakes A126

1983, June 22 Photo. *Perf. 13*
489 A126 31fr Laticauda laticauda 55 24
490 A126 33fr Laticauda colubrina 60 28

7th South Pacific Games, Sept. — A127

1983, Aug. 10 Engr.
491 A127 16fr Volleyball 25 15

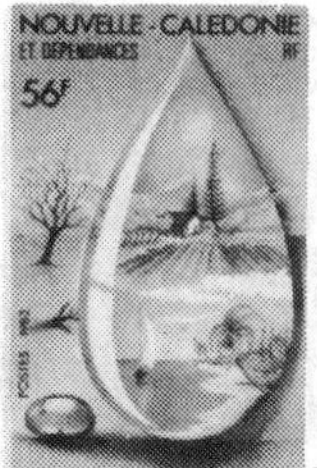

Nature Protection A128

1983, Sept. 8 Photo. *Perf. 12½*
492 A128 56fr multi 70 40

Birds of Prey A129

1983, Nov. 16 Litho. *Perf. 13*
493 A129 34fr Tyto Alba Lifuensis, vert. 40 26
494 A129 37fr Pandion Haliaetus 45 30

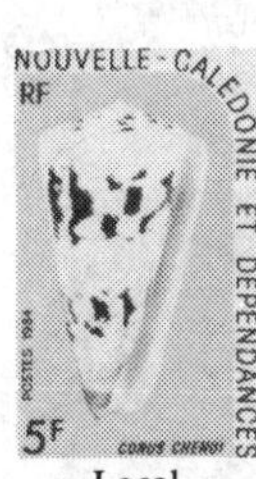

Local Shells — A130

Arms of Noumea — A132

Steamers A131

1984, Jan. 11 Litho. & Engr.
495 A130 5fr Conus chenui 15 15
496 A130 15fr Conus moluccensis 28 15
497 A130 20fr Conus optimus 30 28
Set value 36

See Nos. 521-522.

1984, Feb. 8 **Engr.**
498 A131 18fr St. Joseph 25 20
499 A131 31fr St. Antoine 45 32

1984, Apr. 11 Litho. *Perf. 12½x13*
500 A132 35fr multi 50 38

See No. 546, 607, C214.

Environmental Preservation — A133

1984, May 23 ***Perf. 13***
501 A133 65fr Island scene 60 45

Orchids A134

1984, July 18 Litho. *Perf. 12*
502 A134 16fr Diplocaulobium ou-hinnae 22 15
503 A134 38fr Acianthus atepalus 48 30

Cent. of Public Schooling A135

Kagu A137

1984, Oct. 11 Litho. *Perf. 13½x13*
504 A135 59fr Schoolhouse 60 28

1985-86 **Engr.** ***Perf. 13***
511 A137 1fr brt bl 15 15
512 A137 2fr green 15 15
513 A137 3fr brt org 15 15
514 A137 4fr brt grn 15 15
515 A137 5fr dp rose lil 15 15
516 A137 35fr crimson 28 15
517 A137 38fr vermilion 30 15
518 A137 40fr brt rose ('86) 40 20
Set value 1.20 70

Issue dates: 1fr, 2fr, 5fr, 38fr, May 22. 3fr, 4fr, 35fr, Feb. 13. 40fr, July 30.
See types A179, A179a.

Sea Shell Type of 1984

Lithographed and Engraved

1985, Feb. 27 ***Perf. 13***
521 A130 55fr Conus bullatus 42 20
522 A130 72fr Conus lamberti 55 28

25th World Meteorological Day — A138

1985, Mar. 20 **Litho.**
523 A138 17fr Radio communication, storm 20 15

Red Cross, Medicine Without Frontiers — A139

1985, Apr. 10 ***Perf. 12½***
524 A139 41fr multi 35 15

Electronic Railway Switching Center Inauguration — A140

1985, Apr. 24
525 A140 70fr E 10 B installation 70 38

Marguerite La Foa Suspension Bridge A141

1985, May 10 Engr. *Perf. 13*
526 A141 44fr brt bl & red brn 45 18

Historical Preservation Association.

Le Cagou Philatelic Society — A142

1985, June 15 **Litho.**
527 A142 220fr multi 1.75 85
a. Souvenir sheet, perf. 12½ 1.90 1.90

No. 527a sold for 230fr.

4th Pacific Arts Festival — A143

1985, July 3 ***Perf. 13½***

Black Overprint

528 A143 55fr multi 52 25
529 A143 75fr multi 75 35

Not issued without overprint. Festival was transferred to French Polynesia.

Intl. Youth Year — A144

1985, July 24 Litho. *Perf. 13*
530 A144 59fr multi 60 30

Amedee Lighthouse Electrification — A145

1985, Aug. 13
531 A145 89fr multi 85 42

Environmental Conservation A146

1985, Sept. 18
532 A146 100fr Planting trees 1.00 50

Birds A147

1985, Dec. 18 ***Perf. 12½***
533 A147 50fr Poule sultane 50 25
534 A147 60fr Merle caledonien 60 32

Noumea Aquarium A148

1986, Feb. 19 Litho. *Perf. 12½x13*
535 A148 10fr Pomacanthus imperator 15 15
536 A148 17fr Rhinopias aphanes 20 15
Set value 16

Kanumera Bay, Isle of Pines — A149

1986, Mar. 26 Litho. *Perf. 12½*
537 A149 50fr shown 60 30
538 A149 55fr Inland village 68 35

See Nos. 547-548, 617-618.

Geckos A150

1986, Apr. 16 ***Perf. 12½x13***
539 A150 20fr Bavayia sauvagii 25 15
540 A150 45fr Rhacodactylus leachianus 55 30

1986 World Cup Soccer Championships, Mexico — A151

1986, May 28 ***Perf. 13***
541 A151 60fr multi 75 38

1st Pharmacy in New Caledonia, 120th Anniv. — A152

1986, June 25 Litho. *Perf. 13*
542 A152 80fr multi 95 48

Orchids A153

1986, July 16 ***Perf. 12½x13***
543 A153 44fr Coelogynae licastioides 45 22
544 A153 58fr Calanthe langei 60 30

STAMPEX '86, Adelaide — A154

1986, Aug. 4 ***Perf. 12½***
545 A154 110fr Bird 1.25 65

Arms Type of 1984

1986, Oct. 11 Litho. *Perf. 13½*
546 A132 94fr Mont Dore 1.10 55

Landscape Type of 1986

1986, Oct. 29 Litho. *Perf. 12½*
547 A149 40fr West landscape, vert. 45 24
548 A149 76fr South Landscape 95 52

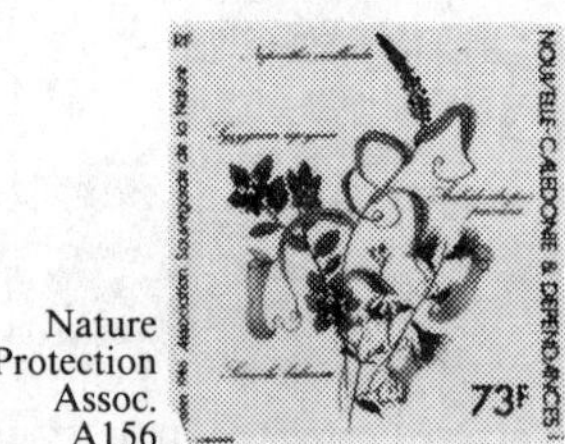

Nature Protection Assoc. A156

Flowers: Niponthes vieillardi, Syzygium ngayense, Archidendropsis Paivana, Scavola balansae.

1986, Nov. 12 ***Perf. 12½***
549 A156 73fr multi 90 45

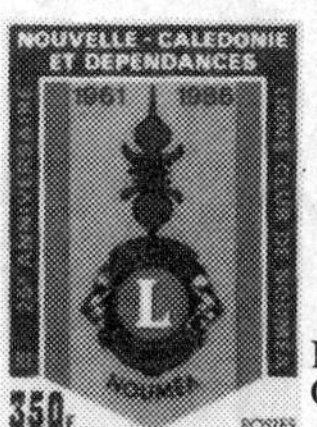

Noumea Lions Club, 25th Anniv. — A157

1986, Nov. 26 ***Perf. 13x12½***
550 A157 350fr Emblem 4.25 2.00

Paintings A158

Designs: 74fr, Moret Point, by A. Sisley. 140fr, Butterfly Chase, by B. Morisot.

1986, Dec. 23 Litho. ***Perf. 13***
551 A158 74fr multi 75 38
552 A158 140fr multi 1.40 70

America's Cup — A159

1987, Jan. 28 ***Perf. 13½***
553 A159 30fr Challenge France 38 18
554 A159 70fr French Kiss 90 45

Plants, Butterflies A160

Designs: 46fr, Anona squamosa, Graphium gelon. 54fr, Albizzia granulosa, Polyura gamma.

1987, Feb. 25 Litho. ***Perf. 13x12½***
555 A160 46fr multi 60 30
556 A160 54fr multi 65 32

Pirogues A161

1987, May 13 Engr. ***Perf. 13x12½***
557 A161 72fr from Isle of Pines 80 40
558 A161 90fr from Ouvea 90 45

New Town Hall, Mont Dore A162

1987, May 23 Litho. ***Perf. 12½x13***
559 A162 92fr multi 1.10 55

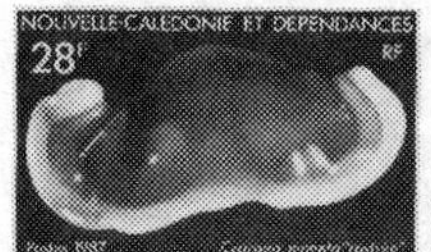

Seashells A163

1987, June 24 ***Perf. 13***
560 A163 28fr Cypraea moneta 35 16
561 A163 36fr Cypraea martini 45 25

8th South Pacific Games — A164

1987, July 8 ***Perf. 12½x13***
562 A164 40fr multi 52 26

Soroptimist Int'l. 13th Convention, Melbourne, July 26-31 — A165

1987, July 22 ***Perf. 13½***
563 A165 270fr multi 3.50 1.75

Birds A166

1987, Aug. 26 ***Perf. 13***
564 A166 18fr Zosterops xanthochroa 26 15
565 A166 21fr Falco peregrinus nesiotes, vert. 28 15
Set value 21

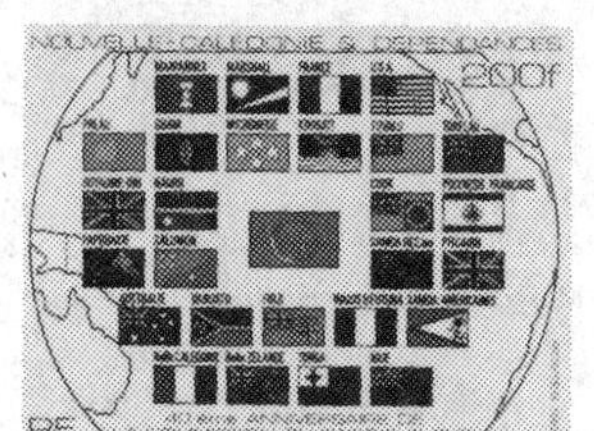

South Pacific Commission, 40th Anniv. — A167

1987, Oct. 14 Litho. ***Perf. 13***
566 A167 200fr multi 2.75 1.40

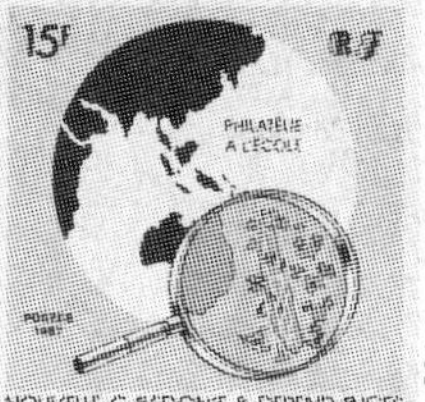

Philately at School A168

1987, Oct. 21 ***Perf. 12½***
567 A168 15fr multi 20 15

8th South Pacific Games, Noumea — A169

1987, Dec. 5 Litho. ***Perf. 12½***
568 A169 20fr Golf 28 15
569 A169 30fr Rugby 40 20
570 A169 100fr Long jump 1.40 70

Map, Ships, La Perouse — A170

1988, Feb. 10 Engr. ***Perf. 13***
571 A170 36fr dark rose lil 48 24

Disappearance of La Perouse expedition, 200th anniv., and Jean-Francois de Galaup (1741-1788), Comte de La Perouse.

French University of the South Pacific at Noumea and Papeete A171

1988, Feb. 24 Litho. ***Perf. 13x12½***
572 A171 400fr multi 5.25 2.75

Tropical Fish A172

1988, Mar. 23 Litho. ***Perf. 13***
573 A172 30fr Pomacanthus semicirculatus 38 20
574 A172 46fr Glyphidodontops cyaneus 60 30

Intl. Red Cross and Red Crescent Organizations, 125th Annivs. — A173

1988, Apr. 27
575 A173 300fr multi 3.75 1.50

Regional Housing A174

Designs: 19fr, Mwaringou, Canala Region, vert. 21fr, Nathalo, Lifou.

1988, Apr. 13 Engr. ***Perf. 13***
576 A174 19fr emer grn, brt blue & red brn 24 15
577 A174 21fr brt blue, emer grn & red brn 28 15

Medicinal Plants A175

1988, May 18 Litho. ***Perf. 13x12½***
578 A175 28fr *Ochrosia elliptica* 38 20
579 A175 64fr *Rauvolfia levenetii* 85 42

No. 579 is airmail.

Living Fossils — A176

1988, June 13 ***Perf. 13***
580 A176 51fr *Gymnocrinus richeri* 70 35

Bourail Museum and Historical Soc. — A177

1988, June 25 Litho. ***Perf. 13***
581 A177 120fr multi 1.50 75

SYDPEX '88 — A178

Designs: No. 582, La Perouse aboard *La Boussole,* gazing through spyglass at the First

Fleet in Botany Bay, Jan. 24, 1788. No. 583, Capt. Phillip and crew ashore on Botany Bay watching the approach of La Perouse's ships *La Boussole* and *L'Astrolabe*.

1988, July 30 Litho. *Perf. 13x12½*

582 A178 42fr multi 50 25
583 A178 42fr multi 50 25
a. Souvenir sheet of 2, #582-583, perf. 13x13½ 1.40 1.40

Nos. 582-583 printed se-tenant with center label picturing SYDPEX '88 emblem.
No. 583a sold for 120fr.

Kagu
A179 A179a

1988-90 Engr. *Perf. 13*

584 A179 1fr bright blue 15 15
585 A179 2fr green 15 15
586 A179 3fr bright orange 15 15
587 A179 4fr bright green 15 15
588 A179 5fr deep rose lilac 15 15
589 A179 28fr orange 55 28
590 A179 40fr bright rose 50 25
Set value 1.35 75

Issue dates: 40fr, Aug. 11. 1fr, 4fr, Jan. 25, 1989. 2fr, 3fr, 5fr, Apr. 19, 1989. 28fr, Jan. 15, 1990.
See Type A137.

1990-92 Engr. *Perf. 13*

591 A179a 1fr bright blue 15 15
592 A179a 2fr bright green 15 15
593 A179a 3fr brt yel org 15 15
594 A179a 4fr dark green 15 15
595 A179a 5fr bright violet 15 15
598 A179a 40fr lilac rose 95 48
599 A179a 50fr red 1.20 60
Set value 2.50 1.30

Issue dates: 50fr, Sept. 6, 1990. 1fr-5fr, Jan. 9, 1991. 40fr, Jan. 16, 1992.
This is an expanding set. Numbers will change if necessary.
See Type A137.

1988 Summer Olympics, Seoul — A180

1988, Sept. 15 *Perf. 12½x12*

600 A180 150fr multi 1.50 75

Pasteur Institute, Noumea, Cent. A181

1988, Sept. 29 Engr. *Perf. 13*

601 A181 100fr blk, brt ultra & dark red 1.50 75

Writers — A182

1988, Oct. 15 Engr. *Perf. 13*

602 A182 72fr Georges Baudoux (1870-1949) 1.35 68
603 A182 73fr Jean Mariotti (1901-1975) 1.40 70

No. 603 is airmail.

WHO, 40th Anniv. A183

1988, Nov. 16 Litho. *Perf. 13x12½*

604 A183 250fr multi 4.75 2.40

Art Type of 1984 Without "ET DEPENDANCES"

Paintings by artists of the Pacific: 54fr, *Land of Men,* by L. Bunckley. 92fr, *The Latin Quarter,* by Marik.

1988, Dec. 7

605 AP113 54fr multi 1.05 52
606 AP113 92fr multi 1.75 88

Arms Type of 1984 Without "ET DEPENDANCES"

1989, Feb. 22 Litho. *Perf. 13½*

607 A132 200fr Koumac 3.65 1.85

Indigenous Flora A184

1989, Mar. 22 Litho. *Perf. 13½*

608 A184 80fr *Parasitaxus ustus,* vert. 1.55 78
609 A184 90fr *Tristaniopsis guillainii* 1.75 88

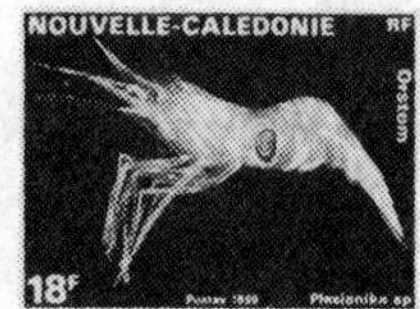

Marine Life A185

1989, May 17 Litho. *Perf. 12½x13*

610 A185 18fr *Plesionika* 38 20
611 A185 66fr *Ocosia apia* 1.35 68
612 A185 110fr *Latiaxis* 2.25 1.25

See Nos. 652-653.

French Revolution, Bicent. — A186

1989, July 7 Litho. *Perf. 13½*

613 A186 40fr Liberty 72 35
614 A186 58fr Equality 1.05 52
615 A186 76fr Fraternity 1.35 68

Souvenir Sheet

616 A186 180fr Liberty, Equality, Fraternity 3.25 3.25

Nos. 614-616 are airmail.

Landscape Type of 1986 Without "ET DEPENDANCES"

1989, Aug. 23 Litho. *Perf. 13*

617 A149 64fr La Poule rookery, Hienghene 1.10 55
618 A149 180fr Ouaieme ferry 3.00 1.50

No. 617 is airmail.

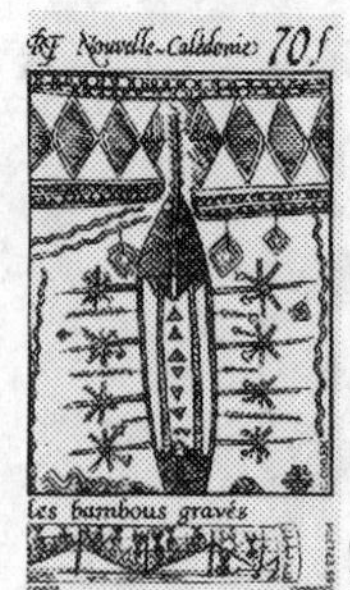

Carved Bamboo — A187

Litho. & Engr.

1989, Sept. 27 *Perf. 12½x13*

619 A187 70fr tan, blk & dark org 1.20 60

See No. C216.

Hobie-Cat 14 10th World Championships, Nov. 3, Noumea — A188

1989, Oct. 25 Litho. *Perf. 13*

620 A188 350fr multicolored 6.00 3.00

Natl. Historical Soc., 20th Anniv. — A189

Cover of *Moeurs: Superstitions of New Caledonians,* cover of book on Melanesian oral literature and historians G. Pisier, R.P. Neyret and A. Surleau.

1989, Nov. 3 Engr.

621 A189 74fr brown & black 1.30 65

Ft. Teremba — A190

1989, Nov. 18 Engr.

622 A190 100fr bl grn & dk org 1.75 88

Marguerite Historical Preservation Soc.

Impressionist Paintings — A191

Designs: 130fr, *The Escape of Rochefort,* by Manet. 270fr, *Self-portrait,* by Courbet.

1989, Dec. 6 Litho. *Perf. 13½*

623 A191 130fr multicolored 2.25 1.15
624 A191 270fr multicolored 4.50 2.25

Fr. Patrick O'Reilly (1900-1988), Writer — A192

1990, Jan. 24 Engr. *Perf. 13x13½*

625 A192 170fr blk & plum 3.25 1.65

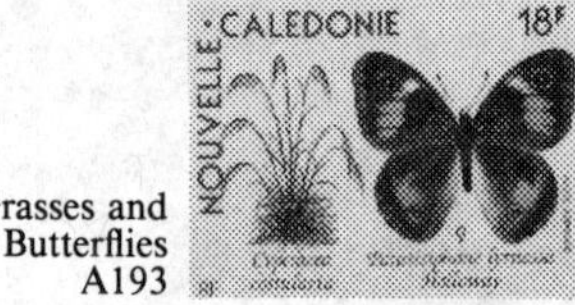

Grasses and Butterflies A193

Various *Cyperacea costularia* and *Paratisiphone lyrnessa:* 18fr, Female. 50fr, Female, diff. 94fr, Male.

1990, Jan. 21 Litho. *Perf. 13½*

626 A193 18fr shown 35 18
627 A193 50fr multicolored 95 48
628 A193 94fr multicolored 1.75 88

Nos. 626 and 628 are airmail.

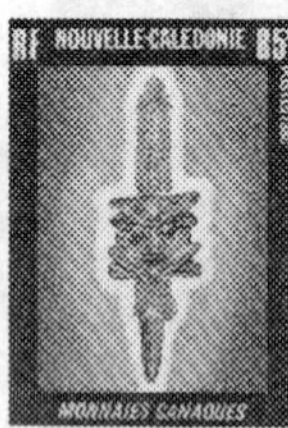

Kanakan Money — A194

1990, Mar. 16 Engr. *Perf. 12½x13*

629 A194 85fr multicolored 1.60 80
630 A194 140fr multi, diff. 2.65 1.35

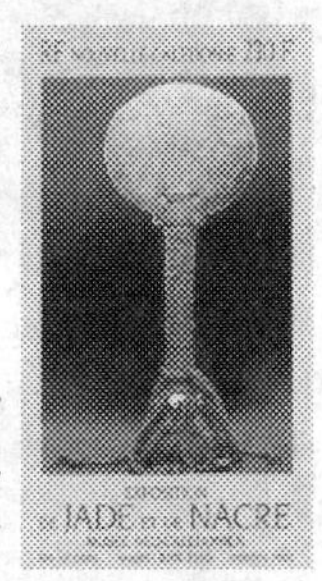
Jade and Mother of Pearl Exhibition, New Caledonian Museum — A195

1990, Mar. 16 Litho. *Perf. 13x13½*
631 A195 230fr multicolored 4.35 2.20

Noumea Aquarium A196

Perf. 13x12½, 12½x13
1990, Apr. 25
632 A196 10fr *Phyllidia ocellata* 20 15
633 A196 42fr *Chromodoris kuniei,* vert. 88 45

Petroglyphs A197

1990, July 11 Engr. *Perf. 13*
634 A197 40fr Neounda 78 40
635 A197 58fr Kassducou 1.10 55

No. 635 is airmail.

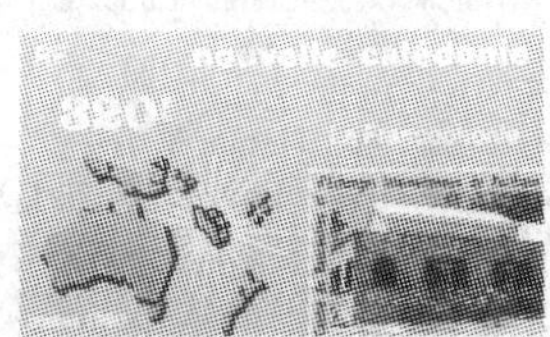
Meeting Center of the Pacific — A198

1990, July 25 Litho. *Perf. 13*
636 A198 320fr multicolored 6.25 3.10

World Cup Soccer Championships, Italy — A199

1990, May 30 Litho. *Perf. 13*
637 A199 240fr multicolored 5.25 2.60

Flowers A200

1990, Nov. 7 *Perf. 13x12½*
638 A200 105fr Gardenia aubryi 1.00 50
639 A200 130fr Hibbertia baudouinii 1.20 60

La Maison Celieres by M. Petron A201

Design: 365fr, Le Mont-Dore de Jade by C. Degroiselle.

1990, Dec. 5 *Perf. 12½*
640 A201 110fr multicolored 2.60 1.30
641 A201 365fr multicolored 8.75 4.35

No. 640 is airmail.

Writers — A202

Designs: #642, Louise Michel (1830-1905). #643, Charles B. Nething (1867-1947).

1991, Mar. 20 Engr. *Perf. 13*
642 A202 125fr rose lil & bl 2.75 1.40
643 A202 125fr brn & bl 2.75 1.40
a. Pair, #642-643 + label 5.50 2.80

Native Huts — A203

1991, May 15 Litho. *Perf. 12*
644 A203 12fr Houailou 25 15
645 A203 35fr Hienghene 75 38

Maps of the Provinces A204

1991, June 17 Litho. *Perf. 13½*
646 A204 45fr Northern 95 48
647 A204 45fr Island 95 48
648 A204 45fr Southern 95 48
a. Strip of 3, #646-648 2.85 1.42

Orchids — A205

1991, July 24 Litho. *Perf. 13*
649 A205 55fr Dendrobium biflorum 1.15 62
650 A205 70fr Dendrobium closterium 1.45 72

French Institute of Scientific Research — A206

1991, Aug. 26
651 A206 170fr multicolored 3.50 1.75

Marine Life Type of 1989

1991, Aug. 26 Litho. *Perf. 12*
652 A185 60fr Monocentris japonicus 1.25 65
653 A185 100fr Tristigenys niphonia 2.10 1.05

9th South Pacific Games, Papua New Guinea A207

1991, Sept. 6 *Perf. 12½*
654 A207 170fr multicolored 3.50 1.75

Vietnamese in New Caledonia, Cent. — A208

1991, Sept. 8 Engr. *Perf. 13x12½*
655 A208 300fr multicolored 7.00 3.50

Lions Club of New Caledonia, 30th Anniv. — A209

1991, Oct. 5 Litho. *Perf. 12½*
656 A209 192fr multicolored 4.25 2.10

First Commercial Harvesting of Sandalwood, 150th Anniv. — A210

1991, Oct. 23 Engr. *Perf. 13*
657 A210 200fr multicolored 4.25 2.10

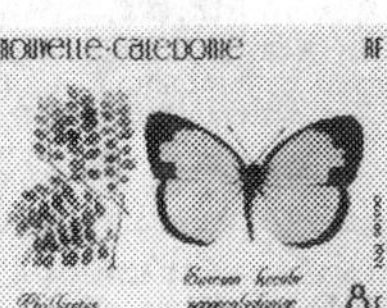
Phila Nippon '91 — A211

Plants and butterflies: 8fr, Phillantus, Eurema hecabe. 15fr, Pipturus incanus, Hypolimnas octocula. 20fr, Stachytarpheta urticaefolia, Precis villida. 26fr, Malaisia scandens, Cyrestis telamon.

Butterflies: No. 662a, Cyrestis telamon, vert. b, Hypolimnas octocula, vert. c, Eurema hecabe, vert. d, Precis villida, vert.

1991, Nov. 16 Litho. *Perf. 12½*
658 A211 8fr multicolored 20 15
659 A211 15fr multicolored 38 18
660 A211 20fr multicolored 50 25
661 A211 26fr multicolored 65 32
a. Strip of 4, #658-661 + label 1.70 85

Souvenir Sheet

662 A211 75fr Sheet of 4, #a.-d. 7.00 7.00

SEMI-POSTAL STAMPS

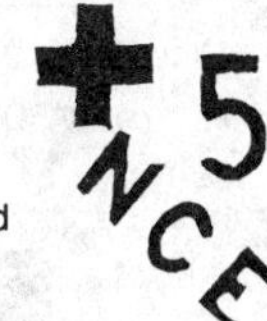
No. 93 Surcharged

1915 Unwmk. *Perf. 14x13½*
B1 A16 10c + 5c car 45 45
a. Inverted surcharge 17.50 17.50
b. Cross omitted 17.50 17.50

Regular Issue of 1905 Surcharged

1917
B2 A16 10c + 5c rose 28 28
a. Double surcharge 30.00 30.00
B3 A16 15c + 5c vio 28 28

Curie Issue
Common Design Type

1938, Oct. 24 *Perf. 13*
B4 CD80 1.75fr + 50c brt ultra 5.75 5.75

French Revolution Issue
Common Design Type

1939, July 5 Photo.
Name and Value Typo. in Black
B5 CD83 45c + 25c grn 3.50 3.50
B6 CD83 70c + 30c brn 3.50 3.50
B7 CD83 90c + 35c red org 3.50 3.50
B8 CD83 1.25fr + 1fr rose pink 3.50 3.50
B9 CD83 2.25fr + 2fr bl 3.50 3.50
Nos. B5-B9 (5) 17.50 17.50

Common Design Type and

Dumont d'Urville's ship, "Zelée" — SP2

New Caledonian Militiaman SP3

1941 Photo. *Perf. 13½*
B10 SP2 1fr + 1fr red 50
B11 CD86 1.50fr + 3fr maroon 50
B12 SP3 2.50fr + 1fr dk blue 50

Nos. B10-B12 were issued by the Vichy government and were not placed on sale in the colony.

In 1944 Nos. 216A-216B were surcharged "OEUVRES COLONIALES" and surtax (including change of denomination of the 2.50fr to 50c). These were issued by the Vichy government and not placed on sale in New Caledonia.

Catalogue values for unused stamps in this section, from this point to the end of the section, are for Never Hinged items.

Red Cross Issue
Common Design Type

1944 ***Perf. 14½x14***
B13 CD90 5fr + 20fr brt scar 45 45

The surtax was for the French Red Cross and national relief.

Tropical Medicine Issue
Common Design Type

1950, May 15 Engr. ***Perf. 13***
B14 CD100 10fr + 2fr red brn & sepia 2.00 2.00

The surtax was for charitable work.

AIR POST STAMPS

Seaplane Over Pacific Ocean AP1

1938-40 Unwmk. Engr. ***Perf. 13***

C1	AP1	65c dp vio	38	38
a.		"65c" omitted	67.50	
C2	AP1	4.50fr red	55	55
C3	AP1	7fr dk bl grn ('40)	38	38
C4	AP1	9fr ultra	1.00	1.00
C5	AP1	20fr dk org ('40)	60	60
C6	AP1	50fr blk ('40)	1.25	1.25
		Nos. C1-C6 (6)	4.16	4.16

V4

Stamps of type AP1, without "RF" monogram, and stamp of the design shown above were issued in 1942 to 1944 by the Vichy Government, but were not placed on sale in the colony.

Common Design Type

1942 Unwmk. ***Perf. 14½x14***

C7	CD87	1fr dk org	28	24
C8	CD87	1.50fr brt red	28	24
C9	CD87	5fr brn red	30	24
C10	CD87	10fr black	50	40
C11	CD87	25fr ultra	55	45
C12	CD87	50fr dk grn	70	60
C13	CD87	100fr plum	95	85
		Nos. C7-C13 (7)	3.56	3.02

Catalogue values for unused stamps in this section, from this point to the end of the section, are for Never Hinged items.

Victory Issue
Common Design Type

1946, May 8 Engr. ***Perf. 12½***
C14 CD92 8fr brt ultra 60 60

Chad to Rhine Issue
Common Design Types

1946, June 6

C15	CD93	5fr black	45	45
C16	CD94	10fr carmine	45	45
C17	CD95	15fr dk bl	48	48
C18	CD96	20fr org brn	48	48
C19	CD97	25fr ol grn	75	75
C20	CD98	50fr dk rose vio	1.10	1.10
		Nos. C15-C20 (6)	3.71	3.71

St. Vincent Bay — AP2

Planes over Islands — AP3

View of Nouméa — AP4

Perf. 13x12½, 12½x13
1948, Mar. 1 Photo. Unwmk.

C21	AP2	50fr org & rose vio	1.90	1.50
C22	AP3	100fr bl grn & sl bl	4.25	2.00
C23	AP4	200fr brn & yel	9.00	4.50

UPU Issue
Common Design Type

1949, July 4 Engr. ***Perf. 13***
C24 CD99 10fr multi 1.90 1.65

Liberation Issue
Common Design Type

1954, June 6
C25 CD102 3fr ind & ultra 1.90 1.65

Conveyor for Nickel Ore — AP5

1955, Nov. 21 Unwmk. ***Perf. 13***
C26 AP5 14fr ind & sep 2.00 70

Rock Formations, Bourail — AP6

1959, Mar. 23
C27 AP6 200fr lt bl, brn & grn 20.00 7.50

Yaté Dam — AP7

1959, Sept. 20 **Engr.**
C28 AP7 50fr grn, brt bl & sep 4.00 2.75

Dedication of Yaté Dam.

Fisherman with Throw-net — AP8

Skin Diver Shooting Bumphead Surgeonfish — AP9

Designs: 20fr, Nautilus shell. 100fr, Yaté rock.

1962 Unwmk. ***Perf. 13***

C29	AP8	15fr red, Prus grn & sep	2.50	90
C30	AP9	20fr dk sl grn & org ver	3.50	1.50
C31	AP9	25fr red brn, gray & bl	5.00	1.50
C32	AP9	100fr dk brn, dk bl & sl grn	14.00	5.25

Telstar Issue
Common Design Type

1962, Dec. 4 Unwmk. ***Perf. 13***
C33 CD111 200fr dk bl, choc & grnsh bl 20.00 9.00

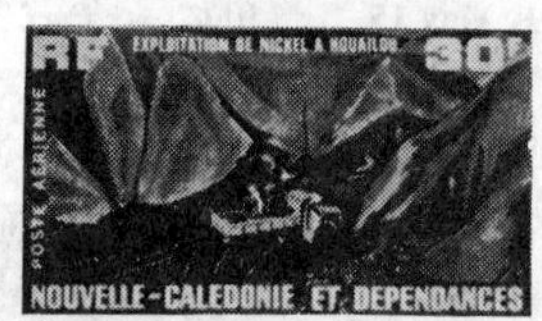
Nickel Mining, Houailou — AP10

1964, May 14 **Photo.**
C34 AP10 30fr multi 2.00 1.25

Isle of Pines AP11

1964, Dec. 7 Engr. ***Perf. 13***
C35 AP11 50fr dk bl, sl grn & choc 2.25 1.50

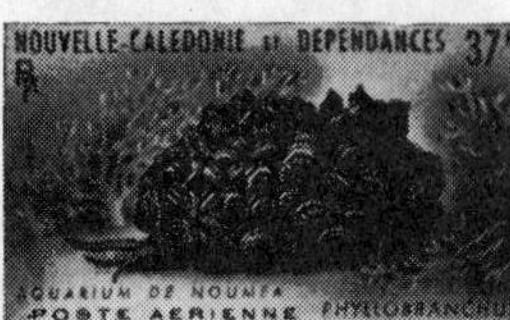
Phyllobranchus — AP12

Design: 27fr, Paracanthurus teuthis (fish).

1964, Dec. 17 **Photo.**

C36	AP12	27fr red brn, yel, dp bl & blk	3.00	1.50
C37	AP12	37fr bl, brn & yel	3.75	2.25

Issued to publicize the Nouméa Aquarium.

Greco-Roman Wrestling — AP13

1964, Dec. 28 **Engr.**
C38 AP13 10fr brt grn, pink & blk 12.50 10.00

18th Olympic Games, Tokyo, Oct. 10-25.

Nimbus Weather Satellite over New Caledonia — AP14

1965, Mar. 23 Photo. ***Perf. 13x12½***
C39 AP14 9fr multi 2.00 1.75

Fifth World Meteorological Day.

ITU Issue
Common Design Type

1965, May 17 Engr. ***Perf. 13***
C40 CD120 40fr lt bl, lil rose & lt brn 5.00 4.25

Coris Angulata (Young Fish) — AP15

Coris Angulata: 15fr, Adolescent fish. 25fr, Adult fish.

1965, Dec. 6 Engr. ***Perf. 13***

C41	AP15	13fr red org, ol bis & blk	1.10	40
C42	AP15	15fr ind, sl grn & bis	1.75	65
C43	AP15	25fr ind & yel grn	2.75	1.75

Issued to publicize the Nouméa Aquarium.

French Satellite A-1 Issue
Common Design Type

Designs: 8fr, Diamant rocket and launching installations. 12fr, A-1 satellite.

1966, Jan. 10 Engr. ***Perf. 13***

C44	CD121	8fr rose brn, ultra & Prus bl	2.00	1.10
C45	CD121	12fr ultra, Prus bl & rose brn	2.50	1.90
a.		Strip of 2, #C44-C45 + label	4.50	3.00

French Satellite D-1 Issue
Common Design Type

1966, May 16 Engr. *Perf. 13*
C46 CD122 10fr dl bl, ocher & sep 1.25 1.10

Port-de-France, 1866 — AP16

1966, June 2
C47 AP16 30fr dk red, bl & ind 2.25 1.90

Centenary of Port-de-France changing name to Noumea.

Bird Type of Regular Issue

Designs: 27fr, Uvea crested parakeet. 37fr, Scarlet honey eater. 50fr, Two cloven-feathered doves.

1966-68 Photo. *Perf. 13*
Size: 26x46mm
C48 A45 27fr pink & multi 3.25 2.00
C49 A45 37fr grn & multi 4.75 2.75
Size: 27x48mm
C49A A45 50fr multi ('68) 5.50 2.75

Issue dates: 50fr, May 14, 1968. Others, Oct. 10, 1966.

Sailboats and Map of New Caledonia-New Zealand Route — AP17

1967, Apr. 15 Engr. *Perf. 13*
C50 AP17 25fr brt grn, dp ultra & red 2.25 1.50

2nd sailboat race from Whangarei, New Zealand, to Noumea, New Caledonia.

Butterfly Type of Regular Issue

Butterflies: 19fr, Danaus plexippus. 29fr, Hippotion celerio. 85fr, Delias elipsis.

1967-68 Engr. *Perf. 13*
Size: 48x27mm
C51 A52 19fr multi ('68) 3.00 1.75
C52 A52 29fr multi ('68) 3.50 2.50
C53 A52 85fr red, dk brn & yel 9.50 4.75

Issue dates: 85fr, Aug. 10. Others, Mar. 26.

Jules Garnier, Garnierite and Mine — AP18

1967, Oct. 9 Engr. *Perf. 13*
C54 AP18 70fr bl gray, brn & yel grn 2.75 2.00

Centenary of the discovery of garnierite (nickel ore).

Lifu Island — AP19

1967, Oct. 28 Photo. *Perf. 13*
C55 AP19 200fr multi 6.00 4.00

Skier, Snowflake and Olympic Emblem — AP20

1967, Nov. 16 Engr. *Perf. 13*
C56 AP20 100fr brn red, sl grn & brt bl 8.00 4.50

10th Winter Olympic Games, Grenoble, France, Feb. 6-18, 1968.

Sea Shell Type of Regular Issue

Designs: 39fr, Conus lienardi. 40fr, Conus cabriti. 70fr, Conus coccineus.

1968, Nov. 9 Engr. *Perf. 13*
C58 A54 39fr bl grn, brn & gray 2.50 1.25
C59 A54 40fr blk, brn red & ol 2.50 1.25
C60 A54 70fr brn, pur & gray 6.00 3.00

Maré Dancers — AP21

1968, Nov. 20 Engr. *Perf. 13*
C61 AP21 60fr grn, ultra & hn brn 3.50 2.25

World Map and Caudron C 600 "Aiglon" — AP22

1969, Mar. 24 Engr. *Perf. 13*
C62 AP22 29fr lil, dk bl & dk car 2.00 1.40

Issued for Stamp Day and to commemorate the first flight from Nouméa to Paris of Henri Martinet and Paul Klein, March 24, 1939.

Concorde Issue
Common Design Type

1969, Apr. 17 Engr. *Perf. 13*
C63 CD129 100fr sl grn & brt grn 14.00 10.00

Cattle Type of Regular Issue

Design: 50fr, Cowboy and herd.

1969, May 10 Engr. *Perf. 13*
Size: 48x27mm
C64 A56 50fr sl grn, dk brn & red brn 3.00 2.00

Shell Type of Regular Issue, 1969

Design: 100fr, Black murex.

1969, June 21 Engr. *Perf. 13*
Size: 48x27mm
C65 A57 100fr lake, bl & blk 13.00 7.00

Sports Type of 1969

Designs: 30fr, Woman diver. 39fr, Shot put (vert.).

1969, Aug. 7 Engr. *Perf. 13*
Size: 48x27mm, 27x48mm
C66 A58 30fr dk brn, bl & blk 2.00 1.25
C67 A58 39fr dk ol, brt grn & ol 2.75 1.65

Napoleon in Coronation Robes, by François P. Gerard AP23

1969, Oct. 2 Photo. *Perf. 12½x12*
C68 AP23 40fr lil & multi 8.50 5.50

200th birth anniv. of Napoleon Bonaparte (1769-1821).

Air France Plane over Outrigger Canoe — AP24

1969, Oct. 2 Engr. *Perf. 13*
C69 AP24 50fr slate grn, sky bl & choc 2.50 2.00

20th anniversary of the inauguration of the Nouméa to Paris airline.

Bird Type of Regular Issue, 1966.

Birds: 39fr, Emerald doves. 100fr, Whistling kite.

1970, Feb. 19 Photo. *Perf. 13*
Size: 27x48mm
C70 A45 39fr multi 3.00 1.40
C71 A45 100r lt bl & multi 8.00 4.00

Planes Circling Globe and Paris-Nouméa Route — AP25

1970, May 6 Engr. *Perf. 13*
C72 AP25 200fr vio, org brn & grnsh bl 8.75 5.00

10th anniversary of the Paris to Nouméa flight: "French Wings Around the World."

Shell Type of Regular Issue

Designs: 22fr, Strombus sinautus humphrey (vert.). 33fr, Argus porcelain shell. 34fr, Strombus vomer (vert.). 60fr, Card porcelain shell.

1970 Engr. *Perf. 13*
Size: 27x48mm, 48x27mm
C73 A59 22fr bl & multi 2.00 1.40
C74 A59 33fr brn & gray bl 3.00 1.75
C75 A59 34fr pur & multi 3.00 1.75
C76 A59 60fr lt grn & brn 6.00 3.00

See Nos. C89-C90.

Bicyclists on Map of New Caledonia — AP26

1970, Aug. 20 Engr. *Perf. 13*
C77 AP26 40fr bl, ultra & choc 1.75 1.25

The 4th Bicycling Race of New Caledonia.

Mt. Fuji and Monorail Train — AP27

Design: 45fr, Map of Japan and Buddha statue.

1970, Sept. 3 Photo. *Perf. 13x12½*
C78 AP27 20fr blk, bl & yel grn 1.10 65
C79 AP27 45fr mar, lt bl & ol 1.90 90

EXPO '70 International Exposition, Osaka, Japan, Mar. 15-Sept. 13.

Racing Yachts AP28

1971, Feb. 23 Engr. *Perf. 13*
C80 AP28 20fr grn, blk & ver 1.25 65

First challenge in New Zealand waters for the One Ton Cup ocean race.

Lt. Col. Broche and Map of Mediterranean — AP29

1971, May 5 Photo. *Perf. 12½*
C81 AP29 60fr multi 3.00 2.25

30th anniversary of Battalion of the Pacific.

Pole Vault — AP30

1971, June 24 Engr. *Perf. 13*
C82 AP30 25fr shown 1.40 90
C83 AP30 100fr Archery 3.75 2.25

4th South Pacific Games, Papeete, French Polynesia, Sept. 8-19.

Port de Plaisance, Nouméa — AP31

1971, Sept. 27 Photo. *Perf. 13*
C84 AP31 200fr multi 10.00 5.00

Golden Eagle and Pilot's Leaflet — AP32

1971, Nov. 20 Engr. *Perf. 13*
C85 AP32 90fr dk brn, org & ind 4.00 2.25

40th anniversary of the first flight from New Caledonia to Australia with Victor Roffey piloting the Golden Eagle.

Skiing and Sapporo '72 Emblem — AP33

1972, Jan. 22 Engr. *Perf. 13*
C86 AP33 50fr brt bl, car & sl grn 2.75 1.40

11th Winter Olympic Games, Sapporo, Japan, Feb. 3-13.

South Pacific Commission Headquarters, Nouméa — AP34

1972, Feb. 5 Photo.
C87 AP34 18fr bl & multi 70 45

South Pacific Commission, 25th anniv.

St. Mark's Basilica, Venice — AP35

1972, Feb. 5 Engr.
C88 AP35 20fr lt grn, bl & grn 1.40 65

UNESCO campaign to save Venice.

Shell Type of Regular Issue, 1970

Designs: 25fr, Orange spider conch (vert.). 50fr, Chiragra spider conch (vert.).

1972, Mar. 4 Engr. *Perf. 13*
Size: 27x48mm
C89 A59 25fr dp car & dk brn 2.25 1.10
C90 A59 50fr grn, brn & rose car 3.50 1.90

Breguet F-ALMV and Globe — AP36

1972, Apr. 5 Engr. *Perf. 13*
C91 AP36 110fr brt rose lil, bl & grn 6.50 4.50

40th anniversary of the first Paris-Nouméa flight, Mar. 9-Apr. 5, 1932.

Round House and Festival Emblem — AP37

1972, May 13
C92 AP37 24fr org, bl & brn 1.25 80

So. Pacific Festival of Arts, Fiji, May 6-20.

Hurdles and Olympic Rings — AP38

1972, Sept. 2 Engr. *Perf. 13*
C93 AP38 72fr vio, bl & red lil 4.00 2.25

20th Olympic Games, Munich, Aug. 26-Sept. 11.

New Post Office, Noumea — AP39

1972, Nov. 25 Engr. *Perf. 13*
C94 AP39 23fr brn, brt bl & grn 1.25 55

Molière and Scenes from Plays — AP40

1973, Feb. 24 Engr. *Perf. 13*
C95 AP40 50fr multi 3.00 1.50

300th anniversary of the death of Molière (Jean Baptiste Poquelin, 1622-1673), French actor and playwright.

Woodlands — AP41

Designs: 18fr, Palm trees on coast (vert.). 21fr, Waterfall (vert.).

1973, Feb. 24 Photo.
C96 AP41 11fr gold & multi 75 50
C97 AP41 18fr gold & multi 1.50 60
C98 AP41 21fr gold & multi 2.00 75

Concorde — AP42

1973, Mar. 15 Engr. *Perf. 13*
C99 AP42 23fr blue 2.75 2.00
a. Booklet pane of 5 25.00

No. C99 issued in booklets only.

El Kantara in Panama Canal — AP43

1973, Mar. 24 Engr. *Perf. 13*
C100 AP43 60fr brn, yel grn & blk 3.50 2.00

50th anniversary of steamship connection Marseilles to Noumea through Panama Canal.

Sun, Earth, Wind God and Satellite — AP44

1973, Mar. 24
C101 AP44 80fr multi 3.00 1.65

Centenary of international meteorological cooperation and 13th World Meteorological Day.

Museum Type of Regular Issue

Designs: 16fr, Carved arrows and arrowhead. 40fr, Carved entrance to chief's house.

1973, Apr. 30 Photo. *Perf. 12½x13*
C102 A66 16fr multi 60 50
C103 A66 40fr multi 1.40 1.00

DC-10 over Map of Route Paris to Noumea — AP45

1973, May 19 Engr. *Perf. 13*
C104 AP45 100fr brn, ultra & sl grn 4.00 2.50

First direct flight by DC-10, Nouméa to Paris.

Fish Type of Regular Issue

Design: 32fr, Old and young olive surgeonfish.

1973, June 23 Photo. *Perf. 13x12½*
C105 A69 32fr multi 3.00 1.75

Coach, 1880 — AP46

1973, Sept. 22 Engr. *Perf. 13*
C106 AP46 15fr choc, bl & sl grn 85 55

Stamp Day 1973.

Landscape — AP47

West Coast Landscapes: 8fr, Rocky path (vert.). 26fr, Trees on shore.

1974, Feb. 23 Photo. *Perf. 13*
C107 AP47 8fr gold & multi 60 25
C108 AP47 22fr gold & multi 1.10 45
C109 AP47 26fr gold & multi 1.65 65

Anse-Vata, Scientific Center, Nouméa — AP48

1974, Mar. 23 Photo. *Perf. 13x12½*
C110 AP48 50fr multi 1.75 80

Ovula Ovum AP49

1974, Mar. 23
C111 AP49 3fr *shown* 22 15
C112 AP49 32fr *Hydatina* 1.40 65
C113 AP49 37fr *Dolium perdix* 2.00 1.00

Nouméa Aquarium.

Capt. Cook, Map of Grande Terre and "Endeavour" — AP50

Designs: 25fr, Jean F. de la Perouse, his ship and map of Grande Terre. 28fr, French sailor, 18th century, on board ship (vert.). 30fr, Antoine R. J. d'Entrecasteaux, ship and map. 36fr, Dumont d'Urville, ship and map of Loyalty Islands.

1974, Sept. 4 Engr. *Perf. 13*
C114 AP50 20fr multi 65 25
C115 AP50 25fr multi 65 45
C116 AP50 28fr multi 85 45

C117 AP50 30fr multi 1.00 55
C118 AP50 36fr multi 1.10 85
Nos. C114-C118 (5) 4.25 2.55

Discovery and exploration of New Caledonia and Loyalty Islands.

UPU Emblem and Symbolic Design — AP51

1974, Oct. 9 **Engr.** ***Perf. 13***
C119 AP51 95fr multi 3.00 2.00

Centenary of Universal Postal Union.

Abstract Design — AP52

1974, Oct. 26 **Photo.** ***Perf. 13***
C120 AP52 80fr bl, blk & org 2.50 1.25

ARPHILA 75, Philatelic Exhibition, Paris, June 6-16, 1975.

Hôtel Château-Royal, Nouméa — AP53

1975, Jan. 20 **Photo.** ***Perf. 13***
C121 AP53 22fr multi 85 50

Cricket AP54

Designs: 25fr, Bougna ceremony (food offering). 31fr, Pilou dance.

1975, Mar. 24 **Photo.** ***Perf. 13***
C122 AP54 3fr bl & multi 32 15
C123 AP54 25fr ol grn & multi 65 35
C124 AP54 31fr yel grn & multi 1.00 45

Tourist publicity.

Orchid Type of 1975

Design: 42fr, Eriaxis rigida.

1975, May 30
C125 A74 42fr grn & multi 2.75 1.75

Globe as "Flower" with "Stamps" and leaves — AP55

1975, June 7 **Engr.** ***Perf. 13***
C126 AP55 105fr multi 3.25 2.00

ARPHILA 75 International Philatelic Exhibition, Paris, June 6-16.

Discus and Games' Emblem — AP56

Design: 50fr, Volleyball and Games' emblem.

1975, Aug. 23 **Photo.** ***Perf. 13x12½***
C127 AP56 24fr emer, pur & dk bl 50 40
C128 AP56 50fr multi 1.40 85

5th South Pacific Games, Guam, Aug. 1-10.

Concorde — AP57

1976, Jan. 21 **Engr.** ***Perf. 13***
C129 AP57 147fr car & ultra 5.50 4.00

First commercial flight of supersonic jet Concorde, Paris-Rio de Janeiro, Jan. 21.
For surcharge see No. C141.

Telephones 1876 and 1976, Satellite — AP58

1976, Mar. 10 **Photo.** ***Perf. 13***
C130 AP58 36fr multi 1.10 55

Centenary of first telephone call by Alexander Graham Bell, Mar. 10, 1876.

Battle Scene — AP59

1976, June 14 **Engr.** ***Perf. 13***
C131 AP59 24fr red brn & ver 75 55

American Bicentennial.

Runners and Maple Leaf — AP60

1976, July 24 **Engr.** ***Perf. 13***
C132 AP60 33fr car, vio & brn 1.10 55

21st Olympic Games, Montreal, Canada, July 17-Aug. 1.

Whimsical Bird as Student and Collector AP61

1976, Aug. 21 **Photo.**
C133 AP61 42fr multi 1.40 1.00

Philately in School, Philatelic Exhibition in La Perouse Lyceum, Nouméa.

Old City Hall, Nouméa — AP62

Design: 125fr, New City Hall, Nouméa.

1976, Oct. 22 **Photo.** ***Perf. 13***
C134 AP62 75fr multi 2.50 1.40
C135 AP62 125fr multi 3.50 2.00

Lagoon, Women and Festival Symbols AP63

1977, Jan. 15 **Photo.** ***Perf. 13x12½***
C136 AP63 11fr multi 45 28

Summer Festival 1977, Nouméa.

Training Children in Toy Cars — AP64

1977, Mar. 12 **Litho.** ***Perf. 13***
C137 AP64 50fr multi 1.40 1.00

Road safety training.

Bird Type of 1977

Design: 42fr, Male frigate bird (horiz.).

1977, Sept. 17 **Photo.** ***Perf. 13***
C138 A89 42fr multi 2.25 1.10

Magenta Airport and Routes — AP65

Design: 57fr, La Tontouta airport.

1977, Oct. 22 **Litho.** ***Perf. 13***
C139 AP65 24fr multi 55 40
C140 AP65 57fr multi 1.65 65

No. C129 Surcharged in Violet Blue: "22.11.77 PARIS NEW YORK"

1977, Nov. 22 **Engr.** ***Perf. 13***
C141 AP57 147fr car & ultra 6.50 5.50

Concorde, 1st commercial flight Paris-NY.

Old Nouméa, by H. Didonna — AP66

Valley of the Settlers, by Jean Kreber — AP67

1977, Nov. 26 **Photo.** ***Perf. 13***
C142 AP66 41fr gold & multi 1.25 55

Engr.

C143 AP67 42fr yel brn & dk brn 1.25 55

"Underwater Carnival," Aubusson Tapestry — AP68

1978, June 17 **Photo.** ***Perf. 13***
C144 AP68 105fr multi 2.50 1.40

"The Hare and the Tortoise" — AP69

1978, Aug. 19 Photo. *Perf. 13x13½*
C145 AP69 35fr multi 1.25 75

School philately.

Bourail School Children, Map and Conus Shell — AP70

1978, Sept. 30 Engr. *Perf. 13*
C146 AP70 41fr multi 1.10 55

Promotion of topical philately in Bourail public schools.

Old and New Candles — AP71

1978, Oct. 21 Photo. *Perf. 13*
C147 AP71 36fr multi 75 45

Third Caledonian Senior Citizens' Day.

Faubourg Blanchot, by Lacouture — AP72

1978, Nov. 25 Photo. *Perf. 13*
C148 AP72 24fr multi 85 60

Type of 1978

Design: 42fr, Amyema scandens (horiz.).

1978, Mar. 17 *Perf. 13x12½*
C149 A91 42fr multi 2.00 90

Orbiting Weather Satellites, WMO Emblem AP73

1979, Mar. 24 Photo. *Perf. 13*
C150 AP73 53fr multi 90 55

First world-wide satellite system in the atmosphere.

Ships and Emblem — AP74

1979, Mar. 31 Engr.
C151 AP74 49fr multi 95 50

Chamber of Commerce and Industry, centenary.

Child's Drawing, IYC Emblem AP75

1979, Apr. 21 Photo. *Perf. 13*
C152 AP75 35fr multi 80 52

International Year of the Child.

Surf Casting AP76

Design: 30fr, Swordfish fishing.

1979, May 26 Litho. *Perf. 12½*
C153 AP76 29fr multi 85 55
C154 AP76 30fr multi 1.00 65

Port-de-France, 1854, and de Montravel — AP77

1979, June 16 Engr. *Perf. 13*
C155 AP77 75fr multi 1.75 1.00

125th anniversary of Noumea, formerly Port-de-France, founded by L. Tardy de Montravel.

The Eel Queen, Kanaka Legend — AP78

1979, July 7 Photo. *Perf. 13*
C156 AP78 42fr multi 1.50 1.00

Nature protection.

Map of New Caledonia, Postmark, Five Races — AP79

1979, Aug. 18 Photo. *Perf. 13*
C157 AP79 27fr multi 50 30

New Caledonian youth and philately.

Orstom Center, Noumea, Orstom Emblem — AP80

1979, Sept. 17 Photo. *Perf. 13*
C158 AP80 25fr multi 45 28

Old Post Office, Noumea, New Caledonia No. 1, Hill — AP81

1979, Nov. 17 Engr.
C159 AP81 150fr multi 3.50 2.25

Sir Rowland Hill (1795-1879), originator of penny postage.

Pirogue AP82

1980, Jan. 26 Engr. *Perf. 13*
C160 AP82 45fr multi 1.00 70

Rotary International, 75th Anniversary — AP83

1980, Feb. 23 Photo. *Perf. 13*
C161 AP83 100fr multi 2.50 1.75

Man Holding Dolphinfish AP84

1980, Oct. 11 Photo. *Perf. 13x12½*
C162 AP84 34fr shown 85 55
C163 AP84 39fr Fishermen, sail fish, vert. 1.00 65

Coral Seas Air Rally — AP85

1980, June 7 Engr. *Perf. 13*
C164 AP85 31fr multi 85 65

Carved Alligator, Boat — AP86

1980, June 21 Photo.
C165 AP86 27fr multi 60 40

South Pacific Arts Festival, Port Moresby, Papua New Guinea.

New Caledonian Kiwanis, 10th Anniversary — AP87

1980, Sept. 10 Photo. *Perf. 13*
C166 AP87 50fr multi 1.00 65

View of Old Noumea — AP88

1980, Oct. 25 Photo. *Perf. 13½*
C167 AP88 33fr multi 65 48

Charles de Gaulle, 10th Anniversary of Death — AP89

1980, Nov. 15 Engr. *Perf. 13*
C168 AP89 120fr multi 3.00 2.00

Fluorescent Coral, Noumea Aquarium AP90

1980, Dec. 13 Photo. *Perf. 13x13½*
C169 AP90 60fr multi 1.25 70

Xeronema Moorei AP91

1981, Mar. 18 Photo. *Perf. 13x12½*
C170 AP91 38fr shown 75 40
C171 AP91 51fr Geissois pruinosa 95 40

Yuri Gagarin and Vostok I — AP92

20th Anniversary of First Space Flights: 155fr, Alan B. Shepard, Freedom 7.

1981, Apr. 8 Engr. *Perf. 13*
C172 AP92 64fr multi 1.40 85
C173 AP92 155fr multi 3.00 1.75
a. Souv. sheet of 2, #C172-C173 5.25 5.25

No. C173a sold for 225fr.

40th Anniv. of Departure of Pacific Batallion — AP93

1981, May 5 Photo. *Perf. 13*
C174 AP93 29fr multi 70 55

Ecinometra Mathaei AP94

1981, Aug. 5 Photo. *Perf. 13x13½*
C175 AP94 38fr shown 65 35
C176 AP94 51fr Prionocidaris verticillata 85 48

No. 4, Post Office Building AP95

1981, Sept. 16 Photo. *Perf. 13x13½*
C177 AP95 41fr multi 75 48

Stamp Day.

Old Noumea Latin Quarter — AP96

1981, Oct. 14 Photo. *Perf. 13½*
C178 AP96 43fr multi 75 48

New Caledonia to Australia Airmail Flight by Victor Roffey, 50th Anniv. AP97

1981, Nov. 21 Engr. *Perf. 13*
C179 AP97 37fr multi 70 40

Rousette AP98

1982, Feb. 17 Engr. *Perf. 13*
C180 AP98 38fr shown 65 35
C181 AP98 51fr Kagu 85 48

See Nos. C188B-C188C.

50th Anniv. of Paris-Noumea Flight — AP99

1982, Apr. 5 Engr. *Perf. 13*
C182 AP99 250fr Pilots, map, plane 4.50 2.50

Scouting Year — AP100

1982, Apr. 21 Photo. *Perf. 13½x13*
C183 AP100 40fr multi 70 40

PHILEXFRANCE '82 Intl. Stamp Show, Paris, June 11-21 — AP101

1982, May 12 Engr. *Perf. 13*
C184 AP101 150fr multi 2.50 2.00

1982 World Cup AP102

1982, June 9 Photo. *Perf. 13x13½*
C185 AP102 74fr multi 1.25 70

French Overseas Possessions Week, Sept. 18-25 AP103

1982, Sept. 17 *Perf. 13x12½*
C186 AP103 100fr Map, kagu, citizens 1.75 85

Gypsum, Poya Mines AP104

1983, Jan. 15 Photo. *Perf. 13x13½*
C187 AP104 44fr shown 55 30
C188 AP104 59fr Silica gel, Kone mine 70 35

World Communications Year — AP104a

Design: WCY emblem, map, globe.

1983, Mar. 9 Litho. *Perf. 13*
C188A AP104a 170fr multi 2.25 1.10

Aircraft Type of 1982

1983, Jul. 6 Engr. *Perf. 13*
C188B AP98 46fr Pou-du-Ciel 80 50
C188C AP98 61fr L'Aiglon Caudron 85 60

Temple and Dancers — AP105

1983, July 20 Litho. *Perf. 12½x12*
C189 AP105 47fr multi 85 55

BANGKOK '83 Intl. Stamp Show, Aug. 4-13.

Oueholle Tribe, Straw Hut — AP106

1983, Sept. 8 Litho. *Perf. 13*
C190 AP106 76fr multi 1.10 75

Loyalty Islander by the Shore, by R. Mascart AP107

Paintings: 350fr, The Guitarist from Mare Island, by P. Neilly.

1983, Dec. 7 Photo. *Perf. 13*
C191 AP107 100fr multi 1.10 75
C192 AP107 350fr multi 4.00 2.75

Noumea Aquarium Fish AP108

1984, Mar. 7 Photo. *Perf. 13*
C193 AP108 46fr Amphiprion clarkii 50 35
C194 AP108 61fr Centropyge bicolor 70 50

Local Plants — AP109

1984, Apr. 25 Litho. *Perf. 12½x13*
C195 AP109 51fr Araucaria columnaris 65 32
C196 AP109 67fr Pritchardiopsis jeanneneyi 85 42

1984 Summer Olympics — AP110

1984, June 20 Photo. *Perf. 13½x13*
C197 AP110 50fr Swimming 55 40
C198 AP110 83fr Wind surfing 95 70
C199 AP110 200fr Running 2.25 1.40

Ausipex '84 — AP111

Army Day — AP112

1984, Sept. 21 Engr. *Perf. 13*
C200 AP111 150fr Exhibition Hall 1.75 1.40
a. Souvenir sheet 1.90 1.90

Se-tenant with label showing exhibition emblem. No. C200a contains No. C200 in changed colors.

1984, Oct. 28 Litho. *Perf. 13½x13*
C201 AP112 51fr multi 60 32

Woman Fishing for Crabs, by Mme. Bonnet de Larbogne — AP113

Painting: 300fr, Cook Discovering New Caledonia, by Pilioko.

1984, Nov. 8 Litho. *Perf. 13x12½*
C202 AP113 120fr multi 1.50 70
C203 AP113 300fr multi 3.50 1.75

See Nos. 605-606.

Transpac Dragon Rapide, Map AP114

1985, Oct. 2 Litho. *Perf. 13½*
C204 AP114 80fr multi 80 40

Internal air services, 30th anniv.

UN, 40th Anniv. AP115

Perf. 12½x13

1985, Oct. 25 Wmk. 385
C205 AP115 250fr multi 2.25 1.10

Jules Garnier High School AP116

1985, Nov. 13 Unwmk. *Perf. 13*
C206 AP116 400fr multi 3.75 1.90

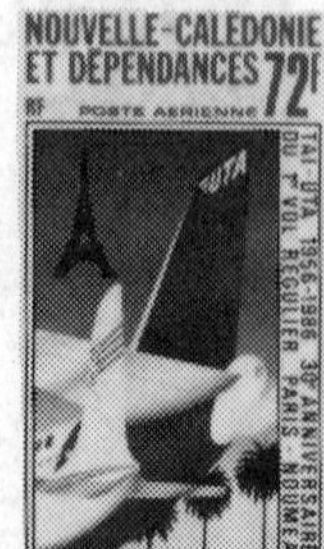

Paris-Noumea Scheduled Flights, 30th Anniv. — AP117

1986, Jan. 6
C207 AP117 72fr multi 75 38

Nou Island Livestock Warehouse — AP118

1986, June 14 Engr. *Perf. 13*
C208 AP118 230fr Prus bl, sep & brn 2.75 1.40

ATR-42 Inaugural Service AP119

1986, Aug. 13 Litho. *Perf. 12½x13*
C209 AP119 18fr multi 20 10

STOCKHOLMIA '86 — AP120

1986, Aug. 29 Engr. *Perf. 13*
C210 AP120 108fr No. 1 1.25 65

Natl. Assoc. of Amateur Radio Operators, 25th Anniv. AP121

1987, Jan. 7 Litho. *Perf. 12½*
C211 AP121 64fr multi 80 40

Nature Conservation, Fight Noise Pollution — AP122

1987, Mar. 25 Litho. *Perf. 13x12½*
C212 AP122 150fr multi 1.90 1.00

French Cricket Federation AP123

1987, Nov. 25 Litho. *Perf. 12½*
C213 AP123 94fr multi 1.40 75

Arms Type of 1984

1988, Jan. 13 *Perf. 12½x13*
C214 A132 76fr Dumbea 1.00 50

Rotary Intl. Anti-Polio Campaign — AP124

1988, Oct. 26 Litho. *Perf. 13½*
C215 AP124 220fr multi 4.00 2.00

Bamboo Type of 1989

Litho. & Engr.

1989, Sept. 27 *Perf. 12½x13*
C216 A187 44fr multi 80 40

De Gaulle's Call For French Resistance, 50th Anniv. AP125

1990, June 20 Litho. *Perf. 12½*
C217 AP125 160fr multicolored 3.50 1.75

Military Cemetery, New Zealand — AP126

Auckland 1990: C219, Brigadier William Walter Dove.

1990, Aug. 24 *Perf. 13*
C218 AP126 80fr multi 1.60 80
C219 AP126 80fr multi 1.60 80
a. Pair, #C218-C219 + label 3.25 1.60

Souvenir Sheet

New Zealand 1990 — AP126a

1990, Aug. 25 Litho. *Perf. 13x12½*
C219B AP126a 150fr multi 3.50 1.75

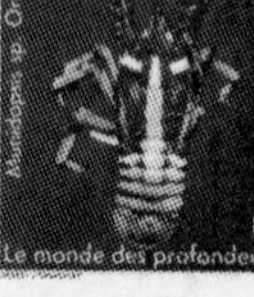

Crustaceans AP127

1990, Oct. 17 Litho. *Perf. 12½x13*
C220 AP127 30fr Munidopsis sp. Orstom 60 30
C221 AP127 60fr Lyreidius tridentatus 1.20 60

30th South Pacific Conference — AP128

1990, Oct. 29 Litho. *Perf. 13*
C222 AP128 85fr multicolored 2.10 1.05

Gen. Charles de Gaulle (1890-1970) AP129

1990, Nov. 21 Engr. *Perf. 13*
C223 AP129 410fr dk blue 10.00 5.00

Scenic Views — AP130

1991, Feb. 13 Litho. *Perf. 13*
C224 AP130 36fr Fayawa-Ouvea Bay 90 45
C225 AP130 90fr shown 2.20 1.10

New Caledonian Cricket Players by Marcel Moutouh — AP131

Design: 435fr, Saint Louis by Janine Goetz.

1991, Dec. 18 *Perf. 13x12½*
C226 AP131 130fr multicolored 3.00 1.50
C227 AP131 435fr multicolored 10.00 5.00

AIR POST SEMI-POSTAL STAMP

French Revolution Issue
Common Design Type
Unwmk.

1939, July 5 Photo. *Perf. 13*
Name and Value Typo. in Orange
CB1 CD83 4.50fr + 4fr brn blk 12.00 12.00

V5

Stamps of the design shown above and stamp of Cameroun type V10 inscribed "Nlle Caledonie" were issued in 1942 by the Vichy Government, but were not placed on sale in the colony.

POSTAGE DUE STAMPS

For a short time in 1894, 5, 10, 15, 20, 25 and 30c postage stamps (Nos. 43, 45, 47, 49, 50 and 52) were overprinted with a "T" in an inverted triangle and used as Postage Due stamps.

French Colonies Postage Due Stamps Overprinted in Carmine, Blue or Silver

1903 Unwmk. *Imperf.*

No.	Type	Description	Unused	Used
J1	D1	5c bl (C)	75	65
J2	D1	10c brn (C)	4.00	2.50
J3	D1	15c yel grn (C)	7.50	3.75
J4	D1	30c car (Bl)	5.75	4.50
J5	D1	50c vio (Bl)	30.00	6.75
J6	D1	60c brn, *buff* (Bl)	95.00	24.00
J7	D1	1fr rose, *buff* (S)	15.00	6.00
J8	D1	2fr red brn (Bl)	525.00	525.00
		Nos. J1-J8 (8)	683.00	573.15

Nos. J1 to J8 are known with the "I" in "TENAIRE" missing.

Commemorating fifty years of French occupation.

Men Poling Boat — D2

Malayan Sambar — D3

1906 Typo. *Perf. 13½x14*

No.	Type	Description	Unused	Used
J9	D2	5c ultra, *azure*	20	20
J10	D2	10c vio brn, *buff*	20	20
J11	D2	15c grn, *greenish*	35	35
J12	D2	20c blk, *yellow*	35	35
J13	D2	30c carmine	48	48
J14	D2	50c ultra, *buff*	60	60
J15	D2	60c brn, *azure*	60	60
J16	D2	1fr dk grn, *straw*	85	85
		Nos. J9-J16 (8)	3.63	3.63

Type of 1906 Issue Surcharged **2F. =**

1926-27

No.	Type	Description	Unused	Used
J17	D2	2fr on 1fr vio	1.50	1.50
J18	D2	3fr on 1fr org brn	1.50	1.50

1928 Typo.

No.	Type	Description	Unused	Used
J19	D3	2c sl bl & dp brn	15	15
J20	D3	4c brn red & bl grn	15	15
J21	D3	5c red org & bl blk	15	15
J22	D3	10c mag & Prus bl	15	15
J23	D3	15c dl grn & scar	15	15
J24	D3	20c mar & ol grn	40	40
J25	D3	25c bis brn & sl bl	28	28
J26	D3	30c bl grn & ol grn	35	35
J27	D3	50c lt brn & dk red	60	60
J28	D3	60c mag & brt rose	60	60
J29	D3	1fr dl bl & Prus grn	70	70
J30	D3	2fr dk red & ol grn	70	70
J31	D3	3fr vio & brn	1.25	1.25
		Nos. J19-J31 (13)	5.63	5.63

Catalogue values for unused stamps in this section, from this point to the end of the section, are for Never Hinged items.

D4

Bat — D5

1948 Unwmk. Photo. *Perf. 13*

No.	Type	Description	Unused	Used
J32	D4	10c violet	15	15
J33	D4	30c brown	15	15
J34	D4	50c bl grn	15	15
J35	D4	1fr orange	15	15
J36	D4	2fr red vio	15	15
J37	D4	3fr red brn	15	15
J38	D4	4fr dl bl	28	28
J39	D4	5fr hn brn	40	40
J40	D4	10fr sl grn	60	60
J41	D4	20fr vio bl	1.25	1.25
		Nos. J32-J41 (10)	3.43	3.43

1983 Litho. *Perf. 13*

No.	Type	Description	Unused	Used
J42	D5	1fr multi	15	15
J43	D5	2fr multi	15	15
J44	D5	3fr multi	15	15
J45	D5	4fr multi	15	15
J46	D5	5fr multi	15	15
J47	D5	10fr multi	22	22
J48	D5	20fr multi	42	42
J49	D5	40fr multi	85	85
J50	D5	50fr multi	1.00	1.00
		Nos. J42-J50 (9)	3.24	3.24

MILITARY STAMPS

Stamps of the above types, although issued by officials, were unauthorized and practically a private speculation.

OFFICIAL STAMPS

Catalogue values for unused stamps in this section are for Never Hinged items.

Ancestor Pole — O1

Carved Wooden Pillow — O2

Various carved ancestor poles.

1959 Unwmk. Typo. *Perf. 14x13*

No.	Type	Description	Unused	Used
O1	O1	1fr org yel	28	15
O2	O1	3fr lt bl grn	28	15
O3	O1	4fr purple	35	20
O4	O1	5fr ultra	45	24
O5	O1	9fr black	50	35
O6	O1	10fr brt vio	65	35
O7	O1	13fr yel grn	75	48
O8	O1	15fr lt bl	85	70
O9	O1	24fr red lil	1.00	85
O10	O1	26fr dp org	1.25	1.00
O11	O1	50fr green	3.00	1.50
O12	O1	100fr chocolate	6.00	3.00
O13	O1	200fr red	11.00	5.25
		Nos. O1-O13 (13)	26.36	14.22

1973-87 Photo. *Perf. 13*
Vignette: Green, Red Brown (2, 29, 31, 35, 38, 65, 76fr), Brown (40fr), Blue (58fr)

No.	Type	Description	Unused	Used
O14	O2	1fr yellow	15	15
O14A	O2	2fr grn ('87)	15	15
O15	O2	3fr tan	20	15
O16	O2	4fr pale vio	20	15
O17	O2	5fr lil rose	28	15
O18	O2	9fr lt bl	35	20
O19	O2	10fr orange	35	24
O20	O2	11fr brt lil	18	15
O21	O2	12fr bl grn ('76)	50	35
O22	O2	15fr grn ('76)	24	15
O23	O2	20fr rose ('76)	28	15
O24	O2	23fr red ('80)	28	15
O25	O2	24fr Prus bl ('76)	32	15
O25A	O2	25fr gray ('81)	32	15
O26	O2	26fr yel ('76)	35	18
O26A	O2	29fr dl grn ('83)	30	15
O26B	O2	31fr yel ('82)	32	16
O26C	O2	35fr yel ('84)	48	24
O27	O2	36fr dp lil rose ('76)	50	20
O27A	O2	38fr tan	28	15
O27B	O2	40fr blue ('87)	52	28
O28	O2	42fr bis ('76)	60	35
O29	O2	50fr bl ('76)	70	60
O29A	O2	58fr blue grn ('87)	75	48
O29B	O2	65fr lil ('84)	75	30
O29C	O2	76fr brt yel ('87)	1.10	52
O30	O2	100fr red ('76)	1.40	1.00
O31	O2	200fr org ('76)	2.75	1.50
		Nos. O14-O31 (28)	14.60	8.55

This is an expanding set. Numbers will change when complete.

PARCEL POST STAMPS

Type of Regular Issue of 1905-28 Surcharged or Overprinted

50c
Colis Postaux

1926 Unwmk. *Perf. 14x13½*

No.	Type	Description	Unused	Used
Q1	A18	50c on 5fr ol, *lav*	50	50
Q2	A18	1fr dp bl	70	70
Q3	A18	2fr car, *bluish*	1.00	1.00

Regular Issue of 1928 Overprinted:

Colis Postaux

1930

No.	Type	Description	Unused	Used
Q4	A20	50c vio & brn	50	50
Q5	A21	1fr dp ol & sal red	60	60
Q6	A21	2fr red org & brn	85	85

NEW HEBRIDES

LOCATION — A group of islands in the South Pacific Ocean lying north of New Caledonia

GOVT. — Condominium under the joint administration of Great Britain and France

AREA — 5,790 sq. mi.

POP. — 100,000 (est. 1976)

CAPITAL — Port-Vila (Vila)

Postage stamps are issued by both Great Britain and France. In 1911 a joint issue was made bearing the coats of arms of both countries. The British stamps bore the coat of arms of Great Britain and the value in British currency on the right and the French coat of arms and values at the left. On the French stamps the positions were reversed. This resulted in some confusion when the value of the French franc decreased following World War I but the situation was corrected by arranging that both series of stamps be sold for their value as expressed in French currency.

12 Pence = 1 Shilling
100 Centimes = 1 Franc
New Hebrides Franc (FNH)--1977

Catalogue values for unused stamps in this country are for Never Hinged items, beginning with Scott 79 in the regular postage section, Scott J16 in the postage due section.

See Vol. I for British issues.

French Issues

Stamps of New Caledonia, 1905, Overprinted in Black or Red **NOUVELLES HÉBRIDES**

1908 Unwmk. *Perf. 14x13½*

No.	Type	Description	Unused	Used
1	A16	5c green	1.50	1.50
2	A16	10c rose	1.75	1.75
3	A17	25c blue, *grnsh* (R)	2.50	2.50
4	A17	50c carmine, *org*	3.25	3.25

Overprinted

NOUVELLES-HEBRIDES

No.	Type	Description	Unused	Used
5	A18	1fr bl, *yel grn* (R)	6.50	6.50
		Nos. 1-5 (5)	15.50	15.50

For overprints and surcharges see Nos. 6-10, 33-35.

Stamps of 1908 with Additional Overprint **CONDOMINIUM**

1910

No.	Type	Description	Unused	Used
6	A16	5c green	60	60
7	A16	10c rose	80	80
8	A17	25c blue, *grnsh* (R)	1.00	1.00
9	A17	50c car, *orange*	2.75	2.75
10	A18	1fr bl, *yel grn* (R)	9.00	9.00
		Nos. 6-10 (5)	14.15	14.15

A2

Wmk. 3
1911, July 12 Engr. *Perf. 14*

No.	Type	Description	Unused	Used
11	A2	5c pale green	35	35
12	A2	10c red	35	35
13	A2	20c gray	1.10	1.10
14	A2	25c ultramarine	1.40	1.10
15	A2	30c vio, *yellow*	1.75	1.60
16	A2	40c red, *yellow*	1.75	1.60
17	A2	50c olive green	1.75	1.60
18	A2	75c brn orange	2.75	2.75
19	A2	1fr brn red, *bl*	1.50	1.50
20	A2	2fr violet	3.00	3.00
21	A2	5fr brn red, *grn*	6.50	6.50
		Nos. 11-21 (11)	22.20	21.45

For surcharges see Nos. 36-37, 43 and British issue No. 30.

1912 Wmk. R F in Sheet

No.	Type	Description	Unused	Used
22	A2	5c pale green	1.25	1.25
23	A2	10c red	1.25	1.25
24	A2	20c gray	1.65	1.65
25	A2	25c ultramarine	1.65	1.65
26	A2	30c vio, *yellow*	1.65	1.65
27	A2	40c red, *yellow*	10.00	10.00
28	A2	50c olive green	5.75	5.75
29	A2	75c brn orange	5.75	5.75
30	A2	1fr brn red, *bl*	3.25	3.25
31	A2	2fr violet	5.75	5.75
32	A2	5fr brn red, *grn*	10.00	10.00
		Nos. 22-32 (11)	47.95	47.95

In the watermark, "R F" (République Française initials) are large double-lined Roman capitals, about 120mm high. About one-fourth of the stamps in each sheet show parts of the watermark. The other stamps are without watermark.

For surcharge see Nos. 38-42 and British issue No. 31.

Nos. 9 and 8 Surcharged **5c.**

1920 Unwmk. *Perf. 14x13½*
33 A17 5c on 50c red, *org* 1.40 1.40
34 A17 10c on 25c bl, *grnsh* 65 65

Same Surcharge on No. 4
35 A17 5c on 50c red, *org* 650.00 650.00

British Issue No. 21 and French Issue No. 15 Surcharged **10c.**

1921 Wmk. 3 *Perf. 14*
36 A1 10c on 5p ol grn 6.25 6.25
37 A2 20c on 30c vio, *yel* 6.25 6.25

Nos. 27 and 26 Surcharged **05c.**

1921 Wmk. R F in Sheet
38 A2 5c on 40c red, *yel* 19.00 19.00
39 A2 20c on 30c vio, *yel* 7.00 7.00

Stamps of 1910-12 Surcharged with New Values as in 1920-21

1924
40 A2 10c on 5c pale grn 60 60
41 A2 30c on 10c red 60 60
42 A2 50c on 25c ultra 1.60 1.60

Wmk. 3
43 A2 50c on 25c ultra 4.50 4.50

A4

The values at the lower right denote the currency and amount for which the stamps were to be sold. The stamps could be purchased at the French post office and used to pay postage at the English rates.

1925 Engr. Wmk. R F in Sheet
44 A4 5c (½p) black 55 55
45 A4 10c (1p) green 40 40
46 A4 20c (2p) grnsh gray 40 40
47 A4 25c (2½p) brown 40 40
48 A4 30c (3p) carmine 40 40
49 A4 40c (4p) car, *org* 60 60
50 A4 50c (5p) ultra 70 70
51 A4 75c (7½p) bis brn 1.10 1.10
52 A4 1fr (10p) car, *blue* 1.90 1.90
53 A4 2fr (1sh 8p) gray vio 1.90 1.90
54 A4 5fr (4sh) car, *grnsh* 4.50 4.50
Nos. 44-54 (11) 12.85 12.85

For overprints see Nos. J1-J5.

Beach Scene A6

1938 *Perf. 12*
55 A6 5c green 40 40
56 A6 10c dark orange 40 40
57 A6 15c violet 40 40
58 A6 20c rose red 40 40
59 A6 25c brown 60 60
60 A6 30c dark blue 60 60
61 A6 40c olive grn 90 90
62 A6 50c brn violet 90 90
63 A6 1fr dk car, *grn* 2.00 2.00
64 A6 2fr blue, *grn* 4.00 4.00
65 A6 5fr red, *yellow* 14.00 14.00
66 A6 10fr vio, *blue* 27.50 27.50
Nos. 55-66 (12) 52.10 52.10

For overprints see Nos. 67-78, J6-J15.

Stamps of 1938 Overprinted in Black

France Libre

1941
67 A6 5c green 6.00 6.00
68 A6 10c dark org 6.00 6.00
69 A6 15c violet 6.00 6.00
70 A6 20c rose red 6.50 6.50
71 A6 25c brown 6.75 6.75
72 A6 30c dark blue 6.75 6.75
73 A6 40c olive grn 6.75 6.75
74 A6 50c brn violet 6.75 6.75
75 A6 1fr dk car, *grn* 8.50 8.50
76 A6 2fr blue, *grn* 8.50 8.50
77 A6 5fr red, *yellow* 10.50 10.50
78 A6 10fr vio, *blue* 16.00 16.00
Nos. 67-78 (12) 95.00 95.00

Catalogue values for unused stamps in this section, from this point to the end of the section, are for Never Hinged items.

UPU Monument, Bern — A7

Wmk. RF in Sheet

1949 Engr. *Perf. 13½x14*
79 A7 10c red org 50 50
80 A7 15c violet 60 60
81 A7 30c vio bl 85 85
82 A7 50c rose vio 1.75 1.75

75th anniv. of the UPU.
Some stamps in each sheet show part of the watermark; others show none.

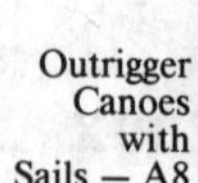

Outrigger Canoes with Sails — A8

Designs: 5c, 10c, 15c, 20c, Canoes with sails. 25c, 30c, 40c, 50c, Native carving. 1fr, 2fr, 5fr, Natives.

1953 *Perf. 12½*
83 A8 5c green 22 22
84 A8 10c red 35 35
85 A8 15c yellow 35 35
86 A8 20c ultramarine 60 60
87 A8 25c olive 60 60
88 A8 30c light brown 90 90
89 A8 40c black brown 90 90
90 A8 50c violet 1.10 1.10
91 A8 1fr deep orange 2.50 2.50
92 A8 2fr red violet 9.00 9.00
93 A8 5fr scarlet 14.00 14.00
Nos. 83-93 (11) 30.52 30.52

For overprints see Nos. J16-J20.

Discovery of New Hebrides, 1606 — A9

Designs: 20c, 50c, Britannia, Marianne, Flags and Mask.

1956 Unwmk. Photo. *Perf. 14½x14*
94 A9 5c emerald 58 58
95 A9 10c crimson 58 58
96 A9 20c ultramarine 80 80
97 A9 50c purple 2.50 2.50

50th anniv. of the establishment of the Anglo-French Condominium.

Port Vila and Iririki Islet — A10

Designs: 25c, 30c, 40c, 50c, Tropical river and spear fisherman. 1fr, 2fr, 5fr, Woman drinking from coconut (inscribed: "Alliance Franco-Britannique 4 Mars 1947").

Wmk. RF in Sheet

1957 Engr. *Perf. 13½x13*
98 A10 5c green 28 28
99 A10 10c red 35 35
100 A10 15c orange yel 45 45
101 A10 20c ultramarine 45 45
102 A10 25c olive 45 45
103 A10 30c light brown 70 70
104 A10 40c sepia 80 80
105 A10 50c violet 1.25 1.25
106 A10 1fr orange 2.50 2.50
107 A10 2fr rose lilac 6.00 6.00
108 A10 5fr black 12.50 12.50
Nos. 98-108 (11) 25.73 25.73

For overprints see Nos. J21-J25.

Wheat Emblem and Globe A10a

1963, Sept. 2 Unwmk. *Perf. 13*
109 A10a 60c org brn & sl grn 2.00 2.00

FAO "Freedom from Hunger" campaign.

Centenary Emblem — A11

1963, Sept. 2 Unwmk.
110 A11 15c org, gray & car 80 80
111 A11 45c bis, gray & car 1.50 1.50

Centenary of International Red Cross.

Copra Industry A12

Designs: 5c, Manganese loading, Forari Wharf. 10c, Cacao. 20c, Map of New Hebrides, tuna, marlin and ships. 25c, Striped triggerfish. 30c, Nautilus. 40c, 60c, Turkeyfish (pterois volitans). 50c, Lined tang (fish). 1fr, Cardinal honeyeater and hibiscus. 2fr, Buff-bellied flycatcher. 3fr, Thicket warbler. 5fr, White-collared kingfisher.

Perf. 12½ (10c, 20c, 40c, 60c); 14 (3fr); 13 (others)

Photo. (10c, 20c, 40c, 60c, 3fr); Engr. (others)

1963-67 Unwmk.
112 A12 5c Prus bl & cl ('66) 40 40
113 A12 10c brt grn, org brn & dk brn ("RF" at left) ('65) 1.40 90
114 A12 15c dk pur, yel & brn 28 28
115 A12 20c brt bl, gray & cit ("RF" at left) ('65) 1.90 1.40
116 A12 25c vio, rose lil & org brn ('66) 55 55
117 A12 30c lil, brn & cit 65 65
118 A12 40c dk bl & ver ('65) 3.25 2.25
119 A12 50c Prus bl, yel & grn 90 90
119A A12 60c dk bl & ver ('67) 1.10 90
120 A12 1fr bl grn, blk & red ('66) 2.00 2.00
121 A12 2fr ol, blk & brn 4.50 4.50
122 A12 3fr org brn, brt grn & blk ("RF" at left) ('65) 9.00 6.50
123 A12 5fr ind, dp bl & gray ('67) 10.00 10.00
Nos. 112-123 (13) 35.93 31.23

See #146-148. For surcharge see #160.

Telegraph, Syncom Satellite and ITU Emblem — A13

1965, May 17 Unwmk. *Perf. 13*
124 A13 15c dk red brn, brt bl & emer 1.00 75
125 A13 60c Prus grn, mag & sl 2.25 1.50

ITU, centenary.

ICY Emblem A14

1965, Oct. 24 Litho. *Perf. 14½*
126 A14 5c bl grn & cl 35 35
127 A14 55c lt vio & grn 90 90

International Cooperation Year.

Winston Churchill and St. Paul's, London, During Air Attack A15

1966, Jan. 24 Photo. *Perf. 14*

Design in Black, Gold and Carmine Rose
128 A15 5c brt blue 20 20
129 A15 15c green 25 25
130 A15 25c brown 55 55
131 A15 30c violet 1.00 1.00

Soccer Player and Rimet Cup A16

1966, July 1 Litho. *Perf. 14*
132 A16 20c multi 60 60
133 A16 40c multi 70 70

World Cup Soccer Championship, Wembley, England, July 11-30.

Inauguration of WHO Headquarters, Geneva — A17

1966, Sept. 20 Litho. *Perf. 14*
134 A17 25c multi 60 60
135 A17 60c multi 80 80

"Education" — A18

UNESCO, 20th anniv.: 30c, "Science" (retort and grain). 45c, "Culture" (lyre and columns).

1966, Dec. 1 Litho. *Perf. 14*

136 A18 15c dp org, yel & dl vio 40 40
137 A18 30c vio, dk ol grn & yel 65 65
138 A18 45c yel, mag & blk 90 90

US Marine, Australian Soldier and Map of South Pacific War Zone — A19

Designs: 15c, The coast watchers. 60c, Australian cruiser Canberra. 1fr, Flying fortress taking off from Bauer Field, and view of Vila.

Perf. 14x13

1967, Sept. 26 Photo. Unwmk.

139 A19 15c lt bl & multi 40 40
140 A19 25c yel & multi 55 55
141 A19 60c multi 80 80
142 A19 1fr pale sal & multi 1.50 1.50

25th anniv. of the Allied Forces' campaign in the South Pacific War Zone.

L. A. de Bougainville, Ship's Figurehead and Bougainvillea A20

Designs: 15c, Globe and world map. 25c, Ships La Boudeuse and L'Etoile and map of Bougainville Strait.

1968, May 23 Engr. *Perf. 13*

143 A20 15c ver, emer & dl vio 22 22
144 A20 25c ultra, ol & brn 45 45
145 A20 60c mag, grn & brn 80 80

200th anniv. of Louis Antoine de Bougainville's (1729-1811) voyage around the world.

Type of 1963-67 Redrawn, "E II R" at left, "RF" at Right

Designs as before.

1968, Aug. 5 Photo. *Perf. 12½*

146 A12 10c brt grn, org brn & dk brn 30 30
147 A12 20c brt bl, gray & cit 42 42

Perf. 14

148 A12 3fr org brn, brt grn & blk 3.50 3.50

On Nos. 113, 115 and 122 "RF" is at left and "E II R" is at right.
For surcharge see No. 160.

Concorde Supersonic Airliner A21

Design: 25c, Concorde seen from above.

1968, Oct. 9 Litho. *Perf. 14x13½*

149 A21 25c vio bl, red & lt bl 2.25 2.00
150 A21 60c red, ultra & blk 4.00 3.50

Development of the Concorde supersonic airliner, a joint Anglo-French project.

Kauri Pine — A22

Land Diver at Start, Pentecost Island — A24

Relay Race, British and French Flags A23

1969, June 30 *Perf. 14½x14*

151 A22 20c brn & multi 40 40

New Hebrides timber industry. Issued in sheets of 9 (3x3) on simulated wood grain background.

1969, Aug. 13 Photo. *Perf. 12½x13*

152 A23 25c shown 60 60
153 A23 1fr Runner at right 1.25 1.25

3rd South Pacific Games, Port Moresby, Papua and New Guinea, Aug. 13-23.

1969, Oct. 15 Litho. *Perf. 12½*

154 A24 15c shown 35 35
155 A24 25c Diver in mid-air 45 45
156 A24 1fr Diver near ground 2.00 2.00

Land divers of Pentecost Island.

UPU Headquarters and Monument, Bern — A25

1970, May 20 Engr. *Perf. 13*

157 A25 1.05fr org, lil & sl 1.20 1.20

New UPU Headquarters, Bern.

Charles de Gaulle — A26

1970, July 20 Photo. *Perf. 13*

158 A26 65c brn & multi 1.20 1.20
159 A26 1.10fr dp bl & multi 2.25 2.25

Rallying of the Free French, 30th anniv.
For overprints see Nos. 163-164.

No. 147 Surcharged

1970, Oct. 15 Photo. *Perf. 12½*

160 A12 35c on 20c multi 80 80

Virgin and Child, by Giovanni Bellini — A27

Design: 50c, Virgin and Child, by Giovanni Cima.

1970, Nov. 30 Litho. *Perf. 14½x14*

161 A27 15c tan & multi 35 22
162 A27 50c lt grn & multi 62 45

Christmas. See Nos. 186-187.

Nos. 158-159 Overprinted "1890-1970 / IN MEMORIAM / 9-11-70" in Gold, 2 Vertical Bars in Black

1971, Jan. 19 Photo. *Perf. 13*

163 A26 65c brn & multi 80 80
164 A26 1.10fr dp bl & multi 2.00 2.00

In memory of Gen. Charles de Gaulle (1890-1970), President of France.

Soccer A28

Design: 65c, Basketball (vert.).

1971, July 13 Photo. *Perf. 12½*

165 A28 20c multi 40 40
166 A28 65c multi 90 70

4th South Pacific Games, Papeete, French Polynesia, Sept. 8-19.

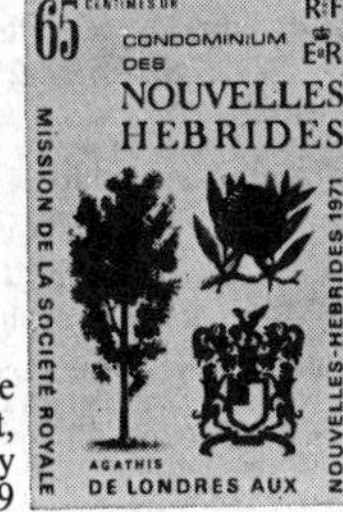

Breadfruit Tree and Fruit, Society Arms — A29

Perf. 14½x14

1971, Sept. 7 Litho. Unwmk.

167 A29 65c multi 80 65

Expedition of the Royal Society of London for the Advancement of Science to study vegetation and fauna, July 1-October.

Adoration of the Shepherds, by Louis Le Nain — A30

Christmas: 50c, Adoration of the Shepherds, by Jacopo Tintoretto.

1971, Nov. 23 *Perf. 14x13½*

168 A30 25c lt grn & multi 45 35
169 A30 50c lt bl & multi 65 60

Drover Mk III A31

Airplanes: 25c, Sandringham seaplane. 30c, Dragon Rapide. 65c, Caravelle.

1972, Feb. 29 Photo. *Perf. 13½x13*

170 A31 20c lt grn & multi 45 35
171 A31 25c ultra & multi 55 40
172 A31 30c org & multi 75 60
173 A31 65c dk bl & multi 2.25 1.75

Headdress, South Malekula — A32

Baker's Pigeon — A33

Artifacts; 15c, Slit gong and carved figure, North Ambrym. 1fr, Carved figures, North Ambrym. 3fr, Ceremonial headdress, South Malekula.
Birds: 20c, Red-headed parrot-finch. 35c, Chestnut-bellied kingfisher. 2fr, Green palm lorikeet.
Sea Shells; 25c, Cribraria fischeri. 30c, Oliva rubrolabiata. 65c, Strombus plicatus. 5fr, Turbo marmoratus.

1972, July 24 Photo. *Perf. 12½x13*

174 A32 5c plum & multi 15 15
175 A33 10c bl & multi 15 15
176 A32 15c red & multi 20 16
177 A33 20c org brn & multi 25 20
178 A32 25c dp bl & multi 30 25
179 A32 30c dk grn & multi 35 30
180 A33 35c gray bl & multi 55 45
181 A32 65c dk grn & multi 75 70
182 A32 1fr org & multi 1.50 1.25
183 A33 2fr multi 2.50 1.75
184 A32 3fr yel & multi 4.25 2.75
185 A32 5fr pink & multi 8.50 6.00
Nos. 174-185 (12) 19.45 14.11

For overprints see Nos. 200-201.

Christmas Type of 1970

Christmas: 25c, Adoration of the Magi (detail), by Bartholomaeus Spranger. 70c, Virgin and Child, by Jan Provoost.

1972, Sept. 25 Litho. *Perf. 14x13½*

186 A27 25c lt grn & multi 45 40
187 A27 70c lt bl & multi 65 62

Queen Elizabeth II and Prince Philip — A34

Perf. 14x14½

1972, Nov. 20 Photo. Wmk. 314

188 A34 35c vio blk & multi 35 28
189 A34 65c olive & multi 65 45

25th anniversary of the marriage of Queen Elizabeth II and Prince Philip.

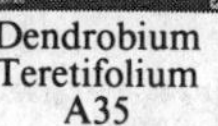
Dendrobium Teretifolium A35

New Wharf, Vila A36

Orchids: 30c, Ephemerantha comata. 35c, Spathoglottis petri. 65c, Dendrobium mohlianum.

Unwmk.

1973, Feb. 26 Litho. *Perf. 14*

190 A35 25c bl vio & multi 32 25
191 A35 30c multi 45 42
192 A35 35c vio & multi 65 50
193 A35 65c dk grn & multi 1.75 1.50

1973, May 14 Litho. *Perf. 14*

194 A36 25c shown 60 40
195 A36 70c New Wharf, horiz. 1.25 1.00

New wharf at Vila, completed Nov. 1972.

Wild Horses, Tanna A37

Design: 70c, Yasur Volcano, Tanna.

1973, Aug. 13 Photo. *Perf. 13x13½*

196 A37 35c multi 65 60
197 A37 70c multi 1.40 1.10

Mother and Child, by Marcel Moutouh — A38

Christmas: 70c, Star over Lagoon, by Tatin D'Avesnieres.

1973, Nov. 19 Litho. *Perf. 14x13½*

198 A38 35c tan & multi 45 28
199 A38 70c lil rose & multi 65 60

Nos. 180, 183 Overprinted in Red or Black: "VISITE ROYALE / 1974"

1974, Feb. 11 Photo. *Perf. 12½x13*

200 A33 35c multi (R) 40 25
201 A33 2fr multi (B) 1.65 1.25

Visit of British Royal Family, Feb. 15-16.

Pacific Dove — A39

Designs: 35c, Night swallowtail. 70c, Green sea turtle. 1.15fr, Flying fox.

1974, Feb. 11 *Perf. 13x12½*

202 A39 25c gray & multi 42 40
203 A39 35c gray & multi 1.00 55
204 A39 70c gray & multi 1.65 1.25
205 A39 1.15fr gray & multi 2.25 1.75

Nature conservation.

Old Post Office, Vila A40

Design: 70c, New Post Office.

Unwmk.

1974, May 6 Photo. *Perf. 12*

206 A40 35c bl & multi 45 32
207 A40 70c red & multi 65 65

Opening of New Post Office, May, 1974. Nos. 206-207 printed se-tenant at the base in sheets of 50.

Capt. Cook and Tanna Island A41

Designs: No. 209, William Wales and boat landing on island. No. 210, William Hodges painting islanders and landscape. 1.15fr, Capt. Cook, "Resolution" and map of New Hebrides.

1974, Aug. 1 Litho. *Perf. 13*

Size: 40x25mm

208 A41 35c multi 1.25 90
209 A41 35c multi 1.25 90
210 A41 35c multi 1.25 90

Size: 58x34mm

Perf. 11

211 A41 1.15fr lil & multi 3.00 1.90

Bicentenary of the discovery of the New Hebrides by Capt. James Cook.

Nos. 208-210 printed se-tenant in continuous design in sheets of 30 (6x5).

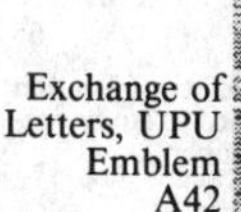

Exchange of Letters, UPU Emblem A42

1974, Oct. 9 Photo. *Perf. 13x12½*

212 A42 70c multi 62 60

Centenary of Universal Postal Union.

Nativity, by Gerard Van Honthorst — A43

Christmas: 35c, Adoration of the Kings, by Velazquez, vert.

1974, Nov. 14 Litho. *Perf. 13½*

213 A43 35c multi 40 35
214 A43 70c multi 60 55

Charolais Bull — A44

1975, Apr. 29 Engr. *Perf. 13*

215 A44 10fr multi 10.00 10.00

Nordjamb Emblem, Kayaks A45

Pitti Madonna, by Michelangelo A46

1975, Aug. 5 Litho. *Perf. 14x13½*

216 A45 25c shown 42 30
217 A45 35c Camp cooks 45 42
218 A45 1fr Map makers 1.10 75
219 A45 5fr Fishermen 6.00 4.75

Nordjamb 75, 14th Boy Scout Jamboree, Lillehammer, Norway, July 29-Aug. 7.

1975, Nov. 11 Litho. *Perf. 14½x14*

Christmas (After Michelangelo): 70c, Bruges Madonna. 2.50fr, Taddei Madonna.

220 A46 35c multi 40 28
221 A46 70c brn & multi 62 45
222 A46 2.50fr bl & multi 2.25 1.90

Concorde, Air France Colors and Emblem — A47

1976, Jan. 30 Typo. *Perf. 13*

223 A47 5fr bl & multi 10.00 6.50

1st commercial flight of supersonic jet Concorde from Paris to Rio, Jan. 21.

Telephones, 1876 and 1976 — A48

Designs: 70c, Alexander Graham Bell. 1.15fr, Noumea Earth Station and satellite.

1976, Mar. 31 Photo. *Perf. 13*

224 A48 25c blk, car & bl 35 28
225 A48 70c blk & multi 65 55
226 A48 1.15fr blk, org & vio bl 1.40 90

Centenary of first telephone call by Alexander Graham Bell, Mar. 10, 1876.

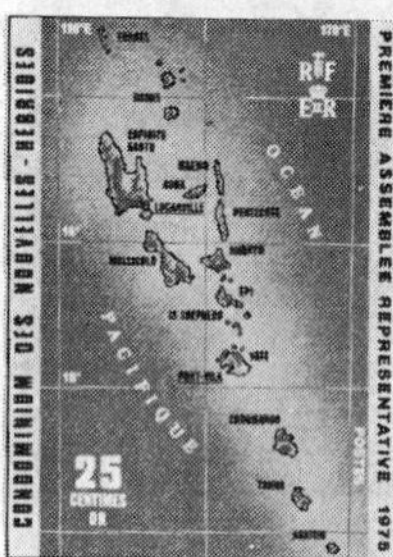

Map of New Hebrides A49

View of Luganville (Santo) A50

Design: 2fr, View of Vila.

1976, June 29 Unwmk. *Perf. 13*

227 A49 25c blue & multi 45 28
228 A50 1fr multi 1.25 65
229 A50 2fr multi 3.00 1.60

Opening of first Representative Assembly, June 29, 1976 (25c); first Luganville (Santo) Municipal Council (1fr); first Vila Municipal Council (2fr).

Nos. 228-229 exist with lower inscription reading "Premiere Assemblee Representative 1975" instead of "Premiere Municipalite de Luganville" on 1fr and "Premiere Municipalite de Port-Vila" on 2fr.

Flight into Egypt, by Francisco Vieira Lusitano — A51

Portuguese 16th Century Paintings: 70c, Adoration of the Shepherds. 2.50fr, Adoration of the Kings.

1976, Nov. 8 Litho. *Perf. 14*

230 A51 35c pur & multi 45 35
231 A51 70c bl & multi 65 60
232 A51 2.50fr multi 2.50 2.00

Christmas 1976.

Queen's Visit, 1974 — A52

Designs: 70c, Imperial State crown. 2fr, The blessing.

1977, Feb. 7 Litho. *Perf. 14x13½*

233 A52 35c lt grn & multi	35	22
234 A52 70c bl & multi	60	40
235 A52 2fr pink & multi	1.60	1.40

Reign of Queen Elizabeth II, 25th anniv.

Nos. 174-185, 215 Surcharged with New Value, "FNH" and Bars

1977, July 1 Photo. *Perf. 12½x13*

236 A32 5fr on 5c multi	22	22
237 A33 10fr on 10c multi	35	35
238 A32 15fr on 15c multi	55	55
239 A33 20fr on 20c multi	60	50
240 A32 25fr on 25c multi	80	80
241 A32 30fr on 30c multi	1.10	1.10
242 A33 35fr on 35c multi	1.10	1.10
243 A32 40fr on 65c multi	1.50	1.50
244 A32 50fr on 1fr multi	2.50	2.50
245 A33 70fr on 2fr multi	4.50	4.50
246 A32 100fr on 3fr multi	6.25	6.25
247 A32 200fr on 5fr multi	11.00	11.00

Engr.

Perf. 13

248 A44 500fr on 10fr multi	25.00	25.00
Nos. 236-248 (13)	55.47	55.37

Surcharged in Paris. Later all except 20fr were surcharged in Vila with slightly different letters and different bars. Of these 12, the 50fr, 70fr and 100fr were reported to have been sold only at the philatelic bureau.

Espiritu Santo and Cattle — A53

Tempi Madonna, by Raphael — A54

Designs: 5fr, Erromango Island and Kaori tree. 10fr, Archipelago and man making copra. 20fr, Efate Island and Post Office, Vila. 25fr, Malakula Island and headdresses. 30fr, Aoba and Maewo Islands and pig tusks. 35fr, Pentecost Island and land diving. 40fr, Tanna Island and Prophet John Frum's Red Cross. 50fr, Shepherd Island and canoe with sail. 70fr, Banks Island and dancers. 100fr, Ambrym Island and carvings. 200fr, Aneityum Island and decorated baskets. 500fr, Torres Islands and fishing with bow and arrow.

1977-78 Litho. *Perf. 14*

258 A53 5fr multi	20	20
259 A53 10fr multi	25	22
260 A53 15fr multi	32	28
261 A53 20fr multi	45	32
262 A53 25fr multi	50	35
263 A53 30fr multi	55	48
264 A53 35fr multi	65	50
265 A53 40fr multi	80	55
266 A53 50fr multi	90	70
267 A53 70fr multi	1.25	1.00
268 A53 100fr multi	2.25	1.50
269 A53 200fr multi	5.00	3.50
270 A53 500fr multi	11.00	8.75
Nos. 258-270 (13)	24.12	18.35

Issue dates: 5fr, 20fr, 50fr, 100fr, 200fr, Sept. 7; 15fr, 25fr, 30fr, 40fr, Nov. 23, 1977; 10fr, 35fr, 70fr, 500fr, May 9, 1978.

1977, Dec. 8 Litho. *Perf. 12*

Christmas: 15fr, Virgin and Child, by Gerard David. 30fr, Virgin and Child, by Pompeo Batoni.

271 A54 10fr multi	30	25
272 A54 15fr multi	38	32
273 A54 30fr multi	80	70

British Airways Concorde over New York — A55

Designs: 20fr, British Airways Concorde over London. 30fr, Air France Concorde over Washington. 40fr, Air France Concorde over Paris.

1978, May 9 Litho. *Perf. 14*

274 A55 10fr multi	60	40
275 A55 20fr multi	1.00	70
276 A55 30fr multi	1.40	1.10
277 A55 40fr multi	2.00	1.50

Souvenir Sheet

White Horse of Hanover — A56

Elizabeth II — A57

Design: No. 278c, Gallic cock.

1978, June 2 Litho. *Perf. 15*

278 Sheet of 6	6.00	6.00
a. A56 40fr grnsh bl & multi	85	85
b. A57 40fr grnsh bl & multi	85	85
c. A56 40fr grnsh bl & multi	85	85

25th anniversary of coronation of Queen Elizabeth II. No. 278 contains 2 se-tenant strips of Nos. 278a-278c, separated by horizontal gutter with commemorative and descriptive inscriptions and showing central part of coronation procession with coach.

Virgin and Child, by Dürer — A58

Paintings by Albrecht Durer (1471-1528): 15fr, Virgin and Child with St. Anne. 30fr, Virgin and Child with Goldfinch. 40fr, Virgin and Child with Pear.

1978, Dec. 1 Litho. *Perf. 14x13½*

279 A58 10fr multi	25	25
280 A58 15fr multi	35	35
281 A58 30fr multi	60	55
282 A58 40fr multi	1.00	80

Christmas.

Type of 1976 Surcharged with New Value, Bars over Old Denomination and Inscription at Right. Longitude changed to "166E."

1979, Jan. 11 Photo. *Perf. 13*

283 A49 10fr on 25c bl & multi	40	28
284 A49 40fr on 25c lt grn & multi	1.10	80

First anniv. of Internal Self-Government.

New Hebrides No. 155 and Hill Statue A59

Rowland Hill and New Hebrides Stamps: 10fr, No. 55. 40fr, No. 46.

1979, Sept. 10 Litho. *Perf. 14*

285 A59 10fr multi	22	16
286 A59 20fr multi	45	35
287 A59 40fr multi	80	62

Sir Rowland Hill (1795-1879), originator of penny postage. A souvenir sheet containing No. 286 and British Issue No. 266 is listed as No. 266a in Volume I, New Hebrides, British Issues.

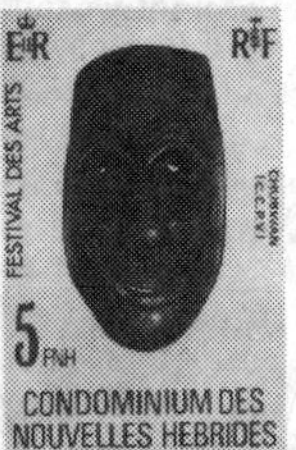
Arts Festival — A60

Designs: 10fr, Clubs and spears. 20fr, Ritual puppet. 40fr, Headdress.

1979, Nov. 16 Litho. *Perf. 14*

288 A60 5fr multi	20	20
289 A60 10fr multi	28	22
290 A60 20fr multi	50	38
291 A60 40fr multi	1.00	62

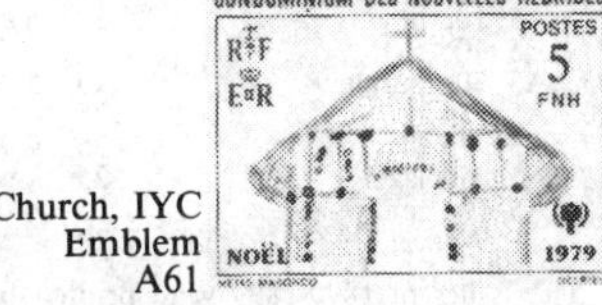
Church, IYC Emblem A61

IYC Emblem, Children's Drawings: 10fr, Father Christmas. 20fr, Cross and Bible, vert. 40fr, Stars, candle and Santa Claus, vert.

1979, Dec. 4 *Perf. 13x13½*

292 A61 5fr multi	20	20
293 A61 10fr multi	28	22
294 A61 20fr multi	50	35
295 A61 40fr multi	1.00	62

Christmas; Intl. Year of the Child.

White-bellied Honeyeater — A62

1980, Feb. 27 Litho. *Perf. 14*

296 A62 10fr shown	40	40
297 A62 20fr Scarlet robins	60	60
298 A62 30fr Yellow white-eyes	1.00	1.00
299 A62 40fr Fan-tailed brush cuckoo	1.50	1.50

Stamps of Vanuatu (Vol. 1) replaced those of New Hebrides in 1980.

POSTAGE DUE STAMPS

French Issues

Regular Issue of 1925 Overprinted CHIFFRE TAXE

1925 Wmk. R F in Sheet *Perf. 14*

J1 A4 10c green	27.50	3.50
J2 A4 20c green	27.50	3.50
J3 A4 30c carmine	27.50	3.50
J4 A4 50c ultramarine	27.50	3.50
J5 A4 1fr carmine, *blue*	27.50	3.50
Nos. J1-J5 (5)	137.50	17.50

Regular Stamps of 1938 Overprinted in Black CHIFFRE TAXE

1938 *Perf. 12*

J6 A6 5c green	1.50	1.50
J7 A6 10c dark orange	1.50	1.50
J8 A6 20c rose red	2.25	2.25
J9 A6 40c olive green	6.25	6.25
J10 A6 1fr dark car, *green*	9.50	9.50
Nos. J6-J10 (5)	21.00	21.00

Postage Due Stamps of 1938 Overprinted **France Libre**

1941

J11 A6 5c green	7.00	7.00
J12 A6 10c dark orange	7.00	7.00
J13 A6 20c rose red	7.00	7.00
J14 A6 40c olive green	7.00	7.00
J15 A6 1fr dk car, *green*	7.00	7.00
Nos. J11-J15 (5)	35.00	35.00

Catalogue values for unused stamps in this section, from this point to the end of the section, are for Never Hinged items.

Regular Stamps of 1953 Overprinted "TIMBRE-TAXE"

1953 Unwmk. *Perf. 12½*

J16 A8 5c green	60	60
J17 A8 10c red	80	80
J18 A8 20c ultramarine	2.00	2.00
J19 A8 40c black brown	4.00	4.00
J20 A8 1fr deep orange	7.00	7.00
Nos. J16-J20 (5)	14.40	14.40

Regular Stamps of 1957 Overprinted "TIMBRE-TAXE"

Wmk. R F in Sheet

1957 Engr. *Perf. 13½x13*

J21 A10 5c green	40	40
J22 A10 10c red	55	55
J23 A10 20c ultramarine	62	62
J24 A10 40c sepia	2.00	2.00
J25 A10 1fr orange	6.00	6.00
Nos. J21-J25 (5)	9.57	9.57

NICARAGUA

LOCATION — Central America, between Honduras and Costa Rica
GOVT. — Republic
AREA — 57,143 sq. mi.
POP. — 2,908,000 (est. 1984)
CAPITAL — Managua

100 Centavos = 1 Peso
100 Centavos = 1 Córdoba (1913)

Catalogue values for unused stamps in this country are for Never Hinged items, beginning with Scott 689 in the regular postage section, Scott C261 in the airpost section, Scott CO37 in the airpost official section, and Scott RA60 in the postal tax section.

Watermarks

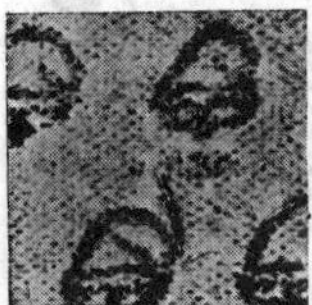
Wmk. 117-Liberty Cap

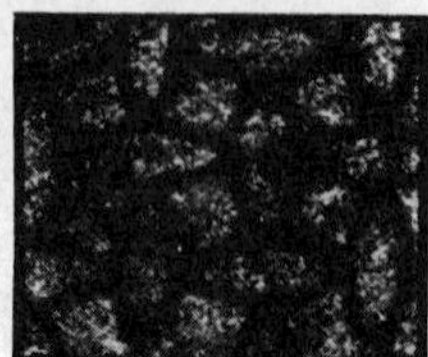

Wmk. 209- Multiple Ovals

Liberty Cap on Mountain Peak; From Seal of Country — A1

A2

A3

Unwmk.

1862, Dec. 2 Engr. *Perf. 12*

Yellowish Paper

1	A1	2c dk bl	75.00	20.00
2	A1	5c black	150.00	50.00

Values are for copies without gum. Copies with gum sell for more. Nos. 1-2 were canceled only by pen.

See No. C509.

1869-71

White Paper

3	A1	1c bis ('71)	2.50	1.25
4	A1	2c blue	2.50	1.25
5	A1	5c black	22.50	1.00
6	A2	10c vermilion	3.75	1.75
7	A3	25c green	6.25	4.00

1878-80 *Rouletted 8½*

8	A1	1c brown	2.00	1.25
9	A1	2c blue	2.00	1.25
10	A1	5c black	10.00	1.00
11	A2	10c ver ('80)	2.50	1.50
12	A3	25c grn ('79)	2.50	4.00

Nos. 3-12 were reprinted in 1892. The corresponding values of the two series are printed in the same shades which is not usually true of the originals. They are, however, similar to some of the original shades and the only certain test is comparison. Originals have thin white gum; reprints have rather thick yellowish gum. Value 50c each.

Seal of Nicaragua — A4

Locomotive and Telegraph Key — A5

1882 Engr. *Perf. 12*

13	A4	1c green	20	25
14	A4	2c carmine	20	25
15	A4	5c blue	20	25
16	A4	10c dl vio	25	75
17	A4	15c yellow	60	*2.50*
18	A4	20c sl gray	90	*5.00*
19	A4	50c dl vio	1.25	*10.00*
		Nos. 13-19 (7)	3.60	

Used Values

of Nos. 13-120 are for stamps with genuine cancellations applied while the stamps were valid. Various counterfeit cancellations exist.

1890 Engr.

20	A5	1c yel brn	20	25
21	A5	2c vermilion	20	25
22	A5	5c dp bl	20	25
23	A5	10c lil gray	20	25
24	A5	20c red	20	*1.75*
25	A5	50c purple	20	*5.00*
26	A5	1p brown	25	*8.50*
27	A5	2p dk grn	25	*9.00*
28	A5	5p lake	25	
29	A5	10p orange	25	
		Nos. 20-29 (10)	2.20	

The issues of 1890-1899 were printed by the Hamilton Bank Note Co., New York, to the order of N. F. Seebeck who held a contract for stamps with the government of Nicaragua. Reprints were made, for sale to collectors, of the 1896, 1897 and 1898, postage, postage due and official stamps. See notes following those issues.

For overprints see Nos. O1-O10.

Goddess of Plenty — A6

Columbus Sighting Land — A7

1891 Litho.

30	A6	1c yel brn	25	35
31	A6	2c red	25	35
32	A6	5c dk bl	25	25
33	A6	10c slate	25	50
34	A6	20c plum	25	*2.00*
35	A6	50c purple	25	*5.00*
36	A6	1p blk brn	25	*5.00*
37	A6	2p green	25	*8.50*
38	A6	5p brn red	25	
39	A6	10p orange	25	
		Nos. 30-39 (10)	2.50	

For overprints see Nos. O11-O20.

1892 Engr.

40	A7	1c yel brn	20	25
41	A7	2c vermilion	20	20
42	A7	5c dk bl	20	20
43	A7	10c slate	20	25
44	A7	20c plum	20	*2.00*
45	A7	50c purple	20	*7.00*
46	A7	1p brown	20	*7.00*
47	A7	2p bl grn	20	*8.50*
48	A7	5p rose lake	20	
49	A7	10p orange	20	
		Nos. 40-49 (10)	2.00	

Commemorative of the 400th anniversary of the discovery of America by Columbus.

Stamps of the 1892 design were printed in other colors than those listed and overprinted "Telegrafos". The 1c blue, 10c orange, 20c slate, 50c plum and 2p vermilion are telegraph stamps which did not receive the overprint.

For overprints see Nos. O21-O30.

Arms A8

"Victory" A9

1893 Engr.

51	A8	1c yel brn	20	20
52	A8	2c vermilion	20	20
53	A8	5c dk bl	20	20
54	A8	10c slate	20	25
55	A8	20c dl red	20	*1.50*
56	A8	50c violet	20	*4.00*
57	A8	1p dk brn	20	*7.00*
58	A8	2p bl grn	20	*8.50*
59	A8	5p rose lake	20	
60	A8	10p orange	20	
		Nos. 51-60 (10)	2.00	

The 1c blue and 2c dark brown are telegraph stamps which did not receive the "Telegrafos" overprint.

For overprints see Nos. O31-O41.

1894 Engr.

61	A9	1c yel brn	20	25
62	A9	2c vermilion	20	30
63	A9	5c dp bl	20	25
64	A9	10c slate	20	30
65	A9	20c lake	20	*1.75*
66	A9	50c purple	20	*4.00*
67	A9	1p brown	20	*7.00*
68	A9	2p green	20	*12.50*
69	A9	5p brn red	20	*15.00*
70	A9	10p orange	20	*20.00*
		Nos. 61-70 (10)	2.00	

Specialists believe the 25c yellow green, type A9, is a telegraph denomination never issued for postal purposes. Stamps in other colors are telegraph stamps without the usual "Telegrafos" overprint.

For overprints see Nos. O42-O51.

Coat of Arms A10

Map of Nicaragua A11

1895 Engr.

71	A10	1c yel brn	20	30
72	A10	2c vermilion	20	30
73	A10	5c dp bl	20	25
74	A10	10c slate	20	25
75	A10	20c claret	20	75
76	A10	50c dl vio	20	*5.00*
77	A10	1p dk brn	20	*5.00*
78	A10	2p dp grn	20	*8.00*
79	A10	5p brn red	20	*11.00*
80	A10	10p orange	20	*16.50*
		Nos. 71-80 (10)	2.00	

Frames of Nos. 71-80 differ for each denomination.

A 50c violet blue exists. Its status is questioned. Value 20c.

For overprints see Nos. O52-O71.

1896 Engr.

81	A11	1c violet	30	*1.00*
82	A11	2c bl grn	30	*50*
83	A11	5c brt rose	30	*30*
84	A11	10c blue	50	*50*
85	A11	20c bis brn	3.00	*4.00*
86	A11	50c bl gray	60	*8.00*
87	A11	1p black	75	*11.00*
88	A11	2p claret	75	*15.00*
89	A11	5p dp bl	75	*15.00*
		Nos. 81-89 (9)	7.25	

See italic note after No. 109M.

For overprints see Nos. O82-O117.

Wmk. 117

89A	A11	1c violet	3.75	90
89B	A11	2c bl grn	3.75	1.25
89C	A11	5c brt rose	15.00	30
89D	A11	10c blue	25.00	90
89E	A11	20c bis brn	3.75	4.25
89F	A11	50c bl gray	42.50	*9.00*
89G	A11	1p black	37.50	*12.50*
89H	A11	2p claret		*18.50*
89I	A11	5p dp bl		*40.00*

Same, dated 1897

1897 Engr. Unwmk.

90	A11	1c violet	50	50
91	A11	2c bl grn	50	62
92	A11	5c brt rose	50	32
93	A11	10c blue	6.25	75
94	A11	20c bis brn	2.50	*3.75*
95	A11	50c bl gray	9.00	*9.50*
96	A11	1p black	9.00	*15.00*
97	A11	2p claret	20.00	*19.00*
98	A11	5p dp bl	20.00	*42.50*
		Nos. 90-98 (9)	68.25	*91.94*

See italic note after No. 109M.

Wmk. 117

98A	A11	1c violet	14.00	50
98B	A11	2c bl grn	14.00	50
98C	A11	5c brt rose	20.00	38
98D	A11	10c blue	22.50	90
98E	A11	20c bis brn	3.75	4.25
98F	A11	50c bl gray	22.50	*8.00*
98G	A11	1p black	25.00	*16.00*
98H	A11	2p claret	25.00	*25.00*
98I	A11	5p dp bl	125.00	*50.00*
		Nos. 98A-98I (9)	271.75	*105.53*

Coat of Arms of "Republic of Central America" — A12

1898 Engr. Wmk. 117

99	A12	1c brown	25	38
100	A12	2c slate	25	38
101	A12	4c red brn	25	50
102	A12	5c ol grn	40.00	22.50
103	A12	10c violet	15.00	62
104	A12	15c ultra	40	1.50
105	A12	20c blue	10.00	2.00
106	A12	50c yellow	10.00	*9.50*
107	A12	1p vio bl	40	*16.00*
108	A12	2p brown	19.00	*22.50*
109	A12	5p orange	25.00	*32.50*
		Nos. 99-109 (11)	120.55	*108.38*

Unwmk.

109A	A12	1c brown	1.25	32
109B	A12	2c slate	1.25	1.25
109D	A12	4c red brn	2.25	62
109E	A12	5c ol grn	25.00	15
109G	A12	10c violet	25.00	62
109H	A12	15c ultra	25.00	
109I	A12	20c blue	25.00	
109J	A12	50c yellow	25.00	
109K	A12	1p dp ultra	25.00	
109L	A12	2p ol brn	25.00	
109M	A12	5p orange	25.00	
		Nos. 109A-109M (11)	204.75	

The paper of Nos. 109A to 109M is slightly thicker and more opaque than that of Nos. 81 to 89 and 90 to 98. The 5c and 10c also exist on very thin, semi-transparent paper.

Many reprints of Nos. 81-109M are on thick, porous paper, with and without watermark. The watermark is sideways. Paper of the originals is thinner for Nos. 81-109 but thicker for Nos. 109A-109M. Value 15 cents each.

In addition, reprints of Nos. 81-89 and 90-98 exist on thin paper, but with shades differing slightly from those of originals.

For overprints see Nos. O118-O128.

"Justice" A13

Mt. Momotombo A14

1899 Litho.

110	A13	1c gray grn	15	*35*
111	A13	2c brown	15	*25*
112	A13	4c dp rose	35	*40*
113	A13	5c dp bl	20	*25*
114	A13	10c buff	20	*30*
115	A13	15c chocolate	20	*65*
116	A13	20c dk grn	35	*75*
117	A13	50c brt rose	20	*3.00*
118	A13	1p red	20	*8.50*

119 A13 2p violet 20 *20.00*
120 A13 5p lt bl 20 *25.00*
Nos. 110-120 (11) 2.40

Nos. 110-120 exist imperf. and in horizontal pairs imperf. between.
For overprints see Nos. O129-O139.

Imprint: "American Bank Note Co. NY"

1900, Jan. 1 **Engr.**
121 A14 1c plum 50 15
122 A14 2c vermilion 50 15
123 A14 3c green 75 25
124 A14 4c ol grn 1.00 25
125 A14 5c dk bl 4.00 20
126 A14 6c car rose 14.00 5.00
127 A14 10c violet 7.00 25
128 A14 15c ultra 8.00 65
129 A14 20c brown 8.00 65
130 A14 50c lake 7.00 1.10
131 A14 1p yellow 12.00 4.00
132 A14 2p salmon 10.00 2.25
133 A14 5p black 10.00 3.00
Nos. 121-133 (13) 82.75 17.90

See Nos. 159-161. For overprints and surcharges see Nos. 134-136, 144-151, 162-163, 175-178, O150-O154, 1L1-1L13, 1L16-1L19, 1L20, 2L1-2L10, 2L16-2L24, 2L36-2L39.

Nos. 131-133 Surcharged in Black or Red

1901
2 Cent.

1901, Mar. 5
134 A14 2c on 1p yel 5.00 3.00
a. Bar below date 14.00 8.00
b. Inverted surcharge 16.50
c. Double surcharge 27.50
135 A14 10c on 5p blk (R) 6.50 4.50
a. Bar below date 14.00 8.00
136 A14 20c on 2p salmon 7.50 7.50
a. Bar below date 14.00 10.00

A 2c surcharge on No. 121, the 1c plum, was not put on sale, nor postally used.
The 2c on 1p yellow without ornaments is a reprint.

Postage Due Stamps of 1900 Overprinted in Black or Gold

Correos
1901

1901, Mar.
137 D3 1c plum 4.50 3.50
138 D3 2c vermilion 4.50 3.50
139 D3 5c dk bl 6.00 3.50
140 D3 10c pur (G) 8.50 5.00
a. Double overprint 14.00 14.00
141 D3 20c org brn 10.00 6.50
142 D3 30c dk grn 10.00 6.50
143 D3 50c lake 8.50 4.00
a. "1091" for "1901" 16.00 16.00
b. "Correo" 37.50
Nos. 137-143 (7) 52.00 32.50

In 1904 an imitation of this overprint was made to fill a dealer's order. The date is at top and "Correos" at bottom. The overprint is printed in black, sideways on the 1c and 2c and upright on the 5c and 10c. Some copies of the 2c were further surcharged "1 Centavo." None of these stamps was ever regularly used.

Nos. 126, 131-133 Surcharged

3 Cent.
1901

Black Surcharge

1901, Oct. 20
144 A14 3c on 6c rose 6.00 5.00
a. Bar below value 7.00 5.50
b. Inverted surcharge 8.00 8.00
c. Double surcharge 8.00 8.00
d. Double surch., one inverted 25.00 25.00
145 A14 4c on 6c rose 5.00 4.00
a. Bar below value 5.50 4.50
b. "1 cent" instead of "4 cent" 8.00 8.00
c. Double surcharge 20.00 20.00
146 A14 5c on 1p yellow 5.00 4.00
a. Three bars below value 6.00 4.50
b. Ornaments at each side of "1901" 6.00 4.50
c. Double surcharge, one in red 15.00 15.00
147 A14 10c on 2p salmon 5.50 4.00
a. Inverted surcharge 12.50 12.50
b. Double surcharge

Blue Surcharge

148 A14 3c on 6c rose 6.00 4.50
a. Bar below value 7.00 5.50
b. Double surcharge 8.00 8.00
149 A14 4c on 6c rose 6.50 5.00
a. Bar below value 7.50 7.50
b. "1 cent" instead of "4 cent" 10.00 10.00
c. Inverted surcharge 20.00 20.00

Red Surcharge

150 A14 5c on 1p yellow 7.50 6.50
a. Three bars below value 9.00 7.00
b. Ornaments at each side of "1901" 9.00 7.00
c. Inverted surcharge 12.00 12.00
d. Double surcharge, inverted 17.50 17.50
151 A14 20c on 5p black 5.00 3.50
a. Inverted surcharge 16.00 16.00
b. Double surcharge 22.50 22.50
c. Triple surcharge
Nos. 144-151 (8) 46.50 36.50

In 1904 a series was surcharged as above, but with "Centavos" spelled out. About the same time No. 122 was surcharged "1 cent." and "1901," "1902" or "1904." All of these surcharges were made to fill a dealer's order and none of the stamps was regularly issued or used.

Postage Due Stamps of 1900 Overprinted in Black

1901
Correos

1901, Oct.
152 D3 1c red violet 1.00 40
a. Ornaments at each side of the stamp 1.10 65
b. Ornaments at each side of "1901" 1.10 65
c. "Correos" in italics 1.50 1.50
d. Double overprint 14.00 14.00
153 D3 2c vermilion 75 40
a. Double overprint 8.50 5.50
154 D3 5c dark blue 1.00 60
a. Double overprint, one inverted
b. Double overprint 7.00 7.00
155 D3 10c purple 1.00 60
b. Double overprint 10.00 10.00
c. Double overprint, one inverted 12.00 12.00
156 D3 20c org brn 1.25 1.25
b. Double overprint 7.00 7.00
157 D3 30c dk grn 1.00 1.10
a. Double overprint 9.00 9.00
b. Inverted overprint 19.00 19.00
158 D3 50c lake 1.00 1.10
a. Triple overprint 25.00 25.00
b. Double overprint 16.50 16.50
Nos. 152-158 (7) 7.00 5.45

One stamp in each group of 25 has the 2nd "o" of "Correos" italic. Value twice normal.

Momotombo Type of 1900 Without Imprint

1902 **Litho.** ***Perf. 14***
159 A14 5c blue 50 25
a. Imperf., pair 3.75
160 A14 5c carmine 50 20
a. Imperf., pair 3.75
161 A14 10c violet 1.50 20
a. Imperf., pair 3.75

No. 161 was privately surcharged 6c, 1p and 5p in black in 1903.

Nos. 121 and 122 Surcharged in Black

15 cvos.
1902

1902, Oct. ***Perf. 12***
162 A14 15c on 2c ver 2.00 75
a. Double surcharge 32.50
b. Blue surcharge 90.00
163 A14 30c on 1c plum 1.00 2.25
a. Double surcharge 9.00
b. Inverted surcharge 27.50

Counterfeits of No. 163 exist in slightly smaller type.

President José Santos Zelaya — A15

1903, Jan. **Engr.**
167 A15 1c emer & blk 35 50
168 A15 2c rose & blk 70 50
169 A15 5c ultra & blk 35 50
170 A15 10c yel & blk 35 85
171 A15 15c lake & blk 60 2.00
172 A15 20c vio & blk 60 2.00
173 A15 50c ol & blk 60 5.00
174 A15 1p red brn & blk 60 6.00
Nos. 167-174 (8) 4.15 17.35

10th anniv. of 1st election of Pres. Zelaya.
The so-called color errors-1c orange yellow and black, 2c ultramarine and black, 5c lake and black and 10c emerald and black-were also delivered to postal authorities. They were intended for official use though not issued as such. Value, $4 each.

A16

A17

No. 161 Surcharged with New Values in Blue

1904-05
175 A16 5c on 10c vio ('05) 1.75 25
a. Inverted surcharge 2.00 1.40
b. Without ornaments 2.00 70
c. Character for "cents" inverted 1.75 40
d. As "b," inverted
e. As "c," inverted 2.75 2.75
f. Double surcharge 8.00 8.00
g. "5" omitted 2.75 2.75
176 A16 15c on 10c vio ('05) 30 30
a. Inverted surcharge 1.40 1.40
b. Without ornaments 1.40 1.40
c. Character for "cents" inverted 1.10 1.10
d. As "b," inverted
e. As "c," inverted 1.75 1.75
f. Imperf. 6.50
h. As "a," imperf. 9.00 9.00
i. Double surcharge 14.00 14.00
177 A17 15c on 10c vio 4.50 2.75
a. Inverted surcharge 6.00 6.00
b. "Centcvos" 6.00 4.50
c. "5" of "15" omitted 7.50
d. As "b," inverted 8.50 8.50
e. Double surcharge 11.00 11.00
f. Double surcharge, inverted 13.00 13.00
g. Imperf., pair 9.00 9.00

There are two settings of the surcharge on No. 175. In the 1st the character for "cents" and the figure "5" are 2mm apart and in the 2nd 4mm.
The 2c vermilion, No. 122, with surcharge "1 cent. / 1904" was not issued.

No. 161 Surcharged in Black

5 CENTS.

1905, June
178 A14 5c on 10c violet 60 35
a. Inverted surcharge 2.75 2.75
b. Double surcharge 4.50 4.50
c. Surcharge in blue 13.00

Coat of Arms — A18

Imprint: "American Bank Note Co. NY"

1905, July 25 **Engr.** ***Perf. 12***
179 A18 1c green 30 20
180 A18 2c car rose 30 20
181 A18 3c violet 45 25
182 A18 4c org red 45 25
183 A18 5c blue 45 15
184 A18 6c slate 60 40
185 A18 10c yel brn 85 25
186 A18 15c brn olive 75 35
187 A18 20c lake 60 30
188 A18 50c orange 3.00 1.50
189 A18 1p black 1.50 1.50
190 A18 2p dk grn 1.50 2.00
191 A18 5p violet 1.75 2.50
Nos. 179-191 (13) 12.50 9.85

See Nos. 202-208, 237-248. For overprints and surcharges see Nos. 193-201, 212-216, 235-236, 249-265, O187-O198, O210-O222, 1L21-1L62, 1L73-1L95, 1LO1-1LO3, 2L26-2L35, 2L42-2L46, 2L48-2L72, 2LO1-2LO4.

Nos. 179-184 and 191 Surcharged in Black or Red Reading Up or Down

Vale 10¢

1906-08
193 A18 10c on 2c car rose (up) 7.00 4.00
a. Surcharge reading down 13.00 13.00
194 A18 10c on 3c vio (up) 60 20
a. "¢" normal 2.75 1.35
b. Double surcharge 4.50 4.50
c. Double surch., up and down 7.00 5.00
d. Pair, one without surcharge 9.50
e. Surcharge reading down 30 20
195 A18 10c on 4c org red (up) ('08) *35.00* *20.00*
a. Surcharge reading down *32.50* *22.50*
196 A18 15c on 1c grn (up) 60 30
a. Double surcharge 7.50 7.50
b. Dbl. surch., one reading down 11.00 11.00
c. Surcharge reading down 40 25
197 A18 20c on 2c car rose (down) ('07) 50 30
a. Double surcharge 13.00 13.00
b. Surcharge reading up 37.50 32.00
c. "V" omitted 10.00 10.00
198 A18 20c on 5c bl (down) 75 50
a. Surcharge reading up 35.00
199 A18 50c on 6c sl (R) (down) 60 50
a. Double surcharge
b. Surcharge reading up 30.00 30.00
c. Yellow brown surcharge 60 40
200 A18 1p on 5p vio (down) ('07) 42.50 25.00

There are several settings of these surcharges and many varieties in the shapes of the figures, the spacing, etc.

Surcharged in Red Vertically Reading Up

Vale 35 cts.

1908, May
201 A18 35c on 6c slate 3.00 2.25
a. Double surcharge (R) 25.00
b. Double surcharge (R + Bk) 65.00
c. Carmine surcharge 3.00 2.25

Arms Type of 1905
Imprint: "Waterlow & Sons, Ltd."

1907, Feb. ***Perf. 14 to 15***
202 A18 1c green 70 40
203 A18 2c rose 80 25
204 A18 4c brn org 2.00 30
205 A18 10c yel brn 3.00 25
206 A18 15c brn olive 4.50 90
207 A18 20c lake 8.00 1.25
208 A18 50c orange 11.00 4.25
Nos. 202-208 (7) 30.00 7.60

Nos. 202-204, 207-208 Surcharged in Black or Blue (Bl) Reading Down

Vale 10¢

1907-08
212 A18 10c on 2c rose 1.50 50
a. Double surcharge 10.00
b. "Vale" only 22.50
c. Surcharge reading up 14.00 6.50
213 A18 10c on 4c brn org (up) ('08) 2.25 85
a. Double surcharge 10.00
b. Surcharge reading down 5.50
214 A18 10c on 20c lake ('08) 3.25 1.40
b. Surcharge reading up 80.00
215 A18 10c on 50c org (Bl) ('08) 2.00 60
216 A18 15c ol 1c grn ('08) 32.50 4.00
Nos. 212-216 (5) 41.50 7.35

Several settings of this surcharge provide varieties of numeral font, spacing, etc.

Revenue Stamps Overprinted "CORREO-1908" — A19

1908, June

217 A19 5c yel & blk 60 40
a. "CORROE" 2.75 2.75
b. Overprint reading down 7.00
c. Double overprint 13.00
218 A19 10c lt bl & blk 50 25
a. Double overprint 4.50 4.50
b. Overprint reading down 50 25
c. Double overprint, up and down 13.00 13.00
219 A19 1p yel brn & blk 50 *2.00*
a. "CORROE" 7.50 7.50
220 A19 2p Pearl gray & blk 50 *2.50*
a. "CORROE" 10.00 10.00

Remainders of Nos. 219-220 were sold.

Revenue Stamps Surcharged Vertically Reading Up in Red, Blue, Green or Orange

CORREO–1908
VALE 2 ₵

221 A19 1c on 5c yel & blk (R) 40 25
a. "1008" 1.50 1.50
b. "8908" 1.50 1.50
c. Surcharge reading down 4.00 4.00
d. Double surcharge 4.00 4.00
222 A19 2c on 5c yel & blk (Bl) 50 30
b. "ORREO" 1.75 1.75
c. "1008" 1.75 1.75
d. "8908" 1.75 1.75
f. Double surcharge 7.00 7.00
g. Double surcharge, one inverted 7.00 7.00
h. Surcharge reading down 9.00 9.00
223 A19 4c on 5c yel & blk (G) 65 35
a. "ORREO" 2.50 2.50
b. "1008" 2.00 2.00
c. "8908" 2.00 2.00
224 A19 15c on 50c ol & blk (R) 60 40
a. "1008" 4.00 4.00
b. "8908" 4.00 4.00
c. Surcharge reading down 10.00 10.00
225 A19 35c on 50c ol & blk (O) 4.00 1.00
a. Double surcharge, one inverted 12.00 12.00
b. Surcharge reading down 12.00 12.00
c. Double surcharge, one in black
Nos. 221-225 (5) 6.15 2.30

For surcharges and overprints see Nos. 225D-225H, 230-234, 266-278, 1L63-1L72A, 1L96-1L106, 2L47.

Revenue Stamps Surcharged Vertically Reading Up in Blue, Black or Orange

CORREOS–1908
VALE 2 ₵

1908, Nov.

225D A19 2c on 5c yel & blk (Bl) 20.00 12.50
e. "9c" instead of "2c" 75.00 75.00
225F A19 10c on 50c ol & blk (Bk) *850.00 325.00*
g. Double surcharge *425.00*
225H A19 35c on 50c ol & blk (O) 17.50 10.00

In this setting there are three types of the character for "cents".

Demand, as well as supply, determines a stamp's market value. One is as important as the other.

CORREOS—1908
VALE 4 ₵
CORREOS—1908

Revenue Stamps Overprinted or Surcharged in Various Colors

1908, Dec.

226 2c org (Bk) 3.50 2.00
a. Double overprint 6.00 6.00
b. Overprint reading up 5.00 5.00
227 4c on 2c org (Bk) 1.75 90
a. Surcharge reading up 5.00 5.00
b. Blue surcharge 80.00 80.00
228 5c on 2c org (Bl) 1.50 60
a. Surcharge reading up 6.00 6.00
229 10c on 2c org (G) 1.50 30
a. "1988" for "1908" 4.00 3.00
b. Surcharge reading up 5.00 5.00
c. "e" inverted 4.00 4.00
d. Double surcharge 7.50

Two printings of No. 229 exist. In the first, the initial of "VALE" is a small capital, and in the second a large capital.

The overprint "Correos-1908." 35mm long, handstamped on 1c blue revenue stamp of type A20, is private and fraudulent.

Revenue Stamps Surcharged in Various Colors

CORREOS 1909
VALE 10 ₵

1909, Feb.

Color: Olive & Black

230 A19 1c on 50c (V) 4.00 1.65
231 A19 2c on 50c (Br) 7.00 3.00
232 A19 4c on 50c (G) 7.00 3.00
233 A19 5c on 50c (C) 4.00 1.75
a. Double surcharge 12.50 12.50
234 A19 10c on 50c (Bk) 1.10 75
Nos. 230-234 (5) 23.10 10.15

Nos. 230 to 234 are found with three types of the character for "cents".

Nos. 190 and 191 Surcharged in Black

VALE 10 ₵

1909, Mar. *Perf. 12*

235 A18 10c on 2p dk grn 20.00 12.00
236 A18 10c on 5p vio *100.00 70.00*

There are three types of the character for "cents."

Arms Type of 1905
Imprint: "American Bank Note Co. NY"

1909, Mar.

237 A18 1c yel grn 35 20
238 A18 2c vermilion 35 20
239 A18 3c red org 35 20
240 A18 4c violet 35 20
241 A18 5c dp bl 35 20
242 A18 6c gray brn 3.00 1.50
243 A18 10c lake 85 15
244 A18 15c black 85 15
245 A18 20c brn olive 85 15
246 A18 50c dp grn 1.25 40
247 A18 1p yellow 1.25 40
248 A18 2p car rose 1.00 40
Nos. 237-248 (12) 10.80 4.15

Nos. 239 and 244, Surcharged in Black or Red

VALE 2 ₵

1910, July

249 A18 2c on 3c red org 2.75 1.10
250 A18 10c on 15c blk (R) 1.25 30
a. "VLEA" 3.50 2.00
b. Double surcharge 17.50 17.50

There are two types of the character for "cents".

Nos. 239, 244, 245 Surcharged in Black or Red

VALE 2 ₵

1910

252 A18 2c on 3c (Bk) 1.50 1.25
a. Double surcharge 6.00 6.00
b. Pair, one without surcharge
c. "Vale" omitted 10.00 10.00
254 A18 5c on 20c (R) 40 30
a. Double surcharge (R) 6.00 5.00
b. Inverted surcharge (R) 3.50 25
c. Black surcharge 100.00
d. Double surcharge (Bk) 135.00
e. Inverted surcharge (Bk) 110.00
255 A18 10c on 15c (Bk) 90 30
a. "c" omitted 2.00 1.10
b. "10c" omitted 2.50 1.50
c. Inverted surcharge 4.00 4.00
d. Double surcharge 6.00 6.00
e. Double surch., one inverted 12.00

There are several minor varieties in this setting, such as italic "L" and "E" and fancy "V" in "VALE", small italic "C", and italic "I" for "1" in "10".

Nos. 239, 244, 246 and 247, Surcharged in Black

Vale
2 cts.

1910, Dec. 10

256 A18 2c on 3c red org 90 50
a. Without period 1.00 75
b. Inverted surcharge 6.00 6.00
c. Double surcharge 6.00 6.00
257 A18 10c on 15c blk 2.00 75
a. Without period 3.50 1.25
b. Double surcharge 3.50 3.00
c. Inverted surcharge 5.00 5.00
258 A18 10c on 50c dp grn 1.25 40
a. Without period 1.50 75
b. Double surcharge 3.00 3.00
c. Inverted surcharge 3.00 3.00
259 A18 10c on 1p yel 90 40
a. Without period 1.25 75
b. Double surcharge 3.00 3.00

The 15c on 50c deep green is a telegraph stamp.

Nos. 240, 244-248 Surcharged in Black

Vale
2 cts.

Surcharge as on Nos. 256-259 but lines wider apart.

1911, Mar.

260 A18 2c on 4c vio 30 20
a. Without period 35 30
b. Double surcharge 35 30
c. Double surcharge, inverted 4.00 4.00
d. Double surcharge, one inverted 3.50 3.50
e. Inverted surcharge 7.50 7.50
261 A18 5c on 20c brn ol 30 20
a. Without period 60 50
b. Double surcharge 2.50 2.50
c. Inverted surcharge 2.50 2.00
d. Double surcharge, one inverted 6.00 6.00
262 A18 10c on 15c blk 40 20
a. Without period 1.00 50
b. "Yale" 12.00 12.00
c. Double surcharge 3.00 3.00
d. Inverted surcharge 3.00 3.00
e. Double surch., one inverted 5.00 4.00
f. Double surch., both inverted 12.00 12.00
263 A18 10c on 50c dp grn 25 20
a. Without period 1.00 50
b. Double surcharge 3.00 2.50
c. Double surcharge, one inverted 5.00 4.00
d. Inverted surcharge 5.00 5.00
264 A18 10c on 1p yel 1.50 40
a. Without period 2.00 1.50
b. Double surcharge 4.00 4.00
c. Double surcharge, one inverted 7.50
265 A18 10c on 2p car rose 60 50
a. Without period 2.00 1.50
b. Double surcharge 2.50 2.50
c. Double surcharge, one inverted 6.00 6.00
d. Inverted surcharge 6.00 6.00
Nos. 260-265 (6) 3.35 1.70

Revenue Stamps Surcharged in Black

Correos
02 cts
1911

1911, Apr. 10 *Perf. 14 to 15*

266 A19 2c on 5p dl bl 1.00 1.25
a. Without period 1.25 1.50
b. Double surcharge 2.50 *2.00*
267 A19 2c on 5p ultra 35 40
a. Without period 75 1.25
b. Double surcharge *3.50*
268 A19 5c on 10p pink 75 40
a. Without period 1.50 1.00
b. "cte" for "cts" 1.50 1.00
c. Double surcharge 4.00 4.00
d. Inverted surcharge 2.50 2.50
269 A19 10c on 25c lil 40 25
a. Without period 1.00 75
b. "cte" for "cts" 1.25 1.00
c. Inverted surcharge 4.00 4.00
d. Double surcharge 2.50 2.50
e. Double surcharge, one inverted 4.00 4.00
270 A19 10c on 2p gray 40 25
a. Without period 1.00 75
b. "cte" for "cts" 1.25 1.00
c. Double surcharge 5.00 5.00
d. Double surcharge, one inverted 4.00 3.00
271 A19 35c on 1p brn 40 30
a. Without period 1.00 75
b. "cte" for "cts" 1.25 1.00
c. "Corre" 1.50 1.50
d. Double surcharge 2.50 2.50
e. Double surcharge, one inverted 2.50 2.50
f. Double surcharge inverted 3.00 3.00
g. Inverted surcharge *5.00*
Nos. 266-271 (6) 3.30 2.85

These surcharges are in settings of twenty-five. One stamp in each setting has a large square period after "cts" and two have no period. One of the 2c has no space between "02" and "cts" and one 5c has a small thin "s" in "Correos."

Surcharged in Black

CORREOS
05 cts.
1911

1911, June

272 A19 5c on 2p gray 1.50 1.00
a. Inverted surcharge 6.00 5.00

In this setting one stamp has a large square period and another has a thick up-right "c" in "cts."

Surcharged in Black

VALE
05 cts
POSTAL
de 1911

1911, June 12

273 A19 5c on 25c lilac 1.50 1.25
274 A19 5c on 50c ol grn 5.00 5.00
275 A19 5c on 5p blue 7.00 7.00
276 A19 5c on 5p ultra 6.00 6.00
a. Inverted surcharge
277 A19 5c on 50p ver 5.00 5.00
278 A19 10c on 50c ol grn 1.50 50
Nos. 273-278 (6) 26.00 24.75

This setting has the large square period and the thick "c" in "cts." Many of the stamps have no period after "cts." Owing to broken type and defective impressions letters sometimes appear to be omitted.

A21

Revenue Stamps Surcharged on the Back in Black:

a	b
vale / **05 cts.** / **CORREO** / **DE 1911**	*Vale* / **05 cts** / **CORREO** / **DE 1911**

Railroad coupon tax stamps (1st class red and 2nd class blue) are the basic stamps of Nos. 279-294. They were first surcharged for revenue use in 1903 in two types: I- "Timbre Fiscal" and "ctvs." II- "TIMBRE FISCAL" and "cents" (originally intended for use in Bluefields).

1911, July

279 A21 (a) 2c on 5c on 2 bl 25 30
a. New value in yellow on face 6.00 6.00
b. New value in black on face 5.00 5.00
c. New value in red on face 60.00
d. Inverted surcharge 75
e. Double surch., one inverted 7.50 7.50
f. "TIMBRE FISCAL" in blk 75 75
280 A21 (b) 2c on 5c on 2 bl 25 30
a. New value in yellow on face 3.00 3.00
b. New value in black on face 4.00 4.00
c. New value in red on face 60.00
d. Inverted surcharge 90 1.00
e. Double surch., one inverted 7.50 7.50
f. "TIMBRE FISCAL" in blk 1.00 1.00
281 A21 (a) 5c on 5c on 2 bl 20 15
a. Inverted surcharge 50 35
b. "TIMBRE FISCAL" in blk 1.00 1.00
c. New value in yellow on face
282 A21 (b) 5c on 5c on 2 bl 25 20
a. Inverted surcharge 40 35
b. "TIMBRE FISCAL" in blk 1.00 1.00
283 A21 (a) 10c on 5c on 2 bl 20 20
a. Inverted surcharge 75 50
b. "TIMBRE FISCAL" in blk 1.00 1.00
c. New value in yellow on face 60.00
284 A21 (b) 10c on 5c on 2 bl 20 20
a. Inverted surcharge 75 50
b. "TIMBRE FISCAL" in blk 1.00 1.00
c. Double surcharge 6.00 6.00
d. New value in yellow on face 65.00
285 A21 (a) 15c on 10c on 1 red 25 25
a. Inverted surcharge 1.00 1.25
b. "Timbre Fiscal" double 5.00
286 A21 (b) 15c on 10c on 1 red 35 35
a. Inverted surcharge 1.00 1.00
b. "Timbre Fiscal" double 5.00
Nos. 279-286 (8) 1.95 1.95

These surcharges are in settings of 20. For listing, they are separated into small and large figures, but there are many other varieties due to type and arrangement.

For overprints and surcharges see Nos. 287-294, O223-O244, 1L107-1L108.

Surcharged on the Face in Black

CORREO
02 centavos

1911, Oct.

287 A21 2c on 10c on 1 red 6.50 6.50
a. Inverted surcharge 1.40 1.40
b. Double surcharge 10.00 10.00
288 A21 20c on 10c on 1 red 4.50 4.50
a. Inverted surcharge 5.25 5.00
289 A21 50c on 10c on 1 red 5.25 4.50
a. Inverted surcharge 10.00 10.00

There are two varieties of the figures "2" and "5" in this setting.

Surcharged on the Back in Black

Vale
10 cts.
CORREO DE
1911

1911, Nov.

289B A21 5c on 10c on 1 red 37.50
c. Inverted surcharge 20.00
289D A21 10c on 10c on 1 red 12.50
e. Inverted surcharge 24.00

Surcharged on the Face

Correo
Vale
2 cts.
1911

1911, Dec.

Dark Blue Postal Surcharge

290 A21 2c on 10c on 1 red 25 20
a. Inverted surcharge 2.50 2.50
b. Double surcharge 5.00 5.00
291 A21 5c on 10c on 1 red 30 20
a. Double surcharge 2.50 2.50
b. Inverted surcharge 2.50 2.50
292 A21 10c on 10c on 1 red 35 20
a. Inverted surcharge 2.50 2.50
b. Double surcharge 2.50 2.50
c. "TIMBRE FISCAL" on back 3.50 3.50

Black Postal Surcharge

293 A21 10c on 10c on 1 red 1.50 1.00
a. Inverted surcharge 7.00 7.00
b. New value surch. on back 12.00 12.00

Red Postal Surcharge

293C A21 5c on 5c on 2 blue 1.40 1.25
d. "TIMBRE FISCAL" in blk 2.50 1.75
e. "5" omitted 3.75 3.75
f. Inverted surcharge 4.75 4.75
Nos. 290-293C (5) 3.80 2.85

Bar Overprinted on No. O234 in Dark Blue

Correo oficial
Vale
10 cts.
1911

294 A21 10c on 10c on 1 red 1.25 1.00
a. Inverted surcharge 2.50 2.50
b. Bar at foot of stamp 5.00 5.00

Nos. 290-294 each have three varieties of the numerals in the surcharge.

"Liberty" A22

Coat of Arms A23

1912, Jan. **Engr.** ***Perf. 14, 15***

295 A22 1c yel grn 30 15
296 A22 2c carmine 40 15
297 A22 3c yel brn 30 20
298 A22 4c brn vio 30 15
299 A22 5c blue & blk 25 15
300 A22 6c olive bister 30 80
301 A22 10c red brn 25 15
302 A22 15c vio 25 15
303 A22 20c red 25 15
304 A22 25c blue grn & blk 30 20
305 A23 35c grn & chnt 2.00 1.50
306 A22 50c lt blue 1.00 40
307 A22 1p org 1.40 2.00
308 A22 2p dark blue grn 1.50 2.25
309 A22 5p blk 3.50 3.50
Nos. 295-309 (15) 12.30 11.90

For overprints and surcharges see Nos. 310-324, 337A-348, 395-396, O245-O259.

No. 305 Surcharged in Violet

Vale 15 cts.
Correos-1913.

1913, Mar.

310 A23 15c on 35c 40 25
a. "ats" for "cts" 6.00 6.00

Stamps of 1912 Surcharged in Red or Black

VALE
medio
centavo
de córdoba
1913

1913-14

311 A22 ½c on 3c yel brn (R) 40 35
a. "Corooba" 2.50 2.50
b. "do" for "de" 2.50 2.50
c. Inverted surcharge 22.50
d. Black surcharge 50.00
312 A22 ½c on 15c vio (R) 25 20
a. "Corooba" 1.00 1.00
b. "do" for "de" 1.25 1.25
c. Black surcharge 25.00
313 A22 ½c on 1p org 25 20
a. "VALB" 1.50 1.00
b. "ALE" 4.00 3.50
c. "LE" 6.00 5.00
d. "VALE" omitted 3.50 3.50
314 A22 1c on 3c yel brn 75 60
315 A22 1c on 4c brn vio 25 20
316 A22 1c on 50c lt blue 25 20
317 A22 1c on 5p blk 25 20
318 A22 2c on 4c brn vio 35 25
a. "do" for "de" 1.25 1.25
319 A22 2c on 20c red 3.50 4.50
a. "do" for "de" 17.50 12.50
320 A22 2c on 25c blue grn & blk 35 20
a. "do" for "de" 3.50 2.50
321 A23 2c on 35c grn & chnt 25 40
a. "9131" 3.00 2.00
b. "do" for "de" 2.50 2.00
322 A22 2c on 50c lt blue 25 20
a. "do" for "de" 1.25 1.25
323 A22 2c on 2p dark blue grn 20 15
a. "VALB" 1.25 75
b. "ALE" 2.50 1.25
c. "VALE" omitted 6.00
d. "VALE" and "dos" omitted 6.00
324 A22 3c on 6c olive bis 20 15
a. "VALB" 35.00

Surcharged on Zelaya Issue of 1912

325 Z2 ½c on 2c ver 60 45
a. "Corooba" 1.25 1.25
b. "do" for "de" 1.25 1.25
326 Z2 1c on 3c org brn 50 20
327 Z2 1c on 4c car 50 20
328 Z2 1c on 6c red brn 40 20
329 Z2 1c on 20c dark vio 50 20
330 Z2 1c on 25c grn & blk 50 20
331 Z2 2c on 1c yel grn ('14) 6.75 1.25
a. "Centavos" 7.50 1.50
332 Z2 2c on 25c grn & blk 2.25 3.00
333 Z2 5c on 35c brn & blk 40 20
334 Z2 5c on 50c ol grn 40 20
a. Double surcharge 22.50
335 Z2 6c on 1p org 40 20
336 Z2 10c on 2p org brn 40 20
337 Z2 1p on 5p dk bl grn 40 40
Nos. 325-337 (13) 14.00 6.90

On No. 331 the surcharge has a space of 2½mm between "Vale" and "dos".

Space between "Vale" and "dos" 2½mm instead of 1mm "de Cordoba" in different type.

1914, Feb.

337A A22 2c on 4c brn vio 27.50 4.00
b. "Ccntavos" 12.00
337C A22 2c on 20c red 13.00 1.25
d. "Ccntavos" 4.00
337E A22 2c on 25c bl grn & blk 6.00
f. "Ccntavos" 12.00
337G A23 2c on 35c grn & chnt 8.50
h. "Ccntavos" 15.00
337I A22 2c on 50c lt bl 22.00 4.00
j. "Ccntavos" 10.00

No. 310 with Additional Surcharge

medio
cvo. Córdoba

1913, Dec.

337K A23 ½c on 15c on 35c *200.00*

The word "Medio" is usually in heavy-faced, shaded letters. It is also in thinner, unshaded letters and in letters from both fonts mixed.

No. 310 Surcharged in Black and Violet

½ cl. Cordoba
Correos 1913.

338 A23 ½c on 15c on 35c 20 15
a. Double surcharge 3.50
b. Inverted surcharge 3.50
c. Surcharged on No. 305 12.00
339 A23 1c on 15c on 35c 25 20
a. Double surcharge 4.00

Official Stamps of 1912 Surcharged

VALE
₡ 0.01

1914, Feb.

340 A22 1c on 25c lt bl 40 25
a. Double surcharge 9.00
341 A23 1c on 35c lt bl 40 25
a. "0.10" for "0.01" 10.00 10.00
341B A22 1c on 50c lt bl *160.00*
342 A22 1c on 1p lt bl 25 20
342A A22 2c on 20c lt bl *160.00* *110.00*
b. "0.12" for "0.02"
343 A22 2c on 50c lt bl 40 20
a. "0.12" for "0.02" 75.00
344 A22 2c on 2p lt bl 40 20
345 A22 2c on 5p lt bl *185.00*
346 A22 5c on 5p lt bl 25 20

Red Surcharge

347 A22 5c on 1p lt bl *55.00*
348 A22 5c on 5p lt bl *325.00*

National Palace, Managua — A24

Leon Cathedral — A25

Various Frames

1914, May 13 **Engr.** ***Perf. 12***

349 A24 ½c lt bl 85 20
350 A24 1c dk grn 85 15
351 A25 2c red org 85 15
352 A24 3c red brn 1.25 30
353 A25 4c scarlet 1.25 40
354 A24 5c gray blk 45 15
355 A25 6c blk brn 9.00 5.50
356 A25 10c org yel 85 20
357 A24 15c dp vio 5.75 2.00
358 A25 20c slate 11.00 5.50
359 A24 25c orange 1.50 45
360 A25 50c pale blue 1.40 40
Nos. 349-360 (12) 35.00 15.40

In 1924 the 5c, 10c, 25c, 50c were issued in slightly larger size, 27x22¾mm. The original set was 26x22½mm.

No. 356 with overprint "Union Panamericana 1890-1940" in green is of private origin.

See Nos. 408-415, 483-495, 513-523, 652-664. For overprints and surcharges see Nos. 361-394, 397-400, 416-419, 427-479, 500, 540-548, 580-586, 600-648, 671-673, 684-685, C1-C3, C9-C13, C49-C66, C92-C105, C121-C134, C147-C149, C155-C163, C174-C185, CO1-CO24, O260-O294, O296-O319, O332-O376, RA1-RA5, RA10-RA11, RA26-RA35, RA39-RA40, RA44, RA47, RA52.

No. 355 Surcharged in Black

VALE
5 cts
de Córdoba
1915

1915, Sept.

361 A25 5c on 6c blk brn 1.50 40
a. Double surcharge 7.00 7.00

Stamps of 1914 Surcharged in Black or Red

Vale
1 centavo
de córdoba

New Value in Figures

1918-19

362 A24 1c on 3c red brn 6.50 2.25
a. Double surch., one invtd. 12.50
363 A25 2c on 4c scar 32.50 22.50
364 A24 5c on 15c dp vio (R) 7.50 1.50
a. Double surcharge 12.00
364C A24 5c on 15c dp vio 350.00

Surcharged in Black

VALE
por 2 centavos
de Córdoba

365 A25 2c on 20c sl 110.00 55.00
a. "ppr" for "por" *120.00*
b. Double surcharge 90.00 30.00
c. "Cordobo" 150.00 110.00
365D A25 5c on 20c sl 325.00 120.00
e. Double surch. (Bk + R) 250.00
f. "Cordobo" 200.00

The surcharge on No. 365 is in blue black, and that on No. 365D usually has an admixture of red.

Surcharged in Black, Red or Violet

Vale
medio centavo
de córdoba

New Value in Words

366 A25 ½c on 6c blk brn 4.00 1.50
a. "Meio" 15.00
b. Double surcharge 12.00
367 A25 ½c on 10c yel 2.50 30
a. "Val" for "Vale" 3.00
b. "Codoba" 3.00
c. Inverted surcharge 5.00
d. Double surch., one inverted 10.00
368 A24 ½c on 15c dp vio 2.50 60
a. Double surcharge 7.50
b. "Codoba" 4.00
c. "Meio" 6.00
369 A24 ½c on 25c org 5.00 2.00
a. Double surcharge 8.00
b. Double surch., one inverted 6.00
370 A25 ½c on 50c pale bl 2.50 30
a. "Meio" 6.00
b. Double surcharge 5.00
c. Double surch., one inverted 7.00
371 A25 ½c on 50c pale bl (R) 4.50 1.50
a. Double surcharge 10.00
372 A24 1c on 3c red brn 3.00 30
a. Double surcharge 3.50
373 A25 1c on 6c blk brn 12.50 3.50
a. Double surcharge 9.00

374 A25 1c on 10c yel 24.00 8.00
a. "nu" for "un" 22.50
375 A24 1c on 15c dp vio 4.50 75
a. Double surcharge 10.00
b. "Codoba" 6.00
376 A25 1c on 20c sl 110.00 55.00
a. Blk surch., normal and red surch. invtd. 80.00
b. Double surch., red & blk 90.00
c. Blue surcharge 110.00
377 A25 1c on 20c sl (V) 110.00 42.50
a. Double surcharge (V + Bk) 80.00
378 A25 1c on 20c sl (R) 2.50 30
a. Double surch., one inverted
b. "Val" for "Vale" 3.50 3.00
379 A24 1c on 25c org 4.50 1.00
a. Double surcharge 11.00
380 A25 1c on 50c pale bl 14.00 4.50
a. Double surcharge 17.50
381 A25 2c on 4c scar 3.50 30
a. Double surcharge 10.00
b. "centavo" 5.00
c. "Val" for "Vale"
382 A25 2c on 6c blk brn 24.00 8.00
a. "Centavoss"
b. "Cordobas"
383 A25 2c on 10c yel 24.00 4.50
a. "centavo"
384 A25 2c on 20c sl (R) 13.00 3.25
a. "pe" for "de" 15.00
b. Double surch., red & blk 27.50
c. "centavo" 12.00
d. Double surcharge (R) 17.50
385 A24 2c on 25c org 5.50 40
a. "Vle" for "Vale" 7.50
b. "Codoba" 7.50
c. Inverted surcharge 10.00
386 A25 5c on 6c blk brn 10.00 4.25
a. Double surcharge 13.50
387 A24 5c on 15c dp vio 3.50 60
a. "cincoun" for "cinco" 15.00
b. "Vle" for "Vale" 12.50
c. "Codoba" 12.50
Nos. 366-387 (22) 389.50 143.35

No. 378 is surcharged in light red and brown red: the latter color is frequently offered as the violet surcharge (No. 377).

Official Stamps of 1915 Surcharged in Black or Blue

Vale dos centavos de cordoba

1919-21

388 A24 1c on 25c lt bl 1.50 25
a. Double surcharge 10.00
b. Inverted surcharge 12.00
389 A25 2c on 50c lt bl 1.50 25
a. "centavo" 4.00 4.00
b. Double surcharge 12.00
390 A25 10c on 20c lt bl 1.40 40
a. "centovos" 5.00 5.00
b. Double surcharge 8.00
390F A25 10c on 20c lt bl (Bl) 65.00

There are numerous varieties of omitted, inverted and italic letters in the foregoing surcharges.

No. 358 Surcharged in Black

VALE 5 Centavos

Types of the numerals:

2 I, 2 II, 2 III
2 IV, 2 V, 2 VI, 2 VII, 2 VIII
5 I, 5 II, 5 III, 5 IV
5 V, 5 VI, 5 VII, 5 VIII

1919, May

391 A25 2c on 20c sl (I) 160.00 110.00
a. Type II
b. Type III
c. Type IV
d. Type VI
e. Type VIII
392 A25 5c on 20c sl (I) 110.00 40.00
a. Type II 110.00 45.00
b. Type III 120.00 50.00
c. Type IV 125.00 50.00
d. Type V 140.00 60.00
e. Type VI 140.00 60.00
f. Type VII 400.00 250.00
h. Double surch., one inverted

No. 358 Surcharged in Black

VALE 2 Cents

393 A25 2 Cents on 20c (I) 135.00
a. Type II
b. Type III
c. Type IV
d. Type V
e. Type VI
f. Type VII
393G A25 5 Cents on 20c sl, (VIII) 135.00 55.00

No. 351 Surcharged in Black

Vale un centavo de córdoba

1920, Jan.

394 A25 1c on 2c red org 1.50 25
a. Inverted surcharge
b. Double surcharge

«Particular»

Official Stamps of 1912 Overprinted in Carmine

1921, Mar.

395 A22 1c lt bl 1.50 60
a. "Parricular" 5.00 5.00
b. Inverted overprint 10.00
396 A22 5c lt bl 1.50 40
a. "Parricular" 5.00 5.00

Official Stamps of 1915 Surcharged in Carmine

Vale un centavo de córdoba

397 A25 ½c on 2c lt bl 50 20
a. "Mddio" 2.50 2.50
398 A25 ½c on 4c lt bl 1.25 20
a. "Mddio" 2.50 2.50
399 A24 1c on 3c lt bl 1.25 30

No. 354 Surcharged in Red

Vale medio centavo

1921, Aug.

400 A24 ½c on 5c gray blk 75 75

Trial printings of this stamp were surcharged in yellow, black and red, and yellow and red. Some of these were used for postage.

Gen. Manuel José Arce — A26

José Cecilio del Valle — A27

Miguel Larreinaga A28

Gen. Fernando Chamorro A29

Gen. Maximo Jerez A30

Gen. Pedro Joaquin Chamorro A31

Rubén Darío — A32

1921, Sept. **Engr.**

401 A26 ½c lt bl & blk 1.00 1.00
402 A27 1c grn & blk 1.00 1.00
403 A28 2c rose red & blk 1.00 1.00
404 A29 5c ultra & blk 1.00 1.00
405 A30 10c org & blk 1.00 1.00
406 A31 25c yel & blk 1.00 1.00
407 A32 50c vio & blk 1.00 1.00
Nos. 401-407 (7) 7.00 7.00

Centenary of independence.
For overprints and surcharges see Nos. 420-421, RA12-RA16, RA19-RA23.

Types of 1914 Issue Various Frames

1922

408 A24 ½c green 20 15
409 A24 1c violet 20 15
410 A25 2c car rose 20 15
411 A24 3c ol gray 30 15
411A A25 4c vermilion 35 25
412 A25 6c red brn 20 15
413 A24 15c brown 35 15
414 A25 20c bis brn 50 20
415 A25 1cor blk brn 90 50
Nos. 408-415 (9) 3.20 1.85

In 1924 Nos. 408-415 were issued in slightly larger size, 27x22¾mm. The original set was 26x22½mm.

Nos. 408, 410 exist with signature controls. See note before No. 600. Same values.

No. 356 Surcharged in Black

Vale 0.01 de córdoba

1922, Nov.

416 A25 1c on 10c org yel 1.00 35
417 A25 2c on 10c org yel 1.00 25

Nos. 354 and 356 Surcharged in Red

Vale 2 centavos de córdoba

1923, Jan.

418 A24 1c on 5c gray blk 1.25 20
419 A25 2c on 10c org yel 1.25 20
a. Inverted surcharge

Nos. 401 and 402 Overprinted in Red

Sello Postal

1923

420 A26 ½c lt bl & blk 7.50 7.50
421 A27 1c grn & blk 2.50 85
a. Double overprint 7.50

Francisco Hernández de Córdoba — A33

1924 **Engr.**

422 A33 1c dp grn 1.50 30
423 A33 2c car rose 1.50 30
424 A33 5c dp bl 1.00 30
425 A33 10c bis brn 1.00 60

400th anniversary of the founding of León and Granada.

For overprint and surcharges see Nos. 499, 536, O295.

Stamps of 1914-22 Overprinted

Resello 1927

Black, Red or Blue Overprint

1927, May 3

427 A24 ½c grn (Bk) 25 20
428 A24 1c vio (R) 20 15
a. Double overprint 3.00
428B A24 1c vio (Bk) 85.00 55.00
429 A25 2c car rose (Bk) 20 15
a. Inverted overprint 5.00
b. Double overprint 5.00
430 A24 3c ol gray (Bk) 1.25 1.25
a. Inverted overprint 5.00
b. Double overprint 6.00
c. Double ovpt., one inverted 9.00 7.00
430D A24 3c ol gray (Bl) 8.00 3.25
431 A25 4c ver (Bk) 16.00 13.00
a. Inverted overprint 30.00
432 A24 5c gray blk (R) 1.25 30
a. Inverted overprint 7.50
432B A24 5c gray blk (Bk) 75 25
c. Double ovpt., one inverted 8.00
d. Double overprint 8.00
433 A25 6c red brn (Bk) 13.00 11.00
a. Inverted overprint 17.50
b. Double overprint
434 A25 10c yel (Bl) 65 40
a. Double overprint 12.50
b. Double ovpt., one inverted 10.00
435 A24 15c brn (Bk) 6.00 2.50
436 A25 20c bis brn (Bk) 6.00 2.50
a. Double overprint 17.50
437 A24 25c org (Bk) 27.50 5.00
438 A25 50c pale bl (Bk) 7.50 3.00
439 A25 1cor blk brn (Bk) 15.00 9.00

Most stamps of this group exist with tall "1" in "1927." Counterfeits exist of normal stamps and errors of Nos. 427-478.

Violet Overprint

1927, May 19

440 A24 ½c green 15 15
a. Inverted overprint 2.00 2.00
b. Double overprint 2.00 2.00
441 A24 1c violet 20 15
a. Double overprint 2.00 2.00
442 A25 2c car rose 15 15
a. Double overprint 2.00 2.00
b. "1927" double 5.00
d. Double ovpt., one inverted 2.00 2.00
443 A24 3c ol gray 25 15
a. Inverted overprint 6.00
b. Overprinted "1927" only 12.00
c. Double ovpt., one inverted 9.00
444 A25 4c vermilion 37.50 27.50
a. Inverted overprint 75.00
445 A24 5c gray blk 1.00 25
a. Double overprint, one inverted 6.00
446 A25 6c red brn 37.50 27.50
a. Inverted overprint 75.00
447 A25 10c yellow 35 20
a. Double overprint 2.00 2.00
448 A24 15c brown 75 30
a. Double overprint 5.00
b. Double overprint, one inverted 8.00
449 A25 20c bis brn 35 20
a. Double overprint
450 A24 25c orange 40 20
451 A25 50c pale bl 40 20
a. Double ovpt., one inverted 4.00 4.00
452 A25 1cor blk brn 75 20
a. Double overprint 3.00
b. "1927" double 5.00
c. Double ovpt., one inverted 6.00
Nos. 440-452 (13) 79.75 57.15

Stamps of 1914-22 Overprinted in Violet

Resello 1928

1928, Jan. 3

453 A24 ½c green 25 20
a. Double overprint 3.00
b. Double overprint, one inverted 4.00
454 A24 1c violet 15 15
a. Inverted overprint 2.00
b. Double overprint 2.00
c. Double overprint, one inverted 2.00
d. "928" for "1928" 2.50
455 A25 2c car rose 20 15
a. Inverted overprint 2.00
b. Double overprint 2.00
c. "1928" omitted 5.00
d. "928" for "1928" 2.50
e. As "d," inverted
f. "19" for "1928"
456 A24 3c ol gray 40 15
457 A25 4c vermilion 20 15
458 A24 5c gray blk 20 15
a. Double overprint 5.00
b. Double overprint, one inverted 5.00
459 A25 6c red brn 20 15
460 A25 10c yellow 25 15
a. Double overprint 2.50
c. Inverted overprint
461 A24 15c brown 35 25
462 A25 20c bis brn 50 25
a. Double overprint
463 A24 25c orange 75 25
a. Double overprint, one inverted 4.00
464 A25 50c pale bl 1.25 15
465 A25 1cor blk brn 1.25 35
Nos. 453-465 (13) 5.95 2.50

Stamps of 1914-22 Overprinted in Violet

Correos 1928

1928, June 11
466 A24 ½c green 20 15
467 A24 1c violet 15 15
a. "928" omitted
469 A24 3c ol gray 75 25
a. Double overprint 6.00
470 A25 4c vermilion 35 15
471 A24 5c gray blk 25 20
a. Double overprint 4.00
472 A25 6c red brn 40 20
a. Double overprint 5.00
473 A25 10c yellow 50 20
474 A24 15c brown 1.75 20
a. Double overprint
475 A25 20c bis brn 2.00 20
476 A24 25c orange 2.00 25
a. Double overprint, one inverted 6.00
477 A25 50c pale bl 2.00 25
478 A25 1cor blk brn 5.00 2.50
a. Double overprint 10.00
Nos. 466-478 (12) 15.35 4.70

No. 410 with above overprint in black was not regularly issued.

No. 470 with Additional Surcharge in Violet — Vale 2 Cts.

1928
479 A25 2c on 4c ver 1.25 35
a. Double surcharge 9.00

A34

Inscribed: "Timbre Telegrafico" Red Surcharge

1928
480 A34 1c on 5c bl & blk 30 20
a. Double surcharge 5.00
b. Double surcharge, one inverted
481 A34 2c on 5c bl & blk 30 20
a. Double surcharge 5.00
482 A34 3c on 5c bl & blk 30 20

Stamps similar to Nos. 481-482, but with surcharge in black and with basic stamp inscribed "Timbre Fiscal," are of private origin.

See designs A36, A37, A44, PT1, PT4, PT6, PT7.

Types of 1914 Issue Various Frames

1928
483 A24 ½c org red 40 15
484 A24 1c orange 40 15
485 A25 2c green 40 15
486 A24 3c dp vio 40 25
487 A25 4c brown 40 25
488 A24 5c yellow 40 20
489 A25 6c lt bl 40 25
490 A25 10c dk bl 90 20
491 A24 15c car rose 1.40 50
492 A25 20c dk grn 1.40 50
493 A24 25c blk brn 27.50 6.00
494 A25 50c bis brn 3.25 1.00
495 A25 1cor dl vio 6.25 3.00
Nos. 483-495 (13) 43.50 12.60

No. 425 Overprinted in Violet — Correos 1928

1929
499 A33 10c bis brn 75 60

No. 408 Overprinted in Red

Correos 1929

1929
500 A24 ½c grn (R) 25 20
a. Inverted overprint 2.50
b. Double overprint 2.50
c. Double overprint, one inverted 3.50

A36

A37

Ovptd. Horiz. in Black "R. de T." Surcharged Vert. in Red

1929
504 A36 1c on 5c bl & blk (R) 25 20
a. Inverted surcharge 3.00
b. Surcharged "0.10" for "0.01" 3.00
c. "0.0" instead of "0.01" 5.00
509 A36 2c on 5c bl & blk (R) 20 15
a. Double surcharge 2.50
b. Double surcharge, one inverted 3.50
c. Inverted surcharge 5.00

Overprinted Horizontally in Black "R. de C." Surcharged Vertically in Red

510 A36 2c on 5c bl & blk (R) 22.50 1.25
a. Dbl. surcharge, one inverted 25.00

Surcharged in Red

511 A37 1c on 10c dk grn & blk (R) 25 20
a. Double surcharge
512 A37 2c on 5c bl & blk (R) 25 15

The varieties tall "1" in "0.01" and "O$" for "C$" are found in this surcharge.

Nos. 500, 504, 509-512 and RA38 were surcharged in red and sold in large quantities to the public. Surcharges in various other colors were distributed only to a favored few and not regularly sold at the post offices.

Types of 1914 Issue Various Frames

1929-31
513 A24 1c ol grn 15 15
514 A24 3c lt bl 30 15
515 A25 4c dk bl ('31) 30 20
516 A24 5c ol brn 40 15
517 A25 6c bis brn ('31) 50 30
518 A25 10c lt brn ('31) 60 20
519 A24 15c org red ('31) 90 25
520 A25 20c org ('31) 1.20 35
521 A24 25c dk vio 25 15
522 A25 50c grn ('31) 50 20
523 A25 1cor yel ('31) 4.50 1.25
Nos. 513-523 (11) 9.60 3.35

Nos. 513-523 exist with signature controls. See note before No. 600. Same values.

New Post Office at Managua — A38

1930, Sept. 15 **Engr.**
525 A38 ½c ol gray 1.20 1.20
526 A38 1c carmine 1.20 1.20
527 A38 2c red org 90 90
528 A38 3c orange 1.75 1.75
529 A38 4c yellow 1.75 1.75
530 A38 5c ol grn 2.25 2.25
531 A38 6c bl grn 2.25 2.25
532 A38 10c black 2.75 2.75
533 A38 25c dp bl 5.50 5.50
534 A38 50c ultra 9.00 9.00
535 A38 1cor dp vio 25.00 25.00
Nos. 525-535 (11) 53.55 53.55

Opening of the new general post office at Managua. The stamps were on sale on day of issuance and for an emergency in April, 1931.

No. 499 Surcharged in Black and Red — C$ 0.02 1931

1931, May 29
536 A33 2c on 10c bis brn 50 1.60
a. Red surcharge omitted 2.50
b. Red surcharge double 5.00
c. Red surcharge inverted 3.50
d. Red surcharge double, one invtd.

Surcharge exists in brown.

Types of 1914-31 Issue Overprinted — 1931

1931, June 11
540 A24 ½c green 35 15
a. Double overprint 80
b. Double ovpt., one inverted 1.40
c. Inverted overprint 80
541 A24 1c ol grn 35 15
a. Double overprint 80
b. Double ovpt., one inverted 1.40
c. Inverted overprint
542 A25 2c car rose 35 15
a. Double overprint 80
b. Double ovpt., both inverted 2.50
c. Inverted overprint 1.40
543 A24 3c lt bl 35 15
a. Double overprint 80
b. Double ovpt., one inverted 1.40
c. Inverted overprint 1.40
544 A24 5c yellow 3.50 2.25
545 A24 5c ol brn 1.00 16
a. Double overprint 1.40
b. Inverted overprint 1.40
546 A24 15c org red 1.20 40
a. Double overprint 3.50
547 A24 25c blk brn 10.00 6.50
a. Double overprint 11.00 7.00
b. Inverted overprint 11.00 7.00
548 A24 25c dk vio 4.00 2.50
a. Double overprint 6.50
Nos. 540-548 (9) 21.10 12.41

Counterfeits exist of the scarcer values. The 4c brown and 6c light blue with this overprint are bogus.

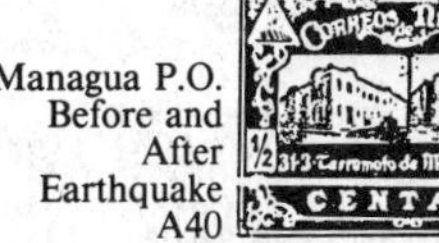
Managua P.O. Before and After Earthquake A40

1932, Jan. 1 **Litho.** ***Perf. 11½***
Soft porous paper, Without gum
556 A40 ½c emerald 1.50
557 A40 1c yel brn 1.90
558 A40 2c dp car 1.50
559 A40 3c ultra 1.50
560 A40 4c dp ultra 1.50
561 A40 5c yel brn 1.60
562 A40 6c gray brn 1.60
563 A40 10c yel brn 2.50
564 A40 15c dl rose 3.75
565 A40 20c orange 3.50
566 A40 25c dk vio 2.50
567 A40 50c emerald 2.50
568 A40 1cor yellow 6.25
Nos. 556-568 (13) 32.10

Issued in commemoration of the earthquake at Managua, Mar. 31, 1931. The stamps were on sale on Jan. 1, 1932, only. The money received from this sale was for the reconstruction of the Post Office building and for the improvement of the postal service. Many shades exist.

Sheets of 10.

Reprints are on thin hard paper and do not have the faint horiz. ribbing that is on the front or back of the originals. Fake cancels abound. Value 75 cents each.

See Nos. C20-C24. For overprints and surcharges see Nos. C32-C43, C47-C48.

Rivas Railroad Issue

"Fill" at El Nacascolo — A41

Designs: 1c, Wharf at San Jorge. 5c, Rivas Station. 10c, San Juan del Sur. 15c, Train at Rivas Station.

1932, Dec. 17 **Litho.** ***Perf. 12***
Soft porous paper
570 A41 1c yellow 16.50
a. 1c ocher 18.00
571 A41 2c carmine 16.50
572 A41 5c blk brn 16.50
573 A41 10c chocolate 16.50
574 A41 15c yellow 16.50
a. 15c dp org 18.00
Nos. 570-574 (5) 82.50

Inauguration of the railroad from San Jorge to San Juan del Sur. On sale only on Dec. 17, 1932.

Sheets of four, without gum. See Nos. C67-C71.

Reprints exist on thin hard paper and do not have the faint horiz. ribbing that is on the front or back of the originals. Value, $1 each.

Leon-Sauce Railroad Issue

Bridge No. 2 at Santa Lucia — A42

Designs: 1c, Environs of El Sauce. 5c, Santa Lucia. 10c, Works at Km. 64. 15c, Rock cut at Santa Lucia.

1932, Dec. 30 ***Perf. 12***
Soft porous paper
575 A42 1c orange 16.50
576 A42 2c carmine 16.50
577 A42 5c blk brn 16.50
578 A42 10c brown 16.50
579 A42 15c orange 16.50
Nos. 575-579 (5) 82.50

Inauguration of the railroad from Leon to El Sauce. On sale only on Dec. 30, 1932.

Sheets of 4, without gum. See Nos. C72-C76.

Reprints exist on thin hard paper and do not have the faint horiz. ribbing that is on the front or back of the originals. Value $1 each.

Nos. 514-515, 543 Surcharged in Red — Vale un centavo

1932, Dec. 10
580 A24 1c on 3c lt bl (514) 35 15
a. Double surcharge 3.50
581 A24 1c on 3c lt bl (543) 4.00 3.50
582 A25 2c on 4c dk bl (515) 25 15
a. Double surcharge 2.50

Nos. 514, 516, 545 and 518 Surcharged in Black or Red — Resello 1933 Vale Un Centavo

1933
583 A24 1c on 3c lt bl (Bk) (514) 16 15
a. "Censavo" 4.00 2.25
b. Double surcharge, one inverted 4.00
584 A24 1c on 5c ol brn (R) (516) 16 15
a. Inverted surcharge
b. Double surcharge
585 A24 1c on 5c ol brn (R) (545) 6.50 5.00
a. Red surcharge double 12.00
586 A25 2c on 10c lt brn (Bk) (518) 16 15
a. Double surcharge 4.00 2.50
b. Inverted surcharge 3.50 3.50
c. Double surcharge, one inverted 4.00 2.50

On No. 586 "Vale Dos" measures 13mm and 14mm.

No. 583 with green surcharge and No. 586 with red surcharge are bogus.

Flag of the Race Issue

Flag with Three Crosses for Three Ships of Columbus — A43

1933, Aug. 3 **Litho.** ***Rouletted 9***
Without gum
587 A43 ½c emerald 1.75 1.75
588 A43 1c green 1.50 1.50
589 A43 2c red 1.50 1.50
590 A43 3c dp rose 1.50 1.50
591 A43 4c orange 1.50 1.50
592 A43 5c yellow 1.75 1.75
593 A43 10c dp brn 1.75 1.75
594 A43 15c dk brn 1.75 1.75
595 A43 20c vio bl 1.75 1.75
596 A43 25c dl bl 1.75 1.75
597 A43 30c violet 4.50 4.50

598 A43 50c red vio 4.50 4.50
599 A43 1cor ol brn 4.50 4.50
Nos. 587-599 (13) 30.00 30.00

Commemorating the raising of the symbolical "Flag of the Race"; also the 441st anniversary of the sailing of Columbus for the New World, Aug. 3, 1492. Printed in sheets of 10.

See Nos. C77-C87, O320-O331.

In October, 1933, various postage, airmail and official stamps of current issues were overprinted with facsimile signatures of the Minister of Public Works and the Postmaster-General. These overprints are control marks.

Nos. 410 and 513 Overprinted in Black

Resello
1935

1935 *Perf. 12*
600 A24 1c ol grn 15 15
a. Inverted overprint 1.40 1.60
b. Double overprint 1.40 1.60
c. Double overprint, one inverted 1.60 1.60
601 A25 2c car rose 15 15
a. Inverted overprint 1.60
b. Double overprint 1.60
c. Double overprint, one inverted 1.60
d. Double overprint, both inverted 2.50 2.25
Set value 24 15

No. 517 Surcharged in Red as in 1932

1936, June
602 A25 ½c on 6c bis brn 35 15
a. "Ccentavo" 80 80
b. Double surcharge 3.50 3.50

Regular Issues of 1929-35 Overprinted in Blue

1935, Dec.
603 A25 ½c on 6c bis brn 65 15
604 A24 1c ol grn (#600) 80 15
605 A25 2c car rose (#601) 80 15
a. Black overprint inverted 6.00
606 A24 3c lt bl 80 22
607 A24 5c ol brn 1.00 25
608 A25 10c lt brn 1.60 80
Nos. 603-608 (6) 5.65 1.72

Nos. 606-608 have signature control overprint. See note before No. 600.

Same Overprint in Red

1936, Jan.
609 A24 ½c dk grn 16 15
610 A25 ½c on 6c bis brn (602) 15 15
a. Double surch., one inverted 6.00 6.00
611 A24 1c ol grn (513) 22 15
612 A24 1c ol grn (600) 25 15
613 A25 2c car rose (410) 50 15
614 A25 2c car rose (601) 25 15
a. Black overprint inverted 2.50 2.50
b. Black ovpt. double, one invtd. 3.50 3.50
615 A24 3c lt bl 25 15
616 A25 4c dk bl 25 15
617 A24 5c ol brn 22 15
618 A25 6c bis brn 25 15
619 A25 10c lt brn 50 16
620 A24 15c org red 15 15
621 A25 20c orange 80 22
622 A24 25c dk vio 25 15
623 A25 50c green 35 20
624 A25 1cor yellow 40 25
Nos. 609-624 (16) 4.95
Set value 1.95

Red or blue "Resello 1935" overprint may be found inverted or double. Red and blue overprints on same stamp are bogus.

Nos. 615-624 have signature control overprint. See note before No. 600.

Regular Issues of 1922-29 Overprinted in Carmine

1936, May
625 A24 ½c green 15 15
626 A24 1c ol grn 16 15
627 A25 2c car rose 50 15
628 A24 3c lt bl 16 15
Set value 35

No. 628 has signature control overprint. See note before No. 600.

Nos. 514, 516 Surcharged in Black

Resello 1936
Vale
Un Centavo

1936, June
629 A24 1c on 3c lt bl 15 15
a. "1396" for "1936" 1.00 1.00
b. "Un" omitted 1.40 1.40
c. Inverted surcharge 1.60 1.60
d. Double surcharge 1.60 1.60
630 A24 2c on 5c ol brn 15 15
a. "1396" for "1936" 1.40 1.40
b. Double surcharge 3.50 3.50
Set value 20

Regular Issues of 1929-31 Surcharged in Black or Red

1936
Vale
Un Centavo

1936
631 A24 ½c on 15c org red (R) 16 15
a. Double surcharge 4.00
632 A25 1c on 4c dk bl (Bk) 22 15
633 A24 1c on 5c ol brn (Bk) 22 16
634 A25 1c on 6c bis brn (Bk) 40 16
a. "1939" instead of "1936" 2.50 1.60
635 A24 1c on 15c org red (Bk) 22 16
a. "1939" instead of "1936" 2.50 1.60
636 A25 1c on 20c org (Bk) 16 15
a. "1939" intead of "1936" 2.50 1.60
b. Double surcharge 4.00
637 A25 1c on 20c org (R) 16 15
638 A25 2c on 10c lt brn (Bk) 25 16
639 A24 2c on 15c org red (Bk) 1.00 80
640 A25 2c on 20c org (Bk) 50 25
641 A24 2c on 25c dk vio (R) 35 16
642 A24 2c on 25c dk vio (Bk) 35 16
a. "1939" instead of "1936" 2.50 1.60
643 A25 2c on 50c grn (Bk) 35 22
a. "1939" instead of "1936" 2.50 1.60
644 A25 2c on 1 cor yel (Bk) 35 22
a. "1939" instead of "1936" 2.50 1.60
645 A25 3c on 4c dk bl (Bk) 65 50
a. "1939" instead of "1936" 2.50 1.60
b. "s" of "Centavos" omitted and "r" of "Tres" inverted 2.50
Nos. 631-645 (15) 5.34 3.55

Nos. 634, 639, 643-644 exist with and without signature controls. Nos. 635-636, 642, 645 do not have signature controls. Others have signature controls. See note before No. 600. Same values for those that come both ways.

Regular Issues of 1929-31 Overprinted in Black

Resello
1936

1936, Aug.
646 A24 3c lt bl 35 20
647 A24 5c ol brn 25 15
648 A25 10c lt brn 50 35

No. 648 bears script control mark.

A44

Surcharged in Red

1936, Oct. 19
649 A44 1c on 5c grn & blk 20 15
650 A44 2c on 5c grn & blk 20 15
Set value 15

Types of 1914

1937, Jan. 1 Engr.
652 A24 ½c black 15 15
653 A24 1c car rose 15 15
654 A25 2c dp bl 15 15
655 A24 3c chocolate 15 15
656 A25 4c yellow 16 15
657 A24 5c org red 15 15
658 A25 6c dl vio 16 15
659 A25 10c ol grn 16 15
660 A24 15c green 15 15
661 A25 20c red brn 25 15
663 A25 50c brown 35 15
664 A25 1cor ultra 60 22
Nos. 652-664 (12) 2.58
Set value 1.25

See note after No. 360.

Mail Carrier — A45

Designs: 1c, Mule carrying mail. 2c, Mail coach. 3c, Sailboat. 5c, Steamship. 7½c, Train.

1937, Dec. Litho. *Perf. 11*
665 A45 ½c green 15 15
666 A45 1c magenta 15 15
667 A45 2c brown 15 15
668 A45 3c purple 15 15
669 A45 5c blue 15 15
670 A45 7½c red org 55 35
Nos. 665-670 (6) 1.30
Set value 75

75th anniversary of the postal service in Nicaragua.

Nos. 665-670 were also issued in sheets of 4, value, set of sheets, $7.

The miniature sheets are ungummed, and also exist imperf. and part-perf.

Nos. 662, 663 and 664 Surcharged in Red

Vale Tres Centavos
1938

1938 *Perf. 12*
671 A24 3c on 25c org 15 15
672 A25 5c on 50c brn 24 15
a. "e" of "Vale" omitted 1.60 1.00
673 A25 6c on 1cor ultra 15 15
Set value 48 25

No. 672 has a script signature control and the surcharge is in three lines.

Dario Park A46

1939, Jan. Engr. *Perf. 12½*
674 A46 1½c yel grn 15 15
675 A46 2c dp rose 15 15
676 A46 3c brt bl 15 15
677 A46 6c brn org 15 15
678 A46 7½c dp grn 15 15
679 A46 10c blk brn 20 15
680 A46 15c orange 20 15
681 A46 25c lt vio 20 15
682 A46 50c brt yel grn 16 15
683 A46 1cor yellow 65 40
Nos. 674-683 (10) 2.16
Set value 1.10

Nos. 660 and 661 Surcharged in Red

Vale un Centavo
1939

1939 *Perf. 12*
684 A24 1c on 15c grn 15 15
a. Inverted surcharge 2.00 2.00
685 A25 1c on 20c red brn 15 15
Set value 17 15

No. C236 Surcharged in Carmine

Servicio ordinario
Vale Diez Centavos
de Córdoba

1941 Unwmk. *Perf. 12*
686 AP14 10c on 1c brt grn 15 15
a. Double surcharge 10.00 2.50
b. Inverted surcharge 10.00 2.50

Ruben Dario A47

1941, Dec. Engr. *Perf. 12½*
687 A47 10c red 35 15
Nos. 687,C257-C260 (5) 1.95 1.05

25th anniversary of the death of Ruben Dario, poet and writer.

No. C236 Surcharged in Carmine

Servicio Ordinario
Vale Diez Centavos

1943 *Perf. 12*
688 AP14 10c on 1c brt grn 4.00 15
a. Inverted surcharge 10.00
b. Double surcharge 10.00

Catalogue values for unused stamps in this section, from this point to the end of the section, are for Never Hinged items.

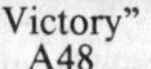
"Victory" A48

Columbus and Lighthouse A49

1943, Dec. 8 Engr.
689 A48 10c vio & cerise 15 15
690 A48 30c org brn & cerise 15 15
Set value 21 15

2nd anniv. of Nicaragua's declaration of war against the Axis. See Nos. C261-C262.

1945, Sept. 1 Unwmk. *Perf. 12½*
691 A49 4c dk grn & blk 20 20
692 A49 6c org & blk 25 25
693 A49 8c dp rose & blk 35 35
694 A49 10c bl & blk 40 40
Nos. 691-694,C266-C271 (10) 6.10 5.35

Issued in honor of the discovery of America by Columbus and the Columbus Lighthouse near Ciudad Trujillo, Dominican Republic.

Franklin D. Roosevelt, Philatelist A50

Roosevelt Signing Declaration of War Against Japan — A51

Designs: 8c, F. D. Roosevelt and Winston Churchill. 16c, Gen. Henri Giraud, Roosevelt, Gen. Charles de Gaulle and Churchill. 32c, Stalin, Roosevelt and Churchill. 50c, Sculptured head of Roosevelt.

Engraved, Center Photogravure
1946, June 15 Unwmk. *Perf. 12½*
Frame in Black

695 A50 4c sl grn 16 16
696 A50 8c violet 28 28
697 A51 10c ultra 32 32
698 A50 16c rose red 40 40
699 A50 32c org brn 28 28
700 A51 50c gray 28 28
Nos. 695-700 (6) 1.72 1.72

Issued to honor U.S. Pres. Franklin D. Roosevelt (1882-1945). See Nos. C272-C276.

Metropolitan Cathedral, Managua — A56

Designs: 5c, Sanitation Building. 6c, Municipal Building. 10c, Projected Provincial Seminary. 75c, Communications Building.

1947, Jan. 10
Frame in Black

701 A56 4c carmine 15 15
702 A56 5c blue 16 15
703 A56 6c green 20 16
704 A56 10c olive 20 16
705 A56 75c gldn brn 28 28
Nos. 701-705 (5) 99 90

Issued to commemorate the centenary of the founding of the city of Managua. See Nos. C277-C282.

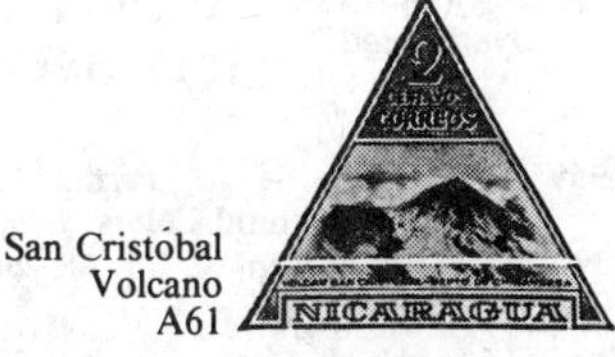

San Cristobal Volcano A61

Designs: 3c, Tomb of Rubén Dario. 4c, Grandstand. 5c, Soldiers' monument. 6c, Sugar cane. 8c, Tropical fruit. 10c, Cotton industry. 20c, Horse race. 30c, Nicaraguan coffee. 50c, Steer. 1cor, Agriculture.

Engraved, Center Photogravure
1947, Aug. 29
Frame in Black

706 A61 2c orange 16 15
707 A61 3c violet 15 15
708 A61 4c gray 22 15
709 A61 5c rose car 55 22
710 A61 6c green 32 15
711 A61 8c org brn 38 15
712 A61 10c red 55 22
713 A61 20c brt ultra 1.90 48
714 A61 30c rose lilac 1.50 48
715 A61 50c dp claret 3.25 95
716 A61 1cor brn org 1.10 48
Nos. 706-716 (11) 10.08 3.58

The frames differ for each denomination.
For surcharge see No. 769.

Softball A62

Boy Scout, Badge and Flag — A63

Designs: 3c, Pole vault. 4c, Diving. 5c, Bicycling. 10c, Proposed stadium. 15c, Baseball. 25c, Boxing. 35c, Basketball. 40c, Regatta. 60c, Table tennis. 1 cor, Soccer. 2 cor, Tennis.

1949, July 15 Photo. *Perf. 12*

717 A62 1c henna brn 15 15
718 A63 2c ultra 75 20
719 A63 3c bl grn 30 15
720 A62 4c dp claret 20 15
721 A63 5c orange 50 15
722 A62 10c emerald 50 15
723 A63 15c cerise 75 18
724 A63 25c brt bl 75 20
725 A63 35c ol grn 1.25 25
726 A62 40c violet 1.75 30
727 A62 60c ol gray 2.00 40
728 A62 1cor scarlet 2.50 1.25
729 A62 2cor red vio 4.50 2.50
Nos. 717-729 (13) 15.90 6.03

Issued to publicize the tenth World Series of Amateur Baseball, 1948.

Each denomination was also issued in a souvenir sheet containing four stamps and marginal inscriptions. Value, set of 13 sheets, $100.

See Nos. C296-C308.

Rowland Hill — A64

Designs: 25c, Heinrich von Stephan. 75c, UPU Monument. 80c, Congress medal, obverse. 4cor, as 80c, reverse.

1950, Nov. 23 Engr. *Perf. 13*
Frame in Black

730 A64 20c car lake 15 15
731 A64 25c yel grn 15 15
732 A64 75c ultra 48 18
733 A64 80c green 22 22
734 A64 4cor blue 90 80
Nos. 730-734 (5) 1.90 1.50

75th anniv. (in 1949) of the UPU.

Each denomination was also issued in a souvenir sheet containing four stamps and marginal inscriptions. Size: 115x123mm. Value, set of 5 sheets, $30.

See Nos. C309-C315, CO45-CO50. For surcharge see No. 771.

Queen Isabella I — A65

Ships of Columbus — A66

Designs: 98c, Santa Maria. 1.20cor, Map. 1.76cor, Portrait facing left.

1952, June 25 *Perf. 11½*

735 A65 10c lil rose 15 15
736 A66 96c dp ultra 75 75
737 A65 98c carmine 75 75
738 A65 1.20cor brown 90 90
739 A65 1.76cor red vio 1.25 1.25
a. Souv. sheet of 5, #735-739 3.75 3.75
Nos. 735-739 (5) 3.80 3.80

500th anniversary of the birth of Queen Isabella I of Spain.

See Nos. C316-C320.

ODECA Flag — A67

Designs: 5c, Map of Central America. 6c, Arms of ODECA. 15c, Presidents of Five Central American Republics. 50c, ODECA Charter and Flags.

1953, Apr. 15 *Perf. 13½x14*

740 A67 4c dk bl 15 15
741 A67 5c emerald 15 15
742 A67 6c lt brn 15 15
743 A67 15c lt ol grn 15 15
744 A67 50c blk brn 15 15
Set value 55 35

Founding of the Organization of the Central American States (ODECA).

See Nos. C321-C325. For surcharge see No. 767.

Pres. Carlos Solorzano — A68

Presidents: 6c, Diego Manuel Chamorro. 8c, Adolfo Diaz. 15c, Gen. Anastasio Somoza. 50c, Gen. Emiliano Chamorro.

Engr. (frames); Photo. (heads)
1953, June 25 *Perf. 12½*
Heads in Gray Black

745 A68 4c dk car rose 15 15
746 A68 6c dp ultra 15 15
747 A68 8c brown 15 15
748 A68 15c car rose 15 15
749 A68 50c bl grn 18 15
Set value 45 35

See Nos. C326-C338. For surcharges see Nos. 768, 853.

Sculptor and UN Emblem — A69

Capt. Dean L. Ray, USAF — A70

Designs: 4c, Arms of Nicaragua. 5c, Globe. 15c, Candle and Charter. 1cor, Flags of Nicaragua and UN.

Perf. 13½
1954, Apr. 30 Engr. Unwmk.

750 A69 3c olive 15 15
751 A69 4c ol grn 15 15
752 A69 5c emerald 18 15
753 A69 15c dp grn 90 18
754 A69 1cor bl grn 75 30
Nos. 750-754 (5) 2.13
Set value 70

Issued to honor the United Nations Organization. See Nos. C339-C345.

Engraved; Center Photogravure
1954, Nov. 5 *Perf. 13*

Designs: 2c, Sabre jet plane. 3c, Plane, type A-20. 4c, B-24 bomber. 5c, Plane, type AT-6. 15c, Gen. Anastasio Somoza. 1cor, Air Force emblem.

Frame in Black

755 A70 1c gray 15 15
756 A70 2c gray 15 15
757 A70 3c dk gray grn 15 15
758 A70 4c orange 15 15
759 A70 5c emerald 15 15
760 A70 15c aqua 15 15
761 A70 1cor purple 20 15
Set value 55 40

Issued to honor the National Air Force. See Nos. C346-C352.

Rotary Slogans and Wreath — A71

Map of the World and Rotary Emblem — A72

Designs: 20c, Handclasp, Rotary emblem and globe. 35c, Flags of Nicaragua and Rotary. 90c, Paul P. Harris.

1955, Aug. 30 Photo. *Perf. 11½*
Granite Paper.

762 A71 15c dp org 15 15
763 A71 20c dk olive grn 15 15
764 A71 35c red vio 15 15
765 A72 40c carmine 20 20
766 A71 90c blk & gray 35 35
a. Souv. sheet of 5, #762-766 4.25 4.25
Nos. 762-766 (5) 1.00 1.00

50th anniversary of Rotary International.

See Nos. C353-C362. For surcharges see Nos. 770, 772, 876.

Issues of 1947-55 Surcharged in Various Colors

Conmemoración
Exposición Nacional
Febrero 4-16, 1956
₡ 0.15

Perf. 13½x14, 12½, 11½, 13
Engraved, Photogravure
1956, Feb. 4 Unwmk.

767 A67 5c on 6c lt brn 15 15
768 A68 5c on 6c ultra & gray blk (Ult) 15 15
769 A61 5c on 8c blk & org brn 15 15
770 A71 15c on 35c red vio (G) 15 15
771 A64 15c on 80c blk & grn 15 15
772 A71 15c on 90c blk & gray (Bl) 15 15
Set value 62 48

Spacing of surcharge varies to fit shape of stamps.

Issued to commemorate the National Exhibition, Feb. 4-16, 1956. See Nos. C363-C366.

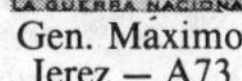

Gen. Maximo Jerez — A73

Battle of San Jacinto — A74

Designs: 10c, Gen. Fernando Chamorro. 25c, Burning of Granada. 50c, Gen. Jose Dolores Estrada.

Perf. 12½x12, 12, 12½
1956, Sept. 14 Engr.

773 A73 5c brown 15 15
774 A73 10c dk car rose 15 15
775 A74 15c bl gray 15 15
776 A74 25c brt red 25 18
777 A73 50c brt red vio 30 20
Set value 84 58

Issued to commemorate the centenary of the National War. See Nos. C367-C371.

Boy Scout — A75

Pres. Luis A. Somoza — A76

Designs: 15c, Cub Scout. 20c, Boy Scout. 25c, Lord Baden-Powell. 50c, Joseph A. Harrison.

Perf. 13½x14

1957, Apr. 9 Photo. Unwmk.

778 A75 10c vio & ol 15 15
779 A75 15c dp plum & gray blk 15 15
780 A75 20c ultra & brn 15 15
781 A75 25c dl red brn & dp bluish grn 15 15
782 A75 50c red & ol 20 16
a. Souv. sheet of 5, #778-782 2.50 2.50
Set value 65 45

Centenary of the birth of Lord Baden-Powell, founder of the Boy Scouts.

See Nos. C377-C386. For surcharge see No. C754.

1957, July 2 *Perf. 14x13½*

Portrait in Dark Brown

783 A76 10c brt red 15 15
784 A76 15c dp bl 15 15
785 A76 35c rose vio 22 15
786 A76 50c brown 30 18
787 A76 75c gray grn 65 55
Nos. 783-787 (5) 1.47
Set value 1.00

Issued to honor President Luis A. Somoza. See Nos. C387-C391.

Managua Cathedral A77

Bishop Pereira y Castellon — A78

Designs: 15c, Archbishop Lezcano y Ortega. 20c, Leon Cathedral. 50c, De la Merced Church, Granada. 1cor, Father Mariano Dubon.

Perf. 13½x14, 14x13½

1957, July 12

Centers in Olive Gray

788 A77 5c dl grn 15 15
789 A78 10c dk pur 15 15
790 A78 15c dk bl 15 15
791 A77 20c dk brn 15 15
792 A77 50c dk sl grn 16 15
793 A78 1cor dk vio 30 28
Set value 70 60

Issued in honor of the Catholic Church in Nicaragua. See Nos. C392-C397.

M. S. Honduras A79

Designs: 5c, Gen. Anastasio Somoza and freighter. 6c, M. S. Guatemala. 10c, M. S. Salvador. 15c, Ship between globes. 50c, Globes and ship.

1957, Oct. 15 Litho. *Perf. 14*

794 A79 4c grn, bl & blk 15 15
795 A79 5c multi 15 15
796 A79 6c red, bl & blk 15 15
797 A79 10c brn, bl grn & blk 15 15
798 A79 15c dk car, ultra & ol brn 24 15
799 A79 50c vio, bl & mar 40 26
Set value 1.00 65

Issued to honor Nicaragua's Merchant Marine. See Nos. C398-C403. For surcharge see No. C691.

Melvin Jones and Lions Emblem A80

Designs: 5c, Arms of Central American Republics. 20c, Dr. Teodoro A. Arias. 50c, Edward G. Barry. 75c, Motto and emblem. 1.50 cor, Map of Central America.

1958, May 8 Unwmk. *Perf. 14*

Emblem in Yellow, Red and Blue

800 A80 5c bl & multi 15 15
801 A80 10c bl & org 15 15
802 A80 20c bl & ol 15 15
803 A80 50c bl & lil 25 20
804 A80 75c bl & pink 35 25
805 A80 1.50cor bl, gray ol & sal 60 45
a. Souv. sheet of 6, #800-805 2.50 2.50
Nos. 800-805 (6) 1.65
Set value 1.10

17th convention of Lions Intl. of Central America, May, 1958.

See Nos. C410-C415. For surcharge see No. C686.

St. Jean Baptiste De La Salle — A81

UN Emblem and Globe — A82

Designs: 5c, Arms of La Salle. 10c, School, Managua (horiz.). 20c, Bro. Carlos. 50c, Bro. Antonio. 75c, Bro. Julio. 1cor, Bro. Argeo.

1958, July 13 Photo. *Perf. 14*

806 A81 5c car, bl & yel 15 15
807 A81 10c emer, blk & ultra 15 15
808 A81 15c red brn, bis & blk 15 15
809 A81 20c car, bis & blk 15 15
810 A81 50c org, bis & brn blk 16 15
811 A81 75c bl, lt grn & dk brn 24 20
812 A81 1cor vio, bis & grnsh blk 32 32
Set value 95 85

Issued to honor the Christian Brothers. See Nos. C416-C423. For surcharges see Nos. C539A, C755-C756.

1958, Dec. 15 Litho. *Perf. 11½*

Designs: 15c, UNESCO building. 25c, 45c, "UNESCO." 40c, UNESCO building and Eiffel tower.

813 A82 10c brt pink & bl 15 15
814 A82 15c bl & brt pink 15 15
815 A82 25c grn & brn 15 15
816 A82 40c red org & blk 15 15
817 A82 45c dk bl & rose lil 15 15
818 A82 50c brn & grn 15 15
a. Min. sheet of 6, #813-818 45 45
Set value 45 35

Opening of UNESCO Headquarters in Paris, Nov. 3. See Nos. C424-C429.

Pope John XXIII and Cardinal Spellman A83

Abraham Lincoln A84

Designs: 10c, Spellman coat of arms. 15c, Cardinal Spellman. 20c, Human rosary and Cardinal (horiz.). 25c, Cardinal with Ruben Dario order.

1959, Nov. 26 Unwmk. *Perf. 12½*

819 A83 5c grnsh bl & brn 15 15
820 A83 10c yel, bl & car 15 15
821 A83 15c dk grn, blk & dk car 15 15
822 A83 20c yel, dk bl & grn 15 15
823 A83 25c ultra, vio & mag 15 15
a. Min. sheet of 5, #819-823, perf. or imperf. 35 35
Set value 30 25

Cardinal Spellman's visit to Managua, Feb. 1958. See Nos. C430-C436. For surcharges see Nos. C638, C747, C752.

1960, Jan. Engr. *Perf. 13x13½*

Center in Black

824 A84 5c dp car 15 15
825 A84 10c green 15 15
826 A84 15c dp org 15 15
827 A84 1cor plum 20 15
828 A84 2cor ultra 35 30
a. Souvenir sheet of 5, #824-828, imperf. 90 90
Set value 70 60

150th anniversary of the birth of Abraham Lincoln. See Nos. C437-C442. For surcharges see Nos. C637, C680, C753.

Nos. 824-828 Overprinted in Red

Resello

1960, Sept. 19

Center in Black

829 A84 5c dp car 15 15
830 A84 10c green 15 15
831 A84 15c dp org 15 15
832 A84 1cor plum 22 20
833 A84 2cor ultra 50 42
Set value 85 75

Issued for the Red Cross to aid earthquake victims in Chile. For overprints and surcharges see Nos. C446-C451, C500, C539.

Gen. Tomas Martinez and Pres. Luis A. Somoza — A85

Arms of Nueva Segovia — A86

Designs: 5c, Official decrees. 10c, Two envelopes.

Perf. 13½

1961, Aug. 29 Unwmk. Litho.

834 A85 5c grnsh bl & lt brn 15 15
835 A85 10c grn & lt brn 15 15
836 A85 15c pink & brn 15 15
Set value 17 15

Issued to commemorate the centenary (in 1960) of the postal rates regulation.

1962, Nov. 22 *Perf. 12½x13*

Coats of Arms: 3c, Leon. 4c, Managua. 5c, Granada. 6c, Rivas.

Arms in Original Colors; Black Inscriptions

837 A86 2c pink 15 15
838 A86 3c lt bl 15 15
839 A86 4c pale lil 15 15
840 A86 5c yellow 15 15
841 A86 6c buff 15 15
Set value 25 25

See Nos. C510-C514. For surcharge see No. 854.

No. RA73 Overprinted in Red: "CORREOS"

1964 Photo. *Perf. 11½*

842 PT13 5c gray, red & org 15 15
a. Inverted overprint

Nos. RA66-RA75 Overprinted

1965 Photo. *Perf. 11½*

Orchids in Natural Colors

843 PT13 5c pale lil & grn 30
844 PT13 5c yel & grn 30
845 PT13 5c pink & grn 30
846 PT13 5c pale vio & grn 30
847 PT13 5c lt grnsh bl & red 30
848 PT13 5c buff & lil 30
849 PT13 5c yel grn & brn 30
850 PT13 5c gray & red 30
851 PT13 5c lt bl & dk bl 30
852 PT13 5c lt grn & brn 30
Nos. 843-852 (10) 3.00

Issued to commemorate the 7th Central American Scout Camporee at El Coyotete. This overprint was also applied to each stamp on souvenir sheet No. C386a.

Use of Nos. 843-852 for postage was authorized by official decree.

Nos. 746 and 841 Surcharged with New Value and "RESELLO"

1968, May Engr. *Perf. 12½*

853 A68 5c on 6c dp ultra & gray blk 50 50

Litho. *Perf. 12½x13*

854 A86 5c on 6c multi 50 50

Nos. RA66-RA67, RA69 and RA71 Overprinted

CORREO

1969 Photo. *Perf. 11½*

Orchids in Natural Colors

855 PT13 5c pale lil & grn 50 50
856 PT13 5c yel & grn 50 50
857 PT13 5c pale vio & grn 50 50
858 PT13 5c buff & lil 50 50

Nos. RA66-RA75 Overprinted

O. I. T.
1919 - 1969

1969 Photo. *Perf. 11½*

Orchids in Natural Colors

859 PT13 5c pale lil & grn 20 20
860 PT13 5c yel & grn 20 20
861 PT13 5c pink & grn 20 20
862 PT13 5c pale vio & grn 20 20
863 PT13 5c lt grnsh bl & red 20 20
864 PT13 5c buff & lil 20 20
865 PT13 5c yel grn & brn 20 20
866 PT13 5c gray & red 20 20
867 PT13 5c lt & dk bl 20 20
868 PT13 5c lt grn & brn 20 20
Nos. 859-868 (10) 2.00 2.00

Issued to commemorate the 50th anniversary of the International Labor Organization.

Pelé, Brazil — A87

Soccer Players: 10c, Ferenc Puskás, Hungary. 15c, Sir Stanley Matthews, England. 40c, Alfredo di Stefano, Argentina. 2cor, Giacinto Facchetti, Italy. 3cor, Lev Yashin, USSR. 5cor, Franz Beckenbauer, West Germany.

1970, May 11 Litho. *Perf. 13½*

869 A87 5c multi 15 15
870 A87 10c multi 15 15
871 A87 15c multi 15 15
872 A87 40c multi 25 18
873 A87 2cor multi 90 75
874 A87 3cor multi 1.25 90
875 A87 5cor multi 1.25 1.25
Nos. 869-875,C712-C716 (12) 7.40 6.23

Issued to honor the winners of the 1970 poll for the International Soccer Hall of

Fame. Names of players and their achievements printed in black on back of stamps.

For surcharges and overprint see Nos. 899-900, C786-C788.

No. 766 Surcharged with New Value and Overprinted "RESELLO" and Bar Through Old Denomination

1971, Mar. Photo. *Perf. 11*

876 A71 30c on 90c blk & gray

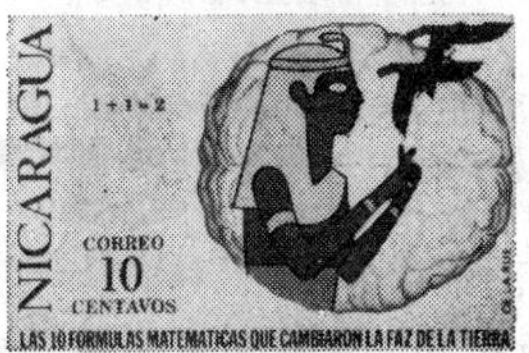

Egyptian Using Fingers to Count — A88

Symbolic Designs of Scientific Formulas: 15c, Newton's law (gravity). 20c, Einstein's theory (relativity). 1cor, Tsiolkovski's law (speed of rockets). 2cor, Maxwell's law (electromagnetism).

1971, May 15 Litho. *Perf. 13½*

877 A88 10c lt bl & multi 15 15
878 A88 15c lt bl & multi 15 15
879 A88 20c lt bl & multi 20 20
880 A88 1cor lt bl & multi 65 60
881 A88 2cor lt bl & multi 1.50 1.25
Nos. 877-881,C761-C765 (10) 4.83 3.96

Mathematical equations which changed the world. On the back of each stamp is a descriptive paragraph.

Symbols of Civilization, Peace Emblem with Globe — A89

1971, Sept. 6 Litho. *Perf. 14*

882 A89 10c blk & bl 15 15
883 A89 15c vio bl, bl & blk 15 15
884 A89 20c brn bl & blk 20 20
885 A89 40c emer, bl & blk 30 30
886 A89 50c mag, bl & blk 40 40
887 A89 80c org, bl & blk 60 60
888 A89 1cor ol, bl & blk 75 75
889 A89 2cor vio, bl & blk 1.50 1.50
Nos. 882-889 (8) 4.05 4.05

"Is there a formula for peace?" issue.

Moses with Tablets of the Law, by Rembrandt A90

The Ten Commandments (Paintings): 15c, Moses and the Burning Bush, by Botticelli (I). 20c, Jephthah's Daughter, by Degas, (II, horiz.). 30c, St. Vincent Ferrer Preaching in Verona, by Domenico Morone (III). 35c, The Nakedness of Noah, by Michelangelo (IV, horiz.). 40c, Cain and Abel, by Francesco Trevisani (V, horiz.). 50c, Potiphar's wife, by Rembrandt (VI). 60c, Isaac Blessing Jacob, by Gerbrand van den Eeckhout (VII, horiz.). 75c, Susanna and the Elders, by Rubens (VIII, horiz.).

1971, Nov. 1 *Perf. 11*

890 A90 10c ocher & multi 15 15
891 A90 15c ocher & multi 15 15
892 A90 20c ocher & multi 15 15
893 A90 30c ocher & multi 18 18
894 A90 35c ocher & multi 24 24
895 A90 40c ocher & multi 24 24
896 A90 50c ocher & multi 35 35
897 A90 60c ocher & multi 48 48
898 A90 75c ocher & multi 75 75
Nos. 890-898,C776-C777 (11) 5.09 3.94

Descriptive inscriptions printed in gray on back of stamps.

Nos. 873-874 Surcharged

¢0.40

OLIMPIADAS
MUNICH 1972

1972, Mar. 20 Litho. *Perf. 13½*

899 A87 40c on 2cor multi 15 15
900 A87 50c on 3cor multi 20 15
Nos. 899-900,C786-C788 (5) 1.75 1.60

20th Olympic Games, Munich, Aug. 26-Sept. 10.

Nos. RA66-RA69, RA71-RA74 Overprinted in Blue

CORREO

1972, July 29 Photo. *Perf. 11½*
Granite Paper

901 PT13 5c (#RA66) 25 25
902 PT13 5c (#RA67) 25 25
903 PT13 5c (#RA68) 25 25
904 PT13 5c (#RA69) 25 25
905 PT13 5c (#RA71) 25 25
906 PT13 5c (#RA72) 25 25
907 PT13 5c (#RA73) 25 25
908 PT13 5c (#RA74) 25 25
Nos. 901-908 (8) 2.00 2.00

Gown by Givenchy, Paris — A91

1973, July 26 Litho. *Perf. 13½*

909 A91 1cor shown 30 24
910 A91 2cor Hartnell, London 55 52
911 A91 5cor Balmain, Paris 1.40 1.20
Set value, #909-911, C839-C844 2.75 2.35

Gowns by famous designers, modeled by Nicaraguan women. Inscriptions on back printed on top of gum give description of gown in Spanish and English.

Nos. 909-911 in perf. 11, see No. C844a.

Christmas A92

Designs: 2c, 5c, Virginia O'Hanlon writing letter, father. 3c, 15c, letter. 4c, 20c, Virginia, father reading letter.

1973, Nov. 15 Litho. *Perf. 15*

912 A92 2c multicolored 15
913 A92 3c multicolored 15
914 A92 4c multicolored 15
915 A92 5c multicolored 15
916 A92 15c multicolored 15
917 A92 20c multicolored 15
Set value, #912-917, C846-C848 2.30

Sir Winston Churchill (1874-1965) A93

Designs: 2c, Churchill speaking. 3c, Military planning. 4c, Cigar, lamp. 5c, Churchill with Roosevert and Stalin. 10c, Churchill walking ashore from landing craft.

1974, Apr. 30 *Perf. 14½*

918 A93 2c multicolored 15
919 A93 3c multicolored 15
920 A93 4c multicolored 15
921 A93 5c multicolored 15
922 A93 10c multicolored 15
Set value, #918-922, C849-C850 3.25

World Cup Soccer Championships, Munich — A94

Scenes from previous World Cup Championships with flags and scores of finalists.

1974, May 8 *Perf. 14½*

923 A94 1c 1930 15
924 A94 2c 1934 15
925 A94 3c 1938 15
926 A94 4c 1950 15
927 A94 5c 1954 15
928 A94 10c 1958 15
929 A94 15c 1962 15
930 A94 20c 1966 15
931 A94 25c 1970 15
Set value, #923-931, C853 3.25

For overprint see No. C856.

Hollyhocks — A95

Wild Flowers and Cacti: 3c, Paguira insignis. 4c, Morning glory. 5c, Pereschia autumnalis. 10c, Cultivated morning glory. 15c, Hibiscus. 20c, Pagoda tree blossoms.

1974, June 11 Litho. *Perf. 14*

932 A95 2c grn & multi 15 15
933 A95 3c grn & multi 15 15
934 A95 4c grn & multi 15 15
935 A95 5c grn & multi 15 15
936 A95 10c grn & multi 15 15
937 A95 15c grn & multi 15 15
938 A95 20c grn & multi 15 15
Set value, #932-938, C854-C855 1.25 1.10

Nicaraguan Stamps — A96

1974, July 10 *Perf. 14½*

939 A96 2c No. 670 15
940 A96 3c No. 669 15
941 A96 4c No. C110, horiz. 15
942 A96 5c No. 667 15
943 A96 10c No. 666 15
944 A96 20c No. 665 15
Set value, #934-944, C855A-C855C 2.75

UPU, Cent.

Four-toed Anteater A97

Designs: 2c, Puma. 3c, Raccoon. 4c, Ocelot. 5c, Kinkajou. 10c, Coypu. 15c, Peccary. 20c, Tapir.

1974, Sept. 10 Litho. *Perf. 14½*

946 A97 1c multi 15 15
947 A97 2c multi 15 15
948 A97 3c multi 15 15
949 A97 4c multi 15 15
950 A97 5c multi 15 15
951 A97 10c multi 15 15
952 A97 15c multi 15 15
953 A97 20c multi 15 15
Set value, #946-953, C857-C858 2.10 1.85

Wild animals from San Diego and London Zoos.

Prophet Zacharias, by Michelangelo A98

Works of Michelangelo: 2c, The Last Judgment. 3c, The Creation of Adam (horiz.). 4c, Sistine Chapel. 5c, Moses. 10c, Mouscron Madonna. 15c, David. 20c, Doni Madonna.

1974, Dec. 15

954 A98 1c dp rose & multi 15 15
955 A98 2c yel & multi 15 15
956 A98 3c sal & multi 15 15
957 A98 4c bl & multi 15 15
958 A98 5c tan & multi 15 15
959 A98 10c multi 15 15
960 A98 15c multi 15 15
961 A98 20c bl & multi 15 15
Set value, #954-961, C859-C862 1.50 1.40

Christmas 1974 and 500th birth anniversary of Michelangelo Buonarroti (1475-1564), Italian painter, sculptor and architect.

Giovanni Martinelli, Othello A99

Opera Singers and Scores: 2c, Tito Gobbi, Simone Boccanegra. 3c, Lotte Lehmann, Der

Rosenkavalier. 4c, Lauritz Melchior, Parsifal. 5c, Nellie Melba, La Traviata. 15c, Jussi Bjoerling, La Boheme. 20c, Birgit Nilsson, Turandot.

1975, Jan. 22 *Perf. 14x13½*

962	A99	1c rose lil & multi	15	15
963	A99	2c brt bl & multi	15	15
964	A99	3c yel & multi	15	15
965	A99	4c dl bl & multi	15	15
966	A99	5c org & multi	15	15
967	A99	15c lake & multi	15	15
968	A99	20c gray & multi	15	15
		Set value, #962-968, C863-C870	3.00	1.60

Famous opera singers.

Jesus Condemned A100

The Spirit of 76, by Archibald M. Willard A101

Stations of the Cross: 2c, Jesus Carries the Cross. 3c, Jesus falls the first time. 4c, Jesus meets his mother. 5c, Simon of Cyrene carries the Cross. 15c, St. Veronica wipes Jesus' face. 20c, Jesus falls the second time. 25c, Jesus meets the women of Jerusalem. 35c, Jesus falls the third time. Designs from Leon Cathedral.

1975, Mar. 20 *Perf. 14½*

969	A100	1c ultra & multi	15	15
970	A100	2c ultra & multi	15	15
971	A100	3c ultra & multi	15	15
972	A100	4c ultra & multi	15	15
973	A100	5c ultra & multi	15	15
974	A100	15c ultra & multi	15	15
975	A100	20c ultra & multi	15	15
976	A100	25c ultra & multi	15	15
977	A100	35c ultra & multi	15	15
		Set value, #969-977, C871-C875	1.80	1.60

Easter 1975.

1975, Apr. 16 *Perf. 14*

Designs: 2c, Pitt Addressing Parliament, by K. A. Hickel. 3c, The Midnight Ride of Paul Revere (horiz.). 4c, Statue of George III Demolished, by W. Walcutt (horiz.). 5c, Boston Massacre. 10c, Colonial coin and seal (horiz.). 15c, Boston Tea Party (horiz.). 20c, Thomas Jefferson, by Rembrandt Peale. 25c, Benjamin Franklin, by Charles Willson Peale. 30c, Signing Declaration of Independence, by John Trumbull (horiz.). 35c, Surrender of Cornwallis, by Trumbull (horiz.).

978	A101	1c tan & multi	15	15
979	A101	2c tan & multi	15	15
980	A101	3c tan & multi	15	15
981	A101	4c tan & multi	15	15
982	A101	5c tan & multi	15	15
983	A101	10c tan & multi	15	15
984	A101	15c tan & multi	15	15
985	A101	20c tan & multi	15	15
986	A101	25c tan & multi	15	15
987	A101	30c tan & multi	16	15
988	A101	35c tan & multi	20	18
		Set value, #978-988, C876-C879	4.20	3.80

American Bicentennial.

Scouts Saluting Flag, Scout Emblems A102

Designs (Scout and Nordjamb Emblems and): 2c, Two-men canoe. 3c, Scouts of various races shaking hands. 4c, Scout cooking. 5c, Entrance to Camp Nicaragua. 20c, Group discussion.

1975, Aug. 15 *Perf. 14½*

989	A102	1c multi	15	15
990	A102	2c multi	15	15
991	A102	3c multi	15	15
992	A102	4c multi	15	15
993	A102	5c multi	15	15
994	A102	20c multi	15	15
		Set value, #989-994, C880-C883	1.90	1.70

Nordjamb 75, 14th World Boy Scout Jamboree, Lillehammer, Norway, July 29-Aug. 7.

Pres. Somoza, Map and Arms of Nicaragua — A103

1975, Sept. 10 *Perf. 14*

995	A103	20c multi	15	15
996	A103	40c org & multi	15	15
		Nos. 995-996,C884-C886 (5)	6.50	5.28

Reelection of Pres. Anastasio Somoza D.

King's College Choir, Cambridge — A104

Famous Choirs: 2c, Einsiedeln Abbey. 3c, Regensburg. 4c, Vienna Choir Boys. 5c, Sistine Chapel. 15c, Westminster Cathedral. 20c, Mormon Tabernacle.

1975, Nov. 15 *Perf. 14½*

997	A104	1c sil & multi	15	15
998	A104	2c sil & multi	15	15
999	A104	3c sil & multi	15	15
1000	A104	4c sil & multi	15	15
1001	A104	5c sil & multi	15	15
1002	A104	15c sil & multi	15	15
1003	A104	20c sil & multi	15	15
		Set value, #997-1003, C887-C890	1.90	1.70

Christmas 1975.

The Chess Players, by Ludovico Carracci A105

History of Chess: 2c, Arabs Playing Chess, by Delacroix. 3c, Cardinals Playing Chess, by Victor Marais-Milton. 4c, Albrecht V of Bavaria and Anne of Austria Playing Chess, by Hans Muelich (vert.). 5c, Chess Players, Persian manuscript, 14th century. 10c, Origin of Chess, Indian miniature, 17th century. 15c, Napoleon Playing Chess at Schönbrunn, by Antoni Uniechowski (vert.). 20c, The Chess Game, by J. E. Hummel.

1976, Jan. 8 *Perf. 14½*

1004	A105	1c brn & multi	15	15
1005	A105	2c lt vio & multi	15	15
1006	A105	3c ocher & multi	15	15
1007	A105	4c multi	15	15
1008	A105	5c multi	15	15
1009	A105	10c multi	15	15
1010	A105	15c bl & multi	15	15
1011	A105	20c ocher & multi	15	15
		Set value, #1004-1011, C891-C893	2.90	2.30

Olympic Rings, Danish Crew, — A107

Winners, Rowing and Sculling Events: 2c, East Germany, 1972. 3c, Italy, 1968. 4c, Great Britain, 1936. 5c, France, 1952. 35c, United States, 1920 (vert.).

1976, Sept. 7 **Litho.** *Perf. 14*

1022	A107	1c bl & multi	15	15
1023	A107	2c bl & multi	15	15
1024	A107	3c bl & multi	15	15
1025	A107	4c bl & multi	15	15
1026	A107	5c bl & multi	15	15
1027	A107	35c bl & multi	15	15
		Nos. 1022-1027,C902-C905 (10)	5.98	5.13

The Smoke Signal, by Frederic Remington — A108

Designs (American Bicentennial Emblem and): No. 1029, Space Signal Monitoring Center. No. 1030, Candlelight. No. 1031, Edison's laboratory and light bulb. No. 1032, Agriculture, 1776. No. 1033, Agriculture, 1976. No. 1034, Harvard College, 1726. No. 1035, Harvard University, 1976. No. 1036, Horse-drawn carriage. No. 1037, Boeing 747.

1976, May 25 **Litho.** *Perf. 13½*

1028	A108	1c gray & multi	15	15
1029	A108	1c gray & multi	15	15
1030	A108	2c gray & multi	15	15
1031	A108	2c gray & multi	15	15
1032	A108	3c gray & multi	15	15
1033	A108	3c gray & multi	15	15
1034	A108	4c gray & multi	15	15
1035	A108	4c gray & multi	15	15
1036	A108	5c gray & multi	15	15
1037	A108	5c gray & multi	15	15
		Set value, #1028-1037, C907-C912	3.30	2.35

American Bicentennial, 200 years of progress. Stamps of same denomination printed se-tenant.

Mauritius No. 2 — A109

Rare Stamps: 2c, Western Australia No. 3a. 3c, Mauritius No. 1. 4c, Jamaica No. 83a. 5c, United States No. C3a. 10c, Basel No. 3L1. 25c, Canada No. 387a.

1976, Dec. *Perf. 14*

1038	A109	1c multi	15	15
1039	A109	2c multi	15	15
1040	A109	3c multi	15	15
1041	A109	4c multi	15	15
1042	A109	5c multi	15	15
1043	A109	10c multi	15	15
1044	A109	25c multi	15	15
		Set value, #1038-1044, C913-C917	2.85	2.60

Back inscriptions printed on top of gum describe illustrated stamp.

Zeppelin in Flight A110

Designs: 1c, Zeppelin in hangar. 3c, Giffard's dirigible airship, 1852. 4c, Zeppelin on raising stilts coming out of hangar. 5c, Zeppelin ready for take-off.

1977, Oct. 31 **Litho.** *Perf. 14½*

1045	A110	1c multi	15	15
1046	A110	2c multi	15	15
1047	A110	3c multi	15	15
1048	A110	4c multi	15	15
1049	A110	5c multi	15	15
		Nos. 1045-1049,C921-C924 (9)	4.23	
		Set value		2.75

75th anniversary of Zeppelin.

Lindbergh, Map of Nicaragua A111

Designs: 2c, Spirit of St. Louis, map of Nicaragua. 3c, Lindbergh (vert.). 4c, Spirit of St. Louis and New York-Paris route. 5c, Lindbergh and Spirit of St. Louis. 20c, Lindbergh, New York-Paris route and plane.

1977, Nov. 30

1050	A111	1c multi	15	15
1051	A111	2c multi	15	15
1052	A111	3c multi	15	15
1053	A111	4c multi	15	15
1054	A111	5c multi	15	15
1055	A111	20c multi	15	15
		Nos. 1050-1055,C926-C929 (10)	3.61	
		Set value		2.40

Charles A. Lindbergh's solo transatlantic flight from New York to Paris, 50th anniversary.

Clara and Snowflakes — A112

Nutcracker Suite: 1c, Christmas party. 2c, Dancing dolls. 4c, Snowflake and prince. 5c, Snowflake dance. 15c, Sugarplum fairy and prince. 40c, Waltz of the flowers. 90c, Chinese tea dance. 1cor, Bonbonniere. 10cor, Arabian coffee dance.

1977, Dec. 12

1056	A112	1c multi	15	15
1057	A112	2c multi	15	15
1058	A112	3c multi	15	15
1059	A112	4c multi	15	15
1060	A112	5c multi	15	15
1061	A112	15c multi	15	15
1062	A112	40c multi	15	15
1063	A112	90c multi	20	20
1064	A112	1cor multi	28	20
1065	A112	10cor multi	2.25	2.00
		Set value	3.00	2.70

Christmas 1977. See No. C931.

Mr. and Mrs. Andrews, by Gainsborough — A113

Paintings: 2c, Giovanna Bacelli, by Gainsborough. 3c, Blue Boy by Gainsborough. 4c, Francis I, by Titian. 5c, Charles V in Battle of Muhlberg, by Titian. 25c, Sacred Love, by Titian.

1978, Jan. 11 **Litho.** *Perf. 14½*

1066	A113	1c multi	15	15
1067	A113	2c multi	15	15
1068	A113	3c multi	15	15
1069	A113	4c multi	15	15
1070	A113	5c multi	15	15
1071	A113	25c multi	15	15

Set value, #1066-1071, C932-C933 3.25 2.75

Thomas Gainsborough (1727-1788), 250th birth anniversary; Titian (1477-1576), 500th birth anniversary.

Gothic Portal, Lower Church, Assisi — A114

Designs: 2c, St. Francis preaching to the birds. 3c, St. Francis, painting. 4c, St. Francis and Franciscan saints, 15th century tapestry. 5c, Portiuncola, cell of St. Francis, now in church of St. Mary of the Angels, Assisi. 15c, Blessing of St. Francis for Brother Leo (parchment). 25c, Stained-glass window, Upper Church of St. Francis, Assisi.

1978, Feb. 23 Litho. *Perf. 14½*

1072 A114 1c red & multi 15 15
1073 A114 2c brt grn & multi 15 15
1074 A114 3c bl grn & multi 15 15
1075 A114 4c ultra & multi 15 15
1076 A114 5c rose & multi 15 15
1077 A114 15c yel & multi 15 15
1078 A114 25c ocher & multi 15 15
Set value, #1072-1078, C935-C936 2.35 2.15

St. Francis of Assisi (1182-1266), 750th anniversary of his canonization, and in honor of Our Lady of the Immaculate Conception, patron saint of Nicaragua.

Passenger and Freight Locomotives — A115

Locomotives: 2c, Lightweight freight. 3c, American. 4c, Heavy freight Baldwin. 5c, Light freight and passenger Baldwin. 15c, Presidential coach.

1978, Apr. 7 Litho. *Perf. 14½*

1079 A115 1c lil & multi 15 15
1080 A115 2c rose lil & multi 15 15
1081 A115 3c bl & multi 15 15
1082 A115 4c ol & multi 15 15
1083 A115 5c yel & multi 15 15
1084 A115 15c dp org & multi 15 15
Set value, #1079-1084, C938-C940 3.60 3.35

Centenary of Nicaraguan railroads.

Michael Strogoff, by Jules Verne — A116

Designs (Jules Verne Books): 2c, The Mysterious Island. 3c, Journey to the Center of the Earth (battle of the sea monsters). 4c, Five Weeks in a Balloon.

1978, Aug. Litho. *Perf. 14½*

1085 A116 1c multi 15 15
1086 A116 2c multi 15 15
1087 A116 3c multi 15 15
1088 A116 4c multi 15 15
Nos. 1085-1088,C942-C943 (6) 2.55
Set value 1.90

Jules Verne (1828-1905), science fiction writer.

Montgolfier Balloon — A117

Designs: 1c, Icarus (horiz.). 3c, Wright Brothers' Flyer A (horiz.). 4c, Orville Wright at control of Flyer, 1908.

1978, Sept. 29 Litho. *Perf. 14½*

1089 A117 1c multi 15 15
1090 A117 2c multi 15 15
1091 A117 3c multi 15 15
1092 A117 4c multi 15 15
Set value, #1089-1092, C945-C946 1.70 1.30

History of aviation and 75th anniversary of first powered flight.

Ernst Ocwirk and Alfredo Di Stefano — A118

St. Peter, by Goya — A119

Soccer Players: 25c, Ralf Edstroem and Oswaldo Piazza.

1978, Oct. 25 Litho. *Perf. 13½x14*

1093 A118 20c multicolored 15 15
1094 A118 25c multicolored 15 15
Set value 15 15

11th World Soccer Cup Championship, Argentina, June 1-25. See Nos. C948-C950.

1978, Dec. 12 Litho. *Perf. 13½x14*

Paintings: 15c, St. Gregory, by Goya.

1095 A119 10c multi 15 15
1096 A119 15c multi 15 15
Set value 15 15

Christmas 1978. See Nos. C951-C953.

San Cristobal Volcano and Map — A120

Designs: No. 1098, Lake Cosiguina. No. 1099, Telica Volcano. No. 1100, Lake Jiloa.

1978, Dec. 29 *Perf. 14x13½*

1097 A120 5c multi 15 15
1098 A120 5c multi 15 15
1099 A120 20c multi 15 15
1100 A120 20c multi 15 15
Nos. 1097-1100,C954-C961 (12) 5.42
Set value 3.35

Volcanos, lakes and their locations. Stamps of same denomination printed se-tenant in sheets of 40.

1980 Overprints

The editors are still gathering data on the 1980 overprints for the listing of these issues.

Souvenir Sheet

Quetzal — A121

1981, May 18 Litho. *Perf. 13*

1101 A121 10cor multi 1.75 1.25

WIPA 1981 Phil. Exhib., Vienna, May 22-31.

1982 World Cup A122

Designs: Various soccer players and stadiums.

1981, June 25 *Perf. 12x12½*

1102 A122 5c multi 15 15
1103 A122 20c multi 15 15
1104 A122 25c multi 15 15
1105 A122 30c multi 15 15
1106 A122 50c multi 15 15
1107 A122 4cor multi 45 26
1108 A122 5cor multi 52 32
1109 A122 10cor multi 1.10 65
Set value 2.30 1.30

Souvenir Sheet

Perf. 13

1110 A122 10cor multi 1.40 1.00

2nd Anniv. of Revolution — A123

1981, July 19 *Perf. 12½x12*

1111 A123 50c Adult education 15 15

See Nos. C973-C975.

20th Anniv. of the FSLN A124

1981, July 23

1112 A124 50c Armed citizen 15 15

See No. C976.

Postal Union of Spain and the Americas, 12th Congress, Managua — A125

1981, Aug. 10

1113 A125 50c Mailman 15 15

See Nos. C977-C979.

Aquatic Flowers (Nymphaea...) A126

1981, Sept. 15 *Perf. 12½*

1114 A126 50c Capensis 15 15
1115 A126 1cor Daubenyana 15 15
1116 A126 1.20cor Marliacea 22 15
1117 A126 1.80cor GT Moore 35 15
1118 A126 2cor Lotus 35 15
1119 A126 2.50cor BG Berry 50 28
Nos. 1114-1119,C981 (7) 3.12 1.93

Tropical Fish A127

1981, Oct. 19

1120 A127 50c Cheirodon axelrodi 15 15
1121 A127 1cor Poecilia reticulata 18 15
1122 A127 1.85cor Anostomus anostomus 35 18
1123 A127 2.10cor Corydoras arcuatus 42 20
1124 A127 2.50cor Cynolebias nigripinnis 48 28
Nos. 1120-1124,C983-C984 (7) 2.61 1.54

Dryocopus Lineatus — A128

1981, Nov. 30 *Perf. 12½*

1125 A128 50c shown 15 15
1126 A128 1.20cor Ramphastos sulfuratus, horiz. 26 15
1127 A128 1.80cor Aratinga finschi, horiz. 40 22
1128 A128 2cor Ara macao 40 26
Nos. 1125-1128,C986-C988 (7) 3.29 1.97

Space Communications A129

Designs: Various communications satellites.

1981, Dec. 15 ***Perf. 13x12½***

1129 A129 50c multi 15 15

1130 A129 1cor multi 15 15

1131 A129 1.50cor multi 25 15

1132 A129 2cor multi 30 20

Nos. 1129-1132,C989-C991 (7) 2.30 1.50

Vaporcito 93 — A130

1981, Dec. 30 ***Perf. 12½***

1133 A130 50c shown 15 15

1134 A130 1cor Vulcan Iron Works, 1946 20 15

1135 A130 1.20cor 1911 25 15

1136 A130 1.80cor Hoist & Derriel, 1909 38 20

1137 A130 2cor U-10B, 1956 38 25

1138 A130 2.50cor Ferrobus, 1945 38 30

Nos. 1133-1138,C992 (7) 2.74 1.75

1982 World Cup — A131

Designs: Various soccer players. 3.50cor horiz.

1982, Jan. 25

1139 A131 5c multi 15 15

1140 A131 20c multi 15 15

1141 A131 25c multi 15 15

1142 A131 2.50cor multi 42 34

1143 A131 3.50cor multi 55 35

Nos. 1139-1143,C993-C994 (7) 3.15

Set value 1.80

Cocker Spaniels A132

1982, Feb. 18

1144 A132 5c shown 15 15

1145 A132 20c German shepherds 15 15

1146 A132 25c English setters 15 15

1147 A132 2.50cor Brittany spaniels 45 28

Nos. 1144-1147,C996-C998 (7) 2.73

Set value 1.40

Dynamine Myrrhina A133

1982, Mar. 26

1148 A133 50c shown 15 15

1149 A133 1.20cor Eunica alcmena 24 15

1150 A133 1.50cor Callizona acesta 28 16

1151 A133 2cor Adelpha leuceria 35 24

Nos. 1148-1151,C1000-C1002 (7) 2.50 1.63

Satellite A134

Designs: Various satellites. 5c, 50c, 1.50cor, 2.50cor horiz.

1982, Apr. 12

1152 A134 5c multi 15 15

1153 A134 15c multi 15 15

1154 A134 50c multi 15 15

1155 A134 1.50cor multi 26 16

1156 A134 2.50cor multi 45 26

Nos. 1152-1156,C1003-C1004 (7) 2.71

Set value 1.45

UPU Membership Centenary — A135

1982, May 1 **Litho.** ***Perf. 13***

1157 A135 50c Mail coach 15 15

1158 A135 1.20cor Ship 16 15

Set value 23 15

See Nos. C1005-C1006.

14th Central American and Caribbean Games (Cuba '82) — A136

1982, May 13

1159 A136 10c Bicycling, vert. 15 15

1160 A136 15c Swimming 15 15

1161 A136 25c Basketball, vert. 15 15

1162 A136 50c Weight lifting, vert. 15 15

Set value, #1159-1162, C1007-C1009 2.45 1.50

3rd Anniv. of Revolution — A137

1982, July 19

1163 A137 50c multi 15 15

See Nos. C1012-C1014.

George Washington (1732-1799) A138

19th Century Paintings. 1cor horiz. Size of 50c: 45x35mm.

Perf. 13x12½, 12½x13

1982, June 20 **Litho.**

1164 A138 50c Mount Vernon 15 15

1165 A138 1cor Signing the Constitution 20 15

1166 A138 2cor Riding through Trenton 38 25

Nos. 1164-1166,C1015-C1018 (7) 3.23 2.10

Flower Arrangement, by R. Penalba — A139

Paintings: 50c, Masked Dancers, by M. Garcia (horiz.). 1cor, The Couple, by R. Perez. 1.20cor, Canales Valley, by A. Mejias (horiz.). 1.85cor, Portrait of Mrs. Castellon, by T. Jerez. 2cor, Street Vendors, by L. Cerrato. 10cor, Cock Fight, by Gallos P. Ortiz.

1982, Aug. 17 ***Perf. 13***

1167 A139 25c multi 15 15

1168 A139 50c multi 15 15

1169 A139 1cor multi 18 15

1170 A139 1.20cor multi 20 15

1171 A139 1.85cor multi 32 20

1172 A139 2cor multi 32 20

Nos. 1167-1172,C1019 (7) 2.57

Set value 1.45

Souvenir Sheet

1173 A139 10cor multi 1.65 1.00

No. 1173 contains one 36x28mm stamp.

George Dimitrov, First Pres. of Bulgaria — A140

1982, Sept. 9

1174 A140 50c Lenin, Dimitrov, 1921 15 15

See Nos. C1020-C1021.

26th Anniv. of End of Dictatorship — A141

1982, Sept. 21 ***Perf. 13x12½***

1175 A141 50c Ausberto Narvaez 15 15

1176 A141 2.50cor Cornelio Silva 52 30

Set value 36

See Nos. C1022-C1023.

Ruins, Leon Viejo A142

1982, Sept. 25 ***Perf. 13***

1177 A142 50c shown 15 15

1178 A142 1cor Ruben Dario Theater and Park 15 15

1179 A142 1.20cor Independence Plaza, Granada 18 15

1180 A142 1.80cor Corn Island 28 16

1181 A142 2cor Santiago Volcano crater, Masaya 30 18

Nos. 1177-1181,C1024-C1025 (7) 1.72

Set value 1.10

Karl Marx (1818-1883) — A143

1982, Oct. 4 ***Perf. 12½***

1182 A143 1cor Marx, birthplace 18 15

Se-tenant with label showing Communist Manifesto titlepage. See No. C1026.

World Food Day (Oct. 16) A144

1982, Oct. 10 ***Perf. 13***

1183 A144 50c Picking fruit 15 15

1184 A144 1cor Farm workers, vert. 15 15

1185 A144 2cor Cutting sugar cane 30 25

1186 A144 10cor Emblems 1.50 1.20

Discovery of America, 490th Anniv. — A145

1982, Oct. 12 *Perf. 12½x13*

1187 A145 50c Santa Maria 15 15
1188 A145 1cor Nina 22 15
1189 A145 1.50cor Pinta 32 20
1190 A145 2cor Columbus, fleet 42 28
Nos. 1187-1190,C1027-C1029 (7) 3.28 2.14

A146

1982, Nov. 13 *Perf. 12½*

1191 A146 50c Lobelia laxiflora 15 15
1192 A146 1.20cor Bombacopsis quinata 25 15
1193 A146 1.80cor Mimosa albida 38 22
1194 A146 2cor Epidendrum alatum 38 25
Nos. 1191-1194,C1031-C1033 (7) 2.81 1.76

A147

1982, Dec. 10 *Perf. 13*

1195 A147 10c Coral snake 15 15
1196 A147 50c Iguana, horiz. 15 15
1197 A147 2cor Lachesis muta, horiz. 38 25
Nos. 1195-1197,C1034-C1037 (7) 2.78 1.82

Telecommunications Day — A148

1982, Dec. 12 **Litho.** *Perf. 12½*

1198 A148 50c Radio transmission station 15 15
1199 A148 1cor Telcor building, Managua 16 15
Set value 25 15

50c airmail.

Jose Marti, Cuban Independence Hero, 130th Birth Anniv. — A149

1983, Jan. 28 *Perf. 13*

1200 A149 1cor multi 25 15

Boxing A150

Local Flowers A151

1983, Jan. 31 *Perf. 12½*

1201 A150 50c shown 15 15
1202 A150 1cor Gymnast 15 15
1203 A150 1.50cor Running 20 15
1204 A150 2cor Weightlifting 25 16
1205 A150 4cor Women's discus 65 35
1206 A150 5cor Basketball 80 40
1207 A150 6cor Bicycling 1.00 50
Nos. 1201-1207 (7) 3.20 1.86

Souvenir Sheet

Perf. 13

1208 A150 15cor Sailing 2.25 1.20

23rd Olympic Games, Los Angeles, July 28-Aug. 12, 1984. Nos. 1205-1208 airmail. No. 1208 contains one 31x39mm stamp.

1983, Feb. 5 *Perf. 12½*

1209 A151 1cor Bixa orellana 16 15
1210 A151 1cor Brassavola nodosa 16 15
1211 A151 1cor Cattleya lueddemanniana 16 15
1212 A151 1cor Cochlospermum spec. 16 15
1213 A151 1cor Hibiscus rosa-sinensis 16 15
1214 A151 1cor Laella spec. 16 15
1215 A151 1cor Malvaviscus arboreus 16 15
1216 A151 1cor Neomarica coerulea 16 15
1217 A151 1cor Plumeria rubra 16 15
1218 A151 1cor Senecio spec. 16 15
1219 A151 1cor Sobralla macrantha 16 15
1220 A151 1cor Stachytarpheta indica 16 15
1221 A151 1cor Tabebula ochraceae 16 15
1222 A151 1cor Tagetes erecta 16 15
1223 A151 1cor Tecoma stans 16 15
1224 A151 1cor Thumbergia alata 16 15
Nos. 1209-1224 (16) 2.56
Set value 1.25

See Nos. 1515-1530, 1592-1607, 1828-1843.

Visit of Pope John Paul II A152

1983, Mar. 4 *Perf. 13*

1225 A152 50c Peace banner 15 15
1226 A152 1cor Map, girl picking coffee beans 24 15
1227 A152 4cor Pres. Rafael Rivas, Pope 95 60
1228 A152 7cor Pope, Managua Cathedral 1.65 95

Souvenir Sheet

1229 A152 15cor Pope, vert. 3.25 1.75

Nos. 1227-1229 airmail. No. 1229 contains one 31x39mm stamp.

Nocturnal Moths — A153

1983, Mar. 10

1230 A153 15c Xilophanes chiron 15 15
1231 A153 50c Protoparce ochus 15 15
1232 A153 65c Pholus lasbruscae 15 15
1233 A153 1cor Amphypterus gannascus 16 15
1234 A153 1.50cor Pholus licaon 20 15
1235 A153 2cor Agrius cingulata 35 16
1236 A153 10cor Rothschildia jurulla, vert. 1.50 75
Nos. 1230-1236 (7) 2.66
Set value 1.20

26th Anniv. of the Anti-Somoza Movement — A154

Various monuments and churches. 2cor, 4cor vert. 4cor airmail.

1983, Mar. 25 *Perf. 12½*

1237 A154 50c Church of Subtiava, Leon 15 15
1238 A154 1cor La Immaculata Castle, Rio San Juan 16 15
1239 A154 2cor La Recoleccion Church, Leon 35 16
1240 A154 4cor Ruben Dario monument, Managua 65 35
Set value 64

Railroad Cars A155

1983, Apr. 15

1241 A155 15c Passenger 15 15
1242 A155 65c Freight 15 15
1243 A155 1cor Tank 15 15
1244 A155 1.50cor Ore 20 15
1245 A155 4cor Passenger, diff. 55 30
1246 A155 5cor Flat 70 35
1247 A155 7cor Rail bus 95 48
Nos. 1241-1247 (7) 2.85
Set value 1.35

Nos. 1245-1247 airmail.

Red Cross Flood Rescue A156

1983, May 8 *Perf. 13*

1248 A156 50c shown 15 15
1249 A156 1cor Putting patient in ambulance 18 15
1250 A156 4cor 1972 earthquake & fire rescue 65 38
1251 A156 5cor Nurse examining soldier, 1979 Liberation War 70 42

4cor, 5cor airmail. 4cor vert.

World Communications Year — A157

1983, May 17

1252 A157 1cor multi 18 15

9th Pan-American Games, Aug. — A158

1983, May 30 **Litho.** *Perf. 13*

1253 A158 15c Baseball 15 15
1254 A158 50c Water polo 15 15
1255 A158 65c Running 15 15
1256 A158 1cor Women's basketball, vert. 16 15
1257 A158 2cor Weightlifting, vert. 35 16
1258 A158 7cor Fencing 1.10 55
1259 A158 8cor Gymnastics 1.20 65
Nos. 1253-1259 (7) 3.26
Set value 1.55

Souvenir Sheet

1260 A158 15cor Boxing 2.25 1.25

Nos. 1258-1260 airmail. No. 1260 contains one 39x31mm stamp.

4th Anniv. of Revolution — A159

1983, July 19 **Litho.** *Perf. 12½*

1261 A159 1cor Port of Corinto 16 15
1262 A159 2cor Telecommunications Bldg., Leon 38 16
Set value 25

Founders of FSLN (Sandinista Party) — A160

1983, July 23 **Litho.** *Perf. 13*

1263 A160 50c multi 15 15
1264 A160 1cor multi 16 15
1265 A160 4cor multi, vert. 60 35
Set value 48

No. 1265, airmail, 33x44mm.

Simon Bolivar, 200th Birth Anniv. A161

1983, July 24 **Litho.** *Perf. 12½*

1266 A161 50c Bolivar and Sandino 15 15
1267 A161 1cor Bolivar on horseback, vert. 15 15
Set value 24 15

14th Winter Olympic Games, Sarajevo, Yugoslavia, Feb. 8-19, 1984 — A162

1983, Aug. 5 Litho. *Perf. 13*

1268 A162 50c Speed skating 15 15
1269 A162 1cor Slalom 15 15
1270 A162 1.50cor Luge 20 15
1271 A162 2cor Ski jumping 35 16
1272 A162 4cor Ice dancing 60 35
1273 A162 5cor Skiing 70 40
1274 A162 6cor Biathlon 90 50
Nos. 1268-1274 (7) 3.05 1.86

Souvenir Sheet

1983, Aug. 25 Litho. *Perf. 13*

1275 A162 15cor Hockey 2.50 1.40

No. 1275 contains one 39x32mm stamp. Nos. 1272-1275 airmail.

Chess Moves — A163

Archaeological Finds — A164

1983, Aug. 20 Litho. *Perf. 13*

1276 A163 15c Pawn 15 15
1277 A163 65c Knight 15 15
1278 A163 1cor Bishop 15 15
1279 A163 2cor Castle 35 16
1280 A163 4cor Queen 60 35
1281 A163 5cor King 70 40
1282 A163 7cor Player 1.00 55
Nos. 1276-1282 (7) 3.10
Set value 1.60

Nos. 1280-1282 airmail.

1983, Aug. 20 *Perf. 13x12½*

1283 A164 50c Stone figurine 15 15
1284 A164 1cor Covered dish 15 15
1285 A164 2cor Vase 35 16
1286 A164 4cor Platter 60 35
Set value 64

No. 1286 airmail.

Madonna of the Chair, by Raphael (1483-1517) A165

Paintings: 1cor, The Eszterhazy Madonna. 1.50cor, Sistine Madonna. 2cor, Madonna of the Linnet. 4cor, Madonna of the Meadow. 5cor, La Belle Jardiniere. 6cor, Adoration of the Kings. 15cor, Madonna de Foligno. 4, 5, 6, 15cor airmail.

1983, Sept. 15

1287 A165 50c multi 15 15
1288 A165 1cor multi 15 15
1289 A165 1.50cor multi 20 15
1290 A165 2cor multi 35 16
1291 A165 4cor multi 60 35
1292 A165 5cor multi 70 40
1293 A165 6cor multi 90 48
Nos. 1287-1293 (7) 3.05 1.84

Souvenir Sheet

1984, Sept. 15 Litho. *Perf. 13*

1293A A165 15cor multi 2.25 1.25

Mining Industry Nationalization — A166

1983, Oct. 2 *Perf. 13*

1294 A166 1cor Pouring molten metal 16 15
1295 A166 4cor Mine headstock, workers 60 40

4cor airmail.

Ship-to-Shore Communications — A167

1983, Oct. 7 *Perf. 12½*

1296 A167 1cor shown 16 15
1297 A167 4cor Radio tower, view 60 40

FRACAP '83, Federation of Central American and Panamanian Radio Amateurs Congress, Oct. 7-9.

Agrarian Reform — A168

1983, Oct. 16

1298 A168 1cor Tobacco 15 15
1299 A168 2cor Cotton 35 15
1300 A168 4cor Corn 60 25
1301 A168 5cor Sugar cane 70 35
1302 A168 6cor Cattle 90 40
1303 A168 7cor Rice paddy 1.00 45
1304 A168 8cor Coffee beans 1.20 55
1305 A168 10cor Bananas 1.50 65
Nos. 1298-1305 (8) 6.40 2.95

See Nos. 1531-1538, 1608-1615.

Fire Engine A169

Various Fire Engines.

1983, Oct. 17 *Perf. 13*

1306 A169 50c multi 15 15
1307 A169 1cor multi 15 15
1308 A169 1.50cor multi 20 15
1309 A169 2cor multi 35 16
1310 A169 4cor multi 60 35
1311 A169 5cor multi 70 40
1312 A169 6cor multi 90 48
Nos. 1306-1312 (7) 3.05 1.84

Nos. 1308-1312 airmail.

Nicaraguan-Cuban Solidarity — A170

1983, Oct. 24

1313 A170 1cor José Marti, Gen. Sandino 16 15
1314 A170 4cor Education, health, industry 60 40

4cor airmail.

Christmas 1983 — A171

Adoration of the Kings Paintings by: 50c, Hugo van der Goes. 1 cor, Ghirlandaio. 2cor, El Greco. 7cor, Konrad von Soest. 7cor airmail.

1983, Dec. 1

1315 A171 50c multi 15 15
1316 A171 1cor multi 15 15
1317 A171 2cor multi 28 15
1318 A171 7cor multi 90 42
Set value 1.30 66

1984 Winter Olympics A172

1984, Jan. 10

1319 A172 50c Biathlon 15 15
1320 A172 50c Bobsledding 15 15
1321 A172 1cor Speed skating 15 15
1322 A172 1cor Slalom 15 15
1323 A172 4cor Downhill skiing 65 35
1324 A172 5cor Ice dancing 80 40
1325 A172 10cor Ski jumping 1.40 75
Nos. 1319-1325 (7) 3.45
Set value 1.75

Souvenir Sheet

1326 A172 15cor Hockey 2.50 1.50

No. 1326 contains one 31x39mm stamp. Nos. 1323-1326 airmail.

Domestic Cats A173

1984, Feb. 15 *Perf. 12½*

1327 A173 50c Chinchilla 15 15
1328 A173 50c Long-haired Angel 15 15
1329 A173 1cor Red tabby 18 15
1330 A173 2cor Tortoiseshell 38 18
1331 A173 3cor Siamese 32 28
1332 A173 4cor Blue Burmese 70 38
1333 A173 7cor Silver long-haired 1.25 60
Nos. 1327-1333 (7) 3.13
Set value 1.55

Nos. 1331, 1333 airmail.

Augusto Cesar Sandino (d. 1934) — A174

1984, Feb. 21

1334 A174 1cor Arms 16 15
1335 A174 4cor Portrait 60 40

4cor airmail.

Intl. Women's Day — A175

1984, Mar. 8

1336 A175 1cor Blanca Arauz 15 15

Bee-pollinated Flowers — A176

1984, Mar. 20

1337 A176 50c Poinsettia 15 15
1338 A176 50c Sunflower 15 15
1339 A176 1cor Antigonan leptopus 16 15
1340 A176 1cor Cassia alata 16 15
1341 A176 3cor Bidens pilosa 42 25
1342 A176 4cor Althea rosea 60 35
1343 A176 5cor Rivea corymbosa 70 40
Nos. 1337-1343 (7) 2.34
Set value 1.25

Nos. 1341-1343 airmail.

Space Annivs. — A177

1984, Apr. 20

1344 A177 50c Soyuz 6,7,8, 1969 15 15
1345 A177 50c Soyuz 6,7,8, diff. 15 15
1346 A177 1cor Apollo 11, 1969 15 15
1347 A177 2cor Luna 1, 1959 35 16
1348 A177 3cor Luna 2, 1959 50 25
1349 A177 4cor Luna 3, 1959 65 35
1350 A177 9cor Painting by Koroliov, 1934 1.40 50
Nos. 1344-1350 (7) 3.35
Set value 1.40

Nos. 1348-1350 airmail.

Noli Me Tangere, by Correggio A178

1984, May 17 Litho. *Perf. 12½*

1351	A178	50c shown	15	15
1352	A178	50c Madonna of San Girolamo	15	15
1353	A178	1cor Allegory of the Virtues	15	15
1354	A178	2cor Allegory of Placer	35	16
1355	A178	3cor Ganimedes	50	25
1356	A178	5cor Danae	80	40
1357	A178	8cor Leda	1.20	65
		Nos. 1351-1357 (7)	3.30	
		Set value		1.60

Souvenir Sheet

1358	A178	15cor St. John the Evangelist	2.25	1.20

No. 1358 contains one 31x39mm stamp. Nos. 1355-1358 airmail.

Vintage Cars A179

1984, May 18

1359	A179	1cor Abadal, 1914	15	15
1360	A179	1cor Daimler, 1886, vert.	15	15
1361	A179	2cor Ford, 1903, vert.	35	16
1362	A179	2cor Renault, 1899, vert.	35	16
1363	A179	3cor Rolls Royce, 1910	50	25
1364	A179	4cor Metallurgique, 1907	65	35
1365	A179	7cor Bugatti Mode 40	1.10	55
		Nos. 1359-1365 (7)	3.25	1.77

Birth sesquicentennial of Gottlieb Daimler. Nos. 1363-1365 airmail.

1984 Summer Olympics A180

1984, July 6

1366	A180	50c Volleyball	15	15
1367	A180	50c Basketball	15	15
1368	A180	1cor Field hockey	15	15
1369	A180	2cor Tennis	35	16
1370	A180	3cor Soccer	50	25
1371	A180	4cor Water polo	65	35
1372	A180	9cor Net ball	1.40	70
		Nos. 1366-1372 (7)	3.35	
		Set value		1.60

Souvenir Sheet

Perf. 13

1373	A180	15cor Baseball	2.25	1.20

No. 1373 contains one 40x31mm stamp. Nos. 1370-1373 airmail and horiz.

5th Anniv. of Revolution — A181

1984, July 19

1374	A181	50c Construction	15	15
1375	A181	1cor Transportation	16	15
1376	A181	4cor Agriculture	65	35
1377	A181	7cor Govt. building	1.20	55
		Set value		1.00

Nos. 1376-1377 airmail.

UNESCO Nature Conservation Campaign A182

1984, Aug. 3 *Perf. 12½x13, 13x12½*

1378	A182	50c Children dependent on nature	15	15
1379	A182	1cor Forest	15	15
1380	A182	2cor River	35	16
1381	A182	10cor Seedlings, field, vert.	1.50	80
		Set value		1.05

No. 1381 airmail.

Nicaraguan Red Cross, 50th Anniv. — A183

1984, Sept. 16 *Perf. 12½x12*

1382	A183	1cor Air ambulance	16	15
1383	A183	7cor Battle field	1.00	55

No. 1383 airmail.

History of Baseball — A184

Portraits and national colors: No. 1384, Ventura Escalante, Dominican Republic. No. 1385, Daniel Herrera, Mexico. No. 1386, Adalberto Herrera, Venezuela. No. 1387, Roberto Clemente, Puerto Rico. No. 1388, Carlos Colas, Cuba. No. 1389, Stanley Cayasso, Nicaragua. No. 1390, Babe Ruth, US.

1984, Oct. 25 Litho. *Perf. 12½*

1384	A184	50c multi	15	15
1385	A184	50c multi	15	15
1386	A184	1cor multi	16	15
1387	A184	1cor multi	16	15
1388	A184	3cor multi	50	20
1389	A184	4cor multi	65	25
1390	A184	5cor multi	80	35
		Nos. 1384-1390 (7)	2.57	
		Set value		1.00

Nos. 1388-1390 are airmail.

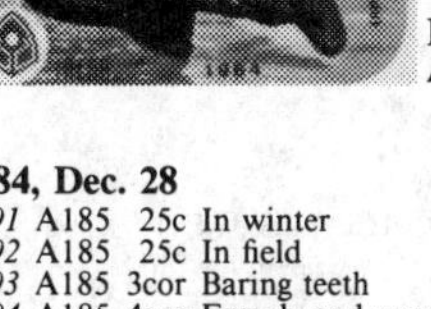

Tapirus Bairdii A185

1984, Dec. 28 *Perf. 13*

1391	A185	25c In winter	15	15
1392	A185	25c In field	15	15
1393	A185	3cor Baring teeth	40	20
1394	A185	4cor Female and young	55	25
		Set value	1.00	50

Wildlife conservation. Nos. 1393-1394 are airmail.

1986 World Cup Soccer Championships, Mexico — A186

Evolution of soccer.

1985, Jan. 20

1395	A186	50c 1314	15	15
1396	A186	50c 1500	15	15
1397	A186	1cor 1846	15	15
1398	A186	1cor 1872	15	15
1399	A186	2cor 1883	20	15
1400	A186	4cor 1890	40	20
1401	A186	6cor 1953	60	30
		Set value	1.50	75

Souvenir Sheet

Perf. 12½

1402	A186	10cor 1985	1.20	80

Nos. 1399-1402 are airmail. No. 1402 contains one 40x32mm stamp.

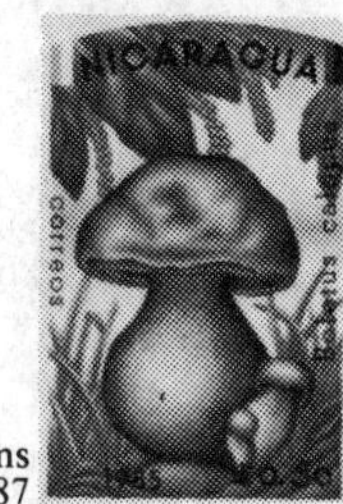

Mushrooms A187

1985, Feb. 20

1403	A187	50c Boletus calopus	15	15
1404	A187	50c Strobilomyces retisporus	15	15
1405	A187	1cor Boletus luridus	15	15
1406	A187	1cor Xerocomus illudens	15	15
1407	A187	4cor Gyrodon merulioides	50	20
1408	A187	5cor Tylopilus plumbeoviolaceus	60	25
1409	A187	8cor Gyroporus castaneus	1.00	40
		Nos. 1403-1409 (7)	2.70	
		Set value		1.00

Nos. 1406-1409 are airmail.

Postal Union of the Americas and Spain, 13th Congress A188

UPAE emblem and: 1cor, Chasqui, mail runner and map of Realejo-Nicaragua route. 7cor, Monoplane and Nicaraguan air network.

1985, Mar. 11 *Perf. 12½x13*

1410	A188	1cor multi	15	15
1411	A188	7cor multi	70	38

No. 1411 is airmail.

City Railway Engine A189

Various locomotives.

1985, Apr. 5 *Perf. 12½*

1412	A189	1cor Electric	15	15
1413	A189	1cor Steam	15	15
1414	A189	9cor shown	52	25
1415	A189	9cor shown	52	25
1416	A189	15cor steam, diff.	85	42
1417	A189	21cor steam, diff.	1.25	35
		Nos. 1412-1417 (6)	3.44	1.57

Souvenir Sheet

Perf. 13

1418	A189	42cor steam, diff.	3.25	1.90

German Railroads, 150th Anniv. No. 1418 also for 100th anniv. of Nicaraguan railroads. No. 1418 contains one 40x32mm stamp. Nos. 1414-1418 are airmail.

Motorcycle Cent. — A190

1985, Apr. 30 Litho. *Perf. 12½*

1419	A190	50c F.N., 1928	15	15
1420	A190	50c Douglas, 1928	15	15
1421	A190	1cor Puch, 1938	15	15
1422	A190	2cor Wanderer, 1939	20	15
1423	A190	4cor Honda, 1949	40	20
1424	A190	5cor BMW, 1984	50	25
1425	A190	7cor Honda, 1984	70	38
		Nos. 1419-1425 (7)	2.25	
		Set value		1.00

Nos. 1419-1425 se-tenant with labels picturing manufacturers' trademarks. Nos. 1422-1425 are airmail.

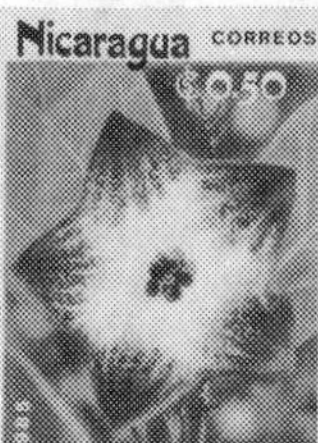

Flowers — A194

1985, May 20 Litho. *Perf. 13*

1454	A194	50c Metelea quirosii	15	15
1455	A194	50c Ipomea nil	15	15
1456	A194	1cor Lysichitum americanum	18	15
1457	A194	2cor Clusia sp.	36	18
1458	A194	4cor Vanilla planifolia	72	36
1459	A194	7cor Stemmadenia obovata	1.25	62
a.		Min. sheet of 6, #1454-1459	2.75	
		Nos. 1454-1459 (6)	2.81	
		Set value		1.35

Nos. 1457-1459 are airmail.

Stamps in No. 1459a do not have white border.

End of World War II, 40th Anniv. — A195

1985, May *Perf. 12x12½, 12½x12*

1460 A195 9.50cor German army surrenders 38 18
1461 A195 28cor Nuremberg trials, horiz. 1.10 52

No. 1461 is airmail.

Lenin, 115th Birth Anniv. A196

Design: 21cor, Lenin speaking to workers.

1985, June **Litho.** *Perf. 12x12½*

1462 A196 4cor multicolored 40 20
1463 A196 21cor multicolored 2.25 1.10

Souvenir Sheet

Argentina '85 — A197

1985, June 5 **Litho.** *Perf. 13*

1464 A197 75cor multicolored 4.25 2.00

World Stamp Exposition.

Birds — A198

1985, Aug. 25

1465 A198 50c Ring-neck pheasant 15 15
1466 A198 50c Chicken 15 15
1467 A198 1cor Guinea hen 20 15
1468 A198 2cor Goose 40 20
1469 A198 6cor Wild turkey 1.25 60
1470 A198 8cor Duck 1.65 80
Nos. 1465-1470 (6) 3.80 2.05

Intl. Music Year A199

1985, Sept. 1

1471 A199 1cor Luis A. Delgadillo, vert. 15 15
1472 A199 1cor shown 15 15
1473 A199 9cor Parade 60 30
1474 A199 9cor Managua Cathedral 60 30
1475 A199 15cor Masked dancer 95 48
1476 A199 21cor Parade, diff. 1.25 65
Nos. 1471-1476 (6) 3.70 2.03

Nos. 1473-1476 are airmail.

Natl. Fire Brigade, 6th Anniv. A200

1985, Oct. 18

1477 A200 1cor Fire station 15 15
1478 A200 1cor Fire truck 15 15
1479 A200 1cor shown 15 15
1480 A200 3cor Ambulance 20 15
1481 A200 9cor Airport fire truck 60 30
1482 A200 15cor Waterfront fire 1.00 50
1483 A200 21cor Hose team, fire 1.40 75
a. Min. sheet of 7, #1474-1483 + 2 labels 3.75
Nos. 1477-1483 (7) 3.65
Set value 1.70

Stamps from No. 1483a have orange borders. Nos. 1480-1483 are airmail.

Halley's Comet — A201

1985, Nov. 26

1484 A201 1cor Edmond Halley 15 15
1485 A201 3cor Map of comet's track, 1910 16 15
1486 A201 3cor Tycho Brahe's observatory 16 15
1487 A201 9cor Astrolabe, map 50 24
1488 A201 15cor Telescopes 80 40
1489 A201 21cor Telescope designs 1.25 60
Nos. 1484-1489 (6) 3.02 1.69

Nos. 1487-1489 are airmail.

Tapirus Bairdii A202

1985, Dec. 30

1490 A202 1cor Eating 15 15
1491 A202 3cor Drinking 32 16
1492 A202 5cor Grazing in field 50 25
1493 A202 9cor With young 95 45

Nos. 1491-1493 are airmail.

Roses — A203

1986, Jan. 15 *Perf. 12½*

1494 A203 1cor Spinosissima 15 15
1495 A203 1cor Canina 15 15
1496 A203 3cor Eglanteria 15 15
1497 A203 5cor Rubrifolia 15 15
1498 A203 9cor Foetida 20 15
1499 A203 100cor Rugosa 2.25 1.10
Nos. 1494-1499 (6) 3.05
Set value 1.25

Nos. 1497-1499 are airmail.

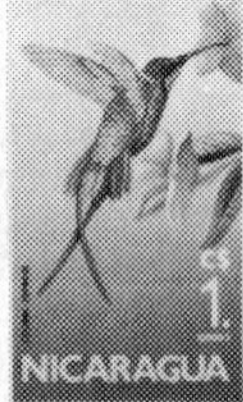

Birds — A204

1986, Feb. 10 *Perf. 13x12½*

1500 A204 1cor Colibri topacio 15 15
1501 A204 3cor Paraulata picodorado 15 15
1502 A204 3cor Troupial 15 15
1503 A204 5cor Vereron pintado 15 15
1504 A204 10cor Tordo ruisenor 24 15
1505 A204 21cor Buho real 50 26
1506 A204 75cor Gran kiskadee 1.75 90
Nos. 1500-1506 (7) 3.09
Set value 1.45

Nos. 1504-1506 are airmail.

World Cup Soccer Championships, Mexico — A205

Designs: Soccer players and pre-Columbian artifacts. No. 1514, Player's foot, ball.

1986, Mar. 20 *Perf. 12½*

Shirt Colors

1507 A205 1cor blue & yel 15 15
1508 A205 1cor yel & green 15 15
1509 A205 3cor blue & white 15 15
1510 A205 3cor red & white 15 15
1511 A205 5cor red 15 15
1512 A205 9cor blk & yel 20 15
1513 A205 100cor red & grn 2.25 1.10
Nos. 1507-1513 (7) 3.20
Set value 1.35

Souvenir Sheet

Perf. 13

1514 A205 100cor multicolored 2.50 1.25

Nos. 1509-1514 are airmail.

Flower Type of 1983

1986, Mar. **Litho.** *Perf. 12½*

1515 A151 5cor like #1209 25 15
1516 A151 5cor like #1210 25 15
1517 A151 5cor like #1211 25 15
1518 A151 5cor like #1212 25 15
1519 A151 5cor like #1213 25 15
1520 A151 5cor like #1214 25 15
1521 A151 5cor like #1215 25 15
1522 A151 5cor like #1216 25 15
1523 A151 5cor like #1217 25 15
1524 A151 5cor like #1218 25 15
1525 A151 5cor like #1219 25 15
1526 A151 5cor like #1220 25 15
1527 A151 5cor like #1221 25 15
1528 A151 5cor like #1222 25 15
1529 A151 5cor like #1223 25 15
1530 A151 5cor like #1224 25 15
Nos. 1515-1530 (16) 4.00
Set value 2.00

Agrarian Reform Type of 1983

1986, Apr. 15 *Perf. 12½*

1531 A168 1cor dk brown 15 15
1532 A168 9cor purple 20 15
1533 A168 15cor rose violet 32 16
1534 A168 21cor dk car rose 45 22
1535 A168 33cor orange 75 35
1536 A168 42cor green 95 45
1537 A168 50cor brown 1.10 55
1538 A168 100cor blue 2.25 1.10
Nos. 1531-1538 (8) 6.17 3.13

Writers A207

1986, Apr. 23 *Perf. 12½x13*

1539 A207 1cor Alfonso Cortes 15 15
1540 A207 3cor Salomon de la Selva 15 15
1541 A207 3cor Azarias H. Pallais 15 15
1542 A207 5cor Ruben Dario 15 15
1543 A207 9cor Pablo Neruda 22 15
1544 A207 15cor Alfonso Reyes 35 18
1545 A207 100cor Pedro Henriquez Urena 2.25 1.10
Nos. 1539-1545 (7) 3.42
Set value 1.55

Nos. 1544-1545 are airmail.

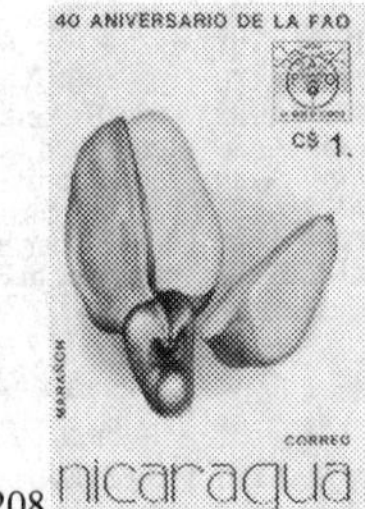

Nuts — A208

1986, June 20 *Perf. 12x12½*

1546 A208 1cor Maranon (cashew) 15 15
1547 A208 1cor Zapote 15 15
1548 A208 3cor Pitahaya 15 15
1549 A208 3cor Granadilla 15 15
1550 A208 5cor Anona 15 15

1551 A208 21cor Melocoton (starfruit) 50 25
1552 A208 100cor Mamey 2.25 1.10
Set value 3.10 1.55

FAO, 40th Anniv. Nos. 1550-1552 are airmail.

Lockheed L-1011 Tristar A209

Airplanes: No. 1554, YAK 40. No. 1555, BAC 1-11. No. 1556, Boeing 747. 9cor, A-300. 15cor, TU-154. No. 1559, Concorde, vert. No. 1560, Fairchild 340.

1986, Aug. 22 ***Perf. 12½***
1553 A209 1cor multicolored 15 15
1554 A209 1cor multicolored 15 15
1555 A209 3cor multicolored 15 15
1556 A209 3cor multicolored 15 15
1557 A209 9cor multicolored 22 15
1558 A209 15cor multicolored 35 20
1559 A209 100cor multicolored 2.25 1.10
Set value 3.10 1.55

Souvenir Sheet

Perf. 13

1560 A209 100cor multicolored 2.50 1.25

Stockholmia '86. No. 1560 contains one 40x32mm stamp.

A210

A210a

Discovery of America, 500th Anniv. (in 1992) — A210b

1986, Oct. 12 ***Perf. 12½x12***
1561 A210 1cor shown 15 15
1562 A210 1cor 2 of Columbus' ships 15 15
a. Pair, #1561-1562 15 15
b. Souv. sheet of 2, #1561-1562 15 15

Perf. 12x12½

1563 A210a 9cor Juan de la Cosa 20 15
1564 A210a 9cor Columbus 20 15
a. Pair, #1563-1564 40 20
1565 A210b 21cor Ferdinand, Isabella 50 25
1566 A210b 100cor Columbus before throne 2.25 1.10
a. Pair, #1565-1566 2.75 1.35
b. Souv. sheet of 4, #1563-1566 3.25 1.55
Nos. 1561-1566 (6) 3.45 1.95

Nos. 1563-1566 are airmail. Nos. 1564a, 1566a have continuous design.

Butterflies A211

1986, Dec. 12 ***Perf. 12½***
1567 A211 10cor Theritas coronata 24 15
1568 A211 15cor Charayes nitebis 35 18
1569 A211 15cor Salamis cacta 35 18
1570 A211 15cor Papilio maacki 35 18
1571 A211 25cor Euphaedro cyparissa 60 30
1572 A211 25cor Palaeochrysophonus hippothoe 60 30
1573 A211 30cor Ritra aurea 70 35
Nos. 1567-1573 (7) 3.19 1.64

Nos. 1568-1573 are airmail.

Ruben Dario Order of Cultural Independence A212

Dario Order Winning Writers: No. 1574, Ernesto Mejia Sanchez. No. 1575, Fernando Gordillo C. No. 1576, Francisco Perez Estrada. 30cor, Julio Cortazar. 60cor, Enrique Fernandez Morales.

1987, Jan. 18 **Litho.** ***Perf. 13***
1574 A212 10cor multicolored 22 15
1575 A212 10cor multicolored 22 15
1576 A212 10cor multicolored 22 15
1577 A212 15cor multicolored 32 16
1578 A212 30cor multicolored 65 32
1579 A212 60cor multicolored 1.25 65
a. Strip of 6, #1574-1579 2.90 1.50
b. Min. sheet of 6, #1574-1579 2.90 2.90
Nos. 1574-1579 (6) 2.88 1.58

1988 Winter Olympics, Calgary — A213

Designs: No. 1580, Speed skating. No. 1581, Ice hockey. No. 1582, Women's figure skating. No. 1583, Ski jumping. 20cor, Biathalon. 30cor, Slalom skiing. 40cor, Downhill skiing. 110cor, Ice hockey, diff., horiz.

1987, Feb. 3 ***Perf. 13***
1580 A213 10cor multi 22 15
1581 A213 10cor multi 22 15
1582 A213 15cor multi 30 15
1583 A213 15cor multi 30 15
1584 A213 20cor multi 40 20
1585 A213 30cor multi 60 30
1586 A213 40cor multi 85 42
Nos. 1580-1586 (7) 2.89 1.52

Souvenir Sheet

Perf. 12½

1587 A213 110cor multi 2.25 2.25

Nos. 1582-1587 are airmail. No. 1587 contains one 40x32mm stamp.

Children's Welfare Campaign A214

1987, Mar. 18 ***Perf. 13***
1588 A214 10cor Growth & development 25 15
1589 A214 25cor Vaccination 60 30
1590 A214 30cor Rehydration 75 35
1591 A214 50cor Breastfeeding 1.25 60

Nos. 1589-1591 are airmail.

Flower Type of 1983

1987, Mar. 25 ***Perf. 12½***
1592 A151 10cor Bixa orellana 20 15
1593 A151 10cor Brassavola nodosa 20 15
1594 A151 10cor Cattleya luedemanniana 20 15
1595 A151 10cor Cochlospermum spec. 20 15
1596 A151 10cor Hibiscus rosasinensis 20 15
1597 A151 10cor Laella spec. 20 15
1598 A151 10cor Malvaviscus arboreus 20 15
1599 A151 10cor Neomarica coerulea 20 15
1600 A151 10cor Plumeria rubra 20 15
1601 A151 10cor Senecio spec. 20 15
1602 A151 10cor Sobralla macrantha 20 15
1603 A151 10cor Stachytarpheta indica 20 15
1604 A151 10cor Tabebula ochraceae 20 15
1605 A151 10cor Tagetes erecta 20 15
1606 A151 10cor Tecoma stans 20 15
1607 A151 10cor Thumbergia alata 20 15
Nos. 1592-1607 (16) 3.20
Set value 1.70

Agrarian Reform Type of 1983 Inscribed "1987"

Designs: No. 1608, Tobacco. No. 1609, Cotton. 15cor, Corn. 25cor, Sugar. 30cor, Cattle. 50cor, Coffee Beans. 60cor, Rice. 100cor, Bananas.

1987, Mar. 25 ***Perf. 12½***
1608 A168 10cor dk brown 28 15
1609 A168 10cor purple 28 15
1610 A168 15cor rose violet 45 22
1611 A168 25cor dk car rose 70 35
1612 A168 30cor orange 85 45
1613 A168 50cor brown 1.40 65
1614 A168 60cor green 1.75 90
1615 A168 100cor blue 2.75 1.40
Nos. 1608-1615 (8) 8.46 4.27

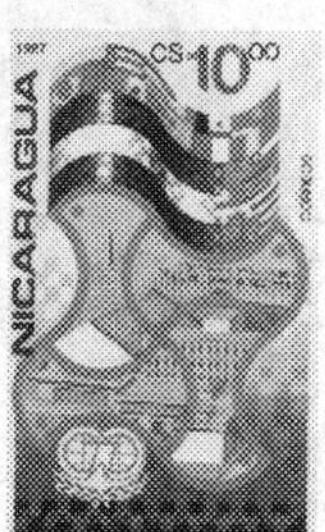

77th Interparliamentary Conf., Managua — A215

1987, Apr. 27
1616 A215 10cor multicolored 18 15

Prehistoric Creatures — A216

1987, May 25 ***Perf. 13***
1617 A216 10cor Mammoth 18 15
1618 A216 10cor Dimetrodon 18 15
1619 A216 10cor Triceratops 18 15
1620 A216 15cor Dinichthys 22 15
1621 A216 15cor Uintaterium 22 15
1622 A216 30cor Pteranodon 55 25
1623 A216 40cor Tilosaurus 75 32
Nos. 1617-1623 (7) 2.28 1.32

Nos. 1620-1623 are airmail.

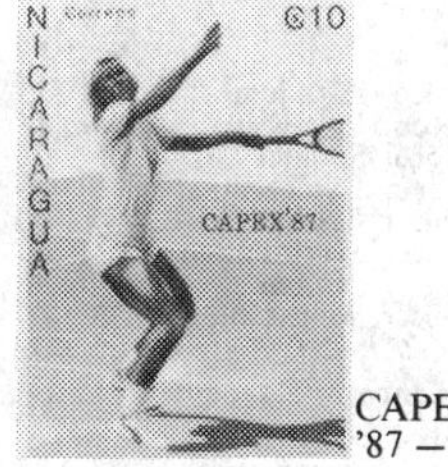

CAPEX '87 — A217

Various tennis players in action.

1987, June 2 ***Perf. 13***
1624 A217 10cor Male player 20 15
1625 A217 10cor Female player 20 15
1626 A217 15cor Player at net 30 15
1627 A217 15cor Female player, diff. 30 15
1628 A217 20cor multi 35 20
1629 A217 30cor multi 60 30
1630 A217 40cor multi 90 40
Nos. 1624-1630 (7) 2.85 1.50

Souvenir Sheet

Perf. 12½

1631 A217 110cor Doubles partners, vert. 2.25 2.25

Nos. 1626-1631 are airmail. No. 1631 contains one 32x40mm stamp.

Dogs — A218

1987, June 25 ***Perf. 13***
1632 A218 10cor Doberman pinscher 20 15
1633 A218 10cor Bulldog 20 15
1634 A218 15cor Pekinese 30 15
1635 A218 15cor Chow 30 15
1636 A218 20cor Chihuahua 40 20
1637 A218 30cor St. Bernard 60 30
1638 A218 40cor West Gotha spitz 85 40
Nos. 1632-1638 (7) 2.85 1.50

Nos. 1634-1638 are airmail.

Cacti A219

1987, July 25 ***Perf. 12½***
1639 A219 10cor Lophocereus schottii 20 15
1640 A219 10cor Opuntia acanthocarpa 20 15
1641 A219 10cor Echinocereus engelmanii 20 15
1642 A219 20cor Lemaireocereus thurberi 40 20
1643 A219 20cor Saguaros 40 20
1644 A219 30cor Opuntia fulgida 60 30
1645 A219 50cor Opuntia ficus 1.00 50
Nos. 1639-1645 (7) 3.00 1.65

Nos. 1642-1645 are airmail.

10th Pan American Games, Indianapolis — A220

1987, Aug. 7 ***Perf. 13***

1646 A220 10cor High jump 30 15
1647 A220 10cor Volleyball 30 15
1648 A220 15cor Sprinter 45 22
1649 A220 15cor Gymnastics 45 22
1650 A220 20cor Baseball 60 30
1651 A220 30cor Synchronized swimming 90 45
1652 A220 40cor Weightlifting 1.25 60
Nos. 1646-1652 (7) 4.25 2.09

Souvenir Sheet

1653 A220 110cor Rhythmic gymnastics 2.25 2.25

Nos. 1648-1653 are airmail. No. 1653 contains one 32x40mm stamp. Nos. 1651-1653 are vert.

Satellites A221

1987, Oct. 4

1654 A221 10cor Sputnik 20 15
1655 A221 10cor Cosmos 20 15
1656 A221 15cor Proton 30 15
1657 A221 25cor Meteor 50 22
1658 A221 25cor Luna 50 22
1659 A221 30cor Electron 60 30
1660 A221 50cor Mars 1 90 50
Nos. 1654-1660 (7) 3.20 1.69

Cosmonauts' Day. Nos. 1656-1660 are airmail.

Fish A222

Designs: No. 1661, Tarpon atlanticus. No. 1662, Cichlasoma managuense. No. 1663, Atractoteus tropicus. No. 1664, Astyana fasciatus. No. 1665, Cichlasoma citrimellum. 20cor, Cichlosoma dowi. 50cor, Caracharhinus nicaraguensis.

1987, Oct. 18 ***Perf. 12½***

1661 A222 10cor multicolored 20 15
1662 A222 10cor multicolored 20 15
1663 A222 10cor multicolored 20 15
1664 A222 15cor multicolored 30 15
1665 A222 15cor multicolored 30 15
1666 A222 20cor multicolored 40 20
1667 A222 50cor multicolored 1.00 50
Nos. 1661-1667 (7) 2.60 1.45

Nos. 1663-1667 are airmail.

October Revolution, 70th Anniv. — A223

Designs: 30cor, Cruiser Aurora, horiz. 50cor, USSR natl. arms.

1987, Nov. 7 ***Perf. 13***

1668 A223 10cor multicolored 25 15
1669 A223 30cor multicolored 70 35
1670 A223 50cor multicolored 1.25 60

Nos. 1669-1670 are airmail.

Christmas Paintings by L. Saenz — A224

1987, Nov. 15 ***Perf. 13***

1671 A224 10cor Nativity 15 15
1672 A224 20cor Adoration of the Magi 30 15
1673 A224 25cor Adoration of the Magi, diff. 35 18
1674 A224 50cor Nativity, diff. 75 35

1988 Winter Olymmpics, Calgary — A225

1988, Jan. 30 **Litho.** ***Perf. 12½***

1675 A225 10cor Biathlon 20 15
1676 A225 10cor Cross-country skiing, vert. 20 15
1677 A225 15cor Hockey, vert. 40 15
1678 A225 20cor Women's figure skating, vert. 55 20
1679 A225 25cor Slalom skiing, vert. 70 30
1680 A225 30cor Ski jumping 80 40
1681 A225 40cor Men's downhill skiing, vert. 1.10 50
Nos. 1675-1681 (7) 3.95 1.85

Souvenir Sheet
Perf. 13

1682 A225 100cor Pairs figure skating 2.00 2.00

Nos. 1675-1681 printed with se-tenant label showing Canadian flag and wildlife.
No. 1682 contains one 40x32mm stamp.

Nicaraguan Journalists Assoc., 10th Anniv. — A226

Design: 5cor, Churches of St. Francis Xavier and Fatima, and speaker addressing journalists, horiz.

1988, Feb. 10

1683 A226 1cor shown 15 15
1684 A226 5cor multicolored 75 40

No. 1684 is airmail.

1988 Summer Olympics, Seoul — A227

1988, Feb. 28

1685 A227 10cor Gymnastics 20 15
1686 A227 10cor Basketball 20 15
1687 A227 15cor Volleyball 40 15
1688 A227 20cor Long jump 55 20
1689 A227 25cor Soccer 70 25
1690 A227 30cor Water polo 80 40
1691 A227 40cor Boxing 1.10 50
Nos. 1685-1691 (7) 3.95 1.80

Souvenir Sheet

1692 A227 100cor Baseball 2.00 2.00

No. 1692 contains one 40x32mm stamp.

European Soccer Championships, Essen — A228

Designs: Various soccer players in action.

Perf. 13x12½, 12½x13

1988, Apr. 14

1693 A228 50c multicolored 15 15
1694 A228 1cor multicolored 15 15
1695 A228 2cor multi, vert. 25 15
1696 A228 3cor multi, vert. 40 22
1697 A228 4cor multi, vert. 55 25
1698 A228 5cor multi, vert. 75 35
1699 A228 6cor multicolored 85 40
Nos. 1693-1699 (7) 3.10 1.67

Souvenir Sheet
Perf. 13

1700 A228 15cor multi, vert. 2.00 2.00

Nos. 1695-1700 are airmail. No. 1700 contains one 32x40mm stamp.

Sandanista Revolution, 9th Anniv. — A229

1988, July 19 ***Perf. 13***

1701 A229 1cor shown 15 15
1702 A229 5cor Volcanoes, dove 60 30

No. 1702 is airmail.

Animals — A230

1988, Mar. 3 ***Perf. 13x12½***

1703 A230 10c Bear, cub 15 15
1704 A230 15c Lion, cubs 15 15
1705 A230 25c Spaniel, pups 15 15
1706 A230 50c Wild boars 15 15
1707 A230 4cor Cheetah, cubs 85 35
1708 A230 7cor Hyenas 1.25 70
1709 A230 8cor Fox, kit 1.50 80
Nos. 1703-1709 (7) 4.20 2.45

Souvenir Sheet
Perf. 12½

1710 A230 15cor House cat, kittens, vert. 2.00 1.65

Nos. 1707-1710 are airmail. No. 1710 contains one 32x40mm stamp.

Helicopters — A231

Illustration reduced.

1988, June 1 ***Perf. 12½x12***

1711 A231 4cor B-206B-JRIII 15 15
1712 A231 12cor BK-117A-3 20 15
1713 A231 16cor B-360 28 15
1714 A231 20cor 109-MRII 35 18
1715 A231 24cor S-61 42 20
1716 A231 28cor SA-365N-D2 50 25
1717 A231 56cor S-76 1.00 50
Nos. 1711-1717 (7) 2.90 1.58

Souvenir Sheet
Perf. 13

1718 A231 120cor NH-90 2.50 2.50

Nos. 1712-1718 are airmail. No. 1718 contains one 40x32mm stamp.

Shells — A232

1988, Sept. 20 ***Perf. 13***

1719 A232 4cor Strombus pugilis 15 15
1720 A232 12cor Polymita picta 24 15
1721 A232 16cor Architectonica maximum 32 16
1722 A232 20cor Pectens laqueatus 40 20
1723 A232 24cor Guildfordia triumphans 50 24
1724 A232 28cor Ranella pustulosa 55 32
1725 A232 50cor Trochus maculatus 1.00 50
Nos. 1719-1725 (7) 3.16 1.72

Nos. 1720-1725 are airmail.

Insects A233

1988, Nov. 10

1726 A233 4cor Chrysina macropus 15 15
1727 A233 12cor Plusiotis victoriana 25 15
1728 A233 16cor Ceratotrupes bolivari 35 16
1729 A233 20cor Gymnetosoma stellata 45 20
1730 A233 24cor Euphoria lineoligera 55 25
1731 A233 28cor Euphoria candezei 60 30
1732 A233 50cor Sulcophanaeus chryseicollis 1.10 50
Nos. 1726-1732 (7) 3.45 1.71

Nos. 1727-1732 are airmail.

Heroes of the Revolution — A234

Designs: 4cor, Casimiro Sotelo Montenegro. 12cor, Ricardo Morales Aviles. 16cor, Silvio Mayorga Delgado. 20cor, Pedro Arauz Palacios. 24cor, Oscar A. Turcios Chavarrias. 28cor, Julio C. Buitrago Urroz. 50cor, Jose B. Escobar Perez. 100cor, Eduardo E. Contreras Escobar.

1988, Aug. 27 ***Perf. 12½x12***

1733	A234	4cor sky blue	15	15
1734	A234	12cor red lilac	24	15
1735	A234	16cor yel grn	32	16
1736	A234	20cor org brown	40	20
1737	A234	24cor brown	45	24
1738	A234	28cor purple	55	32
1739	A234	50cor henna brown	95	50
1740	A234	100cor plum	1.90	95
		Nos. 1733-1740 (8)	4.96	2.67

Nos. 1734-1740 are airmail.

Flowers — A235

Designs: 4cor, Acacia baileyana. 12cor, Anigozanthos manglesii. 16cor, Telopia speciosissima. 20cor, Eucalyptus ficifolia. 24cor, Boronia heterophylla. 28cor, Callistemon speciosus. 30cor, Nymphaea caerulea, horiz. 50cor, Clianthus formosus.

1988, Aug. 30 ***Perf. 13***

1741	A235	4cor multicolored	15	15
1742	A235	12cor multicolored	24	15
1743	A235	16cor multicolored	32	16
1744	A235	20cor multicolored	40	20
1745	A235	24cor multicolored	45	24
1746	A235	28cor multicolored	55	48
1747	A235	30cor multicolored	60	30
1748	A235	50cor multicolored	1.00	45
		Nos. 1741-1748 (8)	3.71	2.13

Nos. 1742-1748 are airmail.

Discovery of America, 500th Anniv. (in 1992) — A236

Pre-Columbian Art: 4cor, Zapotec funeral urn. 12cor, Mochica ceramic kneeling man. 16cor, Mochica ceramic head. 20cor, Taina ceramic vase. 28cor, Nazca cup, horiz. 100cor, Inca pipe, horiz. 120cor, Aztec ceramic vessel, horiz.

Perf. 12x12½, 12½x12

1988, Oct. 12

1749	A236	4cor multicolored	15	15
1750	A236	12cor multicolored	24	15
1751	A236	16cor multicolored	32	16
1752	A236	20cor multicolored	40	20
1753	A236	28cor multicolored	55	28
1754	A236	100cor multicolored	1.90	1.00
		Nos. 1749-1754 (6)	3.56	1.94

Souvenir Sheet

Perf. 13x13½

1755	A236	120cor multicolored	2.25	1.10

Nos. 1750-1755 are airmail. Nos. 1749-1754 printed with se-tenant label. No. 1755 contains one 40x32mm stamp.

Ruben Dario — A237

1988, Oct. 12 ***Perf. 12x12½***

1756	A237	25cor multicolored	45	20

Publication of "Blue," centenary. Printed se-tenant with label.

Tourism — A238

1989, Feb. 5 ***Perf. 12½x12***

1757	A238	4cor Pochomil	15	15
1758	A238	12cor Granada	24	16
1759	A238	20cor Olof Palme Convention Center	40	20
1760	A238	24cor Masaya Volcano Natl. Park	45	24
1761	A238	28cor La Boquita	55	25
1762	A238	30cor Xiloa	60	25
1763	A238	50cor Hotels of Managua	1.00	45
		Nos. 1757-1763 (7)	3.39	1.70

Souvenir Sheet

Perf. 13

1764	A238	160cor Montelimar	2.00	2.00

Nos. 1758-1764 are airmail. No. 1764 contains one 40x32mm stamp.

French Revolution, Bicentennial A240

Designs: 50cor, Procession of the Estates General, Versailles. 300cor, Oath of the Tennis Court. 600cor, 14th of July, vert. 1000cor, Dancing Around the Liberty Tree. 2000cor, Liberty Guiding the People, vert. 3000cor, Storming the Bastille. 5000cor, Lafayette Swearing Allegiance to the Constitution, vert. 9000cor, La Marseillaise, vert.

Perf. 12½x13 (50cor), 13x12½ (600, 2000cor), 12½

1989, July 14

Sizes: 50cor, 40x25mm

600cor, 2000cor, 33x44mm

1773	A240	50cor multicolored	15	15
1774	A240	300cor shown	15	15
1775	A240	600cor multicolored	16	15
1776	A240	1000cor multicolored	28	15
1777	A240	2000cor multicolored	55	28
1778	A240	3000cor multicolored	90	42
1779	A240	5000cor multicolored	1.40	65
		Nos. 1773-1779 (7)	3.59	1.95

Souvenir Sheet

Perf. 12½

1780	A240	9000cor multicolored	2.25	2.25

Philexfrance '89. #1774-1780 are airmail. #1780 contains one 32x40mm stamp.

Ships A241

Designs: 500cor, *Director.* 1000cor, *Independence.* 3000cor, *Orizaba.* 5000cor, SS *Lewis.* 10,000cor, *Golden Rule.* 30,000cor, *Santiago de Cuba.* 75,000cor, *Bahia de Corinto.* 100,000cor, *North Star.*

1990, Apr. 3 ***Perf. 12½x12***

1781	A241	500cor multi	15	15
1782	A241	1000cor multi	15	15
1783	A241	3000cor multi	15	15
1784	A241	5000cor multi	15	15
1785	A241	10,000cor multi	20	15
1786	A241	30,000cor multi	60	30
1787	A241	100,000cor multi	2.00	1.00
		Nos. 1781-1788 (8)	4.90	3.55

Souvenir Sheet

Perf. 12½

1788	A241	75,000cor multi	1.50	1.50

Stamp World London '90. No. 1788 contains one 32x40mm stamp.

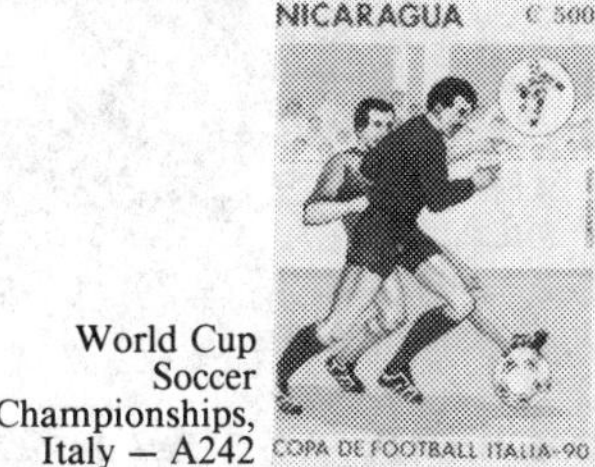

World Cup Soccer Championships, Italy — A242

Designs: Various soccer players in action.

1990, Apr. 30 ***Perf. 13***

1789	A242	500cor multi	15	15
1790	A242	1000cor multi	15	15
1791	A242	3000cor multi	15	15
1792	A242	5000cor multi	15	15
1793	A242	10,000cor multi	30	15
1794	A242	30,000cor multi	85	42
1795	A242	100,000cor multi	3.00	1.50
		Nos. 1789-1795 (7)	4.75	2.67

Souvenir Sheet

Perf. 12½

1796	A242	75,000cor multi	4.00	4.00

No. 1796 contains one 32x40mm stamp.

1992 Winter Olympics, Albertville — A243

Designs: 500cor, Ski jumping. 1000cor, Downhill skiing. 3000cor, Figure skating, vert. 5000cor, Speed skating, vert. 10,000cor, Biathlon, vert. 30,000cor, Cross country skiing, vert. 75,000cor, Two-man bobsled, vert. 100,000cor, Ice hockey, vert.

1990, July 25 ***Perf. 13***

1797	A243	500cor multi	15	15
1798	A243	1000cor multi	15	15
1799	A243	3000cor multi	15	15
1800	A243	5000cor multi	15	15
1801	A243	10,000cor multi	30	15
1802	A243	30,000cor multi	90	45
1803	A243	100,000cor multi	3.00	1.50
		Nos. 1797-1803 (7)	4.80	2.70

Souvenir Sheet

Perf. 12½

1804	A243	75,000cor multi	2.25	2.25

No. 1804 contains one 32x40mm stamp.

1992 Summer Olympics, Barcelona A244

Designs: 500cor, Javelin. 1000cor, Steeplechase. 3000cor, Handball. 5000cor, Basketball. 10,000cor, Gymnastics. 30,000cor, Cycling. 75,000cor, Soccer. 100,000cor, Boxing, horiz.

1990, Aug. 10 ***Perf. 13***

1805	A244	500cor multi	15	15
1806	A244	1000cor multi	15	15
1807	A244	3000cor multi	15	15
1808	A244	5000cor multi	16	15
1809	A244	10,000cor multi	32	16
1810	A244	30,000cor multi	95	48
1811	A244	100,000cor multi	3.25	1.65
		Nos. 1805-1811 (7)	5.13	2.89

Souvenir Sheet

1812	A244	75,000cor multi	2.50	2.50

No. 1812 contains one 32x40mm stamp.

Birds A245

Designs: No. 1813, Apteryx owenii. No. 1814, Notornis mantelli. 10c, Cyanoramphus novaezelandiae. 20c, Gallirallus australis. 30c, Rhynochetus jubatus, vert. 60c, Nestor notabilis. 70c, Strigops habroptilus. 1.50cor, Cygnus atratus.

1990, Aug. 14 **Litho.** ***Perf. 12½***

1813	A245	5c multicolored	15	15
1814	A245	5c multicolored	15	15
1815	A245	10c multicolored	20	15
1816	A245	20c multicolored	42	20
1817	A245	30c multicolored	65	32
1818	A245	60c multicolored	1.30	65
1819	A245	70c multicolored	1.50	75
		Nos. 1813-1819 (7)	4.37	2.37

Souvenir Sheet

1820	A245	1.50cor multicolored	3.25	1.60

New Zealand '90, Intl. Philatelic Exhibition.

Fauna A246

1990, Oct. 10

1821	A246	5c Panthera onca	15	15
1822	A246	5c Felis pardalis, vert.	15	15
1823	A246	10c Atelles geoffrogi, vert.	20	15
1824	A246	20c Tapirus bairdi	42	20
1825	A246	30c Dasypus novencintus	65	32
1826	A246	60c Canis latrans	1.30	65
1827	A246	70c Choloepus hoffmanni	1.50	75
		Nos. 1821-1827 (7)	4.37	2.37

FAO, 45th anniv.

Flower Type of 1983 Redrawn Without Date

1991, Apr. 24 **Litho.** ***Perf. 14x13½***

Size: 19x22mm

1828	A151	1cor like #1220	40	15
1829	A151	2cor like #1212	80	15
1830	A151	3cor like #1218	1.20	15
1831	A151	4cor like #1219	1.60	15
1832	A151	5cor like #1217	2.00	15
1833	A151	6cor like #1210	2.40	15
1834	A151	7cor like #1216	2.80	15
1835	A151	8cor like #1215	3.20	15

1836 A151 9cor like #1211 3.60 15
1837 A151 10cor like #1221 4.00 15
1838 A151 11cor like #1214 4.40 15
1839 A151 12cor like #1222 4.80 15
1840 A151 13cor like #1213 5.20 15
1841 A151 14cor like #1224 5.60 15
1842 A151 15cor like #1223 6.00 15
1843 A151 16cor like #1209 6.40 15
Nos. 1828-1843 (16) 54.40
Set value 1.25

Dr. Pedro Joaquin Chamorro — A247

1991, Apr. 25 ***Perf. 14½x14***
1844 A247 2.25cor multicolored 90 45

1990 World Cup Soccer Championships, Italy — A248

Designs: No. 1845, Two players. No. 1846, Four players, vert. 50c, Two players, referee. 1cor, Germany, five players, vert. 1.50cor, One player, vert. 3cor, Argentina, five players, vert. 3.50cor, Italian players. 7.50cor, German team with trophy.

Perf. 14x14½, 14½x14
1991, July 16
1845 A248 25c multicolored 15 15
1846 A248 25c multicolored 15 15
1847 A248 50c multicolored 20 15
1848 A248 1cor multicolored 40 20
1849 A248 1.50cor multicolored 60 30
1850 A248 3cor multicolored 1.20 60
1851 A248 3.50cor multicolored 1.40 70
Nos. 1845-1851 (7) 4.10 2.25

Souvenir Sheet
1852 A248 7.50cor multicolored 3.00 1.50

Butterflies — A249

Designs: No. 1853, Prepona praeneste. No. 1854, Anartia fatima. 50c, Eryphanis aesacus. 1cor, Heliconius melpomene. 1.50cor, Chlosyne janais. 3cor, Marpesia iole. 3.50cor, Metamorpha epaphus. 7.50cor, Morpho peleides.

1991, July 16 ***Perf. 14½x14***
1853 A249 25c multicolored 15 15
1854 A249 25c multicolored 15 15
1855 A249 50c multicolored 20 15
1856 A249 1cor multicolored 40 20
1857 A249 1.50cor multicolored 60 30
1858 A249 3cor multicolored 1.20 60
1859 A249 3.50cor multicolored 1.40 70
Nos. 1853-1859 (7) 4.10 2.25

Souvenir Sheet
1860 A249 7.50cor multicolored 3.00 1.50

Miniature Sheet

Fauna of Rainforest — A250

Designs: a, Yellow-headed amazon. b, Toucan. c, Scarlet macaw (lapa roja). d, Quetzal. e, Spider monkey (mono arana). f, Capuchin monkey . g, Sloth (cucala). h, Oropendola. i, Violet sabrewing (colibri violeta). j, Tamandua. k, Jaguarundi. l, Boa constrictor. m, Iguana. n, Jaguar. o, White-necked jacobin. p, Doxocopa clothilda. q, Dismorphia deione. r, Golden arrow-poison frog (rana venenosa). s, Callithomia hezia. t, Chameleon.

1991, Aug. 7 Litho. ***Perf. 14x14½***
1861 A250 2.25cor Sheet of 20, #a.-t. 19.00 9.50

America Issue — A251

1991, Oct. 12 ***Perf. 14½x14***
1862 A251 2.25cor Concepcion volcano 95 48

AIR POST STAMPS

Counterfeits exist of almost all scarce surcharges among Nos. C1-C66.

Regular Issues of 1914-28 Overprinted in Red

Correo Aéreo
1929
P.A.A.

1929, May 15 Unwmk. ***Perf. 12***
C1 A24 25c orange 1.75 1.75
a. Double overprint, one inverted 50.00
b. Inverted overprint 50.00
c. Double overprint 50.00
C2 A24 25c blk brn 2.25 2.25
a. Double overprint, one inverted 50.00
b. Double overprint 50.00
c. Inverted overprint 30.00

There are numerous varieties in the setting of the overprint. The most important are: Large "1" in "1929" and large "A" in "Aereo" and "P. A. A."

Similar Overprint on Regular Issue of 1929 in Red
C3 A24 25c dk vio 1.25 75
a. Double overprint 50.00
b. Inverted overprint 50.00
c. Double overprint, one inverted 50.00

The stamps in the bottom row of the sheet have the letters "P. A. A." larger than usual.

Airplanes over Mt. Momotombo AP1

1929, Dec. 15 **Engr.**
C4 AP1 25c olive blk 50 40
C5 AP1 50c blk brn 75 75
C6 AP1 1cor org red 1.00 1.00

See Nos. C18-C19, C164-C168. For surcharges and overprints see Nos. C7-C8, C14-C17, C25-C31, C106-C120, C135-C146, C150-C154, C169-C173, CO25-CO29.

No. C4 Surcharged in Red or Black

Vale
C$ 0.15

1930, May 15
C7 AP1 15c on 25c ol blk (R) 50 40
a. "$" inverted 3.50
b. Double surcharge (R + Bk) 7.00
c. As "b," red normal, blk invtd. 7.00
d. Double red surch., one inverted 7.00
C8 AP1 20c on 25c ol blk (Bk) 75 60
a. "$" inverted 7.00
b. Inverted surcharge 15.00

Nos. C1, C2 and C3 Surcharged in Green

Vale ₡ 0.15
1931

1931, June 7
C9 A24 15c on 25c org 50.00 50.00
C10 A24 15c on 25c blk brn 100.00 100.00
C11 A24 15c on 25c dk vio 15.00 15.00
c. Inverted surcharge 30.00
C12 A24 20c on 25c dk vio 10.00 10.00
c. Inverted surcharge 50.00
d. Double surcharge 50.00
C13 A24 20c on 25c blk brn *375.00*

No. C13 was not regularly issued.

"1391"
C9a A24 15c on 25c
C10a A24 15c on 25c
C11a A24 15c on 25c 60.00
d. As "a," inverted 400.00
C12a A24 20c on 25c 25.00
e. As "a," inverted 400.00
g. As "a," double 400.00
C13a A24 20c on 25c

"1921"
C9b A24 15c on 25c
C10b A24 15c on 25c 400.00
C11b A24 15c on 25c 60.00
e. As "b," inverted 400.00
C12b A24 20c on 25c 25.00
f. As "b," inverted 400.00
h. As "b," double 400.00
C13b A24 20c on 25c

Nos. C8, C4-C6 Surcharged in Blue

1931
₡ 0.15

1931, June
C14 AP1 15c on 20c on 25c 9.00 9.00
b. Blue surcharge inverted 25.00
c. "$" in blk, surch. invtd. 50.00
d. Blue surch. dbl., one invtd. 25.00
C15 AP1 15c on 25c 5.50 5.50
b. Blue surcharge inverted 25.00
c. Double surch., one invtd. 25.00
C16 AP1 15c on 50c 40.00 40.00
C17 AP1 15c on 1cor 100.00 100.00

"1391"
C14a AP1 15c on 20c on 25c 50.00
C15a AP1 15c on 25c 30.00
C16a AP1 15c on 50c 80.00
C17a AP1 15c on 1cor 225.00

Momotombo Type of 1929

1931, July 8
C18 AP1 15c deep violet 16 15
C19 AP1 20c deep green 42 38

Managua Post Office Before and After Earthquake AP2

Without gum, Soft porous paper

1932, Jan. 1 **Litho.** ***Perf. 11***
C20 AP2 15c lilac 1.50 *1.20*
a. 15c violet 22.50
b. Vert. pair, imperf. btwn. 22.50
C21 AP2 20c emerald 1.90
b. Horizontal pair, imperf. between 27.50
C22 AP2 25c yel brn 6.50
b. Vertical pair, imperf. between 60.00
C23 AP2 50c yel brn 8.00
C24 AP2 1cor dp car 12.00
a. Vert. or horiz. pair, imperf. btwn. 80.00
Nos. C20-C24 (5) 29.90

Sheets of 10. See note after No. 568.

For overprint and surcharges see Nos. C44-C46.

Reprints: see note following No. 568. Value $1 each.

Nos. C5 and C6 Surcharged in Red or Black

Vale ₡ 0.30

1932, July 12 ***Perf. 12***
C25 AP1 30c on 50c blk brn (Bk) 1.50 1.50
a. "Valc" 25.00
b. Double surcharge 15.00
c. Double surch., one inverted 15.00
d. Period omitted after "O" 25.00
e. As "a," double 300.00
C26 AP1 35c on 50c blk brn (R) 1.50 1.50
a. "Valc" 30.00
b. Double surcharge 12.00
c. Double surch., one inverted 12.00
d. As "a," double 300.00
C27 AP1 35c on 50c blk brn (Bk) 35.00 35.00
a. "Valc" 250.00
C28 AP1 40c on 1cor org red (Bk) 1.75 1.75
a. "Valc" 25.00
b. Double surcharge 15.00
c. Double surch., one inverted 15.00
d. Inverted surcharge 15.00
e. As "a," inverted 300.00
f. As "a," double 300.00
C29 AP1 55c on 1cor org red (R) 1.75 1.75
a. "Valc" 25.00
b. Double surcharge 12.00
c. Double surch., one inverted 12.00
d. Inverted surcharge 12.00
e. As "a," inverted 300.00
f. As "a," double 300.00
Nos. C25-C29 (5) 41.50 41.50

No. C18 Overprinted in Red

Semana Correo Aéreo
Internacional
11-17 Septiembre 1932

1932, Sept. 11
C30 AP1 15c dp vio 70.00 70.00
a. "Aerreo" 150.00 150.00
b. Invtd. "m" in "Septiembre" 150.00

International Air Mail Week.

No. C6 Surcharged

Inauguracion Interior
12 Octubre 1932
Vale ₡ 0.08

1932, Oct. 12
C31 AP1 8c on 1 cor org red 20.00 20.00
a. "1232" 30.00 30.00
b. Second "u" of "Inauguration" inverted 30.00 30.00

Issued for the inauguration of airmail service to the interior.

Regular Issue of 1932 Overprinted in Red

Correo Aéreo Interior
1932

1932, Oct. 24 ***Perf. 11½***
Without Gum
C32 A40 1c yel brn 20.00 20.00
a. Inverted overprint 125.00 125.00
C33 A40 2c carmine 20.00 20.00
a. Inverted overprint 125.00 125.00
b. Double overprint 100.00 100.00
C34 A40 3c ultra 9.50 9.50
a. Inverted overprint 150.00 150.00
b. As "a," vert. pair, imperf. btwn. 500.00
C35 A40 4c dp ultra 9.50 9.50
a. Inverted overprint 125.00 125.00
b. Double overprint 100.00 100.00
c. Vert. or horiz. pair, imperf. btwn. 300.00

C36 A40 5c yel brn 9.50 9.50
a. Inverted overprint 125.00 125.00
b. Vert. pair, imperf. btwn. 75.00
C37 A40 6c gray brn 9.50 9.50
a. Inverted overprint 100.00 100.00
C38 A40 50c green 9.00 9.00
a. Inverted overprint 125.00 125.00
C39 A40 1cor yellow 9.50 9.50
a. Inverted overprint 125.00 125.00
b. Horiz. pair, imperf. btwn. 200.00
Nos. C32-C39 (8) 96.50 96.50

Nos. C20 and C21 exist overprinted as C32-C39. The editors believe they were not regularly issued.

Surcharged in Red

Correo Aéreo Interior
1932
Vale ₡ 0.16

C40 A40 8c on 10c yel brn 9.00 9.00
a. Inverted surcharge 125.00 125.00
C41 A40 16c on 20c org 9.00 9.00
a. Inverted surcharge 125.00 125.00
C42 A40 24c on 25c dp vio 9.00 9.00
a. Inverted surcharge 125.00 125.00
b. Horiz. pair, imperf. vert. 300.00

Surcharged in Red as No. C40 but without the word "Vale"

C43 A40 80c on 10c yel brn 45.00 45.00
a. Inverted surcharge 125.00 125.00
b. Horiz. pair, imperf. vert. 300.00

No. C22 Overprinted in Red

Interior—1932

C44 AP2 25c yel brn 8.00 8.00
a. Inverted overprint 125.00 125.00

Nos. C23 and C24 Surcharged in Red

Interior—1932
Vale ₡ 0.32

C45 AP2 32c on 50c yel brn 9.50 9.50
a. Inverted surcharge 125.00 125.00
b. "Interior-1932" inverted 150.00 150.00
c. "Vale $0.32" inverted 150.00 150.00
d. Horiz. pair, imperf. btwn. 200.00
C46 AP2 40c on 1cor car 7.00 7.00
a. Inverted surcharge 125.00 125.00
b. "Vale $0.40" inverted 200.00 200.00

Nos. 557-558 Overprinted in Black like Nos. C32 to C39

1932, Nov. 16

C47 A40 1c yel brn 25.00 22.50
a. "1232" 45.00 45.00
b. Inverted overprint 125.00 125.00
c. Double ovpt., one invtd. 125.00 125.00
d. As "a," inverted 500.00
C48 A40 2c dp car 20.00 17.50
a. "1232" 45.00 45.00
b. Inverted overprint 125.00 125.00
c. As "a," inverted 500.00

Excellent counterfeits exist of Nos. C27, C30-C48. Forged overprints and surcharges as on Nos. C32-C48 exist on reprints of Nos. C20-C24.

Regular Issue of 1914-32 Surcharged in Black

Correo Aéreo
Interior-1932
Vale ₡ 0.01

1932 ***Perf. 12***

C49 A25 1c on 2c brt rose 35 30
C50 A24 2c on 3c lt bl 35 30
C51 A25 3c on 4c dk bl 35 30
C52 A24 4c on 5c gray brn 35 30
C53 A25 5c on 6c ol brn 35 30
C54 A25 6c on 10c lt brn 35 30
a. Double surcharge 4.00
C55 A24 8c on 15c org red 35 30
C56 A25 16c on 20c org 35 35
C57 A24 24c on 25c dk vio 1.40 1.00
C58 A24 25c on 25c dk vio 1.40 1.00
a. Double surcharge 25.00
C59 A25 32c on 50c grn 1.40 1.25
C60 A25 40vc on 50c grn 1.60 1.40
C61 A25 50c on 1cor yel 2.25 2.25
C62 A25 1cor on 1cor yel 3.00 3.00
Nos. C49-C62 (14) 13.85 12.35

Nos. C49-C62 exist with inverted surcharge.
In addition to C49 to C62, four other stamps, Type A25, exist with this surcharge.
40c on 50c bister brown, black surcharge.
1cor on 2c bright rose, black surcharge.
1cor on 1cor yellow, red surcharge.
1cor on 1cor dull violet, black surcharge.
The editors believe they were not regularly issued.

Surcharged on Nos. 548, 547

1932

C65 A24 24c on 25c dk vio 45.00 45.00
C66 A24 25c on 25c blk brn 50.00 50.00

Counterfeits of Nos. C65 and C66 are plentiful.

Rivas Railroad Issue

La Chocolata Cut
AP3

El Nacascola — AP4

Designs: 25c, Cuesta cut. 50c, Mole of San Juan del Sur. 1cor, View of El Estero.

1932, Dec. **Litho.**

Soft porous paper

C67 AP3 15c dk vio 20.00
C68 AP4 20c bl grn 20.00
C69 AP4 25c dk brn 20.00
C70 AP4 50c blk brn 20.00
C71 AP4 1cor rose red 20.00
Nos. C67-C71 (5) 100.00

Issued in commemoration of the inauguration of the railroad from San Jorge to San Juan del Sur December 18, 1932. Printed in sheets of four, without gum.

Reprints: see note following No. 574. Value, $1 each.

Leon-Sauce Railroad Issue

"Fill" at Santa Lucia River
AP5

Designs: 15c, Bridge at Santa Lucia. 25c, Malpaicillo Station. 50c, Panoramic view. 1cor, San Andres.

1932, Dec. 30

Soft porous paper

C72 AP5 15c purple 20.00
C73 AP5 20c bl grn 20.00
C74 AP5 25c dk brn 20.00
C75 AP5 50c blk brn 20.00
C76 AP5 1cor rose red 20.00
Nos. C72-C76 (5) 100.00

Issued to commemorate the inauguration of the railroad from Leon to El Sauce, Dec. 30, 1932. Sheets of 4, without gum.

Reprints: see note following No. 579. Value, $16 each.

Flag of the Race Issue

1933, Aug. 3 **Litho.** ***Rouletted 9***

Without gum

C77 A43 1c dk brn 1.50 1.50
C78 A43 2c red vio 1.50 1.50
C79 A43 4c violet 2.50 2.25
C80 A43 5c dl bl 2.25 2.25
C81 A43 6c vio bl 2.25 2.25
C82 A43 8c dp brn 70 70
C83 A43 15c ol brn 70 70
C84 A43 20c yellow 2.25 2.25
a. Horiz. pair, imperf. btwn. 15.00
b. Horiz. pair, imperf. vert. 15.00
C85 A43 25c orange 2.25 2.25
C86 A43 50c rose 2.25 2.25
C87 A43 1cor green 11.00 11.00
Nos. C77-C87 (11) 29.15 28.90

See note after No. 599. Printed in sheets of 10. *Reprints exist, shades differ from postage and official stamps.*

Imperf., Pairs

C78a A43 2c 14.00
C79a A43 4c 10.00
C81a A43 6c 10.00
C82a A43 8c 10.00
C83a A43 15c 10.00
C87a A43 1cor 30.00

AP7

1933, Nov. ***Perf. 12***

C88 AP7 10c bis brn 1.50 1.50
a. Vert. pair, imperf. between 35.00
C89 AP7 15c violet 1.20 1.20
a. Vert. pair, imperf. between 37.50
C90 AP7 25c red 1.40 1.40
a. Horiz. pair, imperf. between 22.50
C91 AP7 50c dp bl 1.50 1.50

International Air Post Week, Nov. 6-11, 1933. Printed in sheets of 4. Counterfeits exist.

Stamps and Types of 1928-31 Surcharged in Black

Correo Aéreo
Interior
Vale ₡ 0.01

1933, Nov. 3

C92 A25 1c on 2c grn 15 15
C93 A24 2c on 3c ol gray 15 15
C94 A25 3c on 4c car rose 15 15
C95 A24 4c on 5c lt bl 15 15
C96 A25 5c on 6c dk bl 15 15
C97 A25 6c on 10c ol brn 15 15
C98 A24 8c on 15c bis brn 20 15
C99 A25 16c on 20c brn 16 15
C100 A24 24c on 25c ver 15 15
C101 A24 25c on 25c org 22 16
C102 A25 32c on 50c vio 20 20
C103 A25 40c on 50c grn 20 15
C104 A25 50c on 1cor yel 16 15
C105 A25 1cor on 1cor org red 35 22
Set value 2.20 1.75

Nos. C100, C102-C105 exist without script control overprint. Value, each $1.50.

Type of Air Post Stamps of 1929 Surcharged in Black

Vale ₡ 0.30

1933, Oct. 28

C106 AP1 30c on 50c org red 22 15
C107 AP1 35c on 50c lt bl 25 16
C108 AP1 40c on 1cor yel 40 16
C109 AP1 55c on 1cor grn 30 22

No. C19 Surcharged in Red

Servicio
Centroamericano
Vale 10 centavos

1934, Mar. 31

C110 AP1 10c on 20c grn 30 25
a. Inverted surcharge 15.00
b. Double surcharge, one inverted 15.00
c. "Ceutroamericano" 10.00

No. C110 with black surcharge is believed to be of private origin.

No. C4 Surcharged in Red

Servicio
Centroamericano
Vale 10 centavos

1935, Aug.

C111 AP1 10c on 25c ol blk 25 25
a. Small "v" in "vale" (R) 5.00
b. "centrvos" (R) 5.00
c. Double surcharge (R) 25.00
d. Inverted surcharge (R) 25.00
g. As "a," inverted 400.00
h. As "a," double 400.00

No. C111 with blue surcharge is believed to be private origin.

The editors do not recognize the Nicaraguan air post stamps overprinted in red "VALIDO 1935" in two lines and with or without script control marks as having been issued primarily for postal purposes.

Nos C4-C6, C18-C19 Overprinted Vertically in Blue, Reading Up:

1935-36

C112 AP1 15c dp vio 1.00 1.00
C113 AP1 20c dp grn 1.75 1.75
C114 AP1 25c ol blk 2.25 2.25
C115 AP1 50c blk brn 5.00 5.00
C116 AP1 1cor org red 40.00 40.00
Nos. C112-C116 (5) 50.00 50.00

Same Overprint on Nos. C106-C109 Reading Up or Down

C117 AP1 30c on 50c org red 1.50 1.40
C118 AP1 35c on 50c lt bl 6.50 6.50
C119 AP1 40c on 1cor yel 6.50 6.50
C120 AP1 55c on 1cor grn 6.50 6.50

Same Overprint in Red on Nos. C92-C105

1936

C121 A25 1c on 2c grn 15 15
C122 A24 2c on 3c ol gray 16 16
C123 A25 3c on 4c car rose 16 16
C124 A24 4c on 5c lt bl 16 16
C125 A25 5c on 6c dk bl 16 16
C126 A25 6c on 10c ol brn 16 16
C127 A24 8c on 15c bis brn 16 16
C128 A25 16c on 20c brn 25 25
C129 A24 24c on 25c ver 35 28
C130 A24 25c on 25c org 22 22
C131 A25 32c on 50c vio 16 16
C132 A25 40c on 50c grn 55 50
C133 A25 50c on 1cor yel 40 25
C134 A25 1cor on 1cor org red 1.40 65
Nos. C121-C134 (14) 4.44 3.42

Nos. C121 to C134 are handstamped with script control mark.

Overprint Reading Down on No. C110

C135 AP1 10c on 20c grn *350.00*

This stamp has been extensively counterfeited.

Overprinted in Red on Nos. C4 to C6, C18 and C19

C136 AP1 15c dp vio 55 15
C137 AP1 20c dp grn 65 60
C138 AP1 25c ol blk 65 55
C139 AP1 50c blk brn 55 55
C140 AP1 1cor org red 1.10 55

On Nos. C106 to C109

C141 AP1 30c on 50c org red 65 60
C142 AP1 35c on 50c lt bl 65 42
C143 AP1 40c on 1cor yel 65 55
C144 AP1 55c on 1cor grn 65 50

Same Overprint in Red or Blue on No. C111 Reading Up or Down

C145 AP1 10c on 25c ol blk (R), down 55 45
a. "Centrvos" 25.00
C146 AP1 10c on 25c ol blk (Bl), up 1.20 1.00
a. "Centrvos" 25.00
Nos. C136-C146 (11) 7.85 5.92

Overprint on No. C145 is at right, on No. C146 in center.

Nos. C92, C93 and C98 Overprinted in Black

Resello
1936

1936

C147	A25	1c on 2c grn	20	16
C148	A24	2c on 3c ol gray	15	15
a.		"Resello 1936" dbl., one invtd.	2.50	
C149	A24	8c on 15c bis brn	22	22

With script control handstamp.

Nos. C5 and C6 Surcharged in Red

1936
Vale
Quince Centavos

C150	AP1	15c on 50c blk brn	20	16
C151	AP1	15c on 1cor org red	20	16

Nos. C18 and C19 Overprinted in Carmine — RESELLO - 1935

C152	AP1	15c dp vio	35	16
C153	AP1	20c dp grn	35	25

Overprint reading up or down.

No. C4 Surcharged and Overprinted in Red

Servicio
Centroamericano
Vale diez centavos
and
RESELLO - 1935

C154	AP1	10c on 25c ol blk	30	30
a.		Surch. and ovpt. inverted	3.50	

Same Overprint in Carmine on Nos. C92 to C99

C155	A25	1c on 2c grn	15	15
C156	A24	2c on 3c ol gray	65	65
C157	A25	3c on 4c car rose	15	15
C158	A24	4c on 5c lt bl	15	15
C159	A25	5c on 6c dk bl	15	15
C160	A25	6c on 10c ol brn	15	15
C161	A24	8c on 15c bis brn	15	15
C162	A25	16c on 20c brn	15	15
		Set value	1.40	1.40

No. 518 Overprinted in Black

Correo Aéreo
Centro-Americano
Resello 1936

C163	A25	10c lt brn	16	16
a.		Overprint inverted	2.25	
b.		Double overprint	2.25	

Two fonts are found in the sheet of No. C163.

Momotombo Type of 1929

1937

C164	AP1	15c yel org	15	15
C165	AP1	20c org red	15	15
C166	AP1	25c black	15	15
C167	AP1	50c violet	22	15
C168	AP1	1cor orange	55	15
		Nos. C164-C168 (5)	1.22	
		Set value		42

Surcharged in Black — Vale ₡ 0.30

1937

C169	AP1	30c on 50c car rose	16	15
C170	AP1	35c on 50c ol grn	20	15
C171	AP1	40c on 1cor grn	22	15
C172	AP1	55c on 1cor bl	20	20
		Set value		42

No. C168 Surcharged in Violet

Servicio
Centroamericano
Vale Diez Centavos

1937 Unwmk. *Perf. 12*

C173	AP1	10c on 1cor org	15	15
a.		"Centauos"	10.00	

No. C98 with Additional Overprint "1937"

C174	A24	8c on 15c bis brn	45	15
a.		"1937" double	6.50	

Nos. C92-C102 with Additional Overprint in Blue reading "HABILITADO 1937"

C175	A25	1c on 2c grn	15	15
a.		Blue overprint double	2.50	
C176	A24	2c on 3c ol gray	15	15
a.		Double surch., one inverted	2.50	
C177	A25	3c on 4c car rose	15	15
C178	A24	4c on 5c lt bl	15	15
C179	A25	5c on 6c dk bl	15	15
C180	A25	6c on 10c ol brn	15	15
C181	A24	8c on 15c bis brn	15	15
a.		"Habilitado 1937" double	3.50	
C182	A25	16c on 20c brn	16	16
a.		Double surcharge	2.50	
C183	A24	24c on 25c ver	16	16
C184	A24	25c on 25c org	22	20
C185	A25	32c on 50c vio	22	22
		Set value, #C175-C185	1.25	1.10

Map of Nicaragua AP8

For Foreign Postage

1937, July 30 Engr.

C186	AP8	10c green	15	15
C187	AP8	15c dp bl	15	15
C188	AP8	20c yellow	20	16
C189	AP8	25c bl vio	20	16
C190	AP8	30c rose car	22	20
C191	AP8	50c org yel	35	20
C192	AP8	1cor ol grn	70	55
		Nos. C186-C192 (7)	1.97	1.57

Presidential Palace AP9

For Domestic Postage

C193	AP9	1c rose car	15	15
C194	AP9	2c dp bl	15	15
C195	AP9	3c ol grn	15	15
C196	AP9	4c black	15	15
C197	AP9	5c dk vio	15	15
C198	AP9	6c chocolate	15	15
C199	AP9	8c bl vio	15	15
C200	AP9	16c org yel	22	20
C201	AP9	24c yellow	15	15
C202	AP9	25c yel grn	25	20
		Set value	1.32	1.00

No. C201 with green overprint "Union Panamericana 1890-1940" is of private origin.

Managua AP10

Designs: 15c, Presidential Palace. 20c, Map of South America. 25c, Map of Central America. 30c, Map of North America. 35c, Lagoon of Tiscapa, Managua. 40c, Road Scene. 45c, Park. 50c, Another park. 55c, Scene in San Juan del Sur. 75c, Tipitapa River. 1cor, Landscape.

Wmk. 209

1937, Sept. 17 Typo. *Perf. 11*

Center in Dark Blue

C203	AP10	10c yel grn	1.60	1.20
C204	AP10	15c orange	1.60	1.40
C205	AP10	20c red	1.00	1.00
C206	AP10	25c vio brn	1.00	1.00
C207	AP10	30c bl grn	1.00	1.00
a.		Great Lakes omitted	40.00	40.00
C208	AP10	35c lemon	50	45
C209	AP10	40c green	40	38
C210	AP10	45c brt vio	40	35
C211	AP10	50c rose lil	40	35
a.		Vert. pair, imperf. btwn.	140.00	
C212	AP10	55c lt bl	40	35
C213	AP10	75c gray grn	40	35

Center in Brown Red

C214	AP10	1cor dk bl	1.00	50
		Nos. C203-C214 (12)	9.70	8.33

150th anniv. of the Constitution of the US.

Diriangen — AP11

Designs: 4c, 10c, Nicarao. 5c, 15c, Bartolome de Las Casas. 8c, 20c, Columbus.

For Domestic Postage
Without gum

1937, Oct. 12 Unwmk. *Perf. 11*

C215	AP11	1c green	15	15
C216	AP11	4c brn car	15	15
C217	AP11	5c dk vio	15	15
a.		Without imprint	40	
C218	AP11	8c dp bl	15	15
a.		Without imprint	50	

For Foreign Postage
Wmk. 209
With Gum

C219	AP11	10c lt brn	15	15
C220	AP11	15c pale bl	15	15
a.		Without imprint	1.00	
C221	AP11	20c pale rose	16	15
		Set value, #C215-C221	75	65

Nos. C215-C221 printed in sheets of 4.

Imperf., Pair

C215a	AP11	1c	16	16
C216a	AP11	4c	20	20
C217b	AP11	5c	20	20
C218b	AP11	8c	20	
C219a	AP11	10c	20	20
C220b	AP11	15c	22	22
C221a	AP11	20c	35	35

Gen. Tomas Martinez — AP11a

Design: 10c, 15c, 25c, 50c, Gen. Anastasio Somoza.

For Domestic Postage
Without Gum

Perf. 11½, Imperf.

1938, Jan. 18 Typo. Unwmk.

Center in Black

C221B	AP11a	1c orange	20	20
C221C	AP11a	5c red vio	20	20
C221D	AP11a	8c dk bl	22	22
C221E	AP11a	16c brown	25	25
f.		Sheet of 4, 1c, 5c, 8c, 16c	1.25	1.25

For Foreign Postage

C221G	AP11a	10c green	22	20
C221H	AP11a	15c dk bl	25	25
C221J	AP11a	25c violet	42	40
C221K	AP11a	50c carmine	50	45
m.		Sheet of 4, 10c, 15c, 25c, 50c	2.00	2.00
		Nos. C221B-C221K (8)	2.26	2.17

75th anniv. of postal service in Nicaragua. Printed in sheets of four.

Stamps of type AP11a exist in changed colors and with inverted centers, double centers and frames printed on the back. These varieties were private fabrications.

Lake Managua AP12

President Anastasio Somoza — AP13

For Domestic Postage

1939 Unwmk. Engr. *Perf. 12½*

C222	AP12	2c dp bl	15	15
C223	AP12	3c green	15	15
C224	AP12	8c pale lil	15	15
C225	AP12	16c orange	15	15
C226	AP12	24c yellow	15	15
C227	AP12	32c dk grn	16	15
C228	AP12	50c dp rose	16	15

For Foreign Postage

C229	AP13	10c dk brn	15	15
C230	AP13	15c dk bl	15	15
C231	AP13	20c org yel	15	16
C232	AP13	25c dk pur	15	15
C233	AP13	30c lake	16	16
C234	AP13	50c dp org	25	20
C235	AP13	1cor dk ol grn	40	35
		Set value, #C222-C235	2.10	1.90

For Domestic Postage

Will Rogers and View of Managua AP14

Designs: 2c, Rogers standing beside plane. 3c, Leaving airport office. 4c, Rogers and US Marines. 5c, Managua after earthquake.

1939, Mar. 31 Engr. *Perf. 12*

C236	AP14	1c brt grn	15	15
C237	AP14	2c org red	15	15
C238	AP14	3c lt ultra	15	15
C239	AP14	4c dk bl	15	15
C240	AP14	5c rose car	15	15
		Set value	28	25

Will Rogers' flight to Managua after the earthquake, Mar. 31, 1931.

For surcharges see Nos. 686, 688.

Pres. Anastasio Somoza in US House of Representatives — AP19

President Somoza and US Capitol AP20

President Somoza, Tower of the Sun and Trylon and Perisphere AP21

For Domestic Postage

1940, Feb. 1

C241	AP19	4c red brn	15	15
C242	AP20	8c blk brn	15	15
C243	AP19	16c grnsh bl	15	15
C244	AP20	20c brt plum	50	30
C245	AP21	32c scarlet	16	16

For Foreign Postage

C246	AP19	25c dp bl	20	15
C247	AP19	30c black	20	15
C248	AP20	50c rose pink	45	38
C249	AP21	60c green	50	30

C250	AP19	65c dk vio brn	50	20
C251	AP19	90c ol grn	65	30
C252	AP21	1cor violet	1.00	55
		Nos. C241-C252 (12)	4.61	
		Set value		2.50

Visit of Pres. Somoza to US in 1939.
For surcharge see No. C636.

L. S. Rowe, Statue of Liberty, Nicaraguan Coastline, Flags of 21 American Republics, US Shield and Arms of Nicaragua — AP22

1940, Aug. 2 **Engr.** ***Perf. 12½***

C253	AP22	1.25cor multi	65	60

50th anniversary of Pan American Union.
For overprint see No. C493.

First Nicaraguan Postage Stamp and Sir Rowland Hill — AP23

1941, Apr. 4

C254	AP23	2cor brown	2.50	80
C255	AP23	3cor dk bl	8.25	1.40
C256	AP23	5cor carmine	22.50	3.50

Centenary of the first postage stamp.
Nos. C254-C256 imperf. are proofs.

Rubén Dario AP24

1941, Dec. 23

C257	AP24	20c pale lil	25	18
C258	AP24	35c yel grn	30	20
C259	AP24	40c org yel	40	22
C260	AP24	60c lt bl	65	30

25th anniversary of the death of Rubén Dario, poet and writer.

Catalogue values for unused stamps in this section, from this point to the end of the section, are for Never Hinged items.

"Victory" — AP25

1943, Dec. 8 ***Perf. 12***

C261	AP25	40c dk bl grn & cer	20	15
C262	AP25	60c lt bl & cer	30	15
		Set value		15

Issued to commemorate the second anniversary of Nicaragua's declaration of war against the Axis.

Red Cross — AP26

Cross and Globes — AP27

Red Cross Workers AP28

1944, Oct. 12 **Engr.**

C263	AP26	25c red lil & car	65	30
C264	AP27	50c ol brn & car	1.00	55
C265	AP28	1cor dk bl grn & car	2.00	2.00

80th anniversary of the International Red Cross Society.

Caravels of Columbus and Columbus Lighthouse AP29

Landing of Columbus AP30

1945, Sept. 1 ***Perf. 12½***

C266	AP29	20c dp grn & gray	15	15
C267	AP29	35c dk car & blk	35	30
C268	AP29	75c ol grn & rose pink	45	40
C269	AP29	90c brick red & aqua	80	75
C270	AP29	1cor blk & pale bl	90	30
C271	AP30	2.50cor dk bl & car rose	2.25	2.25
		Nos. C266-C271 (6)	4.90	4.15

Issued in honor of the discovery of America by Columbus and the Columbus Lighthouse near Ciudad Trujillo, Dominican Republic.

Franklin D. Roosevelt and Winston Churchill AP31

Roosevelt Signing Declaration of War Against Japan — AP32

Designs: 1cor, Gen. Henri Giraud, Roosevelt, Gen. Charles de Gaulle and Churchill. 3cor, Stalin, Roosevelt and Churchill. 5cor, Sculptured head of Roosevelt.

Engraved, Center Photogravure

1946, June 15 ***Perf. 12½***

Frame in Black

C272	AP31	25c orange	15	15
a.		Horiz. pair, imperf. btwn.	225.00	
b.		Imperf., pair	175.00	
C273	AP32	75c carmine	25	25
a.		Imperf., pair	175.00	
C274	AP31	1cor dk grn	40	40
C275	AP31	3cor violet	3.75	3.75
C276	AP32	5cor grnsh bl	5.00	5.00
		Nos. C272-C276 (5)	9.55	9.55

Issued to honor Franklin D. Roosevelt.

Projected Provincial Seminary — AP36

Designs: 20c, Communications Building. 35c, Sanitation Building. 90c, National Bank. 1cor, Municipal Building. 2.50cor, National Palace.

1947, Jan. 10

Frame in Black

C277	AP36	5c violet	15	15
a.		Imperf., pair	125.00	
C278	AP36	20c gray grn	15	15
C279	AP36	35c orange	20	18
C280	AP36	90c red lil	40	30
C281	AP36	1cor brown	60	45
C282	AP36	2.50cor rose lil	1.75	1.50
		Nos. C277-C282 (6)	3.25	2.73

City of Managua centenary.

Rubén Dario Monument — AP42

Designs: 6c, Tapir. 8c, Stone Highway. 10c, Genizaro Dam. 20c, Detail of Dario Monument. 25c, Sulphurous Lake of Nejapa. 35c, Mercedes Airport. 50c, Prinzapolka River delta. 1cor, Tipitapa Spa. 1.50cor, Tipitapa River. 5cor, United States Embassy. 10cor, Indian fruit vendor. 25cor, Franklin D. Roosevelt Monument.

Engraved, Center Photogravure

1947, Aug. 29 **Unwmk.** ***Perf. 12½***

C283	AP42	5c dk bl grn & rose car	15	15
C284	AP42	6c blk & yel	15	15
C285	AP42	8c car & ol	15	15
C286	AP42	10c brn & bl	18	15
C287	AP42	20c bl vio & org	30	30
C288	AP42	25c brn red & emer	35	35
C289	AP42	35c gray & bis	30	30
C290	AP42	50c pur & sep	25	25
C291	AP42	1cor blk & lil rose	75	75
C292	AP42	1.50cor red brn & aqua	80	80
C293	AP42	5cor choc & car rose	6.25	6.25
C294	AP42	10cor vio & dk brn	5.00	5.00
C295	AP42	25cor dk bl grn & yel	10.00	10.00
		Nos. C283-C295 (13)	24.63	24.60

The frames differ for each denomination.
For surcharge see No. C750.

Tennis — AP43

Designs: 2c, Soccer. 3c, Table tennis. 4c, Proposed stadium. 5c, Regatta. 15c, Basketball. 25c, Boxing. 30c, Baseball. 40c, Bicycling. 75c, Diving. 1cor, Pole vault. 2cor, Boy Scouts. 5cor, Softball.

1949, July **Photo.** ***Perf. 12***

C296	AP43	1c cerise	15	15
C297	AP43	2c ol gray	15	15
C298	AP43	3c scarlet	15	15
C299	AP43	4c dk bl gray	15	15
C300	AP43	5c aqua	30	15
C301	AP43	15c bl grn	90	15
C302	AP43	25c red vio	2.00	30
C303	AP43	30c red brn	1.75	30
C304	AP43	40c violet	45	30
C305	AP43	75c magenta	4.50	2.75
C306	AP43	1cor lt bl	5.00	1.35
C307	AP43	2cor brn ol	2.00	1.75
C308	AP43	5cor lt grn	2.25	2.25
a.		Set of 13 souvenir sheets of 4	125.00	125.00
		Nos. C296-C308 (13)	19.75	9.90

Issued to publicize the tenth World Series of Amateur Baseball, 1948.

Rowland Hill — AP44

Designs: 20c, Heinrich von Stephan. 25c, First UPU Bldg. 30c, UPU Bldg., Bern. 85c, UPU Monument. 1.10cor, Congress medal, obverse. 2.14cor, as 1.10cor, reverse.

1950, Nov. 23 **Engr.** ***Perf. 13***

Frames in Black

C309	AP44	16c cerise	15	15
C310	AP44	20c orange	15	15
C311	AP44	25c gray	20	20
C312	AP44	30c cerise	30	15
C313	AP44	85c dk bl grn	65	65
C314	AP44	1.10cor chnt brn	50	45
C315	AP44	2.14cor ol grn	2.25	2.25
		Nos. C309-C315 (7)	4.20	4.00

75th anniv. (in 1949) of the UPU.
Each denomination was also issued in a souvenir sheet containing four stamps and marginal inscriptions. Size: 126x114mm. Value, set of 7 sheets, $35.
For surcharges see Nos. C501, C758.

Queen Isabella I — AP45

Columbus' Ships — AP46

Designs: 2.80cor, Map. 3cor, Santa Maria. 3.60cor, Portrait facing right.

1952, June 25 **Unwmk.** ***Perf. 11½***

C316	AP45	2.30cor rose car	2.00	2.00
C317	AP45	2.80cor red org	1.75	1.75
C318	AP45	3cor green	2.00	2.00
C319	AP46	3.30cor lt bl	2.00	2.00
C320	AP45	3.60cor yel grn	2.25	2.25
a.		Souv. sheet of 5, #C316-C320	10.00	10.00
		Nos. C316-C320 (5)	10.00	10.00

Issued to commemorate the 500th anniversary of the birth of Queen Isabella I of Spain.
For overprint see No. C445.

Arms of ODECA AP47

Designs: 25c, ODECA Flag. 30c, Presidents of five Central American countries. 60c, ODECA Charter and Flags. 1cor, Map of Central America.

1953, Apr. 15 ***Perf. 13½x14***

C321	AP47	20c red lil	15	15
C322	AP47	25c lt bl	15	15
C323	AP47	30c sepia	20	15
C324	AP47	60c dk bl grn	30	25
C325	AP47	1cor dk vio	70	65
		Nos. C321-C325 (5)	1.50	1.35

Issued to commemorate the founding of the Organization of Central American States (ODECA).

Leonardo Arguello — AP48

Presidents: 5c, Gen. Jose Maria Moncada. 20c, Juan Bautista Sacasa. 25c, Gen. Jose Santos Zelaya. 30c, Gen. Anastasio Somoza. 35c, Gen. Tomas Martinez. 40c, Fernando Guzman. 45c, Vicente Cuadra. 50c, Pedro Joaquin Chamorro. 60c, Gen. Joaquin Zavala. 85c, Adan Cardenas. 1.10cor, Evaristo Carazo. 1.20cor, Roberto Sacasa.

Engraved (frames); Photogravure (heads)

1953, June 25 ***Perf. 12½***

Heads in Gray Black

C326	AP48	4c dp car	15	15
C327	AP48	5c dp org	15	15
C328	AP48	20c dk Prus bl	15	15
C329	AP48	25c blue	15	15
C330	AP48	30c red brn	15	15
C331	AP48	35c dp grn	18	18
C332	AP48	40c dk vio brn	22	18
C333	AP48	45c olive	22	22
C334	AP48	50c carmine	28	15
C335	AP48	60c ultra	30	22
C336	AP48	85c brown	38	35
C337	AP48	1.10cor purple	45	45
C338	AP48	1.20cor ol bis	45	45
		Set value	2.80	2.40

For surcharges see Nos. C363-C364, C757.

Torch and UN Emblem AP49

Capt. Dean L. Ray, USAF AP50

Designs: 4c, Raised hands. 5c, Candle and charter. 30c, Flags of Nicaragua and UN. 2cor, Globe. 3cor, Arms of Nicaragua. 5cor, Type A69 inscribed "Aereo."

1954, Apr. 30 **Engr.** ***Perf. 13½***

C339	AP49	3c rose pink	15	15
C340	AP49	4c dp org	15	15
C341	AP49	5c red	15	15
C342	AP49	30c cerise	1.00	20
C343	AP49	2cor magenta	1.35	1.00
C344	AP49	3cor org brn	2.50	1.75
C345	AP49	5cor brn vio	3.00	2.25
		Nos. C339-C345 (7)	8.30	5.65

Honoring the United Nations.
For overprint and surcharge see Nos. C366, C443.

Engraved; Center Photogravure

1954, Nov. 5 ***Perf. 13***

Designs: 15c, Sabre jet plane. 20c, Air Force emblem. 25c, National Air Force hangars. 30c, Gen. A. Somoza. 50c, AT-6's in formation. 1cor, Plane, type P-38.

Frame in Black

C346	AP50	10c gray	15	15
C347	AP50	15c gray	15	15
C348	AP50	20c claret	15	15
C349	AP50	25c red	15	15
C350	AP50	30c ultra	15	15
C351	AP50	50c blue	45	45
C352	AP50	1cor green	35	22
		Set value	1.25	95

Issued to honor the National Air Force.

Paul P. Harris — AP51

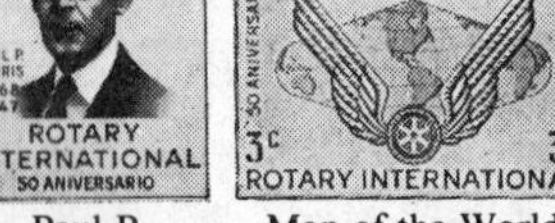

Map of the World and Rotary Emblem — AP52

Designs: 2c, 50c, Handclasp, Rotary emblem and globe. 4c, 30c, Rotary slogans and wreath. 5c, 25c, Flags of Nicaragua and Rotary.

Perf. 11½

1955, Aug. 30 **Unwmk.** **Photo.**

Granite Paper

C353	AP51	1c vermilion	15	15
C354	AP51	2c ultra	15	15
C355	AP52	3c pck grn	15	15
C356	AP51	4c violet	15	15
C357	AP51	5c org brn	15	15
C358	AP51	25c brt grnsh bl	20	18
C359	AP51	30c dl pur	15	15
C360	AP52	45c lil rose	35	30
C361	AP51	50c lt bl grn	25	20
C362	AP51	1cor ultra	35	35
a.		Souv. sheet of 5, #C358-C362	9.50	9.50
		Set value	1.50	1.35

Rotary International, 50th anniversary.
For surcharge see No. C365.

Nos. C331, C333, C360, C345 Surcharged in Green or Black

Conmemoración
Exposición Nacional
Febrero 4-16, 1956
₡ 0.15

Engraved, Photogravure

1956, Feb. 4 ***Perf. 13½x13, 11½***

C363	AP48	30c on 35c (G)	20	18
C364	AP48	30c on 45c (G)	20	18
C365	AP52	30c on 45c	20	15
C366	AP49	2cor on 5cor	80	75

National Exhibition, Feb. 4-16, 1956.
See note after No. 772.

Gen. Jose D. Estrada — AP53

The Stoning of Andres Castro — AP54

Designs: 1.50 cor, Emanuel Mongalo. 2.50 cor, Battle of Rivas. 10 cor, Com. Hiram Paulding.

1956, Sept. 14 **Engr.** ***Perf. 12½***

C367	AP53	30c dk car rose	15	15
C368	AP54	60c chocolate	15	15
C369	AP53	1.50cor green	30	30
C370	AP54	2.50cor dk ultra	50	50
C371	AP53	10cor red org	2.00	2.00
		Nos. C367-C371 (5)	3.10	3.10

Centenary of the National War.
For overprint and surcharge see Nos. C444, C751.

President Somoza — AP55

1957, Feb. 1 **Photo.** ***Perf. 14x13½***

Various Frames: Centers in Black

C372	AP55	15c gray blk	15	15
C373	AP55	30c indigo	20	20
C374	AP55	2cor purple	1.00	1.00
C375	AP55	3cor dk grn	2.00	2.00
C376	AP55	5cor dk brn	3.25	3.25
		Nos. C372-C376 (5)	6.60	6.60

Issued in tribute to President Anastasio Somoza, 1896-1956.

Type of Regular Issue and

Handshake and Globe — AP56

Designs: 4c, Scout emblem, globe and Lord Baden-Powell. 5c, Cub Scout. 6c, Crossed flags and Scout emblem. 8c, Scout symbols. 30c, Joseph A. Harrison. 40c, Pres. Somoza receiving decoration at first Central American Camporee. 75c, Explorer Scout. 85c, Boy Scout. 1cor, Lord Baden-Powell.

1957, Apr. 9 **Unwmk.** ***Perf. 13½x14***

C377	AP56	3c red org & ol	15	15
C378	A75	4c dk brn & dk Prus grn	15	15
C379	A75	5c grn & brn	15	15
C380	A75	6c pur & ol	15	15
C381	A75	8c grnsh blk & red	15	15
C382	A75	30c Prus grn & gray	15	15
C383	AP56	40c dk bl & grysh blk	15	15
C384	A75	75c mar & brn	20	20
C385	A75	85c red & gray	22	22
C386	A75	1cor dl red brn & sl grn	30	28
a.		Souv. sheet of 5, #C382-C386, imperf.	2.50	2.50
		Set value	1.50	1.45

Centenary of the birth of Lord Baden-Powell, founder of the Boy Scouts.
No. C386a with each stamp overprinted "CAMPOREE SCOUT 1965" was issued in 1965 along with Nos. 843-852.
For surcharge see No. C754.

Pres. Luis A. Somoza — AP57

1957, July 2 ***Perf. 14x13½***

Portrait in Dark Brown

C387	AP57	20c dp bl	15	15
C388	AP57	25c lil rose	15	15
C389	AP57	30c blk brn	15	15
C390	AP57	40c grnsh bl	20	20
C391	AP57	2cor brt vio	1.25	1.25
		Nos. C387-C391 (5)	1.90	1.90

Issued to honor President Luis A. Somoza.

Church Types of Regular Issue

Designs: 30c, Archbishop Lezcano y Ortega. 60c, Managua Cathedral. 75c, Bishop Pereira y Castellon. 90c, Leon Cathedral. 1.50cor, De la Merced Church, Granada. 2cor, Father Mariano Dubon.

1957, July 16 **Unwmk.**

Centers in Olive Gray

C392	A78	30c dk grn	15	15
C393	A77	60c chocolate	15	15
C394	A78	75c dk bl	20	20
C395	A77	90c brt red	28	28
C396	A77	1.50cor Prus grn	40	40
C397	A78	2cor brt pur	60	60
		Nos. C392-C397 (6)	1.78	1.78

Merchant Marine Type of 1957

Designs: 25c, M. S. Managua. 30c, Ship's wheel and map. 50c, Pennants. 60c, M. S. Costa Rica. 1 cor, M. S. Nicarao. 2.50 cor, Flag, globe & ship.

1957, Oct. 24 **Litho.** ***Perf. 14***

C398	A79	25c ultra grysh bl & gray	15	15
C399	A79	30c red brn, gray & yel	15	15
C400	A79	50c vio, ol gray & bl	30	30
C401	A79	60c lake, grnsh bl & blk	35	35
C402	A79	1cor crim, brt bl & blk	48	48
C403	A79	2.50cor blk, bl & red brn	1.50	1.50
		Nos. C398-C403 (6)	2.93	2.93

For surcharge see No. C691.

Fair Emblem — AP58

Designs: 30c, 2cor, Arms of Nicaragua. 45c, 10cor, Pavilion of Nicaragua, Brussels.

1958, Apr. 17 **Unwmk.** ***Perf. 14***

C404	AP58	25c bluish grn, blk & yel	15	15
C405	AP58	30c multi	15	15
C406	AP58	45c bis, bl & blk	15	15
C407	AP58	1cor pale brn, lt bl & blk	18	18
C408	AP58	2cor multi	32	32
C409	AP58	10cor pale bl, lil & brn	1.65	1.65
a.		Souv. sheet of 6, #C404-C409	7.50	7.50
		Nos. C404-C409 (6)	2.60	2.60

World's Fair, Brussels, Apr. 17-Oct. 19.

Lions Type of Regular Issue

Designs: 30c, Dr. Teodoro A. Arias. 60c, Arms of Central American Republics. 90c, Edward G. Barry. 1.25cor, Melvin Jones. 2cor, Motto and emblem. 3cor, Map of Central America.

1958, May 8 **Litho.**

Emblem in Yellow, Red and Blue

C410	A80	30c bl & org	15	15
C411	A80	60c multi	25	20
C412	A80	90c blue	35	30
C413	A80	1.25cor bl & ol	45	40
C414	A80	2cor bl & grn	80	70
C415	A80	3cor bl, lil & pink	1.25	1.10
a.		Souv. sheet of 6, #C410-C415	4.25	4.25
		Nos. C410-C415 (6)	3.25	2.85

For surcharge see No. C686.

Chrisyian Brothers Type of 1958

Designs: 30c, Arms of La Salle. 60c, School, Managua (horiz.) 85c, St. Jean Baptiste De La Salle. 90c, Bro. Carlos. 1.25cor, Bro. Julio. 1.50cor, Bro. Antonio. 1.75cor, Bro. Argeo. 2cor, Bro. Eugenio.

1958, July 13 **Photo.** ***Perf. 14***

C416	A81	30c bl, car & yel	15	15
C417	A81	60c gray, brn & lil	28	24
C418	A81	85c red, bl & grnsh blk	32	28
C419	A81	90c ol grn, ocher & blk	40	36
C420	A81	1.25cor car, ocher & blk	55	52
C421	A81	1.50cor lt grn, gray & vio blk	65	55
C422	A81	1.75cor brn, bl & grnsh blk	70	65
C423	A81	2cor ol grn, gray & vio blk	1.00	1.00
		Nos. C416-C423 (8)	4.05	3.75

For surcharges see Nos. C539A, C755-C756.

UNESCO Building, Paris — AP59

Designs: 75c, 5cor, "UNESCO." 90c, 3cor, UNESCO building and Eiffel tower. 1cor, Emblem and globe.

Perf. 11½

1958, Dec. 15 **Unwmk.** **Litho.**

C424	AP59	60c brt pink & bl	15	15
C425	AP59	75c grn & red brn	15	15
C426	AP59	90c lt brn & grn	18	15
C427	AP59	1cor ultra & brt pink	20	20
C428	AP59	3cor gray & org	65	65
C429	AP59	5cor rose lil & dk bl	1.00	95
a.		Min. sheet of 6, #C424-C429	2.50	2.50
		Nos. C424-C429 (6)	2.33	2.25

Opening of UNESCO Headquarters in Paris, Nov. 3.
For overprints see Nos. C494-C499.

Type of Regular Issue, 1959 and

Nicaraguan, Papal and US Flags AP60

Designs: 35c, Pope John XXIII and Cardinal Spellman. 1 cor, Spellman coat of arms. 1.05 cor, Cardinal Spellman. 1.50 cor, Human rosary and Cardinal (horiz.). 2 cor, Cardinal with Ruben Dario order.

1959, Nov. 26 ***Perf. 12½***

C430 AP60 30c vio bl, yel & red 15 15
C431 A83 35c dp org & grnsh blk 15 15
C432 A83 1cor yel, bl & car 22 22
C433 A83 1.05cor red, blk & dk car 28 28
C434 A83 1.50cor dk bl & yel 30 30
C435 A83 2cor multi 40 40
C436 AP60 5cor multi 1.25 90
a. Min. sheet of 7, #C430-C436, perf. or imperf. 3.75 3.75
Nos. C430-C436 (7) 2.75 2.40

Visit of Cardinal Spellman to Managua, Feb. 1958.
For surcharges see Nos. C538, C638, C747, C752, .

Type of Lincoln Regular Issue and

AP61

Perf. 13x13½, 13½x13

1960, Jan. 21 Engr. Unwmk.

Portrait in Black

C437 A84 30c indigo 15 15
C438 A84 35c brt car 15 15
C439 A84 70c plum 15 15
C440 A84 1.05cor emerald 22 22
C441 A84 1.50cor violet 30 30
C442 AP61 5cor int blk & bis 90 90
a. Souv. sheet of 6, #C437-C442, imperf. 3.00 3.00
Nos. C437-C442 (6) 1.87 1.87

150th anniv. of the birth of Abraham Lincoln.
For overprints and surcharges see Nos. C446-C451, C500, C539, C637, C680, C753.

Nos. C343, C370 and C318 Overprinted: "X Aniversario Club Filatelico S.J.-C.R."

1960, July 4 **Engr.**

C443 AP49 2cor magenta 65 70
C444 AP54 2.50cor dk ultra 65 75
C445 AP45 3cor green 85 1.10

10th anniversary of the Philatelic Club of San Jose, Costa Rica.

Nos. C437-C442 Overprinted in Red

Resello

Perf. 13x13½, 13½x13

1960, Sept. 19 Unwmk.

Center in Black

C446 A84 30c indigo 20 16
C447 A84 35c brt car 16 15
C448 A84 70c plum 16 16
C449 A84 1.05cor emerald 22 22
C450 A84 1.50cor violet 38 35
C451 AP61 5cor int blk & bis 1.10 1.10
Nos. C446-C451 (6) 2.22 2.14

Issued for the Red Cross to aid earthquake victims in Chile. The overprint on No. C451 is horizontal and always inverted.

People and World Refugee Year Emblem AP62

Design: 5cor, Crosses, globe and WRY emblem.

1961, Jan. 2 Litho. ***Perf. 11x11½***

C452 AP62 2cor multi 30 30
C453 AP62 5cor multi 65 65
a. Souv. sheet of 2, #C452-C453 2.50 2.50

Issued to commemorate World Refugee Year, July 1, 1959-June 30, 1960.

AP63

Consular Service Stamps Surcharged "Correo Aereo" and New Denomination in Red, Black or Blue

Unwmk.

1961, Feb. 21 Engr. ***Perf. 12***

Red Marginal Number

C454 AP63 20c on 50c dp bl (R) 15 15
C455 AP63 20c on 1cor grnsh blk (R) 15 15
C456 AP63 20c on 2cor grn (R) 15 15
C457 AP63 20c on 3cor dk car 15 15
C458 AP63 20c on 5cor org (Bl) 15 15
C459 AP63 20c on 10cor vio (R) 15 15
C460 AP63 20c on 20cor red brn (R) 15 15
C461 AP63 20c on 50cor brn (R) 15 15
C462 AP63 20c on 100cor mag 15 15
Set value 72 54

See Nos. CO51-CO59, RA63-RA64.

Charles L. Mullins, Anastasio Somoza and Franklin D. Roosevelt AP64

Standard Bearers with Flags of Nicaragua and Academy — AP65

Designs: 25c, 70c, Flags of Nicaragua and Academy. 30c, 1.05cor, Directors of Academy: Fred T. Cruse, LeRoy Bartlett, Jr., John F. Greco, Anastasio Somoza Debayle, Francisco Boza, Elias Monge. 40c, 2cor, Academy Emblem. 45c, 5cor, Anastasio Somoza Debayle and Luis Somoza Debayle.

Perf. 11x11½, 11½x11

1961, Feb. 24 Litho. Unwmk.

C463 AP64 20c rose lil, gray & buff 15 15
C464 AP65 25c bl, red & blk 15 15
C465 AP64 30c bl, gray & yel 15 15
C466 AP65 35c multi 15 15
C467 AP65 40c multi 15 15
C468 AP64 45c pink, gray & buff 15 15
a. Min. sheet of 6, #C463-C468, imperf. 40 40
C469 AP64 60c brn, gray & buff 15 15
C470 AP65 70c multi 15 15
C471 AP64 1.05cor lil, gray & yel 15 15
C472 AP65 1.50cor multi 18 18
C473 AP65 2cor multi 26 25
C474 AP64 5cor gray & buff 70 55
a. Min. sheet of 6, #C469-C474, imperf. 1.65 1.65
Set value 1.80 1.65

20th anniversary (in 1959) of the founding of the Military Academy of Nicaragua.
In 1977, Nos. C468a and C474a were overprinted in black: "1927-1977 50 ANIVERSARIO / Guardia Nacional de Nicaragua." Value, $4.
For surcharges see Nos. C692, C748, C759.

Emblem of Junior Chamber of Commerce — AP66

Designs: 2c, 15c, Globe showing map of Americas (horiz.). 4c, 35c, Globe and initials (horiz.). 5c, 70c, Chamber credo. 6c, 1.05cor, Handclasp. 10c, 5cor, Regional map.

Perf. 11x11½, 11½x11

1961, May 16 Unwmk.

C475 AP66 2c multi 15 15
C476 AP66 3c yel & blk 15 15
C477 AP66 4c multi 15 15
C478 AP66 5c crim & blk 15 15
C479 AP66 6c brn, yel & blk 15 15
C480 AP66 10c red org, blk & bl 15 15
C481 AP66 15c bl, blk & grn 15 15
C482 AP66 30c bl & blk 15 15
C483 AP66 35c multi 15 15
C484 AP66 70c yel, blk & crim 15 15
C485 AP66 1.05cor multi 15 15
C486 AP66 5cor multi 55 55
Set value 1.25 1.15

Issued to commemorate the 13th Regional Congress of the Junior Chamber of Commerce of Nicaragua and the International Junior Chamber of Commerce.
The imperforates of Nos. C475-C486 were not authorized.
For overprints and surcharges see Nos. C504-C508, C537, C634, C687, C749.

Rigoberto Cabezas — AP67

Map of Mosquito Territory and View of Cartago AP68

Designs: 45c, Newspaper. 70c, Building. 2cor, Cabezas quotation. 10cor, Map of lower Nicaragua with Masaya area.

1961, Aug. 29 Litho. ***Perf. 13½***

C487 AP67 20c org & dk bl 15 15
C488 AP68 40c lt bl & cl 15 15
C489 AP68 45c cit & brn 15 15
C490 AP68 70c beige & grn 15 15
C491 AP68 2cor pink & dk bl 32 22
C492 AP68 10cor grnsh bl & cl 1.40 1.10
Nos. C487-C492 (6) 2.32 1.92

Issued to commemorate the centenary of the birth of Rigoberto Cabezas, who acquired the Mosquito Territory (Atlantic Littoral) for Nicaragua.

No. C253 Overprinted in Red: "Convencion Filatelica-Centro-America-Panama-San Salvador-27 Julio 1961"

1961, Aug. 23 Engr. ***Perf. 12½***

C493 AP22 1.25cor multi 42 42
a. Inverted overprint 75.00

Central American Philatelic Convention, San Salvador, July 27.

Nos. C424-C429 Overprinted in Red: "Homenaje a Hammarskjold Sept. 18-1961"

1961 Litho. ***Perf. 11½***

C494 AP59 60c brt pink & bl 25 25
C495 AP59 75c grn & red brn 28 28
C496 AP59 90c lt brn & grn 30 30
C497 AP59 1cor ultra & brt pink 32 32
C498 AP59 3cor gray & org 65 65
C499 AP59 5cor rose lil & dk bl 1.75 1.75
Nos. C494-C499 (6) 3.55 3.55

Issued in memory of Dag Hammarskjold, Secretary General of the United Nations, 1953-61.

RESELLO

Nos. C314 and C440 Surcharged in Red

¢ 1.00

Perf. 13x13½, 13

1962, Jan. 20 Engr.

C500 A84 1cor on 1.05cor 20 18
C501 AP44 1cor on 1.10cor 20 18

UNESCO Emblem and Crowd — AP69

Design: 5cor, UNESCO and UN Emblems.

Unwmk.

1962, Feb. 26 Photo. ***Perf. 12***

C502 AP69 2cor multi 28 25
C503 AP69 5cor multi 70 70
a. Souv. sheet of 2, #C502-C503, imperf. 1.25 1.25

15th anniv. (in 1961) of UNESCO.

Nos. C480 and C483-C486 Overprinted

Perf. 11x11½, 11½x11

1962, July Litho.

C504 AP66 10c red org, blk & bl 22 20
C505 AP66 35c multi 30 20
C506 AP66 70c yel, blk & crim 38 30
C507 AP66 1.05cor multi 50 45
C508 AP66 5cor multi 85 1.40
Nos. C504-C508 (5) 2.25 2.55

WHO drive to eradicate malaria.

Souvenir Sheet

Stamps and Postmarks of 1862 — AP69a

1962, Sept. 9 Litho. ***Imperf.***

C509 AP69a 7cor multi 2.50 2.50

Cent. of Nicaraguan postage stamps.

Arms Type of Regular Issue, 1962

Coats of Arms: 30c, Nueva Segovia. 50c, Leon. 1cor, Managua. 2cor, Granada. 5cor, Rivas.

1962, Nov. 22 *Perf. 12½x13*

Arms in Original Colors; Black Inscriptions

C510 A86 30c rose 15 15
C511 A86 50c salmon 15 15
C512 A86 1cor lt grn 15 15
C513 A86 2cor gray 32 28
C514 A86 5cor lt bl 85 75
Nos. C510-C514 (5) 1.62
Set value 1.25

Liberty Bell AP70

1963, May 15 **Litho.** *Perf. 13x12*

C515 AP70 30c lt bl, blk & ol bis 15 15

Issued to commemorate the sesquicentennial of the first Nicaraguan declaration of Independence (in 1961).

Paulist Brother Comforting Boy AP71

Map of Central America AP72

Designs: 60c, Nun comforting girl. 2cor, St. Vincent de Paul and St. Louisa de Marillac (horiz.).

1963, May 15 **Photo.** *Perf. 13½*

C516 AP71 60c gray & ocher 15 15
C517 AP71 1cor sal & blk 25 22
C518 AP71 2cor crim & blk 50 50

300th anniv. of the deaths of St. Vincent de Paul and St. Louisa de Marillac (in 1960).

Lithographed and Engraved

1963, Aug. 2 **Unwmk.** *Perf. 12*

C519 AP72 1cor bl & yel 20 15

Issued to honor the Federation of Central American Philatelic Societies.

Cross over World AP73

Wheat and Map of Nicaragua AP74

1963, Aug. 6

C520 AP73 20c yel & red 15 15

Issued to commemorate Vatican II, the 21st Ecumenical Council of the Roman Catholic Church.

1963, Aug. 6

Design: 25c, Dead tree on parched earth.

C521 AP74 10c lt grn & grn 15 15
C522 AP74 25c yel & dk brn 15 15
Set value 15 15

FAO "Freedom from Hunger" campaign.

Boxing — AP75

Flags of Central American States — AP75a

Lithographed and Engraved

1963, Dec. 12 **Unwmk.** *Perf. 12*

C523 AP75 2c shown 15 15
C524 AP75 3c Running 15 15
C525 AP75 4c Underwater 15 15
C526 AP75 5c Soccer 15 15
C527 AP75 6c Baseball 15 15
C528 AP75 10c Tennis 15 15
C529 AP75 15c Bicycling 15 15
C530 AP75 20c Motorcycling 15 15
C531 AP75 35c Chess 22 22
C532 AP75 60c Deep-sea fishing 28 28
C533 AP75 1cor Table tennis 42 42
C534 AP75 2cor Basketball 80 80
C535 AP75 5cor Golf 2.00 2.00
Set value 4.25 4.25

Publicizing the 1964 Olympic Games.
For overprints and surcharge see Nos. C553-C558, C635.

Central American Independence Issue

1964, Sept. 15 **Litho.** *Perf. 13x13½*

Size: 27x43mm

C536 AP75a 40c multi 25 25

Nos. C479, C430, C437 and C416 Surcharged in Black or Red

Resello **RESELLO**
₡ 0.15 **₡0.20**
a b

1964 **Litho.** *Perf. 11½x11*

C537 AP66 5c on 6c 25 15

Perf. 12½

C538 AP60 10c on 30c 50 15

Engr.

Perf. 13x13½

C539 A84 15c on 30c (R) 65 15

Photo.

Perf. 14

C539A A81 20c on 30c 15 15
Set value 20

Floating Red Cross Station — AP76

Designs: 5c, Alliance for Progress emblem (vert.). 15c, Highway. 20c, Plowing with tractors, and sun. 25c, Housing development. 30c, Presidents Somoza and Kennedy and World Bank Chairman Eugene Black. 35c, Adult education. 40c, Smokestacks.

1964, Oct. 15 **Litho.** *Perf. 12*

C540 AP76 5c yel, brt bl, grn & gray 15 15
C541 AP76 10c multi 15 15
C542 AP76 15c multi 15 15
C543 AP76 20c org brn, yel & blk 15 15
C544 AP76 25c multi 15 15
C545 AP76 30c dk bl, blk & brn 15 15
C546 AP76 35c lil rose, dk red & blk 18 15
C547 AP76 40c dp car, blk & yel 22 15
Set value 90 52

Alliance for Progress.
For surcharges see Nos. C677, C693.

Map of Central America and Central American States — AP77

Designs (Map of Central America and): 25c, Grain. 40c, Cogwheels. 50c, Heads of cattle.

1964, Nov. 30 **Litho.** *Perf. 12*

C548 AP77 15c ultra & multi 15 15
C549 AP77 25c multi 15 15
C550 AP77 40c multi 15 15
C551 AP77 50c multi 15 15
Set value 36 30

Central American Common Market.
For surcharge see No. C678.

Nos. C523-C525, C527 and C533-C534 Overprinted: "OLIMPIADAS / TOKYO-1964"

Lithographed and Engraved

1964, Dec. 19 **Unwmk.** *Perf. 12*

C553 AP75 2c multi 15 15
C554 AP75 3c multi 15 15
C555 AP75 4c multi 15 15
C556 AP75 6c multi 15 15
C557 AP75 1cor multi 2.00 2.00
C558 AP75 2cor multi 2.50 2.50
Nos. C553-C558 (6) 5.10 5.10

18th Olympic Games, Tokyo, Oct. 10-25.

Blood Transfusion AP78

Stele AP79

Designs: 20c, Volunteers and priest rescuing wounded man. 40c, Landscape during storm. 10cor, Red Cross over map of Nicaragua.

1965, Jan. 28 **Litho.** *Perf. 12*

C559 AP78 20c yel, blk & red 15 15
C560 AP78 25c red, blk & ol bis 15 15
C561 AP78 40c grn, blk & red 15 15
C562 AP78 10cor multi 1.75 1.10
Set value 1.90 1.20

Centenary (in 1963) of the International Red Cross.

Perf. 13½x13, 13x13½

1965, Mar. 24 **Litho.** **Unwmk.**

Antique Indian artifacts: 5c, Three jadeite statuettes (horiz.). 15c, Dog (horiz.). 20c, Talamanca pendant. 25c, Decorated pottery bowl and vase (horiz.). 30c, Stone pestle and mortar on animal base. 35c, Three statuettes (horiz.). 40c, Idol on animal pedestal. 50c, Decorated pottery bowl and vase. 60c, Vase and metate (tripod bowl; horiz.). 1cor, Metate.

Black Margin and Inscription

C563 AP79 5c yel & multi 15 15
C564 AP79 10c multi 15 15
C565 AP79 15c multi 15 15
C566 AP79 20c sal & dk brn 15 15
C567 AP79 25c lil & multi 15 15
C568 AP79 30c lt grn & multi 15 15
C569 AP79 35c multi 15 15
C570 AP79 40c cit & multi 15 15
C571 AP79 50c ocher & multi 15 15
C572 AP79 60c multi 15 15
C573 AP79 1cor car & multi 30 15
Set value 95 55

For surcharges see Nos. C596-597, C679, C688-C690.

Pres. John F. Kennedy — AP80

Photogravure & Lithographed

1965, Apr. 28 *Perf. 12½x13½*

C574 AP80 35c blk & brt grn 20 15
C575 AP80 75c blk & brt pink 35 20
C576 AP80 1.10cor blk & dk bl 50 40
C577 AP80 2cor blk & yel brn 1.25 1.00
Set of 4 souvenir sheets 5.00 5.00

Issued in memory of Pres. John F. Kennedy (1917-63). Nos. C574-C577 each exist in separate imperf. souvenir sheets, each containing one imperf. block of four.
For surcharge see No. C760.

Andrés Bello AP81

1965, Oct. 15 **Litho.** *Perf. 14*

C578 AP81 10c dk brn & red brn 15 15
C579 AP81 15c ind & lt bl 15 15
C580 AP81 45c blk & dl lil 15 15
C581 AP81 80c blk & yel grn 15 15
C582 AP81 1cor dk brn & yel 18 15
C583 AP81 2cor blk & gray 32 30
Set value 80 70

Issued to commemorate the centenary of the death of Andrés Bello (1780?-1864), Venezuelan writer and educator.

Winston Churchill AP82

Pope John XXIII AP83

Winston Churchill: 35c, 1cor, Broadcasting (horiz.). 60c, 3cor, On military inspection. 75c, As young officer.

1966, Feb. 7 **Unwmk.** *Perf. 14*

C584 AP82 20c cer & blk 15 15
C585 AP82 35c dk ol grn & blk 15 15
C586 AP82 60c brn & blk 16 15
C587 AP82 75c rose red 20 16
C588 AP82 1cor vio blk 28 25
C589 AP82 2cor lil & blk 55 50
a. Souv. sheet of 4 1.40 1.40
C590 AP82 3cor ind & blk 85 70
Nos. C584-C590 (7) 2.34 2.06

Sir Winston Spencer Churchill (1874-1965), statesman and World War II leader.
No. C589a contains four imperf. stamps similar to Nos. C586-C589 with simulated perforations.

1966, Dec. 15 **Litho.** *Perf. 13*

Designs: 35c, Pope Paul VI. 1cor, Archbishop Gonzalez y Robleto. 2cor, St. Peter's, Rome. 3cor, Arms of Pope John XXIII and St. Peter's.

C591 AP83 20c multi 15 15
C592 AP83 35c multi 15 15
C593 AP83 1cor multi 22 18
C594 AP83 2cor multi 42 35
C595 AP83 3cor multi 65 50
Nos. C591-C595 (5) 1.59 1.33

Issued to commemorate the closing of the Ecumenical Council, Vatican II.

Nos. C571-C572 Surcharged in Red

RESELLO
C$ 0.10

1967 ***Perf. 13x13½, 13½x13***

C596 AP79 10c on 50c multi 15 15
C597 AP79 15c on 60c multi 15 15
Set value 15 15

Rubén Dario and Birthplace — AP84

Portrait and: 10c, Monument, Managua. 20c, Leon Cathedral, site of Dario's tomb. 40c, Centaurs. 75c, Swans. 1cor, Roman triumphal march. 2cor, St. Francis and the Wolf. 5cor, "Faith" defeating "Death."

1967, Jan. 18 **Litho.** ***Perf. 13***

C598 AP84 5c lt brn, tan & blk 15 15
C599 AP84 10c org, pale org & blk 15 15
C600 AP84 20c vio, lt bl & blk 15 15
C601 AP84 40c grn, dk grn & blk 15 15
a. Souv. sheet of 4, #C598-C601 50 50
C602 AP84 75c ultra, pale bl & blk 15 15
C603 AP84 1cor red, pale red & blk 18 15
C604 AP84 2cor rose pink, car & blk 32 28
C605 AP84 5cor dp ultra, vio bl, & blk 75 65
a. Souv. sheet of 4, #C602-C605 3.50 3.50
Set value 1.60 1.35

Rubén Dario (pen name of Felix Rubén Garcia Sarmiento, 1867-1916), poet, newspaper correspondent and diplomat.
Sheets were issued perf. and imperf.

Megalura Peleus AP85

Designs: Various butterflies. 5c, 10c, 30c, 35c, 50c and 1cor are vertical.

1967, Apr. 20 **Litho.** ***Perf. 14***

C606 AP85 5c multi 15 15
C607 AP85 10c multi 15 15
C608 AP85 15c multi 15 15
C609 AP85 20c multi 15 15
C610 AP85 25c multi 15 15
C611 AP85 30c multi 15 15
C612 AP85 35c multi 20 15
C613 AP85 40c multi 20 15
C614 AP85 50c multi 25 15
C615 AP85 60c multi 25 15
C616 AP85 1cor multi 40 22
C617 AP85 2cor multi 75 45
Set value 2.50 1.50

Com. James McDivitt and Maj. Edward H. White AP86

Gemini 4 Space Flight: 10c, 40c, Rocket launching and astronauts. 15c, 75c, Edward H. White walking in space. 20c, 1cor, Recovery of capsule.

1967, Sept. 20 **Litho.** ***Perf. 13***

C618 AP86 5c red & multi 15 15
C619 AP86 10c org & multi 15 15
C620 AP86 15c multi 15 15
C621 AP86 20c multi 15 15
C622 AP86 35c ol & multi 15 15
C623 AP86 40c ultra & multi 15 15
C624 AP86 75c brn & multi 18 18
C625 AP86 1cor multi 22 22
Set value 75 75

Saquanjoche, National Flower of Nicaragua AP87

Presidents of Nicaragua and Mexico AP88

National Flowers: No. C626, White nun orchid, Guatemala. No. C627, Rose, Honduras. No. C629, Maquilishuat, Salvador. No. C630, Purple guaria orchid, Costa Rica.

1967, Nov. 22 **Litho.** ***Perf. 13½***

C626 AP87 40c multi 15 15
C627 AP87 40c multi 15 15
C628 AP87 40c multi 15 15
C629 AP87 40c multi 15 15
C630 AP87 40c multi 15 15
Nos. C626-C630 (5) 75
Set value 25

5th anniversary of the General Treaty for Central American Economic Integration. Nos. C626-C630 are printed se-tenant in horizontal rows of 5 in sheet of 25 (5x5). Sheet has marginal inscription and control number. Value $5.

1968, Feb. 28 **Litho.** ***Perf. 12½***

Designs: 40c Pres. Gustavo Diaz Ordaz of Mexico and Pres. René Schick of Nicaragua signing statement (horiz.). 1cor, President Diaz.

C631 AP88 20c black 15 15
C632 AP88 40c slate grn 15 15
C633 AP88 1cor dp brn 22 15
Set value 40 22

Issued to commemorate the visit of the President of Mexico, Gustavo Diaz Ordaz.

Nos. C479, C527, C242, C440 and C434 Surcharged "Resello" and New Value in Black, Red or Yellow

1968, May **Litho.; Engr.**

C634 AP66 5c on 6c multi 15 15
C635 AP75 5c on 6c multi 15 15
C636 AP20 5c on 8c blk brn 15 15
C637 A84 1cor on 1.05cor emer & blk (R) 15 15
C638 A83 1cor on 1.50cor dk bl & yel (Y) 15 15
Set value 45 38

Mangos — AP89

1968, May 15 **Litho.** ***Perf. 14***

C639 AP89 5c shown 15 15
C640 AP89 10c Pineapples 15 15
C641 AP89 15c Orange 15 15
C642 AP89 20c Papaya 15 15
C643 AP89 30c Bananas 15 15
C644 AP89 35c Avocado 15 15
C645 AP89 50c Watermelon 15 15
C646 AP89 75c Cashews 25 15
C647 AP89 1cor Sapodilla 38 22
C648 AP89 2cor Cacao 75 45
Set value 1.90 1.15

The Last Judgment, by Michelangelo — AP90

Paintings: 10c, The Crucifixion, by Fra Angelo (horiz.). 35c, Madonna with Child and St. John, by Raphael. 2cor, The Disrobing of Christ, by El Greco. 3cor, The Immaculate Conception, by Murillo. 5cor, Christ of St. John of the Cross, by Salvador Dali.

1968, July 22 **Litho.** ***Perf. 12½***

C649 AP90 10c gold & multi 15 15
C650 AP90 15c gold & multi 15 15
C651 AP90 35c gold & multi 15 15
C652 AP90 2cor gold & multi 45 40
C653 AP90 3cor gold & multi 65 55
Set value 1.25 1.10

Miniature Sheet

C654 AP90 5cor gold & multi 2.75 2.75

Nos. C649-C652 Overprinted: "Visita de S.S. Paulo VI C.E. de Bogota 1968"

1968, Oct. 25 **Litho.** ***Perf. 12½***

C655 AP90 10c gold & multi 15 15
C656 AP90 15c gold & multi 15 15
C657 AP90 35c gold & multi 15 15
C658 AP90 2cor gold & multi 50 45
Set value 68 60

Issued to commemorate the visit of Pope Paul VI to Bogota, Colombia, Aug. 22-24. The overprint has 3 lines on the 10c stamp and 5 lines on others.

Basketball — AP91

Sports: 15c, Fencing (horiz.). 20c, Diving. 35c, Running. 50c, Hurdling (horiz.). 75c, Weight lifting. 1cor, Boxing (horiz.). 2cor, Soccer.

1968, Nov. 28 **Litho.** ***Perf. 14***

C659 AP91 10c multi 15 15
C660 AP91 15c org red, blk & gray 15 15
C661 AP91 20c multi 15 15
C662 AP91 35c multi 15 15
C663 AP91 50c multi 15 15
C664 AP91 75c multi 18 18
C665 AP91 1cor yel & multi 30 30
C666 AP91 2cor gray & multi 80 80
a. Souv. sheet of 4, #C663-C666 1.75 1.75
Set value 1.55 1.55

Issued to commemorate the 19th Olympic Games, Mexico City, Oct. 12-27.

Cichlasoma Citrinellum — AP92

Fish: 15c, Cichlasoma nicaraguensis. 20c, Carp. 30c, Gar (lepisosteus tropicus). 35c, Swordfish. 50c, Phylipnus dormitor (vert.). 75c, Tarpon atlanticus (vert.). 1cor, Eulamia nicaraguensis (vert.). 2cor, Sailfish (vert.). 3cor, Sawfish (vert.).

Perf. 13½x13, 13x13½

1969, Mar. 12 **Litho.**

C667 AP92 10c vio bl & multi 15 15
C668 AP92 15c org & multi 15 15
C669 AP92 20c grn & multi 15 15
C670 AP92 30c pur & multi 15 15
C671 AP92 35c yel & multi 15 15
C672 AP92 50c brn & multi 15 15
C673 AP92 75c ultra & multi 15 15
C674 AP92 1cor org & multi 20 15
C675 AP92 2cor dk bl & multi 40 25
C676 AP92 3cor multi 65 42
a. Min. sheet of 4, #C673-C676 1.75 1.75
Set value 1.70 1.10

Nos. C544, C549, C567 and C439 Surcharged in Black or Red

RESELLO
C$ 0.10

1969, Mar. **Litho.** ***Perf. 12, 13½x13***

C677 AP76 10c on 25c multi 15 15
C678 AP77 10c on 25c multi 15 15
C679 AP79 15c on 25c multi 15 15

Engr.

C680 A84 50c on 70c (R) 15 15
Set value 25 22

Size of 50c surcharge: 11½x9mm.

View, Exhibition Tower and Emblem — AP93

1969, May 30 **Litho.** ***Perf. 13½x13***

C681 AP93 30c dk vio bl & red 15 15
C682 AP93 35c blk & red 15 15
C683 AP93 75c car rose & vio bl 15 15
C684 AP93 1cor dp plum & blk 25 15
C685 AP93 2cor dk brn & blk 45 35
a. Souv. sheet of 4, #C681-C682, C684-C685 1.25 1.25
Set value 92 65

HEMISFAIR 1968 Exhibition.

Nos. C410, C482, C567-C569, C399, C465, C546 Surcharged in Black or Red

RESELLO
C$ 0.20

1969 **Litho.** ***Perfs. as before***

C686 A80 10c on 30c multi 15 15
C687 AP66 10c on 30c bl & blk (R) 15 15
C688 AP79 10c on 25c multi 15 15
C689 AP79 10c on 30c multi 15 15
C690 AP79 15c on 35c multi (R) 15 15
C691 A79 20c on 30c multi 15 15
C692 AP64 20c on 30c multi 15 15
C693 AP76 20c on 35c multi 15 15
Set value 40 40

Fishing AP94

Products of Nicaragua: 5c, Minerals (miner). 15c, Bananas. 20c, Timber (truck). 35c, Coffee. 40c, Sugar cane. 60c, Cotton. 75c, Rice and corn. 1cor, Tobacco. 2cor, Meat.

1969, Sept. 22 Litho. *Perf. 13x13½*

C694 AP94 5c gold & multi 15 15
C695 AP94 10c gold & multi 15 15
C696 AP94 15c gold & multi 15 15
C697 AP94 20c gold & multi 15 15
C698 AP94 35c gold & multi 15 15
C699 AP94 40c gold & multi 15 15
C700 AP94 60c gold & multi 15 15
C701 AP94 75c gold & multi 15 15
C702 AP94 1cor gold & multi 20 15
C703 AP94 2cor gold & multi 42 25
Set value 1.20 75

Woman Carrying Jar, Conference Emblem — AP95

1970, Feb. 26 Litho. *Perf. 13½x14*

C704 AP95 10c multi 15 15
C705 AP95 15c grn & multi 15 15
C706 AP95 20c ultra & multi 15 15
C707 AP95 35c multi 15 15
C708 AP95 50c multi 20 15
C709 AP95 75c multi 25 18
C710 AP95 1cor lil & multi 45 25
C711 AP95 2cor multi 85 50
Nos. C704-C711 (8) 2.35
Set value 1.20

Issued to publicize the 8th Inter-American Conference on Savings and Loans.

Soccer Type of Regular Issue and

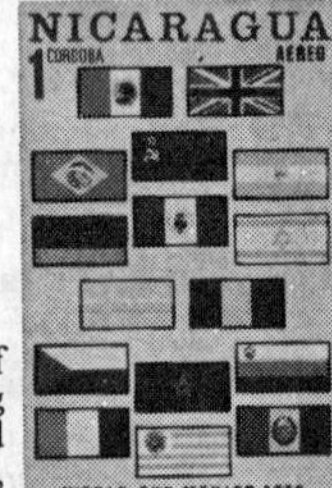

Flags of Participating Nations, World Cup, 1970 — AP96

Soccer Players: 20c, Djalma Santos, Brazil. 80c, Billy Wright, England. 4cor, Jozef Bozsik, Hungary. 5cor, Bobby Charlton, England.

1970, May 11 Litho. *Perf. 13½*

C712 A87 20c multi 15 15
C713 A87 80c multi 22 18
C714 AP96 1cor multi 28 22
C715 A87 4cor multi 1.25 90
C716 A87 5cor multi 1.40 1.25
Nos. C712-C716 (5) 3.30 2.70

Issued to honor the winners of the 1970 poll for the International Soccer Hall of Fame. No. C714 also publicizes the 9th World Soccer Championships for the Jules Rimet Cup, Mexico City, May 30-June 21, 1970.

Names of players and their achievements printed in back on back of stamps.

For overprint and surcharges see Nos. C786-788.

EXPO Emblem, Mt. Fuji and Torii — AP97

1970, July 5 Litho. *Perf. 13½x14*

C717 AP97 25c multi 15 15
C718 AP97 30c multi 15 15
C719 AP97 35c multi 15 15
C720 AP97 75c multi 22 15
C721 AP97 1.50cor multi 42 30
C722 AP97 3cor multi 75 75
a. Souv. sheet of 3, #C720-C722, imperf. 1.00 1.00
Nos. C717-C722 (6) 1.84
Set value 1.35

EXPO '70 International Exhibition, Osaka, Japan, Mar. 15-Sept. 13, 1970.

Moon Landing, Apollo 11 Emblem and Nicaragua Flag — AP98

Designs (Apollo 11 Emblem, Nicaragua Flag and): 40c, 75c, Moon surface and landing capsule. 60c, 1cor, Astronaut planting US flag.

1970, Aug. 12 Litho. *Perf. 14*

C723 AP98 35c multi 15 15
C724 AP98 40c multi 15 15
C725 AP98 60c pink & multi 18 15
C726 AP98 75c yel & multi 22 15
C727 AP98 1cor vio & multi 38 18
C728 AP98 2cor org & multi 65 38
Nos. C723-C728 (6) 1.73
Set value 90

Man's 1st landing on the moon, July 20, 1969. See note after US No. C76.

Franklin D. Roosevelt AP99

Annunciation, by Matthias Grunewald AP100

Roosevelt Portraits: 15c, 1cor, as stamp collector. 20c, 50c, 2cor, Full face.

1970, Oct. 12

C729 AP99 10c blk & bluish blk 15 15
C730 AP99 15c blk & brn vio 15 15
C731 AP99 20c blk & ol grn 15 15
C732 AP99 35c blk & brn vio 15 15
C733 AP99 50c brown 15 15
C734 AP99 75c blue 15 15
C735 AP99 1cor rose red 18 15
C736 AP99 2cor black 38 25
Set value 1.00 70

Franklin Delano Roosevelt (1882-1945).

1970, Dec. 1 Litho. *Perf. 14*

Paintings: No. C737, like 15c. No. C738, 20c, Nativity, by El Greco. No. C739, 35c, Adoration of the Magi, by Albrecht Dürer No. C740, 75c, Virgin and Child, by J. van Hemessen. No. C741, 1cor, Holy Shepherd, Portuguese School, 16th century.

C737 AP100 10c multi 15 15
C738 AP100 10c multi 15 15
C739 AP100 10c multi 15 15
C740 AP100 10c multi 15 15
C741 AP100 10c multi 15 15
C742 AP100 15c multi 15 15
C743 AP100 20c multi 15 15
C744 AP100 35c multi 15 15
C745 AP100 75c multi 18 15
C746 AP100 1cor multi 22 15
Set value 80 60

Christmas 1970. Nos. C737-C741 printed se-tenant.

RESELLO
C$ 0.15

Issues of 1947-67 Surcharged

1971, Mar.

C747 A83 10c on 1.05cor (#C433) 28 28
C748 AP64 10c on 1.05cor (#C471) 28 28
C749 AP66 10c on 1.05cor (#C485) 28 28
C750 AP42 15c on 1.50cor (#C292) 42 42
C751 AP53 15c on 1.50cor (#C369) 42 42
C752 A83 15c on 1.50cor (#C434) 42 42
C753 A84 15c on 1.50cor (#C441) 42 42
C754 A75 20c on 85c (#C385) 55 55
C755 A81 20c on 85c (#C418) 55 55
C756 A81 25c on 90c (#C419) 70 70
C757 AP48 30c on 1.10cor (#C337) 85 85
C758 AP44 40c on 1.10cor (#C314) 1.10 1.10
C759 AP65 40c on 1.50cor (#C472) 1.10 1.10
C760 AP80 1cor on 1.10cor (#C576) 2.75 2.75
Nos. C747-C760 (14) 10.12 10.12

The arrangement of the surcharge differs on each stamp.

Mathematics Type of Regular Issue

Symbolic Designs of Scientific Formulae: 25c, Napier's law (logarithms). 30c, Pythagorean theorem (length of sides of right-angled triangle). 40c, Boltzman's equation (movement of gases). 1cor, Broglie's law (motion of particles of matter). 2cor, Archimedes' principle (displacement of mass).

1971, May 15 Litho. *Perf. 13½*

C761 A88 25c lt bl & multi 15 15
C762 A88 30c lt bl & multi 18 16
C763 A88 40c lt bl & multi 25 20
C764 A88 1cor lt bl & multi 60 35
C765 A88 2cor lt bl & multi 1.00 75
Nos. C761-C765 (5) 2.18 1.61

On the back of each stamp is a descriptive paragraph.

Montezuma Oropendola AP101

Birds: 15c, Turquoise-browed motmot. 20c, Magpie-jay. 25c, Scissor-tailed flycatchers. 30c, Spot-breasted oriole (horiz.). 35c, Rufous-naped wren. 40c, Great kiskadee. 75c, Red-legged honeycreeper (horiz.). 1cor, Great-tailed grackle (horiz.). 2cor, Belted kingfisher.

1971, Oct. 15 Litho. *Perf. 14*

C766 AP101 10c multi 15 15
C767 AP101 15c multi 15 15
C768 AP101 20c gray & multi 15 15
C769 AP101 25c multi 15 15
C770 AP101 30c multi 15 15
C771 AP101 35c multi 15 15
C772 AP101 40c multi 15 15
C773 AP101 75c yel & multi 25 15
C774 AP101 1cor org & multi 30 18
C775 AP101 2cor org & multi 65 32
Set value 1.75 95

Ten Commandments Type of Regular Issue

Designs: 1cor, Bathsheba at her Bath, by Rembrandt (IX). 2cor, Naboth's Vineyard, by James Smetham (X).

1971, Nov. 1 *Perf. 11*

C776 A90 1cor ocher & multi 90 45
C777 A90 2cor ocher & multi 1.50 80

Descriptive inscriptions printed in gray on back of stamps.

U Thant, Anastasio Somoza, UN Emblem AP102

1972, Feb. 15 *Perf. 14x13½*

C778 AP102 10c pink & mar 15 15
C779 AP102 15c green 15 15
C780 AP102 20c blue 15 15
C781 AP102 25c rose cl 15 15
C782 AP102 30c org & brn 15 15
C783 AP102 40c gray & sl grn 15 15
C784 AP102 1cor ol grn 22 15
C785 AP102 2cor brown 45 25
Set value 1.00 65

25th anniv. of the United Nations (in 1970).

Nos. C713, C715, C716 Surcharged or Overprinted Like Nos. 899-900

1972, Mar. 20 Litho. *Perf. 13½*

C786 A87 20c on 80c multi 15 15
C787 A87 60c on 4cor multi 15 15
C788 A87 5cor multi 1.10 1.00

20th Olympic Games, Munich, Aug. 26-Sept. 11.

Ceramic Figure, Map of Nicaragua — AP103

Designs: Pre-Columbian ceramics (700-1200A.D.) found at sites indicated on map of Nicaragua.

1972, Sept. 16 Litho. *Perf. 14x13½*

C789 AP103 10c bl & multi 15 15
C790 AP103 15c bl & multi 15 15
C791 AP103 20c bl & multi 15 15
C792 AP103 25c bl & multi 15 15
C793 AP103 30c bl & multi 15 15
C794 AP103 35c bl & multi 15 15
C795 AP103 40c bl & multi 15 15
C796 AP103 50c bl & multi 15 15
C797 AP103 60c bl & multi 15 15
C798 AP103 80c bl & multi 15 15
C799 AP103 1cor bl & multi 20 15
C800 AP103 2cor bl & multi 38 25
Set value 1.20 90

Lord Peter Wimsey, by Dorothy L. Sayers AP104

Designs (Book and): 10c, Philip Marlowe, by Raymond Chandler. 15c, Sam Spade, by Dashiell Hammett. 20c, Perry Mason, by Erle S. Gardner. 25c, Nero Wolfe, by Rex Stout. 35c, Auguste Dupin, by Edgar Allan Poe. 40c, Ellery Queen, by Frederick Dannay and Manfred B. Lee. 50c, Father Brown, by G. K. Chesterton. 60c, Charlie Chan, by Earl Derr Biggers. 80c, Inspector Maigret, by Georges Simenon. 1cor, Hercule Poirot, by Agatha Christie. 2cor, Sherlock Holmes, by A. Conan Doyle.

1972, Nov. 13 Litho. *Perf. 14x13½*

C801 AP104 5c bl & multi 15 15
C802 AP104 10c bl & multi 15 15
C803 AP104 15c bl & multi 15 15
C804 AP104 20c bl & multi 15 15
C805 AP104 25c bl & multi 16 16
C806 AP104 35c bl & multi 22 22
C807 AP104 40c bl & multi 25 25
C808 AP104 50c bl & multi 32 32
C809 AP104 60c bl & multi 38 38
C810 AP104 80c bl & multi 50 50
C811 AP104 1cor bl & multi 65 65
C812 AP104 2cor bl & multi 1.25 1.25
Nos. C801-C812 (12) 4.33 4.33

50th anniversary of INTERPOL, international police organization. Designs show famous fictional detectives. Inscriptions on back, printed on top of gum, give thumbnail sketch of character and author.

Shepherds Following Star AP105

Legend of the Christmas Rose: 15c, Adoration of the kings and shepherds. 20c, Shepherd girl alone crying. 35c, Angel appears to girl. 40c, Christmas rose (Helleborus niger). 60c, Girl thanks angel. 80c, Girl and Holy Family. 1cor, Girl presents rose to Christ Child. 2cor, Adoration.

1972, Dec. 20

C813 AP105 10c multi 15 15
C814 AP105 15c multi 15 15
C815 AP105 20c multi 15 15
C816 AP105 35c multi 15 15
C817 AP105 40c multi 15 15
C818 AP105 60c multi 15 15
C819 AP105 80c multi 16 15
C820 AP105 1cor multi 18 16
C821 AP105 2cor multi 35 32
a. Souv. sheet of 9, #C813-C821 1.10 1.10
Set value 1.00 90

Christmas 1972.

No. C821a exists with red marginal overprint, "TERREMOTO DESASTRE," for the Managua earthquake of Dec. 22-23, 1972. It was sold abroad, starting in Jan. 1973.

Sir Walter Raleigh, Patent to Settle New World — AP106

Events and Quotations from Contemporary Illustrations: 15c, Mayflower Compact, 1620. 20c, Acquittal of Peter Zenger, 1735 (vert.). 25c, William Pitt, 1766 (vert.). 30c, British revenue stamp for use in America No. RM31 (vert.). 35c, "Join or Die" serpent, 1768. 40c, Boston Massacre and State House, 1770 (vert.). 50c, Boston Tea Party and 3p coin, 1774. 60c, Patrick Henry, 1775 (vert.). 75c, Battle scene ("Our cause is just, our union is perfect," 1775). 80c, Declaration of Independence, 1776. 1cor, Liberty Bell, Philadelphia. 2cor, Seal of United States, 1782 (vert.).

1973, Feb. 22 Photo. *Perf. 13½*

C822 AP106 10c ol & multi 15 15
C823 AP106 15c ol & multi 15 15
C824 AP106 20c ol & multi 15 15
C825 AP106 25c ol & multi 15 15
C826 AP106 30c ol & multi 20 15
C827 AP106 35c ol, gold & blk 35 20
C828 AP106 40c ol & multi 35 20
C829 AP106 50c ol & multi 35 35
C830 AP106 60c ol & multi 40 35
C831 AP106 75c ol & multi 50 40
C832 AP106 80c ol & multi 50 40
C833 AP106 1cor ol & multi 80 50
C834 AP106 2cor ol & multi 1.50 1.00
Nos. C822-C834 (13) 5.55 4.15

Inscriptions on back, printed on top of gum, give brief description of subject and event.

Baseball, Player and Map of Nicaragua — AP107

1973, May 25 Litho. *Perf. 13½x14*

C835 AP107 15c lil & multi 15 15
C836 AP107 20c multi 15 15
C837 AP107 40c multi 15 15
C838 AP107 10cor multi 1.75 1.50
a. Souvenir sheet of 4 2.50 2.50
Set value 1.65

20th International Baseball Championships, Managua, Nov. 15-Dec. 5, 1972. No. C838a contains 4 stamps similar to Nos. C835-C838 with changed background colors (15c, olive; 20c, gray; 40c, lt. green; 10cor, lilac), and 5 labels.

Fashion Type of 1973

1973, July 26 Litho. *Perf. 13½*

C839 A91 10c Lourdes Nicaragua 15 15
C840 A91 15c Halston, New York 15 15
C841 A91 20c Pino Lancetti, Rome 15 15
C842 A91 35c Madame Ges, Paris 15 15
C843 A91 40c Irene Galitzine, Rome 15 15
C844 A91 80c Pedro Rodriguez, Barcelona 18 15
a. Souv. sheet of 9, #909-911, C839-C844, perf. 11 + 3 labels 3.00 3.00
Set value 50 42

Inscriptions on back printed on top of gum give description of gown in Spanish and English.

Type of Air Post Semi-Postal Issue

Design: 2cor, Pediatric surgery.

1973, Sept. 25

C845 SPAP1 2cor multi 40 35
Set value, #C845, CB1-CB11 1.60 1.35

Planned Children's Hospital. Inscription on back, printed on top of gum gives brief description of subject shown.

Christmas Type

Designs: 1cor, Virginia O'Hanlon writing letter, father. 2cor, Letter. 4cor, Virginia, father reading letter.

1973, Nov. 15 Litho. *Perf. 15*

C846 A92 1cor multicolored 30
C847 A92 2cor multicolored 55
C848 A92 4cor multicolored 1.10
a. Souv. sheet of 3, #C846-C848, perf. 14½ 3.75

Churchill Type

Designs: No. C851, Silhouette, Parliament. No. C852, Silhouette, #10 Downing St. 5cor, Showing "V" sign. 6cor, "Bulldog" Churchill protecting England.

1974, Apr. 30 *Perf. 14½*

C849 A93 5cor multicolored 1.40
C850 A93 6cor multicolored 1.70

Souvenir Sheets

Perf. 15

C851 A93 4cor blk, org & bl 1.10
C852 A93 4cor blk, org, & grn 1.10

Nos. C851-C852 contain one 28x42mm stamp.

World Cup Type

Scenes from previous World Cup Championships with flags and scores of finalists.

1974, May 8 *Perf. 14½*

C853 A94 10cor Flags of participants 2.80

Souvenir Sheets

C853A A94 4cor like No. 928 1.10
C853B A94 5cor like No. 930 1.40

For overprint see No. C856.

Flower Type of 1974

Wild Flowers and Cacti: 1 cor, Centrosema. 3 cor, Night-blooming cereus.

1974, June 11 Litho. *Perf. 14*

C854 A95 1cor grn & multi 20 18
C855 A95 3cor grn & multi 65 55

Nicaraguan Stamps Type

1974, July 10 *Perf. 14½*

C855A A96 40c No. 835 20
C855B A96 3cor No. C313, horiz. 90
C855C A96 5cor No. 734 1.40

Souvenir Sheet

Imperf

C855D Sheet of 3 2.05
e. A96 1cor No. 665 30
f. A96 2cor No. C110, horiz. 55
g. A96 4cor Globe, stars 1.20

UPU, Cent.

No. C853 Ovptd. **TRIUMFADOR ALEMANIA OCCIDENTAL**

1974, July 12

C856 A94 10cor Flags 2.80

Animal Type of 1974

Designs: 3cor, Colorado deer. 5cor, Jaguar.

1974, Sept. 10 Litho. *Perf. 14½*

C857 A97 3cor multi 65 55
C858 A97 5cor multi 1.00 90

Christmas Type of 1974

Works of Michelangelo: 40c, Madonna of the Stairs. 80c, Pitti Madonna. 2cor, Pieta. 5cor, Self-portrait.

1974, Dec. 15

C859 A98 40c multi 15 15
C860 A98 80c multi 15 15
C861 A98 2cor multi 28 25
C862 A98 5cor multi 70 65

An imperf. souvenir sheet exists containing 2cor and 5cor stamps.

Opera Type of 1975

Opera Singers and Scores: 25c, Rosa Ponselle, Norma. 35c, Giuseppe de Luca, Rigoletto. 40c, Joan Sutherland, La Figlia del Reggimento. 50c, Ezio Pinza, Don Giovanni. 60c, Kirsten Flagstad, Tristan and Isolde. 80c, Maria Callas, Tosca. 2cor, Fyodor Chaliapin, Boris Godunov. 5cor, Enrico Caruso, La Juive.

1975, Jan. 22 *Perf. 14x13½*

C863 A99 25c grn & multi 15 15
C864 A99 35c multi 15 15
C865 A99 40c multi 15 15
C866 A99 50c org & multi 15 15
C867 A99 60c rose & multi 18 15
C868 A99 80c lake & multi 25 15
C869 A99 2cor sep & multi 50 25
C870 A99 5cor multi 1.25 65
a. Souvenir sheet of 3 2.50
Nos. C863-C870 (8) 2.78
Set value 1.25

No. C870a contains one each of Nos. C869-C870 and a 1cor with design and colors of No. C868. Exists imperf.

Easter Type of 1975

Stations of the Cross: 40c, Jesus stripped of his clothes. 50c, Jesus nailed to the Cross. 80c, Jesus dies on the Cross. 1cor, Descent from the Cross. 5cor, Jesus laid in the tomb.

1975, Mar. 20 *Perf. 14½*

C871 A100 40c ultra & multi 15 15
C872 A100 50c ultra & multi 15 15
C873 A100 80c ultra & multi 15 15
C874 A100 1cor ultra & multi 16 15
C875 A100 5cor ultra & multi 90 80
Nos. C871-C875 (5) 1.51
Set value 1.15

American Bicentennial Type of 1975

Designs: 40c, Washington's Farewell, 1783. 50c, Washington Addressing Continental Congress by J. B. Stearns. 2cor, Washington Arriving for Inauguration. 5cor, Statue of Liberty and flags of 1776 and 1976. 40c, 50c, 2cor, horiz.

1975, Apr. 16 *Perf. 14*

C876 A101 40c tan & multi 18 15
C877 A101 50c tan & multi 25 18
C878 A101 2cor tan & multi 80 75
C879 A101 5cor tan & multi 2.00 1.90

Perf. and imperf. 7cor souv. sheets exist.

Nordjamb 75 Type of 1975

Designs (Scout and Nordjamb Emblems and): 35c, Camp. 40c, Scout musicians. 1cor, Campfire. 10cor, Lord Baden-Powell.

1975, Aug. 15 *Perf. 14½*

C880 A102 35c multi 15 15
C881 A102 40c multi 15 15
C882 A102 1cor multi 15 15
C883 A102 10cor multi 1.40 1.25
Set value 1.45

Two airmail souvenir sheets of 2 exist. One, perf., contains 2cor and 3cor with designs of Nos. 992 and 990. The other, imperf., contains 2cor and 3cor with designs of Nos. 993 and C882. Size: 125x101mm.

Pres. Somoza Type of 1975

1975, Sept. 10 *Perf. 14*

C884 A103 1cor vio & multi 20 18
C885 A103 10cor bl & multi 2.00 1.80
C886 A103 20cor multi 4.00 3.00

Choir Type of 1975

Famous Choirs: 50c, Montserrat Abbey. 1cor, St. Florian Choir Boys. 2cor, Choir Boys of the Wooden Cross (vert.). 5cor, Boys and Pope Paul VI (Pueri Cantores International Federation).

1975, Nov. 15 *Perf. 14½*

C887 A104 50c sil & multi 15 15
C888 A104 1cor sil & multi 20 16
C889 A104 2cor sil & multi 35 32
C890 A104 5cor sil & multi 1.00 85

A 10cor imperf. souvenir sheet exists (Oberndorf Memorial Chapel Choir and score of "Holy Night-Silent Night").

Chess Type of 1976

Designs: 40c, The Chess Players, by Thomas Eakins. 2cor, Bobby Fischer and Boris Spasski in Reykjavik, 1972. 5cor, Shakespeare and Ben Johnson Playing Chess, by Karel van Mander.

1976, Jan. 8 *Perf. 14½*

C891 A105 40c multi 16 15
C892 A105 2cor vio & multi 75 50
C893 A105 5cor multi 1.50 1.25

A souvenir sheet contains one each of Nos. C892-C893, perf. and imperf. Size: 143x67mm.

Olympic Winner Type 1976

Winners, Rowing and Sculling Events: 55c, USSR, 1956, 1960, 1964 (vert.). 70c, New Zealand, 1972 (vert.). 90c, New Zealand, 1968. 10cor, Women's rowing crew, US, 1976 (vert.). 20cor, US, 1956.

1976, Sept. 7 Litho. *Perf. 14*

C902 A107 55c bl & multi 18 15
C903 A107 70c bl & multi 18 15
C904 A107 90c bl & multi 22 18
C905 A107 20cor bl & multi 4.50 3.75

Souvenir Sheet

C906 A107 10cor multi 1.65

No. C906 for the 1st participation of women in Olympic rowing events, size of stamp: 37x50mm.

The overprint "Republica Democratica Alemana Vencedor en 1976" was applied in 1976 to No. C905 in black in 3 lines and to the margin of No. C906 in gold in 2 lines.

Bicentennial Type of 1976

Designs (American Bicentennial Emblem and): No. C907, Philadelphia, 1776. No. C908, Washington, 1976. No. C909, John Paul Jones' ships. No. C910, Atomic submarine. No. C911, Wagon train. No. C912, Diesel train.

1976, May 25 Litho. *Perf. 13½*

C907 A108 80c multi 18 15
C908 A108 80c multi 18 15
C909 A108 2.75cor multi 50 38
C910 A108 2.75cor multi 50 38
C911 A108 4cor multi 65 50
C912 A108 4cor multi 65 50
Nos. C907-C912 (6) 2.66 2.06

Stamps of same denomination printed se-tenant. A souvenir sheet contains two 10cor stamps showing George Washington and Gerald R. Ford with their families. Size: 140x111mm.

Rare Stamps Type of 1976

Rare Stamps: 40c, Hawaii No. 1. 1cor, Great Britain No. 1. 2cor, British Guiana No. 13. 5cor, Honduras No. C12. 10cor, Newfoundland No. C1.

1976, Dec. *Perf. 14*

C913 A109 40c multi 15 15
C914 A109 1cor multi 15 15
C915 A109 2cor multi 28 25
C916 A109 5cor multi 70 65
C917 A109 10cor multi 1.40 1.25
Nos. C913-C917 (5) 2.68 2.45

Inscriptions on back printed on top of gum give description of illustrated stamp. A 4cor imperf. souvenir sheet shows 1881 Great Britain-Nicaragua combination cover. Size: 140x101mm.

Olga Nuñez de Saballos — AP108

Designs: 1cor, Josefa Toledo de Aguerri. 10cor, Hope Portocarrero de Somoza.

1977, Feb. Litho. *Perf. 13½*
C918 AP108 35c multi 15 15
C919 AP108 1cor red & multi 20 18
C920 AP108 10cor multi 2.00 1.75

Famous Nicaraguan women and for International Women's Year (in 1975).

Zeppelin Type of 1977

Designs: 35c, Ville de Paris airship. 70c, Zeppelin "Schwaben." 3cor, Zeppelin in flight. 10cor, Vickers "Mayfly" before take-off. 20cor, Zeppelin with leadlines extended.

1977, Oct. 31 Litho. *Perf. 14½*
C921 A110 35c multi 15 15
C922 A110 70c multi 18 15
C923 A110 3cor multi 65 50
C924 A110 10cor multi 2.50 1.75

Souvenir Sheet

C925 A110 20cor multi 4.50 2.75

Lindbergh Type of 1977

Designs: 55c, Lindbergh's plane approaching Nicaraguan airfield, 1928. 80c, Spirit of St. Louis and map of New York-Paris route. 2cor, Plane flying off Nicaragua's Pacific Coast. 10cor, Lindbergh flying past Momotombo Volcano on way to Managua. 20cor, Spirit of St. Louis.

1977, Nov. 30
C926 A111 55c multi 15 15
C927 A111 80c multi 16 15
C928 A111 2cor multi 40 32
C929 A111 10cor multi 2.00 1.65

Souvenir Sheet

C930 A111 20cor multi 4.50 3.50

Christmas Type of 1977
Souvenir Sheet

Design: 20cor, Finale of Nutcracker Suite.

1977, Dec. 12
C931 A112 20cor multi 4.50 4.50

Painting Type of 1978

Rubens Paintings: 5cor, Hippopotamus and Crocodile Hunt. 100cor, Duke de Lerma on Horseback. 20cor, Self-portrait.

1978, Jan. 11 Litho. *Perf. 14½*
C932 A113 5cor multi 1.00 85
C933 A113 10cor multi 2.00 1.65

Souvenir Sheet

C934 A113 20cor multi 4.75 4.00

Peter Paul Rubens (1577-1640), 400th birth anniversary.

St. Francis Type of 1978

Designs: 80c, St. Francis and the wolf. 10cor, St. Francis, painting. 20cor, Our Lady of Conception, statue in Church of El Viejo.

1978, Feb. 23 Litho. *Perf. 14½*
C935 A114 80c lt brn & multi 16 15
C936 A114 10cor bl & multi 1.90 1.75

Souvenir Sheet

C937 A114 20cor multi 3.50

Railroad Type of 1978

Locomotives: 35c, Light-weight American. 4cor, Heavy Baldwin. 10cor, Juniata, 13-ton. 20cor, Map of route system.

1978, Apr. 7 Litho. *Perf. 14½*
C938 A115 35c lt grn & multi 15 15
C939 A115 4cor dp org & multi 90 75
C940 A115 10cor cit & multi 2.00 1.90

Souvenir Sheet

C941 A115 20cor multi 3.50

Jules Verne Type of 1978

Designs: 90c, 20,000 Leagues under the Sea. 10cor, Around the World in 80 Days. 20cor, From the Earth to the Moon.

1978, Aug. Litho. *Perf. 14½*
C942 A116 90c multi 20 15
C943 A116 10cor multi 1.75 1.50

Souvenir Sheet

C944 A116 20cor multi 5.00

Aviation History Type of 1978

Designs: 55c, Igor Sikorsky in his helicopter, 1913 (horiz.). 10cor, Space shuttle (horiz.). 20cor, Flyer III (horiz.).

1978, Sept. 29 Litho. *Perf. 14½*
C945 A117 55c multi 15 15
C946 A117 10cor multi 1.40 1.00

Souvenir Sheet

C947 A117 20cor multi 5.00

Soccer Type of 1978

Soccer Players: 50c, Denis Law and Franz Beckenbauer. 5cor, Dino Zoff and Pele. 20cor, Dominique Rocheteau and Johan Neeskens.

1978, Oct. 25 Litho. *Perf. 13½x14*
C948 A118 50c multi 15 15
C949 A118 5cor multi 1.00 85

Souvenir Sheet

C950 A118 20cor multi 4.50

Christmas Type of 1978

Paintings: 3cor, Apostles John and Peter, by Dürer. 10cor, Apostles Paul and Mark, by Dürer. 20cor, Virgin and Child with Garlands, by Dürer.

1978, Dec. 12 Litho. *Perf. 13½x14*
C951 A119 3cor multi 42 35
C952 A119 10cor multi 1.40 1.00

Souvenir Sheet

C953 A119 20cor multi 3.50

Volcano Type of 1978

Designs: No. C954, Cerro Negro Volcano. No. C955, Lake Masaya. No. C956, Momotombo Volcano. No. C957, Lake Asososca. No. C958, Mombacho Volcano. No. C959, Lake Apoyo. No. C960, Concepcion Volcano. No. C961, Lake Tiscapa.

1978, Dec. 29 *Perf. 14x13½*
C954 A120 35c multi 15 15
C955 A120 35c multi 15 15
C956 A120 90c multi 16 15
C957 A120 90c multi 16 15
C958 A120 1cor multi 20 15
C959 A120 1cor multi 20 15
C960 A120 10cor multi 1.90 1.35
C961 A120 10cor multi 1.90 1.35
Nos. C954-C961 (8) 4.82 3.60

Stamps of same denomination printed se-tenant in sheets of 40.

Bernardo O'Higgins — AP109

1979, Mar. 7 Litho. *Perf. 14*
C962 AP109 20cor multi 4.25 3.25

Bernardo O'Higgins (1778-1842), Chilean soldier and statesman.

Red Ginger and Rubythroated Hummingbird — AP110

Designs: 55c, Orchid. 70c, Poinsettia. 80c, Flower and bees. 2cor, Lignum vitae and blue morpho butterfly. 4cor, Cattleya.

1979, Apr. 6 Litho. *Perf. 14x13½*
C963 AP110 50c multi 15 15
C964 AP110 55c multi 15 15
C965 AP110 70c multi 16 15
C966 AP110 80c multi 16 15
C967 AP110 2cor multi 35 28
C968 AP110 4cor multi 70 52
Nos. C963-C968 (6) 1.67
Set value 1.00

Revolution Type of 1981

1981, July 19 Litho. *Perf. 12½x12*
C973 A123 2.10cor March 30 15
C974 A123 3cor Construction 42 24
C975 A123 6cor Health programs 80 48

FSLN Type of 1981

1981, July 23
C976 A124 4cor Founder 55 35

Postal Union Type of 1981

1981, Aug. 10
C977 A125 2.10cor Pony express 22 15
C978 A125 3cor Headquarters 30 18
C979 A125 6cor Members' flags 60 35

1300th Anniv. of Bulgaria — AP112

1981, Sept. 2 *Imperf.*
C980 AP112 10cor multi 1.25 1.00

Size: 96x70mm.

Aquatic Flower Type of 1981

1981, Sept. 15 *Perf. 12½*
C981 A126 10cor Nymphaea gladstoniana 1.40 90

Souvenir Sheet

Panda Bear — AP113

1981, Oct. 9 *Perf. 13*
C982 AP113 10cor multi 1.25 1.00

Philatokyo Stamp Exhibition, Tokyo.

Tropical Fish Type of 1981

1981, Oct. 19 *Perf. 12½*
C983 A127 3.50cor Pterolebias longipinnis 48 28
C984 A127 4cor Xiphophorus helleri 55 30

Souvenir Sheet

Frigate — AP114

1981, Nov. 2 *Perf. 13*
C985 AP114 10cor multi 1.40 85

Espamer '81 Stamp Exhibition, Buenos Aires, Nov. 13-22.

Bird Type of 1981

1981, Nov. 30 *Perf. 12½*
C986 A128 3cor Trogon massena 48 26
C987 A128 4cor Campylo-pterus hemileucurus, horiz. 65 38
C988 A128 6cor Momotus momota 95 55

Satellite Type of 1981

1981, Dec. 15 *Perf. 13x12½*
C989 A129 3cor multi 35 22
C990 A129 4cor multi 50 28
C991 A129 5cor multi 60 35

Railroad Type of 1981

1981, Dec. 30 *Perf. 12½*
C992 A130 6cor Ferrobus, 1967 1.00 55

World Cup Type of 1982

1982, Jan. 25
C993 A131 4cor multi 48 30
C994 A131 10cor multi, horiz. 1.25 80

Souvenir Sheet
Perf. 13

C995 A131 10cor multi 1.65 1.10

No. C995 contains one 39x31mm stamp.

Dog Type of 1982

1982, Feb. 18
C996 A132 3cor Boxers 45 28
C997 A132 3.50cor Pointers 48 28
C998 A132 6cor Collies 90 50

Intl. ITU Congress — AP115

1982, Mar. 12
C999 AP115 25cor multi 3.25 2.25

Butterfly Type of 1982

1982, Mar. 26
C1000 A133 3cor Parides iphidamas 45 28
C1001 A133 3.50cor Consul hippona 48 30
C1002 A133 4cor Morpho peleides 55 35

Satellite Type of 1982

1982, Apr. 12
C1003 A134 5cor multi, horiz. 65 40
C1004 A134 6cor multi 90 48

UPU Type of 1982

1982, May 1 Litho. *Perf. 13*
C1005 A135 3.50cor Train 38 22
C1006 A135 10cor Jet 1.10 70

Sports Type of 1982

1982, May 13
C1007 A136 2.50cor Women's volleyball, vert. 38 22
C1008 A136 3cor Boxing 45 30
C1009 A136 9cor Soccer 1.40 80

Souvenir Sheet

C1010 A136 10cor Baseball, vert. 1.50 80

No. C1010 contains one 29x36mm stamp.

Souvenir Sheet

PHILEXFRANCE '82 Intl. Stamp Exhibition, Paris, June 11-21 — AP116

1982, June 9 *Perf. 13x12½*
C1011 AP116 15cor multi 1.65 1.00

Revolution Type of 1982

Designs: Symbolic doves. 2.50cor, 4cor vert.

1982, July 19 *Perf. 13*
C1012 A137 2.50cor multi 38 22
C1013 A137 4cor multi 60 38
C1014 A137 6cor multi 1.00 60

Washington Type of 1982

Perf. 12½x13, 13x12½

1982, June 20 **Litho.**
C1015 A138 2.50cor Crossing the Delaware, horiz. 38 22
C1016 A138 3.50cor At Valley Forge, horiz. 52 35
C1017 A138 4cor Battle of Trenton 60 38
C1018 A138 6cor Washington in Princeton 1.00 60

Painting Type of 1982

1982, Aug. 17 *Perf. 13*
C1019 A139 9cor Seated Woman, by A. Morales 1.25 80

Dimitrov Type of 1982

1982, Sept. 9
C1020 A140 2.50cor Dimitrov, Yikov, Sofia, 1946 38 24
C1021 A140 4cor Portrait, flag 60 38

Dictatorship Type of 1982

1982, Sept. 21 *Perf. 13x12½*
C1022 A141 4cor Rigoberto Lopez Perez 60 38
C1023 A141 6cor Edwin Castro 1.00 60

Tourism Type of 1982

1982, Sept. 25 *Perf. 13*
C1024 A142 2.50cor Coyotepe Fortress, Masaya 28 16
C1025 A142 3.50cor Velazquez Park, Managua 38 24

Marx Type of 1982

1982, Oct. 4 *Perf. 12½*
C1026 A143 4cor Marx, Highgate Monument 55 35

Discovery of America Type of 1982

1982, Oct. 12 *Perf. 12½x13*
C1027 A145 2.50cor Trans-atlantic voyage 42 24
C1028 A145 4cor Landing of Columbus 65 42
C1029 A145 7cor Death of Columbus 1.10 70

Souvenir Sheet

Perf. 13

C1030 A145 10cor Columbus' fleet 1.65 1.00

No. C1030 contains one 31x39mm stamp.

Flower Type of 1982

1982, Nov. 13 *Perf. 12½*
C1031 A146 2.50cor Pasiflora foetida 38 22
C1032 A146 3.50cor Clitoria sp. 52 32
C1033 A146 5cor Russelia sarmentosa 75 45

Reptile Type of 1982

1982, Dec. 10 *Perf. 13*
C1034 A147 2.50cor Turtle, horiz. 38 22
C1035 A147 3cor Boa constrictor 45 28
C1036 A147 3.50cor Crocodile, horiz. 52 32
C1037 A147 5cor Sistrurus catenatus, horiz. 75 45

Non-aligned States Conference, Jan. 12-14 — AP117

1983, Jan. 10 **Litho.** *Perf. 12½x13*
C1038 AP117 4cor multi 60 38

Geothermal Electricity Generating Plant, Momotombo Volcano — AP118

1983, Feb. 25 *Perf. 13*
C1039 AP118 2.50cor multi 38 22

Souvenir Sheet

TEMBAL '83 Philatelic Exhibition, Basel, Switz. AP119

1983, May 21 **Litho.** *Perf. 13*
C1040 AP119 15cor Chamoix 2.25 1.25

Souvenir Sheet

1st Nicaraguan Philatelic Exhibition AP120

1983, July 17 **Litho.** *Perf. 13*
C1041 AP120 10cor Nicaragua Airlines jet 2.25 1.25

Armed Forces — AP121

1983, Sept. 2 **Litho.** *Perf. 13*
C1042 AP121 4cor Frontier guards, watch dog 42 26

Souvenir Sheet

BRASILIANA '83 Intl. Stamp Show, Rio de Janeiro, July 29-Aug. 7 — AP122

1983
C1043 AP122 15cor Jaguar 2.25 1.25

Cuban Revolution, 25th Anniv. AP122a

1984, Jan. 1 **Litho.** *Perf. 13*
C1043A AP122a 4cor shown 60 32
C1043B AP122a 6cor Castro, Guevara, flag 95 45

Souvenir Sheet

Cardinal Infante Don Fernando, by Diego Velazquez AP123

1984, May 2 **Litho.** *Perf. 13*
C1044 AP123 15cor multi 1.75 1.00

ESPANA '84.

Souvenir Sheet

Hamburg '84 AP124

1984, June 19 **Litho.** *Perf. 13*
C1045 AP124 15cor Dirigible 1.75 90

1984 UPU Congress AP125

1984, June 24 *Perf. 12½*
C1046 AP125 15cor Mail transport 1.75 90

Souvenir Sheet

Expofilnic '84 (2nd Natl. Stamp Exhibition) AP126

1984, July 15
C1047 AP126 15cor Communications Museum 1.75 90

Souvenir Sheet

Ausipex '84 — AP127

1984, Sept. 21
C1048 AP127 15cor Explorer ship 1.75 90

Souvenir Sheet

OLYMPHILEX '85 — AP128

1985, Mar. 18 **Litho.** *Perf. 12½*
C1049 AP128 15cor Bicycle race 1.10 60

Souvenir Sheet

ESPAMER '85, Havana, Mar. 19-24 — AP129

1985, Mar. 19
C1050 AP129 10cor Crocodylus rhom-bifer 75 38

Victory of Sandanista Revolution, 6th Anniv. — AP134

1985, July 19 **Litho.** *Perf. 12½*
C1125 AP134 9cor Soldier, flag 1.05 58
C1126 AP134 9cor Sugar mill 1.05 58

Benjamin Zeledon, Birth Cent. — AP135

1985, Oct. 4 **Litho.** *Perf. 12½*
C1127 AP135 15cor multicolored 75 38

Henri Dunant (1828-1910), Founder of Red Cross — AP136

1985, Oct. 10 *Perf. 12½x12*

C1128 AP136 3cor shown 18 15
C1129 AP136 15cor Dunant, air ambulance 90 45
a. Pair, #C1128-C1129 + label 1.10 55

Nicaraguan Stamps, 125th Anniv. AP137

1986, May 22 *Perf. 12½x13*

C1130 AP137 30cor No. C1 65 32
C1131 AP137 40cor No. 174 85 42
C1132 AP137 50cor No. 48 1.10 52
C1133 AP137 100cor No. 1 2.00 1.10

Intl. Peace Year — AP138

1986, July 19 *Perf. 12½*

C1134 AP138 5cor shown 15 15
C1135 AP138 10cor Globe, dove 25 15
Set value 20

Carlos Fonseca, 10th Death Anniv. — AP139

1986, Aug. 11 **Litho.** *Perf. 12½*

C1136 AP139 15cor multicolored 38 20

Formation of the Sandinista Front, 25th anniv.

Animals — AP140

1986, Nov. 20 *Perf. 13*

C1137 AP140 15cor Rhinoceros 32 16
C1138 AP140 15cor Zebra 32 16
C1139 AP140 25cor Elephant 55 28
C1140 AP140 25cor Giraffe 55 28
C1141 AP140 50cor Mandrill 1.10 55
C1142 AP140 50cor Tiger 1.10 55
Nos. C1137-C1142 (6) 3.94 1.98

The only foreign revenue stamps listed in this Catalogue are those authorized for prepayment of postage.

World Cup Soccer Championships, Mexico AP141

Various soccer players and natl. flags.

1986, Dec. 20 *Perf. 13*

Shirt Colors

C1143 AP141 10cor blue 22 15
C1144 AP141 10cor blk & white 22 15
C1145 AP141 10cor blue & white 22 15
C1146 AP141 15cor pink & white 35 18
C1147 AP141 15cor grn & blk 35 18
C1148 AP141 25cor blk & white, red 55 28
C1149 AP141 50cor grn & yel, red, horiz. 1.10 55
Nos. C1143-C1149 (7) 3.01 1.64

Souvenir Sheet

Perf. 12½

C1150 AP141 100cor blk & white, bl & white 2.25 1.10

Vassil Levski, 150th Birth Anniv. — AP142

1987, Apr. 18 *Perf. 13*

C1151 AP142 30cor multicolored 70 32

Intl. Year of Shelter for the Homeless AP143

1987, Aug. 2

C1152 AP143 20cor multicolored 45 22
C1153 AP143 30cor Housing, diff. 70 35

Souvenir Sheet

Berlin, 750th Anniv. — AP144

1987, Sept. 25 **Litho.** *Perf. 13*

C1154 AP144 130cor multi 1.40 70

Discovery of America, 500th Anniv. (in 1992) — AP145

1987, Oct. 12 *Perf. 13*

C1155 AP145 15cor Indian village 32 16
C1156 AP145 15cor Sailing ships 32 16
C1157 AP145 20cor Battle in village 42 22
C1158 AP145 30cor Battle, prisoners 65 32
C1159 AP145 40cor Spanish town 85 42
C1160 AP145 50cor Cathedral 1.00 52
a. Min. sheet of 6, #C1155-C1160 3.75 3.75
Nos. C1155-C1160 (6) 3.56 1.80

Cuban Revolution, 30th Anniv. — AP146

1989, Jan. 1 *Perf. 13*

C1161 AP146 20cor multicolored 45 22

AP147 AP148

Designs: Various soccer players in action.

1989, Feb. 20 *Perf. 13x12½*

C1162 AP147 100cor multi 15 15
C1163 AP147 200cor multi 15 15
C1164 AP147 600cor multi 16 15
C1165 AP147 1000cor multi 26 15
C1166 AP147 2000cor multi 52 46
C1167 AP147 3000cor multi 80 40
C1168 AP147 5000cor multi 1.25 65
Nos. C1162-C1168 (7) 3.29 2.11

Souvenir Sheet

Perf. 13

C1169 AP147 9000cor multi 2.25 2.25

World Cup Soccer Championships, Italy. No. C1169 contains one 32x40mm stamp.

1989, July 19 *Perf. 13*

Design: 9000cor, Concepcion Volcano.

C1170 AP148 300cor multi 15 15

Souvenir Sheet

C1171 AP148 9000cor multi 2.25 2.25

Sandinista Revolution, 10th Anniv. No. C1171 contains one 40x32mm stamp.

Birds — AP149

AP150

Designs: 100cor, Anhinga anhinga. 200cor, Elanoides forficatus. 600cor, Eumomota superciliosa. 1000cor, Setophaga picta. 2000cor, Taraba major, horiz. 3000cor, Onychorhynchus mexicanus. 5000cor, Myrmotherula axillaris, horiz. 9000cor, Amazona ochrocephala.

Perf. 13x12½, 12½x13

1989, July 18

C1172 AP149 100cor multi 15 15
C1173 AP149 200cor multi 15 15
C1174 AP149 600cor multi 18 15
C1175 AP149 1000cor multi 30 15
C1176 AP149 2000cor multi 60 30
C1177 AP149 3000cor multi 90 45
C1178 AP149 5000cor multi 1.50 75
Nos. C1172-C1178 (7) 3.78 2.10

Souvenir Sheet

Perf. 13

C1179 AP149 9000cor multi 1.65 1.65

Brasiliana '89. No. C1179 contains one 32x40mm stamp.

1989, Mar. 25 *Perf. 13*

Designs: 50cor, Downhill skiing. 300cor, Ice hockey. 600cor, Ski jumping. 1000cor, Pairs figure skating. 2000cor, Biathalon. 3000cor, Slalom skiing. 5000cor, Cross country skiing. 9000cor, Two-man luge.

C1180 AP150 50cor multi 15 15
C1181 AP150 300cor multi 15 15
C1182 AP150 600cor multi 15 15
C1183 AP150 1000cor multi 15 15
C1184 AP150 2000cor multi 20 15
C1185 AP150 3000cor multi 30 15
C1186 AP150 5000cor multi 48 24
Set value 1.20 65

Souvenir Sheet

C1187 AP150 9000cor multi 88 45

1992 Winter Olympics, Albertville. No. C1187 contains one 32x40mm stamp.

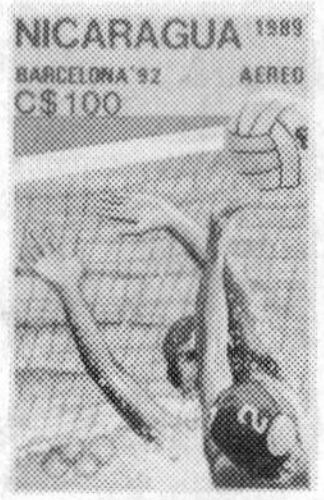

AP151 AP152

Designs: 100cor, Water polo. 200cor, Running. 600cor, Diving. 1000cor, Gymnastics. 2000cor, Weight lifting. 3000cor, Volleyball. 5000cor, Wrestling. 9000cor, Field hockey.

1989, Apr. 23

C1188 AP151 100cor multi 15 15
C1189 AP151 200cor multi 15 15
C1190 AP151 600cor multi 15 15
C1191 AP151 1000cor multi 15 15
C1192 AP151 2000cor multi 20 15
C1193 AP151 3000cor multi 30 15
C1194 AP151 5000cor multi 50 25
Set value 1.20 60

Souvenir Sheet

C1195 AP151 9000cor multi 88 45

1992 Summer Olympics, Barcelona. No. C1195 contains one 32x40mm stamp.

1989, Oct. 12

C1196 AP152 2000cor Vase 68 32

Discovery of America, 500th Anniv. (in 1992).

Mushrooms AP153

Designs: 500cor, Morchella esculenta. 1000cor, Boletus edulis. 5000cor, Lactarius deliciosus. 10,000cor, Panellus stipticus. 20,000cor, Craterellus cornucopioides. 40,000cor, Cantharellus cibarius. 50,000cor, Armillariella mellea.

1990, July 15 ***Perf. 13***

C1197	AP153	500cor multi
C1198	AP153	1000cor multi
C1199	AP153	5000cor multi
C1200	AP153	10,000cor multi
C1201	AP153	20,000cor multi
C1202	AP153	40,000cor multi
C1203	AP153	50,000cor multi

AIR POST SEMI-POSTAL STAMPS

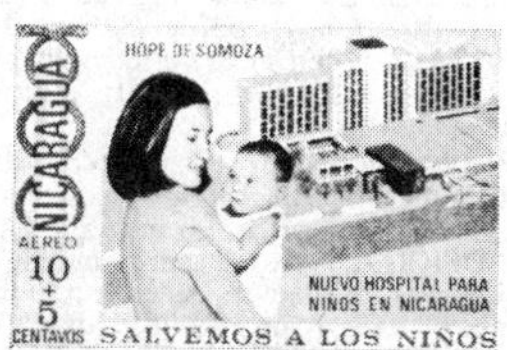

Mrs. Somoza and Children's Hospital — SPAP1

Designs: 5c+5c, Children and weight chart. 15c+5c, Incubator and Da Vinci's "Child in Womb." 20c+5c, Smallpox vaccination. 30c+5c, Water purification. 35c+5c, 1cor+50c, like 10c+5c. 50c+10c, Antibiotics. 60c+15c, Malaria control. 70c+10c, Laboratory. 80c+20c, Gastroenteritis (sick and well babies).

1973, Sept. 25 **Litho.** ***Perf. 13½x14***

CB1	SPAP1	5c + 5c multi	15	15
CB2	SPAP1	10c + 5c multi	15	15
CB3	SPAP1	15c + 5c multi	15	15
CB4	SPAP1	20c + 5c multi	15	15
CB5	SPAP1	30c + 5c multi	15	15
CB6	SPAP1	35c + 5c multi	15	15
CB7	SPAP1	50c + 10c multi	15	15
CB8	SPAP1	60c + 15c multi	15	15
CB9	SPAP1	70c + 10c multi	15	15
CB10	SPAP1	80c + 20c multi	20	18
CB11	SPAP1	1cor + 50c multi	30	25
		Set value	1.20	1.00

The surtax was for hospital building fund. See No. C845. Inscriptions on back, printed on top of gum give brief description of subjects shown.

AIR POST OFFICIAL STAMPS

OA1

"Typewritten" Overprint on #O293

1929, Aug. **Unwmk.** ***Perf. 12***

CO1	OA1	25c orange	50.00	45.00

Excellent counterfeits of No. CO1 are plentiful.

Official Stamps of 1926 Overprinted in Dark Blue

Correo Aéreo

1929, Sept. 15

CO2	A24	25c orange	50	50
a.		Inverted overprint	25.00	
b.		Double overprint	25.00	
CO3	A25	50c pale bl	75	75
a.		Inverted overprint	25.00	
b.		Double overprint	25.00	
c.		Double overprint, one inverted	8.00	

Nos. 519-523 Overprinted in Black

Correo Aéreo
OFICIAL

1932, Feb.

CO4	A24	15c org red	40	40
a.		Inverted overprint	25.00	
b.		Double overprint	25.00	
c.		Double overprint, one inverted	25.00	
CO5	A25	20c orange	45	45
a.		Double overprint	25.00	
CO6	A24	25c dk vio	45	45
CO7	A25	50c green	55	55
CO8	A25	1cor yellow	1.00	1.00
		Nos. CO4-CO8 (5)	2.85	2.85

Nos. CO4-CO5, CO7-CO8 exist with signature control overprint. Value, each, $2.50.

Overprinted on Stamp No. 547

CO9	A24	25c blk brn	42.50	42.50

The varieties "OFICAL", "OFIAIAL" and "CORROE" occur in the setting and are found on each stamp of the series.

Counterfeits of No. CO9 are plentiful.

Stamp No. CO4 with overprint "1931" in addition is believed to be of private origin.

Type of Regular Issue of 1914 Overprinted Like Nos. CO4-CO8

1933

CO10	A24	25c olive	15	15
CO11	A25	50c ol grn	22	22
CO12	A25	1cor org red	40	40

On Stamps of 1914-28

CO13	A24	15c dp vio	15	15
CO14	A25	20c dp grn	15	15
		Nos. CO10-CO14 (5)	1.07	1.07

Nos. CO10-CO14 exist without signature control mark. Value, each $2.50.

Air Post Official Stamps of 1932-33 Overprinted in Blue

RESELLO 1935

1935

CO15	A24	15c dp vio	1.00	80
CO16	A25	20c dp grn	2.00	1.60
CO17	A24	25c olive	3.00	2.50
CO18	A25	50c ol grn	35.00	30.00
CO19	A25	1cor org red	40.00	37.50
		Nos. CO15-CO19 (5)	81.00	72.40

Overprinted in Red

CO20	A24	15c dp vio	25	22
CO21	A25	20c dp grn	25	22
CO22	A24	25c olive	25	25
CO23	A25	50c ol grn	80	80
CO24	A25	1cor org red	80	80
		Nos. CO20-CO24 (5)	2.35	2.29

Nos. CO15 to CO24 are handstamped with script control mark. Counterfeits of blue overprint are plentiful.

The editors do not recognize the Nicaraguan air post Official stamps overprinted in red "VALIDO 1935" in two lines and with or without script control marks as having been issued primarily for postal purposes.

Nos. C164-C168 Overprinted in Black

1937

CO25	AP1	15c yel org	80	55
CO26	AP1	20c org red	80	60
CO27	AP1	25c black	80	70
CO28	AP1	50c violet	80	70
CO29	AP1	1cor orange	80	70
		Nos. CO25-CO29 (5)	4.00	3.25

Pres. Anastasio Somoza — OA2

1939, Feb. 7 **Engr.** ***Perf. 12½***

CO30	OA2	10c brown	25	25
CO31	OA2	15c dk bl	25	25
CO32	OA2	20c yellow	25	25
CO33	OA2	25c dk pur	25	25
CO34	OA2	30c lake	25	25
CO35	OA2	50c dp org	65	65
CO36	OA2	1cor dk ol grn	1.20	1.20
		Nos. CO30-CO36 (7)	3.10	3.10

Catalogue values for unused stamps in this section, from this point to the end of the section, are for Never Hinged items.

Mercedes Airport — OA3

Designs: 10c, Sulphurous Lake of Nejapa. 15c, Ruben Dario Monument. 20c, Tapir. 25c, Genizaro Dam. 50c, Tipitapa Spa. 1cor, Stone Highway. 2.50cor, Franklin D. Roosevelt Monument.

Engraved, Center Photogravure

1947, Aug. 29

Various Frames in Black

CO37	OA3	5c org brn	15	15
CO38	OA3	10c blue	20	20
CO39	OA3	15c violet	15	15
CO40	OA3	20c red org	20	15
CO41	OA3	25c blue	15	15
CO42	OA3	50c car rose	20	20
CO43	OA3	1cor slate	45	45
CO44	OA3	2.50cor red brn	1.25	1.25
		Nos. CO37-CO44 (8)	2.75	2.70

Rowland Hill — OA4

Designs: 10c, Heinrich von Stephan. 25c, 1st UPU Bldg. 50c, UPU Bldg., Bern. 1cor, UPU Monument. 2.60cor, Congress medal, reverse.

1950, Nov. 23 **Engr.** ***Perf. 13***

Frames in Black

CO45	OA4	5c rose vio	15	15
CO46	OA4	10c dp grn	15	15
CO47	OA4	25c rose vio	15	15
CO48	OA4	50c dp org	15	15
CO49	OA4	1cor ultra	28	28
CO50	OA4	2.60cor gray blk	2.25	2.00
		Nos. CO45-CO50 (6)	3.13	2.88

75th anniv. (in 1949) of the UPU.

Each denomination was also issued in a souvenir sheet containing four stamps and marginal inscriptions. Size: 121x96mm. Value, set of 6 sheets, $35.

Consular Service Stamps Surcharged "Oficial Aereo" and New Denomination in Red, Black or Blue

Type AP63 illustrated above No. C454.

1961, Nov. **Unwmk.** **Engr.** ***Perf. 12***

Red Marginal Number

CO51	AP63	10c on 1cor grnsh blk (R)	15	15
CO52	AP63	15c on 20cor red brn (R)	15	15
CO53	AP63	20c on 100cor mag	15	15
CO54	AP63	25c on 50c dp bl (R)	15	15
CO55	AP63	35c on 50cor brn (R)	15	15
CO56	AP63	50c on 3cor dk car	15	15

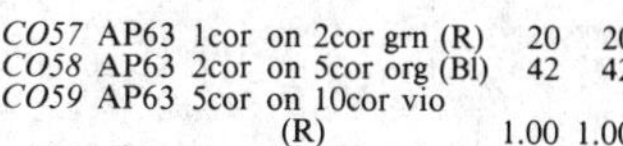

CO57	AP63	1cor on 2cor grn (R)	20	20
CO58	AP63	2cor on 5cor org (Bl)	42	42
CO59	AP63	5cor on 10cor vio (R)	1.00	1.00
		Set value	2.10	2.05

POSTAGE DUE STAMPS

D1

D2

1896 **Unwmk.** **Engr.** ***Perf. 12***

J1	D1	1c orange	50	*1.25*
J2	D1	2c orange	50	*1.25*
J3	D1	5c orange	50	*1.25*
J4	D1	10c orange	50	*1.25*
J5	D1	20c orange	50	*1.25*
J6	D1	30c orange	50	*1.25*
J7	D1	50c orange	50	*1.50*
		Nos. J1-J7 (7)	3.50	*9.00*

Wmk. 117

J8	D1	1c orange	1.00	*1.50*
J9	D1	2c orange	1.00	*1.50*
J10	D1	5c orange	1.00	*1.50*
J11	D1	10c orange	1.00	*1.50*
J12	D1	20c orange	1.25	*1.50*
J13	D1	30c orange	1.00	*1.50*
J14	D1	50c orange	1.00	*1.50*
		Nos. J8-J14 (7)	7.25	*10.50*

1897 **Unwmk.**

J15	D1	1c violet	50	*1.50*
J16	D1	2c violet	50	*1.50*
J17	D1	5c violet	50	*1.50*
J18	D1	10c violet	50	*1.50*
J19	D1	20c violet	1.25	*2.00*
J20	D1	30c violet	50	*1.50*
J21	D1	50c violet	50	*1.50*
		Nos. J15-J21 (7)	4.25	*11.00*

Wmk. 117

J22	D1	1c violet	50	*1.50*
J23	D1	2c violet	50	*1.50*
J24	D1	5c violet	50	*1.50*
J25	D1	10c violet	50	*1.50*
J26	D1	20c violet	1.00	*2.00*
J27	D1	30c violet	50	*1.50*
J28	D1	50c violet	50	*1.50*
		Nos. J22-J28 (7)	4.00	*11.00*

Reprints of Nos. J1-J28 are on thick, porous paper. Color of 1896 reprints, reddish orange; or 1897 reprints, reddish violet. On watermarked reprints, liberty cap is sideways. Value 25c each.

1898 **Litho.** **Unwmk.**

J29	D2	1c bl grn	15	*2.00*
J30	D2	2c bl grn	15	*2.00*
J31	D2	5c bl grn	15	*2.00*
J32	D2	10c bl grn	15	*2.00*
J33	D2	20c bl grn	15	*2.00*
J34	D2	30c bl grn	15	*2.00*
J35	D2	50c bl grn	15	*2.00*
		Nos. J29-J35 (7)	1.05	

1899

J36	D2	1c carmine	15	*2.00*
J37	D2	2c carmine	15	*2.00*
J38	D2	5c carmine	15	*2.00*
J39	D2	10c carmine	15	*2.00*
J40	D2	20c carmine	15	*2.00*
J41	D2	50c carmine	15	*2.00*
		Set value	60	

Some denominations are found in se-tenant pairs.

Various counterfeit cancellations exist on Nos. J1-J41.

D3

1900 **Engr.**

J42	D3	1c plum	1.00
J43	D3	2c vermilion	1.00
J44	D3	5c dk bl	1.00
J45	D3	10c purple	1.00
J46	D3	20c org brn	1.00

No.	Description	Unused	Used
J47	D3 30c dk grn	2.00	
J48	D3 50c lake	2.00	
	Nos. J42-J48 (7)	9.00	

Nos. J42-J48 were not issued without postage overprint. See Nos. 137-143, 152-158. For overprints see Nos. 137-143, 152-158, O72-O81, 2L11-2L15, 2L25, 2L40-2L41.

OFFICIAL STAMPS

Types of Postage Stamps Overprinted in Red Diagonally Reading up

FRANQUEO OFICIAL

1890 **Unwmk.** **Engr.** ***Perf. 12***

No.	Description	Unused	Used
O1	A5 1c ultra	15	*35*
O2	A5 2c ultra	15	*35*
O3	A5 5c ultra	15	*35*
O4	A5 10c ultra	15	*40*
O5	A5 20c ultra	15	*75*
O6	A5 50c ultra	15	*75*
O7	A5 1p ultra	15	*1.25*
O8	A5 2p ultra	15	*1.50*
O9	A5 5p ultra	15	*2.50*
O10	A5 10p ultra	15	*3.25*
	Nos. O1-O10 (10)	1.50	

All values of the 1890 issue are known without overprint and most of them with inverted or double overprint, or without overprint and imperforate. There is no evidence that they were issued in these forms.

Official stamps of 1890-1899 are scarce with genuine cancellations. Forged cancellations are plentiful.

Overprinted Vertically Reading Up

1891 **Litho.**

No.	Description	Unused	Used
O11	A6 1c green	15	*35*
O12	A6 2c green	15	*35*
O13	A6 5c green	15	*35*
O14	A6 10c green	15	*35*
O15	A6 20c green	15	*75*
O16	A6 50c green	15	*1.25*
O17	A6 1p green	15	*1.50*
O18	A6 2p green	15	*1.50*
O19	A6 5p green	15	*2.50*
O20	A6 10p green	15	*4.00*
	Nos. O11-O20 (10)	1.50	

All values of this issue except the 2c and 5p exist without overprint and several with double overprint. They are not known to have been issued in this form.

Many of the denominations may be found in se-tenant pairs.

Overprinted in Dark Blue

FRANQUEO OFICIAL

1892 **Engr.**

No.	Description	Unused	Used
O21	A7 1c yel brn	15	*35*
O22	A7 2c yel brn	15	*35*
O23	A7 5c yel brn	15	*35*
O24	A7 10c yel brn	15	*35*
O25	A7 20c yel brn	15	*75*
O26	A7 50c yel brn	15	*1.00*
O27	A7 1p yel brn	15	*1.50*
O28	A7 2p yel brn	15	*2.00*
O29	A7 5p yel brn	15	*3.00*
O30	A7 10p yel brn	15	*4.00*
	Nos. O21-O30 (10)	1.50	

The 2c and 1p are known without overprint and several values exist with double or inverted overprint. These probably were not regularly issued.

Commemorative of the 400th anniversary of the discovery of America by Christopher Columbus.

Overprinted in Red

FRANQUEO OFICIAL

1893 **Engr.**

No.	Description	Unused	Used
O31	A8 1c slate	15	*35*
O32	A8 2c slate	15	*35*
O33	A8 5c slate	15	*35*
O34	A8 10c slate	15	*35*
O35	A8 20c slate	15	*50*
O36	A8 25c slate	15	
O37	A8 50c slate	15	*85*
O38	A8 1p slate	15	*1.50*
O39	A8 2p slate	15	*2.00*
O40	A8 5p slate	15	*3.00*
O41	A8 10p slate	15	*4.00*
	Nos. O31-O41 (11)	1.65	

The 2, 5, 10, 20, 25, 50c and 5p are known without overprint but probably were not regularly issued. Some values exist with double or inverted overprints.

Overprinted in Black

FRANQUEO OFICIAL

1894

No.	Description	Unused	Used
O42	A9 1c orange	15	*35*
O43	A9 2c orange	15	*35*
O44	A9 5c orange	15	*35*
O45	A9 10c orange	15	*35*
O46	A9 20c orange	15	*50*
O47	A9 50c orange	15	*75*
O48	A9 1p orange	15	*1.50*
O49	A9 2p orange	15	*2.00*
O50	A9 5p orange	15	*3.00*
O51	A9 10p orange	15	*4.00*
	Nos. O42-O51 (10)	1.50	

Reprints are yellow.

1895

Overprinted in Blue

No.	Description	Unused	Used
O52	A10 1c green	15	*35*
O53	A10 2c green	15	*35*
O54	A10 5c green	15	*35*
O55	A10 10c green	15	*35*
O56	A10 20c green	15	*50*
O57	A10 50c green	15	*1.00*
O58	A10 1p green	15	*1.50*
O59	A10 2p green	15	*2.00*
O60	A10 5p green	15	*3.00*
O61	A10 10p green	15	*4.00*
	Nos. O52-O61 (10)	1.50	

Wmk. 117

No.	Description	Unused	Used
O62	A10 1c green		
O63	A10 2c green		
O64	A10 5c green		
O65	A10 10c green		
O66	A10 20c green		
O67	A10 50c green		
O68	A10 1p green		
O69	A10 2p green		
O70	A10 5p green		
O71	A10 10p green		

Nos. O62-O71 probably exist only as reprints. Value, each 15 cents.

Postage Due Stamps of Same Date Handstamped in Violet

Franqueo Oficial

1896 **Unwmk.**

No.	Description	Unused	Used
O72	D1 1c orange	7.00	
O73	D1 2c orange	7.00	
O74	D1 5c orange	5.00	
O75	D1 10c orange	5.00	
O76	D1 20c orange	5.00	
	Set value	29.00	

Wmk. 117

No.	Description	Unused	Used
O77	D1 1c orange	7.00	
O78	D1 2c orange	7.00	
O79	D1 5c orange	4.00	
O80	D1 10c orange	4.00	
O81	D1 20c orange	4.00	
	Set value	26.00	

Nos. O72 to O81 were handstamped in rows of five. Several handstamps were used, one of which had the variety "Oftcial". Most varieties are known inverted and double.

Types of Postage Stamps Overprinted in Red

1896 **Unwmk.**

No.	Description	Unused	Used
O82	A11 1c red	2.50	3.00
O83	A11 2c red	2.50	3.00
O84	A11 5c red	2.50	3.00
O85	A11 10c red	2.50	3.00
O86	A11 20c red	3.00	3.00
O87	A11 50c red	5.00	*5.00*
O88	A11 1p red	12.00	*12.00*
O89	A11 2p red	12.00	*12.00*
O90	A11 5p red	16.00	*16.00*
	Nos. O82-O90 (9)	58.00	*60.00*

Wmk. 117

No.	Description	Unused	Used
O91	A11 1c red	3.00	3.50
O92	A11 2c red	3.00	3.50
O93	A11 5c red	3.00	3.50
O94	A11 10c red	3.00	3.50
O95	A11 20c red	5.00	5.00
O96	A11 50c red	3.00	*5.00*
O97	A11 1p red	14.00	*14.00*
O98	A11 2p red	16.50	*16.50*
O99	A11 5p red	25.00	*25.00*
	Nos. O91-O99 (9)	75.50	*79.50*

Same, Dated 1897

1897 **Unwmk.**

No.	Description	Unused	Used
O100	A11 1c red	3.00	3.00
O101	A11 2c red	3.00	3.00
O102	A11 5c red	3.00	2.50
O103	A11 10c red	3.00	3.00
O104	A11 20c red	3.00	4.00
O105	A11 50c red	5.00	*5.00*
O106	A11 1p red	12.00	*12.00*
O107	A11 2p red	12.00	*12.00*
O108	A11 5p red	16.00	*16.00*
	Nos. O100-O108 (9)	60.00	*60.50*

Wmk. 117

No.	Description	Unused	Used
O109	A11 1c red	5.00	5.00
O110	A11 2c red	5.00	5.00
O111	A11 5c red	5.00	5.00
O112	A11 10c red	10.00	10.00
O113	A11 20c red	10.00	10.00
O114	A11 50c red	12.00	*12.00*
O115	A11 1p red	20.00	*20.00*
O116	A11 2p red	20.00	*20.00*
O117	A11 5p red	20.00	*20.00*
	Nos. O109-O117 (9)	107.00	*107.00*

Overprinted in Blue

1898 **Unwmk.**

No.	Description	Unused	Used
O118	A12 1c carmine	3.25	3.25
O119	A12 2c carmine	3.25	3.25
O120	A12 4c carmine	3.25	3.25
O121	A12 5c carmine	2.50	2.50
O122	A12 10c carmine	4.00	4.00
O123	A12 15c carmine	6.00	6.00
O124	A12 20c carmine	6.00	6.00
O125	A12 50c carmine	8.50	*8.50*
O126	A12 1p carmine	11.00	*11.00*
O127	A12 2p carmine	11.00	*11.00*
O128	A12 5p carmine	11.00	*11.00*
	Nos. O118-O128 (11)	69.75	69.75

Stamps of this set with sideways watermark 117 or with black overprint are reprints. Value 25c each.

Reprints of Nos. O82-O117 are described in notes after No. 109M. Value 15c each.

Overprinted in Dark Blue

1899

No.	Description	Unused	Used
O129	A13 1c gray grn	15	*1.00*
O130	A13 2c bis brn	15	*1.00*
O131	A13 4c lake	15	*1.00*
O132	A13 5c dk bl	15	*50*
O133	A13 10c buff	15	*1.00*
O134	A13 15c chocolate	15	*2.00*
O135	A13 20c dk grn	15	*3.00*
O136	A13 50c car rose	15	*3.00*
O137	A13 1p red	15	*10.00*
O138	A13 2p violet	15	*10.00*
O139	A13 5p lt bl	15	*15.00*
	Set value	1.10	

Counterfeit cancellations on Nos. O129-O139 are plentiful.

"Justice" — O5

1900 **Engr.**

No.	Description	Unused	Used
O140	O5 1c plum	60	60
O141	O5 2c vermilion	50	50
O142	O5 4c ol grn	60	60
O143	O5 5c dk bl	1.25	45
O144	O5 10c purple	1.25	35
O145	O5 20c brown	90	35
O146	O5 50c lake	1.25	50
O147	O5 1p ultra	3.50	2.50
O148	O5 2p brn org	4.00	4.00
O149	O5 5p grnsh blk	5.00	5.00
	Nos. O140-O149 (10)	18.85	14.85

For surcharges see Nos. O155-O157.

Nos. 123, 161 Surcharged in Black

1 1
OFICIAL
1 Centavo

1903 ***Perf. 12, 14***

No.	Description	Unused	Used
O150	A14 1c on 10c vio	25	30
a.	"Centovo"	1.00	
b.	"Contavo"	1.00	
c.	With ornaments	30	
d.	Inverted surcharge	1.00	
e.	"1" omitted at upper left	2.00	
O151	A14 2c on 3c grn	30	40
a.	"Centovos"	1.00	
b.	"Contavos"	1.00	
c.	With ornaments	35	
d.	Inverted surcharge	1.00	
O152	A14 4c on 3c grn	1.25	1.25
a.	"Centovos"	2.50	
b.	"Contavos"	2.50	
c.	With ornaments	2.50	
d.	Inverted surcharge		
O153	A14 4c on 10c vio	1.25	1.25
a.	"Centovos"	2.50	
b.	"Contavos"	2.50	
c.	With ornaments	2.00	
d.	Inverted surcharge		
O154	A14 5c on 3c grn	15	18
a.	"Centovos"	1.00	
b.	"Contavos"	1.00	
c.	With ornaments	30	
d.	Double surcharge	2.00	
e.	Inverted surcharge		
	Nos. O150-O154 (5)	3.20	3.38

These surcharges are set up to cover 25 stamps. Some of the settings have bars or pieces of fancy border type below "OFICIAL." There are 5 varieties on #O150, 3 on #O151, and 1 each on #O152, O153 and O154.

In 1904 #O151 was reprinted to fill a dealer's order. This printing lacks the small figure at the upper right. It includes the variety "OFICILA." At the same time the same setting was printed in carmine on official stamps of 1900, 1c on 10c violet and 2c on 1p ultramarine. Also the 1, 2 and 5p official stamps of 1900 were surcharged with new values and the dates 1901 or 1902 in various colors, inverted, etc. It is doubtful if any of these varieties were ever in Nicaragua and certain that none of them ever did legitimate postal duty.

10 10

No. O145 Surcharged in Black

10 Ctvs.

1904 ***Perf. 12***

No.	Description	Unused	Used
O155	O5 10c on 20c brn	20	20
a.	No period after "Ctvs"	1.00	75
O156	O5 30c on 20c brn	20	20
O157	O5 50c on 20c brn	50	35
a.	Lower "50" omitted	2.50	2.50
b.	Upper figures omitted	2.50	2.50
c.	Top left and lower figures omitted	3.50	3.50

Coat of Arms — O6

1905, July 25 **Engr.**

No.	Description	Unused	Used
O158	O6 1c green	25	25
O159	O6 2c rose	25	25
O160	O6 5c blue	25	25
O161	O6 10c yel brn	25	25
O162	O6 20c orange	25	25
O163	O6 50c brn ol	25	25
O164	O6 1p lake	25	25
O165	O6 2p violet	25	25
O166	O6 5p gray blk	25	25
	Nos. O158-O166 (9)	2.25	2.25

Surcharged Vertically Up or Down

Vale 10

1907

O167 O6 10c on 1c grn 75 75
O168 O6 10c on 2c rose 25.00 22.50
O169 O6 20c on 2c rose 22.50 17.50
O170 O6 50c on 1c grn 1.50 1.50
O171 O6 50c on 2c rose 22.50 12.50

Surcharged **Vale $ 1.00**

O172 O6 1p on 2c rose 1.50 1.50
O173 O6 2p on 2c rose 1.50 1.50
O174 O6 3p on 2c rose 1.50 1.50
O175 O6 4p on 2c rose
O176 O6 4p on 5c blue 2.25 2.25

The setting for this surcharge includes various letters from wrong fonts, the figure "1" for "l" in "Vale" and an "l" for "1" in "$1.00".

Surcharged **Vale 20 cts**

O177 O6 20c on 1c green 1.00 1.00
a. Double surcharge 5.00 5.00
Nos. O167-O174,O176-O177 (10) 80.00 62.50

The preceding surcharges are vertical, reading both up and down.

O7

Revenue Stamps Surcharged

1907 *Perf. 14 to 15*

O178 O7 10c on 2c org (Bk) 15 15
O179 O7 35c on 1c bl (R) 15 15
a. Inverted surcharge 3.00 3.00
O180 O7 70c on 1c bl (V) 15 15
a. Inverted surcharge 3.00 3.00
O181 O7 70c on 1c bl (O) 15 15
a. Inverted surcharge 3.00 3.00
O182 O7 1p on 2c org (G) 15 15
a. Inverted surcharge 2.50 2.50
O183 O7 2p on 2c org (Br) 15 15
O184 O7 3p on 5c brn (Bl) 15 15
O185 O7 4p on 5c brn (G) 20 20
a. Double surcharge 3.00 3.00
O186 O7 5p on 5c brn (G) 20 20
a. Inverted surcharge 3.50 3.50
Nos. O178-O186 (9) 1.45 1.45

Letters and figures from several fonts were mixed in these surcharges.
See Nos. O199-O209.

No. 202 Surcharged **OFICIAL —10 CVS—**

1907, Nov.

Black or Blue Black Surcharge

O187 A18 10c on 1c grn 15.00 13.00
O188 A18 15c on 1c grn 15.00 13.00
O189 A18 20c on 1c grn 15.00 13.00
O190 A18 50c on 1c grn 15.00 13.00

Red Surcharge

O191 A18 1(un)p on 1c grn 14.00 13.00
O192 A18 2(dos)p on 1c grn 14.00 13.00
Nos. O187-O192 (6) 88.00 78.00

No. 181 Surcharged **OFICIAL VALE 10 ₵**

1908 Yellow Surcharge *Perf. 12*

O193 A18 10c on 3c vio 15.00 15.00
O194 A18 15c on 3c vio 15.00 15.00
O195 A18 20c on 3c vio 15.00 15.00
O196 A18 35c on 3c vio 15.00 15.00
O197 A18 50c on 3c vio 15.00 15.00
Nos. O193-O197 (5) 75.00 75.00

Black Surcharge

O198 A18 35c on 3c vio 60.00 60.00

Revenue Stamps Surcharged like 1907 Issue
Dated "1908"

1908 *Perf. 14 to 15*

O199 O7 10c on 1c bl (V) 75 50
a. Inverted surcharge 3.50 3.50
O200 O7 35c on 1c bl (Bk) 75 50
a. Inverted surcharge 3.50 3.50
b. Double surcharge 4.00 4.00
O201 O7 50c on 1c bl (R) 75 50
O202 O7 1p on 1c bl (Br) 37.50 37.50
a. Inverted surcharge 65.00 65.00
O203 O7 2p on 1c bl (G) 90 75
O204 O7 10c on 2c org (Bk) 1.10 65
O205 O7 35c on 2c org (R) 1.10 65
a. Double surcharge 3.50
O206 O7 50c on 2c org (Bk) 1.10 65
O207 O7 70c on 2c org (Bl) 1.10 65
O208 O7 1p on 2c org (G) 1.10 65
O209 O7 2p on 2c org (Br) 1.10 65
Nos. O199-O209 (11) 47.25 43.65

There are several minor varieties in the figures, etc., in these surcharges.

Nos. 243-248 Overprinted in Black **OFICIAL**

1909 *Perf. 12*

O210 A18 10c lake 20 15
a. Double overprint 2.50 2.50
O211 A18 15c black 60 50
O212 A18 20c brn ol 1.00 75
O213 A18 50c dp grn 1.50 1.00
O214 A18 1p yellow 1.75 1.25
O215 A18 2p car rose 2.75 2.00
Nos. O210-O215 (6) 7.80 5.65

Overprinted in Black **OFICIAL**

1910

O216 A18 15c black 1.50 1.25
a. Double overprint 4.00 4.00
O217 A18 20c brn ol 2.50 2.00
O218 A18 50c dp grn 2.50 2.00
O219 A18 1p yellow 2.75 2.50
a. Inverted overprint 7.50 7.50
O220 A18 2p car rose 4.00 3.00
Nos. O216-O220 (5) 13.25 10.75

Nos. 239-240 Surcharged in Black **OFICIAL Vale 10 cts.**

1911

O221 A18 5c on 3c red org 6.00 6.00
O222 A18 10c on 4c vio 5.00 5.00
a. Double surcharge 10.00 10.00
b. Pair, one without new value 20.00

Railroad Stamps Surcharged in Black **Correo oficial Vale 10 cts.**

1911, Nov. *Perf. 14 to 15*

O223 A21 10c on 1 red 3.00 3.00
a. Inverted surcharge 4.50
b. Double surcharge 4.50
O224 A21 15c on 1 red 3.00 3.00
a. Inverted surcharge 5.00
b. Double surcharge 4.50
O225 A21 20c on 1 red 3.00 3.00
a. Inverted surcharge 5.00
O226 A21 50c on 1 red 3.75 3.75
a. Inverted surcharge 4.50
O227 A21 1p on 1 red 5.00 7.00
a. Inverted surcharge 6.00
O228 A21 2p on 1 red 5.50 10.00
a. Inverted surcharge 7.50
b. Double surcharge 7.50
Nos. O223-O228 (6) 23.25 29.75

Surcharged in Black **CORREO OFICIAL 15 centavos**

1911, Nov.

O229 A21 10c on 1 red 22.50
O230 A21 15c on 1 red 22.50
O231 A21 20c on 1 red 22.50
O232 A21 50c on 1 red 16.00

Surcharged in Black **Correo oficial Vale 5 cts. 1911**

1911, Dec.

O233 A21 5c on 1 red 4.50 6.00
a. Double surcharge 7.50
b. Inverted surcharge 7.50
c. "5" omitted 6.00
O234 A21 10c on 1 red 5.50 7.00
O235 A21 15c on 1 red 6.00 7.50
O236 A21 20c on 1 red 6.50 8.50
O237 A21 50c on 1 red 7.50 10.00
Nos. O233-O237 (5) 30.00 39.00

Nos. O233 to O237 have a surcharge on the back like Nos. 285 and 286 with "15 cts" obliterated by a heavy bar.

Surcharged Vertically in Black **Correo Oficial 1912 85 cvs.**

1912

O238 A21 5c on 1 red 8.00 8.00
O239 A21 10c on 1 red 8.00 8.00
O240 A21 15c on 1 red 8.00 8.00
O241 A21 20c on 1 red 8.00 8.00
O242 A21 35c on 1 red 8.00 8.00
O243 A21 50c on 1 red 8.00 8.00
O244 A21 1p on 1 red 8.00 8.00
Nos. O238-O244 (7) 56.00 56.00

Nos. O238 to O244 are printed on Nos. 285 and 286 but the surcharge on the back is obliterated by a vertical bar.

Types of Regular Issue of 1912 Overprinted in Black **OFICIAL**

1912 *Perf. 12*

O245 A22 1c lt bl 15 15
O246 A22 2c lt bl 15 15
O247 A22 3c lt bl 15 15
O248 A22 4c lt bl 15 15
O249 A22 5c lt bl 15 15
O250 A22 6c lt bl 15 15
O251 A22 10c lt bl 15 15
O252 A22 15c lt bl 15 15
O253 A22 20c lt bl 15 15
O254 A22 25c lt bl 20 20
O255 A22 35c lt bl 25 25
O256 A22 50c lt bl 1.50 1.50
O257 A22 1p lt bl 30 30
O258 A22 2p lt bl 35 35
O259 A22 5p lt bl 50 50
Set value 3.85 3.85

On the 35c the overprint is 15½mm wide, on the other values it is 13mm.

Types of Regular Issue of 1914 Overprinted in Black **OFICIAL**

1915, May

O260 A24 1c lt bl 15 15
O261 A25 2c lt bl 15 15
O262 A24 3c lt bl 20 15
O263 A25 4c lt bl 15 15
O264 A24 5c lt bl 15 15
O265 A25 6c lt bl 15 15
O266 A25 10c lt bl 15 15
O267 A24 15c lt bl 20 20
O268 A25 20c lt bl 20 20
O269 A24 25c lt bl 30 30
O270 A25 50c lt bl 60 60
Nos. O260-O270 (11) 2.40 2.35

Regular Issues of 1914-22 Overprinted in Red **Oficial**

1925

O271 A24 ½c dp grn 15 15
a. Double overprint 2.50 2.50
O272 A24 1c violet 15 15
O273 A25 2c car rose 15 15
O274 A24 3c ol grn 15 15
O275 A25 4c vermilion 15 15
a. Double overprint 2.50 2.50
O276 A24 5c black 15 15
a. Double overprint 2.50 2.50
O277 A25 6c red brn 25 25
O278 A25 10c yellow 35 35
a. Double overprint 3.50 3.50
O279 A24 15c red brn 40 40
O280 A25 20c bis brn 50 50
O281 A24 25c orange 60 60
a. Inverted overprint 4.00 4.00
O282 A25 50c pale bl 75 75
a. Double overprint 5.00 5.00
Nos. O271-O282 (12) 3.75 3.75

Type II overprint has "f" and "i" separated. Comes on Nos. O272-O274 and O276.

Regular Issues of 1914-22 Overprinted in Black **OFICIAL**

1926

O283 A24 ½c dk grn 15 15
O284 A24 1c dp vio 15 15
O285 A25 2c car rose 15 15
O286 A24 3c ol gray 15 15
O287 A25 4c vermilion 15 15
O288 A24 5c gray blk 15 15
O289 A25 6c red brn 15 15
O290 A25 10c yellow 15 15
O291 A24 15c dp brn 15 15
O292 A25 20c bis brn 15 15
O293 A24 25c orange 15 18
O294 A25 50c pale bl 25 25
Set value 1.30 1.30

No. 499 Surcharged in Black **OFICIAL ₵ 0.05 1931**

1931

O295 A33 5c on 10c bis brn 20 20

Nos. 517-518 Overprinted in Red **OFICIAL**

1931

O296 A25 6c bis brn 20 20
O297 A25 10c lt brn 20 20

Nos. 541, 543, 545 With Additional Overprint in Black **1931**

O298 A24 1c ol grn 16 16
O299 A24 3c lt bl 16 16
a. "OFICIAL" inverted 80 80
O300 A24 5c gray brn 16 16
a. "1931" double 80 80

Regular Issues of 1914-31 Overprinted in Black **OFICIAL**

1932, Feb. 6

O301 A24 1c ol grn 15 15
a. Double overprint 1.40 1.40
O302 A25 2c brt rose 15 15
a. Double overprint 1.40 1.40
O303 A24 3c lt bl 15 15
a. Double overprint 50 50
O304 A25 4c dk bl 15 15
O305 A24 5c ol brn 15 15
O306 A25 6c bis brn 20 15
a. Double overprint 2.00 2.00
O307 A25 10c lt brn 30 20
O308 A24 15c org red 40 22
a. Double overprint 2.25 2.25
O309 A25 20c orange 65 35
O310 A24 25c dk vio 2.00 50
O311 A25 50c green 15 15
O312 A25 1cor yellow 20 20
Nos. O301-O312 (12) 4.65 2.52

With Additional Overprint in Black **1931**

1932, Feb. 6

O313 A24 1c ol grn 5.50 5.50
O314 A25 2c brt rose 6.50 6.50
a. Double overprint 8.25 8.25
O315 A24 3c lt bl 5.00 5.00
O316 A24 5c ol brn 5.00 5.00
O317 A24 15c org red 65 65
O318 A24 25c blk brn 65 65
O319 A24 25c dk vio 1.50 1.50
Nos. O313-O319 (7) 24.80 24.80

The variety "OFIAIAL" occurs once in each sheet of Nos. O301 to O319 inclusive.

Flag of the Race Issue

1933, Aug. 9 Litho. *Rouletted 9*

Without gum

O320 A43 1c orange 1.00 1.00
O321 A43 2c yellow 1.00 1.00
O322 A43 3c dk brn 1.00 1.00
O323 A43 4c dp brn 1.00 1.00
O324 A43 5c gray brn 1.00 1.00
O325 A43 6c dp ultra 1.20 1.20
O326 A43 10c dp vio 1.20 1.20
O327 A43 15c red vio 1.20 1.20
O328 A43 20c dp grn 1.20 1.20
O329 A43 25c green 2.00 2.00
O330 A43 50c carmine 2.50 2.50
O331 A43 1cor red 4.00 4.00
Nos. O320-O331 (12) 18.30 18.30

See note after No. 599.

Reprints of Nos. O320-O331 exist.

A 25c dull blue exists. Its status is questioned.

Regular Issue of 1914-31 Overprinted in Red **OFICIAL**

1933, Nov. *Perf. 12*

O332 A24 1c ol grn 15 15
O333 A25 2c brt rose 15 15
O334 A24 3c lt bl 15 15
O335 A25 4c dk bl 15 15
O336 A24 5c ol brn 15 15
O337 A25 6c bis brn 15 15
O338 A25 10c lt brn 15 15
O339 A24 15c red org 15 15
O340 A25 20c orange 15 15
O341 A24 25c dk vio 15 15
O342 A25 50c green 16 16
O343 A25 1cor yellow 35 20
Set value 1.00 90

Nos. O332-O343 exist with or without signature control overprint. Values are the same.

Official Stamps of 1933 Overprinted as Nos. CO15-CO19 in Blue

1935, Dec.

O344 A24 1c ol grn 65 42
O345 A25 2c brt rose 65 50
O346 A24 3c lt bl 1.60 50
O347 A25 4c dk bl 1.60 1.60
O348 A24 5c ol brn 1.60 1.60
O349 A25 6c bis brn 2.00 2.00
O350 A25 10c lt brn 2.00 2.00
O351 A24 15c org red 28.00 28.00
O352 A25 20c orange 28.00 28.00
O353 A24 25c dk vio 28.00 28.00
O354 A25 50c green 28.00 28.00
O355 A25 1cor yellow 28.00 28.00
Nos. O344-O355 (12) 150.10 148.62

Nos. O344-O355 have signature control overprints. Counterfeits of overprint abound.

Same Overprinted in Red

1936, Jan.

O356 A24 1c ol grn 15 15
O357 A25 2c brt rose 15 15
O358 A24 3c lt bl 15 15
a. Double overprint
O359 A25 4c dk bl 15 15
O360 A24 5c ol brn 15 15
O361 A25 6c bis brn 15 15
O362 A25 10c lt brn 15 15
O363 A24 15c org red 15 15
O364 A25 20c orange 15 15
O365 A24 25c dk vio 15 15
O366 A25 50c green 16 16
O367 A25 1cor yellow 35 35
Set value 1.35 1.35

Have signature control overprints.

Nos. 653 to 655, 657, 659 660, 662 to 664 Overprinted in Black

1937

O368 A24 1c car rose 20 16
O369 A25 2c dp bl 20 16
O370 A24 3c chocolate 25 22
O371 A24 5c org red 35 25
O372 A25 10c ol grn 65 40
O373 A24 15c green 80 50
O374 A24 25c orange 1.00 65
O375 A24 50c brown 1.40 80
O376 A25 1cor ultra 2.50 1.20
Nos. O368-O376 (9) 7.35 4.34

Islands of the Great Lake
O9

1939, Jan. Engr. *Perf. 12½*

O377 O9 2c rose red 15 15
O378 O9 3c lt bl 15 15
O379 O9 6c brn org 15 15
O380 O9 7½c dp grn 15 15
O381 O9 10c blk brn 15 15
O382 O9 15c orange 15 15
O383 O9 25c dk vio 25 25
O384 O9 50c brt yel grn 40 40
Set value 1.25 1.25

POSTAL TAX STAMPS

Official Stamps of 1915 Surcharged in Black

Vale
un centavo
R de C

1921, July Unwmk. *Perf. 12*

RA1 A24 1c on 5c lt bl 1.50 60
RA2 A25 1c on 6c lt bl 65 20
a. Double surcharge, one inverted
RA3 A25 1c on 10c lt bl 1.00 25
a. Double surcharge 3.50 3.50
RA4 A24 1c on 15c lt bl 1.50 25
a. Double surcharge, one inverted 5.00 5.00

"R de C" signifies "Reconstruccion de Comunicaciones." The stamps were intended to provide a fund for rebuilding the General Post Office which was burned in April, 1921. One stamp was required on each letter or parcel, in addition to the regular postage. In the setting of one hundred there are five stamps with antique "C" and twenty-one with "R" and "C" smaller than in the illustration. One or more stamps in the setting have a dotted bar, as illustrated over No. 388, instead of the double bar.

The use of the "R de C" stamps for the payment of regular postage was not permitted.

Official Stamp of 1915 Overprinted in Black

«Particular»
R de C

RA5 A24 1c light blue 6.00 1.75

This stamp is known with the dotted bar as illustrated over No. 388, instead of the double bar.

Coat of Arms — PT1

PT2

1921, Sept.

Red Surcharge

RA6 PT1 1c on 1c ver & blk 15 15
RA7 PT1 1c on 2c grn & blk 15 15
a. Double surcharge 3.00 3.00
b. Double surcharge, one inverted 4.00 4.00
RA8 PT1 1c on 4c org & blk 15 15
a. Double surcharge 4.00 4.00
RA9 PT1 1c on 15c dk bl & blk 15 15
a. Double surcharge 3.00 3.00
Set value 40

1922, Feb.

Black Surcharge

RA10 PT2 1c on 10c yel 15 15
a. Period after "de" 50 40
b. Double surcharge 2.00 2.00
c. Double inverted surcharge 3.75 3.75
d. Inverted surcharge 3.00 3.00
e. Without period after "C" 1.00 1.00

No. 409 Overprinted in Black **R. de C.**

RA11 A24 1c violet 16 15
a. Double overprint 2.00 2.00

This stamp with the overprint in red is a trial printing.

Nos. 402, 404-407 Surcharged in Black

R. de C.
Vale
un centavo

1922, June

RA12 A27 1c on 1c grn & blk 75 75
RA13 A29 1c on 5c ultra & blk 75 75
RA14 A30 1c on 10c org & blk 75 40
RA15 A31 1c on 25c yel & blk 75 30
a. Inverted surcharge 5.00 5.00
RA16 A32 1c on 50c vio & blk 30 25
a. Double surcharge 4.00 4.00
Nos. RA12-RA16 (5) 3.30 2.45

PT3

Surcharge in Red or Dark Blue

1922, Oct. *Perf. 11½*

RA17 PT3 1c yellow (R) 15 15
a. No period after "C" 1.00 1.00
RA18 PT3 1c violet (DBl) 15 15
a. No period after "C" 1.00 1.00
Set value 24 20

Surcharge is inverted on 22 out of 50 of No. RA17, 23 out of 50 of No. RA18.

Nos. 403-407 Surcharged in Black

R. de C.
Vale
un centavo
de córdoba

1923 *Perf. 12*

RA19 A28 1c on 2c rose red & ultra 50 45
RA20 A29 1c on 5c ultra & blk 55 15
RA21 A30 1c on 10c org & blk 25 20
RA22 A31 1c on 25c yel & blk 35 30
RA23 A32 1c on 50c vio & blk 25 15
Nos. RA19-RA23 (5) 1.90 1.25

The variety no period after "R" occurs twice on each sheet.

Red Surcharge

Wmk. Coat of Arms in Sheet

Perf. 11½

RA24 PT3 1c pale blue 15 15

Unwmk.

Type of 1921 Issue

Without Surcharge of New Value

RA25 PT1 1c ver & blk 15 15
a. Double overprint, one inverted 3.00 3.00

No. 409 Overprinted in Blue **R. de C. 1924**

1924

RA26 A24 1c violet 20 15
a. Double overprint 8.00 8.00

There are two settings of the overprint on No. RA26, with "1924" 5½mm or 6½mm wide.

No. 409 Overprinted in Blue **R. de C. 1925**

1925

RA27 A24 1c violet 15 15

No. 409 Overprinted in Blue **R. de C.**

1926

RA28 A24 1c violet 25 15

No. RA28 Overprinted in Various Colors **Resello 1927**

1927

RA29 A24 1c vio (R) 15 15
a. Double overprint (R) 2.00 2.00
b. Inverted overprint (R) 3.00 3.00
RA30 A24 1c vio (V) 15 15
a. Double overprint 2.50 2.50
b. Inverted overprint 2.50 2.50
RA31 A24 1c vio (Bl) 15 15
a. Double overprint 5.00 5.00
RA32 A24 1c vio (Bk) 15 15
a. Double ovpt., one invtd. 4.25 4.25
b. Double overprint 4.25 4.25

Same Overprint on No. RA27

RA33 A24 1c vio (Bk) 15.00 10.00
Nos. RA29-RA33 (5) 15.60 10.60

No. RA28 Overprinted in Violet **Resello 1928**

1928

RA34 A24 1c violet 15 15
a. Double overprint 2.00 2.00
b. "928" 1.00 1.00

Similar to No. RA34 but 8mm space between "Resello" and "1928"

Black Overprint

RA35 A24 1c violet 40 15
a. "1828" 2.00 2.00

PT4

Inscribed "Timbre Telegrafico"
Horiz. Surch. in Black,
Vert. Surch. in Red

RA36 PT4 1c on 5c bl & blk 60 15
a. Comma after "R" 1.25 1.25
b. No period after "R" 1.25 1.25
c. No periods after "R" and "C" 1.25 1.25

("CORREOS" at right) — PT5

PT6

1928 Engr. *Perf. 12*

RA37 PT5 1c plum 25 15

See Nos. RA41-RA43. For overprints see Nos. RA45-RA46, RA48-RA51.

1929

Surcharged in Red

RA38 PT6 1c on 5c bl & blk 15 15
a. Inverted surcharge 3.00 3.00
b. Double surcharge 2.00 2.00

c. Double surcharge, one inverted 2.00 2.00
d. Period after "de" 1.25 1.25
e. Comma after "R" 1.25 1.25

See note after No. 512.

Regular Issue of 1928 Overprinted in Blue R. de C.

RA39 A24 1c red org 15 15

No. RA39 exists both with and without signature control overprint.

An additional overprint, "1929" in black or blue on No. RA39, is fraudulent.

No. 513 Overprinted in Red R. de C.

1929

RA40 A24 1c ol grn 20 15
a. Double overprint 75 75

No. RA40 is known with overprint in black, and with overprint inverted. These varieties were not regularly issued, but copies have been canceled by favor.

Type of 1928 Issue Inscribed at right "COMUNICACIONES"

1930-37

RA41 PT5 1c carmine 20 15
RA42 PT5 1c org ('33) 15 15
RA43 PT5 1c grn ('37) 15 15
Set value 18

No. RA42 has signature control. See note before No. 600.

No. RA39 Overprinted in Black 1931

1931

RA44 A24 1c red orange 15 15
a. "1931" double overprint 35 35
b. "1931" double ovpt., one invtd. 42 42

No. RA44 exists with signature control overprint. See note before No. 600. Value is the same.

No. RA42 Overprinted Vertically, up or down, in Black Resello 1935

1935

RA45 PT5 1c orange 15 15
a. Double overprint 1.00 1.00
b. Double ovpt., one inverted

No. RA45 and RA45a Overprinted Vertically, Reading Down, in Blue RESELLO-1935

RA46 PT5 1c orange 50 15
a. Black overprint double 2.00 2.00

Same Overprint in Red on Nos. RA39, RA42 and RA45

RA47 A24 1c red org (#RA39) *37.50*
RA48 PT5 1c org (#RA42) 20 15
RA49 PT5 1c org (#RA45) 20 15
a. Black overprint double 80 80

Overprint is horizontal on No. RA47 and vertical, reading down, on Nos. RA48-RA49.

No. RA48 exists with signature control overprint. See note before No. 600. Same values.

No. RA42 Overprinted Vertically, Reading Down, in Carmine

1935 **Unwmk.** ***Perf. 12***

RA50 PT5 1c orange 20 15

No. RA45 with Additional Overprint "1936", Vertically, Reading Down, in Red

1936

RA51 PT5 1c orange 50 16

No. RA39 with Additional Overprint "1936" in Red

RA52 A24 1c red org 50 16

No. RA52 exists only with script control mark.

PT7

Vertical Surcharge in Red

1936

RA53 PT7 1c on 5c grn & blk 15 15
a. "Cenavo" 1.40 1.40
b. "Centavos" 1.40 1.40

Horizontal Surcharge in Red

RA54 PT7 1c on 5c grn & blk 15 15
a. Double surcharge 1.40 1.40
Set value 16

Baseball Player PT8

1937 **Typo.** ***Perf. 11***

RA55 PT8 1c carmine 35 15
RA56 PT8 1c yellow 35 15
RA57 PT8 1c blue 35 15
RA58 PT8 1c green 35 15
b. Sheet of 4, #RA55-RA58 3.00 3.00
Set value 44

Issued for the benefit of the Central American Caribbean Games of 1937.

Control mark in red is variously placed. See dark oval below "OLIMPICO" in illustration.

Tête bêche Pair

RA55a PT8 1c 75 75
RA56a PT8 1c 75 75
RA57a PT8 1c 75 75
RA58a PT8 1c 75 75

Catalogue values for unused stamps in this section, from this point to the end of the section, are for Never Hinged items.

Proposed Natl. Stadium, Managua — PT9

PT10

1949 **Photo.** ***Perf. 12***

RA60 PT9 5c grnsh bl 25 15
a. Souvenir sheet of 4 3.75 3.75

10th World Series of Amateur Baseball, 1948. The tax was used toward the erection of a national stadium at Managua.

Type Similar to 1949, with "Correos" omitted

1952

RA61 PT9 5c magenta 25 15

The tax was used toward the erection of a national stadium at Managua.

1956 **Engr.** ***Perf. 12½x12***

RA62 PT10 5c dp ultra 15 15

The tax was used for social welfare.

PT11

Jesus and Children — PT12

Surcharged in Red or Black

1959 **Unwmk.** ***Perf. 12***

Red Marginal Number

RA63 PT11 5c on 50c vio bl (R) 15 15
RA64 PT11 5c on 50c vio bl (B) 15 15
Set value 24 15

Nos. RA63-RA64 are surcharged on consular revenue stamps. Surcharge reads "Sobre Tasa Postal CO.O5." Vertical surcharge on No. RA63, horizontal on No. RA64.

1959 **Photo.** ***Perf. 16***

RA65 PT12 5c ultra 15 15

Hexisia Bidentata — PT13

Orchids: No. RA67, Schomburgkia tibicinus. No. RA68, Stanhopea ecornuta. No. RA69, Lycaste macrophylla. No. RA70, Maxillaria tenuifolia. No. RA71, Cattleya skinneri. No. RA72, Cycnoches egertonianum. No. RA73, Bletia roezlii. No. RA74, Sobralia pleiantha. No. RA75, Oncidium cebolleta and ascendens.

1962, Feb. **Photo.** ***Perf. 11½***

Granite Paper

Orchids in Natural Colors

RA66 PT13 5c pale lil & grn 15 15
RA67 PT13 5c yel & grn 15 15
RA68 PT13 5c pink & grn 15 15
RA69 PT13 5c pale vio & grn 15 15
RA70 PT13 5c lt grnsh bl & red 15 15
RA71 PT13 5c buff & lil 15 15
RA72 PT13 5c yel grn & brn 15 15
RA73 PT13 5c gray & red 15 15
RA74 PT13 5c lt bl & dk bl 15 15
RA75 PT13 5c lt grn & brn 15 15
Set value 80 80

For overprints see Nos. 842-852, 855-868, 901-908.

PROVINCE OF ZELAYA

(Bluefields)

A province of Nicaragua lying along the eastern coast. Special postage stamps for this section were made necessary because for a period two currencies, which differed materially in value, were in use in Nicaragua. Silver money was used in Zelaya and Cabo Gracias a Dios while the rest of Nicaragua used paper money. Later the money of the entire country was placed on a gold basis.

Dangerous counterfeits exist of most of the Bluefields overprints.

Regular Issues of 1900-05 Handstamped in Black B Dpto Zelaya.

1904-05 **Unwmk.** ***Perf. 12, 14***

On Engraved Stamps of 1900

1L1 A14 1c plum 1.50 75
1L2 A14 2c vermilion 1.50 75
1L3 A14 3c green 1.90 1.50
1L4 A14 4c ol grn 11.00 11.00
1L5 A14 15c ultra 3.00 1.90
1L6 A14 20c brown 3.00 1.90
1L7 A14 50c lake 10.50 7.50
1L8 A14 1p yellow 21.00
1L9 A14 2p salmon 30.00
1L10 A14 5p black 37.50

On Lithographed Stamps of 1902

1L11 A14 5c blue 3.00 75
1L12 A14 5c carmine 1.90 90
1L13 A14 10c violet 1.50 75

On Postage Due Stamps Overprinted "1901 Correos"

1L14 D3 20c brn (No. 156) 4.50 1.90
1L15 D3 50c lake (No. 158)

On Surcharged Stamps of 1904-05

1L16 A16 5c on 10c (#175) 1.50 1.10
1L17 A14 5c on 10c (#178) 4.00 1.50
1L18 A16 15c on 10c vio 1.50 1.50
1L19 A17 15c on 10c vio 14.00 4.50

On Surcharged Stamp of 1901

1L20 A14 20c on 5p blk 18.00 3.00

On Regular Issue of 1905

1906-07 ***Perf. 12***

1L21 A18 1c green 30 30
1L22 A18 2c car rose 30 30
1L23 A18 3c violet 30 30
1L24 A18 4c org red 45 45
1L25 A18 5c blue 22 22
1L26 A18 10c yel brn 3.00 1.50
1L27 A18 15c brn ol 4.50 1.75
1L28 A18 20c lake 9.00 7.50
1L29 A18 50c orange 35.00 30.00
1L30 A18 1p black 30.00 27.50
1L31 A18 2p dk grn 37.50
1L32 A18 5p violet 45.00
Nos. 1L21-1L32 (12) 165.57

On Surcharged Stamps of 1906-08

1L33 A18 10c on 3c vio 38 38
1L34 A18 15c on 1c grn 52 52
1L35 A18 20c on 2c rose 3.50 3.50
1L36 A18 20c on 5c bl 1.50 1.50
1L37 A18 50c on 6c sl (R) 1.50 3.00
Nos. 1L33-1L37 (5) 7.40 8.90

Four or more types exist of the foregoing overprints.

B Dpto. Zelaya   B Dto. Zelaya

Stamps with the above overprints were made to fill dealers' orders but were never regularly issued or used. Stamps with similar overprints handstamped are bogus.

Surcharged Stamps of 1906 Overprinted in Red, Black or Blue B Dpto. Zelaya

1L38 A18 15c on 1c grn (R) 2.75 2.75
a. Red overprint inverted
1L39 A18 20c on 2c rose (Bk) 1.90 1.90
1L40 A18 20c on 5c bl (R) 3.00 3.00
1L41 A18 50c on 6c sl (Bl) 14.00 14.00

Stamps of the 1905 issue overprinted as above No. 1L38 or similarly overprinted but with only 2¼mm space between "B" and "Dpto. Zelaya" were made to fill dealers' orders but not placed in use.

No. 205 Handstamped in Black B Dpto Zelaya.

Perf. 14 to 15

1L42 A18 10c yel brn 24.00 24.00

Stamps of 1907 Overprinted in Red or Black B Dpto Zelaya

1L43 A18 15c brn ol (R) 3.00 3.00
1L44 A18 20c lake 90 90
a. Inverted overprint 11.00 11.00

With Additional Surcharge **5 cent.**

1L45 A18 5c brn org 52 45
a. Inverted surcharge 7.50 7.50

With Additional Surcharge 5 cent.

1L46 A18 5c on 4c brn org 12.00 12.00

On Provisional Postage Stamps of 1907-08

1L47 A18 10c on 2c rose (Bl) 4.50 4.50
1L48 A18 10c on 2c rose (Bk)
1L48A A18 10c on 4c brn org (Bk)
1L49 A18 10c on 20c lake (Bk) 3.00 3.00
1L50 A18 10c on 50c org (Bl) 3.00 2.25

Arms Type of 1907 Overprinted in Black or Violet

"COSTA ATLANTICA"
B.

1907
1L51 A18 1c green 30 22
1L52 A18 2c rose 30 22
1L53 A18 3c violet 38 38
1L54 A18 4c brn org 45 45
1L55 A18 5c blue 4.50 2.25
1L56 A18 10c yel brn 38 30
1L57 A18 15c brn ol 75 38
1L58 A18 20c lake 75 45
1L59 A18 50c orange 2.25 1.50
1L60 A18 1p blk (V) 2.25 1.50
1L61 A18 2p dk grn 2.25 1.90
1L62 A18 5p violet 3.75 2.25
Nos. 1L51-1L62 (12) 18.31 11.80

Nos. 217-225 Overprinted in Green

B
Dpto. Zelaya

1908
1L63 A19 1c on 5c yel & blk (R) 45 38
1L64 A19 2c on 5c yel & blk (Bl) 45 38
1L65 A19 4c on 5c yel & blk (G) 45 38
a. Overprint reading down 11.00 11.00
b. Double overprint, reading up and down 18.00 18.00
1L66 A19 5c yel & blk 45 45
a. "CORROE" 4.50
b. Double overprint 11.00 11.00
c. Double overprint, reading up and down 19.00 19.00
d. "CORREO 1908" double 15.00 15.00
1L67 A19 10c lt bl & blk 45 45
a. Ovpt. reading down 52 52
b. "CORREO 1908" triple 37.50
1L68 A19 15c on 50c ol & blk (R) 90 90
a. "1008" 4.50
b. "8908" 4.50
1L69 A19 35c on 50c ol & blk 1.40 1.40
1L70 A19 1p yel brn & blk 1.90 1.90
a. "CORROE" 12.00 12.00
1L71 A19 2p pearl gray & blk 2.25 2.25
a. "CORROE" 15.00 15.00
Nos. 1L63-1L71 (9) 8.70 8.49

Overprinted Horizontally in Black or Green

1L72 A19 5c yel & blk 9.00 7.50
1L72A A19 2p pearl gray & blk (G)

On Nos. 1L72-1L72A, space between "B" and "Dpto. Zelaya" is 13mm.

Nos. 237-248 Overprinted in Black

B
Dpto. Zelaya

Imprint: "American Bank Note Co. NY"

1909 ***Perf. 12***
1L73 A18 1c yel grn 22 22
1L74 A18 2c vermilion 22 22
a. Inverted overprint
1L75 A18 3c red org 22 22
1L76 A18 4c violet 22 22
1L77 A18 5c dp bl 30 22
a. Inverted overprint 9.00 9.00
b. "B" inverted 7.50 7.50
c. Double overprint 12.00 12.00
1L78 A18 6c gray brn 4.50 3.00
1L79 A18 10c lake 30 28
a. "B" inverted 9.00 9.00
1L80 A18 15c black 45 38
a. "B" inverted 11.00 11.00
b. Inverted overprint 12.00 12.00
c. Double overprint 14.00 14.00
1L81 A18 20c brn ol 52 52
a. "B" inverted 19.00 19.00
1L82 A18 50c dp grn 1.50 1.50
1L83 A18 1p yellow 2.25 2.25
1L84 A18 2p car rose 3.00 3.00
a. Double overprint 27.50 27.50
Nos. 1L73-1L84 (12) 13.70 12.03

One stamp in each sheet has the "o" of "Dpto." sideways.

Overprinted in Black

B
Dpto. Zelaya

1910
1L85 A18 3c red org 38 38
1L86 A18 4c violet 38 38
a. Inverted overprint 14.00 14.00
1L87 A18 15c black 4.50 2.25
1L88 A18 20c brn ol 22 30
1L89 A18 50c dp grn 28 38
1L90 A18 1p yellow 30 45
a. Inverted overprint 7.50
1L91 A18 2p car rose 38 75
Nos. 1L85-1L91 (7) 6.44 4.89

Z1

Black Ovpt., Green Surch., Carmine Block-outs

1910
1L92 Z1 5c on 10c lake 3.75 3.00

There are three types of the letter "B". It is stated that this stamp was used exclusively for postal purposes and not for telegrams.

No. 247 Surcharged in Black

B
Vale
5 cts.

1911
1L93 A18 5c on 1p yel 75 75
a. Double surcharge 14.00
1L94 A18 10c on 1p yel 1.50 1.50
1L95 A18 15c on 1p yel 75 75
a. Inverted surcharge 9.00
b. Double surcharge 9.00
c. Double surcharge, one invtd. 9.00

Revenue Stamps Surcharged in Black

B
CORREOS
05 cts.
1911

Perf. 14 to 15
1L96 A19 5c on 25c lilac 75 1.10
a. Without period 1.50 1.50
b. Inverted surcharge 9.00 9.00
1L97 A19 10c on 1p yel brn 1.10 75
a. Without period 1.90 1.90
b. "01" for "10" 9.00 7.50
c. Inverted surcharge 13.00 13.00

Surcharged in Black

VALE
05 cts.
POSTAL B
de 1911

1L98 A19 5c on 1p yel brn 1.50 1.50
a. Without period 2.25
b. "50" for "05" 14.00 14.00
c. Inverted surcharge 15.00 15.00
1L99 A19 5c on 10p pink 1.50 1.50
a. Without period 2.25 2.25
b. "50" for "05" 11.00 11.00
1L100 A19 10c on 1p yel brn 82.50 82.50
a. Without period 95.00 95.00
1L101 A19 10c on 25p grn 75 75
a. Without period 2.25 2.25
b. "1" for "10" 7.50
1L102 A19 10c on 50p ver 11.00 11.00
a. Without period 16.50
b. "1" for "10" 22.50
Nos. 1L98-1L102 (5) 97.25 97.25

With Additional Overprint "1904"

1L103 A19 5c on 10p pink 14.00 14.00
a. Without period 24.00 24.00
b. "50" for "05" 110.00 110.00
1L104 A19 10c on 2p gray 75 75
a. Without period 1.90
b. "1" for "10" 7.50
1L105 A19 10c on 25p grn 92.50
a. Without period 100.00
1L106 A19 10c on 50p ver 7.50 7.50
a. Without period 14.00
b. "1" for "10" 18.00
c. Inverted surcharge

The surcharges on Nos. 1L96 to 1L106 are in settings of twenty-five. One stamp in each setting has a large square period after "cts" and another has a thick upright "c" in that word. There are two types of "1904".

No. 293C Overprinted

B
Dpto. Zelaya

1911
1L107 A21 5c on 5c on 2c bl (R) 22.50
a. "5" omitted 27.50
b. Red overprint inverted 30.00
c. As "a" and "b" 37.50

Same Overprint On Nos. 290, 291, 292 and 289D with Lines of Surcharge spaced 2½mm apart Reading Down

1L107D A21 2c on 10c on 1c red
e. Overprint reading up
1L107F A21 5c on 10c on 1c red *92.50*
1L107G A21 10c on 10c on 1c red (#292) *125.00*
1L108 A21 10c on 10c on 1c red (#289D) *120.00*

Locomotive — Z2

1912 **Engr.** ***Perf. 14***
1L109 Z2 1c yel grn 75 50
1L110 Z2 2c vermilion 50 25
1L111 Z2 3c org brn 75 45
1L112 Z2 4c carmine 75 30
1L113 Z2 5c dp bl 75 45
1L114 Z2 6c red brn 4.00 2.50
1L115 Z2 10c slate 75 30
1L116 Z2 15c dl lil 75 60
1L117 Z2 20c bl vio 75 60
1L118 Z2 25c grn & blk 1.00 80
1L119 Z2 35c brn & blk 1.25 1.00
1L120 Z2 50c ol grn 1.25 1.00
1L121 Z2 1p orange 1.75 1.50
1L122 Z2 2p org brn 4.00 3.00
1L123 Z2 5p dk bl grn 7.00 6.50
Nos. 1L109-1L123 (15) 26.00 19.75

The stamps of this issue were for use in all places on the Atlantic Coast of Nicaragua where the currency was on a silver basis.

For surcharges see Nos. 325-337.

OFFICIAL STAMPS

Regular Issue of 1909 Overprinted in Black

Oficial
B

1909 **Unwmk.** ***Perf. 12***
1LO1 A18 20c brn ol 11.00 8.00
a. Double overprint 13.00

Official Stamp of 1909 Overprinted in Black

B

1LO2 A18 15c black 11.00 6.50

Same Overprint on Official Stamp of 1911

1911
1LO3 A18 5c on 3c red org 16.00 13.00

CABO GRACIAS A DIOS

A cape and seaport town in the extreme northeast of Nicaragua. The name was coined by Spanish explorers who had great difficulty finding a landing place along the Nicaraguan coast and when eventually locating this harbor expressed their relief by designating the point "Cape Thanks to God". Special postage stamps came into use for the same reasons as the Zelaya issues. (See Zelaya.)

Dangerous counterfeits exist of most of the Cabo Gracias a Dios overprints.

Regular Issues of 1900-04 Handstamped in Violet

CABO

On Engraved Stamps of 1900

1904-05 **Unwmk.** ***Perf. 12, 14***
2L1 A14 1c plum 2.25 1.10
2L2 A14 2c vermilion 4.50 1.20
2L3 A14 3c green 6.00 4.50
2L4 A14 4c ol grn 9.75 9.75
2L5 A14 15c ultra 35.00 22.50
2L6 A14 20c brown 3.00 2.25
Nos. 2L1-2L6 (6) 60.50 41.30

On Lithographed Stamps of 1902

2L7 A14 5c blue 24.00 24.00
2L8 A14 10c violet 24.00 24.00

On Surcharged Stamps of 1904

2L9 A16 5c on 10c vio 22.50 22.50
2L10 A16 15c on 10c vio

On Postage Due Stamps

Violet Handstamp

2L11 D3 20c org brn (#141) 5.00 1.25
2L12 D3 20c org brn (#156) 3.50 1.25
2L13 D3 30c dk grn (#157) 14.00 14.00
2L14 D3 50c lake (#158) 3.75 75

Black Handstamp

2L15 D3 30c dk grn (#157) 24.00 24.00

Stamps of 1900-05 Handstamped in Violet

Cabo

On Engraved Stamps of 1900

2L16 A14 1c plum 2.75 2.25
2L17 A14 2c vermilion 27.50 24.00
2L18 A14 3c green 37.50 27.50
2L19 A14 4c ol grn 40.00 37.50
2L20 A14 15c ultra 45.00 45.00
Nos. 2L16-2L20 (5) 152.75 136.25

On Lithographed Stamps of 1902

2L22 A14 5c dk bl 95.00 50.00
2L23 A14 10c violet 27.50 24.00

On Surcharged Stamp of 1904

2L24 A16 5c on 10c vio

On Postage Due Stamp

2L25 D3 20c org brn (#141)

Cabo

The editors have no evidence that stamps with this handstamp were issued. Copies were sent to the UPU and covers are known.

Stamps of 1900-08 Handstamped in Violet

1905

On Stamps of 1905

2L26	A18	1c green	1.10	1.10
2L27	A18	2c car rose	1.50	1.50
2L28	A18	3c violet	1.50	1.50
2L29	A18	4c org red	3.75	3.75
2L30	A18	5c blue	1.50	1.10
2L31	A18	6c slate	3.75	3.75
2L32	A18	10c yel brn	3.00	1.90
2L33	A18	15c brn ol	4.50	4.50
2L34	A18	1p black	20.00	20.00
2L35	A18	2p dk grn	35.00	35.00
		Nos. 2L26-2L35 (10)	75.60	74.10

Magenta handstamp

2L26a	A18	1c	3.75	3.00
2L27a	A18	2c	3.00	2.75
2L28a	A18	3c	3.75	3.00
2L30a	A18	5c	7.50	6.00
2L33a	A18	15c	13.50	11.00

On Stamps of 1900-04

2L36	A16	5c on 10c vio	14.00	14.00
2L37	A14	10c violet		
2L38	A14	20c brown	12.00	12.00
2L39	A14	20c on 5p blk		95.00

On Postage Due Stamps Overprinted "Correos"

2L40	D3	20c org brn (#141)	9.00	9.00
2L41	D3	20c org brn (#156)	5.00	4.50

On Surcharged Stamps of 1906-08

2L42	A18	10c on 3c vio		
2L43	A18	20c on 5c bl	9.00	9.00
2L44	A18	50c on 6c sl	24.00	24.00

On Stamps of 1907

Perf. 14 to 15

2L44A	A18	2c rose		
2L45	A18	10c yel brn	*100.00*	*75.00*
2L46	A18	15c brn ol	*90.00*	*75.00*

On Provisional Stamp of 1908 in Magenta

2L47	A19	5c yel & blk	7.50	7.50

Stamps with the above large handstamp in black instead of violet, are bogus. There are also excellent counterfeits in violet.

The foregoing overprints being handstamped are found in various positions, especially the last type.

Stamps of 1907 Type A18, Overprinted in Black or Violet

"COSTA ATLANTICA" C.

1907

2L48	A18	1c green	30	30
2L49	A18	2c rose	30	30
2L50	A18	3c violet	30	30
a.		Vert. pair, imperf. btwn.	15.00	
2L51	A18	4c brn org	38	38
2L52	A18	5c blue	50	50
2L53	A18	10c yel brn	38	38
2L54	A18	15c brn ol	75	75
2L55	A18	20c lake	75	75
2L56	A18	50c orange	1.90	1.50
2L57	A18	1p blk (V)	2.25	1.90
2L58	A18	2p dk grn	3.00	2.25
2L59	A18	5p violet	4.50	3.75
		Nos. 2L48-2L59 (12)	15.31	13.06

Nos. 237-248 Overprinted in Black

C

Dpto. Zelaya

Imprint: American Bank Note Co.

1909 ***Perf. 12***

2L60	A18	1c yel grn	35	38
2L61	A18	2c vermilion	35	38
2L62	A18	3c red org	35	38
2L63	A18	4c violet	35	38
2L64	A18	5c dp bl	35	60
2L65	A18	6c gray brn	6.00	6.00
2L66	A18	10c lake	60	75
2L67	A18	15c black	90	90
2L68	A18	20c brn ol	1.00	1.10
2L69	A18	50c dp grn	2.50	2.50
2L70	A18	1p yellow	4.00	4.00
2L71	A18	2p car rose	5.75	5.75
		Nos. 2L60-2L71 (12)	22.50	23.12

No. 199 Overprinted Vertically

CÂBO

2L72	A18	50c on 6c slate (R)	7.50	7.50

OFFICIAL STAMPS

Official Stamps of 1907 Overprinted in Red or Violet

CÂBO

1907

2LO1	A18	10c on 1c grn	*60.00*
2LO2	A18	15c on 1c grn	*75.00*
2LO3	A18	20c on 1c grn	*100.00*
2LO4	A18	50c on 1c grn	*125.00*

NIGER

LOCATION — Northern Africa, directly north of Nigeria
GOVT. — Republic
AREA — 458,075 sq. mi.
POP. — 6,265,000 (est. 1984)
CAPITAL — Niamey

The colony, formed in 1922, was originally a military territory. The Republic of the Niger was proclaimed December 19, 1955. In the period between issues of the colony and the republic, stamps of French West Africa were used.

100 Centimes = 1 Franc

Catalogue values for unused stamps in this country are for Never Hinged items, beginning with Scott 91 in the regular postage section, Scott B14 in the semi-postal section, Scott C14 in the airpost section, Scott J22 in the postage due section, and Scott O1 in the official section.

Camel and Rider — A1

Stamps of Upper Senegal and Niger Type of 1914, Overprinted

1921-26 Unwmk. ***Perf. 13½x14***

1	A1	1c brn vio & vio	15	15
2	A1	2c dk gray & dl vio	15	15
3	A1	4c blk & bl	15	15
4	A1	5c ol brn & dk brn	15	15
5	A1	10c yel grn & bl grn	40	40
6	A1	10c mag, *bluish* ('26)	15	15
7	A1	15c red brn & org	15	15
8	A1	20c brn vio & blk	15	15
9	A1	25c blk & bl grn	15	15
10	A1	30c red org & rose	35	35
11	A1	30c bl grn & red org ('26)	28	28
12	A1	35c rose & vio	20	20
13	A1	40c gray & rose	28	28
14	A1	45c bl & ol brn	28	28
15	A1	50c ultra & bl	35	35
16	A1	50c dk gray & bl vio ('25)	28	28
17	A1	60c org red ('26)	42	42
18	A1	75c yel & ol brn	40	40
19	A1	1fr dk brn & dl vio	50	50
20	A1	2fr grn & bl	55	55
21	A1	5fr vio & blk	1.00	1.00
		Nos. 1-21 (21)	6.49	6.49

Stamps and Type of 1921 Surcharged New Value and Bars in Black or Red

60 = 60

1922-26

22	A1	25c on 15c red brn & org ('25)	20	20
a.		Multiple surcharge	55.00	
b.		"25c" inverted	55.00	
23	A1	25c on 2fr grn & bl (R) ('24)	28	28
24	A1	25c on 5fr vio & blk (R) ('24)	28	28
a.		Double surcharge	55.00	
25	A1	60c on 75c vio,*pnksh*	28	28
26	A1	65c on 45c bl & ol brn ('25)	1.10	1.10
27	A1	85c on 75c yel & ol brn ('25)	1.10	1.10
28	A1	1.25fr on 1fr dp bl & lt bl (R) ('26)	20	20
a.		Surcharge omitted	90.00	
		Nos. 22-28 (7)	3.44	3.44

Nos. 22-24 are surcharged "25c," No. 28, "1f25." Nos. 25-27 are surcharged like illustration.

Drawing Water from Well — A2

Zinder Fortress — A4

Boat on Niger River — A3

Perf. 13x14, 13½x14, 14x13, 14x13½

1926-40 **Typo.**

29	A2	1c lil rose & ol	15	15
30	A2	2c dk gray & dl red	15	15
31	A2	3c red vio & ol gray ('40)	15	15
32	A2	4c umber & gray	15	15
33	A2	5c ver & yel grn	15	15
34	A2	10c dp bl & Prus bl	15	15
35	A2	15c gray grn & yel grn	15	15
36	A2	15c gray lil & lt red ('28)	15	15
37	A3	20c Prus grn & ol brn	15	15
38	A3	25c blk & dl red	15	15
39	A3	30c bl grn & yel grn	22	20
40	A3	30c yel & red vio ('40)	15	15
41	A3	35c brn org & turq bl, *bluish*	15	15
42	A3	35c bl grn & dl grn ('38)	20	20
43	A3	40c red brn & sl	15	15
44	A3	45c yel & red vio	40	40
45	A3	45c bl grn & dl grn ('40)	15	15
46	A3	50c scar & grn,*grnsh*	15	15
47	A3	55c dk car & brn ('38)	40	40
48	A3	60c dk car & brn ('40)	15	15
49	A3	65c ol grn & rose	15	15
50	A3	70c ol grn & rose ('40)	40	40
51	A3	75c grn & vio,*pink*	55	52
52	A3	80c cl & ol grn ('38)	55	55
53	A3	90c brn red & ver	40	40
54	A3	90c brt rose & yel grn ('39)	40	40
55	A4	1fr rose & yel grn	3.50	2.50
56	A4	1fr dk red & red org ('38)	40	32
57	A4	1fr grn & red ('40)	15	15
58	A4	1.10fr ol brn & grn	2.00	1.50
59	A4	1.25fr grn & red ('33)	55	55
60	A4	1.25fr dk red & red org ('39)	20	20
61	A4	1.40fr red vio & dk brn ('40)	20	20
62	A4	1.50fr dp bl & pale bl	15	15
63	A4	1.60fr ol brn & grn ('40)	60	60
64	A4	1.75fr red vio & dk brn ('33)	1.20	1.00
65	A4	1.75fr dk bl & vio bl ('38)	40	40
66	A4	2fr red org & ol brn	15	15
67	A4	2.25fr dk bl & vio bl ('39)	30	30
68	A4	2.50fr blk brn ('40)	30	30
69	A4	3fr dl vio & blk ('27)	28	28
70	A4	5fr vio brn & blk, *pink*	28	28
71	A4	10fr chlky bl & mag	62	62
72	A4	20fr yel grn & red org	62	62
		Nos. 29-72 (44)	17.97	16.14

For surcharges see Nos. B7-B10.

Colonial Exposition Issue

Common Design Types

1931 **Typo.** ***Perf. 12½***

Name of Country in Black

73	CD70	40c dp grn	1.60	1.60
74	CD71	50c violet	1.60	1.60
75	CD72	90c red org	2.00	2.00
76	CD73	1.50fr dl bl	2.00	2.00

Paris International Exposition Issue

Common Design Types

1937 ***Perf. 13***

77	CD74	20c dp vio	45	45
78	CD75	30c dk grn	45	45
79	CD76	40c car rose	45	45
80	CD77	50c dk brn	45	45
81	CD78	90c red	60	60
82	CD79	1.50fr ultra	60	60
		Nos. 77-82 (6)	3.00	3.00

Colonial Arts Exhibition Issue

Souvenir Sheet

Common Design Type

1937 ***Imperf.***

83	CD74	3fr magenta	2.25	2.25

Caillie Issue

Common Design Type

1939 ***Perf. 12½x12***

84	CD81	90c org brn & org	40	40
85	CD81	2fr brt vio	40	40
86	CD81	2.25fr ultra & dk bl	40	40

New York World's Fair Issue

Common Design Type

1939, May 10

87	CD82	1.25fr car lake	40	40
88	CD82	2.25fr ultra	40	40

Zinder Fortress and Marshal Petain — A5

1941 Unwmk. Engr. ***Perf. 12x12½***

89	A5	1fr green	28
90	A5	2.50fr dk bl	28

Nos. 89-90 were issued by the Vichy government and were not placed on sale in the colony.

Catalogue values for unused stamps in this section, from this point to the end of the section, are for Never Hinged items.

Republic of the Niger

Giraffes — A6

Designs: 1fr, 2fr, Crested cranes. 5fr, 7fr, Saddle-billed storks. 15fr, 20fr, Barbary sheep. 25fr, 30fr, Giraffes. 50fr, 60fr, Ostriches. 85fr, 100fr, Lion.

1959-60 Unwmk. Engr. ***Perf. 13***

91	A6	1fr multi	15	15
92	A6	2fr multi	15	15
93	A6	5fr blk, car & ol	15	15
94	A6	7fr grn, blk & red	15	15
95	A6	15fr grnsh bl & dk brn	18	15
96	A6	20fr vio, blk & ind	20	15
97	A6	25fr multi	22	15
98	A6	30fr multi	28	15
99	A6	50fr ind & org brn	50	25
100	A6	60fr dk brn & emer	60	35

101 A6 85fr org brn & bis	75	40
102 A6 100fr bis & yel grn	90	50
Nos. 91-102 (12)	4.23	
Set value		2.00

Issue years: #97, 1959; others, 1960.
For surcharge see No. 103.

Imperforates
Most stamps of the republic exist imperforate in issued and trial colors, and also in small presentation sheets in issued color.

No. 102 Surcharged with New Value and: "Independance 3-8-60"

1960
103 A6 200fr on 100fr org brn & bis 4.00 4.00

Niger's independence.

C.C.T.A. Issue
Common Design Type

1960 Engr. *Perf. 13*
104 CD106 25fr buff & red brn 35 30

Emblem of the Entente — A6a

Pres. Diori Hamani — A7

1960 Photo. *Perf. 13x13½*
105 A6a 25fr multi 35 28

Issued to commemorate the first anniversary of the Entente (Dahomey, Ivory Coast, Niger and Upper Volta).

1960, Dec. 18 Engr. *Perf. 13*
106 A7 25fr ol bis & blk 22 15

Issued to commemorate the second anniversary of the proclamation of the Republic of the Niger.

Common Design Types pictured in section at front of book.

Manatee A8

1962, Jan. 29 Unwmk. *Perf. 13*

107 A8 50c grn & dk sl grn	15	15
108 A8 10fr red brn & dk grn	15	15
Set value	20	15

Abidjan Games Issue
Common Design Type

Designs: 25fr, Basketball and Soccer. 85fr, Track (horiz.).

1962, May 26 Photo. *Perf. 12x12½*

109 CD109 15fr multi	15	15
110 CD109 25fr multi	22	15
111 CD109 85fr multi	65	38

African-Malgache Union Issue
Common Design Type

1962, Sept. 8 *Perf. 12½x12*
112 CD110 30fr multi 30 22

15-Cent Minimum Value
The minimum value for a single stamp is 15 cents. This value reflects the costs of the handlling of inexpensive stamps.

Pres. Diori Hamani and Map of Niger in Africa A10

1962, Dec. 18 Photo. *Perf. 12½x12*
113 A10 25fr multi 22 20

Woman Runner A11

Woodworker A12

Designs: 15fr, Swimming (horiz.). 45fr, Volleyball.

Unwmk.

1963, Apr. 11 Engr. *Perf. 13*

114 A11 15fr brt bl & dk brn	15	15
115 A11 25fr dk brn & red	22	15
116 A11 45fr grn & blk	38	25
Set value		46

Friendship Games, Dakar, Apr. 11-21.

Perf. 12x12½, 12½x12

1963, Aug. 30 Photo.

Designs: 10fr, Tanners (horiz.). 25fr, Goldsmith. 30fr, Mat makers (horiz.). 85fr, Decoy maker.

117 A12 5fr brn & multi	15	15
118 A12 10fr dk grn & multi	15	15
119 A12 25fr blk & multi	22	15
120 A12 30fr vio & multi	28	15
121 A12 85fr dk bl & multi	65	40
Nos. 117-121,C26 (6)	2.25	
Set value		1.20

Berberi (Nuba) Woman's Costume — A13

Costume Museum, Niamey — A14

Costumes: 20fr, Hausa woman. 25fr, Tuareg woman. 30fr, Tuareg man. 60fr, Djerma woman.

Perf. 12x12½, 12½x12

1963, Oct. 15 Photo.

122 A13 15fr multi	15	15
123 A13 20fr blk & bl	18	15
124 A13 25fr multi	25	15
125 A13 30fr multi	28	15
126 A13 60fr multi	60	35
127 A14 85fr multi	70	40
Nos. 122-127 (6)	2.16	1.35

Man, Globe and Scales — A15

Parkinsonia Aculeata — A16

Unwmk.

1963, Dec. 10 Engr. *Perf. 13*
128 A15 25fr lt ol grn, ultra & brn org 25 18

Issued to commemorate the 15th anniversary of the Universal Declaration of Human Rights.

1964-65 Photo. *Perf. 13½x13*

Flowers: 10fr, Russelia equisetiformis. 15fr, Red sage (lantana). 20fr, Argyreia nervosa. 25fr, Luffa cylindrica. 30fr, Hibiscus rosa sinensis. 45fr, Red jasmine (frangipani). 50fr, Catharanthus roseus. 60fr, Caesalpinia pulcherrima.

129 A16 5fr dk red, grn & yel	25	15
130 A16 10fr multi	20	15
131 A16 15fr multi	28	15
132 A16 20fr multi	28	15
133 A16 25fr multi	28	15
134 A16 30fr multi	40	25
135 A16 45fr multi ('65)	48	25
136 A16 50fr dk red, brt pink & grn ('65)	48	25
137 A16 60fr multi ('65)	70	35
Nos. 129-137 (9)	3.35	1.85

Solar Flares and IQSY Emblem — A17

1964, May 12 Engr. *Perf. 13*
138 A17 30fr dp org, vio & blk 30 22

International Quiet Sun Year, 1964-65.

Mobile Medical Unit — A18

Designs: 30fr, Mobile children's clinic. 50fr, Mobile women's clinic. 60fr, Outdoor medical laboratory.

1964, May 26

139 A18 25fr bl, org & ol	25	15
140 A18 30fr multi	28	15
141 A18 50fr vio, org & bl	40	18
142 A18 60fr grnsh bl, org & dk brn	48	22

Issued to publicize the Nigerian mobile health education organization, OMNES (Organisation Medicale Mobile Nigerienne d'Education Sanitaire).

Cooperation Issue
Common Design Type

1964, Nov. 7 Unwmk. *Perf. 13*
143 CD119 50fr vio, dk brn & org 40 25

Tuareg Tent of Azawak A19

Designs: 20fr, Songhai house. 25fr, Wogo and Kourtey tents. 30fr, Djerma house. 60fr, Huts of Sorkawa fishermen. 85fr, Hausa town house.

1964-65 Engr.

144 A19 15fr ultra, dl grn & red brn	15	15
145 A19 20fr multi	18	15
146 A19 25fr Prus bl, dk brn & org brn	20	15
147 A19 30fr multi ('65)	22	15
148 A19 60fr red, grn & bis ('65)	40	18
149 A19 85fr multi ('65)	60	30
Nos. 144-149 (6)	1.75	1.08

Leprosy Examination A20

Abraham Lincoln A21

1964, Dec. 15 Photo. *Perf. 13x12½*
150 A20 50fr multi 35 28

Issued to publicize the fight against leprosy.

1965, Apr. 3 *Perf. 13x12½*
151 A21 50fr vio bl, blk, & ocher 40 35

Centenary of death of Abraham Lincoln.

Teaching with Radio and Pictures — A22

Designs: 25fr, Woman studying arithmetic: "A better life through knowledge." 30fr, Adult education class. 50fr, Map of Niger and 5 tribesmen, "Literacy for adults."

1965, Apr. 16 Engr. *Perf. 13*

152 A22 20fr dk bl, dk brn & ocher	20	15
153 A22 25fr sl grn, brn & ol brn	25	15
154 A22 30fr red, sl grn & vio brn	28	15
155 A22 50fr dp bl, brn & vio brn	45	20

Issued to promote adult education and "a better life through knowledge."

Ader Portable Telephone A23

Runner A24

Designs: 30fr, Wheatstone telegraph interrupter. 50fr, Early telewriter.

1965, May 17 Unwmk. *Perf. 13*

156 A23 25fr red brn, dk grn & ind	25	15
157 A23 30fr lil, sl grn & red	28	15
158 A23 50fr red, sl grn & pur	40	25

Issued to commemorate the centenary of the International Telecommunication Union.

1965, July 1 Engr. *Perf. 13*

Designs: 10fr, Hurdler (horiz.). 20fr, Pole vaulter (horiz.). 30fr, Long jumper.

159 A24 10fr brn, ocher & blk 15 15
160 A24 15fr gray, brn & red 18 15
161 A24 20fr dk grn, brn & vio bl 20 15
162 A24 30fr mar, brn & grn 28 15
Set value 34

African Games, Brazzaville, July 18-25.

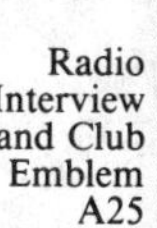

Radio Interview and Club Emblem A25

Designs (Club Emblem and): 45fr, Recording folk music (vert.). 50fr, Group listening to broadcast (vert.). 60fr, Public debate.

1965, Oct. 1 Engr. *Perf. 13*

163 A25 30fr brt vio, emer & red brn 25 15
164 A25 45fr blk, car & buff 35 15
165 A25 50fr dk car, bl & lt brn 38 18
166 A25 60fr bis, ultra & brn 45 22

Issued to promote radio clubs.

Water Cycle A26

1966, Feb. 28 Engr. *Perf. 13*

167 A26 50fr vio, ocher & bl 40 22

Hydrological Decade, 1965-74.

Carvings, Mask and Headdresses A27

Designs: 50fr, Carvings and wall decorations. 60fr, Carvings and arch. 100fr, Architecture and handicraft.

1966, Apr. 12

168 A27 30fr red brn, blk & brt grn 25 15
169 A27 50fr brt bl, ocher & pur 40 20
170 A27 60fr car lake, dl pur & yel brn 50 25
171 A27 100fr brt red, bl & blk 80 35

International Negro Arts Festival, Dakar, Senegal, Apr. 1-24.

Soccer Player — A28

Color Guard — A29

Designs: 50fr, Goalkeeper (horiz.). 60fr, Player kicking ball.

1966, June 17 Engr. *Perf. 13*

172 A28 30fr dk brn, brt bl & rose red 30 15
173 A28 50fr bl, choc & emer 40 15
174 A28 60fr bl, lil & brn 50 25

8th World Soccer Cup Championship, Wembley, England, July 11-30.

Perf. 12½x13, 13x12½

1966, Aug. 23 Photo.

Designs: 20fr, Parachutist (horiz.). 45fr, Tanks (horiz.).

175 A29 20fr multi 20 15
176 A29 30fr multi 25 15
177 A29 45fr multi 35 22
Set value 44

Issued to commemorate the 5th anniversary of the National Armed Forces.

Cow Receiving Injection A30

1966, Sept. 26 Litho. *Perf. 12½x13*

178 A30 45fr org brn, bl & blk 35 18

Campaign against cattle plague.

UNESCO Emblem — A31

1966, Nov. 4 Litho. *Perf. 13x12½*

179 A31 50fr multi 48 18

20th anniversary of UNESCO.

Cement Works Malbaza A32

Designs: 10fr, Furnace (vert.). 20fr, Electric center. 50fr, Handling of raw material.

1966, Dec. 17 Engr. *Perf. 13*

180 A32 10fr ind, brn & org 15 15
181 A32 20fr dk ol grn & dl bl 22 15
182 A32 30fr bl, gray & red brn 28 15
183 A32 50fr ind, bl & brn 40 15
Set value 36

Redbilled Hornbill A33

Birds: 2fr, Pied kingfisher. 30fr, Barbary shrike. 45fr, 65fr, Little weaver and nest.

1967 Engr. *Perf. 13*

184 A33 1fr red, sl grn & dk brn 15 15
185 A33 2fr brn, brt grn & blk 15 15
186 A33 30fr multi 25 15
187 A33 45fr multi 30 15
188 A33 65fr multi ('81) 28 18
189 A33 70fr multi 42 30
Set value 1.30 82

Issue dates: 45fr, 70fr, Nov. 18. Others, Feb. 8. See No. 237.

Villard-de-Lans and Olympic Emblem A34

Lions Emblem and Family A35

Olympic Emblem and Mountains: 45fr, Autrans and ski jump. 60fr, Saint Nizier du Moucherotte and ski jump. 90fr, Chamrousse and course for downhill and slalom races.

1967, Feb. 24

190 A34 30fr grn, ultra & brn 22 15
191 A34 45fr grn, ultra & brn 35 40
192 A34 60fr grn, ultra & brn 42 22
193 A34 90fr grn, ultra & brn 65 35

Issued to publicize the 10th Winter Olympic Games, Grenoble, 1968.

1967, Mar. 4

194 A35 50fr dk grn, brn red & ultra 40 22

Lions International, 50th anniversary.

ITY Emblem, Views, Globe and Plane A36

1967, Apr. 28 Engr. *Perf. 13*

195 A36 45fr vio, brt grn & red lil 35 22

International Tourist Year, 1967.

1967 Jamboree Emblem and Scouts — A37

Red Cross Aides Carrying Sick Man — A38

Designs (Jamboree Emblem and): 45fr, Scouts gathering from all directions (horiz.). 80fr, Campfire.

1967, May 25 Engr. *Perf. 13*

196 A37 30fr mar, Prus bl & ol 22 15
197 A37 45fr org, vio bl & brn ol 32 20
198 A37 80fr multi 60 35

Issued to publicize the 12th Boy Scout World Jamboree, Farragut State Park, Idaho, Aug. 1-9.

1967, July 13 Engr. *Perf. 13*

Designs: 50fr, Nurse, mother and infant. 60fr, Physician examining woman.

199 A38 45fr blk, grn & car 32 15
200 A38 50fr grn, blk & car 38 18
201 A38 60fr blk, grn & car 42 20

Issued for the Red Cross.

Europafrica Issue, 1967

Map of Europe and Africa A39

1967, July 20 Photo. *Perf. 12½x12*

202 A39 50fr multi 40 20

Women and UN Emblem — A40

1967, Oct. 21 Engr. *Perf. 13*

203 A40 50fr brn, brt bl & yel 38 22

UN Commission on Status of Women.

Monetary Union Issue
Common Design Type

1967, Nov. 4 Engr. *Perf. 13*

204 CD125 30fr grn & dk gray 22 15

Human Rights Flame, Globe, People and Statue of Liberty A41

1968, Feb. 19 Engr. *Perf. 13*

205 A41 50fr brn, ind & brt bl 35 20

International Human Rights Year.

Woman Dancing and WHO Emblem — A42

1968, Apr. 8 Engr. *Perf. 13*

206 A42 50fr brt bl, blk & red brn 35 22

20th anniv. of WHO.

Gray Hornbill A43

Birds: 10fr, Woodland kingfisher. 15fr, Senegalese coucal. 20fr, Rose-ringed parakeets. 25fr, Abyssinian roller. 50fr, Cattle egret.

Dated "1968"

1968, Nov. 15 Photo. *Perf. 12½x13*

207 A43 5fr dk grn & multi 15 15
208 A43 10fr grn & multi 15 15
209 A43 15fr bl vio & multi 15 15
210 A43 20fr pink & multi 15 15
211 A43 25fr ol & multi 18 15
212 A43 50fr pur & multi 30 18
Set value 82 55

See Nos. 233-236, 316.

ILO Emblem and "Labor Supporting the World" A44

1969, Apr. 22 Engr. *Perf. 13*
213 A44 30fr yel grn & dk car 22 15
214 A44 50fr dk car & yel grn 35 22

50th anniv. of the World Labor Organization.

Red Crosses, Mother and Child — A45

Designs: 50fr, People, globe, red crosses (horiz.). 70fr, Man with gift parcel and red crosses.

1969, May 5 Engr. *Perf. 13*
215 A45 45fr bl, red & brn ol 30 18
216 A45 50fr dk grn, red & gray 35 18
217 A45 70fr ocher, red & dk brn 42 28

Issued to commemorate the 50th anniversary of the League of Red Cross Societies.

Mouth and Ear — A46

1969, May 20 Photo. *Perf. 12½x12*
218 A46 100fr multi 65 40

First (cultural) Conference of French-speaking Community at Niamey.

National Administration College — A47

1969, July 8 Photo. *Perf. 12½x12*
219 A47 30fr emer & dp org 18 15

Issued to publicize the National Administration College.

Development Bank Issue
Common Design Type

1969, Sept. 10 Engr. *Perf. 13*
220 CD130 30fr pur, grn & ocher 20 15

ASECNA Issue
Common Design Type

1969, Dec. 12 Engr. *Perf. 12*
221 CD132 100fr car rose 65 40

Classical Pavilion, National Museum A48

Pavilions, National Museum: 45fr, Temporary exhibitions. 50fr, Audio-visual. 70fr, Nigerian musical instruments. 100fr, Craftsmanship.

1970, Feb. 23 Engr. *Perf. 13*
222 A48 30fr brt bl, sl grn & brn 20 15
223 A48 45fr emer, Prus bl & brn 28 15
224 A48 50fr sl grn, vio bl & brn 32 15
225 A48 70fr brn, sl grn & lt bl 45 25
226 A48 100fr sl grn, vio bl & brn 65 35
Nos. 222-226 (5) 1.90 1.05

Map of Africa and Vaccination Gun — A49

1970, Mar. 31 Engr. *Perf. 13*
227 A49 50fr ultra, dp yel grn & mag 30 18

Issued to commemorate the 100 millionth smallpox vaccination in West Africa.

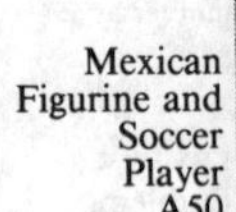

Mexican Figurine and Soccer Player A50

Designs: 70fr, Figurine, globe and soccer ball. 90fr, Figurine and 2 soccer players.

1970, Apr. 25
228 A50 40fr dk brn, red lil & emer 28 18
229 A50 70fr red brn, bl & plum 40 28
230 A50 90fr blk & red 60 40

Issued to publicize the 9th World Soccer Championship for the Jules Rimet Cup, Mexico City, May 29-June 21.

UPU Headquarters Issue
Common Design Type

1970, May 20 Engr. *Perf. 13*
231 CD133 30fr brn, dk gray & dk red 22 15
232 CD133 60fr vio bl, dk car & vio 35 18

Bird Types of 1967-68

Birds: 5fr, Gray hornbill. 10fr, Woodland kingfisher. 15fr, Senegalese coucal. 20fr, Rose-ringed parakeets. 40fr, Red bishop.

Dated "1970"

1970-71 Photo. *Perf. 13*
233 A43 5fr multi ('71) 15 15
234 A43 10fr multi ('71) 15 15
235 A43 15fr multi ('71) 15 15
236 A43 20fr multi ('71) 20 15

Engr.
237 A33 40fr multi 30 22
Set value 75 50

Issue dates: 40fr, Dec. 9; others Jan. 4.

World Map with Niamey in Center A51

1971, Mar. 3 Photo. *Perf. 12½x12*
238 A51 40fr brn & multi 28 15

First anniversary of founding of the cooperative agency of French-speaking countries.
For overprint see No. 289.

Scout Emblem, Merit Badges, Mt. Fuji, Japanese Flag — A52

Designs: 40fr, Boy Scouts and flags (vert.). 45fr, Map of Japan, Boy Scouts and compass rose (vert.). 50fr, Tent and "Jamboree."

1971, July 5 Engr. *Perf. 13*
239 A52 35fr rose lil, dp car & org 22 15
240 A52 40fr dk pur, grn & mar 25 15
241 A52 45fr ultra, cop red & grn 28 18
242 A52 50fr multi 30 18

13th Boy Scout World Jamboree, Asagiri Plain, Japan, Aug. 2-10.

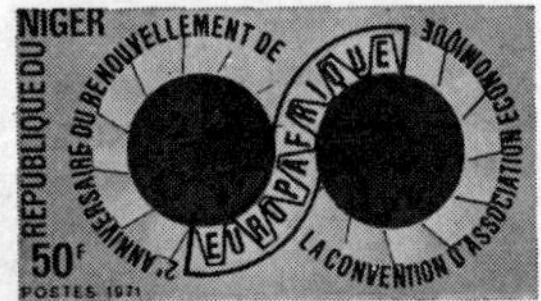
Maps of Europe and Africa — A53

1971, July 29 Photo. *Perf. 13x12*
243 A53 50fr lt bl & multi 35 18

2nd anniversary of the renewal of the agreement on economic association between Europe and Africa.

Broad-tailed Whydah A54

1971, Aug. 17 *Perf. 12½x12*
244 A54 35fr yel grn & multi 32 20

See No. 443.

Garaya, Haoussa A55

UNICEF Emblem, Children of 4 Races A56

Stringed Instruments of Niger: 25fr, Gouroumi, Haoussa. 30fr, Molo, Djerma. 40fr, Godjie, Djerma-Sonrai. 45fr, Inzad, Tuareg. 50fr, Kountigui, Sonrai.

1971-72 Engr. *Perf. 13*
245 A55 25fr red, emer & brn 18 15
246 A55 30fr emer, pur & brn 20 15
247 A55 35fr brn red, emer & ind 18 15
248 A55 40fr emer, org & dk brn 20 15
249 A55 45fr Prus bl, grn & bis 25 18
250 A55 50fr blk, red & brn 32 20
Nos. 245-250 (6) 1.33
Set value 78

Issue dates: 35fr, 40fr, 45fr, Oct. 13, 1971; others, June 16, 1972.

1971, Dec. 11 Photo. *Perf. 11*
251 A56 50fr multi 32 25

25th anniversary of UNICEF.

Star with Globe, Book, UNESCO Emblem A57

Design: 40fr, Boy reading, UNESCO emblem, sailing ship, plane, mosque.

1972, Mar. 27 Engr. *Perf. 13*
252 A57 35fr mag & emer 22 15
253 A57 40fr dk car & Prus bl 25 15
Set value 24

International Book Year 1972.

Cattle Egret — A58

1972, July 31 Photo. *Perf. 12½x12*
254 A58 50fr tan & multi 38 22

See No. 425.

Cattle at Salt Pond of In-Gall A59

1972, Aug. 25 *Perf. 13*
255 A59 35fr shown 22 15
256 A59 40fr Cattle wading in pond 25 15
Set value 24

Salt cure for cattle.
For surcharge see No. 282.

Lottery Drum — A60

1972, Sept. 18
257 A60 35fr multi 22 15

6th anniversary of the national lottery.

West African Monetary Union Issue
Common Design Type

Design: 40fr, African couple, city, village and commemorative coin.

1972, Nov. 2 Engr. *Perf. 13*
258 CD136 40fr brn, lil & gray 25 15

Dromedary Race — A61

Design: 40fr, Horse race.

1972, Dec. 15 Engr. *Perf. 13*
259 A61 35fr brt bl, dk red & brn 22 15
260 A61 40fr sl grn, mar & brn 28 15

Pole Vault, Map of Africa
A62

Knight, Pawn, Chessboard
A63

Designs (Map of Africa and): 40fr, Basketball. 45fr, Boxing. 75fr, Soccer.

1973, Jan. 15 Engr. *Perf. 13*

261 A62 35fr cl & multi 20 15
262 A62 40fr grn & multi 22 15
263 A62 45fr red & multi 25 18
264 A62 75fr dk bl & multi 38 25

2nd African Games, Legos, Nigeria, Jan. 7-18.

1973, Feb. 16 Engr. *Perf. 13*

265 A63 100fr dl red, sl grn & bl 55 35

World Chess Championship, Reykjavik, Iceland, July-Sept. 1972.

Abutilon Pannosum
A64

Interpol Emblem
A65

Rare African Flowers: 45fr, Crotalaria barkae. 60fr, Dichrostachys cinerea. 80fr, Caralluma decaisneana.

1973, Feb. 26 Photo. *Perf. 12x12½*

266 A64 30fr dk vio & multi 18 15
267 A64 45fr red & multi 25 15
268 A64 60fr ultra & multi 32 22
269 A64 80fr ocher & multi 40 25

1973, Mar. 13 Typo. *Perf. 13x12½*

270 A65 50fr brt grn & multi 25 15

50th anniversary of International Criminal Police Organization (INTERPOL).

Dr. Hansen, Microscope and Petri Dish
A66

Nurse Treating Infant, UN and Red Cross Emblems
A67

1973, Mar. 29 Engr. *Perf. 13*

271 A66 50fr vio bl, sl grn & dk brn 28 15

Centenary of the discovery by Dr. Armauer G. Hansen of the Hansen bacillus, the cause of leprosy.

1973, Apr. 3 Engr. *Perf. 13*

272 A67 50fr red, bl & brn 25 15

25th anniversary of WHO.

Crocodile
A68

Animals from W National Park: 35fr, Elephant. 40fr, Hippopotamus. 80fr, Wart hog.

1973, June 5 Typo. *Perf. 12½x13*

273 A68 25fr gray & blk 18 15
274 A68 35fr blk, gold & gray 22 15
275 A68 40fr red, lt bl & blk 25 15
276 A68 80fr multi 40 22
Set value 56

Eclipse over Mountains
A69

1973, June 21 Engr. *Perf. 13*

277 A69 40fr dk vio bl 22 18

Solar eclipse, June 30, 1973.

Palominos — A70

Horses: 75fr, French trotters. 80fr, English thoroughbreds. 100fr, Arabian thoroughbreds.

1973, Aug. 1 Photo. *Perf. 13x12½*

278 A70 50fr ultra & multi 28 15
279 A70 75fr gray & multi 38 20
280 A70 80fr emer & multi 45 25
281 A70 100fr ocher & multi 55 30

No. 255 Surcharged with New Value, 2 Bars, and Overprinted in Ultramarine: "SECHERESSE/SOLIDARITE AFRICAINE"

1973, Aug. 16 *Perf. 13*

282 A59 100fr on 35fr multi 50 35

African solidarity in drought emergency.

Diesel Engine and Rudolf Diesel
A71

Designs: Various Diesel locomotives.

1973, Sept. 7 *Perf. 13x12½*

283 A71 25fr gray, choc & Prus bl 15 15
284 A71 50fr sl bl, gray & dk grn 25 15
285 A71 75fr red lil, sl bl & gray 38 28
286 A71 125fr brt grn, vio bl & car 60 38

60th anniversary of the death of Rudolf Diesel (1858-1913), inventor of an internal combustion engine, later called Diesel engine.

African Postal Union Issue
Common Design Type

1973, Sept. 12 Engr. *Perf. 13*

287 CD137 100fr ol, dk car & sl grn 55 35

TV Set, Map of Niger, Children
A72

1973, Oct. 1 Engr. *Perf. 13*

288 A72 50fr car, ultra & brn 25 18

Educational television.

Type of 1971 Overprinted

3e CONFERENCE DE LA FRANCOPHONIE
LIEGE
OCTOBRE 1973

1973, Oct. 12 Photo. *Perf. 13*

289 A51 40fr red & multi 25 15

3rd Conference of French-speaking countries, Liege, Sept. 15-Oct. 14.

Apollo of Belvedere — A73

Classic Sculpture: No. 291, Venus of Milo. No. 292, Hercules. No. 293, Atlas.

1973, Oct. 15 Engr.

290 A73 50fr brn & sl grn 32 20
291 A73 50fr rose car & pur 32 20
292 A73 50fr red brn & dk brn 32 20
293 A73 50fr red brn & blk 32 20

Beehive, Bees and Globes
A74

1973, Oct. 31 Engr. *Perf. 13*

294 A74 40fr dl red, ocher & dl bl 22 15

World Savings Day.

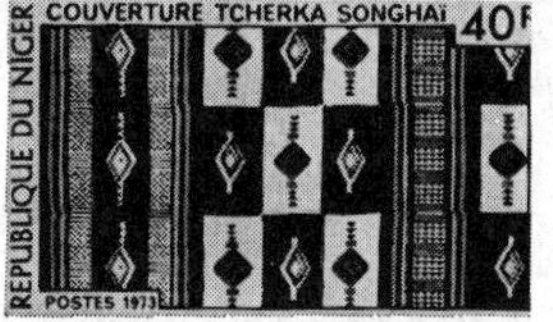

Tcherka Songhai Blanket — A75

Design: 35fr, Kounta Songhai blanket (vert.).

Perf. 12½x13, 13x12½

1973, Dec. 17 Photo.

295 A75 35fr brn & multi 25 15
296 A75 40fr brn & multi 25 18

Textiles of Niger.

WPY Emblem, Infant and Globe
A76

1974, Mar. 4 Engr. *Perf. 13*

297 A76 50fr multi 25 15

World Population Year 1974.

Locomotives, 1938 and 1948 — A77

1974, May 24 Engr. *Perf. 13*

298 A77 50fr shown 25 18
299 A77 75fr Locomotive, 1893 35 22
300 A77 100fr Locomotives, 1866 and 1939 48 35
301 A77 150fr *Locomotives, 1829* 70 55

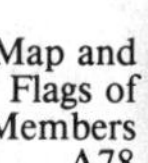

Map and Flags of Members
A78

1974, May 29 Photo. *Perf. 13x12½*

302 A78 40fr bl & multi 20 15

15th anniversary of the Council of Accord.

Marconi Sending Radio Signals to Australia — A79

1974, July 1 Engr. *Perf. 13*

303 A79 50fr pur, bl & dk brn 25 18

Centenary of the birth of Guglielmo Marconi (1874-1937), Italian inventor and physicist.

Hand Holding Sapling — A80

Camel Saddle — A81

1974, Aug. 2 Engr. *Perf. 13*

304 A80 35fr multi 18 15

National Tree Week.

1974, Aug. 20 Engr. *Perf. 13*

Design: 50fr, 3 sculptured horses (horiz.).

305 A81 40fr ol brn, bl & red 20 15
306 A81 50fr ol brn, bl & red 25 15
Set value 22

Chopin and Polish Eagle — A82

Design: No. 308, Ludwig van Beethoven and allegory of Ninth Symphony.

1974
307 A82 100fr multi 48 28
308 A82 100fr multi 48 28

125th anniversary of the death of Frederic Chopin (1810-1849), composer and 150th anniversary of Beethoven's Ninth Symphony, composed 1823.
Issue dates: #307, Sept. 4; #308, Sept. 19.

Don-Don Drum — A83

1974, Nov. 12 Engr. *Perf. 13*
309 A83 60fr multi 30 18

Tenere Tree, Compass Rose and Caravan — A84

1974, Nov. 24 Engr. *Perf. 13*
310 A84 50fr multi 30 20

Tenere tree, a landmark in Sahara Desert, first death anniversary.

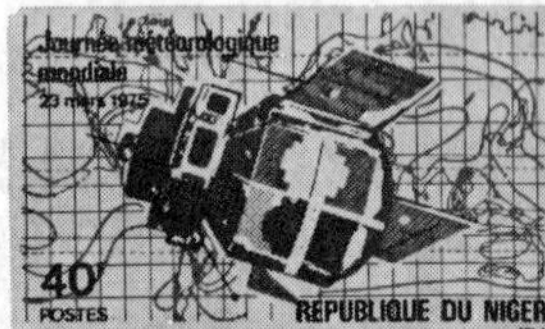
Satellite over World Weather Map — A85

1975, Mar. 23 Litho. *Perf. 13*
311 A85 40fr bl, blk & red 20 15

World Meteorological Day, Mar. 23, 1975.

"City of Truro," English, 1903 — A86

Locomotives and Flags: 75fr, "5.003," Germany, 1937. 100fr, "The General," United States, 1863. 125fr, "Electric BB 15.000," France, 1971.

1975, Apr. 24 Typo. *Perf. 13*
312 A86 50fr org & multi 25 18
313 A86 75fr yel grn & multi 35 22
314 A86 100fr lt bl & multi 48 32
315 A86 125fr multi 65 40

Bird Type of 1968 Dated "1975"

1975, Apr. Photo. *Perf. 13*
316 A43 25fr ol & multi 15 15

Zabira Leather Bag — A87

Handicrafts: 40fr, Damier tapestry. 45fr, Vase. 60fr, Gourd flask.

1975, May 28 Litho. *Perf. 12½*
317 A87 35fr dp bl & multi 18 15
318 A87 40fr dp grn & multi 20 15
319 A87 45fr brn & multi 22 30
320 A87 60fr dp org & multi 28 18

Mother and Child, IWY Emblem — A88

1975, June 9 Engr. *Perf. 13*
321 A88 50fr claret, brn & bl 25 18

International Women's Year 1975.

Dr. Schweitzer and Lambarene Hospital — A89

1975, June 23 Engr. *Perf. 13*
322 A89 100fr brn, grn & blk 42 28

Dr. Albert Schweitzer (1875-1965), medical missionary.

Peugeot, 1892 — A90

Early Autos: 75fr, Daimler, 1895. 100fr, Fiat, 1899. 125fr, Cadillac, 1903.

1975, July 16 Engr. *Perf. 13*
323 A90 50fr rose & vio bl 22 15
324 A90 75fr bl & vio brn 21 20
325 A90 100fr brt grn & mag 40 28
326 A90 125fr brick red & brt grn 55 30

Sun, Tree and Earth — A91

Boxing — A92

1975, Aug. 2 Engr. *Perf. 13*
327 A91 40fr multi 20 15

National Tree Week.

1975, Aug. 25 Engr. *Perf. 13*

Designs: 35fr, Boxing (horiz.). 45fr, Wrestling (horiz.). 50fr, Wrestling.

328 A92 35fr blk, org & brn 18 15
329 A92 40fr bl grn, brn & blk 20 15
330 A92 45fr blk, brt bl & brn 22 15
331 A92 50fr red, brn & blk 25 18

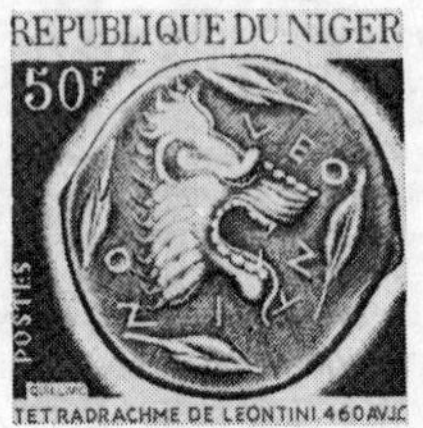
Lion's Head Tetradrachma, Leontini, 460 B.C. — A93

Greek Coins: 75fr, Owl tetradrachma, Athens, 500 B.C. 100fr, Crab diadrachma, Himera, 480 B.C. 125fr, Minotaur tetradrachma, Gela, 460 B.C.

1975, Sept. 12 Engr. *Perf. 13*
332 A93 50fr red, dl bl & blk 22 15
333 A93 75fr lil, brt bl & blk 32 22
334 A93 100fr bl, org & blk 42 28
335 A93 125fr grn, pur & blk 55 32

Starving Family A94

Designs: 45fr, Animal skeletons. 60fr, Truck bringing food.

1975, Oct. 21 Engr. *Perf. 13x12½*
336 A94 40fr multi 20 18
337 A94 45fr ultra & brn 22 15
338 A94 60fr grn, org & dk bl 28 15

Fight against drought.

Niger River Crossing — A95

Designs: 45fr, Entrance to Boubon camp. 50fr, Camp building.

1975, Nov. 10 Litho. *Perf. 12½*
339 A95 40fr multi 18 15
340 A95 45fr multi 20 15
341 A95 50fr multi 22 15

Tourist publicity.

Teacher and Pupils A96

Designs: Each stamp has different inscription in center.

1976, Jan. 12 Photo. *Perf. 13*
342 A96 25fr ol & multi 15 15
343 A96 30fr vio bl & multi 15 15
344 A96 40fr multi 18 15
345 A96 50fr multi 22 15
346 A96 60fr multi 25 18
Nos. 342-346 (5) 95
Set value 65

Literacy campaign 1976.
For overprints see Nos. 371-375.

12th Winter Olympic Games, Innsbruck — A97

1976, Feb. 20 Litho. *Perf. 14x13½*
347 A97 40fr Ice hockey 20 15
348 A97 50fr Luge 28 15
349 A97 150fr Ski jump 75 35
Nos. 347-349,C266-C267 (5) 3.73 1.70

Satellite, Telephone, ITU Emblem — A98

1976, Mar. 10 Litho. *Perf. 13*
350 A98 100fr org, bl & vio bl 42 28

Centenary of first telephone call by Alexander Graham Bell, Mar. 10, 1876.

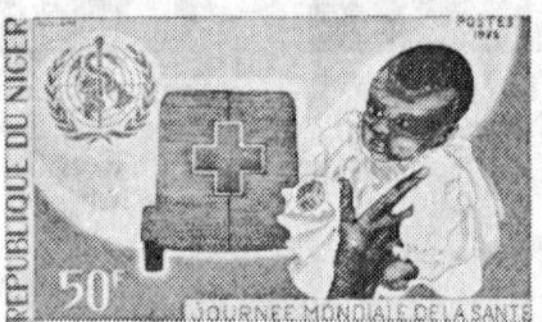
WHO Emblem, Red Cross Truck, Infant — A99

1976, Apr. 7 Engr. *Perf. 13*
351 A99 50fr multi 22 15

World Health Day 1976.

Statue of Liberty and Washington Crossing the Delaware — A100

Design: 50fr, Statue of Liberty and call to arms.

1976, Apr. 8 Litho. *Perf. 14x13½*

352 A100 40fr multi 20 15
353 A100 50fr multi 25 15
Nos. 352-353,C269-C271 (5) 3.55 1.80

American Bicentennial.

The Army Helping in Development — A101

Design: 50fr, Food distribution (vert.).

Perf. 12½x13, 13x12½

1976, Apr. 15 Litho.

354 A101 50fr multi 22 15
355 A101 100fr multi 42 28

National Armed Forces, 2nd anniversary of take-over.

Europafrica Issue 1976

Maps, Concorde, Ship and Grain — A102

1976, June 9 Litho. *Perf. 13*

356 A102 100fr multi 42 28

Road Building A103

Design: 30fr, Rice cultivation.

1976, June 26 *Perf. 12½*

357 A103 25fr multi 15 15
358 A103 30fr multi 15 15
Set value 18

Community labor.

Motobecane 125, France — A104

Motorcycles: 75fr, Norton Challenge, England. 100fr, BMW 90 S, Germany. 125fr, Kawasaki 1000, Japan.

1976, July 16 Engr. *Perf. 13*

359 A104 50fr vio bl & multi 22 15
360 A104 75fr dp grn & multi 21 25
361 A104 100fr dk brn & multi 42 35
362 A104 125fr slate & multi 55 35

Boxing A105

Designs: 50fr, Basketball. 60fr, Soccer. 80fr, Cycling (horiz.). 100fr, Judo (horiz.).

1976, July 17 Litho. *Perf. 14*

363 A105 40fr multi 22 15
364 A105 50fr multi 28 15
365 A105 60fr multi 35 15
366 A105 80fr multi 40 18
367 A105 100fr multi 50 25
Nos. 363-367 (5) 1.75 88

21st Summer Olympic games, Montreal. See No. C279.

Map of Niger, Planting Seedlings A106

Designs: 50fr, Woman watering seedling (vert.). 60fr, Women planting seedlings (vert.).

1976, Aug. 1 Litho. *Perf. 12½x13*

368 A106 40fr org & multi 18 15
369 A106 50fr yel & multi 22 18
370 A106 60fr grn & multi 28 18

Reclamation of Sahel Region.

Nos. 342-346 Overprinted: "JOURNEE / INTERNATIONALE / DE L'ALPHABETISATION"

1976, Sept. 8 Photo. *Perf. 13*

371 A96 25fr ol & multi 15 15
372 A96 30fr vio bl & multi 15 15
373 A96 40fr multi 20 15
374 A96 50fr multi 22 15
375 A96 60fr multi 28 15
Nos. 371-375 (5) 1.00
Set value 55

Literacy campaign.

Hairdresser — A107

Designs: 40fr, Woman weaving straw (vert.). 50fr, Women potters (vert.).

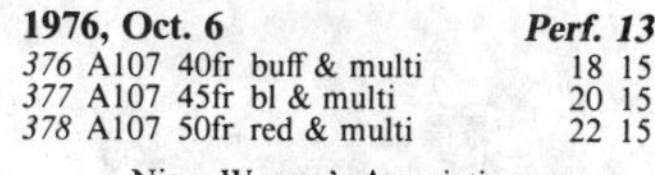

1976, Oct. 6 *Perf. 13*

376 A107 40fr buff & multi 18 15
377 A107 45fr bl & multi 20 15
378 A107 50fr red & multi 22 15

Niger Women's Association.

Rock Carvings A108

Archaeology: 50fr, Neolithic sculptures. 60fr, Dinosaur skeleton.

1976, Nov. 15 Photo. *Perf. 13x12½*

379 A108 40fr blk, sl & yel 18 15
380 A108 50fr blk, red & bis 22 15
381 A108 60fr bis, blk & brn 28 15

Benin Head — A109

Weaver, Dancers and Musicians — A110

1977, Jan. 15 Engr. *Perf. 13*

382 A109 40fr dk brn 20 15
383 A110 50fr gray bl 22 15

2nd World Black and African Festival, Lagos, Nigeria, Jan. 15-Feb. 12.

First Aid, Student, Blackboard and Plow — A111

Midwife — A112

Designs: Inscriptions on blackboard differ on each denomination.

1977, Jan. 23 Photo. *Perf. 12½x13*

384 A111 40fr multi 18 15
385 A111 50fr multi 22 15
386 A111 60fr multi 28 15
Set value 38

Literacy campaign.

1977, Feb. 23 Litho. *Perf. 13*

Design: 50fr, Midwife examining newborn.

387 A112 40fr multi 18 15
388 A112 50fr multi 22 15
Set value 24

Village health service.

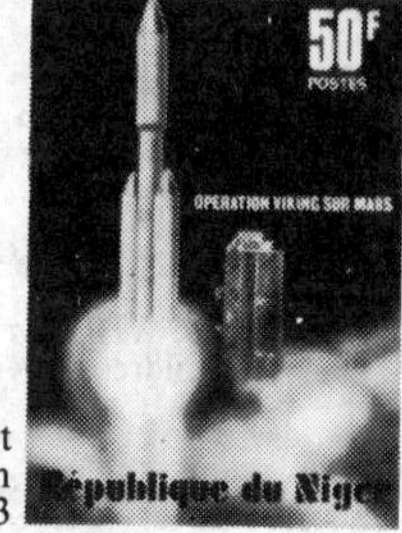

Titan Rocket Launch A113

Design: 80fr, Viking orbiter near Mars (horiz.).

1977, Mar. 15 Litho. *Perf. 14*

389 A113 50fr multi 28 15
390 A113 80fr multi 40 20
Nos. 389-390,C283-C285 (5) 2.93 1.37

Viking Mars project.
For overprints see #497-498, C295-C297.

Marabous A114

Design: 90fr, Harnessed antelopes.

1977, Mar. 18 Engr. *Perf. 13*

391 A114 80fr multi 38 22
392 A114 90fr multi 40 25

Nature protection.

Weather Map, Satellite, WMO Emblem A115

1977, Mar. 23

393 A115 100fr multi 40 28

World Meteorological Day.

Group Gymnastics — A116

Designs: 50fr, High jump. 80fr, Folk singers.

1977, Apr. 7 Litho. *Perf. 13x12½*

394 A116 40fr dl yel & multi 20 15
395 A116 50fr bl & multi 22 15
396 A116 80fr org & multi 35 18

2nd Tahoua Youth Festival, Apr. 7-14.

Red Cross, WHO Emblems and Children — A117

1977, Apr. 25 Engr. *Perf. 13*
397 A117 80fr lil, org & red 35 22

World Health Day: "Immunization means protection of your children."

Eye with WHO Emblem, and Sword Killing Fly — A118

1977, May 7
398 A118 100fr multi 42 28

Fight against onchocerciasis, a roundworm infection, transmitted by flies, causing blindness.

Guirka Tahoua Dance A119

Dances: 50fr, Mailfilafili Gaya. 80fr, Naguihinayan Loga.

1977, June 7 Photo. *Perf. 13x12½*
399 A119 40fr multi 18 15
400 A119 50fr multi 22 15
401 A119 80fr multi 35 20

Popular arts and traditions.

Cavalry — A120

Designs: Traditional chief's cavalry, different groups.

1977, July 7 Litho. *Perf. 13x12½*
402 A120 40fr multi 18 15
403 A120 50fr multi 22 15
404 A120 60fr multi 28 15

Planting and Cultivating — A121

1977, Aug. 10
405 A121 40fr multi 18 15

Reclamation of Sahel Region.

Albert John Luthuli Peace — A122

Designs: 80fr, Maurice Maeterlinck, literature. 100fr, Allan L. Hodgkin, medicine. 150fr, Albert Camus, literature. 200fr, Paul Ehrlich, medicine.

1977, Aug. 20 Litho. *Perf. 14*
406 A122 50fr multi 28 15
407 A122 80fr multi 28 18
408 A122 100fr multi 50 20
409 A122 150fr multi 75 28
410 A122 200fr multi 1.00 40
Nos. 406-410 (5) 2.81 1.21

Nobel prize winners. See No. C287.

Mao Tse-tung — A123

1977, Sept. 9 Engr. *Perf. 13*
411 A123 100fr blk & red 42 28

Argentina '78 Emblem, Soccer Players and Coach, Vittorio Pozzo, Italy — A124

Designs (Argentina '78 emblem, soccer players and coach): 50fr, Vincente Feola, Spain. 80fr, Aymore Moreira, Portugal. 100fr, Sir Alf Ramsey, England. 200fr, Helmut Schoen, Germany. 500fr, Sepp Herberger, Germany.

1977, Oct. 12 Litho. *Perf. 13½*
412 A124 40fr multi 20 15
413 A124 50fr multi 28 15
414 A124 80fr multi 40 20
415 A124 100fr multi 55 25
416 A124 200fr multi 1.10 40
Nos. 412-416 (5) 2.53 1.15

Souvenir Sheet

417 A124 500fr multi 2.50 1.10

World Cup Soccer championship, Argentina '78.
For overprints see Nos. 453-458.

Horse's Head, Parthenon and UNESCO Emblem — A125

1977, Nov. 12 Engr. *Perf. 13*
418 A125 100fr multi 42 28

United Nations, Educational, Scientific and Cultural Organization.

Woman Carrying Water Pots — A126

Design: 50fr, Women pounding corn.

1977, Nov. 23 Photo. *Perf. 12½x13*
419 A126 40fr multi 18 15
420 A126 50fr red & multi 22 15
Set value 22

Niger Women's Association.

Crocodile's Skull, 100 Million Years Old — A127

Design: 80fr, Neolithic flint tools.

1977, Dec. 14 *Perf. 13*
421 A127 50fr multi 22 15
422 A127 80fr multi 35 22

Raoul Follereau and Lepers A128

Design: 40fr, Raoul Follereau and woman leper (vert.).

1978, Jan. 28 Engr. *Perf. 13*
423 A128 40fr multi 18 15
424 A128 50fr multi 22 15

25th anniversary of Leprosy Day. Follereau (1903-1977) was "Apostle to the Lepers" and educator of the blind.

Bird Type of 1972 Redrawn

1978, Feb. Photo. *Perf. 13*
425 A58 50fr tan & multi 22 15

No. 425 is dated "1978" and has only designer's name in imprint. No. 254 has printer's name also.

Assumption, by Rubens A129

Rubens Paintings: 70fr, Rubens and Friends (horiz.). 100fr, History of Marie de Medici. 150fr, Alathea Talbot and Family. 200fr, Marquise de Spinola. 500fr, Virgin and St. Ildefonso.

1978, Feb. 25 Litho. *Perf. 14*
426 A129 50fr multi 28 15
427 A129 70fr multi 32 18
428 A129 100fr multi 50 22
429 A129 150fr multi 75 35
430 A129 200fr multi 1.10 42
Nos. 426-430 (5) 2.95 1.32

Souvenir Sheet

Perf. 13½

431 A129 500fr gold & multi 2.50 1.10

Peter Paul Rubens (1577-1640), 400th birth anniversary.

Shot Put — A130

Designs: 50fr, Volleyball. 60fr, Long jump. 100fr, Javelin.

1978, Mar. 22 Photo. *Perf. 13*
432 A130 40fr multi 18 15
433 A130 50fr multi 22 15
434 A130 60fr multi 28 15
435 A130 100fr multi 42 28

Natl. University Games' Championships.

First Aid and Red Crosses A131

1978, May 13 Litho.
436 A131 40fr red & multi 18 15

Niger Red Cross.

Goudel Earth Station A132

1978, May 23
437 A132 100fr multi 45 28

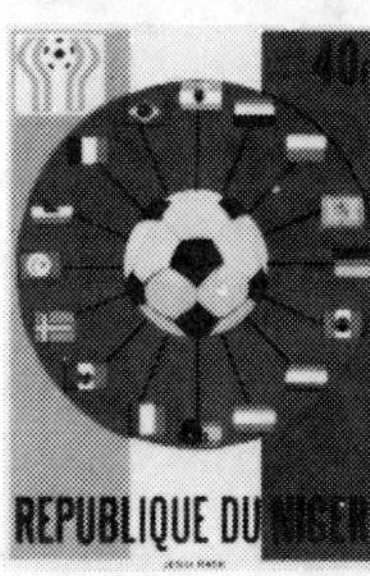

Soccer Ball, Flags of Participants A133

Designs (Argentina '78 Emblem and): 50fr, Ball in net. 100fr, Globe with South America, Soccer field. 200fr, Two players (horiz.). 300fr, Player and globe.

1978, June 18 Litho. *Perf. 13½*
438 A133 40fr multi 20 15
439 A133 50fr multi 30 18
440 A133 100fr multi 50 35
441 A133 200fr multi 1.00 60

Souvenir Sheet

442 A133 300fr multi 1.60 90

11th World Cup Soccer Championship, Argentina, June 1-25.

Bird Type of 1971 Redrawn

1978, June Photo. *Perf. 13*
443 A54 35fr bl & multi 18 15

No. 443 has no year date, nor Delrieu imprint.

Post Office, Niamey — A134

Design: 60fr, Post Office, different view.

1978, Aug. 12 Litho.
444 A134 40fr multi 18 15
445 A134 60fr multi 28 15

Goudel Water Works A135

1978, Sept. 25 Photo. *Perf. 13*
446 A135 100fr multi 42 28

Giraffe — A136

Animals and Wildlife Fund Emblem: 50fr, Ostrich. 70fr, Cheetah. 150fr, Oryx (horiz.). 200fr, Addax (horiz.). 300fr, Hartebeest (horiz.).

1978, Nov. 20 Litho. *Perf. 15*
447 A136 40fr multi 20 15
448 A136 50fr multi 28 15
449 A136 70fr multi 35 20
450 A136 150fr multi 75 40
451 A136 200fr multi 1.00 55
452 A136 300fr multi 1.50 80
Nos. 447-452 (6) 4.08 2.25

Endangered species.

Nos. 412-417 Overprinted in Silver
a. "EQUIPE QUATRIEME: ITALIE"
b. "EQUIPE TROISIEME: BRESIL"
c. "EQUIPE / SECONDE: / PAYS BAS"
d. "EQUIPE VAINQUEUR: ARGENTINE"
e. "ARGENTINE-PAYS BAS 3-1"

1978, Dec. 1 *Perf. 13½*
453 A124(a) 40fr multi 18 15
454 A124(b) 50fr multi 22 15
455 A124(c) 80fr multi 35 22
456 A124(d) 100fr multi 42 28
457 A124(e) 200fr multi 85 55
Nos. 453-457 (5) 2.02 1.35

Souvenir Sheet

458 A124(e) 500fr multi 2.25 90

Winners, World Soccer Cup Championship, Argentina, June 1-25.

Tinguizi — A137

Musicians: No. 460, Dan Gourmou. No. 461, Chetima Ganga (horiz.).

1978, Dec. 11 Litho. *Perf. 13*
459 A137 100fr multi 42 28
460 A137 100fr multi 42 28
461 A137 100fr multi 42 28

Virgin Mary, by Dürer A138

Paintings: 50fr, The Homecoming, by Honore Daumier (1808-79). 150fr, 200fr, 500fr, Virgin and Child, by Albrecht Dürer (1471-1528) (different).

1979, Jan. 31 Litho. *Perf. 13½*
462 A138 50fr multi 30 15
463 A138 100fr multi 50 30
464 A138 150fr multi 75 40
465 A138 200fr multi 1.00 55

Souvenir Sheet

466 A138 500fr multi 2.50 1.10

Solar Panels and Tank — A139

Design: 40fr, Tank and panels on roof (vert.).

Perf. 12½x12, 12x12½

1979, Feb. 28
467 A139 40fr multi 18 15
468 A139 50fr multi 22 15

Hot water from solar heat.

Children with Building Blocks — A140

Children and IYC Emblem: 100fr, Reading books. 150fr, With model plane.

1979, Apr. 10 Litho. *Perf. 13½*
469 A140 40fr multi 22 15
470 A140 100fr multi 50 28
471 A140 150fr multi 75 40

International Year of the Child.

The Langa, Traditional Sport A141

Design: 50fr, The langa (diff.).

1979, Apr. 10 Litho. *Perf. 12½x12*
472 A141 40fr multi 18 15
473 A141 50fr multi 22 15

Rowland Hill, Mail Truck and France No. 8 — A142

Designs (Hill and): 100fr, Canoes and Austria No. P4. 150fr, Air Niger plane and U.S. No. 122. 200fr, Streamlined mail train and Canada type A6. 400fr, Electric train and Niger No. 51.

1979, June 6 Litho. *Perf. 14*
474 A142 40fr multi 18 15
475 A142 100fr multi 42 28
476 A142 150fr multi 65 40
477 A142 200fr multi 85 55

Souvenir Sheet

478 A142 400fr multi 1.90

Sir Rowland Hill (1795-1879), originator of penny postage.

Zabira Handbag and Niger No. 135 — A143

Design: 150fr, Heads with communications waves, world map, UPU emblem and satellite.

1979, June 8 Litho. *Perf. 12x12½*
479 A143 50fr multi 22 15

Engr. *Perf. 13*
480 A143 150fr brt red & ultra 65 80

Philexafrique II, Libreville, Gabon, June 8-17. Nos. 479, 480 each printed in sheets of 10 and 5 labels showing exhibition emblem.

Djermakoye Palace — A144

1979, Sept. 26 Litho. *Perf. 13x12½*
481 A144 100fr multi 42 28

Bororo Festive Headdress — A145

Design: 60fr, Bororo women's traditional costumes (vert.).

Perf. 13x12½, 12½x13

1979, Sept. 26
482 A145 45fr multi 20 15
483 A145 60fr multi 25 18

Annual Bororo Festival.

Olympic Emblem, Flame and Boxers — A146

Designs: 100fr, 150fr, 250fr, 500fr, Olympic emblem, flame and boxers (diff.).

1979, Oct. 6 *Perf. 13½*
484 A146 45fr multi 20 15
485 A146 100fr multi 42 28
486 A146 150fr multi 65 40
487 A146 250fr multi 1.10 65

Souvenir Sheet

488 A146 500fr multi 2.50 1.50

Pre-Olympic Year.

Values quoted in this catalogue are for stamps graded at Fine-Very Fine and with no faults. An illustrated guide to grade is provided in introductory material, beginning on Page 1A.

John Alcock, Arthur Whitten Brown, Vickers-Vimy Biplane — A147

1979, Sept. 3 ***Perf. 13½***
489 A147 100fr multi 45 30

First Transatlantic flight, 60th anniversary.

Road and Traffic Safety — A148

1979, Nov. 20 **Litho.** ***Perf. 12½***
490 A148 45fr multi 20 15

Four-Man Bobsledding, Lake Placid '80 Emblem — A149

Lake Placid '80 Emblem and: 60fr, Downhill skiing. 100fr, Speed skating. 150fr, Two-man bobsledding. 200fr, Figure skating. 300fr, Cross-country skiing.

1979, Dec. 10 ***Perf. 14½***
491 A149 40fr multi 18 15
492 A149 60fr multi 25 18
493 A149 100fr multi 42 30
494 A149 150fr multi 65 40
495 A149 200fr multi 90 55
Nos. 491-495 (5) 2.40 1.58

Souvenir Sheet

496 A149 300fr multi 1.40 90

13th Winter Olympic Games, Lake Placid, NY, Feb. 12-24, 1980.
For overprints see Nos. 501-506.

Nos. 389, 390 Overprinted in Silver or Black "alunissage/apollo XI/juillet 1969" and Emblem

1979, Dec. 20 **Litho.** ***Perf. 14***
497 A113 50fr multi (S) 22 15
498 A113 80fr multi 35 22

Apollo 11 moon landing, 10th anniversary. See Nos. C295-C297.

Court of Sultan of Zinder — A150

1980, Mar. 25 **Litho.** ***Perf. 13x12½***
499 A150 45fr shown 20 15
500 A150 60fr Sultan's court, diff. 25 18

Nos. 491-496 Overprinted
a. VAINQUEUR/R.D.A.
b. VAINQUEUR/STENMARK/SUEDE
c. VAINQUEUR/HEIDEN/Etats-Unis
d. VAINQUEURS/SCHAERER-BENZ/Suisse
e. VAINQUEUR/COUSINS/ Grande Bretagne
f. VAINQUEUR/ZIMIATOV/U.R.S.S.

1980, Mar. 31 **Litho.** ***Perf. 14½***
501 A149 (a) 40fr multi 18 15
502 A149 (b) 60fr multi 25 18
503 A149 (c) 100fr multi 45 28
504 A149 (d) 150fr multi 65 40
505 A149 (e) 200fr multi 90 55
Nos. 501-505 (5) 2.43 1.56

Souvenir Sheet

506 A149 (f) 300fr multi 1.25 80

Javelin, Olympic Rings — A151

Man Smoking Cigarette, Runner — A152

1980, Apr. 17
507 A151 60fr shown 25 18
508 A151 90fr Walking 38 25
509 A151 100fr High jump, horiz. 42 28
510 A151 300fr Marathon runners, horiz. 1.25 80

Souvenir Sheet

511 A151 500fr High jump, diff. 2.25 1.40

22nd Summer Olympic Games, Moscow, July 19-Aug. 3.
For overprints see Nos. 527-531.

1980, Apr. 7 ***Perf. 13***
512 A152 100fr multi 42 28

World Health Day; fight against cigarette smoking.

Health Year A153

1980, May 15 **Photo.** ***Perf. 13x12½***
513 A153 150fr multi 65 40

Shimbashi-Yokohama Locomotive — A154

1980, June **Litho.** ***Perf. 12½***
514 A154 45fr shown 20 15
515 A154 60fr American type 25 18
516 A154 90fr German Reichsbahn series 61 40 25
517 A154 100fr Prussian Staatsbahn P2 42 28
518 A154 130fr L'Aigle 55 35
Nos. 514-518 (5) 1.82 1.21

Souvenir Sheet

519 A154 425fr Stephenson's Rocket 1.80 1.10

For overprint see No. 674.

Steve Biko, 4th Anniversary of Death — A155

1980, Sept. 12 **Litho.** ***Perf. 13***
520 A155 150fr org & blk 65 40

Soccer Players — A156

Designs: Various soccer scenes.

1980, Oct. 15 ***Perf. 12½***
521 A156 45fr multi 20 15
522 A156 60fr multi 25 18
523 A156 90fr multi 38 25
524 A156 100fr multi 42 28
525 A156 130fr multi 55 35
Nos. 521-525 (5) 1.80 1.21

Souvenir Sheet

526 A156 425fr multi 1.90 1.10

World Soccer Cup 1982.

Nos. 507-511 Overprinted in Gold with Winner's Name and Country

1980, Sept. 27 **Litho.** ***Perf. 14½***
527 A151 60fr multi 25 18
528 A151 90fr multi 38 25
529 A151 100fr multi 45 30
530 A151 300fr multi 1.25 80

Souvenir Sheet

531 A151 500fr multi 2.25 1.40

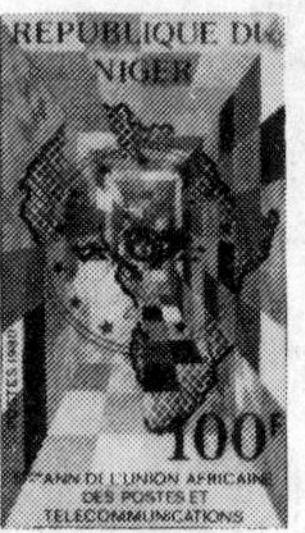

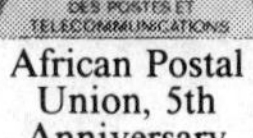

African Postal Union, 5th Anniversary A157

Terra Cotta Kareygorou Head A158

1980, Dec. 24 **Photo.** ***Perf. 13½***
532 A157 100fr multi 45 30

1981, Jan. 23 **Litho.** ***Perf. 13***

Designs: Terra Cotta Kareygorou Statues, 5th-12th cent. 45fr, 150fr, horiz.

533 A158 45fr multi 20 15
534 A158 60fr multi 25 18
535 A158 90fr multi 40 25
536 A158 150fr multi 65 40

Ostrich — A159

1981, Mar. 17 **Litho.** ***Perf. 12½***
537 A159 10fr shown 15 15
538 A159 20fr Oryx 15 15
539 A159 25fr Gazelle 15 15
540 A159 30fr Great bustard 15 15
541 A159 60fr Giraffe 25 18
542 A159 150fr Addax 65 40
Nos. 537-542 (6) 1.50
Set value 85

7th Anniv. of the F.A.N. A160

1981, Apr. 14 **Litho.** ***Perf. 13***
543 A160 100fr multi 45 30

One-armed Archer — A161

1981, Apr. 24 **Engr.**
544 A161 50fr shown 22 15
545 A161 100fr Draftsman 42 28

Intl. Year of the Disabled.

Scene from Mahalba Ballet, 1980 Youth Festival, Dosso A162

1981, May 17 **Litho.**
546 A162 100fr shown 42 28
547 A162 100fr Ballet, diff. 42 28

Prince Charles and Lady Diana, Coach A163

Designs: Couple and coaches.

1981, July 15 **Litho.** ***Perf. 14½***
548 A163 150fr multi 65 40
549 A163 200fr multi 85 55
550 A163 300fr multi 1.25 80

Souvenir Sheet

551 A163 400fr multi 1.75 1.10

Royal wedding.
For overprints see Nos. 595-598.

Hegira 1500th Anniv.
A164

Alexander Fleming (1881-1955)
A165

1981, July 15 ***Perf. 13½x13***
552 A164 100fr multi 45 30

1981, Aug. 6 **Engr.** ***Perf. 13***
553 A165 150fr multi 65 40

25th Intl. Letter Writing Week, Oct. 6-12 — A167

1981, Oct. 9 **Surcharged in Black**
554 A167 65fr on 40fr multi 30 18
555 A167 85fr on 60fr multi 35 25

Nos. 554-555 not issued without surcharge.

World Food Day — A168

1981, Oct. 16 **Litho.**
556 A168 100fr multi 42 30

Espana '82 World Cup Soccer — A169

Designs: Various soccer players.

1981, Nov. 18 **Litho.** ***Perf. 14x13½***
557 A169 40fr multi 18 15
558 A169 65fr multi 28 18
559 A169 85fr multi 35 22
560 A169 150fr multi 65 40
561 A169 300fr multi 1.25 80
Nos. 557-561 (5) 2.71 1.75

Souvenir Sheet

562 A169 500fr multi 2.25 1.40

For overprints see Nos. 603-608.

75th Anniv. of Grand Prix — A170

Designs: Winners and their cars.

1981, Nov. 30 ***Perf. 14***
563 A170 20fr Peugeot, 1912 15 15
564 A170 40fr Bugatti, 1924 18 15
565 A170 65fr Lotus-Climax, 1962 28 18
566 A170 85fr Georges Boillot, 1912 35 22
567 A170 150fr Phil Hill, 1960 65 40
Nos. 563-567 (5) 1.61 1.10

Souvenir Sheet

568 A170 450fr Race 2.00 1.25

For overprint see No. 675.

Christmas 1981 — A171

Designs: Virgin and Child paintings.

1981, Dec. 24
569 A171 100fr Botticelli 42 26
570 A171 200fr Botticini 85 55
571 A171 300fr Botticelli, diff. 1.25 80

School Gardens
A172

1982, Feb. 19 **Litho.** ***Perf. 13x13½***
572 A172 65fr shown 28 18
573 A172 85fr Garden, diff. 35 22

Fruit on a Table, by Edouard Manet (1832-1883) — A173

Anniversaries: 120fr, Arturo Toscanini (1867-1957) (vert.). 200fr, L'Estaque, by Georges Braque (1882-1963). 300fr, George Washington (1732-1799) (vert.). 400fr, Goethe (1749-1832) (vert.). Nos. 579-580, 21st birthday of Diana, Princess of Wales (portraits, vert.).

1982, Mar. 8 **Litho.** ***Perf. 13***
574 A173 120fr multi 55 35
575 A173 140fr multi 65 38
576 A173 200fr multi 85 55
577 A173 300fr multi 1.25 80
578 A173 400fr multi 1.75 1.10
579 A173 500fr multi 2.25 1.40
Nos. 574-579 (6) 7.30 4.58

Souvenir Sheet

580 A173 500fr multi 2.25 1.40

Palace of Congress — A174

1982, Mar. 17
581 A174 150fr multi 65 40

7th Youth Festival, Agadez
A175

Reafforestation Campaign
A176

1982, Apr. 7 ***Perf. 12½***
582 A175 65fr Martial arts, horiz. 28 18
583 A175 100fr Wrestling 42 28

1982, Apr. 16 ***Perf. 13***
584 A176 150fr Tree planting 65 40
585 A176 200fr Trees, Desert 85 55

For overprints see Nos. 668-669.

Scouting Year
A177

1982, May 13
586 A177 65fr Canoeing 28 18
587 A177 85fr Scouts in rubber boat 35 22
588 A177 130fr Canoeing, diff. 55 35
589 A177 200fr Rafting 85 55

Souvenir Sheet

590 A177 400fr Beach scene 1.75 1.10

For overprint see No. 673.

13th Meeting of Islamic Countries Foreign Affairs Ministers, Niamey, Aug. 20-27
A178

1982, June 6
591 A178 100fr multi 42 28

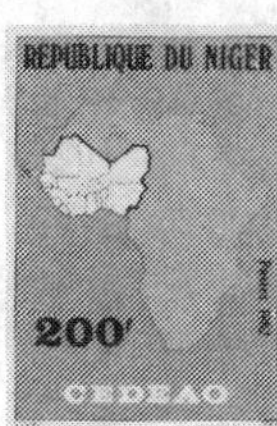

West African Economic Community
A179

1982, June 28
592 A179 200fr Map 85 55

Fishermen in Canoe
A180

1982, July 18 ***Perf. 13x12½***
593 A180 65fr shown 28 18
594 A180 85fr Bringing in nets 35 22

Nos. 548-551 Overprinted in Blue: "NAISSANCE ROYALE 1982"

1982, Aug. 4 ***Perf. 14½***
595 A163 150fr multi 65 40
596 A163 200fr multi 85 55
597 A163 300fr multi 1.25 80

Souvenir Sheet

598 A163 400fr multi 1.75 1.10

Flautist, by Norman Rockwell
A181

1982, Sept. 10 **Litho.** ***Perf. 14***
599 A181 65fr shown 28 18
600 A181 85fr Clerk 35 22
601 A181 110fr Teacher and Pupil 48 30
602 A181 150fr Girl Shopper 65 40

Nos. 557-562 Overprinted with Past and Present Winners in Black on Silver

1982, Sept. 28 ***Perf. 14x13½***
603 A169 40fr multi 18 15
604 A169 65fr multi 28 18
605 A169 85fr multi 35 22
606 A169 150fr multi 65 40
607 A169 300fr multi 1.25 80
Nos. 603-607 (5) 2.71 1.75

Souvenir Sheet

608 A169 500fr multi 2.25 1.40

Italy's victory in 1982 World Cup.

ITU Plenipotentiaries Conference, Nairobi, Sept. — A182

1982, Sept. 28 ***Perf. 13***
609 A182 130fr blk & bl 55 35

Laboratory Workers A183

Various laboratory workers.

1982, Nov. 9 Litho. *Perf. 13*
610 A168 65fr multi 30 18
611 A183 115fr multi 50 30

Self-sufficiency in Food Production — A184

1983, Feb. 16 Litho. *Perf. 13½x13*
612 A184 65fr Rice harvest 28 18
613 A184 85fr Planting rice, vert. 35 22

Grand Ducal Madonna, by Raphael A185

Raphael Paintings: 65fr, Miraculous Catch of Fishes. 100fr, Deliverance of St. Peter. 150fr, Sistine Madonna. 200fr, Christ on the Way to Calvary. 300fr, Deposition. 400fr, Transfiguration. 500fr, St. Michael Slaying the Dragon. 65fr, 100fr, 300fr horiz.

1983, Mar. 30 Litho. *Perf. 14*
614 A185 65fr multi 28 18
615 A185 85fr multi 35 22
616 A185 100fr multi 42 26
617 A185 150fr multi 65 40
618 A185 200fr multi 85 55
619 A185 300fr multi 1.25 80
620 A185 400fr multi 1.75 1.10
621 A185 500fr multi 2.25 1.30
Nos. 614-621 (8) 7.80 4.81

African Economic Commission, 25th Anniv. — A186

1983, Mar. 18 *Perf. 12½x13*
622 A186 120fr multi 55 32
623 A186 200fr multi 85 55

Army Surveyors A187

1983, Apr. 14 *Perf. 13x12½*
624 A187 85fr shown 35 22
625 A187 150fr Road building 65 40

Agadez Court A188

1983, Apr. 26 Litho. *Perf. 13x12½*
626 A188 65fr multi 28 18

Mail Van — A189

1983, June 25 Litho.
627 A189 65fr Van 28 18
628 A189 100fr Van, map 42 25

Palestine Solidarity — A190

1983, Aug. 21 Litho. *Perf. 12½*
629 A190 65fr multi 28 18

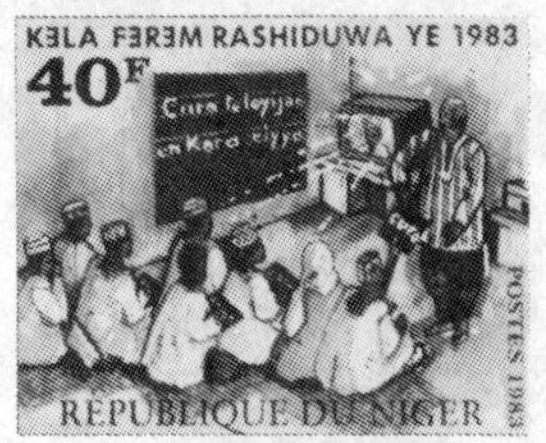
Intl. Literacy Year — A191

Various adult education classes. 65fr, 150fr vert.

Perf. 13½x14½, 14½x13½
1983, Sept. 8 Litho.
630 A191 40fr multi 15 15
631 A191 65fr multi 15 15
632 A191 85fr multi 18 15
633 A191 100fr multi 22 15
634 A191 150fr multi 32 18
Nos. 630-634 (5) 1.02
Set value 58

7th Ballet Festival of Dosso Dept. A192

Various dancers.

1983, Oct. 7 *Perf. 14½x13½*
635 A192 65fr multi 15 15
636 A192 85fr multi 18 15
637 A192 120fr multi 25 16
Set value 36

World Communications Year — A193

Perf. 13x12½, 12½x13
1983, Oct. 18
638 A193 80fr Post Office, mail van 16 15
639 A193 120fr Sorting mail 25 16
640 A193 150fr Emblem, vert. 32 20

Solar Energy for Television — A194

1983, Nov. 26 *Perf. 13*
641 A194 85fr Antenna 18 15
642 A194 130fr Car 28 18

Local Butterflies — A195

1983, Dec. 9 *Perf. 12½*
643 A195 75fr Hypolimnas misippus 18 15
644 A195 120fr Papilio demodocus 32 16
645 A195 250fr Vanessa antiopa 70 35
646 A195 350fr Charesex jasius 90 45
647 A195 500fr Danaus chrisippus 1.40 65
Nos. 643-647 (5) 3.50 1.76

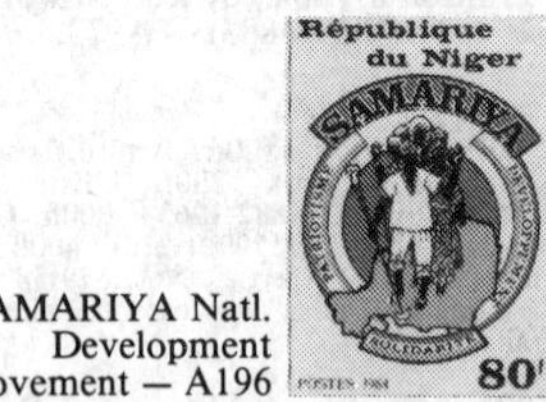
SAMARIYA Natl. Development Movement — A196

1984, Jan. 18 Litho. *Perf. 13x13½*
648 A196 80fr multi 16 15

Alestes Bouboni A197

1984, Mar. 28 Litho. *Perf. 13*
649 A197 120fr multi 32 15

Military Pentathlon A198

1984, Apr. 10
650 A198 120fr Hurdles 32 15
651 A198 140fr Shooting 36 16

Radio Broadcasting Building Opening A199

1984, May 14 Litho. *Perf. 13*
652 A199 120fr multi 32 15

25th Anniv. of Council of Unity — A200

1984, May 29 *Perf. 12½*
653 A200 65fr multi 18 15
654 A200 85fr multi 22 15
Set value 18

Renault, 1902 — A201

Vintage cars (100fr, 140fr, 250fr, 400fr) and ships.

1984, June 12 *Perf. 12½*
655 A201 80fr Paris 22 15
656 A201 100fr Gottlieb Daimler 28 15
657 A201 120fr Three-master Jacques Coeur 32 15
658 A201 140fr shown 36 16
659 A201 150fr Barque Bosphorus 38 18
660 A201 250fr Delage D8 65 35
661 A201 300fr Three-master Comet 80 36
662 A201 400fr Maybach Zeppelin 1.10 48
Nos. 655-662 (8) 4.11 1.98

1984 UPU Congress A202

1984, June 20 Engr. *Perf. 13x12½*
663 A202 300fr Ship, emblems 80 35

Ayerou Market Place A203

1984, July 18 Litho. *Perf. 12½*
664 A203 80fr shown 22 15
665 A203 120fr River scene 32 16

Vipere Echis Leucogaster — A204

1984, Aug. 16 *Perf. 13x12½*
666 A204 80fr multi 22 15

West African Union, CEAO, 10th Anniv. A205

1984, Oct. 26 **Litho.** *Perf. 13½*
667 A205 80fr multi 18 15

UN Disarmament Campaign, 20th Anniv. — A205a

1984, Oct. 31 *Perf. 13*
667A A205a 400fr brt grn & blk 90 48
667B A205a 500fr brt bl & blk 1.25 60

Nos. 584-585 Overprinted "Aide au Sahel 84"

1984 **Litho.** *Perf. 13*
668 A176 150fr multi 32 18
669 A176 200fr multi 45 22

World Tourism Organization, 10th Anniv. — A206

1984, Jan. 2 **Litho.** *Perf. 12½*
670 A206 110fr WTO emblem 25 15

Infant Survival Campaign — A207

1985, Jan. 28 **Litho.** *Perf. 12½*
671 A207 85fr Breastfeeding 18 15
672 A207 110fr Weighing child, giving liquids 24 15
Set value 24

Nos. 590, 519 and 568 Overprinted with Exhibitions in Red Souvenir Sheets

Perf. 13, 12½, 14

1985, Mar. 11 **Litho.**
673 A177 400fr MOPHILA '85 / HAMBOURG 90 50
674 A154 425fr TSUKUBA EXPO '85 90 50
675 A170 450fr ROME, ITALIA '85 emblem 1.10 55

See Nos. C356-C357.

Technical & Cultural Cooperation Agency, 15th Anniv. — A208

1985, Mar. 20 *Perf. 13*
676 A208 110fr vio, brn & car rose 24 15

8th Niamey Festival A209

Gaya Ballet Troupe. No. 678 vert.

1985, Apr. 8 *Perf. 12½x13, 13x12½*
677 A209 85fr multi 18 15
678 A209 110fr multi 24 15
679 A209 150fr multi 32 16
Set value 38

Intl. Youth Year — A210

Authors and scenes from novels: 85fr, Jack London (1876-1916). 105fr, Joseph Kessel (1898-1979). 250fr, Herman Melville. 450fr, Rudyard Kipling.

1985, Apr. 29 *Perf. 13*
680 A210 85fr multi 18 15
681 A210 105fr multi 22 15
682 A210 250fr multi 55 30
683 A210 450fr multi 1.10 55

PHILEXAFRICA '85, Lome, Togo — A211

1985, May 6 *Perf. 13x12½*
684 A211 200fr Tree planting 45 22
685 A211 200fr Industry 45 22

Nos. 684-685 printed se-tenant with center label picturing map of Africa or the UAPT emblem.

Victor Hugo and His Son Francois, by A. de Chatillon — A212

1985, May 22 *Perf. 12½*
686 A212 500fr multi 1.10 55

Europafrica A213

1985, June 3 *Perf. 13*
687 A213 110fr multi 24 15

World Wildlife Fund — A214

Designs: 50fr, 60fr, Addax. 85fr, 110fr, Oryx.

1985, June 15
688 A214 50fr Head, vert. 15 15
689 A214 60fr Grazing 15 15
690 A214 85fr Two adults 18 15
691 A214 110fr Head, vert. 24 15
Set value 35

Environ-destroying Species — A215

1985, July 1 *Perf. 13x12½, 12½x13*
692 A215 85fr Oedaleus sp. 18 15
693 A215 110fr Dysdercus volkeri 24 15
694 A215 150fr Tolyposporium ehrenbergii, Sclerospora graminicola, horiz. 32 16
695 A215 210fr Passer luteus 45 22
696 A215 390fr Quelea quelea 80 40
Nos. 692-696 (5) 1.99 1.08

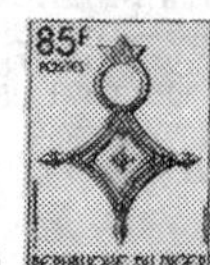

Cross of Agadez — A216

1985, July **Engr.** *Perf. 13*
697 A216 85fr green 18 15
698 A216 110fr brown 24 15
Set value 22

Natl. Independence, 25th Anniv. — A217

1985, Aug. 3 **Litho.** *Perf. 13x12½*
707 A217 110fr multi 24 15

Protected Trees A218

Designs: 30fr, No. 711, Adansonia digitata and pod, vert. 85fr, 210fr, Acacia albida. No. 710, 390fr, Adansonia digitata, diff. Nos. 708-710 inscribed "DES ARBRES POUR LE NIGER."

1985 *Perf. 13x12½, 12½x13*
708 A218 30fr grn & multi 15 15
709 A218 85fr brn & multi 18 15
710 A218 110fr mag & multi 24 15
711 A218 110fr blk & multi 24 15
712 A218 210fr blk & multi 45 22
713 A218 390fr blk & multi 80 40
Nos. 708-713 (6) 2.06
Set value 1.00

Issue dates: Nos. 708-710, Oct. 1. Nos. 711-713, Aug. 19.

Niamey-Bamako Motorboat Race — A219

1985, Sept. 16 *Perf. 13½*
714 A219 110fr Boats on Niger River 24 15
715 A219 150fr Helicopter, competitor 32 16
716 A219 250fr Motorboat, map 55 28

Mushrooms A220

1985, Oct. 3
717 A220 85fr Boletus 24 15
718 A220 110fr Hypholma fasciculare 32 15
719 A220 200fr Coprinus comatus 55 22
720 A220 300fr Agaricus arvensis 85 32
721 A220 400fr Geastrum fimbriatum 1.25 48
Nos. 717-721 (5) 3.21 1.32

Nos. 717-719 vert.

Set Values
A 15-cent minimum now applies to individual stamps and sets. Where the 15-cent minimum per stamp would increase the "value" of a set beyond retail, there is a "Set Value" notation giving the retail value of the set.

PHILEXAFRICA '85, Lome, Togo — A221

1985, Oct. 21 *Perf. 13x12½*

722 A221 250fr Village water pump 55 30
723 A221 250fr Children playing dili 55 30

Nos. 722-723 printed se-tenant with center label picturing map of Africa or UAPT emblem.

61st World Savings Day — A222

1985, Oct. 31 *Perf. 12½x13*

724 A222 210fr multi 44 22

European Music Year A223

Traditional instruments.

1985, Nov. 4 *Perf. 13½*

725 A223 150fr Gouroumi, vert. 32 16
726 A223 210fr Gassou 45 22
727 A223 390fr Algaita, vert. 80 40

Souvenir Sheet

Perf. 12½

728 A223 500fr Biti 1.10 55

Civil Statutes Reform — A224

1986, Jan. 2 **Litho.** *Perf. 13x12½*

729 A224 85fr Natl. identity card 35 18
730 A224 110fr Family services 45 22

Traffic Safety — A225

Artists — A226

1986, Mar. 26 **Litho.** *Perf. 12½x13*

731 A225 85fr Obey signs 35 18
732 A225 110fr Speed restriction 45 22

1986, Apr. 11 *Perf. 12½*

Designs: 60fr, Oumarou Ganda, filmmaker. 85fr, Ida Na Dadaou, entertainer. 100fr, Dan Gourmou, entertainer. 130fr, Koungoui, comedian.

733 A226 60fr multi 24 15
734 A226 85fr multi 35 18
735 A226 100fr multi 42 20
736 A226 130fr multi 45 26

Hunger Relief Campaign, Trucks of Hope — A227

1986, Aug. 27 **Litho.** *Perf. 12½*

737 A227 85fr Relief supply truck 35 18
738 A227 110fr Mother, child, vert. 45 22

Intl. Solidarity Day — A228

Designs: 200fr, Nelson Mandela and Walter Sisulu, Robben Island prison camp. 300fr, Mandela.

1986, Oct. 8 *Perf. 13½*

739 A228 200fr multi 80 42
740 A228 300fr multi 1.25 60

FAO, 40th Anniv. A229

1986, Oct. 16 *Perf. 13*

741 A229 50fr Cooperative peanut farm 20 15
742 A229 60fr Fight desert encroachment 24 15
743 A229 85fr Irrigation management 35 18
744 A229 100fr Breeding livestock 42 20
745 A229 110fr Afforestation 45 22
Nos. 741-745 (5) 1.66 90

Improved Housing for a Healthier Niger — A230

Insects Protecting Growing Crops — A231

1987, Feb. 26 **Litho.** *Perf. 13½*

746 A230 85fr Albarka 35 18
747 A230 110fr Mai Sauki 45 22

1987, Mar. 26 *Perf. 13x12½*

748 A231 85fr Sphodromantis 35 18
749 A231 110fr Delta 45 22
750 A231 120fr Cicindela 50 25

Liptako-Gourma Telecommunications Link Inauguration — A232

1987, Apr. 10 *Perf. 13½*

751 A232 110fr multi 45 22

Samuel Morse — A233

1988 Seoul Summer Olympics — A234

1987, May 21 **Litho.** *Perf. 12x12½*

752 A233 120fr Telegraph key, operator, horiz. 50 25
753 A233 200fr shown 85 40
754 A233 350fr Receiver, horiz. 1.50 75

Invention of the telegraph, 150th anniv.

1987, July 15

755 A234 85fr Tennis 35 18
756 A234 110fr Pole vault 45 22
757 A234 250fr Soccer 1.10 52

Souvenir Sheet

758 A234 500fr Running 2.00 1.10

1988 Winter Olympics, Calgary — A235

1987, July 28 **Litho.** *Perf. 12½*

759 A235 85fr Ice hockey 35 18
760 A235 110fr Speed skating 45 22
761 A235 250fr Pairs figure skating 1.10 52

Souvenir Sheet

762 A235 500fr Downhill skiing 2.00 1.10

For overprints see Nos. 783-785.

African Games, Nairobi — A236

1987, Aug. 5 *Perf. 13*

763 A236 85fr Runners 35 18
764 A236 110fr High jump 45 22
765 A236 200fr Hurdles 85 40
766 A236 400fr Javelin 1.65 85

Natl. Tourism Office, 10th Anniv. A237

1987, Sept. 10 *Perf. 13½*

767 A237 85fr Chief's stool, scepter, vert. 45 22
768 A237 110fr Nomad, caravan, scepter 60 30
769 A237 120fr Moslem village 60 30
770 A237 200fr Bridge over Niger River 1.10 50

Aga Khan Architecture Prize, 1986 — A238

1987, Oct. 7 *Perf. 13*

771 A238 85fr Yaama Mosque, dawn 45 22
772 A238 110fr At night 60 30
773 A238 250fr In daylight 1.40 65

Niamey Court of Appeal A239

1987, Nov. 17 *Perf. 13x12½*

774 A239 85fr multi 45 22
775 A239 110fr multi 60 30
776 A239 140fr multi 75 38

Christmas 1987 — A240

Paintings: 110fr, The Holy Family with Lamb, by Raphael. 500fr, The Adoration of the Magi, by Hans Memling (c. 1430-1494).

Wmk. 385

1987, Dec. 24 **Litho.** *Perf. 12½*

777 A240 110fr multi 60 28

Souvenir Sheet

778 A240 500fr multi 2.50 1.40

No. 778 is airmail.

Modern Services for a Healthy Community — A241

1988, Jan. 21 *Perf. 13*

779 A241 85fr Water drainage 60 30
780 A241 110fr Sewage 78 40
781 A241 165fr Garbage removal 1.20 60

Dan-Gourmou Prize — A242

1988, Feb. 16 Litho. *Perf. 13½*

782 A242 85fr multi 60 30

Natl. modern music competition.

Nos. 759-761 Ovptd. "Medaille d'or" and Name of Winner in Gold

1988, Mar. 29 *Perf. 12½*

783 A235 85fr USSR 62 30
784 A235 110fr Gusafson, Sweden 80 40
785 A235 250fr Gordeeva and Grinkov, USSR 1.80 90

New Market Building, Niamey A243

1988, Apr. 9 Litho. *Perf. 13x12½*

786 A243 85fr multi 60 30

WHO 40th Anniv., Universal Immunization Campaign — A244

1988, May 26 Litho. *Perf. 12½x13*

787 A244 85fr Mother and child 55 28
788 A244 110fr Visiting doctor 72 35

Organization for African Unity (OAU), 25th Anniv. — A245

1988, June 28 *Perf. 12½*

789 A245 85fr multi 55 28

Construction of a Sand Break to Arrest Desert Encroachment — A246

1988, Sept. 27 Litho. *Perf. 12½x13*

790 A246 85fr multi 55 28

Intl. Red Cross and Red Crescent Organizations, 125th Annivs. — A247

1988, Oct. 26 *Perf. 13x12½*

791 A247 85fr multi 55 28
792 A247 110fr multi 72 35

Niger Press Agency A248

1989, Jan. 31 Litho. *Perf. 12½*

793 A248 85fr blk, org & grn 55 28

Fight Against AIDS — A249

1989, Feb. 28 *Perf. 13½*

794 A249 85fr multi 55 28
795 A249 110fr multi 72 35

Intl. Maritime Organization, 30th Anniv. — A250

1989, Mar. 29 Litho. *Perf. 12½x13*

796 A250 100fr multi 65 32
797 A250 120fr multi 78 35

FAN Seizure of Government, 15th Anniv. — A251

1989, Apr. 14

798 A251 85fr Gen. Ali Saibou 55 28
799 A251 110fr Raising of the flag 72 35

PHILEXFRANCE '89 — A252

1989, July 1 Litho. *Perf. 13*

800 A252 100fr Eiffel Tower 60 30
801 A252 200fr Simulated stamps 1.20 60

French Revolution, Bicent. — A253

1989, July 1

802 A253 250fr Planting a tree for liberty 1.50 75

African Development Bank, 25th Anniv. — A254

1989, Aug. 30 Litho. *Perf. 13½*

803 A254 100fr multi 65 32

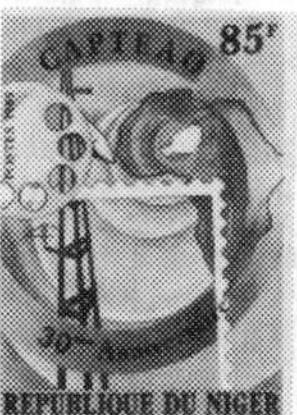

Communication and Postal Organization of West Africa (CAPTEAO), 30th Anniv. — A255

1989, July 3 Litho. *Perf. 13½*

804 A255 85fr multi 55 28

Verdant Field, Field After Locust Plague — A256

1989, Oct. 1 Litho. *Perf. 13*

805 A256 85fr multicolored 55 28

Lumiere Brothers, Film Pioneers A256a

Designs: 150fr, Auguste Lumiere (1862-1954). 250fr, Louis Lumiere (1864-1948).

1989, Nov. 21 Litho. *Perf. 13½*

805A A256a 150fr multicolored 1.05 52
805B A256a 250fr multicolored 1.75 85
805C A256a 400fr multicolored 2.75 1.38

Flora — A257

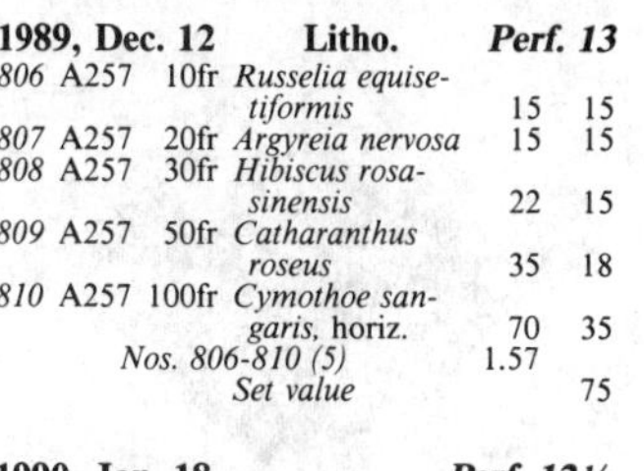

A258

1989, Dec. 12 Litho. *Perf. 13*

806 A257 10fr *Russelia equisetiformis* 15 15
807 A257 20fr *Argyreia nervosa* 15 15
808 A257 30fr *Hibiscus rosa-sinensis* 22 15
809 A257 50fr *Catharanthus roseus* 35 18
810 A257 100fr *Cymothoe sangaris*, horiz. 70 35
Nos. 806-810 (5) 1.57
Set value 75

1990, Jan. 18 *Perf. 12½*

811 A258 120fr multicolored 85 42

Pan-African Postal Union, 10th anniv.

Intl. Literacy Year — A259

OCI Emblem — A260

1990, Feb. 27 *Perf. 13½x13*

812 A259 85fr shown 60 30
813 A259 110fr Class, diff. 78 40

1990, Mar. 15 *Perf. 13x12½*

814 A260 85fr multicolored 60 30

Islamic Conference Organization, 20th anniv.

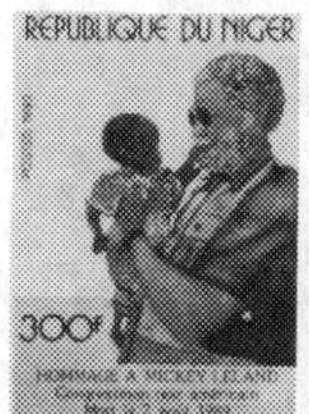

Mickey Leland, US Congressman A261

1990, Mar. 29 Litho. *Perf. 13½*

815 A261 300fr multicolored 2.35 1.20
816 A261 500fr multicolored 4.00 2.00

Congressman Leland died Aug. 7, 1989 in a plane crash on a humanitarian mission.

Natl. Development Society, 1st Anniv. — A262

1990, May 15 Litho. *Perf. 13½*

817 A262 85fr multicolored 60 30

Multinational Postal School, 20th Anniv. — A263

1990, May 31 *Perf. 13x12½*

818 A263 85fr multicolored 60 30

1992 Summer Olympics, Barcelona — A263a

1990, June 4 Litho. *Perf. 13½*

818A	A263a	85fr	Gymnastics	65	32
818B	A263a	110fr	Hurdles	85	42
818C	A263a	250fr	Running	1.95	1.00
818D	A263a	400fr	Equestrian	3.10	1.55
818E	A263a	500fr	Long jump	4.00	2.00
			Nos. 818A-818E (5)	10.55	5.29

Souvenir sheet

819F	A263a	600fr	Cycling	4.65	2.30

Nos. 818D-818F are airmail.

Independence, 30th Anniv. — A264

1990, Aug. 3 *Perf. 12½*

819	A264	85fr	gray grn & multi	60	30
820	A264	110fr	buff & multi	80	40

UN Development Program, 40th Anniv. — A265

1990, Oct. 24 Litho. *Perf. 13½*

821	A265	100fr multicolored	78	40

Butterflies and Mushrooms
A266 A266a

Designs: 85fr, Amanita rubescens. 110fr, Graphum pylades. 200fr, Pseudacraea hostilia. 250fr, Russula virescens. 400fr, Boletus impolitus. 500fr, Precis octavia. 600fr, Cantharellus cibarius & pseudacraea boisduvali.

1991, Jan. 15 Litho. *Perf. 13½*

822	A266	85fr multicolored	65	32
823	A266	110fr multicolored	85	42
824	A266	200fr multicolored	1.55	78
825	A266	250fr multicolored	1.95	1.00
826	A266	400fr multicolored	3.10	1.55
827	A266	500fr multicolored	4.00	2.00
		Nos. 822-827 (6)	12.10	6.07

Souvenir Sheet

828	A266a	600fr multicolored	4.65	2.30

Nos. 826-828 are airmail. No. 828 contains one 30x38mm stamp.

Palestinian Uprising — A267

1991, Mar. 30 Litho. *Perf. 12½*

829	A267	110fr multicolored	90	45

Christopher Columbus (1451-1506) A268

Hypothetical portraits and: 85fr, Santa Maria, 15th cent. 110fr, Frigata, Portuguese caravel, 15th cent. 200fr, Four-masted caravel, 16th cent. 250fr, Estremadura, Spanish caravel, 1511. 400fr, Vija, Portuguese caravel, 1600. 500fr, Pinta, Spanish caravel, 15th cent.

1991, Mar. 19 Litho. *Perf. 13½*

830	A268	85fr multicolored	65	32
831	A268	110fr multicolored	85	42
832	A268	200fr multicolored	1.55	78
833	A268	250fr multicolored	1.95	1.00
834	A268	400fr multicolored	3.10	1.55
835	A268	500fr multicolored	4.00	2.00
		Nos. 830-835 (6)	12.10	6.07

Nos. 834-835 are airmail.

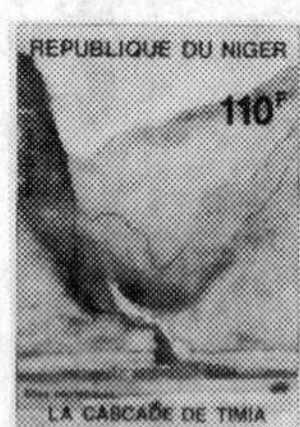

Timia Falls — A269 African Tourism Year — A270

Designs: 85fr, Boubon Market, horiz. 130fr, Ruins of Assode, horiz.

1991, July 10

836	A269	85fr multicolored	65	32
837	A269	110fr multicolored	85	42
838	A269	130fr multicolored	1.00	50
839	A270	200fr multicolored	1.50	75

Native Hairstyles — A271

Women with various hairstyles.

1991

840	A271	85fr multicolored	65	32
841	A271	110fr multicolored	85	42
842	A271	165fr multicolored	1.25	62
843	A271	200fr multicolored	1.50	75

SEMI-POSTAL STAMPS

Curie Issue
Common Design Type

1938 Unwmk. Engr. *Perf. 13*

B1	CD80	1.75fr + 50c brt ultra	8.00	8.00

French Revolution Issue
Common Design Type

1939 Photo. *Perf. 13*
Name and Value Typo. in Black

B2	CD83	45c + 25c grn	3.75	3.75
B3	CD83	70c + 30c brn	3.75	3.75
B4	CD83	90c + 35c red org	3.75	3.75
B5	CD83	1.25fr + 1fr rose pink	3.75	3.75
B6	CD83	2.25fr + 2fr blue	3.75	3.75
		Nos. B2-B6 (5)	18.75	18.75

Stamps of 1926-38, Surcharged in Black

SECOURS
+ 1 fr.
NATIONAL

1941 *Perf. 14x13½, 13½x14*

B7	A3	50c + 1fr scar & grn, *grnsh*	45	45
B8	A3	80c + 2fr cl & ol grn	2.50	2.50
B9	A4	1.50fr + 2fr dp bl & pale bl	3.50	3.50
B10	A4	2fr + 3fr red org & ol brn	3.50	3.50

Common Design Type and

Colonial Cavalry — SP1

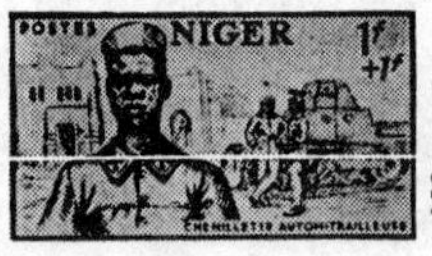

Soldiers and Tank — SP2

1941 Unwmk. Photo. *Perf. 13½*

B11	SP2	1fr + 1fr red	50
B12	CD86	1.50fr + 3fr claret	50
B13	SP1	2.50fr + 1fr blue	50

Nos. B11-B13 were issued by the Vichy government and were not placed on sale in the colony.

Nos. 89-90 were surcharged "OEUVRES COLONIALES" and surtax (including change of denomination of the 2.50fr to 50c). These were issued in 1944 by the Vichy government and were not placed on sale in the colony.

Catalogue values for unused stamps in this section, from this point to the end of the section, are for Never Hinged items.

Republic of the Niger
Anti-Malaria Issue
Common Design Type
Perf. 12½x12

1962, Apr. 7 Engr. Unwmk.

B14	CD108	25fr + 5fr brn	38	38

Freedom from Hunger Issue
Common Design Type

1963, Mar. 21 *Perf. 13*

B15	CD112	25fr + 5fr gray ol, red lil & brn	45	45

Dome of the Rock — SP3

1978, Dec. 11 Litho. *Perf. 12½*

B16	SP3	40fr + 5fr multi	15	15

Surtax was for Palestinian fighters and their families.

AIR POST STAMPS

Common Design Type

1940 Unwmk. Engr. *Perf. 12½x12*

C1	CD85	1.90fr ultra	28	16
C2	CD85	2.90fr dk red	28	16
C3	CD85	4.50fr dk gray grn	60	45
C4	CD85	4.90fr yel bis	40	32
C5	CD85	6.90fr dp org	40	32
		Nos. C1-C5 (5)	1.96	1.41

Common Design Types

1942

C6	CD88	50c car & bl	15
C7	CD88	1fr brn & blk	15
C8	CD88	2fr multi	15
C9	CD88	3fr multi	15
C10	CD88	5fr vio & brn red	15

Frame Engraved, Center Typographed

C11	CD89	10fr multi	28
C12	CD89	20fr multi	35
C13	CD89	50fr multi	65
		Nos. C6-C13 (8)	2.03

There is doubt whether Nos. C6-C13 were officially placed in use. They were issued by the Vichy government.

Catalogue values for unused stamps in this section, from this point to the end of the section, are for Never Hinged items.

Republic of the Niger

Wild Animals, W National Park — AP1

1960, Apr. 11 Engr. *Perf. 13*

C14	AP1	500fr multi	6.50	3.25

For overprint see No. C112.

Nubian Carmine Bee-eater — AP2

1961, Dec. 18 Unwmk. *Perf. 13*

C15	AP2	200fr multi	1.75	1.00

UN Headquarters and Emblem, Niger Flag and Map — AP3

1961, Dec. 16

C20 AP3 25fr multi 22 15
C21 AP3 100fr multi 80 50

Niger's admission to the United Nations. For overprints see Nos. C28-C29.

Air Afrique Issue
Common Design Type

1962, Feb. 17 Unwmk. *Perf. 13*

C22 CD107 100fr multi 80 48

Mosque at Agadez and UPU Emblem — AP4

Designs: 85fr, Gaya Bridge. 100fr, Presidential Palace, Niamey.

1963, June 12 Photo. *Perf. 12½*

C23 AP4 50fr multi 48 18
C24 AP4 85fr multi 70 35
C25 AP4 100fr multi 80 55

2nd anniv. of Niger's admission to the UPU.

Type of Regular Issue, 1963

Design: 100fr, Building boats (kadei), (horiz.).

1963, Aug. 30 *Perf. 12½x12*
Size: 47x27mm

C26 A12 100fr multi 80 40

African Postal Union Issue
Common Design Type

1963, Sept. 8 *Perf. 12½*

C27 CD114 85fr multi 65 35

Nos. C20-C21 Overprinted "Centenaire de la Croix-Rouge" and Cross in Red

1963, Sept. 30 Engr. *Perf. 13*

C28 AP3 25fr multi 32 22
C29 AP3 100fr multi 1.00 55

Centenary of International Red Cross.

White and Black before Rising Sun — AP5

1963, Oct. 25 Photo. *Perf. 12x13*

C30 AP5 50fr multi 65 50

See note after Mauritania No. C28.

Peanut Cultivation — AP6

Designs: 45fr, Camels transporting peanuts to market. 85fr, Men closing bags. 100fr, Loading bags on truck.

1963, Nov. 5 Engr. *Perf. 13*

C31 AP6 20fr grn, bl & red brn 18 15
C32 AP6 45fr red brn, bl & grn 35 18
C33 AP6 85fr multi 65 30
C34 AP6 100fr red brn, ol bis & bl 90 40
a. Souv. sheet of 4, #C31-C34 2.25 2.25

To publicize Niger's peanut industry.

1963 Air Afrique Issue
Common Design Type

1963, Nov. 19 Photo. *Perf. 13x12*

C35 CD115 50fr multi 40 28

Telstar and Capricornus and Sagittarius Constellations — AP7

Design: 100fr, Relay satellite and Leo and Virgo constellations.

1964, Feb. 11 Engr. *Perf. 13*

C36 AP7 25fr ol gray & vio 22 15
C37 AP7 100fr grn & rose cl 70 55

Ramses II Holding Crook and Flail, Abu Simbel — AP8

1964, Mar. 9

C38 AP8 25fr bis brn & dl bl grn 32 25
C39 AP8 30fr dk bl & org brn 36 28
C40 AP8 50fr dp cl & dk bl 65 48

Issued to publicize the UNESCO world campaign to save historic monuments in Nubia.

Tiros I Weather Satellite over Globe and WMO Emblem — AP9

1964, Mar. 23 Unwmk. *Perf. 13*

C41 AP9 50fr emer, dk bl & choc 65 40

4th World Meteorological Day, Mar. 23.

Rocket, Stars and "Stamp" — AP10

1964, June 5 Engr.

C42 AP10 50fr dk bl & mag 55 35

Issued to publicize "PHILATEC," International Philatelic and Postal Techniques Exhibition, Paris, June 5-21, 1964.

Europafrica Issue, 1963
Common Design Type

Design: 50fr, European and African shaking hands, emblems of industry and agriculture.

1964, July 20 Photo. *Perf. 12x13*

C43 CD116 50fr multi 40 22

John F. Kennedy AP11

Discobolus and Discus Thrower AP12

Perf. 12½

1964, Sept. 25 Unwmk. Photo.

C44 AP11 100fr multi 80 60
a. Souvenir sheet of 4 3.25 2.75

Issued in memory of President John F. Kennedy (1917-1963).

1964, Oct. 10 Engr. *Perf. 13*

Designs: 60fr, Water polo (horiz.). 85fr, Relay race (horiz.). 250fr, Torch bearer and Pierre de Coubertin.

C45 AP12 60fr red brn & sl grn 40 30
C46 AP12 85fr ultra & red brn 65 35
C47 AP12 100fr brt grn, dk red & sl 70 45
C48 AP12 250fr yel brn, brt grn & sl 1.65 1.10
a. Min. sheet of 4, #C45-C48 3.50 3.50

Issued to commemorate the 18th Olympic Games, Tokyo, Oct. 10-25.

Pope John XXIII AP13

1965, June 3 Photo. *Perf. 12½x13*

C49 AP13 100fr multi 75 55

Issued in memory of Pope John XXIII (1881-1963).

Hand Crushing Crab — AP14

Sir Winston Churchill — AP15

1965, July 15 Engr. *Perf. 13*

C50 AP14 100fr yel grn, blk & brn 80 42

Issued to publicize the fight against cancer.

Perf. 12½x13

1965, Sept. 3 Photo. Unwmk.

C51 AP15 100fr multi 80 42

Issued to memory of Sir Winston Spencer Churchill (1875-1965), statesman and World War II leader.

Symbols of Agriculture, Industry, Education AP16

Flags and Niamey Fair AP17

1965, Oct. 24 Engr. *Perf. 13*

C52 AP16 50fr hn brn, blk & ol 40 22

International Cooperation Year, 1965.

1965, Dec. 10 Photo. *Perf. 13x12½*

C53 AP17 100fr multi 75 42

International Fair at Niamey.

Dr. Schweitzer, Crippled Hands and Symbols of Medicine, Religion and Music — AP18

1966, Jan. 4 Photo. *Perf. 12½x13*

C54 AP18 50fr multi 40 24

Issued in memory of Dr. Albert Schweitzer (1875-1965), medical missionary, theologian and musician.

Weather Survey Frigate and WMO Emblem — AP19

1966, Mar. 23 **Engr.** ***Perf. 13***
C55 AP19 50fr brt rose lil, dl grn & dk vio bl 42 28

6th World Meteorological Day, Mar. 23.

Edward H. White Floating in Space and Gemini IV — AP20

Design: No. C57, Alexei A. Leonov and Voskhod II.

1966, Mar. 30
C56 AP20 50fr dk red brn, blk & brt grn 42 28
C57 AP20 50fr pur, sl & org 42 28

Issued to honor astronauts Edward H. White and Alexei A. Leonov.

A-1 Satellite and Earth — AP21

Designs: 45fr, Diamant rocket and launching pad (vert.). 90fr, FR-1 satellite. 100fr, D-1 satellite.

1966, May 12 **Photo.** ***Perf. 13***
C58 AP21 45fr multi 36 24
C59 AP21 60fr multi 48 28
C60 AP21 90fr multi 70 36
C61 AP21 100fr multi 85 48

French achievements in space.

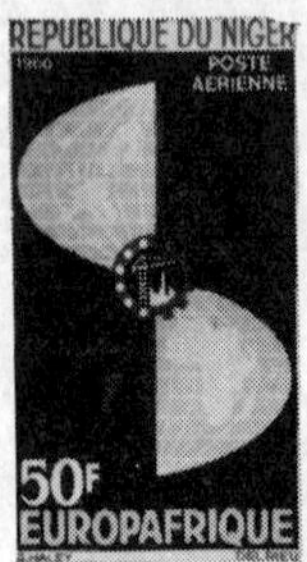

Maps of Europe and Africa and Symbols of Industry — AP22

1966, July 20 **Photo.** ***Perf. 12x13***
C62 AP22 50fr multi 40 26

Third anniversary of economic agreement between the European Economic Community and the African and Malgache Union.

Air Afrique Issue, 1966
Common Design Type

1966, Aug. 31 **Photo.** ***Perf. 13***
C63 CD123 30fr gray, yel grn & blk 22 15

Gemini 6 and 7 — AP23

Design: 50fr, Voskhod 1 (vert.).

1966, Oct. 14 **Engr.** ***Perf. 13***
C64 AP23 50fr red brn, sl & ultra 40 22
C65 AP23 100fr red brn, bl & pur 80 38

Issued to commemorate Russian and American achievements in space.

Torii and Atom Destroying Crab — AP24

1966, Dec. 2 **Photo.** ***Perf. 13***
C66 AP24 100fr dp cl, brn, vio & bl grn 75 42

Issued to commemorate the 9th International Anticancer Congress, Tokyo, Oct. 23-29.

New Mosque, Niamey — AP25

1967, Jan. 11 **Engr.** ***Perf. 13***
C67 AP25 100fr grn & brt bl 70 35

Albrecht Dürer, Self-portrait AP26

Self-portraits: 100fr, Jacques Louis David. 250fr, Ferdinand Delacroix.

1967, Jan. 27 **Photo.** ***Perf. 12½***
C68 AP26 50fr multi 45 30
C69 AP26 100fr multi 75 60
C70 AP26 250fr multi 1.90 1.10

See No. C98.

Maritime Weather Station — AP27

1967, Apr. 28 **Engr.** ***Perf. 13***
C71 AP27 50fr brt bl, dk car rose & blk 65 32

7th World Meteorological Day.

View of EXPO '67, Montreal — AP28

1967, Apr. 28 **Engr.** ***Perf. 13***
C72 AP28 100fr lil, brt bl & blk 70 35

Issued for EXPO '67, International Exhibition, Montreal, Apr. 28-Oct. 27, 1967.

Audio-visual Center, Stylized Eye and People — AP29

1967, June 22 **Engr.** ***Perf. 13***
C73 AP29 100fr brt bl, pur & grn 70 35

National Audio-Visual Center.

Konrad Adenauer — AP30

1967, Aug. 11 **Photo.** ***Perf. 12½***
C74 AP30 100fr dk bl, gray & sep 75 40
a. Souv. sheet of 4 3.00 2.50

Konrad Adenauer (1876-1967), chancellor of West Germany (1949-63).

African Postal Union Issue, 1967
Common Design Type

1967, Sept. 9 **Engr.** ***Perf. 13***
C75 CD124 100fr emer, red & brt lil 70 35

Jesus Teaching in the Temple, by Ingres — AP31

Design: 150fr, Jesus Giving the Keys to St. Peter, by Ingres (vert.).

1967, Oct. 2 **Photo.** ***Perf. 12½***
C76 AP31 100fr multi 1.00 65
C77 AP31 150fr multi 1.50 1.00

Issued to commemorate the centenary of the death of Jean Dominique Ingres (1780-1867), French painter.

Children and UNICEF Emblem — AP32

1967, Dec. 11 **Engr.** ***Perf. 13***
C78 AP32 100fr bl, brn & grn 70 35

21st anniv. of UNICEF.

O.C.A.M. Emblem — AP33

1968, Jan. 12 **Engr.** ***Perf. 13***
C79 AP33 100fr brt bl, grn & org 70 35

Issued to publicize the conference of the Organization Communitée Afrique et Malgache (OCAM) held in Niamey, January 1968.

Vincent van Gogh, Self-portrait AP34

Self-portraits: 50fr, Jean Baptiste Camille Corot. 150fr, Francisco de Goya.

1968, Jan. 29 **Photo.** ***Perf. 12½***
C80 AP34 50fr multi 50 22
C81 AP34 150fr multi 1.20 55
C82 AP34 200fr multi 1.60 80

See No. C98.

Breguet 27 — AP35

Planes: 80fr, Potez 25 on the ground. 100fr, Potez 25 in the air.

1968, Mar. 14 **Engr.** ***Perf. 13***
C83 AP35 45fr ind, car & dk grn 34 22
C84 AP35 80fr ind, bl & brn 60 28
C85 AP35 100fr sky bl, brn blk & dk grn 70 34

Issued to commemorate the 25th anniversary of air mail service between France and Niger.

Splendid Glossy Starling — AP36

Design: 100fr, Amethyst starling (vert.).

1968-69 **Photo.** ***Perf. 13***
C86 AP36 100fr gold & multi ('69) 65 28

Engr.

C87 AP36 250fr mag, sl grn & brt bl 1.40 70

See No. C255.

Dandy Horse, 1818, and Racer, 1968 — AP37

1968, May 17 **Engr.** ***Perf. 13***
C88 AP37 100fr bl grn & red 65 35

Issued to commemorate the 150th anniversary of the invention of the bicycle.

Sheet Bend Knot — AP37a

1968, July 20 **Photo.** ***Perf. 13***
C89 AP37a 50fr gray, blk, red & grn 38 22

Fifth anniversary of economic agreement between the European Economic Community and the African and Malgache Union.

Fencing — AP38

Designs: 100fr, Jackknife dive (vert.). 150fr, Weight lifting (vert.). 200fr, Equestrian.

1968, Sept. 10 **Engr.** ***Perf. 13***
C90 AP38 50fr pur & blk 32 18
C91 AP38 100fr choc, ultra & blk 65 28
C92 AP38 150fr choc & org 90 42
C93 AP38 200fr brn, emer & ind 1.25 65
a. Min. sheet of 4, #C90-C93 3.50 3.50

Issued to publicize the 19th Olympic Games, Mexico City, Oct. 12-27.

No. C93a is folded down the vertical gutter separating Nos. C90-C91 se-tenant at left and Nos. C92-C93 se-tenant at right.

Robert F. Kennedy — AP39

Designs: No. C94, John F. Kennedy. No. C95, Rev. Dr. Martin Luther King, Jr. No. C96, Mahatma Gandhi.

1968, Oct. 4 **Photo.** ***Perf. 12½***
C94 AP39 100fr blk & dl org 65 30
C95 AP39 100fr blk & aqua 65 30
C96 AP39 100fr blk & gray 65 30
C97 AP39 100fr blk & yel 65 30
a. Souv. sheet of 4, #C94-C97 3.00 2.50

Issued to honor proponents of non-violence.

PHILEXAFRIQUE Issue

Painting Type of 1968

Design: 100fr, Interior Minister Paré, by J. L. La Neuville (1748-1826).

1968, Oct. 25 **Photo.** ***Perf. 12½***
C98 AP34 100fr multi 80 80

Issued to publicize PHILEXAFRIQUE, Philatelic Exhibition in Abidjan, Feb. 14-23, 1969. Printed with alternating light blue label.

Arms and Flags of Niger — AP40

1968, Dec. 17 **Litho.** ***Perf. 13***
C99 AP40 100fr multi 65 30

Issued to commemorate the 10th anniversary of the proclamation of the Republic.

Bonaparte as First Consul, by Ingres AP41

Paintings: 100fr, Napoleon Visiting the Plague House in Jaffa, by Antoine Jean Gros. 150fr, Napoleon on the Imperial Throne, by Jean Auguste Dominique Ingres. 200fr, Napoleon's March Through France, by Jean Louis Ernest Meissonier (horiz.).

Perf. 12½x12, 12x12½

1969, Jan. 20 **Photo.**
C100 AP41 50fr multi 80 60
C101 AP41 100fr grn & multi 1.30 1.40
C102 AP41 150fr pur & multi 1.75 1.25
C103 AP41 200fr brn & multi 2.50 1.75

Issued to commemorate the 200th anniversary of the birth of Napoleon Bonaparte (1769-1821).

2nd PHILEXAFRIQUE Issue

Common Design Type

Designs: 50fr, Niger No. 41 and giraffes.

1969, Feb. 14 **Engr.** ***Perf. 13***
C104 CD128 50fr sl, brn & org 40 34

Weather Observation Plane in Storm and Anemometer — AP42

1969, Mar. 23 **Engr.** ***Perf. 13***
C105 AP42 50fr blk, brt bl & grn 35 16

9th World Meteorological Day.

Panhard Levassor, 1900 — AP43

Early Automobiles: 45fr, De Dion Bouton 8, 1904. 50fr, Opel, 1909. 70fr, Daimler, 1910. 100fr, Vermorel 12/16, 1912.

1969, Apr. 15 **Engr.** ***Perf. 13***
C106 AP43 25fr gray, lt grn & bl grn 18 15
C107 AP43 45fr gray, bl & vio 24 15
C108 AP43 50fr gray, yel bis & brn 40 20
C109 AP43 70fr gray, brt pink & brt lil 55 28
C110 AP43 100fr gray, lem & sl grn 70 35
Nos. C106-C110 (5) 2.07 1.13

Apollo 8 Trip around Moon AP44

Embossed on Gold Foil

1969, Mar. 31 ***Die-cut Perf. 10½***
C111 AP44 1000fr gold 7.00 7.00

US Apollo 8 mission, which put the 1st men into orbit around the moon, Dec. 21-27, 1968.

No. C14 Overprinted in Red with Lunar Landing Module and: "L'HOMME / SUR LA LUNE / JUILLET 1969 / APOLLO 11"

1969, July 25 **Engr.** ***Perf. 13***
C112 AP1 500fr multi 3.50 3.50

See note after Mali No. C80.

Toys — AP45

1969, Oct. 13 **Engr.** ***Perf. 13***
C113 AP45 100fr bl, red brn & grn 65 28

International Nuremberg Toy Fair.

Europafrica Issue

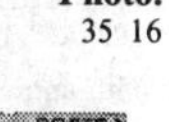
Links AP46

1969, Oct. 30 **Photo.**
C114 AP46 50fr vio, yel & blk 35 16

Camels and Motor Caravan Crossing Desert — AP47

Designs: 100fr, Motor caravan crossing mountainous region. 150fr, Motor caravan in African village. 200fr, Map of Africa showing tour, Citroen B-2 tractor, African and European men shaking hands.

1969, Nov. 22 **Engr.** ***Perf. 13***
C115 AP47 50fr lil, pink & brn 32 15
C116 AP47 100fr dk car rose, lt bl & vio bl 65 28
C117 AP47 150fr multi 90 42
C118 AP47 200fr sl grn, bl & blk 1.20 60

Issued to commemorate the Black Tour across Africa from Colomb-Bechar, Algeria, to Mombassa, Dar es Salaam, Mozambique, Tananarive and the Cape of Good Hope.

EXPO '70 at Osaka — AP48

1970, Mar. 25 **Photo.** ***Perf. 12½***
C119 AP48 100fr multi 65 30

Issued to publicize EXPO '70 International Exhibition, Osaka, Japan, Mar. 15-Sept. 13.

Education Year Emblem and Education Symbols — AP49

1970, Apr. 6 **Engr.** ***Perf. 13***
C120 AP49 100fr plum, red & gray 65 30

Issued for International Education Year.

An enhanced introduction to the Scott Catalogue begins on Page 1A. A thorough understanding of the material presented there will greatly aid your use of the catalogue itself.

Rotary Emblem, Globe and Niamey Club Emblem — AP50

1970, Apr. 30 Photo. *Perf. 12½*

C121 AP50 100fr gold & multi 65 30

65th anniversary of Rotary International.

Modern Plane, Clement Ader and his Flying Machine — AP51

Designs: 100fr, Joseph and Jacques Montgolfier, rocket and balloon. 150fr, Isaac Newton, planetary system and trajectories. 200fr, Galileo Galilei, spaceship and trajectories. 250fr, Leonardo da Vinci, his flying machine, and plane.

1970, May 11 Engr. *Perf. 13*

C122 AP51 50fr bl, cop red & sl 32 15
C123 AP51 100fr cop red, bl & sl 60 30
C124 AP51 150fr brn, grn & ocher 85 45
C125 AP51 200fr dk car rose, dp vio & bis 1.20 60
C126 AP51 250fr cop red, gray & pur 1.60 80
Nos. C122-C126 (5) 4.57 2.30

Pioneers of space research.
For overprints and surcharges see Nos. C129-C130, C141-C142.

Bay of Naples, Buildings, Mt. Vesuvius and Niger No. 97 — AP52

1970, May 5 Photo. *Perf. 12½*

C127 AP52 100fr multi 65 28

Issued to publicize the 10th Europa Philatelic Exhibition, Naples, Italy, May 2-10.

TV Tube, Books, Microscope, Globe and ITU Emblem — AP53

1970, May 16 Engr. *Perf. 13*

C128 AP53 100fr grn, brn & red 65 28

Issued for World Telecommunications Day.

Nos. C123 and C125 Overprinted: "Solidarite Spatiale / Apollo XIII / 11-17 Avril 1970"

1970, June 6 Engr. *Perf. 13*

C129 AP51 100fr multi 65 30
C130 AP51 200fr multi 1.10 55

Issued to commemorate the abortive flight of Apollo 13, Apr. 11-17, 1970.

UN Emblem, Man, Woman and Doves — AP54

1970, June 26 Photo. *Perf. 12½*

C131 AP54 100fr brt bl, dk bl & org 60 28
C132 AP54 150fr multi 1.10 45

25th anniversary of the United Nations.

European and African Men, Globe and Fleur-de-lis — AP55

Lithographed; Embossed on Gold Foil

1970, July 22 *Perf. 12½*

C133 AP55 250fr gold & ultra 1.60 1.60

French Language Cong., Niamey, Mar. 1970.

Europafrica Issue

European and African Women — AP56

1970, July 29 Engr. *Perf. 13*

C134 AP56 50fr sl grn & dl red 32 18

EXPO Emblem, Geisha and Torii — AP57

Design: 150fr, EXPO emblem, exhibition at night and character from Noh play.

1970, Sept. 16 Engr. *Perf. 13*

C135 AP57 100fr multi 60 28
C136 AP57 150fr bl, dk brn & grn 85 42

Issued to commemorate EXPO '70 International Exhibition, Osaka, Japan, Mar. 15-Sept. 13.

Gymnast on Parallel Bars — AP58

Beethoven and Piano — AP59

Sports: 100fr, Vaulting (horiz.). 150fr, Flying jump (horiz.). 200fr, Rings.

1970, Oct. 26 Engr. *Perf. 13*

C137 AP58 50fr brt bl 35 20
C138 AP58 100fr brt grn 65 35
C139 AP58 150fr brt rose lil 1.00 50
C140 AP58 200fr red org 1.25 65

17th World Gymnastics Championships, Ljubljana, Oct. 22-27.

Nos. C124 and C126 Surcharged and Overprinted: "LUNA 16 - Sept. 1970 / PREMIERS PRELEVEMENTS / AUTOMATIQUES SUR LA LUNE"

1970, Nov. 5

C141 AP51 100fr on 150fr multi 65 30
C142 AP51 200fr on 250fr multi 1.25 55

Issued to commemorate the unmanned moon probe of the Russian space ship Luna 16, Sept. 12-24.

1970, Nov. 18 Photo. *Perf. 12½*

Design: 150fr, Beethoven and dancers with dove, symbolic of Ode to Joy.

C143 AP59 100fr multi 65 26
C144 AP59 150fr multi 1.25 55

Issued to commemorate the bicentenary of the birth of Ludwig van Beethoven (1770-1827), composer.

John F. Kennedy Bridge, Niamey — AP60

1970, Dec. 18 Photo. *Perf. 12½*

C145 AP60 100fr multi 60 22

Proclamation of the Republic, 12th anniversary.

Gamal Abdel Nasser — AP61

Design: 200fr, Nasser with raised arm.

1971, Jan. 5 Photo. *Perf. 12½*

C146 AP61 100fr blk, org brn & grn 55 22
C147 AP61 200fr grn, org & blk brn 1.10 60

In memory of Gamal Abdel Nasser (1918-70), President of Egypt.

Charles de Gaulle — AP62

Embossed on Gold Foil

1971, Jan. 22 *Die-cut Perf. 10*

C148 AP62 1000fr gold 14.00 14.00

In memory of Gen. Charles de Gaulle (1890-1970), President of France.

Olympic Rings and "Munich" — AP63

1971, Jan. 29 Engr. *Perf. 13*

C149 AP63 150fr dk bl, rose lil & grn 85 45

Publicity for 1972 Summer Olympic Games in Munich.

Landing Module over Moon — AP64

Masks of Hate — AP65

1971, Feb. 5 Engr. *Perf. 13*

C150 AP64 250fr ultra, sl grn & org 1.40 70

Apollo 14 mission, Jan. 31-Feb. 9.

1971, Mar. 20 Engr. *Perf. 13*

Design: 200fr, People and 4-leaf clover (symbol of unity).

C151 AP65 100fr red, sl & brt bl 65 30
C152 AP65 200fr sl, red & grn 1.10 55

Intl. Year against Racial Discrimination.

Map of Africa and Telecommunications System — AP66

1971, Apr. 6 Photo. *Perf. 12½*

C153 AP66 100fr grn & multi 60 22

Pan-African telecommunications system.

African Mask and Japan No. 580 — AP67

Design: 100fr, Japanese actors, stamps of Niger, No. 95 on cover and No. 170.

1971, Apr. 23 Engr. *Perf. 13*
C154 AP67 50fr dk brn, emer & blk 32 16
C155 AP67 100fr brn & multi 65 28

Philatokyo 71, Tokyo Philatelic Exposition, Apr. 19-29.

Longwood, St. Helena, by Carle Vernet — AP68

Design: 200fr, Napoleon's body on camp bed, by Marryat.

1971, May 5 Photo. *Perf. 13*
C156 AP68 150fr gold & multi 95 42
C157 AP68 200fr gold & multi 1.25 60

Sesquicentennial of the death of Napoleon Bonaparte (1769-1821).

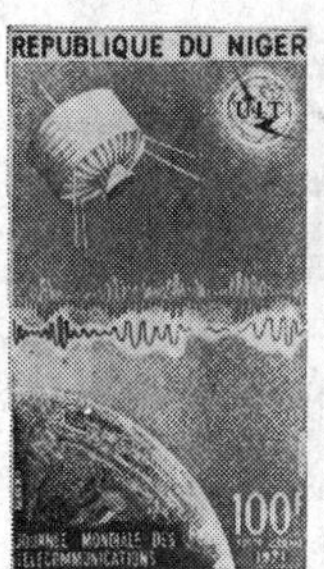

Satellite, Waves and Earth — AP69

Olympic Rings, Athletes and Torch — AP70

1971, May 17 Engr. *Perf. 13*
C158 AP69 100fr org, ultra & dk brn 60 28

3rd World Telecommunications Day.

1971, June 10

Designs: 50fr, Pierre de Coubertin, discus throwers (horiz.). 150fr, Runners (horiz.).

C159 AP70 50fr red & sl 32 15
C160 AP70 100fr sl, brn & grn 65 22
C161 AP70 150fr plum, bl & rose lil 95 42

75th anniv. of modern Olympic Games.

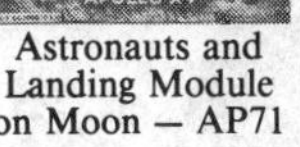

Astronauts and Landing Module on Moon — AP71

Charles de Gaulle — AP72

1971, July 26 Engr. *Perf. 13*
C162 AP71 150fr red brn, pur & sl 85 40

US Apollo 15 moon mission, July 26-Aug. 7, 1971.

1971, Nov. 9 Photo. *Perf. 12½x12*
C163 AP72 250r multi 2.25 1.40

First anniversary of the death of Charles de Gaulle (1890-1970), president of France.

African Postal Union Issue, 1971
Common Design Type

Design: 100fr, Water carrier, cattle and UAMPT headquarters, Brazzaville, Congo.

1971, Nov. 13 Photo. *Perf. 13x13½*
C164 CD135 100fr bl & multi 60 28

Al Hariri Holding Audience, Baghdad, 1237 — AP73

Designs from Mohammedan Miniatures: 150fr, Archangel Israfil, late 14th century (vert.). 200fr, Horsemen, 1210.

1971, Nov. 25 *Perf. 13*
C165 AP73 100fr multi 55 30
C166 AP73 150fr multi 80 45
C167 AP73 200fr multi 1.10 60

Louis Armstrong — AP74

Design: 150fr, Armstrong with trumpet.

1971, Dec. 6
C168 AP74 100fr multi 60 28
C169 AP74 150fr multi 85 42

Louis Armstrong (1900-1971), American jazz musician.

Adoration of the Kings, by Di Bartolo — AP75

Paintings: 150fr, Nativity, by Domenico Ghirlandaio (vert.). 200fr, Adoration of the Shepherds, by Il Perugino.

1971, Dec. 24 Photo. *Perf. 13*
C170 AP75 100fr blk & multi 65 30
C171 AP75 150fr blk & multi 1.00 45
C172 AP75 200fr blk & multi 1.25 60

Christmas 1971. See Nos. C210-C212, C232-C234.

Presidents Pompidou and Diori Hamani, Flags of Niger and France — AP76

1972, Jan. 22
C173 AP76 250fr multi 2.25 1.50

Visit of President Georges Pompidou of France, Jan. 1972.

Snowflakes, Olympic Torch and Emblem — AP77

Design: 100fr, Torii made of ski poles and skis, and dwarf tree (vert.).

1972, Jan. 27 Engr.
C174 AP77 100fr dk vio, grn & car 55 25
C175 AP77 150fr dk vio, lil & red 85 40
a. Souv. sheet of 2, #C174-C175 1.60 1.60

11th Winter Olympic Games, Sapporo, Japan, Feb. 3-13.

The Masked Ball, by Guardi — AP78

Designs: 50fr, 100fr, 150fr, Details from "The Masked Ball," by Francesco Guardi (1712-1793); all vertical.

1972, Feb. 7 Photo.
C176 AP78 50fr gold & multi 32 15
C177 AP78 100fr gold & multi 65 28
C178 AP78 150fr gold & multi 95 42
C179 AP78 200fr gold & multi 1.25 60

UNESCO campaign to save Venice. See Nos. C215-C216.

Johannes Brahms and "Lullaby" AP79

Scout Sign and Tents AP80

1972, Mar. 17 Engr. *Perf. 13*
C180 AP79 100fr brt grn, car rose & sl grn 65 28

75th anniversary of death of Johannes Brahms (1833-1897), German composer.

1972, Mar. 22
C181 AP80 150fr pur, org & sl bl 80 30

World Boy Scout Seminar, Cotonou, Dahomey, March 1972.

Surgical Team, Heart-shaped Globe and Emblem — AP81

1972 Engr. *Perf. 13*
C182 AP81 100fr dp brn & car 65 28

"Your heart is your health," World Health Day.

Bleriot XI Crossing English Channel — AP82

Famous Aircraft: 75fr, Spirit of St. Louis crossing Atlantic. 100fr, First flight of Concorde supersonic jet.

1972, Apr. 24
C183 AP82 50fr dk vio bl, brn & mag 35 18
C184 AP82 75fr brn red, bl & ind 55 30
C185 AP82 100fr dp ultra, mag & grnsh bl 75 45

ITU Emblem, Satellite, Stars and Earth — AP83

1972, May 17 Engr. *Perf. 13*
C186 AP83 100fr pur, car & blk 60 28

4th World Telecommunications Day.

Boxing and Opera House — AP84

Designs: 100fr, Broad jump and City Hall (vert.). 150fr, Soccer and Church of the Theatines (vert.). 200fr, Running and Propylaeum.

1972, May 26
C187 AP84 50fr bl & grn 30 15
C188 AP84 100fr yel grn & dk brn 55 25
C189 AP84 150fr org red & dk brn 80 35
C190 AP84 200fr vio & dk brn 1.10 45
a. Min. sheet of 4. #C187-C190 3.25 2.75

20th Olympic Games, Munich, Aug. 26-Sept. 10.
For overprints see Nos. C196-C199.

"Alexander Graham Bell," Telephone — AP85

1972, July 7
C191 AP85 100fr car, dk pur & sl 60 25

50th anniversary of the death of Alexander Graham Bell (1847-1922), inventor of the telephone. Stamp pictures Samuel F. B. Morse.

Europafrica Issue

Stylized Maps of Africa and Europe — AP86

1972, July 29 Engr. *Perf. 13*
C192 AP86 50fr red brn, bl & grn 30 15

Mail Runner, UPU Emblem — AP87

Designs: 100fr, Mail truck, UPU emblem. 150fr, Mail plane, UPU emblem.

1972, Oct. 9 Engr. *Perf. 13*
C193 AP87 50fr red brn, sl grn & dk brn 30 18
C194 AP87 100fr red brn, ultra & Prus grn 60 30
C195 AP87 150fr red brn, pur & sl grn 85 45

Universal Postal Union Day.

Nos. C187-C190 Overprinted in Red or Violet Blue

a. WELTER / CORREA / MEDAILLE D'OR
b. TRIPLE SAUT / SANEEV / MEDAILLE D'OR
c. FOOTBALL / POLOGNE / MEDAILLE D'OR
d. MARATHON / SHORTER / MEDAILLE D'OR

1972, Nov. 10
C196 AP84(a) 50fr multi (R) 30 15
C197 AP84(b) 100fr multi (R) 60 24
C198 AP84(c) 150fr multi (VBl) 95 38
C199 AP84(d) 200fr multi (R) 1.40 50

Gold medal winners in 20th Olympic Games: Emilio Correa, Cuba, welterweight boxing; Victor Saneev, USSR, triple jump; Poland, soccer; Frank Shorter, US, marathon.

The Crow and The Fox — AP88

Fables: 50fr, The Lion and the Mouse. 75fr, The Monkey and the Leopard.

1972, Nov. 23
C200 AP88 25fr emer, blk & brn 18 15
C201 AP88 50fr brt pink, bl grn & brn 32 15
C202 AP88 75fr lt brn, grn & dk brn 48 28

Jean de La Fontaine (1621-1695), French fabulist.

Astronauts on Moon — AP89

1972, Dec. 12 Photo. *Perf. 13*
C203 AP89 250fr multi 1.40 65

Apollo 17 US moon mission, Dec. 7-19.

Young Athlete AP90

Design: 100fr, Head of Hermes.

1973, Feb. 7 Engr. *Perf. 13*
C204 AP90 50fr dk car 28 15
C205 AP90 100fr purple 55 25

Treasures of antiquity.

Boy Scouts and Radio Transmission — AP91

Niger Boy Scouts: 50fr, Red Cross, first aid. 100fr, Scout and gazelle. 150fr, Scouts with gazelle and bird.

1973, Mar. 21 Engr. *Perf. 13*
C206 AP91 25fr sl grn, choc & dk red 15 15
C207 AP91 50fr grn, red & choc 28 15
C208 AP91 100fr mar, sl grn & choc 55 28
C209 AP91 150fr multi 80 35

For overprints see Nos. C217-C218.

Christmas Type of 1971

Paintings: 50fr, Crucifixion, by Hugo van der Goes (vert.). 100fr, Burial of Christ, by Cima da Conegliano. 150fr, Pieta, by Giovanni Bellini.

1973, Apr. 20 Photo. *Perf. 13*
C210 AP75 50fr gold & multi 32 15
C211 AP75 100fr gold & multi 65 32
C212 AP75 150fr gold & multi 90 42

Easter 1973.

Air Afrique Plane and Mail Truck — AP92

1973, Apr. 30 Engr. *Perf. 13*
C213 AP92 100fr brt grn, choc & car 60 28

Stamp Day 1973.

WMO Emblem, Pyramids with Weather Symbols, Satellite — AP93

1973, May 7
C214 AP93 100fr ol brn, brt grn & brt mag 60 28

Cent. of intl. meteorological cooperation.

Painting Type of 1972

Paintings by Delacroix: 150fr, Prowling lioness. 200fr, Tigress and cub.

1973, May 22 Photo. *Perf. 13x12½*
C215 AP78 150fr blk & multi 85 40
C216 AP78 200fr blk & multi 1.20 60

175th anniversary of the birth of Ferdinand Delacroix (1798-1863), French painter.

Nos. C208-C209 Overprinted: "24 * Conference Mondiale / du Scoutisme / NAIROBI 1973"

1973, July 19 Engr. *Perf. 13*
C217 AP91 100fr multi 55 28
C218 AP91 150fr multi 80 35

Boy Scout 24th World Jamboree, Nairobi, Kenya, July 16-21.

Head and City Hall, Brussels — AP93a

1973, Sept. 17 Engr. *Perf. 13*
C219 AP93a 100fr dk pur, mag & vio bl 60 28

Africa Weeks, Brussels, Sept. 15-30, 1973.

Men Emptying Cornucopia, FAO Emblem, People AP94

1973, Nov. 2 Engr. *Perf. 13*
C220 AP94 50fr ultra, pur & ver 30 15

10th anniversary of the World Food Program.

Copernicus, Sputnik 1, Heliocentric System — AP95

1973, Nov. 12
C221 AP95 150fr mag, vio bl & brn 85 42

500th anniversary of the birth of Nicolaus Copernicus (1473-1543), Polish astronomer.

John F. Kennedy — AP96

1973, Nov. 22 Photo. *Perf. 12½*
C222 AP96 100fr redsh brn & multi 60 30

Souvenir Sheet
Perf. 13

C223 AP96 200fr dp ultra & multi 1.10 1.10

10th anniversary of the death of Pres. John F. Kennedy (1917-63).

Barge on Niger River — AP97

Design: 75fr, Tug Baban Maza.

1974, Jan. 18 Engr. *Perf. 13*
C224 AP97 50fr mar, vio bl & grn 24 15
C225 AP97 75fr yel grn, bl & lil rose 38 20

First anniversary of the upstream voyage of the Flotilla of Hope.

Lenin — AP98

1974, Jan. 21
C226 AP98 50fr dk red brn 25 15

50th anniversary of the death of Lenin (1870-1924), Russian Communist leader.

Skiers AP99

1974, Feb. 8 Engr. *Perf. 11½x11*
C227 AP99 200fr bl, sep & car 1.10 55

50th anniversary of the first Winter Olympic Games, Chamonix, France.

Soccer and Emblem — AP100

Designs: Various views of soccer game.

1974, Apr. 8 Engr. *Perf. 13*
C228 AP100 75fr vio & blk 30 18
C229 AP100 150fr brn, lt & sl grn 52 30
C230 AP100 200fr Prus bl, grn & brn 75 50

Souvenir Sheet
C231 AP100 250fr yel grn, brn & ol brn 1.10 1.10

World Soccer Championship, Munich, June 13-July 7.
For overprint see No. C239.

Christmas Type of 1971

Paintings: 50fr, Crucifixion, by Matthias Grunewald. 75fr, Avignon Pieta, attributed to Enguerrand Quarton. 125fr, Burial of Christ, by G. Isenmann.

1974, Apr. 12 Litho. *Perf. 13x12½*
C232 AP75 50fr blk & multi 26 15
C233 AP75 75fr blk & multi 38 18
C234 AP75 125r blk & multi 65 32

Easter 1974.

21st Chess Olympiad, Nice, June 6-30 — AP101

1974, June 3 Engr. *Perf. 13*
C235 AP101 50fr Knights 28 15
C236 AP101 75fr Kings 38 22

Astronaut and Apollo 11 Badge AP102

1974, July 20 Engr. *Perf. 13*
C237 AP102 150fr multi 70 40

5th anniversary of the first manned moon landing.

Europafrica Issue

The Rhinoceros, by Pietro Longhi AP103

1974, Aug. 10 Photo. *Perf. 12½x13*
C238 AP103 250fr multi 1.40 85

No. C231 Overprinted in Red: "R.F.A. 2 / HOLLANDE 1"

1974, Sept. 27 Engr. *Perf. 13*
Souvenir Sheet
C239 AP100 250fr multi 1.40 1.40

World Cup Soccer Championship, Munich, 1974, victory of German Federal Republic. No. C239 has additional red inscription in margin: "7 JUILLET 1974 / VAINQUEUR REPUBLIQUE FEDERALE ALLEMANDE".

Caucasian Woman, Envelope, UPU Emblem and Jets — AP104

Skylab over Africa — AP105

Designs (UPU emblem, Envelope and): 100fr, Oriental woman and trains. 150fr, Indian woman and ships. 200fr, Black woman and buses.

1974, Oct. 9 Engr. *Perf. 13*
C240 AP104 50fr multi 28 15
C241 AP104 100fr multi 48 28
C242 AP104 150fr bl & multi 70 40
C243 AP104 200fr multi 90 60

Centenary of Universal Postal Union.

1974, Nov. 4 Engr. *Perf. 13*
C244 AP105 100fr multi 48 28

Virgin and Child, by Correggio AP106

Paintings: 150fr, Virgin and Child with St. Hilary, by Filippo Lippi. 200fr, Virgin and Child, by Murillo.

1974, Dec. 24 Litho. *Perf. 12½x13*
C245 AP106 100fr multi 55 22
C246 AP106 150fr multi 75 40
C247 AP106 200fr multi 1.10 60

Christmas 1974. See Nos. C252-C254, C260-C262, C280-C282.

Apollo and Emblem AP107

Designs (Emblem of Soyuz-Apollo Space Docking): 100fr, Docking in space over earth. 150fr, Soyuz in space.

1975, Jan. 31 Engr. *Perf. 13*
C248 AP107 50fr bl & multi 25 15
C249 AP107 100fr multi 45 28
C250 AP107 150fr multi 75 40

Russo-American space cooperation.
For overprints see Nos. C263-C265.

Europafrica Issue

European and African Women, Globe — AP108

1975, Feb. 28 Engr. *Perf. 13*
C251 AP108 250fr brn, lil & red 1.20 70

Painting Type of 1974

Easter: 75fr, Jesus in Garden of Olives, by Delacroix (horiz.). 125fr, Crucifixion, by El Greco. 150fr, Resurrection, by Leonard Limosin.

Perf. 13x12½, 12½x13
1975, Mar. 27 Litho.
C252 AP106 75fr multi 38 15
C253 AP106 125fr multi 60 32
C254 AP106 150fr multi 75 40

Bird Type of 1968-69 Dated "1975"

Design: 100fr, Cinnyricinclus leucogaster (vert.).

1975, Apr. Photo. *Perf. 13*
C255 AP36 100fr gold & multi 42 25

Lt. Col. Seyni Kountche AP109

1975, Apr. 15 Litho. *Perf. 12½x13*
C256 AP109 100fr multi 42 28

Military Government, first anniversary.

Shot Put, Maple Leaf, Montreal Olympic Emblem AP110

Design: 200fr, Gymnast on rings, Canadian flag, Montreal Olympic emblem.

1975, Oct. 6 Engr. *Perf. 13*
C257 AP110 150fr blk & red 65 35
C258 AP110 200fr red & blk 85 55

Pre-Olympic Year 1975.

UN Emblem and Dove — AP111

1975, Nov. 26 Engr. *Perf. 13*
C259 AP111 100fr grn & bl 45 28

United Nations, 30th anniversary.

Painting Type of 1974

Paintings: 50fr, Virgin of Seville, by Murillo. 75fr, Adoration of the Shepherds, by Tintoretto (horiz.). 125fr, Virgin with Angels, Florentine, 15th century.

1975, Dec. 24 Litho. *Perf. 12½x13*
C260 AP106 50fr multi 22 15
C261 AP106 75fr multi 32 25
C262 AP106 125fr multi 55 40

Christmas 1975.

Nos. C248-C250 Overprinted: "JONCTION / 17 Juillet 1975"

1975, Dec. 30 Engr. *Perf. 13*
C263 AP107 50fr bl & multi 22 15
C264 AP107 100fr multi 45 30
C265 AP107 150fr multi 65 42

Apollo-Soyuz link-up in space, July 17, 1975.

12th Winter Olympic Games Type, 1976

Designs: 200fr, Women's figure skating. 300fr, Biathlon. 500fr, Speed skating.

1976, Feb. 20 Litho. *Perf. 14x13½*
C266 A97 200fr multi 1.10 45
C267 A97 300fr multi 1.40 60

Souvenir Sheet
C268 A97 500fr multi 2.50 1.10

American Bicentennial Type, 1976

Design (Statue of Liberty and): 150fr, Joseph Warren, martyr at Bunker Hill. 200fr, John Paul Jones on the bridge of the "Bonhomme Richard." 300fr, Molly Pitcher, Monmouth battle heroine. 500fr, Start of the fighting.

1976, Apr. 8
C269 A100 150fr multi 70 30
C270 A100 200fr multi 90 50
C271 A100 300fr multi 1.50 70

Souvenir Sheet
C272 A100 500fr multi 2.50 1.10

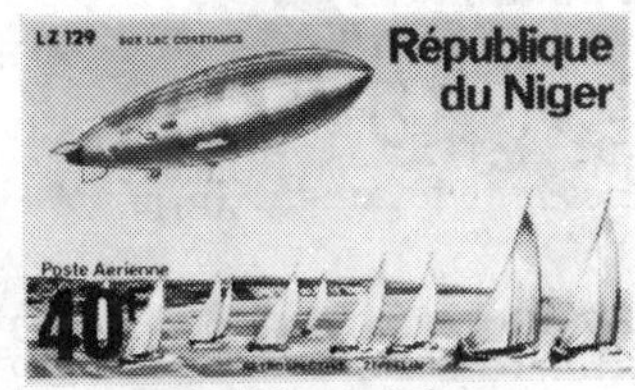
LZ-129 over Lake Constance — AP112

Designs: 50fr, LZ-3 over Würzburg. 150fr, LZ-9 over Friedrichshafen. 200fr, LZ-2 over Rothenburg (vert.). 300fr, LZ-130 over Essen. 500fr, LZ-127 over the Swiss Alps.

1976, May 18 Litho. *Perf. 11*

C273	AP112	40fr multi	20	15
C274	AP112	50fr multi	30	15
C275	AP112	150fr multi	75	40
C276	AP112	200fr multi	1.00	40
C277	AP112	300fr multi	1.50	60
		Nos. C273-C277 (5)	3.75	1.70

Souvenir Sheet

C278	AP112	500fr multi	2.50	1.10

75th anniversary of the Zeppelin.

Olympic Games Type, 1976

Souvenir Sheet

1976, July 17 Litho. *Perf. 14*

C279	A105	150fr Sprint	80	38

Christmas Type of 1974

Paintings: 50fr, Nativity, by Rubens. 100fr, Virgin and Child, by Correggio. 150fr, Adoration of the Kings, by Gerard David (horiz.).

1976, Dec. 24 Litho. *Perf. 12½*

C280	AP106	50fr multi	22	15
C281	AP106	100fr multi	45	28
C282	AP106	150fr multi	65	35

Christmas 1976.

Viking Mars Project Type, 1977

Designs: 100fr, Viking lander and probe (horiz.). 150fr, Descent phases of Viking lander. 200fr, Titan rocket start for Mars. 400fr, Viking orbiter in flight.

1977, Mar. 15 Litho. *Perf. 14*

C283	A113	100fr multi	50	25
C284	A113	150fr multi	75	32
C285	A113	200fr multi	1.00	45

Souvenir Sheet

C286	A113	400fr multi	2.25	80

For overprints see Nos. C295-C297.

Nobel Prize Type, 1977

Souvenir Sheet

Design: 500fr, Theodore Roosevelt, peace.

1977, Aug. 20 Litho. *Perf. 14*

C287	A122	500fr multi	3.00	1.10

Games' Emblem, Wheels and Colors AP113

Design: 150fr, Rings, colors and Games' emblem.

1978, July 13 Litho. *Perf. 12½x13*

C288	AP113	40fr multi	18	15
C289	AP113	150fr multi	65	40

Third African Games, Algiers, July 13-28.

Emblem AP114

1978, Oct. 6 Litho. *Perf. 13*

C290	AP114	150fr multi	65	40

Niger Broadcasting Company, 20th anniversary.

Philexafrique II - Essen Issue

Common Design Types

Designs: No. C291, Giraffes and Niger No. 92. No. C292, Eagle and Oldenburg No. 7.

1978, Nov. 1 Litho. *Perf. 13x12½*

C291	CD138	100fr multi	42	28
C292	CD139	100fr multi	42	28

Nos. C291-C292 printed se-tenant.

View of Campus and Laying Cornerstone — AP115

1978, Dec. 11 Litho. *Perf. 12½*

C293	AP115	100fr multi	42	28

Islamic University of Niger.

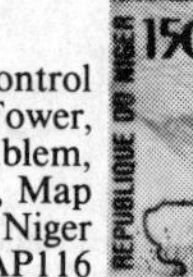

Control Tower, Emblem, Plane, Map of Niger AP116

1979, Dec. 12 Litho. *Perf. 12½*

C294	AP116	150fr multi	65	40

ASECNA (Air Safety Board), 20th anniversary.

Nos. C284-C286 Overprinted in Silver or Black: "alunissage / apollo XI / juillet 1969" and Emblem

1979, Dec. 20 Litho. *Perf. 14*

C295	A113	150fr multi	65	40
C296	A113	200fr multi (S)	85	55

Souvenir Sheet

C297	A113	400fr multi (S)	2.50	1.50

Apollo 11 moon landing, 10th anniversary.

Gaweye Hotel AP117

1980, Jan. 10 Litho. *Perf. 13*

C298	AP117	100fr multi	45	28

Self-portrait, by Rembrandt AP118

Rembrandt Portraits: 90fr, Hendrickje at the Window. 100fr, Old Man. 130fr, Maria Trip. 200fr, Self-portrait (diff.). 400fr, Saskia.

1981, Feb. 12 Litho. *Perf. 12½*

C299	AP118	60fr multi	25	18
C300	AP118	90fr multi	38	25
C301	AP118	100fr multi	42	28
C302	AP118	130fr multi	55	35
C303	AP118	200fr multi	85	55
C304	AP118	400fr multi	1.65	1.10
		Nos. C299-C304 (6)	4.10	2.71

Apollo 11, 1969 — AP119

Space Conquest: Views of Columbia space shuttle, 1981.

1981, Mar. 30 Litho. *Perf. 12½*

C305	AP119	100fr multi	42	28
C306	AP119	150fr multi	65	40
C307	AP119	200fr multi	85	55
C308	AP119	300fr multi	1.20	80

Souvenir Sheet

C309	AP119	500fr multi	2.25	1.40

For overprint see No. C356.

Girl in a Room, by Picasso — AP120

Picasso Birth Centenary: 60fr, Olga in an Armchair. 90fr, Family of Acrobats. 120fr, Three Musicians. 200fr, Paul on a Donkey. All vert.

1981, June 25 Litho. *Perf. 12½*

C310	AP120	60fr multi	25	18
C311	AP120	90fr multi	38	25
C312	AP120	120fr multi	50	32
C313	AP120	200fr multi	85	55
C314	AP120	400fr multi	1.75	1.10
		Nos. C310-C314 (5)	3.73	2.40

Christmas 1982 AP121

Rubens Paintings.

1982, Dec. 24 Litho. *Perf. 14*

C315	AP121	200fr Adoration of the Kings	65	42
C316	AP121	300fr Mystical Marriage of St. Catherine	1.10	80
C317	AP121	400fr Virgin and Child	1.40	90

Manned Flight Bicentenary AP122

1983, Jan. 24

C318	AP122	65fr Montgolfiere balloon, 1783, vert.	28	18
C319	AP122	85fr Hydrogen balloon, 1783, vert.	38	22
C320	AP122	200fr Zeppelin	85	55
C321	AP122	250fr Farman plane	1.10	65
C322	AP122	300fr Concorde	1.25	80
C323	AP122	500fr Apollo 11, vert.	2.25	1.40
		Nos. C318-C323 (6)	6.11	3.80

Pre-Olympic Year — AP123

1983, May 25 Litho. *Perf. 13*

C324	AP123	85fr Javelin	38	22
C325	AP123	200fr Shot put	85	55
C326	AP123	250fr Hammer, vert.	1.10	70
C327	AP123	300fr Discus	1.25	80

Souvenir Sheet

C328	AP123	500fr Shot put, diff.	2.25	1.40

For overprint see No. C357.

Christmas 1983 — AP124

Botticelli Paintings. 120fr, 500fr vert.

Wmk. 385 Cartor

1983 Litho. *Perf. 13*

C329	AP124	120fr Virgin and Child with Angels	25	18
C330	AP124	350fr Adoration of the Kings	75	45
C331	AP124	500fr Virgin of the Pomegranate	1.10	65

1984 Summer Olympics — AP125

Unwmk.

1984, Feb. 22 Litho. *Perf. 13*

C332	AP125	80fr Sprint	18	15
C333	AP125	120fr Pole vault	30	18
C334	AP125	140fr High jump	35	22
C335	AP125	200fr Triple jump, vert.	48	30
C336	AP125	350fr Long jump	85	55
		Nos. C332-C336 (5)	2.16	1.40

Souvenir Sheet

C337	AP125	500fr 110-meter hurdles	1.20	75

1984, Oct. 8 Litho.

Designs: Winners of various track events. Nos. C338-C341 vert.

C338	AP125	80fr Carl Lewis	22	15
C339	AP125	120fr J. Cruz	32	16
C340	AP125	140fr A. Cova	38	18
C341	AP125	300fr Al Joyner	80	40

Souvenir Sheet

C342 AP125 500fr D. Mogenburg, high jump 1.40 65

World Soccer Cup — AP126

1984, Nov. 19 Litho. *Perf. 13*

C345 AP126 150fr multi 32 16
C346 AP126 250fr multi 55 28
C347 AP126 450fr multi 95 50
C348 AP126 500fr multi 1.10 55

Christmas 1984 AP127

Paintings: 100fr, The Visitation, by Ghirlandajo. 200fr, Virgin and Child, by the Master of Santa Verdiana. 400fr, Virgin and Child, by J. Koning.

1984, Dec. 24 Litho. *Perf. 13*

C349 AP127 100fr multi 22 15
C350 AP127 200fr multi 42 22
C351 AP127 400fr multi 85 42

Audubon Birth Bicentennial — AP128

1985, Feb. 6 Litho. *Perf. 13*

C352 AP128 110fr Himantopus mexicanus 25 15
C353 AP128 140fr Phoenicopterus ruber, vert. 30 15
C354 AP128 200fr Fratercula arctica 42 22
C355 AP128 350fr Sterna paradisaea, vert. 75 38

Nos. C309, C328 Ovptd. in Silver with Exhibition Emblems

1985, Mar. 11 Litho. *Perf. 12½, 13*

C356 AP119 500fr ARGENTINA '85 BUENOS AIRES 1.10 55
C357 AP123 500fr OLYMPHILEX '85 LAUSANNE 1.10 55

Religious Paintings by Bartolome Murillo (1617-1682) AP129

1985, Dec. 19 Litho. *Perf. 13*

C358 AP129 110fr Virgin of the Rosary 32 16
C359 AP129 250fr The Immaculate Conception 65 35
C360 AP129 390fr Virgin of Seville 1.10 55

Christmas 1985.

Halley's Comet — AP130

1985, Dec. 26

C361 AP130 110fr Over Paris, 1910 32 16
C362 AP130 130fr Over New York 35 16
C363 AP130 200fr Giotto space probe 55 28
C364 AP130 300fr Vega probe 80 40
C365 AP130 390fr Planet A probe 1.10 55
Nos. C361-C365 (5) 3.12 1.55

Martin Luther King, Jr. (1929-1968), Civil Rights Activist — AP131

1986, Apr. 28 Litho. *Perf. 13½*

C366 AP131 500fr multi 2.00 1.00

1986 World Cup Soccer Championships, Mexico — AP132

Various soccer plays, stamps and labels.

1986, May 21 *Perf. 13*

C367 AP132 130fr No. 228 45 28
C368 AP132 210fr No. 229 90 42
C369 AP132 390fr No. 230 1.65 85
C370 AP132 400fr Aztec drawing 1.65 85

Souvenir Sheet

C371 AP132 500fr World Cup 2.00 1.00

Statue of Liberty, Cent. AP133

1986, June 19

C372 AP133 300fr Bartholdi, statue 1.25 55

1988 Summer Olympics, Seoul AP134

Olympic Rings, Pierre de Coubertin and: 85fr, One-man kayak, vert. 165fr, Crew racing. 200fr, Two-man kayak. 600fr, One-man kayak, diff., vert. 750fr, One-man kayak, diff., vert.

1988, June 22 Litho. *Perf. 13*

C373 AP134 85fr multi 58 30
C374 AP134 165fr multi 1.10 55
C375 AP134 200fr multi 1.35 68
C376 AP134 600fr multi 4.00 2.00

Souvenir Sheet

C377 AP134 750fr multi 5.00 5.00

First Moon Landing, 20th Anniv. AP135

1989, July 27 Litho. *Perf. 13*

C378 AP135 200fr Launch 1.30 65
C379 AP135 300fr Crew 1.90 95
C380 AP135 350fr Lunar experiments 2.25 1.15
C381 AP135 400fr Raising flag 2.55 1.30

1990 World Cup Soccer Championships, Italy — AP136

Various athletes and views or symbols of Italian cities.

1990, Mar. 6 Litho. *Perf. 13*

C382 AP136 130fr Florence 92 45
C383 AP136 210fr Verona 1.50 75
C384 AP136 500fr Bari 3.50 1.75
C385 AP136 600fr Rome 4.25 2.15

1992 Winter Olympics, Albertville — AP138

1991, Mar. 28 Litho. *Perf. 13*

C392 AP138 110fr Speed skating 80 40
C393 AP138 300fr Ice hockey 2.35 1.20
C394 AP138 500fr Downhill skiing 4.00 2.00
C395 AP138 600fr Luge 4.70 2.35

AIR POST SEMI-POSTAL STAMPS

Stamps of Dahomey types V1, V2, V3 and V4 inscribed "Niger" were issued in 1942 by the Vichy Government, but were not placed on sale in the colony.

POSTAGE DUE STAMPS

D1

D2

Postage Due Stamps of Upper Senegal and Niger, 1914, Overprinted

1921 Unwmk. *Perf. 14x13½*

J1 D1 5c green 35 35
J2 D1 10c rose 35 35
J3 D1 15c gray 40 40
J4 D1 20c brown 40 40
J5 D1 30c blue 40 40
J6 D1 50c black 45 45
J7 D1 60c orange 70 70
J8 D1 1fr violet 90 90
Nos. J1-J8 (8) 3.95 3.95

1927 Typo.

J9 D2 2c dk bl & red 15 15
J10 D2 4c ver & blk 15 15
J11 D2 5c org & vio 15 15
J12 D2 10c red brn & blk vio 15 15
J13 D2 15c grn & org 20 20
J14 D2 20c cer & ol brn 28 28
J15 D2 25c blk & ol brn 28 28
J16 D2 30c dl vio & blk 75 75
J17 D2 50c dp red, *grnsh* 35 35
J18 D2 60c gray vio & org, *bluish* 35 35
J19 D2 1fr ind & ultra, *bluish* 35 35
J20 D2 2fr rose red & vio 35 35
J21 D2 3fr org brn & ultra 65 65
Nos. J9-J21 (13) 4.16 4.16

Catalogue values for unused stamps in this section, from this point to the end of the section, are for Never Hinged items.

Republic of the Niger

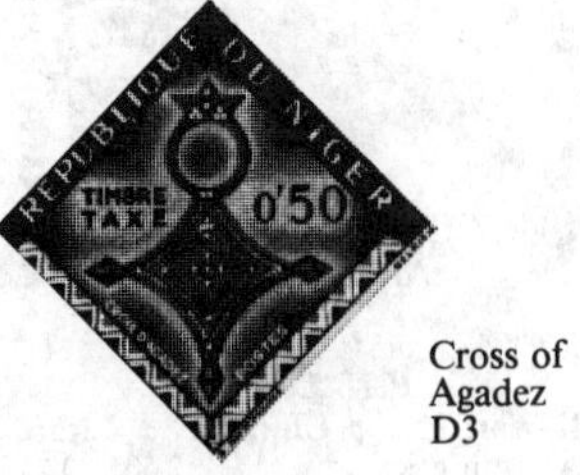

Cross of Agadez D3

Native Metalcraft: 3fr, 5fr, 10fr, Cross of Iferouane. 15fr, 20fr, 50fr, Cross of Tahoua.

Perf. 12½

1962, July 1 Unwmk. Photo.

J22 D3 50c emerald 15 15
J23 D3 1fr violet 15 15
J24 D3 2fr slate green 15 15
J25 D3 3fr lilac rose 15 15
J26 D3 5fr green 15 15
J27 D3 10fr orange 15 15
J28 D3 15fr deep blue 15 15
J29 D3 20fr carmine 15 15
J30 D3 50fr chocolate 28 28
Set value 95 95

OFFICIAL STAMPS

Catalogue values for unused stamps in this section are for Never Hinged items.

Djerma Girl Carrying Jug
O1 O2

Perf. 14x13½

1962-71 Typo. Unwmk.

Denomination in Black

No.	Design	Description	Unused	Used
O1	O1	1fr dark pur	15	15
O2	O1	2fr yel grn	15	15
O3	O1	5fr brt blue	15	15
O4	O1	10fr deep red	15	15
O5	O1	20fr vio blue	16	15
O6	O1	25fr orange	18	15
O7	O1	30fr lt bl ('65)	22	16
O8	O1	35fr pale grn ('71)	28	22
O9	O1	40fr brown ('71)	28	22
O10	O1	50fr black	32	22
O11	O1	60fr rose red	42	28
O12	O1	85fr blue green	58	28
O13	O1	100fr red lilac	65	28
O14	O1	200fr dark blue	1.40	65
		Nos. O1-O14 (14)	5.09	
		Set value		2.70

1988, Nov. Typo. *Perf. 13*

No.	Design	Description	Unused	Used
O15	O2	5fr brt blue	15	15
O16	O2	10fr henna brn	15	15
O17	O2	20fr vio blue	15	15
O18	O2	50fr greenish blk	25	15

1989, Mar.

No.	Design	Description	Unused	Used
O19	O2	15fr bright yellow	15	15
O20	O2	45fr orange	30	15
		Set value, #O15-O20	85	45

This is an expanding set. Numbers will change when complete.

NORTH INGERMANLAND

LOCATION — In Northern Russia lying between the River Neva and Finland

CAPITAL — Kirjasalo

In 1920 the residents of this territory revolted from Russian rule and set up a provisional government. The new State existed only a short period as the revolution was quickly quelled by Soviet troops.

100 Pennia = 1 Markka

Arms — A1

Perf. 11½

1920, Mar. 21 Unwmk. Litho.

No.	Design	Description	Unused	Used
1	A1	5p green	2.50	3.25
2	A1	10p rose red	2.50	3.25
3	A1	25p bister	2.50	3.25
4	A1	50p dark blue	2.50	3.25
5	A1	1m car & black	21.00	30.00
6	A1	5m lilac & black	90.00	115.00
7	A1	10m brown & blk	175.00	210.00
		Nos. 1-7 (7)	296.00	368.00

Imperf., Pair

No.	Design	Description	Unused
1a	A1	5p	17.50
2a	A1	10p	17.50
3a	A1	25p	17.50
4a	A1	50p	17.50
5a	A1	1m	70.00
6a	A1	5m	325.00
7a	A1	10m	625.00

Arms — A2

Peasant — A3

Plowing — A4

Milking — A5

Planting A6

Ruins of Church — A7

Peasants Playing Zithers A8

1920, Aug. 2

No.	Design	Description	Unused	Used
8	A2	10p gray grn & ultra	3.25	*6.50*
9	A3	30p buff & gray grn	3.25	*6.50*
10	A4	50p ultra & red brn	3.25	*6.50*
11	A5	80p claret & slate	3.25	*6.50*
12	A6	1m red & slate	15.00	*32.50*
13	A7	5m dk vio & dl rose	9.00	*13.00*
14	A8	10m brn & violet	9.00	*13.00*
a.		Center inverted	700.00	
		Nos. 8-14 (7)	46.00	*84.50*

Counterfeits abound.

Nos. 8-14 exist imperf. Value for set in pairs, $200.

NORWAY

LOCATION — Western half of the Scandinavian Peninsula in northern Europe

GOVT. — Kingdom

AREA — 125,051 sq. mi.

POP. — 4,134,353 (1984)

CAPITAL — Oslo

120 Skilling = 1 Specie Daler

100 Ore = 1 Krone (1877)

Catalogue values for unused stamps in this country are for Never Hinged items, beginning with Scott 275 in the regular postage section, Scott B27 in the semi-postal section, and Scott O65 in the official section.

Watermarks

Wmk. 159- Lion

Wmk. 160- Post Horn

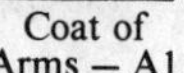

Coat of Arms — A1

King Oscar I — A2

1855 Typo. Wmk. 159 *Imperf.*

No.	Design	Description	Unused	Used
1	A1	4s blue	*4,500.*	100.00
a.		Double foot on right hind leg of lion		2,500.

Only a few genuine unused copies of No. 1 exist. Specimens often offered have had pen-markings removed. The unused catalogue value is for a specimen without gum. Copies with original gum sell for much more.

No. 1 was reprinted in 1914 and 1924 unwatermarked. Lowest value reprint, $75.

Rouletted Reprints

1963: Nos. 1, 2-5, 15. Value each $20.

1965: Nos. 57, 70a, 100, 152, J1, O1. Value each $10.

1969: Nos. 69, 92, 107, 114, 128, J12. Value each $10.

1856-57 Unwmk. *Perf. 13*

No.	Design	Description	Unused	Used
2	A2	2s yellow ('57)	450.00	125.00
3	A2	3s lilac ('57)	275.00	65.00
4	A2	4s blue	165.00	9.00
a.		Imperf.		*9,000.*
b.		Half used as 2s on cover		
5	A2	8s dull lake	800.00	27.50

Nos. 2-5 were reprinted in 1914 and 1924, perf. 13½. Lowest valued reprint, $60 each.

A3

A4

1863 Litho. *Perf. 14½x13½*

No.	Design	Description	Unused	Used
6	A3	2s yellow	450.00	150.00
7	A3	3s gray lilac	500.00	325.00
8	A3	4s blue	65.00	6.00
9	A3	8s rose	575.00	32.50
10	A3	24s brown	40.00	52.50

There are four types of the 2, 3, 8 and 24 skilling and eight types of the 4 skilling. See note on used value of No. 10 following No. 21.

1867-68 Typo.

No.	Design	Description	Unused	Used
11	A4	1s black ('68)	75.00	35.00
12	A4	2s orange	20.00	15.00
13	A4	3s dl lil ('68)	250.00	65.00
14	A4	4s blue	45.00	6.00
15	A4	8s car rose	400.00	30.00
a.		8s rose, clear impression	750.00	300.00

See note on used value of No. 12 following No. 21.

For surcharges see Nos. 59-61, 149.

No. 15 was reprinted in 1914 and 1924, perf. 13½. Lowest valued reprint, $60.

Post Horn and Crown — A5

1872-75 Wmk. 160

No.	Design	Description	Unused	Used
16	A5	1s yel grn ('75)	8.50	9.75
a.		1s deep green ('73)	135.00	45.00
b.		"E.EN"	22.50	27.50
17	A5	2s ultra ('74)	12.00	14.00
a.		2s Prussian blue ('74)	3,750.	3,000.
b.		2s gray blue	12.00	16.00
18	A5	3s rose	40.00	5.00
a.		3s carmine	40.00	5.00
b.		3s car, *bluish* thin paper	125.00	16.00
19	A5	4s lilac ('73)	12.00	14.00
a.		4s dark violet, *bluish* thin paper	375.00	125.00
b.		4s brown violet, *bluish* thin paper ('73)	375.00	125.00
20	A5	6s org brn ('75)	375.00	30.00
21	A5	7s red brn ('73)	30.00	30.00

In this issue there are 12 types each of Nos. 16, 17, 18 and 19; 15 types of No. 20 and 22 types of No. 21. The differences are in the words of value.

Used values of Nos. 10, 12, 16-17, 19 and 21 are for specimens canceled in later period, 1888-1908. Those canceled before 1888 are usually worth considerably more. These six stamps were used until Mar. 31, 1908.

No. 19 comes on thin and thick paper. Same value used. Unused, thick paper ten times given value.

For surcharges see Nos. 62-63.

Post Horn — A6

King Oscar II — A7

"NORGE" in Sans-serif Capitals, Ring of Post Horn Shaded

1877-78

No.	Design	Description	Unused	Used
22	A6	1o drab	4.00	3.00
23	A6	3o orange	70.00	17.50
24	A6	5o ultra	30.00	4.50
a.		5o dull blue	60.00	7.00
b.		5o bright blue	90.00	14.00
c.		No period after "Postfrim"	50.00	8.00
d.		Retouched plate	55.00	8.00
e.		As "c,", retouched plate	85.00	12.00
25	A6	10o rose	50.00	1.00
a.		No period after "Postfrim"	52.50	1.50
b.		Retouched plate	50.00	1.10
26	A6	12o lt green	85.00	13.00
27	A6	20o org brn	230.00	8.75
28	A6	25o lilac	250.00	95.00
29	A6	35o bl grn ('78)	16.00	8.00
a.		Retouched plate	100.00	70.00
30	A6	50o maroon	35.00	8.00
31	A6	60o dk bl ('78)	32.50	8.00
32	A7	1k gray grn & grn ('78)	22.50	6.00
33	A7	1.50k ultra & bl ('78)	60.00	30.00
34	A7	2k rose & mar ('78)	35.00	20.00

There are 6 types each of Nos. 22, 26 and 28 to 34; 12 types each of Nos. 23, 24, 25 and 27. The differences are in the numerals.

A 2nd plate of the 5o ultramarine has 100 types, the 10o, 200 types.

The retouch on 5o, 10o and 35o shows as a thin white line between crown and post horn.

Post Horn — A8

"NORGE" in Sans-serif Capitals, Ring of Horn Unshaded

1882-93 Wmk. 160 *Perf. 14½x13½*

No.	Design	Description	Unused	Used
35	A8	1o blk brn ('86)	16.00	14.00
a.		No period after "Postfrim"	55.00	55.00
b.		Small "N" in "NORGE"	55.00	55.00
36	A8	1o gray ('93)	8.25	8.25
37	A8	2o brn ('90)	3.00	2.00
38	A8	3o org ('83)	47.50	2.75
a.		3o yellow ('89)	47.50	2.75
b.		Perf. 13½x12½ ('89)		1,500.
39	A8	5o bl grn ('89)	40.00	1.10
a.		5o gray green ('86)	55.00	1.75
b.		5o emerald ('88)	150.00	6.00
c.		5o yellow green ('91)	35.00	1.10
d.		Perf. 13½x12½ ('92)		800.00
40	A8	10o rose	40.00	85
a.		10o rose red ('86)	35.00	85
b.		10o carmine ('91)	47.50	85
c.		As "b," imperf., pair	1,000.	1,000.
41	A8	12o grn ('84)	1,500.	300.00
42	A8	12o yel brn ('84)	25.00	13.00
a.		12o bister brown ('83)	40.00	30.00
43	A8	20o brown	75.00	9.00
44	A8	20o blue ('86)	47.50	1.10
a.		20o ultramarine ('83)	105.00	6.50
b.		No period after "Postfrim" ('85)	300.00	12.00
c.		As "a," imperf., pair	1,100.	1,100.
45	A8	25o dl vio ('84)	12.50	9.00

Dies vary from 20 to 21mm high. Numerous types exist due to different production methods, including separate handmade dies for value figures. Many shades exist.

No. 42 and 42a Surcharged in Black **2 Øre.**

1888 *Perf. 14½x13½*

No.	Design	Description	Unused	Used
46	A8	2o on 12o yel brn	1.50	1.50
a.		2o on 12o bister brown	1.50	1.50

Post Horn — A10

"NORGE" in Roman instead of Sans-serif capitals

Perf. 14½x13½

1893-1908 **Wmk. 160**

Size: 16x20mm

No.	Type	Description	Unused	Used
47	A10	1o gray ('99)	2.00	1.10
48	A10	2o pale brn ('99)	2.00	1.10
49	A10	3o org yel	1.50	20
50	A10	5o dp grn ('98)	4.50	15
b.		Booklet pane of 6		
51	A10	10o car rose ('98)	11.50	15
b.		Booklet pane of 6		
52	A10	15o brn ('08)	42.50	4.00
53	A10	20o dp ultra	27.50	20
b.		Booklet pane of 6		
54	A10	25o red vio ('01)	52.50	2.00
55	A10	30o sl gray ('07)	45.00	1.50
56	A10	35o dk bl grn ('98)	12.50	3.50
57	A10	50o maroon ('94)	50.00	1.10
58	A10	60o dk bl ('00)	60.00	12.00
		Nos. 47-58 (12)	311.50	27.00

Two dies exist of each except 2, 25 and 60o.

See Nos. 74-95, 162-166, 187-191, 193, 307-309, 325-326, 416-419, 606, 709-714. For overprints and surcharge see Nos. 99, 207-211, 220-224, 226.

1893-98 **Wmk. 160** ***Perf. 13½x12½***

No.	Type	Description	Unused	Used
47a	A10	1o gray ('95)	10.50	10.50
49a	A10	3o orange ('95)	45.00	4.00
50a	A10	5o green	27.50	90
51a	A10	10o carmine ('95)	27.50	90
c.		10o rose	42.50	90
53a	A10	20o dl ultra ('95)	75.00	3.25
54a	A10	25o red vio ('98)	75.00	20.00
56a	A10	35o dk bl grn ('95)	75.00	20.00
57a	A10	50o maroon ('97)	115.00	13.00

No. 12 Surcharged in Green, Blue or Carmine **Kr. 1.00**

1905 **Unwmk.** ***Perf. 14½x13½***

No.	Type	Description	Unused	Used
59	A4	1k on 2s org (G)	35.00	26.00
60	A4	1.50k on 2s org (Bl)	62.50	62.50
61	A4	2k on 2s org (C)	65.00	47.50

Nos. 19 and 21 Surcharged in Black **30 ØRE**

1906-08 **Wmk. 160** ***Perf. 14½x13½***

No.	Type	Description	Unused	Used
62	A5	15o on 4s lil ('08)	3.00	3.00
a.		15o on 4s violet ('08)	8.00	8.00
63	A5	30o on 7s red brn	5.50	5.50

King Haakon VII — A11

Die A - Background of ruled lines. The coils at the sides are ornamented with fine cross-lines and small dots. Stamps 20¼mm high.

Die B - Background of ruled lines. The coils are ornamented with large white dots and dashes. Stamps 21¼mm high.

Die C - Solid background. The coils are without ornamental marks. Stamps 20¾mm high.

1907 **Typo.** ***Perf. 14½x13½***

Die A

No.	Type	Description	Unused	Used
64	A11	1k yel grn	35.00	30.00
65	A11	1.50k ultra	80.00	80.00
66	A11	2k rose	100.00	100.00

1909-10

Die B

No.	Type	Description	Unused	Used
67	A11	1k green	165.00	100.00
68	A11	1.50k ultra	180.00	*350.00*
69	A11	2k rose	180.00	4.00

1911-18

Die C

No.	Type	Description	Unused	Used
70	A11	1k light grn	70	15
a.		1k dark green	62.50	1.75
71	A11	1.50k ultra	1.75	30
72	A11	2k rose ('15)	2.50	30
73	A11	5k dk vio ('18)	4.25	3.25

Post Horn Type Redrawn

Original Redrawn

In the redrawn stamps the white ring of the post horn is continuous instead of being broken by, a spot of color below the crown. On the 3 and 30 ore the top of the figure "3" in the oval band is rounded instead of flattened.

1910-29 ***Perf. 14½x13½***

No.	Type	Description	Unused	Used
74	A10	1o pale olive	35	18
75	A10	2o pale brn	35	18
76	A10	3o orange	35	18
77	A10	5o green	3.50	15
a.		Booklet pane of 6	80.00	
78	A10	5o magenta ('22)	70	15
79	A10	7o green ('29)	70	15
80	A10	10o car rose	4.50	15
a.		Booklet pane of 6	100.00	
81	A10	10o green ('22)	6.00	18
82	A10	12o purple ('17)	70	45
83	A10	15o brown	4.00	15
a.		Booklet pane of 6	40.00	
84	A10	15o indigo ('20)	4.00	18
85	A10	20o dp ultra	6.50	15
a.		Booklet pane of 6	150.00	
86	A10	20o ol grn ('21)	6.00	18
87	A10	25o red lilac	30.00	18
88	A10	25o car rose ('22)	6.00	80
89	A10	30o slate gray	7.00	24
90	A10	30o lt blue ('27)	10.00	3.00
91	A10	35o dk olive ('20)	10.00	28
92	A10	40o ol grn ('17)	3.00	28
93	A10	40o dp ultra ('22)	22.50	28
94	A10	50o claret	19.00	28
95	A10	60o deep blue	22.50	30
		Nos. 74-95 (22)	167.65	8.07

Constitutional Assembly of 1814 — A12

1914, May 10 **Engr.** ***Perf. 13½***

No.	Type	Description	Unused	Used
96	A12	5o green	1.00	42
97	A12	10o car rose	2.00	42
98	A12	20o deep blue	8.50	3.50

Centenary of Norway's Constitution of May 17, 1814.

No. 87 Surcharged **5 ØRE**

1922, Mar. 1 ***Perf. 14½x13½***

No.	Type	Description	Unused	Used
99	A10	5o on 25o red lil	35	35

Lion Rampant A13

Polar Bear and Airplane A14

"NORGE" in Roman capitals, Line below "Ore"

1922-24 **Typo.** ***Perf. 14½x13½***

No.	Type	Description	Unused	Used
100	A13	10o dp grn ('24)	9.00	28
101	A13	20o dp vio	15.00	15
102	A13	25o scar ('24)	25.00	60
103	A13	45o blue ('24)	1.00	55

For surcharge see No. 129.

1925, Apr. 1

No.	Type	Description	Unused	Used
104	A14	2o yel brn	2.00	2.00
105	A14	3o orange	2.50	2.50
106	A14	5o magenta	5.00	5.00
107	A14	10o yel grn	6.50	6.50
108	A14	15o dk blue	6.50	6.50
109	A14	20o plum	12.00	12.00
110	A14	25o scarlet	1.75	1.75
		Nos. 104-110 (7)	36.25	36.25

Issued to help finance Roald Amundsen's attempted flight to the North Pole.

A15

A16

1925, Aug. 19

No.	Type	Description	Unused	Used
111	A15	10o yel grn	4.00	4.00
112	A15	15o indigo	3.50	3.50
113	A15	20o plum	4.00	1.00
114	A15	45o dark blue	4.00	4.00

Annexation of Spitsbergen (Svalbard). For surcharge see No. 130.

"NORGE" in Sans-serif Capitals, No Line below "Ore"

1926-34 **Wmk. 160**

Size: 16x19½mm

No.	Type	Description	Unused	Used
115	A16	10o yel grn	70	15
116	A16	14o dp org ('29)	1.50	1.50
117	A16	15o olive gray	70	15
118	A16	20o plum	20.00	15
119	A16	20o scar ('27)	70	15
a.		Booklet pane of 6	80.00	
120	A16	25o red	9.00	1.75
121	A16	25o org brn ('27)	1.00	16
122	A16	30o dull bl ('28)	1.00	16
123	A16	35o ol brn ('27)	50.00	16
124	A16	35o red vio ('34)	1.90	16
125	A16	40o dull blue	2.75	90
126	A16	40o slate ('27)	1.90	16
127	A16	50o claret ('27)	1.90	16
128	A16	60o Prus bl ('27)	1.90	16
		Nos. 115-128 (14)	94.95	5.87

See Nos. 167-176, 192, 194-202A, 212-219, 225, 227-234, 237-238, 302-303. For overprints and surcharges see Nos. 131, 212-219, 227-234, 237-238.

Nos. 103 and 114 Surcharged **30 ≡**

1927, June 13

No.	Type	Description	Unused	Used
129	A13	30o on 45o blue	11.00	95
130	A15	30o on 45o dk blue	2.50	2.50

No. 120 Surcharged **20 ≡**

1928

No.	Type	Description	Unused	Used
131	A16	20o on 25o red	1.50	95

See Nos. 302-303.

Henrik Ibsen — A17

Niels Henrik Abel — A18

1928, Mar. 20 **Litho.**

No.	Type	Description	Unused	Used
132	A17	10o yel grn	5.00	1.50
133	A17	15o chnt brn	2.50	1.75
134	A17	20o carmine	2.75	45
135	A17	30o dp ultra	3.25	2.75

Ibsen (1828-1906), dramatist.

Postage Due Stamps of 1889-1923 Overprinted

Post Frimerke

a

POST

b

1929, Jan.

136 D1 (a)	1o gray	38	30
137 D1 (a)	4o lil rose	38	30
138 D1 (a)	10o green	1.50	1.50
139 D1 (b)	15o brown	2.00	2.00
140 D1 (b)	20o dl vio	1.10	50
141 D1 (b)	40o dp ultra	1.90	50
142 D1 (b)	50o maroon	6.50	6.25
143 D1 (a)	100o org yel	3.00	1.50
144 D1 (b)	200o dk vio	4.75	3.00
	Nos. 136-144 (9)	21.51	15.85

1929, Apr. 6 Litho. ***Perf. 14½x13½***

145 A18	10o green	1.75	70
146 A18	15o red brn	2.25	1.65
147 A18	20o rose red	1.40	35
148 A18	30o dp ultra	2.25	1.75

Abel (1802-1829), mathematician.

No. 12 Surcharged **14 ØRE 14**

Perf. 14½x13½

1929, July 1 **Unwmk.**

149 A4	14o on 2s org	2.25	2.25

Saint Olaf A19

Trondheim Cathedral A20

Death of Olaf in Battle of Stiklestad A21

Typo.; Litho. (15o)
Perf. 14½x13½

1930, Apr. 1 **Wmk. 160**

150 A19	10o yel grn	7.50	35
151 A20	15o brn & blk	1.00	45
152 A19	20o scarlet	1.40	30

Engr.
Perf. 13½

153 A21	30o deep blue	3.00	3.00

King Olaf Haraldsson (995-1030), patron saint of Norway.

Björnson A22

Holberg A23

1932, Dec. 8 ***Perf. 14½x13½***

154 A22	10o yel grn	8.25	40
155 A22	15o blk brn	1.25	90
156 A22	20o rose red	1.10	30
157 A22	30o ultra	2.00	2.25

Björnstjerne Björnson (1832-1910), novelist, poet and dramatist.

1934, Nov. 23

158 A23	10o yel grn	1.25	35
159 A23	15o brown	60	60
160 A23	20o rose red	11.00	24
161 A23	30o ultra	2.50	2.25

Ludvig Holberg (1684-1754), Danish man of letters.

Types of 1893-1900, 1926-34
Second Redrawing
Perf. 13x13½

1937 **Wmk. 160** **Photo.**
Size: 17x21mm

162 A10	1o olive	70	50
163 A10	2o yel brn	70	50
164 A10	3o deep org	1.75	1.40
165 A10	5o rose lilac	55	15
a.	Booklet pane of 6	55.00	
166 A10	7o brt grn	70	20
167 A16	10o brt grn	45	15
a.	Booklet pane of 6	50.00	
168 A16	14o dp org	1.90	1.65
169 A16	15o olive bis	1.10	15
170 A16	20o scarlet	1.10	15
a.	Booklet pane of 6	50.00	
171 A16	25o dk org brn	5.50	25
172 A16	30o ultra	2.50	25
173 A16	35o brt vio	2.50	25
174 A16	40o dk sl grn	3.00	25
175 A16	50o dp claret	3.50	40
176 A16	60o Prussian bl	1.50	20
	Nos. 162-176 (15)	27.45	6.45

Nos. 162 to 166 have a solid background inside oval. Nos. 74, 75, 76, 78, 79 have background of vertical lines.

King Haakon VII — A24

1937-38

177 A24	1k dk green	15	18
178 A24	1.50k sapphire ('38)	65	70
179 A24	2k rose red ('38)	65	70
180 A24	5k dl vio ('38)	5.00	5.75

Nos. 177-180, 267, B19, B32-B34 and B38-B41 were demonetized from May 15, 1945 until Sept. 1, 1981. Used values are for stamps canceled after this period. Stamps with dated cancellations prior to May 15, 1945 sell for more. False cancellations exist.

Reindeer A25

Borgund Church A26

Jolster in Sunnfiord A27

Perf. 13x13½, 13½x13

1938, Apr. 20 **Wmk. 160**

181 A25	15o olive brn	60	42
182 A26	20o copper red	4.00	55
183 A27	30o brt ultra	3.75	1.65

1939 **Unwmk.**

184 A25	15o olive brn	38	22
185 A26	20o copper red	52	20
186 A27	30o brt ultra	52	28

Types of 1937
Perf. 13x13½

1940-49 **Unwmk.** **Photo.**
Size: 17x21mm

187 A10	1o ol grn ('41)	16	15
188 A10	2o yel brn ('41)	16	15
189 A10	3o dp org ('41)	16	15
190 A10	5o rose lil ('41)	32	15
a.	Booklet pane of 6, vert.	20.00	
b.	Booklet pane of 10, horiz.	8.00	
191 A10	7o brt grn ('41)	40	15
192 A16	10o brt grn	32	15
a.	Booklet pane of 6, vert.	24.00	
b.	Booklet pane of 10, horiz.	20.00	
193 A10	12o brt vio	80	1.10
194 A16	14o dp org ('41)	1.00	2.00
195 A16	15o olive bis	48	15
a.	Booklet pane of 10	40.00	
196 A16	20o red	45	15
a.	Booklet pane of 6, vert.	24.00	
b.	Booklet pane of 10, horiz.	25.00	
197 A16	25o dk org brn	1.25	15
197A A16	25o scar ('46)	40	15
b.	Booklet pane of 10	24.00	
198 A16	30o brt ultra ('41)	1.25	20
198A A16	30o gray ('49)	5.75	15
199 A16	35o brt vio ('41)	1.50	15
200 A16	40o dk sl grn ('41)	1.00	15
200A A16	40o dp ultra ('46)	1.50	15
201 A16	50o dp claret ('41)	1.00	15
201A A16	55o dp org ('46)	15.00	15
202 A16	60o Prus bl ('41)	1.00	15
202A A16	80o dk org brn ('46)	12.50	15
	Nos. 187-202A (21)	46.40	
	Set value		4.90

Lion Rampant
A28 A29

1940 Unwmk. Photo. ***Perf. 13x13½***

203 A28	1k brt grn	80	15
204 A28	1½k dp blue	1.10	30
205 A28	2k brt red	1.25	90
206 A28	5k dull pur	3.00	2.50

For overprints see Nos. 235-236.

Stamps of 1937-41, Types A10, A16, A28, Overprinted "V" in Black

1941 **Wmk. 160** ***Perf. 13x13½***

207 A10	1o olive	40	*2.75*
208 A10	2o yel brn	40	*2.75*
209 A10	3o orange	2.00	*6.00*
210 A10	5o rose lil	50	*1.40*
211 A10	7o brt grn	50	*2.75*
212 A16	10o brt grn	7.50	*26.00*
213 A16	14o dp org	1.00	*6.00*
214 A16	15o olive bis	30	*95*
215 A16	30o ultra	1.00	*1.50*
216 A16	35o brt vio	75	70
217 A16	40o dk sl grn	7.50	*10.00*
218 A16	50o dp claret	200.00	*375.00*
219 A16	60o Prus bl	75	95
	Nos. 207-217,219 (12)	22.60	*61.75*

Unwmk.

220 A10	1o olive	35	*1.25*
221 A10	2o yel brn	35	*1.25*
222 A10	3o deep org	35	*1.25*
223 A10	5o rose lil	35	30
224 A10	7o brt grn	95	*3.25*
225 A16	10o brt grn	35	15
226 A10	12o brt vio	1.10	*6.50*
227 A16	15o ol bis	1.90	*8.75*
228 A16	20o red	35	15
a.	Inverted overprint	600.00	800.00
229 A16	25o dk org brn	42	32
230 A16	30o brt ultra	70	*65*
231 A16	35o brt vio	70	50
232 A16	40o dk sl grn	70	50
233 A16	50o dp claret	80	*1.25*
234 A16	60o Prus bl	1.90	75
235 A28	1k brt grn	1.25	50
236 A28	1½k dp blue	3.75	*9.00*
237 A16	2k brt red	10.50	*30.00*
238 A16	5k dl pur	19.00	*50.00*

Coil Stamp

239 A29	10o brt grn	1.25	*7.00*
	Nos. 220-239 (20)	47.02	*123.32*

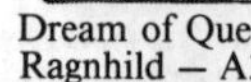
Dream of Queen Ragnhild — A30

Snorri Sturluson — A32

Einar Tambarskjelve in Fight at Svolder — A31

Designs: 30o, King Olaf sailing in wedding procession to Landmerket. 50o, Syipdag's sons and followers going to Hall of Seven Kings. 60o, Before Battle of Stiklestad.

1941 ***Perf. 13½x13, 13x13½***

240 A30	10o bright grn	35	20
241 A31	15o olive brn	38	55
242 A32	20o dark red	35	15
243 A31	30o blue	1.00	1.40
244 A31	50o dull violet	1.10	1.40
245 A31	60o Prussian bl	1.10	1.40
	Nos. 240-245 (6)	4.28	5.10

700th anniversary of the death of Snorri Sturluson, writer and historian.

University of Oslo — A36

1941, Sept. 2 *Perf. 13x13½*
246 A36 1k dk ol grn 32.50 40.00

Centenary of cornerstone laying of University of Oslo building.

Richard (Rikard) Nordraak (1842-66), Composer — A37

"Broad Sails Go over the North Sea" — A38

View of Coast and Lines of National Anthem A39

1942, June 12 *Perf. 13*
247 A37 10o dp grn 1.50 1.50
248 A38 15o dp brn 1.50 1.50
249 A37 20o rose red 1.50 1.50
250 A39 30o sapphire 1.50 1.50

Johan Herman Wessel (1742-1785), Author — A40

1942, Oct. 6
251 A40 15o dl brn 20 20
252 A40 20o henna 20 20

Designs of 1942 and 1855 Stamps of Norway A41

1942, Oct. 12
253 A41 20o henna 25 55
254 A41 30o sapphire 35 1.10

To commemorate the European Postal Congress at Vienna, October, 1942.

Edvard Grieg (1843-1907), Composer A42

Destroyer Sleipner A43

1943, June 15
255 A42 10o dp grn 25 25
256 A42 20o henna 25 25
257 A42 40o grnsh blk 25 25
258 A42 60o dk grnsh bl 25 25

1943-45 Unwmk. Engr. *Perf. 12½*

Designs: 5o, 10o, "Sleipner." 7o, 30o, Convoy under midnight sun. 15o, Plane and pilot. 20o, "We will win." 40o, Ski troops. 60o, King Haakon VII.

259 A43 5o rose vio ('45) 16 15
260 A43 7o grnsh blk ('45) 20 20
261 A43 10o dk bl grn 15 15
262 A43 15o dk ol grn 52 45
263 A43 20o rose red 15 15
264 A43 30o dp ultra 65 75
265 A43 40o olive black 55 55
266 A43 60o dark blue 55 55
Nos. 259-266 (8) 2.93 2.95

Nos. 261-266 were used for correspondence carried on Norwegian ships until after the liberation of Norway, when they became regular postage stamps.
Nos. 261-266 exist with overprint "London 17-5-43" and serial number. Value for set, unused, $1,000; canceled $1,200.

Gran's Plane and Map of His North Sea Flight Route A49

1944, July 30 *Perf. 13*
267 A49 40o dk grnsh bl 40 40

20th anniv. of the 1st flight over the North Sea, made by Tryggve Gran on July 30, 1914.
For used value see note following No. 180.

New National Arms of 1943 — A50

1945, Feb. 15 Typo. *Perf. 13*
268 A50 1½k dark blue 85 40

Henrik Wergeland A51

Lion Rampant A52

1945, July 12 **Photo.**
269 A51 10o dk olive grn 30 30
270 A51 15o dark brown 85 1.00
271 A51 20o dark red 25 30

Henrik Wergeland, poet and playwright, death cent.

1945, Dec. 19
272 A52 10o dk ol grn 35 30
273 A52 20o red 35 30

Founding of the Norwegian Folklore Museum, 50th anniv.

Pilot and Mechanic — A53

King Haakon VII — A54

1946, Mar. 22 Engr. *Perf. 12*
274 A53 15o brn rose 40 75

Issued in honor of Little Norway, training center in Canada for Norwegian pilots.

Catalogue values for unused stamps in this section, from this point to the end of the section, are for Never Hinged items.

1946, June 7 Photo. *Perf. 13*
275 A54 1k bright grn 1.65 15
276 A54 1½k Prussian bl 4.75 15
277 A54 2k henna brn 35.00 15
278 A54 5k violet 21.00 40
Set value 60

Hannibal Sehested — A55

Designs: 10o, Letter carrier, 1700. 15o, Adm. Peter W. Tordenskjold. 25o, Christian Magnus Falsen. 30o, Cleng Peerson and "Restaurationen." 40o, Post ship "Constitution." 45o, First Norwegian locomotive. 50o, Sven Foyn and whaler. 55o, Fridtjof Nansen and Roald Amundsen. 60o, Coronation of King Haakon VII and Queen Maud, 1906. 80o, Return of King Haakon, June 7, 1945.

1947, Apr. 15 Photo. *Perf. 13*
279 A55 5o red lil 65 15
280 A55 10o green 65 15
281 A55 15o brown 65 15
282 A55 25o org red 65 15
283 A55 30o gray 1.00 15
284 A55 40o blue 1.10 15
285 A55 45o violet 2.25 48
286 A55 50o org brn 2.75 15
287 A55 55o orange 6.00 24
288 A55 60o slate gray 4.00 75
289 A55 80o dk brn 3.00 24
Nos. 279-289 (11) 22.70
Set value 2.30

Establishment of the Norwegian Post Office, 300th anniv.

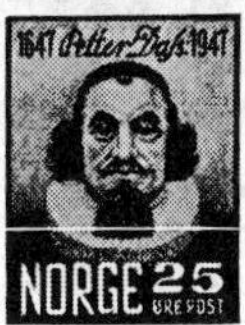

Petter Dass — A66

King Haakon VII — A67

1947, July 1 **Unwmk.**
290 A66 25o brt red 90 55

300th birth anniv. of Petter Dass, poet.

1947, Aug. 2
291 A67 25o org red 90 55

75th birthday of King Haakon.

Axel Heiberg — A68

Alexander L. Kielland — A69

1948, June 15
292 A68 25o dp carmine 1.10 32
293 A68 80o dp red brn 2.25 30

50th anniv. of the Norwegian Society of Forestry; birth cent. of Axel Heiberg, its founder.

1949, May 9
295 A69 25o rose brn 1.65 20
296 A69 40o greenish blue 1.65 50
297 A69 80o org brn 2.00 65

Birth cent. of Alexander L. Kielland, author.

Symbols of UPU Members — A70

Stylized Pigeons and Globe — A71

Symbolical of the UPU A72

1949, Oct. 9 *Perf. 13*
299 A70 10o dk grn & blk 75 60
300 A71 25o scarlet 52 25
301 A72 40o dull blue 55 52

75th anniv. of the formation of the UPU.

Nos. 196 and 200A Surcharged with New Value and Bar in Black

1949 *Perf. 13x13½*
302 A16 25o on 20o red 45 15
303 A16 45o on 40o dp ultra 2.00 28
Set value 36

King Harald Haardraade and Oslo City Hall — A73

1950, May 15 Photo. *Perf. 13*
304 A73 15o green 90 1.00
305 A73 25o red 55 35
306 A73 45o ultramarine 90 75

900th anniversary of Oslo.

Redrawn Post Horn Type of 1937

1950-51 Photo. *Perf. 13x13½*
Size: 17x21mm
307 A10 10o grnsh gray 50 15
a. Booklet pane of 10 6.00
308 A10 15o dark green 2.00 40
a. Booklet pane of 10 22.50
309 A10 20o chnt brn ('51) 5.00 2.25

A little time given to the study of the arrangement of the Scott Catalogue can make it easier to use effectively.

King Haakon VII A74

Arne Garborg A75

1950-51 Photo. *Perf. 13x13½*

310 A74 25o dk red ('50) 90 15
a. Booklet pane of 10 40.00
311 A74 30o gray 9.00 60
312 A74 35o red brn 19.00 15
313 A74 45o brt blue 1.75 85
314 A74 50o olive brn 1.75 15
315 A74 55o orange 1.75 85
316 A74 60o gray blue 10.00 15
317 A74 80o chnt brn 2.75 30
Nos. 310-317 (8) 46.90 3.20

See Nos. 322-324, 345-352.

1951, Jan. 25 *Perf. 13*

318 A75 25o red 65 22
319 A75 45o dull blue 2.25 1.50
320 A75 80o brown 3.50 1.25

Birth cent. of Arne Garborg, poet.

No. 310 Surcharged with New Value in Black

1951 *Perf. 13x13½*

321 A74 30o on 25o dk red 60 15

Haakon Type of 1950-51

1951-52 Photo.

322 A74 25o gray 22.50 15
323 A74 30o dk red ('52) 90 15
a. Booklet pane of 10 35.00
324 A74 55o blue ('52) 1.75 40
Set value 52

Redrawn Post Horn Type of 1937

1952, June 3 *Perf. 13x13½*

325 A10 15o org brn 70 15
a. Booklet pane of 10 12.00
326 A10 20o green 70 15
Set value 15

King Haakon VII — A76

Medieval Sculpture, Nidaros Cathedral — A77

1952, Aug. 3 Unwmk. *Perf. 13*

327 A76 30o red 50 15
328 A76 55o deep blue 1.10 1.00

80th birthday of King Haakon VII.

No. 308 Surcharged with New Value

1952, Nov. 18 *Perf. 13x13½*

329 A10 20o on 15o dk grn 60 15

1953, July 15 *Perf. 13*

330 A77 30o henna brn 60 40

800th anniv. of the creation of the Norwegian Archbishopric of Nidaros.

Train of 1854 and Horse-drawn Sled — A78

Carsten T. Nielsen — A79

Designs: 30o, Diesel train. 55o, Engineer.

1954, Apr. 30 Photo.

331 A78 20o green 85 30
332 A78 30o red 85 18
333 A78 55o ultra 2.00 1.25

Inauguration of the first Norwegian railway, cent.

1954, Dec. 10

Designs: 30o, Government radio towers. 55o, Lineman and telegraph poles in snow.

334 A79 20o ol grn & blk 40 20
335 A79 30o brt red 40 15
336 A79 55o blue 1.50 85

Centenary (in 1955) of the inauguration of the first Norwegian public telegraph line.

Norway No. 1 — A80

Stamp Reproductions: 30o, Post horn type A5. 55o, Lion type A13.

1955, Jan. 3 *Perf. 13*

337 A80 20o dp grn & gray bl 48 28
338 A80 30o red & car 18 15
339 A80 55o gray bl & dp bl 95 55

Centenary of Norway's first postage stamp.

Nos. 337-339 Overprinted in Black

1955, June 4

340 A80 20o dp grn & gray bl 12.00 10.00
341 A80 30o red & car 12.00 10.00
342 A80 55o gray bl & dp bl 12.00 10.00

Norway Philatelic Exhibition, Oslo, 1955. Sold at exhibition post office for face value plus 1kr admission fee.

King Haakon VII and Queen Maud in Coronation Robes — A81

1955, Nov. 25 Photo. *Perf. 13*

343 A81 30o rose red 40 20
344 A81 55o ultra 60 48

Haakon's 50th anniv. as King of Norway.

Haakon Type of 1950-51

1955-57 Unwmk. *Perf. 13x13½*

345 A74 25o dk grn ('56) 1.10 15
346 A74 35o brn red ('56) 4.50 15
a. Booklet pane of 10 62.50
347 A74 40o pale pur 1.90 15
a. Booklet pane of 10 60.00
348 A74 50o bis ('57) 1.50 15
349 A74 65o ultra ('56) 1.65 40
350 A74 70o brn ol ('56) 11.00 15
351 A74 75o mar ('57) 2.25 15
352 A74 90o dp org 1.65 15
Nos. 345-352 (8) 25.55
Set value 1.00

Northern Countries Issue

Whooper Swans — A81a

1956, Oct. 30 Engr. *Perf. 12½*

353 A81a 35o rose red 95 60
354 A81a 65o ultra 95 85

Issued to emphasize the close bonds connecting the northern countries: Denmark, Finland, Iceland, Norway and Sweden.

Jan Mayen Island A82

Map of Spitsbergen A83

King Haakon VII A84

Design: 65o, Map of South Pole with Queen Maud Land.

Perf. 12½x13, 13x12½

1957, July 1 Photo. Unwmk.

355 A82 25o slate grn 65 40
356 A83 35o dk red & gray 65 15
357 A83 65o dk grn & bl 65 50

Intl. Geophysical Year, 1957-58.

1957, Aug. 2 *Perf. 13*

358 A84 35o dk red 35 20
359 A84 65o ultra 85 85

85th birthday of King Haakon VII.

King Olav V A85 A86

1958-60 Photo. *Perf. 13x13½*

360 A85 25o emerald 85 15
a. Booklet pane of 4 150.00
361 A85 30o pur ('59) 1.65 15
361A A85 35o brn car ('60) 1.25 15
362 A85 40o dk red 1.25 15
a. Booklet pane of 10 85.00
363 A85 45o scarlet 1.90 15
a. Booklet pane of 10 55.00
364 A85 50o bis ('59) 6.75 15
365 A85 55o dk gray ('59) 2.25 48
366 A85 65o blue 2.50 35
367 A85 80o org brn ('60) 12.50 20
368 A85 85o ol brn ('59) 2.25 15
369 A85 90o org ('59) 1.90 15
Nos. 360-369 (11) 35.05
Set value 1.55

See Nos. 408-412.

1959, Jan. 12

370 A86 1k green 1.10 15
371 A86 1.50k dark blue 3.50 15
372 A86 2k crimson 3.50 15
373 A86 5k lilac 50.00 15
374 A86 10k dp org 5.00 25
Nos. 370-374 (5) 63.10
Set value 60

See Phosphorescence note following No. 430.

Asbjörn Kloster A87

Agricultural Society Medal A88

1959, Feb. 2

375 A87 45o vio brn 70 25

Centenary of the founding of the Norwegian Temperance Movement; Asbjörn Kloster, its founder.

1959, May 26

376 A88 45o red & ocher 80 25
377 A88 90o bl & gray 2.25 1.65

150th anniversary of the Royal Agricultural Society of Norway.

Sower — A89

Society Seal — A90

Design: 90o, Grain (vert.).

1959, Oct. 1 Photo. *Perf. 13*

378 A89 45o ocher & blk 80 25
379 A89 90o bl & blk 1.25 1.25

Agricultural College of Norway, cent.

1960, Feb. 26 Unwmk.

380 A90 45o carmine 75 25
381 A90 90o dk blue 2.00 1.40

Bicentenary of the Royal Norwegian Society of Sciences, Trondheim.

Viking Ship — A91

Designs: 25o, Caravel and fish. 45o, Sailing ship and nautical knot. 55o, Freighter and oil derricks. 90o, Passenger ship and Statue of Liberty.

1960, Aug. 27 *Perf. 12½x13*

382 A91 20o gray & blk 1.10 65
383 A91 25o yel grn & blk 1.50 1.00
384 A91 45o ver & blk 1.10 18
385 A91 55o ocher & blk 3.50 2.75
386 A91 90o Prus bl & blk 1.50 1.25
Nos. 382-386 (5) 8.70 5.83

Norwegian shipping industry.

Europa Issue, 1960

Common Design Type

1960, Sept. 19 *Perf. 13*

Size: 27x21mm

387 CD3 90o blue 75 75

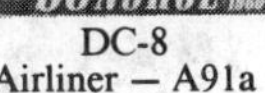

DC-8 Airliner — A91a

Javelin Thrower — A92

1961, Feb. 24 **Photo.** ***Perf. 13***
388 A91a 90o dk bl 1.00 60

10th anniv. of the Scandinavian Airlines System, SAS.

Common Design Types pictured in section at front of book.

1961, Mar. 15
389 A92 20o shown 80 48
390 A92 25o Skater 80 48
391 A92 45o Ski jumper 80 15
392 A92 90o Sailboat 1.40 1.40

Norwegian Sports Federation centenary.

Haakonshallen — A93

1961, May 25 ***Perf. 12½x13***
393 A93 45o mar & gray 70 22
394 A93 1k gray grn & gray 1.10 24

700th anniv. of Haakonshallen, castle in Bergen.

Domus Media, Oslo University A94

1961, Sept. 2 **Photo.** ***Perf. 12½x13***
395 A94 45o dk red 60 22
396 A94 1.50k Prus bl 1.25 24

150th anniversary of Oslo University.

Fridtjof Nansen — A95

1961, Oct. 10 ***Perf. 13***
397 A95 45o org red & gray 50 20
398 A95 90o chlky bl & gray 1.10 85

Birth centenary of Fridtjof Nansen, explorer.

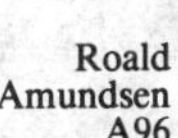
Roald Amundsen A96

Design: 90o, Explorers and tent at Pole.

1961, Nov. 10 **Unwmk.** ***Perf. 13***
399 A96 45o dl red brn & gray 90 20
400 A96 90o dk & lt bl 1.40 70

50th anniversary of Roald Amundsen's arrival at the South Pole.

Frederic Passy, Henri Dunant — A97

Vilhelm Bjerknes — A98

1961, Dec. 9 **Photo.**
401 A97 45o henna brn 45 20
402 A97 1k yel grn 1.25 30

Winners of the first Nobel Peace prize. Frederic Passy, a founder of the Interparliamentary Union, and Henri Dunant, founder of the International Red Cross.

1962, Mar. 14 ***Perf. 13***
403 A98 45o dk red & gray 35 24
404 A98 1.50k dk bl & gray 90 35

Vilhelm Bjerknes (1862-1951), physicist, mathematician, meteorologist, etc.

German Rumpler Taube over Oslo Fjord A99

1962, June 1 **Photo.**
405 A99 1.50k dl bl & blk 1.90 70

50th anniversary of Norwegian aviation.

Fir Branch and Cone — A100

1962, June 15
406 A100 45o sal & blk 75 40
407 A100 1k pale grn & blk 6.75 28

Olav Type of 1958-60

1962 **Unwmk.** ***Perf. 13x13½***
408 A85 25o slate grn 1.25 15
  a. Booklet pane of 4 150.00
  b. Booklet pane of 10 30.00
409 A85 35o emerald 4.25 15
410 A85 40o gray 4.25 75
411 A85 50o scarlet 9.50 15
  a. Booklet pane of 10 125.00
412 A85 60o violet 4.75 42
  Nos. 408-412 (5) 24.00
  Set value 1.35

Europa Issue, 1962
Common Design Type

1962, Sept. 17 **Photo.** ***Perf. 13***
Size: 37x21mm
414 CD5 50o dp rose & mar 42 28
415 CD5 90o bl & dk bl 1.40 1.00

Post Horn Type of 1893-1908 Redrawn and

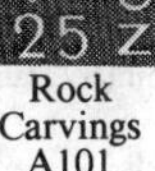

Rock Carvings A101

Boatswain's Knot A102

Designs: 30o, 55o, 85o, Rye and fish. 65o, 80o, Stave church and northern lights.

1962-63 **Engr.** ***Perf. 13x13½***
416 A10 5o rose cl 15 15
  a. Booklet pane of 4, vert. 1.65
  b. Booklet pane of 10, horiz. 8.00
417 A10 10o slate 15 15
  a. Booklet pane of 10 20.00
418 A10 15o org brn 15 15
419 A10 20o green 15 15
  a. Booklet pane of 4 8.00
420 A101 25o gray grn ('63) 1.10 15
  a. Booklet pane of 4 16.00
  b. Booklet pane of 10 20.00
421 A101 30o ol brn ('63) 4.00 2.75
422 A102 35o brt grn ('63) 32 15
423 A101 40o lake ('63) 3.00 15
424 A102 50o vermilion 4.75 15
  a. Booklet pane of 10 65.00
425 A101 55o org brn ('63) 50 45
426 A102 60o dk grnsh gray ('63) 8.50 15
427 A102 65o dk bl ('63) 3.50 15
  a. Booklet pane of 10 62.50
428 A102 80o rose lake ('63) 7.25 2.00
429 A101 85o sepia ('63) 50 22
430 A101 90o blue ('63) 32 15
  Nos. 416-430 (15) 34.34
  Set value 6.00

Nos. 416-419 have been redrawn and are similar to 1910-29 issue, with vertical lines inside oval and horizontal lines in oval frame. See Nos. 462-470, 608-615.

Phosphorescence

Nos. 370-372, 416-419, 423, 425, 428, 430, 462, 466, O65-O68, O75, O78-O82, O83-O84 and O88 have been issued on both ordinary and phosphorescent paper.

Nos. 463-465, 467-468, 510 to last number assigned, O86 and O89-O93 have been issued only on phosphorescent paper.

Camilla Collett (1813-1895), Author — A103

1963, Jan. 23 **Photo.** ***Perf. 13***
431 A103 50o red brn & tan 38 20
432 A103 90o slate & gray 1.50 1.10

Girl in Boat Loaded with Grain — A104

Still Life A105

1963, Mar. 21 **Unwmk.** ***Perf. 13***
433 A104 25o yel brn 35 25
434 A104 35o dk grn 60 45
435 A105 50o dk red 50 35
436 A105 90o dk bl 1.50 1.10

FAO "Freedom from Hunger" campaign.

River Boat A106

Design: 90o, Northern sailboat.

1963, May 20 **Unwmk.** ***Perf. 13***
437 A106 50o brn red 1.50 48
438 A106 90o blue 2.25 1.50

Tercentenary of regular postal service between Northern and Southern Norway.

Ivar Aasen — A107

1963, Aug. 5 **Photo.**
439 A107 50o dk red & gray 60 28
440 A107 90o dk bl & gray 1.25 75

150th birth anniv. of Ivar Aasen, poet and philologist.

Europa Issue, 1963
Common Design Type

1963, Sept. 14 **Unwmk.** ***Perf. 13***
Size: 27x21½mm
441 CD6 50o dl rose & org 75 42
442 CD6 90o bl & yel grn 2.50 1.50

Patterned Fabric A108

1963, Sept. 24
443 A108 25o ol & ol grn 60 40
444 A108 35o Prus bl & dk bl 85 70
445 A108 50o dk car rose & plum 60 40

Norwegian textile industry, 150th anniv.

"Loneliness" A109

Eilert Sundt A110

Paintings by Edvard Munch (1863-1944): 25o, Self-portrait (vert.). 35o, "Fertility." 90o, "Girls on Bridge" (vert.).

1963, Dec. 12 **Litho.** ***Perf. 13***
446 A109 25o black 35 22
447 A109 35o dk grn 45 35
448 A109 50o dp claret 42 32
449 A109 90o gray bl & dk bl 1.25 1.00

1964, Feb. 17 **Photo.**

Design: 50o, Beehive, Workers' Society emblem.

450 A110 25o dk grn 40 45
451 A110 50o dk red brn 38 24

Centenary of the Oslo Workers' Society.

Cato M. Guldberg and Peter Waage by Stinius Fredriksen — A111

1964, Mar. 11 **Unwmk.** ***Perf. 13***
452 A111 35o ol grn 90 45
453 A111 55o bister 2.00 1.75

Centenary of the presentation of the Law of Mass Action (chemistry) by Professors Cato M. Guldberg and Peter Waage in the Oslo Scientific Society.

Eidsvoll Building A112

Design: 90o, Storting (Parliament House).

1964, May 11 **Photo.**
454 A112 50o hn brn & blk 45 30
455 A112 90o Prus bl & dk bl 1.25 1.10

150th anniv. of Norway's constitution.

Church and Ships in Harbor A113

1964, Aug. 17 *Perf. 13*
456 A113 25o dk sl grn & buff 48 40
457 A113 90o dk bl & gray 2.00 1.65

Centenary of the Norwegian Seamen's Mission, which operates 32 stations around the world.

Europa Issue, 1964
Common Design Type

1964, Sept. 14 Photo. *Perf. 13*
458 CD7 90o dark blue 2.00 1.25

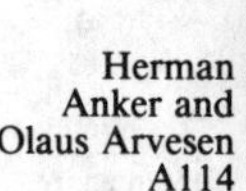

Herman Anker and Olaus Arvesen A114

1964, Oct. 31 Litho. Unwmk.
459 A114 50o rose 65 30
460 A114 90o blue 2.75 1.90

Centenary of the founding of Norwegian schools of higher education (Folk High Schools).

Types of Regular Issue, 1962-63

Designs: 30o, 45o, Rye and fish. 40o, 100o, Rock carvings. 50o, 60o, 65o, 70o, Boatswain's knot.

Two types of 60o:
I - Four twists across bottom of knot.
II - Five twists.

1964-70 Engr. *Perf. 13x13½*

462	A101	30o dl grn	80	15
463	A101	40o lt bl grn ('68)	52	15
464	A101	45o lt yel grn ('68)	1.10	75
465	A102	50o indigo ('68)	52	15
466	A102	60o brick red, II ('75)	2.50	30
a.		Booklet pane of 10	45.00	
b.		Type I	2.75	30
467	A102	65o lake ('68)	65	15
a.		Booklet pane of 10	35.00	
468	A102	70o brn ('70)	52	15
a.		Booklet pane of 10	20.00	
469	A101	100o vio bl ('70)	1.10	15
		Nos. 462-469 (8)	7.71	
		Set value		1.60

See Phosphorescence note following #430.

Coil Stamp

1965 ***Perf. 13½ Horiz.***
470 A101 30p dull grn 4.25 1.25

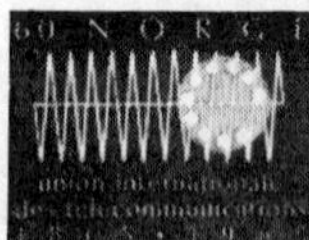

Telephone Dial and Waves — A115

Design: 90o, Television mast and antenna.

1965, Apr. 1 Engr. *Perf. 13*
471 A115 60o redsh brn 38 15
472 A115 90o slate 1.65 1.50

ITU, centenary.

Mountain Scene A116

Design: 90o, Coastal view.

1965, June 4 Unwmk. *Perf. 13*
473 A116 60o brn blk & car 52 35
474 A116 90o slate bl & car 3.75 3.25

Centenary of the Norwegian Red Cross.

Europa Issue, 1965
Common Design Type

1965, Sept. 25 Photo. *Perf. 13*
Size: 27x21mm
475 CD8 60o brick red 50 24
476 CD8 90o blue 1.50 1.40

St. Sunniva and Buildings of Bergen A117

Rondane Mountains by Harold Sohlberg A118

Design: 90o, St. Sunniva and stylized view of Bergen (horiz.).

1965, Oct. 25 ***Perf. 13***
477 A117 30o dk grn & blk 55 30
478 A117 90o bl & blk 1.65 1.25

Issued to commemorate the bicentenary of Bergen's philharmonic society "Harmonien."

1965, Nov. 29 Photo. *Perf. 13*
484 A118 1.50k dk bl 1.75 18

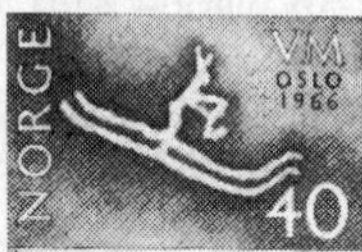

Rock Carving of Skier, Rodoy Island, c. 2000 B.C. — A120

Designs: 55o, Ski jumper. 60o, Cross country skier. 90o, Holmenkollen ski jump (vert.).

1966, Feb. 8 Engr. *Perf. 13*
486 A120 40o sepia 75 70
487 A120 55o dl grn 1.50 1.40
488 A120 60o dl red 60 20
489 A120 90o blue 1.50 1.40

World Ski Championships, Oslo, Feb. 17-27.

Open Bible and Chrismon — A121

1966, May 20 Photo. *Perf. 13*
490 A121 60o dull red 40 15
491 A121 90o slate blue 1.40 1.00

150th anniv. of the Norwegian Bible Society.

Engine-turned Bank Note Design — A122

Bank of Norway — A123

1966, June 14 Engr.
492 A122 30o green 55 32
493 A123 60o dk car rose 55 15

150th anniversary of Bank of Norway.

Johan Sverdrup A124

Nitrogen Molecule in Test Tube A125

1966, July 30 Photo. *Perf. 13*
494 A124 30o green 48 25
495 A124 60o rose lake 48 15
Set value 32

Johan Sverdrup (1816-92), Prime Minister of Norway (1884-89).

Canceled to Order
The Norwegian philatelic agency began in 1966 to sell commemorative and definitive issues canceled to order at face value.

Europa Issue, 1966
Common Design Type

1966, Sept. 26 Engr. *Perf. 13*
Size: 21x27mm
496 CD9 60o dk carmine 60 25
497 CD9 90o bl gray 1.75 1.25

1966, Oct. 29 Photo. *Perf. 13x12½*

Design: 55o, Wheat and laboratory bottle.

498 A125 40o bl & dp bl 1.25 95
499 A125 55o red, org & lil rose 2.25 1.65

Centenary of the birth of Kristian Birkeland (1867-1917), and of Sam Eyde (1866-1940), who together developed the production of nitrates.

EFTA Emblem — A126

1967, Jan. 16 Engr. *Perf. 13*
500 A126 60o rose red 52 18
501 A126 90o dark blue 2.25 1.65

European Free Trade Association. Tariffs were abolished Dec. 31, 1966, among EFTA members: Austria, Denmark, Finland, Great Britain, Norway, Portugal, Sweden, Switzerland.

Sabers, Owl and Oak Leaves A127

1967, Feb. 16 Engr. *Perf. 13*
502 A127 60o chocolate 1.00 35
503 A127 90o black 3.00 2.00

150th anniversary of higher military training in Norway.

Europa Issue, 1967
Common Design Type

1967, May 2 Photo. *Perf. 13*
Size: 21x27mm
504 CD10 60o mag & plum 55 20
505 CD10 90o bl & dk vio bl 1.50 1.25

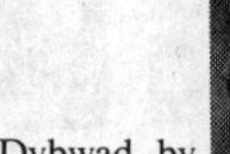

Johanne Dybwad, by Per Ung — A128

1967, Aug. 2 Photo. *Perf. 13*
506 A128 40o slate bl 52 45
507 A128 60o dk car rose 52 15

Johanne Dybwad (1867-1950), actress.

Missionary L.O. Skrefsrud A129

Ebenezer Church, Benagaria, Santal A130

1967, Sept. 26 Engr. *Perf. 13*
508 A129 60o red brn 55 15
509 A130 90o bl gray 1.25 1.10

Norwegian Santal (India) mission, cent.

Mountaineers A131

Designs: 60o, Mountain view. 90o, Glittertind mountain peak.

1968, Jan. 22 Engr. *Perf. 13*
510 A131 40o sepia 95 60
511 A131 60o brn red 52 20
512 A131 90o slate bl 1.25 1.10

Centenary of the Norwegian Mountain Touring Association.

Two Smiths A132

1968, Mar. 30 Photo. *Perf. 12½x13*
513 A132 65o dk car rose & brn 45 20
514 A132 90o bl & brn 1.10 1.10

Issued to honor Norwegian craftsmen.

A. O. Vinje — A133

Cross and Heart — A134

1968, May 21 Engr. *Perf. 13*
515 A133 50o sepia 55 35
516 A133 65o maroon 50 25

Aasmund Olafsson Vinje (1818-1870), poet, journalist and language reformer.

1968, Sept. 16 Photo.
517 A134 40o brt grn & brn red 3.25 1.25
518 A134 65o brn red & vio bl 45 25

Centenary of the Norwegian Lutheran Home Mission Society.

Cathinka Guldberg — A135

1968, Oct. 31 **Engr.** ***Perf. 13***
519 A135 50o brt bl 50 35
520 A135 65o dl red 50 20

Nursing profession; centenary of Deaconess House in Oslo. Cathinka Guldberg was a pioneer of Norwegian nursing and the first deaconess.

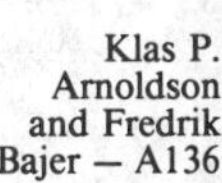

Klas P. Arnoldson and Fredrik Bajer — A136

1968, Dec. 10 **Engr.** ***Perf. 13***
521 A136 65o red brn 42 28
522 A136 90o dk bl 1.00 80

60th anniv. of the awarding of the Nobel Peace prize to Klas P. Arnoldson (1844-1916), Swedish writer and statesman, and to Fredrik Bajer (1837-1922), Danish writer and statesman.

Nordic Cooperation Issue

Five Ancient Ships — A136a

1969, Feb. 28 **Engr.** ***Perf. 13***
523 A136a 65o red 35 28
524 A136a 90o blue 1.25 1.00

Nordic Society's 50th anniversary and centenary of postal cooperation among the northern countries: Denmark, Finland, Iceland, Norway and Sweden.

Ornament from Urnes Stave Church A137

Traena Island A138

1969 **Engr.** ***Perf. 13***
526 A137 1.15k sepia 1.25 50
529 A138 3.50k bluish blk 1.00 20

Issue dates: 1.15k, Jan. 23, 3.50k, June 18.

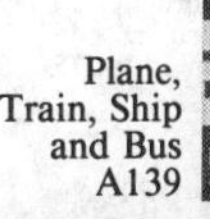

Plane, Train, Ship and Bus A139

Child Crossing Street A140

1969, Mar. 24 **Photo.** ***Perf. 13***
531 A139 50o green 60 30
532 A140 65o sl grn & dk red 42 25

No. 531 for the centenary of the publication of "Rutebok of Norway" (Communications of Norway); No. 532 publicizes traffic safety.

Europa Issue, 1969
Common Design Type
1969, Apr. 28
Size: 37x21mm
533 CD12 65o dk red & gray 65 25
534 CD12 90o chlky bl & gray 1.50 85

Johan Hjort — A141

King Olav V — A142

Design: 90o, different emblem.

1969, May 30 **Engr.** ***Perf. 13***
535 A141 40o brn & bl 90 60
536 A141 90o bl & grn 1.50 1.50

Hjort (1869-1948), zoologist and oceanographer.

1969-83 **Engr.** ***Perf. 13***
537 A142 1k lt ol grn ('70) 85 15
538 A142 1.50k dk bl ('70) 85 15
539 A142 2k dk red ('70) 85 15
540 A142 5k vio bl ('70) 1.75 15
541 A142 10k org brn ('70) 3.50 15
542 A142 20k brown 7.25 35
543 A142 50k dk ol grn ('83) 14.00 3.00
Nos. 537-543 (7) 29.05 4.10

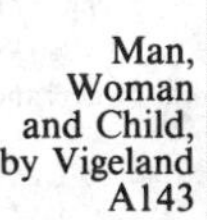

Man, Woman and Child, by Vigeland A143

Design: 65o, Mother and Child, by Gustav Vigeland.

1969, Sept. 8 **Photo.** ***Perf. 13***
545 A143 65o car rose & blk 45 35
546 A143 90o bl & blk 1.10 90

Gustav Vigeland (1869-1943), sculptor.

People A144

1969, Oct. 10
547 A144 65o Punched card 42 35
548 A144 90o shown 1.10 90

1st Norwegian census, 200th anniv.

Queen Maud A145

Pulsatilla Vernalis A146

1969, Nov. 26 **Engr.** ***Perf. 13***
549 A145 65o dk car 45 25
550 A145 90o vio bl 1.10 90

Queen Maud (1869-1938), wife of King Haakon VII.

1970, Apr. 10 **Photo.** ***Perf. 13***

European Nature Conservation Year: 40o, Wolf. 70o, Voringsfossen (waterfall). 100o, White-tailed sea eagle, horiz.

551 A146 40o sep & pale bl 1.25 60
552 A146 60o lt brn & gray 1.40 1.10
553 A146 70o pale bl & brn 1.40 48
554 A146 100o pale bl & brn 1.40 1.10

"V" for Victory A147

"Citizens" A148

Design: 100o, Convoy (horiz.).

Perf. 13x12½, 12½x13
1970, May 8 **Photo.**
555 A147 70o red & lil 1.75 45
556 A147 100o vio bl & brt grn 1.75 1.25

Norway's liberation from the Germans, 25th anniv.

1970, June 23 **Engr.** ***Perf. 13***

Designs: 70o, "The City and the Mountains." 100o, "Ships."

557 A148 40o green 1.25 65
558 A148 70o rose cl 2.50 35
559 A148 100o vio bl 1.90 1.75

City of Bergen, 900th anniversary.

Olive Wreath and Hands Upholding Globe A149

Georg Ossian Sars (1837-1927) A150

1970, Sept. 15 **Engr.** ***Perf. 13***
560 A149 70o dk car rose 2.75 50
561 A149 100o steel bl 1.75 1.25

25th anniversary of the United Nations.

1970, Oct. 15 **Engr.** ***Perf. 13***

Portraits: 50o, Hans Strom (1726-1797). 70o, Johan Ernst Gunnerus (1718-1773). 100o, Michael Sars (1805-1869).

562 A150 40o brown 90 90
563 A150 50o dl pur 1.10 65
564 A150 70o brn red 1.10 40
565 A150 100o brt bl 1.10 1.10

Issued to honor Norwegian zoologists.

Leapfrog — A151

1970, Nov. 17 **Photo.** ***Perf. 13***
566 A151 50o Ball game 55 40
567 A151 70o shown 80 20

Central School of Gymnastics, Oslo, cent.

Seal of Tonsberg A152

1971, Jan. 20 **Photo.** ***Perf. 13***
568 A152 70o dk red 48 35
569 A152 100o bl blk 95 65

City of Tonsberg, 1,100th anniversary.

Parliament A153

1971, Feb. 23
570 A153 70o red brn & lil 48 35
571 A153 100o dk bl & sl grn 95 65

Centenary of annual sessions of Norwegian Parliament.

Hand, Heart and Eye — A154

1971, Mar. 26 **Photo.** ***Perf. 13***
572 A154 50o emer & blk 55 45
573 A154 70o scar & blk 55 30

Joint northern campaign for the benefit of refugees.

"Haugianerne" by Adolph Tiedemand — A155

1971, Apr. 27 **Photo.** ***Perf. 13***
574 A155 60o dk gray 45 25
575 A155 70o brown 45 25

Hans Nielsen Hauge (1771-1824), church reformer.

Worshippers Coming to Church — A156

Design: 70o, Building first church (vert.).

1971, May 21
576 A156 70o blk & dk red 48 32
577 A156 1k blk & bl 1.90 1.25

900th anniversary of the Bishopric of Oslo.

Roald Amundsen, Antarctic Treaty Emblem A157

The Farmer and the Woman A158

1971, June 23 Engr. *Perf. 13*
578 A157 100o bl & org red 3.00 2.50

Antarctic Treaty pledging peaceful uses of and scientific cooperation in Antarctica, 10th anniv.

1971, Nov. 17 Photo. *Perf. 13*

Designs: 50o, The Preacher and the King (vert.). 70o, The Troll and the Girl. Illustrations for legends and folk tales by Erik Werenskiold.

579 A158 40o olive & blk 42 25
580 A158 50o blue & blk 42 25
581 A158 70o magenta & blk 85 25

Engine Turning A159

1972, Apr. 10 Photo. *Perf. 13*
582 A159 80o red & gold 80 35
583 A159 1.20k ultra & gold 80 75

Norwegian Savings Bank sesquicentennial.

Norway #18 — A160

Dragon's Head, Oseberg Viking Ship — A161

Engr. & Photo.

1972, May 6 *Perf. 12*
584 A160 80o shown 48 35
585 A160 1k Norway #17 70 50
a. Souvenir sheet of 2, #584-585 4.75 5.50

Centenary of the post horn stamps. No. 585a sold for 2.50k.

1972, June 7 Engr. *Perf. 13*

Ancient Artifacts: 50o, Horseman from Stone of Alstad. 60o, Horseman, wood carving, stave church, Hemsedal. 1.20k, Sword hilt, found at Lodingen.

586 A161 50o yel grn 60 55
587 A161 60o brown 1.10 1.00
588 A161 80o dl red 1.25 45
589 A161 1.20k ultra 1.10 1.00

1,100th anniversary of unification.

King Haakon VII (1872-1957) A162

"Joy" A163

1972, Aug. 3 Engr. *Perf. 13*
590 A162 80o brown org 90 35
591 A162 1.20k Prussian bl 80 70

1972, Aug. 15 Photo. *Perf. 13x13½*

Design: 1.20k, "Solidarity."

592 A163 80o brt mag 70 30
593 A163 1.20k Prussian bl 80 70

2nd Intl. Youth Stamp Exhib., INTERJUNEX 72, Kristiansand, Aug. 25-Sept. 3.

Same Overprinted "INTERJUNEX 72"

1972, Aug. 25
594 A163 80o brt mag 3.00 2.50
595 A163 1.20k Prussian bl 3.00 2.50

Opening of INTERJUNEX 72. Sold at exhibition only together with 3k entrance ticket.

"Maud" A164

"Little Man" A165

Polar Exploration Ships: 80o, "Fram." 1.20k, "Gjoa."

1972, Sept. 20 *Perf. 13½x13*
596 A164 60o ol & grn 1.25 70
597 A164 80o red & blk 1.75 35
598 A164 1.20k bl & red brn 1.75 1.50

1972, Nov. 15 Litho. *Perf. 13½x13*

Illustrations for folk tales by Theodor Kittelsen (1857-1914): 60o, The Troll who wondered how old he was. 80o, The princess riding the polar bear.

599 A165 50o green & blk 45 20
600 A165 60o blue & blk 45 35
601 A165 80o pink & blk 45 20

Dr. Armauer G. Hansen and Leprosy Bacillus Drawing — A166

Design: 1.40k, Dr. Hansen and leprosy bacillus, microscopic view.

1973, Feb. 28 Engr. *Perf. 13x13½*
602 A166 1k hn brn & bl 52 35
603 A166 1.40k dk bl & dp org 1.10 1.00

Centenary of the discovery of the Hansen bacillus, the cause of leprosy.

Europa Issue 1973
Common Design Type

1973, Apr. 30 Photo. *Perf. 12½x13*
Size: 37x20mm
604 CD16 1k red, org & lil 1.65 35
605 CD16 1.40k dk grn, grn & bl 1.10 75

Types of 1893 and 1962-63

Designs: 75o, 85o, Rye and fish. 80o, 140o, Stave church. 100o, 110o, 120o, 125o, Rock carvings.

1972-75 Engr. *Perf. 13x13½*
606 A10 25o ultra ('74) 15 15
a. Booklet pane of 4 3.00
608 A101 75o green ('73) 45 15
609 A102 80o red brn 75 15
a. Booklet pane of 10 35.00
610 A101 85o bister ('74) 60 25
611 A101 100o red ('73) 1.10 15
a. Booklet pane of 10 15.00
612 A101 110o rose car ('74) 75 15
613 A101 120o gray blue 85 50
614 A101 125o red ('75) 85 15
a. Booklet pane of 10 12.00
615 A102 140o dk bl ('73) 95 40
Nos. 606-615 (9) 6.45
Set value 1.55

Nordic Cooperation Issue

Nordic House, Reykjavik A167

1973, June 26 Engr. *Perf. 12½*
617 A167 1k multi 1.25 40
618 A167 1.40k multi 65 60

A century of postal cooperation among Denmark, Finland, Iceland, Norway and Sweden; Nordic Postal Conference, Reykjavik, Iceland.

King Olav V — A168

Jacob Aall — A169

1973, July 2 Engr. *Perf. 13*
619 A168 1k car & org brn 65 22
620 A168 1.40k bl & org brn 70 65

70th birthday of King Olav V.

1973, Aug. 22 Engr. *Perf. 13*
621 A169 1k dp claret 65 20
622 A169 1.40k dk bl gray 1.00 65

Jacob Aall (1773-1844), mill owner and industrial pioneer.

Blade Decoration A170

Viola Biflora A171

Handicraft from Lapland: 1k, Textile pattern. 1.40k, Decoration made of tin.

1973, Oct. 9 Photo. *Perf. 13x12½*
623 A170 75o blk brn & buff 40 40
624 A170 1k dp car & buff 65 30
625 A170 1.40k blk & dl bl 80 50

1973, Nov. 15 Litho. *Perf. 13*
626 A171 65o shown 48 18
627 A171 70o Speedwell 55 40
628 A171 1k Mountain heath 70 25

Surveyor in Northern Norway, 1907 — A172

Design: 1.40k, Map of South Norway Mountains, 1851.

1973, Dec. 14 Engr. *Perf. 13*
629 A172 1k red org 48 48
630 A172 1.40k slate blue 70 70

Geographical Survey of Norway, bicent.

Lindesnes — A173

Design: 1.40k, North Cape.

1974, Apr. 25 Photo. *Perf. 13*
631 A173 1k olive 80 50
632 A173 1.40k dark blue 1.50 1.50

Ferry in Hardanger Fjord, by A. Tidemand and H. Gude — A174

Classical Norwegian paintings: 1.40k, Stugunoset from Filefjell, by Johan Christian Dahl.

1974, May 21 Litho. *Perf. 13*
633 A174 1k multi 60 20
634 A174 1.40k multi 80 60

Gulating Law Manuscript, 1325 A175

King Magnus VI Lagaböter A176

1974, June 21 Engr.
635 A175 1k red & brn 55 20
636 A176 1.40k ultra & brn 95 75

700th anniv. of the National Code given by King Magnus VI Lagaböter (1238-80).

Saw Blade and Pines — A177

J.H.L. Vogt — A178

Design: 1k, Cog wheel and guard.

1974, Aug. 12 Photo. *Perf. 13*
637 A177 85o grn, ol & dk grn 1.65 1.65
638 A177 1k org, plum & dk red 1.40 60

Safe working conditions.

1974, Sept. 4 Engr. *Perf. 13*

Geologists: 85o, V. M. Goldschmidt. 1k, Theodor Kjerulf. 1.40k, Waldemar C. Brogger.

639 A178 65o ol & red brn 30 20
640 A178 85o mag & red brn 90 75
641 A178 1k org & red brn 45 25
642 A178 1.40k bl & red brn 75 60

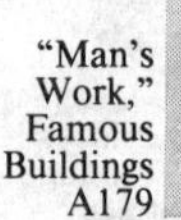

"Man's Work," Famous Buildings A179

Design: 1.40k, "Men, our brethren," people of various races.

1974, Oct. 9 Photo. *Perf. 13*
643 A179 1k grn & brn 52 20
644 A179 1.40k brn & grnsh bl 70 60

Centenary of Universal Postal Union.

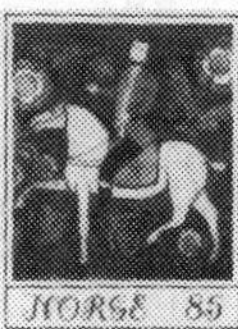

Horseback Rider
A180

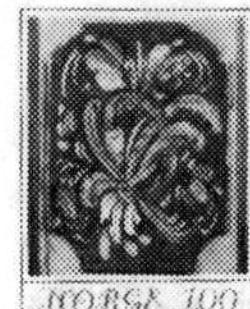

Flowers
A181

1974, Nov. 15 **Litho.** ***Perf. 13***
645 A180 85o multi 42 35
646 A181 1k multi 50 20

Norwegian folk art, rose paintings from furniture decorations.

Woman Skier, c. 1900 — A182

1975, Jan. 15 **Litho.** ***Perf. 13***
647 A182 1k shown 90 20
648 A182 1.40k Telemark turn 90 70

"Norway, homeland of skiing."

Women — A183

Nusfjord Fishing Harbor — A184

Design: Detail from wrought iron gates of Vigeland Park, Oslo.

1975, Mar. 7 **Litho.** ***Perf. 13***
649 A183 1.25k brt rose lil & dk bl 65 25
650 A183 1.40k bl & dk bl 65 65

International Women's Year.

1975, Apr. 17 **Litho.** ***Perf. 13***

Designs: 1.25k, Street in Stavanger. 1.40k, View of Roros.

651 A184 1k yel grn 85 40
652 A184 1.25k dl red 60 15
653 A184 1.40k blue 70 60

European Architectural Heritage Year.

Norwegian Krone, 1875 — A185

Ole Jacob Broch — A186

1975, May 20 **Engr.** ***Perf. 13***
654 A185 1.25k dark car 48 70
655 A186 1.40k blue 70 60

Centenary of Monetary Convention of Norway, Sweden and Denmark (1.25k); and of Intl. Meter Convention, Paris, 1875. Ole Jacob Broch (1818-1889) was first director of Intl. Bureau of Weights and Measures.

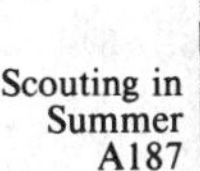

Scouting in Summer
A187

Design: 1.40k, Scouting in winter (skiers).

1975, June 19 **Litho.** ***Perf. 13***
656 A187 1.25k multi 75 35
657 A187 1.40k multi 75 75

Nordjamb 75, 14th Boy Scout Jamboree, Lillehammer, July 29-Aug. 7.

Sod Hut and Settlers
A188

Cleng Peerson and Letter from America, 1874
A189

1975, July 4
658 A188 1.25k red brn 1.00 15
659 A189 1.40k bluish blk 70 65

Sesquicentennial of Norwegian emigration to America.

Templet, Tempelfjord, Spitsbergen
A190

Miners Leaving Coal Pit
A191

Design: 1.40k, Polar bear.

1975, Aug. 14 **Engr.** ***Perf. 13***
660 A190 1k olive blk 80 50
661 A191 1.25k maroon 80 30
662 A191 1.40k Prus bl 2.25 1.75

50th anniversary of union of Spitsbergen (Svalbard) with Norway.

Microphone with Ear Phones
A192

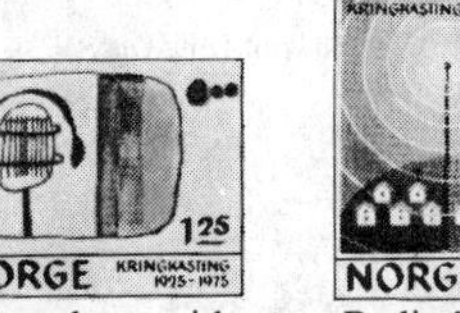

Radio Tower and Houses
A193

Designs after children's drawings.

1975, Oct. 9 **Litho.** ***Perf. 13***
663 A192 1.25k multi 40 35
664 A193 1.40k multi 60 50

50 years of broadcasting in Norway.

Annunciation
A194

Nativity
A195

Designs: 1k, Visitation. 1.40k, Adoration of the Kings. Designs are from painted vault of stave church of Al, 13th century.

1975, Nov. 14
665 A194 80o red & multi 30 20
666 A194 1k red & multi 42 20
667 A195 1.25k red & multi 42 20
668 A195 1.40k red & multi 70 45

Sigurd and Regin
A196

Halling, Hallingdal Dance
A197

1976, Jan. 20 **Engr.** ***Perf. 13***
669 A196 7.50k brown 2.25 50

Norwegian folk tale, Sigurd the Dragon-killer. Design from portal of Hylestad stave church, 13th century.

1976, Feb. 25 **Litho.** ***Perf. 13***

Folk Dances: 1k, Springar, Hordaland region. 1.25k, Gangar, Setesdal.

670 A197 80o blk & multi 45 30
671 A197 1k blk & multi 60 20
672 A197 1.25k blk & multi 60 15

Silver Sugar Shaker, Stavanger, c. 1770 — A198

Design: 1.40k, Goblet, Nostetangen glass, c. 1770.

1976, Mar. 25 **Engr.** ***Perf. 13***
673 A198 1.25k multi 55 42
674 A198 1.40k multi 70 70

Oslo Museum of Applied Art, centenary.

Ceramic Bowl Shaped Like Bishop's Mitre
A199

Europa: 1.40k, Plate and CEPT emblem. Both designs after faience works from Herrebo Potteries, c. 1760.

1976, May 3 **Litho.** ***Perf. 13***
675 A199 1.25k rose mag & brn 80 60
676 A199 1.40k brt bl & vio bl 1.10 95

The Pulpit, Lyse Fjord — A200

Gulleplet (Peak), Sogne Fjord — A201

Perf. 13 on 3 Sides

1976, May 20 **Litho.**
677 A200 1k multi 80 40
a. Booklet pane of 10 5.50
678 A201 1.25k multi 80 25
a. Booklet pane of 10 8.00

Nos. 677-678 issued only in booklets.

Graph Paper, Old and New Subjects — A202

Design: 2k, Graph of national product.

1976, July 1 **Engr.** ***Perf. 13***
679 A202 1.25k red brn 50 20
680 A202 2k dark blue 80 40

Central Bureau of Statistics, centenary.

Olav Duun on Dun Mountain
A203

1976, Sept. 10 **Engr.** ***Perf. 13***
681 A203 1.25k multi 65 20
682 A203 1.40k multi 70 60

Olav Duun (1876-1939), novelist.

"Birches" by Th. Fearnley (1802-1842)
A204

Design: 1.40k, "Gamle Furutraer" (trees), by L. Hertervig (1830-1902).

1976, Oct. 8 **Litho.** ***Perf. 13***
683 A204 1.25k multi 65 25
684 A204 1.40k multi 70 60

"April"
A205

"May"
A206

1.25 NORGE 1.25
Baldishol Tapestry — A207

Design: 80o, 1k, Details from 13th century Baldishol tapestry, found in Baldishol stave church.

1976, Nov. 5 **Litho.** ***Perf. 13***
685 A205 80o multi 45 25
686 A206 1k multi 45 25
687 A207 1.25k multi 60 25

Five Water Lilies — A208

Photo. & Engr.

1977, Feb. 2 ***Perf. 12½***
688 A208 1.25k multi 65 20
689 A208 1.40k multi 65 60

Nordic countries cooperation for protection of the environment and 25th Session of Nordic Council, Helsinki, Feb. 19.

Akershus Castle, Oslo — A209

Steinviksholm Fort, Asen Fjord — A210

Torungen Lighthouses, Arendal — A211

1977, Feb. 24 Engr. *Perf. 13*

690 A209 1.25k red 45 15
691 A210 1.30k olive brn 50 15
692 A211 1.80k blue 65 20
Set value 35

See Nos. 715-724, 772-774.

Europa Issue

Hamnoy, Lofoten, Fishing Village — A212

Huldre Falls, Loen — A213

Perf. 13 on 3 Sides

1977, May 2 Litho.

693 A212 1.25k multi 70 15
a. Booklet pane of 10 8.00
694 A213 1.80k multi 1.00 60
a. Booklet pane of 10 6.00

Nos. 693-694 issued only in booklets.

Norwegian Trees — A214

1977, June 1 Engr. *Perf. 13*

695 A214 1k Spruce 38 25
696 A214 1.25k Fir 45 25
697 A214 1.80k Birch 65 60

"Constitutionen," Norway's 1st Steamship, at Arendal — A215

Designs: 1.25k, "Vesteraalen" off Bodo, 1893. 1.30k, "Kong Haakon," 1904 and "Dronningen," 1893, off Stavanger. 1.80k, "Nordstjernen" and "Harald Jari" at pier, 1970.

1977, June 22

698 A215 1k brown 55 25
699 A215 1.25k red 65 25
700 A215 1.30k green 1.50 1.50
701 A215 1.80k blue 75 65

Norwegian ships serving coastal routes.

Fishermen and Boats A216

Fish and Fishhooks A217

1977, Sept. 22 Engr. *Perf. 13*

702 A216 1.25k buff, lt brn & dk brn 55 20
703 A217 1.80k lt bl, bl & dk bl 75 60

Men, by Halfdan Egedius — A218

Landscape, by August Cappelen A219

1977, Oct. 7 Litho. *Perf. 13*

704 A218 1.25k multi 55 20
705 A219 1.80k multi 75 60

Norwegian classical painting.

David with the Bells — A220

Christmas: 1k, Singing Friars. 1.25k, Virgin and Child (horiz.). Designs from Bible of Bishop Aslak Bolt, 13th century.

1977, Nov. 10 Litho. *Perf. 13*

Size: 21x27mm

706 A220 80o multi 42 20
707 A220 1k multi 42 15

Size: 34x27mm

708 A220 1.25k multi 42 15

Post Horn Type of 1893 and Scenic Types of 1977

Designs: 1k, Austrat Manor, 1650. 1.10k, Trondenes Chruch, early 13th Century. 1.40k, Ruins of Hamar Cathedral, 12th Century. 1.75k, Seamen's Hall, Stavern, 1926 (vert.). 2k, Tofte Estate, Dovre, 16-17th cent. (vert.). 2.25k, Oscarhall, Oslofjord, 1847 (vert.). 2.50k, Log house, Breiland, 1785. 2.75k, Damsgard Building, Lakesvag, 1770. 3k, Selje Monastery, 11th cent. 3.50k, Lighthouse, Lindesnes, 1655.

1978 Engr. *Perf. 13x13½, 13½x13*

709 A10 40o olive 15 15
710 A10 50o dull pur 18 15
711 A10 60o vermilion 22 15
712 A10 70o orange 30 22
713 A10 80o red brn 28 15
714 A10 90o brown 35 22
715 A209 1k green 35 15
716 A209 1.10k rose mag 70 18
717 A209 1.40k dark pur 48 18
718 A211 1.75k grn ('82) 55 18
719 A211 2k brn red ('82) 65 18
720 A211 2.25k dp vio ('82) 80 35
721 A209 2.50k brn red ('83) 80 18
722 A209 2.75k dp mag ('82) 1.00 65
723 A209 3k dk bl ('82) 90 35
724 A209 3.50k dp vio ('83) 1.10 45
Nos. 709-724 (16) 8.81
Set value 3.30

See Nos. 772-774.

Peer Gynt, and Reindeer by Per Krogh — A222

Henrik Ibsen, by Erik Werenskiold, 1895 — A223

1978, Mar. 10 Litho. *Perf. 13*

725 A222 1.25k buff & blk 60 28
726 A223 1.80k multi 70 70

Ibsen (1828-1906), poet and dramatist.

Heddal Stave Church, c. 1250 A224

Lenangstindene and Jaegervasstindene A225

Europa: 1.80k, Borgund stave church.

1978, May 2 Engr. *Perf. 13*

727 A224 1.25k dk brn & red 75 25
728 A224 1.80k sl grn & bl 95 70

Perf. 13 on 3 Sides

1978, June 1 Litho.

Design: 1.25k, Gaustatoppen, mountain, Telemark.

729 A225 1k multi 80 40
a. Booklet pane of 10 6.50
730 A225 1.25k multi 80 25
a. Booklet pane of 10 9.00

Nos. 729-730 issued only in booklets.

Olav V Sailing A226

Design: 1.80k, King Olav delivering royal address in Parliament (vert.).

1978, June 30 Engr. *Perf. 13*

731 A226 1.25k red brn 55 20
732 A226 1.80k vio bl 70 60

75th birthday of King Olav V.

Norway No. 107 — A227

Stamps: b, #108. c, #109. d, #110. e, #111. f, #112. g, #113. h, #114.

Perf. 13 on 3 Sides

1978, Sept. 19 Litho.

733 Booklet pane of 8 8.75 9.50
a.-h. A227 1.25k, any single 1.05 1.10

NORWEX '80 Philatelic Exhibition, Oslo, June 13-22, 1980. Booklet sold for 15k; the additional 5k went for financing the exhibition.

Willow Pipe Player A228

Musical Instruments: 1.25k, Norwegian violin. 1.80k, Norwegian zither. 7.50k, Ram's horn.

1978, Oct. 6 Engr. *Perf. 13*

734 A228 1k deep grn 35 15
735 A228 1.25k dk rose car 55 15
736 A228 1.80k dk vio bl 60 30
737 A228 7.50k gray 2.25 30

Wooden Doll, 1830 A229

Ski Jump, Huseby Hill, c. 1900 A230

Christmas: 1k, Toy town 1896-97. 1.25k, Wooden horse from Torpo in Hallingdal.

1978, Nov. 10 Litho.

738 A229 80o multi 45 20
739 A229 1k multi 45 15
740 A229 1.25k multi 45 15

1979, Mar. 2 Engr. *Perf. 13*

Designs: 1.25k, Crown Prince Olav, Holmenkollen ski jump competition, 1922. 1.80k, Cross-country race, Holmenkollen, 1976.

741 A230 1k green 42 25
742 A230 1.25k red 52 25
743 A230 1.80k blue 70 60

Huseby Hills and Holmenkollen ski competitions, centenary.

Girl, by Mathias Stoltenberg A231

Road to Briksdal Glacier A232

Portrait: 1.80k, Boy, by H. C. F. Hosenfelder.

1979, Apr. 26 Litho. *Perf. 13*

744 A231 1.25k multi 52 25
745 A231 1.80k multi 70 60

International Year of the Child.

1979, June 13 *Perf. 13 on 3 Sides*

Design: 1.25k, Boat on Skjernoysund, near Mandal.

746 A232 1k multi 75 20
a. Booklet pane of 10 5.50
747 A232 1.25k multi 75 25
a. Booklet pane of 10 7.50

Nos. 746-747 issued only in booklets.

Johan Falkberget, by Harald Dal — A233

Kylling Bridge, Verma, 1923 — A234

Design: 1.80k, "Ann-Magritt and the Hovi Bullock" (by Falkberget), monument by Kristofer Leirdal.

1979, Sept. 4 Engr. *Perf. 13*

748 A233 1.25k dp claret 55 25
749 A233 1.80k Prussian bl 70 60

Johan Falkberget (1879-1967), novelist.

1979, Oct. 5

Norwegian Engineering: 2k, Vessingsjo Dam, Nea, 1960. 10k, Stratfjord A, oil drilling platform in North Sea.

750 A234 1.25k gray brn 65 15
751 A234 2k gray bl 1.00 25
752 A234 10k brn ol 3.25 65

Souvenir Sheet

Dornier Wal over Polar Map — A235

Arctic Aviation and Polar Maps: 2k, Dirigible Norge. 2.80k, Loening air yacht amphibian. 4k, Reidar Viking DC-7C.

1979, Oct. 5 Litho. *Perf. 13*
753 Sheet of 4 6.25 6.25
a. A235 1.25k multi 1.40 1.40
b. A235 2k multi 1.40 1.40
c. A235 2.80k multi 1.40 1.40
d. A235 4k multi 1.40 1.40

Norwex '80 Intl. Phil. Exhib., Oslo, June 13-22, 1980. No. 753 sold for 15k.

Buttercup — A236

Mountain Flowers: 1k, Cinquefoil. 1.25k, Twinleaf saxifrage.

1979, Nov. 22 Litho. *Perf. 13½*
754 A236 80o multi 35 15
755 A236 1k multi 55 25
756 A236 1.25k multi 55 15

See Nos. 770-771.

Norwegian Christian Youth Assn. Centenary A237

1980, Feb. 26 Litho. *Perf. 13*
757 A237 100o shown 40 15
758 A237 180o Emblems and doves 70 50

Oyster Catcher — A238

Perf. 13 on 3 Sides

1980, Apr. 18 Litho.
759 A238 100o shown 40 15
760 A238 100o Mallard 40 15
a. Bklt. pane of 10 (5 #759, 5 #760) 4.00
761 A238 125o Dipper 40 15
762 A238 125o Great tit 40 15
a. Bklt. pane of 10 (5 #761, 5 #762) 4.50
Set value 45

Nos. 759-762 issued in booklets only.

Dish Antenna, Old Phone A239

National Telephone Service Centenary: 1.80k, Erecting telephone pole.

1980, May 9 Litho. *Perf. 13½*
763 A239 1.25k multi 48 25
764 A239 1.80k multi 70 52

Souvenir Sheet

Paddle Steamer "Bergen" A240

1980, June 13
765 Sheet of 4, multi 6.00 6.00
a. A240 1.25k shown 1.40 1.40
b. A240 2k Train, 1900 1.40 1.40
c. A240 2.80k Bus, 1940 1.40 1.40
d. A240 4k Boeing 737 1.40 1.40

NORWEX '80 Stamp Exhibition, Oslo, June 13-22. Sold for 15k.

Nordic Cooperation Issue

Vulcan as an Armourer, by Henrich Bech, 1761 — A241

Henrich Bech Cast Iron Stove Ornament: 1.80k, Hercules at a Burning Altar, 1769.

1980, Sept. 9 Engr. *Perf. 13*
766 A241 1.25k dk vio brn 55 25
767 A241 1.80k dark blue 80 50

Self-Portrait, by Christian Skredsvig (1854-1924) A242

Paintings: 1.25k, Fire, by Nikolai Astrup.

1980, Nov. 14 Litho. *Perf. 13½x13*
768 A242 1.25k multi 50 25
769 A242 1.80k multi 75 50

Mountain Flower Type of 1979

1980, Nov. 14 *Perf. 13*
770 A236 80o Sorbus aucuparia 48 15
771 A236 1k Rosa canina 48 15
Set value 24

Scenic Type of 1977

Designs: 1.50k, Stavanger Cathedral, 13th cent. 1.70k, Rosenkrantz Tower, Bergen, 13th-16th cent. 2.20k, Church of Tromsdalen (Arctic Cathedral), 1965.

Perf. 13x13½, 13½x13

1981, Feb. 26 Engr.
772 A211 1.50k brn red 48 15
773 A211 1.70k ol grn 55 25
774 A209 2.20k dk blue 70 50

Lesser White-fronted Goose A243

Nat'l Milk Producers Assn. Centenary A244

Perf. 13 on 3 Sides

1981, Feb. 26 Litho.
775 A243 1.30k shown 35 20
776 A243 1.30k Peregrine falcon 35 20
a. Booklet pane of 10 (5 each) 3.50
777 A243 1.50k Black guillemot 42 18
778 A243 1.50k Puffin 42 18
a. Booklet pane of 10 (5 each) 4.25

Nos. 775-778 issued in booklets. See Nos. 800-801, 821-822.

1981, Mar. 24 Litho. *Perf. 13x13½*
779 A244 1.10k Cow 35 20
780 A244 1.50k Goat 65 15

The Proposal, Painted Box, Nes — A245

Europa: 1.50k, The Mermaid, painted dish, Hol.

1981, May 4 Litho. *Perf. 13*
781 A245 1.50k multi 75 25
782 A245 2.20k multi 90 60

Training Ship Christian Radich — A246

Designs: 1.30k, Weighing anchor. 1.50k, Climbing sail pole (vert.).

1981, May 4 Engr.
783 A246 1.30k dk ol grn 48 25
784 A246 1.50k org red 65 25
785 A246 2.20k dark blue 70 60

Paddle Steamer Skibladner, 1856, Mjosa Lake — A247

Lake Transportation: 1.30k, Victoria, 1882, Bandak Channel. 1.50k, Faemund II, 1905, Fermund Lake. 2.30k, Storegut, 1956, Tinnsjo Lake.

1981, June 11 Engr. *Perf. 13*
786 A247 1.10k dk brown 40 32
787 A247 1.30k green 48 25
788 A247 1.50k red 65 25
789 A247 2.30k dark blue 90 65

Group Walking Arm in Arm — A248

1981, Aug. 25 Engr.
790 A248 1.50k shown 50 25
791 A248 2.20k Group, diff. 75 60

Intl. Year of the Disabled.

Interior in Blue, by Harriet Backer (1845-1932) A249

Painting: Peat Moor on Jaeren, by Kitty Lange Kielland (1843-1914).

1981, Oct. 9 Litho. *Perf. 13*
792 A249 1.50k multi 48 25
793 A249 1.70k multi 65 40

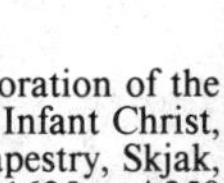

Adoration of the Infant Christ, Tapestry, Skjak, 1625 — A250

Tapestries: 1.10k, One of the Three Kings, Skjak, 1625. 1.50k, The Marriage of Cana, Storen, 18th cent.

1981, Nov. 25 Litho. *Perf. 13½*
794 A250 1.10k multi 40 15
795 A250 1.30k multi 40 15

Size: 29x37mm

796 A250 1.50k multi 55 15
Set value 36

1921 Nobel Prize Winners Christian L. Lange (1869-1938) and Hjalmar Branting (1860-1925) A251

1981, Nov. 25 Engr. *Perf. 13*
797 A251 5k black 1.75 40

World Skiing Championship, Oslo — A252

1982, Feb. 16 *Perf. 13½*
798 A252 2k Poles 65 25
799 A252 3k Skis 1.10 60

Bird Type of 1981

Perf. 13 on 3 Sides

1982, Apr. 1 Litho.
800 A243 2k Blue-throat 55 15
801 A243 2k Robin 55 15
a. Bklt. pane of 10 (5 each) 6.00

Nos. 800-801 issued only in booklets.

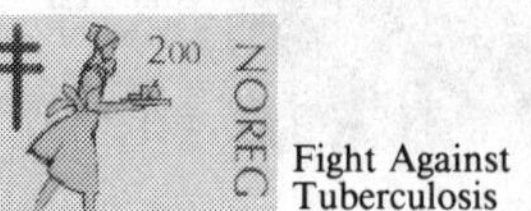

Fight Against Tuberculosis A253

1982, Apr. 1 *Perf. 13*
802 A253 2k Nurse 70 20
803 A253 3k Microscope 1.10 60

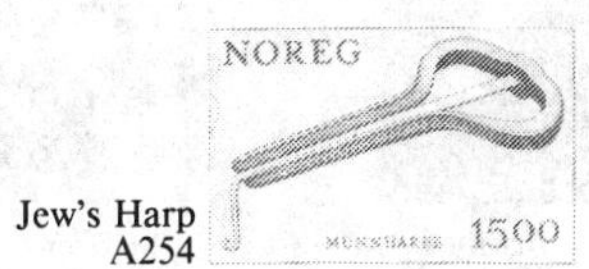

Jew's Harp A254

1982, May 3 Engr. *Perf. 13*
804 A254 15k sepia 4.00 65

Europa 1982 — A255

1982, May 3
805 A255 2k Haakon VII, 1905 85 25
806 A255 3k Prince Olav, King Haakon VII, 1945 1.40 60

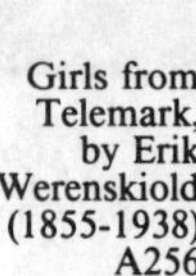

Girls from Telemark, by Erik Werenskiold (1855-1938)
A256

Design: 2k, Tone Veli at the Fence, by Henrik Sorensen (1882-1962) (vert.).

1982, June 23 Litho. *Perf. 13*
807 A256 1.75k multi 70 35
808 A256 2k multi 70 20

Consecration Ceremony, Nidaros Cathedral, Trondheim
A257

Sigrid Undset (1882-1949), Writer, by A.C. Svarstad
A258

1982, Sept. 2 Engr. *Perf. 13x13½*
809 A257 3k blue 1.10 55

Reign of King Olav, 25th anniv.

1982, Oct. 1 Litho. *Perf. 13*

Painting: 1.75k, Bjornstjerne Bjornson (1832-1910), writer, by Erik Werenskiold (horiz.).

810 A258 1.75k multi 65 30
811 A258 2k multi 75 25

A souvenir sheet containing Nos. 810-811 was prepared by the Norwegian Philatelic Association.

Graphical Union of Norway Centenary
A259

1982, Oct. 1
812 A259 2k "A" 65 15
813 A259 3k Type 1.00 42

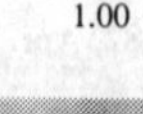

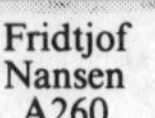
Fridtjof Nansen
A260

Christmas
A261

1982, Nov. 15 Engr. *Perf. 13½x13*
814 A260 3k dark blue 1.10 50

Fridtjof Nansen (1861-1930) polar explorer, 1922 Nobel Peace Prize winner.

Perf. 13 on 3 Sides
1982, Nov. 15 Litho.

Painting: Christmas Tradition, by Adolf Tidemand (1814-1876).

815 A261 1.75k multi 60 32
a. Booklet pane of 10 6.00

Farm Dog — A262

1983, Feb. 16 Litho. *Perf. 13x13½*
816 A262 2k shown 60 15
817 A262 2.50k Elk hound 80 15
818 A262 3.50k Hunting dog 1.10 50

Nordic Cooperation Issue — A263

1983, Mar. 24 Litho. *Perf. 13*
819 A263 2.50k Mountains 90 15
820 A263 3.50k Fjord 1.25 65

Bird Type of 1981
1983, Apr. 14 *Perf. 13 on 3 Sides*
821 A243 2.50k Goose 80 15
822 A243 2.50k Little auk 80 15
a. Bklt. pane of 10 (5 each #821-822) 8.00

Nos. 821-822 issued only in booklets.

Europa
A264

Designs: 2.50k, Edvard Grieg (1843-1907), composer and his Piano Concerto in A-minor. 3.50k, Niels Henrik Abel (1802-1829), mathematician, by Gustav Vigeland (vert.).

1983, May 3 Engr. *Perf. 13*
823 A264 2.50k red org 1.10 15
824 A264 3.50k dk bl & grn 1.65 40

World Communications Year — A265

Symbolic arrow designs.

1983, May 3 Litho.
825 A265 2.50k multi 90 25
826 A265 3.50k multi 1.25 60

80th Birthday of King Olav V, July 2 — A266

1983, June 22 Engr. *Perf. 13x13½*
827 A266 5k green 1.65 40

Jonas Lie (1833-1908), Writer
A267

Northern Ships
A268

1983, Oct. 7 Engr. *Perf. 13½x13*
828 A267 2.50k red 90 15

1983, Oct. 7 Litho.
829 A268 2k Nordlandsfemboring 70 15
830 A268 3k Nordlandsjekt 1.10 50

Christmas 1983 — A269

Paintings: 2k, The Sleigh Ride by Axel Ender (1853-1920). 2.50k, The Guests are Arriving by Gustav Wenzel (1859-1927).

Perf. 13 on 3 sides
1983, Nov. 17 Litho.
831 A269 2k multi 60 15
a. Booklet pane of 10 6.00
832 A269 2.50k multi 90 15
a. Booklet pane of 10 9.00

Postal Services
A270

1984, Feb. 24 Litho. *Perf. 13½x13*
833 A270 2k Counter service 70 20
834 A270 2.50k Sorting 85 15
835 A270 3.50k Delivery 1.10 45

Freshwater Fishing
A271

Christopher Hansteen (1784-1873), Astronomer
A272

1984, Apr. 10 Engr. *Perf. 13*
836 A271 2.50k shown 80 15
837 A271 3k Salmon fishing 1.00 45
838 A271 3.50k Ocean fishing 1.10 45

1984, Apr. 10
839 A272 3.50k Magnetic meridians, parallels, horiz. 1.10 45
840 A272 5k shown 1.50 45

Europa (1959-84)
A273

Produce, Spices
A274

1984, June 4 Litho. *Perf. 13*
841 A273 2.50k multi 80 15
842 A273 3.50k multi 1.10 45

1984, June 4 *Perf. 13*
843 A274 2k shown 60 15
844 A274 2.50k Flowers 75 15
Set value 24

Horticultural Society centenary.

Worker Bees — A275

1984, June 4
845 A275 2.50k shown 80 15
846 A275 2.50k Rooster 80 15
Set value 24

Centenaries: Beekeeping Society (No. 845); Poultry-breeding Society (No. 846).

Ludvig Holberg (1684-1754), Writer, by J.M. Bernigeroth
A276

Illustrations from Children's Stories by Thorbjorn Egner
A278

Norwegian Weekly Press Sesquicentennial
A277

1984, Oct. 5 Engr. *Perf. 13*
847 A276 2.50k lake 80 15

1984, Oct. 5 Litho. & Engr.
848 A277 2.50k Children reading 70 15
849 A277 3.50k First edition 1.10 45

Perf. 13½x13 on 3 sides
1984, Nov. 15 Litho.
850 A278 2k Karius & Baktus 60 15
851 A278 2k Tree Shrew 60 15
a. Bklt. pane of 10 (5 each #850-851) 6.00
852 A278 2.50k Cardamom Rovers 75 15
853 A278 2.50k Chief Constable Bastian 75 15
a. Bklt. pane of 10 (5 each #852-853) 7.50
Set value 48

Nos. 850-853 issued only in booklets.

Parliament Centenary
A279

1984, Nov. 15 Engr. *Perf. 13½x13*
854 A279 7.50k Sverdrup Govt. parliament, 1884 2.25 80

Antarctic Mountains — A280

1985, Apr. 18 Litho. *Perf. 13*
855 A280 2.50k The Saw Blade 70 15
856 A280 3.50k The Chopping Block 1.10 45

Liberation from the German Occupation Forces, 40th Anniv. A281

1985, May 8 Engr. *Perf. 13x13½*

857 A281 3.50k dk bl & red 1.00 45

Norwegian Artillery A282

Anniversaries: 3k, Norwegian Artillery, 300th. 4k, Artillery Officers Training School, 200th.

1985, May 22 Litho. *Perf. 13½x13*

858 A282 3k multi 80 55
859 A282 4k multi 1.10 70

Kongsten Fort, 300th Anniv. A283

1985, May 22

860 A283 2.50k multi 75 25

Europa A284

Intl. Youth Year A285

Designs: 2.50k, Torgeir Augundsson (1801-1872), fiddler. 3.50k, Ole Bull (1810-1880), composer, violinist.

1985, June 19 Engr.

861 A284 2.50k brn lake 75 15
862 A284 3.50k dk bl 1.10 45

1985, June 19 Litho.

Stone and bronze sculptures: 2k, Boy and Girl, detail, Vigeland Museum, Oslo. 3.50k, Fountain, detail, Vigeland Park, Oslo.

863 A285 2k multi 60 25
864 A285 3.50k multi 1.10 70

Electrification of Norway, Cent. — A286

1985, Sept. 6 Engr. *Perf. 13½x13*

865 A286 2.50k Glomfjord Dam penstock 75 20
866 A286 4k Linemen 1.25 70

Public Libraries, 200th Anniv. A287

Designs; 2.50k, Carl Deichman (1705-1780), Public Libraries System founder. 10k, Modern library interior, horiz.

1985, Oct. 4

867 A287 2.50k hn brn & yel brn 65 20
868 A287 10k dk grn 2.50 1.00

Ship Navigation A288

Lithographed & Engraved

1985, Nov. 14 *Perf. 13x13½*

869 A288 2.50k Dredger Berghavn, 1980 75 20
870 A288 5k Sextant and chart, 1791 1.50 70

Port Authorities 250th anniv., Hydrographic Services bicent.

Christmas Wreath A289

Bullfinches A290

Booklet Stamps

Perf. 13½ on 3 Sides

1985, Nov. 14 Litho.

871 A289 2k multi 60 20
a. Booklet pane of 10 6.00
872 A290 2.50k multi 75 20
a. Booklet pane of 10 7.50

World Biathlon Championships, Feb. 18-23 — A291

1986, Feb. 18 *Perf. 13x13½*

873 A291 2.50k shown 65 20
874 A291 3.50k Shooting upright 1.00 70

Ornaments A291

Fauna A292

Mushrooms — A293

Litho. & Engr.

1986-90 *Perf. 13½x13*

875 A291 2.10k Sun 65 45
876 A291 2.30k Fish 68 52
877 A292 2.60k Fox 78 58
878 A291 2.70k Flowers, wheat 78 58
879 A292 2.90k Capercaillie 95 72
880 A292 3k Ermine 90 68
881 A292 3.20k Mute swan 1.00 75
882 A292 3.80k Reindeer 1.20 90
883 A291 4k Star 1.25 82
883A A292 4k Squirrel 1.20 90
883B A292 4.50k Beaver 1.40 1.05
Nos. 875-883B (11) 10.79 7.95

Issue dates: 2.10k, No. 883, Feb. 18. 2.30k, 2.70k, Feb. 12, 1987. 2.90k, 3.80k, Feb. 18, 1988. 2.60k, 3k, No. 883A, Feb. 20, 1989. 3.20k, 4.50k, Feb. 23, 1990.

See Nos. 958-959.

Booklet Stamps

Perf. 13½x13 on 3 Sides

1987-89 Litho.

884 A293 2.70k Cantharellus tubaeformis 80 60
885 A293 2.70k Rozites caperata 80 60
a. Bklt. pane, 5 #884, 5 #885 8.00
886 A293 2.90k Lepista nuda 95 72
887 A293 2.90k Lactarius deterrimus 95 72
a. Bklt. pane, 5 #886, 5 #887 9.50
888 A293 3k Cantharellus cibarius 90 68
889 A293 3k Suillus luteus 90 68
a. Bklt. pane, 5 #888, 5 #889 9.00

Issue dates: 2.70k, May 8, 1987. 2.90k, Apr. 26, 1988. 3k, Feb. 20, 1989.

Natl. Federation of Craftsmen, Cent. — A294

1986, Apr. 11 Engr.

890 A294 2.50k Stone cutter 55 25
891 A294 7k Carpenter 1.65 1.00

Europa A295

1986, Apr. 11 Litho. *Perf. 13*

892 A295 2.50k Bird, industry 55 30
893 A295 3.50k Acid rain 80 35

Nordic Cooperation Issue A296

Sister towns.

1986, May 27 *Perf. 13½x13*

894 A296 2.50k Moss 55 30
895 A296 4k Alesund 95 50

Famous Men — A297

Designs: 2.10k, Hans Poulson Egede (1686-1758), missionary, and map of Norway and Greenland. 2.50k, Herman Wildenvey (1886-1959), poet, and poem carved in Seaman's Commemoration Hall, Stavern. 3k, Tore Orjasaeter (1886-1968), poet, and antique cupboard, Skjak. 4k, Engebret Soot, engineer, and canal lock, Orje.

Engr., Litho. & Engr. (#897)

1986, Oct. 17 *Perf. 13x13½*

896 A297 2.10k multi 48 45
897 A297 2.50k multi 55 52
898 A297 3k multi 65 65
899 A297 4k multi 95 88

Christmas — A298

Stained glass windows by Gabriel Kielland, Nidaros Cathedral, Trondheim: 2.10k, Olav Kyrre Founding The Diocese in Nidaros. 2.50k, The King and the Peasant at Sul.

Perf. 13½ on 3 Sides

1986, Nov. 26 Litho.

Booklet Stamps

900 A298 2.10k multi 57 42
a. Booklet pane of 10 5.75
901 A298 2.50k multi 67 50
a. Booklet pane of 10 6.75

Intl. Peace Year — A299

Lithographed & Engaved

1986, Nov. 26 *Perf. 13½x13*

902 A299 15k brt grn, org & lt bl 3.75 3.00

A300

1987, Feb. 12 Litho. *Perf. 13½*

903 A300 3.50k red, yel & dk bl 1.00 75
904 A300 4.50k bl, yel & grn 1.30 1.00

Europa A301

Modern architecture: 2.70k, Wood. 4.50k, Glass and stone.

1987, Apr. 3 Litho. *Perf. 13½x13*

905 A301 2.70k multi 80 60
906 A301 4.50k multi 1.30 1.00

Odelsting (Norwegian Assembly) Voting on Law Administering Local Councils, 150th Anniv. A302

1987, Apr. 3 Engr. *Perf. 13x13½*

907 A302 12k dk grn 3.50 2.65

Miniature Sheet

Red Crescent-Red Cross Rehabilitation Center, Mogadishu, Somalia — A303

1987, May 8 Litho. Perf. 13½x13
908 A303 4.50k multi 1.40 1.40

See Somalia Nos. 576-577.

Sandvig Collection, Maihaugen Open-air Museum A305

1987, June 10 Engr. Perf. 13x13½
911 A305 2.70k Bjornstad Farm, Vaga 80 60
912 A305 3.50k Horse and Rider, by Christen E. Listad 1.05 80

Churchyard, Inspiration for Valen's Churchyard by the Sea — A306

Designs: 4.50k, Fartein Valen (1887-1952), Composer.

Perf. 13x13½, 13½x13
1987, Aug. 25 Engr.
913 A306 2.30k emer grn & dark blue 65 48
914 A306 4.50k dark brown 1.25 95

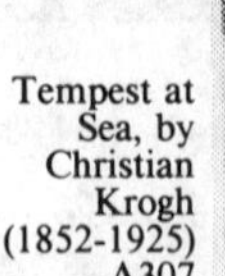

Tempest at Sea, by Christian Krogh (1852-1925) A307

Painting: 5k, The Farm, by Gerhard Munthe (1849-1929).

1987, Oct. 9 Litho. Perf. 13½x13
915 A307 2.70k multi 85 65
916 A307 5k multi 1.60 1.20

Norwegian Horse Breeds A308

Litho. & Engr.
1987, Nov. 12 Perf. 13x13½
917 A308 2.30k Dales 72 58
918 A308 2.70k Fjord 85 65
919 A308 4.50k Nordland 1.40 1.05

Christmas A309

Perf. 13½x13 on 3 sides
1987, Nov. 12 Litho.
920 A309 2.30k Children making tree ornaments 72 58
a. Booklet pane of 10 7.25
921 A309 2.70k Baking ginger-snaps 85 65
a. Booklet pane of 10 8.50

Salvation Army in Norway, Cent. A310

1988, Feb. 18 Perf. 13½
922 A310 2.90k multi 95 72
923 A310 4.80k multi 1.50 1.15

European North-South Solidarity Campaign A311

1988, Apr. 26 Perf. 13x13½
924 A311 25k multi 8.00 6.00

Defense Forces Activities A312

Defense Forces, 300th anniv.: 2.50k, Fortress construction. 2.90k, Army Signal Corps on duty. 4.60k, Pontoon bridge under construction, Corps of Engineers.

1988, Apr. 26 Engr.
925 A312 2.50k dark green 80 60
926 A312 2.90k car lake 95 72
927 A312 4.60k dark blue 1.50 1.15

Europa A313

Transport: 2.90k, *Prinds Gustav* passing Lofoten Isls., 1st passenger steamer in northern Norway, sesquicent. 3.80k, Heroybrua Bridge, between Leinoy and Blankholm, 1976.

Litho. & Engr.
1988, July 1 Perf. 13x13½
928 A313 2.90k blue black & ver 95 72
929 A313 3.80k blue black, pink & ver 1.25 95

A souvenir sheet containing 2 No. 928 exists, though it is invalid for postage. Sold for 30k.

85th Birthday of King Olav V — A314

Reign of King Christian IV (1577-1648), 400th Anniv. — A315

Designs: No. 930, Portrait, c. 1988. No. 931a, Arrival in 1905 after Norway declared independence from Sweden. No. 931b, Olav in snowstorm at Holmenkollen.

1988, July 1 Litho. Perf. 13½x13
930 A314 2.90k multi 95 72

Souvenir Sheet
931 Sheet of 3 2.85 2.85
a. A314 2.90k org red, black & ultra 95 95
b. A314 2.90k multi 95 95
c. A314 2.90k like No. 930, no date 95 95

Litho. & Engr.
1988, Oct. 7 Perf. 13½x13

Designs: 10k, Reverse of a rixdaler struck in Christiania (Oslo), 1628, and excerpt of a mining decree issued by Christian IV.

932 A315 2.50k black & buff 75 58
933 A315 10k multi 3.00 2.25

Miniature Sheet

Handball A316

Ball sports: b, Soccer. c, Basketball. d, Volleyball.

1988, Oct. 7 Litho. Perf. 13½x13
934 Sheet of 4 4.50 4.50
a.-d. A316 2.90k any single 1.10 1.10

Stamp Day. No. 934 sold for 15k.

Christmas — A317

Ludvig, a cartoon character created by Kjell Aukrust: No. 935, With ski pole. No. 936, Reading letter.

Perf. 13½x13 on 3 sides
1988, Nov. 15 Litho.
Booklet Stamps
935 A317 2.90k multi 90 68
936 A317 2.90k multi 90 68
a. Bklt. pane of 10, 5 #935, 5 #936 9.00

World Cross-Country Running Championships, Stavanger, Mar. 19 — A318

1989, Feb. 20 Litho. Perf. 13x13½
937 A318 5k multi 1.50 1.15

Port City Bicentennials A319

Nordic Cooperation Issue A320

Litho. & Engr.
1989, Apr. 20 Perf. 13½x13
938 A319 3k Vardo 90 68
939 A319 4k Hammerfest 1.20 90

1989, Apr. 20 Litho. Perf. 13x13½

Folk costumes.

940 A320 3k Setesdal (woman) 90 68
941 A320 4k Kautokeino (man) 1.20 90

Europa 1989 A321

Public Primary Schools, 250th Anniv. A322

Children's games.

1989, June 7 Litho. Perf. 13x13½
942 A321 3.70k Building snow-man 1.10 82
943 A321 5k Cat's cradle 1.50 1.15

Litho. & Engr.
1989, June 7 Perf. 13½x13
944 A322 2.60k shown 80 60

Engr.
945 A322 3k Child learning to write 90 68

Souvenir Sheet

Winter Olympic Gold Medalists from Norway A323

Portraits: a, Bjoerg Eva Jensen, women's 3000-meter speed skating, 1980. b, Eirik Kvalfoss, 10k biathlon, 1984. c, Tom Sandberg, combined cross-country and ski jumping, 1984. d, Women's Nordic ski team, 20k relay, 1984.

1989, Oct. 6 Litho. Perf. 13½x13
946 Sheet of 4 5.60 5.60
a.-d. A323 4k any single 1.40 1.40

Sold for 20k to benefit Olympic sports promotion.
See Nos. 984, 997.

Souvenir Sheet

Impression of the Countryside, 1982, by Jakob Weidemann — A324

1989, Oct. 6

947 A324 Sheet of 4 4.20 4.20
a.-d. 3k any single 1.05 1.05

Stamp Day. Sold for 15k to benefit philatelic promotion.

Writers A325

Portraits: 3k, Arnulf Overland (1889-1968), poet. 25k, Hanna Winsnes (1789-1872), author.

Litho. & Engr.

1989, Nov. 24 ***Perf. 13x13½***

948 A325 3k dk red & brt bl 85 62
949 A325 25k multi 7.00 5.25

Manors A326

1989, Nov. 24 **Engr.** ***Perf. 13***

950 A326 3k Manor at Larvik 85 62
951 A326 3k Rosendal Barony 85 62

Christmas Decorations — A327

Perf. 13 on 3 sides

1989, Nov. 24 **Litho.**

Booklet Stamps

952 A327 3k Star 85 62
953 A327 3k Round ornament 85 62
a. Bklt. pane of 10, 5 #952, 5 #953 8.50

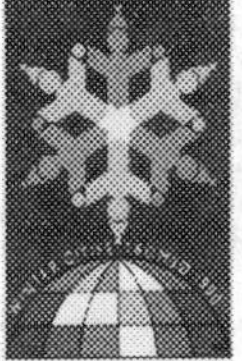

Winter City Events, Tromso — A328

1990, Feb. 23 **Litho.** ***Perf. 13½***

954 A328 5k multicolored 1.55 1.15

Fauna Type of 1988

1991 **Litho. & Engr.** ***Perf. 13***

958 A292 5.50k Lynx 1.75 1.30
959 A292 6.40k Owl 2.00 1.50

Issue date: Feb. 21.

This is an expanding set. Numbers will change if necessary.

Posthorn Type of 1893

1991 **Engr.** ***Perf. 12½x13***

964 A10 6k grn & red vio 1.80 1.35
965 A10 7k red brn & bl 2.10 1.60
966 A10 8k red vio & grn 2.40 1.80
967 A10 9k ultra & red brn 2.65 2.00

Issue date: Nov. 22. This is an expanding set. Numbers may change.

Orchids — A332

Perf. 13½x13 on 3 Sides

1990 **Litho.** **Booklet Stamps**

970 A332 3.20k *Dactylorhiza fuchsii* 1.00 75
971 A332 3.20k *Epipactis atrorubens* 1.00 75
a. Bklt. pane, 5 #970, 5 #971 10.00

Issue dates: Nos. 970-971, Feb. 23.
This is an expanding set. Numbers will change if necessary.

German Invasion of Norway, 40th Anniv. — A334

Designs: 3.20k, King Haakon VII's monogram, merchant navy, air force, Norwegian Home Guard and cannon Moses. 4k, Recapture of Narvik, May 28, 1940, by the Polish, British, Norwegian and French forces.

1990, Apr. 9 **Litho.** ***Perf. 13x13½***

975 A334 3.20k shown 1.00 75
976 A334 4k multicolored 1.25 92

Souvenir Sheet

Penny Black, 150th Anniv. — A335

Stamps on stamps: b, Norway #1.

1990, Apr. 9 ***Perf. 13½x13***

977 Sheet of 2 4.60 4.60
a.-b. A335 5k any single 2.30 2.30

Sold for 15k.

Tordenskiold (Peter Wessel, 1690-1720), Naval Hero — A336

1990, June 14 **Litho. & Engr.**

978 A336 3.20k Portrait 1.00 75
979 A336 5k Coat of arms 1.50 1.15

Europa 1990 — A337

Post offices.

1990, June 14 **Litho.** ***Perf. 13x13½***

980 A337 3.20k Trondheim 1.00 75
981 A337 4k Longyearbyen 1.25 92

Johan Severin Svendsen (1840-1911), Composer — A338

1990, Oct. 5 **Litho. & Engr.** ***Perf. 13***

982 A338 2.70k shown 85 62
983 A338 15k Monument by Fredriksen 4.65 3.50

Winter Olympic Type of 1989

Souvenir Sheet

Gold medal winners: a, Thorleif Haug, skier, 1924. b, Sonja Henie, figure skater, 1928, 1932, 1936. c, Ivar Ballangrud, speed skater, 1928, 1936. d, Hjalmar Andersen, speed skater, 1952.

1990, Oct. 5 **Litho.** ***Perf. 13½x13***

984 Sheet of 4 6.25 6.25
a.-d. A323 4k any single 1.55 1.55

Sold for 20k to benefit Olympic sports promotion.

Lars Olof Jonathan Soderblom (1866-1931), 1930 Nobel Peace Prize Winner A339

Litho & Engr.

1990, Nov. 23 ***Perf. 13***

985 A339 30k bl, brn & car rose 10.00 7.50

Christmas — A340

Children's drawings: No. 987, Church, stars, and Christmas tree.

Perf. 13 on 3 sides

1990, Nov. 23 **Litho.**

986 A340 3.20k multicolored 1.10 80
987 A340 3.20k multicolored 1.10 80
a. Bklt. pane, 5 each #986-987 11.00

Ship Building Industry A341

1991, Feb. 21 **Litho.** ***Perf. 13½x13***

988 A341 5k multicolored 1.60 1.20

Europa — A342

1991, Apr. 16 **Litho.** ***Perf. 13***

989 A342 3.20k ERS-1 90 70
990 A342 4k Andoya rocket range 1.15 85

City of Christiansand, 350th Anniv. A343

Litho. & Engr.

1991, Apr. 16 ***Perf. 13***

991 A343 3.20k Early view 90 70
992 A343 5.50k Modern view 1.55 1.15

Lifeboat Service, Cent. A344

Tourism A345

Designs: 3.20k, Rescue boat, Skomvaer III, horiz. 27k, Sailboat Colin Archer.

1991, June 7 **Litho & Engr.** ***Perf. 13***

993 A344 3.20k multicolored 90 70
994 A344 27k multicolored 7.50 5.65

1991, June 7 **Litho.** ***Perf. 13½x13***

Designs: 3.20k, Fountain, Vigeland Park. 4k, Globe, North Cape.

995 A345 3.20k multicolored 90 70
996 A345 4k multicolored 1.10 85

Winter Olympics Type of 1989

Souvenir Sheet

Gold medal winners: a, Birger Ruud, ski jumping. b, Johan Grottumsbraten, cross country skiing. c, Knut Johannesen, speed skating. d, Magnar Solberg, biathlon.

1991, Oct. 11 **Litho.** ***Perf. 13½x13***

997 Sheet of 4 5.60 5.60
a.-d. A323 4k any single 1.40 1.40

Sold for 20k to benefit Olympic sports promotion.

Souvenir Sheet

Natl. Stamp Day — A346

Designs: a, Hands engraving. b, Magnifying glass above hands. c, View of hands through magnifying glass. d, Printed label being removed from plate.

1991, Oct. 11 ***Perf. 13x13½***

998 Sheet of 4 5.60 5.60
a. A346 2.70k multicolored 1.25 1.25
b. A346 3.20k multicolored 1.00 1.00
c. A346 4k multicolored 1.40 1.40
d. A346 5k multicolored 2.00 2.00

Sold for 20k.

Christmas — A347

Design: No. 1000, People with lantern.

Perf. 13½x13 on 3 Sides

1991, Nov. 22 Litho.

Booklet Stamps

999	A347	3.20k multicolored	95	75
1000	A347	3.20k multicolored	95	75
a.		Bklt. pane, 5 each #999-1000	9.50	

SEMI-POSTAL STAMPS

North Cape Issue

North Cape — SP1

Perf. 13½x14

1930, June 28 Wmk. 160 Photo.

Size: 33¼x21½mm

B1	SP1	15o + 25o blk brn	1.65	1.65
B2	SP1	20o + 25o car	20.00	20.00
B3	SP1	30o + 25o ultra	65.00	65.00

The surtax was given to the Tourist Association. See Nos. B9-B10, B28-B30, B54-B56, B59-B61.

Radium Hospital SP2

1931, Apr. 1 ***Perf. 14½x13½***

B4	SP2	20o + 10o carmine	8.50	2.75

The surtax aided the Norwegian Radium Hospital.

Fridtjof Nansen — SP3

1935, Dec. 13 ***Perf. 13½***

B5	SP3	10o + 10o green	1.25	1.50
B6	SP3	15o + 10o red brn	6.00	7.25
B7	SP3	20o + 10o crimson	95	1.20
B8	SP3	30o + 10o brt ultra	5.00	6.00

The surtax aided the International Nansen Office for Refugees.

North Cape Type of 1930

1938, June 20 ***Perf. 13x13½***

Size: 27x21mm

B9	SP1	20o + 25o brn car	2.75	4.00
B10	SP1	30o + 25o dp ultra	11.00	13.00

Surtax given to the Tourist Assoc.

For unused stamps, more recent issues are valued as never hinged, with the beginning point determined on a country-by-country basis. Notes to show the beginning points are prominently placed in the text.

Queen Maud SP4

Fridtjof Nansen SP5

Perf. 13x13½

1939, July 24 Photo. Unwmk.

B11	SP4	10o + 5o brt grn	40	40
B12	SP4	15o + 5o red brn	40	40
B13	SP4	20o + 5o scarlet	40	40
B14	SP4	30o + 5o brt ultra	40	40

The surtax was used for charities.

1940, Oct. 21

B15	SP5	10o + 10o dk grn	1.25	2.25
B16	SP5	15o + 10o henna brn	1.75	3.25
B17	SP5	20o + 10o dark red	42	1.10
B18	SP5	30o + 10o ultra	1.25	2.25

The surtax was used for war relief work.

Ancient Sailing Craft off Lofoten Islands — SP6

1941, May 16

B19	SP6	15o + 10o deep blue	90	90

Haalogaland Exposition. Surtax for relief fund for families of lost fishermen.

Nos. 177-180, 267, B19, B32-B34 and B38-B41 were demonetized from May 15, 1945 until Sept. 1, 1981. Used values are for stamps canceled after this period. Stamps with dated cancellations prior to May 15, 1945 sell for more. False cancellations exist.

Colin Archer and Lifeboat SP7

Lifeboat SP8

1941, July 9 ***Perf. 13x13½, 13½x13***

B20	SP7	10o + 10o yel grn	95	1.65
B21	SP7	15o + 10o dk ol brn	1.25	1.90
B22	SP8	20o + 10o brt red	38	55
B23	SP8	30o + 10o ultra	2.50	4.00

Norwegian Lifeboat Society, 50th anniv.

Legionary, Norwegian and Finnish Flags SP9

Vidkun Quisling SP10

1941, Aug. 1 ***Perf. 13½x13***

B24	SP9	20o + 80o scar ver	50.00	80.00

The surtax was for the Norwegian Legion.

1942, Feb. 1

B25	SP10	20o + 30o henna	4.00	*13.00*

Overprinted in Red **1–2–1942**

B26	SP10	20o + 30o henna	4.00	*13.00*

Inauguration of Quisling as prime minister.

Catalogue values for unused stamps in this section, from this point to the end of the section, are for Never Hinged items.

Vidkun Quisling SP11

Frontier Guardsmen Emblem SP12

1942, Sept. 26 ***Perf. 13***

B27	SP11	20o + 30o henna	45	*3.00*

8th annual meeting of Nasjonal Samling, Quisling's party. The surtax aided relatives of soldiers killed in action.

North Cape Type of 1930

1943, Apr. 1

Size: 27x21mm

B28	SP1	15o + 25o ol brn	1.25	1.25
B29	SP1	20o + 25o dk car	1.50	1.50
B30	SP1	30o + 25o chlky bl	2.25	2.25

The surtax aided the Tourist Association.

1943, Aug. 2 Unwmk.

B31	SP12	20o + 30o henna	75	*3.25*

The surtax aided the Frontier Guardsmen (Norwegian Nazi Volunteers).

Fishing Village — SP13

Drying Grain — SP14

Barn in Winter — SP15

1943, Nov. 10

B32	SP13	10o + 10o gray grn	1.50	1.00
B33	SP14	20o + 10o henna	1.50	1.00
B34	SP15	40o + 10o grnsh blk	1.50	1.00

The surtax was for winter relief.

The Baroy Sinking SP16

Sanct Svithun Aflame SP17

Design: 20o+10o, "Irma" sinking.

1944, May 20

B35	SP16	10o + 10o gray grn	1.40	*3.50*
B36	SP17	15o + 10o dk olive	1.40	*3.50*
B37	SP16	20o + 10o henna	1.40	*3.50*

The surtax aided victims of wartime ship sinkings, and their families.

Spinning SP19

Plowing SP20

Tree Felling SP21

Child Care SP22

1944, Dec. 1

B38	SP19	5o + 10o dp mag	90	90
B39	SP20	10o + 10o dk yel grn	90	90
B40	SP21	15o + 10o choc	90	90
B41	SP22	20o + 10o henna	90	90

The surtax was for National Welfare.

Red Cross Nurse — SP23

Crown Prince Olav — SP24

1945, Sept. 22

B42	SP23	20o + 10o red	1.00	1.10

80th anniv. of the founding of the Norwegian Red Cross. The surtax was for that institution.

For surcharge see No. B47.

1946, Mar. 4 Unwmk.

B43	SP24	10o + 10o ol grn	45	40
B44	SP24	15o + 10o ol brn	45	40
B45	SP24	20o + 10o dk red	45	40
B46	SP24	30o + 10o brt bl	2.00	1.50

The surtax was for war victims.

No. B42 Surcharged with New Value and Bar in Black

1948, Dec. 1

B47	SP23	25o + 5o on 20o+10o	85	85

The surtax was for Red Cross relief work.

Child Picking Flowers — SP25

1950, Aug. 15 Photo. *Perf. 13*
B48 SP25 25o + 5o brt red 1.90 1.10
B49 SP25 45o + 5o dp bl 5.75 3.50

The surtax was for poliomyelitis victims.

Skater — SP26

Winter Scene SP27

Design: 30o+10o, Ski jumper.

1951, Oct. 1
B50 SP26 15o + 5o ol grn 1.50 1.25
B51 SP26 30o + 10o red 1.50 1.25
B52 SP27 55o + 20o blue 9.00 7.25

Olympic Winter Games, Oslo, Feb. 14-29, 1952.

Kneeling Woman SP28

Crown Princess Martha SP29

1953, June 1 Photo. & Litho.
B53 SP28 30o + 10o red & cr 2.25 2.00

The surtax was for cancer research.

North Cape Type of 1930

1953, June 15 Photo.

Size: 27x21mm

B54 SP1 20o + 10o grn 10.50 8.50
B55 SP1 30o + 15o red 10.50 8.50
B56 SP1 55o + 25o gray bl 17.00 13.00

The surtax aided the Tourist Association.

1956, Mar. 28 *Perf. 13*
B57 SP29 35o + 10o dk red 1.75 1.50
B58 SP29 65o + 10o dk bl 4.25 3.50

The surtax was for the Crown Princess Martha Memorial Fund.

North Cape Type of 1930

1957, May 6

Size: 27x21mm

B59 SP1 25o + 10o grn 4.75 4.00
B60 SP1 35o + 15o red 5.50 5.00
B61 SP1 65o + 25o gray bl 4.75 3.50

The surtax aided the Tourist Association.

White Anemone SP30

Mother, Child, WRY Emblem SP31

Design: 90o+10o, Hepatica.

1960, Jan. 12 Litho. *Perf. 13*
B62 SP30 45o + 10o brt red & grn 2.00 1.90
B63 SP30 90o + 10o bl, org & grn 5.75 5.50

The surtax was for anti-tuberculosis work.

1960, Apr. 7 Photo. Unwmk.
B64 SP31 45o + 25o rose & blk 5.00 3.75
B65 SP31 90o + 25o bl & blk 9.00 6.50

World Refugee Year, July 1, 1959-June 30, 1960. The surtax was for aid to refugees.

Severed Chain and Dove SP32

Design: 60o+10o, Norwegian flags.

1965, May 8 Photo. *Perf. 13*
B66 SP32 30o + 10o grn, blk & tan 75 70
B67 SP32 60o + 10o red & dk bl 75 75

20th anniversary of liberation from the Germans. The surtax was for war cripples.

Souvenir Sheet

Offshore Oil Drilling SP33

Designs: a, Ekofisk Center. b, Treasure Scout drilling rig and Odin Viking supply vessel at Tromsoflaket, 1982. c, Statfjord C oil platform, 1984. d, Men working on deck of Neptune Nordraug.

1985, Oct. 4 Litho. *Perf. 13½x13*
B68 Sheet of 4 2.75 3.50
a.-d. SP33 2k + 1k, any single 65 85

Stamp Day 1985. Surtax for philatelic promotion.

Souvenir Sheet

Paper Industry SP34

Paper mill: a, Wood aging containers. b, Boiling plant. c, Paper-making machine. d, Paper dryer.

1986, Oct. 17 Litho. *Perf. 13½*
B69 Sheet of 4 3.25 3.75
a.-d. SP34 2.50k + 1k, any single 80 90

Surtax for philatelic promotion. Nos. B69a-B69b and B69c-B69d printed in continuous designs.

Souvenir Sheet

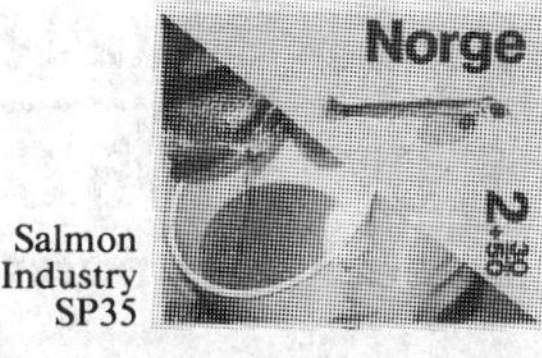

Salmon Industry SP35

Designs: a, Eggs and milt pressed out of fish by hand. b, Cultivation of eggs in tanks. c, Outdoor hatchery. d, Market.

1987, Oct. 9 Litho. *Perf. 13½x13*
B70 Sheet of 4 3.75 3.75
a. SP35 2.30k +50o multi 65 65
b. SP35 2.70k +50o multi 75 75
c. SP35 3.50k +50o multi 95 95
d. SP35 4.50k +50o multi 1.25 1.25

AIR POST STAMPS

Airplane over Akershus Castle
AP1 AP2

Perf. 13½x14½

1927-34 Typo. Wmk. 160
C1 AP1 45o lt bl, strong frame line ('34) 5.00 2.00
a. Faint or broken frame line 13.00 3.75

1937, Aug. 18 Photo. *Perf. 13*
C2 AP2 45o Prussian blue 1.25 55

1941, Nov. 10 Unwmk.
C3 AP2 45o indigo 40 30

POSTAGE DUE STAMPS

Numeral of Value — D1

Perf. 14½x13½

1889-1914 Typo. Wmk. 160

Inscribed "at betale"

J1 D1 1o gray 52 50
J2 D1 4o magenta 1.00 50
J3 D1 10o car rose 4.00 50
a. 10o rose red 47.50 7.50
J4 D1 15o brn ('14) 1.10 50
J5 D1 20o ultra 2.00 50
a. Perf. 13½x12½ 150.00 75.00
J6 D1 50o maroon 4.00 1.75
Nos. J1-J6 (6) 12.62 4.25

See #J7-J12. For overprint see #136-144.

1922-23

Inscribed "a betale"

J7 D1 4o lil rose 5.00 5.00
J8 D1 10o green 1.65 1.50
J9 D1 20o dl violet 3.50 3.25
J10 D1 40o dp ultra 5.50 50
J11 D1 100o org yel 22.50 8.50
J12 D1 200o dk violet 55.00 18.00
Nos. J7-J12 (6) 93.15 36.75

OFFICIAL STAMPS

Coat of Arms
O1 O2

Perf. 14½x13½

1926 Typo. Wmk. 160
O1 O1 5o rose lilac 32 32
O2 O1 10o yellow green 32 15
O3 O1 15o indigo 1.40 1.40
O4 O1 20o plum 32 15
O5 O1 30o slate 4.00 4.00
O6 O1 40o deep blue 1.25 52
O7 O1 60o Prussian blue 4.00 4.00
Nos. O1-O7 (7) 11.61 10.54

Official Stamp of 1926 Surcharged **2 2**

1929, July 1
O8 O1 2o on 5o magenta 40 32

Perf. 14½x13½

1933-34 Litho. Wmk. 160

Size: 35x19¼mm

O9 O2 2o ocher 60 85
O10 O2 5o rose lil 1.65 1.65
O11 O2 7o orange 8.00 5.00
O12 O2 10o green 16.00 65
O13 O2 15o olive 52 42
O14 O2 20o vermilion 16.00 42
O15 O2 25o yel brn 52 42
O16 O2 30o ultra 52 42
O18 O2 40o slate 21.00 52
O19 O2 60o blue 6.50 52
O20 O2 70o ol brn 1.50 1.50
O21 O2 100o violet 2.00 1.10
Nos. O9-O16,O18-O21 (12) 74.81 13.47

On the lithographed stamps, the lion's left leg is shaded.

Typo.

Size: 34x18¾mm

O10a O2 5o rose lilac 85 1.10
O11a O2 7o orange 10.00 7.25
O12a O2 10o green 70 40
O13a O2 15o olive 10.00 12.00
O14a O2 20o vermilion 70 25
O17 O2 35o red vio ('34) 85 50
O18a O2 40o slate 85 50
O19a O2 60o blue 85 50
Nos. O10A-O14A,O17,O18A-O19A (8) 24.80 22.50

Coat of Arms — O3

Norwegian Nazi Party Emblem — O4

1937-38 Photo. *Perf. 13½x13*
O22 O3 5o rose lil ('38) 65 60
O23 O3 7o dp org 65 60
O24 O3 10o brt grn 40 22
O25 O3 15o olive bis 52 52
O26 O3 20o car ('38) 52 15
O27 O3 25o red brn ('38) 1.00 70
O28 O3 30o ultra 1.00 60
O29 O3 35o red vio ('38) 1.00 60
O30 O3 40o Prus grn ('38) 85 40
O31 O3 60o Prus bl ('38) 1.00 60
O32 O3 100o dk vio ('38) 2.00 1.50
Nos. O22-O32 (11) 9.59 6.49

See Nos. O33-O43, O55-O56. For surcharge see No. O57.

1939-47 Unwmk.
O33 O3 5o dp red lil ('41) 40 15
O34 O3 7o dp org ('41) 40 32
O35 O3 10o brt grn ('41) 25 15
O36 O3 15o olive ('45) 40 22
O37 O3 20o carmine 25 15
O38 O3 25o red brn 2.00 3.00
O38A O3 25o scar ('46) 25 15
O39 O3 30o ultra 2.75 1.10
O39A O3 30o dk gray ('47) 65 52
O40 O3 35o brt lil ('41) 52 22
O41 O3 40o grnsh blk ('41) 52 22
O41A O3 40o dp ultra ('46) 1.25 22
O42 O3 60o Prus bl ('41) 65 22
O43 O3 100o dk vio ('41) 65 22
Nos. O33-O43 (14) 10.94 6.86

1942-44
O44 O4 5o magenta 32 *85*
O45 O4 7o yel org 32 *85*
O46 O4 10o emerald 15 15
O47 O4 15o olive ('44) 2.00 *5.00*
O48 O4 20o brt red 15 15
O49 O4 25o red brn ('43) 4.00 *8.50*
O50 O4 30o brt ultra ('44) 3.00 *10.00*
O51 O4 35o brt pur ('43) 3.00 *7.25*
O52 O4 40o grnsh blk ('43) 25 15
O53 O4 60o indigo ('43) 2.25 *5.00*
O54 O4 1k bl vio ('43) 2.25 *7.25*
Nos. O44-O54 (11) 17.69 *45.15*

Type of 1937

1947, Nov. 1
O55 O3 50o deep magenta 75 22
O56 O3 200o orange 3.00 45

No. O37 Surcharged with New Values and Bars in Black

1949, Mar. 15
O57 O3 25o on 20o carmine 25 35

Norway Coat of Arms
O5 O6

1951-52 Unwmk. Photo. *Perf. 13*

No.	Type	Description	Unused	Used
O58	O5	5o rose lilac	60	15
O59	O5	10o dk gray	60	15
O60	O5	15o dp org brn ('52)	60	15
O61	O5	30o scarlet	60	15
O62	O5	35o red brn ('52)	70	45
O63	O5	60o bl gray	70	15
O64	O5	100o vio bl ('52)	1.10	15
		Nos. O58-O64 (7)	4.90	1.35

Catalogue values for unused stamps in this section, from this point to the end of the section, are for Never Hinged items.

1955-61

No.	Type	Description	Unused	Used
O65	O6	5o rose lilac	18	15
O66	O6	10o slate	18	15
O67	O6	15o org brn	1.65	1.10
O68	O6	20o bl grn ('57)	28	15
O69	O6	25o emer ('59)	70	15
O70	O6	30o scarlet	1.65	65
O71	O6	35o brn red	70	15
O72	O6	40o blue lilac	1.10	15
O73	O6	45o scar ('58)	90	15
O74	O6	50o gldn brn ('57)	2.50	22
O75	O6	60o grnsh bl	2.25	32
O76	O6	70o brn olive	3.25	1.10
O77	O6	75o maroon ('57)	8.00	6.00
O78	O6	80o org brn ('58)	3.50	70
O79	O6	90o org ('58)	1.10	20
O80	O6	1k vio ('57)	1.65	15
O81	O6	2k gray grn ('60)	1.75	15
O82	O6	5k red lil ('61)	6.25	85
		Nos. O65-O82 (18)	37.59	12.49

See Phosphorescence note after No. 430.

1962-74 Photo.

No.	Type	Description	Unused	Used
O83	O6	30o grn ('64)	75	15
O84	O6	40o ol grn ('68)	25	15
O85	O6	50o scarlet	1.10	25
O86	O6	50o slate ('69)	18	15
O87	O6	60o dk red ('64)	1.10	15
O88	O6	65o dk red ('68)	1.10	15
O89	O6	70o dk red ('70)	30	15
O90	O6	75o lt grn ('73)	75	75
O91	O6	85o ocher ('74)	95	95
O92	O6	1k dp org ('73)	45	15
O93	O6	1.10k car lake ('74)	75	60
		Nos. O83-O93 (11)	7.68	3.60

Shades exist of several values of type O6.

1975-82 Litho.

No.	Type	Description	Unused	Used
O94	O6	5o rose lil ('80)	60	60
O95	O6	10o bluish gray ('82)	80	80
O96	O6	15o henna brn	1.25	1.25
O97	O6	20o grn ('82)	80	80
O98	O6	25o yel grn	40	15
O99	O6	40o ol grn ('79)	1.00	1.00
O100	O6	50o grnsh gray ('76)	40	15
O101	O6	60o dk grnsh bl	1.00	1.00
O102	O6	70o dk red ('82)	2.00	1.50
O103	O6	80o red brn ('76)	60	15
O104	O6	1k vio ('80)	1.40	35
O105	O6	1.10k red ('80)	1.25	60
O106	O6	1.25k dull red	60	15
O107	O6	1.30k lilac ('81)	1.00	1.00
O108	O6	1.50k red ('81)	70	20
O109	O6	1.75k dl bl grn ('82)	1.40	1.25
O110	O6	2k dk gray grn	1.00	20
O111	O6	2k cerise ('82)	1.40	30
O112	O6	3k purple ('82)	2.00	80
O113	O6	5k lt vio	12.00	2.50
O114	O6	5k blue ('77)	2.75	80
		Nos. O94-O114 (21)	34.35	15.55

In lithographed set, shield's background is dotted; on photogravure stamps it is solid color.

Official stamps invalid as of Apr. 1, 1986.

NOSSI-BE

LOCATION — Island in the Indian Ocean, off the northwest coast of Madagascar
GOVT. — A former French Protectorate
AREA — 130 sq. mi.
POP. — 9,000 (approx. 1900)
CAPITAL — Hellville

In 1896 the island was placed under the authority of the Governor-General of Madagascar and postage stamps of Madagascar were placed in use.

100 Centimes = 1 Franc

Stamps of French Colonies Surcharged in Blue:

25 (a) 25 c (b) 5 c (c)

1889 Unwmk. *Imperf.*

No.	Type	Description	Unused	Used
1	A8 (a)	25 on 40c red, *straw*	1,300.	400.00
a.		Double surcharge		*900.00*
2	A8 (b)	25c on 40c red, *straw*	1,750.	1,000.
		Perf. 14x13½		
3	A9 (b)	5c on 10c blk, *lav*	1,750.	600.00
4	A9 (b)	5c on 20c red, *green*	1,750.	650.00
5	A9 (c)	5c on 10c blk, *lav*	1,600.	500.00
6	A9 (c)	5c on 20c red, *green*	1,750.	1,100.
7	A9 (a)	15 on 20c red, *green*	1,500.	600.00
a.		15 on 30c brown, *bister* (error)	*17,500.*	*11,000.*
8	A9 (a)	25 on 30c brn, *bister*	1,500.	375.00
9	A9 (a)	25 on 40c ver, *straw*	1,500.	400.00

N S B 0 25 (d) N S B 25 c. (f) N S B 25 (g)

Black Surcharge

1890

No.	Type	Description	Unused	Used
10	A9 (d)	0.25 on 20c red, *green*	200.00	140.00
11	A9 (d)	0.25 on 75c car, *rose*	200.00	140.00
12	A9 (d)	0.25 on 1fr brnz grn, *straw*	200.00	140.00
a.		Without ornament		
16	A9 (f)	25c on 20c red, *green*	200.00	140.00
17	A9 (f)	25c on 75c car, *rose*	200.00	140.00
18	A9 (f)	25c on 1fr brnz grn, *straw*	200.00	140.00
19	A9 (g)	25 on 20c red, *green*	550.00	350.00
20	A9 (g)	25 on 75c car, *rose*	550.00	350.00
21	A9 (g)	25 on 1fr brnz grn, *straw*	550.00	350.00

The 25c on 20c with surcharge composed of "25 c." as in "f," "N S B" as in "d," and frame as in "g" is an essay.

Surcharged or Overprinted in Black, Carmine, Vermilion or Blue:

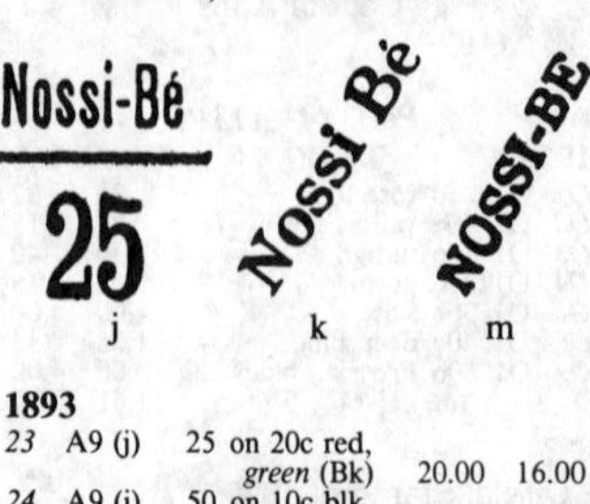

1893

No.	Type	Description	Unused	Used
23	A9 (j)	25 on 20c red, *green* (Bk)	20.00	16.00
24	A9 (j)	50 on 10c blk, *lav* (Bk)	22.50	16.00
a.		Inverted surcharge	150.00	110.00
25	A9 (j)	75 on 15c bl (Bk)	150.00	100.00
26	A9 (j)	1fr on 5c grn, *greenish* (Bk)	52.50	40.00
a.		Inverted surcharge	150.00	125.00
27	A9 (k)	10c blk, *lav* (C)	6.50	5.75
a.		Inverted overprint	45.00	42.50
28	A9 (k)	10c blk, *lav* (V)	6.50	5.75
29	A9 (k)	15c bl (Bk)	6.50	5.75
a.		Inverted overprint	45.00	42.50
30	A9 (k)	20c red, *green* (Bk)	225.00	27.50
a.		Double overprint		
31	A9 (m)	20c red, *green* (Bl)	47.50	21.00
a.		Inverted overprint	65.00	62.50

Counterfeits exist of surcharges and overprints of Nos. 1-31.

Navigation and Commerce — A14

1894 Typo. *Perf. 14x13½*
Name of Colony in Blue or Carmine

No.	Type	Description	Unused	Used
32	A14	1c blk, *lil bl*	55	55
33	A14	2c brn, *buff*	65	62
34	A14	4c cl, *lavender*	80	62
35	A14	5c grn, *greenish*	1.10	80
36	A14	10c blk, *lav*	2.50	1.40
37	A14	15c blue, quadrille paper	3.50	1.75
38	A14	20c red, *green*	3.75	2.25
39	A14	25c blk, *rose*	5.00	3.75
40	A14	30c brn, *bister*	5.75	4.25
41	A14	40c red, *straw*	7.00	5.75
42	A14	50c car, *rose*	7.00	5.75
43	A14	75c dp vio, *orange*	16.00	16.00
44	A14	1fr brnz grn, *straw*	9.00	6.50
		Nos. 32-44 (13)	62.60	49.99

Perf. 13½x14 stamps are counterfeits.

POSTAGE DUE STAMPS

Stamps of French Colonies Surcharged in Black:

Nossi-Bé chiffre-taxe 0.20 A PERCEVOIR (n) Nossi-Bé chiffre-taxe 0.35 A PERCEVOIR (o)

1891 Unwmk. *Perf. 14x13½*

No.	Type	Description	Unused	Used
J1	A9(n)	20 on 1c blk, *lil bl*	180.00	150.00
a.		Inverted surcharge	325.00	250.00
b.		Surcharged vertically	500.00	500.00
c.		Surcharge on back	375.00	375.00
J2	A9(n)	30 on 2c brn, *buff*	180.00	150.00
a.		Inverted surcharge	325.00	250.00
b.		Surcharge on back	400.00	400.00
J3	A9(n)	50 on 30c brn, *bister*	55.00	50.00
a.		Inverted surcharge	325.00	250.00
b.		Surcharge on back	400.00	400.00
J4	A9(o)	35 on 4c cl, *lav*	210.00	160.00
a.		Inverted surcharge	325.00	250.00
b.		Surcharge on back	400.00	400.00
c.		Pair, one without surcharge		
J5	A9(o)	35 on 20c red, *green*	225.00	160.00
a.		Inverted surcharge	325.00	250.00
J6	A9(o)	1fr on 35c vio, *orange*	135.00	90.00
a.		Inverted surcharge	325.00	250.00
b.		Surcharge on back	400.00	400.00

Nossi-Bé 5 C. A PERCEVOIR (p) Nossi-Bé 5 C. A PERCEVOIR (q) Nossi-Bé 0.10 A PERCEVOIR (r)

1891

No.	Type	Description	Unused	Used
J7	A9(p)	5c on 20c red, *green*	120.00	120.00
J8	A9(q)	5c on 20c red, *green*	140.00	140.00
J9	A9(r)	0.10c on 5c grn, *greenish*	9.00	8.00
J10	A9(p)	10c on 15c bl	120.00	120.00
J11	A9(q)	10c on 15c bl	140.00	140.00
J12	A9(p)	15c on 10c blk, *lav*	80.00	80.00
J13	A9(q)	15c on 10c blk, *lav*	90.00	90.00
J14	A9(r)	0.15c on 20c red, *green*	9.00	9.00
a.		25c on 20c red, *grn* (error)	*20,000.*	*20,000.*
J15	A9(p)	25c on 5c grn, *greenish*	80.00	80.00
J16	A9(q)	25c on 5c grn, *greenish*	90.00	90.00
J17	A9(r)	0.25c on 75c car, *rose*	325.00	275.00

Inverted Surcharge

No.	Type	Description	Unused	Used
J7a	A9(p)	5c on 20c	175.00	175.00
J8a	A9(q)	5c on 20c	175.00	175.00
J10a	A9(p)	10c on 15c	190.00	190.00
J11a	A9(q)	10c on 15c	190.00	190.00
J12a	A9(p)	15c on 10c	190.00	190.00
J13a	A9(q)	15c on 10c	190.00	190.00
J15a	A9(p)	25c on 5c	190.00	190.00
J16a	A9(q)	25c on 5c	190.00	190.00
J17a	A9(r)	0.25c on 75c	625.00	600.00

Stamps of Nossi-Be were superseded by those of Madagascar.

Counterfeits exist of surcharges on #J1-J17.

NYASSA

LOCATION — In the northern part of Mozambique in southeast Africa
GOVT. — Part of Portuguese East Africa Colony
AREA — 73,292 sq. mi.
POP. — 3,000,000 (estimated)
CAPITAL — Porto Amelia

The district formerly administered by the Nyassa Company is now a part of Mozambique. Postage stamps of Mozambique are used.

1000 Reis = 1 Milreis
100 Centavos = 1 Escudo (1919)

Mozambique Nos. 24-35 Overprinted in Black

NYASSA

1898 Unwmk. *Perf. 11½, 12½*

No.	Type	Description	Unused	Used
1	A3	5r yellow	2.50	1.75
2	A3	10r redsh vio	2.50	1.75
3	A3	15r chocolate	2.50	1.75
4	A3	20r gray vio	2.50	1.75
5	A3	25r bl grn	2.50	1.75
6	A3	50r light blue	2.50	1.75
a.		Inverted overprint		
b.		Perf. 12½	8.00	6.50
7	A3	75r rose	3.25	2.25
8	A3	80r yel grn	3.25	2.25
9	A3	100r brn, *buff*	3.25	2.25
10	A3	150r car, *rose*	7.25	6.00
11	A3	200r dk bl, *blue*	4.25	3.25
12	A3	300r dk bl, *salmon*	5.25	3.25
		Nos. 1-12 (12)	41.50	29.75

Reprints of Nos. 1, 5, 8, 9, 10 and 12 have white gum and clean-cut perforation 13½. Value of No. 9, $15; others $3 each.

Same Overprint on Mozambique Issue of 1898

1898 *Perf. 11½*

No.	Type	Description	Unused	Used
13	A4	2½r gray	1.75	1.25
14	A4	5r orange	1.75	1.25
15	A4	10r light grn	1.75	1.25
16	A4	15r brown	2.00	1.50
17	A4	20r gray vio	2.00	1.50
18	A4	25r sea green	2.00	1.50
19	A4	50r blue	2.00	1.50
20	A4	75r rose	2.50	1.25
21	A4	80r violet	2.75	2.00
22	A4	100r dk bl, *bl*	2.75	2.00
23	A4	150r brn, *straw*	3.50	2.00
24	A4	200r red lil, *pnksh*	3.50	2.00
25	A4	300r dk blue, *rose*	3.50	2.00
		Nos. 13-25 (13)	31.75	21.00

Giraffe — A5

Camels — A6

Perf. 13½-15 & Compound

1901 **Engr.**

26 A5 2½r blk & red brn 75 45
27 A5 5r blk & violet 75 45
28 A5 10r blk & dp grn 75 45
29 A5 15r blk & org brn 75 45
30 A5 20r blk & org red 75 45
31 A5 25r blk & orange 75 45
32 A5 50r blk & dl bl 75 45
33 A6 75r blk & car lake 1.00 45
34 A6 80r blk & lilac 1.00 45
35 A6 100r blk & brn bis 1.00 50
36 A6 150r blk & dp org 1.25 95
37 A6 200r blk & grnsh bl 1.00 95
38 A6 300r blk & yel grn 1.00 1.10
Nos. 26-38 (13) 11.50 7.55

Nos. 26 to 38 are known with inverted centers but are believed to be purely speculative and never regularly issued. Value $20 each.

For overprints and surcharges see Nos. 39-50, 63-80.

Nos. 34, 36, 38 Surcharged **65 REIS**

1903

39 A6 65r on 80r 70 65
40 A6 115r on 150r 70 65
41 A6 130r on 300r 70 65

Nos. 29, 31 Overprinted **PROVISORIO**

42 A5 15r blk & org brn 70 65
43 A5 25r blk & orange 70 65

Nos. 34, 36, 38 Surcharged 65 réis

44 A6 65r on 80r 32.50 20.00
45 A6 115r on 150r 32.50 20.00
46 A6 130r on 300r 32.50 20.00

Nos. 29, 31 Overprinted PROVISORIO

47 A5 15r blk & org brn 375.00 150.00
48 A5 25r blk & org 300.00 150.00

Forgeries exist of Nos. 44-48.

Nos. 26, 35 Surcharged **5 REIS PROVISORIO**

1910

49 A5 5r on 2½r 85 75
50 A6 50r on 100r 85 75
a. "50 REIS" omitted 90.00

Reprints of Nos. 49-50, made in 1921, have 2mm space between surcharge lines, instead of 1½mm. Value, each 25 cents.

Zebra — A7

Vasco da Gama's Flagship "San Gabriel" — A8

Red Overprint

Designs: Nos. 51-53, Camels. Nos. 57-59, Giraffe and palms.

1911

51 A7 2½r blk & dl vio 1.00 55
52 A7 5r black 1.00 55
53 A7 10r blk & gray grn 1.00 55
54 A7 20r blk & car lake 1.00 55
55 A7 25r blk & vio brn 1.00 55
56 A7 50r blk & dp bl 1.00 55
57 A8 75r blk & brn 1.00 85
58 A8 100r blk & brn, *grn* 1.00 85
59 A8 200r blk & dp grn, *sal* 1.25 1.10
60 A8 300r blk, *blue* 2.00 1.90
61 A8 400r blk & dk brn 2.00 2.25
a. Pair, one without overprint
62 A8 500r ol & vio brn 2.50 2.50
Nos. 51-62 (12) 15.75 12.75

Nos. 51-62 exist without overprint but were not issued in that condition. Value $10 each.

For surcharges see Nos. 81-105.

Stamps of 1901-03 Surcharged **REPUBLICA 1½ C.**

1918

On Nos. 26-38

63 A5 ¼c on 2½r 85.00 65.00
64 A5 ½c on 5r 85.00 65.00
65 A5 1c on 10r 85.00 65.00
66 A5 1½c on 15r 5.50 4.00
67 A5 2c on 20r 3.00 3.00
68 A5 3½c on 25r 3.00 3.00
69 A5 5c on 50r 3.00 3.00
70 A6 7½c on 75r 3.00 3.00
71 A6 8c on 80r 3.00 3.00
72 A6 10c on 100r 3.00 3.00
73 A6 15c on 150r 5.00 3.75
74 A6 20c on 200r 5.00 3.75
75 A6 30c on 300r 3.25 6.50

On Nos. 39-41

76 A6 40c on 65r on 80r 30.00 25.00
77 A6 50c on 115r on 150r 8.50 6.50
78 A6 1e on 130r on 300r 8.50 6.50

On Nos. 42-43

79 A5 1½c on 15r 37.50 30.00
80 A5 3½c on 25r 10.00 7.50
Nos. 63-80 (18) 386.25 306.50

On Nos. 70-78 there is less space between "REPUBLICA" and the new value than on the other stamps of this issue.

On Nos. 76-78 the 1903 surcharge is cancelled by a bar.

The surcharge exists inverted on Nos. 64, 66-70, 72, 76 and 78-80, and double on Nos. 64, 67 and 69.

Nos. 51-62 Surcharged in Black or Red *7½ Centavos*

1921

Lisbon Surcharges

Numerals: The "1" (large or small) is thin, sharp-pointed, and has thin serifs. The "2" is italic, with the tail thin and only slightly wavy. The "3" has a flat top. The "4" is open at the top. The "7" has thin strokes.

Centavos: The letters are shaded, i.e., they are thicker in some parts than in others. The "t" has a thin cross bar ending in a downward stroke at the right. The "s" is flat at the bottom and wider than in the next group.

81 A7 ¼c on 2½r 11.00 11.00
83 A7 ½c on 5r (R) 11.00 11.00
a. ½c on 2½r (R) (error) 150.00 150.00
84 A7 1c on 10r 11.00 11.00
a. Pair, one without surcharge
85 A8 1½c on 300r (R) 16.00 16.00
86 A7 2c on 20r 11.00 11.00
87 A7 2½c on 25r 16.00 16.00
88 A8 3c on 400r 11.00 11.00
a. "Republica" omitted
89 A7 5c on 50r 16.00 16.00
90 A8 7½c on 75r 11.00 11.00
91 A8 10c on 100r 16.00 16.00
92 A8 12c on 500r 10.00 10.00
93 A8 20c on 200r 16.00 16.00
Nos. 81-93 (12) 156.00 156.00

The surcharge exists inverted on Nos. 83-85, 87-88 and 92, and double on Nos. 81, 83 and 86.

Forgeries exist of Nos. 81-93.

London Surcharges

Numerals: The "1" has the vertical stroke and serifs thicker than in the Lisbon printing. The "2" is upright and has a strong wave in the tail. The small "2" is heavily shaded. The "3" has a rounded top. The "4" is closed at the top. The "7" has thick strokes.

Centavos: The letters are heavier than in the Lisbon printing and are of even thickness throughout. The "t" has a thick cross bar with scarcely any down stroke at the end. The "s" is rounded at the bottom and narrower than in the Lisbon printing.

94 A7 ¼c on 2½r 1.25 1.25
95 A7 ½c on 5r (R) 1.25 1.25
96 A7 1c on 10r 1.25 1.25
97 A8 1½c on 300r (R) 1.25 1.25
98 A7 2c on 20r 1.25 1.25
99 A7 2½c on 25r 1.25 1.25
100 A8 3c on 400r 1.25 1.25
101 A7 5c on 50r 1.25 1.25
102 A8 7½c on 75r 1.25 1.25
a. Inverted surcharge
103 A8 10c on 100r 1.25 1.25
104 A8 12c on 500r 1.25 1.25
105 A8 20c on 200r 1.25 1.25
Nos. 94-105 (12) 15.00 15.00

A9

Zebra and Warrior — A10

Designs: 2c-5c, Vasco da Gama. 7½c-20c, "San Gabriel." 2e-5e, Dhow and warrior.

Perf. 12½, 13½-15 & Compound

1921-23 **Engr.**

106 A9 ¼c claret 80 80
107 A9 ½c steel bl 80 80
108 A9 1c grn & blk 80 80
109 A9 1½c blk & ocher 80 80
110 A9 2c red & blk 80 80
111 A9 2½c blk & ol grn 80 80
112 A9 4c blk & org 80 80
113 A9 5c ultra & blk 80 80
114 A9 6c blk & vio 80 80
115 A9 7½c blk & blk brn 80 80
116 A9 8c blk & ol grn 80 80
117 A9 10c blk & red brn 80 80
118 A9 15c blk & carmine 80 80
119 A9 20c blk & pale bl 1.00 1.00
120 A10 30c blk & bister 1.00 1.00
121 A10 40c blk & gray bl 1.00 1.00
122 A10 50c blk & green 1.00 1.00
123 A10 1e blk & red brn 1.00 1.00
124 A10 2e red brn & blk ('23) 3.75 3.75
125 A10 5e ultra & red brn ('23) 2.75 2.75
Nos. 106-125 (20) 21.90 21.90

POSTAGE DUE STAMPS

Giraffe — D1

Designs: ½c, 1c, Giraffe. 2c, 3c, Zebra. 5c, 6c, 10c, "San Gabriel." 20c, 50c, Vasco da Gama.

1924 **Unwmk.** **Engr.** ***Perf. 14***

J1 D1 ½c deep green 75 38
J2 D1 1c gray 75 38
J3 D1 2c red 75 38
J4 D1 3c red orange 75 38
J5 D1 5c dark brown 75 38
J6 D1 6c orange brown 75 38
J7 D1 10c brown violet 85 50
J8 D1 20c carmine 85 50
J9 D1 50c lilac gray 85 50
Nos. J1-J9 (9) 7.05 3.78

NEWSPAPER STAMP

Mozambique No. P6 Overprinted Like Nos. 1-25 in Black

1898 **Unwmk.** ***Perf. 13½***

P1 N3 2½r brown 1.00 85

Reprints have white gum and clean-cut perf. 13½. Value $1.

POSTAL TAX STAMPS

Pombal Issue

Mozambique Nos. RA1-RA3 Overprinted "NYASSA" in Red

1925 **Unwmk.** ***Perf. 12½***

RA1 CD28 15c brn & blk 5.00 5.00
RA2 CD29 15c brn & blk 5.00 5.00
RA3 CD30 15c brn & blk 5.00 5.00

POSTAL TAX DUE STAMPS

Pombal Issue

Mozambique Nos. RAJ1-RAJ3 Overprinted "NYASSA" in Red

1925 **Unwmk.** ***Perf. 12½***

RAJ1 CD31 30c brn & blk 30.00 27.50
RAJ2 CD32 30c brn & blk 30.00 27.50
RAJ3 CD33 30c brn & blk 30.00 27.50

OBOCK

LOCATION — A seaport in eastern Africa on the Gulf of Aden, directly opposite Aden.

Obock was the point of entrance from which French Somaliland was formed. The port was acquired by the French in 1862 but was not actively occupied until 1884 when Sagallo and Tadjoura were ceded to France. In 1888 Djibouti was made into a port and the seat of government moved from Obock to the latter city. In 1902 the name Somali Coast was adopted on the postage stamps of Djibouti, these stamps superseding the individual issues of Obock. See Somali Coast in Vol. IV.

100 Centimes = 1 Franc

Counterfeits exist of Nos. 1-31.

Stamps of French Colonies Handstamped in Black:

OBOCK — Nos. 1-11, J1-J4

OBOCK — Nos. 12-20, J5-J18

1892 **Unwmk.** ***Perf. 14x13½***

1 A9 1c blk, *lil bl* 15.00 12.50
2 A9 2c brn, *buff* 17.00 15.00
3 A9 4c claret, *lav* 225.00 225.00
4 A9 5c grn, *grnsh* 12.00 10.00
5 A9 10c blk, *lavender* 30.00 20.00
6 A9 15c blue 30.00 26.00
7 A9 25c blk, *rose* 40.00 35.00
8 A9 35c vio, *org* 210.00 210.00
9 A9 40c red, *straw* 175.00 175.00
10 A9 75c car, *rose* 200.00 200.00
11 A9 1fr brnz grn, *straw* 240.00 240.00

No. 3 has been reprinted. On the reprints the second "O" of "OBOCK" is 4mm high instead of 3½mm. Value $7.50.

1892

12 A9 4c claret, *lav* 10.00 9.00
13 A9 5c grn, *grnsh* 10.00 9.00
14 A9 10c blk, *lavender* 12.00 11.50
15 A9 15c blue 12.00 11.50
16 A9 20c red, *grn* 20.00 16.00
17 A9 25c blk, *rose* 9.00 8.00
18 A9 40c red, *straw* 25.00 22.50
19 A9 75c car, *rose* 190.00 150.00
20 A9 1fr brnz grn, *straw* 35.00 27.50

Exists inverted or double on all denominations.

Nos. 14, 15, 17, 20 with Additional Surcharge Handstamped in Red, Blue or Black:

Nos, 21-30

No. 31

1892

21	A9	1c on 25c blk, *rose*	5.00	5.00
22	A9	2c on 10c blk, *lav*	32.00	21.00
23	A9	2c on 15c blue	6.25	6.00
24	A9	4c on 15c bl (Bk)	6.25	6.00
25	A9	4c on 25c blk, *rose* (Bk)	7.00	6.25
26	A9	5c on 25c blk, *rose*	10.00	7.00
27	A9	20c on 10c blk, *lav*	45.00	35.00
28	A9	30c on 10c blk, *lav*	60.00	50.00
29	A9	35c on 25c blk, *rose*	45.00	40.00
a.		"3" instead of "35"	400.00	400.00
30	A9	75c on 1fr brnz grn, *straw*	62.50	52.50
b.		"57" instead of "75"	4,500.	4,500.
c.		"55" instead of "75"	4,500.	4,500.
31	A9	5fr on 1fr brnz grn, *straw*(Bl)	500.00	425.00

Exists inverted on most denominations.

Navigation and Commerce
A4

Camel and Rider
A5

1892 **Typo.** ***Perf. 14x13½***

Obock in Red (1c, 5c, 15c, 25c, 75c, 1fr) or Blue

32	A4	1c blk, *lil bl*	1.00	70
33	A4	2c brn, *buff*	60	60
34	A4	4c claret, *lav*	1.00	70
35	A4	5c grn, *grnsh*	1.50	70
36	A4	10c blk, *lavender*	2.75	1.25
37	A4	15c bl, quadrille paper	5.50	3.00
38	A4	20c red, *grn*	11.00	8.00
39	A4	25c blk, *rose*	10.50	8.00
40	A4	30c brn, *bis*	7.75	5.25
41	A4	40c red, *straw*	7.75	5.00
42	A4	50c car, *rose*	9.25	5.25
43	A4	75c vio, *org*	11.00	5.25
a.		Name double	140.00	140.00
b.		Name inverted	1,400.	1,400.
44	A4	1fr brnz grn, *straw*	14.00	11.00

Perf. 13½x14 stamps are counterfeits.

1893 ***Imperf.***

Quadrille Lines Printed on Paper

Size: 32mm at base

44A	A5	2fr brnz grn	26.00	22.50

Size: 45mm at base

45	A5	5fr red	60.00	50.00

Somali Warriors
A7

A8

1894 ***Imperf.***

Quadrille Lines Printed on Paper

46	A7	1c blk & rose	1.10	1.10
47	A7	2c vio brn & grn	1.10	1.10
48	A7	4c brn vio & org	1.10	1.10
49	A7	5c bl grn & brn	1.25	1.10
50	A7	10c blk & grn	4.50	2.75
a.		Half used as 5c on cover		90.00
51	A7	15c bl & rose	3.25	2.25
52	A7	20c brn org & mar	4.50	2.50
a.		Half used as 10c on cover		70.00
53	A7	25c blk & bl	4.50	2.75
a.		Half used on cover		60.00
54	A7	30c bis & yel grn	10.00	6.00
a.		Half used as 15c on cover		850.00
55	A7	40c red & bl grn	7.00	3.50
56	A7	50c rose & bl	6.25	3.50
a.		Half used as 25c on cover		1,500.
57	A7	75c gray lil & org	7.25	4.00
58	A7	1fr ol grn & mar	7.25	5.25

Size: 37mm at base

60	A8	2fr vio & org	62.50	55.00

Size: 42mm at base

61	A8	5fr rose & bl	52.50	42.50

Size: 46mm at base

62	A8	10fr org & red vio	80.00	70.00
63	A8	25fr brn & bl	450.00	450.00
64	A8	50fr red vio & grn	500.00	500.00

Counterfeits exist of Nos. 63-64.

Stamps of Obock were replaced in 1901 by those of Somali Coast. The 5c on 75c, 5c on 25fr and 10c on 50fr of 1902 are listed under Somali Coast.

POSTAGE DUE STAMPS

Postage Due Stamps of French Colonies Handstamped Like #1-20

1892 **Unwmk.** ***Imperf.***

J1	D1	5c black	*6,250.*	
J2	D1	10c black	100.00	110.00
J3	D1	30c black	165.00	190.00
J4	D1	60c black	210.00	225.00
J5	D1	1c black	21.00	21.00
J6	D1	2c black	16.00	16.00
J7	D1	3c black	16.00	16.00
J8	D1	4c black	13.00	13.00
J9	D1	5c black	5.50	5.50
J10	D1	10c black	13.00	13.00
J11	D1	15c black	8.00	8.00
J12	D1	20c black	11.00	11.00
J13	D1	30c black	13.50	13.50
J14	D1	40c black	21.00	21.00
J15	D1	60c black	32.50	32.50
J16	D1	1fr brown	100.00	100.00
J17	D1	2fr brown	100.00	100.00
J18	D1	5fr brown	210.00	210.00

These handstamped overprints may be found double or inverted on some values. Counterfeits exist of Nos. J1-J18.

No. J1 has been reprinted. The overprint on the original measures 12½x3¾mm and on the reprint 12x3¼mm. Value, $120.

OLTRE GIUBA

(Italian Jubaland)

LOCATION — A strip of land, 50 to 100 miles in width, west of and parallel to the Juba River in East Africa
GOVT. — Former Italian Protectorate
AREA — 33,000 sq. mi.
POP. — 12,000
CAPITAL — Kismayu

Oltre Giuba was ceded to Italy by Great Britain in 1924 and in 1926 was incorporated with Italian Somaliland. In 1936 it became part of Italian East Africa.

100 Centesimi = 1 Lira

Italian Stamps of 1901-26 Overprinted

OLTRE GIUBA On #1-15 **OLTRE GIUBA** On #16-20

1925, July 29 **Wmk. 140** ***Perf. 14***

1	A42	1c brown	1.00	1.00
a.		Inverted overprint	65.00	
2	A43	2c yel brown	90	1.00
3	A48	5c green	52	1.00
4	A48	10c claret	52	1.00
5	A48	15c slate	52	1.00
6	A50	20c brn orange	52	1.00
7	A49	25c blue	75	1.00
8	A49	30c org brown	75	1.00
9	A49	40c brown	90	1.00
10	A49	50c violet	90	1.00
11	A49	60c carmine	1.00	1.00
12	A46	1 l brn & green	2.50	2.50
13	A46	2 l dk grn & org	17.50	14.00
14	A46	5 l blue & rose	27.50	17.00
15	A51	10 l gray grn & red	3.75	*7.25*
		Nos. 1-15 (15)	59.53	*51.75*

1925-26

16	A49	20c green	1.65	*3.00*
17	A49	30c gray	2.50	*3.00*
18	A46	75c dk red & rose	12.50	*17.00*
19	A46	1.25 l bl & ultra	16.00	*21.00*
20	A46	2.50 l dk grn & org	20.00	*27.50*
		Nos. 16-20 (5)	52.65	*71.50*

Issue years: #18-20, 1926; others 1925.

Victor Emmanuel Issue

Italian Stamps of 1925 Overprinted

OLTRE GIUBA

1925-26 **Unwmk.** ***Perf. 11***

21	A78	60c brn car	15	*2.00*
a.		Perf. 13½	*2,000.*	
22	A78	1 l dark blue	20	*2.00*
a.		Perf. 13½	80.00	*500.00*
23	A78	1.25 l dk bl ('26)	50	*6.00*
a.		Perf. 13½	50	*7.25*

Saint Francis of Assisi Issue

Italian Stamps and Type of 1926 Overprinted

OLTRE GIUBA

1926, Apr. 12 **Wmk. 140** ***Perf. 14***

24	A79	20c gray green	75	*3.00*
25	A80	40c dark vio	75	*3.00*
26	A81	60c red brown	75	*3.00*

Overprinted in Red **Oltre Giuba**

Unwmk.

27	A82	1.25 l dk bl, perf. 11	75	*3.00*
28	A83	5 l + 2.50 l ol grn, perf. 13½	1.90	*5.50*
		Nos. 24-28 (5)	4.90	

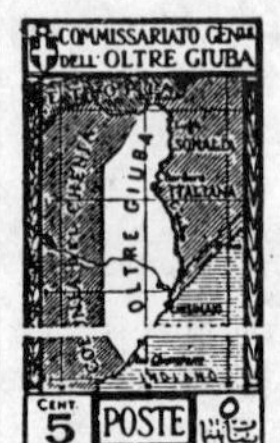

Map of Oltre Giuba — A1

1926, Apr. 21 **Typo.** **Wmk. 140**

29	A1	5c yel brown	30	*1.65*
30	A1	20c blue green	30	*1.65*
31	A1	25c olive brown	30	*1.65*
32	A1	40c dull red	30	*1.65*
33	A1	60c brown vio	30	*1.65*
34	A1	1 l blue	30	*1.65*
35	A1	2 l dark green	30	*1.65*
		Nos. 29-35 (7)	2.10	

Oltre Giuba was incorporated with Italian Somaliland on July 1, 1926, and stamps inscribed "Oltre Giuba" were discontinued.

SEMI-POSTAL STAMPS

Note preceding Italy semi-postals applies to No. 28.

Colonial Institute Issue

"Peace" Substituting Spade for Sword — SP1

Wmk. 140

1926, June 1 **Typo.** ***Perf. 14***

B1	SP1	5c + 5c brown	15	*1.65*
B2	SP1	10c + 5c olive grn	15	*1.65*
B3	SP1	20c + 5c blue grn	15	*1.65*
B4	SP1	40c + 5c brown red	15	*1.65*
B5	SP1	60c + 5c orange	15	*1.65*
B6	SP1	1 l + 5c blue	15	*1.65*
		Nos. B1-B6 (6)	90	

Surtax for Italian Colonial Institute.

SPECIAL DELIVERY STAMPS

Special Delivery Stamps of Italy Overprinted

OLTRE GIUBA

1926 **Wmk. 140** ***Perf. 14***

E1	SD1	70c dull red	8.00	*10.00*
E2	SD2	2.50 l blue & red	12.00	*14.00*

POSTAGE DUE STAMPS

Italian Postage Due Stamps of 1870-1903 Overprinted Like Nos. E1-E2

1925, July 29 **Wmk. 140** ***Perf. 14***

J1	D3	5c buff & mag	5.00	3.50
J2	D3	10c buff & mag	3.50	3.50
J3	D3	20c buff & mag	3.50	3.50
J4	D3	30c buff & mag	3.50	3.50
J5	D3	40c buff & mag	4.25	4.00
J6	D3	50c buff & mag	5.00	5.00
J7	D3	60c buff & brn	5.00	5.00
J8	D3	1 l blue & mag	6.75	6.00
J9	D3	2 l blue & mag	20.00	*20.00*
J10	D3	5 l bl & mag	24.00	*27.50*
		Nos. J1-J10 (10)	80.50	

PARCEL POST STAMPS

These stamps were used by affixing them to the waybill so that one half remained on it following the parcel, the other half staying on the receipt given the sender. Most used halves are right halves. Complete stamps were obtainable canceled, probably to order. Both unused and used values are for complete stamps.

Italian Parcel Post Stamps of 1914-22 Overprinted

OLTRE GIUBA

1925, July 29 **Wmk. 140** ***Perf. 13½***

Q1	PP2	5c brown	5.75	*3.00*
Q2	PP2	10c blue	1.25	*1.50*
Q3	PP2	20c black	1.25	*1.50*
Q4	PP2	25c red	1.25	*1.50*
Q5	PP2	50c orange	3.00	*2.50*
Q6	PP2	1 l violet	2.25	*2.50*
a.		Double overprint	65.00	
Q7	PP2	2 l green	2.25	*2.50*
Q8	PP2	3 l bister	3.00	3.00
Q9	PP2	4 l slate	3.75	4.00
Q10	PP2	10 l rose lilac	16.00	14.00
Q11	PP2	12 l red brown	52.50	50.00
Q12	PP2	15 l olive grn	30.00	32.50
Q13	PP2	20 l brown vio	30.00	32.50
		Nos. Q1-Q13 (13)	152.25	

Halves Used

Q1,Q10	32
Q2-Q6	15
Q7-Q8	15
Q9	15
Q11,Q13	1.00
Q12	80

Colonies, Former Colonies, Offices, Territories Controlled by Parent States

Belgium

Belgian Congo
Ruanda-Urundi

Denmark

Danish West Indies
Faroe Islands
Greenland
Iceland

Finland

Aland Islands

France

COLONIES PAST AND PRESENT, CONTROLLED TERRITORIES

Afars & Issas, Territory of
Alaouites
Alexandretta
Algeria
Alsace & Lorraine
Ajouan
Annam & Tonkin
Benin
Cambodia (Khmer)
Cameroun
Castellorizo
Chad
Cilicia
Cochin China
Comoro Islands
Dahomey
Diego Suarez
Djibouti (Somali Coast)
Fezzan
French Congo
French Equatorial Africa
French Guiana
French Guinea
French India
French Morocco
French Polynesia (Oceania)
French Southern & Antarctic Territories
French Sudan
French West Africa
Gabon
Germany
Ghadames
Grand Comoro
Guadeloupe
Indo-China
Inini
Ivory Coast
Laos
Latakia
Lebanon
Madagascar
Martinique
Mauritania
Mayotte
Memel
Middle Congo
Moheli
New Caledonia
New Hebrides
Niger Territory
Nossi-Be
Obock
Reunion
Rouad, Ile
Ste.-Marie de Madagascar
St. Pierre & Miquelon
Senegal
Senegambia & Niger
Somali Coast
Syria
Tahiti
Togo
Tunisia
Ubangi-Shari
Upper Senegal & Niger
Upper Volta
Viet Nam
Wallis & Futuna Islands

POST OFFICES IN FOREIGN COUNTRIES

China
Crete
Egypt
Turkish Empire
Zanzibar

Germany

EARLY STATES

Baden
Bavaria
Bergedorf
Bremen
Brunswick
Hamburg
Hanover
Lubeck
Mecklenburg-Schwerin
Mecklenburg-Strelitz
Oldenburg
Prussia
Saxony
Schleswig-Holstein
Wurttemberg

FORMER COLONIES

Cameroun (Kamerun)
Caroline Islands
German East Africa
German New Guinea
German South-West Africa
Kiauchau
Mariana Islands
Marshall Islands
Samoa
Togo

Italy

EARLY STATES

Modena
Parma
Romagna
Roman States
Sardinia
Tuscany
Two Sicilies
  Naples
  Neapolitan Provinces
  Sicily

FORMER COLONIES, CONTROLLED TERRITORIES, OCCUPATION AREAS

Aegean Islands
  Calimno (Calino)
  Caso
  Cos (Coo)
  Karki (Carchi)
  Leros (Lero)
  Lipso
  Nisiros (Nisiro)
  Patmos (Patmo)
  Piscopi
  Rodi (Rhodes)
  Scarpanto
  Simi
  Stampalia
Castellorizo
Corfu
Cyrenaica
Eritrea
Ethiopia (Abyssinia)
Fiume
Ionian Islands
  Cephalonia
  Ithaca
  Paxos
Italian East Africa
Libya
Oltre Giuba
Saseno
Somalia (Italian Somaliland)
Tripolitania

POST OFFICES IN FOREIGN COUNTRIES "ESTERO"*

Austria
China
  Peking
  Tientsin
Crete
Tripoli
Turkish Empire
  Constantinople
  Durazzo
  Janina
Jerusalem
Salonika
Scutari
Smyrna
Valona

* Stamps overprinted "ESTERO" were used in various parts of the world.

Netherlands

Aruba
Netherlands Antilles (Curacao)
Netherlands Indies
Netherlands New Guinea
Surinam (Dutch Guiana)

Portugal

COLONIES PAST AND PRESENT, CONTROLLED TERRITORIES

Angola
Angra
Azores
Cape Verde
Funchal
Horta
Inhambane
Kionga
Lourenco Marques
Macao
Madeira
Mozambique
Mozambique Co.
Nyassa
Ponta Delgada
Portuguese Africa
Portuguese Congo
Portuguese Guinea
Portuguese India
Quelimane
St. Thomas & Prince Islands
Tete
Timor
Zambezia

Russia

ALLIED TERRITORIES AND REPUBLICS, OCCUPATION AREAS

Armenia
Aunus (Olonets)
Azerbaijan
Batum
Estonia
Far Eastern Republic
Georgia
Karelia
Latvia
Lithuania
North Ingermanland
Ostland
Russian Turkestan
Siberia
South Russia
Tannu Tuva
Transcaucasian Fed. Republics
Ukraine
Wenden (Livonia)
Western Ukraine

Spain

COLONIES PAST AND PRESENT, CONTROLLED TERRITORIES

Aguera, La
Cape Juby
Cuba
Elobey, Annobon & Corisco
Fernando Po
Ifni
Mariana Islands
Philippines
Puerto Rico
Rio de Oro
Rio Muni
Spanish Guinea
Spanish Morocco
Spanish Sahara
Spanish West Africa

POST OFFICES IN FOREIGN COUNTRIES

Morocco
Tangier
Tetuan

Index and Identifier

1993 Number Changes For Volume 3

Number in 1992 Catalogue	Number in 1993 Catalogue
German States—Bavaria	
J2-J3	J2a-J3a
J2a-J3a	J2-J3
Germany	
1474A-1475	1475-1476
1475A-1475B	1477-1478
1476-1480	1479-1483
1482	1484
1484-1486A	1485-1488
1487-1488	1489-1490
14909	1491
Guinea-Bissau	
626	625A
Honduras	
11, 12, 17	deleted
21, 22	deleted
26-29	deleted
C814	C783A
Iran	
184-187	deleted
286, 287, 289	deleted
Israel	
1002-1003	1014-1015
1015-1017	1016-1018
Italy	
1656A-1658	1657-1659
E34	E34a
E34a	E34
Japan	
1437-1437A	1436-1437
1824-1824B	1822-1824
Japan—Offices in China	
5a, 6a, 8a, 9a, 13a	deleted
25a, 27a, 29a	deleted
Jordan	
520-524	521-521D
525-538	528-528M
574-575	573A-573B
Laos	
266-269	268-268C
Martinique	
11a	deleted
Mexico	
642a, 642b	deleted
644a, 645a	deleted
697	RA13B
1677	1682
Monaco	
1506A-1507	1507-1508
1512-1513A	1510-1512
1514-1514A	1513-1515
1661A-1662	1662-1663
1662A-1663	1664-1665
1663A-1664	1666-1667
1664A-1668	1668-1672
Montenegro	
2N24-2N32	2N24a-2N32a
2N24a-2N32a	2N24-2N32
Morocco	
J13-J13	J13-J14
J14	J12

INDEX TO ADVERTISERS - 1993 VOLUME 3

MENTION SCOTT WHEN RESPONDING TO ADVERTISEMENTS!

Scott Catalogue Philatelic Marketplace

This "Yellow Pages" section of your Scott Catalogue contains advertisements to help you find what you need, when you need it... ...conveniently!